PREFACE

This publication contains the current Bankruptcy Code (11 U.S.C.) and related provisions of the United States Code Titles 18 and 28. Although several bills related to bankruptcy have been introduced in the current Congress, there is no indication at this time of when or if specific bills will be enacted.

This 2019 edition includes the most recent Bankruptcy Court Miscellaneous Fee schedule, effective September 1, 2018, following 28 U.S.C. § 1930, along with the most recent Electronic Public Access Fee Schedule, effective April 1, 2017, following 28 U.S.C. §§ 1913 and 1930 and the most recent Court of Appeals Miscellaneous Fee schedule, effective September 1, 2018, following 28 U.S.C. § 1913. Revised and new Official Forms and Administrative Office Forms effective in 2018 are also included.

Judge William H. Brown and Lawrence R. Ahern, III prepared the "Bankruptcy Highlights" feature, in which they discuss recent bankruptcy law developments, including the 2018 amendments to the Federal Rules of Bankruptcy Procedure and Forms, amendments to the Federal Rules of Civil Procedure, amendments to the Federal Bankruptcy Code, and recent Supreme Court and Circuit Court decisions relevant to bankruptcy practitioners.

The Federal Rules of Civil Procedure and Federal Rules of Evidence, as amended, have been included to provide the practitioner with a "single source" reference for current bankruptcy laws, rules and forms. The Federal Rules of Civil Procedure govern adversary proceedings under Part VII and contested matters under Part IX of the Federal Rules of Bankruptcy Procedure. Bankruptcy Rule 9017 provides that the Federal Rules of Evidence govern evidentiary matters in bankruptcy proceedings.

The Department of Justice regulations relating to the United States Trustees—including United States Trustee Guidelines for Compensation and Reimbursement of Expenses Filed Under 11 U.S.C. § 330—are included, as well.

For comprehensive coverage of all aspects of bankrup   *y Law and Practice*. The *Bankruptcy Code Manual* by Michael J. H   , and John B. Corr contains a section-by-section explanation of Tit   *re Manual* by Lawrence R. Ahern, III and Nancy Fraas MacLean   *ntary and practical advice relating to the Federal Rules of Ba   ns of the Federal Rules of Evidence in bankruptcy proceedings   *y Evidence Manual* by Judge Barry Russell. The *Bankruptcy Exemption Manual* by Judge William H. Brown, Lawrence R. Ahern, III and Nancy Fraas MacLean discusses the use of state and federal exemptions to shelter assets in bankruptcy, and contains a detailed comparison of each state's exemption. Additional bankruptcy forms and commentary are provided in Volumes 6 and 6A of *West's Federal Forms* (by Hon. William Houston Brown, Lawrence R. Ahern, III and Nancy Fraas MacLean) and in Volumes 9 and 9A of *West's Legal Forms* (by Judge William H. Brown, Lawrence R. Ahern III and Nancy Fraas MacLean). *The Law of Debtors and Creditors* by Judge William H. Brown is a two-volume treatise that covers all aspects of the debtor-creditor relationship-from both points of view-and offers in-depth analysis of questions arising in bankruptcy, debt collection, consumer credit, and secured transactions.

For researching bankruptcy cases, see West's Bankruptcy Reporter and West's Bankruptcy Digest. Cross-references to the West Key Number System are provided throughout this 2019 Edition.

PREFACE

CONTACT US

For additional information or research assistance call the Reference Attorneys at 1-800-REF-ATTY (1-800-733-2889). Contact our U.S. legal editorial department directly with your questions and suggestions by e-mail at editors.us-legal@tr.com.

Thank you for subscribing to this product. Should you have any questions regarding this product, please contact Customer Service at 1-800-328-4880 or by fax at 1-800-340-9378. If you would like to inquire about related publications, or to place an order, please contact us at 1-888-728-7677 or visit us at legalsolutions.thomsonreuters.com.

THOMSON REUTERS PROVIEW™

This title is one of many now available on your tablet as an eBook.

Take your research mobile. Powered by the Thomson Reuters ProView™ app, our eBooks deliver the same trusted content as your print resources, but in a compact, on-the-go format.

ProView eBooks are designed for the way you work. You can add your own notes and highlights to the text, and all of your annotations will transfer electronically to every new edition of your eBook.

You can also instantly verify primary authority with built-in links to WestlawNext® and KeyCite®, so you can be confident that you're accessing the most current and accurate information.

To find out more about ProView eBooks and available discounts, call 1-800-344-5009.

TABLE OF CONTENTS

TABLE OF CONTENTS

BANKRUPTCY HIGHLIGHTS

By

William Houston Brown
Brown & Ahern
United States Bankruptcy Judge, 1987-2006
Western District of Tennessee

Lawrence R. Ahern III
Brown & Ahern
Nashville, Tennessee

I.   New Rules and Amendments to the Federal Rules of Bankruptcy Procedure and Federal Rules of Civil Procedure

The following summaries of new and changed bankruptcy and civil rules are adapted from publications for comment and submissions to Congress found on the website maintained by the Administrative Office of the U.S. Courts on behalf of the Federal Judiciary, www.uscourts.gov.

A.   Federal Rules of Bankruptcy Procedure

Absent contrary Congressional action, Federal Rules of Bankruptcy Procedure, Rules 3002.1, 5005, 7004, 7062, 8002, 8006, 8007, 8010, 8011, 8013, 8015, 8016, 8017, 8021, 8022, 9025 were amended in 2018, and a new Rule 8018.1 and Part VIII Appendix were adopted.

Rule 3002.1. Notice Relating to Claims Secured by Security Interest in the Debtor's Principal Residence. Subdivision (b) was amended to authorize courts to modify its requirements for claims arising from home equity lines of credit (HELOCs) and to clarify the procedure for a party in interest to object to a change in a home-mortgage payment amount after receiving notice of the change under subdivision (b)(1). Subdivision (e) was amended to clarify that any party in interest, such as the United States trustee, may seek a determination regarding the validity of any postpetition claimed fee, expense or charge noticed under subdivision (c). These changes are highlighted below:

> (b) Notice of Payment Changes; Objection.
>> (1) *Notice.* The holder of the claim shall file and serve on the debtor, debtor's counsel, and the trustee a notice of any change in the payment amount, including any change that results from an interest‑rate or escrow‑account adjustment, no later than 21 days before a payment in the new amount is due. <u>If the claim arises from a home-equity line of credit, this requirement may be modified by court order.</u>
>> (2) *Objection.* <u>A party in interest who objects to the payment change may file a motion to determine whether the change is required to maintain payments in accordance with § 1322(b)(5) of the Code. If no motion is filed by the day before the new amount is due, the change goes into effect, unless the court orders otherwise.</u>
>
> * * * * *
>
> (e) Determination of Fees, Expenses, or Charges. On motion of <u>a party in interest</u> ~~the debtor or trustee~~ filed within one year after service of a notice under subdivision (c) of this rule, the court shall, after notice and hearing, determine whether payment of any claimed fee, expense, or charge is required by the underlying agreement and applicable nonbankruptcy law to cure a default or maintain payments in accordance with § 1322(b)(5) of the Code.

Rule 5005. Filing and transmittal of papers. Electronic filing in the bankruptcy courts came of age in 2018. New Rule 5005(a)(2) makes it mandatory for most filers, with exceptions primarily for filings by individuals not represented by counsel. It is also now clear that a filing made through an ECF account and authorized by that person, along with that person's name on a signature block, is the person's signature. These changes are highlighted below:

> (a) Filing.
> * * * * *
>> (2) *Electronic Filing and Signing.*~~by Electronic Means~~.
>> (A) *By a Represented Entity—Generally Required; Exceptions.* ~~A court may by local rule permit or require documents to be filed, signed, or verified by electronic means that are consistent with technical standards, if any, that the Judicial Conference of the United States establishes. A local rule may require filing by electronic means only if reasonable exceptions are allowed.~~ <u>An entity represented by an attorney shall file electronically, unless nonelectronic filing is allowed by the court for good cause or is allowed or required by local rule.</u>

(B) *By an Unrepresented Individual—When Allowed or Required.* An individual not represented by an attorney:
(i) may file electronically only if allowed by court order or by local rule; and
(ii) may be required to file electronically only by court order, or by a local rule that includes reasonable exceptions.
(C) *Signing.* A filing made through a person's electronic-filing account and authorized by that person, together with that person's name on a signature block, constitutes the person's signature.
(D) *Same as a Written Paper.* A paper ~~document~~ filed electronically ~~by electronic means in compliance with a local rule constitutes~~ is a written paper for ~~the~~ purposes of ~~applying~~ these rules, the Federal Rules of Civil Procedure made applicable by these rules, and § 107 of the Code.

Rule 7004. Process; Service of Summons, Complaint. Rule 7004(a) was amended to update its cross-reference to Civil Rule 4. The change is highlighted below:

(a) Summons; Service; Proof Of Service.
(1) Except as provided in Rule 7004(a)(2), Rule 4(a), (b), (c)(1), (d)~~(1)~~(5), (e)–(j), (*l*), and (m) F.R.Civ.P. applies in adversary proceedings. Personal service under Rule 4(e)–(j) F.R.Civ.P. may be made by any person at least 18 years of age who is not a party, and the summons may be delivered by the clerk to any such person.
* * * * *

Rule 7062. Stay of Proceedings to Enforce a Judgment. Rule 7062 was amended to retain a 14-day period for the automatic stay of a judgment, while Civil Rule 62(a) now provides for a 30-day stay (accommodating the 28-day periods under the of Civil Rules for filing post-judgment motions and the 30-day period for filing a notice of appeal). The change is highlighted below:

Rule 62 F.R.Civ.P. applies in adversary proceedings, except that proceedings to enforce a judgment are stayed for 14 days after its entry.

Rule 8002. Time for Filing Notice of Appeal.

Subdivisions (a), (b), and (c) of Rule 8002 were clarified in 2018, modeled on parallel provisions of Appellate Rule 4. Paragraph (5) was added to subdivision (a) to clarify the effect of the separate-document requirement of Civil Rule 58(a) on the entry of a judgment, order, or decree for the purpose of determining the time for filing a notice of appeal for adversary proceedings. (Rule 9021, not Rule 58 applies in contested matters.) If Rule 58(a) requires a judgment to be set out in a separate document, the time for filing a notice of appeal runs--subject to subdivisions (b) and (c)--from when the judgment is docketed and the judgment is set out in a separate document or, if no separate document is prepared, from 150 days from when the judgment is entered in the docket. The court's failure to comply with the separate-document requirement of Rule 58(a), however, does not affect the validity of an appeal.

Responding to a circuit split concerning the meaning of "timely" in Appellate Rule 4(a)(4), a clarifying amendment to subdivision (b)(1) adopts the majority approach and rejects the approach taken in *National Ecological Foundation v. Alexander*, 496 F.3d 466 (6th Cir. 2007). A motion made after the time allowed by the Bankruptcy Rules will not qualify as a motion that, under Rule 8002(b)(1), re-starts the appeal time; this is not altered by, e.g., a court order that sets a due date that is later than permitted by the Bankruptcy Rules.

Subdivision (c)(1) was revised to conform to recent amendments of Appellate Rule 4(c)(1), which streamline and clarify the operation of the inmate-filing rule.

These changes are highlighted below:

(a) In General.
* * * * *

    (5) *Entry Defined.*
       (A) A judgment, order, or decree is entered for purposes of this Rule 8002(a):
          (i) when it is entered in the docket under Rule 5003(a), or
          (ii) if Rule 7058 applies and Rule 58(a) F.R.Civ.P. requires a separate document, when the judgment, order, or decree is entered in the docket under Rule 5003(a) and when the earlier of these events occurs:
          • the judgment, order, or decree is set out in a separate document; or
          • 150 days have run from entry of the judgment, order, or decree in the docket under Rule 5003(a).
       (B) A failure to set out a judgment, order, or decree in a separate document when required by Rule 58(a) F.R.Civ.P. does not affect the validity of an appeal from that judgment, order, or decree.
    (b) Effect of a Motion on the Time to Appeal.
       (1) *In General.* If a party ~~timely~~ files in the bankruptcy court any of the following motions and does so within the time allowed by these rules, the time to file an appeal runs for all parties from the entry of the order disposing of the last such remaining motion:
    * * * * *

(c) Appeal by an Inmate Confined in an Institution.

    (1) *In General.* <u>If an institution has a system designed for legal mail, an inmate confined there must use that system to receive the benefit of this Rule 8002(c)(1).</u> If an inmate ~~confined in an institution~~ files a notice of appeal from a judgment, order, or decree of a bankruptcy court, the notice is timely if it is deposited in the institution's internal mail system on or before the last day for filing~~. If the institution has a system designed for legal mail, the inmate must use that system to receive the benefit of this rule. Timely filing may be shown by a declaration in compliance with 28 U.S.C. § 1746 or by a notarized statement, either of which must set forth the date of deposit and state that first-class postage has been prepaid.~~ <u>and:</u>

        <u>(A) it is accompanied by:</u>

            <u>(i) a declaration in compliance with 28 U.S.C. § 1746—or a notarized statement—setting out the date of deposit and stating that first-class postage is being prepaid; or</u>

            <u>(ii) evidence (such as a postmark or date stamp) showing that the notice was so deposited and that postage was prepaid; or</u>

        <u>(B) the appellate court exercises its discretion to permit the later filing of a declaration or notarized statement that satisfies Rule 8002(c)(1)(A)(i).</u>

* * * * *

Rule 8006. Certifying a Direct Appeal to the Court of Appeals. Rule 8006(c) was amended to provide authority for the court to file a statement on the merits of a certification for direct review by the court of appeals when the certification is made jointly by all of the parties to the appeal, while Rule 8006(e)(2) continues to allow a party to file a similar statement. The court may file the supplemental statement within 14 days after the certification. These changes are highlighted below:

    (c) Joint Certification by all Appellants and Appellees.

        (1) *How Accomplished.* A joint certification by all the appellants and appellees under 28 U.S.C. § 158(d)(2)(A) must be made by using the appropriate Official Form. The parties may supplement the certification with a short statement of the basis for the certification, which may include the information listed in subdivision (f)(2).

        <u>(2) *Supplemental Statement by the Court.* Within 14 days after the parties' certification, the bankruptcy court or the court in which the matter is then pending may file a short supplemental statement about the merits of the certification.</u>

* * * * *

Rule 8007. Stay Pending Appeal; Bonds; Suspension of Proceedings. Rule 8007(a)(1)(B), (c) and (d) were amended to conform to amended Civil Rule 62 (made applicable to adversary proceedings by Rule 7062). Rule 62(b) was amended to change its "supersedeas bond" language, now allowing a party to obtain a stay by providing a "bond or other security." These changes are highlighted below:

(a) Initial Motion in the Bankruptcy Court.
    (1) *In General.* Ordinarily, a party must move first in the bankruptcy court for the following relief:
        (A) a stay of a judgment, order, or decree of the bankruptcy court pending appeal;
        (B) the approval of a ~~supersedeas~~ bond <u>or other security provided to obtain a stay of judgment</u>;

* * * * *

(c) Filing a Bond or Other Security. The district court, BAP, or court of appeals may condition relief on filing a bond or other ~~appropriate~~ security with the bankruptcy court.
(d) Bond or Other Security for a Trustee or the United States. The court may require a trustee to file a bond or other ~~appropriate~~ security when the trustee appeals. A bond or other security is not required when an appeal is taken by the United States, its officer, or its agency or by direction of any department of the federal government.

Rule 8010. Completing and Transmitting the Record. Rule 8010(c) was also amended consistent with an amendment of Civil Rule 62 (made applicable in adversary proceedings by Rule 7062). Rule 62(b) was amended to change its "supersedeas bond" language, now allowing a party to obtain a stay by providing a "bond or other security." These changes are highlighted below:

(c) Record for a Preliminary Motion in the District Court, Bap, or Court of Appeals. This subdivision (c) applies if, before the record is transmitted, a party moves in the district court, BAP, or court of appeals for any of the following relief:
    • leave to appeal;
    • dismissal;
    • a stay pending appeal;
    • approval of a ~~supersedeas~~ bond, or <u>other security provided to obtain a stay of judgment</u> ~~additional security on a bond or undertaking on appeal~~; or
    • any other intermediate order.
The bankruptcy clerk must then transmit to the clerk of the court where the relief is sought any parts of the record designated by a party to the appeal or a notice that those parts are available electronically.

Rule 8011. Filing and Service; Signature.

Rule 8011 was amended to conform to the amendments to Appellate Rule 25 on inmate filing, electronic filing, signature, service, and proof of service.

The rules in Part VIII moved toward broad acceptance of electronic filing well ahead of the new Rule 5005 (discussed above). Now, consistent with Rules 5005 and 8001(c), Rule 8011(a)(2) generally makes electronic filing mandatory, with exceptions for persons proceeding without an attorney, exceptions for good cause and variations established by local rule. Rule 8011(c) was amended to authorize electronic service by means of the court's electronic-filing system on registered users without requiring their written consent. All other forms of electronic service require the written consent of the person served. Rule 8011(d) eliminates the requirement of proof of service when service is made through the electronic-filing system. Finally, Rule 8011(e) requires the signature of counsel or an unrepresented party on every document that is filed. A filing made through a person's electronic-filing account and authorized by that person, together with that person's name on a signature block, is the "signature."

These changes are highlighted below:

(a) Filing.
* * * * *

 (2) *Method and Timeliness.*
  (A) *Nonelectronic Filing.*
  (A)(i) *In General.* Filing For a document not filed electronically, filing may be accomplished by transmission mail addressed to the clerk of the district court or BAP. Except as provided in subdivision (a)(2)(B) and (C) (a)(2)(A)(ii) and (iii), filing is timely only if the clerk receives the document within the time fixed for filing.
  (B)(ii) *Brief or Appendix.* A brief or appendix not filed electronically is also timely filed if, on or before the last day for filing, it is:
   (i): mailed to the clerk by first-class mail—or other class of mail that is at least as expeditious—postage prepaid, if the district court's or BAP's procedures permit or require a brief or appendix to be filed by mailing; or
   (ii): dispatched to a third-party commercial carrier for delivery within 3 days to the clerk, if the court's procedures so permit or require.
  (C)(iii) *Inmate Filing.* If an institution has a system designed for legal mail, an inmate confined there must use that system to receive the benefit of this Rule 8011(a)(2)(A)(iii). A document not filed electronically by an inmate confined in an institution is timely if it is deposited in the

institution's internal mailing system on or before the last day for filing. ~~If the institution has a system designed for legal mail, the inmate must use that system to receive the benefit of this rule. Timely filing may be shown by a declaration in compliance with 28 U.S.C. § 1746 or by a notarized statement, either of which must set forth the date of deposit and state that first-class postage has been prepaid.~~ and:

- it is accompanied by a declaration in compliance with 28 U.S.C. § 1746—or a notarized statement—setting out the date of deposit and stating that first-class postage is being prepaid; or evidence (such as a postmark or date stamp) showing that the notice was so deposited and that postage was prepaid; or

- the appellate court exercises its discretion to permit the later filing of a declaration or notarized statement that satisfies this Rule 8011(a)(2)(A)(iii).

(B) *Electronic Filing.*

    (i) *By a Represented Person—Generally Required; Exceptions.* An entity represented by an attorney must file electronically, unless nonelectronic filing is allowed by the court for good cause or is allowed or required by local rule.

    (ii) *By an Unrepresented Individual—When Allowed or Required.* An individual not represented by an attorney:

    - may file electronically only if allowed by court order or by local rule; and

    - may be required to file electronically only by court order, or by a local rule that includes reasonable exceptions.

    (iii) *Same as a Written Paper.* A document filed electronically is a written paper for purposes of these rules.

~~(D)~~(C) *Copies.* If a document is filed electronically, no paper copy is required. If a document is filed by mail or delivery to the district court or BAP, no additional copies are required. But the district court or BAP may require by local rule or by order in a particular case the filing or furnishing of a specified number of paper copies.

* * * * *

(c) Manner of Service.

    (1) *Nonelectronic Service. ~~Methods.~~ ~~Service must be made electronically, unless it is being made by or on an individual who is not represented by counsel or the court's governing rules permit or require service by mail or other means of delivery. Service~~* Nonelectronic service may be made by or on an ~~unrepresented party~~ by any of the following methods:

    (A) personal delivery;

    (B) mail; or

    (C) third-party commercial carrier for delivery within 3 days.

    (2) *Electronic Service.* Electronic service may be made by sending a document to a registered user by filing it with the court's electronic-filing system or by using other electronic means that the person served consented to in writing.

~~(2)~~(3) *When Service ~~is~~ Is Complete.* Service by electronic means is complete on ~~transmission~~ filing or sending, unless the ~~party~~ person making service receives notice that the document was not ~~transmitted successfully~~ received by the person served. Service by mail or by commercial carrier is complete on mailing or delivery to the carrier.

(d) Proof of Service.

    (1) *What ~~is~~ Is Required.* A document presented for filing must contain either of the following if it was served other than through the court's electronic-filing system:

        (A) an acknowledgment of service by the person served; or

        (B) proof of service consisting of a statement by the person who made service certifying:

            (i) the date and manner of service;

            (ii) the names of the persons served; and

            (iii) the mail or electronic address, the fax number, or the address of the place of delivery, as appropriate for the manner of service, for each person served.

* * * * *

(e) Signature. Every document filed electronically must include the electronic signature of the person filing it or, if the person is represented, the electronic signature of counsel. ~~The electronic signature must be provided by electronic means that are consistent with any technical standards that the Judicial Conference of the United States establishes.~~ A filing made through a person's electronic-filing account and authorized by that person, together with that person's name on a signature block, constitutes the person's signature. Every document filed in paper form must be signed by the person filing the document or, if the person is represented, by counsel.

Rule 8013. Motions; Intervention. Rule 8013(f)(3) was amended to conform to Appellate Rule 27(d)(2), by replacing page limits with word limits for motions and responses produced using a computer. Documents produced using a computer must include a certificate of compliance, satisfied by Official Form 417C. Page limits are still the standard for papers prepared without the aid of a computer. These changes are highlighted below:

(f) Form of Documents; ~~Page~~ length Limits; Number of Copies.
    * * * * *

    (2) *Format of an Electronically Filed Document.* A motion, response, or reply filed electronically must comply with the requirements for a paper version regarding covers, line spacing, margins, typeface, and type style. It must also comply with the ~~page~~ length limits under paragraph (3).

(3) ~~Page~~ Length Limits. ~~Unless the district court or BAP orders otherwise:~~ Except by the district court's or BAP's permission, and excluding the accompanying documents authorized by subdivision (a)(2)(C):
  (A) a motion or a response to a motion ~~must not exceed 20 pages, exclusive of the corporate disclosure statement and accompanying documents authorized by subdivision (a)(2)(C)~~ produced using a computer must include a certificate under Rule 8015(h) and not exceed 5,200 words; ~~and~~
  (B) ~~a reply to a response must not exceed 10 pages.~~ a handwritten or typewritten motion or a response to a motion must not exceed 20 pages;
  (C) a reply produced using a computer must include a certificate under Rule 8015(h) and not exceed 2,600 words; and
  (D) a handwritten or typewritten reply must not exceed 10 pages.

Rule 8015. Form and Length of Briefs; Form of Appendices and Other Papers.

Rule 8015 was amended to conform to recent amendments to Appellate Rule 32, reducing the word limits generally allowed for briefs. In a complex case, a party may need to file a longer brief and the drafters stated that "[t]he Committee expects that courts will accommodate those situations by granting leave to exceed the type-volume limitations as appropriate." Thus, Rule 8015(f) was amended to clarify the court's ability to increase the length limits for briefs and other documents extending this authority to all length limits in Part VIII.

Rule 8015(g) was added to set out a global list of items excluded from length computations, replacing the list of exclusions formerly found in Rule 8015(a)(7)(B)(iii). In a similar housekeeping change, the certificate-of-compliance provision was moved from Rule 8015(a)(7)(C) to a new Rule 8015(h); it now applies to filings under all type-volume limits, other than Rule 8014(f)'s word limit. Conforming amendments were made to Official Form 417C.

These changes are highlighted below:

(a) Paper Copies of a Brief. If a paper copy of a brief may or must be filed, the following provisions apply:
    * * * * *
  (7) Length.
    (A) Page limitation. A principal brief must not exceed 30 pages, or a reply brief 15 pages, unless it complies with subparagraph (B) ~~and (C)~~.
    (B) Type-volume limitation.
      (i) A principal brief is acceptable if it contains a certificate under Rule 8015(h) and:

> • ~~it~~ contains no more than ~~14,000~~ 13,000 words; or
> • ~~it~~ uses a monospaced face and contains no more than 1,300 lines of text.
>
> (ii) A reply brief is acceptable if it <u>includes a certificate under Rule 8015(h) and</u> contains no more than half of the type volume specified in item (i).
>
> (iii) ~~Headings, footnotes, and quotations count toward the word and line limitations. The corporate disclosure statement, table of contents, table of citations, statement with respect to oral argument, any addendum containing statutes, rules, or regulations, and any certificates of counsel do not count toward the limitation.~~
>
> ~~(C) *Certificate of Compliance.*~~
>
> ~~(i) A brief submitted under subdivision (a)(7)(B) must include a certificate signed by the attorney, or an unrepresented party, that the brief complies with the type-volume limitation. The person preparing the certificate may rely on the word or line count of the word-processing system used to prepare the brief. The certificate must state either:~~
> ~~• the number of words in the brief; or~~
> ~~• the number of lines of monospaced type in the brief.~~
>
> ~~(ii) The certification requirement is satisfied by a certificate of compliance that conforms substantially to the appropriate Official Form.~~

* * * * *

(f) Local Variation. A district court or BAP must accept documents that comply with the ~~applicable~~ <u>form</u> requirements of this rule <u>and the length limits set by Part VIII of these rules</u>. By local rule <u>or order in a particular case</u>, a district court or BAP may accept documents that do not meet all ~~of~~ the <u>form</u> requirements of this rule <u>or the length limits set by Part VIII of these rules</u>.

<u>(g) Items Excluded from Length. In computing any length limit, headings, footnotes, and quotations count toward the limit, but the following items do not:</u>
<u>• the cover page;</u>
<u>• a corporate disclosure statement;</u>
<u>• a table of contents;</u>
<u>• a table of citations;</u>
<u>• a statement regarding oral argument;</u>
<u>• an addendum containing statutes, rules, or regulations;</u>
<u>• certificates of counsel;</u>
<u>• the signature block;</u>
<u>• the proof of service; and</u>
<u>• any item specifically excluded by these rules or by local rule.</u>

(h) Certificate of Compliance.

<u>(1) *Briefs and Documents That Require a Certificate.* A brief submitted under Rule 8015(a)(7)(B), 8016(d)(2), or 8017(b)(4)—and a document submitted under Rule 8013(f)(3)(A), 8013(f)(3)(C), or 8022(b)(1)—must include a certificate by the attorney, or an unrepresented party, that the document complies with the type-volume limitation. The individual preparing the certificate may rely on the word or line count of the word-processing system</u>

used to prepare the document. The certificate must state the number of words—or the number of lines of monospaced type—in the document.

(2) *Acceptable Form.* The certificate requirement is satisfied by a certificate of compliance that conforms substantially to the appropriate Official Form.

Rule 8016. Cross–Appeals. Rule 8016 was amended to conform to recent amendments to Appellate Rule 28.1, which reduced the word limits generally allowed for briefs in cross-appeals. In a complex case, a party may need to file a brief that exceeds the type-volume limitations specified in these rules and the drafters indicated that "[t]he Committee expects that courts will accommodate those situations by granting leave to exceed the type-volume limitations as appropriate." These changes are highlighted below:

(d) Length.
- (1) *Page Limitation.* Unless it complies with paragraphs (2) and (3), the appellant's principal brief must not exceed 30 pages; the appellee's principal and response brief, 35 pages; the appellant's response and reply brief, 30 pages; and the appellee's reply brief, 15 pages.
- (2) *Type–Volume Limitation.*
  - (A) The appellant's principal brief or the appellant's response and reply brief is acceptable if it includes a certificate under Rule 8015(h) and:
    - (i) it contains no more than 14,000 13,000 words; or
    - (ii) it uses a monospaced face and contains no more than 1,300 lines of text.
  - (B) The appellee's principal and response brief is acceptable if it includes a certificate under Rule 8015(h) and:
    - (i) it contains no more than 16,500 15,300 words; or
    - (ii) it uses a monospaced face and contains no more than 1,500 lines of text.
  - (C) The appellee's reply brief is acceptable if it includes a certificate under Rule 8015(h) and contains no more than half of the type volume specified in subparagraph (A).
  - (D) Headings, footnotes, and quotations count toward the word and line limitations. The corporate disclosure statement, table of contents, table of citations, statement with respect to oral argument, any addendum containing statutes, rules, or regulations, and any certificates of counsel do not count toward the limitation.
- (3) *Certificate of Compliance.* A brief submitted either electronically or in paper form under paragraph (2) must comply with Rule 8015(a)(7)(C).

* * * * *

Rule 8017. Brief of an Amicus Curiae. Rule 8017 was amended to conform to recent amendments to Appellate Rule 29, which now addresses amicus filings in connection with petitions for rehearing, so renumbered Rule 8017(a) states that its provisions apply to amicus filings during the district court's or BAP's initial consideration of a case on the merits. Rule 8017(b) addresses such filings in connection with a motion for rehearing. Rule 8017(b) sets basic guidelines that apply when a district court or BAP does not provide otherwise by local rule or by order in a case. Rule 8017(a)(2) authorizes restrictions on an amicus brief that would result in a judge's disqualification. These changes are highlighted below:

(a) During Initial Consideration of a Case on the Merits.
  (1) *Applicability.* This Rule 8017(a) governs amicus filings during a court's initial consideration of a case on the merits.
  (2) *When Permitted.* The United States or its officer or agency or a state may file an amicus-curiae brief without the consent of the parties or leave of court. Any other amicus curiae may file a brief only by leave of court or if the brief states that all parties have consented to its filing, but a district court or BAP may prohibit the filing of or may strike an amicus brief that would result in a judge's disqualification. On its own motion, and with notice to all parties to an appeal, the district court or BAP may request a brief by an amicus curiae.
  (b)(3) *Motion for Leave to File.* The motion must be accompanied by the proposed brief and state:
    (1)(A) the movant's interest; and
    (2)(B) the reason why an amicus brief is desirable and why the matters asserted are relevant to the disposition of the appeal.
  (c)(4) *Contents and Form.* An amicus brief must comply with Rule 8015. In addition to the requirements of Rule 8015, the cover must identify the party or parties supported and indicate whether the brief supports affirmance or reversal. If an amicus curiae is a corporation, the brief must include a disclosure statement like that required of parties by Rule 8012. An amicus brief need not comply with Rule 8014, but must include the following:
    (1)(A) a table of contents, with page references;
    (2)(B) a table of authorities—cases (alphabetically arranged), statutes, and other authorities—with references to the pages of the brief where they are cited;
    (3)(C) a concise statement of the identity of the amicus curiae, its interest in the case, and the source of its authority to file;
    (4)(D) unless the amicus curiae is one listed in the first sentence of subdivision (a)(2), a statement that indicates whether:
      (A)(i) a party's counsel authored the brief in whole or in part;

(i)(ii) a party or a party's counsel contributed money that was intended to fund preparing or submitting the brief; and

(C)(iii) a person—other than the amicus curiae, its members, or its counsel—contributed money that was intended to fund preparing or submitting the brief and, if so, identifies each such person;

(5)(E) an argument, which may be preceded by a summary and need not include a statement of the applicable standard of review; and

(6)(F) a certificate of compliance, if required by Rule 8015(a)(7)(C) or 8015(b) (h).

(d)(5) *Length.* Except by the district court's or BAP's permission, an amicus brief must be no more than one-half the maximum length authorized by these rules for a party's principal brief. If the court grants a party permission to file a longer brief, that extension does not affect the length of an amicus brief.

(e)(6) *Time for Filing.* An amicus curiae must file its brief, accompanied by a motion for filing when necessary, no later than 7 days after the principal brief of the party being supported is filed. An amicus curiae that does not support either party must file its brief no later than 7 days after the appellant's principal brief is filed. The district court or BAP may grant leave for later filing, specifying the time within which an opposing party may answer.

(f)(7) *Reply Brief.* Except by the district court's or BAP's permission, an amicus curiae may not file a reply brief.

(g)(8) *Oral Argument.* An amicus curiae may participate in oral argument only with the district court's or BAP's permission.

(b) During Consideration of Whether to Grant Rehearing.

(1) *Applicability.* This Rule 8017(b) governs amicus filings during a district court's or BAP's consideration of whether to grant rehearing, unless a local rule or order in a case provides otherwise.

(2) *When Permitted.* The United States or its officer or agency or a state may file an amicus brief without the consent of the parties or leave of court. Any other amicus curiae may file a brief only by leave of court.

(3) *Motion for Leave to File.* Rule 8017(a)(3) applies to a motion for leave.

(4) *Contents, Form, and Length.* Rule 8017(a)(4) applies to the amicus brief. The brief must include a certificate under Rule 8015(h) and not exceed 2,600 words.

(5) *Time for Filing.* An amicus curiae supporting the motion for rehearing or supporting neither party must file its brief, accompanied by a motion for filing when necessary, no later than 7 days after the motion is filed. An amicus curiae opposing the motion for rehearing must file its brief, accompanied by a motion for filing when necessary, no later than the date set by the court for the response.

Rule 8018.1 District–Court Review of a Judgment that the Bankruptcy Court Lacked the Constitutional Authority to Enter *[New]*. New Rule 8018.1 was added to limit the circumstances in which a district court will have to remand an appeal when it determines that the bankruptcy court lacked constitutional authority to enter the judgment, order or decree appealed from. *Executive Benefits Insurance Agency v. Arkison*, 134 S. Ct. 2165 (2014), suggested this approach where the district court may treat the bankruptcy court's judgment as proposed findings of fact and conclusions of law. If the district court makes the determination to proceed in that manner, it may choose to allow the parties to file written objections to specific proposed findings and conclusions and to respond to another party's objections. See Rule 9033. Alternatively, it may treat the parties' briefs as objections and responses or prescribe other procedures. These changes are highlighted below:

> If, on appeal, a district court determines that the bankruptcy court did not have the power under Article III of the Constitution to enter the judgment, order, or decree appealed from, the district court may treat it as proposed findings of fact and conclusions of law.

Rule 8021. Costs. Rule 8021(c) now conforms with the amendment of Civil Rule 62 (made applicable in adversary proceedings by Rule 7062). Rule 62(b) was amended to change its "supersedeas bond" language, now allowing a party to obtain a stay by providing a "bond or other security." These changes are highlighted below:

> (c) Costs on Appeal Taxable in the Bankruptcy Court. The following costs on appeal are taxable in the bankruptcy court for the benefit of the party entitled to costs under this rule:
> (1) the production of any required copies of a brief, appendix, exhibit, or the record;
> (2) the preparation and transmission of the record;
> (3) the reporter's transcript, if needed to determine the appeal;
> (4) premiums paid for a ~~supersedeas~~ bond or other security ~~bonds~~ to preserve rights pending appeal; and
> (5) the fee for filing the notice of appeal.
> * * * * *

Rule 8022. Motion for Rehearing. Rule 8022(b) now conforms to Appellate Rule 40(b), which is one of several appellate rules in which word limits were substituted for page limits for documents prepared by computer. Documents produced using a computer must include the certificate of compliance required by Rule 8015(h) and provided by Official Form 417C. Page limits still apply to papers prepared without the aid of a computer. These changes are highlighted below:

> (b) Form of the Motion; Length. The motion must comply in form with Rule 8013(f)(1) and (2). Copies must be served and filed as provided by Rule 8011. ~~Unless the district court or BAP orders otherwise, a motion for rehearing must not exceed 15 pages.~~ Except by the district court's or BAP's permission:
> (1) a motion for rehearing produced using a computer must include a certificate under Rule 8015(h) and not exceed 3,900 words; and
> (2) a handwritten or typewritten motion must not exceed 15 pages.

Part VIII Appendix. An appendix adopted along with these changes is a chart showing the length limits stated in Part VIII of the Federal Rules of Bankruptcy Procedure.

Rule 9025. Security: Proceedings Against Sureties Security Providers.

Rule 9025 was also amended to reflect the amendment of Civil Rule 62 (made applicable to adversary proceedings by Rule 7062), so as not to limit the rule's enforcement procedures to sureties but instead covering all security providers. These changes are highlighted below:

> Whenever the Code or these rules require or permit ~~the giving of security by a party~~ a party to give security, and security is given ~~in the form of a bond or stipulation or other undertaking~~ with one or more ~~sureties~~ security providers, each ~~surety~~ provider submits to the jurisdiction of the court, and liability may be determined in an adversary proceeding governed by the rules in Part VII.

B.   Federal Rules of Civil Procedure

Absent contrary Congressional action, the Federal Rules of Civil Procedure, Rules 5, 23, 62 (applicable to bankruptcy practice) were amended in 2018. Civil Rule 65.1 was also amended but is inapplicable to bankruptcy practice and so is not detailed here.

Rule 5. Serving and Filing Pleadings and Other Papers.

Civil Rule 5 is applied to adversary proceedings by Bankruptcy Rule 7005. As with Bankruptcy Rule 5005, Rule 5(b) was amended to expand the provisions for electronic service. The amended rule recognizes electronic service through the court's transmission facilities as to any registered user. With the consent of the person served, electronic service also may be made by means that do not utilize the court's facilities. Service is complete when a person files the paper with the court's electronic-filing system for transmission to a registered user, or when one person sends it to another person by other electronic means that the other person has consented to in writing. Because Rule 5(b)(2)(E) now authorizes service through the court's facilities as a uniform national practice, Rule 5(b)(3) was abrogated. Rule 5(d)(1)(B) no longer requires a certificate of service when a paper is served by filing it with the court's electronic-filing system, but when service is not made by filing with the court's electronic-filing system, a certificate of service must still be filed with the paper or within a reasonable time after service, and should specify the date as well as the manner of service. Rule 5(d)(3) recognizes increased reliance on electronic filing by making it generally mandatory but exceptions continue to be available.

As in Bankruptcy Rule 5005, filings by a person proceeding without an attorney are treated separately and a filing made through a person's electronic-filing account and authorized by that person, together with that person's name on a signature block, constitutes the person's signature.

These changes are highlighted below:

(b) Service: How Made.
* * * * *

   (2) *Service in General.* A paper is served under this rule by:
    (A) handing it to the person;
    * * * * *

    (E) sending it to a registered user by filing it with the court's electronic-filing system or sending it by other electronic means that the person consented to in writing—in either of which events service is complete upon filing or sending, but is not effective if the filer or sender learns that it did not reach the person to be served; or
   * * * * *

   (3) *Using Court Facilities.* [Abrogated (Apr.   , 2018, eff. Dec. 1, 2018.)]
 * * * * *

(d) Filing.
   (1) *Required Filings; Certificate of Service.*

(A) *Papers after the Complaint.* Any paper after the complaint that is required to be served——must be filed no later than a reasonable time after service. But disclosures under Rule 26(a)(1) or (2) and the following discovery requests and responses must not be filed until they are used in the proceeding or the court orders filing: depositions, interrogatories, requests for documents or tangible things or to permit entry onto land, and requests for admission.

(B) *Certificate of Service.* No certificate of service is required when a paper is served by filing it with the court's electronic-filing system. When a paper that is required to be served is served by other means:
(i) if the paper is filed, a certificate of service must be filed with it or within a reasonable time after service; and
(ii) if the paper is not filed, a certificate of service need not be filed unless filing is required by court order or by local rule.

(2) *Nonelectronic Filing.* A paper not filed electronically is filed by delivering it:
(A) to the clerk; or
(B) to a judge who agrees to accept it for filing, and who must then note the filing date on the paper and promptly send it to the clerk.

(3) *Electronic Filing and Signing.*
(A) *By a Represented Person—Generally Required; Exceptions.* A person represented by an attorney must file electronically, unless nonelectronic filing is allowed by the court for good cause or is allowed or required by local rule.
(B) *By an Unrepresented Person—When Allowed or Required.* A person not represented by an attorney:
(i) may file electronically only if allowed by court order or by local rule; and
(ii) may be required to file electronically only by court order, or by a local rule that includes reasonable exceptions.
(C) *Signing.* A filing made through a person's electronic-filing account and authorized by that person, together with that person's name on a signature block, constitutes the person's signature.
(D) *Same as a Written Paper.* A paper filed electronically is a written paper for purposes of these rules.

Rule 23. Class Actions.

Rule 23, applied to bankruptcy practice by Bankruptcy Rule 7023, was amended mainly to address issues related to settlement, and also to take account of issues that have emerged since the rule was last amended in 2003. As amended, Rule 23(e)(1) provides that the court must direct notice to the class regarding a proposed class-action settlement only after determining that the prospect of class certification and approval of the proposed settlement justifies giving notice. This decision has been called "preliminary approval" of the proposed class certification in Rule 23(b)(3) actions. It is common to send notice to the class simultaneously under both Rule 23(e)(1) and Rule 23(c)(2)(B), including a provision for class members to decide by a certain date whether to opt out. This amendment recognizes the propriety of this combined notice practice. Subdivision (c)(2) was also amended to recognize contemporary methods of giving notice to class members. Since *Eisen v. Carlisle & Jacquelin*, 417 U.S. 156 (1974) (interpreting individual notice requirement for class members in Rule 23(b)(3) class actions), many courts have read the rule to require notice by first class mail in every case. But technological change since 1974 has introduced other means of communication that may sometimes provide a reliable additional or alternative method for giving notice. Although first class mail may often be the preferred primary method of giving notice, courts and counsel have begun to employ new technology to make notice more effective. Because there is no reason to expect that technological change will cease, when selecting a method or methods of giving notice courts should consider the capacity and limits of current technology, including class members' likely access to such technology. Rule 23(c)(2)(B) was amended to take account of these changes. Instead of preferring any one means of notice, the amended rule relies on courts and counsel to focus on the means or combination of means most likely to be effective in the case before the court.

The introductory paragraph of Rule 23(e) was amended to make explicit that its procedural requirements apply in instances in which the court has not certified a class at the time that a proposed settlement is presented to the court. The notice required under Rule 23(e)(1) then should also satisfy the notice requirements of amended Rule 23(c)(2)(B) for a class to be certified under Rule 23(b)(3), and trigger the class members' time to request exclusion. Information about the opt-out rate could then be available to the court when it considers final approval of the proposed settlement. The submissions required by Rule 23(e)(1) may provide information critical to decisions whether to object or opt out. Objections by class members can provide the court with important information bearing on its determination under Rule 23(e)(2) whether to approve the proposal.

Rule 23(e)(5)(A) was amended to remove the requirement of court approval for every withdrawal of an objection but Rule 23(e)(5)(B)(i) requires court approval of any payment or other consideration in connection with withdrawing the objection.

Rule 23(e)(5)(B) was amended to require approval of withdrawal of an objection under Rule 23(e)(5)(B)(i) only when consideration is involved. If the consideration involves a payment to counsel for an objector, the proper procedure is by motion under Rule 23(h) for an award of fees. Rule 23(e)(5)(B)(ii) applies to consideration in connection with forgoing, dismissing, or abandoning an appeal from a judgment approving the proposal. The rule requires that the motion seeking approval be made to the district court.

Rule 23(f) was amended to make it clear that an appeal under this rule is not permitted until the district court decides whether to certify the class and to extend the time to file a petition for review of a class-action certification order to 45 days whenever a party is the United States, one of its agencies, or a United States officer or employee sued for an act or omission occurring in connection with duties performed on the United States' behalf.

These changes are highlighted below:

(c) Certification Order; Notice to Class Members; Judgment; Issues Classes; Subclasses.
* * * * *
(2) *Notice.*
* * * * *
    (B) *For (b)(3) Classes.* For any class certified under Rule 23(b)(3) —or upon ordering notice under Rule 23(e)(1) to a class proposed to be certified for purposes of settlement under Rule 23(b)(3)—the court must direct to class members the best notice that is practicable under the circumstances, including individual notice to all members who can be identified through reasonable effort. The notice may be by one or more of the following: United States mail, electronic means, or other appropriate means. The notice must clearly and concisely state in plain, easily understood language:
* * * * *
(e) Settlement, Voluntary Dismissal, or Compromise. The claims, issues, or defenses of a certified class—or a class proposed to be certified for purposes of settlement—may be settled, voluntarily dismissed, or compromised only

with the court's approval. The following procedures apply to a proposed settlement, voluntary dismissal, or compromise:

(1) *Notice to the Class.*

    (A) *Information That Parties Must Provide to the Court.* The parties must provide the court with information sufficient to enable it to determine whether to give notice of the proposal to the class.

    (B) *Grounds for a Decision to Give Notice.* The court must direct notice in a reasonable manner to all class members who would be bound by the proposal if giving notice is justified by the parties' showing that the court will likely be able to:

        (i) approve the proposal under Rule 23(e)(2); and

        (ii) certify the class for purposes of judgment on the proposal.

(2) *Approval of the Proposal.* If the proposal would bind class members, the court may approve it only after a hearing and only on finding that it is fair, reasonable, and adequate after considering whether:

    (A) the class representatives and class counsel have adequately represented the class;

    (B) the proposal was negotiated at arm's length;

    (C) the relief provided for the class is adequate, taking into account:

        (i) the costs, risks, and delay of trial and appeal;

        (ii) the effectiveness of any proposed method of distributing relief to the class, including the method of processing class-member claims;

        (iii) the terms of any proposed award of attorney's fees, including timing of payment; and

        (iv) any agreement required to be identified under Rule 23(e)(3); and

    (D) the proposal treats class members equitably relative to each other.

(3) *Identifying Agreements.* The parties seeking approval must file a statement identifying any agreement made in connection with the proposal.

(4) *New Opportunity to Be Excluded.* If the class action was previously certified under Rule 23(b)(3), the court may refuse to approve a settlement unless it affords a new opportunity to request exclusion to individual class members who had an earlier opportunity to request exclusion but did not do so.

(5) *Class–Member Objections.*

    (A) *In General.* Any class member may object to the proposal if it requires court approval under this subdivision (e) The objection must state whether it applies only to the objector, to a specific subset of the class, or to the entire class, and also state with specificity the grounds for the objection.

    (B) *Court Approval Required for Payment in Connection with an Objection.* Unless approved by the court after a hearing, no payment or other consideration may be provided in connection with:

        (i) forgoing or withdrawing an objection, or

        (ii) forgoing, dismissing, or abandoning an appeal from a judgment approving the proposal.

> (C) *Procedure for Approval After an Appeal.* If approval under Rule 23(e)(5)(B) has not been obtained before an appeal is docketed in the court of appeals, the procedure of Rule 62.1 applies while the appeal remains pending.

(f) Appeals. A court of appeals may permit an appeal from an order granting or denying class-action certification under this rule, but not from an order under Rule 23(e)(1). A party must file a petition for permission to appeal with the circuit clerk within 14 days after the order is entered, or within 45 days after the order is entered if any party is the United States, a United States agency, or a United States officer or employee sued for an act or omission occurring in connection with duties performed on the United States' behalf. An appeal does not stay proceedings in the 118 district court unless the district judge or the court of appeals so orders.

Rule 62. Stay of Proceedings to Enforce a Judgment. Rule 62 is applied to bankruptcy practice by Bankruptcy Rule 7062, which was also amended in 2018. Subdivisions (a), (b), (c), and (d) of former Rule 62 were reorganized and the provisions for staying a judgment are revised. The language is revised to include all of the words used in 28 U.S.C. § 1292(a)(1) to describe the right to appeal from interlocutory actions with respect to an injunction, but subdivisions (c) and (d) apply both to interlocutory injunction orders and to final judgments that grant, refuse, or otherwise deal with an injunction. New Rule 62(a) extends the period of the automatic stay to 30 days, necessitating the change in Bankruptcy Rule 7062 described above, and expressly recognizes the court's authority to dissolve the automatic stay or supersede it by a court-ordered stay. Rule 62(b) carries forward in modified form the provisions for supersedeas bonds. These changes are highlighted below:

> (a) Automatic Stay. Except as provided in Rule 62(c) and (d), on a judgment and proceedings to enforce it are stayed for 30 days after its entry, unless the court orders otherwise.
> (b) Stay by Bond or Other Security. At any time after judgment is entered, a party may obtain a stay by providing a bond or other security. The stay takes effect when the court approves the bond or other security and remains in effect for the time specified in the bond or other security.
> (c) Stay of an Injunction, Receivership, or Patent Accounting Order. Unless the court orders otherwise, the following are not stayed after being entered, even if an appeal is taken:
>> (1) an interlocutory or final judgment in an action for an injunction or receivership; or

(2) a judgment or order that directs an accounting in an action for patent infringement.

(d) Injunction Pending an Appeal. While an appeal is pending from an interlocutory order or final judgment that grants, continues, modifies, refuses, dissolves, or refuses to dissolve or modify an injunction, the court may suspend, modify, restore, or grant an injunction on terms for bond or other terms that secure the opposing party's rights. If the judgment appealed from is rendered by a statutory three-judge district court, the order must be made either:

(1) by that court sitting in open session; or

(2) by the assent of all its judges, as evidenced by their signatures.

II. Amendments to Bankruptcy Code – Automatic adjustment in monetary amounts

Under 28 U.S.C.A. § 104(a), it is anticipated that effective April 1, 2019, the three-year automatic adjustment to various monetary amounts in the Bankruptcy Code will occur. The Code sections in Title 11 subject to this automatic adjustment are: sections 101(3), 101(18), 101(19A), 101(51D), 109(e), 303(b), 507(a), 522(d), 522(f)(3) and 522(f)(4), 522(n), 522(p), 522(q), 523(a)(2)(C), 541(b), 547(c)(9), 707(b), 1322(d), 1325(b), and 1326(b)(3). Section 1409(b) of Title 28 is also subject to automatic adjustment. The adjusted amounts will be published by the Judicial Conference of the United States in the Federal Register by March 1, 2019, under the provision of 11 U.S.C.A. § 104(b).

III. Changes to Official Bankruptcy and Director's Forms

A. Changes to Official Bankruptcy Forms effective December 1, 2018

According the website of the Administrative Office of the United States Courts, www.uscourts.gov, several proposed amendments to Official Forms and Director's Forms are on track to be effective December 1, 2018. Proposed amendments to Official Forms 417A and 417B were approved by the Judicial Conference in September 2017, and proposed amendments to Official Forms 411A and 411B were approved by the Judicial Conference in September 2018. New or revised Director's Forms 2000, 3180W and 4170 also take effect December 1, 2018.

The following Committee Notes or brief descriptions explain the form changes.

BANKRUPTCY HIGHLIGHTS

Official Bankruptcy Form 4011A—General Power of Attorney

Committee Note: This form replaces Director's Bankruptcy Form 4011A, which, in turn, was derived from former Official Form 11A in 2015 as part of the Bankruptcy Forms Modernization project.

Parties routinely modify the General Power of Attorney form to conform to state law, the needs of the case, or local practice. Because the exact language of the form is not needed, and Rule 9009, as amended on December 1, 2017, generally restricts alteration of the Official Forms, the form was abrogated as an Official Bankruptcy Form and reissued as a Director's Bankruptcy Form.

Bankruptcy Rule 9010(c), however, requires that "[t]he authority of any agent, attorney in fact, or proxy to represent a creditor for any purpose . . . shall be evidenced by a power of attorney *conforming substantially to the appropriate Official Form*" (emphasis added). The form is therefore reissued as an Official Form. Because only substantial conformity to the Official Form is required by Rule 9010(c), parties will be able to continue modifying the form as needed to conform to state law, the needs of the case, or local practice.

Official Bankruptcy Form 4011B—Special Power of Attorney

Committee Note: This form replaces Director's Bankruptcy Form 4011B, which, in turn, was derived from former Official Form 11B in 2015 as part of the Bankruptcy Forms Modernization project.

Parties routinely modify the Special Power of Attorney form to conform to state law, the needs of the case, or local practice. Because the exact language of the form is not needed, and Rule 9009, as amended on December 1, 2017, generally restricts alteration of the Official Forms, the form was abrogated as an Official Bankruptcy Form and reissued as a Director's Bankruptcy Form.

Bankruptcy Rule 9010(c), however, requires that "[t]he authority of any agent, attorney in fact, or proxy to represent a creditor for any purpose . . . shall be evidenced by a power of attorney *conforming substantially to the appropriate Official Form*" (emphasis added). The form is therefore reissued as an Official Form. Because only substantial conformity to the Official Form is required by Rule 9010(c), parties will be able to continue modifying the form as needed to conform to state law, the needs of the case, or local practice.

Official Bankruptcy Form 417A—Notice of Appeal and Statement of Election

Committee Note: The form is amended to include (at the end of the form) a notice to inmate filers that Director's Form 4170 may be used to provide a declaration under Rule 8002(c)(1) regarding the mailing of a notice of appeal using an institution's legal mail system.

Official Bankruptcy Form 417C—Certificate of Compliance with Type-Volume Limit, Typeface Requirements, and Type-Style Requirements

Committee Note: The form is amended to reflect changes in the length limits specified by Part VIII of the Bankruptcy Rules for appellate documents and the broadened requirement for a certificate of compliance under Rule 8015(h). The rule now requires certification of compliance with the type-volume or word limits for briefs filed under Rule 8015(a)(7)(b), 8016(d)(2), or 8017(b)(4), and documents filed under Rule 8013(f)(3)(A), 8013(f)(3)(C), or 8022(b)(1).

B. Changes to Director's Bankruptcy Forms effective December 1, 2018

In addition to changes to the Official Bankruptcy Forms described above, the following new or amended Director's Forms will go into effect December 1, 2018:

Form 2000--Required Lists, Schedules, Statements and Fees

The language on the form following the checkbox labeled "Chapter 13 Plan" on page 4 is revised to provide: "(Official Form 113), or local form plan (check with your local court for required plan version). Fed. R. Bankr. P. 3015.1. Must be filed with the petition or within 14 days. Fed. R. Bankr. P. 3015."

BANKRUPTCY HIGHLIGHTS

Form 3180W--Order of Discharge in Chapter 13 Case

The bullet point on page 2 of the form, describing certain debts not discharged in Chapter 13, was changed from "debts for most fines, penalties, forfeitures, or criminal restitution obligations" to "debts for restitution, or a criminal fine, included in a sentence on debtor's criminal conviction." The revised language is derived from 11 U.S.C. § 1328(a)(3).

New Director's Form 4170--Declaration of Inmate Filing

The new form is designed to comply with pending Bankruptcy Rule 8002(c)(1)(A), that takes effect December 1, 2018.

IV. Changes to Miscellaneous Bankruptcy Fees

The Miscellaneous Fee schedule was revised by the Administrative Office of United States Courts, effective September 1, 2018, as found on the website of the Administrative Office, www.uscourts.gov and issued in accordance with 28 U.S.C. § 1930.

Bankruptcy Court Miscellaneous Fee Schedule

The fees included in the Bankruptcy Court Miscellaneous Fee Schedule are to be charged for services provided by the bankruptcy courts, effective on: September 1, 2018:

- The United States should not be charged fees under this schedule, with the exception of those specifically prescribed in Items 1, 3 and 5 when the information requested is available through remote electronic access.

- Federal agencies or programs that are funded from judiciary appropriations (agencies, organizations, and individuals providing services authorized by the Criminal Justice Act, 18 U.S.C. § 3006A, and bankruptcy administrators) should not be charged any fees under this schedule.

BANKRUPTCY HIGHLIGHTS

1. a. For reproducing any document and providing a copy in paper form, $.50 per page. This fee applies to services rendered on behalf of the United States if the document requested is available through electronic access.

   b. For reproducing and transmitting in any manner a copy of an electronic record stored outside of the court's electronic case management system, including but not limited to, document files, audio recordings, and video recordings, $31 per record provided. Audio recordings of court proceedings continue to be governed by a separate fee under item 3 of this schedule.

2. For certification of any document, $11.
   For exemplification of any document, $22.

3. For reproduction of an audio recording of a court proceeding, $31. This fee applies to services rendered on behalf of the United States if the recording is available electronically.

4. For filing an amendment to the debtor's schedules of creditors, lists of creditors, or mailing list, $31, except:

   o The bankruptcy judge may, for good cause, waive the charge in any case.

   o This fee must not be charged if -

     ▪ the amendment is to change the address of a creditor or an attorney for a creditor listed on the schedules; or

     ▪ the amendment is to add the name and address of an attorney for a creditor listed on the schedules.

5. For conducting a search of the bankruptcy court records, $31 per name or item searched. This fee applies to services rendered on behalf of the United States if the information requested is available through electronic access.

6. For filing a complaint, $350, except:

- o If the trustee or debtor-in-possession files the complaint, the fee must be paid only by the estate, to the extent there is an estate.

- o This fee must not be charged if -

  - the debtor is the plaintiff; or

  - a child support creditor or representative files the complaint and submits the form required by § 304(g) of the Bankruptcy Reform Act of 1994.

7. For filing any document that is not related to a pending case or proceeding, $47.

8. Administrative fee:

   - o For filing a petition under Chapter 7, 12, or 13, $75.

   - o For filing a petition under Chapter 9, 11, or 15, $550.

   - o When a motion to divide a joint case under Chapter 7, 12, or 13 is filed, $75

   - o When a motion to divide a joint case under Chapter 11 is filed, $550.

9. For payment to trustees pursuant to 11 U.S.C. § 330(b)(2), a $15 fee applies in the following circumstances:

   - o For filing a petition under Chapter 7.

   - o For filing a notice of conversion to a Chapter 7 case.

   - o For filing a motion to convert a case to a Chapter 7 case.

   - o For filing a motion to divide a joint Chapter 7 case.

   - o For filing a motion to reopen a Chapter 7 case.

10. In addition to any fees imposed under Item 9, above, the following fees must be collected:

BANKRUPTCY HIGHLIGHTS

- For filing a motion to convert a Chapter 12 case to a Chapter 7 case or a notice of conversion pursuant to 11 U.S.C. § 1208(a), $45.

- For filing a motion to convert a Chapter 13 case to a Chapter 7 case or a notice of conversion pursuant to 11 U.S.C. § 1307(a), $10.

The fee amounts in this item are derived from the fees prescribed in 28 U.S.C. § 1930(a).

If the trustee files the motion to convert, the fee is payable only from the estate that exists prior to conversion.

If the filing fee for the chapter to which the case is requested to be converted is less than the fee paid at the commencement of the case, no refund may be provided.

11. For filing a motion to reopen, the following fees apply:

- For filing a motion to reopen a Chapter 7 case, $245.

- For filing a motion to reopen a Chapter 9 case, $1167.

- For filing a motion to reopen a Chapter 11 case, $1167.

- For filing a motion to reopen a Chapter 12 case, $200.

- For filing a motion to reopen a Chapter 13 case, $235.

- For filing a motion to reopen a Chapter 15 case, $1167.

The fee amounts in this item are derived from the fees prescribed in 28 U.S.C.§ 1930(a).

The reopening fee must be charged when a case has been closed without a discharge being entered.

The court may waive this fee under appropriate circumstances or may defer payment of the fee from trustees pending discovery of additional assets. If payment is deferred, the fee should be waived if no additional assets are discovered.

The reopening fee must not be charged in the following situations:

- to permit a party to file a complaint to obtain a determination under Rule 4007(b); or

- when a debtor files a motion to reopen a case based upon an alleged violation of the terms of the discharge under 11 U.S.C. § 524; or

- when the reopening is to correct an administrative error.

- to redact a record already filed in a case, pursuant to Fed. R. Bankr. P. 9037, if redaction is the only reason for reopening.

12. For retrieval of one box of records from a Federal Records Center, National Archives, or other storage location removed from the place of business of the court, $64. For retrievals involving multiple boxes, $39 for each additional box. For electronic retrievals, $10 plus any charges assessed by the Federal Records Center, National Archives, or other storage location removed from the place of business of the courts.

13. For any payment returned or denied for insufficient funds, $53.

14. For filing an appeal or cross appeal from a judgment, order, or decree, $293.

> This fee is collected in addition to the statutory fee of $5 that is collected under 28 U.S.C. § 1930 (c) when a notice of appeal is filed.

> Parties filing a joint notice of appeal should pay only one fee.

> If a trustee or debtor-in-possession is the appellant, the fee must be paid only by the estate, to the extent there is an estate.

> Upon notice from the court of appeals that a direct appeal or direct cross-appeal has been authorized, an additional fee of $207 must be collected.

15. For filing a case under Chapter 15 of the Bankruptcy Code, $1167.

    This fee is derived from and equal to the fee prescribed in 28 U.S.C. § 1930(a)(3) for filing a case commenced under Chapter 11 of Title 11.

16. The court may charge and collect fees commensurate with the cost of providing copies of the local rules of court. The court may also distribute copies of the local rules without charge.

17.

   - For handling registry funds deposited with and held by the court, the clerk shall asses a charge from interest earnings, in accordance with the detailed fee schedule issued by the Director of the Administrative Office of the United States Courts.

   - For management of registry funds invested through the Court Registry Investment System, a fee at an annual rate of 10 basis points of assets on deposit shall be assessed from interest earnings, excluding registry funds from disputed ownership interpleader cases deposited under 28 U.S.C. § 1335 and held in a Court Registry Investment System Disputed Ownership Fund.

   - For management of funds deposited under 28 U.S.C. § 1335 and invested in a Disputed Ownership Fund through the Court Registry Investment System, a fee at an annual rate of 20 basis points of assets on deposit shall be assessed from interest earnings.

   - The Director of the Administrative Office has the authority to waive these fees for cause.

18. For a motion filed by the debtor to divide a joint case filed under 11 U.S.C. § 302, the following fees apply:

   - For filing a motion to divide a joint Chapter 7 case, $245.

   - For filing a motion to divide a joint Chapter 11 case, $1167.

- For filing a motion to divide a joint Chapter 12 case, $200.

- For filing a motion to divide a joint Chapter 13 case, $235.

  These fees are derived from and equal to the filing fees prescribed in 28 U.S.C.§ 1930(a).

19. For filing the following motions, $181:

- To terminate, annul, modify or condition the automatic stay;

- To compel abandonment of property of the estate pursuant to Rule 6007(b) of the Federal Rules of Bankruptcy Procedure;

- To withdraw the reference of a case or proceeding under 28 U.S.C. § 157(d); or

- To sell property of the estate free and clear of liens under 11 U.S.C. § 363(f).

  This fee must not be collected in the following situations:

- For a motion for relief from the co-debtor stay;

- For a stipulation for court approval of an agreement for relief from a stay; or

- For a motion filed by a child support creditor or its representative, if the form required by § 304(g) of the Bankruptcy Reform Act of 1994 is filed.

  20. For filing a transfer of claim, $25 per claim transferred.

21. For filing a motion to redact a record, $25 per affected case. The court may waive this fee under appropriate circumstances.

V.   Recent Supreme Court Cases of Interest to Bankruptcy Practitioners

The Supreme Court has handed down three decisions of interest to the bankruptcy bench and bar. Several more are awaiting action on petitions for certiorari and others were returned to the circuits.

BANKRUPTCY HIGHLIGHTS

A.   Bankruptcy decisions

Merit Management Group, LP v. FTI Consulting, Inc., 138 S. Ct. 883, 200 L. Ed. 2d 183, 65 Bankr. Ct. Dec. (CRR) 92, Bankr. L. Rep. (CCH) P 83219 (2018). The trustee of a litigation trust, created pursuant to a confirmed Chapter 11 plan of a debtor that sought to develop a "racino" in Pennsylvania, brought an adversary proceeding seeking to avoid the debtor's allegedly fraudulent transfers to the partial owner of a competitor of the debtor, as part of the debtor's purchase of the competitor's stock. The Supreme Court held that the only relevant transfer for purposes of the Bankruptcy Code's "securities safe harbor" provision, 11 U.S.C.A. § 546(e), is the transfer that the trustee seeks to avoid under a substantive avoiding power, that is, the overarching or end-to-end transfer, not any component part of that transfer, abrogating *In re Quebecor World (USA) Inc.*, 719 F.3d 94 (2d Cir. 2013), *In re QSI Holdings, Inc.*, 571 F.3d 545 (6th Cir. 2009), *Contemporary Indus. Corp. v. Frost*, 564 F.3d 981 (8th Cir. 2009), *In re Resorts Int'l, Inc.*, 181 F.3d 505 (3d Cir. 1999), and *In re Kaiser Steel Corp.*, 952 F.2d 1230 (10th Cir. 1991). Here, the transfer between debtor and transferee was not "made by or to (or for the benefit of)" a financial institution and so fell outside the safe harbor.

U.S. Bank Nat. Ass'n ex rel. CWCapital Asset Management LLC v. Village at Lakeridge, LLC, 138 S. Ct. 960, 200 L. Ed. 2d 218, 65 Bankr. Ct. Dec. (CRR) 91, Bankr. L. Rep. (CCH) P 83220 (2018). In a Chapter 11 case, the trustee moved to designate a creditor's claim and disallow the creditor's vote to confirm the plan. The bankruptcy court held that the creditor did not qualify as a non-statutory insider and the trustee appealed. The Supreme Court affirmed, issuing a limited holding that the bankruptcy court's determination resolved a mixed question of law and fact, subject only to review for clear error.

Lamar, Archer & Cofrin, LLP v. Appling, 138 S. Ct. 1752, 201 L. Ed. 2d 102, 65 Bankr. Ct. Dec. (CRR) 194, Bankr. L. Rep. (CCH) P 83247 (2018). A law firm brought an adversary proceeding to except a Chapter 7 debtor-client's debt from his discharge on the basis of "false pretenses, false representation, or actual fraud." 11 U.S.C.A. § 523(a)(2). The debtor made false statements orally regarding a large tax refund to a law firm providing legal services in reliance on being compensated from the tax refund. The bankruptcy court held that the judgment obtained by the law firm against debtors was nondischargeable and the district court agreed, but the Eleventh Circuit reversed. The Supreme Court affirmed, holding that a statement about a single asset can be a "statement respecting the debtor's financial condition," within meaning of the fraud discharge exception, abrogating *In re Bandi*, 683 F.3d 671 (5th Cir. 2012) and *In re Joelson*, 427 F.3d 700 (10th Cir. 2005). Another circuit decision, not mentioned in the opinion, *In re Lauer*, 371 F.3d 406 (8th Cir. 2004), had also concluded that the phrase "a statement respecting the debtor's ... financial condition" must be construed narrowly, to refer to only those statements about a debtor's overall net worth.

B.   Pending cases

Obduskey v. Wells Fargo, 879 F.3d 1216 (10th Cir. 2018), cert. granted, 138 S. Ct. 2710 (2018). The Court is to review the question of whether the Fair Debt Collection Practices Act applies to non-judicial foreclosure proceedings.

In re Tempnology, LLC, 879 F.3d 389, 65 Bankr. Ct. Dec. (CRR) 23, Bankr. L. Rep. (CCH) P 83196 (1st Cir. 2018), certiorari granted in part, 2018 WL 2939184 (U.S. 2018). The Court of Appeals' holding is discussed in the First Circuit's decisions below.

In re Taggart, 888 F.3d 438, 65 Bankr. Ct. Dec. (CRR) 145, Bankr. L. Rep. (CCH) P 83243 (9th Cir. 2018), cert. docketed, Taggart v. Lorenzen, No. 18-489 (U.S., Oct. 16, 2018). The Court of Appeals' holding is discussed in the Ninth Circuit's decisions below.

C.   Other actions of interest to bankruptcy practitioners

Epic Systems Corp. v. Lewis, 138 S. Ct. 1612, 200 L. Ed. 2d 889, 211 L.R.R.M. (BNA) 3061, 27 Wage & Hour Cas. 2d (BNA) 1197, 168 Lab. Cas. (CCH) P 11091 (2018). This opinion decided three cases involving arbitration clauses in employment contracts. In two (from the Seventh and Ninth Circuits), the employees brought putative collective and class actions, alleged that their employers violated the

Fair Labor Standards Act (FLSA) and state law by misclassifying employees and thereby depriving them of overtime pay. In the third (from the Fifth Circuit), the employer sought review of an order of the National Labor Relations Board (NLRB), finding that the employer had unlawfully required employees to sign arbitration agreements waiving their right to pursue class and collective actions. The Supreme Court, 5-4, upheld and enforced the arbitration agreement, holding that the Federal Arbitration Act (FAA) did not provide a basis for refusing to enforce arbitration agreements waiving collective action procedures for claims under the FLSA or class action procedures for claims under state law. Neither the National Labor Relations Act nor the FLSA displaces the FAA and outlaws class and collective action waivers (abrogating *NLRB v. Alternative Entertainment, Inc.*, 858 F.3d 393 (6th Cir. 2017)). The ruling purports to be limited, merely declining to read into the law "a novel right to class action procedures," which novel right "the Board's own general counsel disclaimed as recently as 2010." 138 S. Ct. at 1630. See also the Court's action denying review of *Anderson v. Credit One Bank N.A. (In re Anderson)*, 884 F.3d 382 (2d Cir. 2018), cert. denied, *Credit One Bank N.A. v. Anderson*, 2018 WL 2876199 (U.S. Oct. 1, 2018), discussed in the Second Circuit's actions, below, where a bankruptcy court denied arbitration of a dispute over violation of the discharge injunction.

In re Whitley, 848 F.3d 205, 63 Bankr. Ct. Dec. (CRR) 178, 77 Collier Bankr. Cas. 2d (MB) 413, Bankr. L. Rep. (CCH) P 83068 (4th Cir. 2017), cert. denied, 138 S. Ct. 314, 199 L. Ed. 2d 207 (2017); Matter of Walldesign, Inc., 872 F.3d 954, 64 Bankr. Ct. Dec. (CRR) 195, Bankr. L. Rep. (CCH) P 83163 (9th Cir. 2017), cert. denied, 138 S. Ct. 2575, 201 L. Ed. 2d 293 (2018). The Supreme Court declined to resolve a circuit split and provide clarification of the definition of a "transfer" or an "initial transferee," on petitions from decisions of the Fourth and Ninth Circuits. In *In re Whitley*, a chapter 7 trustee brought an adversary proceeding to avoid prepetition funds transfers by the debtor (operator of an alleged Ponzi scheme), as actually fraudulent to creditors. The bankruptcy court granted the defendant's motion for summary judgment and the district and circuit courts, affirmed, holding that the trustee could not avoid, as "transfers" of interests of the debtor in property, prepetition deposits and wire transfers into the debtor's unrestricted checking account. *In re Walldesign* is discussed in the Ninth Circuit's decisions, below.

Matter of Jackson, 850 F.3d 816, 63 Bankr. Ct. Dec. (CRR) 231, 77 Collier Bankr. Cas. 2d (MB) 619, Bankr. L. Rep. (CCH) P 83076 (5th Cir. 2017), cert. denied, 138 S. Ct. 506, 199 L. Ed. 2d 386 (2017). The Court of Appeals held that collection of garnished wages earned during the preference period under 11 U.S.C.A. § 547 is a voidable transfer, even if the garnishment order was served prior to the preference period.

In re Sunnyslope Housing Limited Partnership, 859 F.3d 637, 64 Bankr. Ct. Dec. (CRR) 51, 77 Collier Bankr. Cas. 2d (MB) 1338, 77 Collier Bankr. Cas. 2d (MB) 1670, Bankr. L. Rep. (CCH) P 83115 (9th Cir. 2017), as amended, (June 23, 2017) and cert. denied, 138 S. Ct. 648, 199 L. Ed. 2d 530 (2018). The Ninth Circuit applied the Supreme Court's standard in *Associates Commercial Corp. v. Rash*, 520 U.S. 953, 963, 117 S. Ct. 1879, 138 L. Ed. 2d 148 (1997) (holding that replacement value, "rather than a foreclosure sale that will not take place, is the proper guide under a prescription hinged to the property's 'disposition or use'" (quoting *In re Winthrop Old Farm Nurseries, Inc.*, 50 F.3d 72, 75 (1st Cir. 1995)), to rule that the bankruptcy court did not err when it determined a lower value for the debtor's apartment complex by considering low-income housing restrictions included in the liens on the property, even though the restrictions would be released at foreclosure, causing the property to have a higher value at foreclosure.

In re Jemsek Clinic, P.A., 850 F.3d 150, 63 Bankr. Ct. Dec. (CRR) 221 (4th Cir. 2017), cert. dismissed, 138 S. Ct. 1611, 200 L. Ed. 2d 791 (2018). Chapter 11 debtors, after litigating their counterclaims against an insurer for more than a year, learned that the counterclaims were identical to claims asserted against an insurer in an undisclosed class action pending in another forum and that their failure to opt out of class settlement barred them from pursuing the majority of these counterclaims on *res judicata* grounds. They moved to impose sanctions on the insurer for its alleged breach of its disclosure obligations. The bankruptcy court entered an order awarding sanctions, and the insurer appealed. The Court of Appeals vacated and remanded, finding that the bankruptcy court abused its discretion when, as a sanction imposed in the exercise of its inherent authority, it (1) dismissed the insurer's multimillion claim against the estate and (2) awarded attorney fees beyond those incurred by the debtor in the adversary proceeding in bankruptcy court after the class settlement went into effect.

In re Anderson, 884 F.3d 382, 65 Bankr. Ct. Dec. (CRR) 101, Bankr. L. Rep. (CCH) P 83222 (2d Cir. 2018), cert. denied, 2018 WL 2876199 (U.S. 2018). The Court of Appeals' holding is discussed in the Second Circuit's decisions below. See also the discussion of Epic Systems Corp. v. Lewis, in the "other actions of interest to bankruptcy practitioners," below.

Noble Energy, Inc. v. ConocoPhillips Company, 532 S.W.3d 771 (Tex. 2017), cert. denied, 2018 WL 1858882 (U.S. 2018). On a petition for *certiorari* to the Texas Supreme Court, the issues involved the Texas courts' interpretation of federal bankruptcy law regarding blanket assumptions of executory contracts. The purchase of the debtor's assets included an agreement in which bankruptcy debtor had acquired an oil and gas field lease that obligated the debtor to indemnify the oil and gas company for any past or future environmental claims regarding the lease, so the asset purchaser assumed the indemnification liability, even though the lease agreement was not mentioned in the asset-purchase agreement. The purchaser did agree to buy the debtor's assets contained in an exhibit, which listed the property interests that the debtor had acquired from the oil and gas company, the purchaser agreed to buy all rights and interests in all agreements in any way associated with the purchased assets and the purchaser did not specifically reject the lease agreement. The Texas Supreme Court affirmed the trial court's summary judgment for the oil and gas field leaseholder.

VI.   Recent Circuit Court Decisions of Particular Interest to Bankruptcy Practitioners

Most of the following summaries of opinions from the circuit courts are based on the monthly Norton Bankruptcy Law Adviser, as prepared by Bradley, Arant, Boult, Cummings, LLP, Nashville, Tennessee. The March issue of the Adviser each year contains a more extensive summary of appellate bankruptcy decisions for the prior twelve months from each circuit and its bankruptcy appellate panel.

BANKRUPTCY HIGHLIGHTS

A.   First Circuit

In re Fustolo, 896 F.3d 76, 65 Bankr. Ct. Dec. (CRR) 256 (1st Cir. 2018). The plaintiff creditor's request to amend its pleadings to add a new claim for denial of discharge for failure to obey a lawful order of the court was first made two months after trial. The debtor was not put on notice prior to the trial and was prejudiced by this late addition of the new claim.   The opinion reviews requirements under Fed. R. Civ. P. 15(b)(2).

Internal Revenue Service v. Murphy, 892 F.3d 29, 65 Bankr. Ct. Dec. (CRR) 195, 2018-1 U.S. Tax Cas. (CCH) P 50280, 121 A.F.T.R.2d 2018-1996 (1st Cir. 2018). The IRS "willfully violates" a discharge order under 26 U.S.C.A. § 7433(e) when it knows of the discharge order and takes an intentional action that violates the order. Section 7433(e) provides that when the IRS "willfully violates any provision of section 362 (relating to automatic stay) or 524 (relating to effect of discharge) of title 11," the taxpayer may petition to recover damages against the United States. The IRS's good faith belief that it has a right to collect the discharged debts is irrelevant to whether it willfully violated the discharge injunction. The court based its definition of what constitutes a "willful violation" on interpretations of the same phrase under Bankruptcy Code § 362(h) and § 524 both before and after IRC § 7433(e) was enacted and determined that good faith had no relevance in either context. The IRS argued that the doctrine of sovereign immunity required a narrower definition of a "willful violation," but the court held that sovereign immunity principles do not displace the well-established general definition.

In re Montreal, Maine & Atlantic Railway, Ltd., 888 F.3d 1, 65 Bankr. Ct. Dec. (CRR) 143 (1st Cir. 2018). Multiparty transaction for the sale of railroad lines in which the debtor acted only as bailee did not produce proceeds that were recoverable by the trustee in bankruptcy. Debtor purchased the assets of several United States and Canadian railways; however, debtor soon found itself strapped for cash, and received a $34 million loan from the Federal Railroad Administration ("FRA"). In 2010, debtor and the FRA amended their agreement, in which the FRA agreed to provide a "limited waiver" of its senior lien over the lines, which would take effect "upon the closing" of a proposed sale to the State of Maine. The amendment required debtor, upon the closing of the sale, to convey the proceeds to an escrow agent. In January 2011, the State of Maine agreed to pay $21 million for the lines. The First Circuit held the sale proceeds were not property of the estate, because the debtor only held the money as bailee under the agreement, and, therefore, the property was not recoverable by the bankruptcy trustee.

In re Tempnology, LLC, 879 F.3d 389, 65 Bankr. Ct. Dec. (CRR) 23, Bankr. L. Rep. (CCH) P 83196 (1st Cir. 2018), certiorari granted in part, 2018 WL 2939184 (U.S. 2018). Rejection of an executory contract under § 365(a), when the debtor is the licensor of intellectual property, leaves the counter-party with only a prepetition damages' claim; the debtor has no further obligation to perform under either a trademark license or a grant of exclusive distribution rights. The counter-party's right to use the debtor's trademarks did not survive rejection of the contract. The court reasoned that a contract to sell products using debtor's patented technology was not comparable to an exclusive right to exploit the underlying intellectual property. Additionally, the court concluded that trademark licenses should be categorically unprotected from court-approved rejection of a contract, until Congress decides otherwise. Holding otherwise would impair bankruptcy relief from executory obligations.

In re Old Cold LLC, 879 F.3d 376, 65 Bankr. Ct. Dec. (CRR) 22, Bankr. L. Rep. (CCH) P 83198 (1st Cir. 2018). The winning bidder in a § 363(b) asset sale was a good faith purchaser entitled to the protections of § 363(m). The impact of § 363(m) is to render statutorily moot any appellate challenge to a sale to a good faith purchaser that is not stayed. The winning bidder acted in good faith, because the bidder purchased the assets for value and did not have knowledge of adverse claims. The panel found no clear error in the bankruptcy court's findings that there was no collusion or misconduct between the debtor and the purchaser.

In re Financial Oversight and Management Board for Puerto Rico for Puerto Rico, 872 F.3d 57, 64 Bankr. Ct. Dec. (CRR) 173 (1st Cir. 2017). The First Circuit sustains right of official committee of unsecured creditors to intervene in an adversary proceeding within the Commonwealth of Puerto Rico's debt adjustment case under Title

III of the Puerto Rico Oversight, Management, and Economic Stability Act. The court held that § 1109(b) provides an unconditional right to intervene within the meaning of Federal Rule of Civil Procedure 24(a)(1). The First Circuit noted that its holding did not dictate the scope of the committee's participation in the adversary proceeding and empowered the district court on remand to exercise discretion with respect to that issue.

B.　Second Circuit

In re Anderson, 884 F.3d 382, 65 Bankr. Ct. Dec. (CRR) 101, Bankr. L. Rep. (CCH) P 83222 (2d Cir. 2018), cert. denied, 2018 WL 2876199 (U.S. 2018). A chapter 7 debtor filed a putative class action to recover for a credit card issuer's alleged violation of his and others' discharge injunctions by continuing to report, as "charged off," discharged credit card debt. The issuer moved to compel arbitration. The bankruptcy court denied the motion and the district and circuit courts affirmed. The Court of Appeals held that (1) a stipulation by the credit card issuer, that it would update the credit reports for the debtor and other cardholders who had obtained bankruptcy discharges of their credit card debts, did not moot appeal; (2) arbitration of claims that the debtor had brought, even as a putative class action, to recover for the card issuer's alleged violation of the discharge injunction, would seriously jeopardize an integral part of the bankruptcy court's ability to provide debtors with fresh start; and (3) the bankruptcy court did not abuse its discretion in denying the issuer's motion to compel arbitration.

In re Murray, 900 F.3d 53, 66 Bankr. Ct. Dec. (CRR) 12 (2d Cir. 2018). The bankruptcy court did not abuse its discretion in dismissing an involuntary Chapter 7 bankruptcy filed by a judgment creditor in a two-party dispute. The involuntary petition was a judgment enforcement tactic but there were other adequate state-law remedies available to the creditor.

SPV Osus Ltd. v. UBS AG, 882 F.3d 333, 65 Bankr. Ct. Dec. (CRR) 60 (2d Cir. 2018). The Second Circuit explored "related to" jurisdiction, personal jurisdiction and proximate cause in a Ponzi scheme context. An investor brought a state court action alleging that financial services companies acted as accomplices to funnel investments into Bernie Madoff's Ponzi scheme. The defendants removed the case to federal court. The district court denied a motion to remand on the grounds that the federal court had jurisdiction under 28 U.S.C.A. § 1334, which provides federal courts with "original but not exclusive jurisdiction of all civil proceedings arising under title 11, or arising in or related to cases under title 11." The district court then dismissed the complaint for lack of personal jurisdiction and lack of proximate cause. The Second Circuit affirmed. The Second Circuit held it had jurisdiction under § 1334, reasoning that a contingent contribution claim may serve as the basis for "related to" jurisdiction as it may have a "conceivable effect" on the bankruptcy estate. The circuit went on to affirm the lack of personal jurisdiction because defendants lacked sufficient contacts with New York. The Second Circuit also affirmed that the link between the defendants' actions and the harm alleged by the plaintiff was too attenuated to constitute proximate cause—the plaintiff's causation argument was so broad as to implicate one of its own affiliates.

C. Third Circuit

In re Energy Future Holdings Corp., 904 F.3d 298, 66 Bankr. Ct. Dec. (CRR) 66 (3d Cir. 2018). Holding that federal courts have inherent authority to reconsider a prior decision that was not controlled by Fed. R. Civ. P. 60(b)'s one-year limitation, the divided Circuit panel affirmed the bankruptcy court's reconsideration of its prior approval of a $275 million breakup fee in a Chapter 11 case. The bankruptcy court correctly reconsidered under Fed. R. Civ. P. 59(e).

In re W.R. Grace & Co., 900 F.3d 126, 66 Bankr. Ct. Dec. (CRR) 23 (3d Cir. 2018). In the confirmation order, a channeling injunction created a trust to pay asbestos claims, protecting the debtor and insurers from further claims, and the Circuit opinion discusses § 524(g)'s limitations on such injunctions against third party liability.

Tepper v. Amos Financial, LLC, 898 F.3d 364 (3d Cir. 2018). The Third Circuit found that the Supreme Court in *Henson v. Santander Consumer USA, Inc.,* 137 S. Ct. 1718 (2017), did not answer the question of whether one in the principal business of debt collection would be covered by the Fair Debt Collection Practices Act when it was collecting debt that it owned, and the Circuit held that plain text of the statute included such a debt collector. In *Henson,* that issue was not before the Court, and the Third Circuit looked to the Act's application to a "debt collector" who is engaged in the "principal business of which is the collection of any debts" as an alternative to application to one "who regularly collects" debts owed to another party. 15 U.S.C. § 1692a)(6). The term "any debts" in the "principal business" portion of the statute did not distinguish between debts owed to the collector or another party. This creditor's principal business was collecting debts; therefore, it was subject to the FDCPA under that portion of the definition.

In re Philadelphia Entertainment & Development Partners, 879 F.3d 492, 65 Bankr. Ct. Dec. (CRR) 31 (3d Cir. 2018). *Rooker-Feldman* doctrine did not bar the bankruptcy court from deciding whether the revocation of a Chapter 11 debtor's gaming license was a fraudulent transfer under § 548 or § 544 and Pennsylvania's Uniform Fraudulent Transfer Act, when the prepetition decision to revoke the debtor's gaming license was affirmed by the state appellate court on state gaming law grounds. The Third Circuit reasoned, to determine the merits of the fraudulent transfer claims, the bankruptcy court was not required to consider or to review the propriety of the state court proceedings or judgment.

In re Pursuit Capital Management, LLC, 874 F.3d 124, 64 Bankr. Ct. Dec. (CRR) 226, Bankr. L. Rep. (CCH) P 83174 (3d Cir. 2017). Appeal of order approving sale of potential avoidance actions was statutorily moot under § 363(m) because appealing parties failed to obtain stay pending appeal. Bankruptcy court did not clearly err in finding the sale was in good faith, when there was no evidence of collusion between the trustee and the purchaser, and the claims were purchased for fair value. Remedy sought by appealing parties would affect validity of the sale, therefore appeal was statutorily moot.

In Re: J & S Properties, LLC, 872 F.3d 138, 64 Bankr. Ct. Dec. (CRR) 184, Bankr. L. Rep. (CCH) P 83160 (3d Cir. 2017). Bankruptcy trustees are government officials entitled to qualified immunity from 28 U.S.C. § 1983 claims by third parties when the trustee acts in an official capacity in a manner that is not contrary to clearly established law. The trustee did not act in a manner contrary to clearly established law and had qualified immunity from liability to the debtor's tenant when she took control of a commercial leasehold to preserve the estate's asset following burst pipes and flooding of the property.

D.   Fourth Circuit

In re Alpha Natural Resources, Incorporated, 736 Fed. Appx. 412 (4th Cir. 2018). Appellant must have pecuniary interest in appeal's outcome; otherwise, dismissal of appeal by district court is appropriate. A creditor lacked standing to appeal rulings in connection with the creditor's objections to the sufficiency of disclosures by a turnaround advisor employed by Chapter 11 debtors, in the context of confirmation of the debtors' reorganization plan.

No v. Gorman, 891 F.3d 138, 65 Bankr. Ct. Dec. (CRR) 184 (4th Cir. 2018). Bankruptcy court cannot dismiss a Chapter 13 case for failure to timely commence payments without first providing the debtor notice and an opportunity for a hearing. The debtor failed to make payments as required by § 1326. The Chapter 13 trustee filed a motion to dismiss and certification under Local Bankruptcy Rule 3070-1(C), which allows for dismissal based on the certification of noncompliance with § 1326 without a hearing. The bankruptcy court dismissed the case before a hearing on the motion could occur, and the district court affirmed. The Fourth Circuit reversed, holding that the local rule conflicted with the notice and hearing requirement of § 1307.

Burkhart v. Grigsby, 886 F.3d 434, 65 Bankr. Ct. Dec. (CRR) 113 (4th Cir. 2018). Chapter 13 plan can strip off a wholly unsecured junior lien under § 1322(b)(2) without regard to whether a proof of claim has been filed. Trustee argued that § 506(d) prohibits lien avoidance when no proof of claim has been filed. The Fourth Circuit concluded that § 506(d) is not applicable when there is no dispute that the underlying debt is unsecured. Further, a creditor's rights under § 1322(b)(2) turn on whether there is *any* value in the collateral. Rather than pursuing valuation under § 506(a), which would normally require the filing of a formal proof of claim, a Chapter 13 debtor may strip off a worthless lien under § 1322(b) regardless of whether a claim has been filed.

Janvey v. Romero, 883 F.3d 406, 65 Bankr. Ct. Dec. (CRR) 81 (4th Cir. 2018). Although bad faith may constitute "cause" for dismissal under § 707(a), considering the totality of circumstances the bankruptcy court acted within its discretion to deny dismissal when debtor had legitimate reasons to file bankruptcy. The primary reason debtor filed bankruptcy was his wife's health problems, which increased out-of-pocket medical expenses. Additionally, the court found that debtor was candid and cooperative throughout the underlying litigation.

In re Bate Land & Timber LLC, 877 F.3d 188, 65 Bankr. Ct. Dec. (CRR) 2 (4th Cir. 2017). Secured creditor's appeal of unstayed orders confirming partial dirt-for-debt Chapter 11 plan was not equitably moot when equities did not support conclusion that it would be impractical, imprudent, or inequitable to provide relief to secured creditor. Partial dirt-for-debt plan may provide the indubitable equivalent of a secured creditor's claim in certain cases, and bankruptcy court did not clearly err in finding the valuation of eight tracts of land and $1 million in cash was the indubitable equivalent of the secured creditor's claim. Bankruptcy court also did not err in disallowing 266 days of post-petition interest based on conclusion that it would be inequitable to require the debtor to pay interest that accrued through no fault of its own.

E. Fifth Circuit

In re OGA Charters, L.L.C., 901 F.3d 599, 66 Bankr. Ct. Dec. (CRR) 24 (5th Cir. 2018). On direct appeal and affirming the bankruptcy court, under § 541(a)'s broad definition of property of the estate, insurance policies are generally within that scope, and under facts of this case, § 541(a) included policy proceeds.

Matter of Glenn, 900 F.3d 187, 66 Bankr. Ct. Dec. (CRR) 13 (5th Cir. 2018). The Fifth Circuit applied *Associates Commercial Corp. v. Rash,* 520 U.S. 953 (1997), and § 506(a), to hold that when the debtor retained a manufactured home the valuation would not include delivery and setup costs, because those were not services that the debtor would receive as a result of retention. These were not costs of "sales or marketing," but rather were additional costs such as service agreements.

Matter of Lopez, 897 F.3d 663 (5th Cir. 2018). The Fifth Circuit referred to *Harris v. Viegelahn,* 135 S. Ct. 1829 (2015), to hold that § 349(b) required that upon voluntary dismissal of the case, the debtors were to be paid the proceeds of the postpetition sale of their homestead, even though they otherwise had lost the exempt status of those proceeds by failure to reinvest the proceeds in another home under Texas law. Under *Harris* and other Fifth Circuit precedent, "§ 349(b)'s purpose is to undo the bankruptcy case as far as practicable, and to restore all property rights to the position in which they were found at the commencement of the case." Moreover, the trustee had no authority to distribute property to creditors upon dismissal.

Matter of Lindsey, 733 Fed. Appx. 190 (5th Cir. 2018). The Fifth Circuit held that Civil Rule 9(b), applied by Bankruptcy Rule 7009, requires heightened pleading requirements when a complaint alleges fraud under § 523(a)(2)(A).

Fornesa v. Fifth Third Mortgage Company, 897 F.3d 624 (5th Cir. 2018). The Chapter 13 debtor had acquired an equitable interest in his son's real property, and the schedules listed an "equity sharing agreement in son's house," but the property address and mortgage creditor were not listed. The equity sharing agreement by its terms expired and thereafter, the debtor moved into the son's house and obtained a quitclaim deed. The mortgage lender was not notified of the transfer and the debtor did not amend schedules to disclose the transfer. After default on the mortgage, the lender initiated foreclosure. The debtor and his son filed suit, alleging wrongful foreclosure and violation of the automatic stay. The Fifth Circuit affirmed the district court's application of judicial estoppel, stating that the Chapter 13 debtor had a continuing duty to amend schedules to disclose the quitclaim deed and putative claims against the lender.

Matter of Technicool Systems, Incorporated, 896 F.3d 382, 65 Bankr. Ct. Dec. (CRR) 246, Bankr. L. Rep. (CCH) P 83268 (5th Cir. 2018). Owner of debtor corporation lacked standing to appeal bankruptcy court's approval of trustee's application to employ special counsel. Appellant was not a creditor and as an equity holder only had a speculative financial interest if there was a surplus in the estate. Standing for appeal requires a "higher causal nexus between act and injury" than traditional Article III standing. Under the "narrow inquiry for bankruptcy standing," otherwise known as the "person aggrieved" test, a bankruptcy appellant must show that he would be "directly and adversely affected pecuniarily by the order of the bankruptcy court." In other words, "[t]he order must burden his pocket before he burdens a docket."

BANKRUPTCY HIGHLIGHTS

Matter of Houston Regional Sports Network, L.P., 886 F.3d 523, 65 Bankr. Ct. Dec. (CRR) 123 (5th Cir. 2018). Bankruptcy courts have flexibility to select the valuation date for collateral in a Chapter 11 cramdown proceeding so long as the court takes into account the purpose of the valuation and the proposed use or disposition of the collateral. The Fifth Circuit explained the relationship between § 506(a)(1) and the cramdown provision of § 1129(b)(2)(A)(i)(II): § 506(a)(1) instructs the court how to make initial valuations before the present value of collateral is calculated under § 1129. Section 1129 did not require the effective date of a plan of reorganization to be the date of valuation. The court declined to extend to Chapter 11 cramdown, its holding in *Chase Manhattan Bank USA NA v. Stembridge (In re Stembridge)*, 394 F.3d 383 (5th Cir. 2004), that the value of collateral for purposes of plan confirmation in a Chapter 13 case should be determined as of the filing of the petition. The court reasoned that flexibility in valuation timing allows bankruptcy courts to take into account the development of the proceedings, as the value of collateral may vary dramatically based on its proposed use under any given plan. The Fifth Circuit remanded the case to the bankruptcy court for re-valuation of waived media-rights fees in light of their proposed use by the debtor and because subtraction of the fees during the bankruptcy constituted an impermissible surcharge under 11 U.S.C.A. § 506(c).

Matter of DeBerry, 884 F.3d 526, Bankr. L. Rep. (CCH) P 83221 (5th Cir. 2018). Chapter 7 debtor who owns property at the petition and claims a homestead exemption to which no objection is filed, can sell the homestead postpetition without forfeiting the proceeds to the trustee even if the debtor does not reinvest the proceeds in another homestead within six months of the sale. The court reasoned that holding otherwise would inject uncertainty into Chapter 7 cases, because it would lead to arbitrary results as protection for the proceeds of postpetition homestead sales would depend on the aggressiveness of the trustee in closing a case. The court relied on its recent ruling in *Hawk v. Engelhart (In re Hawk)*, 871 F.3d 287 (5th Cir. 2017), that funds withdrawn from an exempt retirement account after the filing of a Chapter 7 bankruptcy did not lose exempt status even if the money was not redeposited in a similar account within 60 days pursuant to Texas' proceeds rule.

BANKRUPTCY HIGHLIGHTS

Matter of JFK Capital Holdings, L.L.C, 880 F.3d 747, 65 Bankr. Ct. Dec. (CRR) 41, Bankr. L. Rep. (CCH) P 83202 (5th Cir. 2018). The Fifth Circuit clarified the standard for "reasonable compensation" of Chapter 7 trustees under §§ 326 and 330. Examining a Chapter 7 trustee's application for fees incurred to litigate the disbursement of a settlement check, the bankruptcy court significantly reduced the requested fee, which had not been contested, without explanation. The district court vacated and remanded. The Fifth Circuit stated that under §§ 326 and 330, courts had struggled to determine the appropriate method to determine "reasonable compensation" for Chapter 7 trustees in light of amendments by the Bankruptcy Abuse Prevention and Consumer Protection Act of 2005. Some courts have held that § 326(a) is a presumptively reasonable fixed commission rate for Chapter 7 trustees, to be reduced only in rare or extraordinary circumstances. A second approach, adopted by the district court, relied on the bankruptcy court's discretion to award reasonable compensation only for actual and necessary services. The Fifth Circuit adopted the first approach, holding that the percentage amounts listed in § 326 are presumptively reasonable because BAPCPA's amendment to § 330(a)(3) directs courts to treat trustee's compensation as a commission, rather than as a factor-based assessment of the trustee's services. The court acknowledged that § 330 still permitted a reduction or denial of compensation in rare and exceptional circumstances.

In Matter of Ayobami, 879 F.3d 152, Bankr. L. Rep. (CCH) P 83197 (5th Cir. 2018). Narrowly answering a certified question, there are circumstances in which a Chapter 13 debtor can claim an exemption under § 522 in "100% interest" in an asset— so long as the value of that interest does not exceed the statutory limit on the exemption claimed. The debtor filed Schedule C claiming an exemption in "100% of fair market value, up to any applicable statutory limit" of specified property. The debtor identified provisions of § 522, which capped the value of the debtor's interest that may be exempted at designated statutory limits. The bankruptcy court certified the question whether a debtor claiming federal exemptions under § 522 may ever exempt a 100% interest in an asset. The Fifth Circuit held that a debtor may exempt a100% interest in an asset because § 522 caps the value of the asset a debtor may exempt, not the debtor's interest in that asset. The Fifth Circuit noted that there would be circumstances when exempting a 100% interest in an asset would not be allowable under § 522, such as when the value of the asset exceeds the statutory cap. The Fifth Circuit declined to address whether claiming an exemption in a 100% interest entitles the debtor to clear title to that asset or whether the debtor may benefit from any postpetition appreciation of that asset.

F.   Sixth Circuit

Re: Jackson Masonry, LLC, 66 Bankr. Ct. Dec. (CRR) 97, 2018 WL 4997779 (6th Cir. 2018). Reviewing circuit authority on finality of orders for appellate purposes, the Sixth Circuit affirmed the district court's dismissal of appeal from a denial of stay relief. Under 28 U.S.C.A. § 158(a), there is a two-part test for finality, and denial of stay relief met the test.

Kentucky Employees Retirement System v. Seven Counties Services, Inc., 901 F.3d 718, 66 Bankr. Ct. Dec. (CRR) 46 (6th Cir. 2018). Under §§ 101(27) and 109(d), the nonprofit community health services provider was not governmental unit and was eligible for Chapter 11 relief, notwithstanding most of its budget source being state funds.

In re Isaacs, 895 F.3d 904, 65 Bankr. Ct. Dec. (CRR) 257, Bankr. L. Rep. (CCH) P 83278 (6th Cir. 2018). *Rooker-Feldman* doctrine barred the bankruptcy court from determining in a Chapter 13 case that the debtor's mortgage lien was discharged in the debtor's previous Chapter 7 case. Between the debtor's Chapter 7 and Chapter 13 cases, a state court issued a foreclosure judgment interpreting the Chapter 7 discharge order not to include the mortgage lien. The Sixth Circuit reasoned that any finding by the bankruptcy court in the Chapter 13 case would be appellate review of the state court's judgment in violation of *Rooker-Feldman*. The *Hamilton* exception to the *Rooker-Feldman* doctrine—which voids state court judgments that incorrectly interpret federal discharge orders, thereby allowing federal court review without violating *Rooker-Feldman*—did not apply because the exception only voids judgments to the extent they determine personal liability, not the existence of liens.

Andrews v. Michigan Unemployment Insurance Agency, 891 F.3d 245, 65 Bankr. Ct. Dec. (CRR) 185, Bankr. L. Rep. (CCH) P 83258, Unempl. Ins. Rep. (CCH) P 22448 (6th Cir. 2018). Penalty assessed by a governmental unit against a debtor due to fraud is nondischargeable under § 523(a)(2). Under *Cohen v. de la Cruz*, 523 U.S. 213, 118 S. Ct. 1212, 140 L. Ed. 2d 341 (1998), "penalties associated with fraud should be regarded as essentially the same as the fraud itself" and are included under § 523(a)(2)'s exception to discharge. Because the subsections of § 523(a) are not mutually exclusive, a debt can be nondischargeable under one subsection and dischargeable under another.

In re Mountain Glacier LLC, 877 F.3d 246, 64 Bankr. Ct. Dec. (CRR) 256, Bankr. L. Rep. (CCH) P 83189 (6th Cir. 2017). Debtor properly preserved unliquidated arbitration claim in confirmed Chapter 11 plan that contained a transfer-of-assets provision specifically identifying the adverse party and transferring the arbitration claim to the reorganized debtor. The Sixth Circuit rejected arguments that more detail regarding the substance of the claim and the potential recovery was required under § 1123(b)(3) for the reorganized debtor to retain a claim. Such disclosures are better controlled by the "adequate information" requirements for a disclosure statement under § 1125. Adverse party did not object to the adequacy of information in the disclosure statement.

G.   Seventh Circuit

Berg v. Social Security Administration, 900 F.3d 864, 66 Bankr. Ct. Dec. (CRR) 35 (7th Cir. 2018). Prior to filing bankruptcy, the debtor had received an overpayment from the Social Security Administration (SSA) and subsequently, the debtor was awarded disability benefits, with the accumulated benefits set off by the prior overpayment. The debtor used § 522(h) to initiate a recovery of the setoff under § 553(b). As stated by the Seventh Circuit, "the SSA had a pre-petition claim against Berg for return of its earlier overpayment; SSA owed a pre-petition debt to Berg because of the award of back-benefits; the obligations were mutual; and both the claim and the debt were valid and enforceable." The issue was whether SSA had improved its position within the 90 days prior to the bankruptcy filing, and the Circuit affirmed on direct appeal a determination that the improved position was $2,015, which was to be returned to the debtor. The underlying issue was when the debtor's Social Security benefits began to accrue, with the debtor arguing that the benefits accrued only when the SSA made its determination of back benefits, which was within the 90 days pre-petition, and under this theory the SSA would have improved its position by the entire setoff of $19,400. The Circuit agreed with the SSA that the benefits began to accrue monthly when the debtor became disabled, even though the SSA did not make its disability determination until later. Under that theory, the SSA improved its position within the 90 days only by $2,015. The Seventh Circuit agreed with the Third Circuit's *Lee v. Schweiker,* 739 F.2d 870 (3d Cir. 1984), concluding that "understanding of Social Security benefits as accruing as soon as the recipient survives the month and is lawfully entitled to them is consistent with the Bankruptcy Code's concepts of 'debt' and 'claim' as they are used in section 553(b)(2)."

Illinois Department of Revenue v. Hanmi Bank, 895 F.3d 465, 65 Bankr. Ct. Dec. (CRR) 247 (7th Cir. 2018). After the bankruptcy court authorized a sale of the principal assets of Chapter 11 debtors under § 363(f), the bankruptcy court correctly held that the sale was free and clear of the right of the Illinois Department of Revenue (IDOR) to pursue the purchaser in a bulk sale for the state taxes owed by the seller. The bankruptcy court correctly concluded that IDOR was entitled to "adequate protection" but that the IDOR's interest in the property was zero because the IDOR did not offer any evidence to show its potential recovery from the sale such that the court could assign a reasonable value to its interest.

Marshall v. Blake, 885 F.3d 1065, Bankr. L. Rep. (CCH) P 83228 (7th Cir. 2018). The bankruptcy court did not err in confirming a Chapter 13 plan that allowed debtor to keep yearly tax credits as long as debtor accounted for the income by proration. The Seventh Circuit confirmed that tax credits are current monthly income under § 101(10A)(A). However, the court also held that § 1325(b)(2) allows a below-median income debtor to retain her tax refund, so long as she prorates it as monthly income and offsets it with reasonable necessary expenses incurred throughout the year. The court reasoned that debtor's plan was consistent with the Supreme Court's interpretation of "projected disposable income," and did not violate good faith and feasibility requirements.

In re Thorpe, 881 F.3d 536, 65 Bankr. Ct. Dec. (CRR) 42 (7th Cir. 2018). The Seventh Circuit held that a debtor's half interest in a former marital home was no longer an asset of his Chapter 7 estate once the divorce court awarded the home to his former spouse. Under Illinois law, divorcing spouses are vested with independent contingent interests in all martial property at the moment the petition is filed. The court concluded that once the divorce court awarded the home to the wife, the wife's contingent interest in the home ripened into a full ownership interest, and the estate's contingent interest in the house disappeared.

In re Veluchamy, 879 F.3d 808, 65 Bankr. Ct. Dec. (CRR) 24, Bankr. L. Rep. (CCH) P 83199 (7th Cir. 2018). In a Chapter 7 case, turnover was available under § 542 to recover $5.5 million transferred to an account held by a family-owned company when the estate sought to regain the debtor's interest. No credible evidence was presented to show that the debtor transferred ownership of the assets to someone else; rather, the debtor simply moved the contested funds to an overseas account the debtor still controlled. The lower courts did not err by failing to join the family-owned company as a necessary party to the litigation under Federal Rule of Civil Procedure 19 because the debtor presented no evidence that the company took title to the funds.

In re OneStar Long Distance, Inc., 872 F.3d 526, 64 Bankr. Ct. Dec. (CRR) 163, Bankr. L. Rep. (CCH) P 83159 (7th Cir. 2017). Sustaining a complete subsequent new value defense in a preferential transfer action, the Seventh Circuit affirmed that the debtor's assignment of debt and contractual rights to its affiliate did not have the effect of repaying the creditor for new value; subsequent new value remained unpaid and the creditor was entitled to the subsequent new value defense. Additionally, the bankruptcy court did not err in allocating new value on a per diem basis when the new value was billed on a monthly basis and was not otherwise identifiable to any particular day.

BANKRUPTCY HIGHLIGHTS

H.   Eighth Circuit

In re Archdiocese of Saint Paul and Minneapolis, 888 F.3d 944, 65 Bankr. Ct. Dec. (CRR) 153, Bankr. L. Rep. (CCH) P 83244 (8th Cir. 2018). An archdiocese in Chapter 11 cannot be substantively consolidated under § 105(a) with over 200 Catholic nonprofit, nondebtor entities, including parishes and schools. Substantively consolidating the targeted entities would pull nonprofit entities into bankruptcy involuntarily in contravention of § 303(a). The court reasoned that § 303(a) protects bona fide nonprofit organizations from involuntary bankruptcy.

In re Wigley, 886 F.3d 681, 65 Bankr. Ct. Dec. (CRR) 114, Bankr. L. Rep. (CCH) P 83233 (8th Cir. 2018). The Eighth Circuit dismissed the appeal of nondebtor spouse of a debtor-guarantor for lack of standing, because the nondebtor was not a "person aggrieved" by bankruptcy court orders that denied confirmation of debtor's proposed plan. The court cited *OpportunityFin., LLC v. Kelley*, 822 F.3d 451, 458 (8th Cir. 2016), that a person has standing if a bankruptcy order diminishes the person's property, increases the person's burdens, or impairs the person's rights. The court reasoned the spouse was not a "person aggrieved" for bankruptcy standing because the bankruptcy orders maintained the *status quo ante* and the harm of potential future litigation was too indirect.

Dahlin v. Lyondell Chemical Company, 881 F.3d 599, 65 Bankr. Ct. Dec. (CRR) 32, Bankr. L. Rep. (CCH) P 83204 (8th Cir. 2018). The Eighth Circuit, joining the Third Circuit, adopted the "reasonably ascertainable" standard, and rejected the "reasonably foreseeable" standard, for finding known creditors for bankruptcy notice purposes. The court held that the plaintiff's wrongful death action was discharged in the debtor's Chapter 11 case when the debtor conducted a reasonably diligent search for creditors and identified over one million reasonably ascertainable creditors. The plaintiff remaining unknown was provided notice by publication that satisfied due process.

BANKRUPTCY HIGHLIGHTS

I.   Ninth Circuit

In re Swintek, 2018 WL 5117193 (9th Cir. 2018). Applying California law on an unusual lien encumbering the debtor's personal property, the Ninth Circuit's divided panel held that the state-law period for executing on the lien was tolled under § 108(c). The dissenting judge found that the lien was a tool of judgment enforcement and did not fall with the statute's language "commencing or continuing a civil action."

Bunker Holdings Ltd. v. Yang Ming Liberia Corp., 2018 WL 4924364 (9th Cir. 2018). Agreeing with the Second, Fifth and Eleventh Circuits, the Ninth Circuit held that a subcontractor providing fuel to a vessel was not entitled to a maritime lien under 46 U.S.C.A. § 31342(a).

Hunsaker v. United States, 902 F.3d 963, 66 Bankr. Ct. Dec. (CRR) 47, 2018-2 U.S. Tax Cas. (CCH) P 50397, 122 A.F.T.R.2d 2018-5711 (9th Cir. 2018). IRS had violated the automatic stay by sending collection notices after the filing of a Chapter 13 case, and the Ninth Circuit considered the interplay between §§ 106(a) and 362(k), holding that the waiver of sovereign immunity found in § 106(a)(3) was broad enough to include an award of emotional distress damages for a willful stay violation. Such damages are not punitive but rather are monetary damages within the scope of the statute's waiver. The opinion noted disagreement with the First Circuit's *In re Rivera Torres,* 432 F.3d 20 (1st Cir. 2005), where that Circuit had adopted a "temporal approach" to waiver, considering whether emotional distress damages were understood by Congress to be available under § 106(a)(1) at the time of the 1994 amendments. The Ninth Circuit rejected that temporal approach for several reasons, including that § 106(a)'s waiver was unambiguous, applying a plain meaning to the statute.

In re Sino Clean Energy, Inc., 901 F.3d 1139, 66 Bankr. Ct. Dec. (CRR) 25 (9th Cir. 2018). The Nevada court had appointed a receiver, with authority to form a new corporate board. The former chief executive then filed Chapter 11, but the case was dismissed. Under Nevada law, the filing party was not a member of the receiver's board and were without authority to file the bankruptcy petition.

Goudelock v. Sixty-01 Association of Apartment Owners, 895 F.3d 633, 65 Bankr. Ct. Dec. (CRR) 248, Bankr. L. Rep. (CCH) P 83276 (9th Cir. 2018). The Ninth

BANKRUPTCY HIGHLIGHTS

Circuit noted that the exceptions from discharge under § 1328(a) do not include § 523(a)(16), and the Court held that the debtor's in personam obligation on condominium association fees that accrued after the case filing were prepetition debts, which were created when she took title to the property. As prepetition debt, the obligation was discharged. The Court agreed with the Seventh Circuit's reasoning in a Chapter 7 case, *Matter of Rosteck,* 899 F.2d 694 (7th Cir. 1990), that such association obligations were unmatured contingent debt that arose prepetition and that merely matured when the assessments became due postpetition. The Court acknowledged that a contrary view was taken in the Fourth Circuit's *In re Rosenfeld,* 23 F.3d 833 (4th Cir. 1994), where that Court held that association assessments ran with the land, arising each month from the debtor's postpetition ownership of the property. Under that rationale, in a Chapter 7 case, the postpetition assessments were not dischargeable. Applying the *Rosteck* reasoning, the condominium association had two state law remedies, an in rem lien, with its right to foreclosure, and in personam remedy for suing the homeowner. The in rem lien and foreclosure right continued, but the in personam obligation was discharged. The debtor's "personal obligation to pay CA assessments was not the result of a separate, post-petition transaction but was created when she took title to the condominium unit. As a result, the debt for the assessments arose pre-petition and is dischargeable under Section 1328(a), unless the Bankruptcy Code provides an exception to discharge."

In re Fagerdala USA-Lompoc, Inc., 891 F.3d 848, 65 Bankr. Ct. Dec. (CRR) 204, Bankr. L. Rep. (CCH) P 83260 (9th Cir. 2018). A creditor's offer to purchase a subset of the claims of a class, as opposed to offering to purchase all claims of the class, for the purpose of blocking the debtor's reorganization plan was insufficient evidence of bad faith to support designation of the creditor's votes cast against the plan under § 1126(e). The creditor was merely acting in its own self-interest and there was no evidence of an ulterior motive necessary for a finding of bad faith.

Matter of Point Center Financial, Inc., 890 F.3d 1188, 65 Bankr. Ct. Dec. (CRR) 197, Bankr. L. Rep. (CCH) P 83259 (9th Cir. 2018). Appellant's failure to attend and object at bankruptcy court hearing had no bearing on the question whether appellant had standing to appeal a bankruptcy court's order. Failure to attend and object may result in a waiver or forfeiture of the right to make certain arguments or object to certain claims, but does not present a jurisdictional standing issue. On remand, the district court should consider whether appellants forfeited their opposition to the motion.

In re Lee, 889 F.3d 639, Bankr. L. Rep. (CCH) P 83249 (9th Cir. 2018). Trustee's fraudulent conveyance complaint satisfied Rule 4003's requirement that a party in interest "file an objection" to a claimed exemption, although the complaint made no mention of Rule 4003 and did not specifically challenge debtor's entitlement to his claimed exemption. Debtor's transfer of the property allowed him to claim the exemption, making the adversary action and an objection under Rule 4003 "inextricably intertwined" such that the adversary action afforded adequate notice that the trustee objected to the exemption. The Ninth Circuit, in determining that the fraudulent transfer complaint satisfied Rule 4003, joined the "well-reasoned conclusion of the Sixth Circuit" in *Liberty State Bank & Trust v. Grosslight (In re Grosslight)*, 757 F.2d 773 (6th Cir. 1985).

In re Taggart, 888 F.3d 438, 65 Bankr. Ct. Dec. (CRR) 145, Bankr. L. Rep. (CCH) P 83243 (9th Cir. 2018). The bankruptcy court erred when it held creditors in contempt for knowingly violating a discharge injunction by seeking attorney fees in a state court proceeding against a debtor. Creditors argued that the debtor had "returned to the fray" by participating in litigation and opposing them in state court. Consistent with its ruling in *Zilog, Inc. v. Corning (In re Zilog, Inc.)*, 450 F.3d 996 (9th Cir. 2006), the Ninth Circuit held that the creditors did not knowingly violate the discharge injunction because they possessed a good faith belief that the injunction did not prevent them from seeking attorney fees. This good faith belief, even if unreasonable, insulated the creditors from a finding of contempt.

Diamond v. Hogan Lovells US LLP, 883 F.3d 1140, 65 Bankr. Ct. Dec. (CRR) 103 (9th Cir. 2018). The Ninth Circuit certified to the District of Columbia Court of Appeals the question whether, under District of Columbia law, a dissociated partner owes a duty to his former law firm to account for profits earned post-departure on legal matters that continued when the partner's former law firm had been hired on an hourly basis and the matters were completed at another law firm that hired the partner. The trustee for a bankrupt law firm brought an adversary proceeding against the firms that hired departing partners, arguing fraudulent transfer and unjust enrichment theories of recovery. The law firms' motion to dismiss was denied by the bankruptcy court. The district court reversed. The Ninth Circuit certified a determinative question to the District of Columbia Court of Appeals, observing that if the D.C. court holds that the dissolved law firm does have a property interest, the circuit will remand the matter to the district court to determine if defendant law firms are liable as subsequent transferees under the fraudulent transfer provisions of §§ 548 and 550.

Matter of Transwest Resort Properties, Inc., 881 F.3d 724, 65 Bankr. Ct. Dec. (CRR) 51, Bankr. L. Rep. (CCH) P 83206 (9th Cir. 2018). The accepting impaired class requirement for confirmation in § 1129(a)(10) applies on a "per plan" not a "per debtor" basis. Also, a due-on-sale clause does not need to be included in a Chapter 11 plan when an undersecured creditor elects to have its claim treated as secured pursuant to § 1111(b)(2). The Ninth Circuit reasoned that neither the plain language of § 1111(b)(2) nor the broader context of Chapter 11 requires that a plan involving an electing creditor contain a due-on-sale clause. The court further held that § 1129(a)(10) applies on a "per plan" basis. The court reasoned that the plain language of the statute makes no distinction between debtors under "the plan" whether the plan involves a single-debtor or multiple debtors. The court stated that once a single impaired class accepts a plan, § 1129(a)(10) is satisfied as to the entire plan.

In re Cherrett, 873 F.3d 1060, 64 Bankr. Ct. Dec. (CRR) 217, Bankr. L. Rep. (CCH) P 83170 (9th Cir. 2017). Joining the majority of circuit courts, bankruptcy court order denying a creditor's motion to dismiss under § 707(b) is a final and appealable order. Additionally, the Ninth Circuit affirmed the bankruptcy court's finding that a loan from the debtor's employer to purchase a condominium in connection with accepting employment was a non-consumer debt when the new employment was in a different state than the debtor's home and family, the debtor accepted the employment as an opportunity to further his career, he considered the condominium as a place holder only for purposes of allowing him to accept the new employment, and the loan likely would not have been available by other means. Employer's motion to dismiss under § 707(b) was denied.

BANKRUPTCY HIGHLIGHTS

Matter of Walldesign, Inc., 872 F.3d 954, 64 Bankr. Ct. Dec. (CRR) 195, Bankr. L. Rep. (CCH) P 83163 (9th Cir. 2017), cert. denied, 138 S. Ct. 2575, 201 L. Ed. 2d 293 (2018). Safe harbor provision in § 550(b) was inapplicable to third party recipients who were initial transferees of voidable payments made by the debtor's sole shareholder, director, and president for his personal expenses. The Ninth Circuit reasoned that under the dominion test, the third party recipients qualified as initial transferees because they were the first parties to have legal title to the fraudulently transferred funds after they left the transferor. The Ninth Circuit held the third party recipients strictly liable to the Committee of Unsecured Creditors as initial transferees. Additionally, the court held the debtor's sole shareholder strictly liable to the Committee, and allowed the Committee to seek single satisfaction from all responsible parties, jointly or severally.

J.   Tenth Circuit

In re Garcia, 2018 WL 5045613 (10th Cir. 2018). In per curiam decision applying its prior *In re Cowen*, 849 F.3d 943 (10th Cir. 2017), the Tenth Circuit held that the automatic stay was not violated by the passive attachment of a statutory worker's compensation lien. As held in *Cowen*, § 362(a)(3) and here § 362(a)(4) require affirmative acts, with the applicable lien attaching automatically and solely by operation of law under the statute.

In re Taylor, 899 F.3d 1126 (10th Cir. 2018). The Tenth Circuit agreed with the First, Third and Eleventh Circuits and the Ninth Circuit Bankruptcy Appellate Panel on the method for calculating a debtor's avoidance of a judicial lien when the debtor owned a one-half interest in homestead property subject to the lien. "Based on the plain language of § 522(f) and the structure of the Bankruptcy Code as a whole, we conclude that the impairment calculation must use the value of other liens on the home corresponding to the debtor's percentage of ownership, rather than the full amount of the liens." The debtor's ex-wife owned one-half interest in the home and she was not a debtor in the Chapter 13 case, which was then converted to Chapter 7. The Tenth Circuit had granted direct appeal from the bankruptcy court's interpretation that § 522(f) permitted avoidance of the disputed lien entirely. The Circuit construed the statute in light of the Supreme Court's emphasis on the "debtor's interest" in property in *Farrey v. Sanderfoot,* 500 U.S. 291 (1991), and "property" in § 522(f)(2)(A)(ii) refers to the "debtor's interest, rather than the undivided whole parcel." Under the debtor's approach, "judicial liens could be avoided in excess of the debtor's homestead exemption," and "interpreting the term 'property' to refer to Taylor's half interest is also consistent with the Bankruptcy Code as a whole," because "property" refers to the "property of the debtor." Quoting the Third Circuit's opinion, *In re Miller,* 299 F.3d 183, 186 (3d Cir. 2002), "the correct approach is to view the debtor as owning one half of the property to which one half of the mortgage debt is thus attributable and therefore to regard 'property' in subsection (ii) to mean the debtor's interest in the property and then to allocate the lien among the interests in the property proportionately."

In re Peeples, 880 F.3d 1207, 65 Bankr. Ct. Dec. (CRR) 33, Bankr. L. Rep. (CCH) P 83203 (10th Cir. 2018). In an adversary proceeding by a judgment creditor to enforce the automatic stay, the Tenth Circuit concluded that the wife of the judgment creditor lacked standing and the judgment creditor's claims were not in the zone of interests of § 362. Prior to the petition date, the debtor's judgment creditor brought an action in state court against the trustee of a trust that the judgment creditor alleged owed the debtor money. The state court dismissed the action, but determined the trustee was entitled to attorney fees and left the case open to determine the amount of fees. In the interim, the debtor filed bankruptcy, and the judgment creditor argued the automatic stay applied to the state court action and stayed the state court from awarding attorney fees. The state court rejected the argument and awarded attorney fees to the trustee against the judgment creditor. The judgment creditor filed an adversary proceeding in the bankruptcy case against the trustee seeking damages and an order that the automatic stay applied to the state court action. The Tenth Circuit first concluded the judgment creditor's spouse lacked standing to bring the adversary proceeding because the judgment for attorney fees was not against her. Additionally, the court dismissed the judgment creditor's claims because the harm the judgment creditor complained of was not within the zone of interests of § 362.

BANKRUPTCY HIGHLIGHTS

K.   Eleventh Circuit

Bennett v. Jefferson County, Alabama, 899 F.3d 1240, 66 Bankr. Ct. Dec. (CRR) 26 (11th Cir. 2018). The doctrine of equitable mootness applies to a confirmation order in a Chapter 9 case, as it does in Chapter 11, and the ratepayers' appeal of confirmation order was dismissed.

In re BFW Liquidation, LLC, 899 F.3d 1178, 66 Bankr. Ct. Dec. (CRR) 27 (11th Cir. 2018). The Eleventh Circuit held that new value is not required to remain unpaid in order to serve as a § 547(c)(4) defense to a preference.

In re Daughtrey, 896 F.3d 1255, 65 Bankr. Ct. Dec. (CRR) 258 (11th Cir. 2018). Debtors filed Chapter 7 for purpose of preventing foreclosure sale of property, and when trustee reached compromise agreement with judgment creditor the debtors moved to convert the case to Chapter 11, but the bankruptcy court denied the motion. In a matter of first impression, the Eleventh Circuit applied the abuse-of-discretion standard to the bankruptcy court's denial of a motion to convert under § 706(a). Cause existed for the bankruptcy court to deny the conversion, and there was no abuse of discretion.

Weakley v. Eagle Logistics, 894 F.3d 1244, 65 Bankr. Ct. Dec. (CRR) 226 (11th Cir. 2018). Judicial estoppel still applied to a cause of action that was not disclosed by the debtor, even though the bankruptcy case was voluntarily dismissed.

First National Bank of Oneida, N.A. v. Brandt, 887 F.3d 1255, 65 Bankr. Ct. Dec. (CRR) 154 (11th Cir. 2018). The Eleventh Circuit remanded to the district court the difficult question whether dismissal of a Chapter 11 case after confirmation but without a discharge affects a creditor's ability to pursue its deficiency claims. While the Eleventh Circuit did not issue a holding, it did note that the bankruptcy court's dismissal of debtor's case without a discharge is a "potentially significant event that may affect the ultimate disposition" of the creditor's deficiency claims. Providing guidance for the district court, the Eleventh Circuit examined the history of § 1141 and whether confirmation of an individual's Chapter 11 plan could discharge obligations without a formal discharge order. On this point, the court stated that "opinions discussing the dismissal of Chapter 13 cases without a discharge could become relevant" in analyzing similar Chapter 11 cases. The court also examined the goal of § 349(b) that dismissal returns the parties to the financial positions they were in before the case was filed. While acknowledging that § 349(b) does not expressly provide that a dismissal without discharge vacates a previously confirmed Chapter 11 plan, the court observed that the statute's "silence does not necessarily mean that the confirmed plan can survive the dismissal."

Cadwell v. Kaufman, Englett & Lynd, PLLC, 886 F.3d 1153, Bankr. L. Rep. (CCH) P 83234 (11th Cir. 2018). To state a claim under the second prohibition in § 526(a)(4), a plaintiff need not allege that advice received from a debt relief agency to incur additional debt to pay bankruptcy-related legal fees was given for an improper purpose. Section 526(a)(4) prohibits a debt relief agency from "advis[ing] an assisted person or prospective assisted person to incur more debt in contemplation of such person filing a case under this title or to pay an attorney or bankruptcy petition preparer a fee or charge for services performed as part of preparing for or representing a debtor in a case under this title." The Supreme Court analyzed § 526(a)(4) in *Gallop & Milavetz, P.A. v. United States*, 599 U.S. 229, 130 S. Ct. 1324, 176 L. Ed. 2d 79 (2010), holding that its first prohibition—against advice to incur more debt—required proof that the advice was given for an invalid purpose designed to manipulate the bankruptcy process. The Court inferred the necessity of proof of invalid purpose from the phrase "in contemplation of," which it explained was a term of art associated with abusive conduct. However, the Court did not decide whether § 526(a)(4)'s second prohibition—advice to pay an attorney—required the same proof. The Eleventh Circuit addressed this question in the context of a complaint dismissed for failure to state a claim, when plaintiff did not assert that advice he received from a debt relief agency to pay his legal bills by credit card was given for an improper purpose. The Eleventh Circuit considered three interpretations of § 526(a)(4), ultimately deciding that the phrase "in contemplation of" was not intended to apply to the second prohibition. Though the phrase was necessary to the first prohibition because the prohibition was so general, the second prohibition concerned specific misconduct that was suspect *per se* because advice that a client should incur additional debt to pay a bankruptcy attorney is inherently abusive.

BANKRUPTCY HIGHLIGHTS

In re Northington, 876 F.3d 1302, Bankr. L. Rep. (CCH) P 83188 (11th Cir. 2017). Chapter 13 plan that provided for redemption of pawned vehicle by payment in full through plan, confirmed after expiration of state law redemption period, did not preclude pawnbroker from stay relief. It was not necessary for pawnbroker to object to confirmation of the plan—the pawnbroker adequately preserved its rights by filing a motion for relief from stay which made the same arguments and sought the same relief. While the vehicle and the debtor's redemption rights entered the bankruptcy estate at the petition, following expiration of the redemption period title to the vehicle automatically passed to the pawnbroker under Georgia law. The Bankruptcy Code did not overcome the ordinary operation of Georgia's pawn statute following expiration of the redemption period: the automatic stay did not toll the redemption period; § 541 did not freeze the assets of the estate as of the filing of the petition; and § 1322(b)(2) was not applicable because at confirmation the redemption period had already expired—the pawnbroker did not have a claim to be modified, instead it had title to the vehicle by operation of Georgia law. When the debtor's redemption period expired, his rights in the vehicle were forfeited, extinguished and vested in the pawnbroker.

In re Horne, 876 F.3d 1076, 65 Bankr. Ct. Dec. (CRR) 3, Bankr. L. Rep. (CCH) P 83183 (11th Cir. 2017). Section 362(k)(1) is a broad fee-shifting statute that permits recovery of costs and attorney fees incurred by debtors in ending a willful violation of the automatic stay, prosecuting a damages violation, and defending those judgments on appeal. District court did not abuse its discretion in awarding reasonable attorney fees to the debtors for their successful defense of appeal of damages award for willful violations of the automatic stay. Eleventh Circuit awarded an additional $30,559.98 for attorney fees and costs in connection with the appeal.

In re Fundamental Long Term Care, Inc., 873 F.3d 1325 (11th Cir. 2017), cert. denied, 2018 WL 3306855 (U.S. 2018). Bankruptcy court had related-to subject matter jurisdiction to issue a permanent injunction prohibiting the plaintiffs from pursuing any claims against a dismissed defendant arising out of the nucleus of facts contained in the adversary complaint because any judgment on those claims from another court would impact the size and administration of the bankruptcy estate. Additionally, the bankruptcy court properly issued the injunction under the Anti-Injunction Act because the relitigation exception to the Anti-Injunction Act applied to the claims brought by plaintiffs in the adversary proceeding that were dismissed with prejudice. Enjoining the plaintiffs from bringing any additional potential claims not brought in the adversary proceeding was necessary in aid of the bankruptcy court's jurisdiction to prevent substantially similar claims from being brought in state court.

VII. Other Developments of Interest to Insolvency Practitioners – The Uniform Commercial Real Estate Receivership Act

In keeping with past Highlights, we note another development outside the Bankruptcy Code and Rules and related caselaw, to alert readers to the Uniform Commercial Real Estate Receivership Act (UCRERA), promulgated by the Uniform Law Commission (ULA) (formerly the National Conference of Commissioners on Uniform State Laws).

As parties to financial difficulties search for ways to resolve financial issues without the cumbersome and expensive procedure under Chapter 11 of the Bankruptcy Code, several states have attempted to address these concerns by providing for state receiverships that contain many of the powers and protections available in Chapter 11 proceedings. Since 2015, one such alternative may be the UCRERA. As promulgated, the uniform act and extensive commentary are available on the website of the ULA. http://www.uniformlaws.org/shared/docs/appointment%20and%20powers%20of%20real %20estate%20receivers/UCRERA_Final%20Act_2016jul29.pdf (last visited Oct 1, 2018). As of October 1, 2018, the proposed act had been enacted by five states (Michigan, Nevada, Oregon, Tennessee and Utah) and introduced in three more (Kentucky, Oklahoma and West Virginia). http://www.uniformlaws.org/LegislativeFactSheet.aspx?title=Commercial%20Real%20E state%20Receivership%20Act (last visited Oct. 1, 2018). The following summary of these extensive new rules governing receiverships involving "commercial" real estate is adapted from the ULA Prefatory Note to the promulgated UCRERA.

BANKRUPTCY HIGHLIGHTS

Before judgment:

The court may appoint a receiver .... to protect a party that demonstrates an apparent right, title, or interest in real property that is the subject of the action, if the property or the property's revenue-producing potential:
(A) is being subjected to or is in danger of waste, loss, dissipation, or impairment; or
(B) has been or is about to be the subject of a voidable transaction ....

UCRERA § 6(a)(1) (citations to UCRERA hereinafter are to section number only).

After judgment, the law as promulgated provides:

The court may appoint a receiver ...
(A) to carry the judgment into effect; or
(B) to preserve nonexempt real property pending appeal or when an execution has been returned unsatisfied and the owner refuses to apply the property in satisfaction of the judgment ....

§ 6(a)(2). The proposed legislation also provides for appointment on equitable grounds, during the time allowed for redemption and in connection with foreclosure. § 4 (a) & (b). The scope of the new rules is broad but not exclusive, leaving other statutes, in place. § 4(d).

(a) Except as otherwise provided in subsection (b) or (c), this chapter applies to a receivership for an interest in real property and any personal property related to or used in operating the real property.
(b) This [act] does not apply to a receivership for an interest in real property improved by one (1) to four (4) dwelling units unless:
   (1) The interest is used for agricultural, commercial, industrial, or mineral-extraction purposes, other than incidental uses by an owner occupying the property as the owner's primary residence;
   (2) The interest secures an obligation incurred at a time when the property was used or planned for use for agricultural, commercial, industrial, or mineral-extraction purposes;
   (3) The owner planned or is planning to develop the property into one (1) or more dwelling units to be sold or leased in the ordinary course of the owner's business; or
   (4) The owner is collecting or has the right to collect rents or other income from the property from a person other than an affiliate of the owner.
(c) This [act] does not apply to a receivership authorized by the law of this state, other than this [act], in which the receiver is a governmental unit or an individual acting in an official capacity on behalf of the governmental unit.

§ 4 (a)-(c).

The provisions of the new uniform act resemble those of the Bankruptcy Code in many ways. For example, the court may enter orders only after notice and opportunity for a hearing as is appropriate under the circumstances, but the court is expressly empowered to issue an order without an actual hearing if no interested party timely requests a hearing or if the particular circumstances require the issuance of an order before a hearing can be held. § 3(a) & (b).

The new act applies to receiverships involving real property but also covers personal property that is related to the real property or is used in its operation. § 4(a). It covers "commercial" receiverships in the sense that it does not govern a receivership for real property improved by only one to four dwelling units, unless one of the exceptions found in § 4(b) (above) applies.

The act as promulgated establishes standards under which a court may appoint a receiver. § 6(a). It also establishes standards under which a petitioning mortgage lienholder is entitled to appointment of a receiver. § 6(b). Where the court appoints a receiver *ex parte*, it may require that security be posted for any damages, etc., caused by an appointment determined later to be unjustified. § 6(c).

Because a receiver holds property for the benefit of all interested parties, the new uniform act requires that the receiver provide sworn evidence of the receiver's independence, subject to an exception to prevent disqualification based on certain pre-existing relationships that are *de minimis* in nature. § 7 (a)-(c). While a party seeking the appointment of a receiver may nominate a person to serve as a receiver, the court is not required to accept the suggestion. § 7(d).

Upon appointment, a receiver has the status of a lien creditor under both Article 9 of the Uniform Commercial Code (as to receivership property that is personal property or fixtures) and other state laws as to receivership property that is real property. § 9. Note that the definition of "lien creditor" in Article 9 of the UCC is very broad, including "a trustee in bankruptcy from the date of the filing of the petition." UCC § 9-101(a)(52)(C). Appointment of a receiver does not affect the validity of a pre-receivership security interest in receivership property, and property acquired after appointment is subject to any pre-receivership security agreement to the same extent as if no receiver had been appointed. § 10. Thus, as in bankruptcy, the priority of a security interest (as opposed to its validity) would appear to be determined as of the date of commencement (of, in this case, the receivership).

The new act sets forth the receiver's presumptive powers, as well as those that the receiver may exercise only with court approval. § 12 (a) & (b). As in Chapter 11, the receiver has broad power to deal with the subject of the receivership in the ordinary course of business:

> Except as limited by court order or the law of this state, other than this [act], a receiver may:
> ...
> (2) Operate a business constituting receivership property, including preservation, use, sale, lease, license, exchange, collection, or disposition of the property in the ordinary course of business; [and]
> (3) In the ordinary course of business, incur unsecured debt and pay expenses incidental to the receiver's preservation, use, sale, lease, license, exchange, collection, or disposition of receivership property ....

§ 12(a). In addition to addressing the receiver's powers in detail, the act as promulgated sets forth duties of the receiver and the owner of receivership property. §§ 12(c) & 13.

Outside the ordinary course of business, and with court approval, the receiver may use, sell, lease, license, exchange or otherwise transfer receivership property. § 16(b) & (c). Unless the agreement of transfer provides otherwise, the transfer is free and clear of rights of redemption and liens other than liens that are senior to the lien of the person who obtained the receiver's appointment. § 16(c). Liens extinguished by the receiver's sale attach to proceeds with the same validity, perfection and priority as they had with respect to the property sold, according to the priority rules established by law other than these new rules. §§ 16(d) & 20(g).The sale may be conducted as a private sale and creditors with valid secured claims may credit bid. § 16(e). The new uniform act also provides a safe harbor for purchasers, in case a party objects to the sale but fails to get a stay of the order approving the sale. § 16(f).

The court may award the receiver from receivership property reasonable and necessary fees and expenses for carrying out the receiver's duties. § 21(a). The official comment to section 21 quotes 2 Clark on Receivers, § 640.1(b) at 1082 (3d ed. 1959), to suggest that this includes proceeds of encumbered property:

A sale by the receiver free from liens is for most practical purposes equivalent to a foreclosure sale and if and when the property is realized under such circumstances and if and when the mortgagees or lienholders avail themselves of the advantage of the receivership to effect the sale of the mortgaged premises, this means they have saved themselves similar expenses in a foreclosure suit or otherwise and, therefore, should pay for the advantage they have received.

In another provision that will be familiar to bankruptcy practitioners but is unusual in state receivership law, the new statute provides that entry of the order of appointment acts as an automatic stay, applicable to all persons, of an act to obtain possession of, exercise control over, or enforce a judgment against receivership property, as well as an act to enforce a lien against receivership property. § 14(a). The court can expand the scope of the stay and grant relief from the stay. § 14 (b) & (c). However, certain actions are outside the scope of the stay. § 14(d). The new act also addresses the consequences of a violation of the stay. § 14(e) & (f).

The act as promulgated authorizes the receiver, with court approval, to engage and pay professionals to assist in the administration of the receivership. § 15.

With court approval, a receiver may "adopt" or reject an executory contract of the owner relating to receivership property and the new uniform act sets out the mechanics for adoption or rejection. § 17 (b) & (c). The receiver may also assign an adopted executory contract to the extent permitted by the contract and applicable law other than this new act, but free of so-called "ipso facto" clauses. § 17(d) & (f). The consequences of a receiver's rejection of an executory contract are prescribed in section 17(e). As is true for a bankruptcy trustee, the receiver's ability to reject the unexpired lease of a tenant is limited. § 17(h).

Consistent with the receiver's status as an officer of the court, the act as promulgated provides the receiver with immunity for acts or omissions within the scope of the receiver's appointment. § 18(a). It also incorporates the *Barton* doctrine, *Barton v. Barbour*, 104 U.S. 126, 128, 26 L. Ed. 672, 1881 WL 19839 (1881), providing that a receiver cannot be sued personally for an act or omission in administering receivership property except with the approval of the appointing court. § 18(b).

BANKRUPTCY HIGHLIGHTS

The new uniform act requires a receiver to notify creditors of the appointment unless the court orders otherwise, § 20(a) & (e), and requires creditors to file claims with the receiver as a precondition to obtaining any distribution from receivership property or the proceeds of such property. § 20(b). It permits a receiver to recommend disallowance of claims. § 20(e). It also authorizes the court to forgo the filing of unsecured claims where the receivership property is likely to be insufficient to satisfy secured claims against the property.

Where a receiver has been appointed by another state, the new act authorizes the court to appoint that person or its designee as an ancillary receiver for the purpose of obtaining possession, custody and control of receivership property located within this state. § 24(a). It also permits the court to enter any order necessary to effectuate an order of a court in another state appointing or directing a receiver. § 24(b).

The appointment of a receiver on request of a mortgagee or assignee of rents triggers special protections under § 25:

(a) A request by a mortgagee for appointment of a receiver, the appointment of a receiver, or application by a mortgagee of receivership property or proceeds to the secured obligation does not:
(1) Make the mortgagee a mortgagee in possession of the real property;
(2) Make the mortgagee an agent of the owner;
(3) Constitute an election of remedies that precludes a later action to enforce the secured obligation;
(4) Make the secured obligation unenforceable;
(5) Limit any right available to the mortgagee with respect to the secured obligation; or
(6) Except as otherwise provided in subsection (b), bar a deficiency judgment pursuant to the law of this state, other than this [act], governing or relating to a deficiency judgment.
(b) If a receiver sells receivership property that pursuant to [§ 16(c)] is free and clear of a lien, the ability of a creditor to enforce an obligation that had been secured by the lien is subject to the law of this state, other than this [act], relating to a deficiency judgment.

VIII. Report of Statistics Required by the Bankruptcy Abuse Prevention and Consumer Protection Act of 2005

BANKRUPTCY HIGHLIGHTS

The following report of statistics, required by the Bankruptcy Abuse Prevention and Consumer Protection Act or 2005 (BAPCPA) (codified as 28 U.S.C.A. § 159(b)), was issued for the calendar year 2017 by the Director of the Administrative Office of United States Courts, and the full report, with accompanying tables, is available at http://www.uscourts.gov/statistics-reports/bapcpa-report-2017 (last visited Oct. 26, 2018).

Introduction

Under 28 U.S.C. § 159(b), enacted as part of the Bankruptcy Abuse Prevention and Consumer Protection Act of 2005 (BAPCPA), the Director of the Administrative Office of the United States Courts (AO) is required to submit an annual report to Congress on certain bankruptcy statistics detailed in 28 U.S.C. § 159(c). Section 159(a) provides that clerks of the bankruptcy courts "shall collect statistics regarding debtors who are individuals with primarily consumer debts seeking relief under chapters 7, 11, and 13 of title 11." The Director of the AO is required to compile this information, analyze it, and make it accessible to the public as well as Congress. This report is prepared to fulfill the statutory requirement. Tables in the report display data nationally, by circuit, and by district.

Summary of Findings

During calendar year 2017, more than 740,000 bankruptcy petitions were filed by individuals with debts that are predominantly consumer in nature ("consumer cases"), 1 percent fewer than in 2016. Approximately 61 percent of the petitions were filed under chapter 7, in which a debtor's assets are liquidated and the nonexempt proceeds distributed to creditors. About 38 percent were filed under chapter 13, in which individuals who have regular income and debts below a statutory threshold make installment payments to creditors under court-confirmed plans. One-tenth of 1 percent of petitions filed by individuals with predominantly consumer debt were filed under chapter 11, which allows businesses and individuals to continue operating while they formulate plans to reorganize and repay their creditors. [Note 1] [Notes appear at the end of this report, in a section entitled "Notes to BAPCPA 2017 Report."]

Approximately 817,000 consumer cases were closed during calendar year 2017. Sixty-one percent of the closed consumer cases had been filed under chapter 7, about 39 percent under chapter 13, and less than 1 percent under chapter 11.

BANKRUPTCY HIGHLIGHTS

Consumer debtors seeking bankruptcy protection under chapters 7, 11, or 13 during 2017 reported holding total assets of $80 billion and total liabilities of $105 billion. Total assets reported by consumer debtors rose 11 percent from 2016. Total liabilities for the same set of cases decreased 45 percent from 2016. The growth in 2016 was primarily due to one debtor in the Western District of Washington (WA-W) who reported total liabilities of $85,122,168,563. Excluding the data for WA-W, the total liabilities decreased by 1 percent. (When considering the magnitude of these decreases, one should keep in mind that annual consumer filings fell 1 percent in 2017.)

The median average monthly income reported by all debtors was $2,741 (3 percent higher than in 2016), and the median average reported monthly expenses was $2,645 (2 percent higher than in 2016) . [Note 2] From filing to closing, chapter 7 consumer cases terminated in 2017 had a mean time interval of 199 days and a median time interval of 114 days. A total of 151,483 reaffirmation agreements were reported as filed in 107,540 chapter 7 consumer cases terminated during 2017. In 40 percent of the chapter 13 cases filed during 2017, debtors reported that they had filed for bankruptcy protection during the previous eight years, 1 percent higher than in 2016.

Tables

In accordance with BAPCPA, the bankruptcy statistics in this report are itemized by chapter of Title 11 (the Bankruptcy Code) and report only data in consumer cases. The tables noted in the list below have been created for this report as specified in 28 U.S.C. § 159(c) (Note that the actual tables are not reproduced here, but are available at the website of the United States Courts, www.uscourt.gov/statistics-reports/bapcappa-report-2017.).

BAPCPA REPORT TABLES		
Code	Description	BAPCPA Table
28 U.S.C. § 159(c)(3)(A) &	Assets and Liabilities Reported by Debtors and	1

BAPCPA REPORT TABLES

Code	Description	BAPCPA Table
28 U.S.C. § 159(c)(3)(C)	Debts Discharged	
28 U.S.C. § 159(c)(3)(B)	Income and Expenses Reported by Debtors	2
28 U.S.C. § 159(c)(3)(D)	Time Interval from Filing to Closing	3
28 U.S.C. § 159(c)(3)(E)	Reaffirmation Agreements	4
28 U.S.C. § 159(c)(3)(F)(i)	Property Valuation Orders	5
28 U.S.C. § 159(c)(3)(F)(ii)	Chapter 13 Cases Closed by Dismissal or Plan Completion and Plan Modifications	6
28 U.S.C. § 159(c)(3)(F)(iii)	Prior/No Prior Filings Reported by Debtors	7
28 U.S.C. § 159(c)(3)(G)	Creditor Misconduct and Punitive Damages	8
28 U.S.C. § 159(c)(3)(H)	Rule 9011 Sanctions Imposed Against Debtors' Attorneys and Damages Awarded	

The naming convention used for the tables in this report provides that the alphabetic character immediately following the table number indicates the chapter(s) of the Bankruptcy Code associated with the cases included in the table. "A" indicates cases under chapter 7 only; "B" indicates cases under chapter 11 only; "D" indicates cases under chapter 13 only; and "X" indicates cases under chapters 7, 11, and 13 combined. For example, Table 1D reports assets and liabilities for cases filed under chapter 13. [Note 3]

Methodology and Data Limitations

Debtor-Provided Data

The U.S. bankruptcy courts send data to the AO when a case is filed, when certain motions are filed in the case, and when the case is closed. The data are then compiled annually for the purpose of this report. Many BAPCPA tables, particularly those reporting data on debtors' assets, liabilities, income, and expenses, rely on data provided by debtors when they submit required forms, schedules, motions, agreements, and other filings to the court. Most of these data, as specified in 28 U.S.C. § 159(c), are provided exclusively by the debtors and are not validated either by the courts or the AO.

With respect to data collected from forms and schedules submitted at filing, debtors may fail to provide some or all of the data required for the BAPCPA tables. Therefore, analyses involving two or more columns in any table may overstate or understate differences. When all required data from a debtor are missing, either because of omission or delayed submission, analyses involving the data and the number of cases become unreliable. Therefore, caution should be used when analyzing columns of data or comparing any column of data to the number of cases filed.

Reliance on debtor-provided data may introduce other sources of error. One likely source of error arises when a debtor inaccurately reports assets, liabilities, income, or expenses at the time of filing. Those inaccuracies, if significant enough, may affect district, circuit, and national totals for the relevant fields in the tables in this report.

Data on Cases Filed and Closed

Another limitation relates to the first column of data in each table, which presents total cases. Some tables include reopened and transferred cases in the totals, but others omit these cases. Reopened and transferred cases are excluded when the data would be duplicative. For example, totals for assets and liabilities at the original filing of a case are the same for each reopening of that case. Counting the cases twice (once at filing and once at reopening) would distort the data on reported assets, liabilities, income, and expenses. In all other instances in which the duplication would not affect the results, these cases are included.

Transaction Data

Transaction data include reports of case-related events such as reaffirmation agreements, valuation orders, creditor misconduct, and attorney sanctions that occur during bankruptcy proceedings (see Tables 4, 5, 8, and 9). Such data are typically captured in the courts' docketing activity.

In many instances, BAPCPA requires a report of the total number of cases in which a specific type of transaction has occurred. This affects the way that transaction data are reported. A case may have more than one occurrence of a particular type of transaction. For this reason, the case must be concluded before the AO can report whether the case meets the requirement to be counted and to ensure that no case is counted more than once. Thus, tables based on transaction data are based only on data from cases closed during the reporting period. These tables are subject to the same limitations noted in the section on cases filed and closed. Case activity that occurred prior to October 17, 2006, in a case that closed during the reporting period would not have been captured, causing transaction data to be underreported.

In addition, because a case may have more than one occurrence of a specific type of transaction, but the characteristics of each transaction may be different, the case must be counted in each column of a table whenever any occurrence meets the criteria for data in that column. If, for example, a debtor enters into three reaffirmation agreements, two of which include certification from the debtor's attorney and one of which does not, the case is counted in the column representing "number of cases with agreements filed pro se" as well as the column representing the "total number of cases with agreements filed." Furthermore, if, in the example above, the court approves one reaffirmation agreement and denies the other two, the case is also counted in the column representing the number of cases with agreements approved."

Because transaction data are captured from docket activity, the collection of accurate transaction data relies on debtors, their attorneys, and other case parties who file motions, agreements, and other documents with the courts to identify them appropriately. If a filer fails to note the correct court event at docketing, the data may not be reported accurately or at all. If the filer submits multiple matters under a single court event, the activities may be undercounted or not counted at all.

Assets and Liabilities Reported by Debtors

Tables 1A, 1B, 1D, and 1X set forth the assets and liabilities reported by debtors in total and by category of assets and liabilities, as well as the total net scheduled debt reported by the debtors on Official Bankruptcy Form 106Sum—Summary of Your Assets and Liabilities and Certain Statistical Information (B 106 Summary). All tables that report assets and liabilities (1A, 1B, 1D, and 1X) present data on cases filed during the reporting period by individual debtors with primarily consumer debt. The data for these tables are provided exclusively by the debtors and cannot be validated by the courts. These data typically are provided by a debtor at the time of filing or within 14 days thereafter as required by Rule 1007 of the Federal Rule of Bankruptcy Procedure (Fed. R. Bankr. P. 1007). They are not typically updated as the case proceeds. Data for reopened and transferred cases are excluded to prevent duplicate reporting.

"Net scheduled debt" is defined as the difference between the total amount of debt and obligations of a debtor reported on the schedules and the amount of such debt reported in categories that are predominantly non-dischargeable. Debt that is predominantly non-dischargeable may include, but is not limited to, domestic support obligations, taxes, student loans, and pension obligations. Thus, net scheduled debt approximates the amount of debt reported by the debtor at the time of filing that may be eligible for discharge (without regard to security interests) during the case and is referred to in 28 U.S.C. § 159(c)(3)(C) as the "aggregate amount of debt discharged in cases filed during the reporting period."

"Net scheduled debt," however, overstates the amount of debt actually discharged by the amount of secured debt (e.g., mortgages on real property and many car loans) that remains after the discharge. A discharge in bankruptcy releases the debtor from personal liability for certain specified types of debts. Although a debtor is not personally liable for discharged debts, a valid lien secured by property that has not been voided in the bankruptcy case will remain in effect as to that secured property after the bankruptcy case has been closed. Therefore, unless the debtor continues repaying the discharged debt, a secured creditor may enforce the lien to recover the property that secures payment of the debt. In determining dischargeable debt, the statute does not provide for a deduction of either real or personal property valuations from the claims by creditors secured by such property.

Table 1X shows that individual debtors with primarily consumer debt seeking bankruptcy protection under chapters 7, 11, or 13, during 2017 reported holding total assets in the aggregate amount of $80 billion. Sixty-two percent of these assets were categorized as real property, and 38 percent as personal property. Apart from districts with fewer than 200 case filings each (the Districts of the Northern Mariana Islands, U.S. Virgin Islands, and Guam), debtors in the Northern District of California (CA-N) and Southern District of Florida (FL-S) reported the highest average assets per petition at $583,000 and $338,000, respectively. Filers in the Western District of Tennessee (TN-W) reported the lowest average assets at $44,000.

Debtors reported total liabilities in the aggregate amount of $105 billion, with 58 percent of liabilities categorized as secured claims, 3 percent as unsecured priority claims, and 40 percent as unsecured non-priority claims. Overall, debtors categorized 90 percent of debts and obligations as dischargeable debt. Excluding districts with fewer than 200 case filings each, debtors in the Eastern District of New York (NY-E) reported the highest average liabilities per filed petition at $445,000, and filers in TN-W had the lowest average liabilities at $69,000.

Income and Expenses Reported by Debtors

Tables 2A, 2B, 2D, and 2X present data on the income and expenses as reported by debtors on Official Bankruptcy Form 106Sum—Summary of Your Assets and Liabilities and Certain Statistical Information (B 106 Summary). Current monthly income data reflect income from all sources. Average monthly income data reflect total income for the last full six months prior to the bankruptcy filing, divided by six. The data for these tables are provided exclusively by the debtors and are not validated by the courts. A debtor typically provides the data at the time of filing or within 14 days of filing as required by Fed. R. Bankr. P. 1007. Only data provided during the initial filing of each case are counted in Tables 2A-2X. Data for reopened and transferred cases are excluded to prevent duplicate reporting. Median values are calculated only when 10 or more cases are reported. [Note 4]

Table 2X shows that 742,323 consumer cases were filed in 2017 under chapters 7, 11, and 13 across the nation and 686,125 debtors completed the forms needed to include their data in these tables. [Note 5] The median current monthly income [Note 6] of debtors who completed the relevant forms was $3,023, slightly more than the $2,934 median current monthly income reported in 2016. The median average monthly income [Note 7] was $2,741, a 3 percent increase from 2016, and the median average expenses [Note 8] were $2,645, an increase of 2 percent from 2016. CA-N had the highest median current monthly income with $4,193, and the District of Puerto Rico (PR) had the lowest median current monthly income with $1,719. Filers in CA-N had the highest median average monthly income with $3,604, and filers in PR had the lowest median average monthly income with $1,827. Filers in CA-N had the highest median average expenses with $3,560, and filers in PR had the lowest with $1,742.

Time Interval from Case Filing to Closing

In accordance with 28 U.S.C. § 159(c)(3)(D), Table 3 reports the mean time interval between case filing and closing of consumer cases filed on or after October 17, 2006, under chapters 7, 11, and 13 and terminated during 2017. [Note 9] The median time interval also has been included to provide perspective on the mean value by reducing the effect of data outliers, although median values are calculated only when 10 or more cases are reported. [Note 10] Reopened cases are excluded from this table because most reopened cases are filed and closed relatively quickly to settle administrative matters and do not proceed in the same way as original filings. [Note 11] For transferred cases, the mean and median time intervals are calculated from the date the case is received at the new location to the closing of the case at that location.

During the 12-month period ending December 31, 2017, a total of 794,571 consumer cases opened on or after October 17, 2006, were closed under chapters 7, 11, and 13, with a mean time interval from filing to closing of 556 days and a median time interval of 146 days. The higher mean closing time (relative to the median time) reflects particularly long-running cases. Both the mean and median are 6 percent lower than for 2016.

Of the 481,250 chapter 7 consumer cases filed on or after October 17, 2006, and closed in 2017, the mean time interval from filing to closing was 199 days (down from 209 days in 2016), and the median time interval was 114 days (down from 115 days in 2016). The Middle District of Louisiana had the highest median of any district at 316 days, and the Southern District of Iowa had the lowest median at 98 days.

A total of 925 chapter 11 consumer cases filed on or after October 17, 2006, were closed in 71 districts during 2017. The mean time interval from filing to closing was 796 days (up from 760 days in 2016), and the median time interval was 587 days (down from 590 days in 2016). Only 21 districts had 10 or more chapter 11 cases closed in 2017. Of those 21 districts, the District of Arizona had the highest median at 1,159 days, and the Northern District of Texas had the lowest median at 325 days.

A total of 312,396 chapter 13 consumer cases filed on or after October 17, 2006, were closed during 2017. The mean time interval from filing to closing was 1,105 days (down from 1,162 days in 2016), and the median time interval was 1,177 days (down from 1,255 days in 2016). The District of Vermont (VT) had the highest median at 1,976 days, and NY-E had the lowest median at 90 days. However, the median and mean do not accurately convey the time required for a typical chapter 13 case; rather, they are proxies for the percent of chapter 13 cases closed by plan completion, as plan completion typically takes much longer than dismissal. [Note 12]

Reaffirmation Agreements

A debtor may enter into a reaffirmation agreement with a creditor to continue paying a dischargeable debt following bankruptcy. This may occur when, for example, a debtor wants to keep an automobile and continue making payments on it. If an attorney represents the debtor during the bankruptcy, the debtor's attorney may or may not represent the debtor during negotiation of a reaffirmation agreement. For purposes of this report, a reaffirmation agreement is considered "pro se" if it was submitted without the certification of an attorney contained in Part IV of Director's Bankruptcy Form 2400A—Reaffirmation Documents (Form B2400A), regardless of whether the debtor was otherwise represented in the case by an attorney.

Table 4 reports only on reaffirmation agreements filed in cases under chapter 7. [Note 13] Varying local practices govern the procedures for approving and denying reaffirmation agreements filed with the courts. In many districts, the court does not issue orders with respect to reaffirmation agreements filed with certification by debtors' attorneys. In these instances, the reaffirmation agreement between the debtor and creditor is implicitly accepted without further court action and may or may not be recorded or otherwise noted in court documentation of the case. As a result, the difference between the number of reaffirmation agreements filed and the number of reaffirmation agreements approved does not represent the number of reaffirmation agreements denied. Moreover, sometimes multiple reaffirmation agreements are submitted together, some with and others without attorney certification, and a court order may fail to specify decisions of the court on the individual reaffirmation agreements. For these reasons, the data reported for approved reaffirmation agreements may not be representative of the total number of valid reaffirmation agreements executed by the parties.

As Table 4 illustrates, a total of 151,483 reaffirmation agreements were reported as filed in 496,637 chapter 7 consumer cases closed during the 12-month period ending December 31, 2017. The Northern District of Illinois had the highest total number of cases in which reaffirmation agreements were filed (5,719), followed by the Central District of California (CA-C) (4,717 cases) and the Middle District of Florida (FL-M) (4,523). Nationwide, 22 percent of chapter 7 cases closed had at least one reaffirmation agreement filed, up 2 percentage points from 2016. The District of Maine reported the highest percentage of cases closed that had at least one reaffirmation agreement filed (41 percent). In 10 percent of cases with reaffirmation agreements filed, one or more agreements were submitted without attorney certification (pro se). The District of Kansas (KS) had the highest number of cases in which at least one pro se reaffirmation agreement was filed (1,097 cases). At least one pro se reaffirmation agreement was filed in 2 percent of chapter 7 cases closed. The Middle District of Alabama (32 percent of cases) and KS (27 percent) had the highest percentage of chapter 7 cases closed in which one or more pro se reaffirmation agreements were filed.

One percent of cases in which a reaffirmation agreement was filed had at least one reaffirmation agreement approved by order of the court. However, as described above, this does not indicate that reaffirmation agreements were denied in 99 percent of the cases. In 2017, The District of Montana reported the highest percentage of cases in which at least one reaffirmation agreement had been approved (90 percent), followed by the District of Colorado (CO) (27 percent), and the District of Alaska (AK) (17 percent). These three districts accounted for 47 percent of the cases in which at least one reaffirmation agreement was approved.

Property Valuation Orders

BANKRUPTCY HIGHLIGHTS

In some cases, motions are made to the court to determine the value of property securing an allowed claim under 11 U.S.C. §§ 506 and 1325 and Federal Rule of Bankruptcy Procedure 3012 . Table 5 shows the number of cases closed in 2017 in which final orders were entered determining the value of property securing a claim in an amount less than the amount of the claim, as well as the number of final orders entered determining the value of property securing a claim. Additional columns of data were added to provide further perspective on the required data.

A total of 318,974 chapter 13 consumer cases were closed in 2017. Final orders determining the value of property securing a claim were entered in 11,242 of the cases. In 7,450 cases, the value of property was reported in one or more final orders; in 4,844 (65 percent) of those cases, at least one final order valued the property at less than the full amount of the claim.

A case may have more than one final order determining the value of property securing a claim. In total, 14,621 final orders were entered in the 11,242 cases. Determinations of the value of property were reported in 10,095 final orders, of which 6,214 (62 percent) were valued below the amount of the claim. FL-S reported that 4,466 final orders had been entered determining the value of property securing a claim, the highest total of any district. Seventy-six percent of the final orders determining the value of property securing a claim (11,174 final orders) were entered in five districts (FL-S, the District of South Carolina, the Eastern District of California, FL-M, and CO); 46 districts reported no final orders determining the value of property securing a claim.

Chapter 13 Cases Closed by Dismissal or Plan Completion

Table 6 shows the number of cases in which plans were completed in chapter 13 consumer cases, separately itemized by the number of modifications made to the plans. Table 6 also reports the number of chapter 13 consumer cases dismissed, the number dismissed for failure to make payments under the plan, and the number refiled after dismissal. For purposes of this table, a chapter 13 consumer case is counted as "refiled after dismissal" if the case was filed during the reporting period by one or more debtors who were party to a separate chapter 13 consumer case that was dismissed no more than 180 days prior to the filing date of the current case. Cases that are reopened are not included in the total for cases refiled after dismissal.

BANKRUPTCY HIGHLIGHTS

A total of 318,751 chapter 13 consumer cases filed on or after October 17, 2006, were closed by dismissal or plan completion in 2017. Table 6 illustrates that 164,417 of these cases were dismissed. In 48 percent of the cases closed (154,334 cases), the debtors were discharged after completing repayment plans, down from 52 percent in 2016. Among districts with at least 10 closed cases, VT had the highest percentage of cases (80 percent) closed by plan completion, followed by the District of Minnesota (78 percent) and District of North Dakota (74 percent). Of the 154,334 chapter 13 consumer cases in which debtors completed repayment plans, 33,388 (22 percent) had plans that were modified at least once prior to plan completion, a slightly higher percentage than in 2016.

Nationwide, failure to make plan payments was cited in 51 percent of cases as the reason for dismissal, down from 53 percent in 2016. Among districts with at least 10 closed cases, the Southern District of Alabama had the greatest percentage of dismissals (87 percent) that were for failure to make payments. The Southern District of Texas had the lowest percentage of its dismissals made for failure to make payments (5 percent), followed by CA-C (10 percent). Table 6 shows that 22,061 cases were refiled after dismissal.

Prior Filings Reported by Debtors

Table 7 reports the number of cases in which individual debtors with primarily consumer debts filed for protection under chapter 13 during the reporting period and stated on the voluntary bankruptcy petition (Official Bankruptcy Form 101) that they previously had filed a case under any chapter of the Bankruptcy Code during the preceding eight years ("prior filings"). For this table, data are captured at the time of filing, and only data on the initial filing of each case are counted. Data on reopened cases are excluded to prevent duplicate reporting. The data for Table 7 are provided exclusively by the debtors and are subject to the limitations described in the section above on debtor-provided data.

In 40 percent of the 285,680 (113,059) chapter 13 cases filed in 2017, debtors stated that they had filed a bankruptcy petition during the previous eight years. In the remaining 172,621 cases, debtors stated that they had not filed for bankruptcy during the previous eight years. In 2017, the District of Utah recorded the highest percentage of cases with prior filings at 59 percent, followed by District of Idaho (59 percent). The districts with the lowest percentage of cases in which debtors indicated prior filings were AK (21 percent of cases) and PR (21 percent).

Creditor Misconduct and Punitive Damages

28 U.S.C. § 159(c)(3)(G) requires the Director of the AO to report on "the number of cases in which creditors were fined for misconduct and any amount of punitive damages awarded by the court for creditor misconduct." Creditor misconduct, however, is not a specific cause of action under the Bankruptcy Code. At least five violations of the Bankruptcy Code could be considered creditor misconduct:

- involuntary petition filed in bad faith (11 U.S.C. § 303(i)(2)) (link is external),

- willful violation of the automatic stay (11 U.S.C. § 362(k)(1)) (link is external),

- collusive bidding (11 U.S.C. § 363(n)) (link is external),

- creditor request for a determination of dischargeability of consumer debt that is subsequently discharged was not substantially justified (11 U.S.C. § 523(d)) (link is external), and

- violation of the injunction against attempting to collect a discharged debt (11 U.S.C. § 524(a)(2) and (3)) (link is external).

At least six other activities related to litigation procedures could also be considered creditor misconduct under certain circumstances:

- improper activity related to pretrial conference and order (Fed. R. Bankr. P. 7016) (link is external),

- sanctionable discovery requests, responses, or objections (Fed. R. Bankr. P. 7026) (link is external),

- failure to make disclosures or cooperate in discovery (Fed. R. Bankr. P. 7037) (link is external),

- failure to prosecute or to comply with court orders and rules (Fed. R. Bankr. P. 7041) (link is external),

- sanctionable filings (Fed. R. Bankr. P. 9011) (link is external), and

- unreasonably or vexatiously multiplying proceedings (28 U.S.C. § 1927) (link is external).

What may be reported as creditor misconduct in one district may not be reported in another. In addition, because a creditor may be reprimanded or penalized for misconduct in many ways, many of which may not be explicitly recorded on a court's docket as a sanction, this table does not provide a comprehensive picture of sanctions imposed against creditors in bankruptcy courts. Moreover, a sanction imposed for creditor misconduct is likely limited to what is sufficient to deter repetition of such conduct or comparable conduct by others similarly situated. Although sanctions may consist of or include directives of a nonmonetary nature, an order to pay a penalty into court, or an order directing payment to the movant of some or all of the reasonable attorneys' fees and other expenses incurred as a direct result of the violation, the Bankruptcy Code and Bankruptcy Rules do not permit the award of punitive damages for every violation classifiable as creditor misconduct. However, only punitive damages are reflected in the Table 8 series.

Table 8X shows that creditors were fined for misconduct in 142 consumer cases closed during 2017 and that orders to pay punitive damages totaling $27,110 were issued in 12 of those cases.

Rule 9011 Sanctions Imposed Against Debtors' Attorneys

Federal Rule of Bankruptcy Procedure 9011 provides that attorneys may be sanctioned for improper or frivolous representations to the court submitted in any petition, pleading, written motion, or other paper. The rule states that "[a] sanction imposed for violation of this rule shall be limited to what is sufficient to deter repetition of such conduct or comparable conduct by others similarly situated." Any "sanction may consist of, or include, directives of a nonmonetary nature, an order to pay a penalty into court, or . . . an order directing payment to the movant of some or all of the reasonable attorneys' fees and other expenses incurred as a direct result of the violation." Fed. R. Bankr. P. 9011(c)(2). The Table 9 series captures only misconduct by debtors' attorneys that rises to the level required for sanctions under Federal Rule of Bankruptcy Procedure 9011. Because a debtor's attorney may be reprimanded or penalized for misconduct in other ways, this table does not provide a comprehensive picture of sanctions imposed against debtors' attorneys in bankruptcy courts.

BANKRUPTCY HIGHLIGHTS

Table 9X shows that of the 816,892 consumer cases filed on or after October 17, 2006, and terminated in 2017, sanctions were imposed against debtors' attorneys in 24 cases, with damages totaling $25,464 awarded in 20 cases.

Notes to BAPCPA 2017 Report

1 Consumer cases filed under chapter 11 are relatively infrequent and are generally believed to result when debtors exceed the debt limits of 11 U.S.C. § 109(e), which in calendar year 2017 restricts chapter 13 to debtors with less than $394,725 in noncontingent, liquidated, unsecured debts and less than $1,184,200 of noncontingent, liquidated, secured debts.

2 Debtors calculate their average monthly incomes and average monthly expenses and report them to the courts on line 10 of Official Bankruptcy Form 106I—Schedule I: Your Income (B 106I) and line 22 of Official Bankruptcy Form 106J—Schedule J Your Expenses (B 106J). The AO then calculates the median of the average monthly incomes reported by debtors for all districts and circuits.

3 "C" is reserved for cases filed under chapter 12, which does not apply to consumer cases.

4 It is not meaningful to calculate medians when the number of cases is small. For this reason, the AO does not calculate medians for fewer than 10 cases at any aggregate level (e.g., district, circuit).

5 The number of cases with completed schedules differs between the Table 1 series and the Table 2 series because those tables draw data from different parts of the summary of schedules. If a debtor completed all necessary fields for inclusion in the Table 1 series, but not the Table 2 series, then that case and its data were included in the appropriate tables in the Table 1 series but not in the Table 2 series, and vice versa.

6 Current monthly income is provided by chapter 7 debtors on line 11 of Official Bankruptcy Form 122A-1—Chapter 7 Statement of Your Current Monthly Income (B 122A-1), by chapter 11 debtors on line 11 of Official Bankruptcy Form 122B—Chapter 11 Statement of Your Current Monthly Income (B 122B), and by chapter 13 debtors on line 11 of Official Bankruptcy Form 122C-1—Chapter 13 Statement of Your Current Monthly Income and Calculation of Commitment Period (B 122C-1).

BANKRUPTCY HIGHLIGHTS

7 See note 2.

8 See note 2.

9 The time interval measures can be influenced by the proportion of cases filed to cases terminated, where a stable proportion creates better comparability year-over-year.

10 See note 6.

11 Tables 4, 5, 6, 8A-8X, and 9A-9X include reopened cases, whereas Table 3 does not include reopened cases. Accordingly, the total for cases closed in Table 3 may differ from the total in other tables.

12 See Table 6.

13 Although reaffirmation agreements are technically possible under other chapters of the Bankruptcy Code, they are found almost exclusively in chapter 7 cases. Because no modification of a secured creditor's rights may be obtained under chapter 7 without consent of the creditor, a debtor who wishes to retain collateral securing a claim must negotiate a reaffirmation agreement acceptable to the creditor. In contrast, under chapters 11, 12, and 13, subject to certain restrictions, the terms of a secured claim may be altered to allow the debtor to retain use of the collateral, thereby obviating the need for a reaffirmation agreement.

UNITED STATES CODE ANNOTATED

TITLE 11

BANKRUPTCY

TABLE I

This Table lists the sections of former Title 11, Bankruptcy, and indicates the sections of Title 11, as revised by Pub.L. 95–598 which cover similar and related subject matter.

Title 11 Former Sections	Title 11 New Sections
1(1)–(3)	Rep.
1(4)	101(12)
1(5)–(7)	Rep.
1(8)	101(8)
1(9), (10)	Rep.
1(11)	101(9)
1(12), (13)	Rep.
1(14)	101(11)
1(15), (16)	Rep.
1(17)	101(17), (18)
1(18)	Rep.
1(19)	101(26)
1(20)–(22)	Rep.
1(23)	101(30)
1(24)	101(31)
1(25), (26)	Rep.
1(27)	101(34)
1(28), (29)	Rep.
1(29a)	101(38)
1(30)	101(40)
1(31)	Rep.
1(32)	101(24)
1(33), (34)	Rep.
1(35)	102(7)
11(a)(1)	109(a)
11(a)(2)	502(j)
11(a)(2A)	505(a), (b)
11(a)(3), (4)	Rep.
11(a)(5)	721
11(a)(6)	Rep.
11(a)(7)	363
11(a)(8)	350
11(a)(9)–(14)	Rep.
11(a)(15)	105
11(a)(16)	Rep.
11(a)(17)	324
11(a)(18)	303(i)
11(a)(19), (20)	Rep.
11(a)(21)	543(b), (c)
11(a)(22)	305(a)(2)
11(b)	Rep.
21	303(h)
22	109(b)
22(a)	301
22(b)	303(a)
23(a)	Rep.
23(b)	303(b)
23(c)–(f)	Rep.
23(g)	723
23(h)–(k)	Rep.
24	522
25(a)(1)	343, 521(4)
25(a)(2)	Rep.
25(a)(3)	521(2)
25(a)(4)	521(3)
25(a)(5)	521(3)
25(a)(6)	521(2)
25(a)(7)	521(2)
25(a)(8), (9)	521(1)
25(a)(10)	343, 344
25(a)(11)	521(3)
25(b)	Rep.
26	541(a)
27, 28	Rep.
29(a)	362
29(b)–(d)	Rep.
29(e)	108(a), (b)
29(f)	108(c)
30, 31	(See former 501–1103)
32(a)	727(a)(10), 1141(d)(4)
32(b)	727(c)
32(c)(1)	727(a)(2), (4)
32(c)(2)	727(a)(3)
32(c)(3)	727(a)(4)
32(c)(4)	727(a)(2)
32(c)(5)	727(a)(8), (9)
32(c)(6)	727(a)(6)
32(c)(7)	727(a)(5)
32(c)(8)	Rep.
32(d), (e)	Rep.
32(f)	524(a)
32(g), (h)	Rep.
33	727(d), (e), 1328(e)
34	524(e)

BANKRUPTCY CODE

Title 11 Former Sections	Title 11 New Sections	Title 11 Former Sections	Title 11 New Sections
35(a)(1)	523(a)(1)	91, 92	341
35(a)(2)	523(a)(2)	93(a)–(c)	Rep.
35(a)(3)	523(a)(3)	93(d)	502(a), (c)
35(a)(4)	523(a)(4)	93(e)	Rep.
35(a)(5), (6)	Rep.	93(f)	502(b)
35(a)(7)	523(a)(5)	93(g)	502(d)
35(a)(8)	523(a)(6)	93(h)	506(a), (b)
35(b)	523(b), 349(a)	93(i)	501(b), 509
35(c)	523(c)	93(j)	724(a)
35(c)(4)	362	93(k)	502(j)
41(a)	Rep.	93(l), (m)	Rep.
41(b)	303(d)	93(n)	501(a), 726(a)(3)
41(c)–(e)	Rep.	93a	Rep.
41(f)	301	94	342
42	Omitted	95(a)	301
43	Rep.	95(b)	303(b)
44(a)	343	95(c), (d)	Rep.
44(b)–(f)	Rep.	95(e)	303(b)
44(g)	549(c)	95(f)	303(c)
44(h)–(l)	Rep.	95(g)	303(j), 707
45–51	Rep.	95(h)	Rep.
52, 53	Rep.	96	547
54	Rep.	96(a)(4)	547(e)(1)(B)
55	Omitted	96(b)	550, 551
61–71	Rep.	96(c)	547(c)(4), 553
72(a)	702	96(d)	329
72(b)	705	96(e)(1)	741
72(c)	327(c)	96(e)(2)	745, 751, 752
73	321	96(e)(3)	753
74	325, 703(a)	96(e)(5)	749
75(a)(1)	704(1)	101	345
75(a)(2)	345	101a	Rep.
75(a)(3)	704(2)	102(a)(1)	503(b)(2)
75(a)(4)	Rep.	102(a)(2)–(4)	Rep.
75(a)(5)	704(2)	102(b)	Rep.
75(a)(6)	Rep.	102(c)	504
75(a)(7)	704(3)	102(d)	Rep.
75(a)(8)	704(4)	103	101(4)
75(a)(9)	704(5)	103(a)(9)	502(b)(7)
75(a)(10)	704(6)	103(c)	365
75(a)(11), (12)	Rep.	103a	Rep.
75(a)(13)	704(8)	104(a)	507
75(a)(14)	Rep.	104(a)(1)	503(b)
75(b), (c)	Rep.	104(a)(2)	507(a)(3)
76(a), (b)	Rep.	104(a)(4)	502(b)(4), 505(a), (b)
76(c)	326(a), 330	104(b)	Rep.
76(d)	Rep.	105(a)–(c)	Rep.
76(e)	326(d)	105(d)	508
76(f), (g)	Rep.	105(e)	Rep.
76a	330	106(a)	347(a)
77	107	106(b)	Rep.
78(a)	Rep.	107(a)	349(b), 547(b), (d), 551
78(b)	322(a)	107(b), (c)	545
78(c)	322(b)(1)	107(c)(1)(A)	545(1)
78(d)	322(b)(2)	107(c)(1)(B)	545(2), 546(b)
78(e)	Rep.	107(c)(1)(C)	545(3), (4)
78(f), (g)	322(b)(2)	107(c)(2)	551
78(h)	Rep.	107(c)(3)	724(b)
78(i)	322(c)	107(d)(1)(a)–(c)	Rep.
78(j)–(l)	Rep.	107(d)(1)(d)	101(26)
78(m)	322(d)	107(d)(1)(e)	Rep.
78(n)	Rep.	107(d)(2)	548(a)
79–82	Rep.	107(d)(3)	550
		107(d)(4)	548(b)
		107(d)(5)	548(d)(1)

Title 11 Former Sections	Title 11 New Sections	Title 11 Former Sections	Title 11 New Sections
107(d)(6)	548(c), 550, 551	405(d)	923
107(d)(7)	Rep.	405(e)	901
107(e), (f)	Rep.	405(e)(1)	922(a)
108	502(b)(3), 553	405(f), (g)	Rep.
109(a)	303(e)	405(h)	901, 926
109(b)	303(i)	406, 407	Rep.
109(c)	Rep.	408(a)	925
109(d)	303(g), 543(b), (c)	408(b)	901
110(a)	541(a)	408(c)	Rep.
110(a)(3)	541(b)	409	901
110(a)(5)	522(d)(7), (8)	410(a)	941, 942
110(b)	365	410(b)	942
110(c)	541(e), 544(a)	411, 412	901
110(d)(1)	549(a)	413	901, 943(a)
110(d)(2), (3)	542(c)	414(a)	901
110(d)(4), (5)	Rep.	414(b)(1)	943(b)(5), (6)
110(e)	544(b)	414(b)(2)	943(b)(2)
110(f)	363	414(b)(3)	Rep.
110(g)–(i)	Rep.	414(b)(4)	943(b)(3)
111, 112	Rep.	414(b)(5)	Rep.
201, 202	(See former 501–1103)	414(b)(6)	943(b)(4)
202a–204	Rep.	415(a)	944(a)
205(a)	Rep.	415(b)(1)	944(b)
205(b)	1171(b), 1172	415(b)(2)	944(c)
205(c)(1)	1163	416(a)	Rep.
205(c)(2)	1166	416(b)	901
205(c)(3)–(5)	Rep.	416(c)	Rep.
205(c)(6)	1169	416(d)	347(b), 901
205(c)(7)–(13)	Rep.	416(e)	945(a)
205(d)	Rep.	416(f)	Rep.
205(e)	1173	417	946
205(f)–(i)	Rep.	418	927
205(j)	1168	501, 502	Rep.
205(k), (l)	Rep.	506(1)	101(4)
205(m)	101(33)	506(2), (3)	Rep.
205(n)	1167, 1171(a)	506(4)	101(9)
205(o)	1170	506(5)	101(12)
205(p)–(s)	Rep.	506(6)	101(11)
205a	Rep.	506(7)	Rep.
206, 207	(See former 501–1103)	506(8)	101(23)
208	Rep.	506(9)	101(31)
301–303	Rep.	506(10)	Rep.
401(1)	101(4)	506(11)	101(35)
401(2)	Rep.	506(12), (13)	Rep.
401(3)	101(9)	507	1124
401(4)	Rep.	511, 512	Rep.
401(5)	101(11)	513	362
401(6)	101(28)	514, 515	Rep.
401(7)	101(30)	516(1)	365
401(8)	101(12)	516(2)	364
401(9)	Rep.	516(3)	363
401(10)	902(2)	516(4)	362
401(11)	903(3)	516(5), (6)	1110
402(a)	Rep.	517–521	Rep.
402(b)(1), (2)	901	526	303(b)
402(b)(3)	Rep.	527	Rep.
402(c)	904	528	Omitted
402(d)	921(b)	529–533	Rep.
403	903	536, 537	303(d)
404	101(29), 109(c)	541–549	Rep.
405(a)	921(a), (c)–(f)	556	1104(a)
405(b)	901, 924	557	327
405(c)	Rep.	558	101(13)
		559	1105
		560	324, 1104(c)

Title 11 Former Sections	Title 11 New Sections	Title 11 Former Sections	Title 11 New Sections
561, 562	Rep.	626	1141(c)
563	1107(a)	627	1142(b)
564	1106(a)(2)	628(1)	1141(d)(1)–(3)
565	Rep.	628(2)–(4)	Rep.
566	107	629(a)	1101(2)
567(1)	1106(a)(3)	629(b)	Rep.
567(2)	Rep.	629(c)	1127(b)
567(3)	1106(a)(4)(A)	636	1112(b)
567(4)	Rep.	637	Rep.
567(5)	1106(a)(4)	638	348
567(6)	Rep.	641(1), (2)	Rep.
568	1104(b), 1106(b)	641(3), (4)	330
569	1106(a)(5)	641(5)	503(b)(4)
570	1121	642(1)	503(b)(3), (5)
571–574	Rep.	642(2)	Rep.
575	1125(d)	642(3)	503(b)(4)
576	1125(b)	643	503(b)(3), (4)
577, 578	Rep.	644(1)	330
579	1126, 1128(a)	644(2)	503(b)(4)
580	1128(b)	644(3)	330
586	541(a)	644(4)	503(b)(3), (4)
587	1106	645–650	Rep.
588	1107(a)	656–659	Rep.
589	1108	661	108(c)
590	Rep.	662	Rep.
591	327	663	362
596	501(a), 1111	664(a)	1145(a)
597	1122	664(b)	1145(b)
598	501(a)	665, 666	Rep.
599	1126(a)	667	1146(c)
600, 601	Rep.	668	346(j)(1)
602	502(b)(7)	669	1129(d)
603	1126(e)	670	346(j)(5)
604	1143	671, 672	Rep.
605	347(b)	676	Rep.
606	1109(b)	701, 702	Rep.
607	1109	706(1), (2)	Rep.
608	1109(a)	706(3)	101(12), 109(d)
609–613	Rep.	706(4)	Rep.
616(1)	1123(b)(1)	706(5)	101(31)
616(2)	1123(a)(5), (b)(4)	707(1)	101(9)
616(3)	Rep.	707(2)	101(4), (11)
616(4)	1123(b)(2)	708	1124
616(5)	1123(a)(3)	711, 712	Rep.
616(6)	1123(a)(2)	713(1)	365
616(7)–(9)	Rep.	713(2)	363
616(10)	1123(a)(5)	713(3)	Rep.
616(11)	1123(a)(7)	714	362
616(12)(a)	1123(a)(6)	715, 716	Rep.
616(12)(b)	Rep.	721–728	Rep.
616(13)	1123(b)(3)	731–733	Rep.
616(14)	1123(b)(5)	734	341
621(1)	1129(a)(1)	735	341
621(2)	1129(a)(7), (11)	735(3)	1128(a)
621(3)	1129(a)(3)	736	341
621(4)	1129(a)(4)	736(2)	501(a)
621(5)	1129(a)(5)	736(3)	343
622	1127	737(1)	Rep.
623	1127(d)	737(2)	1129(a)(9)
624(1)	1141(a)	737(3)	1128(a)
624(2)	1129(a)(6), 1142(a)	738	1102
624(3), (4)	Rep.	739(1)(a)	1103(c)(2)
625	Rep.	739(1)(b)–(e)	1103(c)(3)
		739(1)(f)	1104(c)(5)
		739(2)	503(b)(4), 1103(a)

Title 11 Former Sections	Title 11 New Sections	Title 11 Former Sections	Title 11 New Sections
741	Rep.	831	Rep.
742	1107(a)	832	1104(a)
743	1108	833	Rep.
744	364	834	341
751	1122	835	341, 1128(a)
752	Rep.	836	341
753	502(b)(7)	836(2)	501(a)
754, 755	Rep.	836(3)	343
755a	501(a)	837(1)	1104(a)
756	Rep.	837(2)	Rep.
757(1)	Rep.	837(3)	1128(a)
757(2)	1123(b)(2)	841	Rep.
757(3)–(7)	Rep.	842	1106
757(8)	1123(b)(5)	843	348
761	1129(a)(3)	844	1107(a)
762	Rep.	845	1108
763	1127	846	364
764	1127(d)	851	501(a), 1111
765	1127(c)	852	1122
766(1)	1129(a)(1)	853	Rep.
766(2)	1129(a)(7), (11)	854	501(a)
766(3)	1129(a)(2)	855–857	Rep.
766(4)	1129(a)(3)	858	502(b)(7)
767(1)	1141(a)	859	Rep.
767(2)–(4)	Rep.	861(1)–(3)	Rep.
768–770	Rep.	861(4)	1123(b)(2)
771	1141(d)(1)–(3)	861(5), (6)	Rep.
772	Rep.	861(7)	1123(b)(4)
776, 777	1112(b)	861(8)	Rep.
778	348	861(9)	1123(a)(3)
779–781	Rep.	861(10)	1123(a)(2)
786	1144	861(11)	Rep.
787(1)	1127(b)	861(12)	1123(a)(5)
787(2)	1127(c)	861(13)	1123(b)(5)
787(3)	1127(d)	866	Rep.
787(4)	Rep.	867	1129(a)(3)
791	108(c)	868	Rep.
792	Rep.	869	1127(a), (b)
793(a)	1145(a)	870	1127(d)
793(b)	1145(b)	871	1127(c)
794	Rep.	872(1)	1129(a)(1)
795	346(j)(1)	872(2)	1129(a)(7), (11)
796	346(j)(5)	872(3)	1129(a)(2)
797	Rep.	872(4)	1129(a)(3)
799	Rep.	872(5)	1129(a)(4)
801, 802	Rep.	873(1)	1141(a)
806(1)	Rep.	873(2)	1142(a)
806(2)	101(4)	873(3)	Rep.
806(3), (4)	Rep.	874	1141(c)
806(5)	101(9)	875	1142(b)
806(6)	101(12), 109(d)	876	1141(d)(1)–(3)
806(7)	101(11)	877	Rep.
806(8)	101(23)	881, 882	1112(b)
806(9)	101(31)	883	348
807	1124	884–886	Rep.
811, 812	Rep.	891(1)	Rep.
813(1)	365	891(2), (3)	330
813(2)	363	892(1)	503(b)(3)
813(3)	Rep.	892(2)	Rep.
814	362	892(3)	503(b)(4)
815, 816	Rep.	893(1)	Rep.
821–827	Rep.	893(2)	503(b)(4)
828	362	893(3)	330
		893(4)	503(b)(4)
		894–898	Rep.

For Complete Annotation Materials, see United States Code Annotated

Title 11 Former Sections	Title 11 New Sections
906–909	Rep.
911	1144
916	108(c)
917	362
918(a)	1145(a)
918(b)	1145(b)
919	Rep.
920	346(j)(1)
921	1129(d)
922	346(j)(5)
923	Rep.
926	Rep.
1001, 1002	Rep.
1006(1)	101(4)
1006(2)	101(9)
1006(3)	101(12), 109(e)
1006(4)	101(11)
1006(5)	Rep.
1006(6)	101(31)
1006(7)	Rep.
1006(8)	101(24), 109(e)
1007	Rep.
1011, 1012	Rep.
1013(1)	365
1013(2)	Rep.
1014	362
1015, 1016	Rep.
1021–1026	Rep.
1031	Rep.
1032, 1033	341
1033(1)	343, 501(a)
1033(2)	1321
1033(5)	1324
1036	1303
1037	Rep.
1041–1044	Rep.
1046(1)	1322(b)(1)
1046(2)	1322(b)(2)
1046(3)	1322(a)(2)
1046(4)	1322(a)(1)
1046(5)	1329(a)
1046(6)	1322(b)(7)
1046(7)	1322(b)(10)
1051	1325(a)(3)
1052	Rep.
1053	1323(a)
1054	1323(c)
1055	Rep.
1056(a)(1)	1325(a)(1)
1056(a)(2)	1325(a)(6)
1056(a)(3)	Rep.
1056(a)(4)	1325(a)(3)
1056(b)	502(b)
1057	1327(a)
1058	Rep.
1059	1326(a)
1060	1328(a), (c), (d)
1061	1328(b)
1062	Rep.
1066	348, 1307
1067	348
1068, 1069	Rep.
1071	1330

Title 11 Former Sections	Title 11 New Sections
1076	108(c)
1077–1079	Rep.
1080	1305(a)(1)
1086	Rep.
1101–1103	Rep.
1200–1255	Rep.

Table II

This Table lists the sections of revised Title 11, Bankruptcy, and indicates the sections of former Title 11, which covered similar and related subject matter.

Title 11 New Sections	Title 11 Former Sections
101(1)–(3)	
101(4)	103, 401(1), 506(1), 707(2), 806(2), 1006(1)
101(5)–(7)	
101(8)	1(8)
101(9)	1(11), 401(3), 506(4), 707(1), 806(5), 1062(2)
101(10)	
101(11)	1(14), 401(5), 506(6), 707(2), 806(7), 1006(4)
101(12)	1(4), 401(8), 506(5), 706(3), 806(6), 1006(3)
101(13)	553
101(14)–(16)	
101(17), (18)	1(17)
101(19)–(21)	
101(22)	T. 15 § 77ccc(7)
101(23)	506(8), 806(8)
101(24)	1(32), 1006(8)
101(25)	
101(26)	1(19), 107(d)(1)(d)
101(27)	
101(28)	401(6)
101(29)	404
101(30)	1(23), 401(7)
101(31)	1(24), 506(9), 706(5), 806(9), 1006(6)
101(32)	205(m)
101(33)	
101(34)	1(27)
101(35)	506(11)
101(36), (37)	
101(38)	1(29a)
101(39)	T. 15 § 78c(a)(4), (5)
101(40)	1(30)
102(1)–(6)	
102(7)	1(35)
102(8)	
103, 104	
105	11(a)(15)
106	
107	77, 566
108(a), (b)	29(e)
108(c)	29(f), 661, 791, 1076
109(a)	11(a)(1)
109(b)	22
109(c)	404
109(d)	706(3), 806(6)
109(e)	1006(3), (8)
301	22(a), 41(f), 95(a)

Title 11 New Sections	Title 11 Former Sections	Title 11 New Sections	Title 11 Former Sections
302		501(a)	93(n), 596, 598, 736(2), 755a, 836(2), 851, 854, 1033(1)
303(a)	22(b)		
303(b)	23(b), 95(b), (e), 526	501(b)	93(i)
303(c)	95(f)	501(c), (d)	
303(d)	41(b), 536, 537	502(a)	93(d)
303(e)	109(a)	502(b)	93(f), 1056(b)
303(f)		502(b)(3)	108
303(g)	109(d)	502(b)(4)	104(a)(4)
303(h)	21	502(b)(7)	103(a)(9), 602, 753, 858
303(i)	11(a)(18), 19(b)	502(c)	93(d)
303(j)	95(g)	502(d)	93(g)
303(k)		502(e)–(i)	
304		502(j)	93(k), 11(a)(2)
305(a)(1)		503(a)	
305(a)(2)	11(a)(22)	503(b)	104(a)(1)
305(b), (c)		503(b)(2)	102(a)(1)
306		503(b)(3)	642(1), 643, 644(4), 892(1)
321	73	503(b)(4)	641(5), 642(3), 643, 644(2), (4), 739(2), 892(3), 893(2), (4)
322(a)	78(b)		
322(b)(1)	78(c)	503(b)(5)	642(1)
322(b)(2)	78(d), (f), (g)	504	102(c)
322(c)	78(i)	505(a), (b)	11(a)(2A), 104(a)(4)
322(d)	78(m)	505(c)	
323		506(a), (b)	93(h)
324	11(a)(17), 560	506(c), (d)	
325	74	507	104(a)
326(a)	76(c)	507(a)(3)	104(a)(2)
326(b), (c)		508	105(d)
326(d)	76(e)	509	93(i)
327	557, 591	510	
327(c)	72(c)	521(1)	25(a)(8), (9)
328		521(2)	25(a)(3), (6), (7)
329	96(d)	521(3)	25(a)(4), (5), (11)
330	76(c), 76a, 641(3), (4), 644(1), (3), 891(2), (3), 893(3)	521(4)	25(a)(1)
		522	24
331		523(a)(1)	35(a)(1)
341	91, 92, 734–736, 834–836, 1032, 1033	523(a)(2)	35(a)(2)
		523(a)(3)	35(a)(3)
342	94	523(a)(4)	35(a)(4)
343	44(a), 25(a)(1), (10), 736(3), 836(3), 1033(1)	523(a)(5)	35(a)(7)
		523(a)(6)	35(a)(8)
344	25(a)(10)	523(a)(7)–(9)	
345	101, 75(a)(2)	523(b)	35(b)
346(a)–(i)		523(c)	35(c)
346(j)(1)	668, 795, 920	523(d)	
346(j)(2)–(4)		524(a)	32(f)
346(j)(5)	670, 796, 922	524(b)–(d)	
346(j)(6), (7)		524(e)	34
347(a)	106(a)	525	
347(b)	416(d), 605	541(a)	26, 110(a), 586
348	638, 778, 843, 1066, 1067	541(b)	110(a)(3)
349(a)	35(b)	541(c), (d)	
349(b)	107(a)	541(e)	110(c)
350	11(a)(8)	542(a), (b)	
361		542(c)	110(d)(2), (3)
362	29(a), 35(c)(4), 513, 516(4), 663, 714, 814, 828, 917, 1014	542(d), (e)	
		543(a)	
363	11(a)(7), 110(f), 516(3), 713(2), 813(2)	543(b), (c)	11(a)(21), 109(d)
		543(d)	
364	516(2), 744, 846	544(a)	110(c)
365	103(c), 110(b), 516(1), 713(1), 813(1), 1013(1)	544(b)	110(e)
		545	107(b), (c)
366		545(1)	107(c)(1)(A)
		545(2)	107(c)(1)(B)
		545(3), (4)	107(c)(1)(C)

For Complete Annotation Materials, see United States Code Annotated

Title 11 New Sections	Title 11 Former Sections	Title 11 New Sections	Title 11 Former Sections
546(a)		745	96(e)(2)
546(b)	107(c)(1)(B)	746–748	
546(c).....................		749	96(e)(5)
547........................	96	750	
547(b)	107(a)	751	96(e)(2)
547(c)(4)	96(c)	752	96(e)(2), (3)
547(d)	107(a)	761–766	
547(e)(1)(B)	96(a)(4)	901	402(b)(1), (2), 405(b), (e), (h), 408(b), 409, 411, 412, 413, 414(a), 416(b), (d)
548(a)	107(d)(2)		
548(b)	107(d)(4)		
548(c)	107(d)(6)	902(1).....................	
548(d)(1)	107(d)(5)	902(2).....................	401(10)
548(d)(2)		902(3).....................	401(11)
549(a)	110(d)(1)	902(4).....................	
549(b)		903	403
549(c)	44(g)	904	402(c)
549(d)		921(a)	405(a)
550	96(b), 107(d)(3), (6)	921(b)	402(d)
551	96(b), 107(a)(3), (c)(2), (d)(6), 110(e)(2)	921(c)–(f)	405(a)
		922(a)	405(e)(1)
552........................		922(b)	
553........................	96(c), 108	923	405(d)
554........................		924	405(b)
701........................		925	408(a)
702........................	72(a)	926	405(h)
703(a)	74	927	418
703(b), (c)		941	410(a)
704(1).....................	75(a)(1)	942	410(a), (b)
704(2).....................	75(a)(3), (5)	943(a)	413
704(3).....................	75(a)(7)	943(b)(1)	
704(4).....................	75(a)(8)	943(b)(2)	414(b)(2)
704(5).....................	75(a)(9)	943(b)(3)	414(b)(4)
704(6).....................	75(a)(10)	943(b)(4)	414(b)(6)
704(7).....................		943(b)(5), (6)	414(b)(1)
704(8).....................	75(a)(13)	944(a)	415(a)
705........................	72(b)	944(b)	415(b)(1)
706........................		944(c)	415(b)(2)
707........................	95(g)	945(a)	416(e)
721........................	11(a)(5)	945(b)	
722........................		946	417
723........................	23(g)	1101(1)....................	
724(a)	93(j)	1101(2)....................	629(a)
724(b)	107(c)(3)	1102	738
724(c), (d)		1103(a)...................	739(2)
725........................		1103(b), (c)(1)	
726(a)(1), (2)		1103(c)(2)	739(1)(a)
726(a)(3)	93(n)	1103(c)(3)	739(1)(b)–(e)
726(a)(4)–(6), (b), (c)		1103(c)(4)	
727(a)(1)		1103(c)(5)	739(1)(f)
727(a)(2)	32(c)(1), (4)	1103(d)	
727(a)(3)	32(c)(2)	1104(a)...................	556, 832, 837(1)
727(a)(4)	32(c)(1), (3)	1104(b)	568
727(a)(5)	32(c)(7)	1104(c)	560
727(a)(6)	32(c)(6)	1105	559
727(a)(7)		1106	587, 842
727(a)(8), (9)	32(c)(5)	1106(a)(2)	564
727(a)(10)	32(a)	1106(a)(3)	567(1)
727(b).....................		1106(a)(4)	567(5)
727(c).....................	32(b)	1106(a)(4)(A)	567(3)
727(d), (e)	33	1106(a)(5)	569
728........................		1106(b)	568
741........................	96(e)(1)	1107(a)...................	563, 588, 742, 844
742–744		1107(b)	
		1108	589, 743, 845
		1109	607

For Complete Annotation Materials, see United States Code Annotated

Title 11 New Sections	Title 11 Former Sections	Title 11 New Sections	Title 11 Former Sections
1109(a)	608	1146(a), (b)	
1109(b)	606	1146(c)	667
1110	516(5), (6)	1146(d)	
1111	596, 851	1161, 1162	
1112(a)		1163	205(c)(1)
1112(b)	636, 776, 777, 881, 882	1164, 1165	
1112(c)–(e)		1166	205(c)(2)
1121	570	1167	205(n)
1122	597, 751, 852	1168	205(j)
1123(a)(1)		1169	205(c)(6)
1123(a)(2)	616(6), 861(10)	1170	205(o)
1123(a)(3)	616(5), 861(9)	1171(a)	205(n)
1123(a)(4)		1171(b)	205(b)
1123(a)(5)	616(2), (10), 861(12)	1172	205(b)
1123(a)(6)	616(12)(a)	1173	205(e)
1123(a)(7)	616(11)	1174	
1123(b)(1)	616(1)	1301, 1302	
1123(b)(2)	616(4), 757(2), 861(4)	1303	1036
1123(b)(3)	616(13)	1304	
1123(b)(4)	616(2), 861(7)	1305(a)(1)	1080
1123(b)(5)	616(14), 757(8), 861(13)	1305(a)(2), (b), (c)	
1123(c)		1306	
1124	507, 708, 807	1307	1066
1125(a)		1321	1033(2)
1125(b)	576	1322(a)(1)	1046(4)
1125(c)		1322(a)(2)	1046(3)
1125(d)	575	1322(a)(3)	
1125(e)		1322(b)(1)	1046(1)
1126	579	1322(b)(2)	1046(2)
1126(a)	599	1322(b)(3)–(6)	
1126(e)	603	1322(b)(7)	1046(6)
1127	622, 763	1322(b)(8), (9)	
1127(a)	869	1322(b)(10)	1046(7)
1127(b)	629(c), 787(1), 869	1322(c)	
1127(c)	765, 787(2), (3), 871	1323(a)	1053
1127(d)	623, 764, 870	1323(b)	
1128(a)	579, 735(3), 737(3), 835, 837(3)	1323(c)	1054
1128(b)	580	1324	1033(5)
1129(a)(1)	621(1), 766(1), 872(1)	1325(a)(1)	1056(a)(1)
1129(a)(2)	766(3), 872(3)	1325(a)(2)	
1129(a)(3)	621(3), 761, 766(4), 867, 872(4)	1325(a)(3)	1051, 1056(a)(4)
1129(a)(4)	621(4), 872(5)	1325(a)(4), (5)	
1129(a)(5)	621(5)	1325(a)(6)	1056(a)(2)
1129(a)(6)	624(2)	1325(b)	
1129(a)(7)	621(2), 766(2), 872(2)	1326(a)	1059
1129(a)(8)		1326(b)	
1129(a)(9)	737(2)	1327(a)	1057
1129(a)(10)		1327(b), (c)	
1129(a)(11)	621(2), 766(2), 872(2)	1328(a)	1060
1129(b), (c)		1328(b)	1061
1129(d)	669, 921	1328(c), (d)	1060
1141(a)	624(1), 767(1), 873(1)	1328(e)	33
1141(b)		1329(a)	1046(5)
1141(c)	626, 874	1329(b), (c)	
1141(d)(1)–(3)	628(1), 771, 876	1330	1071
1141(d)(4)	32(a)	1501–151326	
1142(a)	624(2), 873(2)		
1142(b)	627, 875		
1143	604		
1144	786, 911		
1145(a)	664(a), 793(a), 918(a)		
1145(b)	664(b), 793(b), 918(b)		
1145(c), (d)			

HISTORICAL AND STATUTORY NOTES

Enacting Clause

Pub.L. 95–598, Title I, § 101, Nov. 6, 1978, 92 Stat. 2549, provided in part: "The law relating to bankruptcy is codified and enacted as title 11 of the United States Code, entitled 'Bankruptcy', and may be cited as 11 U.S.C. § ___."

Effective and Applicability Provisions

2005 Acts. Amendments by Pub.L. 109–8 effective, except as otherwise provided, 180 days after April 20, 2005, and inapplicable with respect to cases commenced under Title 11 before the effective date, see Pub.L. 109–8, § 1501, set out as a note under 11 U.S.C.A. § 101.

1994 Acts. Amendment by Pub.L. 103–394 effective on Oct. 22, 1994, and not to apply with respect to cases commenced under Title 11 of the United States Code before Oct. 22, 1994, see section 702 of Pub.L. 103–394, set out as a note under section 101 of this title.

1978 Acts. Pub.L. 95–598, Title IV, § 402, Nov. 6, 1978, 92 Stat. 2682, as amended by Pub.L. 98–249, § 1(a), Mar. 31, 1984, 98 Stat. 116; Pub.L. 98–271, § 1(a), Apr. 30, 1984, 98 Stat. 163; Pub.L. 98–299, § 1(a), May 25, 1984, 98 Stat. 214; Pub.L. 98–325, § 1(a), June 20, 1984, 98 Stat. 268; Pub.L. 98–353, Title I, §§ 113, 121(a), July 10, 1984, 98 Stat. 343, 345; Pub.L. 98–454, Title X, § 1001, Oct. 5, 1984, 98 Stat. 1745, provided that:

"**(a)** Except as otherwise provided in this title [sections 401 to 411 of Pub.L. 95–598, this Act [see Tables for classification] shall take effect on October 1, 1979.

"**(b)** Except as provided in subsections (c) and (d) of this section, the amendments made by title II of this Act [sections 201 to 252 of Pub.L. 95–598] shall not be effective.

"**(c)** The amendments made by sections 210, 214, 219, 220, 222, 224, 225, 228, 229, 235, 244, 245, 246, 249, and 251 of this Act shall take effect on October 1, 1979.

"**(d)** The amendments made by sections 217, 218, 230, 247, 302, 314(j), 317, 327, 328, 338, and 411 of this Act shall take effect on the date of enactment of this Act [Nov. 6, 1978]."

[**(e)** Repealed. Pub.L. 98–454, Title X, § 1001, Oct. 5, 1984, 98 Stat. 1745.]

[Section 121(a) of Pub.L. 98–353 purported to amend section 402(b) of Pub.L. 95–598 by substituting "the date of enactment of the Bankruptcy Amendments and Federal Judgeship Act of 1984 [i.e. July 10, 1984]" for "June 28, 1984". This amendment was not executed as the probable intent of Congress in view of the prior amendment to section 402(b) of Pub.L. 95–598 by section 113 of Pub.L. 98–353.]

[Amendment of section 402(b) of Pub.L. 95–598 by section 113 of Pub.L. 98–353 effective June 27, 1984, see section 122(c) of Pub.L. 98–353, set out as an Effective Date note under section 151 of Title 28, Judiciary and Judicial Procedure.]

Repeals

Pub.L. 95–598, Title IV, § 401(a), Nov. 6, 1978, 92 Stat. 2682, provided that: "The Bankruptcy Act [Act July 1, 1898, c. 541, 30 Stat. 544, as amended] is repealed."

Savings Provisions

Pub.L. 95–598, Title IV, § 403, Nov. 6, 1978, 92 Stat. 2683, as amended by Pub.L. 98–353, Title III, § 382, July 10, 1984, 98 Stat. 364, provided that:

"**(a)** A case commenced under the Bankruptcy Act [Act July 1, 1898, c. 541, 30 Stat. 544, as amended], and all matters and proceedings in or relating to any such case, shall be conducted and determined under such Act as if this Act had not been enacted, and the substantive rights of parties in connection with any such bankruptcy case, matter, or proceeding shall continue to be governed by the law applicable to such case, matter, or proceeding as if the [this] Act had not been enacted.

"**(b)** Notwithstanding subsection (a) of this section, sections 1165, 1167, 1168, 1169, and 1171 of title 11 of the United States Code, as enacted by section 101 of this Act, apply to cases pending under section 77 of the Bankruptcy Act ([former] 11 U.S.C. 205) on the date of enactment of this Act [Nov. 6, 1978] in which the trustee has not filed a plan of reorganization.

"**(c)** The repeal made by section 401(a) of this Act [repealing the Bankruptcy Act] does not affect any right of a referee in bankruptcy, United States bankruptcy judge, or survivor of a referee in bankruptcy or United States bankruptcy judge to receive any annuity or other payment under the civil service retirement laws.

"**(d)** The amendments made by section 314 of this Act [see Tables] do not affect the application of chapter 9, chapter 96, section 2516, section 3057, or section 3284 of title 18 of the United States Code to any act of any person—

"**(1)** committed before October 1, 1979; or

"**(2)** committed after October 1, 1979, in connection with a case commenced before such date.

"**(e)** Notwithstanding subsection (a) of this section—

"**(1)** a fee may not be charged under section 40c(2)(a) of the Bankruptcy Act [former 11 U.S.C.A. § 68(c)(2)(a)] in a case pending under such Act after September 30, 1979, to the extent that such fee exceeds $200,000;

"**(2)** a fee may not be charged under section 40c(2)(b) of the Bankruptcy Act in a case in which the plan is confirmed after September 30, 1978, or in which the final determination as to the amount of such fee is made after September 30, 1979, notwithstanding an earlier confirmation date, to the extent that such fee exceeds $100,000;

"**(3)** after September 30, 1979, all moneys collected for payment into the referees' salary and expense fund in cases filed under the Bankruptcy Act shall be collected and paid into the general fund of the Treasury; and

"**(4)** any balance in the referees' salary and expense fund in the Treasury on October 1, 1979, shall be transferred to the general fund of the Treasury and the referees' salary and expense fund account shall be closed."

Pub.L. 98–353, Title III, § 381, July 10, 1984, 98 Stat. 364, provided that: "This subtitle [§§ 381, 382 of Pub.L. 98–353], [amending subsec. (e) of this note] may be cited as the 'Referees Salary and Expense Fund Act of 1984'."

Separability of Provisions

If any provision of or amendment made by Pub.L. 103–394 or the application of such provision or amendment to any person or circumstance is held to be unconstitutional, the remaining provisions of and amendments made by Pub.L. 103–394 and the application of such provisions and amendments to any person or circumstance shall not be affected thereby, see section 701 of Pub.L. 103–394, set out as a note under section 101 of this title.

Commission on the Bankruptcy Laws of the United States

Pub.L. 91–354, §§ 1–6, July 24, 1970, 84 Stat. 468, as amended by Pub.L. 92–251, Mar. 17, 1972, 86 Stat. 63; Pub.L. 93–56, § 1, July 1, 1973, 87 Stat. 140, established the Commission on the Bankruptcy Laws of the United States, to study and recommend changes to this title, which ceased to exist 30 days after the date of submission of its final report which was required prior to July 31, 1973.

History of Bankruptcy Acts

The bankruptcy laws were revised generally and enacted as Title 11, Bankruptcy, by Pub.L. 96–598, Nov. 6, 1978, 92 Stat. 2549.

Earlier bankruptcy laws included the following Acts:

Apr. 4, 1800, c. 19, 2 Stat. 19, repealed Dec. 19, 1803, ch. 6, 2 Stat. 248.

Aug. 19, 1841, c. 9, 5 Stat. 440, repealed Mar. 3, 1843, ch. 82, 5 Stat. 614.

Mar. 2, 1867, c. 176, 14 Stat. 517, the provisions of which were incorporated in Rev.Stat.Title LXI, §§ 4972 to 5132, were materially amended June 22, 1874, c. 390, 18 Stat. 178, and were repealed June 7, 1878, c. 160, 20 Stat. 99.

The Bankruptcy Act of July 1, 1898, c. 541, 30 Stat. 544, as amended, sometimes called the Nelson Act, repealed by Pub.L. 95–598.

The Chandler Act of July 22, 1938, c. 575, 52 Stat. 883, which revised the Bankruptcy Act generally and materially amended the provisions covering corporate reorganizations, repealed by Pub.L. 95–598.

National Bankruptcy Review Commission

Pub.L. 103–394, Title VI, Oct. 22, 1994, 108 Stat. 4147, provided that:

"**Sec. 601. Short title.**

"This title [this note] may be cited as the 'National Bankruptcy Review Commission Act'.

"**Sec. 602. Establishment.**

"There is established the National Bankruptcy Review Commission (referred to as the 'Commission').

"**Sec. 603. Duties of the Commission.**

"The duties of the Commission are—

"(1) to investigate and study issues and problems relating to title 11, United States Code (commonly known as the 'Bankruptcy Code');

"(2) to evaluate the advisability of proposals and current arrangements with respect to such issues and problems;

"(3) to prepare and submit to the Congress, the Chief Justice, and the President a report in accordance with section 608; and

"(4) to solicit divergent views of all parties concerned with the operation of the bankruptcy system.

"**Sec. 604. Membership.**

"(a) **Number and appointment.**—The Commission shall be composed of 9 members as follows:

"(1) Three members appointed by the President, 1 of whom shall be designated as chairman by the President.

"(2) One member shall be appointed by the President pro tempore of the Senate.

"(3) One member shall be appointed by the Minority Leader of the Senate.

"(4) One member shall be appointed by the Speaker of the House of Representatives.

"(5) One member shall be appointed by the Minority Leader of the House of Representatives.

"(6) Two members appointed by the Chief Justice.

Members of Congress, and officers and employees of the executive branch, shall be ineligible for appointment to the Commission.

"(b) **Term.**—Members of the Commission shall be appointed for the life of the Commission.

"(c) **Quorum.**—Five members of the Commission shall constitute a quorum, but a lesser number may conduct meetings.

"(d) **Appointment deadline.**—The first appointments made under subsection (a) shall be made within 60 days after the date of enactment of this Act [Oct. 22, 1994].

"(e) **First meeting.**—The first meeting of the Commission shall be called by the chairman and shall be held within 210 days after the date of enactment of this Act [Oct. 22, 1994].

"(f) **Vacancy.**—A vacancy on the Commission resulting from the death or resignation of a member shall not affect its powers and shall be filled in the same manner in which the original appointment was made.

"(g) **Continuation of membership.**—If any member of the Commission who was appointed to the Commission as an officer or employee of a government leaves that office, or if any member of the Commission who was not appointed in such a capacity becomes an officer or employee of a government, the member may continue as a member of the Commission for not longer than the 90–day period beginning on the date the member leaves that office or becomes such an officer or employee, as the case may be.

"(h) **Consultation prior to appointment.**—Prior to the appointment of members of the Commission, the President, the President pro tempore of the Senate, the Speaker of the House of Representatives, and the Chief Justice shall consult with each other to ensure fair and equitable representation of various points of view in the Commission and its staff.

"**Sec. 605. Compensation of the Commission.**

"(a) **Pay.—**

"(1) **Nongovernment employees.**—Each member of the Commission who is not otherwise employed by the United States Government shall be entitled to receive the daily equivalent of the annual rate of basic pay payable for level IV of the Executive Schedule under section 5315 of title 5, United States Code [section 5315 of Title 5, Government Organization and Employees], for each day (including travel time) during which he or she is engaged in the actual performance of duties as a member of the Commission.

"(2) **Government employees.**—A member of the Commission who is an officer or employee of the United States Government shall serve without additional compensation.

"(b) **Travel.**—Members of the Commission shall be reimbursed for travel, subsistence, and other necessary expenses incurred by them in the performance of their duties.

"**Sec. 606. Staff of Commission; experts and consultants.**

"(a) **Staff.—**

"(1) **Appointment.**—The chairman of the Commission may, without regard to the civil service laws and regulations, appoint, and terminate an executive director and such other personnel as are necessary to enable the Commission to perform its duties. The employment of an executive director shall be subject to confirmation by the Commission.

"(2) **Compensation.**—The chairman of the Commission may fix the compensation of the executive director and other personnel without regard to the provisions of chapter 51 and subchapter II of chapter 53 of title 5, United States Code [sections 5101 et seq. and 5311 et seq. of Title 5], relating to classification of positions and General Schedule pay rates, except that the rate of pay for the executive director and other personnel may not exceed the rate payable for level V of the Executive Schedule under section 5316 of that title [section 5316 of Title 5].

"(b) **Experts and consultants.**—The Commission may procure temporary and intermittent services of experts and consultants under section 3109(b) of title 5, United States Code [section 3109(b) of Title 5].

"**Sec. 607. Powers of the Commission.**

"(a) **Hearings and meetings.**—The Commission or, on authorization of the Commission, a member of the Commission, may hold such hearings, sit and act at such time and places, take such testimony, and receive such evidence, as the Commission considers appropriate. The Commission or a member of the Commission may administer oaths or affirmations to witnesses appearing before it.

"(b) **Official data.**—The Commission may secure directly from any Federal department, agency, or court information necessary to enable it to carry out this title [this note]. Upon request of the chairman of the Commission, the head of a Federal department or agency or chief judge of a Federal court shall furnish such information, consistent with law, to the Commission.

"(c) **Facilities and support services.**—The Administrator of General Services shall provide to the Commission on a reimbursable basis such facilities and support services as the Commission may request. Upon request of the Commission, the head of a Federal department or agency may make any of the facilities or services of the agency available to the Commission to assist the Commission in carrying out its duties under this title [this note].

"(d) **Expenditures and contracts.**—The Commission or, on authorization of the Commission, a member of the Commission may make expenditures and enter into contracts for the procurement of such supplies, services, and property as the Commission or member considers appropriate for the purposes of carrying out the duties of the Commission. Such expenditures and contracts may be made only to such extent or in such amounts as are provided in appropriation Acts.

"(e) **Mails.**—The Commission may use the United States mails in the same manner and under the same conditions as other Federal departments and agencies of the United States.

"(f) **Gifts.**—The Commission may accept, use, and dispose of gifts or donations of services or property.

"**Sec. 608. Report.**

"The Commission shall submit to the Congress, the Chief Justice, and the President a report not later than 2 years after the date of its first meeting. The report shall contain a detailed statement of the findings and conclusions of the Commission, together with its recommendations for such legislative or administrative action as it considers appropriate.

"**Sec. 609. Termination.**

"The Commission shall cease to exist on the date that is 30 days after the date on which it submits its report under section 608.

"**Sec. 610. Authorization of appropriations.**

"There is authorized to be appropriated $1,500,000 to carry out this title [this note]."

CROSS REFERENCES

Additional information on bankruptcy filings required, see 15 USCA § 1681c.

Amount of unfunded vested benefits allocable to employer withdrawn from pension plan as including uncollectible amounts for reasons arising out of cases or proceedings under this title, see 29 USCA § 1391.

Applicability of provisions of Securities Act of 1933 to certain classes of securities exchanged in cases under this title, see 15 USCA § 77c.

Applicability of rules to bankruptcy proceedings,
    Federal Rules of Civil Procedure, see Fed.Rules Civ. Proc. Rule 81, 28 USCA.
    Federal Rules of Evidence, see Fed.Rules Evid. Rule 1101, 28 USCA.
Applicability of this title to district court of,
    Guam, see 48 USCA § 1424–4.
    Northern Mariana Islands, see 48 USCA § 1821.
    Virgin Islands, see 48 USCA § 1614.

Applicability to case under this title of provisions relating to special pay to selected reserve health care professionals in critically short wartime specialties, see 37 USCA § 302g.

Assertion of claim against guarantor providing evidence of financial responsibility in cases where owner or operator is in bankruptcy under this title for corrective action relating to,
    Hazardous waste treatment, storage and disposal facilities, see 42 USCA § 6924.
    Release of hazardous substances from facilities, see 42 USCA § 9608.
    Underground storage tanks, see 42 USCA §§ 6991b and 6991c.

Authority of Attorney General to investigate official acts, records and accounts of trustees in cases under this title, see 28 USCA § 526.

Automatic protection of lands conveyed pursuant to Alaska Native Claims Settlement Act provided such lands are not sold to third parties from judgments resulting from claims arising under this title, see 43 USCA § 1636.

"Bankruptcy Act" defined as this title for purposes of Trust Indenture Act of 1939, see 15 USCA § 77ccc.

Benefit accrual requirements and prohibition on increases where plan sponsor is in bankruptcy, see 29 USCA § 1054.

"Bridge owner" as including bridge in possession or under control of trustee in case under this title for purposes of alteration of bridges over navigable waters, see 33 USCA § 511.

Change of venue in cases or proceedings under this title, see 28 USCA § 1412.

"Company" defined as including trustee in case under this title for purposes of,
    Subchapter I of Investment Advisers Act of 1940, see 15 USCA § 80a–2.
    Subchapter II of Investment Advisers Act of 1940, see 15 USCA § 80b–2.

Compromise, adjustment or cancellation of farm loans upon discharge of indebtedness in proceeding under this title, see 12 USCA § 1150.

Concealment of assets, false oaths or claims, and bribery in cases under this title, see 18 USCA § 152.

Congressional finding of railroad insolvency and reorganization under this title for purposes of enacting Regional Rail Reorganization Act of 1973, see 45 USCA § 701.

Congressional power to establish uniform bankruptcy laws throughout United States, see USCA Const. Art. I § 8, cl. 4.

Coordination of Internal Revenue Code provisions with cases under this title, see 26 USCA § 6658.

Court procedures for cases under this title, see 28 USCA § 157.

Credits against unemployment tax, see 26 USCA § 3302.

"Debtor" defined under this title as having same meaning for purposes of crimes in bankruptcy, see 18 USCA § 151.

Disclosure of confidential tax returns and return information to trustee in cases under this title, see 26 USCA § 6103.

Duties of United States trustees and supervision by Attorney General, see 28 USCA § 586.

Effect of discharge in bankruptcy under this title on discharge of debt arising from,

Advanced educational assistance loan, see 10 USCA § 2005.

Aviation service agreement, see 37 USCA § 301b.

Child support obligation assigned to State, see 42 USCA § 656.

Critical acquisition positions service agreement, see 37 USCA § 317.

Engineering and scientific career service agreement, see 37 USCA § 315.

Enlistment in elements of Ready Reserve, see 37 USCA § 308g.

Health professionals educational assistance, see 38 USCA § 7635.

Indian Health Scholarship, see 25 USCA § 1613a.

Indian health service loan, see 25 USCA § 1616a.

Multiyear retention bonus for medical officers of armed forces, see 37 USCA § 301d.

Nurse officer agreement, see 10 USCA § 2130a.

Prior service enlistment bonus, see 37 USCA § 308i.

Reenlistment, enlistment, or voluntary extension of enlistment in elements of Ready Reserve, see 37 USCA § 308h.

Special pay for dental officers of armed forces, see 37 USCA §§ 302b and 302h.

Special pay for medical officers of armed forces, see 37 USCA § 302.

Special pay for nurse anesthetists, see 37 USCA § 302e.

Special pay for registered nurses, see 37 USCA § 302d.

Effect of Federal debt collection procedure on this title, see 28 USCA § 3003.

Employee protection benefits available under this title deemed waived upon receipt of assistance by employee under,

Milwaukee Railroad Restructuring Act, see 45 USCA § 912.

Rock Island Railroad Transition and Employee Assistance Act, see 45 USCA § 1007.

Employer Retirement Income new reportable events, see 29 USCA § 1343.

Extension of time for paying tax claims in cases under this title, see 26 USCA § 6161.

Fee agreements in cases under this title, see 18 USCA § 155.

"Filing date" as meaning date on which petition filed under this title for purposes of Securities Investor Protection Act of 1970, see 15 USCA § 78lll.

Fraud and consumer issues under this chapter, see 18 USCA § 157.

Immediate assessment for tax deficiencies with respect to certain cases under this title, see 26 USCA § 6871.

Inapplicability of § 421(a) of Title 26 to transfers of stock acquired pursuant to exercise of incentive stock option by debtor in proceeding under this title, see 26 USCA § 422.

Inapplicability to case under this title of provision relating to,

Limitation on net operating loss carry forwards following ownership change for tax purposes, see 26 USCA § 382.

Limitation on pension plan withdrawal liability to employers undergoing reorganization, see 29 USCA § 1405.

Postponement of certain time periods in determining tax liability by reason of service in combat zone, see 26 USCA § 7508.

Priority of government claims, see 31 USCA § 3713.

Transfers to corporation controlled by transferor, see 26 USCA § 351.

Inappropriate transfers included in determining net worth of employer, see 29 USCA § 1362.

Income tax rules relating to individuals' cases under this title, see 26 USCA § 1398.

Inferiority of rights of trustee and other parties under this title to rights of,

Federal Deposit Insurance Corporation as conservator or liquidating agent in connection with avoidance of fraudulent transfers, see 12 USCA § 1821.

National Credit Union Administration Board as conservator or liquidating agent in connection with avoidance of fraudulent transfers, see 12 USCA § 1787.

Insolvency and liquidation of holding companies by trustee pursuant to provisions of this title, see 12 USCA § 1467a.

Interception of wire or oral communications involving fraud under this title, see 18 USCA § 2516.

Intervention by trustee of debtor's estate in case under this title in proceeding before Tax Court to which debtor is party, see 26 USCA § 7464.

Jurisdiction and power of court over Securities Investor Protection Act decrees same as under this title, see 15 USCA § 78eee.

Jurisdiction of district courts in cases under this title, see 28 USCA § 1334.

Jury trials, see 28 USCA § 1411.

Lien of Black Lung Disability Trust Fund treated in same manner as lien for taxes due United States for purposes of this title, see 30 USCA § 934.

Limitations period for concealment of assets of debtor in case under this title begins to run upon final discharge or denial of discharge, see 18 USCA § 3284.

Liquidation proceedings under Securities Investor Protection Act conducted in accordance with Chapters 1, 3, and 5 and subchapters I and II of Chapter 7 of this title, see 15 USCA § 78fff.

No separate taxable entity resulting from commencement of case under this title, see 26 USCA § 1399.

Nonenforcement of guarantee of legal custody and financial ability for certain aliens when sponsor adjudicated bankrupt under this title, see 8 USCA § 1154.

Notice to creditors of commencement of liquidation proceeding for purposes of Securities Investor Protection Act of 1970 given in manner prescribed by this title, see 15 USCA § 78fff–2.

Notice to Secretary of Treasury of qualification as trustee in case under this title for purposes of Internal Revenue Code, see 26 USCA § 6036.

Original and exclusive jurisdiction of courts under this title over civil actions for adjudication of direct payment procedure for purposes of Securities Investor Protection Act of 1970, see 15 USCA § 78fff–4.

Ownership of copyright, see 17 USCA § 201.

Partition of multiemployer pension plan if reduction in amount of aggregate contributions will result from case or proceeding under this title, see 29 USCA § 1413.

"Person" defined as including trustees in cases under this title for purposes of,

  Equal Employment Opportunity Act of 1972, see 42 USCA § 2000e.

  Fair housing, see 42 USCA § 3602.

  Labor–Management Reporting and Disclosure Act of 1959, see 29 USCA § 402.

  National Labor Relations Act, see 29 USCA § 152.

  Walsh–Healey provisions, see 41 USCA § 6501.

"Personal holding company" for income tax purposes defined as excluding corporation subject to jurisdiction of court in cases under this title, see 26 USCA § 542.

Powers and duties of trustee same as under this title for purposes of Securities Investor Protection Act of 1970, see 15 USCA § 78fff–1.

Priority of,

  Claims of United States arising out of any contract authorized by Boulder Canyon Project Act, see 43 USCA § 617p.

  Liens for pension plan contribution of employer in cases under this title, see 29 USCA § 1368.

Procedure on default of housing and small business loans, see 38 USCA § 3732.

Prohibition on benefit increases while sponsor is in bankruptcy, see 26 USCA § 401.

Public disclosure of data in connection with bankruptcy proceedings for purposes of Commodity Exchange Act, see 7 USCA § 12.

"Qualifying event" as including proceeding in case under this title for purposes of,

  Determination of excise taxes for failure to satisfy continuation coverage requirements of group health plans, see 26 USCA § 4980B.

  Providing group health plan continuation coverage under Employee Retirement Income Security Act of 1974, see 29 USCA § 1163.

"Racketeering activity" for purposes of RICO as including any offense involving fraud connected with case under this title, see 18 USCA § 1961.

Reduction in basis of property held by taxpayer by portion of discharge of indebtedness under this title, see 26 USCA § 1017.

Regulations respecting commodity broker debtors notwithstanding provisions of this title, see 7 USCA § 24.

Reimbursements to multiemployer pension plans for payments due from employers uncollectible as result of employer involvement in cases under this title, see 29 USCA § 1402.

Relationship of Regional Rail Reorganization Act of 1973 to this title, see 45 USCA § 791.

"Reorganization" defined as certain transfers by corporation of all or part of its assets to another corporation in case under this title for purposes of income tax provisions relating to corporate organizations and reorganizations, see 26 USCA § 368.

Rules of bankruptcy, power of Supreme Court to prescribe, see 28 USCA § 2075.

Settlement common stock of Alaska native regional corporation not treated as asset under this title, see 43 USCA § 1606.

Suspension of limitations period for assessment and collection of tax, see 26 USCA § 6503.

Suspension of period on tax assessment in cases under this title where notice of qualification of fiduciary required to be given Secretary of Treasury, see 26 USCA § 6872.

Time for filing petition with Tax Court for redetermination of deficiency, see 26 USCA § 6213.

Treatment of income from discharge of indebtedness under this title for purposes of Internal Revenue Code, see 26 USCA § 108.

Trustee in case under this title deemed importer of record of merchandise consigned to insolvent for purposes of customs duties declaration, see 19 USCA § 1485.

Utilization by courts of facilities or services which pertain to parties in cases filed under this title, see 28 USCA § 156.

Venue of,

  Cases under this title, see 28 USCA § 1408.

  Proceedings arising in or related to cases under this title, see 28 USCA § 1409.

CHAPTER 1—GENERAL PROVISIONS

HISTORICAL AND STATUTORY NOTES

Effective and Applicability Provisions

2005 Acts. Amendments by Pub.L. 109–8 effective, except as otherwise provided, 180 days after April 20, 2005, and inapplicable with respect to cases commenced under Title 11 before the effective date, see Pub.L. 109–8, § 1501, set out as a note under 11 U.S.C.A. § 101.

§ 101. Definitions

In this title the following definitions shall apply:

(1) The term "accountant" means accountant authorized under applicable law to practice public accounting, and includes professional accounting association, corporation, or partnership, if so authorized.

(2) The term "affiliate" means—

(A) entity that directly or indirectly owns, controls, or holds with power to vote, 20 percent or more of the outstanding voting securities of the debtor, other than an entity that holds such securities—

(i) in a fiduciary or agency capacity without sole discretionary power to vote such securities; or

(ii) solely to secure a debt, if such entity has not in fact exercised such power to vote;

(B) corporation 20 percent or more of whose outstanding voting securities are directly or indirectly owned, controlled, or held with power to vote, by the debtor, or by an entity that directly or indirectly owns, controls, or holds with power to vote, 20 percent or more of the outstanding voting securities of the debtor, other than an entity that holds such securities—

(i) in a fiduciary or agency capacity without sole discretionary power to vote such securities; or

(ii) solely to secure a debt, if such entity has not in fact exercised such power to vote;

(C) person whose business is operated under a lease or operating agreement by a debtor, or person substantially all of whose property is operated under an operating agreement with the debtor; or

(D) entity that operates the business or substantially all of the property of the debtor under a lease or operating agreement.

(3) The term "assisted person" means any person whose debts consist primarily of consumer debts and the value of whose nonexempt property is less than $192,450 [1].

(4) The term "attorney" means attorney, professional law association, corporation, or partnership, authorized under applicable law to practice law.

(4A) The term "bankruptcy assistance" means any goods or services sold or otherwise provided to an assisted person with the express or implied purpose of providing information, advice, counsel, document preparation, or filing, or attendance at a credi-

tors' meeting or appearing in a case or proceeding on behalf of another or providing legal representation with respect to a case or proceeding under this title.

(5) The term "claim" means—

(A) right to payment, whether or not such right is reduced to judgment, liquidated, unliquidated, fixed, contingent, matured, unmatured, disputed, undisputed, legal, equitable, secured, or unsecured; or

(B) right to an equitable remedy for breach of performance if such breach gives rise to a right to payment, whether or not such right to an equitable remedy is reduced to judgment, fixed, contingent, matured, unmatured, disputed, undisputed, secured, or unsecured.

(6) The term "commodity broker" means futures commission merchant, foreign futures commission merchant, clearing organization, leverage transaction merchant, or commodity options dealer, as defined in section 761 of this title, with respect to which there is a customer, as defined in section 761 of this title.

(7) The term "community claim" means claim that arose before the commencement of the case concerning the debtor for which property of the kind specified in section 541(a)(2) of this title is liable, whether or not there is any such property at the time of the commencement of the case.

(7A) The term "commercial fishing operation" means—

(A) the catching or harvesting of fish, shrimp, lobsters, urchins, seaweed, shellfish, or other aquatic species or products of such species; or

(B) for purposes of section 109 and chapter 12, aquaculture activities consisting of raising for market any species or product described in subparagraph (A).

(7B) The term "commercial fishing vessel" means a vessel used by a family fisherman to carry out a commercial fishing operation.

(8) The term "consumer debt" means debt incurred by an individual primarily for a personal, family, or household purpose.

(9) The term "corporation"—

(A) includes—

(i) association having a power or privilege that a private corporation, but not an individual or a partnership, possesses;

(ii) partnership association organized under a law that makes only the capital subscribed responsible for the debts of such association;

(iii) joint-stock company;

(iv) unincorporated company or association; or

(v) business trust; but

(B) does not include limited partnership.

(10) The term "creditor" means—

(A) entity that has a claim against the debtor that arose at the time of or before the order for relief concerning the debtor;

(B) entity that has a claim against the estate of a kind specified in section 348(d), 502(f), 502(g), 502(h) or 502(i) of this title; or

(C) entity that has a community claim.

(10A) The term "current monthly income"—

(A) means the average monthly income from all sources that the debtor receives (or in a joint case the debtor and the debtor's spouse receive) without regard to whether such income is taxable income, derived during the 6–month period ending on—

(i) the last day of the calendar month immediately preceding the date of the commencement of the case if the debtor files the schedule of current income required by section 521(a)(1)(B)(ii); or

(ii) the date on which current income is determined by the court for purposes of this title if the debtor does not file the schedule of current income required by section 521(a)(1)(B)(ii); and

(B) includes any amount paid by any entity other than the debtor (or in a joint case the debtor and the debtor's spouse), on a regular basis for the household expenses of the debtor or the debtor's dependents (and in a joint case the debtor's spouse if not otherwise a dependent), but excludes benefits received under the Social Security Act, payments to victims of war crimes or crimes against humanity on account of their status as victims of such crimes, and payments to victims of international terrorism (as defined in section 2331 of title 18) or domestic terrorism (as defined in section 2331 of title 18) on account of their status as victims of such terrorism.

(11) The term "custodian" means—

(A) receiver or trustee of any of the property of the debtor, appointed in a case or proceeding not under this title;

(B) assignee under a general assignment for the benefit of the debtor's creditors; or

(C) trustee, receiver, or agent under applicable law, or under a contract, that is appointed or authorized to take charge of property of the debtor for the purpose of enforcing a lien against such property, or for the purpose of general administration of such property for the benefit of the debtor's creditors.

(12) The term "debt" means liability on a claim.

(12A) The term "debt relief agency" means any person who provides any bankruptcy assistance to an assisted person in return for the payment of money or other valuable consideration, or who is a bankruptcy petition preparer under section 110, but does not include—

(A) any person who is an officer, director, employee, or agent of a person who provides such assistance or of the bankruptcy petition preparer;

(B) a nonprofit organization that is exempt from taxation under section 501(c)(3) of the Internal Revenue Code of 1986;

(C) a creditor of such assisted person, to the extent that the creditor is assisting such assisted person to restructure any debt owed by such assisted person to the creditor;

(D) a depository institution (as defined in section 3 of the Federal Deposit Insurance Act) or any Federal credit union or State credit union (as those terms are defined in section 101 of the Federal Credit Union Act), or any affiliate or subsidiary of such depository institution or credit union; or

(E) an author, publisher, distributor, or seller of works subject to copyright protection under title 17, when acting in such capacity.

(13) The term "debtor" means person or municipality concerning which a case under this title has been commenced.

(13A) The term "debtor's principal residence"—

(A) means a residential structure if used as the principal residence by the debtor, including incidental property, without regard to whether that structure is attached to real property; and

(B) includes an individual condominium or cooperative unit, a mobile or manufactured home, or trailer if used as the principal residence by the debtor.

(14) The term "disinterested person" means a person that—

(A) is not a creditor, an equity security holder, or an insider;

(B) is not and was not, within 2 years before the date of the filing of the petition, a director, officer, or employee of the debtor; and

(C) does not have an interest materially adverse to the interest of the estate or of any class of creditors or equity security holders, by reason of any direct or indirect relationship to, connection with, or interest in, the debtor, or for any other reason.

(14A) The term "domestic support obligation" means a debt that accrues before, on, or after the date of the order for relief in a case under this title, including interest that accrues on that debt as provided under applicable nonbankruptcy law notwithstanding any other provision of this title, that is—

(A) owed to or recoverable by—

(i) a spouse, former spouse, or child of the debtor or such child's parent, legal guardian, or responsible relative; or

(ii) a governmental unit;

(B) in the nature of alimony, maintenance, or support (including assistance provided by a governmental unit) of such spouse, former spouse, or child of the debtor or such child's parent, without regard to whether such debt is expressly so designated;

(C) established or subject to establishment before, on, or after the date of the order for relief in a case under this title, by reason of applicable provisions of—

   (i) a separation agreement, divorce decree, or property settlement agreement;

   (ii) an order of a court of record; or

   (iii) a determination made in accordance with applicable nonbankruptcy law by a governmental unit; and

(D) not assigned to a nongovernmental entity, unless that obligation is assigned voluntarily by the spouse, former spouse, child of the debtor, or such child's parent, legal guardian, or responsible relative for the purpose of collecting the debt.

(15) The term "entity" includes person, estate, trust, governmental unit, and United States trustee.

(16) The term "equity security" means—

(A) share in a corporation, whether or not transferable or denominated "stock", or similar security;

(B) interest of a limited partner in a limited partnership; or

(C) warrant or right, other than a right to convert, to purchase, sell, or subscribe to a share, security, or interest of a kind specified in subparagraph (A) or (B) of this paragraph.

(17) The term "equity security holder" means holder of an equity security of the debtor.

(18) The term "family farmer" means—

(A) individual or individual and spouse engaged in a farming operation whose aggregate debts do not exceed $4,153,150 [1] and not less than 50 percent of whose aggregate noncontingent, liquidated debts (excluding a debt for the principal residence of such individual or such individual and spouse unless such debt arises out of a farming operation), on the date the case is filed, arise out of a farming operation owned or operated by such individual or such individual and spouse, and such individual or such individual and spouse receive from such farming operation more than 50 percent of such individual's or such individual and spouse's gross income for—

   (i) the taxable year preceding; or

   (ii) each of the 2d and 3d taxable years preceding;

the taxable year in which the case concerning such individual or such individual and spouse was filed; or

(B) corporation or partnership in which more than 50 percent of the outstanding stock or equity is held by one family, or by one family and the relatives of the members of such family, and such family or such relatives conduct the farming operation, and

   (i) more than 80 percent of the value of its assets consists of assets related to the farming operation;

   (ii) its aggregate debts do not exceed $4,153,150 [1] and not less than 50 percent of its aggregate noncontingent, liquidated debts (excluding a debt for one dwelling which is owned by such corporation or partnership and which a shareholder or partner maintains as a principal residence, unless such debt arises out of a farming operation), on the date the case is filed, arise out of the farming operation owned or operated by such corporation or such partnership; and

   (iii) if such corporation issues stock, such stock is not publicly traded.

(19) The term "family farmer with regular annual income" means family farmer whose annual income is sufficiently stable and regular to enable such family farmer to make payments under a plan under chapter 12 of this title.

(19A) The term "family fisherman" means—

(A) an individual or individual and spouse engaged in a commercial fishing operation—

   (i) whose aggregate debts do not exceed $1,924,550 [1] and not less than 80 percent of whose aggregate noncontingent, liquidated debts (excluding a debt for the principal residence of such individual or such individual and spouse, unless such debt arises out of a commercial fishing operation), on the date the case is filed, arise out of a commercial fishing operation owned or operated by such individual or such individual and spouse; and

   (ii) who receive from such commercial fishing operation more than 50 percent of such individual's or such individual's and spouse's gross income for the taxable year preceding the taxable year in which the case concerning such individual or such individual and spouse was filed; or

(B) a corporation or partnership—

   (i) in which more than 50 percent of the outstanding stock or equity is held by—

     (I) 1 family that conducts the commercial fishing operation; or

     (II) 1 family and the relatives of the members of such family, and such family or such relatives conduct the commercial fishing operation; and

   (ii)(I) more than 80 percent of the value of its assets consists of assets related to the commercial fishing operation;

(II) its aggregate debts do not exceed $1,924,550 [1] and not less than 80 percent of its aggregate noncontingent, liquidated debts (excluding a debt for 1 dwelling which is owned by such corporation or partnership and which a shareholder or partner maintains as a principal residence, unless such debt arises out of a commercial fishing operation), on the date the case is filed, arise out of a commercial fishing operation owned or operated by such corporation or such partnership; and

(III) if such corporation issues stock, such stock is not publicly traded.

(19B) The term "family fisherman with regular annual income" means a family fisherman whose annual income is sufficiently stable and regular to enable such family fisherman to make payments under a plan under chapter 12 of this title.

(20) The term "farmer" means (except when such term appears in the term "family farmer") person that received more than 80 percent of such person's gross income during the taxable year of such person immediately preceding the taxable year of such person during which the case under this title concerning such person was commenced from a farming operation owned or operated by such person.

(21) The term "farming operation" includes farming, tillage of the soil, dairy farming, ranching, production or raising of crops, poultry, or livestock, and production of poultry or livestock products in an unmanufactured state.

(21A) The term "farmout agreement" means a written agreement in which—

(A) the owner of a right to drill, produce, or operate liquid or gaseous hydrocarbons on property agrees or has agreed to transfer or assign all or a part of such right to another entity; and

(B) such other entity (either directly or through its agents or its assigns), as consideration, agrees to perform drilling, reworking, recompleting, testing, or similar or related operations, to develop or produce liquid or gaseous hydrocarbons on the property.

(21B) The term "Federal depository institutions regulatory agency" means—

(A) with respect to an insured depository institution (as defined in section 3(c)(2) of the Federal Deposit Insurance Act) for which no conservator or receiver has been appointed, the appropriate Federal banking agency (as defined in section 3(q) of such Act);

(B) with respect to an insured credit union (including an insured credit union for which the National Credit Union Administration has been appointed conservator or liquidating agent), the National Credit Union Administration;

(C) with respect to any insured depository institution for which the Resolution Trust Corporation

has been appointed conservator or receiver, the Resolution Trust Corporation; and

(D) with respect to any insured depository institution for which the Federal Deposit Insurance Corporation has been appointed conservator or receiver, the Federal Deposit Insurance Corporation.

(22) The term "financial institution" means—

(A) a Federal reserve bank, or an entity that is a commercial or savings bank, industrial savings bank, savings and loan association, trust company, federally-insured credit union, or receiver, liquidating agent, or conservator for such entity and, when any such Federal reserve bank, receiver, liquidating agent, conservator or entity is acting as agent or custodian for a customer (whether or not a "customer", as defined in section 741) in connection with a securities contract (as defined in section 741) such customer; or

(B) in connection with a securities contract (as defined in section 741) an investment company registered under the Investment Company Act of 1940.

(22A) The term "financial participant" means—

(A) an entity that, at the time it enters into a securities contract, commodity contract, swap agreement, repurchase agreement, or forward contract, or at the time of the date of the filing of the petition, has one or more agreements or transactions described in paragraph (1), (2), (3), (4), (5), or (6) of section 561(a) with the debtor or any other entity (other than an affiliate) of a total gross dollar value of not less than $1,000,000,000 in notional or actual principal amount outstanding (aggregated across counterparties) at such time or on any day during the 15–month period preceding the date of the filing of the petition, or has gross mark-to-market positions of not less than $100,000,000 (aggregated across counterparties) in one or more such agreements or transactions with the debtor or any other entity (other than an affiliate) at such time or on any day during the 15–month period preceding the date of the filing of the petition; or

(B) a clearing organization (as defined in section 402 of the Federal Deposit Insurance Corporation Improvement Act of 1991).

(23) The term "foreign proceeding" means a collective judicial or administrative proceeding in a foreign country, including an interim proceeding, under a law relating to insolvency or adjustment of debt in which proceeding the assets and affairs of the debtor are subject to control or supervision by a foreign court, for the purpose of reorganization or liquidation.

(24) The term "foreign representative" means a person or body, including a person or body appointed on an interim basis, authorized in a foreign proceeding to administer the reorganization or the liquidation of the debtor's assets or affairs or to act as a representative of such foreign proceeding.

(25) The term "forward contract" means—

(A) a contract (other than a commodity contract, as defined in section 761) for the purchase, sale, or transfer of a commodity, as defined in section 761(8) of this title, or any similar good, article, service, right, or interest which is presently or in the future becomes the subject of dealing in the forward contract trade, or product or by-product thereof, with a maturity date more than two days after the date the contract is entered into, including, but not limited to, a repurchase or reverse repurchase transaction (whether or not such repurchase or reverse repurchase transaction is a "repurchase agreement", as defined in this section)[2] consignment, lease, swap, hedge transaction, deposit, loan, option, allocated transaction, unallocated transaction, or any other similar agreement;

(B) any combination of agreements or transactions referred to in subparagraphs (A) and (C);

(C) any option to enter into an agreement or transaction referred to in subparagraph (A) or (B);

(D) a master agreement that provides for an agreement or transaction referred to in subparagraph (A), (B), or (C), together with all supplements to any such master agreement, without regard to whether such master agreement provides for an agreement or transaction that is not a forward contract under this paragraph, except that such master agreement shall be considered to be a forward contract under this paragraph only with respect to each agreement or transaction under such master agreement that is referred to in subparagraph (A), (B), or (C); or

(E) any security agreement or arrangement, or other credit enhancement related to any agreement or transaction referred to in subparagraph (A), (B), (C), or (D), including any guarantee or reimbursement obligation by or to a forward contract merchant or financial participant in connection with any agreement or transaction referred to in any such subparagraph, but not to exceed the damages in connection with any such agreement or transaction, measured in accordance with section 562.

(26) The term "forward contract merchant" means a Federal reserve bank, or an entity the business of which consists in whole or in part of entering into forward contracts as or with merchants in a commodity (as defined in section 761) or any similar good, article, service, right, or interest which is presently or in the future becomes the subject of dealing in the forward contract trade.

(27) The term "governmental unit" means United States; State; Commonwealth; District; Territory; municipality; foreign state; department, agency, or instrumentality of the United States (but not a United States trustee while serving as a trustee in a case under this title), a State, a Commonwealth, a District, a Territory, a municipality, or a foreign state; or other foreign or domestic government.

(27A) The term "health care business"—

(A) means any public or private entity (without regard to whether that entity is organized for profit or not for profit) that is primarily engaged in offering to the general public facilities and services for—

(i) the diagnosis or treatment of injury, deformity, or disease; and

(ii) surgical, drug treatment, psychiatric, or obstetric care; and

(B) includes—

(i) any—

(I) general or specialized hospital;

(II) ancillary ambulatory, emergency, or surgical treatment facility;

(III) hospice;

(IV) home health agency; and

(V) other health care institution that is similar to an entity referred to in subclause (I), (II), (III), or (IV); and

(ii) any long-term care facility, including any—

(I) skilled nursing facility;

(II) intermediate care facility;

(III) assisted living facility;

(IV) home for the aged;

(V) domiciliary care facility; and

(VI) health care institution that is related to a facility referred to in subclause (I), (II), (III), (IV), or (V), if that institution is primarily engaged in offering room, board, laundry, or personal assistance with activities of daily living and incidentals to activities of daily living.

(27B) The term "incidental property" means, with respect to a debtor's principal residence—

(A) property commonly conveyed with a principal residence in the area where the real property is located;

(B) all easements, rights, appurtenances, fixtures, rents, royalties, mineral rights, oil or gas rights or profits, water rights, escrow funds, or insurance proceeds; and

(C) all replacements or additions.

(28) The term "indenture" means mortgage, deed of trust, or indenture, under which there is outstanding a security, other than a voting-trust certificate, constituting a claim against the debtor, a claim secured by a lien on any of the debtor's property, or an equity security of the debtor.

(29) The term "indenture trustee" means trustee under an indenture.

(30) The term "individual with regular income" means individual whose income is sufficiently stable and regular to enable such individual to make payments under a plan under chapter 13 of this title, other than a stockbroker or a commodity broker.

(31) The term "insider" includes—

(A) if the debtor is an individual—

    (i) relative of the debtor or of a general partner of the debtor;

    (ii) partnership in which the debtor is a general partner;

    (iii) general partner of the debtor; or

    (iv) corporation of which the debtor is a director, officer, or person in control;

(B) if the debtor is a corporation—

    (i) director of the debtor;

    (ii) officer of the debtor;

    (iii) person in control of the debtor;

    (iv) partnership in which the debtor is a general partner;

    (v) general partner of the debtor; or

    (vi) relative of a general partner, director, officer, or person in control of the debtor;

(C) if the debtor is a partnership—

    (i) general partner in the debtor;

    (ii) relative of a general partner in, general partner of, or person in control of the debtor;

    (iii) partnership in which the debtor is a general partner;

    (iv) general partner of the debtor; or

    (v) person in control of the debtor;

(D) if the debtor is a municipality, elected official of the debtor or relative of an elected official of the debtor;

(E) affiliate, or insider of an affiliate as if such affiliate were the debtor; and

(F) managing agent of the debtor.

(32) The term "insolvent" means—

(A) with reference to an entity other than a partnership and a municipality, financial condition such that the sum of such entity's debts is greater than all of such entity's property, at a fair valuation, exclusive of—

    (i) property transferred, concealed, or removed with intent to hinder, delay, or defraud such entity's creditors; and

    (ii) property that may be exempted from property of the estate under section 522 of this title;

(B) with reference to a partnership, financial condition such that the sum of such partnership's debts is greater than the aggregate of, at a fair valuation—

    (i) all of such partnership's property, exclusive of property of the kind specified in subparagraph (A)(i) of this paragraph; and

    (ii) the sum of the excess of the value of each general partner's nonpartnership property, exclusive of property of the kind specified in subparagraph (A) of this paragraph, over such partner's nonpartnership debts; and

(C) with reference to a municipality, financial condition such that the municipality is—

    (i) generally not paying its debts as they become due unless such debts are the subject of a bona fide dispute; or

    (ii) unable to pay its debts as they become due.

(33) The term "institution-affiliated party"—

(A) with respect to an insured depository institution (as defined in section 3(c)(2) of the Federal Deposit Insurance Act), has the meaning given it in section 3(u) of the Federal Deposit Insurance Act; and

(B) with respect to an insured credit union, has the meaning given it in section 206(r) of the Federal Credit Union Act.

(34) The term "insured credit union" has the meaning given it in section 101(7) of the Federal Credit Union Act.

(35) The term "insured depository institution"—

(A) has the meaning given it in section 3(c)(2) of the Federal Deposit Insurance Act; and

(B) includes an insured credit union (except in the case of paragraphs (21B) and (33)(A) of this subsection).

(35A) The term "intellectual property" means—

(A) trade secret;

(B) invention, process, design, or plant protected under title 35;

(C) patent application;

(D) plant variety;

(E) work of authorship protected under title 17; or

(F) mask work protected under chapter 9 of title 17;

to the extent protected by applicable nonbankruptcy law.

(36) The term "judicial lien" means lien obtained by judgment, levy, sequestration, or other legal or equitable process or proceeding.

(37) The term "lien" means charge against or interest in property to secure payment of a debt or performance of an obligation.

(38) The term "margin payment" means, for purposes of the forward contract provisions of this title, payment or deposit of cash, a security or other property, that is commonly known in the forward contract trade as original margin, initial margin, maintenance margin, or variation margin, including mark-to-market payments, or variation payments.

(38A) The term "master netting agreement"—

(A) means an agreement providing for the exercise of rights, including rights of netting, setoff, liquidation, termination, acceleration, or close out, under or in connection with one or more contracts that are described in any one or more of paragraphs (1) through (5) of section 561(a), or any security agreement or arrangement or other credit enhancement related to one or more of the foregoing, including any guarantee or reimbursement obligation related to 1 or more of the foregoing; and

(B) if the agreement contains provisions relating to agreements or transactions that are not contracts described in paragraphs (1) through (5) of section 561(a), shall be deemed to be a master netting agreement only with respect to those agreements or transactions that are described in any one or more of paragraphs (1) through (5) of section 561(a).

(38B) The term "master netting agreement participant" means an entity that, at any time before the date of the filing of the petition, is a party to an outstanding master netting agreement with the debtor.

(39) The term "mask work" has the meaning given it in section 901(a)(2) of title 17.

(39A) The term "median family income" means for any year—

(A) the median family income both calculated and reported by the Bureau of the Census in the then most recent year; and

(B) if not so calculated and reported in the then current year, adjusted annually after such most recent year until the next year in which median family income is both calculated and reported by the Bureau of the Census, to reflect the percentage change in the Consumer Price Index for All Urban Consumers during the period of years occurring after such most recent year and before such current year.

(40) The term "municipality" means political subdivision or public agency or instrumentality of a State.

(40A) The term "patient" means any individual who obtains or receives services from a health care business.

(40B) The term "patient records" means any record relating to a patient, including a written document or a record recorded in a magnetic, optical, or other form of electronic medium.

(41) The term "person" includes individual, partnership, and corporation, but does not include governmental unit, except that a governmental unit that—

(A) acquires an asset from a person—

(i) as a result of the operation of a loan guarantee agreement; or

(ii) as receiver or liquidating agent of a person;

(B) is a guarantor of a pension benefit payable by or on behalf of the debtor or an affiliate of the debtor; or

(C) is the legal or beneficial owner of an asset of—

(i) an employee pension benefit plan that is a governmental plan, as defined in section 414(d) of the Internal Revenue Code of 1986; or

(ii) an eligible deferred compensation plan, as defined in section 457(b) of the Internal Revenue Code of 1986;

shall be considered, for purposes of section 1102 of this title, to be a person with respect to such asset or such benefit.

(41A) The term "personally identifiable information" means—

(A) if provided by an individual to the debtor in connection with obtaining a product or a service from the debtor primarily for personal, family, or household purposes—

(i) the first name (or initial) and last name of such individual, whether given at birth or time of adoption, or resulting from a lawful change of name;

(ii) the geographical address of a physical place of residence of such individual;

(iii) an electronic address (including an e-mail address) of such individual;

(iv) a telephone number dedicated to contacting such individual at such physical place of residence;

(v) a social security account number issued to such individual; or

(vi) the account number of a credit card issued to such individual; or

(B) if identified in connection with 1 or more of the items of information specified in subparagraph (A)—

(i) a birth date, the number of a certificate of birth or adoption, or a place of birth; or

(ii) any other information concerning an identified individual that, if disclosed, will result in contacting or identifying such individual physically or electronically.

(42) The term "petition" means petition filed under section 301, 302, 303 and [3] 1504 of this title, as the case may be, commencing a case under this title.

(42A) The term "production payment" means a term overriding royalty satisfiable in cash or in kind—

(A) contingent on the production of a liquid or gaseous hydrocarbon from particular real property; and

(B) from a specified volume, or a specified value, from the liquid or gaseous hydrocarbon produced from such property, and determined without regard to production costs.

(43) The term "purchaser" means transferee of a voluntary transfer, and includes immediate or mediate transferee of such a transferee.

(44) The term "railroad" means common carrier by railroad engaged in the transportation of individuals or property or owner of trackage facilities leased by such a common carrier.

(45) The term "relative" means individual related by affinity or consanguinity within the third degree as determined by the common law, or individual in a step or adoptive relationship within such third degree.

(46) The term "repo participant" means an entity that, at any time before the filing of the petition, has an outstanding repurchase agreement with the debtor.

(47) The term "repurchase agreement" (which definition also applies to a reverse repurchase agreement)—

(A) means—

(i) an agreement, including related terms, which provides for the transfer of one or more certificates of deposit, mortgage related securities (as defined in section 3 of the Securities Exchange Act of 1934), mortgage loans, interests in mortgage related securities or mortgage loans, eligible bankers' acceptances, qualified foreign government securities (defined as a security that is a direct obligation of, or that is fully guaranteed by, the central government of a member of the Organization for Economic Cooperation and Development), or securities that are direct obligations of, or that are fully guaranteed by, the United States or any agency of the United States against the transfer of funds by the transferee of such certificates of deposit, eligible bankers' acceptances, securities, mortgage loans, or interests, with a simultaneous agreement by such transferee to transfer to the transferor thereof certificates of deposit, eligible bankers' acceptance, securities, mortgage loans, or interests of the kind described in this clause, at a date certain not later than 1 year after such transfer or on demand, against the transfer of funds;

(ii) any combination of agreements or transactions referred to in clauses (i) and (iii);

(iii) an option to enter into an agreement or transaction referred to in clause (i) or (ii);

(iv) a master agreement that provides for an agreement or transaction referred to in clause (i), (ii), or (iii), together with all supplements to any such master agreement, without regard to whether such master agreement provides for an agreement or transaction that is not a repurchase agreement under this paragraph, except that such master agreement shall be considered to be a repurchase agreement under this paragraph only with respect to each agreement or transaction under the master agreement that is referred to in clause (i), (ii), or (iii); or

(v) any security agreement or arrangement or other credit enhancement related to any agreement or transaction referred to in clause (i), (ii), (iii), or (iv), including any guarantee or reimbursement obligation by or to a repo participant or financial participant in connection with any agreement or transaction referred to in any such clause, but not to exceed the damages in connection with any such agreement or transaction, measured in accordance with section 562 of this title; and

(B) does not include a repurchase obligation under a participation in a commercial mortgage loan.

(48) The term "securities clearing agency" means person that is registered as a clearing agency under section 17A of the Securities Exchange Act of 1934, or exempt from such registration under such section pursuant to an order of the Securities and Exchange Commission, or whose business is confined to the performance of functions of a clearing agency with respect to exempted securities, as defined in section 3(a)(12) of such Act for the purposes of such section 17A.

(48A) The term "securities self regulatory organization" means either a securities association registered with the Securities and Exchange Commission under section 15A of the Securities Exchange Act of 1934 or a national securities exchange registered with the Securities and Exchange Commission under section 6 of the Securities Exchange Act of 1934.

(49) The term "security"—

(A) includes—

(i) note;

(ii) stock;

(iii) treasury stock;

(iv) bond;

(v) debenture;

(vi) collateral trust certificate;

(vii) pre-organization certificate or subscription;

(viii) transferable share;

(ix) voting-trust certificate;

(x) certificate of deposit;

(xi) certificate of deposit for security;

(xii) investment contract or certificate of interest or participation in a profit-sharing agreement or in an oil, gas, or mineral royalty or lease, if such contract or interest is required to be the subject of a registration statement filed with the Securities and Exchange Commission under the provisions of the Securities Act of 1933, or is exempt under section 3(b) of such Act from the requirement to file such a statement;

(xiii) interest of a limited partner in a limited partnership;

(xiv) other claim or interest commonly known as "security"; and

(xv) certificate of interest or participation in, temporary or interim certificate for, receipt for, or warrant or right to subscribe to or purchase or sell, a security; but

(B) does not include—

(i) currency, check, draft, bill of exchange, or bank letter of credit;

(ii) leverage transaction, as defined in section 761 of this title;

(iii) commodity futures contract or forward contract;

(iv) option, warrant, or right to subscribe to or purchase or sell a commodity futures contract;

(v) option to purchase or sell a commodity;

(vi) contract or certificate of a kind specified in subparagraph (A)(xii) of this paragraph that is not required to be the subject of a registration statement filed with the Securities and Exchange Commission and is not exempt under section 3(b) of the Securities Act of 1933 from the requirement to file such a statement; or

(vii) debt or evidence of indebtedness for goods sold and delivered or services rendered.

(50) The term "security agreement" means agreement that creates or provides for a security interest.

(51) The term "security interest" means lien created by an agreement.

(51A) The term "settlement payment" means, for purposes of the forward contract provisions of this title, a preliminary settlement payment, a partial settlement payment, an interim settlement payment, a settlement payment on account, a final settlement payment, a net settlement payment, or any other similar payment commonly used in the forward contract trade.

(51B) The term "single asset real estate" means real property constituting a single property or project, other than residential real property with fewer than 4 residential units, which generates substantially all of the gross income of a debtor who is not a family farmer and on which no substantial business is being conducted by a debtor other than the business of operating the real property and activities incidental thereto.

(51C) The term "small business case" means a case filed under chapter 11 of this title in which the debtor is a small business debtor.

(51D) The term "small business debtor"—

(A) subject to subparagraph (B), means a person engaged in commercial or business activities (including any affiliate of such person that is also a debtor under this title and excluding a person whose primary activity is the business of owning or operating real property or activities incidental thereto) that has aggregate noncontingent liquidated secured and unsecured debts as of the date of the filing of the petition or the date of the order for relief in an amount not more than $2,566,050 [1] (excluding debts owed to 1 or more affiliates or insiders) for a case in which the United States trustee has not appointed under section 1102(a)(1) a committee of unsecured creditors or where the court has determined that the committee of unsecured creditors is not sufficiently active and representative to provide effective oversight of the debtor; and

(B) does not include any member of a group of affiliated debtors that has aggregate noncontingent liquidated secured and unsecured debts in an amount greater than $2,566,050 [1] (excluding debt owed to 1 or more affiliates or insiders).

(52) The term "State" includes the District of Columbia and Puerto Rico, except for the purpose of defining who may be a debtor under chapter 9 of this title.

(53) The term "statutory lien" means lien arising solely by force of a statute on specified circumstances or conditions, or lien of distress for rent, whether or not statutory, but does not include security interest or judicial lien, whether or not such interest or lien is provided by or is dependent on a statute and whether or not such interest or lien is made fully effective by statute.

(53A) The term "stockbroker" means person—

(A) with respect to which there is a customer, as defined in section 741 of this title; and

(B) that is engaged in the business of effecting transactions in securities—

(i) for the account of others; or

(ii) with members of the general public, from or for such person's own account.

(53B) The term "swap agreement"—

(A) means—

(i) any agreement, including the terms and conditions incorporated by reference in such agreement, which is—

(I) an interest rate swap, option, future, or forward agreement, including a rate floor, rate cap, rate collar, cross-currency rate swap, and basis swap;

(II) a spot, same day-tomorrow, tomorrow-next, forward, or other foreign exchange, precious metals, or other commodity agreement;

(III) a currency swap, option, future, or forward agreement;

(IV) an equity index or equity swap, option, future, or forward agreement;

(V) a debt index or debt swap, option, future, or forward agreement;

(VI) a total return, credit spread or credit swap, option, future, or forward agreement;

(VII) a commodity index or a commodity swap, option, future, or forward agreement;

(VIII) a weather swap, option, future, or forward agreement;

(IX) an emissions swap, option, future, or forward agreement; or

(X) an inflation swap, option, future, or forward agreement;

(ii) any agreement or transaction that is similar to any other agreement or transaction referred to in this paragraph and that—

(I) is of a type that has been, is presently, or in the future becomes, the subject of recurrent dealings in the swap or other derivatives markets (including terms and conditions incorporated by reference therein); and

(II) is a forward, swap, future, option, or spot transaction on one or more rates, currencies, commodities, equity securities, or other equity instruments, debt securities or other debt instruments, quantitative measures associated with an occurrence, extent of an occurrence, or contingency associated with a financial, commercial, or economic consequence, or economic or financial indices or measures of economic or financial risk or value;

(iii) any combination of agreements or transactions referred to in this subparagraph;

(iv) any option to enter into an agreement or transaction referred to in this subparagraph;

(v) a master agreement that provides for an agreement or transaction referred to in clause (i), (ii), (iii), or (iv), together with all supplements to any such master agreement, and without regard to whether the master agreement contains an agreement or transaction that is not a swap agreement under this paragraph, except that the master agreement shall be considered to be a swap agreement under this paragraph only with respect to each agreement or transaction under the master agreement that is referred to in clause (i), (ii), (iii), or (iv); or

(vi) any security agreement or arrangement or other credit enhancement related to any agreements or transactions referred to in clause (i) through (v), including any guarantee or reimbursement obligation by or to a swap participant or financial participant in connection with any agreement or transaction referred to in any such clause, but not to exceed the damages in connection with any such agreement or transaction, measured in accordance with section 562; and

(B) is applicable for purposes of this title only, and shall not be construed or applied so as to challenge or affect the characterization, definition, or treatment of any swap agreement under any other statute, regulation, or rule, including the Gramm–Leach–Bliley Act, the Legal Certainty for Bank Products Act of 2000, the securities laws (as such term is defined in section 3(a)(47) of the Securities Exchange Act of 1934) and the Commodity Exchange Act.

(53C) The term "swap participant" means an entity that, at any time before the filing of the petition, has an outstanding swap agreement with the debtor.

(56A) [4] The term "term overriding royalty" means an interest in liquid or gaseous hydrocarbons in place or to be produced from particular real property that entitles the owner thereof to a share of production, or the value thereof, for a term limited by time, quantity, or value realized.

(53D) The term "timeshare plan" means and shall include that interest purchased in any arrangement, plan, scheme, or similar device, but not including exchange programs, whether by membership, agreement, tenancy in common, sale, lease, deed, rental agreement, license, right to use agreement, or by any other means, whereby a purchaser, in exchange for consideration, receives a right to use accommodations, facilities, or recreational sites, whether improved or unimproved, for a specific period of time less than a full year during any given year, but not necessarily for consecutive years, and which extends for a period of more than three years. A "timeshare interest" is that interest purchased in a timeshare plan which grants the purchaser the right to use and occupy accommodations, facilities, or recreational sites, whether improved or unimproved, pursuant to a timeshare plan.

(54) The term "transfer" means—

(A) the creation of a lien;

(B) the retention of title as a security interest;

(C) the foreclosure of a debtor's equity of redemption; or

(D) each mode, direct or indirect, absolute or conditional, voluntary or involuntary, of disposing of or parting with—

(i) property; or

(ii) an interest in property.

(54A) The term "uninsured State member bank" means a State member bank (as defined in section 3 of the Federal Deposit Insurance Act) the deposits of which are not insured by the Federal Deposit Insurance Corporation.

(55) The term "United States", when used in a geographical sense, includes all locations where the judicial jurisdiction of the United States extends, including territories and possessions of the United States.

(Pub.L. 95–598, Nov. 6, 1978, 92 Stat. 2549; Pub.L. 97–222, § 1, July 27, 1982, 96 Stat. 235; Pub.L. 98–353, Title III, §§ 391, 401, 421, July 10, 1984, 98 Stat. 364, 366, 367; Pub.L. 99–554, Title II, §§ 201, 251, 283(a), Oct. 27, 1986, 100 Stat. 3097, 3104, 3116; Pub.L. 100–506, § 1(a), Oct. 18, 1988, 102 Stat. 2538; Pub.L. 100–597, § 1, Nov. 3, 1988, 102 Stat. 3028; Pub.L. 101–311, Title I, § 101, Title II, § 201, June 25, 1990, 104 Stat. 267, 268; Pub.L. 101–647, Title XXV, § 2522(e), Nov. 29, 1990, 104 Stat. 4867; Pub.L. 102–486, Title XXX, § 3017(a), Oct. 24, 1992, 106 Stat. 3130; Pub.L. 103–394, Title I, § 106, Title II, §§ 208(a), 215, 217(a), 218(a), Title III, § 304(a), Title V, § 501(a), (b)(1), (d)(1), Oct. 22, 1994, 108 Stat. 4111, 4124, 4126–4128, 4132, 4141–4143; Pub.L. 106–554, § 1(a)(5) [Title I, § 112(c)(3), (4)], Dec. 21, 2000, 114 Stat. 2763, 2763A–393, 2763A–394; Pub.L. 109–8, Title I, § 102(b), (k), Title II, §§ 211, 226(a), 231(b), Title III, § 306(c), Title IV, §§ 401(a), 414, 432(a), Title VIII, § 802(b), Title IX, § 907(a)(1), (b), (c), Title X, §§ 1004, 1005, 1007(a), Title XI, § 1101(a), (b), Title XII, § 1201, Apr. 20, 2005, 119 Stat. 32, 35, 50, 66, 73, 80, 104, 107, 110, 145, 170, 175, 186, 187, 189, 192; Pub.L. 109–390, § 5(a)(1), Dec. 12, 2006, 120 Stat. 2695; Pub.L. 111–327, § 2(a)(1), Dec. 22, 2010, 124 Stat. 3557.)

1 Dollar amount as adjusted by the Judicial Conference of the United States. See Adjustment of Dollar Amounts notes set out under this section and 11 U.S.C.A. § 104.

2 So in original. A comma should probably appear.

3 So in original. Probably should be "or". See 2010 Amendments note set out under this section.

4 So in original. Par. (56A) was inserted between pars. (53C) and (53D).

HISTORICAL AND STATUTORY NOTES

Revision Notes and Legislative Reports

1978 Acts. Section 101 of title 11 contains 40 definitions:

Paragraph (1) defines "accountant" as an accountant authorized under applicable law to practice accounting. The term includes a professional accounting association, corporation, or partnership if applicable law authorizes such a unit to practice accounting.

Paragraph (2) defines "affiliate." An affiliate is an entity with a close relationship to the debtor. It includes a 20 percent parent or subsidiary of the debtor, whether a corporate, partnership, individual, or estate parent.

The use of "directly or indirectly" in subparagraphs (A) and (B) is intended to cover situations in which there is an opportunity to control, and where the existence of that opportunity operates as indirect control.

"Affiliate" is defined primarily for use in the definition of insider, infra, and for use in the chapter 11 reorganization cases. The definition of "affiliate" does not include an entity acting in a fiduciary or agency capacity if the entity does not have the sole discretionary power to vote 20 percent of the voting securities but hold them solely as security and have not exercised the power to vote. This restriction applies to a corporate affiliate under subparagraph (B) of paragraph (2).

Subsections (C) and (D) of paragraph (2) define affiliate also as those persons and entities whose business or substantially all of whose property is operated under a lease or operating agreement by a debtor and whose business or property is more than 50 percent under the control of the debtor.

The definition of "attorney" in paragraph (3) is similar to the definition of accountant.

Paragraph (4) defines "claim." The effect of the definition is a significant departure from present law. Under present law, "claim" is not defined in straight bankruptcy. Instead it is simply used, along with the concept of provability in section 63 of the Bankruptcy Act [section 103 of former Title 11], to limit the kinds of obligations that are payable in a bankruptcy case. The term is defined in the debtor rehabilitation chapters of present law far more broadly. The definition in paragraph (4) adopts an even broader definition of claim than is found in the present debtor rehabilitation chapters. The definition is any right to payment, whether or not reduced to judgment, liquidated, unliquidated, fixed, contingent, matured, unmatured, disputed, undisputed, legal, equitable, secured, or unsecured. The definition also includes as a claim an equitable right to performance that does not give rise to a right to payment. By this broadest possible definition and by the use of the term throughout the title 11, especially in subchapter I of chapter 5, the bill contemplates that all legal obligations of the debtor, no matter how remote or contingent, will be able to be dealt with in the bankruptcy case. It permits the broadest possible relief in the bankruptcy court.

Paragraph (5) defines "commodity broker" by reference to various terms used and defined in subchapter IV of chapter 7, Commodity Broker Liquidation. The terms are described in connection with section 761, infra.

Paragraph (6) defines "community claim" for those eight States that have community property laws. The definition is keyed to the liability of the debtor's property for a claim against either the debtor or the debtor's spouse. If the debtor's property is liable for a claim against either, that claim is a community claim.

Paragraph (7) defines "consumer debt". The definition is adapted from the definition used in various consumer protection laws. It encompasses only a debt incurred by an individual primarily for a personal, family, or household purpose.

The definition of "corporation" in paragraph (8) is similar to the definition in current law, section 1(8) [section 1(8) of former Title 11]. The term encompasses any association having the power or privilege that a private corporation, but not an individual or partnership, has; partnership associations organized under a law that makes only the capital subscribed responsible for the debts of the partnership; joint-stock company; unincorporated company or association; and business trust. "Unincorporated association" is intended specifically to include a labor union, as well as other bodies that come under that phrase as used under current law. The exclusion of limited partnerships is explicit, and not left to the case law.

Paragraph (9) defines "court" as the bankruptcy judge in the district in which the case is pending except in municipal adjustment and railroad reorganization cases, where "court" means the Federal district judge.

Paragraph (10) defines "creditor" to include holders of prepetition claims against the debtor. However, it also encompasses certain holders of claims that are deemed to arise before the date of the filing of the petition, such as those injured by the rejection of an executory contract or unexpired lease, certain investment tax credit recapture claim holders, "involuntary gap" creditors, and certain holders of the right of setoff. The term also includes the holder of a prepetition community claim. A guarantor of or surety for a claim against the debtor is also a creditor, because he holds a contingent claim against the debtor that becomes fixed when he pays the creditor whose claim he has guaranteed or insured.

Paragraph (11) defines "custodian." There is no similar definition in current law. It is defined to facilitate drafting, and means a prepetition liquidator of the debtor's property, such as an assignee for the benefit of creditors, a receiver of the debtor's property, or administrator of the debtor's property. The definition of custodian to include a receiver or trustee is descriptive, and not meant to be limited to court officers with those titles. The definition is intended to include other officers of the court if their functions are substantially similar to those of a receiver or trustee.

"Debt" is defined in paragraph (12) as a liability on a claim. The terms "debt" and "claim" are coextensive: a creditor has a "claim" against the debtor; the debtor owes a "debt" to the creditor. This definition of "debt" and the definition of "claim" on which it is based, proposed 11 U.S.C. 101(4), does not include a transaction such as a policy loan on an insurance policy. Under that kind of transaction, the debtor is not liable to the insurance company for repayment; the amount owed is merely available to the company for setoff against any benefits that become payable under the policy. As such, the loan is not a claim (it is not a right to payment) that the company can assert against the estate; nor is the debtor's obligation a debt (a liability on a claim) that will be discharged under proposed 11 U.S.C. 523 or 524.

Paragraph (13) defines "debtor." Debtor means person or municipality concerning which a case under title II [probably means 11] has been commenced. This is a change in terminology from present law, which identifies the person by or against whom a petition is filed in a straight bankruptcy liquidation case as the "bankrupt", and a person or municipality that is proceeding under a debtor rehabilitation chapter (chapters VIII through XIII of the Bankruptcy Act) [chapters 8 through 13 of former Title 11] as a "debtor." The term "debtor" is used for both kinds of cases in this bill, for ease of reference in chapters 1, 3, and 5 (which apply to straight bankruptcy and reorganization cases).

Paragraph (14) defines "disinterested person." The definition is adapted from section 158 of chapter X of current law [section 558 of former Title 11], though it is expanded and modified in some respects. A person is a disinterested person if the person is not a creditor, equity security holder, or insider; is not and was not an investment banker of the debtor for any outstanding security of the debtor (the change from underwriter in current law to investment banker is to make the term more descriptive and to avoid conflict with the definition of underwriter in section 2(11) of the Securities Act of 1933 (15 U.S.C. 77b(11)) [15 U.S.C.A. § 77(b)(11)]; has not been an investment banker for a security of the debtor within 3 years before the date of the filing of the petition (the change from five years to three years here conforms the definition with the statute of limitations in the Securities Act of 1933 [15 U.S.C.A. § 77n], or an attorney for such an investment banker; is not an insider of the debtor or of such an investment banker; and does not have an interest materially adverse to the estate.

"Entity" is defined, for convenience, in paragraph (15), to include person, estate, trust, and governmental unit. It is the most inclusive of the various defined terms relating to bodies or units.

Paragraph (16) defines "equity security." The term includes a share or stock in a corporation, a limited partner's interest in a limited partnership, and a warrant or right to subscribe to an equity security. The term does not include a security, such as a convertible debenture, that is convertible into equity security, but has not been converted.

Paragraph (17) defines "equity security holder" for convenience as the holder of an equity securing of the debtor.

Paragraph (18) defines "farmer". It encompasses only those persons for whom farming operations contribute 75 percent or more of their total income.

Paragraphs (19) and (20) define "foreign proceeding" and "foreign representative". A foreign proceeding is a proceeding in another country in which the debtor has some substantial connection for the purpose of liquidating the estate of the debtor or the purpose of financial rehabilitation of the debtor. A foreign representative is the representative of the estate in a foreign proceeding, such as a trustee or administrator.

Paragraph (21) defines "governmental unit" in the broadest sense. The definition encompasses the United States, a State, Commonwealth, District, Territory, municipality, or foreign state, and a department, agency, or instrumentality of any of those entities. "Department, agency, or instrumentality" does not include an entity that owes its existence to State action, such as the granting of a charter or a license but that has no other connection with a State or local government or the Federal Government. The relationship must be an active one in which the department, agency, or instrumentality is actually carrying out some governmental function.

Paragraph (22) defines "indenture." It is similar to the definition of indenture in the Trust Indenture Act of 1939 [15 U.S.C.A. § 77ccc(7)]. An indenture is the instrument under which securities, either debt or equity, of the debtor are outstanding.

Paragraph (23) defines "indenture trustee" as the trustee under an indenture.

Paragraph (24) defines "individual with regular income." The effect of this definition, and of its use in section 109(e), is to expand substantially the kinds of individuals that are eligible for relief under chapter 13, Adjustment of Debts of an Individual with Regular Income. Chapter XIII [chapter 13 of former Title 11] is now available only for wage earners. The definition encompasses all individuals with incomes that are sufficiently stable and regular to enable them to make payments under a chapter 13 plan. Thus, individuals on welfare, social security, fixed pension incomes, or who live on investment incomes, will be able to work out repayment plans with their creditors rather than being forced into straight bankruptcy. Also, self-employed individuals will be eligible to use chapter 13 if they have regular incomes.

However, the definition excludes certain stockbrokers and commodity brokers, in order to prohibit them from proceeding under chapter 13 and avoiding the customer protection provisions of chapter 7.

"Insider", defined in paragraph (25), is a new term. An insider is one who has a sufficiently close relationship with the debtor that his conduct is made subject to closer scrutiny than those dealing at arms length with the debtor. If the debtor is an individual, then a relative of the debtor, a partnership in which the debtor is a general partner, a general partner of the debtor, and a corporation controlled by the debtor are all insiders. If the debtor is a corporation, then a controlling person, a relative of a controlling person, a partnership in which the debtor is a general partner, and a general partner of the debtor are all insiders. If the debtor is a partnership, then a general partner of or in the debtor, a relative of a general partner in the debtor, and a person in control are all insiders. If the debtor is a municipality, then an elected official of the debtor is an insider. In addition, affiliates of the debtor and managing agents are insiders.

The definition of "insolvent" in paragraph (26) is adopted from section 1(19) of current law [section 1(19) of former Title 11]. An entity is insolvent if its debts are greater than its assets, at a fair valuation, exclusive of property exempted or fraudulently transferred. It is the traditional bankruptcy balance sheet test of insolvency. For a partnership, the definition is modified to account for the liability of a general partner for the partnership's debts. The difference in this definition from that in current law is in the exclusion of exempt property for all purposes in the definition of insolvent.

Paragraph (27) defines "judicial lien." It is one of three kinds of liens defined in this section. A judicial lien is a lien obtained by judgment, levy, sequestration, or other legal or equitable process or proceeding.

Paragraph (28) defines "lien." The definition is new and is very broad. A lien is defined as a charge against or interest in property to secure payment of a debt or performance of an obligation. It includes inchoate liens. In general, the concept of lien is divided into three kinds of liens: judicial liens, security interests, and statutory liens. Those three categories are mutually exclusive and are exhaustive except for certain common law liens.

Paragraph (29) defines "municipality." The definition is adapted from the terms used in the chapter IX (municipal bankruptcy) [chapter 9 of former Title 11] amendment to the Bankruptcy Act enacted in 1976 (Pub.L. 94–260). That amendment spoke in terms of "political subdivision or public agency or instrumentality of a State". Bankruptcy Act sec. 84 [section 404 of former Title 11]. The term municipality is defined by those three terms for convenience. It does not include the District of Columbia or any territories of the United States.

"Person" is defined in paragraph (30). The definition is a change in wording, but not in substance, from the definition in section 1(23) of the Bankruptcy Act [section 1(23) of former Title 11]. The definition is also similar to the one contained in 1 U.S.C. sec. 1, but is repeated here for convenience and ease of reference. Person includes individual partnership, and corporation. The exclusion of governmental units is made explicit in order to avoid any confusion that may arise if, for example, a municipality is incorporated and thus is legally a corporation as well as governmental unit. The definition does not include an estate or a trust, which are included only in the definition of "entity" in proposed 11 U.S.C. 101(14).

"Petition" is defined for convenience in paragraph (31). Petition is a petition under section 301, 302, 303, or 304 of the bankruptcy code—that is, a petition that commences a case under title 11.

Paragraph (32) defines purchaser as a transferee of a voluntary transfer, such as a sale or gift, and includes an immediate or mediate transferee of a purchaser.

The definition of "railroad" in paragraph (33) is derived from section 77 of the Bankruptcy Act [section 205 of former

Title 11]. A railroad is a common carrier by railroad engaged in the transportation of individuals or property, or an owner of trackage facilities leased by such a common carrier. The effect of the definition and the use of the term in section 109(d) is to eliminate the limitation now found in section 77 of the Bankruptcy Act that only railroads engaged in interstate commerce may proceed under the railroad reorganization provisions. The limitation may have been inserted because of a doubt that the commerce power could not reach intrastate railroads. Be that as it may, this bill is enacted under the bankruptcy power.

Paragraph (34) defines "relative" as an individual related by affinity or consanguinity within the third degree as determined by the common law, and includes individuals in a step or adoptive relationship. The definition is similar to current law, but adds the latter phrase. This definition should be applied as of the time when the transaction that it concerns took place. Thus, a former spouse is not a relative, but if, for example, for purposes of the preference section, proposed 11 U.S.C. 547(b)(4)(B), the transferee was a spouse of the debtor at the time of the transfer sought to be avoided, then the transferee would be relative and subject to the insider rules, even if the transferee was no longer married to the debtor at the time of the commencement of the case or at the time of the commencement of the preference recovery proceeding.

Paragraph (35) defines "security." The definition is new and is modeled on the most recent draft of the American Law Institute's proposed securities code, with some exceptions. The interest of a limited partner in a limited partnership is included in order to make sure that everything that is defined as an equity security is also a "security." The definition, as with the definition of "entity", "insider", and "person", is open-ended because the term is not susceptible of precise specification. Thus the courts will be able to use the characterization provided in this definition to treat with new kinds of documents on a flexible basis.

Paragraphs (36) and (37) defined "security agreement" and "security interest." A security interest is one of the kinds of liens. It is a lien created by an agreement. Security agreement is defined as the agreement creating the security interest. Though these terms are similar to the same terms in the Uniform Commercial Code, article IX, they are broader. For example, the U.C.C. does not cover real property mortgages. Under this definition, such a mortgage is included, as are all other liens created by agreement, even though not covered by the U.C.C. All U.C.C. security interests and security agreements are, however, security interests and security agreements under this definition. Whether a consignment or a lease constitutes a security interest under the bankruptcy code will depend on whether it constitutes a security interest under applicable State or local law.

Paragraph (38) defines another kind of lien, "statutory lien." The definition, derived from current law, states that a statutory lien is a lien arising solely by force of statute on specified circumstances or conditions and includes a lien of distress for rent (whether statutory, common law, or otherwise). The definition excludes judicial liens and security interests, whether or not they are provided for or are dependent on a statute, and whether or not they are made fully effective by statute. A statutory lien is only one that arises automatically, and is not based on an agreement to give a lien or on judicial action. Mechanics', materialmen's, and warehousemen's liens are examples. Tax liens are also included in the definition of statutory lien.

"Stockbroker" is defined in paragraph (39) as a person engaged in the business of effecting transactions in securities for the account of others or with members of the general public from or for such person's own account, if the person has a customer, as defined. Thus, the definition, derived from a combination of the definitions of "broker" and "dealer" in the Securities Exchange Act of 1934 [15 U.S.C.A. § 78c], encompasses both brokers and dealers. The definition is used in section 109 and in subchapter III of chapter 7, Stockholder Liquidation. The term does not encompass an employee who acts for a principal that "effects" transaction or deals with the public, because such an employee will not have a "customer".

Paragraph (40) defines "transfer." It is derived and adapted, with stylistic changes, from section 1(30) of the Bankruptcy Act [section 1(30) of former Title 11]. A transfer is a disposition of an interest in property. The definition of transfer is as broad as possible. Many of the potentially limiting words in current law are deleted, and the language is simplified. Under this definition, any transfer of an interest in property is a transfer, including a transfer of possession, custody, or control even if there is no transfer of title, because possession, custody, and control are interests in property. A deposit in a bank account or similar account is a transfer. Senate Report No. 95–989.

1982 Acts. House Report No. 97–420, see 1982 U.S. Code Cong. and Adm. News, p. 583.

1984 Acts. Statements by Legislative Leaders, see 1984 U.S. Code Cong. and Adm. News, p. 576.

1986 Acts. House Report No. 99–764 and House Conference Report No. 99–958, see 1986 U.S. Code Cong. and Adm. News, p. 5227.

1988 Acts. Senate Report No. 100–505, see 1988 U.S. Code Cong. and Adm. News, p. 3200.

House Report No. 100–1011, see 1988 U.S. Code Cong. and Adm. News, p. 4115.

1990 Acts. House Report No. 101–484, see 1990 U.S. Code Cong. and Adm. News, p. 223.

House Report No. 101–681(Part I), see 1990 U.S. Code Cong. and Adm. News, p. 6472.

1994 Acts. House Report No. 103–835, see 1994 U.S. Code Cong. and Adm. News, p. 3340.

2000 Acts. House Report No. 106–645 and Statement by President, see 2000 U.S. Code Cong. and Adm. News, p. 2459.

2005 Acts. House Report No. 109–31(Part I), see 2005 U.S. Code Cong. and Adm. News, p. 88.

2006 Acts. House Report No. 109–648(Part I), see 2006 U.S. Code Cong. and Adm. News, p. 1585.

Legislative Statements

Section 101(2) defines "affiliate." The House amendment contains a provision that is a compromise between the definition in the House-passed version of H.R. 8200 and the Senate amendment in the nature of a substitute to H.R. 8200. Subparagraphs (A) and (B) are derived from the Senate amendment and subparagraph (D) is taken from the House bill, while subparagraph (C) represents a compromise, taking the House position with respect to a person whose business is operated under a lease or an operating agreement by the debtor and with respect to a person substantially all of whose property is operated under an operating agreement by the debtor and with respect to a person substantially all of whose property is operated under an operating agreement by the debtor and the Senate position on leased property. Thus, the definition of "affiliate" excludes persons substantially all of whose property is operated under a lease agreement by a debtor, such as a small company which owns equipment all of which is leased to a larger nonrelated company.

Section 101(4)(B) represents a modification of the House-passed bill to include the definition of "claim" a right to an equitable remedy for breach of performance if such breach gives rise to a right to payment. This is intended to cause the liquidation or estimation of contingent rights of payment for which there may be an alternative equitable remedy with the result that the equitable remedy will be susceptible to being discharged in bankruptcy. For example, in some States, a judgment for specific performance may be satisfied by an alternative right to payment, in the event performance is refused; in that event, the creditor entitled to specific performance would have a "claim" for purposes of a proceeding under title 11.

On the other hand, rights to an equitable remedy for a breach of performance with respect to which such breach does not give rise to a right to payment are not "claims" and would therefore not be susceptible to discharge in bankruptcy.

In a case under chapter 9 to title 11, "claim" does not include a right to payment under an industrial development bond issued by a municipality as a matter of convenience for a third party.

Municipalities are authorized, under section 103(c) of the Internal Revenue Code of 1954, as amended [section 103(c) of Title 26, Internal Revenue Code], to issue tax-exempt industrial development revenue bonds to provide for the financing of certain projects for privately owned companies. The bonds are sold on the basis of the credit of the company on whose behalf they are issued, and the principal, interest, and premium, if any, are payable solely from payments made by the company to the trustee under the bond indenture and do not constitute claims on the tax revenues or other funds of the issuing municipalities. The municipality merely acts as the vehicle to enable the bonds to be issued on a tax-exempt basis. Claims that arise by virtue of these bonds are not among the claims defined by this paragraph and amounts owed by private companies to the holders of industrial development revenue bonds are not to be included among the assets of the municipality that would be affected by the plan.

Section 101(6) defines "community claim" as provided by the Senate amendment in order to indicate that a community claim exists whether or not there is community property in the estate as of the commencement of the case.

Section 101(7) of the House amendment contains a definition of consumer debt identical to the definition in the House bill and Senate amendment. A consumer debt does not include a debt to any extent the debt is secured by real property.

Section 101(9) of the Senate amendment contained a definition of "court." The House amendment deletes the provision as unnecessary in light of the pervasive jurisdiction of a bankruptcy court under all chapters of title 11 as indicated in title II of the House amendment to H.R. 8200.

Section 101(11) defines "debt" to mean liability on a claim, as was contained in the House-passed version of H.R. 8200. The Senate amendment contained language indicating that "debt" does not include a policy loan made by a life insurance company to the debtor. That language is deleted in the House amendment as unnecessary since a life insurance company clearly has no right to have a policy loan repaid by the debtor, although such company does have a right of offset with respect to such policy loan. Clearly, then, a "debt" does not include a policy loan made by a life insurance company. Inclusion of the language contained in the Senate amendment would have required elaboration of other legal relationships not arising by a liability on a claim. Further the language would have required clarification that interest on a policy loan made by a life insurance company is a debt, and that the insurance company does have right to payment to that interest.

Section 101(14) adopts the definition of "entity" contained in the Senate-passed version of H.R. 8200. Since the Senate amendment to H.R. 8200 deleted the U.S. trustee, a corresponding definitional change is made in chapter 15 of the House amendment for U.S. trustees under the pilot program. Adoption by the House amendment of a pilot program for U.S. trustees under chapter 15 requires insertion of "United States trustee" in many sections. Several provisions in chapter 15 of the House amendment that relate to the U.S. trustee were not contained in the Senate amendment in the nature of a substitute.

Section 101(17) defines "farmer," as in the Senate amendment with an income limitation percentage of 80 percent instead of 75 percent.

Section 101(18) contains a new definition of "farming operation" derived from present law and the definition of "farmer" in the Senate amendment. This definition gives a broad construction to the term "farming operation".

Section 101(20) contains a definition of "foreign representative". It clarifies the House bill and Senate amendment by indicating that a foreign representative must be duly selected in a foreign proceeding.

Section 101(35) defines "security" as contained in the Senate amendment. H.R. 8200 as adopted by the House excluded certain commercial notes from the definition of "security", and that exclusion is deleted.

Section 101(40) defines "transfer" as in the Senate amendment. The definition contained in H.R. 8200 as passed by the House included "setoff" in the definition of "transfer". Inclusion of "setoff" is deleted. The effect is that a "setoff" is not subject to being set aside as a preferential "transfer" but will be subject to special rules.

References in Text

Chapter 12, referred to in pars. (7A)(B) and (19B), is chapter 12 of this title, which is classified to 11 U.S.C.A. § 1201 et seq.

The Social Security Act, referred to in par. (10A)(B), is Act Aug. 14, 1935, c. 531, 49 Stat. 620, as amended, which is classified generally to chapter 7 of Title 42, 42 U.S.C.A. § 301 et seq.

Section 501(c)(3) of the Internal Revenue Code of 1986, referred to in par. (12A)(B), is classified to 26 U.S.C.A. § 501(c)(3).

Section 3 of the Federal Deposit Insurance Act, referred to in pars. (12A)(D), (21B)(A), (33)(A), (35)(A), and (54A) is Act Sept. 21, 1950, c. 967, § 2 [3], 64 Stat. 873, which is classified to 12 U.S.C.A. § 1813.

Section 101 of the Federal Credit Union Act, referred to in pars. (12A)(D), (34), is Act June 26, 1934, c. 750, Title I, § 101, formerly § 2, 48 Stat. 1216, as amended, which is classified to 12 U.S.C.A. § 1752.

The Investment Company Act of 1940, referred to in par. (22)(B), is Act Aug. 22, 1940, c. 686, Title I, 54 Stat. 789, as amended, which is classified principally to subchapter 1 of chapter 2D of Title 15, 15 U.S.C.A. § 80a–1 et seq. For complete classification, see Short Title set out as 15 U.S.C.A. § 80a–51 and Tables.

Section 402 of the Federal Deposit Insurance Corporation Improvement Act of 1991, referred to in par. (22A)(B), is Pub.L. 102–242, Title IV, § 402, Dec. 19, 1991, 105 Stat. 2372, which is classified to 12 U.S.C.A. § 4402.

Section 206 of the Federal Credit Union Act, referred to in par. (33)(B), is section 206 of Act June 26, 1934, c. 750, Title II, as added Oct. 19, 1970, Pub.L. 91–468, § 1(3), 84 Stat. 1003, which is classified to section 1786 of Title 12.

Sections 414(d) and 457(b) of the Internal Revenue Code of 1986, referred to in par. (41)(C), are sections 414(d) and 457(b), respectively, of Title 26, Internal Revenue Code.

Section 3 of the Securities and Exchange Act of 1934, referred to in par. (47)(A), is Act June 6, 1934, c. 404, Title I, § 3, 48 Stat. 882, which is classified to 15 U.S.C.A. § 78c.

Section 17A of the Securities and Exchange Act of 1934, referred to in par. (48), is section 17A of Act June 6, 1934, c. 404, Title I, as added June 4, 1975, Pub.L. 94–29, § 15, 89 Stat. 141, which is classified to section 78q–1 of Title 15, Commerce and Trade.

Section 3(a)(12) of such Act, referred to in par. (48), is Section 3 of the Securities and Exchange Act of 1934, Act June 6, 1934, c. 404, Title I, 48 Stat. 882, which is classified to 15 U.S.C.A. § 78c(a)(12).

Section 15A of the Securities Exchange Act of 1934, referred to in par. (48A), is June 6, 1934, c. 404, Title I, § 15A, as added June 25, 1938, c. 677, § 1, 52 Stat. 1070, and amended which is classified to 15 U.S.C.A. § 78o–3.

Section 6 of the Securities Exchange Act of 1934, referred to in par. (48A), is June 6, 1934, c. 404, Title I, § 6, 48 Stat. 885, as amended, which is classified to 15 U.S.C.A. § 78c.

The Securities Act of 1933, referred to in par. (49)(A)(xii), is Act May 27, 1933, c. 38, Title I, 48 Stat. 74, as amended, which is classified generally to subchapter I (section 77a et seq.) of chapter 2A of Title 15, Commerce and Trade. For complete classification of this Act to the Code, see section 77a of Title 15 and Tables.

Section 3 of the Securities Act of 1933, referred to in pars. (49)(A)(xii) and (B)(vi), is section 3 of Act May 27, 1933, c. 38, Title I, 48 Stat. 75, which is classified to section 77c of Title 15.

Chapter 11 of this title, referred to in par. (51C), is 11 U.S.C.A. § 1101 et seq.

The Securities Exchange Act of 1934, referred to in par. (53B)(B), is Act June 6, 1934, c. 404, 48 Stat. 881, as amended, which is classified principally to chapter 2B of Title 15, 15 U.S.C.A. § 78a et seq. Section 3(a)(47) of the Act, as amended, is classified to 15 U.S.C.A. § 78c(a)(47). For complete classification, see Short Title set out as 15 U.S.C.A. § 78a and Tables.

The Commodity Exchange Act, referred to in par. (53B)(B), is Act Sept. 21, 1922, c. 369, 42 Stat. 998, as amended, which is classified principally to chapter 1 of Title 7, 7 U.S.C.A. § 1 et seq. For complete classification, see Short Title set out as 7 U.S.C.A. § 1 and Tables.

The Gramm-Leach-Bliley Act, referred to in par. (53B)(B), is Pub.L. 106–102, Nov. 12, 1999, 113 Stat. 1338, also known as the Financial Services Modernization Act of 1999, which principally enacted chapters 93, 94 and 95 of Title 15, 15 U.S.C.A. § 6701 et seq., 15 U.S.C.A. § 6801 et seq., and 15 U.S.C.A. § 6901 et seq., respectively, and amended chapters 16 and 17 of Title 12, 12 U.S.C.A. § 1811 et seq., and 12 U.S.C.A. § 1841 et seq. For complete classification, see Tables.

The Legal Certainty for Bank Products Act of 2000, referred to in par. (53B)(B), is Pub.L. 106–554, § 1(a)(5) [Title IV, §§ 401 to 408], Dec. 21, 2000, 114 Stat. 2763, 2763A–457, which enacted 7 U.S.C.A. §§ 27 and 27a to 27f. For complete classification, see Short Title set out as a note under 7 U.S.C.A. § 1 and Tables.

Effective and Applicability Provisions

2013 Acts. Increase of dollar amounts by Judicial Conference of the United States by notice published Feb. 21, 2013, 78 F.R. 12089 effective April 1, 2013, and increase not applicable to cases commenced before the effective date of the adjustments, i.e., April 1, 2013. See Adjustment of Dollar Amounts notes under 11 U.S.C.A. § 104 and this section.

2010 Acts. Increase of dollar amounts by Judicial Conference of the United States by notice published Feb. 25, 2010, 75 F.R. 8747 effective April 1, 2010, and increase not applicable to cases commenced before the effective date of the adjustments, i.e., April 1, 2010. See Adjustment of Dollar Amounts notes under 11 U.S.C.A. § 104 and this section.

2007 Acts. Increase of dollar amounts by Judicial Conference of the United States by notice published Feb. 14, 2007, 72 F.R. 7082 effective April 1, 2007, and increase not applicable to cases commenced before the effective date of the adjustments, i.e., April 1, 2007. See Adjustment of Dollar Amounts notes under 11 U.S.C.A. § 104 and this section.

2005 Acts. Pub.L. 109–8, Title XV, § 1501, Apr. 20, 2005, 119 Stat. 216, provided that:

"**(a) Effective date.**—Except as otherwise provided in this Act, this Act and the amendments made by this Act [see Tables for classification] shall take effect 180 days after the date of enactment of this Act [Apr. 20, 2005].

"**(b) Application of amendments.**—

"**(1) In general.**—Except as otherwise provided in this Act and paragraph (2), the amendments made by this Act [see Tables for classification] shall not apply with respect to cases commenced under title 11, United States Code, before the effective date of this Act.

"**(2) Certain limitations applicable to debtors.**—The amendments made by sections 308 [amending 11 § 522], 322 [amending 11 U.S.C.A. §§ 104 and 522], and 330 [amending 11 U.S.C.A. §§ 727, 1141, 1228, and 1328] shall apply with respect to cases commenced under title 11, United States Code, on or after the date of the enactment of this Act [Apr. 20, 2005]."

1994 Acts. Section 702 of Pub.L. 103–394 provided that:

"**(a) Effective date.**—Except as provided in subsection (b), this Act [see Short Title of 1994 Amendments set out under this section] shall take effect on the date of the enactment of this Act [Oct. 22, 1994].

"**(b) Application of amendments.**—(1) Except as provided in paragraph (2), the amendments made by this Act shall not apply with respect to cases commenced under title 11 of the United States Code before the date of the enactment of this Act [Oct. 22, 1994].

"**(2)(A)** Paragraph (1) shall not apply with respect to the amendment made by section 111 [enacting subsecs. (g) and (h)

of section 524 of this title and a provision set out as a note under 11 U.S.C.A. § 524].

"**(B)** The amendments made by sections 113 and 117 [amending 11 U.S.C.A. §§ 106 and 330, respectively] shall apply with respect to cases commenced under title 11 of the United States Code before, on, and after the date of the enactment of this Act [Oct. 22, 1994].

"**(C)** Section 1110 of title 11, United States Code, as amended by section 201 of this Act [11 U.S.C.A. § 1110], shall apply with respect to any lease, as defined in such section 1110(c) as so amended, entered into in connection with a settlement of any proceeding in any case pending under title 11 of the United States Code on the date of the enactment of this Act [Oct. 22, 1994].

"**(D)** The amendments made by section 305 [amending 11 U.S.C.A. §§ 1123, 1222, 1322] shall apply only to agreements entered into after the date of enactment of this Act [Oct. 22, 1994]."

1992 Acts. Section 3017(c) of Pub.L. 102–486 provided that:

"**(1)** Except as provided in paragraph (2), the amendments made by this section [amending this section and 11 U.S.C.A. § 541] shall take effect on the date of the enactment of this Act [Oct. 24, 1992].

"**(2)** The amendments made by this section [amending this section and 11 U.S.C.A. § 541] shall not apply with respect to cases commenced under title 11 of the United States Code [this title] before the date of the enactment of this Act [Oct. 24, 1992]."

1988 Acts. Section 12 of Pub.L. 100–597 provided that:

"**(a) Effective date.**—Except as provided in subsection (b), this Act and the amendments made by this Act [enacting 11 U.S.C.A. §§ 927 to 929, amending 11 U.S.C.A. §§ 101, 109, 901, 902, 922, 926, 943, and renumbering former section 927 as 930 of this title] shall take effect on the date of the enactment of this Act [Nov. 3, 1988].

"**(b) Application of amendments.**—The amendments made by this Act shall not apply with respect to cases commenced under title 11 of the United States Code before the date of the enactment of this Act [Nov. 3, 1988]."

Section 2 of Pub.L. 100–506 provided that:

"**(a) Effective date.**—Except as provided in subsection (b), this Act and the amendments made by this Act [amending 11 U.S.C.A. §§ 101 and 365] shall take effect on the date of the enactment of this Act [Oct. 18, 1988].

"**(b) Application of amendments.**—The amendments made by this Act shall not apply with respect to any case commenced under title 11 of the United States Code before the date of the enactment of this Act [Oct. 18, 1988]."

1986 Acts. Amendment by Pub.L. 99–554 effective 30 days after Oct. 27, 1986, except as otherwise provided for, see section 302(a) of Pub.L. 99–554, set out as a note under 28 U.S.C.A. § 581.

Amendment by Pub.L. 99–554, § 201, not to become effective in or with respect to certain specified judicial districts until, or apply to cases while pending in such district before, the expiration of the 270–day period beginning 30 days after Oct. 27, 1986, or of the 30–day period beginning on the date the Attorney General certifies under section 303 of Pub.L. 99–554 the region specified in a paragraph of section 581(a) of Title 28, as amended by section 111(a) of Pub.L. 99–554, that includes such district, whichever occurs first, see section

302(d)(1) of Pub.L. 99–554, set out as a note under 28 U.S.C.A. § 581.

Amendment by Pub.L. 99–554, § 201, not to become effective in or with respect to certain specified judicial districts until, or apply to cases while pending in such district before, the expiration of the 2–year period beginning 30 days after Oct. 27, 1986, or of the 30–day period beginning on the date the Attorney General certifies under section 303 of Pub.L. 99–554 the region specified in a paragraph of section 581(a) of Title 28, as amended by section 111(a) of Pub.L. 99–554, that includes such district, whichever occurs first, see section 302(d)(2) of Pub.L. 99–554, set out as a note under 28 U.S.C.A. § 581.

Amendment by Pub.L. 99–554, § 201, not to become effective in or with respect to judicial districts established for the States of Alabama and North Carolina until, or apply to cases while pending in such district before, such district elects to be included in a bankruptcy region established in section 581(a) of Title 28, as amended by section 111(a) of Pub.L. 99–554, or Oct. 1, 2002, whichever occurs first, and, except as otherwise provided for, with respect to cases under chapters 7, 11, 12, and 13 of Title 11 commenced before 30 days after Oct. 27, 1986, and pending in a judicial district in the States of Alabama or North Carolina before any election made under section 302(d)(3)(A) of Pub.L. 99–554 by such district becomes effective or Oct. 1, 2002, whichever occurs first, amendments, by Pub.L. 99–554 not to apply until Oct. 1, 2003, or the expiration of the 1–year period beginning on the date such election becomes effective, whichever occurs first, and further, in any judicial district in Alabama or North Carolina not making the election described in section 302(d)(3)(A) of Pub.L. 99–554, any person appointed under regulations issued by the Judicial Conference to administer estates in cases under Title 11 authorized to establish, etc., a panel of private trustees, and to supervise cases and trustees in cases under chapters 7, 11, 12, and 13 of Title 11, until amendments by sections 201 to 231 of Pub.L. 99–554 effective in such district, see section 302(d)(3)(A) to (F), (H), (I) of Pub.L. 99–554, set out as a note under 28 U.S.C.A. § 581.

Amendment by Pub.L. 99–554, § 201, except as otherwise provided, with respect to cases under chapters 7, 11, 12, and 13 of Title 11 commenced before 30 days after Oct. 27, 1986, and pending in a judicial district referred to in section 581(a) of Title 28, as amended by section 111(a) of Pub.L. 99–554, for which a United States trustee is not authorized before 30 days after Oct. 27, 1986 to be appointed, not applicable until the expiration of the 3–year period beginning on Oct. 27, 1986, or of the 1–year period beginning on the date the Attorney General certifies section 303 of Pub.L. 99–554 the region specified in a paragraph of such section 581(a) that includes, such district, whichever occurs first, see section 302(e)(1), (2) of Pub.L. 99–554, set out as a note under 28 U.S.C.A. § 581.

Amendments by Pub.L. 99–554, § 251, effective 30 days after Oct. 27, 1986, but not to apply with respect to cases commenced under this title before that date, see section 302(a), (c)(1) of Pub.L. 99–554, set out as a note under 28 U.S.C.A. § 581.

Amendment by Pub.L. 99–554, § 283, effective 30 days after Oct. 27, 1986, see section 302(a) of Pub.L. 99–554, set out as a note under 28 U.S.C.A. § 581.

1984 Acts. Section 552, formerly section 553 of Title III (§§ 301 to 553) of Pub.L. 98–353, as redesignated by Pub.L. 98–531, §§ 1(2), Oct. 19, 1984, 98 Stat. 2704, eff. July 10, 1984, provided that:

"**(a)** Except as otherwise provided in this section the amendments made by this title [see Tables for classification] shall become effective to [sic] cases filed 90 days after the date of enactment of this Act [July 10, 1984].

"**(b)** The amendments made by section 426(b) [amending 11 U.S.C.A. § 303] shall become effective upon the date of enactment of this Act [July 10, 1984].

"**(c)** The amendments made by subtitle J [enacting 11 U.S.C.A. § 1113], shall become effective as provided in section 541(c) [set out as a note under 11 U.S.C.A. § 1113]."

Separability of Provisions

Section 701 of Pub.L. 103–394 provided that: "If any provision of this Act or amendment made by this Act [see Short Title of 1994 Amendments note set out under this section] or the application of such provision or amendment to any person or circumstance is held to be unconstitutional, the remaining provisions of and amendments made by this Act and the application of such other provisions and amendments to any person or circumstance shall not be affected thereby."

Section 551 of Title III (§§ 301 to 553) of Pub.L. 98–353 provided that: "If any provision of this title or any amendment made by this title [see Tables for classification], or the application thereof to any person or circumstance is held invalid, the provisions of every other part, and their application shall not be affected thereby."

Savings Provisions

Pub.L. 109–8, Title IX, § 912, as added by Pub.L. 109–390, § 5(d), Dec. 12, 2006, 120 Stat. 2698, provided that: "The meanings of terms used in this title [Title IX of the Bankruptcy Abuse Prevention and Consumer Protection Act of 2005, Pub.L. 109–8, Title IX (§§ 901 to 912), Apr. 20, 2005, 119 Stat. 146; see Tables for complete classification] are applicable for the purposes of this title only, and shall not be construed or applied so as to challenge or affect the characterization, definition, or treatment of any similar terms under any other statute, regulation, or rule, including the Gramm–Leach–Bliley Act [Pub.L. 106–102, Nov. 12, 1999, 113 Stat. 1338; see Tables for complete classification], the Legal Certainty for Bank Products Act of 2000 [Pub.L. 106–554, § 1(a)(5) (Title IV, §§ 401 to 408), Dec. 21, 2000, 114 Stat. 2763, 2763A–457, which enacted 7 U.S.C.A. §§ 27 and 27a to 27f; for complete classification, see Short Title note set out under 7 U.S.C.A. § 1 and Tables], the securities laws (as such term is defined in section 3(a)(47) of the Securities Exchange Act of 1934) [15 U.S.C.A. § 78c(a)(47)], and the Commodity Exchange Act [Act Sept. 21, 1922, c. 369, 42 Stat. 998, as amended, which is classified principally to chapter 1 of Title 7, 7 U.S.C.A. § 1 et seq.; for complete classification, see Short Title set out as 7 U.S.C.A. § 1 and Tables]."

Short Title

2015 Amendments. Pub.L. 114–107, § 1, Dec. 18, 2015, 129 Stat. 2223, provided that: "This Act [amending provisions set out as a note under 11 U.S.C.A. § 707] may be cited as the 'National Guard and Reservist Debt Relief Extension Act of 2015'."

2011 Amendments. Pub.L. 112–64, § 1, Dec. 13, 2011, 125 Stat. 766, provided that: "This Act [amending provisions set out as a note under 11 U.S.C.A. § 107] may be cited as the 'National Guard and Reservist Debt Relief Extension Act of 2011'."

2010 Amendments. Pub.L. 111–327, § 1, Dec. 22, 2010, 124 Stat. 3557, provided that: "This Act [amending 11 U.S.C.A. §§ 101, 103, 104, 106, 107, 109, 110, 111, 303, 308, 348, 362, 363, 505, 507, 521, 522, 523, 524, 526, 527, 541, 554, 704, 707, 723, 724, 726, 901, 1104, 1106, 1111, 1112, 1127, 1129, 1141, 1145, 1202, 1302, 1304, 1307, 1308, 1322, 1325, 1511, 1519, 1521 and 1529, 18 U.S.C.A. § 157, and 28 U.S.C.A. §§ 158, 159 and 586, and amending provisions set out as a note under 11 U.S.C.A. § 507] may be cited as the 'Bankruptcy Technical Corrections Act of 2010'."

2009 Amendments. Pub.L. 111–16, § 1, May 7, 2009, 123 Stat. 1607, provided that: "This Act [amending section 7 of the Classified Information Procedures Act (18 App. U.S.C.A. § 7), 11 U.S.C.A. §§ 109, 322, 332, 342, 521, 704, and 764, 18 U.S.C.A. §§ 983, 1514, 1963, 2252A, 2339B, 3060, 3432, 3509, and 3771, 21 U.S.C.A. § 853, and 28 U.S.C.A. §§ 636, 1453, and 2107, and enacting provisions set out as a note under 11 U.S.C.A. § 109] may be cited as the 'Statutory Time–Periods Technical Amendments Act of 2009'."

2008 Amendments. Pub.L. 110–438, § 1, Oct. 20, 2008, 122 Stat. 5000, provided that: "This Act [amending 11 U.S.C.A. § 707, and enacting provisions set out as a note under 11 U.S.C.A. § 707] may be cited as the 'National Guard and Reservists Debt Relief Act of 2008'."

2006 Amendments. Pub.L. 109–439, § 1, Dec. 20, 2006, 120 Stat. 3285, provided that: "This Act [amending 11 U.S.C.A. § 1325] may be cited as the 'Religious Liberty and Charitable Donation Clarification Act of 2006'."

Pub.L. 109–390, § 1, Dec. 12, 2006, 120 Stat. 2692, provided that: "This Act [amending this section, 11 U.S.C.A. §§ 362, 546, and 741, 12 U.S.C.A. §§ 1787, 1821, 4403, and 4404, and 15 U.S.C.A. § 78eee, and enacting provisions set out as notes under this section] may be cited as the 'Financial Netting Improvements Act of 2006'."

2005 Amendments. Pub.L. 109–8, § 1(a), Apr. 20, 2005, 119 Stat. 23, provided that: "This Act [see Tables for complete classification] may be cited as the 'Bankruptcy Abuse Prevention and Consumer Protection Act of 2005'." This Act is also commonly known as the BAPCPA.

Pub.L. 109–8, Title III, § 332(a), Apr. 20, 2005, 119 Stat. 103, provided that: "This section [amending 11 U.S.C.A. § 303 and 18 U.S.C.A. § 157] may be cited as the 'Involuntary Bankruptcy Improvement Act of 2005'."

2004 Amendments. Pub.L. 108–369, § 1, Oct. 25, 2004, 118 Stat. 1749, provided that: "This Act [enacting provisions set out as a note under 11 U.S.C.A. § 1201 and amending 11 U.S.C.A. §§ 1201 to 1208, 1221 to 1231, and provisions set out as a note under 11 U.S.C.A. § 1201] may be cited as the 'Family Farmer Bankruptcy Relief Act of 2004'."

2003 Amendments. Pub.L. 108–73, § 1, Aug. 15, 2003, 117 Stat. 891, provided that: "This Act [enacting provisions set out as a note under 11 U.S.C.A. § 1201 and amending 11 U.S.C.A. §§ 1201 to 1208, 1221 to 1231, and provisions set out as a note under 11 U.S.C.A. § 1201] may be cited as the 'Family Farmer Bankruptcy Relief Act of 2003'."

2002 Amendments. Pub.L. 107–377, § 1, Dec. 19, 2002, 116 Stat. 3115, provided that: "This Act [amending 11 U.S.C.A. §§ 1201 to 1208, 1221 to 1231, enacting provisions set out as notes under 11 U.S.C.A. § 1201, and amending provisions set out as notes under 11 U.S.C.A. § 1201] may be cited as the 'Protection of Family Farmers Act of 2002'."

1998 Amendments. Pub.L. 105–183, § 1, June 19, 1998, 112 Stat. 517, provided that: "This Act [amending 11 U.S.C.A.

§§ 544, 546, 548, 707, and 1325 and enacting provisions set out as a note under 11 U.S.C.A. § 544] may be cited as the 'Religious Liberty and Charitable Donation Protection Act of 1998'."

1994 Amendments. Section 1(a) of Pub.L. 103–394 provided that: "This Act [enacting 11 U.S.C.A. § 110 and 18 U.S.C.A. §§ 156, 157, amending 11 U.S.C.A. §§ 101, 104, 105, 106, 109, 303, 322, 326, 330, 341, 342, 345, 346, 348, 349, 362, 363, 364, 365, 502, 503, 507, 522, 523, 524, 525, 541, 542, 543, 546, 547, 548, 549, 550, 552, 553, 555, 556, 559, 706, 723, 724, 726, 741, 742, 743, 745, 761, 1102, 1104, 1106, 1110, 1112, 1121, 1123, 1124, 1125, 1129, 1145, 1166, 1167, 1168, 1222, 1226, 1302, 1322, 1326, and 1328, rule 7004 of the Federal Rules of Bankruptcy Procedure, 12 U.S.C.A. §§ 1787, 1821, 18 U.S.C.A. §§ 152, 153, 154, 1961, and 28 U.S.C.A. §§ 157, 158, 586, 1334, 2073, 2075, and enacting provisions section out as notes preceding 11 U.S.C.A. § 101 and 11 U.S.C.A. §§ 101, 341, 501, 524] may be cited as the 'Bankruptcy Reform Act of 1994'."

1990 Amendments. Pub.L. 101–647, Title XXXI, § 3101, Nov. 29, 1990, 104 Stat. 4916, provided that: "This title [amending 11 U.S.C.A. §§ 523, 1328 and enacting provisions set out as a note under 11 U.S.C.A. § 523] may be cited as the 'Criminal Victims Protection Act of 1990'."

Pub.L. 101–581, § 1, Nov. 15, 1990, 104 Stat. 2865, provided that: "This Act [amending 11 U.S.C.A. §§ 523, 1328 and enacting provisions set out as notes under 11 U.S.C.A. § 523] may be cited as the 'Criminal Victims Protection Act of 1990'."

1988 Amendments. Pub.L. 100–334, § 1, June 16, 1988, 102 Stat. 610, provided that: "This Act [enacting 11 U.S.C.A. § 1114, amending 11 U.S.C.A. § 1129, enacting provisions set out as a note under 11 U.S.C.A. § 1114, and amending and repealing provisions set out as notes under 11 U.S.C.A. § 1106] may be cited as the 'Retiree Benefits Bankruptcy Protection Act of 1988'."

1986 Amendments. Pub.L. 99–554, § 1, Oct. 27, 1986, 100 Stat. 3088, provided that said Act [enacting 11 U.S.C.A. §§ 307, 1201 to 1231 and 28 U.S.C.A. § 589a, amending 11 U.S.C.A. §§ 101 to 103, 105, 108, 109, 303, 321, 322, 324, 326, 327, 329, 330, 341, 343, 345 to 348, 362 to 365, 502, 503, 521 to 524, 546 to 549, 554, 557, 701, 703 to 707, 724, 726 to 728, 743, 1102, 1104 to 1106, 1112, 1121, 1129, 1163, 1202, 1302, 1306, 1307, 1324 to 1326, Bankruptcy Form No. 1, set out in the Appendix to Title 11, 28 U.S.C.A. §§ 49, 96, 152, 156, 157, 526, 581, 582, 584 to 587, 604, 1334, 1930, repealing 11 U.S.C.A. §§ 1201 to 1231, 1501 to 151326, enacting provisions set out as notes under 28 U.S.C.A. §§ 581, 589, amending provisions set out as a note under 28 U.S.C.A. § 152, and repealing provisions set out as a note preceding 28 U.S.C.A. § 581] may be cited as the "Bankruptcy Judges, United States Trustees, and Family Farmer Bankruptcy Act of 1986". See note set out under 28 U.S.C.A. § 581.

1984 Amendments. Section 361 of Subtitle C (§§ 361 to 363) of Title III of Pub.L. 98–353 provided that: "This subtitle [amending this section and 11 U.S.C.A. §§ 362, 365, 541] may be cited as the 'Leasehold Management Bankruptcy Amendments Act of 1983'."

Adjustment of Dollar Amounts

For adjustment of dollar amounts specified in pars. (3), (18), (19A), (51D) of this section by the Judicial Conference of the United States, effective Apr. 1, 2016, see note set out under 11 U.S.C.A. § 104 of this title.

By notice dated Feb. 22, 2016, 81 F.R. 8748, the Judicial Conference of the United States adjusted the dollar amounts in provisions specified in pars. (3), (18), (19A), (51D) of this section, effective Apr. 1, 2016, as follows:

In par. (3) adjusted $186,825 to $192,450.

In par. (18)(A) and (B)(ii) adjusted $4,031,575 (each time it appears) to $4,153,150 (each time it appears).

In par. (19A)(A)(i) and (B)(ii)(II) adjusted $1,868,200 (each time it appears) to $1,924,550 (each time it appears).

In par. (51D) adjusted $2,490,925 (each time it appears) to $2,566,050 (each time it appears).

By notice dated Feb. 21, 2013, 78 F.R. 12089, the Judicial Conference of the United States adjusted the dollar amounts in provisions specified in pars. (3), (18), (19A), (51D) of this section, effective Apr. 1, 2013, as follows:

In par. (3) adjusted $175,750 to $186,825.

In par. (18)(A) and (B)(ii) adjusted $3,792,650 (each time it appears) to $4,031,575 (each time it appears).

In par. (19A)(A)(i) and (B)(ii)(II) adjusted $1,757,475 (each time it appears) to $1,868,200 (each time it appears).

In par. (51D) adjusted $2,343,300 (each time it appears) to $2,490,925 (each time it appears).

By notice dated Feb. 25, 2010, 75 F.R. 8747, the Judicial Conference of the United States adjusted the dollar amounts in provisions specified in pars. (3), (18), (19A), (51D) of this section, effective Apr. 1, 2010, as follows:

In par. (3) adjusted $164,250 to $175,750.

In par. (18)(A) and (B)(ii) adjusted $3,544,525 (each time it appears) to $3,792,650 (each time it appears).

In par. (19A)(A)(i) and (B)(ii)(II) adjusted $1,642,500 (each time it appears) to $1,757,475 (each time it appears).

In par. (51D) adjusted $2,190,000 (each time it appears) to $2,343,300 (each time it appears).

By notice dated Feb. 14, 2007, 72 F.R. 7082, the Judicial Conference of the United States adjusted the dollar amounts in provisions specified in pars. (3), (18), (19A), (51D) of this section, effective Apr. 1, 2007, as follows:

In par. (3) adjusted $150,000 to $164,250.

In par. (18) adjusted $3,237,000 (each time it appears) to $3,544,525 (each time it appears).

In par. (19A) adjusted $1,500,000 (each time it appears) to $1,642,500 (each time it appears).

In par. (51D) adjusted $2,000,000 (each time it appears) to $2,190,000 (each time it appears).

Scope of Application

Pub.L. 109–390, § 7, Dec. 12, 2006, 120 Stat. 2700, provided that: "The amendments made by this Act [amending this section, 11 U.S.C.A. §§ 362, 546, and 741, 12 U.S.C.A. §§ 1787, 1821, 4403, and 4404, and 15 U.S.C.A. § 78eee, and enacting provisions set out as notes under this section] shall not apply to any cases commenced under title 11, United States Code, or appointments made under any Federal or State law, before the date of the enactment of this Act [Dec. 12, 2006]."

Nonlimitation of Information

Pub.L. 109–8, Title I, § 102(e), Apr. 20, 2005, 119 Stat. 33, provided that: "Nothing in this title [see Tables for classification] shall limit the ability of a creditor to provide information to a judge (except for information communicated ex parte, unless otherwise permitted by applicable law), United States trustee (or bankruptcy administrator, if any), or trustee."

[Except as otherwise provided, this note effective 180 days after April 20, 2005, and inapplicable with respect to cases commenced under Title 11 before the effective date, see Pub.L. 109–8, Title XV, § 1501, Apr. 20, 2005, 119 Stat. 216, set out as a note under this section.]

Rules of Construction

Pub.L. 109–8, Title X, § 1007(e), Apr. 20, 2005, 119 Stat. 188, provided that: "**Applicability.**—Nothing in this section [amending this section and 11 U.S.C.A. §§ 109, 1203, 1206, and the chapter heading and table of contents for Chapter 12 of Title 11] shall change, affect, or amend the Fishery Conservation and Management Act of 1976 [officially titled the Magnuson-Stevens Fishery Conservation and Management Act, which is Pub.L. 94–265, Apr. 13, 1976, 90 Stat. 331, as amended, and which is principally classified to chapter 38 of Title 16] (16 U.S.C. § 1801 et seq.)."

Pub.L. 109–8, Title XI, § 1101(c), Apr. 20, 2005, 119 Stat. 189, provided that: "The amendments made by subsection (a) of this section [amending this section by redesignating par. (27A) as par. (27B) and inserting a new par. (27A) and pars. (40A) and (40B)] shall not affect the interpretation of section 109(b) of title 11, United States Code."

[Except as otherwise provided, this note effective 180 days after April 20, 2005, and inapplicable with respect to cases commenced under Title 11 before the effective date, see Pub.L. 109–8, Title XV, § 1501, Apr. 20, 2005, 119 Stat. 216, set out as a note under this section.]

Judicial Education

Pub.L. 109–8, Title XII, § 1226, Apr. 20, 2005, 119 Stat. 199, provided that: "The Director of the Federal Judicial Center, in consultation with the Director of the Executive Office for United States Trustees, shall develop materials and conduct such training as may be useful to courts in implementing this Act [see Short Title 2005 Amendments note set out under this section] and the amendments made by this Act, including the requirements relating to the means test under section 707(b), and reaffirmation agreements under section 524, of title 11 of the United States Code, as amended by this Act."

[Except as otherwise provided, this note effective 180 days after April 20, 2005, and inapplicable with respect to cases commenced under Title 11 before the effective date, see Pub.L. 109–8, Title XV, § 1501, Apr. 20, 2005, 119 Stat. 216, set out as a note under this section.]

CROSS REFERENCES

"Commodity broker", as defined under this section, determining powers and duties of Securities Investor Protection Act trustees, see 15 USCA § 78fff-1.

Crime victims' rights, rights afforded and best efforts to accord rights, procedures to promote compliance, see 18 USCA § 3771.

"Forward contract", "repurchase agreement", and "transfer" defined under this section as having same meaning for purposes of,

Federal credit union insurance, see 12 USCA § 1787.

Federal deposit insurance, see 12 USCA § 1821.

"Insolvent" defined under this section as having same meaning for purposes of Securities Investor Protection Act decrees, see 15 USCA § 78eee.

List of creditors, unsecured claims, see Official Bankr. Form B104, 11 USCA.

"Margin payment" and "settlement payment" as defined under this section determining exclusion of certain setoffs from automatic stay, see 11 USCA § 362.

"Railroad" as defined under this section, determining bankruptcy fees, see 28 USCA § 1930.

Statement of financial affairs, see Official Bankr. Forms B107 and B207, 11 USCA.

§ 102. Rules of construction

In this title—

(1) "after notice and a hearing", or a similar phrase—

(A) means after such notice as is appropriate in the particular circumstances, and such opportunity for a hearing as is appropriate in the particular circumstances; but

(B) authorizes an act without an actual hearing if such notice is given properly and if—

(i) such a hearing is not requested timely by a party in interest; or

(ii) there is insufficient time for a hearing to be commenced before such act must be done, and the court authorizes such act;

(2) "claim against the debtor" includes claim against property of the debtor;

(3) "includes" and "including" are not limiting;

(4) "may not" is prohibitive, and not permissive;

(5) "or" is not exclusive;

(6) "order for relief" means entry of an order for relief;

(7) the singular includes the plural;

(8) a definition, contained in a section of this title that refers to another section of this title, does not, for the purpose of such reference, affect the meaning of a term used in such other section; and

(9) "United States trustee" includes a designee of the United States trustee.

(Pub.L. 95–598, Nov. 6, 1978, 92 Stat. 2554; Pub.L. 98–353, Title III, § 422, July 10, 1984, 98 Stat. 369; Pub.L. 99–554, Title II, § 202, Oct. 27, 1986, 100 Stat. 3097.)

HISTORICAL AND STATUTORY NOTES

Revision Notes and Legislative Reports

1978 Acts. Section 102 provides seven rules of construction. Some are derived from current law; others are derived from 1 U.S.C. 1; a few are new. They apply generally throughout proposed title 11. These are terms that are not appropriate for definition, but that require an explanation.

Paragraph (1) defines the concept of "after notice and a hearing." The concept is central to the bill and to the separation of the administrative and judicial functions of bankruptcy judges. The phrase means after such notice as is appropriate in the particular circumstances (to be prescribed by either the Rules of Bankruptcy Procedure or by the court in individual circumstances that the Rules do not cover. In

many cases, the Rules will provide for combined notice of several proceedings), and such opportunity for a hearing as is appropriate in the particular circumstances. Thus, a hearing will not be necessary in every instance. If there is no objection to the proposed action, the action may go ahead without court action. This is a significant change from present law, which requires the affirmative approval of the bankruptcy judge for almost every action. The change will permit the bankruptcy judge to stay removed from the administration of the bankruptcy or reorganization case, and to become involved only when there is a dispute about a proposed action, that is, only when there is an objection. The phrase "such opportunity for a hearing as is appropriate in the particular circumstances" is designed to permit the Rules and the courts to expedite or dispense with hearings when speed is essential. The language "or similar phrase" is intended to cover the few instances in the bill where "after notice and a hearing" is interrupted by another phrase, such as "after notice to the debtor and a hearing."

Paragraph (2) specifies that "claim against the debtor" includes claim against property of the debtor. This paragraph is intended to cover nonrecourse loan agreements where the creditor's only rights are against property of the debtor, and not against the debtor personally. Thus, such an agreement would give rise to a claim that would be treated as a claim against the debtor personally, for the purposes of the bankruptcy code.

Paragraph (3) is a codification of *American Surety Co. v. Marotta*, 287 U.S. 513 (1933) [53 S.Ct. 260, 77 L.Ed. 466]. It specifies that "includes" and "including" are not limiting.

Paragraph (4) specifies that "may not" is prohibitive and not permissive (such as in "might not").

Paragraph (5) specifies that "or" is not exclusive. Thus, if a party "may do (a) or (b)", then the party may do either or both. The party is not limited to a mutually exclusive choice between the two alternatives.

Paragraph (6) makes clear that "order for relief" means entry of an order for relief. If the court orally orders relief, but the order is not entered until a later time, then any time measurements in the bill are from entry, not from the oral order. In a voluntary case, the entry of the order for relief is the filing of the petition commencing the voluntary case.

Paragraph (7) specifies that the singular includes the plural. The plural, however, generally does not include the singular. The bill uses only the singular, even when the item in question most often is found in plural quantities, in order to avoid the confusion possible if both rules of construction applied. When an item is specified in the plural, the plural is intended. Senate Report No. 95–989.

1984 Acts. Statements by Legislative Leaders, see 1984 U.S.Code Cong. and Adm.News, p. 576.

1986 Acts. House Report No. 99–764 and House Conference Report No. 99–958, see 1986 U.S.Code Cong. and Adm. News, p. 5227.

Legislative Statements

Section 102 specifies various rules of construction but is not exclusive. Other rules of construction that are not set out in title 11 are nevertheless intended to be followed in construing the bankruptcy code. For example, the phrase "on request of a party in interest" or a similar phrase, is used in connection with an action that the court may take in various sections of the Code. The phrase is intended to restrict the court from acting sua sponte. Rules of bankruptcy procedure or court decisions will determine who is a party in interest for the particular purposes of the provision in question, but the court will not be permitted to act on its own.

Although "property" is not construed in this section, it is used consistently throughout the code in its broadest sense, including cash, all interests in property, such as liens, and every kind of consideration including promises to act or forbear to act as in section 548(d).

Section 102(1) expands on a rule of construction contained in H.R. 8200 as passed by the House and in the Senate amendment. The phrase "after notice and a hearing", or a similar phrase, is intended to be construed according to the particular proceeding to mean after such notice as is appropriate in the particular circumstances, and such opportunity, if any, for a hearing as is appropriate in the particular circumstances. If a provision of title 11 authorizes an act to be taken "after notice and a hearing" this means that if appropriate notice is given and no party to whom such notice is sent timely requests a hearing, then the act sought to be taken may be taken without an actual hearing.

In very limited emergency circumstances, there will be insufficient time for a hearing to be commenced before an action must be taken. The action sought to be taken may be taken if authorized by the court at an ex parte hearing of which a record is made in open court. A full hearing after the fact will be available in such an instance.

In some circumstances, such as under section 1128, the bill requires a hearing and the court may act only after a hearing is held. In those circumstances the judge will receive evidence before ruling. In other circumstances, the court may take action "after notice and a hearing," if no party in interest requests a hearing. In that event a court order authorizing the action to be taken is not necessary as the ultimate action taken by the court implies such an authorization.

Section 102(8) is new. It contains a rule of construction indicating that a definition contained in a section in title 11 that refers to another section of title 11 does not, for the purposes of such reference, take the meaning of a term used in the other section. For example, section 522(a)(2) defines "value" for the purposes of section 522. Section 548(d)(2) defines "value" for purposes of section 548. When section 548 is incorporated by reference in section 522, this rule of construction makes clear that the definition of "value" in section 548 governs its meaning in section 522 notwithstanding a different definition of "value" in section 522(a)(2).

Effective and Applicability Provisions

1986 Acts. Amendment by Pub.L. 99–554 effective 30 days after Oct. 27, 1986, except as otherwise provided for, see section 302(a) of Pub.L. 99–554, set out as a note under section 581 of Title 28, Judiciary and Judicial Procedure.

Amendment by Pub.L. 99–554, § 202, not to become effective in or with respect to certain specified judicial districts until, or apply to cases while pending in such district before, the expiration of the 270-day period beginning 30 days after Oct. 27, 1986, or of the 30-day period beginning on the date the Attorney General certifies under section 303 of Pub.L. 99–554 the region specified in a paragraph of section 581(a) of Title 28, as amended by section 111(a) of Pub.L. 99–554, that includes such district, whichever occurs first, see section 302(d)(1) of Pub.L. 99–554, set out as a note under section 581 of Title 28.

Amendment by Pub.L. 99–554, § 202, not to become effective in or with respect to certain specified judicial districts until, or apply to cases while pending in such district before, the expiration of the 2-year period beginning 30 days after Oct. 27, 1986, or of the 30-day period beginning on the date the Attorney General certifies under section 303 of Pub.L. 99–554 the region specified in a paragraph of section 581(a) of Title 28, as amended by section 111(a) of Pub.L. 99–554, that includes such district, whichever occurs first, see section 302(d)(2) of Pub.L. 99–554, set out as a note under section 581 of Title 28.

Amendment by Pub.L. 99–554, § 202, not to become effective in or with respect to judicial districts established for the States of Alabama and North Carolina until, or apply to cases while pending in such district before, such district elects to be included in a bankruptcy region established in section 581(a) of Title 28, as amended by section 111(a) of Pub.L. 99–554, or Oct. 1, 2002, whichever occurs first, and, except as otherwise provided, with respect to cases under chapters 7, 11, 12 and 13 of Title 11 commenced before 30 days after Oct. 27, 1986, and pending in a judicial district in the States of Alabama or North Carolina before any election made under section 302(d)(3)(A) of Pub.L. 99–554 by such district becomes effective or Oct. 1, 2002, whichever occurs first, amendments by Pub.L. 99–554 not to apply until Oct. 1, 2003, or the expiration of the 1-year period beginning on the date such election becomes effective, whichever occurs first, and further, in any judicial district in Alabama or North Carolina not making the election described in section 302(d)(3)(A) of Pub.L. 99–554, any person appointed under regulations issued by the Judicial Conference to administer estates in cases under Title 11 authorized to establish, etc., a panel of private trustees, and to supervise cases and trustees in cases under chapters 7, 11, 12, and 13 of Title 11, until amendments by sections 201 to 231 of Pub.L. 99–554 effective in such district, see section 302(d)(3)(A) to (F), (H), (I) of Pub.L. 99–554, set out as a note under section 581 of Title 28.

Amendment by Pub.L. 99–554, § 202, except as otherwise provided, with respect to cases under chapters 7, 11, 12, and 13 of Title 11 commenced before 30 days after Oct. 27, 1986, and pending in a judicial district referred to in section 581(a) of Title 28, as amended by section 111(a) of Pub.L. 99–554, for which a United States trustee is not authorized before 30 days after Oct. 27, 1986 to be appointed, not applicable until the expiration of the 3-year period beginning on Oct. 27, 1986, or of the 1-year period beginning on the date the Attorney General certifies under section 303 of Pub.L. 99–554 the region specified in a paragraph of such section 581(a) that includes such district, whichever occurs first, see section 302(e)(1), (2) of Pub.L. 99–554, set out as a note under section 581 of Title 28.

1984 Acts. Amendment by Pub.L. 98–353 effective with respect to cases filed 90 days after July 10, 1984, see section 552(a), formerly 553(a) of Pub.L. 98–353, set out as a note under section 101 of this title.

§ 103.   Applicability of chapters

(a) Except as provided in section 1161 of this title, chapters 1, 3, and 5 of this title apply in a case under chapter 7, 11, 12, or 13 of this title, and this chapter, sections 307, 362(*o*), 555 through 557, and 559 through 562 apply in a case under chapter 15.

(b) Subchapters I and II of chapter 7 of this title apply only in a case under such chapter.

(c) Subchapter III of chapter 7 of this title applies only in a case under such chapter concerning a stockbroker.

(d) Subchapter IV of chapter 7 of this title applies only in a case under such chapter concerning a commodity broker.

(e) Scope of application.—Subchapter V of chapter 7 of this title shall apply only in a case under such chapter concerning the liquidation of an uninsured State member bank, or a corporation organized under section 25A of the Federal Reserve Act, which operates, or operates as, a multilateral clearing organization pursuant to section 409 of the Federal Deposit Insurance Corporation Improvement Act of 1991.

(f) Except as provided in section 901 of this title, only chapters 1 and 9 of this title apply in a case under such chapter 9.

(g) Except as provided in section 901 of this title, subchapters I, II, and III of chapter 11 of this title apply only in a case under such chapter.

(h) Subchapter IV of chapter 11 of this title applies only in a case under such chapter concerning a railroad.

(i) Chapter 13 of this title applies only in a case under such chapter.

(j) Chapter 12 of this title applies only in a case under such chapter.

(k) Chapter 15 applies only in a case under such chapter, except that—

(1) sections 1505, 1513, and 1514 apply in all cases under this title; and

(2) section 1509 applies whether or not a case under this title is pending.

(Pub.L. 95–598, Nov. 6, 1978, 92 Stat. 2555; Pub.L. 97–222, § 2, July 27, 1982, 96 Stat. 235; Pub.L. 98–353, Title III, § 423, July 10, 1984, 98 Stat. 369; Pub.L. 99–554, Title II, § 252, Oct. 27, 1986, 100 Stat. 3104; Pub.L. 106–554, § 1(a)(5) [Title I, § 112(c)(5)(A)], Dec. 21, 2000, 114 Stat. 2763, 2763A–394; Pub.L. 109–8, Title VIII, § 802(a), Apr. 20, 2005, 119 Stat. 145; Pub.L. 111–327, § 2(a)(2), Dec. 22, 2010, 124 Stat. 3557.)

HISTORICAL AND STATUTORY NOTES

Revision Notes and Legislative Reports

1978 Acts. Section 103 prescribes which chapters of the proposed bankruptcy code apply in various cases. All cases, other than cases ancillary to foreign proceedings, are filed under chapter 7, 9, 11, or 13, the operative chapters of the proposed bankruptcy code. The general provisions that apply no matter which chapter a case is filed under are found in chapters 1, 3, and 5. Subsection (a) makes this explicit, with an exception for chapter 9. The other provisions, which are self-explanatory, provide the special rules for Stockbroker Liquidations, Commodity Broker Liquidations, Municipal

Debt Adjustments, and Railroad Reorganizations. Senate Report No. 95–989.

1982 Acts. House Report No. 97–420, see 1982 U.S.Code Cong. and Adm.News, p. 583.

1984 Acts. Statements by Legislative Leaders, see 1984 U.S.Code Cong. and Adm.News, p. 576.

1986 Acts. House Report No. 99–764 and House Conference Report No. 99–958, see 1986 U.S.Code Cong. and Adm. News, p. 5227.

2000 Acts. House Report No. 106–645 and Statement by President, see 2000 U.S. Code Cong. and Adm. News, p. 2459.

2005 Acts. House Report No. 109–31(Part I), see 2005 U.S. Code Cong. and Adm. News, p. 88.

References in Text

Chapters 1, 3, and 5 of this title, referred to in subsec. (a), are 11 U.S.C.A. §§ 101 et seq., 301 et seq., and 501 et seq.

Chapter 7, 11, 12, or 13 of this title, referred to in subsec. (a), is 11 U.S.C.A. § 701 et seq., 11 U.S.C.A. § 1101 et seq., 11 U.S.C.A. § 1201 et seq., or 11 U.S.C.A. § 1301 et seq., respectively.

Chapter 15, referred to in subsecs. (a) and (k), is chapter 15 of this title, which is classified to 11 U.S.C.A. § 1501 et seq.

Subchapters I and II of chapter 7 of this title, referred to in subsec. (b), are 11 U.S.C.A. §§ 701 et seq. and 721 et seq., respectively.

Subchapter III of chapter 7 of this title, referred to in subsec. (c), is 11 U.S.C.A. § 741 et seq.

Subchapter IV of chapter 7 of this title, referred to in subsec. (d), is 11 U.S.C.A. § 761 et seq.

Subchapter V of chapter 7 of this title, referred to in subsec. (e), is 11 U.S.C.A. § 781 et seq.

Section 25A of the Federal Reserve Act, referred to in subsec. (e), is Dec. 23, 1913, c. 6, § 25A, formerly § 25(a), as added Dec. 24, 1919, c. 18, 41 Stat. 378, as amended, which is classified to subchapter II of chapter 6 of Title 12, 12 U.S.C.A. § 611 et seq.

Section 409 of the Federal Deposit Insurance Corporation Improvement Act of 1991, referred to in subsec. (e), is Pub.L. 102–242, Title IV, § 409, as added by Pub.L. 106–554, § 1(a)(5) [Title I, § 112(a)(3)], Dec. 21, 2000, 114 Stat. 2763, 2763A–394, which is classified as 12 U.S.C.A. § 4422.

Chapter 13 of this title, referred to in subsec. (i), is 11 U.S.C.A. § 1301 et seq.

Chapter 12 of this title, referred to in subsec. (j), is 11 U.S.C.A. § 1201 et seq.

Effective and Applicability Provisions

2005 Acts. Amendments by Pub.L. 109–8 effective, except as otherwise provided, 180 days after April 20, 2005, and inapplicable with respect to cases commenced under Title 11 before the effective date, see Pub.L. 109–8, § 1501, set out as a note under 11 U.S.C.A. § 101.

1986 Acts. Amendment by Pub.L. 99–554 effective 30 days after Oct. 27, 1986, but not applicable to cases commenced under this title before that date, see section 302(a), (c)(1) of Pub.L. 99–554, set out as a note under section 581 of Title 28, Judiciary and Judicial Procedure.

1984 Acts. Amendment by Pub.L. 98–353 effective with respect to cases filed 90 days after July 10, 1984, see section 552(a), formerly 553(a), of Pub.L. 98–353, set out as a note under section 101 of this title.

Confirmation of Chapter 9 plan complying with provisions of this title made applicable by this section, see 11 USCA § 943.

Terms as defined in this title made applicable to Chapter 9 by this section, see 11 USCA § 901.

Terms "property of the estate" and "trustee" made applicable to Chapter 9 by this section, defined for purposes of such chapter, see 11 USCA § 902.

§ 104. Adjustment of dollar amounts

(a) On April 1, 1998, and at each 3–year interval ending on April 1 thereafter, each dollar amount in effect under sections 101(3), 101(18), 101(19A), 101(51D), 109(e), 303(b), 507(a), 522(d), 522(f)(3) and 522(f)(4), 522(n), 522(p), 522(q), 523(a)(2)(C), 541(b), 547(c)(9), 707(b), 1322(d), 1325(b), and 1326(b)(3) of this title and section 1409(b) of title 28 immediately before such April 1 shall be adjusted—

(1) to reflect the change in the Consumer Price Index for All Urban Consumers, published by the Department of Labor, for the most recent 3–year period ending immediately before January 1 preceding such April 1, and

(2) to round to the nearest $25 the dollar amount that represents such change.

(b) Not later than March 1, 1998, and at each 3–year interval ending on March 1 thereafter, the Judicial Conference of the United States shall publish in the Federal Register the dollar amounts that will become effective on such April 1 under sections 101(3), 101(18), 101(19A), 101(51D), 109(e), 303(b), 507(a), 522(d), 522(f)(3) and 522(f)(4), 522(n), 522(p), 522(q), 523(a)(2)(C), 541(b), 547(c)(9), 707(b), 1322(d), 1325(b), and 1326(b)(3) of this title and section 1409(b) of title 28.

(c) Adjustments made in accordance with subsection (a) shall not apply with respect to cases commenced before the date of such adjustments.

(Pub.L. 95–598, Nov. 6, 1978, 92 Stat. 2555; Pub.L. 103–394, Title I, § 108(e), Oct. 22, 1994, 108 Stat. 4112; Pub.L. 109–8, Title I, § 102(j), Title II, §§ 224(e)(2), 226(b), Title III, § 322(b), Title IV, § 432(c), Title X, § 1002, Title XII, § 1202, Apr. 20, 2005, 119 Stat. 35, 65, 67, 97, 110, 186, 193; Pub.L. 110–406, § 7, Oct. 13, 2008, 122 Stat. 4293.)

HISTORICAL AND STATUTORY NOTES

Revision Notes and Legislative Reports

1978 Acts. This section requires that the Director of the Administrative Office of the U. S. Courts report to Congress and the President before Oct. 1, 1985, and before May 1 every 6 years thereafter a recommendation for adjustment in dollar amounts found in this title. The Committee feels that regular adjustment of the dollar amounts by the Director will conserve congressional time and yet assure that the relative dollar amounts used in the bill are maintained. Changes in the cost of living should be a significant, but not necessarily the only, factor considered by the Director. The fact that there has been an increase in the cost of living does not

necessarily mean that an adjustment of dollar amounts would be needed or warranted. Senate Report No. 95–989.

This section requires the Judicial Conference to report to the Congress every four years after the effective date of the bankruptcy code any changes that have occurred in the cost of living during the preceding four years, and the appropriate adjustments to the dollar amounts in the bill. The dollar amounts are found primarily in the exemption section (11 U.S.C. 522), the wage priority (11 U.S.C. 507), and the eligibility for chapter 13 (11 U.S.C. 109). This section requires that the Conference recommend uniform percentage changes in these amounts based solely on cost of living changes. The dollar amounts in the bill would not change on that recommendation, absent Congressional veto. Instead, Congress is required to take affirmative action, by passing a law amending the appropriate section, if it wishes to accomplish the change.

If the Judicial Conference has policy recommendations concerning the appropriate dollar amounts in the bankruptcy code based other than on cost of living considerations there are adequate channels through which it may communicate its views. This section is solely for the housekeeping function of maintaining the dollar amounts in the code at fairly constant real dollar levels. House Report No. 95–595.

1994 Acts. House Report No. 103–835, see 1994 U.S. Code Cong. and Adm. News, p. 3340.

2005 Acts. House Report No. 109–31(Part I), see 2005 U.S. Code Cong. and Adm. News, p. 88.

Legislative Statements

Section 104 represents a compromise between the House bill and the Senate amendment with respect to the adjustment of dollar amounts in title 11. The House amendment authorizes the Judicial Conference of the United States to transmit a recommendation for the uniform percentage of adjustment for each dollar amount in title 11 and in 28 U.S.C. 1930 to the Congress and to the President before May 1, 1985, and before May 1 of every sixth year thereafter. The requirement in the House bill that each such recommendation be based only on any change in the cost-of-living increase during the period immediately preceding the recommendation is deleted.

Effective and Applicability Provisions

2005 Acts. Amendments by Pub.L. 109–8, § 322, effective, except as otherwise provided, 180 days after April 20, 2005, and applicable with respect to cases commenced under Title 11 on or after April 20, 2005, see Pub.L. 109–8, § 1501, set out as a note under 11 U.S.C.A. § 101.

Amendments by Pub.L. 109–8 effective, except as otherwise provided, 180 days after April 20, 2005, and inapplicable with respect to cases commenced under Title 11 before the effective date, see Pub.L. 109–8, § 1501, set out as a note under 11 U.S.C.A. § 101.

1994 Acts. Amendment by Pub.L. 103–394 effective on Oct. 22, 1994, and not to apply with respect to cases commenced under Title 11 of the United States Code before Oct. 22, 1994, see section 702 of Pub.L. 103–394, set out as a note under section 101 of this title.

Termination of Reporting Requirements

For termination, effective May 15, 2000, of provisions of law requiring submittal to Congress of any annual, semiannual, or other regular periodic report listed in House Document No. 103–7 (in which a report required under subsec. (a) of this section is listed in the 15th item on page 12, which references a note but probably means this section), see section 3003 of Pub. L. 104–66, as amended, set out as a note under 31 U.S.C.A. § 1113.

Separability of Provisions

If any provision of or amendment made by Pub.L. 103–394 or the application of such provision or amendment to any person or circumstance is held to be unconstitutional, the remaining provisions of and amendments made by Pub.L. 103–394 and the application of such provisions and amendments to any person or circumstance shall not be affected thereby, see section 701 of Pub.L. 103–394, set out as a note under section 101 of this title.

Adjustment of Dollar Amounts

By notice published Feb. 22, 2016, 81 F.R. 8748, the Judicial Conference of the United States increased the dollar amounts in provisions specified in subsec. (b) of this section, effective Apr. 1, 2016, and provided also that these increases do not apply to cases commenced before the effective date of the adjustments, i.e., April 1, 2016 The dollar amounts are adjusted as set out in the following chart.

Affected sections of Title 28 U.S.C and the Bankruptcy Code	Dollar amount to be adjusted	New (adjusted) dollar amount [1]
28 U.S.C.		
Section 1409(b)—a trustee may commence a proceeding arising in or related to a case to recover		
(1)—money judgment of or property worth less than	$1,250	$1,3000.
(2)—a consumer debt less than	$18,675	$19,250.
(3)—a non consumer debt against a non insider less than	$12,475	$12,850.
11 U.S.C.		
Section 101(3)—definition of assisted person	$186,825	$192,450.
Section 101(18)—definition of family farmer	$4,031,575 (each time it appears)	$4,153,150 (each time it appears).
Section 101(19A)—definition of family fisherman	$1,868,200 (each time it appears)	$1,924,550 (each time it appears).
Section 101(51D)—definition of small business debtor	$2,490,925 (each time it appears)	$2,566,050 (each time it appears).
Section 109(e)—debt limits for individual filing bankruptcy under chapter 13	$383,175 (each time it appears)	$394,725 (each time it appears).
	$1,149,525 (each time it appears)	$1,184,200 (each time it appears).
Section 303(b)—minimum aggregate claims needed for the commencement of an involuntary chapter 7 or chapter 11 petition		
(1)—in paragraph (1)	$15,325	$15,775.
(2)—in paragraph (2)	$15,325	$15,775.
Section 507(a)—priority expenses and claims		
(1)—in paragraph (4)	$12,475	$12,850.
(2)—in paragraph (5)(B)(i)	$12,475	$12,850.
(3)—in paragraph (6)(B)	$6,150	$6,325.
(4)—in paragraph (7)	$2,775	$2,850.

Affected sections of Title 28 U.S.C and the Bankruptcy Code	Dollar amount to be adjusted	New (adjusted) dollar amount [1]
Section 522(d)—value of property exemptions allowed to the debtor		
(1)—in paragraph (1)	$22,975	$23,675.
(2)—in paragraph (2)	$3,675	$3,775.
(3)—in paragraph (3)	$575	$600.
	$12,250	$12,625.
(4)—in paragraph (4)	$1,550	$1,600.
(5)—in paragraph (5)	$1,225	$1,250.
	$11,500	$11,850.
(6)—in paragraph (6)	$2,300	$2,375.
(7)—in paragraph (8)	$12,250	$12,625.
(8)—in paragraph (11)(D) . . .	$22,975	$23,675.
Section 522(f)(3)—exception to lien avoidance under certain state laws.	$6,225	$6,425.
Section 522(f)(4)—items excluded from definition of household goods for lien avoidance purposes.	$650 (each time it appears)	$675 (each time it appears).
Section 522(n)—maximum aggregate value of assets in individual retirement accounts exempted. . .	$1,245,475	$1,283,025.
Section 522(p)—qualified homestead exemption	$155,675	$160,375.
Section 522(q)—state homestead exemption	$155,675	$160,375.
Section 523(a)(2)(C)—exceptions to discharge		
(1)—in paragraph [sic] (i)(I)—consumer debts for luxury goods or services incurred < 90 days before filing owed to a single creditor in the aggregate.	$650	$675.
(2)—in paragraph [sic] (i)(II)—cash advances incurred < 70 days before filing in the aggregate. . . .	$925	$950.
Section 541(b)—property of the estate exclusions		
(1)—in paragraph (5)(C)— education IRA funds in the aggregate.	$6,225	$6,425.
(2)—in paragraph (6)(C)— pre-purchased tuition credits in the aggregate.	$6,225	$6,425.
Section 547(c)(9)—preferences, trustee may not avoid a transfer if, in a case filed by a debtor whose debts are not primarily consumer debts, the aggregate value of property is less than.	$6,225	$6,425.
Section 707(b)—dismissal of a chapter 7 case or conversion to chapter 11 or 13 (means test)		
(1)—in paragraph (2)(A)(i)(I)	$7,475	$7,700.
(2)—in paragraph (2)(A)(i)(II)	$12,475	$12,850.
(3)—in paragraph (2)(A)(ii)(IV)	$1,875	$1,925.

Affected sections of Title 28 U.S.C and the Bankruptcy Code	Dollar amount to be adjusted	New (adjusted) dollar amount [1]
(4)—in paragraph (2)(B)(iv)(I)	$7,475	$7,700.
(5)—in paragraph (2)(B)(iv)(II)	$12,475	$12,850.
(6)—in paragraph (5)(B)	$1,250	$1,300.
(7)—in paragraph (6)(C)	$675	$700.
(8)—in paragraph (7)(A)(iii)	$675	$700.
Section 1322(d)—contents of chapter 13 plan, monthly income	$675 (each time it appears)	$700 (each time it appears).
Section 1325(b)—chapter 13 confirmation of plan, disposable income	$675 (each time it appears)	$700 (each time it appears).
Section 1326(b)(3)—payments to former chapter 7 trustee	$25	$25.

[1] The New (Adjusted) Dollar Amounts reflect a 3.016 percent increase, rounded to the nearest $25.

Previous adjustments of the dollar amounts in provisions specified in subsec. (b) of this section were contained in the following:

Notice published Feb. 21, 2013, 78 F.R. 12089, effective Apr. 1, 2013.

Notice published Feb. 25, 2010, 75 F.R. 8747, effective Apr. 1, 2010.

Notice published Feb. 14, 2007, 72 F.R. 7082, modified Mar. 30, 2007, 72 F.R. 15162, effective Apr. 1, 2007.

Notice published Feb. 18, 2004, 69 F.R. 8482, effective Apr. 1, 2004.

Notice published Feb. 20, 2001, 66 F.R. 10910, effective Apr. 1, 2001.

Notice published Feb. 3, 1998, 63 F.R. 7179, effective Apr. 1, 1998.

§ 105. Power of court

(a) The court may issue any order, process, or judgment that is necessary or appropriate to carry out the provisions of this title. No provision of this title providing for the raising of an issue by a party in interest shall be construed to preclude the court from, sua sponte, taking any action or making any determination necessary or appropriate to enforce or implement court orders or rules, or to prevent an abuse of process.

(b) Notwithstanding subsection (a) of this section, a court may not appoint a receiver in a case under this title.

(c) The ability of any district judge or other officer or employee of a district court to exercise any of the authority or responsibilities conferred upon the court under this title shall be determined by reference to the provisions relating to such judge, officer, or employee set forth in title 28. This subsection shall not be interpreted to exclude bankruptcy judges and other officers or employees appointed pursuant to chapter 6 of title 28 from its operation.

(d) The court, on its own motion or on the request of a party in interest—

(1) shall hold such status conferences as are necessary to further the expeditious and economical resolution of the case; and

(2) unless inconsistent with another provision of this title or with applicable Federal Rules of Bankruptcy Procedure, may issue an order at any such conference prescribing such limitations and conditions as the court deems appropriate to ensure that the case is handled expeditiously and economically, including an order that—

(A) sets the date by which the trustee must assume or reject an executory contract or unexpired lease; or

(B) in a case under chapter 11 of this title—

(i) sets a date by which the debtor, or trustee if one has been appointed, shall file a disclosure statement and plan;

(ii) sets a date by which the debtor, or trustee if one has been appointed, shall solicit acceptances of a plan;

(iii) sets the date by which a party in interest other than a debtor may file a plan;

(iv) sets a date by which a proponent of a plan, other than the debtor, shall solicit acceptances of such plan;

(v) fixes the scope and format of the notice to be provided regarding the hearing on approval of the disclosure statement; or

(vi) provides that the hearing on approval of the disclosure statement may be combined with the hearing on confirmation of the plan.

(Pub.L. 95–598, Nov. 6, 1978, 92 Stat. 2555; Pub.L. 98–353, Title I, § 118, July 10, 1984, 98 Stat. 344; Pub.L. 99–554, Title II, § 203, Oct. 27, 1986, 100 Stat. 3097; Pub.L. 103–394, Title I, § 104(a), Oct. 22, 1994, 108 Stat. 4108; Pub.L. 109–8, Title IV, § 440, Apr. 20, 2005, 119 Stat. 114; Pub.L. 111–327, § 2(a)(3), Dec. 22, 2010, 124 Stat. 3557.)

HISTORICAL AND STATUTORY NOTES

Revision Notes and Legislative Reports

1978 Acts. Section 105 is derived from section 2a(15) of present law [section 11(a)(15) of former Title 11], with two changes. First, the limitation on the power of a bankruptcy judge (the power to enjoin a court being reserved to the district judge) is removed as inconsistent with the increased powers and jurisdiction of the new bankruptcy court. Second, the bankruptcy judge is prohibited from appointing a receiver in a case under title 11 under any circumstances. The bankruptcy code has ample provision for the appointment of a trustee when needed. Appointment of a receiver would simply circumvent the established procedures.

This section is also an authorization, as required under 28 U.S.C. 2283, for a court of the United States to stay the action of a State court. As such, *Toucey v. New York Life Insurance Company,* 314 U.S. 118 (1941) [62 S.Ct. 139, 86 L.Ed. 100, 137 A.L.R. 967], is overruled. Senate Report No. 95–989.

1984 Acts. Statements by Legislative Leaders, see 1984 U.S.Code Cong. and Adm.News, p. 576.

1986 Acts. House Report No. 99–764 and House Conference Report No. 99–958, see 1986 U.S.Code Cong. and Adm. News, p. 5227.

1994 Acts. House Report No. 103–835, see 1994 U.S. Code Cong. and Adm. News, p. 3340.

2005 Acts. House Report No. 109–31(Part I), see 2005 U.S. Code Cong. and Adm. News, p. 88.

References in Text

The Federal Rules of Bankruptcy Procedure, referred to in subsec. (d)(2), are set out in the Appendix to this title.

Effective and Applicability Provisions

2005 Acts. Amendments by Pub.L. 109–8 effective, except as otherwise provided, 180 days after April 20, 2005, and inapplicable with respect to cases commenced under Title 11 before the effective date, see Pub.L. 109–8, § 1501, set out as a note under 11 U.S.C.A. § 101.

1994 Acts. Amendment by Pub.L. 103–394 effective on Oct. 22, 1994, and not to apply with respect to cases commenced under Title 11 of the United States Code before Oct. 22, 1994, see section 702 of Pub.L. 103–394, set out as a note under section 101 of this title.

1986 Acts. Amendment by Pub.L. 99–554 effective 30 days after Oct. 27, 1986, except as otherwise provided for, see section 302(a) of Pub.L. 99–554, set out as a note under section 581 of Title 28, Judiciary and Judicial Procedure.

Amendment by Pub.L. 99–554, § 203, not to become effective in or with respect to certain specified judicial districts until, or apply to cases while pending in such district before, the expiration of the 270-day period beginning 30 days after Oct. 27, 1986, or of the 30-day period beginning on the date the Attorney General certifies under section 303 of Pub.L.

99–554 the region specified in a paragraph of section 581(a) of Title 28, as amended by section 111(a) of Pub.L. 99–554, that includes such district, whichever occurs first, see section 302(d)(1) of Pub.L. 99–554, set out as a note under section 581 of Title 28.

Amendment by Pub.L. 99–554, § 203, not to become effective in or with respect to certain specified judicial districts until, or apply to cases while pending in such district before, the expiration of the 2-year period beginning 30 days after Oct. 27, 1986, or of the 30-day period beginning on the date the Attorney General certifies under section 303 of Pub.L. 99–554 the region specified in a paragraph of section 581(a) of Title 28, as amended by section 111(a) of Pub.L. 99–554, that includes such district, whichever occurs first, see section 302(d)(2) of Pub.L. 99–554, set out as a note under section 581 of Title 28.

Amendment by Pub.L. 99–554, § 203, not to become effective in or with respect to judicial districts established for the States of Alabama and North Carolina until, or apply to cases while pending in such district before, such district elects to be included in a bankruptcy region established in section 581(a) of Title 28, as amended by section 111(a) of Pub.L. 99–554, or Oct. 1, 2002, whichever occurs first, except that the amendment to subsec. (a) of this section shall become effective as of Dec. 1, 1990, and, except as otherwise provided, with respect to cases under chapters 7, 11, 12, and 13 of Title 11 commenced before 30 days after Oct. 27, 1986, and pending in a judicial district in the States of Alabama or North Carolina before any election made under section 302(d)(3)(A) of Pub.L. 99–554 by such district becomes effective or Oct. 1, 2002, whichever occurs first, amendments by Pub.L. 99–554 not to apply until Oct. 1, 2003, or the expiration of the 1-year period beginning on the date such election becomes effective, whichever occurs first, and further, in any judicial district in Alabama or North Carolina not making the election described in section 302(d)(3)(A) of Pub.L. 99–554, any person appointed under regulations issued by the Judicial Conference to administer estates in cases under Title 11 authorized to establish, etc., a panel of private trustees, and to supervise cases and trustees in cases under chapters 7, 11, 12, and 13 of Title 11, until amendments by sections 201 to 231 of Pub.L. 99–554 effective in such district, see section 302(d)(3)(A) to (F), (H), and (I) of Pub.L. 99–554, set out as a note under section 581 of Title 28.

Amendment by Pub.L. 99–554, § 203, except as otherwise provided, with respect to cases under chapters 7, 11, 12, and 13 of Title 11 commenced before 30 days after Oct. 27, 1986, and pending in a judicial district referred to in section 581(a) of Title 28, as amended by section 111(a) of Pub.L. 99–554, for which a United States trustee is not authorized before 30 days after Oct. 27, 1986 to be appointed, not applicable until the expiration of the 3-year period beginning on Oct. 27, 1986, or of the 1-year period beginning on the date the Attorney General certifies under section 303 of Pub.L. 99–554 the region specified in a paragraph of such section 581(a) that includes such district, whichever occurs first, see section 302(e)(1), (2) of Pub.L. 99–554, set out as a note under section 581 of Title 28.

1984 Acts. Amendment by Pub.L. 98–353 effective July 10, 1984, see section 122(a) of Pub.L. 98–353, set out as a note under section 151 of Title 28, Judiciary and Judicial Procedure.

Separability of Provisions

If any provision of or amendment made by Pub.L. 103–394 or the application of such provision or amendment to any person or circumstance is held to be unconstitutional, the remaining provisions of and amendments made by Pub.L. 103–394 and the application of such provisions and amendments to any person or circumstance shall not be affected thereby, see section 701 of Pub.L. 103–394, set out as a note under section 101 of this title.

CROSS REFERENCES

Bankruptcy investigations, see 18 USCA § 3057.

§ 106.　Waiver of sovereign immunity

(a) Notwithstanding an assertion of sovereign immunity, sovereign immunity is abrogated as to a governmental unit to the extent set forth in this section with respect to the following:

(1) Sections 105, 106, 107, 108, 303, 346, 362, 363, 364, 365, 366, 502, 503, 505, 506, 510, 522, 523, 524, 525, 542, 543, 544, 545, 546, 547, 548, 549, 550, 551, 552, 553, 722, 724, 726, 744, 749, 764, 901, 922, 926, 928, 929, 944, 1107, 1141, 1142, 1143, 1146, 1201, 1203, 1205, 1206, 1227, 1231, 1301, 1303, 1305, and 1327 of this title.

(2) The court may hear and determine any issue arising with respect to the application of such sections to governmental units.

(3) The court may issue against a governmental unit an order, process, or judgment under such sections or the Federal Rules of Bankruptcy Procedure, including an order or judgment awarding a money recovery, but not including an award of punitive damages. Such order or judgment for costs or fees under this title or the Federal Rules of Bankruptcy Procedure against any governmental unit shall be consistent with the provisions and limitations of section 2412(d)(2)(A) of title 28.

(4) The enforcement of any such order, process, or judgment against any governmental unit shall be consistent with appropriate nonbankruptcy law applicable to such governmental unit and, in the case of a money judgment against the United States, shall be paid as if it is a judgment rendered by a district court of the United States.

(5) Nothing in this section shall create any substantive claim for relief or cause of action not otherwise existing under this title, the Federal Rules of Bankruptcy Procedure, or nonbankruptcy law.

(b) A governmental unit that has filed a proof of claim in the case is deemed to have waived sovereign immunity with respect to a claim against such governmental unit that is property of the estate and that arose out of the same transaction or occurrence out of which the claim of such governmental unit arose.

(c) Notwithstanding any assertion of sovereign immunity by a governmental unit, there shall be offset against a claim or interest of a governmental unit any claim against such governmental unit that is property of the estate.

(Pub.L. 95–598, Nov. 6, 1978, 92 Stat. 2555; Pub.L. 103–394, Title I, § 113, Oct. 22, 1994, 108 Stat. 4117; Pub.L. 111–327, § 2(a)(4), Dec. 22, 2010, 124 Stat. 3557.)

HISTORICAL AND STATUTORY NOTES

Revision Notes and Legislative Reports

1978 Acts. Section 106 provides for a limited waiver of sovereign immunity in bankruptcy cases. Though Congress has the power to waive sovereign immunity for the Federal government completely in bankruptcy cases, the policy followed here is designed to achieve approximately the same result that would prevail outside of bankruptcy. Congress does not, however, have the power to waive sovereign immunity completely with respect to claims of a bankrupt estate against a State, though it may exercise its bankruptcy power through the supremacy clause to prevent or prohibit State action that is contrary to bankruptcy policy.

There is, however, a limited change from the result that would prevail in the absence of bankruptcy; the change is two-fold and is within Congress' power vis-a-vis both the Federal Government and the States. First, the filing of a proof of claim against the estate by a governmental unit is a waiver by that governmental unit of sovereign immunity with respect to compulsory counterclaims, as defined in the Federal Rules of Civil Procedure [set out in Title 28, Judiciary and Judicial Procedure], that is, counterclaims arising out of the same transaction or occurrence. The governmental unit cannot receive a distribution from the estate without subjecting itself to any liability it has to the estate within the confines of a compulsory counterclaim rule. Any other result would be one-sided. The counterclaim by the estate against the governmental unit is without limit.

Second, the estate may offset against the allowed claim of a governmental unit, up to the amount of the governmental unit's claim, any claim that the debtor, and thus the estate, has against the governmental unit, without regard to whether the estate's claim arose out of the same transaction or occurrence as the government's claim. Under this provision, the setoff permitted is only to the extent of the governmental unit's claim. No affirmative recovery is permitted. Subsection (a) governs affirmative recovery.

Though this subsection creates a partial waiver of immunity when the governmental unit files a proof of claim, it does not waive immunity if the debtor or trustee, and not the governmental unit, files proof of a governmental unit's claim under proposed 11 U.S.C. 501(c).

This section does not confer sovereign immunity on any governmental unit that does not already have immunity. It simply recognizes any immunity that exists and prescribes the proper treatment of claims by and against that sovereign. Senate Report No. 92–989.

1994 Acts. House Report No. 103–835, see 1994 U.S. Code Cong. and Adm. News, p. 3340.

Legislative Statements

Section 106(c) relating to sovereign immunity is new. The provision indicates that the use of the term "creditor," "entity," or "governmental unit" in title 11 applies to governmental units notwithstanding any assertion of sovereign immunity and that an order of the court binds governmental units. The provision is included to comply with the requirement in case law that an express waiver of sovereign immunity is required in order to be effective. Section 106(c) codifies *In re Gwilliam*, 519 F.2d 407 (9th Cir., 1975), and *In re Dolard*, 519 F.2d 282 (9th Cir., 1975), permitting the bankruptcy court to determine the amount and dischargeability of tax liabilities owing by the debtor or the estate prior to or during a bankruptcy case whether or not the governmental unit to which such taxes are owed files a proof of claim. Except as provided in sections 106(a) and (b) subsection (c) is not limited to those issues, but permits the bankruptcy court to bind governmental units on other matters as well. For example, section 106(c) permits a trustee or debtor in possession to assert avoiding powers under title 11 against a governmental unit; contrary language in the House report to H.R. 8200 is thereby overruled.

References in Text

The Federal Rules of Bankruptcy Procedure, referred to in subsec. (a)(3) and (5), are set out in the Appendix to this title.

Effective and Applicability Provisions

1994 Acts. Amendment by section 113 of Pub.L. 103–394 effective on Oct. 22, 1994, and applicable with respect to cases commenced under Title 11 of the United States Code before, on, and after Oct. 22, 1994, see section 702 of Pub.L. 103–394, set out as a note under section 101 of this title.

Separability of Provisions

If any provision of or amendment made by Pub.L. 103–394 or the application of such provision or amendment to any person or circumstance is held to be unconstitutional, the remaining provisions of and amendments made by Pub.L. 103–394 and the application of such provisions and amendments to any person or circumstance shall not be affected thereby, see section 701 of Pub.L. 103–394, set out as a note under section 101 of this title.

§ 107. Public access to papers

(a) Except as provided in subsections (b) and (c) and subject to section 112, a paper filed in a case under this title and the dockets of a bankruptcy court are public records and open to examination by an entity at reasonable times without charge.

(b) On request of a party in interest, the bankruptcy court shall, and on the bankruptcy court's own motion, the bankruptcy court may—

    (1) protect an entity with respect to a trade secret or confidential research, development, or commercial information; or

    (2) protect a person with respect to scandalous or defamatory matter contained in a paper filed in a case under this title.

(c)(1) The bankruptcy court, for cause, may protect an individual, with respect to the following types of information to the extent the court finds that disclosure of such information would create undue risk of identity theft or other unlawful injury to the individual or the individual's property:

    (A) Any means of identification (as defined in section 1028(d) of title 18) contained in a paper filed, or to be filed, in a case under this title.

    (B) Other information contained in a paper described in subparagraph (A).

(2) Upon ex parte application demonstrating cause, the court shall provide access to information protected pursuant to paragraph (1) to an entity acting pursuant to the police or regulatory power of a domestic governmental unit.

(3) The United States trustee, bankruptcy administrator, trustee, and any auditor serving under section 586(f) of title 28—

    (A) shall have full access to all information contained in any paper filed or submitted in a case under this title; and

    (B) shall not disclose information specifically protected by the court under this title.

(Pub.L. 95–598, Nov. 6, 1978, 92 Stat. 2556; Pub.L. 109–8, Title II, §§ 233(c), 234(a), (c), Apr. 20, 2005, 119 Stat. 74, 75; Pub.L. 111–327, § 2(a)(5), Dec. 22, 2010, 124 Stat. 3557.)

HISTORICAL AND STATUTORY NOTES

Revision Notes and Legislative Reports

1978 Acts. Subsection (a) of this section makes all papers filed in a bankruptcy case and the dockets of the bankruptcy court public and open to examination at reasonable times without charge. "Docket" includes the claims docket, the proceedings docket, and all papers filed in a case.

Subsection (b) permits the court, on its own motion, and requires the court, on the request of a party in interest, to protect trade secrets, confidential research, development, or commercial information, and to protect persons against scandalous or defamatory matter. Senate Report No. 95–989.

2005 Acts. House Report No. 109–31(Part I), see 2005 U.S. Code Cong. and Adm. News, p. 88.

Effective and Applicability Provisions

2005 Acts. Amendments by Pub.L. 109–8 effective, except as otherwise provided, 180 days after April 20, 2005, and inapplicable with respect to cases commenced under Title 11 before the effective date, see Pub.L. 109–8, § 1501, set out as a note under 11 U.S.C.A. § 101.

CROSS REFERENCES

Application for search of records, see Fed. Bankr. Proc. Form B1320, 11 USCA.

Documents relating to adverse interest and conduct of officers of estate, see 18 USCA § 154.

Reporting of obsolete information prohibited, see 15 USCA § 1681c.

§ 108. Extension of time

(a) If applicable nonbankruptcy law, an order entered in a nonbankruptcy proceeding, or an agreement fixes a period within which the debtor may commence an action, and such period has not expired before the date of the filing of the petition, the trustee may commence such action only before the later of—

(1) the end of such period, including any suspension of such period occurring on or after the commencement of the case; or

(2) two years after the order for relief.

(b) Except as provided in subsection (a) of this section, if applicable nonbankruptcy law, an order entered in a nonbankruptcy proceeding, or an agreement fixes a period within which the debtor or an individual protected under section 1201 or 1301 of this title may file any pleading, demand, notice, or proof of claim or loss, cure a default, or perform any other similar act, and such period has not expired before the date of the filing of the petition, the trustee may only file, cure, or perform, as the case may be, before the later of—

(1) the end of such period, including any suspension of such period occurring on or after the commencement of the case; or

(2) 60 days after the order for relief.

(c) Except as provided in section 524 of this title, if applicable nonbankruptcy law, an order entered in a nonbankruptcy proceeding, or an agreement fixes a period for commencing or continuing a civil action in a court other than a bankruptcy court on a claim against the debtor, or against an individual with respect to which such individual is protected under section 1201 or 1301 of this title, and such period has not expired before the date of the filing of the petition, then such period does not expire until the later of—

(1) the end of such period, including any suspension of such period occurring on or after the commencement of the case; or

(2) 30 days after notice of the termination or expiration of the stay under section 362, 922, 1201, or 1301 of this title, as the case may be, with respect to such claim.

(Pub.L. 95–598, Nov. 6, 1978, 92 Stat. 2556; Pub.L. 98–353, Title III, § 424, July 10, 1984, 98 Stat. 369; Pub.L. 99–554, Title II, § 257(b), Oct. 27, 1986, 100 Stat. 3114; Pub.L. 109–8, Title XII, § 1203, Apr. 20, 2005, 119 Stat. 193.)

HISTORICAL AND STATUTORY NOTES

Revision Notes and Legislative Reports

1978 Acts. Subsections (a) and (b), derived from Bankruptcy Act section 11 [section 29 of former Title 11], permit the trustee, when he steps into the shoes of the debtor, an extension of time for filing an action or doing some other act that is required to preserve the debtor's rights. Subsection (a) extends any statute of limitation for commencing or continuing an action by the debtor for two years after the date of the order for relief, unless it would expire later. Subsection (b) gives the trustee 60 days to take other actions not covered under subsection (a), such as filing a pleading, demand, notice, or proof of claim or loss (such as an insurance claim), unless the period for doing the relevant act expires later than 60 days after the date of the order for relief.

Subsection (c) extends the statute of limitations for creditors. Thus, if a creditor is stayed from commencing or continuing an action against the debtor because of the bankruptcy case, then the creditor is permitted an additional 30 days after notice of the event by which the stay is terminated, whether that event be relief from the automatic stay under proposed 11 U.S.C. 362 or 1301, the closing of the bankruptcy case (which terminates the stay), or the exception from discharge of the debts on which the creditor claims.

In the case of Federal tax liabilities, the Internal Revenue Code [Title 26] suspends the statute of limitations on a tax liability of a taxpayer from running while his assets are in the control or custody of a court and for 6 months thereafter (sec. 6503(b) of the Code) [Title 26]. The amendment applies this rule in a title 11 proceeding. Accordingly, the statute of limitations on collection of a nondischargeable Federal tax liability of a debtor will resume running after 6 months following the end of the period during which the debtor's assets are in the control or custody of the bankruptcy court. This rule will provide the Internal Revenue Service adequate time to collect nondischargeable taxes following the end of the title 11 proceedings. Senate Report No. 95–989.

1984 Acts. Statements by Legislative Leaders, see 1984 U.S.Code Cong. and Adm.News, p. 576.

1986 Acts. House Report No. 99–764 and House Conference Report No. 99–958, see 1986 U.S.Code Cong. and Adm. News, p. 5227.

2005 Acts. House Report No. 109–31(Part I), see 2005 U.S. Code Cong. and Adm. News, p. 88.

Legislative Statements

Extension of time: The House amendment adopts section 108(c)(1) of the Senate amendment which expressly includes any special suspensions of statutes of limitation periods on collection outside bankruptcy when assets are under the authority of a court. For example, section 6503(b) of the Internal Revenue Code [Title 26] suspends collection of tax liabilities while the debtor's assets are in the control or custody of a court, and for 6 months thereafter. By adopting the language of the Senate amendment, the House amendment insures not only that the period for collection of the taxes outside bankruptcy will not expire during the title 11 proceedings, but also that such period will not expire until at least 6 months thereafter, which is the minimum suspension period provided by the Internal Revenue Code [Title 26].

Codifications

Amendment by Pub.L. 99–554, § 257(b)(2)(B), which directed amendment of subsec. (c)(2) by inserting "1201," after "722," was incapable of execution.

Effective and Applicability Provisions

2005 Acts. Amendments by Pub.L. 109–8 effective, except as otherwise provided, 180 days after April 20, 2005, and inapplicable with respect to cases commenced under Title 11 before the effective date, see Pub.L. 109–8, § 1501, set out as a note under 11 U.S.C.A. § 101.

1986 Acts. Amendment by Pub.L. 99–554 effective 30 days after Oct. 27, 1986, but not applicable to cases commenced under this title before that date, see section 302(a), (c)(1) of Pub.L. 99–554, set out as a note under section 581 of Title 28, Judiciary and Judicial Procedure.

1984 Acts. Amendment by Pub.L. 98–353 effective with respect to cases filed 90 days after July 10, 1984, see section 552(a), formerly 553(a) of Pub.L. 98–353, set out as a note under section 101 of this title.

§ 109. Who may be a debtor

(a) Notwithstanding any other provision of this section, only a person that resides or has a domicile, a place of business, or property in the United States, or a municipality, may be a debtor under this title.

(b) A person may be a debtor under chapter 7 of this title only if such person is not—

(1) a railroad;

(2) a domestic insurance company, bank, savings bank, cooperative bank, savings and loan association, building and loan association, homestead association, a New Markets Venture Capital company as defined in section 351 of the Small Business Investment Act of 1958, a small business investment company licensed by the Small Business Administration under section 301 of the Small Business Investment Act of 1958, credit union, or industrial bank or similar institution which is an insured bank as defined in section 3(h) of the Federal Deposit Insurance Act, except that an uninsured State member bank, or a corporation organized under section 25A of the Federal Reserve Act, which operates, or operates as, a multilateral clearing organization pursuant to section 409 of the Federal Deposit Insurance Corporation Improvement Act of 1991 may be a debtor if a petition is filed at the direction of the Board of Governors of the Federal Reserve System; or

(3)(A) a foreign insurance company, engaged in such business in the United States; or

(B) a foreign bank, savings bank, cooperative bank, savings and loan association, building and loan association, or credit union, that has a branch or agency (as defined in section 1(b) of the International Banking Act of 1978) in the United States.

(c) An entity may be a debtor under chapter 9 of this title if and only if such entity—

(1) is a municipality;

(2) is specifically authorized, in its capacity as a municipality or by name, to be a debtor under such chapter by State law, or by a governmental officer or organization empowered by State law to authorize such entity to be a debtor under such chapter;

(3) is insolvent;

(4) desires to effect a plan to adjust such debts; and

(5)(A) has obtained the agreement of creditors holding at least a majority in amount of the claims of each class that such entity intends to impair under a plan in a case under such chapter;

(B) has negotiated in good faith with creditors and has failed to obtain the agreement of creditors holding at least a majority in amount of the claims of each class that such entity intends to impair under a plan in a case under such chapter;

(C) is unable to negotiate with creditors because such negotiation is impracticable; or

(D) reasonably believes that a creditor may attempt to obtain a transfer that is avoidable under section 547 of this title.

(d) Only a railroad, a person that may be a debtor under chapter 7 of this title (except a stockbroker or a commodity broker), and an uninsured State member bank, or a corporation organized under section 25A of the Federal Reserve Act, which operates, or operates as, a multilateral clearing organization pursuant to section 409 of the Federal Deposit Insurance Corporation Improvement Act of 1991 may be a debtor under chapter 11 of this title.

(e) Only an individual with regular income that owes, on the date of the filing of the petition, noncontingent, liquidated, unsecured debts of less than $394,725 [1] and noncontingent, liquidated, secured debts of less than $1,184,200 [1], or an individual with regular income and such individual's spouse, except a stockbroker or a commodity broker, that owe, on the date of the filing of the petition, noncontingent, liquidated, unsecured debts that aggregate less than $394,725 [1] and noncontingent, liquidated, secured debts of less than $1,184,200 [1] may be a debtor under chapter 13 of this title.

(f) Only a family farmer or family fisherman with regular annual income may be a debtor under chapter 12 of this title.

(g) Notwithstanding any other provision of this section, no individual or family farmer may be a debtor under this title who has been a debtor in a case pending under this title at any time in the preceding 180 days if—

(1) the case was dismissed by the court for willful failure of the debtor to abide by orders of the court, or to appear before the court in proper prosecution of the case; or

(2) the debtor requested and obtained the voluntary dismissal of the case following the filing of a request for relief from the automatic stay provided by section 362 of this title.

(h)(1) Subject to paragraphs (2) and (3), and notwithstanding any other provision of this section other than paragraph (4) of this subsection, an individual may not be a debtor under this title unless such individual has, during the 180–day period ending on the date of filing of the petition by such individual, received from an approved nonprofit budget and credit counseling agency described in section 111(a) an individual or group briefing (including a briefing conducted by telephone or on the Internet) that outlined the opportunities for available credit counseling and assisted such individual in performing a related budget analysis.

(2)(A) Paragraph (1) shall not apply with respect to a debtor who resides in a district for which the United States trustee (or the bankruptcy administrator, if any) determines that the approved nonprofit budget and credit counseling agencies for such district are not reasonably able to provide adequate services to the additional individuals who would otherwise seek credit counseling from such agencies by reason of the requirements of paragraph (1).

(B) The United States trustee (or the bankruptcy administrator, if any) who makes a determination described in subparagraph (A) shall review such determination not later than 1 year after the date of such determination, and not less frequently than annually thereafter. Notwithstanding the preceding sentence, a nonprofit budget and credit counseling agency may be disapproved by the United States trustee (or the bankruptcy administrator, if any) at any time.

(3)(A) Subject to subparagraph (B), the requirements of paragraph (1) shall not apply with respect to a debtor who submits to the court a certification that—

    (i) describes exigent circumstances that merit a waiver of the requirements of paragraph (1);

    (ii) states that the debtor requested credit counseling services from an approved nonprofit budget and credit counseling agency, but was unable to obtain the services referred to in paragraph (1) during the 7–day period beginning on the date on which the debtor made that request; and

    (iii) is satisfactory to the court.

(B) With respect to a debtor, an exemption under subparagraph (A) shall cease to apply to that debtor on the date on which the debtor meets the requirements of paragraph (1), but in no case may the exemption apply to that debtor after the date that is 30 days after the debtor files a petition, except that the court, for cause, may order an additional 15 days.

(4) The requirements of paragraph (1) shall not apply with respect to a debtor whom the court determines, after notice and hearing, is unable to complete those requirements because of incapacity, disability, or active military duty in a military combat zone. For the purposes of this paragraph, incapacity means that the debtor is impaired by reason of mental illness or mental deficiency so that he is incapable of realizing and making rational decisions with respect to his financial responsibilities; and "disability" means that the debtor is so physically impaired as to be unable, after reasonable effort, to participate in an in person, telephone, or Internet briefing required under paragraph (1).

(Pub.L. 95–598, Nov. 6, 1978, 92 Stat. 2557; Pub.L. 97–320, Title VII, § 703(d), Oct. 15, 1982, 96 Stat. 1539; Pub.L. 98–353, Title III, §§ 301, 425, July 10, 1984, 98 Stat. 352, 369; Pub.L. 99–554, Title II, § 253, Oct. 27, 1986, 100 Stat. 3105; Pub.L. 100–597, § 2, Nov. 3, 1988, 102 Stat. 3028; Pub.L. 103–394, Title I, § 108(a), Title II, § 220, Title IV, § 402, Title V, § 501(d)(2), Oct. 22, 1994, 108 Stat. 4111, 4129, 4141, 4143; Pub.L. 106–554, § 1(a)(5) [Title I, § 112(c)(1), (2)], (8) [§ 1(e)], Dec. 21, 2000, 114 Stat. 2763, 2763A–393, 2763A–665; Pub.L. 109–8, Title I, § 106(a), Title VIII, § 802(d)(1), Title X, § 1007(b), Title XII, § 1204(1), Apr. 20, 2005, 119 Stat. 37, 146, 188, 193; Pub.L. 111–16, § 2(1), May 7, 2009, 123 Stat. 1607; Pub.L. 111–327, § 2(a)(6), Dec. 22, 2010, 124 Stat. 3557.)

1 Dollar amount as adjusted by the Judicial Conference of the United States. See Adjustment of Dollar Amounts notes set out under this section and 11 U.S.C.A. § 104.

HISTORICAL AND STATUTORY NOTES
Revision Notes and Legislative Reports
1978 Acts. This section specifies eligibility to be a debtor under the bankruptcy laws. The first criterion, found in the current Bankruptcy Act section 2a(1) [section 11(a)(1) of former Title 11] requires that the debtor reside or have a domicile, a place of business, or property in the United States.

Subsection (b) defines eligibility for liquidation under chapter 7. All persons are eligible except insurance companies, and certain banking institutions. These exclusions are contained in current law. However, the banking institution exception is expanded in light of changes in various banking laws since the current law was last amended on this point. A change is also made to clarify that the bankruptcy laws cover foreign banks and insurance companies not engaged in the banking or insurance business in the United States but having assets in the United States. Banking institutions and insurance companies engaged in business in this country are excluded from liquidation under the bankruptcy laws because they are bodies for which alternate provision is made for their liquidation under various State or Federal regulatory laws. Conversely, when a foreign bank or insurance company is not engaged in the banking or insurance business in the United States, then those regulatory laws do not apply, and the bankruptcy laws are the only ones available for administration of any assets found in United States.

The first clause of subsection (b) provides that a railroad is not a debtor except where the requirements of section 1174 are met.

Subsection (c) provides that only a person who may be a debtor under chapter 7 and a railroad may also be a debtor under chapter 11, but a stockbroker or commodity broker is eligible for relief only under chapter 7. Subsection (d) establishes dollar limitations on the amount of indebtedness that an individual with regular income can incur and yet file under chapter 13. Senate Report No. 95–989.

Subsection (c) defines eligibility for chapter 9. Only a municipality that is unable to pay its debts as they mature, and that is not prohibited by State law from proceeding under chapter 9, is permitted to be a chapter 9 debtor. The subsection is derived from Bankruptcy Act section 84 [section 404 of former Title 11], with two changes. First, section 84 requires that the municipality be "generally authorized to file a petition under this chapter by the legislature, or by a governmental officer or organization empowered by State law to authorize the filing of a petition." The "generally authorized" language is unclear, and has generated a problem for a Colorado Metropolitan District that attempted to use chapter IX [chapter 9 of former Title 11] in 1976. The "not prohibited" language provides flexibility for both the States and the municipalities involved, while protecting State sovereignty as required by *Ashton v. Cameron County Water District No. 1,* 298 U.S. 513 (1936) [56 S.Ct. 892, 80 L.Ed. 1309, 31 Am.

Bankr.Rep.N.S. 96, rehearing denied 57 S.Ct. 5, 299 U.S. 619, 81 L.Ed. 457] and *Bekins v. United States,* 304 U.S. 27 (1938) [58 S.Ct. 811, 82 L.Ed. 1137, 36 Am.Bankr.Rep.N.S. 187, rehearing denied 58 S.Ct. 1043, 1044, 304 U.S. 589, 82 L.Ed. 1549].

The second change deletes the four prerequisites to filing found in section 84 [section 404 of former Title 11]. The prerequisites require the municipality to have worked out a plan in advance, to have attempted to work out a plan without success, to fear that a creditor will attempt to obtain a preference, or to allege that prior negotiation is impracticable. The loopholes in those prerequisites are larger than the requirement itself. It was a compromise from pre-1976 chapter IX [chapter 9 of former Title 11] under which a municipality could file only if it had worked out an adjustment plan in advance. In the meantime, chapter IX protection was unavailable. There was some controversy at the time of the enactment of current chapter IX concerning deletion of the pre-negotiation requirement. It was argued that deletion would lead to a rash of municipal bankruptcies. The prerequisites now contained in section 84 were inserted to assuage that fear. They are largely cosmetic and precatory, however, and do not offer any significant deterrent to use of chapter IX. Instead, other factors, such as a general reluctance on the part of any debtor, especially a municipality, to use the bankruptcy laws, operates as a much more effective deterrent against capricious use.

Subsection (d) permits a person that may proceed under chapter 7 to be a debtor under chapter 11, Reorganization, with two exceptions. Railroads, which are excluded from chapter 7, are permitted to proceed under chapter 11. Stockbrokers and commodity brokers, which are permitted to be debtors under chapter 7, are excluded from chapter 11. The special rules for treatment of customer accounts that are the essence of stockbroker and commodity broker liquidations are available only in chapter 7. Customers would be unprotected under chapter 11. The special protective rules are unavailable in chapter 11 because their complexity would make reorganization very difficult at best, and unintelligible at worst. The variety of options available in reorganization cases make it extremely difficult to reorganize and continue to provide the special customer protection necessary in these cases.

Subsection (e) specifies eligibility for chapter 13, Adjustment of Debts of an Individual with Regular Income. An individual with regular income, or an individual with regular income and the individual's spouse, may proceed under chapter 13. As noted in connection with the definition of the term "individual with regular income", this represents a significant departure from current law. The change might have been too great, however, without some limitation. Thus, the debtor (or the debtor and spouse) must have unsecured debts that aggregate less than $100,000, and secured debts that aggregate less than $500,000. These figures will permit the small sole proprietor, for whom a chapter 11 reorganization is too cumbersome a procedure, to proceed under chapter 13. It does not create a presumption that any sole proprietor within that range is better off in chapter 13 than chapter 11. The conversion rules found in section 1307 will govern the appropriateness of the two chapters for any particular individual. The figures merely set maximum limits.

Whether a small business operated by a husband and wife, the so-called "mom and pop grocery store," will be a partnership and thus excluded from chapter 13, or a business owned by an individual, will have to be determined on the facts of each case. Even if partnership papers have not been filed, for example, the issue will be whether the assets of the grocery store are for the benefit of all creditors of the debtor or only for business creditors, and whether such assets may be the subject of a chapter 13 proceeding. The intent of the section is to follow current law that a partnership by estoppel may be adjudicated in bankruptcy and therefore would not prevent a chapter 13 debtor from subjecting assets in such a partnership to the reach of all creditors in a chapter 13 case. However, if the partnership is found to be a partnership by agreement, even informal agreement, then a separate entity exists and the assets of that entity would be exempt from a case under chapter 13. House Report No. 95–595.

1982 Acts. Senate Report No. 97–536 and Senate Conference Report No. 97–641, see 1982 U.S. Code Cong. and Adm. News, p. 3054.

1984 Acts. Statements by Legislative Leaders, see 1984 U.S. Code Cong. and Adm. News, p. 576.

1986 Acts. House Report No. 99–764 and House Conference Report No. 99–958, see U.S. Code Cong. and Adm. News, p. 5227.

1988 Acts. House Report No. 100–1011, see 1988 U.S. Code Cong. and Adm. News, p. 4115.

1994 Acts. House Report No. 103–835, see 1994 U.S. Code Cong. and Adm. News, p. 3340.

2000 Acts. House Report No. 106–645 and Statement by President, see 2000 U.S. Code Cong. and Adm. News, p. 2459.

2005 Acts. House Report No. 109–31(Part I), see 2005 U.S. Code Cong. and Adm. News, p. 88.

Legislative Statements

Section 109(b) of the House amendment adopts a provision contained in H.R. 8200 as passed by the House. Railroad liquidations will occur under chapter 11, not chapter 7.

Section 109(c) contains a provision which tracks the Senate amendment as to when a municipality may be a debtor under chapter 11 of title 11. As under the Bankruptcy Act [former Title 11], State law authorization and prepetition negotiation efforts are required.

Section 109(e) represents a compromise between H.R. 8200 as passed by the House and the Senate amendment relating to the dollar amounts restricting eligibility to be a debtor under chapter 13 of title 11. The House amendment adheres to the limit of $100,000 placed on unsecured debts in H.R. 8200 as passed by the House. It adopts a midpoint of $350,000 as a limit on secured claims, a compromise between the level of $500,000 in H.R. 8200 as passed by the House and $200,000 as contained in the Senate amendment.

References in Text

Section 351 of the Small Business Investment Act of 1958, referred to in subsec. (b)(2), is section 351 of Pub.L. 85–699, which is classified to 15 U.S.C.A. § 689.

Section 301 of the Small Business Investment Act of 1958, referred to in subsec. (b)(2), is section 301 of Pub.L. 85–699, Title III, Aug. 21, 1958, which is classified to 15 U.S.C.A. § 681.

Section 3(h) of the Federal Deposit Insurance Act, referred to in subsec. (b)(2), is classified to 12 U.S.C.A. § 1813(h).

Section 25A of the Federal Reserve Act, referred to in subsecs. (b)(2) and (d), is Dec. 23, 1913, c. 6, § 25A, formerly § 25(a), as added Dec. 24, 1919, c. 18, 41 Stat. 378, as amended, which is classified to subchapter II of chapter 6 of Title 12 (12 U.S.C.A. § 611 et seq.).

Section 409 of the Federal Deposit Insurance Corporation Improvement Act of 1991, referred to in subsecs. (b)(2) and (d), is Pub.L. 102–242, Title IV, § 409, as added by Pub.L. 106–554, § 1(a)(5) [Title I, § 112(a)(3)], Dec. 21, 2000, 114 Stat. 2763, 2763A–391, which is classified as 12 U.S.C.A. § 4422.

Section 1(b) of the International Banking Act of 1978, referred to in subsec. (b)(3)(B), is Pub.L. 95–369, § 1(b), Sept. 17, 1978, 92 Stat. 607, as amended, which is classified to 12 U.S.C.A. § 3101.

Chapter 7 of this title, referred to in subsec. (d), is 11 U.S.C.A. § 701 et seq.

Chapter 11 of this title, referred to in subsec. (d), is 11 U.S.C.A. § 1101 et seq.

Effective and Applicability Provisions

2013 Acts. Increase of dollar amounts by Judicial Conference of the United States by notice published Feb. 21, 2013, 78 F.R. 12089 effective April 1, 2013, and increase not applicable to cases commenced before the effective date of the adjustments, i.e., April 1, 2013. See Adjustment of Dollar Amounts notes under 11 U.S.C.A. § 104 and this section.

2010 Acts. Increase of dollar amounts by Judicial Conference of the United States by notice published Feb. 25, 2010, 75 F.R. 8747 effective April 1, 2010, and increase not applicable to cases commenced before the effective date of the adjustments, i.e., April 1, 2010. See Adjustment of Dollar Amounts notes under 11 U.S.C.A. § 104 and this section.

2009 Acts. Pub.L. 111–16, § 7, May 7, 2009, 123 Stat. 1609, provided that: "The amendments made by this Act [amending this section, section 7 of the Classified Information Procedures Act (18 App. U.S.C.A. § 7), 11 U.S.C.A. §§ 322, 332, 342, 521, 704, 749, and 764, 18 U.S.C.A. §§ 983, 1514, 1963, 2252A, 2339B, 3060, 3432, 3509, and 3771, 21 U.S.C.A. § 853, and 28 U.S.C.A. §§ 636, 1453, and 2107] shall take effect on December 1, 2009."

2007 Acts. Increase of dollar amounts by Judicial Conference of the United States by notice published Feb. 14, 2007, 72 F.R. 7082 effective April 1, 2007, and increase not applicable to cases commenced before the effective date of the adjustments, i.e., April 1, 2007. See Adjustment of Dollar Amounts notes under 11 U.S.C.A. § 104 and this section.

2005 Acts. Amendments by Pub.L. 109–8 effective, except as otherwise provided, 180 days after April 20, 2005, and inapplicable with respect to cases commenced under Title 11 before the effective date, see Pub.L. 109–8, § 1501, set out as a note under 11 U.S.C.A. § 101.

2004 Acts. Adjustment of dollar amounts by Judicial Conference of the United States by notice dated Feb. 18, 2004, 69 F.R. 8482 effective April 1, 2004, and adjustment not applicable to cases commenced before the effective date of the adjustments, i.e., April 1, 2004. See Adjustment of Dollar Amounts notes under 11 U.S.C.A. § 104 and this section.

2001 Acts. Adjustment of dollar amounts by Judicial Conference of the United States by notice dated Feb. 20, 2001, 66 F.R. 10910 effective April 1, 2001, and adjustment not applicable to cases commenced before the effective date of the adjustments, i.e., April 1, 2001. See Adjustment of Dollar Amounts notes under 11 U.S.C.A. § 104 and this section.

1998 Acts. Adjustment of dollar amounts by Judicial Conference of the United States by notice dated Feb. 3, 1998, 63 F.R. 7179 effective April 1, 1998, and adjustment not applicable to cases commenced before the effective date of the adjustments, i.e., April 1, 1998. See Adjustment of Dollar Amounts notes under 11 U.S.C.A. § 104 and this section.

1994 Acts. Amendments by Pub.L. 103–394 effective on Oct. 22, 1994, and not to apply with respect to cases commenced under Title 11 of the United States Code before Oct. 22, 1994, see section 702 of Pub.L. 103–394, set out as a note under section 101 of this title.

1988 Acts. Amendment by Pub.L. 100–597 effective Nov. 3, 1988, but not applicable to any case commenced under this title before that date, see section 12 of Pub.L. 100–597, set out as a note under section 101 of this title.

1986 Acts. Amendment by Pub.L. 99–554 effective 30 days after Oct. 27, 1986, but not applicable to cases commended under this title before that date, see section 302(a), (c)(1) of Pub.L. 99–554, set out as a note under section 581 of Title 28, Judiciary and Judicial Procedure.

1984 Acts. Amendment by Pub.L. 98–353 effective with respect to cases filed 90 days after July 10, 1984, see section 552(a), formerly 553(a), of Pub.L. 98–353, set out as a note under section 101 of this title.

Separability of Provisions

If any provision of or amendment made by Pub.L. 103–394 or the application of such provision or amendment to any person or circumstance is held to be unconstitutional, the remaining provisions of and amendments made by Pub.L. 103–394 and the application of such provisions and amendments to any person or circumstance shall not be affected thereby, see section 701 of Pub.L. 103–394, set out as a note under section 101 of this title.

Adjustment of Dollar Amounts

For adjustment of dollar amounts specified in subsec. (e) of this section by the Judicial Conference of the United States, effective Apr. 1, 2016, see note set out under 11 U.S.C.A. § 104.

By notice published Feb. 22, 2016, 81 F.R. 8748, the Judicial Conference of the United States adjusted the dollar amounts in provisions specified in subsec. (e) of this section, effective Apr. 1, 2016, as follows:

> Adjusted $383,175 (each time it appears) to $394,725 (each time it appears).

> Adjusted $1,149,525 (each time it appears) to $1,184,200 (each time it appears).

By notice published Feb. 21, 2013, 78 F.R. 12089, the Judicial Conference of the United States adjusted the dollar amounts in provisions specified in subsec. (e) of this section, effective Apr. 1, 2013, as follows:

> Adjusted $360,475 (each time it appears) to $383,175 (each time it appears).

> Adjusted $1,081,400 (each time it appears) to $1,149,525 (each time it appears).

By notice published Feb. 25, 2010, 75 F.R. 8747, the Judicial Conference of the United States adjusted the dollar amounts in provisions specified in subsec. (e) of this section, effective Apr. 1, 2010, as follows:

> Adjusted $336,900 (each time it appears) to $360,475 (each time it appears).

> Adjusted $1,010,650 (each time it appears) to $1,081,400 (each time it appears).

By notice published Feb. 14, 2007, 72 F.R. 7082, the Judicial Conference of the United States adjusted the dollar amounts in provisions specified in subsec. (e) of this section, effective Apr. 1, 2007, as follows:

Adjusted $307,675 (each time it appears) to $336,900 (each time it appears).

Adjusted $922,975 (each time it appears) to $1,010,650 (each time it appears).

By notice dated Feb. 18, 2004, 69 F.R. 8482, the Judicial Conference of the United States adjusted the dollar amounts in provisions specified in subsec. (e) of this section, effective Apr. 1, 2004, as follows:

Adjusted $290,525 (each time it appears) to $307,675 (each time it appears).

Adjusted $871,550 to $922,975.

By notice dated Feb. 20, 2001, 66 F.R. 10910, the Judicial Conference of the United States adjusted the dollar amounts in provisions specified in subsec. (e) of this section, effective Apr. 1, 2001, as follows:

Adjusted $269,250 (each time it appears) to $290,525 (each time it appears).

Adjusted $807,750 (each time it appears) to $871,550 (each time it appears).

By notice dated Feb. 3, 1998, 63 F.R. 7179, the Judicial Conference of the United States adjusted the dollar amounts in provisions specified in subsec. (e) of this section, effective Apr. 1, 1998, as follows:

Adjusted $250,000 (each time it appears) to $269,250 (each time it appears).

Adjusted $750,000 (each time it appears) to $807,750 (each time it appears).

CROSS REFERENCES

Filing of Chapter 9 petition by certain unincorporated tax or special assessment districts notwithstanding provisions under this section, see 11 USCA § 921.

Nonprejudicial dismissal, except as provided by this section, see 11 USCA § 349.

§ 110. Penalty for persons who negligently or fraudulently prepare bankruptcy petitions

(a) In this section—

(1) "bankruptcy petition preparer" means a person, other than an attorney for the debtor or an employee of such attorney under the direct supervision of such attorney, who prepares for compensation a document for filing; and

(2) "document for filing" means a petition or any other document prepared for filing by a debtor in a United States bankruptcy court or a United States district court in connection with a case under this title.

(b)(1) A bankruptcy petition preparer who prepares a document for filing shall sign the document and print on the document the preparer's name and address. If a bankruptcy petition preparer is not an individual, then an officer, principal, responsible person, or partner of the bankruptcy petition preparer shall be required to—

(A) sign the document for filing; and

(B) print on the document the name and address of that officer, principal, responsible person, or partner.

(2)(A) Before preparing any document for filing or accepting any fees from or on behalf of a debtor, the bankruptcy petition preparer shall provide to the debtor a written notice which shall be on an official form prescribed by the Judicial Conference of the United States in accordance with rule 9009 of the Federal Rules of Bankruptcy Procedure.

(B) The notice under subparagraph (A)—

(i) shall inform the debtor in simple language that a bankruptcy petition preparer is not an attorney and may not practice law or give legal advice;

(ii) may contain a description of examples of legal advice that a bankruptcy petition preparer is not authorized to give, in addition to any advice that the preparer may not give by reason of subsection (e)(2); and

(iii) shall—

(I) be signed by the debtor and, under penalty of perjury, by the bankruptcy petition preparer; and

(II) be filed with any document for filing.

(c)(1) A bankruptcy petition preparer who prepares a document for filing shall place on the document, after the preparer's signature, an identifying number that identifies individuals who prepared the document.

(2)(A) Subject to subparagraph (B), for purposes of this section, the identifying number of a bankruptcy petition preparer shall be the Social Security account number of each individual who prepared the document or assisted in its preparation.

(B) If a bankruptcy petition preparer is not an individual, the identifying number of the bankruptcy petition preparer shall be the Social Security account number of the officer, principal, responsible person, or partner of the bankruptcy petition preparer.

(d) A bankruptcy petition preparer shall, not later than the time at which a document for filing is presented for the debtor's signature, furnish to the debtor a copy of the document.

(e)(1) A bankruptcy petition preparer shall not execute any document on behalf of a debtor.

(2)(A) A bankruptcy petition preparer may not offer a potential bankruptcy debtor any legal advice, including any legal advice described in subparagraph (B).

(B) The legal advice referred to in subparagraph (A) includes advising the debtor—

(i) whether—

(I) to file a petition under this title; or

(II) commencing a case under chapter 7, 11, 12, or 13 is appropriate;

(ii) whether the debtor's debts will be discharged in a case under this title;

(iii) whether the debtor will be able to retain the debtor's home, car, or other property after commencing a case under this title;

(iv) concerning—

(I) the tax consequences of a case brought under this title; or

(II) the dischargeability of tax claims;

(v) whether the debtor may or should promise to repay debts to a creditor or enter into a reaffirmation agreement with a creditor to reaffirm a debt;

(vi) concerning how to characterize the nature of the debtor's interests in property or the debtor's debts; or

(vii) concerning bankruptcy procedures and rights.

(f) A bankruptcy petition preparer shall not use the word "legal" or any similar term in any advertisements, or advertise under any category that includes the word "legal" or any similar term.

(g) A bankruptcy petition preparer shall not collect or receive any payment from the debtor or on behalf of the debtor for the court fees in connection with filing the petition.

(h)(1) The Supreme Court may promulgate rules under section 2075 of title 28, or the Judicial Conference of the United States may prescribe guidelines, for setting a maximum allowable fee chargeable by a bankruptcy petition preparer. A bankruptcy petition preparer shall notify the debtor of any such maximum amount before preparing any document for filing for the debtor or accepting any fee from or on behalf of the debtor.

(2) A declaration under penalty of perjury by the bankruptcy petition preparer shall be filed together with the petition, disclosing any fee received from or on behalf of the debtor within 12 months immediately prior to the filing of the case, and any unpaid fee charged to the debtor. If rules or guidelines setting a maximum fee for services have been promulgated or prescribed under paragraph (1), the declaration under this paragraph shall include a certification that the bankruptcy petition preparer complied with the notification requirement under paragraph (1).

(3)(A) The court shall disallow and order the immediate turnover to the bankruptcy trustee any fee referred to in paragraph (2)—

(i) found to be in excess of the value of any services rendered by the bankruptcy petition preparer during the 12-month period immediately preceding the date of the filing of the petition; or

(ii) found to be in violation of any rule or guideline promulgated or prescribed under paragraph (1).

(B) All fees charged by a bankruptcy petition preparer may be forfeited in any case in which the bankruptcy petition preparer fails to comply with this subsection or subsection (b), (c), (d), (e), (f), or (g).

(C) An individual may exempt any funds recovered under this paragraph under section 522(b).

(4) The debtor, the trustee, a creditor, the United States trustee (or the bankruptcy administrator, if any) or the court, on the initiative of the court, may file a motion for an order under paragraph (3).

(5) A bankruptcy petition preparer shall be fined not more than $500 for each failure to comply with a court order to turn over funds within 30 days of service of such order.

(i)(1) If a bankruptcy petition preparer violates this section or commits any act that the court finds to be fraudulent, unfair, or deceptive, on the motion of the debtor, trustee, United States trustee (or the bankruptcy administrator, if any), and after notice and a hearing, the court shall order the bankruptcy petition preparer to pay to the debtor—

(A) the debtor's actual damages;

(B) the greater of—

(i) $2,000; or

(ii) twice the amount paid by the debtor to the bankruptcy petition preparer for the preparer's services; and

(C) reasonable attorneys' fees and costs in moving for damages under this subsection.

(2) If the trustee or creditor moves for damages on behalf of the debtor under this subsection, the bankruptcy petition preparer shall be ordered to pay the movant the additional amount of $1,000 plus reasonable attorneys' fees and costs incurred.

(j)(1) A debtor for whom a bankruptcy petition preparer has prepared a document for filing, the trustee, a creditor, or the United States trustee in the district in which the bankruptcy petition preparer resides, has conducted business, or the United States trustee in any other district in which the debtor resides may bring a civil action to enjoin a bankruptcy petition preparer from engaging in any conduct in violation of this section or from further acting as a bankruptcy petition preparer.

(2)(A) In an action under paragraph (1), if the court finds that—

(i) a bankruptcy petition preparer has—

(I) engaged in conduct in violation of this section or of any provision of this title;

(II) misrepresented the preparer's experience or education as a bankruptcy petition preparer; or

(III) engaged in any other fraudulent, unfair, or deceptive conduct; and

(ii) injunctive relief is appropriate to prevent the recurrence of such conduct,

the court may enjoin the bankruptcy petition preparer from engaging in such conduct.

(B) If the court finds that a bankruptcy petition preparer has continually engaged in conduct described in subclause (I), (II), or (III) of clause (i) and that an injunction prohibiting such conduct would not be sufficient to prevent such person's interference with the proper administration of this title, has not paid a penalty imposed under this section, or failed to disgorge all fees ordered by the court the court may enjoin the person from acting as a bankruptcy petition preparer.

(3) The court, as part of its contempt power, may enjoin a bankruptcy petition preparer that has failed to comply with a previous order issued under this section. The injunction under this paragraph may be issued on the motion of the court, the trustee, or the United States trustee (or the bankruptcy administrator, if any).

(4) The court shall award to a debtor, trustee, or creditor that brings a successful action under this subsection reasonable attorneys' fees and costs of the action, to be paid by the bankruptcy petition preparer.

(k) Nothing in this section shall be construed to permit activities that are otherwise prohibited by law, including rules and laws that prohibit the unauthorized practice of law.

(_l_)(1) A bankruptcy petition preparer who fails to comply with any provision of subsection (b), (c), (d), (e), (f), (g), or (h) may be fined not more than $500 for each such failure.

(2) The court shall triple the amount of a fine assessed under paragraph (1) in any case in which the court finds that a bankruptcy petition preparer—

(A) advised the debtor to exclude assets or income that should have been included on applicable schedules;

(B) advised the debtor to use a false Social Security account number;

(C) failed to inform the debtor that the debtor was filing for relief under this title; or

(D) prepared a document for filing in a manner that failed to disclose the identity of the bankruptcy petition preparer.

(3) A debtor, trustee, creditor, or United States trustee (or the bankruptcy administrator, if any) may file a motion for an order imposing a fine on the bankruptcy petition preparer for any violation of this section.

(4)(A) Fines imposed under this subsection in judicial districts served by United States trustees shall be paid to the United States trustees, who shall deposit an amount equal to such fines in the United States Trustee Fund.

(B) Fines imposed under this subsection in judicial districts served by bankruptcy administrators shall be deposited as offsetting receipts to the fund established under section 1931 of title 28, and shall remain available until expended to reimburse any appropriation for the amount paid out of such appropriation for expenses of the operation and maintenance of the courts of the United States.

(Added Pub.L. 103–394, Title III, § 308(a), Oct. 22, 1994, 108 Stat. 4135; amended Pub.L. 109–8, Title II, § 221, Title XII, § 1205, Apr. 20, 2005, 119 Stat. 59, 194; Pub.L. 110–161, Div. B, Title II, § 212(b), Dec. 26, 2007, 121 Stat. 1914; Pub.L. 111–327, § 2(a)(7), Dec. 22, 2010, 124 Stat. 3558.)

HISTORICAL AND STATUTORY NOTES

Revision Notes and Legislative Reports

1994 Acts. House Report No. 103–835, see 1994 U.S. Code Cong. and Adm. News, p. 3340.

2005 Acts. House Report No. 109–31(Part I), see 2005 U.S. Code Cong. and Adm. News, p. 88.

2007 Acts. House Report No. 110–197, see 2007 U.S. Code Cong. and Adm. News, p. 661.

Statement by President, see 2007 U.S. Code Cong. and Adm. News, p. S34.

References in Text

The Federal Rules of Bankruptcy Procedure, referred to in subsec. (b)(2)(A), are set out in the Appendix to this title.

Chapter 7, 11, 12, or 13, referred to in subsec. (e)(2)(B)(i)(II), is chapter 7, 11, 12, or 13 of this title, 11 U.S.C.A. § 701 et seq., 11 U.S.C.A. § 1101 et seq., 11 U.S.C.A. § 1201 et seq., or 11 U.S.C.A. § 1301 et seq., respectively.

Effective and Applicability Provisions

2005 Acts. Amendments by Pub.L. 109–8 effective, except as otherwise provided, 180 days after April 20, 2005, and inapplicable with respect to cases commenced under Title 11 before the effective date, see Pub.L. 109–8, § 1501, set out as a note under 11 U.S.C.A. § 101.

1994 Acts. Section effective on Oct. 22, 1994, and not to apply with respect to cases commenced under Title 11 of the United States Code before Oct. 22, 1994, see section 702 of Pub.L. 103–394, set out as a note under section 101 of this title.

Separability of Provisions

If any provision of or amendment made by Pub.L. 103–394 or the application of such provision or amendment to any person or circumstance is held to be unconstitutional, the remaining provisions of and amendments made by Pub.L. 103–394 and the application of such provisions and amendments to any person or circumstance shall not be affected thereby, see section 701 of Pub.L. 103–394, set out as a note under section 101 of this title.

§ 111. Nonprofit budget and credit counseling agencies; financial management instructional courses

(a) The clerk shall maintain a publicly available list of—

---

(1) nonprofit budget and credit counseling agencies that provide 1 or more services described in section 109(h) currently approved by the United States trustee (or the bankruptcy administrator, if any); and

(2) instructional courses concerning personal financial management currently approved by the United States trustee (or the bankruptcy administrator, if any), as applicable.

(b) The United States trustee (or bankruptcy administrator, if any) shall only approve a nonprofit budget and credit counseling agency or an instructional course concerning personal financial management as follows:

(1) The United States trustee (or bankruptcy administrator, if any) shall have thoroughly reviewed the qualifications of the nonprofit budget and credit counseling agency or of the provider of the instructional course under the standards set forth in this section, and the services or instructional courses that will be offered by such agency or such provider, and may require such agency or such provider that has sought approval to provide information with respect to such review.

(2) The United States trustee (or bankruptcy administrator, if any) shall have determined that such agency or such instructional course fully satisfies the applicable standards set forth in this section.

(3) If a nonprofit budget and credit counseling agency or instructional course did not appear on the approved list for the district under subsection (a) immediately before approval under this section, approval under this subsection of such agency or such instructional course shall be for a probationary period not to exceed 6 months.

(4) At the conclusion of the applicable probationary period under paragraph (3), the United States trustee (or bankruptcy administrator, if any) may only approve for an additional 1–year period, and for successive 1–year periods thereafter, an agency or instructional course that has demonstrated during the probationary or applicable subsequent period of approval that such agency or instructional course—

(A) has met the standards set forth under this section during such period; and

(B) can satisfy such standards in the future.

(5) Not later than 30 days after any final decision under paragraph (4), an interested person may seek judicial review of such decision in the appropriate district court of the United States.

(c)(1) The United States trustee (or the bankruptcy administrator, if any) shall only approve a nonprofit budget and credit counseling agency that demonstrates that it will provide qualified counselors, maintain adequate provision for safekeeping and payment of client funds, provide adequate counseling with respect to client credit problems, and deal responsibly and effectively with other matters relating to the quality, effectiveness, and financial security of the services it provides.

(2) To be approved by the United States trustee (or the bankruptcy administrator, if any), a nonprofit budget and credit counseling agency shall, at a minimum—

(A) have a board of directors the majority of which—

(i) are not employed by such agency; and

(ii) will not directly or indirectly benefit financially from the outcome of the counseling services provided by such agency;

(B) if a fee is charged for counseling services, charge a reasonable fee, and provide services without regard to ability to pay the fee;

(C) provide for safekeeping and payment of client funds, including an annual audit of the trust accounts and appropriate employee bonding;

(D) provide full disclosures to a client, including funding sources, counselor qualifications, possible impact on credit reports, and any costs of such program that will be paid by such client and how such costs will be paid;

(E) provide adequate counseling with respect to a client's credit problems that includes an analysis of such client's current financial condition, factors that caused such financial condition, and how such client can develop a plan to respond to the problems without incurring negative amortization of debt;

(F) provide trained counselors who receive no commissions or bonuses based on the outcome of the counseling services provided by such agency, and who have adequate experience, and have been adequately trained to provide counseling services to individuals in financial difficulty, including the matters described in subparagraph (E);

(G) demonstrate adequate experience and background in providing credit counseling; and

(H) have adequate financial resources to provide continuing support services for budgeting plans over the life of any repayment plan.

(d) The United States trustee (or the bankruptcy administrator, if any) shall only approve an instructional course concerning personal financial management—

(1) for an initial probationary period under subsection (b)(3) if the course will provide at a minimum—

(A) trained personnel with adequate experience and training in providing effective instruction and services;

(B) learning materials and teaching methodologies designed to assist debtors in understanding personal financial management and that are consistent with stated objectives directly related to the goals of such instructional course;

(C) adequate facilities situated in reasonably convenient locations at which such instructional course is offered, except that such facilities may include the provision of such instructional course by telephone or through the Internet, if such instructional course is effective;

(D) the preparation and retention of reasonable records (which shall include the debtor's bankruptcy case number) to permit evaluation of the effectiveness of such instructional course, including any evaluation of satisfaction of instructional course requirements for each debtor attending such instructional course, which shall be available for inspection and evaluation by the Executive Office for United States Trustees, the United States trustee (or the bankruptcy administrator, if any), or the chief bankruptcy judge for the district in which such instructional course is offered; and

(E) if a fee is charged for the instructional course, charge a reasonable fee, and provide services without regard to ability to pay the fee; and

(2) for any 1–year period if the provider thereof has demonstrated that the course meets the standards of paragraph (1) and, in addition—

(A) has been effective in assisting a substantial number of debtors to understand personal financial management; and

(B) is otherwise likely to increase substantially the debtor's understanding of personal financial management.

(e) The district court may, at any time, investigate the qualifications of a nonprofit budget and credit counseling agency referred to in subsection (a), and request production of documents to ensure the integrity and effectiveness of such agency. The district court may, at any time, remove from the approved list under subsection (a) a nonprofit budget and credit counseling agency upon finding such agency does not meet the qualifications of subsection (b).

(f) The United States trustee (or the bankruptcy administrator, if any) shall notify the clerk that a nonprofit budget and credit counseling agency or an instructional course is no longer approved, in which case the clerk shall remove it from the list maintained under subsection (a).

(g)(1) No nonprofit budget and credit counseling agency may provide to a credit reporting agency information concerning whether a debtor has received or sought instruction concerning personal financial management from such agency.

(2) A nonprofit budget and credit counseling agency that willfully or negligently fails to comply with any requirement under this title with respect to a debtor shall be liable for damages in an amount equal to the sum of—

(A) any actual damages sustained by the debtor as a result of the violation; and

(B) any court costs or reasonable attorneys' fees (as determined by the court) incurred in an action to recover those damages.

(Added Pub.L. 109–8, Title I, § 106(e)(1), Apr. 20, 2005, 119 Stat. 39; amended Pub.L. 111–327, § 2(a)(8), Dec. 22, 2010, 124 Stat. 3558.)

HISTORICAL AND STATUTORY NOTES

Revision Notes and Legislative Reports

2005 Acts. House Report No. 109–31(Part I), see 2005 U.S. Code Cong. and Adm. News, p. 88.

Effective and Applicability Provisions

2005 Acts. Amendments by Pub.L. 109–8 effective, except as otherwise provided, 180 days after April 20, 2005, and inapplicable with respect to cases commenced under Title 11 before the effective date, see Pub.L. 109–8, § 1501, set out as a note under 11 U.S.C.A. § 101.

Debtor Financial Management Training Test Program

Pub.L. 109–8, Title I, § 105, Apr. 20, 2005, 119 Stat. 36, provided that:

"**(a) Development of financial management and training curriculum and materials.**—The Director of the Executive Office for United States Trustees (in this section referred to as the 'Director') shall consult with a wide range of individuals who are experts in the field of debtor education, including trustees who serve in cases under chapter 13 of title 11, United States Code [11 U.S.C.A. § 1301 et seq.], and who operate financial management education programs for debtors, and shall develop a financial management training curriculum and materials that can be used to educate debtors who are individuals on how to better manage their finances.

"**(b) Test.—**

"**(1) Selection of districts.**—The Director shall select 6 judicial districts of the United States in which to test the effectiveness of the financial management training curriculum and materials developed under subsection (a) [of this note].

"**(2) Use.**—For an 18–month period beginning not later than 270 days after the date of the enactment of this Act [April 20, 2005], such curriculum and materials shall be, for the 6 judicial districts selected under paragraph (1), used as the instructional course concerning personal financial management for purposes of section 111 of title 11, United States Code.

"**(c) Evaluation.—**

"**(1) In general.**—During the 18–month period referred to in subsection (b) [of this note], the Director shall evaluate the effectiveness of—

"**(A)** the financial management training curriculum and materials developed under subsection (a) [of this note]; and

"**(B)** a sample of existing consumer education programs such as those described in the Report of the National Bankruptcy Review Commission (October 20, 1997) that are representative of consumer education programs carried out by the credit industry, by trustees serving under chapter 13 of title 11, United States Code [11 U.S.C.A. § 1301 et seq.], and by consumer counseling groups.

"(2) **Report.**—Not later than 3 months after concluding such evaluation, the Director shall submit a report to the Speaker of the House of Representatives and the President pro tempore of the Senate, for referral to the appropriate committees of the Congress, containing the findings of the Director regarding the effectiveness of such curriculum, such materials, and such programs and their costs."

[Amendments by Pub.L. 109–8 effective, except as otherwise provided, 180 days after April 20, 2005, and inapplicable with respect to cases commenced under Title 11 before the effective date, see Pub.L. 109–8, § 1501, set out as a note under 11 U.S.C.A. § 101.]

§ 112. Prohibition on disclosure of name of minor children

The debtor may be required to provide information regarding a minor child involved in matters under this title but may not be required to disclose in the public records in the case the name of such minor child. The debtor may be required to disclose the name of such minor child in a nonpublic record that is maintained by the court and made available by the court for examination by the United States trustee, the trustee, and the auditor (if any) serving under section 586(f) of title 28, in the case. The court, the United States trustee, the trustee, and such auditor shall not disclose the name of such minor child maintained in such nonpublic record. (Added Pub.L. 109–8, Title II, § 233(a), Apr. 20, 2005, 119 Stat. 74.)

HISTORICAL AND STATUTORY NOTES

Revision Notes and Legislative Reports

2005 Acts. House Report No. 109–31(Part I), see 2005 U.S. Code Cong. and Adm. News, p. 88.

Effective and Applicability Provisions

2005 Acts. Amendments by Pub.L. 109–8 effective, except as otherwise provided, 180 days after April 20, 2005, and inapplicable with respect to cases commenced under Title 11 before the effective date, see Pub.L. 109–8, § 1501, set out as a note under 11 U.S.C.A. § 101.

CHAPTER 3—CASE ADMINISTRATION

HISTORICAL AND STATUTORY NOTES

Effective and Applicability Provisions

2005 Acts. Amendments by Pub.L. 109–8, § 434, effective, 60 days after the date on which rules are prescribed under 28 U.S.C.A. § 2075, to establish forms to be used to comply with 11 U.S.C.A. § 308, see Pub.L. 109–8, § 434(b), set out as a note under 11 U.S.C.A. § 308.

Amendments by Pub.L. 109–8 effective, except as otherwise provided, 180 days after April 20, 2005, and inapplicable with respect to cases commenced under Title 11 before the effective date, see Pub.L. 109–8, § 1501, set out as a note under 11 U.S.C.A. § 101.

CROSS REFERENCES

Applicability of this chapter to,
  Cases under Chapters 7, 11, 12, or 13 of this title, see 11 USCA § 103.
  Investor protection liquidation proceedings, see 15 USCA § 78fff.

SUBCHAPTER I—COMMENCEMENT OF A CASE

§ 301. Voluntary cases

(a) A voluntary case under a chapter of this title is commenced by the filing with the bankruptcy court of a petition under such chapter by an entity that may be a debtor under such chapter.

(b) The commencement of a voluntary case under a chapter of this title constitutes an order for relief under such chapter.

(Pub.L. 95–598, Nov. 6, 1978, 92 Stat. 2558; Pub.L. 109–8, Title V, § 501(b), Apr. 20, 2005, 119 Stat. 118.)

HISTORICAL AND STATUTORY NOTES

Revision Notes and Legislative Reports

1978 Acts. Section 301 specifies the manner in which a voluntary bankruptcy case is commenced. The debtor files a petition under this section under the particular operative chapter of the bankruptcy code under which he wishes to proceed. The filing of the petition constitutes an order for relief in the case under that chapter. The section contains no change from current law, except for the use of the phrase "order for relief" instead of "adjudication." The term adjudication is replaced by a less pejorative phrase in light of the clear power of Congress to permit voluntary bankruptcy without the necessity for an adjudication, as under the 1898 act [former Title 11], which was adopted when voluntary bankruptcy was a concept not thoroughly tested. Senate Report No. 95–989.

2005 Acts. House Report No. 109–31(Part I), see 2005 U.S. Code Cong. and Adm. News, p. 88.

Legislative Statements

Sections 301, 302, 303, and 304, are all modified in the House amendment to adopt an idea contained in sections 301 and 303 of the Senate amendment requiring a petition commencing a case to be filed with the bankruptcy court. The exception contained in section 301 of the Senate bill relating to cases filed under chapter 9 is deleted. Chapter 9 cases will be handled by a bankruptcy court as are other title 11 cases.

Effective and Applicability Provisions

2005 Acts. Amendments by Pub.L. 109–8 effective, except as otherwise provided, 180 days after April 20, 2005, and inapplicable with respect to cases commenced under Title 11

before the effective date, see Pub.L. 109–8, § 1501, set out as a note under 11 U.S.C.A. § 101.

CROSS REFERENCES

Applicability of this section in Chapter 9 cases, see 11 USCA § 901.

Automatic stay, see 11 USCA § 362.

Commencement of Chapter 9 cases concerning certain unincorporated tax or special assessment districts, see 11 USCA § 921.

Exemptions elected in estates administered jointly, see 11 USCA § 522.

Fees, see 28 USCA § 1930.

"Petition" defined, see 11 USCA § 101.

Property of estate, see 11 USCA § 541.

§ 302. Joint cases

(a) A joint case under a chapter of this title is commenced by the filing with the bankruptcy court of a single petition under such chapter by an individual that may be a debtor under such chapter and such individual's spouse. The commencement of a joint case under a chapter of this title constitutes an order for relief under such chapter.

(b) After the commencement of a joint case, the court shall determine the extent, if any, to which the debtors' estates shall be consolidated.

(Pub.L. 95–598, Nov. 6, 1978, 92 Stat. 2558.)

HISTORICAL AND STATUTORY NOTES

Revision Notes and Legislative Reports

1978 Acts. A joint case is a voluntary bankruptcy case concerning a wife and husband. Under current law, there is no explicit provision for joint cases. Very often, however, in the consumer debtor context, a husband and wife are jointly liable on their debts, and jointly hold most of their property. A joint case will facilitate consolidation of their estates, to the benefit of both the debtors and their creditors, because the cost of administration will be reduced, and there will be only one filing fee.

Section 302 specifies that a joint case is commenced by the filing of a petition under an appropriate chapter by an individual and that individual's spouse. Thus, one spouse cannot take the other into bankruptcy without the other's knowledge or consent. The filing of the petition constitutes an order for relief under the chapter selected.

Subsection (b) requires the court to determine the extent, if any, to which the estates of the two debtors will be consolidated; that is, assets and liabilities combined in a single pool to pay creditors. Factors that will be relevant in the court's determination include the extent of jointly held property and the amount of jointly-owned debts. The section, of course, is not license to consolidate in order to avoid other provisions of the title to the detriment of either the debtors or their creditors. It is designed mainly for ease of administration. Senate Report No. 95–989.

CROSS REFERENCES

Automatic stay, see 11 USCA § 362.

Exempt property, see 11 USCA § 522.

Fees, see 28 USCA § 1930.

"Petition" defined, see 11 USCA § 101.

Property of estate, see 11 USCA § 541.

§ 303. Involuntary cases

(a) An involuntary case may be commenced only under chapter 7 or 11 of this title, and only against a person, except a farmer, family farmer, or a corporation that is not a moneyed, business, or commercial corporation, that may be a debtor under the chapter under which such case is commenced.

(b) An involuntary case against a person is commenced by the filing with the bankruptcy court of a petition under chapter 7 or 11 of this title—

(1) by three or more entities, each of which is either a holder of a claim against such person that is not contingent as to liability or the subject of a bona fide dispute as to liability or amount, or an indenture trustee representing such a holder, if such noncontingent, undisputed claims aggregate at least $15,775 [1] more than the value of any lien on property of the debtor securing such claims held by the holders of such claims;

(2) if there are fewer than 12 such holders, excluding any employee or insider of such person and any transferee of a transfer that is voidable under section 544, 545, 547, 548, 549, or 724(a) of this title, by one or more of such holders that hold in the aggregate at least $15,775 [1] of such claims;

(3) if such person is a partnership—

(A) by fewer than all of the general partners in such partnership; or

(B) if relief has been ordered under this title with respect to all of the general partners in such partnership, by a general partner in such partnership, the trustee of such a general partner, or a holder of a claim against such partnership; or

(4) by a foreign representative of the estate in a foreign proceeding concerning such person.

(c) After the filing of a petition under this section but before the case is dismissed or relief is ordered, a creditor holding an unsecured claim that is not contingent, other than a creditor filing under subsection (b) of this section, may join in the petition with the same effect as if such joining creditor were a petitioning creditor under subsection (b) of this section.

(d) The debtor, or a general partner in a partnership debtor that did not join in the petition, may file an answer to a petition under this section.

(e) After notice and a hearing, and for cause, the court may require the petitioners under this section to file a bond to indemnify the debtor for such amounts as the court may later allow under subsection (i) of this section.

(f) Notwithstanding section 363 of this title, except to the extent that the court orders otherwise, and until an order for relief in the case, any business of the debtor may continue to operate, and the debtor may continue to use, acquire, or dispose of property as if an involuntary case concerning the debtor had not been commenced.

(g) At any time after the commencement of an involuntary case under chapter 7 of this title but before an order for relief in the case, the court, on request of a party in interest, after notice to the debtor and a hearing, and if necessary to preserve the property of the estate or to prevent loss to the estate, may order the United States trustee to appoint an interim trustee under section 701 of this title to take possession of the property of the estate and to operate any business of the debtor. Before an order for relief, the debtor may regain possession of property in the possession of a trustee ordered appointed under this subsection if the debtor files such bond as the court requires, conditioned on the debtor's accounting for and delivering to the trustee, if there is an order for relief in the case, such property, or the value, as of the date the debtor regains possession, of such property.

(h) If the petition is not timely controverted, the court shall order relief against the debtor in an involuntary case under the chapter under which the petition was filed. Otherwise, after trial, the court shall order relief against the debtor in an involuntary case under the chapter under which the petition was filed, only if—

(1) the debtor is generally not paying such debtor's debts as such debts become due unless such debts are the subject of a bona fide dispute as to liability or amount; or

(2) within 120 days before the date of the filing of the petition, a custodian, other than a trustee, receiver, or agent appointed or authorized to take charge of less than substantially all of the property of the debtor for the purpose of enforcing a lien against such property, was appointed or took possession.

(i) If the court dismisses a petition under this section other than on consent of all petitioners and the debtor, and if the debtor does not waive the right to judgment under this subsection, the court may grant judgment—

(1) against the petitioners and in favor of the debtor for—

(A) costs; or

(B) a reasonable attorney's fee; or

(2) against any petitioner that filed the petition in bad faith, for—

(A) any damages proximately caused by such filing; or

(B) punitive damages.

(j) Only after notice to all creditors and a hearing may the court dismiss a petition filed under this section—

(1) on the motion of a petitioner;

(2) on consent of all petitioners and the debtor; or

(3) for want of prosecution.

(k)(1) If—

(A) the petition under this section is false or contains any materially false, fictitious, or fraudulent statement;

(B) the debtor is an individual; and

(C) the court dismisses such petition,

the court, upon the motion of the debtor, shall seal all the records of the court relating to such petition, and all references to such petition.

(2) If the debtor is an individual and the court dismisses a petition under this section, the court may enter an order prohibiting all consumer reporting agencies (as defined in section 603(f) of the Fair Credit Reporting Act (15 U.S.C. 1681a(f))) from making any consumer report (as defined in section 603(d) of that Act) that contains any information relating to such petition or to the case commenced by the filing of such petition.

(3) Upon the expiration of the statute of limitations described in section 3282 of title 18, for a violation of section 152 or 157 of such title, the court, upon the motion of the debtor and for good cause, may expunge any records relating to a petition filed under this section.

(Pub.L. 95–598, Nov. 6, 1978, 92 Stat. 2559; Pub. L. 98–353, Title III, §§ 426, 427, July 10, 1984, 98 Stat. 369; Pub.L. 99–554, Title II, §§ 204, 254, 283(b), Oct. 27, 1986, 100 Stat. 3097, 3105, 3116; Pub.L. 103–394, Title I, § 108(b), Oct. 22, 1994, 108 Stat. 4112; Pub.L. 109–8, Title III, § 332(b), Title VIII, § 802(d)(2), Title XII, § 1234(a), Apr. 20, 2005, 119 Stat. 103, 146, 204; Pub.L. 111–327, § 2(a)(9), Dec. 22, 2010, 124 Stat. 3558.)

1 Dollar amount as adjusted by the Judicial Conference of the United States. See Adjustment of Dollar Amounts notes set out under this section and 11 U.S.C.A. § 104.

HISTORICAL AND STATUTORY NOTES

Revision Notes and Legislative Reports

1978 Acts. Section 303 governs the commencement of involuntary cases under title 11. An involuntary case may be commenced only under chapter 7, Liquidation, or chapter 11, Reorganization. Involuntary cases are not permitted for municipalities, because to do so may constitute an invasion of State sovereignty contrary to the 10th amendment, and would constitute bad policy, by permitting the fate of a municipality, governed by officials elected by the people of the municipality, to be determined by a small number of creditors of the municipality. Involuntary chapter 13 cases are not permitted either. To do so would constitute bad policy, because chapter 13 only works when there is a willing debtor that wants to repay his creditors. Short of involuntary servitude, it is difficult to keep a debtor working for his creditors when he does not want to pay them back. See chapter 3, supra.

The exceptions contained in current law that prohibit involuntary cases against farmers, ranchers and eleemosynary institutions are continued. Farmers and ranchers are excepted because of the cyclical nature of their business. One drought year or one year of low prices, as a result of which a farmer is temporarily unable to pay his creditors, should not subject him to involuntary bankruptcy. Eleemosynary institutions, such as churches, schools, and charitable organizations and foundations, likewise are exempt from involuntary bankruptcy.

The provisions for involuntary chapter 11 cases is a slight change from present law, based on the proposed consolidation of the reorganization chapters. Currently, involuntary cases are permitted under chapters X and XII [chapters 10 and 12 of former Title 11] but not under chapter XI [chapter 11 of former Title 11]. The consolidation requires a single rule for all kinds of reorganization proceedings. Because the assets of an insolvent debtor belong equitably to his creditors, the bill permits involuntary cases in order that creditors may realize on their assets through reorganization as well as through liquidation.

Subsection (b) of the section specifies who may file an involuntary petition. As under current law, if the debtor has more than 12 creditors, three creditors must join in the involuntary petition. The dollar amount limitation is changed from current law to $5,000. The new amount applies both to liquidation and reorganization cases in order that there not be an artificial difference between the two chapters that would provide an incentive for one or the other. Subsection (b)(1) makes explicit the right of an indenture trustee to be one of the three petitioning creditors on behalf of the creditors the trustee represents under the indenture. If all of the general partners in a partnership are in bankruptcy, then the trustee of a single general partner may file an involuntary petition against the partnership. Finally, a foreign representative may file an involuntary case concerning the debtor in the foreign proceeding, in order to administer assets in this country. This subsection is not intended to overrule Bankruptcy Rule 104(d), which places certain restrictions on the transfer of claims for the purpose of commencing an involuntary case. That Rule will be continued under section 405(d) of this bill.

Subsection (c) permits creditors other than the original petitioning creditors to join in the petition with the same effect as if the joining creditor had been one of the original petitioning creditors. Thus, if the claim of one of the original petitioning creditors is disallowed, the case will not be dismissed for want of three creditors or want of $5,000 in petitioning claims if the joining creditor suffices to fulfill the statutory requirements.

Subsection (d) permits the debtor to file an answer to an involuntary petition. The subsection also permits a general partner in a partnership debtor to answer an involuntary petition against the partnership if he did not join in the petition. Thus, a partnership petition by less than all of the general partners is treated as an involuntary, not a voluntary, petition.

The court may, under subsection (e), require the petitioners to file a bond to indemnify the debtor for such amounts as the court may later allow under subsection (i). Subsection (i) provides for costs, attorneys fees, and damages in certain circumstances. The bonding requirement will discourage frivolous petitions as well as spiteful petitions based on a desire to embarrass the debtor (who may be a competitor of a petitioning creditor) or to put the debtor out of business without good cause. An involuntary petition may put a debtor out of business even if it is without foundation and is later dismissed.

Subsection (f) is both a clarification and a change from existing law. It permits the debtor to continue to operate any business of the debtor and to dispose of property as if the case had not been commenced. The court is permitted, however, to control the debtor's powers under this subsection by appropriate orders, such as where there is a fear that the debtor may attempt to abscond with assets, dispose of them at less than their fair value, or dismantle his business, all to the detriment of the debtor's creditors.

The court may also, under subsection (g), appoint an interim trustee to take possession of the debtor's property and to operate any business of the debtor, pending trial on the involuntary petition. The court may make such an order only on the request of a party in interest, and after notice to the debtor and a hearing. There must be a showing that a trustee is necessary to preserve the property of the estate or to prevent loss to the estate. The debtor may regain possession by posting a sufficient bond.

Subsection (h) provides the standard for an order for relief on an involuntary petition. If the petition is not timely controverted (the Rules of Bankruptcy Procedure will fix time limits), the court orders relief after a trial, only if the debtor is generally unable to pay its debts as they mature, or if the debtor has failed to pay a major portion of his debts as they become due, or if a custodian was appointed during the 90-day period preceding the filing of the petition. The first two tests are variations of the equity insolvency test. They represent the most significant departure from present law concerning the grounds for involuntary bankruptcy, which requires an act of bankruptcy. Proof of the commission of an act of bankruptcy has frequently required a showing that the debtor was insolvent on a "balance-sheet" test when the act was committed. This bill abolishes the concept of acts of bankruptcy.

The equity insolvency test has been in equity jurisprudence for hundreds of years, and though it is new in the bankruptcy context (except in chapter X [former chapter 10 of former Title 11 (former section 501 et seq. of former Title 11)]), the bankruptcy courts should have no difficulty in applying it. The third test, appointment of a custodian within ninety days before the petition, is provided for simplicity. It is not a partial re-enactment of acts of bankruptcy. If a custodian of all or substantially all of the property of the debtor has been appointed, this paragraph creates an irrebuttable presumption that the debtor is unable to pay its debts as they mature. Moreover, once a proceeding to liquidate assets has been commenced, the debtor's creditors have an absolute right to have the liquidation (or reorganization) proceed in the bankruptcy court and under the bankruptcy laws with all of the appropriate creditor and debtor protections that those laws provide. Ninety days gives creditors ample time in which to seek bankruptcy liquidation after the appointment of a custodian. If they wait beyond the ninety day period, they are not precluded from filing an involuntary petition. They are simply required to prove equity insolvency rather than the more easily provable custodian test.

Subsection (i) permits the court to award costs, reasonable attorney's fees, or damages if an involuntary petition is dismissed other than by consent of all petitioning creditors and the debtor. The damages that the court may award are those that may be caused by the taking of possession of the debtor's property under subsection (g) or section 1104 of the bankruptcy code. In addition, if a petitioning creditor filed the petition in bad faith, the court may award the debtor any damages proximately caused by the filing of the petition. These damages may include such items as loss of business during and after the pendency of the case, and so on. "Or" is not exclusive in this paragraph. The court may grant any or all of the damages provided for under the provision. Dismissal in the best interests of credits under section 305(a)(1) would not give rise to a damages claim.

Under subsection (j), the court may dismiss the petition by consent only after giving notice to all creditors. The purpose of the subsection is to prevent collusive settlements among the debtor and the petitioning creditors while other creditors, that wish to see relief ordered with respect to the debtor but that did not participate in the case, are left without sufficient protection.

Subsection (k) governs involuntary cases against foreign banks that are not engaged in business in the United States but that have assets located here. The subsection prevents a foreign bank from being placed into bankruptcy in this country unless a foreign proceeding against the bank is pending. The special protection afforded by this section is needed to prevent creditors from effectively closing down a foreign bank by the commencement of an involuntary bankruptcy case in this country unless that bank is involved in a proceeding under foreign law. An involuntary case commenced under this subsection gives the foreign representative and alternative to commencing a case ancillary to a foreign proceeding under section 304. Senate Report No. 95–989.

1984 Acts. Statements by Legislative Leaders, see 1984 U.S. Code Cong. and Adm. News, p. 576.

1986 Acts. House Report No. 99–764 and House Conference Report No. 99–958, see 1986 U.S. Code Cong. and Adm. News, p. 5227.

1994 Acts. House Report No. 103–835, see 1994 U.S. Code Cong. and Adm. News, p. 3340.

2005 Acts. House Report No. 109–31(Part I), see 2005 U.S. Code Cong. and Adm. News, p. 88.

Legislative Statements

Section 303(b)(1) is modified to make clear that unsecured claims against the debtor must be determined by taking into account liens securing property held by third parties.

Section 303(b)(3) adopts a provision contained in the Senate amendment indicating that an involuntary petition may be commenced against a partnership by fewer than all of the general partners in such partnership. Such action may be taken by fewer than all of the general partners notwithstanding a contrary agreement between the partners or State or local law.

Section 303(h)(1) in the House amendment is a compromise of standards found in H.R. 8200 as passed by the House and the Senate amendment pertaining to the standards that must be met in order to obtain an order for relief in an involuntary case under title 11. The language specifies that the court will order such relief only if the debtor is generally not paying debtor's debts as they become due.

Section 303(h)(2) reflects a compromise pertaining to section 543 of title 11 relating to turnover of property by a custodian. It provides an alternative test to support an order

for relief in an involuntary case. If a custodian, other than a trustee, receiver, or agent appointed or authorized to take charge of less than substantially all of the property of the debtor for the purpose of enforcing a lien against such property, was appointed or took possession within 120 days before the date of the filing of the petition, then the court may order relief in the involuntary case. The test under section 303(h)(2) differs from section 3a(5) of the Bankruptcy Act [section 21(a)(5) of former Title 11], which requires an involuntary case to be commenced before the earlier of time such custodian was appointed or took possession. The test in section 303(h)(2) authorizes an order for relief to be entered in an involuntary case from the later date on which the custodian was appointed or took possession.

References in Text

Section 603 of the Fair Credit Reporting Act, referred to in subsec. (k)(2), is Pub.L. 90–321, Title VI, § 603, as added Pub.L. 91–508, Title IV, § 601, Oct. 26, 1970, 84 Stat. 1128, and amended, which is classified to 15 U.S.C.A. § 1681a.

Effective and Applicability Provisions

2013 Acts. Increase of dollar amounts by Judicial Conference of the United States by notice published Feb. 21, 2013, 78 F.R. 12089 effective April 1, 2013, and increase not applicable to cases commenced before the effective date of the adjustments, i.e., April 1, 2013. See Adjustment of Dollar Amounts notes under 11 U.S.C.A. § 104 and this section.

2010 Acts. Increase of dollar amounts by Judicial Conference of the United States by notice published Feb. 25, 2010, 75 F.R. 8747 effective April 1, 2010, and increase not applicable to cases commenced before the effective date of the adjustments, i.e., April 1, 2010. See Adjustment of Dollar Amounts notes under 11 U.S.C.A. § 104 and this section.

2007 Acts. Increase of dollar amounts by Judicial Conference of the United States by notice published Feb. 14, 2007, 72 F.R. 7082 effective April 1, 2007, and increase not applicable to cases commenced before the effective date of the adjustments, i.e., April 1, 2007. See Adjustment of Dollar Amounts notes under 11 U.S.C.A. § 104 and this section.

2005 Acts. Pub.L. 109–8, Title XII, § 1234(b), Apr. 20, 2005, 119 Stat. 204, provided that: "This section and the amendments made by this section [amending this section] shall take effect on the date of the enactment of this Act [Apr. 20, 2005] and shall apply with respect to cases commenced under title 11 of the United States Code before, on, and after such date."

Amendments by sections 332(b) and 802(d)(2) of Pub.L. 109–8 effective, except as otherwise provided, 180 days after April 20, 2005, and inapplicable with respect to cases commenced under Title 11 before the effective date, see Pub.L. 109–8, § 1501, set out as a note under 11 U.S.C.A. § 101.

2004 Acts. Adjustment of dollar amounts by Judicial Conference of the United States by notice dated Feb. 18, 2004, 69 F.R. 8482 effective April 1, 2004, and adjustment not applicable to cases commenced before the effective date of the adjustments, i.e., April 1, 2004. See Adjustment of Dollar Amounts notes under 11 U.S.C.A. § 104 and this section.

2001 Acts. Adjustment of dollar amounts by Judicial Conference of the United States by notice dated Feb. 20, 2001, 66 F.R. 10910 effective April 1, 2001, and adjustment not applicable to cases commenced before the effective date of the adjustments, i.e., April 1, 2001. See Adjustment of Dollar Amounts notes under 11 U.S.C.A. § 104 and this section.

1998 Acts. Adjustment of dollar amounts by Judicial Conference of the United States by notice dated Feb. 3, 1998, 63 F.R. 7179 effective April 1, 1998, and adjustment not applicable to cases commenced before the effective date of the adjustments, i.e., April 1, 1998. See Adjustment of Dollar Amounts notes under 11 U.S.C.A. § 104 and this section.

1994 Acts. Amendment by Pub.L. 103–394 effective on Oct. 22, 1994, and not to apply with respect to cases commenced under Title 11 of the United States Code before Oct. 22, 1994, see section 702 of Pub.L. 103–394, set out as a note under section 101 of this title.

1986 Acts. Amendment by Pub.L. 99–554 effective 30 days after Oct. 27, 1986, except as otherwise provided for, see section 302(a) of Pub.L. 99–554, set out as a note under section 581 of Title 28, Judiciary and Judicial Procedure.

Amendment by Pub.L. 99–554, § 204, not to become effective in or with respect to certain specified judicial districts until, or apply to cases while pending in such district before, the expiration of the 270-day period beginning 30 days after Oct. 27, 1986, or of the 30-day period beginning on the date the Attorney General certifies under section 303 of Pub.L. 99–554 the region specified in a paragraph of section 581(a) of Title 28, as amended by section 111(a) of Pub.L. 99–554, that includes such district, whichever occurs first, see section 302(d)(1) of Pub.L. 99–554, set out as a note under section 581 of Title 28.

Amendment by Pub.L. 99–554, § 204, not to become effective in or with respect to certain specified judicial districts until, or apply to cases while pending in such districts before, the expiration of the 2-year period beginning 30 days after Oct. 27, 1986, or of the 30-day period beginning on the date the Attorney General certifies under section 303 of Pub.L. 99–554 the region specified in a paragraph of section 581(a) of Title 28, as amended by section 111(a) of Pub.L. 99–554, that includes such district, whichever occurs first, see section 302(d)(2) of Pub.L. 99–554, set out as a note under section 581 of Title 28.

Amendment by Pub.L. 99–554, § 204, not to become effective in or with respect to judicial districts established for the States of Alabama and North Carolina until, or apply to cases while pending in such district before, such district elects to be included in a bankruptcy region established in section 581(a) of Title 28, as amended by section 111(a) of Pub.L. 99–554, or Oct. 1, 2002, whichever occurs first, and, except as otherwise provided, with respect to cases under chapters 7, 11, 12, and 13 of Title 11 commenced before 30 days after Oct. 27, 1986, and pending in a judicial district in the States of Alabama or North Carolina before any election made under section 302(d)(3)(A) of Pub.L. 99–554 by such district becomes effective or Oct. 1, 2002, whichever occurs first, amendments by Pub.L. 99–554 not to apply until Oct. 1, 2003, or the expiration of the 1-year period beginning on the date such election becomes effective, whichever occurs first, and further, in any judicial district in Alabama or North Carolina not making the election described in section 302(d)(3)(A) of Pub.L. 99–554, any person appointed under regulations issued by the Judicial Conference to administer estates in cases under Title 11 authorized to establish, etc., a panel of private trustees, and to supervise cases and trustees in cases under chapters 7, 11, 12, and 13 of Title 11, until amendments by sections 201 to 231 of Pub.L. 99–554 effective in such district, see section 302(d)(3)(A) to (F), (H), and (I) of Pub.L. 99–554, set out as a note under section 581 of Title 28.

Amendment by Pub.L. 99–554, § 204, except as otherwise provided, with respect to cases under chapters 7, 11, 12, and 13 of Title 11 commenced before 30 days after Oct. 27, 1986, and pending in a judicial district referred to in section 581(a) of Title 28, as amended by section 111(a) of Pub.L. 99–554, for which a United States trustee is not authorized before 30 days after Oct. 27, 1986 to be appointed, not applicable until the expiration of the 3-year period beginning on Oct. 27, 1986, or of the 1-year period beginning on the date the Attorney General certifies under section 303 of Pub.L. 99–554 the region specified in a paragraph of such section 581(a) that includes, such district, whichever occurs first, see section 302(e)(1), (2) of Pub.L. 99–554, set out as a note under section 581 of Title 28.

Amendment by Pub.L. 99–554, § 254, effective 30 days after Oct. 27, 1986, but not applicable to cases commenced under this title before that date, see section 302(a), (c)(1) of Pub.L. 99–554, set out as a note under section 581 of Title 28.

Amendment by Pub.L. 99–554, § 283, effective 30 days after Oct. 27, 1986, see section 302(a) of Pub.L. 99–554, set out as a note under section 581 of Title 28.

1984 Acts. Amendment by sections 426(a) and 427 of Pub.L. 98–353 effective with respect to cases filed 90 days after July 10, 1984, and amendment by section 426(b) of Pub.L. 98–353 effective July 10, 1984, see section 552(a), (b) of Pub.L. 98–353, set out as a note under section 101 of this title.

Separability of Provisions

If any provision of or amendment made by Pub.L. 103–394 or the application of such provision or amendment to any person or circumstance is held to be unconstitutional, the remaining provisions of and amendments made by Pub.L. 103–394 and the application of such provisions and amendments to any person or circumstance shall not be affected thereby, see section 701 of Pub.L. 103–394, set out as a note under section 101 of this title.

Adjustment of Dollar Amounts

For adjustment of dollar amounts specified in subsec. (b)(1), (2) of this section by the Judicial Conference of the United States, effective Apr. 1, 2016, see note set out under 11 U.S.C.A. § 104.

By notice published Feb. 22, 2016, 81 F.R. 8748, the Judicial Conference of the United States adjusted the dollar amounts in provisions specified in subsec. (b)(1), (2) of this section, effective Apr. 1, 2016, as follows:

In subsec. (b)(1) adjusted $15,325 to $15,775.

In subsec. (b)(2) adjusted $15,325 to $15,775.

By notice published Feb. 21, 2013, 78 F.R. 12089, the Judicial Conference of the United States adjusted the dollar amounts in provisions specified in subsec. (b)(1), (2) of this section, effective Apr. 1, 2013, as follows:

In subsec. (b)(1) adjusted $14,425 to $15,325.

In subsec. (b)(2) adjusted $14,425 to $15,325.

By notice published Feb. 25, 2010, 75 F.R. 8747, the Judicial Conference of the United States adjusted the dollar amounts in provisions specified in subsec. (b)(1), (2) of this section, effective Apr. 1, 2010, as follows:

In subsec. (b)(1) adjusted $13,475 to $14,425.

In subsec. (b)(2) adjusted $13,475 to $14,425.

By notice published Feb. 14, 2007, 72 F.R. 7082, the Judicial Conference of the United States adjusted the dollar amounts in provisions specified in subsec. (b)(1), (2) of this section, effective Apr. 1, 2007, as follows:

    In subsec. (b)(1) adjusted $12,300 to $13,475.

    In subsec. (b)(2) adjusted $12,300 to $13,475.

By notice dated Feb. 18, 2004, 69 F.R. 8482, the Judicial Conference of the United States adjusted the dollar amounts in provisions specified in subsec. (b)(1), (2) of this section, effective Apr. 1, 2004, as follows:

    In subsec. (b)(1) adjusted $11,625 to $12,300.

    In subsec. (b)(2) adjusted $11,625 to $12,300.

By notice dated Feb. 20, 2001, 66 F.R. 10910, the Judicial Conference of the United States adjusted the dollar amounts in provisions specified in subsec. (b)(1), (2) of this section, effective Apr. 1, 2001, as follows:

    In subsec. (b)(1) adjusted $10,775 to $11,625.

    In subsec. (b)(2) adjusted $10,775 to $11,625.

By notice dated Feb. 3, 1998, 63 F.R. 7179, the Judicial Conference of the United States adjusted the dollar amounts in provisions specified in subsec. (b)(1), (2) of this section, effective Apr. 1, 1998, as follows:

    In subsec. (b)(1) adjusted $10,000 to $10,775.

    In subsec. (b)(2) adjusted $10,000 to $10,775.

CROSS REFERENCES

Allowance of administrative expenses incurred by creditor filing petition, see 11 USCA § 503.

Automatic stay, see 11 USCA § 362.

Exempt property, see 11 USCA § 522.

Fees, see 28 USCA § 1930.

Involuntary case, future adjustments, see 11 USCA § 104.

Jury trials, see 28 USCA § 1411.

Lists, schedules, statements and fees, see Fed. Bankr. Proc. Form B2000, 11 USCA.

"Petition" defined, see 11 USCA § 101.

Postpetition transactions, see 11 USCA § 549.

Property of estate, see 11 USCA § 541.

Sharing of compensation between attorneys, see 11 USCA § 504.

[§ 304. Repealed. Pub.L. 109–8, Title VIII, § 802(d)(3), Apr. 20, 2005, 119 Stat. 146]

HISTORICAL AND STATUTORY NOTES

Section, Pub.L. 95–598, Nov. 6, 1978, 92 Stat. 2560, related to cases ancillary to foreign proceedings.

See, now, 11 U.S.C.A. § 1501 et seq. and 28 U.S.C.A. § 1410.

Effective Date of Repeal

Repeal effective, except as otherwise provided, 180 days after April 20, 2005, and inapplicable with respect to cases commenced under Title 11 before the effective date, see Pub.L. 109–8, § 1501, set out as a note under 11 U.S.C.A. § 101.

§ 305. Abstention

(a) The court, after notice and a hearing, may dismiss a case under this title, or may suspend all proceedings in a case under this title, at any time if—

    (1) the interests of creditors and the debtor would be better served by such dismissal or suspension; or

    (2)(A) a petition under section 1515 for recognition of a foreign proceeding has been granted; and

    (B) the purposes of chapter 15 of this title would be best served by such dismissal or suspension.

(b) A foreign representative may seek dismissal or suspension under subsection (a)(2) of this section.

(c) An order under subsection (a) of this section dismissing a case or suspending all proceedings in a case, or a decision not so to dismiss or suspend, is not reviewable by appeal or otherwise by the court of appeals under section 158(d), 1291, or 1292 of title 28 or by the Supreme Court of the United States under section 1254 of title 28.

(Pub.L. 95–598, Nov. 6, 1978, 92 Stat. 2561; Pub.L. 101–650, Title III, § 309(a), Dec. 1, 1990, 104 Stat. 5113; Pub.L. 102–198, § 5, Dec. 9, 1991, 105 Stat. 1623; Pub.L. 109–8, Title VIII, § 802(d)(6), Apr. 20, 2005, 119 Stat. 146.)

HISTORICAL AND STATUTORY NOTES

Revision Notes and Legislative Reports

1978 Acts. A principle of the common law requires a court with jurisdiction over a particular matter to take jurisdiction. This section recognizes that there are cases in which it would be appropriate for the court to decline jurisdiction. Abstention under this section, however, is of jurisdiction over the entire case. Abstention from jurisdiction over a particular proceeding in a case is governed by proposed 28 U.S.C. 1471(c). Thus, the court is permitted, if the interests of creditors and the debtor would be better served by dismissal of the case or suspension of all proceedings in the case, to so order. The court may dismiss or suspend under the first paragraph, for example, if an arrangement is being worked out by creditors and the debtor out of court, there is no prejudice to the results of creditors in that arrangement, and an involuntary case has been commenced by a few recalcitrant creditors to provide a basis for future threats to extract full payment. The less expensive out-of-court workout may better serve the interests in the case. Likewise, if there is pending a foreign proceeding concerning the debtor and the factors specified in proposed 11 U.S.C. 304(c) warrant dismissal or suspension, the court may so act.

Subsection (b) gives a foreign representative authority to appear in the bankruptcy court to request dismissal or suspension. Subsection (c) makes the dismissal or suspension order nonreviewable by appeal or otherwise. The bankruptcy court, based on its experience and discretion is vested with the power of decision. Senate Report No. 95–989.

1990 Acts. Senate Report No. 101–416, see 1990 U.S.Code Cong. and Adm.News, p. 6802.

1991 Acts. House Report No. 102–322, see 1991 U.S.Code Cong. and Adm.News, p. 1303.

2005 Acts. House Report No. 109–31(Part I), see 2005 U.S. Code Cong. and Adm. News, p. 88.

References in Text

Chapter 15 of this title, referred to in subsec. (a)(2)(B), is classified to 11 U.S.C.A. § 1501 et seq.

Effective and Applicability Provisions

2005 Acts. Amendments by Pub.L. 109–8 effective, except as otherwise provided, 180 days after April 20, 2005, and inapplicable with respect to cases commenced under Title 11 before the effective date, see Pub.L. 109–8, § 1501, set out as a note under 11 U.S.C.A. § 101.

§ 306. Limited appearance

An appearance in a bankruptcy court by a foreign representative in connection with a petition or request under section 303 or 305 of this title does not submit such foreign representative to the jurisdiction of any court in the United States for any other purpose, but the bankruptcy court may condition any order under section 303 or 305 of this title on compliance by such foreign representative with the orders of such bankruptcy court.

(Pub.L. 95–598, Nov. 6, 1978, 92 Stat. 2561; Pub.L. 109–8, Title VIII, § 802(d)(5), Apr. 20, 2005, 119 Stat. 146.)

HISTORICAL AND STATUTORY NOTES

Revision Notes and Legislative Reports

1978 Acts. Section 306 permits a foreign representative that is seeking dismissal or suspension under section 305 of an ancillary case or that is appearing in connection with a petition under section 303 or 304 to appear without subjecting himself to the jurisdiction of any other court in the United States, including State courts. The protection is necessary to allow the foreign representative to present his case and the case of the foreign estate, without waiving the normal jurisdictional rules of the foreign country. That is, creditors in this country will still have to seek redress against the foreign estate according to the host country's jurisdictional rules. Any other result would permit local creditors to obtain unfair advantage by filing an involuntary case, thus requiring the foreign representative to appear, and then obtaining local jurisdiction over the representative in connection with his appearance in this country. That kind of bankruptcy law would legalize an ambush technique that has frequently been rejected by the common law in other contexts.

However, the bankruptcy court is permitted under section 306 to condition any relief under section 303, 304, or 305 on the compliance by the foreign representative with the orders of the bankruptcy court. The last provision is not carte blanche to the bankruptcy court to require the foreign representative to submit to jurisdiction in other courts contrary to the general policy of the section. It is designed to enable the bankruptcy court to enforce its own orders that are necessary to the appropriate relief granted under section 303, 304, or 305. Senate Report No. 95–989.

2005 Acts. House Report No. 109–31(Part I), see 2005 U.S. Code Cong. and Adm. News, p. 88.

Effective and Applicability Provisions

2005 Acts. Amendments by Pub.L. 109–8 effective, except as otherwise provided, 180 days after April 20, 2005, and inapplicable with respect to cases commenced under Title 11 before the effective date, see Pub.L. 109–8, § 1501, set out as a note under 11 U.S.C.A. § 101.

§ 307. United States trustee

The United States trustee may raise and may appear and be heard on any issue in any case or proceed-ing under this title but may not file a plan pursuant to section 1121(c) of this title.

(Added Pub.L. 99–554, Title II, § 205(a), Oct. 27, 1986, 100 Stat. 3098.)

HISTORICAL AND STATUTORY NOTES

Revision Notes and Legislative Reports

1986 Acts. House Report No. 99–764 and House Conference Report No. 99–958, see 1986 U.S.Code Cong. and Adm. News, p. 5227.

Effective and Applicability Provisions

1986 Acts. Enactment by Pub.L. 99–554, effective 30 days after Oct. 27, 1986, except as otherwise provided for, see section 302(a) of Pub.L. 99–554, set out as a note under section 581 of Title 28, Judiciary and Judicial Procedure.

Enactment by Pub.L. 99–554, § 205(a), not to become effective in or with respect to certain specified judicial districts until, or apply to cases while pending in such district before, the expiration of the 270-day period beginning 30 days after Oct. 27, 1986, or of the 30-day period beginning on the date the Attorney General certifies under section 303 of Pub.L. 99–554 the region specified in a paragraph of section 581(a) of Title 28, as amended by section 111(a) of Pub.L. 99–554, that includes such district, whichever occurs first, see section 302(d)(1) of Pub.L. 99–554, set out as a note under section 581 of Title 28.

Enactment by Pub.L. 99–554, § 205(a), not to become effective in or with respect to certain specified judicial districts until, or apply to cases while pending in such district before, the expiration of the 2-year period beginning 30 days after Oct. 27, 1986, or of the 30-day period beginning on the date the Attorney General certifies under section 303 of Pub.L. 99–554 the region specified in a paragraph of section 581(a) of Title 28, as amended by section 111(a) of Pub.L. 99–554, that includes such district, whichever occurs first, see section 302(d)(2) of Pub.L. 99–554, set out as a note under section 581 of Title 28.

Enactment by Pub.L. 99–554, § 205(a), not to become effective in or with respect to judicial districts established for the States of Alabama and North Carolina until, or apply to cases while pending in such district before, such district elects to be included in a bankruptcy region established in section 581(a) of Title 28, as amended by section 111(a) of Pub.L. 99–554, or Oct. 1, 2002, whichever occurs first, and, except as otherwise provided for, with respect to cases under chapters 7, 11, 12, and 13 of Title 11 commenced before 30 days after Oct. 27, 1986, and pending in a judicial district in the States of Alabama or North Carolina before an election made under section 302(d)(3)(A) of Pub.L. 99–554 by such district becomes effective or Oct. 1, 2002, whichever occurs first, amendments by Pub.L. 99–554 not to apply until Oct. 1, 2003, or the expiration of the 1-year period beginning on the date such election becomes effective, whichever occurs first, and further, in any judicial district in Alabama or North Carolina not making the election described in section 302(d)(3)(A) of Pub.L. 99–554, any person appointed under regulations issued by the Judicial Conference to administer estates in cases under Title 11 authorized to establish, etc., a panel of private trustees, and to supervise cases and trustees in cases under chapters 7, 11, 12, and 13 of Title 11, until amendments by sections 201 to 231 of Pub.L. 99–554 effective in such district, see section

302(d)(3)(A) to (F), (H), and (I), of Pub.L. 99–554, set out as a note under section 581 of Title 28.

Standing and Authority of Bankruptcy Administrator

Pub.L. 101–650, Title III, § 317(b), Dec. 1, 1990, 104 Stat. 5115, provided that: "A bankruptcy administrator may raise and may appear and be heard on any issue in any case under title 11, United States Code, but may not file a plan pursuant to section 1121(c) of such title."

§ 308. Debtor reporting requirements

(a) For purposes of this section, the term "profitability" means, with respect to a debtor, the amount of money that the debtor has earned or lost during current and recent fiscal periods.

(b) A debtor in a small business case shall file periodic financial and other reports containing information including—

(1) the debtor's profitability;

(2) reasonable approximations of the debtor's projected cash receipts and cash disbursements over a reasonable period;

(3) comparisons of actual cash receipts and disbursements with projections in prior reports;

(4) whether the debtor is—

(A) in compliance in all material respects with postpetition requirements imposed by this title and the Federal Rules of Bankruptcy Procedure; and

(B) timely filing tax returns and other required government filings and paying taxes and other administrative expenses when due;

(5) if the debtor is not in compliance with the requirements referred to in paragraph (4)(A) or filing tax returns and other required government filings and making the payments referred to in paragraph (4)(B), what the failures are and how, at what cost, and when the debtor intends to remedy such failures; and

(6) such other matters as are in the best interests of the debtor and creditors, and in the public interest in fair and efficient procedures under chapter 11 of this title.

(Added Pub.L. 109–8, Title IV, § 434(a)(1), Apr. 20, 2005, 119 Stat. 111; amended Pub.L. 111–327, § 2(a)(10), Dec. 22, 2010, 124 Stat. 3558.)

HISTORICAL AND STATUTORY NOTES

Revision Notes and Legislative Reports

2005 Acts. House Report No. 109–31(Part I), see 2005 U.S. Code Cong. and Adm. News, p. 88.

References in Text

The Federal Rules of Bankruptcy Procedure, referred to in subsec. (b)(4)(A), are set out in the Appendix to this title.

Chapter 11 of this title, referred to in subsec. (b)(6), is 11 U.S.C.A. § 1101 et seq.

Effective and Applicability Provisions

2005 Acts. Pub.L. 109–8, Title IV, § 434(b), Apr. 20, 2005, 119 Stat. 111, provided that: "The amendments made by subsection (a) [enacting this section] shall take effect 60 days after the date on which rules are prescribed under section 2075 of title 28, United States Code, to establish forms to be used to comply with section 308 of title 11, United States Code, as added by subsection (a) [enacting this section]. [See Bankruptcy Form No. 25C, eff. Dec. 1, 2008, set out in the Appendix to this title.]"

Amendments by Pub.L. 109–8 effective, except as otherwise provided, 180 days after April 20, 2005, and inapplicable with respect to cases commenced under Title 11 before the effective date, see Pub.L. 109–8, § 1501, set out as a note under 11 U.S.C.A. § 101.

SUBCHAPTER II—OFFICERS

§ 321. Eligibility to serve as trustee

(a) A person may serve as trustee in a case under this title only if such person is—

(1) an individual that is competent to perform the duties of trustee and, in a case under chapter 7, 12, or 13 of this title, resides or has an office in the judicial district within which the case is pending, or in any judicial district adjacent to such district; or

(2) a corporation authorized by such corporation's charter or bylaws to act as trustee, and, in a case under chapter 7, 12, or 13 of this title, having an office in at least one of such districts.

(b) A person that has served as an examiner in the case may not serve as trustee in the case.

(c) The United States trustee for the judicial district in which the case is pending is eligible to serve as trustee in the case if necessary.

(Pub.L. 95–598, Nov. 6, 1978, 92 Stat. 2561; Pub. L. 98–353, Title III, § 428, July 10, 1984, 98 Stat. 369; Pub.L. 99–554, Title II, §§ 206, 257(c), Oct. 27, 1986, 100 Stat. 3098, 3114.)

HISTORICAL AND STATUTORY NOTES

Revision Notes and Legislative Reports

1978 Acts. Section 321 is adapted from current Bankruptcy Act section 45 [section 73 of former Title 11] and Bankruptcy Rule 209. Subsection (a) specifies that an individual may serve as trustee in a bankruptcy case only if he is competent to perform the duties of trustee and resides or has an office in the judicial district within which the case is pending, or in an adjacent judicial district. A corporation must be authorized by its charter or bylaws to act as trustee, and, for chapter 7 or 13 cases, must have an office in any of the above mentioned judicial districts. Senate Report No. 95–989.

1984 Acts. Statements by Legislative Leaders, see 1984 U.S.Code Cong. and Adm.News, p. 576.

1986 Acts. House Report No. 99–764 and House Conference Report No. 99–958, see 1986 U.S.Code Cong. and Adm. News, p. 5227.

Legislative Statements

Section 321 indicates that an examiner may not serve as a trustee in the case.

Effective and Applicability Provisions

1986 Acts. Amendment by Pub.L. 99–554 effective 30 days after Oct. 27, 1986, except as otherwise provided for, see section 302(a) of Pub.L. 99–554, set out as a note under section 581 of Title 28, Judiciary and Judicial Procedure.

Amendment by Pub.L. 99–554, § 206, not to become effective in or with respect to certain specified judicial districts until, or apply to cases while pending in such district before, the expiration of the 270-day period beginning 30 days after Oct. 27, 1986, or of the 30-day period beginning on the date the Attorney General certifies under section 303 of Pub.L. 99–554 the region specified in a paragraph of section 581(a) of Title 28, as amended by section 111(a) of Pub.L. 99–554, that includes such district, whichever occurs first, see section 302(d)(1) of Pub.L. 99–554, set out as a note under section 581 of Title 28.

Amendment by Pub.L. 99–554, § 206, not to become effective in or with respect to certain specified judicial districts until, or apply to cases while pending in such district before, the expiration of the 2-year period beginning 30 days after Oct. 27, 1986, or of the 30-day period beginning on the date the Attorney General certifies under section 303 of Pub.L. 99–554 the region specified in a paragraph of section 581(a) of Title 28, as amended by section 111(a) of Pub.L. 99–554, that includes such district, whichever occurs first, see section 302(d)(2) of Pub.L. 99–554, set out as a note under section 581 of Title 28.

Amendment by Pub.L. 99–554, § 206, not to become effective in or with respect to judicial districts established for the States of Alabama and North Carolina until, or apply to cases while pending in such district before, such district elects to be included in a bankruptcy region established in section 581(a) of Title 28, as amended by section 111(a) of Pub.L. 99–554, or Oct. 1, 2002, whichever occurs first, and, except as otherwise provided for, with respect to cases under chapters 7, 11, 12, and 13 of Title 11 commenced before 30 days after Oct. 27, 1986, and pending in a judicial district in the States of Alabama or North Carolina before any election made under section 302(d)(3)(A) of Pub.L. 99–554 by such district becomes effective or Oct. 1, 2002, whichever occurs first, amendments by Pub.L. 99–554 not to apply until Oct. 1, 2003, or the expiration of the 1-year period beginning on the date such election becomes effective whichever occurs first, and further, in any judicial district in Alabama or North Carolina not making the election described in section 302(d)(3)(A) of Pub.L. 99–554, any person appointed under regulations issued by the Judicial Conference to administer estates in cases under Title 11 authorized to establish, etc., a panel of private trustees, and to supervise cases and trustees in cases under chapters 7, 11, 12, and 13 of Title 11, until amendments by sections 201 to 231 of Pub.L. 99–554 effective in such district, see section 302(d)(3)(A) to (F), (H), and (I) of Pub.L. 99–554, set out as a note under section 581 of Title 28.

Amendment by Pub.L. 99–554, § 206, except as otherwise provided, with respect to cases under chapters, 7, 11, 12, and 13 of Title 11 commenced before 30 days after Oct. 27, 1986, and pending in a judicial district referred to in section 581(a) of Title 28, as amended by section 111(a) of Pub.L. 99–554, for which a United States trustee is not authorized before 30 days after Oct. 27, 1986 to be appointed, not applicable until the expiration of the 3-year period beginning on Oct. 27, 1986, or of the 1-year period beginning on the date the Attorney General certifies under section 303 of Pub.L. 99–554 the region specified in a paragraph of such section 581(a) that

includes, such district, whichever occurs first, see section 302(e)(1), (2) of Pub.L. 99–554, set out as a note under section 581 of Title 28.

Amendment by Pub.L. 99–554, § 257(c) effective 30 days after Oct. 27, 1986, but not applicable with respect to cases commenced under this title before that date, see section 302(a), (c)(1) of Pub.L. 99–554, set out as a note under section 581 of Title 28.

1984 Acts. Amendment by Pub.L. 98–353 effective with respect to cases filed 90 days after July 10, 1984, see section 552(a), formerly 553(a), of Pub.L. 98–353, set out as a note under section 101 of this title.

§ 322. Qualification of trustee

(a) Except as provided in subsection (b)(1), a person selected under section 701, 702, 703, 1104, 1163, 1202, or 1302 of this title to serve as trustee in a case under this title qualifies if before seven days after such selection, and before beginning official duties, such person has filed with the court a bond in favor of the United States conditioned on the faithful performance of such official duties.

(b)(1) The United States trustee qualifies wherever such trustee serves as trustee in a case under this title.

(2) The United States trustee shall determine—

(A) the amount of a bond required to be filed under subsection (a) of this section; and

(B) the sufficiency of the surety on such bond.

(c) A trustee is not liable personally or on such trustee's bond in favor of the United States for any penalty or forfeiture incurred by the debtor.

(d) A proceeding on a trustee's bond may not be commenced after two years after the date on which such trustee was discharged.

(Pub.L. 95–598, Nov. 6, 1978, 92 Stat. 2562; Pub. L. 98–353, Title III, § 429, July 10, 1984, 98 Stat. 369; Pub.L. 99–554, Title II, §§ 207, 257(d), Oct. 27, 1986, 100 Stat. 3098, 3114; Pub.L. 103–394, Title V, § 501(d)(3), Oct. 22, 1994, 108 Stat. 4143; Pub.L. 111–16, § 2(2), May 7, 2009, 123 Stat. 1607.)

HISTORICAL AND STATUTORY NOTES

Revision Notes and Legislative Reports

1978 Acts. A trustee qualifies in a case by filing, within five days after selection, a bond in favor of the United States, conditioned on the faithful performance of his official duties. This section is derived from the Bankruptcy Act section 50b [section 78(b) of former Title 11]. The court is required to determine the amount of the bond and the sufficiency of the surety on the bond. Subsection (c), derived from Bankruptcy Act section 50i [section 78(i) of former Title 11], relieves the trustee from personal liability and from liability on his bond for any penalty or forfeiture incurred by the debtor. Subsection (d), derived from section 50m [section 78(m) of former Title 11], fixes a two-year statute of limitations on any action on a trustee's bond. Finally, subsection (e) dispenses with the bonding requirement for the United States trustee. Senate Report No. 95–989.

1984 Acts. Statements by Legislative Leaders, see 1984 U.S.Code Cong. and Adm.News, p. 576.

1986 Acts. House Report No. 99–764 and House Conference Report No. 99–958, see 1986 U.S.Code Cong. and Adm. News, p. 5227.

1994 Acts. House Report No. 103–835, see 1994 U.S. Code Cong. and Adm. News, p. 3340.

Legislative Statements

Section 322(a) is modified to include a trustee serving in a railroad reorganization under subchapter IV of chapter 11.

Effective and Applicability Provisions

2009 Acts. Amendments by Pub.L. 111–16 effective Dec. 1, 2009, see Pub.L. 111–16, § 7, set out as a note under 11 U.S.C.A. § 109.

1994 Acts. Amendment by Pub.L. 103–394 effective on Oct. 22, 1994, and not to apply with respect to cases commenced under Title 11 of the United States Code before Oct. 22, 1994, see section 702 of Pub.L. 103–394, set out as a note under section 101 of this title.

1986 Acts. Amendment by Pub.L. 99–554 effective 30 days after Oct. 27, 1986, except as otherwise provided for, see section 302(a) of Pub.L. 99–554, set out as a note under section 581 of Title 28, Judiciary and Judicial Procedure.

Amendment by Pub.L. 99–554, § 207, not to become effective in or with respect to certain specified judicial districts until, or apply to cases while pending in such district before, the expiration of the 270-day period beginning 30 days after Oct. 27, 1986, or of the 30-day period beginning on the date the Attorney General certifies under section 303 of Pub.L. 99–554 the region specified in a paragraph of section 581(a) of Title 28, as amended by section 111(a) of Pub.L. 99–554, that includes such district, whichever occurs first, see section 302(d)(1) of Pub.L. 99–554, set out as a note under section 581 of Title 28.

Amendment by Pub.L. 99–554, § 207, not to become effective in or with respect to certain specified judicial districts until, or apply to cases while pending in such district before, the expiration of the 2-year period beginning 30 days after Oct. 27, 1986, or of the 30-day period beginning on the date the Attorney General certifies under section 303 of Pub.L. 99–554 the region specified in a paragraph of section 581(a) of Title 28, as amended by section 111(a) of Pub.L. 99–554, that includes such district, whichever occurs first, see section 302(d)(2) of Pub.L. 99–554, set out as a note under section 581 of Title 28.

Amendment by Pub.L. 99–554, § 207, not to become effective in or with respect to judicial districts established for the States of Alabama and North Carolina until, or apply to cases while pending in such district before, such district elects to be included in a bankruptcy region established in section 581(a) of Title 28, as amended by section 111(a) of Pub.L. 99–554, or Oct. 1, 2002, whichever occurs first, and, except as otherwise provided for, with respect to cases under chapters 7, 11, 12, and 13 of Title 11 commenced before 30 days after Oct. 27, 1986, and pending in a judicial district in the States of Alabama or North Carolina before any election made under section 302(d)(3)(A) of Pub.L. 99–554 by such district becomes effective or Oct. 1, 2002, whichever occurs first, amendments by Pub.L. 99–554 not to apply until Oct. 1, 2003, or the expiration of the 1-year period beginning on the date such election becomes effective, whichever occurs first, and further, in any judicial district in Alabama or North Carolina not making the election described in section 302(d)(3)(A) of Pub.L. 99–554, any person appointed under regulations issued by the Judicial Conference to administer estates in cases under Title 11 authorized to establish, etc., a panel of private trustees, and to supervise cases and trustees in cases under chapters 7, 11, 12, and 13 of Title 11, until amendments by sections 201 to 231 of Pub.L. 99–554 effective in such district, see section 302(d)(3)(A) to (F), (H), and (I) of Pub.L. 99–554, set out as a note under section 581 of Title 28.

Amendment by Pub.L. 99–554, § 207, except as otherwise provided, with respect to cases under chapters 7, 11, 12, and 13 of Title 11 commenced before 30 days after Oct. 27, 1986, and pending in a judicial district referred to in section 581(a) of Title 28, as amended by section 111(a) of Pub.L. 99–554, for which a United States trustee is not authorized before 30 days after Oct. 27, 1986 to be appointed, not applicable until the expiration of the 3-year period beginning on Oct. 27, 1986, or of the 1-year period beginning on the date the Attorney General certifies under section 303 of Pub.L. 99–554 the region specified in a paragraph of such section 581(a) that includes, such district, whichever occurs first, see section 302(e)(1), (2) of Pub.L. 99–554, set out as a note under section 581 of Title 28.

Amendment by Pub.L. 99–554; § 257(d), effective 30 days after Oct. 27, 1986, but not applicable with respect to cases commenced under this title before that date, see section 302(a), (c)(1) of Pub.L. 99–554, set out as a note under section 581 of Title 28.

1984 Acts. Amendment by Pub.L. 98–353 effective with respect to cases filed 90 days after July 10, 1984, see section 552(a), formerly 553(a), of Pub.L. 98–353, set out as a note under section 101 of this title.

Separability of Provisions

If any provision of or amendment made by Pub.L. 103–394 or the application of such provision or amendment to any person or circumstance is held to be unconstitutional, the remaining provisions of and amendments made by Pub.L. 103–394 and the application of such provisions and amendments to any person or circumstance shall not be affected thereby, see section 701 of Pub.L. 103–394, set out as a note under section 101 of this title.

CROSS REFERENCES

Appointment of trustee or examiner upon failure to qualify, see 11 USCA § 1104.

Certain customer transactions affected before qualification of trustee, see 11 USCA § 746.

"Debtor in possession" defined as debtor except when qualified person is serving as trustee under this section, see 11 USCA § 1101.

Interim trustee, see 11 USCA § 701.

Qualification of trustee and attorney in investor protection liquidation proceedings, see 15 USCA § 78eee.

Standing trustee,

 Chapter 12 cases, see 11 USCA § 1202.

 Chapter 13 cases, see 11 USCA § 1302.

Successor trustee, see 11 USCA § 703.

§ 323. Role and capacity of trustee

(a) The trustee in a case under this title is the representative of the estate.

(b) The trustee in a case under this title has capacity to sue and be sued.

(Pub.L. 95–598, Nov. 6, 1978, 92 Stat. 2562.)

HISTORICAL AND STATUTORY NOTES

Revision Notes and Legislative Reports

1978 Acts. Subsection (a) of this section makes the trustee the representative of the estate. Subsection (b) grants the trustee the capacity to sue and to be sued. If the debtor remains in possession in a chapter 11 case, section 1107 gives the debtor in possession these rights of the trustee: the debtor in possession becomes the representative of the estate, and may sue and be sued. The same applies in a chapter 13 case. Senate Report No. 95–989.

§ 324. Removal of trustee or examiner

(a) The court, after notice and a hearing, may remove a trustee, other than the United States trustee, or an examiner, for cause.

(b) Whenever the court removes a trustee or examiner under subsection (a) in a case under this title, such trustee or examiner shall thereby be removed in all other cases under this title in which such trustee or examiner is then serving unless the court orders otherwise.

(Pub.L. 95–598, Nov. 6, 1978, 92 Stat. 2562; Pub.L. 99–554, Title II, § 208, Oct. 27, 1986, 100 Stat. 3098.)

HISTORICAL AND STATUTORY NOTES

Revision Notes and Legislative Reports

1978 Acts. This section permits the court, after notice and a hearing, to remove a trustee for cause. Senate Report No. 95–989.

1986 Acts. House Report No. 99–764 and House Conference Report No. 99–958, see 1986 U.S.Code Cong. and Adm. News, p. 5227.

Effective and Applicability Provisions

1986 Acts. Amendment by Pub.L. 99–554 effective 30 days after Oct. 27, 1986, except as otherwise provided for, see section 302(a) of Pub.L. 99–554, set out as a note under section 581 of Title 28, Judiciary and Judicial Procedure.

Amendment by Pub.L. 99–554, § 208 not to become effective in or with respect to certain specified judicial districts until, or apply to cases while pending in such district before, the expiration of the 270-day period beginning 30 days after Oct. 27, 1986, or of the 30-day period beginning on the date the Attorney General certifies under section 303 of Pub.L. 99–554 the region specified in a paragraph of section 581(a) of Title 28, as amended by section 111(a) of Pub.L. 99–554, that includes such district, whichever occurs first, see section 302(d)(1) of Pub.L. 99–554, set out as a note under section 581 of Title 28.

Amendment by Pub.L. 99–554, § 208, not to become effective in or with respect to certain specified judicial districts until, or apply to cases while pending in such district before, the expiration of the 2-year period beginning 30 days after Oct. 27, 1986, or of the 30-day period beginning on the date the Attorney General certifies under section 303 of Pub.L. 99–554 the region specified in a paragraph of section 581(a) of Title 28, as amended by section 111(a) of Pub.L. 99–554, that includes such district, whichever occurs first, see section

302(d)(2) of Pub.L. 99–554, set out as a note under section 581 of Title 28.

Amendment by Pub.L. 99–554, § 208, not to become effective in or with respect to judicial districts established for the States of Alabama and North Carolina until, or apply to cases while pending in such district before, such district elects to be included in a bankruptcy region established in section 581(a) of Title 28, as amended by section 111(a) of Pub.L. 99–554, or Oct. 1, 2002, whichever occurs first, and, except as otherwise provided for, with respect to cases under chapters 7, 11, 12, and 13 of Title 11 commenced before 30 days after Oct. 27, 1986, and pending in a judicial district in the States of Alabama or North Carolina before any election made under section 302(d)(3)(A) of Pub.L. 99–554 by such district becomes effective or Oct. 1, 2002, whichever occurs first, amendments by Pub.L. 99–554 not to apply until Oct. 1, 2003, or the expiration of the 1-year period beginning on the date such election becomes effective, whichever occurs first, and further, in any judicial district in Alabama or North Carolina not making the election described in section 302(d)(3)(A) of Pub.L. 99–554, any person appointed under regulations issued by the Judicial Conference to administer estates in cases under Title 11 authorized to establish, etc., a panel of private trustees, and to supervise cases and trustees in cases under chapters 7, 11, 12, and 13 of Title 11, until amendments by sections 201 to 231 of Pub.L. 99–554 effective in such district, see section 302(d)(3)(A) to (F), (H), and (I) of Pub.L. 99–554, set out as a note under section 581 of Title 28.

Amendment by Pub.L. 99–554, § 208, except as otherwise provided, with respect to cases under chapters 7, 11, 12, and 13 of Title 11 commenced before 30 days after Oct. 27, 1986, and pending in a judicial district referred to in section 581(a) of Title 28, as amended by section 111(a) of Pub.L. 99–554, for which a United States trustee is not authorized before 30 days after Oct. 27, 1986 to be appointed, not applicable until the expiration of the 3-year period beginning on Oct. 27, 1986, or of the 1-year period beginning on the date the Attorney General certifies under section 303 of Pub.L. 99–554 the region specified in a paragraph of such section 581(a) that includes, such district, whichever occurs first, see section 302(e)(1), (2) of Pub.L. 99–554, set out as a note under section 581 of Title 28.

CROSS REFERENCES

Adverse interest and conduct of officers of estate, see 18 USCA § 154.

Appointment of trustee or examiner upon removal, see 11 USCA § 1104.

Authority of Attorney General to investigate trustees, see 28 USCA § 526.

Embezzlement by trustee, see 18 USCA § 153.

Successor trustee, see 11 USCA § 703.

§ 325. Effect of vacancy

A vacancy in the office of trustee during a case does not abate any pending action or proceeding, and the successor trustee shall be substituted as a party in such action or proceeding.

(Pub.L. 95–598, Nov. 6, 1978, 92 Stat. 2562.)

For Complete Annotation Materials, see United States Code Annotated

HISTORICAL AND STATUTORY NOTES

Revision Notes and Legislative Reports

1978 Acts. Section 325, derived from Bankruptcy Act section 46 [section 74 of former Title 11] and Bankruptcy Rule 221(b), specifies that a vacancy in the office of trustee during a case does not abate any pending action or proceeding. The successor trustee, when selected and qualified, is substituted as a party in any pending action or proceeding. Senate Report No. 95–989.

§ 326. Limitation on compensation of trustee

(a) In a case under chapter 7 or 11, the court may allow reasonable compensation under section 330 of this title of the trustee for the trustee's services, payable after the trustee renders such services, not to exceed 25 percent on the first $5,000 or less, 10 percent on any amount in excess of $5,000 but not in excess of $50,000, 5 percent on any amount in excess of $50,000 but not in excess of $1,000,000, and reasonable compensation not to exceed 3 percent of such moneys in excess of $1,000,000, upon all moneys disbursed or turned over in the case by the trustee to parties in interest, excluding the debtor, but including holders of secured claims.

(b) In a case under chapter 12 or 13 of this title, the court may not allow compensation for services or reimbursement of expenses of the United States trustee or of a standing trustee appointed under section 586(b) of title 28, but may allow reasonable compensation under section 330 of this title of a trustee appointed under section 1202(a) or 1302(a) of this title for the trustee's services, payable after the trustee renders such services, not to exceed five percent upon all payments under the plan.

(c) If more than one person serves as trustee in the case, the aggregate compensation of such persons for such service may not exceed the maximum compensation prescribed for a single trustee by subsection (a) or (b) of this section, as the case may be.

(d) The court may deny allowance of compensation for services or reimbursement of expenses of the trustee if the trustee failed to make diligent inquiry into facts that would permit denial of allowance under section 328(c) of this title or, with knowledge of such facts, employed a professional person under section 327 of this title.

(Pub.L. 95–598, Nov. 6, 1978, 92 Stat. 2562; Pub. L. 98–353, Title III, § 430(a), (b), July 10, 1984, 98 Stat. 369; Pub.L. 99–554, Title II, § 209, Oct. 27, 1986, 100 Stat. 3098; Pub.L. 103–394, Title I, § 107, Oct. 22, 1994, 108 Stat. 4111.)

HISTORICAL AND STATUTORY NOTES

Revision Notes and Legislative Reports

1978 Acts. This section is derived in part from section 48c of the Bankruptcy Act [section 76(c) of former Title 11]. It must be emphasized that this section does not authorize compensation of trustees. This section simply fixes the maximum compensation of a trustee. Proposed 11 U.S.C. section 330 authorizes and fixes the standard of compensation. Un-

der section 48c of current law, the maximum limits have tended to become minimums in many cases. This section is not intended to be so interpreted. The limits in this section, together with the limitations found in section 330, are to be applied as outer limits and not as grants or entitlements to the maximum fees specified.

The maximum fee schedule is derived from section 48c(1) of the present act [section 76(c)(1) of former Title 11], but with a change relating to the bases on which the percentage maxima are computed. The maximum fee schedule is based on decreasing percentages of increasing amounts. The amounts are the amounts of money distributed by the trustee to parties in interest, excluding the debtor, but including secured creditors. These amounts were last amended in 1952. Since then, the cost of living has approximately doubled. Thus, the bases were doubled.

It should be noted that the bases on which the maximum fee is computed includes moneys turned over to secured creditors, to cover the situation where the trustee liquidates property subject to a lien and distributes the proceeds. It does not cover cases in which the trustee simply turns over the property to the secured creditor, nor where the trustee abandons the property and the secured creditor is permitted to foreclose. The provision is also subject to the rights of the secured creditor generally under proposed section 506, especially section 506(c). The $150 discretionary fee provision of current law is retained.

Subsection (b) of this section entitles an operating trustee to a reasonable fee, without any limitation based on the maximum provided for a liquidating trustee as in current law, Bankruptcy Act section 48c(2) [section 76(c)(2) of former Title 11].

Subsection (c) permits a maximum fee of five percent on all payments to creditors under a chapter 13 plan to the trustee appointed in the case.

Subsection (d) provides a limitation not found in current law. Even if more than one trustee serves in the case, the maximum fee payable to all trustees does not change. For example, if an interim trustee is appointed and an elected trustee replaces him, the combined total of the fees payable to the interim trustee and the permanent trustee may not exceed the amount specified in this section. Under current law, very often a receiver receives a full fee and a subsequent trustee also receives a full fee. The resultant "double-dipping", especially in cases in which the receiver and the trustee are the same individual, is detrimental to the interests of creditors, by needlessly increasing the cost of administering bankruptcy estates.

Subsection (e) permits the court to deny compensation to a trustee if the trustee has been derelict in his duty by employing counsel, who is not disinterested. Senate Report No. 95–989.

1984 Acts. Statements by Legislative Leaders, see 1984 U.S.Code Cong. and Adm.News, p. 576.

1986 Acts. House Report No. 99–764 and House Conference Report No. 99–958, see 1986 U.S.Code Cong. and Adm. News, p. 5227.

1994 Acts. House Report No. 103–835, see 1994 U.S. Code Cong. and Adm. News, p. 3340.

Legislative Statements

Section 326(a) of the House amendment modifies a provision as contained in H.R. 8200 as passed by the House. The percentage limitation on the fees of a trustee contained in the House bill is retained, but no additional percentage is specified for cases in which a trustee operates the business of the debtor. Section 326(b) of the Senate amendment, is deleted as an unnecessary restatement of the limitation contained in section 326(a) as modified. The provision contained in section 326(a) of the Senate amendment authorizing a trustee to receive a maximum fee of $150 regardless of the availability of assets in the estate is deleted. It will not be necessary in view of the increase in section 326(a) and the doubling of the minimum fee as provided in section 330(b).

Section 326(b) of the House amendment derives from section 326(c) of H.R. 8200 as passed by the House. It is a conforming amendment to indicate a change with respect to the selection of a trustee in a chapter 13 case under section 1302(a) of Title 11.

Effective and Applicability Provisions

1994 Acts. Amendment by Pub.L. 103–394 effective on Oct. 22, 1994, and not to apply with respect to cases commenced under Title 11 of the United States Code before Oct. 22, 1994, see section 702 of Pub.L. 103–394, set out as a note under section 101 of this title.

1986 Acts. Amendment by Pub.L. 99–554 effective 30 days after Oct. 27, 1986, except as otherwise provided for, see section 302(a) of Pub.L. 99–554, set out as a note under section 581 of Title 28, Judiciary and Judicial Procedure.

Until amendments made by section 209 of Pub.L. 99–554 become effective in a district and apply to a case, for purposes of such case any references in subsec. (b) of this section to chapter 13 of this title, to section 1302(d) of this title, or to section 1302(a) of this title deemed references to other provisions of the Code, see section 302(c)(3)(A)(i) to (iii) of Pub.L. 99–554, set out as a note under section 581 of Title 28.

Amendment by Pub.L. 99–554, § 209, not to become effective in or with respect to certain specified judicial districts until, or apply to cases while pending in such district before, the expiration of the 270-day period beginning 30 days after Oct. 27, 1986, or of the 30-day period beginning on the date the Attorney General certifies under section 303 of Pub.L. 99–554 the region specified in a paragraph of section 581(a) of Title 28, as amended by section 111(a) of Pub.L. 99–554, that includes such district, whichever occurs first, see section 302(d)(1) of Pub.L. 99–554, set out as a note under section 581 of Title 28.

Amendment by Pub.L. 99–554, § 209, not to become effective in or with respect to certain specified judicial districts until, or apply to cases while pending in such district before, the expiration of the 2-year period beginning 30 days after Oct. 27, 1986, or of the 30-day period beginning on the date the Attorney General certifies under section 303 of Pub.L. 99–554 the region specified in a paragraph of section 581(a) of Title 28, as amended by section 111(a) of Pub.L. 99–554, that includes such district, whichever occurs first, see section 302(d)(2) of Pub.L. 99–554, set out as a note under section 581 of Title 28.

Amendment by Pub.L. 99–554, § 209, not to become effective in or with respect to judicial districts established for the States of Alabama and North Carolina until, or apply to cases while pending in such district before, such district elects to be included in a bankruptcy region established in section 581(a) of Title 28, as amended by section 111(a) of Pub.L. 99–554, or Oct. 1, 2002, whichever occurs first, and, except as otherwise provided for, with respect to cases under chapters 7, 11, 12,

and 13 of Title 11 commenced before 30 days after Oct. 27, 1986, and pending in a judicial district in the States of Alabama or North Carolina before any election made under section 302(d)(3)(A) of Pub.L. 99–554 by such district becomes effective or Oct. 1, 2002, whichever occurs first, amendments by Pub.L. 99–554 not to apply until Oct. 1, 2003, or the expiration of the 1-year period beginning on the date such election becomes effective, whichever occurs first, and further, in any judicial district in Alabama or North Carolina not making the election described in section 302(d)(3)(A) of Pub.L. 99–554, any person appointed under regulations issued by the Judicial Conference to administer estates in cases under Title 11 authorized to establish, etc., a panel of private trustees, and to supervise cases and trustees in cases under chapters 7, 11, 12, and 13 of Title 11, until amendments by sections 201 to 231 of Pub.L. 99–554 effective in such district, see section 302(d)(3)(A) to (F), (H), and (I) of Pub.L. 99–554, set out as a note under section 581 of Title 28.

Amendment by Pub.L. 99–554, § 209, except as otherwise provided, with respect to cases under chapters 7, 11, 12, and 13 of Title 11 commenced before 30 days after Oct. 27, 1986, and pending in a judicial district referred to in section 581(a) of Title 28, as amended by section 111(a) of Pub.L. 99–554, for which a United States trustee is not authorized before 30 days after Oct. 27, 1986 to be appointed, not applicable until the expiration of the 3-year period beginning on Oct. 27, 1986, or of the 1-year period beginning on the date the Attorney General certifies under section 303 of Pub.L. 99–554 the region specified in a paragraph of such section 581(a) that includes, such district, whichever occurs first, see section 302(e)(1), (2) of Pub.L. 99–554, set out as a note under section 581 of Title 28.

1984 Acts. Amendment by Pub.L. 98–353 effective with respect to cases filed 90 days after July 10, 1984, see section 552(a), formerly 553(a), of Pub.L. 98–353, set out as a note under section 101 of this title.

Separability of Provisions

If any provision of or amendment made by Pub.L. 103–394 or the application of such provision or amendment to any person or circumstance is held to be unconstitutional, the remaining provisions of and amendments made by Pub.L. 103–394 and the application of such provisions and amendments to any person or circumstance shall not be affected thereby, see section 701 of Pub.L. 103–394, set out as a note under section 101 of this title.

CROSS REFERENCES

Grain storage facility bankruptcies, expedited determinations, see 11 USCA § 557.

§ 327. Employment of professional persons

(a) Except as otherwise provided in this section, the trustee, with the court's approval, may employ one or more attorneys, accountants, appraisers, auctioneers, or other professional persons, that do not hold or represent an interest adverse to the estate, and that are disinterested persons, to represent or assist the trustee in carrying out the trustee's duties under this title.

(b) If the trustee is authorized to operate the business of the debtor under section 721, 1202, or 1108 of this title, and if the debtor has regularly employed attorneys, accountants, or other professional persons on salary, the trustee may retain or replace such professional persons if necessary in the operation of such business.

(c) In a case under chapter 7, 12, or 11 of this title, a person is not disqualified for employment under this section solely because of such person's employment by or representation of a creditor, unless there is objection by another creditor or the United States trustee, in which case the court shall disapprove such employment if there is an actual conflict of interest.

(d) The court may authorize the trustee to act as attorney or accountant for the estate if such authorization is in the best interest of the estate.

(e) The trustee, with the court's approval, may employ, for a specified special purpose, other than to represent the trustee in conducting the case, an attorney that has represented the debtor, if in the best interest of the estate, and if such attorney does not represent or hold any interest adverse to the debtor or to the estate with respect to the matter on which such attorney is to be employed.

(f) The trustee may not employ a person that has served as an examiner in the case.
(Pub.L. 95–598, Nov. 6, 1978, 92 Stat. 2563; Pub. L. 98–353, Title III, § 430(c), July 10, 1984, 98 Stat. 370; Pub.L. 99–554, Title II, §§ 210, 257(e), Oct. 27, 1986, 100 Stat. 3099, 3114.)

HISTORICAL AND STATUTORY NOTES

Revision Notes and Legislative Reports

1978 Acts. This section authorizes the trustee, subject to the court's approval, to employ professional persons, such as attorneys, accountants, appraisers, and auctioneers, to represent or perform services for the estate. The trustee may employ only disinterested persons that do not hold or represent an interest adverse to the estate.

Subsection (b) is an exception, and authorizes the trustee to retain or replace professional persons that the debtor has employed if necessary in the operation of the debtor's business.

Subsection (c) provides a professional person is not disqualified for employment solely because of the person's prior employment by or representation of a secured or unsecured creditor.

Subsection (d) permits the court to authorize the trustee, if qualified to act as his own counsel or accountant.

Subsection (e) permits the trustee, subject to the court's approval, to employ for a specified special purpose an attorney that has represented the debtor, if such employment is in the best interest of the estate and if the attorney does not hold or represent an interest adverse to the debtor of the estate with respect to the matter on which he is to be employed. This subsection does not authorize the employment of the debtor's attorney to represent the estate generally or to represent the trustee in the conduct of the bankruptcy case. The subsection will most likely be used when the debtor is involved in complex litigation, and changing attorneys in the middle of the case after the bankruptcy case has

commenced would be detrimental to the progress of that other litigation. Senate Report No. 95–989.

Subsection (c) is an additional exception. The trustee may employ as his counsel a nondisinterested person if the only reason that the attorney is not disinterested is because of his representation of an unsecured creditor. House Report No. 95–595.

1984 Acts. Statements by Legislative Leaders, see 1984 U.S.Code Cong. and Adm.News, p. 576.

1986 Acts. House Report No. 99–764 and House Conference Report No. 99–958, see 1986 U.S.Code Cong. and Adm. News, p. 5227.

Legislative Statements

Section 327(a) of the House amendment contains a technical amendment indicating that attorneys, and perhaps other officers enumerated therein, represent, rather than assist, the trustee in carrying out the trustee's duties.

Section 327(c) represents a compromise between H.R. 8200 as passed by the House and the Senate amendment. The provision states that former representation of a creditor, whether secured or unsecured, will not automatically disqualify a person from being employed by a trustee, but if such person is employed by the trustee, the person may no longer represent the creditor in connection with the case.

Section 327(f) prevents an examiner from being employed by the trustee.

Codifications

Amendment by Pub.L. 99–554, § 257(e)(1), has been executed to text following "section 721" as the probable intent of Congress, notwithstanding directory language which required amendment to be executed following "section 721,".

Amendment by Pub.L. 99–554, § 257(e)(2), has been executed to text following "chapter 7" as the probable intent of Congress, notwithstanding directory language which required amendment to be executed following "section 7".

Effective and Applicability Provisions

1986 Acts. Amendment by Pub.L. 99–554 effective 30 days after Oct. 27, 1986, except as otherwise provided for, see section 302(a) of Pub.L. 99–554, set out as a note under section 581 of Title 28, Judiciary and Judicial Procedure.

Amendment by Pub.L. 99–554, § 210, not to become effective in or with respect to certain specified judicial districts until, or apply to cases while pending in such district before, the expiration of the 270-day period beginning 30 days after Oct. 27, 1986, or of the 30-day period beginning on the date the Attorney General certifies under section 303 of Pub.L. 99–554 the region specified in a paragraph of section 581(a) of Title 28, as amended by section 111(a) of Pub.L. 99–554, that includes such district, whichever occurs first, see section 302(d)(1) of Pub.L. 99–554, set out as a note under section 581 of Title 28.

Amendment by Pub.L. 99–554, § 210, not to become effective in or with respect to certain specified judicial districts until, or apply to cases while pending in such district before, the expiration of the 2-year period beginning 30 days after Oct. 27, 1986, or of the 30-day period beginning on the date the Attorney General certifies under section 303 of Pub.L. 99–554 the region specified in a paragraph of section 581(a) of Title 28, as amended by section 111(a) of Pub.L. 99–554, that includes such district, whichever occurs first, see section

302(d)(2) of Pub.L. 99–554, set out as a note under section 581 of Title 28.

Amendment by Pub.L. 99–554, § 210, not to become effective in or with respect to judicial districts established for the States of Alabama and North Carolina until, or apply to cases while pending in such district before, such district elects to be included in a bankruptcy region established in section 581(a) of Title 28, as amended by section 111(a) of Pub.L. 99–554, or Oct. 1, 2002, whichever occurs first, and, except as otherwise provided for, with respect to cases under chapters 7, 11, 12, and 13 of Title 11 commenced before 30 days after Oct. 27, 1986, and pending in a judicial district in the States of Alabama or North Carolina before any election made under section 302(d)(3)(A) of Pub.L. 99–554 by such district becomes effective or Oct. 1, 2002, whichever occurs first, amendments by Pub.L. 99–554 not to apply until Oct. 1, 2003, or the expiration of the 1-year period beginning on the date such election becomes effective, whichever occurs first, and further, in any judicial district in Alabama or North Carolina not making the election described in section 302(d)(3)(A) of Pub.L. 99–554, any person appointed under regulations issued by the Judicial Conference to administer estates in cases under Title 11 authorized to establish, etc., a panel of private trustees, and to supervise cases and trustees in cases under chapters 7, 11, 12, and 13 of Title 11, until amendments by sections 201 to 231 of Pub.L. 99–554 effective in such district, see section 302(d)(3)(A) to (F), (H), and (I) of Pub.L. 99–554, set out as a note under section 581 of Title 28.

Amendment by Pub.L. 99–554, § 210, except as otherwise provided, with respect to cases under chapters 7, 11, 12, and 13 of Title 11 commenced before 30 days after Oct. 27, 1986, and pending in a judicial district referred to in section 581(a) of Title 28, as amended by section 111(a) of Pub.L. 99–554, for which a United States trustee is not authorized before 30 days after Oct. 27, 1986 to be appointed, not applicable until the expiration of the 3-year period beginning on Oct. 27, 1986, or of the 1-year period beginning on the date the Attorney General certifies under section 303 of Pub.L. 99–554 the region specified in a paragraph of such section 581(a) that includes, such district, whichever occurs first, see section 302(e)(1), (2) of Pub.L. 99–554, set out as a note under section 581 of Title 28.

Amendment by Pub.L. 99–554, § 257(e), effective 30 days after Oct. 27, 1986, but not applicable to cases commenced under this title before that date, see section 302(a), (c)(1) of Pub.L. 99–554, set out as a note under section 581 of Title 28.

1984 Acts. Amendment by Pub.L. 98–353 effective with respect to cases filed 90 days after July 10, 1984, see section 552(a), formerly 553(a), of Pub.L. 98–353, set out as a note under section 101 of this title.

CROSS REFERENCES

Duty of United States trustee to monitor applications, see 28 USCA § 586.

Qualification for employment by debtor in possession despite prior employment or representation, see 11 USCA § 1107.

§ 328. Limitation on compensation of professional persons

(a) The trustee, or a committee appointed under section 1102 of this title, with the court's approval, may employ or authorize the employment of a professional person under section 327 or 1103 of this title, as the case may be, on any reasonable terms and conditions of employment, including on a retainer, on an hourly basis, on a fixed or percentage fee basis, or on a contingent fee basis. Notwithstanding such terms and conditions, the court may allow compensation different from the compensation provided under such terms and conditions after the conclusion of such employment, if such terms and conditions prove to have been improvident in light of developments not capable of being anticipated at the time of the fixing of such terms and conditions.

(b) If the court has authorized a trustee to serve as an attorney or accountant for the estate under section 327(d) of this title, the court may allow compensation for the trustee's services as such attorney or accountant only to the extent that the trustee performed services as attorney or accountant for the estate and not for performance of any of the trustee's duties that are generally performed by a trustee without the assistance of an attorney or accountant for the estate.

(c) Except as provided in section 327(c), 327(e), or 1107(b) of this title, the court may deny allowance of compensation for services and reimbursement of expenses of a professional person employed under section 327 or 1103 of this title if, at any time during such professional person's employment under section 327 or 1103 of this title, such professional person is not a disinterested person, or represents or holds an interest adverse to the interest of the estate with respect to the matter on which such professional person is employed. (Pub.L. 95–598, Nov. 6, 1978, 92 Stat. 2563; Pub. L. 98–353, Title III, § 431, July 10, 1984, 98 Stat. 370; Pub.L. 109–8, Title XII, § 1206, Apr. 20, 2005, 119 Stat. 194.)

HISTORICAL AND STATUTORY NOTES
Revision Notes and Legislative Reports

1978 Acts. This section, which is parallel to § 326, fixes the maximum compensation allowable to a professional person employed under section 327. It authorizes the trustee, with the court's approval, to employ professional persons on any reasonable terms, including on a retainer, on an hourly or on a contingent fee basis. Subsection (a) further permits the court to allow compensation different from the compensation provided under the trustee's agreement if the prior agreement proves to have been improvident in light of development unanticipatable at the time of the agreement. The court's power includes the power to increase as well as decrease the agreed upon compensation. This provision is permissive, not mandatory, and should not be used by the court if to do so would violate the code of ethics of the professional involved.

Subsection (b) limits a trustee that has been authorized to serve as his own counsel to only one fee for each service. The purpose of permitting the trustee to serve as his own counsel is to reduce costs. It is not included to provide the trustee with a bonus by permitting him to receive two fees for the same service or to avoid the maxima fixed in section 326. Thus, this subsection requires the court to differentiate between the trustee's services as trustee, and his services as trustee's counsel, and to fix compensation accordingly. Services that a trustee normally performs for an estate without assistance of counsel are to be compensated under the limits fixed in section 326. Only services that he performs that are normally performed by trustee's counsel may be compensated under the maxima imposed by this section.

Subsection (c) permits the court to deny compensation for services and reimbursement of expenses if the professional person is not disinterested or if he represents or holds an interest adverse to the estate on the matter on which he is employed. The subsection provides a penalty for conflicts of interest. Senate Report No. 95–989.

1984 Acts. Statements by Legislative Leaders, see 1984 U.S.Code Cong. and Adm.News, p. 576.

2005 Acts. House Report No. 109–31(Part I), see 2005 U.S. Code Cong. and Adm. News, p. 88.

Legislative Statements

Section 328(c) adopts a technical amendment contained in the Senate amendment indicating that an attorney for the debtor in possession is not disqualified for compensation for services and reimbursement of expenses simply because of prior representation of the debtor.

Effective and Applicability Provisions

2005 Acts. Amendments by Pub.L. 109–8 effective, except as otherwise provided, 180 days after April 20, 2005, and inapplicable with respect to cases commenced under Title 11 before the effective date, see Pub.L. 109–8, § 1501, set out as a note under 11 U.S.C.A. § 101.

1984 Acts. Amendment by Pub.L. 98–353 effective with respect to cases filed 90 days after July 10, 1984, see section 552(a), formerly 553 of Pub.L. 98–353, set out as a note under section 101 of this title.

§ 329. Debtor's transactions with attorneys

(a) Any attorney representing a debtor in a case under this title, or in connection with such a case, whether or not such attorney applies for compensation under this title, shall file with the court a statement of the compensation paid or agreed to be paid, if such payment or agreement was made after one year before the date of the filing of the petition, for services rendered or to be rendered in contemplation of or in connection with the case by such attorney, and the source of such compensation.

(b) If such compensation exceeds the reasonable value of any such services, the court may cancel any such agreement, or order the return of any such payment, to the extent excessive, to—

    (1) the estate, if the property transferred—

        (A) would have been property of the estate; or
        (B) was to be paid by or on behalf of the debtor under a plan under chapter 11, 12, or 13 of this title; or

    (2) the entity that made such payment.

(Pub.L. 95–598, Nov. 6, 1978, 92 Stat. 2564; Pub. L. 98–353, Title III, § 432, July 10, 1984, 98 Stat. 370; Pub.L. 99–554, Title II, § 257(c), Oct. 27, 1986, 100 Stat. 3114.)

Revision Notes and Legislative Reports

1978 Acts. This section, derived in large part from current Bankruptcy Act section 60d [section 96(d) of former Title 11], requires the debtor's attorney to file with the court a statement of the compensation paid or agreed to be paid to the attorney for services in contemplation of and in connection with the case, and the source of the compensation. Payments to a debtor's attorney provide serious potential for evasion of creditor protection provisions of the bankruptcy laws, and serious potential for overreaching by the debtor's attorney, and should be subject to careful scrutiny.

Subsection (b) permits the court to deny compensation to the attorney, to cancel an agreement to pay compensation, or to order the return of compensation paid, if the compensation exceeds the reasonable value of the services provided. The return of payments already made are generally to the trustee for the benefit of the estate. However, if the property would not have come into the estate in any event, the court will order it returned to the entity that made the payment.

The Bankruptcy Commission recommended a provision similar to this that would have also permitted an examination of the debtor's transactions with insiders. S. 236, 94th Cong., 1st sess., sec. 4–311(b) (1975). Its exclusion here is to permit it to be dealt with by the Rules of Bankruptcy Procedure. It is not intended that the provision be deleted entirely, only that the flexibility of the rules is more appropriate for such evidentiary matters. Senate Report No. 95–989.

1984 Acts. Statements by Legislative Leaders, see 1984 U.S.Code Cong. and Adm.News, p. 576.

1986 Acts. House Report No. 99–764 and House Conference Report No. 99–958, see 1986 U.S.Code Cong. and Adm. News, p. 5227.

Effective and Applicability Provisions

1986 Acts. Amendment by Pub.L. 99–554 effective 30 days after Oct. 27, 1986, but not applicable to cases commenced under this title before that date, see section 302(a), (c)(1) of Pub.L. 99–554, set out as a note under section 581 of Title 28, Judiciary and Judicial Procedure.

1984 Acts. Amendment by Pub.L. 98–353 effective with respect to cases filed 90 days after July 10, 1984, see section 552(a), formerly 553(a), of Pub.L. 98–353, set out as a note under section 101 of this title.

CROSS REFERENCES

Disclosure of compensation, debtor's attorney, see Fed. Bankr. Proc. Form B2030, 11 USCA.

Fee agreements, see 18 USCA § 155.

Lists, schedules, statements and fees, see Fed. Bankr. Proc. Form B2000, 11 USCA.

Property of estate, see 11 USCA § 541.

§ 330. Compensation of officers

(a)(1) After notice to the parties in interest and the United States Trustee and a hearing, and subject to sections 326, 328, and 329, the court may award to a trustee, a consumer privacy ombudsman appointed under section 332, an examiner, an ombudsman appointed under section 333, or a professional person employed under section 327 or 1103—

(A) reasonable compensation for actual, necessary services rendered by the trustee, examiner, ombudsman, professional person, or attorney and by any paraprofessional person employed by any such person; and

(B) reimbursement for actual, necessary expenses.

(2) The court may, on its own motion or on the motion of the United States Trustee, the United States Trustee for the District or Region, the trustee for the estate, or any other party in interest, award compensation that is less than the amount of compensation that is requested.

(3) In determining the amount of reasonable compensation to be awarded to an examiner, trustee under chapter 11, or professional person, the court shall consider the nature, the extent, and the value of such services, taking into account all relevant factors, including—

(A) the time spent on such services;

(B) the rates charged for such services;

(C) whether the services were necessary to the administration of, or beneficial at the time at which the service was rendered toward the completion of, a case under this title;

(D) whether the services were performed within a reasonable amount of time commensurate with the complexity, importance, and nature of the problem, issue, or task addressed;

(E) with respect to a professional person, whether the person is board certified or otherwise has demonstrated skill and experience in the bankruptcy field; and

(F) whether the compensation is reasonable based on the customary compensation charged by comparably skilled practitioners in cases other than cases under this title.

(4)(A) Except as provided in subparagraph (B), the court shall not allow compensation for—

(i) unnecessary duplication of services; or

(ii) services that were not—

(I) reasonably likely to benefit the debtor's estate; or

(II) necessary to the administration of the case.

(B) In a chapter 12 or chapter 13 case in which the debtor is an individual, the court may allow reasonable compensation to the debtor's attorney for representing the interests of the debtor in connection with the bankruptcy case based on a consideration of the benefit and necessity of such services to the debtor and the other factors set forth in this section.

(5) The court shall reduce the amount of compensation awarded under this section by the amount of any interim compensation awarded under section 331, and, if the amount of such interim compensation exceeds the amount of compensation awarded under this section, may order the return of the excess to the estate.

(6) Any compensation awarded for the preparation of a fee application shall be based on the level and skill reasonably required to prepare the application.

(7) In determining the amount of reasonable compensation to be awarded to a trustee, the court shall treat such compensation as a commission, based on section 326.

(b)(1) There shall be paid from the filing fee in a case under chapter 7 of this title $45 to the trustee serving in such case, after such trustee's services are rendered.

(2) The Judicial Conference of the United States—

(A) shall prescribe additional fees of the same kind as prescribed under section 1914(b) of title 28; and

(B) may prescribe notice of appearance fees and fees charged against distributions in cases under this title;

to pay $15 to trustees serving in cases after such trustees' services are rendered. Beginning 1 year after the date of the enactment of the Bankruptcy Reform Act of 1994, such $15 shall be paid in addition to the amount paid under paragraph (1).

(c) Unless the court orders otherwise, in a case under chapter 12 or 13 of this title the compensation paid to the trustee serving in the case shall not be less than $5 per month from any distribution under the plan during the administration of the plan.

(d) In a case in which the United States trustee serves as trustee, the compensation of the trustee under this section shall be paid to the clerk of the bankruptcy court and deposited by the clerk into the United States Trustee System Fund established by section 589a of title 28.

(Pub.L. 95–598, Nov. 6, 1978, 92 Stat. 2564; Pub.L. 98–353, Title III, §§ 433, 434, July 10, 1984, 98 Stat. 370; Pub.L. 99–554, Title II, §§ 211, 257(f), Oct. 27, 1986, 100 Stat. 3099, 3114; Pub.L. 103–394, Title I, § 117, Title II, § 224(b), Oct. 22, 1994, 108 Stat. 4119, 4130; Pub.L. 109–8, Title II, § 232(b), Title IV, §§ 407, 415, Title XI, § 1104(b), Apr. 20, 2005, 119 Stat. 74, 106, 107, 192.)

HISTORICAL AND STATUTORY NOTES

Revision Notes and Legislative Reports

1978 Acts. Section 330 authorizes the court to award compensation for services and reimbursement of expenses of officers of the estate, and other professionals. The compensation is to be reasonable, for economy in administration is the basic objective. Compensation is to be for actual necessary services, based on the time spent, the nature, the extent and the value of the services rendered, and the cost of comparable services in nonbankruptcy cases. There are the criteria that have been applied by the courts as analytic aids in defining "reasonable" compensation.

The reference to "the cost of comparable services" in a nonbankruptcy case is not intended as a change of existing law. In a bankruptcy cases fees are not a matter for private agreement. There is inherent a "public interest" that "must be considered in awarding fees," *Massachusetts Mutual Life Insurance Co. v. Brock*, 405 F.2d 429, 432 (C.A.5, 1968), cert. denied, 395 U.S. 906 (1969) [89 S.Ct. 1748, 23 L.Ed.2d 220]. An allowance is the result of a balance struck between moderation in the interest of the estate and its security holders and the need to be "generous enough to encourage" lawyers and others to render the necessary and exacting services that bankruptcy cases often require. *In re Yale Express System, Inc.*, 366 F.Supp. 1376, 1381 (S.D.N.Y.1973). The rates for similar kinds of services in private employment is one element, among others, in that balance. Compensation in private employment noted in subsection (a) is a point of reference, not a controlling determinant of what shall be allowed in bankruptcy cases.

One of the major reforms in 1938, especially for reorganization cases, was centralized control over fees in the bankruptcy courts. See *Brown v. Gerdes*, 321 U.S. 178, 182–184 (1944) [64 S.Ct. 487, 88 L.Ed. 659]; *Leiman v. Guttman*, 336 U.S. 1, 4–9, (1949) [69 S.Ct. 371, 93 L.Ed. 453]. It was intended to guard against a recurrence of "the many sordid chapters" in "the history of fees in corporate reorganizations." *Dickinson Industrial Site, Inc. v. Cowan*, 309 U.S. 382, 388 (1940) [60 S.Ct. 595, 84 L.Ed. 819, rehearing denied 60 S.Ct. 806, 309 U.S. 698, 84 L.Ed. 1037]. In the years since then the bankruptcy bar has flourished and prospered, and persons of merit and quality have not eschewed public service in bankruptcy cases merely because bankruptcy courts, in the interest of economy in administration, have not allowed them compensation that may be earned in the private economy of business or the professions. There is no reason to believe that, in generations to come, their successors will be less persuaded by the need to serve in the public interest because of stronger allures of private gain elsewhere.

Subsection (a) provides for compensation of paraprofessional in order to reduce the cost of administering bankruptcy cases. Paraprofessionals can be employed to perform duties which do not require the full range of skills of a qualified professional. Some courts have not hesitated to recognize paraprofessional services as compensable under existing law. An explicit provision to that effect is useful and constructive.

The last sentence of subsection (a) provides that in the case of a public company—defined in section 1101(3)—the court shall refer, after a hearing, all applications to the Securities and Exchange Commission for a report, which shall be advisory only. In Chapter X cases in which the Commission has appeared, it generally filed reports on fee applications. Usually, courts have accorded the SEC's views substantial weight, as representing the opinion of a disinterested agency skilled and experienced in reorganization affairs. The last sentence intends for the advisory assistance of the Commission to be sought only in case of a public company in reorganization under chapter 11.

Subsection (b) reenacts section 249 of Chapter X of the Bankruptcy Act ([former] 11 U.S.C. 649). It is a codification of equitable principles designed to prevent fiduciaries in the case from engaging in the specified transactions since they are in a position to gain inside information or to shape or influence the course of the reorganization. *Wolf v. Weinstein*, 372 U.S. 633 (1963) [83 S.Ct. 969, 10 L.Ed.2d 33, rehearing denied 83 S.Ct. 1522, 373 U.S. 928, 10 L.Ed.2d 427]. The statutory bar of compensation and reimbursement is based on the principle that such transactions involve conflicts of interest. Private gain undoubtedly prompts the purchase or sale of claims or stock interests, while the fiduciary's obligation is to render loyal and disinterested service which his position of trust has imposed upon him. Subsection (b) extends to a trustee, his attorney, committees and their attorneys, or any other persons "acting in the case in a representative or fiduciary capacity." It bars compensation to any of the foregoing, who after assuming to act in such capacity has purchased or sold, directly or indirectly, claims against, or stock in, the debtor. The bar is absolute. It makes no difference whether the transaction brought a gain or loss, or neither, and the court is not authorized to approve a purchase or sale, before or after the transaction. The exception is for an acquisition or transfer "otherwise" than by a voluntary purchase or sale, such as an acquisition by bequest. See *Otis & Co. v. Insurance Bldg. Corp.*, 110 F.2d 333, 335 (C.A.1, 1940).

Subsection (c) is intended for no asset liquidation cases where minimal compensation for trustees is needed. The sum of $20 will be allowed in each case, which is double the amount provided under current law. Senate Report No. 95–989.

Section 330 authorizes compensation for services and reimbursement of expenses of officers of the estate. It also prescribes the standards on which the amount of compensation is to be determined. As noted above, the compensation allowable under this section is subject to the maxima set out in sections 326, 328, and 329. The compensation is to be reasonable, for actual necessary services rendered, based on the time, the nature, the extent, and the value of the services rendered, and on the cost of comparable services other than in a case under the bankruptcy code. The effect of the last provision is to overrule *In re Beverly Crest Convalescent Hospital, Inc.*, 548 F.2d 817 (9th Cir.1976, as amended 1977), which set an arbitrary limit on fees payable, based on the amount of a district judge's salary, and other, similar cases that require fees to be determined based on notions of conservation of the estate and economy of administration. If that case were allowed to stand, attorneys that could earn much higher incomes in other fields would leave the bankruptcy arena. Bankruptcy specialists, who enable the system to operate smoothly, efficiently, and expeditiously, would be driven elsewhere, and the bankruptcy field would be occupied by those who could not find other work and those who practice bankruptcy law only occasionally almost as a public service. Bankruptcy fees that are lower than fees in other areas of the legal profession may operate properly when the attorneys appearing in bankruptcy cases do so intermittently, because a low fee in a small segment of a practice can be absorbed by other work. Bankruptcy specialists, however, if required to accept fees in all of their cases that are consistently lower than fees they could receive elsewhere, will not remain in the bankruptcy field.

This subsection provides for reimbursement of actual, necessary expenses. It further provides for compensation of paraprofessionals employed by professional persons employed by the estate of the debtor. The provision is included to reduce the cost of administering bankruptcy cases. In nonbankruptcy areas, attorneys are able to charge for a paraprofessional's time on an hourly basis, and not include it in overhead. If a similar practice does not pertain in bankruptcy cases then the attorney will be less inclined to use paraprofessionals even where the work involved could easily be handled by an attorney's assistant, at much lower cost to the estate. "This provision is designed to encourage attorneys to use paraprofessional assistance where possible, and to insure that the estate, not the attorney, will bear the cost, to the benefit of both the estate and the attorneys involved. House Report No. 95–595.

1984 Acts. Statements by Legislative Leaders, see 1984 U.S.Code Cong. and Adm.News, p. 576.

1986 Acts. House Report No. 99–764 and House Conference Report No. 99–958, see 1986 U.S.Code Cong. and Adm. News, p. 5227.

1994 Acts. House Report No. 103–835, see 1994 U.S. Code Cong. and Adm. News, p. 3340.

2005 Acts. House Report No. 109–31(Part I), see 2005 U.S. Code Cong. and Adm. News, p. 88.

Legislative Statements

Section 330(a) contains the standard of compensation adopted in H.R. 8200 as passed by the House rather than the contrary standard contained in the Senate amendment. Attorneys' fees in bankruptcy cases can be quite large and should be closely examined by the court. However bankruptcy legal services are entitled to command the same competency of counsel as other cases. In that light, the policy of this section is to compensate attorneys and other professionals serving in a case under title 11 at the same rate as the attorney or other professional would be compensated for performing comparable services other than in a case under title 11. Contrary language in the Senate report accompanying S. 2266 is rejected, and *Massachusetts Mutual Life Insurance Company v. Brock*, 405 F.2d 429, 432 (5th Cir. 1968) is overruled. Notions of economy of the estate in fixing fees are outdated and have no place in a bankruptcy code.

Section 330(a)(2) of the Senate amendment is deleted although the Securities and Exchange Commission retains a right to file an advisory report under section 1109.

Section 330(b) of the Senate amendment is deleted as unnecessary, as the limitations contained therein are covered by section 328(c) of H.R. 8200 as passed by the House and contained in the House amendment.

Section 330(c) of the Senate amendment providing for a trustee to receive a fee of $20 for each estate from the filing fee paid to the clerk is retained as section 330(b) of the House amendment. The section will encourage private trustees to serve in cases under title 11 and in pilot districts will place less of a burden on the U.S. trustee to serve in no-asset cases.

Section 330(b) of H.R. 8200 as passed by the House is retained by the House amendment as section 330(c) [section 15330].

References in Text

The date of the enactment of the Bankruptcy Reform Act of 1994, referred to in subsec. (b)(2), is the date of enactment of Pub.L. 103–394, which was approved Oct. 22, 1994.

Effective and Applicability Provisions

2005 Acts. Amendments by Pub.L. 109–8 effective, except as otherwise provided, 180 days after April 20, 2005, and inapplicable with respect to cases commenced under Title 11 before the effective date, see Pub.L. 109–8, § 1501, set out as a note under 11 U.S.C.A. § 101.

1994 Acts. Amendment by section 117 of Pub.L. 103–394 effective on Oct. 22, 1994, and applicable with respect to cases commenced under Title 11 of the United States Code before, on, and after Oct. 22, 1994, see section 702(a), (b)(2)(B) of

Pub.L. 103–394, set out as a note under section 101 of this title.

Amendment by section 224(b) of Pub.L. 103–394 effective Oct. 22, 1994, and shall not apply with respect to cases commenced under this title before Oct. 22, 1994, see section 702(a), (b)(1) of Pub.L. 103–394, set out as a note under section 101 of this title.

1986 Acts. Amendment by Pub.L. 99–554 effective 30 days after Oct. 27, 1986, except as otherwise provided for, see section 302(a) of Pub.L. 99–554, set out as a note under section 581 of Title 28, Judiciary and Judicial Procedure.

Amendment by Pub.L. 99–554, § 211, not to become effective in or with respect to certain specified judicial districts until, or apply to cases while pending in such district before, the expiration of the 270-day period beginning 30 days after Oct. 27, 1986, or of the 30-day period beginning on the date the Attorney General certifies under section 303 of Pub.L. 99–554 the region specified in a paragraph of section 581(a) of Title 28, as amended by section 111(a) of Pub.L. 99–554, that includes such district, whichever occurs first, see section 302(d)(1) of Pub.L. 99–554, set out as a note under section 581 of Title 28.

Amendment by Pub.L. 99–554, § 211, not to become effective in or with respect to certain specified judicial districts until, or apply to cases while pending in such district before, the expiration of the 2-year period beginning 30 days after Oct. 27, 1986, or of the 30-day period beginning on the date the Attorney General certifies under section 303 of Pub.L. 99–554 the region specified in a paragraph of section 581(a) of Title 28, as amended by section 111(a) of Pub.L. 99–554, that includes such district, whichever occurs first, see section 302(d)(2) of Pub.L. 99–554, set out as a note under section 581 of Title 28.

Amendment by Pub.L. 99–554, § 211, not to become effective in or with respect to judicial districts established for the States of Alabama and North Carolina until, or apply to cases while pending in such district before, such district elects to be included in a bankruptcy region established in section 581(a) of Title 28, as amended by section 111(a) of Pub.L. 99–554, or Oct. 1, 2002, whichever occurs first, and, except as otherwise provided for, with respect to cases under chapters 7, 11, 12, and 13 of Title 11 commenced before 30 days after Oct. 27, 1986, and pending in a judicial district in the States of Alabama or North Carolina before any election made under section 302(d)(3)(A) of Pub.L. 99–554 by such district becomes effective or Oct. 1, 2002, whichever occurs first, amendments by Pub.L. 99–554 not to apply until Oct. 1, 2003, or the expiration of the 1-year period beginning on the date such election becomes effective, whichever occurs first, and further, in any judicial district in Alabama or North Carolina not making the election described in section 302(d)(3)(A) of Pub.L. 99–554, any person appointed under regulations issued by the Judicial Conference to administer estates in cases under Title 11 authorized to establish, etc., a panel of private trustees, and to supervise cases and trustees in cases under chapters 7, 11, 12, and 13 of Title 11, until amendments by sections 201 to 231 of Pub.L. 99–554 effective in such district, see section 302(d)(3)(A) to (F), (H), and (I) of Pub.L. 99–554, set out as a note under section 581 of Title 28.

Amendment by Pub.L. 99–554, § 211, except as otherwise provided, with respect to cases under chapters 7, 11, 12, and 13 of Title 11 commenced before 30 days after Oct. 27, 1986, and pending in a judicial district referred to in section 581(a)

of Title 28, as amended by section 111(a) of Pub.L. 99–554, for which a United States trustee is not authorized before 30 days after Oct. 27, 1986 to be appointed, not applicable until the expiration of the 3-year period beginning on Oct. 27, 1986, or of the 1-year period beginning on the date the Attorney General certifies under section 303 of Pub.L. 99–554 the region specified in a paragraph of such section 581(a) that includes, such district, whichever occurs first, see section 302(e)(1), (2) of Pub.L. 99–554, set out as a note under section 581 of Title 28.

Amendment by Pub.L. 99–554, § 257(f), effective 30 days after Oct. 27, 1986, but not applicable to cases commenced under this title before that date, see section 302(a), (c)(1) of Pub.L. 99–554, set out as a note under section 581 of Title 28.

1984 Acts. Amendment by Pub.L. 98–353 effective with respect to cases filed 90 days after July 10, 1984, see section 552(a), formerly 553(a), of Pub.L. 98–353, set out as a note under section 101 of this title.

Separability of Provisions

If any provision of or amendment made by Pub.L. 103–394 or the application of such provision or amendment to any person or circumstance is held to be unconstitutional, the remaining provisions of and amendments made by Pub.L. 103–394 and the application of such provisions and amendments to any person or circumstance shall not be affected thereby, see section 701 of Pub.L. 103–394, set out as a note under section 101 of this title.

CROSS REFERENCES

Adverse interest and conduct of officers of estate, see 18 USCA § 154.

Allowances to trustee and trustee's attorney in investor protection liquidation proceedings, see 15 USCA § 78eee.

Debtor in possession's right of compensation,

    Chapter 11 cases, see 11 USCA § 1107.

    Chapter 12 cases, see 11 USCA § 1203.

Guidelines for reviewing applications for compensation and reimbursement of expenses, see Fed.Rules Bankr.Proc. Rule 2016, 11 USCA.

Officers' compensation as administrative expense, see 11 USCA § 503.

Supervision by Attorney General, see 28 USCA § 586.

United States Trustee System Fund establishment and purpose, see 28 USCA § 589a.

§ 331. Interim compensation

A trustee, an examiner, a debtor's attorney, or any professional person employed under section 327 or 1103 of this title may apply to the court not more than once every 120 days after an order for relief in a case under this title, or more often if the court permits, for such compensation for services rendered before the date of such an application or reimbursement for expenses incurred before such date as is provided under section 330 of this title. After notice and a hearing, the court may allow and disburse to such applicant such compensation or reimbursement.

(Pub.L. 95–598, Nov. 6, 1978, 92 Stat. 2564.)

HISTORICAL AND STATUTORY NOTES

Revision Notes and Legislative Reports

1978 Acts. Section 331 permits trustees and professional persons to apply to the court not more than once every 120 days for interim compensation and reimbursement payments. The court may permit more frequent applications if the circumstances warrant, such as in very large cases where the legal work is extensive and merits more frequent payments. The court is authorized to allow and order disbursement to the applicant of compensation and reimbursement that is otherwise allowable under section 330. The only effect of this section is to remove any doubt that officers of the estate may apply for, and the court may approve, compensation and reimbursement during the case, instead of being required to wait until the end of the case, which in some instances, may be years. The practice of interim compensation is followed in some courts today, but has been subject to some question. This section explicitly authorizes it.

This section will apply to professionals such as auctioneers and appraisers only if they are not paid on a per job basis. Senate Report No. 95–989.

§ 332. Consumer privacy ombudsman

(a) If a hearing is required under section 363(b)(1)(B), the court shall order the United States trustee to appoint, not later than 7 days before the commencement of the hearing, 1 disinterested person (other than the United States trustee) to serve as the consumer privacy ombudsman in the case and shall require that notice of such hearing be timely given to such ombudsman.

(b) The consumer privacy ombudsman may appear and be heard at such hearing and shall provide to the court information to assist the court in its consideration of the facts, circumstances, and conditions of the proposed sale or lease of personally identifiable information under section 363(b)(1)(B). Such information may include presentation of—

    (1) the debtor's privacy policy;

    (2) the potential losses or gains of privacy to consumers if such sale or such lease is approved by the court;

    (3) the potential costs or benefits to consumers if such sale or such lease is approved by the court; and

    (4) the potential alternatives that would mitigate potential privacy losses or potential costs to consumers.

(c) A consumer privacy ombudsman shall not disclose any personally identifiable information obtained by the ombudsman under this title.

(Added Pub.L. 109–8, Title II, § 232(a), Apr. 20, 2005, 119 Stat. 73; amended Pub.L. 111–16, § 2(3), May 7, 2009, 123 Stat. 1607.)

HISTORICAL AND STATUTORY NOTES

Revision Notes and Legislative Reports

2005 Acts. House Report No. 109–31(Part I), see 2005 U.S. Code Cong. and Adm. News, p. 88.

2009 Amendments. Subsec. (a). Pub.L. 111–16, § 2(3), struck out "5 days" and inserted "7 days".

Effective and Applicability Provisions

2009 Acts. Amendments by Pub.L. 111–16 effective Dec. 1, 2009, see Pub.L. 111–16, § 7, set out as a note under 11 U.S.C.A. § 109.

2005 Acts. Amendments by Pub.L. 109–8 effective, except as otherwise provided, 180 days after April 20, 2005, and inapplicable with respect to cases commenced under Title 11 before the effective date, see Pub.L. 109–8, § 1501, set out as a note under 11 U.S.C.A. § 101.

§ 333. Appointment of patient care ombudsman

(a)(1) If the debtor in a case under chapter 7, 9, or 11 is a health care business, the court shall order, not later than 30 days after the commencement of the case, the appointment of an ombudsman to monitor the quality of patient care and to represent the interests of the patients of the health care business unless the court finds that the appointment of such ombudsman is not necessary for the protection of patients under the specific facts of the case.

(2)(A) If the court orders the appointment of an ombudsman under paragraph (1), the United States trustee shall appoint 1 disinterested person (other than the United States trustee) to serve as such ombudsman.

(B) If the debtor is a health care business that provides long-term care, then the United States trustee may appoint the State Long–Term Care Ombudsman appointed under the Older Americans Act of 1965 for the State in which the case is pending to serve as the ombudsman required by paragraph (1).

(C) If the United States trustee does not appoint a State Long–Term Care Ombudsman under subparagraph (B), the court shall notify the State Long–Term Care Ombudsman appointed under the Older Americans Act of 1965 for the State in which the case is pending, of the name and address of the person who is appointed under subparagraph (A).

(b) An ombudsman appointed under subsection (a) shall—

    (1) monitor the quality of patient care provided to patients of the debtor, to the extent necessary under the circumstances, including interviewing patients and physicians;

    (2) not later than 60 days after the date of appointment, and not less frequently than at 60–day intervals thereafter, report to the court after notice to the parties in interest, at a hearing or in writing, regarding the quality of patient care provided to patients of the debtor; and

    (3) if such ombudsman determines that the quality of patient care provided to patients of the debtor is declining significantly or is otherwise being materially compromised, file with the court a motion or a written report, with notice to the parties in interest immediately upon making such determination.

(c)(1) An ombudsman appointed under subsection (a) shall maintain any information obtained by such ombudsman under this section that relates to patients (including information relating to patient records) as confidential information. Such ombudsman may not review confidential patient records unless the court approves such review in advance and imposes restrictions on such ombudsman to protect the confidentiality of such records.

(2) An ombudsman appointed under subsection (a)(2)(B) shall have access to patient records consistent with authority of such ombudsman under the Older Americans Act of 1965 and under non-Federal laws governing the State Long–Term Care Ombudsman program.

(Added Pub.L. 109–8, Title XI, § 1104(a)(1), Apr. 20, 2005, 119 Stat. 191.)

HISTORICAL AND STATUTORY NOTES

Revision Notes and Legislative Reports

2005 Acts. House Report No. 109–31(Part I), see 2005 U.S. Code Cong. and Adm. News, p. 88.

References in Text

Chapter 7, 9, or 11, referred to in subsec. (a)(1), means chapter 7, 9, or 11 of this title, 11 U.S.C.A. § 701 et seq., 11 U.S.C.A. § 901 et seq., or 11 U.S.C.A. § 1101 et seq., respectively.

The Older Americans Act of 1965, referred to in subsecs. (a)(2)(B), (C) and (c)(2), is Pub.L. 89–73, July 14, 1965, 79 Stat. 218, as amended, which is classified principally to chapter 35 of Title 42, 42 U.S.C.A. § 3001 et seq. For complete classification, see Short Title note set out under 42 U.S.C.A. § 3001 and Tables.

Effective and Applicability Provisions

2005 Acts. Enactment of this section by Pub.L. 109–8 effective, except as otherwise provided, 180 days after April 20, 2005, and inapplicable with respect to cases commenced under Title 11 before the effective date, see Pub.L. 109–8, § 1501, set out as a note under 11 U.S.C.A. § 101.

SUBCHAPTER III—ADMINISTRATION

§ 341. Meetings of creditors and equity security holders

(a) Within a reasonable time after the order for relief in a case under this title, the United States trustee shall convene and preside at a meeting of creditors.

(b) The United States trustee may convene a meeting of any equity security holders.

(c) The court may not preside at, and may not attend, any meeting under this section including any final meeting of creditors. Notwithstanding any local court rule, provision of a State constitution, any otherwise applicable nonbankruptcy law, or any other requirement that representation at the meeting of creditors under subsection (a) be by an attorney, a creditor holding a consumer debt or any representative of the creditor (which may include an entity or an employee of an entity and may be a representative for more than 1 creditor) shall be permitted to appear at and participate in the meeting of creditors in a case under chapter 7 or 13, either alone or in conjunction with an attorney for the creditor. Nothing in this subsection shall be construed to require any creditor to be represented by an attorney at any meeting of creditors.

(d) Prior to the conclusion of the meeting of creditors or equity security holders, the trustee shall orally examine the debtor to ensure that the debtor in a case under chapter 7 of this title is aware of—

(1) the potential consequences of seeking a discharge in bankruptcy, including the effects on credit history;

(2) the debtor's ability to file a petition under a different chapter of this title;

(3) the effect of receiving a discharge of debts under this title; and

(4) the effect of reaffirming a debt, including the debtor's knowledge of the provisions of section 524(d) of this title.

(e) Notwithstanding subsections (a) and (b), the court, on the request of a party in interest and after notice and a hearing, for cause may order that the United States trustee not convene a meeting of creditors or equity security holders if the debtor has filed a plan as to which the debtor solicited acceptances prior to the commencement of the case.

(Pub.L. 95–598, Nov. 6, 1978, 92 Stat. 2564; Pub.L. 99–554, Title II, § 212, Oct. 27, 1986, 100 Stat. 3099; Pub.L. 103–394, Title I, § 115, Oct. 22, 1994, 108 Stat. 4118; Pub.L. 109–8, Title IV, §§ 402, 413, Apr. 20, 2005, 119 Stat. 104, 107.)

HISTORICAL AND STATUTORY NOTES

Revision Notes and Legislative Reports

1978 Acts. Section [subsection] (a) of this section requires that there be a meeting of creditors within a reasonable time after the order for relief in the case. The Bankruptcy Act [former Title 11] and the current Rules of Bankruptcy Procedure provide for a meeting of creditors, and specify the time and manner of the meeting, and the business to be conducted. This bill leaves those matters to the rules. Under section 405(d) of the bill, the present rules will continue to govern until new rules are promulgated. Thus, pending the adoption of different rules, the present procedure for the meeting will continue.

Subsection (b) authorizes the court to order a meeting of equity security holders in cases where such a meeting would be beneficial or useful, for example, in a chapter 11 reorganization case where it may be necessary for the equity security holders to organize in order to be able to participate in the negotiation of a plan of reorganization.

Subsection (c) makes clear that the bankruptcy judge is to preside at the meeting of creditors. Senate Report No. 95–989.

1986 Acts. House Report No. 99–764 and House Conference Report No. 99–958, see 1986 U.S.Code Cong. and Adm. News, p. 5227.

1994 Acts. House Report No. 103–835, see 1994 U.S. Code Cong. and Adm. News, p. 3340.

2005 Acts. House Report No. 109–31(Part I), see 2005 U.S. Code Cong. and Adm. News, p. 88.

Legislative Statements

Section 341(c) of the Senate amendment is deleted and a contrary provision is added indicating that the bankruptcy judge will not preside at or attend the first meeting of creditors or equity security holders but a discharge hearing for all individuals will be held at which the judge will preside.

References in Text

Chapter 7, referred to in subsecs. (c) and (d), is chapter 7 of this title, 11 U.S.C.A. § 701 et seq.

Chapter 13, referred to in subsec. (c), is chapter 13 of this title, 11 U.S.C.A. § 1301 et seq.

Effective and Applicability Provisions

2005 Acts. Amendments by Pub.L. 109–8 effective, except as otherwise provided, 180 days after April 20, 2005, and inapplicable with respect to cases commenced under Title 11 before the effective date, see Pub.L. 109–8, § 1501, set out as a note under 11 U.S.C.A. § 101.

1994 Acts. Amendment by Pub.L. 103–394 effective on Oct. 22, 1994, and not to apply with respect to cases commenced under Title 11 of the United States Code before Oct. 22, 1994, see section 702 of Pub.L. 103–394, set out as a note under section 101 of this title.

1986 Acts. Amendment by Pub.L. 99–554 effective 30 days after Oct. 27, 1986, except as otherwise provided for, see section 302(a) of Pub.L. 99–554, set out as a note under section 581 of Title 28, Judiciary and Judicial Procedure.

Amendment by Pub.L. 99–554, § 212, not to become effective in or with respect to certain specified judicial districts until, or apply to cases while pending in such district before, the expiration of the 270-day period beginning 30 days after Oct. 27, 1986, or of the 30-day period beginning on the date the Attorney General certifies under section 303 of Pub.L. 99–554 the region specified in a paragraph of section 581(a) of Title 28, as amended by section 111(a) of Pub.L. 99–554, that includes such district, whichever occurs first, see section 302(d)(1) of Pub.L. 99–554, set out as a note under section 581 of Title 28.

Amendment by Pub.L. 99–554, § 212, not to become effective in or with respect to certain specified judicial districts until, or apply to cases while pending in such district before, the expiration of the 2-year period beginning 30 days after Oct. 27, 1986, or of the 30-day period beginning on the date the Attorney General certifies under section 303 of Pub.L. 99–554 the region specified in a paragraph of section 581(a) of Title 28, as amended by section 111(a) of Pub.L. 99–554, that includes such district, whichever occurs first, see section 302(d)(2) of Pub.L. 99–554, set out as a note under section 581 of Title 28.

Amendment by Pub.L. 99–554, § 212, not to become effective in or with respect to judicial districts established for the States of Alabama and North Carolina until, or apply to cases while pending in such district before, such district elects to be included in a bankruptcy region established in section 581(a) of Title 28, as amended by section 111(a) of Pub.L. 99–554, or

Oct. 1, 2002, whichever occurs first, and, except as otherwise provided, with respect to cases under chapters 7, 11, 12, and 13 of Title 11 commenced before 30 days after Oct. 27, 1986, and pending in a judicial district in the States of Alabama or North Carolina before any election made under section 302(d)(3)(A) of Pub.L. 99–554 by such district becomes effective or Oct. 1, 2003, whichever occurs first, amendments by Pub.L. 99–554 not to apply until Oct. 1, 1992, or the expiration of the 1-year period beginning on the date such election becomes effective whichever occurs first, and further, in any judicial district in Alabama or North Carolina not making the election described in section 302(d)(3)(A) of Pub.L. 99–554, any person appointed under regulations issued by the Judicial Conference to administer estates in cases under Title 11 authorized to establish, etc., a panel of private trustees, and to supervise cases and trustees in cases under chapters 7, 11, 12, and 13 of Title 11, until amendments by sections 201 to 231 of Pub.L. 99–554 effective in such district, see section 302(d)(3)(A) to (F), (H), and (I) of Pub.L. 99–554, set out as a note under section 581 of Title 28.

Amendment by Pub.L. 99–554, § 212, except as otherwise provided, with respect to cases under chapters 7, 11, 12 and 13 of Title 11 commenced before 30 days after Oct. 27, 1986, and pending in a judicial district referred to in section 581(a) of Title 28, as amended by section 111(a) of Pub.L. 99–554, for which a United States trustee is not authorized before 30 days after Oct. 27, 1986 to be appointed, not applicable until the expiration of the 3-year period beginning on Oct. 27, 1986, or of the 1-year period beginning on the date the Attorney General certifies under section 303 of Pub.L. 99–554 the region specified in a paragraph of such section 581(a) that includes, such district, whichever occurs first, see section 302(e)(1), (2) of Pub.L. 99–554, set out as a note under section 581 of Title 28.

Separability of Provisions

If any provision of or amendment made by Pub.L. 103–394 or the application of such provision or amendment to any person or circumstance is held to be unconstitutional, the remaining provisions of and amendments made by Pub.L. 103–394 and the application of such provisions and amendments to any person or circumstance shall not be affected thereby, see section 701 of Pub.L. 103–394, set out as a note under section 101 of this title.

Participation by Bankruptcy Administrator at Meetings of Creditors and Equity Security Holders

Section 105 of Pub.L. 103–394 provided that:

"(a) **Presiding officer.**—A bankruptcy administrator appointed under section 302(d)(3)(I) of the Bankruptcy Judges, United States Trustees, and Family Farmer Bankruptcy Act of 1986 (28 U.S.C. 581 note; Public Law 99–554; 100 Stat. 3123), as amended by section 317(a) of the Federal Courts Study Committee Implementation Act of 1990 (Public Law 101–650; 104 Stat. 5115), or the bankruptcy administrator's designee may preside at the meeting of creditors convened under section 341(a) of title 11, United States Code [subsec. (a) of this section]. The bankruptcy administrator or the bankruptcy administrator's designee may preside at any meeting of equity security holders convened under section 341(b) of title 11, United States Code [subsec. (b) of this section].

"(b) **Examination of the debtor.**—The bankruptcy administrator or the bankruptcy administrator's designee may examine the debtor at the meeting of creditors and may admin-

ister the oath required under section 343 of title 11, United States Code [section 343 of this title]."

CROSS REFERENCES

Election of,

    Creditors' committee, see 11 USCA § 705.

    Trustee, see 11 USCA § 702.

Inapplicability of this section in railroad reorganization cases, see 11 USCA § 1161.

§ 342.   Notice

(a) There shall be given such notice as is appropriate, including notice to any holder of a community claim, of an order for relief in a case under this title.

(b) Before the commencement of a case under this title by an individual whose debts are primarily consumer debts, the clerk shall give to such individual written notice containing—

    (1) a brief description of—

        (A) chapters 7, 11, 12, and 13 and the general purpose, benefits, and costs of proceeding under each of those chapters; and

        (B) the types of services available from credit counseling agencies; and

    (2) statements specifying that—

        (A) a person who knowingly and fraudulently conceals assets or makes a false oath or statement under penalty of perjury in connection with a case under this title shall be subject to fine, imprisonment, or both; and

        (B) all information supplied by a debtor in connection with a case under this title is subject to examination by the Attorney General.

(c)(1) If notice is required to be given by the debtor to a creditor under this title, any rule, any applicable law, or any order of the court, such notice shall contain the name, address, and last 4 digits of the taxpayer identification number of the debtor. If the notice concerns an amendment that adds a creditor to the schedules of assets and liabilities, the debtor shall include the full taxpayer identification number in the notice sent to that creditor, but the debtor shall include only the last 4 digits of the taxpayer identification number in the copy of the notice filed with the court.

(2)(A) If, within the 90 days before the commencement of a voluntary case, a creditor supplies the debtor in at least 2 communications sent to the debtor with the current account number of the debtor and the address at which such creditor requests to receive correspondence, then any notice required by this title to be sent by the debtor to such creditor shall be sent to such address and shall include such account number.

(B) If a creditor would be in violation of applicable nonbankruptcy law by sending any such communication within such 90-day period and if such creditor supplies the debtor in the last 2 communications with the current account number of the debtor and the address at which such creditor requests to receive correspondence, then any notice required by this title to be sent by the debtor to such creditor shall be sent to such address and shall include such account number.

(d) In a case under chapter 7 of this title in which the debtor is an individual and in which the presumption of abuse arises under section 707(b), the clerk shall give written notice to all creditors not later than 10 days after the date of the filing of the petition that the presumption of abuse has arisen.

(e)(1) In a case under chapter 7 or 13 of this title of a debtor who is an individual, a creditor at any time may both file with the court and serve on the debtor a notice of address to be used to provide notice in such case to such creditor.

(2) Any notice in such case required to be provided to such creditor by the debtor or the court later than 7 days after the court and the debtor receive such creditor's notice of address, shall be provided to such address.

(f)(1) An entity may file with any bankruptcy court a notice of address to be used by all the bankruptcy courts or by particular bankruptcy courts, as so specified by such entity at the time such notice is filed, to provide notice to such entity in all cases under chapters 7 and 13 pending in the courts with respect to which such notice is filed, in which such entity is a creditor.

(2) In any case filed under chapter 7 or 13, any notice required to be provided by a court with respect to which a notice is filed under paragraph (1), to such entity later than 30 days after the filing of such notice under paragraph (1) shall be provided to such address unless with respect to a particular case a different address is specified in a notice filed and served in accordance with subsection (e).

(3) A notice filed under paragraph (1) may be withdrawn by such entity.

(g)(1) Notice provided to a creditor by the debtor or the court other than in accordance with this section (excluding this subsection) shall not be effective notice until such notice is brought to the attention of such creditor. If such creditor designates a person or an organizational subdivision of such creditor to be responsible for receiving notices under this title and establishes reasonable procedures so that such notices receivable by such creditor are to be delivered to such person or such subdivision, then a notice provided to such creditor other than in accordance with this section (excluding this subsection) shall not be considered to have been brought to the attention of such creditor until such notice is received by such person or such subdivision.

(2) A monetary penalty may not be imposed on a creditor for a violation of a stay in effect under section 362(a) (including a monetary penalty imposed under section 362(k)) or for failure to comply with section 542 or 543 unless the conduct that is the basis of such violation or of such failure occurs after such creditor receives notice effective under this section of the order for relief.

(Pub.L. 95–598, Nov. 6, 1978, 92 Stat. 2565; Pub.L. 98–353, Title III, §§ 302, 435, July 10, 1984, 98 Stat. 352, 370; Pub.L. 103–394, Title II, § 225, Oct. 22, 1994, 108 Stat. 4131; Pub.L. 109–8, Title I, §§ 102(d), 104, Title II, § 234(b), Title III, § 315(a), Apr. 20, 2005, 119 Stat. 33, 35, 75, 88; Pub.L. 111–16, § 2(4), May 7, 2009, 123 Stat. 1607.)

HISTORICAL AND STATUTORY NOTES

Revision Notes and Legislative Reports

1978 Acts. Subsection (a) of section 342 requires the clerk of the bankruptcy court to give notice of the order for relief. The rules will prescribe to whom the notice should be sent and in what manner notice will be given. The rules already prescribe such things, and they will continue to govern unless changed as provided in section 404(a) of the bill. Due process will certainly require notice to all creditors and equity security holders. State and Federal governmental representatives responsible for collecting taxes will also receive notice. In cases where the debtor is subject to regulation, the regulatory agency with jurisdiction will receive notice. In order to insure maximum notice to all parties in interest, the Rules will include notice by publication in appropriate cases and for appropriate issues. Other notices will be given as appropriate.

Subsections (b) and (c) are derived from section 21g of the Bankruptcy Act [section 44(g) of former Title 11]. They specify that the trustee may file notice of the commencement of the case in land recording offices in order to give notice of the pendency of the case to potential transferees of the debtor's real property. Such filing is unnecessary in the county in which the bankruptcy case is commenced. If notice is properly filed, a subsequent purchaser of the property will not be a bona fide purchaser. Otherwise, a purchaser, including a purchaser at a judicial sale, that has no knowledge of the case, is not prevented from obtaining the status of a bona fide purchaser by the mere commencement of the case. "County" is defined in title 1 of the United States Code [1 U.S.C.A. § 2] to include other political subdivisions where counties are not used. Senate Report No. 95–989.

1984 Acts. Statements by Legislative Leaders, see 1984 U.S.Code Cong. and Adm.News, p. 576.

1994 Acts. House Report No. 103–835, see 1994 U.S. Code Cong. and Adm. News, p. 3340.

2005 Acts. House Report No. 109–31(Part I), see 2005 U.S. Code Cong. and Adm. News, p. 88.

Legislative Statements

Section 342(b) and (c) of the Senate amendment are adopted in principle but moved to section 549(c), in lieu of section 342(b) of H.R. 8200 as passed by the House.

Section 342(c) of H.R. 8200 as passed by the House is deleted as a matter to be left to the Rules of Bankruptcy Procedure.

References in Text

Chapters 7, 11, 12, and 13, referred to in subsec. (b)(1), are chapters 7, 11, 12, and 13 of this title, 11 U.S.C.A. § 701 et seq., 11 U.S.C.A. § 1101 et seq., 11 U.S.C.A. § 1201 et seq., and 11 U.S.C.A. § 1301 et seq., respectively.

Chapter 7 of this title, referred to in subsec. (d), is 11 U.S.C.A. § 701 et seq.

Chapter 7 or 13, referred to in subsecs. (e)(1), (f)(1), (2), is chapter 7 or 13 of this title, 11 U.S.C.A. § 701 et seq. or 11 U.S.C.A. § 1301 et seq., respectively.

Effective and Applicability Provisions

2009 Acts. Amendments by Pub.L. 111–16 effective Dec. 1, 2009, see Pub.L. 111–16, § 7, set out as a note under 11 U.S.C.A. § 109.

2005 Acts. Amendments by Pub.L. 109–8 effective, except as otherwise provided, 180 days after April 20, 2005, and inapplicable with respect to cases commenced under Title 11 before the effective date, see Pub.L. 109–8, § 1501, set out as a note under 11 U.S.C.A. § 101.

1994 Acts. Amendment by Pub.L. 103–394 effective on Oct. 22, 1994, and not to apply with respect to cases commenced under Title 11 of the United States Code before Oct. 22, 1994, see section 702 of Pub.L. 103–394, set out as a note under section 101 of this title.

1984 Acts. Amendment by Pub.L. 98–353 effective with respect to cases filed 90 days after July 10, 1984, see section 552(a), formerly 553(a), of Pub.L. 98–353, set out as a note under section 101 of this title.

Separability of Provisions

If any provision of or amendment made by Pub.L. 103–394 or the application of such provision or amendment to any person or circumstance is held to be unconstitutional, the remaining provisions of and amendments made by Pub.L. 103–394 and the application of such provisions and amendments to any person or circumstance shall not be affected thereby, see section 701 of Pub.L. 103–394, set out as a note under section 101 of this title.

CROSS REFERENCES

Instructions in notice to customers, see 11 USCA § 765.

"Net equity" defined in relation to payments made by customers to trustee within 60 days after notice, see 11 USCA § 741.

Notice in,

Commodity broker liquidation cases, see 11 USCA § 762.

Investor protection liquidation proceedings, see 15 USCA § 78fff–2.

Stockbroker liquidation cases, see 11 USCA § 743.

§ 343. Examination of the debtor

The debtor shall appear and submit to examination under oath at the meeting of creditors under section 341(a) of this title. Creditors, any indenture trustee, any trustee or examiner in the case, or the United States trustee may examine the debtor. The United States trustee may administer the oath required under this section.

(Pub.L. 95–598, Nov. 6, 1978, 92 Stat. 2565; Pub.L. 98–353, Title III, § 436, July 10, 1984, 98 Stat. 370; Pub.L. 99–554, Title II, § 213, Oct. 27, 1986, 100 Stat. 3099.)

HISTORICAL AND STATUTORY NOTES
Revision Notes and Legislative Reports

1978 Acts. This section, derived from section 21a of the Bankruptcy Act [section 44(a) of former Title 11], requires the debtor to appear at the meeting of creditors and submit to examination under oath. The purpose of the examination is to enable creditors and the trustee to determine if assets have improperly been disposed of or concealed or if there are grounds for objection to discharge. The scope of the examination under this section will be governed by the Rules of Bankruptcy Procedure, as it is today. See rules 205(d), 10–213(c), and 11–26. It is expected that the scope prescribed by these rules for liquidation cases, that is, "only the debtor's acts, conduct, or property, or any matter that may affect the administration of the estate, or the debtor's right to discharge" will remain substantially unchanged. In reorganization cases, the examination would be broader, including inquiry into the liabilities and financial condition of the debtor, the operation of his business, and the desirability of the continuance thereof, and other matters relevant to the case and to the formulation of the plan. Examination of other persons in connection with the bankruptcy case is left completely to the rules, just as examination of witnesses in civil cases is governed by the Federal Rules of Civil Procedure. Senate Report No. 95–989.

1984 Acts. Statements by Legislative Leaders, see 1984 U.S.Code Cong. and Adm.News, p. 576.

1986 Acts. House Report No. 99–764 and House Conference Report No. 99–958, see 1986 U.S.Code Cong. and Adm. News, p. 5227.

Effective and Applicability Provisions

1986 Acts. Amendment by Pub.L. 99–554 effective 30 days after Oct. 27, 1986, except as otherwise provided for, see section 302(a) of Pub.L. 99–554, set out as a note under section 581 of Title 28, Judiciary and Judicial Procedure.

Amendment by Pub.L. 99–554, § 213, not to become effective in or with respect to certain specified judicial districts until, or apply to cases while pending in such district before, the expiration of the 270-day period beginning 30 days after Oct. 27, 1986, or of the 30-day period beginning on the date the Attorney General certifies under section 303 of Pub.L. 99–554 the region specified in a paragraph of section 581(a) of Title 28, as amended by section 111(a) of Pub.L. 99–554, that includes such district, whichever occurs first, see section 302(d)(1) of Pub.L. 99–554, set out as a note under section 581 of Title 28.

Amendment by Pub.L. 99–554, § 213, not to become effective in or with respect to certain specified judicial districts until, or apply to cases while pending in such district before, the expiration of the 2-year period beginning 30 days after Oct. 27, 1986, or of the 30-day period beginning on the date the Attorney General certifies under section 303 of Pub.L. 99–554 the region specified in a paragraph of section 581(a) of Title 28, as amended by section 111(a) of Pub.L. 99–554, that includes such district, whichever occurs first, see section 302(d)(2) of Pub.L. 99–554, set out as a note under section 581 of Title 28.

Amendment by Pub.L. 99–554, § 213, not to become effective in or with respect to judicial districts established for the States of Alabama and North Carolina until, or apply to cases while pending in such district before, such district elects to be included in a bankruptcy region established in section 581(a) of Title 28, as amended by section 111(a) of Pub.L. 99–554, or

Oct. 1, 2002, whichever occurs first, and, except as otherwise provided for, with respect to cases under chapters 7, 11, 12, and 13 of Title 11 commenced before 30 days after Oct. 27, 1986, and pending in a judicial district in the States of Alabama or North Carolina before any election made under section 302(d)(3)(A) of Pub.L. 99–554 by such district becomes effective or Oct. 1, 2002, whichever occurs first, amendments by Pub.L. 99–554 not to apply until Oct. 1, 2003, or the expiration of the 1-year period beginning on the date such election becomes effective, whichever occurs first, and further, in any judicial district in Alabama or North Carolina not making the election described in section 302(d)(3)(A) of Pub.L. 99–554, any person appointed under regulations issued by the Judicial Conference to administer estates in cases under Title 11 authorized to establish, etc., a panel of private trustees, and to supervise cases and trustees in cases under chapters 7, 11, 12, and 13 of Title 11, until amendments by sections 201 to 231 of Pub.L. 99–554 effective in such district, see section 302(d)(3)(A) to (F), (H), and (I) of Pub.L. 99–554, set out as a note under section 581 of Title 28.

Amendment by Pub.L. 99–554, § 213, except as otherwise provided, with respect to cases under chapters 7, 11, 12, and 13 of Title 11 commenced before 30 days after Oct. 27, 1986, and pending in a judicial district referred to in section 581(a) of Title 28, as amended by section 111(a) of Pub.L. 99–554, for which a United States trustee is not authorized before 30 days after Oct. 27, 1986 to be appointed, not applicable until the expiration of the 3-year period beginning on Oct. 27, 1986, or of the 1-year period beginning on the date the Attorney General certifies under section 303 of Pub.L. 99–554 the region specified in a paragraph of such section 581(a) that includes, such district, whichever occurs first, see section 302(e)(1), (2) of Pub.L. 99–554, set out as a note under section 581 of Title 28.

1984 Acts. Amendment by Pub.L. 98–353 effective with respect to cases filed 90 days after July 10, 1984, see section 552(a), formerly 553(a), of Pub.L. 98–353, set out as a note under section 101 of this title.

Participation by Bankruptcy Administrator at Meetings of Creditors and Equity Security Holders

The bankruptcy administrator or the bankruptcy's designee may examine the debtor at the meeting of the creditors and may administer the oath required by this section, see section 105 of Pub.L. 103–394, set out as a note under section 341 of this title.

CROSS REFERENCES

Concealment of assets deemed continuing offense, see 18 USCA § 3284.

Concealment of assets, false oaths and claims, see 18 USCA § 152.

Inapplicability of this section in railroad reorganization cases, see 11 USCA § 1161.

§ 344. Self-incrimination; immunity

Immunity for persons required to submit to examination, to testify, or to provide information in a case under this title may be granted under part V of title 18.

(Pub.L. 95–598, Nov. 6, 1978, 92 Stat. 2565.)

HISTORICAL AND STATUTORY NOTES

Revision Notes and Legislative Reports

1978 Acts. Part V of title 18 of the United States Code [18 U.S.C.A. § 6001 et seq.] governs the granting of immunity to witnesses before Federal tribunals. The immunity provided under part V is only use immunity, not transactional immunity. Part V applies to all proceedings before Federal courts, before Federal grand juries, before administrative agencies, and before Congressional committees. It requires the Attorney General or the U.S. attorney to request or to approve any grant of immunity, whether before a court, grand jury, agency, or congressional committee.

This section carries part V over into bankruptcy cases. Thus, for a witness to be ordered to testify before a bankruptcy court in spite of a claim of privilege, the U.S. attorney for the district in which the court sits would have to request from the district court for that district the immunity order. The rule would apply to both debtors, creditors, and any other witnesses in a bankruptcy case. If the immunity were granted, the witness would be required to testify. If not, he could claim the privilege against self-incrimination.

Part V [section 6001 et seq. of Title 18, Crimes and Criminal Procedure] is a significant departure from current law. Under section 7a(10) of the Bankruptcy Act [section 25(a)(10) of former Title 11] a debtor is required to testify in all circumstances, but any testimony he gives may not be used against him in any criminal proceeding, except testimony given in any hearing on objections to discharge. With that exception, section 7a(10) amounts to a blanket grant of use immunity to all debtors. Immunity for other witnesses in bankruptcy courts today is governed by part V of title 18.

The consequences of a claim of privileges by a debtor under proposed law and under current law differ as well. Under section 14c(6) of current law [section 32(c)(6) of former Title 11], any refusal to answer a material question approved by the court will result in the denial of a discharge, even if the refusal is based on the privilege against self incrimination. Thus, the debtor is confronted with the choice between losing his discharge and opening himself up to possible criminal prosecution.

Under section 727(a)(6) of the proposed title 11, a debtor is only denied a discharge if he refuses to testify after having been granted immunity. If the debtor claims the privilege and the U.S. attorney does not request immunity from the district courts, then the debtor may refuse to testify and still retain his right to a discharge. It removes the Scylla and Charibdis choice for debtors that exists under the Bankruptcy Act [former Title 11]. Senate Report No. 95–989.

CROSS REFERENCES

Applicability of this section in Chapter 9 cases, see 11 USCA § 901.

Debtor's duty to surrender records despite grant of immunity under this section, see 11 USCA § 521.

§ 345. Money of estates

(a) A trustee in a case under this title may make such deposit or investment of the money of the estate for which such trustee serves as will yield the maximum reasonable net return on such money, taking into account the safety of such deposit or investment.

(b) Except with respect to a deposit or investment that is insured or guaranteed by the United States or by a department, agency, or instrumentality of the United States or backed by the full faith and credit of the United States, the trustee shall require from an entity with which such money is deposited or invested—

(1) a bond—

(A) in favor of the United States;

(B) secured by the undertaking of a corporate surety approved by the United States trustee for the district in which the case is pending; and

(C) conditioned on—

(i) a proper accounting for all money so deposited or invested and for any return on such money;

(ii) prompt repayment of such money and return; and

(iii) faithful performance of duties as a depository; or

(2) the deposit of securities of the kind specified in section 9303 of title 31;

unless the court for cause orders otherwise.

(c) An entity with which such moneys are deposited or invested is authorized to deposit or invest such moneys as may be required under this section.

(Pub.L. 95–598, Nov. 6, 1978, 92 Stat. 2565; Pub.L. 97–258, § 3(c), Sept. 13, 1982, 96 Stat. 1064; Pub.L. 98–353, Title III, § 437, July 10, 1984, 98 Stat. 370; Pub.L. 99–554, Title II, § 214, Oct. 27, 1986, 100 Stat. 3099; Pub.L. 103–394, Title II, § 210, Oct. 22, 1994, 108 Stat. 4125.)

HISTORICAL AND STATUTORY NOTES
Revision Notes and Legislative Reports

1978 Acts. This section is a significant departure from section 61 of the Bankruptcy Act [section 101 of former Title 11]. It permits a trustee in a bankruptcy case to make such deposit of investment of the money of the estate for which he serves as will yield the maximum reasonable net return on the money, taking into account the safety of such deposit or investment. Under current law, the trustee is permitted to deposit money only with banking institutions. Thus, the trustee is generally unable to secure a high rate of return on money of estates pending distribution, to the detriment of creditors. Under this section, the trustee may make deposits in savings and loans, may purchase government bonds, or make such other deposit or investment as is appropriate. Under proposed 11 U.S.C. 541(a)(6), and except as provided in subsection (c) of this section, any interest or gain realized on the deposit or investment of funds under this section with become property of the estate, and will thus enhance the recovery of creditors.

In order to protect the creditors, subsection (b) requires certain precautions against loss of the money so deposited or invested. The trustee must require from a person with which he deposits or invests money of an estate a bond in favor of the United States secured by approved corporate surety and conditioned on a proper accounting for all money deposited or invested and for any return on such money. Alternately, the trustee may require the deposit of securities of the kind

specified in section 15 of title 6 of the United States Code [31 U.S.C.A. § 9303], which governs the posting of security by banks that receive public moneys on deposit. These bonding requirements do not apply to deposits or investments that are insured or guaranteed the United States or a department, agency, or instrumentality of the United States, or that are backed by the full faith and credit of the United States.

These provisions do not address the question of aggregation of funds by a private chapter 13 trustee and are not to be construed as excluding such possibility. The Rules of Bankruptcy Procedure may provide for aggregation under appropriate circumstances and adequate safeguards in cases where there is a significant need, such as in districts in which there is a standing chapter 13 trustee. In such case, the interest or return on the funds would help defray the cost of administering the cases in which the standing trustee serves. Senate Report No. 95–989.

1982 Acts. House Report No. 97–651, see 1982 U.S.Code Cong. and Adm.News, p. 1895.

1984 Acts. Statements by Legislative Leaders, see 1984 U.S.Code Cong. and Adm.News, p. 576.

1986 Acts. House Report No. 99–764 and House Conference Report No. 99–958, see 1986 U.S.Code Cong. and Adm. News, p. 5227.

1994 Acts. House Report No. 103–835, see 1994 U.S. Code Cong. and Adm. News, p. 3340.

Legislative Statements

The House amendment moves section 345(c) of the House bill to chapter 15 as part of the pilot program for the U.S. trustees. The bond required by section 345(b) may be a blanket bond posted by the financial depository sufficient to cover deposits by trustees in several cases, as is done under current law.

Effective and Applicability Provisions

1994 Acts. Amendment by Pub.L. 103–394 effective on Oct. 22, 1994, and not to apply with respect to cases commenced under Title 11 of the United States Code before Oct. 22, 1994, see section 702 of Pub.L. 103–394, set out as a note under section 101 of this title.

1986 Acts. Amendment by Pub.L. 99–554 effective 30 days after Oct. 27, 1986, except as otherwise provided for, see section 302(a) of Pub.L. 99–554, set out as a note under section 581 of Title 28, Judiciary and Judicial Procedure.

Amendment by Pub.L. 99–554, § 214, not to become effective in or with respect to certain specified judicial districts until, or apply to cases while pending in such district before, the expiration of the 270-day period beginning 30 days after Oct. 27, 1986, or of the 30-day period beginning on the date the Attorney General certifies under section 303 of Pub.L. 99–554 the region specified in a paragraph of section 581(a) of Title 28, as amended by section 111(a) of Pub.L. 99–554, that includes such district, whichever occurs first, see section 302(d)(1) of Pub.L. 99–554, set out as a note under section 581 of Title 28.

Amendment by Pub.L. 99–554, § 214, not to become effective in or with respect to certain specified judicial districts until, or apply to cases while pending in such district before, the expiration of the 2-year period beginning 30 days after Oct. 27, 1986, or of the 30-day period beginning on the date the Attorney General certifies under section 303 of Pub.L. 99–554 the region specified in a paragraph of section 581(a) of Title 28, as amended by section 111(a) of Pub.L. 99–554, that includes such district, whichever occurs first, see section 302(d)(2) of Pub.L. 99–554, set out as a note under section 581 of Title 28.

Amendment by Pub.L. 99–554, § 214, not to become effective in or with respect to judicial districts established for the States of Alabama and North Carolina until, or apply to cases while pending in such district before, such district elects to be included in a bankruptcy region established in section 581(a) of Title 28, as amended by section 111(a) of Pub.L. 99–554, or Oct. 1, 2002, whichever occurs first, and except as otherwise provided, with respect to cases under chapters 7, 11, 12, and 13 of Title 11 commenced before 30 days after Oct. 27, 1986, and pending in a judicial district in the States of Alabama or North Carolina before any election made under section 302(d)(3)(A) of Pub.L. 99–554 by such district becomes effective or Oct. 1, 2002, whichever occurs first, amendments by Pub.L. 99–554 not to apply until Oct. 1, 2003, or the expiration of the 1-year period beginning on the date such election becomes effective, whichever occurs first, and further, in any judicial district in Alabama or North Carolina not making the election described in section 302(d)(3)(A) of Pub.L. 99–554, any person appointed under regulations issued by the Judicial Conference to administer estates in cases under Title 11 authorized to establish, etc., a panel of private trustees, and to supervise cases and trustees in cases under chapters 7, 11, 12, and 13 of Title 11, until amendments by sections 201 to 231 of Pub.L. 99–554 effective in such district, see section 302(d)(3)(A) to (F), (H), and (I) of Pub.L. 99–554, set out as a note under section 581 of Title 28.

Amendment by Pub.L. 99–554, § 214, except as otherwise provided, with respect to cases under chapters 7, 11, 12, and 13 of Title 11 commenced before 30 days after Oct. 27, 1986, and pending in a judicial district referred to in section 581(a) of Title 28, as amended by section 111(a) of Pub.L. 99–554, for which a United States trustee is not authorized before 30 days after Oct. 27, 1986, to be appointed, not applicable until the expiration of the 3-year period beginning on Oct. 27, 1986, or of the 1-year period beginning on the date the Attorney General certifies under section 303 of Pub.L. 99–554 the region specified in a paragraph of such section 581(a) that includes, such district, whichever occurs first, see section 302(e)(1), (2) of Pub.L. 99–554, set out as a note under section 581 of Title 28.

1984 Acts. Amendment by Pub.L. 98–353 effective with respect to cases filed 90 days after July 10, 1984, see section 552(a), formerly 553(a), of Pub.L. 98–353, set out as a note under section 101 of this title.

Separability of Provisions

If any provision of or amendment made by Pub.L. 103–394 or the application of such provision or amendment to any person or circumstance is held to be unconstitutional, the remaining provisions of and amendments made by Pub.L. 103–394 and the application of such provisions and amendments to any person or circumstance shall not be affected thereby, see section 701 of Pub.L. 103–394, set out as a note under section 101 of this title.

CROSS REFERENCES

Adverse interest and conduct of officers of estate, see 18 USCA § 154.

Duty of United States trustee to deposit or invest money, see 28 USCA § 586.

Embezzlement by trustee, see 18 USCA § 153.

§ 346. Special provisions related to the treatment of State and local taxes

(a) Whenever the Internal Revenue Code of 1986 provides that a separate taxable estate or entity is created in a case concerning a debtor under this title, and the income, gain, loss, deductions, and credits of such estate shall be taxed to or claimed by the estate, a separate taxable estate is also created for purposes of any State and local law imposing a tax on or measured by income and such income, gain, loss, deductions, and credits shall be taxed to or claimed by the estate and may not be taxed to or claimed by the debtor. The preceding sentence shall not apply if the case is dismissed. The trustee shall make tax returns of income required under any such State or local law.

(b) Whenever the Internal Revenue Code of 1986 provides that no separate taxable estate shall be created in a case concerning a debtor under this title, and the income, gain, loss, deductions, and credits of an estate shall be taxed to or claimed by the debtor, such income, gain, loss, deductions, and credits shall be taxed to or claimed by the debtor under a State or local law imposing a tax on or measured by income and may not be taxed to or claimed by the estate. The trustee shall make such tax returns of income of corporations and of partnerships as are required under any State or local law, but with respect to partnerships, shall make such returns only to the extent such returns are also required to be made under such Code. The estate shall be liable for any tax imposed on such corporation or partnership, but not for any tax imposed on partners or members.

(c) With respect to a partnership or any entity treated as a partnership under a State or local law imposing a tax on or measured by income that is a debtor in a case under this title, any gain or loss resulting from a distribution of property from such partnership, or any distributive share of any income, gain, loss, deduction, or credit of a partner or member that is distributed, or considered distributed, from such partnership, after the commencement of the case, is gain, loss, income, deduction, or credit, as the case may be, of the partner or member, and if such partner or member is a debtor in a case under this title, shall be subject to tax in accordance with subsection (a) or (b).

(d) For purposes of any State or local law imposing a tax on or measured by income, the taxable period of a debtor in a case under this title shall terminate only if and to the extent that the taxable period of such debtor terminates under the Internal Revenue Code of 1986.

(e) The estate in any case described in subsection (a) shall use the same accounting method as the debtor used immediately before the commencement of the case, if such method of accounting complies with applicable nonbankruptcy tax law.

(f) For purposes of any State or local law imposing a tax on or measured by income, a transfer of property from the debtor to the estate or from the estate to the debtor shall not be treated as a disposition for purposes of any provision assigning tax consequences to a disposition, except to the extent that such transfer is treated as a disposition under the Internal Revenue Code of 1986.

(g) Whenever a tax is imposed pursuant to a State or local law imposing a tax on or measured by income pursuant to subsection (a) or (b), such tax shall be imposed at rates generally applicable to the same types of entities under such State or local law.

(h) The trustee shall withhold from any payment of claims for wages, salaries, commissions, dividends, interest, or other payments, or collect, any amount required to be withheld or collected under applicable State or local tax law, and shall pay such withheld or collected amount to the appropriate governmental unit at the time and in the manner required by such tax law, and with the same priority as the claim from which such amount was withheld or collected was paid.

(i)(1) To the extent that any State or local law imposing a tax on or measured by income provides for the carryover of any tax attribute from one taxable period to a subsequent taxable period, the estate shall succeed to such tax attribute in any case in which such estate is subject to tax under subsection (a).

(2) After such a case is closed or dismissed, the debtor shall succeed to any tax attribute to which the estate succeeded under paragraph (1) to the extent consistent with the Internal Revenue Code of 1986.

(3) The estate may carry back any loss or tax attribute to a taxable period of the debtor that ended before the date of the order for relief under this title to the extent that—

(A) applicable State or local tax law provides for a carryback in the case of the debtor; and

(B) the same or a similar tax attribute may be carried back by the estate to such a taxable period of the debtor under the Internal Revenue Code of 1986.

(j)(1) For purposes of any State or local law imposing a tax on or measured by income, income is not realized by the estate, the debtor, or a successor to the debtor by reason of discharge of indebtedness in a case under this title, except to the extent, if any, that such income is subject to tax under the Internal Revenue Code of 1986.

(2) Whenever the Internal Revenue Code of 1986 provides that the amount excluded from gross income in respect of the discharge of indebtedness in a case under this title shall be applied to reduce the tax attributes of the debtor or the estate, a similar reduction shall be made under any State or local law imposing a tax on or measured by income to the extent such State or local law recognizes such attributes. Such

State or local law may also provide for the reduction of other attributes to the extent that the full amount of income from the discharge of indebtedness has not been applied.

(k)(1) Except as provided in this section and section 505, the time and manner of filing tax returns and the items of income, gain, loss, deduction, and credit of any taxpayer shall be determined under applicable nonbankruptcy law.

(2) For Federal tax purposes, the provisions of this section are subject to the Internal Revenue Code of 1986 and other applicable Federal nonbankruptcy law. (Pub.L. 95–598, Nov. 6, 1978, 92 Stat. 2565; Pub.L. 98–353, Title III, § 438, July 10, 1984, 98 Stat. 370; Pub.L. 99–554, Title II, §§ 257(g), 283(c), Oct. 27, 1986, 100 Stat. 3114, 3116; Pub.L. 103–394, Title V, § 501(d)(4), Oct. 22, 1994, 108 Stat. 4143; Pub.L. 109–8, Title VII, § 719(a)(1), Apr. 20, 2005, 119 Stat. 131.)

HISTORICAL AND STATUTORY NOTES
Revision Notes and Legislative Reports

1978 Acts. Subsection (a) indicates that subsections (b), (c), (d), (e), (g), (h), (i), and (j) apply notwithstanding any State or local tax law, but are subject to Federal tax law.

Subsection (b)(1) provides that in a case concerning an individual under chapter 7 or 11 of title 11, income of the estate is taxable only to the estate and not to the debtor. The second sentence of the paragraph provides that if such individual is a partner, the tax attributes of the partnership are distributable to the partner's estate rather than to the partner, except to the extent that section 728 of title 11 provides otherwise.

Subsection (b)(2) states a general rule that the estate of an individual is to be taxed as an estate. The paragraph is made subject to the remainder of section 346 and section 728 of title 11.

Subsection (b)(3) requires the accounting method, but not necessarily the accounting period, of the estate to be the same as the method used by the individual debtor.

Subsection (c)(1) states a general rule that the estate of a partnership or a corporated debtor is not a separate entity for tax purposes. The income of the debtor is to be taxed as if the case were not commenced, except as provided in the remainder of section 346 and section 728.

Subsection (c)(2) requires the trustee, except as provided in section 728 of title 11, to file all tax returns on behalf of the partnership or corporation during the case.

Subsection (d) indicates that the estate in a chapter 13 case is not a separate taxable entity and that all income of the estate is to be taxed to the debtor.

Subsection (e) establishes a business deduction consisting of allowed expenses of administration except for tax or capital expenses that are not otherwise deductible. The deduction may be used by the estate when it is a separate taxable entity or by the entity to which the income of the estate is taxed when it is not.

Subsection (f) imposes a duty on the trustee to comply with any Federal, State, or local tax law requiring withholding or collection of taxes from any payment of wages, salaries, commissions, dividends, interest, or other payments. Any amount withheld is to be paid to the taxing authority at the same time and with the same priority as the claim from which such amount withheld was paid.

Subsection (g)(1)(A) indicates that neither gain nor loss is recognized on the transfer by law of property from the debtor or a creditor to the estate. Subparagraph (B) provides a similar policy if the property of the estate is returned from the estate to the debtor other than by a sale of property to debtor. Subparagraph (C) also provides for nonrecognition of gain or loss in a case under chapter 11 if a corporate debtor transfers property to a successor corporation or to an affiliate under a joint plan. An exception is made to enable a taxing authority to cause recognition of gain or loss to the extent provided in IRC section 371 (as amended by section 109 of this bill) [section 371 of Title 26, Internal Revenue Code].

Subsection (g)(2) provides that any of the three kinds of transferees specified in paragraph (1) take the property with the same character, holding period, and basis in the hands of the transferor at the time of such transfer. The transferor's basis may be adjusted under section 346(j)(5) even if the discharge of indebtedness occurs after the transfer of property. Of course, no adjustment will occur if the transfer is from the debtor to the estate or if the transfer is from an entity that is not discharged.

Subsection (h) provides that the creation of the estate of an individual under chapter 7 or 11 of title 11 as a separate taxable entity does not affect the number of taxable years for purposes of computing loss carryovers or carrybacks. The section applies with respect to carryovers or carrybacks of the debtor transferred into the estate under section 346(i)(1) of title 11 or back to the debtor under section 346(i)(2) of title 11.

Subsection (i)(1) states a general rule that an estate that is a separate taxable entity nevertheless succeeds to all tax attributes of the debtor. The six enumerated attributes are illustrative and not exhaustive.

Subsection (i)(2) indicates that attributes passing from the debtor into an estate that is a separate taxable entity will return to the debtor if unused by the estate. The debtor is permitted to use any such attribute as though the case had not been commenced.

Subsection (i)(3) permits an estate that is a separate taxable entity to carryback losses of the estate to a taxable period of the debtor that ended before the case was filed. The estate is treated as if it were the debtor with respect to time limitations and other restrictions. The section makes clear that the debtor may not carryback any loss of his own from a tax year during the pendency of the case to such a period until the case is closed. No tolling of any period of limitation is provided with respect to carrybacks by the debtor of postpetition losses.

Subsection (j) sets forth seven special rules treating with the tax effects of forgiveness or discharge of indebtedness. The terms "forgiveness" and "discharge" are redundant, but are used to clarify that "discharge" in the context of a special tax provision in title 11 includes forgiveness of indebtedness whether or not such indebtedness is "discharged" in the bankruptcy sense.

Paragraph (1) states the general rule that forgiveness of indebtedness is not taxable except as otherwise provided in paragraphs (2)–(7). The paragraph is patterned after sections 268, 395, and 520 of the Bankruptcy Act [sections 668, 795 and 920 of former Title 11].

Paragraph (2) disallows deductions for liabilities of a deductible nature in any year during or after the year of cancellation of such liabilities. For the purposes of this paragraph, "a deduction with respect to a liability" includes a capital loss incurred on the disposition of a capital asset with respect to a liability that was incurred in connection with the acquisition of such asset.

Paragraph (3) causes any net operating loss of a debtor that is an individual or corporation to be reduced by any discharge of indebtedness except as provided in paragraphs (2) or (4). If a deduction is disallowed under paragraph (2), then no double counting occurs. Thus, paragraph (3) will reflect the reduction of losses by liabilities that have been forgiven, including deductible liabilities or nondeductible liabilities such as repayment of principal on borrowed funds.

Paragraph (4) specifically excludes two kinds of indebtedness from reduction of net operating losses under paragraph (3) or from reduction of basis under paragraph (5). Subparagraph (A) excludes items of a deductible nature that were not deducted or that could not be deducted such as gambling losses or liabilities for interest owed to a relative of the debtor. Subparagraph (B) excludes indebtedness of a debtor that is an individual or corporation that resulted in deductions which did not offset income and that did not contribute to an unexpired net operating loss or loss carryover. In these situations, the debtor has derived no tax benefit so there is no need to incur an offsetting reduction.

Paragraph (5) provides a two-point test for reduction of basis. The paragraph replaces sections 270, 396, and 522 of the Bankruptcy Act [sections 670, 796, and 922 of former Title 11]. Subparagraph (A) sets out the maximum amount by which basis may be reduced—the total indebtedness forgiven less adjustments made under paragraphs (2) and (3). This avoids double counting. If a deduction is disallowed under paragraph (2) or a carryover is reduced under paragraph (3) then the tax benefit is neutralized, and there is no need to reduce basis. Subparagraph (B) reduces basis to the extent the debtor's total basis of assets before the discharge exceeds total preexisting liabilities still remaining after discharge of indebtedness. This is a "basis solvency" limitation which differs from the usual test of solvency because it measures against the remaining liabilities the benefit aspect of assets, their basis, rather than their value. Paragraph (5) applies so that any transferee of the debtor's property who is required to use the debtor's basis takes the debtor's basis reduced by the lesser of (A) and (B). Thus, basis will be reduced, but never below a level equal to undischarged liabilities.

Paragraph (6) specifies that basis need not be reduced under paragraph (5) to the extent the debtor treats discharged indebtedness as taxable income. This permits the debtor to elect whether to recognize income, which may be advantageous if the debtor anticipates subsequent net operating losses, rather than to reduce basis.

Paragraph (7) establishes two rules excluding from the category of discharged indebtedness certain indebtedness that is exchanged for an equity security issued under a plan or that is forgiven as a contribution to capital by an equity security holder. Subparagraph (A) creates the first exclusion to the extent indebtedness consisting of items not of a deductible nature is exchanged for an equity security, other than the interests of a limited partner in a limited partnership, issued by the debtor or is forgiven as a contribution to capital by an equity security holder. Subparagraph (B) excludes indebtedness consisting of items of a deductible nature, if the exchange of stock for debts has the same effect as a cash payment equal to the value of the equity security, in the amount of the fair market value of the equity security or, if less, the extent to which such exchange has such effect. The two provisions treat the debtor as if it had originally issued stock instead of debt. Subparagraph (B) rectifies the inequity under current law between a cash basis and accrual basis debtor concerning the issuance of stock in exchange for previous services rendered that were of a greater value than the stock. Subparagraph (B) also changes current law by taxing forgiveness of indebtedness to the extent that stock is exchanged for the accrued interest component of a security, because the recipient of such stock would not be regarded as having received money under the *Carman* doctrine. Senate Report No. 95–989.

1984 Acts. Statements by Legislative Leaders, see 1984 U.S.Code Cong. and Adm.News, p. 576.

1986 Acts. House Report No. 99–764 and House Conference Report No. 99–958, see 1986 U.S.Code Cong. and Adm. News, p. 5227.

1994 Acts. House Report No. 103–835, see 1994 U.S. Code Cong. and Adm. News, p. 3340.

2005 Acts. House Report No. 109–31(Part I), see 2005 U.S. Code Cong. and Adm. News, p. 88.

Legislative Statements

Section 346 of the House amendment, together with sections 728 and 1146, represent special tax provisions applicable in bankruptcy. The policy contained in those sections reflects the policy that should he applied in Federal, State, and local taxes in the view of the House Committee on the Judiciary. The House Ways and Means Committee and the Senate Finance Committee did not have time to process a bankruptcy tax bill during the 95th Congress. It is anticipated that early in the 96th Congress, and before the effective date of the bankruptcy code [Oct. 1, 1979], the tax committees of Congress will have an opportunity to consider action with respect to amendments to the Internal Revenue Code [Title 26] and the special tax provisions in title 11. Since the special tax provisions are likely to be amended during the first part of the 96th Congress, it is anticipated that the bench and bar will also study and comment on these special tax provisions prior to their revision.

Special tax provisions: State and local rules. This section provides special tax provisions dealing with the treatment, under State or local, but not Federal, tax law, of the method of taxing bankruptcy estates of individuals, partnerships, and corporations; survival and allocation of tax attributes between the bankrupt and the estate; return filing requirements; and the tax treatment of income from discharge of indebtedness. The Senate bill removed these rules pending adoption of Federal rules on these issues in the next Congress. The House amendment returns the State and local tax rules to section 346 so that they may be studied by the bankruptcy and tax bars who may wish to submit comments to Congress.

Withholding rules: Both the House bill and Senate amendment provide that the trustee is required to comply with the normal withholding rules applicable to the payment of wages and other payments. The House amendment retains this rule for State and local taxes only. The treatment of withholding of Federal taxes will be considered in the next Congress.

Section 726 of the Senate amendment provides that the rule requiring pro rata payment of all expenses within a priority category does not apply to the payment of amounts withheld by a bankruptcy trustee. The purpose of this rule was to insure that the trustee pay the full amount of the withheld taxes to the appropriate governmental tax authority. The House amendment deletes this rule as unnecessary because the existing practice conforms essentially to that rule. If the trustee fails to pay over in full amounts that he withheld, it is a violation of his trustee's duties which would permit the taxing authority to sue the trustee on his bond.

When taxes considered "incurred": The Senate amendment contained rules of general application dealing with when a tax is "incurred" for purposes of the various tax collection rules affecting the debtor and the estate. The House amendment adopts the substance of these rules and transfers them to section 507 of title 11.

Penalty for failure to pay tax: The Senate amendment contains a rule which relieves the debtor and the trustee from certain tax penalties for failure to make timely payment of a tax to the extent that the bankruptcy rules prevent the trustee or the debtor from paying the tax on time. Since most of these penalties relate to Federal taxes, the House amendment deletes these rules pending consideration of Federal tax rules affecting bankruptcy in the next Congress.

References in Text

The Internal Revenue Code of 1986, referred to in text, is classified to Title 26 of the Code.

Effective and Applicability Provisions

2005 Acts. Amendments by Pub.L. 109–8 effective, except as otherwise provided, 180 days after April 20, 2005, and inapplicable with respect to cases commenced under Title 11 before the effective date, see Pub.L. 109–8, § 1501, set out as a note under 11 U.S.C.A. § 101.

1994 Acts. Amendment by of Pub.L. 103–394 effective on Oct. 22, 1994, and not to apply with respect to cases commenced under Title 11 of the United States Code before Oct. 22, 1994, see section 702 of Pub.L. 103–394, set out as a note under section 101 of this title.

1986 Acts. Amendment by Pub.L. 99–554, § 257(g), effective 30 days after Oct. 27, 1986, but not applicable with respect to cases commenced under this title before that date, see section 302(a), (c)(1) of Pub.L. 99–554, set out as a note under section 581 of Title 28, Judiciary and Judicial Procedure.

Amendment by Pub.L. 99–554, § 283(c), effective 30 days after Oct. 27, 1986, see section 302(a) of Pub.L. 99–554, set out as a note under section 581 of Title 28.

1984 Acts. Amendment by Pub.L. 98–353 effective with respect to cases filed 90 days after July 10, 1984, see section 552(a), formerly 553(a), of Pub.L. 98–353, set out as a note under section 101 of this title.

Separability of Provisions

If any provision of or amendment made by Pub.L. 103–394 or the application of such provision or amendment to any person or circumstance is held to be unconstitutional, the remaining provisions of and amendments made by Pub.L. 103–394 and the application of such provisions and amendments to any person or circumstance shall not be affected thereby, see section 701 of Pub.L. 103–394, set out as a note under section 101 of this title.

CROSS REFERENCES

Request for determination of tax effects of,
  Chapter 12 plan, see 11 USCA § 1231.
  Reorganization plan, see 11 USCA § 1146.

§ 347. Unclaimed property

(a) Ninety days after the final distribution under section 726, 1226, or 1326 of this title in a case under chapter 7, 12, or 13 of this title, as the case may be, the trustee shall stop payment on any check remaining unpaid, and any remaining property of the estate shall be paid into the court and disposed of under chapter 129 of title 28.

(b) Any security, money, or other property remaining unclaimed at the expiration of the time allowed in a case under chapter 9, 11, or 12 of this title for the presentation of a security or the performance of any other act as a condition to participation in the distribution under any plan confirmed under section 943(b), 1129, 1173, or 1225 of this title, as the case may be, becomes the property of the debtor or of the entity acquiring the assets of the debtor under the plan, as the case may be.

(Pub.L. 95–598, Nov. 6, 1978, 92 Stat. 2568; Pub.L. 99–554, Title II, § 257(h), Oct. 27, 1986, 100 Stat. 3114.)

HISTORICAL AND STATUTORY NOTES

Revision Notes and Legislative Reports

1978 Acts. Section 347 is derived from Bankruptcy Act § 66 [section 106 of former Title 11]. Subsection (a) requires the trustee to stop payment on any distribution check that is unpaid 90 days after the final distribution in a case under chapter 7 or 13. The unclaimed funds, and any other property of the estate are paid into the court and disposed of under chapter 129 of title 28 [section 2041 et seq. of Title 28, Judiciary and Judicial Procedure], which requires the clerk of court to hold the funds for their owner for 5 years, after which they escheat to the Treasury.

Subsection (b) specifies that any property remaining unclaimed at the expiration of the time allowed in a chapter 9 or 11 case for presentation (exchange) of securities or the performance of any other act as a condition to participation in the plan reverts to the debtor or the entity acquiring the assets of the debtor under the plan. Conditions to participation under a plan include such acts as cashing a check, surrendering securities for cancellation, and so on. Similar provisions are found in sections 96(d) and 205 [sections 416(d) and 605 of former Title 11] of current law. Senate Report No. 95–989.

1986 Acts. House Report No. 99–764 and House Conference Report No. 99–958, see 1986 U.S.Code Cong. and Adm. News, p. 5227.

Legislative Statements

Section 347(a) of the House amendment adopts a comparable provision contained in the Senate amendment instructing the trustee to stop payment on any check remaining unpaid more than 90 days after the final distribution in a case under Chapter 7 or 13. Technical changes are made in section 347(b) to cover distributions in a railroad reorganization.

Effective and Applicability Provisions

1986 Acts. Amendment by Pub.L. 99–554, § 257(h), effective 30 days after Oct. 27, 1986, but not applicable with respect to cases commenced under this title before that date, see section 302(a), (c)(1) of Pub.L. 99–554, set out as a note under section 581 of Title 28, Judiciary and Judicial Procedure.

CROSS REFERENCES

Applicability of this section in Chapter 9 cases, see 11 USCA § 901.

"Creditor" defined, see 11 USCA § 101.

§ 348. Effect of conversion

(a) Conversion of a case from a case under one chapter of this title to a case under another chapter of this title constitutes an order for relief under the chapter to which the case is converted, but, except as provided in subsections (b) and (c) of this section, does not effect a change in the date of the filing of the petition, the commencement of the case, or the order for relief.

(b) Unless the court for cause orders otherwise, in sections 701(a), 727(a)(10), 727(b), 1102(a), 1110(a)(1), 1121(b), 1121(c), 1141(d)(4), 1201(a), 1221, 1228(a), 1301(a), and 1305(a) of this title, "the order for relief under this chapter" in a chapter to which a case has been converted under section 706, 1112, 1208, or 1307 of this title means the conversion of such case to such chapter.

(c) Sections 342 and 365(d) of this title apply in a case that has been converted under section 706, 1112, 1208, or 1307 of this title, as if the conversion order were the order for relief.

(d) A claim against the estate or the debtor that arises after the order for relief but before conversion in a case that is converted under section 1112, 1208, or 1307 of this title, other than a claim specified in section 503(b) of this title, shall be treated for all purposes as if such claim had arisen immediately before the date of the filing of the petition.

(e) Conversion of a case under section 706, 1112, 1208, or 1307 of this title terminates the service of any trustee or examiner that is serving in the case before such conversion.

(f)(1) Except as provided in paragraph (2), when a case under chapter 13 of this title is converted to a case under another chapter under this title—

    (A) property of the estate in the converted case shall consist of property of the estate, as of the date of filing of the petition, that remains in the possession of or is under the control of the debtor on the date of conversion;

    (B) valuations of property and of allowed secured claims in the chapter 13 case shall apply only in a case converted to a case under chapter 11 or 12, but not in a case converted to a case under chapter 7, with allowed secured claims in cases under chapters 11 and 12 reduced to the extent that they have been paid in accordance with the chapter 13 plan; and

    (C) with respect to cases converted from chapter 13—

(i) the claim of any creditor holding security as of the date of the filing of the petition shall continue to be secured by that security unless the full amount of such claim determined under applicable nonbankruptcy law has been paid in full as of the date of conversion, notwithstanding any valuation or determination of the amount of an allowed secured claim made for the purposes of the case under chapter 13; and

(ii) unless a prebankruptcy default has been fully cured under the plan at the time of conversion, in any proceeding under this title or otherwise, the default shall have the effect given under applicable nonbankruptcy law.

(2) If the debtor converts a case under chapter 13 of this title to a case under another chapter under this title in bad faith, the property of the estate in the converted case shall consist of the property of the estate as of the date of conversion.

(Pub.L. 95–598, Nov. 6, 1978, 92 Stat. 2568; Pub.L. 99–554, Title II, § 257(i), Oct. 27, 1986, 100 Stat. 3115; Pub.L. 103–394, Title III, § 311, Title V, § 501(d)(5); Oct. 22, 1994, 108 Stat. 4138, 4144; Pub.L. 109–8, Title III, § 309(a), Title XII, § 1207, Apr. 20, 2005, 119 Stat. 82, 194; Pub.L. 111–327, § 2(a)(11), Dec. 22, 2010, 124 Stat. 3558.)

HISTORICAL AND STATUTORY NOTES

Revision Notes and Legislative Reports

1978 Acts. This section governs the effect of the conversion of a case from one chapter of the bankruptcy code to another chapter. Subsection (a) specifies that the date of the filing of the petition, the commencement of the case, or the order for relief are unaffected by conversion, with some exceptions specified in subsections (b) and (c).

Subsection (b) lists certain sections in the operative chapters of the bankruptcy code in which there is a reference to "the order for relief under this chapter." In those sections, the reference is to be read as a reference to the conversion order if the case has been converted into the particular chapter. Subsection (c) specifies that notice is to be given of the conversion order the same as notice was given of the order for relief, and that the time the trustee (or debtor in possession) has for assuming or rejecting executory contracts recommences, thus giving an opportunity for a newly appointed trustee to familiarize himself with the case.

Subsection (d) provides for special treatment of claims that arise during chapter 11 or 13 cases before the case is converted to a liquidation case. With the exception of claims specified in proposed 11 U.S.C. 503(b) (administrative expenses), preconversion claims are treated the same as prepetition claims.

Subsection (e) provides that conversion of a case terminates the service of any trustee serving in the case prior to conversion. Senate Report No. 95–989.

1986 Acts. House Report No. 99–764 and House Conference Report No. 99–958, see 1986 U.S.Code Cong. and Adm. News, p. 5227.

1994 Acts. House Report No. 103–835, see 1994 U.S. Code Cong. and Adm. News, p. 3340.

2005 Acts. House Report No. 109–31(Part I), see 2005 U.S. Code Cong. and Adm. News, p. 88.

Legislative Statements

The House amendment adopts section 348(b) of the Senate amendment with slight modifications, as more accurately reflecting sections to which this particular effect of conversion should apply.

Section 348(e) of the House amendment is a stylistic revision of similar provisions contained in H.R. 8200 as passed by the House and in the Senate amendment. Termination of services is expanded to cover any examiner serving in the case before conversion, as done in H.R. 8200 as passed by the House.

References in Text

Chapter 7, 11, 12, or 13, referred to in subsec. (f)(1), is chapter 7, 11, 12, or 13 of this title, 11 U.S.C.A. § 701 et seq., 11 U.S.C.A. § 1101 et seq., 11 U.S.C.A. § 1201 et seq., or 11 U.S.C.A. § 1301 et seq., respectively.

Effective and Applicability Provisions

2005 Acts. Amendments by Pub.L. 109–8 effective, except as otherwise provided, 180 days after April 20, 2005, and inapplicable with respect to cases commenced under Title 11 before the effective date, see Pub.L. 109–8, § 1501, set out as a note under 11 U.S.C.A. § 101.

1994 Acts. Amendments by Pub.L. 103–394 effective on Oct. 22, 1994, and not to apply with respect to cases commenced under Title 11 of the United States Code before Oct. 22, 1994, see section 702 of Pub.L. 103–394, set out as a note under section 101 of this title.

1986 Acts. Amendment by Pub.L. 99–554, effective 30 days after Oct. 27, 1986, but not applicable with respect to cases commenced under this title before that date see section 302(a), (c)(1) of Pub.L. 99–554, set out as a note under section 581 of Title 28, Judiciary and Judicial Procedure.

Separability of Provisions

If any provision of or amendment made by Pub.L. 103–394 or the application of such provision or amendment to any person or circumstance is held to be unconstitutional, the remaining provisions of and amendments made by Pub.L. 103–394 and the application of such provisions and amendments to any person or circumstance shall not be affected thereby, see section 701 of Pub.L. 103–394, set out as a note under section 101 of this title.

§ 349.　Effect of dismissal

(a) Unless the court, for cause, orders otherwise, the dismissal of a case under this title does not bar the discharge, in a later case under this title, of debts that were dischargeable in the case dismissed; nor does the dismissal of a case under this title prejudice the debtor with regard to the filing of a subsequent petition under this title, except as provided in section 109(g) of this title.

(b) Unless the court, for cause, orders otherwise, a dismissal of a case other than under section 742 of this title—

(1) reinstates—

(A) any proceeding or custodianship superseded under section 543 of this title;

(B) any transfer avoided under section 522, 544, 545, 547, 548, 549, or 724(a) of this title, or preserved under section 510(c)(2), 522(i)(2), or 551 of this title; and

(C) any lien voided under section 506(d) of this title;

(2) vacates any order, judgment, or transfer ordered, under section 522(i)(1), 542, 550, or 553 of this title; and

(3) revests the property of the estate in the entity in which such property was vested immediately before the commencement of the case under this title.

(Pub.L. 95–598, Nov. 6, 1978, 92 Stat. 2569; Pub.L. 98–353, Title III, § 303, July 10, 1984, 98 Stat. 352; Pub.L. 103–394, Title V, § 501(d)(6), Oct. 22, 1994, 108 Stat. 4144.)

HISTORICAL AND STATUTORY NOTES

Revision Notes and Legislative Reports

1978 Acts. Subsection (a) specifies that unless the court for cause orders otherwise, the dismissal of a case is without prejudice. The debtor is not barred from receiving a discharge in a later case of debts that were dischargeable in the case dismissed. Of course, this subsection refers only to pre-discharge dismissals. If the debtor has already received a discharge and it is not revoked, then the debtor would be barred under section 727(a) from receiving a discharge in a subsequent liquidation case for six years. Dismissal of an involuntary [sic] on the merits will generally not give rise to adequate cause so as to bar the debtor from further relief.

Subsection (b) specifies that the dismissal reinstates proceedings or custodianships that were superseded by the bankruptcy case, reinstates avoided transfers, reinstates voided liens, vacates any order, judgment, or transfer ordered as a result of the avoidance of a transfer, and revests the property of the estate in the entity in which the property was vested at the commencement of the case. The court is permitted to order a different result for cause. The basic purpose of the subsection is to undo the bankruptcy case, as far as practicable, and to restore all property rights to the position in which they were found at the commencement of the case. This does not necessarily encompass undoing sales of property from the estate to a good faith purchaser. Where there is a question over the scope of the subsection, the court will make the appropriate orders to protect rights acquired in reliance on the bankruptcy case. Senate Report No. 95–989.

1984 Acts. Statements by Legislative Leaders, see 1984 U.S.Code Cong. and Adm.News, p. 576.

1994 Acts. House Report No. 103–835, see 1994 U.S. Code Cong. and Adm. News, p. 3340.

Legislative Statements

Section 349(b)(2) of the House amendment adds a cross reference to section 553 to reflect the new right of recovery of setoffs created under that section. Corresponding changes are made throughout the House amendment.

Effective and Applicability Provisions

1994 Acts. Amendment by Pub.L. 103–394 effective on Oct. 22, 1994, and not to apply with respect to cases commenced under Title 11 of the United States Code before Oct. 22, 1994, see section 702 of Pub.L. 103–394, set out as a note under section 101 of this title.

1984 Acts. Amendment by Pub.L. 98–353 effective with respect to cases filed 90 days after July 10, 1984, see section 552(a), formerly 553(a), of Pub.L. 98–353, set out as a note under section 101 of this title.

Separability of Provisions

If any provision of or amendment made by Pub.L. 103–394 or the application of such provision or amendment to any person or circumstance is held to be unconstitutional, the remaining provisions of and amendments made by Pub.L. 103–394 and the application of such provisions and amendments to any person or circumstance shall not be affected thereby, see section 701 of Pub.L. 103–394, set out as a note under section 101 of this title.

§ 350.   Closing and reopening cases

(a) After an estate is fully administered and the court has discharged the trustee, the court shall close the case.

(b) A case may be reopened in the court in which such case was closed to administer assets, to accord relief to the debtor, or for other cause.

(Pub.L. 95–598, Nov. 6, 1978, 92 Stat. 2569; Pub.L. 98–353, Title III, § 439, July 10, 1984, 98 Stat. 370.)

HISTORICAL AND STATUTORY NOTES

Revision Notes and Legislative Reports

1978 Acts. Subsection (a) requires the court to close a bankruptcy case after the estate is fully administered and the trustee discharged. The Rules of Bankruptcy Procedure will provide the procedure for case closing. Subsection (b) permits reopening of the case to administer assets, to accord relief to the debtor, or for other cause. Though the court may permit reopening of a case so that the trustee may exercise an avoiding power, laches may constitute a bar to an action that has been delayed too long. The case may be reopened in the court in which it was closed. The rules will prescribe the procedure by which a case is reopened and how it will be conducted after reopening. Senate Report No. 95–989.

1984 Acts. Statements by Legislative Leaders, see 1984 U.S.Code Cong. and Adm.News, p. 576.

Effective and Applicability Provisions

1984 Acts. Amendment by Pub.L. 98–353 effective with respect to cases filed 90 days after July 10, 1984, see section 552(a), formerly 553(a), of Pub.L. 98–353, set out as a note under section 101 of this title.

CROSS REFERENCES

Applicability of subsec. (b) of this section in Chapter 9 cases, see 11 USCA § 901.

Scheduled property deemed abandoned, see 11 USCA § 554.

Successor trustee, see 11 USCA § 703.

§ 351.   Disposal of patient records

If a health care business commences a case under chapter 7, 9, or 11, and the trustee does not have a sufficient amount of funds to pay for the storage of patient records in the manner required under applicable Federal or State law, the following requirements shall apply:

(1) The trustee shall—

(A) promptly publish notice, in 1 or more appropriate newspapers, that if patient records are not claimed by the patient or an insurance provider (if applicable law permits the insurance provider to make that claim) by the date that is 365 days after the date of that notification, the trustee will destroy the patient records; and

(B) during the first 180 days of the 365–day period described in subparagraph (A), promptly attempt to notify directly each patient that is the subject of the patient records and appropriate insurance carrier concerning the patient records by mailing to the most recent known address of that patient, or a family member or contact person for that patient, and to the appropriate insurance carrier an appropriate notice regarding the claiming or disposing of patient records.

(2) If, after providing the notification under paragraph (1), patient records are not claimed during the 365–day period described under that paragraph, the trustee shall mail, by certified mail, at the end of such 365–day period a written request to each appropriate Federal agency to request permission from that agency to deposit the patient records with that agency, except that no Federal agency is required to accept patient records under this paragraph.

(3) If, following the 365–day period described in paragraph (2) and after providing the notification under paragraph (1), patient records are not claimed by a patient or insurance provider, or request is not granted by a Federal agency to deposit such records with that agency, the trustee shall destroy those records by—

(A) if the records are written, shredding or burning the records; or

(B) if the records are magnetic, optical, or other electronic records, by otherwise destroying those records so that those records cannot be retrieved.

(Added Pub.L. 109–8, Title XI, § 1102(a), Apr. 20, 2005, 119 Stat. 189.)

HISTORICAL AND STATUTORY NOTES

Revision Notes and Legislative Reports

2005 Acts. House Report No. 109–31(Part I), see 2005 U.S. Code Cong. and Adm. News, p. 88.

References in Text

Chapter 7, 9, or 11, referred to in the introductory paragraph, means chapter 7, 9, or 11 of this title, 11 U.S.C.A. § 701 et seq., 11 U.S.C.A. § 901 et seq., or 11 U.S.C.A. § 1101 et seq., respectively.

Effective and Applicability Provisions

2005 Acts. Enactment of this section by Pub.L. 109–8 effective, except as otherwise provided, 180 days after April 20, 2005, and inapplicable with respect to cases commenced under Title 11 before the effective date, see Pub.L. 109–8, § 1501, set out as a note under 11 U.S.C.A. § 101.

SUBCHAPTER IV—ADMINISTRATIVE POWERS

§ 361. Adequate protection

When adequate protection is required under section 362, 363, or 364 of this title of an interest of an entity in property, such adequate protection may be provided by—

(1) requiring the trustee to make a cash payment or periodic cash payments to such entity, to the extent that the stay under section 362 of this title, use, sale, or lease under section 363 of this title, or any grant of a lien under section 364 of this title results in a decrease in the value of such entity's interest in such property;

(2) providing to such entity an additional or replacement lien to the extent that such stay, use, sale, lease, or grant results in a decrease in the value of such entity's interest in such property; or

(3) granting such other relief, other than entitling such entity to compensation allowable under section 503(b)(1) of this title as an administrative expense, as will result in the realization by such entity of the indubitable equivalent of such entity's interest in such property.

(Pub.L. 95–598, Nov. 6, 1978, 92 Stat. 2569; Pub.L. 98–353, Title III, § 440, July 10, 1984, 98 Stat. 370.)

HISTORICAL AND STATUTORY NOTES

Revision Notes and Legislative Reports

1978 Acts. Sections 362, 363, and 364 require, in certain circumstances, that the court determine in noticed hearings whether the interest of a secured creditor or co-owner of property with the debtor is adequately protected in connection with the sale or use of property. The interests of which the court may provide protection in the ways described in this section include equitable as well as legal interests. For example, a right to enforce a pledge and a right to recover property delivered to a debtor under a consignment agreement or an agreement of sale or return are interests that may be entitled to protection. This section specifies means by which adequate protection may be provided but, to avoid placing the court in an administrative role, does not require the court to provide it. Instead, the trustee or debtor in possession or the creditor will provide or propose a protection method. If the party that is affected by the proposed action objects, the court will determine whether the protection provided is adequate. The purpose of this section is to illustrate means by which it may be provided and to define the limits of the concept.

The concept of adequate protection is derived from the fifth amendment protection of property interests as enunciated by the Supreme Court. See *Wright v. Union Central Life Ins. Co.*, 311 U.S. 273 (1940) [61 S.Ct. 196, 85 L.Ed. 184, rehearing denied 61 S.Ct. 445, 312 U.S. 711, 85 L.Ed. 1142]; *Louisville Joint Stock Land Bank v. Radford*, 295 U.S. 555 (1935) [55 S.Ct. 854, 79 L.Ed. 1593].

The automatic stay also provides creditor protection. Without it, certain creditors would be able to pursue their own remedies against the debtor's property. Those who acted first would obtain payment of the claims in preference to and to the detriment of other creditors. Bankruptcy is designed to provide an orderly liquidation procedure under which all creditors are treated equally. A race of diligence by creditors for the debtor's assets prevents that.

Subsection (a) defines the scope of the automatic stay, by listing the acts that are stayed by the commencement of the case. The commencement or continuation, including the issuance of process, of a judicial, administrative or other proceeding against the debtor that was or could have been commenced before the commencement of the bankruptcy case is stayed under paragraph (1). The scope of this paragraph is broad. All proceedings are stayed, including arbitration, administrative, and judicial proceedings. Proceeding in this sense encompasses civil actions and all proceedings even if they are not before governmental tribunals.

The stay is not permanent. There is adequate provision for relief from the stay elsewhere in the section. However, it is important that the trustee have an opportunity to inventory the debtor's position before proceeding with the administration of the case. Undoubtedly the court will lift the stay for proceedings before specialized or nongovernmental tribunals to allow those proceedings to come to a conclusion. Any party desiring to enforce an order in such a proceeding would thereafter have to come before the bankruptcy court to collect assets. Nevertheless, it will often be more appropriate to permit proceedings to continue in their place of origin, when no great prejudice to the bankruptcy estate would result, in order to leave the parties to their chosen forum and to relieve the bankruptcy court from many duties that may be handled elsewhere.

Paragraph (2) stays the enforcement, against the debtor or against property of the estate, of a judgment obtained before the commencement of the bankruptcy case. Thus, execution and levy against the debtors' prepetition property are stayed, and attempts to collect a judgment from the debtor personally are stayed.

Paragraph (3) stays any act to obtain possession of property of the estate (that is, property of the debtor as of the date of the filing of the petition) or property from the estate (property over which the estate has control or possession). The purpose of this provision is to prevent dismemberment of the estate. Liquidation must proceed in an orderly fashion. Any distribution of property must be by the trustee after he has had an opportunity to familiarize himself with the various rights and interests involved and with the property available for distribution.

Paragraph (4) stays lien creation against property of the estate. Thus, taking possession to perfect a lien or obtaining court process is prohibited. To permit lien creation after bankruptcy would give certain creditors preferential treatment by making them secured instead of unsecured.

Paragraph (5) stays any act to create or enforce a lien against property of the debtor, that is, most property that is acquired after the date of the filing of the petition, property that is exempted, or property that does not pass to the estate, to the extent that the lien secures a prepetition claim. Again, to permit postbankruptcy lien creation or enforcement would permit certain creditors to receive preferential treatment. It may also circumvent the debtors' discharge.

Paragraph (6) prevents creditors from attempting in any way to collect a prepetition debt. Creditors in consumer cases occasionally telephone debtors to encourage repayment in spite of bankruptcy. Inexperienced, frightened, or ill-counseled debtors may succumb to suggestions to repay notwithstanding their bankruptcy. This provision prevents evasion of the purpose of the bankruptcy laws by sophisticated creditors.

Paragraph (7) stays setoffs of mutual debts and credits between the debtor and creditors. As with all other paragraphs of subsection (a), this paragraph does not affect the right of creditors. It simply stays its enforcement pending an orderly examination of the debtor's and creditors' rights.

Subsection (b) lists seven exceptions to the automatic stay. The effect of an exception is not to make the action immune from injunction.

The court has ample other powers to stay actions not covered by the automatic stay. Section 105, of proposed title 11, derived from Bankruptcy Act, § 2a(15), [section 11(a)(15) of former Title 11], grants the power to issue orders necessary or appropriate to carry out the provisions of title 11. The district court and the bankruptcy court as its adjunct have all the traditional injunctive powers of a court of equity, 28 U.S.C. §§ 151 and 164 as proposed in S. 2266, § 201, and 28 U.S.C. § 1334, as proposed in S. 2266, § 216. Stays or injunctions issued under these other sections will not be automatic upon the commencement of the case, but will be granted or issued under the usual rules for the issuance of injunctions. By excepting an act or action from the automatic stay, the bill simply requires that the trustee move the court into action, rather than requiring the stayed party to request relief from the stay. There are some actions, enumerated in the exceptions, that generally should not be stayed automatically upon the commencement of the case, for reasons of either policy or practicality. Thus, the court will have to determine on a case-by-case basis whether a particular action which may be harming the estate should be stayed.

With respect to stays issued under other powers, or the application of the automatic stay, to governmental actions, this section and the other sections mentioned are intended to be an express waiver of sovereign immunity of the Federal Government, and an assertion of the bankruptcy power over State governments under the supremacy clause notwithstanding a State's sovereign immunity.

The first exception is of criminal proceedings against the debtor. The bankruptcy laws are not a haven for criminal offenders, but are designed to give relief from financial overextension. Thus, criminal actions and proceedings may proceed in spite of bankruptcy.

Paragraph (2) excepts from the stay the collection of alimony, maintenance or support from property that is not property of the estate. This will include property acquired after the commencement of the case, exempted property, and property that does not pass to the estate. The automatic stay is one means of protecting the debtor's discharge. Alimony, maintenance and support obligations are excepted from discharge. Staying collection of them, when not to the detriment of other creditors (because the collection effort is against property that is not property of the estate) does not further that goal. Moreover, it could lead to hardship on the part of the protected spouse or children.

Paragraph (3) excepts any act to perfect an interest in property to the extent that the trustee's rights and powers are limited under section 546(a) of the bankruptcy code. That section permits postpetition perfection of certain liens to be effective against the trustee. If the act of perfection, such as filing, were stayed, the section would be nullified.

Paragraph (4) excepts commencement or continuation of actions and proceedings by governmental units to enforce police or regulatory powers. Thus, where a governmental unit is suing a debtor to prevent or stop violation of fraud, environmental protection, consumer protection, safety, or similar police or regulatory laws, or attempting to fix damages for violation of such a law, the action or proceeding is not stayed under the automatic stay.

Paragraph (5) makes clear that the exception extends to permit an injunction and enforcement of an injunction, and to permit the entry of a money judgment, but does not extend to permit enforcement of a money judgment. Since the assets of the debtor are in the possession and control of the bankruptcy court, and since they constitute a fund out of which all creditors are entitled to share, enforcement by a governmental unit of a money judgment would give it preferential treatment to the detriment of all other creditors.

Paragraph (6) excepts the setoff of any mutual debt and claim for commodity transactions.

Paragraph (7) excepts actions by the Secretary of Housing and Urban Development to foreclose or take possession in a case of a loan insured under the National Housing Act [12 U.S.C.A. § 1701 et seq.]. A general exception for such loans is found in current sections 263 and 517 [sections 663 and 917 of former Title 11], the exception allowed by this paragraph is much more limited.

Subsection (c) of section 362 specifies the duration of the automatic stay. Paragraph (1) terminates a stay of an act against property of the estate when the property ceases to be property of the estate, such as by sale, abandonment, or exemption. It does not terminate the stay against property of the debtor if the property leaves the estate and goes to the debtor. Paragraph (2) terminates the stay of any other act on the earliest of the time the case is closed, the time the case is dismissed, or the time a discharge is granted or denied (unless the debtor is a corporation or partnership in a chapter 7 case).

Subsection (c) governs automatic termination of the stay. Subsections (d) through (g) govern termination of the stay by the court on the request of a party in interest.

Subsection (d) requires the court, upon motion of a party in interest, to grant relief from the stay for cause, such as by terminating, annulling, modifying, or conditioning the stay. The lack of adequate protection of an interest in property is one cause for relief, but is not the only cause. Other causes might include the lack of any connection with or interference with the pending bankruptcy case. Generally, proceedings in which the debtor is a fiduciary or involving postpetition activities of the debtor, need not be stayed because they bear no relationship to the purpose of the automatic stay, which is protection of the debtor and his estate from his creditors.

Upon the court's finding that the debtor has no equity in the property subject to the stay and that the property is not necessary to an effective reorganization of the debtor, the subsection requires the court grant relief from the stay. To aid in this determination, guidelines are established where the property subject to the stay is real property. An exception to "the necessary to an effective reorganization" requirement is made for real property on which no business is being conducted other than operating the real property and activities incident thereto. The intent of this exception is to reach the single-asset apartment type cases which involve primarily tax-shelter investments and for which the bankruptcy laws have provided a too facile method to relay conditions, but not the operating shopping center and hotel cases where attempts at reorganization should be permitted. Property in which the debtor has equity but which is not necessary to an effective reorganization of the debtor should be sold under section 363. Hearings under this subsection are given calendar priority to ensure that court congestion will not unduly prejudice the rights of creditors who may be obviously entitled to relief from the operation of the automatic stay.

Subsection (e) provides protection that is not always available under present law. The subsection sets a time certain within which the bankruptcy court must rule on the adequacy of protection provided for the secured creditor's interest. If the court does not rule within 30 days from a request by motion for relief from the stay, the stay is automatically terminated with respect to the property in question. To accommodate more complex cases, the subsection permits the court to make a preliminary ruling after a preliminary hearing. After a preliminary hearing, the court may continue the stay only if there is a reasonable likelihood that the party opposing relief from the stay will prevail at the final hearing. Because the stay is essentially an injunction, the three stages of the stay may be analogized to the three stages of an injunction. The filing of the petition which gives rise to the automatic stay is similar to a temporary restraining order. The preliminary hearing is similar to the hearing on a preliminary injunction, and the final hearing and order are similar to the hearing and issuance or denial of a permanent injunction. The main difference lies in which party must bring the issue before the court. While in the injunction setting, the party seeking the injunction must prosecute the action, in proceeding for relief from the automatic stay, the enjoined party must move. The difference does not, however, shift the burden of proof. Subsection (g) leaves that burden on the party opposing relief from the stay (that is, on the party seeking continuance of the injunction) on the issue of adequate protection and existence of an equity. It is not, however, intended to be confined strictly to the constitutional requirement. This section and the concept of adequate protection are based as much on policy grounds as on constitutional grounds. Secured creditors should not be deprived of the benefit of their bargain. There may be situations in bankruptcy where giving a secured creditor an absolute right to his bargain may be impossible or seriously detrimental to the policy of the bankruptcy laws. Thus, this section recognizes the availability of alternate means of protecting a secured creditor's interest where such steps are a necessary part of the rehabilitative process. Though the creditor might not be able to retain his lien upon the specific collateral held at the time of filing, the purpose of the section is to insure that the secured creditor receives the value for which he bargained.

The section specifies two exclusive means of providing adequate protection, both of which may require an approximate determination of the value of the protected entity's interest in the property involved. The section does not specify how value is to be determined, nor does it specify when it is to be determined. These matters are left to case-by-case interpretation and development. In light of the restrictive approach of the section to the availability of means of providing adequate protection, this flexibility is important to permit the courts to adapt to varying circumstances and changing modes of financing.

Neither is it expected that the courts will construe the term value to mean, in every case, forced sale liquidation value or full going concern value. There is wide latitude between those two extremes although forced sale liquidation value will be a minimum.

In any particular case, especially a reorganization case, the determination of which entity should be entitled to the difference between the going concern value and the liquidation value must be based on equitable considerations arising from the facts of the case. Finally, the determination of value is binding only for the purposes of the specific hearing and is not to have a res judicata effect.

The first method of adequate protection outlined is the making of cash payments to compensate for the expected decrease in value of the opposing entity's interest. This provision is derived from *In re Bermec Corporation*, 445 F.2d 367 (2d Cir. 1971), though in that case it is not clear whether the payments offered were adequate to compensate the secured creditors for their loss. The use of periodic payments may be appropriate where, for example, the property in question is depreciating at a relatively fixed rate. The periodic payments would be to compensate for the depreciation and might, but need not necessarily, be in the same amount as payments due on the secured obligation.

The second method is the fixing of an additional or replacement lien on other property of the debtor to the extent of the decrease in value or actual consumption of the property involved. The purpose of this method is to provide the protected entity with an alternative means of realizing the value of the original property, if it should decline during the case, by granting an interest in additional property from whose value the entity may realize its loss. This is consistent with the view expressed in *Wright v. Union Central Life Ins. Co.*, 311 U.S. 273 (1940) [61 S.Ct. 196, 85 L.Ed. 184, rehearing denied 61 S.Ct. 445, 312 U.S. 711, 85 L.Ed. 1142], where the Court suggested that it was the value of the secured creditor's collateral, and not necessarily his rights in specific collateral, that was entitled to protection.

The section makes no provision for the granting of an administrative priority as a method of providing adequate protection to an entity as was suggested in *In re Yale Express System, Inc.*, 384 F.2d 990 (2d Cir. 1967), because such protection is too uncertain to be meaningful. Senate Report No. 95–989.

The section specifies four means of providing adequate protection. They are neither exclusive nor exhaustive. They all rely, however, on the value of the protected entity's interest in the property involved. The section does not specify how value is to be determined, nor does it specify when it is to be determined. These matters are left to case-by-case interpretation and development. It is expected that the courts will apply the concept in light of facts of each case and general equitable principles. It is not intended that the courts will develop a hard and fast rule that will apply in every case. The time and method of valuation is not specified precisely, in order to avoid that result. There are an infinite number of variations possible in dealings between debtors and creditors, the law is continually developing, and new ideas are continually being implemented in this field. The flexibility is important to permit the courts to adapt to varying circumstances and changing modes of financing.

Neither is it expected that the courts will construe the term value to mean, in every case, forced sale liquidation value or full going concern value. There is wide latitude between

those two extremes. In any particular case, especially a reorganization case, the determination of which entity should be entitled to the difference between the going concern value and the liquidation value must be based on equitable considerations based on the facts of the case. It will frequently be based on negotiation between the parties. Only if they cannot agree will the court become involved.

The first method of adequate protection specified is periodic cash payments by the estate, to the extent of a decrease in value of the opposing entity's interest in the property involved. This provision is derived from *In re Yale Express, Inc.*, 384 F.2d 990 (2d Cir. 1967) (though in that case it is not clear whether the payments required were adequate to compensate the secured creditors for their loss). The use of periodic payments may be appropriate, where for example, the property in question is depreciating at a relatively fixed rate. The periodic payments would be to compensate for the depreciation.

The second method is the provision of an additional or replacement lien on other property to the extent of the decrease in value of the property involved. The purpose of this method is to provide the protected entity with a means of realizing the value of the original property, if it should decline during the case, by granting an interest in additional property from whose value the entity may realize its loss.

The third method is the granting of an administrative expense priority to the protected entity to the extent of his loss. This method, more than the others, requires a prediction as to whether the unencumbered assets that will remain if the case if converted from reorganization to liquidation will be sufficient to pay the protected entity in full. It is clearly the most risky, from the entity's perspective, and should be used only when there is relative certainty that administrative expenses will be able to be paid in full in the event of liquidation.

The fourth method gives the parties and the courts flexibility by allowing such other relief as will result in the realization by the protected entity of the value of its interest in the property involved. Under this provision, the courts will be able to adapt to new methods of financing and to formulate protection that is appropriate to the circumstances of the case if none of the other methods would accomplish the desired result. For example, another form of adequate protection might be the guarantee by a third party outside the judicial process of compensation for any loss incurred in the case. Adequate protection might also, in some circumstances, be provided by permitting a secured creditor to bid in his claim at the sale of the property and to offset the claim against the price bid in.

The paragraph also defines, more clearly than the others, the general concept of adequate protection, by requiring such relief as will result in the realization of value. It is the general category, and as such, is defined by the concept involved rather than any particular method of adequate protection. House Report No. 95–595.

1984 Acts. Statements by Legislative Leaders, see 1984 U.S.Code Cong. and Adm.News, p. 576.

Legislative Statements

Section 361 of the House amendment represents a compromise between H.R. 8200 as passed by the House and the Senate amendment regarding the issue of "adequate protection" of a secured party. The House amendment deletes the provision found in section 361(3) of H.R. 8200 as passed by the House. It would have permitted adequate protection to be provided by giving the secured party an administrative expense regarding any decrease in the value of such party's collateral. In every case there is the uncertainty that the estate will have sufficient property to pay administrative expenses in full.

Section 361(4) of H.R. 8200 as passed by the House is modified in section 361(3) of the House amendment to indicate that the court may grant other forms of adequate protection, other than an administrative expense, which will result in the realization by the secured creditor of the indubitable equivalent of the creditor's interest in property. In the special instance where there is a reserve fund maintained under the security agreement, such as in the typical bondholder case, indubitable equivalent means that the bondholders would be entitled to be protected as to the reserve fund, in addition to the regular payments needed to service the debt. Adequate protection of an interest of an entity in property is intended to protect a creditor's allowed secured claim. To the extent the protection proves to be inadequate after the fact, the creditor is entitled to a first priority administrative expense under section 503(b).

In the special case of a creditor who has elected application of creditor making an election under section 1111(b)(2), that creditor is entitled to adequate protection of the creditor's interest in property to the extent of the value of the collateral not to the extent of the creditor's allowed secured claim, which is inflated to cover a deficiency as a result of such election.

Effective and Applicability Provisions

1984 Acts. Amendment by Pub.L. 98–353 effective with respect to cases filed 90 days after July 10, 1984, see section 552(a), formerly 553(a), of Pub.L. 98–353, set out as a note under section 101 of this title.

CROSS REFERENCES

Applicability of this section in Chapter 9 cases, see 11 USCA § 901.

Inapplicability of this section in Chapter 12 cases, see 11 USCA § 1205.

§ 362. Automatic stay

(a) Except as provided in subsection (b) of this section, a petition filed under section 301, 302, or 303 of this title, or an application filed under section 5(a)(3) of the Securities Investor Protection Act of 1970, operates as a stay, applicable to all entities, of—

(1) the commencement or continuation, including the issuance or employment of process, of a judicial, administrative, or other action or proceeding against the debtor that was or could have been commenced before the commencement of the case under this title, or to recover a claim against the debtor that arose before the commencement of the case under this title;

(2) the enforcement, against the debtor or against property of the estate, of a judgment obtained before the commencement of the case under this title;

(3) any act to obtain possession of property of the estate or of property from the estate or to exercise control over property of the estate;

(4) any act to create, perfect, or enforce any lien against property of the estate;

(5) any act to create, perfect, or enforce against property of the debtor any lien to the extent that such lien secures a claim that arose before the commencement of the case under this title;

(6) any act to collect, assess, or recover a claim against the debtor that arose before the commencement of the case under this title;

(7) the setoff of any debt owing to the debtor that arose before the commencement of the case under this title against any claim against the debtor; and

(8) the commencement or continuation of a proceeding before the United States Tax Court concerning a tax liability of a debtor that is a corporation for a taxable period the bankruptcy court may determine or concerning the tax liability of a debtor who is an individual for a taxable period ending before the date of the order for relief under this title.

(b) The filing of a petition under section 301, 302, or 303 of this title, or of an application under section 5(a)(3) of the Securities Investor Protection Act of 1970, does not operate as a stay—

(1) under subsection (a) of this section, of the commencement or continuation of a criminal action or proceeding against the debtor;

(2) under subsection (a)—

(A) of the commencement or continuation of a civil action or proceeding—

(i) for the establishment of paternity;

(ii) for the establishment or modification of an order for domestic support obligations;

(iii) concerning child custody or visitation;

(iv) for the dissolution of a marriage, except to the extent that such proceeding seeks to determine the division of property that is property of the estate; or

(v) regarding domestic violence;

(B) of the collection of a domestic support obligation from property that is not property of the estate;

(C) with respect to the withholding of income that is property of the estate or property of the debtor for payment of a domestic support obligation under a judicial or administrative order or a statute;

(D) of the withholding, suspension, or restriction of a driver's license, a professional or occupational license, or a recreational license, under State law, as specified in section 466(a)(16) of the Social Security Act;

(E) of the reporting of overdue support owed by a parent to any consumer reporting agency as specified in section 466(a)(7) of the Social Security Act;

   (F) of the interception of a tax refund, as specified in sections 464 and 466(a)(3) of the Social Security Act or under an analogous State law; or

   (G) of the enforcement of a medical obligation, as specified under title IV of the Social Security Act;

(3) under subsection (a) of this section, of any act to perfect, or to maintain or continue the perfection of, an interest in property to the extent that the trustee's rights and powers are subject to such perfection under section 546(b) of this title or to the extent that such act is accomplished within the period provided under section 547(e)(2)(A) of this title;

(4) under paragraph (1), (2), (3), or (6) of subsection (a) of this section, of the commencement or continuation of an action or proceeding by a governmental unit or any organization exercising authority under the Convention on the Prohibition of the Development, Production, Stockpiling and Use of Chemical Weapons and on Their Destruction, opened for signature on January 13, 1993, to enforce such governmental unit's or organization's police and regulatory power, including the enforcement of a judgment other than a money judgment, obtained in an action or proceeding by the governmental unit to enforce such governmental unit's or organization's police or regulatory power;

[(5) Repealed. Pub.L. 105–277, Div. I, Title VI, § 603(1), Oct. 21, 1998, 112 Stat. 2681–886]

(6) under subsection (a) of this section, of the exercise by a commodity broker, forward contract merchant, stockbroker, financial institution, financial participant, or securities clearing agency of any contractual right (as defined in section 555 or 556) under any security agreement or arrangement or other credit enhancement forming a part of or related to any commodity contract, forward contract or securities contract, or of any contractual right (as defined in section 555 or 556) to offset or net out any termination value, payment amount, or other transfer obligation arising under or in connection with 1 or more such contracts, including any master agreement for such contracts;

(7) under subsection (a) of this section, of the exercise by a repo participant or financial participant of any contractual right (as defined in section 559) under any security agreement or arrangement or other credit enhancement forming a part of or related to any repurchase agreement, or of any contractual right (as defined in section 559) to offset or net out any termination value, payment amount, or other transfer obligation arising under or in connection with 1 or more such agreements, including any master agreement for such agreements;

(8) under subsection (a) of this section, of the commencement of any action by the Secretary of Housing and Urban Development to foreclose a mortgage or deed of trust in any case in which the mortgage or deed of trust held by the Secretary is insured or was formerly insured under the National Housing Act and covers property, or combinations of property, consisting of five or more living units;

(9) under subsection (a), of—

   (A) an audit by a governmental unit to determine tax liability;

   (B) the issuance to the debtor by a governmental unit of a notice of tax deficiency;

   (C) a demand for tax returns; or

   (D) the making of an assessment for any tax and issuance of a notice and demand for payment of such an assessment (but any tax lien that would otherwise attach to property of the estate by reason of such an assessment shall not take effect unless such tax is a debt of the debtor that will not be discharged in the case and such property or its proceeds are transferred out of the estate to, or otherwise revested in, the debtor).

(10) under subsection (a) of this section, of any act by a lessor to the debtor under a lease of nonresidential real property that has terminated by the expiration of the stated term of the lease before the commencement of or during a case under this title to obtain possession of such property;

(11) under subsection (a) of this section, of the presentment of a negotiable instrument and the giving of notice of and protesting dishonor of such an instrument;

(12) under subsection (a) of this section, after the date which is 90 days after the filing of such petition, of the commencement or continuation, and conclusion to the entry of final judgment, of an action which involves a debtor subject to reorganization pursuant to chapter 11 of this title and which was brought by the Secretary of Transportation under section 31325 of title 46 (including distribution of any proceeds of sale) to foreclose a preferred ship or fleet mortgage, or a security interest in or relating to a vessel or vessel under construction, held by the Secretary of Transportation under chapter 537 of title 46 or section 109(h) of title 49, or under applicable State law;

(13) under subsection (a) of this section, after the date which is 90 days after the filing of such petition, of the commencement or continuation, and conclusion to the entry of final judgment, of an action which involves a debtor subject to reorganization pursuant to chapter 11 of this title and which was brought by the Secretary of Commerce under section 31325 of title 46 (including distribution of any proceeds of sale) to foreclose a preferred ship or fleet mortgage in a vessel or a mortgage, deed of trust, or other security interest in a fishing facility held by the Secretary of Commerce under chapter 537 of title 46;

(14) under subsection (a) of this section, of any action by an accrediting agency regarding the accreditation status of the debtor as an educational institution;

(15) under subsection (a) of this section, of any action by a State licensing body regarding the licensure of the debtor as an educational institution;

(16) under subsection (a) of this section, of any action by a guaranty agency, as defined in section 435(j) of the Higher Education Act of 1965 or the Secretary of Education regarding the eligibility of the debtor to participate in programs authorized under such Act;

(17) under subsection (a) of this section, of the exercise by a swap participant or financial participant of any contractual right (as defined in section 560) under any security agreement or arrangement or other credit enhancement forming a part of or related to any swap agreement, or of any contractual right (as defined in section 560) to offset or net out any termination value, payment amount, or other transfer obligation arising under or in connection with 1 or more such agreements, including any master agreement for such agreements;

(18) under subsection (a) of the creation or perfection of a statutory lien for an ad valorem property tax, or a special tax or special assessment on real property whether or not ad valorem, imposed by a governmental unit, if such tax or assessment comes due after the date of the filing of the petition;

(19) under subsection (a), of withholding of income from a debtor's wages and collection of amounts withheld, under the debtor's agreement authorizing that withholding and collection for the benefit of a pension, profit-sharing, stock bonus, or other plan established under section 401, 403, 408, 408A, 414, 457, or 501(c) of the Internal Revenue Code of 1986, that is sponsored by the employer of the debtor, or an affiliate, successor, or predecessor of such employer—

(A) to the extent that the amounts withheld and collected are used solely for payments relating to a loan from a plan under section 408(b)(1) of the Employee Retirement Income Security Act of 1974 or is subject to section 72(p) of the Internal Revenue Code of 1986; or

(B) a loan from a thrift savings plan permitted under subchapter III of chapter 84 of title 5, that satisfies the requirements of section 8433(g) of such title;

but nothing in this paragraph may be construed to provide that any loan made under a governmental plan under section 414(d), or a contract or account

under section 403(b), of the Internal Revenue Code of 1986 constitutes a claim or a debt under this title;

(20) under subsection (a), of any act to enforce any lien against or security interest in real property following entry of the order under subsection (d)(4) as to such real property in any prior case under this title, for a period of 2 years after the date of the entry of such an order, except that the debtor, in a subsequent case under this title, may move for relief from such order based upon changed circumstances or for other good cause shown, after notice and a hearing;

(21) under subsection (a), of any act to enforce any lien against or security interest in real property—

(A) if the debtor is ineligible under section 109(g) to be a debtor in a case under this title; or

(B) if the case under this title was filed in violation of a bankruptcy court order in a prior case under this title prohibiting the debtor from being a debtor in another case under this title;

(22) subject to subsection (*l*), under subsection (a)(3), of the continuation of any eviction, unlawful detainer action, or similar proceeding by a lessor against a debtor involving residential property in which the debtor resides as a tenant under a lease or rental agreement and with respect to which the lessor has obtained before the date of the filing of the bankruptcy petition, a judgment for possession of such property against the debtor;

(23) subject to subsection (m), under subsection (a)(3), of an eviction action that seeks possession of the residential property in which the debtor resides as a tenant under a lease or rental agreement based on endangerment of such property or the illegal use of controlled substances on such property, but only if the lessor files with the court, and serves upon the debtor, a certification under penalty of perjury that such an eviction action has been filed, or that the debtor, during the 30–day period preceding the date of the filing of the certification, has endangered property or illegally used or allowed to be used a controlled substance on the property;

(24) under subsection (a), of any transfer that is not avoidable under section 544 and that is not avoidable under section 549;

(25) under subsection (a), of—

(A) the commencement or continuation of an investigation or action by a securities self regulatory organization to enforce such organization's regulatory power;

(B) the enforcement of an order or decision, other than for monetary sanctions, obtained in an action by such securities self regulatory organization to enforce such organization's regulatory power; or

(C) any act taken by such securities self regulatory organization to delist, delete, or refuse to permit quotation of any stock that does not meet applicable regulatory requirements;

(26) under subsection (a), of the setoff under applicable nonbankruptcy law of an income tax refund, by a governmental unit, with respect to a taxable period that ended before the date of the order for relief against an income tax liability for a taxable period that also ended before the date of the order for relief, except that in any case in which the setoff of an income tax refund is not permitted under applicable nonbankruptcy law because of a pending action to determine the amount or legality of a tax liability, the governmental unit may hold the refund pending the resolution of the action, unless the court, on the motion of the trustee and after notice and a hearing, grants the taxing authority adequate protection (within the meaning of section 361) for the secured claim of such authority in the setoff under section 506(a);

(27) under subsection (a) of this section, of the exercise by a master netting agreement participant of any contractual right (as defined in section 555, 556, 559, or 560) under any security agreement or arrangement or other credit enhancement forming a part of or related to any master netting agreement, or of any contractual right (as defined in section 555, 556, 559, or 560) to offset or net out any termination value, payment amount, or other transfer obligation arising under or in connection with 1 or more such master netting agreements to the extent that such participant is eligible to exercise such rights under paragraph (6), (7), or (17) for each individual contract covered by the master netting agreement in issue; and

(28) under subsection (a), of the exclusion by the Secretary of Health and Human Services of the debtor from participation in the medicare program or any other Federal health care program (as defined in section 1128B(f) of the Social Security Act pursuant to title XI or XVIII of such Act).

The provisions of paragraphs (12) and (13) of this subsection shall apply with respect to any such petition filed on or before December 31, 1989.

(c) Except as provided in subsections (d), (e), (f), and (h) of this section—

(1) the stay of an act against property of the estate under subsection (a) of this section continues until such property is no longer property of the estate;

(2) the stay of any other act under subsection (a) of this section continues until the earliest of—

(A) the time the case is closed;

(B) the time the case is dismissed; or

(C) if the case is a case under chapter 7 of this title concerning an individual or a case under chapter 9, 11, 12, or 13 of this title, the time a discharge is granted or denied;

(3) if a single or joint case is filed by or against a debtor who is an individual in a case under chapter 7, 11, or 13, and if a single or joint case of the debtor was pending within the preceding 1–year period but was dismissed, other than a case refiled under a chapter other than chapter 7 after dismissal under section 707(b)—

(A) the stay under subsection (a) with respect to any action taken with respect to a debt or property securing such debt or with respect to any lease shall terminate with respect to the debtor on the 30th day after the filing of the later case;

(B) on the motion of a party in interest for continuation of the automatic stay and upon notice and a hearing, the court may extend the stay in particular cases as to any or all creditors (subject to such conditions or limitations as the court may then impose) after notice and a hearing completed before the expiration of the 30–day period only if the party in interest demonstrates that the filing of the later case is in good faith as to the creditors to be stayed; and

(C) for purposes of subparagraph (B), a case is presumptively filed not in good faith (but such presumption may be rebutted by clear and convincing evidence to the contrary)—

(i) as to all creditors, if—

(I) more than 1 previous case under any of chapters 7, 11, and 13 in which the individual was a debtor was pending within the preceding 1–year period;

(II) a previous case under any of chapters 7, 11, and 13 in which the individual was a debtor was dismissed within such 1–year period, after the debtor failed to—

(aa) file or amend the petition or other documents as required by this title or the court without substantial excuse (but mere inadvertence or negligence shall not be a substantial excuse unless the dismissal was caused by the negligence of the debtor's attorney);

(bb) provide adequate protection as ordered by the court; or

(cc) perform the terms of a plan confirmed by the court; or

(III) there has not been a substantial change in the financial or personal affairs of the debtor since the dismissal of the next most previous case under chapter 7, 11, or 13 or any other reason to conclude that the later case will be concluded—

(aa) if a case under chapter 7, with a discharge; or

(bb) if a case under chapter 11 or 13, with a confirmed plan that will be fully performed; and

(ii) as to any creditor that commenced an action under subsection (d) in a previous case in which the individual was a debtor if, as of the date of dismissal of such case, that action was still pending or had been resolved by terminating, conditioning, or limiting the stay as to actions of such creditor; and

(4)(A)(i) if a single or joint case is filed by or against a debtor who is an individual under this title, and if 2 or more single or joint cases of the debtor were pending within the previous year but were dismissed, other than a case refiled under a chapter other than chapter 7 after dismissal under section 707(b), the stay under subsection (a) shall not go into effect upon the filing of the later case; and

(ii) on request of a party in interest, the court shall promptly enter an order confirming that no stay is in effect;

(B) if, within 30 days after the filing of the later case, a party in interest requests the court may order the stay to take effect in the case as to any or all creditors (subject to such conditions or limitations as the court may impose), after notice and a hearing, only if the party in interest demonstrates that the filing of the later case is in good faith as to the creditors to be stayed;

(C) a stay imposed under subparagraph (B) shall be effective on the date of the entry of the order allowing the stay to go into effect; and

(D) for purposes of subparagraph (B), a case is presumptively filed not in good faith (but such presumption may be rebutted by clear and convincing evidence to the contrary)—

(i) as to all creditors if—

(I) 2 or more previous cases under this title in which the individual was a debtor were pending within the 1-year period;

(II) a previous case under this title in which the individual was a debtor was dismissed within the time period stated in this paragraph after the debtor failed to file or amend the petition or other documents as required by this title or the court without substantial excuse (but mere inadvertence or negligence shall not be substantial excuse unless the dismissal was caused by the negligence of the debtor's attorney), failed to provide adequate protection as ordered by the court, or failed to perform the terms of a plan confirmed by the court; or

(III) there has not been a substantial change in the financial or personal affairs of the debtor since the dismissal of the next most previous case under this title, or any other reason to conclude that the later case will not be concluded, if a case under chapter 7, with a discharge,

and if a case under chapter 11 or 13, with a confirmed plan that will be fully performed; or

(ii) as to any creditor that commenced an action under subsection (d) in a previous case in which the individual was a debtor if, as of the date of dismissal of such case, such action was still pending or had been resolved by terminating, conditioning, or limiting the stay as to such action of such creditor.

(d) On request of a party in interest and after notice and a hearing, the court shall grant relief from the stay provided under subsection (a) of this section, such as by terminating, annulling, modifying, or conditioning such stay—

(1) for cause, including the lack of adequate protection of an interest in property of such party in interest;

(2) with respect to a stay of an act against property under subsection (a) of this section, if—

(A) the debtor does not have an equity in such property; and

(B) such property is not necessary to an effective reorganization;

(3) with respect to a stay of an act against single asset real estate under subsection (a), by a creditor whose claim is secured by an interest in such real estate, unless, not later than the date that is 90 days after the entry of the order for relief (or such later date as the court may determine for cause by order entered within that 90-day period) or 30 days after the court determines that the debtor is subject to this paragraph, whichever is later—

(A) the debtor has filed a plan of reorganization that has a reasonable possibility of being confirmed within a reasonable time; or

(B) the debtor has commenced monthly payments that—

(i) may, in the debtor's sole discretion, notwithstanding section 363(c)(2), be made from rents or other income generated before, on, or after the date of the commencement of the case by or from the property to each creditor whose claim is secured by such real estate (other than a claim secured by a judgment lien or by an unmatured statutory lien); and

(ii) are in an amount equal to interest at the then applicable nondefault contract rate of interest on the value of the creditor's interest in the real estate; or

(4) with respect to a stay of an act against real property under subsection (a), by a creditor whose claim is secured by an interest in such real property, if the court finds that the filing of the petition was part of a scheme to delay, hinder, or defraud creditors that involved either—

(A) transfer of all or part ownership of, or other interest in, such real property without the consent of the secured creditor or court approval; or

(B) multiple bankruptcy filings affecting such real property.

If recorded in compliance with applicable State laws governing notices of interests or liens in real property, an order entered under paragraph (4) shall be binding in any other case under this title purporting to affect such real property filed not later than 2 years after the date of the entry of such order by the court, except that a debtor in a subsequent case under this title may move for relief from such order based upon changed circumstances or for good cause shown, after notice and a hearing. Any Federal, State, or local governmental unit that accepts notices of interests or liens in real property shall accept any certified copy of an order described in this subsection for indexing and recording.

(e)(1) Thirty days after a request under subsection (d) of this section for relief from the stay of any act against property of the estate under subsection (a) of this section, such stay is terminated with respect to the party in interest making such request, unless the court, after notice and a hearing, orders such stay continued in effect pending the conclusion of, or as a result of, a final hearing and determination under subsection (d) of this section. A hearing under this subsection may be a preliminary hearing, or may be consolidated with the final hearing under subsection (d) of this section. The court shall order such stay continued in effect pending the conclusion of the final hearing under subsection (d) of this section if there is a reasonable likelihood that the party opposing relief from such stay will prevail at the conclusion of such final hearing. If the hearing under this subsection is a preliminary hearing, then such final hearing shall be concluded not later than thirty days after the conclusion of such preliminary hearing, unless the 30–day period is extended with the consent of the parties in interest or for a specific time which the court finds is required by compelling circumstances.

(2) Notwithstanding paragraph (1), in a case under chapter 7, 11, or 13 in which the debtor is an individual, the stay under subsection (a) shall terminate on the date that is 60 days after a request is made by a party in interest under subsection (d), unless—

(A) a final decision is rendered by the court during the 60–day period beginning on the date of the request; or

(B) such 60–day period is extended—

(i) by agreement of all parties in interest; or

(ii) by the court for such specific period of time as the court finds is required for good cause, as described in findings made by the court.

(f) Upon request of a party in interest, the court, with or without a hearing, shall grant such relief from the stay provided under subsection (a) of this section as is necessary to prevent irreparable damage to the interest of an entity in property, if such interest will suffer such damage before there is an opportunity for notice and a hearing under subsection (d) or (e) of this section.

(g) In any hearing under subsection (d) or (e) of this section concerning relief from the stay of any act under subsection (a) of this section—

(1) the party requesting such relief has the burden of proof on the issue of the debtor's equity in property; and

(2) the party opposing such relief has the burden of proof on all other issues.

(h)(1) In a case in which the debtor is an individual, the stay provided by subsection (a) is terminated with respect to personal property of the estate or of the debtor securing in whole or in part a claim, or subject to an unexpired lease, and such personal property shall no longer be property of the estate if the debtor fails within the applicable time set by section 521(a)(2)—

(A) to file timely any statement of intention required under section 521(a)(2) with respect to such personal property or to indicate in such statement that the debtor will either surrender such personal property or retain it and, if retaining such personal property, either redeem such personal property pursuant to section 722, enter into an agreement of the kind specified in section 524(c) applicable to the debt secured by such personal property, or assume such unexpired lease pursuant to section 365(p) if the trustee does not do so, as applicable; and

(B) to take timely the action specified in such statement, as it may be amended before expiration of the period for taking action, unless such statement specifies the debtor's intention to reaffirm such debt on the original contract terms and the creditor refuses to agree to the reaffirmation on such terms.

(2) Paragraph (1) does not apply if the court determines, on the motion of the trustee filed before the expiration of the applicable time set by section 521(a)(2), after notice and a hearing, that such personal property is of consequential value or benefit to the estate, and orders appropriate adequate protection of the creditor's interest, and orders the debtor to deliver any collateral in the debtor's possession to the trustee. If the court does not so determine, the stay provided by subsection (a) shall terminate upon the conclusion of the hearing on the motion.

(i) If a case commenced under chapter 7, 11, or 13 is dismissed due to the creation of a debt repayment plan, for purposes of subsection (c)(3), any subsequent case commenced by the debtor under any such chapter shall not be presumed to be filed not in good faith.

(j) On request of a party in interest, the court shall issue an order under subsection (c) confirming that the automatic stay has been terminated.

(k)(1) Except as provided in paragraph (2), an individual injured by any willful violation of a stay provided by this section shall recover actual damages, including costs and attorneys' fees, and, in appropriate circumstances, may recover punitive damages.

(2) If such violation is based on an action taken by an entity in the good faith belief that subsection (h) applies to the debtor, the recovery under paragraph (1) of this subsection against such entity shall be limited to actual damages.

(*l*)(1) Except as otherwise provided in this subsection, subsection (b) (22) shall apply on the date that is 30 days after the date on which the bankruptcy petition is filed, if the debtor files with the petition and serves upon the lessor a certification under penalty of perjury that—

    (A) under nonbankruptcy law applicable in the jurisdiction, there are circumstances under which the debtor would be permitted to cure the entire monetary default that gave rise to the judgment for possession, after that judgment for possession was entered; and

    (B) the debtor (or an adult dependent of the debtor) has deposited with the clerk of the court, any rent that would become due during the 30–day period after the filing of the bankruptcy petition.

(2) If, within the 30–day period after the filing of the bankruptcy petition, the debtor (or an adult dependent of the debtor) complies with paragraph (1) and files with the court and serves upon the lessor a further certification under penalty of perjury that the debtor (or an adult dependent of the debtor) has cured, under nonbankruptcy law applicable in the jurisdiction, the entire monetary default that gave rise to the judgment under which possession is sought by the lessor, subsection (b)(22) shall not apply, unless ordered to apply by the court under paragraph (3).

(3)(A) If the lessor files an objection to any certification filed by the debtor under paragraph (1) or (2), and serves such objection upon the debtor, the court shall hold a hearing within 10 days after the filing and service of such objection to determine if the certification filed by the debtor under paragraph (1) or (2) is true.

    (B) If the court upholds the objection of the lessor filed under subparagraph (A)—

        (i) subsection (b)(22) shall apply immediately and relief from the stay provided under subsection (a)(3) shall not be required to enable the lessor to complete the process to recover full possession of the property; and

        (ii) the clerk of the court shall immediately serve upon the lessor and the debtor a certified copy of the court's order upholding the lessor's objection.

(4) If a debtor, in accordance with paragraph (5), indicates on the petition that there was a judgment for possession of the residential rental property in which the debtor resides and does not file a certification under paragraph (1) or (2)—

    (A) subsection (b)(22) shall apply immediately upon failure to file such certification, and relief from the stay provided under subsection (a)(3) shall not be required to enable the lessor to complete the process to recover full possession of the property; and

    (B) the clerk of the court shall immediately serve upon the lessor and the debtor a certified copy of the docket indicating the absence of a filed certification and the applicability of the exception to the stay under subsection (b)(22).

(5)(A) Where a judgment for possession of residential property in which the debtor resides as a tenant under a lease or rental agreement has been obtained by the lessor, the debtor shall so indicate on the bankruptcy petition and shall provide the name and address of the lessor that obtained that pre-petition judgment on the petition and on any certification filed under this subsection.

    (B) The form of certification filed with the petition, as specified in this subsection, shall provide for the debtor to certify, and the debtor shall certify—

        (i) whether a judgment for possession of residential rental housing in which the debtor resides has been obtained against the debtor before the date of the filing of the petition; and

        (ii) whether the debtor is claiming under paragraph (1) that under nonbankruptcy law applicable in the jurisdiction, there are circumstances under which the debtor would be permitted to cure the entire monetary default that gave rise to the judgment for possession, after that judgment of possession was entered, and has made the appropriate deposit with the court.

    (C) The standard forms (electronic and otherwise) used in a bankruptcy proceeding shall be amended to reflect the requirements of this subsection.

    (D) The clerk of the court shall arrange for the prompt transmittal of the rent deposited in accordance with paragraph (1)(B) to the lessor.

(m)(1) Except as otherwise provided in this subsection, subsection (b) (23) shall apply on the date that is 15 days after the date on which the lessor files and serves a certification described in subsection (b)(23).

(2)(A) If the debtor files with the court an objection to the truth or legal sufficiency of the certification described in subsection (b)(23) and serves such objection upon the lessor, subsection (b)(23) shall not apply, unless ordered to apply by the court under this subsection.

(B) If the debtor files and serves the objection under subparagraph (A), the court shall hold a hearing within 10 days after the filing and service of such objection to determine if the situation giving rise to the lessor's certification under paragraph (1) existed or has been remedied.

(C) If the debtor can demonstrate to the satisfaction of the court that the situation giving rise to the lessor's certification under paragraph (1) did not exist or has been remedied, the stay provided under subsection (a)(3) shall remain in effect until the termination of the stay under this section.

(D) If the debtor cannot demonstrate to the satisfaction of the court that the situation giving rise to the lessor's certification under paragraph (1) did not exist or has been remedied—

    (i) relief from the stay provided under subsection (a)(3) shall not be required to enable the lessor to proceed with the eviction; and

    (ii) the clerk of the court shall immediately serve upon the lessor and the debtor a certified copy of the court's order upholding the lessor's certification.

(3) If the debtor fails to file, within 15 days, an objection under paragraph (2)(A)—

    (A) subsection (b)(23) shall apply immediately upon such failure and relief from the stay provided under subsection (a)(3) shall not be required to enable the lessor to complete the process to recover full possession of the property; and

    (B) the clerk of the court shall immediately serve upon the lessor and the debtor a certified copy of the docket indicating such failure.

(n)(1) Except as provided in paragraph (2), subsection (a) does not apply in a case in which the debtor—

    (A) is a debtor in a small business case pending at the time the petition is filed;

    (B) was a debtor in a small business case that was dismissed for any reason by an order that became final in the 2–year period ending on the date of the order for relief entered with respect to the petition;

    (C) was a debtor in a small business case in which a plan was confirmed in the 2–year period ending on the date of the order for relief entered with respect to the petition; or

    (D) is an entity that has acquired substantially all of the assets or business of a small business debtor described in subparagraph (A), (B), or (C), unless such entity establishes by a preponderance of the evidence that such entity acquired substantially all of the assets or business of such small business debtor in good faith and not for the purpose of evading this paragraph.

(2) Paragraph (1) does not apply—

    (A) to an involuntary case involving no collusion by the debtor with creditors; or

    (B) to the filing of a petition if—

        (i) the debtor proves by a preponderance of the evidence that the filing of the petition resulted from circumstances beyond the control of the debtor not foreseeable at the time the case then pending was filed; and

        (ii) it is more likely than not that the court will confirm a feasible plan, but not a liquidating plan, within a reasonable period of time.

(o) The exercise of rights not subject to the stay arising under subsection (a) pursuant to paragraph (6), (7), (17), or (27) of subsection (b) shall not be stayed by any order of a court or administrative agency in any proceeding under this title.

(Pub.L. 95–598, Nov. 6, 1978, 92 Stat. 2570; Pub.L. 97–222, § 3, July 27, 1982, 96 Stat. 235; Pub.L. 98–353, Title III, §§ 304, 363(b), 392, 441, July 10, 1984, 98 Stat. 352, 363, 365, 371; Pub.L. 99–509, Title V, § 5001(a), Oct. 21, 1986, 100 Stat. 1911; Pub.L. 99–554, Title II, §§ 257(j), 283(d), Oct. 27, 1986, 100 Stat. 3115, 3116; Pub.L. 101–311, Title I, § 102, Title II, § 202, June 25, 1990, 104 Stat. 267, 269; Pub.L. 101–508, Title III, § 3007(a)(1), Nov. 5, 1990, 104 Stat. 1388–28; Pub.L. 103–394, Title I, §§ 101, 116, Title II, §§ 204(a), 218(b), Title III, § 304(b), Title IV, § 401, Title V, § 501(b)(2), (d)(7), Oct. 22, 1994, 108 Stat. 4107, 4119, 4122, 4128, 4132, 4141, 4142, 4144; Pub.L. 105–277, Div. I, Title VI, § 603, Oct. 21, 1998, 112 Stat. 2681–886; Pub.L. 109–8, Title I, § 106(f), Title II, §§ 214, 224(b), Title III, §§ 302, 303, 305(1), 311, 320, Title IV, §§ 401(b), 441, 444, Title VII, §§ 709, 718, Title IX, § 907(d), (o)(1), (2), Title XI, § 1106, Title XII, § 1225, Apr. 20, 2005, 119 Stat. 41, 54, 64, 75, 77, 79, 84, 94, 104, 114, 117, 127, 131, 176, 181, 182, 192, 199; Pub.L. 109–304, § 17(b)(1), Oct. 6, 2006, 120 Stat. 1706; Pub.L. 109–390, § 5(a)(2), Dec. 12, 2006, 120 Stat. 2696; Pub.L. 111–327, § 2(a)(12), Dec. 22, 2010, 124 Stat. 3558.)

HISTORICAL AND STATUTORY NOTES

Revision Notes and Legislative Reports

1978 Acts. The automatic stay is one of the fundamental debtor protections provided by the bankruptcy laws. It gives the debtor a breathing spell from his creditors. It stops all collection efforts, all harassment, and all foreclosure actions. It permits the debtor to attempt a repayment or reorganization plan, or simply to be relieved of the financial pressures that drove him into bankruptcy.

The action commenced by the party seeking relief from the stay is referred to as a motion to make it clear that at the expedited hearing under subsection (e), and at hearings on relief from the stay, the only issue will be the lack of adequate protection, the debtor's equity in the property, and the necessity of the property to an effective reorganization of the debtor, or the existence of other cause for relief from the stay. This hearing will not be the appropriate time at which to bring in other issues, such as counterclaims against the creditor, which, although relevant to the question of the amount of the debt, concern largely collateral or unrelated matters. This approach is consistent with that taken in cases such as *In re Essex Properties, Ltd.*, 430 F.Supp. 1112 (N.D.Cal.1977), that an action seeking relief from the stay is not the assertion of a claim which would give rise to the right or obligation to assert counterclaims. Those counterclaims are not to be handled in the summary fashion that the preliminary hearing under this provision will be. Rather, they will be the subject of more complete proceedings by the trustee to recover property of the estate or to object to the allowance of a claim. However, this would not preclude the party seeking continuance of the stay from presenting evidence on the existence of claims which the court may consider in exercising its discretion. What is precluded is a determination of such collateral claims on the merits at the hearing. Senate Report No. 95–989.

[For additional discussion, see Revision Notes and Legislative Reports, Senate Report No. 95–989, set out under section 361 of this title.]

Paragraph (7) [of subsec. (a)] stays setoffs of mutual debts and credits between the debtor and creditors. As with all other paragraphs of subsection (a), this paragraph does not affect the right of creditors. It simply stays its enforcement pending an orderly examination of the debtor's and creditors' rights.

Subsection (c) governs automatic termination of the stay. Subsections (d) through (g) govern termination of the stay by the court on the request of a party in interest. Subsection (d) requires the court, on request of a party in interest, to grant relief from the stay, such as by terminating, annulling, modifying, or conditioning the stay, for cause. The lack of adequate protection of an interest in property of the party requesting relief from the stay is one cause for relief, but is not the only cause. As noted above, a desire to permit an action to proceed to completion in another tribunal may provide another cause. Other causes might include the lack of any connection with or interference with the pending bankruptcy case. For example, a divorce or child custody proceeding involving the debtor may bear no relation to the bankruptcy case. In that case, it should not be stayed. A probate proceeding in which the debtor is the executor or administrator of another's estate usually will not be related to the bankruptcy case, and should not be stayed. Generally, proceedings in which the debtor is a fiduciary, or involving postpetition activities of the debtor, need not be stayed because they bear no relationship to the purpose of the automatic stay, which is debtor protection from his creditors. The facts of each request will determine whether relief is appropriate under the circumstances.

Subsection (e) provides a protection for secured creditors that is not available under present law. The subsection sets a time certain within which the bankruptcy court must rule on the adequacy of protection provided of the secured creditor's interest. If the court does not rule within 30 days from a request for relief from the stay, the stay is automatically terminated with respect to the property in question. In order to accommodate more complex cases, the subsection permits the court to make a preliminary ruling after a preliminary hearing. After a preliminary hearing, the court may continue the stay only if there is a reasonable likelihood that the party opposing relief from the stay will prevail at the final hearing. Because the stay is essentially an injunction, the three stages of the stay may be analogized to the three stages of an injunction. The filing of the petition which gives rise to the automatic stay is similar to a temporary restraining order. The preliminary hearing is similar to the hearing on a preliminary injunction, and the final hearing and order is similar to a permanent injunction. The main difference lies in which

party must bring the issue before the court. While in the injunction setting, the party seeking the injunction must prosecute the action, in proceedings for relief from the automatic stay, the enjoined party must move. The difference does not, however, shift the burden of proof. Subsection (g) leaves that burden on the party opposing relief from the stay (that is, on the party seeking continuance of the injunction) on the issue of adequate protection.

At the expedited hearing under subsection (e), and at all hearings on relief from the stay, the only issue will be the claim of the creditor and the lack of adequate protection or existence of other cause for relief from the stay. This hearing will not be the appropriate time at which to bring in other issues, such as counterclaims against the creditor on largely unrelated matters. Those counterclaims are not to be handled in the summary fashion that the preliminary hearing under this provision will be. Rather, they will be the subject of more complete proceedings by the trustees to recover property of the estate or to object to the allowance of a claim. House Report No. 95–595.

1982 Acts. House Report No. 97–420, see 1982 U.S. Code Cong. and Adm. News, p. 583.

1984 Acts. Statements by Legislative Leaders, see 1984 U.S. Code Cong. and Adm. News, p. 576.

1986 Acts. House Report No. 99–727, House Conference Report No. 99–1012, and Statement by President, see 1986 U.S. Code Cong. and Adm. News, p. 3607.

House Report No. 99–764 and House Conference Report No. 99–958, see 1986 U.S. Code Cong. and Adm. News, p. 5227.

1990 Acts. House Report No. 101–484, see 1990 U.S. Code Cong. and Adm. News, p. 223.

House Report No. 101–881, House Conference Report No. 101–964, and Statement by President, see 1990 U.S. Code Cong. and Adm. News, p. 2017.

1994 Acts. House Report No. 103–835, see 1994 U.S. Code Cong. and Adm. News, p. 3340.

1998 Acts. Statement by President, see 1998 U.S. Code Cong. and Adm. News, p. 576.

2005 Acts. House Report No. 109–31(Part I), see 2005 U.S. Code Cong. and Adm. News, p. 88.

2006 Acts. House Report No. 109–170, see 2006 U.S. Code Cong. and Adm. News, p. 972.

House Report No. 109–648(Part I), see 2006 U.S. Code Cong. and Adm. News, p. 1585.

Legislative Statements

Section 362(a)(1) of the House amendment adopts the provision contained in the Senate amendment enjoining the commencement or continuation of a judicial, administrative, or other proceeding to recover a claim against the debtor that arose before the commencement of the case. The provision is beneficial and interacts with section 362(a)(6), which also covers assessment, to prevent harassment of the debtor with respect to pre-petition claims.

Section 362(a)(7) contains a provision contained in H.R. 8200 as passed by the House. The differing provision in the Senate amendment was rejected. It is not possible that a debt owing to the debtor may be offset against an interest in the debtor.

Section 362(a)(8) is new. The provision stays the commencement or continuation of any proceeding concerning the debtor before the U.S. Tax Court.

Section 362(b)(4) indicates that the stay under section 362(a)(1) does not apply to affect the commencement or continuation of an action or proceeding by a governmental unit to enforce the governmental unit's police or regulatory power. This section is intended to be given a narrow construction in order to permit governmental units to pursue actions to protect the public health and safety and not to apply to actions by a governmental unit to protect a pecuniary interest in property of the debtor or property of the estate.

Section 362(b)(6) of the House amendment adopts a provision contained in the Senate amendment restricting the exception to the automatic stay with respect to setoffs to permit only the setoff of mutual debts and claims. Traditionally, the right of setoff has been limited to mutual debts and claims and the lack of the clarifying term "mutual" in H.R. 8200 as passed by the House created an unintentional ambiguity. Section 362(b)(7) of the House amendment permits the issuance of a notice of tax deficiency. The House amendment rejects section 362(b)(7) in the Senate amendment. It would have permitted a particular governmental unit to obtain a pecuniary advantage without a hearing on the merits contrary to the exceptions contained in sections 362(b)(4) and (5).

Section 362(d) of the House amendment represents a compromise between comparable provisions in the House bill and Senate amendment. Under section 362(d)(1) of the House amendment, the court may terminate, annul, modify, or condition the automatic stay for cause, including lack of adequate protection of an interest in property of a secured party. It is anticipated that the Rules of Bankruptcy Procedure will provide that those hearings will receive priority on the calendar. Under section 362(d)(2) the court may alternatively terminate, annul, modify, or condition the automatic stay for cause including inadequate protection for the creditor. The court shall grant relief from the stay if there is no equity and it is not necessary to an effective reorganization of the debtor.

The latter requirement is contained in section 362(d)(2). This section is intended to solve the problem of real property mortgage foreclosures of property where the bankruptcy petition is filed on the eve of foreclosure. The section is not intended to apply if the business of the debtor is managing or leasing real property, such as a hotel operation, even though the debtor has no equity if the property is necessary to an effective reorganization of the debtor. Similarly, if the debtor does have an equity in the property, there is no requirement that the property be sold under section 363 of title 11 as would have been required by the Senate amendment.

Section 362(e) of the House amendment represents a modification of provisions in H.R. 8200 as passed by the House and the Senate amendment to make clear that a final hearing must be commenced within 30 days after a preliminary hearing is held to determine whether a creditor will be entitled to relief from the automatic stay. In order to insure that those hearings will in fact occur within such 30-day period, it is anticipated that the rules of bankruptcy procedure provide that such final hearings receive priority on the court calendar.

Section 362(g) places the burden of proof on the issue of the debtor's equity in collateral on the party requesting relief from the automatic stay and the burden on other issues on the debtor.

An amendment has been made to section 362(b) to permit the Secretary of the Department of Housing and Urban Development to commence an action to foreclose a mortgage or deed of trust. The commencement of such an action is necessary for tax purposes. The section is not intended to permit the continuation of such an action after it is commenced nor is the section to be construed to entitle the Secretary to take possession in lieu of foreclosure.

Automatic stay: Sections 362(b)(8) and (9) contained in the Senate amendment are largely deleted in the House amendment. Those provisions add to the list of actions not stayed (a) jeopardy assessments, (b) other assessments, and (c) the issuance of deficiency notices. In the House amendment, jeopardy assessments against property which ceases to be property of the estate is already authorized by section 362(c)(1). Other assessments are specifically stayed under section 362(a)(6), while the issuance of a deficiency notice is specifically permitted. Stay of the assessment and the permission to issue a statutory notice of a tax deficiency will permit the debtor to take his personal tax case to the Tax Court, if the bankruptcy judge authorizes him to do so (as explained more fully in the discussion of section 505.)

References in Text

Chapter 7, 11, or 13, referred to in text, is chapter 7, 11, or 13 of this title, 11 U.S.C.A. § 701 et seq., 11 U.S.C.A. § 1101 et seq., or 11 U.S.C.A. § 1301 et seq., respectively.

Section 5(a)(3) of the Securities Investor Protection Act of 1970, referred to in subsecs. (a) and (b), is section 5(a)(3) of Pub.L. 91–598, Dec. 30, 1970, 84 Stat. 1644, which is classified to section 78eee of Title 15, Commerce and Trade.

Section 466 of the Social Security Act, referred to in subsec. (b)(2)(D) to (F), is Act Aug. 14, 1935, c. 531, Title IV, § 466, as added Aug. 16, 1984, Pub.L. 98–378, § 3(b), 98 Stat. 1306, and amended, which is classified to 42 U.S.C.A. § 666.

Section 464 of the Social Security Act, referred to in subsec. (b)(2)(F), is Act Aug. 14, 1935, c. 531, Title IV, § 464, as added Aug. 13, 1981, Pub.L. 97–35, Title XXIII, § 2331(a), 95 Stat. 860, and amended, which is classified to 42 U.S.C.A. § 664.

Title IV of the Social Security Act, referred to in subsec. (b)(2)(G), is Act Aug. 14, 1935, c. 531, Title IV, § 401 et seq., as added Aug. 22, 1996, Pub.L. 104–193, Title I, § 103(a)(1), 110 Stat. 2113, and amended, which is classified principally to subchapter IV of chapter 7 of Title 42, 42 U.S.C.A. § 601 et seq. For complete classification, see Tables.

The National Housing Act, referred to in subsec. (b)(8), is Act June 27, 1934, c. 847, 48 Stat. 1246, as amended, which is classified principally to chapter 13 (section 1701 et seq.) of Title 12, Banks and Banking. For complete classification of this Act to the Code, see section 1701 of Title 12 and Tables.

Chapter 537 of title 46, referred to in subsecs. (b)(12) and (13), is Loans and Guarantees, 46 U.S.C.A. § 53701 et seq.

The Higher Education Act of 1965, referred to in subsec. (b)(16), is Pub.L. 89–329, Nov. 8, 1965, 79 Stat. 1219, which is classified generally to chapter 28 of Title 20, 20 U.S.C.A. § 1001 et seq. Section 435(j) of the Act is classified to 20 U.S.C.A. § 1085(j). For complete classification, see Short Title note set out under 20 U.S.C.A. § 1001 and Tables.

Section 401, 403, 408, 408A, 414, 457, or 501(c) of the Internal Revenue Code of 1986, referred to in subsec. (b)(19), is classified to 26 U.S.C.A. § 401, 403, 408, 408A, 414, 457, or 501(c).

Section 414(d) or section 403(b) of the Internal Revenue Code, referred to in subsec. (b)(19), is classified to 26 U.S.C.A. § 414(d) or 26 U.S.C.A. § 403(b).

Section 408(b)(1) of the Employee Retirement Income Security Act of 1974, referred to in subsec. (b)(19)(A), is Pub.L. 93–406, Title I, § 408(b)(1), Sept. 2, 1974, 88 Stat. 883, as amended, which is classified to 29 U.S.C.A. § 1108(b)(1).

Section 72(p) of the Internal Revenue Code of 1986, referred to in subsec. (b)(19)(A), is classified to 26 U.S.C.A. § 72(p).

Subchapter III of chapter 84 of title 5, referred to in subsec. (b)(19)(B), is 5 U.S.C.A. § 8431 et seq.

Section 1128B(f) of the Social Security Act, referred to in subsec. (b)(28), is Act Aug. 14, 1935, c. 531, Title XI, § 1128B, formerly Title XVIII, § 1877(d), and Title XIX, § 1909, as added and amended Oct. 30, 1972, Pub.L. 92–603, Title II, §§ 242(c), 278(b)(9), 86 Stat. 1419, 1454, which is classified to 42 U.S.C.A. § 1320a–7b(f).

Title XI of such Act, referred to in subsec. (b)(28), means title XI of the Social Security Act, Act Aug. 14, 1935, c. 531, Title XI, § 1101 et seq., 49 Stat. 647, as amended, which is classified principally to subchapter XI of chapter 7 of Title 42, 42 U.S.C.A. § 1301 et seq.

Title XVIII of such Act, referred to in subsec. (b)(28), means title XVIII of the Social Security Act, Act Aug. 14, 1935, c. 531, Title XVIII, § 1801 et seq., as added July 30, 1965, Pub.L. 89–97, Title I, § 102(a), 79 Stat. 291, and amended, which is classified principally to subchapter XVIII of chapter 7 of Title 42, 42 U.S.C.A. § 1395 et seq.

Chapter 7, 9, 11, 12, or 13 of this title, referred to in subsec. (c)(2)(C), is 11 U.S.C.A. § 701 et seq., 11 U.S.C.A. § 901 et seq., 11 U.S.C.A. § 1101 et seq., 11 U.S.C.A. § 1201 et seq., or 11 U.S.C.A. § 1301 et seq., respectively.

Codifications

Renumbering and conforming amendments by Pub.L. 101–508 failed to take into consideration prior renumbering and conforming amendments by Pub.L. 101–311, thereby resulting in two pars. numbered "(14)". To accommodate such duplication, the renumbering reflects changes by Pub.L. 101–311 set out first, and by Pub.L. 101–508 set out second, but does not reflect the minor conforming amendments.

Effective and Applicability Provisions

2005 Acts. Amendments by Pub.L. 109–8 effective, except as otherwise provided, 180 days after April 20, 2005, and inapplicable with respect to cases commenced under Title 11 before the effective date, see Pub.L. 109–8, § 1501, set out as a note under 11 U.S.C.A. § 101.

1994 Acts. Amendments by Pub.L. 103–394 effective on Oct. 22, 1994, and not to apply with respect to cases commenced under this title before Oct. 22, 1994, see section 702 of Pub.L. 103–394, set out as a note under section 101 of this title.

1990 Acts. Section 3007(a)(3) of Pub.L. 101–508 provided that: "The amendments made by this subsection [amending this section and section 541 this title] shall be effective upon date of enactment of this Act [Nov. 5, 1990]."

Section 3008 of Pub.L. 101–508, which provided that the amendments made by this subtitle [subtitle A (§§ 3001–3008) of Title III of Pub.L. 101–508, amending this section, sections 541 and 1328 of this title, and sections 1078, 1078–1, 1078–7, 1085, 1088, and 1091 of Title 20, Education, and provisions set out as a note under section 1078–1 of Title 20, and enacting provisions set out as notes under this section, and section 1328 of this title, and sections 1001, 1078–1, 1078–7, 1085, and 1088 of Title 20] were to cease to be effective on October 1, 1996,

was repealed by Pub.L. 102–325, Title XV, § 1558, July 23, 1992, 106 Stat. 841.

1986 Acts. Amendment by Pub.L. 99–554, § 257(j), effective 30 days after Oct. 27, 1986, but not applicable with respect to cases commenced under this title before that date, see section 302(a), (a)(1) of Pub.L. 99–554, set out as a note under section 581 of Title 28, Judiciary and Judicial Procedure.

Amendment by Pub.L. 99–554, § 283(d), effective 30 days after Oct. 27, 1986, see section 302(a) of Pub.L. 99–554, set out as a note under section 581 of Title 28.

Section 5001(b) of Pub.L. 99–509 provided that: "The amendments made by subsection (a) of this section [amending this section and enacting a provision set out as a note under this section] shall apply only to petitions filed under section 362 of title 11, United States Code, which are made after August 1, 1986."

1984 Acts. Amendment by Pub.L. 98–353 effective with respect to cases filed 90 days after July 10, 1984, see section 552(a), formerly 553 of Pub.L. 98–353, set out as a note under section 101 of this title.

Separability of Provisions

If any provision of or amendment made by Pub.L. 103–394 or the application of such provision or amendment to any person or circumstance is held to be unconstitutional, the remaining provisions of and amendments made by Pub.L. 103–394 and the application of such provisions and amendments to any person or circumstance shall not be affected thereby, see section 701 of Pub.L. 103–394, set out as a note under section 101 of this title.

CROSS REFERENCES

Abstention of district court from hearing a proceeding based upon State law as cause of action, provision as not limiting applicability of stay under this section, see 28 USCA § 1334.

Adequate protection in Chapter 12 cases, method of obtaining, see 11 USCA § 1205.

Applicability of this section in Chapter 9 cases, see 11 USCA § 901.

Assessment of taxes against estate, see 11 USCA § 505.

Denial of debtor status to debtor who obtained voluntary dismissal following filing of relief from provisions of this section, see 11 USCA § 109.

Effect of this section on subchapter III of Chapter 7, see 11 USCA § 742.

Enforcement of claims against debtor in Chapter 9 cases, automatic stay of, see 11 USCA § 922.

Extension of time, see 11 USCA § 108.

Grain storage facility bankruptcies, expedited determinations, see 11 USCA § 557.

Priorities, see 11 USCA § 507.

Right of possession of party with security interest in,

Aircraft equipment and vessel, see 11 USCA § 1110.

Rolling stock equipment, see 11 USCA § 1168.

Secretary of Commerce or Transportation as mortgagee, see 46 USCA § 31308.

Setoff, see 11 USCA § 553.

Turnover of property to estate, see 11 USCA § 542.

§ 363. Use, sale, or lease of property

(a) In this section, "cash collateral" means cash, negotiable instruments, documents of title, securities, deposit accounts, or other cash equivalents whenever acquired in which the estate and an entity other than the estate have an interest and includes the proceeds, products, offspring, rents, or profits of property and the fees, charges, accounts or other payments for the use or occupancy of rooms and other public facilities in hotels, motels, or other lodging properties subject to a security interest as provided in section 552(b) of this title, whether existing before or after the commencement of a case under this title.

(b)(1) The trustee, after notice and a hearing, may use, sell, or lease, other than in the ordinary course of business, property of the estate, except that if the debtor in connection with offering a product or a service discloses to an individual a policy prohibiting the transfer of personally identifiable information about individuals to persons that are not affiliated with the debtor and if such policy is in effect on the date of the commencement of the case, then the trustee may not sell or lease personally identifiable information to any person unless—

(A) such sale or such lease is consistent with such policy; or

(B) after appointment of a consumer privacy ombudsman in accordance with section 332, and after notice and a hearing, the court approves such sale or such lease—

(i) giving due consideration to the facts, circumstances, and conditions of such sale or such lease; and

(ii) finding that no showing was made that such sale or such lease would violate applicable nonbankruptcy law.

(2) If notification is required under subsection (a) of section 7A of the Clayton Act in the case of a transaction under this subsection, then—

(A) notwithstanding subsection (a) of such section, the notification required by such subsection to be given by the debtor shall be given by the trustee; and

(B) notwithstanding subsection (b) of such section, the required waiting period shall end on the 15th day after the date of the receipt, by the Federal Trade Commission and the Assistant Attorney General in charge of the Antitrust Division of the Department of Justice, of the notification required under such subsection (a), unless such waiting period is extended—

(i) pursuant to subsection (e)(2) of such section, in the same manner as such subsection (e)(2) applies to a cash tender offer;

(ii) pursuant to subsection (g)(2) of such section; or

(iii) by the court after notice and a hearing.

(c)(1) If the business of the debtor is authorized to be operated under section 721, 1108, 1203, 1204, or 1304 of this title and unless the court orders otherwise, the trustee may enter into transactions, including the sale or lease of property of the estate, in the ordinary course of business, without notice or a hearing, and may use property of the estate in the ordinary course of business without notice or a hearing.

(2) The trustee may not use, sell, or lease cash collateral under paragraph (1) of this subsection unless—

(A) each entity that has an interest in such cash collateral consents; or

(B) the court, after notice and a hearing, authorizes such use, sale, or lease in accordance with the provisions of this section.

(3) Any hearing under paragraph (2)(B) of this subsection may be a preliminary hearing or may be consolidated with a hearing under subsection (e) of this section, but shall be scheduled in accordance with the needs of the debtor. If the hearing under paragraph (2)(B) of this subsection is a preliminary hearing, the court may authorize such use, sale, or lease only if there is a reasonable likelihood that the trustee will prevail at the final hearing under subsection (e) of this section. The court shall act promptly on any request for authorization under paragraph (2)(B) of this subsection.

(4) Except as provided in paragraph (2) of this subsection, the trustee shall segregate and account for any cash collateral in the trustee's possession, custody, or control.

(d) The trustee may use, sell, or lease property under subsection (b) or (c) of this section—

(1) in the case of a debtor that is a corporation or trust that is not a moneyed business, commercial corporation, or trust, only in accordance with nonbankruptcy law applicable to the transfer of property by a debtor that is such a corporation or trust; and

(2) only to the extent not inconsistent with any relief granted under subsection (c), (d), (e), or (f) of section 362.

(e) Notwithstanding any other provision of this section, at any time, on request of an entity that has an interest in property used, sold, or leased, or proposed to be used, sold, or leased, by the trustee, the court, with or without a hearing, shall prohibit or condition such use, sale, or lease as is necessary to provide adequate protection of such interest. This subsection also applies to property that is subject to any unexpired lease of personal property (to the exclusion of such property being subject to an order to grant relief from the stay under section 362).

(f) The trustee may sell property under subsection (b) or (c) of this section free and clear of any interest in such property of an entity other than the estate, only if—

    (1) applicable nonbankruptcy law permits sale of such property free and clear of such interest;

    (2) such entity consents;

    (3) such interest is a lien and the price at which such property is to be sold is greater than the aggregate value of all liens on such property;

    (4) such interest is in bona fide dispute; or

    (5) such entity could be compelled, in a legal or equitable proceeding, to accept a money satisfaction of such interest.

(g) Notwithstanding subsection (f) of this section, the trustee may sell property under subsection (b) or (c) of this section free and clear of any vested or contingent right in the nature of dower or curtesy.

(h) Notwithstanding subsection (f) of this section, the trustee may sell both the estate's interest, under subsection (b) or (c) of this section, and the interest of any co-owner in property in which the debtor had, at the time of the commencement of the case, an undivided interest as a tenant in common, joint tenant, or tenant by the entirety, only if—

    (1) partition in kind of such property among the estate and such co-owners is impracticable;

    (2) sale of the estate's undivided interest in such property would realize significantly less for the estate than sale of such property free of the interests of such co-owners;

    (3) the benefit to the estate of a sale of such property free of the interests of co-owners outweighs the detriment, if any, to such co-owners; and

    (4) such property is not used in the production, transmission, or distribution, for sale, of electric energy or of natural or synthetic gas for heat, light, or power.

(i) Before the consummation of a sale of property to which subsection (g) or (h) of this section applies, or of property of the estate that was community property of the debtor and the debtor's spouse immediately before the commencement of the case, the debtor's spouse, or a co-owner of such property, as the case may be, may purchase such property at the price at which such sale is to be consummated.

(j) After a sale of property to which subsection (g) or (h) of this section applies, the trustee shall distribute to the debtor's spouse or the co-owners of such property, as the case may be, and to the estate, the proceeds of such sale, less the costs and expenses, not including any compensation of the trustee, of such sale, according to the interests of such spouse or co-owners, and of the estate.

(k) At a sale under subsection (b) of this section of property that is subject to a lien that secures an allowed claim, unless the court for cause orders otherwise the holder of such claim may bid at such sale, and, if the holder of such claim purchases such property, such holder may offset such claim against the purchase price of such property.

(l) Subject to the provisions of section 365, the trustee may use, sell, or lease property under subsection (b) or (c) of this section, or a plan under chapter 11, 12, or 13 of this title may provide for the use, sale, or lease of property, notwithstanding any provision in a contract, a lease, or applicable law that is conditioned on the insolvency or financial condition of the debtor, on the commencement of a case under this title concerning the debtor, or on the appointment of or the taking possession by a trustee in a case under this title or a custodian, and that effects, or gives an option to effect, a forfeiture, modification, or termination of the debtor's interest in such property.

(m) The reversal or modification on appeal of an authorization under subsection (b) or (c) of this section of a sale or lease of property does not affect the validity of a sale or lease under such authorization to an entity that purchased or leased such property in good faith, whether or not such entity knew of the pendency of the appeal, unless such authorization and such sale or lease were stayed pending appeal.

(n) The trustee may avoid a sale under this section if the sale price was controlled by an agreement among potential bidders at such sale, or may recover from a party to such agreement any amount by which the value of the property sold exceeds the price at which such sale was consummated, and may recover any costs, attorneys' fees, or expenses incurred in avoiding such sale or recovering such amount. In addition to any recovery under the preceding sentence, the court may grant judgment for punitive damages in favor of the estate and against any such party that entered into such an agreement in willful disregard of this subsection.

(o) Notwithstanding subsection (f), if a person purchases any interest in a consumer credit transaction that is subject to the Truth in Lending Act or any interest in a consumer credit contract (as defined in section 433.1 of title 16 of the Code of Federal Regulations (January 1, 2004), as amended from time to time), and if such interest is purchased through a sale under this section, then such person shall remain subject to all claims and defenses that are related to such consumer credit transaction or such consumer credit contract, to the same extent as such person would be subject to such claims and defenses of the consumer had such interest been purchased at a sale not under this section.

(p) In any hearing under this section—

---

(1) the trustee has the burden of proof on the issue of adequate protection; and

(2) the entity asserting an interest in property has the burden of proof on the issue of the validity, priority, or extent of such interest.

(Pub.L. 95–598, Nov. 6, 1978, 92 Stat. 2572; Pub.L. 98–353, Title III, § 442, July 10, 1984, 98 Stat. 371; Pub.L. 99–554, Title II, § 257(k), Oct. 27, 1986, 100 Stat. 3115; Pub.L. 103–394, Title I, § 109, Title II, §§ 214(b), 219(c), Title V, § 501(d)(8), Oct. 22, 1994, 108 Stat. 4113, 4126, 4129, 4144; Pub.L. 109–8, Title II, §§ 204, 231(a), Title XII, § 1221(a), Apr. 20, 2005, 119 Stat. 49, 72, 195; Pub.L. 111–327, § 2(a)(13), Dec. 22, 2010, 124 Stat. 3559.)

HISTORICAL AND STATUTORY NOTES

Revision Notes and Legislative Reports

1978 Acts. This section defines the right and powers of the trustee with respect to the use, sale or lease of property and the rights of other parties that have interests in the property involved. It applies in both liquidation and reorganization cases.

Subsection (a) defines "cash collateral" as cash, negotiable instruments, documents of title, securities, deposit accounts, or other cash equivalents in which the estate and an entity other than the estate have an interest, such as a lien or a co-ownership interest. The definition is not restricted to property of the estate that is cash collateral on the date of the filing of the petition. Thus, if "non-cash" collateral is disposed of and the proceeds come within the definition of "cash collateral" as set forth in this subsection, the proceeds would be cash collateral as long as they remain subject to the original lien on the "non-cash" collateral under section 52(b). To illustrate, rents received from real property before or after the commencement of the case would be cash collateral to the extent that they are subject to a lien.

Subsection (b) permits the trustees to use, sell, or lease, other than in the ordinary course of business, property of the estate upon notice and opportunity for objections and hearing thereon.

Subsection (c) governs use, sale, or lease in the ordinary course of business. If the business of the debtor is authorized to be operated under section 721, 1108, or 1304 of the bankruptcy code, then the trustee may use, sell, or lease property in the ordinary course of business or enter into ordinary course transactions without need for notice and hearing. This power is subject to several limitations. First, the court may restrict the trustee's powers in the order authorizing operation of the business. Second, with respect to cash collateral, the trustee may not use, sell, or lease cash collateral except upon court authorization after notice and a hearing, or with the consent of each entity that has an interest in such cash collateral. The same preliminary hearing procedure in the automatic stay section applies to a hearing under this subsection. In addition, the trustee is required to segregate and account for any cash collateral in the trustee's possession, custody, or control.

Under subsections (d) and (e), the use, sale, or lease of property is further limited by the concept of adequate protection. Sale, use, or lease of property in which an entity other than the estate has an interest may be effected only to the extent not inconsistent with any relief from the stay granted to that interest's holder. Moreover, the court may prohibit or condition the use, sale, or lease as is necessary to provide adequate protection of that interest. Again, the trustee has the burden of proof on the issue of adequate protection. Subsection (e) also provides that where a sale of the property is proposed, an entity that has an interest in such property may bid at the sale thereof and set off against the purchase price up to the amount of such entity's claim. No prior valuation under section 506(a) would limit this bidding right, since the bid at the sale would be determinative of value.

Subsection (f) permits sale of property free and clear of any interest in the property of an entity other than the estate. The trustee may sell free and clear if applicable nonbankruptcy law permits it, if the other entity consents, if the interest is a lien and the sale price of the property is greater than the amount secured by the lien, if the interest is in bona fide dispute, or if the other entity could be compelled to accept a money satisfaction of the interest in a legal or equitable proceeding. Sale under this subsection is subject to the adequate protection requirement. Most often, adequate protection in connection with a sale free and clear of other interests will be to have those interests attach to the proceeds of the sale.

At a sale free and clear of other interests, any holder of any interest in the property being sold will be permitted to bid. If that holder is the high bidder, he will be permitted to offset the value of his interest against the purchase price of the property. Thus, in the most common situation, a holder of a lien on property being sold may bid at the sale and, if successful, may offset the amount owed to him that is secured by the lien on the property (but may not offset other amounts owed to him) against the purchase price, and be liable to the trustee for the balance of the sale price, if any.

Subsection (g) permits the trustee to sell free and clear of any vested or contingent right in the nature of dower or curtesy.

Subsection (h) permits sale of a co-owner's interest in property in which the debtor had an undivided ownership interest such as a joint tenancy, a tenancy in common, or a tenancy by the entirety. Such a sale is permissible only if partition is impracticable, if sale of the estate's interest would realize significantly less for the estate than sale of the property free of the interests of the co-owners, and if the benefit to the estate of such a sale outweighs any detriment to the co-owners. This subsection does not apply to a co-owner's interest in a public utility when a disruption of the utilities services could result.

Subsection (i) provides protections for co-owners and spouses with dower, curtesy, or community property rights. It gives a right of first refusal to the co-owner or spouse at the price at which the sale is to be consummated.

Subsection (j) requires the trustee to distribute to the spouse or co-owner the appropriate portion of the proceeds of the sale, less certain administrative expenses.

Subsection (k) permits the trustee to use, sell, or lease property notwithstanding certain bankruptcy or ipso facto clauses that terminate the debtor's interest in the property or that work a forfeiture or modification of that interest. This subsection is not as broad as the anti-ipso facto provision in proposed 11 U.S.C. 541(c)(1).

Subsection (l) protects good faith purchasers of property sold under this section from a reversal on appeal of the sale authorization, unless the authorization for the sale and the sale itself were stayed pending appeal. The purchaser's knowledge of the appeal is irrelevant to the issue of good faith.

Subsection (m) is directed at collusive bidding on property sold under this section. It permits the trustee to void a sale if the price of the sale was controlled by an agreement among potential bidders. The trustees may also recover the excess of the value of the property over the purchase price, and may recover any costs, attorney's fees, or expenses incurred in voiding the sale or recovering the difference. In addition, the court is authorized to grant judgment in favor of the estate and against the collusive bidder if the agreement controlling the sale price was entered into in willful disregard of this subsection. The subsection does not specify the precise measure of damages, but simply provides for punitive damages, to be fixed in light of the circumstances. Senate Report No. 95–989.

1984 Acts. Statements by Legislative Leaders, see 1984 U.S.Code Cong. and Adm.News, p. 576.

1986 Acts. House Report No. 99–764 and House Conference Report No. 99–958, see 1986 U.S.Code Cong. and Adm. News, p. 5227.

1994 Acts. House Report No. 103–835, see 1994 U.S. Code Cong. and Adm. News, p. 3340.

2005 Acts. House Report No. 109–31(Part I), see 2005 U.S. Code Cong. and Adm. News, p. 88.

Legislative Statements

Section 363(a) of the House amendment defines "cash collateral" as defined in the Senate amendment. The broader definition of "soft collateral" contained in H.R. 8200 as passed by the House is deleted to remove limitations that were placed on the use, lease, or sale of inventory, accounts, contract rights, general intangibles, and chattel paper by the trustee or debtor in possession.

Section 363(c)(2) of the House amendment is derived from the Senate amendment. Similarly, sections 363(c)(3) and (4) are derived from comparable provisions in the Senate amendment in lieu of the contrary procedure contained in section 363(c) as passed by the House. The policy of the House amendment will generally require the court to schedule a preliminary hearing in accordance with the needs of the debtor to authorize the trustee or debtor in possession to use, sell, or lease cash collateral. The trustee or debtor in possession may use, sell, or lease cash collateral in the ordinary course of business only "after notice and a hearing."

Section 363(f) of the House amendment adopts an identical provision contained in the House bill, as opposed to an alternative provision contained in the Senate amendment.

Section 363(h) of the House amendment adopts a new paragraph (4) representing a compromise between the House bill and Senate amendment. The provision adds a limitation indicating that a trustee or debtor in possession sell jointly owned property only if the property is not used in the production, transmission, or distribution for sale, of electric energy or of natural or synthetic gas for heat, light, or power. This limitation is intended to protect public utilities from being deprived of power sources because of the bankruptcy of a joint owner.

Section 363(k) of the House amendment is derived from the third sentence of section 363(e) of the Senate amendment. The provision indicates that a secured creditor may bid in the full amount of the creditor's allowed claim, including the secured portion and any unsecured portion thereof in the event the creditor is undersecured, with respect to property that is subject to a lien that secures the allowed claim of the sale of the property.

References in Text

Section 7A of the Clayton Act, referred to in subsec. (b)(2), is section 7A of Act Oct. 15, 1914, c. 323, as added Sept. 30, 1976, Pub.L. 94–435, Title II, § 201, 90 Stat. 1390, which is classified to section 18a of Title 15, Commerce and Trade.

The Truth in Lending Act, referred to in subsec. (o), is Title I of Pub.L. 90–321, May 29, 1968, 82 Stat. 146, as amended, also known as TILA, which is classified principally to subchapter I of chapter 41 of Title 15, 15 U.S.C.A. § 1601 et seq. For complete classification, see Short Title note set out under 15 U.S.C.A. § 1601 and Tables.

Effective and Applicability Provisions

2005 Acts. Amendments by Pub.L. 109–8 effective, except as otherwise provided, 180 days after April 20, 2005, and inapplicable with respect to cases commenced under Title 11 before the effective date, see Pub.L. 109–8, § 1501, set out as a note under 11 U.S.C.A. § 101.

Pub.L. 109–8, Title XII, § 1221(d), Apr. 20, 2005, 119 Stat. 196, provided that: "The amendments made by this section [amending this section and 11 U.S.C.A. §§ 541 and 1129, and enacting provisions set out as a note under this section] shall apply to a case pending under title 11, United States Code [11 U.S.C.A. § 101 et seq.], on the date of enactment of this Act [Apr. 20, 2005], or filed under that title on or after that date of enactment, except that the court shall not confirm a plan under chapter 11 of title 11, United States Code [11 U.S.C.A. § 1101 et seq.], without considering whether this section would substantially affect the rights of a party in interest who first acquired rights with respect to the debtor after the date of the filing of the petition. The parties who may appear and be heard in a proceeding under this section include the attorney general of the State in which the debtor is incorporated, was formed, or does business."

1994 Acts. Amendments by Pub.L. 103–394 effective on Oct. 22, 1994, and not to apply with respect to cases commenced under this title before Oct. 22, 1994, see section 702 of Pub.L. 103–394, set out as a note under section 101 of this title.

1986 Acts. Amendment by Pub.L. 99–554 effective 30 days after Oct. 27, 1986, but not applicable with respect to cases commenced under this title before that date, see section 302(a), (c)(1) of Pub.L. 99–554, set out as a note under section 581 of Title 28, Judiciary and Judicial Procedure.

1984 Acts. Amendment by Pub.L. 98–353 effective with respect to cases filed 90 days after July 10, 1984, see section 552(a), formerly 553(a) of Pub.L. 98–353, set out as a note under section 101 of this title.

Separability of Provisions

If any provision of or amendment made by Pub.L. 103–394 or the application of such provision or amendment to any person or circumstance is held to be unconstitutional, the remaining provisions of and amendments made by Pub.L. 103–394 and the application of such provisions and amendments to any person or circumstance shall not be affected thereby, see section 701 of Pub.L. 103–394, set out as a note under section 101 of this title.

Rules of Construction

Pub.L. 109–8, Title XII, § 1221(e), Apr. 20, 2005, 119 Stat. 196, provided that: "Nothing in this section [amending this section and 11 U.S.C.A. §§ 541 and 1129, and enacting provisions set out as a note under this section] shall apply to a case pending under title 11, United States Code [11 U.S.C.A. § 101 et seq.] shall be construed to require the court in which a case under chapter 11 of title 11, United States Code [11 U.S.C.A. § 1101 et seq.], is pending to remand or refer any proceeding, issue, or controversy to any other court or to require the approval of any other court for the transfer of property."

CROSS REFERENCES

Adequate protection in Chapter 12 cases, method of obtaining, see 11 USCA § 1205.

Adverse interest and conduct of officers of estate, see 18 USCA § 154.

Confirmation of plan, see 11 USCA § 1129.

Continuity of business operation and use, acquisition or disposition of property by debtor, see 11 USCA § 303.

Grain storage facility bankruptcies, expedited determinations, see 11 USCA § 557.

Identical rights and powers of debtor in Chapter 13 cases, see 11 USCA § 1303.

Postpetition effect of security interest, see 11 USCA § 552.

Priorities, see 11 USCA § 507.

Property of estate, see 11 USCA § 541.

Right of possession of party with security interest in,

    Aircraft equipment and vessels, see 11 USCA § 1110.

    Rolling stock equipment, see 11 USCA § 1168.

Rights and powers of debtor engaged in business, see 11 USCA § 1304.

Sale of property as affecting allowance of claim secured by lien on property of estate, see 11 USCA § 1111.

Sales free of interests, see 11 USCA § 1206.

Setoff, see 11 USCA § 553.

Turnover of property to estate, see 11 USCA § 542.

§ 364. Obtaining credit

(a) If the trustee is authorized to operate the business of the debtor under section 721, 1108, 1203, 1204, or 1304 of this title, unless the court orders otherwise, the trustee may obtain unsecured credit and incur unsecured debt in the ordinary course of business allowable under section 503(b)(1) of this title as an administrative expense.

(b) The court, after notice and a hearing, may authorize the trustee to obtain unsecured credit or to incur unsecured debt other than under subsection (a) of this section, allowable under section 503(b)(1) of this title as an administrative expense.

(c) If the trustee is unable to obtain unsecured credit allowable under section 503(b)(1) of this title as an administrative expense, the court, after notice and a hearing, may authorize the obtaining of credit or the incurring of debt—

(1) with priority over any or all administrative expenses of the kind specified in section 503(b) or 507(b) of this title;

(2) secured by a lien on property of the estate that is not otherwise subject to a lien; or

(3) secured by a junior lien on property of the estate that is subject to a lien.

(d)(1) The court, after notice and a hearing, may authorize the obtaining of credit or the incurring of debt secured by a senior or equal lien on property of the estate that is subject to a lien only if—

(A) the trustee is unable to obtain such credit otherwise; and

(B) there is adequate protection of the interest of the holder of the lien on the property of the estate on which such senior or equal lien is proposed to be granted.

(2) In any hearing under this subsection, the trustee has the burden of proof on the issue of adequate protection.

(e) The reversal or modification on appeal of an authorization under this section to obtain credit or incur debt, or of a grant under this section of a priority or a lien, does not affect the validity of any debt so incurred, or any priority or lien so granted, to an entity that extended such credit in good faith, whether or not such entity knew of the pendency of the appeal, unless such authorization and the incurring of such debt, or the granting of such priority or lien, were stayed pending appeal.

(f) Except with respect to an entity that is an underwriter as defined in section 1145(b) of this title, section 5 of the Securities Act of 1933, the Trust Indenture Act of 1939, and any State or local law requiring registration for offer or sale of a security or registration or licensing of an issuer of, underwriter of, or broker or dealer in, a security does not apply to the offer or sale under this section of a security that is not an equity security.

(Pub.L. 95–598, Nov. 6, 1978, 92 Stat. 2574; Pub.L. 99–554, Title II, § 257(*l*), Oct. 27, 1986, 100 Stat. 3115; Pub.L. 103–394, Title V, § 501(d)(9), Oct. 22, 1994, 108 Stat. 4144.)

HISTORICAL AND STATUTORY NOTES

Revision Notes and Legislative Reports

1978 Acts. This section is derived from provisions in current law governing certificates of indebtedness, but is much broader. It governs all obtaining of credit and incurring of debt by the estate.

Subsection (a) authorizes the obtaining of unsecured credit and the incurring of unsecured debt in the ordinary course of business if the business of the debtor is authorized to be operated under section 721, 1108, or 1304. The debts so incurred are allowable as administrative expenses under section 503(b)(1). The court may limit the estate's ability to incur debt under this subsection.

Subsection (b) permits the court to authorize the trustee to obtain unsecured credit and incur unsecured debts other than in the ordinary course of business, such as in order to wind up a liquidation case, or to obtain a substantial loan in an operating case. Debt incurred under this subsection is allowable as an administrative expense under section 503(b)(1).

Subsection (c) is closer to the concept of certificates of indebtedness in current law. It authorizes the obtaining of credit and the incurring of debt with some special priority, if the trustee is unable to obtain unsecured credit under subsection (a) or (b). The various priorities are (1) with priority over any or all administrative expenses; (2) secured by a lien on unencumbered property of the estate; or (3) secured by a junior lien on encumbered property. The priorities granted under this subsection do not interfere with existing property rights.

Subsection (d) grants the court the authority to authorize the obtaining of credit and the incurring of debt with a superiority [sic], that is a lien on encumbered property that is senior or equal to the existing lien on the property. The court may authorize such a super-priority [sic] only if the trustee is otherwise unable to obtain credit, and if there is adequate protection of the original lien holder's interest. Again, the trustee has the burden of proof on the issue of adequate protection.

Subsection (e) provides the same protection for credit extenders pending an appeal of an authorization to incur debt as is provided under section 363(*l*) for purchasers: the credit is not affected on appeal by reversal of the authorization and the incurring of the debt were stayed pending appeal. The protection runs to a good faith lender, whether or not he knew of the pendency of the appeal.

A claim arising as a result of lending or borrowing under this section will be a priority claim, as defined in proposed section 507(a)(1), even if the claim is granted a super-priority over administrative expenses and is to be paid in advance of other first priority claims. Senate Report No. 95–989.

1986 Acts. House Report No. 99–764 and House Conference Report No. 99–958, see 1986 U.S.Code Cong. and Adm. News, p. 5227.

1994 Acts. House Report No. 103–835, see 1994 U.S. Code Cong. and Adm. News, p. 3340.

Legislative Statements

Section 364(f) of the House amendment is new. This provision continues the exemption found in section 3(a)(7) of the Securities Act of 1933 [15 U.S.C.A. § 77c(a)(7)] for certificates of indebtedness issued by a trustee in bankruptcy. The exemption applies to any debt security issued under section 364 of title 11. The section does not intend to change present law which exempts such securities from the Trust Indenture Act, 15 U.S.C. 77aaa, et seq. (1976).

References in Text

Section 5 of the Securities Act of 1933, referred to in subsec. (f), is section 5 of Act May 27, 1933, c. 38, Title I, 48 Stat. 77, which is classified to section 77e of Title 15, Commerce and Trade.

The Trust Indenture Act of 1939, referred to in subsec. (f), is Title III of Act May 27, 1933, c. 38, as added Aug. 3, 1939, c. 411, 53 Stat. 1149, as amended, which is classified generally to subchapter III (§ 77aaa et seq.) of chapter 2A of Title 15, Commerce and Trade. For complete classification of this Act to the Code, see section 77aaa of Title 15 and Tables.

Effective and Applicability Provisions

1994 Acts. Amendment by Pub.L. 103–394 effective on Oct. 22, 1994, and not to apply with respect to cases commenced under this title before Oct. 22, 1994, see section 702 of Pub.L. 103–394, set out as a note under section 101 of this title.

1986 Acts. Amendment by Pub.L. 99–554 effective 30 days after Oct. 27, 1986, but not applicable with respect to cases commenced under this title before that date, see section 302(a), (c)(1) of Pub.L. 99–554, set out as a note under section 581 of Title 28, Judiciary and Judicial Procedure.

Separability of Provisions

If any provision of or amendment made by Pub.L. 103–394 or the application of such provision or amendment to any person or circumstance is held to be unconstitutional, the remaining provisions of and amendments made by Pub.L. 103–394 and the application of such provisions and amendments to any person or circumstance shall not be affected thereby, see section 701 of Pub.L. 103–394, set out as a note under section 101 of this title.

CROSS REFERENCES

Adequate protection in Chapter 12 cases, method of obtaining, see 11 USCA § 1205.

Applicability of subsecs. (c) to (f) of this section in Chapter 9 cases, see 11 USCA § 901.

Enforcement of claims against debtor in Chapter 9 cases, automatic stay of, see 11 USCA § 922.

Priorities, see 11 USCA § 507.

Reversal on appeal of finding of jurisdiction as affecting validity of debt incurred, see 11 USCA § 921.

Rights and powers of debtor engaged in business, see 11 USCA § 1304.

§ 365. Executory contracts and unexpired leases

(a) Except as provided in sections 765 and 766 of this title and in subsections (b), (c), and (d) of this section, the trustee, subject to the court's approval, may assume or reject any executory contract or unexpired lease of the debtor.

(b)(1) If there has been a default in an executory contract or unexpired lease of the debtor, the trustee may not assume such contract or lease unless, at the time of assumption of such contract or lease, the trustee—

(A) cures, or provides adequate assurance that the trustee will promptly cure, such default other than a default that is a breach of a provision relating to the satisfaction of any provision (other than a penalty rate or penalty provision) relating to a default arising from any failure to perform nonmonetary obligations under an unexpired lease of real property, if it is impossible for the trustee to cure such default by performing nonmonetary acts at and after the time of assumption, except that if such default arises from a failure to operate in accordance with a nonresidential real property lease, then such default shall be cured by performance at and after the time of assumption in accordance with such lease, and pecuniary losses resulting from such default shall be compensated in accordance with the provisions of this paragraph;

(B) compensates, or provides adequate assurance that the trustee will promptly compensate, a party other than the debtor to such contract or lease, for any actual pecuniary loss to such party resulting from such default; and

(C) provides adequate assurance of future performance under such contract or lease.

(2) Paragraph (1) of this subsection does not apply to a default that is a breach of a provision relating to—

(A) the insolvency or financial condition of the debtor at any time before the closing of the case;

(B) the commencement of a case under this title;

(C) the appointment of or taking possession by a trustee in a case under this title or a custodian before such commencement; or

(D) the satisfaction of any penalty rate or penalty provision relating to a default arising from any failure by the debtor to perform nonmonetary obligations under the executory contract or unexpired lease.

(3) For the purposes of paragraph (1) of this subsection and paragraph (2)(B) of subsection (f), adequate assurance of future performance of a lease of real property in a shopping center includes adequate assurance—

(A) of the source of rent and other consideration due under such lease, and in the case of an assignment, that the financial condition and operating performance of the proposed assignee and its guarantors, if any, shall be similar to the financial condition and operating performance of the debtor and its guarantors, if any, as of the time the debtor became the lessee under the lease;

(B) that any percentage rent due under such lease will not decline substantially;

(C) that assumption or assignment of such lease is subject to all the provisions thereof, including (but not limited to) provisions such as a radius, location, use, or exclusivity provision, and will not breach any such provision contained in any other lease, financing agreement, or master agreement relating to such shopping center; and

(D) that assumption or assignment of such lease will not disrupt any tenant mix or balance in such shopping center.

(4) Notwithstanding any other provision of this section, if there has been a default in an unexpired lease of the debtor, other than a default of a kind specified in paragraph (2) of this subsection, the trustee may not require a lessor to provide services or supplies incidental to such lease before assumption of such lease unless the lessor is compensated under the terms of such lease for any services and supplies provided under such lease before assumption of such lease.

(c) The trustee may not assume or assign any executory contract or unexpired lease of the debtor, whether or not such contract or lease prohibits or restricts assignment of rights or delegation of duties, if—

(1)(A) applicable law excuses a party, other than the debtor, to such contract or lease from accepting performance from or rendering performance to an entity other than the debtor or the debtor in possession, whether or not such contract or lease prohibits or restricts assignment of rights or delegation of duties; and

(B) such party does not consent to such assumption or assignment; or

(2) such contract is a contract to make a loan, or extend other debt financing or financial accommodations, to or for the benefit of the debtor, or to issue a security of the debtor; or

(3) such lease is of nonresidential real property and has been terminated under applicable nonbankruptcy law prior to the order for relief.

(d)(1) In a case under chapter 7 of this title, if the trustee does not assume or reject an executory contract or unexpired lease of residential real property or of personal property of the debtor within 60 days after the order for relief, or within such additional time as the court, for cause, within such 60-day period, fixes, then such contract or lease is deemed rejected.

(2) In a case under chapter 9, 11, 12, or 13 of this title, the trustee may assume or reject an executory contract or unexpired lease of residential real property or of personal property of the debtor at any time before the confirmation of a plan but the court, on the request of any party to such contract or lease, may order the trustee to determine within a specified period of time whether to assume or reject such contract or lease.

(3) The trustee shall timely perform all the obligations of the debtor, except those specified in section 365(b)(2), arising from and after the order for relief under any unexpired lease of nonresidential real property, until such lease is assumed or rejected, notwithstanding section 503(b)(1) of this title. The court may extend, for cause, the time for performance of any such obligation that arises within 60 days after the date of the order for relief, but the time for performance shall not be extended beyond such 60-day period. This subsection shall not be deemed to affect the trustee's obligations under the provisions of subsection (b) or (f) of this section. Acceptance of any such performance does not constitute waiver or relinquishment of the lessor's rights under such lease or under this title.

(4)(A) Subject to subparagraph (B), an unexpired lease of nonresidential real property under which the debtor is the lessee shall be deemed rejected, and the trustee shall immediately surrender that nonresidential real property to the lessor, if the trustee does not assume or reject the unexpired lease by the earlier of—

(i) the date that is 120 days after the date of the order for relief; or

(ii) the date of the entry of an order confirming a plan.

(B)(i) The court may extend the period determined under subparagraph (A), prior to the expiration of the 120–day period, for 90 days on the motion of the trustee or lessor for cause.

(ii) If the court grants an extension under clause (i), the court may grant a subsequent extension only upon prior written consent of the lessor in each instance.

(5) The trustee shall timely perform all of the obligations of the debtor, except those specified in section 365(b)(2), first arising from or after 60 days after the order for relief in a case under chapter 11 of this title under an unexpired lease of personal property (other than personal property leased to an individual primarily for personal, family, or household purposes), until such lease is assumed or rejected notwithstanding section 503(b)(1) of this title, unless the court, after notice and a hearing and based on the equities of the case, orders otherwise with respect to the obligations or timely performance thereof. This subsection shall not be deemed to affect the trustee's obligations under the provisions of subsection (b) or (f). Acceptance of any such performance does not constitute waiver or relinquishment of the lessor's rights under such lease or under this title.

(e)(1) Notwithstanding a provision in an executory contract or unexpired lease, or in applicable law, an executory contract or unexpired lease of the debtor may not be terminated or modified, and any right or obligation under such contract or lease may not be terminated or modified, at any time after the commencement of the case solely because of a provision in such contract or lease that is conditioned on—

(A) the insolvency or financial condition of the debtor at any time before the closing of the case;

(B) the commencement of a case under this title; or

(C) the appointment of or taking possession by a trustee in a case under this title or a custodian before such commencement.

(2) Paragraph (1) of this subsection does not apply to an executory contract or unexpired lease of the debtor, whether or not such contract or lease prohibits or restricts assignment of rights or delegation of duties, if—

(A)(i) applicable law excuses a party, other than the debtor, to such contract or lease from accepting performance from or rendering performance to the trustee or to an assignee of such contract or lease, whether or not such contract or lease prohibits or restricts assignment of rights or delegation of duties; and

(ii) such party does not consent to such assumption or assignment; or

(B) such contract is a contract to make a loan, or extend other debt financing or financial accommodations, to or for the benefit of the debtor, or to issue a security of the debtor.

(f)(1) Except as provided in subsections (b) and (c) of this section, notwithstanding a provision in an executory contract or unexpired lease of the debtor, or in applicable law, that prohibits, restricts, or conditions the assignment of such contract or lease, the trustee may assign such contract or lease under paragraph (2) of this subsection.

(2) The trustee may assign an executory contract or unexpired lease of the debtor only if—

(A) the trustee assumes such contract or lease in accordance with the provisions of this section; and

(B) adequate assurance of future performance by the assignee of such contract or lease is provided, whether or not there has been a default in such contract or lease.

(3) Notwithstanding a provision in an executory contract or unexpired lease of the debtor, or in applicable law that terminates or modifies, or permits a party other than the debtor to terminate or modify, such contract or lease or a right or obligation under such contract or lease on account of an assignment of such contract or lease, such contract, lease, right, or obligation may not be terminated or modified under such provision because of the assumption or assignment of such contract or lease by the trustee.

(g) Except as provided in subsections (h)(2) and (i)(2) of this section, the rejection of an executory contract or unexpired lease of the debtor constitutes a breach of such contract or lease—

(1) if such contract or lease has not been assumed under this section or under a plan confirmed under chapter 9, 11, 12, or 13 of this title, immediately before the date of the filing of the petition; or

(2) if such contract or lease has been assumed under this section or under a plan confirmed under chapter 9, 11, 12, or 13 of this title—

(A) if before such rejection the case has not been converted under section 1112, 1208, or 1307 of this title, at the time of such rejection; or

(B) if before such rejection the case has been converted under section 1112, 1208, or 1307 of this title—

(i) immediately before the date of such conversion, if such contract or lease was assumed before such conversion; or

(ii) at the time of such rejection, if such contract or lease was assumed after such conversion.

(h)(1)(A) If the trustee rejects an unexpired lease of real property under which the debtor is the lessor and—

(i) if the rejection by the trustee amounts to such a breach as would entitle the lessee to treat such lease as terminated by virtue of its terms, applicable nonbankruptcy law, or any agreement made by the lessee, then the lessee under such lease may treat such lease as terminated by the rejection; or

(ii) if the term of such lease has commenced, the lessee may retain its rights under such lease (including rights such as those relating to the amount and timing of payment of rent and other amounts payable by the lessee and any right of use, possession, quiet enjoyment, subletting, assignment, or hypothecation) that are in or appurtenant to the real property for the balance of the term of such lease and for any renewal or extension of such rights to the extent that such rights are enforceable under applicable nonbankruptcy law.

(B) If the lessee retains its rights under subparagraph (A)(ii), the lessee may offset against the rent reserved under such lease for the balance of the term after the date of the rejection of such lease and for the term of any renewal or extension of such lease, the value of any damage caused by the nonperformance after the date of such rejection, of any obligation of the debtor under such lease, but the lessee shall not have any other right against the estate or the debtor on account of any damage occurring after such date caused by such nonperformance.

(C) The rejection of a lease of real property in a shopping center with respect to which the lessee elects to retain its rights under subparagraph (A)(ii) does not affect the enforceability under applicable nonbankruptcy law of any provision in the lease pertaining to radius, location, use, exclusivity, or tenant mix or balance.

(D) In this paragraph, "lessee" includes any successor, assign, or mortgagee permitted under the terms of such lease.

(2)(A) If the trustee rejects a timeshare interest under a timeshare plan under which the debtor is the timeshare interest seller and—

(i) if the rejection amounts to such a breach as would entitle the timeshare interest purchaser to treat the timeshare plan as terminated under its terms, applicable nonbankruptcy law, or any agreement made by timeshare interest purchaser, the timeshare interest purchaser under the timeshare plan may treat the timeshare plan as terminated by such rejection; or

(ii) if the term of such timeshare interest has commenced, then the timeshare interest purchaser may retain its rights in such timeshare interest for the balance of such term and for any term of renewal or extension of such timeshare interest to the extent that such rights are enforceable under applicable nonbankruptcy law.

(B) If the timeshare interest purchaser retains its rights under subparagraph (A), such timeshare interest purchaser may offset against the moneys due for such timeshare interest for the balance of the term after the date of the rejection of such timeshare interest, and the term of any renewal or extension of such timeshare interest, the value of any damage caused by the nonperformance after the date of such rejection, of any obligation of the debtor under such timeshare plan, but the timeshare interest purchaser shall not have any right against the estate or the debtor on account of any damage occurring after such date caused by such nonperformance.

(i)(1) If the trustee rejects an executory contract of the debtor for the sale of real property or for the sale of a timeshare interest under a timeshare plan, under which the purchaser is in possession, such purchaser may treat such contract as terminated, or, in the alternative, may remain in possession of such real property or timeshare interest.

(2) If such purchaser remains in possession—

(A) such purchaser shall continue to make all payments due under such contract, but may,[1] offset against such payments any damages occurring after the date of the rejection of such contract caused by the nonperformance of any obligation of the debtor after such date, but such purchaser does not have any rights against the estate on account of any damages arising after such date from such rejection, other than such offset; and

(B) the trustee shall deliver title to such purchaser in accordance with the provisions of such contract, but is relieved of all other obligations to perform under such contract.

(j) A purchaser that treats an executory contract as terminated under subsection (i) of this section, or a party whose executory contract to purchase real property from the debtor is rejected and under which such party is not in possession, has a lien on the interest of the debtor in such property for the recovery of any portion of the purchase price that such purchaser or party has paid.

(k) Assignment by the trustee to an entity of a contract or lease assumed under this section relieves the trustee and the estate from any liability for any breach of such contract or lease occurring after such assignment.

(l) If an unexpired lease under which the debtor is the lessee is assigned pursuant to this section, the lessor of the property may require a deposit or other security for the performance of the debtor's obligations under the lease substantially the same as would have been required by the landlord upon the initial leasing to a similar tenant.

(m) For purposes of this section 365 and sections 541(b)(2) and 362(b)(10), leases of real property shall include any rental agreement to use real property.

(n)(1) If the trustee rejects an executory contract under which the debtor is a licensor of a right to intellectual property, the licensee under such contract may elect—

    (A) to treat such contract as terminated by such rejection if such rejection by the trustee amounts to such a breach as would entitle the licensee to treat such contract as terminated by virtue of its own terms, applicable nonbankruptcy law, or an agreement made by the licensee with another entity; or

    (B) to retain its rights (including a right to enforce any exclusivity provision of such contract, but excluding any other right under applicable nonbankruptcy law to specific performance of such contract) under such contract and under any agreement supplementary to such contract, to such intellectual property (including any embodiment of such intellectual property to the extent protected by applicable nonbankruptcy law), as such rights existed immediately before the case commenced, for—

        (i) the duration of such contract; and

        (ii) any period for which such contract may be extended by the licensee as of right under applicable nonbankruptcy law.

(2) If the licensee elects to retain its rights, as described in paragraph (1)(B) of this subsection, under such contract—

    (A) the trustee shall allow the licensee to exercise such rights;

    (B) the licensee shall make all royalty payments due under such contract for the duration of such contract and for any period described in paragraph (1)(B) of this subsection for which the licensee extends such contract; and

    (C) the licensee shall be deemed to waive—

        (i) any right of setoff it may have with respect to such contract under this title or applicable nonbankruptcy law; and

        (ii) any claim allowable under section 503(b) of this title arising from the performance of such contract.

(3) If the licensee elects to retain its rights, as described in paragraph (1)(B) of this subsection, then on the written request of the licensee the trustee shall—

    (A) to the extent provided in such contract, or any agreement supplementary to such contract, provide to the licensee any intellectual property (including such embodiment) held by the trustee; and

    (B) not interfere with the rights of the licensee as provided in such contract, or any agreement supplementary to such contract, to such intellectual property (including such embodiment) including any right to obtain such intellectual property (or such embodiment) from another entity.

(4) Unless and until the trustee rejects such contract, on the written request of the licensee the trustee shall—

    (A) to the extent provided in such contract or any agreement supplementary to such contract—

        (i) perform such contract; or

        (ii) provide to the licensee such intellectual property (including any embodiment of such intellectual property to the extent protected by applicable nonbankruptcy law) held by the trustee; and

    (B) not interfere with the rights of the licensee as provided in such contract, or any agreement supplementary to such contract, to such intellectual property (including such embodiment), including any right to obtain such intellectual property (or such embodiment) from another entity.

(o) In a case under chapter 11 of this title, the trustee shall be deemed to have assumed (consistent with the debtor's other obligations under section 507), and shall immediately cure any deficit under, any commitment by the debtor to a Federal depository institutions regulatory agency (or predecessor to such agency) to maintain the capital of an insured depository institution, and any claim for a subsequent breach of the obligations thereunder shall be entitled to priority under section 507. This subsection shall not extend any commitment that would otherwise be terminated by any act of such an agency.

(p)(1) If a lease of personal property is rejected or not timely assumed by the trustee under subsection (d), the leased property is no longer property of the estate and the stay under section 362(a) is automatically terminated.

(2)(A) If the debtor in a case under chapter 7 is an individual, the debtor may notify the creditor in writing that the debtor desires to assume the lease. Upon being so notified, the creditor may, at its option, notify the debtor that it is willing to have the lease assumed by the debtor and may condition such assumption on cure of any outstanding default on terms set by the contract.

    (B) If, not later than 30 days after notice is provided under subparagraph (A), the debtor notifies the lessor in writing that the lease is assumed, the liability under the lease will be assumed by the debtor and not by the estate.

    (C) The stay under section 362 and the injunction under section 524(a) (2) shall not be violated by notification of the debtor and negotiation of cure under this subsection.

(3) In a case under chapter 11 in which the debtor is an individual and in a case under chapter 13, if the debtor is the lessee with respect to personal property and the lease is not assumed in the plan confirmed by the court, the lease is deemed rejected as of the conclusion of the hearing on confirmation. If the lease is rejected, the stay under section 362 and any stay under section 1301 is automatically terminated with respect to the property subject to the lease.

(Pub.L. 95–598, Nov. 6, 1978, 92 Stat. 2574; Pub.L. 98–353, Title III, §§ 362, 402–404, July 10, 1984, 98 Stat. 361, 367; Pub.L. 99–554, Title II, §§ 257(j), (m), 283(e), Oct. 27, 1986, 100 Stat. 3115, 3117; Pub.L. 100–506, § 1(b), Oct. 18, 1988, 102 Stat. 2538; Pub.L. 101–647, Title XXV, § 2522(c), Nov. 29, 1990, 104 Stat. 4866; Pub.L. 102–365, § 19(b)–(e), Sept. 3, 1992, 106 Stat. 982–984; Pub.L. 103–394, Title II, §§ 205(a), 219(a), (b), Title V, § 501(d)(10), Oct. 22, 1994, 108 Stat. 4122, 4128, 4145; Pub.L. 103–429, § 1, Oct. 31, 1994, 108 Stat. 4377; Pub.L. 109–8, Title III, §§ 309(b), 328(a), Title IV, § 404, Apr. 20, 2005, 119 Stat. 82, 100, 104.)

1 So in original. The comma probably should not appear.

HISTORICAL AND STATUTORY NOTES

Revision Notes and Legislative Reports

1978 Acts. Subsection (a) of this section authorizes the trustee, subject to the court's approval, to assume or reject an executory contract or unexpired lease. Though there is no precise definition of what contracts are executory, it generally includes contracts on which performance remains due to some extent on both sides. A note is not usually an executory contract if the only performance that remains is repayment. Performance on one side of the contract would have been completed and the contract is no longer executory.

Because of the volatile nature of the commodities markets and the special provisions governing commodity broker liquidations in subchapter IV of chapter 7, the provisions governing distribution in section 765(a) will govern if any conflict between those provisions and the provisions of this section arise.

Subsections (b), (c), and (d) provide limitations on the trustee's powers. Subsection (b) requires the trustee to cure any default in the contract or lease and to provide adequate assurance of future performance if there has been a default, before he may assume. This provision does not apply to defaults under ipso facto or bankruptcy clauses, which is a significant departure from present law.

Subsection (b)(3) permits termination of leases entered into prior to the effective date of this title in liquidation cases if certain other conditions are met.

Subsection (b)(4) prohibits the trustee's assumption of an executory contract requiring the other party to make a loan or deliver equipment to or to issue a security of the debtor. The purpose of this subsection is to make it clear that a party to a transaction which is based upon the financial strength of a debtor should not be required to extend new credit to the debtor whether in the form of loans, lease financing, or the purchase or discount of notes.

Subsection (b)(5) provides that in lease situations common to shopping centers, protections must be provided for the lessor if the trustee assumes the lease, including protection

against decline in percentage rents, breach of agreements with other tenants, and preservation of the tenant mix. Protection for tenant mix will not be required in the office building situation.

Subsection (c) prohibits the trustee from assuming or assigning a contract or lease if applicable nonbankruptcy law excuses the other party from performance to someone other than the debtor, unless the other party consents. This prohibition applies only in the situation in which applicable law excuses the other party from performance independent of any restrictive language in the contract or lease itself.

Subsection (d) places time limits on assumption and rejection. In a liquidation case, the trustee must assume within 60 days (or within an additional 60 days, if the court, for cause, extends the time). If not assumed, the contract or lease is deemed rejected. In a rehabilitation case, the time limit is not fixed in the bill. However, if the other party to the contract or lease requests the court to fix a time, the court may specify a time within which the trustee must act. This provision will prevent parties in contractual or lease relationships with the debtor from being left in doubt concerning their status vis-a-vis the estate.

Subsection (e) invalidates ipso facto or bankruptcy clauses. These clauses, protected under present law, automatically terminate the contract or lease, or permit the other contracting party to terminate the contract or lease, in the event of bankruptcy. This frequently hampers rehabilitation efforts. If the trustee may assume or assign the contract under the limitations imposed by the remainder of the section, the contract or lease may be utilized to assist in the debtor's rehabilitation or liquidation.

The unenforceability of ipso facto or bankruptcy clauses proposed under this section will require the courts to be sensitive to the rights of the nondebtor party to executory contracts and unexpired leases. If the trustee is to assume a contract or lease, the court will have to insure that the trustee's performance under the contract or lease gives the other contracting party the full benefit of his bargain.

This subsection does not limit the application of an ipso facto or bankruptcy clause if a new insolvency or receivership occurs after the bankruptcy case is closed. That is, the clause is not invalidated in toto, but merely made inapplicable during the case for the purposes of disposition of the executory contract or unexpired lease.

Subsection (f) partially invalidates restrictions on assignment of contracts or leases by the trustee to a third party. The subsection imposes two restrictions on the trustee: he must first assume the contract or lease, subject to all the restrictions on assumption found in the section, and adequate assurance of future performance must be provided to the other contracting party. Paragraph (3) of the subsection invalidates contractual provisions that permit termination or modification in the event of an assignment, as contrary to the policy of this subsection.

Subsection (g) defines the time as of which a rejection of an executory contract or unexpired lease constitutes a breach of the contract or lease. Generally, the breach is as of the date immediately preceding the date of the petition. The purpose is to treat rejection claims as prepetition claims. The remainder of the subsection specifies different times for cases that are converted from one chapter to another. The provisions of this subsection are not a substantive authorization to breach or reject an assumed contract. Rather, they prescribe the rules for the allowance of claims in case an assumed contract is breached, or if a case under chapter 11 in which a contract has been assumed is converted to a case under chapter 7 in which the contract is rejected.

Subsection (h) protects real property lessees of the debtor if the trustee rejects an unexpired lease under which the debtor is the lessor (or sublessor). The subsection permits the lessee to remain in possession of the leased property or to treat the lease as terminated by the rejection. The balance of the term of the lease referred to in paragraph (1) will include any renewal terms that are enforceable by the tenant, but not renewal terms if the landlord had an option to terminate. Thus, the tenant will not be deprived of his estate for the term for which he bargained. If the lessee remains in possession, he may offset the rent reserved under the lease against damages caused by the rejection, but does not have any affirmative rights against the estate for any damages after the rejection that result from the rejection.

Subsection (i) gives a purchaser of real property under a land installment sales contract similar protection. The purchaser, if the contract is rejected, may remain in possession or may treat the contract as terminated. If the purchaser remains in possession, he is required to continue to make the payments due, but may offset damages that occur after rejection. The trustee is required to deliver title, but is relieved of all other obligations to perform.

A purchaser that treats the contract as terminated is granted a lien on the property to the extent of the purchase price paid. A party with a contract to purchase land from the debtor has a lien on the property to secure the price already paid, if the contract is rejected and the purchaser is not yet in possession.

Subsection (k) relieves the trustee and the estate of liability for a breach of an assigned contract or lease that occurs after the assignment. Senate Report No. 95–989.

Subsection (c) prohibits the trustee from assuming or assigning a contract or lease if applicable nonbankruptcy law excuses the other party from performance to someone other than the debtor, unless the other party consents. This prohibition applies only in the situation in which applicable law excuses the other party from performance independent of any restrictive language in the contract or lease itself. The purpose of this subsection, at least in part, is to prevent the trustee from requiring new advances of money or other property. The section permits the trustee to continue to use and pay for property already advanced, but is not designed to permit the trustee to demand new loans or additional transfers of property under lease commitments.

Thus, under this provision, contracts such as loan commitments and letters of credit are nonassignable, and may not be assumed by the trustee.

Subsection (e) invalidates ipso facto or bankruptcy clauses. These clauses, protected under present law, automatically terminate the contract or lease, or permit the other contracting party to terminate the contract or lease, in the event of bankruptcy. This frequently hampers rehabilitation efforts. If the trustee may assume or assign the contract under the limitations imposed by the remainder of the section, then the contract or lease may be utilized to assist in the debtor's rehabilitation or liquidation.

The unenforceability of ipso facto or bankruptcy clauses proposed under this section will require the courts to be sensitive to the rights of the nondebtor party to executory contracts and unexpired leases. If the trustee is to assume a contract or lease, the courts will have to insure that the trustee's performance under the contract or lease gives the other contracting party the full benefit of his bargain. An example of the complexity that may arise in these situations and the need for a determination of all aspects of a particular executory contract or unexpired lease is the shopping center lease under which the debtor is a tenant in a shopping center.

A shopping center is often a carefully planned enterprise, and though it consists of numerous individual tenants, the center is planned as a single unit, often subject to a master lease or financing agreement. Under these agreements, the tenant mix in a shopping center may be as important to the lessor as the actual promised rental payments, because certain mixes will attract higher patronage of the stores in the center, and thus a higher rental for the landlord from those stores that are subject to a percentage of gross receipts rental agreement. Thus, in order to assure a landlord of his bargained for exchange, the court would have to consider such factors as the nature of the business to be conducted by the trustee or his assignee, whether that business complies with the requirements of any master agreement, whether the kind of business proposed will generate gross sales in an amount such that the percentage rent specified in the lease is substantially the same as what would have been provided by the debtor, and whether the business proposed to be conducted would result in a breach of other clauses in master agreements relating, for example, to tenant mix and location.

This subsection does not limit the application of an ipso facto or bankruptcy clause to a new insolvency or receivership after the bankruptcy case is closed. That is, the clause is not invalidated in toto, but merely made inapplicable during the case for the purpose of disposition of the executory contract or unexpired lease. House Report No. 95–595.

1984 Acts. Statements by Legislative Leaders, see 1984 U.S.Code Cong. and Adm.News, p. 576.

1986 Acts. House Report No. 99–764 and House Conference Report No. 99–958, see 1986 U.S.Code Cong. and Adm. News, p. 5227.

1988 Acts. Senate Report No. 100–505, see 1988 U.S.Code Cong. and Adm.News, p. 3200.

1990 Acts. House Report No. 101–681(I), see 1990 U.S.Code Cong. and Adm.News, p. 6472.

1992 Acts. House Report No. 102–205, see U.S.Code Cong. and Adm.News, p. 866.

1994 Acts. House Report No. 103–835, see 1994 U.S. Code Cong. and Adm. News, p. 3340.

House Report No. 103–831, see 1994 U.S. Code Cong. and Adm. News, p. 3579.

2005 Acts. House Report No. 109–31(Part I), see 2005 U.S. Code Cong. and Adm. News, p. 88.

Legislative Statements

Section 365(b)(3) represents a compromise between H.R. 8200 as passed by the House and the Senate amendment. The provision adopts standards contained in section 365(b)(5) of the Senate amendment to define adequate assurance of future performance of a lease of real property in a shopping center.

Section 365(b)(4) of the House amendment indicates that after default the trustee may not require a lessor to supply services or materials without assumption unless the lessor is compensated as provided in the lease.

Section 365(c)(2) and (3) likewise represent a compromise between H.R. 8200 as passed by the House and the Senate amendment. Section 365(c)(2) is derived from section 365(b)(4) of the Senate amendment but does not apply to a contract to deliver equipment as provided in the Senate amendment. As contained in the House amendment, the provision prohibits a trustee or debtor in possession from assuming or assigning an executory contract of the debtor to make a loan, or extend other debt financing or financial accommodations, to or for the benefit of the debtor, or the issuance of a security of the debtor.

Section 365(e) is a refinement of comparable provisions contained in the House bill and Senate amendment. Sections 365(e)(1) and (2)(A) restate section 365(e) of H.R. 8200 as passed by the House. Sections 365(e)(2)(B) expands the section to permit termination of an executory contract or unexpired lease of the debtor if such contract is a contract to make a loan, or extend other debt financing or financial accommodations, to or for the benefit of the debtor, or for the issuance of a security of the debtor.

Characterization of contracts to make a loan, or extend other debt financing or financial accommodations, is limited to the extension of cash or a line of credit and is not intended to embrace ordinary leases or contracts to provide goods or services with payments to be made over time.

Section 365(f) is derived from H.R. 8200 as passed by the House. Deletion of language in section 365(f)(3) of the Senate amendment is done as a matter of style. Restrictions with respect to assignment of an executory contract or unexpired lease are superfluous since the debtor may assign an executory contract or unexpired lease of the debtor only if such contract is first assumed under section 364(f)(2)(A) of the House amendment.

Section 363(h) of the House amendment represents a modification of section 365(h) of the Senate amendment. The House amendment makes clear that in the case of a bankrupt lessor, a lessee may remain in possession for the balance of the term of a lease and any renewal or extension of the term only to the extent that such renewal or extension may be obtained by the lessee without the permission of the landlord or some third party under applicable non-bankruptcy law.

References in Text

Chapter 7, referred to in subsec. (p)(2), is chapter 7 of this title, 11 U.S.C.A. § 701 et seq.

Chapter 11 or 13, referred to in subsec. (p)(3), is chapter 11 or 13 of this title, 11 U.S.C.A. § 1101 et seq. or 11 U.S.C.A. § 1301 et seq., respectively.

Codifications

Amendment to subsec. (c)(1)(A) by Pub.L. 99–554, § 283(e)(1)(1), struck out "or an assignee of such contract or lease" as the probable intent of Congress, notwithstanding directory language requiring "or and assignee of such contract or lease" be struck out.

Amendment by section 501(d)(10)(A) of Pub.L. 103–394, purporting to amend subsec. (d)(6)(C) of this section by substituting "section 40102 of title 49" for "the Federal Aviation Act of 1958 (49 U.S.C. 1301)", could not be executed, as the latter phrase did not appear in text.

Amendment by section 1(2) of Pub.L. 103–429, purporting to amend subsec. (p) of this section by substituting "section 40102(a) of title 49" for "section 101(3) of the Federal Aviation Act of 1958", could not be executed, as subsec. (p) had already been stricken out pursuant to section 510(d)(10)(E) of Pub.L. 103–394.

Effective and Applicability Provisions

2005 Acts. Amendments by Pub.L. 109–8 effective, except as otherwise provided, 180 days after April 20, 2005, and inapplicable with respect to cases commenced under Title 11 before the effective date, see Pub.L. 109–8, § 1501, set out as a note under 11 U.S.C.A. § 101.

1994 Acts. Amendments by Pub.L. 103–394 effective on Oct. 22, 1994, and not to apply with respect to cases commenced under this title before Oct. 22, 1994, see section 702 of Pub.L. 103–394, set out as a note under section 101 of this title.

1992 Acts. Section 19(f) of Pub.L. 102–365 provided that:

"The amendments made by this section [amending this section and enacting provisions set out as a note under this section] shall be in effect for the 12–month period that begins on the date of enactment of this Act [Sept. 3, 1992] and shall apply in all proceedings involving an affected air carrier (as defined in section 365(p) of title 11, United States Code, as amended by this section [subsec. (p) of this section]) that are pending during such 12–month period. Not later than 9 months after the date of enactment [Sept. 3, 1992], the Administrator of the Federal Aviation Administration shall report to the Committee on Commerce, Science, and Transportation and Committee on the Judiciary of the Senate and the Committee on the Judiciary and Committee on Public Works and Transportation of the House of Representatives on whether this section shall apply to proceedings that are commenced after such 12–month period."

[Any reference in any provision of law enacted before Jan. 4, 1995, to the Committee on Public Works and Transportation of the House of Representatives treated as referring to the Committee on Transportation and Infrastructure of the House of Representatives, see section 1(a)(9) of Pub.L. 104–14, set out as a note preceding section 21 of Title 2, The Congress.]

1988 Acts. Amendment by Pub.L. 100–506 effective on Oct. 18, 1988, except with respect to any case commenced under this title before such date, see section 2 of Pub.L. 100–506, set out as a note under section 101 of this title.

1986 Acts. Amendment by Pub.L. 99–554, § 257, effective 30 days after Oct. 27, 1986, but not applicable with respect to cases commenced under this title before that date, see section 302(a), (c)(1) of Pub.L. 99–554, set out as a note under section 581 of Title 28, Judiciary and Judicial Procedure.

Amendment by Pub.L. 99–554, § 283, effective 30 days after Oct. 27, 1986, except as otherwise provided for, see section 302(a) of Pub.L. 99–554, set out as a note under section 581 of Title 28.

1984 Acts. Amendment by Pub.L. 98–353 effective with respect to cases filed 90 days after July 10, 1984, see section 552(a), formerly 553(a), of Pub.L. 98–353, set out as a note under section 101 of this title.

Separability of Provisions

If any provision of or amendment made by Pub.L. 103–394 or the application of such provision or amendment to any person or circumstance is held to be unconstitutional, the remaining provisions of and amendments made by Pub.L. 103–394 and the application of such provisions and amendments to any person or circumstance shall not be affected thereby, see section 701 of Pub.L. 103–394, set out as a note under section 101 of this title.

Congressional Findings Concerning Airport Gate Leases

Section 19(a) of Pub.L. 102–365 provided that:

"Congress finds that—

"(1) there are major airports served by an air carrier that has leased a substantial majority of the airport's gates;

"(2) the commerce in the region served by such a major airport can be disrupted if the air carrier that leases most of its gates enters bankruptcy and either discontinues or materially reduces service; and

"(3) it is important that such airports be empowered to continue service in the event of such a disruption."

CROSS REFERENCES

Allowance of claims, see 11 USCA § 502.

Applicability of this section in Chapter 9 cases, see 11 USCA § 901.

Assumption or rejection of certain executory contracts within reasonable time after order for relief, see 11 USCA § 744.

Collective bargaining agreements, see 11 USCA § 1167.

Contents of plan, see 11 USCA § 1222.

Contractual right to liquidate,

Commodities contract or forward contract, see 11 USCA § 556.

Repurchase agreement, see 11 USCA § 559.

Securities contract, see 11 USCA § 555.

Contractual right to terminate a swap agreement, see 11 USCA § 560.

Effect of,

Conversion, see 11 USCA § 348.

Rejection of lease of railroad line, see 11 USCA § 1169.

Grain storage facility bankruptcies, expedited determinations, see 11 USCA § 557.

Impairment of claims or interests by plans which cure certain defaults, see 11 USCA § 1124.

Municipal leases, see 11 USCA § 929.

Provisions in plan for assumption or rejection of certain executory contracts or unexpired leases, see 11 USCA §§ 1123 and 1322.

Right of possession of party with security interest as affected by default,

Aircraft equipment and vessels, see 11 USCA § 1110.

Rolling stock equipment, see 11 USCA § 1168.

Setoff, see 11 USCA § 553.

§ 366. Utility service

(a) Except as provided in subsections (b) and (c) of this section, a utility may not alter, refuse, or discontinue service to, or discriminate against, the trustee or the debtor solely on the basis of the commencement of a case under this title or that a debt owed by the debtor to such utility for service rendered before the order for relief was not paid when due.

(b) Such utility may alter, refuse, or discontinue service if neither the trustee nor the debtor, within 20 days after the date of the order for relief, furnishes adequate assurance of payment, in the form of a deposit or other security, for service after such date. On request of a party in interest and after notice and a hearing, the court may order reasonable modification of the amount of the deposit or other security necessary to provide adequate assurance of payment.

(c)(1)(A) For purposes of this subsection, the term "assurance of payment" means—

(i) a cash deposit;

(ii) a letter of credit;

(iii) a certificate of deposit;

(iv) a surety bond;

(v) a prepayment of utility consumption; or

(vi) another form of security that is mutually agreed on between the utility and the debtor or the trustee.

(B) For purposes of this subsection an administrative expense priority shall not constitute an assurance of payment.

(2) Subject to paragraphs (3) and (4), with respect to a case filed under chapter 11, a utility referred to in subsection (a) may alter, refuse, or discontinue utility service, if during the 30–day period beginning on the date of the filing of the petition, the utility does not receive from the debtor or the trustee adequate assurance of payment for utility service that is satisfactory to the utility.

(3)(A) On request of a party in interest and after notice and a hearing, the court may order modification of the amount of an assurance of payment under paragraph (2).

(B) In making a determination under this paragraph whether an assurance of payment is adequate, the court may not consider—

(i) the absence of security before the date of the filing of the petition;

(ii) the payment by the debtor of charges for utility service in a timely manner before the date of the filing of the petition; or

(iii) the availability of an administrative expense priority.

(4) Notwithstanding any other provision of law, with respect to a case subject to this subsection, a utility may recover or set off against a security deposit provided to the utility by the debtor before the date of the filing of the petition without notice or order of the court.

(Pub.L. 95–598, Nov. 6, 1978, 92 Stat. 2578; Pub.L. 98–353, Title III, § 443, July 10, 1984, 98 Stat. 373; Pub.L. 109–8, Title IV, § 417, Apr. 20, 2005, 119 Stat. 108.)

HISTORICAL AND STATUTORY NOTES

Revision Notes and Legislative Reports

1978 Acts. This section gives debtors protection from a cut-off of service by a utility because of the filing of a bankruptcy case. This section is intended to cover utilities that have some special position with respect to the debtor, such as an electric company, gas supplier, or telephone company that is a monopoly in the area so that the debtor cannot easily obtain comparable service from another utility. The utility may not alter, refuse, or discontinue service because of the nonpayment of a bill that would be discharged in the bankruptcy case. Subsection (b) protects the utility company by requiring the trustee or the debtor to provide, within ten days, adequate assurance of payment for service provided after the date of the petition. Senate Report No. 95–989.

1984 Acts. Statements by Legislative Leaders, see 1984 U.S.Code Cong. and Adm.News, p. 576.

2005 Acts. House Report No. 109–31(Part I), see 2005 U.S. Code Cong. and Adm. News, p. 88.

Legislative Statements

Section 366 of the House amendment represents a compromise between comparable provisions contained in H.R. 8200 as passed by the House and the Senate amendment. Subsection (a) is modified so that the applicable date is the date of the order for relief rather than the date of the filing of the petition. Subsection (b) contains a similar change but is

otherwise derived from section 366(b) of the Senate amendment, with the exception that a time period for continued service of 20 days rather than 10 days is adopted.

References in Text

Chapter 11, referred to in subsec. (c)(2), is chapter 11 of this title, 11 U.S.C.A. § 1101 et seq.

Effective and Applicability Provisions

2005 Acts. Amendments by Pub.L. 109–8 effective, except as otherwise provided, 180 days after April 20, 2005, and inapplicable with respect to cases commenced under Title 11 before the effective date, see Pub.L. 109–8, § 1501, set out as a note under 11 U.S.C.A. § 101.

1984 Acts. Amendment by Pub.L. 98–353 effective with respect to cases filed 90 days after July 10, 1984, see section 552(a), formerly 553(a) of Pub.L. 98–353, set out as a note under section 101 of this title.

CROSS REFERENCES

Applicability of this section in Chapter 9 cases, see 11 USCA § 901.

CHAPTER 5—CREDITORS, THE DEBTOR, AND THE ESTATE

HISTORICAL AND STATUTORY NOTES
Effective and Applicability Provisions

2005 Acts. Amendments by Pub.L. 109–8 effective, except as otherwise provided, 180 days after April 20, 2005, and inapplicable with respect to cases commenced under Title 11 before the effective date, see Pub.L. 109–8, § 1501, set out as a note under 11 U.S.C.A. § 101.

CROSS REFERENCES

Applicability of this chapter to,
 Cases under Chapter 7, 11, 12, or 13 of this title, see 11 USCA § 103.
 Investor protection liquidation proceedings, see 15 USCA § 78fff.

SUBCHAPTER I—CREDITORS AND CLAIMS

§ 501. Filing of proofs of claims or interests

(a) A creditor or an indenture trustee may file a proof of claim. An equity security holder may file a proof of interest.

(b) If a creditor does not timely file a proof of such creditor's claim, an entity that is liable to such creditor with the debtor, or that has secured such creditor, may file a proof of such claim.

(c) If a creditor does not timely file a proof of such creditor's claim, the debtor or the trustee may file a proof of such claim.

(d) A claim of a kind specified in section 502(e)(2), 502(f), 502(g), 502(h) or 502(i) of this title may be filed under subsection (a), (b), or (c) of this section the same as if such claim were a claim against the debtor and had arisen before the date of the filing of the petition.

(e) A claim arising from the liability of a debtor for fuel use tax assessed consistent with the requirements of section 31705 of title 49 may be filed by the base jurisdiction designated pursuant to the International Fuel Tax Agreement (as defined in section 31701 of title 49) and, if so filed, shall be allowed as a single claim.

(Pub.L. 95–598, Nov. 6, 1978, 92 Stat. 2578; Pub.L. 98–353, Title III, § 444, July 10, 1984, 98 Stat. 373; Pub.L. 109–8, Title VII, § 702, Apr. 20, 2005, 119 Stat. 125.)

HISTORICAL AND STATUTORY NOTES
Revision Notes and Legislative Reports

1978 Acts. This section governs the means by which creditors and equity security holders present their claims or interests to the court. Subsection (a) permits a creditor to file a proof of claim or interest. An indenture trustee representing creditors may file a proof of claim on behalf of the creditors he represents.

This subsection is permissive only, and does not require filing of a proof of claim by any creditor. It permits filing where some purpose would be served, such as where a claim that appears on a list filed under proposed 11 U.S.C. 924 or 1111 was incorrectly stated or listed as disputed, contingent, or unliquidated, where a creditor with a lien is undersecured and asserts a claim for the balance of the debt owed him (his unsecured claim, as determined under proposed 11 U.S.C. 506(a)), or in a liquidation case where there will be a distribution of assets to the holders of allowed claims. In other instances, such as in no-asset liquidation cases, in situations where a secured creditor does not assert any claim against the estate and a determination of his claim is not made under proposed 11 U.S.C. 506, or in situations where the claim asserted would be subordinated and the creditor would not recover from the estate in any event, filing of a proof of claim may simply not be necessary. The Rules of Bankruptcy Procedure and practice under the law will guide creditors as to when filing is necessary and when it may be dispensed with. In general, however, unless a claim is listed in a chapter 9 or chapter 11 case and allowed as a result of the list, a proof of claim will be a prerequisite to allowance for unsecured claims, including priority claims and the unsecured portion of a claim asserted by the holder of a lien.

The Rules of Bankruptcy Procedure will set the time limits, the form, and the procedure for filing, which will determine whether claims are timely or tardily filed. The rules governing time limits for filing proofs of claims will continue to apply under section 405(d) of the bill. These provide a 6-month-bar date for the filing of tax claims.

Subsection (b) permits a codebtor, surety, or guarantor to file a proof of claim on behalf of the creditor to which he is liable if the creditor does not timely file a proof of claim.

In liquidation and individual repayment plan cases, the trustee or the debtor may file a proof of claim under subsection (c) if the creditor does not timely file. The purpose of this subsection is mainly to protect the debtor if the creditor's claim is nondischargeable. If the creditor does not file, there would be no distribution on the claim, and the debtor would have a greater debt to repay after the case is closed than if the claim were paid in part or in full in the case or under the plan.

Subsection (d) governs the filing of claims of the kind specified in subsections (f), (g), (h), (i), or (j) of proposed 11 U.S.C. 502. The separation of this provision from the other claim-filing provisions in this section is intended to indicate that claims of the kind specified, which do not become fixed or do not arise until after the commencement of the case, must be treated differently for filing purposes such as the bar date for filing claims. The rules will provide for later filing of claims of these kinds.

Subsection (e) gives governmental units (including tax authorities) at least six months following the date for the first meeting of creditors in a chapter 7 or chapter 13 case within which to file proof of claims. Senate Report No. 95–989.

1984 Acts. Statements by Legislative Leaders, see 1984 U.S.Code Cong. and Adm.News, p. 576.

2005 Acts. House Report No. 109–31(Part I), see 2005 U.S. Code Cong. and Adm. News, p. 88.

Legislative Statements

The House amendment adopts section 501(b) of the Senate amendment leaving the Rules of Bankruptcy Procedure free to determine where a proof of claim must be filed.

Section 501(c) expands language contained in section 501(c) of the House bill and Senate amendment to permit the debtor to file a proof of claim if a creditor does not timely file a proof of the creditor's claim in a case under title 11.

The House amendment deletes section 501(e) of the Senate amendment as a matter to be left to the rules of bankruptcy procedure. It is anticipated that the rules will enable governmental units, like other creditors, to have a reasonable time to file proofs of claim in bankruptcy cases.

For purposes of section 501, a proof of "interest" includes the interest of a general or limited partner in a partnership, the interest of a proprietor in a sole proprietorship, or the interest of a common or preferred stockholder in a corporation.

Effective and Applicability Provisions

2005 Acts. Amendments by Pub.L. 109–8 effective, except as otherwise provided, 180 days after April 20, 2005, and inapplicable with respect to cases commenced under Title 11 before the effective date, see Pub.L. 109–8, § 1501, set out as a note under 11 U.S.C.A. § 101.

1984 Acts. Amendment by Pub.L. 98–353 effective with respect to cases filed 90 days after July 10, 1984, see section 552(a), formerly 553 of Pub.L. 98–353, set out as a note under section 101 of this title.

Child Support Creditors or Their Representatives; Appearance Before Court

Pub.L. 103–394, Title IV, § 304(g), Oct. 22, 1994, 108 Stat. 4134, provided that: "Child support creditors or their representatives shall be permitted to appear and intervene without charge, and without meeting any special local court rule requirement for attorney appearances, in any bankruptcy case or proceeding in any bankruptcy court or district court of the United States if such creditors or representatives file a form in such court that contains information detailing the child support debt, its status, and other characteristics."

CROSS REFERENCES

Applicability of this section in Chapter 9 cases, see 11 USCA § 901.

Binding effect of confirmation whether or not claim is filed or deemed filed, see 11 USCA § 944.

Discharge of,

Debtor after confirmation of plan, see 11 USCA § 1141.

Liabilities on claims whether or not filed, see 11 USCA § 727.

Distribution of property of estate, see 11 USCA § 726.

False oaths and claims, see 18 USCA § 152.

Proof of claim deemed filed in,

Chapter 9 cases, see 11 USCA § 925.

Chapter 11 cases, see 11 USCA § 1111.

§ 502.   Allowance of claims or interests

(a) A claim or interest, proof of which is filed under section 501 of this title, is deemed allowed, unless a party in interest, including a creditor of a general partner in a partnership that is a debtor in a case under chapter 7 of this title, objects.

(b) Except as provided in subsections (e)(2), (f), (g), (h) and (i) of this section, if such objection to a claim is made, the court, after notice and a hearing, shall determine the amount of such claim in lawful currency of the United States as of the date of the filing of the petition, and shall allow such claim in such amount, except to the extent that—

(1) such claim is unenforceable against the debtor and property of the debtor, under any agreement or applicable law for a reason other than because such claim is contingent or unmatured;

(2) such claim is for unmatured interest;

(3) if such claim is for a tax assessed against property of the estate, such claim exceeds the value of the interest of the estate in such property;

(4) if such claim is for services of an insider or attorney of the debtor, such claim exceeds the reasonable value of such services;

(5) such claim is for a debt that is unmatured on the date of the filing of the petition and that is excepted from discharge under section 523(a)(5) of this title;

(6) if such claim is the claim of a lessor for damages resulting from the termination of a lease of real property, such claim exceeds—

    (A) the rent reserved by such lease, without acceleration, for the greater of one year, or 15 percent, not to exceed three years, of the remaining term of such lease, following the earlier of—

        (i) the date of the filing of the petition; and

        (ii) the date on which such lessor repossessed, or the lessee surrendered, the leased property; plus

    (B) any unpaid rent due under such lease, without acceleration, on the earlier of such dates;

(7) if such claim is the claim of an employee for damages resulting from the termination of an employment contract, such claim exceeds—

    (A) the compensation provided by such contract, without acceleration, for one year following the earlier of—

        (i) the date of the filing of the petition; or

        (ii) the date on which the employer directed the employee to terminate, or such employee terminated, performance under such contract; plus

    (B) any unpaid compensation due under such contract, without acceleration, on the earlier of such dates;

(8) such claim results from a reduction, due to late payment, in the amount of an otherwise applicable credit available to the debtor in connection with an employment tax on wages, salaries, or commissions earned from the debtor; or

(9) proof of such claim is not timely filed, except to the extent tardily filed as permitted under paragraph (1), (2), or (3) of section 726(a) of this title or under the Federal Rules of Bankruptcy Procedure, except that a claim of a governmental unit shall be timely filed if it is filed before 180 days after the date of the order for relief or such later time as the Federal Rules of Bankruptcy Procedure may provide, and except that in a case under chapter 13, a claim of a governmental unit for a tax with respect to a return filed under section 1308 shall be timely if the claim is filed on or before the date that is 60 days after the date on which such return was filed as required.

(c) There shall be estimated for purpose of allowance under this section—

    (1) any contingent or unliquidated claim, the fixing or liquidation of which, as the case may be, would unduly delay the administration of the case; or

    (2) any right to payment arising from a right to an equitable remedy for breach of performance.

(d) Notwithstanding subsections (a) and (b) of this section, the court shall disallow any claim of any entity from which property is recoverable under section 542, 543, 550, or 553 of this title or that is a transferee of a transfer avoidable under section 522(f), 522(h), 544, 545, 547, 548, 549, or 724(a) of this title, unless such entity or transferee has paid the amount, or turned over any such property, for which such entity or transferee is liable under section 522(i), 542, 543, 550, or 553 of this title.

(e)(1) Notwithstanding subsections (a), (b), and (c) of this section and paragraph (2) of this subsection, the court shall disallow any claim for reimbursement or contribution of an entity that is liable with the debtor on or has secured the claim of a creditor, to the extent that—

    (A) such creditor's claim against the estate is disallowed;

    (B) such claim for reimbursement or contribution is contingent as of the time of allowance or disallowance of such claim for reimbursement or contribution; or

    (C) such entity asserts a right of subrogation to the rights of such creditor under section 509 of this title.

(2) A claim for reimbursement or contribution of such an entity that becomes fixed after the commencement of the case shall be determined, and shall be allowed under subsection (a), (b), or (c) of this section, or disallowed under subsection (d) of this section, the same as if such claim had become fixed before the date of the filing of the petition.

(f) In an involuntary case, a claim arising in the ordinary course of the debtor's business or financial affairs after the commencement of the case but before the earlier of the appointment of a trustee and the order for relief shall be determined as of the date such claim arises, and shall be allowed under subsection (a), (b), or (c) of this section or disallowed under subsection (d) or (e) of this section, the same as if such claim had arisen before the date of the filing of the petition.

(g)(1) A claim arising from the rejection, under section 365 of this title or under a plan under chapter 9, 11, 12, or 13 of this title, of an executory contract or unexpired lease of the debtor that has not been assumed shall be determined, and shall be allowed under subsection (a), (b), or (c) of this section or disallowed under subsection (d) or (e) of this section, the same as if such claim had arisen before the date of the filing of the petition.

(2) A claim for damages calculated in accordance with section 562 shall be allowed under subsection (a), (b), or (c), or disallowed under subsection (d) or (e), as if such claim had arisen before the date of the filing of the petition.

(h) A claim arising from the recovery of property under section 522, 550, or 553 of this title shall be determined, and shall be allowed under subsection (a), (b), or (c) of this section, or disallowed under subsection (d) or (e) of this section, the same as if such claim had arisen before the date of the filing of the petition.

(i) A claim that does not arise until after the commencement of the case for a tax entitled to priority under section 507(a)(8) of this title shall be determined, and shall be allowed under subsection (a), (b), or (c) of this section, or disallowed under subsection (d) or (e) of this section, the same as if such claim had arisen before the date of the filing of the petition.

(j) A claim that has been allowed or disallowed may be reconsidered for cause. A reconsidered claim may be allowed or disallowed according to the equities of the case. Reconsideration of a claim under this subsection does not affect the validity of any payment or transfer from the estate made to a holder of an allowed claim on account of such allowed claim that is not reconsidered, but if a reconsidered claim is allowed and is of the same class as such holder's claim, such holder may not receive any additional payment or transfer from the estate on account of such holder's allowed claim until the holder of such reconsidered and allowed claim receives payment on account of such claim proportionate in value to that already received by such other holder. This subsection does not alter or modify the trustee's right to recover from a creditor any excess payment or transfer made to such creditor.

(k)(1) The court, on the motion of the debtor and after a hearing, may reduce a claim filed under this section based in whole on an unsecured consumer debt by not more than 20 percent of the claim, if—

　(A) the claim was filed by a creditor who unreasonably refused to negotiate a reasonable alternative repayment schedule proposed on behalf of the debt-

or by an approved nonprofit budget and credit counseling agency described in section 111;

　(B) the offer of the debtor under subparagraph (A)—

　　(i) was made at least 60 days before the date of the filing of the petition; and

　　(ii) provided for payment of at least 60 percent of the amount of the debt over a period not to exceed the repayment period of the loan, or a reasonable extension thereof; and

　(C) no part of the debt under the alternative repayment schedule is nondischargeable.

(2) The debtor shall have the burden of proving, by clear and convincing evidence, that—

　(A) the creditor unreasonably refused to consider the debtor's proposal; and

　(B) the proposed alternative repayment schedule was made prior to expiration of the 60–day period specified in paragraph (1)(B)(i).

(Pub.L. 95–598, Nov. 6, 1978, 92 Stat. 2579; Pub.L. 98–353, Title III, § 445, July 10, 1984, 98 Stat. 373; Pub.L. 99–554, Title II, §§ 257(j), 283(f), Oct. 27, 1986, 100 Stat. 3115, 3117; Pub.L. 103–394, Title II, § 213(a), Title III, § 304(h)(1), Oct. 22, 1994, 108 Stat. 4125, 4134; Pub.L. 109–8, Title II, § 201(a), Title VII, § 716(d), Title IX, § 910(b), Apr. 20, 2005, 119 Stat. 42, 130, 184.)

HISTORICAL AND STATUTORY NOTES

Revision Notes and Legislative Reports

1978 Acts. A proof of claim or interest is prima facie evidence of the claim or interest. Thus, it is allowed under subsection (a) unless a party in interest objects. The rules and case law will determine who is a party in interest for purposes of objection to allowance. The case law is well developed on this subject today. As a result of the change in the liability of a general partner's estate for the debts of this partnership, see proposed 11 U.S.C. 723, the category of persons that are parties in interest in the partnership case will be expanded to include a creditor of a partner against whose estate the trustee of the partnership estate may proceed under proposed 11 U.S.C. 723(c).

Subsection (b) prescribes the grounds on which a claim may be disallowed. The court will apply these standards if there is an objection to a proof of claim. The burden of proof on the issue of allowance is left to the Rules of Bankruptcy Procedure. Under the current chapter XIII [section 1001 et seq. of former Title 11] rules, a creditor is required to prove that his claim is free from usury, rule 13–301. It is expected that the rules will make similar provision for both liquidation and individual repayment plan cases. See Bankruptcy Act § 656(b) [section 1056(b) of former Title 11]; H.R. 31, 94th Cong., 1st sess., sec. 6–104(a) (1975).

Paragraph (1) requires disallowance if the claim is unenforceable against the debtor for any reason (such as usury, unconscionability, or failure of consideration) other than because it is contingent or unmatured. All such contingent or unmatured claims are to be liquidated by the bankruptcy court in order to afford the debtor complete bankruptcy relief; these claims are generally not provable under present law.

Paragraph (2) requires disallowance to the extent that the claim is for unmatured interest as of the date of the petition. Whether interest is matured or unmatured on the date of bankruptcy is to be determined without reference to any ipso facto or bankruptcy clause in the agreement creating the claim. Interest disallowed under this paragraph includes postpetition interest that is not yet due and payable, and any portion of prepaid interest that represents an original discounting of the claim, yet that would not have been earned on the date of bankruptcy. For example, a claim on a $1,000 note issued the day before bankruptcy would only be allowed to the extent of the cash actually advanced. If the original discount was 10 percent so that the cash advanced was only $900, then notwithstanding the face amount of note, only $900 would be allowed. If $900 was advanced under the note some time before bankruptcy, the interest component of the note would have to be prorated and disallowed to the extent it was for interest after the commencement of the case.

Section 502(b) thus contains two principles of present law. First, interest stops accruing at the date of the filing of the petition, because any claim for unmatured interest is disallowed under this paragraph. Second, bankruptcy operates as the acceleration of the principal amount of all claims against the debtor. One unarticulated reason for this is that the discounting factor for claims after the commencement of the case is equivalent to contractual interest rate on the claim. Thus, this paragraph does not cause disallowance of claims that have not been discounted to a present value because of the irrebuttable presumption that the discounting rate and the contractual interest rate (even a zero interest rate) are equivalent.

Paragraph (3) requires disallowance of a claim to the extent that the creditor may offset the claim against a debt owing to the debtor. This will prevent double recovery, and permit the claim to be filed only for the balance due. This follows section 68 of the Bankruptcy Act [section 108 of former Title 11].

Paragraph (4) requires disallowance of a property tax claim to the extent that the tax due exceeds the value of the property. This too follows current law to the extent the property tax is ad valorem.

Paragraph (5) prevents overreaching by the debtor's attorneys and concealing of assets by debtors. It permits the court to examine the claim of a debtor's attorney independently of any other provision of this subsection, and to disallow it to the extent that it exceeds the reasonable value of the attorneys' services.

Postpetition alimony, maintenance or support claims are disallowed under paragraph (6). They are to be paid from the debtor's postpetition property, because the claims are nondischargeable.

Paragraph (7), derived from current law, limits the damages allowable to a landlord of the debtor. The history of this provision is set out at length in *Oldden v. Tonto Realty Co.*, 143 F.2d 916 (2d Cir. 1944). It is designed to compensate the landlord for his loss while not permitting a claim so large (based on a long-term lease) as to prevent other general unsecured creditors from recovering a dividend from the estate. The damages a landlord may assert from termination of a lease are limited to the rent reserved for the greater of one year or ten percent of the remaining lease term, not to exceed three years, after the earlier of the date of the filing of the petition and the date of surrender or repossession in a chapter 7 case and 3 years lease payments in a chapter 9, 11,

or 13 case. The sliding scale formula for chapter 7 cases is new and designed to protect the long-term lessor. This subsection does not apply to limit administrative expense claims for use of the leased premises to which the landlord is otherwise entitled.

This paragraph will not overrule *Oldden,* or the proposition for which it has been read to stand: To the extent that a landlord has a security deposit in excess of the amount of his claim allowed under this paragraph, the excess comes into the estate. Moreover, his allowed claim is for his total damages, as limited by this paragraph. By virtue of proposed 11 U.S.C. 506(a) and 506(d), the claim will be divided into a secured portion and an unsecured portion in those cases in which the deposit that the landlord holds is less than his damages. As under *Oldden,* he will not be permitted to offset his actual damages against his security deposit and then claim for the balance under this paragraph. Rather, his security deposit will be applied in satisfaction of the claim that is allowed under this paragraph.

As used in section 502(b)(7), the phrase "lease of real property" applies only to a "true" or "bona fide" lease and does not apply to financing leases of real property or interests therein, or to leases of such property which are intended as security.

Historically, the limitation on allowable claims of lessors of real property was based on two considerations. First, the amount of the lessor's damages on breach of a real estate lease was considered contingent and difficult to prove. Partly for this reason, claims of a lessor of real estate were not provable prior to the 1934 amendments to the Bankruptcy Act [former Title 11]. Second, in a true lease of real property, the lessor retains all risk and benefits as to the value of the real estate at the termination of the lease. Historically, it was, therefore, considered equitable to limit the claims of a real estate lessor.

However, these considerations are not present in "lease financing" transactions where, in substance, the "lease" involves a sale of the real estate and the rental payments are in substance the payment of principal and interest on a secured loan or sale. In a financing lease the lessor is essentially a secured or unsecured creditor (depending upon whether his interest is perfected or not) of the debtor, and the lessor's claim should not be subject to the 502(b)(7) limitation. Financing "leases" are in substance installment sales or loans. The "lessors" are essentially sellers or lenders and should be treated as such for purposes of the bankruptcy law.

Whether a "lease" is true or bona fide lease or, in the alternative, a financing "lease" or a lease intended as security, depends upon the circumstances of each case. The distinction between a true lease and a financing transaction is based upon the economic substance of the transaction and not, for example, upon the locus of title, the form of the transaction or the fact that the transaction is denominated as a "lease". The fact that the lessee, upon compliance with the terms of the lease, becomes or has the option to become the owner of the leased property for no additional consideration or for nominal consideration indicates that the transaction is a financing lease or lease intended as security. In such cases, the lessor has no substantial interest in the leased property at the expiration of the lease term. In addition, the fact that the lessee assumes and discharges substantially all the risks and obligations ordinarily attributed to the outright ownership of the property is more indicative of a financing transaction than of a true lease. The rental payments in such cases are in substance payments of principal and interest either on a loan secured by the leased real property or on the purchase of the leased real property. See, e.g., Financial Accounting Standards Board Statement No. 13 and SEC Reg. S–X, 17 C.F.R. sec. 210.3–16(q) (1977); cf. *First National Bank of Chicago v. Irving Trust Co.*, 74 F.2d 263 (2nd Cir. 1934); and Albenda and Lief, "Net Lease Financing Transactions Under the Proposed Bankruptcy Act of 1973," 30 Business Lawyer, 713 (1975).

Paragraph (8) is new. It tracks the landlord limitation on damages provision in paragraph (7) for damages resulting from the breach by the debtor of an employment contract, but limits the recovery to the compensation reserved under an employment contract for the year following the earlier of the date of the petition and the termination of employment.

Subsection (c) requires the estimation of any claim liquidation of which would unduly delay the closing of the estate, such as a contingent claim, or any claim for which applicable law provides only an equitable remedy, such as specific performance. This subsection requires that all claims against the debtor be converted into dollar amounts.

Subsection (d) is derived from present law. It requires disallowance of a claim of a transferee of a voidable transfer in toto if the transferee has not paid the amount or turned over the property received as required under the sections under which the transferee's liability arises.

Subsection (e), also derived from present law, requires disallowance of the claim for reimbursement or contribution of a codebtor, surety or guarantor of an obligation of the debtor, unless the claim of the creditor on such obligation has been paid in full. The provision prevents competition between a creditor and his guarantor for the limited proceeds in the estate.

Subsection (f) specifies that "involuntary gap" creditors receive the same treatment as prepetition creditors. Under the allowance provisions of this subsection, knowledge of the commencement of the case will be irrelevant. The claim is to be allowed "the same as if such claim had arisen before the date of the filing of the petition." Under voluntary petition, proposed 11 U.S.C. 303(f), creditors must be permitted to deal with the debtor and be assured that their claims will be paid. For purposes of this subsection, "creditors" include governmental units holding claims for tax liabilities incurred during the period after the petition is filed and before the earlier of the order for relief or appointment of a trustee.

Subsection (g) gives entities injured by the rejection of an executory contract or unexpired lease, either under section 365 or under a plan or reorganization, a prepetition claim for any resulting damages, and requires that the injured entity be treated as a prepetition creditor with respect to that claim.

Subsection (h) gives a transferee of a setoff that is recovered by one trustee a prepetition claim for the amount recovered.

Subsection (i) answers the nonrecourse loan problem and gives the creditor an unsecured claim for the difference between the value of the collateral and the debt in response to the decision in *Great National Life Ins. Co. v. Pine Gate Associates, Ltd.*, Bankruptcy Case No. B75–4345A (N.D.Ga. Sept. 16, 1977).

The bill, as reported, deletes a provision in the bill as originally introduced (former sec. 502(i)) requiring a tax authority to file a proof of claim for recapture of an investment credit where, during title 11 proceedings, the trustee sells or otherwise disposes of property before the title 11 case began. The tax authority should not be required to submit a formal claim for a taxable event (a sale or other disposition of the asset) of whose occurrence the trustee necessarily knows better than the taxing authority. For procedural purposes, the recapture of investment credit is to be treated as an administrative expense, as to which only a request for payment is required. Senate Report No. 95–989.

Paragraph (9) [of subsec. (b)] requires disallowance of certain employment tax claims. These relate to a Federal tax credit for State unemployment insurance taxes which is disallowed if the State tax is paid late. This paragraph disallows the Federal claim for the tax the same as if the credit had been allowed in full on the Federal return. House Report No. 95–595.

1984 Acts. Statements by Legislative Leaders, see 1984 U.S. Code Cong. and Adm. News, p. 576.

1986 Acts. House Report No. 99–764 and House Conference Report No. 99–958, see 1986 U.S. Code Cong. and Adm. News, p. 5227.

1994 Acts. House Report No. 103–835, see 1994 U.S. Code Cong. and Adm. News, p. 3340.

2005 Acts. House Report No. 109–31(Part I), see 2005 U.S. Code Cong. and Adm. News, p. 88.

Legislative Statements

The House amendment adopts a compromise position in section 502(a) between H.R. 8200, as passed by the House, and the Senate amendment. Section 502(a) has been modified to make clear that a party in interest includes a creditor of a partner in a partnership that is a debtor under chapter 7. Since the trustee of the partnership is given an absolute claim against the estate of each general partner under section 723(c), creditors of the partner must have standing to object to claims against the partnership at the partnership level because no opportunity will be afforded at the partner's level for such objection.

The House amendment contains a provision in section 502(b)(1) that requires disallowance of a claim to the extent that such claim is unenforceable against the debtor and unenforceable against property of the debtor. This is intended to result in the disallowance of any claim for deficiency by an undersecured creditor on a non-recourse loan or under a State antideficiency law, special provision for which is made in section 1111, since neither the debtor personally, nor the property of the debtor is liable for such a deficiency. Similarly claims for usurious interest or which could be barred by an agreement between the creditor and the debtor would be disallowed.

Section 502(b)(7)(A) represents a compromise between the House bill and the Senate amendment. The House amendment takes the provision in H.R. 8200 as passed by the House of Representatives but increases the percentage from 10 to 15 percent.

As used in section 502(b)(7), the phrase "lease of real property" applies only to a "true" or "bona fide" lease and does not apply to financing leases of real property or interests therein, or to leases of such property which are intended as security.

Historically, the limitation on allowable claims of lessors of real property was based on two considerations. First, the amount of the lessor's damages on breach of a real estate lease was considered contingent and difficult to prove. Partly

---

for this reason, claims of a lessor of real estate were not provable prior to the 1934 amendments, to the Bankruptcy Act. Second, in a true lease of real property, the lessor retains all risks and benefits as to the value of the real estate at the termination of the lease. Historically, it was, therefore, considered equitable to limit the claims of real estate lessor.

However, these considerations are not present in "lease financing" transactions where, in substance, the "lease" involves a sale of the real estate and the rental payments are in substance the payment of principal and interest on a secured loan or sale. In a financing lease the lessor is essentially a secured or unsecured creditor (depending upon whether his interest is perfected or not) of the debtor, and the lessor's claim should not be subject to the 502(b)(7) limitation. Financing "leases" are in substance installment sales or loans. The "lessors" are essentially sellers or lenders and should be treated as such for purposes of the bankruptcy law.

Whether a "lease" is true or bona fide lease or, in the alternative a financing "lease" or a lease intended as security, depends upon the circumstances of each case. The distinction between a true lease and a financing transaction is based upon the economic substance of the transaction and not, for example, upon the locus of title, the form of the transaction or the fact that the transaction is denominated as a "lease." The fact that the lessee, upon compliance with the terms of the lease, becomes or has the option to become the owner of the leased property for no additional consideration or for nominal consideration indicates that the transaction is a financing lease or lease intended as security. In such cases, the lessor has no substantial interest in the leased property at the expiration of the lease term. In addition, the fact that the lessee assumes and discharges substantially all the risks and obligations ordinarily attributed to the outright ownership of the property is more indicative of a financing transaction than of a true lease. The rental payments in such cases are in substance payments of principal and interest either on a loan secured by the leased real property or on the purchase of the leased real property. See, e.g., Financial Accounting Standards Board Statement No. 13 and SEC Reg. S–X, 17 C.F.R. sec. 210.3–16(q) (1977); cf. First National Bank of Chicago v. Irving Trust Co., 74 F.2d 263 (2nd Cir.1934); and Albenda and Lief, "Net Lease Financing Transactions Under the Proposed Bankruptcy Act of 1973," 30 Business Lawyer, 713 (1975).

Section 502(c) of the House amendment presents a compromise between similar provisions contained in the House bill and the Senate amendment. The compromise language is consistent with an amendment to the definition of "claim" in section 104(4)(B) of the House amendment and requires estimation of any right to an equitable remedy for breach of performance if such breach gives rise to a right to payment. To the extent language in the House and Senate reports indicate otherwise, such language is expressly overruled.

Section 502(e) of the House amendment contains language modifying a similar section in the House bill and Senate amendment. Section 502(e)(1) states the general rule requiring the court to disallow any claim for reimbursement or contribution of an entity that is liable with the debtor on, or that has secured, the claim of a creditor to any extent that the creditor's claim against the estate is disallowed. This adopts a policy that a surety's claim for reimbursement or contribution is entitled to no better status than the claim of the creditor assured by such surety. Section 502(e)(1)(B) alternatively disallows any claim for reimbursement or contribution

by a surety to the extent such claim is contingent as of the time of allowance. Section 502(e)(2) is clear that to the extent a claim for reimbursement or contribution becomes fixed after the commencement of the case that it is to be considered a prepetition claim for purposes of allowance. The combined effect of sections 502(e)(1)(B) and 502(e)(2) is that a surety or codebtor is generally permitted a claim for reimbursement or contribution to the extent the surety or codebtor has paid the assured party at the time of allowance. Section 502(e)(1)(C) alternatively indicates that a claim for reimbursement or contribution of a surety or codebtor is disallowed to the extent the surety or codebtor requests subrogation under section 509 with respect to the rights of the assured party. Thus, the surety or codebtor has a choice; to the extent a claim for contribution or reimbursement would be advantageous, such as in the case where such a claim is secured, a surety or codebtor may opt for reimbursement or contribution under section 502(e). On the other hand, to the extent the claim for such surety or codebtor by way of subrogation is more advantageous, such as where such claim is secured, the surety may elect subrogation under section 509.

The section changes current law by making the election identical in all other respects. To the extent a creditor's claim is satisfied by a surety or codebtor, other creditors should not benefit by the surety's inability to file a claim against the estate merely because such surety or codebtor has failed to pay such creditor's claim in full. On the other hand, to the extent the creditor's claim against the estate is otherwise disallowed, the surety or codebtor should not be entitled to increased rights by way of reimbursement or contribution, to the detriment of competing claims of other unsecured creditors, than would be realized by way of subrogation.

While the foregoing scheme is equitable with respect to other unsecured creditors of the debtor, it is desirable to preserve present law to the extent that a surety or codebtor is not permitted to compete with the creditor he has assured until the assured party's claim has paid in full [sic]. Accordingly, section 509(c) of the House amendment subordinates both a claim by way of subrogation or a claim for reimbursement or contribution of a surety or codebtor to the claim of the assured party until the assured party's claim is paid in full.

Section 502(h) of the House amendment expands similar provisions contained in the House bill and the Senate amendment to indicate that any claim arising from the recovery of property under section 522(i), 550, or 553 shall be determined as though it were a prepetition claim.

Section 502(i) of the House amendment adopts a provision contained in section 502(j) of H.R. 8200 as passed by the House but that was not contained in the Senate amendment.

Section 502(i) of H.R. 8200 as passed by the House, but was not included in the Senate amendment, is deleted as a matter to be left to the bankruptcy tax bill next year.

The House amendment deletes section 502(i) of the Senate bill but adopts the policy of that section to a limited extent for confirmation of a plan of reorganization in section 1111(b) of the House amendment.

Section 502(j) of the House amendment is new. The provision codifies section 57k of the Bankruptcy Act [section 93(k) of former Title 11].

Allowance of Claims or Interest: The House amendment adopts section 502(b)(9) of the House bill which disallows any tax claim resulting from a reduction of the Federal Unemployment Tax Act (FUTA) credit (sec. 3302 of the Internal

Revenue Code [26 U.S.C.A. § 3302]) on account of a tardy contribution to a State unemployment fund if the contribution is attributable to ways or other compensation paid by the debtor before bankruptcy. The Senate amendment allowed this reduction, but would have subordinated it to other claims in the distribution of the estate's assets by treating it as a punitive (nonpecuniary loss) penalty. The House amendment would also not bar reduction of the FUTA credit on account of a trustee's late payment of a contribution to a State unemployment fund if the contribution was attributable to a trustee's payment of compensation earned from the estate.

Section 511 of the Senate amendment is deleted. Its substance is adopted in section 502(b)(9) of the House amendment which reflects an identical provision contained in H.R. 8200 as passed by the House.

References in Text

Chapter 7 of this title, referred to in subsec. (a), is 11 U.S.C.A. § 701 et seq.

The Federal Rules of Bankruptcy Procedure, referred to in subsec. (b)(9), are set out in the Appendix to this title.

Chapter 13, referred to in subsec. (b)(9), is chapter 13 of this title, 11 U.S.C.A. § 1301.

Chapter 9, 11, 12, or 13 of this title, referred to in subsec. (g)(1), is 11 U.S.C.A. § 901 et seq., 11 U.S.C.A. § 1101 et seq., 11 U.S.C.A. § 1201 et seq., or 11 U.S.C.A. § 1301 et seq., respectively.

Effective and Applicability Provisions

2005 Acts. Amendments by Pub.L. 109–8 effective, except as otherwise provided, 180 days after April 20, 2005, and inapplicable with respect to cases commenced under Title 11 before the effective date, see Pub.L. 109–8, § 1501, set out as a note under 11 U.S.C.A. § 101.

1994 Acts. Amendments by Pub.L. 103–394 effective on Oct. 22, 1994, and not to apply with respect to cases commenced under Title 11 of the United States Code before Oct. 22, 1994, see section 702 of Pub.L. 103–394, set out as a note under section 101 of this title.

1986 Acts. Amendments by Pub.L. 99–554, § 257(j) effective 30 days after Oct. 27, 1986, but not to apply with respect to cases commenced under this title before that date, see section 302(a)(c)(1) of Pub.L. 99–554, set out as a note under section 581 of Title 28, Judiciary and Judicial Procedure.

Amendment by Pub.L. 99–554, § 283, effective 30 days after Oct. 27, 1986, except as otherwise provided for, see section 302(a) of Pub.L. 99–554, set out as a note under section 581 of Title 28.

1984 Acts. Amendment by Pub.L. 98–353 effective with respect to cases filed 90 days after July 10, 1984, see section 552(a), formerly 553(a) of Pub.L. 98–353, set out as a note under section 101 of this title.

Separability of Provisions

If any provision of or amendment made by Pub.L. 103–394 or the application of such provision or amendment to any person or circumstance is held to be unconstitutional, the remaining provisions of and amendments made by Pub.L. 103–394 and the application of such provisions and amendments to any person or circumstance shall not be affected thereby, see section 701 of Pub.L. 103–394, set out as a note under section 101 of this title.

CROSS REFERENCES

Acceptance of plan by holders of claims or interests, see 11 USCA § 1126.

Applicability of this section in Chapter 9 cases, see 11 USCA § 901.

Certain claims for which partner and partnership are liable, see 11 USCA § 723.

Claims secured by lien on property of estate, see 11 USCA § 1111.

Creditor as meaning entity having certain claims specified in this section, see 11 USCA § 101.

Deductibility of allowed claim, see 11 USCA § 346.

Discharge of liabilities on claims in,

Chapter 7 cases, see 11 USCA § 727.

Chapter 12 cases, see 11 USCA § 1228.

Chapter 13 cases, see 11 USCA § 1328.

Effect of confirmation in,

Chapter 9 cases, see 11 USCA § 944.

Chapter 11 cases, see 11 USCA § 1141.

Filing and allowance of postpetition claims, see 11 USCA § 1305.

Liability of exempted property for debtor's debt, see 11 USCA § 522.

Municipal leases, see 11 USCA § 929.

Payment of insurance benefits to retired employees, see 11 USCA § 1114.

Setoff, see 11 USCA § 553.

Trustee as lien creditor and as successor to certain creditors and purchasers, see 11 USCA § 544.

§ 503.   Allowance of administrative expenses

(a) An entity may timely file a request for payment of an administrative expense, or may tardily file such request if permitted by the court for cause.

(b) After notice and a hearing, there shall be allowed administrative expenses, other than claims allowed under section 502(f) of this title, including—

(1)(A) the actual, necessary costs and expenses of preserving the estate including—

(i) wages, salaries, and commissions for services rendered after the commencement of the case; and

(ii) wages and benefits awarded pursuant to a judicial proceeding or a proceeding of the National Labor Relations Board as back pay attributable to any period of time occurring after commencement of the case under this title, as a result of a violation of Federal or State law by the debtor, without regard to the time of the occurrence of unlawful conduct on which such award is based or to whether any services were rendered, if the court determines that payment of wages and benefits by reason of the operation of this clause will not substantially increase the probability of layoff or termination of current employees, or of nonpayment of domestic support obligations, during the case under this title;

(B) any tax—

(i) incurred by the estate, whether secured or unsecured, including property taxes for which liability is in rem, in personam, or both, except a tax of a kind specified in section 507(a)(8) of this title; or

(ii) attributable to an excessive allowance of a tentative carryback adjustment that the estate received, whether the taxable year to which such adjustment relates ended before or after the commencement of the case;

(C) any fine, penalty, or reduction in credit relating to a tax of a kind specified in subparagraph (B) of this paragraph; and

(D) notwithstanding the requirements of subsection (a), a governmental unit shall not be required to file a request for the payment of an expense described in subparagraph (B) or (C), as a condition of its being an allowed administrative expense;

(2) compensation and reimbursement awarded under section 330(a) of this title;

(3) the actual, necessary expenses, other than compensation and reimbursement specified in paragraph (4) of this subsection, incurred by—

(A) a creditor that files a petition under section 303 of this title;

(B) a creditor that recovers, after the court's approval, for the benefit of the estate any property transferred or concealed by the debtor;

(C) a creditor in connection with the prosecution of a criminal offense relating to the case or to the business or property of the debtor;

(D) a creditor, an indenture trustee, an equity security holder, or a committee representing creditors or equity security holders other than a committee appointed under section 1102 of this title, in making a substantial contribution in a case under chapter 9 or 11 of this title;

(E) a custodian superseded under section 543 of this title, and compensation for the services of such custodian; or

(F) a member of a committee appointed under section 1102 of this title, if such expenses are incurred in the performance of the duties of such committee;

(4) reasonable compensation for professional services rendered by an attorney or an accountant of an entity whose expense is allowable under subparagraph (A), (B), (C), (D), or (E) of paragraph (3) of this subsection, based on the time, the nature, the extent, and the value of such services, and the cost of comparable services other than in a case under this title, and reimbursement for actual, necessary expenses incurred by such attorney or accountant;

(5) reasonable compensation for services rendered by an indenture trustee in making a substantial contribution in a case under chapter 9 or 11 of this title, based on the time, the nature, the extent, and the value of such services, and the cost of comparable services other than in a case under this title;

(6) the fees and mileage payable under chapter 119 of title 28;

(7) with respect to a nonresidential real property lease previously assumed under section 365, and subsequently rejected, a sum equal to all monetary obligations due, excluding those arising from or relating to a failure to operate or a penalty provision, for the period of 2 years following the later of the rejection date or the date of actual turnover of the premises, without reduction or setoff for any reason whatsoever except for sums actually received or to be received from an entity other than the debtor, and the claim for remaining sums due for the balance of the term of the lease shall be a claim under section 502(b)(6);

(8) the actual, necessary costs and expenses of closing a health care business incurred by a trustee or by a Federal agency (as defined in section 551(1) of title 5) or a department or agency of a State or political subdivision thereof, including any cost or expense incurred—

(A) in disposing of patient records in accordance with section 351; or

(B) in connection with transferring patients from the health care business that is in the process of being closed to another health care business; and

(9) the value of any goods received by the debtor within 20 days before the date of commencement of a case under this title in which the goods have been sold to the debtor in the ordinary course of such debtor's business.

(c) Notwithstanding subsection (b), there shall neither be allowed, nor paid—

(1) a transfer made to, or an obligation incurred for the benefit of, an insider of the debtor for the purpose of inducing such person to remain with the debtor's business, absent a finding by the court based on evidence in the record that—

(A) the transfer or obligation is essential to retention of the person because the individual has a bona fide job offer from another business at the same or greater rate of compensation;

(B) the services provided by the person are essential to the survival of the business; and

(C) either—

(i) the amount of the transfer made to, or obligation incurred for the benefit of, the person is not greater than an amount equal to 10 times the amount of the mean transfer or obligation of a similar kind given to nonmanagement employees for any purpose during the calendar year in which the transfer is made or the obligation is incurred; or

(ii) if no such similar transfers were made to, or obligations were incurred for the benefit of, such nonmanagement employees during such calendar year, the amount of the transfer or obligation is not greater than an amount equal to 25 percent of the amount of any similar transfer or obligation made to or incurred for the benefit of such insider for any purpose during the calendar year before the year in which such transfer is made or obligation is incurred;

(2) a severance payment to an insider of the debtor, unless—

(A) the payment is part of a program that is generally applicable to all full-time employees; and

(B) the amount of the payment is not greater than 10 times the amount of the mean severance pay given to nonmanagement employees during the calendar year in which the payment is made; or

(3) other transfers or obligations that are outside the ordinary course of business and not justified by the facts and circumstances of the case, including transfers made to, or obligations incurred for the benefit of, officers, managers, or consultants hired after the date of the filing of the petition.

(Pub.L. 95–598, Nov. 6, 1978, 92 Stat. 2581; Pub.L. 98–353, Title III, § 446, July 10, 1984, 98 Stat. 374; Pub.L. 99–554, Title II, § 283(g), Oct. 27, 1986, 100 Stat. 3117; Pub.L. 103–394, Title I, § 110, Title II, § 213(c), Title III, § 304(h)(2), Oct. 22, 1994, 108 Stat. 4113, 4126, 4134; Pub.L. 109–8, Title III, §§ 329, 331, Title IV, § 445, Title VII, § 712(b), (c), Title XI, § 1103, Title XII, §§ 1208, 1227(b), Apr. 20, 2005, 119 Stat. 101, 102, 117, 128, 190, 194, 200.)

HISTORICAL AND STATUTORY NOTES

Revision Notes and Legislative Reports

1978 Acts. Subsection (a) of this section permits administrative expense claimants to file with the court a request for payment of an administrative expense. The Rules of Bankruptcy Procedure will specify the time, the form, and the method of such a filing.

Subsection (b) specifies the kinds of administrative expenses that are allowable in a case under the bankruptcy code. The subsection is derived mainly from section 64a(1) of the Bankruptcy Act [section 104(a)(1) of former Title 11], with some changes. The actual, necessary costs and expenses of preserving the estate, including wages, salaries, or commissions for services rendered after the order for relief, and any taxes on, measured by, or withheld from such wages, salaries, or commissions, are allowable as administrative expenses.

In general, administrative expenses include taxes which the trustee incurs in administering the debtor's estate, including taxes on capital gains from sales of property by the trustee and taxes on income earned by the estate during the case. Interest on tax liabilities and certain tax penalties incurred by the trustee are also included in this first priority.

Taxes which the Internal Revenue Service may find due after giving the trustee a so-called "quickie" tax refund and later doing an audit of the refund are also payable as adminis-

trative expenses. The tax code [Title 26, Internal Revenue Code] permits the trustee of an estate which suffers a net operating loss to carry back the loss against an earlier profit year of the estate or of the debtor and to obtain a tentative refund for the earlier year, subject, however, to a later full audit of the loss which led to the refund. The bill, in effect, requires the Internal Revenue Service to issue a tentative refund to the trustee (whether the refund was applied for by the debtor or by the trustee), but if the refund later proves to have been erroneous in amount, the Service can request that the tax attributable to the erroneous refund be payable by the estate as an administrative expense.

Postpetition payments to an individual debtor for services rendered to the estate are administrative expenses, and are not property of the estate when received by the debtor. This situation would most likely arise when the individual was a sole proprietor and was employed by the estate to run the business after the commencement of the case. An individual debtor in possession would be so employed, for example. See *Local Loan v. Hunt*, 292 U.S. 234, 243 (1933) [54 S.Ct. 695, 78 L.Ed. 1230].

Compensation and reimbursement awarded officers of the estate under section 330 are allowable as administrative expenses. Actual, necessary expenses, other than compensation of a professional person, incurred by a creditor that files an involuntary petition, by a creditor that recovers property for the benefit of the estate, by a creditor that acts in connection with the prosecution of a criminal offense relating to the case, by a creditor, indenture, trustee, equity security holder, or committee of creditors or equity security holders (other than official committees) that makes a substantial contribution to a reorganization or municipal debt adjustment case, or by a superseded custodian, are all allowable administrative expenses. The phrase "substantial contribution in the case" is derived from Bankruptcy Act §§ 242 and 243 [sections 642 and 643 of former Title 11]. It does not require a contribution that leads to confirmation of a plan, for in many cases, it will be a substantial contribution if the person involved uncovers facts that would lead to a denial of confirmation, such as fraud in connection with the case.

Paragraph (4) permits reasonable compensation for professional services rendered by an attorney or an accountant of an equity whose expense is compensable under the previous paragraph. Paragraph (5) permits reasonable compensation for an indenture trustee in making a substantial contribution in a reorganization or municipal debt adjustment case. Finally, paragraph (6) permits witness fees and mileage as prescribed under chapter 119 of title 28 [section 1821 et seq. of Title 28, Judiciary and Judicial Procedure]. Senate Report No. 95–989.

1984 Acts. Statements by Legislative Leaders, see 1984 U.S. Code Cong. and Adm. News, p. 576.

1986 Acts. House Report No. 99–764 and House Conference Report No. 99–958, see 1986 U.S. Code Cong. and Adm. News, p. 5227.

1994 Acts. House Report No. 103–835, see 1994 U.S. Code Cong. and Adm. News, p. 3340.

2005 Acts. House Report No. 109–31(Part I), see 2005 U.S. Code Cong. and Adm. News, p. 88.

Legislative Statements

Section 503(a) of the House amendment represents a compromise between similar provisions in the House bill and the

Senate amendment by leaving to the Rules of Bankruptcy Procedure the determination of the location at which a request for payment of an administrative expense may be filed. The preamble to section 503(b) of the House bill makes a similar change with respect to the allowance of administrative expenses.

Section 503(b)(1) adopts the approach taken in the House bill as modified by some provisions contained in the Senate amendment. The preamble to section 503(b) makes clear that none of the paragraphs of section 503(b) apply to claims or expenses of the kind specified in section 502(f) that arise in the ordinary course of the debtor's business or financial affairs and that arise during the gap between the commencement of an involuntary case and the appointment of a trustee or the order for relief, whichever first occurs. The remainder of section 503(b) represents a compromise between H.R. 8200 as passed by the House and the Senate amendments. Section 503(b)(3)(E) codifies present law in cases such as *Randolph v. Scruggs*, 190 U.S. 533, which accords administrative expense status to services rendered by a prepetition custodian or other party to the extent such services actually benefit the estate. Section 503(b)(4) of the House amendment conforms to the provision contained in H.R. 8200 as passed by the House and deletes language contained in the Senate amendment providing a different standard of compensation under section 330 of that amendment.

Effective and Applicability Provisions

2005 Acts. Amendments by Pub.L. 109–8 effective, except as otherwise provided, 180 days after April 20, 2005, and inapplicable with respect to cases commenced under Title 11 before the effective date, see Pub.L. 109–8, § 1501, set out as a note under 11 U.S.C.A. § 101.

1994 Acts. Amendments by Pub.L. 103–394 effective on Oct. 22, 1994, and not to apply with respect to cases commenced under Title 11 of the United States Code before Oct. 22, 1994, see section 702 of Pub.L. 103–394, set out as a note under section 101 of this title.

1986 Acts. Amendment by Pub.L. 99–554 effective 30 days after Oct. 27, 1986, except as otherwise provided for, see section 302(a) of Pub.L. 99–554, set out as a note under section 581 of Title 28, Judiciary and Judicial Procedure.

1984 Acts. Amendment by Pub.L. 98–353 effective with respect to cases filed 90 days after July 10, 1984, see section 552(a), formerly 553(a), of Pub.L. 98–353, set out as a note under section 101 of this title.

Separability of Provisions

If any provision of or amendment made by Pub.L. 103–394 or the application of such provision or amendment to any person or circumstance is held to be unconstitutional, the remaining provisions of and amendments made by Pub.L. 103–394 and the application of such provisions and amendments to any person or circumstance shall not be affected thereby, see section 701 of Pub.L. 103–394, set out as a note under section 101 of this title.

CROSS REFERENCES

Adequate protection, other than granting certain administrative expenses, see 11 USCA § 361.

Applicability of this section in Chapter 9 cases, see 11 USCA § 901.

Claims arising from automatic stay, see 11 USCA § 922.

Discharge of liabilities on claims in Chapter 12 cases, see 11 USCA § 1228.

Deductibility of allowed claim, see 11 USCA § 346.

Deduction of administrative expenses for income tax purposes, see 26 USCA § 1398.

Deduction of administrative expenses from payments received by trustee if plan not confirmed in,

Chapter 12 cases, see 11 USCA § 1226.

Chapter 13 cases, see 11 USCA § 1326.

Distribution of property of estate, see 11 USCA § 726.

Effect of conversion, see 11 USCA § 348.

Grain storage facility bankruptcies, expedited determinations, see 11 USCA § 557.

Method of obtaining adequate protection in Chapter 12 case, see 11 USCA § 1205.

Payment of insurance benefits to retired employees, see 11 USCA § 1114.

Performance of obligations under executory contracts and unexpired leases notwithstanding subsec. (b)(1) of this section, see 11 USCA § 365.

Proof of claim, see Official Bankr. Form B410, 11 USCA.

Unsecured debt as administrative expense or having priority over certain administrative expenses, see 11 USCA § 364.

§ 504. Sharing of compensation

(a) Except as provided in subsection (b) of this section, a person receiving compensation or reimbursement under section 503(b)(2) or 503(b)(4) of this title may not share or agree to share—

(1) any such compensation or reimbursement with another person; or

(2) any compensation or reimbursement received by another person under such sections.

(b)(1) A member, partner, or regular associate in a professional association, corporation, or partnership may share compensation or reimbursement received under section 503(b)(2) or 503(b)(4) of this title with another member, partner, or regular associate in such association, corporation, or partnership, and may share in any compensation or reimbursement received under such sections by another member, partner, or regular associate in such association, corporation, or partnership.

(2) An attorney for a creditor that files a petition under section 303 of this title may share compensation and reimbursement received under section 503(b)(4) of this title with any other attorney contributing to the services rendered or expenses incurred by such creditor's attorney.

(c) This section shall not apply with respect to sharing, or agreeing to share, compensation with a bona fide public service attorney referral program that operates in accordance with non-Federal law regulating attorney referral services and with rules of professional responsibility applicable to attorney acceptance of referrals.

(Pub.L. 95–598, Nov. 6, 1978, 92 Stat. 2582; Pub.L. 109–8, Title III, § 326, Apr. 20, 2005, 119 Stat. 99.)

HISTORICAL AND STATUTORY NOTES

Revision Notes and Legislative Reports

1978 Acts. Section 504 prohibits the sharing of compensation, or fee splitting, among attorneys, other professionals, or trustees. The section provides only two exceptions: partners or associates in the same professional association, partnership, or corporation may share compensation inter se; and attorneys for petitioning creditors that join in a petition commencing an involuntary case may share compensation. Senate Report No. 95–989.

2005 Acts. House Report No. 109–31(Part I), see 2005 U.S. Code Cong. and Adm. News, p. 88.

Effective and Applicability Provisions

2005 Acts. Amendments by Pub.L. 109–8 effective, except as otherwise provided, 180 days after April 20, 2005, and inapplicable with respect to cases commenced under Title 11 before the effective date, see Pub.L. 109–8, § 1501, set out as a note under 11 U.S.C.A. § 101.

CROSS REFERENCES

Applicability of restrictions on sharing of compensation to allowances in investor protection liquidation proceedings, see 15 USCA § 78eee.

Applicability of this section in Chapter 9 cases, see 11 USCA § 901.

§ 505. Determination of tax liability

(a)(1) Except as provided in paragraph (2) of this subsection, the court may determine the amount or legality of any tax, any fine or penalty relating to a tax, or any addition to tax, whether or not previously assessed, whether or not paid, and whether or not contested before and adjudicated by a judicial or administrative tribunal of competent jurisdiction.

(2) The court may not so determine—

(A) the amount or legality of a tax, fine, penalty, or addition to tax if such amount or legality was contested before and adjudicated by a judicial or administrative tribunal of competent jurisdiction before the commencement of the case under this title;

(B) any right of the estate to a tax refund, before the earlier of—

(i) 120 days after the trustee properly requests such refund from the governmental unit from which such refund is claimed; or

(ii) a determination by such governmental unit of such request; or

(C) the amount or legality of any amount arising in connection with an ad valorem tax on real or personal property of the estate, if the applicable period for contesting or redetermining that amount under applicable nonbankruptcy law has expired.

(b)(1)(A) The clerk shall maintain a list under which a Federal, State, or local governmental unit responsible for the collection of taxes within the district may—

(i) designate an address for service of requests under this subsection; and

(ii) describe where further information concerning additional requirements for filing such requests may be found.

(B) If such governmental unit does not designate an address and provide such address to the clerk under subparagraph (A), any request made under this subsection may be served at the address for the filing of a tax return or protest with the appropriate taxing authority of such governmental unit.

(2) A trustee may request a determination of any unpaid liability of the estate for any tax incurred during the administration of the case by submitting a tax return for such tax and a request for such a determination to the governmental unit charged with responsibility for collection or determination of such tax at the address and in the manner designated in paragraph (1). Unless such return is fraudulent, or contains a material misrepresentation, the estate, the trustee, the debtor, and any successor to the debtor are discharged from any liability for such tax—

(A) upon payment of the tax shown on such return, if—

(i) such governmental unit does not notify the trustee, within 60 days after such request, that such return has been selected for examination; or

(ii) such governmental unit does not complete such an examination and notify the trustee of any tax due, within 180 days after such request or within such additional time as the court, for cause, permits;

(B) upon payment of the tax determined by the court, after notice and a hearing, after completion by such governmental unit of such examination; or

(C) upon payment of the tax determined by such governmental unit to be due.

(c) Notwithstanding section 362 of this title, after determination by the court of a tax under this section, the governmental unit charged with responsibility for collection of such tax may assess such tax against the estate, the debtor, or a successor to the debtor, as the case may be, subject to any otherwise applicable law. (Pub.L. 95–598, Nov. 6, 1978, 92 Stat. 2582; Pub.L. 98–353, Title III, § 447, July 10, 1984, 98 Stat. 374; Pub.L. 109–8, Title VII, §§ 701(b), 703, 715, Apr. 20, 2005, 119 Stat. 124, 125, 129; Pub.L. 111–327, § 2(a)(14), Dec. 22, 2010, 124 Stat. 3559.)

HISTORICAL AND STATUTORY NOTES

Revision Notes and Legislative Reports

1978 Acts. Subsections (a) and (b) are derived, with only stylistic changes, from section 2a(2A) of the Bankruptcy Act [section 11(a)(2A) of former Title 11]. They permit determination by the bankruptcy court of any unpaid tax liability of the debtor that has not been contested before or adjudicated by a judicial or administrative tribunal of competent jurisdiction before the bankruptcy case, and the prosecution by the trustee of an appeal from an order of such a body if the time for review or appeal has not expired before the commencement of the bankruptcy case. As under current Bankruptcy Act section 2a(2A), *Arkansas Corporation Commissioner v. Thompson*, 313 U.S. 132 (1941) [61 S.Ct. 888, 85 L.Ed. 1244], remains good law to permit abstention where uniformity of assessment is of significant importance.

Section (c) [sic] deals with procedures for obtaining a prompt audit of tax returns filed by the trustee in a liquidation or reorganization case. Under the bill as originally introduced, a trustee who is "in doubt" concerning tax liabilities of the estate incurred during a title 11 proceeding could obtain a discharge from personal liability for himself and the debtor (but not for the debtor or the debtor's successor in a reorganization), provided that certain administrative procedures were followed. The trustee could request a prompt tax audit by the local, State, or Federal governmental unit. The taxing authority would have to notify the trustee and the court within sixty days whether it accepted the return or desired to audit the returns more fully. If an audit were conducted, the tax office would have to notify the trustee of any tax deficiency within 4 months (subject to an extension of time if the court approved). These procedures would apply only to tax years completed on or before the case was closed and for which the trustee had filed a tax return.

The committee bill eliminates the "in doubt" rule and makes mandatory (rather than optional) the trustee's request for a prompt audit of the estate's tax returns. In many cases, the trustee could not be certain that his returns raised no doubt about possible tax issues. In addition, it is desirable not to create a situation where the taxing authority asserts a tax liability against the debtor (as transferee of surplus assets, if any, return to him) after the case is over; in any such situation, the debtor would be called on to defend a tax return which he did not prepare. Under the amendment, all disputes concerning these returns are to be resolved by the bankruptcy court, and both the trustee and the debtor himself do not then face potential post-bankruptcy tax liabilities based on these returns. This result would occur as to the debtor, however, only in a liquidation case.

In a reorganization in which the debtor or a successor to the debtor continues in existence, the trustee could obtain a discharge from personal liability through the prompt audit procedure, but the Treasury could still claim a deficiency against the debtor (or his successor) for additional taxes due on returns filed during the title 11 proceedings. Senate Report No. 95–989.

Subsection (c) is new. It codifies in part the referee's decision in *In re Statmaster Corp.*, 465 F.2d 987 (5th Cir. 1972). Its purpose is to protect the trustee from personal liability for a tax falling on the estate that is not assessed until after the case is closed. If necessary to permit expeditious closing of the case, the court, on request of the trustee, must order the governmental unit charged with the responsibility for collection or determination of the tax to audit the trustee's return or be barred from attempting later collection. The court will be required to permit sufficient time to perform an audit, if the taxing authority requests it. The final order of the court and the payment of the tax determined in that order discharges the trustee, the debtor, and any successor to the debtor from any further liability for the tax. See Plumb, The Tax Recommendations of the Commission on the Bankruptcy

Laws: Tax Procedures, 88 Harv.L.Rev. 1360, 1423–42 (1975). House Report No. 95–595.

1984 Acts. Statements by Legislative Leaders, see 1984 U.S.Code Cong. and Adm.News, p. 576.

2005 Acts. House Report No. 109–31(Part I), see 2005 U.S. Code Cong. and Adm. News, p. 88.

Legislative Statements

Section 505 of the House amendment adopts a compromise position with respect to the determination of tax liability from the position taken in H.R. 8200 as passed by the House and in the Senate amendment.

Determinations of tax liability: Authority of bankruptcy court to rule on merits of tax claims.—The House amendment authorizes the bankruptcy court to rule on the merits of any tax claim involving an unpaid tax, fine, or penalty relating to a tax, or any addition to a tax, of the debtor or the estate. This authority applies, in general, whether or not the tax, penalty, fine, or addition to tax had been previously assessed or paid. However, the bankruptcy court will not have jurisdiction to rule on the merits of any tax claim which has been previously adjudicated, in a contested proceeding, before a court of competent jurisdiction. For this purpose, a proceeding in the U.S. Tax Court is to be considered "contested" if the debtor filed a petition in the Tax Court by the commencement of the case and the Internal Revenue Service had filed an answer to the petition. Therefore, if a petition and answer were filed in the Tax Court before the title II petition was filed, and if the debtor later defaults in the Tax Court, then, under res judicata principles, the bankruptcy court could not then rule on the debtor's or the estate's liability for the same taxes.

The House amendment adopts the rule of the Senate bill that the bankruptcy court can, under certain conditions, determine the amount of tax refund claim by the trustee. Under the House amendment, if the refund results from an offset or counterclaim to a claim or request for payment by the Internal Revenue Service, or other tax authority, the trustee would not first have to file an administrative claim for refund with the tax authority.

However, if the trustee requests a refund in other situations, he would first have to submit an administrative claim for the refund. Under the House amendment, if the Internal Revenue Service, or other tax authority does not rule on the refund claim within 120 days, then the bankruptcy court may rule on the merits of the refund claim.

Under the Internal Revenue Code [Title 26, Internal Revenue Code], a suit for refund of Federal taxes cannot be filed until 6 months after a claim for refund is filed with the Internal Revenue Service (sec. 6532(a) [26 U.S.C.A. § 6532(a)]). Because of the bankruptcy aim to close the estate as expeditiously as possible, the House amendment shortens to 120 days the period for the Internal Revenue Service to decide the refund claim.

The House amendment also adopts the substance of the Senate bill rule permitting the bankruptcy court to determine the amount of any penalty, whether punitive or pecuniary in nature, relating to taxes over which it has jurisdiction.

Jurisdiction of the tax court in bankruptcy cases: The Senate amendment provided a detailed series of rules concerning the jurisdiction of the U.S. Tax Court, or similar State or local administrative tribunal to determine personal tax liabilities of an individual debtor. The House amendment deletes these specific rules and relies on procedures to be derived from broad general powers of the bankruptcy court.

Under the House amendment, as under present law, a corporation seeking reorganization under chapter 11 is considered to be personally before the bankruptcy court for purposes of giving that court jurisdiction over the debtor's personal liability for a nondischargeable tax.

The rules are more complex where the debtor is an individual under chapter 7, 11, or 13. An individual debtor or the tax authority can, as under section 17c of the present Bankruptcy Act [section 35(c) of former Title 11], file a request that the bankruptcy court determine the debtor's personal liability for the balance of any nondischargeable tax not satisfied from assets of the estate. The House amendment intends to retain these procedures and also adds a rule staying commencement or continuation of any proceeding in the Tax Court after the bankruptcy petition is filed, unless and until that stay is lifted by the bankruptcy judge under section 362(a)(8). The House amendment also stays assessment as well as collection of a prepetition claim against the debtor (sec. 362(a)(6)). A tax authority would not, however, be stayed from issuing a deficiency notice during the bankruptcy case (sec. (b)(7)). The Senate amendment repealed the existing authority of the Internal Revenue Service to make an immediate assessment of taxes upon bankruptcy (sec. 6871(a) of the code [26 U.S.C.A. § 6871(a)]). See section of the Senate bill. As indicated, the substance of that provision, also affecting State and local taxes, is contained in section 362(a)(6) of the House amendment. The statute of limitations is tolled under the House amendment while the bankruptcy case is pending.

Where no proceeding in the Tax Court is pending at the commencement of the bankruptcy case, the tax authority can, under the House amendment, file a claim against the estate for a prepetition tax liability and may also file a request that the bankruptcy court hear arguments and decide the merits of an individual debtor's personal liability for the balance of any nondischargeable tax liability not satisfied from assets of the estate. Bankruptcy terminology refers to the latter type of request as a creditor's complaint to determine the dischargeability of a debt. Where such a complaint is filed, the bankruptcy court will have personal jurisdiction over an individual debtor, and the debtor himself would have no access to the Tax Court, or to any other court, to determine his personal liability for nondischargeable taxes.

If a tax authority decides not to file a claim for taxes which would typically occur where there are few, if any, assets in the estate, normally the tax authority would also not request the bankruptcy court to rule on the debtor's personal liability for a nondischargeable tax. Under the House amendment, the tax authority would then have to follow normal procedures in order to collect a nondischargeable tax. For example, in the case of nondischargeable Federal income taxes, the Internal Revenue Service would be required to issue a deficiency notice to an individual debtor, and the debtor could then file a petition in the Tax Court—or a refund suit in a district court—as the forum in which to litigate his personal liability for a nondischargeable tax.

Under the House amendment, as under present law, an individual debtor can also file a complaint to determine dischargeability. Consequently, where the tax authority does not file a claim or a request that the bankruptcy court determine dischargeability of a specific tax liability, the debtor could file such a request on his own behalf, so that the bankruptcy court would then determine both the validity of the claim against assets in the estate and also the personal liability of the debtor for any nondischargeable tax.

Where a proceeding is pending in the Tax Court at the commencement of the bankruptcy case, the commencement of the bankruptcy case automatically stays further action in the Tax Court case unless and until the stay is lifted by the bankruptcy court. The Senate amendment repealed a provision of the Internal Revenue case barring a debtor from filing a petition in the Tax Court after commencement of a bankruptcy case (sec. 6871(b) of the code) [26 U.S.C.A. § 6871(b)]. See section 321 of the Senate bill. As indicated earlier, the equivalent of the code amendment is embodied in section 362(a)(8) of the House amendment, which automatically stays commencement or continuation of any proceeding in the Tax Court until the stay is lifted or the case is terminated. The stay will permit sufficient time for the bankruptcy trustee to determine if he desires to join the Tax Court proceeding on behalf of the estate. Where the trustee chooses to join the Tax Court proceeding, it is expected that he will seek permission to intervene in the Tax Court case and then request that the stay on the Tax Court proceeding be lifted. In such a case, the merits of the tax liability will be determined by the Tax Court, and its decision will bind both the individual debtor as to any taxes which are nondischargeable and the trustee as to the tax claim against the estate.

Where the trustee does not want to intervene in the Tax Court, but an individual debtor wants to have the Tax Court determine the amount of his personal liability for nondischargeable taxes, the debtor can request the bankruptcy court to lift the automatic stay on existing Tax Court proceedings. If the stay is lifted and the Tax Court reaches its decision before the bankruptcy court's decision on the tax claim against the estate, the decision of the Tax Court would bind the bankruptcy court under principles of res judicata because the decision of the Tax Court affected the personal liability of the debtor. If the trustee does not wish to subject the estate to the decision of the Tax Court if the latter court decides the issues before the bankruptcy court rules, the trustee could resist the lifting of the stay on the existing Tax Court proceeding. If the Internal Revenue Service had issued a deficiency notice to the debtor before the bankruptcy case began, but as of the filing of the bankruptcy petition the 90-day period for filing in the Tax Court was still running, the debtor would be automatically stayed from filing a petition in the Tax Court. If either the debtor or the Internal Revenue Service then files a complaint to determine dischargeability in the bankruptcy court, the decision of the bankruptcy court would bind both the debtor and the Internal Revenue Service.

The bankruptcy judge could, however, lift the stay on the debtor to allow him to petition the Tax Court, while reserving the right to rule on the tax authority's claim against assets of the estate. The bankruptcy court could also, upon request by the trustee, authorize the trustee to intervene in the Tax Court for purposes of having the estate also governed by the decision of the Tax Court.

In essence, under the House amendment, the bankruptcy judge will have authority to determine which court will determine the merits of the tax claim both as to claims against the estate and claims against the debtor concerning his personal liability for nondischargeable taxes. Thus, if the Internal Revenue Service, or a State or local tax authority, files a petition to determine dischargeability, the bankruptcy judge can either rule on the merits of the claim and continue the stay on any pending Tax Court proceeding or lift the stay on the Tax Court and hold the dischargeability complaint in abeyance. If he rules on the merits of the complaint before the decision of the Tax Court is reached, the bankruptcy court's decision would bind the debtor as to nondischargeable taxes and the Tax Court would be governed by that decision under principles of res judicata. If the bankruptcy judge does not rule on the merits of the complaint before the decision of the Tax Court is reached, the bankruptcy court will be bound by the decision of the Tax Court as it affects the amount of any claim against the debtor's estate.

If the Internal Revenue Service does not file a complaint to determine dischargeability and the automatic stay on a pending Tax Court proceeding is not lifted, the bankruptcy court could determine the merits of any tax claim against the estate. That decision will not bind the debtor personally because he would not have been personally before the bankruptcy court unless the debtor himself asks the bankruptcy court to rule on his personal liability. In any such situation where no party filed a dischargeability petition, the debtor would have access to the Tax Court to determine his personal liability for a nondischargeable tax debt. While the Tax Court in such a situation could take into account the ruling of the bankruptcy court on claims against the estate in deciding the debtor's personal liability, the bankruptcy court's ruling would not bind the Tax Court under principles of res judicata, because the debtor, in that situation, would not have been personally before the bankruptcy court.

If neither the debtor nor the Internal Revenue Service files a claim against the estate or a request to rule on the debtor's personal liability, any pending tax court proceeding would be stayed until the closing of the bankruptcy case, at which time the stay on the tax court would cease and the tax court case could continue for purposes of deciding the merits of the debtor's personal liability for nondischargeable taxes.

Audit of trustee's returns: Under both bills, the bankruptcy court could determine the amount of any administrative period taxes. The Senate amendment, however, provided for an expedited audit procedure, which was mandatory in some cases. The House amendment (sec. 505(b)), adopts the provision of the House bill allowing the trustee discretion in all cases whether to ask the Internal Revenue Service, or State or local tax authority for a prompt audit of his returns on behalf of the estate. The House amendment, however, adopts the provision of the Senate bill permitting a prompt audit only on the basis of tax returns filed by the trustee for completed taxable periods. Procedures for a prompt audit set forth in the Senate bill are also adopted in modified form.

Under the procedure, before the case can be closed, the trustee may request a tax audit by the local, State or Federal tax authority of all tax returns filed by the trustee. The taxing authority would have to notify the trustee and the bankruptcy court within 60 days whether it accepts returns or desires to audit the returns more fully. If an audit is conducted, the taxing authority would have to notify the trustee of tax deficiency within 180 days after the original request, subject to extensions of time if the bankruptcy court approves. If the trustee does not agree with the results of the audit, the trustee could ask the bankruptcy court to resolve the dispute. Once the trustee's tax liability for administration period taxes has thus been determined, the legal effect in a case under chapter 7 or 11 would be to discharge the trustee and any predecessor of the trustee, and also the debtor, from any further liability for these taxes.

The prompt audit procedure would not be available with respect to any tax liability as to which any return required to be filed on behalf of the estate is not filed with the proper tax authority. The House amendment also specifies that a discharge of the trustee or the debtor which would otherwise occur will not be granted, or will be void if the return filed on behalf of the estate reflects fraud or material misrepresentation of facts.

For purposes of the above prompt audit procedures, it is intended that the tax authority with which the request for audit is to be filed is, as to Federal taxes, the office of the District Director in the district where the bankruptcy case is pending.

Under the House amendment, if the trustee does not request a prompt audit, the debtor would not be discharged from possible transferee liability if any assets are returned to the debtor.

Assessment after decision: As indicated above, the commencement of a bankruptcy case automatically stays assessment of any tax (sec. 362(a)(6)). However, the House amendment provides (sec. 505(c)) that if the bankruptcy court renders a final judgment with regard to any tax (under the rules discussed above), the tax authority may then make an assessment (if permitted to do so under otherwise applicable tax law) without waiting for termination of the case or confirmation of a reorganization plan.

Trustee's authority to appeal tax cases: The equivalent provision in the House bill (sec. 505(b)) and in the Senate bill (sec. 362(h)) authorizing the trustee to prosecute an appeal or review of a tax case are deleted as unnecessary. Section 541(a) of the House amendment provides that property of the estate is to include all legal or equitable interests of the debtor. These interests include the debtor's causes of action, so that the specific provisions of the House and Senate bills are not needed.

Effective and Applicability Provisions

2005 Acts. Amendments by Pub.L. 109–8 effective, except as otherwise provided, 180 days after April 20, 2005, and inapplicable with respect to cases commenced under Title 11 before the effective date, see Pub.L. 109–8, § 1501, set out as a note under 11 U.S.C.A. § 101.

1984 Acts. Amendment by Pub.L. 98–353 effective with respect to cases filed 90 days after July 10, 1984, see section 552(a), formerly 553(a), of Pub.L. 98–353, set out as a note under section 101 of this title.

CROSS REFERENCES

Declaratory judgments, see 28 USCA § 2201.

§ 506. Determination of secured status

(a)(1) An allowed claim of a creditor secured by a lien on property in which the estate has an interest, or that is subject to setoff under section 553 of this title, is a secured claim to the extent of the value of such creditor's interest in the estate's interest in such property, or to the extent of the amount subject to setoff, as the case may be, and is an unsecured claim to the extent that the value of such creditor's interest or the amount so subject to setoff is less than the amount of such allowed claim. Such value shall be determined in light of the purpose of the valuation and of the proposed disposition or use of such property, and in conjunction with any hearing on such disposition or use or on a plan affecting such creditor's interest.

(2) If the debtor is an individual in a case under chapter 7 or 13, such value with respect to personal property securing an allowed claim shall be determined based on the replacement value of such property as of the date of the filing of the petition without deduction for costs of sale or marketing. With respect to property acquired for personal, family, or household purposes, replacement value shall mean the price a retail merchant would charge for property of that kind considering the age and condition of the property at the time value is determined.

(b) To the extent that an allowed secured claim is secured by property the value of which, after any recovery under subsection (c) of this section, is greater than the amount of such claim, there shall be allowed to the holder of such claim, interest on such claim, and any reasonable fees, costs, or charges provided for under the agreement or State statute under which such claim arose.

(c) The trustee may recover from property securing an allowed secured claim the reasonable, necessary costs and expenses of preserving, or disposing of, such property to the extent of any benefit to the holder of such claim, including the payment of all ad valorem property taxes with respect to the property.

(d) To the extent that a lien secures a claim against the debtor that is not an allowed secured claim, such lien is void, unless—

(1) such claim was disallowed only under section 502(b)(5) or 502(e) of this title; or

(2) such claim is not an allowed secured claim due only to the failure of any entity to file a proof of such claim under section 501 of this title.

(Pub.L. 95–598, Nov. 6, 1978, 92 Stat. 2583; Pub.L. 98–353, Title III, § 448, July 10, 1984, 98 Stat. 374; Pub.L. 109–8, Title III, § 327, Title VII, § 712(d), Apr. 20, 2005, 119 Stat. 99, 128.)

HISTORICAL AND STATUTORY NOTES

Revision Notes and Legislative Reports

1978 Acts. Subsection (a) of this section separates an undersecured creditor's claim into two parts: He has a secured claim to the extent of the value of his collateral; and he has an unsecured claim for the balance of his claim. The subsection also provides for the valuation of claims which involve setoffs under section 553. While courts will have to determine value on a case-by-case basis, the subsection makes it clear that valuation is to be determined in light of the purpose of the valuation and the proposed disposition or use of the subject property. This determination shall be made in conjunction with any hearing on such disposition or use of property or on a plan affecting the creditor's interest. To illustrate, a valuation early in the case in a proceeding under sections 361–363 would not be binding upon the debtor or creditor at the time of confirmation of the plan. Throughout the bill, references to secured claims are only to the claim

determined to be secured under this subsection, and not to the full amount of the creditor's claim. This provision abolishes the use of the terms "secured creditor" and "unsecured creditor" and substitutes in their places the terms "secured claim" and "unsecured claim."

Subsection (b) codifies current law by entitling a creditor with an oversecured claim to any reasonable fees (including attorney's fees), costs, or charges provided under the agreement under which the claim arose. These fees, costs, and charges are secured claims to the extent that the value of the collateral exceeds the amount of the underlying claim.

Subsection (c) also codifies current law by permitting the trustee to recover from property the value of which is greater than the sum of the claims secured by a lien on that property the reasonable, necessary costs and expenses of preserving, or disposing of, the property. The recovery is limited to the extent of any benefit to the holder of such claim.

Subsection (d) provides that to the extent a secured claim is not allowed, its lien is void unless the holder had neither actual notice nor knowledge of the case, the lien was not listed by the debtor in a chapter 9 or 11 case or such claim was disallowed only under section 502(e). Senate Report No. 95–989.

Subsection (d) permits liens to pass through the bankruptcy case unaffected. However, if a party in interest requests the court to determine and allow or disallow the claim secured by the lien under section 502 and the claim is not allowed, then the lien is void to the extent that the claim is not allowed. The voiding provision does not apply to claims disallowed only under section 502(e), which requires disallowance of certain claims against the debtor by a codebtor, surety, or guarantor for contribution or reimbursement. House Report No. 95–595.

1984 Acts. Statements by Legislative Leaders, see 1984 U.S.Code Cong. and Adm.News, p. 576.

2005 Acts. House Report No. 109–31(Part I), see 2005 U.S. Code Cong. and Adm. News, p. 88.

Legislative Statements

Section 506(a) of the House amendment adopts the provision contained in the Senate amendment and rejects a contrary provision as contained in H.R. 8200 as passed by the House. The provision contained in the Senate amendment and adopted by the House amendment recognizes that an amount subject to set-off is sufficient to recognize a secured status in the holder of such right. Additionally a determination of what portion of an allowed claim is secured and what portion is unsecured is binding only for the purpose for which the determination is made. Thus determinations for purposes of adequate protection is not binding for purposes of "cram down" on confirmation in a case under chapter 11.

Section 506(b) of the House amendment adopts language contained in the Senate amendment and rejects language contained in H.R. 8200 as passed by the House. If the security agreement between the parties provides for attorneys' fees, it will be enforceable under title 11, notwithstanding contrary law, and is recoverable from the collateral after any recovery under section 506(c).

Section 506(c) of the House amendment was contained in H.R. 8200 as passed by the House and adopted, verbatim, in the Senate amendment. Any time the trustee or debtor in possession expends money to provide for the reasonable and necessary cost and expenses of preserving or disposing of a secured creditor's collateral, the trustee or debtor in possession is entitled to recover such expenses from the secured party or from the property securing an allowed secured claim held by such party.

Section 506(d) of the House amendment is derived from H.R. 8200 as passed by the House and is adopted in lieu of the alternative test provided in section 506(d) of the Senate amendment. For purposes of section 506(d) of the House amendment, the debtor is a party in interest.

Determination of Secured Status: The House amendment deletes section 506(d)(3) of the Senate amendment, which insures that a tax lien securing a nondischargeable tax claim is not voided because a tax authority with notice or knowledge of the bankruptcy case fails to file a claim for the liability (as it may elect not to do, if it is clear there are insufficient assets to pay the liability). Since the House amendment retains section 506(d) of the House bill that a lien is not voided unless a party in interest has requested that the court determine and allow or disallow the claim, provision of the Senate amendment is not necessary.

References in Text

Chapter 7 or 13, referred to in subsec. (a)(2), is chapter 7 or 13 of this title, 11 U.S.C.A. § 701 et seq. or 11 U.S.C.A. § 1301 et seq.

Effective and Applicability Provisions

2005 Acts. Amendments by Pub.L. 109–8 effective, except as otherwise provided, 180 days after April 20, 2005, and inapplicable with respect to cases commenced under Title 11 before the effective date, see Pub.L. 109–8, § 1501, set out as a note under 11 U.S.C.A. § 101.

1984 Acts. Amendment by Pub.L. 98–353 effective with respect to cases filed 90 days after July 10, 1984, see section 552(a), formerly 553(a), of Pub.L. 98–353, set out as a note under section 101 of this title.

CROSS REFERENCES

Applicability of this section in Chapter 9 cases, see 11 USCA § 901.

Automatic preservation of avoided transfer, see 11 USCA § 551.

Claims secured by lien on property of estate, see 11 USCA § 1111.

Contents of plan and interest on interest, see 11 USCA §§ 1123, 1222, and 1322.

Effect of dismissal, see 11 USCA § 349.

Liability of exempted property for debtor's debt, see 11 USCA § 522.

Postpetition effect of security interest, see 11 USCA § 552.

§ 507. Priorities

(a) The following expenses and claims have priority in the following order:

(1) First:

(A) Allowed unsecured claims for domestic support obligations that, as of the date of the filing of the petition in a case under this title, are owed to or recoverable by a spouse, former spouse, or child of the debtor, or such child's parent, legal guardian, or responsible relative, without regard to whether the claim is filed by such person or is filed by a governmental unit on behalf of such person, on the condition that funds received under this paragraph by a governmental unit under this title after the date of the filing of the petition shall be applied and distributed in accordance with applicable nonbankruptcy law.

(B) Subject to claims under subparagraph (A), allowed unsecured claims for domestic support obligations that, as of the date of the filing of the petition, are assigned by a spouse, former spouse, child of the debtor, or such child's parent, legal guardian, or responsible relative to a governmental unit (unless such obligation is assigned voluntarily by the spouse, former spouse, child, parent, legal guardian, or responsible relative of the child for the purpose of collecting the debt) or are owed directly to or recoverable by a governmental unit under applicable nonbankruptcy law, on the condition that funds received under this paragraph by a governmental unit under this title after the date of the filing of the petition be applied and distributed in accordance with applicable nonbankruptcy law.

(C) If a trustee is appointed or elected under section 701, 702, 703, 1104, 1202, or 1302, the administrative expenses of the trustee allowed under paragraphs (1)(A), (2), and (6) of section 503(b) shall be paid before payment of claims under subparagraphs (A) and (B), to the extent that the trustee administers assets that are otherwise available for the payment of such claims.

(2) Second, administrative expenses allowed under section 503(b) of this title, unsecured claims of any Federal reserve bank related to loans made through programs or facilities authorized under section 13(3) of the Federal Reserve Act (12 U.S.C. 343), and any fees and charges assessed against the estate under chapter 123 of title 28.

(3) Third, unsecured claims allowed under section 502(f) of this title.

(4) Fourth, allowed unsecured claims, but only to the extent of $12,850[1] for each individual or corporation, as the case may be, earned within 180 days before the date of the filing of the petition or the date of the cessation of the debtor's business, whichever occurs first, for—

(A) wages, salaries, or commissions, including vacation, severance, and sick leave pay earned by an individual; or

(B) sales commissions earned by an individual or by a corporation with only 1 employee, acting as an independent contractor in the sale of goods or services for the debtor in the ordinary course of the debtor's business if, and only if, during the 12 months preceding that date, at least 75 percent of the amount that the individual or corporation earned by acting as an independent contractor in the sale of goods or services was earned from the debtor.

(5) Fifth, allowed unsecured claims for contributions to an employee benefit plan—

(A) arising from services rendered within 180 days before the date of the filing of the petition or the date of the cessation of the debtor's business, whichever occurs first; but only

(B) for each such plan, to the extent of—

(i) the number of employees covered by each such plan multiplied by $12,850 [1]; less

(ii) the aggregate amount paid to such employees under paragraph (4) of this subsection, plus the aggregate amount paid by the estate on behalf of such employees to any other employee benefit plan.

(6) Sixth, allowed unsecured claims of persons—

(A) engaged in the production or raising of grain, as defined in section 557(b) of this title, against a debtor who owns or operates a grain storage facility, as defined in section 557(b) of this title, for grain or the proceeds of grain, or

(B) engaged as a United States fisherman against a debtor who has acquired fish or fish produce from a fisherman through a sale or conversion, and who is engaged in operating a fish produce storage or processing facility—

but only to the extent of $6,325 [1] for each such individual.

(7) Seventh, allowed unsecured claims of individuals, to the extent of $2,850 [1] for each such individual, arising from the deposit, before the commencement of the case, of money in connection with the purchase, lease, or rental of property, or the purchase of services, for the personal, family, or household use of such individuals, that were not delivered or provided.

(8) Eighth, allowed unsecured claims of governmental units, only to the extent that such claims are for—

(A) a tax on or measured by income or gross receipts for a taxable year ending on or before the date of the filing of the petition—

(i) for which a return, if required, is last due, including extensions, after three years before the date of the filing of the petition;

(ii) assessed within 240 days before the date of the filing of the petition, exclusive of—

(I) any time during which an offer in compromise with respect to that tax was pending or in effect during that 240–day period, plus 30 days; and

(II) any time during which a stay of proceedings against collections was in effect in a prior case under this title during that 240–day period, plus 90 days; or

(iii) other than a tax of a kind specified in section 523(a)(1)(B) or 523(a)(1)(C) of this title,

not assessed before, but assessable, under applicable law or by agreement, after, the commencement of the case;

(B) a property tax incurred before the commencement of the case and last payable without penalty after one year before the date of the filing of the petition;

(C) a tax required to be collected or withheld and for which the debtor is liable in whatever capacity;

(D) an employment tax on a wage, salary, or commission of a kind specified in paragraph (4) of this subsection earned from the debtor before the date of the filing of the petition, whether or not actually paid before such date, for which a return is last due, under applicable law or under any extension, after three years before the date of the filing of the petition;

(E) an excise tax on—

(i) a transaction occurring before the date of the filing of the petition for which a return, if required, is last due, under applicable law or under any extension, after three years before the date of the filing of the petition; or

(ii) if a return is not required, a transaction occurring during the three years immediately preceding the date of the filing of the petition;

(F) a customs duty arising out of the importation of merchandise—

(i) entered for consumption within one year before the date of the filing of the petition;

(ii) covered by an entry liquidated or reliquidated within one year before the date of the filing of the petition; or

(iii) entered for consumption within four years before the date of the filing of the petition but unliquidated on such date, if the Secretary of the Treasury certifies that failure to liquidate such entry was due to an investigation pending on such date into assessment of antidumping or countervailing duties or fraud, or if information needed for the proper appraisement or classification of such merchandise was not available to the appropriate customs officer before such date; or

(G) a penalty related to a claim of a kind specified in this paragraph and in compensation for actual pecuniary loss.

An otherwise applicable time period specified in this paragraph shall be suspended for any period during which a governmental unit is prohibited under applicable nonbankruptcy law from collecting a tax as a result of a request by the debtor for a hearing and an appeal of any collection action taken or proposed against the debtor, plus 90 days; plus any time during which the stay of proceedings was in effect in a prior case under this title or during which collection was precluded by the existence of 1 or more confirmed plans under this title, plus 90 days.

---

(9) Ninth, allowed unsecured claims based upon any commitment by the debtor to a Federal depository institutions regulatory agency (or predecessor to such agency) to maintain the capital of an insured depository institution.

(10) Tenth, allowed claims for death or personal injury resulting from the operation of a motor vehicle or vessel if such operation was unlawful because the debtor was intoxicated from using alcohol, a drug, or another substance.

(b) If the trustee, under section 362, 363, or 364 of this title, provides adequate protection of the interest of a holder of a claim secured by a lien on property of the debtor and if, notwithstanding such protection, such creditor has a claim allowable under subsection (a)(2) of this section arising from the stay of action against such property under section 362 of this title, from the use, sale, or lease of such property under section 363 of this title, or from the granting of a lien under section 364(d) of this title, then such creditor's claim under such subsection shall have priority over every other claim allowable under such subsection.

(c) For the purpose of subsection (a) of this section, a claim of a governmental unit arising from an erroneous refund or credit of a tax has the same priority as a claim for the tax to which such refund or credit relates.

(d) An entity that is subrogated to the rights of a holder of a claim of a kind specified in subsection (a)(1), (a)(4), (a)(5), (a)(6), (a)(7), (a)(8), or (a)(9) of this section is not subrogated to the right of the holder of such claim to priority under such subsection.

(Pub.L. 95–598, Nov. 6, 1978, 92 Stat. 2583; Pub.L. 98–353, Title III, §§ 350, 449, July 10, 1984, 98 Stat. 358, 374; Pub.L. 101–647, Title XXV, § 2522(d), Nov. 29, 1990, 104 Stat. 4867; Pub.L. 103–394, Title I, § 108(c), Title II, § 207, Title III, § 304(c), Title V, § 501(b)(3), (d)(11), Oct. 22, 1994, 108 Stat. 4112, 4123, 4132, 4142, 4145; Pub.L. 109–8, Title II, §§ 212, 223, Title VII, §§ 705, 706, Title XIV, § 1401, Title XV, § 1502(a)(1), Apr. 20, 2005, 119 Stat. 51, 62, 126, 214, 216; Pub.L. 111–203, Title XI, § 1101(b), July 21, 2010, 124 Stat. 2115; Pub.L. 111–327, § 2(a)(15), Dec. 22, 2010, 124 Stat. 3559.)

¹ Dollar amount as adjusted by the Judicial Conference of the United States. See Adjustment of Dollar Amounts notes set out under this section and 11 U.S.C.A. § 104.

HISTORICAL AND STATUTORY NOTES

Revision Notes and Legislative Reports

1978 Acts. Section 507 specifies the kinds of claims that are entitled to priority in distribution, and the order of their priority. Paragraph (1) grants first priority to allowed administrative expenses and to fees and charges assessed against the estate under chapter 123 of title 28 [section 1911 et seq. of Title 28, Judiciary and Judicial Procedure]. Taxes included as administrative expenses under section 503(b)(1) of the bill generally receive the first priority, but the bill makes certain qualifications: Examples of these specially treated claims are the estate's liability for recapture of an investment tax credit claimed by the debtor before the title 11 case (this liability receives sixth priority) and the estate's employment tax liabilities on wages earned before, but paid after, the petition was filed (this liability generally receives the same priority as the wages).

"Involuntary gap" creditors, granted first priority under current law, are granted second priority by paragraph (2). This priority, covering claims arising in the ordinary course of the debtor's business or financial affairs after a title 11 case has begun but before a trustee is appointed or before the order for relief, includes taxes incurred during the conduct of such activities.

Paragraph (3) expands and increases the wage priority found in current section 64a(2) [section 104(a)(2) of former Title 11]. The amount entitled to priority is raised from $600 to $1800. The former figure was last adjusted in 1926. Inflation has made it nearly meaningless, and the bill brings it more than up to date. The three month limit of current law is retained, but is modified to run from the earlier of the date of the filing of the petition or the date of the cessation of the debtor's business. The priority is expanded to cover vacation, severance, and sick leave pay. The bill adds to the third priority so-called "trust fund" taxes, that is, withheld income taxes and the employees' share of the social security or railroad retirement taxes, but only to the extent that the wages on which taxes are imposed are themselves entitled to third priority.

The employer's share, the employment tax and the employer's share of the social security or railroad retirement tax on third priority compensation, is also included in the third priority category, but only if, and to the extent that the wages and related trust fund taxes have first been paid in full. Because of the claimants urgent need for their wages in the typical cases, the employer's taxes should not be paid before the wage claims entitled to priority, as well as the related trust fund taxes, are fully paid.

Paragraph (4) overrules *United States v. Embassy Restaurant*, 359 U.S. 29 (1958) [79 S.Ct. 554, 3 L.Ed.2d 601], which held that fringe benefits were not entitled to wage priority status. The bill recognizes the realities of labor contract negotiations, where fringe benefits may be substituted for wage demands. The priority granted is limited to claims for contributions to employee benefit plans such as pension plans, health or life insurance plans, and others, arising from services rendered within 120 days before the commencement of the case or the date of cessation of the debtor's business, whichever occurs first. The dollar limit placed on the total of all contributions payable under this paragraph is equal to the difference between the maximum allowable priority under paragraph (3), $1,800, times the number of employees covered by the plan less the actual distributions under paragraph (3) with respect to these employees.

Paragraph (5) is a new priority for consumer creditors—those who have deposited money in connection with the purchase, lease, or rental of property, or the purchase of services, for their personal, family, or household use, that were not delivered or provided. The priority amount is not to exceed $600. In order to reach only those persons most deserving of this special priority, it is limited to individuals whose adjustable gross income from all sources derived does not exceed $20,000. See Senate Hearings, testimony of Prof. Vern Countryman, at pp. 848–849. The income of the husband and wife should be aggregated for the purposes of the $20,000 limit if either or both spouses assert such a priority claim.

The sixth priority is for certain taxes. Priority is given to income taxes for a taxable year that ended on or before the date of the filing of the petition, if the last due date of the return for such year occurred not more than 3 years immediately before the date on which the petition was filed (§ 507(a)(6)(A)(i)). For the purposes of this rule, the last due date of the return is the last date under any extension of time to file the return which the taxing authority may have granted the debtor.

Employment taxes and transfer taxes (including gift, estate, sales, use and other excise taxes) are also given sixth priority if the transaction or event which gave rise to the tax occurred before the petition date, provided that the required return or report of such tax liabilities was last due within 3 years before the petition was filed or was last due after the petition date (§ 507(a)(6)(A)(ii).) The employment taxes covered under this rule are the employer's share of the social security and railroad retirement taxes and required employer payments toward unemployment insurance.

Priority is given to income taxes and other taxes of a kind described in section 507(a)(6)(A)(i) and (ii) which the Federal, State, or local tax authority had assessed within 3 years after the last due date of the return, that is, including any extension of time to file the return, if the debtor filed in title 11 within 240 days after the assessment was made (§ 507(a)(6)(B)(i)). This rule may bring into the sixth priority the debtor's tax liability for some taxable years which would not qualify for priority under the general three-year rule of section 507(a)(6)(A).

The sixth priority category also includes taxes which the tax authority was barred by law from assessing or collecting at any time during the 300 days before the petition under title 11 was filed (§ 507(a)(6)(B)(ii)). In the case of certain Federal taxes, this preserves a priority for tax liabilities for years more than three years before the filing of the petition where the debtor and the Internal Revenue Service were negotiating over an audit of the debtor's returns or were engaged in litigation in the Tax Court. In such situations, the tax law prohibits the service's right to assess a tax deficiency until ninety days after the service sends the taxpayer a deficiency letter or, if the taxpayer files a petition in the Tax Court during that 90-day period, until the outcome of the litigation. A similar priority exists in present law, except that the taxing authority is allowed no time to assess and collect the taxes after the restrictions on assessment (discussed above) are lifted. Some taxpayers have exploited this loophole by filing in bankruptcy immediately after the end of the 90-day period or immediately after the close of Tax Court proceedings. The bill remedies this defect by preserving a priority for taxes the assessment of which was barred by law by giving the tax authority 300 days within which to make the assessment after the lifting of the bar and then to collect or file public notice of its tax lien. Thus, if a taxpayer files a title 11 petition at any time during that 300-day period, the tax deficiency will be entitled to priority. If the petition is filed more than 300 days after the restriction on assessment was lifted, the taxing authority will not have priority for the tax deficiency.

Taxes for which an offer in compromise was withdrawn by the debtor, or rejected by a governmental unit, within 240 days before the petition date (§ 507(a)(6)(B)(iii)) will also receive sixth priority. This rule closes a loophole under present law under which, following an assessment of tax, some taxpayers have submitted a formal offer in compromise, dragged out negotiations with the taxing authority until the

tax liability would lose priority under the three-year priority period of present law, and then filed in bankruptcy before the governmental unit could take collection steps.

Also included are certain taxes for which no return or report is required by law (§ 507(a)(6)(C)), if the taxable transaction occurred within three years before the petition was filed.

Taxes (not covered by the third priority) which the debtor was required by law to withhold or collect from others and for which he is liable in any capacity, regardless of the age of the tax claims (§ 507(a)(6)(D)) are included. This category covers the so-called "trust fund" taxes, that is, income taxes which an employer is required to withhold from the pay of his employees, the employees' shares of social security and railroad retirement taxes, and also Federal unemployment insurance. This category also includes excise taxes which a seller of goods or services is required to collect from a buyer and pay over to a taxing authority.

This category also covers the liability of a responsible corporate officer under the Internal Revenue Code [Title 26] for income taxes or for the employees' share of employment taxes which, under the tax law, the employer was required to withhold from the wages of employees. This priority will operate where a person found to be a responsible officer has himself filed a petition under title 11, and the priority covers the debtor's liability as an officer under the Internal Revenue Code [Title 26], regardless of the age of the tax year to which the tax relates.

The priority rules under the bill governing employment taxes can be summarized as follows: In the case of wages earned and actually paid before the petition under title 11 was filed, the liability for the employees' share of the employment taxes, regardless of the prepetition year in which the wages were earned and paid. The employer's share of the employment taxes on all wages earned and paid before the petition receive sixth priority; generally, these taxes will be those for which a return was due within three years before the petition. With respect to wages earned by employees before the petition but actually paid by the trustee after the title 11 case commenced, taxes required to be withheld receives the same priority as the wages themselves. Thus, the employees' share of taxes on third priority wages also receives third priority. Taxes on the balance of such wages receive no priority and are collectible only as general claims because the wages themselves are payable only as general claims and liability for the taxes arises only to the extent the wages are actually paid. The employer's share of employment taxes on third priority wages earned before the petition but paid after the petition was filed receives third priority, but only if the wages in this category have first been paid in full. Assuming there are sufficient funds to pay third priority wages and the related employer taxes in full, the employer's share of taxes on the balance of wage payments becomes a general claim (because the wages themselves are payable as general claims). Both the employees' and the employer's share of employment taxes on wages earned and paid after the petition was filed receive first priority as administrative expenses.

Also covered by this sixth priority are property taxes required to be assessed within 3 years before the filing of the petition (§ 507(a)(6)(E)).

Taxes attributable to a tentative carryback adjustment received by the debtor before the petition was filed, such as a "quickie refund" received under section 6411 of the Internal Revenue Code [section 6411 of Title 26, Internal Revenue

Code] (§ 507(a)(6)(F)) are included. However, the tax claim against the debtor will rein a prepetition loss year for which the tax return was last due, including extensions, within 3 years before the petition was filed.

Taxes resulting from a recapture, occasioned by a transfer during bankruptcy, of a tax credit or deduction taken during an earlier tax year (§ 507(a)(6)(G)) are included. A typical example occurs when there is a sale by the trustee of depreciable property during the case and depreciation deductions taken in prepetition years are subject to recapture under section 1250 of the Code [section 1250 of Title 26, Internal Revenue Code].

Taxes owed by the debtor as a transferee of assets from another person who is liable for a tax, if the tax claim against the transferor would have received priority in a chapter 11 case commenced by the transferor within 1 year before the date of the petition filed by the transferee (§ 507(a)(6)(H)), are included.

Also included are certain tax payments required to have been made during the 1 year immediately before the petition was filed, where the debtor had previously entered into a deferred payment agreement (including an offer in compromise) to pay an agreed liability in periodic installments but had become delinquent in one or more installments before the petition was filed (§ 507(a)(6)(I)). This priority covers all types of deferred or part payment agreements. The priority covers only installments which first became due during the 1 year before the petition but which remained unpaid at the date of the petition. The priority does not come into play, however, if before the case began or during the case, the debtor and the taxing authority agree to a further extension of time to pay the delinquent amounts.

Certain tax-related liabilities which are not true taxes or which are not collected by regular assessment procedures (§ 507(a)(6)(J)) are included. One type of liability covered in this category is the liability under section 3505 of the Internal Revenue Code [section 3505 of Title 26, Internal Revenue Code] of a lender who pays wages directly to employees of another employer or who supplies funds to an employer for the payment of wages. Another is the liability under section 6332 of the Internal Revenue Code [section 6332 of Title 26, Internal Revenue Code], of a person who fails to turn over money or property of the taxpayer in response to a levy. Since the taxing authority must collect such a liability from the third party by suit rather than normal assessment procedures, an extra year is added to the normal 3-year priority periods. If a suit was commenced by the taxing authority within the four-year period and before the petition was filed, the priority is also preserved, provided that the suit had not terminated more than 1 year before the date of the filing of the petition.

Also included are certain unpaid customs duties which have not grown unreasonably "stale" (§ 507(a)(6)(K)). These include duties on imports entered for consumption with 3 years before the filing of the petition if the duties are still unliquidated on the petition date. If an import entry has been liquidated (in general, liquidation is in an administrative determination of the value and tariff rate of the item) or reliquidated, within two years of the filing of the petition the customs liability is given priority. If the Secretary of the Treasury certifies that customs duties were not liquidated because of an investigation into possible assessment of antidumping or countervailing duties, or because of fraud penalties, duties not liquidated for this reason during the five years

before the importer filed under title 11 also will receive priority.

Subsection (a) of this section also provides specifically that interest on sixth priority tax claims accrued before the filing of the petition is also entitled to sixth priority.

Subsection (b) of this section provides that any fine or penalty which represents compensation for actual pecuniary loss of a governmental unit, and which involves a tax liability entitled to sixth priority, is to receive the same priority.

Subsection (b) also provides that a claim arising from an erroneous refund or credit of tax is to be given the same priority as the tax to which the refund or credit relates. Senate Report No. 95–989.

1984 Acts. Statements by Legislative Leaders, see 1984 U.S. Code Cong. and Adm. News, p. 576.

1990 Acts. House Report No. 101–681(I), see 1990 U.S. Code Cong. and Adm. News, p. 6472.

1994 Acts. House Report No. 103–835, see 1994 U.S. Code Cong. and Adm. News, p. 3340.

2005 Acts. House Report No. 109–31(Part I), see 2005 U.S. Code Cong. and Adm. News, p. 88.

Legislative Statements

Section 507(a)(3) of the House amendment represents a compromise dollar amount and date for the priority between similar provisions contained in H.R. 8200 as passed by the House and the Senate amendments. A similar compromise is contained in section 507(a)(4).

Section 507(a)(5) represents a compromise on amount between the priority as contained in H.R. 8200 as passed by the House and the Senate amendment. The Senate provision for limiting the priority to consumers having less than a fixed gross income is deleted.

Section 507(a)(6) of the House amendment represents a compromise between similar provisions contained in H.R. 8200 as passed by the House and the Senate amendment.

Section 507(b) of the House amendment is new and is derived from the compromise contained in the House amendment with respect to adequate protection under section 361. Subsection (b) provides that to the extent adequate protection of the interest of a holder of a claim proves to be inadequate, then the creditor's claim is given priority over every other allowable claim entitled to distribution under section 507(a). Section 507(b) of the Senate amendment is deleted.

Section 507(c) of the House amendment is new. Section 507(d) of the House amendment prevents subrogation with respect to priority for certain priority claims. Subrogation with respect to priority is intended to be permitted for administrative claims and claims arising during the gap period.

Priorities: Under the House amendment, taxes receive priority as follows:

First. Administration expenses: The amendment generally follows the Senate amendment in providing expressly that taxes incurred during the administration of the estate share the first priority given to administrative expenses generally. Among the taxes which receives first priority, as defined in section 503, are the employees' and the employer's shares of employment taxes on wages earned and paid after the petition is filed. Section 503(b)(1) also includes in administration expenses a tax liability arising from an excessive allowance by a tax authority of a "quickie refund" to the estate. (In the case of Federal taxes, such refunds are allowed under special rules based on net operating loss carrybacks (section 6411 of the Internal Revenue Code) [section 6411 of Title 26, Internal Revenue Code]).

An exception is made to first priority treatment for taxes incurred by the estate with regard to the employer's share of employment taxes on wages earned from the debtor before the petition but paid from the estate after the petition has been filed. In this situation, the employer's tax receives either sixth priority or general claim treatment.

The House amendment also adopts the provisions of the Senate amendment which include in the definition of administrative expenses under section 503 any fine, penalty (including "additions to tax" under applicable tax laws) or reduction in credit imposed on the estate.

Second. "Involuntary gap" claims: "Involuntary gap" creditors are granted second priority by paragraph (2) of section 507(a). This priority includes tax claims arising in the ordinary course of the debtor's business or financial affairs after he has been placed involuntarily in bankruptcy but before a trustee is appointed or before the order for relief.

Third. Certain taxes on prepetition wages: Wage claims entitled to third priority are for compensation which does not exceed $2,000 and was earned during the 90 days before the filing of the bankruptcy petition or the cessation of the debtor's business. Certain employment taxes receive third priority in payment from the estate along with the payment of wages to which the taxes relate. In the case of wages earned before the filing of the petition, but paid by the trustee (rather than by the debtor) after the filing of the petition, claims or the employees' share of the employment taxes (withheld income taxes and the employees' share of the social security or railroad retirement tax) receive third priority to the extent the wage claims themselves are entitled to this priority.

In the case of wages earned from and paid by the debtor before the filing of the petition, the employer's share of the employment taxes on these wages paid by the debtor receives sixth priority or, if not entitled to that priority, are treated only as general claims. Under the House amendment, the employer's share of employment taxes on wages earned by employees of the debtor, but paid by the trustee after the filing of the bankruptcy petition, will also receive sixth priority to the extent that claims for the wages receive third priority. To the extent the claims for wages do not receive third priority, but instead are treated only as general claims, claims for the employer's share of the employment taxes attributable to those wages will also be treated as general claims. In calculating the amounts payable as general wage claims, the trustee must pay the employer's share of employment taxes on such wages.

Sixth priority. The House amendment modifies the provisions of both the House bill and Senate amendment in the case of sixth priority taxes. Under the amendment, the following Federal, State and local taxes are included in the sixth priority:

First. Income and gross receipts taxes incurred before the date of the petition for which the last due date of the return, including all extensions of time granted to file the return, occurred within 3 years before the date on which the petition was filed, or after the petition date. Under this rule, the due date of the return, rather than the date on which the taxes were assessed, determines the priority.

Second. Income and gross receipts taxes assessed at any time within 240 days before the petition date. Under this rule, the date on which the governmental unit assesses the tax, rather than the due date of the return, determines the priority.

If, following assessment of a tax, the debtor submits an offer in compromise to the governmental unit, the House amendment provides that the 240-day period is to be suspended for the duration of the offer and will resume running after the offer is withdrawn or rejected by the governmental unit, but the tax liability will receive priority if the title 11 petition is filed during the balance of the 240-day period or during a minimum of 30 days after the offer is withdrawn or rejected. This rule modifies a provision of the Senate amendment dealing specifically with offers in compromise. Under the modified rule, if, after the assessment, an offer in compromise is submitted by the debtor and is still pending (without having been accepted or rejected) at the date on which a title 11 petition is filed, the underlying liability will receive sixth priority. However, if an assessment of a tax liability is made but the tax is not collected within 240 days, the tax will not receive priority under section 507(a)(6)(A)(i) and the debtor cannot revive a priority for that tax by submitting an offer in compromise.

Third. Income and gross receipts taxes not assessed before the petition date but still permitted, under otherwise applicable tax laws, to be assessed. Thus, for example, a prepetition tax liability is to receive sixth priority under this rule if, under the applicable statute of limitations, the tax liability can still be assessed by the tax authority. This rule also covers situations referred to in section 507(a)(6)(B)(ii) of the Senate amendment where the assessment or collection of a tax was prohibited before the petition pending exhaustion of judicial or administrative remedies, except that the House amendment eliminates the 300-day limitation of the Senate bill. So, for example, if before the petition a debtor was engaged in litigation in the Tax Court, during which the Internal Revenue Code [Title 26] bars the Internal Revenue Service from assessing or collecting the tax, and if the tax court decision is made in favor of the Service before the petition under title 11 is filed, thereby lifting the restrictions on assessment and collection, the tax liability will receive sixth priority even if the tax authority does not make an assessment within 300 days before the petition (provided, of course, that the statute of limitations on assessment has not expired by the petition date).

In light of the above categories of the sixth priority, and tax liability of the debtor (under the Internal Revenue Code [Title 26] or State or local law) as a transferee of property from another person will receive sixth priority without the limitations contained in the Senate amendment so long as the transferee liability had not been assessed by the tax authority by the petition date but could still have been assessed by that date under the applicable tax statute of limitations or, if the transferee liability had been assessed before the petition, the assessment was made no more than 240 days before the petition date.

Also in light of the above categories, the treatment of prepetition tax liabilities arising from an excessive allowance to the debtor of a tentative carryback adjustment, such as a "quickie refund" under section 6411 of the Internal Revenue Code [section 6411 of Title 26, Internal Revenue Code], is revised as follows: If the tax authority has assessed the additional tax before the petition, the tax liability will receive priority if the date of assessment was within 240 days before the petition date. If the tax authority had not assessed the additional tax by the petition, the tax liability will still receive priority so long as, on the petition date, assessment of the liability is not barred by the statute of limitations.

Fourth. Any property tax assessed before the commencement of the case and last payable without penalty within 1 year before the petition, or thereafter.

Fifth. Taxes which the debtor was required by law to withhold or collect from others and for which he is liable in any capacity, regardless of the age of the tax claims. This category covers the so-called "trust fund" taxes, that is, income taxes which an employer is required to withhold from the pay of his employees, and the employees' share of social security taxes.

In addition, this category includes the liability of a responsible officer under the Internal Revenue Code (Sec. 6672 [section 6672 of Title 26, Internal Revenue Code]) for income taxes or for the employees' share of social security taxes which that officer was responsible for withholding from the wages of employees and paying to the Treasury, although he was not himself the employer. This priority will operate when a person found to be a responsible officer has himself filed in title 11, and the priority will cover the debtor's responsible officer liability regardless of the age of the tax year to which the tax relates. The U.S. Supreme Court has interpreted present law to require the same result as will be reached under this rule. *U.S. v. Sotelo,* 436 U.S. 268 (1978) [98 S.Ct. 1795, 56 L.Ed.2d 275, rehearing denied 98 S.Ct. 3126, 438 U.S. 907, 57 L.Ed.2d 1150].

This category also includes the liability under section 3505 of the Internal Revenue Code [section 3505 of Title 26, Internal Revenue Code] of a taxpayer who loans money for the payment of wages or other compensation.

Sixth. The employer's share of employment taxes on wages paid before the petition and on third-priority wages paid postpetition by the estate. The priority rules under the House amendment governing employment taxes can thus be summarized as follows: Claims for the employees' shares of employment taxes attributable to wages both earned and paid before the filing of the petition are to receive sixth priority. In the case of employee wages earned, but not paid, before the filing of the bankruptcy petition, claims for the employees' share of employment taxes receive third priority to the extent the wages themselves receive third priority. Claims which relate to wages earned before the petition, but not paid before the petition (and which are not entitled to the third priority under the rule set out above), will be paid as general claims. Since the related wages will receive no priority, the related employment taxes would also be paid as nonpriority general claims.

The employer's share of the employment taxes on wages earned and paid before the bankruptcy petition will receive sixth priority to the extent the return for these taxes was last due (including extensions of time) within 3 years before the filing of the petition, or was due after the petition was filed. Older tax claims of this nature will be payable as general claims. In the case of wages earned by employees before the petition, but actually paid by the trustee (as claims against the estate) after the title 11 case commenced, the employer's share of the employment taxes on third priority wages will be payable as sixth priority claims and the employer's taxes on prepetition wages which are treated only as general claims will be payable only as general claims. In calculating the amounts payable as general wage claims, the trustee must pay the employer's share of employment taxes on such wages. The House amendment thus deletes the provision of the Senate amendment that certain employer taxes receive third priority and are to be paid immediately after payment of third priority wages and the employees' shares of employment taxes on those wages.

In the case of employment taxes relating to wages earned and paid after the petition, both the employees' shares and the employer's share will receive first priority as administration expenses of the estate.

Seventh. Excise taxes on transactions for which a return, if required, is last due, under otherwise applicable law or under any extension of time to file the return, within 3 years before the petition was filed, or thereafter. If a return is not required with regard to a particular excise tax, priority is given if the transaction or event itself occurred within 3 years before the date on which the title 11 petition was filed. All Federal, State or local taxes generally considered or expressly treated as excises are covered by this category, including sales taxes, estate and gift taxes, gasoline and special fuel taxes, and wagering and truck taxes.

Eighth. Certain unpaid customs duties. The House amendment covers in this category duties on imports entered for consumption within 1 year before the filing of the petition, but which are still unliquidated on the petition date; duties covered by an entry liquidated or reliquidated within 1 year before the petition date; and any duty on merchandise entered for consumption within 4 years before the petition but not liquidated on the petition date, if the Secretary of the Treasury or his delegate certifies that duties were not liquidated because of possible assessment of antidumping or countervailing duties or fraud penalties.

For purposes of the above priority rules, the House amendment adopts the provision of the Senate bill that any tax liability which, under otherwise applicable tax law, is collectible in the form of a "penalty," is to be treated in the same manner as a tax liability. In bankruptcy terminology, such tax liabilities are referred to as pecuniary loss penalties. Thus, any tax liability which under the Internal Revenue Code [Title 26] or State or local tax law is payable as a "penalty," in addition to the liability of a responsible person under section 6672 of the Internal Revenue Code [section 6672 of Title 26, Internal Revenue Code] will be entitled to the priority which the liability would receive if it were expressly labeled as a "tax" under the applicable tax law. However, a tax penalty which is punitive in nature is given subordinated treatment under section 726(a)(4).

The House amendment also adopts the provision of the Senate amendment that a claim arising from an erroneous refund or credit of tax, other than a "quickie refund," is to receive the same priority as the tax to which the refund or credit relates.

The House amendment deletes the express provision of the Senate amendment that a tax liability is to receive sixth priority if it satisfies any one of the subparagraphs of section 507(a)(6) even if the liability fails to satisfy the terms of one or more other subparagraphs. No change of substance is intended by the deletion, however, in light of section 102(5) of the House amendment, providing a rule of construction that the word "or" is not intended to be exclusive.

The House amendment deletes from the express priority categories of the Senate amendment the priority for a debtor's liability as a third party for failing to surrender property or to pay an obligation in response to a levy for taxes of another, and the priority for amounts provided for under deferred payment agreements between a debtor and the tax authority.

The House amendment also adopts the substance of the definition in section 346(a) the Senate amendment of when taxes are to be considered "incurred" except that the House amendment applies these definitions solely for purposes of determining which category of section 507 tests the priority of a particular tax liability. Thus, for example, the House amendment contains a special rule for the treatment of taxes under the 45-day exception to the preference rules under section 547 and the definitions of when a tax is incurred for priority purposes are not to apply to such preference rules. Under the House amendment, for purposes of the priority rules, a tax on income for a particular period is to be considered "incurred" on the last day of the period. A tax on or measured by some event, such as the payment of wages or a transfer by reason of death or gift, or an excise tax on a sale or other transaction, is to be considered "incurred" on the date of the transaction or event.

References in Text

The Federal Reserve Act, referred to in subsec. (a)(2), is Act Dec. 23, 1913, c. 6, 38 Stat. 251, as amended, which is classified principally to chapter 3 of Title 12, 12 U.S.C.A. § 221 et seq. Section 13(3) of such Act is classified to 12 U.S.C.A. § 343. For complete classification, see References in Text note set out under 12 U.S.C.A. § 226 and Tables.

Codifications

Amendments by Pub.L. 109–8, § 1401, to pars. (4) and (5) of subsec. (a) of this section, as amended by section 212 of Pub.L. 109–8, were made to pars. (3) and (4) of subsec. (a) of this section, as the probable intent of Congress. The redesignation of pars. (3) and (4) as pars. (4) and (5) by section 212 of Pub.L. 109–8 does not take effect until 180 days after April 20, 2005.

Effective and Applicability Provisions

2013 Acts. Increase of dollar amounts by Judicial Conference of the United States by notice published Feb. 21, 2013, 78 F.R. 12089 effective April 1, 2013, and increase not applicable to cases commenced before the effective date of the adjustments, i.e., April 1, 2013. See Adjustment of Dollar Amounts notes under 11 U.S.C.A. § 104 and this section.

2010 Acts. Except as otherwise specifically provided, Pub.L. 111–203 and such amendments by Pub.L. 111–203 are effective 1 day after July 21, 2010, see Pub.L. 111–203, § 4, set out as a note under 12 U.S.C.A. § 5301.

Increase of dollar amounts by Judicial Conference of the United States by notice published Feb. 25, 2010, 75 F.R. 8747 effective April 1, 2010, and increase not applicable to cases commenced before the effective date of the adjustments, i.e., April 1, 2010. See Adjustment of Dollar Amounts notes under 11 U.S.C.A. § 104 and this section.

2007 Acts. Increase of dollar amounts by Judicial Conference of the United States by notice published Feb. 14, 2007, 72 F.R. 7082 effective April 1, 2007, and increase not applicable to cases commenced before the effective date of the adjustments, i.e., April 1, 2007. See Adjustment of Dollar Amounts notes under 11 U.S.C.A. § 104 and this section.

2005 Acts. Pub.L. 109–8, Title XIV, § 1406, Apr. 20, 2005, 119 Stat. 215, as amended Pub.L. 111–327, § 3, Dec. 22, 2010, 124 Stat. 3563, provided that:

"**(a) Effective date.**—Except as provided in subsection (b) [of this note], this title and the amendments made by this title [amending this section and 11 U.S.C.A. §§ 523, 548, 1104, 1114, and enacting provisions set out as a note under 11 U.S.C.A. § 523] shall take effect on the date of the enactment of this Act [Apr. 20, 2005].

"**(b) Application of amendments.**—

"**(1) In general.**—Except as provided in paragraph (2), the amendments made by this title [amending this section and 11 U.S.C.A. §§ 523, 548, 1104, 1114, and enacting provisions set out as a note under 11 U.S.C.A. § 523] shall apply only with respect to cases commenced under title 11 of the United States Code [11 U.S.C.A. § 101 et seq.] on or after the date of the enactment of this Act [Apr. 20, 2005].

"**(2) Avoidance period.**—The amendment made by section 1402(1) [amending 11 U.S.C.A. § 548] shall apply only with respect to cases commenced under title 11 of the United States Code more than 1 year after the date of the enactment of this Act [Apr. 20, 2005]."

Amendments by Pub.L. 109–8 effective, except as otherwise provided, 180 days after April 20, 2005, and inapplicable with respect to cases commenced under Title 11 before the effective date, see Pub.L. 109–8, § 1501, set out as a note under 11 U.S.C.A. § 101.

2004 Acts. Adjustment of dollar amounts by Judicial Conference of the United States by notice dated Feb. 18, 2004, 69 F.R. 8482 effective April 1, 2004, and adjustment not applicable to cases commenced before the effective date of the adjustments, i.e., April 1, 2004. See Adjustment of Dollar Amounts notes under 11 U.S.C.A. § 104 and this section.

2001 Acts. Adjustment of dollar amounts by Judicial Conference of the United States by notice dated Feb. 20, 2001, 66 F.R. 10910 effective April 1, 2001, and adjustment not applicable to cases commenced before the effective date of the adjustments, i.e., April 1, 2001. See Adjustment of Dollar Amounts notes under 11 U.S.C.A. § 104 and this section.

1998 Acts. Adjustment of dollar amounts by Judicial Conference of the United States by notice dated Feb. 3, 1998, 63 F.R. 7179 effective April 1, 1998, and adjustment not applicable to cases commenced before the effective date of the adjustments, i.e., April 1, 1998. See Adjustment of Dollar Amounts notes under 11 U.S.C.A. § 104 and this section.

1994 Acts. Amendments by Pub.L. 103–394 effective on Oct. 22, 1994, and not to apply with respect to cases commenced under Title 11 of the United States Code before Oct. 22, 1994, see section 702 of Pub.L. 103–394, set out as a note under section 101 of this title.

1984 Acts. Amendment by Pub.L. 98–353 effective with respect to cases filed 90 days after July 10, 1984, see section 552(a), formerly 553(a) of Pub.L. 98–353, set out as a note under section 101 of this title.

Severability of Provisions

If any provision of Pub.L. 111–203, an amendment made by Pub.L. 111–203, or the application of such provision or amendment to any person or circumstance is held to be unconstitutional, the remainder of Pub.L. 111–203, the amendments made by Pub.L. 111–203, and the application of the provisions of such to any person or circumstance shall not be affected, see 12 U.S.C.A. § 5302.

If any provision of or amendment made by Pub.L. 103–394 or the application of such provision or amendment to any person or circumstance is held to be unconstitutional, the remaining provisions of and amendments made by Pub.L. 103–394 and the application of such provisions and amendments to any person or circumstance shall not be affected thereby, see section 701 of Pub.L. 103–394, set out as a note under section 101 of this title.

Adjustment of Dollar Amounts

For adjustment of dollar amounts specified in subsec. (a)(4), (5)(B)(i), (6)(B), (7) of this section by the Judicial Conference of the United States, effective Apr. 1, 2016, see note set out under 11 U.S.C.A. § 104.

By notice dated Feb. 22, 2016, 81 F.R. 8748, the Judicial Conference of the United States adjusted the dollar amounts in provisions specified in subsec. (a)(4), (5)(B)(i), (6)(B), (7) of this section, effective Apr. 1, 2016, as follows:

In subsec. (a)(4) adjusted $12,475 to $12,850.

In subsec. (a)(5)(B)(i) adjusted $12,475 to $12,850.

In subsec. (a)(6)(B) adjusted $6,150 to $6,325.

In subsec. (a)(7) adjusted $2,775 to $2,850.

By notice dated Feb. 21, 2013, 78 F.R. 12089, the Judicial Conference of the United States adjusted the dollar amounts in provisions specified in subsec. (a)(4), (5), (6), (7) of this section, effective Apr. 1, 2013, as follows:

In subsec. (a)(4) adjusted $11,725 to $12,475.

In subsec. (a)(5) adjusted $11,725 to $12,475.

In subsec. (a)(6) adjusted $5,775 to $6,150.

In subsec. (a)(7) adjusted $2,600 to $2,775.

By notice dated Feb. 25, 2010, 75 F.R. 8747, the Judicial Conference of the United States adjusted the dollar amounts in provisions specified in subsec. (a)(4), (5), (6), (7) of this section, effective Apr. 1, 2010, as follows:

In subsec. (a)(4) adjusted $10,950 to $11,725.

In subsec. (a)(5) adjusted $10,950 to $11,725.

In subsec. (a)(6) adjusted $5,400 to $5,775.

In subsec. (a)(7) adjusted $2,425 to $2,600.

By notice dated Feb. 14, 2007, 72 F.R. 7082, the Judicial Conference of the United States adjusted the dollar amounts in provisions specified in subsec. (a)(4), (5), (6), (7) of this section, effective Apr. 1, 2007, as follows:

In subsec. (a)(4) adjusted $10,000 to $10,950.

In subsec. (a)(5) adjusted $10,000 to $10,950.

In subsec. (a)(6) adjusted $4,925 to $5,400.

In subsec. (a)(7) adjusted $2,225 to $2,425.

By notice dated Feb. 18, 2004, 69 F.R. 8482, the Judicial Conference of the United States adjusted the dollar amounts in provisions specified in subsec. (a)(3), (4)(B)(i), (5), (6) of this section, effective Apr. 1, 2004, as follows:

In subsec. (a)(3) adjusted $4,650 to $4,925.

In subsec. (a)(4)(B)(i) adjusted $4,650 to $4,925.

In subsec. (a)(5) adjusted $4,650 to $4,925.

In subsec. (a)(6) adjusted $2,100 to $2,225.

By notice dated Feb. 20, 2001, 66 F.R. 10910, the Judicial Conference of the United States adjusted the dollar amounts in provisions specified in subsec. (a)(3), (4)(B)(i), (5), (6) of this section, effective Apr. 1, 2001, as follows:

In subsec. (a)(3) adjusted $4,300 to $4,650.

In subsec. (a)(4)(B)(i) adjusted $4,300 to $4,650.

In subsec. (a)(5) adjusted $4,300 to $4,650.

In subsec. (a)(6) adjusted $1,950 to $2,100.

By notice dated Feb. 3, 1998, 63 F.R. 7179, the Judicial Conference of the United States adjusted the dollar amounts in provisions specified in subsec. (a)(3), (4)(B)(i), (5), (6) of this section, effective Apr. 1, 1998, as follows:

In subsec. (a)(3) adjusted $4,000 to $4,300.

In subsec. (a)(4)(B)(i) adjusted $4,000 to $4,300.

In subsec. (a)(5) adjusted $4,000 to $4,300.

In subsec. (a)(6) adjusted $1,800 to $1,950.

CROSS REFERENCES

Applicability of subsec. (a)(1) of this section in Chapter 9 cases, see 11 USCA § 901.

Confirmation upon payment of administrative expenses, fees, and charges, see 11 USCA § 943.

Contents of plan in,

Chapter 12 cases, see 11 USCA § 1222.

Chapter 13 cases, see 11 USCA § 1322.

Designation by plan of classes of claims, see 11 USCA § 1123.

Distribution of,

Certain estate property subject to liens, see 11 USCA § 724.

Customer property in commodity broker liquidation cases, see 11 USCA § 766.

Customer property in stockbroker liquidation cases, see 11 USCA § 752.

Property of estate, see 11 USCA § 726.

Executory contracts and unexpired leases, see 11 USCA § 365.

Involuntary cases future adjustments, see 11 USCA § 104.

Proof of claim, see Official Bankr. Form B 410, 11 USCA.

Recoupment of funds advanced by Securities Investor Protection Corporation as priority administrative expense, see 15 USCA § 78fff.

Tax or customs duty excepted from discharge, see 11 USCA § 523.

Time of payment of administrative expenses, fees and charges in,

Chapter 12 cases, see 11 USCA § 1226.

Chapter 13 cases, see 11 USCA § 1326.

Treatment of certain claims as affecting confirmation of plan, see 11 USCA § 1129.

Unsecured debt having priority over certain administrative expenses, see 11 USCA § 364.

Unsecured priority claims, see Official Bankr. Form B106E/F, 11 USCA.

§ 508.   Effect of distribution other than under this title

If a creditor of a partnership debtor receives, from a general partner that is not a debtor in a case under chapter 7 of this title, payment of, or a transfer of property on account of, a claim that is allowed under this title and that is not secured by a lien on property of such partner, such creditor may not receive any payment under this title on account of such claim until each of the other holders of claims on account of which such holders are entitled to share equally with such creditor under this title has received payment under this title equal in value to the consideration received by such creditor from such general partner.

(Pub.L. 95–598, Nov. 6, 1978, 92 Stat. 2585; Pub.L. 109–8, Title VIII, § 802(d)(7), Apr. 20, 2005, 119 Stat. 146.)

HISTORICAL AND STATUTORY NOTES

Revision Notes and Legislative Reports

1978 Acts. This section prohibits a creditor from receiving any distribution in the bankruptcy case if he has received payment of a portion of his claim in a foreign proceeding, until the other creditors in the bankruptcy case in this country that are entitled to share equally with that creditor have received as much as he has in the foreign proceeding. Senate Report No. 95–989.

2005 Acts. House Report No. 109–31(Part I), see 2005 U.S. Code Cong. and Adm. News, p. 88.

Legislative Statements

Section 508(b) of the House amendment is new and provides an identical rule with respect to a creditor of a partnership who receives payment from a partner, to that of a creditor of a debtor who receives a payment in a foreign proceeding involving the debtor.

Effective and Applicability Provisions

2005 Acts. Amendments by Pub.L. 109–8 effective, except as otherwise provided, 180 days after April 20, 2005, and inapplicable with respect to cases commenced under Title 11 before the effective date, see Pub.L. 109–8, § 1501, set out as a note under 11 U.S.C.A. § 101.

§ 509. Claims of codebtors

(a) Except as provided in subsection (b) or (c) of this section, an entity that is liable with the debtor on, or that has secured, a claim of a creditor against the debtor, and that pays such claim, is subrogated to the rights of such creditor to the extent of such payment.

(b) Such entity is not subrogated to the rights of such creditor to the extent that—

(1) a claim of such entity for reimbursement or contribution on account of such payment of such creditor's claim is—

(A) allowed under section 502 of this title;

(B) disallowed other than under section 502(e) of this title; or

(C) subordinated under section 510 of this title; or

(2) as between the debtor and such entity, such entity received the consideration for the claim held by such creditor.

(c) The court shall subordinate to the claim of a creditor and for the benefit of such creditor an allowed claim, by way of subrogation under this section, or for reimbursement or contribution, of an entity that is liable with the debtor on, or that has secured, such creditor's claim, until such creditor's claim is paid in full, either through payments under this title or otherwise.

(Pub.L. 95–598, Nov. 6, 1978, 92 Stat. 2585; Pub.L. 98–353, Title III, § 450, July 10, 1984, 98 Stat. 375.)

HISTORICAL AND STATUTORY NOTES

Revision Notes and Legislative Reports

1978 Acts. Section 509 deals with codebtors generally, and is in addition to the disallowance provision in section 502(e). This section is based on the notion that the only rights available to a surety, guarantor, or comaker are contribution, reimbursement, and subrogation. The right that applies in a particular situation will depend on the agreement between the debtor and the codebtor, and on whether and how payment was made by the codebtor to the creditor. The claim of a surety or codebtor for contribution or reimbursement is discharged even if the claim is never filed, as is any claim for subrogation even if the surety or codebtor chooses to file a claim for contribution or reimbursement instead.

Subsection (a) subrogates the codebtor (whether as a co-debtor, surety, or guarantor) to the rights of the creditor, to the extent of any payment made by the codebtor to the creditor. Whether the creditor's claim was filed under section 501(a) or 501(b) is irrelevant. The right of subrogation will exist even if the primary creditor's claim is allowed by virtue of being listed under proposed 11 U.S.C. 924 or 1111, and not by reason of a proof of claim.

Subsection (b) permits a subrogated codebtor to receive payments in the bankruptcy case only if the creditor has been paid in full, either through payments under the bankruptcy code or otherwise. Senate Report No. 95–989.

1984 Acts. Statements by Legislative Leaders, see 1984 U.S.Code Cong. and Adm.News, p. 576.

Legislative Statements

Section 509 of the House amendment represents a substantial revision of provisions contained in H.R. 8200 as passed by the House and in the Senate amendment. Section 509(a) states a general rule that a surety or co-debtor is subrogated to the rights of a creditor assured by the surety or codebtor to the extent the surety or codebtor pays such creditor. Section 509(b) states a general exception indicating that subrogation is not granted to the extent that a claim of a surety or co-debtor for reimbursement or contribution is allowed under section 502 or disallowed other than under section 502(e). Additionally, section 509(b)(1)(C) provides that such claims for subrogation are subordinated to the extent that a claim of the surety or co-debtor for reimbursement or contribution is subordinated under section 510(a)(1) or 510(b). Section 509(b)(2) reiterates the well-known rule that prevents a debtor that is ultimately liable on the debt from recovering from a surety or a co-debtor. Although the language in section 509(b)(2) focuses in terms of receipt of consideration, legislative history appearing elsewhere indicates that an agreement to share liabilities should prevail over an agreement to share profits throughout title 11. This is particularly important in the context of codebtors who are partners. Section 509(c) subordinates the claim of a surety or co-debtor to the claim of an assured creditor until the creditor's claim is paid in full.

Effective and Applicability Provisions

1984 Acts. Amendment by Pub.L. 98–353 effective with respect to cases filed 90 days after July 10, 1984, see section 552(a), formerly 553(a) of Pub.L. 98–353, set out as a note under section 101 of this title.

CROSS REFERENCES

Applicability of this section in Chapter 9 cases, see 11 USCA § 901.

§ 510. Subordination

(a) A subordination agreement is enforceable in a case under this title to the same extent that such agreement is enforceable under applicable nonbankruptcy law.

(b) For the purpose of distribution under this title, a claim arising from rescission of a purchase or sale of a security of the debtor or of an affiliate of the debtor, for damages arising from the purchase or sale of such a security, or for reimbursement or contribution allowed under section 502 on account of such a claim, shall be subordinated to all claims or interests that are senior to or equal the claim or interest represented by such security, except that if such security is common stock, such claim has the same priority as common stock.

(c) Notwithstanding subsections (a) and (b) of this section, after notice and a hearing, the court may—

(1) under principles of equitable subordination, subordinate for purposes of distribution all or part of an allowed claim to all or part of another allowed claim or all or part of an allowed interest to all or part of another allowed interest; or

(2) order that any lien securing such a subordinated claim be transferred to the estate.

(Pub.L. 95–598, Nov. 6, 1978, 92 Stat. 2586; Pub.L. 98–353, Title III, § 451, July 10, 1984, 98 Stat. 375.)

HISTORICAL AND STATUTORY NOTES

Revision Notes and Legislative Reports

1978 Acts. Subsection (a) requires the court to enforce subordination agreements. A subordination agreement will not be enforced, however, in a reorganization case in which the class that is the beneficiary of the agreement has accepted, as specified in proposed 11 U.S.C. 1126, a plan that waives their rights under the agreement. Otherwise, the agreement would prevent just what chapter 11 contemplates: that seniors may give up rights to juniors in the interest of confirmation of a plan and rehabilitation of the debtor. The subsection also requires the court to subordinate in payment any claim for rescission of a purchase or sale of a security of the debtor or of an affiliate, or for damages arising from the purchase or sale of such a security, to all claims and interests that are senior to the claim or interest represented by the security. Thus, the later subordination varies with the claim or interest involved. If the security is a debt instrument, the damages or rescission claim will be granted the status of a general unsecured claim. If the security is an equity security, the damages or rescission claim is subordinated to all creditors and treated the same as the equity security itself.

Subsection (b) authorizes the bankruptcy court, in ordering distribution of assets, to subordinate all or any part of any claim to all or any part of another claim, regardless of the priority ranking of either claim. In addition, any lien securing such a subordinated claim may be transferred to the estate. The bill provides, however, that any subordination ordered under this provision must be based on principles of equitable subordination. These principles are defined by case law, and have generally indicated that a claim may normally be subordinated only if its holder is guilty of misconduct. As originally introduced, the bill provided specifically that a tax claim may not be subordinated on equitable grounds. The bill deletes this express exception, but the effect under the amendment should be much the same in most situations since, under the judicial doctrine of equitable subordination, a tax claim would rarely be subordinated. Senate Report No. 95–989.

1984 Acts. Statements by Legislative Leaders, see 1984 U.S.Code Cong. and Adm.News, p. 576.

Legislative Statements

Section 510(c)(1) of the House amendment represents a compromise between similar provisions in the House bill and Senate amendment. After notice and a hearing, the court may, under principles of equitable subordination, subordinate for purposes of distribution all or part of an allowed claim to all or part of another allowed claim or all or part of an allowed interest to all or part of another allowed interest. As a matter of equity, it is reasonable that a court subordinate claims to claims and interests to interests. It is intended that the term "principles of equitable subordination" follow existing case law and leave to the courts development of this principle. To date, under existing law, a claim is generally subordinated only if holder of such claim is guilty of inequitable conduct, or the claim itself is of a status susceptible to subordination, such as a penalty or a claim for damages arising from the purchase or sale of a security of the debtor. The fact that such a claim may be secured is of no consequence to the issue of subordination. However, it is inconceivable that the status of a claim as a secured claim could ever be grounds for justifying equitable subordination.

Subordination: Since the House amendment authorizes subordination of claims only under principles of equitable subordination, and thus incorporates principles of existing case law, a tax claim would rarely be subordinated under this provision of the bill.

Section 511 of the Senate amendment is deleted. Its substance is adopted in section 502(b)(9) of the House amendment which reflects an identical provision contained in H.R. 8200 as passed by the House.

Effective and Applicability Provisions

1984 Acts. Amendment by Pub.L. 98–353 effective with respect to cases filed 90 days after July 10, 1984, see section 552(a), formerly 553(a) of Pub.L. 98–353, set out as a note under section 101 of this title.

CROSS REFERENCES

Applicability of this section in Chapter 9 cases, see 11 USCA § 901.

Certain customer claims in stockbroker liquidation proceedings, see 11 USCA § 747.

Confirmation of plan, see 11 USCA § 1129.

Distribution of,

Customer property, see 11 USCA § 752.

Property of estate, see 11 USCA § 726.

Effect of dismissal, see 11 USCA § 349.

Property of estate, see 11 USCA § 541.

Property recoverable by trustee as exempt, see 11 USCA § 522.

Unpaid portion of certain claims as entitled to distribution, see 11 USCA § 766.

§ 511.   Rate of interest on tax claims

(a) If any provision of this title requires the payment of interest on a tax claim or on an administrative expense tax, or the payment of interest to enable a creditor to receive the present value of the allowed amount of a tax claim, the rate of interest shall be the rate determined under applicable nonbankruptcy law.

(b) In the case of taxes paid under a confirmed plan under this title, the rate of interest shall be determined as of the calendar month in which the plan is confirmed.

(Added Pub.L. 109–8, Title VII, § 704(a), Apr. 20, 2005, 119 Stat. 125.)

HISTORICAL AND STATUTORY NOTES

Revision Notes and Legislative Reports

2005 Acts. House Report No. 109–31(Part I), see 2005 U.S. Code Cong. and Adm. News, p. 88.

Effective and Applicability Provisions

2005 Acts. Section effective, except as otherwise provided, 180 days after April 20, 2005, and inapplicable with respect to cases commenced under Title 11 before the effective date, see Pub.L. 109–8, § 1501, set out as a note under 11 U.S.C.A. § 101.

SUBCHAPTER II—DEBTOR'S DUTIES AND BENEFITS

§ 521.   Debtor's duties

(a) The debtor shall—

(1) file—

(A) a list of creditors; and

(B) unless the court orders otherwise—

(i) a schedule of assets and liabilities;

(ii) a schedule of current income and current expenditures;

(iii) a statement of the debtor's financial affairs and, if section 342(b) applies, a certificate—

(I) of an attorney whose name is indicated on the petition as the attorney for the debtor, or a bankruptcy petition preparer signing the petition under section 110(b)(1), indicating that such attorney or the bankruptcy petition preparer delivered to the debtor the notice required by section 342(b); or

(II) if no attorney is so indicated, and no bankruptcy petition preparer signed the petition, of the debtor that such notice was received and read by the debtor;

(iv) copies of all payment advices or other evidence of payment received within 60 days before the date of the filing of the petition, by the debtor from any employer of the debtor;

(v) a statement of the amount of monthly net income, itemized to show how the amount is calculated; and

(vi) a statement disclosing any reasonably anticipated increase in income or expenditures over the 12–month period following the date of the filing of the petition;

(2) if an individual debtor's schedule of assets and liabilities includes debts which are secured by property of the estate—

(A) within thirty days after the date of the filing of a petition under chapter 7 of this title or on or before the date of the meeting of creditors, whichever is earlier, or within such additional time as the court, for cause, within such period fixes, file with the clerk a statement of his intention with respect to the retention or surrender of such property and, if applicable, specifying that such property is claimed as exempt, that the debtor intends to redeem such property, or that the debtor intends to reaffirm debts secured by such property; and

(B) within 30 days after the first date set for the meeting of creditors under section 341(a), or within such additional time as the court, for cause, within such 30–day period fixes, perform his intention with respect to such property, as specified by subparagraph (A) of this paragraph;

except that nothing in subparagraphs (A) and (B) of this paragraph shall alter the debtor's or the trustee's rights with regard to such property under this title, except as provided in section 362(h);

(3) if a trustee is serving in the case or an auditor is serving under section 586(f) of title 28, cooperate with the trustee as necessary to enable the trustee to perform the trustee's duties under this title;

(4) if a trustee is serving in the case or an auditor is serving under section 586(f) of title 28, surrender to the trustee all property of the estate and any recorded information, including books, documents, records, and papers, relating to property of the estate, whether or not immunity is granted under section 344 of this title;

(5) appear at the hearing required under section 524(d) of this title;

(6) in a case under chapter 7 of this title in which the debtor is an individual, not retain possession of personal property as to which a creditor has an allowed claim for the purchase price secured in whole or in part by an interest in such personal property unless the debtor, not later than 45 days after the first meeting of creditors under section 341(a), either—

(A) enters into an agreement with the creditor pursuant to section 524(c) with respect to the claim secured by such property; or

(B) redeems such property from the security interest pursuant to section 722; and

(7) unless a trustee is serving in the case, continue to perform the obligations required of the administrator (as defined in section 3 of the Employee Retirement Income Security Act of 1974) of an employee benefit plan if at the time of the commencement of the case the debtor (or any entity designated by the debtor) served as such administrator. If the debtor fails to so act within the 45–day period referred to in paragraph (6), the stay under section 362(a) is terminated with respect to the personal property of the estate or of the debtor which is affected, such property shall no longer be property of the estate, and the creditor may take whatever action as to such property as is permitted by applicable nonbankruptcy law, unless the court determines on the motion of the trustee filed before the expiration of such 45–day period, and after notice and a hearing, that such property is of consequential value or benefit to the estate, orders appropriate adequate protection of the creditor's interest, and orders the debtor to deliver any collateral in the debtor's possession to the trustee.

(b) In addition to the requirements under subsection (a), a debtor who is an individual shall file with the court—

(1) a certificate from the approved nonprofit budget and credit counseling agency that provided the debtor services under section 109(h) describing the services provided to the debtor; and

(2) a copy of the debt repayment plan, if any, developed under section 109(h) through the approved nonprofit budget and credit counseling agency referred to in paragraph (1).

(c) In addition to meeting the requirements under subsection (a), a debtor shall file with the court a record of any interest that a debtor has in an education individual retirement account (as defined in section 530(b)(1) of the Internal Revenue Code of 1986), an interest in an account in a qualified ABLE program (as defined in section 529A(b) of such Code, [1] or under a qualified State tuition program (as defined in section 529(b)(1) of such Code).

(d) If the debtor fails timely to take the action specified in subsection (a)(6) of this section, or in paragraphs (1) and (2) of section 362(h), with respect to property which a lessor or bailor owns and has leased, rented, or bailed to the debtor or as to which a creditor holds a security interest not otherwise voidable under section 522(f), 544, 545, 547, 548, or 549, nothing in this title shall prevent or limit the operation of a provision in the underlying lease or agreement that has the effect of placing the debtor in default under such lease or agreement by reason of the occurrence, pendency, or existence of a proceeding under this title or the insolvency of the debtor. Nothing in this subsection shall be deemed to justify limiting such a provision in any other circumstance.

(e)(1) If the debtor in a case under chapter 7 or 13 is an individual and if a creditor files with the court at any time a request to receive a copy of the petition, schedules, and statement of financial affairs filed by the debtor, then the court shall make such petition, such schedules, and such statement available to such creditor.

(2)(A) The debtor shall provide—

(i) not later than 7 days before the date first set for the first meeting of creditors, to the trustee a copy of the Federal income tax return required under applicable law (or at the election of the debtor, a transcript of such return) for the most recent tax year ending immediately before the commencement of the case and for which a Federal income tax return was filed; and

(ii) at the same time the debtor complies with clause (i), a copy of such return (or if elected under clause (i), such transcript) to any creditor that timely requests such copy.

(B) If the debtor fails to comply with clause (i) or (ii) of subparagraph (A), the court shall dismiss the case unless the debtor demonstrates that the failure to so comply is due to circumstances beyond the control of the debtor.

(C) If a creditor requests a copy of such tax return or such transcript and if the debtor fails to provide a copy of such tax return or such transcript to such creditor at the time the debtor provides such tax return or such transcript to the trustee, then the court shall dismiss the case unless the debtor demonstrates that the failure to provide a copy of such tax return or such transcript is due to circumstances beyond the control of the debtor.

(3) If a creditor in a case under chapter 13 files with the court at any time a request to receive a copy of the plan filed by the debtor, then the court shall make available to such creditor a copy of the plan—

(A) at a reasonable cost; and

(B) not later than 7 days after such request is filed.

(f) At the request of the court, the United States trustee, or any party in interest in a case under chapter 7, 11, or 13, a debtor who is an individual shall file with the court—

(1) at the same time filed with the taxing authority, a copy of each Federal income tax return required under applicable law (or at the election of the debtor, a transcript of such tax return) with respect

to each tax year of the debtor ending while the case is pending under such chapter;

(2) at the same time filed with the taxing authority, each Federal income tax return required under applicable law (or at the election of the debtor, a transcript of such tax return) that had not been filed with such authority as of the date of the commencement of the case and that was subsequently filed for any tax year of the debtor ending in the 3–year period ending on the date of the commencement of the case;

(3) a copy of each amendment to any Federal income tax return or transcript filed with the court under paragraph (1) or (2); and

(4) in a case under chapter 13—

(A) on the date that is either 90 days after the end of such tax year or 1 year after the date of the commencement of the case, whichever is later, if a plan is not confirmed before such later date; and

(B) annually after the plan is confirmed and until the case is closed, not later than the date that is 45 days before the anniversary of the confirmation of the plan;

a statement, under penalty of perjury, of the income and expenditures of the debtor during the tax year of the debtor most recently concluded before such statement is filed under this paragraph, and of the monthly income of the debtor, that shows how income, expenditures, and monthly income are calculated.

(g)(1) A statement referred to in subsection (f)(4) shall disclose—

(A) the amount and sources of the income of the debtor;

(B) the identity of any person responsible with the debtor for the support of any dependent of the debtor; and

(C) the identity of any person who contributed, and the amount contributed, to the household in which the debtor resides.

(2) The tax returns, amendments, and statement of income and expenditures described in subsections (e)(2)(A) and (f) shall be available to the United States trustee (or the bankruptcy administrator, if any), the trustee, and any party in interest for inspection and copying, subject to the requirements of section 315(c) of the Bankruptcy Abuse Prevention and Consumer Protection Act of 2005.

(h) If requested by the United States trustee or by the trustee, the debtor shall provide—

(1) a document that establishes the identity of the debtor, including a driver's license, passport, or other document that contains a photograph of the debtor; or

(2) such other personal identifying information relating to the debtor that establishes the identity of the debtor.

(i)(1) Subject to paragraphs (2) and (4) and notwithstanding section 707(a), if an individual debtor in a voluntary case under chapter 7 or 13 fails to file all of the information required under subsection (a)(1) within 45 days after the date of the filing of the petition, the case shall be automatically dismissed effective on the 46th day after the date of the filing of the petition.

(2) Subject to paragraph (4) and with respect to a case described in paragraph (1), any party in interest may request the court to enter an order dismissing the case. If requested, the court shall enter an order of dismissal not later than 7 days after such request.

(3) Subject to paragraph (4) and upon request of the debtor made within 45 days after the date of the filing of the petition described in paragraph (1), the court may allow the debtor an additional period of not to exceed 45 days to file the information required under subsection (a)(1) if the court finds justification for extending the period for the filing.

(4) Notwithstanding any other provision of this subsection, on the motion of the trustee filed before the expiration of the applicable period of time specified in paragraph (1), (2), or (3), and after notice and a hearing, the court may decline to dismiss the case if the court finds that the debtor attempted in good faith to file all the information required by subsection (a)(1)(B)(iv) and that the best interests of creditors would be served by administration of the case.

(j)(1) Notwithstanding any other provision of this title, if the debtor fails to file a tax return that becomes due after the commencement of the case or to properly obtain an extension of the due date for filing such return, the taxing authority may request that the court enter an order converting or dismissing the case.

(2) If the debtor does not file the required return or obtain the extension referred to in paragraph (1) within 90 days after a request is filed by the taxing authority under that paragraph, the court shall convert or dismiss the case, whichever is in the best interests of creditors and the estate.

(Pub.L. 95–598, Nov. 6, 1978, 92 Stat. 2586; Pub.L. 98–353, Title III,¹ §§ 305, 452, July 10, 1984, 98 Stat. 352, 375; Pub.L. 99–554, Title II, § 283(h), Oct. 27, 1986, 100 Stat. 3117; Pub.L. 109–8, Title I, § 106(d), Title II, § 225(b), Title III, §§ 304(1), 305(2), 315(b), 316, Title IV, § 446(a), Title VI, § 603(c), Title VII, § 720, Apr. 20, 2005, 119 Stat. 38, 66, 78, 80, 89, 92, 118, 123, 133; Pub.L. 111–16, § 2(5), (6), May 7, 2009, 123 Stat. 1607; Pub.L. 111–327, § 2(a)(16), Dec. 22, 2010, 124 Stat. 3559; Pub.L. 113–295, Div. B, Title I, § 104(c), Dec. 19, 2014, 128 Stat. 4064.)

1 So in original. A closing parenthesis probably should precede the comma.

HISTORICAL AND STATUTORY NOTES

Revision Notes and Legislative Reports

1978 Acts. This section lists three duties of the debtor in a bankruptcy case. The Rules of Bankruptcy Procedure will specify the means of carrying out these duties. The first duty is to file with the court a list of creditors and, unless the court orders otherwise, a schedule of assets and liabilities and a statement of his financial affairs. Second, the debtor is required to cooperate with the trustee as necessary to enable the trustee to perform the trustee's duties. Finally, the debtor must surrender to the trustee all property of the estate, and any recorded information, including books, documents, records, and papers, relating to property of the estate. This phrase "recorded information, including books, documents, records, and papers," has been used here and throughout the bill as a more general term, and includes such other forms of recorded information as date in computer storage or in other machine readable forms.

The list in this section is not exhaustive of the debtor's duties. Others are listed elsewhere in proposed title 11, such as in section 343, which requires the debtor to submit to examination, or in the Rules of Bankruptcy Procedure, as continued by § 404(a) of S. 2266, such as the duty to attend any hearing on discharge, Rule 402(2). Senate Reports 95–989.

1984 Acts. Statements by Legislative Leaders, see 1984 U.S.Code Cong. and Adm.News, p. 576.

1986 Acts. House Report No. 99–764 and House Conference Report No. 99–958, see 1986 U.S.Code Cong. and Adm. News, p. 5227.

2005 Acts. House Report No. 109–31(Part I), see 2005 U.S. Code Cong. and Adm. News, p. 88.

Legislative Statements

Section 521 of the House amendment modifies a comparable provision contained in the House bill and Senate amendment. The Rules of Bankruptcy Procedure should provide where the list of creditors is to be filed. In addition, the debtor is required to attend the hearing on discharge under section 524(d).

References in Text

Chapter 7, referred to in text, is chapter 7 of this title, 11 U.S.C.A. § 701 et seq.

Chapter 13, referred to in text, is chapter 13 of this title, 11 U.S.C.A. § 1301 et seq.

Section 3 of the Employee Retirement Income Security Act of 1974, referred to in subsec. (a)(7), is Pub.L. 93–406, Title I, § 3, Sept. 2, 1974, 88 Stat. 833, which is classified to 29 U.S.C.A. § 1002.

Section 529A(b) of such Code, referred to in subsec. (c), is classified to 26 U.S.C.A. § 529A(b).

Section 530(b)(1) of the Internal Revenue Code of 1986, referred to in subsec. (c), is classified to 26 U.S.C.A. § 530(b)(1).

Section 529(b)(1) of such Code, referred to in subsec. (c), is classified to 26 U.S.C.A. § 529(b)(1).

Chapter 11, referred to in subsec. (f), is chapter 11 of this title, 11 U.S.C.A. § 1101 et seq.

Section 315(c) of the Bankruptcy Abuse Prevention and Consumer Protection Act of 2005, referred to in subsec. (g)(2), is Pub.L. 109–8, Title III, § 315(c), Apr. 20, 2005, 119 Stat. 91, which is set out as a note under this section.

Effective and Applicability Provisions

2014 Acts. Pub.L. 113–295, Div. B, Title I, § 104(d), Dec. 19, 2014, 128 Stat. 4064, provided that: "The amendments made by this section [amending this section and 11 U.S.C.A. §§ 541 and 707] shall apply with respect to cases commenced under title 11, United States Code, on or after the date of the enactment of this Act [Dec. 19, 2014]."

2009 Acts. Amendments by Pub.L. 111–16 effective Dec. 1, 2009, see Pub.L. 111–16, § 7, set out as a note under 11 U.S.C.A. 109.

2005 Acts. Pub.L. 109–8, Title VI, § 603(e), Apr. 20, 2005, 119 Stat. 123, provided that: "The amendments made by this section [amending this section and 11 U.S.C.A. § 727, and 28 U.S.C.A. § 586, and enacting provisions set out as a note under 28 U.S.C.A. § 586] shall take effect 18 months after the date of enactment of this Act [Apr. 20, 2005]."

Amendments by Pub.L. 109–8 effective, except as otherwise provided, 180 days after April 20, 2005, and inapplicable with respect to cases commenced under Title 11 before the effective date, see Pub.L. 109–8, § 1501, set out as a note under 11 U.S.C.A. § 101.

1986 Acts. Amendment by Pub.L. 99–554 effective 30 days after Oct. 27, 1986, except as otherwise provided for, see section 302(a) of Pub.L. 99–554, set out as a note under section 581 of Title 28, Judiciary and Judicial Procedure.

1984 Acts. Amendment by Pub.L. 98–353 effective with respect to cases filed 90 days after July 10, 1984, see section 552(a), formerly 553(a), of Pub.L. 98–353, set out as a note under section 101 of this title.

Confidentiality of Tax Information

Pub.L. 109–8, Title III, § 315(c), Apr. 20, 2005, 119 Stat. 91, provided that:

"**(1)** Not later than 180 days after the date of the enactment of this Act [Apr. 20, 2005], the Director of the Administrative Office of the United States Courts shall establish procedures for safeguarding the confidentiality of any tax information required to be provided under this section.

"**(2)** The procedures under paragraph (1) shall include restrictions on creditor access to tax information that is required to be provided under this section.

"**(3)** Not later than 540 days after the date of enactment of this Act [Apr. 20, 2005], the director of the administrative office of the United States courts shall prepare and submit to the President pro tempore of the Senate and the speaker of the House of Representatives a report that—

"**(A)** assesses the effectiveness of the procedures established under paragraph (1); and

"**(B)** If appropriate, includes proposed legislation to—

"**(i)** further protect the confidentiality of tax information; and

"**(ii)** provide penalties for the improper use by any person of the tax information required to be provided under this section."

[Amendments by Pub.L. 109–8 effective, except as otherwise provided, 180 days after April 20, 2005, and inapplicable with respect to cases commenced under Title 11 before the effective date, see Pub.L. 109–8, § 1501, set out as a note under 11 U.S.C.A. § 101.]

For Complete Annotation Materials, see United States Code Annotated

Providing Requested Tax Documents to the Court.

Pub.L. 109–8, Title XII, § 1228, Apr. 20, 2005, 119 Stat. 200, provided that:

"(a) **Chapter 7 cases.**—The court shall not grant a discharge in the case of an individual who is a debtor in a case under chapter 7 of title 11, United States Code [11 U.S.C.A. § 701 et seq.], unless requested tax documents have been provided to the court.

"(b) **Chapter 11 and chapter 13 cases.**—The court shall not confirm a plan of reorganization in the case of an individual under chapter 11 or 13 of title 11, United States Code [11 U.S.C.A. § 1101 et seq. or 1301 et seq.], unless requested tax documents have been filed with the court.

"(c) **Document retention.**—The court shall destroy documents submitted in support of a bankruptcy claim not sooner than 3 years after the date of the conclusion of a case filed by an individual under chapter 7, 11, or 13 of title 11, United States Code [11 U.S.C.A. § 701 et seq. or 1101 et seq., or 1301 et seq.]. In the event of a pending audit or enforcement action, the court may extend the time for destruction of such requested tax documents."

[Amendments by Pub.L. 109–8 effective, except as otherwise provided, 180 days after April 20, 2005, and inapplicable with respect to cases commenced under Title 11 before the effective date, see Pub.L. 109–8, § 1501, set out as a note under 11 U.S.C.A. § 101.]

CROSS REFERENCES

Conversion or dismissal of,

Chapter 11 case, see 11 USCA § 1112.

Chapter 13 case, see 11 USCA § 1307.

Debtor's statement of intention, see Official Bankr. Form B108, 11 USCA.

Dismissal of Chapter 7 case, see 11 USCA § 707.

Filing of list, schedule and statement by trustee, see 11 USCA § 1106.

Lists, schedules, statements and fees, see Fed. Bankr. Proc. Form B2000, 11 USCA.

Penalty for persons who negligently or fraudulently prepare bankruptcy petitions or failure to file bankruptcy papers, see 11 USCA § 110.

Proof of claim or interest deemed filed if scheduled, see 11 USCA § 1111.

Property scheduled but unadministered before close of case deemed abandoned, see 11 USCA § 554.

Trustee's duty to ensure performance of debtor's intention as specified in subsec. (2)(B) of this section, see 11 USCA § 704.

§ 522.   Exemptions

(a) In this section—

(1) "dependent" includes spouse, whether or not actually dependent; and

(2) "value" means fair market value as of the date of the filing of the petition or, with respect to property that becomes property of the estate after such date, as of the date such property becomes property of the estate.

(b)(1) Notwithstanding section 541 of this title, an individual debtor may exempt from property of the estate the property listed in either paragraph (2) or, in the alternative, paragraph (3) of this subsection. In joint cases filed under section 302 of this title and individual cases filed under section 301 or 303 of this title by or against debtors who are husband and wife, and whose estates are ordered to be jointly administered under Rule 1015(b) of the Federal Rules of Bankruptcy Procedure, one debtor may not elect to exempt property listed in paragraph (2) and the other debtor elect to exempt property listed in paragraph (3) of this subsection. If the parties cannot agree on the alternative to be elected, they shall be deemed to elect paragraph (2), where such election is permitted under the law of the jurisdiction where the case is filed.

(2) Property listed in this paragraph is property that is specified under subsection (d), unless the State law that is applicable to the debtor under paragraph (3)(A) specifically does not so authorize.

(3) Property listed in this paragraph is—

(A) subject to subsections (o) and (p), any property that is exempt under Federal law, other than subsection (d) of this section, or State or local law that is applicable on the date of the filing of the petition to the place in which the debtor's domicile has been located for the 730 days immediately preceding the date of the filing of the petition or if the debtor's domicile has not been located in a single State for such 730-day period, the place in which the debtor's domicile was located for 180 days immediately preceding the 730-day period or for a longer portion of such 180-day period than in any other place;

(B) any interest in property in which the debtor had, immediately before the commencement of the case, an interest as a tenant by the entirety or joint tenant to the extent that such interest as a tenant by the entirety or joint tenant is exempt from process under applicable nonbankruptcy law; and

(C) retirement funds to the extent that those funds are in a fund or account that is exempt from taxation under section 401, 403, 408, 408A, 414, 457, or 501(a) of the Internal Revenue Code of 1986.

If the effect of the domiciliary requirement under subparagraph (A) is to render the debtor ineligible for any exemption, the debtor may elect to exempt property that is specified under subsection (d).

(4) For purposes of paragraph (3)(C) and subsection (d)(12), the following shall apply:

(A) If the retirement funds are in a retirement fund that has received a favorable determination under section 7805 of the Internal Revenue Code of 1986, and that determination is in effect as of the date of the filing of the petition in a case under this title, those funds shall be presumed to be exempt from the estate.

(B) If the retirement funds are in a retirement fund that has not received a favorable determination under such section 7805, those funds are exempt from the estate if the debtor demonstrates that—

(i) no prior determination to the contrary has been made by a court or the Internal Revenue Service; and

(ii)(I) the retirement fund is in substantial compliance with the applicable requirements of the Internal Revenue Code of 1986; or

(II) the retirement fund fails to be in substantial compliance with the applicable requirements of the Internal Revenue Code of 1986 and the debtor is not materially responsible for that failure.

(C) A direct transfer of retirement funds from 1 fund or account that is exempt from taxation under section 401, 403, 408, 408A, 414, 457, or 501(a) of the Internal Revenue Code of 1986, under section 401(a)(31) of the Internal Revenue Code of 1986, or otherwise, shall not cease to qualify for exemption under paragraph (3)(C) or subsection (d)(12) by reason of such direct transfer.

(D)(i) Any distribution that qualifies as an eligible rollover distribution within the meaning of section 402(c) of the Internal Revenue Code of 1986 or that is described in clause (ii) shall not cease to qualify for exemption under paragraph (3)(C) or subsection (d)(12) by reason of such distribution.

(ii) A distribution described in this clause is an amount that—

(I) has been distributed from a fund or account that is exempt from taxation under section 401, 403, 408, 408A, 414, 457, or 501(a) of the Internal Revenue Code of 1986; and

(II) to the extent allowed by law, is deposited in such a fund or account not later than 60 days after the distribution of such amount.

(c) Unless the case is dismissed, property exempted under this section is not liable during or after the case for any debt of the debtor that arose, or that is determined under section 502 of this title as if such debt had arisen, before the commencement of the case, except—

(1) a debt of a kind specified in paragraph (1) or (5) of section 523(a) (in which case, notwithstanding any provision of applicable nonbankruptcy law to the contrary, such property shall be liable for a debt of a kind specified in such paragraph);

(2) a debt secured by a lien that is—

(A)(i) not avoided under subsection (f) or (g) of this section or under section 544, 545, 547, 548, 549, or 724(a) of this title; and

(ii) not void under section 506(d) of this title; or

(B) a tax lien, notice of which is properly filed;

(3) a debt of a kind specified in section 523(a)(4) or 523(a)(6) of this title owed by an institution-affiliated party of an insured depository institution to a Federal depository institutions regulatory agency acting in its capacity as conservator, receiver, or liquidating agent for such institution; or

(4) a debt in connection with fraud in the obtaining or providing of any scholarship, grant, loan, tuition, discount, award, or other financial assistance for purposes of financing an education at an institution of higher education (as that term is defined in section 101 of the Higher Education Act of 1965 (20 U.S.C. 1001)).

(d) The following property may be exempted under subsection (b)(2) of this section:

(1) The debtor's aggregate interest, not to exceed $23,675 [1] in value, in real property or personal property that the debtor or a dependent of the debtor uses as a residence, in a cooperative that owns property that the debtor or a dependent of the debtor uses as a residence, or in a burial plot for the debtor or a dependent of the debtor.

(2) The debtor's interest, not to exceed $3,775 [1] in value, in one motor vehicle.

(3) The debtor's interest, not to exceed $600 [1] in value in any particular item or $12,625 [1] in aggregate value, in household furnishings, household goods, wearing apparel, appliances, books, animals, crops, or musical instruments, that are held primarily for the personal, family, or household use of the debtor or a dependent of the debtor.

(4) The debtor's aggregate interest, not to exceed $1,600 [1] in value, in jewelry held primarily for the personal, family, or household use of the debtor or a dependent of the debtor.

(5) The debtor's aggregate interest in any property, not to exceed in value $1,250 [1] plus up to $11,850 [1] of any unused amount of the exemption provided under paragraph (1) of this subsection.

(6) The debtor's aggregate interest, not to exceed $2,375 [1] in value, in any implements, professional books, or tools, of the trade of the debtor or the trade of a dependent of the debtor.

(7) Any unmatured life insurance contract owned by the debtor, other than a credit life insurance contract.

(8) The debtor's aggregate interest, not to exceed in value $12,625 [1] less any amount of property of the estate transferred in the manner specified in section 542(d) of this title, in any accrued dividend or interest under, or loan value of, any unmatured life insurance contract owned by the debtor under which the insured is the debtor or an individual of whom the debtor is a dependent.

(9) Professionally prescribed health aids for the debtor or a dependent of the debtor.

(10) The debtor's right to receive—

(A) a social security benefit, unemployment compensation, or a local public assistance benefit;

(B) a veterans' benefit;

(C) a disability, illness, or unemployment benefit;

(D) alimony, support, or separate maintenance, to the extent reasonably necessary for the support of the debtor and any dependent of the debtor;

(E) a payment under a stock bonus, pension, profitsharing, annuity, or similar plan or contract on account of illness, disability, death, age, or length of service, to the extent reasonably necessary for the support of the debtor and any dependent of the debtor, unless—

(i) such plan or contract was established by or under the auspices of an insider that employed the debtor at the time the debtor's rights under such plan or contract arose;

(ii) such payment is on account of age or length of service; and

(iii) such plan or contract does not qualify under section 401(a), 403(a), 403(b), or 408 of the Internal Revenue Code of 1986.

(11) The debtor's right to receive, or property that is traceable to—

(A) an award under a crime victim's reparation law;

(B) a payment on account of the wrongful death of an individual of whom the debtor was a dependent, to the extent reasonably necessary for the support of the debtor and any dependent of the debtor;

(C) a payment under a life insurance contract that insured the life of an individual of whom the debtor was a dependent on the date of such individual's death, to the extent reasonably necessary for the support of the debtor and any dependent of the debtor;

(D) a payment, not to exceed $23,675,[1] on account of personal bodily injury, not including pain and suffering or compensation for actual pecuniary loss, of the debtor or an individual of whom the debtor is a dependent; or

(E) a payment in compensation of loss of future earnings of the debtor or an individual of whom the debtor is or was a dependent, to the extent reasonably necessary for the support of the debtor and any dependent of the debtor.

(12) Retirement funds to the extent that those funds are in a fund or account that is exempt from taxation under section 401, 403, 408, 408A, 414, 457, or 501(a) of the Internal Revenue Code of 1986.

(e) A waiver of an exemption executed in favor of a creditor that holds an unsecured claim against the debtor is unenforceable in a case under this title with respect to such claim against property that the debtor may exempt under subsection (b) of this section. A waiver by the debtor of a power under subsection (f) or (h) of this section to avoid a transfer, under subsection (g) or (i) of this section to exempt property, or under subsection (i) of this section to recover property or to preserve a transfer, is unenforceable in a case under this title.

(f)(1) Notwithstanding any waiver of exemptions but subject to paragraph (3), the debtor may avoid the fixing of a lien on an interest of the debtor in property to the extent that such lien impairs an exemption to which the debtor would have been entitled under subsection (b) of this section, if such lien is—

(A) a judicial lien, other than a judicial lien that secures a debt of a kind that is specified in section 523(a)(5); or

(B) a nonpossessory, nonpurchase-money security interest in any—

(i) household furnishings, household goods, wearing apparel, appliances, books, animals, crops, musical instruments, or jewelry that are held primarily for the personal, family, or household use of the debtor or a dependent of the debtor;

(ii) implements, professional books, or tools, of the trade of the debtor or the trade of a dependent of the debtor; or

(iii) professionally prescribed health aids for the debtor or a dependent of the debtor.

(2)(A) For the purposes of this subsection, a lien shall be considered to impair an exemption to the extent that the sum of—

(i) the lien;

(ii) all other liens on the property; and

(iii) the amount of the exemption that the debtor could claim if there were no liens on the property;

exceeds the value that the debtor's interest in the property would have in the absence of any liens.

(B) In the case of a property subject to more than 1 lien, a lien that has been avoided shall not be considered in making the calculation under subparagraph (A) with respect to other liens.

(C) This paragraph shall not apply with respect to a judgment arising out of a mortgage foreclosure.

(3) In a case in which State law that is applicable to the debtor—

(A) permits a person to voluntarily waive a right to claim exemptions under subsection (d) or prohibits a debtor from claiming exemptions under subsection (d); and

(B) either permits the debtor to claim exemptions under State law without limitation in amount, except to the extent that the debtor has permitted the fixing of a consensual lien on any property or prohibits avoidance of a consensual lien on property otherwise eligible to be claimed as exempt property;

the debtor may not avoid the fixing of a lien on an interest of the debtor or a dependent of the debtor in property if the lien is a nonpossessory, nonpurchasemoney security interest in implements, professional books, or tools of the trade of the debtor or a dependent of the debtor or farm animals or crops of the debtor or a dependent of the debtor to the extent the value of such implements, professional books, tools of the trade, animals, and crops exceeds $6,425 [1].

(4)(A) Subject to subparagraph (B), for purposes of paragraph (1)(B), the term "household goods" means—

  (i) clothing;

  (ii) furniture;

  (iii) appliances;

  (iv) 1 radio;

  (v) 1 television;

  (vi) 1 VCR;

  (vii) linens;

  (viii) china;

  (ix) crockery;

  (x) kitchenware;

  (xi) educational materials and educational equipment primarily for the use of minor dependent children of the debtor;

  (xii) medical equipment and supplies;

  (xiii) furniture exclusively for the use of minor children, or elderly or disabled dependents of the debtor;

  (xiv) personal effects (including the toys and hobby equipment of minor dependent children and wedding rings) of the debtor and the dependents of the debtor; and

  (xv) 1 personal computer and related equipment.

(B) The term "household goods" does not include—

  (i) works of art (unless by or of the debtor, or any relative of the debtor);

  (ii) electronic entertainment equipment with a fair market value of more than $675 [1] in the aggregate (except 1 television, 1 radio, and 1 VCR);

  (iii) items acquired as antiques with a fair market value of more than $675 [1] in the aggregate;

  (iv) jewelry with a fair market value of more than $675 [1] in the aggregate (except wedding rings); and

  (v) a computer (except as otherwise provided for in this section), motor vehicle (including a tractor or lawn tractor), boat, or a motorized recreational device, conveyance, vehicle, watercraft, or aircraft.

(g) Notwithstanding sections 550 and 551 of this title, the debtor may exempt under subsection (b) of this section property that the trustee recovers under section 510(c)(2), 542, 543, 550, 551, or 553 of this title, to the extent that the debtor could have exempted such property under subsection (b) of this section if such property had not been transferred, if—

  (1)(A) such transfer was not a voluntary transfer of such property by the debtor; and

  (B) the debtor did not conceal such property; or

  (2) the debtor could have avoided such transfer under subsection (f)(1)(B) of this section.

(h) The debtor may avoid a transfer of property of the debtor or recover a setoff to the extent that the debtor could have exempted such property under subsection (g)(1) of this section if the trustee had avoided such transfer, if—

  (1) such transfer is avoidable by the trustee under section 544, 545, 547, 548, 549, or 724(a) of this title or recoverable by the trustee under section 553 of this title; and

  (2) the trustee does not attempt to avoid such transfer.

(i)(1) If the debtor avoids a transfer or recovers a setoff under subsection (f) or (h) of this section, the debtor may recover in the manner prescribed by, and subject to the limitations of, section 550 of this title, the same as if the trustee had avoided such transfer, and may exempt any property so recovered under subsection (b) of this section.

(2) Notwithstanding section 551 of this title, a transfer avoided under section 544, 545, 547, 548, 549, or 724(a) of this title, under subsection (f) or (h) of this section, or property recovered under section 553 of this title, may be preserved for the benefit of the debtor to the extent that the debtor may exempt such property under subsection (g) of this section or paragraph (1) of this subsection.

(j) Notwithstanding subsections (g) and (i) of this section, the debtor may exempt a particular kind of property under subsections (g) and (i) of this section only to the extent that the debtor has exempted less property in value of such kind than that to which the debtor is entitled under subsection (b) of this section.

(k) Property that the debtor exempts under this section is not liable for payment of any administrative expense except—

  (1) the aliquot share of the costs and expenses of avoiding a transfer of property that the debtor exempts under subsection (g) of this section, or of recovery of such property, that is attributable to the value of the portion of such property exempted in relation to the value of the property recovered; and

  (2) any costs and expenses of avoiding a transfer under subsection (f) or (h) of this section, or of recovery of property under subsection (i)(1) of this section, that the debtor has not paid.

(*l*) The debtor shall file a list of property that the debtor claims as exempt under subsection (b) of this section. If the debtor does not file such a list, a dependent of the debtor may file such a list, or may claim property as exempt from property of the estate on behalf of the debtor. Unless a party in interest objects, the property claimed as exempt on such list is exempt.

(m) Subject to the limitation in subsection (b), this section shall apply separately with respect to each debtor in a joint case.

(n) For assets in individual retirement accounts described in section 408 or 408A of the Internal Revenue Code of 1986, other than a simplified employee pension under section 408(k) of such Code or a simple retirement account under section 408(p) of such Code, the aggregate value of such assets exempted under this section, without regard to amounts attributable to rollover contributions under section 402(c), 402(e)(6), 403(a)(4), 403(a)(5), and 403(b)(8) of the Internal Revenue Code of 1986, and earnings thereon, shall not exceed $1,283,025 [1] in a case filed by a debtor who is an individual, except that such amount may be increased if the interests of justice so require.

(*o*) For purposes of subsection (b)(3)(A), and notwithstanding subsection (a), the value of an interest in—

(1) real or personal property that the debtor or a dependent of the debtor uses as a residence;

(2) a cooperative that owns property that the debtor or a dependent of the debtor uses as a residence;

(3) a burial plot for the debtor or a dependent of the debtor; or

(4) real or personal property that the debtor or a dependent of the debtor claims as a homestead;

shall be reduced to the extent that such value is attributable to any portion of any property that the debtor disposed of in the 10–year period ending on the date of the filing of the petition with the intent to hinder, delay, or defraud a creditor and that the debtor could not exempt, or that portion that the debtor could not exempt, under subsection (b), if on such date the debtor had held the property so disposed of.

(p)(1) Except as provided in paragraph (2) of this subsection and sections 544 and 548, as a result of electing under subsection (b)(3)(A) to exempt property under State or local law, a debtor may not exempt any amount of interest that was acquired by the debtor during the 1215–day period preceding the date of the filing of the petition that exceeds in the aggregate $160,375 [1] in value in—

(A) real or personal property that the debtor or a dependent of the debtor uses as a residence;

(B) a cooperative that owns property that the debtor or a dependent of the debtor uses as a residence;

(C) a burial plot for the debtor or a dependent of the debtor; or

(D) real or personal property that the debtor or dependent of the debtor claims as a homestead.

(2)(A) The limitation under paragraph (1) shall not apply to an exemption claimed under subsection (b)(3)(A) by a family farmer for the principal residence of such farmer.

(B) For purposes of paragraph (1), any amount of such interest does not include any interest transferred from a debtor's previous principal residence (which was acquired prior to the beginning of such 1215–day period) into the debtor's current principal residence, if the debtor's previous and current residences are located in the same State.

(q)(1) As a result of electing under subsection (b)(3)(A) to exempt property under State or local law, a debtor may not exempt any amount of an interest in property described in subparagraphs (A), (B), (C), and (D) of subsection (p)(1) which exceeds in the aggregate $160,375 [1] if—

(A) the court determines, after notice and a hearing, that the debtor has been convicted of a felony (as defined in section 3156 of title 18), which under the circumstances, demonstrates that the filing of the case was an abuse of the provisions of this title; or

(B) the debtor owes a debt arising from—

(i) any violation of the Federal securities laws (as defined in section 3(a)(47) of the Securities Exchange Act of 1934), any State securities laws, or any regulation or order issued under Federal securities laws or State securities laws;

(ii) fraud, deceit, or manipulation in a fiduciary capacity or in connection with the purchase or sale of any security registered under section 12 or 15(d) of the Securities Exchange Act of 1934 or under section 6 of the Securities Act of 1933;

(iii) any civil remedy under section 1964 of title 18; or

(iv) any criminal act, intentional tort, or willful or reckless misconduct that caused serious physical injury or death to another individual in the preceding 5 years.

(2) Paragraph (1) shall not apply to the extent the amount of an interest in property described in subparagraphs (A), (B), (C), and (D) of subsection (p)(1) is reasonably necessary for the support of the debtor and any dependent of the debtor.

(Pub.L. 95–598, Nov. 6, 1978, 92 Stat. 2586; Pub.L. 98–353, Title III, §§ 306, 453, July 10, 1984, 98 Stat. 353, 375; Pub.L. 99–554, Title II, § 283(i), Oct. 27, 1986, 100 Stat. 3117; Pub.L. 101–647, Title XXV, § 2522(b), Nov. 29, 1990, 104 Stat. 4866; Pub.L. 103–394, Title I, § 108(d), Title III, §§ 303, 304(d),

310, Title V, § 501(d)(12), Oct. 22, 1994, 108 Stat. 4112, 4132, 4133, 4137, 4145; Pub.L. 106–420, § 4, Nov. 1, 2000, 114 Stat. 1868; Pub.L. 109–8, Title II, §§ 216, 224(a), (e)(1), Title III, §§ 307, 308, 313(a), 322(a), Apr. 20, 2005, 119 Stat. 55, 62, 65, 81, 87, 96; Pub.L. 111–327, § 2(a)(17), Dec. 22, 2010, 124 Stat. 3559.)

1 Dollar amount as adjusted by the Judicial Conference of the United States. See Adjustment of Dollar Amounts notes set out under this section and 11 U.S.C.A. § 104.

HISTORICAL AND STATUTORY NOTES

Revision Notes and Legislative Reports

1978 Acts. Subsection (a) of this section defines two terms: "dependent" includes the debtor's spouse, whether or not actually dependent; and "value" means fair market value as of the date of the filing of the petition.

Subsection (b) tracks current law. It permits a debtor the exemptions to which he is entitled under other Federal law and the law of the State of his domicile. Some of the items that may be exempted under Federal laws other than title 11 include:

Foreign Service Retirement and Disability payments, 22 U.S.C. 1104 [1] [section 1104 of Title 22, Foreign Relations and Intercourse];

Social security payments, 42 U.S.C. 407 [section 407 of Title 42, The Public Health and Welfare];

Injury or death compensation payments from war risk hazards, 42 U.S.C. 1717 [section 1717 of Title 42];

Wages of fishermen, seamen, and apprentices, 46 U.S.C. 601 [2] [section 601 of Title 46, Shipping];

Civil service retirement benefits, 5 U.S.C. 729, 2265 [3] [sections 729 and 2265 of Title 5, Government Organization and Employees];

Longshoremen's and Harbor Workers' Compensation Act death and disability benefits, 33 U.S.C. 916 [section 916 of Title 33, Navigation and Navigable Waters];

Railroad Retirement Act annuities and pensions, 45 U.S.C. 228(L) [4] [former section 2281 of Title 45, Railroads];

Veterans benefits, 45 U.S.C. 352(E) [5] [section 352(e) of Title 45];

Special pensions paid to winners of the Congressional Medal of Honor, 38 U.S.C. 3101 [6] [section 3101 of Title 38, Veterans' Benefits]; and

Federal homestead lands on debts contracted before issuance of the patent, 43 U.S.C. 175 [section 175 of Title 43, Public Lands].

He may also exempt an interest in property in which the debtor had an interest as a tenant by the entirety or joint tenant to the extent that interest would have been exempt from process under applicable nonbankruptcy law.

Under proposed section 541, all property of the debtor becomes property of the estate, but the debtor is permitted to exempt certain property from property of the estate under this section. Property may be exempted even if it is subject to a lien, but only the unencumbered portion of the property is to be counted in computing the "value" of the property for the purposes of exemption.

As under current law, the debtor will be permitted to convert nonexempt property into exempt property before filing a bankruptcy petition. The practice is not fraudulent as to creditors, and permits the debtor to make full use of the exemptions to which he is entitled under the law. [Ed. Note: cf. Mickelson v. Anderson, Bkrtcy.Minn.1982, 31 B.R. 635.]

Subsection (c) insulates exempt property from prepetition claims other than tax claims (whether or not dischargeable), and other than alimony, maintenance, or support claims that are excepted from discharge. The bankruptcy discharge does not prevent enforcement of valid liens. The rule of *Long v. Bullard*, 117 U.S. 617 (1886) [6 S.Ct. 917, 29 L.Ed. 1004], is accepted with respect to the enforcement of valid liens on nonexempt property as well as on exempt property. Cf. *Louisville Joint Stock Land Bank v. Radford*, 295 U.S. 555, 583 (1935) [55 S.Ct. 854].

Subsection (c)(3) permits the collection of dischargeable taxes from exempt assets. Only assets exempted from levy under section 6334 of the Internal Revenue Code [section 6334 of Title 26, Internal Revenue Code] or under applicable state or local tax law cannot be applied to satisfy these tax claims. This rule applies to prepetition tax claims against the debtor regardless of whether the claims do or do not receive priority and whether they are dischargeable or nondischargeable. Thus, even if a tax is dischargeable vis-a-vis the debtor's after-acquired assets, it may nevertheless be collectible from exempt property held by the estate. (Taxes incurred by the debtor's estate which are collectible as first priority administrative expenses are not collectible from the debtor's estate which are collectible as first priority administrative expenses are not collectible from the debtor's exempt assets.)

Subsection (d) protects the debtor's exemptions, either Federal or State, by making unenforceable in a bankruptcy case a waiver of exemptions or a waiver of the debtor's avoiding powers under the following subsections.

Subsection (e) protects the debtor's exemptions, his discharge, and thus his fresh start by permitting him to avoid certain liens on exempt property. The debtor may avoid a judicial lien on any property to the extent that the property could have been exempted in the absence of the lien, and may similarly avoid a nonpurchase-money security interest in certain household and personal goods. The avoiding power is independent of any waiver of exemptions.

Subsection (f) gives the debtor the ability to exempt property that the trustee recovers under one of the trustee's avoiding powers if the property was involuntarily transferred away from the debtor (such as by the fixing of a judicial lien) and if the debtor did not conceal the property. The debtor is also permitted to exempt property that the trustee recovers as the result of the avoiding of the fixing of certain security interests to the extent that the debtor could otherwise have exempted the property.

Subsection (g) provides that if the trustee does not exercise an avoiding power to recover a transfer of property that would be exempt, the debtor may exercise it and exempt the property, if the transfer was involuntary and the debtor did not conceal the property. If the debtor wishes to preserve his right to pursue any action under this provision, then he must intervene in any action brought by the trustee based on the same cause of action. It is not intended that the debtor be given an additional opportunity to avoid a transfer or that the transferee should have to defend the same action twice. Rather, the section is primarily designed to give the debtor the rights the trustee could have, but has not, pursued. The debtor is given no greater rights under this provision than the trustee, and thus, the debtor's avoiding powers under proposed sections 544, 545, 547, and 548, are subject to proposed 546, as are the trustee's powers.

For Complete Annotation Materials, see United States Code Annotated

These subsections are cumulative. The debtor is not required to choose which he will use to gain an exemption. Instead, he may use more than one in any particular instance, just as the trustee's avoiding powers are cumulative.

Subsection (h) permits recovery by the debtor of property transferred by an avoided transfer from either the initial or subsequent transferees. It also permits preserving a transfer for the benefit of the debtor. In either event, the debtor may exempt the property recovered or preserved.

Subsection (i) makes clear that the debtor may exempt property under the avoiding subsections (f) and (h) only to the extent he has exempted less property than allowed under subsection (b).

Subsection (j) makes clear that the liability of the debtor's exempt property is limited to the debtor's aliquot share of the costs and expenses recovery of property that the trustee recovers and the debtor later exempts, and any costs and expenses of avoiding a transfer by the debtor that the debtor has not already paid.

Subsection (k) requires the debtor to file a list of property that he claims as exempt from property of the estate. Absent an objection to the list, the property is exempted. A dependent of the debtor may file it and thus be protected if the debtor fails to file the list.

Subsection (*l*) provides the rule for a joint case. Senate Report No. 95–989.

1 Replaced by 22 USCA § 4060(c).

2 Replaced by 46 USCA §§ 11108, 11109.

3 Replaced by 5 USCA § 8346.

4 Replaced by 45 USCA § 231m.

5 Railroad unemployment benefits are covered by 45 USCA § 352(e).

6 Veterans benefits generally are covered by 38 USCA § 5301.

Subsection (a) of this section defines two terms: "dependent" includes the debtor's spouse, whether or not actually dependent; and "value" means fair market value as of the date of the filing of the petition.

Subsection (b), the operative subsection of this section, is a significant departure from present law. It permits an individual debtor in a bankruptcy case a choice between exemption systems. The debtor may choose the Federal exemptions prescribed in subsection (d), or he may choose the exemptions to which he is entitled under other Federal law and the law of the State of his domicile. If the debtor chooses the latter, some of the items that may be exempted under other Federal laws include:

—Foreign Service Retirement and Disability payments, 22 U.S.C. 1104 1 [section 1104 of Title 22, Foreign Relations and Intercourse];

—Social security payments, 42 U.S.C. 407 [section 407 of Title 42, The Public Health and Welfare];

—Injury or death compensation payments from war risk hazards, 42 U.S.C. 1717 [section 1717 of Title 42];

—Wages of fishermen, seamen, and apprentices, 46 U.S.C. 601 [section 601 of Title 46, Shipping];

—Civil service retirement benefits, 5 U.S.C. 729, 2265 2 [sections 729, 2265 of Title 5, Government Organization and Employees];

—Longshoremen's and Harbor Workers' Compensation Act death and disability benefits, 33 U.S.C. 916 [section 916 of Title 33, Navigation and Navigable Waters];

—Railroad Retirement Act annuities and pensions, 45 U.S.C. 228(*l*) 3; [former section 228l of Title 45, Railroads];

—Veterans benefits, 45 U.S.C. 352(E) 4 [section 352(e) of Title 45];

—Special pensions paid to winners of the Congressional Medal of Honor, 38 U.S.C. 3101 [section 3101 of Title 38, Veterans' Benefits]; 5 and

—Federal homestead lands on debts contracted before issuance of the patent, 43 U.S.C. 175 [section 175 of Title 43, Public Lands].

He may also exempt an interest in property in which the debtor had an interest as a tenant by the entirety or joint tenant to the extent that interest would have been exempt from process under applicable nonbankruptcy law. The Rules will provide for the situation where the debtor's choice of exemption, Federal or State, was improvident and should be changed, for example, where the court has ruled against the debtor with respect to a major exemption.

Under proposed 11 U.S.C. 541, all property of the debtor becomes property of the estate, but the debtor is permitted to exempt certain property from property of the estate under this section. Property may be exempted even if it is subject to a lien, but only the unencumbered portion of the property is to be counted in computing the "value" of the property for the purposes of exemption. Thus, for example, a residence worth $30,000 with a mortgage of $25,000 will be exemptable to the extent of $5,000. This follows current law. The remaining value of the property will be dealt with in the bankruptcy case as is any interest in property that is subject to a lien.

As under current law, the debtor will be permitted to convert nonexempt property into exempt property before filing a bankruptcy petition. See Hearings, pt. 3, at 1355–58. The practice is not fraudulent as to creditors and permits the debtor to make full use of the exemptions to which he is entitled under the law.

Subsection (c) insulates exempt property from prepetition claims, except tax and alimony, maintenance, or support claims that are excepted from discharge. The bankruptcy discharge will not prevent enforcement of valid liens. The rule of *Long v. Bullard,* 117 U.S. 617 (1886) [6 S.Ct. 917, 29 L.Ed. 1004], is accepted with respect to the enforcement of valid liens on nonexempt property as well as on exempt property. Cf. *Louisville Joint Stock Land Bank v. Radford,* 295 U.S. 555, 583 (1935) [55 S.Ct. 854].

Subsection (d) specifies the Federal exemptions to which the debtor is entitled. They are derived in large part from the Uniform Exemptions Act, promulgated by the Commissioners of Uniform State Laws in August, 1976. Eleven categories of property are exempted. First is a homestead to the extent of $10,000, which may be claimed in real or personal property that the debtor or a dependent of the debtor uses as a residence. Second, the debtor may exempt a motor vehicle to the extent of $1500. Third, the debtor may exempt household goods, furnishings, clothing, and similar household items, held primarily for the personal, family, or household use of the debtor or a dependent of the debtor. "Animals" includes all animals, such as pets, livestock, poultry, and fish, if they are held primarily for personal, family or household use. The limitation for third category items is $300 on any particular item. The debtor may also exempt up to $750 of personal jewelry.

Paragraph (5) permits the exemption of $500, plus any unused amount of the homestead exemption, in any property, in order not to discriminate against the nonhomeowner. Paragraph (6) grants the debtor up to $1000 in implements, professional books, or tools, of the trade of the debtor a dependent. Paragraph (7) exempts a life insurance contract, other than a credit life insurance contract, owned by the debtor. This paragraph refers to the life insurance contract itself. It does not encompass any other rights under the contract, such as the right to borrow out the loan value. Because of this provision, the trustee may not surrender a life insurance contract, which remains property of the debtor if he chooses the Federal exemptions. Paragraph (8) permits the debtor to exempt up to $5000 in loan value in a life insurance policy owned by the debtor under which the debtor or an individual of whom the debtor is a dependent is the insured. The exemption provided by this paragraph and paragraph (7) will also include the debtor's rights in a group insurance certificate under which the insured is an individual of whom the debtor is a dependent (assuming the debtor has rights in the policy that could be exempted) or the debtor. A trustee is authorized to collect the entire loan value on every life insurance policy owned by the debtor as property of the estate. First, however, the debtor will choose which policy or policies under which the loan value will be exempted. The $5000 figure is reduced by the amount of any automatic premium loan authorized after the date of the filing of the petition under section 542(d). Paragraph (9) exempts professionally prescribed health aids.

Paragraph (10) exempts certain benefits that are akin to future earnings of the debtor. These include social security, unemployment compensation, or public assistance benefits, veteran's benefits, disability, illness, or unemployment benefits, alimony, support, or separate maintenance (but only to the extent reasonably necessary for the support of the debtor and any dependents of the debtor), and benefits under a certain stock bonus, pension, profitsharing, annuity or similar plan based on illness, disability, death, age or length of service. Paragraph (11) allows the debtor to exempt certain compensation for losses. These include crime victim's reparation benefits, wrongful death benefits (with a reasonably necessary for support limitation), life insurance proceeds (same limitation), compensation for bodily injury, not including pain and suffering ($10,000 limitation), and loss of future earnings payments (support limitation). This provision in subparagraph (D)(11) is designed to cover payments in compensation of actual bodily injury, such as the loss of a limb, and is not intended to include the attendant costs that accompany such a loss, such as medical payments, pain and suffering, or loss of earnings. Those items are handled separately by the bill.

Subsection (e) protects the debtor's exemptions, either Federal or State, by making unenforceable in a bankruptcy case a waiver of exemptions or a waiver of the debtor's avoiding powers under the following subsections.

Subsection (f) protects the debtor's exemptions, his discharge, and thus his fresh start by permitting him to avoid certain liens on exempt property. The debtor may avoid a judicial lien on any property to the extent that the property could have been exempted in the absence of the lien, and may similarly avoid a nonpurchase-money security interest in certain household and personal goods. The avoiding power is independent of any waiver of exemptions.

Subsection (g) gives the debtor the ability to exempt property that the trustee recovers under one of the trustee's avoiding powers if the property was involuntarily transferred away from the debtor (such as by the fixing of a judicial lien) and if the debtor did not conceal the property. The debtor is also permitted to exempt property that the trustee recovers as the result of the avoiding of the fixing of certain security interests to the extent that the debtor could otherwise have exempted the property.

If the trustee does not pursue an avoiding power to recover a transfer of property that would be exempt, the debtor may pursue it and exempt the property, if the transfer was involuntary and the debtor did not conceal the property. If the debtor wishes to preserve his right to pursue an action under this provision, then he must intervene in any action brought by the trustee based on the same cause of action. It is not intended that the debtor be given an additional opportunity to avoid a transfer or that the transferee have to defend the same action twice. Rather, the section is primarily designed to give the debtor the rights the trustee could have pursued if the trustee chooses not to pursue them. The debtor is given no greater rights under this provision than the trustee, and thus the debtor's avoiding powers under proposed 11 U.S.C. 544, 545, 547, and 548, are subject to proposed 11 U.S.C. 546, as are the trustee's powers.

These subsections are cumulative. The debtor is not required to choose which he will use to gain an exemption. Instead, he may use more than one in any particular instance, just as the trustee's avoiding powers are cumulative.

Subsection (i) permits recovery by the debtor of property transferred in an avoided transfer from either the initial or subsequent transferees. It also permits preserving a transfer for the benefit of the debtor. Under either case the debtor may exempt the property recovered or preserved.

Subsection (k) makes clear that the debtor's aliquot share of the costs and expenses [for] recovery of property that the trustee recovers and the debtor later exempts, and any costs and expenses of avoiding a transfer by the debtor that the debtor has not already paid.

Subsection (l) requires the debtor to file a list of property that he claims as exempt from property of the estate. Absent an objection to the list, the property is exempted. A dependent of the debtor may file it and thus be protected if the debtor fails to file the list.

Subsection (m) requires the clerk of the bankruptcy court to give notice of any exemptions claimed under subsection (l), in order that parties in interest may have an opportunity to object to the claim.

Subsection (n) provides the rule for a joint case: each debtor is entitled to the Federal exemptions provided under this section or to the State exemptions, whichever the debtor chooses. House Report 95–595.

1 Replaced by 22 USCA § 4060(c).
2 Replaced by 5 USCA § 8346.
3 Replaced by 45 USCA § 231m.
4 Railroad unemployment benefits are covered by 45 USCA § 352(e).
5 Veteran benefits generally are covered by 38 USCA § 5301.

1984 Acts. Statements by Legislative Leaders, see 1984 U.S. Code Cong. and Adm. News, p. 576.

1986 Acts. House Report No. 99–764 and House Conference Report No. 99–958, see 1986 U.S. Code Cong. and Adm. News, p. 5227.

House Conference Report No. 99–841 and Statement by President, see 1986 U.S. Code Cong. and Adm. News, p. 4075.

1990 Acts. House Report No. 101–681(I), see 1990 U.S. Code Cong. and Adm. News, p. 6472.

1994 Acts. House Report No. 103–835, see 1994 U.S. Code Cong. and Adm. News, p. 3340.

2005 Acts. House Report No. 109–31(Part I), see 2005 U.S. Code Cong. and Adm. News, p. 88.

Legislative Statements

Section 522 of the House amendment represents a compromise on the issue of exemptions between the position taken in the House bill, and that taken in the Senate amendment. Dollar amounts specified in section 522(d) of the House bill have been reduced from amounts as contained in H.R. 8200 as passed by the House. The States may, by passing a law, determine whether the Federal exemptions will apply as an alternative to State exemptions in bankruptcy cases.

Section 522(c)(1) tracks the House bill and provides that dischargeable tax claims may not be collected out of exempt property.

Section 522(f)(2) is derived from the Senate amendment restricting the debtor to avoidance of nonpossessory, nonpurchase money security interests.

Exemptions: Section 522(c)(1) of the House amendment adopts a provision contained in the House bill that dischargeable taxes cannot be collected from exempt assets. This changes present law, which allows collection of dischargeable taxes from exempt property, a rule followed in the Senate amendment. Nondischargeable taxes, however, will continue to be [be] collectable [sic] out of exempt property. It is anticipated that in the next session Congress will review the exemptions from levy currently contained in the Internal Revenue Code [Title 26] with a view to increasing the exemptions to more realistic levels.

References in Text

The Federal Rules of Bankruptcy Procedure, referred to in subsec. (b), are set out in the Appendix to this title.

Section 401, 403, 408, 408A, 414, 457, or 501(a) of the Internal Revenue Code of 1986, referred to in subsecs. (b)(3)(C), (4)(C), (D)(ii)(I), (d)(12), is classified to 26 U.S.C.A. § 401, 403, 408, 408A, 414, 457, or 501(a).

Section 7805 of the Internal Revenue Code of 1986, referred to in subsec. (b)(4)(A), (B), is 26 U.S.C.A. § 7805.

The Internal Revenue Code of 1986, referred to in subsec. (b)(4)(B)(ii)(I), (II), is classified to Title 26 of the Code.

Section 402(c) of the Internal Revenue Code of 1986, referred to in subsec. (b)(4)(D)(i), is 26 U.S.C.A. § 402(c).

Section 401(a), 403(a), 403(b), or 408, of the Internal Revenue Code of 1986, referred to in subsec. (d)(10)(E)(iii), is classified to 26 U.S.C.A. § 401(a), 403(a), 403(b), or 408.

Section 408 or 408A of the Internal Revenue Code of 1986, referred to in subsec. (n), is classified to 26 U.S.C.A. § 408 or 408A.

Section 402(c), 402(e)(6), 403(a)(4), 403(a)(5), and 403(b)(8) of the Internal Revenue Code of 1986, referred to in subsec. (n), are classified to 26 U.S.C.A. §§ 402(c), 402(e)(6), 403(a)(4), 403(a)(5), and 403(b)(8).

Section 3(a)(47) of the Securities Exchange Act of 1934, referred to in subsec. (q)(1)(B)(i), is June 6, 1934, c. 404, Title I, § 3(a)(47), 48 Stat. 882, as amended, which is classified to 15 U.S.C.A. § 78c(a)(47).

Section 12 or 15(d) of the Securities Exchange Act of 1934, referred to in subsec. (q)(1)(B)(ii), is June 6, 1934, c. 404, Title I, § 12 or 15, 48 Stat. 892 or 895, as amended, which is classified to 15 U.S.C.A. § 78l or 15 U.S.C.A. § 78o.

Section 6 of the Securities Act of 1933, referred to in subsec. (q)(1)(B)(ii), is Act May 27, 1933, c. 38, Title I, § 6, 48 Stat. 78, which is classified to 15 U.S.C.A. § 77f.

Effective and Applicability Provisions

2013 Acts. Increase of dollar amounts by Judicial Conference of the United States by notice published Feb. 21, 2013, 78 F.R. 12089 effective April 1, 2013, and increase not applicable to cases commenced before the effective date of the adjustments, i.e., April 1, 2013. See Adjustment of Dollar Amounts notes under 11 U.S.C.A. § 104 and this section.

2010 Acts. Increase of dollar amounts by Judicial Conference of the United States by notice published Feb. 25, 2010, 75 F.R. 8747 effective April 1, 2010, and increase not applicable to cases commenced before the effective date of the adjustments, i.e., April 1, 2010. See Adjustment of Dollar Amounts notes under 11 U.S.C.A. § 104 and this section.

2007 Acts. Increase of dollar amounts by Judicial Conference of the United States by notice published Feb. 14, 2007, 72 F.R. 7082 effective April 1, 2007, and increase not applicable to cases commenced before the effective date of the adjustments, i.e., April 1, 2007. See Adjustment of Dollar Amounts notes under 11 U.S.C.A. § 104 and this section.

2005 Acts. Amendments by Pub.L. 109–8 effective 180 days after Apr. 20, 2005, with amendments by sections 216, 224(a), (e)(1), 307, and 313(a) of Pub.L. 109–8 not applicable with respect to cases commenced under this title before such effective date, except as otherwise provided, and amendments by sections 308 and 322(a) of Pub.L. 109–8 applicable with respect to cases commenced under this title on or after Apr. 20, 2005, see Pub.L. 109–8, § 1501, set out as a note under 11 U.S.C.A. § 101.

2004 Acts. Adjustment of dollar amounts by Judicial Conference of the United States by notice dated Feb. 18, 2004, 69 F.R. 8482 effective April 1, 2004, and adjustment not applicable to cases commenced before the effective date of the adjustments, i.e., April 1, 2004. See Adjustment of Dollar Amounts notes under 11 U.S.C.A. § 104 and this section.

2001 Acts. Adjustment of dollar amounts by Judicial Conference of the United States by notice dated Feb. 20, 2001, 66 F.R. 10910 effective April 1, 2001, and adjustment not applicable to cases commenced before the effective date of the adjustments, i.e., April 1, 2001. See Adjustment of Dollar Amounts notes under 11 U.S.C.A. § 104 and this section.

1998 Acts. Adjustment of dollar amounts by Judicial Conference of the United States by notice dated Feb. 3, 1998, 63 F.R. 7179 effective April 1, 1998, and adjustment not applicable to cases commenced before the effective date of the adjustments, i.e., April 1, 1998. See Adjustment of Dollar Amounts notes under 11 U.S.C.A. § 104 and this section.

1994 Acts. Amendments by Pub.L. 103–394 effective on Oct. 22, 1994, and not to apply with respect to cases commenced under Title 11 of the United States Code before Oct. 22, 1994, see section 702 of Pub.L. 103–394, set out as a note under section 101 of this title.

1986 Acts. Amendment by Pub.L. 99–554 effective 30 days after Oct. 27, 1986, except as otherwise provided for, see section 302(a) of Pub.L. 99–554, set out as a note under section 581 of Title 28, Judiciary and Judicial Procedure.

1984 Acts. Amendment by Pub.L. 98–353 effective with respect to cases filed 90 days after July 10, 1984, see section 552(a), formerly 553(a) of Pub.L. 98–353, set out as a note under section 101 of this title.

Separability of Provisions

If any provision of or amendment made by Pub.L. 103–394 or the application of such provision or amendment to any person or circumstance is held to be unconstitutional, the remaining provisions of and amendments made by Pub.L. 103–394 and the application of such provisions and amendments to any person or circumstance shall not be affected thereby, see section 701 of Pub.L. 103–394, set out as a note under section 101 of this title.

Adjustment of Dollar Amounts

For adjustment of dollar amounts specified in subsecs. (d)(1) to (6), (8), (11)(D), (f)(3), (4)(B), (n), (p)(1), (q)(1) of this section by the Judicial Conference of the United States, effective Apr. 1, 2016, see note set out under 11 U.S.C.A. § 104 of this title.

By notice dated Feb. 22, 2016, 81 F.R. 8748, the Judicial Conference of the United States adjusted the dollar amounts in provisions specified in subsecs. (d)(1) to (6), (8), (11)(D), (f)(3), (4)(B), (n), (p)(1), (q)(1) of this section, effective Apr. 1, 2016, as follows:

In subsec. (d)(1) adjusted $22,975 to $23,675.

In subsec. (d)(2) adjusted $3,675 to $3,775.

In subsec. (d)(3) adjusted $575 to $600 and $12,250 to $12,625.

In subsec. (d)(4) adjusted $1,550 to $1,600.

In subsec. (d)(5) adjusted $1,225 to $1,250, and $11,500 to $11,850.

In subsec. (d)(6) adjusted $2,300 to $2,375.

In subsec. (d)(8) adjusted $12,250 to $12,625.

In subsec. (d)(11)(D) adjusted $22,975 to $23,675.

In subsec. (f)(3) adjusted $6,225 to $6,425.

In subsec. (f)(4)(B) adjusted $650 (each time it appears) to $675 (each time it appears).

In subsec. (n) adjusted $1,245,475 to $1,283,025.

In subsec. (p)(1) adjusted $155,675 to $160,375.

In subsec. (q)(1) adjusted $155,675 to $160,375.

By notice dated Feb. 21, 2013, 78 F.R. 12089, the Judicial Conference of the United States adjusted the dollar amounts in provisions specified in subsecs. (d)(1) to (6), (8), (11)(D), (f)(3), (4)(B), (n), (p)(1), (q)(1) of this section, effective Apr. 1, 2013, as follows:

In subsec. (d)(1) adjusted $21,625 to $22,975.

In subsec. (d)(2) adjusted $3,450 to $3,675.

In subsec. (d)(3) adjusted $550 to $575 and $11,525 to $12,250.

In subsec. (d)(4) adjusted $1,450 to $1,550.

In subsec. (d)(5) adjusted $1,150 to $1,225, and $10,825 to $11,500.

In subsec. (d)(6) adjusted $2,175 to $2,300.

In subsec. (d)(8) adjusted $11,525 to $12,250.

In subsec. (d)(11)(D) adjusted $21,625 to $22,975.

In subsec. (f)(3) adjusted $5,850 to $6,225.

In subsec. (f)(4)(B) adjusted $600 (each time it appears) to $650 (each time it appears).

In subsec. (n) adjusted $1,171,650 to $1,245,475.

In subsec. (p)(1) adjusted $146,450 to $155,675.

In subsec. (q)(1) adjusted $146,450 to $155,675.

By notice dated Feb. 25, 2010, 75 F.R. 8747, the Judicial Conference of the United States adjusted the dollar amounts in provisions specified in subsecs. (d)(1) to (6), (8), (11)(D), (f)(3), (4)(B), (n), (p)(1), (q)(1) of this section, effective Apr. 1, 2010, as follows:

In subsec. (d)(1) adjusted $20,200 to $21,625.

In subsec. (d)(2) adjusted $3,225 to $3,450.

In subsec. (d)(3) adjusted $525 to $550 and $10,775 to $11,525.

In subsec. (d)(4) adjusted $1,350 to $1,450.

In subsec. (d)(5) adjusted $1,075 to $1,150, and $10,125 to $10,825.

In subsec. (d)(6) adjusted $2,025 to $2,175.

In subsec. (d)(8) adjusted $10,775 to $11,525.

In subsec. (d)(11)(D) adjusted $20,200 to $21,625.

In subsec. (f)(3) adjusted $5,475 to $5,850.

In subsec. (f)(4)(B) adjusted $550 (each time it appears) to $600 (each time it appears).

In subsec. (n) adjusted $1,095,000 to $1,171,650.

In subsec. (p)(1) adjusted $136,875 to $146,450.

In subsec. (q)(1) adjusted $136,875 to $146,450.

By notice dated Feb. 14, 2007, 72 F.R. 7082, the Judicial Conference of the United States adjusted the dollar amounts in provisions specified in subsecs. (d)(1) to (6), (8), (11)(D), (f)(3), (4), (n), (p), (q) of this section, effective Apr. 1, 2007, as follows:

In subsec. (d)(1) adjusted $18,450 to $20,200.

In subsec. (d)(2) adjusted $2,950 to $3,225.

In subsec. (d)(3) adjusted $475 to $525 and $9,850 to $10,775.

In subsec. (d)(4) adjusted $1,225 to $1,350.

In subsec. (d)(5) adjusted $975 to $1,075, and $9,250 to $10,125.

In subsec. (d)(6) adjusted $1,850 to $2,025.

In subsec. (d)(8) adjusted $9,850 to $10,775.

In subsec. (d)(11)(D) adjusted $18,450 to $20,200.

In subsec. (f)(3) adjusted $5,000 to $5,475.

In subsec. (f)(4) adjusted $500 (each time it appears) to $550 (each time it appears).

In subsec. (n) adjusted $1,000,000 to $1,095,000.

In subsec. (p) adjusted $125,000 to $136,875.

In subsec. (q) adjusted $125,000 to $136,875.

By notice dated Feb. 18, 2004, 69 F.R. 8482, the Judicial Conference of the United States adjusted the dollar amounts in provisions specified in subsec. (d)(1) to (6), (8), (11)(D) of this section, effective Apr. 1, 2004, as follows:

In subsec. (d)(1) adjusted $17,425 to $18,450.

In subsec. (d)(2) adjusted $2,775 to $2,950.

In subsec. (d)(3) adjusted $450 to $475 and $9,300 to $9,850.

In subsec. (d)(4) adjusted $1,150 to $1,225.

In subsec. (d)(5) adjusted $925 to $975, and $8,725 to $9,250.

In subsec. (d)(6) adjusted $1,750 to $1,850.

In subsec. (d)(8) adjusted $9,300 to $9,850.

In subsec. (d)(11)(D) adjusted $17,425 to $18,450.

By notice dated Feb. 20, 2001, 66 F.R. 10910, the Judicial Conference of the United States adjusted the dollar amounts in provisions specified in subsec. (d)(1) to (6), (8), (11)(D) of this section, effective Apr. 1, 2001, as follows:

In subsec. (d)(1) adjusted $16,150 to $17,425.

In subsec. (d)(2) adjusted $2,575 to $2,775.

In subsec. (d)(3) adjusted $425 to $450 and $8,625 to $9,300.

In subsec. (d)(4) adjusted $1,075 to $1,150.

In subsec. (d)(5) adjusted $850 to $925, and $8,075 to $8,725.

In subsec. (d)(6) adjusted $1,625 to $1,750.

In subsec. (d)(8) adjusted $8,625 to $9,300.

In subsec. (d)(11)(D) adjusted $16,150 to $17,425.

By notice dated Feb. 3, 1998, 63 F.R. 7179, the Judicial Conference of the United States adjusted the dollar amounts in provisions specified in subsec. (d)(1) to (6), (8), (11)(D) of this section, effective Apr. 1, 1998, as follows:

In subsec. (d)(1) adjusted $15,000 to $16,150.

In subsec. (d)(2) adjusted $2,400 to $2,575.

In subsec. (d)(3) adjusted $400 to $425 and $8,000 to $8,625.

In subsec. (d)(4) adjusted $1,000 to $1,075.

In subsec. (d)(5) adjusted $800 to $850 and $7,500 to $8,075.

In subsec. (d)(6) adjusted $1,500 to $1,625.

In subsec. (d)(8) adjusted $8,000 to $8,625.

In subsec. (d)(11)(D) adjusted $15,000 to $16,150.

CROSS REFERENCES

Allowance of claims or interests, see 11 USCA § 502.

Automatic preservation of avoided transfer, see 11 USCA § 551.

Effect of dismissal, see 11 USCA § 349.

Election to terminate debtor's taxable year for purposes of Internal Revenue Code not available to debtor with no assets other than property treated as exempt under this section, see 26 USCA § 1398.

Exempt property as including property treated as exempt under this section for purposes of Federal Debt Collection Act, see 28 USCA § 3014.

Insolvent as meaning financial condition wherein entity's debts are greater than entity's property exclusive of property that may be exempted under this section, see 11 USCA § 101.

Involuntary cases and future adjustments, see 11 USCA § 104.

Penalty for persons who negligently or fraudulently prepare bankruptcy petitions and exempt funds, see 11 USCA § 110.

Postpetition effect of security interest, see 11 USCA § 552.

Property claimed as exempt, see Official Bankr. Form B106C, 11 USCA.

Property exempt under this section not subject to enforcement of withdrawal liability for purposes of Employee Retirement Income Security Act Program, see 29 USCA § 1405.

Provisions in plan for use, sale or lease of exempt property, see 11 USCA § 1123.

Redemption, see 11 USCA § 722.

Reduction in basis not allowed for property exempt under this section for purposes of Internal Revenue Code, see 26 USCA § 1017.

Turnover of property to estate, see 11 USCA § 542.

§ 523. Exceptions to discharge

(a) A discharge under section 727, 1141, 1228(a), 1228(b), or 1328(b) of this title does not discharge an individual debtor from any debt—

(1) for a tax or a customs duty—

(A) of the kind and for the periods specified in section 507(a)(3) or 507(a)(8) of this title, whether or not a claim for such tax was filed or allowed;

(B) with respect to which a return, or equivalent report or notice, if required—

(i) was not filed or given; or

(ii) was filed or given after the date on which such return, report, or notice was last due, under applicable law or under any extension, and after two years before the date of the filing of the petition; or

(C) with respect to which the debtor made a fraudulent return or willfully attempted in any manner to evade or defeat such tax;

(2) for money, property, services, or an extension, renewal, or refinancing of credit, to the extent obtained by—

(A) false pretenses, a false representation, or actual fraud, other than a statement respecting the debtor's or an insider's financial condition;

(B) use of a statement in writing—

(i) that is materially false;

(ii) respecting the debtor's or an insider's financial condition;

(iii) on which the creditor to whom the debtor is liable for such money, property, services, or credit reasonably relied; and

(iv) that the debtor caused to be made or published with intent to deceive; or

(C)(i) for purposes of subparagraph (A)—

(I) consumer debts owed to a single creditor and aggregating more than $675 [1] for luxury goods or services incurred by an individual debtor on or within 90 days before the order for relief under this title are presumed to be nondischargeable; and

(II) cash advances aggregating more than $950 [1] that are extensions of consumer credit under an open end credit plan obtained by an individual debtor on or within 70 days before the order for relief under this title, are presumed to be nondischargeable; and

(ii) for purposes of this subparagraph—

(I) the terms "consumer", "credit", and "open end credit plan" have the same meanings as in section 103 of the Truth in Lending Act; and

(II) the term "luxury goods or services" does not include goods or services reasonably necessary for the support or maintenance of the debtor or a dependent of the debtor;

(3) neither listed nor scheduled under section 521(a)(1) of this title, with the name, if known to the debtor, of the creditor to whom such debt is owed, in time to permit—

(A) if such debt is not of a kind specified in paragraph (2), (4), or (6) of this subsection, timely filing of a proof of claim, unless such creditor had notice or actual knowledge of the case in time for such timely filing; or

(B) if such debt is of a kind specified in paragraph (2), (4), or (6) of this subsection, timely filing of a proof of claim and timely request for a determination of dischargeability of such debt under one of such paragraphs, unless such creditor had notice or actual knowledge of the case in time for such timely filing and request;

(4) for fraud or defalcation while acting in a fiduciary capacity, embezzlement, or larceny;

(5) for a domestic support obligation;

(6) for willful and malicious injury by the debtor to another entity or to the property of another entity;

(7) to the extent such debt is for a fine, penalty, or forfeiture payable to and for the benefit of a governmental unit, and is not compensation for actual pecuniary loss, other than a tax penalty—

(A) relating to a tax of a kind not specified in paragraph (1) of this subsection; or

(B) imposed with respect to a transaction or event that occurred before three years before the date of the filing of the petition;

(8) unless excepting such debt from discharge under this paragraph would impose an undue hardship on the debtor and the debtor's dependents, for—

(A)(i) an educational benefit overpayment or loan made, insured, or guaranteed by a governmental unit, or made under any program funded in whole or in part by a governmental unit or nonprofit institution; or

(ii) an obligation to repay funds received as an educational benefit, scholarship, or stipend; or

(B) any other educational loan that is a qualified education loan, as defined in section 221(d)(1) of the Internal Revenue Code of 1986, incurred by a debtor who is an individual;

(9) for death or personal injury caused by the debtor's operation of a motor vehicle, vessel, or aircraft if such operation was unlawful because the debtor was intoxicated from using alcohol, a drug, or another substance;

(10) that was or could have been listed or scheduled by the debtor in a prior case concerning the debtor under this title or under the Bankruptcy Act in which the debtor waived discharge, or was denied a discharge under section 727(a)(2), (3), (4), (5), (6), or (7) of this title, or under section 14c(1), (2), (3), (4), (6), or (7) of such Act;

(11) provided in any final judgment, unreviewable order, or consent order or decree entered in any court of the United States or of any State, issued by a Federal depository institutions regulatory agency, or contained in any settlement agreement entered into by the debtor, arising from any act of fraud or defalcation while acting in a fiduciary capacity committed with respect to any depository institution or insured credit union;

(12) for malicious or reckless failure to fulfill any commitment by the debtor to a Federal depository institutions regulatory agency to maintain the capital of an insured depository institution, except that this paragraph shall not extend any such commitment which would otherwise be terminated due to any act of such agency;

(13) for any payment of an order of restitution issued under title 18, United States Code;

(14) incurred to pay a tax to the United States that would be nondischargeable pursuant to paragraph (1);

(14A) incurred to pay a tax to a governmental unit, other than the United States, that would be nondischargeable under paragraph (1);

(14B) incurred to pay fines or penalties imposed under Federal election law;

(15) to a spouse, former spouse, or child of the debtor and not of the kind described in paragraph (5) that is incurred by the debtor in the course of a divorce or separation or in connection with a separation agreement, divorce decree or other order of a court of record, or a determination made in accordance with State or territorial law by a governmental unit;

(16) for a fee or assessment that becomes due and payable after the order for relief to a membership association with respect to the debtor's interest in a unit that has condominium ownership, in a share of a cooperative corporation, or a lot in a homeowners association, for as long as the debtor or the trustee has a legal, equitable, or possessory ownership interest in such unit, such corporation, or such lot, but nothing in this paragraph shall except from discharge the debt of a debtor for a membership association fee or assessment for a period arising before entry of the order for relief in a pending or subsequent bankruptcy case;

(17) for a fee imposed on a prisoner by any court for the filing of a case, motion, complaint, or appeal, or for other costs and expenses assessed with respect to such filing, regardless of an assertion of poverty by the debtor under subsection (b) or (f)(2) of section 1915 of title 28 (or a similar non–Federal

law), or the debtor's status as a prisoner, as defined in section 1915(h) of title 28 (or a similar non–Federal law);

(18) owed to a pension, profit-sharing, stock bonus, or other plan established under section 401, 403, 408, 408A, 414, 457, or 501(c) of the Internal Revenue Code of 1986, under—

    (A) a loan permitted under section 408(b)(1) of the Employee Retirement Income Security Act of 1974, or subject to section 72(p) of the Internal Revenue Code of 1986; or

    (B) a loan from a thrift savings plan permitted under subchapter III of chapter 84 of title 5, that satisfies the requirements of section 8433(g) of such title;

but nothing in this paragraph may be construed to provide that any loan made under a governmental plan under section 414(d), or a contract or account under section 403(b), of the Internal Revenue Code of 1986 constitutes a claim or a debt under this title; or

(19) that—

    (A) is for—

        (i) the violation of any of the Federal securities laws (as that term is defined in section 3(a)(47) of the Securities Exchange Act of 1934), any of the State securities laws, or any regulation or order issued under such Federal or State securities laws; or

        (ii) common law fraud, deceit, or manipulation in connection with the purchase or sale of any security; and

    (B) results, before, on, or after the date on which the petition was filed, from—

        (i) any judgment, order, consent order, or decree entered in any Federal or State judicial or administrative proceeding;

        (ii) any settlement agreement entered into by the debtor; or

        (iii) any court or administrative order for any damages, fine, penalty, citation, restitutionary payment, disgorgement payment, attorney fee, cost, or other payment owed by the debtor.

For purposes of this subsection, the term "return" means a return that satisfies the requirements of applicable nonbankruptcy law (including applicable filing requirements). Such term includes a return prepared pursuant to section 6020(a) of the Internal Revenue Code of 1986, or similar State or local law, or a written stipulation to a judgment or a final order entered by a nonbankruptcy tribunal, but does not include a return made pursuant to section 6020(b) of the Internal Revenue Code of 1986, or a similar State or local law.

(b) Notwithstanding subsection (a) of this section, a debt that was excepted from discharge under subsection (a)(1), (a)(3), or (a)(8) of this section, under section 17a(1), 17a(3), or 17a(5) of the Bankruptcy Act, under

section 439A of the Higher Education Act of 1965, or under section 733(g) of the Public Health Service Act in a prior case concerning the debtor under this title, or under the Bankruptcy Act, is dischargeable in a case under this title unless, by the terms of subsection (a) of this section, such debt is not dischargeable in the case under this title.

(c)(1) Except as provided in subsection (a)(3)(B) of this section, the debtor shall be discharged from a debt of a kind specified in paragraph (2), (4), or (6) of subsection (a) of this section, unless, on request of the creditor to whom such debt is owed, and after notice and a hearing, the court determines such debt to be excepted from discharge under paragraph (2), (4), or (6), as the case may be, of subsection (a) of this section.

(2) Paragraph (1) shall not apply in the case of a Federal depository institutions regulatory agency seeking, in its capacity as conservator, receiver, or liquidating agent for an insured depository institution, to recover a debt described in subsection (a)(2), (a)(4), (a)(6), or (a)(11) owed to such institution by an institution-affiliated party unless the receiver, conservator, or liquidating agent was appointed in time to reasonably comply, or for a Federal depository institutions regulatory agency acting in its corporate capacity as a successor to such receiver, conservator, or liquidating agent to reasonably comply, with subsection (a)(3)(B) as a creditor of such institution-affiliated party with respect to such debt.

(d) If a creditor requests a determination of dischargeability of a consumer debt under subsection (a)(2) of this section, and such debt is discharged, the court shall grant judgment in favor of the debtor for the costs of, and a reasonable attorney's fee for, the proceeding if the court finds that the position of the creditor was not substantially justified, except that the court shall not award such costs and fees if special circumstances would make the award unjust.

(e) Any institution-affiliated party of an insured depository institution shall be considered to be acting in a fiduciary capacity with respect to the purposes of subsection (a)(4) or (11).

(Pub.L. 95–598, Nov. 6, 1978, 92 Stat. 2590; Pub.L. 96–56, § 3, Aug. 14, 1979, 93 Stat. 387; Pub.L. 97–35, Title XXIII, § 2334(b), Aug. 13, 1981, 95 Stat. 863; Pub.L. 98–353, Title III, §§ 307, 371, 454, July 10, 1984, 98 Stat. 353, 364, 375; Pub.L. 99–554, Title II, §§ 257(n), 281, 283(j), Oct. 27, 1986, 100 Stat. 3115 to 3117; Pub.L. 101–581, § 2(a), Nov. 15, 1990, 104 Stat. 2865; Pub.L. 101–647, Title XXV, § 2522(a), Title XXXI, § 3102(a), Title XXXVI, § 3621, Nov. 29, 1990, 104 Stat. 4865, 4916, 4964; Pub.L. 103–322, Title XXXII, § 320934, Sept. 13, 1994, 108 Stat. 2135; Pub.L. 103–394, Title II, § 221, Title III, §§ 304(e), (h)(3), 306, 309, Title V, § 501(d)(13), Oct. 22, 1994, 108 Stat. 4129, 4133 to 4135, 4137, 4145; Pub.L. 104–134, Title I, § 101[(a)] [Title VIII, § 804(b)], Apr. 26, 1996, 110 Stat. 1321, 1321–74; renumbered Title I Pub.L. 104–140, § 1(a), May 2, 1996, 110 Stat. 1327; amended Pub.L. 104–193, Title III, § 374(a), Aug. 22, 1996,

---

110 Stat. 2255; Pub.L. 105–244, Title IX, § 971(a), Oct. 7, 1998, 112 Stat. 1837; Pub.L. 107–204, Title VIII, § 803, July 30, 2002, 116 Stat. 801; Pub.L. 109–8, Title II, §§ 215, 220, 224(c), Title III, §§ 301, 310, 314(a), Title IV, § 412, Title VII, § 714, Title XII, §§ 1209, 1235, Title XIV, § 1404(a), Title XV, § 1502(a)(2), Apr. 20, 2005, 119 Stat. 54, 59, 64, 75, 84, 88, 107, 128, 194, 204, 215, 216; Pub.L. 111–327, § 2(a)(18), Dec. 22, 2010, 124 Stat. 3559.)

¹ Dollar amount as adjusted by the Judicial Conference of the United States. See Adjustment of Dollar Amounts notes set out under this section and 11 U.S.C.A. § 104.

HISTORICAL AND STATUTORY NOTES

Revision Notes and Legislative Reports

1978 Acts. This section specifies which of the debtor's debts are not discharged in a bankruptcy case, and certain procedures for effectuating the section. The provision in Bankruptcy Act § 17c [section § 35(c) of former Title 11] granting the bankruptcy courts jurisdiction to determine dischargeability is deleted as unnecessary, in view of the comprehensive grant of jurisdiction prescribed in proposed 28 U.S.C. 1334(b), which is adequate to cover the full jurisdiction that the bankruptcy courts have today over dischargeability and related issues under Bankruptcy Act § 17c [section 35(c) of former Title 11]. The Rules of Bankruptcy Procedure will specify, as they do today, who may request determinations of dischargeability, subject, of course, to proposed 11 U.S.C. 523(c), and when such a request may be made. Proposed 11 U.S.C. 350, providing for reopening of cases, provides one possible procedure for a determination of dischargeability and related issues after a case is closed.

Subsection (a) lists nine kinds of debts excepted from discharge. Taxes that are excepted from discharge are set forth in paragraph (1). These include claims against the debtor which receive priority in the second, third and sixth categories (§ 507(a)(3)(B) and (C) and (6)). These categories include taxes for which the tax authority failed to file a claim against the estate or filed its claim late. Whether or not the taxing authority's claim is secured will also not affect the claim's nondischargeability if the tax liability in question is otherwise entitled to priority.

Also included in the nondischargeable debts are taxes for which the debtor had not filed a required return as of the petition date, or for which a return had been filed beyond its last permitted due date (§ 523(a)(1)(B)). For this purpose, the date of the tax year to which the return relates is immaterial. The late return rule applies, however, only to the late returns filed within three years before the petition was filed, and to late returns filed after the petition in title 11 was filed. For this purpose, the taxable year in question need not be one or more of the three years immediately preceding the filing of the petition.

Tax claims with respect to which the debtor filed a fraudulent return, entry or invoice, or fraudulently attempted to evade or defeat any tax (§ 523(a)(1)(C)) are included. The date of the taxable year with regard to which the fraud occurred is immaterial.

Also included are tax payments due under an agreement for deferred payment of taxes, which a debtor had entered into with the Internal Revenue Service (or State or local tax authority) before the filing of the petition and which relate to a prepetition tax liability (§ 523(a)(1)(D)) are also nondischargeable. This classification applies only to tax claims which would have received priority under section 507(a) if the

taxpayer had filed a title 11 petition on the date on which the deferred payment agreement was entered into. This rule also applies only to installment payments which become due during and after the commencement of the title 11 case. Payments which had become due within one year before the filing of the petition receive sixth priority, and will be nondischargeable under the general rule of section 523(a)(1)(A).

The above categories of nondischargeability apply to customs duties as well as to taxes.

Paragraph (2) provides that as under Bankruptcy Act § 17a(2) [section 35(a)(2) of former Title 11], a debt for obtaining money, property, services, or a refinancing extension or renewal of credit by false pretenses, a false representation, or actual fraud, or by use of a statement in writing respecting the debtor's financial condition that is materially false, on which the creditor reasonably relied, and which the debtor made or published with intent to deceive, is excepted from discharge. This provision is modified only slightly from current section 17a(2) [section 35(a)(2) of former Title 11]. First, "actual fraud" is added as a ground for exception from discharge. Second, the creditor must not only have relied on a false statement in writing, but the reliance must have been reasonable. This codifies case law construing present section 17a(2) [section 35(a)(2) of former Title 11]. Third, the phrase "in any manner whatsoever" that appears in current law after "made or published" is deleted as unnecessary, the word "published" is used in the same sense that it is used in defamation cases.

Unscheduled debts are excepted from discharge under paragraph (3). The provision, derived from section 17a(3) [section 35(a)(3) of former Title 11], follows current law, but clarifies some uncertainties generated by the case law construing 17a(3) [section 35(a)(3) of former Title 11]. The debt is excepted from discharge if it was not scheduled in time to permit timely action by the creditor to protect his rights, unless the creditor had notice or actual knowledge of the case.

Paragraph (4) excepts debts for fraud incurred by the debtor while acting in a fiduciary capacity or for defalcation, embezzlement, or misappropriation.

Paragraph (5) [So in original. Probably should be "Paragraph (6)".] provides that debts for willful and malicious conversion or injury by the debtor to another entity or the property of another entity are nondischargeable. Under this paragraph "willful" means deliberate or intentional. To the extent that *Tinker v. Colwell*, 139 U.S. 473 (1902) [24 S.Ct. 505, 48 L.Ed. 754, 11 Am.Bankr.Rep. 568], held that a less strict standard is intended, and to the extent that other cases have relied on *Tinker* to apply a "reckless disregard" standard, they are overruled.

Paragraph (6) [So in original. Probably should be "Paragraph (5)".] excepts from discharge debts to a spouse, former spouse, or child of the debtor for alimony to, maintenance for, or support of the spouse or child. This language, in combination with the repeal of section 456(b) of the Social Security Act (42 U.S.C. 656(b)) [section 656(b) of Title 42, The Public Health and Welfare] by section 326 of the bill, will apply to make nondischargeable only alimony, maintenance, or support owed directly to a spouse or dependent. What constitutes alimony, maintenance, or support, will be determined under the bankruptcy law, not State law. Thus, cases such as *In re Waller*, 494 F.2d 447 (6th Cir. 1974), are overruled, and the result in cases such as *Fife v. Fife*, 1 Utah 2d 281, 265 P.2d 642 (1952) is followed. The proviso, however, makes nondischargeable any debts resulting from an agreement by the debtor to hold the debtor's spouse harmless on joint debts, to the extent that the agreement is in payment of alimony, maintenance, or support of the spouse, as determined under bankruptcy law considerations as to whether a particular agreement to pay money to a spouse is actually alimony or a property settlement.

Paragraph (7) makes nondischargeable certain liabilities for penalties including tax penalties if the underlying tax with respect to which the penalty was imposed is also nondischargeable (sec. 523(a)(7)). These latter liabilities cover those which, but are penal in nature, as distinct from so-called "pecuniary loss" penalties which, in the case of taxes, involve basically the collection of a tax under the label of a "penalty." This provision differs from the bill as introduced, which did not link the nondischarge of a tax penalty with the treatment of the underlying tax. The amended provision reflects the existing position of the Internal Revenue Service as to tax penalties imposed by the Internal Revenue Code [Title 26] (Rev.Rul. 68–574, 1968–2 C.B. 595).

Paragraph (8) follows generally current law and excerpts [sic] from discharge student loans until such loans have been due and owing for five years. Such loans include direct student loans as well as insured and guaranteed loans. This provision is intended to be self-executing and the lender or institution is not required to file a complaint to determine the nondischargeability of any student loan.

Paragraph (9) excepts from discharge debts that the debtor owed before a previous bankruptcy case concerning the debtor in which the debtor was denied a discharge other than on the basis of the six-year bar.

Subsection (b) of this section permits discharge in a bankruptcy case of an unscheduled debt from a prior case. This provision is carried over from Bankruptcy Act § 17b [section 35(b) of former Title 11]. The result dictated by the subsection would probably not be different if the subsection were not included. It is included nevertheless for clarity.

Subsection (c) requires a creditor who is owed a debt that may be excepted from discharge under paragraph (2), (4), or (5), (false statements, defalcation or larceny misappropriation, or willful and malicious injury) to initiate proceedings in the bankruptcy court for an exception to discharge. If the creditor does not act, the debt is discharged. This provision does not change current law.

Subsection (d) is new. It provides protection to a consumer debtor that dealt honestly with a creditor who sought to have a debt excepted from discharge on the ground of falsity in the incurring of the debt. The debtor may be awarded costs and a reasonable attorney's fee for the proceeding to determine the dischargeability of a debt under subsection (a)(2), if the court finds that the proceeding was frivolous or not brought by its creditor in good faith.

The purpose of the provision is to discourage creditors from initiating proceedings to obtaining a false financial statement exception to discharge in the hope of obtaining a settlement from an honest debtor anxious to save attorney's fees. Such practices impair the debtor's fresh start and are contrary to the spirit of the bankruptcy laws. Senate Report 95–989.

Subsection (a) lists eight kinds of debts excepted from discharge. Taxes that are entitled to priority are excepted from discharge under paragraph (1). In addition, taxes with respect to which the debtor made a fraudulent return or willfully attempted to evade or defeat, or with respect to which a return (if required) was not filed or was not filed after the due date and after one year before the bankruptcy case

are excepted from discharge. If the taxing authority's claim has been disallowed, then it would be barred by the more modern rules of collateral estoppel from reasserting that claim against the debtor after the case was closed. See Plumb, The Tax Recommendations of the Commission on the Bankruptcy Laws: Tax Procedures, 88 Harv.L.Rev. 1360, 1388 (1975).

As under Bankruptcy Act § 17a(2) [section 35(a)(2) of former Title 11], a debt for obtaining money, property, services, or an extension or renewal of credit by false pretenses, a false representation, or actual fraud, or by use of a statement in writing respecting the debtor's financial condition that is materially false, on which the creditor reasonably relied, and that the debtor made or published with intent to deceive, is excepted from discharge. This provision is modified only slightly from current section 17a(2). First, "actual fraud" is added as a grounds for exception from discharge. Second, the creditor must not only have relied on a false statement in writing, the reliance must have been reasonable. This codifies case law construing this provision. Third, the phrase "in any manner whatsoever" that appears in current law after "made or published" is deleted as unnecessary. The word "published" is used in the same sense that it is used in slander actions.

Unscheduled debts are excepted from discharge under paragraph (3). The provision, derived from section 17a(3) [section 35(a)(3) of former Title 11], follows current law, but clarifies some uncertainties generated by the case law construing 17a(3). The debt is excepted from discharge if it was not scheduled in time to permit timely action by the creditor to protect his rights, unless the creditor had notice or actual knowledge of the case.

Paragraph (4) excepts debts for embezzlement or larceny. The deletion of willful and malicious conversion from § 17a(2) [section 35(a)(2) of former Title 11] of the Bankruptcy Act is not intended to effect a substantive change. The intent is to include in the category of non-dischargeable debts a conversion under which the debtor willfully and maliciously intends to borrow property for a short period of time with no intent to inflict injury but on which injury is in fact inflicted.

Paragraph (5) excepts from discharge debts to a spouse, former spouse, or child of the debtor for alimony to, maintenance for, or support of, the spouse or child. This language, in combination with the repeal of section 456(b) of the Social Security Act (42 U.S.C. 656(b)) [former section 656(b) of Title 42, The Public Health and Welfare] by section 327 of the bill, will apply to make nondischargeable only alimony, maintenance, or support owed directly to a spouse or dependent. See Hearings, pt. 2, at 942. What constitutes alimony, maintenance, or support, will be determined under the bankruptcy laws, not State law. Thus, cases such as *In re Waller*, 494 F.2d 447 (6th Cir. 1974); Hearings, pt. 3, at 1308–10, are overruled, and the result in cases such as *Fife v. Fife*, 1 Utah 2d 281, 265 P.2d 642 (1952) is followed. This provision will, however, make nondischargeable any debts resulting from an agreement by the debtor to hold the debtor's spouse harmless on joint debts, to the extent that the agreement is in payment of alimony, maintenance, or support of the spouse, as determined under bankruptcy law considerations that are similar to considerations of whether a particular agreement to pay money to a spouse is actually alimony or a property settlement. See Hearings, pt. 3, at 1287–1290.

Paragraph (6) excepts debts for willful and malicious injury by the debtor to another person or to the property of another person. Under this paragraph, "willful" means deliberate or intentional. To the extent that *Tinker v. Colwell*, 193 U.S. 473 (1902) [24 S.Ct. 505, 48 L.Ed. 754, 11 Am.Bankr.Rep. 568], held that a looser standard is intended, and to the extent that other cases have relied on *Tinker* to apply a "reckless disregard" standard, they are overruled.

Paragraph (7) excepts from discharge a debt for a fine, penalty, or forfeiture payable to and for the benefit of a governmental unit, that is not compensation for actual pecuniary loss.

Paragraph (8) [now (9)] excepts from discharge debts that the debtor owed before a previous bankruptcy case concerning the debtor in which the debtor was denied a discharge other than on the basis of the six-year bar.

Subsection (b) of this section permits discharge in a bankruptcy case of an unscheduled debt from a prior case. This provision is carried over from Bankruptcy Act § 17b [section 35(b) of former Title 11]. The result dictated by the subsection would probably not be different if the subsection were not included. It is included nevertheless for clarity.

Subsection (c) requires a creditor who is owed a debt that may be expected from discharge under paragraph (2), (4), or (6) (false statements, embezzlement or larceny, or willful and malicious injury) to initiate proceedings in the bankruptcy court for an exception to discharge. If the creditor does not act, the debt is discharged. This provision does not change current law.

Subsection (d) is new. It provides protection to a consumer debtor that dealt honestly with a creditor who sought to have a debt excepted from discharge on grounds of falsity in the incurring of the debt. The debtor is entitled to costs of and a reasonable attorney's fee for the proceeding to determine the dischargeability of a debt under subsection (a)(2), if the creditor initiated the proceeding and the debt was determined to be dischargeable. The court is permitted to award any actual pecuniary loss that the debtor may have suffered as a result of the proceeding (such as loss of a day's pay). The purpose of the provision is to discourage creditors from initiating false financial statement exception to discharge actions in the hopes of obtaining a settlement from an honest debtor anxious to save attorney's fees. Such practices impair the debtor's fresh start. House Report No. 95–595.

1979 Acts. Senate Report No. 96–230, see 1979 U.S. Code Cong. and Adm. News, p. 936.

1981 Acts. Senate Report No. 97–139 and House Conference Report No. 97–208, see 1981 U.S. Code Cong. and Adm. News, p. 396.

1984 Acts. Statements by Legislative Leaders, see 1984 U.S. Code Cong. and Adm. News, p. 576.

1986 Acts. House Report No. 99–764 and House Conference Report No. 99–958, see 1986 U.S. Code Cong. and Adm. News, p. 5227.

1990 Acts. House Report No. 101–681(Part I), see 1990 U.S. Code Cong. and Adm. News, p. 6472.

Senate Report No. 101–434, see 1990 U.S. Code Cong. and Adm. News, p. 4065.

1994 Acts. House Report No. 103–324, House Report No. 103–489, and House Conference Report No. 103–711, see 1994 U.S. Code Cong. and Adm. News, p. 1801.

House Report No. 103–835, see 1994 U.S. Code Cong. and Adm. News, p. 3340.

1996 Acts. House Report No. 104–651 and House Conference Report No. 104–725, see 1996 U.S. Code Cong. and Adm. News, p. 2183.

1998 Acts. House Conference Report No. 105–750, see 1998 U.S. Code Cong. and Adm. News, p. 417.

2002 Acts. House Conference Report No. 107–610 and Statement by President, see 2002 U.S. Code Cong. and Adm. News, p. 542.

2005 Acts. House Report No. 109–31(Part I), see 2005 U.S. Code Cong. and Adm. News, p. 88.

Legislative Statements

Section 523(a)(1) represents a compromise between the position taken in the House bill and the Senate amendment. Section 523(a)(2) likewise represents a compromise between the position taken in the House bill and the Senate amendment with respect to the false financial statement exception to discharge. In order to clarify that a "renewal of credit" includes a "refinancing of credit", explicit reference to a refinancing of credit is made in the preamble to section 523(a)(2). A renewal of credit or refinancing of credit that was obtained by a false financial statement within the terms of section 523(a)(2) is nondischargeable. However, each of the provisions of section 523(a)(2) must be proved. Thus, under section 523(a)(2)(A) a creditor must prove that the debt was obtained by false pretenses, a false representation, or actual fraud, other than a statement respecting the debtor's or an insider's financial condition. Subparagraph (A) is intended to codify current case law e.g., *Neal v. Clark*, 95 U.S. 704 (1887) [24 L.Ed. 586], which interprets "fraud" to mean actual or positive fraud rather than fraud implied in law. Subparagraph (A) is mutually exclusive from subparagraph (B). Subparagraph (B) pertains to the so-called false financial statement. In order for the debt to be nondischargeable, the creditor must prove that the debt was obtained by the use of a statement in writing (i) that is materially false; (ii) respecting the debtor's or an insider's financial condition; (iii) on which the creditor to whom the debtor is liable for obtaining money, property, services, or credit reasonably relied; (iv) that the debtor caused to be made or published with intent to deceive. Section 523(a)(2)(B)(iv) is not intended to change from present law since the statement that the debtor causes to be made or published with the intent to deceive automatically includes a statement that the debtor actually makes or publishes with an intent to deceive. Section 523(a)(2)(B) is explained in the House report. Under section 523(a)(2)(B)(i) a discharge is barred only as to that portion of a loan with respect to which a false financial statement is materially false.

In many cases, a creditor is required by state law to refinance existing credit on which there has been no default. If the creditor does not forfeit remedies or otherwise rely to his detriment on a false financial statement with respect to existing credit, then an extension, renewal, or refinancing of such credit is nondischargeable only to the extent of the new money advanced; on the other hand, if an existing loan is in default or the creditor otherwise reasonably relies to his detriment on a false financial statement with regard to an existing loan, then the entire debt is nondischargeable under section 523(a)(2)(B). This codifies the reasoning expressed by the second circuit in *In re Danns*, 558 F.2d 114 (2d Cir. 1977).

Section 523(a)(3) of the House amendment is derived from the Senate amendment. The provision is intended to overrule

Birkett v. Columbia Bank, 195 U.S. 345 (1904) [25 S.Ct. 38, 49 L.Ed. 231, 12 Am.Bankr.Rep. 691].

Section 523(a)(4) of the House amendment represents a compromise between the House bill and the Senate amendment.

Section 523(a)(5) is a compromise between the House bill and the Senate amendment. The provision excepts from discharge a debt owed to a spouse, former spouse or child of the debtor, in connection with a separation agreement, divorce decree, or property settlement agreement, for alimony to, maintenance for, or support of such spouse or child but not to the extent that the debt is assigned to another entity. If the debtor has assumed an obligation of the debtor's spouse to a third party in connection with a separation agreement, property settlement agreement, or divorce proceeding, such debt is dischargeable to the extent that payment of the debt by the debtor is not actually in the nature of alimony, maintenance, or support of debtor's spouse, former spouse, or child.

Section 523(a)(6) adopts the position taken in the House bill and rejects the alternative suggested in the Senate amendment. The phrase "willful and malicious injury" covers a willful and malicious conversion.

Section 523(a)(7) of the House amendment adopts the position taken in the Senate amendment and rejects the position taken in the House bill. A penalty relating to a tax cannot be nondischargeable unless the tax itself is nondischargeable.

Section 523(a)(8) represents a compromise between the House bill and the Senate amendment regarding educational loans. This provision is broader than current law which is limited to federally insured loans. Only educational loans owing to a governmental unit or a nonprofit institution of higher education are made nondischargeable under this paragraph.

Section 523(b) is new. The section represents a modification of similar provisions contained in the House bill and the Senate amendment.

Section 523(c) of the House amendment adopts the position taken in the Senate amendment.

Section 523(d) represents a compromise between the position taken in the House bill and the Senate amendment on the issue of attorneys' fees in false financial statement complaints to determine dischargeability. The provision contained in the House bill permitting the court to award damages is eliminated. The court must grant the debtor judgment or a reasonable attorneys' fee unless the granting of judgment would be clearly inequitable.

Nondischargeable debts: The House amendment retains the basic categories of nondischargeable tax liabilities contained in both bills, but restricts the time limits on certain nondischargeable taxes. Under the amendment, nondischargeable taxes cover taxes entitled to priority under section 507(a)(6) of title 11 and, in the case of individual debtors under chapters 7, 11, or 13, tax liabilities with respect to which no required return had been filed or as to which a late return had been filed if the return became last due, including extensions, within 2 years before the date of the petition or became due after the petition or as to which the debtor made a fraudulent return, entry or invoice or fraudulently attempted to evade or defeat the tax.

In the case of individuals in liquidation under chapter 7 or in reorganization under chapter 11 of title 11, section 1141(d)(2) incorporates by reference the exceptions to discharge continued in section 523. Different rules concerning the discharge of taxes where a partnership or corporation reorganizes under chapter 11, apply under section 1141.

The House amendment also deletes the reduction rule contained in section 523(e) of the Senate amendment. Under that rule, the amount of an otherwise nondischargeable tax liability would be reduced by the amount which a governmental tax authority could have collected from the debtor's estate if it had filed a timely claim against the estate but which it did not collect because no such claim was filed. This provision is deleted in order not to effectively compel a tax authority to file claim against the estate in "no asset" cases, along with a dischargeability petition. In no-asset cases, therefore, if the tax authority is not potentially penalized by failing to file a claim, the debtor in such cases will have a better opportunity to choose the prepayment forum, bankruptcy court or the Tax Court, in which to litigate his personal liability for a nondischargeable tax.

The House amendment also adopts the Senate amendment provision limiting the nondischargeability of punitive tax penalties, that is, penalties other than those which represent collection of a principal amount of tax liability through the form of a "penalty." Under the House amendment, tax penalties which are basically punitive in nature are to be nondischargeable only if the penalty is computed by reference to a related tax liability which is nondischargeable or, if the amount of the penalty is not computed by reference to a tax liability, the transaction or event giving rise to the penalty occurred during the 3-year period ending on the date of the petition.

References in Text

Section 6020(a) of the Internal Revenue Code of 1986, referred to in subsec. (a), is classified to 26 U.S.C.A. § 6020(a).

Section 6020(b) of the Internal Revenue Code of 1986, referred to in subsec. (a), is classified to 26 U.S.C.A. § 6020(b).

Section 103 of the Truth in Lending Act, referred to in subsec. (a)(2)(C)(ii)(I), is Pub.L. 90–321, Title I, § 103, May 29, 1968, 82 Stat. 147, as amended, which is classified to 15 U.S.C.A. § 1602.

Section 221(d)(1) of the Internal Revenue Code of 1986, referred to in subsec. (a)(8)(B), is classified to 26 U.S.C.A. § 221(d)(1).

The Bankruptcy Act, referred to in subsecs. (a)(10) and (b), is Act July 1, 1898, c. 541, 30 Stat. 544, as amended, which was classified generally to former Title 11. Sections 14c and 17a of the Bankruptcy Act were classified to sections 32(c) and 35(a) of former Title 11.

Section 401, 403, 408, 408A, 414, 457, or 501(c) of the Internal Revenue Code of 1986, referred to in subsec. (a)(18), is classified to 26 U.S.C.A. § 401, 403, 408, 408A, 414, 457, or 501(c).

Section 408(b)(1) of the Employee Retirement Income Security Act of 1974, referred to in subsec. (a)(18)(A), is Pub.L. 93–406, Title I, § 408(b)(1), Sept. 2, 1974, 88 Stat. 883, as amended, which is classified to 29 U.S.C.A. § 1108(b)(1).

Section 72(p) of the Internal Revenue Code of 1986, referred to in subsec. (a)(18)(A), is classified to 26 U.S.C.A. § 72(p).

Subchapter III of chapter 84 of title 5, referred to in subsec. (a)(18)(B), is 5 U.S.C.A. § 8431 et seq.

Section 414(d) or section 403(b) of the Internal Revenue Code, referred to in the undesignated paragraph following subsec. (a)(18), is classified to 26 U.S.C.A. § 414(d) or 26 U.S.C.A. § 403(b).

Section 3(a)(47) of the Securities Exchange Act of 1934, referred to in subsec. (a)(19)(A)(i), is section 3(a)(47) of Act June 6, 1934, c. 404, Title I, 48 Stat. 882, as amended, which is classified to 15 U.S.C.A. § 78c(a)(47).

Section 439A of the Higher Education Act of 1965, referred to in subsec. (b), is section 439A of Pub.L. 89–329, Title IV, as added Pub.L. 94–482, Title I, § 127(a), Oct. 12, 1976, 90 Stat. 2141, which was classified to section 1087–3 of Title 20, Education, and was repealed by Pub.L. 95–598, Title III, § 317, Nov. 6, 1978, 92 Stat. 2678.

Section 733 of the Public Health Service Act, referred to in subsec. (b), is section 733 of Act July 1, 1944, c. 373, Title VII as added Oct. 12, 1976, Pub.L. 94–484, Title IV, § 401(b)(3), 90 Stat. 2262, which was classified to section 294f of Title 42, The Public Health and Welfare, and which was repealed by Pub.L. 95–598, Title III, § 327, Nov. 6, 1978, 92 Stat. 2679. A subsec. (g), containing similar provisions, was added to section 733 by Pub.L. 97–35, Title XXVII, § 2730, Aug. 13, 1981, 95 Stat. 919. Section 733 was subsequently omitted in the general revision of subchapter V of chapter 6A of Title 42 by Pub.L. 102–408, Title I, § 102, Oct. 13, 1992, 106 Stat. 1992.

Codifications

Amendment by section 215(3) of Pub.L. 109–8, directing the amendment of par. (15) as added by Public Law 103–394, was executed by amending par. (15) of subsec. (a), as the probable intent of Congress.

Amendment by section 304(e) of Pub.L. 103–394, directing the addition of par. (15), was executed by adding par. (15) to subsec. (a), as the probable intent of Congress.

Pub.L. 101–581 and Pub.L. 101–647, § 3102(a), made identical amendments to subsec. (a)(9) of this section. See 1990 Amendments note set out under this section.

Amendment by section 283(j)(1) of Pub.L. 99–554, which redesignated the second par. (9) of subsec. (a) as (10), has been executed by redesignating as (10), par. (9) as enacted by Pub.L. 95–598 as the probable intent of Congress in view of amendment by section 371(2) of Pub.L. 98–353, which directed the addition of par. (9), as presently set out, to follow par. (8).

Effective and Applicability Provisions

2013 Acts. Increase of dollar amounts by Judicial Conference of the United States by notice published Feb. 21, 2013, 78 F.R. 12089 effective April 1, 2013, and increase not applicable to cases commenced before the effective date of the adjustments, i.e., April 1, 2013. See Adjustment of Dollar Amounts notes under 11 U.S.C.A. § 104 and this section.

2010 Acts. Increase of dollar amounts by Judicial Conference of the United States by notice published Feb. 25, 2010, 75 F.R. 8747 effective April 1, 2010, and increase not applicable to cases commenced before the effective date of the adjustments, i.e., April 1, 2010. See Adjustment of Dollar Amounts notes under 11 U.S.C.A. § 104 and this section.

2007 Acts. Increase of dollar amounts by Judicial Conference of the United States by notice published Feb. 14, 2007, 72 F.R. 7082 effective April 1, 2007, and increase not applicable to cases commenced before the effective date of the adjustments, i.e., April 1, 2007. See Adjustment of Dollar Amounts notes under 11 U.S.C.A. § 104 and this section.

2005 Acts. Pub.L. 109–8, Title XIV, § 1404(b), Apr. 20, 2005, 119 Stat. 215, provided that: "**Effective date upon enactment of Sarbanes–Oxley Act.**—The amendment made by subsection (a) [amending subsec. (a)(19)(B) of this section] is effective beginning July 30, 2002."

Amendments by Pub.L. 109–8, Title XIV, effective, except as otherwise provided, on Apr. 20, 2005, and applicable only with respect to cases commenced under Title 11 on or after Apr. 20, 2005, see Pub.L. 109–8, § 1406, set out as a note under 11 U.S.C.A. § 507.

Amendments by Pub.L. 109–8 effective, except as otherwise provided, 180 days after April 20, 2005, and inapplicable with respect to cases commenced under Title 11 before the effective date, see Pub.L. 109–8, § 1501, set out as a note under 11 U.S.C.A. § 101.

2004 Acts. Adjustment of dollar amounts by Judicial Conference of the United States by notice dated Feb. 18, 2004, 69 F.R. 8482 effective April 1, 2004, and adjustment not applicable to cases commenced before the effective date of the adjustments, i.e., April 1, 2004. See Adjustment of Dollar Amounts notes under 11 U.S.C.A. § 104 and this section.

2001 Acts. Adjustment of dollar amounts by Judicial Conference of the United States by notice dated Feb. 20, 2001, 66 F.R. 10910 effective April 1, 2001, and adjustment not applicable to cases commenced before the effective date of the adjustments, i.e., April 1, 2001. See Adjustment of Dollar Amounts notes under 11 U.S.C.A. § 104 and this section.

1998 Acts. Amendment by Pub.L. 105–244 effective Oct. 1, 1998, except as otherwise provided, see section 3 of Pub.L. 105–244, set out as a note under section 1001 of Title 20.

Pub.L. 105–244, Title IX, § 971(b), Oct. 7, 1998, 112 Stat. 1837, provided that: "The amendment made by subsection (a) [amending subsec. (a)(8) of this section] shall apply only with respect to cases commenced under title 11, United States Code, after the date of enactment of this Act [Oct. 7, 1998]."

Adjustment of dollar amounts by Judicial Conference of the United States by notice dated Feb. 3, 1998, 63 F.R. 7179 effective April 1, 1998, and adjustment not applicable to cases commenced before the effective date of the adjustments, i.e., April 1, 1998. See Adjustment of Dollar Amounts notes under 11 U.S.C.A. § 104 and this section.

1996 Acts. For effective date of Title III of Pub.L. 104–193, see section 395(a) to (c) of Pub.L. 104–193, set out as a note under section 654 of Title 42, The Public Health and Welfare.

Section 374(c) of Pub.L. 104–193 provided that: "The amendments made by this section [amending this section and section 656 of Title 42, The Public Health and Welfare] shall apply only with respect to cases commenced under title 11 of the United States Code [this title] after the date of the enactment of this Act [Aug. 22, 1996]."

1994 Acts. Amendments by Pub.L. 103–394 effective on Oct. 22, 1994, and not to apply with respect to cases commenced under Title 11 of the United States Code before Oct. 22, 1994, see section 702 of Pub.L. 103–394, set out as a note under section 101 of this title.

1990 Acts. Section 3104 of Title XXXI of Pub.L. 101–647 provided that:

"(a) Effective date.—This title and the amendments made by this title [amending this section and section 1328 of this title and enacting provisions set out as a note under section 101 of this title] shall take effect on the date of the enactment of this Act [Nov. 29, 1990].

"(b) Application of amendments.—The amendments made by this title [amending this section and section 1328 of this title] shall not apply with respect to cases commenced under title 11 of the United States Code before the date of the enactment of this Act."

Amendment by section 3621 of Pub.L. 101–647 effective 180 days after Nov. 29, 1990, see section 3631 of Pub.L. 101–647, set out as a note under section 3001 of Title 28, Judiciary and Judicial Procedure.

Section 4 of Pub.L. 101–581 provided that:

"(a) Effective date.—This Act and the amendments made by this Act [amending this section and section 1328 of this title and enacting provisions set out as a note under section 101 of this title] shall take effect on the date of the enactment of this Act [Nov. 15, 1990.]"

"(b) Application of amendments.—The amendments made by this Act [amending this section and section 1328 of this title] shall not apply with respect to cases commenced under title 11 of the United States Code [this title] before the date of the enactment of this Act [Nov. 5, 1990.]"

1986 Acts. Amendment by sections 281 and 283 of Pub.L. 99–554 effective 30 days after Oct. 27, 1986, except as otherwise provided for, see section 302(a) of Pub.L. 99–554, set out as a note under section 581 of Title 28, Judiciary and Judicial Procedure.

Amendment by section 257 of Pub.L. 99–554 effective 30 days after Oct. 27, 1986, but not applicable to cases commenced under this title before that date, see section 302(a), (c)(1) of Pub.L. 99–554, set out as a note under section 581 of Title 28.

1984 Acts. Amendment by Pub.L. 98–353 effective with respect to cases filed 90 days after July 10, 1984, see section 552(a), formerly 553 of Pub.L. 98–353, set out as a note under section 101 of this title.

1981 Acts. Amendment by Pub.L. 97–35 effective on Aug. 13, 1981, see section 2334(c) of Pub.L. 97–35, set out as a note under section 656 of Title 42, The Public Health and Welfare.

Separability of Provisions

If any provision of section 101[a] [Title VIII] of Pub.L. 104–134, an amendment made by such Title, or the application of such provision or amendment to any person or circumstance is held to be unconstitutional, the remainder of such Title, the amendments made by such Title, and the application of the provisions of such Title to any person or circumstance not affected thereby, see section 101[a] [Title VIII, § 810] of Pub.L. 104–134, set out as a note under section 3626 of Title 18, Crimes and Criminal Procedure.

If any provision of or amendment made by Pub.L. 103–394 or the application of such provision or amendment to any person or circumstance is held to be unconstitutional, the remaining provisions of and amendments made by Pub.L. 103–394 and the application of such provisions and amendments to any person or circumstance shall not be affected thereby, see section 701 of Pub.L. 103–394, set out as a note under section 101 of this title.

Adjustment of Dollar Amounts

For adjustment of dollar amounts specified in subsec. (a)(2)(C)(i)(I), (II) of this section by the Judicial Conference of the United States, effective Apr. 1, 2016, see note set out under 11 U.S.C.A. § 104.

By notice published Feb. 22, 2016, 81 F.R. 8748, the Judicial Conference of the United States adjusted the dollar amounts in provisions specified in subsec. (a)(2)(C)(i)(I), (II) of this section, effective Apr. 1, 2016, as follows:

In subsec. (a)(2)(C)(i)(I) adjusted $650 to $675.

In subsec. (a)(2)(C)(i)(II) adjusted $925 to $950.

By notice published Feb. 21, 2013, 78 F.R. 12089, the Judicial Conference of the United States adjusted the dollar amounts in provisions specified in subsec. (a)(2)(C)(i)(I), (II) of this section, effective Apr. 1, 2013, as follows:

In subsec. (a)(2)(C)(i)(I) adjusted $600 to $650.

In subsec. (a)(2)(C)(i)(II) adjusted $875 to $925.

By notice published Feb. 25, 2010, 75 F.R. 8747, the Judicial Conference of the United States adjusted the dollar amounts in provisions specified in subsec. (a)(2)(C)(i)(I), (II) of this section, effective Apr. 1, 2010, as follows:

In subsec. (a)(2)(C)(i)(I) adjusted $550 to $600.

In subsec. (a)(2)(C)(i)(II) adjusted $825 to $875.

By notice published Feb. 14, 2007, 72 F.R. 7082, the Judicial Conference of the United States adjusted the dollar amounts in provisions specified in subsec. (a)(2)(C)(i)(I), (II) of this section, effective Apr. 1, 2007, as follows:

In subsec. (a)(2)(C)(i)(I) adjusted $500 to $550.

In subsec. (a)(2)(C)(i)(II) adjusted $750 to $825.

By notice dated Feb. 18, 2004, 69 F.R. 8482, the Judicial Conference of the United States adjusted the dollar amounts in provisions specified in subsec. (a)(2)(C) of this section, effective Apr. 1, 2004, as follows:

Adjusted $1,150 (each time it appears) to $1,225 (each time it appears).

By notice dated Feb. 20, 2001, 66 F.R. 10910, the Judicial Conference of the United States adjusted the dollar amounts in provisions specified in subsec. (a)(2)(C) of this section, effective Apr. 1, 2001, as follows:

Adjusted $1,075 (each time it appears) to $1,150 (each time it appears).

By notice dated Feb. 3, 1998, 63 F.R. 7179, the Judicial Conference of the United States adjusted the dollar amounts in provisions specified in subsec. (a)(2)(C) of this section, effective Apr. 1, 1998, as follows:

Adjusted $1,000 (each time it appears) to $1,075 (each time it appears).

CROSS REFERENCES

Disallowance of claim to extent claim is for unmatured debt and excepted from discharge as debt for alimony, maintenance or support, see 11 USCA § 502.

Discharge of debtor,

Generally, see Official Bankr. Form B318, 11 USCA.

Chapter 7 cases, see 11 USCA § 727.

Chapter 12 cases, see 11 USCA § 1228.

Chapter 13 cases, see 11 USCA § 1328.

Effect of confirmation, see 11 USCA § 1141.

Extent of priorities for unsecured claims of governmental units, see 11 USCA § 507.

Involuntary cases and future adjustments, see 11 USCA § 104.

Notice of filing, creditors and dates, see Official Bankr. Form B309B, 11 USCA.

§ 524. Effect of discharge

(a) A discharge in a case under this title—

(1) voids any judgment at any time obtained, to the extent that such judgment is a determination of the personal liability of the debtor with respect to any debt discharged under section 727, 944, 1141, 1228, or 1328 of this title, whether or not discharge of such debt is waived;

(2) operates as an injunction against the commencement or continuation of an action, the employment of process, or an act, to collect, recover or offset any such debt as a personal liability of the debtor, whether or not discharge of such debt is waived; and

(3) operates as an injunction against the commencement or continuation of an action, the employment of process, or an act, to collect or recover from, or offset against, property of the debtor of the kind specified in section 541(a)(2) of this title that is acquired after the commencement of the case, on account of any allowable community claim, except a community claim that is excepted from discharge under section 523, 1228(a)(1), or 1328(a)(1), or that would be so excepted, determined in accordance with the provisions of sections 523(c) and 523(d) of this title, in a case concerning the debtor's spouse commenced on the date of the filing of the petition in the case concerning the debtor, whether or not discharge of the debt based on such community claim is waived.

(b) Subsection (a)(3) of this section does not apply if—

(1)(A) the debtor's spouse is a debtor in a case under this title, or a bankrupt or a debtor in a case under the Bankruptcy Act, commenced within six years of the date of the filing of the petition in the case concerning the debtor; and

(B) the court does not grant the debtor's spouse a discharge in such case concerning the debtor's spouse; or

(2)(A) the court would not grant the debtor's spouse a discharge in a case under chapter 7 of this title concerning such spouse commenced on the date of the filing of the petition in the case concerning the debtor; and

(B) a determination that the court would not so grant such discharge is made by the bankruptcy court within the time and in the manner provided for a determination under section 727 of this title of whether a debtor is granted a discharge.

(c) An agreement between a holder of a claim and the debtor, the consideration for which, in whole or in part, is based on a debt that is dischargeable in a case under this title is enforceable only to any extent enforceable under applicable nonbankruptcy law, whether or not discharge of such debt is waived, only if—

(1) such agreement was made before the granting of the discharge under section 727, 1141, 1228, or 1328 of this title;

(2) the debtor received the disclosures described in subsection (k) at or before the time at which the debtor signed the agreement;

(3) such agreement has been filed with the court and, if applicable, accompanied by a declaration or an affidavit of the attorney that represented the debtor during the course of negotiating an agreement under this subsection, which states that—

(A) such agreement represents a fully informed and voluntary agreement by the debtor;

(B) such agreement does not impose an undue hardship on the debtor or a dependent of the debtor; and

(C) the attorney fully advised the debtor of the legal effect and consequences of—

(i) an agreement of the kind specified in this subsection; and

(ii) any default under such an agreement;

(4) the debtor has not rescinded such agreement at any time prior to discharge or within sixty days after such agreement is filed with the court, whichever occurs later, by giving notice of rescission to the holder of such claim;

(5) the provisions of subsection (d) of this section have been complied with; and

(6)(A) in a case concerning an individual who was not represented by an attorney during the course of negotiating an agreement under this subsection, the court approves such agreement as—

(i) not imposing an undue hardship on the debtor or a dependent of the debtor; and

(ii) in the best interest of the debtor.

(B) Subparagraph (A) shall not apply to the extent that such debt is a consumer debt secured by real property.

(d) In a case concerning an individual, when the court has determined whether to grant or not to grant a discharge under section 727, 1141, 1228, or 1328 of this title, the court may hold a hearing at which the debtor shall appear in person. At any such hearing, the court shall inform the debtor that a discharge has been granted or the reason why a discharge has not been granted. If a discharge has been granted and if the debtor desires to make an agreement of the kind specified in subsection (c) of this section and was not represented by an attorney during the course of negotiating such agreement, then the court shall hold a hearing at which the debtor shall appear in person and at such hearing the court shall—

(1) inform the debtor—

(A) that such an agreement is not required under this title, under nonbankruptcy law, or under any agreement not made in accordance with the provisions of subsection (c) of this section; and

    (B) of the legal effect and consequences of—

        (i) an agreement of the kind specified in subsection (c) of this section; and

        (ii) a default under such an agreement; and

  (2) determine whether the agreement that the debtor desires to make complies with the requirements of subsection (c)(6) of this section, if the consideration for such agreement is based in whole or in part on a consumer debt that is not secured by real property of the debtor.

(e) Except as provided in subsection (a)(3) of this section, discharge of a debt of the debtor does not affect the liability of any other entity on, or the property of any other entity for, such debt.

(f) Nothing contained in subsection (c) or (d) of this section prevents a debtor from voluntarily repaying any debt.

(g)(1)(A) After notice and hearing, a court that enters an order confirming a plan of reorganization under chapter 11 may issue, in connection with such order, an injunction in accordance with this subsection to supplement the injunctive effect of a discharge under this section.

(B) An injunction may be issued under subparagraph (A) to enjoin entities from taking legal action for the purpose of directly or indirectly collecting, recovering, or receiving payment or recovery with respect to any claim or demand that, under a plan of reorganization, is to be paid in whole or in part by a trust described in paragraph (2)(B)(i), except such legal actions as are expressly allowed by the injunction, the confirmation order, or the plan of reorganization.

(2)(A) Subject to subsection (h), if the requirements of subparagraph (B) are met at the time an injunction described in paragraph (1) is entered, then after entry of such injunction, any proceeding that involves the validity, application, construction, or modification of such injunction, or of this subsection with respect to such injunction, may be commenced only in the district court in which such injunction was entered, and such court shall have exclusive jurisdiction over any such proceeding without regard to the amount in controversy.

(B) The requirements of this subparagraph are that—

  (i) the injunction is to be implemented in connection with a trust that, pursuant to the plan of reorganization—

    (I) is to assume the liabilities of a debtor which at the time of entry of the order for relief has been named as a defendant in personal injury, wrongful death, or property-damage actions seeking recovery for damages allegedly caused by the presence of, or exposure to, asbestos or asbestos-containing products;

    (II) is to be funded in whole or in part by the securities of 1 or more debtors involved in such plan and by the obligation of such debtor or debtors to make future payments, including dividends;

    (III) is to own, or by the exercise of rights granted under such plan would be entitled to own if specified contingencies occur, a majority of the voting shares of—

      (aa) each such debtor;

      (bb) the parent corporation of each such debtor; or

      (cc) a subsidiary of each such debtor that is also a debtor; and

    (IV) is to use its assets or income to pay claims and demands; and

  (ii) subject to subsection (h), the court determines that—

    (I) the debtor is likely to be subject to substantial future demands for payment arising out of the same or similar conduct or events that gave rise to the claims that are addressed by the injunction;

    (II) the actual amounts, numbers, and timing of such future demands cannot be determined;

    (III) pursuit of such demands outside the procedures prescribed by such plan is likely to threaten the plan's purpose to deal equitably with claims and future demands;

    (IV) as part of the process of seeking confirmation of such plan—

      (aa) the terms of the injunction proposed to be issued under paragraph (1)(A), including any provisions barring actions against third parties pursuant to paragraph (4)(A), are set out in such plan and in any disclosure statement supporting the plan; and

      (bb) a separate class or classes of the claimants whose claims are to be addressed by a trust described in clause (i) is established and votes, by at least 75 percent of those voting, in favor of the plan; and

    (V) subject to subsection (h), pursuant to court orders or otherwise, the trust will operate through mechanisms such as structured, periodic, or supplemental payments, pro rata distributions, matrices, or periodic review of estimates of the numbers and values of present claims and future demands, or other comparable mechanisms, that provide reasonable assurance that the trust will value, and be in a financial position to pay, present claims and future demands that involve similar claims in substantially the same manner.

(3)(A) If the requirements of paragraph (2)(B) are met and the order confirming the plan of reorganization was issued or affirmed by the district court that has jurisdiction over the reorganization case, then after the time for appeal of the order that issues or affirms the plan—

(i) the injunction shall be valid and enforceable and may not be revoked or modified by any court except through appeal in accordance with paragraph (6);

(ii) no entity that pursuant to such plan or thereafter becomes a direct or indirect transferee of, or successor to any assets of, a debtor or trust that is the subject of the injunction shall be liable with respect to any claim or demand made against such entity by reason of its becoming such a transferee or successor; and

(iii) no entity that pursuant to such plan or thereafter makes a loan to such a debtor or trust or to such a successor or transferee shall, by reason of making the loan, be liable with respect to any claim or demand made against such entity, nor shall any pledge of assets made in connection with such a loan be upset or impaired for that reason;

(B) Subparagraph (A) shall not be construed to—

(i) imply that an entity described in subparagraph (A)(ii) or (iii) would, if this paragraph were not applicable, necessarily be liable to any entity by reason of any of the acts described in subparagraph (A);

(ii) relieve any such entity of the duty to comply with, or of liability under, any Federal or State law regarding the making of a fraudulent conveyance in a transaction described in subparagraph (A)(ii) or (iii); or

(iii) relieve a debtor of the debtor's obligation to comply with the terms of the plan of reorganization, or affect the power of the court to exercise its authority under sections 1141 and 1142 to compel the debtor to do so.

(4)(A)(i) Subject to subparagraph (B), an injunction described in paragraph (1) shall be valid and enforceable against all entities that it addresses.

(ii) Notwithstanding the provisions of section 524(e), such an injunction may bar any action directed against a third party who is identifiable from the terms of such injunction (by name or as part of an identifiable group) and is alleged to be directly or indirectly liable for the conduct of, claims against, or demands on the debtor to the extent such alleged liability of such third party arises by reason of—

(I) the third party's ownership of a financial interest in the debtor, a past or present affiliate of the debtor, or a predecessor in interest of the debtor;

(II) the third party's involvement in the management of the debtor or a predecessor in interest of the debtor, or service as an officer, director or employee of the debtor or a related party;

(III) the third party's provision of insurance to the debtor or a related party; or

(IV) the third party's involvement in a transaction changing the corporate structure, or in a loan or other financial transaction affecting the financial condition, of the debtor or a related party, including but not limited to—

(aa) involvement in providing financing (debt or equity), or advice to an entity involved in such a transaction; or

(bb) acquiring or selling a financial interest in an entity as part of such a transaction.

(iii) As used in this subparagraph, the term "related party" means—

(I) a past or present affiliate of the debtor;

(II) a predecessor in interest of the debtor; or

(III) any entity that owned a financial interest in—

(aa) the debtor;

(bb) a past or present affiliate of the debtor; or

(cc) a predecessor in interest of the debtor.

(B) Subject to subsection (h), if, under a plan of reorganization, a kind of demand described in such plan is to be paid in whole or in part by a trust described in paragraph (2)(B)(i) in connection with which an injunction described in paragraph (1) is to be implemented, then such injunction shall be valid and enforceable with respect to a demand of such kind made, after such plan is confirmed, against the debtor or debtors involved, or against a third party described in subparagraph (A)(ii), if—

(i) as part of the proceedings leading to issuance of such injunction, the court appoints a legal representative for the purpose of protecting the rights of persons that might subsequently assert demands of such kind, and

(ii) the court determines, before entering the order confirming such plan, that identifying such debtor or debtors, or such third party (by name or as part of an identifiable group), in such injunction with respect to such demands for purposes of this subparagraph is fair and equitable with respect to the persons that might subsequently assert such demands, in light of the benefits provided, or to be provided, to such trust on behalf of such debtor or debtors or such third party.

(5) In this subsection, the term "demand" means a demand for payment, present or future, that—

(A) was not a claim during the proceedings leading to the confirmation of a plan of reorganization;

(B) arises out of the same or similar conduct or events that gave rise to the claims addressed by the injunction issued under paragraph (1); and

(C) pursuant to the plan, is to be paid by a trust described in paragraph (2)(B)(i).

(6) Paragraph (3)(A)(i) does not bar an action taken by or at the direction of an appellate court on appeal of an injunction issued under paragraph (1) or of the order of confirmation that relates to the injunction.

(7) This subsection does not affect the operation of section 1144 or the power of the district court to refer a proceeding under section 157 of title 28 or any reference of a proceeding made prior to the date of the enactment of this subsection.

(h) Application to existing injunctions.—For purposes of subsection (g)—

(1) subject to paragraph (2), if an injunction of the kind described in subsection (g)(1)(B) was issued before the date of the enactment of this Act, as part of a plan of reorganization confirmed by an order entered before such date, then the injunction shall be considered to meet the requirements of subsection (g)(2)(B) for purposes of subsection (g)(2)(A), and to satisfy subsection (g)(4)(A)(ii), if—

(A) the court determined at the time the plan was confirmed that the plan was fair and equitable in accordance with the requirements of section 1129(b);

(B) as part of the proceedings leading to issuance of such injunction and confirmation of such plan, the court had appointed a legal representative for the purpose of protecting the rights of persons that might subsequently assert demands described in subsection (g)(4)(B) with respect to such plan; and

(C) such legal representative did not object to confirmation of such plan or issuance of such injunction; and

(2) for purposes of paragraph (1), if a trust described in subsection (g)(2)(B)(i) is subject to a court order on the date of the enactment of this Act staying such trust from settling or paying further claims—

(A) the requirements of subsection (g)(2)(B)(ii)(V) shall not apply with respect to such trust until such stay is lifted or dissolved; and

(B) if such trust meets such requirements on the date such stay is lifted or dissolved, such trust shall be considered to have met such requirements continuously from the date of the enactment of this Act.

(i) The willful failure of a creditor to credit payments received under a plan confirmed under this title, unless the order confirming the plan is revoked, the plan is in default, or the creditor has not received payments required to be made under the plan in the manner required by the plan (including crediting the amounts required under the plan), shall constitute a violation of an injunction under subsection (a)(2) if the act of the creditor to collect and failure to credit payments in the manner required by the plan caused material injury to the debtor.

(j) Subsection (a)(2) does not operate as an injunction against an act by a creditor that is the holder of a secured claim, if—

(1) such creditor retains a security interest in real property that is the principal residence of the debtor;

(2) such act is in the ordinary course of business between the creditor and the debtor; and

(3) such act is limited to seeking or obtaining periodic payments associated with a valid security interest in lieu of pursuit of in rem relief to enforce the lien.

(k)(1) The disclosures required under subsection (c)(2) shall consist of the disclosure statement described in paragraph (3), completed as required in that paragraph, together with the agreement specified in subsection (c), statement, declaration, motion and order described, respectively, in paragraphs (4) through (8), and shall be the only disclosures required in connection with entering into such agreement.

(2) Disclosures made under paragraph (1) shall be made clearly and conspicuously and in writing. The terms "Amount Reaffirmed" and "Annual Percentage Rate" shall be disclosed more conspicuously than other terms, data or information provided in connection with this disclosure, except that the phrases "Before agreeing to reaffirm a debt, review these important disclosures" and "Summary of Reaffirmation Agreement" may be equally conspicuous. Disclosures may be made in a different order and may use terminology different from that set forth in paragraphs (2) through (8), except that the terms "Amount Reaffirmed" and "Annual Percentage Rate" must be used where indicated.

(3) The disclosure statement required under this paragraph shall consist of the following:

(A) The statement: "Part A: Before agreeing to reaffirm a debt, review these important disclosures:";

(B) Under the heading "Summary of Reaffirmation Agreement", the statement: "This Summary is made pursuant to the requirements of the Bankruptcy Code";

(C) The "Amount Reaffirmed", using that term, which shall be—

(i) the total amount of debt that the debtor agrees to reaffirm by entering into an agreement of the kind specified in subsection (c), and

(ii) the total of any fees and costs accrued as of the date of the disclosure statement, related to such total amount.

(D) In conjunction with the disclosure of the "Amount Reaffirmed", the statements—

(i) "The amount of debt you have agreed to reaffirm"; and

(ii) "Your credit agreement may obligate you to pay additional amounts which may come due after the date of this disclosure. Consult your credit agreement.".

(E) The "Annual Percentage Rate", using that term, which shall be disclosed as—

(i) if, at the time the petition is filed, the debt is an extension of credit under an open end credit plan, as the terms "credit" and "open end credit plan" are defined in section 103 of the Truth in Lending Act, then—

(I) the annual percentage rate determined under paragraphs (5) and (6) of section 127(b) of the Truth in Lending Act, as applicable, as disclosed to the debtor in the most recent periodic statement prior to entering into an agreement of the kind specified in subsection (c) or, if no such periodic statement has been given to the debtor during the prior 6 months, the annual percentage rate as it would have been so disclosed at the time the disclosure statement is given to the debtor, or to the extent this annual percentage rate is not readily available or not applicable, then

(II) the simple interest rate applicable to the amount reaffirmed as of the date the disclosure statement is given to the debtor, or if different simple interest rates apply to different balances, the simple interest rate applicable to each such balance, identifying the amount of each such balance included in the amount reaffirmed, or

(III) if the entity making the disclosure elects, to disclose the annual percentage rate under subclause (I) and the simple interest rate under subclause (II); or

(ii) if, at the time the petition is filed, the debt is an extension of credit other than under an open end credit plan, as the terms "credit" and "open end credit plan" are defined in section 103 of the Truth in Lending Act, then—

(I) the annual percentage rate under section 128(a)(4) of the Truth in Lending Act, as disclosed to the debtor in the most recent disclosure statement given to the debtor prior to the entering into an agreement of the kind specified in subsection (c) with respect to the debt, or, if no such disclosure statement was given to the debtor, the annual percentage rate as it would have been so disclosed at the time the disclosure statement is given to the debtor, or to the extent this annual percentage rate is not readily available or not applicable, then

(II) the simple interest rate applicable to the amount reaffirmed as of the date the disclosure statement is given to the debtor, or if different simple interest rates apply to different balances, the simple interest rate applicable to each such balance, identifying the amount of such balance included in the amount reaffirmed, or

(III) if the entity making the disclosure elects, to disclose the annual percentage rate under (I) and the simple interest rate under (II).

(F) If the underlying debt transaction was disclosed as a variable rate transaction on the most recent disclosure given under the Truth in Lending Act, by stating "The interest rate on your loan may be a variable interest rate which changes from time to time, so that the annual percentage rate disclosed here may be higher or lower."

(G) If the debt is secured by a security interest which has not been waived in whole or in part or determined to be void by a final order of the court at the time of the disclosure, by disclosing that a security interest or lien in goods or property is asserted over some or all of the debts the debtor is reaffirming and listing the items and their original purchase price that are subject to the asserted security interest, or if not a purchase-money security interest then listing by items or types and the original amount of the loan.

(H) At the election of the creditor, a statement of the repayment schedule using 1 or a combination of the following—

(i) by making the statement: "Your first payment in the amount of $___ is due on ___ but the future payment amount may be different. Consult your reaffirmation agreement or credit agreement, as applicable.", and stating the amount of the first payment and the due date of that payment in the places provided;

(ii) by making the statement: "Your payment schedule will be:", and describing the repayment schedule with the number, amount, and due dates or period of payments scheduled to repay the debts reaffirmed to the extent then known by the disclosing party; or

(iii) by describing the debtor's repayment obligations with reasonable specificity to the extent then known by the disclosing party.

(I) The following statement: "Note: When this disclosure refers to what a creditor 'may' do, it does not use the word 'may' to give the creditor specific permission. The word 'may' is used to tell you what might occur if the law permits the creditor to take the action. If you have questions about your reaffirming a debt or what the law requires, consult with the attorney who helped you negotiate this agreement reaffirming a debt. If you don't have an attorney helping you, the judge will explain the effect of your reaffirming a debt when the hearing on the reaffirmation agreement is held.".

(J)(i) The following additional statements:

"Reaffirming a debt is a serious financial decision. The law requires you to take certain steps to make sure the decision is in your best interest. If these steps are not completed, the reaffirmation agreement is not effective, even though you have signed it.

"1. Read the disclosures in this Part A carefully. Consider the decision to reaffirm carefully. Then, if you want to reaffirm, sign the reaffirmation agreement in Part B (or you may use a separate agreement you and your creditor agree on).

"2. Complete and sign Part D and be sure you can afford to make the payments you are agreeing to make and have received a copy of the disclosure statement and a completed and signed reaffirmation agreement.

"3. If you were represented by an attorney during the negotiation of your reaffirmation agreement, the attorney must have signed the certification in Part C.

"4. If you were not represented by an attorney during the negotiation of your reaffirmation agreement, you must have completed and signed Part E.

"5. The original of this disclosure must be filed with the court by you or your creditor. If a separate reaffirmation agreement (other than the one in Part B) has been signed, it must be attached.

"6. If you were represented by an attorney during the negotiation of your reaffirmation agreement, your reaffirmation agreement becomes effective upon filing with the court unless the reaffirmation is presumed to be an undue hardship as explained in Part D.

"7. If you were not represented by an attorney during the negotiation of your reaffirmation agreement, it will not be effective unless the court approves it. The court will notify you of the hearing on your reaffirmation agreement. You must attend this hearing in bankruptcy court where the judge will review your reaffirmation agreement. The bankruptcy court must approve your reaffirmation agreement as consistent with your best interests, except that no court approval is required if your reaffirmation agreement is for a consumer debt secured by a mortgage, deed of trust, security deed, or other lien on your real property, like your home.

"Your right to rescind (cancel) your reaffirmation agreement. You may rescind (cancel) your reaffirmation agreement at any time before the bankruptcy court enters a discharge order, or before the expiration of the 60–day period that begins on the date your reaffirmation agreement is filed with the court, whichever occurs later. To rescind (cancel) your reaffirmation agreement, you must notify the creditor that your reaffirmation agreement is rescinded (or canceled).

"What are your obligations if you reaffirm the debt? A reaffirmed debt remains your personal legal obligation. It is not discharged in your bankruptcy case. That means that if you default on your reaffirmed debt after your bankruptcy case is over, your creditor may

be able to take your property or your wages. Otherwise, your obligations will be determined by the reaffirmation agreement which may have changed the terms of the original agreement. For example, if you are reaffirming an open end credit agreement, the creditor may be permitted by that agreement or applicable law to change the terms of that agreement in the future under certain conditions.

"Are you required to enter into a reaffirmation agreement by any law? No, you are not required to reaffirm a debt by any law. Only agree to reaffirm a debt if it is in your best interest. Be sure you can afford the payments you agree to make.

"What if your creditor has a security interest or lien? Your bankruptcy discharge does not eliminate any lien on your property. A 'lien' is often referred to as a security interest, deed of trust, mortgage or security deed. Even if you do not reaffirm and your personal liability on the debt is discharged, because of the lien your creditor may still have the right to take the property securing the lien if you do not pay the debt or default on it. If the lien is on an item of personal property that is exempt under your State's law or that the trustee has abandoned, you may be able to redeem the item rather than reaffirm the debt. To redeem, you must make a single payment to the creditor equal to the amount of the allowed secured claim, as agreed by the parties or determined by the court.".

(ii) In the case of a reaffirmation under subsection (m)(2), numbered paragraph 6 in the disclosures required by clause (i) of this subparagraph shall read as follows:

"6. If you were represented by an attorney during the negotiation of your reaffirmation agreement, your reaffirmation agreement becomes effective upon filing with the court.".

(4) The form of such agreement required under this paragraph shall consist of the following:

"Part B: Reaffirmation Agreement. I (we) agree to reaffirm the debts arising under the credit agreement described below.

"Brief description of credit agreement:

"Description of any changes to the credit agreement made as part of this reaffirmation agreement:

"Signature: Date:

"Borrower:

"Co-borrower, if also reaffirming these debts:

"Accepted by creditor:

"Date of creditor acceptance:".

(5) The declaration shall consist of the following:

(A) The following certification:

"Part C: Certification by Debtor's Attorney (If Any).

"I hereby certify that (1) this agreement represents a fully informed and voluntary agreement by the debtor; (2) this agreement does not impose an undue hardship on the debtor or any dependent of the debtor; and (3) I have fully advised the debtor of the legal effect and consequences of this agreement and any default under this agreement.

"Signature of Debtor's Attorney: Date:".

(B) If a presumption of undue hardship has been established with respect to such agreement, such certification shall state that, in the opinion of the attorney, the debtor is able to make the payment.

(C) In the case of a reaffirmation agreement under subsection (m)(2), subparagraph (B) is not applicable.

(6)(A) The statement in support of such agreement, which the debtor shall sign and date prior to filing with the court, shall consist of the following:

"Part D: Debtor's Statement in Support of Reaffirmation Agreement.

"1. I believe this reaffirmation agreement will not impose an undue hardship on my dependents or me. I can afford to make the payments on the reaffirmed debt because my monthly income (take home pay plus any other income received) is \$___, and my actual current monthly expenses including monthly payments on post-bankruptcy debt and other reaffirmation agreements total \$___, leaving \$___ to make the required payments on this reaffirmed debt. I understand that if my income less my monthly expenses does not leave enough to make the payments, this reaffirmation agreement is presumed to be an undue hardship on me and must be reviewed by the court. However, this presumption may be overcome if I explain to the satisfaction of the court how I can afford to make the payments here: ___.

"2. I received a copy of the Reaffirmation Disclosure Statement in Part A and a completed and signed reaffirmation agreement.".

(B) Where the debtor is represented by an attorney and is reaffirming a debt owed to a creditor defined in section 19(b)(1)(A)(iv) of the Federal Reserve Act, the statement of support of the reaffirmation agreement, which the debtor shall sign and date prior to filing with the court, shall consist of the following:

"I believe this reaffirmation agreement is in my financial interest. I can afford to make the payments on the reaffirmed debt. I received a copy of the Reaffirmation Disclosure Statement in Part A and a completed and signed reaffirmation agreement.".

(7) The motion that may be used if approval of such agreement by the court is required in order for it to be effective, shall be signed and dated by the movant and shall consist of the following:

"Part E: Motion for Court Approval (To be completed only if the debtor is not represented by an attorney.). I (we), the debtor(s), affirm the following to be true and correct:

"I am not represented by an attorney in connection with this reaffirmation agreement.

"I believe this reaffirmation agreement is in my best interest based on the income and expenses I have disclosed in my Statement in Support of this reaffirmation agreement, and because (provide any additional relevant reasons the court should consider):

"Therefore, I ask the court for an order approving this reaffirmation agreement.".

(8) The court order, which may be used to approve such agreement, shall consist of the following:

"Court Order: The court grants the debtor's motion and approves the reaffirmation agreement described above.".

(*l*) Notwithstanding any other provision of this title the following shall apply:

(1) A creditor may accept payments from a debtor before and after the filing of an agreement of the kind specified in subsection (c) with the court.

(2) A creditor may accept payments from a debtor under such agreement that the creditor believes in good faith to be effective.

(3) The requirements of subsections (c)(2) and (k) shall be satisfied if disclosures required under those subsections are given in good faith.

(m)(1) Until 60 days after an agreement of the kind specified in subsection (c) is filed with the court (or such additional period as the court, after notice and a hearing and for cause, orders before the expiration of such period), it shall be presumed that such agreement is an undue hardship on the debtor if the debtor's monthly income less the debtor's monthly expenses as shown on the debtor's completed and signed statement in support of such agreement required under subsection (k)(6)(A) is less than the scheduled payments on the reaffirmed debt. This presumption shall be reviewed by the court. The presumption may be rebutted in writing by the debtor if the statement includes an explanation that identifies additional sources of funds to make the payments as agreed upon under the terms of such agreement. If the presumption is not rebutted to the satisfaction of the court, the court may disapprove such agreement. No agreement shall be disapproved without notice and a hearing to the debtor and creditor, and such hearing shall be concluded before the entry of the debtor's discharge.

(2) This subsection does not apply to reaffirmation agreements where the creditor is a credit union, as defined in section 19(b)(1)(A)(iv) of the Federal Reserve Act.

(Pub.L. 95–598, Nov. 6, 1978, 92 Stat. 2592; Pub.L. 98–353, Title III, §§ 308, 455, July 10, 1984, 98 Stat. 354, 376; Pub.L. 99–554, Title II, §§ 257(*o*), 282, 283(k), Oct. 27, 1986, 100 Stat.

3115–3117; Pub.L. 103–394, Title I, §§ 103, 111(a), Title V, § 501(d)(14), Oct. 22, 1994, 108 Stat. 4108, 4113, 4145; Pub.L. 109–8, Title II, §§ 202, 203(a), Title XII, § 1210, Apr. 20, 2005, 119 Stat. 43, 194; Pub.L. 111–327, § 2(a)(19), Dec. 22, 2010, 124 Stat. 3559.)

HISTORICAL AND STATUTORY NOTES

Revision Notes and Legislative Reports

1978 Acts. Subsection (a) specifies that a discharge in a bankruptcy case voids any judgment to the extent that it is a determination of the personal liability of the debtor with respect to a prepetition debt, and operates as an injunction against the commencement or continuation of an action, the employment of process, or any act, including telephone calls, letters, and personal contacts, to collect, recover, or offset any discharged debt as a personal liability of the debtor, or from property of the debtor, whether or not the debtor has waived discharge of the debt involved. The injunction is to give complete effect to the discharge and to eliminate any doubt concerning the effect of the discharge as a total prohibition on debt collection efforts. This paragraph has been expanded over a comparable provision in Bankruptcy Act § 14f [section 32(f) of former Title 11] to cover any act to collect, such as dunning by telephone or letter, or indirectly through friends, relatives, or employers, harassment, threats of repossession, and the like. The change is consonant with the new policy forbidding binding reaffirmation agreements under proposed 11 U.S.C. 524(b), and is intended to insure that once a debt is discharged, the debtor will not be pressured in any way to repay it. In effect, the discharge extinguishes the debt, and creditors may not attempt to avoid that. The language "whether or not discharge of such debt is waived" is intended to prevent waiver of discharge of a particular debt from defeating the purposes of this section. It is directed at waiver of discharge of a particular debt, not waiver of discharge in toto as permitted under section 727(a)(9).

Subsection (a) also codifies the split discharge for debtors in community property states. If community property was in the estate and community claims were discharged, the discharge is effective against community creditors of the non-debtor spouse as well as of the debtor spouse.

Subsection (b) gives further effect to the discharge. It prohibits reaffirmation agreements after the commencement of the case with respect to any dischargeable debt. The prohibition extends to agreements the consideration for which in whole or in part is based on a dischargeable debt, and it applies whether or not discharge of the debt involved in the agreement has been waived. Thus, the prohibition on reaffirmation agreements extends to debts that are based on discharged debts. Thus, "second generation" debts, which included all or a part of a discharged debt could not be included in any new agreement for new money. This subsection will not have any effect on reaffirmations of debts discharged under the Bankruptcy Act [former Title 11]. It will only apply to discharges granted if commenced under the new title 11 bankruptcy code.

Subsection (c) grants an exception to the anti-reaffirmation provision. It permits reaffirmation in connection with the settlement of a proceeding to determine the dischargeability of the debt being reaffirmed, or in connection with a redemption agreement permitted under section 722. In either case, the reaffirmation agreement must be entered into in good faith and must be approved by the court.

Subsection (d) provides the discharge of the debtor does not affect co-debtors or guarantors. Senate Report No. 95–989.

1984 Acts. Statements by Legislative Leaders, see 1984 U.S. Code Cong. and Adm. News, p. 576.

1986 Acts. House Report No. 99–764 and House Conference Report No. 99–958, see 1986 U.S. Code Cong. and Adm. News, p. 5227.

1994 Acts. House Report No. 103–835, see 1994 U.S. Code Cong. and Adm. News, p. 3340.

2005 Acts. House Report No. 109–31(Part I), see 2005 U.S. Code Cong. and Adm. News, p. 88.

Legislative Statements

Section 524(a) of the House amendment represents a compromise between the House bill and the Senate amendment. Section 524(b) of the House amendment is new, and represents standards clarifying the operation of section 524(a)(3) with respect to community property.

Sections 524(c) and (d) represent a compromise between the House bill and Senate amendment on the issue of reaffirmation of a debt discharged in bankruptcy. Every reaffirmation to be enforceable must be approved by the court, and any debtor may rescind a reaffirmation for 30 days from the time the reaffirmation becomes enforceable. If the debtor is an individual the court must advise the debtor of various effects of reaffirmation at a hearing. In addition, to any extent the debt is a consumer debt that is not secured by real property of the debtor reaffirmation is permitted only if the court approves the reaffirmation agreement, before granting a discharge under section 727, 1141, or 1328, as not imposing a hardship on the debtor or a dependent of the debtor and in the best interest of the debtor; alternatively, the court may approve an agreement entered into in good faith that is in settlement of litigation of a complaint to determine dischargeability or that is entered into in connection with redemption under section 722. The hearing on discharge under section 524(d) will be held whether or not the debtor desires to reaffirm any debts.

References in Text

The Bankruptcy Act, referred to in subsec. (b)(1), is Act July 1, 1898, c. 541, 30 Stat. 544, as amended, which was classified generally to former Title 11.

The date of enactment of this subsection, referred to in subsec. (g)(7), is the date of enactment of section 111(a) of Pub.L. 103–394, which enacted subsec. (g) of this section and which was approved Oct. 22, 1994.

The date of enactment of this Act, referred to in subsec. (h), probably means the date of enactment of Pub.L. 103–394, known as the Bankruptcy Reform Act of 1994, which was approved Oct. 22, 1994.

The Truth in Lending Act, referred to in subsec. (k), is Title I of Pub.L. 90–321, May 29, 1968, 82 Stat. 146, as amended, which is classified generally to subchapter I (15 U.S.C.A. § 1601 et seq.) of chapter 41 of Title 15. Sections 103, 127(b), and 128(a)(4) of the Act are classified to 15 U.S.C.A. §§ 1602, 1637(b), and 1638(a)(4), respectively. For complete classification, see Short Title note set out under 15 U.S.C.A. § 1601 and Tables.

Section 19(b)(1)(A)(iv) of the Federal Reserve Act, referred to in subsecs. (k)(6)(B), (m)(2), is Act Dec. 23, 1913, c. 6, § 19(b)(1)(A)(iv), 38 Stat. 270, as amended, which is classified to 12 U.S.C.A. § 461(b)(1)(A)(iv).

Effective and Applicability Provisions

2005 Acts. Amendments by Pub.L. 109–8 effective, except as otherwise provided, 180 days after April 20, 2005, and inapplicable with respect to cases commenced under Title 11 before the effective date, see Pub.L. 109–8, § 1501, set out as a note under 11 U.S.C.A. § 101.

1994 Acts. Amendments by sections 103 and 501(d)(14) of Pub.L. 103–394 effective on Oct. 22, 1994, and not to apply with respect to cases commenced under Title 11 of the United States Code before Oct. 22, 1994, see section 702 of Pub.L. 103–394, set out as a note under section 101 of this title.

Amendment by section 111 of Pub.L. 103–394 [enacting subsecs. (g) and (h) of this section and a provision set out as a note under this section] effective Oct. 22, 1994, see section 702 of Pub.L. 103–394, set out as a note under section 101 of this title.

1986 Acts. Amendment by sections 282 and 283 of Pub.L. 99–554 effective 30 days after Oct. 27, 1986, see section 302(a) of Pub.L. 99–554, set out as a note under section 581 of Title 28, Judiciary and Judicial Procedure.

Amendment by section 257 of Pub.L. 99–554 effective 30 days after Oct. 27, 1986, but not applicable to cases commenced under this title before that date, see section 302(a), (c)(1) of Pub.L. 99–554, set out as a note under Section 581 of Title 28.

1984 Acts. Amendment by Pub.L. 98–353 effective with respect to cases filed 90 days after July 10, 1984, see section 552(a), formerly 553(a) of Pub.L. 98–353, set out as a note under section 101 of this title.

Separability of Provisions

If any provision of or amendment made by Pub.L. 103–394 or the application of such provision or amendment to any person or circumstance is held to be unconstitutional, the remaining provisions of and amendments made by Pub.L. 103–394 and the application of such provisions and amendments to any person or circumstance shall not be affected thereby, see section 701 of Pub.L. 103–394, set out as a note under section 101 of this title.

Rules of Construction

Section 111(b) of Pub.L. 103–394 provided that: "Nothing in subsection (a), or in the amendments made by subsection (a) [enacting subsecs. (g) and (h) of this section], shall be construed to modify, impair, or supersede any other authority the court has to issue injunctions in connection with an order confirming a plan of reorganization."

CROSS REFERENCES

Applicability of subsec. (a)(1), (2) of this section in Chapter 9 cases, see 11 USCA § 901.

Cancellation of indebtedness from discharged farm loans, see 12 USCA § 1150.

Extension of time, generally, see 11 USCA § 108.

Meetings of creditors and equity security holders reaffirming a debt, see 11 USCA § 341.

§ 525. Protection against discriminatory treatment

(a) Except as provided in the Perishable Agricultural Commodities Act, 1930, the Packers and Stockyards Act, 1921, and section 1 of the Act entitled "An Act making appropriations for the Department of Agriculture for the fiscal year ending June 30, 1944, and for other purposes," approved July 12, 1943, a governmental unit may not deny, revoke, suspend, or refuse to renew a license, permit, charter, franchise, or other similar grant to, condition such a grant to, discriminate with respect to such a grant against, deny employment to, terminate the employment of, or discriminate with respect to employment against, a person that is or has been a debtor under this title or a bankrupt or a debtor under the Bankruptcy Act, or another person with whom such bankrupt or debtor has been associated, solely because such bankrupt or debtor is or has been a debtor under this title or a bankrupt or debtor under the Bankruptcy Act, has been insolvent before the commencement of the case under this title, or during the case but before the debtor is granted or denied a discharge, or has not paid a debt that is dischargeable in the case under this title or that was discharged under the Bankruptcy Act.

(b) No private employer may terminate the employment of, or discriminate with respect to employment against, an individual who is or has been a debtor under this title, a debtor or bankrupt under the Bankruptcy Act, or an individual associated with such debtor or bankrupt, solely because such debtor or bankrupt—

(1) is or has been a debtor under this title or a debtor or bankrupt under the Bankruptcy Act;

(2) has been insolvent before the commencement of a case under this title or during the case but before the grant or denial of a discharge; or

(3) has not paid a debt that is dischargeable in a case under this title or that was discharged under the Bankruptcy Act.

(c)(1) A governmental unit that operates a student grant or loan program and a person engaged in a business that includes the making of loans guaranteed or insured under a student loan program may not deny a student grant, loan, loan guarantee, or loan insurance to a person that is or has been a debtor under this title or a bankrupt or debtor under the Bankruptcy Act, or another person with whom the debtor or bankrupt has been associated, because the debtor or bankrupt is or has been a debtor under this title or a bankrupt or debtor under the Bankruptcy Act, has been insolvent before the commencement of a case under this title or during the pendency of the case but before the debtor is granted or denied a discharge, or has not paid a debt that is dischargeable in the case under this title or that was discharged under the Bankruptcy Act.

(2) In this section, "student loan program" means any program operated under title IV of the Higher Education Act of 1965 or a similar program operated under State or local law.

(Pub.L. 95–598, Nov. 6, 1978, 92 Stat. 2593; Pub.L. 98–353, Title III, § 309, July 10, 1984, 98 Stat. 354; Pub.L. 103–394,

Title III, § 313, Title V, § 501(d)(15), Oct. 22, 1994, 108 Stat. 4140, 4145; Pub.L. 109–8, Title XII, § 1211, Apr. 20, 2005, 119 Stat. 194.)

HISTORICAL AND STATUTORY NOTES

Revision Notes and Legislative Reports

1978 Acts. This section is additional debtor protection. It codifies the result of *Perez v. Campbell,* 402 U.S. 637 (1971) [91 S.Ct. 1704, 29 L.Ed.2d 233], which held that a State would frustrate the Congressional policy of a fresh start for a debtor if it were permitted to refuse to renew a drivers license because a tort judgment resulting from an automobile accident had been unpaid as a result of a discharge in bankruptcy.

Notwithstanding any other laws, section 525 prohibits a governmental unit from denying, revoking, suspending, or refusing to renew a license, permit, charter, franchise, or other similar grant to, from conditioning such a grant to, from discrimination with respect to such a grant against, deny employment to, terminate the employment of, or discriminate with respect to employment against, a person that is or has been a debtor or that is or has been associated with a debtor. The prohibition extends only to discrimination or other action based solely on the basis of the bankruptcy, on the basis of insolvency before or during bankruptcy prior to a determination of discharge, or on the basis of nonpayment of a debt discharged in the bankruptcy case (the *Perez* situation). It does not prohibit consideration of other factors, such as future financial responsibility or ability, and does not prohibit imposition of requirements such as net capital rules, if applied nondiscriminatorily.

In addition, the section is not exhaustive. The enumeration of various forms of discrimination against former bankrupts is not intended to permit other forms of discrimination. The courts have been developing the *Perez* rule. This section permits further development to prohibit actions by governmental or quasi-governmental organizations that perform licensing functions, such as a State bar association or a medical society, or by other organizations that can seriously affect the debtors' livelihood or fresh start, such as exclusion from a union on the basis of discharge of a debt to the union's credit union.

The effect of the section, and of further interpretations of the *Perez* rule, is to strengthen the anti-reaffirmation policy found in section 524(b). Discrimination based solely on nonpayment could encourage reaffirmations, contrary to the expressed policy.

The section is not so broad as a comparable section proposed by the Bankruptcy Commission, S. 236, 94th Cong., 1st Sess. § 4–508 (1975), which would have extended the prohibition to any discrimination, even by private parties. Nevertheless, it is not limiting either, as noted. The courts will continue to mark the contours of the anti-discrimination provision in pursuit of sound bankruptcy policy. Senate Report No. 95–989.

1984 Acts. Statements by Legislative Leaders, see 1984 U.S. Code Cong. and Adm. News, p. 576.

1994 Acts. House Report No. 103–835, see 1994 U.S. Code Cong. and Adm. News, p. 3340.

2005 Acts. House Report No. 109–31(Part I), see 2005 U.S. Code Cong. and Adm. News, p. 88.

References in Text

The Perishable Agricultural Commodities Act, 1930, referred to in subsec. (a), is Act June 10, 1930, c. 436, 46 Stat. 531, as amended, which is classified principally to chapter 20A of Title 7, 7 U.S.C.A. § 499a et seq. For complete classification of this Act to the Code, see 7 U.S.C.A. § 499a and Tables.

The Packers and Stockyards Act, 1921, referred to in subsec. (a), is Act Aug. 15, 1921, c. 64, 42 Stat. 159, which is classified principally to chapter 9 of Title 7, 7 U.S.C.A. § 181 et seq. For complete classification, see 7 U.S.C.A. § 181 and Tables.

Section 1 of an Act entitled "An Act making appropriations for the Department of Agriculture for the fiscal year ending June 30, 1944, and for other purposes," approved July 12, 1943, referred to in subsec. (a), is section 1 of Act July 12, 1943, c. 215, 57 Stat. 422, which is classified to 7 U.S.C.A. § 204.

The Bankruptcy Act, referred to in subsecs. (a), (b), and (c)(1), is Act July 1, 1898, c. 541, 30 Stat. 544, as amended, which was classified generally to former Title 11.

The Higher Education Act of 1965, referred to in subsec. (c)(2), is Pub.L. 89–329, Nov. 8, 1965, 79 Stat. 1219, as amended, which is classified generally to chapter 28 of Title 20, 20 U.S.C.A. § 1001 et seq. Title IV of the Act is classified generally to subchapter IV of chapter 28 of Title 20, 20 U.S.C.A. § 1070 et seq. For complete classification, see Short Title note set out under 20 U.S.C.A. § 1001 and Tables.

Effective and Applicability Provisions

2005 Acts. Amendments by Pub.L. 109–8 effective, except as otherwise provided, 180 days after April 20, 2005, and inapplicable with respect to cases commenced under Title 11 before the effective date, see Pub.L. 109–8, § 1501, set out as a note under 11 U.S.C.A. § 101.

1994 Acts. Amendments by Pub.L. 103–394 effective on Oct. 22, 1994, and not to apply with respect to cases commenced under Title 11 of the United States Code before Oct. 22, 1994, see section 702 of Pub.L. 103–394, set out as a note under section 101 of this title.

1984 Acts. Amendment by Pub.L. 98–353 effective with respect to cases filed 90 days after July 10, 1984, see section 552(a), formerly 553(a) of Pub.L. 98–353, set out as a note under section 101 of this title.

Separability of Provisions

If any provision of or amendment made by Pub.L. 103–394 or the application of such provision or amendment to any person or circumstance is held to be unconstitutional, the remaining provisions of and amendments made by Pub.L. 103–394 and the application of such provisions and amendments to any person or circumstance shall not be affected thereby, see section 701 of Pub.L. 103–394, set out as a note under section 101 of this title.

CROSS REFERENCES

Reporting of obsolete information prohibited, see 15 USCA § 1681c.

§ 526. Restrictions on debt relief agencies

(a) A debt relief agency shall not—

(1) fail to perform any service that such agency informed an assisted person or prospective assisted

---

person it would provide in connection with a case or proceeding under this title;

(2) make any statement, or counsel or advise any assisted person or prospective assisted person to make a statement in a document filed in a case or proceeding under this title, that is untrue or misleading, or that upon the exercise of reasonable care, should have been known by such agency to be untrue or misleading;

(3) misrepresent to any assisted person or prospective assisted person, directly or indirectly, affirmatively or by material omission, with respect to—

(A) the services that such agency will provide to such person; or

(B) the benefits and risks that may result if such person becomes a debtor in a case under this title; or

(4) advise an assisted person or prospective assisted person to incur more debt in contemplation of such person filing a case under this title or to pay an attorney or bankruptcy petition preparer a fee or charge for services performed as part of preparing for or representing a debtor in a case under this title.

(b) Any waiver by any assisted person of any protection or right provided under this section shall not be enforceable against the debtor by any Federal or State court or any other person, but may be enforced against a debt relief agency.

(c)(1) Any contract for bankruptcy assistance between a debt relief agency and an assisted person that does not comply with the material requirements of this section, section 527, or section 528 shall be void and may not be enforced by any Federal or State court or by any other person, other than such assisted person.

(2) Any debt relief agency shall be liable to an assisted person in the amount of any fees or charges in connection with providing bankruptcy assistance to such person that such debt relief agency has received, for actual damages, and for reasonable attorneys' fees and costs if such agency is found, after notice and a hearing, to have—

(A) intentionally or negligently failed to comply with any provision of this section, section 527, or section 528 with respect to a case or proceeding under this title for such assisted person;

(B) provided bankruptcy assistance to an assisted person in a case or proceeding under this title that is dismissed or converted to a case under another chapter of this title because of such agency's intentional or negligent failure to file any required document including those specified in section 521; or

(C) intentionally or negligently disregarded the material requirements of this title or the Federal Rules of Bankruptcy Procedure applicable to such agency.

(3) In addition to such other remedies as are provided under State law, whenever the chief law enforcement officer of a State, or an official or agency designated by a State, has reason to believe that any person has violated or is violating this section, the State—

(A) may bring an action to enjoin such violation;

(B) may bring an action on behalf of its residents to recover the actual damages of assisted persons arising from such violation, including any liability under paragraph (2); and

(C) in the case of any successful action under subparagraph (A) or (B), shall be awarded the costs of the action and reasonable attorneys' fees as determined by the court.

(4) The district courts of the United States for districts located in the State shall have concurrent jurisdiction of any action under subparagraph (A) or (B) of paragraph (3).

(5) Notwithstanding any other provision of Federal law and in addition to any other remedy provided under Federal or State law, if the court, on its own motion or on the motion of the United States trustee or the debtor, finds that a person intentionally violated this section, or engaged in a clear and consistent pattern or practice of violating this section, the court may—

(A) enjoin the violation of such section; or

(B) impose an appropriate civil penalty against such person.

(d) No provision of this section, section 527, or section 528 shall—

(1) annul, alter, affect, or exempt any person subject to such sections from complying with any law of any State except to the extent that such law is inconsistent with those sections, and then only to the extent of the inconsistency; or

(2) be deemed to limit or curtail the authority or ability—

(A) of a State or subdivision or instrumentality thereof, to determine and enforce qualifications for the practice of law under the laws of that State; or

(B) of a Federal court to determine and enforce the qualifications for the practice of law before that court.

(Added Pub.L. 109–8, Title II, § 227(a), Apr. 20, 2005, 119 Stat. 67; amended Pub.L. 111–327, § 2(a)(20), Dec. 22, 2010, 124 Stat. 3560.)

HISTORICAL AND STATUTORY NOTES

Revision Notes and Legislative Reports

2005 Acts. House Report No. 109–31(Part I), see 2005 U.S. Code Cong. and Adm. News, p. 88.

References in Text

The Federal Rules of Bankruptcy Procedure, referred to in subsec. (c)(2)(C), are set out in the Appendix to this title.

Effective and Applicability Provisions

2005 Acts. Amendments by Pub.L. 109–8 effective, except as otherwise provided, 180 days after April 20, 2005, and inapplicable with respect to cases commenced under Title 11 before the effective date, see Pub.L. 109–8, § 1501, set out as a note under 11 U.S.C.A. § 101.

§ 527. Disclosures

(a) A debt relief agency providing bankruptcy assistance to an assisted person shall provide—

(1) the written notice required under section 342(b)(1); and

(2) to the extent not covered in the written notice described in paragraph (1), and not later than 3 business days after the first date on which a debt relief agency first offers to provide any bankruptcy assistance services to an assisted person, a clear and conspicuous written notice advising assisted persons that—

(A) all information that the assisted person is required to provide with a petition and thereafter during a case under this title is required to be complete, accurate, and truthful;

(B) all assets and all liabilities are required to be completely and accurately disclosed in the documents filed to commence the case, and the replacement value of each asset as defined in section 506 must be stated in those documents where requested after reasonable inquiry to establish such value;

(C) current monthly income, the amounts specified in section 707(b)(2), and, in a case under chapter 13 of this title, disposable income (determined in accordance with section 707(b)(2)), are required to be stated after reasonable inquiry; and

(D) information that an assisted person provides during their case may be audited pursuant to this title, and that failure to provide such information may result in dismissal of the case under this title or other sanction, including a criminal sanction.

(b) A debt relief agency providing bankruptcy assistance to an assisted person shall provide each assisted person at the same time as the notices required under subsection (a)(1) the following statement, to the extent applicable, or one substantially similar. The statement shall be clear and conspicuous and shall be in a single document separate from other documents or notices provided to the assisted person:

"IMPORTANT INFORMATION ABOUT BANKRUPTCY ASSISTANCE SERVICES FROM AN ATTORNEY OR BANKRUPTCY PETITION PREPARER.

"If you decide to seek bankruptcy relief, you can represent yourself, you can hire an attorney to represent you, or you can get help in some localities from a bankruptcy petition preparer who is not an attorney. THE LAW REQUIRES AN ATTORNEY OR BANKRUPTCY PETITION PREPARER TO GIVE YOU A WRITTEN CONTRACT SPECIFYING WHAT THE ATTORNEY OR BANKRUPTCY PETITION PREPARER WILL DO FOR YOU AND HOW MUCH IT WILL COST. Ask to see the contract before you hire anyone.

"The following information helps you understand what must be done in a routine bankruptcy case to help you evaluate how much service you need. Although bankruptcy can be complex, many cases are routine.

"Before filing a bankruptcy case, either you or your attorney should analyze your eligibility for different forms of debt relief available under the Bankruptcy Code and which form of relief is most likely to be beneficial for you. Be sure you understand the relief you can obtain and its limitations. To file a bankruptcy case, documents called a Petition, Schedules, and Statement of Financial Affairs, and in some cases a Statement of Intention, need to be prepared correctly and filed with the bankruptcy court. You will have to pay a filing fee to the bankruptcy court. Once your case starts, you will have to attend the required first meeting of creditors where you may be questioned by a court official called a 'trustee' and by creditors.

"If you choose to file a chapter 7 case, you may be asked by a creditor to reaffirm a debt. You may want help deciding whether to do so. A creditor is not permitted to coerce you into reaffirming your debts.

"If you choose to file a chapter 13 case in which you repay your creditors what you can afford over 3 to 5 years, you may also want help with preparing your chapter 13 plan and with the confirmation hearing on your plan which will be before a bankruptcy judge.

"If you select another type of relief under the Bankruptcy Code other than chapter 7 or chapter 13, you will want to find out what should be done from someone familiar with that type of relief.

"Your bankruptcy case may also involve litigation. You are generally permitted to represent yourself in litigation in bankruptcy court, but only attorneys, not bankruptcy petition preparers, can give you legal advice.".

(c) Except to the extent the debt relief agency provides the required information itself after reasonably diligent inquiry of the assisted person or others so as to obtain such information reasonably accurately for inclusion on the petition, schedules or statement of financial affairs, a debt relief agency providing bankruptcy assistance to an assisted person, to the extent permitted by nonbankruptcy law, shall provide each assisted person at the time required for the notice required under subsection (a)(1) reasonably sufficient information (which shall be provided in a clear and conspicuous writing) to the assisted person on how to provide all the information the assisted person is required to provide under this title pursuant to section 521, including—

(1) how to value assets at replacement value, determine current monthly income, the amounts specified in section 707(b)(2) and, in a chapter 13 case, how to determine disposable income in accordance with section 707(b)(2) and related calculations;

(2) how to complete the list of creditors, including how to determine what amount is owed and what address for the creditor should be shown; and

(3) how to determine what property is exempt and how to value exempt property at replacement value as defined in section 506.

(d) A debt relief agency shall maintain a copy of the notices required under subsection (a) of this section for 2 years after the date on which the notice is given the assisted person.

(Added Pub.L. 109–8, Title II, § 228(a), Apr. 20, 2005, 119 Stat. 69; amended Pub.L. 111–327, § 2(a)(21), Dec. 22, 2010, 124 Stat. 3560.)

HISTORICAL AND STATUTORY NOTES

Revision Notes and Legislative Reports

2005 Acts. House Report No. 109–31(Part I), see 2005 U.S. Code Cong. and Adm. News, p. 88.

References in Text

Chapter 13, referred to in text, is chapter 13 of this title, 11 U.S.C.A. § 1301 et seq.

Chapter 7, referred to in text, is chapter 7 of this title, 11 U.S.C.A. § 701 et seq.

Effective and Applicability Provisions

2005 Acts. Amendments by Pub.L. 109–8 effective, except as otherwise provided, 180 days after April 20, 2005, and inapplicable with respect to cases commenced under Title 11 before the effective date, see Pub.L. 109–8, § 1501, set out as a note under 11 U.S.C.A. § 101.

§ 528. Requirements for debt relief agencies

(a) A debt relief agency shall—

(1) not later than 5 business days after the first date on which such agency provides any bankruptcy assistance services to an assisted person, but prior to such assisted person's petition under this title being filed, execute a written contract with such assisted person that explains clearly and conspicuously—

(A) the services such agency will provide to such assisted person; and

(B) the fees or charges for such services, and the terms of payment;

(2) provide the assisted person with a copy of the fully executed and completed contract;

(3) clearly and conspicuously disclose in any advertisement of bankruptcy assistance services or of the benefits of bankruptcy directed to the general public (whether in general media, seminars or specific mailings, telephonic or electronic messages, or otherwise) that the services or benefits are with respect to bankruptcy relief under this title; and

(4) clearly and conspicuously use the following statement in such advertisement: "We are a debt relief agency. We help people file for bankruptcy relief under the Bankruptcy Code." or a substantially similar statement.

(b)(1) An advertisement of bankruptcy assistance services or of the benefits of bankruptcy directed to the general public includes—

(A) descriptions of bankruptcy assistance in connection with a chapter 13 plan whether or not chapter 13 is specifically mentioned in such advertisement; and

(B) statements such as "federally supervised repayment plan" or "Federal debt restructuring help" or other similar statements that could lead a reasonable consumer to believe that debt counseling was being offered when in fact the services were directed to providing bankruptcy assistance with a chapter 13 plan or other form of bankruptcy relief under this title.

(2) An advertisement, directed to the general public, indicating that the debt relief agency provides assistance with respect to credit defaults, mortgage foreclosures, eviction proceedings, excessive debt, debt collection pressure, or inability to pay any consumer debt shall—

(A) disclose clearly and conspicuously in such advertisement that the assistance may involve bankruptcy relief under this title; and

(B) include the following statement: "We are a debt relief agency. We help people file for bankruptcy relief under the Bankruptcy Code." or a substantially similar statement.

(Added Pub.L. 109–8, Title II, § 229(a), Apr. 20, 2005, 119 Stat. 71.)

HISTORICAL AND STATUTORY NOTES

Revision Notes and Legislative Reports

2005 Acts. House Report No. 109–31(Part I), see 2005 U.S. Code Cong. and Adm. News, p. 88.

References in Text

Chapter 13, referred to in subsec. (b)(1)(A), (B), is chapter 13 of this title, 11 U.S.C.A. § 1301 et seq.

Effective and Applicability Provisions

2005 Acts. Amendments by Pub.L. 109–8 effective, except as otherwise provided, 180 days after April 20, 2005, and inapplicable with respect to cases commenced under Title 11 before the effective date, see Pub.L. 109–8, § 1501, set out as a note under 11 U.S.C.A. § 101.

SUBCHAPTER III—THE ESTATE

§ 541. Property of the estate

(a) The commencement of a case under section 301, 302, or 303 of this title creates an estate. Such estate is comprised of all the following property, wherever located and by whomever held:

(1) Except as provided in subsections (b) and (c)(2) of this section, all legal or equitable interests of the debtor in property as of the commencement of the case.

(2) All interests of the debtor and the debtor's spouse in community property as of the commencement of the case that is—

(A) under the sole, equal, or joint management and control of the debtor; or

(B) liable for an allowable claim against the debtor, or for both an allowable claim against the debtor and an allowable claim against the debtor's spouse, to the extent that such interest is so liable.

(3) Any interest in property that the trustee recovers under section 329(b), 363(n), 543, 550, 553, or 723 of this title.

(4) Any interest in property preserved for the benefit of or ordered transferred to the estate under section 510(c) or 551 of this title.

(5) Any interest in property that would have been property of the estate if such interest had been an interest of the debtor on the date of the filing of the petition, and that the debtor acquires or becomes entitled to acquire within 180 days after such date—

(A) by bequest, devise, or inheritance;

(B) as a result of a property settlement agreement with the debtor's spouse, or of an interlocutory or final divorce decree; or

(C) as a beneficiary of a life insurance policy or of a death benefit plan.

(6) Proceeds, product, offspring, rents, or profits of or from property of the estate, except such as are earnings from services performed by an individual debtor after the commencement of the case.

(7) Any interest in property that the estate acquires after the commencement of the case.

(b) Property of the estate does not include—

(1) any power that the debtor may exercise solely for the benefit of an entity other than the debtor;

(2) any interest of the debtor as a lessee under a lease of nonresidential real property that has terminated at the expiration of the stated term of such lease before the commencement of the case under this title, and ceases to include any interest of the debtor as a lessee under a lease of nonresidential real property that has terminated at the expiration of the stated term of such lease during the case;

(3) any eligibility of the debtor to participate in programs authorized under the Higher Education Act of 1965 (20 U.S.C. 1001 et seq.; 42 U.S.C. 2751 et seq.), or any accreditation status or State licensure of the debtor as an educational institution;

(4) any interest of the debtor in liquid or gaseous hydrocarbons to the extent that—

(A)(i) the debtor has transferred or has agreed to transfer such interest pursuant to a farmout agreement or any written agreement directly related to a farmout agreement; and

(ii) but for the operation of this paragraph, the estate could include the interest referred to in clause (i) only by virtue of section 365 or 544(a)(3) of this title; or

(B)(i) the debtor has transferred such interest pursuant to a written conveyance of a production payment to an entity that does not participate in the operation of the property from which such production payment is transferred; and

(ii) but for the operation of this paragraph, the estate could include the interest referred to in clause (i) only by virtue of section 365 or 542 of this title;

(5) funds placed in an education individual retirement account (as defined in section 530(b)(1) of the Internal Revenue Code of 1986) not later than 365 days before the date of the filing of the petition in a case under this title, but—

(A) only if the designated beneficiary of such account was a child, stepchild, grandchild, or step-grandchild of the debtor for the taxable year for which funds were placed in such account;

(B) only to the extent that such funds—

(i) are not pledged or promised to any entity in connection with any extension of credit; and

(ii) are not excess contributions (as described in section 4973(e) of the Internal Revenue Code of 1986); and

(C) in the case of funds placed in all such accounts having the same designated beneficiary not earlier than 720 days nor later than 365 days before such date, only so much of such funds as does not exceed $6,425 [1];

(6) funds used to purchase a tuition credit or certificate or contributed to an account in accordance with section 529(b)(1)(A) of the Internal Revenue Code of 1986 under a qualified State tuition program (as defined in section 529(b)(1) of such Code) not later than 365 days before the date of the filing of the petition in a case under this title, but—

(A) only if the designated beneficiary of the amounts paid or contributed to such tuition program was a child, stepchild, grandchild, or step-grandchild of the debtor for the taxable year for which funds were paid or contributed;

(B) with respect to the aggregate amount paid or contributed to such program having the same designated beneficiary, only so much of such amount as does not exceed the total contributions permitted under section 529(b)(6) of such Code with respect to such beneficiary, as adjusted beginning on the date of the filing of the petition in a case under this title by the annual increase or decrease (rounded to the nearest tenth of 1 percent) in the education expenditure category of the Consumer Price Index prepared by the Department of Labor; and

(C) in the case of funds paid or contributed to such program having the same designated beneficiary not earlier than 720 days nor later than 365 days before such date, only so much of such funds as does not exceed $6,425 [1];

(7) any amount—

(A) withheld by an employer from the wages of employees for payment as contributions—

(i) to—

(I) an employee benefit plan that is subject to title I of the Employee Retirement Income Security Act of 1974 or under an employee benefit plan which is a governmental plan under section 414(d) of the Internal Revenue Code of 1986;

(II) a deferred compensation plan under section 457 of the Internal Revenue Code of 1986; or

(III) a tax-deferred annuity under section 403(b) of the Internal Revenue Code of 1986;

except that such amount under this subparagraph shall not constitute disposable income as defined in section 1325(b)(2); or

(ii) to a health insurance plan regulated by State law whether or not subject to such title; or

(B) received by an employer from employees for payment as contributions—

(i) to—

(I) an employee benefit plan that is subject to title I of the Employee Retirement Income Security Act of 1974 or under an employee benefit plan which is a governmental plan under section 414(d) of the Internal Revenue Code of 1986;

(II) a deferred compensation plan under section 457 of the Internal Revenue Code of 1986; or

(III) a tax-deferred annuity under section 403(b) of the Internal Revenue Code of 1986;

except that such amount under this subparagraph shall not constitute disposable income, as defined in section 1325(b)(2); or

(ii) to a health insurance plan regulated by State law whether or not subject to such title;

(8) subject to subchapter III of chapter 5, any interest of the debtor in property where the debtor pledged or sold tangible personal property (other than securities or written or printed evidences of indebtedness or title) as collateral for a loan or advance of money given by a person licensed under law to make such loans or advances, where—

(A) the tangible personal property is in the possession of the pledgee or transferee;

(B) the debtor has no obligation to repay the money, redeem the collateral, or buy back the property at a stipulated price; and

(C) neither the debtor nor the trustee have exercised any right to redeem provided under the contract or State law, in a timely manner as provided under State law and section 108(b);

(9) any interest in cash or cash equivalents that constitute proceeds of a sale by the debtor of a money order that is made—

(A) on or after the date that is 14 days prior to the date on which the petition is filed; and

(B) under an agreement with a money order issuer that prohibits the commingling of such proceeds with property of the debtor (notwithstanding that, contrary to the agreement, the proceeds may have been commingled with property of the debtor),

unless the money order issuer had not taken action, prior to the filing of the petition, to require compliance with the prohibition; or

(10) funds placed in an account of a qualified ABLE program (as defined in section 529A(b) of the Internal Revenue Code of 1986) not later than 365 days before the date of the filing of the petition in a case under this title, but—

(A) only if the designated beneficiary of such account was a child, stepchild, grandchild, or stepgrandchild of the debtor for the taxable year for which funds were placed in such account;

(B) only to the extent that such funds—

(i) are not pledged or promised to any entity in connection with any extension of credit; and

(ii) are not excess contributions (as described in section 4973(h) of the Internal Revenue Code of 1986); and

(C) in the case of funds placed in all such accounts having the same designated beneficiary not earlier than 720 days nor later than 365 days before such date, only so much of such funds as does not exceed $6,225.

Paragraph (4) shall not be construed to exclude from the estate any consideration the debtor retains, receives, or is entitled to receive for transferring an interest in liquid or gaseous hydrocarbons pursuant to a farmout agreement.

(c)(1) Except as provided in paragraph (2) of this subsection, an interest of the debtor in property becomes property of the estate under subsection (a)(1), (a)(2), or (a)(5) of this section notwithstanding any provision in an agreement, transfer instrument, or applicable nonbankruptcy law—

(A) that restricts or conditions transfer of such interest by the debtor; or

(B) that is conditioned on the insolvency or financial condition of the debtor, on the commencement of a case under this title, or on the appointment of or taking possession by a trustee in a case under this title or a custodian before such commencement, and that effects or gives an option to effect a forfeiture, modification, or termination of the debtor's interest in property.

(2) A restriction on the transfer of a beneficial interest of the debtor in a trust that is enforceable under applicable nonbankruptcy law is enforceable in a case under this title.

(d) Property in which the debtor holds, as of the commencement of the case, only legal title and not an equitable interest, such as a mortgage secured by real property, or an interest in such a mortgage, sold by the debtor but as to which the debtor retains legal title to service or supervise the servicing of such mortgage or interest, becomes property of the estate under subsection (a)(1) or (2) of this section only to the extent of the debtor's legal title to such property, but not to the extent of any equitable interest in such property that the debtor does not hold.

(e) In determining whether any of the relationships specified in paragraph (5)(A) or (6)(A) of subsection (b) exists, a legally adopted child of an individual (and a child who is a member of an individual's household, if placed with such individual by an authorized placement agency for legal adoption by such individual), or a foster child of an individual (if such child has as the child's principal place of abode the home of the debtor and is a member of the debtor's household) shall be treated as a child of such individual by blood.

(f) Notwithstanding any other provision of this title, property that is held by a debtor that is a corporation described in section 501(c)(3) of the Internal Revenue Code of 1986 and exempt from tax under section 501(a) of such Code may be transferred to an entity that is not such a corporation, but only under the same conditions as would apply if the debtor had not filed a case under this title.

(Pub.L. 95–598, Nov. 6, 1978, 92 Stat. 2594; Pub.L. 98–353, Title III, §§ 363(a), 456, July 10, 1984, 98 Stat. 363, 376; Pub.L. 101–508, Title III, § 3007(a)(2), Nov. 5, 1990, 104 Stat. 1388–28; Pub.L. 102–486, Title XXX, § 3017(b), Oct. 24, 1992, 106 Stat. 3130; Pub.L. 103–394, Title II, §§ 208(b), 223, Oct. 22, 1994, 108 Stat. 4124, 4129; Pub.L. 109–8, Title II, § 225(a), Title III, § 323, Title XII, §§ 1212, 1221(c), 1230, Apr. 20, 2005, 119 Stat. 65, 97, 194, 196, 201; Pub.L. 111–327, § 2(a)(22), Dec. 22, 2010, 124 Stat. 3560; Pub.L. 113–295, Div. B, Title I, § 104(a), Dec. 19, 2014, 128 Stat. 4063.)

1 Dollar amount as adjusted by the Judicial Conference of the United States. See Adjustment of Dollar Amounts notes set out under this section and 11 U.S.C.A. § 104.

HISTORICAL AND STATUTORY NOTES

Revision Notes and Legislative Reports

1978 Acts. This section defines property of the estate, and specifies what property becomes property of the estate. The commencement of a bankruptcy case creates an estate. Under paragraph (1) of subsection (a), the estate is comprised of all legal or equitable interest of the debtor in property, wherever located, as of the commencement of the case. The scope of this paragraph is broad. It includes all kinds of property, including tangible or intangible property, causes of action (see Bankruptcy Act § 70a(6) [section 110(a)(6) of former Title 11]), and all other forms of property currently specified in section 70a of the Bankruptcy Act § 70a [sic] [section 110(a) of former Title 11], as well as property recovered by the trustee under section 542 of proposed title 11, if the property recovered was merely out of the possession of the debtor, yet remained "property of the debtor." The debtor's interest in property also includes "title" to property, which is an interest, just as are a possessory interest, or leasehold interest, for example. The result of *Segal v. Rochelle*, 382 U.S. 375 (1966) [86 S.Ct. 511, 15 L.Ed.2d 428], is followed, and the right to a refund is property of the estate.

Though this paragraph will include choses in action and claims by the debtor against others, it is not intended to expand the debtor's rights against others more than they exist at the commencement of the case. For example, if the debtor has a claim that is barred at the time of the commencement of the case by the statute of limitations, then the trustee would not be able to pursue that claim, because he too would be barred. He could take no greater rights than the debtor himself had. But see proposed 11 U.S.C. 108, which would permit the trustee a tolling of the statute of limitations if it had not run before the date of the filing of the petition.

Paragraph (1) has the effect of overruling *Lockwood v. Exchange Bank*, 190 U.S. 294 (1903) [23 S.Ct. 751, 47 L.Ed. 1061, 10 Am.Bankr.Rep. 107], because it includes as property of the estate all property of the debtor, even that needed for a fresh start. After the property comes into the estate, then the debtor is permitted to exempt it under proposed 11 U.S.C. 522, and the court will have jurisdiction to determine what property may be exempted and what remains as property of the estate. The broad jurisdictional grant in proposed 28 U.S.C. 1334 would have the effect of overruling *Lockwood* independently of the change made by this provision.

Paragraph (1) also has the effect of overruling *Lines v. Frederick*, 400 U.S. 18 (1970) [91 S.Ct. 113, 27 L.Ed.2d 124].

Situations occasionally arise where property ostensibly belonging to the debtor will actually not be property of the debtor, but will be held in trust for another. For example, if the debtor has incurred medical bills that were covered by insurance, and the insurance company had sent the payment of the bills to the debtor before the debtor had paid the bill for which the payment was reimbursement, the payment would actually be held in a constructive trust for the person to whom the bill was owed. This section and proposed 11 U.S.C. 545 also will not affect various statutory provisions that give a creditor of the debtor a lien that is valid outside as well as inside bankruptcy, or that creates a trust fund for the benefit of a creditor of the debtor. See Packers and Stockyards Act § 206, 7 U.S.C. 196 [7 U.S.C.A. § 196].

Bankruptcy Act § 8 [section 26 of former Title 11] has been deleted as unnecessary. Once the estate is created, no interests in property of the estate remain in the debtor. Consequently, if the debtor dies during the case, only property exempted from property of the estate or acquired by the debtor after the commencement of the case and not included as property of the estate will be available to the representative of the debtor's probate estate. The bankruptcy proceeding will continue in rem with respect to property of the state [sic], and the discharge will apply in personam to relieve the debtor, and thus his probate representative, of liability for dischargeable debts.

The estate also includes the interests of the debtor and the debtor's spouse in community property, subject to certain limitations; property that the trustee recovers under the avoiding powers; property that the debtor acquires by bequest, devise, inheritance, a property settlement agreement with the debtor's spouse, or as the beneficiary of a life insurance policy within 180 days after the petition; and proceeds, product, offspring, rents, and profits of or from property of the estate, except such as are earning from services performed by an individual debtor after the commencement of the case. Proceeds here is not used in a confining sense, as defined in the Uniform Commercial Code, but is intended to be a broad term to encompass all proceeds of property of the estate. The conversion in form of property of the estate does not change its character as property of the estate.

Subsection (b) excludes from property of the estate any power, such as a power of appointment, that the debtor may exercise solely for the benefit of an entity other than the debtor. This changes present law which excludes powers solely benefiting other persons but not other entities.

Subsection (c) invalidates restrictions on the transfer of property of the debtor, in order that all of the interests of the debtor in property will become property of the estate. The provisions invalidated are those that restrict or condition transfer of the debtor's interest, and those that are conditioned on the insolvency or financial condition of the debtor, on the commencement of a bankruptcy case, or on the appointment of a custodian of the debtor's property. Paragraph (2) of subsection (c), however, preserves restrictions on a transfer of a spendthrift trust that the restriction is enforceable nonbankruptcy law to the extent of the income reasonably necessary for the support of a debtor and his dependents.

Subsection (d), derived from section 70c of the Bankruptcy Act [section 110(c) of former Title 11], gives the estate the benefit of all defenses available to the debtor as against an entity other than the estate, including such defenses as statutes of limitations, statutes of frauds, usury, and other personal defenses, and makes waiver by the debtor after the commencement of the case ineffective to bind the estate.

Section 541(e) confirms the current status under the Bankruptcy Act [former Title 11] of bona fide secondary mortgage market transactions as the purchase and sale of assets. Mortgages or interests in mortgages sold in the secondary market should not be considered as part of the debtor's estate. To permit the efficient servicing of mortgages or interests in mortgages the seller often retains the original mortgage notes and related documents, and the purchaser records under State recording statutes the purchaser's ownership of the mortgages or interests in mortgages purchased. Section 541(e) makes clear that the seller's retention of the mortgage documents and the purchaser's decision not to record do not impair the asset sale character of secondary mortgage market transactions. The committee notes that in

secondary mortgage market transactions the parties may characterize their relationship as one of trust, agency, or independent contractor. The characterization adopted by the parties should not affect the statutes in bankruptcy on bona fide secondary mortgage market purchases and sales. Senate Report No. 95–989.

1984 Acts. Statements by Legislative Leaders, see 1984 U.S. Code Cong. and Adm. News, p. 576.

1990 Acts. House Report No. 101–881, House Conference Report No. 101–964, and President's Signing Statement, see 1990 U.S. Code Cong. and Adm. News, p. 2017.

1994 Acts. House Report No. 103–835, see 1994 U.S. Code Cong. and Adm. News, p. 3340.

2005 Acts. House Report No. 109–31(Part I), see 2005 U.S. Code Cong. and Adm. News, p. 88.

Legislative Statements

Section 541(a)(7) is new. The provision clarifies that any interest in property that the estate acquires after the commencement of the case is property of the estate; for example, if the estate enters into a contract, after the commencement of the case, such a contract would be property of the estate. The addition of this provision by the House amendment merely clarifies that section 541(a) is an all-embracing definition which includes charges on property, such as liens held by the debtor on property of a third party, or beneficial rights and interests that the debtor may have in property of another. However, only the debtor's interest in such property becomes property of the estate. If the debtor holds bare legal title or holds property in trust for another, only those rights which the debtor would have otherwise had emanating from such interest pass to the estate under section 541. Neither this section nor section 545 will affect various statutory provisions that give a creditor a lien that is valid both inside and outside bankruptcy against a bona fide purchaser of property from the debtor, or that creates a trust fund for the benefit of creditors meeting similar criteria. See Packers and Stockyards Act § 206, 7 U.S.C. 196 (1976) [7 U.S.C.A. § 196].

Section 541(c)(2) follows the position taken in the House bill and rejects the position taken in the Senate amendment with respect to income limitations on a spend-thrift trust.

Section 541(d) of the House amendment is derived from section 541(e) of the Senate amendment and reiterates the general principle that where the debtor holds bare legal title without any equitable interest, that the estate acquires bare legal title without any equitable interest in the property. The purpose of section 541(d) as applied to the secondary mortgage market is identical to the purpose of section 541(e) of the Senate amendment and section 541(d) will accomplish the same result as would have been accomplished by section 541(e). Even if a mortgage seller retains for purposes of servicing legal title to mortgages or interests in mortgages sold in the secondary mortgage market, the trustee would be required by section 541(d) to turn over the mortgages or interests in mortgages to the purchaser of those mortgages.

The seller of mortgages in the secondary mortgage market will often retain the original mortgage notes and related documents and the seller will not endorse the notes to reflect the sale to the purchaser. Similarly, the purchaser will often not record the purchaser's ownership of the mortgages or interests in mortgages under State recording statutes. These facts are irrelevant and the seller's retention of the mortgage documents and the purchaser's decision not to record do not change the trustee's obligation to turn the mortgages or interests in mortgages over to the purchaser. The application of section 541(d) to secondary mortgage market transactions will not be affected by the terms of the servicing agreement between the mortgage servicer and the purchaser of the mortgages. Under section 541(d), the trustee is required to recognize the purchaser's title to the mortgages or interests in mortgages and to turn this property over to the purchaser. It makes no difference whether the servicer and the purchaser characterize their relationship as one of trust, agency, or independent contractor.

The purpose of section 541(d) as applied to the secondary mortgage market is therefore to make certain that secondary mortgage market sales as they are currently structured are not subject to challenge by bankruptcy trustees and that purchasers of mortgages will be able to obtain the mortgages or interests in mortgages which they have purchased from trustees without the trustees asserting that a sale of mortgages is a loan from the purchaser to the seller.

Thus, as section 541(a)(1) clearly states, the estate is comprised of all legal or equitable interests of the debtor in property as of the commencement of the case. To the extent such an interest is limited in the hands of the debtor, it is equally limited in the hands of the estate except to the extent that defenses which are personal against the debtor are not effective against the estate.

Property of the estate: The Senate amendment provided that property of the estate does not include amounts held by the debtor as trustee and any taxes withheld or collected from others before the commencement of the case. The House amendment removes these two provisions. As to property held by the debtor as a trustee, the House amendment provides that property of the estate will include whatever interest the debtor held in the property at the commencement of the case. Thus, where the debtor held only legal title to the property and the beneficial interest in that property belongs to another, such as exists in the case of property held in trust, the property of the estate includes the legal title, but not the beneficial interest in the property.

As to withheld taxes, the House amendment deletes the rule in the Senate bill as unnecessary since property of the estate does not include the beneficial interest in property held by the debtor as a trustee. Under the Internal Revenue Code of 1954 (section 7501 [26 U.S.C.A. § 7501]), the amounts of withheld taxes are held to be a special fund in trust for the United States. Where the Internal Revenue Service can demonstrate that the amounts of taxes withheld are still in the possession of the debtor at the commencement of the case, then if a trust is created, those amounts are not property of the estate. Compare *In re Shakesteers Coffee Shops*, 546 F.2d 821 (9th Cir. 1976) with *In re Glynn Wholesale Building Materials, Inc.* (S.D.Ga.1978) and *In re Progress Tech Colleges, Inc.*, 42 Aftr 2d 78–5573 (S.D.Ohio 1977).

Where it is not possible for the Internal Revenue Service to demonstrate that the amounts of taxes withheld are still in the possession of the debtor at the commencement of the case, present law generally includes amounts of withheld taxes as property of the estate. See, e.g., *United States v. Randall*, 401 U.S. 513 (1973) [91 S.Ct. 991, 28 L.Ed.2d 273] and *In re Tamasha Town and Country Club*, 483 F.2d 1377 (9th Cir. 1973). Nonetheless, a serious problem exists where "trust fund taxes" withheld from others are held to be property of the estate where the withheld amounts are commingled with other assets of the debtor. The courts should permit the use of reasonable assumptions under which the Internal Revenue

Service, and other tax authorities, can demonstrate that amounts of withheld taxes are still in the possession of the debtor at the commencement of the case. For example, where the debtor had commingled that amount of withheld taxes in his general checking account, it might be reasonable to assume that any remaining amounts in that account on the commencement of the case are the withheld taxes. In addition, Congress may consider future amendments to the Internal Revenue Code making clear that amounts of withheld taxes are held by the debtor in a trust relationship and, consequently, that such amounts are not property of the estate.

References in Text

The Higher Education Act of 1965, referred to in subsec. (b)(3), is Pub.L. 89–329, Nov. 8, 1965, 79 Stat. 1219, which is classified generally to chapter 28 of Title 20, 20 U.S.C.A. § 1001 et seq. Part C of title IV of the Act was formerly classified to part C of subchapter I of chapter 34 of Title 42, 42 U.S.C.A. § 2751 et seq., prior to transfer to part C of subchapter IV of chapter 28 of Title 20, 20 U.S.C.A. § 1087–51 et seq. For complete classification, see Short Title note set out under 20 U.S.C.A. § 1001 and Tables.

Section 530(b)(1) of the Internal Revenue Code of 1986, referred to in subsec. (b)(5), is classified to 26 U.S.C.A. § 530(b)(1).

Section 4973(e) of the Internal Revenue Code of 1986, referred to in subsec. (b)(5)(B)(ii), is classified to 26 U.S.C.A. § 4973(e).

"Section 529(b)(1) of such Code" and "section 529(b)(6) of such Code", referred to in subsec. (b)(6), are classified to 26 U.S.C.A. § 529(b)(1) and to 26 U.S.C.A. § 529(b)(6), respectively.

Title I of the Employee Retirement Income Security Act of 1974, referred to in subsec. (b)(7)(A)(i)(I), (B)(i)(I), means Pub.L. 93–406, Title I, Sept. 2, 1974, 88 Stat. 829, which principally enacted subchapter I of chapter 18 of Title 29, 29 U.S.C.A. § 1001 et seq.; see Tables for complete classification.

Section 414(d) of the Internal Revenue Code of 1986, referred to in subsec. (b)(7)(A)(i)(I), (B)(i)(I), is 26 U.S.C.A. § 414(d).

Section 457 of the Internal Revenue Code of 1986, referred to in subsec. (b)(7)(A)(i)(II), (B)(i)(II), is 26 U.S.C.A. § 457.

Section 403(b) of the Internal Revenue Code of 1986, referred to in subsec. (b)(7)(A)(i)(III), (B)(i)(III), is 26 U.S.C.A. § 403(b).

Section 529A(b) of the Internal Revenue Code of 1986, referred to in subsec. (b)(10), is classified to 26 U.S.C.A. § 529A(b).

Section 4973(h) of the Internal Revenue Code of 1986, referred to in subsec. (b)(10)(B)(ii), is classified to 26 U.S.C.A. § 4973(h).

Codifications

Section 223(2) of Pub.L. 103–394, directing that subsec. (b)(4) of this section be amended by striking out the period at the end and inserting "; or", was executed by inserting "or" following the semicolon at the end of subsec. (b)(4)(B)(ii) of this section, as added by section 208(b)(3) of Pub.L. 103–394, as the probable intent of Congress.

Effective and Applicability Provisions

2014 Acts. Amendments by Pub.L. 113–295, Div. B, Title I, § 104 shall apply with respect to cases commenced under Title 11 on or after December 19, 2014, see Pub.L. 113–295, Div. B, Title I, § 104(d), set out as a note under 11 U.S.C.A. § 521.

2013 Acts. Increase of dollar amounts by Judicial Conference of the United States by notice published Feb. 21, 2013, 78 F.R. 12089 effective April 1, 2013, and increase not applicable to cases commenced before the effective date of the adjustments, i.e., April 1, 2013. See Adjustment of Dollar Amounts notes under 11 U.S.C.A. § 104 and this section.

2010 Acts. Increase of dollar amounts by Judicial Conference of the United States by notice published Feb. 25, 2010, 75 F.R. 8747 effective April 1, 2010, and increase not applicable to cases commenced before the effective date of the adjustments, i.e., April 1, 2010. See Adjustment of Dollar Amounts notes under 11 U.S.C.A. § 104 and this section.

2007 Acts. Increase of dollar amounts by Judicial Conference of the United States by notice published Feb. 14, 2007, 72 F.R. 7082 effective April 1, 2007, and increase not applicable to cases commenced before the effective date of the adjustments, i.e., April 1, 2007. See Adjustment of Dollar Amounts notes under 11 U.S.C.A. § 104 and this section.

2005 Acts. Amendments to this section by Pub.L. 109–8, § 1221, applicable to case pending under this title on April 20, 2005, or filed under this title on or after that date, except that the court shall not confirm a plan under chapter 11 of this title without considering whether this section would substantially affect the rights of a party in interest who first acquired rights with respect to the debtor after the date of the filing of the petition, see Pub.L. 109–8, § 1221(d), set out as a note under 11 U.S.C.A. § 363.

Amendments by Pub.L. 109–8 effective, except as otherwise provided, 180 days after April 20, 2005, and inapplicable with respect to cases commenced under Title 11 before the effective date, see Pub.L. 109–8, § 1501, set out as a note under 11 U.S.C.A. § 101.

1994 Acts. Amendment by Pub.L. 103–394 effective on Oct. 22, 1994, and not to apply with respect to cases commenced under Title 11 of the United States Code before Oct. 22, 1994, see section 702 of Pub.L. 103–394, set out as a note under section 101 of this title.

1992 Acts. Enactment of subsec. (b)(4) by Pub.L. 102–486 effective Oct. 24, 1992, see section 3017(c) of Pub.L. 102–486, set out as a note under section 101 of this title.

1990 Acts. Section 3008 of Pub.L. 101–508, which had provided that the amendment to this section by Pub.L. 101–508 was to cease to be effective on Oct. 1, 1996, was repealed by Pub.L. 102–325, Title XV, § 1558, July 23, 1992, 106 Stat. 841.

1984 Acts. Amendment by Pub.L. 98–353 effective with respect to cases filed 90 days after July 10, 1984, see section 552(a), formerly 553(a) of Pub.L. 98–353, set out as a note under section 101 of this title.

Separability of Provisions

If any provision of or amendment made by Pub.L. 103–394 or the application of such provision or amendment to any person or circumstance is held to be unconstitutional, the remaining provisions of and amendments made by Pub.L. 103–394 and the application of such provisions and amendments to any person or circumstance shall not be affected thereby, see section 701 of Pub.L. 103–394, set out as a note under section 101 of this title.

Adjustment of Dollar Amounts

For adjustment of dollar amounts specified in subsec. (b)(5)(C), (6)(C) of this section by the Judicial Conference of the United States, effective Apr. 1, 2016, see note set out under 11 U.S.C.A. § 104.

By notice published Feb. 22, 2016, 81 F.R. 8748, the Judicial Conference of the United States adjusted the dollar amounts in provisions specified in subsec. (b)(5)(C), (6)(C) of this section, effective Apr. 1, 2016, as follows:

In subsec. (b)(5)(C) adjusted $6,225 to $6,425.

In subsec. (b)(6)(C) adjusted $6,225 to $6,425.

By notice published Feb. 21, 2013, 78 F.R. 12089, the Judicial Conference of the United States adjusted the dollar amounts in provisions specified in subsec. (b)(5)(C), (6)(C) of this section, effective Apr. 1, 2013, as follows:

In subsec. (b)(5)(C) adjusted $5,850 to $6,225.

In subsec. (b)(6)(C) adjusted $5,850 to $6,225.

By notice published Feb. 25, 2010, 75 F.R. 8747, the Judicial Conference of the United States adjusted the dollar amounts in provisions specified in subsec. (b)(5)(C), (6)(C) of this section, effective Apr. 1, 2010, as follows:

In subsec. (b)(5)(C) adjusted $5,475 to $5,850.

In subsec. (b)(6)(C) adjusted $5,475 to $5,850.

By notice published Feb. 14, 2007, 72 F.R. 7082, the Judicial Conference of the United States adjusted the dollar amounts in provisions specified in subsec. (b)(5)(C), (6)(C) of this section, effective Apr. 1, 2007, as follows:

In subsec. (b)(5)(C) adjusted $5,000 to $5,475.

In subsec. (b)(6)(C) adjusted $5,000 to $5,475.

CROSS REFERENCES

"Community claim" defined, see 11 USCA § 101.

Distribution of property of estate, see 11 USCA § 726.

Effect of discharge, see 11 USCA § 524.

Executory contracts and unexpired leases, see 11 USCA § 365.

Exemptions, see 11 USCA § 522.

Ownership of copyright, see 17 USCA § 201.

Property of estate in,

Chapter thirteen cases, see 11 USCA § 1306.

Chapter twelve cases, see 11 USCA § 1207.

Trustee considered consignee of merchandise consigned to deceased or insolvent persons, see 19 USCA § 1485.

Venue of action brought under this title by trustee as statutory successor under this section to debtor, see 28 USCA § 1409.

§ 542.   Turnover of property to the estate

(a) Except as provided in subsection (c) or (d) of this section, an entity, other than a custodian, in possession, custody, or control, during the case, of property that the trustee may use, sell, or lease under section 363 of this title, or that the debtor may exempt under section 522 of this title, shall deliver to the trustee, and account for, such property or the value of such property, unless such property is of inconsequential value or benefit to the estate.

(b) Except as provided in subsection (c) or (d) of this section, an entity that owes a debt that is property of the estate and that is matured, payable on demand, or payable on order, shall pay such debt to, or on the order of, the trustee, except to the extent that such debt may be offset under section 553 of this title against a claim against the debtor.

(c) Except as provided in section 362(a)(7) of this title, an entity that has neither actual notice nor actual knowledge of the commencement of the case concerning the debtor may transfer property of the estate, or pay a debt owing to the debtor, in good faith and other than in the manner specified in subsection (d) of this section, to an entity other than the trustee, with the same effect as to the entity making such transfer or payment as if the case under this title concerning the debtor had not been commenced.

(d) A life insurance company may transfer property of the estate or property of the debtor to such company in good faith, with the same effect with respect to such company as if the case under this title concerning the debtor had not been commenced, if such transfer is to pay a premium or to carry out a nonforfeiture insurance option, and is required to be made automatically, under a life insurance contract with such company that was entered into before the date of the filing of the petition and that is property of the estate.

(e) Subject to any applicable privilege, after notice and a hearing, the court may order an attorney, accountant, or other person that holds recorded information, including books, documents, records, and papers, relating to the debtor's property or financial affairs, to turn over or disclose such recorded information to the trustee.

(Pub.L. 95–598, Nov. 6, 1978, 92 Stat. 2595; Pub.L. 98–353, Title III, § 457, July 10, 1984, 98 Stat. 376; Pub.L. 103–394, Title V, § 501(d)(16), Oct. 22, 1994, 108 Stat. 4146.)

HISTORICAL AND STATUTORY NOTES

Revision Notes and Legislative Reports

1978 Acts. Subsection (a) of this section requires anyone holding property of the estate on the date of the filing of the petition, or property that the trustee may use, sell, or lease under section 363, to deliver it to the trustee. The subsection also requires an accounting. The holder of property of the estate is excused from the turnover requirement of this subsection if the property held is of inconsequential value to the estate. However, this provision must be read in conjunction with the remainder of the subsection, so that if the property is of inconsequential monetary value, yet has a significant use value for the estate, the holder of the property would not be excused from turnover.

Subsection (b) requires an entity that owes money to the debtor as of the date of the petition, or that holds money payable on demand or payable on order, to pay the money to the order of the trustee. An exception is made to the extent

that the entity has a valid right of setoff, as recognized by section 553.

Subsection (c) provides an exception to subsections (a) and (b). It protects an entity that has neither actual notice nor actual knowledge of the case and that transfers, in good faith, property that is deliverable or payable to the trustee to someone other than to the estate or on order of the estate. This subsection codifies the result of *Bank of Marin v. England*, 385 U.S. 99 (1966) [87 S.Ct. 274, 17 L.Ed.2d 197], but does not go so far as to permit bank setoff in violation of the automatic stay, proposed 11 U.S.C. 362(a)(7), even if the bank offsetting the debtor's balance has no knowledge of the case.

Subsection (d) protects life insurance companies that are required by contract to make automatic premium loans from property that might otherwise be property of the estate.

Subsection (e) requires an attorney, accountant, or other professional that holds recorded information relating to the debtor's property or financial affairs, to surrender it to the trustee. This duty is subject to any applicable claim of privilege, such as attorney-client privilege. It is a new provision that deprives accountants and attorneys of the leverage that they have today, under State law lien provisions, to receive payment in full ahead of other creditors when the information they hold is necessary to the administration of the estate. Senate Report No. 95–989.

1984 Acts. Statements by Legislative Leaders, see 1984 U.S. Code Cong. and Adm. News, p. 576.

1994 Acts. House Report No. 103–835, see 1994 U.S. Code Cong. and Adm. News, p. 3340.

Legislative Statements

Section 542(a) of the House amendment modifies similar provisions contained in the House bill and the Senate amendment treating with turnover of property to the estate. The section makes clear that any entity, other than a custodian, is required to deliver property of the estate to the trustee or debtor in possession whenever such property is acquired by the entity during the case, if the trustee or debtor in possession may use, sell, or lease the property under section 363, or if the debtor may exempt the property under section 522, unless the property is of inconsequential value or benefit to the estate. This section is not intended to require an entity to deliver property to the trustee if such entity has obtained an order of the court authorizing the entity to retain possession, custody or control of the property.

The House amendment adopts section 542(c) of the House bill in preference to a similar provision contained in section 542(c) of the Senate amendment. Protection afforded by section 542(c) applies only to the transferor or payor and not to a transferee or payee receiving a transfer or payment, as the case may be. Such transferee or payee is treated under section 549 and section 550 of title 11.

The extent to which the attorney client privilege is valid against the trustee is unclear under current law and is left to be determined by the courts on a case by case basis.

Effective and Applicability Provisions

1994 Acts. Amendment by Pub.L. 103–394 effective on Oct. 22, 1994, and not to apply with respect to cases commenced under Title 11 of the United States Code before Oct. 22, 1994, see section 702 of Pub.L. 103–394, set out as a note under section 101 of this title.

1984 Acts. Amendment by Pub.L. 98–353 effective with respect to cases filed 90 days after July 10, 1984, see section 552(a), formerly 553 of Pub.L. 98–353, set out as a note under section 101 of this title.

Separability of Provisions

If any provision of or amendment made by Pub.L. 103–394 or the application of such provision or amendment to any person or circumstance is held to be unconstitutional, the remaining provisions of and amendments made by Pub.L. 103–394 and the application of such provisions and amendments to any person or circumstance shall not be affected thereby, see section 701 of Pub.L. 103–394, set out as a note under section 101 of this title.

CROSS REFERENCES

Assignability or accrual to third persons of farm loan agreements respecting credits or principal and interest, see 42 USCA § 1473.

Concealment of assets, see 18 USCA § 152.

Disallowance of claims of entity from which property is recoverable, see 11 USCA § 502.

Effect of dismissal, see 11 USCA § 349.

Exemptions, see 11 USCA § 522.

§ 543.   Turnover of property by a custodian

(a) A custodian with knowledge of the commencement of a case under this title concerning the debtor may not make any disbursement from, or take any action in the administration of, property of the debtor, proceeds, product, offspring, rents, or profits of such property, or property of the estate, in the possession, custody, or control of such custodian, except such action as is necessary to preserve such property.

(b) A custodian shall—

(1) deliver to the trustee any property of the debtor held by or transferred to such custodian, or proceeds, product, offspring, rents, or profits of such property, that is in such custodian's possession, custody, or control on the date that such custodian acquires knowledge of the commencement of the case; and

(2) file an accounting of any property of the debtor, or proceeds, product, offspring, rents, or profits of such property, that, at any time, came into the possession, custody, or control of such custodian.

(c) The court, after notice and a hearing, shall—

(1) protect all entities to which a custodian has become obligated with respect to such property or proceeds, product, offspring, rents, or profits of such property;

(2) provide for the payment of reasonable compensation for services rendered and costs and expenses incurred by such custodian; and

(3) surcharge such custodian, other than an assignee for the benefit of the debtor's creditors that was appointed or took possession more than 120 days before the date of the filing of the petition, for

any improper or excessive disbursement, other than a disbursement that has been made in accordance with applicable law or that has been approved, after notice and a hearing, by a court of competent jurisdiction before the commencement of the case under this title.

(d) After notice and hearing, the bankruptcy court—

(1) may excuse compliance with subsection (a), (b), or (c) of this section if the interests of creditors and, if the debtor is not insolvent, of equity security holders would be better served by permitting a custodian to continue in possession, custody, or control of such property, and

(2) shall excuse compliance with subsections (a) and (b)(1) of this section if the custodian is an assignee for the benefit of the debtor's creditors that was appointed or took possession more than 120 days before the date of the filing of the petition, unless compliance with such subsections is necessary to prevent fraud or injustice.

(Pub.L. 95–598, Nov. 6, 1978, 92 Stat. 2595; Pub.L. 98–353, Title III, § 458, July 10, 1984, 98 Stat. 376; Pub.L. 103–394, Title V, § 501(d)(17), Oct. 22, 1994, 108 Stat. 4146.)

HISTORICAL AND STATUTORY NOTES

Revision Notes and Legislative Reports

1978 Acts. This section requires a custodian appointed before the bankruptcy case to deliver to the trustee and to account for property that has come into his possession, custody, or control as a custodian. "Property of the debtor" in section (a) [sic] includes property that was property of the debtor at the time the custodian took the property, but the title to which passed to the custodian. The section requires the court to protect any obligations incurred by the custodian, provide for the payment of reasonable compensation for services rendered and costs and expenses incurred by the custodian, and to surcharge the custodian for any improper or excessive disbursement, unless it has been approved by a court of competent jurisdiction. Subsection (d) reinforces the general abstention policy in § 305 by permitting the bankruptcy court to authorize the custodianship to proceed notwithstanding this section. Senate Report No. 95–989.

1984 Acts. Statements by Legislative Leaders, see 1984 U.S. Code Cong. and Adm. News, p. 576.

1994 Acts. House Report No. 103–835, see 1994 U.S. Code Cong. and Adm. News, p. 3340.

Legislative Statements

Section 543(a) is a modification of similar provisions contained in the House bill and the Senate amendment. The provision clarifies that a custodian may always act as is necessary to preserve property of the debtor. Section 543(c)(3) excepts from surcharge a custodian that is an assignee for the benefit of creditors, who was appointed or took possession before 120 days before the date of the filing of the petition, whichever is later. The provision also prevents a custodian from being surcharged in connection with payments made in accordance with applicable law.

Effective and Applicability Provisions

1994 Acts. Amendment by Pub.L. 103–394 effective on Oct. 22, 1994, and not to apply with respect to cases commenced under Title 11 of the United States Code before Oct. 22, 1994, see section 702 of Pub.L. 103–394, set out as a note under section 101 of this title.

1984 Acts. Amendment by Pub.L. 98–353 effective with respect to cases filed 90 days after July 10, 1984, see section 552(a)(7), formerly 553 of Pub.L. 98–353, set out as a note under section 101 of this title.

Separability of Provisions

If any provision of or amendment made by Pub.L. 103–394 or the application of such provision or amendment to any person or circumstance is held to be unconstitutional, the remaining provisions of and amendments made by Pub.L. 103–394 and the application of such provisions and amendments to any person or circumstance shall not be affected thereby, see section 701 of Pub.L. 103–394, set out as a note under section 101 of this title.

CROSS REFERENCES

Administrative expenses of superseded custodians, see 11 USCA § 503.

Concealment of assets, see 18 USCA § 152.

Disallowance of claim of entity from which property is recoverable, see 11 USCA § 502.

Effect of dismissal, see 11 USCA § 349.

Order of payment on claims for expenses of superseded custodians, see 11 USCA § 726.

Property recoverable by trustee as exempt, see 11 USCA § 522.

§ 544. Trustee as lien creditor and as successor to certain creditors and purchasers

(a) The trustee shall have, as of the commencement of the case, and without regard to any knowledge of the trustee or of any creditor, the rights and powers of, or may avoid any transfer of property of the debtor or any obligation incurred by the debtor that is voidable by—

(1) a creditor that extends credit to the debtor at the time of the commencement of the case, and that obtains, at such time and with respect to such credit, a judicial lien on all property on which a creditor on a simple contract could have obtained such a judicial lien, whether or not such a creditor exists;

(2) a creditor that extends credit to the debtor at the time of the commencement of the case, and obtains, at such time and with respect to such credit, an execution against the debtor that is returned unsatisfied at such time, whether or not such a creditor exists; or

(3) a bona fide purchaser of real property, other than fixtures, from the debtor, against whom applicable law permits such transfer to be perfected, that obtains the status of a bona fide purchaser and has perfected such transfer at the time of the commence-

ment of the case, whether or not such a purchaser exists.

(b)(1) Except as provided in paragraph (2), the trustee may avoid any transfer of an interest of the debtor in property or any obligation incurred by the debtor that is voidable under applicable law by a creditor holding an unsecured claim that is allowable under section 502 of this title or that is not allowable only under section 502(e) of this title.

(2) Paragraph (1) shall not apply to a transfer of a charitable contribution (as that term is defined in section 548(d)(3)) that is not covered under section 548(a)(1)(B), by reason of section 548(a)(2). Any claim by any person to recover a transferred contribution described in the preceding sentence under Federal or State law in a Federal or State court shall be preempted by the commencement of the case.

(Pub.L. 95–598, Nov. 6, 1978, 92 Stat. 2596; Pub.L. 98–353, Title III, § 459, July 10, 1984, 98 Stat. 377; Pub.L. 105–183, § 3(b), June 19, 1998, 112 Stat. 518.)

HISTORICAL AND STATUTORY NOTES

Revision Notes and Legislative Reports

1978 Acts. Subsection (a) is the "strong arm clause" of current law, now found in Bankruptcy Act § 70c [section 110(c) of former Title 11]. It gives the trustee the rights of a creditor on a simple contract with a judicial lien on the property of the debtor as of the date of the petition; of a creditor with a writ of execution against the property of the debtor unsatisfied as of the date of the petition; and a bona fide purchaser of the real property of the debtor as of the date of the petition. "Simple contract" as used here is derived from Bankruptcy Act § 60a(4) [section 96(a)(4) of former title 11]. The third status, that of a bona fide purchaser of real property, is new.

Subsection (b) is derived from current section 70e [former § 110(e) of former Title 11]. It gives the trustee the rights of actual unsecured creditors under applicable law to void transfers. It follows *Moore v. Bay*, 284 U.S. 4 (1931) [52 S.Ct. 3, 76 L.Ed. 133, 18 Am.Bankr.Rep.N.S. 675.], and overrules those cases that hold section 70e [section 110(e) of former Title 11] gives the trustee the rights of secured creditors. Senate Report No. 95–989.

1984 Acts. Statements by Legislative Leaders, see 1984 U.S.Code Cong. and Adm.News, p. 576.

1998 Acts. Statement by President, see 1998 U.S. Code Cong. and Adm. News, p. 230.

Legislative Statements

Section 544(a)(3) modifies similar provisions contained in the House bill and Senate amendment so as not to require a creditor to perform the impossible in order to perfect his interest. Both the lien creditor test in section 544(a)(1), and the bona fide purchaser test in section 544(a)(3) should not require a transferee to perfect a transfer against an entity with respect to which applicable law does not permit perfection. The avoiding powers under section 544(a)(1), (2), and (3) are new. In particular, section 544(a)(1) overrules *Pacific Finance Corp. v. Edwards*, 309 F.2d 224 (9th Cir. 1962), and *In re Federals, Inc.*, 553 F.2d 509 (6th Cir. 1977), insofar as those cases held that the trustee did not have the status of a creditor who extended credit immediately prior to the commencement of the case.

The House amendment deletes section 544(c) of the House bill.

Effective and Applicability Provisions

1984 Acts. Amendment by Pub.L. 98–353 effective with respect to cases filed 90 days after July 10, 1984, see section 552(a), formerly 553 of Pub.L. 98–353, set out as a note under section 101 of this title.

Applicability

Pub.L. 105–183, § 5, June 19, 1998, 112 Stat. 518, provided that: "This Act and the amendments made by this Act [amending this section and sections 546, 548, 707, and 1325 of this title and enacting this note and provisions set out as notes under this section and section 101 of this title] shall apply to any case brought under an applicable provision of title 11, United States Code, [this title] that is pending or commenced on or after the date of enactment of this Act [June 19, 1998]."

Rules of Construction

Pub.L. 105–183, § 6, June 19, 1998, 112 Stat. 519, provided that: "Nothing in the amendments made by this Act [amending this section and sections 546, 548, 707, and 1325 of this title and enacting this note and provisions set out as notes under this section and section 101 of this title] is intended to limit the applicability of the Religious Freedom Restoration Act of 1993 (42 U.S.C. 2002bb et seq.)."

CROSS REFERENCES

Applicability of this section in Chapter nine cases, see 11 USCA § 901.

Appointment of trustee upon debtor's refusal to pursue cause of action under this section, see 11 USCA § 926.

Commencement of involuntary cases by transferees of voidable transfer, see 11 USCA § 303.

Disallowance of claims of entity that is transferee of avoidable transfer, see 11 USCA § 502.

Effect of dismissal, see 11 USCA § 349.

Exemptions, see 11 USCA § 522.

Recovery of voidable transfers in investor protection liquidation proceedings, see 15 USCA § 78fff–2.

Venue of action brought under this title by trustee as statutory successor under this section to creditors, see 28 USCA § 1409.

Voidable transfers in,

Commodity broker liquidation cases, see 11 USCA § 764.

Stockbroker liquidation proceedings, see 11 USCA § 749.

§ 545. Statutory liens

The trustee may avoid the fixing of a statutory lien on property of the debtor to the extent that such lien—

(1) first becomes effective against the debtor—

(A) when a case under this title concerning the debtor is commenced;

(B) when an insolvency proceeding other than under this title concerning the debtor is commenced;

(C) when a custodian is appointed or authorized to take or takes possession;

(D) when the debtor becomes insolvent;

(E) when the debtor's financial condition fails to meet a specified standard; or

(F) at the time of an execution against property of the debtor levied at the instance of an entity other than the holder of such statutory lien;

(2) is not perfected or enforceable at the time of the commencement of the case against a bona fide purchaser that purchases such property at the time of the commencement of the case, whether or not such a purchaser exists, except in any case in which a purchaser is a purchaser described in section 6323 of the Internal Revenue Code of 1986, or in any other similar provision of State or local law;

(3) is for rent; or

(4) is a lien of distress for rent.

(Pub.L. 95–598, Nov. 6, 1978, 92 Stat. 2597; Pub.L. 98–353, Title III, § 460, July 10, 1984, 98 Stat. 377; Pub.L. 109–8, Title VII, § 711, Apr. 20, 2005, 119 Stat. 127.)

HISTORICAL AND STATUTORY NOTES

Revision Notes and Legislative Reports

1978 Acts. This section permits the trustee to avoid the fixing of certain statutory liens. It is derived from subsections 67b and 67c of present law [sections 107(b) and (c) former Title 11]. Liens that first become effective on the bankruptcy or insolvency of the debtor are voidable by the trustee. Liens that are not perfected or enforceable on the date of the petition against a bona fide purchaser are voidable. If a transferee is able to perfect under section 546(a) and that perfection relates back to an earlier date, then in spite of the filing of the bankruptcy petition, the trustee would not be able to defeat the lien, because the lien would be perfected and enforceable against a bona fide purchaser that purchased the property on the date of the filing of the petition. Finally, a lien for rent or of distress for rent is voidable, whether the lien is a statutory lien or a common law lien of distress for rent. See proposed 11 U.S.C. 101(37); Bankruptcy Act § 67(c)(1)(C) [section 107(c)(1)(C) of former Title 11]. The trustee may avoid a lien under this section even if the lien has been enforced by sale before the commencement of the case. To that extent, Bankruptcy Act section 67c(5) [section 107(c)(5) of former Title 11] is not followed.

Subsection (b) limits the trustee's power to avoid tax liens under Federal, state, or local law. For example, under section 6323 of the Internal Revenue Code [Title 26]. Once public notice of a tax lien has been filed, the Government is generally entitled to priority over subsequent lienholders. However, certain purchasers who acquire an interest in certain specific kinds of personal property will take free of an existing filed tax lien attaching to such property. Among the specific kinds of personal property which a purchaser can acquire free of an existing tax lien (unless the buyer knows of the existence of the lien) are stocks and securities, motor vehicles, inventory, and certain household goods. Under the present Bankruptcy Act (section 67(c)(1) [section 107(c)(1) of former Title 11]), the trustee may be viewed as a bona fide purchaser, so that he can take over any such designated items free of tax liens even if the tax authority has perfected its lien. However, the reasons for enabling a bona fide purchaser to take these kinds of assets free of an unfiled tax lien, that is, to encourage free movement of these assets in general commerce, do not apply to a trustee in a title 11 case, who is not in the same position as an ordinary bona fide purchaser as to such property. The bill accordingly adds a new subsection (b) to sec. 545 providing, in effect, that a trustee in bankruptcy does not have the right under this section to take otherwise specially treated items of personal property free of a tax lien filed before the filing of the petition. Senate Report No. 95–989.

1984 Acts. Statements by Legislative Leaders, see 1984 U.S.Code Cong. and Adm.News, p. 576.

2005 Acts. House Report No. 109–31(Part I), see 2005 U.S. Code Cong. and Adm. News, p. 88.

Legislative Statements

Section 545 of the House amendment modifies similar provisions contained in the House bill and Senate amendment to make clear that a statutory lien may be avoided under section 545 only to the extent the lien violates the perfection standards of section 545. Thus a Federal tax lien is invalid under section 545(2) with respect to property specified in sections 6323(b) and (c) of the Internal Revenue Code of 1954 [sections 6323(b) and (c) of Title 26, Internal Revenue Code]. As a result of this modification, section 545(b) of the Senate amendment is deleted as unnecessary.

Statutory liens: The House amendment retains the provision of section 545(2) of the House bill giving the trustee in a bankruptcy case the same power which a bona fide purchaser has to take over certain kinds of personal property despite the existence of a tax lien covering that property. The amendment thus retains present law, and deletes section 545(b) of the Senate amendment which would have no longer allowed the trustee to step into the shoes of a bona fide purchaser for this purpose.

References in Text

Section 6323 of the Internal Revenue Code of 1986, referred to in par. (2), is classified to 26 U.S.C.A. § 6323.

Effective and Applicability Provisions

2005 Acts. Amendments by Pub.L. 109–8 effective, except as otherwise provided, 180 days after April 20, 2005, and inapplicable with respect to cases commenced under Title 11 before the effective date, see Pub.L. 109–8, § 1501, set out as a note under 11 U.S.C.A. § 101.

1984 Acts. Amendment by Pub.L. 98–353 effective with respect to cases filed 90 days after July 10, 1984, see section 552(a), formerly 553(a) of Pub.L. 98–353, set out as a note under section 101 of this title.

CROSS REFERENCES

Applicability of this section in Chapter nine cases, see 11 USCA § 901.

Appointment of trustee upon debtor's refusal to pursue cause of action under this section, see 11 USCA § 926.

Commencement of involuntary cases by transferees of voidable transfers, see 11 USCA § 303.

Disallowance of claims of entity that is a transferee of an avoidable transfer, see 11 USCA § 502.

Effect of dismissal, see 11 USCA § 349.

Exemptions, see 11 USCA § 522.

Recovery of voidable transfers in investor protection liquidation proceedings, see 15 USCA § 78fff–2.

Voidable transfers in,

Commodity broker liquidation cases, see 11 USCA § 764.

Stockbroker liquidation cases, see 11 USCA § 749.

§ 546.   Limitations on avoiding powers

(a) An action or proceeding under section 544, 545, 547, 548, or 553 of this title may not be commenced after the earlier of—

(1) the later of—

(A) 2 years after the entry of the order for relief; or

(B) 1 year after the appointment or election of the first trustee under section 702, 1104, 1163, 1202, or 1302 of this title if such appointment or such election occurs before the expiration of the period specified in subparagraph (A); or

(2) the time the case is closed or dismissed.

(b)(1) The rights and powers of a trustee under sections 544, 545, and 549 of this title are subject to any generally applicable law that—

(A) permits perfection of an interest in property to be effective against an entity that acquires rights in such property before the date of perfection; or

(B) provides for the maintenance or continuation of perfection of an interest in property to be effective against an entity that acquires rights in such property before the date on which action is taken to effect such maintenance or continuation.

(2) If—

(A) a law described in paragraph (1) requires seizure of such property or commencement of an action to accomplish such perfection, or maintenance or continuation of perfection of an interest in property; and

(B) such property has not been seized or such an action has not been commenced before the date of the filing of the petition;

such interest in such property shall be perfected, or perfection of such interest shall be maintained or continued, by giving notice within the time fixed by such law for such seizure or such commencement.

(c)(1) Except as provided in subsection (d) of this section and in section 507(c), and subject to the prior rights of a holder of a security interest in such goods or the proceeds thereof, the rights and powers of the trustee under sections 544(a), 545, 547, and 549 are subject to the right of a seller of goods that has sold goods to the debtor, in the ordinary course of such seller's business, to reclaim such goods if the debtor has received such goods while insolvent, within 45 days before the date of the commencement of a case under this title, but such seller may not reclaim such goods unless such seller demands in writing reclamation of such goods—

(A) not later than 45 days after the date of receipt of such goods by the debtor; or

(B) not later than 20 days after the date of commencement of the case, if the 45–day period expires after the commencement of the case.

(2) If a seller of goods fails to provide notice in the manner described in paragraph (1), the seller still may assert the rights contained in section 503(b)(9).

(d) In the case of a seller who is a producer of grain sold to a grain storage facility, owned or operated by the debtor, in the ordinary course of such seller's business (as such terms are defined in section 557 of this title) or in the case of a United States fisherman who has caught fish sold to a fish processing facility owned or operated by the debtor in the ordinary course of such fisherman's business, the rights and powers of the trustee under sections 544(a), 545, 547, and 549 of this title are subject to any statutory or common law right of such producer or fisherman to reclaim such grain or fish if the debtor has received such grain or fish while insolvent, but—

(1) such producer or fisherman may not reclaim any grain or fish unless such producer or fisherman demands, in writing, reclamation of such grain or fish before ten days after receipt thereof by the debtor; and

(2) the court may deny reclamation to such a producer or fisherman with a right of reclamation that has made such a demand only if the court secures such claim by a lien.

(e) Notwithstanding sections 544, 545, 547, 548(a)(1)(B), and 548(b) of this title, the trustee may not avoid a transfer that is a margin payment, as defined in section 101, 741, or 761 of this title, or settlement payment, as defined in section 101 or 741 of this title, made by or to (or for the benefit of) a commodity broker, forward contract merchant, stockbroker, financial institution, financial participant, or securities clearing agency, or that is a transfer made by or to (or for the benefit of) a commodity broker, forward contract merchant, stockbroker, financial institution, financial participant, or securities clearing agency, in connection with a securities contract, as defined in section 741(7), commodity contract, as defined in section 761(4), or forward contract, that is made before the commencement of the case, except under section 548(a)(1)(A) of this title.

(f) Notwithstanding sections 544, 545, 547, 548(a)(1)(B), and 548(b) of this title, the trustee may not avoid a transfer made by or to (or for the benefit of) a repo participant or financial participant, in connection with a repurchase agreement and that is made before the commencement of the case, except under section 548(a)(1)(A) of this title.

(g) Notwithstanding sections 544, 545, 547, 548(a)(1)(B) and 548(b) of this title, the trustee may not

avoid a transfer, made by or to (or for the benefit of) a swap participant or financial participant, under or in connection with any swap agreement and that is made before the commencement of the case, except under section 548(a)(1)(A) of this title.

(h) Notwithstanding the rights and powers of a trustee under sections 544(a), 545, 547, 549, and 553, if the court determines on a motion by the trustee made not later than 120 days after the date of the order for relief in a case under chapter 11 of this title and after notice and a hearing, that a return is in the best interests of the estate, the debtor, with the consent of a creditor and subject to the prior rights of holders of security interests in such goods or the proceeds of such goods, may return goods shipped to the debtor by the creditor before the commencement of the case, and the creditor may offset the purchase price of such goods against any claim of the creditor against the debtor that arose before the commencement of the case.

(i)(1) Notwithstanding paragraphs (2) and (3) of section 545, the trustee may not avoid a warehouseman's lien for storage, transportation, or other costs incidental to the storage and handling of goods.

(2) The prohibition under paragraph (1) shall be applied in a manner consistent with any State statute applicable to such lien that is similar to section 7–209 of the Uniform Commercial Code, as in effect on the date of enactment of the Bankruptcy Abuse Prevention and Consumer Protection Act of 2005, or any successor to such section 7–209.

(j) Notwithstanding sections 544, 545, 547, 548(a)(1)(B), and 548(b) the trustee may not avoid a transfer made by or to (or for the benefit of) a master netting agreement participant under or in connection with any master netting agreement or any individual contract covered thereby that is made before the commencement of the case, except under section 548(a)(1)(A) and except to the extent that the trustee could otherwise avoid such a transfer made under an individual contract covered by such master netting agreement.

(Pub.L. 95–598, Nov. 6, 1978, 92 Stat. 2597; Pub.L. 97–222, § 4, July 27, 1982, 96 Stat. 236; Pub.L. 98–353, Title III, §§ 351, 393, 461, July 10, 1984, 98 Stat. 358, 365, 377; Pub.L. 99–554, Title II, §§ 257(d), 283(*l*), Oct. 27, 1986, 100 Stat. 3114, 3117; Pub.L. 101–311, Title I, § 103, Title II, § 203, June 25, 1990, 104 Stat. 268, 269; Pub.L. 103–394, Title II, §§ 204(b), 209, 216, 222(a), Title V, § 501(b)(4), Oct. 22, 1994, 108 Stat. 4122, 4125, 4126, 4129, 4142; Pub.L. 105–183, § 3(c), June 19, 1998, 112 Stat. 518; Pub.L. 109–8, Title IV, § 406, Title IX, § 907(e), (o)(2), (3), Title XII, § 1227(a), Apr. 20, 2005, 119 Stat. 105, 177, 182, 199; Pub.L. 109–390, § 5(b), Dec. 12, 2006, 120 Stat. 2697.)

HISTORICAL AND STATUTORY NOTES
Revision Notes and Legislative Reports

1978 Acts. The trustee's rights and powers under certain of the avoiding powers are limited by section 546. First, if an interest holder against whom the trustee would have rights still has, under applicable nonbankruptcy law, and as of the date of the petition, the opportunity to perfect his lien against an intervening interest holder, then he may perfect his interest against the trustee. If applicable law requires seizure for perfection, then perfection is by notice to the trustee instead. The rights granted to a creditor under this subsection prevail over the trustee only if the transferee has perfected the transfer in accordance with applicable law, and that perfection relates back to a date that is before the commencement of the case.

The phrase "generally applicable law" relates to those provisions of applicable law that apply both in bankruptcy cases and outside of bankruptcy cases. For example, many State laws, under the Uniform Commercial Code, permit perfection of a purchase-money security interest to relate back to defeat an earlier levy by another creditor if the former was perfected within ten days of delivery of the property. U.C.C. § 9–301(2). Such perfection would then be able to defeat an intervening hypothetical judicial lien creditor on the date of the filing of the petition. The purpose of the subsection is to protect, in spite of the surprise intervention of a bankruptcy petition, those whom State law protects by allowing them to perfect their liens or interests as of an effective date that is earlier than the date of perfection. It is not designed to give the States an opportunity to enact disguised priorities in the form of liens that apply only in bankruptcy cases.

Subsection (b) specifies that the trustee's rights and powers under the strong arm clause, the successor to creditors provision, the preference section, and the postpetition transaction section are all subject to any statutory or common-law right of a seller, in the ordinary course of business, of goods to the debtor to reclaim the goods if the debtor received the goods on credit while insolvent. The seller must demand reclamation within ten days after receipt of the goods by the debtor. As under nonbankruptcy law, the right is subject to any superior rights of secured creditors. The purpose of the provision is to recognize, in part, the validity of section 2–702 of the Uniform Commercial Code, which has generated much litigation, confusion, and divergent decisions in different circuits. The right is subject, however, to the power of the court to deny reclamation and protect the seller by granting him a priority as an administrative expense for his claim arising out of the sale of the goods.

Subsection (c) adds a statute of limitations to the use by the trustee of the avoiding powers. The limitation is two years after his appointment, or the time the case is closed or dismissed, whichever occurs later. Senate Report No. 95–989.

1982 Acts. House Report No. 97–420, see 1982 U.S. Code Cong. and Adm. News, p. 583.

1984 Acts. Statements by Legislative Leaders, see 1984 U.S. Code Cong. and Adm. News, p. 576.

1986 Acts. House Report No. 99–764 and House Conference Report No. 99–958, see 1986 U.S. Code Cong. and Adm. News, p. 5227.

1990 Acts. House Report No. 101–484, see 1990 U.S. Code Cong. and Adm. News, p. 223.

1994 Acts. House Report No. 103–835, see 1994 U.S. Code Cong. and Adm. News, p. 3340.

1998 Acts. Statement by President, see 1998 U.S. Code Cong. and Adm. News, p. 230.

2005 Acts. House Report No. 109–31(Part I), see 2005 U.S. Code Cong. and Adm. News, p. 88.

2006 Acts. House Report No. 109–648(Part I), see 2006 U.S. Code Cong. and Adm. News, p. 1585.

Legislative Statements

Section 546(a) of the House amendment is derived from section 546(c) of the Senate amendment. Section 546(c) of the House amendment is derived from section 546(b) of the Senate amendment. It applies to receipt of goods on credit as well as by cash sales. The section clarifies that a demand for reclamation must be made in writing anytime before 10 days after receipt of the goods by the debtor. The section also permits the court to grant the reclaiming creditor a lien or an administrative expense in lieu of turning over the property.

References in Text

The date of enactment of the Bankruptcy Abuse Prevention and Consumer Protection Act of 2005, referred to in subsec. (i)(2), is April 20, 2005, the approval date of Pub.L. 109–8, 119 Stat. 23.

Codifications

The amendment by Pub.L. 105–183, § 3(c)(3), to subsec. (g) of this section was executed to the first subsec. (g) of this section as the probable intent of Congress since the phrases being amended, "section 548(a)(1)" and "548(a)(2)", appeared only in the first subsec. (g).

Effective and Applicability Provisions

2005 Acts. Amendments by Pub.L. 109–8 effective, except as otherwise provided, 180 days after April 20, 2005, and inapplicable with respect to cases commenced under Title 11 before the effective date, see Pub.L. 109–8, § 1501, set out as a note under 11 U.S.C.A. § 101.

1994 Acts. Amendments by Pub.L. 103–394 effective on Oct. 22, 1994, and not to apply with respect to cases commenced under Title 11 of the United States Code before Oct. 22, 1994, see section 702 of Pub.L. 103–394, set out as a note under section 101 of this title.

1986 Acts. Amendments by Pub.L. 99–554, § 257(d), effective 30 days after Oct. 27, 1986, but not to apply with respect to cases commenced under this title before that date, see section 302(a), (c)(1) of Pub.L. 99–554, set out as a note under section 581 of Title 28, Judiciary and Judicial Procedure.

Amendment by Pub.L. 99–554, § 283, effective 30 days after Oct. 27, 1986, except as otherwise provided for, see section 302(a) of Pub.L. 99–554, set out as a note under section 581 of Title 28.

1984 Acts. Amendment by Pub.L. 98–353 effective with respect to cases filed 90 days after July 10, 1984, see section 552(a), formerly 553 of Pub.L. 98–353, set out as a note under section 101 of this title.

Separability of Provisions

If any provision of or amendment made by Pub.L. 103–394 or the application of such provision or amendment to any person or circumstance is held to be unconstitutional, the remaining provisions of and amendments made by Pub.L. 103–394 and the application of such provisions and amendments to any person or circumstance shall not be affected thereby, see section 701 of Pub.L. 103–394, set out as a note under section 101 of this title.

Applicability

Applicability of amendments made by Pub.L. 105–183 to any case brought under an applicable provision of this title that is pending or commenced on or after June 19, 1998, see Pub.L. 105–183, § 5, June 19, 1998, 112 Stat. 518, set out as a note under section 544 of this title.

Rules of Construction

Amendments made by Pub.L. 105–183 not intended to limit the applicability of the Religious Freedom Restoration Act of 1993 (42 U.S.C. 2002bb et seq.), see Pub.L. 105–183, § 6, June 19, 1998, 112 Stat. 519, set out as a note under section 544 of this title.

CROSS REFERENCES

Applicability of this section in Chapter nine cases, see 11 USCA § 901.'

Automatic stay, see 11 USCA § 362.

Concealment of debtor's assets deemed continuing offense, see 18 USCA § 3284.

§ 547.　Preferences

(a) In this section—

(1) "inventory" means personal property leased or furnished, held for sale or lease, or to be furnished under a contract for service, raw materials, work in process, or materials used or consumed in a business, including farm products such as crops or livestock, held for sale or lease;

(2) "new value" means money or money's worth in goods, services, or new credit, or release by a transferee of property previously transferred to such transferee in a transaction that is neither void nor voidable by the debtor or the trustee under any applicable law, including proceeds of such property, but does not include an obligation substituted for an existing obligation;

(3) "receivable" means right to payment, whether or not such right has been earned by performance; and

(4) a debt for a tax is incurred on the day when such tax is last payable without penalty, including any extension.

(b) Except as provided in subsections (c) and (i) of this section, the trustee may avoid any transfer of an interest of the debtor in property—

(1) to or for the benefit of a creditor;

(2) for or on account of an antecedent debt owed by the debtor before such transfer was made;

(3) made while the debtor was insolvent;

(4) made—

(A) on or within 90 days before the date of the filing of the petition; or

(B) between ninety days and one year before the date of the filing of the petition, if such creditor at the time of such transfer was an insider; and

(5) that enables such creditor to receive more than such creditor would receive if—

(A) the case were a case under chapter 7 of this title;

(B) the transfer had not been made; and

(C) such creditor received payment of such debt to the extent provided by the provisions of this title.

(c) The trustee may not avoid under this section a transfer—

(1) to the extent that such transfer was—

(A) intended by the debtor and the creditor to or for whose benefit such transfer was made to be a contemporaneous exchange for new value given to the debtor; and

(B) in fact a substantially contemporaneous exchange;

(2) to the extent that such transfer was in payment of a debt incurred by the debtor in the ordinary course of business or financial affairs of the debtor and the transferee, and such transfer was—

(A) made in the ordinary course of business or financial affairs of the debtor and the transferee; or

(B) made according to ordinary business terms;

(3) that creates a security interest in property acquired by the debtor—

(A) to the extent such security interest secures new value that was—

(i) given at or after the signing of a security agreement that contains a description of such property as collateral;

(ii) given by or on behalf of the secured party under such agreement;

(iii) given to enable the debtor to acquire such property; and

(iv) in fact used by the debtor to acquire such property; and

(B) that is perfected on or before 30 days after the debtor receives possession of such property;

(4) to or for the benefit of a creditor, to the extent that, after such transfer, such creditor gave new value to or for the benefit of the debtor—

(A) not secured by an otherwise unavoidable security interest; and

(B) on account of which new value the debtor did not make an otherwise unavoidable transfer to or for the benefit of such creditor;

(5) that creates a perfected security interest in inventory or a receivable or the proceeds of either, except to the extent that the aggregate of all such transfers to the transferee caused a reduction, as of the date of the filing of the petition and to the prejudice of other creditors holding unsecured claims, of any amount by which the debt secured by such security interest exceeded the value of all security interests for such debt on the later of—

(A)(i) with respect to a transfer to which subsection (b)(4)(A) of this section applies, 90 days before the date of the filing of the petition; or

(ii) with respect to a transfer to which subsection (b)(4)(B) of this section applies, one year before the date of the filing of the petition; or

(B) the date on which new value was first given under the security agreement creating such security interest;

(6) that is the fixing of a statutory lien that is not avoidable under section 545 of this title;

(7) to the extent such transfer was a bona fide payment of a debt for a domestic support obligation;

(8) if, in a case filed by an individual debtor whose debts are primarily consumer debts, the aggregate value of all property that constitutes or is affected by such transfer is less than $600; or

(9) if, in a case filed by a debtor whose debts are not primarily consumer debts, the aggregate value of all property that constitutes or is affected by such transfer is less than $6,425 [1].

(d) The trustee may avoid a transfer of an interest in property of the debtor transferred to or for the benefit of a surety to secure reimbursement of such a surety that furnished a bond or other obligation to dissolve a judicial lien that would have been avoidable by the trustee under subsection (b) of this section. The liability of such surety under such bond or obligation shall be discharged to the extent of the value of such property recovered by the trustee or the amount paid to the trustee.

(e)(1) For the purposes of this section—

(A) a transfer of real property other than fixtures, but including the interest of a seller or purchaser under a contract for the sale of real property, is perfected when a bona fide purchaser of such property from the debtor against whom applicable law permits such transfer to be perfected cannot acquire an interest that is superior to the interest of the transferee; and

(B) a transfer of a fixture or property other than real property is perfected when a creditor on a simple contract cannot acquire a judicial lien that is superior to the interest of the transferee.

(2) For the purposes of this section, except as provided in paragraph (3) of this subsection, a transfer is made—

(A) at the time such transfer takes effect between the transferor and the transferee, if such transfer is perfected at, or within 30 days after, such time, except as provided in subsection (c)(3)(B);

(B) at the time such transfer is perfected, if such transfer is perfected after such 30 days; or

(C) immediately before the date of the filing of the petition, if such transfer is not perfected at the later of—

(i) the commencement of the case; or

(ii) 30 days after such transfer takes effect between the transferor and the transferee.

(3) For the purposes of this section, a transfer is not made until the debtor has acquired rights in the property transferred.

(f) For the purposes of this section, the debtor is presumed to have been insolvent on and during the 90 days immediately preceding the date of the filing of the petition.

(g) For the purposes of this section, the trustee has the burden of proving the avoidability of a transfer under subsection (b) of this section, and the creditor or party in interest against whom recovery or avoidance is sought has the burden of proving the nonavoidability of a transfer under subsection (c) of this section.

(h) The trustee may not avoid a transfer if such transfer was made as a part of an alternative repayment schedule between the debtor and any creditor of the debtor created by an approved nonprofit budget and credit counseling agency.

(i) If the trustee avoids under subsection (b) a transfer made between 90 days and 1 year before the date of the filing of the petition, by the debtor to an entity that is not an insider for the benefit of a creditor that is an insider, such transfer shall be considered to be avoided under this section only with respect to the creditor that is an insider.

(Pub.L. 95–598, Nov. 6, 1978, 92 Stat. 2597; Pub.L. 98–353, Title III, §§ 310, 462, July 10, 1984, 98 Stat. 355, 377; Pub.L. 99–554, Title II, § 283(m), Oct. 27, 1986, 100 Stat. 3117; Pub.L. 103–394, Title II, § 203, Title III, § 304(f), Oct. 22, 1994, 108 Stat. 4121, 4133; Pub.L. 109–8, Title II, §§ 201(b), 217, Title IV, §§ 403, 409, Title XII, §§ 1213(a), 1222, Apr. 20, 2005, 119 Stat. 42, 55, 104, 106, 194, 196.)

[1] Dollar amount as adjusted by the Judicial Conference of the United States. See Adjustment of Dollar Amounts notes set out under this section and 11 U.S.C.A. § 104.

HISTORICAL AND STATUTORY NOTES

Revision Notes and Legislative Reports

1978 Acts. This section is a substantial modification of present law. It modernizes the preference provisions and brings them more into conformity with commercial practice and the Uniform Commercial Code.

Subsection (a) contains three definitions. Inventory, new value, and receivable are defined in their ordinary senses, but are defined to avoid any confusion or uncertainty surrounding the terms.

Subsection (b) is the operative provision of the section. It authorizes the trustee to avoid a transfer if five conditions are met. These are the five elements of a preference action. First, the transfer must be to or for the benefit of a creditor. Second, the transfer must be for or on account of an antecedent debt owed by the debtor before the transfer was made. Third, the transfer must have been made when the debtor was insolvent. Fourth, the transfer must have been made during the 90 days immediately preceding the commencement of the case. If the transfer was to an insider, the trustee may avoid the transfer if it was made during the period that begins one year before the filing of the petition and ends 90 days before the filing, if the insider to whom the transfer was made had reasonable cause to believe the debtor was insolvent at the time the transfer was made.

Finally, the transfer must enable the creditor to whom or for whose benefit it was made to receive a greater percentage of his claim than he would receive under the distributive provisions of the bankruptcy code. Specifically, the creditor must receive more than he would if the case were a liquidation case, if the transfer had not been made, and if the creditor received payment of the debt to the extent provided by the provisions of the code.

The phrasing of the final element changes the application of the greater percentage test from that employed under current law. Under this language, the court must focus on the relative distribution between classes as well as the amount that will be received by the members of the class of which the creditor is a member. The language also requires the court to focus on the allowability of the claim for which the preference was made. If the claim would have been entirely disallowed, for example, then the test of paragraph (5) will be met, because the creditor would have received nothing under the distributive provisions of the bankruptcy code.

The trustee may avoid a transfer of a lien under this section even if the lien has been enforced by sale before the commencement of the case.

Subsection (b)(2) of this section in effect exempts from the preference rules payments by the debtor of tax liabilities, regardless of their priority status.

Subsection (c) contains exceptions to the trustee's avoiding power. If a creditor can qualify under any one of the exceptions, then he is protected to that extent. If he can qualify under several, he is protected by each to the extent that he can qualify under each.

The first exception is for a transfer that was intended by all parties to be a contemporaneous exchange for new value, and was in fact substantially contemporaneous. Normally, a check is a credit transaction. However, for the purposes of this paragraph, a transfer involving a check is considered to be "intended to be contemporaneous", and if the check is presented for payment in the normal course of affairs, which the Uniform Commercial Code specifies as 30 days, U.C.C. § 3–503(2)(a), that will amount to a transfer that is "in fact substantially contemporaneous."

The second exception protects transfers in the ordinary course of business (or of financial affairs, where a business is not involved) transfers. For the case of a consumer, the paragraph uses the phrase "financial affairs" to include such nonbusiness activities as payment of monthly utility bills. If the debt on account of which the transfer was made was incurred in the ordinary course of both the debtor and the transferee, if the transfer was made not later than 45 days after the debt was incurred, if the transfer itself was made in the ordinary course of both the debtor and the transferee, and if the transfer was made according to ordinary business terms, then the transfer is protected. The purpose of this exception is to leave undisturbed normal financial relations, because it does not detract from the general policy of the preference section to discourage unusual action by either the debtor or his creditors during the debtor's slide into bankruptcy.

The third exception is for enabling loans in connection with which the debtor acquires the property that the loan enabled him to purchase after the loan is actually made.

The fourth exception codifies the net result rule in section 60c of current law [section 96(c) of former Title 11]. If the creditor and the debtor have more than one exchange during the 90-day period, the exchanges are netted out according to the formula in paragraph (4). Any new value that the creditor advances must be unsecured in order for it to qualify under this exception.

Paragraph (5) codifies the improvement in position test, and thereby overrules such cases as *DuBay v. Williams*, 417 F.2d 1277 (C.A.9, 1966), and *Grain Merchants of Indiana, Inc. v. Union Bank and Savings Co.*, 408 F.2d 209 (C.A.7, 1969). A creditor with a security interest in a floating mass, such as inventory or accounts receivable, is subject to preference attack to the extent he improves his position during the 90-day period before bankruptcy. The test is a two-point test, and requires determination of the secured creditor's position 90 days before the petition and on the date of the petition. If new value was first given after 90 days before the case, the date on which it was first given substitutes for the 90-day point.

Paragraph (6) excepts statutory liens validated under section 545 from preference attack. It also protects transfers in satisfaction of such liens, and the fixing of a lien under section 365(j), which protects a vendee whose contract to purchase real property from the debtor is rejected.

Subsection (d), derived from section 67a of the Bankruptcy Act [section 107(a) of former Title 11], permits the trustee to avoid a transfer to reimburse a surety that posts a bond to dissolve a judicial lien that would have been avoidable under this section. The second sentence protects the surety from double liability.

Subsection (e) determines when a transfer is made for the purposes of the preference section. Paragraph (1) defines when a transfer is perfected. For real property, a transfer is perfected when it is valid against a bona fide purchaser. For personal property and fixtures, a transfer is perfected when it is valid against a creditor on a simple contract that obtains a judicial lien after the transfer is perfected. "Simple contract" as used here is derived from Bankruptcy Act § 60a(4) [section 96(a)(4) of former Title 11]. Paragraph (2) specifies that a transfer is made when it takes effect between the transferor and the transferee if it is perfected at or within 10 days after that time. Otherwise, it is made when the transfer is perfected. If it is not perfected before the commencement of the case, it is made immediately before the commencement of the case. Paragraph (3) specifies that a transfer is not made until the debtor has acquired rights in the property transferred. This provision, more than any other in the section, overrules *DuBay and Grain Merchants*, and in combination with subsection (b)(2), overrules *In re King-Porter Co.*, 446 F.2d 722 (5th Cir. 1971).

Subsection (e) is designed to reach the different results under the 1962 version of Article 9 of the U.C.C. and under the 1972 version because different actions are required under each version in order to make a security agreement affective between the parties.

Subsection (f) creates a presumption of insolvency for the 90 days preceding the bankruptcy case. The presumption is as defined in Rule 301 of the Federal Rules of Evidence [Title

28, Judiciary and Judicial Procedure], made applicable in bankruptcy cases by sections 224 and 225 of the bill. The presumption requires the party against whom the presumption exists to come forward with some evidence to rebut the presumption, but the burden of proof remains on the party in whose favor the presumption exists. Senate Report No. 95–989.

1984 Acts. Statements by Legislative Leaders, see 1984 U.S. Code Cong. and Adm. News, p. 576.

1986 Acts. House Report No. 99–764 and House Conference Report No. 99–958, see 1986 U.S. Code Cong. and Adm. News, p. 5227.

1994 Acts. House Report No. 103–835, see 1994 U.S. Code Cong. and Adm. News, p. 3340.

2005 Acts. House Report No. 109–31(Part I), see 2005 U.S. Code Cong. and Adm. News, p. 88.

Legislative Statements

No limitation is provided for payments to commodity brokers as in section 766 of the Senate amendment other than the amendment to section 548 of title 11. Section 547(c)(2) protects most payments.

Section 547(b)(2) of the House amendment adopts a provision contained in the House bill and rejects an alternative contained in the Senate amendment relating to the avoidance of a preferential transfer that is payment of a tax claim owing to a governmental unit. As provided, section 106(c) of the House amendment overrules contrary language in the House report with the result that the Government is subject to avoidance of preferential transfers.

Contrary to language contained in the House report, payment of a debt by means of a check is equivalent to a cash payment, unless the check is dishonored. Payment is considered to be made when the check is delivered for purposes of sections 547(c)(1) and (2).

Section 547(c)(6) of the House bill is deleted and is treated in a different fashion in section 553 of the House amendment.

Section 547(c)(6) represents a modification of a similar provision contained in the House bill and Senate amendment. The exception relating to satisfaction of a statutory lien is deleted. The exception for a lien created under title 11 is deleted since such a lien is a statutory lien that will not be avoidable in a subsequent bankruptcy.

Section 547(e)(1)(B) is adopted from the House bill and Senate amendment without change. It is intended that the simple contract test used in this section will be applied as under section 544(a)(1) not to require a creditor to perfect against a creditor on a simple contract in the event applicable law makes such perfection impossible. For example, a purchaser from a debtor at an improperly noticed bulk sale may take subject to the rights of a creditor on a simple contract of the debtor for 1 year after the bulk sale. Since the purchaser cannot perfect against such a creditor on a simple contract, he should not be held responsible for failing to do the impossible. In the event the debtor goes into bankruptcy within a short time after the bulk sale, the trustee should not be able to use the avoiding powers under section 544(a)(1) or 547 merely because State law has made some transfers of personal property subject to the rights of a creditor on a simple contract to acquire a judicial lien with no opportunity to perfect against such a creditor.

Preferences: The House amendment deletes from the category of transfers on account of antecedent debts which may be avoided under the preference rules, section 547(b)(2), the exception in the Senate amendment for taxes owed to governmental authorities. However, for purposes of the "ordinary course" exception to the preference rules contained in section 547(c)(2), the House amendment specifies that the 45-day period referred to in section 547(c)(2)(B) is to begin running, in the case of taxes from the last due date, including extensions, of the return with respect to which the tax payment was made.

Effective and Applicability Provisions

2013 Acts. Increase of dollar amounts by Judicial Conference of the United States by notice published Feb. 21, 2013, 78 F.R. 12089 effective April 1, 2013, and increase not applicable to cases commenced before the effective date of the adjustments, i.e., April 1, 2013. See Adjustment of Dollar Amounts notes under 11 U.S.C.A. § 104 and this section.

2010 Acts. Increase of dollar amounts by Judicial Conference of the United States by notice published Feb. 25, 2010, 75 F.R. 8747 effective April 1, 2010, and increase not applicable to cases commenced before the effective date of the adjustments, i.e., April 1, 2010. See Adjustment of Dollar Amounts notes under 11 U.S.C.A. § 104 and this section.

2007 Acts. Increase of dollar amounts by Judicial Conference of the United States by notice published Feb. 14, 2007, 72 F.R. 7082 effective April 1, 2007, and increase not applicable to cases commenced before the effective date of the adjustments, i.e., April 1, 2007. See Adjustment of Dollar Amounts notes under 11 U.S.C.A. § 104 and this section.

2005 Acts. Pub.L. 109–8, Title XII, § 1213(b), Apr. 20, 2005, 119 Stat. 195, provided that: "The amendments made by this section [amending this section] shall apply to any case that is pending or commenced on or after the date of enactment of this Act [Apr. 20, 2005]."

Amendments by Pub.L. 109–8 effective, except as otherwise provided, 180 days after April 20, 2005, and inapplicable with respect to cases commenced under Title 11 before the effective date, see Pub.L. 109–8, § 1501, set out as a note under 11 U.S.C.A. § 101.

1994 Acts. Amendments by Pub.L. 103–394 effective on Oct. 22, 1994, and not to apply with respect to cases commenced under Title 11 of the United States Code before Oct. 22, 1994, see section 702 of Pub.L. 103–394, set out as a note under section 101 of this title.

1986 Acts. Amendment by Pub.L. 99–554 effective 30 days after Oct. 27, 1986, except as otherwise provided for, see section 302(a) of Pub.L. 99–554, set out as a note under section 581 of Title 28, Judiciary and Judicial Procedure.

1984 Acts. Amendment by Pub.L. 98–353 effective with respect to cases filed 90 days after July 10, 1984, see section 552(a), formerly 553(a), of Pub.L. 98–353, set out as a note under section 101 of this title.

Separability of Provisions

If any provision of or amendment made by Pub.L. 103–394 or the application of such provision or amendment to any person or circumstance is held to be unconstitutional, the remaining provisions of and amendments made by Pub.L. 103–394 and the application of such provisions and amendments to any person or circumstance shall not be affected thereby, see section 701 of Pub.L. 103–394, set out as a note under section 101 of this title.

Adjustment of Dollar Amounts

For adjustment of dollar amounts specified in subsec. (c)(9) of this section by the Judicial Conference of the United States, effective Apr. 1, 2016, see note set out under 11 U.S.C.A. § 104.

By notice published Feb. 22, 2016, 81 F.R. 8748, the Judicial Conference of the United States adjusted the dollar amounts in provisions specified in subsec. (c)(9) of this section, effective Apr. 1, 2016, as follows:

Adjusted $6,225 to $6,425.

By notice published Feb. 21, 2013, 78 F.R. 12089, the Judicial Conference of the United States adjusted the dollar amounts in provisions specified in subsec. (c)(9) of this section, effective Apr. 1, 2013, as follows:

Adjusted $5,850 to $6,225.

By notice published Feb. 25, 2010, 75 F.R. 8747, the Judicial Conference of the United States adjusted the dollar amounts in provisions specified in subsec. (c)(9) of this section, effective Apr. 1, 2010, as follows:

Adjusted $5,475 to $5,850.

By notice published Feb. 14, 2007, 72 F.R. 7082, the Judicial Conference of the United States adjusted the dollar amounts in provisions specified in subsec. (c)(9) of this section, effective Apr. 1, 2007, as follows:

Adjusted $5,000 to $5,475.

CROSS REFERENCES

Applicability of this section in Chapter nine cases, see 11 USCA § 901.

Appointment of trustee upon debtor's refusal to pursue cause of action under this section, see 11 USCA § 926.

Automatic stay, see 11 USCA § 362.

Commencement of involuntary cases by transferees of voidable transfers, see 11 USCA § 303.

Disallowance of claims of entity that is transferee of avoidable transfer, see 11 USCA § 502.

Effect of dismissal, see 11 USCA § 349.

Exemptions, see 11 USCA § 522.

Persons who may be debtors in Chapter nine case, see 11 USCA § 109.

Recovery of voidable transfers in investor protection liquidation proceedings, see 15 USCA § 78fff–2.

Transfers to defeat cases under this title, see 18 USCA § 152.

Voidable transfers in,

Commodity broker liquidation cases, see 11 USCA § 764.

Stockbroker liquidation cases, see 11 USCA § 749.

§ 548. Fraudulent transfers and obligations

(a)(1) The trustee may avoid any transfer (including any transfer to or for the benefit of an insider under an employment contract) of an interest of the debtor in property, or any obligation (including any obligation to or for the benefit of an insider under an employment contract) incurred by the debtor, that was made or incurred on or within 2 years before the date of the filing of the petition, if the debtor voluntarily or involuntarily—

(A) made such transfer or incurred such obligation with actual intent to hinder, delay, or defraud any entity to which the debtor was or became, on or after the date that such transfer was made or such obligation was incurred, indebted; or

(B)(i) received less than a reasonably equivalent value in exchange for such transfer or obligation; and

(ii)(I) was insolvent on the date that such transfer was made or such obligation was incurred, or became insolvent as a result of such transfer or obligation;

(II) was engaged in business or a transaction, or was about to engage in business or a transaction, for which any property remaining with the debtor was an unreasonably small capital;

(III) intended to incur, or believed that the debtor would incur, debts that would be beyond the debtor's ability to pay as such debts matured; or

(IV) made such transfer to or for the benefit of an insider, or incurred such obligation to or for the benefit of an insider, under an employment contract and not in the ordinary course of business.

(2) A transfer of a charitable contribution to a qualified religious or charitable entity or organization shall not be considered to be a transfer covered under paragraph (1)(B) in any case in which—

(A) the amount of that contribution does not exceed 15 percent of the gross annual income of the debtor for the year in which the transfer of the contribution is made; or

(B) the contribution made by a debtor exceeded the percentage amount of gross annual income specified in subparagraph (A), if the transfer was consistent with the practices of the debtor in making charitable contributions.

(b) The trustee of a partnership debtor may avoid any transfer of an interest of the debtor in property, or any obligation incurred by the debtor, that was made or incurred on or within 2 years before the date of the filing of the petition, to a general partner in the debtor, if the debtor was insolvent on the date such transfer was made or such obligation was incurred, or became insolvent as a result of such transfer or obligation.

(c) Except to the extent that a transfer or obligation voidable under this section is voidable under section 544, 545, or 547 of this title, a transferee or obligee of such a transfer or obligation that takes for value and in good faith has a lien on or may retain any interest transferred or may enforce any obligation incurred, as the case may be, to the extent that such transferee or obligee gave value to the debtor in exchange for such transfer or obligation.

(d)(1) For the purposes of this section, a transfer is made when such transfer is so perfected that a bona fide purchaser from the debtor against whom applicable law permits such transfer to be perfected cannot acquire an interest in the property transferred that is superior to the interest in such property of the transferee, but if such transfer is not so perfected before the commencement of the case, such transfer is made immediately before the date of the filing of the petition.

(2) In this section—

(A) "value" means property, or satisfaction or securing of a present or antecedent debt of the debtor, but does not include an unperformed promise to furnish support to the debtor or to a relative of the debtor;

(B) a commodity broker, forward contract merchant, stockbroker, financial institution, financial participant, or securities clearing agency that receives a margin payment, as defined in section 101, 741, or 761 of this title, or settlement payment, as defined in section 101 or 741 of this title, takes for value to the extent of such payment;

(C) a repo participant or financial participant that receives a margin payment, as defined in section 741 or 761 of this title, or settlement payment, as defined in section 741 of this title, in connection with a repurchase agreement, takes for value to the extent of such payment;

(D) a swap participant or financial participant that receives a transfer in connection with a swap agreement takes for value to the extent of such transfer; and

(E) a master netting agreement participant that receives a transfer in connection with a master netting agreement or any individual contract covered thereby takes for value to the extent of such transfer, except that, with respect to a transfer under any individual contract covered thereby, to the extent that such master netting agreement participant otherwise did not take (or is otherwise not deemed to have taken) such transfer for value.

(3) In this section, the term "charitable contribution" means a charitable contribution, as that term is defined in section 170(c) of the Internal Revenue Code of 1986, if that contribution—

(A) is made by a natural person; and

(B) consists of—

(i) a financial instrument (as that term is defined in section 731(c)(2)(C) of the Internal Revenue Code of 1986); or

(ii) cash.

(4) In this section, the term "qualified religious or charitable entity or organization" means—

(A) an entity described in section 170(c)(1) of the Internal Revenue Code of 1986; or

(B) an entity or organization described in section 170(c)(2) of the Internal Revenue Code of 1986.

(e)(1) In addition to any transfer that the trustee may otherwise avoid, the trustee may avoid any transfer of an interest of the debtor in property that was made on or within 10 years before the date of the filing of the petition, if—

(A) such transfer was made to a self-settled trust or similar device;

(B) such transfer was by the debtor;

(C) the debtor is a beneficiary of such trust or similar device; and

(D) the debtor made such transfer with actual intent to hinder, delay, or defraud any entity to which the debtor was or became, on or after the date that such transfer was made, indebted.

(2) For the purposes of this subsection, a transfer includes a transfer made in anticipation of any money judgment, settlement, civil penalty, equitable order, or criminal fine incurred by, or which the debtor believed would be incurred by—

(A) any violation of the securities laws (as defined in section 3(a)(47) of the Securities Exchange Act of 1934 (15 U.S.C. 78c(a)(47))), any State securities laws, or any regulation or order issued under Federal securities laws or State securities laws; or

(B) fraud, deceit, or manipulation in a fiduciary capacity or in connection with the purchase or sale of any security registered under section 12 or 15(d) of the Securities Exchange Act of 1934 (15 U.S.C. 78l and 78o(d)) or under section 6 of the Securities Act of 1933 (15 U.S.C. 77f).

(Pub.L. 95–598, Nov. 6, 1978, 92 Stat. 2600; Pub.L. 97–222, § 5, July 27, 1982, 96 Stat. 236; Pub.L. 98–353, Title III, §§ 394, 463, July 10, 1984, 98 Stat. 365, 378; Pub.L. 99–554, Title II, § 283(n), Oct. 27, 1986, 100 Stat. 3117; Pub.L. 101–311, Title I, § 104, Title II, § 204, June 25, 1990, 104 Stat. 268, 269; Pub.L. 103–394, Title V, § 501(b)(5), Oct. 22, 1994, 108 Stat. 4142; Pub.L. 105–183, §§ 2, 3(a), June 19, 1998, 112 Stat. 517; Pub.L. 109–8, Title IX, § 907(f), (o)(4) to (6), Title XIV, § 1402, Apr. 20, 2005, 119 Stat. 177, 182, 214.)

HISTORICAL AND STATUTORY NOTES

Revision Notes and Legislative Reports

1978 Acts. This section is derived in large part from section 67d of the Bankruptcy Act [section 107(d) of former Title 11]. It permits the trustee to avoid transfers by the debtor in fraud of his creditors. Its history dates from the statute of 13 Eliz. c. 5 (1570).

The trustee may avoid fraudulent transfers or obligations if made with actual intent to hinder, delay, or defraud a past or future creditor. Transfers made for less than a reasonably equivalent consideration are also vulnerable if the debtor was or thereby becomes insolvent, was engaged in business with an unreasonably small capital, or intended to incur debts that would be beyond his ability to repay.

The trustee of a partnership debtor may avoid any transfer of partnership property to a partner in the debtor if the debtor was or thereby became insolvent.

If a transferee's only liability to the trustee is under this section, and if he takes for value and in good faith, then subsection (c) grants him a lien on the property transferred, or other similar protection.

Subsection (d) specifies that for the purposes of fraudulent transfer section, a transfer is made when it is valid against a subsequent bona fide purchaser. If not made before the commencement of the case, it is considered made immediately before then. Subsection (d) also defines "value" to mean property, or the satisfaction or securing of a present or antecedent debt, but does not include an unperformed promise to furnish support to the debtor or a relative of the debtor. Senate Report No. 95–989.

1982 Acts. House Report No. 97–420, see 1982 U.S. Code Cong. and Adm. News, p. 583.

1984 Acts. Statements by Legislative Leaders, see 1984 U.S. Code Cong. and Adm. News, p. 576.

1986 Acts. House Report No. 99–764 and House Conference Report No. 99–958, see 1986 U.S. Code Cong. and Adm. News, p. 5227.

1990 Acts. House Report No. 101–484, see 1990 U.S. Code Cong. and Adm. News, p. 223.

1994 Acts. House Report No. 103–835, see 1994 U.S. Code Cong. and Adm. News, p. 3340.

1998 Acts. Statement by President, see 1998 U.S. Code Cong. and Adm. News, p. 230.

2005 Acts. House Report No. 109–31(Part I), see 2005 U.S. Code Cong. and Adm. News, p. 88.

Legislative Statements

Section 548(d)(2) is modified to reflect general application of a provision contained in section 766 of the Senate amendment with respect to commodity brokers. In particular, section 548(d)(2)(B) of the House amendment makes clear that a commodity broker who receives a margin payment is considered to receive the margin payment in return for "value" for purposes of section 548.

References in Text

The Internal Revenue Code of 1986, referred to in subsec. (d)(3) and (4), is classified generally to Title 26.

Section 3(a)(47) of the Securities Exchange Act of 1934, referred to in subsec. (e)(2)(A), is June 6, 1934, c. 404, Title I, § 3(a)(47), 48 Stat. 882, as amended, which is classified to 15 U.S.C.A. § 78c(a)(47).

Section 12 of the Securities Exchange Act of 1934, referred to in subsec. (e)(2)(B), is June 6, 1934, c. 404, Title I, § 12, 48 Stat. 892, as amended, which is classified to 15 U.S.C.A. § 78l.

Section 15(d) of the Securities Exchange Act of 1934, referred to in subsec. (e)(2)(B), is June 6, 1934, c. 404, Title I, § 15(d), 48 Stat. 895, as amended, which is classified to 15 U.S.C.A. § 78o.

Section 6 of the Securities Act of 1933, referred to in subsec. (e)(2)(B), is Act May 27, 1933, c. 38, Title I, § 6, 48 Stat. 78, as amended, which is classified to 15 U.S.C.A. § 77f.

Effective and Applicability Provisions

2005 Acts. Amendments by Pub.L. 109–8, Title XIV, effective, except as otherwise provided, on Apr. 20, 2005, and applicable only with respect to cases commenced under Title 11 on or after Apr. 20, 2005. Amendments by Pub.L. 109–8, § 1402(1), to subsecs. (a) and (b) of this section applicable only with respect to cases commenced under Title 11 more than 1 year after April 20, 2005; see Pub.L. 109–8, § 1406, set out as a note under 11 U.S.C.A. § 507.

Amendments by Pub.L. 109–8 effective, except as otherwise provided, 180 days after April 20, 2005, and inapplicable with respect to cases commenced under Title 11 before the effective date, see Pub.L. 109–8, § 1501, set out as a note under 11 U.S.C.A. § 101.

1994 Acts. Amendment by Pub.L. 103–394 effective on Oct. 22, 1994, and not to apply with respect to cases commenced under Title 11 of the United States Code before Oct. 22, 1994, see section 702 of Pub.L. 103–394, set out as a note under section 101 of this title.

1986 Acts. Amendment by Pub.L. 99–554, effective 30 days after Oct. 27, 1986, except as otherwise provided for, see section 302(a) of Pub.L. 99–554, set out as a note under section 581 of Title 28, Judiciary and Judicial Procedure.

1984 Acts. Amendment by Pub.L. 98–353 effective with respect to cases filed 90 days after July 10, 1984, see section 552(a), formerly 553(a), of Pub.L. 98–353, set out as a note under section 101 of this title.

Separability of Provisions

If any provision of or amendment made by Pub.L. 103–394 or the application of such provision or amendment to any person or circumstance is held to be unconstitutional, the remaining provisions of and amendments made by Pub.L. 103–394 and the application of such provisions and amendments to any person or circumstance shall not be affected thereby, see section 701 of Pub.L. 103–394, set out as a note under section 101 of this title.

Applicability

Applicability of amendments made by Pub.L. 105–183 to any case brought under an applicable provision of this title that is pending or commenced on or after June 19, 1998, see Pub.L. 105–183, § 5, June 19, 1998, 112 Stat. 518, set out as a note under section 544 of this title.

Rules of Construction

Amendments made by Pub.L. 105–183 not intended to limit the applicability of the Religious Freedom Restoration Act of 1993 (42 U.S.C. 2002bb et seq.), see Pub.L. 105–183, § 6, June 19, 1998, 112 Stat. 519, set out as a note under section 544 of this title.

CROSS REFERENCES

Applicability of this section in Chapter nine cases, see 11 USCA § 901.

Appointment of trustee upon debtor's refusal to pursue cause of action under this section, see 11 USCA § 926.

Commencement of involuntary cases by transferees of voidable transfers, see 11 USCA § 303.

Disallowance of claims of entity that is transferee of avoidable transfer, see 11 USCA § 502.

Effect of dismissal, see 11 USCA § 349.

Exemptions, see 11 USCA § 522.

Inappropriate transfers included in determining net worth of employer, see 29 USCA § 1362.

Recovery of voidable transfers in investor protection liquidation proceedings, see 15 USCA § 78fff–2.

Transfers to defeat cases under this title, see 18 USCA § 152.

Voidable transfers in,
> Commodity broker liquidation cases, see 11 USCA § 764.
> Stockbroker liquidation cases, see 11 USCA § 749.

§ 549. Postpetition transactions

(a) Except as provided in subsection (b) or (c) of this section, the trustee may avoid a transfer of property of the estate—

> (1) that occurs after the commencement of the case; and

> (2)(A) that is authorized only under section 303(f) or 542(c) of this title; or

> (B) that is not authorized under this title or by the court.

(b) In an involuntary case, the trustee may not avoid under subsection (a) of this section a transfer made after the commencement of such case but before the order for relief to the extent any value, including services, but not including satisfaction or securing of a debt that arose before the commencement of the case, is given after the commencement of the case in exchange for such transfer, notwithstanding any notice or knowledge of the case that the transferee has.

(c) The trustee may not avoid under subsection (a) of this section a transfer of an interest in real property to a good faith purchaser without knowledge of the commencement of the case and for present fair equivalent value unless a copy or notice of the petition was filed, where a transfer of an interest in such real property may be recorded to perfect such transfer, before such transfer is so perfected that a bona fide purchaser of such real property, against whom applicable law permits such transfer to be perfected, could not acquire an interest that is superior to such interest of such good faith purchaser. A good faith purchaser without knowledge of the commencement of the case and for less than present fair equivalent value has a lien on the property transferred to the extent of any present value given, unless a copy or notice of the petition was so filed before such transfer was so perfected.

(d) An action or proceeding under this section may not be commenced after the earlier of—

> (1) two years after the date of the transfer sought to be avoided; or

> (2) the time the case is closed or dismissed.

(Pub.L. 95–598, Nov. 6, 1978, 92 Stat. 2601; Pub.L. 98–353, Title III, § 464, July 10, 1984, 98 Stat. 379; Pub.L. 99–554, Title II, § 283(o), Oct. 27, 1986, 100 Stat. 3117; Pub.L. 103–394, Title V, § 501(d)(18), Oct. 22, 1994, 108 Stat. 4146; Pub.L. 109–8, Title XII, § 1214, Apr. 20, 2005, 119 Stat. 195.)

HISTORICAL AND STATUTORY NOTES

Revision Notes and Legislative Reports

1978 Acts. This section modifies section 70d of current law [section 110(d) of former Title 11]. It permits the trustee to avoid transfers of property that occur after the commencement of the case. The transfer must either have been unauthorized, or authorized under a section that protects only the transferor. Subsection (b) protects "involuntary gap" transferees to the extent of any value (including services, but not including satisfaction of a debt that arose before the commencement of the case), given after commencement in exchange for the transfer. Notice or knowledge of the transferee is irrelevant in determining whether he is protected under this provision. Senate Report No. 95–989.

1984 Acts. Statements by Legislative Leaders, see 1984 U.S. Code Cong. and Adm. News, p. 576.

1986 Acts. House Report No. 99–764 and House Conference Report No. 99–958, see 1986 U.S. Code Cong. and Adm. News, p. 5227.

1994 Acts. House Report No. 103–835, see 1994 U.S. Code Cong. and Adm. News, p. 3340.

2005 Acts. House Report No. 109–31(Part I), see 2005 U.S. Code Cong. and Adm. News, p. 88.

Legislative Statements

Section 549 of the House amendment has been redrafted in order to incorporate section 342(b) and (c) of the Senate amendment. Those sections have been consolidated and redrafted in section 549(c) of the House amendment. Section 549(d) of the House amendment adopts a provision contained in section 549(c) of the Senate amendment.

Effective and Applicability Provisions

2005 Acts. Amendments by Pub.L. 109–8 effective, except as otherwise provided, 180 days after April 20, 2005, and inapplicable with respect to cases commenced under Title 11 before the effective date, see Pub.L. 109–8, § 1501, set out as a note under 11 U.S.C.A. § 101.

1994 Acts. Amendment by Pub.L. 103–394 effective on Oct. 22, 1994, and not to apply with respect to cases commenced under Title 11 of the United States Code before Oct. 22, 1994, see section 702 of Pub.L. 103–394, set out as a note under section 101 of this title.

1986 Acts. Amendment by Pub.L. 99–554 effective 30 days after Oct. 27, 1986, except as otherwise provided for, see section 302(a) of Pub.L. 99–554, set out as a note under section 581 of Title 28, Judiciary and Judicial Procedure.

1984 Acts. Amendment by Pub.L. 98–353 effective with respect to cases filed 90 days after July 10, 1984, see section 552(a), formerly 553(a), of Pub.L. 98–353, set out as a note under section 101 of this title.

Separability of Provisions

If any provision of or amendment made by Pub.L. 103–394 or the application of such provision or amendment to any person or circumstance is held to be unconstitutional, the remaining provisions of and amendments made by Pub.L. 103–394 and the application of such provisions and amendments to any person or circumstance shall not be affected thereby, see section 701 of Pub.L. 103–394, set out as a note under section 101 of this title.

CROSS REFERENCES

Applicability of subsecs. (a), (c) and (d) of this section in Chapter nine cases, see 11 USCA § 901.

Appointment of trustee upon debtor's refusal to pursue cause of action under this section, see 11 USCA § 926.

Commencement of involuntary cases by transferees of voidable transfers, see 11 USCA § 303.

Disallowance of claims of entity that is transferee of avoidable transfer, see 11 USCA § 502.

Effect of dismissal, see 11 USCA § 349.

Exemptions, see 11 USCA § 522.

Inappropriate transfers included in determining net worth of employer, see 29 USCA § 1362.

Recovery of voidable transfers in investor liquidation proceedings, see 15 USCA § 78fff–2.

Voidable transfers in,

Commodity broker liquidation cases, see 11 USCA § 764.

Stockbroker liquidation cases, see 11 USCA § 749.

§ 550. Liability of transferee of avoided transfer

(a) Except as otherwise provided in this section, to the extent that a transfer is avoided under section 544, 545, 547, 548, 549, 553(b), or 724(a) of this title, the trustee may recover, for the benefit of the estate, the property transferred, or, if the court so orders, the value of such property, from—

(1) the initial transferee of such transfer or the entity for whose benefit such transfer was made; or

(2) any immediate or mediate transferee of such initial transferee.

(b) The trustee may not recover under section[1] (a)(2) of this section from—

(1) a transferee that takes for value, including satisfaction or securing of a present or antecedent debt, in good faith, and without knowledge of the voidability of the transfer avoided; or

(2) any immediate or mediate good faith transferee of such transferee.

(c) If a transfer made between 90 days and one year before the filing of the petition—

(1) is avoided under section 547(b) of this title; and

(2) was made for the benefit of a creditor that at the time of such transfer was an insider;

the trustee may not recover under subsection (a) from a transferee that is not an insider.

(d) The trustee is entitled to only a single satisfaction under subsection (a) of this section.

(e)(1) A good faith transferee from whom the trustee may recover under subsection (a) of this section has a lien on the property recovered to secure the lesser of—

(A) the cost, to such transferee, of any improvement made after the transfer, less the amount of any profit realized by or accruing to such transferee from such property; and

(B) any increase in the value of such property as a result of such improvement, of the property transferred.

(2) In this subsection, "improvement" includes—

(A) physical additions or changes to the property transferred;

(B) repairs to such property;

(C) payment of any tax on such property;

(D) payment of any debt secured by a lien on such property that is superior or equal to the rights of the trustee; and

(E) preservation of such property.

(f) An action or proceeding under this section may not be commenced after the earlier of—

(1) one year after the avoidance of the transfer on account of which recovery under this section is sought; or

(2) the time the case is closed or dismissed.

(Pub.L. 95–598, Nov. 6, 1978, 92 Stat. 2601; Pub.L. 98–353, Title III, § 465, July 10, 1984, 98 Stat. 379; Pub.L. 103–394, Title II, § 202, Oct. 22, 1994, 108 Stat. 4121.)

1 So in original. Probably should be "subsection".

HISTORICAL AND STATUTORY NOTES

Revision Notes and Legislative Reports

1978 Acts. Section 550 prescribes the liability of a transferee of an avoided transfer, and enunciates the separation between the concepts of avoiding a transfer and recovering from the transferee. Subsection (a) permits the trustee to recover from the initial transferee of an avoided transfer or from any immediate or mediate transferee of the initial transferee. The words "to the extent that" in the lead in to this subsection are designed to incorporate the protection of transferees found in proposed 11 U.S.C. 549(b) and 548(c). Subsection (b) limits the liability of an immediate or mediate transferee of the initial transferee if such secondary transferee takes for value, in good faith and without knowledge of the voidability of the transfer. An immediate or mediate good faith transferee of a protected secondary transferee is also shielded from liability. This subsection is limited to the trustee's right to recover from subsequent transferees under subsection (a)(2). It does not limit the trustee's rights against the initial transferee under subsection (a)(1). The phrase "good faith" in this paragraph is intended to prevent a transferee from whom the trustee could recover from transferring the recoverable property to an innocent transferee, and receiving a retransfer from him, that is, "washing" the transaction through an innocent third party. In order for the transferee to be excepted from liability under this paragraph, he himself must be a good faith transferee. Subsection (c) is a further limitation on recovery. It specifies that the trustee is entitled to only one satisfactory, under subsection (a), even if more than one transferee is liable.

Subsection (d) protects good faith transferees, either initial or subsequent, to the extent of the lesser of the cost of any improvement the transferee makes in the transferred property and the increase in value of the property as a result of the improvement. Paragraph (2) of the subsection defines improvement to include physical additions or changes to the property, repairs, payment of taxes on the property, payment of a debt secured by a lien on the property, discharge of a lien on the property, and preservation of the property.

Subsection (e) establishes a statute of limitations on avoidance by the Trustee. The limitation is one year after the avoidance of the transfer or the time the case is closed or dismissed, whichever is earlier. Senate Report No. 95–989.

1984 Acts. Statements by Legislative Leaders, see 1984 U.S. Code Cong. and Adm. News, p. 576.

1994 Acts. House Report No. 103–835, see 1994 U.S. Code Cong. and Adm. News, p. 3340.

Legislative Statements

Section 550(a)(1) of the House amendment has been modified in order to permit recovery from an entity for whose benefit an avoided transfer is made in addition to a recovery from the initial transferee of the transfer. Section 550(c) would still apply, and the trustee is entitled only to a single satisfaction. The liability of a transferee under section 550(a) applies only "to the extent that a transfer is avoided". This means that liability is not imposed on a transferee to the extent that a transferee is protected under a provision such as section 548(c) which grants a good faith transferee for value of a transfer that is avoided only as a fraudulent transfer, a lien on the property transferred to the extent of value given.

Section 550(b) of the House amendment is modified to indicate that value includes satisfaction or securing of a present antecedent debt. This means that the trustee may not recover under subsection (a)(2) from a subsequent transferee that takes for "value", provided the subsequent transferee also takes in good faith and without knowledge of the transfer avoided.

Section 550(e) of the House amendment is derived from section 550(e) of the Senate amendment.

Effective and Applicability Provisions

1994 Acts. Amendment by Pub.L. 103–394 effective on Oct. 22, 1994, and not to apply with respect to cases commenced under Title 11 of the United States Code before Oct. 22, 1994, see section 702 of Pub.L. 103–394, set out as a note under section 101 of this title.

1984 Acts. Amendment by Pub.L. 98–353 effective with respect to cases filed 90 days after July 10, 1984, see section 552(a), formerly 553(a), of Pub.L. 98–353, set out as a note under section 101 of this title.

Separability of Provisions

If any provision of or amendment made by Pub.L. 103–394 or the application of such provision or amendment to any person or circumstance is held to be unconstitutional, the remaining provisions of and amendments made by Pub.L. 103–394 and the application of such provisions and amendments to any person or circumstance shall not be affected thereby, see section 701 of Pub.L. 103–394, set out as a note under section 101 of this title.

CROSS REFERENCES

Allowance of claims or interests, see 11 USCA § 502.

Applicability of this section in Chapter nine cases, see 11 USCA § 901.

Appointment of trustee upon debtor's refusal to pursue cause of action under this section, see 11 USCA § 926.

Effect of dismissal, see 11 USCA § 349.

Exemptions, see 11 USCA § 522.

§ 551.   Automatic preservation of avoided transfer

Any transfer avoided under section 522, 544, 545, 547, 548, 549, or 724(a) of this title, or any lien void under section 506(d) of this title, is preserved for the benefit of the estate but only with respect to property of the estate.
(Pub.L. 95–598, Nov. 6, 1978, 92 Stat. 2602.)

HISTORICAL AND STATUTORY NOTES

Revision Notes and Legislative Reports

1978 Acts. This section is a change from present law. It specifies that any avoided transfer is automatically preserved for the benefit of the estate. Under current law, the court must determine whether or not the transfer should be preserved. The operation of the section is automatic, unlike current law, even though preservation may not benefit the estate in every instance. A preserved lien may be abandoned by the trustee under proposed 11 U.S.C. 554 if the preservation does not benefit the estate. The section as a whole prevents junior lienors from improving their position at the expense of the estate when a senior lien is avoided. Senate Report No. 95–989.

1984 Acts. Statements by Legislative Leaders, see 1984 U.S.Code Cong. and Adm.News, p. 576.

Legislative Statements

Section 551 is adopted from the House bill and the alternative in the Senate amendment is rejected. The section is clarified to indicate that a transfer avoided or a lien that is void is preserved for the benefit of the estate, but only with respect to property of the estate. This prevents the trustee from asserting an avoided tax lien against after acquired property of the debtor.

CROSS REFERENCES

Applicability of this section in Chapter nine cases, see 11 USCA § 901.

Effect of dismissal, see 11 USCA § 349.

Exemptions, see 11 USCA § 522.

§ 552.   Postpetition effect of security interest

(a) Except as provided in subsection (b) of this section, property acquired by the estate or by the debtor after the commencement of the case is not subject to any lien resulting from any security agreement entered into by the debtor before the commencement of the case.

(b)(1) Except as provided in sections 363, 506(c), 522, 544, 545, 547, and 548 of this title, if the debtor and an entity entered into a security agreement before the commencement of the case and if the security interest created by such security agreement extends to property of the debtor acquired before the commencement of the case and to proceeds, products, offspring, or profits of such property, then such security interest extends to such proceeds, products, offspring, or profits acquired by the estate after the commencement of the case to the extent provided by such security agreement and by applicable nonbankruptcy law, except to any extent that the court, after notice and a hearing and based on the equities of the case, orders otherwise.

(2) Except as provided in sections 363, 506(c), 522, 544, 545, 547, and 548 of this title, and notwithstanding section 546(b) of this title, if the debtor and an entity entered into a security agreement before the commencement of the case and if the security interest created by such security agreement extends to property of the debtor acquired before the commencement of the case and to amounts paid as rents of such property or the fees, charges, accounts, or other payments for the use or occupancy of rooms and other public facilities in hotels, motels, or other lodging properties, then such security interest extends to such rents and such fees, charges, accounts, or other payments acquired by the estate after the commencement of the case to the extent provided in such security agreement, except to any extent that the court, after notice and a hearing and based on the equities of the case, orders otherwise. (Pub.L. 95–598, Nov. 6, 1978, 92 Stat. 2602; Pub.L. 98–353, Title III, § 466, July 10, 1984, 98 Stat. 380; Pub.L. 103–394, Title II, § 214(a), Oct. 22, 1994, 108 Stat. 4126; Pub.L. 109–8, Title XII, § 1204(2), Apr. 20, 2005, 119 Stat. 194.)

HISTORICAL AND STATUTORY NOTES

Revision Notes and Legislative Reports

1978 Acts. Under the Uniform Commercial Code, article 9, creditors may take security interests in after-acquired property. Section 552 governs the effect of such a prepetition security interest in postpetition property. It applies to all security interests as defined in section 101(37) of the bankruptcy code, not only to U.C.C. security interests.

As a general rule, if a security agreement is entered into before the commencement of the case, then property that the estate acquires is not subject to the security interest created by a provision in the security agreement extending the security interest to after-acquired property. Subsection (b) provides an important exception consistent with the Uniform Commercial Code. If the security agreement extends to proceeds, product, offspring, rents, or profits of the property in question, then the proceeds would continue to be subject to the security interest pursuant to the terms of the security agreement and provisions of applicable law, except to the extent that where the estate acquires the proceeds at the expense of other creditors holding unsecured claims, the expenditure resulted in an improvement in the position of the secured party.

The exception covers the situation where raw materials, for example, are converted into inventory, or inventory into accounts, at some expense to the estate, thus depleting the fund available for general unsecured creditors, but is limited to the benefit inuring to the secured party thereby. Situations in which the estate incurs expense in simply protecting collateral are governed by 11 U.S.C. 506(c). In ordinary circumstances, the risk of loss in continued operations will remain with the estate. Senate Report No. 95–989.

Under the Uniform Commercial Code, Article 9, creditors may take security interests in after-acquired property. This section governs the effect of such a prepetition security interest in postpetition property. It applies to all security interests as defined in section 101 of the bankruptcy code, not only to U.C.C. security interests.

As a general rule, if a security agreement is entered into before the case, then property that the estate acquires is not subject to the security interest created by the security agreement. Subsection (b) provides the only exception. If the security agreement extends to proceeds, product, offspring, rents, or profits of property that the debtor had before the commencement of the case, then the proceeds, etc., continue to be subject to the security interest, except to the extent that the estate acquired the proceeds to the prejudice of other creditors holding unsecured claims. "Extends to" as used here would include an automatically arising security interest in proceeds, as permitted under the 1972 version of the Uniform Commercial Code, as well as an interest in proceeds specifically designated, as required under the 1962 Code or similar statutes covering property not covered by the Code. "Prejudice" is not intended to be a broad term here, but is designed to cover the situation where the estate expends funds that result in an increase in the value of collateral. The exception is to cover the situation where raw materials, for example, are converted into inventory, or inventory into accounts, at some expense to the estate, thus depleting the fund available for general unsecured creditors. The term "proceeds" is not limited to the technical definition of that term in the U.C.C., but covers any property into which property subject to the security interest is converted. House Report No. 95–595.

1984 Acts. Statements by Legislative Leaders, see 1984 U.S. Code Cong. and Adm. News, p. 576.

1994 Acts. House Report No, 103–835, see 1994 U.S. Code Cong. and Adm. News, p. 3340.

2005 Acts. House Report No. 109–31(Part I), see 2005 U.S. Code Cong. and Adm. News, p. 88.

Legislative Statements

Section 552(a) is derived from the House bill and the alternative provision in the Senate amendment is rejected. Section 552(b) represents a compromise between the House bill and the Senate amendment. Proceeds coverage, but not after acquired property clauses, are valid under title 11. The provision allows the court to consider the equities in each case. In the course of such consideration the court may evaluate any expenditures by the estate relating to proceeds and any related improvement in position of the secured party. Although this section grants a secured party a security interest in proceeds, product, offspring, rents, or profits, the section is explicitly subject to other sections of title 11. For example, the trustee or debtor in possession may use, sell, or lease proceeds, product, offspring, rents or profits under section 363.

Effective and Applicability Provisions

2005 Acts. Amendments by Pub.L. 109–8 effective, except as otherwise provided, 180 days after April 20, 2005, and inapplicable with respect to cases commenced under Title 11 before the effective date, see Pub.L. 109–8, § 1501, set out as a note under 11 U.S.C.A. § 101.

1994 Acts. Amendment by Pub.L. 103–394 effective on Oct. 22, 1994, and not to apply with respect to cases commenced under Title 11 of the United States Code before Oct. 22, 1994, see section 702 of Pub.L. 103–394, set out as a note under section 101 of this title.

1984 Acts. Amendment by Pub.L. 98–353 effective with respect to cases filed 90 days after July 10, 1984, see section

552, formerly 553, of Pub.L. 98–353, set out as a note under section 101 of this title.

Separability of Provisions

If any provision of or amendment made by Pub.L. 103–394 or the application of such provision or amendment to any person or circumstance is held to be unconstitutional, the remaining provisions of and amendments made by Pub.L. 103–394 and the application of such provisions and amendments to any person or circumstance shall not be affected thereby, see section 701 of Pub.L. 103–394, set out as a note under section 101 of this title.

CROSS REFERENCES

Applicability of this section in Chapter nine cases, see 11 USCA § 901.

"Cash collateral" as including proceeds, products, offspring, rents or profits of property subject to security interest as provided in this section, see 11 USCA § 363.

Special revenues acquired by debtor after commencement of Chapter nine case subject to security interest, see 11 USCA § 928.

§ 553.　Setoff

(a) Except as otherwise provided in this section and in sections 362 and 363 of this title, this title does not affect any right of a creditor to offset a mutual debt owing by such creditor to the debtor that arose before the commencement of the case under this title against a claim of such creditor against the debtor that arose before the commencement of the case, except to the extent that—

(1) the claim of such creditor against the debtor is disallowed;

(2) such claim was transferred, by an entity other than the debtor, to such creditor—

(A) after the commencement of the case; or

(B)(i) after 90 days before the date of the filing of the petition; and

(ii) while the debtor was insolvent (except for a setoff of a kind described in section 362(b)(6), 362(b)(7), 362(b)(17), 362(b)(27), 555, 556, 559, 560, or 561); or

(3) the debt owed to the debtor by such creditor was incurred by such creditor—

(A) after 90 days before the date of the filing of the petition;

(B) while the debtor was insolvent; and

(C) for the purpose of obtaining a right of setoff against the debtor (except for a setoff of a kind described in section 362(b)(6), 362(b)(7), 362(b)(17), 362(b)(27), 555, 556, 559, 560, or 561).

(b)(1) Except with respect to a setoff of a kind described in section 362(b)(6), 362(b)(7), 362(b)(17), 362(b)(27), 555, 556, 559, 560, 561, 365(h), 546(h), or 365(i)(2) of this title, if a creditor offsets a mutual debt owing to the debtor against a claim against the debtor on or within 90 days before the date of the filing of the petition, then the trustee may recover from such credi-

tor the amount so offset to the extent that any insufficiency on the date of such setoff is less than the insufficiency on the later of—

(A) 90 days before the date of the filing of the petition; and

(B) the first date during the 90 days immediately preceding the date of the filing of the petition on which there is an insufficiency.

(2) In this subsection, "insufficiency" means amount, if any, by which a claim against the debtor exceeds a mutual debt owing to the debtor by the holder of such claim.

(c) For the purposes of this section, the debtor is presumed to have been insolvent on and during the 90 days immediately preceding the date of the filing of the petition.

(Pub.L. 95–598, Nov. 6, 1978, 92 Stat. 2602; Pub.L. 98–353, Title III, §§ 395, 467, July 10, 1984, 98 Stat. 365, 380; Pub.L. 101–311, Title I, § 105, June 25, 1990, 104 Stat. 268; Pub.L. 103–394, Title II, §§ 205(b), 222(b), Title V, § 501(d)(19), Oct. 22, 1994, 108 Stat. 4123, 4129, 4146; Pub.L. 109–8, Title IX, § 907(n), Apr. 20, 2005, 119 Stat. 181.)

HISTORICAL AND STATUTORY NOTES

Revision Notes and Legislative Reports

1978 Acts. This section preserves, with some changes, the right of setoff in bankruptcy cases now found in section 68 of the Bankruptcy Act [section 108 of former Title 11]. One exception to the right is the automatic stay, discussed in connection with proposed 11 U.S.C. 362. Another is the right of the trustee to use property under section 363 that is subject to a right of setoff.

The section states that the right of setoff is unaffected by the bankruptcy code except to the extent that the creditor's claim is disallowed, the creditor acquired (other than from the debtor) the claim during the 90 days preceding the case while the debtor was insolvent, the debt being offset was incurred for the purpose of obtaining a right of setoff, while the debtor was insolvent and during the 90-day prebankruptcy period, or the creditor improved his position in the 90-day period (similar to the improvement in position test found in the preference section 547(c)(5)). Only the last exception is an addition to current law.

As under section 547(f), the debtor is presumed to have been insolvent during the 90 days before the case. Senate Report No. 95–989.

1984 Acts. Statements by Legislative Leaders, see 1984 U.S. Code Cong. and Adm. News, p. 576.

1990 Acts. House Report No. 101–484, see 1990 U.S. Code Cong. and Adm. News, p. 223.

1994 Acts. House Report No. 103–835, see 1994 U.S. Code Cong. and Adm. News, p. 3340.

2005 Acts. House Report No. 109–31(Part I), see 2005 U.S. Code Cong. and Adm. News, p. 88.

Legislative Statements

Section 553 of the House amendment is derived from a similar provision contained in the Senate amendment, but is modified to clarify application of a two-point test with respect to setoffs.

Effective and Applicability Provisions

2005 Acts. Amendments by Pub.L. 109–8 effective, except as otherwise provided, 180 days after April 20, 2005, and inapplicable with respect to cases commenced under Title 11 before the effective date, see Pub.L. 109–8, § 1501, set out as a note under 11 U.S.C.A. § 101.

1994 Acts. Amendments by Pub.L. 103–394 effective on Oct. 22, 1994, and not to apply with respect to cases commenced under Title 11 of the United States Code before Oct. 22, 1994, see section 702 of Pub.L. 103–394, set out as a note under section 101 of this title.

1984 Acts. Amendment by Pub.L. 98–353 effective with respect to cases filed 90 days after July 10, 1984, see section 552(a), formerly 553(a), of Pub.L. 98–353, set out as a note under section 101 of this title.

Separability of Provisions

If any provision of or amendment made by Pub.L. 103–394 or the application of such provision or amendment to any person or circumstance is held to be unconstitutional, the remaining provisions of and amendments made by Pub.L. 103–394 and the application of such provisions and amendments to any person or circumstance shall not be affected thereby, see section 701 of Pub.L. 103–394, set out as a note under section 101 of this title.

CROSS REFERENCES

Allowance of claims or interests, see 11 USCA § 502.

Applicability of this section in Chapter nine cases, see 11 USCA § 901.

Determination of secured status, see 11 USCA § 506.

Effect of dismissal, see 11 USCA § 349.

Recovered property as exempt, see 11 USCA § 522.

Stay of pending actions in investor protection liquidation proceedings, see 15 USCA § 78eee.

§ 554. Abandonment of property of the estate

(a) After notice and a hearing, the trustee may abandon any property of the estate that is burdensome to the estate or that is of inconsequential value and benefit to the estate.

(b) On request of a party in interest and after notice and a hearing, the court may order the trustee to abandon any property of the estate that is burdensome to the estate or that is of inconsequential value and benefit to the estate.

(c) Unless the court orders otherwise, any property scheduled under section 521(a)(1) of this title not otherwise administered at the time of the closing of a case is abandoned to the debtor and administered for purposes of section 350 of this title.

(d) Unless the court orders otherwise, property of the estate that is not abandoned under this section and that is not administered in the case remains property of the estate.

(Pub.L. 95–598, Nov. 6, 1978, 92 Stat. 2603; Pub.L. 98–353, Title III, § 468, July 10, 1984, 98 Stat. 380; Pub.L. 99–554, Title II, § 283(p), Oct. 27, 1986, 100 Stat. 3118; Pub.L. 111–327, § 2(a)(23), Dec. 22, 2010, 124 Stat. 3560.)

HISTORICAL AND STATUTORY NOTES

Revision Notes and Legislative Reports

1978 Acts. Under this section the court may authorize the trustee to abandon any property of the estate that is burdensome to the estate or that is of inconsequential value to the estate. Abandonment may be to any party with a possessory interest in the property abandoned. In order to aid administration of the case, subsection (b) deems the court to have authorized abandonment of any property that is scheduled under section 521(1) and that is not administered before the case is closed. That property is deemed abandoned to the debtor. Subsection (c) specifies that if property is neither abandoned nor administered it remains property of the estate. Senate Report No. 95–989.

1984 Acts. Statements by Legislative Leaders, see 1984 U.S.Code Cong. and Adm.News, p. 576.

1986 Acts. House Report No. 99–764 and House Conference Report No. 99–958, see 1986 U.S.Code Cong. and Adm. News, p. 5227.

Legislative Statements

Section 554(b) is new and permits a party in interest to request the court to order the trustee to abandon property of the estate that is burdensome to the estate or that is of inconsequential value to the estate.

Effective and Applicability Provisions

1986 Acts. Amendment by Pub.L. 99–554 effective 30 days after Oct. 27, 1986, except as otherwise provided, see section 302(a) of Pub.L. 99–554, set out as a note under section 581 of Title 28, Judiciary and Judicial Procedure.

1984 Acts. Amendment by Pub.L. 98–353 effective with respect to cases filed 90 days after July 10, 1984, see section 552(a), formerly 553(a) of Pub.L. 98–353, set out as a note under section 101 of this title.

CROSS REFERENCES

Grain storage facility bankruptcies, expedited determinations, see 11 USCA § 557.

Redemption, see 11 USCA § 722.

§ 555. Contractual right to liquidate, terminate, or accelerate a securities contract

The exercise of a contractual right of a stockbroker, financial institution, financial participant, or securities clearing agency to cause the liquidation, termination, or acceleration of a securities contract, as defined in section 741 of this title, because of a condition of the kind specified in section 365(e)(1) of this title shall not be stayed, avoided, or otherwise limited by operation of any provision of this title or by order of a court or administrative agency in any proceeding under this title unless such order is authorized under the provisions of the Securities Investor Protection Act of 1970 or any statute administered by the Securities and Exchange Commission. As used in this section, the term "contractual right" includes a right set forth in a rule or bylaw of a derivatives clearing organization (as defined in the Commodity Exchange Act), a multilateral clearing organization (as defined in the Federal Deposit Insurance Corporation Improvement Act of

1991), a national securities exchange, a national securities association, a securities clearing agency, a contract market designated under the Commodity Exchange Act, a derivatives transaction execution facility registered under the Commodity Exchange Act, or a board of trade (as defined in the Commodity Exchange Act), or in a resolution of the governing board thereof, and a right, whether or not in writing, arising under common law, under law merchant, or by reason of normal business practice.

(Added Pub.L. 97–222, § 6(a), July 27, 1982, 96 Stat. 236; amended Pub.L. 98–353, Title III, § 469, July 10, 1984, 98 Stat. 380; Pub.L. 103–394, Title V, § 501(b)(6), (d)(20), Oct. 22, 1994, 108 Stat. 4143, 4146; Pub.L. 109–8, Title IX, § 907(g), (o)(7), Apr. 20, 2005, 119 Stat. 177, 182.)

HISTORICAL AND STATUTORY NOTES

Revision Notes and Legislative Reports

1982 Acts. House Report No. 97–420, see 1982 U.S. Code Cong. and Adm. News, p. 583.

1984 Acts. Statements by Legislative Leaders, see 1984 U.S. Code Cong. and Adm. News, p. 576.

1994 Acts. House Report No. 103–835, see 1994 U.S. Code Cong. and Adm. News, p. 3340.

2005 Acts. House Report No. 109–31(Part I), see 2005 U.S. Code Cong. and Adm. News, p. 88.

References in Text

The Securities Investor Protection Act of 1970, referred to in text, is Pub.L. 91–598, Dec. 30, 1970, 84 Stat. 1636, as amended, which is classified generally to chapter 2B–1 (section 78aaa et seq.) of Title 15, Commerce and Trade. For complete classification of this Act to the Code, see section 78aaa of Title 15 and Tables.

The Commodity Exchange Act, referred to in text, is Act Sept. 21, 1922, c. 369, 42 Stat. 998, as amended, which is classified principally to chapter 1 of Title 7, 7 U.S.C.A. § 1 et seq. For complete classification, see Short Title set out as 7 U.S.C.A. § 1 and Tables.

The Federal Deposit Insurance Corporation Improvement Act of 1991, referred to in text, is Pub.L. 102–242, Dec. 19, 1991, 105 Stat. 2236. See Tables for classification.

Effective and Applicability Provisions

2005 Acts. Amendments by Pub.L. 109–8 effective, except as otherwise provided, 180 days after April 20, 2005, and inapplicable with respect to cases commenced under Title 11 before the effective date, see Pub.L. 109–8, § 1501, set out as a note under 11 U.S.C.A. § 101.

1994 Acts. Amendments by Pub.L. 103–394 effective on Oct. 22, 1994, and not to apply with respect to cases commenced under Title 11 of the United States Code before Oct. 22, 1994, see section 702 of Pub.L. 103–394, set out as a note under section 101 of this title.

1984 Acts. Amendment by Pub.L. 98–353 effective with respect to cases filed 90 days after July 10, 1984, see section 552(a), formerly 553(a) of Pub.L. 98–353, set out as a note under section 101 of this title.

Separability of Provisions

If any provision of or amendment made by Pub.L. 103–394 or the application of such provision or amendment to any person or circumstance is held to be unconstitutional, the remaining provisions of and amendments made by Pub.L. 103–394 and the application of such provisions and amendments to any person or circumstance shall not be affected thereby, see section 701 of Pub.L. 103–394, set out as a note under section 101 of this title.

§ 556. Contractual right to liquidate, terminate, or accelerate a commodities contract or forward contract

The contractual right of a commodity broker, financial participant, or forward contract merchant to cause the liquidation, termination, or acceleration of a commodity contract, as defined in section 761 of this title, or forward contract because of a condition of the kind specified in section 365(e)(1) of this title, and the right to a variation or maintenance margin payment received from a trustee with respect to open commodity contracts or forward contracts, shall not be stayed, avoided, or otherwise limited by operation of any provision of this title or by the order of a court in any proceeding under this title.   As used in this section, the term "contractual right" includes a right set forth in a rule or bylaw of a derivatives clearing organization (as defined in the Commodity Exchange Act), a multilateral clearing organization (as defined in the Federal Deposit Insurance Corporation Improvement Act of 1991), a national securities exchange, a national securities association, a securities clearing agency, a contract market designated under the Commodity Exchange Act, a derivatives transaction execution facility registered under the Commodity Exchange Act, or a board of trade (as defined in the Commodity Exchange Act) or in a resolution of the governing board thereof and a right, whether or not evidenced in writing, arising under common law, under law merchant or by reason of normal business practice.

(Added Pub.L. 97–222, § 6(a), July 27, 1982, 96 Stat. 236; amended Pub.L. 101–311, Title II, § 205, June 25, 1990, 104 Stat. 270; Pub.L. 103–394, Title V, § 501(b)(7), Oct. 22, 1994, 108 Stat. 4143; Pub.L. 109–8, Title IX, § 907(h), (o)(8), Apr. 20, 2005, 119 Stat. 178, 182.)

HISTORICAL AND STATUTORY NOTES

Revision Notes and Legislative Reports

1982 Acts. House Report No. 97–420, see 1982 U.S. Code Cong. and Adm. News, p. 583.

1990 Acts. House Report No. 101–484, see 1990 U.S. Code Cong. and Adm. News, p. 223.

1994 Acts. House Report No. 103–835, see 1994 U.S. Code Cong. and Adm. News, p. 3340.

2005 Acts. House Report No. 109–31(Part I), see 2005 U.S. Code Cong. and Adm. News, p. 88.

References in Text

The Commodity Exchange Act, referred to in text, is Act Sept. 21, 1922, c. 369, 42 Stat. 998, as amended, which is classified principally to chapter 1 of Title 7, 7 U.S.C.A. § 1. For complete classification, see Short Title set out as 7 U.S.C.A. § 1 and Tables.

The Federal Deposit Insurance Corporation Improvement Act of 1991, referred to in text, is Pub.L. 102–242, Dec. 19, 1991, 105 Stat. 2236, as amended. For complete classification, see Short Title of 1991 Amendments note set out under 12 U.S.C.A. § 1811 and Tables.

Effective and Applicability Provisions

2005 Acts. Amendments by Pub.L. 109–8 effective, except as otherwise provided, 180 days after April 20, 2005, and inapplicable with respect to cases commenced under Title 11 before the effective date, see Pub.L. 109–8, § 1501, set out as a note under 11 U.S.C.A. § 101.

1994 Acts. Amendment by Pub.L. 103–394 effective on Oct. 22, 1994, and not to apply with respect to cases commenced under Title 11 of the United States Code before Oct. 22, 1994, see section 702 of Pub.L. 103–394, set out as a note under section 101 of this title.

Separability of Provisions

If any provision of or amendment made by Pub.L. 103–394 or the application of such provision or amendment to any person or circumstance is held to be unconstitutional, the remaining provisions of and amendments made by Pub.L. 103–394 and the application of such provisions and amendments to any person or circumstance shall not be affected thereby, see section 701 of Pub.L. 103–394, set out as a note under section 101 of this title.

§ 557. Expedited determination of interests in, and abandonment or other disposition of grain assets

(a) This section applies only in a case concerning a debtor that owns or operates a grain storage facility and only with respect to grain and the proceeds of grain. This section does not affect the application of any other section of this title to property other than grain and proceeds of grain.

(b) In this section—

(1) "grain" means wheat, corn, flaxseed, grain sorghum, barley, oats, rye, soybeans, other dry edible beans, or rice;

(2) "grain storage facility" means a site or physical structure regularly used to store grain for producers, or to store grain acquired from producers for resale; and

(3) "producer" means an entity which engages in the growing of grain.

(c)(1) Notwithstanding sections 362, 363, 365, and 554 of this title, on the court's own motion the court may, and on the request of the trustee or an entity that claims an interest in grain or the proceeds of grain the court shall, expedite the procedures for the determination of interests in and the disposition of grain and the proceeds of grain, by shortening to the greatest extent feasible such time periods as are otherwise applicable for such procedures and by establishing, by order, a timetable having a duration of not to exceed 120 days for the completion of the applicable procedure specified in subsection (d) of this section. Such time periods and such timetable may be modified by the court, for cause, in accordance with subsection (f) of this section.

(2) The court shall determine the extent to which such time periods shall be shortened, based upon—

(A) any need of an entity claiming an interest in such grain or the proceeds of grain for a prompt determination of such interest;

(B) any need of such entity for a prompt disposition of such grain;

(C) the market for such grain;

(D) the conditions under which such grain is stored;

(E) the costs of continued storage or disposition of such grain;

(F) the orderly administration of the estate;

(G) the appropriate opportunity for an entity to assert an interest in such grain; and

(H) such other considerations as are relevant to the need to expedite such procedures in the case.

(d) The procedures that may be expedited under subsection (c) of this section include—

(1) the filing of and response to—

(A) a claim of ownership;

(B) a proof of claim;

(C) a request for abandonment;

(D) a request for relief from the stay of action against property under section 362(a) of this title;

(E) a request for determination of secured status;

(F) a request for determination of whether such grain or the proceeds of grain—

(i) is property of the estate;

(ii) must be turned over to the estate; or

(iii) may be used, sold, or leased; and

(G) any other request for determination of an interest in such grain or the proceeds of grain;

(2) the disposition of such grain or the proceeds of grain, before or after determination of interests in such grain or the proceeds of grain, by way of—

(A) sale of such grain;

(B) abandonment;

(C) distribution; or

(D) such other method as is equitable in the case;

(3) subject to sections 701, 702, 703, 1104, 1202, and 1302 of this title, the appointment of a trustee or examiner and the retention and compensation of any professional person required to assist with respect to matters relevant to the determination of interests in or disposition of such grain or the proceeds of grain; and

(4) the determination of any dispute concerning a matter specified in paragraph (1), (2), or (3) of this subsection.

(e)(1) Any governmental unit that has regulatory jurisdiction over the operation or liquidation of the debtor or the debtor's business shall be given notice of any request made or order entered under subsection (c) of this section.

(2) Any such governmental unit may raise, and may appear and be heard on, any issue relating to grain or the proceeds of grain in a case in which a request is made, or an order is entered, under subsection (c) of this section.

(3) The trustee shall consult with such governmental unit before taking any action relating to the disposition of grain in the possession, custody, or control of the debtor or the estate.

(f) The court may extend the period for final disposition of grain or the proceeds of grain under this section beyond 120 days if the court finds that—

(1) the interests of justice so require in light of the complexity of the case; and

(2) the interests of those claimants entitled to distribution of grain or the proceeds of grain will not be materially injured by such additional delay.

(g) Unless an order establishing an expedited procedure under subsection (c) of this section, or determining any interest in or approving any disposition of grain or the proceeds of grain, is stayed pending appeal—

(1) the reversal or modification of such order on appeal does not affect the validity of any procedure, determination, or disposition that occurs before such reversal or modification, whether or not any entity knew of the pendency of the appeal; and

(2) neither the court nor the trustee may delay, due to the appeal of such order, any proceeding in the case in which such order is issued.

(h)(1) The trustee may recover from grain and the proceeds of grain the reasonable and necessary costs and expenses allowable under section 503(b) of this title attributable to preserving or disposing of grain or the proceeds of grain, but may not recover from such grain or the proceeds of grain any other costs or expenses.

(2) Notwithstanding section 326(a) of this title, the dollar amounts of money specified in such section include the value, as of the date of disposition, of any grain that the trustee distributes in kind.

(i) In all cases where the quantity of a specific type of grain held by a debtor operating a grain storage facility exceeds ten thousand bushels, such grain shall be sold by the trustee and the assets thereof distributed in accordance with the provisions of this section.
(Added Pub.L. 98–353, Title III, § 352(a), July 10, 1984, 98 Stat. 359; amended Pub.L. 99–554, Title II, § 257(p), Oct. 27, 1986, 100 Stat. 3115.)

HISTORICAL AND STATUTORY NOTES

Revision Notes and Legislative Reports

1984 Acts. Statements by Legislative Leaders, see 1984 U.S. Code Cong. and Adm.News, p. 576.

1986 Acts. House Report No. 99–764 and House Conference Report No. 99–958, see 1986 U.S.Code Cong. and Adm. News, p. 5227.

Effective and Applicability Provisions

1986 Acts. Amendment by Pub.L. 99–554 effective 30 days after Oct. 27, 1986, but not applicable to cases commenced under this title before that date, see section 302(a)(c)(1) of Pub.L. 99–554, set out as a note under section 581 of Title 28, Judiciary and Judicial Procedure.

1984 Acts. Section effective with respect to cases filed 90 days after July 10, 1984, see section 552(a), formerly 553(a), of Pub.L. 98–353, set out as a note under section 101 of this title.

CROSS REFERENCES

Applicability of this section in Chapter nine cases, see 11 USCA § 901.

Priorities, see 11 USCA § 507.

Rights and powers of trustee subject to right of seller who is "producer" of "grain" sold to "grain storage facility" owned or operated by debtor, as such terms are defined under this section, see 11 USCA § 546.

§ 558. Defenses of the estate

The estate shall have the benefit of any defense available to the debtor as against any entity other than the estate, including statutes of limitation, statutes of frauds, usury, and other personal defenses. A waiver of any such defense by the debtor after the commencement of the case does not bind the estate.
(Added Pub.L. 98–353, Title III, § 470(a), July 10, 1984, 98 Stat. 380.)

HISTORICAL AND STATUTORY NOTES

Revision Notes and Legislative Reports

1984 Acts. Statements by Legislative Leaders, see 1984 U.S.Code Cong. and Adm.News, p. 576.

Effective and Applicability Provisions

1984 Acts. Section effective with respect to cases filed 90 days after July 10, 1984, see section 552(a), formerly 553(a), of Pub.L. 98–353, set out as a note under section 101 of this title.

§ 559. Contractual right to liquidate, terminate, or accelerate a repurchase agreement

The exercise of a contractual right of a repo participant or financial participant to cause the liquidation, termination, or acceleration of a repurchase agreement because of a condition of the kind specified in section 365(e)(1) of this title shall not be stayed, avoided, or otherwise limited by operation of any provision of this title or by order of a court or administrative agency in any proceeding under this title, unless, where the debtor is a stockbroker or securities clearing agency, such order is authorized under the provisions of the Securities Investor Protection Act of 1970 or any statute administered by the Securities and Exchange Commission. In the event that a repo participant or financial participant liquidates one or more repurchase agreements with a debtor and under the terms of one or more such agreements has agreed to deliver assets subject to repurchase agreements to the debtor, any excess of the market prices received on liquidation of such assets (or if any such assets are not disposed of on the date of liquidation of such repurchase agreements, at the prices available at the time of liquidation of such repurchase agreements from a generally recognized source or the most recent closing bid quotation from such a source) over the sum of the stated repurchase prices and all expenses in connection with the liquidation of such repurchase agreements shall be deemed property of the estate, subject to the available rights of setoff. As used in this section, the term "contractual right" includes a right set forth in a rule or bylaw of a derivatives clearing organization (as defined in the Commodity Exchange Act), a multilateral clearing organization (as defined in the Federal Deposit Insurance Corporation Improvement Act of 1991), a national securities exchange, a national securities association, a securities clearing agency, a contract market designated under the Commodity Exchange Act, a derivatives transaction execution facility registered under the Commodity Exchange Act, or a board of trade (as defined in the Commodity Exchange Act) or in a resolution of the governing board thereof and a right, whether or not evidenced in writing, arising under common law, under law merchant or by reason of normal business practice.

(Added Pub.L. 98–353, Title III, § 396(a), July 10, 1984, 98 Stat. 366; amended Pub.L. 103–394, Title V, § 501(d)(21), Oct. 22, 1994, 108 Stat. 4146; Pub.L. 109–8, Title IX, § 907(i), (o)(9), Apr. 20, 2005, 119 Stat. 178, 182.)

HISTORICAL AND STATUTORY NOTES
Revision Notes and Legislative Reports

1984 Acts. Statements by Legislative Leaders, see 1984 U.S. Code Cong. and Adm. News, p. 576.

1994 Acts. House Report No. 103–835, see 1994 U.S. Code Cong. and Adm. News, p. 3340.

2005 Acts. House Report No. 109–31(Part I), see 2005 U.S. Code Cong. and Adm. News, p. 88.

References in Text

The Securities Investor Protection Act of 1970, referred to in text, is Pub. L. 91–598, Dec. 30, 1970, 84 Stat. 1636, as amended, which is classified generally to chapter 2B–1 (section 78aaa et seq.) of Title 15, Commerce and Trade. For complete classification of this Act to the Code, see section 78aaa of Title 15 and Tables.

The Commodity Exchange Act, referred to in text, is Act Sept. 21, 1922, c. 369, 42 Stat. 998, as amended, which is classified principally to chapter 1 of Title 7, 7 U.S.C.A. § 1. For complete classification, see Short Title set out as 7 U.S.C.A. § 1 and Tables.

The Federal Deposit Insurance Corporation Improvement Act of 1991, referred to in text, is Pub.L. 102–242, Dec. 19,

1991, 105 Stat. 2236, as amended. For complete classification, see Short Title of 1991 Amendments note set out under 12 U.S.C.A. § 1811 and Tables.

Effective and Applicability Provisions

2005 Acts. Amendments by Pub.L. 109–8 effective, except as otherwise provided, 180 days after April 20, 2005, and inapplicable with respect to cases commenced under Title 11 before the effective date, see Pub.L. 109–8, § 1501, set out as a note under 11 U.S.C.A. § 101.

1994 Acts. Amendment by Pub.L. 103–394 effective on Oct. 22, 1994, and not to apply with respect to cases commenced under Title 11 of the United States Code before Oct. 22, 1994, see section 702 of Pub.L. 103–394, set out as a note under section 101 of this title.

1984 Acts. Section effective with respect to cases filed 90 days after July 10, 1984, see section 552(a), formerly 553(a), of Pub.L. 98–353, set out as a note under section 101 of this title.

Separability of Provisions

If any provision of or amendment made by Pub.L. 103–394 or the application of such provision or amendment to any person or circumstance is held to be unconstitutional, the remaining provisions of and amendments made by Pub.L. 103–394 and the application of such provisions and amendments to any person or circumstance shall not be affected thereby, see section 701 of Pub.L. 103–394, set out as a note under section 101 of this title.

§ 560. Contractual right to liquidate, terminate, or accelerate a swap agreement

The exercise of any contractual right of any swap participant or financial participant to cause the liquidation, termination, or acceleration of one or more swap agreements because of a condition of the kind specified in section 365(e)(1) of this title or to offset or net out any termination values or payment amounts arising under or in connection with the termination, liquidation, or acceleration of one or more swap agreements shall not be stayed, avoided, or otherwise limited by operation of any provision of this title or by order of a court or administrative agency in any proceeding under this title. As used in this section, the term "contractual right" includes a right set forth in a rule or bylaw of a derivatives clearing organization (as defined in the Commodity Exchange Act), a multilateral clearing organization (as defined in the Federal Deposit Insurance Corporation Improvement Act of 1991), a national securities exchange, a national securities association, a securities clearing agency, a contract market designated under the Commodity Exchange Act, a derivatives transaction execution facility registered under the Commodity Exchange Act, or a board of trade (as defined in the Commodity Exchange Act) or in a resolution of the governing board thereof and a right, whether or not evidenced in writing, arising under common law, under law merchant, or by reason of normal business practice.

(Added Pub.L. 101–311, Title I, § 106(a), June 25, 1990, 104 Stat. 268; amended Pub.L. 109–8, Title IX, § 907(j), (o)(10), Apr. 20, 2005, 119 Stat. 178, 182.)

HISTORICAL AND STATUTORY NOTES

Revision Notes and Legislative Reports

1990 Acts. House Report No. 101–484, see 1990 U.S.Code Cong. and Adm.News, p. 223.

2005 Acts. House Report No. 109–31(Part I), see 2005 U.S. Code Cong. and Adm. News, p. 88.

References in Text

The Commodity Exchange Act, referred to in text, is Act Sept. 21, 1922, c. 369, 42 Stat. 998, as amended, which is classified principally to chapter 1 of Title 7, 7 U.S.C.A. § 1. For complete classification, see Short Title set out as 7 U.S.C.A. § 1 and Tables.

The Federal Deposit Insurance Corporation Improvement Act of 1991, referred to in text, is Pub.L. 102–242, Dec. 19, 1991, 105 Stat. 2236, as amended. For complete classification, see Short Title of 1991 Amendments note set out under 12 U.S.C.A. § 1811 and Tables.

Effective and Applicability Provisions

2005 Acts. Amendments by Pub.L. 109–8 effective, except as otherwise provided, 180 days after April 20, 2005, and inapplicable with respect to cases commenced under Title 11 before the effective date, see Pub.L. 109–8, § 1501, set out as a note under 11 U.S.C.A. § 101.

§ 561. Contractual right to terminate, liquidate, accelerate, or offset under a master netting agreement and across contracts; proceedings under chapter 15

(a) Subject to subsection (b), the exercise of any contractual right, because of a condition of the kind specified in section 365(e)(1), to cause the termination, liquidation, or acceleration of or to offset or net termination values, payment amounts, or other transfer obligations arising under or in connection with one or more (or the termination, liquidation, or acceleration of one or more)—

    (1) securities contracts, as defined in section 741(7);

    (2) commodity contracts, as defined in section 761(4);

    (3) forward contracts;

    (4) repurchase agreements;

    (5) swap agreements; or

    (6) master netting agreements,

shall not be stayed, avoided, or otherwise limited by operation of any provision of this title or by any order of a court or administrative agency in any proceeding under this title.

(b)(1) A party may exercise a contractual right described in subsection (a) to terminate, liquidate, or accelerate only to the extent that such party could exercise such a right under section 555, 556, 559, or 560 for each individual contract covered by the master netting agreement in issue.

(2) If a debtor is a commodity broker subject to subchapter IV of chapter 7—

    (A) a party may not net or offset an obligation to the debtor arising under, or in connection with, a commodity contract traded on or subject to the rules of a contract market designated under the Commodity Exchange Act or a derivatives transaction execution facility registered under the Commodity Exchange Act against any claim arising under, or in connection with, other instruments, contracts, or agreements listed in subsection (a) except to the extent that the party has positive net equity in the commodity accounts at the debtor, as calculated under such subchapter; and

    (B) another commodity broker may not net or offset an obligation to the debtor arising under, or in connection with, a commodity contract entered into or held on behalf of a customer of the debtor and traded on or subject to the rules of a contract market designated under the Commodity Exchange Act or a derivatives transaction execution facility registered under the Commodity Exchange Act against any claim arising under, or in connection with, other instruments, contracts, or agreements listed in subsection (a).

(3) No provision of subparagraph (A) or (B) of paragraph (2) shall prohibit the offset of claims and obligations that arise under—

    (A) a cross-margining agreement or similar arrangement that has been approved by the Commodity Futures Trading Commission or submitted to the Commodity Futures Trading Commission under paragraph (1) or (2) of section 5c(c) of the Commodity Exchange Act and has not been abrogated or rendered ineffective by the Commodity Futures Trading Commission; or

    (B) any other netting agreement between a clearing organization (as defined in section 761) and another entity that has been approved by the Commodity Futures Trading Commission.

(c) As used in this section, the term "contractual right" includes a right set forth in a rule or bylaw of a derivatives clearing organization (as defined in the Commodity Exchange Act), a multilateral clearing organization (as defined in the Federal Deposit Insurance Corporation Improvement Act of 1991), a national securities exchange, a national securities association, a securities clearing agency, a contract market designated under the Commodity Exchange Act, a derivatives transaction execution facility registered under the Commodity Exchange Act, or a board of trade (as defined in the Commodity Exchange Act) or in a resolution of the governing board thereof, and a right, whether or not evidenced in writing, arising under common law, under law merchant, or by reason of normal business practice.

(d) Any provisions of this title relating to securities contracts, commodity contracts, forward contracts, repurchase agreements, swap agreements, or master netting agreements shall apply in a case under chapter 15, so that enforcement of contractual provisions of such contracts and agreements in accordance with their terms will not be stayed or otherwise limited by operation of any provision of this title or by order of a court in any case under this title, and to limit avoidance powers to the same extent as in a proceeding under chapter 7 or 11 of this title (such enforcement not to be limited based on the presence or absence of assets of the debtor in the United States).

(Added Pub.L. 109–8, Title IX, § 907(k)(1), Apr. 20, 2005, 119 Stat. 179.)

HISTORICAL AND STATUTORY NOTES

Revision Notes and Legislative Reports

2005 Acts. House Report No. 109–31(Part I), see 2005 U.S. Code Cong. and Adm. News, p. 88.

References in Text

Subchapter IV of chapter 7, referred to in subsec. (b)(2), is subchapter IV of chapter 7 of this title, 11 U.S.C.A. § 761 et seq.

The Commodity Exchange Act, referred to in subsecs. (b)(2)(A) and (c), is Act Sept. 21, 1922, c. 369, 42 Stat. 998, as amended, which is classified principally to chapter 1 of Title 7, 7 U.S.C.A. § 1 et seq. For complete classification, see Short Title set out as 7 U.S.C.A. § 1 and Tables.

Section 5c(c) of the Commodity Exchange Act, referred to in subsec. (b)(3)(A), is Act Sept. 21, 1922, c. 369, § 5c, as added and amended Dec. 21, 2000, Pub.L. 106–554, § 1(a)(5) [Title I, § 113, Title II, § 251(h)], 114 Stat. 2763, 2763A-399, 2763a–444, which is classified to 7 U.S.C.A. § 7a–2.

The Federal Deposit Insurance Corporation Improvement Act of 1991, referred to in subsec. (c), is Pub.L. 102–242, Dec. 19, 1991, 105 Stat. 2236, as amended. For complete classification, see Short Title of 1991 Amendments note set out under 12 U.S.C.A. § 1811 and Tables.

Chapter 15, referred to in subsec. (d), is chapter 15 of this title, 11 U.S.C.A. § 1501 et seq.

Chapter 7 or 11 of this title, referred to in subsec. (d), is 11 U.S.C.A. § 701 et seq., or 11 U.S.C.A. § 1101 et seq., respectively.

Effective and Applicability Provisions

2005 Acts. Amendments by Pub.L. 109–8 effective, except as otherwise provided, 180 days after April 20, 2005, and inapplicable with respect to cases commenced under Title 11 before the effective date, see Pub.L. 109–8, § 1501, set out as a note under 11 U.S.C.A. § 101.

§ 562.　Timing of damage measurement in connection with swap agreements, securities contracts, forward contracts, commodity contracts, repurchase agreements, and master netting agreements

(a) If the trustee rejects a swap agreement, securities contract (as defined in section 741), forward contract, commodity contract (as defined in section 761), repurchase agreement, or master netting agreement pursuant to section 365(a), or if a forward contract merchant, stockbroker, financial institution, securities clearing agency, repo participant, financial participant, master netting agreement participant, or swap participant liquidates, terminates, or accelerates such contract or agreement, damages shall be measured as of the earlier of—

(1) the date of such rejection; or

(2) the date or dates of such liquidation, termination, or acceleration.

(b) If there are not any commercially reasonable determinants of value as of any date referred to in paragraph (1) or (2) of subsection (a), damages shall be measured as of the earliest subsequent date or dates on which there are commercially reasonable determinants of value.

(c) For the purposes of subsection (b), if damages are not measured as of the date or dates of rejection, liquidation, termination, or acceleration, and the forward contract merchant, stockbroker, financial institution, securities clearing agency, repo participant, financial participant, master netting agreement participant, or swap participant or the trustee objects to the timing of the measurement of damages—

(1) the trustee, in the case of an objection by a forward contract merchant, stockbroker, financial institution, securities clearing agency, repo participant, financial participant, master netting agreement participant, or swap participant; or

(2) the forward contract merchant, stockbroker, financial institution, securities clearing agency, repo participant, financial participant, master netting agreement participant, or swap participant, in the case of an objection by the trustee,

has the burden of proving that there were no commercially reasonable determinants of value as of such date or dates.

(Added Pub.L. 109–8, Title IX, § 910(a)(1), Apr. 20, 2005, 119 Stat. 184.)

HISTORICAL AND STATUTORY NOTES

Revision Notes and Legislative Reports

2005 Acts. House Report No. 109–31(Part I), see 2005 U.S. Code Cong. and Adm. News, p. 88.

Effective and Applicability Provisions

2005 Acts. Amendments by Pub.L. 109–8 effective, except as otherwise provided, 180 days after April 20, 2005, and inapplicable with respect to cases commenced under Title 11 before the effective date, see Pub.L. 109–8, § 1501, set out as a note under 11 U.S.C.A. § 101.

CHAPTER 7—LIQUIDATION

HISTORICAL AND STATUTORY NOTES

Effective and Applicability Provisions

2005 Acts. Amendments by Pub.L. 109–8 effective, except as otherwise provided, 180 days after April 20, 2005, and inapplicable with respect to cases commenced under Title 11 before the effective date, see Pub.L. 109–8, § 1501, set out as a note under 11 U.S.C.A. § 101.

CROSS REFERENCES

Amount received for claim through liquidation under this chapter as standard for confirmation requirement in,
    Chapter eleven cases, see 11 USCA § 1129.
    Chapter thirteen cases, see 11 USCA § 1325.
    Chapter twelve cases, see 11 USCA § 1225.
Amount received for claim through liquidation under this chapter as standard for discharge requirement in,
    Chapter thirteen cases, see 11 USCA § 1328.
    Chapter twelve cases, see 11 USCA § 1228.
Applicability of income tax provisions to cases under this chapter, see 26 USCA § 1398.
Certain provisions respecting commodity brokers under this chapter, see 7 USCA § 24.
Chapters one, three, and five of this title applicable in case under this chapter, see 11 USCA § 103.
Commencement of involuntary cases, see 11 USCA § 303.
Conversion to this chapter from,
    Chapter eleven, see 11 USCA § 1112.
    Chapter thirteen, see 11 USCA § 1307.
    Chapter twelve, see 11 USCA § 1208.
Debtor's duty under this chapter to file statement of intentions with respect to schedule of assets and liabilities, see 11 USCA § 521.
Denial of discharge under this chapter as affecting operation of injunction, see 11 USCA § 524.
Determination of net worth of person subject to liability for termination of single-employer plans includes improper transfers of assets in cases under this chapter, see 29 USCA § 1362.
Distribution of certain proceeds and property under this chapter as requirement for confirmation of plan, see 11 USCA § 1173.
Duration of automatic stay in case concerning an individual under this chapter, see 11 USCA § 362.
Duties of trustee in investor protection liquidation proceedings same as under this chapter, see 15 USCA § 78fff–1.
Duties of United States trustees, see 28 USCA § 586.
Effect of confirmation, see 11 USCA § 1141.
Effect of distribution other than under this title, see 11 USCA § 508.
Eligibility to serve as trustee, see 11 USCA § 321.

Employment of professional persons, see 11 USCA § 327.

Executory contracts and unexpired leases, see 11 USCA § 365.

Filing fees, see 28 USCA § 1930.

Limitation on compensation of trustee, see 11 USCA § 326.

Liquidation in railroad reorganization case as if under this chapter, see 11 USCA § 1174.

Meetings of creditors and equity security holders and oral examination of debtor, see 11 USCA § 341.

Objection to allowance of claims by creditor of partner in partnership that is debtor under this chapter, see 11 USCA § 502.

Payment of trustee from filing fee, see 11 USCA § 330.

Persons required to make returns of income under this chapter, see 26 USCA § 6012.

Persons who may be debtors under this chapter, see 11 USCA § 109.

Property of estate in cases converted to this chapter from,

Chapter thirteen, see 11 USCA § 1306.

Chapter twelve, see 11 USCA § 1207.

Recommendation by trustee of conversion from Chapter eleven to this chapter, see 11 USCA § 1106.

Special tax provisions, see 11 USCA § 346.

Stay of action against codebtor in cases converted to this chapter from,

Chapter thirteen, see 11 USCA § 1301.

Chapter twelve, see 11 USCA § 1201.

Transfers enabling creditor to receive more than under this chapter, see 11 USCA § 547.

Treatment of debtor's estate in cases under this chapter as taxpayer for certain income tax purposes, see 26 USCA § 108.

Unclaimed property, see 11 USCA § 347.

SUBCHAPTER I—OFFICERS AND ADMINISTRATION

CROSS REFERENCES

Applicability of this subchapter in investor protection liquidation proceedings, see 15 USCA § 78fff.

Subchapter applicable only in case under this chapter, see 11 USCA § 103.

§ 701. Interim trustee

(a)(1) Promptly after the order for relief under this chapter, the United States trustee shall appoint one disinterested person that is a member of the panel of private trustees established under section 586(a)(1) of title 28 or that is serving as trustee in the case immediately before the order for relief under this chapter to serve as interim trustee in the case.

(2) If none of the members of such panel is willing to serve as interim trustee in the case, then the United States trustee may serve as interim trustee in the case.

(b) The service of an interim trustee under this section terminates when a trustee elected or designated under section 702 of this title to serve as trustee in the case qualifies under section 322 of this title.

(c) An interim trustee serving under this section is a trustee in a case under this title.

(Pub.L. 95–598, Nov. 6, 1978, 92 Stat. 2604; Pub.L. 99–554, Title II, § 215, Oct. 27, 1986, 100 Stat. 3100.)

HISTORICAL AND STATUTORY NOTES

Revision Notes and Legislative Reports

1978 Acts. This section requires the court to appoint an interim trustee. The appointment must be made from the panel of private trustees established and maintained by the Director of the Administrative Office under proposed 28 U.S.C. 604(e).

Subsection (a) requires the appointment of an interim trustee to be made promptly after the order for relief, unless a trustee is already serving in the case, such as before a conversion from a reorganization to a liquidation case.

Subsection (b) specifies that the appointment of an interim trustee expires when the permanent trustee is elected or designated under section 702.

Subsection (c) makes clear that an interim trustee is a trustee in a case under the bankruptcy code.

Subsection (d) provides that in a commodity broker case where speed is essential the interim trustee must be appointed by noon of the business day immediately following the order for relief. Senate Report No. 95–989.

1986 Acts. House Report No. 99–764 and House Conference Report No. 99–958, see 1986 U.S.Code Cong. and Adm. News, p. 5227.

Legislative Statements

The House amendment deletes section 701(d) of the Senate amendment. It is anticipated that the Rules of Bankruptcy Procedure will require the appointment of an interim trustee at the earliest practical moment in commodity broker bankruptcies, but no later than noon of the day after the date of the filing of the petition, due to the volatility of such cases.

Effective and Applicability Provisions

1986 Acts. Amendment by Pub.L. 99–554 effective 30 days after Oct. 27, 1986, except as otherwise provided for, see section 302(a) of Pub.L. 99–554, set out as a note under section 581 of Title 28, Judiciary and Judicial Procedure.

Amendment by Pub.L. 99–554, § 215, not to become effective in or with respect to certain specified judicial districts until, or apply to cases while pending in such district before, the expiration of the 270-day period beginning 30 days after Oct. 27, 1986, or of the 30-day period beginning on the date the Attorney General certifies under section 303 of Pub.L. 99–554 the region specified in a paragraph of section 581(a) of Title 28, as amended by section 111(a) of Pub.L. 99–554, that includes such district, whichever occurs first, see section 302(d)(1) of Pub.L. 99–554, set out as a note under section 581 of Title 28.

Amendment by Pub.L. 99–554, § 215, not to become effective in or with respect to certain specified judicial districts until, or apply to cases while pending in such district before, the expiration of the 2-year period beginning 30 days after Oct. 27, 1986, or of the 30-day period beginning on the date the Attorney General certifies under section 303 of Pub.L. 99–554 the region specified in a paragraph of section 581(a) of Title 28, as amended by section 111(a) of Pub.L. 99–554, that includes such district, whichever occurs first, see section

302(d)(2) of Pub.L. 99–554, set out as a note under section 581 of Title 28.

Amendment by Pub.L. 99–554, § 215, not to become effective in or with respect to judicial districts established for the States of Alabama and North Carolina until, or apply to cases while pending in such district before, such district elects to be included in a bankruptcy region established in section 581(a) of Title 28, as amended by section 111(a) of Pub.L. 99–554, or Oct. 1, 2002, whichever occurs first, and, except as otherwise provided, with respect to cases under chapters 7, 11, 12, and 13 of Title 11 commenced before 30 days after Oct. 27, 1986, and pending in a judicial district in the States of Alabama or North Carolina before any election made under section 302(d)(3)(A) of Pub.L. 99–554 by such district becomes effective or Oct. 1, 2002, whichever occurs first, amendments by Pub.L. 99–554 not to apply until Oct. 1, 2003, or the expiration of the 1-year period beginning on the date such election becomes effective, whichever occurs first, and further, in any judicial district in Alabama or North Carolina not making the election described in section 302(d)(3)(A) of Pub.L. 99–554, any person appointed under regulations issued by the Judicial Conference to administer estates in cases under Title 11 authorized to establish, etc., a panel of private trustees, and to supervise cases and trustees in cases under chapters 7, 11, 12 and 13 of Title 11, until amendments by sections 201 to 231 of Pub.L. 99–554 effective in such district, see section 302(d)(3)(A) to (F), (H), and (I) of Pub.L. 99–554, set out as a note under section 581 of Title 28.

Amendment by Pub.L. 99–554, § 215, except as otherwise provided, with respect to cases under chapters 7, 11, 12, and 13 of Title 11 commenced before 30 days after Oct. 27, 1986, and pending in a judicial district referred to in section 581(a) of Title 28, as amended by section 111(a) of Pub.L. 99–554, for which a United States trustee is not authorized before 30 days after Oct. 27, 1986 to be appointed, not applicable until the expiration of the 3-year period beginning on Oct. 27, 1986 or of the 1-year period beginning on the date the Attorney General certifies under section 303 of Pub.L. 99–554 the region specified in a paragraph of such section 581(a) that includes, such district, whichever occurs first, see section 302(e)(1)(2) of Pub.L. 99–554, set out as a note under section 581 of Title 28.

CROSS REFERENCES

Appointment of interim trustee after commencement of involuntary case, see 11 USCA § 303.

Effect of conversion, see 11 USCA § 348.

Grain storage facility bankruptcies, expedited appointment of trustee, see 11 USCA § 557.

Qualification of trustee, see 11 USCA § 322.

§ 702. Election of trustee

(a) A creditor may vote for a candidate for trustee only if such creditor—

(1) holds an allowable, undisputed, fixed, liquidated, unsecured claim of a kind entitled to distribution under section 726(a)(2), 726(a)(3), 726(a)(4), 752(a), 766(h), or 766(i) of this title;

(2) does not have an interest materially adverse, other than an equity interest that is not substantial in relation to such creditor's interest as a creditor, to

the interest of creditors entitled to such distribution; and

(3) is not an insider.

(b) At the meeting of creditors held under section 341 of this title, creditors may elect one person to serve as trustee in the case if election of a trustee is requested by creditors that may vote under subsection (a) of this section, and that hold at least 20 percent in amount of the claims specified in subsection (a)(1) of this section that are held by creditors that may vote under subsection (a) of this section.

(c) A candidate for trustee is elected trustee if—

(1) creditors holding at least 20 percent in amount of the claims of a kind specified in subsection (a)(1) of this section that are held by creditors that may vote under subsection (a) of this section vote; and

(2) such candidate receives the votes of creditors holding a majority in amount of claims specified in subsection (a)(1) of this section that are held by creditors that vote for a trustee.

(d) If a trustee is not elected under this section, then the interim trustee shall serve as trustee in the case.

(Pub.L. 95–598, Nov. 6, 1978, 92 Stat. 2604; Pub.L. 97–222, § 7, July 27, 1982, 96 Stat. 237; Pub.L. 98–353, Title III, § 472, July 10, 1984, 98 Stat. 380.)

HISTORICAL AND STATUTORY NOTES

Revision Notes and Legislative Reports

1978 Acts. Subsection (a) of this section specifies which creditors may vote for a trustee. Only a creditor that holds an allowable, undisputed, fixed, liquidated, unsecured claim that is not entitled to priority, that does not have an interest materially adverse to the interest of general unsecured creditors, and that is not an insider may vote for a trustee. The phrase "materially adverse" is currently used in the Rules of Bankruptcy Procedure, rule 207(d). The application of the standard requires a balancing of various factors, such as the nature of the adversity. A creditor with a very small equity position would not be excluded from voting solely because he holds a small equity in the debtor. The Rules of Bankruptcy Procedure also currently provide for temporary allowance of claims, and will continue to do so for the purposes of determining who is eligible to vote under this provision.

Subsection (b) permits creditors at the meeting of creditors to elect one person to serve as trustee in the case. Creditors holding at least 20 percent in amount of the claims specified in the preceding paragraph must request election before creditors may elect a trustee. Subsection (c) specifies that a candidate for trustee is elected trustee if creditors holding at least 20 percent in amount of those claims actually vote, and if the candidate receives a majority in amount of votes actually cast.

Subsection (d) specifies that if a trustee is not elected, then the interim trustee becomes the permanent trustee and serves in the case permanently. Senate Report No. 95–989.

1982 Acts. House Report No. 97–420, see 1982 U.S.Code Cong. and Adm.News, p. 583.

1984 Acts. Statements by Legislative Leaders, see 1984 U.S.Code Cong. and Adm.News, p. 576.

Legislative Statements

The House amendment adopts section 702(a)(2) of the Senate amendment. An insubstantial equity interest does not disqualify a creditor from voting for a candidate for trustee.

Effective and Applicability Provisions

1984 Acts. Amendment by Pub.L. 98–353 effective with respect to cases filed 90 days after July 10, 1984, see section 552(a), formerly 553(a), of Pub.L. 98–353, set out as a note under section 101 of this title.

CROSS REFERENCES

Grain storage facility bankruptcies, expedited appointment of trustee, see 11 USCA § 557.

Qualification of trustee, see 11 USCA § 322.

Time for bringing action, see 11 USCA § 546.

§ 703. Successor trustee

(a) If a trustee dies or resigns during a case, fails to qualify under section 322 of this title, or is removed under section 324 of this title, creditors may elect, in the manner specified in section 702 of this title, a person to fill the vacancy in the office of trustee.

(b) Pending election of a trustee under subsection (a) of this section, if necessary to preserve or prevent loss to the estate, the United States trustee may appoint an interim trustee in the manner specified in section 701(a).

(c) If creditors do not elect a successor trustee under subsection (a) of this section or if a trustee is needed in a case reopened under section 350 of this title, then the United States trustee—

    (1) shall appoint one disinterested person that is a member of the panel of private trustees established under section 586(a)(1) of title 28 to serve as trustee in the case; or

    (2) may, if none of the disinterested members of such panel is willing to serve as trustee, serve as trustee in the case.

(Pub.L. 95–598, Nov. 6, 1978, 92 Stat. 2605; Pub.L. 98–353, Title III, § 473, July 10, 1984, 98 Stat. 381; Pub.L. 99–554, Title II, § 216, Oct. 27, 1986, 100 Stat. 3100.)

HISTORICAL AND STATUTORY NOTES

Revision Notes and Legislative Reports

1978 Acts. If the office of trustee becomes vacant during the case, this section makes provision for the selection of a successor trustee. The office might become vacant through death, resignation, removal, failure to qualify under section 322 by posting bond, or the reopening of a case. If it does, creditors may elect a successor in the same manner as they may elect a trustee under the previous section. Pending the election of a successor, the court may appoint an interim trustee in the usual manner if necessary to preserve or prevent loss to the estate. If creditors do not elect a successor, or if a trustee is needed in a reopened case, then the

court appoints a disinterested member of the panel of private trustees to serve. Senate Report No. 95–989.

1984 Acts. Statements by Legislative Leaders, see 1984 U.S.Code Cong. and Adm.News, p. 576.

1986 Acts. House Report No. 99–764 and House Conference Report No. 99–958, see 1986 U.S.Code Cong. and Adm. News, p. 5227.

Effective and Applicability Provisions

1986 Acts. Amendment by Pub.L. 99–554 effective 30 days after Oct. 27, 1986, except as otherwise provided for, see section 302(a) of Pub.L. 99–554, set out as a note under section 581 of Title 28, Judiciary and Judicial Procedure.

Amendment by Pub.L. 99–554, § 216, not to become effective in or with respect to certain specified judicial districts until, or apply to cases while pending in such district before, the expiration of the 270-day period beginning 30 days after Oct. 27, 1986, or of the 30-day period beginning on the date the Attorney General certifies under section 303 of Pub.L. 99–554 the region specified in a paragraph of section 581(a) of Title 28, as amended by section 111(a) of Pub.L. 99–554, that includes such district, whichever occurs first, see section 302(d)(1) of Pub.L. 99–554, set out as a note under section 581 of Title 28.

Amendment by Pub.L. 99–554, § 216, not to become effective in or with respect to certain specified judicial districts until, or apply to cases while pending in such district before, the expiration of the 2-year period beginning 30 days after Oct. 27, 1986, or of the 30-day period beginning on the date the Attorney General certifies under section 303 of Pub.L. 99–554 the region specified in a paragraph of section 581(a) of Title 28, as amended by section 111(a) of Pub.L. 99–554, that includes such district, whichever occurs first, see section 302(d)(2) of Pub.L. 99–554, set out as a note under section 581 of Title 28.

Amendment by Pub.L. 99–554, § 216, not to become effective in or with respect to judicial districts established for the States of Alabama and North Carolina until, or apply to cases while pending in such district before, such district elects to be included in a bankruptcy region established in section 581(a) of Title 28, as amended by section 111(a) of Pub.L. 99–554, or Oct. 1, 2002, whichever occurs first, and, except as otherwise provided, with respect to cases under chapters 7, 11, 12, and 13 of Title 11 commenced before 30 days after Oct. 27, 1986, and pending in a judicial district in the States of Alabama or North Carolina before any election made under section 302(d)(3)(A) of Pub.L. 99–554 by such district becomes effective or Oct. 1, 2002, whichever occurs first, amendments by Pub.L. 99–554 not to apply until Oct. 1, 2003, or the expiration of the 1-year period beginning on the date such election becomes effective, whichever occurs first, and further, in any judicial district in Alabama or North Carolina not making the election described in section 302(d)(3)(A) of Pub.L. 99–554, any person appointed under regulations issued by the Judicial Conference to administer estates in cases under Title 11 authorized to establish, etc., a panel of private trustees, and to supervise cases and trustees in cases under chapters 7, 11, 12, and 13 of Title 11, until amendments by sections 201 to 231 of Pub.L. 99–554 effective in such district, see section 302(d)(3)(A) to (F), (H), and (I) of Pub.L. 99–554, set out as a note under section 581 of Title 28.

Amendment by Pub.L. 99–554, § 216, except as otherwise provided, with respect to cases under chapters 7, 11, 12, and 13 of Title 11 commenced before 30 days after Oct. 27, 1986, and pending in a judicial district referred to in section 581(a) of Title 28, as amended by section 111(a) of Pub.L. 99–554, for which a United States trustee is not authorized before 30 days after Oct. 27, 1986 to be appointed, not applicable until the expiration of the 3-year period beginning on Oct. 27, 1986, or of the 1-year period beginning on the date the Attorney General certifies under section 303 of Pub.L. 99–554 the region specified in a paragraph of such section 581(a) that includes, such district, whichever occurs first, see section 302(e)(1), (2) of Pub.L. 99–554, set out as a note under section 581 of Title 28.

1984 Acts. Amendment by Pub.L. 98–353 effective with respect to cases filed 90 days after July 10, 1984, see section 552(a), formerly 553(a), of Pub.L. 98–353, set out as a note under section 101 of this title.

CROSS REFERENCES

Effect of vacancy in office of trustee, see 11 USCA § 325.

Grain storage facility bankruptcies, expedited appointment of trustee, see 11 USCA § 557.

Qualification of trustee, see 11 USCA § 322.

§ 704.   Duties of trustee

(a) The trustee shall—

(1) collect and reduce to money the property of the estate for which such trustee serves, and close such estate as expeditiously as is compatible with the best interests of parties in interest;

(2) be accountable for all property received;

(3) ensure that the debtor shall perform his intention as specified in section 521(a)(2)(B) of this title;

(4) investigate the financial affairs of the debtor;

(5) if a purpose would be served, examine proofs of claims and object to the allowance of any claim that is improper;

(6) if advisable, oppose the discharge of the debtor;

(7) unless the court orders otherwise, furnish such information concerning the estate and the estate's administration as is requested by a party in interest;

(8) if the business of the debtor is authorized to be operated, file with the court, with the United States trustee, and with any governmental unit charged with responsibility for collection or determination of any tax arising out of such operation, periodic reports and summaries of the operation of such business, including a statement of receipts and disbursements, and such other information as the United States trustee or the court requires;

(9) make a final report and file a final account of the administration of the estate with the court and with the United States trustee;

(10) if with respect to the debtor there is a claim for a domestic support obligation, provide the applicable notice specified in subsection (c);

(11) if, at the time of the commencement of the case, the debtor (or any entity designated by the debtor) served as the administrator (as defined in section 3 of the Employee Retirement Income Security Act of 1974) of an employee benefit plan, continue to perform the obligations required of the administrator; and

(12) use all reasonable and best efforts to transfer patients from a health care business that is in the process of being closed to an appropriate health care business that—

(A) is in the vicinity of the health care business that is closing;

(B) provides the patient with services that are substantially similar to those provided by the health care business that is in the process of being closed; and

(C) maintains a reasonable quality of care.

(b)(1) With respect to a debtor who is an individual in a case under this chapter—

(A) the United States trustee (or the bankruptcy administrator, if any) shall review all materials filed by the debtor and, not later than 10 days after the date of the first meeting of creditors, file with the court a statement as to whether the debtor's case would be presumed to be an abuse under section 707(b); and

(B) not later than 7 days after receiving a statement under subparagraph (A), the court shall provide a copy of the statement to all creditors.

(2) The United States trustee (or bankruptcy administrator, if any) shall, not later than 30 days after the date of filing a statement under paragraph (1), either file a motion to dismiss or convert under section 707(b) or file a statement setting forth the reasons the United States trustee (or the bankruptcy administrator, if any) does not consider such a motion to be appropriate, if the United States trustee (or the bankruptcy administrator, if any) determines that the debtor's case should be presumed to be an abuse under section 707(b) and the product of the debtor's current monthly income, multiplied by 12 is not less than—

(A) in the case of a debtor in a household of 1 person, the median family income of the applicable State for 1 earner; or

(B) in the case of a debtor in a household of 2 or more individuals, the highest median family income of the applicable State for a family of the same number or fewer individuals.

(c)(1) In a case described in subsection (a)(10) to which subsection (a)(10) applies, the trustee shall—

(A)(i) provide written notice to the holder of the claim described in subsection (a)(10) of such claim and of the right of such holder to use the services of the State child support enforcement agency established under sections 464 and 466 of the Social

Security Act for the State in which such holder resides, for assistance in collecting child support during and after the case under this title;

(ii) include in the notice provided under clause (i) the address and telephone number of such State child support enforcement agency; and

(iii) include in the notice provided under clause (i) an explanation of the rights of such holder to payment of such claim under this chapter;

(B)(i) provide written notice to such State child support enforcement agency of such claim; and

(ii) include in the notice provided under clause (i) the name, address, and telephone number of such holder; and

(C) at such time as the debtor is granted a discharge under section 727, provide written notice to such holder and to such State child support enforcement agency of—

(i) the granting of the discharge;

(ii) the last recent known address of the debtor;

(iii) the last recent known name and address of the debtor's employer; and

(iv) the name of each creditor that holds a claim that—

(I) is not discharged under paragraph (2), (4), or (14A) of section 523(a); or

(II) was reaffirmed by the debtor under section 524(c).

(2)(A) The holder of a claim described in subsection (a)(10) or the State child support enforcement agency of the State in which such holder resides may request from a creditor described in paragraph (1)(C)(iv) the last known address of the debtor.

(B) Notwithstanding any other provision of law, a creditor that makes a disclosure of a last known address of a debtor in connection with a request made under subparagraph (A) shall not be liable by reason of making such disclosure.

(Pub.L. 95–598, Nov. 6, 1978, 92 Stat. 2605; Pub.L. 98–353, Title III, §§ 311(a), 474, July 10, 1984, 98 Stat. 355, 381; Pub.L. 99–554, Title II, § 217, Oct. 27, 1986, 100 Stat. 3100; Pub.L. 109–8, Title I, § 102(c), Title II, § 219(a), Title IV, § 446(b), Title XI, § 1105(a), Apr. 20, 2005, 119 Stat. 32, 55, 118, 192; Pub.L. 111–16, § 2(7), May 7, 2009, 123 Stat. 1607; Pub.L. 111–327, § 2(a)(24), Dec. 22, 2010, 124 Stat. 3560.)

HISTORICAL AND STATUTORY NOTES

Revision Notes and Legislative Reports

1978 Acts. The essential duties of the trustee are enumerated in this section. Others, or elaborations on these, may be prescribed by the Rules of Bankruptcy Procedure to the extent not inconsistent with those prescribed by this section. The duties are derived from section 47a of the Bankruptcy Act [section 75(a) of former Title 11].

The trustee's principal duty is to collect and reduce to money the property of the estate for which he serves, and to close up the estate as expeditiously as is compatible with the best interests of parties in interest. He must be accountable for all property received, and must investigate the financial affairs of the debtor. If a purpose would be served (such as if there are assets that will be distributed), the trustee is required to examine proofs of claims and object to the allowance of any claim that is improper. If advisable, the trustee must oppose the discharge of the debtor, which is for the benefit of general unsecured creditors whom the trustee represents.

The trustee is responsible to furnish such information concerning the estate and its administration as is requested by a party in interest. If the business of the debtor is authorized to be operated, then the trustee is required to file with governmental units charged with the responsibility for collection or determination of any tax arising out of the operation of the business periodic reports and summaries of the operation, including a statement of receipts and disbursements, and such other information as the court requires. He is required to give constructive notice of the commencement of the case in the manner specified under section 342(b). Senate Report No. 95–989.

1984 Acts. Statements by Legislative Leaders, see 1984 U.S.Code Cong. and Adm.News, p. 576.

1986 Acts. House Report No. 99–764 and House Conference Report No. 99–958, see 1986 U.S.Code Cong. and Adm. News, p. 5227.

2005 Acts. House Report No. 109–31(Part I), see 2005 U.S. Code Cong. and Adm. News, p. 88.

Legislative Statements

Section 704(8) of the Senate amendment is deleted in the House amendment. Trustees should give constructive notice of the commencement of the case in the manner specified under section 549(c) of title 11.

References in Text

Section 3 of the Employee Retirement Income Security Act of 1974, referred to in subsec. (a)(11), is Pub.L. 93–406, Title I, § 3, Sept. 2, 1974, 88 Stat. 833, which is classified to 29 U.S.C.A. § 1002.

Section 464 of the Social Security Act, referred to in subsec. (c)(1)(A)(i), is Act Aug. 14, 1935, c. 531, Title IV, § 464, as added Aug. 13, 1981, Pub.L. 97–35, Title XXIII, § 2331(a), 95 Stat. 860, and amended, which is classified to 42 U.S.C.A. § 664.

Section 466 of the Social Security Act, referred to in subsec. (c)(1)(A)(i), is Act Aug. 14, 1935, c. 531, Title IV, § 466, as added Aug. 16, 1984, Pub.L. 98–378, § 3(b), 98 Stat. 1306, and amended, which is classified to 42 U.S.C.A. § 666.

Effective and Applicability Provisions

2009 Acts. Amendments by Pub.L. 111–16 effective Dec. 1, 2009, see Pub.L. 111–16, § 7, set out as a note under 11 U.S.C.A. § 109.

2005 Acts. Amendments by Pub.L. 109–8 effective, except as otherwise provided, 180 days after April 20, 2005, and inapplicable with respect to cases commenced under Title 11 before the effective date, see Pub.L. 109–8, § 1501, set out as a note under 11 U.S.C.A. § 101.

1986 Acts. Amendment by Pub.L. 99–554 effective 30 days after Oct. 27, 1986, except as otherwise provided for, see section 302(a) of Pub.L. 99–554, set out as a note under section 581 of Title 28, Judiciary and Judicial Procedure.

Amendment by Pub.L. 99–554, § 217, not to become effective in or with respect to certain specified judicial districts until, or apply to cases while pending in such district before, the expiration of the 270-day period beginning 30 days after Oct. 27, 1986, or of the 30-day period beginning on the date the Attorney General certifies under section 303 of Pub.L. 99–554 the region specified in a paragraph of section 581(a) of Title 28, as amended by section 111(a) of Pub.L. 99–554, that includes such district, whichever occurs first, see section 302(d)(1) of Pub.L. 99–554, set out as a note under section 581 of Title 28.

Amendment by Pub.L. 99–554, § 217, not to become effective in or with respect to certain specified judicial districts until, or apply to cases while pending in such district before, the expiration of the 2-year period beginning 30 days after Oct. 27, 1986, or of the 30-day period beginning on the date the Attorney General certifies under section 303 of Pub.L. 99–554 the region specified in a paragraph of section 581(a) of Title 28, as amended by section 111(a) of Pub.L. 99–554, that includes such district, whichever occurs first, see section 302(d)(2) of Pub.L. 99–554, set out as a note under section 581 of Title 28.

Amendment by Pub.L. 99–554, § 217, not to become effective in or with respect to judicial districts established for the States of Alabama and North Carolina until, or apply to cases while pending in such district before, such district elects to be included in a bankruptcy region established in section 581(a) of Title 28, as amended by section 111(a) of Pub.L. 99–554, or Oct. 1, 2002, whichever occurs first and, except as otherwise provided for, with respect to cases under chapters 7, 11, 12 and 13 of Title 11 commenced before 30 days after Oct. 27, 1986, and pending in a judicial district in the States of Alabama or North Carolina before any election made under section 302(d)(3)(A) of Pub.L. 99–554 by such district becomes effective or Oct. 1, 2002, whichever occurs first, amendments by Pub.L. 99–554 not to apply until Oct. 1, 2003, or the expiration of the 1-year period beginning on the date such election becomes effective, whichever occurs first, and further, in any judicial district in Alabama or North Carolina not making the election described in section 302(d)(3)(A) of Pub.L. 99–554, any person appointed under regulations issued by the Judicial Conference to administer estates in cases under Title 11 authorized to establish, etc., a panel of private trustees, and to supervise cases and trustees in cases under chapters 7, 11, 12 and 13 of Title 11, until amendments by sections 201 to 231 of Pub.L. 99–554 effective in such district, see section 302(d)(3)(A) to (F), (H), and (I) of Pub.L. 99–554, set out as a note under section 581 of Title 28.

Amendment by Pub.L. 99–554, § 217, except as otherwise provided, with respect to cases under chapters 7, 11, 12, and 13 of Title 11 commenced before 30 days after Oct. 27, 1986, and pending in a judicial district referred to in section 581(a) of Title 28, as amended by section 111(a) of Pub.L. 99–554, for which a United States trustee is not authorized before 30 days after Oct. 27, 1986 to be appointed, not applicable until the expiration of the 3-year period beginning on Oct. 27, 1986, or of the 1-year period beginning on the date the Attorney General certifies under section 303 of Pub.L. 99–554 the region specified in a paragraph of such section 581(a) that includes, such district, whichever occurs first, see section 302(e)(1), (2) of Pub.L. 99–554, set out as a note under section 581 of Title 28.

1984 Acts. Amendment by Pub.L. 98–353 effective with respect to cases filed 90 days after July 10, 1984, see section

552(a), formerly 553(a), of Pub.L. 98–353, set out as a note under section 101 of this title.

CROSS REFERENCES

Duties of trustee in,

    Chapter eleven cases, see 11 USCA § 1106.

    Chapter thirteen cases, see 11 USCA § 1302.

    Chapter twelve cases, see 11 USCA § 1202.

    Multiemployer plan termination proceedings, see 29 USCA § 1342.

Filing of reports and summaries by debtor engaged in business, see 11 USCA § 1304.

Powers and duties of trustee in investor protection liquidation proceedings, see 15 USCA § 78fff–1.

§ 705. Creditors' committee

(a) At the meeting under section 341(a) of this title, creditors that may vote for a trustee under section 702(a) of this title may elect a committee of not fewer than three, and not more than eleven, creditors, each of whom holds an allowable unsecured claim of a kind entitled to distribution under section 726(a)(2) of this title.

(b) A committee elected under subsection (a) of this section may consult with the trustee or the United States trustee in connection with the administration of the estate, make recommendations to the trustee or the United States trustee respecting the performance of the trustee's duties, and submit to the court or the United States trustee any question affecting the administration of the estate.

(Pub.L. 95–598, Nov. 6, 1978, 92 Stat. 2605; Pub.L. 99–554, Title II, § 218, Oct. 27, 1986, 100 Stat. 3100.)

HISTORICAL AND STATUTORY NOTES

Revision Notes and Legislative Reports

1978 Acts. This section is derived from section 44b of the Bankruptcy Act [section 72(b) of former Title 11] without substantial change. It permits election by general unsecured creditors of a committee of not fewer than 3 members and not more than 11 members to consult with the trustee in connection with the administration of the estate, to make recommendations to the trustee respecting the performance of his duties, and to submit to the court any question affecting the administration of the estate. There is no provision for compensation or reimbursement of its counsel. Senate Report No. 95–989.

1986 Acts. House Report No. 99–764 and House Conference Report No. 99–958, see 1986 U.S.Code Cong. and Adm. News, p. 5227.

Legislative Statements

Section 705(a) of the House amendment adopts a provision contained in the Senate amendment that limits a committee of creditors to not more than 11; the House bill contained no maximum limitation.

Effective and Applicability Provisions

1986 Acts. Amendment by Pub.L. 99–554 effective 30 days after Oct. 27, 1986, except as otherwise provided for, see section 302(a) of Pub.L. 99–554, set out as a note under section 581 of Title 28, Judiciary and Judicial Procedure.

Amendment by Pub.L. 99–554, § 218, not to become effective in or with respect to certain specified judicial districts until, or apply to cases while pending in such district before, the expiration of the 270-day period beginning 30 days after Oct. 27, 1986, or of the 30-day period beginning on the date the Attorney General certifies under section 303 of Pub.L. 99–554 the region specified in a paragraph of section 581(a) of Title 28, as amended by section 111(a) of Pub.L. 99–554, that includes such district, whichever occurs first, see section 302(d)(1) of Pub.L. 99–554, set out as a note under section 581 of Title 28.

Amendment by Pub.L. 99–554, § 218, not to become effective in or with respect to certain specified judicial districts until, or apply to cases while pending in such district before, the expiration of the 2-year period beginning 30 days after Oct. 27, 1986, or of the 30-day period beginning on the date the Attorney General certifies under section 303 of Pub.L. 99–554 the region specified in a paragraph of section 581(a) of Title 28, as amended by section 111(a) of Pub.L. 99–554, that includes such district, whichever occurs first, see section 302(d)(2) of Pub.L. 99–554, set out as a note under section 581 of Title 28.

Amendment by Pub.L. 99–554, § 218, not to become effective in or with respect to judicial districts established for the States of Alabama and North Carolina until, or apply to cases while pending in such district before, such district elects to be included in a bankruptcy region established in section 581(a) of Title 28, as amended by section 111(a) of Pub.L. 99–554, or Oct. 1, 2002, whichever occurs first, and, except as otherwise provided, with respect to cases under chapters 7, 11, 12, and 13 of Title 11 commenced before 30 days after Oct. 27, 1986, and pending in a judicial district in the States of Alabama or North Carolina before any election made under section 302(d)(3)(A) of Pub.L. 99–554 by such district becomes effective or Oct. 1, 2002, whichever occurs first, amendments by Pub.L. 99–554 not to apply until Oct. 1, 2003, or the expiration of the 1-year period beginning on the date such election becomes effective, whichever occurs first, and further, in any judicial district in Alabama or North Carolina not making the election described in section 302(d)(3)(A) of Pub.L. 99–554, any person appointed under regulations issued by the Judicial Conference to administer estates in cases under Title 11 authorized to establish, etc., a panel of private trustees, and to supervise cases and trustees in cases under chapters 7, 11, 12, and 13 of Title 11, until amendments by sections 201 to 231 of Pub.L. 99–554 effective in such district, see section 302(d)(3)(A) to (F), (H), and (I) of Pub.L. 9–554, set out as a note under section 581 of Title 28.

Amendment by Pub.L. 99–554, § 218, except as otherwise provided, with respect to cases under chapters 7, 11, 12, and 13 of Title 11 commenced before 30 days after Oct. 27, 1986, and pending in a judicial district referred to in section 581(a) of Title 28, as amended by section 111(a) of Pub.L. 99–554, for which a United States trustee is not authorized before 30 days after Oct. 27, 1986 to be appointed, not applicable until the expiration of the 3-year period beginning on Oct. 27, 1986, or of the 1-year period beginning on the date the Attorney General certifies under section 303 of Pub.L. 99–554 the region specified in a paragraph of such section 581(a) that includes, such district, whichever occurs first, see section 302(e)(1), (2) of Pub.L. 99–554, set out as a note under section 581 of Title 28.

CROSS REFERENCES

Appointment of creditors' and equity security holders' committees in Chapter eleven cases, see 11 USCA § 1102.

Powers and duties of committees in Chapter eleven cases, see 11 USCA § 1103.

§ 706. Conversion

(a) The debtor may convert a case under this chapter to a case under chapter 11, 12, or 13 of this title at any time, if the case has not been converted under section 1112, 1208, or 1307 of this title. Any waiver of the right to convert a case under this subsection is unenforceable.

(b) On request of a party in interest and after notice and a hearing, the court may convert a case under this chapter to a case under chapter 11 of this title at any time.

(c) The court may not convert a case under this chapter to a case under chapter 12 or 13 of this title unless the debtor requests or consents to such conversion.

(d) Notwithstanding any other provision of this section, a case may not be converted to a case under another chapter of this title unless the debtor may be a debtor under such chapter.

(Pub.L. 95–598, Nov. 6, 1978, 92 Stat. 2606; Pub.L. 99–554, Title II, § 257(q), Oct. 27, 1986, 100 Stat. 3115; Pub.L. 103–394, Title V, § 501(d)(22), Oct. 22, 1994, 108 Stat. 4146; Pub.L. 109–8, Title I, § 101, Apr. 20, 2005, 119 Stat. 27.)

HISTORICAL AND STATUTORY NOTES

Revision Notes and Legislative Reports

1978 Acts. Subsection (a) of this section gives the debtor the one-time absolute right of conversion of a liquidation case to a reorganization or individual repayment plan case. If the case has already once been converted from chapter 11 or 13 to chapter 7, then the debtor does not have that right. The policy of the provision is that the debtor should always be given the opportunity to repay his debts, and a waiver of the right to convert a case is unenforceable.

Subsection (b) permits the court, on request of a party in interest and after notice and a hearing, to convert the case to chapter 11 at any time. The decision whether to convert is left in the sound discretion of the court, based on what will most inure to the benefit of all parties in interest.

Subsection (c) is part of the prohibition against involuntary chapter 13 cases, and prohibits the court from converting a case to chapter 13 without the debtor's consent.

Subsection (d) reinforces section 109 by prohibiting conversion to a chapter unless the debtor is eligible to be a debtor under that chapter. Senate Report No. 95–989.

1986 Acts. House Report No. 99–764 and House Conference Report No. 99–958, see 1986 U.S.Code Cong. and Adm. News, p. 5227.

1994 Acts. House Report No. 103–835, see 1994 U.S. Code Cong. and Adm. News, p. 3340.

2005 Acts. House Report No. 109–31(Part I), see 2005 U.S. Code Cong. and Adm. News, p. 88.

Legislative Statements

Section 706(a) of the House amendment adopts a provision contained in the Senate amendment indicating that a waiver of the right to convert a case under section 706(a) is unenforceable. The explicit reference in title 11 forbidding the waiver of certain rights is not intended to imply that other rights, such as the right to file a voluntary bankruptcy case under section 301, may be waived.

Section 706 of the House amendment adopts a similar provision contained in H.R. 8200 as passed by the House. Competing proposals contained in section 706(c) and section 706(d) of the Senate amendment are rejected.

Effective and Applicability Provisions

2005 Acts. Amendments by Pub.L. 109–8 effective, except as otherwise provided, 180 days after April 20, 2005, and inapplicable with respect to cases commenced under Title 11 before the effective date, see Pub.L. 109–8, § 1501, set out as a note under 11 U.S.C.A. § 101.

1994 Acts. Amendment by Pub.L. 103–394 effective on Oct. 22, 1994, and not to apply with respect to cases commenced under Title 11 of the United States Code before Oct. 22, 1994, see section 702 of Pub.L. 103–394, set out as a note under section 101 of this title.

1986 Acts. Amendment by Pub.L. 99–554 effective 30 days after Oct. 27, 1986, but not applicable to cases commenced under this title before that date, see section 302(a), (c)(1) of Pub.L. 99–554, set out as a note under section 581 of Title 28, Judiciary and Judicial Procedure.

Separability of Provisions

If any provision of or amendment made by Pub.L. 103–394 or the application of such provision or amendment to any person or circumstance is held to be unconstitutional, the remaining provisions of and amendments made by Pub.L. 103–394 and the application of such provisions and amendments to any person or circumstance shall not be affected thereby, see section 701 of Pub.L. 103–394, set out as a note under section 101 of this title.

CROSS REFERENCES

Conversion or dismissal of,

    Chapter eleven cases, see 11 USCA § 1112.

    Chapter thirteen cases, see 11 USCA § 1307.

    Chapter twelve cases, see 11 USCA § 1208.

Effect of conversion, see 11 USCA § 348.

Termination of debtor's taxable period in,

    Chapter eleven cases, see 11 USCA § 1146.

    Chapter twelve cases, see 11 USCA § 1231.

§ 707.   Dismissal of a case or conversion to a case under chapter 11 or 13

(a) The court may dismiss a case under this chapter only after notice and a hearing and only for cause, including—

    (1) unreasonable delay by the debtor that is prejudicial to creditors;

    (2) nonpayment of any fees or charges required under chapter 123 of title 28; and

    (3) failure of the debtor in a voluntary case to file, within fifteen days or such additional time as the court may allow after the filing of the petition commencing such case, the information required by paragraph (1) of section 521(a), but only on a motion by the United States trustee.

(b)(1) After notice and a hearing, the court, on its own motion or on a motion by the United States trustee, trustee (or bankruptcy administrator, if any), or any party in interest, may dismiss a case filed by an individual debtor under this chapter whose debts are primarily consumer debts, or, with the debtor's consent, convert such a case to a case under chapter 11 or 13 of this title, if it finds that the granting of relief would be an abuse of the provisions of this chapter. In making a determination whether to dismiss a case under this section, the court may not take into consideration whether a debtor has made, or continues to make, charitable contributions (that meet the definition of "charitable contribution" under section 548(d)(3)) to any qualified religious or charitable entity or organization (as that term is defined in section 548(d)(4)).

(2)(A)(i) In considering under paragraph (1) whether the granting of relief would be an abuse of the provisions of this chapter, the court shall presume abuse exists if the debtor's current monthly income reduced by the amounts determined under clauses (ii), (iii), and (iv), and multiplied by 60 is not less than the lesser of—

    (I) 25 percent of the debtor's nonpriority unsecured claims in the case, or $7,700 [1], whichever is greater; or

    (II) $12,850 [1].

(ii)(I) The debtor's monthly expenses shall be the debtor's applicable monthly expense amounts specified under the National Standards and Local Standards, and the debtor's actual monthly expenses for the categories specified as Other Necessary Expenses issued by the Internal Revenue Service for the area in which the debtor resides, as in effect on the date of the order for relief, for the debtor, the dependents of the debtor, and the spouse of the debtor in a joint case, if the spouse is not otherwise a dependent. Such expenses shall include reasonably necessary health insurance, disability insurance, and health savings account expenses for the debtor, the spouse of the debtor, or the dependents of the debtor. Notwithstanding any other provision of this clause, the monthly expenses of the debtor shall not include any payments for debts. In addition, the debtor's monthly expenses shall include the debtor's reasonably necessary expenses incurred to maintain the safety of the debtor and the family of the debtor from family violence as identified under section 302 of the Family Violence Prevention and Services Act, or other applicable Federal law. The expenses included in the debtor's monthly expenses described in the preceding sentence shall be kept confidential by the court. In addition, if it is demonstrated that it is reasonable and necessary, the debtor's monthly expenses may also include an additional allowance for food and clothing of up to 5 percent of the food and clothing categories as specified by the National Standards issued by the Internal Revenue Service.

(II) In addition, the debtor's monthly expenses may include, if applicable, the continuation of actual expenses paid by the debtor that are reasonable and necessary for care and support of an elderly, chronically ill, or disabled household member or member of the debtor's immediate family (including parents, grandparents, siblings, children, and grandchildren of the debtor, the dependents of the debtor, and the spouse of the debtor in a joint case who is not a dependent) and who is unable to pay for such reasonable and necessary expenses. Such monthly expenses may include, if applicable, contributions to an account of a qualified ABLE program to the extent such contributions are not excess contributions (as described in section 4973(h) of the Internal Revenue Code of 1986) and if the designated beneficiary of such account is a child, stepchild, grandchild, or stepgrandchild of the debtor.

(III) In addition, for a debtor eligible for chapter 13, the debtor's monthly expenses may include the actual administrative expenses of administering a chapter 13 plan for the district in which the debtor resides, up to an amount of 10 percent of the projected plan payments, as determined under schedules issued by the Executive Office for United States Trustees.

(IV) In addition, the debtor's monthly expenses may include the actual expenses for each dependent child less than 18 years of age, not to exceed $1,925 [1] per year per child, to attend a private or public elementary or secondary school if the debtor provides documentation of such expenses and a detailed explanation of why such expenses are reasonable and necessary, and why such expenses are not already accounted for in the National Standards, Local Standards, or Other Necessary Expenses referred to in subclause (I).

(V) In addition, the debtor's monthly expenses may include an allowance for housing and utilities, in excess of the allowance specified by the Local Standards for housing and utilities issued by the Internal Revenue Service, based on the actual expenses for home energy costs if the debtor provides documentation of such actual expenses and demonstrates that such actual expenses are reasonable and necessary.

(iii) The debtor's average monthly payments on account of secured debts shall be calculated as the sum of—

(I) the total of all amounts scheduled as contractually due to secured creditors in each month

of the 60 months following the date of the filing of the petition; and

(II) any additional payments to secured creditors necessary for the debtor, in filing a plan under chapter 13 of this title, to maintain possession of the debtor's primary residence, motor vehicle, or other property necessary for the support of the debtor and the debtor's dependents, that serves as collateral for secured debts;

divided by 60.

(iv) The debtor's expenses for payment of all priority claims (including priority child support and alimony claims) shall be calculated as the total amount of debts entitled to priority, divided by 60.

(B)(i) In any proceeding brought under this subsection, the presumption of abuse may only be rebutted by demonstrating special circumstances, such as a serious medical condition or a call or order to active duty in the Armed Forces, to the extent such special circumstances that justify additional expenses or adjustments of current monthly income for which there is no reasonable alternative.

(ii) In order to establish special circumstances, the debtor shall be required to itemize each additional expense or adjustment of income and to provide—

(I) documentation for such expense or adjustment to income; and

(II) a detailed explanation of the special circumstances that make such expenses or adjustment to income necessary and reasonable.

(iii) The debtor shall attest under oath to the accuracy of any information provided to demonstrate that additional expenses or adjustments to income are required.

(iv) The presumption of abuse may only be rebutted if the additional expenses or adjustments to income referred to in clause (i) cause the product of the debtor's current monthly income reduced by the amounts determined under clauses (ii), (iii), and (iv) of subparagraph (A) when multiplied by 60 to be less than the lesser of—

(I) 25 percent of the debtor's nonpriority unsecured claims, or $7,700 [1], whichever is greater; or

(II) $12,850 [1].

(C) As part of the schedule of current income and expenditures required under section 521, the debtor shall include a statement of the debtor's current monthly income, and the calculations that determine whether a presumption arises under subparagraph (A)(i), that show how each such amount is calculated.

(D) Subparagraphs (A) through (C) shall not apply, and the court may not dismiss or convert a case based on any form of means testing—

(i) if the debtor is a disabled veteran (as defined in section 3741(1) of title 38), and the indebtedness occurred primarily during a period during which he or she was—

    (I) on active duty (as defined in section 101(d)(1) of title 10); or

    (II) performing a homeland defense activity (as defined in section 901(1) of title 32); or

  (ii) with respect to the debtor, while the debtor is—

    (I) on, and during the 540–day period beginning immediately after the debtor is released from, a period of active duty (as defined in section 101(d)(1) of title 10) of not less than 90 days; or

    (II) performing, and during the 540–day period beginning immediately after the debtor is no longer performing, a homeland defense activity (as defined in section 901(1) of title 32) performed for a period of not less than 90 days;

if after September 11, 2001, the debtor while a member of a reserve component of the Armed Forces or a member of the National Guard, was called to such active duty or performed such homeland defense activity.

(3) In considering under paragraph (1) whether the granting of relief would be an abuse of the provisions of this chapter in a case in which the presumption in paragraph (2)(A)(i) does not arise or is rebutted, the court shall consider—

  (A) whether the debtor filed the petition in bad faith; or

  (B) the totality of the circumstances (including whether the debtor seeks to reject a personal services contract and the financial need for such rejection as sought by the debtor) of the debtor's financial situation demonstrates abuse.

(4)(A) The court, on its own initiative or on the motion of a party in interest, in accordance with the procedures described in rule 9011 of the Federal Rules of Bankruptcy Procedure, may order the attorney for the debtor to reimburse the trustee for all reasonable costs in prosecuting a motion filed under section 707(b), including reasonable attorneys' fees, if—

  (i) a trustee files a motion for dismissal or conversion under this subsection; and

  (ii) the court—

    (I) grants such motion; and

    (II) finds that the action of the attorney for the debtor in filing a case under this chapter violated rule 9011 of the Federal Rules of Bankruptcy Procedure.

(B) If the court finds that the attorney for the debtor violated rule 9011 of the Federal Rules of Bankruptcy Procedure, the court, on its own initiative or on the motion of a party in interest, in accordance with such procedures, may order—

  (i) the assessment of an appropriate civil penalty against the attorney for the debtor; and

  (ii) the payment of such civil penalty to the trustee, the United States trustee (or the bankruptcy administrator, if any).

(C) The signature of an attorney on a petition, pleading, or written motion shall constitute a certification that the attorney has—

  (i) performed a reasonable investigation into the circumstances that gave rise to the petition, pleading, or written motion; and

  (ii) determined that the petition, pleading, or written motion—

    (I) is well grounded in fact; and

    (II) is warranted by existing law or a good faith argument for the extension, modification, or reversal of existing law and does not constitute an abuse under paragraph (1).

(D) The signature of an attorney on the petition shall constitute a certification that the attorney has no knowledge after an inquiry that the information in the schedules filed with such petition is incorrect.

(5)(A) Except as provided in subparagraph (B) and subject to paragraph (6), the court, on its own initiative or on the motion of a party in interest, in accordance with the procedures described in rule 9011 of the Federal Rules of Bankruptcy Procedure, may award a debtor all reasonable costs (including reasonable attorneys' fees) in contesting a motion filed by a party in interest (other than a trustee or United States trustee (or bankruptcy administrator, if any)) under this subsection if—

  (i) the court does not grant the motion; and

  (ii) the court finds that—

    (I) the position of the party that filed the motion violated rule 9011 of the Federal Rules of Bankruptcy Procedure; or

    (II) the attorney (if any) who filed the motion did not comply with the requirements of clauses (i) and (ii) of paragraph (4)(C), and the motion was made solely for the purpose of coercing a debtor into waiving a right guaranteed to the debtor under this title.

(B) A small business that has a claim of an aggregate amount less than $1,300 [1] shall not be subject to subparagraph (A)(ii)(I).

(C) For purposes of this paragraph—

  (i) the term "small business" means an unincorporated business, partnership, corporation, association, or organization that—

    (I) has fewer than 25 full-time employees as determined on the date on which the motion is filed; and

    (II) is engaged in commercial or business activity; and

(ii) the number of employees of a wholly owned subsidiary of a corporation includes the employees of—

(I) a parent corporation; and

(II) any other subsidiary corporation of the parent corporation.

(6) Only the judge or United States trustee (or bankruptcy administrator, if any) may file a motion under section 707(b), if the current monthly income of the debtor, or in a joint case, the debtor and the debtor's spouse, as of the date of the order for relief, when multiplied by 12, is equal to or less than—

(A) in the case of a debtor in a household of 1 person, the median family income of the applicable State for 1 earner;

(B) in the case of a debtor in a household of 2, 3, or 4 individuals, the highest median family income of the applicable State for a family of the same number or fewer individuals; or

(C) in the case of a debtor in a household exceeding 4 individuals, the highest median family income of the applicable State for a family of 4 or fewer individuals, plus $700 [1] per month for each individual in excess of 4.

(7)(A) No judge, United States trustee (or bankruptcy administrator, if any), trustee, or other party in interest may file a motion under paragraph (2) if the current monthly income of the debtor, including a veteran (as that term is defined in section 101 of title 38), and the debtor's spouse combined, as of the date of the order for relief when multiplied by 12, is equal to or less than—

(i) in the case of a debtor in a household of 1 person, the median family income of the applicable State for 1 earner;

(ii) in the case of a debtor in a household of 2, 3, or 4 individuals, the highest median family income of the applicable State for a family of the same number or fewer individuals; or

(iii) in the case of a debtor in a household exceeding 4 individuals, the highest median family income of the applicable State for a family of 4 or fewer individuals, plus $700 [1] per month for each individual in excess of 4.

(B) In a case that is not a joint case, current monthly income of the debtor's spouse shall not be considered for purposes of subparagraph (A) if—

(i)(I) the debtor and the debtor's spouse are separated under applicable nonbankruptcy law; or

(II) the debtor and the debtor's spouse are living separate and apart, other than for the purpose of evading subparagraph (A); and

(ii) the debtor files a statement under penalty of perjury—

(I) specifying that the debtor meets the requirement of subclause (I) or (II) of clause (i); and

(II) disclosing the aggregate, or best estimate of the aggregate, amount of any cash or money payments received from the debtor's spouse attributed to the debtor's current monthly income.

(c)(1) In this subsection—

(A) the term "crime of violence" has the meaning given such term in section 16 of title 18; and

(B) the term "drug trafficking crime" has the meaning given such term in section 924(c)(2) of title 18.

(2) Except as provided in paragraph (3), after notice and a hearing, the court, on a motion by the victim of a crime of violence or a drug trafficking crime, may when it is in the best interest of the victim dismiss a voluntary case filed under this chapter by a debtor who is an individual if such individual was convicted of such crime.

(3) The court may not dismiss a case under paragraph (2) if the debtor establishes by a preponderance of the evidence that the filing of a case under this chapter is necessary to satisfy a claim for a domestic support obligation.

(Pub.L. 95–598, Nov. 6, 1978, 92 Stat. 2606; Pub.L. 98–353, Title III, §§ 312, 475, July 10, 1984, 98 Stat. 355, 381; Pub.L. 99–554, Title II, § 219, Oct. 27, 1986, 100 Stat. 3100; Pub.L. 105–183, § 4(b), June 19, 1998, 112 Stat. 518; Pub.L. 109–8, Title I, § 102(a), (f), Apr. 20, 2005, 119 Stat. 27, 33; Pub.L. 110–438, § 2, Oct. 20, 2008, 122 Stat. 5000; Pub.L. 111–320, Title II, § 202(a), Dec. 20, 2010, 124 Stat. 3509; Pub.L. 111–327, § 2(a)(25), Dec. 22, 2010, 124 Stat. 3560; Pub.L. 113–295, Div. B, Title I, § 104(b), Dec. 19, 2014, 128 Stat. 4064.)

[1] Dollar amount as adjusted by the Judicial Conference of the United States. See Adjustment of Dollar Amounts notes set out under this section and 11 U.S.C.A. § 104.

HISTORICAL AND STATUTORY NOTES

Revision Notes and Legislative Reports

1978 Acts. This section authorizes the court to dismiss a liquidation case only for cause, such as unreasonable delay by the debtor that is prejudicial to creditors or nonpayment of any fees and charges required under chapter 123 of title 28 [section 1911 et seq. of Title 28, Judiciary and Judicial Procedure]. These causes are not exhaustive, but merely illustrative. The section does not contemplate, however, that the ability of the debtor to repay his debts in whole or in part constitutes adequate cause for dismissal. To permit dismissal on that ground would be to enact a non-uniform mandatory chapter 13, in lieu of the remedy of bankruptcy. Senate Report No. 95–989.

1984 Acts. Statements by Legislative Leaders, see 1984 U.S.Code Cong. and Adm.News, p. 576.

1986 Acts. House Report No. 99–764 and House Conference Report No. 99–958, see 1986 U.S.Code Cong. and Adm. News, p. 5227.

1998 Acts. Statement by President, see 1998 U.S. Code Cong. and Adm. News, p. 230.

2005 Acts. House Report No. 109–31(Part I), see 2005 U.S. Code Cong. and Adm. News, p. 88.

Legislative Statements

Section 707 of the House amendment indicates that the court may dismiss a case only after notice and a hearing.

References in Text

Chapter 11 of this title, referred to in subsec. (b)(1), is 11 U.S.C.A. § 1101 et seq.

Chapter 13 of this title, referred to in subsec. (b)(1), (2)(A)(ii)(III), (iii)(II), is 11 U.S.C.A. § 1301 et seq.

The Family Violence Prevention and Services Act, referred to in subsec. (b)(2)(A)(ii)(I), is Pub.L. 98–457, Title III, § 301 et seq., as revised by Pub.L. 111–320, § 201, Dec. 20, 2010, 124 Stat. 3484, which is classified principally to chapter 110 of Title 42, 42 U.S.C.A. § 10401 et seq. Section 302 of the Act is classified to 42 U.S.C.A. § 10402.

Section 4973(h) of the Internal Revenue Code of 1986, referred to in subsec. (b)(2)(A)(ii)(II), is classified to 26 U.S.C.A. § 4973(h).

The Federal Rules of Bankruptcy Procedure, referred to in subsec. (b)(4)(A), (B), (5)(A), are set out in the Appendix to this title.

Effective and Applicability Provisions

2014 Acts. Amendments by Pub.L. 113–295, Div. B, Title I, § 104, shall apply with respect to cases commenced under Title 11 on or after December 19, 2014, see Pub.L. 113–295, Div. B, Title I, § 104(d), set out as a note under 11 U.S.C.A. § 521.

2013 Acts. Increase of dollar amounts by Judicial Conference of the United States by notice published Feb. 21, 2013, 78 F.R. 12089 effective April 1, 2013, and increase not applicable to cases commenced before the effective date of the adjustments, i.e., April 1, 2013. See Adjustment of Dollar Amounts notes under 11 U.S.C.A. § 104 and this section.

2010 Acts. Increase of dollar amounts by Judicial Conference of the United States by notice published Feb. 25, 2010, 75 F.R. 8747 effective April 1, 2010, and increase not applicable to cases commenced before the effective date of the adjustments, i.e., April 1, 2010. See Adjustment of Dollar Amounts notes under 11 U.S.C.A. § 104 and this section.

2008 Acts. Pub.L. 110–438, § 4, Oct. 20, 2008, 122 Stat. 5002, as amended Pub.L. 112–64, § 2, Dec. 13, 2011, 125 Stat. 766; Pub.L. 114–107, § 2, Dec. 18, 2015, 129 Stat. 2223, provided that: provided that:

"(a) **Effective date.**—Except as provided in subsection (b), this Act and the amendments made by this Act [amending this section and enacting provisions set out as a note under 11 U.S.C.A. § 101] shall take effect 60 days after the date of enactment of this Act [Oct. 20, 2008].

"(b) **Application of amendments.**—The amendments made by this Act [amending this section] shall apply only with respect to cases commenced under title 11 of the United States Code [11 U.S.C.A. § 101 et seq.] in the 11–year period beginning on the effective date of this Act [set out in this note]."

2007 Acts. Increase of dollar amounts by Judicial Conference of the United States by notice published Feb. 14, 2007, 72 F.R. 7082, modified Mar. 30, 2007, 72 F.R. 15162, effective April 1, 2007, and increase not applicable to cases commenced before the effective date of the adjustments, i.e., April 1, 2007.

See Adjustment of Dollar Amounts notes under 11 U.S.C.A. § 104 and this section.

2005 Acts. Amendments by Pub.L. 109–8 effective, except as otherwise provided, 180 days after April 20, 2005, and inapplicable with respect to cases commenced under Title 11 before the effective date, see Pub.L. 109–8, § 1501, set out as a note under 11 U.S.C.A. § 101.

1986 Acts. Amendment by Pub.L. 99–554 effective 30 days after Oct. 27, 1986, except as otherwise provided for, see section 302(a) of Pub.L. 99–554, set out as a note under section 581 of Title 28, Judiciary and Judicial Procedure.

Amendment by Pub.L. 99–554, § 219, not to become effective in or with respect to certain specified judicial districts until, or apply to cases while pending in such district before, the expiration of the 270-day period beginning 30 days after Oct. 27, 1986, or of the 30-day period beginning on the date the Attorney General certifies under section 303 of Pub.L. 99–554 the region specified in a paragraph of section 581(a) of Title 28, as amended by section 111(a) of Pub.L. 99–554, that includes such district, whichever occurs first, see section 302(d)(1) of Pub.L. 99–554, set out as a note under section 581 of Title 28.

Amendment by Pub.L. 99–554, § 219, not to become effective in or with respect to certain specified judicial districts until, or apply to cases while pending in such district before, the expiration of the 2-year period beginning 30 days after Oct. 27, 1986, or of the 30-day period beginning on the date the Attorney General certifies under section 303 of Pub.L. 99–554 the region specified in a paragraph of section 581(a) of Title 28, as amended by section 111(a) of Pub.L. 99–554, that includes such district, whichever occurs first, see section 302(d)(2) of Pub.L. 99–554, set out as a note under section 581 of Title 28.

Amendment by Pub.L. 99–554, § 219, not to become effective in or with respect to judicial districts established for the States of Alabama and North Carolina until, or apply to cases while pending in such district before, such district elects to be included in a bankruptcy region established in section 581(a) of Title 28, as amended by section 111(a) of Pub.L. 99–554, or Oct. 1, 2002, whichever occurs first, and, except as otherwise provided, with respect to cases under chapters 7, 11, 12, and 13 of Title 11 commenced before 30 days after Oct. 27, 1986, and pending in a judicial district in the States of Alabama or North Carolina before any election made under section 302(d)(3)(A) of Pub.L. 99–554 by such district becomes effective or Oct. 1, 2002, whichever occurs first, amendments by Pub.L. 99–554 not to apply until Oct. 1, 2003, or the expiration of the 1-year period beginning on the date such election becomes effective, whichever occurs first, and further, in any judicial district in Alabama or North Carolina not making the election described in section 302(d)(3)(A) of Pub.L. 99–554, any person appointed under regulations issued by the Judicial Conference to administer estates in cases under Title 11 authorized to establish, etc., a panel of private trustees, and to supervise cases and trustees in cases under chapters 7, 11, 12, and 13 of Title 11, until amendments by sections 201 to 231 of Pub.L. 99–554 effective in such district, see section 302(d)(3)(A) to (F), (H), and (I) of Pub.L. 99–554, set out as a note under section 581 of Title 28.

Amendment by Pub.L. 99–554, § 219, except as otherwise provided, with respect to cases under chapters 7, 11, 12, and 13 of Title 11 commenced before 30 days after Oct. 27, 1986, and pending in a judicial district referred to in section 581(a) of Title 28, as amended by section 111(a) of Pub.L. 99–554, for which a United States trustee is not authorized before 30 days after Oct. 27, 1986 to be appointed, not applicable until the expiration of the 3-year period beginning on Oct. 27, 1986, or of the 1-year period beginning on the date the Attorney General certifies under section 303 of Pub.L. 99–554 the region specified in a paragraph of such section 581(a) that includes, such district, whichever occurs first, see section 302(e)(1), (2) of Pub.L. 99–554, set out as a note under section 581 of Title 28.

1984 Acts. Amendment by Pub.L. 98–353 effective with respect to cases filed 90 days after July 10, 1984, see section 552(a), formerly 553(a), of Pub.L. 98–353, set out as a note under section 101 of this title.

Applicability

Applicability of amendments made by Pub.L. 105–183 to any case brought under an applicable provision of this title that is pending or commenced on or after June 19, 1998, see Pub.L. 105–153, § 5, June 19, 1998, 112 Stat. 518, set out as a note under section 544 of this title.

Adjustment of Dollar Amounts

For adjustment of dollar amounts specified in subsec. (b)(2)(A)(i)(I), (II), (ii)(IV), (B)(iv)(I), (II), (5)(B), (6)(C), (7)(A)(iii) of this section by the Judicial Conference of the United States, effective Apr. 1, 2016, see note set out under 11 U.S.C.A. § 104 of this title.

By notice dated Feb. 22, 2016, 81 F.R. 8748, the Judicial Conference of the United States adjusted the dollar amounts in provisions specified in subsec. (b)(2)(A)(i)(I), (II), (ii)(IV), (B)(iv)(I), (II), (5)(B), (6)(C), (7)(A)(iii) of this section, effective Apr. 1, 2016, as follows:

In subsec. (b)(2)(A)(i)(I) adjusted $7,475 to $7,700.

In subsec. (b)(2)(A)(i)(II) adjusted $12,475 to $12,850.

In subsec. (b)(2)(A)(ii)(IV) adjusted $1,875 to $1,925.

In subsec. (b)(2)(B)(iv)(I) adjusted $7,475 to $7,700.

In subsec. (b)(2)(B)(iv)(II) adjusted $12,475 to $12,850.

In subsec. (b)(5)(B) adjusted $1,250 to $1,300.

In subsec. (b)(6)(C) adjusted $675 to $700.

In subsec. (b)(7)(A)(iii) adjusted $675 to $700.

By notice dated Feb. 21, 2013, 78 F.R. 12089, the Judicial Conference of the United States adjusted the dollar amounts in provisions specified in subsec. (b)(2)(A)(i)(I), (II), (ii)(IV), (B)(iv)(I), (II), (5)(B), (6)(C), (7)(A)(iii) of this section, effective Apr. 1, 2013, as follows:

In subsec. (b)(2)(A)(i)(I) adjusted $7,025 to $7,475.

In subsec. (b)(2)(A)(i)(II) adjusted $11,725 to $12,475.

In subsec. (b)(2)(A)(ii)(IV) adjusted $1,775 to $1,875.

In subsec. (b)(2)(B)(iv)(I) adjusted $7,025 to $7,475.

In subsec. (b)(2)(B)(iv)(II) adjusted $11,725 to $12,475.

In subsec. (b)(5)(B) adjusted $1,175 to $1,250.

In subsec. (b)(6)(C) adjusted $625 to $675.

In subsec. (b)(7)(A)(iii) adjusted $625 to $675.

By notice dated Feb. 25, 2010, 75 F.R. 8747, the Judicial Conference of the United States adjusted the dollar amounts in provisions specified in subsec. (b)(2)(A)(i)(I), (II), (ii)(IV), (B)(iv)(I), (II), (5)(B), (6)(C), (7)(A)(iii) of this section, effective Apr. 1, 2010, as follows:

In subsec. (b)(2)(A)(i)(I) adjusted $6,575 to $7,025.

In subsec. (b)(2)(A)(i)(II) adjusted $10,950 to $11,725.

In subsec. (b)(2)(A)(ii)(IV) adjusted $1,650 to $1,775.

In subsec. (b)(2)(B)(iv)(I) adjusted $6,575 to $7,025.

In subsec. (b)(2)(B)(iv)(II) adjusted $10,950 to $11,725.

In subsec. (b)(5)(B) adjusted $1,100 to $1,175.

In subsec. (b)(6)(C) adjusted $575 to $625.

In subsec. (b)(7)(A)(iii) adjusted $575 to $625.

By notice dated Feb. 14, 2007, 72 F.R. 7082, modified Mar. 30, 2007, 72 F.R. 15162, the Judicial Conference of the United States adjusted the dollar amounts in provisions specified in subsec. (b)(2)(A)(i)(I), (II), (ii)(IV), (B)(iv)(I), (II), (5)(B), (6)(C), (7)(A)(iii) of this section, effective Apr. 1, 2007, as follows:

In subsec. (b)(2)(A)(i)(I) adjusted $6,000 to $6,575.

In subsec. (b)(2)(A)(i)(II) adjusted $10,000 to $10,950.

In subsec. (b)(2)(A)(ii)(IV) adjusted $1,500 to $1,650.

In subsec. (b)(2)(B)(iv)(I) adjusted $6,000 to $6,575.

In subsec. (b)(2)(B)(iv)(II) adjusted $10,000 to $10,950.

In subsec. (b)(5)(B) adjusted $1,000 to $1,100.

In subsec. (b)(6)(C) adjusted $525 to $575.

In subsec. (b)(7)(A)(iii) adjusted $525 to $575.

Schedules of Reasonable and Necessary Expenses

Pub.L. 109–8, Title I, § 107, Apr. 20, 2005, 119 Stat. 42, provided that: "For purposes of section 707(b) of title 11, United States Code [subsec. (b) of this section], as amended by this Act [Bankruptcy Abuse Prevention and Consumer Protection Act of 2005, Pub.L. 109–8, April 20, 2005, 119 Stat. 23, see Tables for classification], the Director of the Executive Office for United States Trustees shall, not later than 180 days after the date of enactment of this Act [April 20, 2005], issue schedules of reasonable and necessary administrative expenses of administering a chapter 13 plan [chapter 13 of this title is 11 U.S.C.A. § 1301 et seq.] for each judicial district of the United States."

Rules of Construction

Amendments made by Pub.L. 105–183 not intended to limit the applicability of the Religious Freedom Restoration Act of 1993 (42 U.S.C. 2002bb et seq.), see Pub.L. 105–183, § 6, June 19, 1998, 112 Stat. 519, set out as a note under section 544 of this title.

Rules Promulgated by Supreme Court

United States Supreme Court to prescribe general rules implementing the practice and procedure to be followed under subsec. (b) of this section, with section 2075 of Title 28, Judiciary and Judicial Procedure, to apply with respect to such general rules, see section 320 of Pub.L. 98–353, set out as a note under section 2075 of Title 28.

CROSS REFERENCES

Conversion or dismissal of,

Chapter eleven cases, see 11 USCA § 1112.

Chapter thirteen cases, see 11 USCA § 1307.

Crime victims' rights, rights afforded and best efforts to accord rights, procedures to promote compliance, see 18 USCA § 3771.

Dismissal of Chapter nine cases, see 11 USCA § 930.

Effect of dismissal, see 11 USCA § 349.

SUBCHAPTER II—COLLECTION, LIQUIDATION, AND DISTRIBUTION OF THE ESTATE

CROSS REFERENCES

Applicability of this subchapter in investor protection liquidation proceedings, see 15 USCA § 78fff.

Subchapter applicable only in case under this chapter, see 11 USCA § 103.

§ 721. Authorization to operate business

The court may authorize the trustee to operate the business of the debtor for a limited period, if such operation is in the best interest of the estate and consistent with the orderly liquidation of the estate. (Pub.L. 95–598, Nov. 6, 1978, 92 Stat. 2606.)

HISTORICAL AND STATUTORY NOTES

Revision Notes and Legislative Reports

1978 Acts. This section is derived from section 2a(5) of the Bankruptcy Act [section 11(a)(5) of former Title 11]. It permits the court to authorize the operation of any business of the debtor for a limited period, if the operation is in the best interest of the estate and consistent with orderly liquidation of the estate. An example is the operation of a watch company to convert watch movements and cases into completed watches which will bring much higher prices than the component parts would have brought. Senate Report No. 95–989.

CROSS REFERENCES

Authorization to operate business in Chapter eleven cases, see 11 USCA § 1108.

Debtor engaged in business in Chapter thirteen cases, see 11 USCA § 1304.

Executory contracts and unexpired leases, see 11 USCA § 365.

Executory contracts in stockbroker liquidation cases, see 11 USCA § 744.

Obtaining credit, see 11 USCA § 364.

Retention or replacement of professional persons, see 11 USCA § 327.

Treatment of accounts in,
    Commodity broker liquidation cases, see 11 USCA § 763.
    Stockbroker liquidation cases, see 11 USCA § 745.

Use, sale or lease of property, see 11 USCA § 363.

Utility service, see 11 USCA § 366.

§ 722. Redemption

An individual debtor may, whether or not the debtor has waived the right to redeem under this section, redeem tangible personal property intended primarily for personal, family, or household use, from a lien securing a dischargeable consumer debt, if such property is exempted under section 522 of this title or has been abandoned under section 554 of this title, by paying the holder of such lien the amount of the allowed secured claim of such holder that is secured by such lien in full at the time of redemption. (Pub.L. 95–598, Nov. 6, 1978, 92 Stat. 2606; Pub.L. 109–8, Title III, § 304(2), Apr. 20, 2005, 119 Stat. 79.)

HISTORICAL AND STATUTORY NOTES

Revision Notes and Legislative Reports

1978 Acts. This section is new and is broader than rights of redemption under the Uniform Commercial Code. It author-izes an individual debtor to redeem tangible personal property intended primarily for personal, family, or household use, from a lien securing a nonpurchase money dischargeable consumer debt. It applies only if the debtor's interest in the property is exempt or has been abandoned.

This right to redeem is a very substantial change from current law. To prevent abuses such as may occur when the debtor deliberately allows the property to depreciate in value, the debtor will be required to pay the fair market value of the goods or the amount of the claim if the claim is less. The right is personal to the debtor and not assignable. Senate Report No. 95–989.

This section is new and is broader than rights of redemption under the Uniform Commercial Code. It authorizes an individual debtor to redeem tangible personal property intended primarily for personal, family, or household use, from a lien securing a dischargeable consumer debt. It applies only if the debtor's interest in the property is exempt or has been abandoned.

The right to redeem extends to the whole of the property, not just the debtor's exempt interest in it. Thus, for example, if a debtor owned a $2,000 car, subject to a $1,200 lien, the debtor could exempt his $800 interest in the car. The debtor is permitted a $1,500 exemption in a car, proposed 11 U.S.C. 522(d)(2). This section permits him to pay the holder of the lien $1,200 and redeem the entire car, not just the remaining $700 of his exemption. The redemption is accomplished by paying the holder of the lien the amount of the allowed claim secured by the lien. The provision amounts to a right of first refusal for the debtor in consumer goods that might otherwise be repossessed. The right of redemption under this section is not waivable. House Report No. 95–595.

2005 Acts. House Report No. 109–31(Part I), see 2005 U.S. Code Cong. and Adm. News, p. 88.

Legislative Statements

Section 722 of the House amendment adopts the position taken in H.R. 8200 as passed by the House and rejects the alternative contained in section 722 of the Senate amendment.

Effective and Applicability Provisions

2005 Acts. Amendments by Pub.L. 109–8 effective, except as otherwise provided, 180 days after April 20, 2005, and inapplicable with respect to cases commenced under Title 11 before the effective date, see Pub.L. 109–8, § 1501, set out as a note under 11 U.S.C.A. § 101.

§ 723. Rights of partnership trustee against general partners

(a) If there is a deficiency of property of the estate to pay in full all claims which are allowed in a case under this chapter concerning a partnership and with respect to which a general partner of the partnership is personally liable, the trustee shall have a claim against such general partner to the extent that under applicable nonbankruptcy law such general partner is personally liable for such deficiency.

(b) To the extent practicable, the trustee shall first seek recovery of such deficiency from any general partner in such partnership that is not a debtor in a case under this title. Pending determination of such deficiency, the court may order any such partner to provide the estate with indemnity for, or assurance of payment of, any deficiency recoverable from such partner, or not to dispose of property.

(c) The trustee has a claim against the estate of each general partner in such partnership that is a debtor in a case under this title for the full amount of all claims of creditors allowed in the case concerning such partnership. Notwithstanding section 502 of this title, there shall not be allowed in such partner's case a claim against such partner on which both such partner and such partnership are liable, except to any extent that such claim is secured only by property of such partner and not by property of such partnership. The claim of the trustee under this subsection is entitled to distribution in such partner's case under section 726(a) of this title the same as any other claim of a kind specified in such section.

(d) If the aggregate that the trustee recovers from the estates of general partners under subsection (c) of this section is greater than any deficiency not recovered under subsection (b) of this section, the court, after notice and a hearing, shall determine an equitable distribution of the surplus so recovered, and the trustee shall distribute such surplus to the estates of the general partners in such partnership according to such determination.

(Pub.L. 95–598, Nov. 6, 1978, 92 Stat. 2606; Pub.L. 98–353, Title III, § 476, July 10, 1984, 98 Stat. 381; Pub.L. 103–394, Title II, § 212, Oct. 22, 1994, 108 Stat. 4125; Pub.L. 111–327, § 2(a)(26), Dec. 22, 2010, 124 Stat. 3560.)

HISTORICAL AND STATUTORY NOTES

Revision Notes and Legislative Reports

1978 Acts. This section is a significant departure from present law. It repeals the jingle rule, which, for ease of administration, denied partnership creditors their rights against general partners by permitting general partners' individual creditors to share in their estates first to the exclusion of partnership creditors. The result under this section more closely tracks generally applicable partnership law, without a significant administrative burden.

Subsection (a) specifies that each general partner in a partnership debtor is liable to the partnership's trustee for any deficiency of partnership property to pay in full all administrative expenses and all claims against the partnership.

Subsection (b) requires the trustee to seek recovery of the deficiency from any general partner that is not a debtor in a bankruptcy case. The court is empowered to order that partner to indemnify the estate or not to dispose of property pending a determination of the deficiency. The language of the subsection is directed to cases under the bankruptcy code. However, if, during the early stages of the transition period, a partner in a partnership is proceeding under the Bankruptcy Act [former Title 11] while the partnership is proceeding under the bankruptcy code, the trustee should not first seek recovery against the Bankruptcy Act partner. Rather, the Bankruptcy Act partner should be deemed for the purposes of this section and the rights of the trustee to be proceeding under title 11.

Subsection (c) requires the partnership trustee to seek recovery of the full amount of the deficiency from the estate of each general partner that is a debtor in a bankruptcy case. The trustee will share equally with the partners' individual creditors in the assets of the partners' estates. Claims of partnership creditors who may have filed against the partner will be disallowed to avoid double counting.

Subsection (d) provides for the case where the total recovery from all of the bankrupt general partners is greater than the deficiency of which the trustee sought recovery. This case would most likely occur for a partnership with a large number of general partners. If the situation arises, the court is required to determine an equitable redistribution of the surplus to the estate of the general partners. The determination will be based on factors such as the relative liability of each of the general partners under the partnership agreement and the relative rights of each of the general partners in the profits of the enterprise under the partnership agreement. Senate Report No. 95–989.

1984 Acts. Statements by Legislative Leaders, see 1984 U.S.Code Cong. and Adm.News, p. 576.

1994 Acts. House Report No. 103–835, see 1994 U.S. Code Cong. and Adm. News, p. 3340.

Legislative Statements

Section 723(c) of the House amendment is a compromise between similar provisions contained in the House bill and Senate amendment. The section makes clear that the trustee of a partnership has a claim against each general partner for the full amount of all claims of creditors allowed in the case concerning the partnership. By restricting the trustee's rights to claims of "creditors," the trustee of the partnership will not have a claim against the general partners for administrative expenses or claims allowed in the case concerning the partnership. As under present law, sections of the Bankruptcy Act [former title 11] applying to codebtors and sureties apply to the relationship of a partner with respect to a partnership debtor. See sections 501(b), 502(e), 506(d)(2), 509, 524(d), and 1301 of title 11.

Effective and Applicability Provisions

1994 Acts. Amendment by Pub.L. 103–394 effective on Oct. 22, 1994, and not to apply with respect to cases commenced under Title 11 of the United States Code before Oct. 22, 1994, see section 702 of Pub.L. 103–394, set out as a note under section 101 of this title.

1984 Acts. Amendment by Pub.L. 98–353 effective with respect to cases filed 90 days after July 10, 1984, see section 552(a), formerly 553(a), of Pub.L. 98–353, set out as a note under section 101 of this title.

Separability of Provisions

If any provision of or amendment made by Pub.L. 103–394 or the application of such provision or amendment to any person or circumstance is held to be unconstitutional, the remaining provisions of and amendments made by Pub.L. 103–394 and the application of such provisions and amendments to any person or circumstance shall not be affected thereby, see section 701 of Pub.L. 103–394, set out as a note under section 101 of this title.

CROSS REFERENCES

Property of estate, see 11 USCA § 541.

---

§ 724.   Treatment of certain liens

(a) The trustee may avoid a lien that secures a claim of a kind specified in section 726(a)(4) of this title.

(b) Property in which the estate has an interest and that is subject to a lien that is not avoidable under this title (other than to the extent that there is a properly perfected unavoidable tax lien arising in connection with an ad valorem tax on real or personal property of the estate) and that secures an allowed claim for a tax, or proceeds of such property, shall be distributed—

(1) first, to any holder of an allowed claim secured by a lien on such property that is not avoidable under this title and that is senior to such tax lien;

(2) second, to any holder of a claim of a kind specified in section 507(a)(1)(C) or 507(a)(2) (except that such expenses under each such section, other than claims for wages, salaries, or commissions that arise after the date of the filing of the petition, shall be limited to expenses incurred under this chapter and shall not include expenses incurred under chapter 11 of this title), 507(a)(1)(A), 507(a)(1)(B), 507(a)(3), 507(a)(4), 507(a)(5), 507(a)(6), or 507(a)(7) of this title, to the extent of the amount of such allowed tax claim that is secured by such tax lien;

(3) third, to the holder of such tax lien, to any extent that such holder's allowed tax claim that is secured by such tax lien exceeds any amount distributed under paragraph (2) of this subsection;

(4) fourth, to any holder of an allowed claim secured by a lien on such property that is not avoidable under this title and that is junior to such tax lien;

(5) fifth, to the holder of such tax lien, to the extent that such holder's allowed claim secured by such tax lien is not paid under paragraph (3) of this subsection; and

(6) sixth, to the estate.

(c) If more than one holder of a claim is entitled to distribution under a particular paragraph of subsection (b) of this section, distribution to such holders under such paragraph shall be in the same order as distribution to such holders would have been other than under this section.

(d) A statutory lien the priority of which is determined in the same manner as the priority of a tax lien under section 6323 of the Internal Revenue Code of 1986 shall be treated under subsection (b) of this section the same as if such lien were a tax lien.

(e) Before subordinating a tax lien on real or personal property of the estate, the trustee shall—

(1) exhaust the unencumbered assets of the estate; and

(2) in a manner consistent with section 506(c), recover from property securing an allowed secured claim the reasonable, necessary costs and expenses of preserving or disposing of such property.

(f) Notwithstanding the exclusion of ad valorem tax liens under this section and subject to the requirements of subsection (e), the following may be paid from property of the estate which secures a tax lien, or the proceeds of such property:

(1) Claims for wages, salaries, and commissions that are entitled to priority under section 507(a)(4).

(2) Claims for contributions to an employee benefit plan entitled to priority under section 507(a)(5).

(Pub.L. 95–598, Nov. 6, 1978, 92 Stat. 2607; Pub.L. 98–353, Title III, § 477, July 10, 1984, 98 Stat. 381; Pub.L. 99–554, Title II, § 283(r), Oct. 27, 1986, 100 Stat. 3118; Pub.L. 103–394, Title III, § 304(h)(4), Title V, § 501(d)(23), Oct. 22, 1994, 108 Stat. 4134, 4146; Pub.L. 109–8, Title VII, § 701(a), Apr. 20, 2005, 119 Stat. 124; Pub.L. 111–327, § 2(a)(27), Dec. 22, 2010, 124 Stat. 3560.)

HISTORICAL AND STATUTORY NOTES

Revision Notes and Legislative Reports

1978 Acts. Subsection (a) of section 724 permits the trustee to avoid a lien that secures a fine, penalty, forfeiture, or multiple, punitive, or exemplary damages claim to the extent that the claim is not compensation for actual pecuniary loss. The subsection follows the policy found in section 57j of the Bankruptcy Act [section 93(j) of former Title 11] of protecting unsecured creditors from the debtor's wrongdoing, but expands the protection afforded. The lien is made voidable rather than void in chapter 7, in order to permit the lien to be revived if the case is converted to chapter 11 under which penalty liens are not voidable. To make the lien void would be to permit the filing of a chapter 7, the voiding of the lien, and the conversion to a chapter 11, simply to avoid a penalty lien, which should be valid in a reorganization case.

Subsection (b) governs tax liens. This provision retains the rule of present bankruptcy law (section 67(C)(3) of the Bankruptcy Act [section 107(c)(3) of former Title 11]) that a tax lien on personal property, if not avoidable by the trustee, is subordinated in payment to unsecured claims having a higher priority than unsecured tax claims. Those other claims may be satisfied from the amount that would otherwise have been applied to the tax lien, and any excess of the amount of the lien is then applied to the tax. Any personal property (or sale proceeds) remaining is to be used to satisfy claims secured by liens which are junior to the tax lien. Any proceeds remaining are next applied to pay any unpaid balance of the tax lien.

Subsection (d) specifies that any statutory lien whose priority is determined in the same manner as a tax lien is to be treated as a tax lien under this section, even if the lien does not secure a claim for taxes. An example is the ERISA [29 U.S.C.A. § 1001 et seq.] lien. Senate Report No. 95–989.

Subsection (b) governs tax liens. It is derived from section 67c(3) of the Bankruptcy Act [section 107(c)(3) of former Title 11], without substantial modification in result. It subordinates tax liens to administrative expense and wage claims, and solves certain circuity of liens problems that arise in connection with the subordination. The order of distribution of property subject to a tax lien is as follows: First, to holders of liens senior to the tax lien; second, to administrative expenses, wage claims, and consumer creditors that are granted priority, but only to the extent of the amount of the allowed tax claim secured by the lien. In other words, the priority claimants step into the shoes of the tax collector. Third, to the tax claimant, to the extent that priority claimants did not use up his entire claim. Fourth, to junior lien holders. Fifth, to the tax collector to the extent that he was not paid under paragraph (3). Finally, any remaining property goes to the estate. The result of these provisions are to leave senior and junior lienors and holders of unsecured claims undisturbed. If there are any liens that are equal in status to the tax lien, they share pari passu with the tax lien under the distribution provisions of this subsection. House Report No. 95–595.

1984 Acts. Statements by Legislative Leaders, see 1984 U.S.Code Cong. and Adm.News, p. 576.

1986 Acts. House Report No. 99–764 and House Conference Report No. 99–958, see 1986 U.S.Code Cong. and Adm. News, p. 5227.

House Conference Report No. 99–841 and Statement by President, see 1986 U.S.Code Cong. and Adm.News, p. 4075.

1994 Acts. House Report No. 103–835, see 1994 U.S. Code Cong. and Adm. News, p. 3340.

2005 Acts. House Report No. 109–31(Part I), see 2005 U.S. Code Cong. and Adm. News, p. 88.

Legislative Statements

Section 724 of the House amendment adopts the provision taken in the House bill and rejects the provision taken in the Senate amendment. In effect, a tax claim secured by a lien is treated as a claim between the fifth and sixth priority in a case under chapter 7 rather than as a secured claim.

Treatment of certain liens: The House amendment modifies present law by requiring the subordination of tax liens on both real and personal property to the payment of claims having a priority. This means that assets are to be distributed from the debtor's estate to pay higher priority claims before the tax claims are paid, even though the tax claims are properly secured. Under present law and the Senate amendment only tax liens on personal property, but not on real property, are subordinated to the payment of claims having a priority above the priority for tax claims.

References in Text

Chapter 11 of this title, referred to in subsec. (b)(2), is 11 U.S.C.A. § 1101 et seq.

Section 6323 of the Internal Revenue Code of 1986, referred to in subsec. (d), is classified to section 6323 of Title 26, Internal Revenue Code.

Effective and Applicability Provisions

2005 Acts. Amendments by Pub.L. 109–8 effective, except as otherwise provided, 180 days after April 20, 2005, and inapplicable with respect to cases commenced under Title 11 before the effective date, see Pub.L. 109–8, § 1501, set out as a note under 11 U.S.C.A. § 101.

1994 Acts. Amendments by Pub.L. 103–394 effective on Oct. 22, 1994, and not to apply with respect to cases commenced under Title 11 of the United States Code before Oct. 22, 1994, see section 702 of Pub.L. 103–394, set out as a note under section 101 of this title.

1986 Acts. Amendment by Pub.L. 99–554 effective 30 days after Oct. 27, 1986, except as otherwise provided, see section 302(a) of Pub.L. 99–554, set out as a note under section 581 of Title 28, Judiciary and Judicial Procedure.

1984 Acts. Amendment by Pub.L. 98–353 effective with respect to cases filed 90 days after July 10, 1984, see section 552(a), formerly 553(a), of Pub.L. 98–353, set out as a note under section 101 of this title.

Separability of Provisions

If any provision of or amendment made by Pub.L. 103–394 or the application of such provision or amendment to any person or circumstance is held to be unconstitutional, the remaining provisions of and amendments made by Pub.L. 103–394 and the application of such provisions and amendments to any person or circumstance shall not be affected thereby, see section 701 of Pub.L. 103–394, set out as a note under section 101 of this title.

CROSS REFERENCES

Automatic preservation of avoided transfer, see 11 USCA § 551.

Commencement of involuntary cases by transferees of voidable transfers, see 11 USCA § 303.

Disallowance of claims of entity that is transferee of avoidable transfer, see 11 USCA § 502.

Effect of dismissal, see 11 USCA § 349.

Exemptions, see 11 USCA § 522.

Liability of transferee of avoided transfer, see 11 USCA § 550.

Recovery of voidable transfers in investor protection liquidation proceedings, see 15 USCA § 78fff–2.

Voidable transfers in commodity broker liquidation cases, see 11 USCA § 764.

§ 725. Disposition of certain property

After the commencement of a case under this chapter, but before final distribution of property of the estate under section 726 of this title, the trustee, after notice and a hearing, shall dispose of any property in which an entity other than the estate has an interest, such as a lien, and that has not been disposed of under another section of this title.

(Pub.L. 95–598, Nov. 6, 1978, 92 Stat. 2607; Pub.L. 98–353, Title III, § 478, July 10, 1984, 98 Stat. 381.)

HISTORICAL AND STATUTORY NOTES

Revision Notes and Legislative Reports

1978 Acts. This section requires the court to determine the appropriate disposition of property in which the estate and an entity other than the estate have an interest. It would apply, for example, to property subject to a lien or property co-owned by the estate and another entity. The court must make the determination with respect to property that is not disposed of under another section of the bankruptcy code, such as by abandonment under section 554, by sale or distribution under 363, or by allowing foreclosure by a secured creditor by lifting the stay under section 362. The purpose of the section is to give the court appropriate authority to ensure that collateral or its proceeds is returned to the proper secured creditor, that consigned or bailed goods are returned to the consignor or bailor and so on. Current law is curiously silent on this point, though case law has grown to fill the void. The section is in lieu of a section that would direct a certain distribution to secured creditors. It gives the court greater flexibility to meet the circumstances, and it is broader, permitting disposition of property subject to a co-ownership interest. Senate Report No. 95–989.

1984 Acts. Statements by Legislative Leaders, see 1984 U.S.Code Cong. and Adm.News, p. 576.

Legislative Statements

Section 725 of the House amendment adopts the substance contained in both the House bill and Senate amendment but transfers an administrative function to the trustee in accordance with the general thrust of this legislation to separate the administrative and the judicial functions where appropriate.

Effective and Applicability Provisions

1984 Acts. Amendment by Pub.L. 98–353 effective with respect to cases filed 90 days after July 10, 1984, see section 552(a), formerly 553(a), of Pub.L. 98–353, set out as a note under section 101 of this title.

§ 726. Distribution of property of the estate

(a) Except as provided in section 510 of this title, property of the estate shall be distributed—

(1) first, in payment of claims of the kind specified in, and in the order specified in, section 507 of this title, proof of which is timely filed under section 501 of this title or tardily filed on or before the earlier of—

(A) the date that is 10 days after the mailing to creditors of the summary of the trustee's final report; or

(B) the date on which the trustee commences final distribution under this section;

(2) second, in payment of any allowed unsecured claim, other than a claim of a kind specified in paragraph (1), (3), or (4) of this subsection, proof of which is—

(A) timely filed under section 501(a) of this title;

(B) timely filed under section 501(b) or 501(c) of this title; or

(C) tardily filed under section 501(a) of this title, if—

(i) the creditor that holds such claim did not have notice or actual knowledge of the case in time for timely filing of a proof of such claim under section 501(a) of this title; and

(ii) proof of such claim is filed in time to permit payment of such claim;

(3) third, in payment of any allowed unsecured claim proof of which is tardily filed under section 501(a) of this title, other than a claim of the kind specified in paragraph (2)(C) of this subsection;

(4) fourth, in payment of any allowed claim, whether secured or unsecured, for any fine, penalty, or forfeiture, or for multiple, exemplary, or punitive damages, arising before the earlier of the order for relief or the appointment of a trustee, to the extent that such fine, penalty, forfeiture, or damages are not compensation for actual pecuniary loss suffered by the holder of such claim;

(5) fifth, in payment of interest at the legal rate from the date of the filing of the petition, on any claim paid under paragraph (1), (2), (3), or (4) of this subsection; and

(6) sixth, to the debtor.

(b) Payment on claims of a kind specified in paragraph (1), (2), (3), (4), (5), (6), (7), (8), (9), or (10) of section 507(a) of this title, or in paragraph (2), (3), (4), or (5) of subsection (a) of this section, shall be made pro rata among claims of the kind specified in each such particular paragraph, except that in a case that has been converted to this chapter under section 1112, 1208, or 1307 of this title, a claim allowed under section 503(b) of this title incurred under this chapter after such conversion has priority over a claim allowed under section 503(b) of this title incurred under any other chapter of this title or under this chapter before such conversion and over any expenses of a custodian superseded under section 543 of this title.

(c) Notwithstanding subsections (a) and (b) of this section, if there is property of the kind specified in section 541(a)(2) of this title, or proceeds of such property, in the estate, such property or proceeds shall be segregated from other property of the estate, and such property or proceeds and other property of the estate shall be distributed as follows:

(1) Claims allowed under section 503 of this title shall be paid either from property of the kind specified in section 541(a)(2) of this title, or from other property of the estate, as the interest of justice requires.

(2) Allowed claims, other than claims allowed under section 503 of this title, shall be paid in the order specified in subsection (a) of this section, and, with respect to claims of a kind specified in a particular paragraph of section 507 of this title or subsection (a) of this section, in the following order and manner:

(A) First, community claims against the debtor or the debtor's spouse shall be paid from property of the kind specified in section 541(a)(2) of this title, except to the extent that such property is solely liable for debts of the debtor.

(B) Second, to the extent that community claims against the debtor are not paid under subparagraph (A) of this paragraph, such community claims shall be paid from property of the kind specified in section 541(a)(2) of this title that is solely liable for debts of the debtor.

(C) Third, to the extent that all claims against the debtor including community claims against the debtor are not paid under subparagraph (A) or (B) of this paragraph such claims shall be paid from property of the estate other than property of the kind specified in section 541(a)(2) of this title.

(D) Fourth, to the extent that community claims against the debtor or the debtor's spouse are not paid under subparagraph (A), (B), or (C) of this paragraph, such claims shall be paid from all remaining property of the estate.

(Pub.L. 95–598, Nov. 6, 1978, 92 Stat. 2608; Pub.L. 98–353, Title III, § 479, July 10, 1984, 98 Stat. 381; Pub.L. 99–554, Title II, §§ 257(r), 283(s), Oct. 27, 1986, 100 Stat. 3115, 3118; Pub.L. 103–394, Title II, § 213(b), Title III, § 304(h)(5), Title V, § 501(d)(24), Oct. 22, 1994, 108 Stat. 4126, 4134, 4146; Pub.L. 109–8, Title VII, § 713, Title XII, § 1215, Apr. 20, 2005, 119 Stat. 128, 195; Pub.L. 111–327, § 2(a)(28), Dec. 22, 2010, 124 Stat. 3560.)

HISTORICAL AND STATUTORY NOTES

Revision Notes and Legislative Reports

1978 Acts. This section is the general distribution section for liquidation cases. It dictates the order in which distribution of property of the estate, which has usually been reduced to money by the trustee under the requirements of section 704(1).

First, property is distributed among priority claimants, as determined by section 507, and in the order prescribed by section 507. Second, distribution is to general unsecured creditors. This class excludes priority creditors and the two classes of subordinated creditors specified below. The provision is written to permit distribution to creditors that tardily file claims if their tardiness was due to lack of notice or knowledge of the case. Though it is in the interest of the estate to encourage timely filing, when tardy filing is not the result of a failure to act by the creditor, the normal subordination penalty should not apply. Third distribution is to general unsecured creditors who tardily file. Fourth distribution is to holders of fine, penalty, forfeiture, or multiple, punitive, or exemplary damage claims. More of these claims are disallowed entirely under present law. They are simply subordinated here.

Paragraph (4) provides that punitive penalties, including prepetition tax penalties, are subordinated to the payment of all other classes of claims, except claims for interest accruing during the case. In effect, these penalties are payable out of the estate's assets only if and to the extent that a surplus of assets would otherwise remain at the close of the case for distribution back to the debtor.

Paragraph (5) provides that postpetition interest on prepetition claims is also to be paid to the creditor in a subordinated position. Like prepetition penalties, such interest will be paid from the estate only if and to the extent that a surplus of assets would otherwise remain for return to the debtor at the close of the case.

This section also specifies that interest accrued on all claims (including priority and nonpriority tax claims) which accrued before the date of the filing of the title 11 petition is to be paid in the same order of distribution of the estate's assets as the principal amount of the related claims.

Any surplus is paid to the debtor under paragraph (6).

Subsection (b) follows current law. It specifies that claims within a particular class are to be paid pro rata. This provision will apply, of course, only when there are inadequate funds to pay the holders of claims of a particular class in full. The exception found in the section, which also follows current law, specifies that liquidation administrative expenses are to be paid ahead of reorganization administrative expenses if the case has been converted from a reorganization case to a liquidation case, or from an individual repayment plan case to a liquidation case.

Subsection (c) governs distributions in cases in which there is community property and other property of the estate. The section requires the two kinds of property to be segregated. The distribution is as follows: First, administrative expenses are to be paid, as the court determines on any reasonable equitable basis, from both kinds of property. The court will divide administrative expenses according to such factors as the amount of each kind of property in the estate, the cost of preservation and liquidation of each kind of property, and whether any particular administrative expenses are attributable to one kind of property or the other. Second, claims are to be paid as provided under subsection (a) (the normal liquidation case distribution rules) in the following order and manner: First, community claims against the debtor or the debtor's spouse are paid from community property, except such as is liable solely for the debts of the debtor.

Second, community claims against the debtor, to the extent not paid under the first provision, are paid from community property that is solely liable for the debts of the debtor. Third, community claims, to the extent they remain unpaid, and all other claims against the debtor, are paid from noncommunity property. Fourth, if any community claims against the debtor or the debtor's spouse remain unpaid, they are paid from whatever property remains in the estate. This would occur if community claims against the debtor's spouse are large in amount and most of the estate's property is property solely liable, under nonbankruptcy law, for debts of the debtor.

The marshalling rules in this section apply only to property of the estate. However, they will provide a guide to the courts in the interpretation of proposed 11 U.S.C. 725, relating to distribution of collateral, in cases in which there is community property. If a secured creditor has a lien on both community and non-community property, the marshalling rules here—by analogy would dictate that the creditor be satisfied first out of community property, and then out of separate property. Senate Report No. 95–989.

1984 Acts. Statements by Legislative Leaders, see 1984 U.S.Code Cong. and Adm.News, p. 576.

1986 Acts. House Report No. 99–764 and House Conference Report No. 99–958, see 1986 U.S.Code Cong. and Adm. News, p. 5227.

1994 Acts. House Report No. 103–835, see 1994 U.S. Code Cong. and Adm. News, p. 3340.

2005 Acts. House Report No. 109–31(Part I), see 2005 U.S. Code Cong. and Adm. News, p. 88.

Legislative Statements

Section 726(a)(4) adopts a provision contained in the Senate amendment subordinating prepetition penalties and penalties arising in the involuntary gap period to the extent the penalties are not compensation for actual pecuniary laws.

The House amendment deletes a provision following section 726(a)(6) of the Senate amendment providing that the term "claim" includes interest due owed before the date of the filing of the petition as unnecessary since a right to payment for interest due is a right to payment which is within the definition of "claim" in section 101(4) of the House amendment.

Effective and Applicability Provisions

2005 Acts. Amendments by Pub.L. 109–8 effective, except as otherwise provided, 180 days after April 20, 2005, and inapplicable with respect to cases commenced under Title 11 before the effective date, see Pub.L. 109–8, § 1501, set out as a note under 11 U.S.C.A. § 101.

1994 Acts. Amendments by Pub.L. 103–394 effective on Oct. 22, 1994, and not to apply with respect to cases commenced under Title 11 of the United States Code before Oct. 22, 1994, see section 702 of Pub.L. 103–394, set out as a note under section 101 of this title.

1986 Acts. Amendments by Pub.L. 99–554, § 257(r), effective 30 days after Oct. 27, 1986, but not to apply with respect to cases commenced under this title before that date, see section 302(a), (c)(1) of Pub.L. 99–554, set out as a note under section 581 of Title 28, Judiciary and Judicial Procedure.

Amendment by Pub.L. 99–554, § 283, effective 30 days after Oct. 27, 1986, see section 302(a) of Pub.L. 99–554, set out as a note under section 581 of Title 28.

1984 Acts. Amendment by Pub.L. 98–353 effective with respect to cases filed 90 days after July 10, 1984, see section 552(a), formerly 553(a), of Pub.L. 98–353, set out as a note under section 101 of this title.

Separability of Provisions

If any provision of or amendment made by Pub.L. 103–394 or the application of such provision or amendment to any person or circumstance is held to be unconstitutional, the remaining provisions of and amendments made by Pub.L. 103–394 and the application of such provisions and amendments to any person or circumstance shall not be affected thereby, see section 701 of Pub.L. 103–394, set out as a note under section 101 of this title.

CROSS REFERENCES

Customer property, distribution in,

    Commodity broker liquidation cases, see 11 USCA § 766.

    Stockbroker liquidation cases, see 11 USCA § 752.

Distribution in Chapter eleven cases, see 11 USCA § 1143.

Distribution of securities in stockbroker liquidation cases, see 11 USCA § 750.

Election of creditors holding certain claims entitled to distribution to creditors' committee, see 11 USCA § 705.

Election of trustee by creditors holding claims entitled to distribution, see 11 USCA § 702.

Impairment of claims and interests and objection to claims filed untimely, see 11 USCA § 502.

Ownership of copyright, see 17 USCA § 201.

Payment stopped on checks remaining unpaid 90 days after final distribution, see 11 USCA § 347.

Priorities of distribution in investor liquidation proceedings, see 15 USCA § 78fff.

Student Loan Marketing Association of the Robert T. Stafford Student Loan Program deemed person within meaning of this title for purposes of distribution of its property pursuant to this section, see 20 USCA § 1087–2.

§ 727. Discharge

(a) The court shall grant the debtor a discharge, unless—

(1) the debtor is not an individual;

(2) the debtor, with intent to hinder, delay, or defraud a creditor or an officer of the estate charged with custody of property under this title, has transferred, removed, destroyed, mutilated, or concealed, or has permitted to be transferred, removed, destroyed, mutilated, or concealed—

    (A) property of the debtor, within one year before the date of the filing of the petition; or

    (B) property of the estate, after the date of the filing of the petition;

(3) the debtor has concealed, destroyed, mutilated, falsified, or failed to keep or preserve any recorded information, including books, documents, records, and papers, from which the debtor's financial condition or business transactions might be ascertained, unless such act or failure to act was justified under all of the circumstances of the case;

(4) the debtor knowingly and fraudulently, in or in connection with the case—

    (A) made a false oath or account;

    (B) presented or used a false claim;

    (C) gave, offered, received, or attempted to obtain money, property, or advantage, or a promise of money, property, or advantage, for acting or forbearing to act; or

    (D) withheld from an officer of the estate entitled to possession under this title, any recorded information, including books, documents, records, and papers, relating to the debtor's property or financial affairs;

(5) the debtor has failed to explain satisfactorily, before determination of denial of discharge under this paragraph, any loss of assets or deficiency of assets to meet the debtor's liabilities;

(6) the debtor has refused, in the case—

    (A) to obey any lawful order of the court, other than an order to respond to a material question or to testify;

    (B) on the ground of privilege against self-incrimination, to respond to a material question approved by the court or to testify, after the debtor has been granted immunity with respect to the matter concerning which such privilege was invoked; or

    (C) on a ground other than the properly invoked privilege against self-incrimination, to respond to a material question approved by the court or to testify;

(7) the debtor has committed any act specified in paragraph (2), (3), (4), (5), or (6) of this subsection, on or within one year before the date of the filing of the petition, or during the case, in connection with another case, under this title or under the Bankruptcy Act, concerning an insider;

(8) the debtor has been granted a discharge under this section, under section 1141 of this title, or

under section 14, 371, or 476 of the Bankruptcy Act, in a case commenced within 8 years before the date of the filing of the petition;

(9) the debtor has been granted a discharge under section 1228 or 1328 of this title, or under section 660 or 661 of the Bankruptcy Act, in a case commenced within six years before the date of the filing of the petition, unless payments under the plan in such case totaled at least—

(A) 100 percent of the allowed unsecured claims in such case; or

(B)(i) 70 percent of such claims; and

(ii) the plan was proposed by the debtor in good faith, and was the debtor's best effort;

(10) the court approves a written waiver of discharge executed by the debtor after the order for relief under this chapter;

(11) after filing the petition, the debtor failed to complete an instructional course concerning personal financial management described in section 111, except that this paragraph shall not apply with respect to a debtor who is a person described in section 109(h)(4) or who resides in a district for which the United States trustee (or the bankruptcy administrator, if any) determines that the approved instructional courses are not adequate to service the additional individuals who would otherwise be required to complete such instructional courses under this section (The United States trustee (or the bankruptcy administrator, if any) who makes a determination described in this paragraph shall review such determination not later than 1 year after the date of such determination, and not less frequently than annually thereafter.); or

(12) the court after notice and a hearing held not more than 10 days before the date of the entry of the order granting the discharge finds that there is reasonable cause to believe that—

(A) section 522(q)(1) may be applicable to the debtor; and

(B) there is pending any proceeding in which the debtor may be found guilty of a felony of the kind described in section 522(q)(1)(A) or liable for a debt of the kind described in section 522(q)(1)(B).

(b) Except as provided in section 523 of this title, a discharge under subsection (a) of this section discharges the debtor from all debts that arose before the date of the order for relief under this chapter, and any liability on a claim that is determined under section 502 of this title as if such claim had arisen before the commencement of the case, whether or not a proof of claim based on any such debt or liability is filed under section 501 of this title, and whether or not a claim based on any such debt or liability is allowed under section 502 of this title.

(c)(1) The trustee, a creditor, or the United States trustee may object to the granting of a discharge under subsection (a) of this section.

(2) On request of a party in interest, the court may order the trustee to examine the acts and conduct of the debtor to determine whether a ground exists for denial of discharge.

(d) On request of the trustee, a creditor, or the United States trustee, and after notice and a hearing, the court shall revoke a discharge granted under subsection (a) of this section if—

(1) such discharge was obtained through the fraud of the debtor, and the requesting party did not know of such fraud until after the granting of such discharge;

(2) the debtor acquired property that is property of the estate, or became entitled to acquire property that would be property of the estate, and knowingly and fraudulently failed to report the acquisition of or entitlement to such property, or to deliver or surrender such property to the trustee;

(3) the debtor committed an act specified in subsection (a)(6) of this section; or

(4) the debtor has failed to explain satisfactorily—

(A) a material misstatement in an audit referred to in section 586(f) of title 28; or

(B) a failure to make available for inspection all necessary accounts, papers, documents, financial records, files, and all other papers, things, or property belonging to the debtor that are requested for an audit referred to in section 586(f) of title 28.

(e) The trustee, a creditor, or the United States trustee may request a revocation of a discharge—

(1) under subsection (d)(1) of this section within one year after such discharge is granted; or

(2) under subsection (d)(2) or (d)(3) of this section before the later of—

(A) one year after the granting of such discharge; and

(B) the date the case is closed.

(Pub.L. 95–598, Nov. 6, 1978, 92 Stat. 2609; Pub.L. 98–353, Title III, § 480, July 10, 1984, 98 Stat. 382; Pub.L. 99–554, Title II, §§ 220, 257(s), Oct. 27, 1986, 100 Stat. 3101, 3116; Pub.L. 109–8, Title I, § 106(b), Title III, §§ 312(1), 330(a), Title VI, § 603(d), Apr. 20, 2005, 119 Stat. 38, 86, 101, 123.)

HISTORICAL AND STATUTORY NOTES

Revision Notes and Legislative Reports

1978 Acts. This section is the heart of the fresh start provisions of the bankruptcy law. Subsection (a) requires the court to grant a debtor a discharge unless one of nine conditions is met. The first condition is that the debtor is not an individual. This is a change from present law, under which corporations and partnerships may be discharged in liquidation cases, though they rarely are. The change in policy will avoid trafficking in corporate shells and in bankrupt partnerships. "Individual" includes a deceased individual, so that if the debtor dies during the bankruptcy case, he will nevertheless be released from his debts, and his estate will not be liable for them. Creditors will be entitled to only one satisfaction—from the bankruptcy estate and not from the probate estate.

The next three grounds for denial of discharge center on the debtor's wrongdoing in or in connection with the bankruptcy case. They are derived from Bankruptcy Act § 14c [section 32(c) of former Title 11]. If the debtor, with intent to hinder, delay, or defraud his creditors or an officer of the estate, has transferred, removed, destroyed, mutilated, or concealed, or has permitted any such action with respect to, property of the debtor within the year preceding the case, or property of the estate after the commencement of the case, then the debtor is denied discharge. The debtor is also denied discharge if he has concealed, destroyed, mutilated, falsified, or failed to keep or preserve any books and records from which his financial condition might be ascertained, unless the act or failure to act was justified under all the circumstances of the case. The fourth ground for denial of discharge is the commission of a bankruptcy crime, although the standard of proof is preponderance of the evidence rather than proof beyond a reasonable doubt. These crimes include the making of a false oath or account, the use or presentation of a false claim, the giving or receiving of money for acting or forbearing to act, and the withholding from an officer of the estate entitled to possession of books and records relating to the debtor's financial affairs.

The fifth ground for denial of discharge is the failure of the debtor to explain satisfactorily any loss of assets or deficiency of assets to meet the debtor's liabilities. The sixth ground concerns refusal to testify. It is a change from present law, under which the debtor may be denied discharge for legitimately exercising his right against self-incrimination. Under this provision, the debtor may be denied discharge if he refuses to obey any lawful order of the court, or if he refuses to testify after having been granted immunity or after improperly invoking the constitutional privilege against self-incrimination.

The seventh ground for denial of discharge is the commission of an act specified in grounds two through six during the year before the debtor's case in connection with another bankruptcy case concerning an insider.

The eighth ground for denial of discharge is derived from § 14c(5) of the Bankruptcy Act [section 32(c)(5) of former Title 11]. If the debtor has been granted a discharge in a case commenced within 6 years preceding the present bankruptcy case, he is denied discharge. This provision, which is no change from current law with respect to straight bankruptcy, is the 6-year bar to discharge. Discharge under chapter 11 will bar a discharge for 6 years. As under current law, confirmation of a composition wage earner plan under chapter 13 is a basis for invoking the 6-year bar.

The ninth ground is approval by the court of a waiver of discharge.

Subsection (b) specifies that the discharge granted under this section discharges the debtor from all debts that arose before the date of the order for relief. It is irrelevant whether or not a proof of claim was filed with respect to the debt, and whether or not the claim based on the debt was allowed.

Subsection (c) permits the trustee, or a creditor, to object to discharge. It also permits the court, on request of a party

in interest, to order the trustee to examine the acts and conduct of the debtor to determine whether a ground for denial of discharge exists.

Subsection (d) requires the court to revoke a discharge already granted in certain circumstances. If the debtor obtained the discharge through fraud, if he acquired and concealed property of the estate, or if he refused to obey a court order or to testify, the discharge is to be revoked.

Subsection (e) permits the trustee or a creditor to request revocation of a discharge within 1 year after the discharge is granted, on the grounds of fraud, and within one year of discharge or the date of the closing of the case, whichever is later, on other grounds. Senate Report No. 95–989.

1984 Acts. Statements by Legislative Leaders, see 1984 U.S.Code Cong. and Adm.News, p. 576.

1986 Acts. House Report No. 99–764 and House Conference Report No. 99–958, see 1986 U.S.Code Cong. and Adm. News, p. 5227.

2005 Acts. House Report No. 109–31(Part I), see 2005 U.S. Code Cong. and Adm. News, p. 88.

Legislative Statements

Sections 727(a)(8) and (9) of the House amendment represent a compromise between provisions contained in section 727(a)(8) of the House bill and Senate amendment. Section 727(a)(8) of the House amendment adopts section 727(a)(8) of the House bill. However, section 727(a)(9) of the House amendment contains a compromise based on section 727(a)(8) of the Senate amendment with respect to the circumstances under which a plan by way of composition under Chapter XIII of the Bankruptcy Act [chapter 13 of former Title 11 (section 1001 et seq.)] should be a bar to discharge in a subsequent proceeding under Title 11. The paragraph provides that a discharge under section 660 or 661 of the Bankruptcy Act [sections 1060 or 1061 of former Title 11] or section 1328 of Title 11 in a case commenced within 6 years before the date of the filing of the petition in a subsequent case, operates as a bar to discharge unless, first, payments under the plan totaled at least 100 percent of the allowed unsecured claims in the case; or second, payments under the plan totaled at least 70 percent of the allowed unsecured claims in the case and the plan was proposed by the debtor in good faith and was the debtor's best effort.

It is expected that the Rules of Bankruptcy Procedure will contain a provision permitting the debtor to request a determination of whether a plan is the debtor's "best effort" prior to confirmation of a plan in a case under chapter 13 of title 11. In determining whether a plan is the debtor's "best effort" the court will evaluate several factors. Different facts and circumstances in cases under chapter 13 operate to make any rule of thumb of limited usefulness. The court should balance the debtor's assets, including family income, health insurance, retirement benefits, and other wealth, a sum which is generally determinable, against the foreseeable necessary living expenses of the debtor and the debtor's dependents, which unfortunately is rarely quantifiable. In determining the expenses of the debtor and the debtor's dependents, the court should consider the stability of the debtor's employment, if any, the age of the debtor, the number of the debtor's dependents and their ages, the condition of equipment and tools necessary to the debtor's employment or to the operation of his business, and other foreseeable expenses that the debtor will be required to pay during the period of the plan, other than payments to be made to creditors under the plan.

Section 727(a)(10) of the House amendment clarifies a provision contained in section 727(a)(9) of the House bill and Senate amendment indicating that a discharge may be barred if the court approves a waiver of discharge executed in writing by the debtor after the order for relief under chapter 7.

Section 727(b) of the House amendment adopts a similar provision contained in the Senate amendment modifying the effect of discharge. The provision makes clear that the debtor is discharged from all debts that arose before the date of the order for relief under chapter 7 in addition to any debt which is determined under section 502 as if it were a prepetition claim. Thus, if a case is converted from chapter 11 or chapter 13 to a case under chapter 7, all debts prior to the time of conversion are discharged, in addition to debts determined after the date of conversion of a kind specified in section 502, that are to be determined as prepetition claims. This modification is particularly important with respect to an individual debtor who files a petition under chapter 11 or chapter 13 of title 11 if the case is converted to chapter 7. The logical result of the House amendment is to equate the result that obtains whether the case is converted from another chapter to chapter 7, or whether the other chapter proceeding is dismissed and a new case is commenced by filing a petition under chapter 7.

References in Text

The Bankruptcy Act, referred to in subsec. (a)(7), is Act July 1, 1898, c. 541, 30 Stat. 544, as amended, which was classified generally to former Title 11, prior to repeal of such Act by Pub.L. 95–598, Title IV, § 401(a), Nov. 6, 1978, 92 Stat. 2692.

Sections 14, 371, and 476 of the Bankruptcy Act, referred to in subsec. (a)(8), are section 14 of Act July 1, 1898, c. 541, 30 Stat. 550, and sections 371 and 476 of Act July 1, 1898, c. 541, as added June 22, 1938, c. 575, § 1, 52 Stat. 912, 924, which were classified to sections 32, 771, and 876 of former Title 11, respectively.

Sections 660 and 661 of the Bankruptcy Act, referred to in subsec. (a)(9), are sections 660 and 661 of Act July 1, 1898, c. 541, as added June 22, 1938, c. 575, § 1, 52 Stat. 935, 936, which were classified, respectively, to sections 1060 and 1061 of former Title 11.

Effective and Applicability Provisions

2005 Acts. Amendments by sections 106(b), 312(1), and 330(a) of Pub.L. 109–8 effective 180 days after Apr. 20, 2005, with amendments by sections 106(b) and 312(1) of Pub.L. 109–8 not applicable with respect to cases commenced under this title before such effective date, except as otherwise provided, and amendment by section 330(a) of Pub.L. 109–8 applicable with respect to cases commenced under this title on or after Apr. 20, 2005, see Pub.L. 109–8, § 1501, set out as a note under 11 U.S.C.A. § 101.

Amendments by Pub.L. 109–8, § 603, effective 18 months after Apr. 20, 2005, see Pub.L. 109–8, § 603(e), set out as a note under 11 U.S.C.A. § 521.

1986 Acts. Amendment by section 257 Pub.L. 99–554 effective 30 days after Oct. 27, 1986, except as otherwise provided for, see section 302(a) of Pub.L. 99–554, set out as a note under section 581 of Title 28, Judiciary and Judicial Procedure.

Amendment by Pub.L. 99–554, § 220 not to become effective in or with respect to certain specified judicial districts until, or apply to cases while pending in such district before, the expiration of the 270-day period beginning 30 days after Oct. 27, 1986, or of the 30-day period beginning on the date the Attorney General certifies under section 303 of Pub.L. 99–554 the region specified in a paragraph of section 581(a) of Title 28, as amended by section 111(a) of Pub.L. 99–554, that includes such district, whichever occurs first, see section 302(d)(1) of Pub.L. 99–554, set out as a note under section 581 of Title 28.

Amendment by Pub.L. 99–554, § 220, not to become effective in or with respect to certain specified judicial districts until, or apply to cases while pending in such district before, the expiration of the 2-year period beginning 30 days after Oct. 27, 1986, or of the 30-day period beginning on the date the Attorney General certifies under section 303 of Pub.L. 99–554 the region specified in a paragraph of section 581(a) of Title 28, as amended by section 111(a) of Pub.L. 99–554, that includes such district, whichever occurs first, see section 302(d)(2) of Pub.L. 99–554, set out as a note under section 581 of Title 28.

Amendment by Pub.L. 99–554, § 220, not to become effective in or with respect to judicial districts established for the States of Alabama and North Carolina until, or apply to cases while pending in such district before, such district elects to be included in a bankruptcy region established in section 581(a) of Title 28, as amended by section 111(a) of Pub.L. 99–554, or Oct. 1, 2002, whichever occurs first, and, except as otherwise provided, with respect to cases under chapters 7, 11, 12, and 13 of Title 11 commenced before 30 days after Oct. 27, 1986, and pending in a judicial district in the States of Alabama or North Carolina before any election made under section 302(d)(3)(A) of Pub.L. 99–554 by such district becomes effective or Oct. 1, 2002, whichever occurs first, amendments by Pub.L. 99–554 not to apply until Oct. 1, 2003, or the expiration of the 1-year period beginning on the date such election becomes effective, whichever occurs first, and further, in any judicial district in Alabama or North Carolina not making the election described in section 302(d)(3)(A) of Pub.L. 99–554, any person appointed under regulations issued by the Judicial Conference to administer estates in cases under Title 11 authorized to establish, etc., a panel of private trustees, and to supervise cases and trustees in cases under chapters 7, 11, 12, and 13 of Title 11, until amendments by sections 201 to 231 of Pub.L. 99–554 effective in such district, see section 302(d)(3)(A) to (F), (H), and (I) of Pub.L. 99–554, set out as a note under section 581 of Title 28.

Amendment by Pub.L. 99–554, § 220, except as otherwise provided, with respect to cases under chapters 7, 11, 12, and 13 of Title 11 commenced before 30 days after Oct. 27, 1986, and pending in a judicial district referred to in section 581(a) of Title 28, as amended by section 111(a) of Pub.L. 99–554, for which a United States trustee is not authorized before 30 days after Oct. 27, 1986 to be appointed, not applicable until the expiration of the 3-year period beginning on Oct. 27, 1986, or of the 1-year period beginning on the date the Attorney General certifies under section 303 of Pub.L. 99–554 the region specified in a paragraph of such section 581(a) that includes, such district, whichever occurs first, see section 302(e)(1), (2) of Pub.L. 99–554, as amended, set out as a note under section 581 of Title 28.

Amendment by Pub.L. 99–554, § 257(s), effective 30 days after Oct. 27, 1986, but not applicable to cases commenced under this title before that date, see section 302(a), (c)(1) of Pub.L. 99–554, set out as a note under section 581 of Title 28.

1984 Acts. Amendment by Pub.L. 98–353 effective with respect to cases filed 90 days after July 10, 1984, see section 552(a), formerly 553(a), of Pub.L. 98–353, set out as a note under section 101 of this title.

CROSS REFERENCES

Cancellation of indebtedness from discharged farm loans, see 12 USCA § 1150.

Concealment of assets, false oaths and claims, see 18 USCA § 152.

Confirmation of plan as affecting discharge in,

　Chapter eleven cases, see 11 USCA § 1141.

　Chapter nine cases, see 11 USCA § 944.

Discharge in Chapter thirteen cases, see 11 USCA § 1328.

Duty of trustee to oppose discharge, see 11 USCA § 704.

Effect of,

　Conversion, see 11 USCA § 348.

　Discharge, see 11 USCA § 524.

Exceptions to discharge, see 11 USCA § 523.

Nondischargeability of capital improvement loans for multi-family housing projects in proceedings under this section, see 12 USCA § 1715z–1a.

[§ 728. Repealed. Pub.L. 109–8, Title VII, § 719(b)(1), Apr. 20, 2005, 119 Stat. 133]

HISTORICAL AND STATUTORY NOTES

Section, Pub.L. 95–598, Nov. 6, 1978, 92 Stat. 2611; Pub.L. 98–353, Title III, § 481, July 10, 1984, 98 Stat. 382; Pub.L. 99–554, Title II, § 257(t), Oct. 27, 1986, 100 Stat. 3116, related to special tax provisions applying to state and local taxation.

See, now, 11 U.S.C.A. § 346.

Effective Date of Repeal

Amendments by Pub.L. 109–8 effective, except as otherwise provided, 180 days after April 20, 2005, and inapplicable with respect to cases commenced under Title 11 before the effective date, see Pub.L. 109–8, § 1501, set out as a note under 11 U.S.C.A. § 101.

SUBCHAPTER III—STOCKBROKER LIQUIDATION

CROSS REFERENCES

Subchapter applicable only in case under chapter concerning stockholder, see 11 USCA § 103.

§ 741. Definitions for this subchapter

In this subchapter—

(1) "Commission" means Securities and Exchange Commission;

(2) "customer" includes—

　(A) entity with whom a person deals as principal or agent and that has a claim against such person on account of a security received, acquired, or held by such person in the ordinary course of such person's business as a stockbroker, from or for the securities account or accounts of such entity—

　　(i) for safekeeping;

　　(ii) with a view to sale;

　　(iii) to cover a consummated sale;

　　(iv) pursuant to a purchase;

　　(v) as collateral under a security agreement; or

　　(vi) for the purpose of effecting registration of transfer; and

　(B) entity that has a claim against a person arising out of—

　　(i) a sale or conversion of a security received, acquired, or held as specified in subparagraph (A) of this paragraph; or

　　(ii) a deposit of cash, a security, or other property with such person for the purpose of purchasing or selling a security;

(3) "customer name security" means security—

　(A) held for the account of a customer on the date of the filing of the petition by or on behalf of the debtor;

　(B) registered in such customer's name on such date or in the process of being so registered under instructions from the debtor; and

　(C) not in a form transferable by delivery on such date;

(4) "customer property" means cash, security, or other property, and proceeds of such cash, security, or property, received, acquired, or held by or for the account of the debtor, from or for the securities account of a customer—

　(A) including—

　　(i) property that was unlawfully converted from and that is the lawful property of the estate;

　　(ii) a security held as property of the debtor to the extent such security is necessary to meet a net equity claim of a customer based on a security of the same class and series of an issuer;

　　(iii) resources provided through the use or realization of a customer's debit cash balance or a debit item includible in the Formula for Determination of Reserve Requirement for Brokers and Dealers as promulgated by the Commission under the Securities Exchange Act of 1934; and

　　(iv) other property of the debtor that any applicable law, rule, or regulation requires to be set aside or held for the benefit of a customer, unless including such property as customer property would not significantly increase customer property; but

　(B) not including—

(i) a customer name security delivered to or reclaimed by a customer under section 751 of this title; or

(ii) property to the extent that a customer does not have a claim against the debtor based on such property;

(5) "margin payment" means payment or deposit of cash, a security, or other property, that is commonly known to the securities trade as original margin, initial margin, maintenance margin, or variation margin, or as a mark-to-market payment, or that secures an obligation of a participant in a securities clearing agency;

(6) "net equity" means, with respect to all accounts of a customer that such customer has in the same capacity—

(A)(i) aggregate dollar balance that would remain in such accounts after the liquidation, by sale or purchase, at the time of the filing of the petition, of all securities positions in all such accounts, except any customer name securities of such customer; minus

(ii) any claim of the debtor against such customer in such capacity that would have been owing immediately after such liquidation; plus

(B) any payment by such customer to the trustee, within 60 days after notice under section 342 of this title, of any business related claim of the debtor against such customer in such capacity;

(7) "securities contract"—

(A) means—

(i) a contract for the purchase, sale, or loan of a security, a certificate of deposit, a mortgage loan, any interest in a mortgage loan, a group or index of securities, certificates of deposit, or mortgage loans or interests therein (including an interest therein or based on the value thereof), or option on any of the foregoing, including an option to purchase or sell any such security, certificate of deposit, mortgage loan, interest, group or index, or option, and including any repurchase or reverse repurchase transaction on any such security, certificate of deposit, mortgage loan, interest, group or index, or option (whether or not such repurchase or reverse repurchase transaction is a "repurchase agreement", as defined in section 101);

(ii) any option entered into on a national securities exchange relating to foreign currencies;

(iii) the guarantee (including by novation) by or to any securities clearing agency of a settlement of cash, securities, certificates of deposit, mortgage loans or interests therein, group or index of securities, or mortgage loans or interests therein (including any interest therein or based on the value thereof), or option on any of the foregoing, including an option to purchase or

sell any such security, certificate of deposit, mortgage loan, interest, group or index, or option (whether or not such settlement is in connection with any agreement or transaction referred to in clauses (i) through (xi));

(iv) any margin loan;

(v) any extension of credit for the clearance or settlement of securities transactions;

(vi) any loan transaction coupled with a securities collar transaction, any prepaid forward securities transaction, or any total return swap transaction coupled with a securities sale transaction;

(vii) any other agreement or transaction that is similar to an agreement or transaction referred to in this subparagraph;

(viii) any combination of the agreements or transactions referred to in this subparagraph;

(ix) any option to enter into any agreement or transaction referred to in this subparagraph;

(x) a master agreement that provides for an agreement or transaction referred to in clause (i), (ii), (iii), (iv), (v), (vi), (vii), (viii), or (ix), together with all supplements to any such master agreement, without regard to whether the master agreement provides for an agreement or transaction that is not a securities contract under this subparagraph, except that such master agreement shall be considered to be a securities contract under this subparagraph only with respect to each agreement or transaction under such master agreement that is referred to in clause (i), (ii), (iii), (iv), (v), (vi), (vii), (viii), or (ix); or

(xi) any security agreement or arrangement or other credit enhancement related to any agreement or transaction referred to in this subparagraph, including any guarantee or reimbursement obligation by or to a stockbroker, securities clearing agency, financial institution, or financial participant in connection with any agreement or transaction referred to in this subparagraph, but not to exceed the damages in connection with any such agreement or transaction, measured in accordance with section 562; and

(B) does not include any purchase, sale, or repurchase obligation under a participation in a commercial mortgage loan;

(8) "settlement payment" means a preliminary settlement payment, a partial settlement payment, an interim settlement payment, a settlement payment on account, a final settlement payment, or any other similar payment commonly used in the securities trade; and

(9) "SIPC" means Securities Investor Protection Corporation.

(Pub.L. 95–598, Nov. 6, 1978, 92 Stat. 2611; Pub.L. 97–222, § 8, July 27, 1982, 96 Stat. 237; Pub.L. 98–353, Title III, § 482, July 10, 1984, 98 Stat. 382; Pub.L. 103–394, Title V, § 501(d)(25), Oct. 22, 1994, 108 Stat. 4146; Pub.L. 109–8, Title IX, § 907(a)(2), Apr. 20, 2005, 119 Stat. 173; Pub.L. 109–390, § 5(a)(3), Dec. 12, 2006, 120 Stat. 2697.)

HISTORICAL AND STATUTORY NOTES

Revision Notes and Legislative Reports

1978 Acts. Section 741 sets forth definitions for subchapter III of chapter 7.

Paragraph (1) defines "Commission" to mean the Securities and Exchange Commission.

Paragraph (2) defines "customer" to include anybody that interacts with the debtor in a capacity that concerns securities transactions. The term embraces cash or margin customers of a broker or dealer in the broadest sense.

Paragraph (3) defines "customer name security" in a restrictive fashion to include only non-transferrable securities that are registered, or in the process of being registered in a customer's own name. The securities must not be endorsed by the customer and the stockbroker must not be able to legally transfer the securities by delivery, by a power of attorney, or otherwise.

Paragraph (4) defines "customer property" to include all property of the debtor that has been segregated for customers or property that should have been segregated but was unlawfully converted. Clause (i) refers to customer property not properly segregated by the debtor or customer property converted and then recovered so as to become property of the estate. Unlawfully converted property that has been transferred to a third party is excluded until it is recovered as property of the estate by virtue of the avoiding powers. The concept excludes customer name securities that have been delivered to or reclaimed by a customer and any property properly belonging to the stockholder, such as money deposited by a customer to pay for securities that the stockholder has distributed to such customer.

Paragraph (5) defines "net equity" to establish the extent to which a customer will be entitled to share in the single and separate fund. Accounts of a customer are aggregated and offset only to the extent the accounts are held by the customer in the same capacity. Thus, a personal account is separate from an account held as trustee. In a community property state an account held for the community is distinct from an account held as separate property.

The net equity is computed by liquidating all securities positions in the accounts and crediting the account with any amount due to the customer. Regardless of the actual dates, if any, of liquidation, the customer is only entitled to the liquidation value at the time of the filing of the petition. To avoid double counting, the liquidation value of customer name securities belonging to a customer is excluded from net equity. Thus, clause (ii) includes claims against a customer resulting from the liquidation of a security under clause (i). The value of a security on which trading has been suspended at the time of the filing of the petition will be estimated. Once the net liquidation value is computed, any amount that the customer owes to the stockbroker is subtracted including any amount that would be owing after the hypothetical liquidation, such as brokerage fees. Debts owed by the customer to the debtor, other than in a securities related transaction, will not reduce the net equity of the customer. Finally, net equity is increased by any payment by the customer to the debtor actually paid within 60 days after notice. The principal reason a customer would make such a payment is to reclaim customer name securities under § 751.

Paragraph (6) defines "1934 Act" to mean the Securities Exchange Act of 1934 [15 U.S.C.A. § 78a et seq.].

Paragraph (7) defines "SIPC" to mean the Securities Investor Protection Corporation. Senate Report No. 95–989.

1982 Acts. House Report No. 97–420, see 1982 U.S.Code Cong. and Adm.News, p. 583.

1984 Acts. Statements by Legislative Leaders, see 1984 U.S.Code Cong. and Adm.News, p. 576.

1994 Acts. House Report No. 103–835, see 1994 U.S. Code Cong. and Adm. News, p. 3340.

2005 Acts. House Report No. 109–31(Part I), see 2005 U.S. Code Cong. and Adm. News, p. 88.

2006 Acts. House Report No. 109–648(Part I), see 2006 U.S. Code Cong. and Adm. News, p. 1585.

Legislative Statements

Section 741(6) of the House bill and Senate amendment is deleted by the House amendment since the defined term is used only in section 741(4)(A)(iii). A corresponding change is made in that section.

References in Text

The Securities Exchange Act of 1934, referred to in par. (4)(A)(iii), is Act June 6, 1934, c. 404, 48 Stat. 881, as amended, which is classified principally to chapter 2B (section 78a et seq.) of Title 15, Commerce and Trade. For complete classification of this Act to the Code, see section 78l of Title 15 and Tables.

Effective and Applicability Provisions

2005 Acts. Amendments by Pub.L. 109–8 effective, except as otherwise provided, 180 days after April 20, 2005, and inapplicable with respect to cases commenced under Title 11 before the effective date, see Pub.L. 109–8, § 1501, set out as a note under 11 U.S.C.A. § 101.

1994 Acts. Amendment by Pub.L. 103–394 effective on Oct. 22, 1994, and not to apply with respect to cases commenced under Title 11 of the United States Code before Oct. 22, 1994, see section 702 of Pub.L. 103–394, set out as a note under section 101 of this title.

1984 Acts. Amendment by Pub.L. 98–353 effective with respect to cases filed 90 days after July 10, 1984, see section 552(a), formerly 553(a), of Pub.L. 98–353, set out as a note under section 101 of this title.

Separability of Provisions

If any provision of or amendment made by Pub.L. 103–394 or the application of such provision or amendment to any person or circumstance is held to be unconstitutional, the remaining provisions of and amendments made by Pub.L. 103–394 and the application of such provisions and amendments to any person or circumstance shall not be affected thereby, see section 701 of Pub.L. 103–394, set out as a note under section 101 of this title.

CROSS REFERENCES

Certain persons acting as agent or custodian for customer in connection with "securities contract" as defined under this section considered a financial institution for purposes of this title, see 11 USCA § 101.

Contractual right to liquidate "securities contract" as defined under this section not stayed, avoided or limited by operation of any provision of this title, see 11 USCA § 555.

"Customer" defined under this section as determining who is a stockbroker for purposes of this title, see 11 USCA § 101.

Definitions applicable in,

Chapter eleven cases, see 11 USCA § 1101.

Chapter nine cases, see 11 USCA § 902.

Commodity broker liquidation cases, see 11 USCA § 761.

Railroad reorganization cases, see 11 USCA § 1162.

Limitation on power of trustee to avoid transfer of "margin payment" and "settlement payment" as defined under this section, see 11 USCA § 546.

Receipt of "margin payment" or "settlement payment" as defined under this section is taking for value for purposes of avoidance of fraudulent transfers and obligations, see 11 USCA § 548.

"Securities contract" as defined under this section as having same meaning for purposes of,

Federal credit union insurance, see 12 USCA § 1787.

Federal deposit insurance corporation, see 12 USCA § 1821.

Setoff of mutual debt in connection with securities contract, margin payment or settlement payment, not stayed by filing of petitions for voluntary cases, joint cases or involuntary cases or protective decrees in investor protection liquidation proceedings, see 11 USCA § 362.

§ 742. Effect of section 362 of this title in this subchapter

Notwithstanding section 362 of this title, SIPC may file an application for a protective decree under the Securities Investor Protection Act of 1970. The filing of such application stays all proceedings in the case under this title unless and until such application is dismissed. If SIPC completes the liquidation of the debtor, then the court shall dismiss the case.
(Pub.L. 95–598, Nov. 6, 1978, 92 Stat. 2613; Pub.L. 97–222, § 9, July 27, 1982, 96 Stat. 237; Pub.L. 103–394, Title V, § 501(d)(26), Oct. 22, 1994, 108 Stat. 4146.)

HISTORICAL AND STATUTORY NOTES

Revision Notes and Legislative Reports

1978 Acts. Section 742 indicates that the automatic stay does not prevent SIPC from filing an application for a protective decree under SIPA. If SIPA does file such an application, then all bankruptcy proceedings are suspended until the SIPC action is completed. If SIPC completes liquidation of the stockbroker then the bankruptcy case is dismissed. Senate Report No. 95–989.

1982 Acts. House Report No. 97–420, see 1982 U.S.Code Cong. and Adm.News, p. 583.

1994 Acts. House Report No. 103–835, see 1994 U.S. Code Cong. and Adm. News, p. 3340.

Legislative Statements

Section 742 of the House amendment deletes a sentence contained in the Senate amendment requiring the trustee in an interstate stock-brokerage liquidation to comply with the provisions of subchapter IV of chapter 7 if the debtor is also a commodity broker. The House amendment expands the requirement to require the SIPC trustee to perform such duties, if the debtor is a commodity broker, under section 7(b) of the Securities Investor Protection Act [15 U.S.C. 78ggg(b)]. The requirement is deleted from section 742 since the trustee of an intrastate stockbroker will be bound by the provisions of subchapter IV of chapter 7 if the debtor is also a commodity broker by reason of section 103 of title 11.

References in Text

The Securities Investor Protection Act of 1970, referred to in text, is Pub.L. 91–598, Dec. 30, 1970, 84 Stat. 1636, as amended, which is classified generally to chapter 2B–1 (section 78aaa et seq.) of Title 15, Commerce and Trade. For complete classification of this Act to the Code, see section 78aaa of Title 15 and Tables.

Effective and Applicability Provisions

1994 Acts. Amendment by Pub.L. 103–394 effective on Oct. 22, 1994, and not to apply with respect to cases commenced under Title 11 of the United States Code before Oct. 22, 1994, see section 702 of Pub.L. 103–394, set out as a note under section 101 of this title.

Separability of Provisions

If any provision of or amendment made by Pub.L. 103–394 or the application of such provision or amendment to any person or circumstance is held to be unconstitutional, the remaining provisions of and amendments made by Pub.L. 103–394 and the application of such provisions and amendments to any person or circumstance shall not be affected thereby, see section 701 of Pub.L. 103–394, set out as a note under section 101 of this title.

CROSS REFERENCES

Automatic stay of enforcement of claims against debtor in Chapter nine cases, see 11 USCA § 922.

Effect of dismissal, see 11 USCA § 349.

Stay of action against codebtor in Chapter thirteen cases, see 11 USCA § 1301.

§ 743. Notice

The clerk shall give the notice required by section 342 of this title to SIPC and to the Commission.
(Pub.L. 95–598, Nov. 6, 1978, 92 Stat. 2613; Pub.L. 99–554, Title II, § 283(t), Oct. 27, 1986, 100 Stat. 3118; Pub.L. 103–394, Title V, § 501(d)(27), Oct. 22, 1994, 108 Stat. 4146.)

HISTORICAL AND STATUTORY NOTES

Revision Notes and Legislative Reports

1978 Acts. Section 743 requires that notice of the order for relief be given to SIPC and to the SEC in every stockbroker case. Senate Report No. 95–989.

1986 Acts. House Report No. 99–764 and House Conference Report No. 99–958, see 1986 U.S.Code Cong. and Adm. News, p. 5227.

1994 Acts. House Report No. 103–835, see 1994 U.S. Code Cong. and Adm. News, p. 3340.

Codifications

Pub.L. 99–554, Title II, § 283(t), Oct. 27, 1986, 100 Stat. 3118, provided that this section be amended by striking out "(d)", which amendment was incapable of execution in view of present language of text.

Effective and Applicability Provisions

1994 Acts. Amendment by Pub.L. 103–394 effective on Oct. 22, 1994, and not to apply with respect to cases commenced under Title 11 of the United States Code before Oct. 22, 1994, see section 702 of Pub.L. 103–394, set out as a note under section 101 of this title.

Separability of Provisions

If any provision of or amendment made by Pub.L. 103–394 or the application of such provision or amendment to any person or circumstance is held to be unconstitutional, the remaining provisions of and amendments made by Pub.L. 103–394 and the application of such provisions and amendments to any person or circumstance shall not be affected thereby, see section 701 of Pub.L. 103–394, set out as a note under section 101 of this title.

CROSS REFERENCES

Notice in Chapter nine cases, see 11 USCA § 923.

Notice to the Commodity Futures Trading Commission, see 11 USCA § 762.

§ 744. Executory contracts

Notwithstanding section 365(d) (1) of this title, the trustee shall assume or reject, under section 365 of this title, any executory contract of the debtor for the purchase or sale of a security in the ordinary course of the debtor's business, within a reasonable time after the date of the order for relief, but not to exceed 30 days. If the trustee does not assume such a contract within such time, such contract is rejected.

(Pub.L. 95–598, Nov. 6, 1978, 92 Stat. 2613; Pub.L. 97–222, § 10, July 27, 1982, 96 Stat. 238.)

HISTORICAL AND STATUTORY NOTES

Revision Notes and Legislative Reports

1978 Acts. Section 744 instructs the court to give the trustee a reasonable time, not to exceed 30 days, to assume or reject any executory contract of the stockbroker to buy or sell securities. Any contract not assumed within the time fixed by the court is considered to be rejected. Senate Report No. 95–989.

1982 Acts. House Report No. 97–420, see 1982 U.S.Code Cong. and Adm.News, p. 583.

CROSS REFERENCES

Effect of rejection of lease of railroad line, see 11 USCA § 1169.

§ 745. Treatment of accounts

(a) Accounts held by the debtor for a particular customer in separate capacities shall be treated as accounts of separate customers.

(b) If a stockbroker or a bank holds a customer net equity claim against the debtor that arose out of a transaction for a customer of such stockbroker or bank, each such customer of such stockbroker or bank shall be treated as a separate customer of the debtor.

(c) Each trustee's account specified as such on the debtor's books, and supported by a trust deed filed with, and qualified as such by, the Internal Revenue Service, and under the Internal Revenue Code of 1986, shall be treated as a separate customer account for each beneficiary under such trustee account.

(Pub.L. 95–598, Nov. 6, 1978, 92 Stat. 2613; Pub.L. 97–222, § 11, July 27, 1982, 96 Stat. 238; Pub.L. 98–353, Title III, § 483, July 10, 1984, 98 Stat. 383; Pub.L. 103–394, Title V, § 501(d)(28), Oct. 22, 1994, 108 Stat. 4146.)

HISTORICAL AND STATUTORY NOTES

Revision Notes and Legislative Reports

1978 Acts. Section 745(a) indicates that each account held by a customer in a separate capacity is to be considered a separate account. This prevents the offset of accounts held in different capacities.

Subsection (b) indicates that a bank or another stockbroker that is a customer of a debtor is considered to hold its customers accounts in separate capacities. Thus a bank or other stockbroker is not treated as a mutual fund for purposes of bulk investment. This protects unrelated customers of a bank or other stockholder [sic] from having their accounts offset.

Subsection (c) effects the same result with respect to a trust so that each beneficiary is treated as the customer of the debtor rather than the trust itself. This eliminates any doubt whether a trustee holds a personal account in a separate capacity from his trustee's account. Senate Report No. 95–989.

1982 Acts. House Report No. 97–420, see 1982 U.S.Code Cong. and Adm.News, p. 583.

1986 Acts. House Conference Report No. 99–841 and Statement by President, see 1986 U.S.Code Cong. and Adm. News, p. 4075.

1994 Acts. House Report No. 103–835, see 1994 U.S. Code Cong. and Adm. News, p. 3340.

References in Text

The Internal Revenue Code of 1986, referred to in subsec. (c), is classified to Title 26, Internal Revenue Code.

Effective and Applicability Provisions

1994 Acts. Amendment by Pub.L. 103–394 effective on Oct. 22, 1994, and not to apply with respect to cases commenced under Title 11 of the United States Code before Oct. 22, 1994, see section 702 of Pub.L. 103–394, set out as a note under section 101 of this title.

1984 Acts. Amendment by Pub.L. 98–353 effective with respect to cases filed 90 days after July 10, 1984, see section 552(a), formerly 553(a), of Pub.L. 98–353, set out as a note under section 101 of this title.

Separability of Provisions

If any provision of or amendment made by Pub.L. 103–394 or the application of such provision or amendment to any person or circumstance is held to be unconstitutional, the remaining provisions of and amendments made by Pub.L. 103–394 and the application of such provisions and amendments to any person or circumstance shall not be affected thereby, see section 701 of Pub.L. 103–394, set out as a note under section 101 of this title.

CROSS REFERENCES

"Stockbroker" defined, see 11 USCA § 101.

Treatment of accounts in commodity broker liquidation cases, see 11 USCA § 763.

§ 746.　Extent of customer claims

(a) If, after the date of the filing of the petition, an entity enters into a transaction with the debtor, in a manner that would have made such entity a customer had such transaction occurred before the date of the filing of the petition, and such transaction was entered into by such entity in good faith and before the qualification under section 322 of this title of a trustee, such entity shall be deemed a customer, and the date of such transaction shall be deemed to be the date of the filing of the petition for the purpose of determining such entity's net equity.

(b) An entity does not have a claim as a customer to the extent that such entity transferred to the debtor cash or a security that, by contract, agreement, understanding, or operation of law, is—

(1) part of the capital of the debtor; or

(2) subordinated to the claims of any or all creditors.

(Pub.L. 95–598, Nov. 6, 1978, 92 Stat. 2613; Pub.L. 97–222, § 12, July 27, 1982, 96 Stat. 238.)

HISTORICAL AND STATUTORY NOTES

Revision Notes and Legislative Reports

1978 Acts. Section 746(a) protects entities who deal in good faith with the debtor after the filing of the petition and before a trustee is appointed by deeming such entities to be customers. The principal application of this section will be in an involuntary case before the order for relief, because § 701(b) requires prompt appointment of an interim trustee after the order for relief.

Subsection (b) indicates that an entity who holds securities that are either part of the capital of the debtor or that are subordinated to the claims of any creditor of the debtor is not a customer with respect to those securities. This subsection will apply when the stockbroker has sold securities in itself to the customer or when the customer has otherwise placed such securities in an account with the stockbroker. Senate Report No. 95–989.

1982 Acts. House Report No. 97–420, see 1982 U.S.Code Cong. and Adm.News, p. 583.

CROSS REFERENCES

Allowance of claims or interests, see 11 USCA § 502.

§ 747.　Subordination of certain customer claims

Except as provided in section 510 of this title, unless all other customer net equity claims have been paid in full, the trustee may not pay in full or pay in part, directly or indirectly, any net equity claim of a customer that was, on the date the transaction giving rise to such claim occurred—

(1) an insider;

(2) a beneficial owner of at least five percent of any class of equity securities of the debtor, other than—

(A) nonconvertible stock having fixed preferential dividend and liquidation rights; or

(B) interests of limited partners in a limited partnership;

(3) a limited partner with a participation of at least five percent in the net assets or net profits of the debtor; or

(4) an entity that, directly or indirectly, through agreement or otherwise, exercised or had the power to exercise control over the management or policies of the debtor.

(Pub.L. 95–598, Nov. 6, 1978, 92 Stat. 2613; Pub.L. 97–222, § 13, July 27, 1982, 96 Stat. 238.)

HISTORICAL AND STATUTORY NOTES

Revision Notes and Legislative Reports

1978 Acts. Section 747 subordinates to other customer claims, all claims of a customer who is an insider, a five percent owner of the debtor, or otherwise in control of the debtor. Senate Report No. 95–989.

1982 Acts. House Report No. 97–420, see 1982 U.S.Code Cong. and Adm.News, p. 583.

CROSS REFERENCES

"Insider" defined, see 11 USCA § 101.

§ 748.　Reduction of securities to money

As soon as practicable after the date of the order for relief, the trustee shall reduce to money, consistent with good market practice, all securities held as property of the estate, except for customer name securities delivered or reclaimed under section 751 of this title.

(Pub.L. 95–598, Nov. 6, 1978, 92 Stat. 2614.)

HISTORICAL AND STATUTORY NOTES

Revision Notes and Legislative Reports

1978 Acts. Section 748 requires the trustee to liquidate all securities, except for customer name securities, of the estate in a manner consistent with good market practice. The trustee should refrain from flooding a thin market with a large percentage of shares in any one issue. If the trustee holds restricted securities or securities in which trading has been suspended, then the trustee must arrange to liquidate such securities in accordance with the securities laws. A private placement may be the only exemption available with the customer of the debtor the best prospect for such a placement. The subsection does not permit such a customer to bid in his net equity as part of the purchase price; a contrary result would permit a customer to receive a greater percentage on his net equity claim than other customers. Senate Report No. 95–989.

CROSS REFERENCES

Reduction of certain securities and property to money in commodity broker liquidation cases, see 11 USCA § 766.

§ 749.   Voidable transfers

(a) Except as otherwise provided in this section, any transfer of property that, but for such transfer, would have been customer property, may be avoided by the trustee, and such property shall be treated as customer property, if and to the extent that the trustee avoids such transfer under section 544, 545, 547, 548, or 549 of this title. For the purpose of such sections, the property so transferred shall be deemed to have been property of the debtor and, if such transfer was made to a customer or for a customer's benefit, such customer shall be deemed, for the purposes of this section, to have been a creditor.

(b) Notwithstanding sections 544, 545, 547, 548, and 549 of this title, the trustee may not avoid a transfer made before seven days after the order for relief if such transfer is approved by the Commission by rule or order, either before or after such transfer, and if such transfer is—

(1) a transfer of a securities contract entered into or carried by or through the debtor on behalf of a customer, and of any cash, security, or other property margining or securing such securities contract; or

(2) the liquidation of a securities contract entered into or carried by or through the debtor on behalf of a customer.

(Pub.L. 95–598, Nov. 6, 1978, 92 Stat. 2614; Pub.L. 97–222, § 14, July 27, 1982, 96 Stat. 238; Pub.L. 111–16, § 2(8), May 7, 2009, 123 Stat. 1607.)

HISTORICAL AND STATUTORY NOTES

Revision Notes and Legislative Reports

1978 Acts. Section 749 indicates that if the trustee avoids a transfer, property recovered is customer property to any extent it would have been customer property but for the transfer. The section clarifies that a customer who receives a transfer of property of the debtor is a creditor and that property in a customer's account is property of a creditor for purposes of the avoiding powers. Senate Report No. 95–989.

1982 Acts. House Report No. 97–420, see 1982 U.S.Code Cong. and Adm.News, p. 583.

Effective and Applicability Provisions

2009 Acts. Amendments by Pub.L. 111–16 effective Dec. 1, 2009, see Pub.L. 111–16, § 7, set out as a note under 11 U.S.C.A. § 109.

CROSS REFERENCES

Voidable transfers in commodity broker liquidation cases, see 11 USCA § 764.

§ 750.   Distribution of securities

The trustee may not distribute a security except under section 751 of this title.

(Pub.L. 95–598, Nov. 6, 1978, 92 Stat. 2614.)

HISTORICAL AND STATUTORY NOTES

Revision Notes and Legislative Reports

1978 Acts. Section 750 forbids the trustee from distributing a security other than a customer name security. The term "distribution" refers to a distribution to customers in satisfaction of net equity claims and is not intended to preclude the trustee from liquidating securities under proposed 11 U.S.C. 748. Senate Report No. 95–989.

CROSS REFERENCES

Distribution in Chapter eleven cases, see 11 USCA § 1143.

Distribution of property of estate, see 11 USCA § 726.

§ 751.   Customer name securities

The trustee shall deliver any customer name security to or on behalf of the customer entitled to such security, unless such customer has a negative net equity. With the approval of the trustee, a customer may reclaim a customer name security after payment to the trustee, within such period as the trustee allows, of any claim of the debtor against such customer to the extent that such customer will not have a negative net equity after such payment.

(Pub.L. 95–598, Nov. 6, 1978, 92 Stat. 2614.)

HISTORICAL AND STATUTORY NOTES

Revision Notes and Legislative Reports

1978 Acts. Section 751 requires the trustee to deliver a customer name security to the customer entitled to such security unless the customer has a negative net equity. The customer's net equity will be negative when the amount owed by the customer to the stockbroker exceeds the liquidation value of the non-customer name securities in the customer's account. If the customer is a net debtor of the stockbroker, then the trustee may permit the customer to repay debts to the stockbroker so that the customer will no longer be in debt to the stockbroker. If the customer refuses to pay such amount, then the court may order the customer to endorse the security in order that the trustee may liquidate such property. Senate Report No. 95–989.

§ 752.   Customer property

(a) The trustee shall distribute customer property ratably to customers on the basis and to the extent of such customers' allowed net equity claims and in priority to all other claims, except claims of the kind specified in section 507(a)(2) of this title that are attributable to the administration of such customer property.

(b)(1) The trustee shall distribute customer property in excess of that distributed under subsection (a) of this section in accordance with section 726 of this title.

(2) Except as provided in section 510 of this title, if a customer is not paid the full amount of such customer's allowed net equity claim from customer property, the unpaid portion of such claim is a claim entitled to distribution under section 726 of this title.

(c) Any cash or security remaining after the liquidation of a security interest created under a security agreement made by the debtor, excluding property excluded under section 741(4)(B) of this title, shall be apportioned between the general estate and customer property in the same proportion as the general estate of the debtor and customer property were subject to such security interest.

(Pub.L. 95–598, Nov. 6, 1978, 92 Stat. 2614; Pub.L. 97–222, § 15, July 27, 1982, 96 Stat. 238; Pub.L. 98–353, Title III, § 484, July 10, 1984, 98 Stat. 383; Pub.L. 109–8, Title XV, § 1502(a)(3), Apr. 20, 2005, 119 Stat. 216.)

HISTORICAL AND STATUTORY NOTES

Revision Notes and Legislative Reports

1978 Acts. Section 752(a) requires the trustee to distribute customer property to customers based on the amount of their net equity claims. Customer property is to be distributed in priority to all claims except expenses of administration entitled to priority under § 507(1). It is anticipated that the court will apportion such administrative claims on an equitable basis between the general estate and the customer property of the debtor.

Subsection (b)(1) indicates that in the event customer property exceeds customers net equity claims and administrative expenses, the excess pours over into the general estate. This event would occur if the value of securities increased dramatically after the order for relief but before liquidation by the trustee. Subsection (b)(2) indicates that the unpaid portion of a customer's net equity claim is entitled to share in the general estate as an unsecured claim unless subordinated by the court under proposed 11 U.S.C. 501. A net equity claim of a customer that is subordinated under section 747 is entitled to share in distribution under section 726(a)(2) unless subordinated under section 510 independently of the subordination under section 747.

Subsection (c) provides for apportionment between customer property and the general estate of any equity of the debtor in property remaining after a secured creditor liquidates a security interest. This might occur if a stockbroker hypothecates securities of his own and of his customers if the value of the hypothecated securities exceeds the debt owed to the secured party. The apportionment is to be made according to the ratio of customer property and general property of the debtor that comprised the collateral. The subsection refers to cash and securities of customers to include any customer property unlawfully converted by the stockbroker in the course of such a transaction. The apportionment is made subject to section 741(4)(B) to insure that property in a customer's account that is owed to the stockbroker will not be considered customer property. This recognizes the right of the stockbroker to withdraw money that has been erroneously placed in a customer's account or that is otherwise owing to the stockbroker. Senate Report No. 95–989.

1982 Acts. House Report No. 97–420, see 1982 U.S.Code Cong. and Adm.News, p. 583.

1984 Acts. Statements by Legislative Leaders, see 1984 U.S.Code Cong. and Adm.News, p. 576.

2005 Acts. House Report No. 109–31(Part I), see 2005 U.S. Code Cong. and Adm. News, p. 88.

Codifications

Amendment by section 484(a)(3) of Pub.L. 98–353, directing that subsec. (a) of this section be amended by inserting "such" before "customer property", has been executed by inserting "such" before "customer property" following "the administration of" as the probable intent of Congress.

Effective and Applicability Provisions

2005 Acts. Amendments by Pub.L. 109–8 effective, except as otherwise provided, 180 days after April 20, 2005, and inapplicable with respect to cases commenced under Title 11 before the effective date, see Pub.L. 109–8, § 1501, set out as a note under 11 U.S.C.A. § 101.

1984 Acts. Amendment by Pub.L. 98–353 effective with respect to cases filed 90 days after July 10, 1984, see section 552(a), formerly 553(a), of Pub.L. 98–353, set out as a note under section 101 of this title.

CROSS REFERENCES

Distribution in Chapter 11 cases, see 11 USCA § 1143.

Distribution of,

    Customer property in commodity broker liquidation cases, see 11 USCA § 766.

    Property of the estate, see 11 USCA § 726.

Election of trustee by creditors holding claims entitled to distribution, see 11 USCA § 702.

Priorities, see 11 USCA § 507.

§ 753. Stockbroker liquidation and forward contract merchants, commodity brokers, stockbrokers, financial institutions, financial participants, securities clearing agencies, swap participants, repo participants, and master netting agreement participants

Notwithstanding any other provision of this title, the exercise of rights by a forward contract merchant, commodity broker, stockbroker, financial institution, financial participant, securities clearing agency, swap participant, repo participant, or master netting agreement participant under this title shall not affect the priority of any unsecured claim it may have after the exercise of such rights.

(Added Pub.L. 109–8, Title IX, § 907(m), Apr. 20, 2005, 119 Stat. 181.)

HISTORICAL AND STATUTORY NOTES

Revision Notes and Legislative Reports

2005 Acts. House Report No. 109–31(Part I), see 2005 U.S. Code Cong. and Adm. News, p. 88.

Effective and Applicability Provisions

2005 Acts. Amendments by Pub.L. 109–8 effective, except as otherwise provided, 180 days after April 20, 2005, and inapplicable with respect to cases commenced under Title 11 before the effective date, see Pub.L. 109–8, § 1501, set out as a note under 11 U.S.C.A. § 101.

SUBCHAPTER IV—COMMODITY BROKER LIQUIDATION

CROSS REFERENCES

Certain terms defined under this section as having same meaning for purposes of Commodity Exchange Act, see 7 USCA § 24.

Powers and duties of trustee in investor liquidation proceedings, see 15 USCA § 78fff–1.

Subchapter generally applicable only in case under chapter concerning commodity broker, see 11 USCA § 103.

§ 761. Definitions for this subchapter

In this subchapter—

(1) "Act" means Commodity Exchange Act;

(2) "clearing organization" means a derivatives clearing organization registered under the Act;

(3) "Commission" means Commodity Futures Trading Commission;

(4) "commodity contract" means—

(A) with respect to a futures commission merchant, contract for the purchase or sale of a commodity for future delivery on, or subject to the rules of, a contract market or board of trade;

(B) with respect to a foreign futures commission merchant, foreign future;

(C) with respect to a leverage transaction merchant, leverage transaction;

(D) with respect to a clearing organization, contract for the purchase or sale of a commodity for future delivery on, or subject to the rules of, a contract market or board of trade that is cleared by such clearing organization, or commodity option traded on, or subject to the rules of, a contract market or board of trade that is cleared by such clearing organization;

(E) with respect to a commodity options dealer, commodity option;

(F)(i) any other contract, option, agreement, or transaction that is similar to a contract, option, agreement, or transaction referred to in this paragraph; and

(ii) with respect to a futures commission merchant or a clearing organization, any other contract, option, agreement, or transaction, in each case, that is cleared by a clearing organization;

(G) any combination of the agreements or transactions referred to in this paragraph;

(H) any option to enter into an agreement or transaction referred to in this paragraph;

(I) a master agreement that provides for an agreement or transaction referred to in subparagraph (A), (B), (C), (D), (E), (F), (G), or (H), together with all supplements to such master agreement, without regard to whether the master agreement provides for an agreement or transaction that is not a commodity contract under this paragraph, except that the master agreement shall be considered to be a commodity contract under this paragraph only with respect to each agreement or transaction under the master agreement that is referred to in subparagraph (A), (B), (C), (D), (E), (F), (G), or (H); or

(J) any security agreement or arrangement or other credit enhancement related to any agreement or transaction referred to in this paragraph, including any guarantee or reimbursement obligation by or to a commodity broker or financial participant in connection with any agreement or transaction referred to in this paragraph, but not to exceed the damages in connection with any such agreement or transaction, measured in accordance with section 562;

(5) "commodity option" means agreement or transaction subject to regulation under section 4c(b) of the Act;

(6) "commodity options dealer" means person that extends credit to, or that accepts cash, a security, or other property from, a customer of such person for the purchase or sale of an interest in a commodity option;

(7) "contract market" means a registered entity;

(8) "contract of sale", "commodity", "derivatives clearing organization", "future delivery", "board of trade", "registered entity", and "futures commission merchant" have the meanings assigned to those terms in the Act;

(9) "customer" means—

(A) with respect to a futures commission merchant—

(i) entity for or with whom such futures commission merchant deals and that holds a claim against such futures commission merchant on account of a commodity contract made, received, acquired, or held by or through such futures commission merchant in the ordinary course of such futures commission merchant's business as a futures commission merchant from or for a commodity contract account of such entity; or

(ii) entity that holds a claim against such futures commission merchant arising out of—

(I) the making, liquidation, or change in the value of a commodity contract of a kind specified in clause (i) of this subparagraph;

(II) a deposit or payment of cash, a security, or other property with such futures commission merchant for the purpose of making or margining such a commodity contract; or

(III) the making or taking of delivery on such a commodity contract;

(B) with respect to a foreign futures commission merchant—

(i) entity for or with whom such foreign futures commission merchant deals and that holds a claim against such foreign futures commission merchant on account of a commodity contract made, received, acquired, or held by or through such foreign futures commission merchant in the ordinary course of such foreign futures commission merchant's business as a foreign futures commission merchant from or for the foreign futures account of such entity; or

(ii) entity that holds a claim against such foreign futures commission merchant arising out of—

(I) the making, liquidation, or change in value of a commodity contract of a kind specified in clause (i) of this subparagraph;

(II) a deposit or payment of cash, a security, or other property with such foreign futures commission merchant for the purpose of making or margining such a commodity contract; or

(III) the making or taking of delivery on such a commodity contract;

(C) with respect to a leverage transaction merchant—

(i) entity for or with whom such leverage transaction merchant deals and that holds a claim against such leverage transaction merchant on account of a commodity contract engaged in by or with such leverage transaction merchant in the ordinary course of such leverage transaction merchant's business as a leverage transaction merchant from or for the leverage account of such entity; or

(ii) entity that holds a claim against such leverage transaction merchant arising out of—

(I) the making, liquidation, or change in value of a commodity contract of a kind specified in clause (i) of this subparagraph;

(II) a deposit or payment of cash, a security, or other property with such leverage transaction merchant for the purpose of entering into or margining such a commodity contract; or

(III) the making or taking of delivery on such a commodity contract;

(D) with respect to a clearing organization, clearing member of such clearing organization with whom such clearing organization deals and that holds a claim against such clearing organization on account of cash, a security, or other property received by such clearing organization to margin, guarantee, or secure a commodity contract in such clearing member's proprietary account or customers' account; or

(E) with respect to a commodity options dealer—

(i) entity for or with whom such commodity options dealer deals and that holds a claim on account of a commodity contract made, received, acquired, or held by or through such commodity options dealer in the ordinary course of such commodity options dealer's business as a com-

modity options dealer from or for the commodity options account of such entity; or

(ii) entity that holds a claim against such commodity options dealer arising out of—

(I) the making of, liquidation of, exercise of, or a change in value of, a commodity contract of a kind specified in clause (i) of this subparagraph; or

(II) a deposit or payment of cash, a security, or other property with such commodity options dealer for the purpose of making, exercising, or margining such a commodity contract;

(10) "customer property" means cash, a security, or other property, or proceeds of such cash, security, or property, received, acquired, or held by or for the account of the debtor, from or for the account of a customer—

(A) including—

(i) property received, acquired, or held to margin, guarantee, secure, purchase, or sell a commodity contract;

(ii) profits or contractual or other rights accruing to a customer as a result of a commodity contract;

(iii) an open commodity contract;

(iv) specifically identifiable customer property;

(v) warehouse receipt or other document held by the debtor evidencing ownership of or title to property to be delivered to fulfill a commodity contract from or for the account of a customer;

(vi) cash, a security, or other property received by the debtor as payment for a commodity to be delivered to fulfill a commodity contract from or for the account of a customer;

(vii) a security held as property of the debtor to the extent such security is necessary to meet a net equity claim based on a security of the same class and series of an issuer;

(viii) property that was unlawfully converted from and that is the lawful property of the estate; and

(ix) other property of the debtor that any applicable law, rule, or regulation requires to be set aside or held for the benefit of a customer, unless including such property as customer property would not significantly increase customer property; but

(B) not including property to the extent that a customer does not have a claim against the debtor based on such property;

(11) "foreign future" means contract for the purchase or sale of a commodity for future delivery on, or subject to the rules of, a board of trade outside the United States;

(12) "foreign futures commission merchant" means entity engaged in soliciting or accepting or-

ders for the purchase or sale of a foreign future or that, in connection with such a solicitation or acceptance, accepts cash, a security, or other property, or extends credit to margin, guarantee, or secure any trade or contract that results from such a solicitation or acceptance;

(13) "leverage transaction" means agreement that is subject to regulation under section 19 of the Commodity Exchange Act, and that is commonly known to the commodities trade as a margin account, margin contract, leverage account, or leverage contract;

(14) "leverage transaction merchant" means person in the business of engaging in leverage transactions;

(15) "margin payment" means payment or deposit of cash, a security, or other property, that is commonly known to the commodities trade as original margin, initial margin, maintenance margin, or variation margin, including mark-to-market payments, settlement payments, variation payments, daily settlement payments, and final settlement payments made as adjustments to settlement prices;

(16) "member property" means customer property received, acquired, or held by or for the account of a debtor that is a clearing organization, from or for the proprietary account of a customer that is a clearing member of the debtor; and

(17) "net equity" means, subject to such rules and regulations as the Commission promulgates under the Act, with respect to the aggregate of all of a customer's accounts that such customer has in the same capacity—

    (A) the balance remaining in such customer's accounts immediately after—

        (i) all commodity contracts of such customer have been transferred, liquidated, or become identified for delivery; and

        (ii) all obligations of such customer in such capacity to the debtor have been offset; plus

    (B) the value, as of the date of return under section 766 of this title, of any specifically identifiable customer property actually returned to such customer before the date specified in subparagraph (A) of this paragraph; plus

    (C) the value, as of the date of transfer, of—

        (i) any commodity contract to which such customer is entitled that is transferred to another person under section 766 of this title; and

        (ii) any cash, security, or other property of such customer transferred to such other person under section 766 of this title to margin or secure such transferred commodity contract.

(Pub.L. 95–598, Nov. 6, 1978, 92 Stat. 2615; Pub.L. 97–222, § 16, July 27, 1982, 96 Stat. 238; Pub.L. 98–353, Title III, § 485, July 10, 1984, 98 Stat. 383; Pub.L. 103–394, Title V, § 501(d)(29), Oct. 22, 1994, 108 Stat. 4146; Pub.L. 106–554,

§ 1(a)(5) [Title I, § 112(c)(6)], Dec. 21, 2000, 114 Stat. 2763, 2763A–395; Pub.L. 109–8, Title IX, § 907(a)(3), Apr. 20, 2005, 119 Stat. 174; Pub.L. 111–203, Title VII, § 724(b), July 21, 2010, 124 Stat. 1684.)

HISTORICAL AND STATUTORY NOTES

Revision Notes and Legislative Reports

1978 Acts. Paragraph (1) defines "Act" to mean the Commodity Exchange Act [7 U.S.C.A. § 1 et seq.].

Paragraph (2) defines "clearing organization" to mean an organization that clears (i.e., matches purchases and sales) commodity futures contracts made on or subject to the rules of a contract market or commodity options transactions made on or subject to the rules of a commodity option exchange. Although commodity option trading on exchanges is currently prohibited, it is anticipated that CFTC may permit such trading in the future.

Paragraphs (3) and (4) define terms "Commission" and "commodity futures contract".

Paragraph (5) defines "commodity contract". to mean a commodity futures contract (§ 761(4)), a commodity option (§ 761(6)), or a leverage contract (§ 761(15)).

Paragraph (b) [probably should be "(6)" defines "commodity option" by reference to section 4c(b) of the Commodity Exchange Act [7 U.S.C.A. § 6c(b)].

Paragraphs (7), (8), and (9), define "commodity options dealer," "contract market," "contract of sale," "commodity," "future delivery," "board of trade," and "futures commission merchant."

Paragraph (10) defines the term "customer" to mean with respect to a futures commission merchant or a foreign futures commission merchant, the entity for whom the debtor carries a commodity futures contract or foreign future, or with whom such a contract is carried (such as another commodity broker), or from whom the debtor has received, acquired, or holds cash, securities, or other property arising out of or connected with specified transactions involving commodity futures contracts or foreign futures. This section also defines "customer" in the context of leverage transaction merchants, clearing organizations, and commodity options dealers. Persons associated with a commodity broker, such as its employees, officers, or partners, may be customers under this definition.

The definition of "customer" serves to isolate that class of persons entitled to the protection subchapter IV provides to customers. In addition, section 101(5) defines "commodity broker" to mean a futures commission merchant, foreign futures commission merchant, clearing organization, leverage transaction merchant, or commodity options dealer, with respect to which there is a customer. Accordingly, the definition of customer also serves to designate those entities which must utilize chapter 7 and are precluded from reorganizing under chapter 11.

Paragraph (11) defines "customer property" to mean virtually all property or proceeds thereof, received, acquired, or held by or for the account of the debtor for a customer arising out of or in connection with a transaction involving a commodity contract.

Paragraph (12) defines "distribution share" to mean the amount to which a customer is entitled under section 765(a).

Paragraphs (13), (14), (15), and (16), define "foreign future," "foreign futures commission merchant," "leverage transaction," and "leverage transaction merchant."

Paragraph (17) defines "margin payment" to mean a payment or deposit commonly known to the commodities trade as original margin, initial margin, or variation margin.

Paragraph (18) defines "member property."

Paragraph (19) defines "net equity" to be the sum of (A) the value of all customer property remaining in a customer's account immediately after all commodity contracts of such customer have been transferred, liquidated, or become identified for delivery and all obligations of such customer to the debtor have been offset (such as margin payments, whether or not called, and brokerage commissions) plus (B) the value of specifically identifiable customer property previously returned to the customer by the trustee, plus (C) if the trustee has transferred any commodity contract to which the customer is entitled or any margin or security for such contract, the value of such contract and margin or security. Net equity, therefore, will be the total amount of customer property to which a customer is entitled as of the date of the filing of the bankruptcy petition, although valued at subsequent dates. The Commission is given authority to promulgate rules and regulations to further refine this definition. Senate Report No. 95–989.

Paragraph (8) is a dynamic definition of "contractual commitment". The definition will vary depending on the character of the debtor in each case. If the debtor is a futures commission merchant or a clearing organization, then subparagraphs (A) and (D) indicate that the definition means a contract of sale of a commodity for future delivery on a contract market. If the debtor is a foreign futures commission merchant, a leverage transaction merchant, or a commodity options dealer, then subparagraphs (B), (C), and (E) indicate that the definition means foreign future, leverage transaction, or commodity option, respectively.

Paragraph (9) defines "customer" in a similar style. It is anticipated that a debtor with multifaceted characteristics will have separate estates for each different kind of customer. Thus, a debtor that is a leverage transaction merchant and a commodity options dealer would have separate estates for the leverage transaction customers and for the options customers, and a general estate for other creditors. Customers for each kind of commodity broker, except the clearing organization, arise from either of two relationships. In subparagraphs (A), (B), (C), and (E), clause (i) treats with customers to the extent of contractual commitments with the debtor in either a broker or a dealer relationship. Clause (ii) treats with customers to the extent of proceeds from contractual commitments or deposits for the purpose of making contractual commitments. The customer of the clearing organization is a member with a proprietary or customers' account.

Paragraph (10) defines "customer property" to include all property in customer accounts and property that should have been in those accounts but was diverted through conversion or mistake. Clause (i) refers to customer property not properly segregated by the debtor or customer property converted and then recovered so as to become property of the estate. Clause (vii) is intended to exclude property that would cost more to recover from a third party than the value of the property itself. Subparagraph (B) excludes property in a customer's account that belongs to the commodity broker, such as a contract placed in the account by error, or cash due the broker for a margin payment that the broker has made.

Paragraph (15) defines "net equity" to include the value of all contractual commitments at the time of liquidation or transfer less any obligations owed by the customer to the

debtor, such as brokerage fees. In addition, the term includes the value of any specifically identifiable property as of the date of return to the customer and the value of any customer property transferred to another commodity broker as of the date of transfer. This definition places the risk of market fluctuations on the customer until commitments leave the estate. House Report No. 95–595.

1982 Acts. House Report No. 97–420, see 1982 U.S.Code Cong. and Adm.News, p. 583.

1984 Acts. Statements by Legislative Leaders, see 1984 U.S.Code Cong. and Adm.News, p. 576.

1994 Acts. House Report No. 103–835, see 1994 U.S. Code Cong. and Adm. News, p. 3340.

2000 Acts. House Report No. 106–645 and Statement by President, see 2000 U.S. Code Cong. and Adm. News, p. 2459.

2005 Acts. House Report No. 109–31(Part I), see 2005 U.S. Code Cong. and Adm. News, p. 88.

Legislative Statements

Subchapter IV of chapter 7 represents a compromise between similar chapters in the House bill and Senate amendment. Section 761(2) of the House amendment defines "clearing organization" to cover an organization that clears commodity contracts on a contract market or a board of trade; the expansion of the definition is intended to include clearing organizations that clear commodity options. Section 761(4) of the House amendment adopts the term "commodity contract" as used in section 761(5) of the Senate amendment but with the more precise substantive definitions contained in section 761(8) of the House bill. The definition is modified to insert "board of trade" to cover commodity options. Section 761(5) of the House amendment adopts the definition contained in section 761(6) of the Senate amendment in preference to the definition contained in section 761(4) of the House bill which erroneously included onions. Section 761(9) of the House amendment represents a compromise between similar provisions in section 761(10) of the Senate amendment and section 761(9) of the House bill. The compromise adopts the substance contained in the House bill and adopts the terminology of "commodity contract" in lieu of "contractual commitment" as suggested in the Senate amendment. Section 761(10) of the House amendment represents a compromise between similar sections in the House bill and Senate amendment regarding the definition of "customer property." The definition of "distribution share" contained in section 761(12) of the Senate amendment is deleted as unnecessary. Section 761(12) of the House amendment adopts a definition of "foreign futures commission merchant" similar to the definition contained in section 761(14) of the Senate amendment. The definition is modified to cover either an entity engaged in soliciting orders or the purchase or sale of a foreign future, or an entity that accepts cash, a security, or other property for credit in connection with such a solicitation or acceptance. Section 761(13) of the House amendment adopts a definition of "leverage transaction" identical to the definition contained in section 761(15) of the Senate amendment. Section 761(15) of the House amendment adopts the definition of "margin payment" contained in section 761(17) of the Senate amendment. Section 761(17) of the House amendment adopts a definition of "net equity" derived from section 761(15) of the House bill.

References in Text

The Commodity Exchange Act or the Act, referred to in pars. (1), (8), and (17), is Act Sept. 21, 1922, c. 369, 42 Stat. 998, as amended, which is classified generally to chapter 1 (section 1 et seq.) of Title 7, Agriculture. For complete classification of this Act to the Code, see section 1 of Title 7 and Tables.

Section 4c of the Commodity Exchange Act, referred to in par. (5), is section 4c of Act Sept. 21, 1922, c. 369, as added June 15, 1936, c. 545, § 5, 49 Stat. 1494, which is classified to section 6c of Title 7, Agriculture.

Section 19 of the Commodity Exchange Act, referred to in par. (13), is section 19 of Act Sept. 21, 1922, c. 369, as added Sept. 30, 1978, Pub.L. 95–405, § 23, 92 Stat. 876, which is classified to section 23 of Title 7.

Effective and Applicability Provisions

2010 Acts. Unless as otherwise provided, Pub.L. 111–203, Title VII, subtitle A, § 711 et seq., shall take effect on the later of 360 days after July 21, 2010, or, to the extent a provision requires a rulemaking, not less than 60 days after publication of the final rule or regulation, see Pub.L. 111–203, § 754, set out as a note under 7 U.S.C.A. § 1a.

2005 Acts. Amendments by Pub.L. 109–8 effective, except as otherwise provided, 180 days after April 20, 2005, and inapplicable with respect to cases commenced under Title 11 before the effective date, see Pub.L. 109–8, § 1501, set out as a note under 11 U.S.C.A. § 101.

1994 Acts. Amendment by Pub.L. 103–394 effective on Oct. 22, 1994, and not to apply with respect to cases commenced under Title 11 of the United States Code before Oct. 22, 1994, see section 702 of Pub.L. 103–394, set out as a note under section 101 of this title.

1984 Acts. Amendment by Pub.L. 98–353 effective with respect to cases filed 90 days after July 10, 1984, see section 552(a), formerly 553(a), of Pub.L. 98–353, set out as a note under section 101 of this title.

Savings Provisions

Notwithstanding any other provision of Title VII of Pub.L. 111–203, § 701 et seq., nothing in subtitle A of such title, § 701 et seq., shall be construed as divesting any appropriate Federal banking agency of any authority it may have to establish or enforce, with respect to a person for which such agency is the appropriate Federal banking agency, prudential or other standards pursuant to authority by Federal law other than Title VII of Pub.L. 111–203, see 15 U.S.C.A. § 8324.

Unless otherwise provided by the amendments made by Title VII of Pub.L. 111–203, § 711 et seq., the amendments made by that subtitle do not divest any appropriate Federal banking agency, the Commodity Futures Trading Commission, the Securities and Exchange Commission, or other Federal or State agency of any authority derived from any other applicable law, see Pub.L. 111–203, § 743, set out as a note under 7 U.S.C.A. § 1a.

Severability of Provisions

If any provision of Pub.L. 111–203, an amendment made by Pub.L. 111–203, or the application of such provision or amendment to any person or circumstance is held to be unconstitutional, the remainder of Pub.L. 111–203, the amendments made by Pub.L. 111–203, and the application of the provisions of such to any person or circumstance shall not be affected, see 12 U.S.C.A. § 5302.

Separability of Provisions

If any provision of or amendment made by Pub.L. 103–394 or the application of such provision or amendment to any person or circumstance is held to be unconstitutional, the remaining provisions of and amendments made by Pub.L. 103–394 and the application of such provisions and amendments to any person or circumstance shall not be affected thereby, see section 701 of Pub.L. 103–394, set out as a note under section 101 of this title.

CROSS REFERENCES

Certain terms having same meanings as under this section, see 7 USCA § 24.

"Commodity broker" defined, see 11 USCA § 101.

"Commodity contract" defined under this section as having same meaning for purposes of Federal deposit insurance corporation, see 12 USCA § 1821.

Contractual right to liquidate "commodity contract" as defined under this section not stayed, avoided or limited by operation of any provision of this title, see 11 USCA § 556.

Definitions applicable in,

    Chapter eleven cases, see 11 USCA § 1101.

    Chapter nine cases, see 11 USCA § 902.

    Railroad reorganization cases, see 11 USCA § 1162.

    Stockbroker liquidation cases, see 11 USCA § 741.

Limitation on power of trustee to avoid transfer of "margin payment" as defined in this section, see 11 USCA § 546.

Reception of margin payments by commodity brokers or forward contract merchants as taking for value, see 11 USCA § 548.

Setoff of mutual debt in connection with "commodity contract" or "margin payment" not stayed by filing of petitions for voluntary cases, joint cases or involuntary cases or protective decrees in investor protection liquidation proceedings, see 11 USCA § 362.

§ 762. Notice to the Commission and right to be heard

(a) The clerk shall give the notice required by section 342 of this title to the Commission.

(b) The Commission may raise and may appear and be heard on any issue in a case under this chapter.
(Pub.L. 95–598, Nov. 6, 1978, 92 Stat. 2618.)

HISTORICAL AND STATUTORY NOTES

Revision Notes and Legislative Reports

1978 Acts. Section 762 provides that the Commission shall be given such notice as is appropriate of an order for relief in a bankruptcy case and that the Commission may raise and may appear and may be heard on any issue in case involving a commodity broker liquidation. Senate Report No. 95–989.

CROSS REFERENCES

Notice in,

    Chapter nine cases, see 11 USCA § 923.

    Stockbroker liquidation proceedings, see 11 USCA § 743.

§ 763.　Treatment of accounts

(a) Accounts held by the debtor for a particular customer in separate capacities shall be treated as accounts of separate customers.

(b) A member of a clearing organization shall be deemed to hold such member's proprietary account in a separate capacity from such member's customers' account.

(c) The net equity in a customer's account may not be offset against the net equity in the account of any other customer.

(Pub.L. 95–598, Nov. 6, 1978, 92 Stat. 2618; Pub.L. 98–353, Title III, § 486, July 10, 1984, 98 Stat. 383.)

HISTORICAL AND STATUTORY NOTES

Revision Notes and Legislative Reports

1978 Acts. Section 763 provides for separate treatment of accounts held in separate capacities. A deficit in one account held for a customer may not be offset against the net equity in another account held by the same customer in a separate capacity or held by another customer. Senate Report No. 95–989.

1984 Acts. Statements by Legislative Leaders, see 1984 U.S.Code Cong. and Adm.News, p. 576.

Effective and Applicability Provisions

1984 Acts. Amendment by Pub.L. 98–353 effective with respect to cases filed 90 days after July 10, 1984, see section 552(a), formerly 553(a), of Pub.L. 98–353, set out as a note under section 101 of this title.

CROSS REFERENCES

Treatment of accounts in stockbroker liquidation cases, see 11 USCA § 745.

§ 764.　Voidable transfers

(a) Except as otherwise provided in this section, any transfer by the debtor of property that, but for such transfer, would have been customer property, may be avoided by the trustee, and such property shall be treated as customer property, if and to the extent that the trustee avoids such transfer under section 544, 545, 547, 548, 549, or 724(a) of this title. For the purpose of such sections, the property so transferred shall be deemed to have been property of the debtor, and, if such transfer was made to a customer or for a customer's benefit, such customer shall be deemed, for the purposes of this section, to have been a creditor.

(b) Notwithstanding sections 544, 545, 547, 548, 549, and 724(a) of this title, the trustee may not avoid a transfer made before seven days after the order for relief, if such transfer is approved by the Commission by rule or order, either before or after such transfer, and if such transfer is—

(1) a transfer of a commodity contract entered into or carried by or through the debtor on behalf of a customer, and of any cash, securities, or other property margining or securing such commodity contract; or

(2) the liquidation of a commodity contract entered into or carried by or through the debtor on behalf of a customer.

(Pub.L. 95–598, Nov. 6, 1978, 92 Stat. 2618; Pub.L. 97–222, § 17, July 27, 1982, 96 Stat. 240; Pub.L. 98–353, Title III, § 487, July 10, 1984, 98 Stat. 383; Pub.L. 111–16, § 2(9), May 7, 2009, 123 Stat. 1607.)

HISTORICAL AND STATUTORY NOTES

Revision Notes and Legislative Reports

1978 Acts. Section 764 permits the trustee to void any transfer of property that, except for such transfer, would have been customer property, to the extent permitted under section 544, 545, 547, 548, 549, or 724(a). Senate Report No. 95–989.

Section 764 indicates the extent to which the avoiding powers may be used by the trustee under subchapter IV of chapter 7. If property recovered would have been customer property if never transferred, then subsection (a) indicates that it will be so treated when recovered.

Subsection (b) prohibits avoiding any transaction that occurs before or within five days after the petition if the transaction is approved by the Commission and concerns an open contractual commitment. This enables the Commission to exercise its discretion to protect the integrity of the market by insuring that transactions cleared with other brokers will not be undone on a preference or a fraudulent transfer theory.

Subsection (c) insulates variation margin payments and other deposits from the avoiding powers except to the extent of actual fraud under section 548(a)(1). This facilitates prepetition transfers and protects the ordinary course of business in the market. House Report No. 95–595.

1982 Acts. House Report No. 97–420, see 1982 U.S.Code Cong. and Adm.News, p. 583.

1984 Acts. Statements by Legislative Leaders, see 1984 U.S.Code Cong. and Adm.News, p. 576.

Legislative Statements

Section 764 of the House amendment is derived from the House bill.

Effective and Applicability Provisions

2009 Acts. Amendments by Pub.L. 111–16 effective Dec. 1, 2009, see Pub.L. 111–16, § 7, set out as a note under 11 U.S.C.A. § 109.

1984 Acts. Amendment by Pub.L. 98–353 effective with respect to cases filed 90 days after July 10, 1984, see section 552(a), formerly 553(a), of Pub.L. 98–353, set out as a note under section 101 of this title.

CROSS REFERENCES

Voidable transfers in stockbroker liquidation cases, see 11 USCA § 749.

§ 765.　Customer instructions

(a) The notice required by section 342 of this title to customers shall instruct each customer—

(1) to file a proof of such customer's claim promptly, and to specify in such claim any specifical-

ly identifiable security, property, or commodity contract; and

(2) to instruct the trustee of such customer's desired disposition, including transfer under section 766 of this title or liquidation, of any commodity contract specifically identified to such customer.

(b) The trustee shall comply, to the extent practicable, with any instruction received from a customer regarding such customer's desired disposition of any commodity contract specifically identified to such customer. If the trustee has transferred, under section 766 of this title, such a commodity contract, the trustee shall transmit any such instruction to the commodity broker to whom such commodity contract was so transferred.

(Pub.L. 95–598, Nov. 6, 1978, 92 Stat. 2619; Pub.L. 97–222, § 18, July 27, 1982, 96 Stat. 240; Pub.L. 98–353, Title III, § 488, July 10, 1984, 98 Stat. 383.)

HISTORICAL AND STATUTORY NOTES

Revision Notes and Legislative Reports

1978 Acts. For Revision Notes and Legislative Reports for this section, see Revision Notes and Legislative Reports set out under section 766 of this title.

1982 Acts. House Report No. 97–420, see 1982 U.S.Code Cong. and Adm.News, p. 583.

1984 Acts. Statements by Legislative Leaders, see 1984 U.S.Code Cong. and Adm.News, p. 576.

Effective and Applicability Provisions

1984 Acts. Amendment by Pub.L. 98–353 effective with respect to cases filed 90 days after July 10, 1984, see section 552(a), formerly 553(a), of Pub.L. 98–353, set out as a note under section 101 of this title.

CROSS REFERENCES

Executory contracts and unexpired leases, see 11 USCA § 365.

§ 766. Treatment of customer property

(a) The trustee shall answer all margin calls with respect to a specifically identifiable commodity contract of a customer until such time as the trustee returns or transfers such commodity contract, but the trustee may not make a margin payment that has the effect of a distribution to such customer of more than that to which such customer is entitled under subsection (h) or (i) of this section.

(b) The trustee shall prevent any open commodity contract from remaining open after the last day of trading in such commodity contract, or into the first day on which notice of intent to deliver on such commodity contract may be tendered, whichever occurs first. With respect to any commodity contract that has remained open after the last day of trading in such commodity contract or with respect to which delivery must be made or accepted under the rules of the contract market on which such commodity contract was

made, the trustee may operate the business of the debtor for the purpose of—

(1) accepting or making tender of notice of intent to deliver the physical commodity underlying such commodity contract;

(2) facilitating delivery of such commodity; or

(3) disposing of such commodity if a party to such commodity contract defaults.

(c) The trustee shall return promptly to a customer any specifically identifiable security, property, or commodity contract to which such customer is entitled, or shall transfer, on such customer's behalf, such security, property, or commodity contract to a commodity broker that is not a debtor under this title, subject to such rules or regulations as the Commission may prescribe, to the extent that the value of such security, property, or commodity contract does not exceed the amount to which such customer would be entitled under subsection (h) or (i) of this section if such security, property, or commodity contract were not returned or transferred under this subsection.

(d) If the value of a specifically identifiable security, property, or commodity contract exceeds the amount to which the customer of the debtor is entitled under subsection (h) or (i) of this section, then such customer to whom such security, property, or commodity contract is specifically identified may deposit cash with the trustee equal to the difference between the value of such security, property, or commodity contract and such amount, and the trustee then shall—

(1) return promptly such security, property, or commodity contract to such customer; or

(2) transfer, on such customer's behalf, such security, property, or commodity contract to a commodity broker that is not a debtor under this title, subject to such rules or regulations as the Commission may prescribe.

(e) Subject to subsection (b) of this section, the trustee shall liquidate any commodity contract that—

(1) is identified to a particular customer and with respect to which such customer has not timely instructed the trustee as to the desired disposition of such commodity contract;

(2) cannot be transferred under subsection (c) of this section; or

(3) cannot be identified to a particular customer.

(f) As soon as practicable after the commencement of the case, the trustee shall reduce to money, consistent with good market practice, all securities and other property, other than commodity contracts, held as property of the estate, except for specifically identifiable securities or property distributable under subsection (h) or (i) of this section.

(g) The trustee may not distribute a security or other property except under subsection (h) or (i) of this section.

(h) Except as provided in subsection (b) of this section, the trustee shall distribute customer property ratably to customers on the basis and to the extent of such customers' allowed net equity claims, and in priority to all other claims, except claims of a kind specified in section 507(a)(2) of this title that are attributable to the administration of customer property. Such distribution shall be in the form of—

   (1) cash;

   (2) the return or transfer, under subsection (c) or (d) of this section, of specifically identifiable customer securities, property, or commodity contracts; or

   (3) payment of margin calls under subsection (a) of this section.

Notwithstanding any other provision of this subsection, a customer net equity claim based on a proprietary account, as defined by Commission rule, regulation, or order, may not be paid either in whole or in part, directly or indirectly, out of customer property unless all other customer net equity claims have been paid in full.

(i) If the debtor is a clearing organization, the trustee shall distribute—

   (1) customer property, other than member property, ratably to customers on the basis and to the extent of such customers' allowed net equity claims based on such customers' accounts other than proprietary accounts, and in priority to all other claims, except claims of a kind specified in section 507(a)(2) of this title that are attributable to the administration of such customer property; and

   (2) member property ratably to customers on the basis and to the extent of such customers' allowed net equity claims based on such customers' proprietary accounts, and in priority to all other claims, except claims of a kind specified in section 507(a)(2) of this title that are attributable to the administration of member property or customer property.

(j)(1) The trustee shall distribute customer property in excess of that distributed under subsection (h) or (i) of this section in accordance with section 726 of this title.

(2) Except as provided in section 510 of this title, if a customer is not paid the full amount of such customer's allowed net equity claim from customer property, the unpaid portion of such claim is a claim entitled to distribution under section 726 of this title.

(Pub.L. 95–598, Nov. 6, 1978, 92 Stat. 2619; Pub.L. 97–222, § 19, July 27, 1982, 96 Stat. 240; Pub.L. 98–353, Title III, § 489, July 10, 1984, 98 Stat. 383; Pub.L. 109–8, Title XV, § 1502(a)(4), Apr. 20, 2005, 119 Stat. 216.)

HISTORICAL AND STATUTORY NOTES

Revision Notes and Legislative Reports

1978 Acts. [Section 765] Subsection (a) of this section [now section 766(h)] provides that with respect to liquidation of commodity brokers which are not clearing organizations, the trustee shall distribute customer property to customers on the basis and to the extent of such customers' allowed net equity claims, and in priority to all other claims. This section grants customers' claims first priority in the distribution of the estate. Subsection (b) [now section 766(i)] grants the same priority to member property and other customer property in the liquidation of a clearing organization. A fundamental purpose of these provisions is to ensure that the property entrusted by customers to their brokers will not be subject to the risks of the broker's business and will be available for disbursement to customers if the broker becomes bankrupt.

As a result of section 765, a customer need not trace any funds in order to avoid treatment as a general creditor as was required by the Seventh Circuit in *In re Rosenbaum Grain Corporation.*

Section 766 lists certain transfers which are not voidable by the trustee of a commodity broker. Subsection (a) exempts transfers approved by the Commission by rule or order, either before or after the transfer. It is expected that the Commission will use this power sparingly and only when necessary to effectuate the remedial purposes of this legislation, bearing in mind that the immediate transfer of customer accounts from bankrupt commodity brokers to solvent commodity brokers is one of the primary goals of this subchapter. The committee considered and rejected a provision in subsection (b) that would have exempted payments made to a commodity broker. The Commission may not by rule exempt such transfers. The Commission's prompt attention to the promulgation of such rules and regulations is expected.

Subsection (b) [now section 764(c)] provides for the nonavoidability of margin payments made by a commodity broker, other than a clearing organization. If such payments are made by or to a clearing organization, they are nonavoidable pursuant to subsection (c). All other margin payments made by a commodity broker, other than a clearing organization, are nonavoidable if they meet the conditions set forth in subsection (b). Subsections (b)(1) and (b)(2) parallel the requirements for avoidance of fraudulent transfers and obligations under section 548. Subsection (b)(3) adds a requirement that there be collusion between the transferee and transferor in order for such payments to be voidable. It would be unfair to permit recovery from an innocent commodity broker since such brokers are, for the most part, simply conduits for margin payments and do not retain margin for use in their operations. Subsection (b)(4) would permit recovery of a subsequent transferee only if it had actual knowledge at the time of that subsequent transfer of the scheme to defraud. Again it should be noted that if the transfer is a margin payment and the subsequent transferee is a clearing organization, the transfer is nonavoidable under section 766(c).

Subsection (c) [now section 548(d)(2)] overrules *Seligson v. New York Produce Exchange,* and provides as a matter of law that margin payments made by or to a clearing organization are not voidable.

Section 767 sets forth the procedures to be followed by the trustee. It should be emphasized that many of the duties imposed on the trustee are required to be discharged by the trustee immediately upon his appointment. The earlier these duties are discharged the less potential market disruption can result.

The initial duty of the trustee is to endeavor to transfer to another commodity broker or brokers all identified customer accounts together with the customer property margining such accounts, to the extent the trustee deems appropriate. Although it is preferable for all such accounts to be transferred, exigencies may dictate a partial transfer. The requirement that the value of the accounts and property transferred not exceed the customer's distribution share may necessitate a slight delay until the trustee can submit to the court, for its disapproval, an estimate of each customer's distribution share pursuant to section 768.

Subsection (c) [now section 766(e)] provides that contemporaneously with the estimate of the distribution share and the transfer of identified customer accounts and property, subsection (c) provides that the trustee should make arrangements for the liquidation of all commodity contracts maintained by the debtor that are not identifiable to specific customers. These contracts would, of course, include all such contracts held in the debtor's proprietary account.

At approximately the same time, the trustee should notify each customer of the debtor's bankruptcy and instruct each customer immediately to submit a claim including any claim to a specifically identifiable security or other property, and advise the trustee as to the desired disposition of commodity contracts carried by the debtor for the customer.

This requirement is placed upon the trustee to insure that producers who have hedged their production in the commodities market are allowed the opportunity to preserve their positions. The theory of the commodity market is that it exists for producers and buyers of commodities and not for the benefit of the speculators whose transactions now comprise the overwhelming majority of trades. Maintenance of positions by hedges may require them to put up additional margin payments in the hours and days following the commodity broker bankruptcy, which they may be unable or unwilling to do. In such cases, their positions will be quickly liquidated by the trustee, but they must have the opportunity to make those margin payments before they are summarily liquidated out of the market to the detriment of their growing crop. The failure of the customer to advise the trustee as to disposition of the customer's commodity contract will not delay a transfer of a contract pursuant to subsection (b) so long as the contract can otherwise be identified to the customer. Nor will the failure of the customer to submit a claim prevent the customer from recovering the net equity in that customer's account, absent a claim the customer cannot participate in the determination of the net equity in the account.

If the customer submits instructions pursuant to subsection (a) after the customer's commodity contracts are transferred to another commodity broker, the trustee must transmit the instruction to the transferee. If the customer's commodity contracts are not transferred before the customer's instructions are received, the trustee must attempt to comply with the instruction, subject to the provisions of section 767(d).

Under subsection (d) [now section 766(e)], the trustee has discretion to liquidate any commodity contract carried by the debtor at any time. This discretion must be exercised with restraint in such cases, consistent with the purposes of this subchapter and good business practices. The committee intends that hedged accounts will be given special consideration before liquidation as discussed in connection with subsection (c).

Subsection (e) [now section 766(c)] instructs the trustee as to the disposition of any security or other property, not disposed of pursuant to subsection (b) or (d), that is specifically identifiable to a customer and to which the customer is entitled. Such security or other property must be returned to the customer or promptly transferred to another commodity broker for the benefit of the customer. If the value of the security or other property retained or transferred, together with any other distribution made by the trustee to or on behalf of the customer, exceeds the customer's distribution share the customer must deposit cash with the trustee equal to that difference before the return or transfer of the security or other property.

Subsection (f) [now section 766(a)] requires the trustee to answer margin calls on specifically identifiable customer commodity contracts, but only to the extent that the margin payment, together with any other distribution made by the trustee to or on behalf of the customer, does not exceed the customer's distribution share.

Subsection (g) [now section 766(b)] requires the trustee to liquidate all commodity futures contracts prior to the close of trading in that contract, or the first day on which notice of intent to deliver on that contract may be tendered, whichever occurs first. If the customer desires that the contract be kept open for delivery, the contract should be transferred to another commodity broker pursuant to subsection (b).

If for some reason the trustee is unable to transfer a contract on which delivery must be made or accepted and is unable to close out such contract, the trustee is authorized to operate the business of the debtor for the purpose of accepting or making tender of notice of intent to deliver the physical commodity underlying the contract, facilitating delivery of the physical commodity or disposing of the physical commodity in the event of a default. Any property received, not previously held, by the trustee in connection with its operation of the business of the debtor for these purposes, is not by the terms of this subchapter specifically included in the definition of customer property.

Finally, subsection (h) [now section 766(f)] requires the trustee to liquidate the debtor's estate as soon as practicable and consistent with good market practice, except for specifically identifiable securities or other property distributable under subsection (e).

Section 768 is an integral part of the commodity broker liquidation procedures outlined in section 767. Prompt action by the trustee to transfer or liquidate customer commodity contracts is necessary to protect customers, the debtor's estate, and the marketplace generally. However, transfers of customer accounts and property valued in excess of the customer's distribution share are prohibited. Since a determination of the customer's distribution share requires a determination of the customer's net equity and the total dollar value of customer property held by or for the account of the debtor, it is possible that the customer's distribution share will not be determined, and thus the customer's contracts and property will not be transferred, on a timely basis. To avoid this problem, and to expedite transfers of customer property, section 768 permits the trustee to make distributions to customers in accordance with a preliminary estimate of the debtor's customer property and each customer's distribution share.

It is acknowledged that the necessity for prompt action may not allow the trustee to assemble all relevant facts before such an estimate is made. However, the trustee is expected to develop as accurate an estimate as possible based on the available facts. Further, in order to permit expeditious action, section 768 does not require that notice be given to customers or other creditors before the court approves or disapproves the estimate. Nor does section 768 require that customer claims be received pursuant to section 767(a) before the trustee may act upon and in accordance with the estimate. If the estimate is inaccurate, the trustee is absolved of liability for a distribution share so long as the distribution did not exceed the customer's estimated distribution share. However, a trustee may have a claim back against a customer who received more than its actual distribution share. Senate Report No. 95–989.

Section 765(a) indicates that a customer must file a proof of claim, including any claim to specifically identifiable property, within such time as the court fixes.

Subsection (c) [subsec. (c) of section 765 of H. Bill] sets forth the general rule requiring the trustee to liquidate contractual commitments that are either not specifically identifiable or with respect to which a customer has not instructed the trustee during the time fixed by the court. Subsection (d) [subsec. (d) of section 765 of H. Bill] indicates an exception to the time limits in the rule by requiring the trustee to liquidate any open contractual commitment before the last day of trading or the first day during which delivery may be demanded, whichever first occurs, if transfer cannot be effectuated.

Section 766(a) indicates that the trustee may distribute securities or other property only under section 768. This does not preclude a distribution of cash under section 767(a) or distribution of any excess customer property under section 767(c) to the general estate.

Subsection (b) indicates that the trustee shall liquidate all securities and other property that is not specifically identifiable property as soon as practicable after the commencement of the case and in accordance with good market practice. If securities are restricted or trading has been suspended, the trustee will have to make an exempt sale or file a registration statement. In the event of a private placement, a customer is not entitled to "bid in" his net equity claim. To do so would enable him to receive a greater percentage recovery than other customers.

Section 767(a) provides for the trustee to distribute customer property pro rata according to customers' net equity claims. The court will determine an equitable portion of customer property to pay administrative expenses. Paragraphs (2) and (3) indicate that the return of specifically identifiable property constitutes a distribution of net equity.

Subsection (b) indicates that if the debtor is a clearing organization, customer property is to be segregated into customers' accounts and proprietary accounts and distributed accordingly without offset. This protects a member's customers from having their claims offset against the member's proprietary account. Subsection (c)(1) indicates that any excess customer property will pour over into the general estate. This unlikely event would occur only if customers fail to file proofs of claim. Subsection (c)(2) indicates that to the extent customers are not paid in full, they are entitled to share in the general estate as unsecured creditors, unless subordinated by the court under proposed 11 U.S.C. 510.

Section 768(a) requires the trustee to return specifically identifiable property to the extent that such distribution will not exceed a customer's net equity claim. Thus, if the

customer owes money to a commodity broker, this will be offset under section 761(15)(A)(ii). If the value of the specifically identifiable property exceeds the net equity claim, then the customer may deposit cash with the trustee to make up the difference after which the trustee may return or transfer the customer's property.

Subsection (c) permits the trustee to answer all margin calls, to the extent of the customer's net equity claim, with respect to any specifically identifiable open contractual commitment. It should be noted that any payment under subsections (a) or (c) will be considered a reduction of the net equity claim under section 767(a). Thus the customer's net equity claim is a dynamic amount that varies with distributions of specifically identifiable property or margin payments on such property. This approach differs from the priority given to specifically identifiable property under subchapter III of chapter 7 by limiting the priority effect to a right to receive specific property as part of, rather than in addition to, a ratable share of customer property. This policy is designed to protect the small customer who is unlikely to have property in specifically identifiable form as compared with the professional trader. The CFTC is authorized to make rules defining specifically identifiable property under section 302 of the bill, in title III. House Report No. 95–595.

1982 Acts. House Report No. 97–420, see 1982 U.S.Code Cong. and Adm.News, p. 583.

1984 Acts. Statements by Legislative Leaders, see 1984 U.S.Code Cong. and Adm.News, p. 576.

2005 Acts. House Report No. 109–31(Part I), see 2005 U.S. Code Cong. and Adm. News, p. 88.

Legislative Statements

Sections 765 and 766 of the House amendment represent a consolidation and redraft of sections 765, 766, 767, and 768 of the House bill and sections 765, 766, 767, and 768 of the Senate amendment. In particular, section 765(a) of the House amendment is derived from section 765(a) of the House bill and section 767(a) of the Senate amendment. Under section 765(a) of the House amendment customers are notified of the opportunity to immediately file proofs of claim and to identify specifically identifiable securities, property, or commodity contracts. The customer is also afforded an opportunity to instruct the trustee regarding the customer's desires concerning disposition of the customer's commodity contracts. Section 767(b) [probably should be 765(b)] makes clear that the trustee must comply with instructions received to the extent practicable, but in the event the trustee has transferred commodity contracts to a commodity broker, such instructions shall be forwarded to the broker.

Section 766(a) of the House amendment is derived from section 768(c) of the House bill and section 767(f) of the Senate amendment. Section 766(b) of the House amendment is derived from section 765(d) of the House bill, and section 767(g) of the Senate amendment. Section 766(c) of the House amendment is derived from section 768(a) of the House bill and section 767(e) of the Senate amendment. Section 766(d) of the House amendment is derived from section 768(b) of the House bill and the second sentence of section 767(e) of the Senate amendment.

Section 766(e) of the House amendment is derived from section 765(c) of the House bill and sections 767(c) and (d) of the Senate amendment. The provision clarifies that the trustee may liquidate a commodity contract only if the commodity contract cannot be transferred to a commodity broker under section 766(c), cannot be identified to a particular customer, or has been identified with respect to a particular customer, but with respect to which the customer's instructions have not been received.

Section 766(f) of the House amendment is derived from section 766(b) of the House bill and section 767(h) of the Senate amendment. The term "all securities and other property" is not intended to include a commodity contract. Section 766(g) of the House amendment is derived from section 766(a) of the House bill. Section 766(h) of the House amendment is derived from section 767(a) of the House bill and section 765(a) of the Senate amendment. In order to induce private trustees to undertake the difficult and risky job of liquidating a commodity broker, the House amendment contains a provision insuring that a pro rata share of administrative claims will be paid. The provision represents a compromise between the position taken in the House bill, subordinating customer property to all expenses of administration, and the position taken in the Senate amendment requiring the distribution of customer property in advance of any expenses of administration. The position in the Senate amendment is rejected since customers, in any event, would have to pay a brokerage commission or fee in the ordinary course of business. The compromise provision requires customers to pay only those administrative expenses that are attributable to the administration of customer property.

Section 766(i) of the House amendment is derived from section 767(b) of the House bill and contains a similar compromise with respect to expenses of administration as the compromise detailed in connection with section 766(h) of the House amendment. Section 766(j) of the House amendment is derived from section 767(c) of the House bill. No counterpart is contained in the Senate amendment. The provision takes account of the rare case where the estate has customer property in excess of customer claims and administrative expenses attributable to those claims. The section also specifies that to the extent a customer is not paid in full out of customer property, that the unpaid claim will be treated the same as any other general unsecured creditor.

Section 768 of the Senate amendment was deleted from the House amendment as unwise. The provision in the Senate amendment would have permitted the trustee to distribute customer property based upon an estimate of value of the customer's account, with no provision for recapture of excessive disbursements. Moreover, the section would have exonerated the trustee from any liability for such an excessive disbursement. Furthermore, the section is unclear with respect to the customer's rights in the event the trustee makes a distribution less than the share to which the customer is entitled. The provision is deleted in the House amendment so that this difficult problem may be handled on a case-by-case basis by the courts as the facts and circumstances of each case require.

Section 769 of the Senate amendment is deleted in the House amendment as unnecessary. The provision was intended to codify *Board of Trade v. Johnson*, 264 U.S. 1 (1924) [Ill.1924, 44 S.Ct. 232]. *Board of Trade against Johnson* is codified in section 363(f) of the House amendment which indicates the only five circumstances in which property may be sold free and clear of an interest in such property of an entity other than the estate.

Section 770 of the Senate amendment is deleted in the House amendment as unnecessary. That section would have permitted commodity brokers to liquidate commodity contracts, notwithstanding any contrary order of the court. It would require an extraordinary circumstance, such as a threat to the national security, to enjoin a commodity broker from liquidating a commodity contract. However, in those circumstances, an injunction must prevail. Failure of the House amendment to incorporate section 770 of the Senate amendment does not imply that the automatic stay prevents liquidation of commodity contracts by commodity brokers. To the contrary, whenever by contract, or otherwise, a commodity broker is entitled to liquidate a position as a result of a condition specified in a contract, other than a condition or default of the kind specified in section 365(b)(2) of title 11, the commodity broker may engage in such liquidation. To this extent, the commodity broker's contract with his customer is treated no differently than any other contract under section 365 of Title 11.

Effective and Applicability Provisions

2005 Acts. Amendments by Pub.L. 109–8 effective, except as otherwise provided, 180 days after April 20, 2005, and inapplicable with respect to cases commenced under Title 11 before the effective date, see Pub.L. 109–8, § 1501, set out as a note under 11 U.S.C.A. § 101.

1984 Acts. Amendment by Pub.L. 98–353 effective with respect to cases filed 90 days after July 10, 1984, see section 552(a), formerly 553(a), of Pub.L. 98–353, set out as a note under section 101 of this title.

CROSS REFERENCES

Distribution in Chapter eleven cases, see 11 USCA § 1143.

Distribution of,

    Customer property in stockbroker liquidation cases, see 11 USCA § 752.

    Property of estate, see 11 USCA § 726.

Election of trustee by creditors holding claims entitled to distribution, see 11 USCA § 702.

Executory contracts and unexpired leases, see 11 USCA § 365.

Provisions relating to transferability of customer property and commodity contracts, see 7 USCA § 24.

§ 767. Commodity broker liquidation and forward contract merchants, commodity brokers, stockbrokers, financial institutions, financial participants, securities clearing agencies, swap participants, repo participants, and master netting agreement participants

Notwithstanding any other provision of this title, the exercise of rights by a forward contract merchant, commodity broker, stockbroker, financial institution, financial participant, securities clearing agency, swap participant, repo participant, or master netting agreement participant under this title shall not affect the priority of any unsecured claim it may have after the exercise of such rights.

(Added Pub.L. 109–8, Title IX, § 907(*l*), Apr. 20, 2005, 119 Stat. 181.)

HISTORICAL AND STATUTORY NOTES

Revision Notes and Legislative Reports

2005 Acts. House Report No. 109–31(Part I), see 2005 U.S. Code Cong. and Adm. News, p. 88.

Effective and Applicability Provisions

2005 Acts. Amendments by Pub.L. 109–8 effective, except as otherwise provided, 180 days after April 20, 2005, and inapplicable with respect to cases commenced under Title 11 before the effective date, see Pub.L. 109–8, § 1501, set out as a note under 11 U.S.C.A. § 101.

SUBCHAPTER V—CLEARING BANK LIQUIDATION

§ 781. Definitions

For purposes of this subchapter, the following definitions shall apply:

(1) **Board.**—The term "Board" means the Board of Governors of the Federal Reserve System.

(2) **Depository institution.**—The term "depository institution" has the same meaning as in section 3 of the Federal Deposit Insurance Act.

(3) **Clearing bank.**—The term "clearing bank" means an uninsured State member bank, or a corporation organized under section 25A of the Federal Reserve Act, which operates, or operates as, a multilateral clearing organization pursuant to section 409 of the Federal Deposit Insurance Corporation Improvement Act of 1991.

(Added Pub.L. 106–554, § 1(a)(5) [Title I, § 112(c)(5)(B)], Dec. 21, 2000, 114 Stat. 2763, 2763A–394.)

HISTORICAL AND STATUTORY NOTES

Revision Notes and Legislative Reports

2000 Acts. House Report No. 106–645 and Statement by President, see 2000 U.S. Code Cong. and Adm. News, p. 2459.

References in Text

Section 3 of the Federal Deposit Insurance Act, referred to in par. (2), is Act Sept. 21, 1950, c. 967, § 2[3], 64 Stat. 873, which is classified to 12 U.S.C.A. § 1813.

Section 25A of the Federal Reserve Act, referred to in par. (3), is Dec. 23, 1913, c. 6, § 25A, formerly § 25(a), as added Dec. 24, 1919, c. 18, 41 Stat. 378, as amended, which is classified to subchapter II of chapter 6 of Title 12, 12 U.S.C.A. § 611 et seq.

Section 409 of the Federal Deposit Insurance Corporation Improvement Act of 1991, referred to in par. (3), is Pub.L. 102–242, Title IV, § 409, as added by Pub.L. 106–554, § 1(a)(5) [Title I, § 112(a)(3)], Dec. 21, 2000, 114 Stat. 2763, 2763A–392, which is classified as 12 U.S.C.A. § 4422.

§ 782. Selection of trustee

(a) **In general.**—

(1) **Appointment.**—Notwithstanding any other provision of this title, the conservator or receiver who files the petition shall be the trustee under this chapter, unless the Board designates an alternative trustee.

(2) **Successor.**—The Board may designate a successor trustee if required.

(b) **Authority of trustee.**—Whenever the Board appoints or designates a trustee, chapter 3 and sections 704 and 705 of this title shall apply to the Board in the same way and to the same extent that they apply to a United States trustee.

(Added Pub.L. 106–554, § 1(a)(5) [Title I, § 112(c)(5)(B)], Dec. 21, 2000, 114 Stat. 2763, 2763A–394.)

HISTORICAL AND STATUTORY NOTES

Revision Notes and Legislative Reports

2000 Acts. House Report No. 106–645 and Statement by President, see 2000 U.S. Code Cong. and Adm. News, p. 2459.

References in Text

Chapter 3, referred to in subsec. (b), is classified to 11 U.S.C.A. § 301 et seq.

§ 783. Additional powers of trustee

(a) **Distribution of property not of the estate.**—The trustee under this subchapter has power to distribute property not of the estate, including distributions to customers that are mandated by subchapters III and IV of this chapter.

(b) **Disposition of institution.**—The trustee under this subchapter may, after notice and a hearing—

(1) sell the clearing bank to a depository institution or consortium of depository institutions (which consortium may agree on the allocation of the clearing bank among the consortium);

(2) merge the clearing bank with a depository institution;

(3) transfer contracts to the same extent as could a receiver for a depository institution under paragraphs (9) and (10) of section 11(e) of the Federal Deposit Insurance Act;

(4) transfer assets or liabilities to a depository institution; and

(5) transfer assets and liabilities to a bridge depository institution as provided in paragraphs (1), (3)(A), (5), and (6) of section 11(n) of the Federal Deposit Insurance Act, paragraphs (9) through (13) of such section, and subparagraphs (A) through (H) and subparagraph (K) of paragraph (4) of such section 11(n), except that—

(A) the bridge depository institution to which such assets or liabilities are transferred shall be treated as a clearing bank for the purpose of this subsection; and

(B) any references in any such provision of law to the Federal Deposit Insurance Corporation shall be construed to be references to the appointing agency and that references to deposit insurance shall be omitted.

(c) Certain transfers included.—Any reference in this section to transfers of liabilities includes a ratable transfer of liabilities within a priority class.

(Added Pub.L. 106–554, § 1(a)(5) [Title I, § 112(c)(5)(B)], Dec. 21, 2000, 114 Stat. 2763, 2763A–395; amended Pub.L. 110–289, Div. A, Title VI, § 1604(b)(3), July 30, 2008, 122 Stat. 2829.)

HISTORICAL AND STATUTORY NOTES

Revision Notes and Legislative Reports

2000 Acts. House Report No. 106–645 and Statement by President, see 2000 U.S. Code Cong. and Adm. News, p. 2459.

References in Text

Subchapters III and IV of this chapter, referred to in subsec. (a), are 11 U.S.C.A. §§ 741 et seq. and 761 et seq.

Paragraphs (9) and (10) of section 11(e) of the Federal Deposit Insurance Act, referred to in subsec. (b)(3), are classified to 12 U.S.C.A. § 1821(e)(9), (10).

Paragraphs (1), (3)(A), (5), and (6) of section 11(n) of the Federal Deposit Insurance Act, paragraphs (9) through (13) of such section, and subparagraphs (A) through (H) and subparagraph (K) of paragraph (4) of such section 11(n), referred to in subsec. (b)(5), are classified to 12 U.S.C.A. § 1821(n)(1), (3)(A), (5), (6), and (4)(A) to (K).

Codifications

Amendment by Pub.L. 110–289, § 1604(b)(3), which directed striking out "bridge bank" and inserting "bridge depository institution", was executed to both locations where the term appeared in subsec. (b)(5), as the probable intent of Congress. See 2008 Amendments note set out under this section.

§ 784.   Right to be heard

The Board or a Federal reserve bank (in the case of a clearing bank that is a member of that bank) may raise and may appear and be heard on any issue in a case under this subchapter.

(Added Pub.L. 106–554, § 1(a)(5) [Title I, § 112(c)(5)(B)], Dec. 21, 2000, 114 Stat. 2763, 2763A–395.)

HISTORICAL AND STATUTORY NOTES

Revision Notes and Legislative Reports

2000 Acts. House Report No. 106–645 and Statement by President, see 2000 U.S. Code Cong. and Adm. News, p. 2459.

CHAPTER 9—ADJUSTMENT OF DEBTS OF A MUNICIPALITY

SUBCHAPTER I—GENERAL PROVISIONS

CROSS REFERENCES

Allowance of administrative expenses of substantial contributors in cases under this chapter, see 11 USCA § 503.

Chapter one of this title and this chapter solely applicable in cases under this chapter except as provided in § 901 of this title, see 11 USCA § 103.

Claims arising from rejection of executory contracts or unexpired leases under this chapter's plans, see 11 USCA § 502.

Definitions applicable in this title, see 11 USCA § 101.

Duration of automatic stay, see 11 USCA § 362.

Entities which may be debtors under this chapter, see 11 USCA § 109.

Executory contracts and unexpired leases, see 11 USCA § 365.

Filing fees, see 28 USCA § 1930.

Unclaimed property, see 11 USCA § 347.

§ 901. Applicability of other sections of this title

(a) Sections 301, 333, 344, 347(b), 349, 350(b) 351,,[1] 361, 362, 364(c), 364(d), 364(e), 364(f), 365, 366, 501, 502, 503, 504, 506, 507(a)(2), 509, 510, 524(a)(1), 524(a)(2), 544, 545, 546, 547, 548, 549(a), 549(c), 549(d), 550, 551, 552, 553, 555, 556, 557, 559, 560, 561, 562, 1102, 1103, 1109, 1111(b), 1122, 1123(a)(1), 1123(a)(2), 1123(a)(3), 1123(a)(4), 1123(a)(5), 1123(b), 1123(d), 1124, 1125, 1126(a), 1126(b), 1126(c), 1126(e), 1126(f), 1126(g), 1127(d), 1128, 1129(a)(2), 1129(a)(3), 1129(a)(6), 1129(a)(8), 1129(a)(10), 1129(b)(1), 1129(b)(2)(A), 1129(b)(2)(B), 1142(b), 1143, 1144, and 1145 of this title apply in a case under this chapter.

(b) A term used in a section of this title made applicable in a case under this chapter by subsection (a) of this section or section 103(e) of this title has the meaning defined for such term for the purpose of such applicable section, unless such term is otherwise defined in section 902 of this title.

(c) A section made applicable in a case under this chapter by subsection (a) of this section that is operative if the business of the debtor is authorized to be operated is operative in a case under this chapter.

(Pub.L. 95–598, Nov. 6, 1978, 92 Stat. 2621; Pub.L. 98–353, Title III, §§ 353, 490, July 10, 1984, 98 Stat. 361, 383; Pub.L. 100–597, § 3, Nov. 3, 1988, 102 Stat. 3028; Pub.L. 109–8, Title V, § 502, Title XII, § 1216, Title XV, § 1502(a)(5), Apr. 20, 2005, 119 Stat. 118, 195, 216; Pub.L. 111–327, § 2(a)(29), Dec. 22, 2010, 124 Stat. 3560.)

[1] So in original. The second comma probably should follow "350(b)".

HISTORICAL AND STATUTORY NOTES

Revision Notes and Legislative Reports

1978 Acts. Section 901 makes applicable appropriate provisions of other chapters of proposed title 11. The general rule set out in section 103(e) is that only the provisions of chapters 1 and 9 apply in a chapter 9 case. Section 901 is the exception, and specifies other provisions that do apply. They are as follows:

§ 301. Voluntary cases. Application of this section makes clear, as under current chapter IX [former chapter 9 (section 401 et seq.) of former Title 11], that a municipal case can be commenced only by the municipality itself. There are no involuntary chapter 9 cases.

§ 344. Self-incrimination; immunity. Application of this section is of no substantive effect for the administration of the case, but merely provides that the general rules in part V of title 18 [section 6001 et seq. of Title 18, Crimes and Criminal Procedure] govern immunity.

§ 347(b). Unclaimed property. This provision currently appears in section 96(d) of chapter IX [section 416(d) of this former Title 11].

§ 349. Effect of dismissal. This section governs the effect of a dismissal of a chapter 9 case. It provides in substance that rights that existed before the case that were disturbed by the commencement of the case are reinstated. This section does not concern grounds for dismissal, which are found in § 926.

§ 361. Adequate protection. Section 361 provides the general standard for the protection of secured creditors whose property is used in a case under title 11. Its importance lies in its application to sections 362 and 364.

§ 362. Automatic stay. The automatic stay provisions of the general portions of the title are incorporated into chapter 9. There is an automatic stay provided in current Bankruptcy Act section 85(e) [section 405(e) of former title 11]. The thrust of section 362 is the same as that of section 85(e), but, of course, its application in chapter 9 is modernized and drafted to conform with the stay generally applicable under the bankruptcy code. An additional part of the automatic stay applicable only to municipal cases is included in section 922.

§§ 364(c), 364(d), 364(e). Obtaining credit. This section governs the borrowing of money by a municipality in reorganization. It is narrower than a comparable provision in current law, section 82(b)(2) [section 402(b)(2) of former title 11]. The difference lies mainly in the removal under the bill of the authority of the court to supervise borrowing by the municipality in instances in which none of the special bankruptcy powers are involved. That is, if a municipality could borrow money outside of the bankruptcy court, then it should have the same authority in bankruptcy court, under the doctrine of *Ashton v. Cameron Water District No. 1*, 298 U.S. 513 (1936) [Tex.1936, 56 S.Ct. 892, 80 L.Ed. 1309, 31 Am. Bankr.Rep.N.S. 96, rehearing denied 57 S.Ct. 5, 299 U.S. 619, 81 L.Ed. 457] and *National League of Cities v. Usery*, 426 U.S. 833 (1976) [Dist.Col.1976, 96 S.Ct. 2465, 49 L.Ed.2d 245, on remand 429 F.Supp. 703]. Only when the municipality needs special authority, such as subordination of existing liens, or special priority for the borrowed funds, will the court become involved in the authorization.

§ 365. Executory contracts and unexpired leases. The applicability of section 365 incorporates the general power of a bankruptcy court to authorize the assumption or rejection of executory contracts or unexpired leases found in other chapters of the title. This section is comparable to section 82(b)(1) [section 402(b)(1) of former Title 11] of current law.

§ 366. Utility service. This section gives a municipality the same authority as any other debtor with respect to continuation of utility service during the proceeding, provided adequate assurance of future payment is provided. No comparable explicit provision is found in current law, although the case law seems to support the same result.

§ 501. Filing of proofs of claims. This section permits filing of proofs of claims in a chapter 9 case. Note, however, that section 924 permits listing of creditors' claims, as under chapter 11 and under section 85(b) of chapter IX [section 405(b) of former Title 11].

§ 502. Allowance of claims. This section applies the general allowance rules to chapter 9 cases. This is no change from current law.

§ 503. Administrative expenses. Administrative expenses as defined in section 503 will be paid in a chapter 9 case, as provided under section 89(1) of current law [section 409(1) of former Title 11].

§ 504. Sharing of compensation. There is no comparable provision in current law. However, this provision applies generally throughout the proposed law, and will not affect the progress of the case, only the interrelations between attorneys and other professionals that participate in the case.

§ 506. Determination of secured status. Section 506 specifies that claims secured by a lien should be separated, to the extent provided, into secured and unsecured claims. It

applies generally. Current law follows this result, though there is no explicit provision.

§ 507(1). Priorities. Paragraph (1) of section 507 requires that administrative expenses be paid first. This rule will apply in chapter 9 cases. It is presently found in section 89(1) [section 409(1) of former Title 11]. The two other priorities presently found in section 89 have been deleted. The second, for claims arising within 3 months before the case is commenced, is deleted from the statute, but may be within the court's equitable power to award, under the case of *Fosdick v. Schall*, 99 U.S. 235 (1878). Leaving the provision to the courts permits greater flexibility, as under railroad cases, than an absolute three-month rule. The third priority under current law, for claims which are entitled to priority under the laws of the United States, is deleted because of the proposed amendment to section 3466 of the Revised Statutes [former 31 U.S.C.A. § 191, see 31 U.S.C.A. § 3713(a)] contained in section 321(a) of title III of the bill, which previously has given the United States an absolute first priority in Chapter X [former Chapter 10 (section 501 et seq.) of former Title 11] and section 77 [section 205 of former Title 1] cases. Because the priority rules are regularized and brought together in the bankruptcy laws by this bill, the need for incorporation of priorities elsewhere specified is eliminated.

§ 509. Claims of codebtors. This section provides for the treatment of sureties, guarantors, and codebtors. The general rule of postponement found in the other chapters will apply in chapter 9. This section adopts current law.

§ 510. Subordination of claims. This section permits the court to subordinate, on equitable grounds, any claim, and requires enforcement of contractual subordination agreements, and subordination of securities rescission claims. The section recognizes the inherent equitable power of the court under current law, and the practice followed with respect to contractual provisions.

§ 547. Preferences. Incorporation of section 547 will permit the debtor to recover preferences. This power will be used primarily when those who gave the preferences have been replaced by new municipal officers or when creditors coerced preferential payments. Unlike Bankruptcy Act § 85(h) [section 405(h) of former Title 11], the section does not permit the appointment of a trustee for the purpose of pursuing preferences. Moreover, this bill does not incorporate the other avoiding powers of a trustee for chapter 9, found in current section 85(h).

§ 550. Liability of transfers. Incorporation of this section is made necessary by the incorporation of the preference section, and permits recovery by the debtor from a transferee of an avoided preference.

§ 551. Automatic preservation of avoided transfer. Application of section 551 requires preservation of any avoided preference for the benefit of the estate.

§ 552. Postpetition effect of security interest. This section will govern the applicability after the commencement of the case of security interests granted by the debtor before the commencement of the case.

§ 553. Setoff. Under current law, certain setoff is stayed. Application of this section preserves that result, though the setoffs that are permitted under section 553 are better defined than under present law. Application of this section is necessary to stay the setoff and to provide the offsetting creditor with the protection to which he is entitled under present law.

§ 1122. Classification of claims. This section is derived from current section 88(b) [section 408(b) of former Title 11], and is substantially similar.

§ 1123(a)(1)–(4), (b). Contents of plan. The general provisions governing contents of a chapter 11 plan are made applicable here, with two exceptions relating to the rights of stockholders, which are not applicable in chapter 9 cases. This section expands current law by specifying the contents of a plan in some detail. Section 91 of current law [section 411 of former Title 11] speaks only in general terms. The substance of the two sections is substantially the same, however.

§ 1124. Impairment of claims. The confirmation standards adopted in chapter 9 are the same as those of chapter 11. This changes current chapter IX [former chapter 9 (section 401 et seq.) of former Title 11], which requires compliance with the fair and equitable rule. The greater flexibility of proposed chapter 11 is carried over into chapter 9, for there appears to be no reason why the confirmation standards for the two chapters should be different, or why the elimination of the fair and equitable rule from corporate reorganizations should not be followed in municipal debt adjustments. The current chapter IX rule is based on the confirmation rules of current chapter X [chapter 10 of former Title 11]. The change in the latter suggests a corresponding change in the former. Section 1124 is one part of the new confirmation standard. It defines impairment, for use in section 1129.

§ 1125. Postpetition disclosure and solicitation. The change in the confirmation standard necessitates a corresponding change in the disclosure requirements for solicitation of acceptances of a plan. Under current chapter IX [former chapter 9 (section 401 et seq.) of former Title 11] there is no disclosure requirement. Incorporation of section 1125 will insure that creditors receive adequate information before they are required to vote on a plan.

§ 1126(a), (b), (c), (e), (f), (g). Acceptance of plan. Section 1126 incorporates the current chapter IX [former chapter 9 (section 401 et seq.) of former Title 11] acceptance requirement: two-thirds in amount and a majority in number, Bankruptcy Act § 92 [section 412 of former Title 11]. Section 1125 permits exclusion of certain acceptances from the computation if the acceptances were obtained in bad faith or, unlike current law, if there is a conflict of interest motivating the acceptance.

§ 1127(d). Modification of plan. This section governs the change of a creditor's vote on the plan after a modification is proposed. It is derived from current section 92(e) [section 412(e) of former Title 11].

§ 1128. Hearing on confirmation. This section requires a hearing on the confirmation of the plan, and permits parties in interest to object. It is the same as Bankruptcy Act §§ 93 and 94(a) [section 413 and section 414(a) of former Title 11], though the provision, comparable to section 206 of current chapter X [section 606 of former Title 11], permitting a labor organization to appear and be heard on the economic soundness of the plan, has been deleted as more appropriate for the Rules.

§ 1129(a)(2), (3), (8), (b)(1), (2). Confirmation of plan. This section provides the boiler-plate language that the plan be proposed in good faith and that it comply with the provisions of the chapter, and also provides the financial standard for confirmation, which replaces the fair and equitable rule. See § 1124, supra.

§ 1142(b). Execution of plan. Derived from Bankruptcy Act § 96(b) [section 416(b) of former Title 11], this section permits the court to order execution and delivery of instruments in order to execute the plan.

§ 1143. Distribution. This section is the same in substance as section 96(d) [section 416(d) of former Title 11], which requires presentment or delivery of securities within five years, and bars creditors that do not act within that time.

§ 1144. Revocation of order of confirmation. This section permits the court to revoke the order of confirmation and the discharge if the confirmation of the plan was procured by fraud. There is no comparable provision in current chapter IX [former chapter 9 (section 401 et seq.) of former Title 11]. House Report No. 95–595.

1984 Acts. Statements by Legislative Leaders, see 1984 U.S.Code Cong. and Adm.News, p. 576.

1988 Acts. House Report No. 100–1011, see 1988 U.S.Code Cong. and Adm.News, p. 4115.

2005 Acts. House Report No. 109–31(Part I), see 2005 U.S. Code Cong. and Adm. News, p. 88.

Legislative Statements

Chapter 9 of the House amendment represents a compromise between chapter 9 of the House bill and 9 of the Senate amendment. In most respects this chapter follows current law with respect to the adjustment of debts of a municipality. Stylistic changes and minor substantive revisions have been made in order to conform this chapter with other new chapters of the bankruptcy code [this title]. There are few major differences between the House bill and the Senate amendment on this issue. Section 901 indicates the applicability of other sections of title 11 in cases under chapter 9. Included are sections providing for creditors' committees under sections 1102 and 1103.

References in Text

Section 103(e) of this title, referred to in subsec. (b), was redesignated subsec. (f) and a new subsec. (e) was added by Pub.L. 106–554, § 1(a)(5) [Title I, § 112(c)(5)(A)], Dec. 21, 2000, 114 Stat. 2763, 2763A–394.

Effective and Applicability Provisions

2005 Acts. Amendments by Pub.L. 109–8 effective, except as otherwise provided, 180 days after April 20, 2005, and inapplicable with respect to cases commenced under Title 11 before the effective date, see Pub.L. 109–8, § 1501, set out as a note under 11 U.S.C.A. § 101.

1988 Acts. Amendment by Pub.L. 100–597 effective Nov. 3, 1988, but not applicable to any case commenced under this title before that date, see section 12 of Pub.L. 100–597, set out as a note under section 101 of this title.

1984 Acts. Amendment by Pub.L. 98–353 effective with respect to cases filed 90 days after July 10, 1984, see section 552(a), formerly 553(a), of Pub.L. 98–353, set out as a note under section 101 of this title.

CROSS REFERENCES

Chapters one and nine of this title solely applicable in cases under Chapter nine except as provided in this section, see 11 USCA § 103.

Confirmation in Chapter nine cases upon compliance with provisions of this title made applicable by this section, see 11 USCA § 943.

---

§ 902. Definitions for this chapter

In this chapter—

(1) "property of the estate", when used in a section that is made applicable in a case under this chapter by section 103(e) or 901 of this title, means property of the debtor;

(2) "special revenues" means—

(A) receipts derived from the ownership, operation, or disposition of projects or systems of the debtor that are primarily used or intended to be used primarily to provide transportation, utility, or other services, including the proceeds of borrowings to finance the projects or systems;

(B) special excise taxes imposed on particular activities or transactions;

(C) incremental tax receipts from the benefited area in the case of tax-increment financing;

(D) other revenues or receipts derived from particular functions of the debtor, whether or not the debtor has other functions; or

(E) taxes specifically levied to finance one or more projects or systems, excluding receipts from general property, sales, or income taxes (other than tax-increment financing) levied to finance the general purposes of the debtor;

(3) "special tax payer" means record owner or holder of legal or equitable title to real property against which a special assessment or special tax has been levied the proceeds of which are the sole source of payment of an obligation issued by the debtor to defray the cost of an improvement relating to such real property;

(4) "special tax payer affected by the plan" means special tax payer with respect to whose real property the plan proposes to increase the proportion of special assessments or special taxes referred to in paragraph (2) of this section assessed against such real property; and

(5) "trustee", when used in a section that is made applicable in a case under this chapter by section 103(e) or 901 of this title, means debtor, except as provided in section 926 of this title.

(Pub.L. 95–598, Nov. 6, 1978, 92 Stat. 2622; Pub.L. 98–353, Title III, § 491, July 10, 1984, 98 Stat. 383; Pub.L. 100–597, § 4, Nov. 3, 1988, 102 Stat. 3028.)

HISTORICAL AND STATUTORY NOTES

Revision Notes and Legislative Reports

1978 Acts. There are six definitions for use in chapter 9. Paragraph (1) defines what claims are included in a chapter 9 case and adopts the definition now found in section 81(1) [section 401(1) of former Title 11]. All claims against the petitioner generally will be included, with one significant exception. Municipalities are authorized, under section 103(c) of the Internal Revenue Code of 1954 [section 103(c) of Title 26, Internal Revenue Code], as amended, to issue tax-exempt industrial development revenue bonds to provide for the financing of certain projects for privately owned companies.

The bonds are sold on the basis of the credit of the company on whose behalf they are issued, and the principal, interest, and premium, if any, are payable solely from payments made by the company to the trustee under the bond indenture and do not constitute claims on the tax revenues or other funds of the issuing municipalities. The municipality merely acts as the vehicle to enable the bonds to be issued on a tax-exempt basis. Claims that arise by virtue of these bonds are not among the claims defined by this paragraph and amounts owed by private companies to the holders of industrial development revenue bonds are not to be included among the assets of the municipality that would be affected by the plan. See Cong. Record, 94th Cong., 1st Sess. H.R. 12073 (statement by Mr. Don Edwards, floor manager of the bill in the House). Paragraph (2) defines the court which means the federal district court or federal district judge before which the case is pending. Paragraph (3) specifies that when the term "property of the estate" is used in a section in another chapter made applicable in chapter 9 cases, the term means "property of the debtor". Paragraphs (4) and (5) adopt the definition of "special taxpayer affected by the plan" that appears in current sections 81(10) and 81(11) [section 401(10) and (11) of former Title 11] of the Bankruptcy Act. Paragraph (6) provides that "trustee" means "debtor" when used in conjunction with chapter 9. Senate Report No. 95–989.

There are only four definitions for use only in chapter 9. The first specifies that when the term "property of the estate" is used in a section in another chapter made applicable in chapter 9 cases, the term will mean "property of the debtor". Paragraphs (2) and (3) adopt the definition of "special taxpayer affected by the plan" that appears in current section 81(10) and 81(11) [section 401(10) and (11) of former Title 11]. Paragraphs [sic] (4) provides for "trustee" the same treatment as provided for "property of the estate", specifying that it means "debtor" when used in conjunction with chapter 9. House Report No. 95–595.

1984 Acts. Statements by Legislative Leaders, see 1984 U.S.Code Cong. and Adm.News, p. 576.

1988 Acts. House Report No. 100–1011, see 1988 U.S.Code Cong. and Adm.News, p. 4115.

Legislative Statements

Section 902(2) of the Senate amendment is deleted since the bankruptcy court will have jurisdiction over all cases under chapter 9. The concept of a claim being materially and adversely affected reflected in section 902(1) of the Senate amendment has been deleted and replaced with the new concept of "impairment" set forth in section 1124 of the House amendment and incorporated by reference into chapter 9.

References in Text

Section 103(e) of this title, referred to in pars. (1) and (5), was redesignated section 103(f) and a new section 103(e) was added by Pub.L. 106–554, § 1(a)(5) [Title I, § 112(c)(5)(A)], Dec. 21, 2000, 114 Stat. 2763, 2763A–394.

Effective and Applicability Provisions

1988 Acts. Amendment by Pub.L. 100–597 effective Nov. 3, 1988, but not applicable to any case commenced under this title before that date, see section 12 of Pub.L. 100–597, set out as a note under section 101 of this title.

1984 Acts. Amendment by Pub.L. 98–353 effective with respect to cases filed 90 days after July 10, 1984, see section 552(a), formerly 553(a), of Pub.L. 98–353, set out as a note under section 101 of this title.

Definitions applicable in,

Cases under this title, see 11 USCA § 101.

Chapter eleven cases, see 11 USCA § 1101.

Commodity broker liquidation cases, see 11 USCA § 761.

Railroad reorganization cases, see 11 USCA § 1162.

Stockbroker liquidation cases, see 11 USCA § 741.

§ 903. Reservation of State power to control municipalities

This chapter does not limit or impair the power of a State to control, by legislation or otherwise, a municipality of or in such State in the exercise of the political or governmental powers of such municipality, including expenditures for such exercise, but—

(1) a State law prescribing a method of composition of indebtedness of such municipality may not bind any creditor that does not consent to such composition; and

(2) a judgment entered under such a law may not bind a creditor that does not consent to such composition.

(Pub.L. 95–598, Nov. 6, 1978, 92 Stat. 2622; Pub.L. 98–353, Title III, § 492, July 10, 1984, 98 Stat. 383.)

HISTORICAL AND STATUTORY NOTES

Revision Notes and Legislative Reports

1978 Acts. Section 903 is derived, with stylistic changes, from section 83 of current Chapter IX [section 403 of former Title 11]. It sets forth the primary authority of a State, through its constitution, laws, and other powers, over its municipalities. The proviso in section 83, prohibiting State composition procedures for municipalities, is retained. Deletion of the provision would "permit all States to enact their own versions of Chapter IX [former chapter 9 (section 401 et seq.) of former Title 11]", Municipal Insolvency, 50 Am.Bankr. L.J. 55, 65, which would frustrate the constitutional mandate of uniform bankruptcy laws. Constitution of the United States, Art. I, Sec. 8.

This section provides that the municipality can consent to the court's orders in regard to use of its income or property. It is contemplated that such consent will be required by the court for the issuance of certificates of indebtedness under section 364(c). Such consent could extend to enforcement of the conditions attached to the certificates or the municipal services to be provided during the proceedings. Senate Report No. 95–989.

1984 Acts. Statements by Legislative Leaders, see 1984 U.S.Code Cong. and Adm.News, p. 576.

Legislative Statements

Section 903 of the House amendment represents a stylistic revision of section 903 of the Senate amendment. To the extent section 903 of the House bill would have changed present law, such section is rejected.

Effective and Applicability Provisions

1984 Acts. Amendment by Pub.L. 98–353 effective with respect to cases filed 90 days after July 10, 1984, see section

552(a), formerly 553(a), of Pub.L. 98–353, set out as a note under section 101 of this title.

Authorization by State to be debtor under this chapter, see 11 USCA § 109.

§ 904. Limitation on jurisdiction and powers of court

Notwithstanding any power of the court, unless the debtor consents or the plan so provides, the court may not, by any stay, order, or decree, in the case or otherwise, interfere with—

(1) any of the political or governmental powers of the debtor;

(2) any of the property or revenues of the debtor; or

(3) the debtor's use or enjoyment of any income-producing property.

(Pub.L. 95–598, Nov. 6, 1978, 92 Stat. 2622.)

HISTORICAL AND STATUTORY NOTES

Revision Notes and Legislative Reports

1978 Acts. This section adopts the policy of section 82(c) of current law [section 402(c) of former Title 11]. The only change in this section from section 82(c) is to conform the section to the style and cross-references of S. 2266. Senate Report No. 95–989.

This section adopts the policy of section 82(c) of current law [section 402(c) of former Title 11]. The *Usery* case underlines the need for this limitation on the court's powers. The only change in this section from section 82(c) is to conform the section to the style and cross-references of H.R. 8200. This section makes clear that the court may not interfere with the choices a municipality makes as to what services and benefits it will provide to its inhabitants. House Report No. 95–595.

Power of courts, see 11 USCA § 105.

SUBCHAPTER II—ADMINISTRATION

§ 921. Petition and proceedings relating to petition

(a) Notwithstanding sections 109(d) and 301 of this title, a case under this chapter concerning an unincorporated tax or special assessment district that does not have such district's own officials is commenced by the filing under section 301 of this title of a petition under this chapter by such district's governing authority or the board or body having authority to levy taxes or assessments to meet the obligations of such district.

(b) The chief judge of the court of appeals for the circuit embracing the district in which the case is commenced shall designate the bankruptcy judge to conduct the case.

(c) After any objection to the petition, the court, after notice and a hearing, may dismiss the petition if the debtor did not file the petition in good faith or if the petition does not meet the requirements of this title.

(d) If the petition is not dismissed under subsection (c) of this section, the court shall order relief under this chapter notwithstanding section 301(b).

(e) The court may not, on account of an appeal from an order for relief, delay any proceeding under this chapter in the case in which the appeal is being taken; nor shall any court order a stay of such proceeding pending such appeal. The reversal on appeal of a finding of jurisdiction does not affect the validity of any debt incurred that is authorized by the court under section 364(c) or 364(d) of this title.

(Pub.L. 95–598, Nov. 6, 1978, 92 Stat. 2622; Pub.L. 98–353, Title III, § 494, July 10, 1984, 98 Stat. 383; Pub.L. 109–8, Title V, § 501(a), Apr. 20, 2005, 119 Stat. 118.)

HISTORICAL AND STATUTORY NOTES

Revision Notes and Legislative Reports

1978 Acts. Section 905 adopts the procedures for selection of the judge for the chapter 9 case as found in current section 82(d) [section 402(d) of former Title 11]. It is expected that the large chapter 9 case might take up almost all the judicial time of the presiding judge and involve very complex legal questions. Selection should not be left to chance or the luck of the draw. This provision will insure that calendar demands and levels of experience can be considered in the selection of the judge in a chapter 9 case. Senate Report No. 95–989.

Subsection (a) is derived from section 85(a) [section 405(a) of former Title 11], second sentence, of current law. There is no substantive change in the law. The subsection permits a municipality that does not have its own officers to be moved into chapter 9 by the action of the body or board that has authority to levy taxes for the municipality.

Subsection (b) permits a party in interest to object to the filing of the petition not later than 15 days after notice. This provision tracks the third sentence of section 85(a) [section 405(a) of former Title 11], except that the provision for publication in section 85(a) is left to the Rules (See Rule 9–14 [Rules of Bankruptcy Procedure, this title]), and therefore the determinative date is left less definite.

Subsection (c) permits the court to dismiss a petition not filed in good faith or not filed in compliance with the requirements of the chapter. This provision is the fourth sentence of section 85(a) [section 405(a) of former Title 11].

Subsection (d) directs the court to order relief on the petition if it does not dismiss the case under subsection (c).

Subsection (e) contains the fifth and sixth sentences of section 85(a) [section 405(a) of former Title 11]. House Report No. 95–595.

1984 Acts. Statements by Legislative Leaders, see 1984 U.S.Code Cong. and Adm.News, p. 576.

2005 Acts. House Report No. 109–31(Part I), see 2005 U.S. Code Cong. and Adm. News, p. 88.

Legislative Statements

Section 905 of the Senate amendment is incorporated as section 921(b) of the House amendment with the difference that the chief judge of the circuit embracing the district in which the case is commenced designates a bankruptcy judge

to conduct the case in lieu of a district judge as under present law. It is intended that a municipality may commence a case in any district in which the municipality is located, as under present law. Section 906 of the Senate amendment has been adopted in substance in section 109(c) of the House amendment.

Effective and Applicability Provisions

2005 Acts. Amendments by Pub.L. 109–8 effective, except as otherwise provided, 180 days after April 20, 2005, and inapplicable with respect to cases commenced under Title 11 before the effective date, see Pub.L. 109–8, § 1501, set out as a note under 11 U.S.C.A. § 101.

1984 Acts. Amendment by Pub.L. 98–353 effective with respect to cases filed 90 days after July 10, 1984, see section 552(a), formerly 553(a), of Pub.L. 98–353, set out as a note under section 101 of this title.

§ 922. Automatic stay of enforcement of claims against the debtor

(a) A petition filed under this chapter operates as a stay, in addition to the stay provided by section 362 of this title, applicable to all entities, of—

    (1) the commencement or continuation, including the issuance or employment of process, of a judicial, administrative, or other action or proceeding against an officer or inhabitant of the debtor that seeks to enforce a claim against the debtor; and

    (2) the enforcement of a lien on or arising out of taxes or assessments owed to the debtor.

(b) Subsections (c), (d), (e), (f), and (g) of section 362 of this title apply to a stay under subsection (a) of this section the same as such subsections apply to a stay under section 362(a) of this title.

(c) If the debtor provides, under section 362, 364, or 922 of this title, adequate protection of the interest of the holder of a claim secured by a lien on property of the debtor and if, notwithstanding such protection such creditor has a claim arising from the stay of action against such property under section 362 or 922 of this title or from the granting of a lien under section 364(d) of this title, then such claim shall be allowable as an administrative expense under section 503(b) of this title.

(d) Notwithstanding section 362 of this title and subsection (a) of this section, a petition filed under this chapter does not operate as a stay of application of pledged special revenues in a manner consistent with section 927 of this title to payment of indebtedness secured by such revenues.

(Pub.L. 95–598, Nov. 6, 1978, 92 Stat. 2623; Pub.L. 98–353, Title III, § 495, July 10, 1984, 98 Stat. 384; Pub.L. 100–597, § 5, Nov. 3, 1988, 102 Stat. 3029.)

HISTORICAL AND STATUTORY NOTES

Revision Notes and Legislative Reports

1978 Acts. The automatic stay provided under section 362 of title 11 is incomplete for a municipality, because there is the possibility of action by a creditor against an officer or inhabitant of the municipality to collect taxes due the municipality. Section 85(e)(1) of current chapter IX [section 405(e)(1) of former Title 11] stays such actions. Section 922 carries over that protection into the proposed chapter 9. Subsection (b) applies the provisions for relief from the stay that apply generally in section 362 to the stay under section 922. House Report No. 95–595.

1984 Acts. Statements by Legislative Leaders, see 1984 U.S.Code Cong. and Adm.News, p. 576.

1988 Acts. House Report No. 100–1011, see 1988 U.S.Code Cong. and Adm.News, p. 4115.

Effective and Applicability Provisions

1988 Acts. Amendment by Pub.L. 100–597 effective Nov. 3, 1988, but not applicable to any case commenced under this title before that date, see section 12 of Pub.L. 100–597, set out as a note under section 101 of this title.

1984 Acts. Amendment by Pub.L. 98–353 effective with respect to cases filed 90 days after July 10, 1984, see section 552(a), formerly 553(a), of Pub.L. 98–353, set out as a note under section 101 of this title.

CROSS REFERENCES

Effect of § 362 of this title in stockbroker liquidation cases, see 11 USCA § 742.

Extension of time, generally, see 11 USCA § 108.

Stay of action against codebtor in,

Chapter thirteen cases, see 11 USCA § 1301.

Chapter twelve cases, see 11 USCA § 1201.

§ 923. Notice

There shall be given notice of the commencement of a case under this chapter, notice of an order for relief under this chapter, and notice of the dismissal of a case under this chapter. Such notice shall also be published at least once a week for three successive weeks in at least one newspaper of general circulation published within the district in which the case is commenced, and in such other newspaper having a general circulation among bond dealers and bondholders as the court designates.
(Pub.L. 95–598, Nov. 6, 1978, 92 Stat. 2623.)

HISTORICAL AND STATUTORY NOTES

Revision Notes and Legislative Reports

1978 Acts. The notice provisions in section 923 are significantly more sparse than those provided under section 85(d) of chapter IX [section § 405(d) of former Title 11]. The exact contours of the notice to be given under chapter 9 are left to the Rules [Rules of Bankruptcy Procedure, this title]. Because the Rules deal with notice in a municipal case (Rule 9–14), and because section 405(d) of title IV of the bill continues those Rules in effect to the extent not inconsistent with the bill, the notice provisions of current law and Rules would continue to apply. House Report No. 95–595.

Legislative Statements

Section 923 of the House amendment represents a compromise with respect to the notice provisions contained in comparable provisions of the House bill and Senate amendment. As a general matter, title 11 leaves most procedural issues to be determined by the Rules of Bankruptcy Procedure. Section 923 of the House amendment contains certain important aspects of procedure that have been retained from present law. It is anticipated that the Rules of Bankruptcy Procedure will adopt rules similar to the present rules for chapter IX of the Bankruptcy Act [former chapter 9 (section 401 et seq.) of former Title 11].

CROSS REFERENCES

Notice in,

Commodity broker liquidation cases, see 11 USCA § 762.

Stockbroker liquidation cases, see 11 USCA § 743.

Notice of order for relief, see 11 USCA § 342.

§ 924. List of creditors

The debtor shall file a list of creditors.
(Pub.L. 95–598, Nov. 6, 1978, 92 Stat. 2623.)

HISTORICAL AND STATUTORY NOTES

Revision Notes and Legislative Reports

1978 Acts. This section adopts the provision presently contained in section 85(b) of Chapter IX [section 405(b) of former Title 11]. A list of creditors, as complete and accurate as practicable, must be filed with the court. Senate Report No. 95–989.

This section directs the debtor to file a list of creditors with the court. A comparable provision is presently contained in section 85(b) of chapter IX [section 405(b) of former Title 11]. The Rules, [Rules of Bankruptcy Procedure, this title], in Rule 9–7, copy the provisions of section 85(b), with additional matter. As noted above, section 405(d) of title IV will continue those Rules in effect. Because the form, time of filing, and nature of the list, are procedural matters that may call for some flexibility, those details have been left to the Rules. House Report No. 95–595.

Legislative Statements

Section 924 of the House amendment is derived from section 924 of the House bill with the location of the filing of the list of creditors to be determined by the rules of bankruptcy procedure. The detailed requirements of section 724 [924] of the Senate bill are anticipated to be incorporated in the rules of bankruptcy procedure.

CROSS REFERENCES

Duty of,

Debtor to file list of creditors, see 11 USCA § 521.

Trustee to file list of creditors in Chapter eleven cases, see 11 USCA § 1106.

§ 925. Effect of list of claims

A proof of claim is deemed filed under section 501 of this title for any claim that appears in the list filed under section 924 of this title, except a claim that is listed as disputed, contingent, or unliquidated.
(Pub.L. 95–598, Nov. 6, 1978, 92 Stat. 2623.)

HISTORICAL AND STATUTORY NOTES

Revision Notes and Legislative Reports

1978 Acts. Section 926 [now section 925] follows the policy contained in section 88(a) of the present Act [section 408(a) of former Title 11], though certain details are left to the Rules. The language of section 926 is the same as that of proposed 11 U.S.C. 1111, which applies in chapter 11 cases. The list of creditors filed under section 924 is given weight as prima facie evidence of the claims listed (except claims that are listed as disputed, contingent, or unliquidated), which are deemed filed under section 501, obviating the need for listed creditors to file proofs of claim. Senate Report No. 95–989.

Legislative Statements

Section 925 of the Senate amendment regarding venue and fees has been deleted.

§ 926.   Avoiding powers

(a) If the debtor refuses to pursue a cause of action under section 544, 545, 547, 548, 549(a), or 550 of this title, then on request of a creditor, the court may appoint a trustee to pursue such cause of action.

(b) A transfer of property of the debtor to or for the benefit of any holder of a bond or note, on account of such bond or note, may not be avoided under section 547 of this title.

(Pub.L. 95–598, Nov. 6, 1978, 92 Stat. 2623; Pub.L. 100–597, § 6, Nov. 3, 1988, 102 Stat. 3029.)

HISTORICAL AND STATUTORY NOTES

Revision Notes and Legislative Reports

1978 Acts. This section [928 (now section 926)] adopts current section 85(h) [section 405(h) of former Title 11] which provides for a trustee to be appointed for the purpose of pursuing an action under an avoiding power, if the debtor refuses to do so. This section is necessary because a municipality might, by reason of political pressure or desire for future good relations with a particular creditor or class of creditors, make payments to such creditors in the days preceding the petition to the detriment of all other creditors. No change in the elected officials of such a city would automatically occur upon filing of the petition, and it might be very awkward for those same officials to turn around and demand the return of the payments following the filing of the petition. Hence, the need for a trustee for such purpose.

The general avoiding powers are incorporated by reference in section 901 and are broader than under current law. Preferences, fraudulent conveyances, and other kinds of transfers will thus be voidable.

Incorporated by reference also is the power to accept or reject executory contracts and leases (section 365). Within the definition of executory contracts are collective bargaining agreements between the city and its employees. Such contracts may be rejected despite contrary State laws. Courts should readily allow the rejection of such contracts where they are burdensome, the rejection will aid in the municipality's reorganization and in consideration of the equities of each case. On the last point, "[e]quities in favor of the city in chapter 9 will be far more compelling than the equities in favor of the employer in chapter 11. Onerous employment obligations may prevent a city from balancing its budget for some time. The prospect of an unbalanced budget may preclude judicial confirmation of the plan. Unless a city can reject its labor contracts, lack of funds may force cutbacks in police, fire, sanitation, and welfare services, imposing hardships on many citizens. In addition, because cities in the past have often seemed immune to the constraint of "profitability"

faced by private businesses, their wage contracts may be relatively more onerous than those in the private sector." Executory Contracts and Municipal Bankruptcy, 85 Yale L.J. 957, 965 (1976) (footnote omitted). Rejection of the contracts may require the municipalities to renegotiate such contracts by state collective bargaining laws. It is intended that the power to reject collective bargaining agreements will preempt state termination provisions, but not state collective bargaining laws. Thus, a city would not be required to maintain existing employment terms during the renegotiation period. Senate Report No. 95–989.

1988 Acts. House Report No. 100–1011, see 1988 U.S.Code Cong. and Adm.News, p. 4115.

Legislative Statements

Section 926 of the House amendment is derived from section 928 of the Senate bill. The provision enables creditors to request the court to appoint a trustee to pursue avoiding powers if the debtor refuses to exercise those powers. Section 901 of the House amendment makes a corresponding change to incorporate avoiding powers included in the Senate amendment, but excluded from the House bill.

Effective and Applicability Provisions

1988 Acts. Amendment by Pub.L. 100–597 effective Nov. 3, 1988, but not applicable to any case commenced under this title before that date, see section 12 of Pub.L. 100–597, set out as a note under section 101 of this title.

CROSS REFERENCES

Appointment of trustee in,

    Chapter eleven cases, see 11 USCA § 1104.

    Chapter thirteen cases, see 11 USCA § 1302.

    Railroad reorganization cases, see 11 USCA § 1163.

"Trustee" defined when used in sections made applicable to cases under this chapter, see 11 USCA § 902.

§ 927.   Limitation on recourse

The holder of a claim payable solely from special revenues of the debtor under applicable nonbankruptcy law shall not be treated as having recourse against the debtor on account of such claim pursuant to section 1111(b) of this title.

(Added Pub.L. 100–597, § 7(2), Nov. 3, 1988, 102 Stat. 3029.)

HISTORICAL AND STATUTORY NOTES

Revision Notes and Legislative Reports

1988 Acts. House Report No. 100–1011, see 1988 U.S.Code Cong. and Adm.News, p. 4115.

Effective and Applicability Provisions

1988 Acts. Section effective Nov. 3, 1988, but not applicable to any case commenced under this title before that date, see section 12 of Pub.L. 100–597, set out as an Effective Date of 1988 Amendment note under section 101 of this title.

§ 928.   Post petition effect of security interest

(a) Notwithstanding section 552(a) of this title and subject to subsection (b) of this section, special revenues acquired by the debtor after the commencement of the case shall remain subject to any lien resulting from any security agreement entered into by the debtor before the commencement of the case.

(b) Any such lien on special revenues, other than municipal betterment assessments, derived from a project or system shall be subject to the necessary operating expenses of such project or system, as the case may be.

(Added Pub.L. 100–597, § 8, Nov. 3, 1988, 102 Stat. 3029.)

HISTORICAL AND STATUTORY NOTES

Revision Notes and Legislative Reports

1988 Acts. House Report No. 100–1011, see 1988 U.S.Code Cong. and Adm.News, p. 4115.

Effective and Applicability Provisions

1988 Acts. Section effective Nov. 3, 1988, but not applicable to any case commenced under this title before that date, see section 12 of Pub.L. 100–597, set out as an Effective Date of 1988 Amendment note under section 101 of this title.

§ 929. Municipal leases

A lease to a municipality shall not be treated as an executory contract or unexpired lease for the purposes of section 365 or 502(b)(6) of this title solely by reason of its being subject to termination in the event the debtor fails to appropriate rent.

(Added Pub.L. 100–597, § 9, Nov. 3, 1988, 102 Stat. 3030.)

HISTORICAL AND STATUTORY NOTES

Revision Notes and Legislative Reports

1988 Acts. House Report No. 100–1011, see 1988 U.S.Code Cong. and Adm.News, p. 4115.

Effective and Applicability Provisions

1988 Acts. Section effective Nov. 3, 1988, but not applicable to any case commenced under this title before that date, see section 12 of Pub.L. 100–597, set out as an Effective Date of 1988 Amendment note under section 101 of this title.

§ 930. Dismissal

(a) After notice and a hearing, the court may dismiss a case under this chapter for cause, including—

(1) want of prosecution;

(2) unreasonable delay by the debtor that is prejudicial to creditors;

(3) failure to propose a plan within the time fixed under section 941 of this title;

(4) if a plan is not accepted within any time fixed by the court;

(5) denial of confirmation of a plan under section 943(b) of this title and denial of additional time for filing another plan or a modification of a plan; or

(6) if the court has retained jurisdiction after confirmation of a plan—

(A) material default by the debtor with respect to a term of such plan; or

(B) termination of such plan by reason of the occurrence of a condition specified in such plan.

(b) The court shall dismiss a case under this chapter if confirmation of a plan under this chapter is refused. (Pub.L. 95–598, Nov. 6, 1978, 92 Stat. 2623, § 927; Pub.L. 98–353, Title III, § 496, July 10, 1984, 98 Stat. 384; renumbered § 930, Pub.L. 100–597, § 7(1), Nov. 3, 1988, 102 Stat. 3029.)

HISTORICAL AND STATUTORY NOTES

Revision Notes and Legislative Reports

1978 Acts. Section 927 conforms to section 98 [section 418 of former Title 11] of current law. The Section [sic] permits dismissal by the court for unreasonable delay by the debtor, failure to propose a plan, failure of acceptance of a plan, or default by the debtor under a conformed plan. Mandatory dismissal is required if confirmation is refused. Senate Report No. 95–989.

Section 926 [now 927] generally conforms to section 98(a) [section 418(a) of former title 11] of current law. Stylistic changes have been made to conform the language with that used in chapter 11, section 1112. The section permits dismissal by the court for unreasonable delay by the debtor that is prejudicial to creditors, failure to propose a plan, failure of confirmation of a plan, or material default by the debtor under a confirmed plan. The only significant change from current law lies in the second ground. Currently, section 98(a)(2) provides for dismissal if a proposed plan is not accepted, and section 98(b) *requires* dismissal if an accepted plan is not confirmed. In order to provide greater flexibility to the court, the debtor, and creditors, the bill allows the court to permit the debtor to propose another plan if the first plan is not confirmed. In that event the debtor need not, as under current law, commence the case all over again. This could provide savings in time and administrative expenses if a plan is denied confirmation. House Report No. 95–595.

1984 Acts. Statements by Legislative Leaders, see 1984 U.S.Code Cong. and Adm.News, p. 576.

1988 Acts. House Report No. 100–1011, see 1988 U.S.Code Cong. and Adm.News, p. 4115.

Legislative Statements

Section 927(b) of the House amendment is derived from section 927(b) of the Senate bill. The provision requires mandatory dismissal if confirmation of a plan is refused.

The House amendment deletes section 929 of the Senate amendment as unnecessary since the bankruptcy court has original exclusive jurisdiction of all cases under chapter 9.

The House amendment deletes section 930 of the Senate amendment and incorporates section 507(a)(1) by reference.

Effective and Applicability Provisions

1984 Acts. Amendment by Pub.L. 98–353 effective with respect to cases filed 90 days after July 10, 1984, see section 552(a), formerly 553(a), of Pub.L. 98–353, set out as a note under section 101 of this title.

CROSS REFERENCES

Conversion or dismissal of,

Chapter eleven cases, see 11 USCA § 1112.

Chapter thirteen cases, see 11 USCA § 1307.

Dismissal of Chapter seven cases, see 11 USCA § 707.

Effect of dismissal, see 11 USCA § 349.

SUBCHAPTER III—THE PLAN

§ 941.   Filing of plan

The debtor shall file a plan for the adjustment of the debtor's debts. If such a plan is not filed with the petition, the debtor shall file such a plan at such later time as the court fixes.

(Pub.L. 95–598, Nov. 6, 1978, 92 Stat. 2624.)

HISTORICAL AND STATUTORY NOTES

Revision Notes and Legislative Reports

1978 Acts. Section 941 gives the debtor the exclusive right to propose a plan, and directs that the debtor propose one either with the petition or within such time as the court directs. The section follows section 90(a) of current law [section 410(a) of former Title 11]. Senate Report No. 95–989.

1984 Acts. Statements by Legislative Leaders, see 1984 U.S.Code Cong. and Adm.News, p. 576.

CROSS REFERENCES

Dismissal for failure to timely propose plan, see 11 USCA § 930.

Filing of plan in Chapter thirteen cases, see 11 USCA § 1321.

Who may file a plan in Chapter eleven cases, see 11 USCA § 1121.

§ 942.   Modification of plan

The debtor may modify the plan at any time before confirmation, but may not modify the plan so that the plan as modified fails to meet the requirements of this chapter. After the debtor files a modification, the plan as modified becomes the plan.

(Pub.L. 95–598, Nov. 6, 1978, 92 Stat. 2624.)

HISTORICAL AND STATUTORY NOTES

Revision Notes and Legislative Reports

1978 Acts. Section 942 permits the debtor to modify the plan at any time before confirmation, as does section 90(a) of current law [section 410(a) of former Title 11]. Senate Report No.95–989.

Legislative Statements

The House amendment deletes section 942 of the Senate amendment in favor of incorporating section 1125 by cross-reference. Similarly, the House amendment does not incorporate section 944 or 945 of the Senate amendment since incorporation of several sections in chapter 11 in section 901 is sufficient.

CROSS REFERENCES

Modification of plan after confirmation in,

    Chapter thirteen cases, see 11 USCA § 1329.

    Chapter twelve cases, see 11 USCA § 1229.

Modification of plan before confirmation in,

    Chapter thirteen cases, see 11 USCA § 1323.

    Chapter twelve cases, see 11 USCA § 1223.

Modification of plan in Chapter eleven cases, see 11 USCA § 1127.

§ 943.   Confirmation

(a) A special tax payer may object to confirmation of a plan.

(b) The court shall confirm the plan if—

(1) the plan complies with the provisions of this title made applicable by sections 103(e) and 901 of this title;

(2) the plan complies with the provisions of this chapter;

(3) all amounts to be paid by the debtor or by any person for services or expenses in the case or incident to the plan have been fully disclosed and are reasonable;

(4) the debtor is not prohibited by law from taking any action necessary to carry out the plan;

(5) except to the extent that the holder of a particular claim has agreed to a different treatment of such claim, the plan provides that on the effective date of the plan each holder of a claim of a kind specified in section 507(a)(2) of this title will receive on account of such claim cash equal to the allowed amount of such claim;

(6) any regulatory or electoral approval necessary under applicable nonbankruptcy law in order to carry out any provision of the plan has been obtained, or such provision is expressly conditioned on such approval; and

(7) the plan is in the best interests of creditors and is feasible.

(Pub.L. 95–598, Nov. 6, 1978, 92 Stat. 2624; Pub.L. 98–353, Title III, § 497, July 10, 1984, 98 Stat. 384; Pub.L. 100–597, § 10, Nov. 3, 1988, 102 Stat. 3030; Pub.L. 109–8, Title XV, § 1502(a)(6), Apr. 20, 2005, 119 Stat. 216.)

HISTORICAL AND STATUTORY NOTES

Revision Notes and Legislative Reports

1978 Acts. Section 946 [now this section] is adopted from current section 94 [section 414 of former Title 11]. The test for confirmation is whether or not the plan is fair and equitable and feasible. The fair and equitable test tracts current chapter X [former chapter 10 (section 501 et seq.) of this title] and is known as the strict priority rule. Creditors must be provided, under the plan, the going concern value of their claims. The going concern value contemplates a "comparison of revenues and expenditures taking into account the taxing power and the extent to which tax increases are both necessary and feasible" Municipal Insolvency, supra, at p. 64, and is intended to provide more of a return to creditors than the liquidation value if the city's assets could be liquidated like those of a private corporation. Senate Report No. 95–989.

In addition to the confirmation requirements incorporated from section 1129 by section 901, this section specifies additional requirements. Paragraph (1) requires compliance with the provisions of the title made applicable in chapter 9 cases. This provision follows section 94(b)(2) [section 414(b)(2) of former Title 11]. Paragraph (2) requires compliance with the provisions of chapter 9, as does section 94(b)(2) [section 414(b)(2) of former Title 11]. Paragraph (3) adopts section 94(b)(4) [section 414(b)(4) of former Title 11], requiring disclosure and reasonableness of all payments to be made in connection with the plan or the case. Paragraph (4), copied from section 92(b)(6) [probably should be "94(b)(6)", which was section 414(b)(6) of former Title 11], requires that the debtor not be prohibited by law from taking any action necessary to carry out the plan. Paragraph (5) departs from current law by requiring that administrative expenses be paid in full, but not necessarily in cash. Finally, paragraph (6) requires that the plan be in the best interest of creditors and feasible. The best interest test was deleted in section 94(b)(1) of current chapter IX [section 414(b)(1) of former Title 11] from previous chapter IX [former chapter 9 (section 401 et seq.) of former Title 11], because it was redundant with the fair and equitable rule. However, this bill proposes a new confirmation standard generally for reorganization, one element of which is the best interest of creditors test; see section 1129(a)(7). In that section, the test is phrased in terms of liquidation of the debtor. Because that is not possible in a municipal case, the test here is phrased in its more traditional form, using the words of art "best interest of creditors." The best interest of creditors test here is in addition to the financial standards imposed on the plan by section 1129(a)(8) and 1129(b), just as those provisions are in addition to the comparable best interest test in chapter 11, 11 U.S.C. 1129(a)(7). The feasibility requirement, added in the revision of chapter IX [former chapter 9 (section 401 et seq.) of former Title 11] last year, is retained. House Report No. 95–595.

1984 Acts. Statements by Legislative Leaders, see 1984 U.S.Code Cong. and Adm.News, p. 576.

1988 Acts. House Report No. 100–1011, see 1988 U.S.Code Cong. and Adm.News, p. 4115.

2005 Acts. House Report No. 109–31(Part I), see 2005 U.S. Code Cong. and Adm. News, p. 88.

Legislative Statements

Section 943(a) of the House amendment makes clear that a special taxpayer may object to confirmation of a plan. Section 943(b) of the House amendment is derived from section 943 of the House bill respecting confirmation of a plan under chapter 9. It must be emphasized that these standards of confirmation are in addition to standards in section 1129 that are made applicable to chapter 9 by section 901 of the House amendment. In particular, if the requirements of section 1129(a)(8) are not complied with, then the proponent may request application of section 1129(b). The court will then be required to confirm the plan if it complies with the "fair and equitable" test and is in the best interests of creditors. The best interests of creditors test does not mean liquidation value as under chapter XI of the Bankruptcy Act [former chapter 11 (section 701 et seq.) of former Title 11]. In making such a determination, it is expected that the court will be guided by standards set forth in *Kelley v. Everglades Drainage District*, 319 U.S. 415 (1943) [Fla.1943, 63 S.Ct. 1141, 87 L.Ed. 1485, rehearing denied 63 S.Ct. 1444, 320 U.S. 214, 87 L.Ed. 1851, motion denied 64 S.Ct. 783, 321 U.S. 754, 88 L.Ed. 1054] and *Fano v. Newport Heights Irrigation Dist.*, 114 F.2d 563 (9th Cir. 1940), as under present law, the bankruptcy court should make findings as detailed as possible to support a conclusion that this test has been met. However, it must be emphasized that unlike current law, the fair and equitable test under section 1129(b) will not apply if section 1129(a)(8) has been satisfied in addition to the other confirmation standards specified in section 943 and incorporated by reference in section 901 of the House amendment. To the extent that *American United Mutual Life Insurance Co. v. City of Avon Park*, 311 U.S. 138 (1940) [Fla.1940, 61 S.Ct. 157, 85 L.Ed. 91, 136 A.L.R. 860, rehearing denied 61 S.Ct. 395, 311 U.S. 730, 85 L.Ed. 475] and other cases are to the contrary, such cases are overruled to that extent.

References in Text

Section 103(e) of this title, referred to in subsec. (b), was redesignated subsec. (f) and a new subsec. (e) was added by Pub.L. 106–554, § 1(a)(5) [Title I, § 112(c)(5)(A)], Dec. 21, 2000, 114 Stat. 2763, 2763A–394.

Effective and Applicability Provisions

2005 Acts. Amendments by Pub.L. 109–8 effective, except as otherwise provided, 180 days after April 20, 2005, and inapplicable with respect to cases commenced under Title 11 before the effective date, see Pub.L. 109–8, § 1501, set out as a note under 11 U.S.C.A. § 101.

1988 Acts. Amendment by Pub.L. 100–597 effective Nov. 3, 1988, but not applicable to any case commenced under this title before that date, see section 12 of Pub.L. 100–597, set out as a note under section 101 of this title.

1984 Acts. Amendment by Pub.L. 98–353 effective with respect to cases filed 90 days after July 10, 1984, see section 552(a), formerly 553(a), of Pub.L. 98–353, set out as a note under section 101 of this title.

CROSS REFERENCES

Confirmation hearing in,

    Chapter eleven cases, see 11 USCA § 1128.

    Chapter thirteen cases, see 11 USCA § 1324.

    Chapter twelve cases, see 11 USCA § 1224.

Confirmation of plan in,

    Chapter eleven cases, see 11 USCA § 1129.

    Chapter thirteen cases, see 11 USCA § 1325.

    Chapter twelve cases, see 11 USCA § 1225.

    Railroad reorganization cases, see 11 USCA § 1173.

Dismissal for denial of confirmation of plan, see 11 USCA § 930.

Unclaimed property, see 11 USCA § 347.

§ 944. Effect of confirmation

(a) The provisions of a confirmed plan bind the debtor and any creditor, whether or not—

    (1) a proof of such creditor's claim is filed or deemed filed under section 501 of this title;

    (2) such claim is allowed under section 502 of this title; or

    (3) such creditor has accepted the plan.

(b) Except as provided in subsection (c) of this section, the debtor is discharged from all debts as of the time when—

    (1) the plan is confirmed;

(2) the debtor deposits any consideration to be distributed under the plan with a disbursing agent appointed by the court; and

(3) the court has determined—

(A) that any security so deposited will constitute, after distribution, a valid legal obligation of the debtor; and

(B) that any provision made to pay or secure payment of such obligation is valid.

(c) The debtor is not discharged under subsection (b) of this section from any debt—

(1) excepted from discharge by the plan or order confirming the plan; or

(2) owed to an entity that, before confirmation of the plan, had neither notice nor actual knowledge of the case.

(Pub.L. 95–598, Nov. 6, 1978, 92 Stat. 2624.)

HISTORICAL AND STATUTORY NOTES
Revision Notes and Legislative Reports

1978 Acts. [Section 947] Subsection (a) [now section 944(a)] makes the provisions of a confirmed plan binding on the debtor and creditors. It is derived from section 95(a) of chapter 9 [section 415(a) of former Title 11].

Subsections (b) and (c) [now section 944(b) and (c)] provide for the discharge of a municipality. The discharge is essentially the same as that granted under section 95(b) of the Bankruptcy Act [section 415(b) of former Title 11]. Senate Report No. 95–989.

CROSS REFERENCES

Discharge in,

Chapter seven cases, see 11 USCA § 727.

Chapter thirteen cases, see 11 USCA § 1328.

Chapter twelve cases, see 11 USCA § 1228.

Effect of confirmation in,

Chapter eleven cases, see 11 USCA § 1141.

Chapter thirteen cases, see 11 USCA § 1327.

Chapter twelve cases, see 11 USCA § 1227.

Effect of discharge, see 11 USCA § 524.

Exceptions to discharge, see 11 USCA § 523.

§ 945. Continuing jurisdiction and closing of the case

(a) The court may retain jurisdiction over the case for such period of time as is necessary for the successful implementation of the plan.

(b) Except as provided in subsection (a) of this section, the court shall close the case when administration of the case has been completed.

(Pub.L. 95–598, Nov. 6, 1978, 92 Stat. 2625; Pub.L. 98–353, Title III, § 498, July 10, 1984, 98 Stat. 384.)

HISTORICAL AND STATUTORY NOTES
Revision Notes and Legislative Reports

1978 Acts. Section 948 [now this section] permits the court to retain jurisdiction over the case to ensure successful execution of the plan. The provision is the same as that found in section 96(e) of Chapter 9 of the present Act [former section 416(e) of former Title 11]. Senate Report No. 95–989.

1984 Acts. Statements by Legislative Leaders, see 1984 U.S.Code Cong. and Adm.News, p. 576.

Effective and Applicability Provisions

1984 Acts. Amendment by Pub.L. 98–353 effective with respect to cases filed 90 days after July 10, 1984, see section 552(a), formerly 553(a), of Pub.L. 98–353, set out as a note under section 101 of this title.

CROSS REFERENCES

Closing and reopening cases, see 11 USCA § 350.

§ 946. Effect of exchange of securities before the date of the filing of the petition

The exchange of a new security under the plan for a claim covered by the plan, whether such exchange occurred before or after the date of the filing of the petition, does not limit or impair the effectiveness of the plan or of any provision of this chapter. The amount and number specified in section 1126(c) of this title include the amount and number of claims formerly held by a creditor that has participated in any such exchange.

(Pub.L. 95–598, Nov. 6, 1978, 92 Stat. 2625.)

HISTORICAL AND STATUTORY NOTES
Revision Notes and Legislative Reports

1978 Acts. [Section 949] This section [now section 946], which follows section 97 of current law [section 417 of former Title 11], permits an exchange of a security before the case is filed to constitute an acceptance of the plan if the exchange was under a proposal that later becomes the plan. Section Report No. 95–989.

Legislative Statements

The House amendment deletes section 950 of the Senate amendment as unnecessary. The constitutionality of chapter 9 of the House amendment is beyond doubt.

CHAPTER 11—REORGANIZATION

CROSS REFERENCES

Allowance of administrative expenses of substantial contributors to cases under this chapter, see 11 USCA § 503.

Applicability of income tax provisions to cases under this chapter, see 26 USCA § 1398.

Chapters one, three, and five of this title applicable in cases under this chapter except as provided in § 1161 of this title, see 11 USCA § 103.

Claims arising from rejection under chapter plans of executory contracts or unexpired leases, see 11 USCA § 502.

Commencement of involuntary cases, see 11 USCA § 303.

Conversion to this chapter from,

Chapter seven, see 11 USCA § 706.

Chapter thirteen, see 11 USCA § 1307.

Core proceedings, see 28 USCA § 157.

Distress termination of single-employer plans in cases under this chapter, see 29 USCA § 1341.

Duration of automatic stay, see 11 USCA § 362.

Duties of United States trustees, see 28 USCA § 586.

Employment of professional persons, see 11 USCA § 327.

Establishment, operation and termination of Bankruptcy Appellate Panel Service and undue delay or increased costs, see 28 USCA § 158.

Executory contracts and unexpired leases, see 11 USCA § 365.

Filing fees, see 28 USCA § 1930.

Jurisdiction of courts in termination proceedings of employer plans brought by Pension Benefit Guaranty Corporation same as jurisdiction of courts in cases under this chapter, see 29 USCA § 1342.

Limitation on compensation of trustee, see 11 USCA § 326.

Persons required to make returns of income under this chapter, see 26 USCA § 6012.

Persons who may be debtors under this chapter, see 11 USCA § 109.

Powers of Courts to set date to file disclosure, see 11 USCA § 105.

Property of estate in cases converted from Chapter 13, see 11 USCA § 1306.

Provisions concerning reorganization plan of investment companies not to affect or derogate from powers of courts with reference to reorganizations under this title, see 15 USCA § 80a–25.

Return of excessive attorney compensation if transferred property was to be paid by debtor under plan under this chapter, see 11 USCA § 329.

Rights and powers of debtor in Chapter twelve case not encompassing certain duties of trustee serving in case under this chapter, see 11 USCA § 1203.

Special tax provisions, see 11 USCA § 346.

Stay of action against Chapter thirteen codebtor in cases converted to this chapter, see 11 USCA § 1301.

Supplemental injunctions and notice and hearings, see 11 USCA § 524.

Treatment of debtor's estate in cases under this chapter as taxpayer for certain income tax purposes, see 26 USCA § 108.

Unclaimed property, see 11 USCA § 347.

Use, sale or lease of property under plan under this chapter, see 11 USCA § 363.

SUBCHAPTER I—OFFICERS AND ADMINISTRATION

CROSS REFERENCES

Subchapter applicable only in case under this chapter except as provided in § 901 of this title, see 11 USCA § 103.

§ 1101. Definitions for this chapter

In this chapter—

(1) "debtor in possession" means debtor except when a person that has qualified under section 322 of this title is serving as trustee in the case;

(2) "substantial consummation" means—

(A) transfer of all or substantially all of the property proposed by the plan to be transferred;

(B) assumption by the debtor or by the successor to the debtor under the plan of the business or of the management of all or substantially all of the property dealt with by the plan; and

(C) commencement of distribution under the plan.

(Pub.L. 95–598, Nov. 6, 1978, 92 Stat. 2626.)

HISTORICAL AND STATUTORY NOTES

Revision Notes and Legislative Reports

1978 Acts. This section contains definitions of three terms that are used in chapter 11. Paragraph (1) defines debtor in possession to mean the debtor, except when a trustee who has qualified is serving in the case.

Paragraph (2), derived from section 229a of current law [section 629(a) of former Title 11], defines substantial consummation. Substantial consummation of a plan occurs when transfer of all or substantially all of the property proposed by the plan to be transferred is actually transferred; when the debtor (or its successor) has assumed the business of the debtor or the management of all or substantially all of the property dealt with by the plan; and when distribution under the plan has commenced.

Paragraph (3) defines for purposes of Chapter 11 a public company to mean "a debtor who, within 12 months prior to the filing of a petition for relief under this chapter, had outstanding liabilities of $5 million or more, exclusive of liabilities for goods, services, or taxes and not less than 1,000 security holders." There are, as noted, special safeguards for public investors related to the reorganization of a public company, as so defined.

Both requirements must be met: liabilities, excluding tax obligations and trade liabilities, must be $5 million or more; and (2) the number of holders of securities, debt or equity, or both, must be not less than 1,000. The amount and number are to be determined as of any time within 12 months prior to the filing of the petition for reorganization. Senate Report No. 95–989.

CROSS REFERENCES

Definitions applicable in,

Cases under this title, see 11 USCA § 101.

Chapter nine cases, see 11 USCA § 902.

Commodity broker liquidation cases, see 11 USCA § 761.

Railroad reorganization cases, see 11 USCA § 1162.

Stockbroker liquidation cases, see 11 USCA § 741.

§ 1102. Creditors' and equity security holders' committees

(a)(1) Except as provided in paragraph (3), as soon as practicable after the order for relief under chapter 11 of this title, the United States trustee shall appoint a committee of creditors holding unsecured claims and may appoint additional committees of creditors or of equity security holders as the United States trustee deems appropriate.

(2) On request of a party in interest, the court may order the appointment of additional committees of creditors or of equity security holders if necessary to assure adequate representation of creditors or of equity security holders. The United States trustee shall appoint any such committee.

(3) On request of a party in interest in a case in which the debtor is a small business debtor and for cause, the court may order that a committee of creditors not be appointed.

(4) On request of a party in interest and after notice and a hearing, the court may order the United States trustee to change the membership of a committee appointed under this subsection, if the court determines that the change is necessary to ensure adequate representation of creditors or equity security holders. The court may order the United States trustee to increase the number of members of a committee to include a creditor that is a small business concern (as described in section 3(a)(1) of the Small Business Act), if the court determines that the creditor holds claims (of the kind represented by the committee) the aggregate amount of which, in comparison to the annual gross revenue of that creditor, is disproportionately large.

(b)(1) A committee of creditors appointed under subsection (a) of this section shall ordinarily consist of the persons, willing to serve, that hold the seven largest claims against the debtor of the kinds represented on such committee, or of the members of a committee organized by creditors before the commencement of the case under this chapter, if such committee was fairly chosen and is representative of the different kinds of claims to be represented.

(2) A committee of equity security holders appointed under subsection (a)(2) of this section shall ordinarily consist of the persons, willing to serve, that hold the seven largest amounts of equity securities of the debtor of the kinds represented on such committee.

---

(3) A committee appointed under subsection (a) shall—

(A) provide access to information for creditors who—

(i) hold claims of the kind represented by that committee; and

(ii) are not appointed to the committee;

(B) solicit and receive comments from the creditors described in subparagraph (A); and

(C) be subject to a court order that compels any additional report or disclosure to be made to the creditors described in subparagraph (A).

(Pub.L. 95–598, Nov. 6, 1978, 92 Stat. 2626; Pub.L. 98–353, Title III, § 499, July 10, 1984, 98 Stat. 384; Pub.L. 99–554, Title II, § 221, Oct. 27, 1986, 100 Stat. 3101; Pub.L. 103–394, Title II, § 217(b), Oct. 22, 1994, 108 Stat. 4127; Pub.L. 109–8, Title IV, §§ 405, 432(b), Apr. 20, 2005, 119 Stat. 105, 110.)

HISTORICAL AND STATUTORY NOTES

Revision Notes and Legislative Reports

1978 Acts. This section provides for the election and appointment of committees. Subsection (c) provides that this section does not apply in case of a public company, as to which a trustee, appointed under section 1104(a) will have responsibility to administer the estate and to formulate a plan as provided in section 1106(a).

There is no need for the election or appointment of committees for which the appointment of a trustee is mandatory. In the case of a public company there are likely to be several committees, each representing a different class of security holders and seeking authority to retain accountants, lawyers, and other experts, who will expect to be paid. If in the case of a public company creditors or stockholders wish to organize committees, they may do so, as authorized under section 1109(a). Compensation and reimbursement will be allowed for contributions to the reorganization pursuant to section 503(b)(3) and (4). Senate Report No. 95–989.

This section provides for the appointment of creditors' and equity security holders' committees, which will be the primary negotiating bodies for the formulation of the plan of reorganization. They will represent the various classes of creditors and equity security holders from which they are selected. They will also provide supervision of the debtor in possession and of the trustee, and will protect their constituents' interests.

Subsection (a) requires the court to appoint at least one committee. That committee is to be composed of creditors holding unsecured claims. The court is authorized to appoint such additional committees as are necessary to assure adequate representation of creditors and equity security holders. The provision will be relied upon in cases in which the debtor proposes to affect several classes of debt or equity holders under the plan, and in which they need representation.

Subsection (b) contains precatory language directing the court to appoint the persons holding the seven largest claims against the debtor of the kinds represented on a creditors' committee, or the members of a prepetition committee organized by creditors before the order for relief under chapter 11. The court may continue prepetition committee members only if the committee was fairly chosen and is representative of the different kinds of claims to be represented. The court

is restricted to the appointment of persons in order to exclude governmental holders of claims or interests.

Paragraph (2) of subsection (b) requires similar treatment for equity security holders' committees. The seven largest holders are normally to be appointed, but the language is only precatory.

Subsection (c) authorizes the court, on request of a party in interest, to change the size or the membership of a creditors' or equity security holders' committee if the membership of the committee is not representative of the different kinds of claims or interests to be represented. This subsection is intended, along with the nonbinding nature of subsection (b), to afford the court latitude in appointing a committee that is manageable and representative in light of the circumstances of the case. House Report No. 95–595.

1984 Acts. Statements by Legislative Leaders, see 1984 U.S.Code Cong. and Adm.News, p. 576.

1986 Acts. House Report No. 99–764 and House Conference Report No. 99–958, see 1986 U.S.Code Cong. and Adm. News, p. 5227.

1994 Acts. House Report No. 103–835, see 1994 U.S. Code Cong. and Adm. News, p. 3340.

2005 Acts. House Report No. 109–31(Part I), see 2005 U.S. Code Cong. and Adm. News, p. 88.

Legislative Statements

Section 1102(a) of the House amendment adopts a compromise between the House bill and Senate amendment requiring appointment of a committee of creditors holding unsecured claims by the court; the alternative of creditor committee election is rejected.

Section 1102(b) of the House amendment represents a compromise between the House bill and the Senate amendment by preventing the appointment of creditors who are unwilling to serve on a creditors committee.

References in Text

Section 3(a)(1) of the Small Business Act, referred to in subsec. (a)(4), is section 3(a)(1) of Pub.L. 85–536 § 2[3], July 18, 1958, 72 Stat. 384, as amended, which is classified to 15 U.S.C.A. § 632(a)(1). For complete classification, see Short Title note under 15 U.S.C.A. § 631 and Tables.

Effective and Applicability Provisions

2005 Acts. Amendments by Pub.L. 109–8 effective, except as otherwise provided, 180 days after April 20, 2005, and inapplicable with respect to cases commenced under Title 11 before the effective date, see Pub.L. 109–8, § 1501, set out as a note under 11 U.S.C.A. § 101.

1994 Acts. Amendment by Pub.L. 103–394 effective on Oct. 22, 1994, and not to apply with respect to cases commenced under Title 11 of the United States Code before Oct. 22, 1994, see section 702 of Pub.L. 103–394, set out as a note under section 101 of this title.

1986 Acts. Amendment by Pub.L. 99–554 effective 30 days after Oct. 27, 1986, except as otherwise provided for, see section 302(a) of Pub.L. 99–554, set out as a note under section 581 of Title 28, Judiciary and Judicial Procedure.

Amendment by Pub.L. 99–554, § 221, not to become effective in or with respect to certain specified judicial districts until, or apply to cases while pending in such district before, the expiration of the 270–day period beginning 30 days after Oct. 27, 1986, or of the 30–day period beginning on the date the Attorney General certifies under section 303 of Pub.L. 99–554 the region specified in a paragraph of section 581(a) of Title 28, as amended by section 111(a) of Pub.L. 99–554, that includes such district, whichever occurs first, see section 302(d)(1) of Pub.L. 99–554, set out as a note under section 581 of Title 28.

Amendment by Pub.L. 99–554, § 221, not to become effective in or with respect to certain specified judicial districts until, or apply to cases while pending in such district before, the expiration of the 2–year period beginning 30 days after Oct. 27, 1986, or of the 30–day period beginning on the date the Attorney General certifies under section 303 of Pub.L. 99–554 the region specified in a paragraph of section 581(a) of Title 28, as amended by section 111(a) of Pub.L. 99–554, that includes such district, whichever occurs first, see section 302(d)(2) of Pub.L. 99–554, set out as a note under section 581 of Title 28.

Amendment by Pub.L. 99–554, § 221, not to become effective in or with respect to judicial districts established for the States of Alabama and North Carolina until, or apply to cases while pending in such district before, such district elects to be included in a bankruptcy region established in section 581(a) of Title 28, as amended by section 111(a) of Pub.L. 99–554, or Oct. 1, 2002, whichever occurs first, and, except as otherwise provided for, with respect to cases under chapters 7, 11, 12, and 13 of Title 11 commenced before 30 days after Oct. 27, 1986, and pending in a judicial district in the States of Alabama or North Carolina before any election made under section 302(d)(3)(A) of Pub.L. 99–554 by such district becomes effective or Oct. 1, 2002, whichever occurs first, amendments by Pub.L. 99–554 not to apply until Oct. 1, 2003, or the expiration of the 1–year period beginning on the date such election becomes effective, whichever occurs first, and further, in any judicial district in Alabama or North Carolina not making the election described in section 302(d)(3)(A) of Pub.L. 99–554, any person appointed under regulations issued by the Judicial Conference to administer estates in cases under Title 11 authorized to establish, etc., a panel of private trustees, and to supervise cases and trustees in cases under chapters 7, 11, 12 and 13 of Title 11, until amendments by sections 201 to 231 of Pub.L. 99–554 effective in such district, see section 302(d)(3)(A) to (F), (H), (I), of Pub.L. 99–554, set out as a note under section 581 of Title 28.

Amendment by Pub.L. 99–554, § 221, except as otherwise provided, with respect to cases under chapters 7, 11, 12 and 13 of Title 11 commenced before 30 days after Oct. 27, 1986, and pending in a judicial district referred to in section 581(a) of Title 28, as amended by section 111(a) of Pub.L. 99–554, for which a United States trustee is not authorized before 30 days after Oct. 27, 1986 to be appointed, not applicable until the expiration of the 3–year period beginning on Oct. 27, 1986, or of the 1–year period beginning on the date the Attorney General certifies under section 303 of Pub.L. 99–554 the region specified in a paragraph of such section 581(a) that includes, such district, whichever occurs first, see section 302(e)(1), (2) of Pub.L. 99–554, set out as a note under section 581 of Title 28.

1984 Acts. Amendment by Pub.L. 98–353 effective with respect to cases filed 90 days after July 10, 1984, see section 552(a), formerly 553(a), of Pub.L. 98–353, set out as a note under section 101 of this title.

Separability of Provisions

If any provision of or amendment made by Pub.L. 103–394 or the application of such provision or amendment to any person or circumstance is held to be unconstitutional, the remaining provisions of and amendments made by Pub.L. 103–394 and the application of such provisions and amendments to any person or circumstance shall not be affected thereby, see section 701 of Pub.L. 103–394, set out as a note under section 101 of this title.

CROSS REFERENCES

Allowance of creditor committee expenses, see 11 USCA § 503.

Applicability of this section in Chapter nine cases, see 11 USCA § 901.

Creditors' committees in Chapter seven cases, see 11 USCA § 705.

Disallowance of administrative expenses for creditors' and equity security holders' committees, see 11 USCA § 503.

Effect of conversion, see 11 USCA § 348.

Inapplicability of subsec. (a)(1) of this section to railroad reorganization cases, see 11 USCA § 1161.

Limitation on compensation of professional persons, see 11 USCA § 328.

"Person" defined for purposes of this section, see 11 USCA § 101.

§ 1103. Powers and duties of committees

(a) At a scheduled meeting of a committee appointed under section 1102 of this title, at which a majority of the members of such committee are present, and with the court's approval, such committee may select and authorize the employment by such committee of one or more attorneys, accountants, or other agents, to represent or perform services for such committee.

(b) An attorney or accountant employed to represent a committee appointed under section 1102 of this title may not, while employed by such committee, represent any other entity having an adverse interest in connection with the case. Representation of one or more creditors of the same class as represented by the committee shall not per se constitute the representation of an adverse interest.

(c) A committee appointed under section 1102 of this title may—

    (1) consult with the trustee or debtor in possession concerning the administration of the case;

    (2) investigate the acts, conduct, assets, liabilities, and financial condition of the debtor, the operation of the debtor's business and the desirability of the continuance of such business, and any other matter relevant to the case or to the formulation of a plan;

    (3) participate in the formulation of a plan, advise those represented by such committee of such committee's determinations as to any plan formulated, and collect and file with the court acceptances or rejections of a plan;

    (4) request the appointment of a trustee or examiner under section 1104 of this title; and

(5) perform such other services as are in the interest of those represented.

(d) As soon as practicable after the appointment of a committee under section 1102 of this title, the trustee shall meet with such committee to transact such business as may be necessary and proper.

(Pub.L. 95–598, Nov. 6, 1978, 92 Stat. 2627; Pub.L. 98–353, Title III, §§ 324, 500, July 10, 1984, 98 Stat. 358, 384.)

HISTORICAL AND STATUTORY NOTES

Revision Notes and Legislative Reports

1978 Acts. This section defines the powers and duties of a committee elected or appointed under section 1102.

Under subsection (a) the committee may, if authorized by the court, employ one or more attorneys, accountants, or other agents to represent or perform services for the committee. Normally one attorney should suffice; more than one may be authorized for good cause. The same considerations apply to the services of others, if the need for any at all is demonstrated.

Under subsections (c) and (d) the committee, like any party in interest, may confer with the trustee or debtor regarding the administration of the estate; may advise the court on the need for a trustee under section 1104(b). The committee may investigate matters specified in paragraph (2) of subsection (c), but only if authorized by the court and if no trustee or examiner is appointed. Senate Report No. 95–989.

Subsection (a) of this section authorizes a committee appointed under section 1102 to select and authorize the employment of counsel, accountants, or other agents, to represent or perform services for the committee. The committee's selection and authorization is subject to the court's approval, and may only be done at a meeting of the committee at which a majority of its members are present. The subsection provides for the employment of more than one attorney. However, this will be the exception, and not the rule; cause must be shown to depart from the normal standard.

Subsection (b) requires a committee's counsel to cease representation of any other entity in connection with the case after he begins to represent the committee. This will prevent the potential of severe conflicts of interest.

Subsection (c) lists a committee's functions in a chapter 11 case. The committee may consult with the trustee or debtor in possession concerning the administration of the case, may investigate the acts, conduct, assets, liabilities and financial condition of the debtor, the operation of the debtor's business, and the desirability of the continuance of the business, and any other matter relevant to the case or to the formulation of a plan. The committee may participate in the formulation of a plan, advise those it represents of the committee's recommendation with respect to any plan formulated, and collect and file acceptances. These will be its most important functions. The committee may also determine the need for the appointment of a trustee, if one has not previously been appointed, and perform such other services as are in the interest of those represented.

Subsection (d) requires the trustee and each committee to meet as soon as practicable after their appointments to transact such business as may be necessary and proper. House Report No. 95–595.

1984 Acts. Statements by Legislative Leaders, see 1984 U.S.Code Cong. and Adm.News, p. 576.

Effective and Applicability Provisions

1984 Acts. Amendment by Pub.L. 98–353 effective with respect to cases filed 90 days after July 10, 1984, see section 552(a), formerly 553(a), of Pub.L. 98–353, set out as a note under section 101 of this title.

CROSS REFERENCES

Applicability of this section in Chapter nine cases, see 11 USCA § 901.

Compensation of officers, see 11 USCA § 330.

Creditors' committees in Chapter seven cases, see 11 USCA § 705.

Interim compensation for professional persons, see 11 USCA § 331.

Limitation on compensation of professional persons, see 11 USCA § 328.

§ 1104. Appointment of trustee or examiner

(a) At any time after the commencement of the case but before confirmation of a plan, on request of a party in interest or the United States trustee, and after notice and a hearing, the court shall order the appointment of a trustee—

(1) for cause, including fraud, dishonesty, incompetence, or gross mismanagement of the affairs of the debtor by current management, either before or after the commencement of the case, or similar cause, but not including the number of holders of securities of the debtor or the amount of assets or liabilities of the debtor; or

(2) if such appointment is in the interests of creditors, any equity security holders, and other interests of the estate, without regard to the number of holders of securities of the debtor or the amount of assets or liabilities of the debtor.

(b)(1) Except as provided in section 1163 of this title, on the request of a party in interest made not later than 30 days after the court orders the appointment of a trustee under subsection (a), the United States trustee shall convene a meeting of creditors for the purpose of electing one disinterested person to serve as trustee in the case. The election of a trustee shall be conducted in the manner provided in subsections (a), (b), and (c) of section 702 of this title.

(2)(A) If an eligible, disinterested trustee is elected at a meeting of creditors under paragraph (1), the United States trustee shall file a report certifying that election.

(B) Upon the filing of a report under subparagraph (A)—

(i) the trustee elected under paragraph (1) shall be considered to have been selected and appointed for purposes of this section; and

(ii) the service of any trustee appointed under subsection (a) shall terminate.

(C) The court shall resolve any dispute arising out of an election described in subparagraph (A).

(c) If the court does not order the appointment of a trustee under this section, then at any time before the confirmation of a plan, on request of a party in interest or the United States trustee, and after notice and a hearing, the court shall order the appointment of an examiner to conduct such an investigation of the debtor as is appropriate, including an investigation of any allegations of fraud, dishonesty, incompetence, misconduct, mismanagement, or irregularity in the management of the affairs of the debtor of or by current or former management of the debtor, if—

    (1) such appointment is in the interests of creditors, any equity security holders, and other interests of the estate; or

    (2) the debtor's fixed, liquidated, unsecured debts, other than debts for goods, services, or taxes, or owing to an insider, exceed $5,000,000.

(d) If the court orders the appointment of a trustee or an examiner, if a trustee or an examiner dies or resigns during the case or is removed under section 324 of this title, or if a trustee fails to qualify under section 322 of this title, then the United States trustee, after consultation with parties in interest, shall appoint, subject to the court's approval, one disinterested person other than the United States trustee to serve as trustee or examiner, as the case may be, in the case.

(e) The United States trustee shall move for the appointment of a trustee under subsection (a) if there are reasonable grounds to suspect that current members of the governing body of the debtor, the debtor's chief executive or chief financial officer, or members of the governing body who selected the debtor's chief executive or chief financial officer, participated in actual fraud, dishonesty, or criminal conduct in the management of the debtor or the debtor's public financial reporting.

(Pub.L. 95–598, Nov. 6, 1978, 92 Stat. 2627; Pub.L. 99–554, Title II, § 222, Oct. 27, 1986, 100 Stat. 3102; Pub.L. 103–394, Title II, § 211(a), Title V, § 501(d)(30), Oct. 22, 1994, 108 Stat. 4125, 4146; Pub.L. 109–8, Title IV, §§ 416, 442(b), Title XIV, § 1405, Apr. 20, 2005, 119 Stat. 107, 116, 215; Pub.L. 111–327, § 2(a)(30), Dec. 22, 2010, 124 Stat. 3560.)

HISTORICAL AND STATUTORY NOTES

Revision Notes and Legislative Reports

1978 Acts. Subsection (a) provides for the mandatory appointment of a disinterested trustee in the case of a public company, as defined in section 1101(3), within 10 days of the order for relief, or of a successor, in the event of a vacancy, as soon as practicable.

Section 156 of chapter X [section 516 (556) of former Title 11] requires the appointment of a disinterested trustee if the debtor's liabilities are $250,000 or over. Section 1104(a) marks a substantial change. The appointment of a trustee is mandatory only for a public company, which under section 1101(3), has $5 million in liabilities, excluding tax and trade obligations, and 1,000 security holders. In view of past experience, cases involving public companies will under normal circumstances probably be relatively few in number but of vast importance in terms of public investor interest.

In case of a nonpublic company, the appointment or election of a trustee is discretionary if the interests of the estate and its security holders would be served thereby. A test based on probable costs and benefits of a trusteeship is not practical. The appointment may be made at any time prior to confirmation of the plan.

In case of a nonpublic company, if no trustee is appointed, the court may under subsection (c) appoint an examiner, if the appointment would serve the interests of the estate and security holders. The purpose of his appointment is specified in section 1106(b). Senate Report No. 95–989.

Subsection (a) of this section governs the appointment of trustees in reorganization cases. The court is permitted to order the appointment of one trustee at any time after the commencement of the case if a party in interest so requests. The court may order appointment only if the protection afforded by a trustee is needed and the costs and expenses of a trustee would not be disproportionately higher than the value of the protection afforded.

The protection afforded by a trustee would be needed, for example, in cases where the current management of the debtor has been fraudulent or dishonest, or has grossly mismanaged the company, or where the debtor's management has abandoned the business. A trustee would not necessarily be needed to investigate misconduct of former management of the debtor, because an examiner appointed under this section might well be able to serve that function adequately without displacing the current management. Generally, a trustee would not be needed in any case where the protection afforded by a trustee could equally be afforded by an examiner. Though the device of examiner appears in current chapter X [chapter 10 (section 501 et seq.) of former Title 11], it is rarely used because of the nearly absolute presumption in favor of the appointment of a trustee. Its use here will give the courts, debtors, creditors, and equity security holders greater flexibility in handling the affairs of an insolvent debtor, permitting the court to tailor the remedy to the case.

The second test, relating to the costs and expenses of a trustee, is not intended to be a strict cost/benefit analysis. It is included to require the court to have due regard for any additional costs or expenses that the appointment of a trustee would impose on the estate.

Subsection (b) permits the court, at any time after the commencement of the case and on request of a party in interest, to order the appointment of an examiner, if the court has not ordered the appointment of a trustee. The examiner would be appointed to conduct such an investigation of the debtor as is appropriate under the particular circumstances of the case, including an investigation of any allegations of fraud, dishonesty, or gross mismanagement of the debtor of or by current or former management of the debtor. The standards for the appointment of an examiner are the same as those for the appointment of a trustee: the protection must be needed, and the costs and expenses must not be disproportionately high.

By virtue of proposed 11 U.S.C. 1109, an indenture trustee and the Securities and Exchange Commission will be parties in interest for the purpose of requesting the appointment of a trustee or examiner.

Subsection (c) directs that the United States trustee actually select and appoint the trustee or examiner ordered appointed under this section. The United States trustee is required to consult with various parties in interest before selecting and appointing a trustee. He is not bound to select one of the members of the panel of private trustees established under proposed 28 U.S.C. 586(a)(1) which exists only for the purpose of providing trustees for chapter 7 cases. Neither is he precluded from selecting a panel member if the member is qualified to serve as chapter 11 trustee. Appointment by the United States trustee will remove the court from the often criticized practice of appointing an officer that will appear in litigation before the court against an adverse party. House Report No. 95–595.

1986 Acts. House Report No. 99–764 and House Conference Report No. 99–958, see 1986 U.S.Code Cong. and Adm. News, p. 5227.

1994 Acts. House Report No. 103–835, see 1994 U.S. Code Cong. and Adm. News, p. 3340.

2005 Acts. House Report No. 109–31(Part I), see 2005 U.S. Code Cong. and Adm. News, p. 88.

Legislative Statements

Section 1104 of the House amendment represents a compromise between the House bill and the Senate amendment concerning the appointment of a trustee or examiner. The method of appointment rather than election, is derived from the House bill; the two alternative standards of appointment are derived with modifications from the Senate amendment, instead of the standard stated in the House bill. For example, if the current management of the debtor gambled away rental income before the filing of the petition, a trustee should be appointed after the petition, whether or not postpetition mismanagement can be shown. However, under no circumstances will cause include the number of security holders of the debtor or the amount of assets or liabilities of the debtor. The standard also applies to the appointment of an examiner in those circumstances in which mandatory appointment, as previously detailed, is not required.

Effective and Applicability Provisions

2005 Acts. Amendments by Pub.L. 109–8, Title XIV, effective, except as otherwise provided, on Apr. 20, 2005, and applicable only with respect to cases commenced under Title 11 on or after Apr. 20, 2005, see Pub.L. 109–8, § 1406, set out as a note under 11 U.S.C.A. § 507.

Amendments by Pub.L. 109–8 effective, except as otherwise provided, 180 days after April 20, 2005, and inapplicable with respect to cases commenced under Title 11 before the effective date, see Pub.L. 109–8, § 1501, set out as a note under 11 U.S.C.A. § 101.

1994 Acts. Amendments by Pub.L. 103–394 effective on Oct. 22, 1994, and not to apply with respect to cases commenced under Title 11 of the United States Code before Oct. 22, 1994, see section 702 of Pub.L. 103–394, set out as a note under section 101 of this title.

1986 Acts. Amendment by Pub.L. 99–554 effective 30 days after Oct. 27, 1986, except as otherwise provided for, see section 302(a) of Pub.L. 99–554, set out as a note under section 581 of Title 28, Judiciary and Judicial Procedure.

Amendment by Pub.L. 99–554, § 222, not to become effective in or with respect to certain specified judicial districts until, or apply to cases while pending in such district before, the expiration of the 270–day period beginning 30 days after Oct. 27, 1986, or of the 30–day period beginning on the date the Attorney General certifies under section 303 of Pub.L. 99–554 the region specified in a paragraph of section 581(a) of Title 28, as amended by section 111(a) of Pub.L. 99–554, that includes such district, whichever occurs first, see section 302(d)(1) of Pub.L. 99–554, set out as a note under section 581 of Title 28.

Amendment by Pub.L. 99–554, § 222, not to become effective in or with respect to certain specified judicial districts until, or apply to cases while pending in such district before, the expiration of the 2–year period beginning 30 days after Oct. 27, 1986, or of the 30–day period beginning on the date the Attorney General certifies under section 303 of Pub.L. 99–554 the region specified in a paragraph of section 581(a) of Title 28, as amended by section 111(a) of Pub.L. 99–554, that includes such district, whichever occurs first, see section 302(d)(2) of Pub.L. 99–554, set out as a note under section 581 of Title 28.

Amendment by Pub.L. 99–554, § 222, not to become effective in or with respect to judicial districts established for the States of Alabama and North Carolina until, or apply to cases while pending in such district before, such district elects to be included in a bankruptcy region established in section 581(a) of Title 28, as amended by section 111(a) of Pub.L. 99–554, or Oct. 1, 2002, whichever occurs first, and, except as otherwise provided for, with respect to cases under chapters 7, 11, 12, and 13 of Title 11 commenced before 30 days after Oct. 27, 1986, and pending in a judicial district in the States of Alabama or North Carolina before any election made under section 302(d)(3)(A) of Pub.L. 99–554 by such district becomes effective or Oct. 1, 2002, whichever occurs first, amendments by Pub.L. 99–554 not to apply until Oct. 1, 2003, or the expiration of the 1–year period beginning on the date such election becomes effective, whichever occurs first, and further, in any judicial district in Alabama or North Carolina not making the election described in section 302(d)(3)(A) of Pub.L. 99–554, any person appointed under regulations issued by the Judicial Conference to administer estates in cases under Title 11 authorized to establish, etc., a panel of private trustees, and to supervise cases and trustees in cases under chapters 7, 11, 12, and 13 of Title 11, until amendments by sections 201 to 231 of Pub.L. 99–554 effective in such district, see section 302(d)(3)(A) to (F), (H), (I), of Pub.L. 99–554, set out as a note under section 581 of Title 28.

Amendment by Pub.L. 99–554, § 222, except as otherwise provided, with respect to cases under chapters 7, 11, 12, and 13 of Title 11 commenced before 30 days after Oct. 27, 1986, and pending in a judicial district referred to in section 581(a) of Title 28, as amended by section 111(a) of Pub.L. 99–554, for which a United States trustee is not authorized before 30 days after Oct. 27, 1986 to be appointed, not applicable until the expiration of the 3–year period beginning on Oct. 27, 1986, or of the 1–year period beginning on the date the Attorney General certifies under section 303 of Pub.L. 99–554 the region specified in a paragraph of such section 581(a) that includes such district, whichever occurs first, see section 302(e)(1), (2) of Pub.L. 99–554 set out as a note under section 581 of Title 28.

Separability of Provisions

If any provision of or amendment made by Pub.L. 103–394 or the application of such provision or amendment to any person or circumstance is held to be unconstitutional, the remaining provisions of and amendments made by Pub.L.

103–394 and the application of such provisions and amendments to any person or circumstance shall not be affected thereby, see section 701 of Pub.L. 103–394, set out as a note under section 101 of this title.

CROSS REFERENCES

Appointment of Secretary of Transportation as sole trustee, see 46 USCA § 50305.

Appointment of trustee in,

Chapter thirteen cases, see 11 USCA § 1302.

Chapter twelve cases, see 11 USCA § 1202.

Railroad reorganization cases, see 11 USCA § 1163.

Election of trustee in Chapter seven cases, see 11 USCA § 702.

Grain storage facility bankruptcies, expedited appointment of trustee or examiner, see 11 USCA § 557.

Inapplicability of this section to railroad reorganization cases, see 11 USCA § 1161.

Qualification of trustee, see 11 USCA § 322.

Time for bringing action, see 11 USCA § 546.

§ 1105.   Termination of trustee's appointment

At any time before confirmation of a plan, on request of a party in interest or the United States trustee, and after notice and a hearing, the court may terminate the trustee's appointment and restore the debtor to possession and management of the property of the estate and of the operation of the debtor's business.

(Pub.L. 95–598, Nov. 6, 1978, 92 Stat. 2628; Pub.L. 98–353, Title III, § 501, July 10, 1984, 98 Stat. 384; Pub.L. 99–554, Title II, § 223, Oct. 27, 1986, 100 Stat. 3102.)

HISTORICAL AND STATUTORY NOTES

Revision Notes and Legislative Reports

1978 Acts. This section authorizes the court to terminate the trustee's appointment and to restore the debtor to possession and management of the property of the estate and to operation of the debtor's business. Section 1104(a) provides that this section does not apply in the case of a public company, for which the appointment of a trustee is mandatory. Senate Report No. 95–989.

This section authorizes the court to terminate the trustee's appointment and to restore the debtor to possession and management of the property of the estate, and to operation of the debtor's business. This section would permit the court to reverse its decision to order the appointment of a trustee in light of new evidence. House Report No. 95–595.

1984 Acts. Statements by Legislative Leaders, see 1984 U.S.Code Cong. and Adm.News, p. 576.

1986 Acts. House Report No. 99–764 and House Conference Report No. 99–958, see 1986 U.S.Code Cong. and Adm. News, p. 5227.

Effective and Applicability Provisions

1986 Acts. Amendment by Pub.L. 99–554 effective 30 days after Oct. 27, 1986, except as otherwise provided for, see section 302(a) of Pub.L. 99–554, set out as a note under section 581 of Title 28, Judiciary and Judicial Procedure.

Amendment by Pub.L. 99–554, § 223, not to become effective in or with respect to certain specified judicial districts until, or apply to cases while pending in such district before, the expiration of the 270–day period beginning 30 days after Oct. 27, 1986, or of the 30–day period beginning on the date the Attorney General certifies under section 303 of Pub.L. 99–554 the region specified in a paragraph of section 581(a) of Title 28, as amended by section 111(a) of Pub.L. 99–554, that includes such district, whichever occurs first, see section 302(d)(1) of Pub.L. 99–554, set out as a note under section 581 of Title 28.

Amendment by Pub.L. 99–554, § 223, not to become effective in or with respect to certain specified judicial districts until, or apply to cases while pending in such district before, the expiration of the 2–year period beginning 30 days after Oct. 27, 1986, or of the 30–day period beginning on the date the Attorney General certifies under section 303 of Pub.L. 99–554 the region specified in a paragraph of section 581(a) of Title 28, as amended by section 111(a) of Pub.L. 99–554, that includes such district, whichever occurs first, see section 302(d)(2) of Pub.L. 99–554, set out as a note under section 581 of Title 28.

Amendment by Pub.L. 99–554, § 223, not to become effective in or with respect to judicial districts established for the States of Alabama and North Carolina until, or apply to cases while pending in such district before, such district elects to be included in a bankruptcy region established in section 581(a) of Title 28, as amended by section 111(a) of Pub.L. 99–554, or Oct. 1, 2002, whichever occurs first, and, except as otherwise provided for, with respect to cases under chapters 7, 11, 12, and 13 of Title 11 commenced before 30 days after Oct. 27, 1986, and pending in a judicial district in the States of Alabama or North Carolina before any election made under section 302(d)(3)(A) of Pub.L. 99–554 by such district becomes effective or Oct. 1, 2002, whichever occurs first, amendments by Pub.L. 99–554 not to apply until Oct. 1, 2003, or the expiration of the 1–year period beginning on the date such election becomes effective, whichever occurs first, and further, in any judicial district in Alabama or North Carolina not making the election described in section 302(d)(3)(A) of Pub.L. 99–554, any person appointed under regulations issued by the Judicial Conference to administer estates in cases under Title 11 authorized to establish, etc., a panel of private trustees, and to supervise cases and trustees in cases under chapters 7, 11, 12, and 13 of Title 11, until amendments by sections 201 to 231 of Pub.L. 99–554 effective in such district, see section 302(d)(3)(A) to (F), (H), (I) of Pub.L. 99–554, set out as a note under section 581 of Title 28.

Amendment by Pub.L. 99–554, § 223, except as otherwise provided, with respect to cases under chapters 7, 11, 12, and 13 of Title 11 commenced before 30 days after Oct. 27, 1986, and pending in a judicial district referred to in section 581(a) of Title 28, as amended by section 111(a) of Pub.L. 99–554, for which a United States trustee is not authorized before 30 days after Oct. 27, 1986 to be appointed, not applicable until the expiration of the 3–year period beginning on Oct. 27, 1986, or of the 1–year period beginning on the date the Attorney General certifies under section 303 of Pub.L. 99–554, the region specified in a paragraph of such section 581(a) that includes, such district, whichever occurs first, see section 302(e)(1), (2) of Pub.L. 99–554, set out as a note under section 581 of Title 28.

1984 Acts. Amendment by Pub.L. 98–353 effective with respect to cases filed 90 days after July 10, 1984, see section 552(a), formerly 553(a), of Pub.L. 98–353, set out as a note under section 101 of this title.

Effect of vacancy in office of trustee, see 11 USCA § 325.

Inapplicability of this section to railroad reorganization cases, see 11 USCA § 1161.

Removal of trustee, see 11 USCA § 324.

§ 1106. Duties of trustee and examiner

(a) A trustee shall—

(1) perform the duties of the trustee, as specified in paragraphs (2), (5), (7), (8), (9), (10), (11), and (12) of section 704(a);

(2) if the debtor has not done so, file the list, schedule, and statement required under section 521(a)(1) of this title;

(3) except to the extent that the court orders otherwise, investigate the acts, conduct, assets, liabilities, and financial condition of the debtor, the operation of the debtor's business and the desirability of the continuance of such business, and any other matter relevant to the case or to the formulation of a plan;

(4) as soon as practicable—

(A) file a statement of any investigation conducted under paragraph (3) of this subsection, including any fact ascertained pertaining to fraud, dishonesty, incompetence, misconduct, mismanagement, or irregularity in the management of the affairs of the debtor, or to a cause of action available to the estate; and

(B) transmit a copy or a summary of any such statement to any creditors' committee or equity security holders' committee, to any indenture trustee, and to such other entity as the court designates;

(5) as soon as practicable, file a plan under section 1121 of this title, file a report of why the trustee will not file a plan, or recommend conversion of the case to a case under chapter 7, 12, or 13 of this title or dismissal of the case;

(6) for any year for which the debtor has not filed a tax return required by law, furnish, without personal liability, such information as may be required by the governmental unit with which such tax return was to be filed, in light of the condition of the debtor's books and records and the availability of such information;

(7) after confirmation of a plan, file such reports as are necessary or as the court orders; and

(8) if with respect to the debtor there is a claim for a domestic support obligation, provide the applicable notice specified in subsection (c).

(b) An examiner appointed under section 1104(d) of this title shall perform the duties specified in paragraphs (3) and (4) of subsection (a) of this section, and, except to the extent that the court orders otherwise, any other duties of the trustee that the court orders the debtor in possession not to perform.

(c)(1) In a case described in subsection (a)(8) to which subsection (a)(8) applies, the trustee shall—

(A)(i) provide written notice to the holder of the claim described in subsection (a)(8) of such claim and of the right of such holder to use the services of the State child support enforcement agency established under sections 464 and 466 of the Social Security Act for the State in which such holder resides, for assistance in collecting child support during and after the case under this title; and

(ii) include in the notice required by clause (i) the address and telephone number of such State child support enforcement agency;

(B)(i) provide written notice to such State child support enforcement agency of such claim; and

(ii) include in the notice required by clause (i) the name, address, and telephone number of such holder; and

(C) at such time as the debtor is granted a discharge under section 1141, provide written notice to such holder and to such State child support enforcement agency of—

(i) the granting of the discharge;

(ii) the last recent known address of the debtor;

(iii) the last recent known name and address of the debtor's employer; and

(iv) the name of each creditor that holds a claim that—

(I) is not discharged under paragraph (2), (4), or (14A) of section 523(a); or

(II) was reaffirmed by the debtor under section 524(c).

(2)(A) The holder of a claim described in subsection (a)(8) or the State child enforcement support agency of the State in which such holder resides may request from a creditor described in paragraph (1)(C)(iv) the last known address of the debtor.

(B) Notwithstanding any other provision of law, a creditor that makes a disclosure of a last known address of a debtor in connection with a request made under subparagraph (A) shall not be liable by reason of making such disclosure.

(Pub.L. 95–598, Nov. 6, 1978, 92 Stat. 2628; Pub.L. 98–353, Title III, §§ 311(b)(1), 502, July 10, 1984, 98 Stat. 355, 384; Pub.L. 99–554, Title II, § 257(c), Oct. 27, 1986, 100 Stat. 3114; Pub.L. 103–394, Title II, § 211(b), Oct. 22, 1994, 108 Stat. 4125; Pub.L. 109–8, Title II, § 219(b), Title IV, § 446(c), Title XI, § 1105(b), Apr. 20, 2005, 119 Stat. 56, 118, 192; Pub.L. 111–327, § 2(a)(31), Dec. 22, 2010, 124 Stat. 3560.)

HISTORICAL AND STATUTORY NOTES

Revision Notes and Legislative Reports

1978 Acts. Subsection (a) of this section prescribes the trustee's duties. He is required to perform the duties of a trustee in a liquidation case specified in section 704(2), (4), (6), (7), (8), and (9). These include reporting and informational duties, and accountability for all property received. Paragraph (2) of this subsection requires the trustee to file with the court, if the debtor has not done so, the list of creditors, schedule of assets and liabilities, and statement of affairs required under section 521(1).

Paragraph (3) of S. 1106 requires the trustee to investigate the acts, conduct, assets, liabilities, and financial condition of the debtor, the operation of the debtor's business, and the desirability of the continuance of the business, and any other matter relevant to the case or to the formulation of a plan. Paragraph (4) requires the trustee to report the results of his investigation to the court and to creditors' committees, equity security holders' committees, indenture trustees and any other entity the court designates.

Paragraph (5) requires the trustee to file a plan or to report why a plan cannot be formulated, or to recommend conversion to liquidation or to an individual repayment plan case, or dismissal. It is anticipated that the trustee will consult with creditors and other parties in interest in the formulation of a plan, just as the debtor in possession would.

Paragraph (6) [now (7)] requires final reports by the trustee, as the court orders.

Subsection (b) gives the trustee's investigative duties to an examiner, if one is appointed. The court is authorized to give the examiner additional duties as the circumstances warrant.

Paragraphs (3), (4), and (5) of subsection (a) are derived from sections 165 and 169 of chapter X (11 U.S.C. 565, 569) [former sections 565 and 569 of former Title 11, respectively]. Senate Report No. 95–989.

1984 Acts. Statements by Legislative Leaders, see 1984 U.S.Code Cong. and Adm.News, p. 576.

1986 Acts. House Report No. 99–764 and House Conference Report No. 99–958, see 1986 U.S.Code Cong. and Adm. News, p. 5227.

1994 Acts. House Report No. 103–835, see 1994 U.S. Code Cong. and Adm. News, p. 3340.

2005 Acts. House Report No. 109–31(Part I), see 2005 U.S. Code Cong. and Adm. News, p. 88.

References in Text

Section 464 of the Social Security Act, referred to in subsec. (c)(1)(A)(i), is Act Aug. 14, 1935, c. 531, Title IV, § 464, as added Aug. 13, 1981, Pub.L. 97–35, Title XXIII, § 2331(a), 95 Stat. 860, and amended, which is classified to 42 U.S.C.A. § 664.

Section 466 of the Social Security Act, referred to in subsec. (c)(1)(A)(i), is Act Aug. 14, 1935, c. 531, Title IV, § 466, as added Aug. 16, 1984, Pub.L. 98–378, § 3(b), 98 Stat. 1306, and amended, which is classified to 42 U.S.C.A. § 666.

Effective and Applicability Provisions

2005 Acts. Amendments by Pub.L. 109–8 effective, except as otherwise provided, 180 days after April 20, 2005, and inapplicable with respect to cases commenced under Title 11 before the effective date, see Pub.L. 109–8, § 1501, set out as a note under 11 U.S.C.A. § 101.

1994 Acts. Amendment by Pub.L. 103–394 effective on Oct. 22, 1994, and not to apply with respect to cases commenced under Title 11 of the United States Code before Oct. 22, 1994, see section 702 of Pub.L. 103–394, set out as a note under section 101 of this title.

1986 Acts. Amendment by Pub.L. 99–554 effective 30 days after Oct. 27, 1986, but not applicable to cases commenced under this title before that date, see section 302(a), (c)(1), of Pub.L. 99–554, set out as a note under section 581 of Title 28, Judiciary and Judicial Procedure.

1984 Acts. Amendment by Pub.L. 98–353 effective with respect to cases filed 90 days after July 10, 1984, see section 552(a), formerly 553(a), of Pub.L. 98–353, set out as a note under section 101 of this title.

Separability of Provisions

If any provision of or amendment made by Pub.L. 103–394 or the application of such provision or amendment to any person or circumstance is held to be unconstitutional, the remaining provisions of and amendments made by Pub.L. 103–394 and the application of such provisions and amendments to any person or circumstance shall not be affected thereby, see section 701 of Pub.L. 103–394, set out as a note under section 101 of this title.

Payment of Certain Benefits to Retired Former Employees

Pub.L. 99–500, § 101(b) [Title VI, § 608], Oct. 18, 1986, 100 Stat. 1783–39, 1783–74, and Pub.L. 99–591, § 101(b) [Title VI, § 608], Oct. 30, 1986, 100 Stat. 3341–74, as amended by Pub.L. 100–41, May 15, 1987, 101 Stat. 309; Pub.L. 100–99, Aug. 18, 1987, 101 Stat. 716; Pub.L. 100–334, § 3(a), June 16, 1988, 102 Stat. 613, provided that:

"(a)(1) Subject to paragraphs (2), (3), (4), and (5), and notwithstanding title 11 of the United States Code [this title], the trustee shall pay benefits to retired former employees under a plan, fund, or program maintained or established by the debtor prior to filing a petition (through the purchase of insurance or otherwise) for the purpose of providing medical, surgical, or hospital care benefits, or benefits in the event of sickness, accident, disability, or death.

"(2) The level of benefits required to be paid by this subsection may be modified prior to confirmation of a plan under section 1129 of such title [section 1129 of this title] if—

"(A) the trustee and an authorized representative of the former employees with respect to whom such benefits are payable agree to the modification of such benefit payments; or

"(B) the court finds that a modification proposed by the trustee meets the standards of section 1113(b)(1)(A) of such title [section 1113(b)(1)(A) of this title] and the balance of the equities clearly favors the modification.

If such benefits are covered by a collective bargaining agreement, the authorized representative shall be the labor organization that is signatory to such collective bargaining agreement unless there is a conflict of interest.

"(3) The trustee shall pay benefits in accordance with this subsection until—

"(A) the dismissal of the case involved; or

"(B) the effective date of a plan confirmed under section 1129 of such title which provides for the continued payment after confirmation of the plan of all such benefits at the level established under paragraph (2) of this subsection, at any time prior to the confirmation of the plan, for the duration of the period the debtor (as defined in such title) has obligated itself to provide such benefits.

"(4) No such benefits paid between the filing of a petition in a case covered by this section and the time a plan con-

---

firmed under section 1129 of such title with respect to such case becomes effective shall be deducted or offset from the amount allowed as claims for any benefits which remain unpaid, or from the amount to be paid under the plan with respect to such claims for unpaid benefits, whether such claims for unpaid benefits are based upon or arise from a right to future benefits or from any benefit not paid as a result of modifications allowed pursuant to this section.

"(5) No claim for benefits covered by this section shall be limited by section 502(b)(7) of such title [section 502(b)(7) of this title].

"(b)(1) Notwithstanding any provision of title 11 of the United States Code [this title], the trustee shall pay an allowable claim of any person for a benefit paid—

"(A) before the filing of the petition under title 11 of the United States Code; and

"(B) directly or indirectly to a retired former employee under a plan, fund, or program described in subsection (a)(1);

if, as determined by the court, such person is entitled to recover from such employee, or any provider of health care to such employee, directly or indirectly, the amount of such benefit for which such person receives no payment from the debtor.

"(2) For purposes of paragraph (1), the term 'provider of health care' means a person who—

"(A) is the direct provider of health care (including a physician, dentist, nurse, podiatrist, optometrist, physician assistant, or ancillary personnel employed under the supervision of a physician); or

"(B) administers a facility or institution (including a hospital, alcohol and drug abuse treatment facility, outpatient facility, or health maintenance organization) in which health care is provided.

"(c) This section is effective with respect to cases commenced under chapter 11, of title 11, United States Code [this chapter], in which a plan for reorganization has not been confirmed by the court and in which any such benefit is still being paid on October 2, 1986, and in cases that become subject to chapter 11, title 11, United States Code, after October 2, 1986 and before the date of the enactment of the Retiree Benefits Bankruptcy Protection Act of 1988 [June 16, 1988].

"(d) This section shall not apply during any period in which a case is subject to chapter 7, title 11, United States Code [11 U.S.C.A. § 701 et seq.]."

Similar provisions were contained in Pub.L. 99–656, § 2, Nov. 14, 1986, 100 Stat. 3668, as amended by Pub.L. 100–41, May 15, 1987, 101 Stat. 309; Pub.L. 100–99, Aug. 18, 1987, 101 Stat. 716, and were repealed by Pub.L. 100–334, § 3(b), June 16, 1988, 102 Stat. 614.

CROSS REFERENCES

Duties of trustees in,

Chapter thirteen cases, see 11 USCA § 1302.

Chapter twelve cases, see 11 USCA § 1202.

Powers and duties of trustee in investor protection liquidation proceedings, see 15 USCA § 78fff–1.

Rights and powers of debtor in Chapter twelve case not encompassing duties specified in subsec. (a)(3) and (4) of this section, see 11 USCA § 1203.

§ 1107. Rights, powers, and duties of debtor in possession

(a) Subject to any limitations on a trustee serving in a case under this chapter, and to such limitations or conditions as the court prescribes, a debtor in possession shall have all the rights, other than the right to compensation under section 330 of this title, and powers, and shall perform all the functions and duties, except the duties specified in sections 1106(a)(2), (3), and (4) of this title, of a trustee serving in a case under this chapter.

(b) Notwithstanding section 327(a) of this title, a person is not disqualified for employment under section 327 of this title by a debtor in possession solely because of such person's employment by or representation of the debtor before the commencement of the case.

(Pub.L. 95–598, Nov. 6, 1978, 92 Stat. 2628; Pub.L. 98–353, Title III, § 503, July 10, 1984, 98 Stat. 384.)

HISTORICAL AND STATUTORY NOTES

Revision Notes and Legislative Reports

1978 Acts. This section places a debtor in possession in the shoes of a trustee in every way. The debtor is given the rights and powers of a chapter 11 trustee. He is required to perform the functions and duties of a chapter 11 trustee (except the investigative duties). He is also subject to any limitations on a chapter 11 trustee, and to such other limitations and conditions as the court prescribes cf. *Wolf v. Weinstein*, 372 U.S. 633, 649–650 (1963). Senate Report No. 95–989.

1984 Acts. Statements by Legislative Leaders, see 1984 U.S.Code Cong. and Adm.News, p. 576.

Legislative Statements

The House amendment adopts section 1107(b) of the Senate amendment which clarifies a point not covered by the House bill.

Effective and Applicability Provisions

1984 Acts. Amendment by Pub.L. 98–353 effective with respect to cases filed 90 days after July 10, 1984, see section 552(a), formerly 553(a), of Pub.L. 98–353, set out as a note under section 101 of this title.

CROSS REFERENCES

Debtor engaged in business in Chapter thirteen cases, see 11 USCA § 1304.

Debtor's duties, see 11 USCA § 521.

Inapplicability of this section in railroad reorganization cases, see 11 USCA § 1161.

Limitation on compensation of professional persons, see 11 USCA § 328.

Rights and powers of debtor in,

Chapter thirteen cases, see 11 USCA § 1303.

Chapter twelve cases, see 11 USCA § 1203.

§ 1108. Authorization to operate business

Unless the court, on request of a party in interest and after notice and a hearing, orders otherwise, the trustee may operate the debtor's business.

(Pub.L. 95–598, Nov. 6, 1978, 92 Stat. 2629; Pub.L. 98–353, Title III, § 504, July 10, 1984, 98 Stat. 384.)

HISTORICAL AND STATUTORY NOTES

Revision Notes and Legislative Reports

1978 Acts. This section permits the debtor's business to continue to be operated, unless the court orders otherwise. Thus, in a reorganization case, operation of the business will be the rule, and it will not be necessary to go to the court to obtain an order authorizing operation. Senate Report No. 95–989.

This section does not presume that a trustee will be appointed to operate the business of the debtor. Rather, the power granted to trustee under this section is one of the powers that a debtor in possession acquires by virtue of proposed 11 U.S.C. 1107. House Report No. 95–595.

1984 Acts. Statements by Legislative Leaders, see 1984 U.S.Code Cong. and Adm.News, p. 576.

Legislative Statements

The House amendment adopts section 1108 of the House bill in preference to the style of an identical substantive provision contained in the Senate amendment. Throughout title 11 references [sic] to a "trustee" is read to include other parties under various sections of the bill. For example, section 1107 applies to give the debtor in possession all the rights and powers of a trustee in a case under chapter 11; this includes the power of the trustee to operate the debtor's business under section 1108.

Effective and Applicability Provisions

1984 Acts. Amendment by Pub.L. 98–353 effective with respect to cases filed 90 days after July 10, 1984, see section 552(a), formerly 553(a), of Pub.L. 98–353, set out as a note under section 101 of this title.

CROSS REFERENCES

Authorization to operate business in Chapter seven cases, see 11 USCA § 721.

Executory contracts and unexpired leases, see 11 USCA § 365.

Executory contracts in stockbroker liquidation cases, see 11 USCA § 744.

Obtaining credit, see 11 USCA § 364.

Retention or replacement of professional persons, see 11 USCA § 327.

Treatment of accounts in,

Commodity broker liquidation cases, see 11 USCA § 763.

Stockbroker liquidation cases, see 11 USCA § 745.

Use, sale or lease of property, see 11 USCA § 363.

Utility service, see 11 USCA § 366.

§ 1109. Right to be heard

(a) The Securities and Exchange Commission may raise and may appear and be heard on any issue in a case under this chapter, but the Securities and Exchange Commission may not appeal from any judgment, order, or decree entered in the case.

(b) A party in interest, including the debtor, the trustee, a creditors' committee, an equity security holders' committee, a creditor, an equity security holder, or any indenture trustee, may raise and may appear and be heard on any issue in a case under this chapter.

(Pub.L. 95–598, Nov. 6, 1978, 92 Stat. 2629.)

HISTORICAL AND STATUTORY NOTES

Revision Notes and Legislative Reports

1978 Acts. Subsection (a) provides, in unqualified terms, that any creditor, equity security holder, or an indenture trustee shall have the right to be heard as a party in interest under this chapter in person, by an attorney, or by a committee. It is derived from section 206 of chapter X (11 U.S.C. 606) [section 606 of former Title 11].

Subsection (b) provides that the Securities and Exchange Commission may appear by filing an appearance in a case of a public company and may appear in other cases if authorized or requested by the court. As a party in interest in either case, the Commission may raise and be heard on any issue. The Commission may not appeal from a judgment, order, or decree in a case, but may participate in any appeal by any other party in interest. This is the present law under section 208 of chapter X (11 U.S.C. 608) [section 608 of former Title 11]. Senate Report No. 95–989.

Section 1109 authorizes the Securities and Exchange Commission and any indenture trustee to intervene in the case at any time on any issue. They may raise an issue or may appear and be heard on an issue that is raised by someone else. The section, following current law, denies the right of appeal to the Securities and Exchange Commission. It does not, however, prevent the Commission from joining or participating in an appeal taken by a true party in interest. The Commission is merely prevented from initiating the appeal in any capacity. House Report No. 95–595.

Legislative Statements

Section 1109 of the House amendment represents a compromise between comparable provisions in the House bill and Senate amendment. As previously discussed the section gives the Securities and Exchange Commission the right to appear and be heard and to raise any issue in a case under chapter 11; however, the Securities and Exchange Commission is not a party in interest and the Commission may not appeal from any judgment, order, or decree entered in the case. Under section 1109(b) a party in interest, including the debtor, the trustee, creditors' committee, equity securities holders' committee, a creditor, an equity security holder, or an indentured trustee, may raise and may appear and be heard on any issue in a case under chapter 11. Section 1109(c) of the Senate amendment has been moved to subchapter IV pertaining to Railroad Reorganizations.

CROSS REFERENCES

Applicability of this section in Chapter nine cases, see 11 USCA § 901.

Right of Commodity Futures Trading Commission to be heard in commodity broker liquidation cases, see 11 USCA § 762.

Right of Interstate Commerce Commission, Department of Transportation, and State or local regulatory commission to be heard in railroad reorganization, see 11 USCA § 1164.

§ 1110. Aircraft equipment and vessels

(a)(1) Except as provided in paragraph (2) and subject to subsection (b), the right of a secured party with a security interest in equipment described in paragraph (3), or of a lessor or conditional vendor of such equipment, to take possession of such equipment in compliance with a security agreement, lease, or conditional sale contract, and to enforce any of its other rights or remedies, under such security agreement, lease, or conditional sale contract, to sell, lease, or otherwise retain or dispose of such equipment, is not limited or otherwise affected by any other provision of this title or by any power of the court.

(2) The right to take possession and to enforce the other rights and remedies described in paragraph (1) shall be subject to section 362 if—

(A) before the date that is 60 days after the date of the order for relief under this chapter, the trustee, subject to the approval of the court, agrees to perform all obligations of the debtor under such security agreement, lease, or conditional sale contract; and

(B) any default, other than a default of a kind specified in section 365(b)(2), under such security agreement, lease, or conditional sale contract—

    (i) that occurs before the date of the order is cured before the expiration of such 60-day period;

    (ii) that occurs after the date of the order and before the expiration of such 60-day period is cured before the later of—

        (I) the date that is 30 days after the date of the default; or

        (II) the expiration of such 60-day period; and

    (iii) that occurs on or after the expiration of such 60-day period is cured in compliance with the terms of such security agreement, lease, or conditional sale contract, if a cure is permitted under that agreement, lease, or contract.

(3) The equipment described in this paragraph—

    (A) is—

        (i) an aircraft, aircraft engine, propeller, appliance, or spare part (as defined in section 40102 of title 49) that is subject to a security interest granted by, leased to, or conditionally sold to a debtor that, at the time such transaction is entered into, holds an air carrier operating certificate issued pursuant to chapter 447 of title 49 for aircraft capable of carrying 10 or more individuals or 6,000 pounds or more of cargo; or

        (ii) a vessel documented under chapter 121 of title 46 that is subject to a security interest granted by, leased to, or conditionally sold to a debtor

that is a water carrier that, at the time such transaction is entered into, holds a certificate of public convenience and necessity or permit issued by the Department of Transportation; and

    (B) includes all records and documents relating to such equipment that are required, under the terms of the security agreement, lease, or conditional sale contract, to be surrendered or returned by the debtor in connection with the surrender or return of such equipment.

(4) Paragraph (1) applies to a secured party, lessor, or conditional vendor acting in its own behalf or acting as trustee or otherwise in behalf of another party.

(b) The trustee and the secured party, lessor, or conditional vendor whose right to take possession is protected under subsection (a) may agree, subject to the approval of the court, to extend the 60-day period specified in subsection (a)(1).

(c)(1) In any case under this chapter, the trustee shall immediately surrender and return to a secured party, lessor, or conditional vendor, described in subsection (a)(1), equipment described in subsection (a)(3), if at any time after the date of the order for relief under this chapter such secured party, lessor, or conditional vendor is entitled pursuant to subsection (a)(1) to take possession of such equipment and makes a written demand for such possession to the trustee.

(2) At such time as the trustee is required under paragraph (1) to surrender and return equipment described in subsection (a)(3), any lease of such equipment, and any security agreement or conditional sale contract relating to such equipment, if such security agreement or conditional sale contract is an executory contract, shall be deemed rejected.

(d) With respect to equipment first placed in service on or before October 22, 1994, for purposes of this section—

    (1) the term "lease" includes any written agreement with respect to which the lessor and the debtor, as lessee, have expressed in the agreement or in a substantially contemporaneous writing that the agreement is to be treated as a lease for Federal income tax purposes; and

    (2) the term "security interest" means a purchase-money equipment security interest.

(Pub.L. 95–598, Nov. 6, 1978, 92 Stat. 2629; Pub.L. 103–272, § 5(c), July 5, 1994, 108 Stat. 1373; Pub.L. 103–394, Title II, § 201(a), Oct. 22, 1994, 108 Stat. 4119; Pub.L. 106–181, Title VII, § 744(b), Apr. 5, 2000, 114 Stat. 177; Pub.L. 109–304, § 17(b)(2), Oct. 6, 2006, 120 Stat. 1707.)

HISTORICAL AND STATUTORY NOTES

Revision Notes and Legislative Reports

1978 Acts. This section, to a large degree, preserves the protection given lessors and conditional vendors of aircraft to a certificated air carrier or of vessels to a certificated water carrier under sections 116(5) and 116(6) of present Chapter X [sections 516(5) and 516(6) of former Title 11]. It is modified to conform with the consolidation of Chapters X [former chapter 10, section 501 et seq.] and XI [former chapter 11 (section 701 et seq.) of former Title 11] and with the new chapter 11 generally. It is also modified to give the trustee in a reorganization case an opportunity to continue in possession of the equipment in question by curing defaults and by making the required lease or purchase payments. This removes the absolute veto power over a reorganization that lessors and conditional vendors have under present law, while entitling them to protection of their investment.

The section overrides the automatic stay or any power of the court to enjoin taking of possession of certain leased, conditionally sold, or liened equipment, unless, [sic] the trustee agrees to perform the debtor's obligations and cures all prior defaults (other than defaults under ipso facto or bankruptcy clauses) within 60 days after the order for relief. The trustee and the equipment financer are permitted to extend the 60-day period by agreement. During the first 60 days, the automatic stay will apply to prevent foreclosure unless the creditor gets relief from the stay.

The effect of this section will be the same if the debtor has granted the security interest to the financer or if the debtor is leasing equipment from a financer that has leveraged the lease and leased the equipment subject to a security interest of a third party. Senate Report No. 95–989.

1994 Acts. House Report No. 103–180, see 1994 U.S. Code Cong. and Adm. News, p. 818.

House Report No. 103–835, see 1994 U.S. Code Cong. and Adm. News, p. 3340.

2000 Acts. House Conference Report No. 106–513 and Statement by President, see 2000 U.S. Code Cong. and Adm. News, p. 80.

2006 Acts. House Report No. 109–170, see 2006 U.S. Code Cong. and Adm. News, p. 972.

Legislative Statements

Section 1110 of the House amendment adopts an identical provision contained in the House bill without modifications contained in the Senate amendment. This section protects a limited class of financiers of aircraft and vessels and is intended to be narrowly construed to prevent secured parties or lessors from gaining the protection of the section unless the interest of such lessor or secured party is explicitly enumerated therein. It should be emphasized that under section 1110(a) a debtor in possession or trustee is given 60 days after the order for relief in a case under chapter 11, to have an opportunity to comply with the provisions of section 1110(a).

During this time the automatic stay will apply and may not be lifted prior to the expiration of the 60-day period. Under section 1110(b), the debtor and secured party or lessor are given an opportunity to extend the 60-day period, but no right to reduce the period is intended. It should additionally be noted that under section 1110(a) the trustee or debtor in possession is not required to assume the executory contract or unexpired lease under section 1110; rather, if the trustee or debtor in possession complies with the requirements of section 1110(a), the trustee or debtor in possession is entitled to retain the aircraft or vessels subject to the normal requirements of section 365. The discussion regarding aircraft and vessels likewise applies with respect to railroad rolling stock in a railroad reorganization under section 1168.

References in Text

Chapter 447 of title 49, referred to in subsec. (a)(3)(A)(i), is classified to 49 U.S.C.A. § 44701 et seq.

Chapter 121 of title 46, referred to in subsec. (a)(3)(A)(ii), is Documentation of Vessels, 46 U.S.C.A. § 12101 et seq.

Effective and Applicability Provisions

2000 Acts. Amendment by Pub.L. 106–181 applicable only to fiscal years beginning after September 30, 1999, see section 3 of Pub.L. 106–181, set out as a note under section 106 of this title.

1994 Acts. Amendment by Pub.L. 103–394 effective on Oct. 22, 1994, with this section as amended by section 201 of Pub.L. 103–394 applicable with respect to any lease, as defined by subsec. (c) of this section as so amended, entered into in connection with a settlement of any proceeding in any case pending under Title 11 of the United States Code on Oct. 22, 1994, see section 702 of Pub.L. 103–394, set out as a note under section 101 of this title.

Separability of Provisions

If any provision of or amendment made by Pub.L. 103–394 or the application of such provision or amendment to any person or circumstance is held to be unconstitutional, the remaining provisions of and amendments made by Pub.L. 103–394 and the application of such provisions and amendments to any person or circumstance shall not be affected thereby, see section 701 of Pub.L. 103–394, set out as a note under section 101 of this title.

Abolition of Interstate Commerce Commission and Transfer of Functions

Interstate Commerce Commission abolished and functions of Commission transferred, except as otherwise provided in Pub.L. 104–88, to Surface Transportation Board effective Jan. 1, 1996, by 49 U.S.C.A. § 1302, and section 101 of Pub.L. 104–88, set out as a note under 49 U.S.C.A. § 1301. References to Interstate Commerce Commission deemed to refer to Surface Transportation Board, a member or employee of the Board, or Secretary of Transportation, as appropriate, see section 205 of Pub.L. 104–88, set out as a note under 49 U.S.C.A. § 1301.

Aircraft Equipment Settlement Leases Act of 1993

Pub.L. 103–7, Mar. 17, 1993, 107 Stat. 36, provided:

"**Section 1. Short Title.**

"This Act [this note] may be cited as the 'Aircraft Equipment Settlement Leases Act of 1993'.

"**Sec. 2. Treatment of Aircraft Equipment Settlement Leases with the Pension Benefit Guaranty Corporation.**

"In the case of any settlement of liability under title IV of the Employee Retirement Income Security Act of 1974 [29 U.S.C.A. § 1301 et seq.], entered into by the Pension Benefit Guaranty Corporation and one or more other parties, if—

"(1) such settlement was entered into before, on, or after the date of the enactment of this Act [Mar. 17, 1993],

"(2) at least one party to such settlement was a debtor under title 11 of the United States Code [this title], and

"(3) an agreement that is entered into as part of such settlement provides that such agreement is to be treated as a lease,

then such agreement shall be treated as a lease for purposes of section 1110 of such title 11 [this section]."

Termination of Civil Aeronautics Board and Transfer of Certain Functions

All functions, powers, and duties of the Civil Aeronautics Board were terminated or transferred by section 1551 of Title 49, Appendix, Transportation, effective in part on Dec. 31, 1981, in part on Jan. 1, 1983, and in part on Jan. 1, 1985.

CROSS REFERENCES

Effect of conversion, see 11 USCA § 348.

Rights of certain secured parties in rolling stock equipment, see 11 USCA § 1168.

§ 1111. Claims and interests

(a) A proof of claim or interest is deemed filed under section 501 of this title for any claim or interest that appears in the schedules filed under section 521(a)(1) or 1106(a)(2) of this title, except a claim or interest that is scheduled as disputed, contingent, or unliquidated.

(b)(1)(A) A claim secured by a lien on property of the estate shall be allowed or disallowed under section 502 of this title the same as if the holder of such claim had recourse against the debtor on account of such claim, whether or not such holder has such recourse, unless—

(i) the class of which such claim is a part elects, by at least two-thirds in amount and more than half in number of allowed claims of such class, application of paragraph (2) of this subsection; or

(ii) such holder does not have such recourse and such property is sold under section 363 of this title or is to be sold under the plan.

(B) A class of claims may not elect application of paragraph (2) of this subsection if—

(i) the interest on account of such claims of the holders of such claims in such property is of inconsequential value; or

(ii) the holder of a claim of such class has recourse against the debtor on account of such claim and such property is sold under section 363 of this title or is to be sold under the plan.

(2) If such an election is made, then notwithstanding section 506(a) of this title, such claim is a secured claim to the extent that such claim is allowed.

(Pub.L. 95–598, Nov. 6, 1978, 92 Stat. 2630; Pub.L. 111–327, § 2(a)(32), Dec. 22, 2010, 124 Stat. 3561.)

HISTORICAL AND STATUTORY NOTES

Revision Notes and Legislative Reports

1978 Acts. Senate Report No. 95–989 and House Report No. 95–595, see 1978 U.S.Code Cong. and Adm.News, p. 5787.

This section dispenses with the need for every creditor and equity security holder to file a proof of claim or interest in a reorganization case. Usually the debtor's schedules are accurate enough that they will suffice to determine the claims or interests allowable in the case. Thus, the section specifies that any claim or interest included on the debtor's schedules is deemed filed under section 501. This does not apply to claims or interests that are scheduled as disputed, contingent, or unliquidated. Senate Report No. 95–989.

Legislative Statements

A discussion of section 1111(b) of the House amendment is best considered in the context of confirmation and will therefore, [sic] be discussed in connection with section 1129.

CROSS REFERENCES

Applicability of subsec. (b) of this section in Chapter nine cases, see 11 USCA § 901.

Effect of list of claims in Chapter nine cases, see 11 USCA § 925.

Election as affecting confirmation of plan, see 11 USCA § 1129.

Filing and allowance of postpetition claims in Chapter thirteen cases, see 11 USCA § 1305.

Limitation on recourse of claim payable solely from special revenues of debtor, see 11 USCA § 927.

§ 1112. Conversion or dismissal

(a) The debtor may convert a case under this chapter to a case under chapter 7 of this title unless—

(1) the debtor is not a debtor in possession;

(2) the case originally was commenced as an involuntary case under this chapter; or

(3) the case was converted to a case under this chapter other than on the debtor's request.

(b)(1) Except as provided in paragraph (2) and subsection (c), on request of a party in interest, and after notice and a hearing, the court shall convert a case under this chapter to a case under chapter 7 or dismiss a case under this chapter, whichever is in the best interests of creditors and the estate, for cause unless the court determines that the appointment under section 1104(a) of a trustee or an examiner is in the best interests of creditors and the estate.

(2) The court may not convert a case under this chapter to a case under chapter 7 or dismiss a case under this chapter if the court finds and specifically identifies unusual circumstances establishing that converting or dismissing the case is not in the best interests of creditors and the estate, and the debtor or any other party in interest establishes that—

(A) there is a reasonable likelihood that a plan will be confirmed within the timeframes established in sections 1121(e) and 1129(e) of this title, or if such sections do not apply, within a reasonable period of time; and

(B) the grounds for converting or dismissing the case include an act or omission of the debtor other than under paragraph (4)(A)—

(i) for which there exists a reasonable justification for the act or omission; and

(ii) that will be cured within a reasonable period of time fixed by the court.

(3) The court shall commence the hearing on a motion under this subsection not later than 30 days after filing of the motion, and shall decide the motion not later than 15 days after commencement of such hearing, unless the movant expressly consents to a continuance for a specific period of time or compelling circumstances prevent the court from meeting the time limits established by this paragraph.

(4) For purposes of this subsection, the term "cause" includes—

(A) substantial or continuing loss to or diminution of the estate and the absence of a reasonable likelihood of rehabilitation;

(B) gross mismanagement of the estate;

(C) failure to maintain appropriate insurance that poses a risk to the estate or to the public;

(D) unauthorized use of cash collateral substantially harmful to 1 or more creditors;

(E) failure to comply with an order of the court;

(F) unexcused failure to satisfy timely any filing or reporting requirement established by this title or by any rule applicable to a case under this chapter;

(G) failure to attend the meeting of creditors convened under section 341(a) or an examination ordered under rule 2004 of the Federal Rules of Bankruptcy Procedure without good cause shown by the debtor;

(H) failure timely to provide information or attend meetings reasonably requested by the United States trustee (or the bankruptcy administrator, if any);

(I) failure timely to pay taxes owed after the date of the order for relief or to file tax returns due after the date of the order for relief;

(J) failure to file a disclosure statement, or to file or confirm a plan, within the time fixed by this title or by order of the court;

(K) failure to pay any fees or charges required under chapter 123 of title 28;

(L) revocation of an order of confirmation under section 1144;

(M) inability to effectuate substantial consummation of a confirmed plan;

(N) material default by the debtor with respect to a confirmed plan;

(O) termination of a confirmed plan by reason of the occurrence of a condition specified in the plan; and

(P) failure of the debtor to pay any domestic support obligation that first becomes payable after the date of the filing of the petition.

(c) The court may not convert a case under this chapter to a case under chapter 7 of this title if the debtor is a farmer or a corporation that is not a moneyed, business, or commercial corporation, unless the debtor requests such conversion.

(d) The court may convert a case under this chapter to a case under chapter 12 or 13 of this title only if—

(1) the debtor requests such conversion;

(2) the debtor has not been discharged under section 1141(d) of this title; and

(3) if the debtor requests conversion to chapter 12 of this title, such conversion is equitable.

(e) Except as provided in subsections (c) and (f), the court, on request of the United States trustee, may convert a case under this chapter to a case under chapter 7 of this title or may dismiss a case under this chapter, whichever is in the best interest of creditors and the estate if the debtor in a voluntary case fails to file, within fifteen days after the filing of the petition commencing such case or such additional time as the court may allow, the information required by paragraph (1) of section 521(a), including a list containing the names and addresses of the holders of the twenty largest unsecured claims (or of all unsecured claims if there are fewer than twenty unsecured claims), and the approximate dollar amounts of each of such claims.

(f) Notwithstanding any other provision of this section, a case may not be converted to a case under another chapter of this title unless the debtor may be a debtor under such chapter.

(Pub.L. 95–598, Nov. 6, 1978, 92 Stat. 2630; Pub.L. 98–353, Title III, § 505, July 10, 1984, 98 Stat. 384; Pub.L. 99–554, Title II, §§ 224, 256, Oct. 27, 1986, 100 Stat. 3102, 3114; Pub.L. 103–394, Title II, § 217(c), Oct. 22, 1994, 108 Stat. 4127; Pub.L. 109–8, Title IV, § 442(a), Apr. 20, 2005, 119 Stat. 115; Pub.L. 111–327, § 2(a)(33), Dec. 22, 2010, 124 Stat. 3561.)

HISTORICAL AND STATUTORY NOTES

Revision Notes and Legislative Reports

1978 Acts. This section brings together all of the conversion and dismissal rules for chapter 11 cases. Subsection (a) gives the debtor an absolute right to convert a voluntarily commenced chapter 11 case in which the debtor remains in possession to a liquidation case.

Subsection (b) gives wide discretion to the court to make an appropriate disposition of the case sua sponte or upon motion of a party in interest, or the court is permitted to convert a reorganization case to a liquidation case or to dismiss the case, whichever is in the best interest of creditors and the estate, but only for cause. Cause may include the continuing loss to or diminution of the estate of an insolvent debtor, the absence of a reasonable likelihood of rehabilitation, the inability to effectuate a plan, unreasonable delay by the debtor that is prejudicial to creditors, failure to file a plan within the appropriate time limits, denial of confirmation and any opportunity to modify or propose a new plan, revocation of confirmation and denial of confirmation of a modified plan, inability to effectuate substantial consummation of a confirmed plan, material default by the debtor under the plan, and termination of the plan by reason of the occurrence of a condition specified in the plan. This list is not exhaustive. The court will be able to consider other factors as they arise, and to use its equitable powers to reach an appropriate result in individual cases. The power of the court to act sua sponte should be used sparingly and only in emergency situations.

Subsection (c) prohibits the court from converting a case concerning a farmer or an eleemosynary institution to a liquidation case unless the debtor consents.

Subsection (d) prohibits conversion of a reorganization case to a chapter 13 case unless the debtor requests conversion and his discharge had not been granted or has been revoked.

Subsection (e) reinforces section 109 by prohibiting conversion of a chapter 11 case to a case under another chapter proceedings under which the debtor is not permitted to proceed. Senate Report No. 95–989.

1984 Acts. Statements by Legislative Leaders, see 1984 U.S.Code Cong. and Adm.News, p. 576.

1986 Acts. House Report No. 99–764 and House Conference Report No. 99–958, see 1986 U.S.Code Cong. and Adm. News, p. 5227.

1994 Acts. House Report No. 103–835, see 1994 U.S. Code Cong. and Adm. News, p. 3340.

2005 Acts. House Report No. 109–31(Part I), see 2005 U.S. Code Cong. and Adm. News, p. 88.

Legislative Statements

Section 1112 of the House amendment represents a compromise between the House bill and Senate amendment with respect to the factors constituting cause for conversion of a case to chapter 7 or dismissal. The House amendment combines two separate factors contained in section 1112(b)(1) and section 1112(b)(2) of the Senate amendment. Section 1112(b)(1) of the House amendment permits the court to convert a case to a case under chapter 7 or to dismiss the case if there is both a continuing loss to or diminution of the estate and the absence of a reasonable likelihood of rehabilitation; requiring both factors to be present simultaneously represents a compromise from the House bill which eliminated both factors from the list of causes enumerated.

Sections 1112(c) and 1112(d) of the House amendment is derived from the House bill which differs from the Senate amendment only as a matter of style.

References in Text

Chapter 7 of this title, referred to in text, is 11 U.S.C.A. § 701 et seq.

The Federal Rules of Bankruptcy Procedure, referred to in subsec. (b)(4)(G), are set out in the Appendix to this title.

Chapter 123 of title 28, referred to in subsec. (b)(4)(K), is 28 U.S.C.A. § 1911 et seq.

Chapter 12 or 13 of this title, referred to in subsec. (d), is 11 U.S.C.A. § 1201 et seq. or 11 U.S.C.A. § 1301 et seq., respectively.

Effective and Applicability Provisions

2005 Acts. Amendments by Pub.L. 109–8 effective, except as otherwise provided, 180 days after April 20, 2005, and inapplicable with respect to cases commenced under Title 11 before the effective date, see Pub.L. 109–8, § 1501, set out as a note under 11 U.S.C.A. § 101.

1994 Acts. Amendment by Pub.L. 103–394 effective on Oct. 22, 1994, and not to apply with respect to cases commenced under Title 11 of the United States Code before Oct. 22, 1994,

see section 702 of Pub.L. 103–394, set out as a note under section 101 of this title.

1986 Acts. Amendment by Pub.L. 99–554 effective 30 days after Oct. 27, 1986, except as otherwise provided for, see section 302(a) of Pub.L. 99–554, set out as a note under section 581 of Title 28, Judiciary and Judicial Procedure.

Amendment by Pub.L. 99–554, § 224, not to become effective in or with respect to certain specified judicial districts until, or apply to cases while pending in such district before, the expiration of the 270–day period beginning 30 days after Oct. 27, 1986, or of the 30–day period beginning on the date the Attorney General certifies under section 303 of Pub.L. 99–554 the region specified in a paragraph of section 581(a) of Title 28, as amended by section 111(a) of Pub.L. 99–554, that includes such district, whichever occurs first, see section 302(d)(1) of Pub.L. 99–554, set out as a note under section 581 of Title 28.

Amendment by Pub.L. 99–554, § 224, not to become effective in or with respect to certain specified judicial districts until, or apply to cases while pending in such district before, the expiration of the 2–year period beginning 30 days after Oct. 27, 1986, or of the 30–day period beginning on the date the Attorney General certifies under section 303 of Pub.L. 99–554 the region specified in a paragraph of section 581(a) of Title 28, as amended by section 111(a) of Pub.L. 99–554, that includes such district, whichever occurs first, see section 302(d)(2) of Pub.L. 99–554, set out as a note under section 581 of Title 28.

Amendment by Pub.L. 99–554, § 224, not to become effective in or with respect to judicial districts established for the States of Alabama and North Carolina until, or apply to cases while pending in such district before, such district elects to be included in a bankruptcy region established in section 581(a) of Title 28, as amended by section 111(a) of Pub.L. 99–554, or Oct. 1, 2002, whichever occurs first, and, except as otherwise provided for, with respect to cases under chapters 7, 11, 12, and 13 of Title 11 commenced before 30 days after Oct. 27, 1986, and pending in a judicial district in the States of Alabama or North Carolina before any election made under section 302(d)(3)(A) of Pub.L. 99–554 by such district becomes effective or Oct. 1, 2002, whichever occurs first, amendments by Pub.L. 99–554 not to apply until Oct. 1, 2003, or the expiration of the 1–year period beginning on the date such election becomes effective, whichever occurs first, and further, in any judicial district in Alabama or North Carolina not making the election described in section 302(d)(3)(A) of Pub.L. 99–554, any person appointed under regulations issued by the Judicial Conference to administer estates in cases under Title 11 authorized to establish, etc., a panel of private trustees, and to supervise cases and trustees in cases under chapters 7, 11, 12, and 13 of Title 11, until amendments by sections 201 to 231 of Pub.L. 99–554 effective in such district, see section 302(d)(3)(A) to (F), (H), (I) of Pub.L. 99–554, set out as a note under section 581 of Title 28.

Amendment by Pub.L. 99–554, § 224, except as otherwise provided, with respect to cases under chapters 7, 11, 12, and 13 of Title 11 commenced before 30 days after Oct. 27, 1986, and pending in a judicial district referred to in section 581(a) of Title 28, as amended by section 111(a) of Pub.L. 99–554, for which a United States trustee is not authorized before 30 days after Oct. 27, 1986 to be appointed, not applicable until the expiration of the 3–year period beginning on Oct. 27, 1986, or of the 1–year period beginning on the date the Attorney General certifies under section 303 of Pub.L. 99–554 the region specified in a paragraph of such section 581(a) that includes, such district, whichever occurs first, see section 302(e)(1), (2) of Pub.L. 99–554, set out as a note under section 581 of Title 28.

Amendments by Pub.L. 99–554, § 256, not to apply with respect to cases commenced under Title 11, Bankruptcy, before 30 days after Oct. 27, 1986, see section 302(c)(1) of Pub.L. 99–554, set out as a note under section 581 of Title 28.

1984 Acts. Amendment by Pub.L. 98–353 effective with respect to cases filed 90 days after July 10, 1984, see section 552(a), formerly 553(a), of Pub.L. 98–353, set out as a note under section 101 of this title.

Separability of Provisions

If any provision of or amendment made by Pub.L. 103–394 or the application of such provision or amendment to any person or circumstance is held to be unconstitutional, the remaining provisions of and amendments made by Pub.L. 103–394 and the application of such provisions and amendments to any person or circumstance shall not be affected thereby, see section 701 of Pub.L. 103–394, set out as a note under section 101 of this title.

CROSS REFERENCES

Conversion of,

Chapter seven cases, see 11 USCA § 706.

Chapter thirteen cases, see 11 USCA § 1307.

Chapter twelve cases, see 11 USCA § 1208.

Dismissal of,

Chapter nine cases, see 11 USCA § 930.

Chapter seven cases, see 11 USCA § 707.

Distribution of property of estate converted to Chapter seven, see 11 USCA § 726.

Effect of conversion, see 11 USCA § 348.

Effect of dismissal, see 11 USCA § 349.

Executory contracts and unexpired leases, see 11 USCA § 365.

Liquidation of estate in railroad reorganization cases, see 11 USCA § 1174.

Termination of debtor's taxable period for cases converted to Chapter seven, see 11 USCA § 346.

§ 1113. Rejection of collective bargaining agreements

(a) The debtor in possession, or the trustee if one has been appointed under the provisions of this chapter, other than a trustee in a case covered by subchapter IV of this chapter and by title I of the Railway Labor Act, may assume or reject a collective bargaining agreement only in accordance with the provisions of this section.

(b)(1) Subsequent to filing a petition and prior to filing an application seeking rejection of a collective bargaining agreement, the debtor in possession or trustee (hereinafter in this section "trustee" shall include a debtor in possession), shall—

   (A) make a proposal to the authorized representative of the employees covered by such agreement, based on the most complete and reliable information available at the time of such proposal, which provides for those necessary modifications in the employees benefits and protections that are necessary to permit the reorganization of the debtor and assures that all creditors, the debtor and all of the affected parties are treated fairly and equitably; and

   (B) provide, subject to subsection (d)(3), the representative of the employees with such relevant information as is necessary to evaluate the proposal.

(2) During the period beginning on the date of the making of a proposal provided for in paragraph (1) and ending on the date of the hearing provided for in subsection (d)(1), the trustee shall meet, at reasonable times, with the authorized representative to confer in good faith in attempting to reach mutually satisfactory modifications of such agreement.

(c) The court shall approve an application for rejection of a collective bargaining agreement only if the court finds that—

   (1) the trustee has, prior to the hearing, made a proposal that fulfills the requirements of subsection (b)(1);

   (2) the authorized representative of the employees has refused to accept such proposal without good cause; and

   (3) the balance of the equities clearly favors rejection of such agreement.

(d)(1) Upon the filing of an application for rejection the court shall schedule a hearing to be held not later than fourteen days after the date of the filing of such application. All interested parties may appear and be heard at such hearing. Adequate notice shall be provided to such parties at least ten days before the date of such hearing. The court may extend the time for the commencement of such hearing for a period not exceeding seven days where the circumstances of the case, and the interests of justice require such extension, or for additional periods of time to which the trustee and representative agree.

(2) The court shall rule on such application for rejection within thirty days after the date of the commencement of the hearing. In the interests of justice, the court may extend such time for ruling for such additional period as the trustee and the employees' representative may agree to. If the court does not rule on such application within thirty days after the date of the commencement of the hearing, or within such additional time as the trustee and the employees' representative may agree to, the trustee may terminate or alter any provisions of the collective bargaining agreement pending the ruling of the court on such application.

(3) The court may enter such protective orders, consistent with the need of the authorized representative of the employee to evaluate the trustee's proposal and the application for rejection, as may be necessary to prevent disclosure of information provided to such representative where such disclosure could compromise the position of the debtor with respect to its competitors in the industry in which it is engaged.

(e) If during a period when the collective bargaining agreement continues in effect, and if essential to the continuation of the debtor's business, or in order to avoid irreparable damage to the estate, the court, after notice and a hearing, may authorize the trustee to implement interim changes in the terms, conditions, wages, benefits, or work rules provided by a collective bargaining agreement. Any hearing under this paragraph shall be scheduled in accordance with the needs of the trustee. The implementation of such interim changes shall not render the application for rejection moot.

(f) No provision of this title shall be construed to permit a trustee to unilaterally terminate or alter any provisions of a collective bargaining agreement prior to compliance with the provisions of this section.
(Added Pub.L. 98–353, Title III, § 541(a), July 10, 1984, 98 Stat. 390.)

HISTORICAL AND STATUTORY NOTES

Revision Notes and Legislative Reports
1984 Acts. Statements by Legislative Leaders, see 1984 U.S.Code Cong. and Adm.News, p. 576.

References in Text
The Railway Labor Act, referred to in subsec. (a), is Act May 20, 1926, c. 347, 44 Stat. 577, as amended. Title I of the Railway Labor Act is classified principally to subchapter I (§ 151 et seq.) of chapter 8 of Title 45, Railroads. For complete classification of this Act to the Code, see § 151 of Title 45 and Tables.

Effective and Applicability Provisions
1984 Acts. Section 541(c) of Pub.L. 98–353 provided that: "The amendments made by this section [enacting this section] shall become effective upon the date of enactment of this Act [July 10, 1984]; provided that this section shall not apply to cases filed under title 11 of the United States Code [this title] which were commenced prior to the date of enactment of this section [July 10, 1984]."

§ 1114. Payment of insurance benefits to retired employees

(a) For purposes of this section, the term "retiree benefits" means payments to any entity or person for the purpose of providing or reimbursing payments for retired employees and their spouses and dependents, for medical, surgical, or hospital care benefits, or benefits in the event of sickness, accident, disability, or death under any plan, fund, or program (through the purchase of insurance or otherwise) maintained or established in whole or in part by the debtor prior to filing a petition commencing a case under this title.

(b)(1) For purposes of this section, the term "authorized representative" means the authorized representative designated pursuant to subsection (c) for persons receiving any retiree benefits covered by a collective bargaining agreement or subsection (d) in the case of persons receiving retiree benefits not covered by such an agreement.

(2) Committees of retired employees appointed by the court pursuant to this section shall have the same rights, powers, and duties as committees appointed under sections 1102 and 1103 of this title for the purpose of carrying out the purposes of sections 1114 and 1129(a)(13) and, as permitted by the court, shall have the power to enforce the rights of persons under this title as they relate to retiree benefits.

(c)(1) A labor organization shall be, for purposes of this section, the authorized representative of those persons receiving any retiree benefits covered by any collective bargaining agreement to which that labor organization is signatory, unless (A) such labor organization elects not to serve as the authorized representative of such persons, or (B) the court, upon a motion by any party in interest, after notice and hearing, determines that different representation of such persons is appropriate.

(2) In cases where the labor organization referred to in paragraph (1) elects not to serve as the authorized representative of those persons receiving any retiree benefits covered by any collective bargaining agreement to which that labor organization is signatory, or in cases where the court, pursuant to paragraph (1) finds different representation of such persons appropriate, the court, upon a motion by any party in interest, and after notice and a hearing, shall appoint a committee of retired employees if the debtor seeks to modify or not pay the retiree benefits or if the court otherwise determines that it is appropriate, from among such persons, to serve as the authorized representative of such persons under this section.

(d) The court, upon a motion by any party in interest, and after notice and a hearing, shall order the appointment of a committee of retired employees if the debtor seeks to modify or not pay the retiree benefits or if the court otherwise determines that it is appropriate, to serve as the authorized representative, under this section, of those persons receiving any retiree benefits not covered by a collective bargaining agreement. The United States trustee shall appoint any such committee.

(e)(1) Notwithstanding any other provision of this title, the debtor in possession, or the trustee if one has been appointed under the provisions of this chapter (hereinafter in this section "trustee" shall include a debtor in possession), shall timely pay and shall not modify any retiree benefits, except that—

(A) the court, on motion of the trustee or authorized representative, and after notice and a hearing, may order modification of such payments, pursuant to the provisions of subsections (g) and (h) of this section, or

(B) the trustee and the authorized representative of the recipients of those benefits may agree to modification of such payments,

after which such benefits as modified shall continue to be paid by the trustee.

(2) Any payment for retiree benefits required to be made before a plan confirmed under section 1129 of this title is effective has the status of an allowed administrative expense as provided in section 503 of this title.

(f)(1) Subsequent to filing a petition and prior to filing an application seeking modification of the retiree benefits, the trustee shall—

(A) make a proposal to the authorized representative of the retirees, based on the most complete and reliable information available at the time of such proposal, which provides for those necessary modifications in the retiree benefits that are necessary to permit the reorganization of the debtor and assures that all creditors, the debtor and all of the affected parties are treated fairly and equitably; and

(B) provide, subject to subsection (k)(3), the representative of the retirees with such relevant information as is necessary to evaluate the proposal.

(2) During the period beginning on the date of the making of a proposal provided for in paragraph (1), and ending on the date of the hearing provided for in subsection (k)(1), the trustee shall meet, at reasonable times, with the authorized representative to confer in good faith in attempting to reach mutually satisfactory modifications of such retiree benefits.

(g) The court shall enter an order providing for modification in the payment of retiree benefits if the court finds that—

(1) the trustee has, prior to the hearing, made a proposal that fulfills the requirements of subsection (f);

(2) the authorized representative of the retirees has refused to accept such proposal without good cause; and

(3) such modification is necessary to permit the reorganization of the debtor and assures that all creditors, the debtor, and all of the affected parties are treated fairly and equitably, and is clearly favored by the balance of the equities;

except that in no case shall the court enter an order providing for such modification which provides for a modification to a level lower than that proposed by the trustee in the proposal found by the court to have complied with the requirements of this subsection and subsection (f): *Provided, however,* That at any time after an order is entered providing for modification in the payment of retiree benefits, or at any time after an agreement modifying such benefits is made between the trustee and the authorized representative of the recipients of such benefits, the authorized representa-

tive may apply to the court for an order increasing those benefits which order shall be granted if the increase in retiree benefits sought is consistent with the standard set forth in paragraph (3): *Provided further,* That neither the trustee nor the authorized representative is precluded from making more than one motion for a modification order governed by this subsection.

(h)(1) Prior to a court issuing a final order under subsection (g) of this section, if essential to the continuation of the debtor's business, or in order to avoid irreparable damage to the estate, the court, after notice and a hearing, may authorize the trustee to implement interim modifications in retiree benefits.

(2) Any hearing under this subsection shall be scheduled in accordance with the needs of the trustee.

(3) The implementation of such interim changes does not render the motion for modification moot.

(i) No retiree benefits paid between the filing of the petition and the time a plan confirmed under section 1129 of this title becomes effective shall be deducted or offset from the amounts allowed as claims for any benefits which remain unpaid, or from the amounts to be paid under the plan with respect to such claims for unpaid benefits, whether such claims for unpaid benefits are based upon or arise from a right to future unpaid benefits or from any benefits not paid as a result of modifications allowed pursuant to this section.

(j) No claim for retiree benefits shall be limited by section 502(b)(7) of this title.

(k)(1) Upon the filing of an application for modifying retiree benefits, the court shall schedule a hearing to be held not later than fourteen days after the date of the filing of such application. All interested parties may appear and be heard at such hearing. Adequate notice shall be provided to such parties at least ten days before the date of such hearing. The court may extend the time for the commencement of such hearing for a period not exceeding seven days where the circumstances of the case, and the interests of justice require such extension, or for additional periods of time to which the trustee and the authorized representative agree.

(2) The court shall rule on such application for modification within ninety days after the date of the commencement of the hearing. In the interests of justice, the court may extend such time for ruling for such additional period as the trustee and the authorized representative may agree to. If the court does not rule on such application within ninety days after the date of the commencement of the hearing, or within such additional time as the trustee and the authorized representative may agree to, the trustee may implement the proposed modifications pending the ruling of the court on such application.

(3) The court may enter such protective orders, consistent with the need of the authorized representative of the retirees to evaluate the trustee's proposal and the application for modification, as may be necessary to prevent disclosure of information provided to such representative where such disclosure could compromise the position of the debtor with respect to its competitors in the industry in which it is engaged.

(*l*) If the debtor, during the 180–day period ending on the date of the filing of the petition—

(1) modified retiree benefits; and

(2) was insolvent on the date such benefits were modified;

the court, on motion of a party in interest, and after notice and a hearing, shall issue an order reinstating as of the date the modification was made, such benefits as in effect immediately before such date unless the court finds that the balance of the equities clearly favors such modification.

(m) This section shall not apply to any retiree, or the spouse or dependents of such retiree, if such retiree's gross income for the twelve months preceding the filing of the bankruptcy petition equals or exceeds $250,000, unless such retiree can demonstrate to the satisfaction of the court that he is unable to obtain health, medical, life, and disability coverage for himself, his spouse, and his dependents who would otherwise be covered by the employer's insurance plan, comparable to the coverage provided by the employer on the day before the filing of a petition under this title.

(Added Pub.L. 100–334, § 2(a), June 16, 1988, 102 Stat. 610; amended Pub.L. 109–8, Title IV, § 447, Title XIV, § 1403, Apr. 20, 2005, 119 Stat. 118, 215.)

HISTORICAL AND STATUTORY NOTES

Revision Notes and Legislative Reports

1988 Acts. Senate Report No. 100–119, see 1988 U.S.Code Cong. and Adm.News, p. 683.

2005 Acts. House Report No. 109–31(Part I), see 2005 U.S. Code Cong. and Adm. News, p. 88.

Effective and Applicability Provisions

2005 Acts. Amendments by Pub.L. 109–8 effective, except as otherwise provided, 180 days after April 20, 2005, and inapplicable with respect to cases commenced under Title 11 before the effective date, see Pub.L. 109–8, § 1501, set out as a note under 11 U.S.C.A. § 101.

Amendments by Pub.L. 109–8, Title XIV, effective, except as otherwise provided, on Apr. 20, 2005, and applicable only with respect to cases commenced under Title 11 on or after Apr. 20, 2005, see Pub.L. 109–8, § 1406, set out as a note under 11 U.S.C.A. § 507.

1988 Acts. Section 4 of Pub.L. 100–334 provided that:

"(a) **General Effective Date.**—Except as provided in subsection (b), this Act and the amendments made by this Act [enacting this section, amending section 1129 of this title, enacting provisions set out as a note under section 101 of this title, and amending and repealing provisions set out as notes

under section 1106 of this title] shall take effect on the date of the enactment of this Act [June 16, 1988].

"(b) **Application of Amendments.**—The amendments made by section 2 [enacting this section and amending section 1129 of this title] shall not apply with respect to cases commenced under title 11 of the United States Code [this title] before the date of the enactment of this Act [June 16, 1988]."

Payment of Certain Benefits to Retired Former Employees

For payment of benefits by bankruptcy trustee to retired employees in enumerated circumstances with respect to cases commenced under this chapter in which a plan for reorganization had not been confirmed by the court and in which any such benefit was still being paid on October 2, 1986, and in cases that became subject to this chapter after October 2, 1986, and before June 16, 1988, see section 101(b) [title VI, § 608] of Pub.L. 99–500, and Pub.L. 99–591, as amended, set out as a note under section 1106 of this title.

CROSS REFERENCES

Confirmation of plan if plan provides for continuation of "retiree benefits" as defined under this section, see 11 USCA § 1129.

§ 1115. Property of the estate

(a) In a case in which the debtor is an individual, property of the estate includes, in addition to the property specified in section 541—

(1) all property of the kind specified in section 541 that the debtor acquires after the commencement of the case but before the case is closed, dismissed, or converted to a case under chapter 7, 12, or 13, whichever occurs first; and

(2) earnings from services performed by the debtor after the commencement of the case but before the case is closed, dismissed, or converted to a case under chapter 7, 12, or 13, whichever occurs first.

(b) Except as provided in section 1104 or a confirmed plan or order confirming a plan, the debtor shall remain in possession of all property of the estate. (Added Pub.L. 109–8, Title III, § 321(a)(1), Apr. 20, 2005, 119 Stat. 94.)

HISTORICAL AND STATUTORY NOTES

Revision Notes and Legislative Reports

2005 Acts. House Report No. 109–31(Part I), see 2005 U.S. Code Cong. and Adm. News, p. 88.

References in Text

Chapter 7, 12, or 13, referred to in subsec. (a)(1), (2), is chapter 7, 12, or 13 of this title, 11 U.S.C.A. § 701 et seq., 11 U.S.C.A. § 1201 et seq., or 11 U.S.C.A. § 1301 et seq., respectively.

Effective and Applicability Provisions

2005 Acts. Amendments by Pub.L. 109–8 effective, except as otherwise provided, 180 days after April 20, 2005, and inapplicable with respect to cases commenced under Title 11

before the effective date, see Pub.L. 109–8, § 1501, set out as a note under 11 U.S.C.A. § 101.

§ 1116. Duties of trustee or debtor in possession in small business cases

In a small business case, a trustee or the debtor in possession, in addition to the duties provided in this title and as otherwise required by law, shall—

(1) append to the voluntary petition or, in an involuntary case, file not later than 7 days after the date of the order for relief—

(A) its most recent balance sheet, statement of operations, cash-flow statement, and Federal income tax return; or

(B) a statement made under penalty of perjury that no balance sheet, statement of operations, or cash-flow statement has been prepared and no Federal tax return has been filed;

(2) attend, through its senior management personnel and counsel, meetings scheduled by the court or the United States trustee, including initial debtor interviews, scheduling conferences, and meetings of creditors convened under section 341 unless the court, after notice and a hearing, waives that requirement upon a finding of extraordinary and compelling circumstances;

(3) timely file all schedules and statements of financial affairs, unless the court, after notice and a hearing, grants an extension, which shall not extend such time period to a date later than 30 days after the date of the order for relief, absent extraordinary and compelling circumstances;

(4) file all postpetition financial and other reports required by the Federal Rules of Bankruptcy Procedure or by local rule of the district court;

(5) subject to section 363(c)(2), maintain insurance customary and appropriate to the industry;

(6)(A) timely file tax returns and other required government filings; and

(B) subject to section 363(c)(2), timely pay all taxes entitled to administrative expense priority except those being contested by appropriate proceedings being diligently prosecuted; and

(7) allow the United States trustee, or a designated representative of the United States trustee, to inspect the debtor's business premises, books, and records at reasonable times, after reasonable prior written notice, unless notice is waived by the debtor.

(Added Pub.L. 109–8, Title IV, § 436(a), Apr. 20, 2005, 119 Stat. 112.)

HISTORICAL AND STATUTORY NOTES

Revision Notes and Legislative Reports

2005 Acts. House Report No. 109–31(Part I), see 2005 U.S. Code Cong. and Adm. News, p. 88.

References in Text

The Federal Rules of Bankruptcy Procedure, referred to in par. (4), are set out in the Appendix to this title.

Effective and Applicability Provisions

2005 Acts. Amendments by Pub.L. 109–8 effective, except as otherwise provided, 180 days after April 20, 2005, and inapplicable with respect to cases commenced under Title 11 before the effective date, see Pub.L. 109–8, § 1501, set out as a note under 11 U.S.C.A. § 101.

SUBCHAPTER II—THE PLAN

CROSS REFERENCES

Subchapter applicable only in case under this chapter except as provided in § 901 of this title, see 11 USCA § 103.

§ 1121. Who may file a plan

(a) The debtor may file a plan with a petition commencing a voluntary case, or at any time in a voluntary case or an involuntary case.

(b) Except as otherwise provided in this section, only the debtor may file a plan until after 120 days after the date of the order for relief under this chapter.

(c) Any party in interest, including the debtor, the trustee, a creditors' committee, an equity security holders' committee, a creditor, an equity security holder, or any indenture trustee, may file a plan if and only if—

(1) a trustee has been appointed under this chapter;

(2) the debtor has not filed a plan before 120 days after the date of the order for relief under this chapter; or

(3) the debtor has not filed a plan that has been accepted, before 180 days after the date of the order for relief under this chapter, by each class of claims or interests that is impaired under the plan.

(d)(1) Subject to paragraph (2), on request of a party in interest made within the respective periods specified in subsections (b) and (c) of this section and after notice and a hearing, the court may for cause reduce or increase the 120-day period or the 180-day period referred to in this section.

(2)(A) The 120–day period specified in paragraph (1) may not be extended beyond a date that is 18 months after the date of the order for relief under this chapter.

(B) The 180–day period specified in paragraph (1) may not be extended beyond a date that is 20 months after the date of the order for relief under this chapter.

(e) In a small business case—

(1) only the debtor may file a plan until after 180 days after the date of the order for relief, unless that period is—

(A) extended as provided by this subsection, after notice and a hearing; or

(B) the court, for cause, orders otherwise;

(2) the plan and a disclosure statement (if any) shall be filed not later than 300 days after the date of the order for relief; and

(3) the time periods specified in paragraphs (1) and (2), and the time fixed in section 1129(e) within which the plan shall be confirmed, may be extended only if—

(A) the debtor, after providing notice to parties in interest (including the United States trustee), demonstrates by a preponderance of the evidence that it is more likely than not that the court will confirm a plan within a reasonable period of time;

(B) a new deadline is imposed at the time the extension is granted; and

(C) the order extending time is signed before the existing deadline has expired.

(Pub.L. 95–598, Nov. 6, 1978, 92 Stat. 2631; Pub.L. 98–353, Title III, § 506, July 10, 1984, 98 Stat. 385; Pub.L. 99–554, Title II, § 283(u), Oct. 27, 1986, 100 Stat. 3118; Pub.L. 103–394, Title II, § 217(d), Oct. 22, 1994, 108 Stat. 4127; Pub.L. 109–8, Title IV, §§ 411, 437, Apr. 20, 2005, 119 Stat. 106, 113.)

HISTORICAL AND STATUTORY NOTES

Revision Notes and Legislative Reports

1978 Acts. Subsection (a) permits the debtor to file a reorganization plan with a petition commencing a voluntary case or at any time during a voluntary or involuntary case.

Subsection (b) gives the debtor the exclusive right to file a plan during the first 120 days of the case. There are exceptions, however, enumerated in subsection (c). If a trustee has been appointed, if the debtor does not meet the 120-day deadline, or if the debtor fails to obtain the required consent within 180 days after the filing of the petition, any party in interest may propose a plan. This includes the debtor, the trustee, a creditors' committee, an equity security holders' committee, a creditor, an equity security holder, and an indenture trustee. The list is not exhaustive. In the case of a public company, a trustee is appointed within 10 days of the petition. In such a case, for all practical purposes, any party in interest may file a plan.

Subsection (d) permits the court, for cause, to increase or reduce the 120-day and 180-day periods specified. Since, [sic] the debtor has an exclusive privilege for 6 months during which others may not file a plan, the granted extension should be based on a showing of some promise of probable success. An extension should not be employed as a tactical device to put pressure on parties in interest to yield to a plan they consider unsatisfactory. Senate Report No. 95–989.

1984 Acts. Statements by Legislative Leaders, see 1984 U.S.Code Cong. and Adm.News, p. 576.

1986 Acts. House Report No. 99–764 and House Conference Report No. 99–958, see 1986 U.S.Code Cong. and Adm. News, p. 5227.

1994 Acts. House Report No. 103–835, see 1994 U.S. Code Cong. and Adm. News, p. 3340.

2005 Acts. House Report No. 109–31(Part I), see 2005 U.S. Code Cong. and Adm. News, p. 88.

Legislative Statements

Section 1121 of the House amendment is derived from section 1121 of the House bill; section 1121(c)(1) will be satisfied automatically in a case under subchapter IV of title 11.

Effective and Applicability Provisions

2005 Acts. Amendments by Pub.L. 109–8 effective, except as otherwise provided, 180 days after April 20, 2005, and inapplicable with respect to cases commenced under Title 11 before the effective date, see Pub.L. 109–8, § 1501, set out as a note under 11 U.S.C.A. § 101.

1994 Acts. Amendment by Pub.L. 103–394 effective on Oct. 22, 1994, and not to apply with respect to cases commenced under Title 11 of the United States Code before Oct. 22, 1994, see section 702 of Pub.L. 103–394, set out as a note under section 101 of this title.

1986 Acts. Amendment by Pub.L. 99–554 effective 30 days after Oct. 27, 1986, except as otherwise provided for, see section 302(a) of Pub.L. 99–554, set out as a note under section 581 of Title 28, Judiciary and Judicial Procedure.

1984 Acts. Amendment by Pub.L. 98–353 effective with respect to cases filed 90 days after July 10, 1984, see section 552(a), formerly 553(a), of Pub.L. 98–353, set out as a note under section 101 of this title.

Separability of Provisions

If any provision of or amendment made by Pub.L. 103–394 or the application of such provision or amendment to any person or circumstance is held to be unconstitutional, the remaining provisions of and amendments made by Pub.L. 103–394 and the application of such provisions and amendments to any person or circumstance shall not be affected thereby, see section 701 of Pub.L. 103–394, set out as a note under section 101 of this title.

CROSS REFERENCES

Effect of conversion, see 11 USCA § 348.

Failure to propose plan as cause for conversion or dismissal, see 11 USCA § 1112.

Filing of plan by trustee, see 11 USCA § 1106.

Filing of plan in,

    Chapter nine cases, see 11 USCA § 941.

    Chapter thirteen cases, see 11 USCA § 1321.

    Chapter twelve cases, see 11 USCA § 1221.

United States trustee not permitted to file plan, see 11 USCA § 307.

§ 1122.   Classification of claims or interests

(a) Except as provided in subsection (b) of this section, a plan may place a claim or an interest in a particular class only if such claim or interest is substantially similar to the other claims or interests of such class.

(b) A plan may designate a separate class of claims consisting only of every unsecured claim that is less than or reduced to an amount that the court approves as reasonable and necessary for administrative convenience.

(Pub.L. 95–598, Nov. 6, 1978, 92 Stat. 2631.)

HISTORICAL AND STATUTORY NOTES

Revision Notes and Legislative Reports

1978 Acts. This section codifies current case law surrounding the classification of claims and equity securities. It requires classification based on the nature of the claims or interests classified, and permits inclusion of claims or interests in a particular class only if the claim or interest being included is substantially similar to the other claims or interests of the class.

Subsection (b), also a codification of existing practice, contains an exception. The plan may designate a separate class of claims consisting only of every unsecured claim that is less than or reduced to an amount that the court approves as reasonable and necessary for administrative convenience. Senate Report No. 95–989.

CROSS REFERENCES

Applicability of this section in Chapter nine cases, see 11 USCA § 901.

Contents of plan filed in,

　Chapter thirteen cases, see 11 USCA § 1322.

　Chapter twelve cases, see 11 USCA § 1222.

Filing and allowance of postpetition claims in Chapter thirteen cases, see 11 USCA § 1305.

Filing of proofs of claims or interests, see 11 USCA § 501.

§ 1123.　Contents of plan

(a) Notwithstanding any otherwise applicable non-bankruptcy law, a plan shall—

(1) designate, subject to section 1122 of this title, classes of claims, other than claims of a kind specified in section 507(a)(2), 507(a)(3), or 507(a)(8) of this title, and classes of interests;

(2) specify any class of claims or interests that is not impaired under the plan;

(3) specify the treatment of any class of claims or interests that is impaired under the plan;

(4) provide the same treatment for each claim or interest of a particular class, unless the holder of a particular claim or interest agrees to a less favorable treatment of such particular claim or interest;

(5) provide adequate means for the plan's implementation, such as—

　(A) retention by the debtor of all or any part of the property of the estate;

　(B) transfer of all or any part of the property of the estate to one or more entities, whether organized before or after the confirmation of such plan;

　(C) merger or consolidation of the debtor with one or more persons;

　(D) sale of all or any part of the property of the estate, either subject to or free of any lien, or the distribution of all or any part of the property of the estate among those having an interest in such property of the estate;

　(E) satisfaction or modification of any lien;

　(F) cancellation or modification of any indenture or similar instrument;

　(G) curing or waiving of any default;

　(H) extension of a maturity date or a change in an interest rate or other term of outstanding securities;

　(I) amendment of the debtor's charter; or

　(J) issuance of securities of the debtor, or of any entity referred to in subparagraph (B) or (C) of this paragraph, for cash, for property, for existing securities, or in exchange for claims or interests, or for any other appropriate purpose;

(6) provide for the inclusion in the charter of the debtor, if the debtor is a corporation, or of any corporation referred to in paragraph (5)(B) or (5)(C) of this subsection, of a provision prohibiting the issuance of nonvoting equity securities, and providing, as to the several classes of securities possessing voting power, an appropriate distribution of such power among such classes, including, in the case of any class of equity securities having a preference over another class of equity securities with respect to dividends, adequate provisions for the election of directors representing such preferred class in the event of default in the payment of such dividends;

(7) contain only provisions that are consistent with the interests of creditors and equity security holders and with public policy with respect to the manner of selection of any officer, director, or trustee under the plan and any successor to such officer, director, or trustee; and

(8) in a case in which the debtor is an individual, provide for the payment to creditors under the plan of all or such portion of earnings from personal services performed by the debtor after the commencement of the case or other future income of the debtor as is necessary for the execution of the plan.

(b) Subject to subsection (a) of this section, a plan may—

(1) impair or leave unimpaired any class of claims, secured or unsecured, or of interests;

(2) subject to section 365 of this title, provide for the assumption, rejection, or assignment of any executory contract or unexpired lease of the debtor not previously rejected under such section;

(3) provide for—

　(A) the settlement or adjustment of any claim or interest belonging to the debtor or to the estate; or

　(B) the retention and enforcement by the debtor, by the trustee, or by a representative of the estate appointed for such purpose, of any such claim or interest;

(4) provide for the sale of all or substantially all of the property of the estate, and the distribution of the proceeds of such sale among holders of claims or interests;

(5) modify the rights of holders of secured claims, other than a claim secured only by a security interest in real property that is the debtor's principal residence, or of holders of unsecured claims, or leave unaffected the rights of holders of any class of claims; and

(6) include any other appropriate provision not inconsistent with the applicable provisions of this title.

(c) In a case concerning an individual, a plan proposed by an entity other than the debtor may not provide for the use, sale, or lease of property exempted under section 522 of this title, unless the debtor consents to such use, sale, or lease.

(d) Notwithstanding subsection (a) of this section and sections 506(b), 1129(a)(7), and 1129(b) of this title, if it is proposed in a plan to cure a default the amount necessary to cure the default shall be determined in accordance with the underlying agreement and applicable nonbankruptcy law.

(Pub.L. 95–598, Nov. 6, 1978, 92 Stat. 2631; Pub.L. 98–353, Title III, § 507, July 10, 1984, 98 Stat. 385; Pub.L. 103–394, Title II, § 206, Title III, §§ 304(h)(6), 305(a), Title V, § 501(d)(31), Oct. 22, 1994, 108 Stat. 4123, 4134, 4146; Pub.L. 109–8, Title III, § 321(b), Title XV, § 1502(a)(7), Apr. 20, 2005, 119 Stat. 95, 216.)

HISTORICAL AND STATUTORY NOTES

Revision Notes and Legislative Reports

1978 Acts. Subsection (a) specifies what a plan of reorganization must contain. The plan must designate classes of claims and interests, and specify, by class, the claims or interests that are unimpaired under the plan. Priority claims are not required to be classified because they may not have arisen when the plan is filed. The plan must provide the same treatment for each claim or interest of a particular class, unless the holder of a particular claim or interest agrees to a different, but not better, treatment of his claim or interest.

Paragraph (3) applies to claims, not creditors. Thus, if a creditor is undersecured, and thus has a secured claim and an unsecured claim, this paragraph will be applied independently to each of his claims.

Paragraph (4) of subsection (a) is derived from section 216 of chapter X [section 616 of former Title 11] with some modifications. It requires the plan to provide adequate means for the plans [sic] execution. These means may include retention by the debtor of all or any part of the property of the estate, transfer of all or any part of the property of the estate to one or more entities, whether organized pre- or postconfirmation, merger or consolidation of the debtor with one or more persons, sale and distribution of all or any part of the property of the estate, satisfaction or modification of any lien, cancellation or modification of any indenture or similar instrument, curing or waiving of any default, extension of maturity dates or change in interest rates of securities, amendment of the debtor's charter, and issuance of securities.

Subparagraph (C), as it applies in railroad cases, has the effect of overruling *St. Joe Paper Co. v. Atlantic Coast Line R.R.*, 347 U.S. 298 (1954). [Fla.1954, 74 S.Ct. 574, 98 L.Ed. 710, rehearing denied 74 S.Ct. 734, 347 U.S. 980, 98 L.Ed.

1118]. It will allow the trustee or creditors to propose a plan of merger with another railroad without the consent of the debtor, and the debtor will be bound under proposed 11 U.S.C. 1141(a). See Hearings, pt. 3, at 1616. "Similar instrument" referred to in subparagraph (F) might include a deposit with an agent for distribution, other than an indenture trustee, such as an agent under an agreement in a railroad conditional sale or lease financing agreement.

Paragraphs (5) and (6) and subsection (b) are derived substantially from section 216 of Chapter X (11 U.S.C. 616) [section 616 of former Title 11]. Paragraph (5) requires the plan to prohibit the issuance of nonvoting equity securities, and to provide for an appropriate distribution of voting power among the various classes of equity securities. Paragraph (6) requires that the plan contain only provisions that are consistent with the interests of creditors and equity security holders, and with public policy with respect to the selection of officers, directors, and trustees, and their successors.

Subsection (b) specifies the matters that the plan may propose. The plan may impair or leave unimpaired any claim or interest. The plan may provide for the assumption or rejection of executory contracts or unexpired leases not previously rejected under section 365. The plan may also provide for the treatment of claims by the debtor against other entities that are not settled before the confirmation of the plan. The plan may propose settlement or adjustment of any claim or equity security belonging to the estate, or may propose retention and enforcement of such claim or interest by the debtor or by an agent appointed for that purpose.

The plan may also propose the sale of all or substantially all of the property of the estate, and the distribution of the proceeds of the sale among creditors and equity security holders. This would be a liquidating plan. The subsection permits the plan to include any other appropriate provision not inconsistent with the applicable provisions of the bankruptcy code.

Subsection (c) protects an individual debtor's exempt property by prohibiting its use, sale, or lease under a plan proposed by someone other than the debtor, unless the debtor consents. Senate Report No. 95–989.

1984 Acts. Statements by Legislative Leaders, see 1984 U.S.Code Cong. and Adm.News, p. 576.

1994 Acts. House Report No. 103–835, see 1994 U.S. Code Cong. and Adm. News, p. 3340.

2005 Acts. House Report No. 109–31(Part I), see 2005 U.S. Code Cong. and Adm. News, p. 88.

Legislative Statements

Section 1123 of the House amendment represents a compromise between similar provisions in the House bill and Senate amendment. The section has been clarified to clearly indicate that both secured and unsecured claims, or either of them, may be impaired in a case under title 11. In addition assumption or rejection of an executory contract under a plan must comply with section 365 of title 11. Moreover, section 1123(a)(1) has been substantively modified to permit classification of certain kinds of priority claims. This is important for purposes of confirmation under section 1129(a)(9).

Section 1123(a)(5) of the House amendment is derived from a similar provision in the House bill and Senate amendment but deletes the language pertaining to "fair upset price" as an unnecessary restriction. Section 1123 is also intended to indicate that a plan may provide for any action specified in section 1123 in the case of a corporation without a resolution of the board of directors. If the plan is confirmed, then any action proposed in the plan may be taken notwithstanding any otherwise applicable nonbankruptcy law in accordance with section 1142(a) of title 11.

Effective and Applicability Provisions

2005 Acts. Amendments by Pub.L. 109–8 effective, except as otherwise provided, 180 days after April 20, 2005, and inapplicable with respect to cases commenced under Title 11 before the effective date, see Pub.L. 109–8, § 1501, set out as a note under 11 U.S.C.A. § 101.

1994 Acts. Amendments by sections 206, 304(h)(6), and 501(d)(31) of Pub.L. 103–394 effective on Oct. 22, 1994, and not to apply with respect to cases commenced under Title 11 of the United States Code before Oct. 22, 1994, see section 702 of Pub.L. 103–394, set out as a note under section 101 of this title.

Amendment by section 305(a) of Pub.L. 103–394 effective Oct. 22, 1994, and applicable only to agreements entered into after Oct. 22, 1994, see section 702 of Pub.L.103–394, set out as a note under section 101 of this title.

1984 Acts. Amendment by Pub.L. 98–353 effective with respect to cases filed 90 days after July 10, 1984, see section 552(a), formerly 553(a), of Pub.L. 98–353, set out as a note under section 101 of this title.

Separability of Provisions

If any provision of or amendment made by Pub.L. 103–394 or the application of such provision or amendment to any person or circumstance is held to be unconstitutional, the remaining provisions of and amendments made by Pub.L. 103–394 and the application of such provisions and amendments to any person or circumstance shall not be affected thereby, see section 701 of Pub.L. 103–394, set out as a note under section 101 of this title.

CROSS REFERENCES

Applicability of subsecs. (a)(1) to (5) and (b) of this section in Chapter nine cases, see 11 USCA § 901.

Contents of plan filed in,

    Chapter thirteen cases, see 11 USCA § 1322.

    Chapter twelve cases, see 11 USCA § 1222.

    Railroad reorganization cases, see 11 USCA § 1172.

§ 1124.   Impairment of claims or interests

Except as provided in section 1123(a)(4) of this title, a class of claims or interests is impaired under a plan unless, with respect to each claim or interest of such class, the plan—

    (1) leaves unaltered the legal, equitable, and contractual rights to which such claim or interest entitles the holder of such claim or interest; or

    (2) notwithstanding any contractual provision or applicable law that entitles the holder of such claim or interest to demand or receive accelerated payment of such claim or interest after the occurrence of a default—

        (A) cures any such default that occurred before or after the commencement of the case under this title, other than a default of a kind specified in

section 365(b)(2) of this title or of a kind that section 365(b)(2) expressly does not require to be cured;

        (B) reinstates the maturity of such claim or interest as such maturity existed before such default;

        (C) compensates the holder of such claim or interest for any damages incurred as a result of any reasonable reliance by such holder on such contractual provision or such applicable law;

        (D) if such claim or such interest arises from any failure to perform a nonmonetary obligation, other than a default arising from failure to operate a nonresidential real property lease subject to section 365(b)(1)(A), compensates the holder of such claim or such interest (other than the debtor or an insider) for any actual pecuniary loss incurred by such holder as a result of such failure; and

        (E) does not otherwise alter the legal, equitable, or contractual rights to which such claim or interest entitles the holder of such claim or interest.

(Pub.L. 95–598, Nov. 6, 1978, 92 Stat. 2633; Pub.L. 98–353, Title III, § 508, July 10, 1984, 98 Stat. 385; Pub.L. 103–394, Title II, § 213(d), Oct. 22, 1994, 108 Stat. 4126; Pub.L. 109–8, Title III, § 328(b), Apr. 20, 2005, 119 Stat. 100.)

HISTORICAL AND STATUTORY NOTES

Revision Notes and Legislative Reports

1978 Acts. The basic concept underlying this section is not new. It rests essentially on Section [sic] 107 of Chapter X (11 U.S.C. 507) [section 507 of former Title 11], which states that creditors or stockholders or any class thereof "shall be deemed to be 'affected' by a plan only if their or its interest shall be materially and adversely affected thereby."

This section is designed to indicate when contractual rights of creditors or interest holders are not materially affected. It specifies three ways in which the plan may leave a claim or interest unimpaired.

First, the plan may propose not to alter the legal, equitable, or contractual rights to which the claim or interest entitled its holder.

Second, a claim or interest is unimpaired by curing the effect of a default and reinstating the original terms of an obligation when maturity was brought on or accelerated by the default. The intervention of bankruptcy and the defaults represent a temporary crisis which the plan of reorganization is intended to clear away. The holder of a claim or interest who under the plan is restored to his original position, when others receive less or get nothing at all, is fortunate indeed and has no cause to complain. Curing of the default and the assumption of the debt in accordance with its terms is an important reorganization technique for dealing with a particular class of claims, especially secured claims.

Third, a claim or interest is unimpaired if the plan provides for their payment in cash. In the case of a debt liability, the cash payment is for the allowed amount of the claim, which does not include a redemption premium. If it is an equity security with a fixed liquidation preference, such as a preferred stock, the allowed amount is such liquidation preference, with no redemption premium. With respect to any other equity security, such as a common stock, cash payment must be equal to the "value of such holder's interest in the debtor."

Section 1124 does not include payment "in property" other than cash. Except for a rare case, claims or interests are not by their terms payable in property, but a plan may so provide and those affected thereby may accept or reject the proposed plan. They may not be forced to accept a plan declaring the holders' claims or interests to be "unimpaired." Senate Report No. 95–989.

This section is new. It is designed to indicate when contractual rights of creditors or interest holders are not materially affected. The section specifies three ways in which the plan may leave a claim or interest unimpaired.

First, the plan may propose not to alter the legal, equitable, or contractual rights to which the claim or interest entitled its holder.

Second, the plan is permitted to reinstate a claim or interest and thus leave it unimpaired. Reinstatement consists of curing any default (other than a default under an ipso facto or bankruptcy clause) and reinstatement of the maturity of the claim or interest. Further, the plan may not otherwise alter any legal, equitable, or contractual right to which the claim or interest entitles its holder.

Third, the plan may leave a claim or interest unimpaired by paying its amount in full other than in securities of the debtor, an affiliate of the debtor participating in a joint plan, or a successor to the debtor. These securities are excluded because determination of their value would require a valuation of the business being reorganized. Use of them to pay a creditor or equity security holder without his consent may be done only under section 1129(b) and only after a valuation of the debtor. Under this paragraph, the plan must pay the allowed amount of the claim in full, in cash or other property, or, in the case of an equity security, must pay the greatest of any fixed liquidation preference to which the terms of the equity security entitle its holder, any fixed price at which the debtor, under the terms of the equity security may redeem such equity security, and the value, as of the effective date of the plan, of the holder's interest in the debtor. The value of the holder's interest need not be determined precisely by valuing the debtor's business if such value of clearly below redemption or liquidation preference values. If such value would require a full-scale valuation of the business, then such interest should be treated as impaired. But, if the debtor corporation is clearly insolvent, then the value of the common stock holder's interest in the debtor is zero, and offering them nothing under the plan of reorganization will not impair their rights.

"Value, as of the effective date of the plan," as used in paragraph (3) and in proposed 11 U.S.C. 1179(a)(7)(B), 1129(a)(9), 1129(b), 1172(2), 1325(a)(4), 1325(a)(5)(B), and 1328(b), indicates that the promised payment under the plan must be discounted to present value as of the effective date of the plan. The discounting should be based only on the unpaid balance of the amount due under the plan, until that amount, including interest, is paid in full. House Report No. 95–595.

1984 Acts. Statements by Legislative Leaders, see 1984 U.S.Code Cong. and Adm.News, p. 576.

1994 Acts. House Report No. 103–835, see 1994 U.S. Code Cong. and Adm. News, p. 3340.

2005 Acts. House Report No. 109–31(Part I), see 2005 U.S. Code Cong. and Adm. News, p. 88.

Legislative Statements

Section 1124 of the House amendment is derived from a similar provision in the House bill and Senate amendment. The section defines the new concept of "impairment" of claims or interests; the concept differs significantly from the concept of "materially and adversely affected" under the Bankruptcy Act [former Title 11]. Section 1124(3) of the House amendment provides that a holder of a claim or interest is not impaired, if the plan provides that the holder will receive the allowed amount of the holder's claim, or in the case of an interest with a fixed liquidation preference or redemption price, the greater of such price. This adopts the position contained in the House bill and rejects the contrary standard contained in the Senate amendment.

Section 1124(3) of the House amendment rejects a provision contained in section 1124(3)(B)(iii) of the House bill which would have considered a class of interest not to be impaired by virtue of the fact that the plan provided cash or property for the value of the holder's interest in the debtor.

The effect of the House amendment is to permit an interest not to be impaired only if the interest has a fixed liquidation preference or redemption price. Therefore, a class of interests such as common stock, must either accept a plan under section 1129(a)(8), or the plan must satisfy the requirements of section 1129(b)(2)(C) in order for a plan to be confirmed.

A compromise reflected in section 1124(2)(C) of the House amendment indicates that a class of claims is not impaired under the circumstances of section 1124(2) if damages are paid to rectify reasonable reliance engaged in by the holder of a claim or interest arising from the prepetition breach of a contractual provision, such as an ipso facto or bankruptcy clause, or law. Where the rights of third parties are concerned, such as in the case of lease premises which have been rerented to a third party, it is not intended that there will be adequate damages to compensate the third party.

Effective and Applicability Provisions

2005 Acts. Amendments by Pub.L. 109–8 effective, except as otherwise provided, 180 days after April 20, 2005, and inapplicable with respect to cases commenced under Title 11 before the effective date, see Pub.L. 109–8, § 1501, set out as a note under 11 U.S.C.A. § 101.

1994 Acts. Amendment by Pub.L. 103–394 effective on Oct. 22, 1994, and not to apply with respect to cases commenced under Title 11 of the United States Code before Oct. 22, 1994, see section 702 of Pub.L. 103–394, set out as a note under section 101 of this title.

1984 Acts. Amendment by Pub.L. 98–353 effective with respect to cases filed 90 days after July 10, 1984, see section 552(a), formerly 553(a), of Pub.L. 98–353, set out as a note under section 101 of this title.

Separability of Provisions

If any provision of or amendment made by Pub.L. 103–394 or the application of such provision or amendment to any person or circumstance is held to be unconstitutional, the remaining provisions of and amendments made by Pub.L. 103–394 and the application of such provisions and amendments to any person or circumstance shall not be affected thereby, see section 701 of Pub.L. 103–394, set out as a note under section 101 of this title.

For Complete Annotation Materials, see United States Code Annotated

CROSS REFERENCES

Allowance of claims or interests, see 11 USCA § 502.

Applicability of this section in Chapter nine cases, see 11 USCA § 901.

Claims and interests, generally, see 11 USCA § 1111.

Filing of proofs of claims or interests, see 11 USCA § 501.

§ 1125.   Postpetition disclosure and solicitation

(a) In this section—

(1) "adequate information" means information of a kind, and in sufficient detail, as far as is reasonably practicable in light of the nature and history of the debtor and the condition of the debtor's books and records, including a discussion of the potential material Federal tax consequences of the plan to the debtor, any successor to the debtor, and a hypothetical investor typical of the holders of claims or interests in the case, that would enable such a hypothetical investor of the relevant class to make an informed judgment about the plan, but adequate information need not include such information about any other possible or proposed plan and in determining whether a disclosure statement provides adequate information, the court shall consider the complexity of the case, the benefit of additional information to creditors and other parties in interest, and the cost of providing additional information; and

(2) "investor typical of holders of claims or interests of the relevant class" means investor having—

(A) a claim or interest of the relevant class;

(B) such a relationship with the debtor as the holders of other claims or interests of such class generally have; and

(C) such ability to obtain such information from sources other than the disclosure required by this section as holders of claims or interests in such class generally have.

(b) An acceptance or rejection of a plan may not be solicited after the commencement of the case under this title from a holder of a claim or interest with respect to such claim or interest, unless, at the time of or before such solicitation, there is transmitted to such holder the plan or a summary of the plan, and a written disclosure statement approved, after notice and a hearing, by the court as containing adequate information. The court may approve a disclosure statement without a valuation of the debtor or an appraisal of the debtor's assets.

(c) The same disclosure statement shall be transmitted to each holder of a claim or interest of a particular class, but there may be transmitted different disclosure statements, differing in amount, detail, or kind of information, as between classes.

(d) Whether a disclosure statement required under subsection (b) of this section contains adequate information is not governed by any otherwise applicable nonbankruptcy law, rule, or regulation, but an agency or official whose duty is to administer or enforce such a law, rule, or regulation may be heard on the issue of whether a disclosure statement contains adequate information. Such an agency or official may not appeal from, or otherwise seek review of, an order approving a disclosure statement.

(e) A person that solicits acceptance or rejection of a plan, in good faith and in compliance with the applicable provisions of this title, or that participates, in good faith and in compliance with the applicable provisions of this title, in the offer, issuance, sale, or purchase of a security, offered or sold under the plan, of the debtor, of an affiliate participating in a joint plan with the debtor, or of a newly organized successor to the debtor under the plan, is not liable, on account of such solicitation or participation, for violation of any applicable law, rule, or regulation governing solicitation of acceptance or rejection of a plan or the offer, issuance, sale, or purchase of securities.

(f) Notwithstanding subsection (b), in a small business case—

(1) the court may determine that the plan itself provides adequate information and that a separate disclosure statement is not necessary;

(2) the court may approve a disclosure statement submitted on standard forms approved by the court or adopted under section 2075 of title 28; and

(3)(A) the court may conditionally approve a disclosure statement subject to final approval after notice and a hearing;

(B) acceptances and rejections of a plan may be solicited based on a conditionally approved disclosure statement if the debtor provides adequate information to each holder of a claim or interest that is solicited, but a conditionally approved disclosure statement shall be mailed not later than 25 days before the date of the hearing on confirmation of the plan; and

(C) the hearing on the disclosure statement may be combined with the hearing on confirmation of a plan.

(g) Notwithstanding subsection (b), an acceptance or rejection of the plan may be solicited from a holder of a claim or interest if such solicitation complies with applicable nonbankruptcy law and if such holder was solicited before the commencement of the case in a manner complying with applicable nonbankruptcy law.

(Pub.L. 95–598, Nov. 6, 1978, 92 Stat. 2633; Pub.L. 98–353, Title III, § 509, July 10, 1984, 98 Stat. 385; Pub.L. 103–394, Title II, § 217(e), Oct. 22, 1994, 108 Stat. 4127; Pub.L. 109–8, Title IV, §§ 408, 431, Title VII, § 717, Apr. 20, 2005, 119 Stat. 106, 109, 131.)

HISTORICAL AND STATUTORY NOTES

Revision Notes and Legislative Reports

1978 Acts. This section extends disclosure requirements in connection with solicitations to all cases under chapter 11. Heretofore this subject was dealt with by the Bankruptcy Act [former Title 11] mainly in the special contexts of railroad reorganizations and chapter X [former Chapter 10 (section 501 et seq.) of former Title 11 cases.

Subsection (a) defines (1) the subject matter of disclosure as "adequate information" and relates the standard of adequacy to an (2) "investor typical of holders or claims or interests of the relevant class." "Investor" is used broadly here, for it will almost always include a trade creditor or other creditors who originally had no investment intent or interest. It refers to the investment-type decision by those called upon to accept a plan to modify their claims or interests, which typically will involve acceptance of new securities or of a cash payment in lieu thereof.

Both the kind and form of information are left essentially to the judicial discretion of the court, guided by the specification in subparagraph (a)(1) that it be of a kind and in sufficient detail that a reasonable and typical investor can make an informed judgment about the plan. The information required will necessarily be governed by the circumstances of the case.

Reporting and audit standards devised for solvent and continuing businesses do not necessarily fit a debtor in reorganization. Subsection (a)(1) expressly incorporates consideration of the nature and history of the debtor and the condition of its books and records into the determination of what is reasonably practicable to supply. These factors are particularly pertinent to historical data and to discontinued operations of no future relevance.

A plan is necessarily predicated on knowledge of the assets and liabilities being dealt with and on factually supported expectations as to the future course of the business sufficient to meet the feasibility standard in section 1130(a)(11) [now section 1129(a)(11)] of this title. It may thus be necessary to provide estimates or judgments for that purpose. Yet it remains practicable to describe, in such detail as may be relevant and needed, the basis for the plan and the data on which supporters of the plan rely.

Subsection (b) establishes the jurisdiction of the court over this subject by prohibiting solicitation of acceptance or rejection of a plan after the commencement of the case, unless the person solicited receives, before or at the time of the solicitation, a written disclosure statement approved by the court, after notice and hearing, as containing adequate information. As under present law, determinations of value, by appraisal or otherwise, are not required if not needed to accomplish the purpose specified in subsection (a)(1).

Subsection (c) requires that the same disclosure statement be transmitted to each member of a class. It recognizes that the information needed for an informed judgment about the plan may differ among classes. A class whose rights under the plan center on a particular fund or asset would have no use for an extensive description of other matters that could not affect them.

Subsection (d) relieves the court of the need to follow any otherwise applicable Federal or state law in determining the adequacy of the information contained in the disclosure statement submitted for its approval. It authorizes an agency or official, Federal or state, charged with administering cognate laws so preempted to advise the court on the adequacy of

proposed disclosure statement. But they are not authorized to appeal the court's decision.

Solicitations with respect to a plan do not involve just mere requests for opinions. Acceptance of the plan vitally affects creditors and shareholders, and most frequently the solicitation involves an offering of securities in exchange for claims or interests. The present bankruptcy statute [former Title 11] has exempted such offerings under each of its chapters from the registration and disclosure requirements of the Securities Act of 1933 [section 77a et seq. of Title 15, Commerce and Trade], an exemption also continued by section 1145(a)(2) of this title. The extension of the disclosure requirements to all chapter 11 cases justifies the coordinate extension of these exemptions. By the same token, no valid purpose is served not to exempt from the requirements of similar state laws in a matter under the exclusive jurisdiction of the Federal bankruptcy laws.

Subsection (e) exonerates any person who, in good faith and in compliance with this title, solicits or participates in the offer, issuance, sale or purchase, under the plan, of a security from any liability, on account of such solicitation or participation, for violation of any law, rule, or regulation governing the offer, issuance, sale, or purchase of securities. This exoneration is coordinate with the exemption from Federal or State registration or licensing requirements provided by section 1145 of this title.

In the nonpublic case, the court, when approving the disclosure statement, has before it the texts of the plan, a proposed disclosure document, and such other information the plan proponents and other interested parties may present at the hearing. In the final analysis the exoneration which subsection (e) grants must depend on the good faith of the plan proponents and of those who participate in the preparation of the disclosure statement and in the solicitation. Subsection (e) does not affect civil or criminal liability for defects and inadequacies that are beyond the limits of the exoneration that good faith provides.

Section 1125 applies to public companies as well, subject to the qualifications of subsection (f). In case of a public company no solicitations of acceptance is permitted unless authorized by the court upon or after approval of the plan pursuant to section 1128(c). In addition to the documents specified in subsection (b), subsection (f) requires transmission of the opinion and order of the court approving the plan and, if filed, the advisory report of the Securities and Exchange Commission or a summary thereof prepared by the Commission. Senate Report No. 95–989.

This section is new. It is the heart of the consolidation of the various reorganization chapters found in current law. It requires disclosure before solicitation of acceptances of a plan or reorganization.

Subsection (a) contains two definitions. First, "adequate information" is defined to mean information of a kind, and insufficient [sic] detail, as far as is reasonably practical in light of the nature and history of the debtor and the condition of the debtor's books and records, that would enable a hypothetical reasonable investor typical of holders of claims or interests of the relevant class to make an informed judgment about the plan. Second, "investor typical of holders of claims or interests of the relevant class" is defined to mean an investor having a claim or interest of the relevant class, having such a relationship with the debtor as the holders of other claims or interests of the relevant class have, and having such ability to obtain information from sources other than the disclosure statement as holders of claims or interests of the relevant class have, and having such ability to obtain information from sources other than the disclosure statement as holders of claims or interests of the relevant class have. That is, the hypothetical investor against which the disclosure is measured must not be an insider if other members of the class are not insiders, and so on. In other words, the adequacy of disclosure is measured against the typical investor, not an extraordinary one.

The Supreme Court's rulemaking power will not extend to rulemaking that will prescribe what constitutes adequate information. That standard is a substantive standard. Precisely what constitutes adequate information in any particular instance will develop on a case-by-case basis. Courts will take a practical approach as to what is necessary under the circumstances of each case, such as the cost of preparation of the statements, the need for relative speed in solicitation and confirmation, and, of course, the need for investor protection. There will be a balancing of interests in each case. In reorganization cases, there is frequently great uncertainty. Therefore the need for flexibility is greatest.

Subsection (b) is the operative subsection. It prohibits solicitation of acceptances or rejections of a plan after the commencement of the case unless, at the time of the solicitation or before, there is transmitted to the solicitee the plan or a summary of the plan, and a written disclosure statement approved by the court as containing adequate information. The subsection permits approval of the statement without the necessity of a valuation of the debtor or an appraisal of the debtor's assets. However, in some cases, a valuation or appraisal will be necessary to develop adequate information. The court will be able to determine what is necessary in light of the facts and circumstances of each particular case.

Subsection (c) requires that the same disclosure statement go to all members of a particular class, but permits different disclosure to different classes.

Subsection (d) excepts the disclosure statements from the requirements of the securities laws (such as section 14 of the 1934 Act [section 78n of Title 15, Commerce and Trade] and section 5 of the 1933 Act [section 77e of Title 15]), and from similar State securities laws (blue sky laws, for example). The subsection permits an agency or official whose duty is to administer or enforce such laws (such as the Securities and Exchange Commission or State Corporation Commissioners) to appear and be heard on the issue of whether a disclosure statement contains adequate information, but the agencies and officials are not granted the right of appeal from an adverse determination in any capacity. They may join in an appeal by a true party in interest, however.

Subsection (e) is a safe harbor provision, and is necessary to make the exemption provided by subsection (d) effective. Without it, a creditor that solicited an acceptance or rejection in reliance on the court's approval of a disclosure statement would be potentially liable under antifraud sections designed to enforce the very sections of the securities laws from which subsection (d) excuses compliance. The subsection protects only persons that solicit in good faith and in compliance with the applicable provisions of the reorganization chapter. It provides protection from legal liability as well as from equitable liability based on an injunctive action by the SEC [Securities and Exchange Commission] or other agency or official. House Report No. 95–595.

1984 Acts. Statements by Legislative Leaders, see 1984 U.S.Code Cong. and Adm.News, p. 576.

1994 Acts. House Report No. 103–835, see 1994 U.S. Code Cong. and Adm. News, p. 3340.

2005 Acts. House Report No. 109–31(Part I), see 2005 U.S. Code Cong. and Adm. News, p. 88.

Legislative Statements

Section 1125 of the House amendment is derived from section 1125 of the House bill and Senate amendment except with respect to section 1125(f) of the Senate amendment. It will not be necessary for the court to consider the report of the examiner prior to approval of a disclosure statement. The investigation of the examiner is to proceed on an independent basis from the procedure of the reorganization under chapter 11. In order to ensure that the examiner's report will be expeditious and fair, the examiner is precluded from serving as a trustee in the case or from representing a trustee if a trustee is appointed, whether the case remains in chapter 11 or is converted to chapter 7 or 13.

Effective and Applicability Provisions

2005 Acts. Amendments by Pub.L. 109–8 effective, except as otherwise provided, 180 days after April 20, 2005, and inapplicable with respect to cases commenced under Title 11 before the effective date, see Pub.L. 109–8, § 1501, set out as a note under 11 U.S.C.A. § 101.

1994 Acts. Amendment by Pub.L. 103–394 effective on Oct. 22, 1994, and not to apply with respect to cases commenced under Title 11 of the United States Code before Oct. 22, 1994, see section 702 of Pub.L. 103–394, set out as a note under section 101 of this title.

1984 Acts. Amendment by Pub.L. 98–353 effective with respect to cases filed 90 days after July 10, 1984, see section 552(a), formerly 553(a), of Pub.L. 98–353, set out as a note under section 101 of this title.

Separability of Provisions

If any provision of or amendment made by Pub.L. 103–394 or the application of such provision or amendment to any person or circumstance is held to be unconstitutional, the remaining provisions of and amendments made by Pub.L. 103–394 and the application of such provisions and amendments to any person or circumstance shall not be affected thereby, see section 701 of Pub.L. 103–394, set out as a note under section 101 of this title.

CROSS REFERENCES

Applicability of this section in Chapter nine cases, see 11 USCA § 901.

Duty of United States trustee to file comments with respect to plans and disclosure statements filed in connection with hearings under this section, see 28 USCA § 586.

Exemption from securities laws of certain transactions in which disclosure statements are provided, see 11 USCA § 1145.

§ 1126.　Acceptance of plan

(a) The holder of a claim or interest allowed under section 502 of this title may accept or reject a plan. If the United States is a creditor or equity security holder, the Secretary of the Treasury may accept or reject the plan on behalf of the United States.

(b) For the purposes of subsections (c) and (d) of this section, a holder of a claim or interest that has accepted or rejected the plan before the commencement of the case under this title is deemed to have accepted or rejected such plan, as the case may be, if—

(1) the solicitation of such acceptance or rejection was in compliance with any applicable nonbankruptcy law, rule, or regulation governing the adequacy of disclosure in connection with such solicitation; or

(2) if there is not any such law, rule, or regulation, such acceptance or rejection was solicited after disclosure to such holder of adequate information, as defined in section 1125(a) of this title.

(c) A class of claims has accepted a plan if such plan has been accepted by creditors, other than any entity designated under subsection (e) of this section, that hold at least two-thirds in amount and more than one-half in number of the allowed claims of such class held by creditors, other than any entity designated under subsection (e) of this section, that have accepted or rejected such plan.

(d) A class of interests has accepted a plan if such plan has been accepted by holders of such interests, other than any entity designated under subsection (e) of this section, that hold at least two-thirds in amount of the allowed interests of such class held by holders of such interests, other than any entity designated under subsection (e) of this section, that have accepted or rejected such plan.

(e) On request of a party in interest, and after notice and a hearing, the court may designate any entity whose acceptance or rejection of such plan was not in good faith, or was not solicited or procured in good faith or in accordance with the provisions of this title.

(f) Notwithstanding any other provision of this section, a class that is not impaired under a plan, and each holder of a claim or interest of such class, are conclusively presumed to have accepted the plan, and solicitation of acceptances with respect to such class from the holders of claims or interests of such class is not required.

(g) Notwithstanding any other provision of this section, a class is deemed not to have accepted a plan if such plan provides that the claims or interests of such class do not entitle the holders of such claims or interests to receive or retain any property under the plan on account of such claims or interests.

(Pub.L. 95–598, Nov. 6, 1978, 92 Stat. 2634; Pub.L. 98–353, Title III, § 510, July 10, 1984, 98 Stat. 386.)

HISTORICAL AND STATUTORY NOTES

Revision Notes and Legislative Reports

1978 Acts. Subsection (a) of this section permits the holder of a claim or interest allowed under section 502 to accept or reject a proposed plan of reorganization. The subsection also incorporates a provision now found in section 199 of chapter X [section 599 of former Title 11] that authorizes the Secretary of the Treasury to accept or reject a plan on behalf of the United States when the United States is a creditor or equity security holder.

Subsection (b) governs acceptances and rejections of plans obtained before commencement of a reorganization for a nonpublic company. Paragraph (3) expressly states that subsection (b) does not apply to a public company.

Prepetition solicitation is a common practice under chapter XI [former chapter 11 (section 701 et seq.) of former Title 11] today, and chapter IX [former chapter 9 (section 401 et seq.) of former Title 11] current makes explicit provision for it. Section 1126(b) counts a prepetition acceptance or rejection toward the required amounts and number of acceptances only if the solicitation of the acceptance or rejection was in compliance with any applicable nonbankruptcy law, rule, or regulation governing the adequacy of disclosure in connection with such solicitation. If there is not any such applicable law, rule, or regulation, then the acceptance or rejection is counted only if it was solicited after disclosure of adequate information, to the holder, as defined in section 1125(a)(1). This permits the court to ensure that the requirements of section 1125 are not avoided by prepetition solicitation.

Subsection (c) specifies the required amount and number of acceptances for a class of creditors. A class of creditors has accepted a plan if at least two-thirds in amount and more than one-half in number of the allowed claims of the class that are voted are cast in favor of the plan. The amount and number are computed on the basis of claims actually voted for or against the plan, not as under chapter X [former chapter 10 (section 501 et seq.) of former Title 11] on the basis of the allowed claims in the class. Subsection (f) excludes from all these calculations claims not voted in good faith, and claims procured or solicited not in good faith or not in accordance with the provisions of this title.

Subsection (c) requires that the same disclosure statement be transmitted to each member of a class. It recognizes that the information needed for an informed judgment about the plan may differ among classes. A class whose rights under the plan center on a particular fund or asset would have no use for an extensive description of other matters that could not affect them.

Subsection (d) relieves the court of the need to follow any otherwise applicable Federal or state law in determining the adequacy of the information contained in the disclosure statement submitted for its approval. It authorizes an agency or official, Federal or state, charged with administering cognate laws so pre-empted to advise the court on the adequacy of proposed disclosure statement. But they are not authorized to appeal the court's decision.

Solicitations with respect to a plan do not involve just mere requests for opinions. Acceptance of the plan vitally affects creditors and shareholders, and most frequently the solicitation involves an offering of securities in exchange for claims or interests. The present Bankruptcy Act [former Title 11] has exempted such offerings under each of its chapters from the registration and disclosure requirements of the Securities Act of 1933 [section 77a of Title 15, Commerce and Trade], et seq., an exemption also continued by section 1145 of this title. The extension of the disclosure requirements to all chapter 11 cases is justified by the integration of the separate chapters into the single chapter 11. By the same token, no valid purpose is served by failing to provide exemption from the requirements of similar state laws in a matter under the exclusive jurisdiction of the Federal bankruptcy laws.

Under subsection (d), with respect to a class of equity securities, it is sufficient for acceptance of the plan if the amount of securities voting for the plan is at least two-thirds of the total actually voted.

Subsection (e) provides that no acceptances are required from any class whose claims or interests are unimpaired under the plan or in the order confirming the plan.

Subsection (g) provides that any class denied participation under the plan is conclusively deemed to have rejected the plan. There is obviously no need to submit a plan for a vote by a class that is to receive nothing. But under subsection (g) the excluded class is like a class that has not accepted, and is a dissenting class for purposes of confirmation under section 1130. Senate Report No. 95–989.

1984 Acts. Statements by Legislative Leaders, see 1984 U.S.Code Cong. and Adm.News, p. 576.

Legislative Statements

Section 1126 of the House amendment deletes section 1126(e) as contained in the House bill. Section 105 of the bill constitutes sufficient power in the court to designate exclusion of a creditor's claim on the basis of a conflict of interest. Section 1126(f) of the House amendment adopts a provision contained in section 1127(f) of the Senate bill indicating that a class that is not impaired under a plan is deemed to have accepted a plan and solicitation of acceptances from such class is not required.

Effective and Applicability Provisions

1984 Acts. Amendment by Pub.L. 98–353 effective with respect to cases filed 90 days after July 10, 1984, see section 552(a), formerly 553(a), of Pub.L. 98–353, set out as a note under section 101 of this title.

CROSS REFERENCES

Amount and number of claims within class as including claims formerly held by certain creditors, see 11 USCA § 946.

Applicability of subsecs. (a) to (c) and (e) to (g) of this section in Chapter nine cases, see 11 USCA § 901.

§ 1127. Modification of plan

(a) The proponent of a plan may modify such plan at any time before confirmation, but may not modify such plan so that such plan as modified fails to meet the requirements of sections 1122 and 1123 of this title. After the proponent of a plan files a modification of such plan with the court, the plan as modified becomes the plan.

(b) The proponent of a plan or the reorganized debtor may modify such plan at any time after confirmation of such plan and before substantial consummation of such plan, but may not modify such plan so that such plan as modified fails to meet the requirements of sections 1122 and 1123 of this title. Such plan as modified under this subsection becomes the plan only if circumstances warrant such modification and the court, after notice and a hearing, confirms such plan as modified, under section 1129 of this title.

(c) The proponent of a modification shall comply with section 1125 of this title with respect to the plan as modified.

(d) Any holder of a claim or interest that has accepted or rejected a plan is deemed to have accepted or rejected, as the case may be, such plan as modified, unless, within the time fixed by the court, such holder changes such holder's previous acceptance or rejection.

(e) If the debtor is an individual, the plan may be modified at any time after confirmation of the plan but before the completion of payments under the plan, whether or not the plan has been substantially consummated, upon request of the debtor, the trustee, the United States trustee, or the holder of an allowed unsecured claim, to—

    (1) increase or reduce the amount of payments on claims of a particular class provided for by the plan;

    (2) extend or reduce the time period for such payments; or

    (3) alter the amount of the distribution to a creditor whose claim is provided for by the plan to the extent necessary to take account of any payment of such claim made other than under the plan.

(f)(1) Sections 1121 through 1128 and the requirements of section 1129 apply to any modification under subsection (e).

(2) The plan, as modified, shall become the plan only after there has been disclosure under section 1125 as the court may direct, notice and a hearing, and such modification is approved.

(Pub.L. 95–598, Nov. 6, 1978, 92 Stat. 2635; Pub.L. 98–353, Title III, § 511, July 10, 1984, 98 Stat. 386; Pub.L. 109–8, Title III, § 321(e), Apr. 20, 2005, 119 Stat. 96; Pub.L. 111–327, § 2(a)(34), Dec. 22, 2010, 124 Stat. 3561.)

HISTORICAL AND STATUTORY NOTES

Revision Notes and Legislative Reports

1978 Acts. Under subsection (a) the proponent may file a proposal to modify a plan prior to confirmation. In the case of a public company the modifying proposal may be filed prior to approval.

Subsection (b) provides that a party in interest eligible to file a plan may file instead of a plan a proposal to modify a plan filed by another. Under subsection (c) a party in interest objecting to some feature of a plan may submit a proposal to modify the plan to meet the objection.

After a plan has been confirmed, but before its substantial consummation, a plan may be modified by leave of court, which subsection (d) provides shall be granted for good cause. Subsection (e) provides that a proposal to modify a plan is subject to the disclosure requirements of section 1125 and as provided in subsection (f). It provides that a creditor or stockholder who voted for or against a plan is deemed to have accepted or rejected the modifying proposal. But if the modification materially and adversely affects any of their interests, they must be afforded an opportunity to change their vote in accordance with the disclosure and solicitation requirements of section 1125.

Under subsection (g) a plan, if modified prior to confirmation, shall be confirmed if it meets the requirements of section 1130. Senate Report No. 95–989.

Subsection (a) permits the proponent of a plan to modify it at any time before confirmation, subject, of course, to the requirements of sections 1122 and 1123, governing classification and contents of a plan. After the proponent of a plan files a modification with the court, the plan as modified becomes the plan, and is to be treated the same as an original plan.

Subsection (b) permits modification of a plan after confirmation under certain circumstances. The modification must be proposed before substantial consummation of the plan. The requirements of sections 1122 and 1123 continue to apply. The plan as modified under this subsection becomes the plan only if the court confirms the plan as modified under section 1129 and the circumstances warrant the modification.

Subsection (c) requires the proponent of a modification to comply with the disclosure provisions of section 1125. Of course, if the modification were sufficiently minor, the court might determine that additional disclosure was not required under the circumstances.

Subsection (d) simplifies modification procedure by deeming any creditor or equity security holder that has already accepted or rejected the plan to have accepted or rejected the modification, unless, within the time fixed by the court, the creditor or equity security holder changes this previous acceptance or rejection. House Report No. 95–595.

1984 Acts. Statements by Legislative Leaders, see 1984 U.S. Code Cong. and Adm. News, p. 576.

2005 Acts. House Report No. 109–31(Part I), see 2005 U.S. Code Cong. and Adm. News, p. 88.

Legislative Statements

Section 1127(a) of the House amendment adopts a provision contained in the House bill permitting only the proponent of a plan to modify the plan and rejection the alternative of open modification contained in the Senate amendment.

Effective and Applicability Provisions

2005 Acts. Amendments by Pub.L. 109–8 effective, except as otherwise provided, 180 days after April 20, 2005, and inapplicable with respect to cases commenced under Title 11 before the effective date, see Pub.L. 109–8, § 1501, set out as a note under 11 U.S.C.A. § 101.

1984 Acts. Amendment by Pub.L. 98–353 effective with respect to cases filed 90 days after July 10, 1984, see section 552(a), formerly 553(a), of Pub.L. 98–353, set out as a note under section 101 of this title.

CROSS REFERENCES

Applicability of subsec. (d) of this section in Chapter nine cases, see 11 USCA § 901.

Modification of plan after confirmation in,

Chapter thirteen cases, see 11 USCA § 1329.

Chapter twelve cases, see 11 USCA § 1229.

Modification of plan before confirmation in,

Chapter thirteen cases, see 11 USCA § 1323.

Chapter twelve cases, see 11 USCA § 1223.

Modification of plan in Chapter nine cases, see 11 USCA § 942.

§ 1128.   Confirmation hearing

(a) After notice, the court shall hold a hearing on confirmation of a plan.

(b) A party in interest may object to confirmation of a plan.
(Pub.L. 95–598, Nov. 6, 1978, 92 Stat. 2635.)

HISTORICAL AND STATUTORY NOTES

Revision Notes and Legislative Reports

1978 Acts. [Section 1129 (now section 1128)] Subsection (a) requires that there be a hearing in every case on the confirmation of the plan. Notice is required.

Subsection (b) permits any party in interest to object to the confirmation of the plan. The Securities and Exchange Commission and indenture trustees, as parties in interest under section 1109, may object to confirmation of the plan. Senate Report No. 95–989.

CROSS REFERENCES

Applicability of this section in Chapter nine cases, see 11 USCA § 901.

Confirmation hearing in,

Chapter thirteen cases, see 11 USCA § 1324.

Chapter twelve cases, see 11 USCA § 1224.

Duty of United States trustee to file comments with respect to plans and disclosure statements filed in connection with hearings under this section, see 28 USCA § 586.

Right to be heard in cases under this chapter, see 11 USCA § 1109.

§ 1129.   Confirmation of plan

(a) The court shall confirm a plan only if all of the following requirements are met:

(1) The plan complies with the applicable provisions of this title.

(2) The proponent of the plan complies with the applicable provisions of this title.

(3) The plan has been proposed in good faith and not by any means forbidden by law.

(4) Any payment made or to be made by the proponent, by the debtor, or by a person issuing securities or acquiring property under the plan, for services or for costs and expenses in or in connection with the case, or in connection with the plan and incident to the case, has been approved by, or is subject to the approval of, the court as reasonable.

(5)(A)(i) The proponent of the plan has disclosed the identity and affiliations of any individual proposed to serve, after confirmation of the plan, as a director, officer, or voting trustee of the debtor, an affiliate of the debtor participating in a joint plan with the debtor, or a successor to the debtor under the plan; and

(ii) the appointment to, or continuance in, such office of such individual, is consistent with the interests of creditors and equity security holders and with public policy; and

(B) the proponent of the plan has disclosed the identity of any insider that will be employed or retained by the reorganized debtor, and the nature of any compensation for such insider.

(6) Any governmental regulatory commission with jurisdiction, after confirmation of the plan, over the rates of the debtor has approved any rate change provided for in the plan, or such rate change is expressly conditioned on such approval.

(7) With respect to each impaired class of claims or interests—

(A) each holder of a claim or interest of such class—

(i) has accepted the plan; or

(ii) will receive or retain under the plan on account of such claim or interest property of a value, as of the effective date of the plan, that is not less than the amount that such holder would so receive or retain if the debtor were liquidated under chapter 7 of this title on such date; or

(B) if section 1111(b)(2) of this title applies to the claims of such class, each holder of a claim of such class will receive or retain under the plan on account of such claim property of a value, as of the effective date of the plan, that is not less than the value of such holder's interest in the estate's interest in the property that secures such claims.

(8) With respect to each class of claims or interests—

(A) such class has accepted the plan; or

(B) such class is not impaired under the plan.

(9) Except to the extent that the holder of a particular claim has agreed to a different treatment of such claim, the plan provides that—

(A) with respect to a claim of a kind specified in section 507(a)(2) or 507(a)(3) of this title, on the effective date of the plan, the holder of such claim will receive on account of such claim cash equal to the allowed amount of such claim;

(B) with respect to a class of claims of a kind specified in section 507(a)(1), 507(a)(4), 507(a)(5), 507(a)(6), or 507(a)(7) of this title, each holder of a claim of such class will receive—

(i) if such class has accepted the plan, deferred cash payments of a value, as of the effective date of the plan, equal to the allowed amount of such claim; or

(ii) if such class has not accepted the plan, cash on the effective date of the plan equal to the allowed amount of such claim;

(C) with respect to a claim of a kind specified in section 507(a)(8) of this title, the holder of such claim will receive on account of such claim regular installment payments in cash—

(i) of a total value, as of the effective date of the plan, equal to the allowed amount of such claim;

(ii) over a period ending not later than 5 years after the date of the order for relief under section 301, 302, or 303; and

(iii) in a manner not less favorable than the most favored nonpriority unsecured claim provided for by the plan (other than cash payments made to a class of creditors under section 1122(b)); and

(D) with respect to a secured claim which would otherwise meet the description of an unsecured claim of a governmental unit under section 507(a)(8), but for the secured status of that claim, the holder of that claim will receive on account of that claim, cash payments, in the same manner and over the same period, as prescribed in subparagraph (C).

(10) If a class of claims is impaired under the plan, at least one class of claims that is impaired under the plan has accepted the plan, determined without including any acceptance of the plan by any insider.

(11) Confirmation of the plan is not likely to be followed by the liquidation, or the need for further financial reorganization, of the debtor or any successor to the debtor under the plan, unless such liquidation or reorganization is proposed in the plan.

(12) All fees payable under section 1930 of title 28, as determined by the court at the hearing on confirmation of the plan, have been paid or the plan provides for the payment of all such fees on the effective date of the plan.

(13) The plan provides for the continuation after its effective date of payment of all retiree benefits, as that term is defined in section 1114 of this title, at the level established pursuant to subsection (e)(1)(B) or (g) of section 1114 of this title, at any time prior to confirmation of the plan, for the duration of the period the debtor has obligated itself to provide such benefits.

(14) If the debtor is required by a judicial or administrative order, or by statute, to pay a domestic support obligation, the debtor has paid all amounts payable under such order or such statute for such obligation that first become payable after the date of the filing of the petition.

(15) In a case in which the debtor is an individual and in which the holder of an allowed unsecured claim objects to the confirmation of the plan—

(A) the value, as of the effective date of the plan, of the property to be distributed under the plan on account of such claim is not less than the amount of such claim; or

(B) the value of the property to be distributed under the plan is not less than the projected disposable income of the debtor (as defined in section 1325(b)(2)) to be received during the 5–year period beginning on the date that the first payment is due under the plan, or during the period for which the plan provides payments, whichever is longer.

(16) All transfers of property under the plan shall be made in accordance with any applicable provisions of nonbankruptcy law that govern the transfer of property by a corporation or trust that is not a moneyed, business, or commercial corporation or trust.

(b)(1) Notwithstanding section 510(a) of this title, if all of the applicable requirements of subsection (a) of this section other than paragraph (8) are met with respect to a plan, the court, on request of the proponent of the plan, shall confirm the plan notwithstanding the requirements of such paragraph if the plan does not discriminate unfairly, and is fair and equitable, with respect to each class of claims or interests that is impaired under, and has not accepted, the plan.

(2) For the purpose of this subsection, the condition that a plan be fair and equitable with respect to a class includes the following requirements:

(A) With respect to a class of secured claims, the plan provides—

(i)(I) that the holders of such claims retain the liens securing such claims, whether the property subject to such liens is retained by the debtor or transferred to another entity, to the extent of the allowed amount of such claims; and

(II) that each holder of a claim of such class receive on account of such claim deferred cash payments totaling at least the allowed amount of such claim, of a value, as of the effective date of the plan, of at least the value of such holder's interest in the estate's interest in such property;

(ii) for the sale, subject to section 363(k) of this title, of any property that is subject to the liens securing such claims, free and clear of such liens, with such liens to attach to the proceeds of such sale, and the treatment of such liens on proceeds under clause (i) or (iii) of this subparagraph; or

(iii) for the realization by such holders of the indubitable equivalent of such claims.

(B) With respect to a class of unsecured claims—

(i) the plan provides that each holder of a claim of such class receive or retain on account of such claim property of a value, as of the effective date of the plan, equal to the allowed amount of such claim; or

(ii) the holder of any claim or interest that is junior to the claims of such class will not receive or retain under the plan on account of such junior claim or interest any property, except that in a case in which the debtor is an individual, the debtor may retain property included in the estate under section 1115, subject to the requirements of subsection (a)(14) of this section.

(C) With respect to a class of interests—

(i) the plan provides that each holder of an interest of such class receive or retain on account of such interest property of a value, as of the effective date of the plan, equal to the greatest of the allowed amount of any fixed liquidation preference to which such holder is entitled, any fixed redemption price to which such holder is entitled, or the value of such interest; or

(ii) the holder of any interest that is junior to the interests of such class will not receive or retain under the plan on account of such junior interest any property.

(c) Notwithstanding subsections (a) and (b) of this section and except as provided in section 1127(b) of this title, the court may confirm only one plan, unless the order of confirmation in the case has been revoked under section 1144 of this title. If the requirements of subsections (a) and (b) of this section are met with respect to more than one plan, the court shall consider the preferences of creditors and equity security holders in determining which plan to confirm.

(d) Notwithstanding any other provision of this section, on request of a party in interest that is a governmental unit, the court may not confirm a plan if the principal purpose of the plan is the avoidance of taxes or the avoidance of the application of section 5 of the Securities Act of 1933. In any hearing under this subsection, the governmental unit has the burden of proof on the issue of avoidance.

(e) In a small business case, the court shall confirm a plan that complies with the applicable provisions of this title and that is filed in accordance with section 1121(e) not later than 45 days after the plan is filed unless the time for confirmation is extended in accordance with section 1121(e)(3).

(Pub.L. 95–598, Nov. 6, 1978, 92 Stat. 2635; Pub.L. 98–353, Title III, § 512, July 10, 1984, 98 Stat. 386; Pub.L. 99–554, Title II, §§ 225, 283(v), Oct. 27, 1986, 100 Stat. 3102, 3118; Pub.L. 100–334, § 2(b), June 16, 1988, 102 Stat. 613; Pub.L. 103–394, Title III, § 304(h)(7), Title V, § 501(d)(32), Oct. 22, 1994, 108 Stat. 4134, 4146; Pub.L. 109–8, Title II, § 213(1), Title III, § 321(c), Title IV, § 438, Title VII, § 710, Title XII, § 1221(b), Title XV, § 1502(a)(8), Apr. 20, 2005, 119 Stat. 52, 95, 113, 127, 196, 216; Pub.L. 111–327, § 2(a)(35), Dec. 22, 2010, 124 Stat. 3561.)

HISTORICAL AND STATUTORY NOTES
Revision Notes and Legislative Reports

1978 Acts. [Section 1130 (now section 1129)] Subsection (a) enumerates the requirement governing confirmation of a plan. The court is required to confirm a plan if and only if all of the requirements are met.

Paragraph (1) requires that the plan comply with the applicable provisions of chapter 11, such as sections 1122 and 1123, governing classification and contents of plan.

Paragraph (2) requires that the proponent of the plan comply with the applicable provisions of chapter 11, such as section 1125 regarding disclosure.

Paragraph (3) requires that the plan have been proposed in good faith, and not by any means forbidden by law.

Paragraph (4) is derived from section 221 of chapter X [section 621 of former Title 11]. It requires that any payment made or promised by the proponent, the debtor, or person issuing securities or acquiring property under the plan, for services or for costs and expenses in, or in connection with the case, or in connection with the plan and incident to the case, be disclosed to the court. In addition, any payment made before confirmation must have been reasonable, and any payment to be fixed after confirmation must be subject to the approval of the court as reasonable.

Paragraph (5) is also derived from section 221 of chapter X [section 621 of former Title 11]. It requires the plan to disclose the identity and affiliations of any individual proposed to serve, after confirmation, as a director, officer, or voting trustee of the reorganized debtor. The appointment to or continuance in one of these offices by the individual must be consistent with the interests of creditors and equity security holders and with public policy. The plan must also disclose the identity of any insider that will be employed or retained by the reorganized debtor, and the nature of any compensation to be paid to the insider.

Paragraph (6) permits confirmation only if any regulatory commission that will have jurisdiction over the debtor after confirmation of the plan has approved any rate change provided for in the plan. As an alternative, the rate change may be conditioned on such approval.

Paragraph (7) provides that in the case of a public company the court shall confirm the plan if it finds the plan to be fair and equitable and the plan either (1) has been accepted by classes of claims or interests as provided in section 1126, or (2), if not so accepted, satisfies the requirements of subsection (b) of this section.

Paragraphs (8) and (9) apply only in nonpublic cases. Paragraph (8) does not apply the fair and equitable standards in two situations. The first occurs if there is unanimous consent of all affected holders of claims and interests. It is also sufficient for purposes of confirmation if each holder of a claim or interest receives or retains consideration of a value, as of the effective date of the plan, that is not less than each would have or receive if the debtor were liquidated under chapter 7 of this title. This standard adapts the test of "best interest of creditors" as interpreted by the courts under chapter XI [former chapter 11 (section 701 et seq.) of former Title 11]. It is given broader application in chapter 11 of this title since a plan under chapter 11 may affect not only unsecured claims but secured claims and stock as well.

Under paragraph (9)(A), if a class of claims or interests has not accepted the plan, the court will confirm the plan if, for the dissenting class and any class of equal rank, the negotiated plan provides for a plan that is fair and equitable. Such review and determination are not required for any other classes that accepted the plan.

Paragraph 9(A) would permit a senior creditor to adjust his participation for the benefit of stockholders. In such a case, junior creditors, who have not been satisfied in full, may not object if, absent the "give-up", they are receiving all that a fair and equitable plan would give them. To illustrate, suppose the estate is valued at $1.5 million and claims and stock are:

		Claims and stock (millions)	Equity (millions)
(1)	Senior debt	$1.2	$1.2
(2)	Junior debt	.5	.3
(3)	Stock	(1)	—
	Total	1.7	1.5

Under the plan, the senior creditor gives up $100,000 in value for the benefit of stockholders as follows:

		Millions
(1)	Senior debt	$1.1
(2)	Junior debt	.3
(3)	Stock	.1
	Total	1.5

[1] No value.

If the junior creditors dissent, the court may nevertheless confirm the plan since under the fair and equitable standard they had an equity of only $300,000 and the allocation to equity security holders did not affect them.

Paragraph 9(A)[(9)(A)] provides a special alternative with respect to secured claims. A plan may be confirmed against a dissenting class of secured claims if the plan or order of confirmation provides for the realization of their security (1) by the retention of the property subject to such security; (2) by a sale of the property and transfer of the claim to the proceeds of sale if the secured creditors were permitted to bid at the sale and set off against the purchase price up to the allowed amount of their claims; or (3) by such other method

---

that will assure them the realization of the indubitable equivalent of the allowed amount of their secured claims. The indubitable equivalent language is intended to follow the strict approach taken by Judge Learned Hand in *In Re Murel Holding Corp.*, 7 5 [75] F.2d 941 (2nd Cir. 1935).

Paragraph (9)(B) provides that, if a class of claims or interests is excluded from participation under the plan, the court may nevertheless confirm the plan if it determines that no class on a parity with or junior to such participates under the plan. In the previous illustration, no confirmation would be permitted if the negotiated plan would grant a participation to stockholders but nothing for junior creditors. As noted elsewhere, by reason of section 1126(g), an excluded class is a dissenting class under section 1130.

Paragraph (10) states that, to be confirmed, the plan must provide that each holder of a claim under section 507 will receive property, as therein noted, of a value equal to the allowed amount of the claim. There are two exceptions: (A) The holder thereof may agree to a different settlement in part or in whole; (B) where a debtor's business is reorganized under chapter 11, this provision requires that taxes entitled to priority (including administrative claims or taxes) must be paid in cash not later than 120 days after the plan is confirmed, unless the Secretary of the Treasury agrees to other terms or kinds of payment. The bill, as introduced, required full payment in cash within 60 days after the plan is confirmed.

Paragraph (11) requires a determination regarding feasibility of the plan. It is a slight elaboration of the law that has developed in the application of the word "feasible" in Chapter X of the present Act [former chapter 10 (section 501 et seq.) of former Title 11].

Paragraph (12) requires that at least one class must accept the plan, but any claims or interests held by insiders are not to be included for purposes of determining the number and amount of acceptances.

Subsection (b) provides that if, in the case of a public company, the plan meets the requirements of subsection (a) (except paragraphs (8) and (9) which do not apply to such a company), the court is to confirm the plan if the plan or the order of confirmation provides adequate protection for the realization of the value of the claims or interests of each class not accepting the plan. The intent is to incorporate inclusively, as a guide to the meaning of subsection (a) the provisions of section 216(7) (11 U.S.C. 616(7)) [section 616(7) of former Title 11] with respect to claims and section 216(8) (11 U.S.C. 616(8)) [section 616(8) of former Title 11] with respect to equity security interests.

Under subsection (c) the court may confirm only one plan, unless the order of confirmation has been revoked under section 1144. If the requirements for confirmation are met with respect to more than one plan, the court shall consider the preferences of creditors and stockholders in deciding which plan to confirm.

Subsection (d) provides that the bankruptcy court may not confirm a plan of reorganization if its principal purpose is the avoidance of taxes or the avoidance of section 5 of the Securities Act of 1933 (15 U.S.C. 77e) [section 77e of Title 15, Commerce and Trade]. This rule modifies a similar provision of present law (section 269 of the Bankruptcy Act) [section 669 of former title 11]. Senate Report No. 95–989.

Paragraph (7) [of subsec. (a)] incorporates the former "best interest of creditors" test found in chapter 11, but spells out precisely what is intended. With respect to each class, the

holders of the claims or interests of that class must receive or retain under the plan on account of those claims or interest property of a value, as of the effective date of the plan, that is not less than the amount that they would so receive or retain if the debtor were liquidated under chapter 7 on the effective date of the plan.

In order to determine the hypothetical distribution in a liquidation, the court will have to consider the various subordination provisions of proposed 11 U.S.C. 510, 726(a)(3), 726(a)(4), and the postponement provisions of proposed 11 U.S.C. 724. Also applicable in appropriate cases will be the rules governing partnership distributions under proposed 11 U.S.C. 723, and distributions of community property under proposed 11 U.S.C. 726(c). Under subparagraph (A), a particular holder is permitted to accept less than liquidation value, but his acceptance does not bind the class.

Property under subparagraph (B) may include securities of the debtor. Thus, the provision will apply in cases in which the plan in confirmed under proposed 11 U.S.C. 1129(b).

Paragraph (8) is central to the confirmation standards. It requires that each class either have accepted the plan or be unimpaired.

Paragraph (9) augments the requirements of paragraph (8) by requiring payment of each priority claim in full. It permits payments over time and payment other than in cash, but payment in securities is not intended to be permitted without consent of the priority claimant even if the class has consented. It also permits a particular claimant to accept less than full payment.

Subsection (b) permits the court to confirm a plan notwithstanding failure of compliance with paragraph (8) of subsection (a). The plan must comply with all other paragraphs of subsection (a), including paragraph (9). This subsection contains the so-called cramdown. It requires simply that the plan meet certain standards of fairness to dissenting creditors or equity security holders. The general principle of the subsection permits confirmation notwithstanding nonacceptance by an impaired class if that class and all below it in priority are treated according to the absolute priority rule. The dissenting class must be paid in full before any junior class may share under the plan. If it is paid in full, then junior classes may share. Treatment of classes of secured creditors is slightly different because they do not fall in the priority ladder, but the principle is the same.

Specifically, the court may confirm a plan over the objection of a class of secured claims if the members of that class are unimpaired or if they are to receive under the plan property of a value equal to the allowed amount of their secured claims, as determined under proposed 11 U.S.C. 506(a). The property is to be valued as of the effective date of the plan, thus recognizing the time-value of money. As used throughout this subsection, "property" includes both tangible and intangible property, such as a security of the debtor or a successor to the debtor under a reorganization plan.

The court may confirm over the dissent of a class of unsecured claims, including priority claims, only if the members of the class are unimpaired, if they will receive under the plan property of a value equal to the allowed amount of their unsecured claims, or if no class junior will share under the plan. That is, if the class is impaired, then they must be paid in full or, if paid less than in full, then no class junior may receive anything under the plan. This codifies the absolute priority rule from the dissenting class on down.

With respect to classes of equity, the court may confirm over a dissent if the members of the class are unimpaired, if they receive their liquidation preference or redemption rights, if any, or if no class junior shares under the plan. This, too, is a codification of the absolute priority rule with respect to equity. If a partnership agreement subordinates limited partners to general partners to any degree, then the general principles of paragraph (3) of this subsection would apply to prevent the general partners from being squeezed out.

One requirement applies generally to all classes before the court may confirm under this subsection. No class may be paid more than in full.

The partial codification of the absolute priority rule here is not intended to deprive senior creditor [sic] of compensation for being required to take securities in the reorganized debtor that are of an equal priority with the securities offered to a junior class. Under current law, seniors are entitled to compensation for their loss of priority, and the increased risk put upon them by being required to give up their priority will be reflected in a lower value of the securities given to them than the value of comparable securities given to juniors that have not lost a priority position.

Finally, the proponent must request use of this subsection. The court may not confirm notwithstanding nonacceptance unless the proponent requests and the court may then confirm only if subsection (b) is complied with. The court may not rewrite the plan.

A more detailed explanation follows:

The test to be applied by the court is set forth in the various paragraphs of section 1129(b). The elements of the test are new [,] departing from both the absolute priority rule and the best interests of creditors tests found under the Bankruptcy Act [former Title 11]. The court is not permitted to alter the terms of the plan. It must merely decide whether the plan complies with the requirements of section 1129(b). If so, the plan is confirmed, if not the plan is denied confirmation.

The procedure followed is simple. The court examines each class of claims or interests designated under section 1123(a)(1) to see if the requirements of section 1129(b) are met. If the class is a class of secured claims, then paragraph (1) contains two tests that must be complied with in order for confirmation to occur. First, under subparagraph (A), the court must be able to find that the consideration given under the plan on account of the secured claim does not exceed the allowed amount of the claim. This condition is not prescribed as a matter of law under section 1129(a), because if the secured claim is compensated in securities of the debtor, a valuation of the business would be necessary to determine the value of the consideration. While section 1129(a) does not contemplate a valuation of the debtor's business, such a valuation will almost always be required under section 1129(b) in order to determine the value of the consideration to be distributed under the plan. Once the valuation is performed, it becomes a simple matter to impose the criterion that no claim will be paid more than in full.

Application of the test under subparagraph (A) also requires a valuation of the consideration "as of the effective date of the plan". This contemplates a present value analysis that will discount value to be received in the future; of course, if the interest rate paid is equivalent to the discount rate used, the present value and face future value will be identical. On the other hand, if no interest is proposed to be paid, the present value will be less than the face future value. For example, consider an allowed secured claim of $1,000 in a class by itself. One plan could propose to pay $1,000 on account of this claim as of the effective date of the plan. Another plan could propose to give a note with a $1,000 face amount due five years after the effective date of the plan on account of this claim. A third plan could propose to give a note in a face amount of $1,000 due five years from the effective date of the plan plus six percent annual interest commencing on the effective date of the plan on account of this claim. The first plan clearly meets the requirements of subparagraph (A) because the amount received on account of the second claim has an equivalent present value as of the effective date of the plan equal to the allowed amount of such claim.

The second plan also meets the requirements of subparagraph (A) because the present value of the five years note as of the effective date of the plan will never exceed the allowed amount of the secured claim; the higher the discount rate, the less present value the note will have. Whether the third plan complies with subparagraph (A) depends on whether the discount rate is less than six percent. Normally, the interest rate used in the plan will be prima facie evidence of the discount rate because the interest rate will reflect an arms length determination of the risk of the security involved and feasibility considerations will tend to understate interest payments. If the court found the discount rate to be greater than or equal to the interest rate used in the plan, then subparagraph (A) would be complied with because the value of the note as of the effective date of the plan would not exceed the allowed amount of the second claim. If, however, the court found the discount rate to be less than the interest rate proposed under the plan, then the present value of the note would exceed $1,000 and the plan would fail of confirmation. On the other hand, it is important to recognize that the future principal amount of a note in excess of the allowed amount of a secured claim may have a present value less than such allowed amount, if the interest rate under the plan is correspondingly less than the discount rate.

Even if the requirements of subparagraph (A) are complied with, the class of secured claims must satisfy one of the three clauses in paragraph (B) in order to pass muster. It is sufficient for confirmation if the class has accepted the plan, or if the claims of the class are unimpaired, or if each holder of a secured claim in the class will receive property of a value as of the effective date of the plan equal to the allowed amount of such claim (unless he has agreed to accept less). It is important to note that under section 506(a), the allowed amount of the secured claim will not include any extent to which the amount of such claim exceeds the value of the property securing such claim. Thus, instead of focusing on secured creditors or unsecured creditors, the statute focuses on secured claims and unsecured claims.

After the court has applied paragraph (1) to each class of secured claims, it then applies paragraph (2) to each class of unsecured claims. Again two separate components must be tested. Subparagraph (A) is identical with the test under section 1129(b)(1)(A) insofar as the holder of an unsecured claim is not permitted to receive property of a value as of the effective date of the plan on account of such claim that is greater than the allowed amount of such claim. In addition, subparagraph (B) requires compliance with one of four conditions. The conditions in clauses (i)–(iii) mirror the conditions of acceptance unimpairment, or full value found in connection with secured claims in section 1129(b)(1)(B).

The condition contained in section 1129(b)(2)(B)(iv) provides another basis for confirming the plan with respect to a class of unsecured claims. It will be of greatest use when an impaired class that has not accepted the plan is to receive less than full value under the plan. The plan may be confirmed under clause (iv) in those circumstances if the class is not unfairly discriminated against with respect to equal classes and if junior classes will receive nothing under the plan. The second criterion is the easier to understand. It is designed to prevent a senior class from giving up consideration to a junior class unless every intermediate class consents, is paid in full, or is unimpaired. This gives intermediate creditors a great deal of leverage in negotiating with senior or secured creditors who wish to have a plan that gives value to equity. One aspect of this test that is not obvious is that whether one class is senior, equal, or junior to another class is relative and not absolute. Thus from the perspective of trade creditors holding unsecured claims, claims of senior and subordinated debentures may be entitled to share on an equal basis with the trade claims. However, from the perspective of the senior unsecured debt, the subordinated debentures are junior.

This point illustrates the lack of precision in the first criterion which demands that a class not be unfairly discriminated against with respect to equal classes. From the perspective of unsecured trade claims, there is no unfair discrimination as long as the total consideration given all other classes of equal rank does not exceed the amount that would result from an exact aliquot distribution. Thus if trade creditors, senior debt, and subordinate debt are each owed $100 and the plan proposes to pay the trade debt $15, the senior debt $30, and the junior debt $0, the plan would not unfairly discriminate against the trade debt nor would any other allocation of consideration under the plan between the senior and junior debt be unfair as to the trade debt as long as the aggregate consideration is less than $30. The senior debt could take $25 and give up $5 to the junior debt and the trade debt would have no cause to complain because as far as it is concerned the junior debt is an equal class.

However, in this latter case the senior debt would have been unfairly discriminated against because the trade debt was being unfairly over-compensated; of course the plan would also fail unless the senior debt was unimpaired, received full value, or accepted the plan, because from its perspective a junior class received property under the plan. Application of the test from the perspective of senior debt is best illustrated by the plan that proposes to pay trade debt $15, senior debt $25, and junior debt $0. Here the senior debt is being unfairly discriminated against with respect to the equal trade debt even though the trade debt receives less than the senior debt. The discrimination arises from the fact that the senior debt is entitled to the rights of the junior debt which in this example entitle the senior debt to share on a 2:1 basis with the trade debt.

Finally, it is necessary to interpret the first criterion from the perspective of subordinated debt. The junior debt is subrogated to the rights of senior debt once the senior debt is paid in full. Thus, while the plan that pays trade debt $15, senior debt $25, and junior debt $0 is not unfairly discriminatory against the junior debt, a plan that proposes to pay trade debt $55, senior debt $100, and junior debt $1, would be unfairly discriminatory. In order to avoid discriminatory treatment against the junior debt, at least $10 would have to be received by such debt under those facts.

The criterion of unfair discrimination is not derived from the fair and equitable rule or from the best interests of creditors test. Rather it preserves just treatment of a dissenting class from the class's own perspective.

If each class of secured claims satisfies the requirements of section 1129(b)(1) and each class of unsecured claims satisfies the requirements of section 1129(b)(2), then the court must still see if each class of interests satisfies section 1129(b)(3) before the plan may be confirmed. Again, two separate criteria must be met. Under subparagraph (A) if the interest entitles the holder thereof to a fixed liquidation preference or if such interest may be redeemed at a fixed price, then the holder of such interest must not receive under the plan on account of such interest property of a value as of the effective date of the plan greater than the greater of these two values of the interest. Preferred stock would be an example of an interest likely to have liquidation preference or redemption price.

If an interest such as most common stock or the interest of a general partnership has neither a fixed liquidation preference nor a fixed redemption price, then the criterion in subparagraph (A) is automatically fulfilled. In addition subparagraph (B) contains five clauses that impose alternative conditions of which at least one must be satisfied in order to warrant confirmation. The first two clauses contain requirements of acceptance or unimpairment similar to the first two clauses in paragraphs (1)(B) and (2)(B). Clause (iii) is similar to the unimpairment test contained in section 1124(3)(B), except that it will apply to cover the issuance securities of the debtor of a value as of the effective date of the plan equal to the greater of any fixed liquidation preference or redemption price. The fourth clause allows confirmation if junior interests are not compensated under the plan and the fifth clause allows confirmation if there are no junior interests. These clauses recognized that as long as senior classes receive no more than full payment, the objection of a junior class will not defeat confirmation unless a class junior to it is receiving value under the plan and the objecting class is impaired. While a determination of impairment may be made under section 1124(3)(B)(iii) without a precise valuation of the business when common stock is clearly under water, once section 1129(b) is used, a more detailed valuation is a necessary byproduct. Thus, if no property is given to a holder of an interest under the plan, the interest should be clearly worthless in order to find unimpairment under section 1124(3)(B)(iii) and section 1129(a)(8); otherwise, since a class of interests receiving no property is deemed to object under section 1126(g), the more precise valuation of section 1129(b) should be used.

If all of the requirements of section 1129(b) are complied with, then the court may confirm the plan subject to other limitations such as those found in section 1129(a) and (d).

Subsection (c) of section 1129 governs confirmation when more than one plan meets the requirements of the section. The court must consider the preferences of creditors and equity security holders in determining which plan to confirm.

Subsection (d) requires the court to deny confirmation if the principal purpose of the plan is the avoidance of taxes (through use of sections 346 and 1146, and applicable provisions of State law or the Internal Revenue Code [Title 26] governing bankruptcy reorganizations) or the avoidance of section 5 of the Securities Act of 1933 [section 77e of Title 15, Commerce and Trade] (through use of section 1145). House Report No. 95–595.

1984 Acts. Statements by Legislative Leaders, see 1984 U.S.Code Cong. and Adm.News, p. 576.

1986 Acts. House Report No. 99–764 and House Conference Report No. 99–958, see 1986 U.S.Code Cong. and Adm. News, p. 5227.

1988 Acts. Senate Report No. 100–119, see 1988 U.S.Code Cong. and Adm.News, p. 683.

1994 Acts. House Report No. 103–835, see 1994 U.S. Code Cong. and Adm. News, p. 3340.

2005 Acts. House Report No. 109–31(Part I), see 2005 U.S. Code Cong. and Adm. News, p. 88.

Legislative Statements

Section 1129 of the House amendment relates to confirmation of a plan in a case under chapter 11. Section 1129(a)(3) of the House amendment adopts the position taken in the Senate amendment and section 1129(a)(5) takes the position adopted in the House bill. Section 1129(a)(7) adopts the position taken in the House bill in order to insure that the dissenting members of an accepting class will receive at least what they would otherwise receive under the best interest of creditors test; it also requires that even the members of a class that has rejected the plan be protected by the best interest of creditors test for those rare cramdown cases where a class of creditors would receive more on liquidation than under reorganization of the debtor. Section 1129(a)(7)(C) is discussed in connection with section 1129(b) and section 1111(b). Section 1129(a)(8) of the House amendment adopts the provision taken in the House bill which permits confirmation of a plan as to a particular class without resort to the fair and equitable test if the class has accepted a plan or is unimpaired under the plan.

Section 1129(a)(9) represents a compromise between a similar provision contained in the House bill and the Senate amendment. Under subparagraph (A) claims entitled to priority under section 507(a)(1) or (2) are entitled to receive cash on the effective date of the plan equal to the amount of the claim. Under subparagraph (B) claims entitled to priority under section 507(a)(3), (4), or (5), are entitled to receive deferred cash payments of a present value as of the effective date of the plan equal to the amount of the claims if the class has accepted the plan or cash payments on the effective date of the plan otherwise. Tax claims entitled to priority under section 507(a)(6) of different governmental units may not be contained in one class although all claims of one such unit may be combined and such unit may be required to take deferred cash payments over a period not to exceed 6 years after the date of assessment of the tax with the present value equal to the amount of the claim.

Section 1129(a)(10) is derived from section 1130(a)(12) of the Senate amendment.

Section 1129(b) is new. Together with section 1111(b) and section 1129(a)(7)(C), this section provides when a plan may be confirmed, notwithstanding the failure of an impaired class to accept the plan under section 1129(a)(8). Before discussing section 1129(b) an understanding of section 1111(b) is necessary. Section 1111(b)(1), the general rule that a secured claim is to be treated as a recourse claim in chapter 11 whether or not the claim is nonrecourse by agreement or applicable law. This preferred status for a nonrecourse loan terminates if the property securing the loan is sold under section 363 or is to be sold under the plan.

The preferred status also terminates if the class of which the secured claim is a part elects application of section

1111(b)(2). Section 1111(b)(2) provides that an allowed claim is a secured claim to the full extent the claim is allowed rather than to the extent of the collateral as under section 506(a). A class may elect application of paragraph (2) only if the security is not of inconsequential value and, if the creditor is a recourse creditor, the collateral is not sold under section 363 or to be sold under the plan. Sale of property under section 363 or under the plan is excluded from treatment under section 1111(b) because of the secured party's right to bid in the full amount of his allowed claim at any sale of collateral under section 363(k) of the House amendment.

As previously noted, section 1129(b) sets forth a standard by which a plan may be confirmed notwithstanding the failure of an impaired class to accept the plan.

Paragraph (1) makes clear that this alternative confirmation standard, referred to as "cram down," will be called into play only on the request of the proponent of the plan. Under this cramdown test, the court must confirm the plan if the plan does not discriminate unfairly, and is "fair and equitable," with respect to each class of claims or interests that is impaired under, and has not accepted, the plan. The requirement of the House bill that a plan not "discriminate unfairly" with respect to a class is included for clarity; the language in the House report interpreting that requirement, in the context of subordinated debentures, applies equally under the requirements of section 1129(b)(1) of the House amendment.

Although many of the factors interpreting "fair and equitable" are specified in paragraph (2), others, which were explicated in the description of section 1129(b) in the House report, were omitted from the House amendment to avoid statutory complexity and because they would undoubtedly be found by a court to be fundamental to "fair and equitable" treatment of a dissenting class. For example, a dissenting class should be assured that no senior class receives more than 100 percent of the amount of its claims. While that requirement was explicitly included in the House bill, the deletion is intended to be one of style and not one of substance.

Paragraph (2) provides guidelines for a court to determine whether a plan is fair and equitable with respect to a dissenting class. It must be emphasized that the fair and equitable requirement applies only with respect to dissenting classes. Therefore, unlike the fair and equitable rule contained in chapter X [former chapter 10 (section 501 et seq.) of former Title 11] and section 77 of the Bankruptcy Act [section 205 of former Title 11] under section 1129(b)(2), senior accepting classes are permitted to give up value to junior classes as long as no dissenting intervening class receives less than the amount of its claims in full. If there is no dissenting intervening class and the only dissent is from a class junior to the class to which value have [sic] been given up, then the plan may still be fair and equitable with respect to the dissenting class, as long as no class senior to the dissenting class has received more than 100 percent of the amount of its claims.

Paragraph (2) contains three subparagraphs, each of which applies to a particular kind of class of claims or interests that is impaired and has not accepted the plan. Subparagraph (A) applies when a class of secured claims is impaired and has not accepted the plan. The provision applies whether or not section 1111(b) applies. The plan may be crammed down notwithstanding the dissent of a secured class only if the plan complies with clause (i), (ii), or (iii).

Clause (i) permits cramdown if the dissenting class of secured claims will retain its lien on the property whether the property is retained by the debtor or transferred. It should be noted that the lien secures the allowed secured claim held by such holder. The meaning of "allowed secured claim" will vary depending on whether section 1111(b)(2) applies to such class.

If section 1111(b)(2) applies then the "electing" class is entitled to have the entire allowed amount of the debt related to such property secured by a lien even if the value of the collateral is less than the amount of the debt. In addition, the plan must provide for the holder to receive, on account of the allowed secured claims, payments, either present or deferred, of a principal face amount equal to the amount of the debt and of a present value equal to the value of the collateral.

For example, if a creditor loaned $15,000,000 to a debtor secured by real property worth $18,000,000 and the value of the real property had dropped to $12,000,000 by the date when the debtor commenced a proceeding under chapter 11, the plan could be confirmed notwithstanding the dissent of the creditor as long as the lien remains on the collateral to secure a $15,000,000 debt, the face amount of present or extended payments to be made to the creditor under the plan is at least $15,000,000, and the present value of the present or deferred payments is not less than $12,000,000. The House report accompanying the House bill described what is meant by "present value".

Clause (ii) is self explanatory. Clause (iii) requires the court to confirm the plan notwithstanding the dissent of the electing secured class if the plan provides for the realization by the secured class of the indubitable equivalents of the secured claims. The standard of "indubitable equivalents" is taken from *In re Murel Holding Corp.*, 75 F.2d 941 (2d Cir. 1935) (Learned Hand, Jr.).

Abandonment of the collateral to the creditor would clearly satisfy indubitable equivalence, as would a lien on similar collateral. However, present cash payments less than the secured claim would not satisfy the standard because the creditor is deprived of an opportunity to gain from a future increase in value of the collateral. Unsecured notes as to the secured claim or equity securities of the debtor would not be the indubitable equivalent. With respect to an oversecured creditor, the secured claim will never exceed the allowed claim.

Although the same language applies, a different result pertains with respect to a class of secured claims to which section 1111(b)(2) does not apply. This will apply to all claims secured by a right of setoff. The court must confirm the plan notwithstanding the dissent of such a class of secured claims if any of three alternative requirements is met. Under clause (i) the plan may be confirmed if the class retains a right of setoff or a lien securing the allowed secured claims of the class and the holders will receive payments of a present value equal to the allowed amount of their secured claims. Contrary to electing classes of secured creditors who retain a lien under subparagraph (A)(i)(I) to the extent of the entire claims secured by such lien, nonelecting creditors retain a lien on collateral only to the extent of their allowed secured claims and not to the extent of any deficiency, and such secured creditors must receive present or deferred payments with a present value equal to the allowed secured claim, which in turn is only the equivalent of the value of the collateral under section 506(a).

Any deficiency claim of a nonelecting class of secured claims is treated as an unsecured claim and is not provided for under subparagraph (A). The plan may be confirmed

under clause (ii) if the plan proposes to sell the property free and clear of the secured party's lien as long as the lien will attach to the proceeds and will receive treatment under clause (i) or (iii). Clause (iii) permits confirmation if the plan provides for the realization by the dissenting nonelecting class of secured claims of the indubitable equivalent of the secured claims of such class.

Contrary to an "electing" class to which section 1111(b)(2) applies, the nonelecting class need not be protected with respect to any future appreciation in value of the collateral since the secured claim of such a class is never undersecured by reason of section 506(a). Thus the lien secures only the value of interest of such creditor in the collateral. To the extent deferred payments exceed that amount, they represent interest. In the event of a subsequent default, the portion of the face amount of deferred payments representing unaccrued interest will not be secured by the lien.

Subparagraph (B) applies to a dissenting class of unsecured claims. The court must confirm the plan notwithstanding the dissent of a class of impaired unsecured claims if the plan provides for such claims to receive property with a present value equal to the allowed amount of the claims. Unsecured claims may receive any kind of "property," which is used in its broadest sense, as long as the present value of the property given to the holders of unsecured claims is equal to the allowed amount of the claims. Some kinds of property, such as securities, may require difficult valuations by the court; in such circumstances the court need only determine that there is a reasonable likelihood that the property given the dissenting class of impaired unsecured claims equals the present value of such allowed claims.

Alternatively, under clause (ii), the court must confirm the plan if the plan provides that holders of any claims or interests junior to the interests of the dissenting class of impaired unsecured claims will not receive any property under the plan on account of such junior claims or interests. As long as senior creditors have not been paid more than in full, and classes of equal claims are being treated so that the dissenting class of impaired unsecured claims is not being discriminated against unfairly, the plan may be confirmed if the impaired class of unsecured claims receives less than 100 cents on the dollar (or nothing at all) as long as no class junior to the dissenting class receives anything at all. Such an impaired dissenting class may not prevent confirmation of a plan by objection merely because a senior class has elected to give up value to a junior class that is higher in priority than the impaired dissenting class of unsecured claims as long as the above safeguards are met.

Subparagraph (C) applies to a dissenting class of impaired interests. Such interests may include the interests of general or limited partners in a partnership, the interests of a sole proprietor in a proprietorship, or the interest of common or preferred stockholders in a corporation. If the holders of such interests are entitled to a fixed liquidation preference or fixed redemption price on account of such interests then the plan may be confirmed notwithstanding the dissent of such class of interests as long as it provides the holders property of a present value equal to the greatest of the fixed redemption price, or the value of such interests. In the event there is no fixed liquidation preference or redemption price, then the plan may be confirmed as long as it provides the holders of such interests property of a present value equal to the value of such interests. If the interests are "under water" then they will be valueless and the plan may be confirmed notwithstanding the dissent of that class of interests even if the plan provides that the holders of such interests will not receive any property on account of such interests.

Alternatively, under clause (ii), the court must confirm the plan notwithstanding the dissent of a class of interests if the plan provides that holders of any interests junior to the dissenting class of interests will not receive or retain any property on account of such junior interests. Clearly, if there are no junior interests junior to the class of dissenting interests, then the condition of clause (ii) is satisfied. The safeguards that no claim or interest receive more than 100 percent of the allowed amount of such claim or interest and that no class be discriminated against unfairly will insure that the plan is fair and equitable with respect to the dissenting class of interests.

Except to the extent of the treatment of secured claims under subparagraph (A) of this statement, the House report remains an accurate description of confirmation of section 1129(b). Contrary to the example contained in the Senate report, a senior class will not be able to give up value to a junior class over the dissent of an intervening class unless the intervening class receives the full amount, as opposed to value, of its claims or interests.

One last point deserves explanation with respect to the admittedly complex subject of confirmation. Section 1129(a)(7)(C) in effect exempts secured creditors making an election under section 1111(b)(2) from application of the best interest of creditors test. In the absence of an election the amount such creditors receive in a plan of liquidation would be the value of their collateral plus any amount recovered on the deficiency in the case of a recourse loan. However, under section 1111(b)(2), the creditors are given an allowed secured claim to the full extent the claim is allowed and have no unsecured deficiency. Since section 1129(b)(2)(A) makes clear that an electing class need receive payments of a present value only equal to the value of the collateral, it is conceivable that under such a "cram down" the electing creditors would receive nothing with respect to their deficiency. The advantage to the electing creditors is that they have a lien securing the full amount of the allowed claim so that if the value of the collateral increases after the case is closed, the deferred payments will be secured claims. Thus it is both reasonable and necessary to exempt such electing class from application of section 1129(a)(7) as a logical consequence of permitting election under section 1111(b)(2).

Section 1131 of the Senate amendment is deleted as unnecessary in light of the protection given a secured creditor under section 1129(b) of the House amendment.

Payment of taxes in reorganizations: Under the provisions of section 1141 as revised by the House amendment, an individual in reorganization under chapter 11 will not be discharged from any debt, including prepetition tax liabilities, which are nondischargeable under section 523. Thus, an individual debtor whose plan of reorganization is confirmed under chapter 11 will remain liable for prepetition priority taxes, as defined in section 507, and for tax liabilities which receive no priority but are nondischargeable under section 523, including no return, late return, and fraud liabilities.

In the case of a partnership or a corporation in reorganization under chapter 11 of title 11, section 1141(d)(1) of the House amendment adopts a provision limiting the taxes that must be provided for in a plan before a plan can be confirmed to taxes which receive priority under section 507. In addition, the House amendment makes dischargeable, in effect, tax

liabilities attributable to no return, late return, or fraud situations. The amendment thus does not adopt a shareholder continuity test such as was contained in section 1141(d)(2)(A)(iii) of the Senate amendment. However, the House amendment amends section 1106, relating to duties of the trustee, to require the trustee to furnish, on request of a tax authority and without personal liability, information available to the trustee concerning potential prepetition tax liabilities for unfiled returns of the debtor. Depending on the condition of the debtor's books and records, this information may include schedules and files available to the business. The House amendment also does not prohibit a tax authority from disallowing any tax benefit claimed after the reorganization if the item originated in a deduction, credit, or other item improperly reported before the reorganization occurred. It may also be appropriate for the Congress to consider in the future imposing civil or criminal liability on corporate officers for preparing a false or fraudulent tax return. The House amendment also contemplates that the Internal Revenue Service will monitor the relief from liabilities under this provision and advise the Congress if, and to the extent, any significant tax abuse may be resulting from the provision.

Medium of payment of taxes: Federal, State, and local taxes incurred during the administration period of the estate, and during the "gap" period in an involuntary case, are to be paid solely in cash. Taxes relating to third priority wages are to be paid, under the general rules, in cash on the effective date of the plan, if the class has not accepted the plan, in an amount equal to the allowed amount of the claim. If the class has accepted the plan, the taxes must be paid in cash but the payments must be made at the time the wages are paid which may be paid in deferred periodic installments having a value, on the effective date of the plan, equal to the allowed amount of the tax claims. Prepetition taxes entitled to sixth priority under section 507(a)(6) also must be paid in cash, but the plan may also permit the debtor whether a corporation, partnership, or an individual, to pay the allowed taxes in installments over a period not to exceed 6 years following the date on which the tax authority assesses the tax liability, provided the value of the deferred payments representing principal and interest, as of the effective date of the plan, equals the allowed amount of the tax claim.

The House amendment also modifies the provisions of both bills dealing with the time when tax liabilities of a debtor in reorganization may be assessed by the tax authority. The House amendment follows the Senate amendment in deleting the limitation in present law under which a priority tax assessed after a reorganization plan is confirmed must be assessed within 1 year after the date of the filing of the petition. The House amendment specifies broadly that after the bankruptcy court determines the liability of the estate for a prepetition tax or for an administration period tax, the governmental unit may thereafter assess the tax against the estate, debtor, or successor to the debtor. The party to be assessed will, of course, depend on whether the case is under chapter 7, 11, or 13, whether the debtor is an individual, partnership, or a corporation, and whether the court is determining an individual debtor's personal liability for a nondischargeable tax. Assessment of the tax may only be made, however, within the limits of otherwise applicable law, such as the statute of limitations under the tax law.

Tax avoidance purpose: The House bill provided that no reorganization plan may be approved if the principal purpose of the plan is the avoidance of taxes. The Senate amendment modified the rule so that the bankruptcy court need make a determination of tax avoidance purpose only if it is asked to do so by the appropriate tax authority. Under the Senate amendment, if the tax authority does not request the bankruptcy court to rule on the purpose of the plan, the tax authority would not be barred from later asserting a tax avoidance motive with respect to allowance of a deduction or other tax benefit claimed after the reorganization. The House amendment adopts the substance of the Senate amendment, but does not provide a basis by which a tax authority may collaterally attack confirmation of a plan of reorganization other than under section 1144.

References in Text

Section 5 of the Securities Act of 1933, referred to in subsec. (d), is section 5 of Act May 27, 1933, c. 38, Title I, 48 Stat. 77, which is classified to section 77e of Title 15, Commerce and Trade.

Effective and Applicability Provisions

2005 Acts. Amendments to this section by Pub.L. 109–8, § 1221, applicable to case pending under this title on Apr. 20, 2005, or filed under this title on or after that date, except that the court shall not confirm a plan under chapter 11 of this title without considering whether this section would substantially affect the rights of a party in interest who first acquired rights with respect to the debtor after the date of the filing of the petition, see Pub.L. 109–8, § 1221(d), set out as a note under 11 U.S.C.A. § 363.

Amendments by Pub.L. 109–8 effective, except as otherwise provided, 180 days after April 20, 2005, and inapplicable with respect to cases commenced under Title 11 before the effective date, see Pub.L. 109–8, § 1501, set out as a note under 11 U.S.C.A. § 101.

1994 Acts. Amendments by Pub.L. 103–394 effective on Oct. 22, 1994, and not to apply with respect to cases commenced under Title 11 of the United States Code before Oct. 22, 1994, see section 702 of Pub.L. 103–394, set out as a note under section 101 of this title.

1988 Acts. Amendment by Pub.L. 100–334 effective on June 16, 1988, but not applicable to cases commenced under this title before that date, see section 4 of Pub.L. 100–334, set out as an Effective Date note under section 1114 of this title.

1986 Acts. Amendment by Pub.L. 99–554 effective 30 days after Oct. 27, 1986, except as otherwise provided for, see section 302(a) of Pub.L. 99–554, set out as a note under section 581 of Title 28, Judiciary and Judicial Procedure.

Amendment by Pub.L. 99–554, § 225, not to become effective in or with respect to certain specified judicial districts until, or apply to cases while pending in such district before, the expiration of the 270–day period beginning 30 days after Oct. 27, 1986, or of the 30–day period beginning on the date the Attorney General certifies under section 303 of Pub.L. 99–554 the region specified in a paragraph of section 581(a) of Title 28, as amended by section 111(a) of Pub.L. 99–554, that includes such district, whichever occurs first, see section 302(d)(1) of Pub.L. 99–554, set out as a note under section 581 of Title 28.

Amendment by Pub.L. 99–554, § 225, not to become effective in or with respect to certain specified judicial districts until, or apply to cases while pending in such district before, the expiration of the 2–year period beginning 30 days after Oct. 27, 1986, or of the 30–day period beginning on the date the Attorney General certifies under section 303 of Pub.L.

99–554 the region specified in a paragraph of section 581(a) of Title 28, as amended by section 111(a) of Pub.L. 99–554, that includes such district, whichever occurs first, see section 302(d)(2) of Pub.L. 99–554, set out as a note under section 581 of Title 28.

Amendment by Pub.L. 99–554, § 225, not to become effective in or with respect to judicial districts established for the States of Alabama and North Carolina until, or apply to cases while pending in such district before, such district elects to be included in a bankruptcy region established in section 581(a) of Title 28, as amended by section 111(a) of Pub.L. 99–554, or Oct. 1, 2002, whichever occurs first, and, except as otherwise provided for, with respect to cases under chapters 7, 11, 12, and 13 of Title 11 commenced before 30 days after Oct. 27, 1986, and pending in a judicial district in the States of Alabama or North Carolina before any election made under section 302(d)(3)(A) of Pub.L. 99–554 by such district becomes effective or Oct. 1, 2002, whichever occurs first, amendments by Pub.L. 99–554 not to apply until Oct. 1, 2003, or the expiration of the 1–year period beginning on the date such election becomes effective, whichever occurs first, and further, in any judicial district in Alabama or North Carolina not making the election described in section 302(d)(3)(A) of Pub.L. 99–554, any person appointed under regulations issued by the Judicial Conference to administer estates in cases under Title 11 authorized to establish, etc., a panel of private trustees, and to supervise cases and trustees in cases under chapters 7, 11, 12, and 13 of Title 11, until amendments by sections 201 to 231 of Pub.L. 99–554 effective in such district, see section 302(d)(3)(A) to (F), (H), (I) of Pub.L. 99–554, set out as a note under section 581 of Title 28.

Amendment by Pub.L. 99–554, § 225, except as otherwise provided, with respect to cases under chapters 7, 11, 12, and 13 of Title 11 commenced before 30 days after Oct. 27, 1986, and pending in a judicial district referred to in section 581(a) of Title 28, as amended by section 111(a) of Pub.L. 99–554, for which a United States trustee is not authorized before 30 days after Oct. 27, 1986 to be appointed, not applicable until the expiration of the 3–year period beginning on Oct. 27, 1986, or of the 1–year period beginning on the date the Attorney General certifies under section 303 of Pub.L. 99–554 the region specified in a paragraph of such section 581(a) that includes, such district, whichever occurs first, see section 302(e)(1), (2) of Pub.L. 99–554, set out as a note under section 581 of Title 28.

1984 Acts. Amendment by Pub.L. 98–353 effective with respect to cases filed 90 days after July 10, 1984, see section 552(a), formerly 553(a), of Pub.L. 98–353, set out as a note under section 101 of this title.

Separability of Provisions

If any provision of or amendment made by Pub.L. 103–394 or the application of such provision or amendment to any person or circumstance is held to be unconstitutional, the remaining provisions of and amendments made by Pub.L. 103–394 and the application of such provisions and amendments to any person or circumstance shall not be affected thereby, see section 701 of Pub.L. 103–394, set out as a note under section 101 of this title.

CROSS REFERENCES

Applicability of subsecs. (a)(2), (3), (6), (8), (10) and (b)(1), (2)(A), (2)(B) of this section in Chapter nine cases, see 11 USCA § 901.

Confirmation of plan in,

Chapter nine cases, see 11 USCA § 943.

Chapter thirteen cases, see 11 USCA § 1325.

Chapter twelve cases, see 11 USCA § 1225.

Railroad reorganization cases, see 11 USCA § 1173.

Denial of confirmation of plan as cause for conversion or dismissal, see 11 USCA § 1112.

Effect of confirmation in cases under this chapter, see 11 USCA § 1141.

Inapplicability of subsecs. (a)(7) and (c) of this section in railroad reorganization cases, see 11 USCA § 1161.

Payment of insurance benefits to retired employees, see 11 USCA § 1114.

Revocation of order of confirmation in cases under this chapter, see 11 USCA § 1144.

Special tax provisions for certain dispositions of securities or instruments under confirmed plan, see 11 USCA § 1146.

Supplemental injunctions and plan fair and equitable, see 11 USCA § 524.

Unclaimed property, see 11 USCA § 347.

SUBCHAPTER III—POSTCONFIRMATION MATTERS

CROSS REFERENCES

Subchapter applicable only in case under this chapter except as provided in § 901 of this title, see 11 USCA § 103.

§ 1141.   Effect of confirmation

(a) Except as provided in subsections (d)(2) and (d)(3) of this section, the provisions of a confirmed plan bind the debtor, any entity issuing securities under the plan, any entity acquiring property under the plan, and any creditor, equity security holder, or general partner in the debtor, whether or not the claim or interest of such creditor, equity security holder, or general partner is impaired under the plan and whether or not such creditor, equity security holder, or general partner has accepted the plan.

(b) Except as otherwise provided in the plan or the order confirming the plan, the confirmation of a plan vests all of the property of the estate in the debtor.

(c) Except as provided in subsections (d)(2) and (d)(3) of this section and except as otherwise provided in the plan or in the order confirming the plan, after confirmation of a plan, the property dealt with by the plan is free and clear of all claims and interests of creditors, equity security holders, and of general partners in the debtor.

(d)(1) Except as otherwise provided in this subsection, in the plan, or in the order confirming the plan, the confirmation of a plan—

(A) discharges the debtor from any debt that arose before the date of such confirmation, and any debt of a kind specified in section 502(g), 502(h), or 502(i) of this title, whether or not—

(i) a proof of the claim based on such debt is filed or deemed filed under section 501 of this title;

(ii) such claim is allowed under section 502 of this title; or

(iii) the holder of such claim has accepted the plan; and

(B) terminates all rights and interests of equity security holders and general partners provided for by the plan.

(2) A discharge under this chapter does not discharge a debtor who is an individual from any debt excepted from discharge under section 523 of this title.

(3) The confirmation of a plan does not discharge a debtor if—

(A) the plan provides for the liquidation of all or substantially all of the property of the estate;

(B) the debtor does not engage in business after consummation of the plan; and

(C) the debtor would be denied a discharge under section 727(a) of this title if the case were a case under chapter 7 of this title.

(4) The court may approve a written waiver of discharge executed by the debtor after the order for relief under this chapter.

(5) In a case in which the debtor is an individual—

(A) unless after notice and a hearing the court orders otherwise for cause, confirmation of the plan does not discharge any debt provided for in the plan until the court grants a discharge on completion of all payments under the plan;

(B) at any time after the confirmation of the plan, and after notice and a hearing, the court may grant a discharge to the debtor who has not completed payments under the plan if—

(i) the value, as of the effective date of the plan, of property actually distributed under the plan on account of each allowed unsecured claim is not less than the amount that would have been paid on such claim if the estate of the debtor had been liquidated under chapter 7 on such date;

(ii) modification of the plan under section 1127 is not practicable; and

(iii) subparagraph (C) permits the court to grant a discharge; and

(C) the court may grant a discharge if, after notice and a hearing held not more than 10 days before the date of the entry of the order granting the discharge, the court finds that there is no reasonable cause to believe that—

(i) section 522(q)(1) may be applicable to the debtor; and

(ii) there is pending any proceeding in which the debtor may be found guilty of a felony of the kind described in section 522(q)(1)(A) or liable for a debt of the kind described in section 522(q)(1)(B);

and if the requirements of subparagraph (A) or (B) are met.

(6) Notwithstanding paragraph (1), the confirmation of a plan does not discharge a debtor that is a corporation from any debt—

(A) of a kind specified in paragraph (2)(A) or (2)(B) of section 523(a) that is owed to a domestic governmental unit, or owed to a person as the result of an action filed under subchapter III of chapter 37 of title 31 or any similar State statute; or

(B) for a tax or customs duty with respect to which the debtor—

(i) made a fraudulent return; or

(ii) willfully attempted in any manner to evade or to defeat such tax or such customs duty.

(Pub.L. 95–598, Nov. 6, 1978, 92 Stat. 2638; Pub.L. 98–353, Title III, § 513, July 10, 1984, 98 Stat. 387; Pub.L. 109–8, Title III, §§ 321(d), 330(b), Title VII, § 708, Apr. 20, 2005, 119 Stat. 95, 101, 126; Pub.L. 111–327, § 2(a)(36), Dec. 22, 2010, 124 Stat. 3561.)

HISTORICAL AND STATUTORY NOTES

Revision Notes and Legislative Reports

1978 Acts. Subsection (a) of this section makes the provisions of a confirmed plan binding on the debtor, any entity issuing securities under the plan, any entity acquiring property under the plan, and any creditor, equity security holder, or general partner in the debtor, whether or not the claim or interest of the creditor, equity security holder, or partner is impaired under the plan and whether or not he has accepted the plan. There are two exceptions, enumerated in paragraph (2) and (3) of subsection (d).

Unless the plan or the order confirming the plan provides otherwise, the confirmation of a plan vests all of the property of the estate in the debtor and releases it from all claims and interests of creditors, equity security holders and general partners.

Subsection (d) contains the discharge for a reorganized debtor. Paragraph (1) specifies that the confirmation of a plan discharges the debtor from any debt that arose before the date of the order for relief unless the plan or the order confirming the plan provides otherwise. The discharge is effective against those claims whether or not proof of the claim is filed (or deemed filed), and whether or not the claim is allowed. The discharge also terminates all rights and interests of equity security holders and general partners provided for by the plan. The paragraph permits the plan or the order confirming the plan to provide otherwise, and excepts certain debts from the discharge as provided in paragraphs (2) and (3).

Paragraph (2) of subsection (d) makes clear what taxes remain nondischargeable in the case of a corporate debtor emerging from a reorganization under chapter 11. Nondischargeable taxes in such a reorganization are the priority taxes (under section 507) and tax payments which come due during and after the proceeding under a deferred or part-payment agreement which the debtor had entered into with the tax authority before the bankruptcy proceedings began. On the other hand, a corporation which is taken over by its creditors through a plan of reorganization will not continue to be liable for nonpriority taxes arising from the corporation's

prepetition fraud, failure to file a return, or failure to file a timely return, since the creditors who take over the reorganized company should not bear the burden of acts for which the creditors were not at fault.

Paragraph (3) specifies that the debtor is not discharged by the confirmation of a plan if the plan is a liquidating plan and if the debtor would be denied discharge in a liquidation case under section 727. Specifically, if all or substantially all of the distribution under the plan is of all or substantially all of the property of the estate or the proceeds of it, if the business, if any, of the debtor does not continue, and if the debtor would be denied a discharge under section 727 (such as if the debtor were not an individual or if he had committed an act that would lead to a denial of discharge), the chapter 11 discharge is not granted.

Paragraph (4) authorizes the court to approve a waiver of discharge by the debtor. Senate Report No. 95–989.

Paragraph (2) [of subsec. (d)] makes applicable to an individual debtor the general exceptions to discharge that are enumerated in section 523(a) of the bankruptcy code [this title]. House Report No. 95–595.

1984 Acts. Statements by Legislative Leaders, see 1984 U.S.Code Cong. and Adm.News, p. 576.

2005 Acts. House Report No. 109–31(Part I), see 2005 U.S. Code Cong. and Adm. News, p. 88.

Legislative Statements

Section 1141(d) of the House amendment is derived from a comparable provision contained in the Senate amendment. However, section 1141(d)(2) of the House amendment is derived from the House bill as preferable to the Senate amendment. It is necessary for a corporation or partnership undergoing reorganization to be able to present its creditors with a fixed list of liabilities upon which the creditors or third parties can make intelligent decisions. Retaining an exception for discharge with respect to nondischargeable taxes would leave an undesirable uncertainty surrounding reorganizations that is unacceptable. Section 1141(d)(3) is derived from the Senate amendment. Section 1141(d)(4) is likewise derived from the Senate amendment.

References in Text

Chapter 7, referred to in subsec. (d)(5)(B)(i), is chapter 7 of this title, 11 U.S.C.A. § 701 et seq.

Subchapter III of chapter 37 of title 31, referred to in subsec. (d)(6)(A), is 31 U.S.C.A. § 3721 et seq.

Codifications

Amendment by Pub.L. 109–8, § 330(b), adding a new subparagraph (C) "at the end" of subsection (d) "as amended by section 321 [of Pub.L. 109–8, which added a new paragraph (5) to subsection (d) of this section]" was executed by adding the new subparagraph to the end of paragraph (5) of subsection (d), as the probable intent of Congress.

Effective and Applicability Provisions

2005 Acts. Amendments by Pub.L. 109–8 effective 180 days after Apr. 20, 2005, with amendments by sections 321(d) and 708 of Pub.L. 109–8 not applicable with respect to cases commenced under this title before such effective date, except as otherwise provided, and amendment by section 330(b) of Pub.L. 109–8 applicable with respect to cases commenced under this title on or after Apr. 20, 2005, see Pub.L. 109–8, § 1501, set out as a note under 11 U.S.C.A. § 101.

1984 Acts. Amendment by Pub.L. 98–353 effective with respect to cases filed 90 days after July 10, 1984, see section 552(a), formerly 553(a), of Pub.L. 98–353, set out as a note under section 101 of this title.

CROSS REFERENCES

Confirmation of plan filed under this chapter, see 11 USCA § 1129.

Discharge under Chapter seven, see 11 USCA § 727.

Effect of confirmation of plans filed in,

    Chapter nine cases, see 11 USCA § 944.

    Chapter thirteen cases, see 11 USCA § 1327.

    Chapter twelve cases, see 11 USCA § 1227.

Effect of conversion, see 11 USCA § 348.

Effect of discharge, see 11 USCA § 524.

Exceptions to discharge, see 11 USCA § 523.

Failure of discharge as cause for conversion, see 11 USCA § 1112.

Nondischargeability of capital improvement loans for multi-family housing projects in proceedings under this section, see 12 USCA § 1715z–1a.

Supplemental injunctions, debtor and plan of reorganization, see 11 USCA § 524.

§ 1142.   Implementation of plan

(a) Notwithstanding any otherwise applicable non-bankruptcy law, rule, or regulation relating to financial condition, the debtor and any entity organized or to be organized for the purpose of carrying out the plan shall carry out the plan and shall comply with any orders of the court.

(b) The court may direct the debtor and any other necessary party to execute or deliver or to join in the execution or delivery of any instrument required to effect a transfer of property dealt with by a confirmed plan, and to perform any other act, including the satisfaction of any lien, that is necessary for the consummation of the plan.

(Pub.L. 95–598, Nov. 6, 1978, 92 Stat. 2639; Pub.L. 98–353, Title III, § 514(a), (c), (d), July 10, 1984, 98 Stat. 387.)

HISTORICAL AND STATUTORY NOTES

Revision Notes and Legislative Reports

1978 Acts. Senate Report No. 95–989 and House Report No. 95–595, see 1978 U.S.Code Cong. and Adm.News, p. 5787.

1984 Acts. Statements by Legislative Leaders, see 1984 U.S.Code Cong. and Adm.News, p. 576.

Effective and Applicability Provisions

1984 Acts. Amendment by Pub.L. 98–353 effective with respect to cases filed 90 days after July 10, 1984, see section 552(a), formerly 553 of Pub.L. 98–353, set out as a note under section 101 of this title.

CROSS REFERENCES

Applicability of subsec. (b) of this section in Chapter nine cases, see 11 USCA § 901.

Supplemental injunctions, debtor and plan of reorganization, see 11 USCA § 524.

§ 1143.   Distribution

If a plan requires presentment or surrender of a security or the performance of any other act as a condition to participation in distribution under the plan, such action shall be taken not later than five years after the date of the entry of the order of confirmation. Any entity that has not within such time presented or surrendered such entity's security or taken any such other action that the plan requires may not participate in distribution under the plan.

(Pub.L. 95–598, Nov. 6, 1978, 92 Stat. 2639.)

HISTORICAL AND STATUTORY NOTES

Revision Notes and Legislative Reports

1978 Acts. Section 1143 fixes a 5-year limitation on presentment or surrender of securities or the performance of any other act that is a condition to participation in distribution under the plan. The 5 years runs from the date of the entry of the order of confirmation. Any entity that does not take the appropriate action with the 5-year period is barred from participation in the distribution under the plan. Senate Report No. 95–989.

CROSS REFERENCES

Applicability of this section in Chapter nine cases, see 11 USCA § 901.

Distribution of property of estate in Chapter seven cases, see 11 USCA § 726.

Distribution of securities in stockbroker liquidation cases, see 11 USCA § 750.

Ownership of copyright, see 17 USCA § 201.

§ 1144.   Revocation of an order of confirmation

On request of a party in interest at any time before 180 days after the date of the entry of the order of confirmation, and after notice and a hearing, the court may revoke such order if and only if such order was procured by fraud. An order under this section revoking an order of confirmation shall—

    (1) contain such provisions as are necessary to protect any entity acquiring rights in good faith reliance on the order of confirmation; and

    (2) revoke the discharge of the debtor.

(Pub.L. 95–598, Nov. 6, 1978, 92 Stat. 2639; Pub.L. 98–353, Title III, § 515, July 10, 1984, 98 Stat. 387.)

HISTORICAL AND STATUTORY NOTES

Revision Notes and Legislative Reports

1978 Acts. If an order of confirmation was procured by fraud, then the court may revoke the order on request of a party in interest if the request is made before 180 days after the date of the entry of the order of confirmation. The order revoking the order of confirmation must revoke the discharge of the debtor, and contain such provisions as are necessary to protect any entity acquiring rights in good faith reliance on the order of confirmation. Senate Report No. 95–989.

1984 Acts. Statements by Legislative Leaders, see 1984 U.S.Code Cong. and Adm.News, p. 576.

Effective and Applicability Provisions

1984 Acts. Amendment by Pub.L. 98–353 effective with respect to cases filed 90 days after July 10, 1984, see section 552(a), formerly 553(a), of Pub.L. 98–353, set out as a note under section 101 of this title.

CROSS REFERENCES

Applicability of this section in Chapter nine cases, see 11 USCA § 901.

Confirmation of one plan as affected by revocation, see 11 USCA § 1129.

Revocation of confirmation order as cause for conversion or dismissal, see 11 USCA § 1112.

Revocation of order of confirmation in,

Chapter thirteen cases, see 11 USCA § 1330.

Chapter twelve cases, see 11 USCA § 1230.

Supplemental injunctions, see 11 USCA § 524.

§ 1145.   Exemption from securities laws

(a) Except with respect to an entity that is an underwriter as defined in subsection (b) of this section, section 5 of the Securities Act of 1933 and any State or local law requiring registration for offer or sale of a security or registration or licensing of an issuer of, underwriter of, or broker or dealer in, a security do not apply to—

(1) the offer or sale under a plan of a security of the debtor, of an affiliate participating in a joint plan with the debtor, or of a successor to the debtor under the plan—

(A) in exchange for a claim against, an interest in, or a claim for an administrative expense in the case concerning, the debtor or such affiliate; or

(B) principally in such exchange and partly for cash or property;

(2) the offer of a security through any warrant, option, right to subscribe, or conversion privilege that was sold in the manner specified in paragraph (1) of this subsection, or the sale of a security upon the exercise of such a warrant, option, right, or privilege;

(3) the offer or sale, other than under a plan, of a security of an issuer other than the debtor or an affiliate, if—

(A) such security was owned by the debtor on the date of the filing of the petition;

(B) the issuer of such security is—

(i) required to file reports under section 13 or 15(d) of the Securities Exchange Act of 1934; and

(ii) in compliance with the disclosure and reporting provision of such applicable section; and

(C) such offer or sale is of securities that do not exceed—

(i) during the two-year period immediately following the date of the filing of the petition, four percent of the securities of such class outstanding on such date; and

(ii) during any 180-day period following such two-year period, one percent of the securities outstanding at the beginning of such 180-day period; or

(4) a transaction by a stockbroker in a security that is executed after a transaction of a kind specified in paragraph (1) or (2) of this subsection in such security and before the expiration of 40 days after the first date on which such security was bona fide offered to the public by the issuer or by or through an underwriter, if such stockbroker provides, at the time of or before such transaction by such stockbroker, a disclosure statement approved under section 1125 of this title, and, if the court orders, information supplementing such disclosure statement.

(b)(1) Except as provided in paragraph (2) of this subsection and except with respect to ordinary trading transactions of an entity that is not an issuer, an entity is an underwriter under section 2(a)(11) of the Securities Act of 1933, if such entity—

(A) purchases a claim against, interest in, or claim for an administrative expense in the case concerning, the debtor, if such purchase is with a view to distribution of any security received or to be received in exchange for such a claim or interest;

(B) offers to sell securities offered or sold under the plan for the holders of such securities;

(C) offers to buy securities offered or sold under the plan from the holders of such securities, if such offer to buy is—

(i) with a view to distribution of such securities; and

(ii) under an agreement made in connection with the plan, with the consummation of the plan, or with the offer or sale of securities under the plan; or

(D) is an issuer, as used in such section 2(a)(11), with respect to such securities.

(2) An entity is not an underwriter under section 2(a)(11) of the Securities Act of 1933 or under paragraph (1) of this subsection with respect to an agreement that provides only for—

(A)(i) the matching or combining of fractional interests in securities offered or sold under the plan into whole interests; or

(ii) the purchase or sale of such fractional interests from or to entities receiving such fractional interests under the plan; or

(B) the purchase or sale for such entities of such fractional or whole interests as are necessary to adjust for any remaining fractional interests after such matching.

(3) An entity other than an entity of the kind specified in paragraph (1) of this subsection is not an underwriter under section 2(a)(11) of the Securities Act

of 1933 with respect to any securities offered or sold to such entity in the manner specified in subsection (a)(1) of this section.

(c) An offer or sale of securities of the kind and in the manner specified under subsection (a)(1) of this section is deemed to be a public offering.

(d) The Trust Indenture Act of 1939 does not apply to a note issued under the plan that matures not later than one year after the effective date of the plan. (Pub.L. 95–598, Nov. 6, 1978, 92 Stat. 2639; Pub.L. 98–353, Title III, § 516, July 10, 1984, 98 Stat. 387; Pub.L. 103–394, Title V, § 501(d)(33), Oct. 22, 1994, 108 Stat. 4146; Pub.L. 111–327, § 2(a)(37), Dec. 22, 2010, 124 Stat. 3561.)

HISTORICAL AND STATUTORY NOTES

Revision Notes and Legislative Reports

1978 Acts. This section, derived from similar provisions found in sections 264, 393, and 518 of the Bankruptcy Act [sections 664, 793, and 918 of former title 11], provides a limited exemption from the securities laws for securities issued under a plan of reorganization and for certain other securities. Subsection (a) exempts from the requirements of section 5 of the Securities Act of 1933 [section 77e of Title 15, Commerce and Trade] and from any State or local law requiring registration or licensing of an issuer of, underwriter of, or broker or dealer in, a security, the offer or sale of certain securities.

Paragraph (1) of subsection (a) exempts the offer or sale under section 364 of any security that is not an equity security or convertible into an equity security. This paragraph is designed to facilitate the issuance of certificates of indebtedness, and should be read in light of the amendment made in section 306 of title III to section 3(a)(7) of the 1933 act [section 77c(a)(7) of Title 15, Commerce and Trade].

Paragraph (2) of subsection (a) exempts the offer or sale of any security of the debtor, a successor to the debtor, or an affiliate in a joint plan, distributed under a plan if such security is exchanged in principal part for securities of the debtor or for allowed claims or administrative expenses. This exemption is carried over from present law, except as to administrative claims, but is limited to prevent distribution of securities to other than claim holders or equity security holders of the debtor or the estate.

Paragraph (3) of subsection (a) exempts the offer or sale of any security that arises from the exercise of a subscription right or from the exercise of a conversion privilege when such subscription right or conversion privilege was issued under a plan. This exemption is necessary in order to enhance the marketability of subscription rights or conversion privileges, including warrants, offered or sold under a plan. This is present law.

Paragraph (4) of subsection (a) exempts sales of portfolio securities, excluding securities of the debtor or its affiliate, owned by the debtor on the date of the filing of the petition. The purpose of this exemption is to allow the debtor or trustee to sell or distribute, without allowing manipulation schemes, restricted portfolio securities held or acquired by the debtor. Subparagraph (B) of section 1145(a)(4) limits the exemption to securities of a company that is required to file reports under section 13 of the Securities Act [section 78m of Title 15, Commerce and Trade] and that is in compliance with all requirements for the continuance of trading those securi-

ties. This limitation effectively prevents selling into the market "cats and dogs" of a nonreporting company. Subparagraph (C) places a limitation on the amount of restricted securities that may be distributed. During the case, the trustee may sell up to 4 percent of each class of restricted securities at any time during the first 2 years and 1 percent during any 180-day period thereafter. This relaxation of the resale rules for debtors in holding restricted securities is similar to but less extensive than the relaxation in SEC [Securities and Exchange Commission] Rule 114(c)(3)(v) for the estates of deceased holders of securities.

Paragraph (5) contains an exemption for brokers and dealers (stockbrokers, as defined in title 11) akin to the exemption provided by section 4(3)(A) of the Securities Act of 1933 [section 77d(3)(A) of Title 15, Commerce and Trade]. Instead of being required to supply a prospectus, however, the stockbroker is required to supply the approved disclosure statement, and if the court orders, information supplementing the disclosure statement. Under present law, the stockholders is not required to supply anything.

Subsection (b) is new. The subsection should be read in light of the amendment in section 306 of Title III to the 1933 act [section 77c(a)(7), (9), (10) of Title 15, Commerce and Trade]. It specifies the standards under which a creditor, equity security holder, or other entity acquiring securities under the plan may resell them. The Securities Act places limitations on sales by underwriters. This subsection defines who is an underwriter, and thus restricted, and who is free to resell. Paragraph (1) enumerates real underwriters that participate in a classical underwriting. A person is an underwriter if he purchases a claim against, interest in, or claim for an administrative expense in the case concerning, the debtor, with a view to distribution or interest. This provision covers the purchase of a certificate of indebtedness issued under proposed 11 U.S.C. 364 and purchased from the debtor, if the purchase of the certificate was with a view to distribution.

A person is also an underwriter if he offers to sell securities offered or sold under the plan for the holders of such securities, or offers to buy securities offered or sold under the plan from the holders of such securities, if the offer to buy is with a view to distribution of the securities and under an agreement made in connection with the plan, with the consummation of the plan or with the offer or sale of securities under the plan. Finally, a person is an underwriter if he is an issuer, as used in section 2(11) of the Securities Act of 1933 [section 77b(11) of Title 15, Commerce and Trade].

Paragraph (2) of subsection (b) exempts from the definition of underwriter any entity to the extent that any agreement that would bring the entity under the definition in paragraph (1) provides only for the matching combination of fractional interests in the covered securities or the purchase or sale of fractional interests. This paragraph and paragraph (1) are modeled after former rule 133 of the Securities and Exchange Commission.

Paragraph (3) specifies that if an entity is not an underwriter under the provisions of paragraph (1), as limited by paragraph (2), then the entity is not an underwriter for the purposes of the Securities Act of 1933 [section 77a et seq. of Title 15, Commerce and Trade] with respect to the covered securities, that is, those offered or sold in an exempt transaction specified in subsection (a)(2). This makes clear that the current definition of underwriter in section 2(11) of the Securities Act of 1933 [section 77b(11) of Title 15] does not apply to such a creditor. The definition in that section technically applies to any person that purchases securities with "a view to distribution." If literally applied, it would prevent any creditor in a bankruptcy case from selling securities received without filing a registration statement or finding another exemption.

Subsection (b) is a first run transaction exemption and does not exempt a creditor that, for example, some years later becomes an underwriter by reacquiring securities originally issued under a plan.

Subsection (c) makes an offer or sale of securities under the plan in an exempt transaction (as specified in subsection (a)(2)) a public offering, in order to prevent characterization of the distribution as a "private placement" which would result in restrictions, under rule 144 of the SEC [Securities and Exchange Commission] on the resale of the securities. Senate Report No. 95–989.

1984 Acts. Statements by Legislative Leaders, see 1984 U.S. Code Cong. and Adm. News, p. 576.

1994 Acts. House Report No. 103–835, see 1994 U.S. Code Cong. and Adm. News, p. 3340.

Legislative Statements

Section 1145 of the House amendment deletes a provision contained in section 1145(a)(1) of the House bill in favor of a more adequate provision contained in section 364(f) of the House amendment. In addition, section 1145(d) has been added to indicate that the Trust Indenture Act [section 77aaa et seq. of Title 15, Commerce and Trade] does not apply to a commercial note issued under a plan, if the note matures not later than 1 year after the effective date of the plan. Some commercial notes receive such an exemption under 304(a)(4) of the Trust Indenture Act of 1939 (15 U.S.C. § 77ddd(a)(4)) [section 77ddd(a)(4) of Title 15] and others may receive protection by incorporation by reference into the Trust indenture Act of securities exempt under section 3a(3), (7), (9), or (10) of the Securities Act of 1933 [section 77c(a)(3), (7), (9) and (10) of Title 15, respectively].

In light of the amendments made to the Securities Act of 1933 [section 77a et seq. of Title 15, Commerce and Trade] in title III of the House amendment to H.R. 8200, a specific exemption from the Trust Indenture Act [section 77aaa et seq. of Title 15, Commerce and Trade] is required in order to create certainty regarding plans of reorganization. Section 1145(d) is not intended to imply that commercial notes issued under a plan that matures more than 1 year after the effective date of the plan are automatically covered by the Trust Indenture Act of 1939 since such notes may fall within another exemption thereto.

One other point with respect to Section [sic] 1145 deserves comment. Section 1145(a)(3) grants a debtor in possession or trustee in chapter 11 an extremely narrow portfolio security exemption from section 5 of the Securities Act of 1933 [section 77e of Title 15, Commerce and Trade] or any comparable State law. The provision was considered by Congress and adopted after much study. The exemption is reasonable and is more restrictive than comparable provisions under the Securities Act [section 77a et seq. of Title 15, Commerce and Trade] relating to the estates of decedents. Subsequent to passage of H.R. 8200 by the House of Representatives, the Securities and Exchange Commission promulgated Rule 148 to treat with this problem under existing law. Members of Congress received opinions from attorneys indicating dissatisfaction with the Commission's rule although the rule has been amended, the ultimate limitation of 1 percent promulgated by the Commission is wholly unacceptable.

The Commission rule would permit a trustee or debtor in possession to distribute securities at the rate of 1 percent every 6 months. Section 1145(a)(3) permits the trustee to distribute 4 percent of the securities during the 2-year period immediately following the date of the filing of the petition. In addition, the security must be of a reporting company under section 13 of the Securities and Exchange Act of 1934 [section 78m of Title 15, Commerce and Trade], and must be in compliance with all applicable requirements for the continuing of trading in the security on the date that the trustee offers or sells the security.

With these safeguards the trustee or debtor in possession should be able to distribute 4 percent of the securities of a class at any time during the 2-year period immediately following the date of the filing of the petition in the interests of expediting bankruptcy administration. The same rationale that applies in expeditiously terminating decedents' estates applies no less to an estate under title 11.

References in Text

Section 5 of the Securities Act of 1933, referred to in subsec. (a), is section 5 of Act May 27, 1933, c. 38, Title I, 48 Stat. 77, which is classified to section 77e of Title 15, Commerce and Trade.

Section 13 or 15 of the Securities Exchange Act of 1934, referred to in subsec. (a)(3)(B)(i), are section 13 and 15 of Act June 6, 1934, c. 404, Title I, 48 Stat. 894, 895, which are classified to sections 78m and 78o, respectively, of Title 15.

Section 2(a)(11) of the Securities Act of 1933, referred to in subsec. (b), is subsec. (a)(11) of section 2 of Act May 27, 1933, c. 38, Title I, 48 Stat. 74, as amended, which is classified to 15 U.S.C.A. § 77b(a)(11).

The Trust Indenture Act of 1939, referred to in subsec. (d), is Title III of Act May 27, 1933, ch. 38, as added Aug. 3, 1939, ch. 411, 53 Stat. 1149, as amended, which is classified generally to subchapter III (section 77aaa et seq.) of chapter 2A of Title 15. For complete classification of this Act to the Code, see section 77aaa of Title 15 and Tables.

Effective and Applicability Provisions

1994 Acts. Amendment by Pub.L. 103–394 effective on Oct. 22, 1994, and not to apply with respect to cases commenced under Title 11 of the United States Code before Oct. 22, 1994, see section 702 of Pub.L. 103–394, set out as a note under section 101 of this title.

1984 Acts. Amendment by Pub.L. 98–353 effective with respect to cases filed 90 days after July 10, 1984, see section 552(a), formerly 553(a), of Pub.L. 98–353, set out as a note under section 101 of this title.

Separability of Provisions

If any provision of or amendment made by Pub.L. 103–394 or the application of such provision or amendment to any person or circumstance is held to be unconstitutional, the remaining provisions of and amendments made by Pub.L. 103–394 and the application of such provisions and amendments to any person or circumstance shall not be affected thereby, see section 701 of Pub.L. 103–394, set out as a note under section 101 of this title.

Applicability of term security to offers or sales under § 364 of this title to underwriters, see 11 USCA § 364.

Applicability of this section in Chapter nine cases, see 11 USCA § 901.

Protection of securities customers, see 15 USCA § 78eee.

"Racketeering activity" defined as offense involving fraud in sale of securities in case under this title, see 18 USCA § 1961.

Securities exempted from Securities Act of 1933, see 15 USCA § 77c.

§ 1146. Special tax provisions

(a) The issuance, transfer, or exchange of a security, or the making or delivery of an instrument of transfer under a plan confirmed under section 1129 of this title, may not be taxed under any law imposing a stamp tax or similar tax.

(b) The court may authorize the proponent of a plan to request a determination, limited to questions of law, by a State or local governmental unit charged with responsibility for collection or determination of a tax on or measured by income, of the tax effects, under section 346 of this title and under the law imposing such tax, of the plan. In the event of an actual controversy, the court may declare such effects after the earlier of—

(1) the date on which such governmental unit responds to the request under this subsection; or

(2) 270 days after such request.

(Pub.L. 95–598, Nov. 6, 1978, 92 Stat. 2641; Pub.L. 98–353, Title III, § 517, July 10, 1984, 98 Stat. 388; Pub.L. 109–8, Title VII, § 719(b)(3), Apr. 20, 2005, 119 Stat. 133.)

HISTORICAL AND STATUTORY NOTES

Revision Notes and Legislative Reports

1978 Acts. Section 1146 provides special tax rules applicable to Title 11 reorganizations. Subsection (a) provides that the taxable period of an individual debtor terminates on the date of the order for relief, unless the case has been converted into a reorganization from a liquidation proceeding.

Subsection (b) requires the trustee of the estate of an individual debtor in a reorganization to file a tax return for each taxable period while the case is pending after the order for relief. For corporations in chapter 11, the trustee is required to file the tax returns due while the case is pending (section 346(c)(2)).

Subsection (c) exempts from Federal, State, or local stamp taxes the issuance, transfer, or exchange of a security, or the making or delivery of an instrument of transfer under a plan. This subsection is derived from section 267 of the present Bankruptcy Act [section 667 of former Title 11].

Subsection (d) permits the court to authorize the proponent of a reorganization plan to request from the Internal Revenue Service (or State or local tax authority) an advance ruling on the tax effects of the proposed plan. If a ruling is not obtained within 270 days after the request was made, or if a ruling is obtained but the proponent of the plan disagrees with the ruling, the bankruptcy court may resolve the dispute and determine the tax effects of the proposed plan.

Subsection (e) provides that prepetition taxes which are nondischargeable in a reorganization, and all taxes arising during the administration period of the case, may be assessed and collected from the debtor or the debtor's successor in a reorganization (see sec. 505(c) of the bill). Senate Report No. 95–989.

Section 1146 of title 11 specifies five subsections which embody special tax provisions that apply in a case under chapter 11 of title 11. Subsection (a) indicates that the tax year of an individual debtor terminates on the date of the order for relief under chapter 11. Termination of the taxable year of the debtor commences the tax period of the estate. If the case was converted from chapter 7 of title 11 then the estate is created as a separate taxable entity dating from the order for relief under chapter 7. If multiple conversion of the case occurs, then the estate is treated as a separate taxable entity on the date of the order for relief under the first chapter under which the estate is a separate taxable entity.

Subsection (d) permits the court to authorize the proponent of a plan to request a taxing authority to declare the tax effects of such plan. In the event of an actual controversy, the court may declare the tax effects of the plan of reorganization at any time after the earlier of action by such taxing authority or 270 days after the request. Such a declaration, unless appealed, becomes a final judgment and binds any tax authority that was requested by the proponent to determine the tax effects of the plan. House Report No. 95–595.

1984 Acts. Statements by Legislative Leaders, see 1984 U.S.Code Cong. and Adm.News, p. 576.

2005 Acts. House Report No. 109–31(Part I), see 2005 U.S. Code Cong. and Adm. News, p. 88.

Legislative Statements

Section 1146 of the House amendment represents a compromise between the House bill and Senate amendment.

Special tax provisions: reorganization: The House bill provided rules on the effect of bankruptcy on the taxable year of the debtor and on tax return filing requirements for State and local taxes only. The House bill also exempted from State or local stamp taxes the issuance, transfer, or exchange of a security, or the making or delivery of an instrument of transfer under a plan. The House bill also authorized the bankruptcy court to declare the tax effects of a reorganization plan after the proponent of the plan had requested a ruling from State or local tax authority and either had received an unfavorable ruling or the tax authority had not issued a ruling within 270 days.

The Senate amendment deleted the rules concerning the taxable years of the debtor and tax return filing requirements since the Federal rules were to be considered in the next Congress. It broadened the rule exempting transfers of securities to include Federal stamp or similar taxes, if any. In addition, the Senate amendment deleted the provision which permitted the bankruptcy court to determine the tax effects of a plan.

The House amendment retains the State and local rules in the House bill with one modification. Under the House amendment, the power of the bankruptcy court to declare the tax effects of the plan is limited to issues of law and not to questions of fact such as the allowance of specific deductions. Thus, the bankruptcy court could declare whether the reorganization qualified for taxfree status under State or local tax rules, but it could not declare the dollar amount of any tax attributes that survive the reorganization.

Effective and Applicability Provisions

2005 Acts. Amendments by Pub.L. 109–8 effective, except as otherwise provided, 180 days after April 20, 2005, and inapplicable with respect to cases commenced under Title 11 before the effective date, see Pub.L. 109–8, § 1501, set out as a note under 11 U.S.C.A. § 101.

1984 Acts. Amendment by Pub.L. 98–353 effective with respect to cases filed 90 days after July 10, 1984, see section 552(a), formerly 553(a), of Pub.L. 98–353, set out as a note under section 101 of this title.

CROSS REFERENCES

Declaratory judgments, see 28 USCA § 2201.

Determination of,

　Number of taxable periods during which debtor may use loss carryover or carryback, see 11 USCA § 346.

　Tax liability, see 11 USCA § 505.

Effect of conversion, see 11 USCA § 348.

Special tax provisions in Chapter seven cases, see 11 USCA § 346.

SUBCHAPTER IV—RAILROAD REORGANIZATION

CROSS REFERENCES

"Carrier subject to liquidation" as meaning carrier subject to proceeding under this subchapter, see 45 USCA § 915.

Collective bargaining agreement, manner of assumption or rejection by trustee other than a trustee in a case covered by this subchapter, see 11 USCA § 1113.

Subchapter applicable only in cases under this chapter concerning railroad, see 11 USCA § 103.

Temporary operating approval granted to carrier subject to this subchapter as of January 14, 1983, see 45 USCA § 1017.

§ 1161.　Inapplicability of other sections

Sections 341, 343, 1102(a)(1), 1104, 1105, 1107, 1129(a)(7), and 1129(c) of this title do not apply in a case concerning a railroad.

(Pub.L. 95–598, Nov. 6, 1978, 92 Stat. 2641.)

HISTORICAL AND STATUTORY NOTES

Revision Notes and Legislative Reports

1978 Acts. This section makes inapplicable sections of the bill which are either inappropriate in railroad reorganizations, or relate to matters which are otherwise dealt with in subchapter IV. Senate Report No. 95–989.

CROSS REFERENCES

Applicability of Chapters one, three, and five of this title to cases under Chapters seven, eleven, or thirteen of this title except as provided in this section, see 11 USCA § 103.

§ 1162.　Definition

In this subchapter, "Board" means the "Surface Transportation Board".

(Added Pub.L. 104–88, Title III, § 302(1), Dec. 29, 1995, 109 Stat. 943.)

HISTORICAL AND STATUTORY NOTES

Revision Notes and Legislative Reports

1995 Acts. House Report No. 104–311 and House Conference Report No. 104–422, see 1995 U.S. Code Cong. and Adm. News, p. 793.

Effective and Applicability Provisions

1995 Acts. Section effective Jan. 1, 1996, see section 2 of Pub.L. 104–88, set out as a note under 49 U.S.C.A. § 1301.

§ 1163.　Appointment of trustee

As soon as practicable after the order for relief the Secretary of Transportation shall submit a list of five disinterested persons that are qualified and willing to serve as trustees in the case. The United States trustee shall appoint one of such persons to serve as trustee in the case.

(Pub.L. 95–598, Nov. 6, 1978, 92 Stat. 2641; Pub.L. 99–554, Title II, § 226, Oct. 27, 1986, 100 Stat. 3102.)

HISTORICAL AND STATUTORY NOTES

Revision Notes and Legislative Reports

1978 Acts. [Section 1166 (now section 1163)] Requires the court to appoint a trustee in every case. Since the trustee may employ whatever help he needs, multiple trusteeships are unnecessary and add to the cost of administration. The present requirement of section 77(c)(1) [section 205(c)(1) of former Title 11] that the trustee be approved by the Interstate Commerce Commission is unnecessary, since the trustee will be selected either from the panel established under section 606(f) of title 28 [section 606(f) of Title 28, Judiciary and Judicial Procedure], or someone certified by the Director of the Administrative Office of the United States Courts as qualified to become a member of that panel. Senate Report No. 95–989.

[Section 1162] This section [now section 1163] requires the appointment of an independent trustee in a railroad reorganization case. The court may appoint one or more disinterested persons to serve as trustee in the case. House Report No. 95–595.

1986 Acts. House Report No. 99–764 and House Conference Report No. 99–958, see 1986 U.S.Code Cong. and Adm. News, p. 5227.

Legislative Statements

Section 1163 of the House amendment represents a compromise between the House bill and Senate amendment with respect to the appointment of a trustee in a railroad reorganization. As soon as practicable after the order for relief, the Secretary of Transportation is required to submit a list of five disinterested persons who are qualified to serve as trustee and the court will then appoint one trustee from the list to serve as trustee in the case.

The House amendment deletes section 1163 of the Senate amendment in order to cover intrastate railroads in a case under subchapter IV of chapter 11. The bill does not confer jurisdiction on the Interstate Commerce Commission with respect to intrastate railroads.

Effective and Applicability Provisions

1986 Acts. Amendment by Pub.L. 99–554 effective 30 days after Oct. 27, 1986, except as otherwise provided for, see section 302(a) of Pub.L. 99–554, set out as a note under section 581 of Title 28, Judiciary and Judicial Procedure.

Amendment by Pub.L. 99–554, § 226, not to become effective in or with respect to certain specified judicial districts until, or apply to cases while pending in such district before, the expiration of the 270–day period beginning 30 days after Oct. 27, 1986, or of the 30–day period beginning on the date the Attorney General certifies under section 303 of Pub.L. 99–554 the region specified in a paragraph of section 581(a) of Title 28, as amended by section 111(a) of Pub.L. 99–554, that includes such district, whichever occurs first, see section 302(d)(1) of Pub.L. 99–554, set out as a note under section 581 of Title 28.

Amendment by Pub.L. 99–554, § 226, not to become effective in or with respect to certain specified judicial districts until, or apply to cases while pending in such district before, the expiration of the 2–year period beginning 30 days after Oct. 27, 1986, or of the 30–day period beginning on the date the Attorney General certifies under section 303 of Pub.L. 99–554 the region specified in a paragraph of section 581(a) of Title 28, as amended by section 111(a) of Pub.L. 99–554, that includes such district, whichever occurs first, see section 302(d)(2) of Pub.L. 99–554, set out as a note under section 581 of Title 28.

Amendment by Pub.L. 99–554, § 226, not to become effective in or with respect to judicial districts established for the States of Alabama and North Carolina until, or apply to cases while pending in such district before, such district elects to be included in a bankruptcy region established in section 581(a) of Title 28, as amended by section 111(a) of Pub.L. 99–554, or Oct. 1, 2002, whichever occurs first, and, except as otherwise provided for, with respect to cases under chapters 7, 11, 12, and 13 of Title 11 commenced before 30 days after Oct. 27, 1986, and pending in a judicial district in the States of Alabama or North Carolina before any election made under section 302(d)(3)(A) of Pub.L. 99–554 by such district becomes effective or Oct. 1, 2002, whichever occurs first, amendments by Pub.L. 99–554 not to apply until Oct. 1, 2003, or the expiration of the 1–year period beginning on the date such election becomes effective, whichever occurs first, and further, in any judicial district in Alabama or North Carolina not making the election described in section 302(d)(3)(A) of Pub.L. 99–554, any person appointed under regulations issued by the Judicial Conference to administer estates in cases under Title 11 authorized to establish, etc., a panel of private trustees, and to supervise cases and trustees in cases under chapters 7, 11, 12, and 13 of Title 11, until amendments by sections 201 to 231 of Pub.L. 99–554 effective in such district, see section 302(d)(3)(A) to (F), (H), (I) of Pub.L. 99–554, set out as a note under section 581 of Title 28.

Amendment by Pub.L. 99–554, § 226, except as otherwise provided, with respect to cases under chapters 7, 11, 12, and 13 of Title 11 commenced before 30 days after Oct. 27, 1986, and pending in a judicial district referred to in section 581(a) of Title 28, as amended by section 111(a) of Pub.L. 99–554, for which a United States trustee is not authorized before 30 days after Oct. 27, 1986 to be appointed, not applicable until the expiration of the 3–year period beginning on Oct. 27, 1986, or of the 1–year period beginning on the date the Attorney General certifies under section 303 of Pub.L. 99–554 the region specified in a paragraph of such section 581(a) that

includes, such district, whichever occurs first, see section 302(e)(1), (2) of Pub.L. 99–554, set out as a note under section 581 of Title 28.

§ 1164.   Right to be heard

The Board, the Department of Transportation, and any State or local commission having regulatory jurisdiction over the debtor may raise and may appear and be heard on any issue in a case under this chapter, but may not appeal from any judgment, order, or decree entered in the case.

(Pub.L. 95–598, Nov. 6, 1978, 92 Stat. 2641; Pub.L. 104–88, Title III, § 302(2), Dec. 29, 1995, 109 Stat. 943.)

HISTORICAL AND STATUTORY NOTES

Revision Notes and Legislative Reports

1978 Acts. [Section 1163] This section [now section 1164] gives the same right to raise, and appear and be heard on, any issue in a railroad reorganization case to the Interstate Commerce Commission, the Department of Transportation, and any State or local commission having regulatory jurisdiction over the debtor as is given to the SEC [Securities and Exchange Commission] and indenture trustees under section 1109 in ordinary reorganization cases. The right of appeal is denied the ICC [Interstate Commerce Commission], the Department of Transportation, and State and local regulatory agencies, the same as it is denied the SEC. House Report No. 95–595.

1995 Acts. House Report No. 104–311 and House Conference Report No. 104–422, see 1995 U.S. Code Cong. and Adm. News, p. 793.

Legislative Statements

Section 1164 of the Senate amendment is deleted as a matter to be left to the Rules of Bankruptcy Procedure. It is anticipated that the rules will require a petition in a railroad reorganization to be filed with the Interstate Commerce Commission and the Secretary of Transportation in a case concerning an interstate railroad.

Section 1164 of the House amendment is derived from section 1163 of the House bill. The section makes clear that the Interstate Commerce Commission, the Department of Transportation, and any State or local commission having regulatory jurisdiction over the debtor may raise and appear and be heard on any issue in a case under subchapter IV of chapter 11, but may not appeal from any judgment, order, or decree in the case. As under section 1109 of title 11, such intervening parties are not parties in interest.

Effective and Applicability Provisions

1995 Acts. Amendment by Pub.L. 104–88 effective Jan. 1, 1996, see section 2 of Pub.L. 104–88, set out as a note under 49 U.S.C.A. § 1301.

CROSS REFERENCES

Right of Commodity Futures Trading Commission to be heard, see 11 USCA § 762.

Right of Securities and Exchange Commission and party in interest to be heard in case under this chapter, see 11 USCA § 1109.

§ 1165. Protection of the public interest

In applying sections 1166, 1167, 1169, 1170, 1171, 1172, 1173, and 1174 of this title, the court and the trustee shall consider the public interest in addition to the interests of the debtor, creditors, and equity security holders.

(Pub.L. 95–598, Nov. 6, 1978, 92 Stat. 2641.)

HISTORICAL AND STATUTORY NOTES

Revision Notes and Legislative Reports

1978 Acts. Section 1165 requires the court, in consideration of the relief to be granted upon the filing of an involuntary petition, to take into account the "public interest" in the preservation of the debtor's rail service. This is an important factor in railroad reorganization, which distinguishes them from other business reorganizations. Hence, this section modifies the provisions in sections 303 and 305 that govern generally when the business of a debtor may continue to operate, when relief under the Act sought should be granted, and when the petition should be dismissed.

Section 1167 [now section 1165] imposes on the trustee the obligations, in addition to his other duties and responsibilities, to take into account the "public interest" in the preservation of the debtor's rail service. Senate Report No. 95–989.

Legislative Statements

Section 1165 of the House amendment represents a modification of sections 1165 and 1167 of the Senate amendment requiring the court and the trustee to consider the broad, general public interest in addition to the interests of the debtor, creditors, and equity security holders in applying specific sections of the subchapter.

Savings Provisions

Section to apply to cases pending under section 77 of the Bankruptcy Act [section 205 of former Title 11] on Nov. 6, 1978, in which the trustee had not filed a plan of reorganization, see section 403(b) of Pub. L. 95–598, set out as a note preceding section 101 of this title.

§ 1166. Effect of subtitle IV of title 49 and of Federal, State, or local regulations

Except with respect to abandonment under section 1170 of this title, or merger, modification of the financial structure of the debtor, or issuance or sale of securities under a plan, the trustee and the debtor are subject to the provisions of subtitle IV of title 49 that are applicable to railroads, and the trustee is subject to orders of any Federal, State, or local regulatory body to the same extent as the debtor would be if a petition commencing the case under this chapter had not been filed, but—

(1) any such order that would require the expenditure, or the incurring of an obligation for the expenditure, of money from the estate is not effective unless approved by the court; and

(2) the provisions of this chapter are subject to section 601(b) of the Regional Rail Reorganization Act of 1973.

(Pub.L. 95–598, Nov. 6, 1978, 92 Stat. 2642; Pub.L. 97–449, § 5(a)(2), Jan. 12, 1983, 96 Stat. 2442; Pub.L. 98–353, Title III, § 518, July 10, 1984, 98 Stat. 388; Pub.L. 103–394, Title V, § 501(d)(34), Oct. 22, 1994, 108 Stat. 4146.)

HISTORICAL AND STATUTORY NOTES

Revision Notes and Legislative Reports

1978 Acts. Section 1168 [now this section] makes the trustee subject to the Interstate Commerce Act [section 10101 et seq. of Title 49, Transportation] and to lawful orders of the Interstate Commerce Commission, the U.S. Department of Transportation, and State and regulatory bodies. The approval of the court is required, however, if the order requires the expenditure of money or the incurring of an expenditure other than the payment of certain interline accounts. The limitation of "lawful orders" of State commissions to those involving "safety, location of tracks, and terminal facilities," which is contained in present section 77(c)(2) [section 205(c)(2) of former Title 11], is eliminated.

Subsection (1) further provides that the debtor must pay in cash all amounts owed other carriers for current balances owed for interline freight, passenger and per diem, including incentive per diem, for periods both prior and subsequent to the filing of the petition, without the necessity of court approval.

Subsection (2) makes the provisions of the chapter subject to section 601(b) of the Regional Rail Reorganization Act [section 791(b) of Title 45, Railroads], which excludes the Interstate Commerce Commission from any participation in the reorganization of certain northeast railroads that have transferred their rail properties to Consolidated Rail Corporation (Conrail). Senate Report No. 95–989.

Section 1164 [now 1166] makes the debtor railroad subject to the provisions of the Interstate Commerce Act [section 10101 et seq. of Title 49, Transportation] that are applicable to railroads, and the trustee subject to the orders of the Interstate Commerce Commission to the same extent as the debtor would have been if the case had not been commenced. There are several exceptions. The section does not apply with respect to abandonment of rail lines, which is provided for under section 1169, or with respect to merger under a plan, modification of the financial structure of the debtor by reason of the plan, or the issuance or sale of securities under a plan. Further, the orders of the ICC [Interstate Commerce Commission] are not effective if the order would require the expenditure or the incurring of an obligation for the expenditure of money from the estate, unless approved by the court, and the provisions of this chapter are subject to section 601(b) of the Regional Rail Reorganization Act of 1973 [section 791(b) of Title 45, Railroads].

[Section 1165 (now section 1166)] The same rules apply with respect to Federal, State, or local regulations. The trustee is subject to the orders of a Federal, State, or local regulatory body to the same extent as the debtor would be if the case had not been commenced. However, any order that would require the expenditure, or the incurring of an obligation for the expenditure, of money is not effective under [until] approved by the court. House Report No. 95–595.

1983 Acts. Detailed Explanation prepared by the Office of the Law Revision Counsel, see 1982 U.S.Code Cong. and Adm.News, p. 4220.

1984 Acts. Statements by Legislative Leaders, see 1984 U.S.Code Cong. and Adm.News, p. 576.

1994 Acts. House Report No. 103–835, see 1994 U.S. Code Cong. and Adm. News, p. 3340.

Legislative Statements

Section 1166 of the House amendment is derived from sections 1164 and 1165 of the House bill. An alternative proposal contained in section 1168(1) of the Senate bill is rejected as violative of the principle or [sic] equal treatment of all creditors under title 11.

References in Text

Section 601(b) of Regional Rail Reorganization Act of 1973, referred to in par. (2), is section 601(b) of Pub.L. 93–236, Title VI, Jan. 2, 1974, 87 Stat. 1021, which is classified to section 791(b) of Title 45, Railroads.

Codifications

Pub.L. 98–353, Title III, § 518, July 10, 1984, 98 Stat. 388, substituted "subtitle IV of title 49" for "the Interstate Commerce Act (49 U.S.C. 1 et seq.)", which amendment was previously made by Pub.L. 97–449, thereby requiring no further change in text.

Effective and Applicability Provisions

1994 Acts. Amendment by Pub.L. 103–394 effective on Oct. 22, 1994, and not to apply with respect to cases commenced under Title 11 of the United States Code before Oct. 22, 1994, see section 702 of Pub.L. 103–394, set out as a note under section 101 of this title.

1984 Acts. Amendment by Pub.L. 98–353 effective with respect to cases filed 90 days after July 10, 1984, see section 552(a), formerly 553(a), of Pub.L. 98–353, set out as a note under section 101 of this title.

Separability of Provisions

If any provision of or amendment made by Pub.L. 103–394 or the application of such provision or amendment to any person or circumstance is held to be unconstitutional, the remaining provisions of and amendments made by Pub.L. 103–394 and the application of such provisions and amendments to any person or circumstance shall not be affected thereby, see section 701 of Pub.L. 103–394, set out as a note under section 101 of this title.

CROSS REFERENCES

Management and operation of property according to State law, see 28 USCA § 959.

§ 1167. Collective bargaining agreements

Notwithstanding section 365 of this title, neither the court nor the trustee may change the wages or work-ing conditions of employees of the debtor established by a collective bargaining agreement that is subject to the Railway Labor Act except in accordance with section 6 of such Act.

(Pub.L. 95–598, Nov. 6, 1978, 92 Stat. 2642; Pub.L. 103–394, Title V, § 501(d)(35), Oct. 22, 1994, 108 Stat. 4146.)

HISTORICAL AND STATUTORY NOTES

Revision Notes and Legislative Reports

1978 Acts. Section 1176 [now this section] is derived from present section 77(n) [section 205(n) of former Title 11]. . It provides that notwithstanding the general section governing the rejection of executory contracts (section 365), neither the court nor the trustee may change the wages or working conditions of employees of the debtor established by a collective bargaining agreement that is subject to the Railway Labor Act [section 151 et seq. of Title 45, Railroads], except in accordance with section 6 of that Act [section 156 of Title 45]. As reported by the subcommittee this section provided that wages and salaries of rail employees could not be affected by the trustee, but that work rules could be rejected by the trustee. The reorganization court was given the authority to review the trustee's decisions and to settle any disputes arising from the rejection. This provision was withdrawn by the full committee, and hearings will be conducted next year by the Human Resources Committee in the area of rail labor contracts and the trustee's ability to reject them in a bankruptcy situation. Senate Report No. 95–989.

Section 1167 is derived from present section 77(n) [section 205(n) of former title 11]. It provides that notwithstanding the general section governing the rejection of executory contracts (section 365), neither the court nor the trustee may change the wages or working conditions of employees of the debtor established by a collective bargaining agreement that is subject to the Railway Labor Act [section 151 et seq. of Title 45, Railroads], except in accordance with section 6 of that Act [section 156 of Title 45]. The subject of railway labor is too delicate and has too long a history for this code to upset established relationships. The balance has been struck over the years. This provision continues that balance unchanged. House Report No. 95–595.

1994 Acts. House Report No. 103–835, see 1994 U.S. Code Cong. and Adm. News, p. 3340.

References in Text

The Railway Labor Act, referred to in text, is Act May 20, 1926, c. 347, 44 Stat. 577, as amended, which is classified principally to chapter 8 (section 151 et seq.) of Title 45, Railroads. Section 6 of such Act is classified to section 156 of Title 15. For complete classification of this Act to the Code, see section 151 of Title 45 and Tables.

Effective and Applicability Provisions

1994 Acts. Amendment by Pub.L. 103–394 effective on Oct. 22, 1994, and not to apply with respect to cases commenced under Title 11 of the United States Code before Oct. 22, 1994, see section 702 of Pub.L. 103–394, set out as a note under section 101 of this title.

Savings Provisions

Section to apply to cases pending under section 77 of the Bankruptcy Act [section 205 of former Title 11] on Nov. 6, 1978, in which the trustee had not filed a plan of reorganization, see section 403(b) of Pub. L. 95–598, set out as a note preceding section 101 of this title.

Separability of Provisions

If any provision of or amendment made by Pub.L. 103–394 or the application of such provision or amendment to any person or circumstance is held to be unconstitutional, the remaining provisions of and amendments made by Pub.L. 103–394 and the application of such provisions and amendments to any person or circumstance shall not be affected thereby, see section 701 of Pub.L. 103–394, set out as a note under section 101 of this title.

CROSS REFERENCES

Authorization of trustee to operate business, see 11 USCA § 1108.

§ 1168. Rolling stock equipment

(a)(1) The right of a secured party with a security interest in or of a lessor or conditional vendor of equipment described in paragraph (2) to take possession of such equipment in compliance with an equipment security agreement, lease, or conditional sale contract, and to enforce any of its other rights or remedies under such security agreement, lease, or conditional sale contract, to sell, lease, or otherwise retain or dispose of such equipment, is not limited or otherwise affected by any other provision of this title or by any power of the court, except that right to take possession and enforce those other rights and remedies shall be subject to section 362, if—

(A) before the date that is 60 days after the date of commencement of a case under this chapter, the trustee, subject to the court's approval, agrees to perform all obligations of the debtor under such security agreement, lease, or conditional sale contract; and

(B) any default, other than a default of a kind described in section 365(b)(2), under such security agreement, lease, or conditional sale contract—

   (i) that occurs before the date of commencement of the case and is an event of default therewith is cured before the expiration of such 60–day period;

   (ii) that occurs or becomes an event of default after the date of commencement of the case and before the expiration of such 60–day period is cured before the later of—

     (I) the date that is 30 days after the date of the default or event of the default; or

     (II) the expiration of such 60–day period; and

   (iii) that occurs on or after the expiration of such 60–day period is cured in accordance with the terms of such security agreement, lease, or conditional sale contract, if cure is permitted under that agreement, lease, or conditional sale contract.

(2) The equipment described in this paragraph—

(A) is rolling stock equipment or accessories used on rolling stock equipment, including superstructures or racks, that is subject to a security interest granted by, leased to, or conditionally sold to a debtor; and

(B) includes all records and documents relating to such equipment that are required, under the terms of the security agreement, lease, or conditional sale contract, that is to be surrendered or returned by the debtor in connection with the surrender or return of such equipment.

(3) Paragraph (1) applies to a secured party, lessor, or conditional vendor acting in its own behalf or acting as trustee or otherwise in behalf of another party.

(b) The trustee and the secured party, lessor, or conditional vendor whose right to take possession is protected under subsection (a) may agree, subject to the court's approval, to extend the 60–day period specified in subsection (a)(1).

(c)(1) In any case under this chapter, the trustee shall immediately surrender and return to a secured party, lessor, or conditional vendor, described in subsection (a)(1), equipment described in subsection (a)(2), if at any time after the date of commencement of the case under this chapter such secured party, lessor, or conditional vendor is entitled pursuant to subsection (a)(1) to take possession of such equipment and makes a written demand for such possession of the trustee.

(2) At such time as the trustee is required under paragraph (1) to surrender and return equipment described in subsection (a)(2), any lease of such equipment, and any security agreement or conditional sale contract relating to such equipment, if such security agreement or conditional sale contract is an executory contract, shall be deemed rejected.

(d) With respect to equipment first placed in service on or prior to October 22, 1994, for purposes of this section—

   (1) the term "lease" includes any written agreement with respect to which the lessor and the debtor, as lessee, have expressed in the agreement or in a substantially contemporaneous writing that the agreement is to be treated as a lease for Federal income tax purposes; and

   (2) the term "security interest" means a purchase- money equipment security interest.

(e) With respect to equipment first placed in service after October 22, 1994, for purposes of this section, the term "rolling stock equipment" includes rolling stock equipment that is substantially rebuilt and accessories used on such equipment.

(Pub.L. 95–598, Nov. 6, 1978, 92 Stat. 2642; Pub.L. 98–353, Title III, § 519, July 10, 1984, 98 Stat. 388; Pub.L. 103–394, Title II, § 201(b), Oct. 22, 1994, 108 Stat. 4120; Pub.L. 106–181, Title VII, § 744(a), Apr. 5, 2000, 114 Stat. 175.)

HISTORICAL AND STATUTORY NOTES
Revision Notes and Legislative Reports

1978 Acts. Section 1175 [now this section] continues the protection accorded in present section 77(j) [section 205(j) of former Title 11] to the rights of holders of purchase-money equipment security, and of lessors or conditional vendors of railroad rolling stock, but accords to the trustee a limited period within which to assume the debtor's obligation and to cure any defaults. The rights of such lenders are not affected by the automatic stay and related provisions of sections 362 and 363, or by any power of the court, unless (1) within 60 days after the commencement of the case (or such longer period as may be agreed to by the secured party, lessor or conditional vendor) the trustees, with the approval of the court, agrees [sic] to perform all of the debtor's obligations under the security agreement, lease or conditional sale contract, and (2) all defaults are cured within the 60-day period. Defaults described in section 365(b)(2)—defaults which are breaches of provisions relating to the insolvency or financial condition of the debtor, or the commencement of a case under this title, or the appointment of a trustee—are for obvious reasons, excepted. Senate Report No. 95–989.

[Section 1166] This section, [now section 1168] derived with changes from the last sentence of present section 77(j) [section 205(j) of former Title 11], protects the interests of rolling stock equipment financers, while providing the trustee with some opportunity to cure defaults, agree to make payments, and retain and use the equipment. The provision is parallel to section 1110, concerning aircraft equipment and vessels. House Report No. 95–595.

1984 Acts. Statements by Legislative Leaders, see 1984 U.S.Code Cong. and Adm.News, p. 576.

1994 Acts. House Report No. 103–835, see 1994 U.S. Code Cong. and Adm. News, p. 3340.

2000 Acts. House Conference Report No. 106–513 and Statement by President, see 2000 U.S. Code Cong. and Adm. News, p. 80.

Legislative Statements

Section 1168 of the House amendment incorporates a provision contained in section 1166 of the House bill instead of the provision contained in section 1175 of the Senate amendment for the reasons stated in connection with the discussion of section 1110 of the House amendment.

Effective and Applicability Provisions

2000 Acts. Amendment by Pub.L. 106–181 applicable only to fiscal years beginning after September 30, 1999, see section 3 of Pub.L. 106–181, set out as a note under section 106 of this title.

1994 Acts. Amendment by Pub.L. 103–394 effective on Oct. 22, 1994, and not to apply with respect to cases commenced under Title 11 of the United States Code before Oct. 22, 1994, see section 702 of Pub.L. 103–394, set out as a note under section 101 of this title.

1984 Acts. Amendment by Pub.L. 98–353 effective with respect to cases filed 90 days after July 10, 1984, see section 552(a), formerly 553(a), of Pub.L. 98–353, set out as a note under section 101 of this title.

Savings Provisions

Section to apply to cases pending under section 77 of the Bankruptcy Act [section 205 of former Title 11] on Nov. 6, 1978, in which the trustee had not filed a plan of reorganiza-tion, see section 403(b) of Pub. L. 95–598, set out as a note preceding section 101 of this title.

Separability of Provisions

If any provision of or amendment made by Pub.L. 103–394 or the application of such provision or amendment to any person or circumstance is held to be unconstitutional, the remaining provisions of and amendments made by Pub.L. 103–394 and the application of such provisions and amendments to any person or circumstance shall not be affected thereby, see section 701 of Pub.L. 103–394, set out as a note under section 101 of this title.

CROSS REFERENCES

Rights of certain secured parties in aircraft equipment and vessels, see 11 USCA § 1110.

§ 1169. Effect of rejection of lease of railroad line

(a) Except as provided in subsection (b) of this section, if a lease of a line of railroad under which the debtor is the lessee is rejected under section 365 of this title, and if the trustee, within such time as the court fixes, and with the court's approval, elects not to operate the leased line, the lessor under such lease, after such approval, shall operate the line.

(b) If operation of such line by such lessor is impracticable or contrary to the public interest, the court, on request of such lessor, and after notice and a hearing, shall order the trustee to continue operation of such line for the account of such lessor until abandonment is ordered under section 1170 of this title, or until such operation is otherwise lawfully terminated, whichever occurs first.

(c) During any such operation, such lessor is deemed a carrier subject to the provisions of subtitle IV of title 49 that are applicable to railroads.

(Pub.L. 95–598, Nov. 6, 1978, 92 Stat. 2643; Pub.L. 97–449, § 5(a)(3), Jan. 12, 1983, 96 Stat. 2442; Pub.L. 98–353, Title III, § 520, July 10, 1984, 98 Stat. 388.)

HISTORICAL AND STATUTORY NOTES
Revision Notes and Legislative Reports

1978 Acts. Section 1177 [now this section] continues, essentially without change, the provisions relating to the rejection by the trustee of a lease of a line of railroad now contained in section 77(c)(6) [section 205(c)(6) of former Title 11]. Subsection (a) requires the lessor of a line of railroad to operate it if the lease is rejected by the trustee and the trustee, with the approval of the court, elects not to operate the leased line. Subsection (b), however, further provides that if operation by the lessor is impractical or contrary to the public interest, the court shall require the trustee to operate the line for the account of the lessor until the operation is lawfully terminated. Subsection (c) provides that during such operation, the lessor is a carrier subject to the Interstate Commerce Act [section 10101 et seq. of Title 49, Transportation]. Senate Report No. 95–989.

[Section 1168] This section [now section 1169] governs the effect of the rejection by the trustee of an unexpired lease of railroad line under which the debtor is the lessee. If the trustee rejects such a lease, and if the trustee, within such time as the court allows, and with the approval of the court, elects not to operate the leased line, then the lessor under the lease must operate the line.

Subsection (b) excuses the lessor from the requirement to operate the line under certain circumstances. If operation of the line by the lessor is impracticable or contrary to the public interest, the court, on request of the lessor, must order the trustee to continue operation of the line for the account of the lessor until abandonment is ordered under section 1169, governing abandonments generally, or until the operation is otherwise lawfully terminated, such as by an order of the ICC.

Subsection (c) deems the lessor a carrier subject to the provisions of the Interstate Commerce Act [section 10101 et seq. of Title 49, Transportation] during the operation of the line before abandonment. House Report No. 95–595.

1983 Acts. Detailed Explanation prepared by the Office of the Law Revision Counsel, see 1982 U.S.Code Cong. and Adm.News, p. 4220.

1984 Acts. Statements by Legislative Leaders, see 1984 U.S.Code Cong. and Adm.News, p. 576.

Legislative Statements

Section 1169 of the Senate amendment is deleted from the House amendment as unnecessary since 28 U.S.C. 1407 [section 1407 of Title 28, Judiciary and Judicial Procedure] treating with the judicial panel on multi-district litigation will apply by its terms to cases under title 11.

Codifications

Pub.L. 98–353, Title III, § 520, July 10, 1984, 98 Stat. 388, substituted "subtitle IV of title 49" for "the Interstate Commerce Act (49 U.S.C. 1 et seq.)", which amendment was previously made by Pub.L. 97–449, thereby requiring no further change in text.

Effective and Applicability Provisions

1984 Acts. Amendment by Pub.L. 98–353 effective with respect to cases filed 90 days after July 10, 1984, see section 552(a), formerly 553(a), of Pub.L. 98–353, set out as a note under section 101 of this title.

Savings Provisions

Section to apply to cases pending under section 77 of the Bankruptcy Act [section 205 of former Title 11] on Nov. 6, 1978, in which the trustee had not filed a plan of reorganization, see section 403(b) of Pub. L. 95–598, set out as a note preceding section 101 of this title.

CROSS REFERENCES

Executory contracts in stockbroker liquidation cases, see 11 USCA § 744.

§ 1170. Abandonment of railroad line

(a) The court, after notice and a hearing, may authorize the abandonment of all or a portion of a railroad line if such abandonment is—

    (1)(A) in the best interest of the estate; or

    (B) essential to the formulation of a plan; and

    (2) consistent with the public interest.

(b) If, except for the pendency of the case under this chapter, such abandonment would require approval by the Board under a law of the United States, the trustee shall initiate an appropriate application for such abandonment with the Board. The court may fix a time within which the Board shall report to the court on such application.

(c) After the court receives the report of the Board, or the expiration of the time fixed under subsection (b) of this section, whichever occurs first, the court may authorize such abandonment, after notice to the Board, the Secretary of Transportation, the trustee, any party in interest that has requested notice, any affected shipper or community, and any other entity prescribed by the court, and a hearing.

(d)(1) Enforcement of an order authorizing such abandonment shall be stayed until the time for taking an appeal has expired, or, if an appeal is timely taken, until such order has become final.

(2) If an order authorizing such abandonment is appealed, the court, on request of a party in interest, may authorize suspension of service on a line or a portion of a line pending the determination of such appeal, after notice to the Board, the Secretary of Transportation, the trustee, any party in interest that has requested notice, any affected shipper or community, and any other entity prescribed by the court, and a hearing. An appellant may not obtain a stay of the enforcement of an order authorizing such suspension by the giving of a supersedeas bond or otherwise, during the pendency of such appeal.

(e)(1) In authorizing any abandonment of a railroad line under this section, the court shall require the rail carrier to provide a fair arrangement at least as protective of the interests of employees as that established under section 11326(a) of title 49.

(2) Nothing in this subsection shall be deemed to affect the priorities or timing of payment of employee protection which might have existed in the absence of this subsection.

(Pub.L. 95–598, Nov. 6, 1978, 92 Stat. 2643; Pub.L. 96–448, Title II, § 227(a), Oct. 14, 1980, 94 Stat. 1931; Pub.L. 98–353, Title III, § 521, July 10, 1984, 98 Stat. 388; Pub.L. 104–88, Title III, § 302(2), Dec. 29, 1995, 109 Stat. 943; Pub.L. 109–8, Title XII, § 1217, Apr. 20, 2005, 119 Stat. 195.)

HISTORICAL AND STATUTORY NOTES

Revision Notes and Legislative Reports

1978 Acts. Subsection (a) of section 1178 [now this section] permits the court to authorize the abandonment of a railroad line if the abandonment is consistent with the public interest and either in the best interest of the estate or essential to the formulation of a plan. This avoids the normal abandonment requirements of generally applicable railroad regulatory law.

Subsection (b) permits some participation by the Interstate Commerce Commission in the abandonment process. The Commission's role, however, is only advisory. The Commission will represent the public interest, while the trustee and various creditors and equity security holders will represent the interests of those who have invested money in the enterprise. The court will balance the various interests and make an appropriate decision. The subsection specifies that if, except for the pendency of the railroad reorganization case, the proposed abandonment would require Commission approval, then the trustee, with the approval of the court, must initiate an application for the abandonment with the Commission. The court may then fix a time within which the Commission must report to the court on the application.

Subsection (c) permits the court to act after it has received the report of the Commission or the time fixed under subsection (b) has expired, whichever occurs first. The court may then authorize the abandonment after notice and a hearing. The notice must go to the Commission, the Secretary of Transportation, the trustee, and party in interest that has requested notice, any affected shipper or community, and any other entity that the court specifies.

Subsection (d) stays the enforcement of an abandonment until the time for taking an appeal has expired, or if an appeal has been taken, until the order has become final. However, the court may, and after notice and a hearing, on request of a party in interest authorize termination of service on the line or a portion of the line pending the determination of the appeal. The notice required is the same as that required under subsection (c). If the court authorizes termination of service pending determination of the appeal, an appellant may not obtain a stay of the enforcement of the order authorizing termination, either by the giving of a supersedeas bond or otherwise, during the pendency of the appeal. Senate Report No. 95–989.

1980 Acts. House Report No. 96–1035 and House Conference Report No. 96–1430, see 1980 U.S.Code Cong. and Adm.News, p. 3978.

1984 Acts. Statements by Legislative Leaders, see 1984 U.S.Code Cong. and Adm.News, p. 576.

1995 Acts. House Report No. 104–311 and House Conference Report No. 104–422, see 1995 U.S. Code Cong. and Adm. News, p. 793.

2005 Acts. House Report No. 109–31(Part I), see 2005 U.S. Code Cong. and Adm. News, p. 88.

Effective and Applicability Provisions

2005 Acts. Amendments by Pub.L. 109–8 effective, except as otherwise provided, 180 days after April 20, 2005, and inapplicable with respect to cases commenced under Title 11 before the effective date, see Pub.L. 109–8, § 1501, set out as a note under 11 U.S.C.A. § 101.

1995 Acts. Amendment by Pub.L. 104–88 effective Jan. 1, 1996, see section 2 of Pub.L. 104–88, set out as a note under 49 U.S.C.A. § 1301.

1984 Acts. Amendment by Pub.L. 98–353 effective with respect to cases filed 90 days after July 10, 1984, see section 552(a), formerly 553(a), of Pub.L. 98–353, set out as a note under section 101 of this title.

1980 Acts. Section 710 of Pub.L. 96–448 provided that:

"(a) Except as provided in subsections (b), (c), and (d) of this section, the provisions of this Act and the amendments made by this Act shall take effect on October 1, 1980.

"(b) Section 206 of this Act [enacting former section 10712 of Title 49, Transportation], shall take effect on January 1, 1981.

"(c) Section 218(b) of this Act [amending former section 10705 of Title 49] shall take effect on October 1, 1983.

"(d) Section 701 of this Act [enacting section 1018 of Title 45, Railroads and amending sections 231, 825, 906, 913, 914, 1002, 1005, 1007, and 1008 of Title 45] shall take effect on the date of enactment of this Act [Oct. 14, 1980]."

CROSS REFERENCES

Abandonment of lines of Milwaukee Railroad in cases pending under § 77 of Bankruptcy Act on November 4, 1979, see 45 USCA § 915.

Abandonment of lines of Milwaukee Railroad under this section, see 45 USCA § 904.

Abandonment of property of estate, see 11 USCA § 554.

§ 1171. Priority claims

(a) There shall be paid as an administrative expense any claim of an individual or of the personal representative of a deceased individual against the debtor or the estate, for personal injury to or death of such individual arising out of the operation of the debtor or the estate, whether such claim arose before or after the commencement of the case.

(b) Any unsecured claim against the debtor that would have been entitled to priority if a receiver in equity of the property of the debtor had been appointed by a Federal court on the date of the order for relief under this title shall be entitled to the same priority in the case under this chapter.

(Pub.L. 95–598, Nov. 6, 1978, 92 Stat. 2643; Pub.L. 98–353, Title III, § 522, July 10, 1984, 98 Stat. 388.)

HISTORICAL AND STATUTORY NOTES

Revision Notes and Legislative Reports

1978 Acts. [Section 1170] This section [now section 1171] is derived from current law. Subsection (a) grants an administrative expense priority to the claim of any individual (or of the personal representative of a deceased individual) against the debtor or the estate for personal injury to or death of the individual arising out of the operation of the debtor railroad or the estate, whether the claim arose before or after commencement of the case. The priority under current law, found in section 77(n) [section 205(n) of former Title 11], applies only to employees of the debtor. This subsection expands the protection provided.

Subsection (b) follows present section 77(b) of the Bankruptcy Act [section 205(b) of former Title] by giving priority to any unsecured claims that would be entitled to priority if a receiver in equity of the property of the debtor had been appointed by a Federal court on the date of the order for relief under the bankruptcy laws. As under current law, the courts will determine the precise contours of the priority recognized by this subsection in each case. House Report No. 95–595.

1984 Acts. Statements by Legislative Leaders, see 1984 U.S.Code Cong. and Adm.News, p. 576.

Legislative Statements

Section 1171 of the House amendment is derived from section 1170 of the House bill in lieu of section 1173(a)(9) of the Senate amendment.

Effective and Applicability Provisions

1984 Acts. Amendment by Pub.L. 98–353 effective with respect to cases filed 90 days after July 10, 1984, see section 552(a), formerly 553(a), of Pub.L. 98–353, set out as a note under section 101 of this title.

Savings Provisions

Section to apply to cases pending under section 77 of the Bankruptcy Act [section 205 of former Title 11] on Nov. 6, 1978, in which the trustee had not filed a plan of reorganization, see section 403(b) of Pub. L. 95–598, set out as a note preceding section 101 of this title.

CROSS REFERENCES

Allowance of administrative expenses, see 11 USCA § 503.

Priorities, see 11 USCA § 507.

§ 1172.　Contents of plan

(a) In addition to the provisions required or permitted under section 1123 of this title, a plan—

(1) shall specify the extent to and the means by which the debtor's rail service is proposed to be continued, and the extent to which any of the debtor's rail service is proposed to be terminated; and

(2) may include a provision for—

(A) the transfer of any or all of the operating railroad lines of the debtor to another operating railroad; or

(B) abandonment of any railroad line in accordance with section 1170 of this title.

(b) If, except for the pendency of the case under this chapter, transfer of, or operation of or over, any of the debtor's rail lines by an entity other than the debtor or a successor to the debtor under the plan would require approval by the Board under a law of the United States, then a plan may not propose such a transfer or such operation unless the proponent of the plan initiates an appropriate application for such a transfer or such operation with the Board and, within such time as the court may fix, not exceeding 180 days, the Board, with or without a hearing, as the Board may determine, and with or without modification or condition, approves such application, or does not act on such application. Any action or order of the Board approving, modifying, conditioning, or disapproving such application is subject to review by the court only under sections 706(2)(A), 706(2)(B), 706(2)(C), and 706(2)(D) of title 5.

(c)(1) In approving an application under subsection (b) of this section, the Board shall require the rail carrier to provide a fair arrangement at least as protective of the interests of employees as that established under section 11326(a) of title 49.

(2) Nothing in this subsection shall be deemed to affect the priorities or timing of payment of employee protection which might have existed in the absence of this subsection.

(Pub.L. 95–598, Nov. 6, 1978, 92 Stat. 2644; Pub.L. 96–448, Title II, § 227(b), Oct. 14, 1980, 94 Stat. 1931; Pub.L. 104–88, Title III, § 302(2), Dec. 29, 1995, 109 Stat. 943; Pub.L. 109–8, Title XII, § 1218, Apr. 20, 2005, 119 Stat. 195.)

HISTORICAL AND STATUTORY NOTES

Revision Notes and Legislative Reports

1978 Acts. Section 1170 [now this section] adds to the general provisions required or permitted in reorganization plans by section 1123. Subsection (1) requires that a reorganization plan under the railroad subchapter specify the means by which the value of the claims of creditors and the interests of equity holders which are materially and adversely affected by the plan are to be realized. Subsection (2) permits a plan to include provisions for the issuance of warrants. Subsection (3) requires that the plan provide for fixed charges by probable earnings for their payment. Subsection (4) requires that the plan specify the means by which, and the extent to which, the debtor's rail service is to be continued, and shall identify any rail service to be terminated. Subsection (5) permits other appropriate provisions not inconsistent with the chapter. With the exception of subsection (4), the requirements are comparable to those of present section 77(b) [section 205(b) of former Title 11]; subsection (4) emphasizes the public interest in the preservation of rail transportation.

Section 1171 imposes on the court, rather than the Interstate Commerce Commission, as in present section 77 [section 205 of former title 11], the responsibility for the plan of reorganization. The Commission is empowered to make final decisions subject only to review by the court under the standards of the Administrative Procedure Act [sections 551 et seq. and 701 et seq. of Title 5, Government Organization and Employees] as to any part of the plan which deals with transportation matters, such as the grant of operating rights of or over, or transfer of, the debtor's rail lines to other carriers.

Subsection (a) requires the trustee to file a plan of reorganization within 18 months after the petition is filed, and permits the court, for good cause shown, to extend such time limit. Subsection (b) permits a plan to be proposed by any interested person, and permits the trustee to revise his plan at any time before it is approved by the court.

Subsections (c), (d) and (e) require the court, when a plan is submitted by the trustee or, if the court deems it worthy of consideration, a plan submitted is proposed by any other person proposes the transfer of, or operation of or over, any of the debtor's lines by other carriers, to refer to such provisions of the plan to the Interstate Commerce Commission. The Commission, within 240 days, and after a hearing if the Commission so determines, is to report to the court the effects of such provisions of the plan in the light of national transportation policy and sections 5(3)(f)(A), (B), and (D), (F)–(I) of the Interstate Commerce Act [section 11350(b)(1), (2), (4), (6)–(9) of Title 49, Transportation]. The report of the Commission is conclusive in all further hearings on the plan by the court, subject only to review pursuant to 5 U.S.C. 706(2)(A)–(D). Senate Report no. 95–989.

[Section 1171 (now section 1172)] A plan in a railroad reorganization case may include provisions in addition to those required and permitted under an ordinary reorganization plan. It may provide for the transfer of any or all of the operating railroad lines of the debtor to another operating railroad.

Paragraph (1) contemplates a liquidating plan for the debtor's rail lines, much as occurred in the Penn Central case by transfer of operating lines to ConRail. Such a liquidating plan is not per se contrary to the public interest, and the court will have to determine on a case-by-case basis, with the guidance of the Interstate Commerce Commission and of other parties in interest, whether the particular plan proposed is in the public interest, as required under proposed 11 U.S.C. 1172(3).

The plan may also provide for abandonment in accordance with section 1169, governing abandonment generally. Neither of these provisions in a plan, transfer or abandonment of lines, requires ICC approval. Confirmation of the plan by the court authorizes the debtor to comply with the plan in accordance with section 1142(a) notwithstanding any bankruptcy law to the contrary. House Report No. 95–595.

1980 Acts. House Report No. 96–1035 and House Conference Report No. 96–1430, see 1980 U.S.Code Cong. and Adm.News, p. 3978.

1995 Acts. House Report No. 104–311 and House Conference Report No. 104–422, see 1995 U.S. Code Cong. and Adm. News, p. 793.

2005 Acts. House Report No. 109–31(Part I), see 2005 U.S. Code Cong. and Adm. News, p. 88.

Legislative Statements

Section 1172 of the House amendment is derived from section 1171 of the House bill in preference to section 1170 of the Senate amendment with the exception that section 1170(4) of the Senate amendment is incorporated into section 1172(a)(1) of the House amendment.

Section 1172(b) of the House amendment is derived from section 1171(c) of the Senate amendment. The section gives the Interstate Commerce Commission the exclusive power to approve or disapprove the transfer of, or operation of or over, any of the debtor's rail lines over which the Commission has jurisdiction, subject to review under the Administrative Procedures Act [sections 551 et seq. and 701 et seq. of Title 5, Government Organization and Employees]. The section does not apply to a transfer of railroad lines to a successor of the debtor under a plan of reorganization by merger or otherwise.

The House amendment deletes section 1171(a) of the Senate amendment as a matter to be determined by the Rules of Bankruptcy Procedure. It is anticipated that the rules will specify the period of time, such as 18 months, within which a trustee must file with the court a proposed plan of reorganization for the debtor or a report why a plan cannot be formulated. Incorporation by reference of section 1121 in section 1161 of title 11 means that a party in interest will also have a right to file a plan of reorganization. This differs from the position taken in the Senate amendment which would have permitted the Interstate Commerce Commission to file a plan of reorganization.

Effective and Applicability Provisions

2005 Acts. Amendments by Pub.L. 109–8 effective, except as otherwise provided, 180 days after April 20, 2005, and inapplicable with respect to cases commenced under Title 11 before the effective date, see Pub.L. 109–8, § 1501, set out as a note under 11 U.S.C.A. § 101.

1995 Acts. Amendment by Pub.L. 104–88 effective Jan. 1, 1996, see section 2 of Pub.L. 104–88, set out as a note under 49 U.S.C.A. § 1301.

1980 Acts. Amendment by Pub.L. 96–448 effective Oct. 1, 1980, see section 710(a) of Pub.L. 96–448, set out as a note under section 1170 of Title 11, Bankruptcy.

Nonapplication of Bankruptcy Law Provision

For provision that subsec. (c) of this section does not apply to Amtrak and its employees, see section 142(d) of Pub.L. 105–134, set out in a note under 49 U.S.C.A. § 24706.

CROSS REFERENCES

Contents of plan filed in,
> Chapter thirteen cases, see 11 USCA § 1322.
> Chapter twelve cases, see 11 USCA § 1222.

§ 1173.   Confirmation of plan

(a) The court shall confirm a plan if—

(1) the applicable requirements of section 1129 of this title have been met;

(2) each creditor or equity security holder will receive or retain under the plan property of a value, as of the effective date of the plan, that is not less than the value of property that each such creditor or equity security holder would so receive or retain if all of the operating railroad lines of the debtor were sold, and the proceeds of such sale, and the other property of the estate, were distributed under chapter 7 of this title on such date;

(3) in light of the debtor's past earnings and the probable prospective earnings of the reorganized debtor, there will be adequate coverage by such prospective earnings of any fixed charges, such as interest on debt, amortization of funded debt, and rent for leased railroads, provided for by the plan; and

(4) the plan is consistent with the public interest.

(b) If the requirements of subsection (a) of this section are met with respect to more than one plan, the court shall confirm the plan that is most likely to maintain adequate rail service in the public interest. (Pub.L. 95–598, Nov. 6, 1978, 92 Stat. 2644; Pub.L. 98–353, Title III, § 523, July 10, 1984, 98 Stat. 388.)

HISTORICAL AND STATUTORY NOTES

Revision Notes and Legislative Reports

1978 Acts. Section 1173 adapts the provisions dealing with reorganization plans generally contained in section 1130 to the particular requirements of railroad reorganization plans, as set out in present section 77(e) [section 205(e) of former Title 11]. Subsection (a) specifies the findings which the court must make before approving a plan: (1) The plan complies with the applicable provisions of the chapter; (2) the proponent of the plan complies with the applicable provisions of the chapter; (3) the plan has been proposed in good faith; (4) any payments for services or for costs or expenses in connection with the case or the plan are disclosed to the court and are reasonable, or, if to be paid later, are subject to the approval of the court as reasonable; (5) the proponent of the plan has disclosed the identity and affiliations of the individuals who will serve as directors, officers, or voting trustees, such appointments or continuations in office are consistent with the interests of creditors, equity security holders, and the proponent the public, and has disclosed the identity and compensation of any insider who will be employed or retained under the plan; (6) that rate changes proposed in the plan have been approved by the appropriate regulatory commission, or that the plan is contingent on such approval; (7) that confirmation of the plan is not likely to be followed by further reorganization or liquidation, unless it is contemplated by the plan; (8) that the plan, if there is more than one, is the one most likely to maintain adequate rail service and (9) that the plan provides the priority traditionally accorded by section 77(b) [section 205(b) of former Title 11] to claims by rail creditors for necessary services rendered during the 6 months preceding the filing of the petition in bankruptcy.

Subsection (b) continues the present power of the court in section 77(e) [section 205(e) of former Title 11] to confirm a plan over the objections of creditors or equity security holders who are materially and adversely affected. The subsection also confirms the authority of the court to approve a transfer of all or part of a debtor's property or its merger over the objections of equity security holders if it finds (1) that the "public interest" in continued rail transportation outweighs any adverse effect on creditors and equity security holders, and (2) that the plan is fair and equitable, affords due recognition to the rights of each class, and does not discriminate unfairly against any class.

Subsection (c) permits modification of a plan confirmed by a final order only for fraud. Senate Report No. 95–989.

[Section 1172] This section [now section 1173] requires the court to confirm a plan if the applicable requirements of section 1129 (relating to confirmation of reorganization plans generally) are met, if the best interest test is met, and if the plan is compatible with the public interest.

The test in this paragraph is similar to the test prescribed for ordinary corporate reorganizations. However, since a railroad cannot liquidate its assets and sell them for scrap to satisfy its creditors, the test focuses on the value of the railroad as a going concern. That is, the test is based on what the assets, sold as operating rail lines, would bring.

The public interest requirement, found in current law, will now be decided by the court, with the ICC [Interstate Commerce Commission] representing the public interest before the court, rather than in the first instance by the ICC. Liquidation of the debtor is not, per se, contrary to the public interest. House Report No. 95–595.

1984 Acts. Statements by Legislative Leaders, see 1984 U.S.Code Cong. and Adm.News, p. 576.

Legislative Statements

Section 1173 of the House amendment concerns confirmation of a plan of railroad reorganization and is derived from section 1172 of the House bill as modified. In particular, section 1173(a)(3) of the House amendment is derived from section 1170(3) of the Senate amendment. Section 1173(b) is derived from section 1173(a)(8) of the Senate amendment.

Effective and Applicability Provisions

1984 Acts. Amendment by Pub.L. 98–353 effective with respect to cases filed 90 days after July 10, 1984, see section 552(a), formerly 553(a), of Pub.L. 98–353, set out as a note under section 101 of this title.

CROSS REFERENCES

Confirmation of plan in,

Chapter nine cases, see 11 USCA § 943.

Chapter thirteen cases, see 11 USCA § 1325.

Chapter twelve cases, see 11 USCA § 1225.

Effect of confirmation in cases under this chapter, see 11 USCA § 1141.

Nonrecognition of gain or loss for income tax purposes of exchanges of stock and securities in reorganizations confirmed under this section, see 26 USCA § 354.

Revocation of order of confirmation in cases under this chapter, see 11 USCA § 1144.

Unclaimed property, see 11 USCA § 347.

§ 1174. Liquidation

On request of a party in interest and after notice and a hearing, the court may, or, if a plan has not been confirmed under section 1173 of this title before five years after the date of the order for relief, the court shall, order the trustee to cease the debtor's operation and to collect and reduce to money all of the property of the estate in the same manner as if the case were a case under chapter 7 of this title.

(Pub.L. 95–598, Nov. 6, 1978, 92 Stat. 2644.)

HISTORICAL AND STATUTORY NOTES

Revision Notes and Legislative Reports

1978 Acts. Section 1174 permits the court to convert the case to a liquidation under chapter 7 if the court finds that the debtor cannot be reorganized, or if various time limits specified in the subchapter are not met. Section 77 [section 205 of former Title 11] does not authorize a liquidation of a railroad under the Bankruptcy Act [former Title 11]. If the railroad is not reorganizable, the only action open to the court is to dismiss the petition, which would in all likelihood be followed by a State court receivership, with all of its attendant disadvantages. If reorganization is impossible, the debtor should be liquidated under the Bankruptcy Act. Senate Report No. 95–989.

Legislative Statements

Section 1174 of the House amendment represents a compromise between the House bill and Senate amendment on the issue of liquidation of a railroad. The provision permits a party in interest at any time to request liquidation. In addition, if a plan has not been confirmed under section 1173 of the House amendment before 5 years after the date of order for relief, the court must order the trustee to cease the debtor's operation and to collect and reduce to money all of the property of the estate in the same manner as if the case were a case under chapter 7 of title 11. The approach differs from the conversion to chapter 7 under section 1174 of the Senate bill in order to make special provisions contained in subchapter IV of chapter 11 applicable to liquidation. However, maintaining liquidation in the context of chapter 11 is not intended to delay liquidation of the railroad to a different extent than if the case were converted to chapter 7.

Although the House amendment does not adopt provisions contained in section 1170(1), (2), (3), or (5), of the Senate amendment such provisions are contained explicitly or implicitly in section 1123 of the House amendment.

CROSS REFERENCES

Conversion of,

    Chapter eleven cases, see 11 USCA § 1112.

    Chapter seven cases, see 11 USCA § 706.

Chapter thirteen cases, see 11 USCA § 1307.

Chapter twelve cases, see 11 USCA § 1208.

Dismissal of,

    Chapter nine cases, see 11 USCA § 930.

    Chapter seven cases, see 11 USCA § 707.

CHAPTER 12—ADJUSTMENT OF DEBTS OF A FAMILY FARMER OR FISHERMAN WITH REGULAR ANNUAL INCOME

HISTORICAL AND STATUTORY NOTES

Effective and Applicability Provisions

2005 Acts. Amendments by Pub.L. 109–8 effective, except as otherwise provided, 180 days after April 20, 2005, and inapplicable with respect to cases commenced under Title 11 before the effective date, see Pub.L. 109–8, § 1501, set out as a note under 11 U.S.C.A. § 101.

Reenactment of Chapter

This chapter as in effect on June 30, 2005, reenacted effective July 1, 2005, see Pub.L. 109–8, § 1001(a), set out as a note under 11 U.S.C.A. § 1201.

Repeal of chapter; extension of provisions

Pub.L. 99–554, Title III, § 302(f), Oct. 27, 1986, 100 Stat. 3124, as amended Pub.L. 103–65, § 1, Aug. 6, 1993, 107 Stat. 311, which provided that, effective Oct. 1, 1998, this chapter is repealed, but that all cases commenced or pending under this chapter, and all matters and proceedings in or relating to such cases, shall be conducted and determined under this chapter as if such chapter had not been repealed, and that the substantive rights of parties in connection with such cases, matters, and proceedings shall continue to be governed under the laws applicable to such cases, matters, and proceedings as if such chapter had not been repealed, was superceded by the reenactment of this chapter by Pub.L. 109–8, Title X, § 1001(a), Apr. 20, 2005, 119 Stat. 185, set out as a note under 11 U.S.C.A. § 1201.

Pub.L. 105–277, Div. C, Title I, § 149, Oct. 21, 1998, 112 Stat. 2681–610, as amended Pub.L. 106–5, §§ 1, 2, Mar. 30, 1999, 113 Stat. 9; Pub.L. 106–70, §§ 1, 2, Oct. 9, 1999, 113 Stat. 1031; Pub.L. 107–8, §§ 1, 2, May 11, 2001, 115 Stat. 10; Pub.L. 107–17, §§ 1, 2, June 26, 2001, 115 Stat. 151; Pub.L. 107–170, §§ 1, 2, May 7, 2002, 116 Stat. 133; Pub.L. 107–171, Title X, § 10814, May 13, 2002, 116 St. 532; Pub.L. 107–377, § 2, Dec. 19, 2002, 116 Stat. 3115; Pub.L. 108–73, § 2(a), Aug. 15, 2003, 117 Stat. 891; Pub.L. 108–369, § 2(a), Oct. 25, 2004, 118 Stat. 1749, provided that, to take effect on January 1, 2004, chapter 12 of Title 11 [this chapter; 11 U.S.C.A. § 1201 et seq.], as in effect on December 31, 2003, is reenacted for the period beginning on January 1, 2004, and ending on July 1, 2005, but that all cases commenced or pending under this chapter 12, as reenacted under section 149(a) of Pub.L. 105–277, and all matters and proceedings in or relating to such cases, shall be conducted and determined under such chapter as if such chapter were continued in effect after July 1, 2005, and that the substantive rights of parties in connection with such cases, matters, and proceedings shall continue to be governed under the law applicable to such cases, matters, and proceedings as if such chapter were continued in effect after July 1, 2005, was superceded by the reenactment of this chapter by Pub.L. 109–8, Title X, § 1001(a), Apr. 20, 2005, 119 Stat. 185, set out as a note under 11 U.S.C.A. § 1201.

SUBCHAPTER I—OFFICERS, ADMINISTRATION, AND THE ESTATE

§ 1201. Stay of action against codebtor

(a) Except as provided in subsections (b) and (c) of this section, after the order for relief under this chapter, a creditor may not act, or commence or continue any civil action, to collect all or any part of a consumer debt of the debtor from any individual that is liable on such debt with the debtor, or that secured such debt, unless—

(1) such individual became liable on or secured such debt in the ordinary course of such individual's business; or

(2) the case is closed, dismissed, or converted to a case under chapter 7 of this title.

(b) A creditor may present a negotiable instrument, and may give notice of dishonor of such an instrument.

(c) On request of a party in interest and after notice and a hearing, the court shall grant relief from the stay provided by subsection (a) of this section with respect to a creditor, to the extent that—

(1) as between the debtor and the individual protected under subsection (a) of this section, such individual received the consideration for the claim held by such creditor;

(2) the plan filed by the debtor proposes not to pay such claim; or

(3) such creditor's interest would be irreparably harmed by continuation of such stay.

(d) Twenty days after the filing of a request under subsection (c)(2) of this section for relief from the stay provided by subsection (a) of this section, such stay is terminated with respect to the party in interest making such request, unless the debtor or any individual that is liable on such debt with the debtor files and serves upon such party in interest a written objection to the taking of the proposed action.

(Added and amended Pub.L. 99–554, Title II, § 255, Title III, § 302(f), Oct. 27, 1986, 100 Stat. 3105, 3124; Pub.L. 103–65, § 1, Aug. 6, 1993, 107 Stat. 311; Pub.L. 105–277, Div. C, Title I, § 149(a), Oct. 21, 1998, 112 Stat. 2681–610; Pub.L. 106–5, § 1(1),(2), Mar. 30, 1999, 113 Stat. 9; Pub.L. 106–70, § 1, Oct. 9, 1999, 113 Stat. 1031; Pub.L. 107–8, § 1, May 11, 2001, 115 Stat. 10; Pub.L. 107–17, § 1, June 26, 2001, 115 Stat. 151; Pub.L. 107–170, § 1, May 7, 2002, 116 Stat. 133; Pub.L. 107–171, Title X, § 10814(a), May 13, 2002, 116 Stat. 532; Pub.L. 107–377, § 2(a), Dec. 19, 2002, 116 Stat. 3115; Pub.L. 108–73, § 2(a), Aug. 15, 2003, 117 Stat. 891; Pub.L. 108–369, § 2(a), Oct. 25, 2004, 118 Stat. 1749; Pub.L. 109–8, Title X, § 1001(a)(1), Apr. 20, 2005, 119 Stat. 185.)

HISTORICAL AND STATUTORY NOTES

Revision Notes and Legislative Reports

1986 Acts. House Report No. 99–764 and House Conference Report No. 99–958, see 1986 U.S. Code Cong. and Adm. News, p. 5227.

1993 Acts. House Report No. 103–32, see 1993 U.S. Code Cong. and Adm. News, p. 373.

1998 Acts. Statement by President, see 1998 U.S. Code Cong. and Adm. News, p. 582.

1999 Acts. Statement by President, see 1999 U.S. Code Cong. and Adm. News, p. 4.

Statement by President, see 1999 U.S. Code Cong. and Adm. News, p. 102.

2001 Acts. House Report No. 107–2, see 2001 U.S. Code Cong. and Adm. News, p. 6.

2005 Acts. House Report No. 109–31(Part I), see 2005 U.S. Code Cong. and Adm. News, p. 88.

Codifications

For repeal of section effective Oct. 1, 1998, and subsequent reenactment of section, see note set out under this section.

Effective and Applicability Provisions

2005 Acts. Amendments by Pub.L. 109–8 effective, except as otherwise provided, 180 days after April 20, 2005, and inapplicable with respect to cases commenced under Title 11 before the effective date, see Pub.L. 109–8, § 1501, set out as a note under 11 U.S.C.A. § 101.

2004 Acts. Pub.L. 108–369, § 2(b), Oct. 25, 2004, 118 Stat. 1749, provided that: "The amendments made by subsection (a) [amending this section, 11 U.S.C.A. §§ 1202 to 1208, 1221 to 1231, and provisions set out as a note under this section] are deemed to have taken effect on January 1, 2004."

2003 Acts. Pub.L. 108–73, § 2(b), Aug. 15, 2003, 117 Stat. 891, provided that: "The amendments made by subsection (a) [amending this section, 11 U.S.C.A. §§ 1202 to 1208, 1221 to 1231, and provisions set out as a note under this section] take effect on July 1, 2003."

2002 Acts. Pub.L. 107–377, § 2(b), Dec. 19, 2002, 116 Stat. 3115, provided that: "The amendments made by subsection (a) [amending this section and 11 U.S.C.A. §§ 1202 to 1208, 1221 to 1231] shall take effect on January 1, 2003."

Pub.L. 107–171, Title X, § 10814(b), May 13, 2002, 116 Stat. 532, provided that: "The amendments made by subsection (a) [amending this section, 11 U.S.C.A. §§ 1202 to 1208, 1221 to 1231, and provisions set out as a note under this section] shall take effect on June 1, 2002."

Pub.L. 107–170, § 2, May 7, 2002, 116 Stat. 133, provided that: "The amendments made by section 1 [amending this section, 11 U.S.C.A. §§ 1202 to 1208, 1221 to 1231, and provisions set out as a note under this section] shall take effect on October 1, 2001."

2001 Acts. Pub.L. 107–17, § 2, June 26, 2001, 115 Stat. 151, provided that: "The amendments made by section 1 [amending this section, 11 U.S.C.A. §§ 1202 to 1208, 1221 to 1231, and provisions set out as a note under this section] shall take effect on June 1, 2001."

Pub.L. 107–8, § 2, May 11, 2001, 115 Stat. 10, provided that: "The amendments made by section 1 [amending this section, 11 U.S.C.A. §§ 1202 to 1208, 1221 to 1231, and provisions set out as a note under this section] shall take effect on July 1, 2000."

1999 Acts. Section 2 of Pub.L. 106–70 provided that: "The amendments made by section 1 [amending this section, 11 U.S.C.A. §§ 1202 to 1208, 1221 to 1231, and provisions set out as a note under this section] shall take effect on October 1, 1999."

Section 2 of Pub.L. 106–5 provided that: "The amendments made by section 1 [amending this section and 11 U.S.C.A. §§ 1202 to 1208, 1221 to 1231, and provisions set out as a note under this section] shall take effect on April 1, 1999."

1998 Acts. Section 149 of Pub.L. 105–277, as amended Pub.L. 106–5, § 1, Mar. 30, 1999, 113 Stat. 9; Pub.L. 106–70, § 1, Oct. 9, 1999, 113 Stat. 1031; Pub.L. 107–8, § 1, May 11, 2001, 115 Stat. 10; Pub.L. 107–17, § 1, June 26, 2001, 115 Stat. 151; Pub.L. 107–170, § 1, May 7, 2002, 116 Stat. 133; Pub.L.107–171, Title X, § 10814(a), May 13, 2002, 116 Stat. 532; Pub.L. 107–377, § 2(a), Dec. 19, 2002, 116 Stat. 3115; Pub.L. 108–73, § 2(a), Aug. 15, 2003, 117 Stat. 891; Pub.L. 108–369, § 2(a), Oct. 25, 2004, 118 Stat. 1749, provided that:

"**(a)** Chapter 12 of title 11 of the United States Code [this chapter; 11 U.S.C.A. § 1201 et seq.], as in effect on December 31, 2003, is hereby reenacted for the period beginning on January 1, 2004, and ending on July 1, 2005.

"**(b)** All cases commenced or pending under chapter 12 of title 11, United States Code [this chapter; 11 U.S.C.A. § 1201 et seq.], as reenacted under subsection (a) [of this note], and all matters and proceedings in or relating to such cases, shall be conducted and determined under such chapter as if such chapter were continued in effect after July 1, 2004. The substantive rights of parties in connection with such cases, matters, and proceedings shall continue to be governed under the law applicable to such cases, matters, and proceedings as if such chapter were continued in effect after July 1, 2005.

"**(c)** [Repealed. Pub.L. 106–5, § 1(3), March 30, 1999, 113 Stat. 9.]"

1993 Acts. Amendment by Pub.L. 103–65, extending to Oct. 1, 1998 the date of repeal of this chapter, to take effect Aug. 6, 1993, see section 3 of Pub.L. 103–65, set out as a note under 11 U.S.C.A. § 1221.

1986 Acts. Section repealed effective Oct. 1, 1998, see section 302(f) of Pub.L. 99–554, as amended, set out in a note under section 581 of Title 28. However, for extension of provisions, see section 149 of Pub.L. 105–277, set out as a note under this section.

Section effective 30 days after Oct. 27, 1986, but not applicable to cases commenced under this title before that date, see section 302(a), (c)(1) of Pub.L. 99–554, set out as a note under 28 U.S.C.A. § 581.

Reenactment of Chapter 12

Pub.L. 109–8, Title X, § 1001(a), (b), Apr. 20, 2005, 119 Stat. 185, 186, provided that:

"(a) **Reenactment.**—

"(1) **In general.**—Chapter 12 of title 11, United States Code [this chapter], as reenacted by section 149 of division C of the Omnibus Consolidated and Emergency Supplemental Appropriations Act, 1999 (Public Law 105–277) [Pub.L. 105–277, Div. C, Title I, § 149, Oct. 21, 1998, 112 Stat. 2681–610, as amended, set out as a note under this section], and as in effect on June 30, 2005, is hereby reenacted.

"(2) **Effective date of reenactment.**—Paragraph (1) shall take effect on July 1, 2005.

"(b) **Amendments.**—Chapter 12 of title 11, United States Code, as reenacted by subsection (a) [of this note], is amended by this Act [Pub.L. 109–8, Apr. 20, 2005, 119 Stat. 23; see Tables for classifications]."

Repeal of Chapter; Extension of Provisions

Pub.L. 99–554, Title III, § 302(f), Oct. 27, 1986, 100 Stat. 3124, as amended Pub.L. 103–65, § 1, Aug. 6, 1993, 107 Stat. 311, which provided that, effective Oct. 1, 1998, this chapter is repealed, but that all cases commenced or pending under this chapter, and all matters and proceedings in or relating to such cases, shall be conducted and determined under this chapter as if such chapter had not been repealed, and that the substantive rights of parties in connection with such cases, matters, and proceedings shall continue to be governed under the laws applicable to such cases, matters, and proceedings as if such chapter had not been repealed, was superceded by the reenactment of this chapter by Pub.L. 109–8, Title X, § 1001(a), Apr. 20, 2005, 119 Stat. 185, set out as a note under this section.

Pub.L. 105–277, Div. C, Title I, § 149, Oct. 21, 1998, 112 Stat. 2681–610, as amended Pub.L. 106–5, §§ 1, 2, Mar. 30, 1999, 113 Stat. 9; Pub.L. 106–70, §§ 1, 2, Oct. 9, 1999, 113 Stat. 1031; Pub.L. 107–8, §§ 1, 2, May 11, 2001, 115 Stat. 10; Pub.L. 107–17, §§ 1, 2, June 26, 2001, 115 Stat. 151; Pub.L. 107–170, §§ 1, 2, May 7, 2002, 116 Stat. 133; Pub.L. 107–171, Title X, § 10814, May 13, 2002, 116 St. 532; Pub.L. 107–377, § 2, Dec. 19, 2002, 116 Stat. 3115; Pub.L. 108–73, § 2(a), Aug. 15, 2003, 117 Stat. 891; Pub.L. 108–369, § 2(a), Oct. 25, 2004, 118 Stat. 1749, which provided that, to take effect on January 1, 2004, chapter 12 of Title 11 [this chapter; 11 U.S.C.A. § 1201 et seq.], as in effect on December 31, 2003, is reenacted for the period beginning on January 1, 2004, and ending on July 1, 2005, but that all cases commenced or pending under this chapter 12, as reenacted under section 149(a) of Pub.L. 105–277, and all matters and proceedings in or relating to such cases, shall be conducted and determined under such chapter as if such chapter were continued in effect after July 1, 2005, and that the substantive rights of parties in connection with such cases, matters, and proceedings shall continue to be governed under the law applicable to such cases, mat-

ters, and proceedings as if such chapter were continued in effect after July 1, 2005, was superceded by the reenactment of this chapter by Pub.L. 109–8, Title X, § 1001(a), Apr. 20, 2005, 119 Stat. 185, set out as a note under this section.

§ 1202. Trustee

(a) If the United States trustee has appointed an individual under section 586(b) of title 28 to serve as standing trustee in cases under this chapter and if such individual qualifies as a trustee under section 322 of this title, then such individual shall serve as trustee in any case filed under this chapter. Otherwise, the United States trustee shall appoint one disinterested person to serve as trustee in the case or the United States trustee may serve as trustee in the case if necessary.

(b) The trustee shall—

(1) perform the duties specified in sections 704(a)(2), 704(a)(3), 704(a)(5), 704(a)(6), 704(a)(7), and 704(a)(9) of this title;

(2) perform the duties specified in section 1106(a)(3) and 1106(a)(4) of this title if the court, for cause and on request of a party in interest, the trustee, or the United States trustee, so orders;

(3) appear and be heard at any hearing that concerns—

(A) the value of property subject to a lien;

(B) confirmation of a plan;

(C) modification of the plan after confirmation; or

(D) the sale of property of the estate;

(4) ensure that the debtor commences making timely payments required by a confirmed plan;

(5) if the debtor ceases to be a debtor in possession, perform the duties specified in sections 704(a)(8), 1106(a)(1), 1106(a)(2), 1106(a)(6), 1106(a)(7), and 1203; and

(6) if with respect to the debtor there is a claim for a domestic support obligation, provide the applicable notice specified in subsection (c).

(c)(1) In a case described in subsection (b)(6) to which subsection (b)(6) applies, the trustee shall—

(A)(i) provide written notice to the holder of the claim described in subsection (b)(6) of such claim and of the right of such holder to use the services of the State child support enforcement agency established under sections 464 and 466 of the Social Security Act for the State in which such holder resides, for assistance in collecting child support during and after the case under this title; and

(ii) include in the notice provided under clause (i) the address and telephone number of such State child support enforcement agency;

(B)(i) provide written notice to such State child support enforcement agency of such claim; and

(ii) include in the notice provided under clause (i) the name, address, and telephone number of such holder; and

(C) at such time as the debtor is granted a discharge under section 1228, provide written notice to such holder and to such State child support enforcement agency of—

(i) the granting of the discharge;

(ii) the last recent known address of the debtor;

(iii) the last recent known name and address of the debtor's employer; and

(iv) the name of each creditor that holds a claim that—

(I) is not discharged under paragraph (2), (4), or (14A) of section 523(a); or

(II) was reaffirmed by the debtor under section 524(c).

(2)(A) The holder of a claim described in subsection (b)(6) or the State child support enforcement agency of the State in which such holder resides may request from a creditor described in paragraph (1)(C)(iv) the last known address of the debtor.

(B) Notwithstanding any other provision of law, a creditor that makes a disclosure of a last known address of a debtor in connection with a request made under subparagraph (A) shall not be liable by reason of making that disclosure.

(Added and amended Pub.L. 99–554, Title II, §§ 227, 255, Title III, § 302(f), Oct. 27, 1986, 100 Stat. 3103, 3106, 3124; Pub.L. 103–65, § 1, Aug. 6, 1993, 107 Stat. 311; Pub.L. 105–277, Div. C, Title I, § 149(a), Oct. 21, 1998, 112 Stat. 2681–610; Pub.L. 106–5, § 1(1), (2), Mar. 30, 1999, 113 Stat. 9; Pub.L. 106–70, § 1, Oct. 9, 1999, 113 Stat. 1031; Pub.L. 107–8, § 1, May 11, 2001, 115 Stat. 10; Pub.L. 107–17, § 1, June 26, 2001, 115 Stat. 151; Pub.L. 107–170, § 1, May 7, 2002, 116 Stat. 133; Pub.L. 107–171, Title X, § 10814(a), May 13, 2002, 116 Stat. 532; Pub.L. 107–377, § 2(a), Dec. 19, 2002, 116 Stat. 3115; Pub.L. 108–73, § 2(a), Aug. 15, 2003, 117 Stat. 891; Pub.L. 108–369, § 2(a), Oct. 25, 2004, 118 Stat. 1749; Pub.L. 109–8, Title II, § 219(c), Title X, § 1001(a)(1), Apr. 20, 2005, 119 Stat. 57, 185; Pub.L. 111–327, § 2(a)(38), Dec. 22, 2010, 124 Stat. 3561.)

HISTORICAL AND STATUTORY NOTES

Revision Notes and Legislative Reports

1986 Acts. House Report No. 99–764 and House Conference Report No. 99–958, see 1986 U.S. Code Cong. and Adm. News, p. 5227.

1993 Acts. House Report No. 103–32, see 1993 U.S. Code Cong. and Adm. News, p. 373.

1998 Acts. Statement by President, see 1998 U.S. Code Cong. and Adm. News, p. 582.

1999 Acts. Statement by President, see 1999 U.S. Code Cong. and Adm. News, p. 4.

Statement by President, see 1999 U.S. Code Cong. and Adm. News, p. 102.

2001 Acts. House Report No. 107–2, see 2001 U.S. Code Cong. and Adm. News, p. 6.

2005 Acts. House Report No. 109–31(Part I), see 2005 U.S. Code Cong. and Adm. News, p. 88.

References in Text

Section 464 of the Social Security Act, referred to in subsec. (c)(1)(A)(i), is Act Aug. 14, 1935, c. 531, Title IV, § 464, as added Aug. 13, 1981, Pub.L. 97–35, Title XXIII, § 2331(a), 95 Stat. 860, and amended, which is classified to 42 U.S.C.A. § 664.

Section 466 of the Social Security Act, referred to in subsec. (c)(1)(A)(i), is Act Aug. 14, 1935, c. 531, Title IV, § 466, as added Aug. 16, 1984, Pub.L. 98–378, § 3(b), 98 Stat. 1306, and amended, which is classified to 42 U.S.C.A. § 666.

Codifications

For repeal of section effective Oct. 1, 1998, and subsequent reenactment of section, see note set out preceding 11 U.S.C.A. § 1201.

Effective and Applicability Provisions

2005 Acts. Amendments by Pub.L. 109–8 effective, except as otherwise provided, 180 days after April 20, 2005, and inapplicable with respect to cases commenced under Title 11 before the effective date, see Pub.L. 109–8, § 1501, set out as a note under 11 U.S.C.A. § 101.

2004 Acts. Amendment by Pub.L. 108–369, § 2(a), extending to July 1, 2005, the date of repeal of this chapter, to take effect Jan. 1, 2004, see Pub.L. 108–369, § 2(b), set out as a note under 11 U.S.C.A. § 1201.

2003 Acts. Amendment by Pub.L. 108–73, § 2(a), extending to Jan. 1, 2004, the date of repeal of this chapter, to take effect July 1, 2003, see Pub.L. 108–73, § 2(b), set out as a note under 11 U.S.C.A. § 1201.

2002 Acts. Amendment by Pub.L. 107–377, § 2(a), extending to July 1, 2003, the date of repeal of this chapter, to take effect Jan. 1, 2003, see Pub.L. 107–377, § 2(b), set out as a note under 11 U.S.C.A. § 1201.

Amendment by Pub.L. 107–171, extending to Jan. 1, 2003, the date of repeal of this chapter, to take effect June 1, 2002, see section 10814(b) of Pub.L. 107–171, set out as a note under 11 U.S.C.A. § 1201.

Amendment by Pub.L. 107–170, extending to June 1, 2002, the date of repeal of this chapter, to take effect October 1, 2001, see section 2 of Pub.L. 107–170, set out as a note under 11 U.S.C.A. § 1201.

2001 Acts. Amendment by Pub.L. 107–17, extending to October 1, 2001, the date of repeal of this chapter, to take effect June 1, 2001, see section 2 of Pub.L. 107–17, set out as a note under 11 U.S.C.A. § 1201.

Amendment by Pub.L. 107–8, extending to June 1, 2001, the date of repeal of this chapter, to take effect July 1, 2000, see section 2 of Pub.L. 107–8, set out as a note under 11 U.S.C.A. § 1201.

1999 Acts. Amendment by Pub.L. 106–70, extending to July 1, 2000, the date of repeal of this chapter, to take effect Oct. 1, 1999, see section 2 of Pub.L. 106–70, set out as a note under section 1201 of this title.

Amendment by Pub.L. 106–5, extending to Oct. 1, 1999 the date of repeal of this chapter, to take effect Apr. 1, 1999, see section 2 of Pub.L. 106–5, set out as a note under section 1201 of this title.

1998 Acts. Section reenacted, eff. Oct. 1, 1998, for the period beginning on Oct. 1, 1998, and ending on Apr. 1, 1999, but all cases commenced or pending under this chapter 12, as reenacted under section 149(a) of Pub.L. 105–277, and all matters and proceedings in or relating to such cases, to be conducted and determined under such chapter as if such chapter were continued in effect after Apr. 1, 1999, and the substantive rights of parties in connection with such cases, matters, and proceedings to continue to be governed under the law applicable to such cases, matters, and proceedings as if such chapter were continued in effect after Apr. 1, 1999, see section 149 of Pub.L. 105–277, set out as a note under section 1201 of this title.

1993 Acts. Amendment by Pub.L. 103–65, extending to Oct. 1, 1998 the date of repeal of this chapter, to take effect Aug. 6, 1993, see section 3 of Pub.L. 103–65, set out as a note under section 1221 of this title.

1986 Acts. Section repealed effective Oct. 1, 1998, see section 302(f) of Pub.L. 99–554, as amended, set out in a note under section 581 of Title 28. However, for extension of provisions, see section 149 of Pub.L. 105–277, set out as a note under section 1201 of this title.

Enactment by Pub.L. 99–554 effective 30 days after Oct. 27, 1986, except as otherwise provided for, see section 302(a) of Pub.L. 99–554, set out as a note under section 581 of Title 28, Judiciary and Judicial Procedure.

Enactment by Pub.L. 99–554, § 255, not to apply with respect to cases commenced under Title 11, Bankruptcy, before 30 days after Oct. 27, 1986, see section 302(c)(1) of Pub.L. 99–554, set out as a note under section 581 of Title 28.

Enactment by section 255 of Pub.L. 99–554 to take effect 30 days after Oct. 27, 1986, and before amendment made by section 227 of Pub.L. 99–554, striking out subsecs. (c) and (d) of this section, see section 302(c)(2) of Pub.L. 99–554, set out as a note under section 581 of Title 28.

Amendment by Pub.L. 99–554, § 227, not to become effective in or with respect to certain specified judicial districts until, or apply to cases while pending in such district before, the expiration of the 270–day period beginning 30 days after Oct. 27, 1986, or of the 30–day period beginning on the date the Attorney General certifies under section 303 of Pub.L. 99–554 the region specified in a paragraph of section 581(a) of Title 28, as amended by section 111(a) of Pub.L. 99–554, that includes such district, whichever occurs first, see section 302(d)(1) of Pub.L. 99–554, set out as a note under section 581 of Title 28.

Amendment by Pub.L. 99–554, § 227, not to become effective in or with respect to certain specified judicial districts until, or apply to cases while pending in such district before, the expiration of the 2–year period beginning 30 days after Oct. 27, 1986, or of the 30–day period beginning on the date the Attorney General certifies under section 303 of Pub.L. 99–554 the region specified in a paragraph of section 581(a) of Title 28, as amended by section 111(a) of Pub.L. 99–554, that includes such district, whichever occurs first, see section

302(d)(2) of Pub.L. 99–554, set out as a note under section 581 of Title 28.

Amendment by Pub.L. 99–554, § 227, not to become effective in or with respect to judicial districts established for the States of Alabama and North Carolina until, or apply to cases while pending in such district before, such district elects to be included in a bankruptcy region established in section 581(a) of Title 28, as amended by section 111(a) of Pub.L. 99–554, or Oct. 1, 2002, whichever occurs first, and except as otherwise provided for, with respect to cases under chapters 7, 11, 12, and 13 of Title 11 commenced before 30 days after Oct. 27, 1986, and pending in a judicial district in the States of Alabama or North Carolina before any election made under section 302(d)(3)(A) of Pub.L. 99–554 by such district becomes effective or Oct. 1, 2002, whichever occurs first, amendments by Pub.L. 99–554 not to apply until Oct. 1, 2003, or the expiration of the 1–year period beginning on the date such election becomes effective, whichever occurs first, and further, in any judicial district in Alabama or North Carolina not making the election described in section 302(d)(3)(A) of Pub.L. 99–554, any person appointed under regulations issued by the Judicial Conference to administer estates in cases under Title 11 authorized to establish, etc., a panel of private trustees, and to supervise cases and trustees in cases under chapters 7, 11, 12, and 13 of Title 11, until amendments by section 201 to 231 of Pub.L. 99–554 becomes effective in such district, see section 302(d)(3)(A) to (F), (H), (I) of Pub.L. 99–554, set out as a note under section 581 of Title 28.

Amendment by Pub.L. 99–554, § 227, except as otherwise provided, with respect to cases under chapters 7, 11, 12, and 13 of Title 11 commenced before 30 days after Oct. 27, 1986, and pending in a judicial district referred to in section 581(a) of Title 28, as amended by section 111(a) of Pub.L. 99–554, for which a United States trustee is not authorized before 30 days after Oct. 27, 1986 to be appointed, not applicable until the expiration of the 3–year period beginning on Oct. 27, 1986, or of the 1–year period beginning on the date the Attorney General certifies under section 303 of Pub.L. 99–554 the region specified in a paragraph of such section 581(a) that includes, such district, whichever occurs first, see section 302(e)(1), (2) of Pub.L. 99–554, set out as a note under section 581 of Title 28.

Reenactment of Chapter

This section as in effect on June 30, 2005, reenacted effective July 1, 2005, see Pub.L. 109–8, § 1001(a), set out as a note under 11 U.S.C.A. § 1201.

Repeal of Chapter; Extension of Provisions

Pub.L. 99–554, Title III, § 302(f), Oct. 27, 1986, 100 Stat. 3124, as amended Pub.L. 103–65, § 1, Aug. 6, 1993, 107 Stat. 311, which provided that, effective Oct. 1, 1998, this chapter is repealed, but that all cases commenced or pending under this chapter, and all matters and proceedings in or relating to such cases, shall be conducted and determined under this chapter as if such chapter had not been repealed, and that the substantive rights of parties in connection with such cases, matters, and proceedings shall continue to be governed under the laws applicable to such cases, matters, and proceedings as if such chapter had not been repealed, was superceded by the reenactment of this chapter by Pub.L. 109–8, Title X, § 1001(a), Apr. 20, 2005, 119 Stat. 185, set out as a note under 11 U.S.C.A. § 1201.

Pub.L. 105–277, Div. C, Title I, § 149, Oct. 21, 1998, 112 Stat. 2681–610, as amended Pub.L. 106–5, §§ 1, 2, Mar. 30,

1999, 113 Stat. 9; Pub.L. 106–70, §§ 1, 2, Oct. 9, 1999, 113 Stat. 1031; Pub.L. 107–8, §§ 1, 2, May 11, 2001, 115 Stat. 10; Pub.L. 107–17, §§ 1, 2, June 26, 2001, 115 Stat. 151; Pub.L. 107–170, §§ 1, 2, May 7, 2002, 116 Stat. 133; Pub.L. 107–171, Title X, § 10814, May 13, 2002, 116 St. 532; Pub.L. 107–377, § 2, Dec. 19, 2002, 116 Stat. 3115; Pub.L. 108–73, § 2(a), Aug. 15, 2003, 117 Stat. 891; Pub.L. 108–369, § 2(a), Oct. 25, 2004, 118 Stat. 1749, provided that, to take effect on January 1, 2004, chapter 12 of Title 11 [this chapter; 11 U.S.C.A. § 1201 et seq.], as in effect on December 31, 2003, is reenacted for the period beginning on January 1, 2004, and ending on July 1, 2005, but that all cases commenced or pending under this chapter 12, as reenacted under section 149(a) of Pub.L. 105–277, and all matters and proceedings in or relating to such cases, shall be conducted and determined under such chapter as if such chapter were continued in effect after July 1, 2005, and that the substantive rights of parties in connection with such cases, matters, and proceedings shall continue to be governed under the law applicable to such cases, matters, and proceedings as if such chapter were continued in effect after July 1, 2005, was superceded by the reenactment of this chapter by Pub.L. 109–8, Title X, § 1001(a), Apr. 20, 2005, 119 Stat. 185, set out as a note under 11 U.S.C.A. § 1201.

References in Subsection (a) Temporarily Deemed to be References to Other Provisions

Until the amendments made by subtitle A (sections 201 to 231) of Title II of Pub.L. 99–554 become effective in a district and apply to a case, in subsec. (a) of this section—

(1) the first two references to the United States trustee are deemed to be references to the court, and

(2) any reference to section 586(b) of Title 28, Judiciary and Judicial Procedure, is deemed to be a reference to subsec. (c) of this section,

see section 302(c)(3)(B), (d), (e) of Pub.L. 99–554, set out as an Effective Date note under section 581 of Title 28.

CROSS REFERENCES

Appointment of trustee in,

    Chapter eleven cases, see 11 USCA § 1104.

    Chapter thirteen cases, see 11 USCA § 1302.

    Railroad reorganization cases, see 11 USCA § 1163.

Compensation of officers, see 11 USCA § 330.

Election of trustee in Chapter seven case, see 11 USCA § 702.

Eligibility to serve as trustee, see 11 USCA § 321.

Grain storage facility bankruptcies, expedited appointment of trustee or examiner, see 11 USCA § 557.

Limitation on compensation of trustee, see 11 USCA § 326.

Qualification of trustee, see 11 USCA § 322.

Removal of trustee, see 11 USCA § 324.

Retention or replacement of professional persons, see 11 USCA § 327.

Role and capacity of trustee, see 11 USCA § 323.

Time of bringing action, see 11 USCA § 546.

Time of payment of percentage fee fixed for standing trustee, see 11 USCA § 1226.

§ 1203.   Rights and powers of debtor

Subject to such limitations as the court may prescribe, a debtor in possession shall have all the rights, other than the right to compensation under section 330, and powers, and shall perform all the functions and duties, except the duties specified in paragraphs (3) and (4) of section 1106(a), of a trustee serving in a case under chapter 11, including operating the debtor's farm or commercial fishing operation.

(Added and amended Pub.L. 99–554, Title II, § 255, Title III, § 302(f), Oct. 27, 1986, 100 Stat. 3107, 3124; Pub.L. 103–65, § 1, Aug. 6, 1993, 107 Stat. 311; Pub.L. 105–277, Div. C, Title I, § 149(a), Oct. 21, 1998, 112 Stat. 2681–610; Pub.L. 106–5, § 1(1), (2), Mar. 30, 1999, 113 Stat. 9; Pub.L. 106–70, § 1, Oct. 9, 1999, 113 Stat. 1031; Pub.L. 107–8, § 1, May 11, 2001, 115 Stat. 10; Pub.L. 107–17, § 1, June 26, 2001, 115 Stat. 151; Pub.L. 107–170, § 1, May 7, 2002, 116 Stat. 133; Pub.L. 107–171, Title X, § 10814(a), May 13, 2002, 116 Stat. 532; Pub.L. 107–377, § 2(a), Dec. 19, 2002, 116 Stat. 3115; Pub.L. 108–73, § 2(a), Aug. 15, 2003, 117 Stat. 891; Pub.L. 108–369, § 2(a), Oct. 25, 2004, 118 Stat. 1749; Pub.L. 109–8, Title X, §§ 1001(a)(1), 1007(c)(2), Apr. 20, 2005, 119 Stat. 185, 188.)

HISTORICAL AND STATUTORY NOTES

Revision Notes and Legislative Reports

1986 Acts. House Report No. 99–764 and House Conference Report No. 99–958, see 1986 U.S. Code Cong. and Adm. News, p. 5227.

1993 Acts. House Report No. 103–32, see 1993 U.S. Code Cong. and Adm. News, p. 373.

1998 Acts. Statement by President, see 1998 U.S. Code Cong. and Adm. News, p. 582.

1999 Acts. Statement by President, see 1999 U.S. Code Cong. and Adm. News, p. 4.

Statement by President, see 1999 U.S. Code Cong. and Adm. News, p. 102.

2001 Acts. House Report No. 107–2, see 2001 U.S. Code Cong. and Adm. News, p. 6.

2005 Acts. House Report No. 109–31(Part I), see 2005 U.S. Code Cong. and Adm. News, p. 88.

Codifications

For repeal of section effective Oct. 1, 1998, and subsequent reenactment of section, see note set out preceding 11 U.S.C.A. § 1201.

Effective and Applicability Provisions

2005 Acts. Amendments by Pub.L. 109–8 effective, except as otherwise provided, 180 days after April 20, 2005, and inapplicable with respect to cases commenced under Title 11 before the effective date, see Pub.L. 109–8, § 1501, set out as a note under 11 U.S.C.A. § 101.

2004 Acts. Amendment by Pub.L. 108–369, § 2(a), extending to July 1, 2005, the date of repeal of this chapter, to take effect Jan. 1, 2004, see Pub.L. 108–369, § 2(b), set out as a note under 11 U.S.C.A. § 1201.

2003 Acts. Amendment by Pub.L. 108–73, § 2(a), extending to Jan. 1, 2004, the date of repeal of this chapter, to take effect July 1, 2003, see Pub.L. 108–73, § 2(b), set out as a note under 11 U.S.C.A. § 1201.

2002 Acts. Amendment by Pub.L. 107–377, § 2(a), extending to July 1, 2003, the date of repeal of this chapter, to take effect Jan. 1, 2003, see Pub.L. 107–377, § 2(b), set out as a note under 11 U.S.C.A. § 1201.

Amendment by Pub.L. 107–171, extending to Jan. 1, 2003, the date of repeal of this chapter, to take effect June 1, 2002, see section 10814(b) of Pub.L. 107–171, set out as a note under 11 U.S.C.A. § 1201.

Amendment by Pub.L. 107–170, extending to June 1, 2002, the date of repeal of this chapter, to take effect October 1, 2001, see section 2 of Pub.L. 107–170, set out as a note under 11 U.S.C.A. § 1201.

2001 Acts. Amendment by Pub.L. 107–17, extending to October 1, 2001, the date of repeal of this chapter, to take effect June 1, 2001, see section 2 of Pub.L. 107–17, set out as a note under 11 U.S.C.A. § 1201.

Amendment by Pub.L. 107–8, extending to June 1, 2001, the date of repeal of this chapter, to take effect July 1, 2000, see section 2 of Pub.L. 107–8, set out as a note under 11 U.S.C.A. § 1201.

1999 Acts. Amendment by Pub.L. 106–70, extending to July 1, 2000, the date of repeal of this chapter, to take effect Oct. 1, 1999, see section 2 of Pub.L. 106–70, set out as a note under section 1201 of this title.

Amendment by Pub.L. 106–5, extending to Oct. 1, 1999 the date of repeal of this chapter, to take effect Apr. 1, 1999, see section 2 of Pub.L. 106–5, set out as a note under section 1201 of this title.

1998 Acts. Section reenacted, eff. Oct. 1, 1998, for the period beginning on Oct. 1, 1998, and ending on Apr. 1, 1999, but all cases commenced or pending under this chapter 12, as reenacted under section 149(a) of Pub.L. 105–277, and all matters and proceedings in or relating to such cases, to be conducted and determined under such chapter as if such chapter were continued in effect after Apr. 1, 1999, and the substantive rights of parties in connection with such cases, matters, and proceedings to continue to be governed under the law applicable to such cases, matters, and proceedings as if such chapter were continued in effect after Apr. 1, 1999, see section 149 of Pub.L. 105–277, set out as a note under section 1201 of this title.

1993 Acts. Amendment by Pub.L. 103–65, extending to Oct. 1, 1998 the date of repeal of this chapter, to take effect Aug. 6, 1993, see section 3 of Pub.L. 103–65, set out as a note under section 1221 of this title.

1986 Acts. Section repealed effective Oct. 1, 1998, see section 302(f) of Pub.L. 99–554, as amended, set out in a note under section 581 of Title 28. However, for extension of provisions, see section 149 of Pub.L. 105–277, set out as a note under section 1201 of this title.

Section effective 30 days after Oct. 27, 1986, but not applicable to cases commenced under this title before that date, see section 302(a), (c)(1) of Pub.L. 99–554, set out as a note under section 581 of Title 28, Judiciary and Judicial Procedure.

Reenactment of Chapter

This section as in effect on June 30, 2005, reenacted effective July 1, 2005, see Pub.L. 109–8, § 1001(a), set out as a note under 11 U.S.C.A. § 1201.

Repeal of Chapter; Extension of Provisions

Pub.L. 99–554, Title III, § 302(f), Oct. 27, 1986, 100 Stat. 3124, as amended Pub.L. 103–65, § 1, Aug. 6, 1993, 107 Stat. 311, which provided that, effective Oct. 1, 1998, this chapter is repealed, but that all cases commenced or pending under this chapter, and all matters and proceedings in or relating to such cases, shall be conducted and determined under this chapter as if such chapter had not been repealed, and that the substantive rights of parties in connection with such cases, matters, and proceedings shall continue to be governed under the laws applicable to such cases, matters, and proceedings as if such chapter had not been repealed, was superceded by the reenactment of this chapter by Pub.L. 109–8, Title X, § 1001(a), Apr. 20, 2005, 119 Stat. 185, set out as a note under 11 U.S.C.A. § 1201.

Pub.L. 105–277, Div. C, Title I, § 149, Oct. 21, 1998, 112 Stat. 2681–610, as amended Pub.L. 106–5, §§ 1, 2, Mar. 30, 1999, 113 Stat. 9; Pub.L. 106–70, §§ 1, 2, Oct. 9, 1999, 113 Stat. 1031; Pub.L. 107–8, §§ 1, 2, May 11, 2001, 115 Stat. 10; Pub.L. 107–17, §§ 1, 2, June 26, 2001, 115 Stat. 151; Pub.L. 107–170, §§ 1, 2, May 7, 2002, 116 Stat. 133; Pub.L. 107–171, Title X, § 10814, May 13, 2002, 116 St. 532; Pub.L. 107–377, § 2, Dec. 19, 2002, 116 Stat. 3115; Pub.L. 108–73, § 2(a), Aug. 15, 2003, 117 Stat. 891; Pub.L. 108–369, § 2(a), Oct. 25, 2004, 118 Stat. 1749, provided that, to take effect on January 1, 2004, chapter 12 of Title 11 [this chapter; 11 U.S.C.A. § 1201 et seq.], as in effect on December 31, 2003, is reenacted for the period beginning on January 1, 2004, and ending on July 1, 2005, but that all cases commenced or pending under this chapter 12, as reenacted under section 149(a) of Pub.L. 105–277, and all matters and proceedings in or relating to such cases, shall be conducted and determined under such chapter as if such chapter were continued in effect after July 1, 2005, and that the substantive rights of parties in connection with such cases, matters, and proceedings shall continue to be governed under the law applicable to such cases, matters, and proceedings as if such chapter were continued in effect after July 1, 2005, was superceded by the reenactment of this chapter by Pub.L. 109–8, Title X, § 1001(a), Apr. 20, 2005, 119 Stat. 185, set out as a note under 11 U.S.C.A. § 1201.

CROSS REFERENCES

Obtaining credit, see 11 USCA § 364.

Rights and powers of debtor in,

Chapter eleven cases, see 11 USCA § 1107.

Chapter thirteen cases, see 11 USCA § 1303.

Use, sale or lease of property, see 11 USCA § 363.

§ 1204. Removal of debtor as debtor in possession

(a) On request of a party in interest, and after notice and a hearing, the court shall order that the debtor shall not be a debtor in possession for cause, including fraud, dishonesty, incompetence, or gross mismanagement of the affairs of the debtor, either before or after the commencement of the case.

(b) On request of a party in interest, and after notice and a hearing, the court may reinstate the debtor in possession.

(Added and amended Pub.L. 99–554, Title II, § 255, Title III, § 302(f), Oct. 27, 1986, 100 Stat. 3107, 3124; Pub.L. 103–65, § 1, Aug. 6, 1993, 107 Stat. 311; Pub.L. 105–277, Div. C, Title I, § 149(a), Oct. 21, 1998, 112 Stat. 2681–610; Pub.L. 106–5, § 1(1), (2), Mar. 30, 1999, 113 Stat. 9; Pub.L. 106–70, § 1, Oct. 9, 1999, 113 Stat. 1031; Pub.L. 107–8, § 1, May 11, 2001, 115

Stat. 10; Pub.L. 107–17, § 1, June 26, 2001, 115 Stat. 151; Pub.L. 107–170, § 1, May 7, 2002, 116 Stat. 133; Pub.L. 107–171, Title X, § 10814(a), May 13, 2002, 116 Stat. 532; Pub.L. 107–377, § 2(a), Dec. 19, 2002, 116 Stat. 3115; Pub.L. 108–73, § 2(a), Aug. 15, 2003, 117 Stat. 891; Pub.L. 108–369, § 2(a), Oct. 25, 2004, 118 Stat. 1749; Pub.L. 109–8, Title X, § 1001(a)(1), Apr. 20, 2005, 119 Stat. 185.)

HISTORICAL AND STATUTORY NOTES

Revision Notes and Legislative Reports

1986 Acts. House Report No. 99–764 and House Conference Report No. 99–958, see 1986 U.S. Code Cong. and Adm. News, p. 5227.

1993 Acts. House Report No. 103–32, see 1993 U.S. Code Cong. and Adm. News, p. 373.

1998 Acts. Statement by President, see 1998 U.S. Code Cong. and Adm. News, p. 582.

1999 Acts. Statement by President, see 1999 U.S. Code Cong. and Adm. News, p. 4.

Statement by President, see 1999 U.S. Code Cong. and Adm. News, p. 102.

2001 Acts. House Report No. 107–2, see 2001 U.S. Code Cong. and Adm. News, p. 6.

2005 Acts. House Report No. 109–31(Part I), see 2005 U.S. Code Cong. and Adm. News, p. 88.

Codifications

For repeal of section effective Oct. 1, 1998, and subsequent reenactment of section, see note set out preceding 11 U.S.C.A. § 1201.

Effective and Applicability Provisions

2005 Acts. Amendments by Pub.L. 109–8 effective, except as otherwise provided, 180 days after April 20, 2005, and inapplicable with respect to cases commenced under Title 11 before the effective date, see Pub.L. 109–8, § 1501, set out as a note under 11 U.S.C.A. § 101.

2004 Acts. Amendment by Pub.L. 108–369, § 2(a), extending to July 1, 2005, the date of repeal of this chapter, to take effect Jan. 1, 2004, see Pub.L. 108–369, § 2(b), set out as a note under 11 U.S.C.A. § 1201.

2003 Acts. Amendment by Pub.L. 108–73, § 2(a), extending to Jan. 1, 2004, the date of repeal of this chapter, to take effect July 1, 2003, see Pub.L. 108–73, § 2(b), set out as a note under 11 U.S.C.A. § 1201.

2002 Acts. Amendment by Pub.L. 107–377, § 2(a), extending to July 1, 2003, the date of repeal of this chapter, to take effect Jan. 1, 2003, see Pub.L. 107–377, § 2(b), set out as a note under 11 U.S.C.A. § 1201.

Amendment by Pub.L. 107–171, extending to Jan. 1, 2003, the date of repeal of this chapter, to take effect June 1, 2002, see section 10814(b) of Pub.L. 107–171, set out as a note under 11 U.S.C.A. § 1201.

Amendment by Pub.L. 107–170, extending to June 1, 2002, the date of repeal of this chapter, to take effect October 1, 2001, see section 2 of Pub.L. 107–170, set out as a note under 11 U.S.C.A. § 1201.

2001 Acts. Amendment by Pub.L. 107–17, extending to October 1, 2001, the date of repeal of this chapter, to take effect June 1, 2001, see section 2 of Pub.L. 107–17, set out as a note under 11 U.S.C.A. § 1201.

Amendment by Pub.L. 107–8, extending to June 1, 2001, the date of repeal of this chapter, to take effect July 1, 2000, see section 2 of Pub.L. 107–8, set out as a note under 11 U.S.C.A. § 1201.

1999 Acts. Amendment by Pub.L. 106–70, extending to July 1, 2000, the date of repeal of this chapter, to take effect Oct. 1, 1999, see section 2 of Pub.L. 106–70, set out as a note under section 1201 of this title.

Amendment by Pub.L. 106–5, extending to Oct. 1, 1999 the date of repeal of this chapter, to take effect Apr. 1, 1999, see section 2 of Pub.L. 106–5, set out as a note under section 1201 of this title.

1998 Acts. Section reenacted, eff. Oct. 1, 1998, for the period beginning on Oct. 1, 1998, and ending on Apr. 1, 1999, but all cases commenced or pending under this chapter 12, as reenacted under section 149(a) of Pub.L. 105–277, and all matters and proceedings in or relating to such cases, to be conducted and determined under such chapter as if such chapter were continued in effect after Apr. 1, 1999, and the substantive rights of parties in connection with such cases, matters, and proceedings to continue to be governed under the law applicable to such cases, matters, and proceedings as if such chapter were continued in effect after Apr. 1, 1999, see section 149 of Pub.L. 105–277, set out as a note under section 1201 of this title.

1993 Acts. Amendment by Pub.L. 103–65, extending to Oct. 1, 1998 the date of repeal of this chapter, to take effect Aug. 6, 1993, see section 3 of Pub.L. 103–65, set out as a note under section 1221 of this title.

1986 Acts. Section repealed effective Oct. 1, 1998, see section 302(f) of Pub.L. 99–554, as amended, set out in a note under section 581 of Title 28. However, for extension of provisions, see section 149 of Pub.L. 105–277, set out as a note under section 1201 of this title.

Section effective 30 days after Oct. 27, 1986, but not applicable to cases commenced under this title before that date, see section 302(a), (c)(1) of Pub.L. 99–554, set out as a note under section 581 of Title 28, Judiciary and Judicial Procedure.

Reenactment of Chapter

This section as in effect on June 30, 2005, reenacted effective July 1, 2005, see Pub.L. 109–8, § 1001(a), set out as a note under 11 U.S.C.A. § 1201.

Repeal of Chapter; Extension of Provisions

Pub.L. 99–554, Title III, § 302(f), Oct. 27, 1986, 100 Stat. 3124, as amended Pub.L. 103–65, § 1, Aug. 6, 1993, 107 Stat. 311, which provided that, effective Oct. 1, 1998, this chapter is repealed, but that all cases commenced or pending under this chapter, and all matters and proceedings in or relating to such cases, shall be conducted and determined under this chapter as if such chapter had not been repealed, and that the substantive rights of parties in connection with such cases, matters, and proceedings shall continue to be governed under the laws applicable to such cases, matters, and proceedings as if such chapter had not been repealed, was superceded by the reenactment of this chapter by Pub.L. 109–8, Title X, § 1001(a), Apr. 20, 2005, 119 Stat. 185, set out as a note under 11 U.S.C.A. § 1201.

Pub.L. 105–277, Div. C, Title I, § 149, Oct. 21, 1998, 112 Stat. 2681–610, as amended Pub.L. 106–5, §§ 1, 2, Mar. 30, 1999, 113 Stat. 9; Pub.L. 106–70, §§ 1, 2, Oct. 9, 1999, 113 Stat. 1031; Pub.L. 107–8, §§ 1, 2, May 11, 2001, 115 Stat. 10;

Pub.L. 107–17, §§ 1, 2, June 26, 2001, 115 Stat. 151; Pub.L. 107–170, §§ 1, 2, May 7, 2002, 116 Stat. 133; Pub.L. 107–171, Title X, § 10814, May 13, 2002, 116 St. 532; Pub.L. 107–377, § 2, Dec. 19, 2002, 116 Stat. 3115; Pub.L. 108–73, § 2(a), Aug. 15, 2003, 117 Stat. 891; Pub.L. 108–369, § 2(a), Oct. 25, 2004, 118 Stat. 1749, provided that, to take effect on January 1, 2004, chapter 12 of Title 11 [this chapter; 11 U.S.C.A. § 1201 et seq.], as in effect on December 31, 2003, is reenacted for the period beginning on January 1, 2004, and ending on July 1, 2005, but that all cases commenced or pending under this chapter 12, as reenacted under section 149(a) of Pub.L. 105–277, and all matters and proceedings in or relating to such cases, shall be conducted and determined under such chapter as if such chapter were continued in effect after July 1, 2005, and that the substantive rights of parties in connection with such cases, matters, and proceedings shall continue to be governed under the law applicable to such cases, matters, and proceedings as if such chapter were continued in effect after July 1, 2005, was superceded by the reenactment of this chapter by Pub.L. 109–8, Title X, § 1001(a), Apr. 20, 2005, 119 Stat. 185, set out as a note under 11 U.S.C.A. § 1201.

CROSS REFERENCES

Obtaining credit, see 11 USCA § 364.

Revocation of an order of confirmation, see 11 USCA § 1230.

Use, sale or lease of property, see 11 USCA § 363.

§ 1205. Adequate protection

(a) Section 361 does not apply in a case under this chapter.

(b) In a case under this chapter, when adequate protection is required under section 362, 363, or 364 of this title of an interest of an entity in property, such adequate protection may be provided by—

(1) requiring the trustee to make a cash payment or periodic cash payments to such entity, to the extent that the stay under section 362 of this title, use, sale, or lease under section 363 of this title, or any grant of a lien under section 364 of this title results in a decrease in the value of property securing a claim or of an entity's ownership interest in property;

(2) providing to such entity an additional or replacement lien to the extent that such stay, use, sale, lease, or grant results in a decrease in the value of property securing a claim or of an entity's ownership interest in property;

(3) paying to such entity for the use of farmland the reasonable rent customary in the community where the property is located, based upon the rental value, net income, and earning capacity of the property; or

(4) granting such other relief, other than entitling such entity to compensation allowable under section 503(b)(1) of this title as an administrative expense, as will adequately protect the value of property secur-

ing a claim or of such entity's ownership interest in property.

(Added and amended Pub.L. 99–554, Title II, § 255, Title III, § 302(f), Oct. 27, 1986, 100 Stat. 3107, 3124; Pub.L. 103–65, § 1, Aug. 6, 1993, 107 Stat. 311; Pub.L. 105–277, Div. C, Title I, § 149(a), Oct. 21, 1998, 112 Stat. 2681–610; Pub.L. 106–5, § 1(1), (2), Mar. 30, 1999, 113 Stat. 9; Pub.L. 106–70, § 1, Oct. 9, 1999, 113 Stat. 1031; Pub.L. 107–8, § 1, May 11, 2001, 115 Stat. 10; Pub.L. 107–17, § 1, June 26, 2001, 115 Stat. 151; Pub.L. 107–170, § 1, May 7, 2002, 116 Stat. 133; Pub.L. 107–171, Title X, § 10814(a), May 13, 2002, 116 Stat. 532; Pub.L. 107–377, § 2(a), Dec. 19, 2002, 116 Stat. 3115; Pub.L. 108–73, § 2(a), Aug. 15, 2003, 117 Stat. 891; Pub.L. 108–369, § 2(a), Oct. 25, 2004, 118 Stat. 1749; Pub.L. 109–8, Title X, § 1001(a)(1), Apr. 20, 2005, 119 Stat. 185.)

HISTORICAL AND STATUTORY NOTES

Revision Notes and Legislative Reports

1986 Acts. House Report No. 99–764 and House Conference Report No. 99–958, see 1986 U.S. Code Cong. and Adm. News, p. 5227.

1993 Acts. House Report No. 103–32, see 1993 U.S. Code Cong. and Adm. News, p. 373.

1998 Acts. Statement by President, see 1998 U.S. Code Cong. and Adm. News, p. 582.

1999 Acts. Statement by President, see 1999 U.S. Code Cong. and Adm. News, p. 4.

Statement by President, see 1999 U.S. Code Cong. and Adm. News, p. 102.

2001 Acts. House Report No. 107–2, see 2001 U.S. Code Cong. and Adm. News, p. 6.

2005 Acts. House Report No. 109–31(Part I), see 2005 U.S. Code Cong. and Adm. News, p. 88.

Codifications

For repeal of section effective Oct. 1, 1998, and subsequent reenactment of section, see note set out preceding 11 U.S.C.A. § 1201.

Effective and Applicability Provisions

2005 Acts. Amendments by Pub.L. 109–8 effective, except as otherwise provided, 180 days after April 20, 2005, and inapplicable with respect to cases commenced under Title 11 before the effective date, see Pub.L. 109–8, § 1501, set out as a note under 11 U.S.C.A. § 101.

2004 Acts. Amendment by Pub.L. 108–369, § 2(a), extending to July 1, 2005, the date of repeal of this chapter, to take effect Jan. 1, 2004, see Pub.L. 108–369, § 2(b), set out as a note under 11 U.S.C.A. § 1201.

2003 Acts. Amendment by Pub.L. 108–73, § 2(a), extending to Jan. 1, 2004, the date of repeal of this chapter, to take effect July 1, 2003, see Pub.L. 108–73, § 2(b), set out as a note under 11 U.S.C.A. § 1201.

2002 Acts. Amendment by Pub.L. 107–377, § 2(a), extending to July 1, 2003, the date of repeal of this chapter, to take effect Jan. 1, 2003, see Pub.L. 107–377, § 2(b), set out as a note under 11 U.S.C.A. § 1201.

Amendment by Pub.L. 107–171, extending to Jan. 1, 2003, the date of repeal of this chapter, to take effect June 1, 2002, see section 10814(b) of Pub.L. 107–171, set out as a note under 11 U.S.C.A. § 1201.

Amendment by Pub.L. 107–170, extending to June 1, 2002, the date of repeal of this chapter, to take effect October 1, 2001, see section 2 of Pub.L. 107–170, set out as a note under 11 U.S.C.A. § 1201.

2001 Acts. Amendment by Pub.L. 107–17, extending to October 1, 2001, the date of repeal of this chapter, to take effect June 1, 2001, see section 2 of Pub.L. 107–17, set out as a note under 11 U.S.C.A. § 1201.

Amendment by Pub.L. 107–8, extending to June 1, 2001, the date of repeal of this chapter, to take effect July 1, 2000, see section 2 of Pub.L. 107–8, set out as a note under 11 U.S.C.A. § 1201.

1999 Acts. Amendment by Pub.L. 106–70, extending to July 1, 2000, the date of repeal of this chapter, to take effect Oct. 1, 1999, see section 2 of Pub.L. 106–70, set out as a note under section 1201 of this title.

Amendment by Pub.L. 106–5, extending to Oct. 1, 1999 the date of repeal of this chapter, to take effect Apr. 1, 1999, see section 2 of Pub.L. 106–5, set out as a note under section 1201 of this title.

1998 Acts. Section reenacted, eff. Oct. 1, 1998, for the period beginning on Oct. 1, 1998, and ending on Apr. 1, 1999, but all cases commenced or pending under this chapter 12, as reenacted under section 149(a) of Pub.L. 105–277, and all matters and proceedings in or relating to such cases, to be conducted and determined under such chapter as if such chapter were continued in effect after Apr. 1, 1999, and the substantive rights of parties in connection with such cases, matters, and proceedings to continue to be governed under the law applicable to such cases, matters, and proceedings as if such chapter were continued in effect after Apr. 1, 1999, see section 149 of Pub.L. 105–277, set out as a note under section 1201 of this title.

1993 Acts. Amendment by Pub.L. 103–65, extending to Oct. 1, 1998 the date of repeal of this chapter, to take effect Aug. 6, 1993, see section 3 of Pub.L. 103–65, set out as a note under section 1221 of this title.

1986 Acts. Section repealed effective Oct. 1, 1998, see section 302(f) of Pub.L. 99–554, as amended, set out in a note under section 581 of Title 28. However, for extension of provisions, see section 149 of Pub.L. 105–277, set out as a note under section 1201 of this title.

Section effective 30 days after Oct. 27, 1986, but not applicable to cases commenced under this title before that date, see section 302(a), (c)(1) of Pub.L. 99–554, set out as a note under section 581 of Title 28, Judiciary and Judicial Procedure.

Reenactment of Chapter

This section as in effect on June 30, 2005, reenacted effective July 1, 2005, see Pub.L. 109–8, § 1001(a), set out as a note under 11 U.S.C.A. § 1201.

Repeal of Chapter; Extension of Provisions

Pub.L. 99–554, Title III, § 302(f), Oct. 27, 1986, 100 Stat. 3124, as amended Pub.L. 103–65, § 1, Aug. 6, 1993, 107 Stat. 311, which provided that, effective Oct. 1, 1998, this chapter is repealed, but that all cases commenced or pending under this chapter, and all matters and proceedings in or relating to such cases, shall be conducted and determined under this chapter as if such chapter had not been repealed, and that the substantive rights of parties in connection with such cases, matters, and proceedings shall continue to be governed under the laws applicable to such cases, matters, and proceedings as

if such chapter had not been repealed, was superceded by the reenactment of this chapter by Pub.L. 109–8, Title X, § 1001(a), Apr. 20, 2005, 119 Stat. 185, set out as a note under 11 U.S.C.A. § 1201.

Pub.L. 105–277, Div. C, Title I, § 149, Oct. 21, 1998, 112 Stat. 2681–610, as amended Pub.L. 106–5, §§ 1, 2, Mar. 30, 1999, 113 Stat. 9; Pub.L. 106–70, §§ 1, 2, Oct. 9, 1999, 113 Stat. 1031; Pub.L. 107–8, §§ 1, 2, May 11, 2001, 115 Stat. 10; Pub.L. 107–17, §§ 1, 2, June 26, 2001, 115 Stat. 151; Pub.L. 107–170, §§ 1, 2, May 7, 2002, 116 Stat. 133; Pub.L. 107–171, Title X, § 10814, May 13, 2002, 116 St. 532; Pub.L. 107–377, § 2, Dec. 19, 2002, 116 Stat. 3115; Pub.L. 108–73, § 2(a), Aug. 15, 2003, 117 Stat. 891; Pub.L. 108–369, § 2(a), Oct. 25, 2004, 118 Stat. 1749, provided that, to take effect on January 1, 2004, chapter 12 of Title 11 [this chapter; 11 U.S.C.A. § 1201 et seq.], as in effect on December 31, 2003, is reenacted for the period beginning on January 1, 2004, and ending on July 1, 2005, but that all cases commenced or pending under this chapter 12, as reenacted under section 149(a) of Pub.L. 105–277, and all matters and proceedings in or relating to such cases, shall be conducted and determined under such chapter as if such chapter were continued in effect after July 1, 2005, and that the substantive rights of parties in connection with such cases, matters, and proceedings shall continue to be governed under the law applicable to such cases, matters, and proceedings as if such chapter were continued in effect after July 1, 2005, was superceded by the reenactment of this chapter by Pub.L. 109–8, Title X, § 1001(a), Apr. 20, 2005, 119 Stat. 185, set out as a note under 11 U.S.C.A. § 1201.

§ 1206.　Sales free of interests

After notice and a hearing, in addition to the authorization contained in section 363(f), the trustee in a case under this chapter may sell property under section 363(b) and (c) free and clear of any interest in such property of an entity other than the estate if the property is farmland, farm equipment, or property used to carry out a commercial fishing operation (including a commercial fishing vessel), except that the proceeds of such sale shall be subject to such interest.

(Added and amended Pub.L. 99–554, Title II, § 255, Title III, § 302(f), Oct. 27, 1986, 100 Stat. 3108, 3124; Pub.L. 103–65, § 1, Aug. 6, 1993, 107 Stat. 311; Pub.L. 105–277, Div. C, Title I, § 149(a), Oct. 21, 1998, 112 Stat. 2681–610; Pub.L. 106–5, § 1(1), (2), Mar. 30, 1999, 113 Stat. 9; Pub.L. 106–70, § 1, Oct. 9, 1999, 113 Stat. 1031; Pub.L. 107–8, § 1, May 11, 2001, 115 Stat. 10; Pub.L. 107–17, § 1, June 26, 2001, 115 Stat. 151; Pub.L. 107–170, § 1, May 7, 2002, 116 Stat. 133; Pub.L. 107–171, Title X, § 10814(a), May 13, 2002, 116 Stat. 532; Pub.L. 107–377, § 2(a), Dec. 19, 2002, 116 Stat. 3115; Pub.L. 108–73, § 2(a), Aug. 15, 2003, 117 Stat. 891; Pub.L. 108–369, § 2(a), Oct. 25, 2004, 118 Stat. 1749; Pub.L. 109–8, Title X, §§ 1001(a)(1), 1007(c)(3), Apr. 20, 2005, 119 Stat. 185, 188.)

HISTORICAL AND STATUTORY NOTES

Revision Notes and Legislative Reports

1986 Acts. House Report No. 99–764 and House Conference Report No. 99–958, see 1986 U.S. Code Cong. and Adm. News, p. 5227.

1993 Acts. House Report No. 103–32, see 1993 U.S. Code Cong. and Adm. News, p. 373.

1998 Acts. Statement by President, see 1998 U.S. Code Cong. and Adm. News, p. 582.

1999 Acts. Statement by President, see 1999 U.S. Code Cong. and Adm. News, p. 4.

Statement by President, see 1999 U.S. Code Cong. and Adm. News, p. 102.

2001 Acts. House Report No. 107–2, see 2001 U.S. Code Cong. and Adm. News, p. 6.

2005 Acts. House Report No. 109–31(Part I), see 2005 U.S. Code Cong. and Adm. News, p. 88.

Codifications

For repeal of section effective Oct. 1, 1998, and subsequent reenactment of section, see note set out preceding 11 U.S.C.A. § 1201.

Effective and Applicability Provisions

2005 Acts. Amendments by Pub.L. 109–8 effective, except as otherwise provided, 180 days after April 20, 2005, and inapplicable with respect to cases commenced under Title 11 before the effective date, see Pub.L. 109–8, § 1501, set out as a note under 11 U.S.C.A. § 101.

2004 Acts. Amendment by Pub.L. 108–369, § 2(a), extending to July 1, 2005, the date of repeal of this chapter, to take effect Jan. 1, 2004, see Pub.L. 108–369, § 2(b), set out as a note under 11 U.S.C.A. § 1201.

2003 Acts. Amendment by Pub.L. 108–73, § 2(a), extending to Jan. 1, 2004, the date of repeal of this chapter, to take effect July 1, 2003, see Pub.L. 108–73, § 2(b), set out as a note under 11 U.S.C.A. § 1201.

2002 Acts. Amendment by Pub.L. 107–377, § 2(a), extending to July 1, 2003, the date of repeal of this chapter, to take effect Jan. 1, 2003, see Pub.L. 107–377, § 2(b), set out as a note under 11 U.S.C.A. § 1201.

Amendment by Pub.L. 107–171, extending to Jan. 1, 2003, the date of repeal of this chapter, to take effect June 1, 2002, see section 10814(b) of Pub.L. 107–171, set out as a note under 11 U.S.C.A. § 1201.

Amendment by Pub.L. 107–170, extending to June 1, 2002, the date of repeal of this chapter, to take effect October 1, 2001, see section 2 of Pub.L. 107–170, set out as a note under 11 U.S.C.A. § 1201.

2001 Acts. Amendment by Pub.L. 107–17, extending to October 1, 2001, the date of repeal of this chapter, to take effect June 1, 2001, see section 2 of Pub.L. 107–17, set out as a note under 11 U.S.C.A. § 1201.

Amendment by Pub.L. 107–8, extending to June 1, 2001, the date of repeal of this chapter, to take effect July 1, 2000, see section 2 of Pub.L. 107–8, set out as a note under 11 U.S.C.A. § 1201.

1999 Acts. Amendment by Pub.L. 106–70, extending to July 1, 2000, the date of repeal of this chapter, to take effect Oct. 1, 1999, see section 2 of Pub.L. 106–70, set out as a note under section 1201 of this title.

Amendment by Pub.L. 106–5, extending to Oct. 1, 1999 the date of repeal of this chapter, to take effect Apr. 1, 1999, see section 2 of Pub.L. 106–5, set out as a note under section 1201 of this title.

1998 Acts. Section reenacted, eff. Oct. 1, 1998, for the period beginning on Oct. 1, 1998, and ending on Apr. 1, 1999, but all cases commenced or pending under this chapter 12, as reenacted under section 149(a) of Pub.L. 105–277, and all matters and proceedings in or relating to such cases, to be conducted and determined under such chapter as if such chapter were continued in effect after Apr. 1, 1999, and the substantive rights of parties in connection with such cases, matters, and proceedings to continue to be governed under the law applicable to such cases, matters, and proceedings as if such chapter were continued in effect after Apr. 1, 1999, see section 149 of Pub.L. 105–277, set out as a note under section 1201 of this title.

1993 Acts. Amendment by Pub.L. 103–65, extending to Oct. 1, 1998 the date of repeal of this chapter, to take effect Aug. 6, 1993, see section 3 of Pub.L. 103–65, set out as a note under section 1221 of this title.

1986 Acts. Section repealed effective Oct. 1, 1998, see section 302(f) of Pub.L. 99–554, as amended, set out in a note under section 581 of Title 28. However, for extension of provisions, see section 149 of Pub.L. 105–277, set out as a note under section 1201 of this title.

Section effective 30 days after Oct. 27, 1986, but not applicable to cases commenced under this title before that date, see section 302(a), (c)(1) of Pub.L. 99–554, set out as a note under section 581 of Title 28, Judiciary and Judicial Procedure.

Reenactment of Chapter

This section as in effect on June 30, 2005, reenacted effective July 1, 2005, see Pub.L. 109–8, § 1001(a), set out as a note under 11 U.S.C.A. § 1201.

Repeal of Chapter; Extension of Provisions

Pub.L. 99–554, Title III, § 302(f), Oct. 27, 1986, 100 Stat. 3124, as amended Pub.L. 103–65, § 1, Aug. 6, 1993, 107 Stat. 311, which provided that, effective Oct. 1, 1998, this chapter is repealed, but that all cases commenced or pending under this chapter, and all matters and proceedings in or relating to such cases, shall be conducted and determined under this chapter as if such chapter had not been repealed, and that the substantive rights of parties in connection with such cases, matters, and proceedings shall continue to be governed under the laws applicable to such cases, matters, and proceedings as if such chapter had not been repealed, was superceded by the reenactment of this chapter by Pub.L. 109–8, Title X, § 1001(a), Apr. 20, 2005, 119 Stat. 185, set out as a note under 11 U.S.C.A. § 1201.

Pub.L. 105–277, Div. C, Title I, § 149, Oct. 21, 1998, 112 Stat. 2681–610, as amended Pub.L. 106–5, §§ 1, 2, Mar. 30, 1999, 113 Stat. 9; Pub.L. 106–70, §§ 1, 2, Oct. 9, 1999, 113 Stat. 1031; Pub.L. 107–8, §§ 1, 2, May 11, 2001, 115 Stat. 10; Pub.L. 107–17, §§ 1, 2, June 26, 2001, 115 Stat. 151; Pub.L. 107–170, §§ 1, 2, May 7, 2002, 116 Stat. 133; Pub.L. 107–171, Title X, § 10814, May 13, 2002, 116 St. 532; Pub.L. 107–377, § 2, Dec. 19, 2002, 116 Stat. 3115; Pub.L. 108–73, § 2(a), Aug. 15, 2003, 117 Stat. 891; Pub.L. 108–369, § 2(a), Oct. 25, 2004, 118 Stat. 1749, provided that, to take effect on January 1, 2004, chapter 12 of Title 11 [this chapter; 11 U.S.C.A. § 1201 et seq.], as in effect on December 31, 2003, is reenacted for the period beginning on January 1, 2004, and ending on July 1, 2005, but that all cases commenced or pending under this chapter 12, as reenacted under section 149(a) of Pub.L. 105–277, and all matters and proceedings in or relating to such cases, shall be conducted and determined under such chapter as if such chapter were continued in effect after July 1, 2005, and that the substantive rights of parties in connection with such cases, matters, and proceedings shall continue to be governed under the law applicable to such cases, matters, and proceedings as if such chapter were continued in effect after July 1, 2005, was superceded by the reenactment of this chapter by Pub.L. 109–8, Title X, § 1001(a), Apr. 20, 2005, 119 Stat. 185, set out as a note under 11 U.S.C.A. § 1201.

§ 1207. Property of the estate

(a) Property of the estate includes, in addition to the property specified in section 541 of this title—

(1) all property of the kind specified in such section that the debtor acquires after the commencement of the case but before the case is closed, dismissed, or converted to a case under chapter 7 of this title, whichever occurs first; and

(2) earnings from services performed by the debtor after the commencement of the case but before the case is closed, dismissed, or converted to a case under chapter 7 of this title, whichever occurs first.

(b) Except as provided in section 1204, a confirmed plan, or an order confirming a plan, the debtor shall remain in possession of all property of the estate. (Added and amended Pub.L. 99–554, Title II, § 255, Title III, § 302(f), Oct. 27, 1986, 100 Stat. 3108, 3124; Pub.L. 103–65, § 1, Aug. 6, 1993, 107 Stat. 311; Pub.L. 105–277, Div. C, Title I, § 149(a), Oct. 21, 1998, 112 Stat. 2681–610; Pub.L. 106–5, § 1(1), (2), Mar. 30, 1999, 113 Stat. 9; Pub.L. 106–70, § 1, Oct. 9, 1999, 113 Stat. 1031; Pub.L. 107–8, § 1, May 11, 2001, 115 Stat. 10; Pub.L. 107–17, § 1, June 26, 2001, 115 Stat. 151; Pub.L. 107–170, § 1, May 7, 2002, 116 Stat. 133; Pub.L. 107–171, Title X, § 10814(a), May 13, 2002, 116 Stat. 532; Pub.L. 107–377, § 2(a), Dec. 19, 2002, 116 Stat. 3115; Pub.L. 108–73, § 2(a), Aug. 15, 2003, 117 Stat. 891; Pub.L. 108–369, § 2(a), Oct. 25, 2004, 118 Stat. 1749; Pub.L. 109–8, Title X, § 1001(a)(1), Apr. 20, 2005, 119 Stat. 185.)

HISTORICAL AND STATUTORY NOTES

Revision Notes and Legislative Reports

1986 Acts. House Report No. 99–764 and House Conference Report No. 99–958, see 1986 U.S. Code Cong. and Adm. News, p. 5227.

1993 Acts. House Report No. 103–32, see 1993 U.S. Code Cong. and Adm. News, p. 373.

1998 Acts. Statement by President, see 1998 U.S. Code Cong. and Adm. News, p. 582.

1999 Acts. Statement by President, see 1999 U.S. Code Cong. and Adm. News, p. 4.

Statement by President, see 1999 U.S. Code Cong. and Adm. News, p. 102.

2001 Acts. House Report No. 107–2, see 2001 U.S. Code Cong. and Adm. News, p. 6.

2005 Acts. House Report No. 109–31(Part I), see 2005 U.S. Code Cong. and Adm. News, p. 88.

Codifications

For repeal of section effective Oct. 1, 1998, and subsequent reenactment of section, see note set out preceding 11 U.S.C.A. § 1201.

Effective and Applicability Provisions

2005 Acts. Amendments by Pub.L. 109–8 effective, except as otherwise provided, 180 days after April 20, 2005, and

inapplicable with respect to cases commenced under Title 11 before the effective date, see Pub.L. 109–8, § 1501, set out as a note under 11 U.S.C.A. § 101.

2004 Acts. Amendment by Pub.L. 108–369, § 2(a), extending to July 1, 2005, the date of repeal of this chapter, to take effect Jan. 1, 2004, see Pub.L. 108–369, § 2(b), set out as a note under 11 U.S.C.A. § 1201.

2003 Acts. Amendment by Pub.L. 108–73, § 2(a), extending to Jan. 1, 2004, the date of repeal of this chapter, to take effect July 1, 2003, see Pub.L. 108–73, § 2(b), set out as a note under 11 U.S.C.A. § 1201.

2002 Acts. Amendment by Pub.L. 107–377, § 2(a), extending to July 1, 2003, the date of repeal of this chapter, to take effect Jan. 1, 2003, see Pub.L. 107–377, § 2(b), set out as a note under 11 U.S.C.A. § 1201.

Amendment by Pub.L. 107–171, extending to Jan. 1, 2003, the date of repeal of this chapter, to take effect June 1, 2002, see section 10814(b) of Pub.L. 107–171, set out as a note under 11 U.S.C.A. § 1201.

Amendment by Pub.L. 107–170, extending to June 1, 2002, the date of repeal of this chapter, to take effect October 1, 2001, see section 2 of Pub.L. 107–170, set out as a note under 11 U.S.C.A. § 1201.

2001 Acts. Amendment by Pub.L. 107–17, extending to October 1, 2001, the date of repeal of this chapter, to take effect June 1, 2001, see section 2 of Pub.L. 107–17, set out as a note under 11 U.S.C.A. § 1201.

Amendment by Pub.L. 107–8, extending to June 1, 2001, the date of repeal of this chapter, to take effect July 1, 2000, see section 2 of Pub.L. 107–8, set out as a note under 11 U.S.C.A. § 1201.

1999 Acts. Amendment by Pub.L. 106–70, extending to July 1, 2000, the date of repeal of this chapter, to take effect Oct. 1, 1999, see section 2 of Pub.L. 106–70, set out as a note under section 1201 of this title.

Amendment by Pub.L. 106–5, extending to Oct. 1, 1999 the date of repeal of this chapter, to take effect Apr. 1, 1999, see section 2 of Pub.L. 106–5, set out as a note under section 1201 of this title.

1998 Acts. Section reenacted, eff. Oct. 1, 1998, for the period beginning on Oct. 1, 1998, and ending on Apr. 1, 1999, but all cases commenced or pending under this chapter 12, as reenacted under section 149(a) of Pub.L. 105–277, and all matters and proceedings in or relating to such cases, to be conducted and determined under such chapter as if such chapter were continued in effect after Apr. 1, 1999, and the substantive rights of parties in connection with such cases, matters, and proceedings to continue to be governed under the law applicable to such cases, matters, and proceedings as if such chapter were continued in effect after Apr. 1, 1999, see section 149 of Pub.L. 105–277, set out as a note under section 1201 of this title.

1993 Acts. Amendment by Pub.L. 103–65, extending to Oct. 1, 1998 the date of repeal of this chapter, to take effect Aug. 6, 1993, see section 3 of Pub.L. 103–65, set out as a note under section 1221 of this title.

1986 Acts. Section repealed effective Oct. 1, 1998, see section 302(f) of Pub.L. 99–554, as amended, set out in a note under section 581 of Title 28. However, for extension of provisions, see section 149 of Pub.L. 105–277, set out as a note under section 1201 of this title.

Section effective 30 days after Oct. 27, 1986, but not applicable to cases commenced under this title before that date, see section 302(a), (c)(1) of Pub.L. 99–554, set out as a note under section 581 of Title 28, Judiciary and Judicial Procedure.

Reenactment of Chapter

This section as in effect on June 30, 2005, reenacted effective July 1, 2005, see Pub.L. 109–8, § 1001(a), set out as a note under 11 U.S.C.A. § 1201.

Repeal of Chapter; Extension of Provisions

Pub.L. 99–554, Title III, § 302(f), Oct. 27, 1986, 100 Stat. 3124, as amended Pub.L. 103–65, § 1, Aug. 6, 1993, 107 Stat. 311, which provided that, effective Oct. 1, 1998, this chapter is repealed, but that all cases commenced or pending under this chapter, and all matters and proceedings in or relating to such cases, shall be conducted and determined under this chapter as if such chapter had not been repealed, and that the substantive rights of parties in connection with such cases, matters, and proceedings shall continue to be governed under the laws applicable to such cases, matters, and proceedings as if such chapter had not been repealed, was superceded by the reenactment of this chapter by Pub.L. 109–8, Title X, § 1001(a), Apr. 20, 2005, 119 Stat. 185, set out as a note under 11 U.S.C.A. § 1201.

Pub.L. 105–277, Div. C, Title I, § 149, Oct. 21, 1998, 112 Stat. 2681–610, as amended Pub.L. 106–5, §§ 1, 2, Mar. 30, 1999, 113 Stat. 9; Pub.L. 106–70, §§ 1, 2, Oct. 9, 1999, 113 Stat. 1031; Pub.L. 107–8, §§ 1, 2, May 11, 2001, 115 Stat. 10; Pub.L. 107–17, §§ 1, 2, June 26, 2001, 115 Stat. 151; Pub.L. 107–170, §§ 1, 2, May 7, 2002, 116 Stat. 133; Pub.L. 107–171, Title X, § 10814, May 13, 2002, 116 St. 532; Pub.L. 107–377, § 2, Dec. 19, 2002, 116 Stat. 3115; Pub.L. 108–73, § 2(a), Aug. 15, 2003, 117 Stat. 891; Pub.L. 108–369, § 2(a), Oct. 25, 2004, 118 Stat. 1749, provided that, to take effect on January 1, 2004, chapter 12 of Title 11 [this chapter; 11 U.S.C.A. § 1201 et seq.], as in effect on December 31, 2003, is reenacted for the period beginning on January 1, 2004, and ending on July 1, 2005, but that all cases commenced or pending under this chapter 12, as reenacted under section 149(a) of Pub.L. 105–277, and all matters and proceedings in or relating to such cases, shall be conducted and determined under such chapter as if such chapter were continued in effect after July 1, 2005, and that the substantive rights of parties in connection with such cases, matters, and proceedings shall continue to be governed under the law applicable to such cases, matters, and proceedings as if such chapter were continued in effect after July 1, 2005, was superceded by the reenactment of this chapter by Pub.L. 109–8, Title X, § 1001(a), Apr. 20, 2005, 119 Stat. 185, set out as a note under 11 U.S.C.A. § 1201.

§ 1208. Conversion or dismissal

(a) The debtor may convert a case under this chapter to a case under chapter 7 of this title at any time. Any waiver of the right to convert under this subsection is unenforceable.

(b) On request of the debtor at any time, if the case has not been converted under section 706 or 1112 of this title, the court shall dismiss a case under this chapter. Any waiver of the right to dismiss under this subsection is unenforceable.

(c) On request of a party in interest, and after notice and a hearing, the court may dismiss a case under this chapter for cause, including—

(1) unreasonable delay, or gross mismanagement, by the debtor that is prejudicial to creditors;

(2) nonpayment of any fees and charges required under chapter 123 of title 28;

(3) failure to file a plan timely under section 1221 of this title;

(4) failure to commence making timely payments required by a confirmed plan;

(5) denial of confirmation of a plan under section 1225 of this title and denial of a request made for additional time for filing another plan or a modification of a plan;

(6) material default by the debtor with respect to a term of a confirmed plan;

(7) revocation of the order of confirmation under section 1230 of this title, and denial of confirmation of a modified plan under section 1229 of this title;

(8) termination of a confirmed plan by reason of the occurrence of a condition specified in the plan;

(9) continuing loss to or diminution of the estate and absence of a reasonable likelihood of rehabilitation; and

(10) failure of the debtor to pay any domestic support obligation that first becomes payable after the date of the filing of the petition.

(d) On request of a party in interest, and after notice and a hearing, the court may dismiss a case under this chapter or convert a case under this chapter to a case under chapter 7 of this title upon a showing that the debtor has committed fraud in connection with the case.

(e) Notwithstanding any other provision of this section, a case may not be converted to a case under another chapter of this title unless the debtor may be a debtor under such chapter.

(Added and amended Pub.L. 99–554, Title II, § 255, Title III, § 302(f), Oct. 27, 1986, 100 Stat. 3108, 3124; Pub.L. 103–65, § 1, Aug. 6, 1993, 107 Stat. 311; Pub.L. 105–277, Div. C, Title I, § 149(a), Oct. 21, 1998, 112 Stat. 2681–610; Pub.L. 106–5, § 1(1), (2), Mar. 30, 1999, 113 Stat. 9; Pub.L. 106–70, § 1, Oct. 9, 1999, 113 Stat. 1031; Pub.L. 107–8, § 1, May 11, 2001, 115 Stat. 10; Pub.L. 107–17, § 1, June 26, 2001, 115 Stat. 151; Pub.L. 107–170, § 1, May 7, 2002, 116 Stat. 133; Pub.L. 107–171, Title X, § 10814(a), May 13, 2002, 116 Stat. 532; Pub.L. 107–377, § 2(a), Dec. 19, 2002, 116 Stat. 3115; Pub.L. 108–73, § 2(a), Aug. 15, 2003, 117 Stat. 891; Pub.L. 108–369, § 2(a), Oct. 25, 2004, 118 Stat. 1749; Pub.L. 109–8, Title II, § 213(2), Title X, § 1001(a)(1), Apr. 20, 2005, 119 Stat. 52, 185.)

HISTORICAL AND STATUTORY NOTES
Revision Notes and Legislative Reports

1986 Acts. House Report No. 99–764 and House Conference Report No. 99–958, see 1986 U.S. Code Cong. and Adm. News, p. 5227.

1993 Acts. House Report No. 103–32, see 1993 U.S. Code Cong. and Adm. News, p. 373.

1998 Acts. Statement by President, see 1998 U.S. Code Cong. and Adm. News, p. 582.

1999 Acts. Statement by President, see 1999 U.S. Code Cong. and Adm. News, p. 4.

Statement by President, see 1999 U.S. Code Cong. and Adm. News, p. 102.

2001 Acts. House Report No. 107–2, see 2001 U.S. Code Cong. and Adm. News, p. 6.

2005 Acts. House Report No. 109–31(Part I), see 2005 U.S. Code Cong. and Adm. News, p. 88.

Codifications

For repeal of section effective Oct. 1, 1998, and subsequent reenactment of section, see note set out preceding 11 U.S.C.A. § 1201.

Effective and Applicability Provisions

2005 Acts. Amendments by Pub.L. 109–8 effective, except as otherwise provided, 180 days after April 20, 2005, and inapplicable with respect to cases commenced under Title 11 before the effective date, see Pub.L. 109–8, § 1501, set out as a note under 11 U.S.C.A. § 101.

2004 Acts. Amendment by Pub.L. 108–369, § 2(a), extending to July 1, 2005, the date of repeal of this chapter, to take effect Jan. 1, 2004, see Pub.L. 108–369, § 2(b), set out as a note under 11 U.S.C.A. § 1201.

2003 Acts. Amendment by Pub.L. 108–73, § 2(a), extending to Jan. 1, 2004, the date of repeal of this chapter, to take effect July 1, 2003, see Pub.L. 108–73, § 2(b), set out as a note under 11 U.S.C.A. § 1201.

2002 Acts. Amendment by Pub.L. 107–377, § 2(a), extending to July 1, 2003, the date of repeal of this chapter, to take effect Jan. 1, 2003, see Pub.L. 107–377, § 2(b), set out as a note under 11 U.S.C.A. § 1201.

Amendment by Pub.L. 107–171, extending to Jan. 1, 2003, the date of repeal of this chapter, to take effect June 1, 2002, see section 10814(b) of Pub.L. 107–171, set out as a note under 11 U.S.C.A. § 1201.

Amendment by Pub.L. 107–170, extending to June 1, 2002, the date of repeal of this chapter, to take effect Oct. 1, 2001, see section 2 of Pub.L. 107–170, set out as a note under 11 U.S.C.A. § 1201.

2001 Acts. Amendment by Pub.L. 107–17, extending to Oct. 1, 2001, the date of repeal of this chapter, to take effect June 1, 2001, see section 2 of Pub.L. 107–17, set out as a note under 11 U.S.C.A. § 1201.

Amendment by Pub.L. 107–8, extending to June 1, 2001, the date of repeal of this chapter, to take effect July 1, 2000, see section 2 of Pub.L. 107–8, set out as a note under 11 U.S.C.A. § 1201.

1999 Acts. Amendment by Pub.L. 106–70, extending to July 1, 2000, the date of repeal of this chapter, to take effect Oct. 1, 1999, see section 2 of Pub.L. 106–70, set out as a note under section 1201 of this title.

Amendment by Pub.L. 106–5, extending to Oct. 1, 1999, the date of repeal of this chapter, to take effect Apr. 1, 1999, see section 2 of Pub.L. 106–5, set out as a note under section 1201 of this title.

1998 Acts. Section reenacted, eff. Oct. 1, 1998, for the period beginning on Oct. 1, 1998, and ending on Apr. 1, 1999, but all cases commenced or pending under this chapter 12, as reenacted under section 149(a) of Pub.L. 105–277, and all matters and proceedings in or relating to such cases, to be conducted and determined under such chapter as if such chapter were continued in effect after Apr. 1, 1999, and the substantive rights of parties in connection with such cases, matters, and proceedings to continue to be governed under the law applicable to such cases, matters, and proceedings as if such chapter were continued in effect after Apr. 1, 1999, see section 149 of Pub.L. 105–277, set out as a note under section 1201 of this title.

1993 Acts. Amendment by Pub.L. 103–65, extending to Oct. 1, 1998 the date of repeal of this chapter, to take effect Aug. 6, 1993, see section 3 of Pub.L. 103–65, set out as a note under section 1221 of this title.

1986 Acts. Section repealed effective Oct. 1, 1998, see section 302(f) of Pub.L. 99–554, as amended, set out in a note under section 581 of Title 28. However, for extension of provisions, see section 149 of Pub.L. 105–277, set out as a note under section 1201 of this title.

Section effective 30 days after Oct. 27, 1986, but not applicable to cases commenced under this title before that date, see section 302(a), (c)(1) of Pub.L. 99–554, set out as a note under section 581 of Title 28, Judiciary and Judicial Procedure.

Reenactment of Chapter

This section as in effect on June 30, 2005, reenacted effective July 1, 2005, see Pub.L. 109–8, § 1001(a), set out as a note under 11 U.S.C.A. § 1201.

Repeal of Chapter; Extension of Provisions

Pub.L. 99–554, Title III, § 302(f), Oct. 27, 1986, 100 Stat. 3124, as amended Pub.L. 103–65, § 1, Aug. 6, 1993, 107 Stat. 311, which provided that, effective Oct. 1, 1998, this chapter is repealed, but that all cases commenced or pending under this chapter, and all matters and proceedings in or relating to such cases, shall be conducted and determined under this chapter as if such chapter had not been repealed, and that the substantive rights of parties in connection with such cases, matters, and proceedings shall continue to be governed under the laws applicable to such cases, matters, and proceedings as if such chapter had not been repealed, was superceded by the reenactment of this chapter by Pub.L. 109–8, Title X, § 1001(a), Apr. 20, 2005, 119 Stat. 185, set out as a note under 11 U.S.C.A. § 1201.

Pub.L. 105–277, Div. C, Title I, § 149, Oct. 21, 1998, 112 Stat. 2681–610, as amended Pub.L. 106–5, §§ 1, 2, Mar. 30, 1999, 113 Stat. 9; Pub.L. 106–70, §§ 1, 2, Oct. 9, 1999, 113 Stat. 1031; Pub.L. 107–8, §§ 1, 2, May 11, 2001, 115 Stat. 10; Pub.L. 107–17, §§ 1, 2, June 26, 2001, 115 Stat. 151; Pub.L. 107–170, §§ 1, 2, May 7, 2002, 116 Stat. 133; Pub.L. 107–171, Title X, § 10814, May 13, 2002, 116 St. 532; Pub.L. 107–377, § 2, Dec. 19, 2002, 116 Stat. 3115; Pub.L. 108–73, § 2(a), Aug. 15, 2003, 117 Stat. 891; Pub.L. 108–369, § 2(a), Oct. 25, 2004, 118 Stat. 1749, provided that, to take effect on January 1, 2004, chapter 12 of Title 11 [this chapter; 11 U.S.C.A. § 1201 et seq.], as in effect on December 31, 2003, is reenacted for the period beginning on January 1, 2004, and ending on July 1, 2005, but that all cases commenced or pending under this chapter 12, as reenacted under section 149(a) of Pub.L. 105–277, and all matters and proceedings in or relating to such cases, shall be conducted and determined under such chapter as if such chapter were continued in effect after July

1, 2005, and that the substantive rights of parties in connection with such cases, matters, and proceedings shall continue to be governed under the law applicable to such cases, matters, and proceedings as if such chapter were continued in effect after July 1, 2005, was superceded by the reenactment of this chapter by Pub.L. 109–8, Title X, § 1001(a), Apr. 20, 2005, 119 Stat. 185, set out as a note under 11 U.S.C.A. § 1201.

CROSS REFERENCES

Conversion from Chapter seven, see 11 USCA § 706.

Dismissal of Chapter thirteen cases where not converted under this section, see 11 USCA § 1307.

Distribution of property of estate converted to Chapter seven, see 11 USCA § 726.

Effect of,

Conversion, see 11 USCA § 348.

Dismissal, see 11 USCA § 349.

Executory contracts and unexpired leases, see 11 USCA § 365.

Liquidation of estate in railroad reorganization cases, see 11 USCA § 1174.

Termination of debtor's taxable period for cases converted to Chapter seven, see 11 USCA § 346.

SUBCHAPTER II—THE PLAN

§ 1221. Filing of plan

The debtor shall file a plan not later than 90 days after the order for relief under this chapter, except that the court may extend such period if the need for an extension is attributable to circumstances for which the debtor should not justly be held accountable.

(Added and amended Pub.L. 99–554, Title II, § 255, Title III, § 302(f), Oct. 27, 1986, 100 Stat. 3109, 3124; Pub.L. 103–65, §§ 1, 2, Aug. 6, 1993, 107 Stat. 311; Pub.L. 105–277, Div. C, Title I, § 149(a), Oct. 21, 1998, 112 Stat. 2681–610; Pub.L. 106–5, § 1(1), (2), Mar. 30, 1999, 113 Stat. 9; Pub.L. 106–70, § 1, Oct. 9, 1999, 113 Stat. 1031; Pub.L. 107–8, § 1, May 11, 2001, 115 Stat. 10; Pub.L. 107–17, § 1, June 26, 2001, 115 Stat. 151; Pub.L. 107–170, § 1, May 7, 2002, 116 Stat. 133; Pub.L. 107–171, Title X, § 10814(a), May 13, 2002, 116 Stat. 532; Pub.L. 107–377, § 2(a), Dec. 19, 2002, 116 Stat. 3115; Pub.L. 108–73, § 2(a), Aug. 15, 2003, 117 Stat. 891; Pub.L. 108–369, § 2(a), Oct. 25, 2004, 118 Stat. 1749; Pub.L. 109–8, Title X, § 1001(a)(1), Apr. 20, 2005, 119 Stat. 185.)

HISTORICAL AND STATUTORY NOTES

Revision Notes and Legislative Reports

1986 Acts. House Report No. 99–764 and House Conference Report No. 99–958, see 1986 U.S. Code Cong. and Adm. News, p. 5227.

1993 Acts. House Report No. 103–32, see 1993 U.S. Code Cong. and Adm. News, p. 373.

1998 Acts. Statement by President, see 1998 U.S. Code Cong. and Adm. News, p. 582.

1999 Acts. Statement by President, see 1999 U.S. Code Cong. and Adm. News, p. 4.

Statement by President, see 1999 U.S. Code Cong. and Adm. News, p. 102.

2001 Acts. House Report No. 107–2, see 2001 U.S. Code Cong. and Adm. News, p. 6.

2005 Acts. House Report No. 109–31(Part I), see 2005 U.S. Code Cong. and Adm. News, p. 88.

Codifications

For repeal of section effective Oct. 1, 1998, and subsequent reenactment of section, see note set out preceding 11 U.S.C.A. § 1201.

Effective and Applicability Provisions

2005 Acts. Amendments by Pub.L. 109–8 effective, except as otherwise provided, 180 days after April 20, 2005, and inapplicable with respect to cases commenced under Title 11 before the effective date, see Pub.L. 109–8, § 1501, set out as a note under 11 U.S.C.A. § 101.

2004 Acts. Amendment by Pub.L. 108–369, § 2(a), extending to July 1, 2005, the date of repeal of this chapter, to take effect Jan. 1, 2004, see Pub.L. 108–369, § 2(b), set out as a note under 11 U.S.C.A. § 1201.

2003 Acts. Amendment by Pub.L. 108–73, § 2(a), extending to Jan. 1, 2004, the date of repeal of this chapter, to take effect July 1, 2003, see Pub.L. 108–73, § 2(b), set out as a note under 11 U.S.C.A. § 1201.

2002 Acts. Amendment by Pub.L. 107–377, § 2(a), extending to July 1, 2003, the date of repeal of this chapter, to take effect Jan. 1, 2003, see Pub.L. 107–377, § 2(b), set out as a note under 11 U.S.C.A. § 1201.

Amendment by Pub.L. 107–171, extending to Jan. 1, 2003, the date of repeal of this chapter, to take effect June 1, 2002, see section 10814(b) of Pub.L. 107–171, set out as a note under 11 U.S.C.A. § 1201.

Amendment by Pub.L. 107–170, extending to June 1, 2002, the date of repeal of this chapter, to take effect October 1, 2001, see section 2 of Pub.L. 107–170, set out as a note under 11 U.S.C.A. § 1201.

2001 Acts. Amendment by Pub.L. 107–17, extending to October 1, 2001, the date of repeal of this chapter, to take effect June 1, 2001, see section 2 of Pub.L. 107–17, set out as a note under 11 U.S.C.A. § 1201.

Amendment by Pub.L. 107–8, extending to June 1, 2001, the date of repeal of this chapter, to take effect July 1, 2000, see section 2 of Pub.L. 107–8, set out as a note under 11 U.S.C.A. § 1201.

1999 Acts. Amendment by Pub.L. 106–70, extending to July 1, 2000, the date of repeal of this chapter, to take effect Oct. 1, 1999, see section 2 of Pub.L. 106–70, set out as a note under section 1201 of this title.

Amendment by Pub.L. 106–5, extending to Oct. 1, 1999 the date of repeal of this chapter, to take effect Apr. 1, 1999, see section 2 of Pub.L. 106–5, set out as a note under section 1201 of this title.

1998 Acts. Section reenacted, eff. Oct. 1, 1998, for the period beginning on Oct. 1, 1998, and ending on Apr. 1, 1999, but all cases commenced or pending under this chapter 12, as reenacted under section 149(a) of Pub.L. 105–277, and all matters and proceedings in or relating to such cases, to be conducted and determined under such chapter as if such chapter were continued in effect after Apr. 1, 1999, and the substantive rights of parties in connection with such cases, matters, and proceedings to continue to be governed under the law applicable to such cases, matters, and proceedings as if such chapter were continued in effect after Apr. 1, 1999, see section 149 of Pub.L. 105–277, set out as a note under 11 U.S.C.A. § 1201.

1993 Acts. Section 3 of Pub.L. 103–65 provided that:

"(a) **Effective date.**—Except as provided in subsection (b), this Act and the amendments made by this Act [amending this section and provisions set out as a note under 28 U.S.C.A. § 581, and extending the date of repeal of this chapter to Oct. 1, 1998] shall take effect on the date of the enactment of this Act [Aug. 6, 1993].

"(b) **Application of amendment made by section 2.**—The amendment made by section 2 [amending this section] shall not apply with respect to cases commenced under title 11 of the United States Code [this title] before the date of the enactment of this Act [Aug. 6, 1993]."

1986 Acts. Section repealed effective Oct. 1, 1998, see section 302(f) of Pub.L. 99–554, as amended, set out as a note under 28 U.S.C.A. § 581. However, for extension of provisions, see section 149 of Pub.L. 105–277, set out as a note under 11 U.S.C.A. § 1201.

Section effective 30 days after Oct. 27, 1986, but not applicable to cases commenced under this title before that date, see section 302(a), (c)(1) of Pub.L. 99–554, set out as a note under 28 U.S.C.A. § 581.

Reenactment of Chapter

This section as in effect on June 30, 2005, reenacted effective July 1, 2005, see Pub.L. 109–8, § 1001(a), set out as a note under 11 U.S.C.A. § 1201.

Repeal of Chapter; Extension of Provisions

Pub.L. 99–554, Title III, § 302(f), Oct. 27, 1986, 100 Stat. 3124, as amended Pub.L. 103–65, § 1, Aug. 6, 1993, 107 Stat. 311, which provided that, effective Oct. 1, 1998, this chapter is repealed, but that all cases commenced or pending under this chapter, and all matters and proceedings in or relating to such cases, shall be conducted and determined under this chapter as if such chapter had not been repealed, and that the substantive rights of parties in connection with such cases, matters, and proceedings shall continue to be governed under the laws applicable to such cases, matters, and proceedings as if such chapter had not been repealed, was superceded by the reenactment of this chapter by Pub.L. 109–8, Title X, § 1001(a), Apr. 20, 2005, 119 Stat. 185, set out as a note under 11 U.S.C.A. § 1201.

Pub.L. 105–277, Div. C, Title I, § 149, Oct. 21, 1998, 112 Stat. 2681–610, as amended Pub.L. 106–5, §§ 1, 2, Mar. 30, 1999, 113 Stat. 9; Pub.L. 106–70, §§ 1, 2, Oct. 9, 1999, 113 Stat. 1031; Pub.L. 107–8, §§ 1, 2, May 11, 2001, 115 Stat. 10; Pub.L. 107–17, §§ 1, 2, June 26, 2001, 115 Stat. 151; Pub.L. 107–170, §§ 1, 2, May 7, 2002, 116 Stat. 133; Pub.L. 107–171, Title X, § 10814, May 13, 2002, 116 St. 532; Pub.L. 107–377, § 2, Dec. 19, 2002, 116 Stat. 3115; Pub.L. 108–73, § 2(a), Aug. 15, 2003, 117 Stat. 891; Pub.L. 108–369, § 2(a), Oct. 25, 2004, 118 Stat. 1749, provided that, to take effect on January 1, 2004, chapter 12 of Title 11 [this chapter; 11 U.S.C.A. § 1201 et seq.], as in effect on December 31, 2003, is reenacted for the period beginning on January 1, 2004, and ending on July 1, 2005, but that all cases commenced or pending under this chapter 12, as reenacted under section 149(a) of Pub.L. 105–277, and all matters and proceedings in or relating to such cases, shall be conducted and determined under such chapter as if such chapter were continued in effect after July 1, 2005, and that the substantive rights of parties in connection with such cases, matters, and proceedings shall continue

to be governed under the law applicable to such cases, matters, and proceedings as if such chapter were continued in effect after July 1, 2005, was superceded by the reenactment of this chapter by Pub.L. 109–8, Title X, § 1001(a), Apr. 20, 2005, 119 Stat. 185, set out as a note under 11 U.S.C.A. § 1201.

CROSS REFERENCES

Conversion or dismissal for failure to timely file plan, see 11 USCA § 1208.

Effect of conversion, see 11 USCA § 348.

Filing of plan in,

Chapter nine cases, see 11 USCA § 941.

Chapter thirteen cases, see 11 USCA § 1321.

Who may file plan in Chapter eleven cases, see 11 USCA § 1121.

§ 1222. Contents of plan

(a) The plan shall—

(1) provide for the submission of all or such portion of future earnings or other future income of the debtor to the supervision and control of the trustee as is necessary for the execution of the plan;

(2) provide for the full payment, in deferred cash payments, of all claims entitled to priority under section 507, unless the holder of a particular claim agrees to a different treatment of that claim;

(3) if the plan classifies claims and interests, provide the same treatment for each claim or interest within a particular class unless the holder of a particular claim or interest agrees to less favorable treatment;

(4) notwithstanding any other provision of this section, a plan may provide for less than full payment of all amounts owed for a claim entitled to priority under section 507(a)(1)(B) only if the plan provides that all of the debtor's projected disposable income for a 5–year period beginning on the date that the first payment is due under the plan will be applied to make payments under the plan; and

(5) subject to section 1232, provide for the treatment of any claim by a governmental unit of a kind described in section 1232(a).

(b) Subject to subsections (a) and (c) of this section, the plan may—

(1) designate a class or classes of unsecured claims, as provided in section 1122 of this title, but may not discriminate unfairly against any class so designated; however, such plan may treat claims for a consumer debt of the debtor if an individual is liable on such consumer debt with the debtor differently than other unsecured claims;

(2) modify the rights of holders of secured claims, or of holders of unsecured claims, or leave unaffected the rights of holders of any class of claims;

(3) provide for the curing or waiving of any default;

(4) provide for payments on any unsecured claim to be made concurrently with payments on any secured claim or any other unsecured claim;

(5) provide for the curing of any default within a reasonable time and maintenance of payments while the case is pending on any unsecured claim or secured claim on which the last payment is due after the date on which the final payment under the plan is due;

(6) subject to section 365 of this title, provide for the assumption, rejection, or assignment of any executory contract or unexpired lease of the debtor not previously rejected under such section;

(7) provide for the payment of all or part of a claim against the debtor from property of the estate or property of the debtor;

(8) provide for the sale of all or any part of the property of the estate or the distribution of all or any part of the property of the estate among those having an interest in such property;

(9) provide for payment of allowed secured claims consistent with section 1225(a)(5) of this title, over a period exceeding the period permitted under section 1222(c);

(10) provide for the vesting of property of the estate, on confirmation of the plan or at a later time, in the debtor or in any other entity;

(11) provide for the payment of interest accruing after the date of the filing of the petition on unsecured claims that are nondischargeable under section 1228(a), except that such interest may be paid only to the extent that the debtor has disposable income available to pay such interest after making provision for full payment of all allowed claims; and

(12) include any other appropriate provision not inconsistent with this title.

(c) Except as provided in subsections (b)(5) and (b)(9), the plan may not provide for payments over a period that is longer than three years unless the court for cause approves a longer period, but the court may not approve a period that is longer than five years.

(d) Notwithstanding subsection (b)(2) of this section and sections 506(b) and 1225(a)(5) of this title, if it is proposed in a plan to cure a default, the amount necessary to cure the default, shall be determined in accordance with the underlying agreement and applicable nonbankruptcy law.

(Added and amended Pub.L. 99–554, Title II, § 255, Title III, § 302(f), Oct. 27, 1986, 100 Stat. 3109, 3124; Pub.L. 103–65, § 1, Aug. 6, 1993, 107 Stat. 311; Pub.L. 103–394, Title III, § 305(b), Oct. 22, 1994, 108 Stat. 4134; Pub.L. 105–277, Div. C, Title I, § 149(a), Oct. 21, 1998, 112 Stat. 2681–610; Pub.L. 106–5, § 1(1), (2), Mar. 30, 1999, 113 Stat. 9; Pub.L. 106–70, § 1, Oct. 9, 1999, 113 Stat. 1031; Pub.L. 107–8, § 1, May 11,

2001, 115 Stat. 10; Pub.L. 107–17, § 1, June 26, 2001, 115 Stat. 151; Pub.L. 107–170, § 1, May 7, 2002, 116 Stat. 133; Pub.L. 107–171, Title X, § 10814(a), May 13, 2002, 116 Stat. 532; Pub.L. 107–377, § 2(a), Dec. 19, 2002, 116 Stat. 3115; Pub.L. 108–73, § 2(a), Aug. 15, 2003, 117 Stat. 891; Pub.L. 108–369, § 2(a), Oct. 25, 2004, 118 Stat. 1749; Pub.L. 109–8, Title II, § 213(3), (4), Title X, §§ 1001(a)(1), 1003(a), Apr. 20, 2005, 119 Stat. 52, 185, 186; Pub.L. 115–72, Div. B, § 1005(b)(1)(A), Oct. 26, 2017, 131 Stat. 1233.)

HISTORICAL AND STATUTORY NOTES

Revision Notes and Legislative Reports

1986 Acts. House Report No. 99–764 and House Conference Report No. 99–958, see 1986 U.S. Code Cong. and Adm. News, p. 5227.

1993 Acts. House Report No. 103–32, see 1993 U.S. Code Cong. and Adm. News, p. 373.

1994 Acts. House Report No. 103–835, see 1994 U.S. Code Cong. and Adm. News, p. 3340.

1998 Acts. Statement by President, see 1998 U.S. Code Cong. and Adm. News, p. 582.

1999 Acts. Statement by President, see 1999 U.S. Code Cong. and Adm. News, p. 4.

Statement by President, see 1999 U.S. Code Cong. and Adm. News, p. 102.

2001 Acts. House Report No. 107–2, see 2001 U.S. Code Cong. and Adm. News, p. 6.

2005 Acts. House Report No. 109–31(Part I), see 2005 U.S. Code Cong. and Adm. News, p. 88.

Codifications

For repeal of section effective Oct. 1, 1998, and subsequent reenactment of section, see note set out preceding 11 U.S.C.A. § 1201.

Effective and Applicability Provisions

2017 Acts. Pub.L. 115–72, Div. B, § 1005(c), Oct. 26, 2017, 131 Stat. 1234, provided that:

"The amendments made by this section [enacting 11 U.S.C.A. § 1232, and amending this section and 11 U.S.C.A. §§ 1228 and 1229] shall apply to—

"(1) any bankruptcy case—

"(A) that is pending on the date of enactment of this Act [Oct. 26, 2017];

"(B) in which the plan under chapter 12 of title 11, United States Code [11 U.S.C.A. § 1201 et seq.], has not been confirmed on the date of enactment of this Act [Oct. 26, 2017]; and

"(C) relating to which an order of discharge under section 1228 of title 11, United States Code, has not been entered; and

"(2) any bankruptcy case that commences on or after the date of enactment of this Act [Oct. 26, 2017]."

2005 Acts. Pub.L. 109–8, Title X, § 1003(c), Apr. 20, 2005, 119 Stat. 186, provided that: "This section and the amendments made by this section [amending subsec. (a)(2) of this section and 11 U.S.C.A. § 1231(b)] shall take effect on the date of the enactment of this Act [Apr. 20, 2005] and shall not apply with respect to cases commenced under title 11 of the United States Code before such date."

Amendment by section 213(3), (4), Pub.L. 109–8 effective, except as otherwise provided, 180 days after April 20, 2005, and inapplicable with respect to cases commenced under Title 11 before the effective date, see Pub.L. 109–8, § 1501, set out as a note under 11 U.S.C.A. § 101.

2004 Acts. Amendment by Pub.L. 108–369, § 2(a), extending to July 1, 2005, the date of repeal of this chapter, to take effect Jan. 1, 2004, see Pub.L. 108–369, § 2(b), set out as a note under 11 U.S.C.A. § 1201.

2003 Acts. Amendment by Pub.L. 108–73, § 2(a), extending to Jan. 1, 2004, the date of repeal of this chapter, to take effect July 1, 2003, see Pub.L. 108–73, § 2(b), set out as a note under 11 U.S.C.A. § 1201.

2002 Acts. Amendment by Pub.L. 107–377, § 2(a), extending to July 1, 2003, the date of repeal of this chapter, to take effect Jan. 1, 2003, see Pub.L. 107–377, § 2(b), set out as a note under 11 U.S.C.A. § 1201.

Amendment by Pub.L. 107–171, extending to Jan. 1, 2003, the date of repeal of this chapter, to take effect June 1, 2002, see section 10814(b) of Pub.L. 107–171, set out as a note under 11 U.S.C.A. § 1201.

Amendment by Pub.L. 107–170, extending to June 1, 2002, the date of repeal of this chapter, to take effect October 1, 2001, see section 2 of Pub.L. 107–170, set out as a note under 11 U.S.C.A. § 1201.

2001 Acts. Amendment by Pub.L. 107–17, extending to October 1, 2001, the date of repeal of this chapter, to take effect June 1, 2001, see section 2 of Pub.L. 107–17, set out as a note under 11 U.S.C.A. § 1201.

Amendment by Pub.L. 107–8, extending to June 1, 2001, the date of repeal of this chapter, to take effect July 1, 2000, see section 2 of Pub.L. 107–8, set out as a note under 11 U.S.C.A. § 1201.

1999 Acts. Amendment by Pub.L. 106–70, extending to July 1, 2000, the date of repeal of this chapter, to take effect Oct. 1, 1999, see section 2 of Pub.L. 106–70, set out as a note under section 1201 of this title.

Amendment by Pub.L. 106–5, extending to Oct. 1, 1999 the date of repeal of this chapter, to take effect Apr. 1, 1999, see section 2 of Pub.L. 106–5, set out as a note under section 1201 of this title.

1998 Acts. Section reenacted, eff. Oct. 1, 1998, for the period beginning on Oct. 1, 1998, and ending on Apr. 1, 1999, but all cases commenced or pending under this chapter 12, as reenacted under section 149(a) of Pub.L. 105–277, and all matters and proceedings in or relating to such cases, to be conducted and determined under such chapter as if such chapter were continued in effect after Apr. 1, 1999, and the substantive rights of parties in connection with such cases, matters, and proceedings to continue to be governed under the law applicable to such cases, matters, and proceedings as if such chapter were continued in effect after Apr. 1, 1999, see section 149 of Pub.L. 105–277, set out as a note under 11 U.S.C.A. § 1201.

1994 Acts. Amendment by Pub.L. 103–394 effective on Oct. 22, 1994, and applicable only to agreements entered into after Oct. 22, 1994, see section 702 of Pub.L. 103–394, set out as a note under 11 U.S.C.A. § 101.

1993 Acts. Amendment by Pub.L. 103–65, extending to Oct. 1, 1998 the date of repeal of this chapter, to take effect Aug. 6, 1993, see section 3 of Pub.L. 103–65, set out as a note under 11 U.S.C.A. § 1221.

1986 Acts. Section repealed effective Oct. 1, 1998, see section 302(f) of Pub.L. 99–554, as amended, set out in a note

under 28 U.S.C.A. § 581. However, for extension of provisions, see section 149 of Pub.L. 105–277, set out as a note under 11 U.S.C.A. § 1201.

Section effective 30 days after Oct. 27, 1986, but not applicable to cases commenced under this title before that date, see section 302(a), (c)(1) of Pub.L. 99–554, set out as a note under section 581 of Title 28, Judiciary and Judicial Procedure.

Separability of Provisions

If any provision of or amendment made by Pub.L. 103–394 or the application of such provision or amendment to any person or circumstance is held to be unconstitutional, the remaining provisions of and amendments made by Pub.L. 103–394 and the application of such provisions and amendments to any person or circumstance shall not be affected thereby, see section 701 of Pub.L. 103–394, set out as a note under section 101 of this title.

Reenactment of Chapter

This section as in effect on June 30, 2005, reenacted effective July 1, 2005, see Pub.L. 109–8, § 1001(a), set out as a note under 11 U.S.C.A. § 1201.

Repeal of Chapter; Extension of Provisions

Pub.L. 99–554, Title III, § 302(f), Oct. 27, 1986, 100 Stat. 3124, as amended Pub.L. 103–65, § 1, Aug. 6, 1993, 107 Stat. 311, which provided that, effective Oct. 1, 1998, this chapter is repealed, but that all cases commenced or pending under this chapter, and all matters and proceedings in or relating to such cases, shall be conducted and determined under this chapter as if such chapter had not been repealed, and that the substantive rights of parties in connection with such cases, matters, and proceedings shall continue to be governed under the laws applicable to such cases, matters, and proceedings as if such chapter had not been repealed, was superceded by the reenactment of this chapter by Pub.L. 109–8, Title X, § 1001(a), Apr. 20, 2005, 119 Stat. 185, set out as a note under 11 U.S.C.A. § 1201.

Pub.L. 105–277, Div. C, Title I, § 149, Oct. 21, 1998, 112 Stat. 2681–610, as amended Pub.L. 106–5, §§ 1, 2, Mar. 30, 1999, 113 Stat. 9; Pub.L. 106–70, §§ 1, 2, Oct. 9, 1999, 113 Stat. 1031; Pub.L. 107–8, §§ 1, 2, May 11, 2001, 115 Stat. 10; Pub.L. 107–17, §§ 1, 2, June 26, 2001, 115 Stat. 151; Pub.L. 107–170, §§ 1, 2, May 7, 2002, 116 Stat. 133; Pub.L. 107–171, Title X, § 10814, May 13, 2002, 116 St. 532; Pub.L. 107–377, § 2, Dec. 19, 2002, 116 Stat. 3115; Pub.L. 108–73, § 2(a), Aug. 15, 2003, 117 Stat. 891; Pub.L. 108–369, § 2(a), Oct. 25, 2004, 118 Stat. 1749, provided that, to take effect on January 1, 2004, chapter 12 of Title 11 [this chapter; 11 U.S.C.A. § 1201 et seq.], as in effect on December 31, 2003, is reenacted for the period beginning on January 1, 2004, and ending on July 1, 2005, but that all cases commenced or pending under this chapter 12, as reenacted under section 149(a) of Pub.L. 105–277, and all matters and proceedings in or relating to such cases, shall be conducted and determined under such chapter as if such chapter were continued in effect after July 1, 2005, and that the substantive rights of parties in connection with such cases, matters, and proceedings shall continue to be governed under the law applicable to such cases, matters, and proceedings as if such chapter were continued in effect after July 1, 2005, was superceded by the reenactment of this chapter by Pub.L. 109–8, Title X, § 1001(a), Apr. 20, 2005, 119 Stat. 185, set out as a note under 11 U.S.C.A. § 1201.

Contents of plan filed in,

Chapter eleven cases, see 11 USCA § 1123.

Chapter thirteen cases, see 11 USCA § 1322.

Railroad reorganization cases, see 11 USCA § 1172.

§ 1223. Modification of plan before confirmation

(a) The debtor may modify the plan at any time before confirmation, but may not modify the plan so that the plan as modified fails to meet the requirements of section 1222 of this title.

(b) After the debtor files a modification under this section, the plan as modified becomes the plan.

(c) Any holder of a secured claim that has accepted or rejected the plan is deemed to have accepted or rejected, as the case may be, the plan as modified, unless the modification provides for a change in the rights of such holder from what such rights were under the plan before modification, and such holder changes such holder's previous acceptance or rejection.

(Added and amended Pub.L. 99–554, Title II, § 255, Title III, § 302(f), Oct. 27, 1986, 100 Stat. 3110, 3124; Pub.L. 103–65, § 1, Aug. 6, 1993, 107 Stat. 311; Pub.L. 105–277, Div. C, Title I, § 149(a), Oct. 21, 1998, 112 Stat. 2681–610; Pub.L. 106–5, § 1(1), (2), Mar. 30, 1999, 113 Stat. 9; Pub.L. 106–70, § 1, Oct. 9, 1999, 113 Stat. 1031; Pub.L. 107–8, § 1, May 11, 2001, 115 Stat. 10; Pub.L. 107–17, § 1, June 26, 2001, 115 Stat. 151; Pub.L. 107–170, § 1, May 7, 2002, 116 Stat. 133; Pub.L. 107–171, Title X, § 10814(a), May 13, 2002, 116 Stat. 532; Pub.L. 107–377, § 2(a), Dec. 19, 2002, 116 Stat. 3115; Pub.L. 108–73, § 2(a), Aug. 15, 2003, 117 Stat. 891; Pub.L. 108–369, § 2(a), Oct. 25, 2004, 118 Stat. 1749; Pub.L. 109–8, Title X, § 1001(a)(1), Apr. 20, 2005, 119 Stat. 185.)

HISTORICAL AND STATUTORY NOTES

Revision Notes and Legislative Reports

1986 Acts. House Report No. 99–764 and House Conference Report No. 99–958, see 1986 U.S. Code Cong. and Adm. News, p. 5227.

1993 Acts. House Report No. 103–32, see 1993 U.S. Code Cong. and Adm. News, p. 373.

1998 Acts. Statement by President, see 1998 U.S. Code Cong. and Adm. News, p. 582.

1999 Acts. Statement by President, see 1999 U.S. Code Cong. and Adm. News, p. 4.

Statement by President, see 1999 U.S. Code Cong. and Adm. News, p. 102.

2001 Acts. House Report No. 107–2, see 2001 U.S. Code Cong. and Adm. News, p. 6.

2005 Acts. House Report No. 109–31(Part I), see 2005 U.S. Code Cong. and Adm. News, p. 88.

Codifications

For repeal of section effective Oct. 1, 1998, and subsequent reenactment of section, see note set out preceding 11 U.S.C.A. § 1201.

Effective and Applicability Provisions

2005 Acts. Amendments by Pub.L. 109–8 effective, except as otherwise provided, 180 days after April 20, 2005, and inapplicable with respect to cases commenced under Title 11 before the effective date, see Pub.L. 109–8, § 1501, set out as a note under 11 U.S.C.A. § 101.

2004 Acts. Amendment by Pub.L. 108–369, § 2(a), extending to July 1, 2005, the date of repeal of this chapter, to take effect Jan. 1, 2004, see Pub.L. 108–369, § 2(b), set out as a note under 11 U.S.C.A. § 1201.

2003 Acts. Amendment by Pub.L. 108–73, § 2(a), extending to Jan. 1, 2004, the date of repeal of this chapter, to take effect July 1, 2003, see Pub.L. 108–73, § 2(b), set out as a note under 11 U.S.C.A. § 1201.

2002 Acts. Amendment by Pub.L. 107–377, § 2(a), extending to July 1, 2003, the date of repeal of this chapter, to take effect Jan. 1, 2003, see Pub.L. 107–377, § 2(b), set out as a note under 11 U.S.C.A. § 1201.

Amendment by Pub.L. 107–171, extending to Jan. 1, 2003, the date of repeal of this chapter, to take effect June 1, 2002, see section 10814(b) of Pub.L. 107–171, set out as a note under 11 U.S.C.A. § 1201.

Amendment by Pub.L. 107–170, extending to June 1, 2002, the date of repeal of this chapter, to take effect October 1, 2001, see section 2 of Pub.L. 107–170, set out as a note under 11 U.S.C.A. § 1201.

2001 Acts. Amendment by Pub.L. 107–17, extending to October 1, 2001, the date of repeal of this chapter, to take effect June 1, 2001, see section 2 of Pub.L. 107–17, set out as a note under 11 U.S.C.A. § 1201.

Amendment by Pub.L. 107–8, extending to June 1, 2001, the date of repeal of this chapter, to take effect July 1, 2000, see section 2 of Pub.L. 107–8, set out as a note under 11 U.S.C.A. § 1201.

1999 Acts. Amendment by Pub.L. 106–70, extending to July 1, 2000, the date of repeal of this chapter, to take effect Oct. 1, 1999, see section 2 of Pub.L. 106–70, set out as a note under 11 U.S.C.A. § 1201.

Amendment by Pub.L. 106–5, extending to Oct. 1, 1999 the date of repeal of this chapter, to take effect Apr. 1, 1999, see section 2 of Pub.L. 106–5, set out as a note under 11 U.S.C.A. § 1201.

1998 Acts. Section reenacted, eff. Oct. 1, 1998, for the period beginning on Oct. 1, 1998, and ending on Apr. 1, 1999, but all cases commenced or pending under this chapter 12, as reenacted under section 149(a) of Pub.L. 105–277, and all matters and proceedings in or relating to such cases, to be conducted and determined under such chapter as if such chapter were continued in effect after Apr. 1, 1999, and the substantive rights of parties in connection with such cases, matters, and proceedings to continue to be governed under the law applicable to such cases, matters, and proceedings as if such chapter were continued in effect after Apr. 1, 1999, see section 149 of Pub.L. 105–277, set out as a note under 11 U.S.C.A. § 1201.

1993 Acts. Amendment by Pub.L. 103–65, extending to Oct. 1, 1998 the date of repeal of this chapter, to take effect Aug. 6, 1993, see section 3 of Pub.L. 103–65, set out as a note under 11 U.S.C.A. § 1221.

1986 Acts. Section repealed effective Oct. 1, 1998, see section 302(f) of Pub.L. 99–554, as amended, set out in a note under 28 U.S.C.A. § 581. However, for extension of provisions, see section 149 of Pub.L. 105–277, set out as a note under 11 U.S.C.A. § 1201.

Section effective 30 days after Oct. 27, 1986, but not applicable to cases commenced under this title before that date, see section 302(a), (c)(1) of Pub.L. 99–554, set out as a note under 28 U.S.C.A. § 581.

Reenactment of Chapter

This section as in effect on June 30, 2005, reenacted effective July 1, 2005, see Pub.L. 109–8, § 1001(a), set out as a note under 11 U.S.C.A. § 1201.

Repeal of Chapter; Extension of Provisions

Pub.L. 99–554, Title III, § 302(f), Oct. 27, 1986, 100 Stat. 3124, as amended Pub.L. 103–65, § 1, Aug. 6, 1993, 107 Stat. 311, which provided that, effective Oct. 1, 1998, this chapter is repealed, but that all cases commenced or pending under this chapter, and all matters and proceedings in or relating to such cases, shall be conducted and determined under this chapter as if such chapter had not been repealed, and that the substantive rights of parties in connection with such cases, matters, and proceedings shall continue to be governed under the laws applicable to such cases, matters, and proceedings as if such chapter had not been repealed, was superceded by the reenactment of this chapter by Pub.L. 109–8, Title X, § 1001(a), Apr. 20, 2005, 119 Stat. 185, set out as a note under 11 U.S.C.A. § 1201.

Pub.L. 105–277, Div. C, Title I, § 149, Oct. 21, 1998, 112 Stat. 2681–610, as amended Pub.L. 106–5, §§ 1, 2, Mar. 30, 1999, 113 Stat. 9; Pub.L. 106–70, §§ 1, 2, Oct. 9, 1999, 113 Stat. 1031; Pub.L. 107–8, §§ 1, 2, May 11, 2001, 115 Stat. 10; Pub.L. 107–17, §§ 1, 2, June 26, 2001, 115 Stat. 151; Pub.L. 107–170, §§ 1, 2, May 7, 2002, 116 Stat. 133; Pub.L. 107–171, Title X, § 10814, May 13, 2002, 116 St. 532; Pub.L. 107–377, § 2, Dec. 19, 2002, 116 Stat. 3115; Pub.L. 108–73, § 2(a), Aug. 15, 2003, 117 Stat. 891; Pub.L. 108–369, § 2(a), Oct. 25, 2004, 118 Stat. 1749, provided that, to take effect on January 1, 2004, chapter 12 of Title 11 [this chapter; 11 U.S.C.A. § 1201 et seq.], as in effect on December 31, 2003, is reenacted for the period beginning on January 1, 2004, and ending on July 1, 2005, but that all cases commenced or pending under this chapter 12, as reenacted under section 149(a) of Pub.L. 105–277, and all matters and proceedings in or relating to such cases, shall be conducted and determined under such chapter as if such chapter were continued in effect after July 1, 2005, and that the substantive rights of parties in connection with such cases, matters, and proceedings shall continue to be governed under the law applicable to such cases, matters, and proceedings as if such chapter were continued in effect after July 1, 2005, was superceded by the reenactment of this chapter by Pub.L. 109–8, Title X, § 1001(a), Apr. 20, 2005, 119 Stat. 185, set out as a note under 11 U.S.C.A. § 1201.

CROSS REFERENCES

Modification of plan filed in,

Chapter eleven cases, see 11 USCA § 1127.

Chapter nine cases, see 11 USCA § 942.

Chapter thirteen cases, see 11 USCA § 1323.

§ 1224. Confirmation hearing

After expedited notice, the court shall hold a hearing on confirmation of the plan. A party in interest, the trustee, or the United States trustee may object to the confirmation of the plan. Except for cause, the hearing shall be concluded not later than 45 days after the filing of the plan.

(Added and amended Pub.L. 99–554, Title II, § 255, Title III, § 302(f), Oct. 27, 1986, 100 Stat. 3110, 3124; Pub.L. 103–65, § 1, Aug. 6, 1993, 107 Stat. 311; Pub.L. 105–277, Div. C, Title I, § 149(a), Oct. 21, 1998, 112 Stat. 2681–610; Pub.L. 106–5, § 1(1), (2), Mar. 30, 1999, 113 Stat. 9; Pub.L. 106–70, § 1, Oct. 9, 1999, 113 Stat. 1031; Pub.L. 107–8, § 1, May 11, 2001, 115 Stat. 10; Pub.L. 107–17, § 1, June 26, 2001, 115 Stat. 151; Pub.L. 107–170, § 1, May 7, 2002, 116 Stat. 133; Pub.L. 107–171, Title X, § 10814(a), May 13, 2002, 116 Stat. 532; Pub.L. 107–377, § 2(a), Dec. 19, 2002, 116 Stat. 3115; Pub.L. 108–73, § 2(a), Aug. 15, 2003, 117 Stat. 891; Pub.L. 108–369, § 2(a), Oct. 25, 2004, 118 Stat. 1749; Pub.L. 109–8, Title X, § 1001(a)(1), Apr. 20, 2005, 119 Stat. 185.)

HISTORICAL AND STATUTORY NOTES

Revision Notes and Legislative Reports

1986 Acts. House Report No. 99–764 and House Conference Report No. 99–958, see 1986 U.S. Code Cong. and Adm. News, p. 5227.

1993 Acts. House Report No. 103–32, see 1993 U.S. Code Cong. and Adm. News, p. 373.

1998 Acts. Statement by President, see 1998 U.S. Code Cong. and Adm. News, p. 582.

1999 Acts. Statement by President, see 1999 U.S. Code Cong. and Adm. News, p. 4.

Statement by President, see 1999 U.S. Code Cong. and Adm. News, p. 102.

2001 Acts. House Report No. 107–2, see 2001 U.S. Code Cong. and Adm. News, p. 6.

2005 Acts. House Report No. 109–31(Part I), see 2005 U.S. Code Cong. and Adm. News, p. 88.

Codifications

For repeal of section effective Oct. 1, 1998, and subsequent reenactment of section, see note set out preceding 11 U.S.C.A. § 1201.

Effective and Applicability Provisions

2005 Acts. Amendments by Pub.L. 109–8 effective, except as otherwise provided, 180 days after April 20, 2005, and inapplicable with respect to cases commenced under Title 11 before the effective date, see Pub.L. 109–8, § 1501, set out as a note under 11 U.S.C.A. § 101.

2004 Acts. Amendment by Pub.L. 108–369, § 2(a), extending to July 1, 2005, the date of repeal of this chapter, to take effect Jan. 1, 2004, see Pub.L. 108–369, § 2(b), set out as a note under 11 U.S.C.A. § 1201.

2003 Acts. Amendment by Pub.L. 108–73, § 2(a), extending to Jan. 1, 2004, the date of repeal of this chapter, to take effect July 1, 2003, see Pub.L. 108–73, § 2(b), set out as a note under 11 U.S.C.A. § 1201.

2002 Acts. Amendment by Pub.L. 107–377, § 2(a), extending to July 1, 2003, the date of repeal of this chapter, to take effect Jan. 1, 2003, see Pub.L. 107–377, § 2(b), set out as a note under 11 U.S.C.A. § 1201.

Amendment by Pub.L. 107–171, extending to Jan. 1, 2003, the date of repeal of this chapter, to take effect June 1, 2002, see section 10814(b) of Pub.L. 107–171, set out as a note under 11 U.S.C.A. § 1201.

Amendment by Pub.L. 107–170, extending to June 1, 2002, the date of repeal of this chapter, to take effect October 1, 2001, see section 2 of Pub.L. 107–170, set out as a note under 11 U.S.C.A. § 1201.

2001 Acts. Amendment by Pub.L. 107–17, extending to October 1, 2001, the date of repeal of this chapter, to take effect June 1, 2001, see section 2 of Pub.L. 107–17, set out as a note under 11 U.S.C.A. § 1201.

Amendment by Pub.L. 107–8, extending to June 1, 2001, the date of repeal of this chapter, to take effect July 1, 2000, see section 2 of Pub.L. 107–8, set out as a note under 11 U.S.C.A. § 1201.

1999 Acts. Amendment by Pub.L. 106–70, extending to July 1, 2000, the date of repeal of this chapter, to take effect Oct. 1, 1999, see section 2 of Pub.L. 106–70, set out as a note under 11 U.S.C.A. § 1201.

Amendment by Pub.L. 106–5, extending to Oct. 1, 1999 the date of repeal of this chapter, to take effect Apr. 1, 1999, see section 2 of Pub.L. 106–5, set out as a note under 11 U.S.C.A. § 1201.

1998 Acts. Section reenacted, eff. Oct. 1, 1998, for the period beginning on Oct. 1, 1998, and ending on Apr. 1, 1999, but all cases commenced or pending under this chapter 12, as reenacted under section 149(a) of Pub.L. 105–277, and all matters and proceedings in or relating to such cases, to be conducted and determined under such chapter as if such chapter were continued in effect after Apr. 1, 1999, and the substantive rights of parties in connection with such cases, matters, and proceedings to continue to be governed under the law applicable to such cases, matters, and proceedings as if such chapter were continued in effect after Apr. 1, 1999, see section 149 of Pub.L. 105–277, set out as a note under 11 U.S.C.A. § 1201.

1993 Acts. Amendment by Pub.L. 103–65, extending to Oct. 1, 1998 the date of repeal of this chapter, to take effect Aug. 6, 1993, see section 3 of Pub.L. 103–65, set out as a note under 11 U.S.C.A. § 1221.

1986 Acts. Section repealed effective Oct. 1, 1998, see section 302(f) of Pub.L. 99–554, as amended, set out in a note under 28 U.S.C.A. § 581. However, for extension of provisions, see section 149 of Pub.L. 105–277, set out as a note under 11 U.S.C.A. § 1201.

Section effective 30 days after Oct. 27, 1986, but not applicable to cases commenced under this title before that date, see section 302(a), (c)(1) of Pub.L. 99–554, set out as a note under 28 U.S.C.A. § 581.

Reenactment of Chapter

This section as in effect on June 30, 2005, reenacted effective July 1, 2005, see Pub.L. 109–8, § 1001(a), set out as a note under 11 U.S.C.A. § 1201.

Repeal of Chapter; Extension of Provisions

Pub.L. 99–554, Title III, § 302(f), Oct. 27, 1986, 100 Stat. 3124, as amended Pub.L. 103–65, § 1, Aug. 6, 1993, 107 Stat. 311, which provided that, effective Oct. 1, 1998, this chapter is repealed, but that all cases commenced or pending under this chapter, and all matters and proceedings in or relating to such cases, shall be conducted and determined under this chapter as if such chapter had not been repealed, and that the substantive rights of parties in connection with such cases, matters, and proceedings shall continue to be governed under

the laws applicable to such cases, matters, and proceedings as if such chapter had not been repealed, was superceded by the reenactment of this chapter by Pub.L. 109–8, Title X, § 1001(a), Apr. 20, 2005, 119 Stat. 185, set out as a note under 11 U.S.C.A. § 1201.

Pub.L. 105–277, Div. C, Title I, § 149, Oct. 21, 1998, 112 Stat. 2681–610, as amended Pub.L. 106–5, §§ 1, 2, Mar. 30, 1999, 113 Stat. 9; Pub.L. 106–70, §§ 1, 2, Oct. 9, 1999, 113 Stat. 1031; Pub.L. 107–8, §§ 1, 2, May 11, 2001, 115 Stat. 10; Pub.L. 107–17, §§ 1, 2, June 26, 2001, 115 Stat. 151; Pub.L. 107–170, §§ 1, 2, May 7, 2002, 116 Stat. 133; Pub.L. 107–171, Title X, § 10814, May 13, 2002, 116 St. 532; Pub.L. 107–377, § 2, Dec. 19, 2002, 116 Stat. 3115; Pub.L. 108–73, § 2(a), Aug. 15, 2003, 117 Stat. 891; Pub.L. 108–369, § 2(a), Oct. 25, 2004, 118 Stat. 1749, provided that, to take effect on January 1, 2004, chapter 12 of Title 11 [this chapter; 11 U.S.C.A. § 1201 et seq.], as in effect on December 31, 2003, is reenacted for the period beginning on January 1, 2004, and ending on July 1, 2005, but that all cases commenced or pending under this chapter 12, as reenacted under section 149(a) of Pub.L. 105–277, and all matters and proceedings in or relating to such cases, shall be conducted and determined under such chapter as if such chapter were continued in effect after July 1, 2005, and that the substantive rights of parties in connection with such cases, matters, and proceedings shall continue to be governed under the law applicable to such cases, matters, and proceedings as if such chapter were continued in effect after July 1, 2005, was superceded by the reenactment of this chapter by Pub.L. 109–8, Title X, § 1001(a), Apr. 20, 2005, 119 Stat. 185, set out as a note under 11 U.S.C.A. § 1201.

CROSS REFERENCES

Confirmation hearing in,

Chapter eleven cases, see 11 USCA § 1128.

Chapter thirteen cases, see 11 USCA § 1324.

Duties of United States trustee, see 28 USCA § 586.

§ 1225. Confirmation of plan

(a) Except as provided in subsection (b), the court shall confirm a plan if—

(1) the plan complies with the provisions of this chapter and with the other applicable provisions of this title;

(2) any fee, charge, or amount required under chapter 123 of title 28, or by the plan, to be paid before confirmation, has been paid;

(3) the plan has been proposed in good faith and not by any means forbidden by law;

(4) the value, as of the effective date of the plan, of property to be distributed under the plan on account of each allowed unsecured claim is not less than the amount that would be paid on such claim if the estate of the debtor were liquidated under chapter 7 of this title on such date;

(5) with respect to each allowed secured claim provided for by the plan—

(A) the holder of such claim has accepted the plan;

(B)(i) the plan provides that the holder of such claim retain the lien securing such claim; and

(ii) the value, as of the effective date of the plan, of property to be distributed by the trustee or the debtor under the plan on account of such claim is not less than the allowed amount of such claim; or

(C) the debtor surrenders the property securing such claim to such holder;

(6) the debtor will be able to make all payments under the plan and to comply with the plan; and

(7) the debtor has paid all amounts that are required to be paid under a domestic support obligation and that first become payable after the date of the filing of the petition if the debtor is required by a judicial or administrative order, or by statute, to pay such domestic support obligation.

(b)(1) If the trustee or the holder of an allowed unsecured claim objects to the confirmation of the plan, then the court may not approve the plan unless, as of the effective date of the plan—

(A) the value of the property to be distributed under the plan on account of such claim is not less than the amount of such claim;

(B) the plan provides that all of the debtor's projected disposable income to be received in the three-year period, or such longer period as the court may approve under section 1222(c), beginning on the date that the first payment is due under the plan will be applied to make payments under the plan; or

(C) the value of the property to be distributed under the plan in the 3–year period, or such longer period as the court may approve under section 1222(c), beginning on the date that the first distribution is due under the plan is not less than the debtor's projected disposable income for such period.

(2) For purposes of this subsection, "disposable income" means income which is received by the debtor and which is not reasonably necessary to be expended—

(A) for the maintenance or support of the debtor or a dependent of the debtor or for a domestic support obligation that first becomes payable after the date of the filing of the petition; or

(B) for the payment of expenditures necessary for the continuation, preservation, and operation of the debtor's business.

(c) After confirmation of a plan, the court may order any entity from whom the debtor receives income to pay all or any part of such income to the trustee.

(Added and amended Pub.L. 99–554, Title II, § 255, Title III, § 302(f), Oct. 27, 1986, 100 Stat. 3110, 3124; Pub.L. 103–65, § 1, Aug. 6, 1993, 107 Stat. 311; Pub.L. 105–277, Div. C, Title I, § 149(a), Oct. 21, 1998, 112 Stat. 2681–610; Pub.L. 106–5, § 1(1), (2), Mar. 30, 1999, 113 Stat. 9; Pub.L. 106–70, § 1, Oct. 9, 1999, 113 Stat. 1031; Pub.L. 107–8, § 1, May 11, 2001, 115 Stat. 10; Pub.L. 107–17, § 1, June 26, 2001, 115 Stat. 151;

Pub.L. 107–170, § 1, May 7, 2002, 116 Stat. 133; Pub.L. 107–171, Title X, § 10814(a), May 13, 2002, 116 Stat. 532; Pub.L. 107–377, § 2(a), Dec. 19, 2002, 116 Stat. 3115; Pub.L. 108–73, § 2(a), Aug. 15, 2003, 117 Stat. 891; Pub.L. 108–369, § 2(a), Oct. 25, 2004, 118 Stat. 1749; Pub.L. 109–8, Title II, §§ 213(5), 218, Title X, §§ 1001(a)(1), 1006(a), Apr. 20, 2005, 119 Stat. 52, 55, 185, 187.)

HISTORICAL AND STATUTORY NOTES

Revision Notes and Legislative Reports

1986 Acts. House Report No. 99–764 and House Conference Report No. 99–958, see 1986 U.S. Code Cong. and Adm. News, p. 5227.

1993 Acts. House Report No. 103–32, see 1993 U.S. Code Cong. and Adm. News, p. 373.

1998 Acts. Statement by President, see 1998 U.S. Code Cong. and Adm. News, p. 582.

1999 Acts. Statement by President, see 1999 U.S. Code Cong. and Adm. News, p. 4.

Statement by President, see 1999 U.S. Code Cong. and Adm. News, p. 102.

2001 Acts. House Report No. 107–2, see 2001 U.S. Code Cong. and Adm. News, p. 6.

2005 Acts. House Report No. 109–31(Part I), see 2005 U.S. Code Cong. and Adm. News, p. 88.

Codifications

For repeal of section effective Oct. 1, 1998, and subsequent reenactment of section, see note set out preceding 11 U.S.C.A. § 1201.

Effective and Applicability Provisions

2005 Acts. Amendments by Pub.L. 109–8 effective, except as otherwise provided, 180 days after April 20, 2005, and inapplicable with respect to cases commenced under Title 11 before the effective date, see Pub.L. 109–8, § 1501, set out as a note under 11 U.S.C.A. § 101.

2004 Acts. Amendment by Pub.L. 108–369, § 2(a), extending to July 1, 2005, the date of repeal of this chapter, to take effect Jan. 1, 2004, see Pub.L. 108–369, § 2(b), set out as a note under 11 U.S.C.A. § 1201.

2003 Acts. Amendment by Pub.L. 108–73, § 2(a), extending to Jan. 1, 2004, the date of repeal of this chapter, to take effect July 1, 2003, see Pub.L. 108–73, § 2(b), set out as a note under 11 U.S.C.A. § 1201.

2002 Acts. Amendment by Pub.L. 107–377, § 2(a), extending to July 1, 2003, the date of repeal of this chapter, to take effect Jan. 1, 2003, see Pub.L. 107–377, § 2(b), set out as a note under 11 U.S.C.A. § 1201.

Amendment by Pub.L. 107–171, extending to Jan. 1, 2003, the date of repeal of this chapter, to take effect June 1, 2002, see section 10814(b) of Pub.L. 107–171, set out as a note under 11 U.S.C.A. § 1201.

Amendment by Pub.L. 107–170, extending to June 1, 2002, the date of repeal of this chapter, to take effect October 1, 2001, see section 2 of Pub.L. 107–170, set out as a note under 11 U.S.C.A. § 1201.

2001 Acts. Amendment by Pub.L. 107–17, extending to October 1, 2001, the date of repeal of this chapter, to take effect June 1, 2001, see section 2 of Pub.L. 107–17, set out as a note under 11 U.S.C.A. § 1201.

Amendment by Pub.L. 107–8, extending to June 1, 2001, the date of repeal of this chapter, to take effect July 1, 2000, see section 2 of Pub.L. 107–8, set out as a note under 11 U.S.C.A. § 1201.

1999 Acts. Amendment by Pub.L. 106–70, extending to July 1, 2000, the date of repeal of this chapter, to take effect Oct. 1, 1999, see section 2 of Pub.L. 106–70, set out as a note under 11 U.S.C.A. § 1201.

Amendment by Pub.L. 106–5, extending to Oct. 1, 1999 the date of repeal of this chapter, to take effect Apr. 1, 1999, see section 2 of Pub.L. 106–5, set out as a note under 11 U.S.C.A. § 1201.

1998 Acts. Section reenacted, eff. Oct. 1, 1998, for the period beginning on Oct. 1, 1998, and ending on Apr. 1, 1999, but all cases commenced or pending under this chapter 12, as reenacted under section 149(a) of Pub.L. 105–277, and all matters and proceedings in or relating to such cases, to be conducted and determined under such chapter as if such chapter were continued in effect after Apr. 1, 1999, and the substantive rights of parties in connection with such cases, matters, and proceedings to continue to be governed under the law applicable to such cases, matters, and proceedings as if such chapter were continued in effect after Apr. 1, 1999, see section 149 of Pub.L. 105–277, set out as a note under 11 U.S.C.A. § 1201.

1993 Acts. Amendment by Pub.L. 103–65, extending to Oct. 1, 1998 the date of repeal of this chapter, to take effect Aug. 6, 1993, see section 3 of Pub.L. 103–65, set out as a note under 11 U.S.C.A. § 1221.

1986 Acts. Section repealed effective Oct. 1, 1998, see section 302(f) of Pub.L. 99–554, as amended, set out in a note under 28 U.S.C.A. § 581. However, for extension of provisions, see section 149 of Pub.L. 105–277, set out as a note under 28 U.S.C.A. § 1201.

Section effective 30 days after Oct. 27, 1986, but not applicable to cases commenced under this title before that date, see section 302(a), (c)(1) of Pub.L. 99–554, set out as a note under 28 U.S.C.A. § 581.

Reenactment of Chapter

This section as in effect on June 30, 2005, reenacted effective July 1, 2005, see Pub.L. 109–8, § 1001(a), set out as a note under 11 U.S.C.A. § 1201.

Repeal of Chapter; Extension of Provisions

Pub.L. 99–554, Title III, § 302(f), Oct. 27, 1986, 100 Stat. 3124, as amended Pub.L. 103–65, § 1, Aug. 6, 1993, 107 Stat. 311, which provided that, effective Oct. 1, 1998, this chapter is repealed, but that all cases commenced or pending under this chapter, and all matters and proceedings in or relating to such cases, shall be conducted and determined under this chapter as if such chapter had not been repealed, and that the substantive rights of parties in connection with such cases, matters, and proceedings shall continue to be governed under the laws applicable to such cases, matters, and proceedings as if such chapter had not been repealed, was superceded by the reenactment of this chapter by Pub.L. 109–8, Title X, § 1001(a), Apr. 20, 2005, 119 Stat. 185, set out as a note under 11 U.S.C.A. § 1201.

Pub.L. 105–277, Div. C, Title I, § 149, Oct. 21, 1998, 112 Stat. 2681–610, as amended Pub.L. 106–5, §§ 1, 2, Mar. 30, 1999, 113 Stat. 9; Pub.L. 106–70, §§ 1, 2, Oct. 9, 1999, 113 Stat. 1031; Pub.L. 107–8, §§ 1, 2, May 11, 2001, 115 Stat. 10; Pub.L. 107–17, §§ 1, 2, June 26, 2001, 115 Stat. 151; Pub.L.

107–170, §§ 1, 2, May 7, 2002, 116 Stat. 133; Pub.L. 107–171, Title X, § 10814, May 13, 2002, 116 St. 532; Pub.L. 107–377, § 2, Dec. 19, 2002, 116 Stat. 3115; Pub.L. 108–73, § 2(a), Aug. 15, 2003, 117 Stat. 891; Pub.L. 108–369, § 2(a), Oct. 25, 2004, 118 Stat. 1749, provided that, to take effect on January 1, 2004, chapter 12 of Title 11 [this chapter; 11 U.S.C.A. § 1201 et seq.], as in effect on December 31, 2003, is reenacted for the period beginning on January 1, 2004, and ending on July 1, 2005, but that all cases commenced or pending under this chapter 12, as reenacted under section 149(a) of Pub.L. 105–277, and all matters and proceedings in or relating to such cases, shall be conducted and determined under such chapter as if such chapter were continued in effect after July 1, 2005, and that the substantive rights of parties in connection with such cases, matters, and proceedings shall continue to be governed under the law applicable to such cases, matters, and proceedings as if such chapter were continued in effect after July 1, 2005, was superceded by the reenactment of this chapter by Pub.L. 109–8, Title X, § 1001(a), Apr. 20, 2005, 119 Stat. 185, set out as a note under 11 U.S.C.A. § 1201.

CROSS REFERENCES

Confirmation of plan in,
    Chapter eleven cases, see 11 USCA § 1129.
    Chapter nine cases, see 11 USCA § 943.
    Chapter thirteen cases, see 11 USCA § 1325.
    Railroad reorganization cases, see 11 USCA § 1173.
Conversion or dismissal, see 11 USCA § 1208.
Unclaimed property, see 11 USCA § 347.

§ 1226.   Payments

(a) Payments and funds received by the trustee shall be retained by the trustee until confirmation or denial of confirmation of a plan. If a plan is confirmed, the trustee shall distribute any such payment in accordance with the plan. If a plan is not confirmed, the trustee shall return any such payments to the debtor, after deducting—

    (1) any unpaid claim allowed under section 503(b) of this title; and

    (2) if a standing trustee is serving in the case, the percentage fee fixed for such standing trustee.

(b) Before or at the time of each payment to creditors under the plan, there shall be paid—

    (1) any unpaid claim of the kind specified in section 507(a)(2) of this title; and

    (2) if a standing trustee appointed under section 1202(c) of this title is serving in the case, the percentage fee fixed for such standing trustee under section 1202(d) of this title.

(c) Except as otherwise provided in the plan or in the order confirming the plan, the trustee shall make payments to creditors under the plan.

(Added and amended Pub.L. 99–554, Title II, § 255, Title III, § 302(f), Oct. 27, 1986, 100 Stat. 3111, 3124; Pub.L. 103–65, § 1, Aug. 6, 1993, 107 Stat. 311; Pub.L. 103–394, Title V, § 501(d)(36), Oct. 22, 1994, 108 Stat. 4147; Pub.L. 105–277,

Div. C, Title I, § 149(a), Oct. 21, 1998, 112 Stat. 2681–610; Pub.L. 106–5, § 1(1), (2), Mar. 30, 1999, 113 Stat. 9; Pub.L. 106–70, § 1, Oct. 9, 1999, 113 Stat. 1031; Pub.L. 107–8, § 1, May 11, 2001, 115 Stat. 10; Pub.L. 107–17, § 1, June 26, 2001, 115 Stat. 151; Pub.L. 107–170, § 1, May 7, 2002, 116 Stat. 133; Pub.L. 107–171, Title X, § 10814(a), May 13, 2002, 116 Stat. 532; Pub.L. 107–377, § 2(a), Dec. 19, 2002, 116 Stat. 3115; Pub.L. 108–73, § 2(a), Aug. 15, 2003, 117 Stat. 891; Pub.L. 108–369, § 2(a), Oct. 25, 2004, 118 Stat. 1749; Pub.L. 109–8, Title X, § 1001(a)(1), Title XV, § 1502(a)(9), Apr. 20, 2005, 119 Stat. 185, 217.)

HISTORICAL AND STATUTORY NOTES

Revision Notes and Legislative Reports

1986 Acts. House Report No. 99–764 and House Conference Report No. 99–958, see 1986 U.S. Code Cong. and Adm. News, p. 5227.

1993 Acts. House Report No. 103–32, see 1993 U.S. Code Cong. and Adm. News, p. 373.

1994 Acts. House Report No. 103–835, see 1994 U.S. Code Cong. and Adm. News, p. 3340.

1998 Acts. Statement by President, see 1998 U.S. Code Cong. and Adm. News, p. 582.

1999 Acts. Statement by President, see 1999 U.S. Code Cong. and Adm. News, p. 4.

Statement by President, see 1999 U.S. Code Cong. and Adm. News, p. 102.

2001 Acts. House Report No. 107–2, see 2001 U.S. Code Cong. and Adm. News, p. 6.

2005 Acts. House Report No. 109–31(Part I), see 2005 U.S. Code Cong. and Adm. News, p. 88.

References in Text

Section 1202(c) and (d) of this title, referred to in subsec. (b)(2), were repealed by section 227 of Pub.L. 99–554, and provisions relating to appointment of and fixing percentage fees for standing trustees are contained in section 586(b) and (e) of Title 28, Judiciary and Judicial Procedure, as amended by section 113(b) and (c) of Pub.L. 99–554.

Codifications

For repeal of section effective Oct. 1, 1998, and subsequent reenactment of section, see note set out preceding 11 U.S.C.A. § 1201.

Effective and Applicability Provisions

2005 Acts. Amendments by Pub.L. 109–8 effective, except as otherwise provided, 180 days after April 20, 2005, and inapplicable with respect to cases commenced under Title 11 before the effective date, see Pub.L. 109–8, § 1501, set out as a note under 11 U.S.C.A. § 101.

2004 Acts. Amendment by Pub.L. 108–369, § 2(a), extending to July 1, 2005, the date of repeal of this chapter, to take effect Jan. 1, 2004, see Pub.L. 108–369, § 2(b), set out as a note under 11 U.S.C.A. § 1201.

2003 Acts. Amendment by Pub.L. 108–73, § 2(a), extending to Jan. 1, 2004, the date of repeal of this chapter, to take effect July 1, 2003, see Pub.L. 108–73, § 2(b), set out as a note under 11 U.S.C.A. § 1201.

2002 Acts. Amendment by Pub.L. 107–377, § 2(a), extending to July 1, 2003, the date of repeal of this chapter, to take effect Jan. 1, 2003, see Pub.L. 107–377, § 2(b), set out as a note under 11 U.S.C.A. § 1201.

Amendment by Pub.L. 107–171, extending to Jan. 1, 2003, the date of repeal of this chapter, to take effect June 1, 2002, see section 10814(b) of Pub.L. 107–171, set out as a note under 11 U.S.C.A. § 1201.

Amendment by Pub.L. 107–170, extending to June 1, 2002, the date of repeal of this chapter, to take effect October 1, 2001, see section 2 of Pub.L. 107–170, set out as a note under 11 U.S.C.A. § 1201.

2001 Acts. Amendment by Pub.L. 107–17, extending to October 1, 2001, the date of repeal of this chapter, to take effect June 1, 2001, see section 2 of Pub.L. 107–17, set out as a note under 11 U.S.C.A. § 1201.

Amendment by Pub.L. 107–8, extending to June 1, 2001, the date of repeal of this chapter, to take effect July 1, 2000, see section 2 of Pub.L. 107–8, set out as a note under 11 U.S.C.A. § 1201.

1999 Acts. Amendment by Pub.L. 106–70, extending to July 1, 2000, the date of repeal of this chapter, to take effect Oct. 1, 1999, see section 2 of Pub.L. 106–70, set out as a note under 11 U.S.C.A. § 1201.

Amendment by Pub.L. 106–5, extending to Oct. 1, 1999 the date of repeal of this chapter, to take effect Apr. 1, 1999, see section 2 of Pub.L. 106–5, set out as a note under 11 U.S.C.A. § 1201.

1998 Acts. Section reenacted, eff. Oct. 1, 1998, for the period beginning on Oct. 1, 1998, and ending on Apr. 1, 1999, but all cases commenced or pending under this chapter 12, as reenacted under section 149(a) of Pub.L. 105–277, and all matters and proceedings in or relating to such cases, to be conducted and determined under such chapter as if such chapter were continued in effect after Apr. 1, 1999, and the substantive rights of parties in connection with such cases, matters, and proceedings to continue to be governed under the law applicable to such cases, matters, and proceedings as if such chapter were continued in effect after Apr. 1, 1999, see section 149 of Pub.L. 105–277, set out as a note under 11 U.S.C.A. § 1201.

1994 Acts. Amendment by Pub.L. 103–394 effective on Oct. 22, 1994, and not to apply with respect to cases commenced under Title 11 of the United States Code before Oct. 22, 1994, see section 702 of Pub.L. 103–394, set out as a note under 11 U.S.C.A. § 101.

1993 Acts. Amendment by Pub.L. 103–65, extending to Oct. 1, 1998 the date of repeal of this chapter, to take effect Aug. 6, 1993, see section 3 of Pub.L. 103–65, set out as a note under 11 U.S.C.A. § 1221.

1986 Acts. Section repealed effective Oct. 1, 1998, see section 302(f) of Pub.L. 99–554, as amended, set out in a note under 28 U.S.C.A. § 581. However, for extension of provisions, see section 149 of Pub.L. 105–277, set out as a note under 11 U.S.C.A. § 1201.

Section effective 30 days after Oct. 27, 1986, but not applicable to cases commenced under this title before that date, see section 302(a), (c)(1) of Pub.L. 99–554, set out as a note under 28 U.S.C.A. § 581.

Separability of Provisions

If any provision of or amendment made by Pub.L. 103–394 or the application of such provision or amendment to any person or circumstance is held to be unconstitutional, the remaining provisions of and amendments made by Pub.L. 103–394 and the application of such provisions and amendments to any person or circumstance shall not be affected thereby, see section 701 of Pub.L. 103–394, set out as a note under 11 U.S.C.A. § 101.

Reenactment of Chapter

This section as in effect on June 30, 2005, reenacted effective July 1, 2005, see Pub.L. 109–8, § 1001(a), set out as a note under 11 U.S.C.A. § 1201.

Repeal of Chapter; Extension of Provisions

Pub.L. 99–554, Title III, § 302(f), Oct. 27, 1986, 100 Stat. 3124, as amended Pub.L. 103–65, § 1, Aug. 6, 1993, 107 Stat. 311, which provided that, effective Oct. 1, 1998, this chapter is repealed, but that all cases commenced or pending under this chapter, and all matters and proceedings in or relating to such cases, shall be conducted and determined under this chapter as if such chapter had not been repealed, and that the substantive rights of parties in connection with such cases, matters, and proceedings shall continue to be governed under the laws applicable to such cases, matters, and proceedings as if such chapter had not been repealed, was superceded by the reenactment of this chapter by Pub.L. 109–8, Title X, § 1001(a), Apr. 20, 2005, 119 Stat. 185, set out as a note under 11 U.S.C.A. § 1201.

Pub.L. 105–277, Div. C, Title I, § 149, Oct. 21, 1998, 112 Stat. 2681–610, as amended Pub.L. 106–5, §§ 1, 2, Mar. 30, 1999, 113 Stat. 9; Pub.L. 106–70, §§ 1, 2, Oct. 9, 1999, 113 Stat. 1031; Pub.L. 107–8, §§ 1, 2, May 11, 2001, 115 Stat. 10; Pub.L. 107–17, §§ 1, 2, June 26, 2001, 115 Stat. 151; Pub.L. 107–170, §§ 1, 2, May 7, 2002, 116 Stat. 133; Pub.L. 107–171, Title X, § 10814, May 13, 2002, 116 St. 532; Pub.L. 107–377, § 2, Dec. 19, 2002, 116 Stat. 3115; Pub.L. 108–73, § 2(a), Aug. 15, 2003, 117 Stat. 891; Pub.L. 108–369, § 2(a), Oct. 25, 2004, 118 Stat. 1749, provided that, to take effect on January 1, 2004, chapter 12 of Title 11 [this chapter; 11 U.S.C.A. § 1201 et seq.], as in effect on December 31, 2003, is reenacted for the period beginning on January 1, 2004, and ending on July 1, 2005, but that all cases commenced or pending under this chapter 12, as reenacted under section 149(a) of Pub.L. 105–277, and all matters and proceedings in or relating to such cases, shall be conducted and determined under such chapter as if such chapter were continued in effect after July 1, 2005, and that the substantive rights of parties in connection with such cases, matters, and proceedings shall continue to be governed under the law applicable to such cases, matters, and proceedings as if such chapter were continued in effect after July 1, 2005, was superceded by the reenactment of this chapter by Pub.L. 109–8, Title X, § 1001(a), Apr. 20, 2005, 119 Stat. 185, set out as a note under 11 U.S.C.A. § 1201.

CROSS REFERENCES

Payment stopped on checks remaining unpaid 90 days after final distribution, see 11 USCA § 347.

Payments in Chapter thirteen cases, see 11 USCA § 1326.

§ 1227. Effect of confirmation

(a) Except as provided in section 1228(a) of this title, the provisions of a confirmed plan bind the debtor, each creditor, each equity security holder, and each general partner in the debtor, whether or not the claim of such creditor, such equity security holder, or such general partner in the debtor is provided for by the plan, and whether or not such creditor, such equity

security holder, or such general partner in the debtor has objected to, has accepted, or has rejected the plan.

(b) Except as otherwise provided in the plan or the order confirming the plan, the confirmation of a plan vests all of the property of the estate in the debtor.

(c) Except as provided in section 1228(a) of this title and except as otherwise provided in the plan or in the order confirming the plan, the property vesting in the debtor under subsection (b) of this section is free and clear of any claim or interest of any creditor provided for by the plan.

(Added and amended Pub.L. 99–554, Title II, § 255, Title III, § 302(f), Oct. 27, 1986, 100 Stat. 3112, 3124; Pub.L. 103–65, § 1, Aug. 6, 1993, 107 Stat. 311; Pub.L. 105–277, Div. C, Title I, § 149(a), Oct. 21, 1998, 112 Stat. 2681–610; Pub.L. 106–5, § 1(1), (2), Mar. 30, 1999, 113 Stat. 9; Pub.L. 106–70, § 1, Oct. 9, 1999, 113 Stat. 1031; Pub.L. 107–8, § 1, May 11, 2001, 115 Stat. 10; Pub.L. 107–17, § 1, June 26, 2001, 115 Stat. 151; Pub.L. 107–170, § 1, May 7, 2002, 116 Stat. 133; Pub.L. 107–171, Title X, § 10814(a), May 13, 2002, 116 Stat. 532; Pub.L. 107–377, § 2(a), Dec. 19, 2002, 116 Stat. 3115; Pub.L. 108–73, § 2(a), Aug. 15, 2003, 117 Stat. 891; Pub.L. 108–369, § 2(a), Oct. 25, 2004, 118 Stat. 1749; Pub.L. 109–8, Title X, § 1001(a)(1), Apr. 20, 2005, 119 Stat. 185.)

HISTORICAL AND STATUTORY NOTES

Revision Notes and Legislative Reports

1986 Acts. House Report No. 99–764 and House Conference Report No. 99–958, see 1986 U.S. Code Cong. and Adm. News, p. 5227.

1993 Acts. House Report No. 103–32, see 1993 U.S. Code Cong. and Adm. News, p. 373.

1998 Acts. Statement by President, see 1998 U.S. Code Cong. and Adm. News, p. 582.

1999 Acts. Statement by President, see 1999 U.S. Code Cong. and Adm. News, p. 4.

Statement by President, see 1999 U.S. Code Cong. and Adm. News, p. 102.

2001 Acts. House Report No. 107–2, see 2001 U.S. Code Cong. and Adm. News, p. 6.

2005 Acts. House Report No. 109–31(Part I), see 2005 U.S. Code Cong. and Adm. News, p. 88.

Codifications

For repeal of section effective Oct. 1, 1998, and subsequent reenactment of section, see note set out preceding 11 U.S.C.A. § 1201.

Effective and Applicability Provisions

2005 Acts. Amendments by Pub.L. 109–8 effective, except as otherwise provided, 180 days after April 20, 2005, and inapplicable with respect to cases commenced under Title 11 before the effective date, see Pub.L. 109–8, § 1501, set out as a note under 11 U.S.C.A. § 101.

2004 Acts. Amendment by Pub.L. 108–369, § 2(a), extending to July 1, 2005, the date of repeal of this chapter, to take effect Jan. 1, 2004, see Pub.L. 108–369, § 2(b), set out as a note under 11 U.S.C.A. § 1201.

2003 Acts. Amendment by Pub.L. 108–73, § 2(a), extending to Jan. 1, 2004, the date of repeal of this chapter, to take effect July 1, 2003, see Pub.L. 108–73, § 2(b), set out as a note under 11 U.S.C.A. § 1201.

2002 Acts. Amendment by Pub.L. 107–377, § 2(a), extending to July 1, 2003, the date of repeal of this chapter, to take effect Jan. 1, 2003, see Pub.L. 107–377, § 2(b), set out as a note under 11 U.S.C.A. § 1201.

Amendment by Pub.L. 107–171, extending to Jan. 1, 2003, the date of repeal of this chapter, to take effect June 1, 2002, see section 10814(b) of Pub.L. 107–171, set out as a note under 11 U.S.C.A. § 1201.

Amendment by Pub.L. 107–170, extending to June 1, 2002, the date of repeal of this chapter, to take effect October 1, 2001, see section 2 of Pub.L. 107–170, set out as a note under 11 U.S.C.A. § 1201.

2001 Acts. Amendment by Pub.L. 107–17, extending to October 1, 2001, the date of repeal of this chapter, to take effect June 1, 2001, see section 2 of Pub.L. 107–17, set out as a note under 11 U.S.C.A. § 1201.

Amendment by Pub.L. 107–8, extending to June 1, 2001, the date of repeal of this chapter, to take effect July 1, 2000, see section 2 of Pub.L. 107–8, set out as a note under 11 U.S.C.A. § 1201.

1999 Acts. Amendment by Pub.L. 106–70, extending to July 1, 2000, the date of repeal of this chapter, to take effect Oct. 1, 1999, see section 2 of Pub.L. 106–70, set out as a note under 11 U.S.C.A. § 1201.

Amendment by Pub.L. 106–5, extending to Oct. 1, 1999 the date of repeal of this chapter, to take effect Apr. 1, 1999, see section 2 of Pub.L. 106–5, set out as a note under 11 U.S.C.A. § 1201.

1998 Acts. Section reenacted, eff. Oct. 1, 1998, for the period beginning on Oct. 1, 1998, and ending on Apr. 1, 1999, but all cases commenced or pending under this chapter 12, as reenacted under section 149(a) of Pub.L. 105–277, and all matters and proceedings in or relating to such cases, to be conducted and determined under such chapter as if such chapter were continued in effect after Apr. 1, 1999, and the substantive rights of parties in connection with such cases, matters, and proceedings to continue to be governed under the law applicable to such cases, matters, and proceedings as if such chapter were continued in effect after Apr. 1, 1999, see section 149 of Pub.L. 105–277, set out as a note under 11 U.S.C.A. § 1201.

1993 Acts. Amendment by Pub.L. 103–65, extending to Oct. 1, 1998 the date of repeal of this chapter, to take effect Aug. 6, 1993, see section 3 of Pub.L. 103–65, set out as a note under 11 U.S.C.A. § 1221.

1986 Acts. Section repealed effective Oct. 1, 1998, see section 302(f) of Pub.L. 99–554, as amended, set out in a note under 28 U.S.C.A. § 581. However, for extension of provisions, see section 149 of Pub.L. 105–277, set out as a note under 11 U.S.C.A. § 1201.

Section effective 30 days after Oct. 27, 1986, but not applicable to cases commenced under this title before that date, see section 302(a), (c)(1) of Pub.L. 99–554, set out as a note under 28 U.S.C.A. § 581.

Reenactment of Chapter

This section as in effect on June 30, 2005, reenacted effective July 1, 2005, see Pub.L. 109–8, § 1001(a), set out as a note under 11 U.S.C.A. § 1201.

Repeal of Chapter; Extension of Provisions

Pub.L. 99–554, Title III, § 302(f), Oct. 27, 1986, 100 Stat. 3124, as amended Pub.L. 103–65, § 1, Aug. 6, 1993, 107 Stat. 311, which provided that, effective Oct. 1, 1998, this chapter is repealed, but that all cases commenced or pending under this chapter, and all matters and proceedings in or relating to such cases, shall be conducted and determined under this chapter as if such chapter had not been repealed, and that the substantive rights of parties in connection with such cases, matters, and proceedings shall continue to be governed under the laws applicable to such cases, matters, and proceedings as if such chapter had not been repealed, was superceded by the reenactment of this chapter by Pub.L. 109–8, Title X, § 1001(a), Apr. 20, 2005, 119 Stat. 185, set out as a note under 11 U.S.C.A. § 1201.

Pub.L. 105–277, Div. C, Title I, § 149, Oct. 21, 1998, 112 Stat. 2681–610, as amended Pub.L. 106–5, §§ 1, 2, Mar. 30, 1999, 113 Stat. 9; Pub.L. 106–70, §§ 1, 2, Oct. 9, 1999, 113 Stat. 1031; Pub.L. 107–8, §§ 1, 2, May 11, 2001, 115 Stat. 10; Pub.L. 107–17, §§ 1, 2, June 26, 2001, 115 Stat. 151; Pub.L. 107–170, §§ 1, 2, May 7, 2002, 116 Stat. 133; Pub.L. 107–171, Title X, § 10814, May 13, 2002, 116 St. 532; Pub.L. 107–377, § 2, Dec. 19, 2002, 116 Stat. 3115; Pub.L. 108–73, § 2(a), Aug. 15, 2003, 117 Stat. 891; Pub.L. 108–369, § 2(a), Oct. 25, 2004, 118 Stat. 1749, provided that, to take effect on January 1, 2004, chapter 12 of Title 11 [this chapter; 11 U.S.C.A. § 1201 et seq.], as in effect on December 31, 2003, is reenacted for the period beginning on January 1, 2004, and ending on July 1, 2005, but that all cases commenced or pending under this chapter 12, as reenacted under section 149(a) of Pub.L. 105–277, and all matters and proceedings in or relating to such cases, shall be conducted and determined under such chapter as if such chapter were continued in effect after July 1, 2005, and that the substantive rights of parties in connection with such cases, matters, and proceedings shall continue to be governed under the law applicable to such cases, matters, and proceedings as if such chapter were continued in effect after July 1, 2005, was superceded by the reenactment of this chapter by Pub.L. 109–8, Title X, § 1001(a), Apr. 20, 2005, 119 Stat. 185, set out as a note under 11 U.S.C.A. § 1201.

CROSS REFERENCES

Effect of confirmation in,
>Chapter eleven cases, see 11 USCA § 1141.
>Chapter nine cases, see 11 USCA § 944.
>Chapter thirteen cases, see 11 USCA § 1327.

§ 1228. Discharge

(a) Subject to subsection (d), as soon as practicable after completion by the debtor of all payments under the plan, and in the case of a debtor who is required by a judicial or administrative order, or by statute, to pay a domestic support obligation, after such debtor certifies that all amounts payable under such order or such statute that are due on or before the date of the certification (including amounts due before the petition was filed, but only to the extent provided for by the plan) have been paid, other than payments to holders of allowed claims provided for under section 1222(b)(5) or 1222(b)(9) of this title, unless the court approves a written waiver of discharge executed by the debtor after the order for relief under this chapter, the court shall grant the debtor a discharge of all debts provided for by the plan, allowed under section 503 of this title, or disallowed under section 502 of this title, except any debt—

(1) provided for under section 1222(b)(5) or 1222(b)(9) of this title; or

(2) of a kind specified in section 523(a) of this title, except as provided in section 1232(c).

(b) Subject to subsection (d), at any time after the confirmation of the plan and after notice and a hearing, the court may grant a discharge to a debtor that has not completed payments under the plan only if—

(1) the debtor's failure to complete such payments is due to circumstances for which the debtor should not justly be held accountable;

(2) the value, as of the effective date of the plan, of property actually distributed under the plan on account of each allowed unsecured claim is not less than the amount that would have been paid on such claim if the estate of the debtor had been liquidated under chapter 7 of this title on such date; and

(3) modification of the plan under section 1229 of this title is not practicable.

(c) A discharge granted under subsection (b) of this section discharges the debtor from all unsecured debts provided for by the plan or disallowed under section 502 of this title, except any debt—

(1) provided for under section 1222(b)(5) or 1222(b)(9) of this title; or

(2) of a kind specified in section 523(a) of this title, except as provided in section 1232(c).

(d) On request of a party in interest before one year after a discharge under this section is granted, and after notice and a hearing, the court may revoke such discharge only if—

(1) such discharge was obtained by the debtor through fraud; and

(2) the requesting party did not know of such fraud until after such discharge was granted.

(e) After the debtor is granted a discharge, the court shall terminate the services of any trustee serving in the case.

(f) The court may not grant a discharge under this chapter unless the court after notice and a hearing held not more than 10 days before the date of the entry of the order granting the discharge finds that there is no reasonable cause to believe that—

(1) section 522(q)(1) may be applicable to the debtor; and

(2) there is pending any proceeding in which the debtor may be found guilty of a felony of the kind described in section 522(q)(1)(A) or liable for a debt of the kind described in section 522(q)(1)(B).

(Added and amended Pub.L. 99–554, Title II, § 255, Title III, § 302(f), Oct. 27, 1986, 100 Stat. 3112, 3124; Pub.L. 103–65, § 1, Aug. 6, 1993, 107 Stat. 311; Pub.L. 105–277, Div. C, Title I, § 149(a), Oct. 21, 1998, 112 Stat. 2681–610; Pub.L. 106–5, § 1(1), (2), Mar. 30, 1999, 113 Stat. 9; Pub.L. 106–70, § 1, Oct. 9, 1999, 113 Stat. 1031; Pub.L. 106–518, Title II, § 208, Nov. 13, 2000, 114 Stat. 2415; Pub.L. 107–8, § 1, May 11, 2001, 115 Stat. 10; Pub.L. 107–17, § 1, June 26, 2001, 115 Stat. 151; Pub.L. 107–170, § 1, May 7, 2002, 116 Stat. 133; Pub.L. 107–171, Title X, § 10814(a), May 13, 2002, 116 Stat. 532; Pub.L. 107–377, § 2(a), Dec. 19, 2002, 116 Stat. 3115; Pub.L. 108–73, § 2(a), Aug. 15, 2003, 117 Stat. 891; Pub.L. 108–369, § 2(a), Oct. 25, 2004, 118 Stat. 1749; Pub.L. 109–8, Title II, § 213(6), Title III, § 330(c), Title X, § 1001(a)(1), Apr. 20, 2005, 119 Stat. 53, 101, 102, 185; Pub.L. 115–72, Div. B, § 1005(b)(1)(B), Oct. 26, 2017, 131 Stat. 1233.)

HISTORICAL AND STATUTORY NOTES

Revision Notes and Legislative Reports

1986 Acts. House Report No. 99–764 and House Conference Report No. 99–958, see 1986 U.S. Code Cong. and Adm. News, p. 5227.

1993 Acts. House Report No. 103–32, see 1993 U.S. Code Cong. and Adm. News, p. 373.

1998 Acts. Statement by President, see 1998 U.S. Code Cong. and Adm. News, p. 582.

1999 Acts. Statement by President, see 1999 U.S. Code Cong. and Adm. News, p. 4.

Statement by President, see 1999 U.S. Code Cong. and Adm. News, p. 102.

2001 Acts. House Report No. 107–2, see 2001 U.S. Code Cong. and Adm. News, p. 6.

2005 Acts. House Report No. 109–31(Part I), see 2005 U.S. Code Cong. and Adm. News, p. 88.

Codifications

For repeal of section effective Oct. 1, 1998, and subsequent reenactment of section, see note set out preceding 11 U.S.C.A. § 1201.

Effective and Applicability Provisions

2017 Acts. Amendments by Pub.L. 115–72, Div. B, § 1005, applicable to any bankruptcy case that is pending on Oct. 26, 2017, in which the plan under chapter 12 of this title has not been confirmed on Oct. 26, 2017, and to which an order of discharge under 11 U.S.C.A. § 1228 has not been entered; and applicable to any bankruptcy case that commences on or after Oct. 26, 2017, see Pub.L. 115–72, Div. B, § 1005(c), set out as a note under 11 U.S.C.A. § 1222.

2005 Acts. Amendments by sections 213(6) and 330(c) of Pub.L. 109–8 effective 180 days after Apr. 20, 2005, with amendments by section 213(6) of Pub.L. 109–8 not applicable with respect to cases commenced under this title before such effective date, except as otherwise provided, and amendment by section 330(c) of Pub.L. 109–8 applicable with respect to cases commenced under this title on or after Apr. 20, 2005, see Pub.L. 109–8, § 1501, set out as a note under 11 U.S.C.A. § 101.

2004 Acts. Amendment by Pub.L. 108–369, § 2(a), extending to July 1, 2005, the date of repeal of this chapter, to take effect Jan. 1, 2004, see Pub.L. 108–369, § 2(b), set out as a note under 11 U.S.C.A. § 1201.

2003 Acts. Amendment by Pub.L. 108–73, § 2(a), extending to Jan. 1, 2004, the date of repeal of this chapter, to take effect July 1, 2003, see Pub.L. 108–73, § 2(b), set out as a note under 11 U.S.C.A. § 1201.

2002 Acts. Amendment by Pub.L. 107–377, § 2(a), extending to July 1, 2003, the date of repeal of this chapter, to take effect Jan. 1, 2003, see Pub.L. 107–377, § 2(b), set out as a note under 11 U.S.C.A. § 1201.

Amendment by Pub.L. 107–171, extending to Jan. 1, 2003, the date of repeal of this chapter, to take effect June 1, 2002, see section 10814(b) of Pub.L. 107–171, set out as a note under 11 U.S.C.A. § 1201.

Amendment by Pub.L. 107–170, extending to June 1, 2002, the date of repeal of this chapter, to take effect October 1, 2001, see section 2 of Pub.L. 107–170, set out as a note under 11 U.S.C.A. § 1201.

2001 Acts. Amendment by Pub.L. 107–17, extending to October 1, 2001, the date of repeal of this chapter, to take effect June 1, 2001, see section 2 of Pub.L. 107–17, set out as a note under 11 U.S.C.A. § 1201.

Amendment by Pub.L. 107–8, extending to June 1, 2001, the date of repeal of this chapter, to take effect July 1, 2000, see section 2 of Pub.L. 107–8, set out as a note under 11 U.S.C.A. § 1201.

1999 Acts. Amendment by Pub.L. 106–70, extending to July 1, 2000, the date of repeal of this chapter, to take effect Oct. 1, 1999, see section 2 of Pub.L. 106–70, set out as a note under 11 U.S.C.A. § 1201.

Amendment by Pub.L. 106–5, extending to Oct. 1, 1999 the date of repeal of this chapter, to take effect Apr. 1, 1999, see section 2 of Pub.L. 106–5, set out as a note under 11 U.S.C.A. § 1201.

1998 Acts. Section reenacted, eff. Oct. 1, 1998, for the period beginning on Oct. 1, 1998, and ending on Apr. 1, 1999, but all cases commenced or pending under this chapter 12, as reenacted under section 149(a) of Pub.L. 105–277, and all matters and proceedings in or relating to such cases, to be conducted and determined under such chapter as if such chapter were continued in effect after Apr. 1, 1999, and the substantive rights of parties in connection with such cases, matters, and proceedings to continue to be governed under the law applicable to such cases, matters, and proceedings as if such chapter were continued in effect after Apr. 1, 1999, see section 149 of Pub.L. 105–277, set out as a note under 11 U.S.C.A. § 1201.

1993 Acts. Amendment by Pub.L. 103–65, extending to Oct. 1, 1998 the date of repeal of this chapter, to take effect Aug. 6, 1993, see section 3 of Pub.L. 103–65, set out as a note under 11 U.S.C.A. § 1221.

1986 Acts. Section repealed effective Oct. 1, 1998, see section 302(f) of Pub.L. 99–554, as amended, set out in a note under 28 U.S.C.A. § 581. However, for extension of provisions, see section 149 of Pub.L. 105–277, set out as a note under 11 U.S.C.A. § 1201.

Section effective 30 days after Oct. 27, 1986, but not applicable to cases commenced under this title before that date, see section 302(a), (c)(1) of Pub.L. 99–554, set out as a note under 28 U.S.C.A. § 581.

Reenactment of Chapter

This section as in effect on June 30, 2005, reenacted effective July 1, 2005, see Pub.L. 109–8, § 1001(a), set out as a note under 11 U.S.C.A. § 1201.

Repeal of Chapter; Extension of Provisions

Pub.L. 99–554, Title III, § 302(f), Oct. 27, 1986, 100 Stat. 3124, as amended Pub.L. 103–65, § 1, Aug. 6, 1993, 107 Stat. 311, which provided that, effective Oct. 1, 1998, this chapter is repealed, but that all cases commenced or pending under this chapter, and all matters and proceedings in or relating to such cases, shall be conducted and determined under this chapter as if such chapter had not been repealed, and that the substantive rights of parties in connection with such cases, matters, and proceedings shall continue to be governed under the laws applicable to such cases, matters, and proceedings as if such chapter had not been repealed, was superceded by the reenactment of this chapter by Pub.L. 109–8, Title X, § 1001(a), Apr. 20, 2005, 119 Stat. 185, set out as a note under 11 U.S.C.A. § 1201.

Pub.L. 105–277, Div. C, Title I, § 149, Oct. 21, 1998, 112 Stat. 2681–610, as amended Pub.L. 106–5, §§ 1, 2, Mar. 30, 1999, 113 Stat. 9; Pub.L. 106–70, §§ 1, 2, Oct. 9, 1999, 113 Stat. 1031; Pub.L. 107–8, §§ 1, 2, May 11, 2001, 115 Stat. 10; Pub.L. 107–17, §§ 1, 2, June 26, 2001, 115 Stat. 151; Pub.L. 107–170, §§ 1, 2, May 7, 2002, 116 Stat. 133; Pub.L. 107–171, Title X, § 10814, May 13, 2002, 116 St. 532; Pub.L. 107–377, § 2, Dec. 19, 2002, 116 Stat. 3115; Pub.L. 108–73, § 2(a), Aug. 15, 2003, 117 Stat. 891; Pub.L. 108–369, § 2(a), Oct. 25, 2004, 118 Stat. 1749, provided that, to take effect on January 1, 2004, chapter 12 of Title 11 [this chapter; 11 U.S.C.A. § 1201 et seq.], as in effect on December 31, 2003, is reenacted for the period beginning on January 1, 2004, and ending on July 1, 2005, but that all cases commenced or pending under this chapter 12, as reenacted under section 149(a) of Pub.L. 105–277, and all matters and proceedings in or relating to such cases, shall be conducted and determined under such chapter as if such chapter were continued in effect after July 1, 2005, and that the substantive rights of parties in connection with such cases, matters, and proceedings shall continue to be governed under the law applicable to such cases, matters, and proceedings as if such chapter were continued in effect after July 1, 2005, was superceded by the reenactment of this chapter by Pub.L. 109–8, Title X, § 1001(a), Apr. 20, 2005, 119 Stat. 185, set out as a note under 11 U.S.C.A. § 1201.

CROSS REFERENCES

Cancellation of indebtedness from discharged farm loans, see 12 USCA § 1150.

Discharge in,

Chapter seven cases, see 11 USCA § 727.

Chapter thirteen cases, see 11 USCA § 1328.

Effect of,

Conversion, see 11 USCA § 348.

Discharge, see 11 USCA § 524.

Exceptions to discharge, see 11 USCA § 523.

§ 1229. Modification of plan after confirmation

(a) At any time after confirmation of the plan but before the completion of payments under such plan, the plan may be modified, on request of the debtor, the trustee, or the holder of an allowed unsecured claim, to—

(1) increase or reduce the amount of payments on claims of a particular class provided for by the plan;

(2) extend or reduce the time for such payments;

(3) alter the amount of the distribution to a creditor whose claim is provided for by the plan to the extent necessary to take account of any payment of such claim other than under the plan; or

(4) provide for the payment of a claim described in section 1232(a) that arose after the date on which the petition was filed.

(b)(1) Sections 1222(a), 1222(b), and 1223(c) of this title and the requirements of section 1225(a) of this title apply to any modification under subsection (a) of this section.

(2) The plan as modified becomes the plan unless, after notice and a hearing, such modification is disapproved.

(c) A plan modified under this section may not provide for payments over a period that expires after three years after the time that the first payment under the original confirmed plan was due, unless the court, for cause, approves a longer period, but the court may not approve a period that expires after five years after such time.

(d) A plan may not be modified under this section—

(1) to increase the amount of any payment due before the plan as modified becomes the plan;

(2) by anyone except the debtor, based on an increase in the debtor's disposable income, to increase the amount of payments to unsecured creditors required for a particular month so that the aggregate of such payments exceeds the debtor's disposable income for such month; or

(3) in the last year of the plan by anyone except the debtor, to require payments that would leave the debtor with insufficient funds to carry on the farming operation after the plan is completed.

(Added and amended Pub.L. 99–554, Title II, § 255, Title III, § 302(f), Oct. 27, 1986, 100 Stat. 3113, 3124; Pub.L. 103–65, § 1, Aug. 6, 1993, 107 Stat. 311; Pub.L. 105–277, Div. C, Title I, § 149(a), Oct. 21, 1998, 112 Stat. 2681–610; Pub.L. 106–5, § 1(1), (2), Mar. 30, 1999, 113 Stat. 9; Pub.L. 106–70, § 1, Oct. 9, 1999, 113 Stat. 1031; Pub.L. 107–8, § 1, May 11, 2001, 115 Stat. 10; Pub.L. 107–17, § 1, June 26, 2001, 115 Stat. 151; Pub.L. 107–170, § 1, May 7, 2002, 116 Stat. 133; Pub.L. 107–171, Title X, § 10814(a), May 13, 2002, 116 Stat. 532; Pub.L. 107–377, § 2(a), Dec. 19, 2002, 116 Stat. 3115; Pub.L. 108–73, § 2(a), Aug. 15, 2003, 117 Stat. 891; Pub.L. 108–369, § 2(a), Oct. 25, 2004, 118 Stat. 1749; Pub.L. 109–8, Title X, §§ 1001(a)(1), 1006(b), Apr. 20, 2005, 119 Stat. 185, 187; Pub.L. 115–72, Div. B, § 1005(b)(1)(C), Oct. 26, 2017, 131 Stat. 1234.)

HISTORICAL AND STATUTORY NOTES
Revision Notes and Legislative Reports

1986 Acts. House Report No. 99–764 and House Conference Report No. 99–958, see 1986 U.S. Code Cong. and Adm. News, p. 5227.

1993 Acts. House Report No. 103–32, see 1993 U.S. Code Cong. and Adm. News, p. 373.

1998 Acts. Statement by President, see 1998 U.S. Code Cong. and Adm. News, p. 582.

1999 Acts. Statement by President, see 1999 U.S. Code Cong. and Adm. News, p. 4.

Statement by President, see 1999 U.S. Code Cong. and Adm. News, p. 102.

2001 Acts. House Report No. 107–2, see 2001 U.S. Code Cong. and Adm. News, p. 6.

2005 Acts. House Report No. 109–31(Part I), see 2005 U.S. Code Cong. and Adm. News, p. 88.

Codifications

For repeal of section effective Oct. 1, 1998, and subsequent reenactment of section, see note set out preceding 11 U.S.C.A. § 1201.

Effective and Applicability Provisions

2017 Acts. Amendments by Pub.L. 115–72, Div. B, § 1005, applicable to any bankruptcy case that is pending on Oct. 26, 2017, in which the plan under chapter 12 of this title has not been confirmed on Oct. 26, 2017, and to which an order of discharge under 11 U.S.C.A. § 1228 has not been entered; and applicable to any bankruptcy case that commences on or after Oct. 26, 2017, see Pub.L. 115–72, Div. B, § 1005(c), set out as a note under 11 U.S.C.A. § 1222.

2005 Acts. Amendments by Pub.L. 109–8 effective, except as otherwise provided, 180 days after April 20, 2005, and inapplicable with respect to cases commenced under Title 11 before the effective date, see Pub.L. 109–8, § 1501, set out as a note under 11 U.S.C.A. § 101.

2004 Acts. Amendment by Pub.L. 108–369, § 2(a), extending to July 1, 2005, the date of repeal of this chapter, to take effect Jan. 1, 2004, see Pub.L. 108–369, § 2(b), set out as a note under 11 U.S.C.A. § 1201.

2003 Acts. Amendment by Pub.L. 108–73, § 2(a), extending to Jan. 1, 2004, the date of repeal of this chapter, to take effect July 1, 2003, see Pub.L. 108–73, § 2(b), set out as a note under 11 U.S.C.A. § 1201.

2002 Acts. Amendment by Pub.L. 107–377, § 2(a), extending to July 1, 2003, the date of repeal of this chapter, to take effect Jan. 1, 2003, see Pub.L. 107–377, § 2(b), set out as a note under 11 U.S.C.A. § 1201.

Amendment by Pub.L. 107–171, extending to Jan. 1, 2003, the date of repeal of this chapter, to take effect June 1, 2002, see section 10814(b) of Pub.L. 107–171, set out as a note under 11 U.S.C.A. § 1201.

Amendment by Pub.L. 107–170, extending to June 1, 2002, the date of repeal of this chapter, to take effect October 1, 2001, see section 2 of Pub.L. 107–170, set out as a note under 11 U.S.C.A. § 1201.

2001 Acts. Amendment by Pub.L. 107–17, extending to October 1, 2001, the date of repeal of this chapter, to take effect June 1, 2001, see section 2 of Pub.L. 107–17, set out as a note under 11 U.S.C.A. § 1201.

Amendment by Pub.L. 107–8, extending to June 1, 2001, the date of repeal of this chapter, to take effect July 1, 2000, see section 2 of Pub.L. 107–8, set out as a note under 11 U.S.C.A. § 1201.

1999 Acts. Amendment by Pub.L. 106–70, extending to July 1, 2000, the date of repeal of this chapter, to take effect Oct. 1, 1999, see section 2 of Pub.L. 106–70, set out as a note under 11 U.S.C.A. § 1201.

Amendment by Pub.L. 106–5, extending to Oct. 1, 1999, the date of repeal of this chapter, to take effect Apr. 1, 1999, see section 2 of Pub.L. 106–5, set out as a note under 11 U.S.C.A. § 1201.

1998 Acts. Section reenacted, eff. Oct. 1, 1998, for the period beginning on Oct. 1, 1998, and ending on Apr. 1, 1999, but all cases commenced or pending under this chapter 12, as reenacted under section 149(a) of Pub.L. 105–277, and all matters and proceedings in or relating to such cases, to be conducted and determined under such chapter as if such chapter were continued in effect after Apr. 1, 1999, and the substantive rights of parties in connection with such cases, matters, and proceedings to continue to be governed under the law applicable to such cases, matters, and proceedings as if such chapter were continued in effect after Apr. 1, 1999, see section 149 of Pub.L. 105–277, set out as a note under 11 U.S.C.A. § 1201.

1993 Acts. Amendment by Pub.L. 103–65, extending to Oct. 1, 1998, the date of repeal of this chapter, to take effect Aug. 6, 1993, see section 3 of Pub.L. 103–65, set out as a note under 11 U.S.C.A. § 1221.

1986 Acts. Section repealed effective Oct. 1, 1998, see section 302(f) of Pub.L. 99–554, as amended, set out in a note under 28 U.S.C.A. § 581. However, for extension of provisions, see section 149 of Pub.L. 105–277, set out as a note under 11 U.S.C.A. § 1201.

Section effective 30 days after Oct. 27, 1986, but not applicable to cases commenced under this title before that date, see section 302(a), (c)(1) of Pub.L. 99–554, set out as a note under 28 U.S.C.A. § 581.

Reenactment of Chapter

This section as in effect on June 30, 2005, reenacted effective July 1, 2005, see Pub.L. 109–8, § 1001(a), set out as a note under 11 U.S.C.A. § 1201.

Repeal of Chapter; Extension of Provisions

Pub.L. 99–554, Title III, § 302(f), Oct. 27, 1986, 100 Stat. 3124, as amended Pub.L. 103–65, § 1, Aug. 6, 1993, 107 Stat. 311, which provided that, effective Oct. 1, 1998, this chapter is repealed, but that all cases commenced or pending under this chapter, and all matters and proceedings in or relating to such cases, shall be conducted and determined under this chapter as if such chapter had not been repealed, and that the substantive rights of parties in connection with such cases, matters, and proceedings shall continue to be governed under the laws applicable to such cases, matters, and proceedings as if such chapter had not been repealed, was superceded by the reenactment of this chapter by Pub.L. 109–8, Title X, § 1001(a), Apr. 20, 2005, 119 Stat. 185, set out as a note under 11 U.S.C.A. § 1201.

Pub.L. 105–277, Div. C, Title I, § 149, Oct. 21, 1998, 112 Stat. 2681–610, as amended Pub.L. 106–5, §§ 1, 2, Mar. 30, 1999, 113 Stat. 9; Pub.L. 106–70, §§ 1, 2, Oct. 9, 1999, 113 Stat. 1031; Pub.L. 107–8, §§ 1, 2, May 11, 2001, 115 Stat. 10; Pub.L. 107–17, §§ 1, 2, June 26, 2001, 115 Stat. 151; Pub.L. 107–170, §§ 1, 2, May 7, 2002, 116 Stat. 133; Pub.L. 107–171, Title X, § 10814, May 13, 2002, 116 St. 532; Pub.L. 107–377, § 2, Dec. 19, 2002, 116 Stat. 3115; Pub.L. 108–73, § 2(a), Aug. 15, 2003, 117 Stat. 891; Pub.L. 108–369, § 2(a), Oct. 25, 2004, 118 Stat. 1749, provided that, to take effect on January 1, 2004, chapter 12 of Title 11 [this chapter; 11 U.S.C.A. § 1201 et seq.], as in effect on December 31, 2003, is reenacted for the period beginning on January 1, 2004, and ending on July

1, 2005, but that all cases commenced or pending under this chapter 12, as reenacted under section 149(a) of Pub.L. 105–277, and all matters and proceedings in or relating to such cases, shall be conducted and determined under such chapter as if such chapter were continued in effect after July 1, 2005, and that the substantive rights of parties in connection with such cases, matters, and proceedings shall continue to be governed under the law applicable to such cases, matters, and proceedings as if such chapter were continued in effect after July 1, 2005, was superceded by the reenactment of this chapter by Pub.L. 109–8, Title X, § 1001(a), Apr. 20, 2005, 119 Stat. 185, set out as a note under 11 U.S.C.A. § 1201.

CROSS REFERENCES

Conversion or dismissal upon denial of confirmation of modified plan, see 11 USCA § 1208.

Duties of United States trustee, see 28 USCA § 586.

Modification of plan in,

    Chapter eleven cases, see 11 USCA § 1127.

    Chapter nine cases, see 11 USCA § 942.

    Chapter thirteen cases, see 11 USCA § 1329.

§ 1230.   Revocation of an order of confirmation

(a) On request of a party in interest at any time within 180 days after the date of the entry of an order of confirmation under section 1225 of this title, and after notice and a hearing, the court may revoke such order if such order was procured by fraud.

(b) If the court revokes an order of confirmation under subsection (a) of this section, the court shall dispose of the case under section 1207 of this title, unless, within the time fixed by the court, the debtor proposes and the court confirms a modification of the plan under section 1229 of this title.

(Added and amended Pub.L. 99–554, Title II, § 255, Title III, § 302(f), Oct. 27, 1986, 100 Stat. 3113, 3124; Pub.L. 103–65, § 1, Aug. 6, 1993, 107 Stat. 311; Pub.L. 105–277, Div. C, Title I, § 149(a), Oct. 21, 1998, 112 Stat. 2681–610; Pub.L. 106–5, § 1(1), (2), Mar. 30, 1999, 113 Stat. 9; Pub.L. 106–70, § 1, Oct. 9, 1999, 113 Stat. 1031; Pub.L. 107–8, § 1, May 11, 2001, 115 Stat. 10; Pub.L. 107–17, § 1, June 26, 2001, 115 Stat. 151; Pub.L. 107–170, § 1, May 7, 2002, 116 Stat. 133; Pub.L. 107–171, Title X, § 10814(a), May 13, 2002, 116 Stat. 532; Pub.L. 107–377, § 2(a), Dec. 19, 2002, 116 Stat. 3115; Pub.L. 108–73, § 2(a), Aug. 15, 2003, 117 Stat. 891; Pub.L. 108–369, § 2(a), Oct. 25, 2004, 118 Stat. 1749; Pub.L. 109–8, Title X, § 1001(a)(1), Apr. 20, 2005, 119 Stat. 185.)

HISTORICAL AND STATUTORY NOTES

Revision Notes and Legislative Reports

1986 Acts. House Report No. 99–764 and House Conference Report No. 99–958, see 1986 U.S. Code Cong. and Adm. News, p. 5227.

1993 Acts. House Report No. 103–32, see 1993 U.S. Code Cong. and Adm. News, p. 373.

1998 Acts. Statement by President, see 1998 U.S. Code Cong. and Adm. News, p. 582.

1999 Acts. Statement by President, see 1999 U.S. Code Cong. and Adm. News, p. 4.

Statement by President, see 1999 U.S. Code Cong. and Adm. News, p. 102.

2001 Acts. House Report No. 107–2, see 2001 U.S. Code Cong. and Adm. News, p. 6.

2005 Acts. House Report No. 109–31(Part I), see 2005 U.S. Code Cong. and Adm. News, p. 88.

Codifications

For repeal of section effective Oct. 1, 1998, and subsequent reenactment of section, see note set out preceding 11 U.S.C.A. § 1201.

Effective and Applicability Provisions

2005 Acts. Amendments by Pub.L. 109–8 effective, except as otherwise provided, 180 days after April 20, 2005, and inapplicable with respect to cases commenced under Title 11 before the effective date, see Pub.L. 109–8, § 1501, set out as a note under 11 U.S.C.A. § 101.

2004 Acts. Amendment by Pub.L. 108–369, § 2(a), extending to July 1, 2005, the date of repeal of this chapter, to take effect Jan. 1, 2004, see Pub.L. 108–369, § 2(b), set out as a note under 11 U.S.C.A. § 1201.

2003 Acts. Amendment by Pub.L. 108–73, § 2(a), extending to Jan. 1, 2004, the date of repeal of this chapter, to take effect July 1, 2003, see Pub.L. 108–73, § 2(b), set out as a note under 11 U.S.C.A. § 1201.

2002 Acts. Amendment by Pub.L. 107–377, § 2(a), extending to July 1, 2003, the date of repeal of this chapter, to take effect Jan. 1, 2003, see Pub.L. 107–377, § 2(b), set out as a note under 11 U.S.C.A. § 1201.

Amendment by Pub.L. 107–171, extending to Jan. 1, 2003, the date of repeal of this chapter, to take effect June 1, 2002, see section 10814(b) of Pub.L. 107–171, set out as a note under 11 U.S.C.A. § 1201.

Amendment by Pub.L. 107–170, extending to June 1, 2002, the date of repeal of this chapter, to take effect October 1, 2001, see section 2 of Pub.L. 107–170, set out as a note under 11 U.S.C.A. § 1201.

2001 Acts. Amendment by Pub.L. 107–17, extending to October 1, 2001, the date of repeal of this chapter, to take effect June 1, 2001, see section 2 of Pub.L. 107–17, set out as a note under 11 U.S.C.A. § 1201.

Amendment by Pub.L. 107–8, extending to June 1, 2001, the date of repeal of this chapter, to take effect July 1, 2000, see section 2 of Pub.L. 107–8, set out as a note under 11 U.S.C.A. § 1201.

1999 Acts. Amendment by Pub.L. 106–70, extending to July 1, 2000, the date of repeal of this chapter, to take effect Oct. 1, 1999, see section 2 of Pub.L. 106–70, set out as a note under 11 U.S.C.A. § 1201.

Amendment by Pub.L. 106–5, extending to Oct. 1, 1999, the date of repeal of this chapter, to take effect Apr. 1, 1999, see section 2 of Pub.L. 106–5, set out as a note under 11 U.S.C.A. § 1201.

1998 Acts. Section reenacted, eff. Oct. 1, 1998, for the period beginning on Oct. 1, 1998, and ending on Apr. 1, 1999, but all cases commenced or pending under this chapter 12, as reenacted under section 149(a) of Pub.L. 105–277, and all matters and proceedings in or relating to such cases, to be conducted and determined under such chapter as if such chapter were continued in effect after Apr. 1, 1999, and the substantive rights of parties in connection with such cases, matters, and proceedings to continue to be governed under the law applicable to such cases, matters, and proceedings as if such chapter were continued in effect after Apr. 1, 1999, see section 149 of Pub.L. 105–277, set out as a note under 11 U.S.C.A. § 1201.

1993 Acts. Amendment by Pub.L. 103–65, extending to Oct. 1, 1998, the date of repeal of this chapter, to take effect Aug. 6, 1993, see section 3 of Pub.L. 103–65, set out as a note under 11 U.S.C.A. § 1221.

1986 Acts. Section repealed effective Oct. 1, 1998, see section 302(f) of Pub.L. 99–554, as amended, set out in a note under 28 U.S.C.A. § 581. However, for extension of provisions, see section 149 of Pub.L. 105–277, set out as a note under 11 U.S.C.A. § 1201.

Section effective 30 days after Oct. 27, 1986, but not applicable to cases commenced under this title before that date, see section 302(a), (c)(1) of Pub.L. 99–554, set out as a note under 28 U.S.C.A. § 581.

Reenactment of Chapter

This section as in effect on June 30, 2005, reenacted effective July 1, 2005, see Pub.L. 109–8, § 1001(a), set out as a note under 11 U.S.C.A. § 1201.

Repeal of Chapter; Extension of Provisions

Pub.L. 99–554, Title III, § 302(f), Oct. 27, 1986, 100 Stat. 3124, as amended Pub.L. 103–65, § 1, Aug. 6, 1993, 107 Stat. 311, which provided that, effective Oct. 1, 1998, this chapter is repealed, but that all cases commenced or pending under this chapter, and all matters and proceedings in or relating to such cases, shall be conducted and determined under this chapter as if such chapter had not been repealed, and that the substantive rights of parties in connection with such cases, matters, and proceedings shall continue to be governed under the laws applicable to such cases, matters, and proceedings as if such chapter had not been repealed, was superceded by the reenactment of this chapter by Pub.L. 109–8, Title X, § 1001(a), Apr. 20, 2005, 119 Stat. 185, set out as a note under 11 U.S.C.A. § 1201.

Pub.L. 105–277, Div. C, Title I, § 149, Oct. 21, 1998, 112 Stat. 2681–610, as amended Pub.L. 106–5, §§ 1, 2, Mar. 30, 1999, 113 Stat. 9; Pub.L. 106–70, §§ 1, 2, Oct. 9, 1999, 113 Stat. 1031; Pub.L. 107–8, §§ 1, 2, May 11, 2001, 115 Stat. 10; Pub.L. 107–17, §§ 1, 2, June 26, 2001, 115 Stat. 151; Pub.L. 107–170, §§ 1, 2, May 7, 2002, 116 Stat. 133; Pub.L. 107–171, Title X, § 10814, May 13, 2002, 116 St. 532; Pub.L. 107–377, § 2, Dec. 19, 2002, 116 Stat. 3115; Pub.L. 108–73, § 2(a), Aug. 15, 2003, 117 Stat. 891; Pub.L. 108–369, § 2(a), Oct. 25, 2004, 118 Stat. 1749, provided that, to take effect on January 1, 2004, chapter 12 of Title 11 [this chapter; 11 U.S.C.A. § 1201 et seq.], as in effect on December 31, 2003, is reenacted for the period beginning on January 1, 2004, and ending on July 1, 2005, but that all cases commenced or pending under this chapter 12, as reenacted under section 149(a) of Pub.L. 105–277, and all matters and proceedings in or relating to such cases, shall be conducted and determined under such chapter as if such chapter were continued in effect after July 1, 2005, and that the substantive rights of parties in connection with such cases, matters, and proceedings shall continue to be governed under the law applicable to such cases, matters, and proceedings as if such chapter were continued in effect after July 1, 2005, was superceded by the reenactment of this chapter by Pub.L. 109–8, Title X, § 1001(a), Apr. 20, 2005, 119 Stat. 185, set out as a note under 11 U.S.C.A. § 1201.

Conversion or dismissal upon denial of confirmation of modified plan, see 11 USCA § 1208.

Revocation of order of confirmation in,

Chapter eleven cases, see 11 USCA § 1144.

Chapter thirteen cases, see 11 USCA § 1330.

§ 1231. Special tax provisions

(a) The issuance, transfer, or exchange of a security, or the making or delivery of an instrument of transfer under a plan confirmed under section 1225 of this title, may not be taxed under any law imposing a stamp tax or similar tax.

(b) The court may authorize the proponent of a plan to request a determination, limited to questions of law, by any governmental unit charged with responsibility for collection or determination of a tax on or measured by income, of the tax effects, under section 346 of this title and under the law imposing such tax, of the plan. In the event of an actual controversy, the court may declare such effects after the earlier of—

(1) the date on which such governmental unit responds to the request under this subsection; or

(2) 270 days after such request.

(Added and amended Pub.L. 99–554, Title II, § 255, Title III, § 302(f), Oct. 27, 1986, 100 Stat. 3113, 3124; Pub.L. 103–65, § 1, Aug. 6, 1993, 107 Stat. 311; Pub.L. 105–277, Div. C, Title I, § 149(a), Oct. 21, 1998, 112 Stat. 2681–610; Pub.L. 106–5, § 1(1), (2), Mar. 30, 1999, 113 Stat. 9; Pub.L. 106–70, § 1, Oct. 9, 1999, 113 Stat. 1031; Pub.L. 107–8, § 1, May 11, 2001, 115 Stat. 10; Pub.L. 107–17, § 1, June 26, 2001, 115 Stat. 151; Pub.L. 107–170, § 1, May 7, 2002, 116 Stat. 133; Pub.L. 107–171, Title X, § 10814(a), May 13, 2002, 116 Stat. 532; Pub.L. 107–377, § 2(a), Dec. 19, 2002, 116 Stat. 3115; Pub.L. 108–73, § 2(a), Aug. 15, 2003, 117 Stat. 891; Pub.L. 108–369, § 2(a), Oct. 25, 2004, 118 Stat. 1749; Pub.L. 109–8, Title VII, § 719(b)(4), Title X, §§ 1001(a)(1), 1003(b), Apr. 20, 2005, 119 Stat. 133, 185, 186.)

HISTORICAL AND STATUTORY NOTES

Revision Notes and Legislative Reports

1986 Acts. House Report No. 99–764 and House Conference Report No. 99–958, see 1986 U.S. Code Cong. and Adm. News, p. 5227.

1993 Acts. House Report No. 103–32, see 1993 U.S. Code Cong. and Adm. News, p. 373.

1998 Acts. Statement by President, see 1998 U.S. Code Cong. and Adm. News, p. 582.

1999 Acts. Statement by President, see 1999 U.S. Code Cong. and Adm. News, p. 4.

Statement by President, see 1999 U.S. Code Cong. and Adm. News, p. 102.

2001 Acts. House Report No. 107–2, see 2001 U.S. Code Cong. and Adm. News, p. 6.

2005 Acts. House Report No. 109–31(Part I), see 2005 U.S. Code Cong. and Adm. News, p. 88.

Effective and Applicability Provisions

2005 Acts. Amendment to subsec. (b) of this section, which was formerly designated as subsec. (d) of this section, effective Apr. 20, 2005, and not applicable with respect to cases commenced under this title before that date, see Pub.L. 109–8, § 1003(c), set out as a note under 11 U.S.C.A. § 1222.

Amendments by Pub.L. 109–8 effective, except as otherwise provided, 180 days after April 20, 2005, and inapplicable with respect to cases commenced under Title 11 before the effective date, see Pub.L. 109–8, § 1501, set out as a note under 11 U.S.C.A. § 101.

2004 Acts. Amendment by Pub.L. 108–369, § 2(a), extending to July 1, 2005, the date of repeal of this chapter, to take effect Jan. 1, 2004, see Pub.L. 108–369, § 2(b), set out as a note under 11 U.S.C.A. § 1201.

2003 Acts. Amendment by Pub.L. 108–73, § 2(a), extending to Jan. 1, 2004, the date of repeal of this chapter, to take effect July 1, 2003, see Pub.L. 108–73, § 2(b), set out as a note under 11 U.S.C.A. § 1201.

2002 Acts. Amendment by Pub.L. 107–377, § 2(a), extending to July 1, 2003, the date of repeal of this chapter, to take effect Jan. 1, 2003, see Pub.L. 107–377, § 2(b), set out as a note under 11 U.S.C.A. § 1201.

Amendment by Pub.L. 107–171, extending to Jan. 1, 2003, the date of repeal of this chapter, to take effect June 1, 2002, see section 10814(b) of Pub.L. 107–171, set out as a note under 11 U.S.C.A. § 1201.

Amendment by Pub.L. 107–170, extending to June 1, 2002, the date of repeal of this chapter, to take effect October 1, 2001, see section 2 of Pub.L. 107–170, set out as a note under 11 U.S.C.A. § 1201.

2001 Acts. Amendment by Pub.L. 107–17, extending to October 1, 2001, the date of repeal of this chapter, to take effect June 1, 2001, see section 2 of Pub.L. 107–17, set out as a note under 11 U.S.C.A. § 1201.

Amendment by Pub.L. 107–8, extending to June 1, 2001, the date of repeal of this chapter, to take effect July 1, 2000, see section 2 of Pub.L. 107–8, set out as a note under 11 U.S.C.A. § 1201.

1999 Acts. Amendment by Pub.L. 106–70, extending to July 1, 2000, the date of repeal of this chapter, to take effect Oct. 1, 1999, see section 2 of Pub.L. 106–70, set out as a note under 11 U.S.C.A. § 1201.

Amendment by Pub.L. 106–5, extending to Oct. 1, 1999, the date of repeal of this chapter, to take effect Apr. 1, 1999, see section 2 of Pub.L. 106–5, set out as a note under 11 U.S.C.A. § 1201.

1998 Acts. Section reenacted, eff. Oct. 1, 1998, for the period beginning on Oct. 1, 1998, and ending on Apr. 1, 1999, but all cases commenced or pending under this chapter 12, as reenacted under section 149(a) of Pub.L. 105–277, and all matters and proceedings in or relating to such cases, to be conducted and determined under such chapter as if such chapter were continued in effect after Apr. 1, 1999, and the substantive rights of parties in connection with such cases, matters, and proceedings to continue to be governed under the law applicable to such cases, matters, and proceedings as if such chapter were continued in effect after Apr. 1, 1999, see section 149 of Pub.L. 105–277, set out as a note under 11 U.S.C.A. § 1201.

1993 Acts. Amendment by Pub.L. 103–65, extending to Oct. 1, 1998, the date of repeal of this chapter, to take effect Aug.

6, 1993, see section 3 of Pub.L. 103–65, set out as a note under 11 U.S.C.A. § 1221.

1986 Acts. Section repealed effective Oct. 1, 1998, see section 302(f) of Pub.L. 99–554, as amended, set out in a note under 28 U.S.C.A. § 581. However, for extension of provisions, see section 149 of Pub.L. 105–277, set out as a note under 11 U.S.C.A. § 1201.

Section effective 30 days after Oct. 27, 1986, but not applicable to cases commenced under this title before that date, see section 302(a), (c)(1) of Pub.L. 99–554, set out as a note under 28 U.S.C.A. § 581.

Reenactment of Chapter

This section as in effect on June 30, 2005, reenacted effective July 1, 2005, see Pub.L. 109–8, § 1001(a), set out as a note under 11 U.S.C.A. § 1201.

Repeal of Chapter; Extension of Provisions

Pub.L. 99–554, Title III, § 302(f), Oct. 27, 1986, 100 Stat. 3124, as amended Pub.L. 103–65, § 1, Aug. 6, 1993, 107 Stat. 311, which provided that, effective Oct. 1, 1998, this chapter is repealed, but that all cases commenced or pending under this chapter, and all matters and proceedings in or relating to such cases, shall be conducted and determined under this chapter as if such chapter had not been repealed, and that the substantive rights of parties in connection with such cases, matters, and proceedings shall continue to be governed under the laws applicable to such cases, matters, and proceedings as if such chapter had not been repealed, was superceded by the reenactment of this chapter by Pub.L. 109–8, Title X, § 1001(a), Apr. 20, 2005, 119 Stat. 185, set out as a note under 11 U.S.C.A. § 1201.

Pub.L. 105–277, Div. C, Title I, § 149, Oct. 21, 1998, 112 Stat. 2681–610, as amended Pub.L. 106–5, §§ 1, 2, Mar. 30, 1999, 113 Stat. 9; Pub.L. 106–70, §§ 1, 2, Oct. 9, 1999, 113 Stat. 1031; Pub.L. 107–8, §§ 1, 2, May 11, 2001, 115 Stat. 10; Pub.L. 107–17, §§ 1, 2, June 26, 2001, 115 Stat. 151; Pub.L. 107–170, §§ 1, 2, May 7, 2002, 116 Stat. 133; Pub.L. 107–171, Title X, § 10814, May 13, 2002, 116 St. 532; Pub.L. 107–377, § 2, Dec. 19, 2002, 116 Stat. 3115; Pub.L. 108–73, § 2(a), Aug. 15, 2003, 117 Stat. 891; Pub.L. 108–369, § 2(a), Oct. 25, 2004, 118 Stat. 1749, provided that, to take effect on January 1, 2004, chapter 12 of Title 11 [this chapter; 11 U.S.C.A. § 1201 et seq.], as in effect on December 31, 2003, is reenacted for the period beginning on January 1, 2004, and ending on July 1, 2005, but that all cases commenced or pending under this chapter 12, as reenacted under section 149(a) of Pub.L. 105–277, and all matters and proceedings in or relating to such cases, shall be conducted and determined under such chapter as if such chapter were continued in effect after July 1, 2005, and that the substantive rights of parties in connection with such cases, matters, and proceedings shall continue to be governed under the law applicable to such cases, matters, and proceedings as if such chapter were continued in effect after July 1, 2005, was superceded by the reenactment of this chapter by Pub.L. 109–8, Title X, § 1001(a), Apr. 20, 2005, 119 Stat. 185, set out as a note under 11 U.S.C.A. § 1201.

§ 1232. Claim by a governmental unit based on the disposition of property used in a farming operation

(a) Any unsecured claim of a governmental unit against the debtor or the estate that arises before the filing of the petition, or that arises after the filing of the petition and before the debtor's discharge under section 1228, as a result of the sale, transfer, exchange, or other disposition of any property used in the debtor's farming operation—

    (1) shall be treated as an unsecured claim arising before the date on which the petition is filed;

    (2) shall not be entitled to priority under section 507;

    (3) shall be provided for under a plan; and

    (4) shall be discharged in accordance with section 1228.

(b) For purposes of applying sections 1225(a)(4), 1228(b)(2), and 1229(b)(1) to a claim described in subsection (a) of this section, the amount that would be paid on such claim if the estate of the debtor were liquidated in a case under chapter 7 of this title shall be the amount that would be paid by the estate in a chapter 7 case if the claim were an unsecured claim arising before the date on which the petition was filed and were not entitled to priority under section 507.

(c) For purposes of applying sections 523(a), 1228(a)(2), and 1228(c)(2) to a claim described in subsection (a) of this section, the claim shall not be treated as a claim of a kind specified in subparagraph (A) or (B) of section 523(a)(1).

(d)(1) A governmental unit may file a proof of claim for a claim described in subsection (a) that arises after the date on which the petition is filed.

(2) If a debtor files a tax return after the filing of the petition for a period in which a claim described in subsection (a) arises, and the claim relates to the tax return, the debtor shall serve notice of the claim on the governmental unit charged with the responsibility for the collection of the tax at the address and in the manner designated in section 505(b)(1). Notice under this paragraph shall state that the debtor has filed a petition under this chapter, state the name and location of the court in which the case under this chapter is pending, state the amount of the claim, and include a copy of the filed tax return and documentation supporting the calculation of the claim.

(3) If notice of a claim has been served on the governmental unit in accordance with paragraph (2), the governmental unit may file a proof of claim not later than 180 days after the date on which such notice was served. If the governmental unit has not filed a timely proof of the claim, the debtor or trustee may file proof of the claim that is consistent with the notice served under paragraph (2). If a proof of claim is filed by the debtor or trustee under this paragraph, the governmental unit may not amend the proof of claim.

(4) A claim filed under this subsection shall be determined and shall be allowed under subsection (a), (b), or (c) of section 502, or disallowed under subsection (d) or (e) of section 502, in the same manner as if the claim had arisen immediately before the date of the filing of the petition.

(Added Pub.L. 115–72, Div. B, § 1005(a), Oct. 26, 2017, 131 Stat. 1232.)

HISTORICAL AND STATUTORY NOTES

References in Text

Chapter 7 of this title, referred to in subsec. (b), is classified to 11 U.S.C.A. § 701 et seq.

Effective and Applicability Provisions

2017 Acts. Amendments by Pub.L. 115–72, Div. B, § 1005, applicable to any bankruptcy case that is pending on Oct. 26, 2017, in which the plan under chapter 12 of this title has not been confirmed on Oct. 26, 2017, and to which an order of discharge under 11 U.S.C.A. § 1228 has not been entered; and applicable to any bankruptcy case that commences on or after Oct. 26, 2017, see Pub.L. 115–72, Div. B, § 1005(c), set out as a note under 11 U.S.C.A. § 1222.

CHAPTER 13—ADJUSTMENT OF DEBTS OF AN INDIVIDUAL WITH REGULAR INCOME

HISTORICAL AND STATUTORY NOTES

Effective and Applicability Provisions

2005 Acts. Amendments by Pub.L. 109–8 effective, except as otherwise provided, 180 days after April 20, 2005, and inapplicable with respect to cases commenced under Title 11 before the effective date, see Pub.L. 109–8, § 1501, set out as a note under 11 U.S.C.A. § 101.

CROSS REFERENCES

Chapters one, three, and five of this title applicable in cases under this chapter, see 11 USCA § 103.

Claims arising from rejection of executory contracts or unexpired leases by plans under this chapter, see 11 USCA § 502.

Compensation of trustee, see 11 USCA § 330.

Conversion from,

Chapter eleven, see 11 USCA § 1112.

Chapter seven, see 11 USCA § 706.

Chapter thirteen, see 11 USCA § 348.

Core proceedings, see 28 USCA § 157.

Duration of automatic stay, see 11 USCA § 362.

Eligibility to serve as trustee, see 11 USCA § 321.

Executory contracts and unexpired leases, see 11 USCA § 365.

Filing fees, see 28 USCA § 1930.

Inapplicability of restrictions on garnishment to orders of bankruptcy courts under this chapter, see 15 USCA § 1673.

"Individual with regular income" defined, see 11 USCA § 101.

Individuals who may be debtors under this chapter, see 11 USCA § 109.

Limitation on compensation of trustee, see 11 USCA § 326.

Recommendation by trustee of conversion from Chapter eleven to this chapter, see 11 USCA § 1106.

Return of excessive attorney compensation if transferred property was to be paid by debtor under plan under this chapter, see 11 USCA § 329.

Special tax provisions, see 11 USCA § 346.

Supervision of United States trustees' duties by Attorney General, see 28 USCA § 586.

Unclaimed property, see 11 USCA § 347.

Use, sale or lease of property under plan under this chapter, see 11 USCA § 363.

SUBCHAPTER I—OFFICERS, ADMINISTRATION, AND THE ESTATE

§ 1301. Stay of action against codebtor

(a) Except as provided in subsections (b) and (c) of this section, after the order for relief under this chapter, a creditor may not act, or commence or continue any civil action, to collect all or any part of a consumer debt of the debtor from any individual that is liable on such debt with the debtor, or that secured such debt, unless—

(1) such individual became liable on or secured such debt in the ordinary course of such individual's business; or

(2) the case is closed, dismissed, or converted to a case under chapter 7 or 11 of this title.

(b) A creditor may present a negotiable instrument, and may give notice of dishonor of such an instrument.

(c) On request of a party in interest and after notice and a hearing, the court shall grant relief from the stay provided by subsection (a) of this section with respect to a creditor, to the extent that—

(1) as between the debtor and the individual protected under subsection (a) of this section, such individual received the consideration for the claim held by such creditor;

(2) the plan filed by the debtor proposes not to pay such claim; or

(3) such creditor's interest would be irreparably harmed by continuation of such stay.

(d) Twenty days after the filing of a request under subsection (c)(2) of this section for relief from the stay provided by subsection (a) of this section, such stay is terminated with respect to the party in interest making such request, unless the debtor or any individual that is liable on such debt with the debtor files and serves upon such party in interest a written objection to the taking of the proposed action.

(Pub.L. 95–598, Nov. 6, 1978, 92 Stat. 2645; Pub.L. 98–353, Title III, §§ 313, 524, July 10, 1984, 98 Stat. 355, 388.)

HISTORICAL AND STATUTORY NOTES

Revision Notes and Legislative Reports

1978 Acts. Subsection (a) automatically stays the holder of a claim based on a consumer debt of the chapter 13 debtor from acting or proceeding in any way, except as authorized pursuant to subsections (b) and (c), against an individual or the property of an individual liable with the chapter 13 debtor, unless such codebtor became liable in the ordinary course of his business, or unless the case is closed, dismissed, or converted to another chapter.

Under the terms of the agreement with the codebtor who is not in bankruptcy, the creditor has a right to collect all payments to the extent they are not made by the debtor at the time they are due. To the extent to which a chapter 13 plan does not propose to pay a creditor his claims, the creditor may obtain relief from the court from the automatic stay and collect such claims from the codebtor. Conversely, a codebtor obtains the benefit of any payments made to the creditor under the plan. If a debtor defaults on scheduled payments under the plan, then the codebtor would be liable for the remaining deficiency; otherwise, payments not made under the plan may never be made by the codebtor. The obligation of the codebtor to make the creditor whole at the time payments are due remains.

The automatic stay under this section pertains only to the collection of a consumer debt, defined by section 101(7) of this title to mean a debt incurred by an individual primarily for a personal, family, or household purpose. Therefore, not all debts owed by a chapter 13 debtor will be subject to the stay of the codebtor, particularly those business debts incurred by an individual with regular income, as defined by section 101(24) of this title, engaged in business, that is permitted by virtue of section 109(b) and section 1304 to obtain chapter 13 relief.

Subsection (b) excepts the giving of notice of dishonor of a negotiable instrument from the reach of the codebtor stay.

Under subsection (c), if the codebtor has property out of which the creditor's claim can be satisfied, the court can grant relief from the stay absent the transfer of a security interest in that property by the codebtor to the creditor. Correspondingly, if there is reasonable cause to believe that property is about to be disposed of by the codebtor which could be used to satisfy his obligation to the creditor, the court should lift the stay to allow the creditor to perfect his rights against such property. Likewise, if property is subject to rapid depreciation or decrease in value the stay should be lifted to allow the creditor to protect his rights to reach such property. Otherwise, the creditor's interest would be irreparably harmed by such stay. Property which could be used to satisfy the claim could be disposed of or encumbered and placed beyond the reach of the creditor. The creditor should be allowed to protect his rights to reach property which could satisfy his claim and prevent its erosion in value, disposal, or encumbrance. Senate Report No. 95–989.

This section is new. It is designed to protect a debtor operating under a chapter 13 individual repayment plan case by insulating him from indirect pressures from his creditors exerted through friends or relatives that may have cosigned an obligation of the debtor. The protection is limited, however, to ensure that the creditor involved does not lose the benefit of the bargain he made for a cosigner. He is entitled to full compensation, including any interest, fees, and costs provided for by the agreement under which the debtor obtained his loan. The creditor is simply required to share with other creditors to the extent that the debtor will repay him under the chapter 13 plan. The creditor is delayed, but his substantive rights are not affected.

Subsection (a) is the operative subsection. It stays action by a creditor after an order for relief under chapter 13. The creditor may not act, or commence or continue any civil action, to collect all or any part of a consumer debt of the debtor from any individual that is liable on such debt with the debtor, or that has secured the debt, unless the individual became liable or secured the debt in the ordinary course of his business, or the case is closed, dismissed, or converted to chapter 7 or 11.

Subsection (b) permits the creditor, notwithstanding the stay, to present a negotiable instrument and to give notice of dishonor of the instrument, in order to preserve his substantive rights against the codebtor as required by applicable nonbankruptcy law.

Subsection (c) requires the court to grant relief from the stay in certain circumstances. The court must grant relief to the extent that the debtor does not propose to pay, under the plan, the amount owed to the creditor. The court must also grant relief to the extent that the debtor was really the codebtor in the transaction, that is, to the extent that the nondebtor party actually received the consideration for the claim held by the creditor. Finally, the court must grant relief to the extent that the creditor's interest would be irreparably harmed by the stay, for example, where the codebtor filed bankruptcy himself, or threatened to leave the locale, or lost his job. House Report No. 95–595.

1984 Acts. Statements by Legislative Leaders, see 1984 U.S.Code Cong. and Adm.News, p. 576.

Legislative Statements

Section 1301 of the House amendment is identical with the provision contained in section 1301 of the House bill and adopted by the Senate amendment. Section 1301(c)(1) indicates that a basis for lifting the stay is that the debtor did not receive consideration for the claim by the creditor, or in other words, the debtor is really the "codebtor." As with other sections in title 11, the standard of receiving consideration is a general rule, but where two co-debtors have agreed to share liabilities in a different manner than profits it is the individual who does not ultimately bear the liability that is protected by the stay under section 1301.

Effective and Applicability Provisions

1984 Acts. Amendment by Pub.L. 98–353 effective with respect to cases filed 90 days after July 10, 1984, see section 552(a), formerly 553(a), of Pub.L. 98–353, set out as a note under 11 U.S.C.A. § 101.

CROSS REFERENCES

Automatic stay, see 11 USCA § 362.

Automatic stay of enforcement of claims against debtor in Chapter nine cases, see 11 USCA § 922.

Claims of codebtors, see 11 USCA § 509.

Effect of conversion, see 11 USCA § 348.

Effect of § 362 of this title in stockbroker liquidation cases, see 11 USCA § 742.

Extension of time, generally, see 11 USCA § 108.

§ 1302. Trustee

(a) If the United States trustee appoints an individual under section 586(b) of title 28 to serve as standing trustee in cases under this chapter and if such individual qualifies under section 322 of this title, then such individual shall serve as trustee in the case. Otherwise, the United States trustee shall appoint one disinterested person to serve as trustee in the case or the United States trustee may serve as a trustee in the case.

(b) The trustee shall—

(1) perform the duties specified in sections 704(a)(2), 704(a)(3), 704(a)(4), 704(a)(5), 704(a)(6), 704(a)(7), and 704(a)(9) of this title;

(2) appear and be heard at any hearing that concerns—

(A) the value of property subject to a lien;

(B) confirmation of a plan; or

(C) modification of the plan after confirmation;

(3) dispose of, under regulations issued by the Director of the Administrative Office of the United States Courts, moneys received or to be received in a case under chapter XIII of the Bankruptcy Act;

(4) advise, other than on legal matters, and assist the debtor in performance under the plan;

(5) ensure that the debtor commences making timely payments under section 1326 of this title; and

(6) if with respect to the debtor there is a claim for a domestic support obligation, provide the applicable notice specified in subsection (d).

(c) If the debtor is engaged in business, then in addition to the duties specified in subsection (b) of this section, the trustee shall perform the duties specified in sections 1106(a)(3) and 1106(a)(4) of this title.

(d)(1) In a case described in subsection (b)(6) to which subsection (b)(6) applies, the trustee shall—

(A)(i) provide written notice to the holder of the claim described in subsection (b)(6) of such claim and of the right of such holder to use the services of the State child support enforcement agency established under sections 464 and 466 of the Social Security Act for the State in which such holder resides, for assistance in collecting child support during and after the case under this title; and

(ii) include in the notice provided under clause (i) the address and telephone number of such State child support enforcement agency;

(B)(i) provide written notice to such State child support enforcement agency of such claim; and

(ii) include in the notice provided under clause (i) the name, address, and telephone number of such holder; and

(C) at such time as the debtor is granted a discharge under section 1328, provide written notice to such holder and to such State child support enforcement agency of—

(i) the granting of the discharge;

(ii) the last recent known address of the debtor;

(iii) the last recent known name and address of the debtor's employer; and

(iv) the name of each creditor that holds a claim that—

(I) is not discharged under paragraph (2) or (4) of section 523(a); or

(II) was reaffirmed by the debtor under section 524(c).

(2)(A) The holder of a claim described in subsection (b)(6) or the State child support enforcement agency of the State in which such holder resides may request from a creditor described in paragraph (1)(C)(iv) the last known address of the debtor.

(B) Notwithstanding any other provision of law, a creditor that makes a disclosure of a last known address of a debtor in connection with a request made under subparagraph (A) shall not be liable by reason of making that disclosure.

(Pub.L. 95–598, Nov. 6, 1978, 92 Stat. 2645; Pub.L. 98–353, Title III, §§ 314, 525, July 10, 1984, 98 Stat. 356, 388; Pub.L. 99–554, Title II, §§ 228, 283(w), Oct. 27, 1986, 100 Stat. 3103, 3118; Pub.L. 103–394, Title V, § 501(d)(37), Oct. 22, 1994, 108 Stat. 4147; Pub.L. 109–8, Title II, § 219(d), Apr. 20, 2005, 119 Stat. 58; Pub.L. 111–327, § 2(a)(39), Dec. 22, 2010, 124 Stat. 3561.)

HISTORICAL AND STATUTORY NOTES

Revision Notes and Legislative Reports

1978 Acts. The principal administrator in a chapter 13 case is the chapter 13 trustee. Experience under chapter XIII of the Bankruptcy Act [former chapter 13 (section 1001 et seq.) of former Title 11] has shown that the more efficient and effective wage earner programs have been conducted by standing chapter XIII trustees who exercise a broad range of responsibilities in both the design and the effectuation of debtor plans.

Subsection (a) provides administrative flexibility by permitting the bankruptcy judge to appoint an individual from the panel of trustees established pursuant to 28 U.S.C. § 604(f) and qualified under section 322 of title 11, either to serve as a standing trustee in all chapter 13 cases filed in the district or a portion thereof, or to serve in a single case.

Subsection (b)(1) makes it clear that the chapter 13 trustee is no mere disbursing agent of the monies paid to him by the debtor under the plan [section 1322(a)(1)], by imposing upon him certain relevant duties of a liquidation trustee prescribed by section 704 of this title.

Subsection (b)(2) requires the chapter 13 trustee to appear before and be heard by the bankruptcy court whenever the value of property secured by a lien or the confirmation or modification of a plan after confirmation as provided by sections 1323–1325 is considered by the court.

Subsection (b)(3) requires the chapter 13 trustee to advise and counsel the debtor while under chapter 13, except on matters more appropriately left to the attorney for the debtor. The chapter 13 trustee must also assist the debtor in performance under the plan by attempting to tailor the requirements of the plan to the changing needs and circumstances of the debtor during the extension period.

Subsection (c) imposes on the trustee in a chapter 13 case filed by a debtor engaged in business the investigative and reporting duties normally required of a chapter 11 debtor or trustee as prescribed by section 1106(a)(3) and (4). Notes of Committee on the Judiciary, Senate Report No. 95–989.

Subsection (d) gives the trustee an additional duty if the debtor is engaged in business, as defined in section 1304. The trustee must perform the duties specified in sections 1106(a)(3) and 1106(a)(4), relating to investigation of the debtor. House Report No. 95–595.

1984 Acts. Statements by Legislative Leaders, see 1984 U.S.Code Cong. and Adm.News, p. 576.

1986 Acts. House Report No. 99–764 and House Conference Report No. 99–958, see 1986 U.S.Code Cong. and Adm. News, p. 5227.

1994 Acts. House Report No. 103–835, see 1994 U.S. Code Cong. and Adm. News, p. 3340.

2005 Acts. House Report No. 109–31(Part I), see 2005 U.S. Code Cong. and Adm. News, p. 88.

Legislative Statements

Section 1302 of the House amendment adopts a provision contained in the Senate amendment instead of the position taken in the House bill. Sections 1302(d) and (e) are modeled on the standing trustee system contained in the House bill with the court assuming supervisory functions in districts not under the pilot program.

References in Text

Chapter XIII of the Bankruptcy Act, referred to in subsec. (b)(3), is chapter XIII of Act July 1, 1898, c. 541, as added June 22, 1938, c. 575, § 1, 52 Stat. 930, which was classified to chapter 13 (section 1001 et seq.) of former Title 11.

Section 464 of the Social Security Act, referred to in subsec. (d)(1)(A)(i), is Act Aug. 14, 1935, c. 531, Title IV, § 464, as added Aug. 13, 1981, Pub.L. 97–35, Title XXIII, § 2331(a), 95 Stat. 860, and amended, which is classified to 42 U.S.C.A. § 664.

Section 466 of the Social Security Act, referred to in subsec. (d)(1)(A)(i), is Act Aug. 14, 1935, c. 531, Title IV, § 466, as added Aug. 16, 1984, Pub.L. 98–378, § 3(b), 98 Stat. 1306, and amended, which is classified to 42 U.S.C.A. § 666.

Effective and Applicability Provisions

2005 Acts. Amendments by Pub.L. 109–8 effective, except as otherwise provided, 180 days after April 20, 2005, and inapplicable with respect to cases commenced under Title 11 before the effective date, see Pub.L. 109–8, § 1501, set out as a note under 11 U.S.C.A. § 101.

1994 Acts. Amendment by Pub.L. 103–394 effective on Oct. 22, 1994, and not to apply with respect to cases commenced under Title 11 of the United States Code before Oct. 22, 1994, see section 702 of Pub.L. 103–394, set out as a note under section 101 of this title.

1986 Acts. Amendment by section 283 of Pub.L. 99–554 effective 30 days after Oct. 27, 1986, except as otherwise provided for, see section 302(a) of Pub.L. 99–554, set out as a note under section 581 of Title 28, Judiciary and Judicial Procedure.

Amendment by Pub.L. 99–554, § 228, not to become effective in or with respect to certain specified judicial districts until, or apply to cases while pending in such district before, the expiration of the 270–day period beginning 30 days after Oct. 27, 1986, or of the 30–day period beginning on the date the Attorney General certifies under section 303 of Pub.L. 99–554 the region specified in a paragraph of section 581(a) of Title 28, as amended by section 111(a) of Pub.L. 99–554, that includes such district, whichever occurs first, see section 302(d)(1) of Pub.L. 99–554, set out as a note under section 581 of Title 28.

Amendment by Pub.L. 99–554, § 228, not to become effective in or with respect to certain specified judicial districts until, or apply to cases while pending in such district before, the expiration of the 2–year period beginning 30 days after Oct. 27, 1986, or of the 30–day period beginning on the date the Attorney General certifies under section 303 of Pub.L. 99–554 the region specified in a paragraph of section 581(a) of Title 28, as amended by section 111(a) of Pub.L. 99–554, that includes such district, whichever occurs first, see section 302(d)(2) of Pub.L. 99–554, set out as a note under section 581 of Title 28.

Amendment by Pub.L. 99–554, § 228, not to become effective in or with respect to judicial districts established for the States of Alabama and North Carolina until, or apply to cases while pending in such district before, such district elects to be included in a bankruptcy region established in section 581(a) of Title 28, as amended by section 111(a) of Pub.L. 99–554, or Oct. 1, 2002, whichever occurs first, and, except as otherwise provided for, with respect to cases under chapters 7, 11, 12, and 13 of Title 11 commenced before 30 days after Oct. 27, 1986, and pending in a judicial district in the States of Alabama or North Carolina before any election made under section 302(d)(3)(A) of Pub.L. 99–554 by such district becomes effective or Oct. 1, 2002, whichever occurs first, amendments by Pub.L. 99–554 not to apply until Oct. 1, 2003, or the expiration of the 1–year period beginning on the date such election becomes effective, whichever occurs first, and further, in any judicial district in Alabama or North Carolina not making the election described in section 302(d)(3)(A) of Pub.L. 99–554, any person appointed under regulations issued by the Judicial Conference to administer estates in cases under Title 11 authorized to establish, etc., a panel of private trustees, and to supervise cases and trustees in cases under chapters 7, 11, 12, and 13 of Title 11, until amendments by sections 201 to 231 of Pub.L. 99–554 effective in such district, see section 302(d)(3)(A) to (F), (H), (I) of Pub.L. 99–554, set out as a note under section 581 of Title 28.

Amendment by Pub.L. 99–554, § 228, except as otherwise provided, with respect to cases under chapters 7, 11, 12, and 13 of Title 11 commenced before 30 days after Oct. 27, 1986, and pending in a judicial district referred to in section 581(a) of Title 28, as amended by section 111(a) of Pub.L. 99–554, for which a United States trustee is not authorized before 30 days after Oct. 27, 1986 to be appointed, not applicable until the expiration of the 3–year period beginning on Oct. 27, 1986, or of the 1–year period beginning on the date the Attorney General certifies under section 303 of Pub.L. 99–554 the region specified in a paragraph of such section 581(a) that includes, such district, whichever occurs first, see section 302(e)(1), (2) of Pub.L. 99–554, set out as a note under section 581 of Title 28.

1984 Acts. Amendment by Pub.L. 98–353 effective with respect to cases filed 90 days after July 10, 1984, see section 552(a), formerly 553(a), of Pub.L. 98–353, set out as a note under section 101 of this title.

Separability of Provisions

If any provision of or amendment made by Pub.L. 103–394 or the application of such provision or amendment to any person or circumstance is held to be unconstitutional, the remaining provisions of and amendments made by Pub.L. 103–394 and the application of such provisions and amendments to any person or circumstance shall not be affected thereby, see section 701 of Pub.L. 103–394, set out as a note under section 101 of this title.

CROSS REFERENCES

Appointment of trustee in,

Chapter eleven cases, see 11 USCA § 1104.

Chapter twelve cases, see 11 USCA § 1202.

Railroad reorganization cases, see 11 USCA § 1163.

Compensation of officers, see 11 USCA § 330.

Election of trustee, see 11 USCA § 702.

Eligibility to serve as trustee, see 11 USCA § 321.

Grain storage facility bankruptcies, expedited appointment of trustee or examiner, see 11 USCA § 557.

Limitation on compensation of trustee, see 11 USCA § 326.

Qualification of trustee, see 11 USCA § 322.

Removal of trustee, see 11 USCA § 324.

Role and capacity of trustee, see 11 USCA § 323.

Time of bringing action, see 11 USCA § 546.

§ 1303. Rights and powers of debtor

Subject to any limitations on a trustee under this chapter, the debtor shall have, exclusive of the trustee, the rights and powers of a trustee under sections 363(b), 363(d), 363(e), 363(f), and 363(l), of this title.
(Pub.L. 95–598, Nov. 6, 1978, 92 Stat. 2646.)

HISTORICAL AND STATUTORY NOTES

Revision Notes and Legislative Reports

1978 Acts. A chapter 13 debtor is vested with the identical rights and powers, and is subject to the same limitations in regard to their exercise, as those given a liquidation trustee by virtue of section 363(b), (d), (e), (f), and (h) of title 11, relating to the sale, use or lease of property. Notes of Committee on the Judiciary, Senate Report No. 95–989.

Legislative Statements

Section 1303 of the House amendment specifies rights and powers that the debtor has exclusive of the trustees. The section does not imply that the debtor does not also possess other powers concurrently with the trustee. For example, although section 1323 is not specified in section 1303, certainly it is intended that the debtor has the power to sue and be sued.

CROSS REFERENCES

Rights and powers of debtor in,

Chapter eleven cases, see 11 USCA § 1107.

Chapter twelve cases, see 11 USCA § 1203.

§ 1304. Debtor engaged in business

(a) A debtor that is self-employed and incurs trade credit in the production of income from such employment is engaged in business.

(b) Unless the court orders otherwise, a debtor engaged in business may operate the business of the debtor and, subject to any limitations on a trustee under sections 363(c) and 364 of this title and to such limitations or conditions as the court prescribes, shall have, exclusive of the trustee, the rights and powers of the trustee under such sections.

(c) A debtor engaged in business shall perform the duties of the trustee specified in section 704(a)(8) of this title.
(Pub.L. 95–598, Nov. 6, 1978, 92 Stat. 2646; Pub.L. 98–353, Title III, §§ 311(b)(2), 526, July 10, 1984, 98 Stat. 355, 389; Pub.L. 111–327, § 2(a)(40), Dec. 22, 2010, 124 Stat. 3562.)

HISTORICAL AND STATUTORY NOTES

Revision Notes and Legislative Reports

1978 Acts. Increased access to the simpler, speedier, and less expensive debtor relief provisions of chapter 13 is accomplished by permitting debtors engaged in business to proceed under chapter 13, provided their income is sufficiently stable and regular to permit compliance with a chapter 13 plan [section 101(24)] and that the debtor (or the debtor and spouse) do not owe liquidated, noncontingent unsecured debts of $50,000, or liquidated, noncontingent secured debts of $200,000 (§ 109(d)).

Section 1304(a) states that a self-employed individual who incurs trade credit in the production of income is a debtor engaged in business.

Subsection (b) empowers a chapter 13 debtor engaged in business to operate his business, subject to the rights, powers and limitations that pertain to a trustee under sections 363(c) and 364 of title 11, and subject to such further limitations and conditions as the court may prescribe.

Subsection (c) requires a chapter 13 debtor engaged in business to file with the court certain financial statements relating to the operation of the business. Notes of Committee on the Judiciary, Senate Report No. 95–989.

1984 Acts. Statements by Legislative Leaders, see 1984 U.S.Code Cong. and Adm.News, p. 576.

Legislative Statements

Section 1304(b) of the House amendment adopts the approach taken in the comparable section of the Senate amendment as preferable to the position taken in the House bill.

Effective and Applicability Provisions

1984 Acts. Amendment by Pub.L. 98–353 effective with respect to cases filed 90 days after July 10, 1984, see section 552(a), formerly 553(a), of Pub.L. 98–353, set out as a note under section 101 of this title.

CROSS REFERENCES

Authorization of trustee to operate business in,

Chapter eleven cases, see 11 USCA § 1108.

Chapter seven cases, see 11 USCA § 721.

Obtaining credit, see 11 USCA § 364.

Rights, powers and duties of debtor in possession in Chapter eleven cases, see 11 USCA § 1107.

Use, sale or lease of property, see 11 USCA § 363.

§ 1305. Filing and allowance of postpetition claims

(a) A proof of claim may be filed by any entity that holds a claim against the debtor—

(1) for taxes that become payable to a governmental unit while the case is pending; or

(2) that is a consumer debt, that arises after the date of the order for relief under this chapter, and that is for property or services necessary for the debtor's performance under the plan.

(b) Except as provided in subsection (c) of this section, a claim filed under subsection (a) of this section shall be allowed or disallowed under section 502 of this title, but shall be determined as of the date such claim arises, and shall be allowed under section 502(a), 502(b), or 502(c) of this title, or disallowed under section 502(d) or 502(e) of this title, the same as if such claim had arisen before the date of the filing of the petition.

(c) A claim filed under subsection (a)(2) of this section shall be disallowed if the holder of such claim knew or should have known that prior approval by the trustee of the debtor's incurring the obligation was practicable and was not obtained.

(Pub.L. 95–598, Nov. 6, 1978, 92 Stat. 2647.)

HISTORICAL AND STATUTORY NOTES

Revision Notes and Legislative Reports

1978 Acts. Section 1305, exclusively applicable in chapter 13 cases, supplements the provisions of sections 501–511 of title 11, dealing with the filing and allowance of claims. Sections 501–511 apply in chapter 13 cases by virtue of section 103(a) of this title. Section 1305(a) provides for the filing of a proof of claim for taxes and other obligations incurred after the filing of the chapter 13 case. Subsection (b) prescribes that section 502 of title 11 governs the allowance of section 1305(a) claims, except that its standards shall be applied as of the date of allowance of the claim, rather than the date of filing of the petition. Subsection (c) requires the disallowance of a postpetition claim for property or services necessary for the debtor's performance under the plan, if the holder of the claim knew or should have known that prior approval by the trustee of the debtor's incurring of the obligation was practicable and was not obtained. Senate Report No. 95–989.

Subsection (a) permits the filing of a proof of a claim against the debtor that is for taxes that become payable to a governmental unit while the case is pending, or that arises after the date of the filing of the petition for property or services that are necessary for the debtor's performance under the plan, such as auto repairs in order that the debtor

will be able to get to work, or medical bills. The effect of the latter provision, in paragraph (2), is to treat postpetition credit extended to a chapter 13 debtor the same as a prepetition claim for purposes of allowance, distribution, and so on. House Report No. 95–595.

Legislative Statements

Section 1305(a)(2) of the House amendment modifies similar provisions contained in the House and Senate bills by restricting application of the paragraph to a consumer debt. Debts of the debtor that are not consumer debts should not be subjected to section 1305(c) or section 1328(d) of the House amendment.

Section 1305(b) of the House amendment represents a technical modification of similar provisions contained in the House bill and Senate amendment.

The House amendment deletes section 1305(d) of the Senate amendment as unnecessary. Section 502(b)(1) is sufficient to disallow any claim to the extent the claim represents the usurious interest or any other charge forbidden by applicable law. It is anticipated that the Rules of Bankruptcy Procedure may require a creditor filing a proof of claim in a case under chapter 13 to include an affirmative statement as contemplated by section 1305(d) of the Senate amendment.

CROSS REFERENCES

Allowance and filing of claims and interests in Chapter eleven cases, see 11 USCA § 1111.

Discharge of certain consumer debts, see 11 USCA § 1328.

Effect of conversion, see 11 USCA § 348.

Filing of proofs of claims or interests, see 11 USCA § 501.

Provisions in plans for payment of claims, see 11 USCA § 1322.

§ 1306. Property of the estate

(a) Property of the estate includes, in addition to the property specified in section 541 of this title—

(1) all property of the kind specified in such section that the debtor acquires after the commencement of the case but before the case is closed, dismissed, or converted to a case under chapter 7, 11, or 12 of this title, whichever occurs first; and

(2) earnings from services performed by the debtor after the commencement of the case but before the case is closed, dismissed, or converted to a case under chapter 7, 11, or 12 of this title, whichever occurs first.

(b) Except as provided in a confirmed plan or order confirming a plan, the debtor shall remain in possession of all property of the estate.

(Pub.L. 95–598, Nov. 6, 1978, 92 Stat. 2647; Pub.L. 99–554, Title II, § 257(u), Oct. 27, 1986, 100 Stat. 3116.)

HISTORICAL AND STATUTORY NOTES

Revision Notes and Legislative Reports

1978 Acts. Section 541 is expressly made applicable to chapter 13 cases by section 103(a). Section 1306 broadens the definition of property of the estate for chapter 13 purposes to include all property acquired and all earnings from services performed by the debtor after the commencement of the case.

Subsection (b) nullifies the effect of section 521(3), otherwise applicable, by providing that a chapter 13 debtor need not surrender possession of property of the estate, unless required by the plan or order of confirmation. Notes of Committee on the Judiciary, Senate Report No. 95–989.

1986 Acts. House Report No. 99–764 and House Conference Report No. 99–958, see 1986 U.S.Code Cong. and Adm. News, p. 5227.

Legislative Statements

Section 1306(a)(2) adopts a provision contained in the Senate amendment in preference to a similar provision contained in the House bill.

Effective and Applicability Provisions

1986 Acts. Amendment by Pub.L. 99–554 effective 30 days after Oct. 27, 1986, but not applicable to cases commenced under this title before that date, see section 302(a), (c)(1) of Pub.L. 99–554, set out as a note under section 581 of Title 28, Judiciary and Judicial Procedure.

CROSS REFERENCES

Ownership of copyright, see 17 USCA § 201.

§ 1307. Conversion or dismissal

(a) The debtor may convert a case under this chapter to a case under chapter 7 of this title at any time. Any waiver of the right to convert under this subsection is unenforceable.

(b) On request of the debtor at any time, if the case has not been converted under section 706, 1112, or 1208 of this title, the court shall dismiss a case under this chapter. Any waiver of the right to dismiss under this subsection is unenforceable.

(c) Except as provided in subsection (f) of this section, on request of a party in interest or the United States trustee and after notice and a hearing, the court may convert a case under this chapter to a case under chapter 7 of this title, or may dismiss a case under this chapter, whichever is in the best interests of creditors and the estate, for cause, including—

    (1) unreasonable delay by the debtor that is prejudicial to creditors;

    (2) nonpayment of any fees and charges required under chapter 123 of title 28;

    (3) failure to file a plan timely under section 1321 of this title;

    (4) failure to commence making timely payments under section 1326 of this title;

    (5) denial of confirmation of a plan under section 1325 of this title and denial of a request made for additional time for filing another plan or a modification of a plan;

    (6) material default by the debtor with respect to a term of a confirmed plan;

    (7) revocation of the order of confirmation under section 1330 of this title, and denial of confirmation of a modified plan under section 1329 of this title;

    (8) termination of a confirmed plan by reason of the occurrence of a condition specified in the plan other than completion of payments under the plan;

    (9) only on request of the United States trustee, failure of the debtor to file, within fifteen days, or such additional time as the court may allow, after the filing of the petition commencing such case, the information required by paragraph (1) of section 521(a);

    (10) only on request of the United States trustee, failure to timely file the information required by paragraph (2) of section 521(a); or

    (11) failure of the debtor to pay any domestic support obligation that first becomes payable after the date of the filing of the petition.

(d) Except as provided in subsection (f) of this section, at any time before the confirmation of a plan under section 1325 of this title, on request of a party in interest or the United States trustee and after notice and a hearing, the court may convert a case under this chapter to a case under chapter 11 or 12 of this title.

(e) Upon the failure of the debtor to file a tax return under section 1308, on request of a party in interest or the United States trustee and after notice and a hearing, the court shall dismiss a case or convert a case under this chapter to a case under chapter 7 of this title, whichever is in the best interest of the creditors and the estate.

(f) The court may not convert a case under this chapter to a case under chapter 7, 11, or 12 of this title if the debtor is a farmer, unless the debtor requests such conversion.

(g) Notwithstanding any other provision of this section, a case may not be converted to a case under another chapter of this title unless the debtor may be a debtor under such chapter.

(Pub.L. 95–598, Nov. 6, 1978, 92 Stat. 2647; Pub.L. 98–353, Title III, §§ 315, 527, July 10, 1984, 98 Stat. 356, 389; Pub.L. 99–554, Title II, §§ 229, 257(v), Oct. 27, 1986, 100 Stat. 3103, 3116; Pub.L. 109–8, Title II, § 213(7), Title VII, § 716(c), Apr. 20, 2005, 119 Stat. 53, 130; Pub.L. 111–327, § 2(a)(41), Dec. 22, 2010, 124 Stat. 3562.)

HISTORICAL AND STATUTORY NOTES

Revision Notes and Legislative Reports

1978 Acts. Subsections (a) and (b) confirm, without qualification, the rights of a chapter 13 debtor to convert the case to a liquidating bankruptcy case under chapter 7 of title 11, at any time, or to have the chapter 13 case dismissed. Waiver of any such right is unenforceable. Subsection (c) specifies various conditions for the exercise of the power of the court to convert a chapter 13 case to one under chapter 7 or to dismiss the case. Subsection (d) deals with the conversion of a chapter 13 case to one under chapter 11. Subsection (e) prohibits conversion of the chapter 13 case filed by a farmer to chapter 7 or 11 except at the request of the debtor. No case is to be converted from chapter 13 to any other chapter, unless the debtor is an eligible debtor under the new chapter. Senate Report No. 95–989.

Subsection (f) reinforces section 109 by prohibiting conversion to a chapter under which the debtor is not eligible to proceed. House Report No. 95–595.

1984 Acts. Statements by Legislative Leaders, see 1984 U.S.Code Cong. and Adm.News, p. 576.

1986 Acts. House Report No. 99–764 and House Conference Report No. 99–958, see 1986 U.S.Code Cong. and Adm. News, p. 5227.

2005 Acts. House Report No. 109–31(Part I), see 2005 U.S. Code Cong. and Adm. News, p. 88.

Legislative Statements

Section 1307(a) is derived from the Senate amendment in preference to a comparable provision contained in the House bill.

References in Text

Chapter 7 of this title, referred to in text, is 11 U.S.C.A. § 701 et seq.

Effective and Applicability Provisions

2005 Acts. Amendments by Pub.L. 109–8 effective, except as otherwise provided, 180 days after April 20, 2005, and inapplicable with respect to cases commenced under Title 11 before the effective date, see Pub.L. 109–8, § 1501, set out as a note under 11 U.S.C.A. § 101.

1986 Acts. Amendment by Pub.L. 99–554 effective 30 days after Oct. 27, 1986, except as otherwise provided for, see section 302(a) of Pub.L. 99–554, set out as a note under section 581 of Title 28, Judiciary and Judicial Procedure.

Amendment by Pub.L. 99–554, § 229, not to become effective in or with respect to certain specified judicial districts until, or apply to cases while pending in such district before, the expiration of the 270–day period beginning 30 days after Oct. 27, 1986, or of the 30–day period beginning on the date the Attorney General certifies under section 303 of Pub.L. 99–554 the region specified in a paragraph of section 581(a) of Title 28, as amended by section 111(a) of Pub.L. 99–554, that includes such district, whichever occurs first, see section 302(d)(1) of Pub.L. 99–554, set out as a note under section 581 of Title 28.

Amendment by Pub.L. 99–554, § 229, not to become effective in or with respect to certain specified judicial districts until, or apply to cases while pending in such district before, the expiration of the 2–year period beginning 30 days after Oct. 27, 1986, or of the 30–day period beginning on the date the Attorney General certifies under section 303 of Pub.L. 99–554 the region specified in a paragraph of section 581(a) of Title 28, as amended by section 111(a) of Pub.L. 99–554, that includes such district, whichever occurs first, see section 302(d)(2) of Pub.L. 99–554, set out as a note under section 581 of Title 28.

Amendment by Pub.L. 99–554, § 229, not to become effective in or with respect to judicial districts established for the States of Alabama and North Carolina until, or apply to cases while pending in such district before, such district elects to be included in a bankruptcy region established in section 581(a) of Title 28, as amended by section 111(a) of Pub.L. 99–554, or Oct. 1, 2002, whichever occurs first, and, except as otherwise provided for, with respect to cases under chapters 7, 11, 12,

and 13 of Title 11 commenced before 30 days after Oct. 27, 1986, and pending in a judicial district in the States of Alabama or North Carolina before any election made under section 302(d)(3)(A) of Pub.L. 99–554 by such district becomes effective or Oct. 1, 2002, whichever occurs first, amendments by Pub.L. 99–554 not to apply, until Oct. 1, 2003, or the expiration of the 1–year period beginning on the date such election becomes effective, whichever occurs first, and further, in any judicial district in Alabama or North Carolina not making the election described in section 302(d)(3)(A) of Pub.L. 99–554, any person appointed under regulations issued by the Judicial Conference to administer estates in cases under Title 11 authorized to establish, etc., a panel of private trustees, and to supervise cases and trustees in cases under chapters 7, 11, 12, and 13 of Title 11, until amendments by sections 201 to 231 of Pub.L. 99–554 effective in such district, see section 302(d)(3)(A) to (F), (H), (I) of Pub.L. 99–554, set out as a note under section 581 of Title 28.

Amendments by Pub.L. 99–554, § 257(v), not to apply with respect to cases commenced under Title 11, Bankruptcy, before 30 days after Oct. 27 1986, see section 302(c)(1) of Pub.L. 99–554, set out as a note under section 581 of Title 28.

Amendment by Pub.L. 99–554, § 229 except as otherwise provided, with respect to cases under chapters 7, 11, 12, and 13 of Title 11 commenced before 30 days after Oct. 27, 1986, and pending in a judicial district referred to in section 581(a) of Title 28, as amended by section 111(a) of Pub.L. 99–554, for which a United States trustee is not authorized before 30 days after Oct. 27, 1986 to be appointed, not applicable until the expiration of the 3–year period beginning on Oct. 27, 1986, or of the 1–year period beginning on the date the Attorney General certifies under section 303 of Pub.L. 99–554 the region specified in a paragraph of such section 581(a) that includes, such district, whichever occurs first, see section 302(e)(1), (2) of Pub.L. 99–554, set out as a note under section 581 of Title 28.

1984 Acts. Amendment by Pub.L. 98–353 effective as to cases filed 90 days after July 10, 1984, see section 552(a), formerly 553(a), of Pub.L. 98–353, set out as a note under section 101 of this title.

CROSS REFERENCES

Conversion from Chapter seven, see 11 USCA § 706.

Conversion or dismissal upon revocation of order of confirmation, see 11 USCA § 1330.

Dismissal of,

    Chapter nine cases, see 11 USCA § 930.

    Chapter seven case, see 11 USCA § 707.

Distribution of property of estate converted to Chapter seven, see 11 USCA § 726.

Effect of,

    Conversion, see 11 USCA § 348.

    Dismissal, see 11 USCA § 349.

Executory contracts and unexpired leases, see 11 USCA § 365.

Liquidation of estate in railroad reorganization case, see 11 USCA § 1174.

§ 1308. Filing of prepetition tax returns

(a) Not later than the day before the date on which the meeting of the creditors is first scheduled to be held under section 341(a), if the debtor was required to file a tax return under applicable nonbankruptcy law, the debtor shall file with appropriate tax authorities all tax returns for all taxable periods ending during the 4–year period ending on the date of the filing of the petition.

(b)(1) Subject to paragraph (2), if the tax returns required by subsection (a) have not been filed by the date on which the meeting of creditors is first scheduled to be held under section 341(a), the trustee may hold open that meeting for a reasonable period of time to allow the debtor an additional period of time to file any unfiled returns, but such additional period of time shall not extend beyond—

(A) for any return that is past due as of the date of the filing of the petition, the date that is 120 days after the date of that meeting; or

(B) for any return that is not past due as of the date of the filing of the petition, the later of—

(i) the date that is 120 days after the date of that meeting; or

(ii) the date on which the return is due under the last automatic extension of time for filing that return to which the debtor is entitled, and for which request is timely made, in accordance with applicable nonbankruptcy law.

(2) After notice and a hearing, and order entered before the tolling of any applicable filing period determined under paragraph (1), if the debtor demonstrates by a preponderance of the evidence that the failure to file a return as required under paragraph (1) is attributable to circumstances beyond the control of the debtor, the court may extend the filing period established by the trustee under paragraph (1) for—

(A) a period of not more than 30 days for returns described in paragraph (1)(A); and

(B) a period not to extend after the applicable extended due date for a return described in paragraph (1)(B).

(c) For purposes of this section, the term "return" includes a return prepared pursuant to subsection (a) or (b) of section 6020 of the Internal Revenue Code of 1986, or a similar State or local law, or a written stipulation to a judgment or a final order entered by a nonbankruptcy tribunal.

(Added Pub.L. 109–8, Title VII, § 716(b)(1), Apr. 20, 2005, 119 Stat. 129; amended Pub.L. 111–327, § 2(a)(42), Dec. 22, 2010, 124 Stat. 3562.)

HISTORICAL AND STATUTORY NOTES

Revision Notes and Legislative Reports

2005 Acts. House Report No. 109–31(Part I), see 2005 U.S. Code Cong. and Adm. News, p. 88.

References in Text

Subsection (a) or (b) of section 6020 of the Internal Revenue Code of 1986, referred to in subsec. (c), is classified to 26 U.S.C.A. § 6020(a) or (b).

Effective and Applicability Provisions

2005 Acts. Amendments by Pub.L. 109–8 effective, except as otherwise provided, 180 days after April 20, 2005, and inapplicable with respect to cases commenced under Title 11 before the effective date, see Pub.L. 109–8, § 1501, set out as a note under 11 U.S.C.A. § 101.

SUBCHAPTER II—THE PLAN

§ 1321. Filing of plan

The debtor shall file a plan.

(Pub.L. 95–598, Nov. 6, 1978, 92 Stat. 2648.)

HISTORICAL AND STATUTORY NOTES

Revision Notes and Legislative Reports

1978 Acts. Chapter 13 contemplates the filing of a plan only by the debtor. Senate Report No. 95–989.

CROSS REFERENCES

Conversion or dismissal for failure to timely file plan, see 11 USCA § 1307.

Filing of plan in,

Chapter nine cases, see 11 USCA § 941.

Chapter twelve cases, see 11 USCA § 1221.

Who may file plan in Chapter eleven cases, see 11 USCA § 1121.

§ 1322. Contents of plan

(a) The plan—

(1) shall provide for the submission of all or such portion of future earnings or other future income of the debtor to the supervision and control of the trustee as is necessary for the execution of the plan;

(2) shall provide for the full payment, in deferred cash payments, of all claims entitled to priority under section 507 of this title, unless the holder of a particular claim agrees to a different treatment of such claim;

(3) if the plan classifies claims, shall provide the same treatment for each claim within a particular class; and

(4) notwithstanding any other provision of this section, may provide for less than full payment of all amounts owed for a claim entitled to priority under section 507(a)(1)(B) only if the plan provides that all of the debtor's projected disposable income for a 5–year period beginning on the date that the first payment is due under the plan will be applied to make payments under the plan.

(b) Subject to subsections (a) and (c) of this section, the plan may—

(1) designate a class or classes of unsecured claims, as provided in section 1122 of this title, but may not discriminate unfairly against any class so designated; however, such plan may treat claims for a consumer debt of the debtor if an individual is liable on such consumer debt with the debtor differently than other unsecured claims;

(2) modify the rights of holders of secured claims, other than a claim secured only by a security interest in real property that is the debtor's principal residence, or of holders of unsecured claims, or leave unaffected the rights of holders of any class of claims;

(3) provide for the curing or waiving of any default;

(4) provide for payments on any unsecured claim to be made concurrently with payments on any secured claim or any other unsecured claim;

(5) notwithstanding paragraph (2) of this subsection, provide for the curing of any default within a reasonable time and maintenance of payments while the case is pending on any unsecured claim or secured claim on which the last payment is due after the date on which the final payment under the plan is due;

(6) provide for the payment of all or any part of any claim allowed under section 1305 of this title;

(7) subject to section 365 of this title, provide for the assumption, rejection, or assignment of any executory contract or unexpired lease of the debtor not previously rejected under such section;

(8) provide for the payment of all or part of a claim against the debtor from property of the estate or property of the debtor;

(9) provide for the vesting of property of the estate, on confirmation of the plan or at a later time, in the debtor or in any other entity;

(10) provide for the payment of interest accruing after the date of the filing of the petition on unsecured claims that are nondischargeable under section 1328(a), except that such interest may be paid only to the extent that the debtor has disposable income available to pay such interest after making provision for full payment of all allowed claims; and

(11) include any other appropriate provision not inconsistent with this title.

(c) Notwithstanding subsection (b)(2) and applicable nonbankruptcy law—

(1) a default with respect to, or that gave rise to, a lien on the debtor's principal residence may be cured under paragraph (3) or (5) of subsection (b) until such residence is sold at a foreclosure sale that is conducted in accordance with applicable nonbankruptcy law; and

(2) in a case in which the last payment on the original payment schedule for a claim secured only by a security interest in real property that is the debtor's principal residence is due before the date on which the final payment under the plan is due, the plan may provide for the payment of the claim as modified pursuant to section 1325(a)(5) of this title.

(d)(1) If the current monthly income of the debtor and the debtor's spouse combined, when multiplied by 12, is not less than—

(A) in the case of a debtor in a household of 1 person, the median family income of the applicable State for 1 earner;

(B) in the case of a debtor in a household of 2, 3, or 4 individuals, the highest median family income of the applicable State for a family of the same number or fewer individuals; or

(C) in the case of a debtor in a household exceeding 4 individuals, the highest median family income of the applicable State for a family of 4 or fewer individuals, plus $700 [1] per month for each individual in excess of 4,

the plan may not provide for payments over a period that is longer than 5 years.

(2) If the current monthly income of the debtor and the debtor's spouse combined, when multiplied by 12, is less than—

(A) in the case of a debtor in a household of 1 person, the median family income of the applicable State for 1 earner;

(B) in the case of a debtor in a household of 2, 3, or 4 individuals, the highest median family income of the applicable State for a family of the same number or fewer individuals; or

(C) in the case of a debtor in a household exceeding 4 individuals, the highest median family income of the applicable State for a family of 4 or fewer individuals, plus $700 [1] per month for each individual in excess of 4,

the plan may not provide for payments over a period that is longer than 3 years, unless the court, for cause, approves a longer period, but the court may not approve a period that is longer than 5 years.

(e) Notwithstanding subsection (b)(2) of this section and sections 506(b) and 1325(a)(5) of this title, if it is proposed in a plan to cure a default, the amount necessary to cure the default, shall be determined in accordance with the underlying agreement and applicable nonbankruptcy law.

(f) A plan may not materially alter the terms of a loan described in section 362(b)(19) and any amounts required to repay such loan shall not constitute "disposable income" under section 1325.

(Pub.L. 95–598, Nov. 6, 1978, 92 Stat. 2648; Pub.L. 98–353, Title III, §§ 316, 528, July 10, 1984, 98 Stat. 356, 389; Pub.L. 103–394, Title III, §§ 301, 305(c), Oct. 22, 1994, 108 Stat. 4131, 4134; Pub.L. 109–8, Title II, §§ 213(8), (9), 224(d), Title III,

§ 318(1), Apr. 20, 2005, 119 Stat. 53, 65, 93; Pub.L. 111–327, § 2(a)(43), Dec. 22, 2010, 124 Stat. 3562.)

¹ Dollar amount as adjusted by the Judicial Conference of the United States. See Adjustment of Dollar Amounts notes set out under this section and 11 U.S.C.A. § 104.

HISTORICAL AND STATUTORY NOTES

Revision Notes and Legislative Reports

1978 Acts. Chapter 13 is designed to serve as a flexible vehicle for the repayment of part or all of the allowed claims of the debtor. Section 1322 emphasizes that purpose by fixing a minimum of mandatory plan provisions.

Subsection (a) requires that the plan submit whatever portion of the future income of the debtor is necessary to implement the plan to the control of the trustee, mandates payment in full of all section 507 priority claims, and requires identical treatment for all claims of a particular class.

Subsection (b) permits a chapter 13 plan to (1) divide unsecured claims not entitled to priority under section 507 into classes in the manner authorized for chapter 11 claims; (2) modify the rights of holders of secured and unsecured claims, except claims wholly secured by real estate mortgages; (3) cure or waive any default; (4) propose payments on unsecured claims concurrently with payments on any secured claim or any other class of unsecured claims; (5) provide for curing any default on any secured or unsecured claim on which the final payment is due after the proposed final payment under the plan; (6) provide for payment of any allowed postpetition claim; (7) assume or reject any previously unrejected executory contract or unexpired lease of the debtor; (8) propose the payment of all or any part of any claim from property of the estate or of the debtor; (9) provide for the vesting of property of the estate; and (10) include any other provision not inconsistent with other provisions of title 11.

Subsection (c) limits the payment period under the plan to 3 years, except that a 4-year payment period may be permitted by the court. Senate Report No. 95–989.

1984 Acts. Statements by Legislative Leaders, see 1984 U.S.Code Cong. and Adm.News, p. 576.

1994 Acts. House Report No. 103–835, see 1994 U.S. Code Cong. and Adm. News, p. 3340.

2005 Acts. House Report No. 109–31(Part I), see 2005 U.S. Code Cong. and Adm. News, p. 88.

Legislative Statements

Section 1322(b)(2) of the House amendment represents a compromise agreement between similar provisions in the House bill and Senate amendment. Under the House amendment, the plan may modify the rights of holders of secured claims other than a claim secured by a security interest in real property that is the debtor's principal residence. It is intended that a claim secured by the debtor's principal residence may be treated with under section 1322(b)(5) of the House amendment.

Section 1322(c) adopts a 5-year period derived from the House bill in preference to a 4-year period contained in the Senate amendment. A conforming change is made in section 1329(c) adopting the provision in the House bill in preference to a comparable provision in the Senate amendment.

Tax payments in wage earner plans: The House bill provided that a wage earner plan had to provide that all priority claims would be paid in full. The Senate amendment contained a special rule in section 1325(c) requiring that Federal tax claims must be paid in cash, but that such tax claims can be paid in deferred cash installments under the general rules applicable to the payment of debts in a wage earner plan, unless the Internal Revenue Service negotiates with the debtor for some different medium or time for payment of the tax liability.

The House bill adopts the substance of the Senate amendment rule under section 1322(a)(2) of the House amendment. A wage earner plan must provide for full payment in deferred cash payments, of all priority claims, unless the holder of a particular claim agrees with a different treatment of such claim.

Effective and Applicability Provisions

2013 Acts. Increase of dollar amounts by Judicial Conference of the United States by notice published Feb. 21, 2013, 78 F.R. 12089 effective April 1, 2013, and increase not applicable to cases commenced before the effective date of the adjustments, i.e., April 1, 2013. See Adjustment of Dollar Amounts notes under 11 U.S.C.A. § 104 and this section.

2010 Acts. Increase of dollar amounts by Judicial Conference of the United States by notice published Feb. 25, 2010, 75 F.R. 8747 effective April 1, 2010, and increase not applicable to cases commenced before the effective date of the adjustments, i.e., April 1, 2010. See Adjustment of Dollar Amounts notes under 11 U.S.C.A. § 104 and this section.

2007 Acts. Increase of dollar amounts by Judicial Conference of the United States by notice published Feb. 14, 2007, 72 F.R. 7082 effective April 1, 2007, and increase not applicable to cases commenced before the effective date of the adjustments, i.e., April 1, 2007. See Adjustment of Dollar Amounts notes under 11 U.S.C.A. § 104 and this section.

2005 Acts. Amendments by Pub.L. 109–8 effective, except as otherwise provided, 180 days after April 20, 2005, and inapplicable with respect to cases commenced under Title 11 before the effective date, see Pub.L. 109–8, § 1501, set out as a note under 11 U.S.C.A. § 101.

1994 Acts. Amendment by section 301 of Pub.L. 103–394 [enacting subsec. (c) of this section and redesignating former subsec. (c) as (d)] effective on Oct. 22, 1994, and not to apply with respect to cases commenced under Title 11 of the United States Code before Oct. 22, 1994, see section 702 of Pub.L. 103–394, set out as a note under section 101 of this title.

Amendment by section 305(c) of Pub.L. 103–394 [enacting subsec. (e) of this section] effective Oct. 22, 1994, and applicable only to agreements entered into after Oct. 22, 1994, see section 702 of Pub.L. 103–394, set out as a note under section 101 of this title.

1984 Acts. Amendment by Pub. L. 98–353 effective as to cases filed 90 days after July 10, 1984, see section 552(a), formerly 553(a), of Pub. L. 98–353, set out as a note under section 101 of this title.

Separability of Provisions

If any provision of or amendment made by Pub.L. 103–394 or the application of such provision or amendment to any person or circumstance is held to be unconstitutional, the remaining provisions of and amendments made by Pub.L. 103–394 and the application of such provisions and amendments to any person or circumstance shall not be affected thereby, see section 701 of Pub.L. 103–394, set out as a note under section 101 of this title.

Adjustment of Dollar Amounts

For adjustment of dollar amounts specified in subsec. (d)(1)(C), (2)(C) of this section by the Judicial Conference of the United States, effective Apr. 1, 2016, see note set out under 11 U.S.C.A. § 104.

By notice published Feb. 22, 2016, 81 F.R. 8748, the Judicial Conference of the United States adjusted the dollar amounts in provisions specified in subsec. (d)(1)(C) and (2)(C) of this section, effective Apr. 1, 2016, as follows:

Adjusted $675 (each time it appears) to $700 (each time it appears).

By notice published Feb. 21, 2013, 78 F.R. 12089, the Judicial Conference of the United States adjusted the dollar amounts in provisions specified in subsec. (d)(1)(C) and (2)(C) of this section, effective Apr. 1, 2013, as follows:

Adjusted $625 (each time it appears) to $675 (each time it appears).

By notice published Feb. 25, 2010, 75 F.R. 8747, the Judicial Conference of the United States adjusted the dollar amounts in provisions specified in subsec. (d)(1)(C) and (2)(C) of this section, effective Apr. 1, 2010, as follows:

Adjusted $575 (each time it appears) to $625 (each time it appears).

By notice published Feb. 14, 2007, 72 F.R. 7082, the Judicial Conference of the United States adjusted the dollar amounts in provisions specified in subsec. (d) of this section, effective Apr. 1, 2007, as follows:

Adjusted $525 (each time it appears) to $575 (each time it appears).

CROSS REFERENCES

Contents of plan filed in,

Chapter eleven cases, see 11 USCA § 1123.

Chapter twelve cases, see 11 USCA § 1222.

Railroad reorganization cases, see 11 USCA § 1172.

§ 1323. Modification of plan before confirmation

(a) The debtor may modify the plan at any time before confirmation, but may not modify the plan so that the plan as modified fails to meet the requirements of section 1322 of this title.

(b) After the debtor files a modification under this section, the plan as modified becomes the plan.

(c) Any holder of a secured claim that has accepted or rejected the plan is deemed to have accepted or rejected, as the case may be, the plan as modified, unless the modification provides for a change in the rights of such holder from what such rights were under the plan before modification, and such holder changes such holder's previous acceptance or rejection.

(Pub.L. 95–598, Nov. 6, 1978, 92 Stat. 2649.)

HISTORICAL AND STATUTORY NOTES

Revision Notes and Legislative Reports

1978 Acts. The debtor is permitted to modify the plan before confirmation without court approval so long as the modified plan, which becomes the plan on filing, complies with the requirements of section 1322.

The original acceptance or rejection of a plan by the holder of a secured claim remains binding unless the modified plan changes the rights of the holder and the holder withdraws or alters its earlier acceptance or rejection. Senate Report No. 95–989.

CROSS REFERENCES

Modification of plan filed in,

Chapter eleven cases, see 11 USCA § 1127.

Chapter nine cases, see 11 USCA § 942.

Chapter twelve cases, see 11 USCA § 1223.

§ 1324. Confirmation hearing

(a) Except as provided in subsection (b) and after notice, the court shall hold a hearing on confirmation of the plan. A party in interest may object to confirmation of the plan.

(b) The hearing on confirmation of the plan may be held not earlier than 20 days and not later than 45 days after the date of the meeting of creditors under section 341(a), unless the court determines that it would be in the best interests of the creditors and the estate to hold such hearing at an earlier date and there is no objection to such earlier date.

(Pub.L. 95–598, Nov. 6, 1978, 92 Stat. 2649; Pub.L. 98–353, Title III, § 529, July 10, 1984, 98 Stat. 389; Pub.L. 99–554, Title II, § 283(x), Oct. 27, 1986, 100 Stat. 3118; Pub.L. 109–8, Title III, § 317, Apr. 20, 2005, 119 Stat. 92.)

HISTORICAL AND STATUTORY NOTES

Revision Notes and Legislative Reports

1978 Acts. Any party in interest may object to the confirmation of a plan, as distinguished from merely rejecting a plan. An objection to confirmation is predicated on failure of the plan or the procedures employed prior to confirmation to conform with the requirements of chapter 13. The bankruptcy judge is required to provide notice and an opportunity for hearing any such objection to confirmation. Senate Report No. 95–989.

1984 Acts. Statements by Legislative Leaders, see 1984 U.S.Code Cong. and Adm.News, p. 576.

1986 Acts. House Report No. 99–764 and House Conference Report No. 99–958, see 1986 U.S.Code Cong. and Adm. News, p. 5227.

2005 Acts. House Report No. 109–31(Part I), see 2005 U.S. Code Cong. and Adm. News, p. 88.

Effective and Applicability Provisions

2005 Acts. Amendments by Pub.L. 109–8 effective, except as otherwise provided, 180 days after April 20, 2005, and inapplicable with respect to cases commenced under Title 11 before the effective date, see Pub.L. 109–8, § 1501, set out as a note under 11 U.S.C.A. § 101.

1986 Acts. Amendment by Pub.L. 99–554 effective 30 days after Oct. 27, 1986, see section 302(a) of Pub.L. 99–554, set out as a note under section 581 of Title 28, Judiciary and Judicial Procedure.

1984 Acts. Amendment by Pub.L. 98–353 effective with respect to cases filed 90 days after July 10, 1984, see section

552(a), formerly 553(a), of Pub.L. 98–353, set out as a note under section 101 of this title.

CROSS REFERENCES

Confirmation hearing in,

Chapter eleven cases, see 11 USCA § 1128.

Chapter twelve cases, see 11 USCA § 1224.

Duties of United States trustee, see 28 USCA § 586.

§ 1325. Confirmation of plan

(a) Except as provided in subsection (b), the court shall confirm a plan if—

(1) The plan complies with the provisions of this chapter and with the other applicable provisions of this title;

(2) any fee, charge, or amount required under chapter 123 of title 28, or by the plan, to be paid before confirmation, has been paid;

(3) the plan has been proposed in good faith and not by any means forbidden by law;

(4) the value, as of the effective date of the plan, of property to be distributed under the plan on account of each allowed unsecured claim is not less than the amount that would be paid on such claim if the estate of the debtor were liquidated under chapter 7 of this title on such date;

(5) with respect to each allowed secured claim provided for by the plan—

(A) the holder of such claim has accepted the plan;

(B)(i) the plan provides that—

(I) the holder of such claim retain the lien securing such claim until the earlier of—

(aa) the payment of the underlying debt determined under nonbankruptcy law; or

(bb) discharge under section 1328; and

(II) if the case under this chapter is dismissed or converted without completion of the plan, such lien shall also be retained by such holder to the extent recognized by applicable nonbankruptcy law;

(ii) the value, as of the effective date of the plan, of property to be distributed under the plan on account of such claim is not less than the allowed amount of such claim; and

(iii) if—

(I) property to be distributed pursuant to this subsection is in the form of periodic payments, such payments shall be in equal monthly amounts; and

(II) the holder of the claim is secured by personal property, the amount of such payments shall not be less than an amount sufficient to provide to the holder of such claim adequate protection during the period of the plan; or

(C) the debtor surrenders the property securing such claim to such holder;

(6) the debtor will be able to make all payments under the plan and to comply with the plan;

(7) the action of the debtor in filing the petition was in good faith;

(8) the debtor has paid all amounts that are required to be paid under a domestic support obligation and that first become payable after the date of the filing of the petition if the debtor is required by a judicial or administrative order, or by statute, to pay such domestic support obligation; and

(9) the debtor has filed all applicable Federal, State, and local tax returns as required by section 1308.

For purposes of paragraph (5), section 506 shall not apply to a claim described in that paragraph if the creditor has a purchase money security interest securing the debt that is the subject of the claim, the debt was incurred within the 910–day period preceding the date of the filing of the petition, and the collateral for that debt consists of a motor vehicle (as defined in section 30102 of title 49) acquired for the personal use of the debtor, or if collateral for that debt consists of any other thing of value, if the debt was incurred during the 1–year period preceding that filing.

(b)(1) If the trustee or the holder of an allowed unsecured claim objects to the confirmation of the plan, then the court may not approve the plan unless, as of the effective date of the plan—

(A) the value of the property to be distributed under the plan on account of such claim is not less than the amount of such claim; or

(B) the plan provides that all of the debtor's projected disposable income to be received in the applicable commitment period beginning on the date that the first payment is due under the plan will be applied to make payments to unsecured creditors under the plan.

(2) For purposes of this subsection, the term "disposable income" means current monthly income received by the debtor (other than child support payments, foster care payments, or disability payments for a dependent child made in accordance with applicable nonbankruptcy law to the extent reasonably necessary to be expended for such child) less amounts reasonably necessary to be expended—

(A)(i) for the maintenance or support of the debtor or a dependent of the debtor, or for a domestic support obligation, that first becomes payable after the date the petition is filed; and

(ii) for charitable contributions (that meet the definition of "charitable contribution" under section 548(d)(3)) to a qualified religious or charitable entity or organization (as defined in section 548(d)(4)) in an amount not to exceed 15 percent of gross income of the debtor for the year in which the contributions are made; and

(B) if the debtor is engaged in business, for the payment of expenditures necessary for the continuation, preservation, and operation of such business.

(3) Amounts reasonably necessary to be expended under paragraph (2), other than subparagraph (A)(ii) of paragraph (2), shall be determined in accordance with subparagraphs (A) and (B) of section 707(b)(2), if the debtor has current monthly income, when multiplied by 12, greater than—

(A) in the case of a debtor in a household of 1 person, the median family income of the applicable State for 1 earner;

(B) in the case of a debtor in a household of 2, 3, or 4 individuals, the highest median family income of the applicable State for a family of the same number or fewer individuals; or

(C) in the case of a debtor in a household exceeding 4 individuals, the highest median family income of the applicable State for a family of 4 or fewer individuals, plus $700 [1] per month for each individual in excess of 4.

(4) For purposes of this subsection, the "applicable commitment period"—

(A) subject to subparagraph (B), shall be—

(i) 3 years; or

(ii) not less than 5 years, if the current monthly income of the debtor and the debtor's spouse combined, when multiplied by 12, is not less than—

(I) in the case of a debtor in a household of 1 person, the median family income of the applicable State for 1 earner;

(II) in the case of a debtor in a household of 2, 3, or 4 individuals, the highest median family income of the applicable State for a family of the same number or fewer individuals; or

(III) in the case of a debtor in a household exceeding 4 individuals, the highest median family income of the applicable State for a family of 4 or fewer individuals, plus $700 [1] per month for each individual in excess of 4; and

(B) may be less than 3 or 5 years, whichever is applicable under subparagraph (A), but only if the plan provides for payment in full of all allowed unsecured claims over a shorter period.

(c) After confirmation of a plan, the court may order any entity from whom the debtor receives income to pay all or any part of such income to the trustee. (Pub.L. 95–598, Nov. 6, 1978, 92 Stat. 2649; Pub.L. 98–353, Title III, §§ 317, 530, July 10, 1984, 98 Stat. 356, 389; Pub.L. 99–554, Title II, § 283(y), Oct. 27, 1986, 100 Stat. 3118; Pub.L. 105–183, § 4(a), June 19, 1998, 112 Stat. 518; Pub.L. 109–8, Title I, § 102(g), (h), Title II, § 213(10), Title III, §§ 306(a), (b), 309(c)(1), 318(2), (3), Title VII, § 716(a), Apr. 20, 2005, 119 Stat. 33, 53, 80, 83, 93, 129; Pub.L. 109–439, § 2,

Dec. 20, 2006, 120 Stat. 3285; Pub.L. 111–327, § 2(a)(44), Dec. 22, 2010, 124 Stat. 3562.)

[1] Dollar amount as adjusted by the Judicial Conference of the United States. See Adjustment of Dollar Amounts notes set out under this section and 11 U.S.C.A. § 104.

HISTORICAL AND STATUTORY NOTES

Revision Notes and Legislative Reports

1978 Acts. The bankruptcy court must confirm a plan if (1) the plan satisfies the provisions of chapter 13 and other applicable provisions of title 11; (2) it is proposed in good faith; (3) it is in the best interests of creditors, and defined by subsection (a)(4) of Section 1325; (4) it has been accepted by the holder of each allowed secured claim provided for the plan or where the holder of any such secured claim is to receive value under the plan not less than the amount of the allowed secured claim, or where the debtor surrenders to the holder the collateral securing any such allowed secured claim; (5) the plan is feasible; and (6) the requisite fees and charges have been paid.

Subsection (b) authorizes the court to order an entity, as defined by section 101(15), to pay any income of the debtor to the trustee. Any governmental unit is an entity subject to such an order. Senate Report No. 95–989.

1984 Acts. Statements by Legislative Leaders, see 1984 U.S.Code Cong. and Adm.News, p. 576.

1986 Acts. House Report No. 99–764 and House Conference Report No. 99–958, see 1986 U.S.Code Cong. and Adm. News, p. 5227.

1998 Acts. Statement by President, see 1998 U.S. Code Cong. and Adm. News, p. 230.

2005 Acts. House Report No. 109–31(Part I), see 2005 U.S. Code Cong. and Adm. News, p. 88.

Legislative Statements

Section 1325(a)(5)(B) of the House amendment modifies the House bill and Senate amendment to significantly protect secured creditors in chapter 13. Unless the secured creditor accepts the plan, the plan must provide that the secured creditor retain the lien securing the creditor's allowed secured claim in addition to receiving value, as of the effective date of the plan of property to be distributed under the plan on account of the claim not less than the allowed amount of the claim. To this extent, a secured creditor in a case under chapter 13 is treated identically with a recourse creditor under section 1111(b)(1) of the House amendment except that the secured creditor in a case under chapter 13 may receive any property of a value as of the effective date of the plan equal to the allowed amount of the creditor's secured claim rather than being restricted to receiving deferred cash payments. Of course, the secured creditors' lien only secures the value of the collateral and to the extent property is distributed of a present value equal to the allowed amount of the creditor's secured claim the creditor's lien will have been satisfied in full. Thus the lien created under section 1325(a)(5)(B)(i) is effective only to secure deferred payments to the extent of the amount of the allowed secured claim. To the extent the deferred payments exceed the value of the allowed amount of the secured claim and the debtor subsequently defaults, the lien will not secure unaccrued interest represented in such deferred payments.

Effective and Applicability Provisions

2013 Acts. Increase of dollar amounts by Judicial Conference of the United States by notice published Feb. 21, 2013, 78 F.R. 12089 effective April 1, 2013, and increase not applicable to cases commenced before the effective date of the adjustments, i.e., April 1, 2013. See Adjustment of Dollar Amounts notes under 11 U.S.C.A. § 104 and this section.

2010 Acts. Increase of dollar amounts by Judicial Conference of the United States by notice published Feb. 25, 2010, 75 F.R. 8747 effective April 1, 2010, and increase not applicable to cases commenced before the effective date of the adjustments, i.e., April 1, 2010. See Adjustment of Dollar Amounts notes under 11 U.S.C.A. § 104 and this section.

2007 Acts. Increase of dollar amounts by Judicial Conference of the United States by notice published Feb. 14, 2007, 72 F.R. 7082 effective April 1, 2007, and increase not applicable to cases commenced before the effective date of the adjustments, i.e., April 1, 2007. See Adjustment of Dollar Amounts notes under 11 U.S.C.A. § 104 and this section.

2005 Acts. Amendments by Pub.L. 109–8 effective, except as otherwise provided, 180 days after April 20, 2005, and inapplicable with respect to cases commenced under Title 11 before the effective date, see Pub.L. 109–8, § 1501, set out as a note under 11 U.S.C.A. § 101.

1986 Acts. Amendment by Pub.L. 99–554 effective 30 days after Oct. 27, 1986, see section 302(a) of Pub.L. 99–554, set out as a note under section 581 of Title 28, Judiciary and Judicial Procedure.

1984 Acts. Amendment by Pub.L. 98–353 effective with respect to cases filed 90 days after July 10, 1984, see section 552(a), formerly 553(a), of Pub.L. 98–353, set out as a note under section 101 of this title.

Adjustment of Dollar Amounts

For adjustment of dollar amounts specified in subsec. (b)(3) and (4) of this section by the Judicial Conference of the United States, effective Apr. 1, 2016, see note set out under 11 U.S.C.A. § 104.

By notice published Feb. 22, 2016, 81 F.R. 8748, the Judicial Conference of the United States adjusted the dollar amounts in provisions specified in subsec. (b)(3) and (4) of this section, effective Apr. 1, 2016, as follows:

Adjusted $675 (each time it appears) to $700 (each time it appears).

By notice published Feb. 21, 2013, 78 F.R. 12089, the Judicial Conference of the United States adjusted the dollar amounts in provisions specified in subsec. (b)(3) and (4) of this section, effective Apr. 1, 2013, as follows:

Adjusted $625 (each time it appears) to $675 (each time it appears).

By notice published Feb. 25, 2010, 75 F.R. 8747, the Judicial Conference of the United States adjusted the dollar amounts in provisions specified in subsec. (b)(3) and (4) of this section, effective Apr. 1, 2010, as follows:

Adjusted $575 (each time it appears) to $625 (each time it appears).

By notice published Feb. 14, 2007, 72 F.R. 7082, the Judicial Conference of the United States adjusted the dollar amounts in provisions specified in subsec. (b) of this section, effective Apr. 1, 2007, as follows:

Adjusted $525 (each time it appears) to $575 (each time it appears).

Applicability

Applicability of amendments made by Pub.L. 105–183 to any case brought under an applicable provision of this title that is pending or commenced on or after June 19, 1998, see Pub.L. 105–183, § 5, June 19, 1998, 112 Stat. 518, set out as a note under section 544 of this title.

Rules of Construction

Amendments made by Pub.L. 105–183 not intended to limit the applicability of the Religious Freedom Restoration Act of 1993 (42 U.S.C. 2002bb et seq.), see Pub.L. 105–183, § 6, June 19, 1998, 112 Stat. 519, set out as a note under section 544 of this title.

CROSS REFERENCES

Confirmation of plan in,

    Chapter eleven cases, see 11 USCA § 1129.

    Chapter nine cases, see 11 USCA § 943.

    Chapter twelve cases, see 11 USCA § 1225.

    Railroad reorganization cases, see 11 USCA § 1173.

Conversion or dismissal, see 11 USCA § 1307.

§ 1326. Payments

(a)(1) Unless the court orders otherwise, the debtor shall commence making payments not later than 30 days after the date of the filing of the plan or the order for relief, whichever is earlier, in the amount—

(A) proposed by the plan to the trustee;

(B) scheduled in a lease of personal property directly to the lessor for that portion of the obligation that becomes due after the order for relief, reducing the payments under subparagraph (A) by the amount so paid and providing the trustee with evidence of such payment, including the amount and date of payment; and

(C) that provides adequate protection directly to a creditor holding an allowed claim secured by personal property to the extent the claim is attributable to the purchase of such property by the debtor for that portion of the obligation that becomes due after the order for relief, reducing the payments under subparagraph (A) by the amount so paid and providing the trustee with evidence of such payment, including the amount and date of payment.

(2) A payment made under paragraph (1)(A) shall be retained by the trustee until confirmation or denial of confirmation. If a plan is confirmed, the trustee shall distribute any such payment in accordance with the plan as soon as is practicable. If a plan is not confirmed, the trustee shall return any such payments not previously paid and not yet due and owing to creditors pursuant to paragraph (3) to the debtor, after deducting any unpaid claim allowed under section 503(b).

(3) Subject to section 363, the court may, upon notice and a hearing, modify, increase, or reduce the payments required under this subsection pending confirmation of a plan.

(4) Not later than 60 days after the date of filing of a case under this chapter, a debtor retaining possession of personal property subject to a lease or securing a claim attributable in whole or in part to the purchase price of such property shall provide the lessor or secured creditor reasonable evidence of the maintenance of any required insurance coverage with respect to the use or ownership of such property and continue to do so for so long as the debtor retains possession of such property.

(b) Before or at the time of each payment to creditors under the plan, there shall be paid—

(1) any unpaid claim of the kind specified in section 507(a)(2) of this title;

(2) if a standing trustee appointed under section 586(b) of title 28 is serving in the case, the percentage fee fixed for such standing trustee under section 586(e)(1)(B) of title 28; and

(3) if a chapter 7 trustee has been allowed compensation due to the conversion or dismissal of the debtor's prior case pursuant to section 707(b), and some portion of that compensation remains unpaid in a case converted to this chapter or in the case dismissed under section 707(b) and refiled under this chapter, the amount of any such unpaid compensation, which shall be paid monthly—

(A) by prorating such amount over the remaining duration of the plan; and

(B) by monthly payments not to exceed the greater of—

(i) $25 [1]; or

(ii) the amount payable to unsecured nonpriority creditors, as provided by the plan, multiplied by 5 percent, and the result divided by the number of months in the plan.

(c) Except as otherwise provided in the plan or in the order confirming the plan, the trustee shall make payments to creditors under the plan.

(d) Notwithstanding any other provision of this title—

(1) compensation referred to in subsection (b)(3) is payable and may be collected by the trustee under that paragraph, even if such amount has been discharged in a prior case under this title; and

(2) such compensation is payable in a case under this chapter only to the extent permitted by subsection (b)(3).

(Pub.L. 95–598, Nov. 6, 1978, 92 Stat. 2650; Pub.L. 98–353, Title III, §§ 318(a), 531, July 10, 1984, 98 Stat. 357, 389; Pub.L. 99–554, Title II, §§ 230, 283(z), Oct. 27, 1986, 100 Stat. 3103, 3118; Pub.L. 103–394, Title III, § 307, Oct. 22, 1994, 108 Stat. 4135; Pub.L. 109–8, Title III, § 309(c)(2), Title XII, § 1224, Title XV, § 1502(a)(10), Apr. 20, 2005, 119 Stat. 83, 199, 217.)

[1] Dollar amount as adjusted by the Judicial Conference of the United States. See Adjustment of Dollar Amounts notes set out under this section and 11 U.S.C.A. § 104.

HISTORICAL AND STATUTORY NOTES

Revision Notes and Legislative Reports

1978 Acts. Section 1326 supplements the priorities provisions of section 507. Subsection (a) requires accrued costs of administration and filing fees, as well as fees due the chapter 13 trustee, to be disbursed before payments to creditors under the plan. Subsection (b) makes it clear that the chapter 13 trustee is normally to make distribution to creditors of the payments made under the plan by the debtor. Senate Report No. 95–989.

Subsection (a) requires that before or at the time of each payment any outstanding administrative expenses [and] any percentage fee due for a private standing chapter 13 trustee be paid in full. House Report No. 95–595.

1984 Acts. Statements by Legislative Leaders, see 1984 U.S.Code Cong. and Adm.News, p. 576.

1986 Acts. House Report No. 99–764 and House Conference Report No. 99–958, see 1986 U.S.Code Cong. and Adm. News, p. 5227.

1994 Acts. House Report No. 103–835, see 1994 U.S. Code Cong. and Adm. News, p. 3340.

2005 Acts. House Report No. 109–31(Part I), see 2005 U.S. Code Cong. and Adm. News, p. 88.

Legislative Statements

Section 1326(a)(2) of the House amendment adopts a comparable provision contained in the House bill providing for standing trustees.

Effective and Applicability Provisions

2013 Acts. Increase of dollar amounts by Judicial Conference of the United States by notice published Feb. 21, 2013, 78 F.R. 12089 effective April 1, 2013, and increase not applicable to cases commenced before the effective date of the adjustments, i.e., April 1, 2013. See Adjustment of Dollar Amounts notes under 11 U.S.C.A. § 104 and this section.

2010 Acts. Increase of dollar amounts by Judicial Conference of the United States by notice published Feb. 25, 2010, 75 F.R. 8747 effective April 1, 2010, and increase not applicable to cases commenced before the effective date of the adjustments, i.e., April 1, 2010. See Adjustment of Dollar Amounts notes under 11 U.S.C.A. § 104 and this section.

2007 Acts. Increase of dollar amounts by Judicial Conference of the United States by notice published Feb. 14, 2007, 72 F.R. 7082 effective April 1, 2007, and increase not applicable to cases commenced before the effective date of the adjustments, i.e., April 1, 2007. See Adjustment of Dollar Amounts notes under 11 U.S.C.A. § 104 and this section.

2005 Acts. Amendments by Pub.L. 109–8 effective, except as otherwise provided, 180 days after April 20, 2005, and inapplicable with respect to cases commenced under Title 11 before the effective date, see Pub.L. 109–8, § 1501, set out as a note under 11 U.S.C.A. § 101.

1994 Acts. Amendment by Pub.L. 103–394 effective on Oct. 22, 1994, and not to apply with respect to cases commenced under Title 11 of the United States Code before Oct. 22, 1994, see section 702 of Pub.L. 103–394, set out as a note under section 101 of this title.

1986 Acts. Amendment by section 283 of Pub.L. 99–554 effective 30 days after Oct. 27, 1986, except as otherwise provided for, see section 302(a) of Pub.L. 99–554, set out as a note under section 581 of Title 28, Judiciary and Judicial Procedure.

Amendment by Pub.L. 99–554, § 230, not to become effective in or with respect to certain specified judicial districts until, or apply to cases while pending in such district before, the expiration of the 270–day period beginning 30 days after Oct. 27, 1986, or of the 30–day period beginning on the date the Attorney General certifies under section 303 of Pub.L. 99–554 the region specified in a paragraph of section 581(a) of Title 28, as amended by section 111(a) of Pub.L. 99–554, that includes such district, whichever occurs first, see section 302(d)(1) of Pub.L. 99–554, set out as a note under section 581 of Title 28.

Amendment by Pub.L. 99–554, § 230, not to become effective in or with respect to certain specified judicial districts until, or apply to cases while pending in such district before, the expiration of the 2–year period beginning 30 days after Oct. 27, 1986, or of the 30–day period beginning on the date the Attorney General certifies under section 303 of Pub.L. 99–554 the region specified in a paragraph of section 581(a) of Title 28, as amended by section 111(a) of Pub.L. 99–554, that includes such district, whichever occurs first, see section 302(d)(2) of Pub.L. 99–554, set out as a note under section 581 of Title 28.

Amendment by Pub.L. 99–554, § 230, not to become effective in or with respect to judicial districts established for the States of Alabama and North Carolina until, or apply to cases while pending in such district before, such district elects to be included in a bankruptcy region established in section 581(a) of Title 28, as amended by section 111(a) of Pub.L. 99–554, or Oct. 1, 2002, whichever occurs first, and, except as otherwise provided for, with respect to cases under chapters 7, 11, 12, and 13 of Title 11 commenced before 30 days after Oct. 27, 1986, and pending in a judicial district in the States of Alabama or North Carolina before any election made under section 302(d)(3)(A) of Pub.L. 99–554 by such district becomes effective or Oct. 1, 2002, whichever occurs first, amendments by Pub.L. 99–554 not to apply until Oct. 1, 2003, or the expiration of the 1–year period beginning on the date such election becomes effective, whichever occurs first, and further, in any judicial district in Alabama or North Carolina not making the election described in section 302(d)(3)(A) of Pub.L. 99–554, any person appointed under regulations issued by the Judicial Conference to administer estates in cases under Title 11 authorized to establish, etc., a panel of private trustees, and to supervise cases and trustees in cases under chapters 7, 11, 12, and 13 of Title 11, until amendments by sections 201 to 231 of Pub.L. 99–554 effective in such district, see section 302(d)(3)(A) to (F), (H), (I) of Pub.L. 99–554, set out as a note under section 581 of Title 28.

Amendment by Pub.L. 99–554, § 230, except as otherwise provided, with respect to cases under chapters 7, 11, 12, and 13 of Title 11 commenced before 30 days after Oct. 27, 1986, and pending in a judicial district referred to in section 581(a) of Title 28, as amended by section 111(a) of Pub.L. 99–554, for which a United States trustee is not authorized before 30 days after Oct. 27, 1986 to be appointed, not applicable until the expiration of the 3–year period beginning on Oct. 27, 1986, or of the 1–year period beginning on the date the Attorney General certifies under section 303 of Pub.L. 99–554 the region specified in a paragraph of such section 581(a) that includes, such district, whichever occurs first, see section 302(e)(1), (2) of Pub.L. 99–554, set out as a note under section 581 of Title 28.

1984 Acts. Amendment by Pub.L. 98–353 effective with respect to cases filed 90 days after July 10, 1984, see section 552(a), formerly 553(a), of Pub.L. 98–353, set out as a note under section 101 of this title.

Separability of Provisions

If any provision of or amendment made by Pub.L. 103–394 or the application of such provision or amendment to any person or circumstance is held to be unconstitutional, the remaining provisions of and amendments made by Pub.L. 103–394 and the application of such provisions and amendments to any person or circumstance shall not be affected thereby, see section 701 of Pub.L. 103–394, set out as a note under section 101 of this title.

Adjustment of Dollar Amounts

For adjustment of dollar amounts specified in subsec. (b)(3)(B) of this section by the Judicial Conference of the United States, effective Apr. 1, 2016, see note set out under 11 U.S.C.A. § 104.

By notice published Feb. 22, 2016, 81 F.R. 8748, the Judicial Conference of the United States purported to adjust the dollar amounts in provisions specified in subsec. (b)(3)(B) of this section, effective Apr. 1, 2016, as follows:

Adjusted $25 to $25 [resulting in no change in text].

By notice published Feb. 21, 2013, 78 F.R. 12089, the Judicial Conference of the United States purported to adjust the dollar amounts in provisions specified in subsec. (b)(3)(B) of this section, effective Apr. 1, 2013, as follows:

Adjusted $25 to $25 [resulting in no change in text].

By notice published Feb. 25, 2010, 75 F.R. 8747, the Judicial Conference of the United States purported to adjust the dollar amounts in provisions specified in subsec. (b)(3)(B) of this section, effective Apr. 1, 2010, as follows:

Adjusted $25 to $25 [resulting in no change in text].

By notice published Feb. 14, 2007, 72 F.R. 7082, the Judicial Conference of the United States purported to adjust the dollar amounts in provisions specified in subsec. (b)(3) of this section, effective Apr. 1, 2007, as follows:

Adjusted $25 to $25 [resulting in no change in text].

CROSS REFERENCES

Conversion or dismissal for failure to commence making timely payments under this section, see 11 USCA § 1307.

Duty of trustee to ensure that debtor commences making timely payments under this section, see 11 USCA § 1302.

Payment stopped on checks remaining unpaid 90 days after final distribution, see 11 USCA § 347.

§ 1327.   Effect of confirmation

(a) The provisions of a confirmed plan bind the debtor and each creditor, whether or not the claim of such creditor is provided for by the plan, and whether or not such creditor has objected to, has accepted, or has rejected the plan.

(b) Except as otherwise provided in the plan or the order confirming the plan, the confirmation of a plan vests all of the property of the estate in the debtor.

(c) Except as otherwise provided in the plan or in the order confirming the plan, the property vesting in the debtor under subsection (b) of this section is free and clear of any claim or interest of any creditor provided for by the plan.

(Pub.L. 95–598, Nov. 6, 1978, 92 Stat. 2650.)

HISTORICAL AND STATUTORY NOTES

Revision Notes and Legislative Reports

1978 Acts. Subsection (a) binds the debtor and each creditor to the provisions of a confirmed plan, whether or not the claim of the creditor is provided for by the plan and whether or not the creditor has accepted, rejected, or objected to the plan. Unless the plan itself or the order confirming the plan otherwise provides, confirmation is deemed to vest all property of the estate in the debtor, free and clear of any claim or interest of any creditor provided for by the plan. Senate Report No. 95–989.

CROSS REFERENCES

Effect of confirmation in,

    Chapter eleven cases, see 11 USCA § 1141.

    Chapter nine cases, see 11 USCA § 944.

    Chapter twelve cases, see 11 USCA § 1227.

§ 1328. Discharge

(a) Subject to subsection (d), as soon as practicable after completion by the debtor of all payments under the plan, and in the case of a debtor who is required by a judicial or administrative order, or by statute, to pay a domestic support obligation, after such debtor certifies that all amounts payable under such order or such statute that are due on or before the date of the certification (including amounts due before the petition was filed, but only to the extent provided for by the plan) have been paid, unless the court approves a written waiver of discharge executed by the debtor after the order for relief under this chapter, the court shall grant the debtor a discharge of all debts provided for by the plan or disallowed under section 502 of this title, except any debt—

    (1) provided for under section 1322(b)(5);

    (2) of the kind specified in section 507(a)(8)(C) or in paragraph (1)(B), (1)(C), (2), (3), (4), (5), (8), or (9) of section 523(a);

    (3) for restitution, or a criminal fine, included in a sentence on the debtor's conviction of a crime; or

    (4) for restitution, or damages, awarded in a civil action against the debtor as a result of willful or malicious injury by the debtor that caused personal injury to an individual or the death of an individual.

(b) Subject to subsection (d), at any time after the confirmation of the plan and after notice and a hearing, the court may grant a discharge to a debtor that has not completed payments under the plan only if—

    (1) the debtor's failure to complete such payments is due to circumstances for which the debtor should not justly be held accountable;

    (2) the value, as of the effective date of the plan, of property actually distributed under the plan on account of each allowed unsecured claim is not less than the amount that would have been paid on such claim if the estate of the debtor had been liquidated under chapter 7 of this title on such date; and

    (3) modification of the plan under section 1329 of this title is not practicable.

(c) A discharge granted under subsection (b) of this section discharges the debtor from all unsecured debts provided for by the plan or disallowed under section 502 of this title, except any debt—

    (1) provided for under section 1322(b)(5) of this title; or

    (2) of a kind specified in section 523(a) of this title.

(d) Notwithstanding any other provision of this section, a discharge granted under this section does not discharge the debtor from any debt based on an allowed claim filed under section 1305(a)(2) of this title if prior approval by the trustee of the debtor's incurring such debt was practicable and was not obtained.

(e) On request of a party in interest before one year after a discharge under this section is granted, and after notice and a hearing, the court may revoke such discharge only if—

    (1) such discharge was obtained by the debtor through fraud; and

    (2) the requesting party did not know of such fraud until after such discharge was granted.

(f) Notwithstanding subsections (a) and (b), the court shall not grant a discharge of all debts provided for in the plan or disallowed under section 502, if the debtor has received a discharge—

    (1) in a case filed under chapter 7, 11, or 12 of this title during the 4–year period preceding the date of the order for relief under this chapter, or

    (2) in a case filed under chapter 13 of this title during the 2–year period preceding the date of such order.

(g)(1) The court shall not grant a discharge under this section to a debtor unless after filing a petition the debtor has completed an instructional course concerning personal financial management described in section 111.

(2) Paragraph (1) shall not apply with respect to a debtor who is a person described in section 109(h)(4) or who resides in a district for which the United States trustee (or the bankruptcy administrator, if any) determines that the approved instructional courses are not adequate to service the additional individuals who would otherwise be required to complete such instructional course by reason of the requirements of paragraph (1).

(3) The United States trustee (or the bankruptcy administrator, if any) who makes a determination de-

scribed in paragraph (2) shall review such determination not later than 1 year after the date of such determination, and not less frequently than annually thereafter.

(h) The court may not grant a discharge under this chapter unless the court after notice and a hearing held not more than 10 days before the date of the entry of the order granting the discharge finds that there is no reasonable cause to believe that—

(1) section 522(q)(1) may be applicable to the debtor; and

(2) there is pending any proceeding in which the debtor may be found guilty of a felony of the kind described in section 522(q)(1)(A) or liable for a debt of the kind described in section 522(q)(1)(B).

(Pub.L. 95–598, Nov. 6, 1978, 92 Stat. 2650; Pub.L. 98–353, Title III, § 532, July 10, 1984, 98 Stat. 389; Pub.L. 101–508, Title III, § 3007(b)(1), Nov. 5, 1990, 104 Stat. 1388–28; Pub.L. 101–581, §§ 2(b), 3, Nov. 15, 1990, 104 Stat. 2865; Pub.L. 101–647, Title XXXI, §§ 3102(b), 3103, Nov. 29, 1990, 104 Stat. 4916; Pub.L. 103–394, Title III, § 302, Title V, § 501(d)(38), Oct. 22, 1994, 108 Stat. 4132, 4147; Pub.L. 109–8, Title I, § 106(c), Title II, § 213(11), Title III, §§ 312(2), 314(b), 330(d), Title VII, § 707, Apr. 20, 2005, 119 Stat. 38, 53, 87, 88, 102, 126.)

HISTORICAL AND STATUTORY NOTES

Revision Notes and Legislative Reports

1978 Acts. The court is to enter a discharge, unless waived, as soon as practicable after completion of payments under the plan. The debtor is to be discharged of all debts provided for by the plan or disallowed under section 502, except a debt provided for under the plan the last payment on which was not due until after the completion of the plan, or a debt incurred for willful and malicious conversion of or injury to the property or person of another.

Subsection (b) is the successor to Bankruptcy Act Section [sic] 661 [Section 1061 of former title 11]. This subsection permits the bankruptcy judge to grant the debtor a discharge at any time after confirmation of a plan, if the court determines, after notice and hearing, that the failure to complete payments under the plan is due to circumstances for which the debtor should not justly be held accountable, the distributions made to each creditor under the plan equal in value the amount that would have been paid to the creditor had the estate been liquidated under chapter 7 of title 11 at the date of the hearing under this subsection, and that modification of the plan is impracticable. The discharge granted under subsection (b) relieves the debtor from all unsecured debts provided for by the plan or disallowed under section 502, except nondischargeable debts described in section 523(a) of title 11 or debts of the type covered by section 1322(b)(5).

Subsection (d) excepts from any chapter 13 discharge a debt based on an allowed section 1305(a)(2) postpetition claim, if prior trustee approval of the incurring of the debt was practicable but was not obtained.

A chapter 13 discharge obtained through fraud and before the moving party gained knowledge of the fraud may be revoked by the court under subsection (e), after notice and hearing, at the request of any party in interest made within 1 year after the discharge was granted. Senate Report No. 95–989.

1984 Acts. Statements by Legislative Leaders, see 1984 U.S.Code Cong. and Adm.News, p. 576.

1990 Acts. House Report No. 101–681(I), see 1990 U.S.Code Cong. and Adm.News, p. 6472.

Senate Report No. 101–434, see 1990 U.S.Code Cong. and Adm.News, p. 4065.

House Report No. 101–881, House Conference Report No. 101–964, and President's Signing Statement, see 1990 U.S.Code Cong. and Adm.News, p. 2017.

1994 Acts. House Report No. 103–835, see 1994 U.S. Code Cong. and Adm. News, p. 3340.

2005 Acts. House Report No. 109–31(Part I), see 2005 U.S. Code Cong. and Adm. News, p. 88.

Legislative Statements

Section 1328(a) adopts a provision contained in the Senate amendment permitting the court to approve a waiver of discharge by the debtor. It is anticipated that such a waiver must be in writing executed after the order for relief in a case under chapter 13.

References in Text

Chapter 7, 11, or 12 of this title, referred to in subsec. (f)(1), is 11 U.S.C.A. § 701 et seq., 11 U.S.C.A. § 1101 et seq., or 11 U.S.C.A. § 1201 et seq., respectively.

Chapter 13 of this title, referred to in subsec. (f)(2), is 11 U.S.C.A. § 1301 et seq.

Codifications

Pub.L. 101–581, §§ 2(b), 3(1) to (3) and Pub.L. 101–647, §§ 3102(b), 3103(1)–(3), contained identical amendments to subsec. (a)(2) and (a)(1)–(3) of this section.

Amendments by Pub.L. 101–581, § 2(b), and Pub.L. 101–647, § 3102(b), which both inserted "or 523(a)(9)" following "523(a)(5)", were incapable of literal execution in view of prior amendment by Pub.L. 101–508, which substituted "paragraph (5) or (8) of section 523(a)" for "section 523(a)(5)", thereby deleting language subsequently amended. See also 1990 Amendments note set out under this section.

Effective and Applicability Provisions

2005 Acts. Amendments Pub.L. 109–8 effective 180 days after Apr. 20, 2005, with amendments by sections 106(c), 213(11), 312(2), 314(b), and 707 of Pub.L. 109–8 not applicable with respect to cases commenced under this title before such effective date, except as otherwise provided, and amendment by section 330(d) of Pub.L. 109–8 applicable with respect to cases commenced under this title on or after Apr. 20, 2005, see Pub.L. 109–8, § 1501, set out as a note under 11 U.S.C.A. § 101.

1994 Acts. Amendments by Pub.L. 103–394 effective on Oct. 22, 1994, and not to apply with respect to cases commenced under Title 11 of the United States Code before Oct. 22, 1994, see section 702 of Pub.L. 103–394, set out as a note under section 101 of this title.

1990 Acts. Amendment by Pub.L. 101–647 effective Nov. 29, 1990, but not applicable with respect to cases commenced under this title before Nov. 29, 1990, see section 3104 of Pub.L. 101–647, set out as an Effective Date of 1990 Amendments note under section 523 of this title.

Amendment by Pub.L. 101–581 effective Nov. 15, 1990, but not applicable with respect to cases commenced under this title before Nov. 15, 1990, see section 4 of Pub.L. 101–581, set out as an Effective Date of 1990 Amendment note under section 523 of this title.

Section 3007(b)(2) of Pub.L. 101–508 provided that: "The amendment made by paragraph (1) [amending this section] shall not apply to any case under the provisions of title 11, United States Code, commenced before the date of the enactment of this Act [Nov. 5, 1990]."

Section 3008 of Pub.L. 101–508, which had provided that the amendment to this section by Pub.L. 101–508 was to cease to be effective on Oct. 1, 1996, was repealed by Pub.L. 102–325, Title XV, § 1558, July 23, 1992, 106 Stat. 841.

1984 Acts. Amendment by Pub.L. 98–353 effective with respect to cases filed 90 days after July 10, 1984, see section 552(a), formerly 553(a), of Pub.L. 98–353, set out as a note under section 101 of this title.

Separability of Provisions

If any provision of or amendment made by Pub.L. 103–394 or the application of such provision or amendment to any person or circumstance is held to be unconstitutional, the remaining provisions of and amendments made by Pub.L. 103–394 and the application of such provisions and amendments to any person or circumstance shall not be affected thereby, see section 701 of Pub.L. 103–394, set out as a note under section 101 of this title.

CROSS REFERENCES

Cancellation of indebtedness from discharged farm loans, see 12 USCA § 1150.

Discharge in,

Chapter seven cases, see 11 USCA § 727.

Chapter twelve cases, see 11 USCA § 1228.

Effect of discharge, see 11 USCA § 524.

Exceptions to discharge, see 11 USCA § 523.

Nondischargeability of capital improvement loans for multi-family housing projects in proceedings under this section, see 12 USCA § 1715z–1a.

§ 1329. Modification of plan after confirmation

(a) At any time after confirmation of the plan but before the completion of payments under such plan, the plan may be modified, upon request of the debtor, the trustee, or the holder of an allowed unsecured claim, to—

(1) increase or reduce the amount of payments on claims of a particular class provided for by the plan;

(2) extend or reduce the time for such payments;

(3) alter the amount of the distribution to a creditor whose claim is provided for by the plan to the extent necessary to take account of any payment of such claim other than under the plan; or

(4) reduce amounts to be paid under the plan by the actual amount expended by the debtor to purchase health insurance for the debtor (and for any dependent of the debtor if such dependent does not otherwise have health insurance coverage) if the debtor documents the cost of such insurance and demonstrates that—

(A) such expenses are reasonable and necessary;

(B)(i) if the debtor previously paid for health insurance, the amount is not materially larger than the cost the debtor previously paid or the cost necessary to maintain the lapsed policy; or

(ii) if the debtor did not have health insurance, the amount is not materially larger than the reasonable cost that would be incurred by a debtor who purchases health insurance, who has similar income, expenses, age, and health status, and who lives in the same geographical location with the same number of dependents who do not otherwise have health insurance coverage; and

(C) the amount is not otherwise allowed for purposes of determining disposable income under section 1325(b) of this title;

and upon request of any party in interest, files proof that a health insurance policy was purchased.

(b)(1) Sections 1322(a), 1322(b), and 1323(c) of this title and the requirements of section 1325(a) of this title apply to any modification under subsection (a) of this section.

(2) The plan as modified becomes the plan unless, after notice and a hearing, such modification is disapproved.

(c) A plan modified under this section may not provide for payments over a period that expires after the applicable commitment period under section 1325(b)(1)(B) after the time that the first payment under the original confirmed plan was due, unless the court, for cause, approves a longer period, but the court may not approve a period that expires after five years after such time.

(Pub.L. 95–598, Nov. 6, 1978, 92 Stat. 2651; Pub.L. 98–353, Title III, §§ 319, 533, July 10, 1984, 98 Stat. 357, 389; Pub.L. 109–8, Title I, § 102(i), Title III, § 318(4), Apr. 20, 2005, 119 Stat. 34, 94.)

HISTORICAL AND STATUTORY NOTES

Revision Notes and Legislative Reports

1978 Acts. At any time prior to the completion of payments under a confirmed plan, the plan may be modified, after notice and hearing, to change the amount of payments to creditors or a particular class of creditors and to extend or reduce the payment period. A modified plan may not contain any provision which could not be included in an original plan as prescribed by section 1322. A modified plan may not call for payments to be made beyond four years as measured from the date of the commencement of payments under the original plan. Senate Report No. 95–989.

1984 Acts. Statements by Legislative Leaders, see 1984 U.S.Code Cong. and Adm.News, p. 576.

2005 Acts. House Report No. 109–31(Part I), see 2005 U.S. Code Cong. and Adm. News, p. 88.

Effective and Applicability Provisions

2005 Acts. Amendments by Pub.L. 109–8 effective, except as otherwise provided, 180 days after April 20, 2005, and inapplicable with respect to cases commenced under Title 11 before the effective date, see Pub.L. 109–8, § 1501, set out as a note under 11 U.S.C.A. § 101.

1984 Acts. Amendment by Pub.L. 98–353 effective with respect to cases filed 90 days after July 10, 1984, see section 552(a), formerly 553(a), of Pub.L. 98–353, set out as a note under section 101 of this title.

CROSS REFERENCES

Conversion or dismissal upon denial of confirmation of modified plan, see 11 USCA § 1307.

Duties of United States trustee, see 28 USCA § 586.

Modification of plan in,

Chapter eleven cases, see 11 USCA § 1127.

Chapter nine cases, see 11 USCA § 942.

Chapter twelve cases, see 11 USCA § 1229.

§ 1330. Revocation of an order of confirmation

(a) On request of a party in interest at any time within 180 days after the date of the entry of an order of confirmation under section 1325 of this title, and after notice and a hearing, the court may revoke such order if such order was procured by fraud.

(b) If the court revokes an order of confirmation under subsection (a) of this section, the court shall dispose of the case under section 1307 of this title, unless, within the time fixed by the court, the debtor proposes and the court confirms a modification of the plan under section 1329 of this title.

(Pub.L. 95–598, Nov. 6, 1978, 92 Stat. 2651.)

HISTORICAL AND STATUTORY NOTES

Revision Notes and Legislative Reports

1978 Acts. The court may revoke an order of confirmation procured by fraud, after notice and hearing, on application of a party in interest filed within 180 days after the entry of the order. Thereafter, unless a modified plan is confirmed, the court is to convert or dismiss the chapter 13 case as provided in section 1307. Senate Report No. 95–989.

Legislative Statements

Section 1331 of the House bill and Senate amendment is deleted in the House amendment.

Special tax provision: Section 1331 of title 11 of the House bill and the comparable provisions in sections 1322 and 1327(d) of the Senate amendment, pertaining to assessment and collection of taxes in wage earner plans, are deleted, and the governing rule is placed in section 505(c) of the House amendment. The provisions of both bills allowing assessment and collection of taxes after confirmation of the wage-earner plan are modified to allow assessment and collection after the court fixes the fact and amount of a tax liability, including administrative period taxes, regardless of whether this occurs before or after confirmation of the plan. The provision of the House bill limiting the collection of taxes to those assessed before one year after the filing of the petition is eliminated, thereby leaving the period of limitations on assessment of these nondischargeable tax liabilities the usual period provided by the Internal Revenue Code [Title 26].

CROSS REFERENCES

Conversion or dismissal upon revocation of order of confirmation, see 11 USCA § 1307.

Revocation of order of confirmation in,

Chapter eleven cases, see 11 USCA § 1144.

Chapter twelve cases, see 11 USCA § 1230.

CHAPTER 15—ANCILLARY AND OTHER CROSS–BORDER CASES

§ 1501.   Purpose and scope of application

(a) The purpose of this chapter is to incorporate the Model Law on Cross–Border Insolvency so as to provide effective mechanisms for dealing with cases of cross-border insolvency with the objectives of—

(1) cooperation between—

(A) courts of the United States, United States trustees, trustees, examiners, debtors, and debtors in possession; and

(B) the courts and other competent authorities of foreign countries involved in cross-border insolvency cases;

(2) greater legal certainty for trade and investment;

(3) fair and efficient administration of cross-border insolvencies that protects the interests of all creditors, and other interested entities, including the debtor;

(4) protection and maximization of the value of the debtor's assets; and

(5) facilitation of the rescue of financially troubled businesses, thereby protecting investment and preserving employment.

(b) This chapter applies where—

(1) assistance is sought in the United States by a foreign court or a foreign representative in connection with a foreign proceeding;

(2) assistance is sought in a foreign country in connection with a case under this title;

(3) a foreign proceeding and a case under this title with respect to the same debtor are pending concurrently; or

(4) creditors or other interested persons in a foreign country have an interest in requesting the commencement of, or participating in, a case or proceeding under this title.

(c) This chapter does not apply to—

(1) a proceeding concerning an entity, other than a foreign insurance company, identified by exclusion in section 109(b);

(2) an individual, or to an individual and such individual's spouse, who have debts within the limits specified in section 109(e) and who are citizens of the United States or aliens lawfully admitted for permanent residence in the United States; or

(3) an entity subject to a proceeding under the Securities Investor Protection Act of 1970, a stockbroker subject to subchapter III of chapter 7 of this title, or a commodity broker subject to subchapter IV of chapter 7 of this title.

(d) The court may not grant relief under this chapter with respect to any deposit, escrow, trust fund, or other security required or permitted under any applicable State insurance law or regulation for the benefit of claim holders in the United States.

(Added Pub.L. 109–8, Title VIII, § 801(a), Apr. 20, 2005, 119 Stat. 135.)

HISTORICAL AND STATUTORY NOTES

Revision Notes and Legislative Reports

2005 Acts. House Report No. 109–31(Part I), see 2005 U.S. Code Cong. and Adm. News, p. 88.

References in Text

The Securities Investor Protection Act of 1970, referred to in subsec. (c)(3), is Pub.L. 91–598, Dec. 30, 1970, 84 Stat. 1636, also known as SIPA, which is classified principally to chapter 2B–1 of Title 15, 15 U.S.C.A. § 78aaa et seq.

Subchapter III of chapter 7 of this title, referred to in subsec. (c)(3), is 11 U.S.C.A. § 741 et seq.

Subchapter IV of chapter 7 of this title, referred to in subsec. (c)(3), is 11 U.S.C.A. § 761 et seq.

Effective and Applicability Provisions

2005 Acts. Amendments by Pub.L. 109–8 effective, except as otherwise provided, 180 days after April 20, 2005, and inapplicable with respect to cases commenced under Title 11 before the effective date, see Pub.L. 109–8, § 1501, set out as a note under 11 U.S.C.A. § 101.

SUBCHAPTER I—GENERAL PROVISIONS

§ 1502. Definitions

For the purposes of this chapter, the term—

(1) "debtor" means an entity that is the subject of a foreign proceeding;

(2) "establishment" means any place of operations where the debtor carries out a nontransitory economic activity;

(3) "foreign court" means a judicial or other authority competent to control or supervise a foreign proceeding;

(4) "foreign main proceeding" means a foreign proceeding pending in the country where the debtor has the center of its main interests;

(5) "foreign nonmain proceeding" means a foreign proceeding, other than a foreign main proceeding, pending in a country where the debtor has an establishment;

(6) "trustee" includes a trustee, a debtor in possession in a case under any chapter of this title, or a debtor under chapter 9 of this title;

(7) "recognition" means the entry of an order granting recognition of a foreign main proceeding or foreign nonmain proceeding under this chapter; and

(8) "within the territorial jurisdiction of the United States", when used with reference to property of a debtor, refers to tangible property located within the territory of the United States and intangible property deemed under applicable nonbankruptcy law to be located within that territory, including any property subject to attachment or garnishment that may properly be seized or garnished by an action in a Federal or State court in the United States.

(Added Pub.L. 109–8, Title VIII, § 801(a), Apr. 20, 2005, 119 Stat. 135.)

HISTORICAL AND STATUTORY NOTES

Revision Notes and Legislative Reports

2005 Acts. House Report No. 109–31(Part I), see 2005 U.S. Code Cong. and Adm. News, p. 88.

References in Text

Chapter 9 of this title, referred to in par. (6), is 11 U.S.C.A. § 901 et seq.

Effective and Applicability Provisions

2005 Acts. Amendments by Pub.L. 109–8 effective, except as otherwise provided, 180 days after April 20, 2005, and inapplicable with respect to cases commenced under Title 11 before the effective date, see Pub.L. 109–8, § 1501, set out as a note under 11 U.S.C.A. § 101.

§ 1503. International obligations of the United States

To the extent that this chapter conflicts with an obligation of the United States arising out of any treaty or other form of agreement to which it is a party with one or more other countries, the requirements of the treaty or agreement prevail.

(Added Pub.L. 109–8, Title VIII, § 801(a), Apr. 20, 2005, 119 Stat. 136.)

HISTORICAL AND STATUTORY NOTES

Revision Notes and Legislative Reports

2005 Acts. House Report No. 109–31(Part I), see 2005 U.S. Code Cong. and Adm. News, p. 88.

Effective and Applicability Provisions

2005 Acts. Amendments by Pub.L. 109–8 effective, except as otherwise provided, 180 days after April 20, 2005, and inapplicable with respect to cases commenced under Title 11 before the effective date, see Pub.L. 109–8, § 1501, set out as a note under 11 U.S.C.A. § 101.

§ 1504. Commencement of ancillary case

A case under this chapter is commenced by the filing of a petition for recognition of a foreign proceeding under section 1515.

(Added Pub.L. 109–8, Title VIII, § 801(a), Apr. 20, 2005, 119 Stat. 136.)

HISTORICAL AND STATUTORY NOTES

Revision Notes and Legislative Reports

2005 Acts. House Report No. 109–31(Part I), see 2005 U.S. Code Cong. and Adm. News, p. 88.

Effective and Applicability Provisions

2005 Acts. Amendments by Pub.L. 109–8 effective, except as otherwise provided, 180 days after April 20, 2005, and inapplicable with respect to cases commenced under Title 11 before the effective date, see Pub.L. 109–8, § 1501, set out as a note under 11 U.S.C.A. § 101.

§ 1505. Authorization to act in a foreign country

A trustee or another entity (including an examiner) may be authorized by the court to act in a foreign country on behalf of an estate created under section 541. An entity authorized to act under this section may act in any way permitted by the applicable foreign law.

(Added Pub.L. 109–8, Title VIII, § 801(a), Apr. 20, 2005, 119 Stat. 136.)

HISTORICAL AND STATUTORY NOTES

Revision Notes and Legislative Reports

2005 Acts. House Report No. 109–31(Part I), see 2005 U.S. Code Cong. and Adm. News, p. 88.

Effective and Applicability Provisions

2005 Acts. Amendments by Pub.L. 109–8 effective, except as otherwise provided, 180 days after April 20, 2005, and inapplicable with respect to cases commenced under Title 11 before the effective date, see Pub.L. 109–8, § 1501, set out as a note under 11 U.S.C.A. § 101.

§ 1506. Public policy exception

Nothing in this chapter prevents the court from refusing to take an action governed by this chapter if the action would be manifestly contrary to the public policy of the United States.

(Added Pub.L. 109–8, Title VIII, § 801(a), Apr. 20, 2005, 119 Stat. 136.)

HISTORICAL AND STATUTORY NOTES

Revision Notes and Legislative Reports

2005 Acts. House Report No. 109–31(Part I), see 2005 U.S. Code Cong. and Adm. News, p. 88.

Effective and Applicability Provisions

2005 Acts. Amendments by Pub.L. 109–8 effective, except as otherwise provided, 180 days after April 20, 2005, and inapplicable with respect to cases commenced under Title 11 before the effective date, see Pub.L. 109–8, § 1501, set out as a note under 11 U.S.C.A. § 101.

§ 1507. Additional assistance

(a) Subject to the specific limitations stated elsewhere in this chapter the court, if recognition is granted, may provide additional assistance to a foreign representative under this title or under other laws of the United States.

(b) In determining whether to provide additional assistance under this title or under other laws of the United States, the court shall consider whether such additional assistance, consistent with the principles of comity, will reasonably assure—

(1) just treatment of all holders of claims against or interests in the debtor's property;

(2) protection of claim holders in the United States against prejudice and inconvenience in the processing of claims in such foreign proceeding;

(3) prevention of preferential or fraudulent dispositions of property of the debtor;

(4) distribution of proceeds of the debtor's property substantially in accordance with the order prescribed by this title; and

(5) if appropriate, the provision of an opportunity for a fresh start for the individual that such foreign proceeding concerns.

(Added Pub.L. 109–8, Title VIII, § 801(a), Apr. 20, 2005, 119 Stat. 136.)

HISTORICAL AND STATUTORY NOTES

Revision Notes and Legislative Reports

2005 Acts. House Report No. 109–31(Part I), see 2005 U.S. Code Cong. and Adm. News, p. 88.

Effective and Applicability Provisions

2005 Acts. Amendments by Pub.L. 109–8 effective, except as otherwise provided, 180 days after April 20, 2005, and inapplicable with respect to cases commenced under Title 11 before the effective date, see Pub.L. 109–8, § 1501, set out as a note under 11 U.S.C.A. § 101.

§ 1508. Interpretation

In interpreting this chapter, the court shall consider its international origin, and the need to promote an application of this chapter that is consistent with the application of similar statutes adopted by foreign jurisdictions.

(Added Pub.L. 109–8, Title VIII, § 801(a), Apr. 20, 2005, 119 Stat. 137.)

HISTORICAL AND STATUTORY NOTES

Revision Notes and Legislative Reports

2005 Acts. House Report No. 109–31(Part I), see 2005 U.S. Code Cong. and Adm. News, p. 88.

Effective and Applicability Provisions

2005 Acts. Amendments by Pub.L. 109–8 effective, except as otherwise provided, 180 days after April 20, 2005, and inapplicable with respect to cases commenced under Title 11 before the effective date, see Pub.L. 109–8, § 1501, set out as a note under 11 U.S.C.A. § 101.

SUBCHAPTER II—ACCESS OF FOREIGN REPRESENTATIVES AND CREDITORS TO THE COURT

§ 1509. Right of direct access

(a) A foreign representative may commence a case under section 1504 by filing directly with the court a petition for recognition of a foreign proceeding under section 1515.

(b) If the court grants recognition under section 1517, and subject to any limitations that the court may impose consistent with the policy of this chapter—

(1) the foreign representative has the capacity to sue and be sued in a court in the United States;

(2) the foreign representative may apply directly to a court in the United States for appropriate relief in that court; and

(3) a court in the United States shall grant comity or cooperation to the foreign representative.

(c) A request for comity or cooperation by a foreign representative in a court in the United States other than the court which granted recognition shall be accompanied by a certified copy of an order granting recognition under section 1517.

(d) If the court denies recognition under this chapter, the court may issue any appropriate order necessary to prevent the foreign representative from obtaining comity or cooperation from courts in the United States.

(e) Whether or not the court grants recognition, and subject to sections 306 and 1510, a foreign representative is subject to applicable nonbankruptcy law.

(f) Notwithstanding any other provision of this section, the failure of a foreign representative to commence a case or to obtain recognition under this chapter does not affect any right the foreign representative may have to sue in a court in the United States to collect or recover a claim which is the property of the debtor.

(Added Pub.L. 109–8, Title VIII, § 801(a), Apr. 20, 2005, 119 Stat. 137.)

HISTORICAL AND STATUTORY NOTES

Revision Notes and Legislative Reports

2005 Acts. House Report No. 109–31(Part I), see 2005 U.S. Code Cong. and Adm. News, p. 88.

Effective and Applicability Provisions

2005 Acts. Amendments by Pub.L. 109–8 effective, except as otherwise provided, 180 days after April 20, 2005, and inapplicable with respect to cases commenced under Title 11 before the effective date, see Pub.L. 109–8, § 1501, set out as a note under 11 U.S.C.A. § 101.

§ 1510. Limited jurisdiction

The sole fact that a foreign representative files a petition under section 1515 does not subject the foreign representative to the jurisdiction of any court in the United States for any other purpose.

(Added Pub.L. 109–8, Title VIII, § 801(a), Apr. 20, 2005, 119 Stat. 138.)

HISTORICAL AND STATUTORY NOTES

Revision Notes and Legislative Reports

2005 Acts. House Report No. 109–31(Part I), see 2005 U.S. Code Cong. and Adm. News, p. 88.

Effective and Applicability Provisions

2005 Acts. Amendments by Pub.L. 109–8 effective, except as otherwise provided, 180 days after April 20, 2005, and inapplicable with respect to cases commenced under Title 11 before the effective date, see Pub.L. 109–8, § 1501, set out as a note under 11 U.S.C.A. § 101.

§ 1511. Commencement of case under section 301, 302, or 303

(a) Upon recognition, a foreign representative may commence—

(1) an involuntary case under section 303; or

(2) a voluntary case under section 301 or 302, if the foreign proceeding is a foreign main proceeding.

(b) The petition commencing a case under subsection (a) must be accompanied by a certified copy of an order granting recognition. The court where the petition for recognition has been filed must be advised of the foreign representative's intent to commence a case under subsection (a) prior to such commencement.

(Added Pub.L. 109–8, Title VIII, § 801(a), Apr. 20, 2005, 119 Stat. 138; amended Pub.L. 111–327, § 2(a)(45), Dec. 22, 2010, 124 Stat. 3562.)

HISTORICAL AND STATUTORY NOTES

Revision Notes and Legislative Reports

2005 Acts. House Report No. 109–31(Part I), see 2005 U.S. Code Cong. and Adm. News, p. 88.

Effective and Applicability Provisions

2005 Acts. Amendments by Pub.L. 109–8 effective, except as otherwise provided, 180 days after April 20, 2005, and inapplicable with respect to cases commenced under Title 11 before the effective date, see Pub.L. 109–8, § 1501, set out as a note under 11 U.S.C.A. § 101.

§ 1512. Participation of a foreign representative in a case under this title

Upon recognition of a foreign proceeding, the foreign representative in the recognized proceeding is entitled to participate as a party in interest in a case regarding the debtor under this title.

(Added Pub.L. 109–8, Title VIII, § 801(a), Apr. 20, 2005, 119 Stat. 138.)

HISTORICAL AND STATUTORY NOTES

Revision Notes and Legislative Reports

2005 Acts. House Report No. 109–31(Part I), see 2005 U.S. Code Cong. and Adm. News, p. 88.

Effective and Applicability Provisions

2005 Acts. Amendments by Pub.L. 109–8 effective, except as otherwise provided, 180 days after April 20, 2005, and inapplicable with respect to cases commenced under Title 11 before the effective date, see Pub.L. 109–8, § 1501, set out as a note under 11 U.S.C.A. § 101.

§ 1513. Access of foreign creditors to a case under this title

(a) Foreign creditors have the same rights regarding the commencement of, and participation in, a case under this title as domestic creditors.

(b)(1) Subsection (a) does not change or codify present law as to the priority of claims under section 507 or 726, except that the claim of a foreign creditor under those sections shall not be given a lower priority than that of general unsecured claims without priority solely because the holder of such claim is a foreign creditor.

(2)(A) Subsection (a) and paragraph (1) do not change or codify present law as to the allowability of foreign revenue claims or other foreign public law claims in a proceeding under this title.

(B) Allowance and priority as to a foreign tax claim or other foreign public law claim shall be governed by any applicable tax treaty of the United States, under the conditions and circumstances specified therein.

(Added Pub.L. 109–8, Title VIII, § 801(a), Apr. 20, 2005, 119 Stat. 138.)

HISTORICAL AND STATUTORY NOTES

Revision Notes and Legislative Reports

2005 Acts. House Report No. 109–31(Part I), see 2005 U.S. Code Cong. and Adm. News, p. 88.

Effective and Applicability Provisions

2005 Acts. Amendments by Pub.L. 109–8 effective, except as otherwise provided, 180 days after April 20, 2005, and inapplicable with respect to cases commenced under Title 11 before the effective date, see Pub.L. 109–8, § 1501, set out as a note under 11 U.S.C.A. § 101.

§ 1514. Notification to foreign creditors concerning a case under this title

(a) Whenever in a case under this title notice is to be given to creditors generally or to any class or category of creditors, such notice shall also be given to the known creditors generally, or to creditors in the notified class or category, that do not have addresses in the United States. The court may order that appropriate steps be taken with a view to notifying any creditor whose address is not yet known.

(b) Such notification to creditors with foreign addresses described in subsection (a) shall be given individually, unless the court considers that, under the circumstances, some other form of notification would be more appropriate. No letter or other formality is required.

(c) When a notification of commencement of a case is to be given to foreign creditors, such notification shall—

(1) indicate the time period for filing proofs of claim and specify the place for filing such proofs of claim;

(2) indicate whether secured creditors need to file proofs of claim; and

(3) contain any other information required to be included in such notification to creditors under this title and the orders of the court.

(d) Any rule of procedure or order of the court as to notice or the filing of a proof of claim shall provide such additional time to creditors with foreign addresses as is reasonable under the circumstances.

(Added Pub.L. 109–8, Title VIII, § 801(a), Apr. 20, 2005, 119 Stat. 138.)

HISTORICAL AND STATUTORY NOTES

Revision Notes and Legislative Reports

2005 Acts. House Report No. 109–31(Part I), see 2005 U.S. Code Cong. and Adm. News, p. 88.

Effective and Applicability Provisions

2005 Acts. Amendments by Pub.L. 109–8 effective, except as otherwise provided, 180 days after April 20, 2005, and inapplicable with respect to cases commenced under Title 11 before the effective date, see Pub.L. 109–8, § 1501, set out as a note under 11 U.S.C.A. § 101.

SUBCHAPTER III—RECOGNITION OF A FOREIGN PROCEEDING AND RELIEF

§ 1515. Application for recognition

(a) A foreign representative applies to the court for recognition of a foreign proceeding in which the foreign representative has been appointed by filing a petition for recognition.

(b) A petition for recognition shall be accompanied by—

(1) a certified copy of the decision commencing such foreign proceeding and appointing the foreign representative;

(2) a certificate from the foreign court affirming the existence of such foreign proceeding and of the appointment of the foreign representative; or

(3) in the absence of evidence referred to in paragraphs (1) and (2), any other evidence acceptable to the court of the existence of such foreign proceeding and of the appointment of the foreign representative.

(c) A petition for recognition shall also be accompanied by a statement identifying all foreign proceedings with respect to the debtor that are known to the foreign representative.

(d) The documents referred to in paragraphs (1) and (2) of subsection (b) shall be translated into English. The court may require a translation into English of additional documents.

(Added Pub.L. 109–8, Title VIII, § 801(a), Apr. 20, 2005, 119 Stat. 139.)

HISTORICAL AND STATUTORY NOTES

Revision Notes and Legislative Reports

2005 Acts. House Report No. 109–31(Part I), see 2005 U.S. Code Cong. and Adm. News, p. 88.

Effective and Applicability Provisions

2005 Acts. Amendments by Pub.L. 109–8 effective, except as otherwise provided, 180 days after April 20, 2005, and inapplicable with respect to cases commenced under Title 11 before the effective date, see Pub.L. 109–8, § 1501, set out as a note under 11 U.S.C.A. § 101.

§ 1516.   Presumptions concerning recognition

(a) If the decision or certificate referred to in section 1515(b) indicates that the foreign proceeding is a foreign proceeding and that the person or body is a foreign representative, the court is entitled to so presume.

(b) The court is entitled to presume that documents submitted in support of the petition for recognition are authentic, whether or not they have been legalized.

(c) In the absence of evidence to the contrary, the debtor's registered office, or habitual residence in the case of an individual, is presumed to be the center of the debtor's main interests.

(Added Pub.L. 109–8, Title VIII, § 801(a), Apr. 20, 2005, 119 Stat. 139.)

HISTORICAL AND STATUTORY NOTES

Revision Notes and Legislative Reports

2005 Acts. House Report No. 109–31(Part I), see 2005 U.S. Code Cong. and Adm. News, p. 88.

Effective and Applicability Provisions

2005 Acts. Amendments by Pub.L. 109–8 effective, except as otherwise provided, 180 days after April 20, 2005, and inapplicable with respect to cases commenced under Title 11 before the effective date, see Pub.L. 109–8, § 1501, set out as a note under 11 U.S.C.A. § 101.

§ 1517.   Order granting recognition

(a) Subject to section 1506, after notice and a hearing, an order recognizing a foreign proceeding shall be entered if—

(1) such foreign proceeding for which recognition is sought is a foreign main proceeding or foreign nonmain proceeding within the meaning of section 1502;

(2) the foreign representative applying for recognition is a person or body; and

(3) the petition meets the requirements of section 1515.

(b) Such foreign proceeding shall be recognized—

(1) as a foreign main proceeding if it is pending in the country where the debtor has the center of its main interests; or

(2) as a foreign nonmain proceeding if the debtor has an establishment within the meaning of section 1502 in the foreign country where the proceeding is pending.

(c) A petition for recognition of a foreign proceeding shall be decided upon at the earliest possible time. Entry of an order recognizing a foreign proceeding constitutes recognition under this chapter.

(d) The provisions of this subchapter do not prevent modification or termination of recognition if it is shown that the grounds for granting it were fully or partially lacking or have ceased to exist, but in considering such action the court shall give due weight to possible prejudice to parties that have relied upon the order granting recognition. A case under this chapter may be closed in the manner prescribed under section 350.

(Added Pub.L. 109–8, Title VIII, § 801(a), Apr. 20, 2005, 119 Stat. 139.)

HISTORICAL AND STATUTORY NOTES

Revision Notes and Legislative Reports

2005 Acts. House Report No. 109–31(Part I), see 2005 U.S. Code Cong. and Adm. News, p. 88.

Effective and Applicability Provisions

2005 Acts. Amendments by Pub.L. 109–8 effective, except as otherwise provided, 180 days after April 20, 2005, and inapplicable with respect to cases commenced under Title 11 before the effective date, see Pub.L. 109–8, § 1501, set out as a note under 11 U.S.C.A. § 101.

§ 1518.   Subsequent information

From the time of filing the petition for recognition of a foreign proceeding, the foreign representative shall file with the court promptly a notice of change of status concerning—

(1) any substantial change in the status of such foreign proceeding or the status of the foreign representative's appointment; and

(2) any other foreign proceeding regarding the debtor that becomes known to the foreign representative.

(Added Pub.L. 109–8, Title VIII, § 801(a), Apr. 20, 2005, 119 Stat. 140.)

HISTORICAL AND STATUTORY NOTES

Revision Notes and Legislative Reports

2005 Acts. House Report No. 109–31(Part I), see 2005 U.S. Code Cong. and Adm. News, p. 88.

Effective and Applicability Provisions

2005 Acts. Amendments by Pub.L. 109–8 effective, except as otherwise provided, 180 days after April 20, 2005, and inapplicable with respect to cases commenced under Title 11 before the effective date, see Pub.L. 109–8, § 1501, set out as a note under 11 U.S.C.A. § 101.

§ 1519.   Relief that may be granted upon filing petition for recognition

(a) From the time of filing a petition for recognition until the court rules on the petition, the court may, at the request of the foreign representative, where relief is urgently needed to protect the assets of the debtor or the interests of the creditors, grant relief of a provisional nature, including—

(1) staying execution against the debtor's assets;

(2) entrusting the administration or realization of all or part of the debtor's assets located in the United States to the foreign representative or another person authorized by the court, including an examiner, in order to protect and preserve the value of assets that, by their nature or because of other circumstances, are perishable, susceptible to devaluation or otherwise in jeopardy; and

(3) any relief referred to in paragraph (3), (4), or (7) of section 1521(a).

(b) Unless extended under section 1521(a)(6), the relief granted under this section terminates when the petition for recognition is granted.

(c) It is a ground for denial of relief under this section that such relief would interfere with the administration of a foreign main proceeding.

(d) The court may not enjoin a police or regulatory act of a governmental unit, including a criminal action or proceeding, under this section.

(e) The standards, procedures, and limitations applicable to an injunction shall apply to relief under this section.

(f) The exercise of rights not subject to the stay arising under section 362(a) pursuant to paragraph (6), (7), (17), or (27) of section 362(b) or pursuant to section 362(o) shall not be stayed by any order of a court or administrative agency in any proceeding under this chapter.

(Added Pub.L. 109–8, Title VIII, § 801(a), Apr. 20, 2005, 119 Stat. 140; amended Pub.L. 111–327, § 2(a)(46), Dec. 22, 2010, 124 Stat. 3562.)

HISTORICAL AND STATUTORY NOTES

Revision Notes and Legislative Reports

2005 Acts. House Report No. 109–31(Part I), see 2005 U.S. Code Cong. and Adm. News, p. 88.

Effective and Applicability Provisions

2005 Acts. Amendments by Pub.L. 109–8 effective, except as otherwise provided, 180 days after April 20, 2005, and inapplicable with respect to cases commenced under Title 11 before the effective date, see Pub.L. 109–8, § 1501, set out as a note under 11 U.S.C.A. § 101.

§ 1520.   Effects of recognition of a foreign main proceeding

(a) Upon recognition of a foreign proceeding that is a foreign main proceeding—

(1) sections 361 and 362 apply with respect to the debtor and the property of the debtor that is within the territorial jurisdiction of the United States;

(2) sections 363, 549, and 552 apply to a transfer of an interest of the debtor in property that is within the territorial jurisdiction of the United States to the same extent that the sections would apply to property of an estate;

(3) unless the court orders otherwise, the foreign representative may operate the debtor's business and may exercise the rights and powers of a trustee under and to the extent provided by sections 363 and 552; and

(4) section 552 applies to property of the debtor that is within the territorial jurisdiction of the United States.

(b) Subsection (a) does not affect the right to commence an individual action or proceeding in a foreign country to the extent necessary to preserve a claim against the debtor.

(c) Subsection (a) does not affect the right of a foreign representative or an entity to file a petition commencing a case under this title or the right of any party to file claims or take other proper actions in such a case.

(Added Pub.L. 109–8, Title VIII, § 801(a), Apr. 20, 2005, 119 Stat. 141.)

HISTORICAL AND STATUTORY NOTES

Revision Notes and Legislative Reports

2005 Acts. House Report No. 109–31(Part I), see 2005 U.S. Code Cong. and Adm. News, p. 88.

Effective and Applicability Provisions

2005 Acts. Amendments by Pub.L. 109–8 effective, except as otherwise provided, 180 days after April 20, 2005, and inapplicable with respect to cases commenced under Title 11 before the effective date, see Pub.L. 109–8, § 1501, set out as a note under 11 U.S.C.A. § 101.

§ 1521.   Relief that may be granted upon recognition

(a) Upon recognition of a foreign proceeding, whether main or nonmain, where necessary to effectuate the purpose of this chapter and to protect the assets of the debtor or the interests of the creditors, the court may, at the request of the foreign representative, grant any appropriate relief, including—

(1) staying the commencement or continuation of an individual action or proceeding concerning the debtor's assets, rights, obligations or liabilities to the extent they have not been stayed under section 1520(a);

(2) staying execution against the debtor's assets to the extent it has not been stayed under section 1520(a);

(3) suspending the right to transfer, encumber or otherwise dispose of any assets of the debtor to the extent this right has not been suspended under section 1520(a);

(4) providing for the examination of witnesses, the taking of evidence or the delivery of information concerning the debtor's assets, affairs, rights, obligations or liabilities;

(5) entrusting the administration or realization of all or part of the debtor's assets within the territorial jurisdiction of the United States to the foreign representative or another person, including an examiner, authorized by the court;

(6) extending relief granted under section 1519(a); and

(7) granting any additional relief that may be available to a trustee, except for relief available under sections 522, 544, 545, 547, 548, 550, and 724(a).

(b) Upon recognition of a foreign proceeding, whether main or nonmain, the court may, at the request of the foreign representative, entrust the distribution of all or part of the debtor's assets located in the United States to the foreign representative or another person, including an examiner, authorized by the court, provided that the court is satisfied that the interests of creditors in the United States are sufficiently protected.

(c) In granting relief under this section to a representative of a foreign nonmain proceeding, the court must be satisfied that the relief relates to assets that, under the law of the United States, should be administered in the foreign nonmain proceeding or concerns information required in that proceeding.

(d) The court may not enjoin a police or regulatory act of a governmental unit, including a criminal action or proceeding, under this section.

(e) The standards, procedures, and limitations applicable to an injunction shall apply to relief under paragraphs (1), (2), (3), and (6) of subsection (a).

(f) The exercise of rights not subject to the stay arising under section 362(a) pursuant to paragraph (6), (7), (17), or (27) of section 362(b) or pursuant to section 362(o) shall not be stayed by any order of a court or administrative agency in any proceeding under this chapter.

(Added Pub.L. 109–8, Title VIII, § 801(a), Apr. 20, 2005, 119 Stat. 141; amended Pub.L. 111–327, § 2(a)(47), Dec. 22, 2010, 124 Stat. 3562.)

HISTORICAL AND STATUTORY NOTES

Revision Notes and Legislative Reports

2005 Acts. House Report No. 109–31(Part I), see 2005 U.S. Code Cong. and Adm. News, p. 88.

Effective and Applicability Provisions

2005 Acts. Amendments by Pub.L. 109–8 effective, except as otherwise provided, 180 days after April 20, 2005, and inapplicable with respect to cases commenced under Title 11 before the effective date, see Pub.L. 109–8, § 1501, set out as a note under 11 U.S.C.A. § 101.

§ 1522. Protection of creditors and other interested persons

(a) The court may grant relief under section 1519 or 1521, or may modify or terminate relief under subsection (c), only if the interests of the creditors and other interested entities, including the debtor, are sufficiently protected.

(b) The court may subject relief granted under section 1519 or 1521, or the operation of the debtor's business under section 1520(a)(3), to conditions it considers appropriate, including the giving of security or the filing of a bond.

(c) The court may, at the request of the foreign representative or an entity affected by relief granted under section 1519 or 1521, or at its own motion, modify or terminate such relief.

(d) Section 1104(d) shall apply to the appointment of an examiner under this chapter. Any examiner shall comply with the qualification requirements imposed on a trustee by section 322.

(Added Pub.L. 109–8, Title VIII, § 801(a), Apr. 20, 2005, 119 Stat. 142.)

HISTORICAL AND STATUTORY NOTES

Revision Notes and Legislative Reports

2005 Acts. House Report No. 109–31(Part I), see 2005 U.S. Code Cong. and Adm. News, p. 88.

Effective and Applicability Provisions

2005 Acts. Amendments by Pub.L. 109–8 effective, except as otherwise provided, 180 days after April 20, 2005, and inapplicable with respect to cases commenced under Title 11 before the effective date, see Pub.L. 109–8, § 1501, set out as a note under 11 U.S.C.A. § 101.

§ 1523. Actions to avoid acts detrimental to creditors

(a) Upon recognition of a foreign proceeding, the foreign representative has standing in a case concerning the debtor pending under another chapter of this title to initiate actions under sections 522, 544, 545, 547, 548, 550, 553, and 724(a).

(b) When a foreign proceeding is a foreign nonmain proceeding, the court must be satisfied that an action under subsection (a) relates to assets that, under United States law, should be administered in the foreign nonmain proceeding.

(Added Pub.L. 109–8, Title VIII, § 801(a), Apr. 20, 2005, 119 Stat. 142.)

HISTORICAL AND STATUTORY NOTES

Revision Notes and Legislative Reports

2005 Acts. House Report No. 109–31(Part I), see 2005 U.S. Code Cong. and Adm. News, p. 88.

Effective and Applicability Provisions

2005 Acts. Amendments by Pub.L. 109–8 effective, except as otherwise provided, 180 days after April 20, 2005, and inapplicable with respect to cases commenced under Title 11 before the effective date, see Pub.L. 109–8, § 1501, set out as a note under 11 U.S.C.A. § 101.

§ 1524.   Intervention by a foreign representative

Upon recognition of a foreign proceeding, the foreign representative may intervene in any proceedings in a State or Federal court in the United States in which the debtor is a party.

(Added Pub.L. 109–8, Title VIII, § 801(a), Apr. 20, 2005, 119 Stat. 142.)

HISTORICAL AND STATUTORY NOTES

Revision Notes and Legislative Reports

2005 Acts. House Report No. 109–31(Part I), see 2005 U.S. Code Cong. and Adm. News, p. 88.

Effective and Applicability Provisions

2005 Acts. Amendments by Pub.L. 109–8 effective, except as otherwise provided, 180 days after April 20, 2005, and inapplicable with respect to cases commenced under Title 11 before the effective date, see Pub.L. 109–8, § 1501, set out as a note under 11 U.S.C.A. § 101.

SUBCHAPTER IV—COOPERATION WITH FOREIGN COURTS AND FOREIGN REPRESENTATIVES

§ 1525.   Cooperation and direct communication between the court and foreign courts or foreign representatives

(a) Consistent with section 1501, the court shall cooperate to the maximum extent possible with a foreign court or a foreign representative, either directly or through the trustee.

(b) The court is entitled to communicate directly with, or to request information or assistance directly from, a foreign court or a foreign representative, subject to the rights of a party in interest to notice and participation.

(Added Pub.L. 109–8, Title VIII, § 801(a), Apr. 20, 2005, 119 Stat. 143.)

HISTORICAL AND STATUTORY NOTES

Revision Notes and Legislative Reports

2005 Acts. House Report No. 109–31(Part I), see 2005 U.S. Code Cong. and Adm. News, p. 88.

Effective and Applicability Provisions

2005 Acts. Amendments by Pub.L. 109–8 effective, except as otherwise provided, 180 days after April 20, 2005, and inapplicable with respect to cases commenced under Title 11 before the effective date, see Pub.L. 109–8, § 1501, set out as a note under 11 U.S.C.A. § 101.

§ 1526.   Cooperation and direct communication between the trustee and foreign courts or foreign representatives

(a) Consistent with section 1501, the trustee or other person, including an examiner, authorized by the court, shall, subject to the supervision of the court, cooperate to the maximum extent possible with a foreign court or a foreign representative.

(b) The trustee or other person, including an examiner, authorized by the court is entitled, subject to the supervision of the court, to communicate directly with a foreign court or a foreign representative.

(Added Pub.L. 109–8, Title VIII, § 801(a), Apr. 20, 2005, 119 Stat. 143.)

HISTORICAL AND STATUTORY NOTES

Revision Notes and Legislative Reports

2005 Acts. House Report No. 109–31(Part I), see 2005 U.S. Code Cong. and Adm. News, p. 88.

Effective and Applicability Provisions

2005 Acts. Amendments by Pub.L. 109–8 effective, except as otherwise provided, 180 days after April 20, 2005, and inapplicable with respect to cases commenced under Title 11 before the effective date, see Pub.L. 109–8, § 1501, set out as a note under 11 U.S.C.A. § 101.

§ 1527.   Forms of cooperation

Cooperation referred to in sections 1525 and 1526 may be implemented by any appropriate means, including—

(1) appointment of a person or body, including an examiner, to act at the direction of the court;

(2) communication of information by any means considered appropriate by the court;

(3) coordination of the administration and supervision of the debtor's assets and affairs;

(4) approval or implementation of agreements concerning the coordination of proceedings; and

(5) coordination of concurrent proceedings regarding the same debtor.

(Added Pub.L. 109–8, Title VIII, § 801(a), Apr. 20, 2005, 119 Stat. 143.)

HISTORICAL AND STATUTORY NOTES

Revision Notes and Legislative Reports

2005 Acts. House Report No. 109–31(Part I), see 2005 U.S. Code Cong. and Adm. News, p. 88.

Effective and Applicability Provisions

2005 Acts. Amendments by Pub.L. 109–8 effective, except as otherwise provided, 180 days after April 20, 2005, and inapplicable with respect to cases commenced under Title 11 before the effective date, see Pub.L. 109–8, § 1501, set out as a note under 11 U.S.C.A. § 101.

SUBCHAPTER V—CONCURRENT PROCEEDINGS

§ 1528.   Commencement of a case under this title after recognition of a foreign main proceeding

After recognition of a foreign main proceeding, a case under another chapter of this title may be commenced only if the debtor has assets in the United States. The effects of such case shall be restricted to the assets of the debtor that are within the territorial jurisdiction of the United States and, to the extent necessary to implement cooperation and coordination under sections 1525, 1526, and 1527, to other assets of the debtor that are within the jurisdiction of the court under sections 541(a) of this title, and 1334(e) of title 28, to the extent that such other assets are not subject to the jurisdiction and control of a foreign proceeding that has been recognized under this chapter.

(Added Pub.L. 109–8, Title VIII, § 801(a), Apr. 20, 2005, 119 Stat. 143.)

HISTORICAL AND STATUTORY NOTES

Revision Notes and Legislative Reports

2005 Acts. House Report No. 109–31(Part I), see 2005 U.S. Code Cong. and Adm. News, p. 88.

Effective and Applicability Provisions

2005 Acts. Amendments by Pub.L. 109–8 effective, except as otherwise provided, 180 days after April 20, 2005, and inapplicable with respect to cases commenced under Title 11 before the effective date, see Pub.L. 109–8, § 1501, set out as a note under 11 U.S.C.A. § 101.

§ 1529. Coordination of a case under this title and a foreign proceeding

If a foreign proceeding and a case under another chapter of this title are pending concurrently regarding the same debtor, the court shall seek cooperation and coordination under sections 1525, 1526, and 1527, and the following shall apply:

(1) If the case in the United States is pending at the time the petition for recognition of such foreign proceeding is filed—

(A) any relief granted under section 1519 or 1521 must be consistent with the relief granted in the case in the United States; and

(B) section 1520 does not apply even if such foreign proceeding is recognized as a foreign main proceeding.

(2) If a case in the United States under this title commences after recognition, or after the date of the filing of the petition for recognition, of such foreign proceeding—

(A) any relief in effect under section 1519 or 1521 shall be reviewed by the court and shall be modified or terminated if inconsistent with the case in the United States; and

(B) if such foreign proceeding is a foreign main proceeding, the stay and suspension referred to in section 1520(a) shall be modified or terminated if inconsistent with the relief granted in the case in the United States.

(3) In granting, extending, or modifying relief granted to a representative of a foreign nonmain proceeding, the court must be satisfied that the relief relates to assets that, under the laws of the United States, should be administered in the foreign nonmain proceeding or concerns information required in that proceeding.

(4) In achieving cooperation and coordination under sections 1528 and 1529, the court may grant any of the relief authorized under section 305.

(Added Pub.L. 109–8, Title VIII, § 801(a), Apr. 20, 2005, 119 Stat. 144; amended Pub.L. 111–327, § 2(a)(48), Dec. 22, 2010, 124 Stat. 3562.)

HISTORICAL AND STATUTORY NOTES

Revision Notes and Legislative Reports

2005 Acts. House Report No. 109–31(Part I), see 2005 U.S. Code Cong. and Adm. News, p. 88.

Effective and Applicability Provisions

2005 Acts. Amendments by Pub.L. 109–8 effective, except as otherwise provided, 180 days after April 20, 2005, and inapplicable with respect to cases commenced under Title 11 before the effective date, see Pub.L. 109–8, § 1501, set out as a note under 11 U.S.C.A. § 101.

§ 1530. Coordination of more than 1 foreign proceeding

In matters referred to in section 1501, with respect to more than 1 foreign proceeding regarding the debtor, the court shall seek cooperation and coordination under sections 1525, 1526, and 1527, and the following shall apply:

(1) Any relief granted under section 1519 or 1521 to a representative of a foreign nonmain proceeding after recognition of a foreign main proceeding must be consistent with the foreign main proceeding.

(2) If a foreign main proceeding is recognized after recognition, or after the filing of a petition for recognition, of a foreign nonmain proceeding, any relief in effect under section 1519 or 1521 shall be reviewed by the court and shall be modified or terminated if inconsistent with the foreign main proceeding.

(3) If, after recognition of a foreign nonmain proceeding, another foreign nonmain proceeding is recognized, the court shall grant, modify, or terminate relief for the purpose of facilitating coordination of the proceedings.

(Added Pub.L. 109–8, Title VIII, § 801(a), Apr. 20, 2005, 119 Stat. 144.)

HISTORICAL AND STATUTORY NOTES

Revision Notes and Legislative Reports

2005 Acts. House Report No. 109–31(Part I), see 2005 U.S. Code Cong. and Adm. News, p. 88.

Effective and Applicability Provisions

2005 Acts. Amendments by Pub.L. 109–8 effective, except as otherwise provided, 180 days after April 20, 2005, and inapplicable with respect to cases commenced under Title 11 before the effective date, see Pub.L. 109–8, § 1501, set out as a note under 11 U.S.C.A. § 101.

§ 1531. Presumption of insolvency based on recognition of a foreign main proceeding

In the absence of evidence to the contrary, recognition of a foreign main proceeding is, for the purpose of commencing a proceeding under section 303, proof that the debtor is generally not paying its debts as such debts become due.

(Added Pub.L. 109–8, Title VIII, § 801(a), Apr. 20, 2005, 119 Stat. 144.)

HISTORICAL AND STATUTORY NOTES

Revision Notes and Legislative Reports

2005 Acts. House Report No. 109–31(Part I), see 2005 U.S. Code Cong. and Adm. News, p. 88.

Effective and Applicability Provisions

2005 Acts. Amendments by Pub.L. 109–8 effective, except as otherwise provided, 180 days after April 20, 2005, and inapplicable with respect to cases commenced under Title 11 before the effective date, see Pub.L. 109–8, § 1501, set out as a note under 11 U.S.C.A. § 101.

§ 1532. Rule of payment in concurrent proceedings

Without prejudice to secured claims or rights in rem, a creditor who has received payment with respect to its claim in a foreign proceeding pursuant to a law relating to insolvency may not receive a payment for the same claim in a case under any other chapter of this title regarding the debtor, so long as the payment to other creditors of the same class is proportionately less than the payment the creditor has already received.

(Added Pub.L. 109–8, Title VIII, § 801(a), Apr. 20, 2005, 119 Stat. 145.)

HISTORICAL AND STATUTORY NOTES

Revision Notes and Legislative Reports

2005 Acts. House Report No. 109–31(Part I), see 2005 U.S. Code Cong. and Adm. News, p. 88.

Effective and Applicability Provisions

2005 Acts. Amendments by Pub.L. 109–8 effective, except as otherwise provided, 180 days after April 20, 2005, and inapplicable with respect to cases commenced under Title 11 before the effective date, see Pub.L. 109–8, § 1501, set out as a note under 11 U.S.C.A. § 101.

[§§ 15101 to 151326. Repealed. Pub.L. 99–554, Title II, § 231, Oct. 27, 1986, 100 Stat. 3103]

HISTORICAL AND STATUTORY NOTES

Section 15101, Pub.L. 95–598, Nov. 6, 1978, 92 Stat. 2652, defined terms "entity" and "governmental unit".

Section 15102, Pub.L. 95–598, Nov. 6, 1978, 92 Stat. 2652, set forth rule of construction.

Section 15103, Pub.L. 95–598, Nov. 6, 1978, 92 Stat. 2652; Pub.L. 98–353, Title III, §§ 311(b)(3), 318(b), July 10, 1984, 98 Stat. 355, 357, set forth applicability of subchapters and sections.

Section 15303, Pub.L. 95–598, Nov. 6, 1978, 92 Stat. 2653, set forth provisions relating to involuntary cases.

Section 15321, Pub.L. 95–598, Nov. 6, 1978, 92 Stat. 2653, related to eligibility to serve as trustee.

Section 15322, Pub.L. 95–598, Nov. 6, 1978, 92 Stat. 2653, related to qualifications of trustees.

Section 15324, Pub.L. 95–598, Nov. 6, 1978, 92 Stat. 2653, related to removal of trustee or examiner.

Section 15326, Pub.L. 95–598, Nov. 6, 1978, 92 Stat. 2653, related to limitation on compensation of trustees.

Section 15330, Pub.L. 95–598, Nov. 6, 1978, 92 Stat. 2653, set forth compensation of officers.

Section 15343, Pub.L. 95–598, Nov. 6, 1978, 92 Stat. 2653, related to examination of the debtor.

Section 15345, Pub.L. 95–598, Nov. 6, 1978, 92 Stat. 2654; Pub.L. 97–258, § 3(c), Sept. 13, 1982, 96 Stat. 1064, related to money of estates.

Section 15701, Pub.L. 95–598, Nov. 6, 1978, 92 Stat. 2654, related to appointment, etc., of interim trustee.

Section 15703, Pub.L. 95–598, Nov. 6, 1978, 92 Stat. 2654, related to successor trustee.

Section 15704, Pub.L. 95–598, Nov. 6, 1978, 92 Stat. 2655, related to duties of trustees.

Section 15727, Pub.L. 95–598, Nov. 6, 1978, 92 Stat. 2655, set forth provisions relating to discharge under section 727(a) of this title.

Section 151102, Pub.L. 95–598, Nov. 6, 1978, 92 Stat. 2655, set forth provisions relating to creditors' and equity security holders' committees.

Section 151104, Pub.L. 95–598, Nov. 6, 1978, 92 Stat. 2655, related to appointment of trustee or examiner in reorganization matters.

Section 151105, Pub.L. 95–598, Nov. 6, 1978, 92 Stat. 2656, related to termination of trustee's appointment.

Section 151163, Pub.L. 95–598, Nov. 6, 1978, 92 Stat. 2656, related to appointment of trustee.

Section 151302, Pub.L. 95–598, Nov. 6, 1978, 92 Stat. 2656; Pub.L. 98–353, Title III, §§ 311(b)(4), 534, July 10, 1984, 98 Stat. 355, 390, related to functions of trustee with respect to adjustment of debts of an individual with regular income.

Section 151326, Pub.L. 95–598, Nov. 6, 1978, 92 Stat. 2657, set forth provisions relating to payments.

Effective and Applicability Provisions of Repeal

Repeal of sections by Pub.L. 99–554 effective 30 days after Oct. 27, 1986, except as otherwise provided for, see section 302 of Pub.L. 99–554, set out as a note under section 581 of Title 28, Judiciary and Judicial Procedure.

Repeal of sections not applicable in or with respect to Northern District of Alabama until March 1, 1987, or the effective date of any election made under section 302(d)(3)(A) of Pub.L. 99–554, whichever occurs first, see section 302(d)(3)(H) of Pub.L. 99–554, set out as a note under section 581 of Title 28.

Pub.L. 95–598, Title IV, § 408(c), Nov. 6, 1978, 92 Stat. 2687, as amended Pub.L. 98–166, Title II, § 200, Nov. 28, 1983, 97 Stat. 1081; Pub.L. 98–353, Title III, § 323, July 10, 1984, 98 Stat. 358; Pub.L. 99–429, Sept. 30, 1986, 100 Stat. 985; Pub.L. 99–500, § 101(b) [Title II, § 200], Oct. 18, 1986, 100 Stat. 1783–39, 1783–45, and Pub.L. 99–591, § 101(b) [Title II, § 200], Oct. 30, 1986, 100 Stat. 3341–39, 3341–45; Pub.L.

99–554, Title III, § 307(a), Oct. 27, 1986, 100 Stat. 3125, which provided for the repeal of this chapter at a prospective date, was repealed by Pub.L. 99–554, Title III, § 307(b), Oct. 27, 1986, 100 Stat. 3125.

RELATED PROVISIONS
OF
U.S. CODE TITLES 18 AND 28

TITLE 18
CRIMES AND CRIMINAL PROCEDURE

PART I—CRIMES
CHAPTER 9—BANKRUPTCY

§ 151. Definition

As used in this chapter, the term "debtor" means a debtor concerning whom a petition has been filed under Title 11.

(June 25, 1948, c. 645, 62 Stat. 689; Pub.L. 95–598, Title III, § 314(b)(1), Nov. 6, 1978, 92 Stat. 2676; Pub.L. 103–322, Title XXXIII, § 330008(5), Sept. 13, 1994, 108 Stat. 2143.)

HISTORICAL AND STATUTORY NOTES

Revision Notes and Legislative Reports

1948 Acts. Based on § 52(f) of Title 11, U.S.C., 1940, ed., Bankruptcy (July 1, 1898, c. 541, § 29f as added June 22, 1938, c. 575, § 1, 52 Stat. 857).

Definition of "bankruptcy" was added to avoid repetitious references to said Title 11.

Minor changes in phraseology were made. 80th Congress House Report No. 304.

1994 Acts. House Report No. 103–324, House Report No. 103–489, and House Conference Report No. 103–711, see 1994 U.S. Code Cong. and Adm. News, p. 1801.

Effective and Applicability Provisions

1978 Acts. Amendment by Pub.L. 95–598 effective Oct. 1, 1979, see section 402(a) of Pub.L. 95–598, set out as a note preceding section 101 of Title 11, Bankruptcy.

Savings Provisions

Amendment by section 314 of Pub. L. 95–598 not to affect the application of this chapter to any act of any person (1) committed before Oct. 1, 1979, or (2) committed after Oct. 1, 1979, in connection with a case commenced before such date, see section 403(d) of Pub. L. 95–598, set out preceding section 101 of Title 11, Bankruptcy.

CROSS REFERENCES

Meaning of words and phrases in bankruptcy proceedings, see 11 USCA § 101.

§ 152. Concealment of assets; false oaths and claims; bribery

A person who—

(1) knowingly and fraudulently conceals from a custodian, trustee, marshal, or other officer of the court charged with the control or custody of property, or, in connection with a case under title 11, from creditors or the United States Trustee, any property belonging to the estate of a debtor;

(2) knowingly and fraudulently makes a false oath or account in or in relation to any case under title 11;

(3) knowingly and fraudulently makes a false declaration, certificate, verification, or statement under penalty of perjury as permitted under section 1746 of title 28, in or in relation to any case under title 11;

(4) knowingly and fraudulently presents any false claim for proof against the estate of a debtor, or uses any such claim in any case under title 11, in a personal capacity or as or through an agent, proxy, or attorney;

(5) knowingly and fraudulently receives any material amount of property from a debtor after the filing of a case under title 11, with intent to defeat the provisions of title 11;

(6) knowingly and fraudulently gives, offers, receives, or attempts to obtain any money or property, remuneration, compensation, reward, advantage, or

promise thereof for acting or forbearing to act in any case under title 11;

(7) in a personal capacity or as an agent or officer of any person or corporation, in contemplation of a case under title 11 by or against the person or any other person or corporation, or with intent to defeat the provisions of title 11, knowingly and fraudulently transfers or conceals any of his property or the property of such other person or corporation;

(8) after the filing of a case under title 11 or in contemplation thereof, knowingly and fraudulently conceals, destroys, mutilates, falsifies, or makes a false entry in any recorded information (including books, documents, records, and papers) relating to the property or financial affairs of a debtor; or

(9) after the filing of a case under title 11, knowingly and fraudulently withholds from a custodian, trustee, marshal, or other officer of the court or a United States Trustee entitled to its possession, any recorded information (including books, documents, records, and papers) relating to the property or financial affairs of a debtor,

shall be fined under this title, imprisoned not more than 5 years, or both.

(June 25, 1948, c. 645, 62 Stat. 689; Pub.L. 86–519, § 2, June 12, 1960, 74 Stat. 217; Pub.L. 86–701, Sept. 2, 1960, 74 Stat. 753; Pub.L. 94–550, § 4, Oct. 18, 1976, 90 Stat. 2535; Pub.L. 95–598, Title III, § 314(a), (c), Nov. 6, 1978, 92 Stat. 2676, 2677; Pub.L. 100–690, Title VII, § 7017, Nov. 18, 1988, 102 Stat. 4395; Pub.L. 103–322, Title XXXIII, § 330016(1)(K), Sept. 13, 1994, 108 Stat. 2147; Pub.L. 103–394, Title III, § 312(a)(1)(A), Oct. 22, 1994, 108 Stat. 4138; Pub.L. 104–294, Title VI, § 601(a)(1), Oct. 11, 1996, 110 Stat. 3497.)

HISTORICAL AND STATUTORY NOTES
Revision Notes and Legislative Reports

1948 Acts. Based on § 52(b) of Title 11, U.S.C., 1940 ed., Bankruptcy (July 1, 1898, c. 541, § 29b, 30 Stat. 554; May 27, 1926, c. 406, § 11 (part), 44 Stat. 665; June 22, 1938, c. 575, § 1 (part), 52 Stat. 855).

Section was broadened to apply to one who gives or offers a bribe.

Minor changes were made in phraseology. 80th Congress House Report No. 304.

1960 Acts. Senate Report No. 1477, see 1960 U.S. Code Cong. and Adm. News, p. 2396.

Senate Report No. 974, see 1960 U.S. Code Cong. and Adm. News, p. 3307.

1976 Acts. House Report No. 94–1616, see 1976 U.S. Code Cong. and Adm. News, p. 5644.

1988 Acts. For Related Reports, see 1988 U.S. Code Cong. and Adm. News, p. 5937.

1994 Acts. House Report No. 103–324, House Report No. 103–489, and House Conference Report No. 103–711, see 1994 U.S. Code Cong. and Adm. News, p. 1801.

House Report No. 103–835, see 1994 U.S. Code Cong. and Adm. News, p. 3340.

1996 Acts. House Report No. 104–788, see 1996 U.S. Code Cong. and Adm. News, p. 4021.

Effective and Applicability Provisions

1994 Acts. Amendment by Pub.L. 103–394 effective on Oct. 22, 1994, and not to apply with respect to cases commenced under Title 11 of the United States Code before Oct. 22, 1994, see section 702 of Pub.L. 103–394, set out as a note under section 101 of Title 11, Bankruptcy.

1978 Acts. Amendment by Pub.L. 95–598 effective Oct. 1, 1979, see section 402(a) of Pub.L. 95–598, set out as a note preceding section 101 of Title 11, Bankruptcy.

Separability of Provisions

If any provision of or amendment made by Pub.L. 103–394 or the application of such provision or amendment to any person or circumstance is held to be unconstitutional, the remaining provisions of and amendments made by Pub.L. 103–394 and the application of such provisions and amendments to any person or circumstance shall not be affected thereby, see section 701 of Pub.L. 103–394, set out as a note under section 101 of Title 11, Bankruptcy.

Savings Provisions

Amendment by section 314 of Pub. L. 95–598 not to affect the application of this chapter to any act of any person (1) committed before Oct. 1, 1979, or (2) committed after Oct. 1, 1979, in connection with a case commenced before such date, see section 403(d) of Pub. L. 95–598, set out preceding section 101 of Title 11, Bankruptcy.

CROSS REFERENCES

Bankruptcy investigations, duties of United States attorney, see 18 USCA § 3057.

Discharges, refusal to grant when offense committed under this section, see 11 USCA § 727.

Examination of bankrupt, evidence as inadmissible in criminal proceedings, see 11 USCA § 521.

Limitation of prosecutions, see 18 USCA §§ 3282 and 3284.

§ 153.   Embezzlement against estate

(a) Offense.—A person described in subsection (b) who knowingly and fraudulently appropriates to the person's own use, embezzles, spends, or transfers any property or secretes or destroys any document belonging to the estate of a debtor shall be fined under this title, imprisoned not more than 5 years, or both.

(b) Person to whom section applies.—A person described in this subsection is one who has access to property or documents belonging to an estate by virtue of the person's participation in the administration of the estate as a trustee, custodian, marshal, attorney, or other officer of the court or as an agent, employee, or other person engaged by such an officer to perform a service with respect to the estate.

(June 25, 1948, c. 645, 62 Stat. 690; Pub.L. 95–598, Title III, § 314(a)(1), (d)(1), (2), Nov. 6, 1978, 92 Stat. 2676, 2677; Pub.L. 103–322, Title XXXIII, § 330016(1)(K), Sept. 13, 1994, 108 Stat. 2147; Pub.L. 103–394, Title III, § 312(a)(1)(A), Oct. 22, 1994, 108 Stat. 4139; Pub.L. 104–294, Title VI, § 601(a)(1), Oct. 11, 1996, 110 Stat. 3497.)

HISTORICAL AND STATUTORY NOTES

Revision Notes and Legislative Reports

1948 Acts. Based on § 52(a) of Title 11, U.S.C., 1940 ed., Bankruptcy (July 1, 1898, c. 541, § 29a, 30 Stat. 554; May 27, 1926, c. 406, § 11 (part), 44 Stat. 665; June 22, 1938, c. 575, § 1 (part), 52 Stat. 855).

Minor changes were made in phraseology. 80th Congress House Report No. 304.

1960 Acts. Senate Report No. 1477, see 1960 U.S. Code Cong. and Adm. News, p. 2396.

Senate Report No. 974, see 1960 U.S. Code Cong. and Adm. News, p. 3307.

1994 Acts. House Report No. 103–324, House Report No. 103–489, and House Conference Report No. 103–711, see 1994 U.S. Code Cong. and Adm. News, p. 1801.

House Report No. 103–835, see 1994 U.S. Code Cong. and Adm. News, p. 3340.

1996 Acts. House Report No. 104–788, see 1996 U.S. Code Cong. and Adm. News, p. 4021.

Effective and Applicability Provisions

1994 Acts. Amendment by Pub.L. 103–394 effective on Oct. 22, 1994, and not to apply with respect to cases commenced under Title 11 of the United States Code before Oct. 22, 1994, see section 702 of Pub.L. 103–394, set out as a note under section 101 of Title 11, Bankruptcy.

1978 Acts. Amendment by Pub.L. 95–598 effective Oct. 1, 1979, see section 402(a) of Pub.L. 95–598, set out as a note preceding section 101 of Title 11, Bankruptcy.

Savings Provisions

Amendment by section 314 of Pub. L. 95–598 not to affect the application of this chapter to any act of any person (1) committed before Oct. 1, 1979, or (2) committed after Oct. 1, 1979, in connection with a case commenced before such date, see section 403(d) of Pub. L. 95–598, set out preceding section 101 of Title 11, Bankruptcy.

Separability of Provisions

If any provision of or amendment made by Pub.L. 103–394 or the application of such provision or amendment to any person or circumstance is held to be unconstitutional, the remaining provisions of and amendments made by Pub.L. 103–394 and the application of such provisions and amendments to any person or circumstance shall not be affected thereby, see section 701 of Pub.L. 103–394, set out as a note under section 101 of Title 11, Bankruptcy.

CROSS REFERENCES

Debts of bankrupt created by fraud, embezzlement, misappropriation or defalcation while acting as an officer or in any fiduciary capacity as not affected by a discharge, see 11 USCA § 523.

Embezzlement by court officers, generally, see 18 USCA § 645.

§ 154. Adverse interest and conduct of officers

A person who, being a custodian, trustee, marshal, or other officer of the court—

(1) knowingly purchases, directly or indirectly, any property of the estate of which the person is such an officer in a case under title 11;

(2) knowingly refuses to permit a reasonable opportunity for the inspection by parties in interest of the documents and accounts relating to the affairs of estates in the person's charge by parties when directed by the court to do so; or

(3) knowingly refuses to permit a reasonable opportunity for the inspection by the United States Trustee of the documents and accounts relating to the affairs of an estate in the person's charge,

shall be fined under this title and shall forfeit the person's office, which shall thereupon become vacant.

(June 25, 1948, c. 645, 62 Stat. 690; Pub.L. 95–598, Title III, § 314(a)(2), (e)(1), (2), Nov. 6, 1978, 92 Stat. 2676, 2677; Pub.L. 103–322, Title XXXIII, § 330016(1)(G), Sept. 13, 1994, 108 Stat. 2147; Pub.L. 103–394, Title III, § 312(a)(1)(A), Oct. 22, 1994, 108 Stat. 4139; Pub.L. 104–294, Title VI, § 601(a)(1), Oct. 11, 1996, 110 Stat. 3497.)

HISTORICAL AND STATUTORY NOTES

Revision Notes and Legislative Reports

1948 Acts. Based on § 52(c) of Title 11, U.S.C., 1940 ed., Bankruptcy (July 1, 1898, c. 541, § 29c, 30 Stat. 554; June 22, 1938, c. 575, § 1, (part), 52 Stat. 856).

Minor changes were made in phraseology. 80th Congress House Report No. 304.

1994 Acts. House Report No. 103–324, House Report No. 103–489, and House Conference Report No. 103–711, see 1994 U.S. Code Cong. and Adm. News, p. 1801.

House Report No. 103–835, see 1994 U.S. Code Cong. and Adm. News, p. 3340.

1996 Acts. House Report No. 104–788, see 1996 U.S. Code Cong. and Adm. News, p. 4021.

Effective and Applicability Provisions

1994 Acts. Amendment by Pub.L. 103–394 effective on Oct. 22, 1994, and not to apply with respect to cases commenced under Title 11 of the United States Code before Oct. 22, 1994, see section 702 of Pub.L. 103–394, set out as a note under section 101 of Title 11, Bankruptcy.

1978 Acts. Amendment by Pub.L. 95–598 effective Oct. 1, 1979, see section 402(a) of Pub.L. 95–598, set out as a note preceding section 101 of Title 11, Bankruptcy.

Savings Provisions

Amendment by section 314 of Pub. L. 95–598 not to affect the application of this chapter to any act of any person (1) committed before Oct. 1, 1979, or (2) committed after Oct. 1, 1979, in connection with a case commenced before such date, see section 403(d) of Pub. L. 95–598, set out preceding section 101 of Title 11, Bankruptcy.

Separability of Provisions

If any provision of or amendment made by Pub.L. 103–394 or the application of such provision or amendment to any person or circumstance is held to be unconstitutional, the remaining provisions of and amendments made by Pub.L. 103–394 and the application of such provisions and amendments to any person or circumstance shall not be affected thereby, see section 701 of Pub.L. 103–394, set out as a note under section 101 of Title 11, Bankruptcy.

§ 155. Fee agreements in cases under title 11 and receiverships

Whoever, being a party in interest, whether as a debtor, creditor, receiver, trustee or representative of any of them, or attorney for any such party in interest, in any receivership or case under title 11 in any United States court or under its supervision, knowingly and fraudulently enters into any agreement, express or implied, with another such party in interest or attorney for another such party in interest, for the purpose of fixing the fees or other compensation to be paid to any party in interest or to any attorney for any party in interest for services rendered in connection therewith, from the assets of the estate, shall be fined under this title or imprisoned not more than one year, or both.
(June 25, 1948, c. 645, 62 Stat. 690; May 24, 1949, c. 139, § 4, 63 Stat. 90; Pub.L. 95–598, Title III, § 314(f)(1), (2), Nov. 6, 1978, 92 Stat. 2677; Pub.L. 103–322, Title XXXIII, § 330016(1)(K), Sept. 13, 1994, 108 Stat. 2147.)

HISTORICAL AND STATUTORY NOTES

Revision Notes and Legislative Reports

1948 Acts. Based on § 572a of Title 28, U.S.C., 1940 ed., Judicial Code and Judiciary (Aug. 25, 1937, c. 777, 50 Stat. 810.

Words "upon conviction" were deleted as surplusage since punishment can be imposed only after a conviction.

A fine of "$5,000" was substituted for "$10,000" and "one year" for "five years", to reduce the offense to the grade of a misdemeanor and the punishment to an amount and term proportionate to the gravity of the offense.

Minor changes were made in phraseology. 80th Congress House Report No. 304.

1949 Acts. This amendment [see section 4] clarifies section 155 of Title 18, U.S.C., by restating the first paragraph thereof in closer conformity with the original law, as it existed at the time of the enactment of the revision of Title 18.

Senate Report No. 303 and House Report No. 352, see 1949 U.S. Code Cong. Service, p. 1248.

1994 Acts. House Report No. 103–324, House Report No. 103–489, and House Conference Report No. 103–711, see 1994 U.S. Code Cong. and Adm. News, p. 1801.

Effective and Applicability Provisions

1978 Acts. Amendment by Pub.L. 95–598 effective Oct. 1, 1979, see section 402(a) of Pub.L. 95–598, set out as a note preceding section 101 of Title 11, Bankruptcy.

Savings Provisions

Amendment by section 314 of Pub. L. 95–598 not to affect the application of this chapter to any act of any person (1) committed before Oct. 1, 1979, or (2) committed after Oct. 1, 1979, in connection with a case commenced before such date, see section 403(d) of Pub. L. 95–598, set out preceding section 101 of Title 11, Bankruptcy.

§ 156. Knowing disregard of bankruptcy law or rule

(a) Definitions.—In this section—

(1) the term "bankruptcy petition preparer" means a person, other than the debtor's attorney or an employee of such an attorney, who prepares for compensation a document for filing; and

(2) the term "document for filing" means a petition or any other document prepared for filing by a debtor in a United States bankruptcy court or a United States district court in connection with a case under title 11.

(b) Offense.—If a bankruptcy case or related proceeding is dismissed because of a knowing attempt by a bankruptcy petition preparer in any manner to disregard the requirements of title 11, United States Code, or the Federal Rules of Bankruptcy Procedure, the bankruptcy petition preparer shall be fined under this title, imprisoned not more than 1 year, or both.
(Added Pub.L. 103–394, Title III, § 312(a)(1)(B), Oct. 22, 1994, 108 Stat. 4140; amended Pub.L. 109–8, Title XII, § 1220, Apr. 20, 2005, 119 Stat. 195.)

HISTORICAL AND STATUTORY NOTES

Revision Notes and Legislative Reports

1994 Acts. House Report No. 103–835, see 1994 U.S. Code Cong. and Adm. News, p. 3340.

2005 Acts. House Report No. 109–31(Part I), see 2005 U.S. Code Cong. and Adm. News, p. 88.

References in Text

The Federal Rules of Bankruptcy Procedure, referred to in subsec. (b), are set out in the Appendix to Title 11, Bankruptcy.

Effective and Applicability Provisions

2005 Acts. Except as otherwise provided, amendments by Pub.L. 109–8 effective 180 days after April 20, 2005, and inapplicable with respect to cases commenced under Title 11 before the effective date, see Pub.L. 109–8, § 1501, set out as a note under 11 U.S.C.A. § 101.

1994 Acts. Section effective on Oct. 22, 1994, and not to apply with respect to cases commenced under Title 11 of the United States Code before Oct. 22, 1994, see section 702 of Pub.L. 103–394, set out as a note under section 101 of Title 11, Bankruptcy.

Separability of Provisions

If any provision of or amendment made by Pub.L. 103–394 or the application of such provision or amendment to any person or circumstance is held to be unconstitutional, the remaining provisions of and amendments made by Pub.L. 103–394 and the application of such provisions and amendments to any person or circumstance shall not be affected thereby, see section 701 of Pub.L. 103–394, set out as a note under section 101 of Title 11, Bankruptcy.

§ 157. Bankruptcy fraud

A person who, having devised or intending to devise a scheme or artifice to defraud and for the purpose of executing or concealing such a scheme or artifice or attempting to do so—

(1) files a petition under title 11, including a fraudulent involuntary petition under section 303 of such title;

(2) files a document in a proceeding under title 11; or

(3) makes a false or fraudulent representation, claim, or promise concerning or in relation to a proceeding under title 11, at any time before or after the filing of the petition, or in relation to a proceeding falsely asserted to be pending under such title,

shall be fined under this title, imprisoned not more than 5 years, or both.

(Added Pub.L. 103–394, Title III, § 312(a)(1)(B), Oct. 22, 1994, 108 Stat. 4140; amended Pub.L. 109–8, Title III, § 332(c), Apr. 20, 2005, 119 Stat. 103; Pub.L. 111–327, § 2(b), Dec. 22, 2010, 124 Stat. 3562.)

HISTORICAL AND STATUTORY NOTES

Revision Notes and Legislative Reports

1994 Acts. House Report No. 103–835, see 1994 U.S. Code Cong. and Adm. News, p. 3340.

2005 Acts. House Report No. 109–31(Part I), see 2005 U.S. Code Cong. and Adm. News, p. 88.

Effective and Applicability Provisions

2005 Acts. Except as otherwise provided, amendments by Pub.L. 109–8 effective 180 days after April 20, 2005, and inapplicable with respect to cases commenced under Title 11 before the effective date, see Pub.L. 109–8, § 1501, set out as a note under 11 U.S.C.A. § 101.

1994 Acts. Section effective on Oct. 22, 1994, and not to apply with respect to cases commenced under Title 11 of the United States Code before Oct. 22, 1994, see section 702 of Pub.L. 103–394, set out as a note under section 101 of Title 11, Bankruptcy.

Separability of Provisions

If any provision of or amendment made by Pub.L. 103–394 or the application of such provision or amendment to any person or circumstance is held to be unconstitutional, the remaining provisions of and amendments made by Pub.L. 103–394 and the application of such provisions and amendments to any person or circumstance shall not be affected thereby, see section 701 of Pub.L. 103–394, set out as a note under section 101 of Title 11, Bankruptcy.

§ 158. Designation of United States attorneys and agents of the Federal Bureau of Investigation to address abusive reaffirmations of debt and materially fraudulent statements in bankruptcy schedules

(a) In general.—The Attorney General of the United States shall designate the individuals described in subsection (b) to have primary responsibility in carrying out enforcement activities in addressing violations of section 152 or 157 relating to abusive reaffirmations of debt. In addition to addressing the violations referred to in the preceding sentence, the individuals described under subsection (b) shall address violations of section 152 or 157 relating to materially fraudulent statements in bankruptcy schedules that are intentionally false or intentionally misleading.

(b) United States attorneys and agents of the Federal Bureau of Investigation.—The individuals referred to in subsection (a) are—

(1) the United States attorney for each judicial district of the United States; and

(2) an agent of the Federal Bureau of Investigation for each field office of the Federal Bureau of Investigation.

(c) Bankruptcy investigations.—Each United States attorney designated under this section shall, in addition to any other responsibilities, have primary responsibility for carrying out the duties of a United States attorney under section 3057.

(d) Bankruptcy procedures.—The bankruptcy courts shall establish procedures for referring any case that may contain a materially fraudulent statement in a bankruptcy schedule to the individuals designated under this section.

(Added Pub.L. 109–8, Title II, § 203(b)(1), Apr. 20, 2005, 119 Stat. 49.)

HISTORICAL AND STATUTORY NOTES

Revision Notes and Legislative Reports

2005 Acts. House Report No. 109–31(Part I), see 2005 U.S. Code Cong. and Adm. News, p. 88.

Effective and Applicability Provisions

2005 Acts. Except as otherwise provided, amendments by Pub.L. 109–8 effective 180 days after April 20, 2005, and inapplicable with respect to cases commenced under Title 11 before the effective date, see Pub.L. 109–8, § 1501, set out as a note under 11 U.S.C.A. § 101.

CHAPTER 73—OBSTRUCTION OF JUSTICE

§ 1519. Destruction, alteration, or falsification of records in Federal investigations and bankruptcy

Whoever knowingly alters, destroys, mutilates, conceals, covers up, falsifies, or makes a false entry in any record, document, or tangible object with the intent to impede, obstruct, or influence the investigation or proper administration of any matter within the jurisdiction of any department or agency of the United States or any case filed under title 11, or in relation to or contemplation of any such matter or case, shall be fined under this title, imprisoned not more than 20 years, or both.

(Added Pub.L. 107–204, Title VIII, § 802(a), July 30, 2002, 116 Stat. 800.)

HISTORICAL AND STATUTORY NOTES

Revision Notes and Legislative Reports

2002 Acts. House Conference Report No. 107–610 and Statement by President, see 2002 U.S. Code Cong. and Adm. News, p. 542.

For Complete Annotation Materials, see United States Code Annotated

CHAPTER 96—RACKETEER INFLUENCED AND CORRUPT ORGANIZATIONS

§ 1961. Definitions

As used in this chapter—

(1) "racketeering activity" means (A) any act or threat involving murder, kidnapping, gambling, arson, robbery, bribery, extortion, dealing in obscene matter, or dealing in a controlled substance or listed chemical (as defined in section 102 of the Controlled Substances Act), which is chargeable under State law and punishable by imprisonment for more than one year; (B) any act which is indictable under any of the following provisions of title 18, United States Code: Section 201 (relating to bribery), section 224 (relating to sports bribery), sections 471, 472, and 473 (relating to counterfeiting), section 659 (relating to theft from interstate shipment) if the act indictable under section 659 is felonious, section 664 (relating to embezzlement from pension and welfare funds), sections 891–894 (relating to extortionate credit transactions), section 1028 (relating to fraud and related activity in connection with identification documents), section 1029 (relating to fraud and related activity in connection with access devices), section 1084 (relating to the transmission of gambling information), section 1341 (relating to mail fraud), section 1343 (relating to wire fraud), section 1344 (relating to financial institution fraud), section 1351 (relating to fraud in foreign labor contracting), section 1425 (relating to the procurement of citizenship or nationalization unlawfully), section 1426 (relating to the reproduction of naturalization or citizenship papers), section 1427 (relating to the sale of naturalization or citizenship papers), sections 1461–1465 (relating to obscene matter), section 1503 (relating to obstruction of justice), section 1510 (relating to obstruction of criminal investigations), section 1511 (relating to the obstruction of State or local law enforcement), section 1512 (relating to tampering with a witness, victim, or an informant), section 1513 (relating to retaliating against a witness, victim, or an informant), section 1542 (relating to false statement in application and use of passport), section 1543 (relating to forgery or false use of passport), section 1544 (relating to misuse of passport), section 1546 (relating to fraud and misuse of visas, permits, and other documents), sections 1581–1592 (relating to peonage, slavery, and trafficking in persons).,[1] sections 1831 and 1832 (relating to economic espionage and theft of trade secrets), section 1951 (relating to interference with commerce, robbery, or extortion), section 1952 (relating to racketeering), section 1953 (relating to interstate transportation of wagering paraphernalia), section 1954 (relating to unlawful welfare fund payments), section 1955 (relating to the prohibition of illegal gambling businesses), section 1956 (relating to the laundering of monetary instruments), section 1957 (relating to engaging in monetary transactions in property derived from specified unlawful activity), section 1958 (relating to use of interstate commerce facilities in the commission of murder-for-hire), section 1960 (relating to illegal money transmitters), sections 2251, 2251A, 2252, and 2260 (relating to sexual exploitation of children), sections 2312 and 2313 (relating to interstate transportation of stolen motor vehicles), sections 2314 and 2315 (relating to interstate transportation of stolen property), section 2318 (relating to trafficking in counterfeit labels for phonorecords, computer programs or computer program documentation or packaging and copies of motion pictures or other audiovisual works), section 2319 (relating to criminal infringement of a copyright), section 2319A (relating to unauthorized fixation of and trafficking in sound recordings and music videos of live musical performances), section 2320 (relating to trafficking in goods or services bearing counterfeit marks), section 2321 (relating to trafficking in certain motor vehicles or motor vehicle parts), sections 2341–2346 (relating to trafficking in contraband cigarettes), sections 2421–24 (relating to white slave traffic), sections 175–178 (relating to biological weapons), sections 229–229F (relating to chemical weapons), section 831 (relating to nuclear materials), (C) any act which is indictable under title 29, United States Code, section 186 (dealing with restrictions on payments and loans to labor organizations) or section 501(c) (relating to embezzlement from union funds), (D) any offense involving fraud connected with a case under title 11 (except a case under section 157 of this title), fraud in the sale of securities, or the felonious manufacture, importation, receiving, concealment, buying, selling, or otherwise dealing in a controlled substance or listed chemical (as defined in section 102 of the Controlled Substances Act), punishable under any law of the United States, (E) any act which is indictable under the Currency and Foreign Transactions Reporting Act, (F) any act which is indictable under the Immigration and Nationality Act, section 274 (relating to bringing in and harboring certain aliens), section 277 (relating to aiding or assisting certain aliens to enter the United States), or section 278 (relating to importation of alien for immoral purpose) if the act indictable under such section of such Act was committed for the purpose of financial gain, or (G) any act that is indictable under any provision listed in section 2332b(g)(5)(B);

(2) "State" means any State of the United States, the District of Columbia, the Commonwealth of Puerto Rico, any territory or possession of the United States, any political subdivision, or any department, agency, or instrumentality thereof;

(3) "person" includes any individual or entity capable of holding a legal or beneficial interest in property;

(4) "enterprise" includes any individual, partnership, corporation, association, or other legal entity, and any union or group of individuals associated in fact although not a legal entity;

(5) "pattern of racketeering activity" requires at least two acts of racketeering activity, one of which occurred after the effective date of this chapter and the last of which occurred within ten years (excluding any period of imprisonment) after the commission of a prior act of racketeering activity;

(6) "unlawful debt" means a debt (A) incurred or contracted in gambling activity which was in violation of the law of the United States, a State or political subdivision thereof, or which is unenforceable under State or Federal law in whole or in part as to principal or interest because of the laws relating to usury, and (B) which was incurred in connection with the business of gambling in violation of the law of the United States, a State or political subdivision thereof, or the business of lending money or a thing of value at a rate usurious under State or Federal law, where the usurious rate is at least twice the enforceable rate;

(7) "racketeering investigator" means any attorney or investigator so designated by the Attorney General and charged with the duty of enforcing or carrying into effect this chapter;

(8) "racketeering investigation" means any inquiry conducted by any racketeering investigator for the purpose of ascertaining whether any person has been involved in any violation of this chapter or of any final order, judgment, or decree of any court of the United States, duly entered in any case or proceeding arising under this chapter;

(9) "documentary material" includes any book, paper, document, record, recording, or other material; and

(10) "Attorney General" includes the Attorney General of the United States, the Deputy Attorney General of the United States, the Associate Attorney General of the United States, any Assistant Attorney General of the United States, or any employee of the Department of Justice or any employee of any department or agency of the United States so designated by the Attorney General to carry out the powers conferred on the Attorney General by this chapter. Any department or agency so designated may use in investigations authorized by this chapter either the investigative provisions of this chapter or the investigative power of such department or agency otherwise conferred by law.

(Added Pub.L. 91–452, Title IX, § 901(a), Oct. 15, 1970, 84 Stat. 941; amended Pub.L. 95–575, § 3(c), Nov. 2, 1978, 92 Stat. 2465; Pub.L. 95–598, Title III, § 314(g), Nov. 6, 1978, 92

Stat. 2677; Pub.L. 98–473, Title II, §§ 901(g), 1020, Oct. 12, 1984, 98 Stat. 2136, 2143; Pub.L. 98–547, Title II, § 205, Oct. 25, 1984, 98 Stat. 2770; Pub.L. 99–570, Title I, § 1365(b), Oct. 27, 1986, 100 Stat. 3207–35; Pub.L. 99–646, § 50(a), Nov. 10, 1986, 100 Stat. 3605; Pub.L. 100–690, Title VII, §§ 7013, 7020(c), 7032, 7054, 7514, Nov. 18, 1988, 102 Stat. 4395, 4396, 4398, 4402, 4489; Pub.L. 101–73, Title IX, § 968, Aug. 9, 1989, 103 Stat. 506; Pub.L. 101–647, Title XXXV, § 3560, Nov. 29, 1990, 104 Stat. 4927; Pub.L. 103–322, Title IX, § 90104, Title XVI, § 160001(f), Title XXXIII, § 330021(1), Sept. 13, 1994, 108 Stat. 1987, 2037, 2150; Pub.L. 103–394, Title III, § 312(b), Oct. 22, 1994, 108 Stat. 4140; Pub.L. 104–132, Title IV, § 433, Apr. 24, 1996, 110 Stat. 1274; Pub.L. 104–153, § 3, July 2, 1996, 110 Stat. 1386; Pub.L. 104–208, Div. C, Title II, § 202, Sept. 30, 1996, 110 Stat. 3009–565; Pub.L. 104–294, Title VI, §§ 601(b)(3), (i)(3), 604(b)(6), Oct. 11, 1996, 110 Stat. 3499, 3501, 3506; Pub.L. 107–56, Title VIII, § 813, Oct. 26, 2001, 115 Stat. 382; Pub.L. 107–273, Div. B, Title IV, § 4005(f)(1), Nov. 2, 2002, 116 Stat. 1813; Pub.L. 108–193, § 5(b), Dec. 19, 2003, 117 Stat. 2879; Pub.L. 108–458, Title VI, § 6802(e), Dec. 17, 2004, 118 Stat. 3767; Pub.L. 109–164, Title I, § 103(c), Jan. 10, 2006, 119 Stat. 3563; Pub.L. 109–177, Title IV, § 403(a), Mar. 9, 2006, 120 Stat. 243; Pub.L. 113–4, Title XII, § 1211(a), Mar. 7, 2013, 127 Stat. 142; Pub.L. 114–153, § 3(b), May 11, 2016, 130 Stat. 382.)

1 So in original.

HISTORICAL AND STATUTORY NOTES

Revision Notes and Legislative Reports

1970 Acts. House Report No. 91–1549, see 1970 U.S. Code Cong. and Adm. News, p. 4007.

1978 Acts. Senate Report No. 95–962 and House Conference Report No. 95–1778, see 1978 U.S. Code Cong. and Adm. News, p. 5518.

1984 Acts. House Report No. 98–1030 and House Conference Report No. 98–1159, see 1984 U.S. Code Cong. and Adm. News, p. 3182.

House Report No. 98–1087, see 1984 U.S. Code Cong. and Adm. News, p. 4628.

1986 Acts. Statement by President, see 1986 U.S. Code Cong. and Adm. News, p. 5393.

House Report No. 99–797, see 1986 U.S. Code Cong. and Adm. News, p. 6138.

1988 Acts. For Related Reports, see 1988 U.S. Code Cong. and Adm. News, p. 5937.

1989 Acts. House Report No. 101–54(Parts I–VII) and House Conference Report No. 101–222, see 1989 Code Cong. and Adm. News, p. 86.

1990 Acts. House Report Nos. 101–681(Parts I and II), 101–736, Senate Report No. 101–460, and Statement by President, see 1990 U.S. Code Cong. and Adm. News, p. 6472.

1994 Acts. House Report Nos. 103–324, 103–489, and House Conference Report No. 103–711, see 1994 U.S. Code Cong. and Adm. News, p. 1801.

House Report No. 103–835, see 1994 U.S. Code Cong. and Adm. News, p. 3340.

1996 Acts. Senate Report No. 104–179 and House Conference Report No. 104–518, see 1996 U.S. Code Cong. and Adm. News, p. 924.

House Report No. 104–556, see 1996 U.S. Code Cong. and Adm. News, p. 1074.

House Report No. 104–788, see 1996 U.S. Code Cong. and Adm. News, p. 4021.

2002 Acts. House Conference Report No. 107–685 and Statement by President, see 2002 U.S. Code Cong. and Adm. News, p. 1120.

2003 Acts. House Report No. 108–264(Parts I and II), see 2003 U.S. Code Cong. and Adm. News, p. 2408.

2004 Acts. House Conference Report No. 108–796, see 2004 U.S. Code Cong. and Adm. News, p. 3178.

Statement by President, see 2004 U.S. Code Cong. and Adm. News, p. S51.

2006 Acts. House Report No. 109–317(Parts I and II), see 2005 U.S. Code Cong. and Adm. News, p. 1888.

Statement by President, see 2005 U.S. Code Cong. and Adm. News, p. S56.

House Conference Report No. 109–333, see 2006 U.S. Code Cong. and Adm. News, p. 184.

Statement by President, see 2006 U.S. Code Cong. and Adm. News, p. S7.

References in Text

Section 102 of the Controlled Substances Act, referred to in par. (1), is section 102 of Pub.L. 91–513, Title II, Oct. 27, 1970, 84 Stat. 1242, as amended, which is classified to 21 U.S.C.A. § 802.

The Currency and Foreign Transactions Reporting Act, referred to in par. (1)(E), is Title II of Pub.L. 91–508, Oct. 26, 1970, 84 Stat. 1118, which was repealed and reenacted as subchapter II of chapter 53 of Title 31, 31 U.S.C.A. § 5311 et seq., by Pub.L. 97–258, § 4(b), Sept. 13, 1982, 96 Stat. 1067, the first section of which enacted Title 31.

The Immigration and Nationality Act and such Act, referred to in par. (1)(F), is Act June 27, 1952, c. 477, 66 Stat. 163, as amended, which is classified principally to chapter 12 (section 1101 et seq.) of Title 8, Aliens and Nationality. Sections 274, 277 and 278 of such Act are classified to sections 1324, 1327 and 1328 of Title 8, respectively. For complete classification of this Act to the Code, see Tables.

The effective date of this chapter, referred to in par. (5), is Oct. 15, 1970.

Codifications

Section 5(b) of Pub.L. 108–193, which directed that paragraph (1)(A) of this section be amended by striking "sections 1581–1588 (relating to peonage and slavery)" and inserting "sections 1581–1591 (relating to peonage, slavery, and trafficking in persons)", was executed to paragraph (1)(B) of this section as the probable intent of Congress.

Effective and Applicability Provisions

2002 Acts. Amendment by section 4005(f)(1) of Pub.L. 107–273, as therein provided, effective Oct. 26, 2001, which is the date of enactment of Pub.L. 107–56, to which such amendment relates.

1996 Acts. Amendment by section 604 of Pub.L. 104–294 effective Sept. 13, 1994, see section 604(d) of Pub.L. 104–294, set out as a note under section 13 of this title.

1994 Acts. Amendment by Pub.L. 103–394 effective on Oct. 22, 1994, and not to apply with respect to cases commenced under Title 11 of the United States Code before Oct. 22, 1994, see section 702 of Pub.L. 103–394, set out as a note under section 101 of Title 11, Bankruptcy.

1978 Acts. Amendment by Pub.L. 95–598 effective Oct. 1, 1979, see section 402(a) of Pub.L. 95–598, set out as an Effective Date note preceding section 101 of Title 11, Bankruptcy.

Amendment by Pub.L. 95–575 effective Nov. 2, 1978, see section 4 of Pub.L. 95–575, set out as an Effective Date note under section 2341 of this title.

Savings Provisions

Amendment by section 314 of Pub.L. 95–598 not to affect the application of chapter 9 (18 U.S.C.A. § 151 et seq.), chapter 96 (18 U.S.C.A. § 1961 et seq.), or 18 U.S.C.A. §§ 2516, 3057, or 3284 to any act of any person (1) committed before Oct. 1, 1979, or (2) committed after Oct. 1, 1979, in connection with a case commenced before such date, see section 403(d) of Pub.L. 95–598, set out as a note preceding 11 U.S.C.A. § 101.

Severability of Provisions

If any provision of Division C of Pub.L. 104–208 or the application of such provision to any person or circumstances is held to be unconstitutional, the remainder of Division C of Pub.L. 104–208 and the application of the provisions of Division C of Pub.L. 104–208 to any person or circumstance not to be affected thereby, see section 1(e) of Pub.L. 104–208, set out as a note under section 1101 of Title 8, Aliens and Nationality.

If any provision of or amendment made by Pub.L. 103–394 or the application of such provision or amendment to any person or circumstance is held to be unconstitutional, the remaining provisions of and amendments made by Pub.L. 103–394 and the application of such provisions and amendments to any person or circumstance shall not be affected thereby, see section 701 of Pub.L. 103–394, set out as a note under section 101 of Title 11, Bankruptcy.

If any provision of Pub.L. 101–73 or the application thereof to any person or circumstance is held invalid, the remainder of Pub.L. 101–73 and the application of the provision to other persons not similarly situated or to other circumstances not to be affected thereby, see section 1221 of Pub.L. 101–73, set out as a note under section 1811 of Title 12, Banks and Banking.

Section 1301 of Pub.L. 91–452 provided that: "If the provisions of any part of this Act [see Short Title note set out above] or the application thereof to any person or circumstances be held invalid, the provisions of the other parts and their application to other persons or circumstances shall not be affected thereby."

Short Title

1984 Amendments. Pub.L. 98–473, Title II, § 301, Oct. 12, 1984, 98 Stat. 2040, provided that: "This title [probably means chapter III of title II of Pub.L. 98–473 which enacted sections 853, 854, and 970 of Title 21, Food and Drugs, and sections 1589, 1600, 1613a, and 1616 of Title 19, Customs Duties, amended section 1963 of this title and sections 1602, 1605, 1606, 1607, 1608, 1609, 1610, 1611, 1612, 1613, 1614, 1615, 1618, 1619, and 1644 of Title 19, sections 824, 848, and 881 of Title 21, and section 524 of Title 28, Judiciary and Judicial Procedure, and repealed section 7607 of Title 26, Internal Revenue Code] may be cited as the 'Comprehensive Forfeiture Act of 1984'."

1970 Acts. Section 1 of Pub.L. 91–452 provided in part that: "This Act [enacting sections 841 to 848, 1511, 1623, 1955, 1961 to 1968, 3331 to 3334, 3503, 3504, 3575 to 3578, and 6001 to 6005 of this title, and section 1826 of Title 28, Judiciary and Judicial Procedure, amending sections 835, 1073, 1505, 1954,

2424, 2516, 2517, 3148, 3486, and 3500 of this title, sections 15, 87f, 135c, 499m, and 2115 of Title 7, Agriculture, section 25 of Title 11, Bankruptcy, section 1820 of Title 12, Banks and Banking, sections 49, 77v, 78u, 79r, 80a–41, 80b–9, 155, 717m, 1271, and 1714 of Title 15, Commerce and Trade, section 825f of Title 16, Conservation, section 1333 of Title 19, Customs Duties, section 373 of Title 21, Food and Drugs, section 161 of Title 29, Labor, section 506 of Title 33, Navigation and Navigable Waters, sections 405 and 2201 of Title 42, The Public Health and Welfare, sections 157 and 362 of Title 45, Railroads, section 1124 of Title 46, Shipping, section 409 of Title 47, Telegraphs, Telephones, and Radio telegraphs, sections 9, 43, 46, 916, 1017, and 1484 of former Title 49, Transportation, sections 792 and 4555 of Title 50, and former sections 643a, 1152, and 2026 of the former Appendix to Title 50, repealing sections 837, 895, 1406, and 2514 of this title, sections 32 and 33 of Title 15; sections 4874 and 7493 of Title 26, Internal Revenue Code, section 827 of Title 46, sections 47 and 48 of former Title 49, and sections 121 to 144 of Title 50, enacting provisions set out as notes under this section and sections 841, 1511, 1955, preceding 3331, preceding 3481, 3504, and 6001 of this title, and repealing provisions set out as a note under section 2510 of this title] may be cited as the 'Organized Crime Control Act of 1970'."

This chapter is commonly known as the Racketeer Influenced and Corrupt Organizations Act or RICO.

References to Coupons, Authorization Cards, or Access Devices under Food and Nutrition Act of 2008

References in any Federal, State, tribal, or local law to a "coupon", "authorization card", or other access device provided under the Food and Nutrition Act of 2008, 7 U.S.C.A. § 2011 et seq., considered to be a reference to a "benefit" provided under that Act, see Pub.L. 110–234, § 4115(d), and Pub.L. 110–246, § 4115(d), set out as a note under 7 U.S.C.A. § 2012.

President's Commission on Organized Crime; Taking of Testimony and Receipt of Evidence

Pub.L. 98–368, July 17, 1984, 98 Stat. 490, provided for the Commission established by Ex. Ord. No. 12435, formerly set out below, authority relating to taking of testimony, receipt of evidence, subpoena power, testimony of persons in custody, immunity, service of process, witness fees, access to other records and information, Federal protection for members and staff, closure of meetings, rules, and procedures, for the period of July 17, 1984, until the earlier of 2 years or the expiration of the Commission.

Congressional Statement of Findings and Purpose

Section 1 of Pub.L. 91–452 provided in part that: "The Congress finds that (1) organized crime in the United States is a highly sophisticated, diversified, and widespread activity that annually drains billions of dollars from America's economy by unlawful conduct and the illegal use of force, fraud, and corruption; (2) organized crime derives a major portion of its power through money obtained from such illegal endeavors as syndicated gambling, loan sharking, the theft and fencing of property, the importation and distribution of narcotics and other dangerous drugs, and other forms of social exploitation; (3) this money and power are increasingly used to infiltrate and corrupt legitimate business and labor unions and to subvert and corrupt our democratic processes; (4) organized crime activities in the United States weaken the stability of the Nation's economic system, harm innocent investors and competing organizations, interfere with free competition, seriously burden interstate and foreign commerce, threaten the domestic security, and undermine the general welfare of the Nation and its citizens; and (5) organized crime continues to grow because of defects in the evidence-gathering process of the law inhibiting the development of the legally admissible evidence necessary to bring criminal and other sanctions or remedies to bear the unlawful activities of those engaged in organized crime and because the sanctions and remedies available to the Government are unnecessarily limited in scope and impact.

"It is the purpose of this Act [see Short Title note above] to seek the eradication of organized crime in the United States by strengthening the legal tools in the evidence-gathering process, by establishing new penal prohibitions, and by providing enhanced sanctions and new remedies to deal with the unlawful activities of those engaged in organized crime."

Liberal Construction of Provisions; Supersedure of Federal or State Laws; Authority of Attorneys Representing United States

Section 904 of Pub.L. 91–452 provided that:

"(a) The provisions of this title [enacting this chapter and amending sections 1505, 2516, and 2517 of this title] shall be liberally construed to effectuate its remedial purposes.

"(b) Nothing in this title shall supersede any provision of Federal, State, or other law imposing criminal penalties or affording civil remedies in addition to those provided for in this title.

"(c) Nothing contained in this title shall impair the authority of any attorney representing the United States to—

"(1) lay before any grand jury impaneled by any district court of the United States any evidence concerning any alleged racketeering violation of law;

"(2) invoke the power of any such court to compel the production of any evidence before any such grand jury; or

"(3) institute any proceeding to enforce any order or process issued in execution of such power or to punish disobedience of any such order or process by any person."

EXECUTIVE ORDERS

EXECUTIVE ORDER NO. 12435

Ex. Ord. No. 12503, July 28, 1983, 48 F.R. 34723, as amended by Ex. Ord. No. 12507, March 22, 1985, 50 F.R. 11835, which related to the establishment, functions, administration and termination of the President's Commission on Organized Crime, was revoked by Ex. Ord. No. 12610, Sept. 30, 1987, 52 F.R. 36901.

CHAPTER 119—WIRE AND ELECTRONIC COMMUNICATIONS INTERCEPTION AND INTERCEPTION OF ORAL COMMUNICATIONS

§ 2516. Authorization for interception of wire, oral, or electronic communications

(1) The Attorney General, Deputy Attorney General, Associate Attorney General,[1] or any Assistant Attorney General, any acting Assistant Attorney General, or any Deputy Assistant Attorney General or acting Deputy Assistant Attorney General in the Criminal Division or National Security Division specially designated by the Attorney General, may authorize an application to a Federal judge of competent jurisdiction for, and such judge may grant in conformity with section 2518 of this chapter an order authorizing or approving the interception of wire or oral communications by the Federal Bureau of Investigation, or a Federal agency having responsibility for the investigation of the offense as to which the application is made, when such interception may provide or has provided evidence of—

(a) any offense punishable by death or by imprisonment for more than one year under sections 2122 and 2274 through 2277 of title 42 of the United States Code (relating to the enforcement of the Atomic Energy Act of 1954), section 2284 of title 42 of the United States Code (relating to sabotage of nuclear facilities or fuel), or under the following chapters of this title: chapter 10 (relating to biological weapons), chapter 37 (relating to espionage), chapter 55 (relating to kidnapping), chapter 90 (relating to protection of trade secrets), chapter 105 (relating to sabotage), chapter 115 (relating to treason), chapter 102 (relating to riots), chapter 65 (relating to malicious mischief), chapter 111 (relating to destruction of vessels), or chapter 81 (relating to piracy);

(b) a violation of section 186 or section 501(c) of title 29, United States Code (dealing with restrictions on payments and loans to labor organizations), or any offense which involves murder, kidnapping, robbery, or extortion, and which is punishable under this title;

(c) any offense which is punishable under the following sections of this title: section 37 (relating to violence at international airports), section 43 (relating to animal enterprise terrorism), section 81 (arson within special maritime and territorial jurisdiction), section 201 (bribery of public officials and witnesses), section 215 (relating to bribery of bank officials), section 224 (bribery in sporting contests), subsection (d), (e), (f), (g), (h), or (i) of section 844 (unlawful use of explosives), section 1032 (relating to concealment of assets), section 1084 (transmission of wagering information), section 751 (relating to escape), section 832 (relating to nuclear and weapons of mass destruction threats), section 842 (relating to explosive

materials), section 930 (relating to possession of weapons in Federal facilities), section 1014 (relating to loans and credit applications generally; renewals and discounts), section 1114 (relating to officers and employees of the United States), section 1116 (relating to protection of foreign officials), sections 1503, 1512, and 1513 (influencing or injuring an officer, juror, or witness generally), section 1510 (obstruction of criminal investigations), section 1511 (obstruction of State or local law enforcement), section 1581 (peonage), section 1584 (involuntary servitude), section 1589 (forced labor), section 1590 (trafficking with respect to peonage, slavery, involuntary servitude, or forced labor), section 1591 (sex trafficking of children by force, fraud, or coercion), section 1592 (unlawful conduct with respect to documents in furtherance of trafficking, peonage, slavery, involuntary servitude, or forced labor), section 1751 (Presidential and Presidential staff assassination, kidnapping, and assault), section 1951 (interference with commerce by threats or violence), section 1952 (interstate and foreign travel or transportation in aid of racketeering enterprises), section 1958 (relating to use of interstate commerce facilities in the commission of murder for hire), section 1959 (relating to violent crimes in aid of racketeering activity), section 1954 (offer, acceptance, or solicitation to influence operations of employee benefit plan), section 1955 (prohibition of business enterprises of gambling), section 1956 (laundering of monetary instruments), section 1957 (relating to engaging in monetary transactions in property derived from specified unlawful activity), section 659 (theft from interstate shipment), section 664 (embezzlement from pension and welfare funds), section 1343 (fraud by wire, radio, or television), section 1344 (relating to bank fraud), section 1992 (relating to terrorist attacks against mass transportation), sections 2251 and 2252 (sexual exploitation of children), section 2251A (selling or buying of children), section 2252A (relating to material constituting or containing child pornography), section 1466A (relating to child obscenity), section 2260 (production of sexually explicit depictions of a minor for importation into the United States), sections 2421, 2422, 2423, and 2425 (relating to transportation for illegal sexual activity and related crimes), sections 2312, 2313, 2314, and 2315 (interstate transportation of stolen property), section 2321 (relating to trafficking in certain motor vehicles or motor vehicle parts), section 2340A (relating to torture), section 1203 (relating to hostage taking), section 1029 (relating to fraud and related activity in connection with access devices), section 3146 (relating to penalty for failure to appear), section 3521(b)(3) (relating to witness relocation and assistance), section 32 (relating to destruction of aircraft or aircraft facilities), section 38 (relating to aircraft parts fraud), section 1963 (violations with respect to racketeer influenced and corrupt organizations), section 115 (relating to threatening or retaliating against a Federal official), section 1341 (relating to mail fraud), a felony violation of section 1030 (relating to computer fraud and abuse), section 351 (violations with respect to congressional, Cabinet, or Supreme Court assassinations, kidnapping, and assault), section 831 (relating to prohibited transactions involving nuclear materials), section 33 (relating to destruction of motor vehicles or motor vehicle facilities), section 175 (relating to biological weapons), section 175c (relating to variola virus), section 956 (conspiracy to harm persons or property overseas), a felony violation of section 1028 (relating to production of false identification documentation), section 1425 (relating to the procurement of citizenship or nationalization unlawfully), section 1426 (relating to the reproduction of naturalization or citizenship papers), section 1427 (relating to the sale of naturalization or citizenship papers), section 1541 (relating to passport issuance without authority), section 1542 (relating to false statements in passport applications), section 1543 (relating to forgery or false use of passports), section 1544 (relating to misuse of passports), section 1546 (relating to fraud and misuse of visas, permits, and other documents), or section 555 (relating to construction or use of international border tunnels);

(d) any offense involving counterfeiting punishable under section 471, 472, or 473 of this title;

(e) any offense involving fraud connected with a case under title 11 or the manufacture, importation, receiving, concealment, buying, selling, or otherwise dealing in narcotic drugs, marihuana, or other dangerous drugs, punishable under any law of the United States;

(f) any offense including extortionate credit transactions under sections 892, 893, or 894 of this title;

(g) a violation of section 5322 of title 31, United States Code (dealing with the reporting of currency transactions), or section 5324 of title 31, United States Code (relating to structuring transactions to evade reporting requirement prohibited);

(h) any felony violation of sections 2511 and 2512 (relating to interception and disclosure of certain communications and to certain intercepting devices) of this title;

(i) any felony violation of chapter 71 (relating to obscenity) of this title;

(j) any violation of section 60123(b) (relating to destruction of a natural gas pipeline), section 46502 (relating to aircraft piracy), the second sentence of section 46504 (relating to assault on a flight crew with dangerous weapon), or section 46505(b)(3) or (c) (relating to explosive or incendiary devices, or endangerment of human life, by means of weapons on aircraft) of title 49;

(k) any criminal violation of section 2778 of title 22 (relating to the Arms Export Control Act);

(*l*) the location of any fugitive from justice from an offense described in this section;

(m) a violation of section 274, 277, or 278 of the Immigration and Nationality Act (8 U.S.C. 1324, 1327, or 1328) (relating to the smuggling of aliens);

(n) any felony violation of sections 922 and 924 of title 18, United States Code (relating to firearms);

(o) any violation of section 5861 of the Internal Revenue Code of 1986 (relating to firearms);

(p) a felony violation of section 1028 (relating to production of false identification documents), section 1542 (relating to false statements in passport applications), section 1546 (relating to fraud and misuse of visas, permits, and other documents), section 1028A (relating to aggravated identity theft) of this title or a violation of section 274, 277, or 278 of the Immigration and Nationality Act (relating to the smuggling of aliens); or [2]

(q) any criminal violation of section 229 (relating to chemical weapons) or section 2332, 2332a, 2332b, 2332d, 2332f, 2332g, 2332h [3] 2339, 2339A, 2339B, 2339C, or 2339D of this title (relating to terrorism);

(r) any criminal violation of section 1 (relating to illegal restraints of trade or commerce), 2 (relating to illegal monopolizing of trade or commerce), or 3 (relating to illegal restraints of trade or commerce in territories or the District of Columbia) of the Sherman Act (15 U.S.C. 1, 2, 3);

(s) any violation of section 670 (relating to theft of medical products);

(t) any violation of the Export Control Reform Act of 2018; or

(u) any conspiracy to commit any offense described in any subparagraph of this paragraph.

(2) The principal prosecuting attorney of any State, or the principal prosecuting attorney of any political subdivision thereof, if such attorney is authorized by a statute of that State to make application to a State court judge of competent jurisdiction for an order authorizing or approving the interception of wire, oral, or electronic communications, may apply to such judge for, and such judge may grant in conformity with section 2518 of this chapter and with the applicable State statute an order authorizing, or approving the interception of wire, oral, or electronic communications by investigative or law enforcement officers having responsibility for the investigation of the offense as to which the application is made, when such interception may provide or has provided evidence of the commis-

sion of the offense of murder, kidnapping[3] human trafficking, child sexual exploitation, child pornography production,,[4] gambling, robbery, bribery, extortion, or dealing in narcotic drugs, marihuana or other dangerous drugs, or other crime dangerous to life, limb, or property, and punishable by imprisonment for more than one year, designated in any applicable State statute authorizing such interception, or any conspiracy to commit any of the foregoing offenses.

(3) Any attorney for the Government (as such term is defined for the purposes of the Federal Rules of Criminal Procedure) may authorize an application to a Federal judge of competent jurisdiction for, and such judge may grant, in conformity with section 2518 of this title, an order authorizing or approving the interception of electronic communications by an investigative or law enforcement officer having responsibility for the investigation of the offense as to which the application is made, when such interception may provide or has provided evidence of any Federal felony.

(Added Pub.L. 90–351, Title III, § 802, June 19, 1968, 82 Stat. 216; amended Pub.L. 91–452, Title VIII, § 810, Title IX, § 902(a), Title XI, § 1103, Oct. 15, 1970, 84 Stat. 940, 947, 959; Pub.L. 91–644, Title IV, § 16, Jan. 2, 1971, 84 Stat. 1891; Pub.L. 95–598, Title III, § 314(h), Nov. 6, 1978, 92 Stat. 2677; Pub.L. 97–285, §§ 2(e), 4(e), Oct. 6, 1982, 96 Stat. 1220, 1221; Pub.L. 98–292, § 8, May 21, 1984, 98 Stat. 206; Pub.L. 98–473, Title II, § 1203(c), Oct. 12, 1984, 98 Stat. 2152; Pub.L. 99–508, Title I, §§ 101(c)(1)(A), 104, 105, Oct. 21, 1986, 100 Stat. 1851, 1855; Pub.L. 99–570, Title I, § 1365(c), Oct. 27, 1986, 100 Stat. 3207–35; Pub.L. 100–690, Title VI, § 6461, Title VII, §§ 7036, 7053(d), 7525, Nov. 18, 1988, 102 Stat. 4374, 4399, 4402, 4502; Pub.L. 101–298, § 3(b), May 22, 1990, 104 Stat. 203; Pub.L. 101–647, Title XXV, § 2531, Title XXXV, § 3568, Nov. 29, 1990, 104 Stat. 4879, 4928; Pub.L. 103–272, § 5(e)(11), July 5, 1994, 108 Stat. 1374; Pub.L. 103–322, Title XXXIII, §§ 330011(c)(1), (q)(1), (r), 330021(1), Sept. 13, 1994, 108 Stat. 2144, 2145, 2150; Pub.L. 103–414, Title II, § 208, Oct. 25, 1994, 108 Stat. 4292; Pub.L. 103–429, § 7(a)(4)(A), Oct. 31, 1994, 108 Stat. 4389; Pub.L. 104–132, Title IV, § 434, Apr. 24, 1996, 110 Stat. 1274; Pub.L. 104–208, Div. C, Title II, § 201, Sept. 30, 1996, 110 Stat. 3009–564; Pub.L. 104–287, § 6(a)(2), Oct. 11, 1996, 110 Stat. 3398; Pub.L. 104–294, Title I, § 102, Title VI, § 601(d), Oct. 11, 1996, 110 Stat. 3491, 3499; Pub.L. 105–318, § 6(b), Oct. 30, 1998, 112 Stat. 3011; Pub.L. 106–181, Title V, § 506(c)(2)(B), Apr. 5, 2000, 114 Stat. 139; Pub.L. 107–56, Title II, §§ 201, 202, Oct. 26, 2001, 115 Stat. 278; Pub.L. 107–197, Title III, § 301(a), June 25, 2002, 116 Stat. 728; Pub.L. 107–273, Div. B, Title IV, §§ 4002(c)(1), 4005(a)(1), Nov. 2, 2002, 116 Stat. 1808, 1812; Pub.L. 108–21, Title II, § 201, Apr. 30, 2003, 117 Stat. 659; Pub.L. 108–458, Title VI, § 6907, Dec. 17, 2004, 118 Stat. 3774; Pub.L. 109–162, Title XI, § 1171(b), Jan. 5, 2006, 119 Stat. 3123; Pub.L. 109–177, Title I, §§ 110(b)(3)(C), 113, Title V, § 506(a)(6), Mar. 9, 2006, 120 Stat. 208, 209, 248; Pub.L. 112–127, § 4, June 5, 2012, 126 Stat. 371; Pub.L. 112–186, § 5, Oct. 5, 2012, 126 Stat. 1429; Pub.L. 114–22, Title I, § 106, May 29, 2015, 129 Stat. 238; Pub.L. 115–232, Div. A, Title XVII, § 1761(f), Aug. 13, 2018, 132 Stat. 2228.)

[1] See 1984 Amendments note set out under this section.
[2] So in original. The word "or" probably should not appear.

[3] So in original. A comma probably should appear.
[4] So in original.

HISTORICAL AND STATUTORY NOTES

Revision Notes and Legislative Reports

1968 Acts. Senate Report No. 90–1097, see 1968 U.S. Code Cong. and Adm. News, p. 2112.

1970 Acts. House Report No. 91–1549, see 1970 U.S. Code Cong. and Adm. News, p. 4007.

1971 Acts. Senate Report No. 91–1253 and Conference Report No. 91–1768, see 1970 U.S. Code Cong. and Adm. News, p. 5804.

1982 Acts. House Report No. 97–803, see 1982 U.S. Code Cong. and Adm. News, p. 2428.

1984 Acts. House Report No. 98–536, see 1984 U.S. Code Cong. and Adm. News, p. 492.

House Report No. 98–1030 and House Conference Report No. 98–1159, see 1984 U.S. Code Cong. and Adm. News, p. 3182.

1986 Acts. Senate Report No. 99–541, see 1986 U.S. Code Cong. and Adm. News, p. 3555.

Statement by President, see 1986 U.S. Code Cong. and Adm. News, p. 5393.

1988 Acts. For Related Reports, see 1988 U.S. Code Cong. and Adm. News, p. 5937.

1990 Acts. Senate Report No. 101–210, and Statement by President, see 1990 U.S. Code Cong. and Adm. News, p. 186.

1994 Acts. House Report No. 103–180, see 1994 U.S. Code Cong. and Adm. News, p. 818.

House Report Nos. 103–324, 103–489, and House Conference Report No. 103–711, see 1994 U.S. Code Cong. and Adm. News, p. 1801.

House Report No. 103–827, see 1994 U.S. Code Cong. and Adm. News, p. 3489.

House Report No. 103–831, see 1994 U.S. Code Cong. and Adm. News, p. 3579.

1996 Acts. Senate Report No. 104–179 and House Conference Report No. 104–518, see 1996 U.S. Code Cong. and Adm. News, p. 924.

House Report No. 104–573, see 1996 U.S. Code Cong. and Adm. News, p. 3831.

House Report No. 104–788, see 1996 U.S. Code Cong. and Adm. News, p. 4021.

1998 Acts. Statement by President, see 1998 U.S. Code Cong. and Adm. News, p. 709.

2000 Acts. House Conference Report No. 106–513 and Statement by President, see 2000 U.S. Code Cong. and Adm. News, p. 80.

2002 Acts. House Report No. 107–307 and Statement by President, see 2002 U.S. Code Cong. and Adm. News, p. 521.

House Conference Report No. 107–685 and Statement by President, see 2002 U.S. Code Cong. and Adm. News, p. 1120.

2003 Acts. House Conference Report No. 108–66 and Statement by President, see 2003 U.S. Code Cong. and Adm. News, p. 683.

2004 Acts. House Conference Report No. 108–796, see 2004 U.S. Code Cong. and Adm. News, p. 3178.

Statement by President, see 2004 U.S. Code Cong. and Adm. News, p. S51.

2006 Acts. House Report No. 109–233, see 2005 U.S. Code Cong. and Adm. News, p. 1636.

House Conference Report No. 109–333, see 2006 U.S. Code Cong. and Adm. News, p. 184.

Statement by President, see 2006 U.S. Code Cong. and Adm. News, p. S7.

References in Text

The Atomic Energy Act of 1954, referred to in par. (1)(a), is Act Aug. 1, 1946, c. 724, as added by Act Aug. 30, 1954, c. 1073, § 1, 68 Stat. 919, which is classified principally to chapter 23 of Title 42, 42 U.S.C.A. § 2011 et seq. For complete classification, see Short Title note set out under 42 U.S.C.A. § 2011 and Tables.

Chapters 10, 37, 55, 90, 105, 115, 102, 65, 111, and 81, referred to in par. (1)(a), are 18 U.S.C.A. §§ 175 et seq., 791 et seq., 1201 et seq., 1831 et seq., 2151 et seq., 2381 et seq., 2101 et seq., 1361 et seq., 2271 et seq., and 1651 et seq., respectively.

The Arms Export Control Act, referred to in par. (1)(k), is Pub.L. 90–629, Oct. 22, 1968, 82 Stat. 1320, as amended, which is classified generally to chapter 39 of Title 22, Foreign Relations and Intercourse (22 U.S.C.A. § 2751 et seq.). For complete classification of this Act to the Code, see Short Title note set out under 22 U.S.C.A. § 2751 and Tables.

Section 5861 of the Internal Revenue Code of 1986, referred to in par. (1)(o), is classified to 26 U.S.C.A. § 5861.

Sections 274, 277, and 278 of the Immigration and Nationality Act, referred to in par. (1)(m) and (p), are sections 274, 277, and 278 of Act June 27, 1952, c. 477, 66 Stat. 163, as amended, which are classified to 8 U.S.C.A. §§ 1324, 1327, and 1328.

Sections 1, 2, or 3 of the Sherman Act, referred to in par. (1)(r), are sections 1, 2, or 3, of Act July 2, 1890, c. 647, 26 Stat. 209, also known as the Sherman Anti-Trust Act, which are classified to 15 U.S.C.A. § 1, 2, or 3.

The Federal Rules of Criminal Procedure, referred to in par. (3), are set out in the Appendix to this title.

Codifications

Pub.L. 98–473, § 1203(c)(4), which directed the amendment of the first paragraph of par. (1) by inserting "Deputy Attorney General, Associate Attorney General," after "Attorney General." was executed by making the insertion after the first reference to "Attorney General," to reflect the probable intent of Congress.

Section 102 of Pub.L. 104–294, which directed that par. (1)(c) of this section be amended by inserting "chapter 90 (relating to protection of trade secrets)," following "chapter 37 (relating to espionage),", could not be executed to text, as par. (1)(c) does not contain phrase "chapter 37 (relating to espionage),".

Amendment to par. (1)(c) by section 1365(c) of Pub.L. 99–570 was executed by inserting "section 1956 (laundering of monetary instruments), section 1957 (relating to engaging in monetary transactions in property derived from specified unlawful activity)," after "section 1955 (prohibition of business enterprises of gambling)," as the probable intent of Congress.

Amendment by section 601(d)(1) of Pub.L. 104–294, which directed that "or" be struck out after the semicolon in par. (1)(l), could not be executed in view of prior identical amendment by section 201(2) of Pub.L. 104–208.

Amendment by section 601(d)(2) of Pub.L. 104–294, which directed that "or" be substituted for "and" following the semicolon in par. (1)(n), could not be executed as the word "and" does not appear at the end of par. (1)(n). See also 2002 Amendments notes set out under this section.

Effective and Applicability Provisions

2002 Acts. Amendment made by section 4002(c)(1) of Pub.L. 107–273, as therein provided, effective Oct. 11, 1996, which is the date of enactment of Pub.L. 104–294, to which such amendment relates.

2000 Acts. Amendment by Pub.L. 106–181 applicable only to fiscal years beginning after September 30, 1999, see section 3 of Pub.L. 106–181, set out as a note under section 106 of Title 49.

1996 Acts. Section 6(a) of Pub.L. 104–287 provided in part that amendment by such section 6(a), amending this section and section 6101 of Title 31, Money and Finance, was effective July 5, 1994.

1994 Acts. Section 7(a) of Pub.L. 103–429 provided in part that amendment of this section by section 7(a) of Pub.L. 103–429 is effective July 5, 1994.

Section 330011(c)(1) of Pub.L. 103–322 provided in part that the amendment made by such section, amending section 3(b) of Pub.L. 101–298, was to take effect on the date on which section 3(b) of Pub.L. 101–298 took effect [section 3(b) of Pub.L. 101–298 took effect on the date of enactment of Pub.L. 101–298, which was approved May 22, 1990].

Section 330011(q)(1) of Pub.L. 103–322 provided in part that the amendment made by such section, repealing section 3568 of Pub.L. 101–647, was to take effect on the date section 3568 of Pub.L. 101–647 took effect [section 3568 of Pub.L. 101–647 took effect on the date of enactment of Pub.L. 101–647, which was approved Nov. 29, 1990].

Section 330011(r) of Pub.L. 103–322 provided in part that the amendment made by such section, amending language of section 2531(3) of Pub.L. 101–647, was to take effect on the date section 2531(3) of Pub.L. 101–647 took effect [section 2531(3) of Pub.L. 101–647 took effect on the date of enactment of Pub.L. 101–647, which was approved Nov. 29, 1990].

1986 Acts. Amendment by sections 101(c)(1)(A) and 105 of Pub.L. 99–508 effective 90 days after Oct. 21, 1986, and, in case of conduct pursuant to court order or extension, applicable only with respect to court orders and extensions made after such date, with special rule for State authorizations of interceptions pursuant to section 2516(2) of this title, and amendment by section 104 of Pub.L. 99–508 effective Oct. 21, 1986, see section 111 of Pub.L. 99–508, set out as a note under 18 U.S.C.A. § 2510.

1978 Acts. Amendment by Pub.L. 95–598 effective Oct. 1, 1979, see section 402(a) of Pub.L. 95–598, set out as a note preceding section 101 of Title 11, Bankruptcy.

Sunset Provisions

Provision that amendments by Pub.L. 107–56, Title II, Oct. 26, 2001, 115 Stat. 278, with certain exclusions, shall cease to have effect on March 10, 2006, except with respect to any particular foreign intelligence investigation that began before that date, or with respect to any particular offense or potential offense that began or occurred before that, such provisions to continue in effect, was repealed by Pub.L. 109–177, § 102(a), see Pub.L. 107–56, § 224, as amended, set out as a note under 18 U.S.C.A. § 2510.

Repeals

Section 3568 of Pub.L. 101–647, which made an identical amendment to par. (1)(j) of this section as did section 2531(3) of Pub.L. 101–647, was repealed by section 330011(q)(1) of Pub.L. 103–322.

Paragraph (2) of section 601(d) of Pub.L. 104–294, cited in the credit of this section, was repealed by section 4002(c)(1) of Pub.L. 107–273, effective Oct. 11, 1996.

Savings Provisions

Amendment by section 314 of Pub.L. 95–598 not to affect the application of chapter 9 (18 U.S.C.A. § 151 et seq.), chapter 96 (18 U.S.C.A. § 1961 et seq.), or 18 U.S.C.A. § 2516, 3057, or 3284 to any act of any person (1) committed before Oct. 1, 1979, or (2) committed after Oct. 1, 1979, in connection with a case commenced before such date, see section 403(d) of Pub.L. 95–598, set out as a note preceding 11 U.S.C.A. § 101.

Severability of Provisions

If any provision of Division C of Pub.L. 104–208 or the application of such provision to any person or circumstances is held to be unconstitutional, the remainder of Division C of Pub.L. 104–208 and the application of the provisions of Division C of Pub.L. 104–208 to any person or circumstance not to be affected thereby, see section 1(e) of Pub.L. 104–208, set out as a note under section 1101 of Title 8, Aliens and Nationality.

References to Coupons, Authorization Cards, or Access Devices under Food and Nutrition Act of 2008

References in any Federal, State, tribal, or local law to a "coupon", "authorization card", or other access device provided under the Food and Nutrition Act of 2008, 7 U.S.C.A. § 2011 et seq., considered to be a reference to a "benefit" provided under that Act, see Pub.L. 110–234, § 4115(d), and Pub.L. 110–246, § 4115(d), set out as a note under 7 U.S.C.A. § 2012.

PART II—CRIMINAL PROCEDURE

CHAPTER 203—ARREST AND COMMITMENT

§ 3057. Bankruptcy investigations

(a) Any judge, receiver, or trustee having reasonable grounds for believing that any violation under chapter 9 of this title or other laws of the United States relating to insolvent debtors, receiverships or reorganization plans has been committed, or that an investigation should be had in connection therewith, shall report to the appropriate United States attorney all the facts and circumstances of the case, the names of the witnesses and the offense or offenses believed to have been committed. Where one of such officers has made such report, the others need not do so.

(b) The United States attorney thereupon shall inquire into the facts and report thereon to the judge, and if it appears probable that any such offense has been committed, shall without delay, present the matter to the grand jury, unless upon inquiry and examination he decides that the ends of public justice do not require investigation or prosecution, in which case he shall report the facts to the Attorney General for his direction.

(June 25, 1948, c. 645, 62 Stat. 818; May 24, 1949, c. 139, § 48, 63 Stat. 96; Pub.L. 95–598, Title III, § 314(i), Nov. 6, 1978, 92 Stat. 2677.)

HISTORICAL AND STATUTORY NOTES

Revision Notes and Legislative Reports

1948 Acts. Based on section 52(e)(1), (2) of Title 11, U.S.C., 1940 ed., Bankruptcy (July 1, 1898, c. 541, § 29e(1), (2), as added by May 27, 1926, c. 406, § 11, 44 Stat. 665, 666; June 22, 1938, c. 575, § 1, 52 Stat. 840, 856).

Remaining provisions of section 52 of Title 11, U.S.C., 1940 ed., Bankruptcy, constitute sections 151 to 154, and 3284 of this title.

The words "or laws relating to insolvent debtors, receiverships, or reorganization plans" were inserted to avoid reference to "Title 11".

Minor changes were made in phraseology.

1949 Acts. This section [section 48] clarifies the meaning of section 3057 of Title 18, U.S.C., by expressly limiting to laws "of the United States", violations of laws which are to be reported to the United States attorney.

Senate Report No. 303 and House Report No. 352, see 1949 U.S. Code Cong. Service, p. 1248.

1978 Acts. Senate Report No. 95–989 and House Report No. 95–595, see 1978 U.S. Code Cong. and Adm. News, p. 5787.

Effective and Applicability Provisions

1978 Acts. Amendment by Pub.L. 95–598 effective Oct. 1, 1979, see section 402(a) of Pub.L. 95–598, set out as an Effective Dates note preceding section 101 of Title 11, Bankruptcy.

Savings Provisions of Pub.L. 95–598

Amendment by Pub.L. 95–598 not to affect the application of chapter 9 (18 U.S.C.A. § 151 et seq.), chapter 96 (18 U.S.C.A. § 1961 et seq.), or 18 U.S.C.A. §§ 2516, 3057, or 3284 to any act of any person (1) committed before Oct. 1, 1979, or (2) committed after Oct. 1, 1979, in connection with a case commenced before such date, see section 403(d) of Pub.L. 95–598, set out as a note preceding 11 U.S.C.A. § 101.

Transfer of Functions

All functions of all other officers of the Department of Justice and all functions of all agencies and employees of such Department were, with a few exceptions, transferred to the Attorney General, with power vested in him to authorize their performance or the performance of any of his functions by any of such officers, agencies, and employees, by Reorg. Plan No. 2, of 1950, §§ 1, 2, eff. May 24, 1950, 15 F.R. 3173, 64 Stat. 1261, set out in Appendix 1 to Title 5, Government Organization and Employees.

CHAPTER 213—LIMITATIONS

§ 3284. Concealment of bankrupt's assets

The concealment of assets of a debtor in a case under title 11 shall be deemed to be a continuing offense until the debtor shall have been finally discharged or a discharge denied, and the period of limitations shall not begin to run until such final discharge or denial of discharge.

(June 25, 1948, c. 645, 62 Stat. 828; Pub.L. 95–598, Title III, § 314(k), Nov. 6, 1978, 92 Stat. 2678.)

HISTORICAL AND STATUTORY NOTES

Revision Notes and Legislative Reports

1948 Acts. Based on section 52(d) of Title 11, U.S.C., 1940 ed., Bankruptcy (May 27, 1926, c. 406, § 11(d), 44 Stat. 665; June 22, 1938, c. 575, § 1, 52 Stat. 856).

The 3-year-limitation provision was omitted as unnecessary in view of the general statute, section 3282 of this title.

The words "or a discharge denied" and "or denial of discharge" were added on the recommendation of the Department of Justice to supply an omission in existing law.

Other subsections of said section 52 of Title 11, U.S.C., 1940 ed., are incorporated in sections 151–154 and 3057 of this title.

Other minor changes of phraseology were made.

1978 Acts. Senate Report No. 95–989 and House Report No. 95–595, see 1978 U.S. Code Cong. and Adm. News, p. 5787.

Effective and Applicability Provisions

1978 Acts. Amendment by Pub.L. 95–598 effective Oct. 1, 1979, see section 402(a) of Pub.L. 95–598, set out as an Effective Date note preceding section 101 of Title 11, Bankruptcy.

Savings Provisions

Amendment by section 314 of Pub.L. 95–598 not to affect the application of this section to any act of any person (1) committed before Oct. 1, 1979, or (2) committed after Oct. 1, 1979, in connection with a case commenced before such date, see section 403(d) of Pub.L. 95–598, set out preceding section 101 of Title 11, Bankruptcy.

CROSS REFERENCES

Bankruptcy investigations, see 18 USCA § 3057.

Five-year limitation on offenses relating to bankruptcy, see 18 USCA § 3282.

Offenses relating to bankruptcy, see 18 USCA § 151 et seq.

TITLE 28

JUDICIARY AND JUDICIAL PROCEDURE

PART I—ORGANIZATION OF COURTS

CHAPTER 6—BANKRUPTCY JUDGES

[1] So in original. Does not conform to section catchline.

Effective and Applicability Provisions

2005 Acts. Amendments by Pub.L. 109–8, Title VI, § 601, effective 18 months after Apr. 20, 2005, see Pub.L. 109–8, § 601(c), set out as a note under 28 U.S.C.A. § 159.

Except as otherwise provided, amendments by Pub.L. 109–8 effective 180 days after April 20, 2005, and inapplicable with respect to cases commenced under Title 11 before the effective date, see Pub.L. 109–8, § 1501, set out as a note under 11 U.S.C.A. § 101.

§ 151. Designation of bankruptcy courts

In each judicial district, the bankruptcy judges in regular active service shall constitute a unit of the district court to be known as the bankruptcy court for that district. Each bankruptcy judge, as a judicial officer of the district court, may exercise the authority conferred under this chapter with respect to any action, suit, or proceeding and may preside alone and hold a regular or special session of the court, except as otherwise provided by law or by rule or order of the district court.

(Added Pub.L. 98–353, Title I, § 104(a), July 10, 1984, 98 Stat. 336.)

HISTORICAL AND STATUTORY NOTES

Revision Notes and Legislative Reports

1984 Acts. Statements by Legislative Leaders, see 1984 U.S.Code Cong. and Adm.News, p. 576.

Codifications

This section as added by Pub.L. 95–598, Title II, § 201(a), Nov. 6, 1978, 92 Stat. 2657, effective June 28, 1984, pursuant to Pub.L. 95–598, Title IV, § 402(b), Nov. 6, 1978, 92 Stat. 2682, as amended by Pub.L. 98–249, § 1(a), Mar. 31, 1984, 98 Stat. 116; Pub.L. 98–271, § 1(a), Apr. 30, 1984, 98 Stat. 163; Pub.L. 98–299, § 1(a), May 25, 1984, 98 Stat. 214; Pub.L. 98–325, § 1(a), June 20, 1984, 98 Stat. 268, set out as a note preceding section 101 of Title 11, Bankruptcy, read as follows:

§ 151. Creation and composition of bankruptcy courts

(a) There shall be in each judicial district, as an adjunct to the district court for such district, a bankruptcy court which shall be a court of record known as the United States Bankruptcy Court for the district.

(b) Each bankruptcy court shall consist of the bankruptcy judge or judges for the district in regular active service. Justices or judges designated and assigned shall be competent to sit as judges of the bankruptcy court.

(c) Except as otherwise provided by law, or rule or order of court, the judicial power of a bankruptcy court with respect to any action, suit or proceeding may be exercised by a single bankruptcy judge, who may preside alone and hold a regular or special session of court at the same time other sessions are held by other bankruptcy judges.

Section 402(b) of Pub.L. 95–598 was amended by section 113 of Pub.L. 98–353 by substituting "shall not be effective" for "shall take effect on June 28, 1984", thereby eliminating the addition of section 151 by section 201(a) of Pub.L. 95–598, effective June 27, 1984, pursuant to section 122(c) of Pub.L. 98–353, set out as an Effective and Applicability Provisions note under this section.

Section 121(a) of Pub.L. 98–353 directed that section 402(b) of Pub.L. 95–598 be amended by substituting "the date of enactment of the Bankruptcy Amendments and Federal Judgeship Act of 1984 [i.e. July 10, 1984]" for "June 28, 1984". This amendment was not executed in view of the prior amendment to section 402(b) of Pub.L. 95–598 by section 113 of Pub.L. 98–353.

Effective and Applicability Provisions

1984 Acts. Section 122 of Title I of Pub.L. 98–353 provided that:

"(a) Except as otherwise provided in this section, this title and the amendments made by this title [Title I of Pub.L. 98–353, enacting this chapter, and sections 1408 to 1412 and 1452 of this title, amending sections 372, 634, 957, 1334, 1360, and 1930 of this title, sections 8331, 8334, 8336, 8339, 8341, and 8344 of Title 5, Government Organization and Employees, and section 105 of Title 11, Bankruptcy, enacting provisions set out as notes preceding section 151 of this title and under sections 151, 152, 153, 634, and 1334 of this title and section 8331 of Title 5, amending provisions set out as notes preceding sections 151 and 1471 of this title and section 101 of Title 11, and repealing provisions set out as notes preceding this section and section 1471 of this title] shall take effect on the date of the enactment of this Act [July 10, 1984].

"(b) Section 1334(c)(2) of title 28, United States Code [section 1334(c)(2) of this title], and section 1411(a) of title 28, United States Code, as added by this Act [section 1411(a) of this title], shall not apply with respect to cases under title 11 of the United States Code [Title 11] that are pending on the date of enactment of this Act [July 10, 1984], or to proceedings arising in or related to such cases.

"**(c)** Sections 108(b) [enacting provisions set out as a note under section 634 of this title], 113 [amending section 402(b) of Pub.L. 95–598, set out as a note preceding section 101 of Title 11], and 121(e) [enacting provisions set out as a note preceding section 151 of this title] shall take effect on June 27, 1984."

Separability of Provisions

Section 119 of Pub.L. 98–353 provided that: "If any provision of this Act [see Short Title of 1984 Amendments note set out under this section] or the application thereof to any person or circumstance is held invalid, the remainder of this Act, or the application of that provision to persons or circumstances other than those as to which it is held invalid, is not affected thereby."

Short Title

1984 Amendments. Section 1 of Pub.L. 98–353 provided: That this Act [enacting this chapter and sections 1408 to 1412 and 1452 of this title and sections 557, 558, 559, and 1113 of Title 11, Bankruptcy, amending sections 44, 98, 131, 133, 371, 372, 634, 957, 1334, 1360, and 1930 of this title, sections 8331, 8334, 8336, 8339, 8341, 8344, 8701, 8706, 8714a, and 8714b of Title 5, Government Organization and Employees, and sections 101, 102, 103, 105, 108, 109, 303, 321, 322, 326, 327, 328, 329, 330, 342, 343, 345, 346, 349, 350, 361, 362, 363, 365, 366, 501, 502, 503, 505, 506, 507, 509, 510, 521, 522, 523, 524, 525, 541, 542, 543, 544, 545, 546, 547, 548, 549, 550, 552, 553, 554, 555, 702, 703, 704, 707, 723, 724, 725, 726, 727, 728, 741, 745, 752, 761, 763, 764, 765, 766, 901, 902, 903, 921, 922, 927, 943, 945, 1102, 1103, 1105, 1106, 1107, 1108, 1112, 1121, 1123, 1124, 1125, 1126, 1127, 1129, 1141, 1142, 1144, 1145, 1146, 1166, 1168, 1169, 1170, 1171, 1173, 1301, 1302, 1304, 1307, 1322, 1324, 1325, 1326, 1328, 1329, 15103, and 151302 of Title 11, Bankruptcy Rules 2002 and 3001, Title 11, and Bankruptcy Form No. 1, Title 11, enacting provisions set out as notes preceding section 151 of this title and under sections 44, 133, 151, 152, 153, 371, 634, 1334, and 2075 of this title, sections 8331 and 8706 of Title 5, and preceding section 101 and sections 101, 365, and 1113 of Title 11, amending provisions set out as notes preceding sections 151, 581 and 1471 of this title and section 101 of Title 11, and repealing provisions set out as notes preceding this section and section 1471 of this title] may be cited as the 'Bankruptcy Amendments and Federal Judgeship Act of 1984'."

§ 152.   Appointment of bankruptcy judges

(a)(1) Each bankruptcy judge to be appointed for a judicial district, as provided in paragraph (2), shall be appointed by the court of appeals of the United States for the circuit in which such district is located. Such appointments shall be made after considering the recommendations of the Judicial Conference submitted pursuant to subsection (b). Each bankruptcy judge shall be appointed for a term of fourteen years, subject to the provisions of subsection (e). However, upon the expiration of the term, a bankruptcy judge may, with the approval of the judicial council of the circuit, continue to perform the duties of the office until the earlier of the date which is 180 days after the expiration of the term or the date of the appointment of a successor. Bankruptcy judges shall serve as judicial officers of the United States district court established under Article III of the Constitution.

(2) The bankruptcy judges appointed pursuant to this section shall be appointed for the several judicial districts as follows:

Districts	Judges
Alabama:	
Northern	5
Middle	2
Southern	2
Alaska	2
Arizona	7
Arkansas:	
Eastern and Western	3
California:	
Northern	9
Eastern	6
Central	21
Southern	4
Colorado	5
Connecticut	3
Delaware	1
District of Columbia	1
Florida:	
Northern	1
Middle	8
Southern	5
Georgia:	
Northern	8
Middle	3
Southern	2
Hawaii	1
Idaho	2
Illinois:	
Northern	10
Central	3
Southern	1
Indiana:	
Northern	3
Southern	4
Iowa:	
Northern	2
Southern	2
Kansas	4
Kentucky:	
Eastern	2
Western	3
Louisiana:	
Eastern	2
Middle	1
Western	3
Maine	2
Maryland	4
Massachusetts	5
Michigan:	

Districts	Judges
Eastern	4
Western	3
Minnesota	4
Mississippi:	
Northern	1
Southern	2
Missouri:	
Eastern	3
Western	3
Montana	1
Nebraska	2
Nevada	3
New Hampshire	1
New Jersey	8
New Mexico	2
New York:	
Northern	2
Southern	9
Eastern	6
Western	3
North Carolina:	
Eastern	2
Middle	2
Western	2
North Dakota	1
Ohio:	
Northern	8
Southern	7
Oklahoma:	
Northern	2
Eastern	1
Western	3
Oregon	5

Districts	Judges
Pennsylvania:	
Eastern	5
Middle	2
Western	4
Puerto Rico	2
Rhode Island	1
South Carolina	2
South Dakota	2
Tennessee:	
Eastern	3
Middle	3
Western	4
Texas:	
Northern	6
Eastern	2
Southern	6
Western	4
Utah	3
Vermont	1
Virginia:	
Eastern	5
Western	3
Washington:	
Eastern	2
Western	5
West Virginia:	
Northern	1
Southern	1
Wisconsin:	
Eastern	4
Western	2
Wyoming	1

(3) Whenever a majority of the judges of any court of appeals cannot agree upon the appointment of a bankruptcy judge, the chief judge of such court shall make such appointment.

(4) The judges of the district courts for the territories shall serve as the bankruptcy judges for such courts. The United States court of appeals for the circuit within which such a territorial district court is located may appoint bankruptcy judges under this chapter for such district if authorized to do so by the Congress of the United States under this section.

(b)(1) The Judicial Conference of the United States shall, from time to time, and after considering the recommendations submitted by the Director of the Administrative Office of the United States Courts after such Director has consulted with the judicial council of the circuit involved, determine the official duty stations of bankruptcy judges and places of holding court.

(2) The Judicial Conference shall, from time to time, submit recommendations to the Congress regarding the number of bankruptcy judges needed and the districts in which such judges are needed.

(3) Not later than December 31, 1994, and not later than the end of each 2–year period thereafter, the Judicial Conference of the United States shall conduct a comprehensive review of all judicial districts to assess the continuing need for the bankruptcy judges authorized by this section, and shall report to the Congress its findings and any recommendations for the elimination of any authorized position which can be eliminated when a vacancy exists by reason of resignation, retirement, removal, or death.

(c)(1) Each bankruptcy judge may hold court at such places within the judicial district, in addition to the official duty station of such judge, as the business of the court may require.

(2)(A) Bankruptcy judges may hold court at such places within the United States outside the judicial district as the nature of the business of the court may require, and upon such notice as the court orders, upon a finding by either the chief judge of the bankruptcy court (or, if the chief judge is unavailable, the most senior available bankruptcy judge) or by the judicial council of the circuit that, because of emergency conditions, no location within the district is reasonably available where the bankruptcy judges could hold court.

(B) Bankruptcy judges may transact any business at special sessions of court held outside the district pursuant to this paragraph that might be transacted at a regular session.

(C) If a bankruptcy court issues an order exercising its authority under subparagraph (A), the court—

(i) through the Administrative Office of the United States Courts, shall—

(I) send notice of such order, including the reasons for the issuance of such order, to the Committee on the Judiciary of the Senate and the Committee on the Judiciary of the House of Representatives; and

(II) not later than 180 days after the expiration of such court order submit a brief report to the Committee on the Judiciary of the Senate and the Committee on the Judiciary of the House of Representatives describing the impact of such order, including—

(aa) the reasons for the issuance of such order;

(bb) the duration of such order;

(cc) the impact of such order on litigants; and

(dd) the costs to the judiciary resulting from such order; and

(ii) shall provide reasonable notice to the United States Marshals Service before the commencement of any special session held pursuant to such order.

(d) With the approval of the Judicial Conference and of each of the judicial councils involved, a bankruptcy judge may be designated to serve in any district adjacent to or near the district for which such bankruptcy judge was appointed.

(e) A bankruptcy judge may be removed during the term for which such bankruptcy judge is appointed, only for incompetence, misconduct, neglect of duty, or physical or mental disability and only by the judicial council of the circuit in which the judge's official duty station is located. Removal may not occur unless a majority of all of the judges of such council concur in the order of removal. Before any order of removal may be entered, a full specification of charges shall be furnished to such bankruptcy judge who shall be accorded an opportunity to be heard on such charges.

(Added Pub.L. 98–353, Title I, § 104(a), July 10, 1984, 98 Stat. 336; amended Pub.L. 99–554, Title I, § 101, Oct. 27, 1986, 100 Stat. 3088; Pub.L. 100–587, Nov. 3, 1988, 102 Stat. 2982; Pub.L. 101–650, Title III, § 304, Dec. 1, 1990, 104 Stat. 5105; Pub.L. 102–361, §§ 2, 4, Aug. 26, 1992, 106 Stat. 965, 966; Pub.L. 109–8, Title XII, § 1223(d), Apr. 20, 2005, 119 Stat. 198; Pub.L. 109–63, § 2(c), Sept. 9, 2005, 119 Stat. 1994.)

HISTORICAL AND STATUTORY NOTES

Revision Notes and Legislative Reports

1984 Acts. Statements by Legislative Leaders, see 1984 U.S. Code Cong. and Adm. News, p. 576.

1986 Acts. House Report No. 99–764 and House Conference Report No. 99–958, see 1986 U.S. Code Cong. and Adm. News, p. 5227.

1988 Acts. House Report No. 100–756, see 1988 U.S. Code Cong. and Adm. News, p. 3979.

1990 Acts. Senate Report No. 101–416, Related House Reports, and Statement by President, see 1990 U.S. Code Cong. and Adm. News, p. 6802.

1992 Acts. House Report No. 102–825, see 1992 U.S. Code Cong. and Adm. News, p. 855.

2005 Acts. House Report No. 109–31(Part I), see 2005 U.S. Code Cong. and Adm. News, p. 88.

Codifications

This section as added by Pub.L. 95–598, Title II, § 201(a), Nov. 6, 1978, 92 Stat. 2657, effective June 28, 1984, pursuant to Pub.L. 95–598, Title IV, § 402(b), Nov. 6, 1978, 92 Stat. 2682, as amended by Pub.L. 98–249, § 1(a), Mar. 31, 1984, 98 Stat. 116; Pub.L. 98–271, § 1(a), Apr. 30, 1984, 98 Stat. 163; Pub.L. 98–299, § 1(a), May 25, 1984, 98 Stat. 214; Pub.L. 98–325, § 1(a), June 20, 1984, 98 Stat. 268, set out as a note preceding section 101 of Title 11, Bankruptcy, read as follows:

"**§ 152. Appointment of bankruptcy judges**

"The President shall appoint, by and with the advice and consent of the Senate, bankruptcy judges for the several judicial districts. In each instance, the President shall give due consideration to the recommended nominee or nominees of the Judicial Council of the Circuit within which an appointment is to be made."

Section 402(b) of Pub.L. 95–598 was amended by section 113 of Pub.L. 98–353 by substituting "shall not be effective" for "shall take effect on June 28, 1984", thereby eliminating the addition of section 152 by section 201(a) of Pub.L. 95–598, effective June 27, 1984, pursuant to section 122(c) of Pub.L. 98–353, set out as an Effective and Applicability Provisions note under 28 U.S.C.A. § 151.

Section 121(a) of Pub.L. 98–353 directed that section 402(b) of Pub.L. 95–598 be amended by substituting "the date of enactment of the Bankruptcy Amendments and Federal Judgeship Act of 1984 [i.e. July 10, 1984]" for "June 28, 1984". This amendment was not executed in view of the prior amendment to section 402(b) of Pub.L. 95–598 by section 113 of Pub.L. 98–353.

Effective and Applicability Provisions

2005 Acts. Pub.L. 109–8, Title XII, § 1223(e), Apr. 20, 2005, 119 Stat. 198, provided that: "The amendments made by this section [amending this section and enacting provisions set out as notes under this section and 28 U.S.C.A. § 1] shall take effect on the date of the enactment of this Act [Apr. 20, 2005]."

Except as otherwise provided, amendments by Pub.L. 109–8 effective 180 days after April 20, 2005, and inapplicable with respect to cases commenced under Title 11 before the effective date, see Pub.L. 109–8, § 1501, set out as a note under 11 U.S.C.A. § 101.

1986 Acts. Amendment by Pub.L. 99–554 effective on Oct. 27, 1986, see section 302(b) of Pub.L. 99–554, set out as a note under section 581 of this title.

1984 Acts. Section effective July 10, 1984, see section 122(a) of Pub.L. 98–353, set out as a note under section 151 of this title.

Termination of Reporting Requirements

For termination of reporting provisions of subsec. (b)(2) of this section, effective May 15, 2000, see Pub.L. 104–66, § 3003, as amended, set out as a note under 31 U.S.C.A. § 1113, and the 16th item on page 12 of House Document No. 103–7.

Extension of Temporary Office of Bankruptcy Judges in Certain Judicial Districts

Pub.L. 115–72, Div. B, § 1002, Oct. 26, 2017, 131 Stat. 1229, provided that:

"**(a) Temporary office of bankruptcy judges authorized by the Bankruptcy Judgeship Act of 2005.—**

"**(1) Extensions.—**The temporary office of bankruptcy judges authorized for the following districts by subsection (b) of the Bankruptcy Judgeship Act of 2005 (28 U.S.C. 152 note) [Pub.L. 109-8, Title XII, § 1223(b), Apr. 20, 1005, 119 Stat. 196, set out as a note under this section] are extended until the applicable vacancy specified in paragraph (2) in the office of a bankruptcy judge for the respective district occurs:

"**(A)** The district of Delaware.

"**(B)** The southern district of Florida.

"**(C)** The district of Maryland.

"**(D)** The eastern district of Michigan.

"**(E)** The district of Nevada.

"**(F)** The eastern district of North Carolina.

"**(G)** The district of Puerto Rico.

"**(H)** The eastern district of Virginia.

"**(2) Vacancies.—**

"**(A) Single vacancies.—**Except as provided in subparagraphs (B), (C), and (D), the 1st vacancy in the office of a bankruptcy judge for each district specified in paragraph (1)—

"**(i)** occurring more than 5 years after the date of the enactment of this Act [Oct. 26, 2017]; and

"**(ii)** resulting from the death, retirement, resignation, or removal of a bankruptcy judge,

"shall not be filled.

"**(B) District of Delaware.—**The 1st, 2d, 3d, and 4th vacancies in the office of a bankruptcy judge for the district of Delaware—

"**(i)** occurring 5 years or more after the date of the enactment of this Act [Oct. 26, 2017]; and

"**(ii)** resulting from the death, retirement, resignation, or removal of a bankruptcy judge,

"shall not be filled.

"**(C) District of Maryland.—**

"**(i)** The 1st vacancy in the office of a bankruptcy judge for the district of Maryland—

"**(I)** occurring more than 5 years after the date of the enactment of this Act [Oct. 26, 2017]; and

"**(II)** resulting from the death, retirement, resignation, or removal of a bankruptcy judge,

"shall not be filled.

"**(ii)** The 2d and 3d vacancies in the office of a bankruptcy judge for the district of Maryland resulting from the death, retirement, resignation, or removal of a bankruptcy judge, shall not be filled.

"**(D) Southern district of Florida.—**The 1st and 2d vacancies in the office of a bankruptcy judge for the southern district of Florida—

"**(i)** occurring more than 5 years after the date of the enactment of this Act [Oct. 26, 2017]; and

"**(ii)** resulting from the death, retirement, resignation, or removal of a bankruptcy judge,

"shall not be filled.

"**(3) Applicability of provisions.—**Except as provided in paragraphs (1) and (2), all other provisions of subsection (b) of the Bankruptcy Judgeship Act of 2005 (28 U.S.C. 152 note) [Pub.L. 109-8, Title XII, § 1223(b), Apr. 20, 1005, 119 Stat. 196, set out as a note under this section] and section 2 of the Temporary Bankruptcy Judgeships Extension Act of 2012 (28 U.S.C. 152 note) [Pub.L. 112-121, § 2, May 25, 2012, 126 Stat. 346, set out as a note under this section] remain applicable to the temporary office of bankruptcy judges referred to in paragraph (1).

"**(b) Temporary office of bankruptcy judges extended by the Bankruptcy Judgeship Act of 2005 and the Temporary Bankruptcy Judgeships Extension Act of 2012.—**

"**(1) Extensions.—**The temporary office of bankruptcy judges authorized by section 3 of the Bankruptcy Judgeship Act of 1992 (28 U.S.C. 152 note) [Pub.L. 102-361, § 3, Aug. 26, 1992, 106 Stat. 965, set out as a note under this section] and extended by subsection (c) of the Bankruptcy Judgeship Act of 2005 (28 U.S.C. 152 note) [Pub.L. 109-8, Title XII, § 1223(c), Apr. 20, 1005, 119 Stat. 198, set out as a note under this section] and further extended by section 2 of the Temporary Bankruptcy Judgeships Extension Act of 2012 (28 U.S.C. 152 note) [Pub.L. 112-121, § 2, May 25, 2012, 126 Stat. 346, set out as a note under this section] for the district of Delaware and the district of Puerto Rico are extended until the applicable vacancy specified in paragraph (2) in the office of a bankruptcy judge for the respective district occurs.

"**(2) Vacancies.—**

"**(A) District of Delaware.—**The 5th vacancy in the office of a bankruptcy judge for the district of Delaware—

"**(i)** occurring more than 5 years after the date of the enactment of this Act [Oct. 26, 2017]; and

"**(ii)** resulting from the death, retirement, resignation, or removal of a bankruptcy judge,

"shall not be filled.

"**(B) District of Puerto Rico.—**The 2d vacancy in the office of a bankruptcy judge for the district of Puerto Rico—

"**(i)** occurring more than 5 years after the date of the enactment of this Act [Oct. 26, 2017]; and

"**(ii)** resulting from the death, retirement, resignation, or removal of a bankruptcy judge,

"shall not be filled.

"**(3) Applicability of other provisions.—**Except as provided in paragraphs (1) and (2), all other provisions of section 3 of the Bankruptcy Judgeship Act of 1992 (28 U.S.C. 152 note) [Pub.L. 102-361, § 3, Aug. 26, 1992, 106 Stat. 965, set out as a note under this section], subsection

(c) of the Bankruptcy Judgeship Act of 2005 (28 U.S.C. 152 note) [Pub.L. 109-8, Title XII, § 1223(c), Apr. 20, 1005, 119 Stat. 198, set out as a note under this section], and section 2 of the Temporary Bankruptcy Judgeships Extension Act of 2012 (28 U.S.C. 152 note) [Pub.L. 112-121, § 2, May 25, 2012, 126 Stat. 346, set out as a note under this section] remain applicable to the temporary office of bankruptcy judges referred to in paragraph (1)."

Temporary Office of Bankruptcy Judge Authorized

Pub.L. 115–72, Div. B, § 1003, Oct. 26, 2017, 131 Stat. 1231, provided that:

"(a) **Appointments.**—The following bankruptcy judges shall be appointed in the manner prescribed in section 152(a)(1) of title 28, United States Code, for the appointment of bankruptcy judges provided for in section 152(a)(2) of that title:

"(1) Two additional bankruptcy judges for the district of Delaware.

"(2) One additional bankruptcy judge for the middle district of Florida.

"(3) One additional bankruptcy judge for the eastern district of Michigan.

"(b) **Vacancies.—**

"(1) **District of Delaware.**—The 6th and 7th vacancies in the office of a bankruptcy judge for the district of Delaware—

"(A) occurring 5 years or more after the appointment date of the bankruptcy judge appointed under subsection (a)(1) to such office; and

"(B) resulting from the death, retirement, resignation, or removal of a bankruptcy judge,

"shall not be filled.

"(2) **Middle district of Florida.**—The 1st vacancy in the office of a bankruptcy judge for the middle district of Florida—

"(A) occurring 5 years or more after the appointment date of the bankruptcy judge appointed under subsection (a)(2) to such office; and

"(B) resulting from the death, retirement, resignation, or removal of a bankruptcy judge,

"shall not be filled.

"(3) **Eastern district of Michigan.**—The 2d vacancy in the office of a bankruptcy judge for the eastern district of Michigan—

"(A) occurring 5 years or more after the appointment date of the bankruptcy judge appointed under subsection (a)(3) to such office; and

"(B) resulting from the death, retirement, resignation, or removal of a bankruptcy judge,

"shall not be filled."

Temporary Appointment of Additional Judges

Pub.L. 112–121, § 2, May 25, 2012, 126 Stat. 346, as amended Pub.L. 115–31, Div. E, Title III, § 307, May 5, 2017, 131 Stat. 347, provided that:

"(a) **Temporary office of bankruptcy judges authorized by Public Law 109-8.—**

"(1) **Extensions.**—The temporary office of bankruptcy judges authorized for the following districts by section 1223(b) of Public Law 109-8 (28 U.S.C. 152 note [Pub.L. 109-8, § 1223(b), set out in a note under this heading]) are extended until the applicable vacancy specified in para-

graph (2) in the office of a bankruptcy judge for the respective district occurs:

"(A) The central district of California.

"(B) The eastern district of California.

"(C) The district of Delaware.

"(D) The southern district of Florida.

"(E) The southern district of Georgia.

"(F) The district of Maryland.

"(G) The eastern district of Michigan.

"(H) The district of New Jersey.

"(I) The northern district of New York.

"(J) The eastern district of North Carolina.

"(K) The eastern district of Pennsylvania.

"(L) The middle district of Pennsylvania.

"(M) The district of Puerto Rico.

"(N) The district of South Carolina.

"(O) The western district of Tennessee.

"(P) The eastern district of Virginia.

"(Q) The district of Nevada.

"(2) **Vacancies.—**

"(A) **Single vacancies.**—Except as provided in subparagraphs (B), (C), (D), (E), (F), (G), and (H), the 1st vacancy in the office of a bankruptcy judge for each district specified in paragraph (1)—

"(i) occurring more than 5 years after the date of the enactment of this Act [May 25, 2012], and

"(ii) resulting from the death, retirement, resignation, or removal of a bankruptcy judge,

"shall not be filled.

"(B) **Central district of California.**—The 1st, 2d, and 3d vacancies in the office of a bankruptcy judge for the central district of California—

"(i) occurring 5 years or more after the date of the enactment of this Act [May 25, 2012], and

"(ii) resulting from the death, retirement, resignation, or removal of a bankruptcy judge,

"shall not be filled.

"(C) **District of Delaware.**—The 1st, 2d, 3d, and 4th vacancies in the office of a bankruptcy judge for the district of Delaware—

"(i) in the case of the 1st and 2d vacancies, occurring more than 6 years after the date of the enactment of this Act [May 25, 2012],

"(ii) in the case of the 3d and 4th vacancies, occurring more than 5 years after the date of the enactment of this Act [May 25, 2012], and

"(iii) resulting from the death, retirement, resignation, or removal of a bankruptcy judge,

"shall not be filled.

"(D) **Southern district of Florida.**—The 1st and 2d vacancies in the office of a bankruptcy judge for the southern district of Florida—

"(i) occurring more than 6 years after the date of the enactment of this Act [May 25, 2012], and

"(ii) resulting from the death, retirement, resignation, or removal of a bankruptcy judge,

"shall not be filled.

"**(E) District of Maryland.**—The 1st, 2d, and 3d vacancies in the office of a bankruptcy judge for the district of Maryland—

"**(i)** occurring more than 5 years after the date of the enactment of this Act [May 25, 2012], and

"**(ii)** resulting from the death, retirement, resignation, or removal of a bankruptcy judge,

"shall not be filled.

"**(F) Eastern district of Michigan.**—The 1st vacancy in the office of a bankruptcy judge for the eastern district of Michigan—

"**(i)** occurring 6 years or more after the date of the enactment of this Act [May 25, 2012], and

"**(ii)** resulting from the death, retirement, resignation, or removal of a bankruptcy judge, shall not be filled.

"**(G) District of Puerto Rico.**—The 1st vacancy in the office of a bankruptcy judge for the district of Puerto Rico—

"**(i)** occurring 6 years or more after the date of the enactment of this Act [May 25, 2012], and

"**(ii)** resulting from the death, retirement, resignation, or removal of a bankruptcy judge, shall not be filled.

"**(H) Eastern district of Virginia.**—The 1st vacancy in the office of a bankruptcy judge for the eastern district of Virginia—

"**(i)** occurring 6 years or more after the date of the enactment of this Act [May 25, 2012], and

"**(ii)** resulting from the death, retirement, resignation, or removal of a bankruptcy judge, shall not be filled.

"**(3) Applicability of other provisions.**—Except as provided in paragraphs (1) and (2), all other provisions of section 1223(b) of Public Law 109–8 (28 U.S.C. 152 note [Pub.L. 109–8, § 1223(b), set out in a note under this heading]) remain applicable to the temporary office of bankruptcy judges referred to in paragraph (1).

"**(b) Temporary office of bankruptcy judges extended by Public Law 109–8.**—

"**(1) Extensions.**—The temporary office of bankruptcy judges authorized by section 3 of the Bankruptcy Judgeship Act of 1992 (28 U.S.C. 152 note) and extended by section 1223(c) of Public Law 109–8 (28 U.S.C. 152 note [Pub.L. 109–8, § 1223(c), set out in a note under this heading]) for the district of Delaware, the district of Puerto Rico, and the eastern district of Tennessee are extended until the applicable vacancy specified in paragraph (2) in the office of a bankruptcy judge for the respective district occurs.

"**(2) Vacancies.**—

"**(A) District of Delaware.**—The 5th vacancy in the office of a bankruptcy judge for the district of Delaware—

"**(i)** occurring more than 5 years after the date of the enactment of this Act [May 25, 2012], and

"**(ii)** resulting from the death, retirement, resignation, or removal of a bankruptcy judge,

"shall not be filled.

"**(B) District of Puerto Rico.**—The 2d vacancy in the office of a bankruptcy judge for the district of Puerto Rico—

"**(i)** occurring more than 5 years after the date of the enactment of this Act [May 25, 2012], and

"**(ii)** resulting from the death, retirement, resignation, or removal of a bankruptcy judge,

"shall not be filled.

"**(C) Eastern district of Tennessee.**—The 1st vacancy in the office of a bankruptcy judge for the eastern district of Tennessee—

"**(i)** occurring more than 5 years after the date of the enactment of this Act [May 25, 2012], and

"**(ii)** resulting from the death, retirement, resignation, or removal of a bankruptcy judge,

"shall not be filled.

"**(3) Applicability of other provisions.**—Except as provided in paragraphs (1) and (2), all other provisions of section 3 of the Bankruptcy Judgeship Act of 1992 (28 U.S.C. 152 note [Pub.L. 102–361, § 3, set out as a note under this heading]) and section 1223(c) of Public Law 109–8 (28 U.S.C. 152 note [Pub.L. 109–8, § 1223(c), set out in a note under this heading]) remain applicable to the temporary office of bankruptcy judges referred to in paragraph (1).

"**(c) Temporary office of the bankruptcy judge authorized by Public Law 102–361 for the middle district of North Carolina.**—

"**(1) Extension.**—The temporary office of the bankruptcy judge authorized by section 3 of the Bankruptcy Judgeship Act of 1992 (28 U.S.C. 152 note [Pub.L. 102–361, § 3, set out as a note under this heading]) for the middle district of North Carolina is extended until the vacancy specified in paragraph (2) occurs.

"**(2) Vacancy.**—The 1st vacancy in the office of a bankruptcy judge for the middle district of North Carolina—

"**(A)** occurring more than 5 years after the date of the enactment of this Act [May 25, 2012], and

"**(B)** resulting from the death, retirement, resignation, or removal of a bankruptcy judge,

"shall not be filled.

"**(3) Applicability of other provisions.**—Except as provided in paragraphs (1) and (2), all other provisions of section 3 of the Bankruptcy Judgeship Act of 1992 (28 U.S.C. 152 note [Pub.L. 102–361, § 3, set out as a note under this heading]) remain applicable to the temporary office of the bankruptcy judge referred to in paragraph (1)."

Pub.L. 109–8, Title XII, § 1223(b), (c), Apr. 20, 2005, 119 Stat. 196, 198, provided that:

"**(b) Temporary Judgeships.**—

"**(1) Appointments.**—The following bankruptcy judges shall be appointed in the manner prescribed in section 152(a)(1) of title 28, United States Code, for the appointment of bankruptcy judges provided for in section 152(a)(2) of such title:

"**(A)** One additional bankruptcy judge for the eastern district of California.

"**(B)** Three additional bankruptcy judges for the central district of California.

"**(C)** Four additional bankruptcy judges for the district of Delaware.

"**(D)** Two additional bankruptcy judges for the southern district of Florida.

"**(E)** One additional bankruptcy judge for the southern district of Georgia.

"**(F)** Three additional bankruptcy judges for the district of Maryland.

"**(G)** One additional bankruptcy judge for the eastern district of Michigan.

"**(H)** One additional bankruptcy judge for the southern district of Mississippi.

"**(I)** One additional bankruptcy judge for the district of New Jersey.

"**(J)** One additional bankruptcy judge for the eastern district of New York.

"**(K)** One additional bankruptcy judge for the northern district of New York.

"**(L)** One additional bankruptcy judge for the southern district of New York.

"**(M)** One additional bankruptcy judge for the eastern district of North Carolina.

"**(N)** One additional bankruptcy judge for the eastern district of Pennsylvania.

"**(O)** One additional bankruptcy judge for the middle district of Pennsylvania.

"**(P)** One additional bankruptcy judge for the district of Puerto Rico.

"**(Q)** One additional bankruptcy judge for the western district of Tennessee.

"**(R)** One additional bankruptcy judge for the eastern district of Virginia.

"**(S)** One additional bankruptcy judge for the district of South Carolina.

"**(T)** One additional bankruptcy judge for the district of Nevada.

"**(2) Vacancies.—**

"**(A) Districts with single appointments.**—Except as provided in subparagraphs (B), (C), (D), and (E), the first vacancy occurring in the office of bankruptcy judge in each of the judicial districts set forth in paragraph (1)—

"**(i)** occurring 5 years or more after the appointment date of the bankruptcy judge appointed under paragraph (1) to such office; and

"**(ii)** resulting from the death, retirement, resignation, or removal of a bankruptcy judge;

"shall not be filled.

"**(B) Central district of California.**—The 1st, 2d, and 3d vacancies in the office of bankruptcy judge in the central district of California—

"**(i)** occurring 5 years or more after the respective 1st, 2d, and 3d appointment dates of the bankruptcy judges appointed under paragraph (1)(B); and

"**(ii)** resulting from the death, retirement, resignation, or removal of a bankruptcy judge;

"shall not be filled.

"**(C) District of Delaware.**—The 1st, 2d, 3d, and 4th vacancies in the office of bankruptcy judge in the district of Delaware—

"**(i)** occurring 5 years or more after the respective 1st, 2d, 3d, and 4th appointment dates of the bankruptcy judges appointed under paragraph (1)(F); and

"**(ii)** resulting from the death, retirement, resignation, or removal of a bankruptcy judge;

"shall not be filled.

"**(D) Southern district of Florida.**—The 1st and 2d vacancies in the office of bankruptcy judge in the southern district of Florida—

"**(i)** occurring 5 years or more after the respective 1st and 2d appointment dates of the bankruptcy judges appointed under paragraph (1)(D); and

"**(ii)** resulting from the death, retirement, resignation, or removal of a bankruptcy judge;

"shall not be filled.

"**(E) District of Maryland.**—The 1st, 2d, and 3d vacancies in the office of bankruptcy judge in the district of Maryland—

"**(i)** occurring 5 years or more after the respective 1st, 2d, and 3d appointment dates of the bankruptcy judges appointed under paragraph (1)(F); and

"**(ii)** resulting from the death, retirement, resignation, or removal of a bankruptcy judge;

"shall not be filled.

"**(c) Extensions.—**

"**(1) In general.**—The temporary office of bankruptcy judges authorized for the northern district of Alabama, the district of Delaware, the district of Puerto Rico, and the eastern district of Tennessee under paragraphs (1), (3), (7), and (9) of section 3(a) of the Bankruptcy Judgeship Act of 1992 (28 U.S.C. 152 note) are extended until the first vacancy occurring in the office of a bankruptcy judge in the applicable district resulting from the death, retirement, resignation, or removal of a bankruptcy judge and occurring 5 years after the date of the enactment of this Act [April 20, 2005].

"**(2) Applicability of other provisions.**—All other provisions of section 3 of the Bankruptcy Judgeship Act of 1992 (28 U.S.C. 152 note) remain applicable to the temporary office of bankruptcy judges referred to in this subsection."

[Amendments by Pub.L. 109–8, § 1223, effective Apr. 20, 2005, see Pub.L. 109–8, § 1223(e), set out as a note under this section.]

Section 3 of Pub.L. 102–361, as amended Pub.L. 104–317, Title III, § 307, Oct. 19, 1996, 110 Stat. 3852, provided that:

"**(a) Appointments.**—The following bankruptcy judges shall be appointed in the manner prescribed in section 152(a)(1) of title 28, United States Code [subsec. (a)(1) of this section]:

"**(1)** 1 additional bankruptcy judge for the northern district of Alabama.

"**(2)** 1 additional bankruptcy judge for the district of Colorado.

"**(3)** 1 additional bankruptcy judge for the district of Delaware.

"**(4)** 1 additional bankruptcy judge for the southern district of Illinois.

"**(5)** 1 additional bankruptcy judge for the district of New Hampshire.

"**(6)** 1 additional bankruptcy judge for the middle district of North Carolina.

"**(7)** 1 additional bankruptcy judge for the district of Puerto Rico.

"**(8)** 1 additional bankruptcy judge for the district of South Carolina.

"**(9)** 1 additional bankruptcy judge for the eastern district of Tennessee.

"**(10)** 1 additional bankruptcy judge for the western district of Texas.

"**(b) Vacancies.**—The first vacancy in the office of bankruptcy judge in each of the judicial districts set forth in subsection (a), resulting from the death, retirement, resignation, or removal of a bankruptcy judge, and occurring 5 years or more after the appointment date of the judge named to fill the temporary judgeship position shall not be filled. In the case of a vacancy resulting from the expiration of the term of a bankruptcy judge not described in the preceding sentence, that judge shall be eligible for reappointment as a bankruptcy judge in that district."

Subsequent Reauthorizations

Pub.L. 112–121, § 4, May 25, 2012, 126 Stat. 349, provided that: "Prior to further reauthorization of any judgeship authorized by this Act [Pub.L. 112–121, May 25, 2012, 126 Stat. 346, known as the Temporary Bankruptcy Judgeships Extension Act of 2012; for classification, see Short Title note set out under 28 U.S.C.A. § 1], the Committee on the Judiciary of the Senate and House of Representatives shall conduct a review of the bankruptcy judgeships authorized by this Act to determine the need, if any, for continued reauthorization of each judgeship, to evaluate any changes in all bankruptcy case filings and their effect, if any, on filing fee revenue, and to require the Administrative Office of the Courts to submit a report to the Committee on the Judiciary of the Senate and House of Representatives on bankruptcy case workload, bankruptcy judgeship costs, and filing fee revenue."

Appointment to Fill Vacancies; Nominations; Qualifications

Section 120 of Pub.L. 98–353, as amended Pub.L. 99–554, Title I, § 102, Oct. 22, 1986, 100 Stat. 3089; Pub.L. 104–317, Title III, § 303, Oct. 19, 1996, 110 Stat. 3852, provided that:

"**(a)(1)** Whenever a court of appeals is authorized to fill a vacancy that occurs on a bankruptcy court of the United States, such court of appeals shall appoint to fill that vacancy a person whose character, experience, ability, and impartiality qualify such person to serve in the Federal judiciary.

"**(2)** It is the sense of the Congress that the courts of appeals should consider for appointment under section 152 of title 28, United States Code [this section], to the first vacancy which arises after the date of the enactment of this Act [July 10, 1984] in the office of each bankruptcy judge, the bankruptcy judge who holds such office immediately before such vacancy arises, if such bankruptcy judge requests to be considered for such appointment.

"**(3)** When filling vacancies, the court of appeals may consider reappointing incumbent bankruptcy judges under procedures prescribed by regulations issued by the Judicial Conference of the United States.

"**(b)** The judicial council of the circuit involved shall assist the court of appeals by evaluating potential nominees and by recommending to such court for consideration for appointment to each vacancy on the bankruptcy court persons who are qualified to be bankruptcy judges under regulations prescribed by the Judicial Conference of the United States. In the case of the first vacancy which arises after the date of the enactment of this Act [July 10, 1984] in the office of each bankruptcy judge, such potential nominees shall include the bankruptcy judge who holds such office immediately before such vacancy arises, if such bankruptcy judge requests to be considered for such appointment and the judicial council

determines that such judge is qualified under subsection (c) of this section to continue to serve. Such potential nominees shall receive consideration equal to that given all other potential nominees for such position. All incumbent nominees seeking reappointment thereafter may be considered for such a reappointment, pursuant to a majority vote of the judges of the appointing court of appeals, under procedures authorized under subsection (a)(3).

"**(c)** Before transmitting to the court of appeals the names of the persons the judicial council for the circuit deems best qualified to fill any existing vacancy, the judicial council shall have determined that—

"**(1)** public notice of such vacancy has been given and an effort has been made, in the case of each such vacancy, to identify qualified candidates, without regard to race, color, sex, religion, or national origin,

"**(2)** such persons are members in good standing of at least one State bar, the District of Columbia bar, or the bar of the Commonwealth of Puerto Rico, and members in good standing of every other bar of which they are members,

"**(3)** such persons possess, and have a reputation for, integrity and good character,

"**(4)** such persons are of sound physical and mental health,

"**(5)** such persons possess and have demonstrated commitment to equal justice under law,

"**(6)** such persons possess and have demonstrated outstanding legal ability and competence, as evidenced by substantial legal experience, ability to deal with complex legal problems, aptitude for legal scholarship and writing, and familiarity with courts and court processes, and

"**(7)** such persons [sic] demeanor, character, and personality indicate that they would exhibit judicial temperament if appointed to the position of United States bankruptcy judge."

Extension and Termination of Term of Office of Bankruptcy Judge and Part-Time Bankruptcy Judge Serving on July 10, 1984; Practice of Law by Part-Time Bankruptcy Judge

Section 106 of Pub.L. 98–353 provided that:

"**(a)** Notwithstanding section 152 of title 28, United States Code, as added by this Act [this section], the term of office of a bankruptcy judge who is serving on the date of enactment of this Act [July 10, 1984] is extended to and expires four years after the date such bankruptcy judge was last appointed to such office or on October 1, 1986, whichever is later.

"**(b)(1)** Notwithstanding section 153(a) of title 28, United States Code, as added by this Act [section 153(a) of this title], and notwithstanding subsection (a) of this section, a bankruptcy judge serving on a part-time basis on the date of enactment of this Act [July 10, 1984] may continue to serve on such basis for a period not to exceed two years from the date of enactment of this Act [July 10, 1984].

"**(2)** Notwithstanding the provisions of section 153(b) of title 28, United States Code [section 153(b) of this title], a bankruptcy judge serving on a part-time basis may engage in the practice of law but may not engage in any other practice, business, occupation, or employment inconsistent with the expeditious, proper, and impartial performance of such bankruptcy judge's duties as a judicial officer. The Judicial Conference of the United States may promulgate appropriate rules and regulations to implement this paragraph."

Extension and Termination of Term of Office of Part-Time Bankruptcy Judge Serving on July 2, 1986, In District of Oregon, Western District of Michigan, and Eastern District of Oklahoma

Pub.L. 99–349, Title I, July 2, 1986, 100 Stat. 718, provided that: "Notwithstanding the provisions of section 106(b)(1) of the Bankruptcy Amendments and Federal Judgeship Act of 1984 [section 106(b)(1) of Pub.L. 98–353, set out as a note under this section], a bankruptcy judge serving on a part-time basis on the date of enactment of this Act [July 2, 1986] may continue to serve as a part-time judge for such district until December 31, 1986, or until such time as a full-time bankruptcy judge for such district is appointed, whichever is earlier: *Provided,* That these provisions shall apply only to part-time bankruptcy judges serving in the district of Oregon, the western district of Michigan, and the eastern district of Oklahoma."

CROSS REFERENCES

Appeals, hearing of, see 28 USCA § 158.

Definition of "bankruptcy judge" as including a judge appointed under this section for purposes of civil service retirement, see 5 USCA § 8331.

Removal of judges for disability to be in accordance with provisions of this section, see 28 USCA § 372.

Retirement of bankruptcy judges and magistrates, see 28 USCA § 377.

§ 153. Salaries; character of service

(a) Each bankruptcy judge shall serve on a full-time basis and shall receive as full compensation for his services, a salary at an annual rate that is equal to 92 percent of the salary of a judge of the district court of the United States as determined pursuant to section 135, to be paid at such times as the Judicial Conference of the United States determines.

(b) A bankruptcy judge may not engage in the practice of law and may not engage in any other practice, business, occupation, or employment inconsistent with the expeditious, proper, and impartial performance of such bankruptcy judge's duties as a judicial officer. The Conference may promulgate appropriate rules and regulations to implement this subsection.

(c) Each individual appointed under this chapter shall take the oath or affirmation prescribed by section 453 of this title before performing the duties of the office of bankruptcy judge.

(d) A bankruptcy judge appointed under this chapter shall be exempt from the provisions of subchapter I of chapter 63 of title 5.

(Added Pub.L. 98–353, Title I, § 104(a), July 10, 1984, 98 Stat. 338; amended Pub.L. 100–202, § 101(a) [Title IV, § 408(a)], Dec. 22, 1987, 101 Stat. 1329–26; Pub.L. 100–702, Title X, § 1003(a)(1), Nov. 19, 1988, 102 Stat. 4665.)

HISTORICAL AND STATUTORY NOTES

Revision Notes and Legislative Reports

1984 Acts. Statements by Legislative Leaders, see 1984 U.S.Code Cong. and Adm.News, p. 576.

1988 Acts. House Report No. 100–889, see 1988 U.S.Code Cong. and Adm.News, p. 5982.

Codifications

This section as added by Pub.L. 95–598, Title II, § 201(a), Nov. 6, 1978, 92 Stat. 2657, effective June 28, 1984, pursuant to Pub.L. 95–598, Title IV, § 402(b), Nov. 6, 1978, 92 Stat. 2682, as amended by Pub.L. 98–249, § 1(a), Mar. 31, 1984, 98 Stat. 116; Pub.L. 98–271, § 1(a), Apr. 30, 1984, 98 Stat. 163; Pub.L. 98–299, § 1(a), May 25, 1984, 98 Stat. 214; Pub.L. 98–325, § 1(a), June 20, 1984, 98 Stat. 268, set out as a note preceding section 101 of Title 11, Bankruptcy, read as follows:

§ 153. Tenure and residence of bankruptcy judges

(a) Each bankruptcy judge shall hold office for a term of 14 years, but may continue to perform the duties of his office until his successor takes office, unless such office has been eliminated.

(b) Removal of a bankruptcy judge during the term for which he is appointed shall be only for incompetency, misconduct, neglect of duty, or physical or mental disability. Removal shall be by the judicial council of the circuit or circuits in which the bankruptcy judge serves, but removal may not occur unless a majority of all the judges of such circuit council or councils concur in the order of removal. Before any order of removal may be entered, a full specification of the charges shall be furnished to the bankruptcy judge, and he shall be accorded an opportunity to be heard on the charges. Any cause for removal of any bankruptcy judge coming to the knowledge of the Director of the Administrative Office of the United States Courts shall be reported by him to the chief judge of the circuit or circuits in which he serves, and a copy of the report shall at the same time be transmitted to the circuit council or councils and to the bankruptcy judge.

(c) Each bankruptcy judge shall reside in the district or one of the districts for which he is appointed, or within 20 miles of his official station.

(d) If the public interest and the nature of the business of a bankruptcy court require that a bankruptcy judge should maintain his abode at or near a particular part of the district the judicial council of the circuit may so declare and may make an appropriate order. If the bankruptcy judges of such a district are unable to agree as to which of them shall maintain his abode at or near the place or within the area specified in such an order the judicial council of the circuit may decide which of them shall do so.

Section 402(b) of Pub.L. 95–598 was amended by section 113 of Pub.L. 98–353 by substituting "shall not be effective" for "shall take effect on June 28, 1984", thereby eliminating the addition of section 153 by section 201(a) of Pub.L. 95–598, effective June 27, 1984, pursuant to section 122(c) of Pub.L. 98–353, set out as an Effective Date note under section 151 of this title.

Section 121(a) of Pub.L. 98–353 directed that section 402(b) of Pub.L. 95–598 be amended by substituting "the date of enactment of the Bankruptcy Amendments and Federal Judgeship Act of 1984 [i.e. July 10, 1984]" for "June 28, 1984". This amendment was not executed in view of the prior amendment to section 402(b) of Pub.L. 95–598 by section 113 of Pub.L. 98–353.

Effective and Applicability Provisions

1987 Acts. Section 101(a) [Title IV, § 408(d)] of Pub.L. 100–202 provided that: "This section [amending this section,

section 634 of this title, and section 356 of Title 2, The Congress] shall become effective October 1, 1988, and any salary affected by the provisions of this section shall be adjusted at the beginning of the first applicable pay period commencing on or after such date of enactment [probably should read "such date", meaning Oct. 1, 1988]."

1984 Acts. Section effective July 10, 1984, see section 122(a) of Pub.L. 98–353, set out as a note under section 151 of this title.

Continuation of Salaries of Bankruptcy Judges in Effect on June 27, 1984

Section 105(a) of Pub.L. 98–353 provided that: "The salary of a bankruptcy judge in effect on June 27, 1984, shall remain in effect until changed as a result of a determination or adjustment made pursuant to section 153(a) of title 28, United States Code, as added by this Act [subsec. (a) of this section]."

Increase in Salaries

1988—Salaries of bankruptcy judges continued at $72,500 per annum by Ex. Ord. No. 12622, Dec. 31, 1987, 53 F.R. 222, formerly set out as a note under section 5332 of Title 5, Government Organization and Employees.

1987—Salaries of bankruptcy judges increased to $72,500 per annum, on recommendation of the President of the United States, see note set out under section 358 of Title 2, The Congress.

Salaries of bankruptcy judges increased to $70,500 effective on the first day of the first pay period beginning on or after January 1, 1987, by Ex. Ord. No. 12578, Dec. 31, 1986, 52 F.R. 505, formerly set out as a note under section 5332 of Title 5.

1985—Salaries of bankruptcy judges increased to $68,400 effective on the first day of the first pay period beginning on or after Jan. 1, 1985, by Ex. Ord. No. 12496, Dec. 28, 1984, 50 F.R. 211, as amended by Ex. Ord. No. 12540, Dec. 30, 1985, 51 F.R. 577, formerly set out as a note under section 5332 of Title 5.

1984—Salaries of bankruptcy judges (full-time) and bankruptcy judges (part-time) (maximum rate) increased to $66,100 and $33,100, respectively, effective on the first day of the first pay period beginning on or after Jan. 1, 1984, by Ex. Ord. No. 12456, Dec. 30, 1983, 49 F.R. 347, as amended Ex. Ord. No. 12477, May 23, 1984, 49 F.R. 22041; Ex. Ord. No. 12487, Sept. 14, 1984, 49 F.R. 36493, formerly set out as a note under section 5332 of Title 5.

1982—Salaries of bankruptcy judges and referees in bankruptcy (full-time), or referees in bankruptcy (part-time) (maximum rate) increased to $63,600 and $31,800, respectively, effective on the first day of the first pay period beginning on or after Oct. 1, 1982, by Ex. Ord. No. 12387, Oct. 8, 1982, 47 F.R. 44981, formerly set out as a note under section 5332 of Title 5, Government Organization and Employees. Ex. Ord. No. 12387 further provided that pursuant to section 101(e) of Pub.L. 97–276 funds are not available to pay a salary at a rate which exceeds the rate in effect on Sept. 30, 1982, which was $58,500 for bankruptcy judges and referees in bankruptcy (full-time), and $30,600 for referees in bankruptcy (part-time) (maximum rate).

Maximum rate payable to bankruptcy judges after Dec. 17, 1982, increased from $58,500 to $63,600, see Pub.L. 97–377, Title I, § 129(b)–(d), Dec. 21, 1982, 96 Stat. 1914, set out as a note under section 5318 of Title 5.

1981—Salaries of bankruptcy judges and referees in bankruptcy (full-time), or referees in bankruptcy (part-time) (maxi-

mum rate) increased to $61,200 and $30,600, respectively, effective on the first day of the first pay period beginning on or after Oct. 1, 1981, by Ex. Ord. No. 12330, Oct. 15, 1981, 46 F.R. 50921, formerly set out as a note under section 5332 of Title 5. Ex. Ord. No. 12330 further provided that pursuant to section 101(c) of Pub.L. 97–51 funds are not available to pay a salary at a rate which exceeds the rate in effect on Sept. 30, 1981, which was $51,167.50 for bankruptcy judges and referees in bankruptcy (full-time), and $25,583.75 for referees in bankruptcy (part-time) (maximum rate).

1980—Salaries of bankruptcy judges and referees in bankruptcy (full-time), or referees in bankruptcy (part-time) (maximum rate) increased to $58,400 and $29,200, respectively, effective on the first day of the first pay period beginning on or after Oct. 1, 1980, by Ex. Ord. No. 12248, Oct. 16, 1980, 45 F.R. 69199, formerly set out as a note under section 5332 of Title 5. Ex. Ord. No. 12248 further provided that pursuant to section 101(c) of Pub.L. 96–369 funds are not available to pay a salary which exceeds the rate in effect on Sept. 30, 1980, which was $51,167.50 for bankruptcy judges and referees in bankruptcy (full-time), and $25,583.75 for referees in bankruptcy (part-time) (maximum rate).

For limitations on use of funds for period Oct. 1, 1980 through June 5, 1981, appropriated by any Act to pay the salary or pay of any individual in legislative, executive, or judicial branch in position equal to or above level V of the Executive Schedule, see section 101(c) of Pub.L. 96–369 and section 101(c) of Pub.L. 96–536, set out as notes under section 5318 of Title 5.

1979—Salaries of bankruptcy judges increased to $53,500 effective on the first day of the first applicable pay period beginning on or after Oct. 1, 1979, by Ex. Ord. No. 12165, Oct. 9, 1979, 44 F.R. 58671, as amended by Ex. Ord. No. 12200, Mar. 12, 1980, 45 F.R. 16443, formerly set out as a note under section 5332 of Title 5. Ex. Ord. No. 12165 further provided that pursuant to Pub.L. 96–86 funds appropriated for fiscal year 1980 may not be used to pay a salary at a rate which exceeds an increase of 5.5 percent over the applicable rate payable for such position or office in effect on Sept. 30, 1978, which was $51,167.50 for bankruptcy judges.

Part–Time Bankruptcy Judges

For provision that notwithstanding subsecs. (a) and (b) of this section, a bankruptcy judge serving on a part-time basis on July 10, 1984, may continue to serve on such basis for two years from such date, and may engage in the practice of law, see section 106 of Pub.L. 98–353, set out as a note under section 152 of this title.

Transition Provisions

Section 1003(b) of Pub.L. 100–702 provided that:

"(1) If an individual who is exempted from the Leave Act by operation of amendments under this section [amending this section and sections 156, 631, 634, 712, 752, and 794 of this title] and who was previously subject to the provisions of subchapter I of chapter 63 of title 5, United States Code [section 6301 et seq. of Title 5, Government Organization and Employees], without a break in service, again becomes subject to this subchapter on completion of his service as an exempted officer, the unused annual leave and sick leave standing to his credit when he was exempted from this subchapter is deemed to have remained to his credit.

"(2) In computing an annuity under section 8339 of title 5, United States Code [section 8339 of Title 5], the total service of a person specified in paragraph (1) of this subsection who retired on an immediate annuity or dies leaving a survivor or survivors entitled to an annuity includes, without regard to the limitations imposed by subsection (f) of section 8339 of title 5, United States Code [section 8339(f) of Title 5], the days of unused sick leave standing to his credit when he was exempted from subchapter I of chapter 63 of title 5, United States Code [section 6301 et seq. of Title 5], except that these days will not be counted in determining average pay or annuity eligibility."

§ 154. Division of businesses; chief judge

(a) Each bankruptcy court for a district having more than one bankruptcy judge shall by majority vote promulgate rules for the division of business among the bankruptcy judges to the extent that the division of business is not otherwise provided for by the rules of the district court.

(b) In each district court having more than one bankruptcy judge the district court shall designate one judge to serve as chief judge of such bankruptcy court. Whenever a majority of the judges of such district court cannot agree upon the designation as chief judge, the chief judge of such district court shall make such designation. The chief judge of the bankruptcy court shall ensure that the rules of the bankruptcy court and of the district court are observed and that the business of the bankruptcy court is handled effectively and expeditiously.

(Added Pub.L. 98–353, Title I, § 104(a), July 10, 1984, 98 Stat. 339.)

HISTORICAL AND STATUTORY NOTES

Revision Notes and Legislative Reports

1984 Acts. Statements by Legislative Leaders, see 1984 U.S.Code Cong. and Adm.News, p. 576.

Codifications

This section as added by Pub.L. 95–598, Title II, § 201(a), Nov. 6, 1978, 92 Stat. 2657, effective June 28, 1984, pursuant to Pub.L. 95–598, Title IV, § 402(b), Nov. 6, 1978, 92 Stat. 2682, as amended by Pub.L. 98–249, § 1(a), Mar. 31, 1984, 98 Stat. 116; Pub.L. 98–271, § 1(a), Apr. 30, 1984, 98 Stat. 163; Pub.L. 98–299, § 1(a), May 25, 1984, 98 Stat. 214; Pub.L. 98–325, § 1(a), June 20, 1984, 98 Stat. 268, set out as a note preceding section 101 of Title 11, Bankruptcy, read as follows:

§ 154. Salaries of bankruptcy judges

Each judge of a bankruptcy court shall receive a salary at an annual rate of $50,000, subject to adjustment under section 225 of the Federal Salary Act of 1967 (2 U.S.C. 351–361), and section 461 of this title.

Section 402(b) of Pub.L. 95–598 was amended by section 113 of Pub.L. 98–353 by substituting "shall not be effective" for "shall take effect on June 28, 1984", thereby eliminating the addition of section 154 by section 201(a) of Pub.L. 95–598, effective June 27, 1984, pursuant to section 122(c) of Pub.L. 98–353, set out as an Effective Date note under section 151 of this title.

Section 121(a) of Pub.L. 98–353 directed that section 402(b) of Pub.L. 95–598 be amended by substituting "the date of enactment of the Bankruptcy Amendments and Federal Judgeship Act of 1984 [i.e. July 10, 1984]" for "June 28, 1984".

This amendment was not executed in view of the prior amendment to section 402(b) of Pub.L. 95–598 by section 113 of Pub.L. 98–353.

Effective and Applicability Provisions

1984 Acts. Section effective July 10, 1984, see section 122(a) of Pub.L. 98–353, set out as a note under section 151 of this title.

§ 155. Temporary transfer of bankruptcy judges

(a) A bankruptcy judge may be transferred to serve temporarily as a bankruptcy judge in any judicial district other than the judicial district for which such bankruptcy judge was appointed upon the approval of the judicial council of each of the circuits involved.

(b) A bankruptcy judge who has retired may, upon consent, be recalled to serve as a bankruptcy judge in any judicial district by the judicial council of the circuit within which such district is located. Upon recall, a bankruptcy judge may receive a salary for such service in accordance with regulations promulgated by the Judicial Conference of the United States, subject to the restrictions on the payment of an annuity in section 377 of this title or in subchapter III of chapter 83, and chapter 84, of title 5 which are applicable to such judge.

(Added Pub.L. 98–353, Title I, § 104(a), July 10, 1984, 98 Stat. 339; amended Pub.L. 99–651, Title II, § 202(a), Nov. 14, 1986, 100 Stat. 3648; Pub.L. 100–659, § 4(a), Nov. 15, 1988, 102 Stat. 3918.)

HISTORICAL AND STATUTORY NOTES

Revision Notes and Legislative Reports

1984 Acts. Statements by Legislative Leaders, see 1984 U.S.Code Cong. and Adm.News, p. 576.

1986 Acts. House Report No. 99–417, see 1986 U.S.Code Cong. and Adm.News, p. 6165.

1988 Acts. Senate Report No. 100–293, and House Conference Report No. 100–1072, see 1988 U.S.Code Cong. and Adm.News, p. 5564.

Codifications

This section as added by Pub.L. 95–598, Title II, § 201(a), Nov. 6, 1978, 92 Stat. 2658, effective June 28, 1984, pursuant to Pub.L. 95–598, Title IV, § 402(b), Nov. 6, 1978, 92 Stat. 2682, as amended by Pub.L. 98–249, § 1(a), Mar. 31, 1984, 98 Stat. 116; Pub.L. 98–271, § 1(a), Apr. 30, 1984, 98 Stat. 163; Pub.L. 98–299, § 1(a), May 25, 1984, 98 Stat. 214; Pub.L. 98–325, § 1(a), June 20, 1984, 98 Stat. 268, set out as a note preceding section 101 of Title 11, Bankruptcy, read as follows:

§ 155. Chief judge; precedence of bankruptcy judges

(a) In each district having more than one judge the bankruptcy judge in regular active service who is senior in commission and under seventy years of age shall be the chief judge of the bankruptcy court. If all the bankruptcy judges in regular active service are 70 years of age or older the youngest shall act as chief judge until a judge has been appointed and qualified who is under 70 years of age, but a judge may not act as chief judge until he has served as a bankruptcy judge for one year.

(b) The chief judge shall have precedence and preside at any session which he attends.

Other bankruptcy judges shall have precedence and preside according to the seniority of their commissions. Judges whose commissions bear the same date shall have precedence according to seniority in age.

(c) A judge whose commission extends over more than one district shall be junior to all bankruptcy judges except in the district in which he resided at the time he entered upon the duties of his office.

(d) If a chief judge desires to be relieved of his duties as chief judge while retaining his active status as a bankruptcy judge, he may so certify to the chief judge of the court of appeals for the circuit in which the bankruptcy judge serves, and thereafter the bankruptcy judge in active service next in precedence and willing to serve shall be designated by the chief judge of the court of appeals as the chief judge of the bankruptcy court.

(e) If a chief judge is temporarily unable to perform his duties as such, they shall be performed by the bankruptcy judge in active service, present in the district and able and qualified to act, who is next in precedence.

(f) Service as a referee in bankruptcy or as a bankruptcy judge under the Bankruptcy Act shall be taken into account in the determination of seniority of commission under this section.

Section 402(b) of Pub.L. 95–598 was amended by section 113 of Pub.L. 98–353 by substituting "shall not be effective" for "shall take effect on June 28, 1984", thereby eliminating the addition of section 155 by section 201(a) of Pub.L. 95–598, effective June 27, 1984, pursuant to section 122(c) of Pub.L. 98–353, set out as an Effective Date note under section 151 of this title.

Section 121(a) of Pub.L. 98–353 directed that section 402(b) of Pub.L. 95–598 be amended by substituting "the date of enactment of the Bankruptcy Amendments and Federal Judgeship Act of 1984 [i.e. July 10, 1984]" for "June 28, 1984". This amendment was not executed in view of the prior amendment to section 402(b) of Pub.L. 95–598 by section 113 of Pub.L. 98–353.

Effective and Applicability Provisions

1988 Acts. Amendment to this section by Pub.L. 100–659 to take effect on Nov. 15, 1988, and shall apply to bankruptcy judges and magistrates who retire on or after Nov. 15, 1988, with special election provisions for bankruptcy judges, etc., who left office on or after July 31, 1987, and before Nov. 15, 1988, see section 9 of Pub.L. 100–659, set out as a note under section 377 of this title.

1986 Acts. Section 203 of Title II of Pub.L. 99–651 provided that: "This title and the amendments made by this title [enacting section 375 of this title, and amending sections 155, 374, 631, 633, 636, and 797 of this title] take effect on January 1, 1987."

1984 Acts. Section effective July 10, 1984, see section 122(a) of Pub.L. 98–353, set out as a note under section 151 of this title.

CROSS REFERENCES

Recall of retired judges,

Generally, see 28 USCA § 375.

Actual abode deemed official station for purposes of residency, see 28 USCA § 374.

Practicing attorney not eligible for recall, see 28 USCA § 377.

§ 156. Staff; expenses

(a) Each bankruptcy judge may appoint a secretary, a law clerk, and such additional assistants as the Director of the Administrative Office of the United States Courts determines to be necessary. A law clerk appointed under this section shall be exempt from the provisions of subchapter I of chapter 63 of title 5, unless specifically included by the appointing judge or by local rule of court.

(b) Upon certification to the judicial council of the circuit involved and to the Director of the Administrative Office of the United States Courts that the number of cases and proceedings pending within the jurisdiction under section 1334 of this title within a judicial district so warrants, the bankruptcy judges for such district may appoint an individual to serve as clerk of such bankruptcy court. The clerk may appoint, with the approval of such bankruptcy judges, and in such number as may be approved by the Director, necessary deputies, and may remove such deputies with the approval of such bankruptcy judges.

(c) Any court may utilize facilities or services, either on or off the court's premises, which pertain to the provision of notices, dockets, calendars, and other administrative information to parties in cases filed under the provisions of title 11, United States Code, where the costs of such facilities or services are paid for out of the assets of the estate and are not charged to the United States. The utilization of such facilities or services shall be subject to such conditions and limitations as the pertinent circuit council may prescribe.

(d) No office of the bankruptcy clerk of court may be consolidated with the district clerk of court office without the prior approval of the Judicial Conference and the Congress.

(e) In a judicial district where a bankruptcy clerk has been appointed pursuant to subsection (b), the bankruptcy clerk shall be the official custodian of the records and dockets of the bankruptcy court.

(f) For purposes of financial accountability in a district where a bankruptcy clerk has been certified, such clerk shall be accountable for and pay into the Treasury all fees, costs, and other monies collected by such clerk except uncollected fees not required by an Act of Congress to be prepaid. Such clerk shall make returns thereof to the Director of the Administrative Office of the United States Courts and the Director of the Executive Office For United States Trustees, under regulations prescribed by such Directors.

(Added Pub.L. 98–353, Title I, § 104(a), July 10, 1984, 98 Stat. 339; amended Pub.L. 99–554, Title I, §§ 103, 142, 144(a), Oct. 27, 1986, 100 Stat. 3090, 3096; Pub.L. 100–702, Title X, § 1003(a)(3), Nov. 19, 1988, 102 Stat. 4665.)

Revision Notes and Legislative Reports

1984 Acts. Statements by Legislative Leaders, see 1984 U.S. Code Cong. and Adm. News, p. 576.

1986 Acts. House Report No. 99–764 and House Conference Report No. 99–958, see 1986 U.S. Code Cong. and Adm. News, p. 5227.

1988 Acts. House Report No. 100–889, see 1988 U.S. Code Cong. and Adm. News, p. 5982.

Codifications

This section as added by Pub.L. 95–598, Title II, § 201(a), Nov. 6, 1978, 92 Stat. 2659, effective June 28, 1984, pursuant to Pub.L. 95–598, Title IV, § 402(b), Nov. 6, 1978, 92 Stat. 2682, as amended by Pub.L. 98–249, § 1(a), Mar. 31, 1984, 98 Stat. 116; Pub.L. 98–271, § 1(a), Apr. 30, 1984, 98 Stat. 163; Pub.L. 98–299, § 1(a), May 25, 1984, 98 Stat. 214; Pub.L. 98–325, § 1(a), June 20, 1984, 98 Stat. 268, set out as a note preceding section 101 of Title 11, Bankruptcy, read as follows:

§ 156. Division of business among bankruptcy judges

The business of a bankruptcy court having more than one judge shall be divided among the judges as provided by the rules and orders of the court.

The chief judge of the bankruptcy court shall be responsible for the observance of such rules and orders, and shall divide the business and assign the cases so far as such rules and orders do not otherwise prescribe.

If the bankruptcy judges in any district are unable to agree upon the adoption of rules or orders for that purpose the judicial council of the circuit shall make the necessary orders.

Section 402(b) of Pub.L. 95–598 was amended by section 113 of Pub.L. 98–353 by substituting "shall not be effective" for "shall take effect on June 28, 1984", thereby eliminating the addition of section 156 by section 201(a) of Pub.L. 95–598, effective June 27, 1984, pursuant to section 122(c) of Pub.L. 98–353, set out as an Effective Date note under section 151 of this title.

Section 121(a) of Pub.L. 98–353 directed that section 402(b) of Pub.L. 95–598 be amended by substituting "the date of enactment of the Bankruptcy Amendments and Federal Judgeship Act of 1984 [i.e. July 10, 1984]" for "June 28, 1984". This amendment was not executed in view of the prior amendment to section 402(b) of Pub.L. 95–598 by section 113 of Pub.L. 98–353.

Effective and Applicability Provisions

1986 Acts. Amendment of subsec. (d) by section 103 of Pub.L. 99–554 effective on Oct. 27, 1986, see section 302(b) of Pub.L. 99–554, set out as a note under section 581 of this title.

Enactment of subsecs. (e) and (f) by sections 142 and 144(a) of Pub.L. 99–554 effective 30 days after Oct. 27, 1986, except as otherwise provided for, see section 302(a) of Pub.L. 99–554, set out as a note under section 581 of this title.

1984 Acts. Section effective July 10, 1984, see section 122(a) of Pub.L. 98–353, set out as a note under section 151 of this title.

CROSS REFERENCES

Conversion fees in bankruptcy, see 28 USCA § 1930.

§ 157. Procedures

(a) Each district court may provide that any or all cases under title 11 and any or all proceedings arising under title 11 or arising in or related to a case under title 11 shall be referred to the bankruptcy judges for the district.

(b)(1) Bankruptcy judges may hear and determine all cases under title 11 and all core proceedings arising under title 11, or arising in a case under title 11, referred under subsection (a) of this section, and may enter appropriate orders and judgments, subject to review under section 158 of this title.

(2) Core proceedings include, but are not limited to—

(A) matters concerning the administration of the estate;

(B) allowance or disallowance of claims against the estate or exemptions from property of the estate, and estimation of claims or interests for the purposes of confirming a plan under chapter 11, 12, or 13 of title 11 but not the liquidation or estimation of contingent or unliquidated personal injury tort or wrongful death claims against the estate for purposes of distribution in a case under title 11;

(C) counterclaims by the estate against persons filing claims against the estate;

(D) orders in respect to obtaining credit;

(E) orders to turn over property of the estate;

(F) proceedings to determine, avoid, or recover preferences;

(G) motions to terminate, annul, or modify the automatic stay;

(H) proceedings to determine, avoid, or recover fraudulent conveyances;

(I) determinations as to the dischargeability of particular debts;

(J) objections to discharges;

(K) determinations of the validity, extent, or priority of liens;

(L) confirmations of plans;

(M) orders approving the use or lease of property, including the use of cash collateral;

(N) orders approving the sale of property other than property resulting from claims brought by the estate against persons who have not filed claims against the estate;

(O) other proceedings affecting the liquidation of the assets of the estate or the adjustment of the debtor-creditor or the equity security holder relationship, except personal injury tort or wrongful death claims; and

(P) recognition of foreign proceedings and other matters under chapter 15 of title 11.

(3) The bankruptcy judge shall determine, on the judge's own motion or on timely motion of a party, whether a proceeding is a core proceeding under this subsection or is a proceeding that is otherwise related to a case under title 11. A determination that a proceeding is not a core proceeding shall not be made solely on the basis that its resolution may be affected by State law.

(4) Non-core proceedings under section 157(b)(2)(B) of title 28, United States Code, shall not be subject to the mandatory abstention provisions of section 1334(c)(2).

(5) The district court shall order that personal injury tort and wrongful death claims shall be tried in the district court in which the bankruptcy case is pending, or in the district court in the district in which the claim arose, as determined by the district court in which the bankruptcy case is pending.

(c)(1) A bankruptcy judge may hear a proceeding that is not a core proceeding but that is otherwise related to a case under title 11. In such proceeding, the bankruptcy judge shall submit proposed findings of fact and conclusions of law to the district court, and any final order or judgment shall be entered by the district judge after considering the bankruptcy judge's proposed findings and conclusions and after reviewing de novo those matters to which any party has timely and specifically objected.

(2) Notwithstanding the provisions of paragraph (1) of this subsection, the district court, with the consent of all the parties to the proceeding, may refer a proceeding related to a case under title 11 to a bankruptcy judge to hear and determine and to enter appropriate orders and judgments, subject to review under section 158 of this title.

(d) The district court may withdraw, in whole or in part, any case or proceeding referred under this section, on its own motion or on timely motion of any party, for cause shown. The district court shall, on timely motion of a party, so withdraw a proceeding if the court determines that resolution of the proceeding requires consideration of both title 11 and other laws of the United States regulating organizations or activities affecting interstate commerce.

(e) If the right to a jury trial applies in a proceeding that may be heard under this section by a bankruptcy judge, the bankruptcy judge may conduct the jury trial if specially designated to exercise such jurisdiction by the district court and with the express consent of all the parties.

(Added Pub.L. 98–353, Title I, § 104(a), July 10, 1984, 98 Stat. 340; amended Pub.L. 99–554, Title I, §§ 143, 144(b), Oct. 27, 1986, 100 Stat. 3096; Pub.L. 103–394, Title I, § 112, Oct. 22, 1994, 108 Stat. 4117; Pub.L. 109–8, Title VIII, § 802(c)(1), Apr. 20, 2005, 119 Stat. 145.)

Validity

The United States Supreme Court has held that certain provisions of this section, as added by section 104(a) of Pub.L. 98–353 (28 U.S.C.A. § 157(b)(2)(C)), are unconstitutional as applied to certain core, non-core and related proceedings. Stern v. Marshall, U.S. 2011, 564 U.S. 462, 131 S.Ct. 2594, 180 L.Ed.2d 475.

HISTORICAL AND STATUTORY NOTES

Revision Notes and Legislative Reports

1984 Acts. Statements by Legislative Leaders, see 1984 U.S. Code Cong. and Adm. News, p. 576.

1986 Acts. House Report No. 99–764 and House Conference Report No. 99–958, see 1986 U.S. Code Cong. and Adm. News, p. 5227.

1994 Acts. House Report No. 103–835, see 1994 U.S. Code Cong. and Adm. News, p. 3340.

2005 Acts. House Report No. 109–31(Part I), see 2005 U.S. Code Cong. and Adm. News, p. 88.

References in Text

Chapter 11, 12, or 13 of title 11, referred to in subsec. (b)(2)(B), is 11 U.S.C.A. § 1101 et seq., 11 U.S.C.A. § 1201 et seq., or 11 U.S.C.A. § 1301 et seq., respectively.

Chapter 15 of title 11, referred to in subsec. (b)(2)(P), is 11 U.S.C.A. § 1501 et seq.

Codifications

This section as added by Pub.L. 95–598, Title II, § 201(a), Nov. 6, 1978, 92 Stat. 2659, effective June 28, 1984, pursuant to Pub.L. 95–598, Title IV, § 402(b), Nov. 6, 1978, 92 Stat. 2682, as amended by Pub.L. 98–249, § 1(a), Mar. 31, 1984, 98 Stat. 116; Pub.L. 98–271, § 1(a), Apr. 30, 1984, 98 Stat. 163; Pub.L. 98–299, § 1(a), May 25, 1984, 98 Stat. 214; Pub.L. 98–325, § 1(a), June 20, 1984, 98 Stat. 268, set out as a note preceding section 101 of Title 11, Bankruptcy, read as follows:

"**§ 157. Times of holding court**

"**(a)** The bankruptcy court at each designated location shall be deemed to be in continuous session on all business days throughout the year.

"**(b)** Each bankruptcy court may establish by local rule or order schedules of court sessions at designated places of holding court other than the headquarters office of the court. Such schedules may be pretermitted by order of the court.

"**(c)** Bankruptcy court may be held at any place within the territory served, in any case, on order of the bankruptcy court, for the convenience of the parties, on such notice as the bankruptcy court orders."

Section 402(b) of Pub.L. 95–598 was amended by section 113 of Pub.L. 98–353 by substituting "shall not be effective" for "shall take effect on June 28, 1984", thereby eliminating the addition of section 157 by section 201(a) of Pub.L. 95–598, effective June 27, 1984, pursuant to section 122(c) of Pub.L. 98–353, set out as an Effective Date note under section 151 of this title.

Section 121(a) of Pub.L. 98–353 directed that section 402(b) of Pub.L. 95–598 be amended by substituting "the date of enactment of the Bankruptcy Amendments and Federal Judgeship Act of 1984 [i.e. July 10, 1984]" for "June 28, 1984". This amendment was not executed in view of the prior amendment to section 402(b) of Pub.L. 95–598 by section 113 of Pub.L. 98–353.

Effective and Applicability Provisions

2005 Acts. Except as otherwise provided, amendments by Pub.L. 109–8 effective 180 days after April 20, 2005, and inapplicable with respect to cases commenced under Title 11 before the effective date, see Pub.L. 109–8, § 1501, set out as a note under 11 U.S.C.A. § 101.

1994 Acts. Amendment by Pub.L. 103–394 effective on Oct. 22, 1994, and not to apply with respect to cases commenced under Title 11 of the United States Code before Oct. 22, 1994, see section 702 of Pub.L. 103–394, set out as a note under section 101 of Title 11, Bankruptcy.

1986 Acts. Amendment by Pub.L. 99–554 effective 30 days after Oct. 27, 1986, except as otherwise provided for, see section 302(a) of Pub.L. 99–554, set out as a note under section 581 of this title.

1984 Acts. Section effective July 10, 1984, see section 122(a) of Pub.L. 98–353, set out as a note under section 151 of this title.

Separability of Provisions

If any provision of or amendment made by Pub.L. 103–394 or the application of such provision or amendment to any person or circumstance is held to be unconstitutional, the remaining provisions of and amendments made by Pub.L. 103–394 and the application of such provisions and amendments to any person or circumstance shall not be affected thereby, see section 701 of Pub.L. 103–394, set out as a note under section 101 of Title 11, Bankruptcy.

CROSS REFERENCES

Supplemental injunctions and power of district court to refer proceedings, see 11 USCA § 524.

§ 158.   Appeals

(a) The district courts of the United States shall have jurisdiction to hear appeals [1]

     (1) from final judgments, orders, and decrees;

     (2) from interlocutory orders and decrees issued under section 1121(d) of title 11 increasing or reducing the time periods referred to in section 1121 of such title; and

     (3) with leave of the court, from other interlocutory orders and decrees;

of bankruptcy judges entered in cases and proceedings referred to the bankruptcy judges under section 157 of this title. An appeal under this subsection shall be taken only to the district court for the judicial district in which the bankruptcy judge is serving.

(b)(1) The judicial council of a circuit shall establish a bankruptcy appellate panel service composed of bankruptcy judges of the districts in the circuit who are appointed by the judicial council in accordance with paragraph (3), to hear and determine, with the consent of all the parties, appeals under subsection (a) unless the judicial council finds that—

     (A) there are insufficient judicial resources available in the circuit; or

     (B) establishment of such service would result in undue delay or increased cost to parties in cases under title 11.

Not later than 90 days after making the finding, the judicial council shall submit to the Judicial Conference of the United States a report containing the factual basis of such finding.

(2)(A) A judicial council may reconsider, at any time, the finding described in paragraph (1).

(B) On the request of a majority of the district judges in a circuit for which a bankruptcy appellate panel service is established under paragraph (1), made after the expiration of the 1–year period beginning on the date such service is established, the judicial council of the circuit shall determine whether a circumstance specified in subparagraph (A) or (B) of such paragraph exists.

(C) On its own motion, after the expiration of the 3–year period beginning on the date a bankruptcy appellate panel service is established under paragraph (1), the judicial council of the circuit may determine whether a circumstance specified in subparagraph (A) or (B) of such paragraph exists.

(D) If the judicial council finds that either of such circumstances exists, the judicial council may provide for the completion of the appeals then pending before such service and the orderly termination of such service.

(3) Bankruptcy judges appointed under paragraph (1) shall be appointed and may be reappointed under such paragraph.

(4) If authorized by the Judicial Conference of the United States, the judicial councils of 2 or more circuits may establish a joint bankruptcy appellate panel comprised of bankruptcy judges from the districts within the circuits for which such panel is established, to hear and determine, upon the consent of all the parties, appeals under subsection (a) of this section.

(5) An appeal to be heard under this subsection shall be heard by a panel of 3 members of the bankruptcy appellate panel service, except that a member of such service may not hear an appeal originating in the district for which such member is appointed or designated under section 152 of this title.

(6) Appeals may not be heard under this subsection by a panel of the bankruptcy appellate panel service unless the district judges for the district in which the appeals occur, by majority vote, have authorized such service to hear and determine appeals originating in such district.

(c)(1) Subject to subsections (b) and (d)(2), each appeal under subsection (a) shall be heard by a 3–judge panel of the bankruptcy appellate panel service established under subsection (b)(1) unless—

     (A) the appellant elects at the time of filing the appeal; or

(B) any other party elects, not later than 30 days after service of notice of the appeal;

to have such appeal heard by the district court.

(2) An appeal under subsections (a) and (b) of this section shall be taken in the same manner as appeals in civil proceedings generally are taken to the courts of appeals from the district courts and in the time provided by Rule 8002 of the Bankruptcy Rules.

(d)(1) The courts of appeals shall have jurisdiction of appeals from all final decisions, judgments, orders, and decrees entered under subsections (a) and (b) of this section.

(2)(A) The appropriate court of appeals shall have jurisdiction of appeals described in the first sentence of subsection (a) if the bankruptcy court, the district court, or the bankruptcy appellate panel involved, acting on its own motion or on the request of a party to the judgment, order, or decree described in such first sentence, or all the appellants and appellees (if any) acting jointly, certify that—

    (i) the judgment, order, or decree involves a question of law as to which there is no controlling decision of the court of appeals for the circuit or of the Supreme Court of the United States, or involves a matter of public importance;

    (ii) the judgment, order, or decree involves a question of law requiring resolution of conflicting decisions; or

    (iii) an immediate appeal from the judgment, order, or decree may materially advance the progress of the case or proceeding in which the appeal is taken;

and if the court of appeals authorizes the direct appeal of the judgment, order, or decree.

(B) If the bankruptcy court, the district court, or the bankruptcy appellate panel—

    (i) on its own motion or on the request of a party, determines that a circumstance specified in clause (i), (ii), or (iii) of subparagraph (A) exists; or

    (ii) receives a request made by a majority of the appellants and a majority of appellees (if any) to make the certification described in subparagraph (A);

then the bankruptcy court, the district court, or the bankruptcy appellate panel shall make the certification described in subparagraph (A).

(C) The parties may supplement the certification with a short statement of the basis for the certification.

(D) An appeal under this paragraph does not stay any proceeding of the bankruptcy court, the district court, or the bankruptcy appellate panel from which the appeal is taken, unless the respective bankruptcy court, district court, or bankruptcy appellate panel, or the court of appeals in which the appeal is pending, issues a stay of such proceeding pending the appeal.

(E) Any request under subparagraph (B) for certification shall be made not later than 60 days after the entry of the judgment, order, or decree.

(Added Pub.L. 98–353, Title I, § 104(a), July 10, 1984, 98 Stat. 341; amended Pub.L. 101–650, Title III, § 305, Dec. 1, 1990, 104 Stat. 5105; Pub.L. 103–394, Title I, §§ 102, 104(c), (d), Oct. 22, 1994, 108 Stat. 4108–4110; Pub.L. 109–8, Title XII, § 1233(a), Apr. 20, 2005, 119 Stat. 202; Pub.L. 111–327, § 2(c)(1), Dec. 22, 2010, 124 Stat. 3563.)

¹ So in original. Probably should be followed by a dash.

HISTORICAL AND STATUTORY NOTES

Revision Notes and Legislative Reports

1984 Acts. Statements by Legislative Leaders, see 1984 U.S. Code Cong. and Adm. News, p. 576.

1990 Acts. Senate Report No. 101–416, Related House Reports, and Statement by President, see 1990 U.S. Code Cong. and Adm. News, p. 6802.

1994 Acts. House Report No. 103–835, see 1994 U.S. Code Cong. and Adm. News, p. 3340.

2005 Acts. House Report No. 109–31(Part I), see 2005 U.S. Code Cong. and Adm. News, p. 88.

Codifications

Pub.L. 103–394, § 102 directed that subsec. (a) be amended by striking "from" the first place it appeared and all that followed through "decrees," and inserting pars. (1) to (3). This amendment was executed by making the insertion as so indicated and by striking the language beginning with "from" the first place it appeared and all that followed through "decrees," the second place it appeared, which resulted in the striking, following "have jurisdiction to hear appeals", of the phrase "from final judgments, orders, and decrees, and, with leave of the court, from interlocutory orders and decrees,", as the probable intent of Congress.

This section (section 158) and section 159 as added by Pub.L. 95–598, Title II, § 201(a), Nov. 6, 1978, 92 Stat. 2659, and section 160, as added by Pub.L. 95–598, Title II, § 201(a), Nov. 6, 1978, 92 Stat. 2659, and amended Pub.L. 97–164, Title I, § 110(d), Apr. 2, 1982, 96 Stat. 29, effective June 28, 1984, pursuant to Pub.L. 95–598, Title IV, § 402(b), Nov. 6, 1978, 92 Stat. 2682, as amended by Pub.L. 98–249, § 1(a), Mar. 31, 1984, 98 Stat. 116; Pub.L. 98–271, § 1(a), Apr. 30, 1984, 98 Stat. 163; Pub.L. 98–299, § 1(a), May 25, 1984, 98 Stat. 214; Pub.L. 98–325, § 1(a), June 20, 1984, 98 Stat. 268, set out as a note preceding section 101 of Title II, Bankruptcy, read as follows:

"§ 158.   Accommodations at places for holding court

"Court shall be held only at places where Federal quarters and accommodations are available, or suitable quarters and accommodations are furnished without cost to the United States. The foregoing restrictions shall not, however, preclude the Administrator of General Services, at the request of the Director of the Administrative Office of the United States Courts, from providing such court quarters and accommodations as the Administrator determines can appropriately be made available at places where court is authorized by law to be held, but only if such court quarters and accommodations have been approved as necessary by the judicial council of the appropriate circuit.

"§ 159.   Vacant judgeship as affecting proceedings

"When the office of a bankruptcy judge becomes vacant, all pending process, pleadings and proceedings shall, when necessary, be continued by the clerk until a judge is appointed or designated to hold such court.

"**§ 160. Appellate panels**

"**(a)** If the circuit council of a circuit orders application of this section to a district within such circuit, the chief judge of each circuit shall designate panels of three bankruptcy judges to hear appeals from judgments, orders, and decrees of the bankruptcy court of the United States for such district. Except as provided in section 293(b) of this title, a panel shall be composed only of bankruptcy judges for districts located in the circuit in which the appeal arises. The chief judge shall designate a sufficient number of such panels so that appeals may be heard and disposed of expeditiously.

"**(b)** A panel designated under subsection (a) of this section may not hear an appeal from a judgment, order, or decree entered by a member of the panel.

"**(c)** When hearing an appeal, a panel designated under subsection (a) of this section shall sit at a place convenient to the parties to the appeal."

Section 402(b) of Pub.L. 95–598 was amended by section 113 of Pub.L. 98–353 by substituting "shall not be effective" for "shall take effect on June 28, 1984", thereby eliminating the additions of sections 158 to 160 by section 201(a) of Pub.L. 95–598, effective June 27, 1984, pursuant to section 122(c) of Pub.L. 98–353, set out as an Effective Date note under section 151 of this title.

Section 121(a) of Pub.L. 98–353 directed that section 402(b) of Pub.L. 95–598 be amended by substituting "the date of enactment of the Bankruptcy Amendments and Federal Judgeship Act of 1984 [i.e. July 10, 1984]" for "June 28, 1984". This amendment was not executed in view of the prior amendment to section 402(b) of Pub.L. 95–598 by section 113 of Pub.L. 98–353.

Effective and Applicability Provisions

2005 Acts. Except as otherwise provided, amendments by Pub.L. 109–8 effective 180 days after April 20, 2005, and inapplicable with respect to cases commenced under Title 11 before the effective date, see Pub.L. 109–8, § 1501, set out as a note under 11 U.S.C.A. § 101.

1994 Acts. Amendments by Pub.L. 103–394 effective on Oct. 22, 1994, and not to apply with respect to cases commenced under Title 11 of the United States Code before Oct. 22, 1994, see section 702 of Pub.L. 103–394, set out as a note under 11 U.S.C.A. § 101.

1984 Acts. Section effective July 10, 1984, see section 122(a) of Pub.L. 98–353, set out as a note under 28 U.S.C.A. § 151.

Separability of Provisions

If any provision of or amendment made by Pub.L. 103–394 or the application of such provision or amendment to any person or circumstance is held to be unconstitutional, the remaining provisions of and amendments made by Pub.L. 103–394 and the application of such provisions and amendments to any person or circumstance shall not be affected thereby, see section 701 of Pub.L. 103–394, set out as a note under 11 U.S.C.A. § 101.

Procedural Rules

Pub.L. 109–8, Title XII, § 1233(b), Apr. 20, 2005, 119 Stat. 203, provided that:

"**(1) Temporary application.**—A provision of this subsection shall apply to appeals under section 158(d)(2) of title 28, United States Code, until a rule of practice and procedure relating to such provision and such appeals is promulgated or amended under chapter 131 of such title [28 U.S.C.A. § 2071 et seq.].

"**(2) Certification.**—A district court, a bankruptcy court, or a bankruptcy appellate panel may make a certification under section 158(d)(2) of title 28, United States Code, only with respect to matters pending in the respective bankruptcy court, district court, or bankruptcy appellate panel.

"**(3) Procedure.**—Subject to any other provision of this subsection, an appeal authorized by the court of appeals under section 158(d)(2)(A) of title 28, United States Code, shall be taken in the manner prescribed in subdivisions (a)(1), (b), (c), and (d) of rule 5 of the Federal Rules of Appellate Procedure. For purposes of subdivision (a)(1) of rule 5—

"**(A)** a reference in such subdivision to a district court shall be deemed to include a reference to a bankruptcy court and a bankruptcy appellate panel, as appropriate; and

"**(B)** a reference in such subdivision to the parties requesting permission to appeal to be served with the petition shall be deemed to include a reference to the parties to the judgment, order, or decree from which the appeal is taken.

"**(4) Filing of petition with attachment.**—A petition requesting permission to appeal, that is based on a certification made under subparagraph (A) or (B) of section 158(d)(2) shall—

"**(A)** be filed with the circuit clerk not later than 10 days after the certification is entered on the docket of the bankruptcy court, the district court, or the bankruptcy appellate panel from which the appeal is taken; and

"**(B)** have attached a copy of such certification.

"**(5) References in rule 5.**—For purposes of rule 5 of the Federal Rules of Appellate Procedure—

"**(A)** a reference in such rule to a district court shall be deemed to include a reference to a bankruptcy court and to a bankruptcy appellate panel; and

"**(B)** a reference in such rule to a district clerk shall be deemed to include a reference to a clerk of a bankruptcy court and to a clerk of a bankruptcy appellate panel.

"**(6) Application of rules.**—The Federal Rules of Appellate Procedure [set out in Title 28, Judiciary and Judicial Procedure] shall apply in the courts of appeals with respect to appeals authorized under section 158(d)(2)(A), to the extent relevant and as if such appeals were taken from final judgments, orders, or decrees of the district courts or bankruptcy appellate panels exercising appellate jurisdiction under subsection (a) or (b) of section 158 of title 28, United States Code."

[Except as otherwise provided, amendments by Pub.L. 109–8 effective 180 days after April 20, 2005, and inapplicable with respect to cases commenced under Title 11 before the effective date, see Pub.L. 109–8, § 1501, set out as a note under 11 U.S.C.A. § 101.]

CROSS REFERENCES

Orders and decisions not reviewable under this section,

Abstention from exercising jurisdiction, generally, see 28 USCA § 1334.

Dismissal or suspension of bankruptcy case on abstention grounds, see 11 USCA § 305.

Remand orders, see 28 USCA § 1452.

§ 159. Bankruptcy statistics

(a) The clerk of the district court, or the clerk of the bankruptcy court if one is certified pursuant to section 156(b) of this title, shall collect statistics regarding debtors who are individuals with primarily consumer debts seeking relief under chapters 7, 11, and 13 of title 11. Those statistics shall be in a standardized format prescribed by the Director of the Administrative Office of the United States Courts (referred to in this section as the "Director").

(b) The Director shall—

(1) compile the statistics referred to in subsection (a);

(2) make the statistics available to the public; and

(3) not later than July 1, 2008, and annually thereafter, prepare, and submit to Congress a report concerning the information collected under subsection (a) that contains an analysis of the information.

(c) The compilation required under subsection (b) shall—

(1) be itemized, by chapter, with respect to title 11;

(2) be presented in the aggregate and for each district; and

(3) include information concerning—

(A) the total assets and total liabilities of the debtors described in subsection (a), and in each category of assets and liabilities, as reported in the schedules prescribed pursuant to section 2075 of this title and filed by debtors;

(B) the current monthly income, average income, and average expenses of debtors as reported on the schedules and statements that each such debtor files under sections 521 and 1322 of title 11;

(C) the aggregate amount of debt discharged in cases filed during the reporting period, determined as the difference between the total amount of debt and obligations of a debtor reported on the schedules and the amount of such debt reported in categories which are predominantly nondischargeable;

(D) the average period of time between the date of the filing of the petition and the closing of the case for cases closed during the reporting period;

(E) for cases closed during the reporting period—

(i) the number of cases in which a reaffirmation agreement was filed; and

(ii)(I) the total number of reaffirmation agreements filed;

(II) of those cases in which a reaffirmation agreement was filed, the number of cases in which the debtor was not represented by an attorney; and

(III) of those cases in which a reaffirmation agreement was filed, the number of cases in which the reaffirmation agreement was approved by the court;

(F) with respect to cases filed under chapter 13 of title 11, for the reporting period—

(i)(I) the number of cases in which a final order was entered determining the value of property securing a claim in an amount less than the amount of the claim; and

(II) the number of final orders entered determining the value of property securing a claim;

(ii) the number of cases dismissed, the number of cases dismissed for failure to make payments under the plan, the number of cases refiled after dismissal, and the number of cases in which the plan was completed, separately itemized with respect to the number of modifications made before completion of the plan, if any; and

(iii) the number of cases in which the debtor filed another case during the 6–year period preceding the filing;

(G) the number of cases in which creditors were fined for misconduct and any amount of punitive damages awarded by the court for creditor misconduct; and

(H) the number of cases in which sanctions under rule 9011 of the Federal Rules of Bankruptcy Procedure were imposed against the debtor's attorney or damages awarded under such Rule.

(Added Pub.L. 109–8, Title VI, § 601(a), Apr. 20, 2005, 119 Stat. 119; amended Pub.L. 111–327, § 2(c)(2), Dec. 22, 2010, 124 Stat. 3563.)

HISTORICAL AND STATUTORY NOTES

Revision Notes and Legislative Reports

2005 Acts. House Report No. 109–31(Part I), see 2005 U.S. Code Cong. and Adm. News, p. 88.

References in Text

Chapters 7 and 11 of title 11, referred to in subsec. (a), are 11 U.S.C.A. § 701 et seq. and 11 U.S.C.A. § 1101 et seq., respectively.

Chapter 13 of title 11, referred to in subsecs. (a) and (c)(3)(F), is 11 U.S.C.A. § 1301 et seq.

The Federal Rules of Bankruptcy Procedure, referred to in subsec. (c)(3)(H), are set out in Title 11.

Effective and Applicability Provisions

2005 Acts. Pub.L. 109–8, Title VI, § 601(c), Apr. 20, 2005, 119 Stat. 120, provided that: "The amendments made by this section [enacting this section] shall take effect 18 months after the date of enactment of this Act [April 20, 2005]."

Except as otherwise provided, amendments by Pub.L. 109–8 effective 180 days after April 20, 2005, and inapplicable with respect to cases commenced under Title 11 before the effective date, see Pub.L. 109–8, § 1501, set out as a note under 11 U.S.C.A. § 101.

CHAPTER 17—RESIGNATION AND RETIREMENT OF JUSTICES AND JUDGES

§ 372. Retirement for disability; substitute judge on failure to retire

(a) Any justice or judge of the United States appointed to hold office during good behavior who becomes permanently disabled from performing his duties may retire from regular active service, and the President shall, by and with the advice and consent of the Senate, appoint a successor.

Any justice or judge of the United States desiring to retire under this section shall certify to the President his disability in writing.

Whenever an associate justice of the Supreme Court, a chief judge of a circuit or the chief judge of the Court of International Trade, desires to retire under this section, he shall furnish to the President a certificate of disability signed by the Chief Justice of the United States.

A circuit or district judge, desiring to retire under this section, shall furnish to the President a certificate of disability signed by the chief judge of his circuit.

A judge of the Court of International Trade desiring to retire under this section, shall furnish to the President a certificate of disability signed by the chief judge of his court.

Each justice or judge retiring under this section after serving ten years continuously or otherwise shall, during the remainder of his lifetime, receive the salary of the office. A justice or judge retiring under this section who has served less than ten years in all shall, during the remainder of his lifetime, receive one-half the salary of the office.

(b) Whenever any judge of the United States appointed to hold office during good behavior who is eligible to retire under this section does not do so and a certificate of his disability signed by a majority of the members of the Judicial Council of his circuit in the case of a circuit or district judge, or by the Chief Justice of the United States in the case of the Chief Judge of the Court of International Trade, or by the chief judge of his court in the case of a judge of the Court of International Trade, is presented to the President and the President finds that such judge is unable to discharge efficiently all the duties of his office by reason of permanent mental or physical disability and that the appointment of an additional judge is necessary for the efficient dispatch of business, the President may make such appointment by and with the advice and consent of the Senate. Whenever any such additional judge is appointed, the vacancy subsequently caused by the death, resignation, or retirement of the disabled judge shall not be filled. Any judge whose disability causes the appointment of an additional judge shall, for purpose of precedence, service as chief judge, or temporary performance of the duties of that office, be treated as junior in commission to the other judges of the circuit, district, or court.

(June 25, 1948, c. 646, 62 Stat. 903; May 24, 1949, c. 139, § 67, 63 Stat. 99; Feb. 10, 1954, c. 6, § 4(a), 68 Stat. 12; Pub.L. 85–261, Sept. 2, 1957, 71 Stat. 586; Pub.L. 96–417, Title V, § 501(9), Oct. 10, 1980, 94 Stat. 1742; Pub.L. 96–458, § 3(a), (b), Oct. 15, 1980, 94 Stat. 2036, 2040; Pub.L. 97–164, Title I, § 112, Apr. 2, 1982, 96 Stat. 29; Pub.L. 98–353, Title I, § 107, July 10, 1984, 98 Stat. 342; Pub.L. 100–702, Title IV, § 403(c), Nov. 19, 1988, 102 Stat. 4651; Pub.L. 101–650, Title IV, § 402, Dec. 1, 1990, 104 Stat. 5117, 5122; Pub.L. 102–572, Title IX, § 902(b)(1), Oct. 29, 1992, 106 Stat. 4516; Pub.L. 107–273, Div. C, Title I, § 11043(a)(1), Nov. 2, 2002, 116 Stat. 1855.)

HISTORICAL AND STATUTORY NOTES

Revision Notes and Legislative Reports

1948 Acts. Based on Title 28, U.S.C., 1940 ed., §§ 375b, 375c, and 375d (Aug. 5, 1939, c. 433, §§ 1 to 3, 53 Stat. 1204, 1205).

This section consolidates sections 375b, 375c, and 375d of Title 28, U.S.C., 1940 ed.

Said section 375e of Title 28, U.S.C., 1940 ed. providing that term "senior circuit judge" includes the Chief Justice of the United States Court of Appeals for the District of Columbia, and the term "judicial circuit" includes the District of Columbia, was omitted from this revision as unnecessary. Such district is included as a judicial circuit by section 41 of this title.

Words "justice or judge of the United States" were used to describe members of all courts who hold office during good behavior. (See reviser's note [now Revision Notes and Legislative Reports] under section 371 of this title.)

Term "chief judge" was substituted for "Chief Justice" of the Court of Claims, "presiding judge" of the Court of Customs and Patent Appeals and "senior circuit judge." (See reviser's note [now Revision Notes and Legislative Reports] under section 136 of this title.)

For clarity and convenience the requirement that certificates of disability be submitted "to the President," was made explicit.

The revised section requires a judge of the Customs Court to furnish a certificate of disability signed by the chief judge of his court, instead of by the chief judge of the Court of Customs and Patent Appeals as in said section 375c of Title 28, U.S.C., 1940 ed. This change insures signing of the certificate of disability by the chief judge possessing knowledge of the facts.

Changes were made in phraseology and arrangement. 80th Congress House Report No. 308.

1949 Acts. Subsection (a) of this section amends section 372 of Title 28, U.S.C., to express the requirement that appointment of successors to justices or judges must be made with confirmation by the Senate. Subsection (b) of this section clarifies the intent of section 372 of Title 28, U.S.C., and conforms with the language of section 371 of such title.

1954 Acts. House Report No. 1005 and Conference Report No. 1133, see 1954 U.S. Code Cong. and Adm. News p. 2006.

1957 Acts. Senate Report No. 1094, see 1957 U.S. Code Cong. and Adm. News, p. 1833.

1980 Acts. House Report No. 96–1235, see 1980 U.S. Code Cong. and Adm. News, p. 3729.

Senate Report No. 96–362, see 1980 U.S. Code Cong. and Adm. News, p. 4315.

1982 Acts. Senate Report No. 97–275, see 1982 U.S. Code Cong. and Adm. News, p. 11.

1984 Acts. Statements by Legislative Leaders, see 1984 U.S. Code Cong. and Adm. News, p. 576.

1988 Acts. House Report No. 100–889, see 1988 U.S. Code Cong. and Adm. News, p. 5982.

1990 Acts. Senate Report No. 101–416, related House Reports, and President's Signing Statement, see 1990 U.S. Code Cong. and Adm. News, p. 6802.

2002 Acts. House Conference Report No. 107–685 and Statement by President, see 2002 U.S. Code Cong. and Adm. News, p. 1120.

Effective and Applicability Provisions

1992 Acts. Amendment by Pub.L. 102–572 effective Oct. 29, 1992, see section 911 of Pub.L. 102–572, set out as a note under section 171 of this title.

1990 Acts. Amendment by section 402 of Pub.L. 101–650 effective 90 days after Dec. 1, 1990, see section 407 of Pub.L. 101–650, set out as a note under section 332 of this title.

1988 Acts. Amendment by Pub.L. 100–702 effective Dec. 1, 1988, see section 407 of Pub.L. 100–702, set out as a note under section 2071 of this title.

1984 Acts. Amendment by Pub.L. 98–353 effective July 10, 1984, see section 122(a) of Pub.L. 98–353, set out as a note under section 151 of this title.

1982 Acts. Amendment by Pub.L. 97–164 effective Oct. 1, 1982, see section 402 of Pub.L. 97–164, set out as a note under section 171 of this title.

1980 Acts. Amendment by Pub.L. 96–458 effective Oct. 1, 1981, see section 7 of Pub.L. 96–458, set out as a note under section 331 of this title.

Amendment by Pub.L. 96–417 effective on Nov. 1, 1980, and applicable with respect to civil actions pending on or commenced on or after such date, see section 701(a) of Pub.L. 96–417, as amended, set out as a note under section 251 of this title.

Transfer of Functions

Any reference in any provision of law enacted before Jan. 4, 1995, to a function, duty, or authority of the Clerk of the House of Representatives treated as referring, with respect to that function, duty, or authority, to the officer of the House of Representatives exercising that function, duty, or authority, as determined by the Committee on House Oversight of the House of Representatives, see section 2(1) of Pub.L. 104–14, set out as a note preceding section 21 of Title 2, The Congress.

Computation of Judicial Service, District of Alaska

Inclusion of service as judge of the District Court for the Territory of Alaska in the computation of years of judicial service for judges of the United States District Court for the District of Alaska, see Pub.L. 89–70, July 8, 1965, 79 Stat. 213, set out as a note under section 371 of this title.

Extension of Time For Report by National Commission on Judicial Discipline and Removal

Pub.L. 102–368, Title I, Sept. 23, 1992, 106 Stat. 1118, provided in part that: "Notwithstanding the requirement of section 415 of Public Law 101–650 [set out as a note under this section] to submit the report mandated by said section not later than one year after the date of the Commission's first meeting, the National Commission on Judicial Discipline and Removal shall submit to each House of Congress, the Chief Justice of the United States, and the President, the report mandated in said section no later than August 1, 1993."

Judicial Service in Hawaii

Certain judicial service in Hawaii as included within computation of aggregate years of judicial service, see section 14(d) of Pub.L. 86–3, Mar. 18, 1959, 73 Stat. 10, set out as a note under section 371 of this title.

National Commission on Judicial Discipline and Removal

Subtitle II (sections 408 to 418) of Title IV of Pub.L. 101–650, as amended Pub.L. 102–198, § 8(a),(b)(2), Dec. 9, 1991, 105 Stat. 1625, 1626, provided that:

"**Sec. 408. Short Title.**

"This subtitle [subtitle II of Title IV of Pub.L. 101–650] may be cited as the 'National Commission on Judicial Discipline and Removal Act'.

"**Sec. 409. Establishment.**

"There is hereby established a commission to be known as the 'National Commission on Judicial Discipline and Removal' (hereinafter in this subtitle referred to as the 'Commission').

"**Sec. 410. Duties of Commission.**

"The duties of the Commission are—

"(1) to investigate and study the problems and issues involved in the tenure (including discipline and removal) of an article III judge;

"(2) to evaluate the advisability of proposing alternatives to current arrangements with respect to such problems and issues, including alternatives for discipline or removal of judges that would require amendment to the Constitution; and

"(3) to prepare and submit to the Congress, the Chief Justice of the United States, and the President a report in accordance with section 415.

"**Sec. 411. Membership.**

"(a) **Number and appointment.**—The Commission shall be composed of 13 members as follows:

"(1) Three appointed by the President pro tempore of the Senate.

"(2) Three appointed by the Speaker of the House of Representatives.

"(3) Three appointed by the Chief Justice of the United States.

"(4) Three appointed by the President.

"(5) One appointed by the Conference of Chief Justices of the States of the United States.

"**(b) Term.**—Members of the Commission shall be appointed for the life of the Commission.

"**(c) Quorum.**—Six members of the Commission shall constitute a quorum, but a lesser number may conduct meetings.

"**(d) Chairman.**—The members of the Commission shall select one of the members to be the Chairman.

"**(e) Vacancy.**—A vacancy on the Commission resulting from the death or resignation of a member shall not affect its powers and shall be filled in the same manner in which the original appointment was made.

"**(f) Continuation of membership.**—If any member of the Commission who was appointed to the Commission as a Member of Congress or as an officer or employee of a government leaves that office, or if any member of the Commission who was appointed from persons who are not officers or employees of a government becomes an officer or employee of a government, the member may continue as a member of the Commission for not longer than the 90-day period beginning on the date the member leaves that office or becomes such an officer or employee, as the case may be.

"**Sec. 412. Compensation of the Commission.**

"**(a) Pay.**—(1) Except as provided in paragraph (2), each member of the Commission who is not otherwise employed by the United States Government shall be entitled to receive the daily equivalent of the annual rate of basic pay payable for GS-18 of the General Schedule under section 5332 of title 5, United States Code [section 5332 of Title 5, Government Organization and Employees], for each day (including travel time) during which he or she is engaged in the actual performance of duties as a member of the Commission.

"(2) A member of the Commission who is an officer or employee of the United States Government shall serve without additional compensation.

"**(b) Travel.**—All members of the Commission shall be reimbursed for travel, subsistence, and other necessary expenses incurred by them in the performance of their duties.

"**Sec. 413. Director and staff of Commission; experts and consultants.**

"**(a) Director.**—The Commission shall, without regard to section 5311(b) of title 5, United States Code [section 5311(b) of Title 5], have a Director who shall be appointed by the Chairman and who shall be paid at a rate not to exceed the rate of basic pay payable for level V of the Executive Schedule under section 5316 of such title [section 5316 of Title 5].

"**(b) Staff.**—The Chairman of the Commission may appoint and fix the pay of such additional personnel as the Chairman finds necessary to enable the Commission to carry out its duties. Such personnel may be appointed without regard to the provisions of title 5, United States Code [Title 5], governing appointments in the competitive service, and may be paid without regard to the provisions of chapter 51 and subchapter III of chapter 53 of such title [section 5101 et seq. and section 5331 et seq. of Title 5] relating to classification and General Schedule pay rates, except that the annual rate of pay for any individual so appointed may not exceed a rate equal to the annual rate of basic pay payable for GS-18 of the General Schedule under section 5332 of such title [section 5332 of Title 5].

"**(c) Experts and consultants.**—The Commission may procure temporary and intermittent services of experts and consultants under section 3109(b) of title 5, United States Code [section 3109(b) of Title 5].

"**Sec. 414. Powers of Commission.**

"**(a) Hearings and sessions.**—The Commission or, on authorization of the Commission, a member of the Commission may, for the purpose of carrying out this subtitle, hold such hearings, sit and act at such times and places, take such testimony, and receive such evidence, as the Commission considers appropriate. The Commission may administer oaths or affirmations to witnesses appearing before it.

"**(b) Obtaining official data.**—The Commission may secure directly from any department, agency, or entity within the executive or judicial branch of the Federal Government information necessary to enable it to carry out this subtitle. Upon request of the Chairman of the Commission, the head of such department or agency shall furnish such information to the Commission.

"**(c) Facilities and support services.**—The Administrator of General Services shall provide to the Commission on a reimbursable basis such facilities and support services as the Commission may request. Upon request of the Commission, the head of any Federal agency is authorized to make any of the facilities and services of such agency available to the Commission to assist the Commission in carrying out its duties under this subtitle.

"**(d) Expenditures and contracts.**—The Commission or, on authorization of the Commission, a member of the Commission may make expenditures and enter into contracts for the procurement of such supplies, services, and property as the Commission or member considers appropriate for the purposes of carrying out the duties of the Commission. Such expenditures and contracts may be made only to such extent or in such amounts as are provided in appropriation Acts.

"**(e) Mails.**—The Commission may use the United States mails in the same manner and under the same conditions as other departments and agencies of the United States.

"**(f) Gifts.**—The Commission may accept, use, and dispose of gifts or donations of services or property.

"**Sec. 415. Report.**

"The Commission shall submit to each House of Congress, the Chief Justice of the United States, and the President a report not later than one year after the date of its first meeting. The report shall contain a detailed statement of the findings and conclusions of the Commission, together with its recommendations for such legislative or administrative action as it considers appropriate.

"**Sec. 416. Termination.**

"The Commission shall cease to exist on the date 30 days after the date it submits its report to the President and the Congress under section 415.

"**Sec. 417. Authorization of appropriations.**

"There is authorized to be appropriated the sum of $750,000 to carry out the provisions of this subtitle.

"**Sec. 418. Effective date.**

"This subtitle shall take effect on the date of the enactment of this Act [Dec. 1, 1990]."

[References in laws to the rates of pay for GS-16, 17, or 18, or to maximum rates of pay under the General Schedule, to be considered references to rates payable under specified sections of Title 5, Government Organization and Employees, see section 529 [Title I, § 101(c)(1)] of Pub.L. 101-509, set out in a note under section 5376 of Title 5.]

[For provisions extending the time for submission by the National Commission on Judicial Discipline and Removal of the report required by section 415 of Pub.L. 101-650, see

Pub.L. 102–368, Title 1, Sept. 23, 1992, 106 Stat. 1118, set out as a note under this section.]

[For termination, effective May 15, 2000, of reporting provisions pertaining to the findings and conclusions of the Commission of Pub.L. 101–650, § 415 set out above, see Pub.L. 104–66, § 3003, as amended, set out as a note under 31 U.S.C.A. § 1113, and the 4th item on page 181 of House Document No. 103–7.]

CROSS REFERENCES

Assignment of retired justices or judges to active duty, see 28 USCA § 294.

Court of Federal Claims judges election of annuity payments upon retirement not entitled to receive annuity or salary in senior status under this section, see 28 USCA § 178.

Duties of Director of Administrative Office of United States Courts, see 28 USCA § 604.

"Employee" defined as including retired judge under this section for purposes of life insurance for Federal employees, see 5 USCA § 8701.

Judicial Conference of the United States, see 28 USCA § 331.

Justices and judges appointed to hold office during good behavior,

Court of Appeals, see USCA Const. Art. III § 1.

Court of International Trade, see 28 USCA § 252.

District Courts, see USCA Const. Art. III § 1.

Supreme Court, see USCA Const. Art. III § 1.

Thrift Savings Fund, see 5 USCA § 8440a.

CHAPTER 21—GENERAL PROVISIONS APPLICABLE TO COURTS AND JUDGES

§ 455. Disqualification of justice, judge, or magistrate judge

(a) Any justice, judge, or magistrate judge of the United States shall disqualify himself in any proceeding in which his impartiality might reasonably be questioned.

(b) He shall also disqualify himself in the following circumstances:

(1) Where he has a personal bias or prejudice concerning a party, or personal knowledge of disputed evidentiary facts concerning the proceeding;

(2) Where in private practice he served as lawyer in the matter in controversy, or a lawyer with whom he previously practiced law served during such association as a lawyer concerning the matter, or the judge or such lawyer has been a material witness concerning it;

(3) Where he has served in governmental employment and in such capacity participated as counsel, adviser or material witness concerning the proceeding or expressed an opinion concerning the merits of the particular case in controversy;

(4) He knows that he, individually or as a fiduciary, or his spouse or minor child residing in his household, has a financial interest in the subject matter in controversy or in a party to the proceeding, or any other interest that could be substantially affected by the outcome of the proceeding;

(5) He or his spouse, or a person within the third degree of relationship to either of them, or the spouse of such a person:

(i) Is a party to the proceeding, or an officer, director, or trustee of a party;

(ii) Is acting as a lawyer in the proceeding;

(iii) Is known by the judge to have an interest that could be substantially affected by the outcome of the proceeding;

(iv) Is to the judge's knowledge likely to be a material witness in the proceeding.

(c) A judge should inform himself about his personal and fiduciary financial interests, and make a reasonable effort to inform himself about the personal financial interests of his spouse and minor children residing in his household.

(d) For the purposes of this section the following words or phrases shall have the meaning indicated:

(1) "proceeding" includes pretrial, trial, appellate review, or other stages of litigation;

(2) the degree of relationship is calculated according to the civil law system;

(3) "fiduciary" includes such relationships as executor, administrator, trustee, and guardian;

(4) "financial interest" means ownership of a legal or equitable interest, however small, or a relationship as director, adviser, or other active participant in the affairs of a party, except that:

(i) Ownership in a mutual or common investment fund that holds securities is not a "financial interest" in such securities unless the judge participates in the management of the fund;

(ii) An office in an educational, religious, charitable, fraternal, or civic organization is not a "financial interest" in securities held by the organization;

(iii) The proprietary interest of a policyholder in a mutual insurance company, of a depositor in a mutual savings association, or a similar proprietary interest, is a "financial interest" in the organization only if the outcome of the proceeding could substantially affect the value of the interest;

(iv) Ownership of government securities is a "financial interest" in the issuer only if the outcome of the proceeding could substantially affect the value of the securities.

(e) No justice, judge, or magistrate judge shall accept from the parties to the proceeding a waiver of any ground for disqualification enumerated in subsection (b). Where the ground for disqualification arises only under subsection (a), waiver may be accepted provided it is preceded by a full disclosure on the record of the basis for disqualification.

(f) Notwithstanding the preceding provisions of this section, if any justice, judge, magistrate judge, or bankruptcy judge to whom a matter has been assigned would be disqualified, after substantial judicial time has been devoted to the matter, because of the appearance or discovery, after the matter was assigned to him or her, that he or she individually or as a fiduciary, or his or her spouse or minor child residing in his or her household, has a financial interest in a party (other than an interest that could be substantially affected by the outcome), disqualification is not required if the justice, judge, magistrate judge, bankruptcy judge, spouse or minor child, as the case may be, divests himself or herself of the interest that provides the grounds for the disqualification.

(June 25, 1948, c. 646, 62 Stat. 908; Pub.L. 93–512, § 1, Dec. 5, 1974, 88 Stat. 1609; Pub.L. 95–598, Title II, § 214(a), (b), Nov. 6, 1978, 92 Stat. 2661; Pub.L. 100–702, Title X, § 1007, Nov. 19, 1988, 102 Stat. 4667; Pub.L. 101–650, Title III, § 321, Dec. 1, 1990, 104 Stat. 5117.)

HISTORICAL AND STATUTORY NOTES

Revision Notes and Legislative Reports

1948 Acts. Based on Title 28, U.S.C., 1940 ed., § 24 (Mar. 3, 1911, c. 231, § 20, 36 Stat. 1090 [Derived from R.S. § 601]).

Section 24 of Title 28, U.S.C., 1940 ed., applied only to district judges. The revised section is made applicable to all justices and judges of the United States.

The phrase "in which he has a substantial interest" was substituted for "concerned in interest in any suit."

The provision of section 24 of Title 28, U.S.C., 1940 ed., as to giving notice of disqualification to the "senior circuit judge," and words "and thereupon such proceedings shall be had as are provided in sections 17 and 18 of this title," were omitted as unnecessary and covered by section 291 et seq. of this title relating to designation and assignment of judges. Such provision is not made by statute in case of disqualification or incapacity, for other cause. See sections 140, 143, and 144 of this title. If a judge or clerk of court is remiss in

failing to notify the chief judge of the district or circuit, the judicial council of the circuit has ample power under section 332 of this title to apply a remedy.

Relationship to a party's attorney is included in the revised section as a basis of disqualification in conformity with the views of judges cognizant of the grave possibility of undesirable consequences resulting from a less inclusive rule.

Changes were made in phraseology. 80th Congress House Report No. 308.

1974 Acts. House Report No. 93–1453, see 1974 U.S.Code Cong. and Adm.News, p. 6351.

1978 Acts. Senate Report No. 95–989 and House Report No. 95–595, see 1978 U.S. Code Cong. and Adm. News, p. 5787.

1988 Acts. House Report No. 100–889, see 1988 U.S.Code Cong. and Adm.News, p. 5982.

Change of Name

"United States magistrate judge" substituted for "United States magistrate" in text pursuant to section 321 of Pub.L. 101–650, set out as a note under 28 U.S.C.A. § 631.

Effective and Applicability Provisions

1978 Acts. Amendment by Pub.L. 95–598 effective Oct. 1, 1979, see section 402(c) of Pub.L. 95–598, set out as a note preceding section 101 of Title 11, Bankruptcy. For procedures relating to bankruptcy matters during transition period, see note preceding section 151 of this title.

1974 Acts. Section 3 of Pub.L. 93–512 provided that: "This Act [amending this section] shall not apply to the trial of any proceeding commenced prior to the date of this Act [Dec. 5, 1974], nor to appellate review of any proceeding which was fully submitted to the reviewing court prior to the date of this Act."

CROSS REFERENCES

Application to other courts, see 28 USCA § 460.

Arbitrators subject to disqualification rules under this section, see 28 USCA § 656.

Bias or prejudice of judge, see 28 USCA § 144.

Disqualification of trial judge to hear appeal, see 28 USCA § 47.

United States Court of Veterans Affairs, judges and proceedings of subject to this section, see 38 USCA § 7264.

PART II—DEPARTMENT OF JUSTICE
CHAPTER 39—UNITED STATES TRUSTEES

HISTORICAL AND STATUTORY NOTES

Effective and Applicability Provisions

2005 Acts. Except as otherwise provided, amendments by Pub.L. 109–8 effective 180 days after April 20, 2005, and inapplicable with respect to cases commenced under Title 11

before the effective date, see Pub.L. 109–8, § 1501, set out as a note under 11 U.S.C.A. § 101.

United States Trustee Pilot; Repeal of Bankruptcy Provisions Relating to United States Trustees

Pub.L. 95–598, Title IV, § 408, Nov. 6, 1978, 92 Stat. 2686, as amended Pub.L. 98–166, Title II, § 200, Nov. 28, 1983, 97 Stat. 1081; Pub.L. 98–353, Title III, § 323, July 10, 1984, 98 Stat. 358; Pub.L. 99–429, Sept. 30, 1986, 100 Stat. 985; Pub.L. 99–500, Title I, § 101(b) [Title II, § 200], Oct. 18, 1986, 100 Stat. 1783–39, 1783–45, and Pub.L. 99–591, Title I, § 101(b), [Title II, § 2001, Oct. 30, 1986, 100 Stat. 3341–45; Pub.L. 99–554, Title III, § 307(a), Oct. 27, 1986, 100 Stat. 3125, which provided that the Attorney General conduct such studies and surveys as necessary to evaluate the needs, feasibility, and effectiveness of the United States trustee system, and report the result of such studies and surveys to the Congress, the President, and the Judicial Conference of the United States, beginning on or before January 3, 1980, and annually thereafter during the transition period; that not later than January 3, 1984, the Attorney General report to the Congress, the President, and the Judicial Conference of the United States, as to the feasibility, projected annual cost and effectiveness of the United States trustee system, as determined on the basis of the studies and surveys respecting the operation of the United States trustee system in the districts, together with recommendations as to the desirability and method of proceeding with implementation of the United States trustee system in all judicial districts of the United States; and that chapter 15 of title 11 of the United States Code [section 1501 et seq. of Title 11, Bankruptcy] and chapter 39 of title 28 of the United States Code [this chapter] are repealed, and all references to the United States trustee contained in title 28 of the United States Code [this title] are deleted, as of 30 days after the effective date of the Bankruptcy Judges, United States Trustees, and Family Farmer Bankruptcy Act of 1986 [see section 302 of Pub.L. 99–554, set out as a note under 28 U.S.C.A. § 581], with service of any United States trustee, of any assistant United States trustee, and of any employee employed or appointed under the authority of such chapter 39 is terminated on such date, was repealed by Pub.L. 99–554, Title III, § 307(b), Oct. 27, 1986, 100 Stat. 3125 [set out as a note under 28 U.S.C.A. § 581].

§ 581.　United States trustees

(a) The Attorney General shall appoint one United States trustee for each of the following regions composed of Federal judicial districts (without regard to section 451):

(1) The judicial districts established for the States of Maine, Massachusetts, New Hampshire, and Rhode Island.

(2) The judicial districts established for the States of Connecticut, New York, and Vermont.

(3) The judicial districts established for the States of Delaware, New Jersey, and Pennsylvania.

(4) The judicial districts established for the States of Maryland, North Carolina, South Carolina, Virginia, and West Virginia and for the District of Columbia.

(5) The judicial districts established for the States of Louisiana and Mississippi.

(6) The Northern District of Texas and the Eastern District of Texas.

(7) The Southern District of Texas and the Western District of Texas.

(8) The judicial districts established for the States of Kentucky and Tennessee.

(9) The judicial districts established for the States of Michigan and Ohio.

(10) The Central District of Illinois and the Southern District of Illinois; and the judicial districts established for the State of Indiana.

(11) The Northern District of Illinois; and the judicial districts established for the State of Wisconsin.

(12) The judicial districts established for the States of Minnesota, Iowa, North Dakota, and South Dakota.

(13) The judicial districts established for the States of Arkansas, Nebraska, and Missouri.

(14) The District of Arizona.

(15) The Southern District of California; and the judicial districts established for the State of Hawaii, and for Guam and the Commonwealth of the Northern Mariana Islands.

(16) The Central District of California.

(17) The Eastern District of California and the Northern District of California; and the judicial district established for the State of Nevada.

(18) The judicial districts established for the States of Alaska, Idaho (exclusive of Yellowstone National Park), Montana (exclusive of Yellowstone National Park), Oregon, and Washington.

(19) The judicial districts established for the States of Colorado, Utah, and Wyoming (including those portions of Yellowstone National Park situated in the States of Montana and Idaho).

(20) The judicial districts established for the States of Kansas, New Mexico, and Oklahoma.

(21) The judicial districts established for the States of Alabama, Florida, and Georgia and for the Commonwealth of Puerto Rico and the Virgin Islands of the United States.

(b) Each United States trustee shall be appointed for a term of five years. On the expiration of his term, a United States trustee shall continue to perform the duties of his office until his successor is appointed and qualifies.

(c) Each United States trustee is subject to removal by the Attorney General.

(Added Pub.L. 95–598, Title II, § 224(a), Nov. 6, 1978, 92 Stat. 2662; amended Pub.L. 99–554, Title I, § 111(a) to (c), Oct. 27, 1986, 100 Stat. 3090, 3091.)

HISTORICAL AND STATUTORY NOTES

Revision Notes and Legislative Reports

1978 Acts. Senate Report No. 95–989 and House Report No. 95–595, see 1978 U.S. Code Cong. and Adm. News, p. 5787.

1986 Acts. House Report No. 99–764 and House Conference Report No. 99–958, see 1986 U.S. Code Cong. and Adm. News, p. 5227.

Codifications

Section 408(c) of Pub.L. 95–598, as amended, which provided for the repeal of this section and the deletion of any references to United States Trustees in this title at a prospective date, was repealed by section 307(b) of Pub.L. 99–554. See note set out preceding this section.

Effective and Applicability Provisions

1978 Acts. Section effective Oct. 1, 1979, see section 402(c) of Pub.L. 95–598, as amended, set out as a note preceding 11 U.S.C.A. § 101.

Short Title

1986 Amendments. Section 1 of Pub.L. 99–554 provided: "That this Act [enacting section 589a of this title and sections 307, and 1201 to 1231 of Title 11, Bankruptcy, amending sections 49, 96, 152, 156, 157, 528, 581, 582, 584 to 587, 604, 1334, and 1930 of this title and sections 101 to 103, 105, 108, 109, 303, 321, 322, 324, 326, 327, 329, 330, 341, 343, 345 to 348, 362 to 365, 502, 503, 521 to 524, 546 to 549, 554, 557, 701, 703 to 707, 724, 726 to 728, 743, 1102, 1104 to 1106, 1112, 1121, 1129, 1163, 1202, 1302, 1306, 1307, and 1324 to 1326 of Title 11, Bankruptcy Form No. 1, set out in the Appendix to Title 11, repealing sections 1201 to 1231 and 1501 to 151326 of Title 11, enacting provisions set out as notes under sections 581 and 589 of this title, amending provisions set out as a note under section 152 of this title and preceding section 581 of this title, and repealing provisions set out as notes under preceding section 581 of this title] may be cited as the 'Bankruptcy Judges, United States Trustees, and Family Farmer Bankruptcy Act of 1986'."

Bankruptcy Crimes

Pub.L. 109–162, Title XI, § 1175, Jan. 5, 2006, 119 Stat. 3125, provided that:

"The Director of the Executive Office for United States Trustees shall prepare an annual report to the Congress detailing—

"(1) the number and types of criminal referrals made by the United States Trustee Program;

"(2) the outcomes of each criminal referral;

"(3) for any year in which the number of criminal referrals is less than for the prior year, an explanation of the decrease; and

"(4) the United States Trustee Program's efforts to prevent bankruptcy fraud and abuse, particularly with respect to the establishment of uniform internal controls to detect common, higher risk frauds, such as a debtor's failure to disclose all assets."

CROSS REFERENCES

Appointment of acting United States trustee by Attorney General to serve until vacancy is filled by appointment under this section, see 28 USCA § 585.

§ 582. Assistant United States trustees

(a) The Attorney General may appoint one or more assistant United States trustees in any region when the public interest so requires.

(b) Each assistant United States trustee is subject to removal by the Attorney General.

(Added Pub.L. 95–598, Title II, § 224(a), Nov. 6, 1978, 92 Stat. 2663; amended Pub.L. 99–554, Title I, § 111(d), Oct. 27, 1986, 100 Stat. 3091.)

HISTORICAL AND STATUTORY NOTES

Revision Notes and Legislative Reports

1978 Acts. Senate Report No. 95–989 and House Report No. 95–595, see 1978 U.S.Code Cong. and Adm.News, p. 5787.

1986 Acts. House Report No. 99–764 and House Conference Report No. 99–958, see 1986 U.S.Code Cong. and Adm. News, p. 5227.

Codifications

Section 408(c) of Pub.L. 95–598, as amended, which provided for the repeal of this section and the deletion of any references to United States Trustees in this title at a prospective date, was repealed by section 307(b) of Pub.L. 99–554. See note set out preceding section 581 of this title.

Effective and Applicability Provisions

1986 Acts. Amendment by Pub.L. 99–554 effective 30 days after Oct. 27, 1986, except as otherwise provided, see section 302(a) of Pub.L. 99–554, as amended, set out as a note under section 581 of this title.

1978 Acts. Section effective Oct. 1, 1979, see section 402(c) of Pub.L. 95–598, as amended, set out as a note preceding section 101 of Title 11, Bankruptcy.

Appointment of United States Trustees by Attorney General

Appointment of United States Trustees by the Attorney General of individuals otherwise qualified, serving as estate administrators under Title 11, Bankruptcy, before effective date of Pub.L. 99–554, see section 309 of Pub.L. 99–554, as amended; set out as a note under section 581 of this title.

§ 583. Oath of office

Each United States trustee and assistant United States trustee, before taking office, shall take an oath to execute faithfully his duties.

(Added Pub.L. 95–598, Title II, § 224(a), Nov. 6, 1978, 92 Stat. 2663.)

HISTORICAL AND STATUTORY NOTES

Revision Notes and Legislative Reports

1978 Acts. Senate Report No. 95–989 and House Report No. 95–595, see 1978 U.S.Code Cong. and Adm.News, p. 5787.

Codifications

Section 408(c) of Pub.L. 95–598, as amended, which provided for the repeal of this section and the deletion of any references to United States Trustees in this title at a prospective date, was repealed by section 307(b) of Pub.L. 99–554. See note set out preceding section 581 of this title.

Effective and Applicability Provisions

1978 Acts. Section effective Oct. 1, 1979, see section 402(c) of Pub.L. 95–598, as amended, set out as a note preceding section 101 of Title 11, Bankruptcy.

§ 584. Official stations

The Attorney General may determine the official stations of the United States trustees and assistant United States trustees within the regions for which they were appointed.

(Added Pub.L. 95–598, Title II, § 224(a), Nov. 6, 1978, 92 Stat. 2663; amended Pub.L. 99–554, Title I, § 144(d), Oct. 27, 1986, 100 Stat. 3096.)

HISTORICAL AND STATUTORY NOTES

Revision Notes and Legislative Reports

1978 Acts. Senate Report No. 95–989 and House Report No. 95–595, see 1978 U.S.Code Cong. and Adm.News, p. 5787.

1986 Acts. House Report No. 99–764 and House Conference Report No. 99–958, see 1986 U.S.Code Cong. and Adm. News, p. 5227.

Codifications

Section 408(c) of Pub.L. 95–598, as amended, which provided for the repeal of this section and the deletion of any references to United States Trustees in this title at a prospective date, was repealed by section 307(b) of Pub.L. 99–554. See note set out preceding section 581 of this title.

Effective and Applicability Provisions

1986 Acts. Amendment by Pub.L. 99–554 effective 30 days after Oct. 27, 1986, except as otherwise provided, see section 302(a) of Pub.L. 99–554, as amended, set out as a note under section 581 of this title.

1978 Acts. Section effective Oct. 1, 1979, see section 402(c) of Pub.L. 95–598, as amended, set out as a note preceding section 101 of Title 11, Bankruptcy.

§ 585. Vacancies

(a) The Attorney General may appoint an acting United States trustee for a region in which the office of the United States trustee is vacant. The individual so appointed may serve until the date on which the vacancy is filled by appointment under section 581 of this title or by designation under subsection (b) of this section.

(b) The Attorney General may designate a United States trustee to serve in not more than two regions for such time as the public interest requires.

(Added Pub.L. 95–598, Title II, § 224(a), Nov. 6, 1978, 92 Stat. 2663; amended Pub.L. 99–554, Title I, § 112, Oct. 27, 1986, 100 Stat. 3091.)

HISTORICAL AND STATUTORY NOTES

Revision Notes and Legislative Reports

1978 Acts. Senate Report No. 95–989 and House Report No. 95–595, see 1978 U.S. Code Cong. and Adm. News, p. 5787.

1986 Acts. House Report No. 99–764 and House Conference Report No. 99–958, see 1986 U.S. Code Cong. and Adm. News, p. 5227.

Codifications

Section 408(c) of Pub.L. 95–598, as amended, which provided for the repeal of this section and the deletion of any references to United States Trustees in this title at a prospective date, was repealed by section 307(b) of Pub.L. 99–554. See note set out preceding section 581 of this title.

Effective and Applicability Provisions

1986 Acts. Amendment by Pub.L. 99–554 effective 30 days after Oct. 27, 1986, except as otherwise provided, see section 302(a) of Pub.L. 99–554, as amended, set out as a note under section 581 of this title.

1978 Acts. Section effective Oct. 1, 1979, see section 402(c) of Pub.L. 95–598, as amended, set out as a note preceding section 101 of Title 11, Bankruptcy.

§ 586. Duties; supervision by Attorney General

(a) Each United States trustee, within the region for which such United States trustee is appointed, shall—

(1) establish, maintain, and supervise a panel of private trustees that are eligible and available to serve as trustees in cases under chapter 7 of title 11;

(2) serve as and perform the duties of a trustee in a case under title 11 when required under title 11 to serve as trustee in such a case;

(3) supervise the administration of cases and trustees in cases under chapter 7, 11, 12, 13, or 15 of title 11 by, whenever the United States trustee considers it to be appropriate—

(A)(i) reviewing, in accordance with procedural guidelines adopted by the Executive Office of the United States Trustee (which guidelines shall be applied uniformly by the United States trustee except when circumstances warrant different treatment), applications filed for compensation and reimbursement under section 330 of title 11; and

(ii) filing with the court comments with respect to such application and, if the United States Trustee considers it to be appropriate, objections to such application;

(B) monitoring plans and disclosure statements filed in cases under chapter 11 of title 11 and filing with the court, in connection with hearings under sections 1125 and 1128 of such title, comments with respect to such plans and disclosure statements;

(C) monitoring plans filed under chapters 12 and 13 of title 11 and filing with the court, in connection with hearings under sections 1224, 1229, 1324, and 1329 of such title, comments with respect to such plans;

(D) taking such action as the United States trustee deems to be appropriate to ensure that all reports, schedules, and fees required to be filed under title 11 and this title by the debtor are properly and timely filed;

(E) monitoring creditors' committees appointed under title 11;

(F) notifying the appropriate United States attorney of matters which relate to the occurrence of any action which may constitute a crime under the laws of the United States and, on the request of the United States attorney, assisting the United States attorney in carrying out prosecutions based on such action;

(G) monitoring the progress of cases under title 11 and taking such actions as the United States trustee deems to be appropriate to prevent undue delay in such progress;

(H) in small business cases (as defined in section 101 of title 11), performing the additional duties specified in title 11 pertaining to such cases; and

(I) monitoring applications filed under section 327 of title 11 and, whenever the United States trustee deems it to be appropriate, filing with the court comments with respect to the approval of such applications;

(4) deposit or invest under section 345 of title 11 money received as trustee in cases under title 11;

(5) perform the duties prescribed for the United States trustee under title 11 and this title, and such duties consistent with title 11 and this title as the Attorney General may prescribe;

(6) make such reports as the Attorney General directs, including the results of audits performed under section 603(a) of the Bankruptcy Abuse Prevention and Consumer Protection Act of 2005;

(7) in each of such small business cases—

(A) conduct an initial debtor interview as soon as practicable after the date of the order for relief but before the first meeting scheduled under section 341(a) of title 11, at which time the United States trustee shall—

(i) begin to investigate the debtor's viability;

(ii) inquire about the debtor's business plan;

(iii) explain the debtor's obligations to file monthly operating reports and other required reports;

(iv) attempt to develop an agreed scheduling order; and

(v) inform the debtor of other obligations;

(B) if determined to be appropriate and advisable, visit the appropriate business premises of the debtor, ascertain the state of the debtor's books and records, and verify that the debtor has filed its tax returns; and

(C) review and monitor diligently the debtor's activities, to determine as promptly as possible whether the debtor will be unable to confirm a plan; and

(8) in any case in which the United States trustee finds material grounds for any relief under section 1112 of title 11, apply promptly after making that finding to the court for relief.

(b) If the number of cases under chapter 12 or 13 of title 11 commenced in a particular region so warrants, the United States trustee for such region may, subject to the approval of the Attorney General, appoint one or more individuals to serve as standing trustee, or designate one or more assistant United States trustees to serve in cases under such chapter. The United States trustee for such region shall supervise any such individual appointed as standing trustee in the performance of the duties of standing trustee.

(c) Each United States trustee shall be under the general supervision of the Attorney General, who shall provide general coordination and assistance to the United States trustees.

(d)(1) The Attorney General shall prescribe by rule qualifications for membership on the panels established by United States trustees under paragraph (a)(1) of this section, and qualifications for appointment under subsection (b) of this section to serve as standing trustee in cases under chapter 12 or 13 of title 11. The Attorney General may not require that an individual be an attorney in order to qualify for appointment under subsection (b) of this section to serve as standing trustee in cases under chapter 12 or 13 of title 11.

(2) A trustee whose appointment under subsection (a)(1) or under subsection (b) is terminated or who ceases to be assigned to cases filed under title 11, United States Code, may obtain judicial review of the final agency decision by commencing an action in the district court of the United States for the district for which the panel to which the trustee is appointed under subsection (a)(1), or in the district court of the United States for the district in which the trustee is appointed under subsection (b) resides, after first exhausting all available administrative remedies, which if the trustee so elects, shall also include an administrative hearing on the record. Unless the trustee elects to have an administrative hearing on the record, the trustee shall be deemed to have exhausted all administrative remedies for purposes of this paragraph if the agency fails to make a final agency decision within 90 days after the trustee requests administrative remedies. The Attorney General shall prescribe procedures to implement this paragraph. The decision of the agency shall be affirmed by the district court unless it is unreasonable and without cause based on the administrative record before the agency.

(e)(1) The Attorney General, after consultation with a United States trustee that has appointed an individual under subsection (b) of this section to serve as standing trustee in cases under chapter 12 or 13 of title 11, shall fix—

(A) a maximum annual compensation for such individual consisting of—

(i) an amount not to exceed the highest annual rate of basic pay in effect for level V of the Executive Schedule; and

(ii) the cash value of employment benefits comparable to the employment benefits provided by the United States to individuals who are employed by the United States at the same rate of basic pay to perform similar services during the same period of time; and

(B) a percentage fee not to exceed—

(i) in the case of a debtor who is not a family farmer, ten percent; or

(ii) in the case of a debtor who is a family farmer, the sum of—

(I) not to exceed ten percent of the payments made under the plan of such debtor, with respect to payments in an aggregate amount not to exceed $450,000; and

(II) three percent of payments made under the plan of such debtor, with respect to payments made after the aggregate amount of payments made under the plan exceeds $450,000;

based on such maximum annual compensation and the actual, necessary expenses incurred by such individual as standing trustee.

(2) Such individual shall collect such percentage fee from all payments received by such individual under plans in the cases under chapter 12 or 13 of title 11 for which such individual serves as standing trustee. Such individual shall pay to the United States trustee, and the United States trustee shall deposit in the United States Trustee System Fund—

(A) any amount by which the actual compensation of such individual exceeds 5 per centum upon all payments received under plans in cases under chapter 12 or 13 of title 11 for which such individual serves as standing trustee; and

(B) any amount by which the percentage for all such cases exceeds—

(i) such individual's actual compensation for such cases, as adjusted under subparagraph (A) of paragraph (1); plus

(ii) the actual, necessary expenses incurred by such individual as standing trustee in such cases. Subject to the approval of the Attorney General, any or all of the interest earned from the deposit of payments under plans by such individual may be utilized to pay actual, necessary expenses without regard to the percentage limitation contained in subparagraph (d)(1)(B) of this section.

(3) After first exhausting all available administrative remedies, an individual appointed under subsection (b) may obtain judicial review of final agency action to deny a claim of actual, necessary expenses under this subsection by commencing an action in the district court of the United States for the district where the individual resides. The decision of the agency shall be affirmed by the district court unless it is unreasonable and without cause based upon the administrative record before the agency.

(4) The Attorney General shall prescribe procedures to implement this subsection.

(f)(1) The United States trustee for each district is authorized to contract with auditors to perform audits in cases designated by the United States trustee, in accordance with the procedures established under section 603(a) of the Bankruptcy Abuse Prevention and Consumer Protection Act of 2005.

(2)(A) The report of each audit referred to in paragraph (1) shall be filed with the court and transmitted to the United States trustee. Each report shall clearly and conspicuously specify any material misstatement of income or expenditures or of assets identified by the person performing the audit. In any case in which a material misstatement of income or expenditures or of assets has been reported, the clerk of the district court (or the clerk of the bankruptcy court if one is certified under section 156(b) of this title) shall give notice of the misstatement to the creditors in the case.

(B) If a material misstatement of income or expenditures or of assets is reported, the United States trustee shall—

(i) report the material misstatement, if appropriate, to the United States Attorney pursuant to section 3057 of title 18; and

(ii) if advisable, take appropriate action, including but not limited to commencing an adversary proceeding to revoke the debtor's discharge pursuant to section 727(d) of title 11.

(Added Pub.L. 95–598, Title II, § 224(a), Nov. 6, 1978, 92 Stat. 2663; amended Pub.L. 99–554, Title I, § 113, Oct. 27, 1986, 100 Stat. 3091; Pub.L. 101–509, Title V, § 529 [Title I, § 110(a)], Nov. 5, 1990, 104 Stat. 1427, 1452; Pub.L. 103–394, Title II, § 224(a), Title V, § 502, Oct. 22, 1994, 108 Stat. 4130, 4147; Pub.L. 109–8, Title IV, § 439, Title VI, § 603(b), Title VIII, § 802(c)(3), Title XII, § 1231, Apr. 20, 2005, 119 Stat. 113, 122, 146, 201; Pub.L. 111–327, § 2(c)(3), Dec. 22, 2010, 124 Stat. 3563.)

HISTORICAL AND STATUTORY NOTES

Revision Notes and Legislative Reports

1978 Acts. Senate Report No. 95–989 and House Report No. 95–595, see 1978 U.S. Code Cong. and Adm. News, p. 5787.

1986 Acts. House Report No. 99–764 and House Conference Report No. 99–958, see 1986 U.S. Code Cong. and Adm. News, p. 5227.

1994 Acts. House Report No. 103–835, see 1994 U.S. Code Cong. and Adm. News, p. 3340.

2005 Acts. House Report No. 109–31(Part I), see 2005 U.S. Code Cong. and Adm. News, p. 88.

References in Text

Chapter 12 or 13 of title 11, referred to in text, is 11 U.S.C.A. § 1201 et seq. or 11 U.S.C.A. § 1301 et seq., respectively.

Chapter 7, 11, 12, 13, or 15 of title 11, referred to in subsec. (a)(3), is 11 U.S.C.A. § 701 et seq., 11 U.S.C.A. § 1101 et seq., 11 U.S.C.A. § 1201 et seq., 11 U.S.C.A. § 1301 et seq., or 11 U.S.C.A. § 1501 et seq., respectively.

Section 603(a) of the Bankruptcy Abuse Prevention and Consumer Protection Act of 2005, referred to in subsecs. (a)(6) and (f)(1), is Pub.L. 109–8, Title VII, § 603(a), Apr. 20, 2005, 119 Stat. 122, which is set out as a note under this section.

Level V of the Executive Schedule, referred to in subsec. (e)(1)(A)(i), is set out in section 5316 of Title 5, Government Organization and Employees.

Codifications

Section 408(c) of Pub.L. 95–598, as amended, which provided for the repeal of this section and the deletion of any references to United States Trustees in this title at a prospective date, was repealed by section 307(b) of Pub.L. 99–554. See note set out preceding section 581 of this title.

Effective and Applicability Provisions

2005 Acts. Amendments by Pub.L. 109–8, § 603, effective 18 months after Apr. 20, 2005, see Pub.L. 109–8, § 603(e), set out as a note under 11 U.S.C.A. 521.

Except as otherwise provided, amendments by Pub.L. 109–8 effective 180 days after April 20, 2005, and inapplicable with respect to cases commenced under Title 11 before the effective date, see Pub.L. 109–8, § 1501, set out as a note under 11 U.S.C.A. § 101.

1994 Acts. Amendments by Pub.L. 103–394 effective on Oct. 22, 1994, and not to apply with respect to cases commenced under Title 11 of the United States Code before Oct. 22, 1994, see section 702 of Pub.L. 103–394, set out as a note under section 101 of Title 11, Bankruptcy.

1990 Acts. Amendment by Pub.L. 101–509 effective on such date as the President shall determine, but not earlier than 90 days, and not later than 180 days, after Nov. 5, 1990, see section 529 [Title III, § 305] of Pub.L. 101–509, set out as a note under section 5301 of Title 5, Government Organization and Employees. [See also related provisions in Ex. Ord. No. 12748, Feb. 1, 1991, 56 F.R. 4521, set out under that section.]

1986 Acts. Effective date and applicability of amendment by Pub.L. 99–554 dependent upon the judicial district involved, see section 302(d), (e) of Pub.L. 99–554, set out as a note under section 581 of this title.

1978 Acts. Section effective Oct. 1, 1979, see section 402(c) of Pub.L. 95–598, as amended, set out as a note preceding section 101 of Title 11, Bankruptcy.

Separability of Provisions

If any provision of or amendment made by Pub.L. 103–394 or the application of such provision or amendment to any person or circumstance is held to be unconstitutional, the remaining provisions of and amendments made by Pub.L. 103–394 and the application of such provisions and amendments to any person or circumstance shall not be affected thereby, see section 701 of Pub.L. 103–394, set out as a note under section 101 of Title 11, Bankruptcy.

Audit Procedures

Pub.L. 109–8, Title VI, § 603(a), Apr. 20, 2005, 119 Stat. 122, provided that:

"(a) In general.—

"(1) **Establishment of procedures.**—The Attorney General (in judicial districts served by United States trustees) and the Judicial Conference of the United States (in judicial districts served by bankruptcy administrators) shall establish procedures to determine the accuracy, veracity, and completeness of petitions, schedules, and other information that the debtor is required to provide under sections 521 and 1322 of title 11, United States Code, and, if applicable, section 111 of such title [11 U.S.C.A. § 111], in cases filed under chapter 7 or 13 of such title [11 U.S.C.A. § 701 or 1301 et seq.] in which the debtor is an individual. Such audits shall be in accordance with generally accepted auditing standards and performed by independent certified public accountants or independent licensed public accountants, provided that the Attorney General and the Judicial Conference, as appropriate, may develop alternative auditing standards not later than 2 years after the date of enactment of this Act [April 20, 2005].

"(2) **Procedures.**—Those procedures required by paragraph (1) shall—

"(A) establish a method of selecting appropriate qualified persons to contract to perform those audits;

"(B) establish a method of randomly selecting cases to be audited, except that not less than 1 out of every 250 cases in each Federal judicial district shall be selected for audit;

"(C) require audits of schedules of income and expenses that reflect greater than average variances from the statistical norm of the district in which the schedules were filed if those variances occur by reason of higher income or higher expenses than the statistical norm of the district in which the schedules were filed; and

"(D) establish procedures for providing, not less frequently than annually, public information concerning the aggregate results of such audits including the percentage of cases, by district, in which a material misstatement of income or expenditures is reported."

[Enactment of this note by Pub.L. 109–8, § 603, effective 18 months after Apr. 20, 2005, see Pub.L. 109–8, § 603(e), set out as a note under 11 U.S.C.A. § 521.]

[Except as otherwise provided, amendments by Pub.L. 109–8 effective 180 days after April 20, 2005, and inapplicable with respect to cases commenced under Title 11 before the effective date, see Pub.L. 109–8, § 1501, set out as a note under 11 U.S.C.A. § 101.]

Application to All Standing Trustees

Section 529 [Title I, § 110(b)] of Pub.L. 101–509 provided that: "The amendment made by subsection (a) [amending this section] shall apply to any trustee to whom the provisions of section 302(d)(3) of the Bankruptcy Judges, United States Trustees, and Family Farmer Bankruptcy Act of 1986 (Public Law 99–54 [Pub.L. 99–554]; 100 Stat. 3121) [set out in a note under section 581 of this title] apply."

CROSS REFERENCES

Appointment of disinterested person from panel of private trustees established under this section to serve as,

Interim trustee, see 11 USCA § 701.

Successor trustee, see 11 USCA § 703.

Appointment of standing trustee to serve in cases under,

Chapter thirteen of Bankruptcy, see 11 USCA § 1302.

Chapter twelve of Bankruptcy, see 11 USCA § 1202.

Compensation for services or reimbursement of expenses not allowable for standing trustee appointed under this section, see 11 USCA § 326.

Payments to standing trustee, percentage fee fixed under this section, see 11 USCA § 1326.

§ 587. Salaries

Subject to sections 5315 through 5317 of title 5, the Attorney General shall fix the annual salaries of United States trustees and assistant United States trustees at rates of compensation not in excess of the rate of basic compensation provided for Executive Level IV of the Executive Schedule set forth in section 5315 of title 5, United States Code.

(Added Pub.L. 95–598, Title II, § 224(a), Nov. 6, 1978, 92 Stat. 2664; amended Pub.L. 99–554, Title I, § 114(a), Oct. 27, 1986, 100 Stat. 3093.)

HISTORICAL AND STATUTORY NOTES

Revision Notes and Legislative Reports

1978 Acts. Senate Report No. 95–989 and House Report No. 95–595, see 1978 U.S.Code Cong. and Adm.News, p. 5787.

1986 Acts. House Report No. 99–764 and House Conference Report No. 99–958, see 1986 U.S.Code Cong. and Adm. News, p. 5227.

Codifications

Section 408(c) of Pub.L. 95–598, as amended, which provided for the repeal of this section and the deletion of any references to United States Trustees in this title at a prospective date, was repealed by section 307(b) of Pub.L. 99–554. See note set out preceding section 581 of this title.

Effective and Applicability Provisions

1986 Acts. Amendment by Pub.L. 99–554 effective 30 days after Oct. 27, 1986, except as otherwise provided, see section 302(a) of Pub.L. 99–554, as amended, set out as a note under section 581 of this title.

1978 Acts. Section effective Oct. 1, 1979, see section 402(c) of Pub.L. 95–598, as amended, set out as a note preceding section 101 of Title 11, Bankruptcy.

§ 588. Expenses

Necessary office expenses of the United States trustee shall be allowed when authorized by the Attorney General.

(Added Pub.L. 95–598, Title II, § 224(a), Nov. 6, 1978, 92 Stat. 2664.)

HISTORICAL AND STATUTORY NOTES

Revision Notes and Legislative Reports

1978 Acts. Senate Report No. 95–989 and House Report No. 95–595, see 1978 U.S.Code Cong. and Adm.News, p. 5787.

Codifications

Section 408(c) of Pub.L. 95–598, as amended, which provided for the repeal of this section and the deletion of any references to United States Trustees in this title at a prospec-

tive date, was repealed by section 307(b) of Pub.L. 99–554. See note set out preceding section 581 of this title.

Effective and Applicability Provisions

1978 Acts. Section effective Oct. 1, 1979, see section 402(c) of Pub.L. 95–598, as amended, set out as a note preceding section 101 of Title 11, Bankruptcy.

§ 589. Staff and other employees

The United States trustee may employ staff and other employees on approval of the Attorney General. (Added Pub.L. 95–598, Title II, § 224(a), Nov. 6, 1978, 92 Stat. 2664.)

HISTORICAL AND STATUTORY NOTES

Revision Notes and Legislative Reports

1978 Acts. Senate Report No. 95–989 and House Report No. 95–595, see 1978 U.S.Code Cong. and Adm.News, p. 5787.

Codifications

Section 408(c) of Pub.L. 95–598, as amended, which provided for the repeal of this section and the deletion of any references to United States Trustees in this title at a prospective date, was repealed by section 307(b) of Pub.L. 99–554. See note set out preceding section 581 of this title.

Effective and Applicability Provisions

1978 Acts. Section effective Oct. 1, 1979, see section 402(c) of Pub.L. 95–598, as amended, set out as a note preceding section 101 of Title 11, Bankruptcy.

Temporary Suspension of Limitation on Appointments

Pub.L. 99–554, Title I, § 114(b), Oct. 27, 1986, 100 Stat. 3093, provided that: "During the period beginning on the effective date of this Act [see section 302 of Pub.L. 99–554, as amended, set out as a note under section 581 of this title], and ending on October 1, 1989, the provisions of title 5 of the United States Code [Title 5, Government Organization and Employees] governing appointments in the competitive service shall not apply with respect to appointments under section 589 of title 28, United States Code [this section]."

§ 589a. United States Trustee System Fund

(a) There is hereby established in the Treasury of the United States a special fund to be known as the "United States Trustee System Fund" (hereinafter in this section referred to as the "Fund"). Monies in the Fund shall be available to the Attorney General without fiscal year limitation in such amounts as may be specified in appropriations Acts for the following purposes in connection with the operations of United States trustees—

(1) salaries and related employee benefits;

(2) travel and transportation;

(3) rental of space;

(4) communication, utilities, and miscellaneous computer charges;

(5) security investigations and audits;

(6) supplies, books, and other materials for legal research;

(7) furniture and equipment;

(8) miscellaneous services, including those obtained by contract; and

(9) printing.

(b) For the purpose of recovering the cost of services of the United States Trustee System, there shall be deposited as offsetting collections to the appropriation "United States Trustee System Fund", to remain available until expended, the following—

(1)(A) 40.46 percent of the fees collected under section 1930(a)(1)(A); and

(B) 28.33 percent of the fees collected under section 1930(a)(1)(B);

(2) 48.89 percent of the fees collected under section 1930(a)(3) of this title;

(3) one-half of the fees collected under section 1930(a)(4) of this title;

(4) one-half of the fees collected under section 1930(a)(5) of this title;

(5) 100 percent of the fees collected under section 1930(a)(6) of this title;

(6) three-fourths of the fees collected under the last sentence of section 1930(a) of this title;

(7) the compensation of trustees received under section 330(d) of title 11 by the clerks of the bankruptcy courts;

(8) excess fees collected under section 586(e)(2) of this title;

(9) interest earned on Fund investment; and

(10) fines imposed under section 110(*l*) of title 11, United States Code.

(c) Amounts in the Fund which are not currently needed for the purposes specified in subsection (a) shall be kept on deposit or invested in obligations of, or guaranteed by, the United States.

(d) The Attorney General shall transmit to the Congress, not later than 120 days after the end of each fiscal year, a detailed report on the amounts deposited in the Fund and a description of expenditures made under this section.

(e) There are authorized to be appropriated to the Fund for any fiscal year such sums as may be necessary to supplement amounts deposited under subsection (b) for the purposes specified in subsection (a). (Added Pub.L. 99–554, Title I, § 115(a), Oct. 27, 1986, 100 Stat. 3094; amended Pub.L. 101–162, Title IV, § 406(c), Nov. 21, 1989, 103 Stat. 1016; Pub.L. 102–140, Title I, § 111(b), (c), Oct. 28, 1991, 105 Stat. 795; Pub.L. 103–121, Title I, § 111(a)(2), (b)(2), (3), Oct. 27, 1993, 107 Stat. 1164; Pub.L. 104–91, Title I, § 101(a), Jan. 6, 1996, 110 Stat. 11, as amended Pub.L. 104–99, Title II, § 211, Jan. 26, 1996, 110 Stat. 37; Pub.L. 104–208, Div. A, Title I, § 101(a) [Title I, § 109(b)], Sept. 30, 1996, 110 Stat. 3009–18; Pub.L. 106–113, Div. B, § 1000(a)(1) [Title I, § 113], Nov. 29, 1999, 113 Stat. 1535, 1501A–6, 1501A–20; Pub.L. 109–8, Title III, § 325(b), Apr. 20,

2005, 119 Stat. 99; Pub.L. 109–13, Div. A, Title VI, § 6058(a), May 11, 2005, 119 Stat. 297; Pub.L. 110–161, Div. B, Title II, § 212(a), Dec. 26, 2007, 121 Stat. 1914; Pub.L. 112–121, § 3(b), May 25, 2012, 126 Stat. 348.)

HISTORICAL AND STATUTORY NOTES

Revision Notes and Legislative Reports

1986 Acts. House Report No. 99–764 and House Conference Report No. 99–958, see 1986 U.S. Code Cong. and Adm. News, p. 5227.

1989 Acts. Statement by President, see 1989 U.S. Code Cong. and Adm. News, p. 733–3.

1999 Acts. Statement by President, see 1999 U.S. Code Cong. and Adm. News, p. 290.

2005 Acts. House Report No. 109–31(Part I), see 2005 U.S. Code Cong. and Adm. News, p. 88.

House Conference Report No. 109–72, see 2005 U.S. Code Cong. and Adm. News, p. 240.

2007 Acts. House Report No. 110–197, see 2007 U.S. Code Cong. and Adm. News, p. 661.

Statement by President, see 2007 U.S. Code Cong. and Adm. News, p. S34.

Codifications

Section 101(a) of Pub.L. 104–91, as amended by section 211 of Pub.L. 104–99, provided in part that section 111(b) and (c) of the General Provisions for the Department of Justice in Title I of the Departments of Commerce, Justice, and State, the Judiciary, and Related Agencies Appropriations Act, 1996 (H.R. 2076) as passed by the House of Representatives on Dec. 6, 1995, was enacted into permanent law. Such section 111(b) and (c) of H.R. 2076 amended subsecs. (b) and (f) of this section. See 1996 Amendments notes set out under this section.

Effective and Applicability Provisions

2012 Acts. Pub.L. 112–121, § 3(e), May 25, 2012, 126 Stat. 349, provided that: "This section and the amendments made by this section [amending this section and 28 U.S.C.A. § 1930, enacting provisions set out as a note under 28 U.S.C.A. § 1931, and amending provisions set out as a note under 28 U.S.C.A. § 1931] shall take effect 180 days after the date of enactment of this Act [May 25, 2012]."

2005 Acts. Pub.L. 109–13, Div. A, Title VI, § 6058(b), May 11, 2005, 119 Stat. 297, provided that: "This section [amending this section and 28 U.S.C.A. § 1930, enacting provisions set out as a note under this section, and amending provisions set out as notes under this section and 28 U.S.C.A. §§ 1930 and 1931] and the amendment made by this section shall take effect immediately after the enactment of the Bankruptcy Abuse Prevention and Consumer Protection Act of 2005 [Pub.L. 109–8, approved Apr. 20, 2005]."

Except as otherwise provided, amendments by Pub.L. 109–8 effective 180 days after April 20, 2005, and inapplicable with respect to cases commenced under Title 11 before the effective date, see Pub.L. 109–8, § 1501, set out as a note under 11 U.S.C.A. § 101.

1999 Acts. Pub.L. 106–113, Div. B, § 1000(a)(1), [Title I, § 113], Nov. 29, 1999, 113 Stat. 1535, 1501A–20, provided in part that section 113 (amending this section and section 1930 of this title and provisions set out as a note under section 1931 of this title) is "[e]ffective 30 days after the enactment of this

Act [Department of Commerce, Justice, and State, the Judiciary and Related Agencies Appropriations Act, 2000, Pub.L. 106–113, Div. B, § 1000(a)(1), Nov. 29, 1999, 113 Stat. 1535, 1501A–3; see Tables for complete classification]".

1996 Acts. Pub.L. 104–208, Div. A, Title I, § 101(a) [Title I, § 109(c)], Sept. 30, 1996, 110 Stat. 3009–19, provided that: "Notwithstanding any other provision of law or of this Act [Pub.L. 104–208, Sept. 30, 1996, 110 Stat. 3009, see Tables for classification] the amendments to 28 U.S.C. 589a [this section] made by subsection (b) of this section shall take effect upon enactment of this Act [probably means the date of enactment of Pub.L. 104–208, 110 Stat. 3009, which was approved Sept. 30, 1996]."

1993 Acts. Section 111(a) of Pub.L. 103–121 provided in part that amendment by section 111(a)(2) of Pub.L. 103–121, amending subsec. (b)(1) of this section, is effective 30 days after Oct. 27, 1993.

Section 111(b) of Pub.L. 103–121 provided in part that amendment by section 111(b)(2) and (3) of Pub.L. 103–121, amending subsecs. (b)(2) and (f)(1) of this section, is effective 30 days after Oct. 27, 1993.

1991 Acts. Section 111 of Pub.L. 102–140 provided that the amendment made by that section is effective 60 days after Oct. 28, 1991.

1986 Acts. Enactment by Pub.L. 99–554 effective 30 days after Oct. 27, 1986, except as otherwise provided, see section 302(a) of Pub.L. 99–554, as amended, set out as a note under section 581 of this title.

Sunset Provisions

Pub.L. 109–8, Title III, § 325(d), Apr. 20, 2005, 119 Stat. 99, as amended Pub.L. 109–13, Div. A, Title VI, § 6058(b), May 11, 2005, 119 Stat. 297, which set forth a two-year effective period for the original amendments by Pub.L. 109–8 to this section, has been omitted. The amendment by Pub.L. 109–13, § 6058(a), to Pub.L. 109–8, § 325, omitted this note in the reenactment of the section, to take effect immediately after the enactment of the Bankruptcy Abuse Prevention and Consumer Protection Act of 2005 [Pub.L. 109–8, Apr. 20, 2005, 119 Stat. 23], see Pub.L. 109–13, § 6058(b), set out as an Effective and Applicability Provisions note under this section.

Termination of Reporting Requirements

For termination of reporting provisions of this section, effective May 15, 2000, see Pub.L. 104–66, § 3003, as amended, set out as a note under 31 U.S.C.A. § 1113, and the 9th item on page 119 of House Document No. 103–7.

Reporting requirement of subsec. (d) of this section excepted from termination under Pub.L. 104–66, § 3003(a)(1), as amended, set out in a note under 31 U.S.C.A. § 1113, see Pub.L. 106–197, § 1, set out as a note under 31 U.S.C.A. § 1113.

Deposits of Certain Fees for Fiscal Years 2018 through 2022

Pub.L. 115–72, Div. B, § 1004(b), Oct. 26, 2017, 131 Stat. 1232, provided that:

"Notwithstanding section 589a(b) of title 28, United States Code [subsec. (b) of this section], for each of fiscal years 2018 through 2022—

"(1) 98 percent of the fees collected under section 1930(a)(6) of such title shall be deposited as offsetting collections to the appropriation 'United States Trustee System Fund', to remain available until expended; and

"(2) 2 percent of the fees collected under section 1930(a)(6) of such title shall be deposited in the general fund of the Treasury."

CROSS REFERENCES

Compensation of Bankruptcy trustee to be deposited by clerk of bankruptcy court into Fund established by this section, see 11 USCA § 330.

§ 589b. Bankruptcy data

(a) Rules.—The Attorney General shall, within a reasonable time after the effective date of this section, issue rules requiring uniform forms for (and from time to time thereafter to appropriately modify and approve)—

(1) final reports by trustees in cases under chapters 7, 12, and 13 of title 11; and

(2) periodic reports by debtors in possession or trustees in cases under chapter 11 of title 11.

(b) Reports.—Each report referred to in subsection (a) shall be designed (and the requirements as to place and manner of filing shall be established) so as to facilitate compilation of data and maximum possible access of the public, both by physical inspection at one or more central filing locations, and by electronic access through the Internet or other appropriate media.

(c) Required information.—The information required to be filed in the reports referred to in subsection (b) shall be that which is in the best interests of debtors and creditors, and in the public interest in reasonable and adequate information to evaluate the efficiency and practicality of the Federal bankruptcy system. In issuing rules proposing the forms referred to in subsection (a), the Attorney General shall strike the best achievable practical balance between—

(1) the reasonable needs of the public for information about the operational results of the Federal bankruptcy system;

(2) economy, simplicity, and lack of undue burden on persons with a duty to file reports; and

(3) appropriate privacy concerns and safeguards.

(d) Final reports.—The uniform forms for final reports required under subsection (a) for use by trustees under chapters 7, 12, and 13 of title 11 shall, in addition to such other matters as are required by law or as the Attorney General in the discretion of the Attorney General shall propose, include with respect to a case under such title—

(1) information about the length of time the case was pending;

(2) assets abandoned;

(3) assets exempted;

(4) receipts and disbursements of the estate;

(5) expenses of administration, including for use under section 707(b), actual costs of administering cases under chapter 13 of title 11;

(6) claims asserted;

(7) claims allowed; and

(8) distributions to claimants and claims discharged without payment,

in each case by appropriate category and, in cases under chapters 12 and 13 of title 11, date of confirmation of the plan, each modification thereto, and defaults by the debtor in performance under the plan.

(e) **Periodic reports.**—The uniform forms for periodic reports required under subsection (a) for use by trustees or debtors in possession under chapter 11 of title 11 shall, in addition to such other matters as are required by law or as the Attorney General in the discretion of the Attorney General shall propose, include—

(1) information about the industry classification, published by the Department of Commerce, for the businesses conducted by the debtor;

(2) length of time the case has been pending;

(3) number of full-time employees as of the date of the order for relief and at the end of each reporting period since the case was filed;

(4) cash receipts, cash disbursements and profitability of the debtor for the most recent period and cumulatively since the date of the order for relief;

(5) compliance with title 11, whether or not tax returns and tax payments since the date of the order for relief have been timely filed and made;

(6) all professional fees approved by the court in the case for the most recent period and cumulatively since the date of the order for relief (separately reported, for the professional fees incurred by or on behalf of the debtor, between those that would have been incurred absent a bankruptcy case and those not); and

(7) plans of reorganization filed and confirmed and, with respect thereto, by class, the recoveries of the holders, expressed in aggregate dollar values and, in the case of claims, as a percentage of total claims of the class allowed.

(Added Pub.L. 109–8, Title VI, § 602(a), Apr. 20, 2005, 119 Stat. 120.)

HISTORICAL AND STATUTORY NOTES

Revision Notes and Legislative Reports

2005 Acts. House Report No. 109–31(Part I), see 2005 U.S. Code Cong. and Adm. News, p. 88.

References in Text

The effective date of this section, referred to in subsec. (a), means 180 days after April 20, 2005. See Pub.L. 109–8, § 1501, set out as an Effective and Applicability Provisions note for 2005 Acts under 11 U.S.C.A. § 101.

Chapters 7, 12, and 13 of title 11, referred to in subsecs. (a)(1) and (d), are 11 U.S.C.A. § 701 et seq., 11 U.S.C.A. § 1201 et seq., and 11 U.S.C.A. § 1301 et seq., respectively.

Chapter 11 of title 11, referred to in subsecs. (a)(2) and (e), is 11 U.S.C.A. § 1101 et seq.

Effective and Applicability Provisions

2005 Acts. Except as otherwise provided, amendments by Pub.L. 109–8 effective 180 days after April 20, 2005, and inapplicable with respect to cases commenced under Title 11 before the effective date, see Pub.L. 109–8, § 1501, set out as a note under 11 U.S.C.A. § 101.

PART III—COURT OFFICERS AND EMPLOYEES

CHAPTER 41—ADMINISTRATIVE OFFICE OF UNITED STATES COURTS

§ 604.   Duties of Director generally

(a) The Director shall be the administrative officer of the courts, and under the supervision and direction of the Judicial Conference of the United States, shall:

(1) Supervise all administrative matters relating to the offices of clerks and other clerical and administrative personnel of the courts;

(2) Examine the state of the dockets of the courts; secure information as to the courts' need of assistance; prepare and transmit semiannually to the chief judges of the circuits, statistical data and reports as to the business of the courts;

(3) Submit to the annual meeting of the Judicial Conference of the United States, at least two weeks prior thereto, a report of the activities of the Administrative Office and the state of the business of the courts, together with the statistical data submitted

to the chief judges of the circuits under paragraph (a)(2) of this section, and the Director's recommendations, which report, data and recommendations shall be public documents.

(4) Submit to Congress and the Attorney General copies of the report, data and recommendations required by paragraph (a)(3) of this section;

(5) Fix the compensation of clerks of court, deputies, librarians, criers, messengers, law clerks, secretaries, stenographers, clerical assistants, and other employees of the courts whose compensation is not otherwise fixed by law, and, notwithstanding any other provision of law, pay on behalf of Justices and judges of the United States appointed to hold office during good behavior, United States magistrate judges, bankruptcy judges appointed under chapter

6 of this title, judges of the District Court of Guam, judges of the District Court for the Northern Mariana Islands, judges of the District Court of the Virgin Islands, bankruptcy judges and magistrate judges retired under section 377 of this title, and judges retired under section 373 of this title, who are, [1] aged 65 or over, any increases in the cost of Federal Employees' Group Life Insurance imposed after April 24, 1999, including any expenses generated by such payments, as authorized by the Judicial Conference of the United States;

(6) Determine and pay necessary office expenses of courts, judges, and those court officials whose expenses are by law allowable, and the lawful fees of United States magistrate judges;

(7) Regulate and pay annuities to widows and surviving dependent children of justices and judges of the United States, judges of the United States Court of Federal Claims, bankruptcy judges, United States magistrate judges, Directors of the Federal Judicial Center, and Directors of the Administrative Office, and necessary travel and subsistence expenses incurred by judges, court officers and employees, and officers and employees of the Administrative Office, and the Federal Judicial Center, while absent from their official stations on official business, without regard to the per diem allowances and amounts for reimbursement of actual and necessary expenses established by the Administrator of General Services under section 5702 of title 5, except that the reimbursement of subsistence expenses may not exceed that authorized by the Director for judges of the United States under section 456 of this title;

(8) Disburse appropriations and other funds for the maintenance and operation of the courts;

(9) Establish pretrial services pursuant to section 3152 of title 18, United States Code;

(10) (A) Purchase, exchange, transfer, distribute, and assign the custody of lawbooks, equipment, supplies, and other personal property for the judicial branch of Government (except the Supreme Court unless otherwise provided pursuant to paragraph (17)); (B) provide or make available readily to each court appropriate equipment for the interpretation of proceedings in accordance with section 1828 of this title; and (C) enter into and perform contracts and other transactions upon such terms as the Director may deem appropriate as may be necessary to the conduct of the work of the judicial branch of Government (except the Supreme Court unless otherwise provided pursuant to paragraph (17)), and contracts for nonpersonal services providing pretrial services, agencies for the interpretation of proceedings, and for the provision of special interpretation services pursuant to section 1828 of this title may be awarded without regard to section 6101(b) to (d) of title 41;

(11) Audit vouchers and accounts of the courts, the Federal Judicial Center, the offices providing pretrial services, and their clerical and administrative personnel;

(12) Provide accommodations for the courts, the Federal Judicial Center, the offices providing pretrial services and their clerical and administrative personnel;

(13) Lay before Congress, annually, statistical tables that will accurately reflect the business transacted by the several bankruptcy courts, and all other pertinent data relating to such courts;

(14) Pursuant to section 1827 of this title, establish a program for the certification and utilization of interpreters in courts of the United States;

(15) Pursuant to section 1828 of this title, establish a program for the provision of special interpretation services in courts of the United States;

(16) (A) In those districts where the Director considers it advisable based on the need for interpreters, authorize the full-time or part-time employment by the court of certified interpreters; (B) where the Director considers it advisable based on the need for interpreters, appoint certified interpreters on a full-time or part-time basis, for services in various courts when he determines that such appointments will result in the economical provision of interpretation services; and (C) pay out of moneys appropriated for the judiciary interpreters' salaries, fees, and expenses, and other costs which may accrue in accordance with the provisions of sections 1827 and 1828 of this title;

(17) In the Director's discretion, (A) accept and utilize voluntary and uncompensated (gratuitous) services, including services as authorized by section 3102(b) of title 5, United States Code; and (B) accept, hold, administer, and utilize gifts and bequests of personal property for the purpose of aiding or facilitating the work of the judicial branch of Government, but gifts or bequests of money shall be covered into the Treasury;

(18) Establish procedures and mechanisms within the judicial branch for processing fines, restitution, forfeitures of bail bonds or collateral, and assessments;

(19) Regulate and pay annuities to bankruptcy judges and United States magistrate judges in accordance with section 377 of this title and paragraphs (1)(B) and (2) of section 2(c) of the Retirement and Survivors' Annuities for Bankruptcy Judges and Magistrates Act of 1988;

(20) Periodically compile—

(A) the rules which are prescribed under section 2071 of this title by courts other than the Supreme Court;

(B) the rules which are prescribed under section 358 of this title; and

(C) the orders which are required to be publicly available under section 360(b) of this title;

so as to provide a current record of such rules and orders;

(21) Establish a program of incentive awards for employees of the judicial branch of the United States Government, other than any judge who is entitled to hold office during good behavior;

(22) Receive and expend, either directly or by transfer to the United States Marshals Service or other Government agency, funds appropriated for the procurement, installation, and maintenance of security equipment and protective services for the United States Courts in courtrooms and adjacent areas, including building ingress/egress control, inspection of packages, directed security patrols, and other similar activities;

(23) Regulate and pay annuities to judges of the United States Court of Federal Claims in accordance with section 178 of this title; and

(24) Perform such other duties as may be assigned to him by the Supreme Court or the Judicial Conference of the United States.

(b) The clerical and administrative personnel of the courts shall comply with all requests by the Director for information or statistical data as to the state of court dockets.

(c) Inspection of court dockets outside the continental United States may be made through United States officials residing within the jurisdiction where the inspection is made.

(d) The Director, under the supervision and direction of the conference, shall:

(1) supervise all administrative matters relating to the offices of the United States magistrate judges;

(2) gather, compile, and evaluate all statistical and other information required for the performance of his duties and the duties of the conference with respect to such officers;

(3) lay before Congress annually statistical tables and other information which will accurately reflect the business which has come before the various United States magistrate judges, including (A) the number of matters in which the parties consented to the exercise of jurisdiction by a magistrate judge, (B) the number of appeals taken pursuant to the decisions of magistrate judges and the disposition of such appeals, and (C) the professional background and qualifications of individuals appointed under section 631 of this title to serve as magistrate judges;

(4) prepare and distribute a manual, with annual supplements and periodic revisions, for the use of such officers, which shall set forth their powers and duties, describe all categories of proceedings that may arise before them, and contain such other information as may be required to enable them to discharge their powers and duties promptly, effectively, and impartially.

(e) The Director may promulgate appropriate rules and regulations approved by the conference and not inconsistent with any provision of law, to assist him in the performance of the duties conferred upon him by subsection (d) of this section. Magistrate judges shall keep such records and make such reports as are specified in such rules and regulations.

(f) The Director may make, promulgate, issue, rescind, and amend rules and regulations (including regulations prescribing standards of conduct for Administrative Office employees) as may be necessary to carry out the Director's functions, powers, duties, and authority. The Director may publish in the Federal Register such rules, regulations, and notices for the judicial branch of Government as the Director determines to be of public interest; and the Director of the Federal Register hereby is authorized to accept and shall publish such materials.

(g)(1) When authorized to exchange personal property, the Director may exchange or sell similar items and may apply the exchange allowance or proceeds of sale in such cases in whole or in part payment for the property acquired, but any transaction carried out under the authority of this subsection shall be evidenced in writing.

(2) The Director hereby is authorized to enter into contracts for public utility services and related terminal equipment for periods not exceeding ten years.

(3)(A) In order to promote the recycling and reuse of recyclable materials, the Director may provide for the sale or disposal of recyclable scrap materials from paper products and other consumable office supplies held by an entity within the judicial branch.

(B) The sale or disposal of recyclable materials under subparagraph (A) shall be consistent with the procedures provided in sections 541–555 of title 40 for the sale of surplus property.

(C) Proceeds from the sale of recyclable materials under subparagraph (A) shall be deposited as offsetting collections to the fund established under section 1931 of this title and shall remain available until expended to reimburse any appropriations for the operation and maintenance of the judicial branch.

(4) The Director is hereby authorized:

(A) to enter into contracts for the acquisition of severable services for a period that begins in one fiscal year and ends in the next fiscal year to the same extent as the head of an executive agency under the authority of section 253*l* of Title 41, United States Code;

(B) to enter into contracts for multiple years for the acquisition of property and services to the same extent as executive agencies under the authority of section 254c of Title 41, United States Code; and

(C) to make advance, partial, progress or other payments under contracts for property or services to the same extent as executive agencies under the authority of section 255 of title 41, United States Code.

(h)(1) The Director shall, out of funds appropriated for the operation and maintenance of the courts, provide facilities and pay necessary expenses incurred by the judicial councils of the circuits and the Judicial Conference under chapter 16 of this title, including mileage allowance and witness fees, at the same rate as provided in section 1821 of this title. Administrative and professional assistance from the Administrative Office of the United States Courts may be requested by each judicial council and the Judicial Conference for purposes of discharging their duties under chapter 16 of this title.

(2) The Director of the Administrative Office of the United States Courts shall include in his annual report filed with the Congress under this section a summary of the number of complaints filed with each judicial council under chapter 16 of this title, indicating the general nature of such complaints and the disposition of those complaints in which action has been taken.
(June 25, 1948, c. 646, 62 Stat. 914; Aug. 3, 1956, c. 944, § 3, 70 Stat. 1026; Pub.L. 90–219, Title II, § 203, Dec. 20, 1967, 81 Stat. 669; Pub.L. 90–578, Title II, § 201, Title IV, § 402(b)(2), Oct. 17, 1968, 82 Stat. 1114, 1118; Pub.L. 92–397, § 4, Aug. 22, 1972, 86 Stat. 580; Pub.L. 93–619, Title II, § 204, Jan. 3, 1975, 88 Stat. 2089; Pub.L. 95–539, §§ 3, 4, Oct. 28, 1978, 92 Stat. 2043; Pub.L. 95–598, Title II, § 225, Nov. 6, 1978, 92 Stat. 2664; Pub.L. 96–82, § 5, Oct. 10, 1979, 93 Stat. 645; Pub.L. 96–458, § 5, Oct. 15, 1980, 94 Stat. 2040; Pub.L. 96–523, § 1(c)(1), Dec. 12, 1980, 94 Stat. 3040; Pub.L. 97–267, § 7, Sept. 27, 1982, 96 Stat. 1139; Pub.L. 99–554, Title I, § 116, Oct. 27, 1986, 100 Stat. 3095; Pub.L. 100–185, § 2, Dec. 11, 1987, 101 Stat. 1279; Pub.L. 100–659, § 6(a), Nov. 15, 1988, 102 Stat. 3918; Pub.L. 100–702, Title IV, § 402(a), Title X, §§ 1008, 1010, 1011, 1020(a)(2), Nov. 19, 1988, 102 Stat. 4650, 4667, 4668, 4671; Pub.L. 101–474, § 5(r), Oct. 30, 1990, 104 Stat. 1101; Pub.L. 101–647, Title XXV, § 2548, Nov. 29, 1990, 104 Stat. 4888; Pub.L. 101–650, Title III, §§ 306(e)(1), 321, 325(c)(1), Dec. 1, 1990, 104 Stat. 5111, 5117, 5121; Pub.L. 102–572, Title V, § 503, Title IX, § 902(b)(1), Oct. 29, 1992, 106 Stat. 4513, 4516; Pub.L. 106–113, § 1000(a)(1) [Title III, § 305], Nov. 29, 1999, 113 Stat. 1535, 1501A–37; Pub.L. 106–518, Title II, § 204, Title III, § 304(d), Nov. 13, 2000, 114 Stat. 2414, 2418; Pub.L. 107–217, § 3(g)(1), Aug. 21, 2002, 116 Stat. 1299; Pub.L. 107–273, Div. C, Title I, § 11043(e), Nov. 2, 2002, 116 Stat. 1855; Pub.L. 109–115, Div. A, Title IV, § 407(a), Nov. 30, 2005, 119 Stat. 2470; Pub.L. 110–177, Title V, § 502(a), Jan. 7, 2008, 121 Stat. 2542; Pub.L. 111–8, Div. D, Title III, § 307(a), Mar. 11, 2009, 123 Stat. 648; Pub.L. 111–350, § 5(g)(2), Jan. 4, 2011, 124 Stat. 3848.)

¹ So in original. The comma probably should not appear.

HISTORICAL AND STATUTORY NOTES
Revision Notes and Legislative Reports
1948 Acts. Based on sections 726–1 and 726a of Title 18, U.S.C., 1940 ed., Criminal Code and Criminal Procedure, and sections 1130(a), (b), and 1131 of Title 26, U.S.C., 1940 ed., Internal Revenue Code, Title 28, U.S.C., 1940 ed., §§ 9, 128, 222a, 245, 268a, 278a, 302–306, 374b, 446, 447, 450, 544, 545, 547, 557, 558, 560, 561, 561a, 562, 563, 565, 566, 595, and 596 and sections 11–204 and 11–403, District of Columbia Code, 1940 ed. (R.S. §§ 1075, 1085; Mar. 3, 1891, c. 517, §§ 2, 9, 26 Stat. 826, 829; Feb. 9, 1893, c. 74, § 4, 27 Stat. 435; July 30, 1894, c. 172, § 1, 28 Stat. 160; Mar. 3, 1901, c. 854, § 224, 31 Stat. 1224; June 30, 1902, c. 1329, 32 Stat. 528; Mar. 3, 1905, c. 1487, 33 Stat. 1259; Mar. 3, 1911, c. 231, § 5, 36 Stat. 1088; Mar. 3, 1911, c. 231, § 118a, as added June 17, 1930, c. 509, 46 Stat. 774; Mar. 3, 1911, c. 231, § 118b, as added Feb. 17, 1936, c. 75, 49 Stat. 1140; Mar. 3, 1911, c. 231, §§ 140, 163, 171, 189–193, 291, 36 Stat. 1136, 1140, 1141, 1143, 1167; Mar. 3, 1911, c. 231, §§ 304, 305, 308, as added Aug. 7, 1939, c. 501, § 1, 53 Stat. 1223; Aug. 23, 1912, c. 350, 37 Stat. 412; Feb. 26, 1919, c. 49, §§ 1, 2, 3, 4, 5, 7, 8, 40 Stat. 1182; July 19, 1919, c. 24, § 1, 41 Stat. 210; Nov. 4, 1919, c. 93, § 1, 41 Stat. 338; Feb. 11, 1921, c. 46, 41 Stat. 1099; Feb. 22, 1921, c. 70, § 7, 41 Stat. 1144; Mar. 4, 1921, c. 161, 41 Stat. 1412; June 1, 1922, c. 204, Title II, 42 Stat. 616; Jan. 3, 1923, c. 21, Title II, 42 Stat. 1084; Mar. 4, 1923, c. 265, 42 Stat. 1488; May 28, 1924, c. 204, Title II, 43 Stat. 221; Feb. 27, 1925, c. 364, Title II, 43 Stat. 1030; Apr. 29, 1926, c. 195, Title II, 44 Stat. 346, 347; May 21, 1928, c. 659, 45 Stat. 645; Mar. 2, 1929, c. 488, § 1, 45 Stat. 1475; June 16, 1930, c. 494, 46 Stat. 589; May 17, 1932, c. 190, 47 Stat. 158; June 25, 1936, c. 804, 49 Stat. 1921; Apr. 27, 1938, c. 180, Title II, § 1, 52 Stat. 264; Feb. 10, 1939, c. 2, §§ 1130(a), (b), 1131, 53 Stat. 162, 163; June 29, 1939, c. 248, Title II, 53 Stat. 902; May 14, 1940, c. 189, Titles III, IV, 54 Stat. 204, 209, 210; June 28, 1941, c. 258, Title IV, 55 Stat. 300–302; July 2, 1942, c. 472, Title IV, 56 Stat. 503, 504; June 28, 1943, c. 173, Title II, § 201, 57 Stat. 242, 243; June 26, 1944, c. 277, Title II, § 201, 58 Stat. 357; Dec. 7, 1944, c. 522, § 1, 58 Stat. 796; May 21, 1945, c. 129, Titles II, IV, 59 Stat. 184, 199; July 5, 1946, c. 541, Title IV, 60 Stat. 478, 479).

For purposes of uniformity, all provisions of law governing the regulation and allowance of office, travel, and subsistence expenses of all officers and employees of the courts, except those provisions relating to Supreme Court officers and employees, are incorporated in subsection (a)(6)(7) of this section. Likewise the provisions respecting the compensation of court officers and employees, except those of the Supreme Court, are incorporated in subsection (a)(5). In each instance the power to fix and determine such salaries and expenses is transferred to the Director of the Administrative Office of the United States Courts. This change is in conformity with the Administrative Office Act 1939 included in this chapter.

Compensation of bailiffs however is provided by sections 713 and 755 of this title and that of court reporters by section 753 of this title.

Salaries and travel expenses of Court of Claims Commissioners are covered by section 792 of this title.

The language "and the lawful fees of United States Commissioners" in subsection (a)(6) and "the offices of the United States Commissioners" in subsection (a)(9) is new. It conforms with sections 633, 636 and 639 of this title.

Subsection (a)(5)(7) covers the provisions of section 726–1 and 726a of Title 18, U.S.C., 1940 ed., which provided that probation officers' salaries, should not be less than $1,800 nor more than $3,600 per annum and their traveling expenses should not exceed more than 4 cents per mile.

Words, "and officers and employees of the Administrative Office" were added in subsection (a)(7) to expressly authorize travel and subsistence expenses of such officers and employees.

The power to fix such pay and allowances is transferred to the Director as above indicated, and conforms with the Administrative Office Act of 1939. For further explanation of the general supervision of probation officers, see reviser's note [now Revision Notes and Legislative Reports] under section 3654, H.Rept. to accompany H.R. 3190 for revision of Title 18, U.S.C.

Subsection (a)(8) covers the provisions of section 1131 of Title 26, U.S.C., 1940 ed. Such section 1131 authorized the Tax Court, successor to the Board of Tax Appeals, to make expenditures for personal services, rent, law books, reference books, periodicals, and provided that all expenditures should be paid out of appropriations for the Tax Court, on itemized vouchers approved by the court.

Two reference to "officials and employees covered by this chapter" were changed to "clerical and administrative personnel," following the language of paragraph (a)(1), conferring general power to supervise such personnel as respects administrative matters.

Similar language was used in paragraph (b) instead of "The clerks of the district courts, their deputies and assistants, and all other employees of said courts."

The provisions of section 374b of Title 28, U.S.C., 1940 ed., based on successive Acts relating to classification and compensation of secretaries and law clerks were omitted as temporary and unnecessary in revision, in view of subsection (a)(5) of this section under which the salaries of all personnel are necessarily limited by current appropriation Acts.

For increases in basic rates of compensation for other judicial officers and employees see, also, section 521 of Act June 30, 1945, c. 212.

The designation "senior circuit judges" was changed to "chief judges of the circuits" in conformity with section 45 of this title.

Provisions of section 11–204 of District of Columbia Code, 1940 ed., relating to appointment of clerk of the United States Court of Appeals for the District of Columbia, and deputy clerk, crier, and messenger thereof, and the provisions relating to accounting for fees, are incorporated in sections 711 and 713 of this title. Provisions of said section, requiring the clerk of such court to give bond, were omitted as covered by section 952 of this title. Provisions of said section, relating to regulation of clerk's fees by such court were omitted so as to render uniform the method of such regulation as prescribed by section 1913 of this title, and the provisions of said section, placing a maximum of five hundred dollars per year on the office expenditures of the clerk of such court, were omitted as inconsistent with this consolidated section.

For distribution of other provisions of sections on which this section is based, see Distribution Table.

Changes were made in phraseology and arrangement. 80th Congress House Report No. 308.

By Senate amendment, all provisions relating to the Tax Court were eliminated, therefore, as finally enacted, sections 1130(a)(b) and 1131 of Title 26 U.S.C., Internal Revenue Code [1940 ed.], did not constitute part of the source of this section.

However, no change in the text of the section was necessary. See 80th Congress Senate Report No. 1559.

As finally enacted, part of Act July 9, 1947, c. 211, Title IV, 61 Stat. 304, 305, which was classified to Title 28 U.S.C., 1946 ed., § 374b, became one of the sources of this section and was accordingly included in the schedule of repeals by Senate amendment. See 80th Congress Senate Report No. 1559.

1956 Acts. House Report No. 2170 and Conference Report No. 2934, see 1956 U.S. Code Cong. and Adm. News, p. 4354.

1967 Acts. Senate Report No. 781 and Conference Report No. 996, see 1967 U.S. Code Cong. and Adm. News, p. 2402.

1968 Acts. House Report No. 1629, see 1968 U.S. Code Cong. and Adm. News, p. 4252.

1972 Acts. House Report No. 92–1148, see 1972 U.S. Code Cong. and Adm. News, p. 3007.

1975 Acts. House Report No. 93–1508, see 1974 U.S. Code Cong. and Adm. News, p. 7401.

1978 Acts. House Report No. 95–1687, see 1978 U.S. Code Cong. and Adm. News, p. 4652.

Senate Report No. 95–989 and House Report No. 95–595, see 1978 U.S. Code Cong. and Adm. News, p. 5787.

1979 Acts. Senate Report No. 96–74 and House Conference Report No. 96–444, see 1979 U.S. Code Cong. and Adm. News, p. 1469.

1980 Acts. Senate Report No. 96–362, see 1980 U.S. Code Cong. and Adm. News, p. 4315.

House Report No. 96–1279, see 1980 U.S. Code Cong. and Adm. News, p. 6530.

1982 Acts. Senate Report No. 97–77 and House Conference Report No. 97–792, see 1982 U.S. Code Cong. and Adm. News, p. 2377.

1986 Acts. House Report No. 99–764 and House Conference Report No. 99–958, see 1986 U.S. Code Cong. and Adm. News, p. 5227.

1987 Acts. House Report No. 100–390, see 1987 U.S. Code Cong. and Adm. News, p. 2137.

1988 Acts. Senate Report No. 100–293 and House Conference Report No. 100–1072, see 1988 U.S. Code Cong. and Adm. News, p. 5564.

House Report No. 100–889, see 1988 U.S. Code Cong. and Adm. News, p. 5982.

1990 Acts. House Report No. 101–770, see 1990 U.S. Code Cong. and Adm. News, p. 1709.

House Report No. 101–681(Part I), see 1990 U.S. Code Cong. and Adm. News, p. 6472.

Senate Report No. 101–416, Related House Reports, and President's Signing Statement, see 1990 U.S. Code Cong. and Adm. News, p. 6802.

1992 Acts. House Report No. 102–1006, see 1992 U.S. Code Cong. and Adm. News, p. 3921.

1999 Acts. Statement by President, see 1999 U.S. Code Cong. and Adm. News, p. 290.

2002 Acts. House Report No. 107–479, see 2002 U.S. Code Cong. and Adm. News, p. 827.

House Conference Report No. 107–685 and Statement by President, see 2002 U.S. Code Cong. and Adm. News, p. 1120.

2005 Acts. House Conference Report No. 109–307, see 2005 U.S. Code Cong. and Adm. News, p. 1260.

Statement by President, see 2005 U.S. Code Cong. and Adm. News, p. S42.

2008 Acts. House Report No. 110–218(Part I), see 2007 U.S. Code Cong. and Adm. News, p. 827.

2009 Acts. Statement by President, see 2009 U.S. Code Cong. and Adm. News, p. S11.

References in Text

Chapter 6 of this title, referred to in subsec. (a)(5), is chapter 6 of part I of this title, which is classified to 28 U.S.C.A. § 151 et seq.

Section 2(c) of the Retirement and Survivors' Annuities for Bankruptcy Judges and Magistrates Act of 1988, referred to in subsec. (a)(19), is section 2(c) of Pub.L. 100–659, Nov. 15, 1988, 102 Stat. 3916, which is set out as a note under section 377 of this title.

Section 253*l* of Title 41, United States Code, referred to in subsec. (g)(4)(A), probably means section 303L of Act June 30, 1949, c. 288, which was classified to section 253*l* of former Title 41, Public Contracts, and was repealed and restated as section 3902 of Title 41, Public Contracts, by Pub.L. 111–350, §§ 3, 7(b), Jan. 4, 2011, 124 Stat. 3677, 3855.

Section 254c of Title 41, United States Code, referred to in subsec. (g)(4)(B), probably means section 304B of Act June 30, 1949, c. 288, which was classified to section 254c of former Title 41, Public Contracts, and was repealed and restated as section 3903 of Title 41, Public Contracts, by Pub.L. 111–350, §§ 3, 7(b), Jan. 4, 2011, 124 Stat. 3677, 3855.

Section 255 of Title 41, referred to in subsec. (g)(4)(C), probably means section 305 of Act June 30, 1949, c. 288, which was classified to section 255 of former Title 41, Public Contracts, and was repealed and restated as chapter 45 (§ 4501 et seq.) of Title 41, Public Contracts, by Pub. L. 111–350, §§ 3, 7(b), Jan. 4, 2011, 124 Stat. 3677, 3855.

Codifications

Pub.L. 101–650, § 306(e)(1)(A), directing amendment of Pub.L. 100–702, § 402(1), probably intended amendment of section 402(a)(1) of pub.L. 100–702, which provided for redesignation of subsec. (a)(19) to be subsec. (a)(23) of this section, redesignated as subsec. (a)(24) by Pub.L. 101–650, § 306(e)(1)(B)(ii).

Amendment by Pub.L. 109–115, Div. A, § 407(a), which directed that this section is amended by adding "section (4) at the end of section '(g)'" was executed by adding par. (4) to the end of subsec. (g), as the probable intent of Congress.

Effective and Applicability Provisions

2009 Acts. Pub.L. 111–8, Div. D, Title III, § 307(c), Mar. 11, 2009, 123 Stat. 649, provided that: "Subsection (b) [enacting provisions set out as a note under 5 U.S.C.A. § 8701] and the amendment made by subsection (a) [amending this section] shall apply with respect to any payment made on or after the first day of the first applicable pay period beginning on or after the date of the enactment of Public Law 110–177 [Jan. 7, 2008]."

2008 Acts. Pub.L. 110–177, Title V, § 502(c), Jan. 7, 2008, 121 Stat. 2542, provided that: "Subsection (b) [enacting provisions set out as a note under 5 U.S.C.A. § 8701] and the amendment made by subsection (a) [amending this section] shall apply with respect to any payment made on or after the first day of the first applicable pay period beginning on or after the date of enactment of this Act [Jan. 7, 2008]."

1992 Acts. Amendment by section 902(b)(1) of Pub.L. 102–572 effective Oct. 29, 1992, see section 911 of Pub.L. 102–572, set out as a note under section 171 of this title.

Amendment by Pub.L. 102–572 effective Jan. 1, 1993, see section 1101(a) of Pub.L. 102–572, set out as a note under section 905 of Title 2, The Congress.

1990 Acts. Amendment by section 306(e)(1) of Pub.L. 101–650 applicable to judges of, and senior judges in active service with, the United States Court of Federal Claims on or after Dec. 1, 1990, see section 306(f) of Pub.L. 101–650, set out as a note under section 8331 of Title 5, Government Organization and Employees.

1988 Acts. Amendment by section 402(a) of Pub.L. 100–702 effective Dec. 1, 1988, see section 407 of Pub.L. 100–702, set out as a note under section 2071 of this title.

Amendment to this section by Pub.L. 100–659 to take effect on Nov. 15, 1988, and shall apply to bankruptcy judges and magistrates who retire on or after Nov. 15, 1988, with special election provisions for bankruptcy judges, etc., who left office on or after July 31, 1987, and before Nov. 15, 1988, see section 9 of Pub.L. 100–659, set out as a note under section 377 of this title.

1986 Acts. Amendment by Pub.L. 99–554 effective 30 days after Oct. 27, 1986, except as otherwise provided, see section 302(a) of Pub.L. 99–554, as amended, set out as a note under section 581 of this title.

1980 Acts. Amendment by Pub.L. 96–523 effective sixty days after Dec. 12, 1980, see section 3 of Pub.L. 96–523, set out as a note under section 3102 of Title 5, Government Organization and Employees.

Amendment by Pub.L. 96–458 effective Oct. 1, 1981, see section 7 of Pub.L. 96–458, set out as a note under section 331 of this title.

1978 Acts. Amendment by Pub.L. 95–598 effective Oct. 1, 1979, see section 402(c) of Pub.L. 95–598, as amended, set out as a note preceding section 101 of Title 11, Bankruptcy.

Amendment by Pub.L. 95–539 effective Oct. 28, 1978, see section 10(a) of Pub.L. 95–539, set out as a note under section 602 of this title.

1968 Acts. Amendment by Pub.L. 90–578 effective Oct. 17, 1968, except when a later effective date is applicable, which is the earlier of date when implementation of amendment by appointment of magistrates and assumption of office takes place or third anniversary of enactment of Pub.L. 90–578 on Oct. 17, 1968, see section 403 of Pub.L. 90–578, set out as a note under section 631 of this title.

Termination of Reporting Requirements

For termination, effective May 15, 2000, of provisions in subsecs. (a)(4), (d)(3), and (h)(2) of this section relating to reporting certain information annually to Congress, see Pub.L. 104–66, § 3003, as amended, set out as a note under 31 U.S.C.A. § 1113 and page 12 of House Document No. 103–7.

Change of Name

"United States magistrate judge" substituted for "United States magistrate" in text pursuant to section 321 of Pub.L. 101–650, set out as a note under 28 U.S.C.A. § 631. Previously, United States commissioners, referred to in text, were replaced by United States magistrates pursuant to Pub.L. 90–578, Oct. 17, 1968, 82 Stat. 1118. See chapter 43 of Title 28, 28 U.S.C.A. § 631 et seq.

Authority; Termination

Pub.L. 109–115, Div. A, Title IV, § 407(c), Nov. 30, 2005, 119 Stat. 2471, which provided that the authorities granted in

---

this section [Pub.L. 109–115, Div. A, Title IV, § 407, 119 Stat. 2470, which amended subsec. (g)(4) of this section and 28 U.S.C.A. § 612] shall expire on September 30, 2010, was repealed by Pub.L. 111–8, Div. D, Title III, § 308, Mar. 11, 2009, 123 Stat. 649.

Compensation and Appointment of Secretaries and Law Clerks

Provisions authorizing the appointment and compensation of secretaries and law clerks to circuit and district judges in such number and at such rates of compensation as may be determined by the Judicial Conference of the United States were contained in the following appropriation Acts:

Dec. 12, 1985, Pub.L. 99–180, Title IV, § 400, 99 Stat. 1154.

Aug. 30, 1984, Pub.L. 98–411, Title IV, § 400, 98 Stat. 1571.

Nov. 28, 1983, Pub.L. 98–166, Title IV, § 400, 97 Stat. 1099.

Dec. 21, 1982, Pub.L. 97–377, § 101(d) [S. 2956, Title IV, § 400], 96 Stat. 1866.

Dec. 15, 1981, Pub.L. 97–92, § 101(h) [incorporating Pub.L. 96–536, § 101(o); H.R. 7584, Title IV, § 400], 95 Stat. 1190.

Dec. 16, 1980, Pub.L. 96–536, § 101(o) [H.R. 7584, Title IV, § 400], 94 Stat. 3169.

Sept. 24, 1979, Pub.L. 96–68, Title IV, § 400, 93 Stat. 428.

Oct. 10, 1978, Pub.L. 95–431, Title IV, § 401, 92 Stat. 1037.

Aug. 2, 1977, Pub.L. 95–86, Title IV, § 401, 91 Stat. 435.

July 14, 1976, Pub.L. 94–362, Title IV, § 401, 90 Stat. 953.

Oct. 21, 1975, Pub.L. 94–121, Title IV, § 401, 89 Stat. 630.

Oct. 5, 1974, Pub.L. 93–433, Title IV, § 401, 88 Stat. 1202.

Nov. 27, 1973, Pub.L. 93–162, Title IV, § 401, 87 Stat. 651.

Oct. 25, 1972, Pub.L. 92–544, Title IV, § 401, 86 Stat. 1126.

Aug. 10, 1971, Pub.L. 92–77, Title IV, § 401, 85 Stat. 262.

Oct. 21, 1970, Pub.L. 91–472, Title IV, § 401, 84 Stat. 1056.

Dec. 24, 1969, Pub.L. 91–153, Title IV, § 401, 83 Stat. 419.

Aug. 9, 1968, Pub.L. 90–470, Title IV, § 401, 82 Stat. 685.

Nov. 8, 1967, Pub.L. 90–133, Title IV, § 401, 81 Stat. 427.

Nov. 8, 1966, Pub.L. 89–797, Title IV, § 401, 80 Stat. 1499.

Sept. 2, 1965, Pub.L. 89–164, Title IV, § 401, 79 Stat. 638.

Aug. 31, 1964, Pub.L. 88–527, Title IV, § 401, 78 Stat. 729.

Dec. 30, 1963, Pub.L. 88–245, Title IV, § 401, 77 Stat. 795.

Oct. 18, 1962, Pub.L. 87–843, Title IV, § 401, 76 Stat. 1099.

Sept. 21, 1961, Pub.L. 87–264, Title III, § 301, 75 Stat. 555.

Aug. 31, 1960, Pub.L. 86–678, Title III, § 301, 74 Stat. 566.

July 13, 1959, Pub.L. 86–84, Title III, § 301, 73 Stat. 192.

June 30, 1958, Pub.L. 85–474, Title III, § 301, 72 Stat. 254.

June 11, 1957, Pub.L. 85–40, Title III, § 301, 70 Stat. 65.

June 20, 1956, c. 414, Title III, § 301, 70 Stat. 310.

July 7, 1955, c. 279, Title III, § 301, 69 Stat. 276.

July 2, 1954, c. 455, Title II, § 201, 68 Stat. 410.

Aug. 1, 1953, c. 304, Title II, § 201, 67 Stat. 334.

July 10, 1952, c. 651, Title IV, § 401, 66 Stat. 569.

Oct. 22, 1951, c. 533, Title IV, § 401, 65 Stat. 596.

Sept. 6, 1950, c. 896, ch. III, Title IV, § 401, 64 Stat. 631.

Increases in Compensation Rates

Increases in rates of basic compensation fixed pursuant to subsec. (a)(5) of this section, see notes under section 603 of this title.

Limitation on Aggregate Salaries of Secretaries and Law Clerks

1967—Pub.L. 90–206, Title II, § 213(b), Dec. 16, 1967, 81 Stat. 635, provided that: "The limitations provided by applicable law on the effective date of this section [see Effective and Applicability Provisions of 1967 amendments note set out under section 5332 of Title 5, Government Organization and Employees] with respect to the aggregate salaries payable to secretaries and law clerks of circuit and district judges are hereby increased by amounts which reflect the respective applicable increases provided by section 202(a) of this title [amending section 5332(a) of Title 5] in corresponding rates of compensation for officers and employees subject to section 5332 of title 5, United States Code [section 5332 of Title 5]."

Section 213(b) of Pub.L. 90–206 effective as of the beginning of the first pay period which begins on or after Oct. 1, 1967, see section 220(a)(2) of Pub.L. 90–206, set out as a note under section 5332 of Title 5, Government Organization and Employees.

1966—Pub.L. 89–504, Title II, § 202(b), July 18, 1966, 80 Stat. 294, provided that: "The limitations provided by applicable law on the effective date of this section with respect to the aggregate salaries payable to secretaries and law clerks of circuit and district judges are hereby increased by amounts which reflect the respective applicable increases provided by section 102(a) of title I of this Act [amending section 1113(b) of former Title 5, Executive Departments and Government Officers and Employees] in corresponding rates of compensation for officers and employees subject to the Classification Act of 1949, as amended [chapter 51 and subchapter III of chapter 53 of Title 5, Government Organization and Employees]."

Provision effective the first day of the first pay period which begins on or after July 1, 1966, see section 203 of Pub.L. 89–504, set out as a note under section 603 of this title.

1965—Pub.L. 89–301, § 12(b), Oct. 29, 1965, 79 Stat. 1122, provided that: "The limitations provided by applicable law on the effective date of this section with respect to the aggregate salaries payable to secretaries and law clerks of circuit and district judges are hereby increased by amounts which reflect the respective applicable increases provided by section 2(a) of this Act [amending section 1113(b) of former Title 5, Executive Departments and Government Officers and Employees] in corresponding rates of compensation for officers and employees subject to the Classification Act of 1949, as amended [chapter 51 and subchapter III of chapter 53 of Title 5, Government Organization and Employees]."

1964—Pub.L. 88–426, Title IV, § 402(b), Aug. 14, 1964, 78 Stat. 433, provided that: "The limitations provided by applicable law on the effective date of this section with respect to the aggregate salaries payable to secretaries and law clerks of circuit and district judges are hereby increased by amounts which reflect the respective applicable increases provided by title I of this Act in corresponding rates of compensation for officers and employees subject to the Classification Act of 1949, as amended [chapter 51 and subchapter III of chapter 53 of Title 5, Government Organization and Employees]."

1962—Pub.L. 87–793, Title VI, § 1004(b), Oct. 11, 1962, 76 Stat. 866, provided that: "The limitations provided by applicable law on the effective date of this section with respect to the aggregate salaries payable to secretaries and law clerks of circuit and district judges are hereby increased by two amounts, the first amount to be effective for the period beginning as of the first day of the first pay period which begins on or after the date of enactment of this Act [Oct. 11, 1962], and ending immediately prior to the first day of the first pay period which begins on or after January 1, 1964, and the second amount to be effective on the first day of the first pay period which begins on or after January 1, 1964, and thereafter, which reflect the respective applicable increases provided by title II of this part in corresponding rates of compensation for officers and employees subject to the Classification Act of 1949, as amended [chapter 51 and subchapter III of chapter 53 of Title 5, Government Organization and Employees]."

1960—Pub.L. 86–568, Title I, § 116(b), July 1, 1960, 74 Stat. 303, provided that: "The limitations provided by applicable law on the effective date of this section with respect to the aggregate salaries payable to secretaries and law clerks of circuit and district judges are hereby increased by the amounts necessary to pay the additional basic compensation provided by this part."

Words "this part", referred to in section 116(b) of Pub.L. 86–568 [this note], means Part B of Pub.L. 86–568, which enacted section 932e of former Title 5, Executive Departments and Government Officers and Employees, amended section 753 of this title, sections 1113, 2091, 2252 and 3002 of former Title 5, sections 867 and 870 of Title 22, Foreign Relations and Intercourse, and sections 4103, 4107 and 4108 of Title 38, Veterans' Benefits and enacted notes set out under sections 603 and 604 of this title, sections 60a and 60f of Title 2, The Congress, sections 1113 and 2252 of former Title 5, section 590h of Title 16, Conservation, and section 867 of Title 22.

1958—Pub.L. 85–462, § 3(b), June 20, 1958, 72 Stat. 207, provided that: "The limitations of $13,485 and $18,010 with respect to the aggregate salaries payable to secretaries and law clerks of circuit and district judges, contained in the paragraph designated "Salaries of supporting personnel" in the Judiciary Appropriation Act, 1958 (71 Stat. 65; Public Law 85–49), or any subsequent appropriation Act, shall be increased by the amounts necessary to pay the additional basic compensation provided by this Act."

1955—Act June 28, 1955, c. 189, § 3(b), 69 Stat. 175, provided that: "The limitations of $10,560 and $14,355 with respect to the aggregate salaries payable to secretaries and law clerks of circuit and district judges, contained in the paragraph under the heading 'SALARIES OF SUPPORTING PERSONNEL' in the Judiciary Appropriation Act, 1955 (Public Law 470, Eighty-third Congress), or in any subsequent appropriation Act, shall be increased by the amounts necessary to pay the additional basic compensation provided by this Act."

1951—Act Oct. 24, 1951, c. 554, § 1(d), 65 Stat. 613, provided that: "The limitations of $9,600 and $13,050 with respect to the aggregate salaries payable to secretaries and law clerks of circuit and district judges, contained in the sixteenth paragraph under the head 'Miscellaneous salaries' in the Judiciary Appropriation Act, 1951 (Public Law 759, Eighty-first Congress), or in any subsequent appropriation Act, shall be increased by the amounts necessary to pay the additional basic compensation provided by this Act."

The particular paragraph of the "Judiciary Appropriation Act, 1951 (Public Law 759, Eighty-first Congress)", referred to in section 1(d) of Act Oct. 24, 1951, c. 554 [this note], is Act Sept. 6, 1950, c. 896, ch. III, Title IV, § 401 (part), 64 Stat. 631. The salary limitations therein, also referred to above, were identical with those in the Judiciary Appropriation Act, 1952 (Act Oct. 22, 1951, c. 533, Title IV, § 401 (part), 65 Stat. 596).

1970 Increase in Pay Rates of Judicial Branch Employees Whose Rates of Pay Are Fixed by Administrative Action

Adjustment of rates of pay of judicial branch employees whose rates of pay are fixed by administrative action by not to exceed the amounts of the adjustment for corresponding rates for employees subject to section 2(a) of Pub.L. 91–231, which raised corresponding rates by 6 percent, effective on the first day of the first pay period which begins on or after Dec. 27, 1969, see Pub.L. 91–231, set out as a note under section 5332 of Title 5, Government Organization and Employees.

Reports by Director of Administrative Office of United States Courts

For requirement that Director of Administrative Office of the United States Courts include statistical information about implementation of chapter 44 of this title in annual report under section 604(a)(3) of this title, see section 903(a) of Pub.L. 100–702, set out as a note under section 651 of this title.

Travel and Subsistence Expenses

Pub.L. 87–139, § 6, Aug. 14, 1961, 75 Stat. 340, provided that: "The Director of the Administrative Office of the United States Courts shall promulgate, in accordance with section 604(a)(7) and section 456 of title 28 of the United States Code [subsec. (a)(7) of this section and section 456 of this title], such regulations as he may deem necessary to effectuate the increases provided by this Act [amending section 553 of this title, section 68b of Title 2, The Congress, sections 73b–2, 836 and 837 of former Title 5, Executive Departments and Government Officers and Employees, and sections 287o, 287q and 1471 of Title 22, Foreign Relations and Intercourse]."

CROSS REFERENCES

Actual abode of recalled judge or magistrate deemed official station for purposes of this section, see 28 USCA § 374.

Annual report to Judicial Conference under this section to include administration and operation pretrial services for previous year, see 18 USCA § 3155.

Classification and general schedule pay rates, see 5 USCA §§ 5101 et seq. and 5331 et seq.

Duties of Supreme Court marshal, see 28 USCA § 672.

Expenses of judges and United States attorneys, see 28 USCA §§ 456, 460, 549, and 566.

Juror travel allowance not to exceed maximum rate per mile that Director prescribes pursuant to this section, see 28 USCA § 1871.

Notification to Attorney General of receipt of payment of unpaid fines, see 18 USCA § 3612.

Office expenses of clerks of court, see 28 USCA § 961.

Overtime pay, see 5 USCA § 5541 et seq.

Specification by Director in payment of fine as provided under this section, see 18 USCA § 3611.

Supreme Court officers and employees, compensation and disbursement, see 28 USCA § 671 et seq.

CHAPTER 44—ALTERNATIVE DISPUTE RESOLUTION

§ 651. Authorization of alternative dispute resolution

(a) **Definition.**—For purposes of this chapter, an alternative dispute resolution process includes any process or procedure, other than an adjudication by a presiding judge, in which a neutral third party participates to assist in the resolution of issues in controversy, through processes such as early neutral evaluation, mediation, minitrial, and arbitration as provided in sections 654 through 658.

(b) **Authority.**—Each United States district court shall authorize, by local rule adopted under section 2071(a), the use of alternative dispute resolution processes in all civil actions, including adversary proceedings in bankruptcy, in accordance with this chapter, except that the use of arbitration may be authorized only as provided in section 654. Each United States district court shall devise and implement its own alternative dispute resolution program, by local rule adopted under section 2071(a), to encourage and promote the use of alternative dispute resolution in its district.

(c) **Existing alternative dispute resolution programs.**—In those courts where an alternative dispute resolution program is in place on the date of the enactment of the Alternative Dispute Resolution Act of 1998, the court shall examine the effectiveness of that program and adopt such improvements to the program as are consistent with the provisions and purposes of this chapter.

(d) **Administration of alternative dispute resolution programs.**—Each United States district court shall designate an employee, or a judicial officer, who is knowledgeable in alternative dispute resolution practices and processes to implement, administer, oversee, and evaluate the court's alternative dispute resolution program. Such person may also be responsible for recruiting, screening, and training attorneys to serve as neutrals and arbitrators in the court's alternative dispute resolution program.

(e) **Title 9 not affected.**—This chapter shall not affect title 9, United States Code.

(f) **Program support.**—The Federal Judicial Center and the Administrative Office of the United States Courts are authorized to assist the district courts in the establishment and improvement of alternative dispute resolution programs by identifying particular practices employed in successful programs and providing additional assistance as needed and appropriate.
(Added Pub.L. 100–702, Title IX, § 901(a), Nov. 19, 1988, 102 Stat. 4659; amended Pub.L. 105–315, § 3, Oct. 30, 1998, 112 Stat. 2993.)

HISTORICAL AND STATUTORY NOTES

Revision Notes and Legislative Reports

1988 Acts. House Report No. 100–889, see 1988 U.S. Code Cong. and Adm. News, p. 5982.

References in Text

The enactment of the Alternative Dispute Resolution Act of 1998, referred to in subsec. (c), is the enactment of Pub.L. 105–315, 112 Stat. 2993, which was approved Oct. 30, 1998.

Effective and Applicability Provisions

1988 Acts. Section 906 of Title IX of Pub.L. 100–702, as amended Pub.L. 103–192, § 1(a), Dec. 14, 1993, 107 Stat. 2292, which provided that, effective December 31, 1994, this chapter, as added by section 901 of Pub.L. 100–702, and the item relating to this chapter in the table of chapters at the beginning of part III of this title, were repealed, except that the provisions of this chapter were to continue to apply through final disposition of all actions in which referral to arbitration was made before the date of repeal, was itself repealed by Pub.L. 103–420, § 3(b), Oct. 25, 1994, 108 Stat. 4345.

Section 907 of Title IX of Pub.L. 100–702 provided that: "This title and the amendments made by this title [enacting this chapter, provisions set out as notes under this section and section 652 of this title] shall take effect 180 days after the date of enactment of this Act [Nov. 19, 1988]."

Findings and Declaration of Policy

Pub.L. 105–315, § 2, Oct. 30, 1998, 112 Stat. 2993, provided that:

"Congress finds that—

"(1) alternative dispute resolution, when supported by the bench and bar, and utilizing properly trained neutrals in a program adequately administered by the court, has the potential to provide a variety of benefits, including greater satisfaction of the parties, innovative methods of resolving disputes, and greater efficiency in achieving settlements;

"(2) certain forms of alternative dispute resolution, including mediation, early neutral evaluation, minitrials, and voluntary arbitration, may have potential to reduce the large backlog of cases now pending in some Federal courts throughout the United States, thereby allowing the courts to process their remaining cases more efficiently; and

"(3) the continued growth of Federal appellate court-annexed mediation programs suggests that this form of alternative dispute resolution can be equally effective in resolving disputes in the Federal trial courts; therefore, the district courts should consider including mediation in their local alternative dispute resolution programs."

Authorization of Appropriations

Pub.L. 105–315, § 11, Oct. 30, 1998, 112 Stat. 2998, provided that: "There are authorized to be appropriated for each fiscal year such sums as may be necessary to carry out chapter 44 of title 28, United States Code [28 U.S.C.A. § 651 et seq.], as amended by this Act [Alternative Dispute Resolution Act of 1998, Pub.L. 105–315, Oct. 30, 1998, 112 Stat. 2993, amending sections 651 to 658 of this title, amending a provision set out as a note under section 652 of this title, and enacting notes set out under this section]." ·

Section 905 of Title IX of Pub.L. 100–702, as amended Pub.L. 103–192, § 1(b), Dec. 14, 1993, 107 Stat. 2292; Pub.L. 103–420, § 3(a), Oct. 25, 1994, 108 Stat. 4345; Pub.L. 105–53, § 1, Oct. 6, 1997, 111 Stat. 1173, provided that: "There are authorized to be appropriated for each fiscal year to the judicial branch such sums as may be necessary to carry out the purposes of chapter 44 [this chapter], as added by section 901 of this Act. Funds appropriated under this section shall be allocated by the Administrative Office of the United States Courts to Federal judicial districts and the Federal Judicial Center. The funds so appropriated are authorized to remain available until expended."

Effect on Judicial Rulemaking Powers

Section 904 of Title IX of Pub.L. 100–702 provided that: "Nothing in this title [enacting this chapter and provisions set out as notes under this section and section 652 of this title], or in chapter 44 [this chapter], as added by section 901 of this Act, is intended to abridge, modify, or enlarge the rule making powers of the Federal judiciary."

Model Procedures

Section 902 of Title IX of Pub.L. 100–702 provided that: "The Judicial Conference of the United States may develop model rules relating to procedures for arbitration under chapter 44 [this chapter], as added by section 901 of this Act. No model rule may supersede any provision of such chapter 44, this title [enacting this chapter and provisions set out as notes under this section and section 652 of this title], or any law of the United States."

Reports by Director of Administrative Office of United States Courts and by Federal Judicial Center

Pub.L. 100–702, Title IX, § 903, Nov. 19, 1988, 102 Stat. 4663, provided that:

"(a) **Annual Report by Director of Administrative Office of the United States Courts.**—The Director of the Administrative Office of the United States Courts shall include in the annual report of the activities of the Administrative Office required under section 604(a)(3) [section 604(a)(3) of this title], statistical information about the implementation of chapter 44 [this chapter], as added by section 901 of this Act."

"(b) **Report by Federal Judicial Center.**—Not later than 5 years after the date of enactment of this Act [Nov. 19, 1988],

the Federal Judicial Center, in consultation with the Director of the Administrative Office of the United States Courts, shall submit to the Congress a report on the implementation of chapter 44 [this chapter], as added by section 901 of this Act, which shall include the following:

"(1) A description of the arbitration programs authorized by such chapter, as conceived and as implemented in the judicial districts in which such programs are authorized.

"(2) A determination of the level of satisfaction with the arbitration programs in those judicial districts by a sampling of court personnel, attorneys, and litigants whose cases have been referred to arbitration.

"(3) A summary of those program features that can be identified as being related to program acceptance both within and across judicial districts.

"(4) A description of the levels of satisfaction relative to the cost per hearing of each program.

"(5) Recommendations to the Congress on whether to terminate or continue chapter 44, or alternatively, to enact an arbitration provision in title 28, United States Code [this title], authorizing arbitration in all Federal district courts."

[For termination, effective May 15, 2000, of reporting provisions of this note, see Pub.L. 104–66, § 3003, as amended, set out as a note under 31 U.S.C.A. § 1113, and the 11th item on page 12 of House Document No. 103–7.]

Treatment of Expired Provisions

Pub.L. 103–192, § 2, Dec. 14, 1993, 107 Stat. 2292, provided that: "Chapter 44 of title 28, United States Code [this chapter], and the item relating to that chapter in the table of chapters at the beginning of part III of such title [analysis preceding section 601 of this title], shall be effective on or after the date of the enactment of this Act [Dec. 14, 1993] as if such chapter and item had not been repealed by section 906 of the Judicial Improvements and Access to Justice Act [section 906 of Pub.L. 100–702, set out as an Effective Date of Repeal note under this section] as such section was in effect on the day before the date of the enactment of this Act [Dec. 14, 1993]."

§ 652. Jurisdiction

(a) Consideration of alternative dispute resolution in appropriate cases.—Notwithstanding any provision of law to the contrary and except as provided in subsections (b) and (c), each district court shall, by local rule adopted under section 2071(a), require that litigants in all civil cases consider the use of an alternative dispute resolution process at an appropriate stage in the litigation. Each district court shall provide litigants in all civil cases with at least one alternative dispute resolution process, including, but not limited to, mediation, early neutral evaluation, minitrial, and arbitration as authorized in sections 654 through 658. Any district court that elects to require the use of alternative dispute resolution in certain cases may do so only with respect to mediation, early neutral evaluation, and, if the parties consent, arbitration.

(b) Actions exempted from consideration of alternative dispute resolution.—Each district court may exempt from the requirements of this section specific cases or categories of cases in which use of alternative dispute resolution would not be appropriate. In defining these exemptions, each district court shall consult with members of the bar, including the United States Attorney for that district.

(c) Authority of the Attorney General.—Nothing in this section shall alter or conflict with the authority of the Attorney General to conduct litigation on behalf of the United States, with the authority of any Federal agency authorized to conduct litigation in the United States courts, or with any delegation of litigation authority by the Attorney General.

(d) Confidentiality provisions.—Until such time as rules are adopted under chapter 131 of this title providing for the confidentiality of alternative dispute resolution processes under this chapter, each district court shall, by local rule adopted under section 2071(a), provide for the confidentiality of the alternative dispute resolution processes and to prohibit disclosure of confidential dispute resolution communications.

(Added Pub.L. 100–702, Title IX, § 901(a), Nov. 19, 1988, 102 Stat. 4659; amended Pub.L. 105–315, § 4, Oct. 30, 1998, 112 Stat. 2994.)

HISTORICAL AND STATUTORY NOTES

Revision Notes and Legislative Reports

1988 Acts. House Report No. 100–889, see 1988 U.S.Code Cong. and Adm.News, p. 5982.

Effective and Applicability Provisions

1988 Acts. Section 906 of Pub.L. 100–702, as amended, which provided that, effective Dec. 31, 1994, this section was repealed, with certain exceptions, was itself repealed by Pub.L. 103–420, § 3(b), Oct. 25, 1994, 108 Stat. 4345. See section 906 of Pub.L. 100–702, set out as a note under section 651 of this title.

Section effective 180 days after Nov. 19, 1988, see section 907 of Pub.L. 100–702, set out as a note under section 651 of this title.

Treatment of Expired Provisions

This section to continue to be effective on or after Dec. 14, 1993 as if it had not been repealed by section 906 of Pub.L. 100–702, as such section was in effect on the day before such date, see Treatment of Expired Provisions note set out under section 651 of this title.

Exception to Limitation on Money Damages

Section 901(c) of Pub.L. 100–702, which provided that notwithstanding this section a district court listed in section 658 of this title whose local rule on Nov. 19, 1988 provided for a limitation on money damages with respect to cases referred to arbitration of not more than $150,000 may continue to apply the higher limitation, was repealed by Pub.L. 105–315, § 12(a), Oct. 30, 1998, 112 Stat. 2998.

§ 653.   Neutrals

(a) Panel of neutrals.—Each district court that authorizes the use of alternative dispute resolution processes shall adopt appropriate processes for making neutrals available for use by the parties for each category of process offered. Each district court shall promulgate its own procedures and criteria for the selection of neutrals on its panels.

(b) Qualifications and training.—Each person serving as a neutral in an alternative dispute resolution process should be qualified and trained to serve as a neutral in the appropriate alternative dispute resolution process. For this purpose, the district court may use, among others, magistrate judges who have been trained to serve as neutrals in alternative dispute resolution processes, professional neutrals from the private sector, and persons who have been trained to serve as neutrals in alternative dispute resolution processes. Until such time as rules are adopted under chapter 131 of this title relating to the disqualification of neutrals, each district court shall issue rules under section 2071(a) relating to the disqualification of neutrals (including, where appropriate, disqualification under section 455 of this title, other applicable law, and professional responsibility standards).

(Added Pub.L. 100–702, Title IX, § 901(a), Nov. 19, 1988, 102 Stat. 4660; amended Pub.L. 105–315, § 5, Oct. 30, 1998, 112 Stat. 2995.)

HISTORICAL AND STATUTORY NOTES

Revision Notes and Legislative Reports

1988 Acts. House Report No. 100–889, see 1988 U.S.Code Cong. and Adm. News, p. 5982.

Effective and Applicability Provisions

1988 Acts. Section 906 of Pub.L. 100–702, as amended, which provided that, effective Dec. 31, 1994, this section was repealed, with certain exceptions, was itself repealed by Pub.L. 103–420, § 3(b), Oct. 25, 1994, 108 Stat. 4345. See section 906 of Pub.L. 100–702, set out as a note under section 651 of this title.

Section effective 180 days after Nov. 19, 1988, see section 907 of Pub.L. 100–702, set out as a note under section 651 of this title.

Treatment of Expired Provisions

This section to continue to be effective on or after Dec. 14, 1993 as if it had not been repealed by section 906 of Pub.L. 100–702 as such section was in effect on the day before such date, see Treatment of Expired Provisions note set out under section 651 of this title.

§ 654.   Arbitration

(a) Referral of actions to arbitration.—Notwithstanding any provision of law to the contrary and except as provided in subsections (a), (b), and (c) of section 652 and subsection (d) of this section, a district court may allow the referral to arbitration of any civil action (including any adversary proceeding in bankruptcy) pending before it when the parties consent, except that referral to arbitration may not be made where—

(1) the action is based on an alleged violation of a right secured by the Constitution of the United States;

(2) jurisdiction is based in whole or in part on section 1343 of this title; or

(3) the relief sought consists of money damages in an amount greater than $150,000.

(b) Safeguards in consent cases.—Until such time as rules are adopted under chapter 131 of this title relating to procedures described in this subsection, the district court shall, by local rule adopted under section 2071(a), establish procedures to ensure that any civil action in which arbitration by consent is allowed under subsection (a)—

(1) consent to arbitration is freely and knowingly obtained; and

(2) no party or attorney is prejudiced for refusing to participate in arbitration.

(c) Presumptions.—For purposes of subsection (a)(3), a district court may presume damages are not in excess of $150,000 unless counsel certifies that damages exceed such amount.

(d) Existing programs.—Nothing in this chapter is deemed to affect any program in which arbitration is conducted pursuant to section [1] title IX of the Judicial Improvements and Access to Justice Act (Public Law 100–702), as amended by section 1 of Public Law 105–53.

(Added Pub.L. 100–702, Title IX, § 901(a), Nov. 19, 1988, 102 Stat. 4660; amended Pub.L. 105–315, § 6, Oct. 30, 1998, 112 Stat. 2995.)

[1] So in original. The word "section" probably should not appear.

HISTORICAL AND STATUTORY NOTES

Revision Notes and Legislative Reports

1988 Acts. House Report No. 100–889, see 1988 U.S. Code Cong. and Adm. News, p. 5982.

References in Text

Title IX of the Judicial Improvements and Access to Justice Act, referred to in subsec. (d), is Pub.L. 100–702, Title IX, Nov. 19, 1988, 102 Stat. 4663. See Codifications note under this section.

Codifications

Section title IX of the Judicial Improvements and Access to Justice Act, referred to in subsec. (d), probably should read section 905 of title IX of the Judicial Improvements and Access to Justice Act, which is Pub.L. 100–702, Title IX, § 905, Nov. 19, 1988, 102 Stat. 4663, set out as a note under section 651 of this title.

Effective and Applicability Provisions

1988 Acts. Section 906 of Pub.L. 100–702, as amended, which provided that, effective Dec. 31, 1994, this section was repealed, with certain exceptions, was itself repealed by Pub.L. 103–420, § 3(b), Oct. 25, 1994, 108 Stat. 4345. See section 906 of Pub.L. 100–702, set out as a note under section 651 of this title.

Section effective 180 days after Nov. 19, 1988, see section 907 of Pub.L. 100–702, set out as a note under section 651 of this title.

Treatment of Expired Provisions

This section to continue to be effective on or after Dec. 14, 1993 as if it had not been repealed by section 906 of Pub.L. 100–702 as such section was in effect on the day before such date, see Treatment of Expired Provisions note set out under section 651 of this title.

§ 655.　Arbitrators

(a) Powers of arbitrators.—An arbitrator to whom an action is referred under section 654 shall have the power, within the judicial district of the district court which referred the action to arbitration—

(1) to conduct arbitration hearings;

(2) to administer oaths and affirmations; and

(3) to make awards.

(b) Standards for certification.—Each district court that authorizes arbitration shall establish standards for the certification of arbitrators and shall certify arbitrators to perform services in accordance with such standards and this chapter. The standards shall include provisions requiring that any arbitrator—

(1) shall take the oath or affirmation described in section 453; and

(2) shall be subject to the disqualification rules under section 455.

(c) Immunity.—All individuals serving as arbitrators in an alternative dispute resolution program under this chapter are performing quasi-judicial functions and are entitled to the immunities and protections that the law accords to persons serving in such capacity.

(Added Pub.L. 100–702, Title IX, § 901(a), Nov. 19, 1988, 102 Stat. 4661; amended Pub.L. 105–315, § 7, Oct. 30, 1998, 112 Stat. 2996.)

HISTORICAL AND STATUTORY NOTES

Revision Notes and Legislative Reports

1988 Acts. House Report No. 100–889, see 1988 U.S.Code Cong. and Adm.News, p. 5982.

Effective and Applicability Provisions

1988 Acts. Section 906 of Pub.L. 100–702, as amended, which provided that, effective Dec. 31, 1994, this section was repealed, with certain exceptions, was itself repealed by Pub.L. 103–420, § 3(b), Oct. 25, 1994, 108 Stat. 4345. See section 906 of Pub.L. 100–702, set out as a note under section 651 of this title.

Section effective 180 days after Nov. 19, 1988, see section 907 of Pub.L. 100–702, set out as a note under section 651 of this title.

Treatment of Expired Provisions

This section to continue to be effective on or after Dec. 14, 1993 as if it had not been repealed by section 906 of Pub.L. 100–702 as such section was in effect on the day before such date, see Treatment of Expired Provisions note set out under section 651 of this title.

---

§ 656. Subpoenas

Rule 45 of the Federal Rules of Civil Procedure (relating to subpoenas) applies to subpoenas for the attendance of witnesses and the production of documentary evidence at an arbitration hearing under this chapter.

(Added Pub.L. 100–702, Title IX, § 901(a), Nov. 19, 1988, 102 Stat. 4662; amended Pub.L. 105–315, § 8, Oct. 30, 1998, 112 Stat. 2996.)

HISTORICAL AND STATUTORY NOTES

Revision Notes and Legislative Reports

1988 Acts. House Report No. 100–889, see 1988 U.S.Code Cong. and Adm.News, p. 5982.

References in Text

The Federal Rules of Civil Procedure, referred to in text, are set out in the Appendix to this title, Fed.Rules Civ.Proc. Rule 1 et seq., 28 U.S.C.A.

Effective and Applicability Provisions

1988 Acts. Section 906 of Pub.L. 100–702, as amended, which provided that, effective Dec. 31, 1994, this section was repealed, with certain exceptions, was itself repealed by Pub.L. 103–420, § 3(b), Oct. 25, 1994, 108 Stat. 4345. See section 906 of Pub.L. 100–702, set out as a note under section 651 of this title.

Section effective 180 days after Nov. 19, 1988, see section 907 of Pub.L. 100–702, set out as a note under section 651 of this title.

Treatment of Expired Provisions

This section to continue to be effective on or after Dec. 14, 1993 as if it had not been repealed by section 906 of Pub.L. 100–702 as such section was in effect on the day before such date, see Treatment of Expired Provisions note set out under section 651 of this title.

§ 657. Arbitration award and judgment

(a) Filing and effect of arbitration award.—An arbitration award made by an arbitrator under this chapter, along with proof of service of such award on the other party by the prevailing party or by the plaintiff, shall be filed promptly after the arbitration hearing is concluded with the clerk of the district court that referred the case to arbitration. Such award shall be entered as the judgment of the court after the time has expired for requesting a trial de novo. The judgment so entered shall be subject to the same provisions of law and shall have the same force and effect as a judgment of the court in a civil action, except that the judgment shall not be subject to review in any other court by appeal or otherwise.

(b) Sealing of arbitration award.—The district court shall provide, by local rule adopted under section 2071(a), that the contents of any arbitration award made under this chapter shall not be made known to any judge who might be assigned to the case until the district court has entered final judgment in the action or the action has otherwise terminated.

(c) Trial de novo of arbitration awards.—

(1) Time for filing demand.—Within 30 days after the filing of an arbitration award with a district court under subsection (a), any party may file a written demand for a trial de novo in the district court.

(2) Action restored to court docket.—Upon a demand for a trial de novo, the action shall be restored to the docket of the court and treated for all purposes as if it had not been referred to arbitration.

(3) Exclusion of evidence of arbitration.—The court shall not admit at the trial de novo any evidence that there has been an arbitration proceeding, the nature or amount of any award, or any other matter concerning the conduct of the arbitration proceeding, unless—

    (A) the evidence would otherwise be admissible in the court under the Federal Rules of Evidence; or

    (B) the parties have otherwise stipulated.

(Added Pub.L. 100–702, Title IX, § 901(a), Nov. 19, 1988, 102 Stat. 4662; amended Pub.L. 105–315, § 9, Oct. 30, 1998, 112 Stat. 2997.)

HISTORICAL AND STATUTORY NOTES

Revision Notes and Legislative Reports

1988 Acts. House Report No. 100–889, see 1988 U.S. Code Cong. and Adm. News, p. 5982.

Effective and Applicability Provisions

1988 Acts. Section 906 of Pub.L. 100–702, as amended, which provided that, effective Dec. 31, 1994, this section was repealed, with certain exceptions, was itself repealed by Pub.L. 103–420, § 3(b), Oct. 25, 1994, 108 Stat. 4345. See section 906 of Pub.L. 100–702, set out as a note under section 651 of this title.

Section effective 180 days after Nov. 19, 1988, see section 907 of Pub.L. 100–702, set out as a note under section 651 of this title.

Treatment of Expired Provisions

This section to continue to be effective on or after Dec. 14, 1993 as if it had not been repealed by section 906 of Pub.L. 100–702 as such section was in effect on the day before such date, see Treatment of Expired Provisions note set out under section 651 of this title.

§ 658. Compensation of arbitrators and neutrals

(a) Compensation.—The district court shall, subject to regulations approved by the Judicial Conference of the United States, establish the amount of compensation, if any, that each arbitrator or neutral shall receive for services rendered in each case under this chapter.

(b) Transportation allowances.—Under regulations prescribed by the Director of the Administrative Office of the United States Courts, a district court may reimburse arbitrators and other neutrals for actual transportation expenses necessarily incurred in the performance of duties under this chapter.

(Added Pub.L. 100–702, Title IX, § 901(a), Nov. 19, 1988, 102 Stat. 4662; amended Pub.L. 105–315, § 10, Oct. 30, 1998, 112 Stat. 2997.)

HISTORICAL AND STATUTORY NOTES

Effective and Applicability Provisions

1988 Acts. Section 906 of Pub.L. 100–702, as amended, which provided that, effective Dec. 31, 1994, this section was repealed, with certain exceptions, was itself repealed by Pub.L. 103–420, § 3(b), Oct. 25, 1994, 108 Stat. 4345. See

section 906 of Pub.L. 100–702, set out as a note under section 651 of this title.

Section effective 180 days after Nov. 19, 1988, see section 907 of Pub.L. 100–702, set out as a note under section 651 of this title.

Treatment of Expired Provisions

This section to continue to be effective on or after Dec. 14, 1993 as if it had not been repealed by section 906 of Pub.L. 100–702 as such section was in effect on the day before such date, see Treatment of Expired Provisions note set out under section 651 of this title.

CHAPTER 57—GENERAL PROVISIONS APPLICABLE TO COURT OFFICERS AND EMPLOYEES

§ 959. Trustees and receivers suable; management; State laws

(a) Trustees, receivers or managers of any property, including debtors in possession, may be sued, without leave of the court appointing them, with respect to any of their acts or transactions in carrying on business connected with such property. Such actions shall be subject to the general equity power of such court so far as the same may be necessary to the ends of justice, but this shall not deprive a litigant of his right to trial by jury.

(b) Except as provided in section 1166 of title 11, a trustee, receiver or manager appointed in any cause pending in any court of the United States, including a debtor in possession, shall manage and operate the property in his possession as such trustee, receiver or manager according to the requirements of the valid laws of the State in which such property is situated, in the same manner that the owner or possessor thereof would be bound to do if in possession thereof.

(June 25, 1948, c. 646, 62 Stat. 926; Pub.L. 95–598, Title II, § 235, Nov. 6, 1978, 92 Stat. 2667.)

HISTORICAL AND STATUTORY NOTES

Revision Notes and Legislative Reports

1948 Acts. Based on Title 28, U.S.C., 1940 ed., §§ 124, 125 (Mar. 3, 1911, c. 231, §§ 65, 66, 36 Stat. 1104).

Section consolidates part of section 124 of Title 28, U.S.C., 1940 ed., with section 125 of the same title. The criminal penalty for violation of said section 124 is incorporated in section 1911 of Title 18, Crimes and Criminal Procedure (H.R. 1600, 80th Cong.).

Section was extended and made applicable to trustees and debtors in possession. The provision at the end of subsection (a) for preserving the right to a jury trial was added to clarify the intent of section 125 of Title 28, U.S.C., 1940 ed., as construed in *Vany v. Receiver of Toledo, St. L. and K.C.R.R. Co.*, C.C.1895, 67 F. 379.

Changes in phraseology were made. 80th Congress House Report No. 308.

1978 Acts. Senate Report No. 95–989 and House Report No. 95–595, see 1978 U.S.Code Cong. and Adm.News, p. 5787.

Effective and Applicability Provisions

1978 Acts. Amendment by Pub.L. 95–598 effective Oct. 1, 1979, see section 402(c) of Pub.L. 95–598, as amended, set out as a note preceding section 101 of Title 11, Bankruptcy.

CROSS REFERENCES

Capacity to sue or be sued, see Fed.Rules Civ.Proc. Rule 17, 28 USCA.

Mismanagement of property by receiver, criminal penalty, see 18 USCA § 1911.

Process and orders affecting property in different districts, see 28 USCA § 1692.

Receivers of property in different districts, jurisdiction, see 28 USCA § 754.

PART IV—JURISDICTION AND VENUE

CHAPTER 85—DISTRICT COURTS; JURISDICTION

§ 1334. Bankruptcy cases and proceedings

(a) Except as provided in subsection (b) of this section, the district courts shall have original and exclusive jurisdiction of all cases under title 11.

(b) Except as provided in subsection (e)(2), and notwithstanding any Act of Congress that confers exclusive jurisdiction on a court or courts other than the

district courts, the district courts shall have original but not exclusive jurisdiction of all civil proceedings arising under title 11, or arising in or related to cases under title 11.

(c)(1) Except with respect to a case under chapter 15 of title 11, nothing in this section prevents a district court in the interest of justice, or in the interest of comity with State courts or respect for State law, from abstaining from hearing a particular proceeding arising under title 11 or arising in or related to a case under title 11.

(2) Upon timely motion of a party in a proceeding based upon a State law claim or State law cause of action, related to a case under title 11 but not arising under title 11 or arising in a case under title 11, with respect to which an action could not have been commenced in a court of the United States absent jurisdiction under this section, the district court shall abstain from hearing such proceeding if an action is commenced, and can be timely adjudicated, in a State forum of appropriate jurisdiction.

(d) Any decision to abstain or not to abstain made under subsection (c) (other than a decision not to abstain in a proceeding described in subsection (c)(2)) is not reviewable by appeal or otherwise by the court of appeals under section 158(d), 1291, or 1292 of this title or by the Supreme Court of the United States under section 1254 of this title. Subsection (c) and this subsection shall not be construed to limit the applicability of the stay provided for by section 362 of title 11, United States Code, as such section applies to an action affecting the property of the estate in bankruptcy.

(e) The district court in which a case under title 11 is commenced or is pending shall have exclusive jurisdiction—

(1) of all the property, wherever located, of the debtor as of the commencement of such case, and of property of the estate; and

(2) over all claims or causes of action that involve construction of section 327 of title 11, United States Code, or rules relating to disclosure requirements under section 327.

(June 25, 1948, c. 646, 62 Stat. 931; Pub.L. 95–598, Title II, § 238(a), Nov. 6, 1978, 92 Stat. 2667; Pub.L. 98–353, Title I, § 101(a), July 10, 1984, 98 Stat. 333; Pub.L. 99–554, Title I, § 144(e), Oct. 27, 1986, 100 Stat. 3096; Pub.L. 101–650, Title III, § 309(b), Dec. 1, 1990, 104 Stat. 5113; Pub.L. 103–394, Title I, § 104(b), Oct. 22, 1994, 108 Stat. 4109; Pub.L. 109–8, Title III, § 324(a), Title VIII, § 802(c)(2), Title XII, § 1219, Apr. 20, 2005, 119 Stat. 98, 145, 195.)

HISTORICAL AND STATUTORY NOTES

Revision Notes and Legislative Reports

1948 Acts. Based on Title 28, U.S.C., 1940 ed., §§ 41(19) and 371(6) (Mar. 3, 1911, c. 231, §§ 24, par. 19, 256, par. 6, 36 Stat. 1093, 1160).

Changes in phraseology were made.

1984 Acts. Statements by Legislative Leaders, see 1984 U.S. Code Cong. and Adm. News, p. 576.

1986 Acts. House Report No. 99–764 and House Conference Report No. 99–958, see 1986 U.S. Code Cong. and Adm. News, p. 5227.

1990 Acts. Senate Report No. 101–416, House Report Nos. 101–123, 101–512, 101–514, 101–734, and 101–735, and State-

ment by President, see 1990 U.S. Code Cong. and Adm. News, p. 6802.

1994 Acts. House Report No. 103–835, see 1994 U.S. Code Cong. and Adm. News, p. 3340.

2005 Acts. House Report No. 109–31(Part I), see 2005 U.S. Code Cong. and Adm. News, p. 88.

References in Text

Chapter 15 of title 11, referred to in subsec. (c), is 11 U.S.C.A. § 1501 et seq.

Codifications

This section was amended by Pub.L. 95–598, Title II, § 238(a), Nov. 6, 1978, 92 Stat. 2668, effective June 28, 1984, pursuant to Pub.L. 95–598, Title IV, § 402(b), Nov. 6, 1978, 92 Stat. 2682, as amended by Pub.L. 98–249, § 1(a), Mar. 31, 1984, 98 Stat. 116; Pub.L. 98–271, § 1(a), Apr. 30, 1984, 98 Stat. 163; Pub.L. 98–299, § 1(a), May 25, 1984, 98 Stat. 214; Pub.L. 98–325, § 1(a), June 20, 1984, 98 Stat. 268, set out as an Effective and Applicability Provisions note preceding section 101 of Title 11, Bankruptcy, to read as follows:

"**§ 1334.　Bankruptcy appeals**

"**(a)** The district courts for districts for which panels have not been ordered appointed under section 160 of this title shall have jurisdiction of appeals from all final judgments, orders, and decrees of bankruptcy courts.

"**(b)** The district courts for such districts shall have jurisdiction of appeals from interlocutory orders and decrees of bankruptcy courts, but only by leave of the district court to which the appeal is taken.

"**(c)** A district court may not refer an appeal under that section to a magistrate or to a special master."

Section 402(b) of Pub.L. 95–598 was amended by section 113 of Pub.L. 98–353 by substituting "shall not be effective" for "shall take effect on June 28, 1984", thereby eliminating the amendment by section 238(a) of Pub.L. 95–598, effective June 27, 1984, pursuant to section 122(c) of Pub.L. 98–353, set out as an Effective and Applicability Provisions note under 28 U.S.C.A. § 151.

Section 121(a) of Pub.L. 98–353 directed that section 402(b) of Pub.L. 95–598 be amended by substituting "the date of enactment of the Bankruptcy Amendments and Federal Judgeship Act of 1984 [i.e. July 10, 1984]" for "June 28, 1984". This amendment was not executed in view of the prior amendment to section 402(b) of Pub.L. 95–598 by section 113 of Pub.L. 98–353.

Effective and Applicability Provisions

2005 Acts. Pub.L. 109–8, Title III, § 324(b), Apr. 20, 2005, 119 Stat. 98, provided that: "This section [amending subsecs. (b) and (e) of this section] shall only apply to cases filed after the date of enactment of this Act [Apr. 20, 2005]."

Except as otherwise provided, amendments by Pub.L. 109–8 effective 180 days after April 20, 2005, and inapplicable with respect to cases commenced under Title 11 before the effective date, see Pub.L. 109–8, § 1501, set out as a note under 11 U.S.C.A. § 101.

1994 Acts. Amendment by Pub.L. 103–394 effective on Oct. 22, 1994, and not to apply with respect to cases commenced under Title 11 of the United States Code before Oct. 22, 1994, see section 702 of Pub.L. 103–394, set out as a note under section 101 of Title 11, Bankruptcy.

1986 Acts. Amendment by Pub.L. 99–554 effective 30 days after Oct. 27, 1986, except as otherwise provided for, see section 302(a) of Pub.L. 99–554, as amended, set out as a note under section 581 of this title.

1984 Acts. Amendment by Pub.L. 98–353, except for subsec. (c)(2), effective July 10, 1984, see section 122(a) of Pub.L. 98–353, set out as a note under section 151 of this title.

Subsec. (c)(2) not applicable with respect to cases under Title 11, Bankruptcy, that are pending on July 10, 1984, or to proceedings arising in or related to such cases, see section 122(b) of Pub.L. 98–353, set out as a note under section 151 of this title.

Separability of Provisions

If any provision of or amendment made by Pub.L. 103–394 or the application of such provision or amendment to any person or circumstance is held to be unconstitutional, the remaining provisions of and amendments made by Pub.L. 103–394 and the application of such provisions and amendments to any person or circumstance shall not be affected thereby, see section 701 of Pub.L. 103–394, set out as a note under section 101 of Title 11, Bankruptcy.

Jurisdiction Over and Transfer of Bankruptcy Cases and Proceedings

Section 115 of Pub.L. 98–353 provided that:

"**(a)** On the date of the enactment of this Act [July 10, 1984] the appropriate district court of the United States shall have jurisdiction of—

"**(1)** cases, and matters and proceedings in cases, under the Bankruptcy Act [former Title 11, Bankruptcy] that are pending immediately before such date in the bankruptcy courts continued by section 404(a) of the Act of November 6, 1978 (Public Law 95–598; 92 Stat. 2687) [Pub.L. 95–598, Title IV, § 404(a), Nov. 6, 1978, 92 Stat. 2683, formerly set out as a note preceding section 151 of this title], and

"**(2)** cases under title 11 of the United States Code [Title 11, Bankruptcy], and proceedings arising under title 11 of the United States Code or arising in or related to cases under title 11 of the United States Code, that are pending immediately before such date in the bankruptcy courts continued by section 404(a) of the Act of November 6, 1978 (Public Law 95–598; 92 Stat. 2687).

"**(b)** On the date of the enactment of this Act [July 10, 1984], there shall be transferred to the appropriate district court of the United States appeals from final judgments, orders, and decrees of the bankruptcy courts pending immediately before such date in the bankruptcy appellate panels appointed under section 405(c) of the Act of November 6, 1978 (Public Law 95–598; 92 Stat. 2685) [formerly set out as a note preceding section 1471 of this title]."

CROSS REFERENCES

Appointment of clerk for bankruptcy court where warranted by number of cases and proceedings pending, see 28 USCA § 156.

Non-core proceedings not subject to mandatory abstention provisions, see 28 USCA § 157.

Removal of claims related to bankruptcy cases, see 28 USCA § 1452.

Venue, see 28 USCA §§ 1408 and 1409.

CHAPTER 87—DISTRICT COURTS; VENUE

CROSS REFERENCES

Criminal cases, venue, see 18 USCA § 3235 et seq.

Fair housing actions venue determined in accordance with this chapter, see 42 USCA § 3612.

Jurisdiction of district courts, see 28 USCA § 1331 et seq.

Process, see 28 USCA § 1691 et seq.

Venue, see Fed.Rules Cr.Proc. Rules 18, 20, and 21, 18 USCA.

§ 1408. Venue of cases under title 11

Except as provided in section 1410 of this title, a case under title 11 may be commenced in the district court for the district—

(1) in which the domicile, residence, principal place of business in the United States, or principal assets in the United States, of the person or entity that is the subject of such case have been located for the one hundred and eighty days immediately preceding such commencement, or for a longer portion of such one-hundred-and-eighty-day period than the domicile, residence, or principal place of business, in the United States, or principal assets in the United States, of such person were located in any other district; or

(2) in which there is pending a case under title 11 concerning such person's affiliate, general partner, or partnership.

(Added Pub.L. 98–353, Title I, § 102(a), July 10, 1984, 98 Stat. 334.)

HISTORICAL AND STATUTORY NOTES

Revision Notes and Legislative Reports

1984 Acts. Statements by Legislative Leaders, see 1984 U.S. Code Cong. and Adm. News, p. 576.

Effective and Applicability Provisions

1984 Acts. Section effective July 10, 1984, see section 122(a) of Pub.L. 98–353, set out as a note under section 151 of this title.

§ 1409. Venue of proceedings arising under title 11 or arising in or related to cases under title 11

(a) Except as otherwise provided in subsections (b) and (d), a proceeding arising under title 11 or arising in or related to a case under title 11 may be commenced in the district court in which such case is pending.

(b) Except as provided in subsection (d) of this section, a trustee in a case under title 11 may commence a proceeding arising in or related to such case to recover a money judgment of or property worth less than $1,300 [1] or a consumer debt of less than $19,250 [1], or a debt (excluding a consumer debt) against a noninsider of less than $12,850 [1], only in the district court for the district in which the defendant resides.

(c) Except as provided in subsection (b) of this section, a trustee in a case under title 11 may commence a proceeding arising in or related to such case as statutory successor to the debtor or creditors under section 541 or 544(b) of title 11 in the district court for the district where the State or Federal court sits in which, under applicable nonbankruptcy venue provisions, the debtor or creditors, as the case may be, may have commenced an action on which such proceeding is based if the case under title 11 had not been commenced.

(d) A trustee may commence a proceeding arising under title 11 or arising in or related to a case under title 11 based on a claim arising after the commencement of such case from the operation of the business of the debtor only in the district court for the district where a State or Federal court sits in which, under applicable nonbankruptcy venue provisions, an action on such claim may have been brought.

(e) A proceeding arising under title 11 or arising in or related to a case under title 11, based on a claim arising after the commencement of such case from the operation of the business of the debtor, may be commenced against the representative of the estate in such case in the district court for the district where the State or Federal court sits in which the party commencing such proceeding may, under applicable nonbankruptcy venue provisions, have brought an action on such claim, or in the district court in which such case is pending.

(Added Pub.L. 98–353, Title I, § 102(a), July 10, 1984, 98 Stat. 334; amended Pub.L. 109–8, Title IV, § 410, Apr. 20, 2005, 119 Stat. 106.)

[1] Dollar amount as adjusted by the Judicial Conference of the United States. See Adjustment of Dollar Amounts notes set out under this section and 11 U.S.C.A. § 104.

HISTORICAL AND STATUTORY NOTES

Revision Notes and Legislative Reports

1984 Acts. Statements by Legislative Leaders, see 1984 U.S. Code Cong. and Adm. News, p. 576.

2005 Acts. House Report No. 109–31(Part I), see 2005 U.S. Code Cong. and Adm. News, p. 88.

Effective and Applicability Provisions

2013 Acts. Increase of dollar amounts by Judicial Conference of the United States by notice published Feb. 21, 2013, 78 F.R. 12089 effective April 1, 2013, and increase not applica-

ble to cases commenced before the effective date of the adjustments, i.e., April 1, 2013. See Adjustment of Dollar Amounts notes under 11 U.S.C.A. § 104 and this section.

2010 Acts. Increase of dollar amounts by Judicial Conference of the United States by notice published Feb. 25, 2010, 75 F.R. 8747 effective April 1, 2010, and increase not applicable to cases commenced before the effective date of the adjustments, i.e., April 1, 2010. See Adjustment of Dollar Amounts notes under 11 U.S.C.A. § 104 and this section.

2007 Acts. Increase of dollar amounts by Judicial Conference of the United States by notice published Feb. 14, 2007, 72 F.R. 7082 effective April 1, 2007, and increase not applicable to cases commenced before the effective date of the adjustments, i.e., April 1, 2007. See Adjustment of Dollar Amounts notes under 11 U.S.C.A. § 104 and this section.

2005 Acts. Except as otherwise provided, amendments by Pub.L. 109–8 effective 180 days after April 20, 2005, and inapplicable with respect to cases commenced under Title 11 before the effective date, see Pub.L. 109–8, § 1501, set out as a note under 11 U.S.C.A. § 101.

1984 Acts. Section effective July 10, 1984, see section 122(a) of Pub.L. 98–353, set out as a note under section 151 of this title.

Adjustment of Dollar Amounts

For adjustment of dollar amounts specified in subsec. (b) of this section by the Judicial Conference of the United States, effective Apr. 1, 2016, see note set out under 11 U.S.C.A. § 104.

By notice published Feb. 22, 2016, 81 F.R. 8748, the Judicial Conference of the United States adjusted the dollar amounts in provisions specified in subsec. (b) of this section, effective Apr. 1, 2016, as follows:

    Adjusted $1,250 to $1,300.

    Adjusted $18,675 to $19,250.

    Adjusted $12,475 to $12,850.

By notice published Feb. 21, 2013, 78 F.R. 12089, the Judicial Conference of the United States adjusted the dollar amounts in provisions specified in subsec. (b) of this section, effective Apr. 1, 2013, as follows:

    Adjusted $1,175 to $1,250.

    Adjusted $17,575 to $18,675.

    Adjusted $11,725 to $12,475.

By notice published Feb. 25, 2010, 75 F.R. 8747, the Judicial Conference of the United States adjusted the dollar amounts in provisions specified in subsec. (b) of this section, effective Apr. 1, 2010, as follows:

    Adjusted $1,100 to $1,175.

    Adjusted $16,425 to $17,575.

    Adjusted $10,950 to $11,725.

By notice published Feb. 14, 2007, 72 F.R. 7082, the Judicial Conference of the United States adjusted the dollar amounts in provisions specified in subsec. (b) of this section, effective Apr. 1, 2007, as follows:

    Adjusted $1,000 to $1,100.

    Adjusted $15,000 to $16,425.

    Adjusted $10,000 to $10,950.

§ 1410. Venue of cases ancillary to foreign proceedings

A case under chapter 15 of title 11 may be commenced in the district court of the United States for the district—

(1) in which the debtor has its principal place of business or principal assets in the United States;

(2) if the debtor does not have a place of business or assets in the United States, in which there is pending against the debtor an action or proceeding in a Federal or State court; or

(3) in a case other than those specified in paragraph (1) or (2), in which venue will be consistent with the interests of justice and the convenience of the parties, having regard to the relief sought by the foreign representative.

(Added Pub.L. 98–353, Title I, § 102(a), July 10, 1984, 98 Stat. 335; amended Pub.L. 109–8, Title VIII, § 802(c)(4), Apr. 20, 2005, 119 Stat. 146.)

HISTORICAL AND STATUTORY NOTES

Revision Notes and Legislative Reports

1984 Acts. Statements by Legislative Leaders, see 1984 U.S. Code Cong. and Adm. News, p. 576.

2005 Acts. House Report No. 109–31(Part I), see 2005 U.S. Code Cong. and Adm. News, p. 88.

References in Text

Chapter 15 of title 11, referred to in text, is 11 U.S.C.A. § 1501 et seq.

Effective and Applicability Provisions

2005 Acts. Except as otherwise provided, amendments by Pub.L. 109–8 effective 180 days after April 20, 2005, and inapplicable with respect to cases commenced under Title 11 before the effective date, see Pub.L. 109–8, § 1501, set out as a note under 11 U.S.C.A. § 101.

1984 Acts. Section effective July 10, 1984, see section 122(a) of Pub.L. 98–353, set out as a note under section 151 of this title.

CROSS REFERENCES

Commencement of bankruptcy cases in district courts having venue except as provided by this section, see 28 USCA § 1408.

§ 1411. Jury trials

(a) Except as provided in subsection (b) of this section, this chapter and title 11 do not affect any right to trial by jury that an individual has under applicable nonbankruptcy law with regard to a personal injury or wrongful death tort claim.

(b) The district court may order the issues arising under section 303 of title 11 to be tried without a jury. (Added Pub.L. 98–353, Title I, § 102(a), July 10, 1984, 98 Stat. 335.)

HISTORICAL AND STATUTORY NOTES

Revision Notes and Legislative Reports

1984 Acts. Statements by Legislative Leaders, see 1984 U.S. Code Cong. and Adm. News, p. 576.

Effective and Applicability Provisions

1984 Acts. Section, except subsec. (a), effective July 10, 1984, see section 122(a) of Pub.L. 98–353, set out as a note under section 151 of this title.

Subsec. (a) not applicable with respect to cases under Title 11, Bankruptcy, that are pending on July 10, 1984, or to proceedings arising in or related to such cases, see section 122(b) of Pub.L. 98–353, set out as a note under section 151 of this title.

§ 1412. Change of venue

A district court may transfer a case or proceeding under title 11 to a district court for another district, in the interest of justice or for the convenience of the parties.

(Added Pub.L. 98–353, Title I, § 102(a), July 10, 1984, 98 Stat. 335.)

HISTORICAL AND STATUTORY NOTES

Revision Notes and Legislative Reports

1984 Acts. Statements by Legislative Leaders, see 1984 U.S. Code Cong. and Adm. News, p. 576.

Effective and Applicability Provisions

1984 Acts. Section effective July 10, 1984, see section 122(a) of Pub.L. 98–353, set out as a note under section 151 of this title.

CHAPTER 89—DISTRICT COURTS; REMOVAL OF CASES FROM STATE COURTS

§ 1452. Removal of claims related to bankruptcy cases

(a) A party may remove any claim or cause of action in a civil action other than a proceeding before the United States Tax Court or a civil action by a governmental unit to enforce such governmental unit's police or regulatory power, to the district court for the district where such civil action is pending, if such district court has jurisdiction of such claim or cause of action under section 1334 of this title.

(b) The court to which such claim or cause of action is removed may remand such claim or cause of action on any equitable ground. An order entered under this subsection remanding a claim or cause of action, or a decision to not remand, is not reviewable by appeal or otherwise by the court of appeals under section 158(d), 1291, or 1292 of this title or by the Supreme Court of the United States under section 1254 of this title. (Added Pub.L. 98–353, Title I, § 103(a), July 10, 1984, 98 Stat. 335; amended Pub.L. 101–650, Title III, § 309(c), Dec. 1, 1990, 104 Stat. 5113.)

HISTORICAL AND STATUTORY NOTES

Revision Notes and Legislative Reports

1984 **Acts**. Statements by Legislative Leaders, see 1984 U.S. Code Cong. and Adm. News, p. 576.

1990 **Acts**. Senate Report No. 101–416, House Report Nos. 101–123, 101–512, 101–514, 101–734, and 101–735, and State-ment by President, see 1990 U.S. Code Cong. and Adm. News, p. 6802.

Effective and Applicability Provisions

1984 **Acts**. Section effective July 10, 1984, see section 122(a) of Pub.L. 98–353, set out as a note under section 151 of this title.

PART V—PROCEDURE

CHAPTER 123—FEES AND COSTS

§ 1913. Courts of appeals

The fees and costs to be charged and collected in each court of appeals shall be prescribed from time to time by the Judicial Conference of the United States. Such fees and costs shall be reasonable and uniform in all the circuits.

(June 25, 1948, c. 646, 62 Stat. 954.)

JUDICIAL CONFERENCE SCHEDULE OF FEES

Court of Appeals Miscellaneous Fee Schedule

(Issued in accordance with 28 U.S.C. § 1913)

(Effective on: September 1, 2018)

The fees included in the Court of Appeals Miscellaneous Fee Schedule are to be charged for services provided by the courts of appeals, including relevant services [Item 13 does not apply to bankruptcy appellate panels.] provided by the bankruptcy appellate panels established under 28 U.S.C. § 158(b)(1).

- The United States should not be charged fees under this schedule, except as prescribed in Items 2, 4, and 5 when the information requested is available through remote electronic access.

- Federal agencies or programs that are funded from judiciary appropriations (agencies, organizations, and individuals providing services authorized by the Criminal Justice Act, 18 U.S.C. § 3006A, and bankruptcy administrators) should not be charged any fees under this schedule.

(1) For docketing a case on appeal or review, or docketing any other proceeding, $500.

- Each party filing a notice of appeal pays a separate fee to the district court, but parties filing a joint notice of appeal pay only one fee.

- There is no docketing fee for an application for an interlocutory appeal under 28 U.S.C. § 1292(b) or other petition for permission to appeal under Fed. R. App. P. 5, unless the appeal is allowed.

- There is no docketing fee for a direct bankruptcy appeal or a direct bankruptcy cross appeal, when the fee has been collected by the bankruptcy court in accordance with item 14 of the Bankruptcy Court Miscellaneous Fee Schedule.

- This fee is collected in addition to the statutory fee of $5 that is collected under 28 U.S.C. § 1917.

(2) For conducting a search of the court of appeals or bankruptcy appellate panel records, $31 per name or item searched. This fee applies to services rendered on behalf of the United States if the information requested is available through remote electronic access.

(3) For certification of any document, $11.

(4)

    a. For reproducing any document and providing a copy in paper form, $.50 per page. This fee applies to services rendered on behalf of the United States if the document requested is available through remote electronic access.

    b. For reproducing and transmitting in any manner a copy of an electronic record stored outside of the court's electronic case management system, including but not limited to, document files, audio and video recordings (other than a recording of a court proceeding), $31 per record provided.

(5) For reproducing recordings of proceedings, regardless of the medium, $31, including the cost of materials. This fee applies to services rendered on behalf of the United States if the recording is available through remote electronic access.

(6) For reproducing the record in any appeal in which the court of appeals does not require an appendix pursuant to Fed. R. App. P.30(f), (or, in appeals before a bankruptcy appellate panel, pursuant to Fed. R. Bankr. P. 8018(e)), $86.

(7) For retrieval of one box of records from a Federal Records Center, National Archives, or other storage location removed from the place of business of the court, $64. For retrievals involving multiple boxes, $39 for each additional box. For electronic retrievals, $10 plus any charges assessed by the Federal Records Center, National Archives, or other storage location removed from the place of business of the courts.

(8) For any payment returned or denied for insufficient funds, $53.

(9) For copies of opinions, a fee commensurate with the cost of printing, as fixed by each court of appeals.

(10) For copies of the local rules of court, a fee commensurate with the cost of distributing the copies. The court may also distribute copies of the local rules without charge.

(11) For filing:

- Any separate or joint notice of appeal or application for appeal from the bankruptcy appellate panel, $5;

- A notice of the allowance of an appeal from the bankruptcy appellate panel, $5.

(12) For counsel's requested use of the court's videoconferencing equipment in connection with each oral argument, the court may charge and collect a fee of $200 per remote location.

(13) For original admission of attorney to practice, including a certificate of admission, $181. For a duplicate certificate of admission or certificate of good standing, $19.

Electronic Public Access Fee Schedule

The fees included in the Electronic Public Access Fee Schedule are to be charged for providing electronic public access to court records.

Published on: August 2, 2017

Effective on: April 1, 2017

(Issued in accordance with 28 U.S.C. §§ 1913, 1914, 1926, 1930, 1932)

Fees for Public Access to Court Electronic Records (PACER)

1. Except as provided below, for electronic access to any case document, docket sheet, or case-specific report via PACER: $0.10 per page, not to exceed the fee for thirty pages.

2. For electronic access to transcripts and non-case specific reports via PACER (such as reports obtained from the PACER Case Locator or docket activity reports): $0.10 per page.

3. For electronic access to an audio file of a court hearing via PACER: $2.40 per audio file.

Fees for Courthouse Electronic Access

4. For printing copies of any record or document accessed electronically at a public terminal in a courthouse: $0.10 per page.

PACER Service Center Fees

5. For every search of court records conducted by the PACER Service Center, $30 per name or item searched.

6. For the PACER Service Center to reproduce on paper any record pertaining to a PACER account, if this information is remotely available through electronic access: $0.50 per page.

7. For any payment returned or denied for insufficient funds, $53.

Free Access and Exemptions

8. Automatic Fee Exemptions:

• No fee is owed for electronic access to court data or audio files via PACER until an account holder accrues charges of more than $15.00 in a quarterly billing cycle.

• Parties in a case (including *pro se* litigants) and attorneys of record receive one free electronic copy, via the notice of electronic filing or notice of docket activity, of all documents filed electronically, if receipt is required by law or directed by the filer.

• No fee is charged for access to judicial opinions.

• No fee is charged for viewing case information or documents at courthouse public access terminals.

• No fee is charged for Chapter 13 bankruptcy trustees to download quarterly (i.e., once every 90 days) a list of the trustee's cases from the PACER Case Locator.

9. Discretionary Fee Exemptions:

• Courts may exempt certain persons or classes of persons from payment of the user access fee. Examples of individuals and groups that a court may consider exempting include: indigents, bankruptcy case trustees, *pro bono* attorneys, *pro bono* alternative dispute resolution neutrals, Section 501(c)(3) not-for-profit organizations, and individual researchers associated with educational institutions. Courts should not, however, exempt individuals or groups that have the ability to pay the statutorily established access fee. Examples of individuals and groups that a court should not exempt include: local, state or federal government agencies, members of the media, privately paid attorneys or others who have the ability to pay the fee.

• In considering granting an exemption, courts must find:

• that those seeking an exemption have demonstrated that an exemption is necessary in order to avoid unreasonable burdens and to promote public access to information;

• that individual researchers requesting an exemption have shown that the defined research project is intended for scholarly research, that it is limited in scope, and that it is not intended for redistribution on the internet or for commercial purposes.

• If the court grants an exemption:

• the user receiving the exemption must agree not to sell the data obtained as a result, and must not transfer any data obtained as the result of a fee exemption, unless expressly authorized by the court; and

• the exemption should be granted for a definite period of time, should be limited in scope, and may be revoked at the discretion of the court granting the exemption.

• Courts may provide local court information at no cost (e.g., local rules, court forms, news items, court calendars, and other information) to benefit the public.

Applicability to the United States and State and Local Governments

10. Unless otherwise authorized by the Judicial Conference, these fees must be charged to the United States, except to federal agencies or programs that are funded from judiciary appropriations (including, but not limited to, agencies, organizations, and individuals providing services authorized by the Criminal Justice Act [18 U.S.C. § 3006A], and bankruptcy administrators).

11. The fee for printing copies of any record or document accessed electronically at a public terminal ($0.10 per page) described in (4) above does not apply to services rendered on behalf of the United States if the record requested is not remotely available through electronic access.

12. The fee for local, state, and federal government entities, shall be $0.08 per page until April 1, 2015, after which time, the fee shall be $0.10 per page.

JUDICIAL CONFERENCE POLICY NOTES

The Electronic Public Access (EPA) fee and its exemptions are directly related to the requirement that the judiciary charge user-based fees for the development and maintenance of electronic public access services. The fee schedule provides examples of users that may not be able to afford reasonable user fees (such as indigents, bankruptcy case trustees, individual researchers associated with educational institutions, 501(c)(3) not-for-profit organizations, and court-appointed pro bono attorneys), but requires those seeking an exemption to demonstrate that an exemption is limited in scope and is necessary in order to avoid an unreasonable burden. In addition, the fee schedule includes examples of other entities that courts should not exempt from the fee (such as local, state or federal government agencies, members of the media, and attorneys). The goal is to provide courts with guidance in evaluating a requestor's ability to pay the fee.

Judicial Conference policy also limits exemptions in other ways. First, it requires exempted users to agree not to sell the data they receive through an exemption (unless expressly authorized by the court). This prohibition is not intended to bar a quote or reference to information received as a result of a fee exemption in a scholarly or other similar work. Second, it permits courts to grant exemptions for a definite period of time, to limit the scope of the exemptions, and to revoke exemptions. Third, it cautions that exemptions should be granted as the exception, not the rule, and prohibits courts from exempting all users from EPA fees.

HISTORICAL AND STATUTORY NOTES

Revision Notes and Legislative Reports

1948 Acts. Based on Title 28, U.S.C., 1940 ed., § 543 (Mar. 3, 1891, c. 517, § 2, 26 Stat. 826; Feb. 19, 1897, c. 263, 29 Stat. 536; Sept. 27, 1944, c. 413, 58 Stat. 743).

Words "and in the United States Circuit Court of Appeals for the District of Columbia" were omitted as covered by "each court of appeals."

Judicial Conference of Senior Circuit Judges was changed to Judicial Conference "of the United States" in conformity with section 331 of this title.

Changes were made in phraseology. 80th Congress House Report No. 308.

Appeals Filed in Courts of Appeals

Pub.L. 109–171, Title X, § 10001(b), Feb. 8, 2006, 120 Stat. 183, provided that: "The $250 fee for docketing a case on appeal or review, or docketing any other proceeding, in a court of appeals, as prescribed by the Judicial Conference, effective as of January 1, 2005, under section 1913 of title 28, United States Code [this section], shall be increased to $450."

[This note effective 60 days after Feb. 8, 2006, see Pub.L. 109–171, § 10001(d), set out as a note under 28 U.S.C.A. § 1914]

Court Fees for Electronic Access to Information

Pub.L. 102–140, Title III, § 303, Oct. 28, 1991, 105 Stat. 810, as amended Pub.L. 104–317, Title IV, § 403(b), Oct. 19, 1996, 110 Stat. 3854; Pub.L. 107–347, Title II, § 205(e), Dec. 17, 2002, 116 Stat. 2915, provided that:

"**(a)** The Judicial Conference may, only to the extent necessary, prescribe reasonable fees, pursuant to sections 1913, 1914, 1926, 1930, and 1932 of title 28, United States Code [this section and sections 1914, 1926, 1930, and 1932 of this title], for collection by the courts under those sections for access to information available through automatic data processing equipment. These fees may distinguish between classes of persons, and shall provide for exempting persons or classes of persons from the fees, in order to avoid unreasonable burdens and to promote public access to such information. The Director of the Administrative Office of the United States Courts, under the direction of the Judicial Conference of the United States, shall prescribe a schedule of reasonable fees for electronic access to information which the Director is required to maintain and make available to the public.

"**(b)** The Judicial Conference and the Director shall transmit each schedule of fees prescribed under paragraph (a) to the Congress at least 30 days before the schedule becomes effective. All fees hereafter collected by the Judiciary under paragraph (a) as a charge for services rendered shall be deposited as offsetting collections to the Judiciary Automation Fund pursuant to 28 U.S.C. 612(c)(1)(A) [section 612(c)(1)(A) of this title] to reimburse expenses incurred in providing these services."

[Amendment by Pub.L. 107–347, § 205, effective 120 days after Dec. 17, 2002, see section 402(a) of Pub.L. 107–347, set out as a note under 44 U.S.C.A. § 3601.]

Similar provisions were contained in the following prior appropriation Act:

Pub.L. 101–515, Title IV, § 404, Nov. 5, 1990, 104 Stat. 2132.

CROSS REFERENCES

Fees for sales of copies of rules of various Courts of Appeals, see 28 USCA § 2077.

Power of Judicial Conference of the United States, see 28 USCA § 331.

§ 1930. Bankruptcy fees

(a) The parties commencing a case under title 11 shall pay to the clerk of the district court or the clerk of the bankruptcy court, if one has been certified pursuant to section 156(b) of this title, the following filing fees:

  (1) For a case commenced under—

    (A) chapter 7 of title 11, $245, and

    (B) chapter 13 of title 11, $235.

  (2) For a case commenced under chapter 9 of title 11, equal to the fee specified in paragraph (3) for filing a case under chapter 11 of title 11. The amount by which the fee payable under this paragraph exceeds $300 shall be deposited in the fund established under section 1931 of this title.

  (3) For a case commenced under chapter 11 of title 11 that does not concern a railroad, as defined in section 101 of title 11, $1,167.

  (4) For a case commenced under chapter 11 of title 11 concerning a railroad, as so defined, $1,000.

  (5) For a case commenced under chapter 12 of title 11, $200.

  (6)(A) Except as provided in subparagraph (B), in addition to the filing fee paid to the clerk, a quarterly fee shall be paid to the United States trustee, for deposit in the Treasury, in each case under chapter 11 of title 11 for each quarter (including any fraction thereof) until the case is converted or dismissed, whichever occurs first. The fee shall be $325 for each quarter in which disbursements total less than $15,000; $650 for each quarter in which disbursements total $15,000 or more but less than $75,000; $975 for each quarter in which disbursements total $75,000 or more but less than $150,000; $1,625 for each quarter in which disbursements total $150,000 or more but less than $225,000; $1,950 for each quarter in which disbursements total $225,000 or more but less than $300,000; $4,875 for each quarter in which disbursements total $300,000 or more but less than $1,000,000; $6,500 for each quarter in which disbursements total $1,000,000 or more but less than $2,000,000; $9,750 for each quarter in which disbursements total $2,000,000 or more but less than $3,000,000; $10,400 for each quarter in which disbursements total $3,000,000 or more but less than $5,000,000; $13,000 for each quarter in which disbursements total $5,000,000 or more but less than $15,000,000; $20,000 for each quarter in which disbursements total $15,000,000 or more but less than $30,000,000; $30,000 for each quarter in which disbursements total more than $30,000,000. The fee shall be payable on the last day of the calendar month following the calendar quarter for which the fee is owed.

(B) During each of fiscal years 2018 through 2022, if the balance in the United States Trustee System Fund as of September 30 of the most recent full fiscal year is less than $200,000,000, the quarterly fee payable for a quarter in which disbursements equal or exceed $1,000,000 shall be the lesser of 1 percent of such disbursements or $250,000.

(7) In districts that are not part of a United States trustee region as defined in section 581 of this title, the Judicial Conference of the United States may require the debtor in a case under chapter 11 of title 11 to pay fees equal to those imposed by paragraph (6) of this subsection. Such fees shall be deposited as offsetting receipts to the fund established under section 1931 of this title and shall remain available until expended.

An individual commencing a voluntary case or a joint case under title 11 may pay such fee in installments. For converting, on request of the debtor, a case under chapter 7, or 13 of title 11, to a case under chapter 11 of title 11, the debtor shall pay to the clerk of the district court or the clerk of the bankruptcy court, if one has been certified pursuant to section 156(b) of this title, a fee of the amount equal to the difference between the fee specified in paragraph (3) and the fee specified in paragraph (1).

(b) The Judicial Conference of the United States may prescribe additional fees in cases under title 11 of the same kind as the Judicial Conference prescribes under section 1914(b) of this title.

(c) Upon the filing of any separate or joint notice of appeal or application for appeal or upon the receipt of any order allowing, or notice of the allowance of, an appeal or a writ of certiorari $5 shall be paid to the clerk of the court, by the appellant or petitioner.

(d) Whenever any case or proceeding is dismissed in any bankruptcy court for want of jurisdiction, such court may order the payment of just costs.

(e) The clerk of the court may collect only the fees prescribed under this section.

(f)(1) Under the procedures prescribed by the Judicial Conference of the United States, the district court or the bankruptcy court may waive the filing fee in a case under chapter 7 of title 11 for an individual if the court determines that such individual has income less than 150 percent of the income official poverty line (as defined by the Office of Management and Budget, and

revised annually in accordance with section 673(2) of the Omnibus Budget Reconciliation Act of 1981) applicable to a family of the size involved and is unable to pay that fee in installments. For purposes of this paragraph, the term "filing fee" means the filing fee required by subsection (a), or any other fee prescribed by the Judicial Conference under subsections (b) and (c) that is payable to the clerk upon the commencement of a case under chapter 7.

(2) The district court or the bankruptcy court may waive for such debtors other fees prescribed under subsections (b) and (c).

(3) This subsection does not restrict the district court or the bankruptcy court from waiving, in accordance with Judicial Conference policy, fees prescribed under this section for other debtors and creditors. (Added Pub.L. 95–598, Title II, § 246(a), Nov. 6, 1978, 92 Stat. 2671; amended Pub.L. 98–353, Title I, § 111(a), (b), July 10, 1984, 98 Stat. 342; Pub.L. 99–500, Title I, § 101(b) [Title IV, § 407(b)], Oct. 18, 1986, 100 Stat. 1783–39, 1783–64; Pub.L. 99–591, Title I, § 101(b) [Title IV, § 407(b)], Oct. 30, 1986, 100 Stat. 3341–39, 3341–64; Pub.L. 99–554, Title I, §§ 117, 144(f), Oct. 27, 1986, 100 Stat. 3095, 3097; Pub.L. 101–162, Title IV, § 406(a), Nov. 21, 1989, 103 Stat. 1016; Pub.L. 102–140, Title I, § 111(a), Oct. 28, 1991, 105 Stat. 795; Pub.L. 103–121, Title I, § 111(a)(1), (b)(1), Oct. 27, 1993, 107 Stat. 1164; Pub.L. 104–91, Title I, § 101(a), Jan. 6, 1996, 110 Stat. 11; Pub.L. 104–99, Title II, § 211, Jan. 26, 1996, 110 Stat. 37; Pub.L. 104–208, Div. A, Title I, § 101(a) [Title I, § 109(a)], Sept. 30, 1996, 110 Stat. 3009, 3009–18; Pub.L. 106–113, Div. B, § 1000(a)(1) [Title I, § 113], Nov. 29, 1999, 113 Stat. 1535, 1501A–20; Pub.L. 106–518, Title I, §§ 103 to 105, Nov. 13, 2000, 114 Stat. 2411; Pub.L. 109–8, Title III, § 325(a), Title IV, § 418, Apr. 20, 2005, 119 Stat. 98, 108; Pub.L. 109–13, Div. A, Title VI, § 6058(a), May 11, 2005, 119 Stat. 297; Pub.L. 109–171, Title X, § 10101(a), Feb. 8, 2006, 120 Stat. 184; Pub.L. 110–161, Div. B, Title II, § 213(a), Dec. 26, 2007, 121 Stat. 1914; Pub.L. 112–121, § 3(a), May 25, 2012, 126 Stat. 348; Pub.L. 115–72, Div. B, § 1004(a), Oct. 26, 2017, 131 Stat. 1232.)

JUDICIAL CONFERENCE SCHEDULE OF FEES

Bankruptcy Court Miscellaneous Fee Schedule (28 U.S.C. § 1930)

(Issued in accordance with 28 U.S.C. § 1930.)

(Effective on: September 1, 2018)

The fees included in the Bankruptcy Court Miscellaneous Fee Schedule are to be charged for services provided by the bankruptcy courts.

● The United States should not be charged fees under this schedule, with the exception of those specifically prescribed in Items 1, 3 and 5 when the information requested is available through remote electronic access.

● Federal agencies or programs that are funded from judiciary appropriations (agencies, organizations, and individuals providing services authorized by the Criminal Justice Act, 18 U.S.C. § 3006A, and bankruptcy administrators) should not be charged any fees under this schedule.

1. a. For reproducing any document and providing a copy in paper form, $.50 per page. This fee applies to

services rendered on behalf of the United States if the document requested is available through electronic access.

b. For reproducing and transmitting in any manner a copy of an electronic record stored outside of the court's electronic case management system, including but not limited to, document files, audio recordings, and video recordings, $31 per record provided. Audio recordings of court proceedings continue to be governed by a separate fee under item 3 of this schedule.

2. For certification of any document, $11.

For exemplification of any document, $22.

3. For reproduction of an audio recording of a court proceeding, $31. This fee applies to services rendered on behalf of the United States if the recording is available electronically.

4. For filing an amendment to the debtor's schedules of creditors, lists of creditors, or mailing list, $31, except:

- The bankruptcy judge may, for good cause, waive the charge in any case.
- This fee must not be charged if—
  - the amendment is to change the address of a creditor or an attorney for a creditor listed on the schedules; or
  - the amendment is to add the name and address of an attorney for a creditor listed on the schedules.

5. For conducting a search of the bankruptcy court records, $31 per name or item searched. This fee applies to services rendered on behalf of the United States if the information requested is available through electronic access.

6. For filing a complaint, $350, except:

- If the trustee or debtor-in-possession files the complaint, the fee must be paid only by the estate, to the extent there is an estate.
- This fee must not be charged if—
  - the debtor is the plaintiff; or
- a child support creditor or representative files the complaint and submits the form required by § 304(g) of the Bankruptcy Reform Act of 1994.

7. For filing any document that is not related to a pending case or proceeding, $47.

8. Administrative fee:

- For filing a petition under Chapter 7, 12, or 13, $75.
- For filing a petition under Chapter 9, 11, or 15, $550.
- When a motion to divide a joint case under Chapter 7, 12, or 13 is filed, $75
- When a motion to divide a joint case under Chapter 11 is filed, $550.

9. For payment to trustees pursuant to 11 U.S.C. § 330(b)(2), a $15 fee applies in the following circumstances:

- For filing a petition under Chapter 7.
- For filing a notice of conversion to a Chapter 7 case.
- For filing a motion to convert a case to a Chapter 7 case.
- For filing a motion to divide a joint Chapter 7 case.
- For filing a motion to reopen a Chapter 7 case.

10. In addition to any fees imposed under Item 9, above, the following fees must be collected:

- For filing a motion to convert a Chapter 12 case to a Chapter 7 case or a notice of conversion pursuant to 11 U.S.C. § 1208(a), $45.

- For filing a motion to convert a Chapter 13 case to a Chapter 7 case or a notice of conversion pursuant to 11 U.S.C. § 1307(a), $10.

The fee amounts in this item are derived from the fees prescribed in 28 U.S.C. § 1930(a).

If the trustee files the motion to convert, the fee is payable only from the estate that exists prior to conversion.

If the filing fee for the chapter to which the case is requested to be converted is less than the fee paid at the commencement of the case, no refund may be provided.

11. For filing a motion to reopen, the following fees apply:

- For filing a motion to reopen a Chapter 7 case, $245.
- For filing a motion to reopen a Chapter 9 case, $1167.
- For filing a motion to reopen a Chapter 11 case, $1167.
- For filing a motion to reopen a Chapter 12 case, $200.
- For filing a motion to reopen a Chapter 13 case, $235.
- For filing a motion to reopen a Chapter 15 case, $1167.

The fee amounts in this item are derived from the fees prescribed in 28 U.S.C. § 1930(a).

The reopening fee must be charged when a case has been closed without a discharge being entered.

The court may waive this fee under appropriate circumstances or may defer payment of the fee from trustees pending discovery of additional assets. If payment is deferred, the fee should be waived if no additional assets are discovered.

The reopening fee must not be charged in the following situations:

- to permit a party to file a complaint to obtain a determination under Rule 4007(b); or
- when a debtor files a motion to reopen a case based upon an alleged violation of the terms of the discharge under 11 U.S.C. § 524; or
- when the reopening is to correct an administrative error.
- to redact a record already filed in a case, pursuant to Fed. R. Bankr. P. 9037, if redaction is the only reason for reopening.

12. For retrieval of one box of records from a Federal Records Center, National Archives, or other storage location removed from the place of business of the court, $64. For retrievals involving multiple boxes, $39 for each additional box. For electronic retrievals, $10 plus any charges assessed by the Federal Records Center, National Archives, or other storage location removed from the place of business of the courts.

13. For any payment returned or denied for insufficient funds, $53.

14. For filing an appeal or cross appeal from a judgment, order, or decree, $293.

This fee is collected in addition to the statutory fee of $5 that is collected under 28 U.S.C. § 1930(c) when a notice of appeal is filed.

Parties filing a joint notice of appeal should pay only one fee.

If a trustee or debtor-in-possession is the appellant, the fee must be paid only by the estate, to the extent there is an estate.

Upon notice from the court of appeals that a direct appeal or direct cross-appeal has been authorized, an additional fee of $207 must be collected.

15. For filing a case under Chapter 15 of the Bankruptcy Code, $1167.

This fee is derived from and equal to the fee prescribed in 28 U.S.C. § 1930(a)(3) for filing a case commenced under Chapter 11 of Title 11.

16. The court may charge and collect fees commensurate with the cost of providing copies of the local rules of court. The court may also distribute copies of the local rules without charge.

17.

• For handling registry funds deposited with and held by the court, the clerk shall asses [sic] a charge from interest earnings, in accordance with the detailed fee schedule issued by the Director of the Administrative Office of the United States Courts.

• For management of registry funds invested through the Court Registry Investment System, a fee at an annual rate of 10 basis points of assets on deposit shall be assessed from interest earnings, excluding registry funds from disputed ownership interpleader cases deposited under 28 U.S.C. § 1335 and held in a Court Registry Investment System Disputed Ownership Fund.

• For management of funds deposited under 28 U.S.C. § 1335 and invested in a Disputed Ownership Fund through the Court Registry Investment System, a fee at an annual rate of 20 basis points of assets on deposit shall be assessed from interest earnings.

• The Director of the Administrative Office has the authority to waive these fees for cause.

18. For a motion filed by the debtor to divide a joint case filed under 11 U.S.C. § 302, the following fees apply:

• For filing a motion to divide a joint Chapter 7 case, $245.

• For filing a motion to divide a joint Chapter 11 case, $1167.

• For filing a motion to divide a joint Chapter 12 case, $200.

• For filing a motion to divide a joint Chapter 13 case, $235.

These fees are derived from and equal to the filing fees prescribed in 28 U.S.C. § 1930(a).

19. For filing the following motions, $181:

• To terminate, annul, modify or condition the automatic stay;

• To compel abandonment of property of the estate pursuant to Rule 6007(b) of the Federal Rules of Bankruptcy Procedure;

• To withdraw the reference of a case or proceeding under 28 U.S.C. § 157(d); or

• To sell property of the estate free and clear of liens under 11 U.S.C. § 363(f).

This fee must not be collected in the following situations:

• For a motion for relief from the co-debtor stay;

• For a stipulation for court approval of an agreement for relief from a stay; or

• For a motion filed by a child support creditor or its representative, if the form required by § 304(g) of the Bankruptcy Reform Act of 1994 is filed.

20. For filing a transfer of claim, $25 per claim transferred.

21. For filing a motion to redact a record, $25 per affected case. The court may waive this fee under appropriate circumstances.

Electronic Public Access Fee Schedule

The fees included in the Electronic Public Access Fee Schedule are to be charged for providing electronic public access to court records.

Published on: August 2, 2017
Effective on: April 1, 2017

*(Issued in accordance with 28 U.S.C.
§§ 1913, 1914, 1926, 1930, 1932)*

Fees for Public Access to Court Electronic Records (PACER)

1. Except as provided below, for electronic access to any case document, docket sheet, or case-specific report via PACER: $0.10 per page, not to exceed the fee for thirty pages.

2. For electronic access to transcripts and non-case specific reports via PACER (such as reports obtained from the PACER Case Locator or docket activity reports): $0.10 per page.

3. For electronic access to an audio file of a court hearing via PACER: $2.40 per audio file.

Fees for Courthouse Electronic Access

4. For printing copies of any record or document accessed electronically at a public terminal in a courthouse: $0.10 per page.

PACER Service Center Fees

5. For every search of court records conducted by the PACER Service Center, $30 per name or item searched.

6. For the PACER Service Center to reproduce on paper any record pertaining to a PACER account, if this information is remotely available through electronic access: $0.50 per page.

7. For any payment returned or denied for insufficient funds, $53.

Free Access and Exemptions

8. Automatic Fee Exemptions:

• No fee is owed for electronic access to court data or audio files via PACER until an account holder accrues charges of more than $15.00 in a quarterly billing cycle.

• Parties in a case (including *pro se* litigants) and attorneys of record receive one free electronic copy, via the notice of electronic filing or notice of docket activity, of all documents filed electronically, if receipt is required by law or directed by the filer.

• No fee is charged for access to judicial opinions.

• No fee is charged for viewing case information or documents at courthouse public access terminals.

• No fee is charged for Chapter 13 bankruptcy trustees to download quarterly (i.e., once every 90 days) a list of the trustee's cases from the PACER Case Locator.

9. Discretionary Fee Exemptions:

• Courts may exempt certain persons or classes of persons from payment of the user access fee. Examples of individuals and groups that a court may consider exempting include: indigents, bankruptcy case trustees, *pro bono* attorneys, *pro bono* alternative dispute resolution neutrals, Section 501(c)(3) not-for-profit organizations, and individual researchers associated with educational institutions. Courts should not, however, exempt individuals or groups that have the ability to pay the statutorily established access fee. Examples of individuals and groups that a court should not exempt include: local, state or federal government agencies, members of the media, privately paid attorneys or others who have the ability to pay the fee.

● In considering granting an exemption, courts must find:

● that those seeking an exemption have demonstrated that an exemption is necessary in order to avoid unreasonable burdens and to promote public access to information;

● that individual researchers requesting an exemption have shown that the defined research project is intended for scholarly research, that it is limited in scope, and that it is not intended for redistribution on the internet or for commercial purposes.

● If the court grants an exemption:

● the user receiving the exemption must agree not to sell the data obtained as a result, and must not transfer any data obtained as the result of a fee exemption, unless expressly authorized by the court; and

● the exemption should be granted for a definite period of time, should be limited in scope, and may be revoked at the discretion of the court granting the exemption.

● Courts may provide local court information at no cost (e.g., local rules, court forms, news items, court calendars, and other information) to benefit the public.

Applicability to the United States and State and Local Governments

10. Unless otherwise authorized by the Judicial Conference, these fees must be charged to the United States, except to federal agencies or programs that are funded from judiciary appropriations (including, but not limited to, agencies, organizations, and individuals providing services authorized by the Criminal Justice Act [18 U.S.C. § 3006A], and bankruptcy administrators).

11. The fee for printing copies of any record or document accessed electronically at a public terminal ($0.10 per page) described in (4) above does not apply to services rendered on behalf of the United States if the record requested is not remotely available through electronic access.

12. The fee for local, state, and federal government entities, shall be $0.08 per page until April 1, 2015, after which time, the fee shall be $0.10 per page.

JUDICIAL CONFERENCE POLICY NOTES

The Electronic Public Access (EPA) fee and its exemptions are directly related to the requirement that the judiciary charge user-based fees for the development and maintenance of electronic public access services. The fee schedule provides examples of users that may not be able to afford reasonable user fees (such as indigents, bankruptcy case trustees, individual researchers associated with educational institutions, 501(c)(3) not-for-profit organizations, and court-appointed pro bono attorneys), but requires those seeking an exemption to demonstrate that an exemption is limited in scope and is necessary in order to avoid an unreasonable burden. In addition, the fee schedule includes examples of other entities that courts should not exempt from the fee (such as local, state or federal government agencies, members of the media, and attorneys). The goal is to provide courts with guidance in evaluating a requestor's ability to pay the fee.

Judicial Conference policy also limits exemptions in other ways. First, it requires exempted users to agree not to sell the data they receive through an exemption (unless expressly

authorized by the court). This prohibition is not intended to bar a quote or reference to information received as a result of a fee exemption in a scholarly or other similar work. Second, it permits courts to grant exemptions for a definite period of time, to limit the scope of the exemptions, and to revoke exemptions. Third, it cautions that exemptions should be granted as the exception, not the rule, and prohibits courts from exempting all users from EPA fees.

STATEMENT RESPECTING 1988 AMENDMENTS FROM ADMINISTRATIVE OFFICE OF UNITED STATES COURTS

The Director of the Administrative Office of the United States Courts in a memorandum to the Chief Judges of the United States Courts of Appeals, United States District Courts, and United States Bankruptcy Courts, dated April 19, 1988, provided in part that: "The amendment establishing a fee for filing a petition ancillary to a foreign proceeding under § 304 of the Bankruptcy Code will become effective May 1, 1988. The amendment expanding the exemption for services rendered 'to the United States' to include services rendered to bankruptcy administrators simply expresses a policy which has been in effect since the creation of the bankruptcy administrator program by Congress in the Bankruptcy Judges, United States Trustees and Family Farmer Bankruptcy Act of 1986. [Pub.L. No. 99–554, § 302(d)(3)(I).]"

Statement from 1989 Meeting of Judicial Conference

The Judicial Conference, at the September 20, 1989 meeting, provided in part that Item 21 takes effect on December 21, 1989. The Conference further provided that: "The remaining fees, Items 20 and 22, take effect on January 11, 1990, pending approval of the Appropriations Committees."

Registry Fund Fees—Item 19
(54 FR 20407, May 11, 1989)

Effective June 12, 1989, a fee will be assessed for handling funds deposited in noncriminal proceedings with the court and held in interest bearing accounts or instruments pursuant to 28 U.S.C. § 2041 and Federal Rules of Civil Procedure rule 67. For new accounts, i.e., investments made on or after June 12, 1989, the fee will be equal to the first 45 days income earned on the deposit. Each subsequent deposit of new principal in the same case or proceeding will be subject to the fee. Reinvestment of prior deposits will not be subject to the fee. For existing accounts, i.e., investments held by the court prior to June 12, 1989, a fee will be assessed equal to the first 45 days of income earned beginning 30 days after June 12, 1989. Subsequent deposits of new principal in the same account will be subject to the fee. Subsequent reinvestment of existing deposits will not be subject to the fee.

The fee will apply only once to each sum deposited regardless of the length of time deposits are held and will not exceed income actually earned on the account.

The fee does not apply in the District Courts of Guam, Northern Mariana Islands, the Virgin Islands, the United States Claims Court, or other courts whose fees are not set under 28 U.S.C. § 1930.

Registry Fund Fees—Item 19
(55 F.R. 42867, October 24, 1990)

Effective December 1, 1990, the registry fee assessment provisions were revised and converted from a one-time charge equal to all income earned in the first 45 days of the investment to a charge of 10 percent of the income earned while funds are held in the court registry. Additionally, the fee was extended to any funds placed in the court's registry and invested regardless of the nature of the action underlying the deposit.

The new method will not be applied on investments in cases from which a fee has been exacted based on the prior method (interest earned in the first 45 days the funds were invested or the first 45 days following July 12, 1989). The new method will also not be applied in cases where the investment instrument has a maturity date greater than one year, but where a fee under the prior method applies but has not been deducted.

The fee does not apply in the District Courts of Guam, the Northern Mariana Islands, the Virgin Islands, the United States Claims Court, or any other federal court whose fees are not set under 28 U.S.C. §§ 1913, 1914, and 1930.

Registry Fund Fees—Item 19
(56 F.R. 56356, November 4, 1991)

Effective February 3, 1992, the registry fee assessment provisions are revised and converted from a charge equal to 10 percent of the income earned while funds are held in the court's registry to a variable rate based on the amount deposited with the court and, in certain cases, the length of time funds are held in the court's registry.

The revised fee will be a fee of 10 percent of the total income received during each income period from investments of less than $100,000,000 of registry funds in income-bearing accounts. On investments exceeding $100,000,000 the 10 percent fee shall be reduced by one percent for each increment of $50,000,000 over the initial $100,000,000. For those deposits where funds are placed in the registry by court order for a time certain, for example, by the terms of an adjudicated trust, the fee will be further reduced. This further reduction will amount to 2.5 percent for each five-year interval or part thereof. The total minimum fee to be charged will be no less than two percent of the income on investments.

The following table sets out the fee schedule promulgated by this notice:

REGISTRY—SCHEDULE OF FEES

[% of income earned]

Amount of deposit *	0–5 yrs.	>5–10 yrs.	>10–15 yrs.	>15 yrs.
less than 100M	10	7.5	5.0	2.5
100M–<150M	9	6.5	4.0	2.0
150M–<200M	8	5.5	3.0	2.0
200M–<250M	7	4.5	2.0	2.0
250M–<300M	6	3.5	2.0	2.0
300M–<350M	5	2.5	2.0	2.0
350M–<400M	4	2.0	2.0	2.0
400M–<450M	3	2.0	2.0	2.0
over 450M	2	2.0	2.0	2.0

The new fee applies to all earnings applied to investments on and after the effective date of this change, except for earnings on investments in cases being administered under the provisions of the May 11, 1989 notice [54 FR 20407], i.e., to which the fee equal to the first 45 days income is applicable.

The fee, as modified herein, will continue to apply to any case where the court has authorized the investment of funds placed in its custody or held by it in trust in its registry regardless of the nature of the underlying action.

The fee does not apply in the District Court of Guam, the Northern Mariana Islands, the Virgin Islands, the United States Claims Court, or any other Federal court whose fees are not set under 28 U.S.C. §§ 1913, 1914, and 1930.

HISTORICAL AND STATUTORY NOTES

Revision Notes and Legislative Reports

1978 Acts. Senate Report No. 95–989 and House Report No. 95–595, see 1978 U.S. Code Cong. and Adm. News, p. 5787.

1984 Acts. Statements by Legislative Leaders, see 1984 U.S. Code Cong. and Adm. News, p. 576.

1986 Acts. House Report No. 99–764 and House Conference Report No. 99–958, see 1986 U.S. Code Cong. and Adm. News, p. 5227.

Statement by President, see 1986 U.S. Code Cong. and Adm. News, p. 5627.

1989 Acts. Statement by President, see 1989 U.S. Code Cong. and Adm. News, p. 733–3.

1991 Acts. Statement by President, see 1991 U.S. Code Cong. and Adm. News, p. 507.

1999 Acts. Statement by President, see 1999 U.S. Code Cong. and Adm. News, p. 290.

2005 Acts. House Report No. 109–31(Part I), see 2005 U.S. Code Cong. and Adm. News, p. 88.

House Conference Report No. 109–72, see 2005 U.S. Code Cong. and Adm. News, p. 240.

2006 Acts. House Conference Report No. 109–362, see 2006 U.S. Code Cong. and Adm. News, p. 3.

Statement by President, see 2006 U.S. Code Cong. and Adm. News, p. S3.

2007 Acts. House Report No. 110–197, see 2007 U.S. Code Cong. and Adm. News, p. 661.

Statement by President, see 2007 U.S. Code Cong. and Adm. News, p. S34.

References in Text

Chapter 7, 11, 12, or 13 of title 11, referred to in text, is 11 U.S.C.A. § 701 et seq., 11 U.S.C.A. § 1101 et seq., 11 U.S.C.A. § 1201 et seq., or 11 U.S.C.A. § 1301 et seq., respectively.

Section 673(2) of the Omnibus Budget Reconciliation Act of 1981, referred to in subsec. (f)(1), is Pub.L. 97–35, Title VI, § 673(2), Aug. 13, 1981, as added Pub.L. 105–285, Title II, § 201, Oct. 27, 1998, 112 Stat. 2729, which is classified to 42 U.S.C.A. § 9902(2).

Codifications

Pub.L. 99–591 is a corrected version of Pub.L. 99–500.

The Chapter 11 filing fee will not change from its current amount of $1,000. It appears that Congress intended to increase chapter 11 filing fees from $1,000 to $2,750. However, there is a drafting error in the language of the Deficit Reduction Act of 2005 which references the incorrect statutory subsection [Pub.L. 109–171, Title X, § 10101(a)(2), Feb. 8, 2006, 120 Stat. 184]. Thus, the chapter 11 fee, at this time, is unaltered. See 2006 Amendments note set out under this section.

Section 101(a) of Pub.L. 104–91, as amended by section 211 of Pub.L. 104–99, provided in part that section 111(a) of the General Provisions for the Department of Justice in Title I of the Departments of Commerce, Justice, and State, the Judiciary, and Related Agencies Appropriations Act, 1996 (H.R. 2076) as passed by the House of Representatives on Dec. 6, 1995, was enacted into permanent law. Such section 111(a) of H.R. 2076 amended subsec. (a)(6) of this section. See 1996 Amendments note set out under this section.

Effective and Applicability Provisions

2017 Acts. Pub.L. 115-72, Div. B, § 1004(c), Oct. 26, 2017, 131 Stat. 1232, provided that: "The amendments made by this section [amending this section] shall apply to quarterly fees payable under section 1930(a)(6) of title 28, United States Code, as amended by this section, for disbursements made in any calendar quarter that begins on or after the date of enactment of this Act [Oct. 26, 2017]."

2012 Acts. Pub.L. 112-121, § 3, and amendments made by Pub.L. 112-121, § 3, shall take effect 180 days after May 25, 2012, see Pub.L. 112-121, § 3(e), set out as a note under 28 U.S.C.A. § 589a.

2007 Acts. Pub.L. 110-161, Div. B, Title II, § 213(b), Dec. 26, 2007, 121 Stat. 1914, provided that: "This section and the amendment made by this section [amending this section] shall take effect January 1, 2008, or the date of the enactment of this Act [Dec. 26, 2007], whichever is later."

2006 Acts. Pub.L. 109-171, Title X, § 10101(c), Feb. 8, 2006, 120 Stat. 184, provided that: "This section and the amendments made by this section [amending this section and enacting provisions set out as a note under 28 U.S.C.A. § 1931] shall take effect 60 days after the date of the enactment of this Act [Feb. 8, 2006]."

2005 Acts. Amendment by Pub.L. 109-13, § 6058(a), amending Pub.L. 109-8, § 325, which amended this section, effective immediately after the enactment of the Bankruptcy Abuse Prevention and Consumer Protection Act of 2005 [Pub.L. 109-8, Apr. 20, 2005, 119 Stat. 23], see Pub.L. 109-13, § 6058(b), set out as a note under 28 U.S.C.A. § 589a.

Except as otherwise provided, amendments by Pub.L. 109-8 effective 180 days after April 20, 2005, and inapplicable with respect to cases commenced under Title 11 before the effective date, see Pub.L. 109-8, § 1501, set out as a note under 11 U.S.C.A. § 101.

1999 Acts. Amendment by Pub.L. 106-113, [§ 113], effective 30 days after Nov. 29, 1999, see Pub.L. 106-113, [§ 113], set out as a note under section 589a of this title.

1993 Acts. Section 111(a) of Pub.L. 103-121 provided in part that amendment by section 111(a)(1) of Pub.L. 103-121, amending subsec. (a)(1) of this section, is effective 30 days after Oct. 27, 1993.

Section 111(b) of Pub.L. 103-121 provided in part that amendment by section 111(b)(1) of Pub.L. 103-121, amending subsec. (a)(3) of this section, is effective 30 days after Oct. 27, 1993.

1991 Acts. Amendment by Pub.L. 102-140 effective 60 days after the date of the enactment of Pub.L. 102-140, which was approved Oct. 28, 1991, see section 111(a) of Pub.L. 102-140, set out as a note under section 589a of this title.

1986 Acts. Amendment by Pub.L. 99-554 effective 30 days after Oct. 27, 1986, except as otherwise provided for, see section 302(a) of Pub.L. 99-554, set out as a note under section 581 of this title.

Amendment by Pub.L. 99-554, § 117(4), not to become effective in or with respect to certain specified judicial districts until, or apply to cases while pending in such district before, the expiration of the 270-day period beginning 30 days

after Oct. 27, 1986, or of the 30-day period beginning on the date the Attorney General certifies under section 303 of Pub.L. 99-554 the region specified in a paragraph of section 581(a) of Title 28, as amended by section 111(a) of Pub.L. 99-554, that includes such district, whichever occurs first, see section 302(d)(1) of Pub.L. 99-554, set out as a note under section 581 of this title.

Amendment by Pub.L. 99-554, § 117(4), not to become effective in or with respect to certain specified judicial districts until, or apply to cases while pending in such district before, the expiration of the 2-year period beginning 30 days after Oct. 27, 1986, or of the 30-day period beginning on the date the Attorney General certifies under section 303 of Pub.L. 99-554 the region specified in a paragraph of section 581(a) of Title 28, as amended by section 111(a) of Pub.L. 99-554, that includes such district, whichever occurs first, see section 302(d)(2) of Pub.L. 99-554, set out as a note under section 581 of this title.

Amendment by Pub.L. 99-554, § 117(4), not to become effective in or with respect to judicial districts established for the States of Alabama and North Carolina until, or apply to cases while pending in such district before, such district elects to be included in a bankruptcy region established in section 581(a) of Title 28, as amended by section 111(a) of Pub.L. 99-554, or Oct. 1, 2002, whichever occurs first, and, except as otherwise provided for, with respect to cases under chapters 7, 11, 12, and 13 of Title 11 commenced before 30 days after Oct. 27, 1986, and pending in a judicial district in the States of Alabama or North Carolina before any election made under section 302(d)(3)(A) of Pub.L. 99-554 by such district becomes effective or Oct. 1, 2002, whichever occurs first, amendments by Pub.L. 99-554 not to apply until Oct. 1, 2003, or the expiration of the 1-year period beginning on the date such election becomes effective, whichever occurs first, and further, in any judicial district in Alabama or North Carolina not making the election described in section 302(d)(3)(A) of Pub.L. 99-554, any person appointed under regulations issued by the Judicial Conference to administer estates in cases under Title 11 authorized to establish, etc., a panel of private trustees, and to supervise cases and trustees in cases under chapters 7, 11, 12, and 13 of Title 11, until amendments by sections 201 to 231 of Pub.L. 99-554 effective in such district, see section 302(d)(3)(A) to (F), (H), (I) of Pub.L. 99-554, set out as a note under section 581 of this title.

Deposit in the general receipts of the Treasury of funds collected as a result of the amendments made by section 117 of Pub.L. 99-554 in a judicial district in the States of Alabama or North Carolina under section 1930(a) of Title 28 before the date the amendments made by sections 201 to 231 of Pub.L. 99-554 take effect in such districts, and notwithstanding section 589a of Title 28, see section 302(d)(3)(G) of Pub.L. 99-554, set out as a note under section 581 of this title.

Amendment by Pub.L. 99-554, § 117(4), except as otherwise provided, with respect to cases under chapters 7, 11, 12, and 13 of Title 11 commenced before 30 days after Oct. 27, 1986, and pending in a judicial district referred to in section 581(a) of Title 28, as amended by section 111(a) of Pub.L. 99-554, for which a United States trustee is not authorized before 30 days after Oct. 27, 1986 to be appointed, not applicable until the expiration of the 3-year period beginning on Oct. 27, 1986, or of the 1-year period beginning on the date the Attorney General certifies under section 303 of Pub.L. 99-554 the region specified in a paragraph of such section 581(a) that includes, such district, whichever occurs first, see section 302(e)(1), (2) of Pub.L. 99–554, set out as a note under section 581 of this title.

Rule of construction regarding fees for cases under Title 11 for any conduct or period occurring before section 1930(a)(6) of Title 28 becomes effective in the district in which such case is pending, see section 302(e)(3) of Pub.L. 99–554, set out as a note under section 581 of this title.

1984 Acts. Amendment by Pub.L. 98–353 effective July 10, 1984, see section 122(a) of Pub.L. 98–353, set out as a note under section 151 of this title.

1979 Acts. Section effective Oct. 1, 1979, see section 402(c) of Pub.L. 95–598, set out as a note preceding section 101 of Title 11, Bankruptcy.

Use of Increased Receipts

Pub.L. 109–8, Title III, § 325(e), Apr. 20, 2005, 119 Stat. 99, which pertained to the use of increased receipts from fees under subsec. (a) of this section, was omitted in the general amendment of Pub.L. 109–8, § 325, by Pub.L. 109–13, Div. A, Title VI, § 6058(a), May 11, 2005, 119 Stat. 297. Such amendment by Pub.L. 109–13, § 6058(a), effective immediately after the enactment of the Bankruptcy Abuse Prevention and Consumer Protection Act of 2005 [Pub.L. 109–8, Apr. 20, 2005, 119 Stat. 23], see Pub.L. 109–13, § 6058(b), set out as a note under 28 U.S.C.A. § 589a.

[Except as otherwise provided, amendments by Pub.L. 109–8 effective 180 days after April 20, 2005, and inapplicable with respect to cases commenced under Title 11 before the effective date, see Pub.L. 109–8, § 1501, set out as a note under 11 U.S.C.A. § 101.]

Miscellaneous Fees

Section 406(a) of Pub.L. 101–162 provided in part that: "Pursuant to section 1930(b) of title 28 [subsec. (b) of this section] the Judicial Conference of the United States shall prescribe a fee of $60 on motions seeking relief from the automatic stay under 11 U.S.C. section 362(b) [section 362(b) of Title 11, Bankruptcy] and motions to compel abandonment of property of the estate. The fees established pursuant to the preceding two sentences shall take effect 30 days after the enactment of this Act [Nov. 21, 1989]."

Accrual and Payment of Quarterly Fees in Chapter 11 Cases After Jan. 27, 1996; Confirmation Status of Plans

Section 101(a) of Pub.L. 104–91, as amended Pub.L. 104–99, Title II, § 211, Jan. 26, 1996, 110 Stat. 37; Pub.L. 104–208, Div. A, Title I, § 101(a) [Title I, § 109(d)], Sept. 30, 1996, 110 Stat. 3009–19, provided, in part: "That, notwithstanding any other provision of law, the fees under 28 U.S.C. 1930(a)(6) [subsec. (a)(6) of this section] shall accrue and be payable from and after January 27, 1996, in all cases (including, without limitation, any cases pending as of that date), regardless of confirmation status of their plans."

Collection and Disposition of Fees in Bankruptcy Cases

Section 404(a) of Pub. L. 101–162 provided that: "For fiscal year 1990 and hereafter, such fees as shall be collected for the preparation and mailing of notices in bankruptcy cases as prescribed by the Judicial Conference of the United States pursuant to 28 U.S.C. 1930(b) [subsec. (b) of this section] shall be deposited to the 'Courts of Appeals, District Courts, and Other Judicial Services, Salaries and Expenses' appropriation to be used for salaries and other expenses incurred in providing these services."

Court Fees for Electronic Access to Information

Judicial Conference to prescribe reasonable fees for collection by courts under this section for access to information available through automatic data processing equipment and fees to be deposited in Judiciary Automation Fund, see section 303 of Pub.L. 102–140, set out as a note under section 1913 of this title.

Issuance of Notices to Creditors and Other Interested Parties

Section 403 of Pub.L. 101–162 provided that: "Notwithstanding any other provision of law, for fiscal year 1990 and hereafter, (a) The Administrative Office of the United States Courts, or any other agency or instrumentality of the United States, is prohibited from restricting solely to staff of the Clerks of the United States Bankruptcy Courts the issuance of notices to creditors and other interested parties. (b) The Administrative Office shall permit and encourage the preparation and mailing of such notices to be performed by or at the expense of the debtors, trustees or such other interested parties as the Court may direct and approve. (c) The Director of the Administrative Office of the United States Courts shall make appropriate provisions for the use of and accounting for any postage required pursuant to such directives."

Report on Bankruptcy Fees

Section 111(d) of Pub.L. 103–121 provided that:

"**(1) Report required.**—Not later than March 31, 1998, the Judicial Conference of the United States shall submit to the Committees on the Judiciary of the House of Representatives and the Senate, a report relating to the bankruptcy fee system and the impact of such system on various participants in bankruptcy cases.

"**(2) Contents of report.**—Such report shall include—

"**(A)(i)** an estimate of the costs and benefits that would result from waiving bankruptcy fees payable by debtors who are individuals, and

"**(ii)** recommendations regarding various revenue sources to offset the net cost of waiving such fees; and

"**(B)(i)** an evaluation of the effects that would result in cases under chapters 11 and 13 of title 11, United States Code [sections 1101 et seq. and 1301 et seq., respectively, of Title 11, Bankruptcy], from using a graduated bankruptcy fee system based on assets, liabilities, or both of the debtor, and

"**(ii)** recommendations regarding various methods to implement such a graduated bankruptcy fee system.

"**(3) Waiver of fees in selected districts.**—For purposes of carrying out paragraphs (1) and (2), the Judicial Conference of the United States shall carry out in not more than six judicial districts, throughout the 3–year period beginning on October 1, 1994, a program under which fees payable under section 1930 of title 28, United States Code [this section], may be waived in cases under chapter 7 of title 11, United States Code [section 701 et seq. of Title 11], for debtors who are individuals unable to pay such fees in installments.

"**(4) Study of graduated fee system.**—For purposes of carrying out paragraphs (1) and (2), the Judicial Conference of the United States shall carry out, in not fewer than six judicial districts, a study to estimate the results that would occur in cases under chapters 11 and 13 of title 11, United States Code [sections 1101 et seq. and 1301 et seq., respectively, of Title 11], if filing fees payable under section 1930 of title 28, United States Code [this section], were paid on a graduated scale based on assets, liabilities, or both of the debtor."

CROSS REFERENCES

Confirmation of reorganization plan contingent on payment of fees, see 11 USCA § 1129.

Recommendation for adjustment of dollar amounts of fees, see 11 USCA § 104.

United States Trustee System Fund, depositing of bankruptcy fees into Fund, see 28 USCA § 589a.

CHAPTER 131—RULES OF COURTS

§ 2075. Bankruptcy rules

The Supreme Court shall have the power to prescribe by general rules, the forms of process, writs, pleadings, and motions, and the practice and procedure in cases under title 11.

Such rules shall not abridge, enlarge, or modify any substantive right.

The Supreme Court shall transmit to Congress not later than May 1 of the year in which a rule prescribed under this section is to become effective a copy of the proposed rule. The rule shall take effect no earlier than December 1 of the year in which it is transmitted to Congress unless otherwise provided by law.

The bankruptcy rules promulgated under this section shall prescribe a form for the statement required under section 707(b)(2)(C) of title 11 and may provide general rules on the content of such statement.

(Added Pub.L. 88–623, § 1, Oct. 3, 1964, 78 Stat. 1001; amended Pub.L. 95–598, Title II, § 247, Nov. 6, 1978, 92 Stat. 2672; Pub.L. 103–394, Title I, § 104(f), Oct. 22, 1994, 108 Stat. 4110; Pub.L. 109–8, Title XII, § 1232, Apr. 20, 2005, 119 Stat. 202.)

HISTORICAL AND STATUTORY NOTES

Revision Notes and Legislative Reports

1964 Acts. Senate Report No. 1561, see 1964 U.S. Code Cong. and Adm. News, p. 3804.

1978 Acts. Senate Report No. 95–989 and House Report No. 95–595, see 1978 U.S. Code Cong. and Adm. News, p. 5787.

1994 Acts. House Report No. 103–835, see 1994 U.S. Code Cong. and Adm. News, p. 3340.

2005 Acts. House Report No. 109–31(Part I), see 2005 U.S. Code Cong. and Adm. News, p. 88.

Effective and Applicability Provisions

2005 Acts. Except as otherwise provided, amendments by Pub.L. 109–8 effective 180 days after April 20, 2005, and inapplicable with respect to cases commenced under Title 11 before the effective date, see Pub.L. 109–8, § 1501, set out as a note under 11 U.S.C.A. § 101.

1994 Acts. Amendment by Pub.L. 103–394 effective on Oct. 22, 1994, and not to apply with respect to cases commenced under Title 11 of the United States Code before Oct. 22, 1994, see section 702 of Pub.L. 103–394, set out as a note under section 101 of Title 11, Bankruptcy.

1978 Acts. Amendment by Pub.L. 95–598 effective Nov. 6, 1978, see section 402(d) of Pub.L. 95–598, set out as a note preceding section 101 of Title 11, Bankruptcy.

Separability of Provisions

If any provision of or amendment made by Pub.L. 103–394 or the application of such provision or amendment to any person or circumstance is held to be unconstitutional, the remaining provisions of and amendments made by Pub.L. 103–394 and the application of such provisions and amendments to any person or circumstance shall not be affected thereby, see section 701 of Pub.L. 103–394, set out as a note under section 101 of Title 11, Bankruptcy.

Additional Rulemaking Power

Pub.L. 95–598, Title IV, § 410, Nov. 6, 1978, 92 Stat. 2687, provided that: "The Supreme Court may issue such additional rules of procedure, consistent with Acts of Congress, as may be necessary for the orderly transfer of functions and records and the orderly transition to the new bankruptcy court system created by this Act [see Tables for complete classification of Pub.L. 95–598]."

Applicability of Rules to Cases Under Title 11

Pub.L. 95–598, Title IV, § 405(d), Nov. 6, 1978, 92 Stat. 2685, provided that: "The rules prescribed under section 2075 of title 28 of the United States Code and in effect on September 30, 1979, shall apply to cases under title 11, to the extent not inconsistent with the amendments made by this Act, or with this Act [see Tables for complete classification of Pub.L. 95–598], until such rules are repealed or superseded by rules prescribed and effective under such section, as amended by section 248 of this Act."

Rules Promulgated by Supreme Court

Pub.L. 98–353, Title III, § 320, July 10, 1984, 98 Stat. 357, provided that: "The Supreme Court shall prescribe general rules implementing the practice and procedure to be followed under section 707(b) of title 11, United States Code [section 707(b) of Title 11, Bankruptcy]. Section 2075 of title 28, United States Code [this section], shall apply with respect to the general rules prescribed under this section."

FEDERAL RULES OF BANKRUPTCY PROCEDURE

Amendments received to December 1, 2018

ORDER OF APRIL 26, 2004

1. That the Federal Rules of Bankruptcy Procedure be, and they hereby are, amended by including therein amendments to Bankruptcy Rules 1011, 2002, and 9014.

2. That the foregoing amendments to the Federal Rules of Bankruptcy Procedure shall take effect on December 1, 2004, and shall govern in all proceedings in bankruptcy cases thereafter commenced and, insofar as just and practicable, all proceedings then pending.

3. That THE CHIEF JUSTICE be, and hereby is, authorized to transmit to the Congress the foregoing amendments to the Federal Rules of Bankruptcy Procedure in accordance with the provisions of Section 2075 of Title 28, United States Code.

ORDER OF APRIL 25, 2005

1. That the Federal Rules of Bankruptcy Procedure be, and they hereby are, amended by including therein amendments to Bankruptcy Rules 1007, 2002, 3004, 3005, 7004, 9001, 9006, and 9036.

2. That the foregoing amendments to the Federal Rules of Bankruptcy Procedure shall take effect on December 1, 2005, and shall govern in all proceedings in bankruptcy cases thereafter commenced and, insofar as just and practicable, all proceedings then pending.

3. That THE CHIEF JUSTICE be, and hereby is, authorized to transmit to the Congress the foregoing amendments to the Federal Rules of Bankruptcy Procedure in accordance with the provisions of Section 2075 of Title 28, United States Code.

ORDER OF APRIL 12, 2006

1. That the Federal Rules of Bankruptcy Procedure be, and they hereby are, amended by including therein amendments to Bankruptcy Rules 1009, 5005, and 7004.

2. That the foregoing amendments to the Federal Rules of Bankruptcy Procedure shall take effect on December 1, 2006, and shall govern in all proceedings in bankruptcy cases thereafter commenced and, insofar as just and practicable, all proceedings then pending.

3. That THE CHIEF JUSTICE be, and hereby is, authorized to transmit to the Congress the foregoing amendments to the Federal Rules of Bankruptcy Procedure in accordance with the provisions of Section 2075 of Title 28, United States Code.

ORDER OF APRIL 30, 2007

1. That the Federal Rules of Bankruptcy Procedure be, and they hereby are, amended by including therein amendments to Bankruptcy Rules 1014, 3007, 4001, 6006, 7007.1, and new Rules 6003, 9005.1, and 9037.

2. That the foregoing amendments to the Federal Rules of Bankruptcy Procedure shall take effect on December 1, 2007, and shall govern in all proceedings in bankruptcy cases thereafter commenced and, insofar as just and practicable, all proceedings then pending.

3. That THE CHIEF JUSTICE be, and hereby is, authorized to transmit to the Congress the foregoing amendments to the Federal Rules of Bankruptcy Procedure in accordance with the provisions of Section 2075 of Title 28, United States Code.

ORDER OF APRIL 23, 2008

1. That the Federal Rules of Bankruptcy Procedure be, and they hereby are, amended by including therein amendments to Bankruptcy Rules 1005, 1006, 1007, 1009, 1010, 1011, 1015, 1017, 1019, 1020, 2002, 2003, 2007.1, 2015, 3002, 3003, 3016, 3017.1, 3019, 4002, 4003, 4004, 4006, 4007, 4008, 5001, 5003, 6004, 7012, 7022, 7023.1, 8001, 8003, 9006, 9009, and 9024, and new Rules 1021, 2007.2, 2015.1, 2015.2, 2015.3, 5008, and 6011.

2. That the foregoing amendments to the Federal Rules of Bankruptcy Procedure shall take effect on December 1, 2008, and shall govern in all proceedings in bankruptcy cases thereafter commenced and, insofar as just and practicable, all proceedings then pending.

3. That THE CHIEF JUSTICE be, and hereby is, authorized to transmit to the Congress the foregoing amendments to the Federal Rules of Bankruptcy Procedure in accordance with the provisions of Section 2075 of Title 28, United States Code.

ORDER OF MARCH 26, 2009

1. That the Federal Rules of Bankruptcy Procedure be, and they hereby are, amended by including therein amendments to Bankruptcy Rules 1007, 1011, 1019, 1020, 2002, 2003, 2006, 2007, 2007.2, 2008, 2015, 2015.1, 2015.2, 2015.3, 2016, 3001, 3015, 3017, 3019, 3020, 4001, 4002, 4004, 4008, 6003, 6004, 6006, 6007, 7004, 7012, 7052, 8001, 8002, 8003, 8006, 8009, 8015, 8017, 9006, 9015, 9021, 9023, 9027, and 9033, and new Rule 7058.

2. That the foregoing amendments to the Federal Rules of Bankruptcy Procedure shall take effect on December 1, 2009, and shall govern in all proceedings in bankruptcy cases thereafter commenced and, insofar as just and practicable, all proceedings then pending.

3. That THE CHIEF JUSTICE be, and hereby is, authorized to transmit to the Congress the foregoing amendments to the Federal Rules of Bankruptcy Procedure in accordance with the provisions of Section 2075 of Title 28, United States Code.

ORDER OF APRIL 28, 2010

1. That the Federal Rules of Bankruptcy Procedure be, and they hereby are, amended by including therein amendments to Bankruptcy Rules 1007, 1014, 1015, 1018, 1019, 4001, 4004, 5009, 7001, and 9001, and new Rule 5012.

[See amendments made thereby under respective rules, post.]

2. That the foregoing amendments to the Federal Rules of Bankruptcy Procedure shall take effect on December 1, 2010, and shall govern in all proceedings in bankruptcy cases thereafter commenced and, insofar as just and practicable, all proceedings then pending.

3. That THE CHIEF JUSTICE be, and hereby is, authorized to transmit to the Congress the foregoing amendments to the Federal Rules of Bankruptcy Procedure in accordance with the provisions of Section 2075 of Title 28, United States Code.

ORDER OF APRIL 26, 2011

1. That the Federal Rules of Bankruptcy Procedure be, and they hereby are, amended by including therein amendments to Bankruptcy Rules 2003, 2019, 3001, 4004, and 6003, and new Rules 1004.2 and 3002.1.

[See amendments made thereby under respective rules, post]

2. That the foregoing amendments to the Federal Rules of Bankruptcy Procedure shall take effect on December 1, 2011, and shall govern in all proceedings in bankruptcy cases thereafter commenced and, insofar as just and practicable, all proceedings then pending.

3. That THE CHIEF JUSTICE be, and hereby is, authorized to transmit to the Congress the foregoing amendments to the Federal Rules of Bankruptcy Procedure in accordance with the provisions of Section 2075 of Title 28, United States Code.

ORDER OF APRIL 23, 2012

1. That the Federal Rules of Bankruptcy Procedure be, and they hereby are, amended by including therein amendments to Bankruptcy Rules 1007, 2015, 3001, 7054, and 7056.

[See amendments made thereby under respective rules, post]

2. That the foregoing amendments to the Federal Rules of Bankruptcy Procedure shall take effect on December 1, 2012, and shall govern in all proceedings in bankruptcy cases thereafter commenced and, insofar as just and practicable, all proceedings then pending.

3. That THE CHIEF JUSTICE be, and hereby is, authorized to transmit to the Congress the foregoing amendments to the Federal Rules of Bankruptcy Procedure in

accordance with the provisions of Section 2075 of Title 28, United States Code.

ORDER OF APRIL 16, 2013

1. That the Federal Rules of Bankruptcy Procedure be, and they hereby are, amended by including therein amendments to Bankruptcy Rules 1007, 4004, 5009, 9006, 9013, and 9014.

[See amendments made thereby under respective rules, post]

2. That the foregoing amendments to the Federal Rules of Bankruptcy Procedure shall take effect on December 1, 2013, and shall govern in all proceedings in bankruptcy cases thereafter commenced and, insofar as just and practicable, all proceedings then pending.

3. That THE CHIEF JUSTICE be, and hereby is, authorized to transmit to the Congress the foregoing amendments to the Federal Rules of Bankruptcy Procedure in accordance with the provisions of Section 2075 of Title 28, United States Code.

ORDER OF APRIL 25, 2014

1. That the Federal Rules of Bankruptcy Procedure be, and they hereby are, amended by including therein amendments to Bankruptcy Rules 1014, 7004, 7008, 7054, 8001–8028, 9023, and 9024.

[See amendments made thereby under respective rules, post]

2. That the foregoing amendments to the Federal Rules of Bankruptcy Procedure shall take effect on December 1, 2014, and shall govern in all proceedings in bankruptcy cases thereafter commenced and, insofar as just and practicable, all proceedings then pending.

3. That THE CHIEF JUSTICE be, and hereby is, authorized to transmit to the Congress the foregoing amendments to the Federal Rules of Bankruptcy Procedure in accordance with the provisions of Section 2075 of Title 28, United States Code.

ORDER OF APRIL 29, 2015

1. That the Federal Rules of Bankruptcy Procedure be, and they hereby are, amended by including therein amendments to Bankruptcy Rule 1007.

[See amendments made thereby under rule, post]

2. That the foregoing amendments to the Federal Rules of Bankruptcy Procedure shall take effect on December 1, 2015, and shall govern in all proceedings in bankruptcy cases thereafter commenced and, insofar as just and practicable, all proceedings then pending.

3. That THE CHIEF JUSTICE be, and hereby is, authorized to transmit to the Congress the foregoing amendments to the Federal Rules of Bankruptcy Procedure in accordance with the provisions of Section 2075 of Title 28, United States Code.

ORDER OF APRIL 28, 2016

1. That the Federal Rules of Bankruptcy Procedure be, and they hereby are, amended by including therein amendments to Bankruptcy Rules 1010, 1011, 2002, 3002.1, 7008, 7012, 7016, 9006, 9027, and 9033, and new Rule 1012.

[See amendments made thereby under respective rules, post]

2. That the foregoing amendments to the Federal Rules of Bankruptcy Procedure shall take effect on December 1, 2016, and shall govern in all proceedings in bankruptcy cases thereafter commenced and, insofar as just and practicable, all proceedings then pending.

3. That THE CHIEF JUSTICE be, and hereby is, authorized to transmit to the Congress the foregoing amendments to the Federal Rules of Bankruptcy Procedure in accordance with the provisions of Section 2075 of Title 28, United States Code.

ORDER OF APRIL 27, 2017

1. That the Federal Rules of Bankruptcy Procedure be, and they hereby are, amended by including therein amendments to Bankruptcy Rules 1001, 1006, 1015, 2002, 3002, 3007, 3012, 3015, 4003, 5009, 7001, and 9009, and new Rule 3015.1.

[See amendments made thereby under respective rules, post]

2. That the foregoing amendments to the Federal Rules of Bankruptcy Procedure shall take effect on December 1, 2017, and shall govern in all proceedings in bankruptcy cases thereafter commenced and, insofar as just and practicable, all proceedings then pending.

3. That THE CHIEF JUSTICE be, and hereby is, authorized to transmit to the Congress the foregoing amendments to the Federal Rules of Bankruptcy Procedure in accordance with the provisions of Section 2075 of Title 28, United States Code.

ORDER OF APRIL 26, 2018

1. That the Federal Rules of Bankruptcy Procedure be, and they hereby are, amended by including therein amendments to Bankruptcy Rules 3002.1, 5005, 7004, 7062, 8002, 8006, 8007, 8010, 8011, 8013, 8015, 8016, 8017, 8021, 8022, 9025, and new Rule 8018.1, and new Part VIII Appendix.

[See amendments made thereby under respective rules, post]

2. That the foregoing amendments to the Federal Rules of Bankruptcy Procedure shall take effect on December 1, 2018, and shall govern in all proceedings in bankruptcy cases thereafter commenced and, insofar as just and practicable, all proceedings then pending.

3. That THE CHIEF JUSTICE be, and hereby is, authorized to transmit to the Congress the foregoing amendments to the Federal Rules of Bankruptcy Procedure in accordance with the provisions of Section 2075 of Title 28, United States Code.

Rule 1001. Scope of Rules and Forms; Short Title

The Bankruptcy Rules and Forms govern procedure in cases under title 11 of the United States Code. The rules shall be cited as the Federal Rules of Bankruptcy Procedure and the forms as the Official Bankruptcy Forms. These rules shall be construed, administered, and employed by the court and the parties to secure the just, speedy, and inexpensive determination of every case and proceeding.

(As amended Mar. 30, 1987, eff. Aug. 1, 1987; Apr. 30, 1991, eff. Aug. 1, 1991; Apr. 27, 2017, eff. Dec. 1, 2017.)

ADVISORY COMMITTEE NOTES

Section 247 of Public Law 95–598, 92 Stat. 2549 amended 28 U.S.C. § 2075 by omitting the last sentence. The effect of the amendment is to require that procedural rules promulgated pursuant to 28 U.S.C. § 2075 be consistent with the bankruptcy statute, both titles 11 and 28 U.S.C. Thus, although Rule 1001 sets forth the scope of the bankruptcy rules and forms, any procedural matters contained in title 11 or 28 U.S.C. with respect to cases filed under 11 U.S.C. would control. See 1 Collier, Bankruptcy ¶3.04[2][c] (15th ed. 1980).

28 U.S.C. § 151 establishes a United States Bankruptcy Court in each district as an adjunct to the district court. This provision does not, however, become effective until April 1, 1984. Public Law 95–598, § 402(b). From October 1, 1979 through March 31, 1984, the courts of bankruptcy as defined in § 1(10) of the Bankruptcy Act [former § 1(10) of this title], and created in § 2a of that Act [former § 11(a) of this title], continue to be the courts of bankruptcy. Public Law 95–598, § 404(a). From their effective date these rules and forms are to be applicable in cases filed under chapters 7, 9, 11 and 13 of title 11 regardless of whether the court is established by the Bankruptcy Act or by 28 U.S.C. § 151. Rule 9001 contains a broad and general definition of "bankruptcy court," "court" and "United States Bankruptcy Court" for this purpose.

"Bankruptcy Code" or "Code" as used in these rules means title 11 of the United States Code, the codification of the bankruptcy law. Public Law 95–598, § 101. See Rule 9001.

"Bankruptcy Act" as used in the notes to these rules means the Bankruptcy Act of 1898 as amended which was repealed by § 401(a) of Public Law 95–598.

These rules apply to all cases filed under the Code except as otherwise specifically stated.

The final sentence of the rule is derived from former Bankruptcy Rule 903. The objective of "expeditious and economical administration" of cases under the Code has frequently been recognized by the courts to be "a chief purpose of the bankruptcy laws." See Katchen v. Landy, 382 U.S. 323, 328 (1966); Bailey v. Glover, 88 U.S. (21 Wall.) 342, 346–47 (1874); Ex parte Christy, 44 U.S. (3 How.) 292, 312–14, 320–22 (1845). The rule also incorporates the wholesome mandate of the last sentence of Rule 1 of the Federal Rules of Civil Procedure. 2 Moore, Federal Practice ¶1.13 (2d ed. 1980); 4 Wright & Miller, Federal Practice and Procedure—Civil § 1029 (1969).

1987 Amendments

Title I of the Bankruptcy Amendments and Federal Judgeship Act of 1984, Pub.L. No. 98–353, 98 Stat. 333 (hereinafter the 1984 amendments), created a new bankruptcy judicial system in which the role of the district court was substantially increased. 28 U.S.C. § 1334 confers on the United States district courts original and exclusive jurisdiction over all cases under title 11 of the United States Code and original but not exclusive jurisdiction over civil proceedings arising under title 11 and civil proceedings arising in or related to a case under title 11.

Pursuant to 28 U.S.C. § 157(a) the district court may but need not refer cases and proceedings within the district court's jurisdiction to the bankruptcy judges for the district. Judgments or orders of the bankruptcy judges entered pursuant to 28 U.S.C. § 157(b)(1) and (c)(2) are subject to appellate review by the district courts or bankruptcy appellate panels under 28 U.S.C. § 158(a).

Rule 81(a)(1) F.R.Civ.P. provides that the civil rules do not apply to proceedings in bankruptcy, except as they may be made applicable by rules promulgated by the Supreme Court, *e.g.,* Part VII of these rules. This amended Bankruptcy Rule 1001 makes the Bankruptcy Rules applicable to cases and proceedings under title 11, whether before the district judges or the bankruptcy judges of the district.

1991 Amendments

The citation to these rules is amended to conform to the citation form of the Federal Rules of Civil Procedure, Federal Rules of Appellate Procedure, and Federal Rules of Criminal Procedure.

2017 Amendments

The last sentence of the rule is amended to incorporate the changes to Rule 1 F.R.Civ.P. made in 1993 and 2015.

The word "administered" is added to recognize the affirmative duty of the court to exercise the authority conferred by these rules to ensure that bankruptcy cases and the proceedings within them are resolved not only fairly, but also without undue cost or delay. As officers of the court, attorneys share

this responsibility with the judge to whom the case is assigned.

The addition of the phrase "employed by the court and the parties" emphasizes that parties share in the duty of using the rules to secure the just, speedy, and inexpensive determination of every case and proceeding. Achievement of this goal depends upon cooperative and proportional use of procedure by lawyers and parties.

This amendment does not create a new or independent source of sanctions. Nor does it abridge the scope of any other of these rules.

CROSS REFERENCES

Promulgation of bankruptcy rules by Supreme Court, see 28 USCA § 2075.

Scope of rules, see Federal Rules of Appellate Procedure Rule 1, 28 USCA.

Applicability of rules, see Fed.Rules Civ.Proc. Rule 81, 28 USCA.

Scope of rules, see Fed.Rules Civ.Proc. Rule 1, 28 USCA.

Applicability of rules, see Fed.Rules Evid. Rule 1101, 28 USCA.

Scope of rules, see Fed.Rules Evid. Rule 101, 28 USCA.

PART I—COMMENCEMENT OF CASE; PROCEEDINGS RELATING TO PETITION AND ORDER FOR RELIEF

Rule 1002. Commencement of Case

(a) Petition

A petition commencing a case under the Code shall be filed with the clerk.

(b) Transmission to United States trustee

The clerk shall forthwith transmit to the United States trustee a copy of the petition filed pursuant to subdivision (a) of this rule.

(As amended Mar. 30, 1987, eff. Aug. 1, 1987; Apr. 30, 1991, eff. Aug. 1, 1991.)

ADVISORY COMMITTEE NOTES

Under §§ 301–303 of the Code, a voluntary or involuntary case is commenced by filing a petition with the bankruptcy court. The voluntary petition may request relief under chapter 7, 9, 11, or 13 whereas an involuntary petition may be filed under only chapter 7 or 11. Section 109 of the Code specifies the types of debtors for whom the different forms of relief are available and § 303(a) indicates the persons against whom involuntary petitions may be filed.

The rule in subdivision (a) is in harmony with the Code in that it requires the filing to be with the bankruptcy court.

The number of copies of the petition to be filed is specified in this rule but a local rule may require additional copies. This rule provides for filing sufficient copies for the court's files and for the trustee in a chapter 7 or 13 case.

Official Form No. 1 may be used to seek relief voluntarily under any of the chapters. Only the original need be signed and verified, but the copies must be conformed to the original. See Rules 1008 and 9011(c). As provided in § 362(a) of the Code, the filing of a petition acts as a stay of certain acts and proceedings against the debtor, property of the debtor, and property of the estate.

1987 Amendments

Rules 1002(a), governing a voluntary petition, 1003(a), governing an involuntary petition, and 1003(e), governing a petition in a case ancillary to a foreign proceedings, are combined into this Rule 1002. If a bankruptcy clerk has been appointed for the district, the petition is filed with the bankruptcy clerk. Otherwise, the petition is filed with the clerk of the district court.

The elimination of the reference to the Official Forms of the petition is not intended to change the practice. Rule 9009 provides that the Official Forms "shall be observed and used" in cases and proceedings under the Code.

Subdivision (b) which provided for the distribution of copies of the petition to agencies of the United States has been deleted. Some of these agencies no longer wish to receive copies of the petition, while others not included in subdivision (b) have now requested copies. The Director of the Administrative Office will determine on an ongoing basis which government agencies will be provided a copy of the petition.

The number of copies of a petition that must be filed is a matter for local rule.

1991 Amendments

Subdivision (b) is derived from Rule X–1002(a). The duties of the United States trustee pursuant to the Code and 28 U.S.C. § 586(a) require that the United States trustee be apprised of the commencement of every case under chapters 7, 11, 12 and 13 and this is most easily accomplished by providing that office with a copy of the petition. Although 28 U.S.C. § 586(a) does not give the United States trustee an administrative role in chapter 9 cases, § 1102 of the Code requires the United States trustee to appoint committees and that section is applicable in chapter 9 cases pursuant to § 901(a). It is therefore appropriate that the United States trustee receive a copy of every chapter 9 petition.

Notwithstanding subdivision (b), pursuant to Rule 5005(b)(3), the clerk is not required to transmit a copy of the petition to the United States trustee if the United States trustee requests that it not be transmitted. Many rules require the clerk to transmit a certain document to the United States trustee, but Rule 5005(b)(3) relieves the clerk of that duty under this or any other rule if the United States trustee requests that such document not be transmitted.

CROSS REFERENCES

Commencement of voluntary cases, see 11 USCA § 301.

Debtors for whom relief available, see 11 USCA § 109.

Joint cases, see 11 USCA § 302.

Number of copies,
  Involuntary petition, see Fed.Rules Bankr.Proc. Rule 1003, 11 USCA.
  Schedules, statements, and lists, see Fed.Rules Bankr. Proc. Rule 1007, 11 USCA.

Signing and verification of petitions, see Fed.Rules Bankr. Proc. Rule 1008 and Rule 9011, 11 USCA.

Stay of acts and proceedings against debtor and estate property, see 11 USCA § 362.

Rule 1003. Involuntary Petition

(a) Transferor or transferee of claim

A transferor or transferee of a claim shall annex to the original and each copy of the petition a copy of all documents evidencing the transfer, whether transferred unconditionally, for security, or otherwise, and a signed statement that the claim was not transferred for the purpose of commencing the case and setting forth the consideration for and terms of the transfer. An entity that has transferred or acquired a claim for the purpose of commencing a case for liquidation under chapter 7 or for reorganization under chapter 11 shall not be a qualified petitioner.

(b) Joinder of petitioners after filing

If the answer to an involuntary petition filed by fewer than three creditors avers the existence of 12 or more creditors, the debtor shall file with the answer a list of all creditors with their addresses, a brief statement of the nature of their claims, and the amounts thereof. If it appears that there are 12 or more creditors as provided in § 303(b) of the Code, the court shall afford a reasonable opportunity for other creditors to join in the petition before a hearing is held thereon.

(As amended Mar. 30, 1987, eff. Aug. 1, 1987.)

ADVISORY COMMITTEE NOTES

Subdivision (a). Official Form No. 11 (Involuntary Case: Creditors' Petition), is prescribed for use by petitioning creditors to have a debtor's assets liquidated under chapter 7 of the Code or the business reorganized under chapter 11. It contains the required allegations as specified in § 303(b) of the Code. Official Form 12 is prescribed for use by fewer than all the general partners to obtain relief for the partnership as governed by § 303(b)(3) of the Code and Rule 1004(b).

Although the number of copies to be filed is specified in Rule 1002, a local rule may require additional copies.

Only the original need be signed and verified, but the copies must be conformed to the original. See Rules 1008 and 9011(c). The petition must be filed with the bankruptcy court. This provision implements § 303(b) which provides that an involuntary case is commenced by filing the petition with the court.

As provided in § 362 of the Code, the filing of the petition acts as a stay of certain acts and proceedings against the debtor, the debtor's property and property of the estate.

Subdivision (c) retains the explicitness of former Bankruptcy Rule 104(d) that a transfer of a claim for the purpose of commencing a case under the Code is a ground for disqualification of a party to the transfer as a petitioner.

Section 303(b) "is not intended to overrule Bankruptcy Rule 104(d), which places certain restrictions on the transfer of claims for the purpose of commencing an involuntary case."

House Report No. 95–595, 95th Cong., 1st Sess. (1977) 322; Senate Report No. 95–989, 95th Cong., 2d Sess. (1978) 33.

The subdivision requires disclosure of any transfer of the petitioner's claim as well as a transfer to the petitioner and applies to transfers for security as well as unconditional transfers. Cf. In re 69th & Crandon Bldg. Corp., 97 F.2d 392, 395 (7th Cir.), cert. denied, 305 U.S. 629 (1938), recognizing the right of a creditor to sign a bankruptcy petition notwithstanding a prior assignment of his claim for the purpose of security. This rule does not, however, qualify the requirement of § 303(b)(1) that a petitioning creditor must have a claim not contingent as to liability.

Subdivision (d). Section 303(c) of the Code permits a creditor to join in the petition at any time before the case is dismissed or relief is ordered. While this rule does not require the court to give all creditors notice of the petition, the list of creditors filed by the debtor affords a petitioner the information needed to enable him to give notice for the purpose of obtaining the co-petitioners required to make the petition sufficient. After a reasonable opportunity has been afforded other creditors to join in an involuntary petition, the hearing on the petition should be held without further delay.

Subdivision (e). This subdivision implements § 304. A petition for relief under § 304 may only be filed by a foreign representative who is defined in § 101(20) generally as a representative of an estate in a foreign proceeding. The term "foreign proceeding" is defined in § 101(19).

Section 304(b) permits a petition filed thereunder to be contested by a party in interest. Subdivision (e)(2) therefore requires that the summons and petition be served on any person against whom the relief permitted by § 304(b) is sought as well as on any other party the court may direct.

The rules applicable to the procedure when an involuntary petition is filed are made applicable generally when a case ancillary to a foreign proceeding is commenced. These rules include Rule 1010 with respect to issuance and service of a summons, Rule 1011 concerning responsive pleadings and motions, and Rule 1018 which makes various rules in Part VII applicable in proceedings on contested petitions.

The venue for a case ancillary to a foreign proceeding is provided in 28 U.S.C. § 1474.

1987 Amendments

The subject matter of subdivisions (a), (b), and (e) has been incorporated in Rules 1002, 1010, 1011, and 1018.

CROSS REFERENCES

Case ancillary to foreign proceeding,

Commencement of and contested petitions, see 11 USCA § 1501 et seq. and 28 USCA § 1410.

"Foreign proceeding" and "foreign representative" defined, see 11 USCA § 101.

Debtors for whom relief available, see 11 USCA § 109.

Number of copies, voluntary petition, see Fed.Rules Bankr. Proc. Rule 1002, 11 USCA.

Requisite allegations and joinder of parties, see 11 USCA § 303.

Signing and verification of petitions, see Fed.Rules Bankr. Proc. Rule 1008 and Rule 9011, 11 USCA.

Stay of acts and proceedings against debtor and estate property, see 11 USCA § 362.

Rule 1004. Involuntary Petition Against a Partnership

After filing of an involuntary petition under § 303(b)(3) of the Code, (1) the petitioning partners or other petitioners shall promptly send to or serve on each general partner who is not a petitioner a copy of the petition; and (2) the clerk shall promptly issue a summons for service on each general partner who is not a petitioner. Rule 1010 applies to the form and service of the summons.

(As amended Apr. 29, 2002, eff. Dec. 1, 2002.)

ADVISORY COMMITTEE NOTES

This rule is adapted from former Bankruptcy Rule 105 and complements §§ 301 and 303(b)(3) of the Code.

Subdivision (a) specifies that while all general partners must consent to the filing of a voluntary petition, it is not necessary that they all execute the petition. It may be executed and filed on behalf of the partnership by fewer than all.

Subdivision (b) implements § 303(b)(3) of the Code which provides that an involuntary petition may be filed by fewer than all the general partners or, when all the general partners are debtors, by a general partner, trustee of the partner or creditors of the partnership. Rule 1010, which governs service of a petition and summons in an involuntary case, specifies the time and mode of service on the partnership. When a petition is filed against a partnership under § 303(b)(3), this rule requires an additional service on the nonfiling general partners. It is the purpose of this subdivision to protect the interests of the nonpetitioning partners and the partnership.

2002 Amendments

Section 303(b)(3)(A) of the Code provides that fewer than all of the general partners in a partnership may commence an involuntary case against the partnership. There is no counterpart provision in the Code setting out the manner in which a partnership commences a voluntary case. The Supreme Court has held in the corporate context that applicable nonbankruptcy law determines whether authority exists for a particular debtor to commence a bankruptcy case. See Price v. Gurney, 324 U.S. 100 (1945). The lower courts have followed this rule in the partnership context as well. See, e.g., Jolly v. Pittore, 170 B.R. 793 (S.D.N.Y. 1994); Union Planters National Bank v. Hunters Horn Associates, 158 B.R. 729 (Bankr. M.D. Tenn. 1993); In re Channel 64 Joint Venture, 61 B.R. 255 (Bankr. S.D. Oh. 1986). Rule 1004(a) could be construed as requiring the consent of all of the general partners to the filing of a voluntary petition, even if fewer than all of the general partners would have the authority under applicable nonbankruptcy law to commence a bankruptcy case for the partnership. Since this is a matter of substantive law beyond the scope of these rules, Rule 1004(a) is deleted as the designation of subdivision (b).

The rule is retitled to reflect that it applies only to involuntary petitions filed against partnerships.

Changes Made After Publication and Comments. No changes since publication.

CROSS REFERENCES

Commencement of,

    Involuntary cases, see 11 USCA § 303.

    Voluntary cases, see 11 USCA § 301.

Contested petition by general partners, see Fed.Rules Bankr.Proc. Rule 1011, 11 USCA.

No change in status for purposes of State or local income tax law, see 11 USCA § 346.

"Person" defined to include partnership, see 11 USCA § 101.

Rule 1004.1.   Petition for an Infant or Incompetent Person

If an infant or incompetent person has a representative, including a general guardian, committee, conservator, or similar fiduciary, the representative may file a voluntary petition on behalf of the infant or incompetent person. An infant or incompetent person who does not have a duly appointed representative may file a voluntary petition by next friend or guardian ad litem. The court shall appoint a guardian ad litem for an infant or incompetent person who is a debtor and is not otherwise represented or shall make any other order to protect the infant or incompetent debtor.

(Added Apr. 29, 2002, eff. Dec. 1, 2002.)

ADVISORY COMMITTEE NOTES

2002 Adoption

This rule is derived from Rule 17(c) F.R. Civ. P. It does not address the commencement of a case filed on behalf of a missing person. *See, e.g., In re King*, 234 B.R. 515 (Bankr. D.N.M. 1999).

Changes Made After Publication and Comments. No changes were made.

Rule 1004.2.   Petition in Chapter 15 Cases

(a) Designating center of main interests

A petition for recognition of a foreign proceeding under chapter 15 of the Code shall state the country where the debtor has its center of main interests. The petition shall also identify each country in which a foreign proceeding by, regarding, or against the debtor is pending.

(b) Challenging designation

The United States trustee or a party in interest may file a motion for a determination that the debtor's center of main interests is other than as stated in the petition for recognition commencing the chapter 15 case. Unless the court orders otherwise, the motion shall be filed no later than seven days before the date set for the hearing on the petition. The motion shall be transmitted to the United States trustee and served on the debtor, all persons or bodies authorized to administer foreign proceedings of the debtor, all entities against whom provisional relief is being sought under § 1519 of the Code, all parties to litigation pending in the United States in which the debtor was a party as of the time the petition was filed, and such other entities as the court may direct.

(Added Apr. 26, 2011, eff. Dec. 1, 2011.)

ADVISORY COMMITTEE NOTES

2011 Adoption

This rule is new. Subdivision (a) directs any entity that files a petition for recognition of a foreign proceeding under chapter 15 of the Code to state in the petition the center of the debtor's main interests. The petition must also list each country in which a foreign proceeding involving the debtor is pending. This information will assist the court and parties in interest in determining whether the foreign proceeding is a foreign main or nonmain proceeding.

Subdivision (b) sets a deadline of seven days before the date set for the hearing on the petition for recognition for filing a motion challenging the statement in the petition as to the country in which the debtor's center of main interests is located.

Rule 1005.   Caption of Petition

The caption of a petition commencing a case under the Code shall contain the name of the court, the title of the case, and the docket number. The title of the case shall include the following information about the debtor: name, employer identification number, last four digits of the social-security number or individual debtor's taxpayer-identification number, any other federal taxpayer-identification number, and all other names used within eight years before filing the petition. If the petition is not filed by the debtor, it shall include all names used by the debtor which are known to the petitioners.

(As amended Mar. 30, 1987, eff. Aug. 1, 1987; Mar. 27, 2003, eff. Dec. 1, 2003; Apr. 23, 2008, eff. Dec. 1, 2008.)

ADVISORY COMMITTEE NOTES

The title of the case should include all names used by the debtor, such as trade names, former married names and maiden name. See also Official Form No. 1 and the Advisory Committee Note to that Form. Additional names of the debtor are also required to appear in the caption of each notice to creditors. See Rule 2002(m).

2003 Amendments

The rule is amended to implement the Judicial Conference policy to limit the disclosure of a party's social security number and similar identifiers. Under the rule, as amended, only the last four digits of the debtor's social security number need be disclosed. Publication of the employer identification number does not present the same identity theft or privacy protection issues. Therefore, the caption must include the full employer identification number.

Debtors must submit with the petition a statement setting out their social security numbers. This enables the clerk to include the full social security number on the notice of the section 341 meeting of creditors, but the statement itself is not submitted in the case or maintained in the case file.

2008 Amendments

The rule is amended to require the disclosure of all names used by the debtor in the past eight years. Section 727(a)(8) was amended in 2005 to extend the time between chapter 7 discharges from six to eight years, and the rule is amended to implement that change. The rule also is amended to require the disclosure of the last four digits of an individual debtor's taxpayer-identification number. This truncation of the number applies only to individual debtors. This is consistent with the requirements of Rule 9037.

CROSS REFERENCES

Conformance of captions of creditor notices with this rule, see Fed.Rules Bankr.Proc. Rule 2002, 11 USCA.

General requirements of form for petition, see Fed.Rules Bankr.Proc. Rule 9004, 11 USCA.

Rule 1006.   Filing Fee

(a) General requirement

Every petition shall be accompanied by the filing fee except as provided in subdivisions (b) and (c) of this rule. For the purpose of this rule, "filing fee" means the filing fee prescribed by 28 U.S.C. § 1930(a)(1)–(a)(5) and any other fee prescribed by the Judicial Conference of the United States under 28 U.S.C. § 1930(b) that is payable to the clerk upon the commencement of a case under the Code.

(b) Payment of filing fee in installments

(1) Application to pay filing fee in installments

A voluntary petition by an individual shall be accepted for filing, regardless of whether any portion of the filing fee is paid, if accompanied by the debtor's signed application, prepared as prescribed by the appropriate Official Form, stating that the debtor is unable to pay the filing fee except in installments.

(2) Action on application

Prior to the meeting of creditors, the court may order the filing fee paid to the clerk or grant leave to pay in installments and fix the number, amount and dates of payment. The number of installments shall not exceed four, and the final installment shall be payable not later than 120 days after filing the petition. For cause shown, the court may extend the time of any installment, provided the last installment is paid not later than 180 days after filing the petition.

(3) Postponement of attorney's fees

All installments of the filing fee must be paid in full before the debtor or chapter 13 trustee may make further payments to an attorney or any other person who renders services to the debtor in connection with the case.

(c) Waiver of filing fee

A voluntary chapter 7 petition filed by an individual shall be accepted for filing if accompanied by the debtor's application requesting a waiver under 28 U.S.C. § 1930(f), prepared as prescribed by the appropriate Official Form.

(As amended Mar. 30, 1987, eff. Aug. 1, 1987; Apr. 23, 1996, eff. Dec. 1, 1996; Apr. 23, 2008, eff. Dec. 1, 2008; Apr. 27, 2017, eff. Dec. 1, 2017.)

ADVISORY COMMITTEE NOTES

1983 Enactments

28 U.S.C. § 1930 specifies the filing fees for petitions under chapters 7, 9, 11 and 13 of the Code. It also permits the payment in installments by individual debtors.

Subdivision (b) is adapted from former Bankruptcy Rule 107. The administrative cost of installments in excess of four is disproportionate to the benefits conferred. Prolonging the period beyond 180 days after the commencement of the case causes undesirable delays in administration. Paragraph (2) accordingly continues the imposition of a maximum of four on the number of installments and retains the maximum period of installment payments allowable on an original application at 120 days. Only in extraordinary cases should it be necessary to give an applicant an extension beyond the four months. The requirement of paragraph (3) that filing fees be paid in full before the debtor may pay an attorney for services in connection with the case codifies the rule declared in In re Latham, 271 Fed. 538 (N.D.N.Y.1921), and In re Darr, 232 Fed. 415 (N.D.Cal.1916).

1987 Amendments

Subdivision (b)(3) is expanded to prohibit payments by the debtor or the chapter 13 trustee not only to attorneys but to any person who renders services to the debtor in connection with the case.

1996 Amendments

The Judicial Conference prescribes miscellaneous fees pursuant to 28 U.S.C. § 1930(b). In 1992, a $30 miscellaneous administrative fee was prescribed for all chapter 7 and chapter 13 cases. The Judicial Conference fee schedule was amended in 1993 to provide that an individual debtor may pay this fee in installments.

Subdivision (a) of this rule is amended to clarify that every petition must be accompanied by any fee prescribed under 28 U.S.C. § 1930(b) that is required to be paid when a petition is filed, as well as the filing fee prescribed by 28 U.S.C. § 1930(a). By defining "filing fee" to include Judicial Conference fees, the procedures set forth in subdivision (b) for paying the filing fee in installments will also apply with respect to any Judicial Conference fee required to be paid at the commencement of the case.

GAP Report on Rule 1006. No changes since publication, except for a stylistic change in subdivision (a).

2008 Amendments

Subdivision (a) is amended to include a reference to new subdivision (c), which deals with fee waivers under 28 U.S.C. § 1930(f), which was added in 2005.

Subdivision (b)(1) is amended to delete the sentence requiring a disclosure that the debtor has not paid an attorney or other person in connection with the case. Inability to pay the filing fee in installments is one of the requirements for a fee waiver under the 2005 revisions to 28 U.S.C. § 1930(f). If the attorney payment prohibition were retained, payment of an attorney's fee would render many debtors ineligible for installment payments and thus enhance their eligibility for the fee waiver. The deletion of this prohibition from the rule, which was not statutorily required, ensures that debtors who have the financial ability to pay the fee in installments will do so rather than request a waiver.

Subdivision (b)(3) is amended in conformance with the changes to subdivision (b)(1) to reflect the 2005 amendments. The change is meant to clarify that subdivision (b)(3) refers to payments made after the debtor has filed the bankruptcy case and after the debtor has received permission to pay the fee in installments. Otherwise, the subdivision may conflict with the intent and effect of the amendments to subdivision (b)(1).

2017 Amendments

Subdivision (b)(1) is amended to clarify that an individual debtor's voluntary petition, accompanied by an application to pay the filing fee in installments, must be accepted for filing, even if the court requires the initial installment to be paid at the time the petition is filed and the debtor fails to make that payment. Because the debtor's bankruptcy case is commenced upon the filing of the petition, dismissal of the case due to the debtor's failure to make the initial or a subsequent installment payment is governed by Rule 1017(b)(1).

CROSS REFERENCES

District court, filing and miscellaneous fees, rules of court, see 28 USCA § 1914.

Enlargement of time for payment of filing fee installments permitted as limited under this rule, see Fed.Rules Bankr. Proc. Rule 9006, 11 USCA.

Specific amount of fee, see 28 USCA § 1930.

Rule 1007. Lists, Schedules, Statements, and Other Documents; Time Limits

(a) Corporate ownership statement, list of creditors and equity security holders, and other lists

(1) Voluntary case

In a voluntary case, the debtor shall file with the petition a list containing the name and address of each entity included or to be included on Schedules D, E/F, G, and H as prescribed by the Official Forms. If the debtor is a corporation, other than a governmental unit, the debtor shall file with the petition a corporate ownership statement containing the information described in Rule 7007.1. The debtor shall file a supplemental statement promptly upon any change in circumstances that renders the corporate ownership statement inaccurate.

(2) Involuntary case

In an involuntary case, the debtor shall file, within seven days after entry of the order for relief, a list containing the name and address of each entity included or to be included on Schedules D, E/F, G, and H as prescribed by the Official Forms.

(3) Equity security holders

In a chapter 11 reorganization case, unless the court orders otherwise, the debtor shall file within 14 days after entry of the order for relief a list of the debtor's equity security holders of each class showing the number and kind of interests registered in the name of each holder, and the last known address or place of business of each holder.

(4) Chapter 15 case

In addition to the documents required under § 1515 of the Code, a foreign representative filing a petition for recognition under chapter 15 shall file with the petition: (A) a corporate ownership statement containing the information described in Rule 7007.1; and (B) unless the court orders otherwise, a list containing the names and addresses of all persons or bodies authorized to administer foreign proceedings of the debtor, all parties to litigation pending in the United States in which the debtor is a party at the time of the filing of the petition, and all entities against whom provisional relief is being sought under § 1519 of the Code.

(5) Extension of time

Any extension of time for the filing of the lists required by this subdivision may be granted only on motion for cause shown and on notice to the United States trustee and to any trustee, committee elected under § 705 or appointed under § 1102 of the Code, or other party as the court may direct.

(b) Schedules, statements, and other documents required

(1) Except in a chapter 9 municipality case, the debtor, unless the court orders otherwise, shall file the following schedules, statements, and other documents, prepared as prescribed by the appropriate Official Forms, if any:

(A) schedules of assets and liabilities;

(B) a schedule of current income and expenditures;

(C) a schedule of executory contracts and unexpired leases;

(D) a statement of financial affairs;

(E) copies of all payment advices or other evidence of payment, if any, received by the debtor from an employer within 60 days before the filing of the petition, with redaction of all but the last four digits of the debtor's social-security number or individual taxpayer-identification number; and

(F) a record of any interest that the debtor has in an account or program of the type specified in § 521(c) of the Code.

(2) An individual debtor in a chapter 7 case shall file a statement of intention as required by § 521(a) of the Code, prepared as prescribed by the appropriate Official Form. A copy of the statement of intention shall be served on the trustee and the creditors named in the statement on or before the filing of the statement.

(3) Unless the United States trustee has determined that the credit counseling requirement of § 109(h) does not apply in the district, an individual debtor must file a statement of compliance with the credit counseling requirement, prepared as prescribed by the appropriate Official Form which must include one of the following:

    (A) an attached certificate and debt repayment plan, if any, required by § 521(b);

    (B) a statement that the debtor has received the credit counseling briefing required by § 109(h)(1) but does not have the certificate required by § 521(b);

    (C) a certification under § 109(h)(3); or

    (D) a request for a determination by the court under § 109(h)(4).

(4) Unless § 707(b)(2)(D) applies, an individual debtor in a chapter 7 case shall file a statement of current monthly income prepared as prescribed by the appropriate Official Form, and, if the current monthly income exceeds the median family income for the applicable state and household size, the information, including calculations, required by § 707(b), prepared as prescribed by the appropriate Official Form.

(5) An individual debtor in a chapter 11 case shall file a statement of current monthly income, prepared as prescribed by the appropriate Official Form.

(6) A debtor in a chapter 13 case shall file a statement of current monthly income, prepared as prescribed by the appropriate Official Form, and, if the current monthly income exceeds the median family income for the applicable state and household size, a calculation of disposable income made in accordance with § 1325(b)(3), prepared as prescribed by the appropriate Official Form.

(7) Unless an approved provider of an instructional course concerning personal financial management has notified the court that a debtor has completed the course after filing the petition:

    (A) An individual debtor in a chapter 7 or chapter 13 case shall file a statement of completion of the course, prepared as prescribed by the appropriate Official Form; and

    (B) An individual debtor in a chapter 11 case shall file the statement if § 1141(d)(3) applies.

(8) If an individual debtor in a chapter 11, 12, or 13 case has claimed an exemption under § 522(b)(3)(A) in property of the kind described in § 522(p)(1) with a value in excess of the amount set out in § 522(q)(1), the debtor shall file a statement as to whether there is any proceeding pending in which the debtor may be found guilty of a felony of a kind described in § 522(q)(1)(A) or found liable for a debt of the kind described in § 522(q)(1)(B).

(c) Time limits

In a voluntary case, the schedules, statements, and other documents required by subdivision (b)(1), (4), (5), and (6) shall be filed with the petition or within 14 days thereafter, except as otherwise provided in subdivisions (d), (e), (f), and (h) of this rule. In an involuntary case, the schedules, statements, and other documents required by subdivision (b)(1) shall be filed by the debtor within 14 days after the entry of the order for relief. In a voluntary case, the documents required by paragraphs (A), (C), and (D) of subdivision (b)(3) shall be filed with the petition. Unless the court orders otherwise, a debtor who has filed a statement under subdivision (b)(3)(B), shall file the documents required by subdivision (b)(3)(A) within 14 days of the order for relief. In a chapter 7 case, the debtor shall file the statement required by subdivision (b)(7) within 60 days after the first date set for the meeting of creditors under § 341 of the Code, and in a chapter 11 or 13 case no later than the date when the last payment was made by the debtor as required by the plan or the filing of a motion for a discharge under § 1141(d)(5)(B) or § 1328(b) of the Code. The court may, at any time and in its discretion, enlarge the time to file the statement required by subdivision (b)(7). The debtor shall file the statement required by subdivision (b)(8) no earlier than the date of the last payment made under the plan or the date of the filing of a motion for a discharge under §§[1] 1141(d)(5)(B), 1228(b), or 1328(b) of the Code. Lists, schedules, statements, and other documents filed prior to the conversion of a case to another chapter shall be deemed filed in the converted case unless the court directs otherwise. Except as provided in § 1116(3), any extension of time to file schedules, statements, and other documents required under this rule may be granted only on motion for cause shown and on notice to the United States trustee, any committee elected under § 705 or appointed under § 1102 of the Code, trustee, examiner, or other party as the court may direct. Notice of an extension shall be given to the United States trustee and to any committee, trustee, or other party as the court may direct.

(d) List of 20 largest creditors in chapter 9 municipality case or chapter 11 reorganization case

In addition to the list required by subdivision (a) of this rule, a debtor in a chapter 9 municipality case or a debtor in a voluntary chapter 11 reorganization case shall file with the petition a list containing the name, address and claim of the creditors that hold the 20 largest unsecured claims, excluding insiders, as prescribed by the appropriate Official Form. In an involuntary chapter 11 reorganization case, such list shall be filed by the debtor within 2 days after entry of the order for relief under § 303(h) of the Code.

(e) List in chapter 9 municipality cases

The list required by subdivision (a) of this rule shall be filed by the debtor in a chapter 9 municipality case within such time as the court shall fix. If a proposed plan requires a revision of assessments so that the proportion of special assessments or special taxes to be assessed against some real property will be different from the proportion in effect at the date the petition is filed, the debtor shall also file a list showing the name and address of each known holder of title, legal or equitable, to real property adversely affected. On motion for cause shown, the court may modify the requirements of this subdivision and subdivision (a) of this rule.

(f) Statement of social security number

An individual debtor shall submit a verified statement that sets out the debtor's social security number, or states that the debtor does not have a social security number. In a voluntary case, the debtor shall submit the statement with the petition. In an involuntary case, the debtor shall submit the statement within 14 days after the entry of the order for relief.

(g) Partnership and partners

The general partners of a debtor partnership shall prepare and file the list required under subdivision (a), schedules of the assets and liabilities, schedule of current income and expenditures, schedule of executory contracts and unexpired leases, and statement of financial affairs of the partnership. The court may order any general partner to file a statement of personal assets and liabilities within such time as the court may fix.

(h) Interests acquired or arising after petition

If, as provided by § 541(a)(5) of the Code, the debtor acquires or becomes entitled to acquire any interest in property, the debtor shall within 14 days after the information comes to the debtor's knowledge or within such further time the court may allow, file a supplemental schedule in the chapter 7 liquidation case, chapter 11 reorganization case, chapter 12 family farmer's debt adjustment case, or chapter 13 individual debt adjustment case. If any of the property required to be reported under this subdivision is claimed by the debtor as exempt, the debtor shall claim the exemptions in the supplemental schedule. The duty to file a supplemental schedule in accordance with this subdivision continues notwithstanding the closing of the case, except that the schedule need not be filed in a chapter 11, chapter 12, or chapter 13 case with respect to property acquired after entry of the order confirming a chapter 11 plan or discharging the debtor in a chapter 12 or chapter 13 case.

(i) Disclosure of list of security holders

After notice and hearing and for cause shown, the court may direct an entity other than the debtor or trustee to disclose any list of security holders of the debtor in its possession or under its control, indicating the name, address and security held by any of them. The entity possessing this list may be required either to produce the list or a true copy thereof, or permit inspection or copying, or otherwise disclose the information contained on the list.

(j) Impounding of lists

On motion of a party in interest and for cause shown the court may direct the impounding of the lists filed under this rule, and may refuse to permit inspection by any entity. The court may permit inspection or use of the lists, however, by any party in interest on terms prescribed by the court.

(k) Preparation of list, schedules, or statements on default of debtor

If a list, schedule, or statement, other than a statement of intention, is not prepared and filed as required by this rule, the court may order the trustee, a petitioning creditor, committee, or other party to prepare and file any of these papers within a time fixed by the court. The court may approve reimbursement of the cost incurred in complying with such an order as an administrative expense.

(*l*)[1] Transmission to United States trustee

The clerk shall forthwith transmit to the United States trustee a copy of every list, schedule, and statement filed pursuant to subdivision (a)(1), (a)(2), (b), (d), or (h) of this rule.

(m) Infants and incompetent persons

If the debtor knows that a person on the list of creditors or schedules is an infant or incompetent person, the debtor also shall include the name, address, and legal relationship of any person upon whom process would be served in an adversary proceeding against the infant or incompetent person in accordance with Rule 7004(b)(2).

(As amended Mar. 30, 1987, eff. Aug. 1, 1987; Apr. 30, 1991, eff. Aug. 1, 1991; Apr. 23, 1996, eff. Dec. 1, 1996; Apr. 23, 2001, eff. Dec. 1, 2001; Mar. 27, 2003, eff. Dec. 1, 2003; Apr. 25, 2005, eff. Dec. 1, 2005; Apr. 23, 2008, eff. Dec. 1, 2008; Mar. 26, 2009, eff. Dec. 1, 2009; Apr. 28, 2010, eff. Dec. 1, 2010; Apr. 23, 2012, eff. Dec. 1, 2012; Apr. 16, 2013, eff. Dec. 1, 2013; Apr. 29, 2015, eff. Dec. 1, 2015.)

1 So in original. Probably should be only one section symbol.

ADVISORY COMMITTEE NOTES

1983 Enactments

This rule is an adaptation of former Rules 108, 8–106, 10–108 and 11–11. As specified in the rule, it is applicable in all types of cases filed under the Code.

Subdivision (a) requires at least a list of creditors with their names and addresses to be filed with the petition. This list is needed for notice of the meeting of creditors (Rule 2002) and notice of the order for relief (§ 342 of the Code). The list will also serve to meet the requirements of § 521(1) of the Code. Subdivision (a) recognizes that it may be impossible to file the schedules required by § 521(1) and subdivision (b) of the rule at the time the petition is filed but in order for the case to proceed expeditiously and efficiently it is necessary that the clerk have the names and addresses of creditors. It should be noted that subdivision (d) of the rule requires a special list of the 20 largest unsecured creditors in chapter 9 and 11 cases. That list is for the purpose of selecting a committee of unsecured creditors.

Subdivision (b) is derived from former Rule 11–11 and conforms with § 521. This subdivision indicates the forms to be used. The court may dispense with the filing of schedules and the statement of affairs pursuant to § 521.

Subdivisions (c) and (f) specify the time periods for filing the papers required by the rule as well as the number of copies. The provisions dealing with an involuntary case are derived from former Bankruptcy Rule 108. Under the Code, a chapter 11 case may be commenced by an involuntary petition (§ 303(a)), whereas under the Act [former Title 11], a Chapter XI [former § 1101 et seq. of this title] case could have been commenced only by a voluntary petition. A motion for an extension of time to file the schedules and statements is required to be made on notice to parties, as the court may direct, including a creditors' committee if one has been appointed under § 1102 of the Code and a trustee or examiner if one has been appointed pursuant to § 1104 of the Code. Although written notice is preferable, it is not required by the rule; in proper circumstances the notice may be by telephone or otherwise.

Subdivision (d) is new and requires that a list of the 20 largest unsecured creditors, excluding insiders as defined in § 101(25) of the Code, be filed with the petition. The court, pursuant to § 1102 of the Code, is required to appoint a committee of unsecured creditors as soon as practicable after the order for relief. That committee generally is to consist of the seven largest unsecured creditors who are willing to serve. The list should, as indicated on Official Form No. 9, specify the nature and amount of the claim. It is important for the court to be aware of the different types of claims existing in the case and this form should supply such information.

Subdivision (e) applies only in chapter 9 municipality cases. It gives greater discretion to the court to determine the time for filing a list of creditors and any other matter related to the list. A list of creditors must at some point be filed since one is required by § 924 of the Code. When the plan affects special assessments, the definitions in § 902(2) and (3) for "special tax payer" and "special tax payer affected by the plan" become relevant.

Subdivision (g) is derived from former Rules 108(c) and 11–11. Nondebtor general partners are liable to the partnership's trustee for any deficiency in the partnership's estate to pay creditors in full as provided by § 723 of the Code. Subdivision (g) authorizes the court to require a partner to file a statement of personal assets and liabilities to provide the trustee with the relevant information.

Subdivision (h) is derived from former Bankruptcy Rule 108(e) for chapter 7, 11 and 13 purposes. It implements the provisions in and language of § 541(a)(5) of the Code.

Subdivisions (i) and (j) are adapted from §§ 165 and 166 of the Act [former §§ 565 and 566 of this title] and former Rule 10–108(b) and (c) without change in substance. The term "party in interest" is not defined in the Code or the rules, but reference may be made to § 1109(b) of the Code.

In the context of this subdivision, the term would include the debtor, the trustee, any indenture trustee, creditor, equity security holder or committee appointed pursuant to § 1102 of the Code.

Subdivision (k) is derived from former Rules 108(d) and 10–108(a).

1987 Amendments

Subdivisions (b), (c), and (g) are amended to provide for the filing of a schedule of current income and current expenditures and the individual debtor's statement of intention. These documents are required by the 1984 amendments to § 521 of the Code. Official Form No. 6A is prescribed for use by an individual debtor for filing a schedule of current income and current expenditures in a chapter 7 or chapter 11 case. Although a partnership or corporation is also required by § 521(1) to file a schedule of current income and current expenditures, no Official Form is prescribed therefor.

The time for filing the statement of intention is governed by § 521(2)(A). A copy of the statement of intention must be served on the trustee and the creditors named in the statement within the same time. The provisions of subdivision (c) governing the time for filing when a chapter 11 or chapter 13 case is converted to a chapter 7 case have been omitted from subdivision (c) as amended. Filing after conversion is now governed exclusively by Rule 1019.

Subdivision (f) has been abrogated. The number of copies of the documents required by this rule will be determined by local rule.

Subdivision (h) is amended to include a direct reference to § 541(a)(5).

Subdivision (k) provides that the court may not order an entity other than the debtor to prepare and file the statement of intention.

1991 Amendments

References to Official Form numbers and to the Chapter 13 Statement are deleted and subdivision (b) is amended in anticipation of future revision and renumbering of the Official Forms. The debtor in a chapter 12 or chapter 13 case shall file the list, schedules and statements required in subdivisions (a)(1), (b)(1), and (h). It is expected that the information currently provided in the Chapter 13 Statement will be included in the schedules and statements as revised not later than the effective date of these rule amendments.

Subdivisions (a)(4) and (c) are amended to provide the United States trustee with notice of any motion to extend the time for the filing of any lists, schedules, or statements. Such notice enables the United States trustee to take appropriate steps to avoid undue delay in the administration of the case. See 28 U.S.C. § 586(a)(3)(G). Subdivisions (a)(4) and (c) are amended further to provide notice to committees elected under § 705 or appointed pursuant to § 1102 of the Code. Committees of retired employees appointed pursuant to § 1114 are not included.

The additions of references to unexpired leases in subdivisions (b)(1) and (g) indicate that the schedule requires the inclusion of unexpired leases as well as other executory contracts.

The words "with the court" in subdivisions (b)(1), (e), and (g) are deleted as unnecessary. See Rules 5005(a) and 9001(3).

Subdivision (*l*), which is derived from Rule X–1002(a), provides the United States trustee with the information required to perform certain administrative duties such as the appointment of a committee of unsecured creditors. In a chapter 7 case, the United States trustee should be aware of the debtor's intention with respect to collateral that secures a consumer debt so that the United States trustee may monitor the progress of the case. Pursuant to § 307 of the Code, the United States trustee has standing to raise, appear and be heard on issues and the lists, schedules and statements contain information that, when provided to the United States trustee, enable that office to participate effectively in the case. The United States trustee has standing to move to dismiss a chapter 7 or 13 case for failure to file timely the list, schedules or statement required by § 521(*l*) of the Code. See §§ 707(a)(3) and 1307(c)(9). It is therefore necessary for the United States trustee to receive notice of any extension of time to file such documents. Upon request, the United States trustee also may receive from the trustee or debtor in possession a list of equity security holders.

1996 Amendments

Subdivision (c) is amended to provide that schedules and statements filed prior to the conversion of a case to another chapter shall be deemed filed in the converted case, whether or not the case was a chapter 7 case prior to conversion. This amendment is in recognition of the 1991 amendments to the Official Forms that abrogated the Chapter 13 Statement and made the same forms for schedules and statements applicable in all cases.

This subdivision also contains a technical correction. The phrase "superseded case" creates the erroneous impression that conversion of a case results in a new case that is distinct from the original case. The effect of conversion of a case is governed by § 348 of the Code.

GAP Report on Rule 1007(c). No changes since publication, except for stylistic changes.

2001 Amendments

Subdivision (m) is added to enable the person required to mail notices under Rule 2002 to mail them to the appropriate guardian or other representative when the debtor knows that a creditor or other person listed is an infant or incompetent person.

The proper mailing address of the representative is determined in accordance with Rule 7004(b)(2), which requires mailing to the person's dwelling house or usual place of abode or at the place where the person regularly conducts a business or profession.

Changes Made After Publication and Comments. No changes were made.

2003 Amendments

This rule is amended to require the debtor to file a corporate ownership statement setting out the information described in Rule 7007.1. Requiring debtors to file the statement provides the court with an opportunity to make judicial disqualification determinations at the outset of the case. This could reduce problems later in the case by preventing the initial assignment of the case to a judge who holds a financial interest in a parent company of the debtor or some other entity that holds a significant ownership interest in the debtor. Moreover, by including the disclosure statement filing requirement at the commencement of the case, the debtor does not have to make the same disclosure filing each time it is involved in an adversary proceeding throughout the case. The debtor also must file supplemental statements as changes in ownership might arise.

The rule is amended to add a requirement that a debtor submit a statement setting out the debtor's social security number. The addition is necessary because of the corresponding amendment to Rule 1005 which now provides that the caption of the petition includes only the final four digits of the debtor's social security number. The debtor submits the statement, but it is not filed, nor is it included in the case file. The statement provides the information necessary to include on the service copy of the notice required under Rule 2002(a)(1). It will also provide the information to facilitate the ability of creditors to search the court record by a search of a social security number already in the creditor's possession.

2005 Amendments

Notice to creditors and other parties in interest is essential to the operation of the bankruptcy system. Sending notice requires a convenient listing of the names and addresses of the entities to whom notice must be sent, and virtually all of the bankruptcy courts have adopted a local rule requiring the submission of a list of these entities with the petition and in a particular format. These lists are commonly called the "mailing matrix."

Given the universal adoption of these local rules, the need for such lists in all cases is apparent. Consequently, the rule is amended to require the debtor to submit such a list at the commencement of the case. This list may be amended when necessary. See Rule 1009(a).

The content of the list is described by reference to Schedules D through H of the Official Forms rather than by reference to creditors or persons holding claims. The cross reference to the Schedules as the source of the names for inclusion in the list ensures that persons such as codebtors or nondebtor parties to executory contracts and unexpired leases will receive appropriate notices in the case.

While this rule renders unnecessary, in part, local rules on the subject, this rule does not direct any particular format or form for the list to take. Local rules still may govern those particulars of the list.

Subdivision (c) is amended to reflect that subdivision (a)(1) no longer requires the debtor to file a schedule of liabilities with the petition in lieu of a list of creditors. The filing of the list is mandatory, and subdivision (b) of the rule requires the filing of schedules. Thus, subdivision (c) no longer needs to account for the possibility that the debtor can delay filing a schedule of liabilities when the petition is accompanied by a list of creditors. Subdivision (c) simply addresses the situation in which the debtor does not file schedules or statements with the petition, and the procedure for seeking an extension of time for filing.

Other changes are stylistic.

2008 Amendments

The title of this rule is expanded to refer to "documents" in conformity with the 2005 amendments to § 521 and related provisions of the Bankruptcy Code that include a wider range of documentary requirements.

Subdivision (a) is amended to require that any foreign representative filing a petition for recognition to commence a case under chapter 15, which was added to the Code in 2005, file a list of entities with whom the debtor is engaged in litigation in the United States. The foreign representative filing the petition for recognition must also list any entities against whom provisional relief is being sought as well as all persons or bodies authorized to administer foreign proceedings of the debtor. This should ensure that entities most interested in the case, or their representatives, will receive notice of the petition under Rule 2002(q).

Subdivision (a)(4) is amended to require the foreign representative who files a petition for recognition under chapter 15 to file the documents described in § 1515 of the Code as well as a corporate ownership statement. The subdivision is also amended to identify the foreign representative in language that more closely follows the text of the Code. Former subdivision (a)(4) is renumbered as subdivision (a)(5) and stylistic changes were made to the subdivision.

Subdivision (b)(1) addresses schedules, statements, and other documents that the debtor must file unless the court orders otherwise and other than in a case under chapter 9. This subdivision is amended to include documentary requirements added by the 2005 amendments to § 521 that apply to the same group of debtors and have the same time limits as the existing requirements of (b)(1). Consistent with the E–Government Act of 2002, Pub. L. No. 107–347, the payment advices should be redacted before they are filed.

Subdivision (b)(2) is amended to conform to the renumbering of the subsections of § 521.

Subdivisions (b)(3) through (b)(8) are new and implement the 2005 amendments to the Code. Subdivision (b)(3) provides for the filing of a document relating to the credit counseling requirement provided by the 2005 amendments to § 109 in the context of an Official Form that warns the debtor of the consequences of failing to comply with the credit counseling requirement.

Subdivision (b)(4) addresses the filing of information about current monthly income, as defined in § 101, for certain chapter 7 debtors and, if required, additional calculations of expenses required by the 2005 amendments to § 707(b).

Subdivision (b)(5) addresses the filing of information about current monthly income, as defined in § 101, for individual chapter 11 debtors. The 2005 amendments to § 1129(a)(15) condition plan confirmation for individual debtors on the commitment of disposable income, as defined in § 1325(b)(2), which is based on current monthly income.

Subdivision (b)(6) addresses the filing of information about current monthly income, as defined in § 101, for chapter 13 debtors and, if required, additional calculations of expenses. These changes are necessary because the 2005 amendments to § 1325 require that the determination of disposable income begin with current monthly income.

Subdivision (b)(7) reflects the 2005 amendments to §§ 727 and 1328 of the Code that condition the receipt of a discharge on the completion of a personal financial management course, with certain exceptions. Certain individual chapter 11 debtors may also be required to complete a personal financial management course under § 727(a)(11) as incorporated by § 1141(d)(3)(C). To evidence compliance with that requirement, the subdivision requires the debtor to file the appropriate Official Form certifying that the debtor has completed the personal financial management course.

Subdivision (b)(8) requires an individual debtor in a case under chapter 11, 12, or 13 to file a statement that there are no reasonable grounds to believe that the restrictions on a homestead exemption as set out in § 522(q) of the Code are applicable. Sections 1141(d)(5)(C), 1228(f), and 1328(h) each provide that the court shall not enter a discharge order unless it finds that there is no reasonable cause to believe that § 522(q) applies. Requiring the debtor to submit a statement to that effect in cases under chapters 11, 12, and 13 in which an exemption is claimed in excess of the amount allowed under § 522(q)(1) provides the court with a basis to conclude, in the absence of any contrary information, that § 522(q) does not apply. Creditors receive notice under Rule 2002(f)(11) of the time to request postponement of the entry of the discharge to permit an opportunity to challenge the debtor's assertions in the Rule 1007(b)(8) statement in appropriate cases.

Subdivision (c) is amended to include time limits for the filing requirements added to subdivision (b) due to the 2005 amendments to the Code, and to make conforming amendments. Separate time limits are provided for the documentation of credit counseling and for the statement of the completion of the financial management course. While most documents relating to credit counseling must be filed with the voluntary petition, the credit counseling certificate and debt repayment plan can be filed within 15 days of the filing of a voluntary petition if the debtor files a statement under subdivision (b)(3)(B) with the petition. Sections 727(a)(11), 1141(d)(3), and 1328(g) of the Code require individual debtors to complete a personal financial management course prior to the entry of a discharge. The amendment allows the court to enlarge the deadline for the debtor to file the statement of completion. Because no party is harmed by the enlargement, no specific restriction is placed on the court's discretion to enlarge the deadline, even after its expiration.

Subdivision (c) of the rule is also amended to recognize the limitation on the extension of time to file schedules and statements when the debtor is a small business debtor. Section 1116(3), added to the Code in 2005, establishes a specific standard for courts to apply in the event that the debtor in possession or the trustee seeks an extension for filing these forms for a period beyond 30 days after the order for relief.

2009 Amendments

The rule is amended to implement changes in connection with the amendment to Rule 9006(a) and the manner by which time is computed under the rules. Each deadline in the rule of fewer than 30 days is amended to substitute a deadline that is a multiple of seven days. Throughout the rules, deadlines are amended in the following manner:

- 5–day periods become 7–day periods
- 10–day periods become 14–day periods
- 15–day periods become 14–day periods
- 20–day periods become 21–day periods
- 25–day periods become 28–day periods

2010 Amendments

Subdivision (a)(2). Subdivision (a)(2) is amended to shorten the time for a debtor to file a list of the creditors included on the various schedules filed or to be filed in the case. This list provides the information necessary for the clerk to provide notice of the § 341 meeting of creditors in a timely manner.

Subdivision (c). Subdivision (c) is amended to provide additional time for individual debtors in chapter 7 to file the statement of completion of a course in personal financial management. This change is made in conjunction with an amendment to Rule 5009 requiring the clerk to provide notice to debtors of the consequences of not filing the statement in a timely manner.

2012 Amendments

Subdivision (c). In subdivision (c), the time limit for a debtor in an involuntary case to file the list required by subdivision (a)(2) is deleted as unnecessary. Subdivision (a)(2) provides that the list must be filed within seven days after the entry of the order for relief. The other change to subdivision (c) is stylistic.

Because this amendment is being made to conform to an amendment to Rule 1007(a)(2) that took effect on December 1, 2010, final approval is sought without publication.

2013 Amendments

Subdivision (b)(7) is amended to relieve an individual debtor of the obligation to file a statement of completion of a personal financial management course if the course provider notifies the court that the debtor has completed the course. Course providers approved under § 111 of the Code may be permitted to file this notification electronically with the court immediately upon the debtor's completion of the course. If the provider does not notify the court, the debtor must file the statement, prepared as prescribed by the appropriate Official Form, within the time period specified by subdivision (c).

2015 Amendments

In subdivisions (a)(1) and (a)(2), the references to Schedules are amended to reflect the new designations adopted as part of the Forms Modernization Project.

CROSS REFERENCES

Committee of seven unsecured creditors appointed in reorganization case, see 11 USCA § 1102.

Compliance with this rule upon conversion to liquidation case, see Fed.Rules Bankr.Proc. Rule 1019, 11 USCA.

Duty of debtor to,

Inform trustee as to property location and name and address of money and property obligors, see Fed.Rules Bankr.Proc. Rule 4002, 11 USCA.

Prepare and file schedule and statement, see 11 USCA § 521.

Enlargement of time for filing list of twenty largest unsecured creditors not permitted, see Fed.Rules Bankr.Proc. Rule 9006, 11 USCA.

Filing of proof of interest by equity security holder obviated by list filed by debtor, see Fed.Rules Bankr.Proc. Rule 3003, 11 USCA.

Immunity from self-incrimination, see 11 USCA § 344.

"Insider" for purposes of list of 20 unsecured claims defined, see 11 USCA § 101.

List of exempt property to be filed,

By dependent of debtor, see Fed.Rules Bankr.Proc. Rule 4003, 11 USCA.

With schedule of assets, see Fed.Rules Bankr.Proc. Rule 4003, 11 USCA.

Motions, form and service, see Fed.Rules Bankr.Proc. Rule 9013, 11 USCA.

Notice required for,

Creditors' meetings, see Fed.Rules Bankr.Proc. Rule 2002, 11 USCA.

Order for relief, see 11 USCA § 342.

Rule 1008. Verification of Petitions and Accompanying Papers

All petitions, lists, schedules, statements and amendments thereto shall be verified or contain an unsworn declaration as provided in 28 U.S.C. § 1746.

(As amended Apr. 30, 1991, eff. Aug. 1, 1991.)

ADVISORY COMMITTEE NOTES

This rule retains the requirement under the Bankruptcy Act [former Title 11] and rules that petitions and accompanying papers must be verified. Only the original need be signed and verified, but the copies must be conformed to the original. See Rule 9011(c).

The verification may be replaced by an unsworn declaration as provided in 28 U.S.C. § 1746. See also, Official Form No. 1 and Advisory Committee Note.

1991 Amendments

The amendments to this rule are stylistic.

CROSS REFERENCES

Signing and verification of papers, see Fed.Rules Bankr. Proc. Rule 9011, 11 USCA.

Rule 1009. Amendments of Voluntary Petitions, Lists, Schedules and Statements

(a) General right to amend

A voluntary petition, list, schedule, or statement may be amended by the debtor as a matter of course at any time before the case is closed. The debtor shall give notice of the amendment to the trustee and to any entity affected thereby. On motion of a party in interest, after notice and a hearing, the court may order any voluntary petition, list, schedule, or statement to be amended and the clerk shall give notice of the amendment to entities designated by the court.

(b) Statement of intention

The statement of intention may be amended by the debtor at any time before the expiration of the period provided in § 521(a) of the Code. The debtor shall give notice of the amendment to the trustee and to any entity affected thereby.

(c) Statement of social security number

If a debtor becomes aware that the statement of social security number submitted under Rule 1007(f) is incorrect, the debtor shall promptly submit an amended verified statement setting forth the correct social security number. The debtor shall give notice of the amendment to all of the entities required to be included on the list filed under Rule 1007(a)(1) or (a)(2).

(d) Transmission to United States trustee

The clerk shall promptly transmit to the United States trustee a copy of every amendment filed or submitted under subdivision (a), (b), or (c) of this rule. (As amended Mar. 30, 1987, eff. Aug. 1, 1987; Apr. 30, 1991, eff. Aug. 1, 1991; Apr. 12, 2006, eff. Dec. 1, 2006; Apr. 23, 2008, eff. Dec. 1, 2008.)

ADVISORY COMMITTEE NOTES

This rule continues the permissive approach adopted by former Bankruptcy Rule 110 to amendments of voluntary petitions and accompanying papers. Notice of any amendment is required to be given to the trustee. This is particularly important with respect to any amendment of the schedule of property affecting the debtor's claim of exemptions. Notice of any amendment of the schedule of liabilities is to be given to any creditor whose claim is changed or newly listed.

The rule does not continue the provision permitting the court to order an amendment on its own initiative. Absent a request in some form by a party in interest, the court should not be involved in administrative matters affecting the estate.

If a list or schedule is amended to include an additional creditor, the effect on the dischargeability of the creditor's claim is governed by the provisions of § 523(a)(3) of the Code.

1987 Amendments

Subdivision (a) is amended to require notice and a hearing in the event a party in interest other than the debtor seeks to amend. The number of copies of the amendment will be determined by local rule of court.

Subdivision (b) is added to treat amendments of the statement of intention separately from other amendments. The intention of the individual debtor must be performed within 45 days of the filing of the statement, unless the court extends the period. Subdivision (b) limits the time for amendment to the time for performance under § 521(2)(B) of the Code or any extension granted by the court.

1991 Amendments

The amendments to subdivision (a) are stylistic.

Subdivision (c) is derived from Rule X-1002(a) and is designed to provide the United States trustee with current information to enable that office to participate effectively in the case.

2006 Amendments

Subdivision (c). Rule 2002(a)(1) provides that the notice of the § 341 meeting of creditors include the debtor's social security number. It provides creditors with the full number while limiting publication of the social security number otherwise to the final four digits of the number to protect the debtor's identity from others who do not have the same need for that information. If, however, the social security number that the debtor submitted under Rule 1007(f) is incorrect, then the only notice to the entities contained on the list filed under Rule 1007(a)(1) or (a)(2) would be incorrect. This

amendment adds a new subdivision (c) that directs the debtor to submit a verified amended statement of social security number and to give notice of the new statement to all entities in the case who received the notice containing the erroneous social security number.

Subdivision (d). Former subdivision (c) becomes subdivision (d) and is amended to include new subdivision (c) amendments in the list of documents that the clerk must transmit to the United States trustee.

Other amendments are stylistic.

2008 Amendments

Subdivision (b) is amended to conform to the 2005 amendments to § 521 of the Code.

CROSS REFERENCES

Amended and supplemental pleadings, see Fed.Rules Civ. Proc. Rule 15, 28 USCA.

Dischargeability of debts added to list or schedule, see 11 USCA § 523.

Motions, form and service, see Fed.Rules Bankr.Proc. Rule 9013, 11 USCA.

Rule 1010. Service of Involuntary Petition and Summons

(a) Service of involuntary petition and summons

On the filing of an involuntary petition, the clerk shall forthwith issue a summons for service. When an involuntary petition is filed, service shall be made on the debtor. The summons shall be served with a copy of the petition in the manner provided for service of a summons and complaint by Rule 7004(a) or (b). If service cannot be so made, the court may order that the summons and petition be served by mailing copies to the party's last known address, and by at least one publication in a manner and form directed by the court. The summons and petition may be served on the party anywhere. Rule 7004(e) and Rule 4(*l*) F.R.Civ.P. apply when service is made or attempted under this rule.

(b) Corporate ownership statement

Each petitioner that is a corporation shall file with the involuntary petition a corporate ownership statement containing the information described in Rule 7007.1.

(As amended Mar. 30, 1987, eff. Aug. 1, 1987; Apr. 30, 1991, eff. Aug. 1, 1991; Apr. 22, 1993, eff. Aug. 1, 1993; Apr. 11, 1997, eff. Dec. 1, 1997; Apr. 23, 2008, eff. Dec. 1, 2008; Apr. 28, 2016, eff. Dec. 1, 2016.)

ADVISORY COMMITTEE NOTES

This rule provides the procedure for service of the involuntary petition and summons. It does not deal with service of a summons and complaint instituting an adversary proceeding pursuant to Part VII.

While this rule is similar to former Bankruptcy Rule 111, it substitutes the clerk of the bankruptcy court for the clerk of the district court as the person who is to issue the summons.

The modes of service prescribed by the rule are personal or by mail, when service can be effected in one of these ways in the United States. Such service is to be made in the manner prescribed in adversary proceedings by Rule 7004(a) and (b). If service must be made in a foreign country, the mode of service is one of that set forth in Rule 4(i) F.R.Civ.P.

When the method set out in Rule 7004(a) and (b) cannot be utilized, service by publication coupled with mailing to the last known address is authorized. Cf. Rule 7004(c). The court determines the form and manner of publication as provided in Rule 9007. The publication need not set out the petition or the order directing service by publication. In order to apprise the debtor fairly, however, the publication should include all the information required to be in the summons by Official Form No. 13 and a notice indicating how service is being effected and how a copy of the petition may be obtained.

There are no territorial limits on the service authorized by this rule, which continues the practice under the former rules and Act. There must, however, be a basis for jurisdiction pursuant to § 109(a) of the Code for the court to order relief. Venue provisions are set forth in 28 U.S.C. § 1472.

Subdivision (f) of Rule 7004 and subdivisions (g) and (h) of Rule 4 F.R.Civ.P. govern time and proof of service and amendment of process or of proof of service.

Rule 1004 provides for transmission to nonpetitioning partners of a petition filed against the partnership by fewer than all the general partners.

1987 Amendments

The rule has been broadened to include service of a petition commencing a case ancillary to a foreign proceeding, previously included in Rule 1003(e)(2).

1991 Amendments

Reference to the Official Form number is deleted in anticipation of future revision and renumbering of the Official Forms.

Rule 4(g) and (h) F.R.Civ.P. made applicable by this rule refers to Rule 4(g) and (h) F.R.Civ.P. in effect on January 1, 1990, notwithstanding any subsequent amendment thereto. See Rule 7004(g).

1993 Amendments

This rule is amended to delete the reference to the Official Form. The Official Form for the summons was abrogated in 1991. Other amendments are stylistic and make no substantive change.

1997 Amendments

The amendments to this rule are technical, are promulgated solely to conform to changes in subdivision designations in Rule 4, F.R.Civ.P., and in Rule 7004, and are not intended to effectuate any material change in substance.

In 1996, the letter designation of subdivision (f) of Rule 7004 (Summons; Time Limit for Service) was changed to subdivision (e). In 1993, the provisions of Rule 4, F.R.Civ.P., relating to proof of service contained in Rule 4(g) (Return) and Rule 4(h) (Amendments), were placed in the new subdivision (*l*) of Rule 4 (Proof of Service). The technical amendments to Rule 1010 are designed solely to conform to these new subdivision designations.

The 1996 amendments to Rule 7004 and the 1993 amendments to Rule 4, F.R.Civ.P., have not affected the availability of service by first class mail in accordance with Rule 7004(b) for the service of a summons and petition in an involuntary case commenced under § 303 or an ancillary case commenced under § 304 of the Code.

GAP Report on Rule 1010. These amendments, which are technical and conforming, were not published for comment.

2008 Amendments

This rule is amended to implement the 2005 amendments to the Code, which repealed § 304 and replaced it with chapter 15 governing ancillary and other cross-border cases. Under chapter 15, a foreign representative commences a case by filing a petition for recognition of a pending foreign nonmain proceeding. The amendment requires service of the summons and petition on the debtor and any entity against whom the representative is seeking provisional relief. Until the court enters a recognition order under § 1517, no stay is in effect unless the court enters some form of provisional relief under § 1519. Thus, only those entities against whom specific provisional relief is sought need to be served. The court may, however, direct that service be made on additional entities as appropriate.

This rule does not apply to a petition for recognition of a foreign main proceeding.

The rule is also amended by renumbering the prior rule as subdivision (a) and adding a new subdivision (b) requiring any corporate creditor that files or joins an involuntary petition to file a corporate ownership statement.

2016 Amendments

Subdivision (a) of this rule is amended to remove provisions regarding the issuance of a summons for service in certain chapter 15 proceedings. The requirements for notice and service in chapter 15 proceedings are found in Rule 2002(q).

CROSS REFERENCES

Applicability of this rule to,

> Involuntary case ancillary to foreign proceeding, see Fed. Rules Bankr.Proc. Rule 1003, 11 USCA.

> Involuntary partnership petitions, see Fed.Rules Bankr. Proc. Rule 1004, 11 USCA.

Form and manner of service by publication, see Fed.Rules Bankr.Proc. Rule 9007 and Rule 9008, 11 USCA.

Jurisdictional basis for service, see 11 USCA § 109.

Process, see Fed.Rules Civ.Proc. Rule 4, 28 USCA.

Rule 1011.   Responsive Pleading or Motion in Involuntary Cases

(a) Who may contest petition

The debtor named in an involuntary petition may contest the petition. In the case of a petition against a partnership under Rule 1004, a nonpetitioning general partner, or a person who is alleged to be a general partner but denies the allegation, may contest the petition.

(b) Defenses and objections; when presented

Defenses and objections to the petition shall be presented in the manner prescribed by Rule 12 F.R.Civ.P. and shall be filed and served within 21 days after service of the summons, except that if service is made by publication on a party or partner not residing or found within the state in which the court sits, the court shall prescribe the time for filing and serving the response.

(c) Effect of motion

Service of a motion under Rule 12(b) F.R.Civ.P. shall extend the time for filing and serving a responsive pleading as permitted by Rule 12(a) F.R.Civ.P.

(d) Claims against petitioners

A claim against a petitioning creditor may not be asserted in the answer except for the purpose of defeating the petition.

(e) Other pleadings

No other pleadings shall be permitted, except that the court may order a reply to an answer and prescribe the time for filing and service.

(f) Corporate ownership statement

If the entity responding to the involuntary petition is a corporation, the entity shall file with its first appearance, pleading, motion, response, or other request addressed to the court a corporate ownership statement containing the information described in Rule 7007.1. (As amended Mar. 30, 1987, eff. Aug. 1, 1987; Apr. 26, 2004, eff. Dec. 1, 2004; Apr. 23, 2008, eff. Dec. 1, 2008; Mar. 26, 2009, eff. Dec. 1, 2009; Apr. 28, 2016, eff. Dec. 1, 2016.)

ADVISORY COMMITTEE NOTES

This rule is derived from former Bankruptcy Rule 112. A petition filed by fewer than all the general partners under Rule 1004(b) to have an order for relief entered with respect to the partnership is referred to as a petition against the partnership because of the adversary character of the proceeding it commences. Cf. § 303(b)(3) of the Code; 2 Collier Bankruptcy ¶303.05[5][a] (15th ed.1981); id. ¶¶18.33[2], 18.46 (14th ed.1966). One who denies an allegation of membership in the firm is nevertheless recognized as a party entitled to contest a petition filed against a partnership under subdivision (b) of Rule 1004 in view of the possible consequences to him of an order for relief against the entity alleged to include him as a member. See § 723 of the Code; Francis v. McNeal, 228 U.S. 695 (1913); Manson v. Williams, 213 U.S. 453 (1909); Carter v. Whisler, 275 Fed. 743, 746–747 (8th Cir.1921). The rule preserves the features of the former Act and Rule 112 and the Code permitting no response by creditors to an involuntary petition or petition against a partnership under rule 1004(b).

Subdivision (b). Rule 12 F.R.Civ.P. has been looked to by the courts as prescribing the mode of making a defense or objection to a petition in bankruptcy. See Fada of New York, Inc. v. Organization Service Co., Inc., 125 F.2d 120 (2d Cir.1942); In the Matter of McDougald, 17 F.R.D. 2, 5 (W.D.Ark.1955); In the Matter of Miller, 6 Fed.Rules Serv. 12f.26, Case No. 1 (N.D.Ohio 1942); Tatum v. Acadian Pro-

duction Corp. of La., 35 F.Supp. 40, 50 (E.D.La.1940); 2 Collier, supra ¶303.07 (15th ed.1981); 2 id. at 134–40 (14th ed.1966). As pointed out in the Note accompanying former Bankruptcy rule 915 an objection that a debtor is neither entitled to the benefits of the Code nor amenable to an involuntary petition goes to jurisdiction of the subject matter and may be made at any time consistent with Rule 12(h)(3) F.R.Civ.P. Nothing in this rule recognizes standing in a creditor or any other person not authorized to contest a petition to raise an objection that a person eligible to file a voluntary petition cannot be the subject of an order for relief on an involuntary petition. See Seligson & King, Jurisdiction and Venue in Bankruptcy, 36 Ref.J. 36, 38–40 (1962).

As Collier has pointed out with respect to the Bankruptcy Act, "the mechanics of the provisions in § 18a and b relating to time for appearance and pleading are unnecessarily confusing. . . . It would seem, though, to be more straightforward to provide, as does Federal Rule 12(a), that the time to respond runs from the date of service rather than the date of issuance of process." 2 Collier, supra at 119. The time normally allowed for the service and filing of an answer or motion under Rule 1011 runs from the date of the issuance of the summons. Compare Rule 7012. Service of the summons and petition will ordinarily be made by mail under Rule 1010 and must be made within 10 days of the issuance of the summons under Rule 7004(e), which governs the time of service. When service is made by publication, the court should fix the time for service and filing of the response in the light of all the circumstances so as to afford a fair opportunity to the debtor to enter a defense or objection without unduly delaying the hearing on the petition. Cf. Rule 12(a) F.R.Civ.P.

Subdivision (c). Under subdivision (c), the timely service of a motion permitted by Rule 12(b), (e), (f), or (h) F.R.Civ.P. alters the time within which an answer must be filed. If the court denies a motion or postpones its disposition until trial on the merits, the answer must be served within 10 days after notice of the court's action. If the court grants a motion for a more definite statement, the answer may be served any time within 10 days after the service of the more definite statement.

Many of the rules governing adversary proceedings apply to proceedings on a contested petition unless the court otherwise directs as provided in Rule 1018. The specific provisions of this Rule 1011 or 7005, however, govern the filing of an answer or motion responsive to a petition. The rules of Part VII are adaptations of the corresponding Federal Rules of Civil Procedure, and the effect of Rule 1018 is thus to make the provisions of Civil Rules 5, 8, 9, 15, and 56, inter alia, generally applicable to the making of defenses and objections to the petition. Rule 1018 follows prior law and practice in this respect. See 2 Collier, Bankruptcy ¶¶18.39–18.41 (14th ed.1966).

Subdivision (d). This subdivision adopts the position taken in many cases that an affirmative judgment against a petitioning creditor cannot be sought by a counterclaim filed in an answer to an involuntary petition. See, e.g., Georgia Jewelers, Inc., v. Bulova Watch Co., 302 F.2d 362, 369–70 (5th Cir.1962); Associated Electronic Supply Co. of Omaha v. C.B.S. Electronic Sales Corp., 288 F.2d 683, 684–85 (8th Cir. 1961). The subdivision follows Harris v. Capehart-Farnsworth Corp., 225 F.2d 268 (8th Cir.1955), in permitting the debtor to challenge the standing of a petitioner by filing a counterclaim against him. It does not foreclose the court from rejecting a counterclaim that cannot be determined without unduly delaying the decision upon the petition. See In the Matter of Bichel Optical Laboratories, Inc., 299 F.Supp. 545 (D.Minn.1969).

Subdivision (e). This subdivision makes it clear that no reply needs to be made to an answer, including one asserting a counterclaim, unless the court orders otherwise.

1987 Amendments

The rule has been broadened to make applicable in ancillary cases the provisions concerning responsive pleadings to involuntary petitions.

2004 Amendments

The amendment to Rule 1004 that became effective on December 1, 2002, deleted former subdivision (a) of that rule leaving only the provisions relating to involuntary petitions against partnerships. The rule no longer includes subdivisions. Therefore, this technical amendment changes the reference to Rule 1004(b) to Rule 1004.

2008 Amendments

The rule is amended to reflect the 2005 amendments to the Code, which repealed § 304 and added chapter 15. Section 304 covered cases ancillary to foreign proceedings, while chapter 15 governs ancillary and other cross-border cases and introduces the concept of a petition for recognition of a foreign proceeding.

The rule is also amended in tandem with the amendment to Rule 1010 to require the parties responding to an involuntary petition and a petition for recognition of a foreign proceeding to file corporate ownership statements to assist the court in determining whether recusal is necessary.

2009 Amendments

The rule is amended to implement changes in connection with the amendment to Rule 9006(a) and the manner by which time is computed under the rules. The deadline in the rule is amended to substitute a deadline that is a multiple of seven days. Throughout the rules, deadlines are amended in the following manner:

- 5–day periods become 7–day periods
- 10–day periods become 14–day periods
- 15–day periods become 14–day periods
- 20–day periods become 21–day periods
- 25–day periods become 28–day periods

2016 Amendments

This rule is amended to remove provisions regarding chapter 15 proceedings. The requirements for responses to a petition for recognition of a foreign proceeding are found in Rule 1012.

CROSS REFERENCES

Applicability of this rule to involuntary case ancillary to foreign proceeding, see Fed.Rules Bankr.Proc. Rule 1003, 11 USCA.

Entry of default upon failure to plead within time, see Fed.Rules Bankr.Proc. Rule 1013, 11 USCA.

Motions, form and service, see Fed.Rules Bankr.Proc. Rule 9013, 11 USCA.

Pleadings,

Amended and supplemental, see Fed.Rules Civ.Proc. Rule 15, 28 USCA.

Capacity, fraud, and other special matters, see Fed.Rules Civ.Proc. Rule 9, 28 USCA.

General rules, see Fed.Rules Civ.Proc. Rule 8, 28 USCA.

Service and filing, see Fed.Rules Civ.Proc. Rule 5, 28 USCA.

Responsive pleadings, see 11 USCA § 303.

Summary judgment, see Fed.Rules Civ.Proc. Rule 56, 28 USCA.

Rule 1012. Responsive Pleading in Cross–Border Cases

(a) Who may contest petition

The debtor or any party in interest may contest a petition for recognition of a foreign proceeding.

(b) Objections and responses; when presented

Objections and other responses to the petition shall be presented no later than seven days before the date set for the hearing on the petition, unless the court prescribes some other time or manner for responses.

(c) Corporate ownership statement

If the entity responding to the petition is a corporation, then the entity shall file a corporate ownership statement containing the information described in Rule 7007.1 with its first appearance, pleading, motion, response, or other request addressed to the court. (Added April 28, 2016, eff. Dec. 1, 2016.)

ADVISORY COMMITTEE NOTES

2016 Amendments

This rule is added to govern responses to petitions for recognition in cross-border cases. It incorporates provisions formerly found in Rule 1011. Subdivision (a) provides that the debtor or a party in interest may contest the petition. Subdivision (b) provides for presentation of responses no later than 7 days before the hearing on the petition, unless the court directs otherwise. Subdivision (c) governs the filing of corporate ownership statements by entities responding to the petition.

Rule 1013. Hearing and Disposition of a Petition in an Involuntary Case

(a) Contested petition

The court shall determine the issues of a contested petition at the earliest practicable time and forthwith enter an order for relief, dismiss the petition, or enter any other appropriate order.

(b) Default

If no pleading or other defense to a petition is filed within the time provided by Rule 1011, the court, on the next day, or as soon thereafter as practicable, shall enter an order for the relief requested in the petition.

(c) [Abrogated]

(As amended Apr. 30, 1991, eff. Aug. 1, 1991; Apr. 22, 1993, eff. Aug. 1, 1993.)

ADVISORY COMMITTEE NOTES

This rule is adapted from former Bankruptcy Rule 115(a) and (c) and applies in chapter 7 and 11 cases. The right to trial by jury under § 19a of the Bankruptcy Act [former § 42(a) of this title] has been abrogated and the availability of a trial by jury is within the discretion of the bankruptcy judge pursuant to 28 U.S.C. § 1480(b). Rule 9015 governs the demand for a jury trial.

Subdivision (b) of Rule 1013 is derived from former Bankruptcy Rule 115(c) and § 18(e) of the Bankruptcy Act [former § 41(e) of this title]. If an order for relief is not entered on default, dismissal will ordinarily be appropriate but the court may postpone definitive action. See also Rule 9024 with respect to setting aside an order for relief on default for cause.

Subdivision (e) of former Bankruptcy Rule 115 has not been carried over because its provisions are covered by § 303(i) of the Code.

1991 Amendments

Reference to the Official Form number is deleted in anticipation of future revision and renumbering of the Official Forms.

1993 Amendments

Subdivision (c) is abrogated because the official form for the order for relief was abrogated in 1991. Other amendments are stylistic and make no substantive change.

CROSS REFERENCES

Costs, counsel fees, expenses and damages upon dismissal of petition, see 11 USCA § 303.

Instructions to jury, objection, see Fed.Rules Civ.Proc. Rule 51, 28 USCA.

Juries of less than twelve, majority verdict, see Fed.Rules Civ.Proc. Rule 48, 28 USCA.

Jurors, see Fed.Rules Civ.Proc. Rule 47, 28 USCA.

Jury trial of right, see Fed.Rules Civ.Proc. Rule 38, 28 USCA.

Motion for directed verdict and for judgment notwithstanding verdict, see Fed.Rules Civ.Proc. Rule 50, 28 USCA.

Power of court to render judgments, see 11 USCA § 105.

Setting aside default for cause, see Fed.Rules Bankr.Proc. Rule 9024, 11 USCA.

Special verdicts and interrogatories, see Fed.Rules Civ. Proc. Rule 49, 28 USCA.

Trial by jury or by court, see Fed.Rules Civ.Proc. Rule 39, 28 USCA.

Rule 1014. Dismissal and Change of Venue

(a) Dismissal and transfer of cases

(1) Cases filed in proper district

If a petition is filed in the proper district, the court, on the timely motion of a party in interest or on its own motion, and after hearing on notice to the petitioners, the United States trustee, and other entities as directed by the court, may transfer the case to any other district if the court determines that the transfer is in the interest of justice or for the convenience of the parties.

(2) Cases filed in improper district

If a petition is filed in an improper district, the court, on the timely motion of a party in interest or on its own motion, and after hearing on notice to the petitioners, the United States trustee, and other entities as directed by the court, may dismiss the case or transfer it to any other district if the court determines that transfer is in the interest of justice or for the convenience of the parties.

(b) Procedure when petitions involving the same debtor or related debtors are filed in different courts

If petitions commencing cases under the Code or seeking recognition under chapter 15 are filed in different districts by, regarding, or against (1) the same debtor, (2) a partnership and one or more of its general partners, (3) two or more general partners, or (4) a debtor and an affiliate, the court in the district in which the first-filed petition is pending may determine, in the interest of justice or for the convenience of the parties, the district or districts in which any of the cases should proceed. The court may so determine on motion and after a hearing, with notice to the following entities in the affected cases: the United States trustee, entities entitled to notice under Rule 2002(a), and other entities as the court directs. The court may order the parties to the later-filed cases not to proceed further until it makes the determination.

(As amended Mar. 30, 1987, eff. Aug. 1, 1987; Apr. 30, 1991, eff. Aug. 1, 1991; Apr. 30, 2007, eff. Dec. 1, 2007; Apr. 28, 2010, eff. Dec. 1, 2010; Apr. 25, 2014, eff. Dec. 1, 2014.)

ADVISORY COMMITTEE NOTES

This rule is derived from former Bankruptcy Rule 116 which contained venue as well as transfer provisions. Public Law 95–598, however, placed the venue provisions in 28 U.S.C. § 1472, and no purpose is served by repeating them in this rule. Transfer of cases is provided in 28 U.S.C. § 1475 but this rule adds the procedure for obtaining transfer. Pursuant to 28 U.S.C. § 1472, proper venue for cases filed under the Code is either the district of domicile, residence, principal place of business, or location of principal assets for 180 days or the longer portion thereof immediately preceding the petition. 28 U.S.C. § 1475 permits the court to transfer a case in the interest of justice and for the convenience of the parties. If the venue is improper, the court may retain or transfer the case in the interest of justice and for the convenience of the parties pursuant to 28 U.S.C. § 1477.

Subdivision (a) of the rule is derived from former Bankruptcy Rule 116(b). It implements 28 U.S.C. §§ 1475 and 1477 and clarifies the procedure to be followed in requesting and effecting transfer of a case. Subdivision (a) protects the parties against being subjected to a transfer except on a timely motion of a party in interest. If the transfer would result in fragmentation or duplication of administration, increase expense, or delay closing the estate, such a factor would bear on the timeliness of the motion as well as on the propriety of the transfer under the standards prescribed in subdivision (a). Subdivision (a) of the rule requires the interest of justice and the convenience of the parties to be the grounds of any transfer of a case or of the retention of a case filed in an improper district as does 28 U.S.C. § 1477. Cf. 28 U.S.C. § 1404(a) (district court may transfer any civil action "[f]or the convenience of parties and witnesses, in the interest of justice"). It also expressly requires a hearing on notice to the petitioner or petitioners before the transfer of any case may be ordered. Under this rule, a motion by a party in interest is necessary. There is no provision for the court to act on its own initiative.

Subdivision (b) is derived from former Bankruptcy Rule 116(c). It authorizes the court in which the first petition is filed under the Code by or against a debtor to entertain a motion seeking a determination whether the case so commenced should continue or be transferred and consolidated or administered jointly with another case commenced by or against the same or related person in another court under a different chapter of the Code. Subdivision (b) is correlated with 28 U.S.C. § 1472 which authorizes petitioners to file cases involving a partnership and partners or affiliated debtors.

The reference in subdivision (b) to petitions filed "by" a partner or "by" any other of the persons mentioned is to be understood as referring to voluntary petitions. It is not the purpose of this subdivision to permit more than one case to be filed in the same court because a creditor signing an involuntary petition happens to be a partner, a partnership, or an affiliate of a debtor.

Transfers of adversary proceedings in cases under title 11 are governed by Rule 7087 and 28 U.S.C. § 1475.

1987 Amendments

Both paragraphs 1 and 2 of subdivision (a) are amended to conform to the standard for transfer in 28 U.S.C. § 1412. Formerly, 28 U.S.C. § 1477 authorized a court either to transfer or retain a case which had been commenced in a district where venue was improper. However, 28 U.S.C. § 1412, which supersedes 28 U.S.C. § 1477, authorizes only the transfer of a case. The rule is amended to delete the reference to retention of a case commenced in the improper district. Dismissal of a case commenced in the improper district as authorized by 28 U.S.C. § 1406 has been added to the rule. If a timely motion to dismiss for improper venue is not filed, the right to object to venue is waived.

The last sentence of the rule has been deleted as unnecessary.

1991 Amendments

Subdivision (b) is amended to provide that a motion for transfer of venue under this subdivision shall be filed in the district in which the first petition is pending. If the case commenced by the first petition has been transferred to another district prior to the filing of a motion to transfer a related case under this subdivision, the motion must be filed in the district to which the first petition had been transferred.

The other amendments to this rule are consistent with the responsibilities of the United States trustee in the supervision and administration of cases pursuant to 28 U.S.C. § 586(a)(3).

The United States trustee may appear and be heard on issues relating to the transfer of the case or dismissal due to improper venue. See § 307 of the Code.

2007 Amendments

Courts have generally held that they have the authority to dismiss or transfer cases on their own motion. The amendment recognizes this authority and also provides that dismissal or transfer of the case may take place only after notice and a hearing.

Other amendments are stylistic.

2010 Amendments

Subdivision (b). Subdivision (b) of the rule is amended to provide that petitions for recognition of a foreign proceeding are included among those that are governed by the procedure for determining where cases should go forward when multiple petitions involving the same debtor are filed. The amendment adds a specific reference to chapter 15 petitions and also provides that the rule governs proceedings regarding a debtor as well as those that are filed by or against a debtor.

Other changes are stylistic.

2014 Amendments

Subdivision (b) provides a practical solution for resolving venue issues when related cases are filed in different districts. It designates the court in which the first-filed petition is pending as the decision maker if a party seeks a determination of where the related cases should proceed. Subdivision (b) is amended to clarify when proceedings in the subsequently filed cases are stayed. It requires an order of the court in which the first-filed petition is pending to stay proceedings in the related cases. Requiring a court order to trigger the stay will prevent the disruption of other cases unless there is a judicial determination that this subdivision of the rule applies and that a stay of related cases is needed while the court makes its venue determination.

Notice of the hearing must be given to all debtors, trustees, creditors, indenture trustees, and United States trustees in the affected cases, as well as any other entity that the court directs. Because the clerk of the court that makes the determination often may lack access to the names and addresses of entities in other cases, a court may order the moving party to provide notice.

The other changes to subdivision (b) are stylistic.

Changes Made After Publication. The only change made after publication was stylistic.

CROSS REFERENCES

Change of venue, see 28 USCA § 1404.

Motions, form and service, see Fed.Rules Bankr.Proc. Rule 9013, 11 USCA.

Transfer of adversary proceeding, see Fed.Rules Bankr. Proc. Rule 7087, 11 USCA.

Rule 1015. Consolidation or Joint Administration of Cases Pending in Same Court

(a) Cases involving same debtor

If two or more petitions by, regarding, or against the same debtor are pending in the same court, the court may order consolidation of the cases.

(b) Cases involving two or more related debtors

If a joint petition or two or more petitions are pending in the same court by or against (1) spouses, or (2) a partnership and one or more of its general partners, or (3) two or more general partners, or (4) a debtor and an affiliate, the court may order a joint administration of the estates. Prior to entering an order the court shall give consideration to protecting creditors of different estates against potential conflicts of interest. An order directing joint administration of individual cases of spouses shall, if one spouse has elected the exemptions under § 522(b)(2) of the Code and the other has elected the exemptions under § 522(b)(3), fix a reasonable time within which either may amend the election so that both shall have elected the same exemptions. The order shall notify the debtors that unless they elect the same exemptions within the time fixed by the court, they will be deemed to have elected the exemptions provided by § 522(b)(2).

(c) Expediting and protective orders

When an order for consolidation or joint administration of a joint case or two or more cases is entered pursuant to this rule, while protecting the rights of the parties under the Code, the court may enter orders as may tend to avoid unnecessary costs and delay.

(As amended Mar. 30, 1987, eff. Aug. 1, 1987; Apr. 23, 2008, eff. Dec. 1, 2008; Apr. 28, 2010, eff. Dec. 1, 2010; Apr. 27, 2017, eff. Dec. 1, 2017.)

ADVISORY COMMITTEE NOTES

Subdivision (a) of this rule is derived from former Bankruptcy Rule 117(a). It applies to cases when the same debtor is named in both voluntary and involuntary petitions, when husband and wife have filed a joint petition pursuant to § 302 of the Code, and when two or more involuntary petitions are filed against the same debtor. It also applies when cases are pending in the same court by virtue of a transfer of one or more petitions from another court. Subdivision (c) allows the court discretion regarding the order of trial of issues raised by two or more involuntary petitions against the same debtor.

Subdivision (b) recognizes the propriety of joint administration of estates in certain kinds of cases. The election or appointment of one trustee for two or more jointly administered estates is authorized by Rule 2009. The authority of the court to order joint administration under subdivision (b) extends equally to the situation when the petitions are filed under different sections, e.g., when one petition is voluntary and the other involuntary, and when all of the petitions are filed under the same section of the Code.

Consolidation of cases implies a unitary administration of the estate and will ordinarily be indicated under the circumstances to which subdivision (a) applies. This rule does not deal with the consolidation of cases involving two or more separate debtors. Consolidation of the estates of separate debtors may sometimes be appropriate, as when the affairs of an individual and a corporation owned or controlled by that individual are so intermingled that the court cannot separate their assets and liabilities. Consolidation, as distinguished from joint administration, is neither authorized nor prohibited by this rule since the propriety of consolidation depends on substantive considerations and affects the substantive rights of the creditors of the different estates. For illustrations of the substantive consolidation of separate estates, see Sampsell v. Imperial Paper & Color Corp., 313 U.S. 215 [61 S.Ct. 904, 85 L.Ed. 1293] (1941). See also Chemical Bank N.Y. Trust Co. v. Kheel, 369 F.2d 845 (2d Cir. 1966); Seligson & Mandell, Multi-Debtor Petition—Consolidation of Debtors and Due Process of Law, 73 Com.L.J. 341 (1968); Kennedy, Insolvency and the Corporate Veil in the United States in Proceedings of the 8th International Symposium on Comparative Law 232, 248–55 (1971).

Joint administration as distinguished from consolidation may include combining the estates by using a single docket for the matters occurring in the administration, including the listing of filed claims, the combining of notices to creditors of the different estates, and the joint handling of other purely administrative matters that may aid in expediting the cases and rendering the process less costly.

Subdivision (c) is an adaptation of the provisions of Rule 42(a) F.R.Civ.P. for the purposes of administration of estates under this rule. The rule does not deal with filing fees when an order for the consolidation of cases or joint administration of estates is made.

A joint petition of husband and wife, requiring the payment of a single filing fee, is permitted by § 302 of the Code. Consolidation of such a case, however, rests in the discretion of the court; see § 302(b) of the Code.

1987 Amendments

The amendment to subdivision (b) implements the provisions of § 522(b) of the Code, as enacted by the 1984 amendments.

2008 Amendments

The rule is amended to conform to the change in the numbering of § 522(b) of the Code that was made as a part of the 2005 amendments. Former subsections (b)(1) and (b)(2) of § 522 were renumbered as subsections (b)(2) and (b)(3), respectively. The rule is amended to make the parallel change.

2010 Amendments

Subdivision (a). By amending subdivision (a) to include cases regarding the same debtor, the rule explicitly recognizes that the court's authority to consolidate cases when more than one petition is filed includes the authority to consolidate cases when one or more of the petitions is filed under chapter 15. This amendment is made in conjunction with the amendment to Rule 1014(b), which also governs petitions filed under chapter 15 regarding the same debtor as well as those filed by or against the debtor.

2017 Amendments

Subdivision (b) is amended to replace "a husband and wife" with "spouses" in light of the Supreme Court's decision in *Obergefell v. Hodges*, 135 S. Ct. 2584 (2015).

Consolidation, see Fed.Rules Civ.Proc. Rule 42, 28 USCA.

Election of trustees in liquidation cases when joint administration ordered, see Fed.Rules Bankr.Proc. Rule 2009, 11 USCA.

Joint cases, see 11 USCA § 302.

Rule 1016. Death or Incompetency of Debtor

Death or incompetency of the debtor shall not abate a liquidation case under chapter 7 of the Code. In such event the estate shall be administered and the case concluded in the same manner, so far as possible, as though the death or incompetency had not occurred. If a reorganization, family farmer's debt adjustment, or individual's debt adjustment case is pending under chapter 11, chapter 12, or chapter 13, the case may be dismissed; or if further administration is possible and in the best interest of the parties, the case may proceed and be concluded in the same manner, so far as possible, as though the death or incompetency had not occurred.

(As amended Apr. 30, 1991, eff. Aug. 1, 1991.)

ADVISORY COMMITTEE NOTES

This rule is derived from former Rules 118 and 11–16. In a chapter 11 reorganization case or chapter 13 individual's debt adjustment case, the likelihood is that the case will be dismissed.

1991 Amendments

This rule is amended to conform to 25 F.R.Civ.P. and to include chapter 12 cases.

CROSS REFERENCES

Exemptions, see 11 USCA § 522.

Property of estate, see 11 USCA § 541.

Rule 1017. Dismissal or Conversion of Case; Suspension

(a) Voluntary dismissal; dismissal for want of prosecution or other cause

Except as provided in §§ 707(a)(3), 707(b), 1208(b), and 1307(b) of the Code, and in Rule 1017(b), (c), and (e), a case shall not be dismissed on motion of the petitioner, for want of prosecution or other cause, or by consent of the parties, before a hearing on notice as provided in Rule 2002. For the purpose of the notice, the debtor shall file a list of creditors with their addresses within the time fixed by the court unless the list was previously filed. If the debtor fails to file the list, the court may order the debtor or another entity to prepare and file it.

(b) Dismissal for failure to pay filing fee

(1) If any installment of the filing fee has not been paid, the court may, after a hearing on notice to the debtor and the trustee, dismiss the case.

(2) If the case is dismissed or closed without full payment of the filing fee, the installments collected shall be distributed in the same manner and proportions as if the filing fee had been paid in full.

(c) Dismissal of voluntary chapter 7 or chapter 13 case for failure to timely file list of creditors, schedules, and statement of financial affairs

The court may dismiss a voluntary chapter 7 or chapter 13 case under § 707(a)(3) or § 1307(c)(9) after a hearing on notice served by the United States trustee on the debtor, the trustee, and any other entities as the court directs.

(d) Suspension

The court shall not dismiss a case or suspend proceedings under § 305 before a hearing on notice as provided in Rule 2002(a).

(e) Dismissal of an individual debtor's chapter 7 case, or conversion to a case under chapter 11 or 13, for abuse

The court may dismiss or, with the debtor's consent, convert an individual debtor's case for abuse under § 707(b) only on motion and after a hearing on notice to the debtor, the trustee, the United States trustee, and any other entity as the court directs.

(1) Except as otherwise provided in § 704(b)(2), a motion to dismiss a case for abuse under § 707(b) or (c) may be filed only within 60 days after the first date set for the meeting of creditors under § 341(a), unless, on request filed before the time has expired, the court for cause extends the time for filing the motion to dismiss. The party filing the motion shall set forth in the motion all matters to be considered at the hearing. In addition, a motion to dismiss under § 707(b)(1) and (3) shall state with particularity the circumstances alleged to constitute abuse.

(2) If the hearing is set on the court's own motion, notice of the hearing shall be served on the debtor no later than 60 days after the first date set for the meeting of creditors under § 341(a). The notice shall set forth all matters to be considered by the court at the hearing.

(f) Procedure for dismissal, conversion, or suspension

(1) Rule 9014 governs a proceeding to dismiss or suspend a case, or to convert a case to another chapter, except under §§ 706(a), 1112(a), 1208(a) or (b), or 1307(a) or (b).

(2) Conversion or dismissal under §§ 706(a), 1112(a), 1208(b), or 1307(b) shall be on motion filed and served as required by Rule 9013.

(3) A chapter 12 or chapter 13 case shall be converted without court order when the debtor files a notice of conversion under §§ 1208(a) or 1307(a). The filing date of the notice becomes the date of the

conversion order for the purposes of applying § 348(c) and Rule 1019. The clerk shall promptly transmit a copy of the notice to the United States trustee.

(As amended Mar. 30, 1987, eff. Aug. 1, 1987; Apr. 30, 1991, eff. Aug. 1, 1991; Apr. 22, 1993, eff. Aug. 1, 1993; Apr. 26, 1999, eff. Dec. 1, 1999; Apr. 17, 2000, eff. Dec. 1, 2000; Apr. 23, 2008, eff. Dec. 1, 2008.)

ADVISORY COMMITTEE NOTES

Subdivision (a) of this rule is derived from former Bankruptcy Rule 120(a). While the rule applies to voluntary and involuntary cases, the "consent of the parties" referred to is that of petitioning creditors and the debtor in an involuntary case. The last sentence recognizes that the court should not be confined to petitioning creditors in its choice of parties on whom to call for assistance in preparing the list of creditors when the debtor fails to do so. This subdivision implements §§ 303(j), 707, 1112 and 1307 of the Code by specifying the manner of and persons to whom notice shall be given and requiring the court to hold a hearing on the issue of dismissal.

Subdivision (b) is derived from former Bankruptcy Rule 120(b). A dismissal under this subdivision can occur only when the petition has been permitted to be filed pursuant to Rule 1006(b). The provision for notice in paragraph (3) is correlated with the provision in Rule 4006 when there is a waiver, denial, or revocation of a discharge. As pointed out in the Note accompanying Rule 4008, the purpose of notifying creditors of a debtor that no discharge has been granted is to correct their assumption to the contrary so that they can take appropriate steps to protect their claims.

Subdivision (c) is new and specifies the notice required for a hearing on dismissal or suspension pursuant to § 305 of the Code. The suspension to which this subdivision refers is that of the case; it does not concern abstention of the court in hearing an adversary proceeding pursuant to 28 U.S.C. § 1478(b).

Subdivision (d). Any proceeding, whether by a debtor or other party, to dismiss or convert a case under §§ 706, 707, 1112, or 1307 is commenced by a motion pursuant to Rule 9014.

1987 Amendments

Subdivision (d) is amended to provide that dismissal or conversion pursuant to §§ 706(a), 707(b), 1112(a), and 1307(b) is not automatically a contested matter under Rule 9014. Conversion or dismissal under these sections is initiated by the filing and serving of a motion as required by Rule 9013. No hearing is required on these motions unless the court directs.

Conversion of a chapter 13 case to a chapter 7 case as authorized by § 1307(a) is accomplished by the filing of a notice of conversion. The notice of conversion procedure is modeled on the voluntary dismissal provision of Rule 41(a)(1) F.R.Civ.P. Conversion occurs on the filing of the notice. No court order is required.

Subdivision (e) is new and provides the procedure to be followed when a court on its own motion has made a preliminary determination that an individual debtor's chapter 7 case may be dismissed pursuant to § 707(b) of the Code, which was added by the 1984 amendments. A debtor's failure to attend the hearing is not a ground for dismissal pursuant to § 707(b).

1991 Amendments

Subdivision (a) is amended to clarify that all entities required to receive notice under Rule 2002, including but not limited to creditors, are entitled to the 20 day notice of the hearing to dismiss the case. The United States trustee receives the notice pursuant to Rule 2002(k).

The word "petition" is changed to "case" in subdivisions (a), (b), and (c) to conform to §§ 707, 930, 1112, 1208, and 1307.

Subdivision (d) is amended to conform to § 348(c) of the Code which refers to the "conversion order."

Subdivisions (a) and (d) are amended to provide procedures for dismissal or conversion of a chapter 12 case. Procedures for dismissal or conversion under § 1208(a) and (b) are the same as the procedures for dismissal or conversion of a chapter 13 case under § 1307(a) and (b).

Subdivision (e) is amended to conform to the 1986 amendment to § 707(b) of the Code which permits the United States trustee to make a motion to dismiss a case for substantial abuse. The time limit for such a motion is added by this subdivision. In general, the facts that are the basis for a motion to dismiss under § 707(b) exist at the time the case is commenced and usually can be discovered early in the case by reviewing the debtor's schedules and examining the debtor at the meeting of creditors. Since dismissal for substantial abuse has the effect of denying the debtor a discharge in the chapter 7 case based on matters which may be discovered early, a motion to dismiss under § 707(b) is analogous to an objection to discharge pursuant to Rule 4004 and, therefore, should be required to be made within a specified time period. If matters relating to substantial abuse are not discovered within the time period specified in subdivision (e) because of the debtor's false testimony, refusal to obey a court order, fraudulent schedules or other fraud, and the debtor receives a discharge, the debtor's conduct may constitute the basis for revocation of the discharge under § 727(d) and (e) of the Code.

1993 Amendments

Subdivision (d) is amended to clarify that the date of the filing of a notice of conversion in a chapter 12 or chapter 13 case is treated as the date of the conversion order for the purpose of applying Rule 1019. Other amendments are stylistic and make no substantive change.

1999 Amendments

Subdivision (b)(3), which provides that notice of dismissal for failure to pay the filing fee shall be sent to all creditors within 30 days after the dismissal, is deleted as unnecessary. Rule 2002(f) provides for notice to creditors of the dismissal of a case.

Rule 2002(a) and this rule currently require notice to all creditors of a hearing on dismissal of a voluntary chapter 7 case for the debtor's failure to file a list of creditors, schedules, and statement of financial affairs within the time provided in § 707(a)(3) of the Code. A new subdivision (c) is added to provide that the United States trustee, who is the only entity with standing to file a motion to dismiss under § 707(a)(3) or § 1307(c)(9), is required to serve the motion on only the debtor, the trustee, and any other entities as the court directs. This amendment, and the amendment to Rule

2002, will have the effect of avoiding the expense of sending notices of the motion to all creditors in a chapter 7 case.

New subdivision (f) is the same as current subdivision (d), except that it provides that a motion to suspend all proceedings in a case or to dismiss a case for substantial abuse of chapter 7 under § 707(b) is governed by Rule 9014.

Other amendments to this rule are stylistic or for clarification.

GAP Report on Rule 1017. No changes since publication, except for stylistic changes in Rule 1017(e) and (f).

2000 Amendments

This rule is amended to permit the court to grant a timely request filed by the United States trustee for an extension of time to file a motion to dismiss a chapter 7 case under § 707(b), whether the court rules on the request before or after the expiration of the 60–day period.

Reporter's Note on Text of Rule 1017(e). The above text of Rule 1017(e) is not based on the text of the rule in effect on this date. The above text embodies amendments that have been promulgated by the Supreme Court in April 1999 and, unless Congress acts with respect to the amendments, will become effective on December 1, 1999.

GAP Report on Rule 1017(e). No changes since publication.

2008 Amendments

Subdivision (e) is amended to implement the 2005 amendments to § 707 of the Code. These statutory amendments permit conversion of a chapter 7 case to a case under chapter 11 or 13, change the basis for dismissal or conversion from "substantial abuse" to "abuse," authorize parties other than the United States trustee to bring motions under § 707(b) under certain circumstances, and add § 707(c) to create an explicit ground for dismissal based on the request of a victim of a crime of violence or drug trafficking. The conforming amendments to subdivision (e) preserve the time limits already in place for § 707(b) motions, except to the extent that § 704(b)(2) sets the deadline for the United States trustee to act. In contrast to the grounds for a motion to dismiss under § 707(b)(2), which are quite specific, the grounds under § 707(b)(1) and (3) are very general. Therefore, to enable the debtor to respond, subdivision (e) requires that motions to dismiss under § 707(b)(1) and (3) state with particularity the circumstances alleged to constitute abuse.

CROSS REFERENCES

Conversion of,
    Individual debt adjustment case, see 11 USCA § 1307.
    Liquidation case, see 11 USCA § 706.
    Reorganization case, see 11 USCA § 1112.
Dismissal of,
    Individual debt adjustment case, see 11 USCA § 1307.
    Involuntary petition, see 11 USCA § 303.
    Liquidation case, see 11 USCA § 707.
    Reorganization case, see 11 USCA § 1112.
Enlargement of thirty-day period for notice of dismissal for failure to pay filing fee not permitted, see Fed.Rules Bankr. Proc. Rule 9006, 11 USCA.
    Motions, form and service, see Fed.Rules Bankr.Proc. Rule 9013, 11 USCA.

Rule 1018. Contested Involuntary Petitions; Contested Petitions Commencing Chapter 15 Cases; Proceedings to Vacate Order for Relief; Applicability of Rules in Part VII Governing Adversary Proceedings

Unless the court otherwise directs and except as otherwise prescribed in Part I of these rules, the following rules in Part VII apply to all proceedings contesting an involuntary petition or a chapter 15 petition for recognition, and to all proceedings to vacate an order for relief: Rules 7005, 7008–7010, 7015, 7016, 7024–7026, 7028–7037, 7052, 7054, 7056, and 7062. The court may direct that other rules in Part VII shall also apply. For the purposes of this rule a reference in the Part VII rules to adversary proceedings shall be read as a reference to proceedings contesting an involuntary petition or a chapter 15 petition for recognition, or proceedings to vacate an order for relief. Reference in the Federal Rules of Civil Procedure to the complaint shall be read as a reference to the petition.

(As amended Mar. 30, 1987, eff. Aug. 1, 1987; Apr. 28, 2010, eff. Dec. 1, 2010.)

ADVISORY COMMITTEE NOTES

The rules in Part VII to which this rule refers are adaptations of the Federal Rules of Civil Procedure for the purpose of governing the procedure in adversary proceedings in cases under the Code. See the Note accompanying Rule 7001 infra. Because of the special need for dispatch and expedition in the determination of the issues in an involuntary petition, see Acme Harvester Co. v. Beekman Lumber Co., 222 U.S. 300, 309 (1911), the objective of some of the Federal Rules of Civil Procedure and their adaptations in Part VII to facilitate the settlement of multiple controversies involving many persons in a single lawsuit is not compatible with the exigencies of bankruptcy administration. See United States F. & G. Co. v. Bray, 225 U.S. 205, 218 (1912). For that reason Rules 7013, 7014 and 7018–7023 will rarely be appropriate in a proceeding on a contested petition.

Certain terms used in the Federal Rules of Civil Procedure have altered meanings when they are made applicable in cases under the Code by these rules. See Rule 9002 infra. This Rule 1018 requires that the terms "adversary proceedings" when used in the rules in Part VII and "complaint" when used in the Federal Rules of Civil Procedure be given altered meanings when they are made applicable to proceedings relating to a contested petition or proceedings to vacate any order for relief. A motion to vacate an order for relief, whether or not made on a petition that was or could have been contested, is governed by the rules in Part VII referred to in this Rule 1018.

1987 Amendments

Rule 1018 is amended to include within its terms a petition commencing an ancillary case when it is contested. This provision was formerly included in Rule 1003(e)(4).

Although this rule does not contain an explicit authorization for the entry of an order for relief when a debtor refuses to cooperate in discovery relating to a contested involuntary petition, the court has ample power under Rule 37(b) F.R.Civ. P., as incorporated by Rule 7037, to enter an order for relief under appropriate circumstances. Rule 37(b) authorizes the court to enter judgment by default or an order that "facts shall be taken as established."

2010 Amendments

The rule is amended to reflect the enactment of chapter 15 of the Code in 2005. As to chapter 15 cases, the rule applies to contests over the petition for recognition and not to all matters that arise in the case. Thus, proceedings governed by § 1519(e) and § 1521(e) of the Code must comply with Rules 7001(7) and 7065, which provide that actions for injunctive relief are adversary proceedings governed by Part VII of the rules. The rule is also amended to clarify that it applies to contests over an involuntary petition, and not to matters merely "relating to" a contested involuntary petition. Matters that may arise in a chapter 15 case or an involuntary case, other than contests over the petition itself, are governed by the otherwise applicable rules.

Other changes are stylistic.

CROSS REFERENCES

Applicability of this rule to involuntary case ancillary to foreign proceeding, see Fed.Rules Bankr.Proc. Rule 1003, 11 USCA.

Effect of amendment of Federal Rules of Civil Procedure, see Fed.Rules Bankr.Proc. Rule 9032, 11 USCA.

Rule 1019. **Conversion of a Chapter 11 Reorganization Case, Chapter 12 Family Farmer's Debt Adjustment Case, or Chapter 13 Individual's Debt Adjustment Case to a Chapter 7 Liquidation Case**

When a chapter 11, chapter 12, or chapter 13 case has been converted or reconverted to a chapter 7 case:

(1) Filing of lists, inventories, schedules, statements

(A) Lists, inventories, schedules, and statements of financial affairs theretofore filed shall be deemed to be filed in the chapter 7 case, unless the court directs otherwise. If they have not been previously filed, the debtor shall comply with Rule 1007 as if an order for relief had been entered on an involuntary petition on the date of the entry of the order directing that the case continue under chapter 7.

(B) If a statement of intention is required, it shall be filed within 30 days after entry of the order of conversion or before the first date set for the meeting of creditors, whichever is earlier. The court may grant an extension of time for cause only on written motion filed, or oral request made during a hearing, before the time has expired. Notice of an extension shall be given to the United States trustee and to any committee, trustee, or other party as the court may direct.

(2) New filing periods

(A) A new time period for filing a motion under § 707(b) or (c), a claim, a complaint objecting to discharge, or a complaint to obtain a determination of dischargeability of any debt shall commence under Rules[1] 1017, 3002, 4004, or 4007, but a new time period shall not commence if a chapter 7 case had been converted to a chapter 11, 12, or 13 case and thereafter reconverted to a chapter 7 case and the time for filing a motion under § 707(b) or (c), a claim, a complaint objecting to discharge, or a complaint to obtain a determination of the dischargeability of any debt, or any extension thereof, expired in the original chapter 7 case.

(B) A new time period for filing an objection to a claim of exemptions shall commence under Rule 4003(b) after conversion of a case to chapter 7 unless:

    (i) the case was converted to chapter 7 more than one year after the entry of the first order confirming a plan under chapter 11, 12, or 13; or

    (ii) the case was previously pending in chapter 7 and the time to object to a claimed exemption had expired in the original chapter 7 case.

(3) Claims filed before conversion

All claims actually filed by a creditor before conversion of the case are deemed filed in the chapter 7 case.

(4) Turnover of records and property

After qualification of, or assumption of duties by the chapter 7 trustee, any debtor in possession or trustee previously acting in the chapter 11, 12, or 13 case shall, forthwith, unless otherwise ordered, turn over to the chapter 7 trustee all records and property of the estate in the possession or control of the debtor in possession or trustee.

(5) Filing final report and schedule of postpetition debts

(A) Conversion of chapter 11 or chapter 12 case

Unless the court directs otherwise, if a chapter 11 or chapter 12 case is converted to chapter 7, the debtor in possession or, if the debtor is not a debtor in possession, the trustee serving at the time of conversion, shall:

    (i) not later than 14 days after conversion of the case, file a schedule of unpaid debts incurred after the filing of the petition and before conversion of the case, including the name and address of each holder of a claim; and

    (ii) not later than 30 days after conversion of the case, file and transmit to the United States trustee a final report and account;

(B) Conversion of chapter 13 case

Unless the court directs otherwise, if a chapter 13 case is converted to chapter 7,

(i) the debtor, not later than 14 days after conversion of the case, shall file a schedule of unpaid debts incurred after the filing of the petition and before conversion of the case, including the name and address of each holder of a claim; and

(ii) the trustee, not later than 30 days after conversion of the case, shall file and transmit to the United States trustee a final report and account;

(C) Conversion after confirmation of a plan

Unless the court orders otherwise, if a chapter 11, chapter 12, or chapter 13 case is converted to chapter 7 after confirmation of a plan, the debtor shall file:

(i) a schedule of property not listed in the final report and account acquired after the filing of the petition but before conversion, except if the case is converted from chapter 13 to chapter 7 and § 348(f)(2) does not apply;

(ii) a schedule of unpaid debts not listed in the final report and account incurred after confirmation but before the conversion; and

(iii) a schedule of executory contracts and unexpired leases entered into or assumed after the filing of the petition but before conversion.

(D) Transmission to United States trustee

The clerk shall forthwith transmit to the United States trustee a copy of every schedule filed pursuant to Rule 1019(5).

(6) Postpetition claims; preconversion administrative expenses; notice

A request for payment of an administrative expense incurred before conversion of the case is timely filed under § 503(a) of the Code if it is filed before conversion or a time fixed by the court. If the request is filed by a governmental unit, it is timely if it is filed before conversion or within the later of a time fixed by the court or 180 days after the date of the conversion. A claim of a kind specified in § 348(d) may be filed in accordance with Rules 3001(a)–(d) and 3002. Upon the filing of the schedule of unpaid debts incurred after commencement of the case and before conversion, the clerk, or some other person as the court may direct, shall give notice to those entities listed on the schedule of the time for filing a request for payment of an administrative expense and, unless a notice of insufficient assets to pay a dividend is mailed in accordance with Rule 2002(e), the time for filing a claim of a kind specified in § 348(d).

(7) [Abrogated]

(As amended Mar. 30, 1987, eff. Aug. 1, 1987; Apr. 30, 1991, eff. Aug. 1, 1991; Apr. 23, 1996, eff. Dec. 1, 1996; Apr. 11, 1997, eff. Dec. 1, 1997; Apr. 26, 1999, eff. Dec. 1, 1999; Apr. 23, 2008, eff. Dec. 1, 2008; Mar. 26, 2009, eff. Dec. 1, 2009; Apr. 28, 2010, eff. Dec. 1, 2010.)

1 So in original. Probably should be "Rule".

ADVISORY COMMITTEE NOTES
1983 Enactments

This rule is derived from former Bankruptcy Rule 122 and implements § 348 of the Code. The rule applies to proceedings in a chapter 7 case following supersession of a case commenced under chapter 11 or 13, whether the latter was initiated by an original petition or was converted from a pending chapter 7 or another chapter case. The rule is not intended to invalidate any action taken in the superseded case before its conversion to chapter 7.

Paragraph (1). If requirements applicable in the superseded case respecting the filing of schedules of debts and property, or lists of creditors and inventory, and of statements of financial affairs have been complied with before the order directing conversion to liquidation, these documents will ordinarily provide all the information about the debts, property, financial affairs, and contracts of the debtor needed for the administration of the estate. If the information submitted in the superseded case is inadequate for the purposes of administration, however, the court may direct the preparation of further informational material and the manner and time of its submission pursuant to paragraph (1). If no schedules, lists, inventories, or statements were filed in the superseded case, this paragraph imposes the duty on the debtor to file schedules and a statement of affairs pursuant to Rule 1007 as if an involuntary petition had been filed on the date when the court directed the conversion of the case to a liquidation case.

Paragraphs (2) and (3). Paragraph (2) requires notice to be given to all creditors of the order of conversion. The notice is to be included in the notice of the meeting of creditors and Official Form No. 16 may be adapted for use. A meeting of creditors may have been held in the superseded case as required by § 341(a) of the Code but that would not dispense with the need to hold one in the ensuing liquidation case. Section 701(a) of the Code permits the court to appoint the trustee acting in the chapter 11 or 13 case as interim trustee in the chapter 7 case. Section 702(a) of the Code allows creditors to elect a trustee but only at the meeting of creditors held under § 341. The right to elect a trustee is not lost because the chapter 7 case follows a chapter 11 or 13 case. Thus a meeting of creditors is necessary. The date fixed for the meeting of creditors will control at least the time for filing claims pursuant to Rule 3002(c). That time will remain applicable in the ensuing chapter 7 case except as paragraph (3) provides, if that time had expired in an earlier chapter 7 case which was converted to the chapter 11 or 13 case, it is not revived in the subsequent chapter 7 case. The same is true if the time for filing a complaint objecting to discharge or to determine nondischargeability of a debt had expired. Paragraph (3), however, recognizes that such time may be extended by the court under Rule 4004 or 4007 on motion made within the original prescribed time.

Paragraph (4) renders it unnecessary to file anew claims that had been filed in the chapter 11 or 13 case before conversion to chapter 7.

Paragraph (5) contemplates that typically, after the court orders conversion of a chapter case to liquidation, a trustee under chapter 7 will forthwith take charge of the property of the estate and proceed expeditiously to liquidate it. The court may appoint the interim trustee in the chapter 7 case pursuant to § 701(a) of the Code. If creditors do not elect a trustee under § 702, the interim trustee becomes the trustee.

Paragraph (6) requires the trustee or debtor in possession acting in the chapter 11 or 13 case to file a final report and schedule of debts incurred in that case. This schedule will provide the information necessary for giving the notice required by paragraph (7) of the rule.

Paragraph (7) requires that claims that arose in the chapter 11 or 13 case be filed within 60 days after entry of the order converting the case to one under chapter 7. Claims not scheduled pursuant to paragraph (6) of the rule or arising from the rejection of an executory contract entered into during the chapter case may be filed within a time fixed by the court. Pursuant to § 348(c) of the Code, the conversion order is treated as the order for relief to fix the time for the trustee to assume or reject executory contracts under § 365(d).

Paragraph (8) permits the extension of the time for filing claims when claims are not timely filed but only with respect to any surplus that may remain in the estate. See also § 726(a)(2)(C) and (3) of the Code.

1987 Amendments

Paragraph (1) is amended to provide for the filing of a statement of intention in a case converted to chapter 7. Paragraph (1)(B) is added to provide for the filing of the statement of intention when a case is converted to chapter 7. The time for filing the statement of intention and for an extension of that time is governed by § 521(2)(A) of the Code. An extension of time for other required filings is governed by Rule 1007(c), which paragraph (1)(A) incorporates by reference. Because of the amendment to Rule 1007(c), the filing of new lists, schedules, and statements is now governed exclusively by Rule 1019(1).

Paragraph (3) of the rule is expanded to include the effect of conversion of a chapter 11 or 13 case to a chapter 7 case. On conversion of a case from chapter 11 or 13 to a chapter 7 case, parties have a new period within which to file claims or complaints relating to the granting of the discharge or the dischargeability of a debt. This amendment is consistent with the holding and reasoning of the court in *F & M Marquette Nat'l Bank v. Richards,* 780 F.2d 24 (8th Cir.1985).

Paragraph (4) is amended to deal directly with the status of claims which are properly listed on the schedules filed in a chapter 11 case and deemed filed pursuant to § 1111(a) of the Code. Section 1111(a) is only applicable to the chapter 11 case. On conversion of the chapter 11 case to a chapter 7 case, paragraph (4) governs the status of claims filed in the chapter 11 case. The Third Circuit properly construed paragraph (4) as applicable to claims deemed filed in the superseded chapter 11 case. *In re Crouthamel Potato Chip Co.,* 786 F.2d 141 (3d Cir.1986).

The amendment to paragraph (4) changes that result by providing that only claims that are actually filed in the chapter 11 case are treated as filed in the superseding chapter 7 case. When chapter 11 cases are converted to chapter 7 cases, difficulties in obtaining and verifying the debtors' records are common. It is unfair to the chapter 7 trustee and creditors to require that they be bound by schedules which may not be subject to verification.

Paragraph (6) is amended to place the obligation on the chapter 13 debtor to file a schedule of unpaid debts incurred during the superseded chapter 13 case.

1991 Amendments

This rule is amended to include conversion of a case from chapter 12 to chapter 7 and to implement the United States trustee system.

The amendments to paragraph (1)(A) are stylistic. Reference to the statement of executory contracts is deleted to conform to the amendment to Rule 1007(b)(1) which changes the statement to a schedule of executory contracts and unexpired leases.

Paragraph (1)(B) is amended to enable the United States trustee to monitor the progress of the case and to take appropriate action to enforce the debtor's obligation to perform the statement of intention in a timely manner.

Paragraph (2) is deleted because notice of conversion of the case is required by Rules 1017(d), 2002(f)(2), and 9022. The United States trustee, who supervises trustees pursuant to 28 U.S.C. § 586(a), may give notice of the conversion to the trustee in the superseded case.

Paragraph (6), renumbered as paragraph (5), is amended to reduce to 15 days the time for filing a schedule of postpetition debts and requires inclusion of the name and address of each creditor in connection with the postpetition debt. These changes will enable the clerk to send postpetition creditors a timely notice of the meeting of creditors held pursuant to § 341(a) of the Code. The amendments to this paragraph also provide the United States trustee with the final report and account of the superseded case, and with a copy of every schedule filed after conversion of the case. Conversion to chapter 7 terminates the service of the trustee in the superseded case pursuant to § 348(e) of the Code. Sections 704(a)(9), 1106(a)(1), 1107(a), 1202(b)(1), 1203 and 1302(b)(1) of the Code require the trustee or debtor in possession to file a final report and account with the court and the United States trustee. The words "with the court" are deleted as unnecessary. See Rules 5005(a) and 9001(3).

Paragraph (7), renumbered as paragraph (6), is amended to conform the time for filing postpetition claims to the time for filing prepetition claims pursuant to paragraph (3) (renumbered as paragraph (2)) of this rule and Rule 3002(c). This paragraph is also amended to eliminate the need for a court order to provide notice of the time for filing claims. It is anticipated that this notice will be given together with the notice of the meeting of creditors. It is amended further to avoid the need to fix a time for filing claims arising under § 365(d) if it is a no asset case upon conversion. If assets become available for distribution, the court may fix a time for filing such claims pursuant to Rule 3002(c)(4).

The additions of references to unexpired leases in paragraph (1)(A) and in paragraphs (6) and (7) (renumbered as paragraphs (5) and (6)) are technical amendments to clarify that unexpired leases are included as well as other executory contracts.

1996 Amendments

Subdivision (7) is abrogated to conform to the abrogation of Rule 3002(c)(6).

GAP Report on Rule 1019. No changes were made to the text of the rule. The Committee Note was changed to conform to the proposed changes to Rule 3002 (see GAP Report on Rule 3002 below).

1997 Amendments

The amendments to subdivisions (3) and (5) are technical corrections and stylistic changes. The phrase "superseded case" is deleted because it creates the erroneous impression that conversion of a case results in a new case that is distinct from the original case. Similarly, the phrase "original petition" is deleted because it erroneously implies that there is a second petition with respect to a converted case. See § 348 of the Code.

GAP Report on Rule 1019. No changes to the published draft.

1999 Amendments

Paragraph (1)(B) is amended to clarify that a motion for an extension of time to file a statement of intention must be made by written motion filed before the time expires, or by oral request made at a hearing before the time expires.

Subdivision (6) is amended to provide that a holder of an administrative expense claim incurred after the commencement of the case, but before conversion to chapter 7, is required to file a request for payment under § 503(a) within a time fixed by the court, rather than a proof of claim under § 501 and Rules 3001(a)-(d) and 3002. The 180-day period applicable to governmental units is intended to conform to § 502(b)(9) of the Code and Rule 3002(c)(1). It is unnecessary for the court to fix a time for filing requests for payment if it appears that there are not sufficient assets to pay preconversion administrative expenses. If a time for filing a request for payment of an administrative expense is fixed by the court, it may be enlarged as provided in Rule 9006(b). If an administrative expense claimant fails to timely file the request, it may be tardily filed under § 503(a) if permitted by the court for cause.

The final sentence of Rule 1019(6) is deleted because it is unnecessary in view of the other amendments to this paragraph. If a party has entered into a postpetition contract or lease with the trustee or debtor that constitutes an administrative expense, a timely request for payment must be filed in accordance with this paragraph and § 503(b) of the Code. The time for filing a proof of claim in connection with the rejection of any other executory contract or unexpired lease is governed by Rule 3002(c)(4).

The phrase "including the United States, any state, or any subdivision thereof" is deleted as unnecessary. Other amendments to this rule are stylistic.

GAP Report on Rule 1019. The proposed amendments to Rule 1019(6) were changed to delete the deadline for filing requests for payment of preconversion administrative expenses that would be applicable in all cases, and to provide instead that the court may fix such a deadline. The committee note was revised to clarify that it is not necessary for the court to fix a deadline where there are insufficient assets to pay preconversion administrative expenses.

2008 Amendments

Subdivision (2) is amended to include a new filing period for motions under § 707(b) and (c) of the Code when a case is converted to chapter 7. The establishment of a deadline for filing such motions is not intended to express a position as to whether such motions are permitted under the Code.

2009 Amendments

The rule is amended to implement changes in connection with the amendment to Rule 9006(a) and the manner by which time is computed under the rules. The deadlines in the rule are amended to substitute a deadline that is a multiple of seven days. Throughout the rules, deadlines are amended in the following manner:

- 5-day periods become 7-day periods
- 10-day periods become 14-day periods
- 15-day periods become 14-day periods
- 20-day periods become 21-day periods
- 25-day periods become 28-day periods

2010 Amendments

Subdivision (2). Subdivision (2) is redesignated as subdivision (2)(A), and a new subdivision (2)(B) is added to the rule. Subdivision (2)(B) provides that a new time period to object to a claim of exemption arises when a case is converted to chapter 7 from chapter 11, 12, or 13. The new time period does not arise, however, if the conversion occurs more than one year after the first order confirming a plan, even if the plan was subsequently modified. A new objection period also does not arise if the case was previously pending under chapter 7 and the objection period had expired in the prior chapter 7 case.

CROSS REFERENCES

Appointment of interim trustee, see Fed.Rules Bankr.Proc. Rule 2001, 11 USCA.

Election of trustee, see 11 USCA § 702.

Enlargement of twenty-day period for notice of order of conversion to liquidation case not permitted, see Fed.Rules Bankr.Proc. Rule 9006, 11 USCA.

Failure to effect plan or substantial consummation of confirmed plan, see 11 USCA § 1112.

Meeting of creditors or equity security holders, see Fed. Rules Bankr.Proc. Rule 2003, 11 USCA.

Rule 1020. Small Business Chapter 11 Reorganization Case

(a) Small business debtor designation

In a voluntary chapter 11 case, the debtor shall state in the petition whether the debtor is a small business debtor. In an involuntary chapter 11 case, the debtor shall file within 14 days after entry of the order for relief a statement as to whether the debtor is a small business debtor. Except as provided in subdivision (c), the status of the case as a small business case shall be in accordance with the debtor's statement under this subdivision, unless and until the court enters an order finding that the debtor's statement is incorrect.

(b) Objecting to designation

Except as provided in subdivision (c), the United States trustee or a party in interest may file an objection to the debtor's statement under subdivision

(a) no later than 30 days after the conclusion of the meeting of creditors held under § 341(a) of the Code, or within 30 days after any amendment to the statement, whichever is later.

(c) Appointment of committee of unsecured creditors

If a committee of unsecured creditors has been appointed under § 1102(a)(1), the case shall proceed as a small business case only if, and from the time when, the court enters an order determining that the committee has not been sufficiently active and representative to provide effective oversight of the debtor and that the debtor satisfies all the other requirements for being a small business. A request for a determination under this subdivision may be filed by the United States trustee or a party in interest only within a reasonable time after the failure of the committee to be sufficiently active and representative. The debtor may file a request for a determination at any time as to whether the committee has been sufficiently active and representative.

(d) Procedure for objection or determination

Any objection or request for a determination under this rule shall be governed by Rule 9014 and served on: the debtor; the debtor's attorney; the United States trustee; the trustee; any committee appointed under § 1102 or its authorized agent, or, if no committee of unsecured creditors has been appointed under § 1102, the creditors included on the list filed under Rule 1007(d); and any other entity as the court directs. (Added Apr. 11, 1997, eff. Dec. 1, 1997; amended Apr. 23, 2008, eff. Dec. 1, 2008; Mar. 26, 2009, eff. Dec. 1, 2009.)

ADVISORY COMMITTEE NOTES
1997 Amendments

This rule is designed to implement §§ 1121(e) and 1125(f), which were added to the Code by the Bankruptcy Reform Act of 1994.

GAP Report on Rule 1020. The phrase "or by a later date as the court, for cause, may fix" at the end of the published draft was deleted. The general provisions on reducing or extending time periods under Rule 9006 will be applicable.

2008 Amendments

Under the Code, as amended in 2005, there are no longer any provisions permitting or requiring a small business debtor to elect to be treated as a small business. Therefore, the election provisions in the rule are eliminated.

The 2005 amendments to the Code include several provisions relating to small business cases under chapter 11. Section 101 includes definitions of "small business debtor" and "small business case." The purpose of the new language in this rule is to provide a procedure for informing the parties, the United States trustee, and the court of whether the debtor is a small business debtor, and to provide procedures for resolving disputes regarding the proper characterization of the debtor. Because it is important to resolve such dis-

putes early in the case, a time limit for objecting to the debtor's self-designation is imposed. Rule 9006(b)(1), which governs enlargement of time, is applicable to the time limits set forth in this rule.

An important factor in determining whether the debtor is a small business debtor is whether the United States trustee has appointed a committee of unsecured creditors under § 1102, and whether such a committee is sufficiently active and representative. Subdivision (c), relating to the appointment and activity of a committee of unsecured creditors, is designed to be consistent with the Code's definition of "small business debtor."

2009 Amendments

The rule is amended to implement changes in connection with the amendment to Rule 9006(a) and the manner by which time is computed under the rules. The deadline in the rule is amended to substitute a deadline that is a multiple of seven days. Throughout the rules, deadlines are amended in the following manner:

- 5–day periods become 7–day periods
- 10–day periods become 14–day periods
- 15–day periods become 14–day periods
- 20–day periods become 21–day periods
- 25–day periods become 28–day periods

Rule 1021. Health Care Business Case

(a) Health care business designation

Unless the court orders otherwise, if a petition in a case under chapter 7, chapter 9, or chapter 11 states that the debtor is a health care business, the case shall proceed as a case in which the debtor is a health care business.

(b) Motion

The United States trustee or a party in interest may file a motion to determine whether the debtor is a health care business. The motion shall be transmitted to the United States trustee and served on: the debtor; the trustee; any committee elected under § 705 or appointed under § 1102 of the Code or its authorized agent, or, if the case is a chapter 9 municipality case or a chapter 11 reorganization case and no committee of unsecured creditors has been appointed under § 1102, the creditors included on the list filed under Rule 1007(d); and any other entity as the court directs. The motion shall be governed by Rule 9014. (Added Apr. 23, 2008, eff. Dec. 1, 2008.)

ADVISORY COMMITTEE NOTES
2008 Adoption

Section 101(27A) of the Code, added by the 2005 amendments, defines a health care business. This rule provides procedures for designating the debtor as a health care business. The debtor in a voluntary case, or petitioning creditors in an involuntary case, make that designation by checking the appropriate box on the petition. The rule also provides procedures for resolving disputes regarding the status of the debtor as a health care business.

Rule 2001. Appointment of Interim Trustee Before Order for Relief in a Chapter 7 Liquidation Case

(a) Appointment

At any time following the commencement of an involuntary liquidation case and before an order for relief, the court on written motion of a party in interest may order the appointment of an interim trustee under § 303(g) of the Code. The motion shall set forth the necessity for the appointment and may be granted only after hearing on notice to the debtor, the petitioning creditors, the United States trustee, and other parties in interest as the court may designate.

(b) Bond of movant

An interim trustee may not be appointed under this rule unless the movant furnishes a bond in an amount approved by the court, conditioned to indemnify the debtor for costs, attorney's fee, expenses, and damages allowable under § 303(i) of the Code.

(c) Order of Appointment

The order directing the appointment of an interim trustee shall state the reason the appointment is necessary and shall specify the trustee's duties.

(d) Turnover and report

Following qualification of the trustee selected under § 702 of the Code, the interim trustee, unless otherwise ordered, shall (1) forthwith deliver to the trustee all the records and property of the estate in possession or subject to control of the interim trustee and, (2) within 30 days thereafter file a final report and account.

(As amended Mar. 30, 1987, eff. Aug. 1, 1987; Apr. 30, 1991, eff. Aug. 1, 1991.)

ADVISORY COMMITTEE NOTES

This rule is adapted from former Bankruptcy Rule 201. See also former Chapter X Rule 10–201. In conformity with title 11 of the United States Code, this rule substitutes "interim trustee" for "receiver." Subdivision (a) and (e) of Rule 201 are not included because the provisions contained therein are found in detail in § 303(g) of the Code, or they are inconsistent with § 701 of the Code. Similarly, the provisions in Rule 201(d) relating to a debtor's counterbond are not included because of their presence in § 303(g).

Subdivision (a) makes it clear that the court may not on its own motion order the appointment of an interim trustee before an order for relief is entered. Appointment may be ordered only on motion of a party in interest.

Subdivision (b) requires those seeking the appointment of an interim trustee to furnish a bond. The bond may be the same one required of petitioning creditors under § 303(e) of the Code to indemnify the debtor for damages allowed by the court under § 303(i).

Subdivision (c) requires that the order specify which duties enumerated in § 303(g) shall be performed by the interim trustee. Reference should be made to Rule 2015 for additional duties required of an interim trustee including keeping records and filing periodic reports with the court.

Subdivision (d) requires turnover of records and property to the trustee selected under § 702 of the Code, after qualification. That trustee may be the interim trustee who becomes the trustee because of the failure of creditors to elect one under § 702(d) or the trustee elected by creditors under § 702(b), (c).

1991 Amendments

This rule is amended to conform to § 303(g) of the Code which provides that the United States trustee appoints the interim trustee. See Rule X–1003. This rule does not apply to the exercise by the court of the power to act sua sponte pursuant to § 105(a) of the Code.

CROSS REFERENCES

Duty to keep and file records and reports, see Fed.Rules Bankr.Proc. Rule 2015, 11 USCA.

Interim trustee, see 11 USCA § 701.

Motions, form and service, see Fed.Rules Bankr.Proc. Rule 9013, 11 USCA.

Security, proceedings against sureties, see Fed.Rules Bankr.Proc. Rule 9025, 11 USCA.

Rule 2002.　Notices to Creditors, Equity Security Holders, Administrators in Foreign Proceedings, Persons Against Whom Provisional Relief Is Sought in Ancillary and Other Cross–Border Cases, United States, and United States Trustee

(a) Twenty–one–day notices to parties in interest

Except as provided in subdivisions (h), (i), (*l*), (p), and (q) of this rule, the clerk, or some other person as the court may direct, shall give the debtor, the trustee, all creditors and indenture trustees at least 21 days' notice by mail of:

(1) the meeting of creditors under § 341 or § 1104(b) of the Code, which notice, unless the court orders otherwise, shall include the debtor's employer identification number, social security number, and any other federal taxpayer identification number;

(2) a proposed use, sale, or lease of property of the estate other than in the ordinary course of business, unless the court for cause shown shortens the time or directs another method of giving notice;

(3) the hearing on approval of a compromise or settlement of a controversy other than approval of an agreement pursuant to Rule 4001(d), unless the court for cause shown directs that notice not be sent;

(4) in a chapter 7 liquidation, a chapter 11 reorganization case, or a chapter 12 family farmer debt adjustment case, the hearing on the dismissal of the case or the conversion of the case to another chapter, unless the hearing is under § 707(a)(3) or § 707(b) or is on dismissal of the case for failure to pay the filing fee;

(5) the time fixed to accept or reject a proposed modification of a plan;

(6) a hearing on any entity's request for compensation or reimbursement of expenses if the request exceeds $1,000;

(7) the time fixed for filing proofs of claims pursuant to Rule 3003(c);

(8) the time fixed for filing objections and the hearing to consider confirmation of a chapter 12 plan; and

(9) the time fixed for filing objections to confirmation of a chapter 13 plan.

(b) Twenty–eight–day notices to parties in interest

Except as provided in subdivision (*l*) of this rule, the clerk, or some other person as the court may direct, shall give the debtor, the trustee, all creditors and indenture trustees not less than 28 days' notice by mail of the time fixed (1) for filing objections and the hearing to consider approval of a disclosure statement or, under § 1125(f), to make a final determination whether the plan provides adequate information so that a separate disclosure statement is not necessary; (2) for filing objections and the hearing to consider confirmation of a chapter 9 or chapter 11 plan; and (3) for the hearing to consider confirmation of a chapter 13 plan.

(c) Content of notice

(1) Proposed use, sale, or lease of property

Subject to Rule 6004, the notice of a proposed use, sale, or lease of property required by subdivision (a)(2) of this rule shall include the time and place of any public sale, the terms and conditions of any private sale and the time fixed for filing objections. The notice of a proposed use, sale, or lease of property, including real estate, is sufficient if it generally describes the property. The notice of a proposed sale or lease of personally identifiable information under § 363(b)(1) of the Code shall state whether the sale is consistent with any policy prohibiting the transfer of the information.

(2) Notice of hearing on compensation

The notice of a hearing on an application for compensation or reimbursement of expenses required by subdivision (a)(6) of this rule shall identify the applicant and the amounts requested.

(3) Notice of hearing on confirmation when plan provides for an injunction

If a plan provides for an injunction against conduct not otherwise enjoined under the Code, the notice required under Rule 2002(b)(2) shall:

(A) include in conspicuous language (bold, italic, or underlined text) a statement that the plan proposes an injunction;

(B) describe briefly the nature of the injunction; and

(C) identify the entities that would be subject to the injunction.

(d) Notice to equity security holders

In a chapter 11 reorganization case, unless otherwise ordered by the court, the clerk, or some other person as the court may direct, shall in the manner and form directed by the court give notice to all equity security holders of (1) the order for relief; (2) any meeting of equity security holders held pursuant to § 341 of the Code; (3) the hearing on the proposed sale of all or substantially all of the debtor's assets; (4) the hearing on the dismissal or conversion of a case to another chapter; (5) the time fixed for filing objections to and the hearing to consider approval of a disclosure statement; (6) the time fixed for filing objections to and the hearing to consider confirmation of a plan; and (7) the time fixed to accept or reject a proposed modification of a plan.

(e) Notice of no dividend

In a chapter 7 liquidation case, if it appears from the schedules that there are no assets from which a dividend can be paid, the notice of the meeting of creditors may include a statement to that effect; that it is unnecessary to file claims; and that if sufficient assets become available for the payment of a dividend, further notice will be given for the filing of claims.

(f) Other notices

Except as provided in subdivision (*l*) of this rule, the clerk, or some other person as the court may direct, shall give the debtor, all creditors, and indenture trustees notice by mail of:

(1) the order for relief;

(2) the dismissal or the conversion of the case to another chapter, or the suspension of proceedings under § 305;

(3) the time allowed for filing claims pursuant to Rule 3002;

(4) the time fixed for filing a complaint objecting to the debtor's discharge pursuant to § 727 of the Code as provided in Rule 4004;

(5) the time fixed for filing a complaint to determine the dischargeability of a debt pursuant to § 523 of the Code as provided in Rule 4007;

(6) the waiver, denial, or revocation of a discharge as provided in Rule 4006;

(7) entry of an order confirming a chapter 9, 11, or 12 plan;

(8) a summary of the trustee's final report in a chapter 7 case if the net proceeds realized exceed $1,500;

(9) a notice under Rule 5008 regarding the presumption of abuse;

(10) a statement under § 704(b)(1) as to whether the debtor's case would be presumed to be an abuse under § 707(b); and

(11) the time to request a delay in the entry of the discharge under §§ 1141(d)(5)(C), 1228(f), and 1328(h). Notice of the time fixed for accepting or rejecting a plan pursuant to Rule 3017(c) shall be given in accordance with Rule 3017(d).

(g) Addressing notices

(1) Notices required to be mailed under Rule 2002 to a creditor, indenture trustee, or equity security holder shall be addressed as such entity or an authorized agent has directed in its last request filed in the particular case. For the purposes of this subdivision—

(A) a proof of claim filed by a creditor or indenture trustee that designates a mailing address constitutes a filed request to mail notices to that address, unless a notice of no dividend has been given under Rule 2002(e) and a later notice of possible dividend under Rule 3002(c)(5) has not been given; and

(B) a proof of interest filed by an equity security holder that designates a mailing address constitutes a filed request to mail notices to that address.

(2) Except as provided in § 342(f) of the Code, if a creditor or indenture trustee has not filed a request designating a mailing address under Rule 2002(g)(1) or Rule 5003(e), the notices shall be mailed to the address shown on the list of creditors or schedule of liabilities, whichever is filed later. If an equity security holder has not filed a request designating a mailing address under Rule 2002(g)(1) or Rule 5003(e), the notices shall be mailed to the address shown on the list of equity security holders.

(3) If a list or schedule filed under Rule 1007 includes the name and address of a legal representative of an infant or incompetent person, and a person other than that representative files a request or proof of claim designating a name and mailing address that differs from the name and address of the representative included in the list or schedule, unless the court orders otherwise, notices under Rule 2002 shall be mailed to the representative included in the list or schedules and to the name and address designated in the request or proof of claim.

(4) Notwithstanding Rule 2002(g)(1)–(3), an entity and a notice provider may agree that when the notice provider is directed by the court to give a notice, the notice provider shall give the notice to the entity in the manner agreed to and at the address or addresses the entity supplies to the notice provider. That address is conclusively presumed to be a proper address for the notice. The notice provider's failure to use the supplied address does not invalidate any notice that is otherwise effective under applicable law.

(5) A creditor may treat a notice as not having been brought to the creditor's attention under § 342(g)(1) only if, prior to issuance of the notice,

the creditor has filed a statement that designates the name and address of the person or organizational subdivision of the creditor responsible for receiving notices under the Code, and that describes the procedures established by the creditor to cause such notices to be delivered to the designated person or subdivision.

(h) Notices to creditors whose claims are filed

In a chapter 7 case, after 90 days following the first date set for the meeting of creditors under § 341 of the Code, the court may direct that all notices required by subdivision (a) of this rule be mailed only to the debtor, the trustee, all indenture trustees, creditors that hold claims for which proofs of claim have been filed, and creditors, if any, that are still permitted to file claims by reason of an extension granted pursuant to Rule 3002(c)(1) or (c)(2). In a case where notice of insufficient assets to pay a dividend has been given to creditors pursuant to subdivision (e) of this rule, after 90 days following the mailing of a notice of the time for filing claims pursuant to Rule 3002(c)(5), the court may direct that notices be mailed only to the entities specified in the preceding sentence.

(i) Notices to committees

Copies of all notices required to be mailed pursuant to this rule shall be mailed to the committees elected under § 705 or appointed under § 1102 of the Code or to their authorized agents. Notwithstanding the foregoing subdivisions, the court may order that notices required by subdivision (a)(2), (3) and (6) of this rule be transmitted to the United States trustee and be mailed only to the committees elected under § 705 or appointed under § 1102 of the Code or to their authorized agents and to the creditors and equity security holders who serve on the trustee or debtor in possession and file a request that all notices be mailed to them. A committee appointed under § 1114 shall receive copies of all notices required by subdivisions (a)(1), (a)(5), (b), (f)(2), and (f)(7), and such other notices as the court may direct.

(j) Notices to the United States

Copies of notices required to be mailed to all creditors under this rule shall be mailed (1) in a chapter 11 reorganization case, to the Securities and Exchange Commission at any place the Commission designates, if the Commission has filed either a notice of appearance in the case or a written request to receive notices; (2) in a commodity broker case, to the Commodity Futures Trading Commission at Washington, D.C.; (3) in a chapter 11 case, to the Internal Revenue Service at its address set out in the register maintained under Rule 5003(e) for the district in which the case is pending; (4) if the papers in the case disclose a debt to the United States other than for taxes, to the United States attorney for the district in which the case is pending and to the department, agency, or instrumentality of the United States through which the debtor became indebted; or (5) if the filed papers disclose a stock interest of the United States, to the Secretary of the Treasury at Washington, D.C.

(k) Notices to United States trustee

Unless the case is a chapter 9 municipality case or unless the United States trustee requests otherwise, the clerk, or some other person as the court may direct, shall transmit to the United States trustee notice of the matters described in subdivisions (a)(2), (a)(3), (a)(4), (a)(8), (b), (f)(1), (f)(2), (f)(4), (f)(6), (f)(7), (f)(8), and (q) of this rule and notice of hearings on all applications for compensation or reimbursement of expenses. Notices to the United States trustee shall be transmitted within the time prescribed in subdivision (a) or (b) of this rule. The United States trustee shall also receive notice of any other matter if such notice is requested by the United States trustee or ordered by the court. Nothing in these rules requires the clerk or any other person to transmit to the United States trustee any notice, schedule, report, application or other document in a case under the Securities Investor Protection Act, 15 U.S.C. § 78aaa et.[1] seq.

(l) Notice by publication

The court may order notice by publication if it finds that notice by mail is impracticable or that it is desirable to supplement the notice.

(m) Orders designating matter of notices

The court may from time to time enter orders designating the matters in respect to which, the entity to whom, and the form and manner in which notices shall be sent except as otherwise provided by these rules.

(n) Caption

The caption of every notice given under this rule shall comply with Rule 1005. The caption of every notice required to be given by the debtor to a creditor shall include the information required to be in the notice by § 342(c) of the Code.

(o) Notice of order for relief in consumer case

In a voluntary case commenced by an individual debtor whose debts are primarily consumer debts, the clerk or some other person as the court may direct shall give the trustee and all creditors notice by mail of the order for relief within 21 days from the date thereof.

(p) Notice to a creditor with a foreign address

(1) If, at the request of the United States trustee or a party in interest, or on its own initiative, the court finds that a notice mailed within the time prescribed by these rules would not be sufficient to give a creditor with a foreign address to which notices under these rules are mailed reasonable no-

tice under the circumstances, the court may order that the notice be supplemented with notice by other means or that the time prescribed for the notice by mail be enlarged.

(2) Unless the court for cause orders otherwise, a creditor with a foreign address to which notices under this rule are mailed shall be given at least 30 days' notice of the time fixed for filing a proof of claim under Rule 3002(c) or Rule 3003(c).

(3) Unless the court for cause orders otherwise, the mailing address of a creditor with a foreign address shall be determined under Rule 2002(g).

(q) Notice of petition for recognition of foreign proceeding and of court's intention to communicate with foreign courts and foreign representatives

(1) Notice of petition for recognition

After the filing of a petition for recognition of a foreign proceeding, the court shall promptly schedule and hold a hearing on the petition. The clerk, or some other person as the court may direct, shall forthwith give the debtor, all persons or bodies authorized to administer foreign proceedings of the debtor, all entities against whom provisional relief is being sought under § 1519 of the Code, all parties to litigation pending in the United States in which the debtor is a party at the time of the filing of the petition, and such other entities as the court may direct, at least 21 days' notice by mail of the hearing. The notice shall state whether the petition seeks recognition as a foreign main proceeding or foreign nonmain proceeding and shall include the petition and any other document the court may require. If the court consolidates the hearing on the petition with the hearing on a request for provisional relief, the court may set a shorter notice period, with notice to the entities listed in this subdivision.

(2) Notice of court's intention to communicate with foreign courts and foreign representatives

The clerk, or some other person as the court may direct, shall give the debtor, all persons or bodies authorized to administer foreign proceedings of the debtor, all entities against whom provisional relief is being sought under § 1519 of the Code, all parties to litigation pending in the United States in which the debtor is a party at the time of the filing of the petition, and such other entities as the court may direct, notice by mail of the court's intention to communicate with a foreign court or foreign representative.

(As amended Pub.L. 98–91, § 2(a), Aug. 30, 1983, 97 Stat. 607; Pub.L. 98–353, Title III, § 321, July 10, 1984, 98 Stat. 357; Mar. 30, 1987, eff. Aug. 1, 1987; Apr. 30, 1991, eff. Aug. 1, 1991; Apr. 22, 1993, eff. Aug. 1, 1993; Apr. 23, 1996, eff. Dec. 1, 1996; Apr. 11, 1997, eff. Dec. 1, 1997; Apr. 26, 1999, eff. Dec. 1, 1999; Apr. 17, 2000, eff. Dec. 1, 2000; Apr. 23, 2001,

eff. Dec. 1, 2001; Mar. 27, 2003, eff. Dec. 1, 2003; Apr. 26, 2004, eff. Dec. 1, 2004; Apr. 25, 2005, eff. Dec. 1, 2005; Apr. 23, 2008, eff. Dec. 1, 2008; Mar. 26, 2009, eff. Dec. 1, 2009; Apr. 28, 2016, eff. Dec. 1, 2016; Apr. 27, 2017, eff. Dec. 1, 2017.)

1 So in original. Period probably should not appear.

ADVISORY COMMITTEE NOTES

1983 Enactments

Some of the notices required by this rule may be given either by the clerk or as the court may otherwise direct. For example, the court may order the trustee or debtor in possession to transmit one or more of the notices required by this rule, such as, notice of a proposed sale of property. See § 363(b) of the Code. When publication of notices is required or desirable, reference should be made to Rule 9008.

Notice of the order for relief is required to be given by § 342 of the Code and by subdivision (f)(1) of this rule. That notice may be combined with the notice of the meeting of creditors as indicated in Official Form No. 16, the notice and order of the meeting of creditors.

Subdivision (a) sets forth the requirement that 20 days notice be given of the significant events in a case under the Bankruptcy Code. The former Act and Rules provided a ten day notice in bankruptcy and Chapter XI [former § 701 et seq. of this title] cases, and a 20 day notice in a Chapter X [former § 501 et seq. of this title] case. This rule generally makes uniform the 20 day notice provision except that subdivision (b) contains a 25 day period for certain events in a chapter 9, 11, or 13 case. Generally, Rule 9006 permits reduction of time periods. Since notice by mail is complete on mailing, the requirement of subdivision (a) is satisfied if the notices are deposited in the mail at least 20 days before the event. See Rule 9006(e). The exceptions referred to in the introductory phrase include the modifications in the notice procedure permitted by subdivision (h) as to non-filing creditors, subdivision (i) as to cases where a committee is functioning, and subdivision (k) where compliance with subdivision (a) is impracticable.

The notice of a proposed sale affords creditors an opportunity to object to the sale and raise a dispute for the court's attention. Section 363(b) of the Code permits the trustee or debtor in possession to sell property, other than in the ordinary course of business, only after notice and hearing. If no objection is raised after notice, § 102(1) provides that there need not be an actual hearing. Thus, absent objection, there would be no court involvement with respect to a trustee's sale. Once an objection is raised, only the court may pass on it.

Prior to the Code the court could shorten the notice period for a proposed sale of property or dispense with notice. This subdivision (a), permits the 20 day period to be shortened in appropriate circumstances but the rule does not contain a provision allowing the court to dispense with notice. The rule is thus consistent with the Code, §§ 363(b) and 102(1)(A) of the Code. See 28 U.S.C. § 2075. It may be necessary, in certain circumstances, however, to use a method of notice other than mail. Subdivision (a)(2) vests the court with discretion, on cause shown, to order a different method. Reference should also be made to Rule 6004 which allows a different type of notice of proposed sales when the property is of little value.

Notice of the hearing on an application for compensation or reimbursement of expenses totalling $100 or less need not be given. In chapter 13 cases relatively small amounts are sometimes allowed for post-confirmation services and it would not serve a useful purpose to require advance notice.

Subdivision (b) is similar to subdivision (a) but lengthens the notice time to 25 days with respect to those events particularly significant in chapter 9, 11 and 13 cases. The additional time may be necessary to formulate objections to a disclosure statement or confirmation of a plan and preparation for the hearing on approval of the disclosure statement or confirmation. The disclosure statement and hearing thereon is only applicable in chapter 9 cases (§ 901(a) of the Code), and chapter 11 cases (§ 1125 of the Code).

Subdivision (c) specifies certain matters that should be included in the notice of a proposed sale of property and notice of the hearing on an application for allowances. Rule 6004 fixes the time within which parties in interest may file objections to a proposed sale of property.

Subdivision (d) relates exclusively to the notices given to equity security holders in chapter 11 cases. Under chapter 11, a plan may impair the interests of the debtor's shareholders or a plan may be a relatively simple restructuring of unsecured debt. In some cases, it is necessary that equity interest holders receive various notices and in other cases there is no purpose to be served. This subdivision indicates that the court is not mandated to order notices but rather that the matter should be treated with some flexibility. The court may decide whether notice is to be given and how it is to be given. Under § 341(b) of the Code, a meeting of equity security holders is not required in each case, only when it is ordered by the court. Thus subdivision (d)(2) requires notice only when the court orders a meeting.

In addition to the notices specified in this subdivision, there may be other events or matters arising in a case as to which equity security holders should receive notice. These are situations left to determination by the court.

Subdivision (e), authorizing a notice of the apparent insufficiency of assets for the payment of any dividend, is correlated with Rule 3002(c)(5), which provides for the issuance of an additional notice to creditors if the possibility of a payment later materializes.

Subdivision (f) provides for the transmission of other notices to which no time period applies. Clause (1) requires notice of the order for relief; this complements the mandate of § 342 of the Code requiring such notice as is appropriate of the order for relief. This notice may be combined with the notice of the meeting of creditors to avoid the necessity of more than one mailing. See Official Form No. 16, notice of meeting of creditors.

Subdivision (g) recognizes that an agent authorized to receive notices for a creditor may, without a court order, designate where notices to the creditor he represents should be addressed. Agent includes an officer of a corporation, an attorney at law, or an attorney in fact if the requisite authority has been given him. It should be noted that Official Forms Nos. 17 and 18 do not include an authorization of the holder of a power of attorney to receive notices for the creditor. Neither these forms nor this rule carries any implication that such an authorization may not be given in a power of attorney or that a request for notices to be addressed to both the creditor or his duly authorized agent may not be filed.

Subdivision (h). After the time for filing claims has expired in a chapter 7 case, creditors who have not filed their claims in accordance with Rule 3002(c) are not entitled to share in the estate except as they may come within the special provisions of § 726 of the Code or Rule 3002(c)(6). The elimination of notice to creditors who have no recognized stake in the estate may permit economies in time and expense. Reduction of the list of creditors to receive notices under this subdivision is discretionary. This subdivision does not apply to the notice of the meeting of creditors.

Subdivision (i) contains a list of matters of which notice may be given a creditors' committee or to its authorized agent in lieu of notice to the creditors. Such notice may serve every practical purpose of a notice to all the creditors and save delay and expense. In re Schulte-United, Inc., 59 F.2d 553, 561 (8th Cir.1932).

Subdivision (j). The premise for the requirement that the district director of internal revenue receive copies of notices that all creditors receive in a chapter 11 case is that every debtor is potentially a tax debtor of the United States. Notice to the district director alerts him to the possibility that a tax debtor's estate is about to be liquidated or reorganized and that the debtor may be discharged. When other indebtedness to the United States is indicated, the United States attorney is notified as the person in the best position to protect the interests of the government. In addition, the provision requires notice by mail to the head of any department, agency, or instrumentality of the United States through whose action the debtor became indebted to the United States. This rule is not intended to preclude a local rule from requiring a state or local tax authority to receive some or all of the notices to creditors under these rules.

Subdivision (k) specifies two kinds of situations in which notice by publication may be appropriate: (1) when notice by mail is impracticable; and (2) when notice by mail alone is less than adequate. Notice by mail may be impracticable when, for example, the debtor has disappeared or his records have been destroyed and the names and addresses of his creditors are unavailable, or when the number of creditors with nominal claims is very large and the estate to be distributed may be insufficient to defray the costs of issuing the notices. Supplementing notice by mail is also indicated when the debtor's records are incomplete or inaccurate and it is reasonable to believe that publication may reach some of the creditors who would otherwise be missed. Rule 9008 applies when the court directs notice by publication under this rule. Neither clause (2) of subdivision (a) nor subdivision (k) of this rule is concerned with the publication of advertisement to the general public of a sale of property of the estate at public auction under Rule 6004(b). See 3 Collier, Bankruptcy 522–23 (14th ed. 1971); 4B id. 1165–67 (1967); 2 id. ¶363.03 (15th ed. 1981).

Subdivision (m). Inclusion in notices to creditors of information as to other names used by the debtor as required by Rule 1005 will assist them in the preparation of their proofs of claim and in deciding whether to file a complaint objecting to the debtor's discharge. Additional names may be listed by the debtor on his statement of affairs when he did not file the petition. The mailing of notices should not be postponed to await a delayed filing of the statement of financial affairs.

1987 Amendments

Subdivision (a) is amended to provide that notice of a hearing on an application for compensation must be given only when the amount requested is in excess of $500.

Subdivision (d). A new notice requirement is added as clause (3). When a proposed sale is of all or substantially all of the debtor's assets, it is appropriate that equity security holders be given notice of the proposed sale. The clauses of subdivision (d) are renumbered to accommodate this addition.

Subdivision (f). Clause (7) is eliminated. Mailing of a copy of the discharge order is governed by Rule 4004(g).

Subdivision (g) is amended to relieve the clerk of the duty to mail notices to the address shown in a proof of claim when a notice of no dividend has been given pursuant to Rule 2002. This amendment avoids the necessity of the clerk searching proofs of claim which are filed in no dividend cases to ascertain whether a different address is shown.

Subdivision (n) was enacted by § 321 of the 1984 amendments.

1991 Amendments

Subdivision (a)(3) is amended to exclude compromise or settlement agreements concerning adequate protection or which modify or terminate the automatic stay, provide for use of cash collateral, or create a senior or equal lien on collateral to obtain credit. Notice requirements relating to approval of such agreements are governed by Rule 4001(d).

Subdivision (a)(5) is amended to include a hearing on dismissal or conversion of a chapter 12 case. This subdivision does not apply when a hearing is not required. It is also amended to avoid the necessity of giving notice to all creditors of a hearing on the dismissal of a consumer debtor's case based on substantial abuse of chapter 7. Such hearings on dismissal under § 707(b) of the Code are governed by Rule 1017(e).

Subdivision (a)(9) is added to provide for notice of the time fixed for filing objections and the hearing to consider confirmation of a plan in a chapter 12 case. Section 1224 of the Code requires "expedited notice" of the confirmation hearing in a chapter 12 case and requires that the hearing be concluded not later than 45 days after the filing of the plan unless the time is extended for cause. This amendment establishes 20 days as the notice period. The court may shorten this time on its own motion or on motion of a party in interest. The notice includes both the date of the hearing and the date for filing objections, and must be accompanied by a copy of the plan or a summary of the plan in accordance with Rule 3015(d).

Subdivision (b) is amended to delete as unnecessary the references to subdivisions (h) and (i).

Subdivision (d) does not require notice to equity security holders in a chapter 12 case. The procedural burden of requiring such notice is outweighed by the likelihood that all equity security holders of a family farmer will be informed of the progress of the case without formal notice. Subdivision (d) is amended to recognize that the United States trustee may convene a meeting of equity security holders pursuant to § 341(b).

Subdivision (f)(2) is amended and subdivision (f)(4) is deleted to require notice of any conversion of the case, whether the conversion is by court order or is effectuated by the debtor filing a notice of conversion pursuant to §§ 1208(a) or 1307(a). Subdivision (f)(8), renumbered (f)(7), is amended to include entry of an order confirming a chapter 12 plan. Subdivision (f)(9) is amended to increase the amount to $1,500.

Subdivisions (g) and (j) are amended to delete the words "with the court" and subdivision (i) is amended to delete the words "with the clerk" because these phrases are unnecessary. See Rules 5005(a) and 9001(3).

Subdivision (i) is amended to require that the United States trustee receive notices required by subdivision (a)(2), (3) and (7) of this rule notwithstanding a court order limiting such notice to committees and to creditors and equity security holders who request such notices. Subdivision (i) is amended further to include committees elected pursuant to § 705 of the Code and to provide that committees of retired employees appointed in chapter 11 cases receive certain notices.

Subdivision (k) is derived from Rule X-1008. The administrative functions of the United States trustee pursuant to 28 U.S.C. § 586(a) and standing to be heard on issues under § 307 and other sections of the Code require that the United States trustee be informed of developments and issues in every case except chapter 9 cases. The rule omits those notices described in subdivision (a)(1) because a meeting of creditors is convened only by the United States trustee, and those notices described in subdivision (a)(4) (date fixed for filing claims against a surplus), subdivision (a)(6) (time fixed to accept or reject proposed modification of a plan), subdivision (a)(8) (time fixed for filing proofs of claims in chapter 11 cases), subdivision (f)(3) (time fixed for filing claims in chapter 7, 12, and 13 cases), and subdivision (f)(5) (time fixed for filing complaint to determine dischargeability of debt) because these notices do not relate to matters that generally involve the United States trustee. Nonetheless, the omission of these notices does not prevent the United States trustee from receiving such notices upon request. The United States trustee also receives notice of hearings on applications for compensation or reimbursement without regard to the $500 limitation contained in subdivision (a)(7) of this rule. This rule is intended to be flexible in that it permits the United States trustee in a particular judicial district to request notices in certain categories, and to request not to receive notices in other categories, when the practice in that district makes that desirable.

1993 Amendments

Subdivision (j) is amended to avoid the necessity of sending an additional notice to the Washington, D.C. address of the Securities and Exchange Commission if the Commission prefers to have notices sent only to a local office. This change also clarifies that notices required to be mailed pursuant to this rule must be sent to the Securities and Exchange Commission only if it has filed a notice of appearance or has filed a written request. Other amendments are stylistic and make no substantive change.

1996 Amendments

Paragraph (a)(4) is abrogated to conform to the abrogation of Rule 3002(c)(6). The remaining paragraphs of subdivision (a) are renumbered, and references to these paragraphs contained in other subdivisions of this rule are amended accordingly.

Paragraph (f)(8) is amended so that a summary of the trustee's final account, which is prepared after distribution of property, does not have to be mailed to the debtor, all creditors, and indenture trustees in a chapter 7 case. Parties are sufficiently protected by receiving a summary of the trustee's final report that informs parties of the proposed distribution of property.

Subdivision (h) is amended (1) to provide that an order under this subdivision may not be issued if a notice of no dividend is given pursuant to Rule 2002(e) and the time for filing claims has not expired as provided in Rule 3002(c)(5); (2) to clarify that notices required to be mailed by subdivision (a) to parties other than creditors must be mailed to those entities despite an order issued pursuant to subdivision (h); (3) to provide that if the court, pursuant to Rule 3002(c)(1) or 3002(c)(2), has granted an extension of time to file a proof of claim, the creditor for whom the extension has been granted must continue to receive notices despite an order issued pursuant to subdivision (h); and (4) to delete references to subdivision (a)(4) and Rule 3002(c)(6), which have been abrogated.

Other amendments to this rule are stylistic.

GAP Report on Rule 2002. No changes since publication, except for stylistic changes and the correction of a typographical error in the committee note.

1997 Amendments

Paragraph (a)(1) is amended to include notice of a meeting of creditors convened under § 1104(b) of the Code for the purpose of electing a trustee in a chapter 11 case. The court for cause shown may order the 20–day period reduced pursuant to Rule 9006(c)(1).

Subdivision (n) is amended to conform to the 1994 amendment to § 342 of the Code. As provided in § 342(c), the failure of a notice given by the debtor to a creditor to contain the information required by § 342(c) does not invalidate the legal effect of the notice.

GAP Report on Rule 2002. No changes to the published draft.

1999 Amendments

Paragraph (a)(4) is amended to conform to the amendments to Rule 1017. If the United States trustee files a motion to dismiss a case for the debtor's failure to file the list of creditors, schedules, or the statement of financial affairs within the time specified in § 707(a)(3), the amendments to this rule and to Rule 1017 eliminate the requirement that all creditors receive notice of the hearing.

Paragraph (a)(4) is amended further to conform to Rule 1017(b), which requires that notice of the hearing on dismissal of a case for failure to pay the filing fee be served on only the debtor and the trustee.

Paragraph (f)(2) is amended to provide for notice of the suspension of proceedings under § 305.

GAP Report on Rule 2002. No changes since publication.

2000 Amendments

Paragraph (a)(6) is amended to increase the dollar amount from $500 to $1,000. The amount was last amended in 1987, when it was changed from $100 to $500. The amendment also clarifies that the notice is required only if a particular entity is requesting more than $1,000 as compensation or reimbursement of expenses. If several professionals are requesting compensation or reimbursement, and only one hearing will be held on all applications, notice under paragraph (a)(6) is required only with respect to the entities that have requested more than $1,000. If each applicant requests $1,000 or less, notice under paragraph (a)(6) is not required even though the aggregate amount of all applications to be considered at the hearing is more than $1,000.

If a particular entity had filed prior applications or had received compensation or reimbursement of expenses at an earlier time in the case, the amounts previously requested or awarded are not considered when determining whether the present application exceeds $1,000 for the purpose of applying this rule.

GAP Report on Rule 2002(a). No changes since publication.

2001 Amendments

Subdivision (c)(3) is added to assure that parties given notice of a hearing to consider confirmation of a plan under subdivision (b) are given adequate notice of an injunction provided for in the plan if it would enjoin conduct that is not otherwise enjoined by operation of the Code. The validity and effect of any injunction provided for in a plan are substantive law matters that are beyond the scope of these rules.

The notice requirement of subdivision (c)(3) is not applicable to an injunction contained in a plan if it is substantially the same as an injunction provided under the Code. For example, if a plan contains an injunction against acts to collect a discharged debt from the debtor, Rule 2002(c)(3) would not apply because that conduct would be enjoined under § 524(a)(2) upon the debtor's discharge. But if a plan provides that creditors will be enjoined from asserting claims against persons who are not debtors in the case, the notice of the confirmation hearing must include the information required under Rule 2002(c)(3) because that conduct would not be enjoined by operation of the Code. *See* § 524(e).

The requirement that the notice identify the entities that would be subject to the injunction requires only reasonable identification under the circumstances. If the entities that would be subject to the injunction cannot be identified by name, the notice may describe them by class or category if reasonable under the circumstances. For example, it may be sufficient for the notice to identify the entities as "all creditors of the debtor" and for the notice to be published in a manner that satisfies due process requirements.

Subdivision (g) has been revised to clarify that where a creditor or indenture trustee files both a proof of claim which includes a mailing address and a separate request designating a mailing address, the last paper filed determines the proper address. The amendments also clarify that a request designating a mailing address is effective only with respect to a particular case.

Under Rule 2002(g), a duly filed proof of claim is considered a request designating a mailing address if a notice of no dividend has been given under Rule 2002(e), but has been superseded by a subsequent notice of possible dividend under Rule 3002(c)(5). A duly filed proof of interest is considered a request designating a mailing address of an equity security holder.

Rule 2002(g)(3) is added to assure that notices to an infant or incompetent person under this rule are mailed to the appropriate guardian or other legal representative. Under Rule 1007(m), if the debtor knows that a creditor is an infant or incompetent person, the debtor is required to include in the list and schedule of creditors the name and address of the person upon whom process would be served in an adversary proceeding in accordance with Rule 7004(b)(2). If the infant or incompetent person, or another person, files a request or proof of claim designating a different name and mailing address, the notices would have to be mailed to both names and addresses until the court resolved the issue as to the proper mailing address.

The other amendments to Rule 2002(g) are stylistic.

Changes Made After Publication and Comments. In Rule 2002(c)(3), the word "highlighted" was replaced with "underlined" because highlighted documents are difficult to scan electronically for inclusion in the clerks' files. The Committee Note was revised to put in a more prominent position the statement that the validity and effect of any injunction provided for in a plan are substantive matters beyond the scope of the rules.

In Rule 2002(g), no changes were made.

2003 Amendments

Subdivision (a)(1) of the rule is amended to direct the clerk or other person giving notice of the § 341 or § 1104(b) meeting of creditors to include the debtor's full social security number on the notice. Official Form 9, the form of the notice of the meeting of creditors that will become a part of the court's file in the case, will include only the last four digits of the debtor's social security number. This rule, however, directs the clerk to include the full social security number on the notice that is served on the creditors and other identified parties, unless the court orders otherwise in a particular case. This will enable creditors and other parties in interest who are in possession of the debtor's social security number to verify the debtor's identity and proceed accordingly. The filed Official Form 9, however, will not include the debtor's full social security number. This will prevent the full social security number from becoming a part of the court's file in the case, and the number will not be included in the court's electronic records. Creditors who already have the debtor's social security number will be able to verify the existence of a case under the debtor's social security number, but any person searching the electronic case files without the number will not be able to acquire the debtor's social security number.

2004 Amendments

The rule is amended to reflect that the structure of the Internal Revenue Service no longer includes a District Director. Thus, rather than sending notice to the District Director, the rule now requires that the notices be sent to the location designated by the Service and set out in the register of addresses maintained by the clerk under Rule 5003(e). The other change is stylistic.

2005 Amendments

A new paragraph (g)(4) is inserted in the rule. The new paragraph authorizes an entity and a notice provider to agree that the notice provider will give notices to the entity at the address or addresses set out in their agreement. Rule 9001(9) sets out the definition of a notice provider.

The business of many entities is national in scope, and technology currently exists to direct the transmission of notice (both electronically and in paper form) to those entities in an accurate and much more efficient manner than by sending individual notices to the same creditor by separate mailings. The rule authorizes an entity and a notice provider to determine the manner of the service as well as to set the address or addresses to which the notices must be sent. For example, they could agree that all notices sent by the notice provider to the entity must be sent to a single, nationwide electronic or

postal address. They could also establish local or regional addresses to which notices would be sent in matters pending in specific districts. Since the entity and notice provider also can agree on the date of the commencement of service under the agreement, there is no need to set a date in the rule after which notices would have to be sent to the address or addresses that the entity establishes. Furthermore, since the entity supplies the address to the notice provider, use of that address is conclusively presumed to be proper. Nonetheless, if that address is not used, the notice still may be effective if the notice is otherwise effective under applicable law. This is the same treatment given under Rule 5003(e) to notices sent to governmental units at addresses other than those set out in that register of addresses.

The remaining subdivisions of Rule 2002(g) continue to govern the addressing of a notice that is not sent pursuant to an agreement described in Rule 2002(g)(4).

2008 Amendments

Subdivision (b) is amended to provide for 25 days' notice of the time for the court to make a final determination whether the plan in a small business case can serve as a disclosure statement. Conditional approval of a disclosure statement in a small business case is governed by Rule 3017.1 and does not require 25 days' notice. The court may consider this matter in a hearing combined with the confirmation hearing in a small business case.

Because of the requirements of Rule 6004(g), subdivision (c)(1) is amended to require that a trustee leasing or selling personally identifiable information under § 363(b)(1)(A) or (B) of the Code, as amended in 2005, include in the notice of the lease or sale transaction a statement as to whether the lease or sale is consistent with a policy prohibiting the transfer of the information.

Subdivisions (f)(9) and (10) are new. They reflect the 2005 amendments to §§ 342(d) and 704(b) of the Code. Section 342(d) requires the clerk to give notice to creditors shortly after the commencement of the case as to whether a presumption of abuse exists. Subdivision (f)(9) adds this notice to the list of notices that the clerk must give. Subdivision (f)(10) implements the amendment to § 704(b), which requires the court to provide a copy to all creditors of a statement by the United States trustee or bankruptcy administrator as to whether the debtor's case would be presumed to be an abuse under § 707(b) not later than five days after receiving it.

Subdivision (f)(11) is also added to provide notice to creditors of the debtor's filing of a statement in a chapter 11, 12, or 13 case that there is no reasonable cause to believe that § 522(q) applies in the case. This allows a creditor who disputes that assertion to request a delay of the entry of the discharge in the case.

Subdivision (g)(2) of the rule is amended because the 2005 amendments to § 342(f) of the Code permit creditors in chapter 7 and 13 individual debtor cases to file a notice with any bankruptcy court of the address to which the creditor wishes all notices to be sent. The amendment to Rule 2002(g)(2) therefore only limits application of the subdivision when a creditor files a notice under § 342(f).

New subdivision (g)(5) implements § 342(g)(1) which was added to the Code in 2005. Section 342(g)(1) allows a creditor to treat a notice as not having been brought to the creditor's attention, and so potentially ineffective, until it is received by a person or organizational subdivision that the creditor has designated to receive notices under the Bankruptcy Code. Under that section, the creditor must have established reasonable procedures for such notices to be delivered to the designated person or subdivision. The rule provides that, in order to challenge a notice under § 342(g)(1), a creditor must have filed the name and address of the designated notice recipient, as well as a description of the procedures for directing notices to that recipient, prior to the time that the challenged notice was issued. The filing required by the rule may be made as part of a creditor's filing under § 342(f), which allows a creditor to file a notice of the address to be used by all bankruptcy courts or by particular bankruptcy courts to provide notice to the creditor in cases under chapters 7 and 13. Filing the name and address of the designated notice recipient and the procedures for directing notices to that recipient will reduce uncertainty as to the proper party for receiving notice and limit factual disputes as to whether a notice recipient has been designated and as to the nature of procedures adopted to direct notices to the recipient.

Subdivision (k) is amended to add notices given under subdivision (q) to the list of notices which must be served on the United States trustee.

Section 1514(d) of the Code, added by the 2005 amendments, requires that such additional time as is reasonable under the circumstances be given to creditors with foreign addresses with respect to notices and the filing of a proof of claim. Thus, subdivision (p)(1) is added to this rule to give the court flexibility to direct that notice by other means shall supplement notice by mail, or to enlarge the notice period, for creditors with foreign addresses. If cause exists, such as likely delays in the delivery of mailed notices in particular locations, the court may order that notice also be given by email, facsimile, or private courier. Alternatively, the court may enlarge the notice period for a creditor with a foreign address. It is expected that in most situations involving foreign creditors, fairness will not require any additional notice or extension of the notice period. This rule recognizes that the court has discretion to establish procedures to determine, on its own initiative, whether relief under subdivision (p) is appropriate, but that the court is not required to establish such procedures and may decide to act only on request of a party in interest.

Subdivision (p)(2) is added to the rule to grant creditors with a foreign address to which notices are mailed at least 30 days' notice of the time within which to file proofs of claims if notice is mailed to the foreign address, unless the court orders otherwise. If cause exists, such as likely delays in the delivery of notices in particular locations, the court may extend the notice period for creditors with foreign addresses. The court may also shorten the additional notice time if circumstances so warrant. For example, if the court in a chapter 11 case determines that supplementing the notice to a foreign creditor with notice by electronic means, such as email or facsimile, would give the creditor reasonable notice, the court may order that the creditor be given only 20 days' notice in accordance with Rule 2002(a)(7).

Subdivision (p)(3) is added to provide that the court may, for cause, override a creditor's designation of a foreign address under Rule 2002(g). For example, if a party in interest believes that a creditor has wrongfully designated a foreign address to obtain additional time when it has a significant presence in the United States, the party can ask the court to order that notices to that creditor be sent to an address other than the one designated by the foreign creditor.

Subdivision (q) is added to require that notice of the hearing on the petition for recognition of a foreign proceeding be given to the debtor, all administrators in foreign proceedings of the debtor, entities against whom provisional relief is sought, and entities with whom the debtor is engaged in litigation at the time of the commencement of the case. There is no need at this stage of the proceedings to provide notice to all creditors. If the foreign representative should take action to commence a case under another chapter of the Code, the rules governing those proceedings will operate to provide that notice is given to all creditors.

The rule also requires notice of the court's intention to communicate with a foreign court or foreign representative.

2009 Amendments

The rule is amended to implement changes in connection with the amendment to Rule 9006(a) and the manner by which time is computed under the rules. The deadlines in the rule are amended to substitute a deadline that is a multiple of seven days. Throughout the rules, deadlines are amended in the following manner:

- 5–day periods become 7–day periods
- 10–day periods become 14–day periods
- 15–day periods become 14–day periods
- 20–day periods become 21–day periods
- 25–day periods become 28–day periods

2016 Amendments

Subdivision (q) is amended to clarify the procedures for giving notice in cross-border proceedings. The amended rule provides, in keeping with Code § 1517(c), for the court to schedule a hearing to be held promptly on the petition for recognition of a foreign proceeding. The amended rule contemplates that a hearing on a request for provisional relief may sometimes overlap substantially with the merits of the petition for recognition. In that case, the court may choose to consolidate the hearing on the request for provisional relief with the hearing on the petition for recognition, see Rules 1018 and 7065, and accordingly shorten the usual 21–day notice period.

2017 Amendments

Subdivisions (a) and (b) are amended and reorganized to alter the provisions governing notice under this rule in chapter 13 cases. Subdivision (a)(9) is added to require at least 21 days' notice of the time for filing objections to confirmation of a chapter 13 plan. Subdivision (b)(3) is added to provide separately for 28 days' notice of the date of the confirmation hearing in a chapter 13 case. These amendments conform to amended Rule 3015, which governs the time for presenting objections to confirmation of a chapter 13 plan. Other changes are stylistic.

HISTORICAL NOTES

Effective and Applicability Provisions

1984 Acts. Amendment by Pub.L. 98–353 effective with respect to cases filed 90 days after July 10, 1984, see section 553 of Pub.L. 98–353, set out as a note under section 101 of this title.

1983 Acts. Section 1 of Pub.L. 98–91 provided: "That rule 2002(f) of the Bankruptcy Rules, as proposed by the United States Supreme Court in the order of April 25, 1983, of the court, shall take effect on August 1, 1983, except as otherwise provided in section 2 [amending subd. (f) of this rule and enacting a provision set out as a note below]."

Section 2(b) of Pub.L. 98–91 provided that: "The amendment made by subsection (a) [amending subd. (f) of this rule] shall take effect on August 1, 1983."

CROSS REFERENCES

Form and manner of publication of notices, see Fed.Rules Bankr.Proc. Rule 9008, 11 USCA.

General requirements of form for creditors' notices, see Fed.Rules Bankr.Proc. Rule 9004, 11 USCA.

Hearing on disclosure statement in municipality debt adjustment and reorganization cases, see Fed.Rules Bankr.Proc. Rule 3017, 11 USCA.

Notice by mail complete on mailing, see Fed.Rules Bankr. Proc. Rule 9006, 11 USCA.

Notice of,

Dismissal for failure to pay filing fees, see Fed.Rules Bankr.Proc. Rule 1017, 11 USCA.

Dividend and of time to file proof of claim in liquidation case, see Fed.Rules Bankr.Proc. Rule 3002, 11 USCA.

Hearing on compromise or settlement to creditors, debtor, indenture trustees, and others designated by court, see Fed.Rules Bankr.Proc. Rule 9019, 11 USCA.

Hearing on confirmation of individual debt adjustment plan to include plan or summary, see Fed.Rules Bankr. Proc. Rule 3015, 11 USCA.

Hearing on dismissal of case, see Fed.Rules Bankr.Proc. Rule 1017, 11 USCA.

Order of conversion to liquidation case, see Fed.Rules Bankr.Proc. Rule 1019, 11 USCA.

Reduction in time periods, generally, see Fed.Rules Bankr.Proc. Rule 9006, 11 USCA.

Time extended to file claims against surplus in converted liquidation case, see Fed.Rules Bankr.Proc. Rule 1019, 11 USCA.

Time fixed for filing complaint objecting to discharge in reorganization case, see Fed.Rules Bankr.Proc. Rule 4004, 11 USCA.

Time fixed for filing complaint to determine debt's dischargeability, see Fed.Rules Bankr.Proc. Rule 4007, 11 USCA.

Use, sale, or lease of property other than in ordinary course, see Fed.Rules Bankr.Proc. Rule 6004, 11 USCA.

Waiver, denial, or revocation of discharge, see Fed.Rules Bankr.Proc. Rule 4006, 11 USCA.

Reduction in twenty-day period for notice to file claims not permitted,

Against surplus in estate in liquidation case, see Fed. Rules Bankr.Proc. Rule 9006, 11 USCA.

In municipality debt adjustment or reorganization cases, see Fed.Rules Bankr.Proc. Rule 9006, 11 USCA.

Review by court on plan's confirmation after notice and hearing pursuant to, see Fed.Rules Bankr.Proc. Rule 3020, 11 USCA.

Rule 2003. Meeting of Creditors or Equity Security Holders

(a) Date and place

Except as otherwise provided in § 341(e) of the Code, in a chapter 7 liquidation or a chapter 11 reorganization case, the United States trustee shall call a meeting of creditors to be held no fewer than 21 and no more than 40 days after the order for relief. In a chapter 12 family farmer debt adjustment case, the United States trustee shall call a meeting of creditors to be held no fewer than 21 and no more than 35 days after the order for relief. In a chapter 13 individual's debt adjustment case, the United States trustee shall call a meeting of creditors to be held no fewer than 21 and no more than 50 days after the order for relief. If there is an appeal from or a motion to vacate the order for relief, or if there is a motion to dismiss the case, the United States trustee may set a later date for the meeting. The meeting may be held at a regular place for holding court or at any other place designated by the United States trustee within the district convenient for the parties in interest. If the United States trustee designates a place for the meeting which is not regularly staffed by the United States trustee or an assistant who may preside at the meeting, the meeting may be held not more than 60 days after the order for relief.

(b) Order of meeting

(1) Meeting of creditors

The United States trustee shall preside at the meeting of creditors. The business of the meeting shall include the examination of the debtor under oath and, in a chapter 7 liquidation case, may include the election of a creditors' committee and, if the case is not under subchapter V of chapter 7, the election of a trustee. The presiding officer shall have the authority to administer oaths.

(2) Meeting of equity security holders

If the United States trustee convenes a meeting of equity security holders pursuant to § 341(b) of the Code, the United States trustee shall fix a date for the meeting and shall preside.

(3) Right to vote

In a chapter 7 liquidation case, a creditor is entitled to vote at a meeting if, at or before the meeting, the creditor has filed a proof of claim or a writing setting forth facts evidencing a right to vote pursuant to § 702(a) of the Code unless objection is made to the claim or the proof of claim is insufficient on its face. A creditor of a partnership may file a proof of claim or writing evidencing a right to vote for the trustee for the estate of a general partner notwithstanding that a trustee for the estate of the partnership has previously qualified. In the event of an objection to the amount or allowability of a claim for the purpose of voting, unless the court orders otherwise, the United States trustee shall tabulate the votes for each alternative presented by the dispute and, if resolution of such dispute is necessary to determine the result of the election, the tabulations for each alternative shall be reported to the court.

(c) Record of meeting

Any examination under oath at the meeting of creditors held pursuant to § 341(a) of the Code shall be recorded verbatim by the United States trustee using electronic sound recording equipment or other means of recording, and such record shall be preserved by the United States trustee and available for public access until two years after the conclusion of the meeting of creditors. Upon request of any entity, the United States trustee shall certify and provide a copy or transcript of such recording at the entity's expense.

(d) Report of election and resolution of disputes in a chapter 7 case

(1) Report of undisputed election

In a chapter 7 case, if the election of a trustee or a member of a creditors' committee is not disputed, the United States trustee shall promptly file a report of the election, including the name and address of the person or entity elected and a statement that the election is undisputed.

(2) Disputed election

If the election is disputed, the United States trustee shall promptly file a report stating that the election is disputed, informing the court of the nature of the dispute, and listing the name and address of any candidate elected under any alternative presented by the dispute. No later than the date on which the report is filed, the United States trustee shall mail a copy of the report to any party in interest that has made a request to receive a copy of the report. Pending disposition by the court of a disputed election for trustee, the interim trustee shall continue in office. Unless a motion for the resolution of the dispute is filed no later than 14 days after the United States trustee files a report of a disputed election for trustee, the interim trustee shall serve as trustee in the case.

(e) Adjournment

The meeting may be adjourned from time to time by announcement at the meeting of the adjourned date and time. The presiding official shall promptly file a statement specifying the date and time to which the meeting is adjourned.

(f) Special meetings

The United States trustee may call a special meeting of creditors on request of a party in interest or on the United States trustee's own initiative.

(g) Final meeting

If the United States trustee calls a final meeting of creditors in a case in which the net proceeds realized exceed $1,500, the clerk shall mail a summary of the trustee's final account to the creditors with a notice of the meeting, together with a statement of the amount of the claims allowed. The trustee shall attend the final meeting and shall, if requested, report on the administration of the estate.

(As amended Mar. 30, 1987, eff. Aug. 1, 1987; Apr. 30, 1991, eff. Aug. 1, 1991; Apr. 22, 1993, eff. Aug. 1, 1993; Apr. 26, 1999, eff. Dec. 1, 1999; Mar. 27, 2003, eff. Dec. 1, 2003; Apr. 23, 2008, eff. Dec. 1, 2008; Mar. 26, 2009, eff. Dec. 1, 2009; Apr. 26, 2011, eff. Dec. 1, 2011.)

ADVISORY COMMITTEE NOTES

Section 341(a) of the Code requires a meeting of creditors in a chapter 7, 11 or 13 case, and § 341(b) permits the court to order a meeting of equity security holders. A major change from prior law, however, prohibits the judge from attending or presiding over the meeting. Section 341(c).

This rule does not apply either in a case for the reorganization of a railroad or for the adjustment of debts of a municipality. Sections 1161 and 901 render §§ 341 and 343 inapplicable in these types of cases. Section 341 sets the requirement for a meeting of creditors and § 343 provides for the examination of the debtor.

Subdivision (a). The meeting is to be held between 20 and 40 days after the date of the order for relief. In a voluntary case, the date of the order for relief is the date of the filing of the petition (§ 301 of the Code); in an involuntary case, it is the date of an actual order (§ 303(i) of the Code).

Subdivision (b) provides flexibility as to who will preside at the meeting of creditors. The court may designate a person to serve as presiding officer, such as the interim trustee appointed under § 701 of the Code. If the court does not designate anyone, the clerk will preside. In either case, creditors may elect a person of their own choosing. In any event, the clerk may remain to record the proceedings and take appearances. Use of the clerk is not contrary to the legislative policy of § 341(c). The judge remains insulated from any information coming forth at the meeting and any information obtained by the clerk must not be relayed to the judge.

Although the clerk may preside at the meeting, the clerk is not performing any kind of judicial role, nor should the clerk give any semblance of performing such a role. It would be pretentious for the clerk to ascend the bench, don a robe or be addressed as "your honor". The clerk should not appear to parties or others as any type of judicial officer.

In a chapter 11 case, if a committee of unsecured creditors has been appointed pursuant to § 1102(a)(1) of the Code and a chairman has been selected, the chairman will preside or a person, such as the attorney for the committee, may be designated to preside by the chairman.

Since the judge must fix the bond of the trustee but cannot be present at the meeting, the rule allows the creditors to recommend the amount of the bond. They should be able to obtain relevant information concerning the extent of assets of the debtor at the meeting.

Paragraph (1) authorizes the presiding officer to administer oaths. This is important because the debtor's examination must be under oath.

Paragraph (3) of subdivision (b) has application only in a chapter 7 case. That is the only type of case under the Code that permits election of a trustee or committee. In all other cases, no vote is taken at the meeting of creditors. If it is necessary for the court to make a determination with respect to a claim, the meeting may be adjourned until the objection or dispute is resolved.

The second sentence recognizes that partnership creditors may vote for a trustee of a partner's estate along with the separate creditors of the partner. Although § 723(c) gives the trustee of a partnership a claim against a partner's estate for the full amount of partnership creditors' claims allowed, the purpose and function of this provision are to simplify distribution and prevent double proof, not to disfranchise partnership creditors in electing a trustee of an estate against which they hold allowable claims.

Subdivision (c) requires minutes and a record of the meeting to be maintained by the presiding officer. A verbatim record must be made of the debtor's examination but the rule is flexible as to the means used to record the examination.

Subdivision (d) recognizes that the court must be informed immediately about the election or nonelection of a trustee in a chapter 7 case. Pursuant to Rule 2008, the clerk officially informs the trustee of his election or appointment and how he is to qualify. The presiding person has no authority to resolve a disputed election.

For purposes of expediency, the results of the election should be obtained for each alternative presented by the dispute and immediately reported to the court. Thus, when an interested party presents the dispute to the court, its prompt resolution by the court will determine the dispute and a new or adjourned meeting to conduct the election may be avoided. The clerk is not an interested party.

A creditors' committee may be elected only in a chapter 7 case. In chapter 11 cases, a creditors' committee is appointed pursuant to § 1102.

While a final meeting is not required, Rule 2002(f)(10) provides for the trustee's final account to be sent to creditors.

1987 Amendments

Subdivision (a). Many courts schedule meetings of creditors at various locations in the district. Because the clerk must schedule meetings at those locations, an additional 20 days for scheduling the meetings is provided under the amended rule.

1991 Amendments

The amendment to subdivision (a) relating to the calling of the meeting of creditors in a chapter 12 case is consistent with the expedited procedures of chapter 12. Subdivision (a) is also amended to clarify that the United States trustee does not call a meeting of creditors in a chapter 9 case. Pursuant to § 901(a) of the Code, § 341 is inapplicable in chapter 9 cases. The other amendments to subdivisions (a), (b)(1), and (b)(2) and the additions of subdivisions (f) and (g) are derived from Rule X–1006 and conform to the 1986 amendments to § 341 of the Code. The second sentence of subdivision (b)(3) is amended because Rule 2009(e) is abrogated. Although the United States trustee fixes the date for the meeting, the clerk

of the bankruptcy court transmits the notice of the meeting unless the court orders otherwise, as prescribed in Rule 2002(a)(1).

Pursuant to § 702 and § 705 of the Code, creditors may elect a trustee and a committee in a chapter 7 case. Subdivision (b) of this rule provides that the United States trustee shall preside over any election that is held under those sections. The deletion of the last sentence of subdivision (b)(1) does not preclude creditors from recommending to the United States trustee the amount of the trustee's bond when a trustee is elected. Trustees and committees are not elected in chapter 11, 12, and 13 cases.

If an election is disputed, the United States trustee shall not resolve the dispute. For purposes of expediency, the United States trustee shall tabulate the results of the election for each alternative presented by the dispute. However, if the court finds that such tabulation is not feasible under the circumstances, the United States trustee need not tabulate the votes. If such tabulation is feasible and if the disputed vote or votes would affect the result of the election, the tabulations of votes for each alternative presented by the dispute shall be reported to the court. If a motion is made for resolution of the dispute in accordance with subdivision (d) of this rule, the court will determine the issue and another meeting to conduct the election may not be necessary.

Subdivisions (f) and (g) are derived from Rule X–1006(d) and (e), except that the amount is increased to $1,500 to conform to the amendment to Rule 2002(f).

1993 Amendments

Subdivision (a) is amended to extend by ten days the time for holding the meeting of creditors in a chapter 13 case. This extension will provide more flexibility for scheduling the meeting of creditors. Other amendments are stylistic and make no substantive change.

1999 Amendments

Subdivision (d) is amended to require the United States trustee to mail a copy of a report of a disputed election to any party in interest that has requested a copy of it. Also, if the election is for a trustee, the rule as amended will give a party in interest ten days from the filing of the report, rather than from the date of the meeting of creditors, to file a motion to resolve the dispute.

The substitution of "United States trustee" for "presiding officer" is stylistic. Section 341(a) of the Code provides that the United States trustee shall preside at the meeting of creditors. Other amendments are designed to conform to the style of Rule 2007.1(b)(3) regarding the election of a trustee in a chapter 11 case.

GAP Report on Rule 2003. No changes since publication.

2003 Amendments

The rule is amended to reflect the enactment of subchapter V of chapter 7 of the Code governing multilateral clearing organization liquidations. Section 782 of the Code provides that the designation of a trustee or alternative trustee for the case is made by the Federal Reserve Board. Therefore, the meeting of creditors in those cases cannot include the election of a trustee.

2008 Amendments

If the debtor has solicited acceptances to a plan before commencement of the case, § 341(e), which was added to the Code by the 2005 amendments, authorizes the court, on request of a party in interest and after notice and a hearing, to order that a meeting of creditors not be convened. The rule is amended to recognize that a meeting of creditors might not be held in those cases.

2009 Amendments

The rule is amended to implement changes in connection with the amendment to Rule 9006(a) and the manner by which time is computed under the rules. The deadlines in the rule are amended to substitute a deadline that is a multiple of seven days. Throughout the rules, deadlines are amended in the following manner:

- 5–day periods become 7–day periods
- 10–day periods become 14–day periods
- 15–day periods become 14–day periods
- 20–day periods become 21–day periods
- 25–day periods become 28–day periods

2011 Amendments

Subdivision (e). Subdivision (e) is amended to require the presiding official to file a statement after the adjournment of a meeting of creditors or equity security holders designating the period of the adjournment. The presiding official is the United States trustee or the United States trustee's designee. This requirement will provide notice to parties in interest not present at the initial meeting of the date and time to which the meeting has been continued. An adjourned meeting is "held open" as permitted by § 1308(b)(1) of the Code. The filing of this statement will also discourage premature motions to dismiss or convert the case under § 1307(e).

CROSS REFERENCES

Affirmations, see Fed.Rules Bankr.Proc. Rule 9012, 11 USCA.

Election of creditors' committee in liquidation case, see 11 USCA § 705.

Eligibility to serve as and qualification of trustee, see 11 USCA §§ 321 and 322.

Enlargement of time not permitted,

  Date of meeting of creditors, see Fed.Rules Bankr.Proc. Rule 9006, 11 USCA.

  Motion for resolution of trustee election dispute, see Fed.Rules Bankr.Proc. Rule 9006, 11 USCA.

Holders of multiple proxies to file list of proxies to be voted, see Fed.Rules Bankr.Proc. Rule 2006, 11 USCA.

Inapplicability of this rule to,

  Municipality debt adjustment case, see 11 USCA § 901.

  Railroad reorganization case, see 11 USCA § 1161.

Interim trustee in liquidation case, see Fed.Rules Bankr. Proc. Rule 2001, 11 USCA, and 11 USCA § 701.

Motions, form and service, see Fed.Rules Bankr.Proc. Rule 9013, 11 USCA.

Reduction of twenty-day period for date of meeting of creditors not permitted, see Fed.Rules Bankr.Proc. Rule 9006, 11 USCA.

Selection and substitution of trustees, see Fed.Rules Bankr. Proc. Rule 2008 and Rule 2012, 11 USCA.

Time for objections to property claimed to be exempt, see Fed.Rules Bankr.Proc. Rule 4003, 11 USCA.

Rule 2004.   Examination

(a) Examination on motion

On motion of any party in interest, the court may order the examination of any entity.

(b) Scope of examination

The examination of an entity under this rule or of the debtor under § 343 of the Code may relate only to the acts, conduct, or property or to the liabilities and financial condition of the debtor, or to any matter which may affect the administration of the debtor's estate, or to the debtor's right to a discharge. In a family farmer's debt adjustment case under chapter 12, an individual's debt adjustment case under chapter 13, or a reorganization case under chapter 11 of the Code, other than for the reorganization of a railroad, the examination may also relate to the operation of any business and the desirability of its continuance, the source of any money or property acquired or to be acquired by the debtor for purposes of consummating a plan and the consideration given or offered therefor, and any other matter relevant to the case or to the formulation of a plan.

(c) Compelling attendance and production of documents

The attendance of an entity for examination and for the production of documents, whether the examination is to be conducted within or without the district in which the case is pending, may be compelled as provided in Rule 9016 for the attendance of a witness at a hearing or trial. As an officer of the court, an attorney may issue and sign a subpoena on behalf of the court for the district in which the examination is to be held if the attorney is admitted to practice in that court or in the court in which the case is pending.

(d) Time and place of examination of debtor

The court may for cause shown and on terms as it may impose order the debtor to be examined under this rule at any time or place it designates, whether within or without the district wherein the case is pending.

(e) Mileage

An entity other than a debtor shall not be required to attend as a witness unless lawful mileage and witness fee for one day's attendance shall be first tendered. If the debtor resides more than 100 miles from the place of examination when required to appear for an examination under this rule, the mileage allowed by law to a witness shall be tendered for any distance more than 100 miles from the debtor's residence at the date of the filing of the first petition commencing a case under the Code or the residence at the time the debtor is required to appear for the examination, whichever is the lesser.

(As amended Mar. 30, 1987, eff. Aug. 1, 1987; Apr. 30, 1991, eff. Aug. 1, 1991; Apr. 29, 2002, eff. Dec. 1, 2002.)

ADVISORY COMMITTEE NOTES

Subdivision (a) of this rule is derived from former Bankruptcy Rule 205(a). See generally 2 Collier, Bankruptcy ¶¶343.02, 343.08, 343.13 (15th ed. 1981). It specifies the manner of moving for an examination. The motion may be heard ex parte or it may be heard on notice.

Subdivision (b) is derived from former Bankruptcy Rules 205(d) and 11–26.

Subdivision (c) specifies the mode of compelling attendance of a witness or party for an examination and for the production of evidence under this rule. The subdivision is substantially declaratory of the practice that had developed under § 21a of the Act [former § 44(a) of this title]. See 2 Collier, supra ¶343.11.

This subdivision will be applicable for the most part to the examination of a person other than the debtor. The debtor is required to appear at the meeting of creditors for examination. The word "person" includes the debtor and this subdivision may be used if necessary to obtain the debtor's attendance for examination.

Subdivision (d) is derived from former Bankruptcy Rule 205(f) and is not a limitation on subdivision (c). Any person, including the debtor, served with a subpoena within the range of a subpoena must attend for examination pursuant to subdivision (c). Subdivision (d) applies only to the debtor and a subpoena need not be issued. There are no territorial limits on the service of an order on the debtor. See, e.g., In re Totem Lodge & Country Club, Inc., 134 F.Supp. 158 (S.D.N.Y.1955).

Subdivision (e) is derived from former Bankruptcy Rule 205(g). The lawful mileage and fee for attendance at a United States court as a witness are prescribed by 28 U.S.C. § 1821.

Definition of debtor. The word "debtor" as used in this rule includes the persons specified in the definition in Rule 9001(5).

Spousal privilege. The limitation on the spousal privilege formerly contained in § 21a of the Act [former § 44(a) of this title] is not carried over in the Code. For privileges generally, see Rule 501 of the Federal Rules of Evidence made applicable in cases under the Code by Rule 1101 thereof.

1991 Amendments

This rule is amended to allow the examination in a chapter 12 case to cover the same matters that may be covered in an examination in a chapter 11 or 13 case.

2002 Amendments

Subdivision (c) is amended to clarify that an examination ordered under Rule 2004(a) may be held outside the district in which the case is pending if the subpoena is issued by the court for the district in which the examination is to be held and is served in the manner provided in Rule 45 F.R.Civ.P., made applicable by Rule 9016.

The subdivision is amended further to clarify that, in addition to the procedures for the issuance of a subpoena set forth in Rule 45 F.R.Civ.P., an attorney may issue and sign a subpoena on behalf of the court for the district in which a Rule 2004 examination is to be held if the attorney is authorized to practice, even if admitted pro hac vice, either in the court in which the case is pending or in the court for the district in which the examination is to be held. This provision supplements the procedures for the issuance of a subpoena set forth in Rule 45(a)(3)(A) and (B) F.R.Civ.P. and is consistent with one of the purposes of the 1991 amendments to Rule 45, to ease the burdens of interdistrict law practice.

Changes Made After Publication and Comments. The typographical error was corrected, but no other changes were made.

CROSS REFERENCES

Allowances and travel expenses of witnesses, see 28 USCA § 1821.

Apprehension and removal of debtor to compel attendance for examination, see Fed.Rules Bankr.Proc. Rule 2005, 11 USCA.

Debtor as corporation or partnership for purposes of this rule, see Fed.Rules Bankr.Proc. Rule 9001, 11 USCA.

Duty of bankrupt to,

Attend hearing on right to discharge, see 11 USCA § 524.

Submit to examination, see Fed.Rules Bankr.Proc. Rule 4002, 11 USCA.

Duty of trustee to investigate debtor,

Individual debt adjustment case, see 11 USCA § 1302.

Liquidation case, see 11 USCA § 704.

Examination of debtor concerning compensation agreements with attorney, see Fed.Rules Bankr.Proc. Rule 2017, 11 USCA.

Immunity from self-incrimination, see 11 USCA § 344.

Motions, form and service, see Fed.Rules Bankr.Proc. Rule 9013, 11 USCA.

Privileges, see Fed.Rules Evid. Rule 501, 28 USCA.

Subpoena, see Fed.Rules Civ.Proc. Rule 45, 28 USCA.

Rule 2005. Apprehension and Removal of Debtor to Compel Attendance for Examination

(a) Order to compel attendance for examination

On motion of any party in interest supported by an affidavit alleging (1) that the examination of the debtor is necessary for the proper administration of the estate and that there is reasonable cause to believe that the debtor is about to leave or has left the debtor's residence or principal place of business to avoid examination, or (2) that the debtor has evaded service of a subpoena or of an order to attend for examination, or (3) that the debtor has willfully disobeyed a subpoena or order to attend for examination, duly served, the court may issue to the marshal, or some other officer authorized by law, an order directing the officer to bring the debtor before the court without unnecessary delay. If, after hearing, the court finds the allegations to be true, the court shall thereupon cause the debtor to be examined forthwith. If necessary, the court shall fix conditions for further examination and for the debtor's obedience to all orders made in reference thereto.

(b) Removal

Whenever any order to bring the debtor before the court is issued under this rule and the debtor is found in a district other than that of the court issuing the order, the debtor may be taken into custody under the order and removed in accordance with the following rules:

(1) If the debtor is taken into custody under the order at a place less than 100 miles from the place of issue of the order, the debtor shall be brought forthwith before the court that issued the order.

(2) If the debtor is taken into custody under the order at a place 100 miles or more from the place of issue of the order, the debtor shall be brought without unnecessary delay before the nearest available United States magistrate judge, bankruptcy judge, or district judge. If, after hearing, the magistrate judge, bankruptcy judge, or district judge finds that an order has issued under this rule and that the person in custody is the debtor, or if the person in custody waives a hearing, the magistrate judge, bankruptcy judge, or district judge shall order removal, and the person in custody shall be released on conditions ensuring prompt appearance before the court that issued the order to compel the attendance.

(c) Conditions of release

In determining what conditions will reasonably assure attendance or obedience under subdivision (a) of this rule or appearance under subdivision (b) of this rule, the court shall be governed by the provisions and policies of title 18, U.S.C., § 3146(a) and (b).

(As amended Mar. 30, 1987, eff. Aug. 1, 1987; Apr. 22, 1993, eff. Aug. 1, 1993.)

ADVISORY COMMITTEE NOTES

This rule is derived from former Bankruptcy Rule 206. The rule requires the debtor to be examined as soon as possible if allegations of the movant for compulsory examination under this rule are found to be true after a hearing. Subdivision (b) includes in paragraphs (1) and (2) provisions adapted from subdivisions (a) and (b) of Rule 40 of the Federal Rules of Criminal Procedure, which governs the handling of a person arrested in one district on a warrant issued in another. Subdivision (c) incorporates by reference the features of subdivisions (a) and (b) of 18 U.S.C. § 3146, which prescribe standards, procedures and factors to be considered in determining conditions of release of accused persons in noncapital cases prior to trial. The word "debtor" as used in this rule includes the persons named in Rule 9001(5).

The affidavit required to be submitted in support of the motion may be subscribed by the unsworn declaration provided for in 28 U.S.C. § 1746.

1993 Amendments

Subdivision (b)(2) is amended to conform to § 321 of the Judicial Improvements Act of 1990, Pub. L. No. 101–650, which changed the title of "United States magistrate" to "United States magistrate judge." Other amendments are stylistic and make no substantive change.

Change of Name

United States magistrate appointed under section 631 of Title 28, Judiciary and Judicial Procedure, to be known as United States magistrate judge after Dec. 1, 1990, with any reference to United States magistrate or magistrate in Title 28, in any other Federal statute, etc., deemed a reference to United States magistrate judge appointed under section 631 of Title 28, see section 321 of Pub.L. 101–650, set out as a note under section 631 of Title 28.

CROSS REFERENCES

Commitment to another district, removal, see Fed.Rules Cr.Proc. Rule 40, 18 USCA.

Debtor as corporation or partnership for purposes of this rule, see Fed.Rules Bankr.Proc. Rule 9001, 11 USCA.

Motions, form and service, see Fed.Rules Bankr.Proc. Rule 9013, 11 USCA.

Rule 2006. Solicitation and Voting of Proxies in Chapter 7 Liquidation Cases

(a) Applicability

This rule applies only in a liquidation case pending under chapter 7 of the Code.

(b) Definitions

(1) Proxy

A proxy is a written power of attorney authorizing any entity to vote the claim or otherwise act as the owner's attorney in fact in connection with the administration of the estate.

(2) Solicitation of proxy

The solicitation of a proxy is any communication, other than one from an attorney to a regular client who owns a claim or from an attorney to the owner of a claim who has requested the attorney to represent the owner, by which a creditor is asked, directly or indirectly, to give a proxy after or in contemplation of the filing of a petition by or against the debtor.

(c) Authorized solicitation

(1) A proxy may be solicited only by (A) a creditor owning an allowable unsecured claim against the estate on the date of the filing of the petition; (B) a committee elected pursuant to § 705 of the Code; (C) a committee of creditors selected by a majority in number and amount of claims of creditors (i) whose claims are not contingent or unliquidated, (ii) who are not disqualified from voting under § 702(a) of the Code and (iii) who were present or represented at a meeting of which all creditors having claims of over $500 or the 100 creditors having the largest claims had at least

seven days' notice in writing and of which meeting written minutes were kept and are available reporting the names of the creditors present or represented and voting and the amounts of their claims; or (D) a bona fide trade or credit association, but such association may solicit only creditors who were its members or subscribers in good standing and had allowable unsecured claims on the date of the filing of the petition.

(2) A proxy may be solicited only in writing.

(d) Solicitation not authorized

This rule does not permit solicitation (1) in any interest other than that of general creditors; (2) by or on behalf of any custodian; (3) by the interim trustee or by or on behalf of any entity not qualified to vote under § 702(a) of the Code; (4) by or on behalf of an attorney at law; or (5) by or on behalf of a transferee of a claim for collection only.

(e) Data required from holders of multiple proxies

At any time before the voting commences at any meeting of creditors pursuant to § 341(a) of the Code, or at any other time as the court may direct, a holder of two or more proxies shall file and transmit to the United States trustee a verified list of the proxies to be voted and a verified statement of the pertinent facts and circumstances in connection with the execution and delivery of each proxy, including:

(1) a copy of the solicitation;

(2) identification of the solicitor, the forwarder, if the forwarder is neither the solicitor nor the owner of the claim, and the proxyholder, including their connections with the debtor and with each other. If the solicitor, forwarder, or proxyholder is an association, there shall also be included a statement that the creditors whose claims have been solicited and the creditors whose claims are to be voted were members or subscribers in good standing and had allowable unsecured claims on the date of the filing of the petition. If the solicitor, forwarder, or proxyholder is a committee of creditors, the statement shall also set forth the date and place the committee was organized, that the committee was organized in accordance with clause (B) or (C) of paragraph (c)(1) of this rule, the members of the committee, the amounts of their claims, when the claims were acquired, the amounts paid therefor, and the extent to which the claims of the committee members are secured or entitled to priority;

(3) a statement that no consideration has been paid or promised by the proxyholder for the proxy;

(4) a statement as to whether there is any agreement and, if so, the particulars thereof, between the proxyholder and any other entity for the payment of any consideration in connection with voting the proxy, or for the sharing of compensation with any entity, other than a member or regular associate of the proxyholder's law firm, which may be allowed the trustee or any entity for services rendered in the case, or for the employment of any person as attorney, accountant, appraiser, auctioneer, or other employee for the estate;

(5) if the proxy was solicited by an entity other than the proxyholder, or forwarded to the holder by an entity who is neither a solicitor of the proxy nor the owner of the claim, a statement signed and verified by the solicitor or forwarder that no consideration has been paid or promised for the proxy, and whether there is any agreement, and, if so, the particulars thereof, between the solicitor or forwarder and any other entity for the payment of any consideration in connection with voting the proxy, or for sharing compensation with any entity, other than a member or regular associate of the solicitor's or forwarder's law firm which may be allowed the trustee or any entity for services rendered in the case, or for the employment of any person as attorney, accountant, appraiser, auctioneer, or other employee for the estate;

(6) if the solicitor, forwarder, or proxyholder is a committee, a statement signed and verified by each member as to the amount and source of any consideration paid or to be paid to such member in connection with the case other than by way of dividend on the member's claim.

(f) Enforcement of restrictions on solicitation

On motion of any party in interest or on its own initiative, the court may determine whether there has been a failure to comply with the provisions of this rule or any other impropriety in connection with the solicitation or voting of a proxy. After notice and a hearing the court may reject any proxy for cause, vacate any order entered in consequence of the voting of any proxy which should have been rejected, or take any other appropriate action.

(As amended Mar. 30, 1987, eff. Aug. 1, 1987; Apr. 30, 1991, eff. Aug. 1, 1991; Mar. 26, 2009, eff. Dec. 1, 2009.)

ADVISORY COMMITTEE NOTES

This rule is a comprehensive regulation of solicitation and voting of proxies in liquidation cases. It is derived from former Bankruptcy Rule 208. The rule applies only in chapter 7 cases because no voting occurs, other than on a plan, in a chapter 11 case. Former Bankruptcy Rule 208 did not apply to solicitations of acceptances of plans.

Creditor control was a basic feature of the Act and is continued, in part, by the Code. Creditor democracy is perverted and the congressional objective frustrated, however, if control of administration falls into the hands of persons whose principal interest is not in what the estate can be made to yield to the unsecured creditors but in what it can yield to those involved in its administration or in other ulterior objectives.

Subdivision (b). The definition of proxy in the first paragraph of subdivision (b) is derived from former Bankruptcy Rule 208.

Subdivision (c). The purpose of the rule is to protect creditors against loss of control of administration of their debtors' estates to holders of proxies having interests that differ from those of the creditors. The rule does not prohibit solicitation but restricts it to those who were creditors at the commencement of the case or their freely and fairly selected representatives. The special role occupied by credit and trade associations is recognized in the last clause of subdivision (c)(1). On the assumption that members or subscribers may have affiliated with an association in part for the purpose of obtaining its services as a representative in liquidation proceedings, an established association is authorized to solicit its own members, or its regular customers or clients, who were creditors on the date of the filing of the petition. Although the association may not solicit nonmembers or nonsubscribers for proxies, it may sponsor a meeting of creditors at which a committee entitled to solicit proxies may be selected in accordance with clause (C) of subdivision (c)(1).

Under certain circumstances, the relationship of a creditor, creditors' committee, or association to the estate or the case may be such as to warrant rejection of any proxy solicited by such a person or group. Thus a person who is forbidden by the Code to vote his own claim should be equally disabled to solicit proxies from creditors. Solicitation by or on behalf of the debtor has been uniformly condemned, e.g., In re White, 15 F.2d 371 (9th Cir. 1926), as has solicitation on behalf of a preferred creditor, Matter of Law, 13 Am.B.R. 650 (S.D.Ill. 1905). The prohibition on solicitation by a receiver or his attorney made explicit by General Order 39 has been collaterally supported by rulings rejecting proxies solicited by a receiver in equity, In re Western States Bldg.-Loan Ass'n, 54 F.2d 415 (S.D.Cal.1931), and by an assignee for the benefit of creditors, Lines v. Falstaff Brewing Co., 233 F.2d 927 (9th Cir. 1956).

Subdivision (d) prohibits solicitation by any person or group having a relationship described in the preceding paragraph. It also makes no exception for attorneys or transferees of claims for collection. The rule does not undertake to regulate communications between an attorney and his regular client or between an attorney and a creditor who has asked the attorney to represent him in a proceeding under the Code, but any other communication by an attorney or any other person or group requesting a proxy from the owner of a claim constitutes a regulated solicitation. Solicitation by an attorney of a proxy from a creditor who was not a client prior to the solicitation is objectionable not only as unethical conduct as recognized by such cases as In the Matter of Darland Company, 184 F.Supp. 760 (S.D.Iowa 1960) but also and more importantly because the practice carries a substantial risk that administration will fall into the hands of those whose interest is in obtaining fees from the estate rather than securing dividends for creditors. The same risk attaches to solicitation by the holder of a claim for collection only.

Subdivision (e). The regulation of solicitation and voting of proxies is achieved by the rule principally through the imposition of requirements of disclosure on the holders of two or more proxies. The disclosures must be made to the clerk before the meeting at which the proxies are to be voted to afford the clerk or a party in interest an opportunity to examine the circumstances accompanying the acquisition of the proxies in advance of any exercise of the proxies. In the light of the examination the clerk or a party in interest should bring to the attention of the judge any question that arises and the judge may permit the proxies that comply with the rule to be voted and reject those that do not unless the holders can effect or establish compliance in such manner as the court shall prescribe. The holders of single proxies are excused from the disclosure requirements because of the insubstantiality of the risk that such proxies have been solicited, or will be voted, in an interest other than that of general creditors.

Every holder of two or more proxies must include in the submission a verified statement that no consideration has been paid or promised for the proxy, either by the proxyholder or the solicitor or any forwarder of the proxy. Any payment or promise of consideration for a proxy would be conclusive evidence of a purpose to acquire control of the administration of an estate for an ulterior purpose. The holder of multiple proxies must also include in the submission a verified statement as to whether there is any agreement by the holder, the solicitor, or any forwarder of the proxy for the employment of any person in the administration of an estate or for the sharing of any compensation allowed in connection with the administration of the estate. The provisions requiring these statements implement the policy of the Code expressed in § 504 as well as the policy of this rule to deter the acquisition of proxies for the purpose of obtaining a share in the outlays for administration. Finally the facts as to any consideration moving or promised to any member of a committee which functions as a solicitor, forwarder, or proxyholder must be disclosed by the proxyholder. Such information would be of significance to the court in evaluating the purpose of the committee in obtaining, transmitting, or voting proxies.

Subdivision (f) has counterparts in the local rules referred to in the Advisory Committee's Note to former Bankruptcy Rule 208. Courts have been accorded a wide range of discretion in the handling of disputes involving proxies. Thus the referee was allowed to reject proxies and to proceed forthwith to hold a scheduled election at the same meeting. E.g., In re Portage Wholesale Co., 183 F.2d 959 (7th Cir. 1950); In re McGill, 106 Fed. 57 (6th Cir. 1901); In re Deena Woolen Mills, Inc., 114 F.Supp. 260, 273 (D.Me.1953); In re Finlay, 3 Am.B.R. 738 (S.D.N.Y.1900). The bankruptcy judge may postpone an election to permit a determination of issues presented by a dispute as to proxies and to afford those creditors whose proxies are rejected an opportunity to give new proxies or to attend an adjourned meeting to vote their own claims. Cf. In the Matter of Lenrick Sales, Inc., 369 F.2d 439, 442–43 (3d Cir.), cert. denied, 389 U.S. 822 (1967); In the Matter of Construction Supply Corp., 221 F.Supp. 124, 128 (E.D.Va.1963). This rule is not intended to restrict the scope of the court's discretion in the handling of disputes as to proxies.

1991 Amendments

This rule is amended to give the United States trustee information in connection with proxies so that the United States trustee may perform responsibilities as presiding officer at the § 341 meeting of creditors. See Rule 2003.

The words "with the clerk" are deleted as unnecessary. See Rules 5005(a) and 9001(3).

2009 Amendments

The rule is amended to implement changes in connection with the amendment to Rule 9006(a) and the manner by which time is computed under the rules. The deadline in the rule is amended to substitute a deadline that is a multiple of seven days. Throughout the rules, deadlines are amended in the following manner:

- 5–day periods become 7–day periods
- 10–day periods become 14–day periods
- 15–day periods become 14–day periods
- 20–day periods become 21–day periods
- 25–day periods become 28–day periods

CROSS REFERENCES

Committee of unsecured creditors selected before order for relief, solicitation pursuant to this rule, see Fed.Rules Bankr. Proc. Rule 2007, 11 USCA.

Motions, form and service, see Fed.Rules Bankr.Proc. Rule 9013, 11 USCA.

Signing and verification of papers, see Fed.Rules Bankr. Proc. Rule 9011, 11 USCA.

Rule 2007. Review of Appointment of Creditors' Committee Organized Before Commencement of the Case

(a) Motion to review appointment

If a committee appointed by the United States trustee pursuant to § 1102(a) of the Code consists of the members of a committee organized by creditors before the commencement of a chapter 9 or chapter 11 case, on motion of a party in interest and after a hearing on notice to the United States trustee and other entities as the court may direct, the court may determine whether the appointment of the committee satisfies the requirements of § 1102(b)(1) of the Code.

(b) Selection of members of committee

The court may find that a committee organized by unsecured creditors before the commencement of a chapter 9 or chapter 11 case was fairly chosen if:

(1) it was selected by a majority in number and amount of claims of unsecured creditors who may vote under § 702(a) of the Code and were present in person or represented at a meeting of which all creditors having unsecured claims of over $1,000 or the 100 unsecured creditors having the largest claims had at least seven days' notice in writing, and of which meeting written minutes reporting the names of the creditors present or represented and voting and the amounts of their claims were kept and are available for inspection;

(2) all proxies voted at the meeting for the elected committee were solicited pursuant to Rule 2006 and the lists and statements required by subdivision (e) thereof have been transmitted to the United States trustee; and

(3) the organization of the committee was in all other respects fair and proper.

(c) Failure to comply with requirements for appointment

After a hearing on notice pursuant to subdivision (a) of this rule, the court shall direct the United States trustee to vacate the appointment of the committee and may order other appropriate action if the court finds that such appointment failed to satisfy the requirements of § 1102(b)(1) of the Code.

(As amended Mar. 30, 1987, eff. Aug. 1, 1987; Apr. 30, 1991, eff. Aug. 1, 1991; Mar. 26, 2009, eff. Dec. 1, 2009.)

ADVISORY COMMITTEE NOTES

Section 1102(b)(1) of the Code permits the court to appoint as the unsecured creditors' committee, the committee that was selected by creditors before the order for relief. This provision recognizes the propriety of continuing a "prepetition" committee in an official capacity. Such a committee, however, must be found to have been fairly chosen and representative of the different kinds of claims to be represented.

Subdivision (a) does not necessarily require a hearing but does require a party in interest to bring to the court's attention the fact that a prepetition committee had been organized and should be appointed. An application would suffice for this purpose. Party in interest would include the committee, any member of the committee, or any of its agents acting for the committee. Whether or not notice of the application should be given to any other party is left to the discretion of the court.

Subdivision (b) implements § 1102(b)(1). The Code provision allows the court to appoint, as the official § 1102(a) committee, a "prepetition" committee if its members were fairly chosen and the committee is representative of the different kinds of claims. This subdivision of the rule indicates some of the factors the court may consider in determining whether the requirements of § 1102(b)(1) have been satisfied. In effect, the subdivision provides various factors which are similar to those set forth in Rule 2006 with respect to the solicitation and voting of proxies in a chapter 7 liquidation case.

1987 Amendments

The rule is amended to conform to the 1984 amendments to § 1102(b)(1) of the Code.

1991 Amendments

This rule is amended to conform to the 1986 amendments to § 1102(a). The United States trustee appoints committees pursuant to § 1102 in chapter 11 cases. Section 1102 is applicable in chapter 9 cases pursuant to § 901(a).

Although § 1102(b)(1) of the Code permits the United States trustee to appoint a prepetition committee as the statutory committee if its members were fairly chosen and it is representative of the different kinds of claims to be represented, the amendment to this rule provides a procedure for judicial review of the appointment. The factors that may be considered by the court in determining whether the committee was fairly chosen are not new. A finding that a prepetition committee has not been fairly chosen does not prohibit the appointment of some or all of its members to the creditors' committee. Although this rule deals only with judicial review of the appointment of prepetition committees, it does not preclude judicial review under Rule 2020 regarding the appointment of other committees.

The rule is amended to implement changes in connection with the amendment to Rule 9006(a) and the manner by which time is computed under the rules. The deadline in the rule is amended to substitute a deadline that is a multiple of seven days. Throughout the rules, deadlines are amended in the following manner:

- 5–day periods become 7–day periods
- 10–day periods become 14–day periods
- 15–day periods become 14–day periods
- 20–day periods become 21–day periods
- 25–day periods become 28–day periods

CROSS REFERENCES

Representation of creditors and equity security holders in municipality debt adjustment and reorganization cases, see Fed.Rules Bankr.Proc. Rule 2019, 11 USCA.

Rule 2007.1. Appointment of Trustee or Examiner in a Chapter 11 Reorganization Case

(a) Order to appoint trustee or examiner

In a chapter 11 reorganization case, a motion for an order to appoint a trustee or an examiner under § 1104(a) or § 1104(c) of the Code shall be made in accordance with Rule 9014.

(b) Election of trustee

(1) Request for an election

A request to convene a meeting of creditors for the purpose of electing a trustee in a chapter 11 reorganization case shall be filed and transmitted to the United States trustee in accordance with Rule 5005 within the time prescribed by § 1104(b) of the Code. Pending court approval of the person elected, any person appointed by the United States trustee under § 1104(d) and approved in accordance with subdivision (c) of this rule shall serve as trustee.

(2) Manner of election and notice

An election of a trustee under § 1104(b) of the Code shall be conducted in the manner provided in Rules 2003(b)(3) and 2006. Notice of the meeting of creditors convened under § 1104(b) shall be given as provided in Rule 2002. The United States trustee shall preside at the meeting. A proxy for the purpose of voting in the election may be solicited only by a committee of creditors appointed under § 1102 of the Code or by any other party entitled to solicit a proxy pursuant to Rule 2006.

(3) Report of election and resolution of disputes

(A) Report of undisputed election

If no dispute arises out of the election, the United States trustee shall promptly file a report certifying the election, including the name and address of the person elected and a statement that the election is undisputed. The report shall be accompanied by a verified statement of the person elected setting forth that person's connections with the debtor, creditors, any other party in interest, their respective attorneys and accountants, the United States trustee, or any person employed in the office of the United States trustee.

(B) Dispute arising out of an election

If a dispute arises out of an election, the United States trustee shall promptly file a report stating that the election is disputed, informing the court of the nature of the dispute, and listing the name and address of any candidate elected under any alternative presented by the dispute. The report shall be accompanied by a verified statement by each candidate elected under each alternative presented by the dispute, setting forth the person's connections with the debtor, creditors, any other party in interest, their respective attorneys and accountants, the United States trustee, or any person employed in the office of the United States trustee. Not later than the date on which the report of the disputed election is filed, the United States trustee shall mail a copy of the report and each verified statement to any party in interest that has made a request to convene a meeting under § 1104(b) or to receive a copy of the report, and to any committee appointed under § 1102 of the Code.

(c) Approval of appointment

An order approving the appointment of a trustee or an examiner under § 1104(d) of the Code shall be made on application of the United States trustee. The application shall state the name of the person appointed and, to the best of the applicant's knowledge, all the person's connections with the debtor, creditors, any other parties in interest, their respective attorneys and accountants, the United States trustee, or persons employed in the office of the United States trustee. The application shall state the names of the parties in interest with whom the United States trustee consulted regarding the appointment. The application shall be accompanied by a verified statement of the person appointed setting forth the person's connections with the debtor, creditors, any other party in interest, their respective attorneys and accountants, the United States trustee, or any person employed in the office of the United States trustee.

(Added Apr. 30, 1991, eff. Aug. 1, 1991; amended Apr. 11, 1997, eff. Dec. 1, 1997; Apr. 23, 2008, eff. Dec. 1, 2008.)

ADVISORY COMMITTEE NOTES

1991 Adoption

This rule is added to implement the 1986 amendments to § 1104 of the Code regarding the appointment of a trustee or examiner in a chapter 11 case. A motion for an order to appoint a trustee or examiner is a contested matter. Although the court decides whether the appointment is warranted under the particular facts of the case, it is the United States trustee who makes the appointment pursuant to § 1104(c) of the Code. The appointment is subject to approval of the court, however, which may be obtained by application of the United States trustee. Section 1104(c) of the Code requires that the appointment be made after consultation with parties in interest and that the person appointed be disinterested.

The requirement that connections with the United States trustee or persons employed in the United States trustee's office be revealed is not intended to enlarge the definition of "disinterested person" in § 101(13) of the Code, to supersede executive regulations or other laws relating to appointments by United States trustees, or to otherwise restrict the United States trustee's discretion in making appointments. This information is required, however, in the interest of full disclosure and confidence in the appointment process and to give the court all information that may be relevant to the exercise of judicial discretion in approving the appointment of a trustee or examiner in a chapter 11 case.

1997 Amendments

This rule is amended to implement the 1994 amendments to § 1104 of the Code regarding the election of a trustee in a chapter 11 case.

Eligibility for voting in an election for a chapter 11 trustee is determined in accordance with Rule 2003(b)(3). Creditors whose claims are deemed filed under § 1111(a) are treated for voting purposes as creditors who have filed proofs of claim.

Proxies for the purpose of voting in the election may be solicited only by a creditors' committee appointed under § 1102 or by any other party entitled to solicit proxies pursuant to Rule 2006. Therefore, a trustee or examiner who has served in the case, or a committee of equity security holders appointed under § 1102, may not solicit proxies.

The procedures for reporting disputes to the court derive from similar provisions in Rule 2003(d) applicable to chapter 7 cases. An election may be disputed by a party in interest or by the United States trustee. For example, if the United States trustee believes that the person elected is ineligible to serve as trustee because the person is not "disinterested," the United States trustee should file a report disputing the election.

The word "only" is deleted from subdivision (b), redesignated as subdivision (c), to avoid any negative inference with respect to the availability of procedures for obtaining review of the United States trustee's acts or failure to act pursuant to Rule 2020.

GAP Report on Rule 2007.1. The published draft of proposed new subdivision (b)(3) of Rule 2007.1, and the Committee Note, was substantially revised to implement Mr. Patchan's recommendations (described above), to clarify how a disputed election will be reported, and to make stylistic improvements.

2008 Amendments

Under § 1104(b)(2) of the Code, as amended in 2005, if an eligible, disinterested person is elected to serve as trustee in a chapter 11 case, the United States trustee is directed to file a report certifying the election. The person elected does not have to be appointed to the position. Rather, the filing of the report certifying the election itself constitutes the appointment. The section further provides that in the event of a dispute in the election of a trustee, the court must resolve the matter. The rule is amended to be consistent with § 1104(b)(2).

When the United States trustee files a report certifying the election of a trustee, the person elected must provide a verified statement, similar to the statement required of professional persons under Rule 2014, disclosing connections with parties in interest and certain other persons connected with the case. Although court approval of the person elected is not required, the disclosure of the person's connections will enable parties in interest to determine whether the person is disinterested.

Rule 2007.2. Appointment of Patient Care Ombudsman in a Health Care Business Case

(a) Order to appoint patient care ombudsman

In a chapter 7, chapter 9, or chapter 11 case in which the debtor is a health care business, the court shall order the appointment of a patient care ombudsman under § 333 of the Code, unless the court, on motion of the United States trustee or a party in interest filed no later than 21 days after the commencement of the case or within another time fixed by the court, finds that the appointment of a patient care ombudsman is not necessary under the specific circumstances of the case for the protection of patients.

(b) Motion for order to appoint ombudsman

If the court has found that the appointment of an ombudsman is not necessary, or has terminated the appointment, the court, on motion of the United States trustee or a party in interest, may order the appointment at a later time if it finds that the appointment has become necessary to protect patients.

(c) Notice of appointment

If a patient care ombudsman is appointed under § 333, the United States trustee shall promptly file a notice of the appointment, including the name and address of the person appointed. Unless the person appointed is a State Long–Term Care Ombudsman, the notice shall be accompanied by a verified statement of the person appointed setting forth the person's connections with the debtor, creditors, patients, any other party in interest, their respective attorneys and accountants, the United States trustee, and any person employed in the office of the United States trustee.

(d) Termination of appointment

On motion of the United States trustee or a party in interest, the court may terminate the appointment of a patient care ombudsman if the court finds that the appointment is not necessary to protect patients.

(e) Motion

A motion under this rule shall be governed by Rule 9014. The motion shall be transmitted to the United States trustee and served on: the debtor; the trustee; any committee elected under § 705 or appointed under § 1102 of the Code or its authorized agent, or, if the case is a chapter 9 municipality case or a chapter 11 reorganization case and no committee of unsecured creditors has been appointed under § 1102, on the creditors included on the list filed under Rule 1007(d); and such other entities as the court may direct.

(Added Apr. 23, 2008, eff. Dec. 1, 2008. As amended Mar. 26, 2009, eff. Dec. 1, 2009.)

ADVISORY COMMITTEE NOTES

2008 Adoption

Section 333 of the Code, added by the 2005 amendments, requires the court to order the appointment of a health care ombudsman within the first 30 days of a health care business case, unless the court finds that the appointment is not necessary for the protection of patients. The rule recognizes this requirement and provides a procedure by which a party may obtain a court order finding that the appointment of a patient care ombudsman is unnecessary. In the absence of a timely motion under subdivision (a) of this rule, the court will enter an order directing the United States trustee to appoint the ombudsman.

Subdivision (b) recognizes that, despite a previous order finding that a patient care ombudsman is not necessary, circumstances of the case may change or newly discovered evidence may demonstrate the necessity of an ombudsman to protect the interests of patients. In that event, a party may move the court for an order directing the appointment of an ombudsman.

When the appointment of a patient care ombudsman is ordered, the United States trustee is required to appoint a disinterested person to serve in that capacity. Court approval of the appointment is not required, but subdivision (c) requires the person appointed, if not a State Long–Term Care Ombudsman, to file a verified statement similar to the statement filed by professional persons under Rule 2014 so that parties in interest will have information relevant to disinterestedness. If a party believes that the person appointed is not disinterested, it may file a motion asking the court to find that the person is not eligible to serve.

Subdivision (d) permits parties in interest to move for the termination of the appointment of a patient care ombudsman. If the movant can show that there no longer is any need for the ombudsman, the court may order the termination of the appointment.

2009 Amendments

The rule is amended to implement changes in connection with the amendment to Rule 9006(a) and the manner by which time is computed under the rules. The deadline in the rule is amended to substitute a deadline that is a multiple of seven days. Throughout the rules, deadlines are amended in the following manner:

- 5–day periods become 7–day periods
- 10–day periods become 14–day periods
- 15–day periods become 14–day periods
- 20–day periods become 21–day periods
- 25–day periods become 28–day periods

Rule 2008.   Notice to Trustee of Selection

The United States trustee shall immediately notify the person selected as trustee how to qualify and, if applicable, the amount of the trustee's bond. A trustee that has filed a blanket bond pursuant to Rule 2010 and has been selected as trustee in a chapter 7, chapter 12, or chapter 13 case that does not notify the court and the United States trustee in writing of rejection of the office within seven days after receipt of notice of selection shall be deemed to have accepted the office. Any other person selected as trustee shall notify the court and the United States trustee in writing of acceptance of the office within seven days after receipt of notice of selection or shall be deemed to have rejected the office.

(As amended Mar. 30, 1987, eff. Aug. 1, 1987; Apr. 30, 1991, eff. Aug. 1, 1991; Mar. 26, 2009, eff. Dec. 1, 2009.)

ADVISORY COMMITTEE NOTES

This rule is adapted from former Bankruptcy Rule 209(c). The remainder of that rule is inapplicable because its provisions are covered by §§ 701–703, 321 of the Code.

If the person selected as trustee accepts the office, he must qualify within five days after his selection, as required by § 322(a) of the Code.

In districts having a standing trustee for chapter 13 cases, a blanket acceptance of the appointment would be sufficient for compliance by the standing trustee with this rule.

1987 Amendments

The rule is amended to eliminate the need for a standing chapter 13 trustee or member of the panel of chapter 7 trustees to accept or reject an appointment.

1991 Amendments

The amendments to this rule relating to the United States trustee are derived from Rule X–1004(a) and conform to the 1986 amendments to the Code and 28 U.S.C. § 586 which provide that the United States trustee appoints and supervises trustees, and in a chapter 7 case presides over any election of a trustee. This rule applies when a trustee is either appointed or elected. This rule is also amended to provide for chapter 12 cases.

2009 Amendments

The rule is amended to implement changes in connection with the amendment to Rule 9006(a) and the manner by which time is computed under the rules. The deadline in the rule is amended to substitute a deadline that is a multiple of seven days. Throughout the rules, deadlines are amended in the following manner:

- 5–day periods become 7–day periods
- 10–day periods become 14–day periods
- 15–day periods become 14–day periods
- 20–day periods become 21–day periods
- 25–day periods become 28–day periods

CROSS REFERENCES

Appointment of trustees,

Individual debt adjustment case, see 11 USCA § 1302.

Railroad reorganization case, see 11 USCA § 1163.

Reorganization case, see 11 USCA § 1104.

Bonds of trustees, see 11 USCA § 322.

Election of trustee in liquidation case, see 11 USCA § 702.

Eligibility to serve as trustee, see 11 USCA § 321.

Limited purpose of trustee appointed in municipality debt adjustment case, see 11 USCA § 926.

Representation of creditors and equity security holders in municipality debt adjustment and reorganization cases, see Fed.Rules Bankr.Proc. Rule 2019, 11 USCA.

Right of creditors to elect single trustee when joint administration ordered, see Fed.Rules Bankr.Proc. Rule 2009, 11 USCA.

Rule 2009. Trustees for Estates When Joint Administration Ordered

(a) Election of single trustee for estates being jointly administered

If the court orders a joint administration of two or more estates under Rule 1015(b), creditors may elect a single trustee for the estates being jointly administered, unless the case is under subchapter V of chapter 7 of the Code.

(b) Right of creditors to elect separate trustee

Notwithstanding entry of an order for joint administration under Rule 1015(b), the creditors of any debtor may elect a separate trustee for the estate of the debtor as provided in § 702 of the Code, unless the case is under subchapter V of chapter 7.

(c) Appointment of trustees for estates being jointly administered

(1) Chapter 7 liquidation cases

Except in a case governed by subchapter V of chapter 7, the United States trustee may appoint one or more interim trustees for estates being jointly administered in chapter 7 cases.

(2) Chapter 11 reorganization cases

If the appointment of a trustee is ordered, the United States trustee may appoint one or more trustees for estates being jointly administered in chapter 11 cases.

(3) Chapter 12 family farmer's debt adjustment cases

The United States trustee may appoint one or more trustees for estates being jointly administered in chapter 12 cases.

(4) Chapter 13 individual's debt adjustment cases

The United States trustee may appoint one or more trustees for estates being jointly administered in chapter 13 cases.

(d) Potential conflicts of interest

On a showing that creditors or equity security holders of the different estates will be prejudiced by conflicts of interest of a common trustee who has been elected or appointed, the court shall order the selection of separate trustees for estates being jointly administered.

(e) Separate accounts

The trustee or trustees of estates being jointly administered shall keep separate accounts of the property and distribution of each estate.

(As amended Mar. 30, 1987, eff. Aug. 1, 1987; Apr. 30, 1991, eff. Aug. 1, 1991; Mar. 27, 2003, eff. Dec. 1, 2003.)

ADVISORY COMMITTEE NOTES

This rule is applicable in chapter 7 cases and, in part, in chapter 11 and 13 cases. The provisions in subdivisions (a) and (b) concerning creditor election of a trustee apply only in a chapter 7 case because it is only pursuant to § 702 of the Code that creditors may elect a trustee. Subdivision (c) of the rule applies in chapter 11 and 13 as well as chapter 7 cases; pursuant to § 1104 of the Code, the court may order the appointment of a trustee on application of a party in interest and, pursuant to § 1163 of the Code, the court must appoint a trustee in a railroad reorganization case. Subdivision (c) should not be taken as an indication that more than one trustee may be appointed for a single debtor. Section 1104(c) permits only one trustee for each estate. In a chapter 13 case, if there is no standing trustee, the court is to appoint a person to serve as trustee pursuant to § 1302 of the Code. There is no provision for a trustee in a chapter 9 case, except for a very limited purpose; see § 926 of the Code.

This rule recognizes that economical and expeditious administration of two or more estates may be facilitated not only by the selection of a single trustee for a partnership and its partners, but by such selection whenever estates are being jointly administered pursuant to Rule 1015. See In the Matter of International Oil Co., 427 F.2d 186, 187 (2d Cir. 1970). The rule is derived from former § 5c of the Act [former § 23(c) of this title] and former Bankruptcy Rule 210. The premise of § 5c of the Act was that notwithstanding the potentiality of conflict between the interests of the creditors of the partners and those of the creditors of the partnership, the conflict is not sufficiently serious or frequent in most cases to warrant the selection of separate trustees for the firm and the several partners. Even before the proviso was added to § 5c of the Act in 1938 to permit the creditors of a general partner to elect their separate trustee for his estate, it was held that the court had discretion to permit such an election or to make a separate appointment when a conflict of interest was recognized. In re Wood, 248 Fed. 246, 249–50 (6th Cir.), cert. denied, 247 U.S. 512 (1918); 4 Collier, Bankruptcy ¶723.04 (15th ed.1980). The rule retains in subdivision (e) the features of the practice respecting the selection of a trustee that was developed under § 5 of the Act [former § 23 of this title]. Subdivisions (a) and (c) permit the court to authorize election of a single trustee or to make a single appointment when joint administration of estates of other kinds of debtors is ordered, but subdivision (d) requires the court to make a preliminary evaluation of the risks of conflict of interest. If after the election or appointment of a common trustee a conflict of interest materializes, the court must take appropriate action to deal with it.

Subdivision (f) is derived from § 5e of the Act [former § 23(e) of this title] and former Bankruptcy Rule 210(f) and requires that the common trustee keep a separate account for each estate in all cases that are jointly administered.

1991 Amendments

One or more trustees may be appointed for estates being jointly administered in chapter 12 cases.

The amendments to this rule are derived from Rule X–1005 and are necessary because the United States trustee, rather than the court, has responsibility for appointing trustees pursuant to §§ 701, 1104, 1202, and 1302 of the Code.

If separate trustees are ordered for chapter 7 estates pursuant to subdivision (d), separate and successor trustees should be chosen as prescribed in § 703 of the Code. If the occasion for another election arises, the United States trustee should call a meeting of creditors for this purpose. An order to select separate trustees does not disqualify an appointed or elected trustee from serving for one of the estates.

Subdivision (e) is abrogated because the exercise of discretion by the United States trustee, who is in the Executive Branch, is not subject to advance restriction by rule of court. United States v. Cox, 342 F.2d 167 (5th Cir.1965), *cert. denied,* 365 U.S. 863 (1965); United States v. Frumento, 409 F.Supp. 136, 141 (E.D.Pa.), *aff'd,* 563 F.2d 1083 (3d Cir.1977), *cert. denied,* 434 U.S. 1072 (1977); see, Smith v. United States, 375 F.2d 243 (5th Cir.1967); House Report No. 95–595, 95th Cong., 1st Sess. 110 (1977). However, a trustee appointed by the United States trustee may be removed by the court for cause. See § 324 of the Code. Subdivision (d) of this rule, as amended, is consistent with § 324. Subdivision (f) is redesignated as subdivision (e).

2003 Amendments

The rule is amended to reflect the enactment of subchapter V of chapter 7 of the Code governing multilateral clearing organization liquidations. Section 782 of the Code provides that the designation of a trustee or alternative trustee for the case is made by the Federal Reserve Board. Therefore, neither the United States trustee nor the creditors can appoint or elect a trustee in these cases.

Other amendments are stylistic.

CROSS REFERENCES

Rule 2010.   Qualification by Trustee; Proceeding on Bond

(a) Blanket bond

The United States trustee may authorize a blanket bond in favor of the United States conditioned on the faithful performance of official duties by the trustee or trustees to cover (1) a person who qualifies as trustee in a number of cases, and (2) a number of trustees each of whom qualifies in a different case.

(b) Proceeding on bond

A proceeding on the trustee's bond may be brought by any party in interest in the name of the United States for the use of the entity injured by the breach of the condition.

(As amended Mar. 30, 1987, eff. Aug. 1, 1987; Apr. 30, 1991, eff. Aug. 1, 1991.)

ADVISORY COMMITTEE NOTES

Subdivisions (a) and (b). Subdivision (a) gives authority for approval by the court of a single bond to cover (1) a person who qualifies as trustee in a number of cases, and (2) a number of trustees each of whom qualifies in a different case. The cases need not be related in any way. Substantial economies can be effected if a single bond covering a number of different cases can be issued and approved at one time. When a blanket bond is filed, the trustee qualifies under subdivision (b) of the rule by filing an acceptance of the office.

Subdivision (c) prescribes the evidentiary effect of a certified copy of an order approving the trustee's bond given by a trustee under this rule or, when a blanket bond has been authorized, of a certified copy of acceptance. This rule supplements the Federal Rules of Evidence, which apply in bankruptcy cases. See Rule 1101 of the Federal Rules of Evidence. The order of approval should conform to Official Form No. 25. See, however, § 549(c) of the Code which provides only for the filing of the petition in the real estate records of serve as constructive notice of the pendency of the case. See also Rule 2011 which prescribes the evidentiary effect of a certificate that the debtor is a debtor in possession.

Subdivision (d) is derived from former Bankruptcy Rule 212(f). Reference should be made to § 322(a) and (d) of the Code which requires the bond to be filed with the bankruptcy court and places a two year limitation for the commencement of a proceeding on the bond. A bond filed under this rule should conform to Official Form No. 25. A proceeding on the bond of a trustee is governed by the rules in Part VII. See the Note accompanying Rule 7001. See also Rule 9025.

1987 Amendments

Subdivision (b) is deleted because of the amendment to Rule 2008.

1991 Amendments

This rule is amended to conform to the 1986 amendment of § 322 of the Code. The United States trustee determines the amount and sufficiency of the trustee's bond. The amendment to subdivision (a) is derived from Rule X–1004(b).

Subdivision (b) is abrogated because an order approving a bond is no longer necessary in view of the 1986 amendments to § 322 of the Code. Subdivision (c) is redesignated as subdivision (b).

CROSS REFERENCES

Proceeding on trustee's bond as exception to procedural rule of prosecution in name of real party in interest, see Fed.Rules Bankr.Proc. Rule 7017, 11 USCA.

Security, proceedings against sureties, see Fed.Rules Bankr.Proc. Rule 9025, 11 USCA and Fed.Rules Civ.Proc. Rule 65.1, 28 USCA.

Two-year limitations period on bond proceeding, see 11 USCA § 322.

Rule 2011. Evidence of Debtor in Possession or Qualification of Trustee

(a) Whenever evidence is required that a debtor is a debtor in possession or that a trustee has qualified, the clerk may so certify and the certificate shall constitute conclusive evidence of that fact.

(b) If a person elected or appointed as trustee does not qualify within the time prescribed by § 322(a) of the Code, the clerk shall so notify the court and the United States trustee.

(As amended Apr. 30, 1991, eff. Aug. 1, 1991.)

ADVISORY COMMITTEE NOTES

This rule prescribes the evidentiary effect of a certificate issued by the clerk that the debtor is a debtor in possession. See Official Form No. 26. Only chapter 11 of the Code provides for a debtor in possession. See § 1107(a) of the Code. If, however, a trustee is appointed in the chapter 11 case, there will not be a debtor in possession. See §§ 1101(1), 1105 of the Code.

1991 Amendments

This rule is amended to provide a procedure for proving that a trustee has qualified in accordance with § 322 of the Code. *Subdivision (b)* is added so that the court and the United States trustee will be informed if the person selected as trustee pursuant to §§ 701, 702, 1104, 1202, 1302, or 1163 fails to qualify within the time prescribed in § 322(a).

CROSS REFERENCES

"Debtor in possession" for purposes of reorganization case defined as debtor except when trustee is serving, see 11 USCA § 1101.

Rule 2012. Substitution of Trustee or Successor Trustee; Accounting

(a) Trustee

If a trustee is appointed in a chapter 11 case or the debtor is removed as debtor in possession in a chapter 12 case, the trustee is substituted automatically for the debtor in possession as a party in any pending action, proceeding, or matter.

(b) Successor trustee

When a trustee dies, resigns, is removed, or otherwise ceases to hold office during the pendency of a case under the Code (1) the successor is automatically substituted as a party in any pending action, proceeding, or matter; and (2) the successor trustee shall prepare,

file, and transmit to the United States trustee an accounting of the prior administration of the estate. (As amended Mar. 30, 1987, eff. Aug. 1, 1987; Apr. 30, 1991, eff. Aug. 1, 1991.)

ADVISORY COMMITTEE NOTES

Paragraph (1) of this rule implements § 325 of the Code. It provides that a pending action or proceeding continues without abatement and that the trustee's successor is automatically substituted as a party whether it be another trustee or the debtor returned to possession, as such party.

Paragraph (2) places it within the responsibility of a successor trustee to file an accounting of the prior administration of the estate. If an accounting is impossible to obtain from the prior trustee because of death or lack of cooperation, prior reports submitted in the earlier administration may be updated.

1987 Amendments

Subdivision (a) is new. The subdivision provides for the substitution of a trustee appointed in a chapter 11 case for the debtor in possession in any pending litigation.

The original provisions of the rule are now in subdivision (b).

1991 Amendments

Subdivision (a) is amended to include any chapter 12 case in which the debtor is removed as debtor in possession pursuant to § 1204(a) of the Code.

Subdivision (b) is amended to require that the accounting of the prior administration which must be filed with the court is also transmitted to the United States trustee who is responsible for supervising the administration of cases and trustees. See 28 U.S.C. § 586(a)(3). Because a court order is not required for the appointment of a successor trustee, requiring the court to fix a time for filing the accounting is inefficient and unnecessary. The United States trustee has supervisory powers over trustees and may require the successor trustee to file the accounting within a certain time period. If the successor trustee fails to file the accounting within a reasonable time, the United States trustee or a party in interest may take appropriate steps including a request for an appropriate court order. See 28 U.S.C. § 586(a)(3)(G). The words "with the court" are deleted in subdivision (b)(2) as unnecessary. See Rules 5005(a) and 9001(3).

CROSS REFERENCES

Abatement of suit or proceeding upon death or removal of trustee, see 11 USCA § 325.

Election by creditors of successor trustee in liquidation case, see 11 USCA § 703.

Exception to procedural rule for substitution of parties, see Fed.Rules Bankr.Proc. Rule 7025, 11 USCA.

Power of court to remove trustee, see 11 USCA § 324.

Substitution of public officer on death or separation from office, see Fed.Rules Civ.Proc. Rule 25, 28 USCA.

Rule 2013. Public Record of Compensation Awarded to Trustees, Examiners, and Professionals

(a) Record to be kept

The clerk shall maintain a public record listing fees awarded by the court (1) to trustees and attorneys, accountants, appraisers, auctioneers and other professionals employed by trustees, and (2) to examiners. The record shall include the name and docket number of the case, the name of the individual or firm receiving the fee and the amount of the fee awarded. The record shall be maintained chronologically and shall be kept current and open to examination by the public without charge. "Trustees," as used in this rule, does not include debtors in possession.

(b) Summary of record

At the close of each annual period, the clerk shall prepare a summary of the public record by individual or firm name, to reflect total fees awarded during the preceding year. The summary shall be open to examination by the public without charge. The clerk shall transmit a copy of the summary to the United States trustee.

(As amended Mar. 30, 1987, eff. Aug. 1, 1987; Apr. 30, 1991, eff. Aug. 1, 1991.)

ADVISORY COMMITTEE NOTES

This rule is adapted from former Rule 213. The first sentence of that rule is omitted because of the provisions in 28 U.S.C. §§ 586 and 604(f) creating panels of private trustees.

The rule is not applicable to standing trustees serving in chapter 13 cases. See § 1302 of the Code.

A basic purpose of the rule is to prevent what Congress has defined as "cronyism." Appointment or employment, whether in a chapter 7 or 11 case, should not center among a small select group of individuals unless the circumstances are such that it would be warranted. The public record of appointments to be kept by the clerk will provide a means for monitoring the appointment process.

Subdivision (b) provides a convenient source for public review of fees paid from debtors' estates in the bankruptcy courts. Thus, public recognition of appointments, fairly distributed and based on professional qualifications and expertise, will be promoted and notions of improper favor dispelled. This rule is in keeping with the findings of the Congressional subcommittees as set forth in the House Report of the Committee on the Judiciary, No. 95–595, 95th Cong., 1st Sess. 89–99 (1977). These findings included the observations that there were frequent appointments of the same person, contacts developed between the bankruptcy bar and the courts, and an unusually close relationship between the bar and the judges developed over the years. A major purpose of the new statute is to dilute these practices and instill greater public confidence in the system. Rule 2013 implements that laudatory purpose.

1987 Amendments

In subdivisions (b) and (c) the word awarded is substituted for the word paid. While clerks do not know if fees are paid, they can determine what fees are awarded by the court.

1991 Amendments

Subdivision (a) is deleted. The matter contained in this subdivision is more properly left for regulation by the United States trustee. When appointing trustees and examiners and when monitoring applications for employment of auctioneers, appraisers and other professionals, the United States trustee should be sensitive to disproportionate or excessive fees received by any person.

Subdivision (b), redesignated as subdivision (a), is amended to reflect the fact that the United States trustee appoints examiners subject to court approval.

Subdivision (c), redesignated as subdivision (b), is amended to furnish the United States trustee with a copy of the annual summary which may assist that office in the performance of its responsibilities under 28 U.S.C. § 586 and the Code.

The rule is not applicable to standing trustees serving in chapter 12 cases. See § 1202 of the Code.

CROSS REFERENCES

Compensation of officers to reimburse actual and necessary services, see 11 USCA § 330.

Limitation on compensation of trustee, see 11 USCA § 326.

Rule 2014. Employment of Professional Persons

(a) Application for an order of employment

An order approving the employment of attorneys, accountants, appraisers, auctioneers, agents, or other professionals pursuant to § 327, § 1103, or § 1114 of the Code shall be made only on application of the trustee or committee. The application shall be filed and, unless the case is a chapter 9 municipality case, a copy of the application shall be transmitted by the applicant to the United States trustee. The application shall state the specific facts showing the necessity for the employment, the name of the person to be employed, the reasons for the selection, the professional services to be rendered, any proposed arrangement for compensation, and, to the best of the applicant's knowledge, all of the person's connections with the debtor, creditors, any other party in interest, their respective attorneys and accountants, the United States trustee, or any person employed in the office of the United States trustee. The application shall be accompanied by a verified statement of the person to be employed setting forth the person's connections with the debtor, creditors, any other party in interest, their respective attorneys and accountants, the United States trustee, or any person employed in the office of the United States trustee.

(b) Services rendered by member or associate of firm of attorneys or accountants

If, under the Code and this rule, a law partnership or corporation is employed as an attorney, or an accounting partnership or corporation is employed as an accountant, or if a named attorney or accountant is employed, any partner, member, or regular associate of the partnership, corporation or individual may act as attorney or accountant so employed, without further order of the court.

(As amended Mar. 30, 1987, eff. Aug. 1, 1987; Apr. 30, 1991, eff. Aug. 1, 1991.)

ADVISORY COMMITTEE NOTES

Subdivision (a) is adapted from the second sentence of former Bankruptcy Rule 215(a). The remainder of that rule is covered by § 327 of the Code.

Subdivision (b) is derived from former Bankruptcy Rule 215(f). The compensation provisions are set forth in § 504 of the Code.

1991 Amendments

This rule is amended to include retention of professionals by committees of retired employees pursuant to § 1114 of the Code.

The United States trustee monitors applications filed under § 327 of the Code and may file with the court comments with respect to the approval of such applications. See 28 U.S.C. § 586(a)(3)(H). The United States trustee also monitors creditors' committees in accordance with 28 U.S.C. § 586(a)(3)(E). The addition of the second sentence of subdivision (a) is designed to enable the United States trustee to perform these duties.

Subdivision (a) is also amended to require disclosure of the professional's connections with the United States trustee or persons employed in the United States trustee's office. This requirement is not intended to prohibit the employment of such persons in all cases or to enlarge the definition of "disinterested person" in § 101(13) of the Code. However, the court may consider a connection with the United States trustee's office as a factor when exercising its discretion. Also, this information should be revealed in the interest of full disclosure and confidence in the bankruptcy system, especially since the United States trustee monitors and may be heard on applications for compensation and reimbursement of professionals employed under this rule.

The United States trustee appoints committees pursuant to § 1102 of the Code which is applicable in chapter 9 cases under § 901. In the interest of full disclosure and confidence in the bankruptcy system, a connection between the United States trustee and a professional employed by the committee should be revealed in every case, including a chapter 9 case. However, since the United States trustee does not have any role in the employment of professionals in chapter 9 cases, it is not necessary in such cases to transmit to the United States trustee a copy of the application under subdivision (a) of this rule. See 28 U.S.C. § 586(a)(3)(H).

CROSS REFERENCES

Application for compensation or reimbursement, see Fed. Rules Bankr.Proc. Rule 2016, 11 USCA.

Compensation for services and reimbursement of costs, see 11 USCA § 503.

Compensation of professional persons,

Actual, necessary services, see 11 USCA § 330.

Limitation on, see 11 USCA § 328.

Sharing of, see 11 USCA § 504.

Rule 2015. Duty to Keep Records, Make Reports, and Give Notice of Case or Change of Status

(a) Trustee or debtor in possession

A trustee or debtor in possession shall:

(1) in a chapter 7 liquidation case and, if the court directs, in a chapter 11 reorganization case file and transmit to the United States trustee a complete inventory of the property of the debtor within 30 days after qualifying as a trustee or debtor in possession, unless such an inventory has already been filed;

(2) keep a record of receipts and the disposition of money and property received;

(3) file the reports and summaries required by § 704(a)(8) of the Code, which shall include a statement, if payments are made to employees, of the amounts of deductions for all taxes required to be withheld or paid for and in behalf of employees and the place where these amounts are deposited;

(4) as soon as possible after the commencement of the case, give notice of the case to every entity known to be holding money or property subject to withdrawal or order of the debtor, including every bank, savings or building and loan association, public utility company, and landlord with whom the debtor has a deposit, and to every insurance company which has issued a policy having a cash surrender value payable to the debtor, except that notice need not be given to any entity who has knowledge or has previously been notified of the case;

(5) in a chapter 11 reorganization case, on or before the last day of the month after each calendar quarter during which there is a duty to pay fees under 28 U.S.C. § 1930(a)(6), file and transmit to the United States trustee a statement of any disbursements made during that quarter and of any fees payable under 28 U.S.C. § 1930(a)(6) for that quarter; and

(6) in a chapter 11 small business case, unless the court, for cause, sets another reporting interval, file and transmit to the United States trustee for each calendar month after the order for relief, on the appropriate Official Form, the report required by § 308. If the order for relief is within the first 15 days of a calendar month, a report shall be filed for the portion of the month that follows the order for relief. If the order for relief is after the 15th day of a calendar month, the period for the remainder of the month shall be included in the report for the next calendar month. Each report shall be filed no later than 21 days after the last day of the calendar month following the month covered by the report. The obligation to file reports under this subparagraph terminates on the effective date of the plan, or conversion or dismissal of the case.

(b) Chapter 12 trustee and debtor in possession

In a chapter 12 family farmer's debt adjustment case, the debtor in possession shall perform the duties prescribed in clauses (2)–(4) of subdivision (a) of this rule and, if the court directs, shall file and transmit to the United States trustee a complete inventory of the property of the debtor within the time fixed by the court. If the debtor is removed as debtor in possession, the trustee shall perform the duties of the debtor in possession prescribed in this paragraph.

(c) Chapter 13 trustee and debtor

(1) Business cases

In a chapter 13 individual's debt adjustment case, when the debtor is engaged in business, the debtor shall perform the duties prescribed by clauses (2)–(4) of subdivision (a) of this rule and, if the court directs, shall file and transmit to the United States trustee a complete inventory of the property of the debtor within the time fixed by the court.

(2) Nonbusiness cases

In a chapter 13 individual's debt adjustment case, when the debtor is not engaged in business, the trustee shall perform the duties prescribed by clause (2) of subdivision (a) of this rule.

(d) Foreign representative

In a case in which the court has granted recognition of a foreign proceeding under chapter 15, the foreign representative shall file any notice required under § 1518 of the Code within 14 days after the date when the representative becomes aware of the subsequent information.

(e) Transmission of reports

In a chapter 11 case the court may direct that copies or summaries of annual reports and copies or summaries of other reports shall be mailed to the creditors, equity security holders, and indenture trustees. The court may also direct the publication of summaries of any such reports. A copy of every report or summary mailed or published pursuant to this subdivision shall be transmitted to the United States trustee.

(As amended Mar. 30, 1987, eff. Aug. 1, 1987; Apr. 30, 1991, eff. Aug. 1, 1991; Apr. 23, 1996, eff. Dec. 1, 1996; Apr. 29, 2002, eff. Dec. 1, 2002; Apr. 23, 2008, eff. Dec. 1, 2008; Mar. 26, 2009, eff. Dec. 1, 2009; Apr. 23, 2012, eff. Dec. 1, 2012.)

ADVISORY COMMITTEE NOTES

This rule combines the provisions found in former Rules 218, 10–208, 11–30 and 13–208 of the Rules of Bankruptcy Procedure. It specifies various duties which are in addition to those required by §§ 704, 1106, 1302 and 1304 of the Code.

In **subdivision (a)** the times permitted to be fixed by the court in clause (3) for the filing of reports and summaries may be fixed by local rule or order.

Subdivision (b). This subdivision prescribes duties on either the debtor or trustee in chapter 13 cases, depending on whether or not the debtor is engaged in business (§ 1304 of the Code). The duty of giving notice prescribed by subdivision (a)(4) is not included in a nonbusiness case because of its impracticability.

Subdivision (c) is derived from former Chapter X Rule 10–208(c) which, in turn, was derived from § 190 of the Act [former § 590 of this title]. The equity security holders to whom the reports should be sent are those of record at the time of transmittal of such reports.

1987 Amendments

Subdivision (a) is amended to add as a duty of the trustee or debtor in possession the filing of a notice of or a copy of the petition. The filing of such notice or a copy of the petition is essential to the protection of the estate from unauthorized post-petition conveyances of real property. Section 549(c) of the Code protects the title of a good faith purchaser for fair equivalent value unless the notice or copy of the petition is filed.

1991 Amendments

This rule is amended to provide the United States trustee with information needed to perform supervisory responsibilities in accordance with 28 U.S.C. § 586(a)(3) and to exercise the right to raise, appear and be heard on issues pursuant to § 307 of the Code.

Subdivision (a)(3) is amended to conform to the 1986 amendments to § 704(8) of the Code and the United States trustee system. It may not be necessary for the court to fix a time to file reports if the United States trustee requests that they be filed within a specified time and there is no dispute regarding such time.

Subdivision (a)(5) is deleted because the filing of a notice of or copy of the petition to protect real property against unauthorized postpetition transfers in a particular case is within the discretion of the trustee.

The new subdivision (a)(5) was added to enable the United States trustee, parties in interest, and the court to determine the appropriate quarterly fee required by 28 U.S.C. § 1930(a)(6). The requirements of subdivision (a)(5) should be satisfied whenever possible by including this information in other reports filed by the trustee or debtor in possession. Nonpayment of the fee may result in dismissal or conversion of the case pursuant to § 1112(b) of the Code.

Rule X–1007(b), which provides that the trustee or debtor in possession shall cooperate with the United States trustee by furnishing information that the United States trustee reasonably requires, is deleted as unnecessary. The deletion of Rule X–1007(b) should not be construed as a limitation of the powers of the United States trustee or of the duty of the trustee or debtor in possession to cooperate with the United States trustee in the performance of the statutory responsibilities of that office.

Subdivision (a)(6) is abrogated as unnecessary. See § 1106(a)(7) of the Code.

Subdivision (a)(7) is abrogated. The closing of a chapter 11 case is governed by Rule 3022.

New **subdivision (b)**, which prescribes the duties of the debtor in possession and trustee in a chapter 12 case, does not prohibit additional reporting requirements pursuant to local rule or court order.

1996 Amendments

Subdivision (a)(1) provides that the trustee in a chapter 7 case and, if the court directs, the trustee or debtor in possession in a chapter 11 case, is required to file and transmit to the United States trustee a complete inventory of the debtor's property within 30 days after qualifying as trustee or debtor in possession, unless such an inventory has already been filed. Subdivisions (b) and (c) are amended to clarify that a debtor in possession and trustee in a chapter 12 case, and a debtor in a chapter 13 case where the debtor is engaged in business, are not required to file and transmit to the United States trustee a complete inventory of the property of the debtor unless the court so directs. If the court so directs, the court also fixes the time limit for filing and transmitting the inventory.

GAP Report on Rule 2015. No changes since publication, except for a stylistic change in the first sentence of the committee note.

2002 Amendments

Subdivision (a)(5) is amended to provide that the duty to file quarterly disbursement reports continues only so long as there is an obligation to make quarterly payments to the United States trustee under 28 U.S.C. § 1930(a)(6).

Other amendments are stylistic.

Changes Made After Publication and Comments. No changes were made.

2008 Amendments

Subparagraph (a)(6) implements § 308 of the Code, added by the 2005 amendments. That section requires small business chapter 11 debtors to file periodic financial and operating reports, and the rule sets the time for filing those reports and requires the use of an Official Form for the report. The obligation to file reports under this rule does not relieve the trustee or debtor of any other obligations to provide information or documents to the United States trustee.

The rule also is amended to fix the time for the filing of notices under § 1518, added to the Code in 2005. Former subdivision (d) is renumbered as subdivision (e).

Other changes are stylistic.

2009 Amendments

The rule is amended to implement changes in connection with the amendment to Rule 9006(a) and the manner by which time is computed under the rules. The deadlines in the rule are amended to substitute a deadline that is a multiple of seven days. Throughout the rules, deadlines are amended in the following manner:

- 5–day periods become 7–day periods
- 10–day periods become 14–day periods
- 15–day periods become 14–day periods
- 20–day periods become 21–day periods
- 25–day periods become 28–day periods

2012 Amendments

Subdivision (a)(3). Subdivision (a)(3) is amended to correct the reference to § 704. The 2005 amendments to the Code expanded § 704 and created subsections within it. The provision that was previously § 704(8) became § 704(a)(8). The other change to (a)(3) is stylistic.

Final approval of this technical amendment is sought without publication.

CROSS REFERENCES

Duties of trustee,

Individual debt adjustment case, see 11 USCA § 1302.

Reorganization case, see 11 USCA § 1106.

Operation of business by debtor, see 11 USCA § 1304.

Public access to papers filed in case under this title, see 11 USCA § 107.

Rule 2015.1. Patient Care Ombudsman

(a) Reports

A patient care ombudsman, at least 14 days before making a report under § 333(b)(2) of the Code, shall give notice that the report will be made to the court, unless the court orders otherwise. The notice shall be transmitted to the United States trustee, posted conspicuously at the health care facility that is the subject of the report, and served on: the debtor; the trustee; all patients; and any committee elected under § 705 or appointed under § 1102 of the Code or its authorized agent, or, if the case is a chapter 9 municipality case or a chapter 11 reorganization case and no committee of unsecured creditors has been appointed under § 1102, on the creditors included on the list filed under Rule 1007(d); and such other entities as the court may direct. The notice shall state the date and time when the report will be made, the manner in which the report will be made, and, if the report is in writing, the name, address, telephone number, email address, and website, if any, of the person from whom a copy of the report may be obtained at the debtor's expense.

(b) Authorization to review confidential patient records

A motion by a patient care ombudsman under § 333(c) to review confidential patient records shall be governed by Rule 9014, served on the patient and any family member or other contact person whose name and address have been given to the trustee or the debtor for the purpose of providing information regarding the patient's health care, and transmitted to the United States trustee subject to applicable nonbankruptcy law relating to patient privacy. Unless the court orders otherwise, a hearing on the motion may not be commenced earlier than 14 days after service of the motion.

(Added Apr. 23, 2008, eff. Dec. 1, 2008; amended Mar. 26, 2009, eff. Dec. 1, 2009.)

ADVISORY COMMITTEE NOTES

2008 Adoption

This rule is new and implements § 333 of the Code, added by the 2005 amendments. Subdivision (a) is designed to give parties in interest, including patients or their representatives, sufficient notice so that they will be able to review written reports or attend hearings at which reports are made. The rule permits a notice to relate to a single report or to periodic reports to be given during the case. For example, the ombudsman may give notice that reports will be made at specified intervals or dates during the case.

Subdivision (a) of the rule also requires that the notice be posted conspicuously at the health care facility in a place where it will be seen by patients and their families or others visiting the patients. This may require posting in common areas and patient rooms within the facility. Because health care facilities and the patients they serve can vary greatly, the locations of the posted notice should be tailored to the specific facility that is the subject of the report.

Subdivision (b) requires the ombudsman to notify the patient and the United States trustee that the ombudsman is seeking access to confidential patient records so that they will be able to appear and be heard on the matter. This procedure should assist the court in reaching its decision both as to access to the records and appropriate restrictions on that access to ensure continued confidentiality. Notices given under this rule are subject to the provisions of applicable federal and state law that relate to the protection of patients' privacy, such as the Health Insurance Portability and Accountability Act of 1996, Pub. L. No. 104–191 (HIPAA).

2009 Amendments

The rule is amended to implement changes in connection with the amendment to Rule 9006(a) and the manner by which time is computed under the rules. The deadlines in the rule are amended to substitute a deadline that is a multiple of seven days. Throughout the rules, deadlines are amended in the following manner:

- 5–day periods become 7–day periods
- 10–day periods become 14–day periods
- 15–day periods become 14–day periods
- 20–day periods become 21–day periods
- 25–day periods become 28–day periods

Rule 2015.2. Transfer of Patient in Health Care Business Case

Unless the court orders otherwise, if the debtor is a health care business, the trustee may not transfer a patient to another health care business under § 704(a)(12) of the Code unless the trustee gives at least 14 days' notice of the transfer to the patient care ombudsman, if any, the patient, and any family member or other contact person whose name and address has been given to the trustee or the debtor for the purpose of providing information regarding the patient's health care. The notice is subject to applicable nonbankruptcy law relating to patient privacy.
(Added Apr. 23, 2008, eff. Dec. 1, 2008; amended Mar. 26, 2009, eff. Dec. 1, 2009.)

ADVISORY COMMITTEE NOTES

2008 Adoption

This rule is new. Section 704(a)(12), added to the Code by the 2005 amendments, authorizes the trustee to relocate patients when a health care business debtor's facility is in the process of being closed. The Code permits the trustee to take this action without the need for any court order, but the notice required by this rule will enable a patient care ombudsman appointed under § 333, or a patient who contends that

the trustee's actions violate § 704(a)(12), to have those issues resolved before the patient is transferred.

This rule also permits the court to enter an order dispensing with or altering the notice requirement in proper circumstances. For example, a facility could be closed immediately, or very quickly, such that 10 days' notice would not be possible in some instances. In that event, the court may shorten the time required for notice.

Notices given under this rule are subject to the provisions of applicable federal and state law that relate to the protection of patients' privacy, such as the Health Insurance Portability and Accountability Act of 1996, Pub. L. No. 104–191 (HIPAA).

2009 Amendments

The rule is amended to implement changes in connection with the amendment to Rule 9006(a) and the manner by which time is computed under the rules. The deadline in the rule is amended to substitute a deadline that is a multiple of seven days. Throughout the rules, deadlines are amended in the following manner:

- 5–day periods become 7–day periods
- 10–day periods become 14–day periods
- 15–day periods become 14–day periods
- 20–day periods become 21–day periods
- 25–day periods become 28–day periods

Rule 2015.3. Reports of Financial Information on Entities in Which a Chapter 11 Estate Holds a Controlling or Substantial Interest

(a) Reporting requirement

In a chapter 11 case, the trustee or debtor in possession shall file periodic financial reports of the value, operations, and profitability of each entity that is not a publicly traded corporation or a debtor in a case under title 11, and in which the estate holds a substantial or controlling interest. The reports shall be prepared as prescribed by the appropriate Official Form, and shall be based upon the most recent information reasonably available to the trustee or debtor in possession.

(b) Time for filing; service

The first report required by this rule shall be filed no later than seven days before the first date set for the meeting of creditors under § 341 of the Code. Subsequent reports shall be filed no less frequently than every six months thereafter, until the effective date of a plan or the case is dismissed or converted. Copies of the report shall be served on the United States trustee, any committee appointed under § 1102 of the Code, and any other party in interest that has filed a request therefor.

(c) Presumption of substantial or controlling interest; judicial determination

For purposes of this rule, an entity of which the estate controls or owns at least a 20 percent interest, shall be presumed to be an entity in which the estate has a substantial or controlling interest. An entity in which the estate controls or owns less than a 20 percent interest shall be presumed not to be an entity in which the estate has a substantial or controlling interest. Upon motion, the entity, any holder of an interest therein, the United States trustee, or any other party in interest may seek to rebut either presumption, and the court shall, after notice and a hearing, determine whether the estate's interest in the entity is substantial or controlling.

(d) Modification of reporting requirement

The court may, after notice and a hearing, vary the reporting requirement established by subdivision (a) of this rule for cause, including that the trustee or debtor in possession is not able, after a good faith effort, to comply with those reporting requirements, or that the information required by subdivision (a) is publicly available.

(e) Notice and protective orders

No later than 14 days before filing the first report required by this rule, the trustee or debtor in possession shall send notice to the entity in which the estate has a substantial or controlling interest, and to all holders—known to the trustee or debtor in possession—of an interest in that entity, that the trustee or debtor in possession expects to file and serve financial information relating to the entity in accordance with this rule. The entity in which the estate has a substantial or controlling interest, or a person holding an interest in that entity, may request protection of the information under § 107 of the Code.

(f) Effect of request

Unless the court orders otherwise, the pendency of a request under subdivisions (c), (d), or (e) of this rule shall not alter or stay the requirements of subdivision (a).

(Added Apr. 23, 2008, eff. Dec. 1, 2008; amended Mar. 26, 2009, eff. Dec. 1, 2009.)

ADVISORY COMMITTEE NOTES

2008 Adoption

This rule implements § 419 of the Bankruptcy Abuse Prevention and Consumer Protection Act of 2005 ("BAPCPA"). Reports are to be made on the appropriate Official Form. While § 419 of BAPCPA places the obligation to report upon the "debtor," this rule extends the obligation to include cases in which a trustee has been appointed. The court can order that the reports not be filed in appropriate circumstances, such as when the information that would be included in these reports is already available to interested parties.

2009 Amendments

The rule is amended to implement changes in connection with the amendment to Rule 9006(a) and the manner by which time is computed under the rules. The deadline in the rule is amended to substitute a deadline that is a multiple of seven days. Throughout the rules, deadlines are amended in the following manner:

- 5–day periods become 7–day periods
- 10–day periods become 14–day periods
- 15–day periods become 14–day periods
- 20–day periods become 21–day periods
- 25–day periods become 28–day periods

Rule 2016. Compensation for Services Rendered and Reimbursement of Expenses

(a) Application for compensation or reimbursement

An entity seeking interim or final compensation for services, or reimbursement of necessary expenses, from the estate shall file an application setting forth a detailed statement of (1) the services rendered, time expended and expenses incurred, and (2) the amounts requested. An application for compensation shall include a statement as to what payments have theretofore been made or promised to the applicant for services rendered or to be rendered in any capacity whatsoever in connection with the case, the source of the compensation so paid or promised, whether any compensation previously received has been shared and whether an agreement or understanding exists between the applicant and any other entity for the sharing of compensation received or to be received for services rendered in or in connection with the case, and the particulars of any sharing of compensation or agreement or understanding therefor, except that details of any agreement by the applicant for the sharing of compensation as a member or regular associate of a firm of lawyers or accountants shall not be required. The requirements of this subdivision shall apply to an application for compensation for services rendered by an attorney or accountant even though the application is filed by a creditor or other entity. Unless the case is a chapter 9 municipality case, the applicant shall transmit to the United States trustee a copy of the application.

(b) Disclosure of compensation paid or promised to attorney for debtor

Every attorney for a debtor, whether or not the attorney applies for compensation, shall file and transmit to the United States trustee within 14 days after the order for relief, or at another time as the court may direct, the statement required by § 329 of the Code including whether the attorney has shared or agreed to share the compensation with any other entity. The statement shall include the particulars of any such sharing or agreement to share by the attorney, but the details of any agreement for the sharing of the compensation with a member or regular associate of the attorney's law firm shall not be required. A supplemental statement shall be filed and transmitted to the United States trustee within 14 days after any payment or agreement not previously disclosed.

(c) Disclosure of compensation paid or promised to bankruptcy petition preparer

Before a petition is filed, every bankruptcy petition preparer for a debtor shall deliver to the debtor, the declaration under penalty of perjury required by § 110(h)(2). The declaration shall disclose any fee, and the source of any fee, received from or on behalf of the debtor within 12 months of the filing of the case and all unpaid fees charged to the debtor. The declaration shall also describe the services performed and documents prepared or caused to be prepared by the bankruptcy petition preparer. The declaration shall be filed with the petition. The petition preparer shall file a supplemental statement within 14 days after any payment or agreement not previously disclosed.

(As amended Mar. 30, 1987, eff. Aug. 1, 1987; Apr. 30, 1991, eff. Aug. 1, 1991; Mar. 27, 2003, eff. Dec. 1, 2003; Mar. 26, 2009, eff. Dec. 1, 2009.)

ADVISORY COMMITTEE NOTES

This rule is derived from former Rule 219. Many of the former rule's requirements are, however, set forth in the Code. Section 329 requires disclosure by an attorney of transactions with the debtor, § 330 sets forth the bases for allowing compensation, and § 504 prohibits sharing of compensation. This rule implements those various provisions.

Subdivision (a) includes within its provisions a committee, member thereof, agent, attorney or accountant for the committee when compensation or reimbursement of expenses is sought from the estate.

Regular associate of a law firm is defined in Rule 9001(9) to include any attorney regularly employed by, associated with, or counsel to that law firm. Firm is defined in Rule 9001(6) to include a partnership or professional corporation.

1987 Amendments

Subdivision (a) is amended to change "person" to "entity." There are occasions in which a governmental unit may be entitled to file an application under this rule. The requirement that the application contain a "detailed statement of services rendered, time expended and expenses incurred" gives to the court authority to ensure that the application is both comprehensive and detailed. No amendments are made to delineate further the requirements of the application because the amount of detail to be furnished is a function of the nature of the services rendered and the complexity of the case.

Subdivision (b) is amended to require that the attorney for the debtor file the § 329 statement before the meeting of creditors. This will assist the parties in conducting the examination of the debtor. In addition, the amended rule requires the attorney to supplement the § 329 statement if an undisclosed payment is made to the attorney or a new or amended agreement is entered into by the debtor and the attorney.

1991 Amendments

Subdivision (a) is amended to enable the United States trustee to perform the duty to monitor applications for compensation and reimbursement filed under § 330 of the Code. See 28 U.S.C. § 586(a)(3)(A).

Subdivision (b) is amended to give the United States trustee the information needed to determine whether to request appropriate relief based on excessive fees under § 329(b) of the Code. See Rule 2017.

The words "with the court" are deleted in subdivisions (a) and (b) as unnecessary. See Rules 5005(a) and 9001(3).

2003 Amendments

This rule is amended by adding subdivision (c) to implement § 110(h)(1) of the Code.

2009 Amendments

The rule is amended to implement changes in connection with the amendment to Rule 9006(a) and the manner by which time is computed under the rules. The deadline in the rule is amended to substitute a deadline that is a multiple of seven days. Throughout the rules, deadlines are amended in the following manner:

- 5–day periods become 7–day periods
- 10–day periods become 14–day periods
- 15–day periods become 14–day periods
- 20–day periods become 21–day periods
- 25–day periods become 28–day periods

Subdivision (c) is amended to reflect the 2005 amendment to § 110(h)(1) of the Bankruptcy Code which now requires that the declaration be filed with the petition. The statute previously required that the petition preparer file the declaration within 10 days after the filing of the petition. The amendment to the rule also corrects the cross reference to § 110(h)(1), which was redesignated as subparagraph (h)(2) of § 110 by the 2005 amendment to the Code.

Other changes are stylistic.

HISTORICAL NOTES

Guidelines for Reviewing Applications for Compensation and Reimbursement of Expenses Filed Under 11 U.S.C. § 330

(a) General Information. (1) The Bankruptcy Reform Act of 1994 amended the responsibilities of the United States Trustees under 28 U.S.C. 586(a)(3)(A) to provide that, whenever they deem appropriate, United States Trustees will review applications for compensation and reimbursement of expenses under section 330 of the Bankruptcy Code, 11 U.S.C. 101, et seq. ("Code"), in accordance with procedural guidelines ("Guidelines") adopted by the Executive Office for United States Trustees ("Executive Office"). The following Guidelines have been adopted by the Executive Office and are to be uniformly applied by the United States Trustees except when circumstances warrant different treatment.

(2) The United States Trustees shall use these Guidelines in all cases commenced on or after October 22, 1994.

(3) The Guidelines are not intended to supersede local rules of court, but should be read as complementing the procedures set forth in local rules.

(4) Nothing in the Guidelines should be construed:

(i) To limit the United States Trustee's discretion to request additional information necessary for the review of a particular application or type of application or to refer any information provided to the United States Trustee to any investigatory or prosecutorial authority of the United States or a state;

(ii) To limit the United States Trustee's discretion to determine whether to file comments or objections to applications; or

(iii) To create any private right of action on the part of any person enforceable in litigation with the United States Trustee or the United States.

(5) Recognizing that the final authority to award compensation and reimbursement under section 330 of the Code is vested in the Court, the Guidelines focus on the disclosure of information relevant to a proper award under the law. In evaluating fees for professional services, it is relevant to consider various factors including the following: the time spent; the rates charged; whether the services were necessary to the administration of, or beneficial towards the completion of, the case at the time they were rendered; whether services were performed within a reasonable time commensurate with the complexity, importance, and nature of the problem, issue, or task addressed; and whether compensation is reasonable based on the customary compensation charged by comparably skilled practitioners in non-bankruptcy cases. The Guidelines thus reflect standards and procedures articulated in section 330 of the Code and Rule 2016 of the Federal Rules of Bankruptcy Procedure for awarding compensation to trustees and to professionals employed under section 327 or 1103. Applications that contain the information requested in these Guidelines will facilitate review by the Court, the parties, and the United States Trustee.

(6) Fee applications submitted by trustees are subject to the same standard of review as are applications of other professionals and will be evaluated according to the principles articulated in these Guidelines. Each United States Trustee should establish whether and to what extent trustees can deviate from the format specified in these Guidelines without substantially affecting the ability of the United States Trustee to review and comment on their fee applications in a manner consistent with the requirements of the law.

(b) Contents of Applications for Compensation and Reimbursement of Expenses. All applications should include sufficient detail to demonstrate compliance with the standards set forth in 11 U.S.C. § 330. The fee application should also contain sufficient information about the case and the applicant so that the Court, the creditors, and the United States Trustee can review it without searching for relevant information in other documents. The following will facilitate review of the application.

(1) Information about the Applicant and the Application. The following information should be provided in every fee application:

(i) Date the bankruptcy petition was filed, date of the order approving employment, identity of the party represented, date services commenced, and whether the applicant is seeking compensation under a provision of the Bankruptcy Code other than section 330.

(ii) Terms and conditions of employment and compensation, source of compensation, existence and terms controlling use of a retainer, and any budgetary or other limitations on fees.

(iii) Names and hourly rates of all applicant's professionals and paraprofessionals who billed time, explanation of any changes in hourly rates from those previously charged, and statement of whether the compensation is based on the customary compensation charged by comparably skilled practitioners in cases other than cases under title 11.

(iv) Whether the application is interim or final, and the dates of previous orders on interim compensation or reimbursement of expenses along with the amounts requested and the amounts allowed or disallowed, amounts of all previous payments, and amount of any allowed fees and expenses remaining unpaid.

(v) Whether the person on whose behalf the applicant is employed has been given the opportunity to review the application and whether that person has approved the requested amount.

(vi) When an application is filed less than 120 days after the order for relief or after a prior application to the Court, the date and terms of the order allowing leave to file at shortened intervals.

(vii) Time period of the services or expenses covered by the application.

(2) Case Status. The following information should be provided to the extent that it is known to or can be reasonably ascertained by the applicant:

(i) In a chapter 7 case, a summary of the administration of the case including all moneys received and disbursed in the case, when the case is expected to close, and, if applicant is seeking an interim award, whether it is feasible to make an interim distribution to creditors without prejudicing the rights of any creditor holding a claim of equal or higher priority.

(ii) In a chapter 11 case, whether a plan and disclosure statement have been filed and, if not yet filed, when the plan and disclosure statement are expected to be filed; whether all quarterly fees have been paid to the United States Trustee; and whether all monthly operating reports have been filed.

(iii) In every case, the amount of cash on hand or on deposit, the amount and nature of accrued unpaid administrative expenses, and the amount of unencumbered funds in the estate.

(iv) Any material changes in the status of the case that occur after the filing of the fee application should be raised, orally or in writing, at the hearing on the application or, if a hearing is not required, prior to the expiration of the time period for objection.

(3) Summary Sheet. All applications should contain a summary or cover sheet that provides a synopsis of the following information:

(i) Total compensation and expenses requested and any amount(s) previously requested;

(ii) Total compensation and expenses previously awarded by the court;

(iii) Name and applicable billing rate for each person who billed time during the period, and date of bar admission for each attorney;

(iv) Total hours billed and total amount of billing for each person who billed time during billing period; and

(v) Computation of blended hourly rate for persons who billed time during period, excluding paralegal or other paraprofessional time.

(4) Project Billing Format. (i) To facilitate effective review of the application, all time and service entries should be arranged by project categories. The project categories set forth in Exhibit A should be used to the extent applicable. A separate project category should be used for administrative matters and, if payment is requested, for fee application preparation.

(ii) The United States Trustee has discretion to determine that the project billing format is not necessary in a particular case or in a particular class of cases. Applicants should be encouraged to consult with the United States Trustee if there is a question as to the need for project billing in any particular case.

(iii) Each project category should contain a narrative summary of the following information:

(A) a description of the project, its necessity and benefit to the estate, and the status of the project including all pending litigation for which compensation and reimbursement are requested;

(B) identification of each person providing services on the project; and

(C) a statement of the number of hours spent and the amount of compensation requested for each professional and paraprofessional on the project.

(iv) Time and service entries are to be reported in chronological order under the appropriate project category.

(v) Time entries should be kept contemporaneously with the services rendered in time periods of tenths of an hour. Services should be noted in detail and not combined or "lumped" together, with each service showing a separate time entry; however, tasks performed in a project which total a de minimis amount of time can be combined or lumped together if they do not exceed .5 hours on a daily aggregate. Time entries for telephone calls, letters, and other communications should give sufficient detail to identify the parties to and the nature of the communication. Time entries for court hearings and conferences should identify the subject of the hearing or conference. If more than one professional from the applicant firm attends a hearing or conference, the applicant should explain the need for multiple attendees.

(5) **Reimbursement for Actual, Necessary Expenses.** Any expense for which reimbursement is sought must be actual and necessary and supported by documentation as appropriate. Factors relevant to a determination that the expense is proper include the following:

(i) Whether the expense is reasonable and economical. For example, first class and other luxurious travel mode or accommodations will normally be objectionable.

(ii) Whether the requested expenses are customarily charged to non-bankruptcy clients of the applicant.

(iii) Whether applicant has provided a detailed itemization of all expenses including the date incurred, description of expense (e.g., type of travel, type of fare, rate, destination), method of computation, and, where relevant, name of the person incurring the expense and purpose of the expense. Itemized expenses should be identified by their nature (e.g., long distance telephone, copy costs, messengers, computer research, airline travel, etc.) and by the month incurred. Unusual items require more detailed explanations and should be allocated, where practicable, to specific projects.

(iv) Whether applicant has prorated expenses where appropriate between the estate and other cases (e.g., travel expenses applicable to more than one case) and has adequately explained the basis for any such proration.

(v) Whether expenses incurred by the applicant to third parties are limited to the actual amounts billed to, or paid by, the applicant on behalf of the estate.

(vi) Whether applicant can demonstrate that the amount requested for expenses incurred in-house reflect the actual cost of such expenses to the applicant. The United States Trustee may establish an objection ceiling for any in-house expenses that are routinely incurred and for which the actual cost cannot easily be determined by most professionals (e.g., photocopies, facsimile charges, and mileage).

(vii) Whether the expenses appear to be in the nature nonreimbursable overhead. Overhead consists of all continuous administrative or general costs incident to the operation of the applicant's office and not particularly attributable to an individual client or case. Overhead includes, but is not limited to, word processing, proofreading, secretarial and other clerical services, rent, utilities, office equipment and furnishings, insurance, taxes, local telephones and monthly car phone charges, lighting, heating and cooling, and library and publication charges.

(viii) Whether applicant has adhered to allowable rates for expenses as fixed by local rule or order of the Court.

Exhibit A—Project Categories

Here is a list of suggested project categories for use in most bankruptcy cases. Only one category should be used for a given activity. Professionals should make their best effort to be consistent in their use of categories, whether within a particular firm or by different firms working on the same case. It would be appropriate for all professionals to discuss the categories in advance and agree generally on how activities will be categorized. This list is not exclusive. The application may contain additional categories as the case requires. They are generally more applicable to attorneys in chapter 7 and chapter 11, but may be used by all professionals as appropriate.

Asset Analysis and Recovery: Identification and review of potential assets including causes of action and non-litigation recoveries.

Asset Disposition: Sales, leases (§ 365 matters), abandonment and related transaction work.

Business Operations: Issues related to debtor-in-possession operating in chapter 11 such as employee, vendor, tenant issues and other similar problems.

Case Administration: Coordination and compliance activities, including preparation of statement of financial affairs; schedules; list of contracts; United States Trustee interim statements and operating reports; contacts with the United States Trustee; general creditor inquiries.

Claims Administration and Objections: Specific claim inquiries; bar date motions; analyses, objections and allowances of claims.

Employee Benefits/Pensions: Review issues such as severance, retention, 401K coverage and continuance of pension plan.

Fee/Employment Applicants: Preparation of employment and fee applications for self or others; motions to establish interim procedures.

Fee/Employment Objections: Review of and objections to the employment and fee applications of others.

Financing: Matters under §§ 361, 363 and 364 including cash collateral and secured claims; loan document analysis.

Litigation: There should be a separate category established for each matter (e.g., XYZ Litigation).

Meetings of Creditors: Preparing for and attending the conference of creditors, the § 341(a) meeting and other creditors' committee meetings.

Plan and Disclosure Statement: Formulation, presentation and confirmation; compliance with the plan confirmation order, related orders and rules; disbursement and case closing activities, except those related to the allowance and objections to allowance of claims.

Relief From Stay Proceedings: Matters relating to termination or continuation of automatic stay under § 362.

The following categories are generally more applicable to accountants and financial advisors, but may be used by all professionals as appropriate.

Accounting/Auditing: Activities related to maintaining and auditing books of account, preparation of financial statements and account analysis.

Business Analysis: Preparation and review of company business plan; development and review of strategies; preparation and review of cash flow forecasts and feasibility studies.

Corporate Finance: Review financial aspects of potential mergers, acquisitions and disposition of company or subsidiaries.

Data Analysis: Management information systems review, installation and analysis, construction, maintenance and reporting of significant case financial data, lease rejection, claims, etc.

Litigation Consulting: Providing consulting and expert witness services relating to various bankruptcy matters such as insolvency, feasibility, avoiding actions, forensic accounting, etc.

Reconstruction Accounting: Reconstructing books and records from past transactions and bringing accounting current.

Tax Issues: Analysis of tax issues and preparation of state and federal tax returns.

Valuation: Appraise or review appraisals of assets.

[61 FR 24890, May 17, 1996]

CROSS REFERENCES

Compensation of professional persons,

Actual, necessary services, see 11 USCA § 330.

Limitation on, see 11 USCA § 328.

Sharing of, see 11 USCA § 504.

Definition of,

"Firm" to include partnership or professional corporation, see Fed.Rules Bankr.Proc. Rule 9001, 11 USCA.

"Regular associate" to mean attorney employed by, associated with, as counsel to firm or individual, see Fed. Rules Bankr.Proc. Rule 9001, 11 USCA.

Employment of professional persons, see Fed.Rules Bankr. Proc. Rule 2014, 11 USCA.

Rule 2017. Examination of Debtor's Transactions With Debtor's Attorney

(a) Payment or transfer to attorney before order for relief

On motion by any party in interest or on the court's own initiative, the court after notice and a hearing may determine whether any payment of money or any transfer of property by the debtor, made directly or indirectly and in contemplation of the filing of a petition under the Code by or against the debtor or before entry of the order for relief in an involuntary case, to an attorney for services rendered or to be rendered is excessive.

(b) Payment or transfer to attorney after order for relief

On motion by the debtor, the United States trustee, or on the court's own initiative, the court after notice and a hearing may determine whether any payment of money or any transfer of property, or any agreement therefor, by the debtor to an attorney after entry of an order for relief in a case under the Code is excessive, whether the payment or transfer is made or is to be made directly or indirectly, if the payment, transfer, or agreement therefor is for services in any way related to the case.

(As amended Mar. 30, 1987, eff. Aug. 1, 1987; Apr. 30, 1991, eff. Aug. 1, 1991.)

ADVISORY COMMITTEE NOTES

This rule is derived from § 60d of the Act [former § 96(d) of this title] and former Bankruptcy Rule 220 and implements § 329 of the Code. Information required to be disclosed by the attorney for a debtor by § 329 of the Code and by the debtor in his Statement of Financial Affairs (Item #15 of Form No. 7, Item #20 of Form No. 8) will assist the court in determining whether to proceed under this rule. Section 60d was enacted in recognition of "the temptation of a failing debtor to deal too liberally with his property in employing counsel to protect him in view of financial reverses and probable failure." In re Wood & Henderson, 210 U.S. 246, 253 (1908). This rule, like § 60d of the Act and § 329 of the Code, is premised on the need for and appropriateness of judicial scrutiny of arrangements between a debtor and his attorney to protect the creditors of the estate and the debtor against overreaching by an officer of the court who is in a peculiarly advantageous position to impose on both the creditors and his client. 2 Collier, Bankruptcy ¶329.02 (15th ed. 1980); MacLachlan, Bankruptcy 318 (1956). Rule 9014 applies to any contested matter arising under this rule.

This rule is not to be construed to permit post-petition payments or transfers which may be avoided under other provisions of the Code.

1991 Amendments

This rule is amended to include within subdivision (a) a payment or transfer of property by the debtor to an attorney after the filing of an involuntary petition but before the order for relief. Any party in interest should be able to make a motion for a determination of whether such payment or transfer is excessive because the funds or property transferred may be property of the estate.

The United States trustee supervises and monitors the administration of bankruptcy cases other than chapter 9 cases and pursuant to § 307 of the Code may raise, appear and be heard on issues relating to fees paid to the debtor's attorney. It is consistent with that role to expect the United States trustee to review statements filed under Rule 2016(b) and to file motions relating to excessive fees pursuant to § 329 of the Code.

CROSS REFERENCES

Court filing of compensation paid or agreed to be paid, see 11 USCA § 329.

Motions, form and service, see Fed.Rules Bankr.Proc. Rule 9013, 11 USCA.

Proceedings under this rule as nonadversarial proceedings, see Fed.Rules Bankr.Proc. Rule 7001, 11 USCA.

Process, service of summons, complaint, see Fed.Rules Bankr.Proc. Rule 7004, 11 USCA.

Rule 2018.   Intervention; Right to Be Heard

(a) Permissive intervention

In a case under the Code, after hearing on such notice as the court directs and for cause shown, the court may permit any interested entity to intervene generally or with respect to any specified matter.

(b) Intervention by Attorney General of a State

In a chapter 7, 11, 12, or 13 case, the Attorney General of a State may appear and be heard on behalf of consumer creditors if the court determines the appearance is in the public interest, but the Attorney General may not appeal from any judgment, order, or decree in the case.

(c) Chapter 9 municipality case

The Secretary of the Treasury of the United States may, or if requested by the court shall, intervene in a chapter 9 case. Representatives of the state in which the debtor is located may intervene in a chapter 9 case with respect to matters specified by the court.

(d) Labor unions

In a chapter 9, 11, or 12 case, a labor union or employees' association, representative of employees of the debtor, shall have the right to be heard on the economic soundness of a plan affecting the interests of the employees. A labor union or employees' association which exercises its right to be heard under this subdivision shall not be entitled to appeal any judgment, order, or decree relating to the plan, unless otherwise permitted by law.

(e) Service on entities covered by this rule

The court may enter orders governing the service of notice and papers on entities permitted to intervene or be heard pursuant to this rule.

(As amended Mar. 30, 1987, eff. Aug. 1, 1987; Apr. 30, 1991, eff. Aug. 1, 1991.)

ADVISORY COMMITTEE NOTES

This rule is derived from former Rules 8–210, 9–15 and 10–210 and it implements §§ 1109 and 1164 of the Code.

Pursuant to § 1109 of the Code, parties in interest have a right to be heard and the Securities and Exchange Commission may raise and be heard on any issue but it may not take an appeal. That section is applicable in chapter 9 cases (§ 901 of the Code) and in chapter 11 cases, including cases under subchapter IV thereof for the reorganization of a railroad.

In a railroad reorganization case under subchapter IV of chapter 11, § 1164 also gives the right to be heard to the Interstate Commerce Commission, the Department of Transportation and any state or local regulatory commission with jurisdiction over the debtor, but these entities may not appeal.

This rule does not apply in adversary proceedings. For intervention in adversary proceedings, see Rule 7024. The rules do not provide any right of compensation to or reimbursement of expenses for intervenors or others covered by this rule. Section 503(b)(3)(D) and (4) is not applicable to the entities covered by this rule.

Subdivision (a) is derived from former Chapter VIII Rule 8–210 and former Chapter X Rule 10–210. It permits intervention of an entity (see § 101(14), (21) of the Code) not otherwise entitled to do so under the Code or this rule. Such a party seeking to intervene must show cause therefor.

Subdivision (b) specifically grants the appropriate state's attorney General the right to appear and be heard on behalf of consumer creditors when it is in the public interest. See House Rep. No. 95–595, 95th Cong., 1st Sess. (1977) 189. While "consumer creditor" is not defined in the Code or elsewhere, it would include the type of individual entitled to priority under § 507(a)(5) of the Code, that is, an individual who has deposited money for the purchase, lease or rental of property or the purchase of services for the personal, family, or household use of the individual. It would also include individuals who purchased or leased property for such purposes in connection with which there may exist claims for breach of warranty.

This subdivision does not grant the Attorney General the status of party in interest. In other contexts, the Attorney General will, of course, be a party in interest as for example, in representing a state in connection with a tax claim.

Subdivision (c) recognizes the possible interests of the Secretary of the Treasury or of the state of the debtor's locale when a municipality is the debtor. It is derived from former Chapter IX Rule 9–15 and § 85(d) of the Act [former § 405(d) of this title].

Subdivision (d) is derived from former Chapter X Rule 10–210 which, in turn, was derived from § 206 of the Act [former § 606 of this title]. Section 206 has no counter-part in the Code.

Subdivision (e) is derived from former Chapter VIII Rule 8–210(d). It gives the court flexibility in directing the type of future notices to be given intervenors.

1987 Amendments

Subdivision (d) is amended to make it clear that the prohibition against appeals by labor unions is limited only to their participation in connection with the hearings on the plan as provided in subdivision (d). If a labor union would otherwise have the right to file an appeal or to be a party to an appeal, this rule does not preclude the labor union from exercising that right.

Subdivisions **(b)** and **(d)** are amended to include chapter 12.

CROSS REFERENCES

"Consumer debt" defined as debt primarily for personal, family, or household purpose, see 11 USCA § 101.

Definitions for purposes of this rule of,

"Entity", see 11 USCA § 101.

"Governmental unit", see 11 USCA § 101.

"Person", see 11 USCA § 101.

Intervention in adversary proceedings, see Fed.Rules Bankr.Proc. Rule 7024, 11 USCA.

Intervention of,

Department of Transportation, see 11 USCA § 1164.

Interstate Commerce Commission, see 11 USCA § 1164.

Party in interest, see 11 USCA § 1109.

Securities and Exchange Commission, see 11 USCA § 1109.

State or local regulatory commission, see 11 USCA § 1164.

Rule 2019. Disclosure Regarding Creditors and Equity Security Holders in Chapter 9 and Chapter 11 Cases

(a) Definitions

In this rule the following terms have the meanings indicated:

(1) "Disclosable economic interest" means any claim, interest, pledge, lien, option, participation, derivative instrument, or any other right or derivative right granting the holder an economic interest that is affected by the value, acquisition, or disposition of a claim or interest.

(2) "Represent" or "represents" means to take a position before the court or to solicit votes regarding the confirmation of a plan on behalf of another.

(b) Disclosure by groups, committees, and entities

(1) In a chapter 9 or 11 case, a verified statement setting forth the information specified in subdivision (c) of this rule shall be filed by every group or committee that consists of or represents, and every entity that represents, multiple creditors or equity security holders that are (A) acting in concert to advance their common interests, and (B) not composed entirely of affiliates or insiders of one another.

(2) Unless the court orders otherwise, an entity is not required to file the verified statement described in paragraph (1) of this subdivision solely because of its status as:

(A) an indenture trustee;

(B) an agent for one or more other entities under an agreement for the extension of credit;

(C) a class action representative; or

(D) a governmental unit that is not a person.

(c) Information required

The verified statement shall include:

(1) the pertinent facts and circumstances concerning:

(A) with respect to a group or committee, other than a committee appointed under § 1102 or § 1114 of the Code, the formation of the group or committee, including the name of each entity at whose instance the group or committee was formed or for whom the group or committee has agreed to act; or

(B) with respect to an entity, the employment of the entity, including the name of each creditor or equity security holder at whose instance the employment was arranged;

(2) if not disclosed under subdivision (c)(1), with respect to an entity, and with respect to each member of a group or committee:

(A) name and address;

(B) the nature and amount of each disclosable economic interest held in relation to the debtor as of the date the entity was employed or the group or committee was formed; and

(C) with respect to each member of a group or committee that claims to represent any entity in addition to the members of the group or committee, other than a committee appointed under § 1102 or § 1114 of the Code, the date of acquisition by quarter and year of each disclosable economic interest, unless acquired more than one year before the petition was filed;

(3) if not disclosed under subdivision (c)(1) or (c)(2), with respect to each creditor or equity security holder represented by an entity, group, or committee, other than a committee appointed under § 1102 or § 1114 of the Code:

(A) name and address; and

(B) the nature and amount of each disclosable economic interest held in relation to the debtor as of the date of the statement; and

(4) a copy of the instrument, if any, authorizing the entity, group, or committee to act on behalf of creditors or equity security holders.

(d) Supplemental statements

If any fact disclosed in its most recently filed statement has changed materially, an entity, group, or committee shall file a verified supplemental statement whenever it takes a position before the court or solicits votes on the confirmation of a plan. The supplemental statement shall set forth the material changes in the facts required by subdivision (c) to be disclosed.

(e) Determination of failure to comply; sanctions

(1) On motion of any party in interest, or on its own motion, the court may determine whether there has been a failure to comply with any provision of this rule.

(2) If the court finds such a failure to comply, it may:

(A) refuse to permit the entity, group, or committee to be heard or to intervene in the case;

(B) hold invalid any authority, acceptance, rejection, or objection given, procured, or received by the entity, group, or committee; or

(C) grant other appropriate relief.

(As amended Mar. 30, 1987, eff. Aug. 1, 1987; Apr. 30, 1991, eff. Aug. 1, 1991; Apr. 26, 2011, eff. Dec. 1, 2011.)

ADVISORY COMMITTEE NOTES

This rule is a comprehensive regulation of representation in chapter 9 municipality and in chapter 11 reorganization cases. It is derived from §§ 209 to 213 of the Act [former §§ 609 to 613 of this title] and former Chapter X Rule 10–211.

Subdivision (b) is derived from §§ 212, 213 of the Act [former §§ 612 and 613 of this title]. As used in clause (2), "other authorization" would include a power or warrant of attorney which are specifically mentioned in § 212 of the Act. This rule deals with representation provisions in mortgages, trust deeds, etc. to protect the beneficiaries from unfair practices and the like. It does not deal with the validation or invalidation of security interests generally. If immediate compliance is not possible, the court may permit a representative to be heard on a specific matter, but there is no implicit waiver of compliance on a permanent basis.

1991 Amendments

Subdivision (a) is amended to exclude from the requirements of this rule committees of retired employees appointed pursuant to § 1114 of the Code. The words "with the clerk" are deleted as unnecessary. See Rules 5005(a) and 9001(3).

2011 Amendments

The rule is substantially amended to expand the scope of its coverage and the content of its disclosure requirements. Stylistic and organizational changes are also made in order to provide greater clarity. Because the rule no longer applies only to representatives of creditors and equity security holders, the title of the rule has been changed to reflect its broadened focus on disclosure of financial information in chapter 9 and chapter 11 cases.

Subdivision (a). The content of subdivision (a) is new. It sets forth a definition of the term "disclosable economic interest," which is used in subdivisions (c)(2), (c)(3), (d), and (e). The definition of the term is intended to be sufficiently broad to cover any economic interest that could affect the legal and strategic positions a stakeholder takes in a chapter 9 or chapter 11 case. A disclosable economic interest extends beyond claims and interests owned by a stakeholder and includes, among other types of holdings, short positions, credit default swaps, and total return swaps.

The second definition is of "represent" or "represents." The definition provides that representation requires active participation in the case or in a proceeding on behalf of another entity—either by taking a position on a matter before the court or by soliciting votes on the confirmation of a plan. Thus, for example, an attorney who is retained and consulted by a creditor or equity security holder to monitor the case, but who does not advocate any position before the court or engage in solicitation activities on behalf of that client, does not represent the creditor or equity security holder for purposes of this rule.

Subdivision (b). Subdivision (b)(1) specifies who is covered by the rule's disclosure requirements. In addition to an entity, group, or committee that *represents* more than one creditor or equity security holder, the amendment extends the rule's coverage to groups or committees that *consist* of more than one creditor or equity security holder. The rule no longer excludes official committees, except as specifically indicated. The rule applies to a group of creditors or equity security holders that act in concert to advance common interests (except when the group consists exclusively of affiliates or insiders of one another), even if the group does not call itself a committee.

Subdivision (b)(2) excludes certain entities from the rule's coverage. Even though these entities may represent multiple creditors or equity security holders, they do so under formal legal arrangements of trust or contact law that preclude them from acting on the basis of conflicting economic interests. For example, an indenture trustee's responsibilities are defined by the indenture, and individual interests of bondholders would not affect the trustee's representation.

Subdivision (c). Subdivision (c) sets forth the information that must be included in a verified statement required to be filed under this rule. Subdivision (c)(1) continues to require disclosure concerning the employment of an entity or indenture trustee and the formation of a committee or group, other than an official committee, and the employment of an entity.

Subdivision (c)(2) specifies information that must be disclosed with respect to the entity and each member of the committee and group filing the statement. In the case of a committee or group, the information about the nature and amount of a disclosable economic interest must be specifically provided on a member-by-member basis, and not in the aggregate. The quarter and year in which each disclosable economic interest was acquired by each member of a committee or group (other than an official committee) that claims to represent others must also be specifically provided, except for a disclosable economic interest acquired more than a year before the filing of the petition. Although the rule no longer requires the disclosure of the precise date of acquisition or the amount paid for disclosable economic interests, nothing in this rule precludes either the discovery of that information or its disclosure when ordered by the court pursuant to authority outside this rule.

Subdivision (c)(3) specifies information that must be disclosed with respect to creditors or equity security holders that are represented by an entity, group, committee, or indenture trustee. This provision does not apply with respect to those represented by official committees. The information required to be disclosed under subdivision (c)(3) parallels that required to be disclosed under subdivision (c)(2)(A) and (B). The amendment also clarifies that under (c)(3) the nature and amount of each disclosable economic interest of represented creditors and shareholders must be stated as of the date of the verified statement.

Subdivision (c)(4) requires the attachment of any instrument authorizing the filer of the verified statement to act on behalf of creditors or equity security holders.

Subdivision (d). Subdivision (d) requires the filing of a supplemental statement at the time an entity, group, or committee takes a position before the court or solicits votes on a plan if there has been a material change in any of the information contained in its last filed statement. The supplemental verified statement must set forth the material changes that have occurred regarding the information required to be disclosed by subdivision (c) of this rule.

Subdivision (e). Subdivision (e) addresses the court's authority to determine whether there has been a violation of this rule and to impose a sanction for any violation. It no longer addresses the court's authority to determine violations of other applicable laws regulating the activities and personnel of an entity, group, or committee.

CROSS REFERENCES

Appointment of creditors' committee organized before order for relief, see Fed.Rules Bankr.Proc. Rule 2007, 11 USCA.

Motions, form and service, see Fed.Rules Bankr.Proc. Rule 9013, 11 USCA.

Trustees for estates when joint administration ordered, see Fed.Rules Bankr.Proc. Rule 2009, 11 USCA.

Rule 2020. Review of Acts by United States Trustee

A proceeding to contest any act or failure to act by the United States trustee is governed by Rule 9014.

(Added Apr. 30, 1991, eff. Aug. 1, 1991.)

ADVISORY COMMITTEE NOTES

The United States trustee performs administrative functions, such as the convening of the meeting of creditors and the appointment of trustees and committees. Most of the acts of the United States trustee are not controversial and will go unchallenged. However, the United States trustee is not a judicial officer and does not resolve disputes regarding the propriety of its own actions. This rule, which is new, provides a procedure for judicial review of the United States trustee's acts or failure to act in connection with the administration of the case. For example, if the United States trustee schedules a § 341 meeting to be held 90 days after the petition is filed, and a party in interest wishes to challenge the propriety of that act in view of § 341(a) of the Code and Rule 2003 which requires that the meeting be held not more than 40 days after the order for relief, this rule permits the party to do so by motion.

This rule provides for review of acts already committed by the United States trustee, but does not provide for advisory opinions in advance of the act. This rule is not intended to limit the discretion of the United States trustee, provided that the United States trustee's act is authorized by, and in compliance with, the Code, title 28, these rules, and other applicable law.

PART III—CLAIMS AND DISTRIBUTION TO CREDITORS AND EQUITY INTEREST HOLDERS; PLANS

Rule 3001. Proof of Claim

(a) Form and content

A proof of claim is a written statement setting forth a creditor's claim. A proof of claim shall conform substantially to the appropriate Official Form.

(b) Who may execute

A proof of claim shall be executed by the creditor or the creditor's authorized agent except as provided in Rules 3004 and 3005.

(c) Supporting information

(1) Claim based on a writing

Except for a claim governed by paragraph (3) of this subdivision, when a claim, or an interest in property of the debtor securing the claim, is based on a writing, a copy of the writing shall be filed with the proof of claim. If the writing has been lost or destroyed, a statement of the circumstances of the loss or destruction shall be filed with the claim.

(2) Additional requirements in an individual debtor case: sanctions for failure to comply

In a case in which the debtor is an individual:

(A) If, in addition to its principal amount, a claim includes interest, fees, expenses, or other charges incurred before the petition was filed, an itemized statement of the interest, fees, expenses, or charges shall be filed with the proof of claim.

(B) If a security interest is claimed in the debtor's property, a statement of the amount necessary to cure any default as of the date of the petition shall be filed with the proof of claim.

(C) If a security interest is claimed in property that is the debtor's principal residence, the attachment prescribed by the appropriate Official Form shall be filed with the proof of claim. If an escrow account has been established in connection with the claim, an escrow account statement prepared as of the date the petition was filed and in a form consistent with applicable nonbankruptcy law shall be filed with the attachment to the proof of claim.

(D) If the holder of a claim fails to provide any information required by this subdivision (c), the court may, after notice and hearing, take either or both of the following actions:

(i) preclude the holder from presenting the omitted information, in any form, as evidence in any contested matter or adversary proceeding in the case, unless the court determines that the failure was substantially justified or is harmless; or

(ii) award other appropriate relief, including reasonable expenses and attorney's fees caused by the failure.

(3) Claim based on an open-end or revolving consumer credit agreement

(A) When a claim is based on an open-end or revolving consumer credit agreement—except one for which a security interest is claimed in the debtor's real property—a statement shall be filed with the proof of claim, including all of the following information that applies to the account:

(i) the name of the entity from whom the creditor purchased the account;

(ii) the name of the entity to whom the debt was owed at the time of an account holder's last transaction on the account;

(iii) the date of an account holder's last transaction;

(iv) the date of the last payment on the account; and

(v) the date on which the account was charged to profit and loss.

(B) On written request by a party in interest, the holder of a claim based on an open-end or revolving consumer credit agreement shall, within 30 days after the request is sent, provide the requesting party a copy of the writing specified in paragraph (1) of this subdivision.

(d) Evidence of perfection of security interest

If a security interest in property of the debtor is claimed, the proof of claim shall be accompanied by evidence that the security interest has been perfected.

(e) Transferred claim

(1) Transfer of claim other than for security before proof filed

If a claim has been transferred other than for security before proof of the claim has been filed, the proof of claim may be filed only by the transferee or an indenture trustee.

(2) Transfer of claim other than for security after proof filed

If a claim other than one based on a publicly traded note, bond, or debenture has been transferred other than for security after the proof of claim has been filed, evidence of the transfer shall be filed by the transferee. The clerk shall immediately notify the alleged transferor by mail of the filing of the evidence of transfer and that objection thereto, if any, must be filed within 21 days of the mailing of the notice or within any additional time allowed by the court. If the alleged transferor files a timely objection and the court finds, after notice and a hearing, that the claim has been transferred other than for security, it shall enter an order substituting the transferee for the transferor. If a timely objection is not filed by the alleged transferor, the transferee shall be substituted for the transferor.

(3) Transfer of claim for security before proof filed

If a claim other than one based on a publicly traded note, bond, or debenture has been transferred for security before proof of the claim has been

filed, the transferor or transferee or both may file a proof of claim for the full amount. The proof shall be supported by a statement setting forth the terms of the transfer. If either the transferor or the transferee files a proof of claim, the clerk shall immediately notify the other by mail of the right to join in the filed claim. If both transferor and transferee file proofs of the same claim, the proofs shall be consolidated. If the transferor or transferee does not file an agreement regarding its relative rights respecting voting of the claim, payment of dividends thereon, or participation in the administration of the estate, on motion by a party in interest and after notice and a hearing, the court shall enter such orders respecting these matters as may be appropriate.

(4) Transfer of claim for security after proof filed

If a claim other than one based on a publicly traded note, bond, or debenture has been transferred for security after the proof of claim has been filed, evidence of the terms of the transfer shall be filed by the transferee. The clerk shall immediately notify the alleged transferor by mail of the filing of the evidence of transfer and that objection thereto, if any, must be filed within 21 days of the mailing of the notice or within any additional time allowed by the court. If a timely objection is filed by the alleged transferor, the court, after notice and a hearing, shall determine whether the claim has been transferred for security. If the transferor or transferee does not file an agreement regarding its relative rights respecting voting of the claim, payment of dividends thereon, or participation in the administration of the estate, on motion by a party in interest and after notice and a hearing, the court shall enter such orders respecting these matters as may be appropriate.

(5) Service of objection or motion; notice of hearing

A copy of an objection filed pursuant to paragraph (2) or (4) or a motion filed pursuant to paragraph (3) or (4) of this subdivision together with a notice of a hearing shall be mailed or otherwise delivered to the transferor or transferee, whichever is appropriate, at least 30 days prior to the hearing.

(f) Evidentiary effect

A proof of claim executed and filed in accordance with these rules shall constitute prima facie evidence of the validity and amount of the claim.

(g)[1] To the extent not inconsistent with the United States Warehouse Act or applicable State law, a warehouse receipt, scale ticket, or similar document of the type routinely issued as evidence of title by a grain storage facility, as defined in section 557 of title 11, shall constitute prima facie evidence of the validity and amount of a claim of ownership of a quantity of grain. (As amended Pub.L. 98–353, Title III, § 354, July 10, 1984, 98 Stat. 361; Apr. 30, 1991, eff. Aug. 1, 1991; Mar. 26, 2009, eff. Dec. 1, 2009; Apr. 26, 2011, eff. Dec. 1, 2011; Apr. 23, 2012, eff. Dec. 1, 2012.)

1 So in original. Subsec. (g) was enacted without a catchline.

ADVISORY COMMITTEE NOTES

This rule is adapted from former Bankruptcy Rules 301 and 302. The Federal Rules of Evidence, made applicable to cases under the Code by Rule 1101, do not prescribe the evidentiary effect to be accorded particular documents. Subdivision (f) of this rule supplements the Federal Rules of Evidence as they apply to cases under the Code.

Subdivision (c). This subdivision is similar to former Bankruptcy Rule 302(c) and continues the requirement for the filing of any written security agreement and provides that the filing of a duplicate of a writing underlying a claim authenticates the claim with the same effect as the filing of the original writing. Cf. Rules 1001(4) and 1003 of F.R. of Evid. Subdivision (d) together with the requirement in the first sentence of subdivision (c) for the filing of any written security agreement, is designed to facilitate the determination whether the claim is secured and properly perfected so as to be valid against the trustee.

Subdivision (d). "Satisfactory evidence" of perfection, which is to accompany the proof of claim, would include a duplicate of an instrument filed or recorded, a duplicate of a certificate of title when a security interest is perfected by notation on such a certificate, a statement that pledged property has been in possession of the secured party since a specified date, or a statement of the reasons why no action was necessary for perfection. The secured creditor may not be required to file a proof of claim under this rule if he is not seeking allowance of a claim for a deficiency. But see § 506(d) of the Code.

Subdivision (e). The rule recognizes the differences between an unconditional transfer of a claim and a transfer for the purpose of security and prescribes a procedure for dealing with the rights of the transferor and transferee when the transfer is for security. The rule clarifies the procedure to be followed when a transfer precedes or follows the filing of the petition. The interests of sound administration are served by requiring the post-petition transferee to file with the proof of claim a statement of the transferor acknowledging the transfer and the consideration for the transfer. Such a disclosure will assist the court in dealing with evils that may arise out of post-bankruptcy traffic in claims against an estate. Monroe v. Scofield, 135 F.2d 725 (10th Cir. 1943); In re Philadelphia & Western Ry., 64 F.Supp. 738 (E.D.Pa.1946); cf. In re Latham Lithographic Corp., 107 F.2d 749 (2d Cir. 1939). Both paragraphs (1) and (3) of this subdivision, which deal with a transfer before the filing of a proof of claim, recognize that the transferee may be unable to obtain the required statement from the transferor, but in that event a sound reason for such inability must accompany the proof of claim filed by the transferee.

Paragraphs (3) and (4) clarify the status of a claim transferred for the purpose of security. An assignee for security has been recognized as a rightful claimant in bankruptcy. Feder v. John Engelhorn & Sons, 202 F.2d 411 (2d Cir. 1953). An assignor's right to file a claim notwithstanding the assignment was sustained in In re R & L Engineering Co., 182

F.Supp. 317 (S.D.Cal.1960). Facilitation of the filing of proofs by both claimants as holders of interests in a single claim is consonant with equitable treatment of the parties and sound administration. See In re Latham Lithographic Corp., 107 F.2d 749 (2d Cir. 1939).

Paragraphs (2) and (4) of subdivision (e) deal with the transfer of a claim after proof has been filed. Evidence of the terms of the transfer required to be disclosed to the court will facilitate the court's determination of the appropriate order to be entered because of the transfer.

Paragraph (5) describes the procedure to be followed when an objection is made by the transferor to the transferee's filed evidence of transfer.

The United States Warehouse Act, referred to in subd. (g), is Part C of Act Aug. 11, 1916, c. 313, 39 Stat. 486, as amended, which is classified generally to chapter 10 (§ 241 et seq.) of Title 7, Agriculture. For complete classification of this Act to the Code, see section 241 of Title 7 and Tables.

1984 Amendments

Subdivision (g) was added by § 354 of the 1984 amendments:

Subd. (g). Pub.L. 98–353 added subd. (g).

1984 Acts

Amendment by Pub.L. 98–353 effective with respect to cases filed 90 days after July 10, 1984, see section 553 of Pub.L. 98–353, set out as a note under section 101 of this title.

1991 Amendments

Subdivision (a) is amended in anticipation of future revision and renumbering of the Official Forms.

Subdivision (e) is amended to limit the court's role to the adjudication of disputes regarding transfers of claims. If a claim has been transferred prior to the filing of a proof of claim, there is no need to state the consideration for the transfer or to submit other evidence of the transfer. If a claim has been transferred other than for security after a proof of claim has been filed, the transferee is substituted for the transferor in the absence of a timely objection by the alleged transferor. In that event, the clerk should note the transfer without the need for court approval. If a timely objection is filed, the court's role is to determine whether a transfer has been made that is enforceable under nonbankruptcy law. This rule is not intended either to encourage or discourage postpetition transfers of claims or to affect any remedies otherwise available under nonbankruptcy law to a transferor or transferee such as for misrepresentation in connection with the transfer of a claim. "After notice and a hearing" as used in subdivision (e) shall be construed in accordance with paragraph (5).

The words "with the clerk" in subdivision (e)(2) and (e)(4) are deleted as unnecessary. See Rules 5005(a) and 9001(3).

2009 Amendments

The rule is amended to implement changes in connection with the amendment to Rule 9006(a) and the manner by which time is computed under the rules. The deadlines in the rule are amended to substitute a deadline that is a multiple of seven days. Throughout the rules, deadlines are amended in the following manner:

- 5–day periods become 7–day periods
- 10–day periods become 14–day periods
- 15–day periods become 14–day periods
- 20–day periods become 21–day periods
- 25–day periods become 28–day periods

2011 Amendments

Subdivision (c). Subdivision (c) is amended to prescribe with greater specificity the supporting information required to accompany certain proofs of claim and, in cases in which the debtor is an individual, the consequences of failing to provide the required information.

Existing subdivision (c) is redesignated as (c)(1).

Subdivision (c)(2) is added to require additional information to accompany proofs of claim filed in cases in which the debtor is an individual. When the holder of a claim seeks to recover-in addition to the principal amount of a debt-interest, fees, expenses, or other charges, the proof of claim must be accompanied by a statement itemizing these additional amounts with sufficient specificity to make clear the basis for the claimed amount.

If a claim is secured by a security interest in the property of the debtor and the debtor defaulted on the claim prior to the filing of the petition, the proof of claim must be accompanied by a statement of the amount required to cure the prepetition default.

If the claim is secured by a security interest in the debtor's principal residence, the proof of claim must be accompanied by the attachment prescribed by the appropriate Official Form. In that attachment, the holder of the claim must provide the information required by subparagraphs (A) and (B) of this paragraph (2). In addition, if an escrow account has been established in connection with the claim, an escrow account statement showing the account balance, and any amount owed, as of the date the petition was filed must be submitted in accordance with subparagraph (C). The statement must be prepared in a form consistent with the requirements of nonbankruptcy law. *See, e.g.*, 12 U.S.C. § 2601 *et seq.* (Real Estate Settlement Procedure Act). Thus the holder of the claim may provide the escrow account statement using the same form it uses outside of bankruptcy for this purpose.

Subparagraph (D) of subdivision (c)(2) sets forth sanctions that the court may impose on a creditor in an individual debtor case that fails to provide information required by subdivision (c). Failure to provide the required information does not itself constitute a ground for disallowance of a claim. See § 502(b) of the Code. But when an objection to the allowance of a claim is made or other litigation arises concerning the status or treatment of a claim, if the holder of that claim has not complied with the requirements of this subdivision, the court may preclude it from presenting as evidence any of the omitted information, unless the failure to comply with this subdivision was substantially justified or harmless. The court retains discretion to allow an amendment to a proof of claim under appropriate circumstances or to impose a sanction different from or in addition to the preclusion of the introduction of evidence.

2012 Amendments

Subdivision (c). Subdivision (c) is amended in several respects. The former requirement in paragraph (1) to file an original or duplicate of a supporting document is amended to reflect the current practice of filing only copies. The proof of claim form instructs claimants not to file the original of a document because it may be destroyed by the clerk's office after scanning.

Subdivision (c) is further amended to add paragraph (3). Except with respect to claims secured by a security interest in the debtor's real property (such as a home equity line of credit), paragraph (3) specifies information that must be provided in support of a claim based on an open-end or revolving consumer credit agreement (such as an agreement underlying the issuance of a credit card). Because a claim of this type may have been sold one or more times prior to the debtor's bankruptcy, the debtor may not recognize the name of the person filing the proof of claim. Disclosure of the information required by paragraph (3) will assist the debtor in associating the claim with a known account. It will also provide a basis for assessing the timeliness of the claim. The date, if any, on which the account was charged to profit and loss ("charge-off" date) under subparagraph (A)(v) should be determined in accordance with applicable standards for the classification and account management of consumer credit. A proof of claim executed and filed in accordance with subparagraph (A), as well as the applicable provisions of subdivisions (a), (b), (c)(2), and (e), constitutes prima facie evidence of the validity and amount of the claim under subdivision (f).

To the extent that paragraph (3) applies to a claim, paragraph (1) of subdivision (c) is not applicable. A party in interest, however, may obtain the writing on which an open-end or revolving consumer credit claim is based by requesting in writing that documentation from the holder of the claim. The holder of the claim must provide the documentation within 30 days after the request is sent. The court, for cause, may extend or reduce that time period under Rule 9006.

Changes Made After Publication

Subdivision (c)(1). The requirement for the attachment of a writing on which a claim is based was changed to require that a copy, rather than the original or a duplicate, of the writing be provided.

Subdivision (c)(3). An exception to subparagraph (A) was added for open-end or revolving consumer credit agreements that are secured by the debtor's real property.

A time limit of 30 days for responding to a written request under subparagraph (B) was added.

Committee Note. A statement was added to clarify that if a proof of claim complies with subdivision (c)(3)(A), as well as with subdivisions (a), (b), (c)(2), and (e), it constitutes prima facie evidence of the validity and amount of the claim under subdivision (f).

Other changes. Stylistic changes were also made to the rule.

CROSS REFERENCES

Admissibility of duplicates, see Fed.Rules Evid. Rule 1003, 28 USCA.

Filed claims or interests deemed allowed, see 11 USCA § 502.

Filing of proofs of claims or interests, see 11 USCA § 501.

Notice to claimants in converted liquidation case, see Fed. Rules Bankr.Proc. Rule 1019, 11 USCA.

Rule 3002.   Filing Proof of Claim or Interest

(a) Necessity for filing

A secured creditor, unsecured creditor, or equity security holder must file a proof of claim or interest for the claim or interest to be allowed, except as provided in Rules 1019(3), 3003, 3004, and 3005. A lien that secures a claim against the debtor is not void due only to the failure of any entity to file a proof of claim.

(b) Place of filing

A proof of claim or interest shall be filed in accordance with Rule 5005.

(c) Time for filing

In a voluntary chapter 7 case, chapter 12 case, or chapter 13 case, a proof of claim is timely filed if it is filed not later than 70 days after the order for relief under that chapter or the date of the order of conversion to a case under chapter 12 or chapter 13. In an involuntary chapter 7 case, a proof of claim is timely filed if it is filed not later than 90 days after the order for relief under that chapter is entered. But in all these cases, the following exceptions apply:

(1) A proof of claim filed by a governmental unit, other than for a claim resulting from a tax return filed under § 1308, is timely filed if it is filed not later than 180 days after the date of the order for relief. A proof of claim filed by a governmental unit for a claim resulting from a tax return filed under § 1308 is timely filed if it is filed no later than 180 days after the date of the order for relief or 60 days after the date of the filing of the tax return. The court may, for cause, enlarge the time for a governmental unit to file a proof of claim only upon motion of the governmental unit made before expiration of the period for filing a timely proof of claim.

(2) In the interest of justice and if it will not unduly delay the administration of the case, the court may extend the time for filing a proof of claim by an infant or incompetent person or the representative of either.

(3) An unsecured claim which arises in favor of an entity or becomes allowable as a result of a judgment may be filed within 30 days after the judgment becomes final if the judgment is for the recovery of money or property from that entity or denies or avoids the entity's interest in property. If the judgment imposes a liability which is not satisfied, or a duty which is not performed within such period or such further time as the court may permit, the claim shall not be allowed.

(4) A claim arising from the rejection of an executory contract or unexpired lease of the debtor may be filed within such time as the court may direct.

(5) If notice of insufficient assets to pay a dividend was given to creditors under Rule 2002(e), and subsequently the trustee notifies the court that payment of a dividend appears possible, the clerk shall give at least 90 days' notice by mail to creditors of that fact and of the date by which proofs of claim must be filed.

(6) On motion filed by a creditor before or after the expiration of the time to file a proof of claim, the court may extend the time by not more than 60 days from the date of the order granting the motion. The motion may be granted if the court finds that:

(A) the notice was insufficient under the circumstances to give the creditor a reasonable time to file a proof of claim because the debtor failed to timely file the list of creditors' names and addresses required by Rule 1007(a); or

(B) the notice was insufficient under the circumstances to give the creditor a reasonable time to file a proof of claim, and the notice was mailed to the creditor at a foreign address.

(7) A proof of claim filed by the holder of a claim that is secured by a security interest in the debtor's principal residence is timely filed if:

(A) the proof of claim, together with the attachments required by Rule 3001(c)(2)(C), is filed not later than 70 days after the order for relief is entered; and

(B) any attachments required by Rule 3001(c)(1) and (d) are filed as a supplement to the holder's claim not later than 120 days after the order for relief is entered.

(As amended Mar. 30, 1987, eff. Aug. 1, 1987; Apr. 30, 1991, eff. Aug. 1, 1991; Apr. 23, 1996, eff. Dec. 1, 1996; Apr. 23, 2008, eff. Dec. 1, 2008; Apr. 27, 2017, eff. Dec. 1, 2017.)

ADVISORY COMMITTEE NOTES

Subdivision (a) of this rule is substantially a restatement of the general requirement that claims be proved and filed. The exceptions refer to Rule 3003 providing for the filing of claims in chapter 9 and 11 cases, and to Rules 3004 and 3005 authorizing claims to be filed by the debtor or trustee and the filing of a claim by a contingent creditor of the debtor.

A secured claim need not be filed or allowed under § 502 or § 506(d) unless a party in interest has requested a determination and allowance or disallowance under § 502.

Subdivision (c) is adapted from former Bankruptcy Rule 302(e) but changes the time limits on the filing of claims in chapter 7 and 13 cases from six months to 90 days after the first date set for the meeting of creditors. The special rule for early filing by a secured creditor in a chapter 13 case, in former Rule 13–302(e)(1) is not continued.

Although the claim of a secured creditor may have arisen before the petition, a judgment avoiding the security interest may not have been entered until after the time for filing claims has expired. Under Rule 3002(c)(3) the creditor who did not file a secured claim may nevertheless file an unsecured claim within the time prescribed. A judgment does not become final for the purpose of starting the 30 day period provided for by paragraph (3) until the time for appeal has expired or, if an appeal is taken, until the appeal has been disposed of. In re Tapp, 61 F.Supp. 594 (W.D.Ky.1945).

Paragraph (1) is derived from former Bankruptcy Rule 302(e). The governmental unit may move for an extension of the 90 day period. Pursuant to § 501(c) of the Code, if the government does not file its claim within the proper time period, the debtor or trustee may file on its behalf. An extension is not needed by the debtor or trustee because the right to file does not arise until the government's time has expired.

Paragraph (4) is derived from former chapter rules. See, e.g., Rule 11–33(a)(2)(B). In light of the reduced time it is necessary that a party with a claim arising from the rejection of an executory contract have sufficient time to file that claim. This clause allows the court to fix an appropriate time.

Paragraph (5) of subdivision (c) is correlated with the provision in Rule 2002(e) authorizing notification to creditors of estates from which no dividends are anticipated. The clause permits creditors who have refrained from filing claims after receiving notification to be given an opportunity to file when subsequent developments indicate the possibility of a dividend. The notice required by this clause must be given in the manner provided in Rule 2002. The information relating to the discovery of assets will usually be obtained by the clerk from the trustee's interim reports or special notification by the trustee.

Provision is made in Rule 2002(a) and (h) for notifying all creditors of the fixing of a time for filing claims against a surplus under paragraph (6). This paragraph does not deal with the distribution of the surplus. Reference must also be made to § 726(a)(2)(C) and (3) which permits distribution on late filed claims.

Paragraph (6) is only operative in a chapter 7 case. In chapter 13 cases, the plan itself provides the distribution to creditors which is not necessarily dependent on the size of the estate.

1987 Amendments

Subdivision (a) is amended by adding a reference to Rule 1019(4). Rule 1019(4) provides that claims actually filed by a creditor in a chapter 11 or 13 case shall be treated as filed in a superseding chapter 7 case. Claims deemed filed in a chapter 11 case pursuant to § 1111(a) of the Code are not considered as filed in a superseding chapter 7 case. The creditor must file a claim in the superseding chapter 7 case.

1991 Amendments

Subdivision (a) is amended to conform to the renumbering of subdivisions of Rule 1019. Subdivision (c) is amended to include chapter 12 cases. Subdivision (c)(4) is amended to clarify that it includes a claim arising from the rejection of an unexpired lease.

1996 Amendments

The amendments are designed to conform to §§ 502(b)(9) and 726(a) of the Code as amended by the Bankruptcy Reform Act of 1994.

The Reform Act amended § 726(a)(1) and added § 502(b)(9) to the Code to govern the effects of a tardily filed claim. Under § 502(b)(9), a tardily filed claim must be disallowed if an objection to the proof of claim is filed, except to the extent that a holder of a tardily filed claim is entitled to distribution under § 726(a)(1), (2), or (3).

The phrase "in accordance with this rule" is deleted from Rule 3002(a) to clarify that the effect of filing a proof of claim after the expiration of the time prescribed in Rule 3002(c) is governed by § 502(b)(9) of the Code, rather than by this rule.

Section 502(b)(9) of the Code provides that a claim of a governmental unit shall be timely filed if it is filed "before 180 days after the date of the order for relief" or such later time as the Bankruptcy Rules provide. To avoid any confusion as to whether a governmental unit's proof of claim is timely filed under § 502(b)(9) if it is filed on the 180th day after the order for relief, paragraph (1) of subdivision (c) provides that a governmental unit's claim is timely if it is filed not later than 180 days after the order for relief.

References to "the United States, a state, or subdivision thereof" in paragraph (1) of subdivision (c) are changed to "governmental unit" to avoid different treatment among foreign and domestic governments.

GAP Report on Rule 3002. After publication of the proposed amendments, the Bankruptcy Reform Act of 1994 amended sections 726 and 502(b) of the Code to clarify the rights of creditors who tardily file a proof of claim. In view of the Reform Act, proposed new subdivision (d) of Rule 3002 has been deleted from the proposed amendments because it is no longer necessary. In addition, subdivisions (a) and (c) have been changed after publication to clarify that the effect of tardily filing a proof of claim is governed by § 502(b)(9) of the Code, rather than by this rule.

The amendments to § 502(b) also provide that a governmental unit's proof of claim is timely filed if it is filed before 180 days after the order for relief. Proposed amendments to Rule 3002(c)(1) were added to the published amendments to conform to this statutory change and to avoid any confusion as to whether a claim by a governmental unit is timely if it is filed on the 180th day.

The committee note has been re-written to explain the rule changes designed to conform to the Reform Act.

2008 Amendments

Subdivision (c)(1) is amended to reflect the addition of § 1308 to the Bankruptcy Code in 2005. This provision requires that chapter 13 debtors file tax returns during the pendency of the case, and imposes bankruptcy-related consequences if debtors fail to do so. Subdivision (c)(1) provides additional time for governmental units to file a proof of claim for tax obligations with respect to tax returns filed during the pendency of a chapter 13 case. The amendment also allows the governmental unit to move for additional time to file a proof of claim prior to expiration of the applicable filing period.

Subdivision (c)(5) of the rule is amended to set a new period for providing notice to creditors that they may file a proof of claim in a case in which they were previously informed that there was no need to file a claim. Under Rule 2002(e), if it appears that there will be no distribution to creditors, the creditors are notified of this fact and are informed that if assets are later discovered and a distribution is likely that a new notice will be given to the creditors. This second notice is prescribed by Rule 3002(c)(5). The rule is amended to direct the clerk to give at least 90 days' notice of the time within which creditors may file a proof of claim. Setting the deadline in this manner allows the notices being sent to creditors to be more accurate regarding the deadline than was possible under the prior rule. The rule previously began the 90 day notice period from the time of the mailing of the notice, a date that could vary and generally would not even be known to the creditor. Under the amended rule, the notice will identify a specific bar date for filing proofs of claim thereby being more helpful to the creditors.

Subdivision (c)(6) is added to give the court discretion to extend the time for filing a proof of claim for a creditor who received notice of the time to file the claim at a foreign address, if the court finds that the notice was not sufficient, under the particular circumstances, to give the foreign creditor a reasonable time to file a proof of claim. This amendment is designed to comply with § 1514(d), added to the Code by the 2005 amendments, and requires that the rules and orders of the court provide such additional time as is reasonable under the circumstances for foreign creditors to file claims in cases under all chapters of the Code.

Other changes are stylistic.

2017 Amendments

Subdivision (a) is amended to clarify that a creditor, including a secured creditor, must file a proof of claim in order to have an allowed claim. The amendment also clarifies, in accordance with § 506(d), that the failure of a secured creditor to file a proof of claim does not render the creditor's lien void. The inclusion of language from § 506(d) is not intended to effect any change of law with respect to claims subject to setoff under § 553. The amendment preserves the existing exceptions to this rule under Rules 1019(3), 3003, 3004, and 3005. Under Rule 1019(3), a creditor does not need to file another proof of claim after conversion of a case to chapter 7. Rule 3003 governs the filing of a proof of claim in chapter 9 and chapter 11 cases. Rules 3004 and 3005 govern the filing of a proof of claim by the debtor, trustee, or another entity if a creditor does not do so in a timely manner.

Subdivision (c) is amended to alter the calculation of the bar date for proofs of claim in chapter 7, chapter 12, and chapter 13 cases. The amendment changes the time for filing a proof of claim in a voluntary chapter 7 case, a chapter 12 case, or a chapter 13 case from 90 days after the § 341 meeting of creditors to 70 days after the petition date. If a case is converted to chapter 12 or chapter 13, the 70–day time for filing runs from the order of conversion. If a case is converted to chapter 7, Rule 1019(2) provides that a new time period for filing a claim commences under Rule 3002. In an involuntary chapter 7 case, a 90–day time for filing applies and runs from the entry of the order for relief.

Subdivision (c)(6) is amended to expand the exception to the bar date for cases in which a creditor received insufficient notice of the time to file a proof of claim. The amendment provides that the court may extend the time to file a proof of claim if the debtor fails to file a timely list of names and addresses of creditors as required by Rule 1007(a). The amendment also clarifies that if a court grants a creditor's motion under this rule to extend the time to file a proof of claim, the extension runs from the date of the court's decision on the motion.

Subdivision (c)(7) is added to provide a two-stage deadline for filing mortgage proofs of claim secured by an interest in the debtor's principal residence. Those proofs of claim must be filed with the appropriate Official Form mortgage attachment within 70 days of the order for relief. The claim will be timely if any additional documents evidencing the claim, as required by Rule 3001(c)(1) and (d), are filed within 120 days of the order for relief. The order for relief is the commencement of the case upon filing a petition, except in an involuntary case. See § 301 and § 303(h). The confirmation of a plan within the 120–day period set forth in subdivision (c)(7)(B) does not prohibit an objection to any proof of claim.

CROSS REFERENCES

Filed claims or interests deemed allowed, see 11 USCA § 502.

Filing of,

Claims by debtor or trustee, see Fed.Rules Bankr.Proc. Rule 3004, 11 USCA.

Claims by guarantor, surety, indorser, or other codebtor, see Fed.Rules Bankr.Proc. Rule 3005, 11 USCA.

Proofs of claims or interests, see 11 USCA § 501.

Filing proof of claim in liquidation or individual debt adjustment case, ninety-day period,

Enlargement permitted as limited in this rule, see Fed.Rules Bankr.Proc. Rule 9006, 11 USCA.

Reduction not permitted, see Fed.Rules Bankr.Proc. Rule 9006, 11 USCA.

Motions, form and service, see Fed.Rules Bankr.Proc. Rule 9013, 11 USCA.

Notice by mail of time allowed to file claims, see Fed.Rules Bankr.Proc. Rule 2002, 11 USCA.

Time extended to file claims against surplus,

Converted liquidation case, see Fed.Rules Bankr.Proc. Rule 1019, 11 USCA.

Notice to creditors in liquidation case, see Fed.Rules Bankr.Proc. Rule 2002, 11 USCA.

Twenty-day notice of time to file claims against surplus, see Fed.Rules Bankr.Proc. Rule 2002, 11 USCA.

Rule 3002.1. Notice Relating to Claims Secured by Security Interest in the Debtor's Principal Residence

(a) In general

This rule applies in a chapter 13 case to claims (1) that are secured by a security interest in the debtor's principal residence, and (2) for which the plan provides that either the trustee or the debtor will make contractual installment payments. Unless the court orders otherwise, the notice requirements of this rule cease to apply when an order terminating or annulling the automatic stay becomes effective with respect to the residence that secures the claim.

(b) Notice of payment changes; objection

(1) Notice

The holder of the claim shall file and serve on the debtor, debtor's counsel, and the trustee a notice of any change in the payment amount, including any change that results from an interest-rate or escrow-account adjustment, no later than 21 days before a payment in the new amount is due. If the claim arises from a home-equity line of credit, this requirement may be modified by court order.

(2) Objection

A party in interest who objects to the payment change may file a motion to determine whether the change is required to maintain payments in accordance with § 1322(b)(5) of the Code. If no motion is filed by the day before the new amount is due, the change goes into effect, unless the court orders otherwise.

(c) Notice of fees, expenses, and charges

The holder of the claim shall file and serve on the debtor, debtor's counsel, and the trustee a notice itemizing all fees, expenses, or charges (1) that were incurred in connection with the claim after the bankruptcy case was filed, and (2) that the holder asserts are recoverable against the debtor or against the debtor's principal residence. The notice shall be served within 180 days after the date on which the fees, expenses, or charges are incurred.

(d) Form and content

A notice filed and served under subdivision (b) or (c) of this rule shall be prepared as prescribed by the appropriate Official Form, and filed as a supplement to the holder's proof of claim. The notice is not subject to Rule 3001(f).

(e) Determination of fees, expenses, or charges

On motion of a party in interest filed within one year after service of a notice under subdivision (c) of this rule, the court shall, after notice and hearing, determine whether payment of any claimed fee, expense, or charge is required by the underlying agreement and applicable nonbankruptcy law to cure a default or maintain payments in accordance with § 1322(b)(5) of the Code.

(f) Notice of final cure payment

Within 30 days after the debtor completes all payments under the plan, the trustee shall file and serve on the holder of the claim, the debtor, and debtor's counsel a notice stating that the debtor has paid in full the amount required to cure any default on the claim. The notice shall also inform the holder of its obligation to file and serve a response under subdivision (g). If the debtor contends that final cure payment has been made and all plan payments have been completed, and the trustee does not timely file and serve the notice required by this subdivision, the debtor may file and serve the notice.

(g) Response to notice of final cure payment

Within 21 days after service of the notice under subdivision (f) of this rule, the holder shall file and serve on the debtor, debtor's counsel, and the trustee a statement indicating (1) whether it agrees that the debtor has paid in full the amount required to cure the default on the claim, and (2) whether the debtor is otherwise current on all payments consistent with § 1322(b)(5) of the Code. The statement shall itemize the required cure or postpetition amounts, if any, that the holder contends remain unpaid as of the date of the statement. The statement shall be filed as a supplement to the holder's proof of claim and is not subject to Rule 3001(f).

(h) Determination of final cure and payment

On motion of the debtor or trustee filed within 21 days after service of the statement under subdivision (g) of this rule, the court shall, after notice and hearing, determine whether the debtor has cured the default and paid all required postpetition amounts.

(i) Failure to notify

If the holder of a claim fails to provide any information as required by subdivision (b), (c), or (g) of this rule, the court may, after notice and hearing, take either or both of the following actions:

(1) preclude the holder from presenting the omitted information, in any form, as evidence in any contested matter or adversary proceeding in the case, unless the court determines that the failure was substantially justified or is harmless; or

(2) award other appropriate relief, including reasonable expenses and attorney's fees caused by the failure.

(Added Apr. 26, 2011, eff. Dec. 1, 2011. As amended Apr. 28, 2016, eff. Dec. 1, 2016; Apr. 26, 2018, eff. Dec. 1, 2018.)

ADVISORY COMMITTEE NOTES

2011 Adoption

This rule is new. It is added to aid in the implementation of § 1322(b)(5), which permits a chapter 13 debtor to cure a default and maintain payments of a home mortgage over the course of the debtor's plan. It applies regardless of whether the trustee or the debtor is the disbursing agent for postpetition mortgage payments.

In order to be able to fulfill the obligations of § 1322(b)(5), a debtor and the trustee must be informed of the exact amount needed to cure any prepetition arrearage, *see* Rule 3001(c)(2), and the amount of the postpetition payment obligations. If the latter amount changes over time, due to the adjustment of the interest rate, escrow account adjustments, or the assessment of fees, expenses, or other charges, notice of any change in payment amount needs to be conveyed to the debtor and trustee. Timely notice of these changes will permit the debtor or trustee to challenge the validity of any such charges, if necessary, and to adjust postpetition mortgage payments to cover any properly claimed adjustment. Compliance with the notice provision of the rule should also eliminate any concern on the part of the holder of the claim that informing a debtor of a change in postpetition payment obligations might violate the automatic stay.

Subdivision (a). Subdivision (a) specifies that this rule applies only in a chapter 13 case to claims secured by a security interest in the debtor's principal residence.

Subdivision (b). Subdivision (b) requires the holder of a claim to notify the debtor, debtor's counsel, and the trustee of any postpetition change in the mortgage payment amount at least 21 days before the new payment amount is due.

Subdivision (c). Subdivision (c) requires an itemized notice to be given, within 180 days of incurrence, of any postpetition fees, expenses, or charges that the holder of the claim asserts are recoverable in connection with a claim secured by the debtor's principal residence. This amount might include, for example, inspection fees, late charges, or attorney's fees.

Subdivision (d). Subdivision (d) provides the method of giving the notice under subdivisions (b) and (c). In both instances, the holder of the claim must give notice of the change as prescribed by the appropriate Official Form. In addition to serving the debtor, debtor's counsel, and the trustee, the holder of the claim must also file the notice on the claims register in the case as a supplement to its proof of claim. Rule 300 I (f) does not apply to any notice given under subdivision (b) or (c), and therefore the notice will not constitute prima facie evidence of the validity and amount of the payment change or of the fee, expense, or charge.

Subdivision (e). Subdivision (e) permits the debtor or trustee, within a year after service of a notice under subdivision (c), to seek a determination by the court as to whether the fees, expenses, or charges set forth in the notice are required by the underlying agreement or applicable nonbankruptcy law to cure a default or maintain payments.

Subdivision (f). Subdivision (f) requires the trustee to issue a notice to the holder of the claim, the debtor, and the debtor's attorney within 30 days after completion of payments under the plan. The notice must (1) indicate that all amounts required to cure a default on a claim secured by the debtor's principal residence have been paid, and (2) direct the holder to comply with subdivision (g). If the trustee fails to file this notice within the required time, this subdivision also permits the debtor to file and serve the notice on the trustee and the holder of the claim.

Subdivision (g). Subdivision (g) governs the response of the holder of the claim to the trustee's or debtor's notice under subdivision (f). Within 21 days after service of notice of the final cure payment, the holder of the claim must file and serve a statement indicating whether the prepetition default has been fully cured and also whether the debtor is current on all payments in accordance with § 1322(b)(5) of the Code. If the holder of the claim contends that all cure payments have not been made or that the debtor is not current on other payments required by § 1322(b)(5), the response must itemize all amounts, other than regular future installment payments, that the holder contends are due.

Subdivision (h). Subdivision (h) provides a procedure for the judicial resolution of any disputes that may arise about payment of a claim secured by the debtor's principal residence. Within 21 days after the service of the statement under (g), the trustee or debtor may move for a determination by the court of whether any default has been cured and whether any other non-current obligations remain outstanding.

Subdivision (i). Subdivision (i) specifies sanctions that may be imposed if the holder of a claim fails to provide any of the information as required by subdivisions (b), (c), or (g).

If, after the chapter 13 debtor has completed payments under the plan and the case has been closed, the holder of a claim secured by the debtor's principal residence seeks to recover amounts that should have been but were not disclosed under this rule, the debtor may move to have the case reopened in order to seek sanctions against the holder of the claim under subdivision (i).

2016 Amendments

Subdivision (a) is amended to clarify the applicability of the rule. Its provisions apply whenever a chapter 13 plan provides that contractual payments on the debtor's home mortgage will be maintained, whether they will be paid by the trustee or directly by the debtor. The reference to § 1322(b)(5) of the Code is deleted to make clear that the rule applies even if there is no prepetition arrearage to be cured. So long as a creditor has a claim that is secured by a security interest in the debtor's principal residence and the plan provides that contractual payments on the claim will be maintained, the rule applies.

Subdivision (a) is further amended to provide that, unless the court orders otherwise, the notice obligations imposed by this rule cease on the effective date of an order granting relief from the automatic stay with regard to the debtor's principal residence. Debtors and trustees typically do not make payments on mortgages after the stay relief is granted, so there is generally no need for the holder of the claim to continue providing the notices required by this rule. Sometimes, however, there may be reasons for the debtor to continue receiving mortgage information after stay relief. For example, the debtor may intend to seek a mortgage modification or to cure the default. When the court determines that the debtor has a need for the information required by this rule, the court is authorized to order that the notice obligations remain in effect or be reinstated after the relief from the stay is granted.

2018 Amendments

Subdivision (b) is subdivided and amended in two respects. First, it is amended in what is now subdivision (b)(1) to authorize courts to modify its requirements for claims arising from home equity lines of credit (HELOCs). Because payments on HELOCs may adjust frequently and in small amounts, the rule provides flexibility for courts to specify alternative procedures for keeping the person who is maintaining payments on the loan apprised of the current payment amount. Courts may specify alternative requirements for providing notice of changes in HELOC payment amounts by local rules or orders in individual cases.

Second, what is now subdivision (b)(2) is amended to acknowledge the right of the trustee, debtor, or other party in interest, such as the United States trustee, to object to a change in a home-mortgage payment amount after receiving notice of the change under subdivision (b)(1). The amended rule does not set a deadline for filing a motion for a determination of the validity of the payment change, but it provides as a general matter—subject to a contrary court order—that if no motion has been filed on or before the day before the change is to take effect, the announced change goes into effect. If there is a later motion and a determination that the payment change was not required to maintain payments under § 1322(b)(5), appropriate adjustments will have to be made to reflect any overpayments. If, however, a motion is made during the time specified in subdivision (b)(2), leading to a suspension of the payment change, a determination that the payment change was valid will require the debtor to cure the resulting default in order to be current on the mortgage at the end of the bankruptcy case.

Subdivision (e) is amended to allow parties in interest in addition to the debtor or trustee, such as the United States trustee, to seek a determination regarding the validity of any claimed fee, expense, or charge.

Rule 3003. Filing Proof of Claim or Equity Security Interest in Chapter 9 Municipality or Chapter 11 Reorganization Cases

(a) Applicability of rule

This rule applies in chapter 9 and 11 cases.

(b) Schedule of liabilities and list of equity security holders

(1) Schedule of liabilities

The schedule of liabilities filed pursuant to § 521(1) of the Code shall constitute prima facie evidence of the validity and amount of the claims of creditors, unless they are scheduled as disputed, contingent, or unliquidated. It shall not be necessary for a creditor or equity security holder to file a proof of claim or interest except as provided in subdivision (c)(2) of this rule.

(2) List of equity security holders

The list of equity security holders filed pursuant to Rule 1007(a)(3) shall constitute prima facie evidence of the validity and amount of the equity security interests and it shall not be necessary for the holders of such interests to file a proof of interest.

(c) Filing of proof of claim

(1) Who may file

Any creditor or indenture trustee may file a proof of claim within the time prescribed by subdivision (c)(3) of this rule.

(2) Who must file

Any creditor or equity security holder whose claim or interest is not scheduled or scheduled as disputed, contingent, or unliquidated shall file a proof of claim or interest within the time prescribed by subdivision (c)(3) of this rule; any creditor who fails to do so shall not be treated as a creditor with respect to such claim for the purposes of voting and distribution.

(3) Time for filing

The court shall fix and for cause shown may extend the time within which proofs of claim or interest may be filed. Notwithstanding the expiration of such time, a proof of claim may be filed to the extent and under the conditions stated in Rule 3002(c)(2), (c)(3), (c)(4), and (c)(6).

(4) Effect of filing claim or interest

A proof of claim or interest executed and filed in accordance with this subdivision shall supersede any scheduling of that claim or interest pursuant to § 521(a)(1) of the Code.

(5) Filing by indenture trustee

An indenture trustee may file a claim on behalf of all known or unknown holders of securities issued pursuant to the trust instrument under which it is trustee.

(d) Proof of right to record status

For the purposes of Rules 3017, 3018 and 3021 and for receiving notices, an entity who is not the record holder of a security may file a statement setting forth facts which entitle that entity to be treated as the record holder. An objection to the statement may be filed by any party in interest.

(As amended Mar. 30, 1987, eff. Aug. 1, 1987; Apr. 30, 1991, eff. Aug. 1, 1991; Apr. 23, 2008, eff. Dec. 1, 2008.)

ADVISORY COMMITTEE NOTES

Subdivision (a). This rule applies only in chapter 9 and chapter 11 cases. It is adapted from former Chapter X Rule 10–401 and provides an exception to the requirement for filing proofs of claim and interest as expressed in §§ 925 and 1111(a) of the Code.

Subdivision (b). This general statement implements §§ 925 and 1111(a) of the Code.

Subdivision (c). This subdivision permits, in paragraph (1), the filing of a proof of claim but does not make it mandatory. Paragraph (2) requires, as does the Code, filing when a claim is scheduled as disputed, contingent, or unliquidated as to amount. It is the creditor's responsibility to determine if the claim is accurately listed. Notice of the provision of this rule is provided for in Official Form No. 16, the order for the meeting of creditors. In an appropriate case the court may order creditors whose claims are scheduled as disputed, contingent, or unliquidated be notified of that fact but the procedure is left to the discretion of the court.

Subdivision (d) is derived from former Chapter X Rule 10–401(f).

Except with respect to the need and time for filing claims, the other aspects concerning claims covered by Rules 3001 and 3002 are applicable in chapter 9 and 11 cases.

Holders of equity security interests need not file proofs of interest. Voting and distribution participation is dependent on ownership as disclosed by the appropriate records of a transfer agent or the corporate or other business records at the time prescribed in Rules 3017 and 3021.

1991 Amendments

Paragraph (3) of subdivision (c) is amended to permit the late filing of claims by infants or incompetent persons under the same circumstances that permit late filings in cases under chapter 7, 12, or 13. The amendment also provides sufficient time in which to file a claim that arises from a postpetition judgment against the claimant for the recovery of money or property or the avoidance of a lien. It also provides for purposes of clarification that upon rejection of an executory contract or unexpired lease, the court shall set a time for filing a claim arising therefrom despite prior expiration of the time set for filing proofs of claim.

The caption of paragraph (4) of subdivision (c) is amended to indicate that it applies to a proof of claim.

2008 Amendments

Subdivision (c)(3) is amended to implement § 1514(d) of the Code, which was added by the 2005 amendments. It makes the new Rule 3002(c)(6) applicable in chapter 9 and chapter 11 cases. This change was necessary so that creditors with foreign addresses be provided such additional time as is reasonable under the circumstances to file proofs of claims.

CROSS REFERENCES

Acceptance or rejection of municipality debt adjustment or reorganization plan by obligor filing creditor's claim, see Fed.Rules Bankr.Proc. Rule 3005, 11 USCA.

Distribution under confirmed plan to indenture trustee filing under this rule, see Fed.Rules Bankr.Proc. Rule 3021, 11 USCA.

Exception to filing requirement for,

    Municipality debt adjustment case, see 11 USCA § 925.

    Reorganization case, see 11 USCA § 1111.

Filing of claims by,

    Debtor or trustee, see Fed.Rules Bankr.Proc. Rule 3004, 11 USCA.

    Guarantor, surety, indorser, or other codebtor, see Fed. Rules Bankr.Proc. Rule 3005, 11 USCA.

Twenty-day notice of time fixed to file proof of claim, see Fed.Rules Bankr.Proc. Rule 2002, 11 USCA.

Rule 3004.   Filing of Claims by Debtor or Trustee

If a creditor does not timely file a proof of claim under Rule 3002(c) or 3003(c), the debtor or trustee may file a proof of the claim within 30 days after the expiration of the time for filing claims prescribed by Rule 3002(c) or 3003(c), whichever is applicable. The clerk shall forthwith give notice of the filing to the creditor, the debtor and the trustee.

(As amended Mar. 30, 1987, eff. Aug. 1, 1987; Apr. 25, 2005, eff. Dec. 1, 2005.)

ADVISORY COMMITTEE NOTES

This rule is adapted from former Bankruptcy Rule 303 but conforms with the changes made by § 501(c) of the Code. Rule 303 permitted only the filing of tax and wage claims by the debtor. Section 501(c) of the Code, however, permits the filing by the debtor or trustee on behalf of any creditor.

It is the policy of the Code that debtors' estates should be administered for the benefit of creditors without regard to the dischargeability of their claims. After their estates have been closed, however, discharged debtors may find themselves saddled with liabilities, particularly for taxes, which remain unpaid because of the failure of creditors holding nondischargeable claims to file proofs of claim and receive distributions thereon. The result is that the debtor is deprived of an important benefit of the Code without any fault or omission on the debtor's part and without any objective of the Code being served thereby.

Section 501(c) of the Code authorizes a debtor or trustee to file a proof of claim for any holder of a claim. Although all claims may not be nondischargeable, it may be difficult to determine, in particular, whether tax claims survive discharge. See Plumb, Federal Tax Liens and Priorities in Bankruptcy, 43 Ref.J. 37, 43–44 (1969); 1 Collier, Bankruptcy

¶17.14 (14th ed. 1967); 3 id. ¶523.06 (15th ed. 1979). To eliminate the necessity of the resolution of this troublesome issue, the option accorded the debtor by the Code does not depend on the nondischargeability of the claim. No serious administrative problems and no unfairness to creditors seemed to develop from adoption of Rule 303, the forerunner to § 501(c). The authority to file is conditioned on the creditor's failure to file the proof of claim on or before the first date set for the meeting of creditors, which is the date a claim must ordinarily be filed in order to be voted in a chapter 7 case. Notice to the creditor is provided to enable him to file a proof of claim pursuant to Rule 3002, which proof, when filed, would supersede the proof filed by the debtor or trustee. Notice to the trustee would serve to alert the trustee to the special character of the proof and the possible need for supplementary evidence of the validity and amount of the claim. If the trustee does not qualify until after a proof of claim is filed by the debtor pursuant to this rule, he should be notified as soon as practicable thereafter.

To the extent the claim is allowed and dividends paid thereon, it will be reduced or perhaps paid in full. If the claim is also filed pursuant to Rule 3005, only one distribution thereon may be made. As expressly required by Rule 3005 and by the purpose of this rule such distribution must diminish the claim.

1987 Amendments

Under the rule as amended, the debtor or trustee in a chapter 7 or 13 case has 120 days from the first date set for the meeting of creditors to file a claim for the creditor. During the first 90 days of that period the creditor in a Chapter 7 or 13 case may file a claim as provided by Rule 3002(c). If the creditor fails to file a claim, the debtor or trustee shall have an additional 30 days thereafter to file the claim. A proof of claim filed by a creditor supersedes a claim filed by the debtor or trustee only if it is timely filed within the 90 days allowed under Rule 3002(c).

2005 Amendments

The rule is amended to conform to § 501(c) of the Code. Under that provision, the debtor or trustee may file proof of a claim if the creditor fails to do so in a timely fashion. The rule previously authorized the debtor and the trustee to file a claim as early as the day after the first date set for the meeting of creditors under § 341(a). Under the amended rule, the debtor and trustee must wait until the creditor's opportunity to file a claim has expired. Providing the debtor and the trustee with the opportunity to file a claim ensures that the claim will participate in any distribution in the case. This is particularly important for claims that are nondischargeable.

Since the debtor and trustee cannot file a proof of claim until after the creditor's time to file has expired, the rule no longer permits the creditor to file a proof of claim that will supersede the claim filed by the debtor or trustee. The rule leaves to the courts the issue of whether to permit subsequent amendment of such proof of claim.

Other changes are stylistic.

CROSS REFERENCES

Exception to execution of proof of claim by creditor or agent, see Fed.Rules Bankr.Proc. Rule 3001, 11 USCA.

Filing of claims by debtor or trustee, see 11 USCA § 501.

Rule 3005. Filing of Claim, Acceptance, or Rejection by Guarantor, Surety, Indorser, or Other Codebtor

(a) Filing of claim

If a creditor does not timely file a proof of claim under Rule 3002(c) or 3003(c), any entity that is or may be liable with the debtor to that creditor, or who has secured that creditor, may file a proof of the claim within 30 days after the expiration of the time for filing claims prescribed by Rule 3002(c) or Rule 3003(c) whichever is applicable. No distribution shall be made on the claim except on satisfactory proof that the original debt will be diminished by the amount of distribution.

(b) Filing of acceptance or rejection; substitution of creditor

An entity which has filed a claim pursuant to the first sentence of subdivision (a) of this rule may file an acceptance or rejection of a plan in the name of the creditor, if known, or if unknown, in the entity's own name but if the creditor files a proof of claim within the time permitted by Rule 3003(c) or files a notice prior to confirmation of a plan of the creditor's intention to act in the creditor's own behalf, the creditor shall be substituted for the obligor with respect to that claim.

(As amended Mar. 30, 1987, eff. Aug. 1, 1987; Apr. 30, 1991, eff. Aug. 1, 1991; Apr. 25, 2005, eff. Dec. 1, 2005.)

ADVISORY COMMITTEE NOTES

This rule is adapted from former Rules 304 and 10–402. Together with § 501(b) of the Code, the rule makes clear that anyone who may be liable on a debt of the debtor, including a surety, guarantor, indorser, or other codebtor, is authorized to file in the name of the creditor of the debtor.

Subdivision (a). Rule 3002(c) provides the time period for filing proofs of claim in chapter 7 and 13 cases; Rule 3003(c) provides the time, when necessary, for filing claims in a chapter 9 or 11 case.

Subdivision (b). This subdivision applies in chapter 9 and 11 cases as distinguished from chapter 7 cases. It permits voting for or against a plan by an obligor who files a claim in place of the creditor.

1991 Amendments

The words "with the court" in subdivision (b) are deleted as unnecessary. See Rules 5005(a) and 9001(3).

2005 Amendments

The rule is amended to delete the last sentence of subdivision (a). The sentence is unnecessary because if a creditor has filed a timely claim under Rule 3002 or 3003(c), the codebtor cannot file a proof of such claim. The codebtor, consistent with § 501(b) of the Code, may file a proof of such claim only after the creditor's time to file has expired. Therefore, the rule no longer permits the creditor to file a superseding claim. The rule leaves to the courts the issue of whether to permit subsequent amendment of the proof of claim.

The amendment conforms the rule to § 501(b) by deleting language providing that the codebtor files proof of the claim in the name of the creditor.

Other amendments are stylistic.

CROSS REFERENCES

Exception to execution of proof of claim by creditor or agent, see Fed.Rules Bankr.Proc. Rule 3001, 11 USCA.

Rule 3006. Withdrawal of Claim; Effect on Acceptance or Rejection of Plan

A creditor may withdraw a claim as of right by filing a notice of withdrawal, except as provided in this rule. If after a creditor has filed a proof of claim an objection is filed thereto or a complaint is filed against that creditor in an adversary proceeding, or the creditor has accepted or rejected the plan or otherwise has participated significantly in the case, the creditor may not withdraw the claim except on order of the court after a hearing on notice to the trustee or debtor in possession, and any creditors' committee elected pursuant to § 705(a) or appointed pursuant to § 1102 of the Code. The order of the court shall contain such terms and conditions as the court deems proper. Unless the court orders otherwise, an authorized withdrawal of a claim shall constitute withdrawal of any related acceptance or rejection of a plan.

(As amended Apr. 30, 1991, eff. Aug. 1, 1991.)

ADVISORY COMMITTEE NOTES

This rule is derived from former Rules 305 and 10–404.

Since 1938 it has generally been held that Rule 41 F.R.Civ.P. governs the withdrawal of a proof of claim. In re Empire Coal Sales Corp., 45 F.Supp. 974, 976 (S.C.N.Y.), aff'd sub nom. Kleid v. Ruthbell Coal Co., 131 F.2d 372, 373 (2d Cir.1942); Kelso v. MacLaren, 122 F.2d 867, 870 (8th Cir. 1941); In re Hills, 35 F.Supp. 532, 533 (W.D.Wash.1940). Accordingly the cited cases held that after an objection has been filed a proof of claim may be withdrawn only subject to approval by the court. This constitutes a restriction of the right of withdrawal as recognized by some though by no means all of the cases antedating the promulgation of the Federal Rules of Civil Procedure. See 3 Collier, Bankruptcy ¶57.12 (14th ed. 1961); Note, 20 Bost.U.L.Rev. 121 (1940).

The filing of a claim does not commence an adversary proceeding but the filing of an objection to the claim initiates a contest that must be disposed of by the court. This rule recognizes the applicability of the considerations underlying Rule 41(a) F.R.Civ.P. to the withdrawal of a claim after it has been put in issue by an objection. Rule 41(a)(2) F.R.Civ.P. requires leave of court to obtain dismissal over the objection of a defendant who has pleaded a counterclaim prior to the service of the plaintiff's motion to dismiss. Although the applicability of this provision to the withdrawal of a claim was assumed in Conway v. Union Bank of Switzerland, 204 F.2d 603, 608 (2d Cir.1953), Kleid v. Ruthbell Coal Co., supra, Kelso v. MacLaren, supra, and In re Hills, supra, this rule vests discretion in the court to grant, deny, or condition the request of a creditor to withdraw, without regard to whether the trustee has filed a merely defensive objection or a complaint seeking an affirmative recovery of money or property from the creditor.

A number of pre-1938 cases sustained denial of a creditor's request to withdraw proof of claim on the ground of estoppel or election of remedies. 2 Remington, Bankruptcy 186 (Henderson ed. 1956); cf. 3 Collier, supra ¶57.12, at 201 (1964). Voting a claim for a trustee was an important factor in the denial of a request to withdraw in Standard Varnish Works v. Haydock, 143 Fed. 318, 319–20 (6th Cir.1906), and In re Cann, 47 F.2d 661, 662 (W.D.Pa.1931). And it has frequently been recognized that a creditor should not be allowed to withdraw a claim after accepting a dividend. In re Friedmann, 1 Am.B.R. 510, 512 (Ref., S.D.N.Y.1899); 3 Collier 205 (1964); cf. In re O'Gara Coal Co., 12 F.2d 426, 429 (7th Cir.), cert. denied, 271 U.S. 683 (1926). It was held in Industrial Credit Co. v. Hazen, 222 F.2d 225 (8th Cir.1955), however, that although a claimant had participated in the first meeting of creditors and in the examination of witnesses, the creditor was entitled under Rule 41(a)(1) F.R.Civ.P. to withdraw the claim as of right by filing a notice of withdrawal before the trustee filed an objection under § 57g of the Act. While this rule incorporates the post-1938 case law referred to in the first paragraph of this note, it rejects the inference drawn in the Hazen case that Rule 41(a) F.R.Civ.P. supersedes the pre-1938 case law that vests discretion in the court to deny or restrict withdrawal of a claim by a creditor on the ground of estoppel or election of remedies. While purely formal or technical participation in a case by a creditor who has filed a claim should not deprive the creditor of the right to withdraw the claim, a creditor who has accepted a dividend or who has voted in the election of a trustee or otherwise participated actively in proceedings in a case should be permitted to withdraw only with the approval of the court on terms it deems appropriate after notice to the trustee. 3 Collier 205–06 (1964).

1991 Amendments

This amendment is stylistic. Notice of the hearing need not be given to committees of equity security holders appointed pursuant to § 1102 or committees of retired employees appointed pursuant to § 1114 of the Code.

CROSS REFERENCES

Dismissal of actions, see Fed.Rules Civ.Proc. Rule 41, 28 USCA.

Rule 3007. Objections to Claims

(a) Time and manner of service

(1) Time of service

An objection to the allowance of a claim and a notice of objection that substantially conforms to the appropriate Official Form shall be filed and served at least 30 days before any scheduled hearing on the objection or any deadline for the claimant to request a hearing.

(2) Manner of service

(A) The objection and notice shall be served on a claimant by first-class mail to the person most recently designated on the claimant's original or amended proof of claim as the person to receive notices, at the address so indicated; and

   (i) if the objection is to a claim of the United States, or any of its officers or agencies, in the manner provided for service of a summons and complaint by Rule 7004(b)(4) or (5); or

   (ii) if the objection is to a claim of an insured depository institution, in the manner provided by Rule 7004(h).

(B) Service of the objection and notice shall also be made by first-class mail or other permitted means on the debtor or debtor in possession, the trustee, and, if applicable, the entity filing the proof of claim under Rule 3005.

(b) Demand for relief requiring an adversary proceeding

A party in interest shall not include a demand for relief of a kind specified in Rule 7001 in an objection to the allowance of a claim, but may include the objection in an adversary proceeding.

(c) Limitation on joinder of claims objections

Unless otherwise ordered by the court or permitted by subdivision (d), objections to more than one claim shall not be joined in a single objection.

(d) Omnibus objection

Subject to subdivision (e), objections to more than one claim may be joined in an omnibus objection if all the claims were filed by the same entity, or the objections are based solely on the grounds that the claims should be disallowed, in whole or in part, because:

   (1) they duplicate other claims;

   (2) they have been filed in the wrong case;

   (3) they have been amended by subsequently filed proofs of claim;

   (4) they were not timely filed;

   (5) they have been satisfied or released during the case in accordance with the Code, applicable rules, or a court order;

   (6) they were presented in a form that does not comply with applicable rules, and the objection states that the objector is unable to determine the validity of the claim because of the noncompliance;

   (7) they are interests, rather than claims; or

   (8) they assert priority in an amount that exceeds the maximum amount under § 507 of the Code.

(e) Requirements for omnibus objection

An omnibus objection shall:

   (1) state in a conspicuous place that claimants receiving the objection should locate their names and claims in the objection;

   (2) list claimants alphabetically, provide a cross-reference to claim numbers, and, if appropriate, list claimants by category of claims;

   (3) state the grounds of the objection to each claim and provide a cross-reference to the pages in the omnibus objection pertinent to the stated grounds;

(4) state in the title the identity of the objector and the grounds for the objections;

(5) be numbered consecutively with other omnibus objections filed by the same objector; and

(6) contain objections to no more than 100 claims.

(f) Finality of objection

The finality of any order regarding a claim objection included in an omnibus objection shall be determined as though the claim had been subject to an individual objection.

(As amended Apr. 30, 1991, eff. Aug. 1, 1991; Apr. 30, 2007, eff. Dec. 1, 2007; Apr. 27, 2017, eff. Dec. 1, 2017.)

ADVISORY COMMITTEE NOTES

This rule is derived from § 47a(8) of the Act [former § 75(a)(8) of this title] and former Bankruptcy Rule 306. It prescribes the manner in which an objection to a claim shall be made and notice of the hearing thereon given to the claimant. The requirement of a writing does not apply to an objection to the allowance of a claim for the purpose of voting for a trustee or creditors' committee in a chapter 7 case. See Rule 2003.

The contested matter initiated by an objection to a claim is governed by rule 9014, unless a counterclaim by the trustee is joined with the objection to the claim. The filing of a counterclaim ordinarily commences an adversary proceeding subject to the rules in Part VII.

While the debtor's other creditors may make objections to the allowance of a claim, the demands of orderly and expeditious administration have led to a recognition that the right to object is generally exercised by the trustee. Pursuant to § 502(a) of the Code, however, any party in interest may object to a claim. But under § 704 the trustee, if any purpose would be served thereby, has the duty to examine proofs of claim and object to improper claims.

By virtue of the automatic allowance of a claim not objected to, a dividend may be paid on a claim which may thereafter be disallowed on objection made pursuant to this rule. The amount of the dividend paid before the disallowance in such event would be recoverable by the trustee in an adversary proceeding.

1991 Amendments

The words "with the court" are deleted as unnecessary. See Rules 5005(a) and 9001(3).

2007 Amendments

The rule is amended in a number of ways. First, the amendment prohibits a party in interest from including in a claim objection a request for relief that requires an adversary proceeding. A party in interest may, however, include an objection to the allowance of a claim in an adversary proceeding. Unlike a contested matter, an adversary proceeding requires the service of a summons and complaint, which puts the defendant on notice of the potential for an affirmative recovery. Permitting the plaintiff in the adversary proceeding to include an objection to a claim would not unfairly surprise the defendant as might be the case if the action were brought as a contested matter that included an action to obtain relief of a kind specified in Rule 7001.

The rule as amended does not require that a party include an objection to the allowance of a claim in an adversary proceeding. If a claim objection is filed separately from a related adversary proceeding, the court may consolidate the objection with the adversary proceeding under Rule 7042.

The rule also is amended to authorize the filing of a pleading that joins objections to more than one claim. Such filings present a significant opportunity for the efficient administration of large cases, but the rule includes restrictions on the use of these omnibus objections to ensure the protection of the due process rights of the claimants.

Unless the court orders otherwise, objections to more than one claim may be joined in a single pleading only if all of the claims were filed by the same entity, or if the objections are based solely on the grounds set out in subdivision (d) of the rule. Objections of the type listed in subdivision (d) often can be resolved without material factual or legal disputes. Objections to multiple claims permitted under the rule must comply with the procedural requirements set forth in subdivision (e). Among those requirements is the requirement in subdivision (e)(5) that these omnibus objections be consecutively numbered. Since these objections may not join more than 100 objections in any one omnibus objection, there may be a need for several omnibus objections to be filed in a particular case. Consecutive numbering of each omnibus objection and the identification of the objector in the title of the objection is essential to keep track of the objections on the court's docket. For example, the objections could be titled Debtor in Possession's First Omnibus Objection to Claims, Debtor in Possession's Second Omnibus Objection to Claims, Creditors' Committee's First Omnibus Objection to Claims, and so on. Titling the objections in this manner should avoid confusion and aid in tracking the objections on the docket.

Subdivision (f) provides that an order resolving an objection to any particular claim is treated, for purposes of finality, as if the claim had been the subject of an individual objection. A party seeking to appeal any such order is neither required, nor permitted, to await the court's resolution of all other joined objections. The rule permits the joinder of objections for convenience, and that convenience should not impede timely review of a court's decision with respect to each claim. Whether the court's action as to a particular objection is final, and the consequences of that finality, are not addressed by this amendment. Moreover, use of an omnibus objection generally does not preclude the objecting party from raising a subsequent objection to the claim on other grounds. See Restatement (Second) of Judgments § 26(1)(d) (1982) (generally applicable rule barring multiple actions based on same transaction or series of transactions is overridden when a statutory scheme permits splitting of claims).

2017 Amendments

Subdivision (a) is amended to specify the manner in which an objection to a claim and notice of the objection must be served. It clarifies that Rule 7004 does not apply to the service of most claim objections. Instead, a claimant must be served by first-class mail addressed to the person whom the claimant most recently designated on its proof of claim to receive notices, at the address so indicated. If, however, the claimant is the United States, an officer or agency of the United States, or an insured depository institution, service must also be made according to the method prescribed by the appropriate provision of Rule 7004. The service methods for the depository institutions are statutorily mandated, and the size and dispersal of the decision-making and litigation authority of the federal government necessitate service on the appropriate United States attorney's office and the Attorney General, as well as the person designated on the proof of claim.

As amended, subdivision (a) no longer requires that a hearing be scheduled or held on every objection. The rule requires the objecting party to provide notice and an opportunity for a hearing on the objection, but, by deleting from the subdivision references to "the hearing," it permits local practices that require a claimant to timely request a hearing or file a response in order to obtain a hearing. The official notice form served with a copy of the objection will inform the claimant of any actions it must take. However, while a local rule may require the claimant to respond to the objection to a proof of claim, the court will still need to determine if the claim is valid, even if the claimant does not file a response to a claim objection or request a hearing.

CROSS REFERENCES

Allowance of claims or interests after objection, see 11 USCA § 502.

Contested matters, see Fed.Rules Bankr.Proc. Rule 9014, 11 USCA.

Duty of trustee to examine proofs of claims and to object to improper claims,

Individual debt adjustment case, see 11 USCA § 1302.

Liquidation case, see 11 USCA § 704.

Reorganization case, see 11 USCA § 1106.

Objection to claim for purpose of voting for trustee or creditors' committee in liquidation case, see Fed.Rules Bankr. Proc. Rule 2003, 11 USCA.

Rule 3008.   Reconsideration of Claims

A party in interest may move for reconsideration of an order allowing or disallowing a claim against the estate. The court after a hearing on notice shall enter an appropriate order.

ADVISORY COMMITTEE NOTES

Section 502(j) of the Code deals only with the reconsideration of allowed claims as did former § 57k of the Act [former § 93(k) of this title] and General Order 21(b). It had sometimes been held that a referee had no jurisdiction to reconsider a disallowed claim, or the amount or priority of an allowed claim, at the instance of the claimant. See, e.g., In re Gouse, 7 F.Supp. 106 (M.D.Pa.1934); In re Tomlinson & Dye, Inc., 3 F.Supp. 800 (N.D.Okla.1933). This view disregarded § 2a(2) of the Act [former § 11(a)(2) of this title] and the "ancient and elementary power" of a referee as a court to reconsider orders. In re Pottasch Bros. Co., Inc., 79 F.2d 613, 616 (2d Cir.1935); Castaner v. Mora, 234 F.2d 710 (1st Cir.1956). This rule recognizes, as did former Bankruptcy Rule 307, the power of the court to reconsider an order of disallowance on appropriate motion.

Reconsideration of a claim that has been previously allowed or disallowed after objection is discretionary with the court. The right to seek reconsideration of an allowed claim, like the right to object to its allowance, is generally exercised by the trustee if one has qualified and is performing the duties of

that office with reasonable diligence and fidelity. A request for reconsideration of a disallowance would, on the other hand, ordinarily come from the claimant.

A proof of claim executed and filed in accordance with the rules in this Part III is prima facie evidence of the validity and the amount of the claim notwithstanding a motion for reconsideration of an order of allowance. Failure to respond does not constitute an admission, though it may be deemed a consent to a reconsideration. In re Goble Boat Co., 190 Fed. 92 (N.D.N.Y.1911). The court may decline to reconsider an order of allowance or disallowance without notice to any adverse party and without affording any hearing to the movant. If a motion to reconsider is granted, notice and hearing must be afforded to parties in interest before the previous action in the claim taken in respect to the claim may be vacated or modified. After reconsideration, the court may allow or disallow the claim, increase or decrease the amount of a prior allowance, accord the claim a priority different from that originally assigned it, or enter any other appropriate order.

The rule expands § 502(j) which provides for reconsideration of an allowance only before the case is closed. Authorities have disagreed as to whether reconsideration may be had after a case has been reopened. Compare 3 Collier, Bankruptcy ¶57.23[4] (14th ed. 1964), see generally 3 id. ¶502.10 (15th ed. 1979), with 2 Remington, Bankruptcy 498 (Henderson ed. 1956). If a case is reopened as provided in § 350(b) of the Code, reconsideration of the allowance or disallowance of a claim may be sought and granted in accordance with this rule.

CROSS REFERENCES

Closing and reopening cases, see 11 USCA § 350.

Exception to procedural rule on new trials and amendment of judgments, see Fed.Rules Bankr.Proc. Rule 9023, 11 USCA.

Motions, form and service, see Fed.Rules Bankr.Proc. Rule 9013, 11 USCA.

Reconsideration of claim prior to closing of case, see 11 USCA § 502.

Rule 3009.   Declaration and Payment of Dividends in a Chapter 7 Liquidation Case

In a chapter 7 case, dividends to creditors shall be paid as promptly as practicable. Dividend checks shall be made payable to and mailed to each creditor whose claim has been allowed, unless a power of attorney authorizing another entity to receive dividends has been executed and filed in accordance with Rule 9010. In that event, dividend checks shall be made payable to the creditor and to the other entity and shall be mailed to the other entity.

(As amended Mar. 30, 1987, eff. Aug. 1, 1987; Apr. 22, 1993, eff. Aug. 1, 1993.)

ADVISORY COMMITTEE NOTES

This rule is derived from former Rules 308 and 11–35(a). The preparation of records showing dividends declared and to whom payable is subject to prescription by the Director of the Administrative Office pursuant to Rule 5003(e). The rule

---

governs distributions to creditors having priority as well as to general unsecured creditors. Notwithstanding the detailed statutory provisions regulating the declaration of dividends, a necessarily wide discretion over this matter has been recognized to reside in the court. See 3A Collier, Bankruptcy ¶65.03 (14th ed. 1975): 1 Proceedings of Seminar for Newly Appointed Referees in Bankruptcy 173 (1964). Although the rule leaves to the discretion of the court the amount and the times of dividend payments, it recognizes the creditors' right to as prompt payment as practicable.

The second and third sentences of the rule make explicit the method of payment of dividends and afford protection of the interests of the creditor and the holder of a power of attorney authorized to receive payment.

The rule does not permit variance at local option. This represents a marked change from former Bankruptcy Rule 308.

1993 Amendments

This rule is amended to delete the requirement that the court approve the amounts and times of distributions in chapter 7 cases. This change recognizes the role of the United States trustee in supervising trustees. Other amendments are stylistic and make no substantive change.

CROSS REFERENCES

Dividend records kept by clerk, see Fed.Rules Bankr.Proc. Rule 5003, 11 USCA.

Unclaimed dividends, see 11 USCA § 347.

Rule 3010. Small Dividends and Payments in Chapter 7 Liquidation, Chapter 12 Family Farmer's Debt Adjustment, and Chapter 13 Individual's Debt Adjustment Cases

(a) Chapter 7 cases

In a chapter 7 case no dividend in an amount less than $5 shall be distributed by the trustee to any creditor unless authorized by local rule or order of the court. Any dividend not distributed to a creditor shall be treated in the same manner as unclaimed funds as provided in § 347 of the Code.

(b) Chapter 12 and chapter 13 cases

In a chapter 12 or chapter 13 case no payment in an amount less than $15 shall be distributed by the trustee to any creditor unless authorized by local rule or order of the court. Funds not distributed because of this subdivision shall accumulate and shall be paid whenever the accumulation aggregates $15. Any funds remaining shall be distributed with the final payment.

(As amended Mar. 30, 1987, eff. Aug. 1, 1987; Apr. 30, 1991, eff. Aug. 1, 1991.)

ADVISORY COMMITTEE NOTES

This rule permits a court to eliminate the disproportionate expense and inconvenience incurred by the issuance of a dividend check of less than $5 (or $15 in a chapter 13 case). Creditors are more irritated than pleased to receive such small dividends, but the money is held subject to their specific request as are unclaimed dividends under § 347(a) of the Code. When the trustee deposits undistributed dividends pursuant to a direction in accordance with this rule the trustee should file with the clerk a list of the names and addresses, so far as known, of the persons entitled to the money so deposited and the respective amounts payable to them pursuant to Rule 3011. In a chapter 13 case, the small dividend will accumulate and will be payable at the latest, with the final dividend. Local rule or order may change the practice permitted in this rule and, in that connection, the order may be incorporated in the order confirming a chapter 13 plan.

1991 Amendments

Subdivision (b) is amended to include chapter 12 cases.

Rule 3011. Unclaimed Funds in Chapter 7 Liquidation, Chapter 12 Family Farmer's Debt Adjustment, and Chapter 13 Individual's Debt Adjustment Cases

The trustee shall file a list of all known names and addresses of the entities and the amounts which they are entitled to be paid from remaining property of the estate that is paid into court pursuant to § 347(a) of the Code.

(As amended Mar. 30, 1987, eff. Aug. 1, 1987; Apr. 30, 1991, eff. Aug. 1, 1991.)

ADVISORY COMMITTEE NOTES

This rule is derived from former Bankruptcy Rule 310. The operative provisions of that rule, however, are contained in § 347(a) of the Code, requiring the trustee to stop payment of checks remaining unpaid 90 days after distribution. The rule adds the requirement of filing a list of the names and addresses of the persons entitled to these dividends. This rule applies in a chapter 7 or 13 case but not in a chapter 9 or 11 case. The latter cases are governed by § 347(b) of the Code which provides for unclaimed distributions to be returned to the debtor or other entity acquiring the assets of the debtor.

1991 Amendments

The title of this rule is amended to include chapter 12 cases. The words "with the clerk" are deleted as unnecessary. See Rules 5005(a) and 9001(3).

CROSS REFERENCES

Treatment of small dividends as unclaimed funds, see Fed. Rules Bankr.Proc. Rule 3010, 11 USCA.

Rule 3012. Determining the Amount of Secured and Priority Claims

(a) Determination of amount of claim

On request by a party in interest and after notice— to the holder of the claim and any other entity the court designates—and a hearing, the court may determine:

(1) the amount of a secured claim under § 506(a) of the Code; or

(2) the amount of a claim entitled to priority under § 507 of the Code.

(b) Request for determination; how made

Except as provided in subdivision (c), a request to determine the amount of a secured claim may be made by motion, in a claim objection, or in a plan filed in a chapter 12 or chapter 13 case. When the request is made in a chapter 12 or chapter 13 plan, the plan shall be served on the holder of the claim and any other entity the court designates in the manner provided for service of a summons and complaint by Rule 7004. A request to determine the amount of a claim entitled to priority may be made only by motion after a claim is filed or in a claim objection.

(c) Claims of governmental units

A request to determine the amount of a secured claim of a governmental unit may be made only by motion or in a claim objection after the governmental unit files a proof of claim or after the time for filing one under Rule 3002(c)(1) has expired.

(As amended Mar. 30, 1987, eff. Aug. 1, 1987; Apr. 27, 2017, eff. Dec. 1, 2017.)

ADVISORY COMMITTEE NOTES

Pursuant to § 506(a) of the Code, secured claims are to be valued and allowed as secured to the extent of the value of the collateral and unsecured, to the extent it is enforceable, for the excess over such value. The valuation of secured claims may become important in different contexts, e.g., to determine the issue of adequate protection under § 361, impairment under § 1124, or treatment of the claim in a plan pursuant to § 1129(b) of the Code. This rule permits the issue to be raised on motion by a party in interest. The secured creditor is entitled to notice of the hearing on the motion and the court may direct that others in the case also receive such notice.

An adversary proceeding is commenced when the validity, priority, or extent of a lien is at issue as prescribed by Rule 7001. That proceeding is relevant to the basis of the lien itself while valuation under Rule 3012 would be for the purposes indicated above.

2017 Amendments

This rule is amended and reorganized.

Subdivision (a) provides, in keeping with the former version of this rule, that a party in interest may seek a determination of the amount of a secured claim. The amended rule provides that the amount of a claim entitled to priority may also be determined by the court.

Subdivision (b) is added to provide that a request to determine the amount of a secured claim may be made in a chapter 12 or chapter 13 plan, as well as by a motion or a claim objection. When the request is made in a plan, the plan must be served on the holder of the claim and any other entities the court designates according to Rule 7004. Secured claims of governmental units are not included in this subdivision and are governed by subdivision (c). The amount of a claim

entitled to priority may be determined through a motion or a claim objection.

Subdivision (c) clarifies that a determination under this rule with respect to a secured claim of a governmental unit may be made only by motion or in a claim objection, but not until the governmental unit has filed a proof of claim or its time for filing a proof of claim has expired.

CROSS REFERENCES

Definition of,

"Lien", see 11 USCA § 101.

"Security", see 11 USCA § 101.

"Security interest", see 11 USCA § 101.

Determination of secured status, see 11 USCA § 506.

Motions, form and service, see Fed.Rules Bankr.Proc. Rule 9013, 11 USCA.

Rule 3013. Classification of Claims and Interests

For the purposes of the plan and its acceptance, the court may, on motion after hearing on notice as the court may direct, determine classes of creditors and equity security holders pursuant to §§ 1122, 1222(b)(1), and 1322(b)(1) of the Code.

(As amended Apr. 30, 1991, eff. Aug. 1, 1991.)

ADVISORY COMMITTEE NOTES

Sections 1122 and 1322(b)(1) set the standards for classifying claims and interests but provide that such classification is accomplished in the plan. This rule does not change the standards; rather it recognizes that it may be desirable or necessary to establish proper classification before a plan can be formulated. It provides for a court hearing on such notice as the court may direct.

1991 Amendments

This rule is amended to include chapter 12 cases.

CROSS REFERENCES

Motions, form and service, see Fed.Rules Bankr.Proc. Rule 9013, 11 USCA.

Rule 3014. Election Under § 1111(b) by Secured Creditor in Chapter 9 Municipality or Chapter 11 Reorganization Case

An election of application of § 1111(b)(2) of the Code by a class of secured creditors in a chapter 9 or 11 case may be made at any time prior to the conclusion of the hearing on the disclosure statement or within such later time as the court may fix. If the disclosure statement is conditionally approved pursuant to Rule 3017.1, and a final hearing on the disclosure statement is not held, the election of application of § 1111(b)(2) may be made not later than the date fixed pursuant to Rule 3017.1(a)(2) or another date the court may fix. The election shall be in writing and signed unless made at the hearing on the disclosure statement. The election, if made by the majorities required by

§ 1111(b)(1)(A)(i), shall be binding on all members of the class with respect to the plan.

(As amended Apr. 11, 1997, eff. Dec. 1, 1997.)

ADVISORY COMMITTEE NOTES

Pursuant to § 1111(b)(1) of the Code, a nonrecourse secured loan is converted, automatically, into a recourse loan thereby entitling the creditor to an unsecured deficiency claim if the value of the collateral is less than the debt. The class, however, may retain the loan as a nonrecourse loan by electing application of § 1111(b)(2) by the majorities stated in § 1111(b)(1)(A)(i). That section does not specify any time periods for making the election.

Rule 3014 provides that if no agreement is negotiated, the election of § 1111(b)(2) of the Code may be made at any time prior to conclusion of the hearing on the disclosure statement. Once the hearing has been concluded, it would be too late for a secured creditor class to demand different treatment unless the court has fixed a later time. This would be the case if, for example, a public class of secured creditors should have an approved disclosure statement prior to electing under § 1111(b).

Generally it is important that the proponent of a plan ascertain the position of the secured creditor class before a plan is proposed. The secured creditor class must know the prospects of its treatment under the plan before it can intelligently determine its rights under § 1111(b). The rule recognizes that there may be negotiations between the proponent of the plan and the secured creditor leading to a representation of desired treatment under § 1111(b). If that treatment is approved by the requisite majorities of the class and culminates in a written, signed statement filed with the court, that statement becomes binding and the class may not thereafter demand different treatment under § 1111(b) with respect to that plan. The proponent of the plan is thus enabled to seek approval of the disclosure statement and transmit the plan for voting in anticipation of confirmation. Only if that plan is not confirmed may the class of secured creditors thereafter change its prior election.

While this rule and the Code refer to a class of secured creditors it should be noted that ordinarily each secured creditor is in a separate and distinct class. In that event, the secured creditor has the sole power to determine application of § 1111(b) with respect to that claim.

1997 Amendments

This amendment provides a deadline for electing application of § 1111(b)(2) in a small business case in which a conditionally approved disclosure statement is finally approved without a hearing.

GAP Report on Rule 3014. No changes to the published draft.

CROSS REFERENCES

Hearing on disclosure statement, see Fed.Rules Bankr. Proc. Rule 3017, 11 USCA.

Reduction of time for election pursuant to § 1111(b) not permitted, see Fed.Rules Bankr.Proc. Rule 9006, 11 USCA.

Rule 3015. Filing, Objection to Confirmation, Effect of Confirmation, and Modification of a Plan in a Chapter 12 or a Chapter 13 Case

(a) Filing a chapter 12 plan

The debtor may file a chapter 12 plan with the petition. If a plan is not filed with the petition, it shall be filed within the time prescribed by § 1221 of the Code.

(b) Filing a chapter 13 plan

The debtor may file a chapter 13 plan with the petition. If a plan is not filed with the petition, it shall be filed within 14 days thereafter, and such time may not be further extended except for cause shown and on notice as the court may direct. If a case is converted to chapter 13, a plan shall be filed within 14 days thereafter, and such time may not be further extended except for cause shown and on notice as the court may direct.

(c) Form of chapter 13 plan

If there is an Official Form for a plan filed in a chapter 13 case, that form must be used unless a Local Form has been adopted in compliance with Rule 3015.1. With either the Official Form or a Local Form, a nonstandard provision is effective only if it is included in a section of the form designated for nonstandard provisions and is also identified in accordance with any other requirements of the form. As used in this rule and the Official Form or a Local Form, "nonstandard provision" means a provision not otherwise included in the Official or Local Form or deviating from it.

(d) Notice

If the plan is not included with the notice of the hearing on confirmation mailed under Rule 2002, the debtor shall serve the plan on the trustee and all creditors when it is filed with the court.

(e) Transmission to United States trustee

The clerk shall forthwith transmit to the United States trustee a copy of the plan and any modification thereof filed under subdivision (a) or (b) of this rule.

(f) Objection to confirmation; determination of good faith in the absence of an objection

An objection to confirmation of a plan shall be filed and served on the debtor, the trustee, and any other entity designated by the court, and shall be transmitted to the United States trustee, at least seven days before the date set for the hearing on confirmation, unless the court orders otherwise. An objection to confirmation is governed by Rule 9014. If no objection is timely filed, the court may determine that the plan has been proposed in good faith and not by any means forbidden by law without receiving evidence on such issues.

(g) Effect of confirmation

Upon the confirmation of a chapter 12 or chapter 13 plan:

(1) any determination in the plan made under Rule 3012 about the amount of a secured claim is binding on the holder of the claim, even if the holder files a contrary proof of claim or the debtor schedules that claim, and regardless of whether an objection to the claim has been filed; and

(2) any request in the plan to terminate the stay imposed by § 362(a), § 1201(a), or § 1301(a) is granted.

(h) Modification of plan after confirmation

A request to modify a plan under § 1229 or § 1329 of the Code shall identify the proponent and shall be filed together with the proposed modification. The clerk, or some other person as the court may direct, shall give the debtor, the trustee, and all creditors not less than 21 days' notice by mail of the time fixed for filing objections and, if an objection is filed, the hearing to consider the proposed modification, unless the court orders otherwise with respect to creditors who are not affected by the proposed modification. A copy of the notice shall be transmitted to the United States trustee. A copy of the proposed modification, or a summary thereof, shall be included with the notice. Any objection to the proposed modification shall be filed and served on the debtor, the trustee, and any other entity designated by the court, and shall be transmitted to the United States trustee. An objection to a proposed modification is governed by Rule 9014.

(As amended Apr. 30, 1991, eff. Aug. 1, 1991; Apr. 22, 1993, eff. Aug. 1, 1993; Mar. 26, 2009, eff. Dec. 1, 2009; Apr. 27, 2017, eff. Dec. 1, 2017.)

ADVISORY COMMITTEE NOTES

Section 1321 provides only that the "debtor shall file a plan." No time periods are specified, nor is any other detail provided. The rule requires a chapter 13 plan to be filed either with the petition or within 15 days thereafter. The court may, for cause, extend the time. The rule permits a summary of the plan to be transmitted with the notice of the hearing on confirmation. The court may, however, require the plan itself to be transmitted and the debtor to supply enough copies for this purpose. In the former rules under Chapter XIII [former § 1001 et seq. of this title] the plan would accompany the notice of the first meeting of creditors. It is more important for the plan or a summary of its terms to be sent with the notice of the confirmation hearing. At that hearing objections to the plan will be heard by the court.

1991 Amendments

This rule is amended to include chapter 12 plans. Section 1221 of the Code requires the debtor to file a chapter 12 plan not later than 90 days after the order for relief, except that

the court may extend the period if an extension is "substantially justified."

Subdivision (e) enables the United States trustee to monitor chapter 12 and chapter 13 plans pursuant to 28 U.S.C. § 586(a)(3)(C).

1993 Amendments

Subdivision (b) is amended to provide a time limit for filing a plan after a case has been converted to chapter 13. The substitution of "may" for "shall" is stylistic and makes no substantive change.

Subdivision (d) is amended to clarify that the plan or a summary of the plan must be included with each notice of the confirmation hearing in a chapter 12 case pursuant to Rule 2002(a).

Subdivision (f) is added to expand the scope of the rule to govern objections to confirmation in chapter 12 and chapter 13 cases. The subdivision also is amended to include a provision that permits the court, in the absence of an objection, to determine that the plan has been proposed in good faith and not by any means forbidden by law without the need to receive evidence on these issues. These matters are now governed by Rule 3020.

Subdivision (g) is added to provide a procedure for postconfirmation modification of chapter 12 and chapter 13 plans. These procedures are designed to be similar to the procedures for confirmation of plans. However, if no objection is filed with respect to a proposed modification of a plan after confirmation, the court is not required to hold a hearing. *See* § 1229(b)(2) and § 1329(b)(2) which provide that the plan as modified becomes the plan unless, after notice and a hearing, such modification is disapproved. *See* § 102(1). The notice of the time fixed for filing objections to the proposed modification should set a date for a hearing to be held in the event that an objection is filed.

Amendments to the title of this rule are stylistic and make no substantive change.

2009 Amendments

The rule is amended to implement changes in connection with the amendment to Rule 9006(a) and the manner by which time is computed under the rules. The deadlines in the rule are amended to substitute a deadline that is a multiple of seven days. Throughout the rules, deadlines are amended in the following manner:

- 5–day periods become 7–day periods
- 10–day periods become 14–day periods
- 15–day periods become 14–day periods
- 20–day periods become 21–day periods
- 25–day periods become 28–day periods

2017 Amendments

This rule is amended and reorganized.

Subdivision (c) is amended to require use of an Official Form if one is adopted for chapter 13 plans unless a Local Form has been adopted consistent with Rule 3015.1. Subdivision (c) also provides that nonstandard provisions in a chapter 13 plan must be set out in the section of the Official or Local Form specifically designated for such provisions and must be identified in the manner required by the Official or Local Form.

Subdivision (d) is amended to ensure that the trustee and creditors are served with the plan before confirmation. Service may be made either at the time the plan is filed or with the notice under Rule 2002 of the hearing to consider confirmation of the plan.

Subdivision (f) is amended to require service of an objection to confirmation at least seven days before the hearing to consider confirmation of a plan, unless the court orders otherwise.

Subdivision (g) is amended to set out two effects of confirmation. Subdivision (g)(1) provides that the amount of a secured claim under § 506(a) may be determined through a chapter 12 or chapter 13 plan in accordance with Rule 3012. That determination, unlike the amount of any current installment payments or arrearages, controls over a contrary proof of claim, without the need for a claim objection under Rule 3007, and over the schedule submitted by the debtor under § 521(a). The amount of a secured claim of a governmental unit, however, may not be determined through a chapter 12 or chapter 13 plan under Rule 3012. Subdivision (g)(2) provides for termination of the automatic stay under §§ 362, 1201, and 1301 as requested in the plan.

Subdivision (h) was formerly subdivision (g). It is redesignated and is amended to reflect that often the party proposing a plan modification is responsible for serving the proposed modification on other parties. The option to serve a summary of the proposed modification has been retained. Unless required by another rule, service under this subdivision does not need to be made in the manner provided for service of a summons and complaint by Rule 7004.

CROSS REFERENCES

Acceptance or rejection of plans, see Fed.Rules Bankr.Proc. Rule 3018, 11 USCA.

Deposit, confirmation of plan, see Fed.Rules Bankr.Proc. Rule 3020, 11 USCA.

Reduction of time for filing plan not permitted, see Fed. Rules Bankr.Proc. Rule 9006, 11 USCA.

Rule 3015.1. Requirements for a Local Form for Plans Filed in a Chapter 13 Case

Notwithstanding Rule 9029(a)(1), a district may require that a Local Form for a plan filed in a chapter 13 case be used instead of an Official Form adopted for that purpose if the following conditions are satisfied:

(a) a single Local Form is adopted for the district after public notice and an opportunity for public comment;

(b) each paragraph is numbered and labeled in boldface type with a heading stating the general subject matter of the paragraph;

(c) the Local Form includes an initial paragraph for the debtor to indicate that the plan does or does not:

(1) contain any nonstandard provision;

(2) limit the amount of a secured claim based on a valuation of the collateral for the claim; or

(3) avoid a security interest or lien;

(d) the Local Form contains separate paragraphs for:

(1) curing any default and maintaining payments on a claim secured by the debtor's principal residence;

(2) paying a domestic-support obligation;

(3) paying a claim described in the final paragraph of § 1325(a) of the Bankruptcy Code; and

(4) surrendering property that secures a claim with a request that the stay under §§ 362(a) and 1301(a) be terminated as to the surrendered collateral; and

(e) the Local Form contains a final paragraph for:

(1) the placement of nonstandard provisions, as defined in Rule 3015(c), along with a statement that any nonstandard provision placed elsewhere in the plan is void; and

(2) certification by the debtor's attorney or by an unrepresented debtor that the plan contains no nonstandard provision other than those set out in the final paragraph.

(Added Apr. 27, 2017, eff. Dec. 1, 2017.)

ADVISORY COMMITTEE NOTES

2017 Amendments

This rule is new. It sets out features required for all Local Forms for plans in chapter 13 cases. If a Local Form does not comply with this rule, it may not be used in lieu of the Official Chapter 13 Plan Form. See Rule 3015(c).

Under the rule only one Local Form may be adopted in a district. The rule does not specify the method of adoption, but it does require that adoption of a Local Form be preceded by a public notice and comment period.

To promote consistency among Local Forms and clarity of content of chapter 13 plans, the rule prescribes several formatting and disclosure requirements. Paragraphs in such a form must be numbered and labeled in bold type, and the form must contain separate paragraphs for the cure and maintenance of home mortgages, payment of domestic support obligations, treatment of secured claims covered by the "hanging paragraph" of § 1325(a), and surrender of property securing a claim. Whether those portions of the Local Form are used in a given chapter 13 case will depend on the debtor's individual circumstances.

The rule requires that a Local Form begin with a paragraph for the debtor to call attention to the fact that the plan contains a nonstandard provision; limits the amount of a secured claim based on a valuation of the collateral, as authorized by Rule 3012(b); or avoids a lien, as authorized by Rule 4003(d).

The last paragraph of a Local Form must be for the inclusion of any nonstandard provisions, as defined by Rule 3015(c), and must include a statement that nonstandard provisions placed elsewhere in the plan are void. This part gives the debtor the opportunity to propose provisions that are not otherwise in, or that deviate from, the Local Form. The form must also require a certification by the debtor's attorney or unrepresented debtor that there are no nonstandard provisions other than those placed in the final paragraph.

Rule 3016. Filing of Plan and Disclosure Statement in a Chapter 9 Municipality or Chapter 11 Reorganization Case

(a) Identification of plan

Every proposed plan and any modification thereof shall be dated and, in a chapter 11 case, identified with the name of the entity or entities submitting or filing it.

(b) Disclosure statement

In a chapter 9 or 11 case, a disclosure statement under § 1125 of the Code or evidence showing compliance with § 1126(b) shall be filed with the plan or within a time fixed by the court, unless the plan is intended to provide adequate information under § 1125(f)(1). If the plan is intended to provide adequate information under § 1125(f)(1), it shall be so designated and Rule 3017.1 shall apply as if the plan is a disclosure statement.

(c) Injunction under a plan

If a plan provides for an injunction against conduct not otherwise enjoined under the Code, the plan and disclosure statement shall describe in specific and conspicuous language (bold, italic, or underlined text) all acts to be enjoined and identify the entities that would be subject to the injunction.

(d) Standard form small business disclosure statement and plan

In a small business case, the court may approve a disclosure statement and may confirm a plan that conform substantially to the appropriate Official Forms or other standard forms approved by the court.

(As amended Mar. 30, 1987, eff. Aug. 1, 1987; Apr. 30, 1991, eff. Aug. 1, 1991; Apr. 23, 1996, eff. Dec. 1, 1996; Apr. 23, 2001, eff. Dec. 1, 2001; Apr. 23, 2008, eff. Dec. 1, 2008.)

ADVISORY COMMITTEE NOTES

This rule implements the Code provisions concerning the filing of plans in chapters 9 and 11.

Chapter 9 Cases. Section 941 provides that the debtor may file a plan with the petition or thereafter but within a time fixed by the court. A rule, therefore, is unnecessary to specify the time for filing chapter 9 plans.

Chapter 11 Nonrailroad Cases. Section 1121 contains detailed provisions with respect to who may file a chapter 11 plan and, in part, the time period. Section 1121(a) permits a debtor to file a plan with the petition or at any time during the case. Section 1121(b) and (c) grants exclusive periods of 120 days and 180 days for the debtor to file and obtain acceptance of a plan. Failure to take advantage of these periods or the appointment of a trustee would permit other parties in interest to file a plan. These statutory provisions are not repeated in the rules.

Chapter 11 Railroad Cases. Pursuant to subchapter IV of chapter 11, § 1121 of the Code is applicable in railroad cases; see §§ 1161, 103(g). A trustee, however, is to be appointed in every case; thus, pursuant to § 1121(c), any party in interest may file a plan. See discussion of subdivision (a) of this rule, infra.

Subdivision (a). Section 1121(c), while permitting parties in interest a limited right to file plans, does not provide any time limitation. This subdivision sets as the deadline, the conclusion of the hearing on the disclosure statement. The court may, however, grant additional time. It is derived from former Chapter X Rule 10–301(c)(2) which used, as the cut-off time, the conclusion of the hearing on approval of a plan. As indicated, supra, § 1121(a) permits a debtor to file a plan at any time during the chapter 11 case. Under § 1121(c), parties other than a debtor may file a plan only after a trustee is appointed or the debtor's exclusive time expires.

Subdivision (b) requires plans to be properly identified.

Subdivision (c). This provision is new. In chapter 9 and 11 cases (including railroad reorganization cases) postpetition solicitation of votes on a plan requires transmittal of a disclosure statement, the contents of which have been approved by the court. See § 1125 of the Code. A prepetition solicitation must either have been in conformity with applicable nonbankruptcy law or, if none, the disclosure must have been of adequate information as set forth in § 1125 of the Code. See § 1126(b). Subdivision (c) of this rule provides the time for filing the disclosure statement or evidence of compliance with § 1126(b) which ordinarily will be with the plan but the court may allow a later time or the court may, pursuant to the last sentence, fix a time certain. Rule 3017 deals with the hearing on the disclosure statement. The disclosure statement, pursuant to § 1125 is to contain adequate information. "Adequate information" is defined in § 1125(a) as information that would permit a reasonable creditor or equity security holder to make an informed judgment on the plan.

1991 Amendments

Subdivision (a) is amended to enlarge the time for filing competing plans. A party in interest may not file a plan without leave of court only if an order approving a disclosure statement relating to another plan has been entered and a decision on confirmation of the plan has not been entered. This subdivision does not fix a deadline beyond which a debtor may not file a plan.

1996 Amendments

Section 1121(c) gives a party in interest the right to file a chapter 11 plan after expiration of the period when only the debtor may file a plan. Under § 1121(d), the exclusive period in which only the debtor may file a plan may be extended, but only if a party in interest so requests and the court, after notice and a hearing, finds cause for an extension. Subdivision (a) is abrogated because it could have the effect of extending the debtor's exclusive period for filing a plan without satisfying the requirements of § 1121(d). The abrogation of subdivision (a) does not affect the court's discretion with respect to the scheduling of hearings on the approval of disclosure statements when more than one plan has been filed.

The amendment to subdivision (c), redesignated as subdivision (b), is stylistic.

GAP Report on Rule 3016. No changes since publication, except for a stylistic change.

2001 Amendments

Subdivision (c) is added to assure that entities whose conduct would be enjoined under a plan, rather than by operation of the Code, are given adequate notice of the proposed injunction. The validity and effect of any injunction are substantive law matters that are beyond the scope of these rules.

Specific and conspicuous language is not necessary if the injunction contained in the plan is substantially the same as an injunction provided under the Code. For example, if a plan contains an injunction against acts to collect a discharged debt from the debtor, Rule 3016(c) would not apply because that conduct would be enjoined nonetheless under § 524(a)(2). But if a plan provides that creditors will be permanently enjoined from asserting claims against persons who are not debtors in the case, the plan and disclosure statement must highlight the injunctive language and comply with the requirements of Rule 3016(c). *See* § 524(e).

The requirement in this rule that the plan and disclosure statement identify the entities that would be subject to the injunction requires reasonable identification under the circumstances. If the entities that would be subject to the injunction cannot be identified by name, the plan and disclosure statement may describe them by class or category. For example, it may be sufficient to identify the subjects of the injunction as "all creditors of the debtor."

Changes Made After Publication and Comments. The word "highlighted" in the parenthesis was replaced with "underlined" because highlighted documents are difficult to scan electronically for inclusion in the clerks' files. The Committee Note was revised to put in a more prominent position the statement that the validity and effect of any injunction provided for in a plan are substantive matters beyond the scope of the rules. Other stylistic changes were made to the Committee Note.

2008 Amendments

Subdivision (b) is amended to recognize that, in 2005, § 1125(f)(1) was added to the Code to provide that the plan proponent in a small business case need not file a disclosure statement if the plan itself includes adequate information and the court finds that a separate disclosure statement is unnecessary. If the plan is intended to provide adequate information in a small business case, it may be conditionally approved as a disclosure statement under Rule 3017.1 and is subject to all other rules applicable to disclosure statements in small business cases.

Subdivision (d) is added to the rule to implement § 433 of the Bankruptcy Abuse Prevention and Consumer Protection Act of 2005 which requires the promulgation of Official Forms for plans and disclosure statements in small business cases. Section 1125(f)(2) of the Code provides that the court may approve a disclosure statement submitted on the appropriate Official Form or on a standard form approved by the court. The rule takes no position on whether a court may require a local standard form disclosure statement or plan of reorganization in lieu of the Official Forms.

Other amendments are stylistic.

CROSS REFERENCES

Filing of municipality debt adjustment plan, see 11 USCA § 941.

Hearing on disclosure statement, see Fed.Rules Bankr. Proc. Rule 3017, 11 USCA.

Rule 3017. Court Consideration of Disclosure Statement in a Chapter 9 Municipality or Chapter 11 Reorganization Case

(a) Hearing on disclosure statement and objections

Except as provided in Rule 3017.1, after a disclosure statement is filed in accordance with Rule 3016(b), the court shall hold a hearing on at least 28 days' notice to the debtor, creditors, equity security holders and other parties in interest as provided in Rule 2002 to consider the disclosure statement and any objections or modifications thereto. The plan and the disclosure statement shall be mailed with the notice of the hearing only to the debtor, any trustee or committee appointed under the Code, the Securities and Exchange Commission and any party in interest who requests in writing a copy of the statement or plan. Objections to the disclosure statement shall be filed and served on the debtor, the trustee, any committee appointed under the Code, and any other entity designated by the court, at any time before the disclosure statement is approved or by an earlier date as the court may fix. In a chapter 11 reorganization case, every notice, plan, disclosure statement, and objection required to be served or mailed pursuant to this subdivision shall be transmitted to the United States trustee within the time provided in this subdivision.

(b) Determination on disclosure statement

Following the hearing the court shall determine whether the disclosure statement should be approved.

(c) Dates fixed for voting on plan and confirmation

On or before approval of the disclosure statement, the court shall fix a time within which the holders of claims and interests may accept or reject the plan and may fix a date for the hearing on confirmation.

(d) Transmission and notice to United States trustee, creditors and equity security holders

Upon approval of a disclosure statement,[1]—except to the extent that the court orders otherwise with respect to one or more unimpaired classes of creditors or equity security holders—the debtor in possession, trustee, proponent of the plan, or clerk as the court orders shall mail to all creditors and equity security holders, and in a chapter 11 reorganization case shall transmit to the United States trustee,

(1) the plan or a court-approved summary of the plan;

(2) the disclosure statement approved by the court;

(3) notice of the time within which acceptances and rejections of the plan may be filed; and

---

(4) any other information as the court may direct, including any court opinion approving the disclosure statement or a court-approved summary of the opinion.

In addition, notice of the time fixed for filing objections and the hearing on confirmation shall be mailed to all creditors and equity security holders in accordance with Rule 2002(b), and a form of ballot conforming to the appropriate Official Form shall be mailed to creditors and equity security holders entitled to vote on the plan. If the court opinion is not transmitted or only a summary of the plan is transmitted, the court opinion or the plan shall be provided on request of a party in interest at the plan proponent's expense. If the court orders that the disclosure statement and the plan or a summary of the plan shall not be mailed to any unimpaired class, notice that the class is designated in the plan as unimpaired and notice of the name and address of the person from whom the plan or summary of the plan and disclosure statement may be obtained upon request and at the plan proponent's expense, shall be mailed to members of the unimpaired class together with the notice of the time fixed for filing objections to and the hearing on confirmation. For the purposes of this subdivision, creditors and equity security holders shall include holders of stock, bonds, debentures, notes, and other securities of record on the date the order approving the disclosure statement is entered or another date fixed by the court, for cause, after notice and a hearing.

(e) Transmission to beneficial holders of securities

At the hearing held pursuant to subdivision (a) of this rule, the court shall consider the procedures for transmitting the documents and information required by subdivision (d) of this rule to beneficial holders of stock, bonds, debentures, notes, and other securities, determine the adequacy of the procedures, and enter any orders the court deems appropriate.

(f) Notice and transmission of documents to entities subject to an injunction under a plan

If a plan provides for an injunction against conduct not otherwise enjoined under the Code and an entity that would be subject to the injunction is not a creditor or equity security holder, at the hearing held under Rule 3017(a), the court shall consider procedures for providing the entity with:

(1) at least 28 days' notice of the time fixed for filing objections and the hearing on confirmation of the plan containing the information described in Rule 2002(c)(3); and

(2) to the extent feasible, a copy of the plan and disclosure statement.

(As amended Mar. 30, 1987, eff. Aug. 1, 1987; Apr. 30, 1991, eff. Aug. 1, 1991; Apr. 11, 1997, eff. Dec. 1, 1997; Apr. 23, 2001, eff. Dec. 1, 2001; Mar. 26, 2009, eff. Dec. 1, 2009.)

¹ So in original. The comma probably should not appear.

ADVISORY COMMITTEE NOTES

This rule is adapted from former Rule 10–303 which dealt with the approval of a Chapter X plan by the court. There is no requirement for plan approval in a chapter 9 or 11 case under the Code but there is the requirement that a disclosure statement containing adequate financial information be approved by the court after notice and a hearing before votes on a plan are solicited. Section 1125(b) of the Code is made applicable in chapter 9 cases by § 901(a). It is also applicable in railroad reorganization cases under subchapter IV of chapter 11; see § 1161 of the Code.

Subdivision (a) of this rule provides for the hearing on the disclosure statement. Thus, a hearing would be required in all cases; whether it may be ex parte would depend on the circumstances of the case, but a mere absence of objections would not eliminate the need for a hearing; see § 102(1) of the Code.

No provision similar to former Rule 10–303(f) is included. That subdivision together with former Rule 10–304 prohibited solicitation of votes until after entry of an order approving the plan. Section 1125(b) of the Code explicitly provides that votes on a plan may not be solicited until a disclosure statement approved by the court is transmitted. Pursuant to the change in rulemaking power, a comparable provision in this rule is unnecessary. 28 U.S.C. § 2075.

Copies of the disclosure statement and plan need not be mailed with the notice of the hearing or otherwise transmitted prior to the hearing except with respect to the parties explicitly set forth in the subdivision.

It should be noted that, by construction, the singular includes the plural. Therefore, the phrase "plan or plans" or "disclosure statement or statements" has not been used although the possibility of multiple plans and statements is recognized.

Subdivision (d) permits the court to require a party other than the clerk of the bankruptcy court to bear the responsibility for transmitting the notices and documents specified in the rule when votes on the plan are solicited. Ordinarily the person responsible for such mailing will be the proponent of the plan. In rare cases the clerk may be directed to mail these documents, particularly when the trustee would have the responsibility but there is insufficient money in the estate to enable the trustee to perform this task.

1987 Amendments

Subdivision (d). Section 1125(c) of the Code requires that the entire approved disclosure statement be provided in connection with voting on a plan. The court is authorized by § 1125(c) to approve different disclosure statements for different classes. Although the rule does not permit the mailing of a summary of the disclosure statement in place of the approved disclosure statement, the court may approve a summary of the disclosure statement to be mailed with the complete disclosure statement to those voting on the plan.

1991 Amendments

This rule is amended to enable the United States trustee to monitor and comment with regard to chapter 11 disclosure statements and plans. The United States trustee does not perform these functions in a chapter 9 municipal debt adjustment case. See 28 U.S.C. § 586(a)(3)(B).

Subdivision (d) is amended to give the court the discretion to direct that one or more unimpaired classes shall not receive disclosure statements, plans, or summaries of plans. Members of unimpaired classes are not entitled to vote on the plan. Although disclosure statements enable members of unimpaired classes to make informed judgments as to whether to object to confirmation because of lack of feasibility or other grounds, in an unusual case the court may direct that disclosure statements shall not be sent to such classes if to do so would not be feasible considering the size of the unimpaired classes and the expense of printing and mailing. In any event, all creditors are entitled to notice of the time fixed for filing objections and notice of the hearing to consider confirmation of the plan pursuant to Rule 2002(b) and the requirement of such notice may not be excused with respect to unimpaired classes. The amendment to subdivision (d) also ensures that the members of unimpaired classes who do not receive such documents will have sufficient information so that they may request these documents in advance of the hearing on confirmation. The amendment to subdivision (d) is not intended to give the court the discretion to dispense with the mailing of the plan and disclosure statement to governmental units holding claims entitled to priority under § 507(a)(7) because they may not be classified. See § 1123(a)(1).

The words "with the court" in subdivision (a) are deleted as unnecessary. See Rules 5005(a) and 9001(3). Reference to the Official Form number in subdivision (d) is deleted in anticipation of future revision and renumbering of the Official Forms.

Subdivision (e) is designed to ensure that appropriate measures are taken for the plan, disclosure statement, ballot and other materials which are required to be transmitted to creditors and equity security holders under this rule to reach the beneficial holders of securities held in nominee name. Such measures may include orders directing the trustee or debtor in possession to reimburse the nominees out of the funds of the estate for the expenses incurred by them in distributing materials to beneficial holders. In most cases, the plan proponent will not know the identities of the beneficial holders and therefore it will be necessary to rely on the nominal holders of the securities to distribute the plan materials to the beneficial owners.

1997 Amendments

Subdivision (a) is amended to provide that it does not apply to the extent provided in new Rule 3017.1, which applies in small business cases.

Subdivision (d) is amended to provide flexibility in fixing the record date for the purpose of determining the holders of securities who are entitled to receive documents pursuant to this subdivision. For example, if there may be a delay between the oral announcement of the judge's order approving the disclosure statement and entry of the order on the court docket, the court may fix the date on which the judge orally approves the disclosure statement as the record date so that the parties may expedite preparation of the lists necessary to facilitate the distribution of the plan, disclosure statement, ballots, and other related documents.

The court may set a record date pursuant to subdivision (d) only after notice and a hearing as provided in § 102(1) of the Code. Notice of a request for an order fixing the record date may be included in the notice of the hearing to consider approval of the disclosure statement mailed pursuant to Rule 2002(b).

If the court fixes a record date pursuant to subdivision (d) with respect to the holders of securities, and the holders are impaired by the plan, the judge also should order that the same record date applies for the purpose of determining eligibility for voting pursuant to Rule 3018(a).

Other amendments to this rule are stylistic.

GAP Report on Rule 3017. No changes to the published draft.

2001 Amendments

Subdivision (f) is added to assure that entities whose conduct would be enjoined under a plan, rather than by operation of the Code, and who will not receive the documents listed in subdivision (d) because they are neither creditors nor equity security holders, are provided with adequate notice of the proposed injunction. It does not address any substantive law issues relating to the validity or effect of any injunction provided under a plan, or any due process or other constitutional issues relating to notice. These issues are beyond the scope of these rules and are left for judicial determination.

This rule recognizes the need for adequate notice to subjects of an injunction, but that reasonable flexibility under the circumstances may be required. If a known and identifiable entity would be subject to the injunction, and the notice, plan, and disclosure statement could be mailed to that entity, the court should require that they be mailed at the same time that the plan, disclosure statement and related documents are mailed to creditors under Rule 3017(d). If mailing notices and other documents is not feasible because the entities subject to the injunction are described in the plan and disclosure statement by class or category and they cannot be identified individually by name and address, the court may require that notice under Rule 3017(f)(1) be published.

Changes Made After Publication and Comments. No changes were made in the text of the proposed amendments since publication. The Committee Note was revised to put in a more prominent position the statement that the rule does not address related substantive law issues which are beyond the scope of the rules.

2009 Amendments

The rule is amended to implement changes in connection with the amendment to Rule 9006(a) and the manner by which time is computed under the rules. The deadlines in the rule are amended to substitute a deadline that is a multiple of seven days. Throughout the rules, deadlines are amended in the following manner:

- 5–day periods become 7–day periods
- 10–day periods become 14–day periods
- 15–day periods become 14–day periods
- 20–day periods become 21–day periods
- 25–day periods become 28–day periods

CROSS REFERENCES

Acceptance or rejection of plan,

Eligible persons, see Fed.Rules Bankr.Proc. Rule 3018, 11 USCA.

Preference among more than one plan, see Fed.Rules Bankr.Proc. Rule 3018, 11 USCA.

Disclosure statement,

> Different statements as between different classes of claims, see 11 USCA § 1125.

> Right to be heard on adequacy of information, see 11 USCA § 1125.

> Solicitation of plan's acceptance, see 11 USCA § 1125.

Notice of time fixed for plan's acceptance or rejection in accord with this rule, see Fed.Rules Bankr.Proc. Rule 2002, 11 USCA.

Proof of right to record status filed by security holder, see Fed.Rules Bankr.Proc. Rule 3003, 11 USCA.

Rule 3017.1. Court Consideration of Disclosure Statement in a Small Business Case

(a) Conditional approval of disclosure statement

In a small business case, the court may, on application of the plan proponent or on its own initiative, conditionally approve a disclosure statement filed in accordance with Rule 3016. On or before conditional approval of the disclosure statement, the court shall:

(1) fix a time within which the holders of claims and interests may accept or reject the plan;

(2) fix a time for filing objections to the disclosure statement;

(3) fix a date for the hearing on final approval of the disclosure statement to be held if a timely objection is filed; and

(4) fix a date for the hearing on confirmation.

(b) Application of Rule 3017

Rule 3017(a), (b), (c), and (e) do not apply to a conditionally approved disclosure statement. Rule 3017(d) applies to a conditionally approved disclosure statement, except that conditional approval is considered approval of the disclosure statement for the purpose of applying Rule 3017(d).

(c) Final approval

(1) Notice

Notice of the time fixed for filing objections and the hearing to consider final approval of the disclosure statement shall be given in accordance with Rule 2002 and may be combined with notice of the hearing on confirmation of the plan.

(2) Objections

Objections to the disclosure statement shall be filed, transmitted to the United States trustee, and served on the debtor, the trustee, any committee appointed under the Code and any other entity designated by the court at any time before final approval of the disclosure statement or by an earlier date as the court may fix.

(3) Hearing

If a timely objection to the disclosure statement is filed, the court shall hold a hearing to consider final approval before or combined with the hearing on confirmation of the plan.

(Added Apr. 11, 1997, eff. Dec. 1, 1997; amended Apr. 23, 2008, eff. Dec. 1, 2008.)

ADVISORY COMMITTEE NOTES

1997 Amendment

This rule is added to implement § 1125(f), which was added to the Code by the Bankruptcy Reform Act of 1994.

The procedures for electing to be considered a small business are set forth in Rule 1020. If the debtor is a small business and has elected to be considered a small business, § 1125(f) permits the court to conditionally approve a disclosure statement subject to final approval after notice and a hearing. If a disclosure statement is conditionally approved, and no timely objection to the disclosure statement is filed, it is not necessary for the court to hold a hearing on final approval.

GAP Report on Rule 3017.1. No changes to the published draft.

2008 Amendments

Section 101 of the Code, as amended in 2005, defines a "small business case" and "small business debtor," and eliminates any need to elect that status. Therefore, the reference in the rule to an election is deleted.

As provided in the amendment to Rule 3016(b), a plan intended to provide adequate information in a small business case under § 1125(f)(1) may be conditionally approved and is otherwise treated as a disclosure statement under this rule.

Rule 3018. Acceptance or Rejection of Plan in a Chapter 9 Municipality or a Chapter 11 Reorganization Case

(a) Entities entitled to accept or reject plan; time for acceptance or rejection

A plan may be accepted or rejected in accordance with § 1126 of the Code within the time fixed by the court pursuant to Rule 3017. Subject to subdivision (b) of this rule, an equity security holder or creditor whose claim is based on a security of record shall not be entitled to accept or reject a plan unless the equity security holder or creditor is the holder of record of the security on the date the order approving the disclosure statement is entered or on another date fixed by the court, for cause, after notice and a hearing. For cause shown, the court after notice and hearing may permit a creditor or equity security holder to change or withdraw an acceptance or rejection. Notwithstanding objection to a claim or interest, the court after notice and hearing may temporarily allow the claim or interest in an amount which the court deems proper for the purpose of accepting or rejecting a plan.

(b) Acceptances or rejections obtained before petition

An equity security holder or creditor whose claim is based on a security of record who accepted or rejected the plan before the commencement of the case shall not be deemed to have accepted or rejected the plan pursuant to § 1126(b) of the Code unless the equity security holder or creditor was the holder of record of the security on the date specified in the solicitation of such acceptance or rejection for the purposes of such solicitation. A holder of a claim or interest who has accepted or rejected a plan before the commencement of the case under the Code shall not be deemed to have accepted or rejected the plan if the court finds after notice and hearing that the plan was not transmitted to substantially all creditors and equity security holders of the same class, that an unreasonably short time was prescribed for such creditors and equity security holders to accept or reject the plan, or that the solicitation was not in compliance with § 1126(b) of the Code.

(c) Form of acceptance or rejection

An acceptance or rejection shall be in writing, identify the plan or plans accepted or rejected, be signed by the creditor or equity security holder or an authorized agent, and conform to the appropriate Official Form. If more than one plan is transmitted pursuant to Rule 3017, an acceptance or rejection may be filed by each creditor or equity security holder for any number of plans transmitted and if acceptances are filed for more than one plan, the creditor or equity security holder may indicate a preference or preferences among the plans so accepted.

(d) Acceptance or rejection by partially secured creditor

A creditor whose claim has been allowed in part as a secured claim and in part as an unsecured claim shall be entitled to accept or reject a plan in both capacities. (As amended Mar. 30, 1987, eff. Aug. 1, 1987; Apr. 30, 1991, eff. Aug. 1, 1991; Apr. 22, 1993, eff. Aug. 1, 1993; Apr. 11, 1997, eff. Dec. 1, 1997.)

ADVISORY COMMITTEE NOTES

This rule applies in chapter 9, 11 and 13 cases under the Code. The references in the rule to equity security holders will not, however, be relevant in chapter 9 or 13 cases. The rule will be of little utility in a chapter 13 case because only secured creditors may be requested to vote on a plan; unsecured creditors are not entitled to vote; see § 1325(a)(4), (5) of the Code.

Subdivision (a) is derived from former Rule 10–305(a). It substitutes, in a reorganization case, entry of the order approving the disclosure statement for the order approving a plan in conformity with the differences between Chapter X [former § 501 et seq. of this title] and chapter 11. In keeping with the underlying theory, it continues to recognize that the lapse of time between the filing of the petition and entry of such order will normally be significant and, during that interim, bonds and equity interests can change ownership.

Subdivision (b) recognizes the former Chapter XI [former § 701 et seq. of this title] practice permitting a plan and acceptances to be filed with the petition, as does § 1126(b) of the Code. However, because a plan under chapter 11 may affect shareholder interests, there should be reference to a record date of ownership. In this instance the appropriate record date is that used in the prepetition solicitation materials because it is those acceptances or rejections which are being submitted to the court.

While § 1126(c), (d), and (e) prohibits use of an acceptance or rejection not procured in good faith, the added provision in subdivision (b) of the rule is somewhat more detailed. It would prohibit use of prepetition acceptances or rejections when some but not all impaired creditors or equity security holders are solicited or when they are not given a reasonable opportunity to submit their acceptances or rejections. This provision together with § 1126(e) gives the court the power to nullify abusive solicitation procedures.

Subdivision (c). It is possible that multiple plans may be before the court for confirmation. Pursuant to § 1129(c) of the Code, the court may confirm only one plan but is required to consider the preferences expressed by those accepting the plans in determining which one to confirm.

Subdivisions (d) and (e) of former Rule 10–305 are not continued since comparable provisions are contained in the statute; see § 1126(c), (d), (e).

It should be noted that while the singular "plan" is used throughout, by construction the plural is included; see § 102(7).

1991 Amendments

Subdivisions (a) and (b) are amended to delete provisions that duplicate § 1126 of the Code. An entity who is not a record holder of a security, but who claims that it is entitled to be treated as a record holder, may file a statement pursuant to Rule 3003(d).

Subdivision (a) is amended further to allow the court to permit a creditor or equity security holder to change or withdraw an acceptance or rejection for cause shown whether or not the time fixed for voting has expired.

Subdivision (b) is also amended to give effect to a prepetition acceptance or rejection if solicitation requirements were satisfied with respect to substantially all members of the same class, instead of requiring proper solicitation with respect to substantially all members of all classes.

Subdivision (c) is amended to delete the Official Form number in anticipation of future revision and renumbering of the Official Forms.

1993 Amendments

The title of this rule is amended to indicate that it applies only in a chapter 9 or a chapter 11 case. The amendment of the word "Plans" to "Plan" is stylistic.

1997 Amendments

Subdivision (a) is amended to provide flexibility in fixing the record date for the purpose of determining the holders of securities who are entitled to vote on the plan. For example, if there may be a delay between the oral announcement of the judge's decision approving the disclosure statement and entry of the order on the court docket, the court may fix the date on which the judge orally approves the disclosure statement as the record date for voting purposes so that the parties may expedite preparation of the lists necessary to facilitate the distribution of the plan, disclosure statement, ballots, and other related documents in connection with the solicitation of votes.

The court may set a record date pursuant to subdivision (a) only after notice and a hearing as provided in § 102(1) of the Code. Notice of a request for an order fixing the record date may be included in the notice of the hearing to consider approval of the disclosure statement mailed pursuant to Rule 2002(b).

If the court fixes the record date for voting purposes, the judge also should order that the same record date shall apply for the purpose of distributing the documents required to be distributed pursuant to Rule 3017(d).

GAP Report on Rule 3018. No changes to the published draft.

CROSS REFERENCES

Acceptance of altered or modified plan, see 11 USCA § 1127.

Disqualification of votes on acceptance in absence of good faith, see 11 USCA § 1126.

Filing of plan in,

Individual debt adjustment case, see Fed.Rules Bankr. Proc. Rule 3015, 11 USCA.

Municipality debt adjustment and reorganization cases, with disclosure statement, see Fed.Rules Bankr.Proc. Rule 3016, 11 USCA.

Proof of right to record status filed by security holder, see Fed.Rules Bankr.Proc. Rule 3003, 11 USCA.

Rule 3019. Modification of Accepted Plan in a Chapter 9 Municipality or a Chapter 11 Reorganization Case

(a) Modification of plan before confirmation

In a chapter 9 or chapter 11 case, after a plan has been accepted and before its confirmation, the proponent may file a modification of the plan. If the court finds after hearing on notice to the trustee, any committee appointed under the Code, and any other entity designated by the court that the proposed modification does not adversely change the treatment of the claim of any creditor or the interest of any equity security holder who has not accepted in writing the modification, it shall be deemed accepted by all creditors and equity security holders who have previously accepted the plan.

(b) Modification of plan after confirmation in individual debtor case

If the debtor is an individual, a request to modify the plan under § 1127(e) of the Code is governed by Rule 9014. The request shall identify the proponent and shall be filed together with the proposed modification. The clerk, or some other person as the court may direct, shall give the debtor, the trustee, and all creditors not less than 21 days' notice by mail of the time fixed to file objections and, if an objection is filed, the

hearing to consider the proposed modification, unless the court orders otherwise with respect to creditors who are not affected by the proposed modification. A copy of the notice shall be transmitted to the United States trustee, together with a copy of the proposed modification. Any objection to the proposed modification shall be filed and served on the debtor, the proponent of the modification, the trustee, and any other entity designated by the court, and shall be transmitted to the United States trustee.

(As amended Mar. 30, 1987, eff. Aug. 1, 1987; Apr. 22, 1993, eff. Aug. 1, 1993; Apr. 23, 2008, eff. Dec. 1, 2008; Mar. 26, 2009, eff. Dec. 1, 2009.)

ADVISORY COMMITTEE NOTES

This rule implements §§ 942, 1127 and 1323 of the Code. For example, § 1127 provides for modification before and after confirmation but does not deal with the minor modifications that do not adversely change any rights. The rule makes clear that a modification may be made, after acceptance of the plan without submission to creditors and equity security holders if their interests are not affected. To come within this rule, the modification should be one that does not change the rights of a creditor or equity security holder as fixed in the plan before modification.

1993 Amendments

This rule is amended to limit its application to chapter 9 and chapter 11 cases. Modification of plans after confirmation in chapter 12 and chapter 13 cases is governed by Rule 3015. The addition of the comma in the second sentence is stylistic and makes no substantive change.

2008 Amendments

The 2005 amendments to § 1127 of the Code provide for modification of a confirmed plan in an individual debtor chapter 11 case. Therefore, the rule is amended to establish the procedure for filing and objecting to a proposed modification of a confirmed plan.

2009 Amendments

The rule is amended to implement changes in connection with the amendment to Rule 9006(a) and the manner by which time is computed under the rules. The deadline in the rule is amended to substitute a deadline that is a multiple of seven days. Throughout the rules, deadlines are amended in the following manner:

- 5–day periods become 7–day periods
- 10–day periods become 14–day periods
- 15–day periods become 14–day periods
- 20–day periods become 21–day periods
- 25–day periods become 28–day periods

CROSS REFERENCES

Acceptance or rejection of plans, see Fed.Rules Bankr.Proc. Rule 3018, 11 USCA.

Modification of plan in,

Individual debt adjustment case, see 11 USCA § 1323.

Municipality debt adjustment case, see 11 USCA § 942.

Reorganization case, see 11 USCA § 1127.

Rule 3020. Deposit; Confirmation of Plan in a Chapter 9 Municipality or Chapter 11 Reorganization Case

(a) Deposit

In a chapter 11 case, prior to entry of the order confirming the plan, the court may order the deposit with the trustee or debtor in possession of the consideration required by the plan to be distributed on confirmation. Any money deposited shall be kept in a special account established for the exclusive purpose of making the distribution.

(b) Objection to and hearing on confirmation in a Chapter 9 or Chapter 11 case

(1) Objection

An objection to confirmation of the plan shall be filed and served on the debtor, the trustee, the proponent of the plan, any committee appointed under the Code, and any other entity designated by the court, within a time fixed by the court. Unless the case is a chapter 9 municipality case, a copy of every objection to confirmation shall be transmitted by the objecting party to the United States trustee within the time fixed for filing objections. An objection to confirmation is governed by Rule 9014.

(2) Hearing

The court shall rule on confirmation of the plan after notice and hearing as provided in Rule 2002. If no objection is timely filed, the court may determine that the plan has been proposed in good faith and not by any means forbidden by law without receiving evidence on such issues.

(c) Order of confirmation

(1) The order of confirmation shall conform to the appropriate Official Form. If the plan provides for an injunction against conduct not otherwise enjoined under the Code, the order of confirmation shall (1) describe in reasonable detail all acts enjoined; (2) be specific in its terms regarding the injunction; and (3) identify the entities subject to the injunction.

(2) Notice of entry of the order of confirmation shall be mailed promptly to the debtor, the trustee, creditors, equity security holders, other parties in interest, and, if known, to any identified entity subject to an injunction provided for in the plan against conduct not otherwise enjoined under the Code.

(3) Except in a chapter 9 municipality case, notice of entry of the order of confirmation shall be transmitted to the United States trustee as provided in Rule 2002(k).

(d) Retained power

Notwithstanding the entry of the order of confirmation, the court may issue any other order necessary to administer the estate.

(e) Stay of confirmation order

An order confirming a plan is stayed until the expiration of 14 days after the entry of the order, unless the court orders otherwise.

(As amended Mar. 30, 1987, eff. Aug. 1, 1987; Apr. 30, 1991, eff. Aug. 1, 1991; Apr. 22, 1993, eff. Aug. 1, 1993; Apr. 26, 1999, eff. Dec. 1, 1999; Apr. 23, 2001, eff. Dec. 1, 2001; Mar. 26, 2009, eff. Dec. 1, 2009.)

ADVISORY COMMITTEE NOTES

This rule is adapted from former Rules 10–307, 11–38, and 13–213. It applies to cases filed under chapters 9, 11 and 13. Certain subdivisions of the earlier rules have not been included, such as, a subdivision revesting title in the debtor because § 541 of the Code does not transfer title out of the debtor as did § 70a of the Bankruptcy Act [former § 110(a) of this title]; see also §§ 1141(b), 1327(b). Subdivision (b) of former Rule 13–213 is not included because its provisions are contained in the statute; see §§ 1322, 1325(b), 105.

Subdivision (a) gives discretion to the court to require in chapter 11 cases the deposit of any consideration to be distributed on confirmation. If money is to be distributed, it is to be deposited in a special account to assure that it will not be used for any other purpose. The Code is silent in chapter 11 with respect to the need to make a deposit or the person with whom any deposit is to be made. Consequently, there is no statutory authority for any person to act in a capacity similar to the disbursing agent under former Chapter XI [former § 701 et seq. of this title] practice. This rule provides that only the debtor in possession or trustee should be appointed as the recipient of the deposit. Any consideration other than money, e.g., notes or stock may be given directly to the debtor in possession or trustee and need not be left in any kind of special account. In chapter 9 cases, § 944(b) provides for deposit with a disbursing agent appointed by the court of any consideration to be distributed under the plan.

Subdivision (d) clarifies the authority of the court to conclude matters pending before it prior to confirmation and to continue to administer the estate as necessary, e.g., resolving objections to claims.

1991 Amendments

The United States trustee monitors chapter 11, chapter 12, and chapter 13 plans and has standing to be heard regarding confirmation of a plan. See 28 U.S.C. § 586(a)(3). The amendments to subdivisions (b)(1) and (c) of this rule facilitate that role of the United States trustee. Subdivision (b)(1) is also amended to require service on the proponent of the plan of objections to confirmation. The words "with the court" in subdivision (b)(1) are deleted as unnecessary. See Rules 5005(a) and 9001(3).

In a chapter 12 case, the court is required to conduct and conclude the hearing on confirmation of the plan within the time prescribed in § 1224 of the Code.

Subdivision (c) is also amended to require that the confirmation order be mailed to the trustee. Reference to the Official Form number is deleted in anticipation of future revision and renumbering of the Official Forms.

1993 Amendments

This rule is amended to limit its application to chapter 9 and chapter 11 cases. The procedures relating to confirmation of plans in chapter 12 and chapter 13 cases are provided in rule 3015. Other amendments are stylistic and make no substantive change.

1999 Amendments

Subdivision (e) is added to provide sufficient time for a party to request a stay pending appeal of an order confirming a plan under chapter 9 or chapter 11 of the Code before the plan is implemented and an appeal becomes moot. Unless the court orders otherwise, any transfer of assets, issuance of securities, and cash distributions provided for in the plan may not be made before the expiration of the 10–day period. The stay of the confirmation order under subdivision (e) does not affect the time for filing a notice of appeal from the confirmation order in accordance with Rule 8002.

The court may, in its discretion, order that Rule 3020(e) is not applicable so that the plan may be implemented and distributions may be made immediately. Alternatively, the court may order that the stay under Rule 3020(e) is for a fixed period less than 10 days.

GAP Report on Rule 3020. No changes since publication.

2001 Amendments

Subdivision (c) is amended to provide notice to an entity subject to an injunction provided for in a plan against conduct not otherwise enjoined by operation of the Code. This requirement is not applicable to an injunction contained in a plan if it is substantially the same as an injunction provided under the Code. The validity and effect of any injunction provided for in a plan are substantive law matters that are beyond the scope of these rules.

The requirement that the order of confirmation identify the entities subject to the injunction requires only reasonable identification under the circumstances. If the entities that would be subject to the injunction cannot be identified by name, the order may describe them by class or category if reasonable under the circumstances. For example, it may be sufficient to identify the entities as "all creditors of the debtor."

Changes Made After Publication and Comments. No changes were made in the text of the proposed amendments. The Committee Note was revised to put in a more prominent position the statement that the validity and effect of injunctions provided for in plans is beyond the scope of the rules.

2009 Amendments

The rule is amended to implement changes in connection with the amendment to Rule 9006(a) and the manner by which time is computed under the rules. The deadline in the rule is amended to substitute a deadline that is a multiple of seven days. Throughout the rules, deadlines are amended in the following manner:

- 5–day periods become 7–day periods
- 10–day periods become 14–day periods
- 15–day periods become 14–day periods
- 20–day periods become 21–day periods
- 25–day periods become 28–day periods

CROSS REFERENCES

Modification of accepted plan before confirmation, see Fed. Rules Bankr.Proc. Rule 3019, 11 USCA.

Rule 3021.   Distribution Under Plan

Except as provided in Rule 3020(e), after a plan is confirmed, distribution shall be made to creditors whose claims have been allowed, to interest holders whose interests have not been disallowed, and to indenture trustees who have filed claims under Rule 3003(c)(5) that have been allowed. For purposes of this rule, creditors include holders of bonds, debentures, notes, and other debt securities, and interest holders include the holders of stock and other equity securities, of record at the time of commencement of distribution, unless a different time is fixed by the plan or the order confirming the plan.

(As amended Apr. 11, 1997, eff. Dec. 1, 1997; Apr. 29, 1999, eff. Dec. 1, 1999.)

ADVISORY COMMITTEE NOTES

This rule is derived from former Chapter X Rule 10–405(a). Subdivision (b) of that rule is covered by § 1143 of the Code.

1997 Amendments

This rule is amended to provide flexibility in fixing the record date for the purpose of making distributions to holders of securities of record. In a large case, it may be impractical for the debtor to determine the holders of record with respect to publicly held securities and also to make distributions to those holders at the same time. Under this amendment, the plan or the order confirming the plan may fix a record date for distributions that is earlier than the date on which distributions commence.

This rule also is amended to treat holders of bonds, debentures, notes, and other debt securities the same as any other creditors by providing that they shall receive a distribution only if their claims have been allowed. Finally, the amendments clarify that distributions are to be made to all interest holders—not only those that are within the definition of "equity security holders" under § 101 of the Code—whose interests have not been disallowed.

GAP Report on Rule 3021. No changes to the published draft.

1999 Amendments

This amendment is to conform to the amendments to Rule 3020 regarding the ten-day stay of an order confirming a plan in a chapter 9 or chapter 11 case. The other amendments are stylistic.

GAP Report on Rule 3021. No changes since publication.

CROSS REFERENCES

Disposition of unclaimed property, see 11 USCA § 347.

Power of court to require transfers of property, see 11 USCA § 1142.

Proof of right to record status filed by security holder, see Fed.Rules Bankr.Proc. Rule 3003, 11 USCA.

Time for surrender of security or performance of required act under reorganization plan, see 11 USCA § 1143.

Rule 3022.   Final Decree in Chapter 11 Reorganization Case

After an estate is fully administered in a chapter 11 reorganization case, the court, on its own motion or on motion of a party in interest, shall enter a final decree closing the case.

(As amended Mar. 30, 1987, eff. Aug. 1, 1987; Apr. 30, 1991, eff. Aug. 1, 1991.)

ADVISORY COMMITTEE NOTES

Section 350 of the Code requires the court to close the case after the estate is fully administered and the trustee has been discharged. Section 1143 places a five year limitation on the surrender of securities when required for participation under a plan but this provision should not delay entry of the final decree.

1991 Amendments

Entry of a final decree closing a chapter 11 case should not be delayed solely because the payments required by the plan have not been completed. Factors that the court should consider in determining whether the estate has been fully administered include (1) whether the order confirming the plan has become final, (2) whether deposits required by the plan have been distributed, (3) whether the property proposed by the plan to be transferred has been transferred, (4) whether the debtor or the successor of the debtor under the plan has assumed the business or the management of the property dealt with by the plan, (5) whether payments under the plan have commenced, and (6) whether all motions, contested matters, and adversary proceedings have been finally resolved.

The court should not keep the case open only because of the possibility that the court's jurisdiction may be invoked in the future. A final decree closing the case after the estate is fully administered does not deprive the court of jurisdiction to enforce or interpret its own orders and does not prevent the court from reopening the case for cause pursuant to § 350(b) of the Code. For example, on motion of a party in interest, the court may reopen the case to revoke an order of confirmation procured by fraud under § 1144 of the Code. If the plan or confirmation order provides that the case shall remain open until a certain date or event because of the likelihood that the court's jurisdiction may be required for specific purposes prior thereto, the case should remain open until that date or event.

CROSS REFERENCES

Close of case after trustee's discharge, see 11 USCA § 350.

Surrender of security or performance of required act under reorganization plan, denial of distribution, see 11 USCA § 1143.

PART IV—THE DEBTOR: DUTIES AND BENEFITS

Rule 4001. Relief From Automatic Stay; Prohibiting or Conditioning the Use, Sale, or Lease of Property; Use of Cash Collateral; Obtaining Credit; Agreements

(a) Relief from stay; prohibiting or conditioning the use, sale, or lease of property

(1) Motion

A motion for relief from an automatic stay provided by the Code or a motion to prohibit or condition the use, sale, or lease of property pursuant to § 363(e) shall be made in accordance with Rule 9014 and shall be served on any committee elected pursuant to § 705 or appointed pursuant to § 1102 of the Code or its authorized agent, or, if the case is a chapter 9 municipality case or a chapter 11 reorganization case and no committee of unsecured creditors has been appointed pursuant to § 1102, on the creditors included on the list filed pursuant to Rule 1007(d), and on such other entities as the court may direct.

(2) Ex parte relief

Relief from a stay under § 362(a) or a request to prohibit or condition the use, sale, or lease of property pursuant to § 363(e) may be granted without prior notice only if (A) it clearly appears from specific facts shown by affidavit or by a verified motion that immediate and irreparable injury, loss, or damage will result to the movant before the adverse party or the attorney for the adverse party can be heard in opposition, and (B) the movant's attorney certifies to the court in writing the efforts, if any, which have been made to give notice and the reasons why notice should not be required. The party obtaining relief under this subdivision and § 362(f) or § 363(e) shall immediately give oral notice thereof to the trustee or debtor in possession and to the debtor and forthwith mail or otherwise transmit to such adverse party or parties a copy of the order granting relief. On two days notice to the party who obtained relief from the stay without notice or on shorter notice to that party as the court may prescribe, the adverse party may appear and move reinstatement of the stay or reconsideration of the order prohibiting or conditioning the use, sale, or lease of property. In that event, the court shall proceed expeditiously to hear and determine the motion.

(3) Stay of order

An order granting a motion for relief from an automatic stay made in accordance with Rule 4001(a)(1) is stayed until the expiration of 14 days after the entry of the order, unless the court orders otherwise.

(b) Use of cash collateral

(1) Motion; service

(A) Motion

A motion for authority to use cash collateral shall be made in accordance with Rule 9014 and shall be accompanied by a proposed form of order.

(B) Contents

The motion shall consist of or (if the motion is more than five pages in length) begin with a concise statement of the relief requested, not to exceed five pages, that lists or summarizes, and sets out the location within the relevant documents of, all material provisions, including:

(i) the name of each entity with an interest in the cash collateral;

(ii) the purposes for the use of the cash collateral;

(iii) the material terms, including duration, of the use of the cash collateral; and

(iv) any liens, cash payments, or other adequate protection that will be provided to each entity with an interest in the cash collateral or, if no additional adequate protection is proposed, an explanation of why each entity's interest is adequately protected.

(C) Service

The motion shall be served on: (1) any entity with an interest in the cash collateral; (2) any committee elected under § 705 or appointed under § 1102 of the Code, or its authorized agent, or, if the case is a chapter 9 municipality case or a chapter 11 reorganization case and no committee of unsecured creditors has been appointed under § 1102, the creditors included on the list filed under Rule 1007(d); and (3) any other entity that the court directs.

(2) Hearing

The court may commence a final hearing on a motion for authorization to use cash collateral no earlier than 14 days after service of the motion. If the motion so requests, the court may conduct a preliminary hearing before such 14–day period expires, but the court may authorize the use of only that amount of cash collateral as is necessary to avoid immediate and irreparable harm to the estate pending a final hearing.

(3) Notice

Notice of hearing pursuant to this subdivision shall be given to the parties on whom service of the motion is required by paragraph (1) of this subdivision and to such other entities as the court may direct.

(c) Obtaining credit

(1) Motion; service

(A) Motion

A motion for authority to obtain credit shall be made in accordance with Rule 9014 and shall be accompanied by a copy of the credit agreement and a proposed form of order.

(B) Contents

The motion shall consist of or (if the motion is more than five pages in length) begin with a concise statement of the relief requested, not to exceed five pages, that lists or summarizes, and sets out the location within the relevant documents of, all material provisions of the proposed credit agreement and form of order, including interest rate, maturity, events of default, liens, borrowing limits, and borrowing conditions. If the proposed credit agreement or form of order includes any of the provisions listed below, the concise statement shall also: briefly list or summarize each one; identify its specific location in the proposed agreement and form of order; and identify any such provision that is proposed to remain in effect if interim approval is granted, but final relief is denied, as provided under Rule 4001(c)(2). In addition, the motion shall describe the nature and extent of each provision listed below:

(i) a grant of priority or a lien on property of the estate under § 364(c) or (d);

(ii) the providing of adequate protection or priority for a claim that arose before the commencement of the case, including the granting of a lien on property of the estate to secure the claim, or the use of property of the estate or credit obtained under § 364 to make cash payments on account of the claim;

(iii) a determination of the validity, enforceability, priority, or amount of a claim that arose before the commencement of the case, or of any lien securing the claim;

(iv) a waiver or modification of Code provisions or applicable rules relating to the automatic stay;

(v) a waiver or modification of any entity's authority or right to file a plan, seek an extension of time in which the debtor has the exclusive right to file a plan, request the use of cash collateral under § 363(c), or request authority to obtain credit under § 364;

(vi) the establishment of deadlines for filing a plan of reorganization, for approval of a disclosure statement, for a hearing on confirmation, or for entry of a confirmation order;

(vii) a waiver or modification of the applicability of nonbankruptcy law relating to the perfection of a lien on property of the estate, or on the foreclosure or other enforcement of the lien;

(viii) a release, waiver, or limitation on any claim or other cause of action belonging to the estate or the trustee, including any modification of the statute of limitations or other deadline to commence an action;

(ix) the indemnification of any entity;

(x) a release, waiver, or limitation of any right under § 506(c); or

(xi) the granting of a lien on any claim or cause of action arising under §§[1] 544, 545, 547, 548, 549, 553(b), 723(a), or 724(a).

(C) Service

The motion shall be served on: (1) any committee elected under § 705 or appointed under § 1102 of the Code, or its authorized agent, or, if the case is a chapter 9 municipality case or a chapter 11 reorganization case and no committee of unsecured creditors has been appointed under § 1102, on the creditors included on the list filed under Rule 1007(d); and (2) on any other entity that the court directs.

(2) Hearing

The court may commence a final hearing on a motion for authority to obtain credit no earlier than 14 days after service of the motion. If the motion so requests, the court may conduct a hearing before such 14–day period expires, but the court may authorize the obtaining of credit only to the extent necessary to avoid immediate and irreparable harm to the estate pending a final hearing.

(3) Notice

Notice of hearing pursuant to this subdivision shall be given to the parties on whom service of the motion is required by paragraph (1) of this subdivision and to such other entities as the court may direct.

(d) Agreement relating to relief from the automatic stay, prohibiting or conditioning the use, sale, or lease of property, providing adequate protection, use of cash collateral, and obtaining credit

(1) Motion; service

(A) Motion

A motion for approval of any of the following shall be accompanied by a copy of the agreement and a proposed form of order:

(i) an agreement to provide adequate protection;

(ii) an agreement to prohibit or condition the use, sale, or lease of property;

(iii) an agreement to modify or terminate the stay provided for in § 362;

(iv) an agreement to use cash collateral; or

(v) an agreement between the debtor and an entity that has a lien or interest in property of the estate pursuant to which the entity consents to the creation of a lien senior or equal to the entity's lien or interest in such property.

(B) Contents

The motion shall consist of or (if the motion is more than five pages in length) begin with a concise statement of the relief requested, not to exceed five pages, that lists or summarizes, and sets out the location within the relevant documents of, all material provisions of the agreement. In addition, the concise statement shall briefly list or summarize, and identify the specific location of, each provision in the proposed form of order, agreement, or other document of the type listed in subdivision (c)(1)(B). The motion shall also describe the nature and extent of each such provision.

(C) Service

The motion shall be served on: (1) any committee elected under § 705 or appointed under § 1102 of the Code, or its authorized agent, or, if the case is a chapter 9 municipality case or a chapter 11 reorganization case and no committee of unsecured creditors has been appointed under § 1102, on the creditors included on the list filed under Rule 1007(d); and (2) on any other entity the court directs.

(2) Objection

Notice of the motion and the time within which objections may be filed and served on the debtor in possession or trustee shall be mailed to the parties on whom service is required by paragraph (1) of this subdivision and to such other entities as the court may direct. Unless the court fixes a different time, objections may be filed within 14 days of the mailing of the notice.

(3) Disposition; hearing

If no objection is filed, the court may enter an order approving or disapproving the agreement without conducting a hearing. If an objection is filed or if the court determines a hearing is appropriate, the court shall hold a hearing on no less than seven days' notice to the objector, the movant, the parties on whom service is required by paragraph (1) of this subdivision and such other entities as the court may direct.

(4) Agreement in settlement of motion

The court may direct that the procedures prescribed in paragraphs (1), (2), and (3) of this subdivision shall not apply and the agreement may be approved without further notice if the court determines that a motion made pursuant to subdivisions (a), (b), or (c) of this rule was sufficient to afford reasonable notice of the material provisions of the agreement and opportunity for a hearing.

(As amended Mar. 30, 1987, eff. Aug. 1, 1987; Apr. 30, 1991, eff. Aug. 1, 1991; Apr. 26, 1999, eff. Dec. 1, 1999; Apr. 30, 2007, eff. Dec. 1, 2007; Mar. 26, 2009, eff. Dec. 1, 2009; Apr. 28, 2010, eff. Dec. 1, 2010.)

1 So in original. Probably should be only one section symbol.

ADVISORY COMMITTEE NOTES

This rule implements § 362 of the Code which sets forth provisions regarding the automatic stay that arises on the filing of a petition. That section and this rule are applicable in chapter 7, 9, 11 and 13 cases. It also implements § 363(c)(2) concerning use of cash collateral.

Subdivision (a) transforms with respect to the automatic stay what was an adversary proceeding under the former rules to motion practice. The Code provides automatic stays in several sections, e.g., §§ 362(a), 1301(a), and in § 362(d) provides some grounds for relief from the stay. This rule specifies that the pleading seeking relief is by means of a motion. Thus the time period in Rule 7012 to answer a complaint would not be applicable and shorter periods may be fixed. Section 362(e) requires the preliminary hearing to be concluded within 30 days of its inception, rendering ordinary complaint and answer practice inappropriate.

This subdivision also makes clear that a motion under Rule 9014 is the proper procedure for a debtor to seek court permission to use cash collateral. See § 363(c)(2). Pursuant to Rule 5005, the motion should be filed in the court in which the case is pending. The court or local rule may specify the persons to be served with the motion for relief from the stay; see Rule 9013.

Subdivision (b) of the rule fills a procedural void left by § 362. Pursuant to § 362(e), the automatic stay is terminated 30 days after a motion for relief is made unless the court continues the stay as a result of a final hearing or, pending final hearing, after a preliminary hearing. If a preliminary hearing is held, § 362(e) requires the final hearing to be commenced within 30 days after the preliminary hearing. Although the expressed legislative intent is to require expeditious resolution of a secured party's motion for relief, § 362 is silent as to the time within which the final hearing must be concluded. Subdivision (b) imposes a 30 day deadline on the court to resolve the dispute.

At the final hearing, the stay is to be terminated, modified, annulled, or conditioned for cause, which includes, inter alia, lack of adequate protection; § 362(d). The burden of proving adequate protection is on the party opposing relief from the stay; § 362(g)(2). Adequate protection is exemplified in § 361.

Subdivision (c) implements § 362(f) which permits ex parte relief from the stay when there will be irreparable damage. This subdivision sets forth the procedure to be followed when relief is sought under § 362(f). It is derived from former Bankruptcy Rule 601(d).

1987 Amendments

The scope of this rule is expanded and the former subdivisions (a), (b) and (c) are now combined in subdivision (a). The new subdivision (a)(2) is amended to conform to the 1984 amendments to § 362(e) of the Code.

Subdivision (b) deals explicitly with the procedures which follow after a motion to use cash collateral is made and served. Filing shall be pursuant to Rule 5005. Service of the motion may be made by any method authorized by Rule 7004 and, if service is by mail, service is complete on mailing. Rule 9006(e). Under subdivision (b)(2), the court may commence a final hearing on the motion within 15 days of service. Rule 9006(f) does not extend this 15 day period when service of the motion is by mail because the party served is not required to act within the 15 day period. In addition to service of the motion, notice of the hearing must be given. Rule 9007 authorizes the court to direct the form and manner of giving notice that is appropriate to the circumstances.

Section 363(c)(3) authorizes the court to conduct a preliminary hearing and to authorize the use of cash collateral "if there is a reasonable likelihood that the trustee will prevail at a final hearing." Subdivision (b)(2) of the rule permits a preliminary hearing to be held earlier than 15 days after service. Any order authorizing the use of cash collateral shall be limited to the amount necessary to protect the estate until a final hearing is held.

The objective of subdivision (b) is to accommodate both the immediate need of the debtor and the interest of the secured creditor in the cash collateral. The time for holding the final hearing may be enlarged beyond the 15 days prescribed when required by the circumstances.

The motion for authority to use cash collateral shall include (1) the amount of cash collateral sought to be used; (2) the name and address of each entity having an interest in the cash collateral; (3) the name and address of the entity in control or having possession of the cash collateral; (4) the facts demonstrating the need to use the cash collateral; and (5) the nature of the protection to be provided those having an interest in the cash collateral. If a preliminary hearing is requested, the motion shall also include the amount of cash collateral sought to be used pending final hearing and the protection to be provided.

Notice of the preliminary and final hearings may be combined. This rule does not limit the authority of the court under § 363(c)(2)(B) and § 102(1).

Subdivision (c) is new. The service, hearing, and notice requirements are similar to those imposed by subdivision (b). The motion to obtain credit shall include the amount and type of the credit to be extended, the name and address of the

lender, the terms of the agreement, the need to obtain the credit, and the efforts made to obtain credit from other sources. If the motion is to obtain credit pursuant to § 364(c) or (d), the motion shall describe the collateral, if any, and the protection for any existing interest in the collateral which may be affected by the proposed agreement.

Subdivision (d) is new. In the event the 15 day period for filing objections to the approval of an agreement of the parties described in this subdivision is too long, the parties either may move for a reduction of the period under Rule 9006(c)(1) or proceed under subdivision (b) or (c), if applicable. Rule 9006(c)(1) requires that cause be shown for the reduction of the period in which to object. In applying this criterion the court may consider the option of proceeding under subdivision (b) or (c) and grant a preliminary hearing and relief pending final hearing.

1991 Amendments

Subdivision (a) is expanded to include a request to prohibit or condition the use, sale, or lease of property as is necessary to provide adequate protection of a property interest pursuant to § 363(e) of the Code.

Notice of the motion for relief from the automatic stay or to prohibit or condition the use, sale, or lease of property must be served on the entities entitled to receive notice of a motion to approve an agreement pursuant to subdivision (d). If the movant and the adverse party agree to settle the motion and the terms of the agreement do not materially differ from the terms set forth in the movant's motion papers, the court may approve the agreement without further notice pursuant to subdivision (d)(4).

Subdivision (a)(2) is deleted as unnecessary because of § 362(e) of the Code.

Subdivisions (b)(1), (c)(1), and (d)(1) are amended to require service on committees that are elected in chapter 7 cases. Service on committees of retired employees appointed under § 1114 of the Code is not required. These subdivisions are amended further to clarify that, in the absence of a creditors' committee, service on the creditors included on the list filed pursuant to Rule 1007(d) is required only in chapter 9 and chapter 11 cases. The other amendments to subdivision (d)(1) are for consistency of style and are not substantive.

Subdivision (d)(4) is added to avoid the necessity of further notice and delay for the approval of an agreement in settlement of a motion for relief from an automatic stay, to prohibit or condition the use, sale, or lease of property, for use of cash collateral, or for authority to obtain credit if the entities entitled to notice have already received sufficient notice of the scope of the proposed agreement in the motion papers and have had an opportunity to be heard. For example, if a trustee makes a motion to use cash collateral and proposes in the original motion papers to provide adequate protection of the interest of the secured party by granting a lien on certain equipment, and the secured creditor subsequently agrees to terms that are within the scope of those proposed in the motion, the court may enter an order approving the agreement without further notice if the entities that received the original motion papers have had a reasonable opportunity to object to the granting of the motion to use cash collateral.

If the motion papers served under subdivision (a), (b), or (c) do not afford notice sufficient to inform the recipients of the material provisions of the proposed agreement and opportunity for a hearing, approval of the settlement agreement may not be obtained unless the procedural requirements of subdivision (d)(1), (d)(2), and (d)(3) are satisfied. If the 15 day period for filing objections to the approval of the settlement agreement is too long under the particular circumstances of the case, the court may shorten the time for cause under Rule 9006(c)(1).

1999 Amendments

Paragraph (a)(3) is added to provide sufficient time for a party to request a stay pending appeal of an order granting relief from an automatic stay before the order is enforced or implemented. The stay under paragraph (a)(3) is not applicable to orders granted ex parte in accordance with Rule 4001(a)(2).

The stay of the order does not affect the time for filing a notice of appeal in accordance with Rule 8002. While the enforcement and implementation of an order granting relief from the automatic stay is temporarily stayed under paragraph (a)(3), the automatic stay continues to protect the debtor, and the moving party may not foreclose on collateral or take any other steps that would violate the automatic stay.

The court may, in its discretion, order that Rule 4001(a)(3) is not applicable so that the prevailing party may immediately enforce and implement the order granting relief from the automatic stay. Alternatively, the court may order that the stay under Rule 4001(a)(3) is for a fixed period less than 10 days.

GAP Report on Rule 4001. No changes since publication.

2007 Amendments

The rule is amended to require that parties seeking authority to use cash collateral, to obtain credit, and to obtain approval of agreements to provide adequate protection, modify or terminate the stay, or to grant a senior or equal lien on property, submit with those requests a proposed order granting the relief, and that they provide more extensive notice to interested parties of a number of specified terms. The motion must either not exceed five pages in length, or, if it is longer, begin with a concise statement of five pages or less, that summarizes or lists the material provisions and which will assist the court and interested parties in understanding the nature of the relief requested. The concise statement must also set out the location within the documents of the summarized or listed provisions. The parties to agreements and lending offers frequently have concise summaries of their transactions that contain a list of the material provisions of the agreements, even if the agreements themselves are very lengthy. A similar summary should allow the court and interested parties to understand the relief requested.

In addition to the concise statement, the rule requires that motions under subdivisions (c) and (d) state whether the movant is seeking approval of any of the provisions listed in subdivision (c)(1)(B), and where those provisions are located in the documents. The rule is intended to enhance the ability of the court and interested parties to find and evaluate those provisions.

The rule also provides that any motion for authority to obtain credit must identify any provision listed in subdivision (c)(1)(B)(i)-(xi) that is proposed to remain effective if the court grants the motion on an interim basis under Rule 4001 (c)(2), but later denies final relief.

Other amendments are stylistic.

2009 Amendments

The rule is amended to implement changes in connection with the amendment to Rule 9006(a) and the manner by which time is computed under the rules. The deadlines in the rule are amended to substitute a deadline that is a multiple of seven days. Throughout the rules, deadlines are amended in the following manner:

- 5–day periods become 7–day periods
- 10–day periods become 14–day periods
- 15–day periods become 14–day periods
- 20–day periods become 21–day periods
- 25–day periods become 28–day periods

2010 Amendments

Subdivision (d). Subdivision (d) is amended to implement changes in connection with the 2009 amendment to Rule 9006(a) and the manner by which time is computed under the rules. The deadlines in subdivision (d)(2) and (d)(3) are amended to substitute deadlines that are multiples of seven days. Throughout the rules, deadlines have been amended in the following manner:

- 5 day periods become 7 day periods
- 10 day periods become 14 day periods
- 15 day periods become 14 day periods
- 20 day periods become 21 day periods
- 25 day periods become 28 day periods

CROSS REFERENCES

Enlargement of thirty-day period after which stay will expire following commencement of final hearing not permitted, see Fed.Rules Bankr.Proc. Rule 9006, 11 USCA.

Extension of time for trustee to redeem debtor's property, see 11 USCA § 108.

Methods for providing adequate protection, see 11 USCA § 361.

Motions,

> For relief from stay filed with court in which case is pending, see Fed.Rules Bankr.Proc. Rule 5005, 11 USCA.

> Form and service, see Fed.Rules Bankr.Proc. Rule 9013, 11 USCA.

Signing and verification of papers, see Fed.Rules Bankr. Proc. Rule 9011, 11 USCA.

Stay of actions on claims against, codebtor in individual debt adjustment case, see 11 USCA § 1301.

Rule 4002. Duties of Debtor

(a) In general

In addition to performing other duties prescribed by the Code and rules, the debtor shall:

(1) attend and submit to an examination at the times ordered by the court;

(2) attend the hearing on a complaint objecting to discharge and testify, if called as a witness;

(3) inform the trustee immediately in writing as to the location of real property in which the debtor

has an interest and the name and address of every person holding money or property subject to the debtor's withdrawal or order if a schedule of property has not yet been filed pursuant to Rule 1007;

(4) cooperate with the trustee in the preparation of an inventory, the examination of proofs of claim, and the administration of the estate; and

(5) file a statement of any change of the debtor's address.

(b) Individual debtor's duty to provide documentation

(1) Personal identification

Every individual debtor shall bring to the meeting of creditors under § 341:

(A) a picture identification issued by a governmental unit, or other personal identifying information that establishes the debtor's identity; and

(B) evidence of social-security number(s), or a written statement that such documentation does not exist.

(2) Financial information

Every individual debtor shall bring to the meeting of creditors under § 341, and make available to the trustee, the following documents or copies of them, or provide a written statement that the documentation does not exist or is not in the debtor's possession:

(A) evidence of current income such as the most recent payment advice;

(B) unless the trustee or the United States trustee instructs otherwise, statements for each of the debtor's depository and investment accounts, including checking, savings, and money market accounts, mutual funds and brokerage accounts for the time period that includes the date of the filing of the petition; and

(C) documentation of monthly expenses claimed by the debtor if required by § 707(b)(2)(A) or (B).

(3) Tax return

At least 7 days before the first date set for the meeting of creditors under § 341, the debtor shall provide to the trustee a copy of the debtor's federal income tax return for the most recent tax year ending immediately before the commencement of the case and for which a return was filed, including any attachments, or a transcript of the tax return, or provide a written statement that the documentation does not exist.

(4) Tax returns provided to creditors

If a creditor, at least 14 days before the first date set for the meeting of creditors under § 341, requests a copy of the debtor's tax return that is to be provided to the trustee under subdivision (b)(3), the debtor, at least 7 days before the first date set for the meeting of creditors under § 341, shall provide to the requesting creditor a copy of the return, including any attachments, or a transcript of the tax return, or provide a written statement that the documentation does not exist.

(5) Confidentiality of tax information

The debtor's obligation to provide tax returns under Rule 4002(b)(3) and (b)(4) is subject to procedures for safeguarding the confidentiality of tax information established by the Director of the Administrative Office of the United States Courts.

(As amended Mar. 30, 1987, eff. Aug. 1, 1987; Apr. 23, 2008, eff. Dec. 1, 2008; Mar. 26, 2009, eff. Dec. 1, 2009.)

ADVISORY COMMITTEE NOTES

This rule should be read together with §§ 343 and 521 of the Code and Rule 1007, all of which impose duties on the debtor. Clause (3) of this rule implements the provisions of Rule 2015(a).

1987 Amendments

New clause (5) of the rule imposes on the debtor the duty to advise the clerk of any change of the debtor's address.

2008 Amendments

This rule is amended to implement § 521(a)(1)(B)(iv) and (e)(2), added to the Code by the 2005 amendments. These Code amendments expressly require the debtor to file with the court, or provide to the trustee, specific documents. The amendments to the rule implement these obligations and establish a time frame for creditors to make requests for a copy of the debtor's Federal income tax return. The rule also requires the debtor to provide documentation in support of claimed expenses under § 707(b)(2)(A) and (B).

Subdivision (b) of the rule is also amended to require the debtor to cooperate with the trustee by providing materials and documents necessary to assist the trustee in the performance of the trustee's duties. Nothing in the rule, however, is intended to limit or restrict the debtor's duties under § 521, or to limit the access of the Attorney General to any information provided by the debtor in the case. Subdivision (b)(2) does not require that the debtor create documents or obtain documents from third parties; rather, the debtor's obligation is to bring to the meeting of creditors under § 341 the documents which the debtor possesses. Under subdivision (b)(2)(B), the trustee or the United States trustee can instruct debtors that they need not provide the documents described in that subdivision. Under subdivisions (b)(3) and (b)(4), the debtor must obtain and provide copies of tax returns or tax transcripts to the appropriate person, unless no such documents exist. Any written statement that the debtor provides indicating either that documents do not exist or are not in the debtor's possession must be verified or contain an unsworn declaration as required under Rule 1008.

Because the amendment implements the debtor's duty to cooperate with the trustee, the materials provided to the trustee would not be made available to any other party in interest at the § 341 meeting of creditors other than the Attorney General. Some of the documents may contain otherwise private information that should not be disseminated. For example, pay stubs and financial account statements might include the social-security numbers of the debtor and the debtor's spouse and dependents, as well as the names of the debtor's children. The debtor should redact all but the last four digits of all social-security numbers and the names of any minors when they appear in these documents. This type of information would not usually be needed by creditors and others who may be attending the meeting. If a creditor perceives a need to review specific documents or other evidence, the creditor may proceed under Rule 2004.

Tax information produced under this rule is subject to procedures for safeguarding confidentiality established by the Director of the Administrative Office of the United States Courts.

2009 Amendments

The rule is amended to implement changes in connection with the amendment to Rule 9006(a) and the manner by which time is computed under the rules. The deadline in the rule is amended to substitute a deadline that is a multiple of seven days. Throughout the rules, deadlines are amended in the following manner:

- 5–day periods become 7–day periods
- 10–day periods become 14–day periods
- 15–day periods become 14–day periods
- 20–day periods become 21–day periods
- 25–day periods become 28–day periods

CROSS REFERENCES

Debtor's duties to,

Appear at meeting of creditors, see 11 USCA § 343.

File list of creditors and assets, cooperate with trustee, and appear at discharge hearing, see 11 USCA § 521.

File lists, schedules, and statements, see Fed.Rules Bankr.Proc. Rule 1007, 11 USCA.

Keep records, make reports, and give notice, see Fed. Rules Bankr.Proc. Rule 2015, 11 USCA.

Immunity from self-incrimination, see 11 USCA § 344.

Rule 4003. Exemptions

(a) Claim of exemptions

A debtor shall list the property claimed as exempt under § 522 of the Code on the schedule of assets required to be filed by Rule 1007. If the debtor fails to claim exemptions or file the schedule within the time specified in Rule 1007, a dependent of the debtor may file the list within 30 days thereafter.

(b) Objecting to a claim of exemptions

(1) Except as provided in paragraphs (2) and (3), a party in interest may file an objection to the list of property claimed as exempt within 30 days after the meeting of creditors held under § 341(a) is concluded or within 30 days after any amendment to the list or supplemental schedules is filed, whichever is later. The court may, for cause, extend the time for filing objections if, before the time to object expires, a party in interest files a request for an extension.

(2) The trustee may file an objection to a claim of exemption at any time prior to one year after the

closing of the case if the debtor fraudulently asserted the claim of exemption. The trustee shall deliver or mail the objection to the debtor and the debtor's attorney, and to any person filing the list of exempt property and that person's attorney.

(3) An objection to a claim of exemption based on § 522(q) shall be filed before the closing of the case. If an exemption is first claimed after a case is reopened, an objection shall be filed before the reopened case is closed.

(4) A copy of any objection shall be delivered or mailed to the trustee, the debtor and the debtor's attorney, and the person filing the list and that person's attorney.

(c) Burden of proof

In any hearing under this rule, the objecting party has the burden of proving that the exemptions are not properly claimed. After hearing on notice, the court shall determine the issues presented by the objections.

(d) Avoidance by debtor of transfers of exempt property

A proceeding under § 522(f) to avoid a lien or other transfer of property exempt under the Code shall be commenced by motion in the manner provided by Rule 9014, or by serving a chapter 12 or chapter 13 plan on the affected creditors in the manner provided by Rule 7004 for service of a summons and complaint. Notwithstanding the provisions of subdivision (b), a creditor may object to a request under § 522(f) by challenging the validity of the exemption asserted to be impaired by the lien.

(As amended Mar. 30, 1987, eff. Aug. 1, 1987; Apr. 30, 1991, eff. Aug. 1, 1991; Apr. 17, 2000, eff. Dec. 1, 2000; Apr. 23, 2008, eff. Dec. 1, 2008; Apr. 27, 2017, eff. Dec. 1, 2017.)

ADVISORY COMMITTEE NOTES

This rule is derived from § 522(l) of the Code and, in part, former Bankruptcy Rule 403. The Code changes the thrust of that rule by making it the burden of the debtor to list his exemptions and the burden of parties in interest to raise objections in the absence of which "the property claimed as exempt on such list is exempt;" § 522(l).

Subdivision (a). While § 522(l) refers to a list of property claimed as exempt, the rule incorporates such a list as part of Official Form No. 6, the schedule of the debtor's assets, rather than requiring a separate list and filing. Rule 1007, to which subdivision (a) refers, requires that schedule to be filed within 15 days after the order for relief, unless the court extends the time.

Section 522(l) also provides that a dependent of the debtor may file the list if the debtor fails to do so. Subdivision (a) of the rule allows such filing from the expiration of the debtor's time until 30 days thereafter. Dependent is defined in § 522(a)(1).

Subdivision (d) provides that a proceeding by the debtor, permitted by § 522(f) of the Code, is a contested matter rather than the more formal adversary proceeding. Proceedings within the scope of this subdivision are distinguished from proceedings brought by the trustee to avoid transfers. The latter are classified as adversary proceedings by Rule 7001.

1991 Amendments

Subdivision (b) is amended to facilitate the filing of objections to exemptions claimed on a supplemental schedule filed under Rule 1007(h).

2000 Amendments

This rule is amended to permit the court to grant a timely request for an extension of time to file objections to the list of claimed exemptions, whether the court rules on the request before or after the expiration of the 30–day period. The purpose of this amendment is to avoid the harshness of the present rule which has been construed to deprive a bankruptcy court of jurisdiction to grant a timely request for an extension if it has failed to rule on the request within the 30–day period. See *In re Laurain*, 113 F.3d 595 (6th Cir. 1997); *Matter of Stoulig*, 45 F.3d 957 (5th Cir. 1995); *In re Brayshaw*, 912 F.2d 1255 (10th Cir. 1990). The amendments clarify that the extension may be granted only for cause. The amendments also conform the rule to § 522(*l*) of the Code by recognizing that any party in interest may file an objection or request for an extension of time under this rule. Other amendments are stylistic.

GAP Report on Rule 4003(b). The words "trustee or creditor" were replaced by "party in interest" to conform to § 522(*l*) of the Bankruptcy Code which permits any party in interest to object to claimed exemptions. Style revisions also were made to the published draft.

2008 Amendments

Subdivision (b) is rewritten to include four paragraphs.

Subdivision (b)(2) is added to the rule to permit the trustee to object to an exemption at any time up to one year after the closing of the case if the debtor fraudulently claimed the exemption. Extending the deadline for trustees to object to an exemption when the exemption claim has been fraudulently made will permit the court to review and, in proper circumstances, deny improperly claimed exemptions, thereby protecting the legitimate interests of creditors and the bankruptcy estate. However, similar to the deadline set in § 727(e) of the Code for revoking a discharge which was fraudulently obtained, an objection to an exemption that was fraudulently claimed must be filed within one year after the closing of the case. Subdivision (b)(2) extends the objection deadline only for trustees.

Subdivision (b)(3) is added to the rule to reflect the addition of subsection (q) to § 522 of the Code by the 2005 Act. Section 522(q) imposes a $136,875 limit on a state homestead exemption if the debtor has been convicted of a felony or owes a debt arising from certain causes of action. Other revised provisions of the Code, such as § 727(a)(12) and § 1328(h), suggest that the court may consider issues relating to § 522(q) late in the case, and the 30–day period for objections would not be appropriate for this provision.

Subdivision (d) is amended to clarify that a creditor with a lien on property that the debtor is attempting to avoid on the grounds that the lien impairs an exemption may raise in defense to the lien avoidance action any objection to the debtor's claimed exemption. The right to object is limited to an objection to the exemption of the property subject to the lien and for purposes of the lien avoidance action only. The creditor may not object to other exemption claims made by the debtor. Those objections, if any, are governed by Rule 4003(b).

Other changes are stylistic.

2017 Amendments

Subdivision (d) is amended to provide that a request under § 522(f) to avoid a lien or other transfer of exempt property may be made by motion or by a chapter 12 or chapter 13 plan. A plan that proposes lien avoidance in accordance with this rule must be served as provided under Rule 7004 for service of a summons and complaint. Lien avoidance not governed by this rule requires an adversary proceeding.

CROSS REFERENCES

Automatic preservation of avoided property transfers for benefit of estate, see 11 USCA § 551.

Enlargement of thirty-day period for filing objections to property claimed as exempt permitted as limited in this rule, see Fed.Rules Bankr.Proc. Rule 9006, 11 USCA.

Motions, form and service, see Fed.Rules Bankr.Proc. Rule 9013, 11 USCA.

Proceedings to avoid transfers of exempt property as non-adversarial proceedings, see Fed.Rules Bankr.Proc. Rule 7001, 11 USCA.

Reduction of time to claim property as exempt by dependent not permitted, see Fed.Rules Bankr.Proc. Rule 9006, 11 USCA.

Right of debtor's redemption of personal property from lien securing dischargeable consumer debt, see 11 USCA § 722.

Rule 4004. Grant or Denial of Discharge

(a) Time for objecting to discharge; notice of time fixed

In a chapter 7 case, a complaint, or a motion under § 727(a)(8) or (a)(9) of the Code, objecting to the debtor's discharge shall be filed no later than 60 days after the first date set for the meeting of creditors under § 341(a). In a chapter 11 case, the complaint shall be filed no later than the first date set for the hearing on confirmation. In a chapter 13 case, a motion objecting to the debtor's discharge under § 1328(f) shall be filed no later than 60 days after the first date set for the meeting of creditors under § 341(a). At least 28 days' notice of the time so fixed shall be given to the United States trustee and all creditors as provided in Rule 2002(f) and (k) and to the trustee and the trustee's attorney.

(b) Extension of Time

(1) On motion of any party in interest, after notice and hearing, the court may for cause extend the time to object to discharge. Except as provided in subdivision (b)(2), the motion shall be filed before the time has expired.

(2) A motion to extend the time to object to discharge may be filed after the time for objection

has expired and before discharge is granted if (A) the objection is based on facts that, if learned after the discharge, would provide a basis for revocation under § 727(d) of the Code, and (B) the movant did not have knowledge of those facts in time to permit an objection. The motion shall be filed promptly after the movant discovers the facts on which the objection is based.

(c) Grant of discharge

(1) In a chapter 7 case, on expiration of the times fixed for objecting to discharge and for filing a motion to dismiss the case under Rule 1017(e), the court shall forthwith grant the discharge, except that the court shall not grant the discharge if:

(A) the debtor is not an individual;

(B) a complaint, or a motion under § 727(a)(8) or (a)(9), objecting to the discharge has been filed and not decided in the debtor's favor;

(C) the debtor has filed a waiver under § 727(a)(10);

(D) a motion to dismiss the case under § 707 is pending;

(E) a motion to extend the time for filing a complaint objecting to the discharge is pending;

(F) a motion to extend the time for filing a motion to dismiss the case under Rule 1017(e)(1) is pending;

(G) the debtor has not paid in full the filing fee prescribed by 28 U.S.C. § 1930(a) and any other fee prescribed by the Judicial Conference of the United States under 28 U.S.C. § 1930(b) that is payable to the clerk upon the commencement of a case under the Code, unless the court has waived the fees under 28 U.S.C. § 1930(f);

(H) the debtor has not filed with the court a statement of completion of a course concerning personal financial management if required by Rule 1007(b)(7);

(I) a motion to delay or postpone discharge under § 727(a)(12) is pending;

(J) a motion to enlarge the time to file a reaffirmation agreement under Rule 4008(a) is pending;

(K) a presumption is in effect under § 524(m) that a reaffirmation agreement is an undue hardship and the court has not concluded a hearing on the presumption; or

(L) a motion is pending to delay discharge because the debtor has not filed with the court all tax documents required to be filed under § 521(f).

(2) Notwithstanding Rule 4004(c)(1), on motion of the debtor, the court may defer the entry of an order granting a discharge for 30 days and, on motion within that period, the court may defer entry of the order to a date certain.

(3) If the debtor is required to file a statement under Rule 1007(b)(8), the court shall not grant a discharge earlier than 30 days after the statement is filed.

(4) In a chapter 11 case in which the debtor is an individual, or a chapter 13 case, the court shall not grant a discharge if the debtor has not filed any statement required by Rule 1007(b)(7).

(d) Applicability of rules in Part VII and Rule 9014

An objection to discharge is governed by Part VII of these rules, except that an objection to discharge under §§[1] 727(a)(8), (a)(9), or 1328(f) is commenced by motion and governed by Rule 9014.

(e) Order of discharge

An order of discharge shall conform to the appropriate Official Form.

(f) Registration in other districts

An order of discharge that has become final may be registered in any other district by filing a certified copy of the order in the office of the clerk of that district. When so registered the order of discharge shall have the same effect as an order of the court of the district where registered.

(g) Notice of discharge

The clerk shall promptly mail a copy of the final order of discharge to those specified in subdivision (a) of this rule.

(As amended Mar. 30, 1987, eff. Aug. 1, 1987; Apr. 30, 1991, eff. Aug. 1, 1991; Apr. 23, 1996, eff. Dec. 1, 1996; Apr. 26, 1999, eff. Dec. 1, 1999; Apr. 17, 2000, eff. Dec. 1, 2000; Apr. 29, 2002, eff. Dec. 1, 2002; Apr. 23, 2008, eff. Dec. 1, 2008; Mar. 26, 2009, eff. Dec. 1, 2009; Apr. 28, 2010, eff. Dec. 1, 2010; Apr. 26, 2011, eff. Dec. 1, 2011; Apr. 16, 2013, eff. Dec. 1, 2013.)

[1] So in original. Probably should be only one section symbol.

ADVISORY COMMITTEE NOTES

This rule is adapted from former Bankruptcy Rule 404.

Subdivisions (a) and (b) of this rule prescribe the procedure for determining whether a discharge will be granted pursuant to § 727 of the Code. The time fixed by subdivision (a) may be enlarged as provided in subdivision (b).

The notice referred to in subdivision (a) is required to be given by mail and addressed to creditors as provided in Rule 2002.

An extension granted on a motion pursuant to subdivision (b) of the rule would ordinarily benefit only the movant, but its scope and effect would depend on the terms of the extension.

Subdivision (c). If a complaint objecting to discharge is filed, the court's grant or denial of the discharge will be entered at the conclusion of the proceeding as a judgment in accordance with Rule 9021. The inclusion of the clause in subdivision (c) qualifying the duty of the court to grant a discharge when a waiver has been filed is in accord with the construction of the Code. 4 Collier, Bankruptcy ¶727.12 (15th ed. 1979).

The last sentence of subdivision (c) takes cognizance of § 524(c) of the Code which authorizes a debtor to enter into enforceable reaffirmation agreements only prior to entry of the order of discharge. Immediate entry of that order after expiration of the time fixed for filing complaints objecting to discharge may render it more difficult for a debtor to settle pending litigation to determine the dischargeability of a debt and execute a reaffirmation agreement as part of a settlement.

Subdivision (d). An objection to discharge is required to be made by a complaint, which initiates an adversary proceeding as provided in Rule 7003. Pursuant to Rule 5005, the complaint should be filed in the court in which the case is pending.

Subdivision (e). Official Form No. 27 to which subdivision (e) refers, includes notice of the effects of a discharge specified in § 524(a) of the Code.

Subdivision (f). Registration may facilitate the enforcement of the order of discharge in a district other than that in which it was entered. See 2 Moore's Federal Practice ¶1.04[2] (2d ed. 1967). Because of the nationwide service of process authorized by Rule 7004, however, registration of the order of discharge is not necessary under these rules to enable a discharged debtor to obtain relief against a creditor proceeding anywhere in the United States in disregard of the injunctive provisions of the order of discharge.

Subdivision (g). Notice of discharge should be mailed promptly after the order becomes final so that creditors may be informed of entry of the order and of its injunctive provisions. Rule 2002 specifies the manner of the notice and persons to whom the notice is to be given.

1991 Amendments

This rule is amended to conform to § 727(c) which gives the United States trustee the right to object to discharge. This amendment is derived from Rule X–1008(a)(1) and is consistent with Rule 2002. The amendment to subdivision (c) is to prevent a timely motion to dismiss a chapter 7 case for substantial abuse from becoming moot merely because a discharge order has been entered. Reference to the Official Form number in subdivision (e) is deleted in anticipation of future revision and renumbering of the Official Forms.

1996 Amendments

Subsection (c) is amended to delay entry of the order of discharge if a motion pursuant to Rule 4004(b) to extend the time for filing a complaint objecting to discharge is pending. Also, this subdivision is amended to delay entry of the discharge order if the debtor has not paid in full the filing fee and the administrative fee required to be paid upon the commencement of the case. If the debtor is authorized to pay the fees in installments in accordance with Rule 1006, the discharge order will not be entered until the final installment has been paid.

The other amendments to this rule are stylistic.

GAP Report on Rule 4004. No changes have been made since publication, except for stylistic changes.

1999 Amendments

Subdivision (a) is amended to clarify that, in a chapter 7 case, the deadline for filing a complaint objecting to discharge under § 727(a) is 60 days after the first date set for the meeting of creditors, whether or not the meeting is held on that date. The time for filing the complaint is not affected by any delay in the commencement or conclusion of the meeting of creditors. This amendment does not affect the right of any party in interest to file a motion for an extension of time to file a complaint objecting to discharge in accordance with Rule 4004(b).

The substitution of the word "filed" for "made" in subdivision (b) is intended to avoid confusion regarding the time when a motion is "made" for the purpose of applying these rules. See, e.g., In re Coggin, 30 F.3d 1443 (11th Cir. 1994). As amended, this rule requires that a motion for an extension of time for filing a complaint objecting to discharge be *filed* before the time has expired.

Other amendments to this rule are stylistic.

GAP Report on Rule 4004. No changes since publication.

2000 Amendments

Subdivision (c) is amended so that a discharge will not be granted while a motion requesting an extension of time to file a motion to dismiss the case under § 707(b) is pending. Other amendments are stylistic.

GAP Report on Rule 4004(c). No changes since publication except for style revisions.

2002 Amendments

Subdivision (c)(1)(D) is amended to provide that the filing of a motion to dismiss under § 707 of the Bankruptcy Code postpones the entry of the discharge. Under the present version of the rule, only motions to dismiss brought under § 707(b) cause the postponement of the discharge. This amendment would change the result in cases such as In re Tanenbaum, 210 B.R. 182 (Bankr. D. Colo. 1997).

Changes Made After Publication and Comments. No changes were made.

2008 Amendments

Subdivision (c)(1)(G) is amended to reflect the fee waiver provision in 28 U.S.C. § 1930, added by the 2005 amendments.

Subdivision (c)(1)(H) is new. It reflects the 2005 addition to the Code of §§ 727(a)(11) and 1328(g), which require that individual debtors complete a course in personal financial management as a condition to the entry of a discharge. Including this requirement in the rule helps prevent the inadvertent entry of a discharge when the debtor has not complied with this requirement. If a debtor fails to file the required statement regarding a personal financial management course, the clerk will close the bankruptcy case without the entry of a discharge.

Subdivision (c)(1)(I) is new. It reflects the 2005 addition to the Code of § 727(a)(12). This provision is linked to § 522(q). Section 522(q) limits the availability of the homestead exemption for individuals who have been convicted of a felony or who owe a debt arising from certain causes of action within a particular time frame. The existence of reasonable cause to believe that § 522(q) may be applicable to the debtor constitutes grounds for withholding the discharge.

Subdivision (c)(1)(J) is new. It accommodates the deadline for filing a reaffirmation agreement established by Rule 4008(a).

Subdivision (c)(1)(K) is new. It reflects the 2005 revisions to § 524 of the Code that alter the requirements for approval of reaffirmation agreements. Section 524(m) sets forth circumstances under which a reaffirmation agreement is presumed to be an undue hardship. This triggers an obligation to review the presumption and may require notice and a hearing. Subdivision (c)(1)(J) has been added to prevent the discharge from being entered until the court approves or disapproves the reaffirmation agreement in accordance with § 524(m).

Subdivision (c)(1)(L) is new. It implements § 1228(a) of Public Law Number 109–8, an uncodified provision of the Bankruptcy Abuse Prevention and Consumer Protection Act of 2005, which prohibits entry of a discharge unless required tax documents have been provided to the court.

Subdivision (c)(3) is new. It postpones the entry of the discharge of an individual debtor in a case under chapter 11, 12, or 13 if there is a question as to the applicability of § 522(q) of the Code. The postponement provides an opportunity for a creditor to file a motion to limit the debtor's exemption under that provision.

Other changes are stylistic.

2009 Amendments

The rule is amended to implement changes in connection with the amendment to Rule 9006(a) and the manner by which time is computed under the rules. The deadline in the rule is amended to substitute a deadline that is a multiple of seven days. Throughout the rules, deadlines are amended in the following manner:

- 5–day periods become 7–day periods
- 10–day periods become 14–day periods
- 15–day periods become 14–day periods
- 20–day periods become 21–day periods
- 25–day periods become 28–day periods

2010 Amendments

Subdivision (a). Subdivision (a) is amended to include a deadline for filing a motion objecting to a debtor's discharge under §§ 727(a)(8), (a)(9), or 1328(f) of the Code. These sections establish time limits on the issuance of discharges in successive bankruptcy cases by the same debtor.

Subdivision (c). Subdivision (c)(1) is amended because a corresponding amendment to subdivision (d) directs certain objections to discharge to be brought by motion rather than by complaint. Subparagraph (c)(1)(B) directs the court not to grant a discharge if a motion or complaint objecting to discharge has been filed unless the objection has been decided in the debtor's favor.

Subdivision (c)(4) is new. It directs the court in chapter 11 and 13 cases to withhold the entry of the discharge if an individual debtor has not filed a statement of completion of a course concerning personal financial management as required by Rule 1007(b)(7).

Subdivision (d). Subdivision (d) is amended to direct that objections to discharge under §§ 727(a)(8), (a)(9), and 1328(f) be commenced by motion rather than by complaint. Objections under the specified provisions are contested matters governed by Rule 9014. The title of the subdivision is also amended to reflect this change.

2011 Amendments

Subdivision (b). Subdivision (b) is amended to allow a party, under certain specified circumstances, to seek an extension of time to object to discharge after the time for filing has expired. This amendment addresses the situation in which there is a gap between the expiration of the time for objecting to discharge and the entry of the discharge order. If, during that period, a party discovers facts that would provide grounds for revocation of discharge, it may not be able to seek revocation under § 727(d) of the Code because the facts would have been known prior to the granting of the discharge. Furthermore, during that period the debtor may commit an act that provides a basis for both denial and revocation of the discharge. In those situations, subdivision (b)(2) allows a party to file a motion for an extension of time to object to discharge based on those facts so long as they were not known to the party before expiration of the deadline for objecting. The motion must be filed promptly after discovery of those facts.

2013 Amendments

Subdivision (c)(1) is amended in several respects. The introductory language of paragraph (1) is revised to emphasize that the listed circumstances do not just relieve the court of the obligation to enter the discharge promptly but that they prevent the court from entering a discharge.

Subdivision (c)(1)(H) is amended to reflect the simultaneous amendment of Rule 1007(b)(7). The amendment of the latter rule relieves a debtor of the obligation to file a statement of completion of a course concerning personal financial management if the course provider notifies the court directly that the debtor has completed the course. Subparagraph (H) now requires postponement of the discharge when a debtor fails to file a statement of course completion only if the debtor has an obligation to file the statement.

Subdivision (c)(1)(K) is amended to make clear that the prohibition on entering a discharge due to a presumption of undue hardship under § 524(m) of the Code ceases when the presumption expires or the court concludes a hearing on the presumption.

Because this amendment is being made to conform to a simultaneous amendment of Rule 1007(b)(7) and is otherwise technical in nature, final approval is sought without publication.

CROSS REFERENCES

Discharge,

    Effect of, see 11 USCA § 524.

    Exceptions to, see 11 USCA § 523.

Filing complaint to object to discharge, sixty-day period,

    Enlargement permitted as limited in this rule, see Fed. Rules Bankr.Proc. Rule 9006, 11 USCA.

    Reduction not permitted, see Fed.Rules Bankr.Proc. Rule 9006, 11 USCA.

Motions, form and service, see Fed.Rules Bankr.Proc. Rule 9013, 11 USCA.

Notice by mail,

    Order of discharge, see Fed.Rules Bankr.Proc. Rule 2002, 11 USCA.

    Time fixed to file complaint objecting to discharge, see Fed.Rules Bankr.Proc. Rule 2002, 11 USCA.

Time for filing complaint in reconverted liquidation case revived or extended as under this rule, see Fed.Rules Bankr. Proc. Rule 1019, 11 USCA.

Transfer of claim before or after proof of claim filed, see Fed.Rules Bankr.Proc. Rule 3001, 11 USCA.

Rule 4005. Burden of Proof in Objecting to Discharge

At the trial on a complaint objecting to a discharge, the plaintiff has the burden of proving the objection. (As amended Mar. 30, 1987, eff. Aug. 1, 1987.)

ADVISORY COMMITTEE NOTES

This rule does not address the burden of going forward with the evidence. Subject to the allocation by the rule of the initial burden of producing evidence and the ultimate burden of persuasion, the rule leaves to the courts the formulation of rules governing the shift of the burden of going forward with the evidence in the light of considerations such as the difficulty of proving the nonexistence of a fact and of establishing a fact as to which the evidence is likely to be more accessible to the debtor than to the objector. See, e.g., In re Haggerty, 165 F.2d 977, 979–80 (2d Cir. 1948); Federal Provision Co. v. Ershowsky, 94 F.2d 574, 575 (2d Cir.1938); In re Riceputo, 41 F.Supp. 926, 927–28 (E.D.N.Y. 1941).

Rule 4006. Notice of No Discharge

If an order is entered: denying a discharge; revoking a discharge; approving a waiver of discharge; or, in the case of an individual debtor, closing the case without the entry of a discharge, the clerk shall promptly notify all parties in interest in the manner provided by Rule 2002.
(As amended Mar. 30, 1987, eff. Aug. 1, 1987; Apr. 23, 2008, eff. Dec. 1, 2008.)

ADVISORY COMMITTEE NOTES

The suspension by § 108(c) of the Code of the statute of limitations affecting any debt of a debtor terminates within 30 days after the debtor is denied a discharge or otherwise loses his right to a discharge. If, however, a debtor's failure to receive a discharge does not come to the attention of his creditors until after the statutes of limitations have run, the debtor obtains substantially the same benefits from his bankruptcy as a debtor who is discharged.

This rule requires the clerk to notify creditors if a debtor fails to obtain a discharge because a waiver of discharge was filed under § 727(a)(10) or as a result of an order denying or revoking the discharge under § 727(a) or (d).

2008 Amendments

This amendment was necessary because the 2005 amendments to the Code require that individual debtors in a chapter 7 or 13 case complete a course in personal financial management as a condition to the entry of a discharge. If the debtor fails to complete the course, the case may be closed and no discharge will be entered. Reopening the case is governed by § 350 and Rule 5010. The rule is amended to provide notice to parties in interest, including the debtor, that no discharge was entered.

CROSS REFERENCES

Notice by mail, see Fed.Rules Bankr.Proc. Rule 2002, 11 USCA.

Suspension of statute of limitations on debts of debtor, see 11 USCA § 108.

Rule 4007. Determination of Dischargeability of a Debt

(a) Persons entitled to file complaint

A debtor or any creditor may file a complaint to obtain a determination of the dischargeability of any debt.

(b) Time for commencing proceeding other than under § 523(c) of the Code

A complaint other than under § 523(c) may be filed at any time. A case may be reopened without payment of an additional filing fee for the purpose of filing a complaint to obtain a determination under this rule.

(c) Time for filing complaint under § 523(c) in a chapter 7 liquidation, chapter 11 reorganization, chapter 12 family farmer's debt adjustment case, or chapter 13 individual's debt adjustment case; notice of time fixed

Except as otherwise provided in subdivision (d), a complaint to determine the dischargeability of a debt under § 523(c) shall be filed no later than 60 days after the first date set for the meeting of creditors under § 341(a). The court shall give all creditors no less than 30 days' notice of the time so fixed in the manner provided in Rule 2002. On motion of a party in interest, after hearing on notice, the court may for cause extend the time fixed under this subdivision. The motion shall be filed before the time has expired.

(d) Time for filing complaint under § 523(a)(6) in a chapter 13 individual's debt adjustment case; notice of time fixed

On motion by a debtor for a discharge under § 1328(b), the court shall enter an order fixing the time to file a complaint to determine the dischargeability of any debt under § 523(a)(6) and shall give no less than 30 days' notice of the time fixed to all creditors in the manner provided in Rule 2002. On motion of any party in interest, after hearing on notice, the court may for cause extend the time fixed under this subdivision. The motion shall be filed before the time has expired.

(e) Applicability of Rules in Part VII

A proceeding commenced by a complaint filed under this rule is governed by Part VII of these rules.
(As amended Mar. 30, 1987, eff. Aug. 1, 1987; Apr. 30, 1991, eff. Aug. 1, 1991; Apr. 26, 1999, eff. Dec. 1, 1999; Apr. 23, 2008, eff. Dec. 1, 2008.)

ADVISORY COMMITTEE NOTES

This rule prescribes the procedure to be followed when a party requests the court to determine dischargeability of a debt pursuant to § 523 of the Code.

Although a complaint that comes within § 523(c) must ordinarily be filed before determining whether the debtor will be discharged, the court need not determine the issues presented by the complaint filed under this rule until the question of discharge has been determined under Rule 4004. A complaint filed under this rule initiates an adversary proceeding as provided in Rule 7003.

Subdivision (b) does not contain a time limit for filing a complaint to determine the dischargeability of a type of debt listed as nondischargeable under § 523(a)(1), (3), (5), (7), (8), or (9). Jurisdiction over this issue on these debts is held concurrently by the bankruptcy court and any appropriate nonbankruptcy forum.

Subdivision (c) differs from subdivision (b) by imposing a deadline for filing complaints to determine the issue of dischargeability of debts set out in § 523(a)(2), (4) or (6) of the Code. The bankruptcy court has exclusive jurisdiction to determine dischargeability of these debts. If a complaint is not timely filed, the debt is discharged. See § 523(c).

Subdivision (e). The complaint required by this subdivision should be filed in the court in which the case is pending pursuant to Rule 5005.

1991 Amendments

Subdivision (a) is amended to delete the words "with the court" as unnecessary. See Rules 5005(a) and 9001(3).

Subdivision (c) is amended to apply in chapter 12 cases the same time period that applies in chapter 7 and 11 cases for filing a complaint under § 523(c) of the Code to determine dischargeability of certain debts. Under § 1228(a) of the Code, a chapter 12 discharge does not discharge the debts specified in § 523(a) of the Code.

1999 Amendments

Subdivision (c) is amended to clarify that the deadline for filing a complaint to determine the dischargeability of a debt under § 523(c) of the Code is 60 days after the first date set for the meeting of creditors, whether or not the meeting is held on that date. The time for filing the complaint is not affected by any delay in the commencement or conclusion of the meeting of creditors. This amendment does not affect the right of any party in interest to file a motion for an extension of time to file a complaint to determine the dischargeability of a debt in accordance with this rule.

The substitution of the word "filed" for "made" in the final sentences of subdivisions (c) and (d) is intended to avoid confusion regarding the time when a motion is "made" for the purpose of applying these rules. *See, e.g., In re Coggin*, 30 F.3d 1443 (11th Cir. 1994). As amended, these subdivisions require that a motion for an extension of time be *filed* before the time has expired.

The other amendments to this rule are stylistic.

GAP Report on Rule 4007. No changes since publication, except for stylistic changes in the heading of Rule 4007(d).

2008 Amendments

Subdivision (c) is amended because of the 2005 amendments to § 1328(a) of the Code. This revision expands the exceptions to discharge upon completion of a chapter 13 plan. Subdivision (c) extends to chapter 13 the same time limits applicable to other chapters of the Code with respect to the two exceptions to discharge that have been added to § 1328(a) and that are within § 523(c).

The amendment to subdivision (d) reflects the 2005 amendments to § 1328(a) that expands the exceptions to discharge upon completion of a chapter 13 plan, including two out of three of the provisions that fall within § 523(c). However, the 2005 revisions to § 1328(a) do not include a reference to § 523(a)(6), which is the third provision to which § 523(c) refers. Thus, subdivision (d) is now limited to that provision.

CROSS REFERENCES

Costs and attorney fees to consumer debtor upon discharge of debt, see 11 USCA § 523.

Effect of dismissal on dischargeability of debt, see 11 USCA § 349.

Filing complaint to determine dischargeability of debt, sixty-day period,

> Enlargement permitted as limited in this rule, see Fed. Rules Bankr.Proc. Rule 9006, 11 USCA.

> Reduction not permitted, see Fed.Rules Bankr.Proc. Rule 9006, 11 USCA.

Motions, form and service, see Fed.Rules Bankr.Proc. Rule 9013, 11 USCA.

Notice by mail of time fixed to file complaint, see Fed.Rules Bankr.Proc. Rule 2002, 11 USCA.

Time for filing complaint in reconverted liquidation case revived or extended as under this rule, see Fed.Rules Bankr. Proc. Rule 1019, 11 USCA.

Rule 4008.   Filing of Reaffirmation Agreement; Statement in Support of Reaffirmation Agreement

(a) Filing of reaffirmation agreement

A reaffirmation agreement shall be filed no later than 60 days after the first date set for the meeting of creditors under § 341(a) of the Code. The reaffirmation agreement shall be accompanied by a cover sheet, prepared as prescribed by the appropriate Official Form. The court may, at any time and in its discretion, enlarge the time to file a reaffirmation agreement.

(b) Statement in support of reaffirmation agreement

The debtor's statement required under § 524(k)(6)(A) of the Code shall be accompanied by a statement of the total income and expenses stated on schedules I and J. If there is a difference between the total income and expenses stated on those schedules and the statement required under § 524(k)(6)(A), the statement required by this subdivision shall include an explanation of the difference.

(As amended Apr. 30, 1991, eff. Aug. 1, 1991; Apr. 23, 2008, eff. Dec. 1, 2008; Mar. 26, 2009, eff. Dec. 1, 2009.)

ADVISORY COMMITTEE NOTES

Section 524(d) of the Code requires the court to hold a hearing to inform an individual debtor concerning the granting or denial of discharge and the law applicable to reaffirmation agreements.

The notice of the § 524(d) hearing may be combined with the notice of the meeting of creditors or entered as a separate order.

The expression "not more than" contained in the first sentence of the rule is for the explicit purpose of requiring the hearing to occur within that time period and cannot be extended.

1991 Amendments

This rule is changed to conform to § 524(d) of the Code as amended in 1986. A hearing under § 524(d) is not mandatory unless the debtor desires to enter into a reaffirmation agreement.

2008 Amendments

This rule is amended to establish a deadline for filing reaffirmation agreements. The Code sets out a number of prerequisites to the enforceability of reaffirmation agreements. Among those requirements, § 524(k)(6)(A) provides that each reaffirmation agreement must be accompanied by a statement indicating the debtor's ability to make the payments called for by the agreement. In the event that this statement reflects an insufficient income to allow payment of the reaffirmed debt, § 524(m) provides that a presumption of undue hardship arises, allowing the court to disapprove the reaffirmation agreement, but only after a hearing conducted prior to the entry of discharge. Rule 4004(c)(1)(K) accommodates this provision by delaying the entry of discharge where a presumption of undue hardship arises. However, in order for that rule to be effective, the reaffirmation agreement itself must be filed before the entry of discharge. Under Rule 4004(c)(1) discharge is to be entered promptly after the expiration of the time for filing a complaint objecting to discharge, which, under Rule 4004(a), is 60 days after the first date set for the meeting of creditors under § 341(a). Accordingly, that date is set as the deadline for filing a reaffirmation agreement.

Any party may file the agreement with the court. Thus, whichever party has a greater incentive to enforce the agreement usually will file it. In the event that the parties are unable to file a reaffirmation agreement in a timely fashion, the rule grants the court broad discretion to permit a late filing. A corresponding change to Rule 4004(c)(1)(J) accommodates such an extension by providing for a delay in the entry of discharge during the pendency of a motion to extend the time for filing a reaffirmation agreement.

Rule 4008 is also amended by deleting provisions regarding the timing of any reaffirmation and discharge hearing. As noted above, § 524(m) itself requires that hearings on undue hardship be conducted prior to the entry of discharge. In other respects, including hearings to approve reaffirmation agreements of unrepresented debtors under § 524(c)(6), the rule leaves discretion to the court to set the hearing at a time appropriate for the particular circumstances presented in the case and consistent with the scheduling needs of the parties.

2009 Amendments

Subdivision (a) of the rule is amended to require that the entity filing the reaffirmation agreement with the court also include Official Form 27, the Reaffirmation Agreement Cover Sheet. The form includes information necessary for the court to determine whether the proposed reaffirmation agreement is presumed to be an undue hardship for the debtor under § 524(m) of the Code.

CROSS REFERENCES

Confirmation of reorganization plan, see Fed.Rules Bankr. Proc. Rule 3020, 11 USCA.

Motions, form and service, see Fed.Rules Bankr.Proc. Rule 9013, 11 USCA.

PART V—BANKRUPTCY COURTS AND CLERKS

Rule 5001. Courts and Clerks' Offices

(a) Courts always open

The courts shall be deemed always open for the purpose of filing any pleading or other proper paper, issuing and returning process, and filing, making, or entering motions, orders and rules.

(b) Trials and hearings; orders in chambers

All trials and hearings shall be conducted in open court and so far as convenient in a regular court room. Except as otherwise provided in 28 U.S.C. § 152(c), all other acts or proceedings may be done or conducted by a judge in chambers and at any place either within or without the district; but no hearing, other than one ex parte, shall be conducted outside the district without the consent of all parties affected thereby.

(c) Clerk's office

The clerk's office with the clerk or a deputy in attendance shall be open during business hours on all days except Saturdays, Sundays and the legal holidays listed in Rule 9006(a).

(As amended Mar. 30, 1987, eff. Aug. 1, 1987; Apr. 30, 1991, eff. Aug. 1, 1991; Apr. 23, 2008, eff. Dec. 1, 2008.)

ADVISORY COMMITTEE NOTES

This rule is adapted from subdivisions (a), (b) and (c) of Rule 77 F.R.Civ.P.

1987 Amendments

Rule 9001, as amended, defines court to mean the bankruptcy judge or district judge before whom a case or proceeding is pending. Clerk means the bankruptcy clerk, if one has been appointed for the district; if a bankruptcy clerk has not been appointed, clerk means clerk of the district court.

1991 Amendments

Subdivision (c) is amended to refer to Rule 9006(a) for a list of legal holidays. Reference to F.R.Civ.P. is not necessary for this purpose.

2008 Amendments

The rule is amended to permit bankruptcy judges to hold hearings outside of the district in which the case is pending to the extent that the circumstances lead to the authorization of the court to take such action under the 2005 amendment to 28 U.S.C. § 152(c). Under that provision, bankruptcy judges may hold court outside of their districts in emergency situations and when the business of the court otherwise so requires. This amendment to the rule is intended to implement the legislation.

CROSS REFERENCES

"Legal holiday" defined, see Fed.Rules Bankr.Proc. Rule 9006, 11 USCA.

Rule 5002. Restrictions on Approval of Appointments

(a) Approval of appointment of relatives prohibited

The appointment of an individual as a trustee or examiner pursuant to § 1104 of the Code shall not be approved by the court if the individual is a relative of the bankruptcy judge approving the appointment or the United States trustee in the region in which the case is pending. The employment of an individual as an attorney, accountant, appraiser, auctioneer, or other professional person pursuant to §§ 327, 1103, or 1114 shall not be approved by the court if the individual is a relative of the bankruptcy judge approving the employment. The employment of an individual as attorney, accountant, appraiser, auctioneer, or other professional person pursuant to §§ 327, 1103, or 1114 may be approved by the court if the individual is a relative of the United States trustee in the region in which the case is pending, unless the court finds that the relationship with the United States trustee renders the employment improper under the circumstances of the case. Whenever under this subdivision an individual may not be approved for appointment or employment, the individual's firm, partnership, corporation, or any other form of business association or relationship, and all members, associates and professional employees thereof also may not be approved for appointment or employment.

(b) Judicial determination that approval of appointment or employment is improper

A bankruptcy judge may not approve the appointment of a person as a trustee or examiner pursuant to § 1104 of the Code or approve the employment of a person as an attorney, accountant, appraiser, auctioneer, or other professional person pursuant to §§ 327, 1103, or 1114 of the Code if that person is or has been so connected with such judge or the United States trustee as to render the appointment or employment improper.

(As amended Apr. 29, 1985, eff. Aug. 1, 1985; Apr. 30, 1991, eff. Aug. 1, 1991.)

ADVISORY COMMITTEE NOTES

This rule is adapted from former Bankruptcy Rule 505(a). The scope of the prohibition on appointment or employment is expanded to include an examiner appointed under § 1104 of the Code and attorneys and other professional persons whose employment must be approved by the court under § 327 or § 1103.

The rule supplements two statutory provisions. Under 18 U.S.C. § 1910, it is a criminal offense for a judge to appoint a relative as a trustee and, under 28 U.S.C. § 458, a person may not be "appointed to or employed in any office or duty in any court" if he is a relative of any judge of that court. The rule prohibits the appointment or employment of a relative of a bankruptcy judge in a case pending before that bankruptcy judge or before other bankruptcy judges sitting within the district.

A relative is defined in § 101(34) of the Code to be an "individual related by affinity or consanguinity within the third degree as determined by the common law, or individual in a step or adoptive relationship within such third degree." Persons within the third degree under the common law system are as follows: first degree—parents, brothers and sisters, and children; second degree—grandparents, uncles and aunts, first cousins, nephews and nieces, and grandchildren; third degree—great grandparents, great uncles and aunts, first cousins once removed, second cousins, grand nephews and nieces, great grandchildren. Rule 9001 incorporates the definitions of § 101 of the Code.

In order for the policy of this rule to be meaningfully implemented, it is necessary to extend the prohibition against appointment or employment to the firm or other business association of the ineligible person and to those affiliated with the firm or business association. "Firm" is defined in Rule 9001 to include a professional partnership or corporation of attorneys or accountants. All other types of business and professional associations and relationships are covered by this rule.

1985 Amendments

The amended rule is divided into two subdivisions. Subdivision (a) applies to relatives of bankruptcy judges and subdivision (b) applies to persons who are or have been connected with bankruptcy judges. Subdivision (a) permits no judicial discretion; subdivision (b) allows judicial discretion. In both subdivisions of the amended rule "bankruptcy judge" has been substituted for "judge." The amended rule makes clear that it only applies to relatives of, or persons connected with, the bankruptcy judge. *See In re Hilltop Sand and Gravel, Inc.*, 35 B.R. 412 (N.D.Ohio 1983).

Subd. (a). The original rule prohibited all bankruptcy judges in a district from appointing or approving the employment of (i) a relative of any bankruptcy judge serving in the district, (ii) the firm or business association of any ineligible relative and (iii) any member or professional employee of the firm or business association of an ineligible relative. In addition, the definition of relative, the third degree relationship under the common law, is quite broad. The restriction

on the employment opportunities of relatives of bankruptcy judges was magnified by the fact that many law and accounting firms have practices and offices spanning the nation.

Relatives are not eligible for appointment or employment when the bankruptcy judge to whom they are related makes the appointment or approves the employment. Canon 3(b)(4) of the Code of Judicial Conduct, which provides that the judge "shall exercise his power of appointment only on the basis of merit, avoiding nepotism and favoritism," should guide a bankruptcy judge when a relative of a judge of the same bankruptcy court is considered for appointment or employment.

Subd. (b), derived from clause (2) of the original rule, makes a person ineligible for appointment or employment if the person is so connected with a bankruptcy judge making the appointment or approving the employment as to render the appointment or approval of employment improper. The caption and text of the subdivision emphasize that application of the connection test is committed to the sound discretion of the bankruptcy judge who is to make the appointment or approve the employment. All relevant circumstances are to be taken into account by the court. The most important of those circumstances include: the nature and duration of the connection with the bankruptcy judge; whether the connection still exists, and, if not, when it was terminated; and the type of appointment or employment. These and other considerations must be carefully evaluated by the bankruptcy judge.

The policy underlying subdivision (b) is essentially the same as the policy embodied in the Code of Judicial Conduct. Canon 2 of the Code of Judicial Conduct instructs a judge to avoid impropriety and the appearance of impropriety, and Canon 3(b)(4) provides that the judge "should exercise his power of appointment only on the basis of merit, avoiding nepotism and favoritism." Subdivision (b) alerts the potential appointee or employee and party seeking approval of employment to consider the possible relevance or impact of subdivision (b) and indicates to them that appropriate disclosure must be made to the bankruptcy court before accepting appointment or employment. The information required may be made a part of the application for approval of employment. See Rule 2014(a).

Subdivision (b) departs from the former rule in an important respect: a firm or business association is not prohibited from appointment or employment merely because an individual member or employee of the firm or business association is ineligible under subdivision (b).

The emphasis given to the bankruptcy court's judicial discretion in applying subdivision (b) and the absence of a *per se* extension of ineligibility to the firm or business association or any ineligible individual complement the amendments to subdivision (a). The change is intended to moderate the prior limitation on the employment opportunities of attorneys, accountants and other professional persons who are or who have been connected in some way with the bankruptcy judge. For example, in all but the most unusual situations service as a law clerk to a bankruptcy judge is not the type of connection which alone precludes appointment or employment. Even if a bankruptcy judge determines that it is improper to appoint or approve the employment of a former law clerk in the period immediately after completion of the former law clerk's service with the judge, the firm which employs the former law clerk will, absent other circumstances, be eligible for employment. In each instance all the facts must be considered by the bankruptcy judge.

Subdivision (b) applies to persons connected with a bankruptcy judge. "Person" is defined in § 101 of the Bankruptcy Code to include an "individual, partnership and corporation." A partnership or corporation may be appointed or employed to serve in a bankruptcy case. If a bankruptcy judge is connected in some way with a partnership or corporation, it is necessary for the court to determine whether the appointment or employment of that partnership or corporation is proper.

The amended rule does not regulate professional relationships which do not require approval of a bankruptcy judge. Disqualification of the bankruptcy judge pursuant to 28 U.S.C. § 455 may, however, be appropriate. Under Rule 5004(a), a bankruptcy judge may find that disqualification from only some aspect of the case, rather than the entire case, is necessary. A situation may also arise in which the disqualifying circumstance only comes to light after services have been performed. Rule 5004(b) provides that if compensation from the estate is sought for these services, the bankruptcy judge is disqualified from awarding compensation.

1991 Amendments

The 1986 amendments to the Code provide that the United States trustee shall appoint trustees in chapter 7, chapter 12, and chapter 13 cases without the necessity of court approval. This rule is not intended to apply to the appointment of trustees in those cases because it would be inappropriate for a court rule to restrict in advance the exercise of discretion by the executive branch. See Committee Note to Rule 2009.

In chapter 11 cases, a trustee or examiner is appointed by the United States trustee after consultation with parties in interest and subject to court approval. Subdivision (a), as amended, prohibits the approval of the appointment of an individual as a trustee or examiner if the person is a relative of the United States trustee making the appointment or the bankruptcy judge approving the appointment.

The United States trustee neither appoints nor approves the employment of professional persons employed pursuant to §§ 327, 1103, or 1114 of the Code. Therefore, subdivision (a) is not a prohibition against judicial approval of employment of a professional person who is a relative of the United States trustee. However, the United States trustee monitors applications for compensation and reimbursement of expenses and may raise, appear and be heard on issues in the case. Employment of relatives of the United States trustee may be approved unless the court finds, after considering the relationship and the particular circumstances of the case, that the relationship would cause the employment to be improper. As used in this rule, "improper" includes the appearance of impropriety.

United States trustee is defined to include a designee or assistant United States trustee. See Rule 9001. Therefore, subdivision (a) is applicable if the person appointed as trustee or examiner or the professional to be employed is a relative of a designee of the United States trustee or any assistant United States trustee in the region in which the case is pending.

This rule is not exclusive of other laws or rules regulating ethical conduct. See, e.g., 28 CFR § 45.735–5.

CROSS REFERENCES

Appointment of trustee or examiner, see 11 USCA § 1104.

Definition of "relative", see 11 USCA § 101.

Nepotism in appointment of receiver or trustee, see 18 USCA § 1910.

Relative of justice or judge ineligible to appointment, see 28 USCA § 458.

Rule 5003. Records Kept by the Clerk

(a) Bankruptcy dockets

The clerk shall keep a docket in each case under the Code and shall enter thereon each judgment, order, and activity in that case as prescribed by the Director of the Administrative Office of the United States Courts. The entry of a judgment or order in a docket shall show the date the entry is made.

(b) Claims register

The clerk shall keep in a claims register a list of claims filed in a case when it appears that there will be a distribution to unsecured creditors.

(c) Judgments and orders

The clerk shall keep, in the form and manner as the Director of the Administrative Office of the United States Courts may prescribe, a correct copy of every final judgment or order affecting title to or lien on real property or for the recovery of money or property, and any other order which the court may direct to be kept. On request of the prevailing party, a correct copy of every judgment or order affecting title to or lien upon real or personal property or for the recovery of money or property shall be kept and indexed with the civil judgments of the district court.

(d) Index of cases; certificate of search

The clerk shall keep indices of all cases and adversary proceedings as prescribed by the Director of the Administrative Office of the United States Courts. On request, the clerk shall make a search of any index and papers in the clerk's custody and certify whether a case or proceeding has been filed in or transferred to the court or if a discharge has been entered in its records.

(e) Register of mailing addresses of federal and state governmental units and certain taxing authorities

The United States or the state or territory in which the court is located may file a statement designating its mailing address. The United States, state, territory, or local governmental unit responsible for collecting taxes within the district in which the case is pending may also file a statement designating an address for service of requests under § 505(b) of the Code, and the designation shall describe where further information concerning additional requirements for filing such requests may be found. The clerk shall keep, in the form and manner as the Director of the Administrative Office of the United States Courts may prescribe, a register that includes the mailing addresses designated under the first sentence of this subdivision, and a separate register of the addresses designated for the service of requests under § 505(b) of the Code. The clerk is not required to include in any single register more than one mailing address for each department, agency, or instrumentality of the United States or the state or territory. If more than one address for a department, agency, or instrumentality is included in the register, the clerk shall also include information that would enable a user of the register to determine the circumstances when each address is applicable, and mailing notice to only one applicable address is sufficient to provide effective notice. The clerk shall update the register annually, effective January 2 of each year. The mailing address in the register is conclusively presumed to be a proper address for the governmental unit, but the failure to use that mailing address does not invalidate any notice that is otherwise effective under applicable law.

(f) Other books and records of the clerk

The clerk shall keep any other books and records required by the Director of the Administrative Office of the United States Courts.

(As amended Mar. 30, 1987, eff. Aug. 1, 1987; Apr. 17, 2000, eff. Dec. 1, 2000; Apr. 23, 2008, eff. Dec. 1, 2008.)

ADVISORY COMMITTEE NOTES

This rule consolidates former Bankruptcy Rules 504 and 507. The record-keeping duties of the referee under former Bankruptcy Rule 504 are transferred to the clerk. Subdivisions (a), (c), (d) and (e) are similar to subdivisions (a)–(d) of Rule 79 F.R.Civ.P.

Subdivision (b) requires that filed claims be listed on a claims register only when there may be a distribution to unsecured creditors. Compilation of the list for no asset or nominal asset cases would serve no purpose.

Rule 2013 requires the clerk to maintain a public record of fees paid from the estate and an annual summary thereof.

Former Bankruptcy Rules 507(d) and 508, which made materials in the clerk's office and files available to the public, are not necessary because § 107 of the Code guarantees public access to files and dockets of cases under the Code.

1987 Amendments

Subdivision (a) has been made more specific.

Subdivision (c) is amended to require that on the request of the prevailing party the clerk of the district court shall keep and index bankruptcy judgments and orders affecting title to or lien upon real or personal property or for the recovery of money or property with the civil judgments of the district court. This requirement is derived from former Rule 9021(b). The Director of the Administrative Office will provide guidance to the bankruptcy and district court clerks regarding appropriate paperwork and retention procedures.

2000 Amendments

Subdivision (e) is added to provide a source where debtors, their attorneys, and other parties may go to determine whether the United States or the state or territory in which the

court is located has filed a statement designating a mailing address for notice purposes. By using the address in the register—which must be available to the public—the sender is assured that the mailing address is proper. But the use of an address that differs from the address included in the register does not invalidate the notice if it is otherwise effective under applicable law.

The register may include a separate mailing address for each department, agency, or instrumentality of the United States or the state or territory. This rule does not require that addresses of municipalities or other local governmental units be included in the register, but the clerk may include them.

Although it is important for the register to be kept current, debtors, their attorneys, and other parties should be able to rely on mailing addresses listed in the register without the need to continuously inquire as to new or amended addresses. Therefore, the clerk must update the register, but only once each year.

To avoid unnecessary cost and burden on the clerk and to keep the register a reasonable length, the clerk is not required to include more than one mailing address for a particular agency, department, or instrumentality of the United States or the state or territory. But if more than one address is included, the clerk is required to include information so that a person using the register could determine when each address should be used. In any event, the inclusion of more than one address for a particular department, agency, or instrumentality does not impose on a person sending a notice the duty to send it to more than one address.

GAP Report on Rule 5003. No changes since publication.

2008 Amendments

The rule is amended to implement § 505(b)(1) of the Code added by the 2005 amendments, which allows a taxing authority to designate an address to use for the service of requests under that subsection. Under the amendment, the clerk is directed to maintain a separate register for mailing addresses of governmental units solely for the service of requests under § 505(b). This register is in addition to the register of addresses of governmental units already maintained by the clerk. The clerk is required to keep only one address for a governmental unit in each register.

CROSS REFERENCES

Books and records kept by Clerk and entries therein, see Fed.Rules Civ.Proc. Rule 79, 28 USCA.

Judgment effective when entered as provided in this rule, see Fed.Rules Bankr.Proc. Rule 9021, 11 USCA.

Public access to case dockets, see 11 USCA § 107.

Public record of estate fees to be kept by clerk, see Fed.Rules Bankr.Proc. Rule 2013, 11 USCA.

Rule 5004.   Disqualification

(a) Disqualification of judge

A bankruptcy judge shall be governed by 28 U.S.C. § 455, and disqualified from presiding over the proceeding or contested matter in which the disqualifying circumstances[1] arises or, if appropriate, shall be disqualified from presiding over the case.

(b) Disqualification of judge from allowing compensation

A bankruptcy judge shall be disqualified from allowing compensation to a person who is a relative of the bankruptcy judge or with whom the judge is so connected as to render it improper for the judge to authorize such compensation.

(As amended Apr. 29, 1985, eff. Aug. 1, 1985; Mar. 30, 1987, eff. Aug. 1, 1987.)

1 So in original. Probably should be "circumstance".

ADVISORY COMMITTEE NOTES

Subdivision (a). Disqualification of a bankruptcy judge is governed by 28 U.S.C. § 455. That section provides that the judge "shall disqualify himself in any proceeding in which his impartiality might reasonably be questioned" or under certain other circumstances. In a case under the Code it is possible that the disqualifying circumstance will be isolated to an adversary proceeding or contested matter. The rule makes it clear that when the disqualifying circumstance is limited in that way the judge need only disqualify himself from presiding over that adversary proceeding or contested matter.

It is possible, however, that even if the disqualifying circumstance arises in connection with an adversary proceeding, the effect will be so pervasive that disqualification from presiding over the case is appropriate. This distinction is consistent with the definition of "proceeding" in 28 U.S.C. § 455(d)(1).

Subdivision (b) precludes a bankruptcy judge from allowing compensation from the estate to a relative or other person closely associated with the judge. The subdivision applies where the judge has not appointed or approved the employment of the person requesting compensation. Perhaps the most frequent application of the subdivision will be in the allowance of administrative expenses under § 503(b)(3) to (5) of the Code. For example, if an attorney or accountant is retained by an indenture trustee who thereafter makes a substantial contribution in a chapter 11 case, the attorney or accountant may seek compensation under § 503(b)(4). If the attorney or accountant is a relative of or associated with the bankruptcy judge, the judge may not allow compensation to the attorney or accountant. Section 101(34) defines relative and Rule 9001 incorporates the definitions of the Code. See the Advisory Committee's Note to Rule 5002.

1985 Amendments

Subdivision (a) was affected by the Bankruptcy Amendments and Federal Judgeship Act of 1984, P.L. 98–353, 98 Stat. 333. The 1978 Bankruptcy Reform Act, P.L. 95–598, included bankruptcy judges in the definition of United States judges in 28 U.S.C. § 451 and they were therefore subject to the provisions of 28 U.S.C. § 455. This was to become effective on April 1, 1984, P.L. 95–598, § 404(b). Section 113 of P.L. 98–353, however, appears to have rendered the amendment to 28 U.S.C. § 451 ineffective. Subdivision (a) of the rule retains the substance and intent of the earlier draft by making bankruptcy judges subject to 28 U.S.C. § 455.

The word "associated" in subdivision (b) has been changed to "connected" in order to conform with Rule 5002(b).

1987 Amendments

The rule is amended to be gender neutral. The bankruptcy judge before whom the matter is pending determines whether disqualification is required.

CROSS REFERENCES

Definition of "relative", see 11 USCA § 101.

Prohibited appointments, see Fed.Rules Bankr.Proc. Rule 5002, 11 USCA.

Rule 5005.   Filing and Transmittal of Papers

(a) Filing

(1) Place of filing

The lists, schedules, statements, proofs of claim or interest, complaints, motions, applications, objections and other papers required to be filed by these rules, except as provided in 28 U.S.C. § 1409, shall be filed with the clerk in the district where the case under the Code is pending. The judge of that court may permit the papers to be filed with the judge, in which event the filing date shall be noted thereon, and they shall be forthwith transmitted to the clerk. The clerk shall not refuse to accept for filing any petition or other paper presented for the purpose of filing solely because it is not presented in proper form as required by these rules or any local rules or practices.

(2) Electronic filing and signing

(A) By a Represented Entity—Generally Required; Exceptions. An entity represented by an attorney shall file electronically, unless nonelectronic filing is allowed by the court for good cause or is allowed or required by local rule.

(B) By an Unrepresented Individual—When Allowed or Required. An individual not represented by an attorney:

(i) may file electronically only if allowed by court order or by local rule; and

(ii) may be required to file electronically only by court order, or by a local rule that includes reasonable exceptions.

(C) Signing. A filing made through a person's electronic-filing account and authorized by that person, together with that person's name on a signature block, constitutes the person's signature.

(D) Same as a Written Paper. A paper filed electronically is a written paper for purposes of these rules, the Federal Rules of Civil Procedure made applicable by these rules, and § 107 of the Code.

(b) Transmittal to the United States trustee

(1) The complaints, motions, applications, objections and other papers required to be transmitted to the United States trustee by these rules shall be mailed or delivered to an office of the United States trustee, or to another place designated by the United

States trustee, in the district where the case under the Code is pending.

(2) The entity, other than the clerk, transmitting a paper to the United States trustee shall promptly file as proof of such transmittal a verified statement identifying the paper and stating the date on which it was transmitted to the United States trustee.

(3) Nothing in these rules shall require the clerk to transmit any paper to the United States trustee if the United States trustee requests in writing that the paper not be transmitted.

(c) Error in filing or transmittal

A paper intended to be filed with the clerk but erroneously delivered to the United States trustee, the trustee, the attorney for the trustee, a bankruptcy judge, a district judge, the clerk of the bankruptcy appellate panel, or the clerk of the district court shall, after the date of its receipt has been noted thereon, be transmitted forthwith to the clerk of the bankruptcy court. A paper intended to be transmitted to the United States trustee but erroneously delivered to the clerk, the trustee, the attorney for the trustee, a bankruptcy judge, a district judge, the clerk of the bankruptcy appellate panel, or the clerk of the district court shall, after the date of its receipt has been noted thereon, be transmitted forthwith to the United States trustee. In the interest of justice, the court may order that a paper erroneously delivered shall be deemed filed with the clerk or transmitted to the United States trustee as of the date of its original delivery.

(As amended Mar. 30, 1987, eff. Aug. 1, 1987; Apr. 30, 1991, eff. Aug. 1, 1991; Apr. 22, 1993, eff. Aug. 1, 1993; Apr. 23, 1996, eff. Dec. 1, 1996; Apr. 12, 2006, eff. Dec. 1, 2006; Apr. 26, 2018, eff. Dec. 1, 2018.)

ADVISORY COMMITTEE NOTES

Subdivision (a) is an adaptation of Rule 5(e) F.R.Civ.P. §§ 301–304 of the Code and Rules 1002 and 1003 require that cases under the Code be commenced by filing a petition "with the bankruptcy court." Other sections of the Code and other rules refer to or contemplate filing but there is no specific reference to filing with the bankruptcy court. For example, § 501 of the Code requires filing of proofs of claim and Rule 3016(c) requires the filing of a disclosure statement. This subdivision applies to all situations in which filing is required. Except when filing in another district is authorized by 28 U.S.C. § 1473, all papers, including complaints commencing adversary proceedings, must be filed in the court where the case under the Code is pending.

Subdivision (b) is the same as former Bankruptcy Rule 509(c).

1987 Amendments

Subdivision (a) is amended to conform with the 1984 amendments.

1991 Amendments

Subdivision (b)(1) is flexible in that it permits the United States trustee to designate a place or places for receiving papers within the district in which the case is pending. Transmittal of papers to the United States trustee may be accomplished by mail or delivery, including delivery by courier, and the technical requirements for service of process are not applicable. Although papers relating to a proceeding commenced in another district pursuant to 28 U.S.C. § 1409 must be filed with the clerk in that district, the papers required to be transmitted to the United States trustee must be mailed or delivered to the United States trustee in the district in which the case under the Code is pending. The United States trustee in the district in which the case is pending monitors the progress of the case and should be informed of all developments in the case wherever the developments take place.

Subdivision (b)(2) requires that proof of transmittal to the United States trustee be filed with the clerk. If papers are served on the United States trustee by mail or otherwise, the filing of proof of service would satisfy the requirements of this subdivision. This requirement enables the court to assure that papers are actually transmitted to the United States trustee in compliance with the rules. When the rules require that a paper be transmitted to the United States trustee and proof of transmittal has not been filed with the clerk, the court should not schedule a hearing or should take other appropriate action to assure that the paper is transmitted to the United States trustee. The filing of the verified statement with the clerk also enables other parties in interest to determine whether a paper has been transmitted to the United States trustee.

Subdivision (b)(3) is designed to relieve the clerk of any obligation under these rules to transmit any paper to the United States trustee if the United States trustee does not wish to receive it.

Subdivision (c) is amended to include the erroneous delivery of papers intended to be transmitted to the United States trustee.

1993 Amendments

Subdivision (a) is amended to conform to the 1991 amendment to Rule 5(e) F.R.Civ.P. It is not a suitable role for the office of the clerk to refuse to accept for filing papers not conforming to requirements of form imposed by these rules or by local rules or practices. The enforcement of these rules and local rules is a role for a judge. This amendment does not require the clerk to accept for filing papers sent to the clerk's office by facsimile transmission.

1996 Amendments

The rule is amended to permit, but not require, courts to adopt local rules that allow filing, signing, or verifying of documents by electronic means. However, such local rules must be consistent with technical standards, if any, promulgated by the Judicial Conference of the United States.

An important benefit to be derived by permitting filing by electronic means is that the extensive volume of paper received and maintained as records in the clerk's office will be reduced substantially. With the receipt of electronic data transmissions by computer, the clerk may maintain records electronically without the need to reproduce them in tangible paper form.

Judicial Conference standards governing the technological aspects of electronic filing will result in uniformity among judicial districts to accommodate an increasingly national bar.

By delegating to the Judicial Conference the establishment and future amendment of national standards for electronic filing, the Supreme Court and Congress will be relieved of the burden of reviewing and promulgating detailed rules dealing with complex technological standards. Another reason for leaving to the Judicial Conference the formulation of technological standards for electronic filing is that advances in computer technology occur often, and changes in the technological standards may have to be implemented more frequently than would be feasible by rule amendment under the Rules Enabling Act process.

It is anticipated that standards established by the Judicial Conference will govern technical specifications for electronic data transmission, such as requirements relating to the formatting of data, speed of transmission, means to transmit copies of supporting documentation, and security of communication procedures. In addition, before procedures for electronic filing are implemented, standards must be established to assure the proper maintenance and integrity of the record and to provide appropriate access and retrieval mechanisms. These matters will be governed by local rules until system-wide standards are adopted by the Judicial Conference.

Rule 9009 requires that the Official Forms shall be observed and used "with alterations as may be appropriate." Compliance with local rules and any Judicial Conference standards with respect to the formatting or presentation of electronically transmitted data, to the extent that they do not conform to the Official Forms, would be an appropriate alteration within the meaning of Rule 9009.

These rules require that certain documents be in writing. For example, Rule 3001 states that a proof of claim is a "written statement." Similarly, Rule 3007 provides that an objection to a claim "shall be in writing." Pursuant to the new subdivision (a)(2), any requirement under these rules that a paper be written may be satisfied by filing the document by electronic means, notwithstanding the fact that the clerk neither receives nor prints a paper reproduction of the electronic data.

Section 107(a) of the Code provides that a "paper" filed in a case is a public record open to examination by an entity at reasonable times without charge, except as provided in § 107(b). The amendment to subdivision (a)(2) provides that an electronically filed document is to be treated as such a public record.

Although under subdivision (a)(2) electronically filed documents may be treated as written papers or as signed or verified writings, it is important to emphasize that such treatment is only for the purpose of applying these rules. In addition, local rules and Judicial Conference standards regarding verification must satisfy the requirements of 28 U.S.C. § 1746.

GAP Report on Rule 5005. No changes since publication.

2006 Amendments

Subdivision (a). Amended Rule 5005(a)(2) acknowledges that many courts have required electronic filing by means of a standing order, procedures manual, or local rule. These local practices reflect the advantages that courts and most litigants realize from electronic filings. Courts requiring electronic filing must make reasonable exceptions for persons for whom electronic filing of documents constitutes an unreasonable denial of access to the courts. Experience with the rule will facilitate convergence on uniform exceptions in an amended Rule 5005(a)(2).

Subdivision (c). The rule is amended to include the clerk of the bankruptcy appellate panel among the list of persons required to transmit to the proper person erroneously filed or transmitted papers. The amendment is necessary because the bankruptcy appellate panels were not in existence at the time of the original promulgation of the rule. The amendment also inserts the district judge on the list of persons required to transmit papers intended for the United States trustee but erroneously sent to another person. The district judge is included in the list of persons who must transmit papers to the clerk of the bankruptcy court in the first part of the rule, and there is no reason to exclude the district judge from the list of persons who must transmit erroneously filed papers to the United States trustee.

2018 Amendments

Electronic filing has matured. Most districts have adopted local rules that require electronic filing and allow reasonable exceptions as required by the former rule. The time has come to seize the advantages of electronic filing by making it mandatory in all districts, except for filings made by an individual not represented by an attorney. But exceptions continue to be available. Paper filing must be allowed for good cause. And a local rule may allow or require paper filing for other reasons.

Filings by an individual not represented by an attorney are treated separately. It is not yet possible to rely on an assumption that pro se litigants are generally able to seize the advantages of electronic filing. Encounters with the court's system may prove overwhelming to some. Attempts to work within the system may generate substantial burdens on a pro se party, on other parties, and on the court. Rather than mandate electronic filing, filing by pro se litigants is left for governing by local rules or court order. Efficiently handled electronic filing works to the advantage of all parties and the court. Many courts now allow electronic filing by pro se litigants with the court's permission. Such approaches may expand with growing experience in these and other courts, along with the growing availability of the systems required for electronic filing and the increasing familiarity of most people with electronic communication. Room is also left for a court to require electronic filing by a pro se litigant by court order or by local rule. Care should be taken to ensure that an order to file electronically does not impede access to the court, and reasonable exceptions must be included in a local rule that requires electronic filing by a pro se litigant.

A filing made through a person's electronic-filing account and authorized by that person, together with that person's name on a signature block, constitutes the person's signature. A person's electronic-filing account means an account established by the court for use of the court's electronic-filing system, which account the person accesses with the user name and password (or other credentials) issued to that person by the court.

HISTORICAL NOTES

References in Text

The Federal Rules of Civil Procedure, referred to in subd. (a)(2), are set out in Title 28.

Filing of pleadings and other papers with court, see Fed. Rules Civ.Proc. Rule 5, 28 USCA.

Rule 5006. Certification of Copies of Papers

The clerk shall issue a certified copy of the record of any proceeding in a case under the Code or of any paper filed with the clerk on payment of any prescribed fee.

(As amended Apr. 30, 1991, eff. Aug. 1, 1991.)

ADVISORY COMMITTEE NOTES

Fees for certification and copying are fixed by the Judicial Conference under 28 U.S.C. § 1930(b).

Rule 1101 F.R.Evid. makes the Federal Rules of Evidence applicable to cases under the Code. Rule 1005 F.R.Evid. allows the contents of an official record or of a paper filed with the court to be proved by a duly certified copy. A copy certified and issued in accordance with Rule 5006 is accorded authenticity by Rule 902(4) F.R.Evid.

CROSS REFERENCES

Public records, see Fed.Rules Evid. Rule 1005, 28 USCA.

Rule 5007. Record of Proceedings and Transcripts

(a) Filing of record or transcript

The reporter or operator of a recording device shall certify the original notes of testimony, tape recording, or other original record of the proceeding and promptly file them with the clerk. The person preparing any transcript shall promptly file a certified copy.

(b) Transcript fees

The fees for copies of transcripts shall be charged at rates prescribed by the Judicial Conference of the United States. No fee may be charged for the certified copy filed with the clerk.

(c) Admissibility of record in evidence

A certified sound recording or a transcript of a proceeding shall be admissible as prima facie evidence to establish the record.

(As amended Mar. 30, 1987, eff. Aug. 1, 1987; Apr. 30, 1991, eff. Aug. 1, 1991.)

ADVISORY COMMITTEE NOTES

This rule supplements 28 U.S.C. § 773. A record of proceedings before the bankruptcy judge is to be made whenever practicable. By whatever means the record is made, subdivision (a) requires that the preparer of the record certify and file the original notes, tape recording, or other form of sound recording of the proceedings. Similarly, if a transcript is requested, the preparer is to file a certified copy with the clerk.

Subdivision (b) is derived from 28 U.S.C. § 753(f).

Subdivision (c) is derived from former Bankruptcy Rule 511(c). This subdivision extends to a sound recording the

same evidentiary status as a transcript under 28 U.S.C. § 773(b).

1991 Amendments

The words "with the clerk" in the final sentence of subdivision (a) are deleted as unnecessary. See Rules 5005(a) and 9001(3).

CROSS REFERENCES

Reporters, see 28 USCA § 753.

Stenographer, stenographic report or transcript as evidence, see Fed.Rules Civ.Proc. Rule 80, 28 USCA.

Rule 5008. Notice Regarding Presumption of Abuse in Chapter 7 Cases of Individual Debtors

If a presumption of abuse has arisen under § 707(b) in a chapter 7 case of an individual with primarily consumer debts, the clerk shall within 10 days after the date of the filing of the petition notify creditors of the presumption of abuse in accordance with Rule 2002. If the debtor has not filed a statement indicating whether a presumption of abuse has arisen, the clerk shall within 10 days after the date of the filing of the petition notify creditors that the debtor has not filed the statement and that further notice will be given if a later filed statement indicates that a presumption of abuse has arisen. If a debtor later files a statement indicating that a presumption of abuse has arisen, the clerk shall notify creditors of the presumption of abuse as promptly as practicable.

(Added Apr. 23, 2008, eff. Dec. 1, 2008.)

ADVISORY COMMITTEE NOTES

2008 Amendments

This rule is new. The 2005 amendments to § 342 of the Code require that clerks give written notice to all creditors not later than 10 days after the date of the filing of the petition that a presumption of abuse has arisen under § 707(b). A statement filed by the debtor will be the source of the clerk's information about the presumption of abuse. This rule enables the clerk to meet its obligation to send the notice within the statutory time period set forth in § 342. In the event that the court receives the debtor's statement after the clerk has sent the first notice, and the debtor's statement indicates a presumption of abuse, the rule requires that the clerk send a second notice.

Rule 5009. Closing Chapter 7, Chapter 12, Chapter 13, and Chapter 15 Cases; Order Declaring Lien Satisfied

(a) Closing of cases under chapters 7, 12, and 13

If in a chapter 7, chapter 12, or chapter 13 case the trustee has filed a final report and final account and has certified that the estate has been fully administered, and if within 30 days no objection has been filed by the United States trustee or a party in interest, there shall be a presumption that the estate has been fully administered.

(b) Notice of failure to file Rule 1007(b)(7) statement

If an individual debtor in a chapter 7 or 13 case is required to file a statement under Rule 1007(b)(7) and fails to do so within 45 days after the first date set for the meeting of creditors under § 341(a) of the Code, the clerk shall promptly notify the debtor that the case will be closed without entry of a discharge unless the required statement is filed within the applicable time limit under Rule 1007(c).

(c) Cases under chapter 15

A foreign representative in a proceeding recognized under § 1517 of the Code shall file a final report when the purpose of the representative's appearance in the court is completed. The report shall describe the nature and results of the representative's activities in the court. The foreign representative shall transmit the report to the United States trustee, and give notice of its filing to the debtor, all persons or bodies authorized to administer foreign proceedings of the debtor, all parties to litigation pending in the United States in which the debtor was a party at the time of the filing of the petition, and such other entities as the court may direct. The foreign representative shall file a certificate with the court that notice has been given. If no objection has been filed by the United States trustee or a party in interest within 30 days after the certificate is filed, there shall be a presumption that the case has been fully administered.

(d) Order declaring lien satisfied

In a chapter 12 or chapter 13 case, if a claim that was secured by property of the estate is subject to a lien under applicable nonbankruptcy law, the debtor may request entry of an order declaring that the secured claim has been satisfied and the lien has been released under the terms of a confirmed plan. The request shall be made by motion and shall be served on the holder of the claim and any other entity the court designates in the manner provided by Rule 7004 for service of a summons and complaint.

(As amended Apr. 30, 1991, eff. Aug. 1, 1991; Apr. 28, 2010, eff. Dec. 1, 2010; Apr. 16, 2013, eff. Dec. 1, 2013; Apr. 27, 2017, eff. Dec. 1, 2017.)

ADVISORY COMMITTEE NOTES

This rule is the same as § 350(a) of the Code. An estate may be closed even though the period allowed by Rule 3002(c) for filing claims has not expired. The closing of a case may be expedited when a notice of no dividends is given under Rule 2002(e). Dismissal of a case for want of prosecution or failure to pay filing fees is governed by Rule 1017.

1991 Amendments

The final report and account of the trustee is required to be filed with the court and the United States trustee under §§ 704(9), 1202(b)(1), and 1302(b)(1) of the Code. This amendment facilitates the United States trustee's performance of statutory duties to supervise trustees and administer cases under chapters 7, 12, and 13 pursuant to 28 U.S.C. § 586. In the absence of a timely objection by the United States trustee or a party in interest, the court may discharge the trustee and close the case pursuant to § 350(a) without the need to review the final report and account or to determine the merits of the trustee's certification that the estate has been fully administered.

Rule 3022 governs the closing of chapter 11 cases.

2010 Amendments

Subdivisions (a) and (b). The rule is amended to redesignate the former rule as subdivision (a) and to add new subdivisions (b) and (c) to the rule, Subdivision (b) requires the clerk to provide notice to an individual debtor in a chapter 7 or 13 case that the case may be closed without the entry of a discharge due to the failure of the debtor to file a timely statement of completion of a personal financial management course. The purpose of the notice is to provide the debtor with an opportunity to complete the course and file the appropriate document prior to the filing deadline. Timely filing of the document avoids the need for a motion to extend the time retroactively. It also avoids the potential for closing the case without discharge, and the possible need to pay an additional fee in connection with reopening. Timely filing also benefits the clerk's office by reducing the number of instances in which cases must be reopened.

Subdivision (c). Subdivision (c) requires a foreign representative in a chapter 15 case to file a final report setting out the foreign representative's actions and results obtained in the United States court. It also requires the foreign representative to give notice of the filing of the report, and provides interested parties with 30 days to object to the report after the foreign representative has certified that notice has been given. In the absence of a timely objection, a presumption arises that the case is fully administered, and the case may be closed.

2013 Amendments

Subdivision (b) is amended to conform to the amendment of Rule 1007(b)(7). Rule 1007(b)(7) relieves an individual debtor of the obligation to file a statement of completion of a personal financial management course if the course provider notifies the court that the debtor has completed the course. The clerk's duty under subdivision (b) to notify the debtor of the possible closure of the case without discharge if the statement is not timely filed therefore applies only if the course provider has not already notified the court of the debtor's completion of the course.

Changes Made After Publication and Comments. No changes were made.

2017 Amendments

Subdivision (d) is added to provide a procedure by which a debtor in a chapter 12 or chapter 13 case may request an order declaring a secured claim satisfied and a lien released under the terms of a confirmed plan. A debtor may need documentation for title purposes of the elimination of a second mortgage or other lien that was secured by property of the estate. Although requests for such orders are likely to be made at the time the case is being closed, the rule does not prohibit a request at another time if the lien has been released and any other requirements for entry of the order have been met.

Other changes to this rule are stylistic.

CROSS REFERENCES

Debtor to succeed to any tax attributes of estate, see 11 USCA § 346.

Dismissal of case, suspension, see Fed.Rules Bankr.Proc. Rule 1017, 11 USCA.

Final decree, see Fed.Rules Bankr.Proc. Rule 3022, 11 USCA.

Postpetition transfers of estate property not avoidable by trustee after case closed, see 11 USCA § 549.

Scheduled property not administered before case closed deemed abandoned, see 11 USCA § 554.

Rule 5010.   Reopening Cases

A case may be reopened on motion of the debtor or other party in interest pursuant to § 350(b) of the Code. In a chapter 7, 12, or 13 case a trustee shall not be appointed by the United States trustee unless the court determines that a trustee is necessary to protect the interests of creditors and the debtor or to insure efficient administration of the case.

(As amended Mar. 30, 1987, eff. Aug. 1, 1987; Apr. 30, 1991, eff. Aug. 1, 1991.)

ADVISORY COMMITTEE NOTES

Section 350(b) of the Code provides: "A case may be reopened in the court in which such case was closed to administer assets, to accord relief to the debtor, or for other cause."

Rule 9024, which incorporates Rule 60 F.R.Civ.P., exempts motions to reopen cases under the Code from the one year limitation of Rule 60(b).

Although a case has been closed the court may sometimes act without reopening the case. Under Rule 9024, clerical errors in judgments, orders, or other parts of the record or errors therein caused by oversight or omission may be corrected. A judgment determined to be non-dischargeable pursuant to Rule 4007 may be enforced after a case is closed by a writ of execution obtained pursuant to Rule 7069.

1987 Amendments

In order to avoid unnecessary cost and delay, the rule is amended to permit reopening of a case without the appointment of a trustee when the services of a trustee are not needed.

1991 Amendments

This rule is amended to conform to the 1986 amendments to the Code that give the United States trustee the duty to appoint trustees in chapter 7, 12 and 13 cases. See §§ 701, 702(d), 1202(a), and 1302(a) of the Code. In most reopened cases, a trustee is not needed because there are no assets to be administered. Therefore, in the interest of judicial economy, this rule is amended so that a motion will not be

necessary unless the United States trustee or a party in interest seeks the appointment of a trustee in the reopened case.

CROSS REFERENCES

Motions, form and service, see Fed.Rules Bankr.Proc. Rule 9013, 11 USCA.

Relief from judgment or order, see Fed.Rules Bankr.Proc. Rule 9024, 11 USCA.

Rule 5011.   Withdrawal and Abstention From Hearing a Proceeding

(a) Withdrawal

A motion for withdrawal of a case or proceeding shall be heard by a district judge.

(b) Abstention from hearing a proceeding

A motion for abstention pursuant to 28 U.S.C. § 1334(c) shall be governed by Rule 9014 and shall be served on the parties to the proceeding.

(c) Effect of filing of motion for withdrawal or abstention

The filing of a motion for withdrawal of a case or proceeding or for abstention pursuant to 28 U.S.C. § 1334(c) shall not stay the administration of the case or any proceeding therein before the bankruptcy judge except that the bankruptcy judge may stay, on such terms and conditions as are proper, proceedings pending disposition of the motion. A motion for a stay ordinarily shall be presented first to the bankruptcy judge. A motion for a stay or relief from a stay filed in the district court shall state why it has not been presented to or obtained from the bankruptcy judge. Relief granted by the district judge shall be on such terms and conditions as the judge deems proper.

(Added Mar. 30, 1987, eff. Aug. 1, 1987 and amended Apr. 30, 1991, eff. Aug. 1, 1991.)

ADVISORY COMMITTEE NOTES

Motions for withdrawal pursuant to 28 U.S.C. § 157(d) or abstention pursuant to 28 U.S.C. § 1334(c), like all other motions, are to be filed with the clerk as required by Rule 5005(a). If a bankruptcy clerk has been appointed for the district, all motions are filed with the bankruptcy clerk. The method for forwarding withdrawal motions to the district court will be established by administrative procedures.

Subdivision (a). Section 157(d) permits the district court to order withdrawal on its own motion or the motion of a party. Subdivision (a) of this rule makes it clear that the bankruptcy judge will not conduct hearings on a withdrawal motion. The withdrawal decision is committed exclusively to the district court.

Subdivision (b). A decision to abstain under 28 U.S.C. § 1334(c) is not appealable. The district court is vested originally with jurisdiction and the decision to relinquish that jurisdiction must ultimately be a matter for the district court. The bankruptcy judge ordinarily will be in the best position to evaluate the grounds asserted for abstention. This subdivision (b) provides that the initial hearing on the motion is before the bankruptcy judge. The procedure for review of the report and recommendation are governed by Rule 9033.

This rule does not apply to motions under § 305 of the Code for abstention from hearing a case. Judicial decisions will determine the scope of the bankruptcy judge's authority under § 305.

Subdivision (c). Unless the court so orders, proceedings are not stayed when motions are filed for withdrawal or for abstention from hearing a proceeding. Because of the district court's authority over cases and proceedings, the subdivision authorizes the district court to order a stay or modify a stay ordered by the bankruptcy judge.

1991 Amendments

Subdivision (b) is amended to delete the restriction that limits the role of the bankruptcy court to the filing of a report and recommendation for disposition of a motion for abstention under 28 U.S.C. § 1334(c)(2). This amendment is consistent with § 309(b) of the Judicial Improvements Act of 1990 which amended § 1334(c)(2) so that it allows an appeal to the district court of a bankruptcy court's order determining an abstention motion. This subdivision is also amended to clarify that the motion is a contested matter governed by Rule 9014 and that it must be served on all parties to the proceeding with is the subject of the motion.

Rule 5012. Agreements Concerning Coordination of Proceedings in Chapter 15 Cases

Approval of an agreement under § 1527(4) of the Code shall be sought by motion. The movant shall attach to the motion a copy of the proposed agreement or protocol and, unless the court directs otherwise, give at least 30 days' notice of any hearing on the motion by transmitting the motion to the United States trustee, and serving it on the debtor, all persons or bodies authorized to administer foreign proceedings of the debtor, all entities against whom provisional relief is being sought under § 1519, all parties to litigation pending in the United States in which the debtor was a party at the time of the filing of the petition, and such other entities as the court may direct.

(Added Apr. 28, 2010, eff. Dec. 1, 2010.)

ADVISORY COMMITTEE NOTES

2010 Adoption

This rule is new. In chapter 15 cases, any party in interest may seek approval of an agreement, frequently referred to as a "protocol," that will assist with the conduct of the case. Because the needs of the courts and the parties may vary greatly from case to case, the rule does not attempt to limit the form or scope of a protocol. Rather, the rule simply requires that approval of a particular protocol be sought by motion, and designates the persons entitled to notice of the hearing on the motion. These agreements, or protocols, drafted entirely by parties in interest in the case, are intended to provide valuable assistance to the court in the management of the case. Interested parties may find guidelines published by organizations, such as the American Law Institute and the International Insolvency Institute, helpful in crafting agreements or protocols to apply in a particular case.

PART VI—COLLECTION AND LIQUIDATION OF THE ESTATE

Rule

6001. Burden of Proof as to Validity of Postpetition Transfer.
6002. Accounting by Prior Custodian of Property of the Estate.
6003. Interim and Final Relief Immediately Following the Commencement of the Case—Applications for Employment; Motions for Use, Sale, or Lease of Property; and Motions for Assumption or Assignment of Executory Contracts.
6004. Use, Sale, or Lease of Property.
6005. Appraisers and Auctioneers.
6006. Assumption, Rejection or Assignment of an Executory Contract or Unexpired Lease.
6007. Abandonment or Disposition of Property.
6008. Redemption of Property From Lien or Sale.
6009. Prosecution and Defense of Proceedings by Trustee or Debtor in Possession.
6010. Proceeding to Avoid Indemnifying Lien or Transfer to Surety.
6011. Disposal of Patient Records in Health Care Business Case.

Rule 6001. Burden of Proof as to Validity of Postpetition Transfer

Any entity asserting the validity of a transfer under § 549 of the Code shall have the burden of proof.

ADVISORY COMMITTEE NOTES

This rule is derived from former Bankruptcy Rule 603. The Act contained, in § 70d [former § 110(d) of this title], a provision placing the burden of proof on the same person as did Rule 603. The Code does not contain any directive with respect to the burden of proof. This omission, in all probability, resulted from the intention to leave matters affecting evidence to these rules. See H.Rep. No. 95–595, 95th Cong. 1st Sess. (1977) 293.

Rule 6002. Accounting by Prior Custodian of Property of the Estate

(a) Accounting required

Any custodian required by the Code to deliver property in the custodian's possession or control to the trustee shall promptly file and transmit to the United States trustee a report and account with respect to the property of the estate and the administration thereof.

(b) Examination of administration

On the filing and transmittal of the report and account required by subdivision (a) of this rule and after an examination has been made into the superseded administration, after notice and a hearing, the court shall determine the propriety of the administration, including the reasonableness of all disbursements.

(As amended Mar. 30, 1987, eff. Aug. 1, 1987; Apr. 30, 1991, eff. Aug. 1, 1991; Apr. 22, 1993, eff. Aug. 1, 1993.)

ADVISORY COMMITTEE NOTES

"Custodian" is defined in § 101(10) of the Code. The definition includes a trustee or receiver appointed in proceedings not under the Code, as well as an assignee for the benefit of creditors.

This rule prescribes the procedure to be followed by a custodian who under § 543 of the Code is required to deliver property to the trustee and to account for its disposition. The examination under subdivision (b) may be initiated (1) on the motion of the custodian required to account under subdivision (a) for an approval of his account and discharge thereon, (2) on the motion of, or the filing of an objection to the custodian's account by, the trustee or any other party in interest, or (3) on the court's own initiative. Rule 9014 applies to any contested matter arising under this rule.

Section 543(d) is similar to an abstention provision. It grants the bankruptcy court discretion to permit the custodian to remain in possession and control of the property. In that event, the custodian is excused from complying with § 543(a)(c) and thus would not be required to turn over the property to the trustee. When there is no duty to turn over to the trustee, Rule 6002 would not be applicable.

1991 Amendments

This rule is amended to enable the United States trustee to review, object to, or to otherwise be heard regarding the custodian's report and accounting. See §§ 307 and 543 of the Code.

1993 Amendments

Subdivision (b) is amended to conform to the language of § 102(1) of the Code.

CROSS REFERENCES

Accountability of prior custodians for estate property, see 11 USCA § 543.

Definition of "custodian", see 11 USCA § 101.

Proceedings under this rule as nonadversarial proceedings, see Fed.Rules Bankr.Proc. Rule 7001, 11 USCA.

Property of estate, see 11 USCA § 541.

Rule 6003. Interim and Final Relief Immediately Following the Commencement of the Case—Applications for Employment; Motions for Use, Sale, or Lease of Property; and Motions for Assumption or Assignment of Executory Contracts

Except to the extent that relief is necessary to avoid immediate and irreparable harm, the court shall not, within 21 days after the filing of the petition, issue an order granting the following:

(a) an application under Rule 2014;

(b) a motion to use, sell, lease, or otherwise incur an obligation regarding property of the estate, including a motion to pay all or part of a claim that arose before the filing of the petition, but not a motion under Rule 4001; or

(c) a motion to assume or assign an executory contract or unexpired lease in accordance with § 365. (Added Apr. 30, 2007, eff. Dec. 1, 2007; amended Mar. 26, 2009, eff. Dec. 1, 2009; Apr. 26, 2011, eff. Dec. 1, 2011.)

ADVISORY COMMITTEE NOTES

2007 Adoption

There can be a flurry of activity during the first days of a bankruptcy case. This activity frequently takes place prior to the formation of a creditors' committee, and it also can include substantial amounts of materials for the court and parties in interest to review and evaluate. This rule is intended to alleviate some of the time pressures present at the start of a case so that full and close consideration can be given to matters that may have a fundamental impact on the case.

The rule provides that the court cannot grant relief on applications for the employment of professional persons, motions for the use, sale, or lease of property of the estate other than such a motion under Rule 4001, and motions to assume or assign executory contracts and unexpired leases for the first 20 days of the case, unless granting relief is necessary to avoid immediate and irreparable harm. This standard is taken from Rule 4001(b)(2) and (c)(2), and decisions under those provisions should provide guidance for the application of this provision.

This rule does not govern motions and applications made more than 20 days after the filing of the petition.

2009 Amendments

The rule is amended to implement changes in connection with the amendment to Rule 9006(a) and the manner by which time is computed under the rules. The deadline in the rule is amended to substitute a deadline that is a multiple of seven days. Throughout the rules, deadlines are amended in the following manner:

- 5–day periods become 7–day periods
- 10–day periods become 14–day periods
- 15–day periods become 14–day periods
- 20–day periods become 21–day periods
- 25–day periods become 28–day periods

2011 Amendments

The rule is amended to clarify that it limits the timing of the entry of certain orders, but does not prevent the court from providing an effective date for such an order that may relate back to the time of the filing of the application or motion, or to some other date. For example, while the rule prohibits, absent immediate and irreparable harm, the court from authorizing the employment of counsel during the first 21 days of a case, it does not prevent the court from providing in an order entered after expiration of the 21–day period that the relief requested in the motion or application is effective as of a date earlier than the issuance of the order. Nor does it prohibit the filing of an application or motion for relief prior to expiration of the 21–day period. Nothing in the rule prevents a professional from representing the trustee or a debtor in possession pending the approval of an application for the approval of the employment under Rule 2014.

The amendment also clarifies that the scope of the rule is limited to granting the specifically identified relief set out in the subdivisions of the rule. Deleting "regarding" from the rule clarifies that the rule does not prohibit the court from entering orders in the first 21 days of the case that may relate to the motions and applications set out in (a), (b), and (c); it is only prohibited from granting the relief requested by those motions or applications. For example, in the first 21 days of the case, the court could grant the relief requested in a motion to establish bidding procedures for the sale of property of the estate, but it could not, absent immediate and irreparable harm, grant a motion to approve the sale of property.

Rule 6004.   Use, Sale, or Lease of Property

(a) Notice of proposed use, sale, or lease of property

Notice of a proposed use, sale, or lease of property, other than cash collateral, not in the ordinary course of business shall be given pursuant to Rule 2002(a)(2), (c)(1), (i), and (k) and, if applicable, in accordance with § 363(b)(2) of the Code.

(b) Objection to proposal

Except as provided in subdivisions (c) and (d) of this rule, an objection to a proposed use, sale, or lease of property shall be filed and served not less than seven days before the date set for the proposed action or within the time fixed by the court. An objection to the proposed use, sale, or lease of property is governed by Rule 9014.

(c) Sale free and clear of liens and other interests

A motion for authority to sell property free and clear of liens or other interests shall be made in accordance with Rule 9014 and shall be served on the parties who have liens or other interests in the property to be sold. The notice required by subdivision (a) of this rule shall include the date of the hearing on the motion and the time within which objections may be filed and served on the debtor in possession or trustee.

(d) Sale of property under $2,500

Notwithstanding subdivision (a) of this rule, when all of the nonexempt property of the estate has an aggregate gross value less than $2,500, it shall be sufficient to give a general notice of intent to sell such property other than in the ordinary course of business to all creditors, indenture trustees, committees appointed or elected pursuant to the Code, the United States trustee and other persons as the court may direct. An objection to any such sale may be filed and served by a party in interest within 14 days of the mailing of the notice, or within the time fixed by the court. An objection is governed by Rule 9014.

(e) Hearing

If a timely objection is made pursuant to subdivision (b) or (d) of this rule, the date of the hearing thereon may be set in the notice given pursuant to subdivision (a) of this rule.

(f) Conduct of sale not in the ordinary course of business
(1) Public or private sale

All sales not in the ordinary course of business may be by private sale or by public auction. Unless it is impracticable, an itemized statement of the property sold, the name of each purchaser, and the price received for each item or lot or for the property as a whole if sold in bulk shall be filed on completion of a sale. If the property is sold by an auctioneer, the auctioneer shall file the statement, transmit a copy thereof to the United States trustee, and furnish a copy to the trustee, debtor in possession, or chapter 13 debtor. If the property is not sold by an auctioneer, the trustee, debtor in possession, or chapter 13 debtor shall file the statement and transmit a copy thereof to the United States trustee.

(2) Execution of instruments

After a sale in accordance with this rule the debtor, the trustee, or debtor in possession, as the case may be, shall execute any instrument necessary or ordered by the court to effectuate the transfer to the purchaser.

(g) Sale of personally identifiable information
(1) Motion

A motion for authority to sell or lease personally identifiable information under § 363(b)(1)(B) shall include a request for an order directing the United States trustee to appoint a consumer privacy ombudsman under § 332. Rule 9014 governs the motion which shall be served on: any committee elected under § 705 or appointed under § 1102 of the Code, or if the case is a chapter 11 reorganization case and no committee of unsecured creditors has been appointed under § 1102, on the creditors included on the list of creditors filed under Rule 1007(d); and on such other entities as the court may direct. The motion shall be transmitted to the United States trustee.

(2) Appointment

If a consumer privacy ombudsman is appointed under § 332, no later than seven days before the hearing on the motion under § 363(b)(1)(B), the United States trustee shall file a notice of the appointment, including the name and address of the person appointed. The United States trustee's notice shall be accompanied by a verified statement of the person appointed setting forth the person's connections with the debtor, creditors, any other party in interest, their respective attorneys and accountants, the United States trustee, or any person employed in the office of the United States trustee.

(h) Stay of order authorizing use, sale, or lease of property

An order authorizing the use, sale, or lease of property other than cash collateral is stayed until the expiration of 14 days after entry of the order, unless the court orders otherwise.

(As amended Mar. 30, 1987, eff. Aug. 1, 1987; Apr. 30, 1991, eff. Aug. 1, 1991; Apr. 26, 1999, eff. Dec. 1, 1999; Apr. 23, 2008, eff. Dec. 1, 2008; Mar. 26, 2009, eff. Dec. 1, 2009.)

ADVISORY COMMITTEE NOTES

Subdivisions (a) and (b). Pursuant to § 363(b) of the Code, a trustee or debtor in possession may use, sell, or lease property other than in the ordinary course of business only after notice and hearing. Rule 2002(a), (c) and (i) specifies the time when notice of sale is to be given, the contents of the notice and the persons to whom notice is to be given of sales of property. Subdivision (a) makes those provisions applicable as well to notices for proposed use and lease of property.

The Code does not provide the time within which parties may file objections to a proposed sale. Subdivision (b) of the rule requires the objection to be in writing and filed not less than five days before the proposed action is to take place. The objection should also be served within that time on the person who is proposing to take the action which would be either the trustee or debtor in possession. This time period is subject to change by the court. In some instances there is a need to conduct a sale in a short period of time and the court is given discretion to tailor the requirements to the circumstances.

Subdivision (c). In some situations a notice of sale for different pieces of property to all persons specified in Rule 2002(a) may be uneconomic and inefficient. This is particularly true in some chapter 7 liquidation cases when there is property of relatively little value which must be sold by the trustee. Subdivision (c) allows a general notice of intent to sell when the aggregate value of the estate's property is less than $2,500. The gross value is the value of the property without regard to the amount of any debt secured by a lien on the property. It is not necessary to give a detailed notice specifying the time and place of a particular sale. Thus, the requirements of Rule 2002(c) need not be met. If this method of providing notice of sales is used, the subdivision specifies that parties in interest may serve and file objections to the proposed sale of any property within the class and the time for service and filing is fixed at not later than 15 days after mailing the notice. The court may fix a different time. Subdivision (c) would have little utility in chapter 11 cases. Pursuant to Rule 2002(i), the court can limit notices of sale to the creditors' committee appointed under § 1102 of the Code and the same burdens present in a small chapter 7 case would not exist.

Subdivision (d). If a timely objection is filed, a hearing is required with respect to the use, sale, or lease of property. Subdivision (d) renders the filing of an objection tantamount to requesting a hearing so as to require a hearing pursuant to §§ 363(b) and 102(1)(B)(i).

Subdivision (e) is derived in part from former Bankruptcy Rule 606(b) but does not carry forward the requirement of that rule that court approval be obtained for sales of property.

Pursuant to § 363(b) court approval is not required unless timely objection is made to the proposed sale. The itemized statement or information required by the subdivision is not necessary when it would be impracticable to prepare it or set forth the information. For example, a liquidation sale of retail goods although not in the ordinary course of business may be on a daily ongoing basis and only summaries may be available.

The duty imposed by paragraph (2) does not affect the power of the bankruptcy court to order third persons to execute instruments transferring property purchased at a sale under this subdivision. See, e.g., In re Rosenberg, 138 F.2d 409 (7th Cir. 1943).

1987 Amendments

Subdivision (a) is amended to conform to the 1984 amendments to § 363(b)(2) of the Code.

Subdivision (b) is amended to provide that an objection to a proposed use, sale, or lease of property creates a contested matter governed by Rule 9014. A similar amendment is made to subdivision (d), which was formerly subdivision (c).

Subdivision (c) is new. Section 363(f) provides that sales free and clear of liens or other interests are only permitted if one of the five statutory requirements is satisfied. Rule 9013 requires that a motion state with particularity the grounds relied upon by the movant. A motion for approval of a sale free and clear of liens or other interests is subject to Rule 9014, service must be made on the parties holding liens or other interests in the property, and notice of the hearing on the motion and the time for filing objections must be included in the notice given under subdivision (a).

1991 Amendments

This rule is amended to provide notice to the United States trustee of a proposed use, sale or lease of property not in the ordinary course of business. See Rule 2002(k). Subdivision (f)(1) is amended to enable the United States trustee to monitor the progress of the case in accordance with 28 U.S.C. § 586(a)(3)(G).

The words "with the clerk" in subdivision (f)(1) are deleted as unnecessary. See Rules 5005(a) and 9001(3).

1999 Amendments

Subdivision (g) is added to provide sufficient time for a party to request a stay pending appeal of an order authorizing the use, sale, or lease of property under § 363(b) of the Code before the order is implemented. It does not affect the time for filing a notice of appeal in accordance with Rule 8002.

Rule 6004(g) does not apply to orders regarding the use of cash collateral and does not affect the trustee's right to use, sell, or lease property without a court order to the extent permitted under § 363 of the Code.

The court may, in its discretion, order that Rule 6004(g) is not applicable so that the property may be used, sold, or leased immediately in accordance with the order entered by the court. Alternatively, the court may order that the stay under Rule 6004(g) is for a fixed period less than 10 days.

GAP Report on Rule 6004. No changes since publication.

2008 Amendments

The rule is amended by inserting a new subdivision (g) to implement §§ 332 and 363(b)(1)(B) of the Code, added by the 2005 amendments. This rule governs the proposed transfer of personally identifiable information in a manner inconsistent with any policy covering the transfer of the information. Rule 2002(c)(1) requires the seller to state in the notice of the sale or lease whether the transfer is consistent with and policy governing the transfer of the information.

Under § 332 of the Code, the consumer privacy ombudsman must be appointed at least five days prior to the hearing on a sale or lease of personally identifiable information. In an appropriate case, the consumer privacy ombudsman may seek a continuance of the hearing on the proposed sale to perform the tasks required of the ombudsman by § 332 of the Code.

Former subdivision (g) is redesignated as subdivision (h).

2009 Amendments

The rule is amended to implement changes in connection with the amendment to Rule 9006(a) and the manner by which time is computed under the rules. The deadlines in the rule are amended to substitute a deadline that is a multiple of seven days. Throughout the rules, deadlines are amended in the following manner:

- 5–day periods become 7–day periods
- 10–day periods become 14–day periods
- 15–day periods become 14–day periods
- 20–day periods become 21–day periods
- 25–day periods become 28–day periods

CROSS REFERENCES

Appraisers and auctioneers, see Fed.Rules Bankr.Proc. Rule 6005, 11 USCA.

Authorization to operate debtor's business,

    Individual debt adjustment case, see 11 USCA § 1304.

    Liquidation case, see 11 USCA § 721.

    Reorganization case, see 11 USCA § 1108.

Twenty-day notice of property disposition to include certain information, see Fed.Rules Bankr.Proc. Rule 2002, 11 USCA.

Rule 6005.   Appraisers and Auctioneers

The order of the court approving the employment of an appraiser or auctioneer shall fix the amount or rate of compensation. No officer or employee of the Judicial Branch of the United States or the United States Department of Justice shall be eligible to act as appraiser or auctioneer. No residence or licensing requirement shall disqualify an appraiser or auctioneer from employment.

(As amended Mar. 30, 1987, eff. Aug. 1, 1987; Apr. 30, 1991, eff. Aug. 1, 1991.)

ADVISORY COMMITTEE NOTES

This rule is derived from former Bankruptcy Rule 606(c) and implements § 327 of the Code. Pursuant to § 327, the trustee or debtor in possession may employ one or more appraisers or auctioneers, subject to court approval. This rule requires the court order approving such employment to fix the amount or rate of compensation. The second sentence of the former rule is retained to continue to safeguard against imputations of favoritism which detract from public confidence in bankruptcy administration. The final sentence is to guard against imposition of parochial requirements not warranted by any consideration having to do with sound bankruptcy administration.

Reference should also be made to Rule 2013(a) regarding the limitation on employment of appraisers and auctioneers, and Rule 2014(a) regarding the application for appointment of an appraiser or auctioneer.

CROSS REFERENCES

Employment,

Application for, see Fed.Rules Bankr.Proc. Rule 2014, 11 USCA.

Limitation on appointment, see Fed.Rules Bankr.Proc. Rule 2013, 11 USCA.

Professional persons, see 11 USCA § 327.

Sharing of compensation prohibited, see 11 USCA § 504.

Rule 6006. Assumption, Rejection or Assignment of an Executory Contract or Unexpired Lease

(a) Proceeding to assume, reject, or assign

A proceeding to assume, reject, or assign an executory contract or unexpired lease, other than as part of a plan, is governed by Rule 9014.

(b) Proceeding to require trustee to act

A proceeding by a party to an executory contract or unexpired lease in a chapter 9 municipality case, chapter 11 reorganization case, chapter 12 family farmer's debt adjustment case, or chapter 13 individual's debt adjustment case, to require the trustee, debtor in possession, or debtor to determine whether to assume or reject the contract or lease is governed by Rule 9014.

(c) Notice

Notice of a motion made pursuant to subdivision (a) or (b) of this rule shall be given to the other party to the contract or lease, to other parties in interest as the court may direct, and, except in a chapter 9 municipality case, to the United States trustee.

(d) Stay of order authorizing assignment

An order authorizing the trustee to assign an executory contract or unexpired lease under § 365(f) is stayed until the expiration of 14 days after the entry of the order, unless the court orders otherwise.

(e) Limitations

The trustee shall not seek authority to assume or assign multiple executory contracts or unexpired leases in one motion unless: (1) all executory contracts or unexpired leases to be assumed or assigned are between the same parties or are to be assigned to the same assignee; (2) the trustee seeks to assume, but not assign to more than one assignee, unexpired leases of real property; or (3) the court otherwise authorizes the motion to be filed. Subject to subdivision (f), the trus-

tee may join requests for authority to reject multiple executory contracts or unexpired leases in one motion.

(f) Omnibus Motions

A motion to reject or, if permitted under subdivision (e), a motion to assume or assign multiple executory contracts or unexpired leases that are not between the same parties shall:

(1) state in a conspicuous place that parties receiving the omnibus motion should locate their names and their contracts or leases listed in the motion;

(2) list parties alphabetically and identify the corresponding contract or lease;

(3) specify the terms, including the curing of defaults, for each requested assumption or assignment;

(4) specify the terms, including the identity of each assignee and the adequate assurance of future performance by each assignee, for each requested assignment;

(5) be numbered consecutively with other omnibus motions to assume, assign, or reject executory contracts or unexpired leases; and

(6) be limited to no more than 100 executory contracts or unexpired leases.

(g) Finality of Determination

The finality of any order respecting an executory contract or unexpired lease included in an omnibus motion shall be determined as though such contract or lease had been the subject of a separate motion.

(As amended Mar. 30, 1987, eff. Aug. 1, 1987; Apr. 30, 1991, eff. Aug. 1, 1991; Apr. 22, 1993, eff. Aug. 1, 1993; Apr. 26, 1999, eff. Dec. 1, 1999; Apr. 30, 2007, eff. Dec. 1, 2007; Mar. 26, 2009, eff. Dec. 1, 2009.)

ADVISORY COMMITTEE NOTES

Section 365(a) of the Code requires court approval for the assumption or rejection of an executory contract by the trustee or debtor in possession. The trustee or debtor in possession may also assign an executory contract, § 365(f)(1), but must first assume the contract, § 365(f)(2). Rule 6006 provides a procedure for obtaining court approval. It does not apply to the automatic rejection of contracts which are not assumed in chapter 7 liquidation cases within 60 days after the order for relief, or to the assumption or rejection of contracts in a plan pursuant to § 1123(b)(2) or § 1322(b)(7).

Subdivision (a) by referring to Rule 9014 requires a motion to be brought for the assumption, rejection, or assignment of an executory contract. Normally, the motion will be brought by the trustee, debtor in possession or debtor in a chapter 9 or chapter 13 case. The authorization to assume a contract and to assign it may be sought in a single motion and determined by a single order.

Subdivision (b) makes applicable the same motion procedure when the other party to the contract seeks to require the chapter officer to take some action. Section 365(d)(2) recognizes that this procedure is available to these contractual parties. This provision of the Code and subdivision of the rule apply only in chapter 9, 11 and 13 cases. A motion is not necessary in chapter 7 cases because in those cases a contract is deemed rejected if the trustee does not timely assume it.

Subdivision (c) provides for the court to set a hearing on a motion made under subdivision (a) or (b). The other party to the contract should be given appropriate notice of the hearing and the court may order that other parties in interest, such as a creditors' committee, also be given notice.

1987 Amendments

Subdivisions (a) and (b) are amended to conform to the 1984 amendment to § 365 of the Code, which governs assumption or rejection of time share interests.

Section 1113, governing collective bargaining agreements, was added to the Code in 1984. It sets out requirements that must be met before a collective bargaining agreement may be rejected. The application to reject a collective bargaining agreement referred to in § 1113 shall be made by motion. The motion to reject creates a contested matter under Rule 9014, and service is made pursuant to Rule 7004 on the representative of the employees. The time periods set forth in § 1113(d) govern the scheduling of the hearing and disposition of a motion to reject the agreement.

1991 Amendments

References to time share interests are deleted as unnecessary. Time share interests are within the scope of this rule to the extent that they are governed by § 365 of the Code.

Subdivision (b) is amended to include chapter 12 cases.

Subdivision (c) is amended to enable the United States trustee to appear and be heard on the issues relating to the assumption or rejection of executory contracts and unexpired leases. See §§ 307, 365, and 1113 of the Code.

1993 Amendments

This rule is amended to delete the requirement for an actual hearing when no request for a hearing is made. See rule 9014.

1999 Amendments

Subdivision (d) is added to provide sufficient time for a party to request a stay pending appeal of an order authorizing the assignment of an executory contract or unexpired lease under § 365(f) of the Code before the assignment is consummated. The stay under subdivision (d) does not affect the time for filing a notice of appeal in accordance with Rule 8002.

The court may, in its discretion, order that Rule 6006(d) is not applicable so that the executory contract or unexpired lease may be assigned immediately in accordance with the order entered by the court. Alternatively, the court may order that the stay under Rule 6006(d) is for a fixed period less than 10 days.

GAP Report on Rule 6006. No changes since publication.

2007 Amendments

The rule is amended to authorize the use of omnibus motions to reject multiple executory contracts and unexpired leases. In some cases there may be numerous executory contracts and unexpired leases, and this rule permits the combining of up to one hundred of these contracts and leases in a single motion to initiate the contested matter.

The rule also is amended to authorize the use of a single motion to assume or assign executory contracts and unexpired leases (i) when such contracts and leases are with a single nondebtor party, (ii) when such contracts and leases are being assigned to the same assignee, (iii) when the trustee proposes to assume, but not assign to more than one assignee, real property leases, or (iv) the court authorizes the filing of a joint motion to assume or to assume and assign executory contracts and unexpired leases under other circumstances that are not specifically recognized in the rule.

An omnibus motion to assume, assign, or reject multiple executory contracts and unexpired leases must comply with the procedural requirements set forth in subdivision (f) of the rule, unless the court orders otherwise. These requirements are intended to ensure that the nondebtor parties to the contracts and leases receive effective notice of the motion. Among those requirements is the requirement in subdivision (f)(5) that these motions be consecutively numbered (e.g., Debtor in Possession's First Omnibus Motion for Authority to Assume Executory Contracts and Unexpired Leases, Debtor in Possession's Second Omnibus Motion for Authority to Assume Executory Contracts and Unexpired Leases, etc.). There may be a need for several of these motions in a particular case. Numbering the motions consecutively is essential to keep track of these motions on the court's docket and should avoid confusion that might otherwise result from similar or identically-titled motions.

Subdivision (g) of the rule provides that the finality of any order respecting an executory contract or unexpired lease included in an omnibus motion shall be determined as though such contract or lease had been the subject of a separate motion. A party seeking to appeal any such order is neither required, nor permitted, to await the court's resolution of all other contracts or leases included in the omnibus motion to obtain appellate review of the order. The rule permits the listing of multiple contracts or leases for convenience, and that convenience should not impede timely review of the court's decision with respect to each contract or lease.

2009 Amendments

The rule is amended to implement changes in connection with the amendment to Rule 9006(a) and the manner by which time is computed under the rules. The deadline in the rule is amended to substitute a deadline that is a multiple of seven days. Throughout the rules, deadlines are amended in the following manner:

- 5–day periods become 7–day periods
- 10–day periods become 14–day periods
- 15–day periods become 14–day periods
- 20–day periods become 21–day periods
- 25–day periods become 28–day periods

CROSS REFERENCES

Assumption or rejection of executory contracts by trustee, see 11 USCA § 365.

Commodity contracts,

Compliance by trustee with customer's instructions, see 11 USCA § 765.

Definition of, see 11 USCA § 761.

Treatment of customer property, see 11 USCA § 766.

Motions, form and service, see Fed.Rules Bankr.Proc. Rule 9013, 11 USCA.

Provisions in plan for assumption or rejection of certain executory contracts or unexpired leases, see 11 USCA §§ 1123 and 1322.

Rule 6007. Abandonment or Disposition of Property

(a) Notice of proposed abandonment or disposition; objections; hearing

Unless otherwise directed by the court, the trustee or debtor in possession shall give notice of a proposed abandonment or disposition of property to the United States trustee, all creditors, indenture trustees, and committees elected pursuant to § 705 or appointed pursuant to § 1102 of the Code. A party in interest may file and serve an objection within 14 days of the mailing of the notice, or within the time fixed by the court. If a timely objection is made, the court shall set a hearing on notice to the United States trustee and to other entities as the court may direct.

(b) Motion by party in interest

A party in interest may file and serve a motion requiring the trustee or debtor in possession to abandon property of the estate.

(c) [Abrogated]

(As amended Mar. 30, 1987, eff. Aug. 1, 1987; Apr. 30, 1991, eff. Aug. 1, 1991; Apr. 22, 1993, eff. Aug. 1, 1993; Mar. 26, 2009, eff. Dec. 1, 2009.)

ADVISORY COMMITTEE NOTES

Sections 554 and 725 of the Code permit and require abandonment and disposition of property of the estate. Pursuant to § 554, the trustee may abandon property but only after notice and hearing. This section is applicable in chapter 7, 11 and 13 cases. Section 725 requires the trustee to dispose of property in which someone other than the estate has an interest, prior to final distribution. It applies only in chapter 7 cases. Notice and hearing are also required conditions. Section 102(1) provides that "notice and hearing" is construed to mean appropriate notice and an opportunity for a hearing. Neither § 554 nor § 725 specify to whom the notices are to be sent. This rule does not apply to § 554(c). Pursuant to that subsection, property is deemed abandoned if it is not administered. A hearing is not required by the statute.

Subdivision (a) requires the notices to be sent to all creditors, indenture trustees, and committees elected under § 705 or appointed under § 1102 of the Code. This may appear burdensome, expensive and inefficient but the subdivision is in keeping with the Code's requirement for notice and the Code's intent to remove the bankruptcy judge from undisputed matters. The burden, expense and inefficiency can be alleviated in large measure by incorporating the notice into or together with the notice of the meeting of creditors so that separate notices would not be required.

Subdivision (b) implements § 554(b) which specifies that a party in interest may request an order that the trustee abandon property. The rule specifies that the request be by motion and, pursuant to the Code, lists the parties who should receive notice.

Subdivision (c) requires a hearing when an objection under subdivision (a) is filed or a motion under subdivision (b) is made. Filing of an objection is sufficient to require a hearing; a separate or joined request for a hearing is unnecessary since the objection itself is tantamount to such a request.

1991 Amendments

This rule is amended to conform to the 1986 amendments to 28 U.S.C. § 586(a) and to the Code. The United States trustee monitors the progress of the case and has standing to raise, appear and be heard on the issues relating to the abandonment or other disposition of property. See §§ 307 and 554 of the Code. Committees of retired employees appointed under § 1114 are not entitled to notice under subdivision (a) of this rule.

1993 Amendments

This rule is amended to clarify that when a motion is made pursuant to subdivision (b), a hearing is not required if a hearing is not requested or if there is no opposition to the motion. *See* Rule 9014. Other amendments are stylistic and make no substantive change.

2009 Amendments

The rule is amended to implement changes in connection with the amendment to Rule 9006(a) and the manner by which time is computed under the rules. The deadline in the rule is amended to substitute a deadline that is a multiple of seven days. Throughout the rules, deadlines are amended in the following manner:

- 5–day periods become 7–day periods
- 10–day periods become 14–day periods
- 15–day periods become 14–day periods
- 20–day periods become 21–day periods
- 25–day periods become 28–day periods

CROSS REFERENCES

Abandonment of property burdensome or of little value to estate, see 11 USCA § 554.

Abandonment of railroad line,

Authorization by court, see 11 USCA § 1170.

Provision of plan, see 11 USCA § 1172.

Disposition of property with lien in liquidation case, see 11 USCA § 725.

Motions, form and service, see Fed.Rules Bankr.Proc. Rule 9013, 11 USCA.

Rule 6008. Redemption of Property From Lien or Sale

On motion by the debtor, trustee, or debtor in possession and after hearing on notice as the court may direct, the court may authorize the redemption of property from a lien or from a sale to enforce a lien in accordance with applicable law.

ADVISORY COMMITTEE NOTES

This rule is derived from former Bankruptcy Rule 609. No provision in the Code addresses the trustee's right of redemption. Ordinarily the secured creditor should be given notice of the trustee's motion so that any objection may be raised to the proposed redemption.

The rule applies also to a debtor exercising a right of redemption pursuant to § 722. A proceeding under that section is governed by Rule 9014.

CROSS REFERENCES

Motions, form and service, see Fed.Rules Bankr.Proc. Rule 9013, 11 USCA.

Tangible personal property,

     Enforceability of agreement between holder of claim and debtor having consideration based on dischargeable debt, see 11 USCA § 524.

     Redemption of exempt or abandoned property from lien securing dischargeable consumer debt, see 11 USCA § 722.

Rule 6009.   Prosecution and Defense of Proceedings by Trustee or Debtor in Possession

With or without court approval, the trustee or debtor in possession may prosecute or may enter an appearance and defend any pending action or proceeding by or against the debtor, or commence and prosecute any action or proceeding in behalf of the estate before any tribunal.

ADVISORY COMMITTEE NOTES

This rule is derived from former Bankruptcy Rule 610.

CROSS REFERENCES

Suspension of statutes of limitations, see 11 USCA § 108.

Voluntary or involuntary petition filed to operate as automatic stay on other proceedings, see 11 USCA § 362.

Rule 6010.   Proceeding to Avoid Indemnifying Lien or Transfer to Surety

If a lien voidable under § 547 of the Code has been dissolved by the furnishing of a bond or other obligation and the surety thereon has been indemnified by the transfer of, or the creation of a lien upon, nonexempt property of the debtor, the surety shall be joined as a defendant in any proceeding to avoid the indemnifying transfer or lien. Such proceeding is governed by the rules in Part VII.

(As amended Apr. 30, 1991, eff. Aug. 1, 1991.)

ADVISORY COMMITTEE NOTES

This rule is derived from former Bankruptcy Rule 612.

1991 Amendments

This rule is amended to conform to § 550(a) of the Code which provides that the trustee may recover the property transferred in a voidable transfer. The value of the property may be recovered in lieu of the property itself only if the court so orders.

CROSS REFERENCES

Motions, form and service, see Fed.Rules Bankr.Proc. Rule 9013, 11 USCA.

Rule 6011.   Disposal of Patient Records in Health Care Business Case

(a) Notice by publication under § 351(1)(A)

A notice regarding the claiming or disposing of patient records under § 351(1)(A) shall not identify any patient by name or other identifying information, but shall:

     (1) identify with particularity the health care facility whose patient records the trustee proposes to destroy;

     (2) state the name, address, telephone number, email address, and website, if any, of a person from whom information about the patient records may be obtained;

     (3) state how to claim the patient records; and

     (4) state the date by which patient records must be claimed, and that if they are not so claimed the records will be destroyed.

(b) Notice by mail under § 351(1)(B)

Subject to applicable nonbankruptcy law relating to patient privacy, a notice regarding the claiming or disposing of patient records under § 351(1)(B) shall, in addition to including the information in subdivision (a), direct that a patient's family member or other representative who receives the notice inform the patient of the notice. Any notice under this subdivision shall be mailed to the patient and any family member or other contact person whose name and address have been given to the trustee or the debtor for the purpose of providing information regarding the patient's health care, to the Attorney General of the State where the health care facility is located, and to any insurance company known to have provided health care insurance to the patient.

(c) Proof of compliance with notice requirement

Unless the court orders the trustee to file proof of compliance with § 351(1)(B) under seal, the trustee shall not file, but shall maintain, the proof of compliance for a reasonable time.

(d) Report of destruction of records

The trustee shall file, no later than 30 days after the destruction of patient records under § 351(3), a report certifying that the unclaimed records have been destroyed and explaining the method used to effect the destruction. The report shall not identify any patient by name or other identifying information.

(Added Apr. 23, 2008, eff. Dec. 1, 2008.)

ADVISORY COMMITTEE NOTES

2008 Adoption

This rule is new. It implements § 351(1), which was added to the Code by the 2005 amendments. That provision requires the trustee to notify patients that their patient records will be destroyed if they remain unclaimed for one year after the publication of a notice in an appropriate newspaper. The Code provision also requires that individualized notice be sent to each patient and to the patient's family member or other contact person.

The variety of health care businesses and the range of current and former patients present the need for flexibility in the creation and publication of the notices that will be given. Nevertheless, there are some matters that must be included in any notice being given to patients, their family members, and contact persons to ensure that sufficient information is provided to these persons regarding the trustee's intent to dispose of patient records. Subdivision (a) of this rule lists the minimum requirements for notices given under § 351(1)(A), and subdivision (b) governs the form of notices under § 351(1)(B). Notices given under this rule are subject to provisions under applicable federal and state law that relate to the protection of patients' privacy, such as the Health Insurance Portability and Accountability Act of 1996, Pub. L. No. 104–191 (HIPAA).

Subdivision (c) directs the trustee to maintain proof of compliance with § 351(1)(B), but because the proof of compliance may contain patient names that should or must remain confidential, it prohibits filing the proof of compliance unless the court orders the trustee to file it under seal.

Subdivision (d) requires the trustee to file a report with the court regarding the destruction of patient records. This certification is intended to ensure that the trustee properly completed the destruction process. However, because the report will be filed with the court and ordinarily will be available to the public under § 107, the names, addresses, and other identifying information of patients are not to be included in the report to protect patient privacy.

PART VII—ADVERSARY PROCEEDINGS

Rule 7001. Scope of Rules of Part VII

An adversary proceeding is governed by the rules of this Part VII. The following are adversary proceedings:

(1) a proceeding to recover money or property, other than a proceeding to compel the debtor to deliver property to the trustee, or a proceeding under § 554(b) or § 725 of the Code, Rule 2017, or Rule 6002;

(2) a proceeding to determine the validity, priority, or extent of a lien or other interest in property, but not a proceeding under Rule 3012 or Rule 4003(d);

(3) a proceeding to obtain approval under § 363(h) for the sale of both the interest of the estate and of a co-owner in property;

(4) a proceeding to object to or revoke a discharge, other than an objection to discharge under §§[1] 727(a)(8), (a)(9), or 1328(f);

(5) a proceeding to revoke an order of confirmation of a chapter 11, chapter 12, or chapter 13 plan;

(6) a proceeding to determine the dischargeability of a debt;

(7) a proceeding to obtain an injunction or other equitable relief, except when a chapter 9, chapter 11, chapter 12, or chapter 13 plan provides for the relief;

(8) a proceeding to subordinate any allowed claim or interest, except when a chapter 9, chapter 11, chapter 12, or chapter 13 plan provides for subordination;

(9) a proceeding to obtain a declaratory judgment relating to any of the foregoing; or

(10) a proceeding to determine a claim or cause of action removed under 28 U.S.C. § 1452.

(As amended Mar. 30, 1987, eff. Aug. 1, 1987; Apr. 30, 1991, eff. Aug. 1, 1991; Apr. 26, 1999, eff. Dec. 1, 1999; Apr. 28, 2010, eff. Dec. 1, 2010; Apr. 27, 2017, eff. Dec. 1, 2017.)

[1] So in original. Probably should be only one section symbol.

ADVISORY COMMITTEE NOTES

The rules in Part VII govern the procedural aspects of litigation involving the matters referred to in this Rule 7001. Under Rule 9014 some of the Part VII rules also apply to contested matters.

These Part VII rules are based on the premise that to the extent possible practice before the bankruptcy courts and the district courts should be the same. These rules either incorporate or are adaptations of most of the Federal Rules of Civil Procedure. Although the Part VII rules of the former

Bankruptcy Rules also relied heavily on the F.R.Civ.P., the former Part VII rules departed from the civil practice in two significant ways: a trial or pretrial conference had to be scheduled as soon as the adversary proceeding was filed and pleadings had to be filed within periods shorter than those established by the F.R.Civ.P. These departures from the civil practice have been eliminated.

The content and numbering of these Part VII rules correlate to the content and numbering of the F.R.Civ.P. Most, but not all, of the F.R.Civ.P. have a comparable Part VII rule. When there is no Part VII rule with a number corresponding to a particular F.R.Civ.P., Parts V and IX of these rules must be consulted to determine if one of the rules in those parts deals with the subject. The list below indicates the F.R.Civ. P., or subdivision thereof, covered by a rule in either Part V or Part IX.

F.R.Civ.P.	Rule in Part V or IX
6	9006
7(b)	9013
10(a)	9004(b)
11	9011
38, 39	9015(a)–(e)
47–51	9015(f)
43, 44, 44.1	9017
45	9016
58	9021
59	9023
60	9024
61	9005
63	9028
77(a), (b), (c)	5001
77(d)	9022(d)
79(a)–(d)	5003
81(c)	9027
83	9029
92	9030

Proceedings to which the rules in Part VII apply directly include those brought to avoid transfers by the debtor under §§ 544, 545, 547, 548 and 549 of the Code; subject to important exceptions, proceedings to recover money or property; proceedings on bonds under Rules 5008(d) and 9025; proceedings under Rule 4004 to determine whether a discharge in a chapter 7 or 11 case should be denied because of an objection grounded on § 727 and proceedings in a chapter 7 or 13 case to revoke a discharge as provided in §§ 727(d) or 1328(e); and proceedings initiated pursuant to § 523(c) of the Code to determine the dischargeability of a particular debt. Those proceedings were classified as adversary proceedings under former Bankruptcy Rule 701.

Also included as adversary proceedings are proceedings to revoke an order of confirmation of a plan in a chapter 11 or 13 case as provided in §§ 1144 and 1330, to subordinate under § 510(c), other than as part of a plan, an allowed claim or interest, and to sell under § 363(h) both the interest of the estate and a co-owner in property.

Declaratory judgments with respect to the subject matter of the various adversary proceedings are also adversary proceedings.

Any claim or cause of action removed to a bankruptcy court pursuant to 28 U.S.C. § 1478 is also an adversary proceeding.

Unlike former Bankruptcy Rule 701, requests for relief from an automatic stay do not commence an adversary proceeding. Section 362(e) of the Code and Rule 4001 establish an expedited schedule for judicial disposition of requests for relief from the automatic stay. The formalities of the adversary proceeding process and the time for serving pleadings are not well suited to the expedited schedule. The motion practice prescribed in Rule 4001 is best suited to such requests because the court has the flexibility to fix hearing dates and other deadlines appropriate to the particular situation.

Clause (1) contains important exceptions. A person with an interest in property in the possession of the trustee or debtor in possession may seek to recover or reclaim that property under § 554(b) or § 725 of the Code. Since many attempts to recover or reclaim property under these two sections do not generate disputes, application of the formalities of the Part VII Rules is not appropriate. Also excluded from adversary proceedings is litigation arising from an examination under Rule 2017 of a debtor's payments of money or transfers of property to an attorney representing the debtor in a case under the Code or an examination of a superseded administration under Rule 6002.

Exemptions and objections thereto are governed by Rule 4003. Filing of proofs of claim and the allowances thereof are governed by Rules 3001–3005, and objections to claims are governed by Rule 3007. When an objection to a claim is joined with a demand for relief of the kind specified in this Rule 7001, the matter becomes an adversary proceeding. See Rule 3007.

1987 Amendment

Another exception is added to clause (1). A trustee may proceed by motion to recover property from the debtor.

1991 Amendment

Clauses (5) and (8) are amended to include chapter 12 plans.

1999 Amendments

This rule is amended to recognize that an adversary proceeding is not necessary to obtain injunctive or other equitable relief that is provided for in a plan under circumstances in which substantive law permits the relief. Other amendments are stylistic.

GAP Report on Rule 7001. No changes since publication, except for stylistic changes.

2010 Amendments

Paragraph (4) of the rule is amended to create an exception for objections to discharge under §§ 727(a)(8), (a)(9), and 1328(f) of the Code. Because objections to discharge on these grounds typically present issues more easily resolved than other objections to discharge, the more formal procedures applicable to adversary proceedings, such as commencement by a complaint, are not required. Instead, objections on these three grounds are governed by Rule 4004(d). In an appropriate case, however, Rule 9014(c) allows the court to order that additional provisions of Part VII of the rules apply to these matters.

Subdivision (2) is amended to provide that the determination of the amount of a secured claim under Rule 3012, like a proceeding by the debtor to avoid a lien on or other transfer of exempt property under Rule 4003(d), does not require an adversary proceeding. The determination of the amount of a secured claim may be sought by motion or through a chapter 12 or chapter 13 plan in accordance with Rule 3012. An adversary proceeding continues to be required for lien avoidance not governed by Rule 4003(d).

CROSS REFERENCES

Adversarial nature of proceeding,

Avoidance of indemnifying lien or transfer to surety, see Fed.Rules Bankr.Proc. Rule 6010, 11 USCA.

Commenced by complaint objecting to discharge, see Fed.Rules Bankr.Proc. Rule 4004, 11 USCA.

Commenced by complaint to obtain determination of debt's dischargeability, see Fed.Rules Bankr.Proc. Rule 4007, 11 USCA.

Joinder of objection to claim with demand for relief, see Fed.Rules Bankr.Proc. Rule 3007, 11 USCA.

Liability of sureties on bond or stipulation or other undertaking, see Fed.Rules Bankr.Proc. Rule 9025, 11 USCA.

Applicability of rules of this part to removed claim or cause of action, see Fed.Rules Bankr.Proc. Rule 9027, 11 USCA.

Contested matters, applicability of and notice to parties of applicability of rules of this part, see Fed.Rules Bankr.Proc. Rule 9014, 11 USCA.

Effect of amendment of Federal Rules of Civil Procedure, see Fed.Rules Bankr.Proc. Rule 9032, 11 USCA.

Meanings of words in Federal Rules of Civil Procedure when applicable, see Fed.Rules Bankr.Proc. Rule 9002, 11 USCA.

Rule 7002. References to Federal Rules of Civil Procedure

Whenever a Federal Rule of Civil Procedure applicable to adversary proceedings makes reference to another Federal Rule of Civil Procedure, the reference shall be read as a reference to the Federal Rule of Civil Procedure as modified in this Part VII.

ADVISORY COMMITTEE NOTES

Rules 5, 12, 13, 14, 25, 27, 30, 41 and 52 F.R.Civ.P. are made applicable to adversary proceedings by Part VII. Each of those rules contains a cross reference to another Federal Rule; however, the Part VII rule which incorporates the cross-referenced Federal Rule modifies the Federal Rule in some way. Under this Rule 7002 the cross reference is to the Federal Rule as modified by Part VII. For example, Rule 5 F.R.Civ.P., which is made applicable to adversary proceedings by Rule 7005, contains a reference to Rule 4 F.R.Civ.P. Under this Rule 7002, the cross reference is to Rule 4 F.R.Civ.P. as modified by Rule 7004.

Rules 7, 10, 12, 13, 14, 19, 22, 23.2, 24–37, 41, 45, 49, 50, 52, 55, 59, 60, 62 F.R.Civ.P. are made applicable to adversary proceedings by Part VII or generally to cases under the Code by Part IX. Each of those Federal Rules contains a cross reference to another Federal Rule which is not modified by the Part VII or Part IX rule which makes the cross-referenced Federal Rule applicable. Since the cross-referenced rule is not modified by a Part VII rule this Rule 7002 does not apply.

Rule 7003. Commencement of Adversary Proceeding

Rule 3 F.R.Civ.P. applies in adversary proceedings.

ADVISORY COMMITTEE NOTES

Rule 5005(a) requires that a complaint commencing an adversary proceeding be filed with the court in which the case under the Code is pending unless 28 U.S.C. § 1473 authorizes the filing of the complaint in another district.

CROSS REFERENCES

Complaint filed with court in which case is pending, see Fed.Rules Bankr.Proc. Rule 5005, 11 USCA.

Rule 7004. Process; Service of Summons, Complaint

(a) Summons; service; proof of service

(1) Except as provided in Rule 7004(a)(2), Rule 4(a), (b), (c)(1), (d)(5), (e)–(j), (*l*), and (m) F.R.Civ.P. applies in adversary proceedings. Personal service under Rule 4(e)–(j) F.R.Civ.P. may be made by any person at least 18 years of age who is not a party, and the summons may be delivered by the clerk to any such person.

(2) The clerk may sign, seal, and issue a summons electronically by putting an "s/" before the clerk's name and including the court's seal on the summons.

(b) Service by first class mail

Except as provided in subdivision (h), in addition to the methods of service authorized by Rule 4(e)–(j) F.R.Civ.P., service may be made within the United States by first class mail postage prepaid as follows:

(1) Upon an individual other than an infant or incompetent, by mailing a copy of the summons and complaint to the individual's dwelling house or usual place of abode or to the place where the individual regularly conducts a business or profession.

(2) Upon an infant or an incompetent person, by mailing a copy of the summons and complaint to the person upon whom process is prescribed to be served by the law of the state in which service is made when an action is brought against such a defendant in the courts of general jurisdiction of that state. The summons and complaint in that case shall be addressed to the person required to be served at that person's dwelling house or usual place of abode or at the place where the person regularly conducts a business or profession.

(3) Upon a domestic or foreign corporation or upon a partnership or other unincorporated association, by mailing a copy of the summons and com-

plaint to the attention of an officer, a managing or general agent, or to any other agent authorized by appointment or by law to receive service of process and, if the agent is one authorized by statute to receive service and the statute so requires, by also mailing a copy to the defendant.

(4) Upon the United States, by mailing a copy of the summons and complaint addressed to the civil process clerk at the office of the United States attorney for the district in which the action is brought and by mailing a copy of the summons and complaint to the Attorney General of the United States at Washington, District of Columbia, and in any action attacking the validity of an order of an officer or an agency of the United States not made a party, by also mailing a copy of the summons and complaint to that officer or agency. The court shall allow a reasonable time for service pursuant to this subdivision for the purpose of curing the failure to mail a copy of the summons and complaint to multiple officers, agencies, or corporations of the United States if the plaintiff has mailed a copy of the summons and complaint either to the civil process clerk at the office of the United States attorney or to the Attorney General of the United States.

(5) Upon any officer or agency of the United States, by mailing a copy of the summons and complaint to the United States as prescribed in paragraph (4) of this subdivision and also to the officer or agency. If the agency is a corporation, the mailing shall be as prescribed in paragraph (3) of this subdivision of this rule. The court shall allow a reasonable time for service pursuant to this subdivision for the purpose of curing the failure to mail a copy of the summons and complaint to multiple officers, agencies, or corporations of the United States if the plaintiff has mailed a copy of the summons and complaint either to the civil process clerk at the office of the United States attorney or to the Attorney General of the United States. If the United States trustee is the trustee in the case and service is made upon the United States trustee solely as trustee, service may be made as prescribed in paragraph (10) of this subdivision of this rule.

(6) Upon a state or municipal corporation or other governmental organization thereof subject to suit, by mailing a copy of the summons and complaint to the person or office upon whom process is prescribed to be served by the law of the state in which service is made when an action is brought against such a defendant in the courts of general jurisdiction of that state, or in the absence of the designation of any such person or office by state law, then to the chief executive officer thereof.

(7) Upon a defendant of any class referred to in paragraph (1) or (3) of this subdivision of this rule, it is also sufficient if a copy of the summons and complaint is mailed to the entity upon whom service is prescribed to be served by any statute of the United States or by the law of the state in which service is made when an action is brought against such a defendant in the court of general jurisdiction of that state.

(8) Upon any defendant, it is also sufficient if a copy of the summons and complaint is mailed to an agent of such defendant authorized by appointment or by law to receive service of process, at the agent's dwelling house or usual place of abode or at the place where the agent regularly carries on a business or profession and, if the authorization so requires, by mailing also a copy of the summons and complaint to the defendant as provided in this subdivision.

(9) Upon the debtor, after a petition has been filed by or served upon the debtor and until the case is dismissed or closed, by mailing a copy of the summons and complaint to the debtor at the address shown in the petition or to such other address as the debtor may designate in a filed writing.

(10) Upon the United States trustee, when the United States trustee is the trustee in the case and service is made upon the United States trustee solely as trustee, by mailing a copy of the summons and complaint to an office of the United States trustee or another place designated by the United States trustee in the district where the case under the Code is pending.

(c) Service by publication

If a party to an adversary proceeding to determine or protect rights in property in the custody of the court cannot be served as provided in Rule 4(e)–(j) F.R.Civ.P. or subdivision (b) of this rule, the court may order the summons and complaint to be served by mailing copies thereof by first class mail, postage prepaid, to the party's last known address, and by at least one publication in such manner and form as the court may direct.

(d) Nationwide service of process

The summons and complaint and all other process except a subpoena may be served anywhere in the United States.

(e) Summons: time limit for service within the United States

Service made under Rule 4(e), (g), (h)(1), (i), or (j)(2) F.R.Civ.P. shall be by delivery of the summons and complaint within 7 days after the summons is issued. If service is by any authorized form of mail, the summons and complaint shall be deposited in the mail within 7 days after the summons is issued. If a summons is not timely delivered or mailed, another summons will be issued for service. This subdivision does not apply to service in a foreign country.

(f) Personal jurisdiction

If the exercise of jurisdiction is consistent with the Constitution and laws of the United States, serving a summons or filing a waiver of service in accordance with this rule or the subdivisions of Rule 4 F.R.Civ.P. made applicable by these rules is effective to establish personal jurisdiction over the person of any defendant with respect to a case under the Code or a civil proceeding arising under the Code, or arising in or related to a case under the Code.

(g) Service on debtor's attorney

If the debtor is represented by an attorney, whenever service is made upon the debtor under this Rule, service shall also be made upon the debtor's attorney by any means authorized under Rule 5(b) F.R.Civ.P.

(h) Service of process on an insured depository institution

Service on an insured depository institution (as defined in section 3 of the Federal Deposit Insurance Act) in a contested matter or adversary proceeding shall be made by certified mail addressed to an officer of the institution unless—

(1) the institution has appeared by its attorney, in which case the attorney shall be served by first class mail;

(2) the court orders otherwise after service upon the institution by certified mail of notice of an application to permit service on the institution by first class mail sent to an officer of the institution designated by the institution; or

(3) the institution has waived in writing its entitlement to service by certified mail by designating an officer to receive service.

(As amended Mar. 30, 1987, eff. Aug. 1, 1987; Apr. 30, 1991, eff. Aug. 1, 1991; Oct. 22, 1994, Pub.L. 103–394, Title I, § 114, 108 Stat. 4118; Apr. 23, 1996, eff. Dec. 1, 1996; Apr. 26, 1999, eff. Dec. 1, 1999; Apr. 25, 2005, eff. Dec. 1, 2005; Apr. 12, 2006, eff. Dec. 1, 2006; Mar. 26, 2009, eff. Dec. 1, 2009; Apr. 25, 2014, eff. Dec. 1, 2014; Apr. 26, 2018, eff. Dec. 1, 2018.)

ADVISORY COMMITTEE NOTES

Subdivision (a) of the rule, by incorporation of Rule 4(a), (b), (d), (e) and (g)–(i) F.R.Civ.P., governs the mechanics of issuance of a summons and its form, the manner of service on parties and their representatives, and service in foreign countries.

Subdivision (b), which is the same as former Rule 704(c), authorizes service of process by first class mail postage prepaid. This rule retains the modes of service contained in former Bankruptcy Rule 704. The former practice, in effect since 1976, has proven satisfactory.

Subdivision (c) is derived from former Bankruptcy Rule 704(d)(2).

Subdivision (d). Nationwide service of process is authorized by subdivision (d).

Subdivision (e) authorizes service by delivery on individuals and corporations in foreign countries if the party to be served is the debtor or any person required to perform the duties of the debtor and certain other persons, the adversary proceeding involves property in the custody of the bankruptcy court, or if federal or state law authorizes such service in a foreign country.

Subdivision (f). The requirement of former Bankruptcy Rule 704 that the summons be served within 10 days is carried over into these rules by subdivision (f).

1987 Amendment

Subdivision (a) is amended to make Rule 4(j) F.R.Civ.P. applicable to service of the summons. If service is not completed within 120 days of the filing of the complaint, the complaint may be dismissed.

Technical amendments are made to subdivisions (a), (b), (e), and (f) to conform to recent amendments to Rule 4 F.R.Civ.P.

1991 Amendment

The United States trustee may serve as trustee in a case pursuant to 28 U.S.C. § 586(a)(2) and §§ 701(a)(2), 1202(a), and 1302(a) of the Code. This rule is amended to avoid the necessity of mailing copies of a summons and complaint or other pleadings to the Attorney General and to the United States attorney when service on the United States trustee is required only because the United States trustee is acting as a case trustee. For example, a proceeding commenced by a creditor to dismiss a case for unreasonable delay under § 707(a) is governed by Rule 9014 which requires service on the trustee pursuant to the requirements of Rule 7004 for the service of a summons and complaint. The Attorney General and the United States attorney would have no interest in receiving a copy of the motion to dismiss. Mailing to the office of the United States trustee when acting as the case trustee is sufficient in such cases.

The words "with the court" in subdivision (b)(9) are deleted as unnecessary. See Rules 5005(a) and 9001(3).

The new paragraph (10) of subdivision (b) does not affect requirements for service of process on the United States trustee when sued or otherwise a party to a litigation unrelated to its capacity as a trustee. If a proceeding is commenced against the United States trustee which is unrelated to the United States trustee's role as trustee, the requirements of paragraph (5) of subdivision (b) of this rule would apply.

Subdivision (g) is added in anticipation of substantial amendment to, and restructuring of subdivisions of, Rule 4 F.R.Civ.P. Any amendment to Rule 4 will not affect service in bankruptcy cases and proceedings until further amendment to the Bankruptcy Rules. On January 1, 1990, Rule 4 F.R.Civ.P. read as follows:

Rule 4 F.R.Civ.P.

PROCESS

(a) Summons: issuance. Upon the filing of the complaint the clerk shall forthwith issue a summons and deliver the summons of the plaintiff or the plaintiff's attorney, who shall be responsible for prompt service of the summons and a copy of the complaint. Upon request of the plaintiff separate or additional summons shall issue against any defendants.

(b) Same: form. The summons shall be signed by the clerk, be under the seal of the court, contain the name of the court and the names of the parties, be directed to the defendant, state the name and address of the plaintiff's attorney, if any, otherwise the plaintiff's address, and the time within which these rules require the defendant to appear and defend, and shall notify the defendant that in case of the defendant's failure to do so judgment by default will be rendered against the defendant for the relief demanded in the complaint. When, under Rule 4(e), service is made pursuant to a statute or rule of court of a state, the summons, or notice, or order in lieu of summons shall correspond as nearly as may be to that required by the statute or rule.

(c) Service

(1) [Not applicable.]

(2)(A) [Not applicable.]

(B) [Not applicable.]

(C) A summons and complaint may be served upon a defendant of any class referred to in paragraph (1) or (3) of subdivision (d) of this rule—

(i) pursuant to the law of the State in which the district court held for the service of summons or other like process upon such defendant in an action brought in the courts of general jurisdiction of that State, or

(ii) [Not applicable.]

(D) [Not applicable.]

(E) [Not applicable.]

(3) [Not applicable.]

(d) Summons and complaint: person to be served. The summons and complaint shall be served together. The plaintiff shall furnish the person making service with such copies as are necessary. Service shall be made as follows:

(1) Upon an individual other than an infant or an incompetent person, by delivering a copy of the summons and of the complaint to the individual personally or by leaving copies thereof at the individual's dwelling house or usual place of abode with some person of suitable age and discretion then residing therein or by delivering a copy of the summons and of the complaint to an agent authorized by appointment or by law to receive service of process.

(2) Upon an infant or an incompetent person, by serving the summons and complaint in the manner prescribed by the law of the state in which the service is made for the service of summons or other like process upon any such defendant in an action brought in the courts of general jurisdiction of that state.

(3) Upon a domestic or foreign corporation or upon a partnership or other unincorporated association which the subject to suit under a common name, by delivering a copy of the summons and of the complaint to an officer, a managing or general agent, or to any other agent authorized by appointment or by law to receive service of process and, if the agent is one authorized by statute to receive service and the statute so requires, by also mailing a copy to the defendant.

(4) Upon the United States, by delivering a copy of the summons and of the complaint to the United States attorney for the district in which the action is brought or to an assistant United States attorney or clerical employee designated by the United States attorney in a writing filed with the clerk of the court and by sending a copy of the summons and of the complaint by registered or certified mail to the Attorney General of the United States at Washington, District of Columbia, and in any action attacking the validity of an order of an officer or agency of the United States not made a party, by also sending a copy of the summons and of the complaint by registered or certified mail to such officer or agency.

(5) Upon an officer or agency of the United States, by serving the United States and by sending a copy of the summons and of the complaint by registered or certified mail to such officer or agency. If the agency is a corporation the copy shall be delivered as provided in paragraph (3) of this subdivision of this rule.

(6) Upon a state or municipal corporation or other governmental organization thereof subject to suit, by delivering a copy of the summons and of the complaint to the chief executive officer thereof or by serving the summons and complaint in the manner prescribed by the law of that state for the service of summons or other like process upon any such defendant.

(e) Summons: service upon party not inhabitant of or found within state. Whenever a statute of the United States or an order of court thereunder provides for service of a summons, or of a notice, or of an order in lieu of summons upon a party not an inhabitant of or found within the state in which the district court is held, service may be made under the circumstances and in the manner prescribed by the statute or order, or, if there is no provision therein prescribing the manner of service, in a manner stated in this rule. Whenever a statute or rule of court of the state in which the district court is held provides (1) for service of a summons, or of a notice, or of an order in lieu of summons upon a party not an inhabitant of or found within the state, or (2) for service upon or notice to such a party to appear and respond or defend in an action by reason of the attachment or garnishment or similar seizure of the party's property located within the state, service may in either case be made under the circumstances and in the manner prescribed in the statute or rule.

(f) [Not applicable.]

(g) Return. The person serving the process shall make proof of service to the court promptly and in any event within the time during which the person served must respond to the process. If service is made by a person other than a United States marshal or deputy United States marshal, such person shall make affidavit thereof. If service is made under subdivision (c)(2)(C)(ii) of this rule, return shall be made by the sender's filing with the court the acknowledgement received pursuant to such subdivision. Failure to make proof of service does not affect the validity of the service.

(h) Amendment. At any time in its discretion and upon such terms as it deems just, the court may allow any process or proof of service thereof to be amended, unless it clearly appears that material prejudice would result to the substantial rights of the party against whom the process issued.

(i) Alternative provisions for service in a foreign country.

(1) Manner. When the federal or state law referred to in subdivision (e) of this rule authorizes service upon a party not an inhabitant of or found within the state in which the district court is held, and service is to be effected upon the party in a foreign country, it is also sufficient if service of the summons and complaint is made: (A) in the manner prescribed by the law of the foreign country for service in that country in an action in any of its courts of general jurisdiction; or (B) as directed by the foreign authority in response to a letter rogatory, when service in either case is reasonably calculated to give actual notice; or (C) upon an individual, by delivery to the individual personally, and upon a corporation or partnership or association, by delivery to an officer, a managing or general agent; or (D) by any form of mail, requiring a signed receipt, to be addressed and dispatched by the clerk of the court to the party to be served; or (E) above may be made by any person who is not a party and is not less than 18 years of age or who is designated by order of the district court or by the foreign court. On request, the clerk shall deliver the summons to the plaintiff for transmission to the person or the foreign court or officer who will make the service.

(2) **Return.** Proof of service may be made as prescribed by subdivision (g) of this rule, or by the law of the foreign country, or by order of the court. When service is made pursuant to subparagraph (1)(D) of this subdivision, proof of service shall include a receipt signed by the addressee or other evidence of delivery to the addressee satisfactory to the court.

(j) Summons: time limit for service. If a service of the summons and complaint is not made upon a defendant within 120 days after the filing of the complaint and the party on whose behalf such service was required cannot show good cause why such service was not made within that period, the action shall be dismissed as to that defendant without prejudice upon the court's own initiative with notice to such party or upon motion. This subdivision shall not apply to service in a foreign country pursuant to subdivision (i) of this rule.

1996 Amendments

The purpose of these amendments is to conform the rule to the 1993 revisions of Rule 4 F.R.Civ.P. and to make stylistic improvements. Rule 7004, as amended, continues to provide for service by first class mail as an alternative to the methods of personal service provided in Rule 4 F.R.Civ.P., except as provided in the new subdivision (h).

Rule 4(d)(2) F.R.Civ.P. provides a procedure by which the plaintiff may request by first class mail that the defendant waive service of the summons. This procedure is not applicable in adversary proceedings because it is not necessary in view of the availability of service by mail pursuant to Rule 7004(b). However, if a written waiver of service of a summons is made in an adversary proceeding, Rule 4(d)(1) F.R.Civ.P. applies so that the defendant does not thereby waive any objection to the venue or the jurisdiction of the court over the person of the defendant.

Subdivisions (b)(4) and (b)(5) are amended to conform to the 1993 amendments to Rule 4(i)(3) F.R.Civ.P., which protect the plaintiff from the hazard of losing a substantive right because of failure to comply with the requirements of multiple service when the United States or an officer, agency, or corporation of the United States is a defendant. These subdivisions also are amended to require that the summons and complaint be addressed to the civil process clerk at the office of the United States attorney.

Subdivision (e), which has governed service in a foreign country, is abrogated and Rule 4(f) and (h)(2) F.R.Civ.P., as substantially revised in 1993, are made applicable in adversary proceedings.

The new subdivision (f) is consistent with the 1993 amendments to F.R.Civ.P. 4(k)(2). It clarifies that service or filing a waiver of service in accordance with this rule or the applicable subdivisions of F.R.Civ.P. 4 is sufficient to establish personal jurisdiction over the defendant. See the committee note to the 1993 amendments to Rule 4 F.R.Civ.P.

Subdivision (g) is abrogated. This subdivision was promulgated in 1991 so that anticipated revisions to Rule 4 F.R.Civ.P. would not affect service of process in adversary proceedings until further amendment to Rule 7004.

Subdivision (h) and the first phrase of subdivision (b) were added by § 114 of the Bankruptcy Reform Act of 1994, Pub.L. No. 103–394, 108 Stat. 4106.

GAP Report on Rule 7004. After publication of the proposed amendments, Rule 7004(b) was amended and Rule 7004(h) was added by the Bankruptcy Reform Act of 1994 to provide for service by certified mail on an insured depository institution. The above draft includes those statutory amendments (without underlining new language or striking former language). No other changes have been made since publication, except for stylistic changes.

1999 Amendments

Subdivision (e) is amended so that the ten-day time limit for service of a summons does not apply if the summons is served in a foreign country.

GAP Report on Rule 7004. No changes since publication.

2005 Amendments

This amendment specifically authorizes the clerk to issue a summons electronically. In some bankruptcy cases the trustee or debtor in possession may commence hundreds of adversary proceedings simultaneously, and permitting the electronic signing and sealing of the summonses for those proceedings increases the efficiency of the clerk's office without any negative impact on any party. The rule only authorizes electronic issuance of the summons. It does not address the service requirements for the summons. Those requirements are set out elsewhere in Rule 7004, and nothing in Rule 7004(a)(2) should be construed as authorizing electronic service of a summons.

2006 Amendments

Under current Rule 7004, an entity may serve a summons and complaint upon the debtor by personal service or by mail. If the entity chooses to serve the debtor by mail, it must also serve a copy of the summons and complaint on the debtor's attorney by mail. If the entity effects personal service on the debtor, there is no requirement that the debtor's attorney also be served.

Subdivision (b)(9). The rule is amended to delete the reference in subdivision (b)(9) to the debtor's address as set forth in the statement of financial affairs. In 1991, the Official Form of the statement of financial affairs was revised and no longer includes a question regarding the debtor's current residence. Since that time, Official Form 1, the petition, has required the debtor to list both the debtor's residence and mailing address. Therefore, the subdivision is amended to delete the statement of financial affairs as a document that might contain an address at which the debtor can be served.

Subdivision (g). The rule is amended to require service on the debtor's attorney whenever the debtor is served with a summons and complaint. The amendment makes this change by deleting that portion of Rule 7004(b)(9) that requires service on the debtor's attorney when the debtor is served by mail, and relocates the obligation to serve the debtor's attorney into new subdivision (g). Service on the debtor's attorney is not limited to mail service, but may be accomplished by any means permitted under Rule 5(b) F.R.Civ.P.

2009 Amendments

The rule is amended to implement changes in connection with the amendment to Rule 9006(a) and the manner by which time is computed under the rules. The deadlines in the rule are amended to substitute a deadline that is a multiple of seven days. Throughout the rules, deadlines are amended in the following manner:

- 5–day periods become 7–day periods
- 10–day periods become 14–day periods
- 15–day periods become 14–day periods
- 20–day periods become 21–day periods
- 25–day periods become 28–day periods

2014 Amendments

Subdivision (e) is amended to alter the period of time during which service of the summons and complaint must be made. The amendment reduces that period from fourteen days to seven days after issuance of the summons. Because Rule 7012 provides that the defendant's time to answer the complaint is calculated from the date the summons is issued, a lengthy delay between issuance and service of the summons may unduly shorten the defendant's time to respond. The amendment is therefore intended to encourage prompt service after issuance of a summons. If service of the summons within any seven-day period is impracticable, a court retains the discretion to enlarge that period of time under Rule 9006(b).

Changes Made After Publication. A new sentence referring to the availability of an enlargement of time under Rule 9006(b) was added to the Committee Note. The only other change made after publication was stylistic.

2018 Amendments

In 1996, Rule 7004(a) was amended to incorporate by reference Rule 4(d)(1) of the Federal Rules of Civil Procedure. Civil Rule 4(d)(1) addresses the effect of a defendant's waiver of service. In 2007, Civil Rule 4 was amended, and the language of old Civil Rule 4(d)(1) was modified and renumbered as Civil Rule 4(d)(5). Accordingly, Rule 7004(a) is amended to update the cross-reference to Civil Rule 4.

HISTORICAL NOTES

Revision Notes and Legislative Reports

1994 Acts. For legislative history and purpose of Pub.L. 103–394, see 1994 U.S. Code Cong. and Adm. News, p. 3340.

References in Text

Section 3 of the Federal Deposit Insurance Act, referred to in subd. (h), is Act Sept. 21, 1950, c. 967, § 2[3], 64 Stat. 873, as amended, which is classified to section 1813 of Title 12, Banks and Banking.

Effective and Applicability Provisions

1994 Acts. Amendment by Pub.L. 103–394 effective on Oct. 22, 1994, and not to apply with respect to cases commenced under Title 11 of the United States Code before Oct. 22, 1994, see section 702 of Pub.L. 103–394, set out as a note under section 101 of Title 11, Bankruptcy.

Severability of Provisions

If any provision of or amendment made by Pub.L. 103–394 or the application of such provision or amendment to any person or circumstance is held to be unconstitutional, the remaining provisions of and amendments made by Pub.L. 103–394 and the application of such provisions and amendments to any person or circumstance shall not be affected thereby, see section 701 of Pub.L. 103–394, set out as a note under section 101 of Title 11, Bankruptcy.

CROSS REFERENCES

Contested matters, request for relief by motion served in manner provided in this rule, see Fed.Rules Bankr.Proc. Rule 9014, 11 USCA.

Form of pleadings, see Fed.Rules Bankr.Proc. Rule 7010, 11 USCA.

Service of,

Motion for substitution of parties, see Fed.Rules Bankr. Proc. Rule 7025, 11 USCA.

Notice of depositions before adversary proceedings or pending appeal, see Fed.Rules Bankr.Proc. Rule 7027, 11 USCA.

Pleadings and other papers, see Fed.Rules Bankr.Proc. Rule 7005, 11 USCA.

Summons and involuntary petition,

Manner of service, see Fed.Rules Bankr.Proc. Rule 1010, 11 USCA.

Time limitations, see Fed.Rules Bankr.Proc. Rule 1010, 11 USCA.

Rule 7005. Service and Filing of Pleadings and Other Papers

Rule 5 F.R.Civ.P. applies in adversary proceedings.

ADVISORY COMMITTEE NOTES

Rule 5 F.R.Civ.P. refers to Rule 4 F.R.Civ.P. Pursuant to Rule 7002 this reference is to Rule 4 F.R.Civ.P. as incorporated and modified by Rule 7004.

CROSS REFERENCES

Applicability of this rule in proceedings on contested involuntary petition and to vacate order for relief, see Fed.Rules Bankr.Proc. Rule 1018, 11 USCA.

Form of pleadings, see Fed.Rules Bankr.Proc. Rule 7010, 11 USCA.

Service of,

Motion for substitution, see Fed.Rules Bankr.Proc. Rule 7025, 11 USCA.

Motion to intervene, see Fed.Rules Bankr. Proc. Rule 7024, 11 USCA.

Notice of judgment or order, see Fed.Rules Bankr.Proc. Rule 9022, 11 USCA.

Requests for depositions and discovery, see Fed.Rules Bankr.Proc. Rule 7027 et seq., 11 USCA.

Rule 7007. Pleadings Allowed

Rule 7 F.R.Civ.P. applies in adversary proceedings.

CROSS REFERENCES

Amended and supplemental pleadings, see Fed.Rules Bankr.Proc. Rule 7015, 11 USCA.

Counterclaim and cross-claim, see Fed.Rules Bankr.Proc. Rule 7013, 11 USCA.

Form of pleadings, see Fed.Rules Bankr.Proc. Rule 7010, 11 USCA.

Service and filing of pleadings and other papers, see Fed. Rules Bankr.Proc. Rule 7005, 11 USCA.

Third-party practice, see Fed.Rules Bankr.Proc. Rule 7014, 11 USCA.

Rule 7007.1.   Corporate Ownership Statement

(a) Required disclosure

Any corporation that is a party to an adversary proceeding, other than the debtor or a governmental unit, shall file two copies of a statement that identifies any corporation, other than a governmental unit, that directly or indirectly owns 10% or more of any class of the corporation's equity interests, or states that there are no entities to report under this subdivision.

(b) Time for Filing

A party shall file the statement required under Rule 7007.1(a) with its first appearance, pleading, motion, response, or other request addressed to the court. A party shall file a supplemental statement promptly upon any change in circumstances that this rule requires the party to identify or disclose.

(Added Mar. 27, 2003, eff. Dec. 1, 2003. As amended Apr. 30, 2007, eff. Dec. 1, 2007.)

ADVISORY COMMITTEE NOTES

2003 Adoption

This rule is derived from Rule 26.1 of the Federal Rules of Appellate Procedure. The information that parties shall supply will support properly informed disqualification decisions in situations that call for automatic disqualification under Canon 3C(1)(c) of the Code of Conduct for United States Judges. This rule does not cover all of the circumstances that may call for disqualification under the subjective financial interest standard of Canon 3C, and does not deal at all with other circumstances that may call for disqualification. Nevertheless, the required disclosures are calculated to reach the majority of circumstances that are likely to call for disqualification under Canon 3C(1)(c).

The rule directs nongovernmental corporate parties to list those corporations that hold significant ownership interests in them. This includes listing membership interests in limited liability companies and similar entities that fall under the definition of a corporation in Bankruptcy Code § 101.

Under subdivision (b), parties must file the statement with the first document that they file in any adversary proceeding. The rule also requires parties and other persons to file supplemental statements promptly whenever changed circumstances require disclosure of new or additional information.

The rule does not prohibit the adoption of local rules requiring disclosures beyond those called for in Rule 7007.1.

2007 Amendments

The rule is amended to clarify that a party must file a corporate ownership statement with its initial paper filed with the court in an adversary proceeding. The party's initial filing may be a document that is not a "pleading" as defined in Rule 7 F.R.Civ.P., which is made applicable in adversary proceedings by Rule 7007. The amendment also brings Rule 7007.1 more closely in line with Rule 7.1 F.R.Civ.P.

Rule 7008.   General Rules of Pleading

Rule 8 F.R.Civ.P. applies in adversary proceedings. The allegation of jurisdiction required by Rule 8(a) shall also contain a reference to the name, number, and chapter of the case under the Code to which the adversary proceeding relates and to the district and division where the case under the Code is pending. In an adversary proceeding before a bankruptcy court, the complaint, counterclaim, cross-claim, or third-party complaint shall contain a statement that the pleader does or does not consent to entry of final orders or judgment by the bankruptcy court.

(As amended Mar. 30, 1987, eff. Aug. 1, 1987; Apr. 25, 2014, eff. Dec. 1, 2014; Apr. 28, 2016, eff. Dec. 1, 2016.)

ADVISORY COMMITTEE NOTES

1987 Amendment

Proceedings before a bankruptcy judge are either core or non-core. 28 U.S.C. § 157. A bankruptcy judge may enter a final order or judgment in a core proceeding. In a non-core proceeding, absent consent of the parties, the bankruptcy judge may not enter a final order or judgment but may only submit proposed findings of fact and conclusions of law to the district judge who will enter the final order or judgment. 28 U.S.C. § 157(c)(1). The amendment to subdivision (a) of this rule requires an allegation as to whether a proceeding is core or non-core. A party who alleges that the proceeding is non-core shall state whether the party does or does not consent to the entry of a final order or judgment by the bankruptcy judge. Failure to include the statement of consent does not constitute consent. Only express consent in the pleadings or otherwise is effective to authorize entry of a final order or judgment by the bankruptcy judge in a non-core proceeding. Amendments to Rule 7012 require that the defendant admit or deny the allegation as to whether the proceeding is core or non-core.

2014 Amendments

The rule is amended to delete subdivision (b), which required a request for attorney's fees always to be pleaded as a claim in an allowed pleading. That requirement, which differed from the practice under the Federal Rules of Civil Procedure, had the potential to serve as a trap for the unwary.

The procedures for seeking an award of attorney's fees are now set out in Rule 7054(b)(2), which makes applicable most of the provisions of Rule 54(d)(2) F.R.Civ.P. As specified by Rule 54(d)(2)(A) and (B) F.R.Civ.P., a claim for attorney's fees must be made by a motion filed no later than 14 days after entry of the judgment unless the governing substantive law requires those fees to be proved at trial as an element of damages. When fees are an element of damages, such as when the terms of a contract provide for the recovery of fees incurred prior to the instant adversary proceeding, the general pleading requirements of this rule still apply.

Changes Made After Publication and Comment. No changes were made after publication and comment.

2016 Amendments

The rule is amended to remove the requirement that the pleader state whether the proceeding is core or non-core and to require in all proceedings that the pleader state whether the party does or does not consent to the entry of final orders or judgment by the bankruptcy court. Some proceedings that satisfy the statutory definition of core proceedings, 28 U.S.C. § 157(b)(2), may remain beyond the constitutional power of a bankruptcy judge to adjudicate finally. The amended rule calls for the pleader to make a statement regarding consent, whether or not a proceeding is termed non-core. Rule 7012(b) has been amended to require a similar statement in a responsive pleading. The bankruptcy judge will then determine the appropriate course of proceedings under Rule 7016.

CROSS REFERENCES

Amended and supplemental pleadings, see Fed.Rules Bankr.Proc. Rule 7015, 11 USCA.

Applicability of this rule in proceedings on contested involuntary petition and to vacate order for relief, see Fed.Rules Bankr.Proc. Rule 1018, 11 USCA.

Defenses and objections, see Fed.Rules Bankr.Proc. Rule 7012, 11 USCA.

Joinder of claims and remedies, see Fed.Rules Bankr.Proc. Rule 7018, 11 USCA.

Rule 7009. Pleading Special Matters

Rule 9 F.R.Civ.P. applies in adversary proceedings.

CROSS REFERENCES

Applicability of this rule in proceedings on contested involuntary petition and to vacate order for relief, see Fed.Rules Bankr.Proc. Rule 1018, 11 USCA.

Parties plaintiff and defendant, capacity, see Fed.Rules Bankr.Proc. Rule 7017, 11 USCA.

Pleading affirmative defenses, see Fed.Rules Bankr.Proc. Rule 7008, 11 USCA.

Rule 7010. Form of Pleadings

Rule 10 F.R.Civ.P. applies in adversary proceedings, except that the caption of each pleading in such a proceeding shall conform substantially to the appropriate Official Form.

(As amended Apr. 30, 1991, eff. Aug. 1, 1991.)

ADVISORY COMMITTEE NOTES

1991 Amendment

Reference to the Official Form number is deleted in anticipation of future revision and renumbering of the Official Forms.

CROSS REFERENCES

Applicability of this rule in proceedings on contested involuntary petition and to vacate order for relief, see Fed.Rules Bankr.Proc. Rule 1018, 11 USCA.

General requirements of form for adversarial pleading or paper, see Fed.Rules Bankr.Proc. Rule 9004, 11 USCA.

Rule 7012. Defenses and Objections—When and How Presented—By Pleading or Motion—Motion for Judgment on the Pleadings

(a) When presented

If a complaint is duly served, the defendant shall serve an answer within 30 days after the issuance of the summons, except when a different time is prescribed by the court. The court shall prescribe the time for service of the answer when service of a complaint is made by publication or upon a party in a foreign country. A party served with a pleading stating a cross-claim shall serve an answer thereto within 21 days after service. The plaintiff shall serve a reply to a counterclaim in the answer within 21 days after service of the answer or, if a reply is ordered by the court, within 21 days after service of the order, unless the order otherwise directs. The United States or an officer or agency thereof shall serve an answer to a complaint within 35 days after the issuance of the summons, and shall serve an answer to a cross-claim, or a reply to a counterclaim, within 35 days after service upon the United States attorney of the pleading in which the claim is asserted. The service of a motion permitted under this rule alters these periods of time as follows, unless a different time is fixed by order of the court: (1) if the court denies the motion or postpones its disposition until the trial on the merits, the responsive pleading shall be served within 14 days after notice of the court's action; (2) if the court grants a motion for a more definite statement, the responsive pleading shall be served within 14 days after the service of a more definite statement.

(b) Applicability of Rule 12(b)–(i) F.R.Civ.P.

Rule 12(b)–(i) F.R.Civ.P. applies in adversary proceedings. A responsive pleading shall include a statement that the party does or does not consent to entry of final orders or judgment by the bankruptcy court. (As amended Mar. 30, 1987, eff. Aug. 1, 1987; Apr. 23, 2008, eff. Dec. 1, 2008; Mar. 26, 2009, eff. Dec. 1, 2009; Apr. 28, 2016, eff. Dec. 1, 2016.)

ADVISORY COMMITTEE NOTES

Subdivision (a) continues the practice of former Bankruptcy Rule 712(a) by requiring that the answer to a complaint be filed within 30 days after the issuance of the summons. Under Rule 7004(f), the summons must be served within 10 days of issuance. The other pleading periods in adversary proceedings are the same as those in civil actions before the district courts, except that the United States is allowed 35 rather than 60 days to respond.

For Complete Annotation Materials, see United States Code Annotated

Rule 12(b)(7) and (h)(2) F.R.Civ.P. refers to Rule 19 F.R.Civ.P. Pursuant to Rule 7002 these references are to Rule 19 F.R.Civ.P. as incorporated and modified by Rule 7019.

1987 Amendment

The amendment to subdivision (b) requires a response to the allegation that the proceeding is core or non-core. A final order of judgment may not be entered in a non-core proceeding heard by a bankruptcy judge unless all parties expressly consent. 28 U.S.C. § 157(c).

2008 Amendments

The rule is amended to conform to the changes made to the Federal Rules of Civil Procedure through the restyling of those rules effective on December 1, 2007.

2009 Amendments

The rule is amended to implement changes in connection with the amendment to Rule 9006(a) and the manner by which time is computed under the rules. The deadlines in the rule are amended to substitute a deadline that is a multiple of seven days. Throughout the rules, deadlines are amended in the following manner:

- 5–day periods become 7–day periods
- 10–day periods become 14–day periods
- 15–day periods become 14–day periods
- 20–day periods become 21–day periods
- 25–day periods become 28–day periods

2016 Amendments

Subdivision (b) is amended to remove the requirement that the pleader state whether the proceeding is core or noncore and to require in all proceedings that the pleader state whether the party does or does not consent to the entry of final orders or judgment by the bankruptcy court. The amended rule also removes the provision requiring express consent before the entry of final orders and judgments in non-core proceedings. Some proceedings that satisfy the statutory definition of core proceedings, 28 U.S.C. § 157(b)(2), may remain beyond the constitutional power of a bankruptcy judge to adjudicate finally. The amended rule calls for the pleader to make a statement regarding consent, whether or not a proceeding is termed non-core. This amendment complements the requirements of amended Rule 7008(a). The bankruptcy judge's subsequent determination of the appropriate course of proceedings, including whether to enter final orders and judgments or to issue proposed findings of fact and conclusions of law, is a pretrial matter now provided for in amended Rule 7016.

CROSS REFERENCES

Averments of defense in separate statements, see Fed. Rules Bankr.Proc. Rule 7010, 11 USCA.

Counterclaim and cross-claim, see Fed.Rules Bankr.Proc. Rule 7013, 11 USCA.

Defenses of third-party defendant, see Fed.Rules Bankr. Proc. Rule 7014, 11 USCA.

Pleadings allowed, see Fed.Rules Bankr.Proc. Rule 7007, 11 USCA.

Removed actions, see Fed.Rules Bankr.Proc. Rule 9027, 11 USCA.

Waiver of sovereign immunity, see 11 USCA § 106.

Rule 7013.   Counterclaim and Cross–Claim

Rule 13 F.R.Civ.P. applies in adversary proceedings, except that a party sued by a trustee or debtor in possession need not state as a counterclaim any claim that the party has against the debtor, the debtor's property, or the estate, unless the claim arose after the entry of an order for relief. A trustee or debtor in possession who fails to plead a counterclaim through oversight, inadvertence, or excusable neglect, or when justice so requires, may by leave of court amend the pleading, or commence a new adversary proceeding or separate action.

(As amended Mar. 30, 1987, eff. Aug. 1, 1987.)

ADVISORY COMMITTEE NOTES

Rule 13(h) F.R.Civ.P. refers to Rule 19 F.R.Civ.P. Pursuant to Rule 7002 this reference is to Rule 19 F.R.Civ.P. as incorporated and modified by Rule 7019.

CROSS REFERENCES

Amended and supplemental pleadings, see Fed.Rules Bankr.Proc. Rule 7015, 11 USCA.

Counterclaims and cross-claims of third-party defendant, see Fed.Rules Bankr.Proc. Rule 7014, 11 USCA.

Default judgment against counterclaimants and cross-claimants, see Fed.Rules Bankr.Proc. Rule 7055, 11 USCA.

Dismissal of counterclaims and cross-claims, see Fed.Rules Bankr.Proc. Rule 7041, 11 USCA.

Separate trial of counterclaims and cross-claims, see Fed. Rules Bankr.Proc. Rule 7042, 11 USCA.

Rule 7014.   Third–Party Practice

Rule 14 F.R.Civ.P. applies in adversary proceedings.

ADVISORY COMMITTEE NOTES

This rule does not purport to deal with questions of jurisdiction. The scope of the jurisdictional grant under 28 U.S.C. § 1471 and whether the doctrines of pendent or ancillary jurisdiction are applicable to adversary proceedings will be determined by the courts.

Rule 14 F.R.Civ.P. refers to Rules 12 and 13 F.R.Civ.P. Pursuant to Rule 7002 those references are to Rules 12 and 13 as incorporated and modified by Rules 7012 and 7013.

CROSS REFERENCES

Default judgment against third-party plaintiff, see Fed. Rules Bankr.Proc. Rule 7055, 11 USCA.

Joinder of claims, see Fed.Rules Bankr.Proc. Rule 7018, 11 USCA.

Requisites of pleading, see Fed.Rules Bankr.Proc. Rule 7008, 11 USCA.

Separate trial of third-party claim, see Fed.Rules Bankr. Proc. Rule 7042, 11 USCA.

Rule 7015. Amended and Supplemental Pleadings

Rule 15 F.R.Civ.P. applies in adversary proceedings.

CROSS REFERENCES

Amendments to pleadings considered at pre-trial conference, see Fed.Rules Bankr.Proc. Rule 7016, 11 USCA.

Applicability of this rule in proceedings on contested involuntary petition and to vacate order for relief, see Fed.Rules Bankr.Proc. Rule 1018, 11 USCA.

Substitution of parties, see Fed.Rules Bankr.Proc. Rule 7025, 11 USCA.

Rule 7016. Pre–Trial Procedures

(a) Pretrial conferences; scheduling; management

Rule 16 F.R.Civ.P. applies in adversary proceedings.

(b) Determining procedure

The bankruptcy court shall decide, on its own motion or a party's timely motion, whether:

(1) to hear and determine the proceeding;

(2) to hear the proceeding and issue proposed findings of fact and conclusions of law; or

(3) to take some other action.

(As amended Apr. 28, 2016, eff. Dec. 1, 2016.)

ADVISORY COMMITTEE NOTES

2016 Amendments

This rule is amended to create a new subdivision (b) that provides for the bankruptcy court to enter final orders and judgment, issue proposed findings and conclusions, or take some other action in a proceeding. The rule leaves the decision as to the appropriate course of proceedings to the bankruptcy court. The court's decision will be informed by the parties' statements, required under Rules 7008(a), 7012(b), and 9027(a) and (e), regarding consent to the entry of final orders and judgment. If the bankruptcy court chooses to issue proposed findings of fact and conclusions of law, Rule 9033 applies.

CROSS REFERENCES

Amended and supplemental pleadings, see Fed.Rules Bankr.Proc. Rule 7015, 11 USCA.

Applicability of this rule in proceedings on contested involuntary petition and to vacate order for relief, see Fed.Rules Bankr.Proc. Rule 1018, 11 USCA.

Preliminary hearing before trial to determine merit of defenses, see Fed.Rules Bankr.Proc. Rule 7012, 11 USCA.

Rule 7017. Parties Plaintiff and Defendant; Capacity

Rule 17 F.R.Civ.P. applies in adversary proceedings, except as provided in Rule 2010(b).

(As amended Apr. 30, 1991, eff. Aug. 1, 1991.)

ADVISORY COMMITTEE NOTES

Rules 2010(d) and 5008(d), which implement §§ 322 and 345 of the Code, authorize a party in interest to prosecute a claim on the bond of a trustee or depository in the name of the United States.

1991 Amendment

Reference to Rule 5008(d) is deleted because of the abrogation of Rule 5008.

CROSS REFERENCES

Bond requirement for deposit or investment by trustee of estate money, see 11 USCA § 345.

Filing by trustee of bond in favor of United States as qualification to serve, see 11 USCA § 322.

Service upon infants or incompetent persons of,

Notice of application for depositions before adversary proceedings or pending appeal, see Fed.Rules Bankr. Proc. Rule 7027, 11 USCA.

Summons and complaint, see Fed.Rules Bankr.Proc. Rule 7004, 11 USCA.

Rule 7018. Joinder of Claims and Remedies

Rule 18 F.R.Civ.P. applies in adversary proceedings.

CROSS REFERENCES

Joinder of parties,

Misjoinder and non-joinder, see Fed.Rules Bankr.Proc. Rule 7021, 11 USCA.

Permissive joinder, see Fed.Rules Bankr.Proc. Rule 7020, 11 USCA.

Persons needed for just determination, see Fed.Rules Bankr.Proc. Rule 7019, 11 USCA.

Rule 7019. Joinder of Persons Needed for Just Determination

Rule 19 F.R.Civ.P. applies in adversary proceedings, except that (1) if an entity joined as a party raises the defense that the court lacks jurisdiction over the subject matter and the defense is sustained, the court shall dismiss such entity from the adversary proceeding and (2) if an entity joined as a party properly and timely raises the defense of improper venue, the court shall determine, as provided in 28 U.S.C. § 1412, whether that part of the proceeding involving the joined party shall be transferred to another district, or whether the entire adversary proceeding shall be transferred to another district.

(As amended Mar. 30, 1987, eff. Aug. 1, 1987.)

ADVISORY COMMITTEE NOTES

This rule addresses a situation different from that encountered by the district court when its jurisdiction is based on diversity of citizenship under 28 U.S.C. § 1332. Joining of a party whose citizenship is the same as that of an adversary destroys the district court's jurisdiction over the entire civil action but under 28 U.S.C. § 1471 the attempted joinder of such a person would not affect the bankruptcy court's jurisdiction over the original adversary proceeding.

For Complete Annotation Materials, see United States Code Annotated

1987 Amendment

The rule is amended to delete the reference to retention of the adversary proceeding if venue is improper. See 28 U.S.C. § 1412.

CROSS REFERENCES

Additional parties for determination of counterclaim or cross-claim, see Fed.Rules Bankr.Proc. Rule 7013, 11 USCA.

Exception to procedural rule on transfer by court of adversary proceeding, see Fed.Rules Bankr.Proc. Rule 7087, 11 USCA.

Parties,

Permissive joinder, see Fed.Rules Bankr.Proc. Rule 7020, 11 USCA.

Substitution of, see Fed.Rules Bankr.Proc. Rule 7025, 11 USCA.

Rule 7020.   Permissive Joinder of Parties

Rule 20 F.R.Civ.P. applies in adversary proceedings.

CROSS REFERENCES

Additional parties for determination of counterclaim or cross-claim, see Fed.Rules Bankr.Proc. Rule 7013, 11 USCA.

Parties,

Joinder of persons needed for just determination, see Fed.Rules Bankr.Proc. Rule 7019, 11 USCA.

Substitution of, see Fed.Rules Bankr.Proc. Rule 7025, 11 USCA.

Rule 7021.   Misjoinder and Non–Joinder of Parties

Rule 21 F.R.Civ.P. applies in adversary proceedings.

CROSS REFERENCES

Applicability of this rule in contested matters not otherwise provided for, see Fed.Rules Bankr.Proc. Rule 9014, 11 USCA.

Judgment on counterclaim or cross-claim rendered in separate trials, see Fed.Rules Bankr.Proc. Rule 7013, 11 USCA.

Separate trials,

In furtherance of convenience or to avoid prejudice, see Fed.Rules Bankr.Proc. Rule 7042, 11 USCA.

Of parties joined permissively, see Fed.Rules Bankr.Proc. Rule 7020, 11 USCA.

Rule 7022.   Interpleader

Rule 22(a) F.R.Civ.P. applies in adversary proceedings. This rule supplements—and does not limit—the joinder of parties allowed by Rule 7020.
(As amended Apr. 23, 2008, eff. Dec. 1, 2008.)

ADVISORY COMMITTEE NOTES

2008 Amendments

The rule is amended to conform to the changes made to the Federal Rules of Civil Procedure through the restyling of those rules effective on December 1, 2007.

CROSS REFERENCES

Preliminary injunction in interpleader actions, see Fed. Rules Bankr.Proc. Rule 7065, 11 USCA.

Rule 7023.   Class Proceedings

Rule 23 F.R.Civ.P. applies in adversary proceedings.

CROSS REFERENCES

Exception of class actions from procedural rule of necessary joinder of parties, see Fed.Rules Bankr.Proc. Rule 7019, 11 USCA.

Rule 7023.1.   Derivative Actions

Rule 23.1 F.R.Civ.P. applies in adversary proceedings.
(As amended Apr. 23, 2008, eff. Dec. 1, 2008.)

ADVISORY COMMITTEE NOTES

2008 Amendments

The rule is amended to conform to the changes made to the Federal Rules of Civil Procedure through the restyling of those rules effective on December 1, 2007.

Rule 7023.2.   Adversary Proceedings Relating to Unincorporated Associations

Rule 23.2 F.R.Civ.P. applies in adversary proceedings.

CROSS REFERENCES

Capacity of unincorporated association to sue or be sued, see Fed.Rules Bankr.Proc. Rule 7017, 11 USCA.

Derivative actions by shareholders, see Fed.Rules Bankr. Proc. Rule 7023.1, 11 USCA.

Rule 7024.   Intervention

Rule 24 F.R.Civ.P. applies in adversary proceedings.

ADVISORY COMMITTEE NOTES

A person may seek to intervene in the case under the Code or in an adversary proceeding relating to the case under the Code. Intervention in a case under the Code is governed by Rule 2018 and intervention in an adversary proceeding is governed by this rule. Intervention in a case and intervention in an adversary proceeding must be sought separately.

CROSS REFERENCES

Applicability of this rule in proceedings on contested involuntary petition and to vacate order for relief, see Fed.Rules Bankr.Proc. Rule 1018, 11 USCA.

Intervention in case under this title, see Fed.Rules Bankr. Proc. Rule 2018, 11 USCA.

Rule 7025.   Substitution of Parties

Subject to the provisions of Rule 2012, Rule 25 F.R.Civ.P. applies in adversary proceedings.

ADVISORY COMMITTEE NOTES

Rule 25 F.R.Civ.P. refers to Rule 4 F.R.Civ.P. Pursuant to Rule 7002 that reference is to Rule 4 as incorporated and modified by Rule 7004.

CROSS REFERENCES

Applicability of this rule in,

Contested matters not otherwise provided for, see Fed. Rules Bankr.Proc. Rule 9014, 11 USCA.

Proceedings on contested involuntary petition and to vacate order for relief, see Fed.Rules Bankr.Proc. Rule 1018, 11 USCA.

Right to use depositions previously taken, see Fed.Rules Bankr.Proc. Rule 7026, 11 USCA.

Rule 7026. General Provisions Governing Discovery

Rule 26 F.R.Civ.P. applies in adversary proceedings.

CROSS REFERENCES

Applicability of this rule in,

Contested matters not otherwise provided for, see Fed. Rules Bankr.Proc. Rule 9014, 11 USCA.

Proceedings on contested involuntary petition and to vacate order for relief, see Fed.Rules Bankr.Proc. Rule 1018, 11 USCA.

Failure to make discovery, sanctions, see Fed.Rules Bankr. Proc. Rule 7037, 11 USCA.

Subpoena for taking depositions, place of examination, see Fed.Rules Bankr.Proc. Rule 9016, 11 USCA.

Rule 7027. Depositions Before Adversary Proceedings or Pending Appeal

Rule 27 F.R.Civ.P. applies to adversary proceedings.

ADVISORY COMMITTEE NOTES

Rule 27(a)(2) F.R.Civ.P. refers to Rule 4 F.R.Civ.P. Pursuant to Rule 7002 the reference is to Rule 4 F.R.Civ.P. as incorporated and modified by Rule 7004.

CROSS REFERENCES

Applicability of this rule in contested matters not otherwise provided for, see Fed.Rules Bankr.Proc. Rule 9014, 11 USCA.

Rule 7028. Persons Before Whom Depositions May Be Taken

Rule 28 F.R.Civ.P. applies in adversary proceedings.

CROSS REFERENCES

Affirmations, see Fed.Rules Bankr.Proc. Rule 9012, 11 USCA.

Applicability of this rule in,

Contested matters not otherwise provided for, see Fed. Rules Bankr.Proc. Rule 9014, 11 USCA.

Proceedings on contested involuntary petition and to vacate order for relief, see Fed.Rules Bankr.Proc. Rule 1018, 11 USCA.

Rule 7029. Stipulations Regarding Discovery Procedure

Rule 29 F.R.Civ.P. applies in adversary proceedings.

CROSS REFERENCES

Applicability of this rule in,

Contested matters not otherwise provided for, see Fed. Rules Bankr.Proc. Rule 9014, 11 USCA.

Proceedings on contested involuntary petition and to vacate order for relief, see Fed.Rules Bankr.Proc. Rule 1018, 11 USCA.

Rule 7030. Depositions Upon Oral Examination

Rule 30 F.R.Civ.P. applies in adversary proceedings.

ADVISORY COMMITTEE NOTES

Rule 30 F.R.Civ.P. refers to Rule 4 F.R.Civ.P. Pursuant to Rule 7002 that reference is a reference to Rule 4 F.R.Civ.P. as incorporated and modified by Rule 7004.

CROSS REFERENCES

Applicability of this rule in,

Contested matters not otherwise provided for, see Fed. Rules Bankr.Proc. Rule 9014, 11 USCA.

Proceedings on contested involuntary petition and to vacate order for relief, see Fed.Rules Bankr.Proc. Rule 1018, 11 USCA.

Failure to make discovery, sanctions, see Fed.Rules Bankr. Proc. Rule 7037, 11 USCA.

Subpoena for taking depositions, place of examination, see Fed.Rules Bankr.Proc. Rule 9016, 11 USCA.

Rule 7031. Deposition Upon Written Questions

Rule 31 F.R.Civ.P. applies in adversary proceedings.

CROSS REFERENCES

Applicability of this rule in,

Contested matters not otherwise provided for, see Fed. Rules Bankr.Proc. Rule 9014, 11 USCA.

Proceedings on contested involuntary petition and to vacate order for relief, see Fed.Rules Bankr.Proc. Rule 1018, 11 USCA.

Failure to make discovery, sanctions, see Fed.Rules Bankr. Proc. Rule 7037, 11 USCA.

Rule 7032. Use of Depositions in Adversary Proceedings

Rule 32 F.R.Civ.P. applies in adversary proceedings.

CROSS REFERENCES

Applicability of this rule in,

Contested matters not otherwise provided for, see Fed. Rules Bankr.Proc. Rule 9014, 11 USCA.

Proceedings on contested involuntary petition and to vacate order for relief, see Fed.Rules Bankr.Proc. Rule 1018, 11 USCA.

Rule 7033. Interrogatories to Parties

Rule 33 F.R.Civ.P. applies in adversary proceedings.

CROSS REFERENCES

Applicability of this rule in,

Contested matters not otherwise provided for, see Fed. Rules Bankr.Proc. Rule 9014, 11 USCA.

Proceedings on contested involuntary petition and to vacate order for relief, see Fed.Rules Bankr.Proc. Rule 1018, 11 USCA.

Failure to make discovery, sanctions, see Fed.Rules Bankr. Proc. Rule 7037, 11 USCA.

Rule 7034. Production of Documents and Things and Entry Upon Land for Inspection and Other Purposes

Rule 34 F.R.Civ.P. applies in adversary proceedings.

CROSS REFERENCES

Applicability of this rule in,

Contested matters not otherwise provided for, see Fed. Rules Bankr.Proc. Rule 9014, 11 USCA.

Proceedings on contested involuntary petition and to vacate order for relief, see Fed.Rules Bankr.Proc. Rule 1018, 11 USCA.

Failure to make discovery, sanctions, see Fed.Rules Bankr. Proc. Rule 7037, 11 USCA.

Subpoena for production of documentary evidence, see Fed. Rules Bankr.Proc. Rule 9016, 11 USCA.

Rule 7035. Physical and Mental Examination of Persons

Rule 35 F.R.Civ.P. applies in adversary proceedings.

CROSS REFERENCES

Applicability of this rule in,

Contested matters not otherwise provided for, see Fed. Rules Bankr.Proc. Rule 9014, 11 USCA.

Proceedings on contested involuntary petition and to vacate order for relief, see Fed.Rules Bankr.Proc. Rule 1018, 11 USCA.

Failure to make discovery, sanctions, see Fed.Rules Bankr. Proc. Rule 7037, 11 USCA.

Rule 7036. Requests for Admission

Rule 36 F.R.Civ.P. applies in adversary proceedings.

CROSS REFERENCES

Applicability of this rule in,

Contested matters not otherwise provided for, see Fed. Rules Bankr.Proc. Rule 9014, 11 USCA.

Proceedings on contested involuntary petition and to vacate order for relief, see Fed.Rules Bankr.Proc. Rule 1018, 11 USCA.

Pre-trial conference to obtain admissions of facts and documents, see Fed.Rules Bankr.Proc. Rule 7016, 11 USCA.

Rule 7037. Failure to Make Discovery: Sanctions

Rule 37 F.R.Civ.P. applies in adversary proceedings.

CROSS REFERENCES

Applicability of this rule in,

Contested matters not otherwise provided for, see Fed. Rules Bankr.Proc. Rule 9014, 11 USCA.

Proceedings on contested involuntary petition and to vacate order for relief, see Fed.Rules Bankr.Proc. Rule 1018, 11 USCA.

Rule 7040. Assignment of Cases for Trial

Rule 40 F.R.Civ.P. applies in adversary proceedings.

CROSS REFERENCES

Local bankruptcy rules on practice and procedure not inconsistent with these rules, see Fed.Rules Bankr.Proc. Rule 9029, 11 USCA.

Rule 7041. Dismissal of Adversary Proceedings

Rule 41 F.R.Civ.P. applies in adversary proceedings, except that a complaint objecting to the debtor's discharge shall not be dismissed at the plaintiff's instance without notice to the trustee, the United States trustee, and such other persons as the court may direct, and only on order of the court containing terms and conditions which the court deems proper.

(As amended Apr. 30, 1991, eff. Aug. 1, 1991.)

ADVISORY COMMITTEE NOTES

Dismissal of a complaint objecting to a discharge raises special concerns because the plaintiff may have been induced to dismiss by an advantage given or promised by the debtor or someone acting in his interest. Some courts by local rule or order have required the debtor and his attorney or the plaintiff to file an affidavit that nothing has been promised to the plaintiff in consideration of the withdrawal of the objection. By specifically authorizing the court to impose conditions in the order of dismissal this rule permits the continuation of this salutary practice.

Rule 41 F.R.Civ.P. refers to Rule 19 F.R.Civ.P. Pursuant to Rule 7002 that reference is to Rule 19 F.R.Civ.P. as incorporated and modified by Rule 7019.

1991 Amendment

The United States trustee has standing to object to the debtor's discharge pursuant to § 727(c) and may have refrained from commencing an adversary proceeding objecting to discharge within the time limits provided in Rule 4004 only because another party commenced such a proceeding. The United States trustee may oppose dismissal of the original proceeding.

The rule is also amended to clarify that the court may direct that other persons receive notice of a plaintiff's motion to dismiss a complaint objecting to discharge.

CROSS REFERENCES

Applicability of this rule in contested matters not otherwise provided for, see Fed.Rules Bankr.Proc. Rule 9014, 11 USCA.

Findings by court necessary when judgment rendered on merits of motion to dismiss after trial on facts, see Fed.Rules Bankr.Proc. Rule 7052, 11 USCA.

Sanction for failure to attend deposition, to answer interrogatories, or to respond to inspection request, see Fed.Rules Bankr.Proc. Rule 7037, 11 USCA.

Rule 7042. Consolidation of Adversary Proceedings; Separate Trials

Rule 42 F.R.Civ.P. applies in adversary proceedings.

CROSS REFERENCES

Applicability of this rule in contested matters not otherwise provided for, see Fed.Rules Bankr.Proc. Rule 9014, 11 USCA.

Separate trials,
> Joinder of party against whom no claim exists, see Fed. Rules Bankr.Proc. Rule 7020, 11 USCA.

> Separate judgments rendered on counterclaim or cross-claim, see Fed.Rules Bankr.Proc. Rule 7013, 11 USCA.

Rule 7052. Findings by the Court

Rule 52 F.R.Civ.P. applies in adversary proceedings, except that any motion under subdivision (b) of that rule for amended or additional findings shall be filed no later than 14 days after entry of judgment. In these proceedings, the reference in Rule 52 F.R.Civ.P. to the entry of judgment under Rule 58 F.R.Civ.P. shall be read as a reference to the entry of a judgment or order under Rule 5003(a).

(As amended Mar. 26, 2009, eff. Dec. 1, 2009.)

ADVISORY COMMITTEE NOTES

Rule 52(a) F.R.Civ.P. refers to Rule 12 F.R.Civ.P. Pursuant to Rule 7002 this reference is to Rule 12 F.R.Civ.P. as incorporated and modified by Rule 7012.

2009 Amendments

The rule is amended to clarify that the reference in Rule 52 F.R.Civ.P. to Rule 58 F.R.Civ.P. and its provisions is construed as a reference to the entry of a judgment or order under Rule 5003(a).

The rule is amended by limiting the time for filing post judgment motions for amended or additional findings. In 2009, Rule 52 F.R.Civ.P. was amended to extend the deadline for filing those post judgment motions to no later than 28 days after entry of the judgment. That deadline corresponds to the 30–day deadline for filing a notice of appeal in a civil case under Rule 4(a)(1)(A) F.R.App.P. In a bankruptcy case, the deadline for filing a notice of appeal is 14 days. Therefore, the 28–day deadline for filing a motion for amended or additional findings would effectively override the notice of appeal deadline under Rule 8002(a) but for this amendment.

CROSS REFERENCES

Amendment of findings,
> On motion for new trial, see Fed.Rules Bankr.Proc. Rule 9023, 11 USCA.

> Stay of proceedings to enforce judgment pending disposition of motion to amend, see Fed.Rules Bankr.Proc. Rule 7062, 11 USCA.

Applicability of this rule in,
> Contested matters not otherwise provided for, see Fed. Rules Bankr.Proc. Rule 9014, 11 USCA.

> Proceedings on contested involuntary petition and to vacate order for relief, see Fed.Rules Bankr.Proc. Rule 1018, 11 USCA.

Effect of motion to amend or to add fact findings on time for appeal, see Fed.Rules Bankr.Proc. Rule 8002, 11 USCA.

Enlargement of ten-day period for motion to amend findings of court not permitted, see Fed.Rules Bankr.Proc. Rule 9006, 11 USCA.

Rule 7054. Judgments; Costs

(a) Judgments

Rule 54(a)–(c) F.R.Civ.P. applies in adversary proceedings.

(b) Costs; Attorney's Fees

(1) Costs Other Than Attorney's Fees. The court may allow costs to the prevailing party except when a statute of the United States or these rules otherwise provides. Costs against the United States, its officers and agencies shall be imposed only to the extent permitted by law. Costs may be taxed by the clerk on 14 days' notice; on motion served within seven days thereafter, the action of the clerk may be reviewed by the court.

(2) Attorney's Fees.

(A) Rule 54(d)(2)(A)–(C) and (E) F.R.Civ.P. applies in adversary proceedings except for the reference in Rule 54(d)(2)(C) to Rule 78.

(B) By local rule, the court may establish special procedures to resolve fee-related issues without extensive evidentiary hearings.

(As amended Apr. 23, 2012, eff. Dec. 1, 2012; Apr. 25, 2014, eff. Dec. 1, 2014.)

ADVISORY COMMITTEE NOTES

2012 Amendments

Subdivision (b). Subdivision (b) is amended to provide more time for a party to respond to the prevailing party's bill of costs. The former rule's provision of one day's notice was unrealistically short. The change to 14 days conforms to the change made to Civil Rule 54(d). Extension from five to seven days of the time for serving a motion for court review of the clerk's action implements changes in connection with the December 1, 2009, amendment to Rule 9006(a) and the manner by which time is computed under the rules. Throughout the rules, deadlines have been amended in the following manner:

- 5–day periods became 7–day periods.
- 10–day periods became 14–day periods.
- 15–day periods became 14–day periods.
- 20–day periods became 21–day periods.
- 25–day periods became 28–day periods.

Changes Made After Publication and Comments. No changes were made.

2014 Amendments

Subdivision (b) is amended to prescribe the procedure for seeking an award of attorney's fees and related nontaxable expenses in adversary proceedings. It does so by adding new paragraph (2) that incorporates most of the provisions of Rule 54(d)(2) F.R.Civ.P. The title of subdivision (b) is amended to reflect the new content, and the previously existing provision governing costs is renumbered as paragraph (1) and re-titled.

As provided in Rule 54(d)(2)(A), new subsection (b)(2) does not apply to fees recoverable as an element of damages, as when sought under the terms of a contract providing for the recovery of fees incurred prior to the instant adversary proceeding. Such fees typically are required to be claimed in a pleading.

Rule 54(d)(2)(D) F.R.Civ.P. does not apply in adversary proceedings insofar as it authorizes the referral of fee matters to a master or a magistrate judge. The use of masters is not authorized in bankruptcy cases, see Rule 9031, and 28 U.S.C. § 636 does not authorize a magistrate judge to exercise jurisdiction upon referral by a bankruptcy judge. The remaining provision of Rule 54(d)(2)(D) is expressed in subdivision (b)(2)(B) of this rule.

Rule 54(d)(2)(C) refers to Rule 78 F.R.Civ.P., which is not applicable in adversary proceedings. Accordingly, that reference is not incorporated by this rule.

Changes Made After Publication. No changes were made after publication.

CROSS REFERENCES

Amendment or alteration,

Stay of proceedings pending disposition of motion for, see Fed.Rules Bankr.Proc. Rule 7062, 11 USCA.

Time for service of motion, see Fed.Rules Bankr.Proc. Rule 9023, 11 USCA.

Applicability of this rule in,

Contested matters not otherwise provided for, see Fed. Rules Bankr.Proc. Rule 9014, 11 USCA.

Proceedings on contested involuntary petition and to vacate order for relief, see Fed.Rules Bankr.Proc. Rule 1018, 11 USCA.

Entry of judgment, district court record of judgment, see Fed.Rules Bankr.Proc. Rule 9021, 11 USCA.

Relief from judgment or order, see Fed.Rules Bankr.Proc. Rule 9024, 11 USCA.

Rule 7055.   Default

Rule 55 F.R.Civ.P. applies in adversary proceedings.

CROSS REFERENCES

Applicability of this rule in contested matters not otherwise provided for, see Fed.Rules Bankr.Proc. Rule 9014, 11 USCA.

Demand for judgment, see Fed.Rules Bankr.Proc. Rule 7054, 11 USCA.

Rule 7056.   Summary Judgment

Rule 56 F.R.Civ.P. applies in adversary proceedings, except that any motion for summary judgment must be made at least 30 days before the initial date set for an evidentiary hearing on any issue for which summary judgment is sought, unless a different time is set by local rule or the court orders otherwise.

(As amended Apr. 23, 2012, eff. Dec. 1, 2012.)

ADVISORY COMMITTEE NOTES

2012 Amendments

The only exception to complete adoption of Rule 56 F.R.Civ.P. involves the default deadline for filing a summary judgment motion. Rule 56(c)(1)(A) makes the default deadline 30 days after the close of all discovery. Because in bankruptcy cases hearings can occur shortly after the close of discovery, a default deadline based on the scheduled hearing date, rather than the close of discovery, is adopted. As with Rule 56(c)(1), the deadline can be altered either by local rule or court order.

Changes Made After Publication and Comments. No changes were made.

CROSS REFERENCES

Applicability of this rule in,

Contested matters, not otherwise provided for, see Fed. Rules Bankr.Proc. Rule 9014, 11 USCA.

Proceedings on contested involuntary petition and to vacate order for relief, see Fed.Rules Bankr.Proc. Rule 1018, 11 USCA.

Rule 7058.   Entering Judgment in Adversary Proceeding

Rule 58 F.R.Civ.P. applies in adversary proceedings. In these proceedings, the reference in Rule 58 F.R.Civ.P. to the civil docket shall be read as a reference to the docket maintained by the clerk under Rule 5003(a).

(Added Mar. 26, 2009, eff. Dec. 1, 2009.)

ADVISORY COMMITTEE NOTES

2009 Adoption

This rule makes Rule 58 F.R.Civ.P. applicable in adversary proceedings and is added in connection with the amendments to Rule 9021.

Rule 7062.   Stay of Proceedings to Enforce a Judgment

Rule 62 F.R.Civ.P. applies in adversary proceedings, except that proceedings to enforce a judgment are stayed for 14 days after its entry.

(As amended Apr. 30, 1991, eff. Aug. 1, 1991; Apr. 26, 1999, eff. Dec. 1, 1999; Apr. 26, 2018, eff. Dec. 1, 2018.)

ADVISORY COMMITTEE NOTES

The additional exceptions set forth in this rule make applicable to those matters the consequences contained in Rule 62(c) and (d) with respect to orders in actions for injunctions.

1991 Amendment

This rule is amended to include as additional exceptions to Rule 62(a) an order granting relief from the automatic stay of actions against codebtors provided by § 1201 of the Code, the sale or lease of property of the estate under § 363, and the assumption or assignment of an executory contract under § 365.

1999 Amendments

The additional exceptions to Rule 62(a) consist of orders that are issued in contested matters. These exceptions are deleted from this rule because of the amendment to Rule 9014 that renders this rule inapplicable in contested matters unless the court orders otherwise. See also the amendments to Rules 3020, 3021, 4001, 6004, and 6006 that delay the implementation of certain types of orders for a period of ten days unless the court otherwise directs.

GAP Report on Rule 7062. No changes since publication.

2018 Amendments

The rule is amended to retain a 14–day period for the automatic stay of a judgment. F.R.Civ.P. 62(a) now provides for a 30–day stay to accommodate the 28–day time periods under the Federal Rules of Civil Procedure for filing post-judgment motions and the 30–day period for filing a notice of appeal. Under the Bankruptcy Rules, however, those periods are limited to 14 days. *See* Rules 7052, 8002, 9015, and 9023.

CROSS REFERENCES

Applicability of this rule in,

Contested matters not otherwise provided for, see Fed. Rules Bankr.Proc. Rule 9014, 11 USCA.

Proceedings on contested involuntary petition and to vacate order for relief, see Fed.Rules Bankr.Proc. Rule 1018, 11 USCA.

Effect of entry of judgment on availability of relief under this rule, see Fed.Rules Bankr.Proc. Rule 9021, 11 USCA.

Power of court to suspend or to order continuation of other proceedings pending appeal, see Fed.Rules Bankr.Proc. Rule 8005, 11 USCA.

Security, proceedings against sureties, see Fed.Rules Bankr.Proc. Rule 9025, 11 USCA.

Stay of new proceedings until payment of costs of previously dismissed action, see Fed.Rules Bankr.Proc. Rule 7041, 11 USCA.

Rule 7064. Seizure of Person or Property

Rule 64 F.R.Civ.P. applies in adversary proceedings.

CROSS REFERENCES

Applicability of this rule in contested matters not otherwise provided for, see Fed.Rules Bankr.Proc. Rule 9014, 11 USCA.

Writ of attachment or sequestration issued against property ordered by judgment to be conveyed, see Fed.Rules Bankr. Proc. Rule 7070, 11 USCA.

Rule 7065. Injunctions

Rule 65 F.R.Civ.P. applies in adversary proceedings, except that a temporary restraining order or preliminary injunction may be issued on application of a debtor, trustee, or debtor in possession without compliance with Rule 65(c).

CROSS REFERENCES

Injunction pending appeal of interlocutory or final judgment concerning injunction, see Fed.Rules Bankr.Proc. Rule 7062, 11 USCA.

Security, proceedings against sureties, see Fed.Rules Bankr.Proc. Rule 9025, 11 USCA.

Signing and verification of papers, see Fed.Rules Bankr. Proc. Rule 9011, 11 USCA.

Rule 7067. Deposit in Court

Rule 67 F.R.Civ.P. applies in adversary proceedings.

Rule 7068. Offer of Judgment

Rule 68 F.R.Civ.P. applies in adversary proceedings.

Rule 7069. Execution

Rule 69 F.R.Civ.P. applies in adversary proceedings.

CROSS REFERENCES

Applicability of this rule in contested matters not otherwise provided for, see Fed.Rules Bankr.Proc. Rule 9014, 11 USCA.

Effect of entry of judgment on availability of process to enforce judgment, see Fed.Rules Bankr.Proc. Rule 9021, 11 USCA.

Writ of execution to enforce judgment to deliver possession of property, see Fed.Rules Bankr.Proc. Rule 7070, 11 USCA.

Rule 7070. Judgment for Specific Acts; Vesting Title

Rule 70 F.R.Civ.P. applies in adversary proceedings and the court may enter a judgment divesting the title of any party and vesting title in others whenever the real or personal property involved is within the jurisdiction of the court.

(As amended Mar. 30, 1987, eff. Aug. 1, 1987.)

ADVISORY COMMITTEE NOTES
1987 Amendment

The reference to court is used in the amendment because the district court may preside over an adversary proceeding.

CROSS REFERENCES

Effect of entry of judgment on availability of relief under this rule, see Fed.Rules Bankr.Proc. Rule 9021, 11 USCA.

Rule 7071. Process in Behalf of and Against Persons Not Parties

Rule 71 F.R.Civ.P. applies in adversary proceedings.

CROSS REFERENCES

Applicability of this rule in contested matters not otherwise provided for, see Fed.Rules Bankr.Proc. Rule 9014, 11 USCA.

Rule 7087. Transfer of Adversary Proceeding

On motion and after a hearing, the court may transfer an adversary proceeding or any part thereof to

---

another district pursuant to 28 U.S.C. § 1412, except as provided in Rule 7019(2).

(As amended Mar. 30, 1987, eff. Aug. 1, 1987.)

ADVISORY COMMITTEE NOTES

1987 Amendment

The reference to the venue section of title 28 is amended to conform to the 1984 amendments to title 28.

Rule 8001. Scope of Part VIII Rules; Definition of "BAP"; Method of Transmission

(a) General scope

These Part VIII rules govern the procedure in a United States district court and a bankruptcy appellate panel on appeal from a judgment, order, or decree of a bankruptcy court. They also govern certain procedures on appeal to a United States court of appeals under 28 U.S.C. § 158(d).

(b) Definition of "BAP"

"BAP" means a bankruptcy appellate panel established by a circuit's judicial council and authorized to hear appeals from a bankruptcy court under 28 U.S.C. § 158.

(c) Method of transmitting documents

A document must be sent electronically under these Part VIII rules, unless it is being sent by or to an individual who is not represented by counsel or the court's governing rules permit or require mailing or other means of delivery.

(As amended Mar. 30, 1987, eff. Aug. 1, 1987; Apr. 30, 1991, eff. Aug. 1, 1991; Apr. 11, 1997, eff. Dec. 1, 1997; Apr. 23, 2008, eff. Dec. 1, 2008; Mar. 26, 2009, eff. Dec. 1, 2009; Apr. 25, 2014, eff. Dec. 1, 2014.)

ADVISORY COMMITTEE NOTES

These rules in Part VIII apply only to appeals to the district courts or bankruptcy appellate panels. Subsequent appeals to the courts of appeals, or direct appeals by agreement of the parties under 28 U.S.C. § 1293(b), are governed by Federal Rules of Appellate Procedure.

Subdivisions (a) and (b) require that a notice of appeal be filed whenever a litigant seeks to secure appellate review by the district court or bankruptcy appellate panel. An appeal from an interlocutory order which will be heard only if leave is granted under 28 U.S.C. §§ 1334(b) or 1482(b) is taken by filing a notice of appeal accompanied by a motion for leave to appeal which complies with the requirements set forth in Rule 8003. Rule 8003 also governs other aspects of interlocutory appeals.

Subdivision (c) is an adaptation of Rule 42 F.R.App.P.

Subdivision (d) deals with the situation in which an appellant perfects an appeal to the district court or a bankruptcy appellate panel and also a direct appeal pursuant to 28 U.S.C. § 1293(b) to the court of appeals. This subdivision provides that once the appeal to the court of appeals is taken, a notice of appeal to the district court or bankruptcy appellate panel shall be dismissed and, if the first appeal is to the district court or bankruptcy appellate panel, the first appeal shall be dismissed. Paragraph (3) gives an appellant or cross appellant an opportunity to file an appeal to the district court or bankruptcy appellate panel if the court of appeals dismisses the direct appeal because the judgment, order, or decree appealed from is not final. Since the court of appeals has determined the judgment, order, or decree is not final, the new appeal is an appeal for which leave is necessary.

1987 Amendment

Subdivisions (a) and (b) are amended to conform to the 1984 amendments.

Subdivision (d) is abrogated because there is no direct appeal to the court of appeals under 28 U.S.C. § 158, as enacted by the 1984 amendments.

Subdivision (e) is new. Section 158(b)(1) of title 28 authorizes the circuit councils to establish bankruptcy appellate panels. Appeals may not be heard by these panels unless the district court authorizes the referral and all parties to the appeal consent. This rule requires that the parties consent to such an appeal; however, the method of consenting to an appeal may be the subject of a rule promulgated by a circuit council under Rule 8018.

1991 Amendment

Reference to the Official Form number is deleted in anticipation of future revision and renumbering of the Official Forms.

1997 Amendment

This rule is amended to conform to the Bankruptcy Reform Act of 1994 which amended 28 U.S.C. § 158. As amended, a party may—without obtaining leave of the court—appeal from an interlocutory order or decree of the bankruptcy court issued under § 1121(d) of the Code increasing or reducing the time periods referred to in § 1121.

Subdivision (e) is amended to provide the procedure for electing under 28 U.S.C. § 158(c)(1) to have an appeal heard by the district court instead of the bankruptcy appellate panel service. This subdivision is applicable only if a bankruptcy appellate panel service is authorized under 28 U.S.C. § 158(b) to hear the appeal.

GAP Report on Rule 8001. The heading of subdivision (e) is amended to clarify that it applies to the election to have an appeal heard by the district court instead of the BAP. The final paragraph of the Committee Note is revised to clarify that subdivision (e) is applicable only if a BAP is authorized to hear the appeal.

2008 Amendments

Subdivision (e) is amended by redesignating the subdivision as (e)(1) and adding new subdivision (e)(2). Subdivision (e)(2) explicitly recognizes the district court's authority to transfer an appeal to the bankruptcy appellate panel on two conditions: first, all of the parties to the appeal must have agreed to request the withdrawal of the election to have the district court hear the appeal; and, second, the district court must decide whether to grant the request for withdrawal. The district court has discretion either to keep the case or transfer it to the bankruptcy appellate panel, which will prevent strategic behavior by parties and avoid the wasting of judicial resources.

Subdivision (f) is added to the rule to implement the 2005 amendments to 28 U.S.C. § 158(d). That section authorizes appeals directly to the court of appeals, with that court's consent, upon certification that a ground for the appeal exists under § 158(d)(2)(A)(i)–(iii). Certification can be made by the court on its own initiative under subdivision (f)(4), or in response to a request of a party or a majority of the appellants and appellees (if any) under subdivision (f)(3). Certification also can be made by all of the appellants and appellees under subdivision (f)(2)(B). Under subdivision (f)(1), certification is effective only when a timely appeal is commenced under subdivision (a) or (b), and a notice of appeal has been timely filed under Rule 8002. These actions will provide sufficient notice of the appeal to the circuit clerk, so the rule dispenses with the uncodified temporary procedural requirements set out in § 1233(b)(4) of the Bankruptcy Abuse Prevention and Consumer Protection Act of 2005, Pub. L. No. 109–8.

The rule adopts a bright-line test for identifying the court in which a matter is pending. Under subdivision (f)(2), the bright-line chosen is the "docketing" under Rule 8007(b) of an appeal of an interlocutory order or decree under 28 U.S.C. § 158(a)(2) or a final judgment, order or decree under 28 U.S.C. § 158(a)(1), or the granting of leave to appeal any other interlocutory judgment, order or decree under 28 U.S.C. § 158(a)(3), whichever is earlier.

To ensure that parties are aware of a certification, the rule requires either that it be made on the Official Form (if being made by all of the parties to the appeal) or on a separate document (whether the certification is made on the court's own initiative or in response to a request by a party). This is particularly important because the rule adopts the bankruptcy practice established by Rule 8001(a) and (b) of requiring a notice of appeal in every instance, including interlocutory orders, of appeals from bankruptcy court orders, judgments, and decrees. Because this requirement is satisfied by filing the notice of appeal that takes the appeal to the district court or bankruptcy appellate panel in the first instance, the rule does not require a separate notice of appeal if a certification occurs after a district court or bankruptcy appellate panel decision.

A certification under subdivision (f)(1) does not place the appeal in the circuit court. Rather, the court of appeals must first authorize the direct appeal. Subdivision (f)(5) therefore provides that any party intending to pursue the appeal in the court of appeals must seek that permission under Rule 5 of the Federal Rules of Appellate Procedure. Subdivision (f)(5) requires that the petition for permission to appeal be filed within 30 days after an effective certification.

2009 Amendments

The rule is amended to implement changes in connection with the amendment to Rule 9006(a) and the manner by which time is computed under the rules. The deadlines in the rule are amended to substitute a deadline that is a multiple of seven days. Throughout the rules, deadlines are amended in the following manner:

- 5–day periods become 7–day periods
- 10–day periods become 14–day periods
- 15–day periods become 14–day periods
- 20–day periods become 21–day periods
- 25–day periods become 28–day periods

2014 Amendments

These Part VIII rules apply to appeals under 28 U.S.C. § 158(a) from bankruptcy courts to district courts and BAPs. The Federal Rules of Appellate Procedure generally govern bankruptcy appeals to courts of appeals.

Eight of the Part VIII rules do, however, relate to appeals to courts of appeals. Rule 8004(e) provides that the authorization by a court of appeals of a direct appeal of a bankruptcy court's interlocutory order or decree constitutes a grant of leave to appeal. Rule 8006 governs the procedure for certification under 28 U.S.C. § 158(d)(2) of a direct appeal from a judgment, order, or decree of a bankruptcy court to a court of appeals. Rule 8007 addresses stays pending a direct appeal to a court of appeals. Rule 8008 authorizes a bankruptcy court to issue an indicative ruling while an appeal is pending in a court of appeals. Rules 8009 and 8010 govern the record on appeal in a direct appeal to a court of appeals. Rule 8025 governs the granting of a stay of a district court or BAP judgment pending an appeal to the court of appeals. And Rule 8028 authorizes the court of appeals to suspend applicable Part VIII rules in a particular case, subject to certain enumerated exceptions.

These rules take account of the evolving technology in the federal courts for the electronic filing, storage, and transmission of documents. Except as applied to pro se parties, the Part VIII rules require documents to be sent electronically, unless applicable court rules or orders expressly require or permit another means of sending a particular document.

Changes Made After Publication. No changes were made after publication.

Rule 8002. Time for Filing Notice of Appeal

(a) In general

(1) Fourteen-day period

Except as provided in subdivisions (b) and (c), a notice of appeal must be filed with the bankruptcy clerk within 14 days after entry of the judgment, order, or decree being appealed.

(2) Filing before the entry of judgment

A notice of appeal filed after the bankruptcy court announces a decision or order—but before entry of the judgment, order, or decree—is treated as filed on the date of and after the entry.

(3) Multiple appeals

If one party files a timely notice of appeal, any other party may file a notice of appeal within 14 days after the date when the first notice was filed, or within the time otherwise allowed by this rule, whichever period ends later.

(4) Mistaken filing in another court

If a notice of appeal is mistakenly filed in a district court, BAP, or court of appeals, the clerk of that court must state on the notice the date on which it was received and transmit it to the bankruptcy clerk. The notice of appeal is then considered filed in the bankruptcy court on the date so stated.

(5) Entry defined

(A) A judgment, order, or decree is entered for purposes of this Rule 8002(a):

(i) when it is entered in the docket under Rule 5003(a), or

(ii) if Rule 7058 applies and Rule 58(a) F.R.Civ.P. requires a separate document, when the judgment, order, or decree is entered in the docket under Rule 5003(a) and when the earlier of these events occurs:

• the judgment, order, or decree is set out in a separate document; or

• 150 days have run from entry of the judgment, order, or decree in the docket under Rule 5003(a).

(B) A failure to set out a judgment, order, or decree in a separate document when required by

Rule 58(a) F.R.Civ.P. does not affect the validity of an appeal from that judgment, order, or decree.

(b) Effect of a motion on the time to appeal

(1) In general

If a party files in the bankruptcy court any of the following motions and does so within the time allowed by these rules, the time to file an appeal runs for all parties from the entry of the order disposing of the last such remaining motion:

(A) to amend or make additional findings under Rule 7052, whether or not granting the motion would alter the judgment;

(B) to alter or amend the judgment under Rule 9023;

(C) for a new trial under Rule 9023; or

(D) for relief under Rule 9024 if the motion is filed within 14 days after the judgment is entered.

(2) Filing an appeal before the motion is decided

If a party files a notice of appeal after the court announces or enters a judgment, order, or decree—but before it disposes of any motion listed in subdivision (b)(1)—the notice becomes effective when the order disposing of the last such remaining motion is entered.

(3) Appealing the ruling on the motion

If a party intends to challenge an order disposing of any motion listed in subdivision (b)(1)—or the alteration or amendment of a judgment, order, or decree upon the motion—the party must file a notice of appeal or an amended notice of appeal. The notice or amended notice must comply with Rule 8003 or 8004 and be filed within the time prescribed by this rule, measured from the entry of the order disposing of the last such remaining motion.

(4) No additional fee

No additional fee is required to file an amended notice of appeal.

(c) Appeal by an inmate confined in an institution

(1) In general

If an institution has a system designed for legal mail, an inmate confined there must use that system to receive the benefit of this Rule 8002(c)(1). If an inmate files a notice of appeal from a judgment, order, or decree of a bankruptcy court, the notice is timely if it is deposited in the institution's internal mail system on or before the last day for filing and:

(A) it is accompanied by:

(i) a declaration in compliance with 28 U.S.C. § 1746—or a notarized statement—setting out the date of deposit and stating that first-class postage is being prepaid; or

(ii) evidence (such as a postmark or date stamp) showing that the notice was so deposited and that postage was prepaid; or

(B) the appellate court exercises its discretion to permit the later filing of a declaration or notarized statement that satisfies Rule 8002(c)(1)(A)(i).

(2) Multiple appeals

If an inmate files under this subdivision the first notice of appeal, the 14–day period provided in subdivision (a)(3) for another party to file a notice of appeal runs from the date when the bankruptcy clerk dockets the first notice.

(d) Extending the time to appeal
(1) When the time may be extended

Except as provided in subdivision (d)(2), the bankruptcy court may extend the time to file a notice of appeal upon a party's motion that is filed:

(A) within the time prescribed by this rule; or

(B) within 21 days after that time, if the party shows excusable neglect.

(2) When the time may not be extended

The bankruptcy court may not extend the time to file a notice of appeal if the judgment, order, or decree appealed from:

(A) grants relief from an automatic stay under § 362, 922, 1201, or 1301 of the Code;

(B) authorizes the sale or lease of property or the use of cash collateral under § 363 of the Code;

(C) authorizes the obtaining of credit under § 364 of the Code;

(D) authorizes the assumption or assignment of an executory contract or unexpired lease under § 365 of the Code;

(E) approves a disclosure statement under § 1125 of the Code; or

(F) confirms a plan under § 943, 1129, 1225, or 1325 of the Code.

(3) Time limits on an extension

No extension of time may exceed 21 days after the time prescribed by this rule, or 14 days after the order granting the motion to extend time is entered, whichever is later.

(As amended Mar. 30, 1987, eff. Aug. 1, 1987; Apr. 30, 1991, eff. Aug. 1, 1991; Apr. 29, 1994, eff. Aug. 1, 1994; Apr. 11, 1997, eff. Dec. 1, 1997; Mar. 26, 2009, eff. Dec. 1, 2009; Apr. 25, 2014, eff. Dec. 1, 2014; Apr. 26, 2018, eff. Dec. 1, 2018.)

ADVISORY COMMITTEE NOTES

This rule is an adaptation of Rule 4(a) F.R.App.P. The time to appeal from a judgment, order, or decree of a bankruptcy judge is 10 days, rather than the 30 days provided for in the civil practice. The shortened time is specified in order to obtain prompt appellate review, often important to the administration of a case under the Code. If a timely notice of appeal is filed, other parties have an additional 10 days within which to file a notice of appeal. A notice of appeal filed within the additional 10 day period by an appellee is a cross appeal, but there is a separate appeal if a non-appellee files a notice of appeal within that 10 day period.

The district courts and bankruptcy appellate panels have inherent authority to consolidate appeals.

Subdivision (b) is essentially the same as Rule 4(a)(4) of the F.R.App.P.

Subdivision (c) is similar to former Bankruptcy Rule 802(c). To expedite the disposition of appeals the maximum extension of time is 20 days instead of the 30 days provided by Rule 4(a)(5) of the F.R.App.P. Subject to the exceptions set forth in subdivision (c), the court may extend the time for taking an appeal when a motion for extension is filed after the expiration of the original 10 day period but no later than 20 days after the expiration of the original 10 day period. Orders of the bankruptcy court relating to the sale of property, extension of credit, confirmation of a plan, dismissal or conversion of the case, and approval of the disclosure statement are of such significance to the administration of the case, the parties in interest, and third parties that this subdivision requires that either an appeal or a motion for extension be filed within the original 10 day period.

If a timely notice of appeal is not filed, no appeal may be taken later. Former Bankruptcy Rule 803, which provided that a referee's judgment became final when the appeal period expired, has been omitted as unnecessary.

1991 Amendment

Subdivision (a) is amended to conform to F.R.App.P. 4(a)(2) which is designed to avoid the loss of the right to appeal when a notice of appeal is filed prematurely.

Subdivision (b)(1) is deleted because Rule 9015 was abrogated in 1987.

1994 Amendments

These amendments are intended to conform to the 1993 amendments to F.R.App.P. 4(a)(4) and 6(b)(2)(i).

This rule as amended provides that a notice of appeal filed before the disposition of a specified postjudgment motion will become effective upon disposition of the motion. A notice filed before the filing of one of the specified motions or after the filing of a motion but before disposition of the motion is, in effect, suspended until the motion is disposed of, whereupon the previously filed notice effectively places jurisdiction in the district court or bankruptcy appellate panel.

Because a notice of appeal will ripen into an effective appeal upon disposition of a postjudgment motion, in some instances there will be an appeal from a judgment that has been altered substantially because the motion was granted in whole or in part. The appeal may be dismissed for want of prosecution when the appellant fails to meet the briefing schedule. But, the appellee may also move to strike the appeal. When responding to such a motion, the appellant would have an opportunity to state that, even though some relief sought in a postjudgment motion was granted, the appellant still plans to pursue the appeal. Because the appellant's response would provide the appellee with sufficient notice of the appellant's intentions, the rule does not require an additional notice of appeal in that situation.

The amendment provides that a notice of appeal filed before the disposition of a postjudgment tolling motion is sufficient to bring the judgment, order, or decree specified in the original notice of appeal to the district court or bankruptcy appellate panel. If the judgment is altered upon disposition of a postjudgment motion, however, and if a party who has previously filed a notice of appeal wishes to appeal from the disposition of the motion, the party must amend the notice to so indicate. When a party files an amended notice, no additional fees are required because the notice is an amendment of the original and not a new notice of appeal.

Subdivision (b) is also amended to include, among motions that extend the time for filing a notice of appeal, a motion under Rule 9024 that is filed within 10 days after entry of a judgment. The addition of this motion conforms to a similar amendment to F.R.App.P. 4(a)(4) made in 1993, except that a Rule 9024 motion does not toll the time to appeal unless it is filed within the 10-day period. The reason for providing that the motion extends the time to appeal only if it is <u>filed</u> within the 10-day period is to enable the court and the parties in interest to determine solely from the court records whether the time to appeal has been extended by a motion for relief under Rule 9024.

1997 Amendment

Subdivision (c) is amended to provide that a request for an extension of time to file a notice of appeal must be filed within the applicable time period. This amendment will avoid uncertainty as to whether the mailing of a motion or an oral request in court is sufficient to request an extension of time, and will enable the court and the parties in interest to determine solely from the court records whether a timely request for an extension has been made.

The amendments also give the court discretion to permit a party to file a notice of appeal more than 20 days after expiration of the time to appeal otherwise prescribed, but only if the motion was timely filed and the notice of appeal is filed within a period not exceeding 10 days after entry of the order extending the time. This amendment is designed to protect parties that file timely motions to extend the time to appeal from the harshness of the present rule as demonstrated in In re Mouradick, 13 F.3d 326 (9th Cir.1994), where the court held that a notice of appeal filed within the 3–day period expressly prescribed by an order granting a timely motion for an extension of time did not confer jurisdiction on the appellate court because the notice of appeal was not filed within the 20–day period specified in subdivision (c).

The subdivision is amended further to prohibit any extension of time to file a notice of appeal—even if the motion for an extension is filed before the expiration of the original time to appeal—if the order appealed from grants relief from the automatic stay, authorizes the sale or lease of property, use of cash collateral, obtaining of credit, or assumption or assignment of an executory contract or unexpired lease under § 365, or approves a disclosure statement or confirms a plan. These types of orders are often relied upon immediately after they are entered and should not be reviewable on appeal after the expiration of the original appeal period under Rule 8002(a) and (b).

GAP Report on Rule 8002. No changes to the published draft.

2009 Amendments

The rule is amended to implement changes in connection with the amendment to Rule 9006(a) and the manner by which time is computed under the rules. The deadlines in the rule are amended to substitute a deadline that is a multiple of seven days. Throughout the rules, deadlines are amended in the following manner:

- 5–day periods become 7–day periods
- 10–day periods become 14–day periods
- 15–day periods become 14–day periods
- 20–day periods become 21–day periods
- 25–day periods become 28–day periods

2014 Amendments

This rule is derived from former Rule 8002 and F.R.App.P. 4(a) and (c). With the exception of subdivision (c), the changes to the former rule are stylistic. The rule retains the former rule's 14–day time period for filing a notice of appeal, as opposed to the longer periods permitted for appeals in civil cases under F.R.App.P. 4(a).

Subdivision (a) continues to allow any other party to file a notice of appeal within 14 days after the first notice of appeal is filed, or thereafter to the extent otherwise authorized by this rule. Subdivision (a) also retains provisions of the former rule that prescribe the date the notice of appeal is deemed filed if the appellant files it prematurely or in the wrong court.

Subdivision (b), like former Rule 8002(b) and F.R.App.P. 4(a), tolls the time for filing a notice of appeal when certain postjudgment motions are filed, and it prescribes the effective date of a notice of appeal that is filed before the court disposes of all of the specified motions. As under the former rule, a party that wants to appeal the court's disposition of the motion or the alteration or amendment of a judgment, order, or decree in response to such a motion must file a notice of appeal or, if it has already filed one, an amended notice of appeal.

Although Rule 8003(a)(3)(C) requires a notice of appeal to be accompanied by the required fee, no additional fee is required for the filing of an amended notice of appeal.

Subdivision (c) mirrors the provisions of F.R.App.P. 4(c)(1) and (2), which specify timing rules for a notice of appeal filed by an inmate confined in an institution.

Subdivision (d) continues to allow the court to grant an extension of time to file a notice of appeal, except with respect to certain specified judgments, orders, and decrees.

Changes Made After Publication. Stylistic changes were made to the title of subdivision (b)(3) and to subdivision (c)(1).

2018 Amendments

Clarifying amendments are made to subdivisions (a), (b), and (c) of the rule. They are modeled on parallel provisions of F.R.App.P. 4.

Paragraph (5) is added to subdivision (a) to clarify the effect of the separate-document requirement of F.R.Civ.P. 58(a) on the entry of a judgment, order, or decree for the purpose of determining the time for filing a notice of appeal.

Rule 7058 adopts F.R.Civ.P. 58 for adversary proceedings. If Rule 58(a) requires a judgment to be set out in a separate document, the time for filing a notice of appeal runs—subject to subdivisions (b) and (c)—from when the judgment is docketed and the judgment is set out in a separate document or, if no separate document is prepared, from 150 days from when the judgment is entered in the docket. The court's failure to comply with the separate-document requirement of Rule 58(a), however, does not affect the validity of an appeal.

Rule 58 does not apply in contested matters. Instead, under Rule 9021, a separate document is not required, and a judgment or order is effective when it is entered in the docket. The time for filing a notice of appeal under subdivision (a) therefore begins to run upon docket entry in contested matters, as well as in adversary proceedings for which Rule 58 does not require a separate document.

A clarifying amendment is made to subdivision (b)(1) to conform to a recent amendment to F.R.App.P. 4(a)(4)—from which Rule 8002(b)(1) is derived. Former Rule 8002(b)(1) provided that "[i]f a party timely files in the bankruptcy court" certain post-judgment motions, "the time to file an appeal runs for all parties from the entry of the order disposing of the last such remaining motion." Responding to a circuit split concerning the meaning of "timely" in F.R.App.P. 4(a)(4), the amendment adopts the majority approach and rejects the approach taken in *National Ecological Foundation v. Alexander*, 496 F.3d 466 (6th Cir. 2007). A motion made after the time allowed by the Bankruptcy Rules will not qualify as a motion that, under Rule 8002(b)(1), re-starts the appeal time—and that fact is not altered by, for example, a court order that sets a due date that is later than permitted by the Bankruptcy Rules, another party's consent or failure to object to the motion's lateness, or the court's disposition of the motion without explicit reliance on untimeliness.

Subdivision (c)(1) is revised to conform to F.R.App.P. 4(c)(1), which was recently amended to streamline and clarify the operation of the inmate-filing rule. The rule requires the inmate to show timely deposit and prepayment of postage. It is amended to specify that a notice is timely if it is accompanied by a declaration or notarized statement stating the date the notice was deposited in the institution's mail system and attesting to the prepayment of first-class postage. The declaration must state that first-class postage "is being prepaid," not (as directed by the former rule) that first-class postage "has been prepaid." This change reflects the fact that inmates may need to rely upon the institution to affix postage after the inmate has deposited the document in the institution's mail system. A new Director's Form sets out a suggested form of the declaration.

The amended rule also provides that a notice is timely without a declaration or notarized statement if other evidence accompanying the notice shows that the notice was deposited on or before the due date and that postage was prepaid. If the notice is not accompanied by evidence that establishes timely deposit and prepayment of postage, then the appellate court—district court, BAP, or court of appeals in the case of a direct appeal—has discretion to accept a declaration or notarized statement at a later date. The rule uses the phrase "exercises its discretion to permit"—rather than simply "permits"—to help ensure that pro se inmates are aware that a court will not necessarily forgive a failure to provide the declaration initially.

Rule 8003. Appeal as of Right—How Taken; Docketing the Appeal

(a) Filing the notice of appeal

(1) In general

An appeal from a judgment, order, or decree of a bankruptcy court to a district court or BAP under 28 U.S.C. § 158(a)(1) or (a)(2) may be taken only by filing a notice of appeal with the bankruptcy clerk within the time allowed by Rule 8002.

(2) Effect of not taking other steps

An appellant's failure to take any step other than the timely filing of a notice of appeal does not affect the validity of the appeal, but is ground only for the district court or BAP to act as it considers appropriate, including dismissing the appeal.

(3) Contents

The notice of appeal must:

(A) conform substantially to the appropriate Official Form;

(B) be accompanied by the judgment, order, or decree, or the part of it, being appealed; and

(C) be accompanied by the prescribed fee.

(4) Additional copies

If requested to do so, the appellant must furnish the bankruptcy clerk with enough copies of the notice to enable the clerk to comply with subdivision (c).

(b) Joint or consolidated appeals

(1) Joint notice of appeal

When two or more parties are entitled to appeal from a judgment, order, or decree of a bankruptcy court and their interests make joinder practicable, they may file a joint notice of appeal. They may then proceed on appeal as a single appellant.

(2) Consolidating appeals

When parties have separately filed timely notices of appeal, the district court or BAP may join or consolidate the appeals.

(c) Serving the notice of appeal

(1) Serving parties and transmitting to the United States trustee

The bankruptcy clerk must serve the notice of appeal on counsel of record for each party to the appeal, excluding the appellant, and transmit it to the United States trustee. If a party is proceeding pro se, the clerk must send the notice of appeal to the party's last known address. The clerk must note, on each copy, the date when the notice of appeal was filed.

(2) Effect of failing to serve or transmit notice

The bankruptcy clerk's failure to serve notice on a party or transmit notice to the United States trustee does not affect the validity of the appeal.

(3) Noting service on the docket

The clerk must note on the docket the names of the parties served and the date and method of the service.

(d) Transmitting the notice of appeal to the district court or BAP; docketing the appeal

(1) Transmitting the notice

The bankruptcy clerk must promptly transmit the notice of appeal to the BAP clerk if a BAP has been established for appeals from that district and the appellant has not elected to have the district court hear the appeal. Otherwise, the bankruptcy clerk must promptly transmit the notice to the district clerk.

(2) Docketing in the district court or BAP

Upon receiving the notice of appeal, the district or BAP clerk must docket the appeal under the title of the bankruptcy case and the title of any adversary proceeding, and must identify the appellant, adding the appellant's name if necessary.

(As amended Mar. 30, 1987, eff. Aug. 1, 1987; Apr. 23, 2008, eff. Dec. 1, 2008; Mar. 26, 2009, eff. Dec. 1, 2009; Apr. 25, 2014, eff. Dec. 1, 2014.)

ADVISORY COMMITTEE NOTES

Subdivisions (a) and (b) of this rule are derived from Rules 5 and 6 F.R.App.P. The motion for leave to appeal is addressed to the district court or the bankruptcy appellate panel, although filed with the clerk of the bankruptcy court.

Subdivision (c) provides that if a party mistakenly believes the order appealed from is final and files only a notice of appeal, the appeal is not automatically dismissed. The district court or bankruptcy appellate panel has the options to direct that a motion be filed, to decide exclusively on the papers already filed to grant leave to appeal, or to deny leave to appeal. Cf. 28 U.S.C. § 2103.

2008 Amendments

The rule is amended to add subdivision (d) to solve the jurisdictional problem that could otherwise ensue when a district court or bankruptcy appellate panel has not granted leave to appeal under 28 U.S.C. § 158(a)(3). If the court of appeals accepts the appeal, the requirement of leave to appeal is deemed satisfied. However, if the court of appeals does not authorize a direct appeal, the question of whether to grant leave to appeal remains a matter to be resolved by the district court or the bankruptcy appellate panel.

2009 Amendments

The rule is amended to implement changes in connection with the amendment to Rule 9006(a) and the manner by which time is computed under the rules. The deadlines in the rule are amended to substitute a deadline that is a multiple of seven days. Throughout the rules, deadlines are amended in the following manner:

- 5-day periods become 7-day periods
- 10-day periods become 14-day periods
- 15-day periods become 14-day periods
- 20-day periods become 21-day periods
- 25-day periods become 28-day periods

2014 Amendments

This rule is derived from several former Bankruptcy Rule and Appellate Rule provisions. It addresses appeals as of right, joint and consolidated appeals, service of the notice of appeal, and the timing of the docketing of an appeal in the district court or BAP.

Subdivision (a) incorporates, with stylistic changes, much of the content of former Rule 8001(a) regarding the taking of an appeal as of right under 28 U.S.C. § 158(a)(1) or (2). The rule now requires that the judgment, order, or decree being appealed be attached to the notice of appeal.

Subdivision (b), which is an adaptation of F.R.App.P. 3(b), permits the filing of a joint notice of appeal by multiple appellants that have sufficiently similar interests that their joinder is practicable. It also allows the district court or BAP to consolidate appeals taken separately by two or more parties.

Subdivision (c) is derived from former Rule 8004 and F.R.App.P. 3(d). Under Rule 8001(c), the former rule's requirement that service of the notice of appeal be accomplished by mailing is generally modified to require that the bankruptcy clerk serve counsel by electronic means. Service on pro se parties must be made by sending the notice to the address most recently provided to the court.

Subdivision (d) modifies the provision of former Rule 8007(b), which delayed the docketing of an appeal by the district court or BAP until the record was complete and the bankruptcy clerk transmitted it. The new provision, adapted from F.R.App.P. 3(d) and 12(a), requires the bankruptcy clerk to promptly transmit the notice of appeal to the clerk of the district court or BAP. Upon receipt of the notice of appeal, the district or BAP clerk must docket the appeal. Under this procedure, motions filed in the district court or BAP prior to completion and transmission of the record can generally be placed on the docket of an already pending appeal.

Changes Made After Publication. In subdivision (d)(2), the direction for docketing a bankruptcy appeal was changed to reflect the fact that many bankruptcy appeals have dual titles—the bankruptcy case itself and the adversary proceeding that is the subject of the appeal. Stylistic changes were made to subdivision (c)(1). Conforming changes were made to the Committee Note.

Rule 8004. Appeal by Leave—How Taken; Docketing the Appeal

(a) Notice of appeal and motion for leave to appeal

To appeal from an interlocutory order or decree of a bankruptcy court under 28 U.S.C. § 158(a)(3), a party must file with the bankruptcy clerk a notice of appeal as prescribed by Rule 8003(a). The notice must:

(1) be filed within the time allowed by Rule 8002;

(2) be accompanied by a motion for leave to appeal prepared in accordance with subdivision (b); and

(3) unless served electronically using the court's transmission equipment, include proof of service in accordance with Rule 8011(d).

(b) Contents of the motion; response
(1) Contents

A motion for leave to appeal under 28 U.S.C. § 158(a)(3) must include the following:

(A) the facts necessary to understand the question presented;

(B) the question itself;

(C) the relief sought;

(D) the reasons why leave to appeal should be granted; and

(E) a copy of the interlocutory order or decree and any related opinion or memorandum.

(2) Response

A party may file with the district or BAP clerk a response in opposition or a cross-motion within 14 days after the motion is served.

(c) Transmitting the notice of appeal and the motion; docketing the appeal; determining the motion

(1) Transmitting to the district court or BAP

The bankruptcy clerk must promptly transmit the notice of appeal and the motion for leave to the BAP clerk if a BAP has been established for appeals from that district and the appellant has not elected to have the district court hear the appeal. Otherwise, the bankruptcy clerk must promptly transmit the notice and motion to the district clerk.

(2) Docketing in the district court or BAP

Upon receiving the notice and motion, the district or BAP clerk must docket the appeal under the title of the bankruptcy case and the title of any adversary proceeding, and must identify the appellant, adding the appellant's name if necessary.

(3) Oral argument not required

The motion and any response or cross-motion are submitted without oral argument unless the district court or BAP orders otherwise.

(d) Failure to file a motion with a notice of appeal

If an appellant timely files a notice of appeal under this rule but does not include a motion for leave, the district court or BAP may order the appellant to file a motion for leave, or treat the notice of appeal as a motion for leave and either grant or deny it. If the court orders that a motion for leave be filed, the appellant must do so within 14 days after the order is entered, unless the order provides otherwise.

(e) Direct appeal to a court of appeals

If leave to appeal an interlocutory order or decree is required under 28 U.S.C. § 158(a)(3), an authorization of a direct appeal by the court of appeals under 28 U.S.C. § 158(d)(2) satisfies the requirement.

(As amended Mar. 30, 1987, eff. Aug. 1, 1987; Apr. 30, 1991, eff. Aug. 1, 1991; Apr. 25, 2014, eff. Dec. 1, 2014.)

ADVISORY COMMITTEE NOTES

This rule is an adaptation of Rule 3(d) F.R.App.P.

1991 Amendment

This rule is amended to keep the United States trustee informed of the progress of the case.

2014 Amendments

This rule is derived from former Rules 8001(b) and 8003 and F.R.App.P. 5. It retains the practice for interlocutory bankruptcy appeals of requiring a notice of appeal to be filed along with a motion for leave to appeal. Like current Rule 8003, it alters the timing of the docketing of the appeal in the district court or BAP.

Subdivision (a) requires a party seeking leave to appeal under 28 U.S.C. § 158(a)(3) to file with the bankruptcy clerk both a notice of appeal and a motion for leave to appeal.

Subdivision (b) prescribes the contents of the motion, retaining the requirements of former Rule 8003(a). It also continues to allow another party to file a cross-motion or response to the appellant's motion. Because of the prompt docketing of the appeal under the current rule, the cross-motion or response must be filed in the district court or BAP, rather than in the bankruptcy court as the former rule required.

Subdivision (c) requires the bankruptcy clerk to transmit promptly to the district court or BAP the notice of appeal and the motion for leave to appeal. Upon receipt of the notice and the motion, the district or BAP clerk must docket the appeal. Unless the district court or BAP orders otherwise, no oral argument will be held on the motion.

Subdivision (d) retains the provisions of former Rule 8003(c). It provides that if the appellant timely files a notice of appeal, but fails to file a motion for leave to appeal, the court can either direct that a motion be filed or treat the notice of appeal as the motion and either grant or deny leave.

Subdivision (e), like former Rule 8003(d), treats the authorization of a direct appeal by the court of appeals as a grant of leave to appeal under 28 U.S.C. § 158(a)(3) if the district court or BAP has not already granted leave. Thus, a separate order granting leave to appeal is not required. If the court of appeals grants permission to appeal, the record must be assembled and transmitted in accordance with Rules 8009 and 8010.

Changes Made After Publication. In subdivision (c)(2), the direction for docketing a bankruptcy appeal was changed to reflect the fact that many bankruptcy appeals have dual titles-the bankruptcy case itself and the adversary proceeding that is the subject of the appeal. As published, subdivision (c)(3) stated that the court must dismiss the appeal if the motion for leave to appeal is denied. That sentence was deleted.

Rule 8005.   **Election to Have an Appeal Heard by the District Court Instead of the BAP**

(a) Filing of a statement of election

To elect to have an appeal heard by the district court, a party must:

(1) file a statement of election that conforms substantially to the appropriate Official Form; and

(2) do so within the time prescribed by 28 U.S.C. § 158(c)(1).

(b) Transmitting the documents related to the appeal

Upon receiving an appellant's timely statement of election, the bankruptcy clerk must transmit to the district clerk all documents related to the appeal. Upon receiving a timely statement of election by a party other than the appellant, the BAP clerk must transmit to the district clerk all documents related to the appeal and notify the bankruptcy clerk of the transmission.

(c) Determining the validity of an election

A party seeking a determination of the validity of an election must file a motion in the court where the appeal is then pending. The motion must be filed within 14 days after the statement of election is filed.

(d) Motion for leave without a notice of appeal—effect on the timing of an election

If an appellant moves for leave to appeal under Rule 8004 but fails to file a separate notice of appeal with the motion, the motion must be treated as a notice of appeal for purposes of determining the timeliness of a statement of election.

(As amended Mar. 30, 1987, eff. Aug. 1, 1987; Apr. 25, 2014, eff. Dec. 1, 2014.)

ADVISORY COMMITTEE NOTES

The first, third, and fourth sentences of this rule are adaptations of Rule 8(a) and (b) F.R.App.P. The second sentence of the rule is derived from § 39(c) of the Bankruptcy Act [former § 67(c) of this title] and confers on the bankruptcy judge discretion respecting the stay or continuation of other proceedings in the case while an appeal is pending.

The last sentence of the rule, which specifically subjects a trustee to the same kind of security requirements as other litigants, is derived from former Bankruptcy Rule 805. The exemption of the United States from the bond or security requirements is the same as the exemption contained in Rule 62(e) F.R.Civ.P.

Sections 363(m) and 364(e) of the Code provide that unless an order approving a sale of property, or authorizing the obtaining of credit or the incurring of debt is stayed pending appeal, the sale of property to a good faith purchaser or a good faith extension of credit, with or without any priority or lien, shall not be affected by the reversal or modification of such order on appeal, whether or not the purchaser or creditor knows of the pendency of the appeal.

2014 Amendments

This rule, which implements 28 U.S.C. § 158(c)(1), is derived from former Rule 8001(e). It applies only in districts in which an appeal to a BAP is authorized.

As the former rule required, **subdivision (a)** provides that an appellant that elects to have a district court, rather than a BAP, hear its appeal must file with the bankruptcy clerk a statement of election when it files its notice of appeal. The statement must conform substantially to the appropriate Official Form. For appellants, that statement is included in the Notice of Appeal Official Form. If a BAP has been established for appeals from the bankruptcy court and the appellant does not file a timely statement of election, any other party that elects to have the district court hear the appeal

must file a statement of election with the BAP clerk no later than 30 days after service of the notice of appeal.

Subdivision (b) requires the bankruptcy clerk to transmit all appeal documents to the district clerk if the appellant files a timely statement of election. If the appellant does not make that election, the bankruptcy clerk must transmit those documents to the BAP clerk. Upon a timely election by any other party, the BAP clerk must promptly transmit the appeal documents to the district clerk and notify the bankruptcy clerk that the appeal has been transferred.

Subdivision (c) provides a new procedure for the resolution of disputes regarding the validity of an election. A motion seeking the determination of the validity of an election must be filed no later than 14 days after the statement of election is filed. Nothing in this rule prevents a court from determining the validity of an election on its own motion.

Subdivision (d) provides that, in the case of an appeal by leave, if the appellant files a motion for leave to appeal but fails to file a notice of appeal, the filing and service of the motion will be treated for timing purposes under this rule as the filing and service of the notice of appeal.

Changes Made After Publication. In subdivision (b), a requirement was added that the BAP clerk notify the bankruptcy clerk if an appeal is transferred from the BAP to the district court upon the election of an appellee. Conforming and clarifying changes were made to the Committee Note.

Rule 8006. Certifying a Direct Appeal to the Court of Appeals

(a) Effective date of a certification

A certification of a judgment, order, or decree of a bankruptcy court for direct review in a court of appeals under 28 U.S.C. § 158(d)(2) is effective when:

(1) the certification has been filed;

(2) a timely appeal has been taken under Rule 8003 or 8004; and

(3) the notice of appeal has become effective under Rule 8002.

(b) Filing the certification

The certification must be filed with the clerk of the court where the matter is pending. For purposes of this rule, a matter remains pending in the bankruptcy court for 30 days after the effective date under Rule 8002 of the first notice of appeal from the judgment, order, or decree for which direct review is sought. A matter is pending in the district court or BAP thereafter.

(c) Joint certification by all appellants and appellees

(1) How accomplished

A joint certification by all the appellants and appellees under 28 U.S.C. § 158(d)(2)(A) must be made by using the appropriate Official Form. The parties may supplement the certification with a short statement of the basis for the certification, which may include the information listed in subdivision (f)(2).

(2) Supplemental statement by the court

Within 14 days after the parties' certification, the bankruptcy court or the court in which the matter is then pending may file a short supplemental statement about the merits of the certification.

(d) The court that may make the certification

Only the court where the matter is pending, as provided in subdivision (b), may certify a direct review on request of parties or on its own motion.

(e) Certification on the court's own motion

(1) How accomplished

A certification on the court's own motion must be set forth in a separate document. The clerk of the certifying court must serve it on the parties to the appeal in the manner required for service of a notice of appeal under Rule 8003(c)(1). The certification must be accompanied by an opinion or memorandum that contains the information required by subdivision (f)(2)(A)-(D).

(2) Supplemental statement by a party

Within 14 days after the court's certification, a party may file with the clerk of the certifying court a short supplemental statement regarding the merits of certification.

(f) Certification by the court on request

(1) How requested

A request by a party for certification that a circumstance specified in 28 U.S.C. §158(d)(2)(A)(i)–(iii) applies—or a request by a majority of the appellants and a majority of the appellees—must be filed with the clerk of the court where the matter is pending within 60 days after the entry of the judgment, order, or decree.

(2) Service and contents

The request must be served on all parties to the appeal in the manner required for service of a notice of appeal under Rule 8003(c)(1), and it must include the following:

   (A) the facts necessary to understand the question presented;

   (B) the question itself;

   (C) the relief sought;

   (D) the reasons why the direct appeal should be allowed, including which circumstance specified in 28 U.S.C. § 158(d)(2)(A)(i)-(iii) applies; and

   (E) a copy of the judgment, order, or decree and any related opinion or memorandum.

(3) Time to file a response or a cross-request

A party may file a response to the request within 14 days after the request is served, or such other time as the court where the matter is pending allows. A party may file a cross-request for certification within 14 days after the request is served, or

within 60 days after the entry of the judgment, order, or decree, whichever occurs first.

(4) Oral argument not required

The request, cross-request, and any response are submitted without oral argument unless the court where the matter is pending orders otherwise.

(5) Form and service of the certification

If the court certifies a direct appeal in response to the request, it must do so in a separate document. The certification must be served on the parties to the appeal in the manner required for service of a notice of appeal under Rule 8003(c)(1).

(g) Proceeding in the court of appeals following a certification

Within 30 days after the date the certification becomes effective under subdivision (a), a request for permission to take a direct appeal to the court of appeals must be filed with the circuit clerk in accordance with F.R.App.P. 6(c).

(As amended Mar. 30, 1987, eff. Aug. 1, 1987; Apr. 30, 1991, eff. Aug. 1, 1991; Apr. 29, 1994, eff. Aug. 1, 1994; Mar. 26, 2009, eff. Dec. 1, 2009; Apr. 25, 2014, eff. Dec. 1, 2014; Apr. 26, 2018, eff. Dec. 1, 2018.)

ADVISORY COMMITTEE NOTES

This rule is an adaptation of Rule 10(b) F.R.App.P. The last sentence of the rule is derived from Rule 11(a) F.R.App.P.

1991 Amendment

The seven-day time periods are changed to 10 days to conform to Rule 75(b)(2) F.R.Civ.P. and Rule 10(b)(3) F.R.App.P. The amendment requiring a party to provide a copy of the items designated for the record is to facilitate the amendments to Rule 8007 providing for retention by the bankruptcy clerk of the original record.

1994 Amendments

The amendment to the first sentence of this rule is made together with the amendment to Rule 8002(b), which provides, in essence, that certain specified postjudgment motions suspend a filed notice of appeal until the disposition of the last of such motions. The purpose of this amendment is to suspend the 10-day period for filing and serving a designation of the record and statement of the issues if a timely postjudgment motion is made and a notice of appeal is suspended under Rule 8002(b). The 10-day period set forth in the first sentence of this rule begins to run when the order disposing of the last of such postjudgment motions outstanding is entered. The other amendments to this rule are stylistic.

2009 Amendments

The rule is amended to implement changes in connection with the amendment to Rule 9006(a) and the manner by which time is computed under the rules. The deadlines in the rule are amended to substitute a deadline that is a multiple of seven days. Throughout the rules, deadlines are amended in the following manner:

- 5–day periods become 7–day periods
- 10–day periods become 14–day periods
- 15–day periods become 14–day periods
- 20–day periods become 21–day periods
- 25–day periods become 28–day periods

2014 Amendments

This rule is derived from former Rule 8001(f), and it provides the procedures for the certification of a direct appeal of a judgment, order, or decree of a bankruptcy court to the court of appeals under 28 U.S.C. § 158(d)(2). Once a case has been certified in the bankruptcy court, the district court, or the BAP for direct appeal and a request for permission to appeal has been timely filed with the circuit clerk, the Federal Rules of Appellate Procedure govern further proceedings in the court of appeals.

Subdivision (a), like the former rule, requires that an appeal be properly taken—now under Rule 8003 or 8004—before a certification for direct review in the court of appeals takes effect. This rule requires the timely filing of a notice of appeal under Rule 8002 and accounts for the delayed effectiveness of a notice of appeal under the circumstances specified in that rule. Ordinarily, a notice of appeal is effective when it is filed in the bankruptcy court. Rule 8002, however, delays the effectiveness of a notice of appeal when (1) it is filed after the announcement of a decision or order but prior to the entry of the judgment, order, or decree; or (2) it is filed after the announcement or entry of a judgment, order, or decree but before the bankruptcy court disposes of certain post-judgment motions.

When the bankruptcy court enters an interlocutory order or decree that is appealable under 28 U.S.C. § 158(a)(3), certification for direct review in the court of appeals may take effect before the district court or BAP grants leave to appeal. The certification is effective when the actions specified in subdivision (a) have occurred. Rule 8004(e) provides that if the court of appeals grants permission to take a direct appeal before leave to appeal an interlocutory ruling has been granted, the authorization by the court of appeals is treated as the granting of leave to appeal.

Subdivision (b) provides that a certification must be filed in the court where the matter is pending, as determined by this subdivision. This provision modifies the former rule. Because of the prompt docketing of appeals in the district court or BAP under Rules 8003 and 8004, a matter is deemed—for purposes of this rule only—to remain pending in the bankruptcy court for 30 days after the effective date of the notice of appeal. This provision will in appropriate cases give the bankruptcy judge, who will be familiar with the matter being appealed, an opportunity to decide whether certification for direct review is appropriate. Similarly, subdivision (d) provides that only the court where the matter is then pending according to subdivision (b) may make a certification on its own motion or on the request of one or more parties.

Section 158(d)(2) provides three different ways in which an appeal may be certified for direct review. Implementing these options, the rule provides in subdivision (c) for the joint certification by all appellants and appellees; in subdivision (e) for the bankruptcy court's, district court's, or BAP's certification on its own motion; and in subdivision (f) for the bankruptcy court's, district court's, or BAP's certification on request of a party or a majority of appellants and a majority of appellees.

Subdivision (g) requires that, once a certification for direct review is made, a request to the court of appeals for permission to take a direct appeal to that court must be filed with the clerk of the court of appeals no later than 30 days after the effective date of the certification. Federal Rule of Appellate Procedure 6(c), which incorporates all of F.R.App.P. 5 except subdivision (a)(3), prescribes the procedure for requesting the permission of the court of appeals and governs proceedings that take place thereafter in that court.

Changes Made After Publication. In subdivisions (b) and (g), cross-references were added. In subdivision (f)(4), the statement regarding the inapplicability of Rule 9014 was deleted as unnecessary. A clarifying change was made to the first paragraph of the Committee Note.

2018 Amendments

Subdivision (c) is amended to provide authority for the court to file a statement on the merits of a certification for direct review by the court of appeals when the certification is made jointly by all of the parties to the appeal. It is a counterpart to subdivision (e)(2), which allows a party to file a similar statement when the court certifies direct review on the court's own motion.

The bankruptcy court may file a supplemental statement within 14 days after the certification, even if the appeal is no longer pending before it according to subdivision (b). If the appeal is pending in the district court or BAP during that 14–day period, the appellate court is authorized to file a statement. In all cases, the filing of a statement by the court is discretionary.

HISTORICAL AND STATUTORY NOTES

References in Text

The Federal Rules of Appellate Procedure, referred to in subd. (g), are set out in the Appendix to Title 28.

Rule 8007. Stay Pending Appeal; Bonds; Suspension of Proceedings

(a) Initial motion in the Bankruptcy Court

(1) In general

Ordinarily, a party must move first in the bankruptcy court for the following relief:

(A) a stay of a judgment, order, or decree of the bankruptcy court pending appeal;

(B) the approval of a bond or other security provided to obtain a stay of judgment;

(C) an order suspending, modifying, restoring, or granting an injunction while an appeal is pending; or

(D) the suspension or continuation of proceedings in a case or other relief permitted by subdivision (e).

(2) Time to file

The motion may be made either before or after the notice of appeal is filed.

(b) Motion in the district court, the BAP, or the Court of Appeals on direct appeal

(1) Request for relief

A motion for the relief specified in subdivision (a)(1)—or to vacate or modify a bankruptcy court's order granting such relief—may be made in the court where the appeal is pending.

(2) Showing or statement required

The motion must:

(A) show that moving first in the bankruptcy court would be impracticable; or

(B) if a motion was made in the bankruptcy court, either state that the court has not yet ruled on the motion, or state that the court has ruled and set out any reasons given for the ruling.

(3) Additional content

The motion must also include:

(A) the reasons for granting the relief requested and the facts relied upon;

(B) affidavits or other sworn statements supporting facts subject to dispute; and

(C) relevant parts of the record.

(4) Serving notice

The movant must give reasonable notice of the motion to all parties.

(c) Filing a bond or other security

The district court, BAP, or court of appeals may condition relief on filing a bond or other security with the bankruptcy court.

(d) Bond or other security for a trustee or the United States

The court may require a trustee to file a bond or other security when the trustee appeals. A bond or other security is not required when an appeal is taken by the United States, its officer, or its agency or by direction of any department of the federal government.

(e) Continuation of proceedings in the bankruptcy court

Despite Rule 7062 and subject to the authority of the district court, BAP, or court of appeals, the bankruptcy court may:

(1) suspend or order the continuation of other proceedings in the case; or

(2) issue any other appropriate orders during the pendency of an appeal to protect the rights of all parties in interest.

(As amended Mar. 30, 1987, eff. Aug. 1, 1987; Apr. 30, 1991, eff. Aug. 1, 1991; Apr. 25, 2014, eff. Dec. 1, 2014; Apr. 26, 2018, eff. Dec. 1, 2018.)

ADVISORY COMMITTEE NOTES

Subdivision (a) is an adaptation of Rule 11(b) F.R.App.P.

Subdivision (b) is similar to former Bankruptcy Rule 807. The duty of the clerk of the bankruptcy court to transmit the record as soon as the record is complete is derived from the second paragraph of Rule 11(b) F.R.App.P. The last sentence of the subdivision applies to appeals to bankruptcy appellate panels. Additional copies of the record may be needed when the appendix to the brief required under Rule 8009(b) is not adequate in the judgment of the bankruptcy appellate panel for disposition of the appeal. If additional copies are required, the appellant will arrange for the production of the copies; if the appellant fails to do so, the clerk of the bankruptcy appellate panel shall prepare the copies at the expense of the appellant.

Subdivision (c) is derived from subdivisions (c), (e) and (f) of Rule 11 F.R.App.P. and subdivision (d) is essentially the same as Rule 11(b) F.R.App.P.

1991 Amendment

This rule is amended to require that the bankruptcy clerk retain the original record and transmit a copy of the record to the clerk of the district court or bankruptcy appellate panel. Transmission of the original documents may cause disruption in the continuing administration of the case in the bankruptcy court.

2014 Amendments

This rule is derived from former Rule 8005 and F.R.App.P. 8. It now applies to direct appeals in courts of appeals.

Subdivision (a), like the former rule, requires a party ordinarily to seek relief pending an appeal in the bankruptcy court. Subdivision (a)(1) expands the list of relief enumerated in F.R.App.P. 8(a)(1) to reflect bankruptcy practice. It includes the suspension or continuation of other proceedings in the bankruptcy case, as authorized by subdivision (e). Subdivision (a)(2) clarifies that a motion for a stay pending appeal, approval of a supersedeas bond, or any other relief specified in paragraph (1) may be made in the bankruptcy court before or after the filing of a notice of appeal.

Subdivision (b) authorizes a party to seek the relief specified in (a)(1), or the vacation or modification of the granting of such relief, by means of a motion filed in the court where the appeal is pending—district court, BAP, or the court of appeals on direct appeal. Accordingly, a notice of appeal need not be filed with respect to a bankruptcy court's order granting or denying such a motion. The motion for relief in the district court, BAP, or court of appeals must state why it was impracticable to seek relief initially in the bankruptcy court, if a motion was not filed there, or why the bankruptcy court denied the relief sought.

Subdivisions (c) and **(d)** retain the provisions of the former rule that permit the district court or BAP—and now the court of appeals—to condition the granting of relief on the posting of a bond by the appellant, except when that party is a federal government entity. Rule 9025 governs proceedings against sureties.

Subdivision (e) retains the provision of the former rule that authorizes the bankruptcy court to decide whether to suspend or allow the continuation of other proceedings in the bankruptcy case while the matter for which a stay has been sought is pending on appeal.

Changes Made After Publication. The clause "or where it will be taken" was deleted in subdivision (b)(1). Stylistic changes were made to the titles of subdivisions (b) and (e) and in subdivision (e)(1). A discussion of subdivision (e) was added to the Committee Note.

2018 Amendments

The amendments to subdivisions (a)(1)(B), (c), and (d) conform this rule with the amendment of Rule 62 F.R.Civ.P., which is made applicable to adversary proceedings by Rule 7062. Rule 62 formerly required a party to provide a "supersedeas bond" to obtain a stay of the judgment and proceedings to enforce the judgment. As amended, Rule 62(b) allows a party to obtain a stay by providing a "bond or other security."

Rule 8008. Indicative Rulings

(a) Relief pending appeal

If a party files a timely motion in the bankruptcy court for relief that the court lacks authority to grant because of an appeal that has been docketed and is pending, the bankruptcy court may:

    (1) defer considering the motion;

    (2) deny the motion; or

    (3) state that the court would grant the motion if the court where the appeal is pending remands for that purpose, or state that the motion raises a substantial issue.

(b) Notice to the court where the appeal is pending

The movant must promptly notify the clerk of the court where the appeal is pending if the bankruptcy court states that it would grant the motion or that the motion raises a substantial issue.

(c) Remand after an indicative ruling

If the bankruptcy court states that it would grant the motion or that the motion raises a substantial issue, the district court or BAP may remand for further proceedings, but it retains jurisdiction unless it expressly dismisses the appeal. If the district court or BAP remands but retains jurisdiction, the parties must promptly notify the clerk of that court when the bankruptcy court has decided the motion on remand.

(As amended Mar. 30, 1987, eff. Aug. 1, 1987; Apr. 23, 1996, eff. Dec. 1, 1996; Apr. 25, 2014, eff. Dec. 1, 2014.)

ADVISORY COMMITTEE NOTES

This rule is an adaptation of Rule 25 F.R.App.P. Motions, briefs, appendices when required, statements, and any other filed paper must be accompanied by the specified number of copies. Rules 8001 and 8004 govern the number of copies of the notice of appeal which must be filed.

1996 Amendment

This rule is amended to permit, but not require, district courts and, where bankruptcy appellate panels have been authorized, circuit councils to adopt local rules that allow filing of documents by electronic means, subject to the limitations contained in Rule 5005(a)(2). See the committee note to the amendments to Rule 5005. Other amendments to this rule are stylistic.

GAP Report on Rule 8008. No changes since publication, except for stylistic changes.

2014 Amendments

This rule is an adaptation of F.R.Civ.P. 62.1 and F.R.App.P. 12.1. It provides a procedure for the issuance of an indicative ruling when a bankruptcy court determines that, because of a pending appeal, the court lacks jurisdiction to grant a request for relief that the court concludes is meritorious or raises a substantial issue. The rule does not attempt to define the circumstances in which an appeal limits or defeats the bankruptcy court's authority to act in the face of a pending appeal. In contrast, Rule 8002(b) identifies motions that, if filed within the relevant time limit, suspend the effect of a notice of appeal filed before the last such motion is resolved. In those circumstances, the bankruptcy court has authority to resolve the motion without resorting to the indicative ruling procedure.

Subdivision (b) requires the movant to notify the court where an appeal is pending if the bankruptcy court states that it would grant the motion or that it raises a substantial issue. This provision applies to appeals pending in the district court, the BAP, or the court of appeals.

Federal Rules of Appellate Procedure 6 and 12.1 govern the procedure in the court of appeals following notification of the bankruptcy court's indicative ruling.

Subdivision (c) of this rule governs the procedure in the district court or BAP upon notification that the bankruptcy court has issued an indicative ruling. The district court or BAP may remand to the bankruptcy court for a ruling on the motion for relief. The district court or BAP may also remand all proceedings, thereby terminating the initial appeal, if it expressly states that it is dismissing the appeal. It should do so, however, only when the appellant has stated clearly its intention to abandon the appeal. Otherwise, the district court or BAP may remand for the purpose of ruling on the motion, while retaining jurisdiction to proceed with the appeal after the bankruptcy court rules, provided that the appeal is not then moot and a party wishes to proceed.

Changes Made After Publication. No changes were made after publication.

Rule 8009. Record on Appeal; Sealed Documents

(a) Designating the record on appeal; statement of the issues

(1) Appellant

    (A) The appellant must file with the bankruptcy clerk and serve on the appellee a designation of the items to be included in the record on appeal and a statement of the issues to be presented.

    (B) The appellant must file and serve the designation and statement within 14 days after:

        (i) the appellant's notice of appeal as of right becomes effective under Rule 8002; or

        (ii) an order granting leave to appeal is entered.

    A designation and statement served prematurely must be treated as served on the first day on which filing is timely.

(2) Appellee and cross-appellant

Within 14 days after being served, the appellee may file with the bankruptcy clerk and serve on the appellant a designation of additional items to be included in the record. An appellee who files a cross-appeal must file and serve a designation of additional items to be included in the record and a statement of the issues to be presented on the cross-appeal.

(3) Cross-appellee

Within 14 days after service of the cross-appellant's designation and statement, a cross-appellee may file with the bankruptcy clerk and serve on the cross-appellant a designation of additional items to be included in the record.

(4) Record on appeal

The record on appeal must include the following:

- docket entries kept by the bankruptcy clerk;
- items designated by the parties;
- the notice of appeal;
- the judgment, order, or decree being appealed;
- any order granting leave to appeal;
- any certification required for a direct appeal to the court of appeals;
- any opinion, findings of fact, and conclusions of law relating to the issues on appeal, including transcripts of all oral rulings;
- any transcript ordered under subdivision (b);
- any statement required by subdivision (c); and
- any additional items from the record that the court where the appeal is pending orders.

(5) Copies for the Bankruptcy Clerk

If paper copies are needed, a party filing a designation of items must provide a copy of any of those items that the bankruptcy clerk requests. If the party fails to do so, the bankruptcy clerk must prepare the copy at the party's expense.

(b) Transcript of Proceedings

(1) Appellant's duty to order

Within the time period prescribed by subdivision (a)(1), the appellant must:

(A) order in writing from the reporter, as defined in Rule 8010(a)(1), a transcript of such parts of the proceedings not already on file as the appellant considers necessary for the appeal, and file a copy of the order with the bankruptcy clerk; or

(B) file with the bankruptcy clerk a certificate stating that the appellant is not ordering a transcript.

(2) Cross-appellant's duty to order

Within 14 days after the appellant files a copy of the transcript order or a certificate of not ordering a transcript, the appellee as cross-appellant must:

(A) order in writing from the reporter, as defined in Rule 8010(a)(1), a transcript of such additional parts of the proceedings as the cross-appellant considers necessary for the appeal, and file a copy of the order with the bankruptcy clerk; or

(B) file with the bankruptcy clerk a certificate stating that the cross-appellant is not ordering a transcript.

(3) Appellee's or cross-appellee's right to order

Within 14 days after the appellant or cross-appellant files a copy of a transcript order or certificate of not ordering a transcript, the appellee or cross-appellee may order in writing from the reporter a transcript of such additional parts of the proceedings as the appellee or cross-appellee considers necessary for the appeal. A copy of the order must be filed with the bankruptcy clerk.

(4) Payment

At the time of ordering, a party must make satisfactory arrangements with the reporter for paying the cost of the transcript.

(5) Unsupported finding or conclusion

If the appellant intends to argue on appeal that a finding or conclusion is unsupported by the evidence or is contrary to the evidence, the appellant must include in the record a transcript of all relevant testimony and copies of all relevant exhibits.

(c) Statement of the evidence when a transcript is unavailable

If a transcript of a hearing or trial is unavailable, the appellant may prepare a statement of the evidence or proceedings from the best available means, including the appellant's recollection. The statement must be filed within the time prescribed by subdivision (a)(1) and served on the appellee, who may serve objections or proposed amendments within 14 days after being served. The statement and any objections or proposed amendments must then be submitted to the bankruptcy court for settlement and approval. As settled and approved, the statement must be included by the bankruptcy clerk in the record on appeal.

(d) Agreed statement as the record on appeal

Instead of the record on appeal as defined in subdivision (a), the parties may prepare, sign, and submit to the bankruptcy court a statement of the case showing how the issues presented by the appeal arose and were decided in the bankruptcy court. The statement must set forth only those facts alleged and proved or sought to be proved that are essential to the court's resolution of the issues. If the statement is accurate, it—together with any additions that the bankruptcy court may consider necessary to a full presentation of the issues on appeal—must be approved by the bankruptcy court and must then be certified to the court where the appeal is pending as the record on appeal. The bankruptcy clerk must then transmit it to the clerk of that court within the time provided by Rule 8010. A copy of the agreed statement may be filed in place of the appendix required by Rule 8018(b) or, in the case of a direct appeal to the court of appeals, by F.R.App.P. 30.

(e) Correcting or modifying the record

(1) Submitting to the Bankruptcy Court

If any difference arises about whether the record accurately discloses what occurred in the bankruptcy court, the difference must be submitted to and settled by the bankruptcy court and the record conformed accordingly. If an item has been improperly designated as part of the record on appeal, a party may move to strike that item.

(2) Correcting in other ways

If anything material to either party is omitted from or misstated in the record by error or accident, the omission or misstatement may be corrected, and a supplemental record may be certified and transmitted:

(A) on stipulation of the parties;

(B) by the bankruptcy court before or after the record has been forwarded; or

(C) by the court where the appeal is pending.

(3) Remaining questions

All other questions as to the form and content of the record must be presented to the court where the appeal is pending.

(f) Sealed documents

A document placed under seal by the bankruptcy court may be designated as part of the record on appeal. In doing so, a party must identify it without revealing confidential or secret information, but the bankruptcy clerk must not transmit it to the clerk of the court where the appeal is pending as part of the record. Instead, a party must file a motion with the court where the appeal is pending to accept the document under seal. If the motion is granted, the movant must notify the bankruptcy court of the ruling, and the bankruptcy clerk must promptly transmit the sealed document to the clerk of the court where the appeal is pending.

(g) Other necessary actions

All parties to an appeal must take any other action necessary to enable the bankruptcy clerk to assemble and transmit the record.

(As amended Mar. 30, 1987, eff. Aug. 1, 1987; Mar. 26, 2009, eff. Dec. 1, 2009; Apr. 25, 2014, eff. Dec. 1, 2014.)

ADVISORY COMMITTEE NOTES

Subdivision (a) of this rule is adapted from Rules 28(a) and 31(a) F.R.App.P. The introductory clause of the rule recognizes the desirability of allowing local and individual variation in the filing of briefs. The numbered paragraphs prescribe

shorter periods than the corresponding periods allowed by Rule 31(a) F.R.App.P.

Subdivision (b), which is similar to an interim rule for bankruptcy appellate panels promulgated by the Ninth Circuit, applies only when an appeal is to an appellate panel. The appellant must prepare an appendix to the brief which contains the documents relevant to the appeal. With the appendix available to each member of the appellate panel, it is unlikely that multiple copies of the record will be necessary. The last sentence of the subdivision enables the appellee to correct an omission of the appellant.

Rule 30 F.R.App.P., which governs the preparation of the appendix in appeals taken to the courts of appeals, specifies fewer documents which must be included in the appendix but permits the parties to include any other material.

1987 Amendment

The amendment to Rule 8007(c) permits a rule of the bankruptcy appellate panel to provide that the record is to be retained rather than transmitted. The new paragraph (9) of subdivision (b) of this rule complements Rule 8007(c) by authorizing a rule of the panel to require inclusion of the transcript or a portion thereof in the appendix.

2009 Amendments

The rule is amended to implement changes in connection with the amendment to Rule 9006(a) and the manner by which time is computed under the rules. The deadlines in the rule are amended to substitute a deadline that is a multiple of seven days. Throughout the rules, deadlines are amended in the following manner:

- 5–day periods become 7–day periods
- 10–day periods become 14–day periods
- 15–day periods become 14–day periods
- 20–day periods become 21–day periods
- 25–day periods become 28–day periods

2014 Amendments

This rule is derived from former Rule 8006 and F.R.App.P. 10 and 11(a). The provisions of this rule and Rule 8010 are applicable to appeals taken directly to a court of appeals under 28 U.S.C. § 158(d)(2), as well as to appeals to a district court or BAP. See F.R.App.P. 6(c)(2)(A) and (B).

The rule retains the practice of former Rule 8006 of requiring the parties to designate items to be included in the record on appeal. In this respect, the bankruptcy rule differs from the appellate rule. Among other things, F.R.App.P. 10(a) provides that the record on appeal consists of all the documents and exhibits filed in the case. This requirement would often be unworkable in a bankruptcy context because thousands of items might have been filed in the overall bankruptcy case.

Subdivision (a) provides the time period for an appellant to file a designation of items to be included in the record on appeal and a statement of the issues to be presented. It then provides for the designation of additional items by the appellee, cross-appellant, and cross-appellee, as well as for the cross-appellant's statement of the issues to be presented in its appeal. Subdivision (a)(4) prescribes the content of the record on appeal. Ordinarily, the bankruptcy clerk will not need to have paper copies of the designated items because the clerk will either transmit them to the appellate court electronically or otherwise make them available electronically. If the bankruptcy clerk requires a paper copy of some or all of the items designated as part of the record, the clerk may request the party that designated the item to provide the necessary copies, and the party must comply with the request or bear the cost of the clerk's copying.

Subdivision (b) governs the process for ordering a complete or partial transcript of the bankruptcy court proceedings. In situations in which a transcript is unavailable, subdivision (c) allows for the parties' preparation of a statement of the evidence or proceedings, which must be approved by the bankruptcy court.

Subdivision (d) adopts the practice of F.R.App.P. 10(d) of permitting the parties to agree on a statement of the case in place of the record on appeal. The statement must show how the issues on appeal arose and were decided in the bankruptcy court. It must be approved by the bankruptcy court in order to be certified as the record on appeal.

Subdivision (e), modeled on F.R.App.P. 10(e), provides a procedure for correcting the record on appeal if an item is improperly designated, omitted, or misstated.

Subdivision (f) is a new provision that governs the handling of any document that remains sealed by the bankruptcy court and that a party wants to include in the record on appeal. The party must request the court where the appeal is pending to accept the document under seal, and that motion must be granted before the bankruptcy clerk may transmit the sealed document to the district, BAP, or circuit clerk.

Subdivision (g) requires the parties' cooperation with the bankruptcy clerk in assembling and transmitting the record. It retains the requirement of former Rule 8006, which was adapted from F.R.App.P. 11(a).

Changes Made After Publication. In subdivision (a)(2) and (3), the place of filing was clarified. "Docket entries kept by the bankruptcy clerk" was added to the list in subdivision (a)(4).

HISTORICAL AND STATUTORY NOTES

References in Text

The Federal Rules of Appellate Procedure, referred to in subd. (d), are set out in the Appendix to Title 28.

Rule 8010.   Completing and Transmitting the Record

(a) Reporter's duties

(1) Proceedings recorded without a reporter present

If proceedings were recorded without a reporter being present, the person or service selected under bankruptcy court procedures to transcribe the recording is the reporter for purposes of this rule.

(2) Preparing and filing the transcript

The reporter must prepare and file a transcript as follows:

(A) Upon receiving an order for a transcript in accordance with Rule 8009(b), the reporter must file in the bankruptcy court an acknowledgment of the request that shows when it was received, and

when the reporter expects to have the transcript completed.

(B) After completing the transcript, the reporter must file it with the bankruptcy clerk, who will notify the district, BAP, or circuit clerk of its filing.

(C) If the transcript cannot be completed within 30 days after receiving the order, the reporter must request an extension of time from the bankruptcy clerk. The clerk must enter on the docket and notify the parties whether the extension is granted.

(D) If the reporter does not file the transcript on time, the bankruptcy clerk must notify the bankruptcy judge.

(b) Clerk's duties

(1) Transmitting the record—in general

Subject to Rule 8009(f) and subdivision (b)(5) of this rule, when the record is complete, the bankruptcy clerk must transmit to the clerk of the court where the appeal is pending either the record or a notice that the record is available electronically.

(2) Multiple appeals

If there are multiple appeals from a judgment, order, or decree, the bankruptcy clerk must transmit a single record.

(3) Receiving the record

Upon receiving the record or notice that it is available electronically, the district, BAP, or circuit clerk must enter that information on the docket and promptly notify all parties to the appeal.

(4) If paper copies are ordered

If the court where the appeal is pending directs that paper copies of the record be provided, the clerk of that court must so notify the appellant. If the appellant fails to provide them, the bankruptcy clerk must prepare them at the appellant's expense.

(5) When leave to appeal is requested

Subject to subdivision (c), if a motion for leave to appeal has been filed under Rule 8004, the bankruptcy clerk must prepare and transmit the record only after the district court, BAP, or court of appeals grants leave.

(c) Record for a preliminary motion in the district court, BAP, or court of appeals

This subdivision (c) applies if, before the record is transmitted, a party moves in the district court, BAP, or court of appeals for any of the following relief:

- leave to appeal;
- dismissal;
- a stay pending appeal;

• approval of a bond or other security provided to obtain a stay of judgment; or

• any other intermediate order.

The bankruptcy clerk must then transmit to the clerk of the court where the relief is sought any parts of the record designated by a party to the appeal or a notice that those parts are available electronically. (As amended Apr. 25, 2014, eff. Dec. 1, 2014; Apr. 26, 2018, eff. Dec. 1, 2018.)

ADVISORY COMMITTEE NOTES

This rule is derived from subdivisions (a), (b), (c), and (f) of Rule 28 F.R.App.P.

When an appeal is to a bankruptcy appellate panel and an appendix is filed pursuant to Rule 8009(b) and reference is made in a brief to parts of the record included in the appendix, the reference should be to the appropriate pages of the appendix at which those parts appear.

2014 Amendments

This rule is derived from former Rule 8007 and F.R.App.P. 11. It applies to an appeal taken directly to a court of appeals under 28 U.S.C. § 158(d)(2), as well as to an appeal to a district court or BAP.

Subdivision (a) generally retains the procedure of former Rule 8007(a) regarding the reporter's duty to prepare and file a transcript if a party requests one. It clarifies that the person or service that transcribes the recording of a proceeding is considered the reporter under this rule if the proceeding is recorded without a reporter being present in the courtroom. It also makes clear that the reporter must file with the bankruptcy court the acknowledgment of the request for a transcript and statement of the expected completion date, the completed transcript, and any request for an extension of time beyond 30 days for completion of the transcript.

Subdivision (b) requires the bankruptcy clerk to transmit the record to the district, BAP or circuit clerk when the record is complete and, in the case of appeals under 28 U.S.C. § 158(a)(3), leave to appeal has been granted. This transmission will be made electronically, either by sending the record itself or sending notice that the record can be accessed electronically. The court where the appeal is pending may, however, require that a paper copy of some or all of the record be furnished, in which case the clerk of that court will direct the appellant to provide the copies. If the appellant does not do so, the bankruptcy clerk must prepare the copies at the appellant's expense.

In a change from former Rule 8007 (b), subdivision (b) of this rule no longer directs the clerk of the appellate court to docket the appeal upon receipt of the record from the bankruptcy clerk. Instead, under Rules 8003(d) and 8004(c) and F.R.App.P. 12(a), the district, BAP, or circuit clerk dockets the appeal upon receipt of the notice of appeal or, in the case of appeals under 28 U.S.C. § 158(a)(3), the notice of appeal and the motion for leave to appeal. Accordingly, by the time the district, BAP, or circuit clerk receives the record, the appeal will already be docketed in that court. The clerk of the appellate court must indicate on the docket and give notice to the parties to the appeal when the transmission of the record is received. Under Rule 8018(a) and F.R.App.P. 31, the briefing schedule is generally based on that date.

Subdivision (c) is derived from former Rule 8007(c) and F.R.App.P. 11(g). It provides for the transmission of parts of the record that the parties designate for consideration by the district court, BAP, or court of appeals in ruling on specified preliminary motions filed prior to the preparation and transmission of the record on appeal.

Changes Made After Publication. Subdivision (a)(1) was revised to more accurately reflect the way in which transcription services are selected. A cross-reference to Rule 8009(b) was added to subdivision (a)(2)(A).

2018 Amendments

The amendment of subdivision (c) conforms this rule with the amendment of Rule 62 F.R.Civ.P., which is made applicable in adversary proceedings by Rule 7062. Rule 62 formerly required a party to provide a "supersedeas bond" to obtain a stay of the judgment and proceedings to enforce the judgment. As amended, Rule 62(b) allows a party to obtain a stay by providing a "bond or other security."

Rule 8011. Filing and Service; Signature

(a) Filing
(1) With the clerk

A document required or permitted to be filed in a district court or BAP must be filed with the clerk of that court.

(2) Method and timeliness

(A) Nonelectronic filing
(i) In general

For a document not filed electronically, filing may be accomplished by mail addressed to the clerk of the district court or BAP. Except as provided in subdivision (a)(2)(A)(ii) and (iii), filing is timely only if the clerk receives the document within the time fixed for filing.

(ii) Brief or appendix

A brief or appendix not filed electronically is also timely filed if, on or before the last day for filing, it is:

• mailed to the clerk by first-class mail—or other class of mail that is at least as expeditious—postage prepaid; or

• dispatched to a third-party commercial carrier for delivery within 3 days to the clerk.

(iii) Inmate filing

If an institution has a system designed for legal mail, an inmate confined there must use that system to receive the benefit of this Rule 8011(a)(2)(A)(iii). A document not filed electronically by an inmate confined in an institution is timely if it is deposited in the institution's internal mailing system on or before the last day for filing and:

• it is accompanied by a declaration in compliance with 28 U.S.C. § 1746—or a notarized statement—setting out the date of deposit and stating that first-class postage is being prepaid; or evidence (such as a postmark or date stamp) showing that the notice was so deposited and that postage was prepaid; or

- the appellate court exercises its discretion to permit the later filing of a declaration or notarized statement that satisfies this Rule 8011(a)(2)(A)(iii).

(B) Electronic filing

(i) By a represented person—generally required; exceptions

An entity represented by an attorney must file electronically, unless nonelectronic filing is allowed by the court for good cause or is allowed or required by local rule.

(ii) By an unrepresented individual—when allowed or required

An individual not represented by an attorney:

- may file electronically only if allowed by court order or by local rule; and

- may be required to file electronically only by court order, or by a local rule that includes reasonable exceptions.

(iii) Same as a written paper

A document filed electronically is a written paper for purposes of these rules.

(C) Copies

If a document is filed electronically, no paper copy is required. If a document is filed by mail or delivery to the district court or BAP, no additional copies are required. But the district court or BAP may require by local rule or by order in a particular case the filing or furnishing of a specified number of paper copies.

(3) Clerk's refusal of documents

The court's clerk must not refuse to accept for filing any document transmitted for that purpose solely because it is not presented in proper form as required by these rules or by any local rule or practice.

(b) Service of all documents required

Unless a rule requires service by the clerk, a party must, at or before the time of the filing of a document, serve it on the other parties to the appeal. Service on a party represented by counsel must be made on the party's counsel.

(c) Manner of service

(1) Nonelectronic service

Nonelectronic service may be by any of the following:

(A) personal delivery;

(B) mail; or

(C) third-party commercial carrier for delivery within 3 days.

(2) Electronic service

Electronic service may be made by sending a document to a registered user by filing it with the court's electronic-filing system or by using other electronic means that the person served consented to in writing.

(3) When service is complete

Service by electronic means is complete on filing or sending, unless the person making service receives notice that the document was not received by the person served. Service by mail or by commercial carrier is complete on mailing or delivery to the carrier.

(d) Proof of service

(1) What is required

A document presented for filing must contain either of the following if it was served other than through the court's electronic-filing system:

(A) an acknowledgment of service by the person served; or

(B) proof of service consisting of a statement by the person who made service certifying:

(i) the date and manner of service;

(ii) the names of the persons served; and

(iii) the mail or electronic address, the fax number, or the address of the place of delivery, as appropriate for the manner of service, for each person served.

(2) Delayed proof

The district or BAP clerk may permit documents to be filed without acknowledgment or proof of service, but must require the acknowledgment or proof to be filed promptly thereafter.

(3) Brief or appendix

When a brief or appendix is filed, the proof of service must also state the date and manner by which it was filed.

(e) Signature

Every document filed electronically must include the electronic signature of the person filing it or, if the person is represented, the electronic signature of counsel. A filing made through a person's electronic-filing account and authorized by that person, together with that person's name on a signature block, constitutes the person's signature. Every document filed in paper form must be signed by the person filing the document or, if the person is represented, by counsel.

(As amended Apr. 25, 2014, eff. Dec. 1, 2014; Apr. 26, 2018, eff. Dec. 1, 2018.)

ADVISORY COMMITTEE NOTES

Subdivisions (a), (b) and (e) of this rule conform substantially to subdivisions (a), (b) and (c) of Rule 27 F.R.App.P. Subdivisions (c) and (d) are taken from Rule 13(c) and (d) of the Rules of the First Circuit governing appeals to bankruptcy appellate panels.

2014 Amendments

This rule is derived from former Rule 8008 and F.R.App.P. 25. It adopts some of the additional details of the appellate rule, and it provides greater recognition of the possibility of electronic filing and service.

Subdivision (a) governs the filing of documents in the district court or BAP. Consistent with other provisions of these Part VIII rules, subdivision (a)(2) requires electronic filing of documents, including briefs and appendices, unless the district court's or BAP's procedures permit or require other methods of delivery to the court. An electronic filing is timely if it is received by the district or BAP clerk within the time fixed for filing. No additional copies need to be submitted when documents are filed electronically, by mail, or by delivery unless the district court or BAP requires them.

Subdivision (a)(3) provides that the district or BAP clerk may not refuse to accept a document for filing solely because its form does not comply with these rules or any local rule or practice. The district court or BAP may, however, direct the correction of any deficiency in any document that does not conform to the requirements of these rules or applicable local rules, and may prescribe such other relief as the court deems appropriate.

Subdivisions (b) and **(c)** address the service of documents in the district court or BAP. Except for documents that the district or BAP clerk must serve, a party that makes a filing must serve copies of the document on the other parties to the appeal. Service on represented parties must be made on counsel. Subdivision (c) expresses the general requirement under these Part VIII rules that documents be sent electronically. See Rule 8001(c). Local court rules, however, may provide for other means of service, and subdivision (c) specifies non-electronic methods of service by or on an unrepresented party. Electronic service is complete upon transmission, unless the party making service receives notice that the transmission did not reach the person intended to be served in a readable form.

Subdivision (d) retains the former rule's provisions regarding proof of service of a document filed in the district court or BAP. In addition, it provides that a certificate of service must state the mail or electronic address or fax number to which service was made.

Subdivision (e) is a new provision that requires an electronic signature of counsel or an unrepresented filer for documents that are filed electronically in the district court or BAP. A local rule may specify a method of providing an electronic signature that is consistent with any standards established by the Judicial Conference of the United States. Paper copies of documents filed in the district court or BAP must bear an actual signature of counsel or the filer. By requiring a signature, subdivision (e) ensures that a readily identifiable attorney or party takes responsibility for every document that is filed.

Changes Made After Publication. No changes were made after publication.

2018 Amendments

The rule is amended to conform to the amendments to F.R.App.P. 25 on inmate filing, electronic filing, signature, service, and proof of service.

Consistent with Rule 8001(c), subdivision (a)(2) generally makes electronic filing mandatory. The rule recognizes exceptions for persons proceeding without an attorney, exceptions for good cause, and variations established by local rule.

Subdivision (a)(2)(A)(iii) is revised to conform to F.R.App.P. 25(a)(2)(A)(iii), which was recently amended to streamline and clarify the operation of the inmate-filing rule. The rule requires the inmate to show timely deposit and prepayment of postage. It is amended to specify that a notice is timely if it is accompanied by a declaration or notarized statement stating the date the notice was deposited in the institution's mail system and attesting to the prepayment of first-class postage. The declaration must state that first-class postage "is being prepaid," not (as directed by the former rule) that first-class postage "has been prepaid." This change reflects the fact that inmates may need to rely upon the institution to affix postage after the inmate has deposited the document in the institution's mail system. A new Director's Form sets out a suggested form of the declaration.

The amended rule also provides that a notice is timely without a declaration or notarized statement if other evidence accompanying the notice shows that the notice was deposited on or before the due date and that postage was prepaid. If the notice is not accompanied by evidence that establishes timely deposit and prepayment of postage, then the appellate court—district court, BAP, or court of appeals in the case of a direct appeal—has discretion to accept a declaration or notarized statement at a later date. The rule uses the phrase "exercises its discretion to permit"—rather than simply "permits"—to help ensure that pro se inmates are aware that a court will not necessarily forgive a failure to provide the declaration initially.

Subdivision (c) is amended to authorize electronic service by means of the court's electronic-filing system on registered users without requiring their written consent. All other forms of electronic service require the written consent of the person served.

Service is complete when a person files the paper with the court's electronic-filing system for transmission to a registered user, or when one person sends it to another person by other electronic means that the other person has consented to in writing. But service is not effective if the person who filed with the court or the person who sent by other agreed-upon electronic means receives notice that the paper did not reach the person to be served. The rule does not make the court responsible for notifying a person who filed the paper with the court's electronic-filing system that an attempted transmission by the court's system failed. But a filer who receives notice that the transmission failed is responsible for making effective service.

As amended, subdivision (d) eliminates the requirement of proof of service when service is made through the electronic-filing system. The notice of electronic filing generated by the system serves that purpose.

Subdivision (e) requires the signature of counsel or an unrepresented party on every document that is filed. A filing made through a person's electronic-filing account and authorized by that person, together with that person's name on a signature block, constitutes the person's signature. A person's electronic-filing account means an account established by the court for use of the court's electronic-filing system, which account the person accesses with the user name and password (or other credentials) issued to that person by the court.

Rule 8012.   Corporate Disclosure Statement

(a) Who must file

Any nongovernmental corporate party appearing in the district court or BAP must file a statement that identifies any parent corporation and any publicly held corporation that owns 10% or more of its stock or states that there is no such corporation.

(b) Time to file; supplemental filing

A party must file the statement with its principal brief or upon filing a motion, response, petition, or answer in the district court or BAP, whichever occurs first, unless a local rule requires earlier filing. Even if the statement has already been filed, the party's principal brief must include a statement before the table of contents. A party must supplement its statement whenever the required information changes.

(As amended Apr. 25, 2014, eff. Dec. 1, 2014.)

ADVISORY COMMITTEE NOTES

This rule is derived from Rule 34(a) F.R.App.P. The other details of oral argument which are covered by the remaining subdivisions of Rule 34 F.R.App.P. are not in these rules and are left to local rule or order of the court.

2014 Amendments

This rule is derived from F.R.App.P. 26.1. It requires the filing of corporate disclosure statements and supplemental statements in order to assist district court and BAP judges in determining whether they should recuse themselves. Rule 9001 makes the definitions in § 101 of the Code applicable to these rules. Under § 101(9) the word "corporation" includes a limited liability company, limited liability partnership, business trust, and certain other entities that are not designated under applicable law as corporations.

If filed separately from a brief, motion, response, petition, or answer, the statement must be filed and served in accordance with Rule 8011. Under Rule 8015(a)(7)(B)(iii), the corporate disclosure statement is not included in calculating applicable word-count limitations.

Changes Made After Publication. A sentence was added to the Committee Note to draw attention to the broad definition of "corporation" under § 101(9) of the Bankruptcy Code.

Rule 8013.   Motions; Intervention

(a) Contents of a motion; response; reply

(1) Request for relief

A request for an order or other relief is made by filing a motion with the district or BAP clerk, with proof of service on the other parties to the appeal.

(2) Contents of a motion

(A) Grounds and the relief sought

A motion must state with particularity the grounds for the motion, the relief sought, and the legal argument necessary to support it.

(B) Motion to expedite an appeal

A motion to expedite an appeal must explain what justifies considering the appeal ahead of other matters. If the district court or BAP grants the motion, it may accelerate the time to transmit the record, the deadline for filing briefs and other documents, oral argument, and the resolution of the appeal. A motion to expedite an appeal may be filed as an emergency motion under subdivision (d).

(C) Accompanying documents

(i) Any affidavit or other document necessary to support a motion must be served and filed with the motion.

(ii) An affidavit must contain only factual information, not legal argument.

(iii) A motion seeking substantive relief must include a copy of the bankruptcy court's judgment, order, or decree, and any accompanying opinion as a separate exhibit.

(D) Documents barred or not required

(i) A separate brief supporting or responding to a motion must not be filed.

(ii) Unless the court orders otherwise, a notice of motion or a proposed order is not required.

(3) Response and reply; time to file

Unless the district court or BAP orders otherwise,

(A) any party to the appeal may file a response to the motion within 7 days after service of the motion; and

(B) the movant may file a reply to a response within 7 days after service of the response, but may only address matters raised in the response.

(b) Disposition of a motion for a procedural order

The district court or BAP may rule on a motion for a procedural order—including a motion under Rule 9006(b) or (c)—at any time without awaiting a response. A party adversely affected by the ruling may move to reconsider, vacate, or modify it within 7 days after the procedural order is served.

(c) Oral argument

A motion will be decided without oral argument unless the district court or BAP orders otherwise.

(d) Emergency motion

(1) Noting the emergency

When a movant requests expedited action on a motion because irreparable harm would occur during the time needed to consider a response, the movant must insert the word "Emergency" before the title of the motion.

(2) Contents of the motion

The emergency motion must

(A) be accompanied by an affidavit setting out the nature of the emergency;

(B) state whether all grounds for it were submitted to the bankruptcy court and, if not, why the motion should not be remanded for the bankruptcy court to consider;

(C) include the e-mail addresses, office addresses, and telephone numbers of moving counsel and, when known, of opposing counsel and any unrepresented parties to the appeal; and

(D) be served as prescribed by Rule 8011.

(3) Notifying opposing parties

Before filing an emergency motion, the movant must make every practicable effort to notify opposing counsel and any unrepresented parties in time for them to respond. The affidavit accompanying the emergency motion must state when and how notice was given or state why giving it was impracticable.

(e) Power of a single BAP judge to entertain a motion

(1) Single judge's authority

A BAP judge may act alone on any motion, but may not dismiss or otherwise determine an appeal, deny a motion for leave to appeal, or deny a motion for a stay pending appeal if denial would make the appeal moot.

(2) Reviewing a single judge's action

The BAP may review a single judge's action, either on its own motion or on a party's motion.

(f) Form of documents; length limits; number of copies

(1) Format of a paper document

Rule 27(d)(1) F.R.App.P. applies in the district court or BAP to a paper version of a motion, response, or reply.

(2) Format of an electronically filed document

A motion, response, or reply filed electronically must comply with the requirements for a paper version regarding covers, line spacing, margins, typeface, and type style. It must also comply with the length limits under paragraph (3).

(3) Length limits

Except by the district court's or BAP's permission, and excluding the accompanying documents authorized by subdivision (a)(2)(C):

(A) a motion or a response to a motion produced using a computer must include a certificate under Rule 8015(h) and not exceed 5,200 words;

(B) a handwritten or typewritten motion or a response to a motion must not exceed 20 pages;

(C) a reply produced using a computer must include a certificate under Rule 8015(h) and not exceed 2,600 words; and

(D) a handwritten or typewritten reply must not exceed 10 pages.

(4) Paper copies

Paper copies must be provided only if required by local rule or by an order in a particular case.

(g) Intervening in an appeal

Unless a statute provides otherwise, an entity that seeks to intervene in an appeal pending in the district court or BAP must move for leave to intervene and serve a copy of the motion on the parties to the appeal. The motion or other notice of intervention authorized by statute must be filed within 30 days after the appeal is docketed. It must concisely state the movant's interest, the grounds for intervention, whether intervention was sought in the bankruptcy court, why intervention is being sought at this stage of the proceeding, and why participating as an amicus curiae would not be adequate.

(As amended Mar. 30, 1987, eff. Aug. 1, 1987; Apr. 25, 2014, eff. Dec. 1, 2014; Apr. 26, 2018, eff. Dec. 1, 2018.)

ADVISORY COMMITTEE NOTES

This rule accords to the findings of a bankruptcy judge the same weight given the findings of a district judge under Rule 52 F.R.Civ.P. See also Rules 7052(a) and 9014.

1987 Amendment

The amendment to this rule conforms the appellate review standard to Rule 52 F.R.Civ.P., as amended in August 1985.

2014 Amendments

This rule is derived from former Rule 8011 and F.R.App.P. 15(d) and 27. It adopts many of the provisions of the appellate rules that specify the form and page limits of motions and accompanying documents, while also adjusting those requirements for electronic filing. In addition, it prescribes the procedure for seeking to intervene in the district court or BAP.

Subdivision (a) retains much of the content of former Rule 8011(a) regarding the contents of a motion, response, and reply. It also specifies the documents that may accompany a motion. Unlike the former rule, which allowed the filing of separate briefs supporting a motion, subdivision (a) now adopts the practice of F.R.App.P. 27(a) of prohibiting the filing of briefs supporting or responding to a motion. The motion or response itself must include the party's legal arguments.

Subdivision (a)(2)(B) clarifies the procedure for seeking to expedite an appeal. A motion under this provision seeks to expedite the time for the disposition of the appeal as a whole, whereas an emergency motion—which is addressed by subdivision (d)—typically involves an urgent request for relief short of disposing of the entire appeal (for example, an emergency request for a stay pending appeal to prevent imminent mootness). In appropriate cases—such as when there is an urgent need to resolve the appeal quickly to prevent harm—a party may file a motion to expedite the appeal as an emergency motion.

Subdivision (b) retains the substance of former Rule 8011 (b). It authorizes the district court or BAP to act on a motion for a procedural order without awaiting a response to the motion. It specifies that a party seeking reconsideration, vacation, or modification of the order must file a motion within 7 days after service of the order.

Subdivision (c) continues the practice of former Rule 8011(c) and F.R.App.P. 27(e) of dispensing with oral argument of motions in the district court or BAP unless the court orders otherwise.

Subdivision (d), which carries forward the content of former Rule 8011(d), governs emergency motions that the district court or BAP may rule on without awaiting a response when necessary to prevent irreparable harm. A party seeking expedited action on a motion in the district court or BAP must explain the nature of the emergency, whether all grounds in support of the motion were first presented to the bankruptcy court, and, if not, why the district court or BAP should not remand for reconsideration. The moving party must also explain the steps taken to notify opposing counsel and any unrepresented parties in advance of filing the emergency motion and, if they were not notified, why it was impracticable to do so.

Subdivision (e), like former Rule 8011(e) and similar to F.R.App.P. 27(c), authorizes a single BAP judge to rule on certain motions. This authority, however, does not extend to issuing rulings that would dispose of the appeal. For that reason, the rule now prohibits a single BAP judge from denying a motion for a stay pending appeal when the effect of that ruling would be to require dismissal of the appeal as moot. A ruling by a single judge is subject to review by the BAP.

Subdivision (f) incorporates by reference the formatting and appearance requirements of F.R.App.P. 27(d)(1). When paper versions of the listed documents are filed, they must comply with the requirements of the specified rules regarding reproduction, covers, binding, appearance, and format. When these documents are filed electronically, they must comply with the relevant requirements of the specified rules regarding covers and format. Subdivision (f) also specifies page limits for motions, responses, and replies, which is a matter that former Rule 8011 did not address.

Subdivision (g) clarifies the procedure for seeking to intervene in a proceeding that has been appealed. It is based on F.R.App.P. 15(d), but it also requires the moving party to explain why intervention is being sought at the appellate stage. The former Part VIII rules did not address intervention.

Changes After Publication. Subdivision (a)(2)(D) was changed to allow the court to require a notice of motion or proposed order. A stylistic change was made to subdivision (d)(2)(B).

2018 Amendments

Subdivision (f)(3) is amended to conform to F.R.App.P. 27(d)(2), which was recently amended to replace page limits with word limits for motions and responses produced using a computer. The word limits were derived from the current page limits, using the assumption that one page is equivalent to 260 words. Documents produced using a computer must include the certificate of compliance required by Rule 8015(h); Official Form 417C suffices to meet that requirement. Page limits are retained for papers prepared without the aid of a computer (i.e., handwritten or typewritten papers). For both the word limit and the page limit, the calculation excludes the accompanying documents required by Rule 8013(a)(2)(C) and any items listed in Rule 8015(h).

HISTORICAL AND STATUTORY NOTES
References in Text

The Federal Rules of Appellate Procedure, referred to in subd. (f)(1), are set out in the Appendix to Title 28.

Rule 8014. Briefs

(a) Appellant's brief

The appellant's brief must contain the following under appropriate headings and in the order indicated:

(1) a corporate disclosure statement, if required by Rule 8012;

(2) a table of contents, with page references;

(3) a table of authorities—cases (alphabetically arranged), statutes, and other authorities—with references to the pages of the brief where they are cited;

(4) a jurisdictional statement, including:

(A) the basis for the bankruptcy court's subject-matter jurisdiction, with citations to applicable statutory provisions and stating relevant facts establishing jurisdiction;

(B) the basis for the district court's or BAP's jurisdiction, with citations to applicable statutory provisions and stating relevant facts establishing jurisdiction;

(C) the filing dates establishing the timeliness of the appeal; and

(D) an assertion that the appeal is from a final judgment, order, or decree, or information establishing the district court's or BAP's jurisdiction on another basis;

(5) a statement of the issues presented and, for each one, a concise statement of the applicable standard of appellate review;

(6) a concise statement of the case setting out the facts relevant to the issues submitted for review, describing the relevant procedural history, and identifying the rulings presented for review, with appropriate references to the record;

(7) a summary of the argument, which must contain a succinct, clear, and accurate statement of the arguments made in the body of the brief, and which must not merely repeat the argument headings;

(8) the argument, which must contain the appellant's contentions and the reasons for them, with citations to the authorities and parts of the record on which the appellant relies;

(9) a short conclusion stating the precise relief sought; and

(10) the certificate of compliance, if required by Rule 8015(a)(7) or (b).

(b) Appellee's brief

The appellee's brief must conform to the requirements of subdivision (a)(1)–(8) and (10), except that none of the following need appear unless the appellee is dissatisfied with the appellant's statement:

(1) the jurisdictional statement;

(2) the statement of the issues and the applicable standard of appellate review; and

(3) the statement of the case.

(c) Reply brief

The appellant may file a brief in reply to the appellee's brief. A reply brief must comply with the requirements of subdivision (a)(2)–(3).

(d) Statutes, rules, regulations, or similar authority

If the court's determination of the issues presented requires the study of the Code or other statutes, rules, regulations, or similar authority, the relevant parts must be set out in the brief or in an addendum.

(e) Briefs in a case involving multiple appellants or appellees

In a case involving more than one appellant or appellee, including consolidated cases, any number of appellants or appellees may join in a brief, and any party may adopt by reference a part of another's brief. Parties may also join in reply briefs.

(f) Citation of supplemental authorities

If pertinent and significant authorities come to a party's attention after the party's brief has been filed—or after oral argument but before a decision—a party may promptly advise the district or BAP clerk by a signed submission setting forth the citations. The submission, which must be served on the other parties to the appeal, must state the reasons for the supplemental citations, referring either to the pertinent page of a brief or to a point argued orally. The body of the submission must not exceed 350 words. Any response must be made within 7 days after the party is served, unless the court orders otherwise, and must be similarly limited.

(As amended Mar. 30, 1987, eff. Aug. 1, 1987; Apr. 25, 2014, eff. Dec. 1, 2014.)

ADVISORY COMMITTEE NOTES

This rule is an adaptation of Rule 39(a), (c) and (e) of the F.R.App.P. Under this rule all costs are taxed by the clerk of the bankruptcy court.

2014 Amendments

This rule is derived from former Rule 8010(a) and (b) and F.R.App.P. 28. Adopting much of the content of Rule 28, it provides greater detail than former Rule 8010 contained regarding appellate briefs.

Subdivision (a) prescribes the content and structure of the appellant's brief. It largely follows former Rule 8010(a)(1), but, to ensure national uniformity, it eliminates the provision authorizing a district court or BAP to alter these requirements. Subdivision (a)(1) provides that when Rule 8012 requires an appellant to file a corporate disclosure statement, it must be placed at the beginning of the appellant's brief. Subdivision (a)(10) is new. It implements the requirement under Rule 8015(a)(7)(C) and (b) for the filing of a certificate of compliance with the limit on the number of words or lines allowed to be in a brief.

Subdivision (b) carries forward the provisions of former Rule 8010(a)(2).

Subdivision (c) is derived from F.R.App.P. 28(c). It authorizes an appellant to file a reply brief, which will generally complete the briefing process.

Subdivision (d) is similar to former Rule 8010(b), but it is reworded to reflect the likelihood that briefs will generally be filed electronically rather than in paper form.

Subdivision (e) mirrors F.R.App.P. 28(i). It authorizes multiple appellants or appellees to join in a single brief. It also allows a party to incorporate by reference portions of another party's brief.

Subdivision (f) adopts the procedures of F.R.App.P. 28(j) with respect to the filing of supplemental authorities with the district court or BAP after a brief has been filed or after oral argument. Unlike the appellate rule, it specifies a period of 7 days for filing a response to a submission of supplemental authorities. The supplemental submission and response must comply with the signature requirements of Rule 8011(e).

Changes Made After Publication. No changes were made after publication.

Rule 8015. Form and Length of Briefs; Form of Appendices and Other Papers

(a) Paper copies of a brief

If a paper copy of a brief may or must be filed, the following provisions apply:

(1) Reproduction

(A) A brief may be reproduced by any process that yields a clear black image on light paper. The paper must be opaque and unglazed. Only one side of the paper may be used.

(B) Text must be reproduced with a clarity that equals or exceeds the output of a laser printer.

(C) Photographs, illustrations, and tables may be reproduced by any method that results in a good copy of the original. A glossy finish is acceptable if the original is glossy.

(2) Cover

The front cover of a brief must contain:

(A) the number of the case centered at the top;

(B) the name of the court;

(C) the title of the case as prescribed by Rule 8003(d)(2) or 8004(c)(2);

(D) the nature of the proceeding and the name of the court below;

(E) the title of the brief, identifying the party or parties for whom the brief is filed; and

(F) the name, office address, telephone number, and e-mail address of counsel representing the party for whom the brief is filed.

(3) Binding

The brief must be bound in any manner that is secure, does not obscure the text, and permits the brief to lie reasonably flat when open.

(4) Paper size, line spacing, and margins

The brief must be on 8 1/2-by-11 inch paper. The text must be double-spaced, but quotations more than two lines long may be indented and single-spaced. Headings and footnotes may be single-spaced. Margins must be at least one inch on all four sides. Page numbers may be placed in the margins, but no text may appear there.

(5) Typeface

Either a proportionally spaced or monospaced face may be used.

(A) A proportionally spaced face must include serifs, but sans-serif type may be used in headings and captions. A proportionally spaced face must be 14-point or larger.

(B) A monospaced face may not contain more than 10 1/2 characters per inch.

(6) Type styles

A brief must be set in plain, roman style, although italics or boldface may be used for emphasis. Case names must be italicized or underlined.

(7) Length

(A) Page limitation

A principal brief must not exceed 30 pages, or a reply brief 15 pages, unless it complies with subparagraph (B).

(B) Type-volume limitation

(i) A principal brief is acceptable if it contains a certificate under Rule 8015(h) and:

• contains no more than 13,000 words; or

• uses a monospaced face and contains no more than 1,300 lines of text.

(ii) A reply brief is acceptable if it includes a certificate under Rule 8015(h) and contains no more than half of the type volume specified in item (i).

(b) Electronically filed briefs

A brief filed electronically must comply with subdivision (a), except for (a)(1), (a)(3), and the paper requirement of (a)(4).

(c) Paper copies of appendices

A paper copy of an appendix must comply with subdivision (a)(1), (2), (3), and (4), with the following exceptions:

(1) An appendix may include a legible photocopy of any document found in the record or of a printed decision.

(2) When necessary to facilitate inclusion of odd-sized documents such as technical drawings, an appendix may be a size other than 8 1/2-by-11 inches, and need not lie reasonably flat when opened.

(d) Electronically filed appendices

An appendix filed electronically must comply with subdivision (a)(2) and (4), except for the paper requirement of (a)(4).

(e) Other documents

(1) Motion

Rule 8013(f) governs the form of a motion, response, or reply.

(2) Paper copies of other documents

A paper copy of any other document, other than a submission under Rule 8014(f), must comply with subdivision (a), with the following exceptions:

(A) A cover is not necessary if the caption and signature page together contain the information required by subdivision (a)(2).

(B) Subdivision (a)(7) does not apply.

(3) Other documents filed electronically

Any other document filed electronically, other than a submission under Rule 8014(f), must comply with the appearance requirements of paragraph (2).

(f) Local variation

A district court or BAP must accept documents that comply with the form requirements of this rule and the length limits set by Part VIII of these rules. By local rule or order in a particular case, a district court or BAP may accept documents that do not meet all the form requirements of this rule or the length limits set by Part VIII of these rules.

(g) Items excluded from length

In computing any length limit, headings, footnotes, and quotations count toward the limit, but the following items do not:

- the cover page;
- a corporate disclosure statement;
- a table of contents;
- a table of citations;
- a statement regarding oral argument;
- an addendum containing statutes, rules, or regulations;
- certificates of counsel;
- the signature block;
- the proof of service; and
- any item specifically excluded by these rules or by local rule.

(h) Certificate of compliance

(1) Briefs and documents that require a certificate

A brief submitted under Rule 8015(a)(7)(B), 8016(d)(2), or 8017(b)(4)—and a document submitted under Rule 8013(f)(3)(A), 8013(f)(3)(C), or 8022(b)(1)—must include a certificate by the attorney, or an unrepresented party, that the document complies with the type-volume limitation. The individual preparing the certificate may rely on the word or line count of the word-processing system used to prepare the document. The certificate must state the number of words—or the number of lines of monospaced type—in the document.

(2) Acceptable form

The certificate requirement is satisfied by a certificate of compliance that conforms substantially to the appropriate Official Form.

(As amended Mar. 30, 1987, eff. Aug. 1, 1987; Mar. 26, 2009, eff. Dec. 1, 2009; Apr. 25, 2014, eff. Dec. 1, 2014; Apr. 26, 2018, eff. Dec. 1, 2018.)

ADVISORY COMMITTEE NOTES

This is an adaptation of the first sentence of Rule 40(a) F.R.App.P. The filing of a motion for rehearing does not toll the time for taking an appeal to the court of appeals from the district court or the bankruptcy appellate panel. Appeals from a district court or a bankruptcy appellate panel are to the appropriate court of appeals. Under Rule 4(a)(4) F.R.App.P. the filing of post-trial motions in the district court has the effect of vitiating any prior notice of appeal and, on the district court's disposition of those post-trial motions, a new appeal period starts. Rule 4 F.R.App.P. does not, however, contain any provision which stays or otherwise alters the time for taking an appeal to the court of appeals when a motion for rehearing is filed under Rule 8015 with the district court or bankruptcy appellate panel.

1987 Amendment

The amendment, which is derived from Rule 8002(b), Rule 4(a)(4) F.R.App.P., and Rule 11.1 Sup.Ct.R., clarifies the effect of the filing of a timely motion for rehearing. If a timely motion is filed, the appeal period to the court of appeals begins to run on the entry of an order denying the motion or the entry of a subsequent judgment.

2009 Amendments

The rule is amended to implement changes in connection with the amendment to Rule 9006(a) and the manner by which time is computed under the rules. The deadline in the rule is amended to substitute a deadline that is a multiple of seven days. Throughout the rules, deadlines are amended in the following manner:

- 5–day periods become 7–day periods
- 10–day periods become 14–day periods
- 15–day periods become 14–day periods
- 20–day periods become 21–day periods
- 25–day periods become 28–day periods

2014 Amendments

This rule is derived primarily from F.R.App.P. 32. Former Rule 8010(c) prescribed page limits for principal briefs and reply briefs. Those limits are now addressed by subdivision (a)(7) of this rule. In addition, the rule incorporates most of the detail of F.R.App.P. 32 regarding the appearance and format of briefs, appendices, and other documents, along with new provisions that apply when those documents are filed electronically.

Subdivision (a) prescribes the form requirements for briefs that are filed in paper form. It incorporates F.R.App.P. 32(a), except it does not include color requirements for brief covers, it requires the cover of a brief to include counsel's email address, and cross-references to the appropriate bankruptcy rules are substituted for references to the Federal Rules of Appellate Procedure.

Subdivision (a)(7) decreases the length of briefs, as measured by the number of pages, that was permitted by former Rule 8010(c). Page limits are reduced from 50 to 30 pages for a principal brief and from 25 to 15 for a reply brief in order to achieve consistency with F.R.App.P. 32(a)(7). But as permitted by the appellate rule, subdivision (a)(7) also permits the limits on the length of a brief to be measured by a word or line count, as an alternative to a page limit. Basing the calculation of brief length on either of the type-volume methods specified in subdivision (a)(7)(B) will result in briefs that may exceed the designated page limits in (a)(7)(A) and that may be approximately as long as allowed by the prior page limits.

Subdivision (b) adapts for briefs that are electronically filed subdivision (a)'s form requirements. With the use of electronic filing, the method of reproduction, method of binding, and use of paper become irrelevant. But information required on the cover, formatting requirements, and limits on brief length remain the same.

Subdivisions (c) and **(d)** prescribe the form requirements for appendices. Subdivision (c), applicable to paper appendices, is derived from F.R.App.P. 32(b), and subdivision (d) adapts those requirements for electronically filed appendices.

Subdivision (e), which is based on F.R.App.P. 32(c), addresses the form required for documents—in paper form or electronically filed—that these rules do not otherwise cover.

Subdivision (f), like F.R.App.P. 32(e), provides assurance to lawyers and parties that compliance with this rule's form requirements will allow a brief or other document to be accepted by any district court or BAP. A court may, however, by local rule or, under Rule 8028 by order in a particular case, choose to accept briefs and documents that do not comply with all of this rule's requirements. The decision whether to accept a brief that appears not to be in compliance with the rules must be made by the court. Under Rule 8011(a)(3), the clerk may not refuse to accept a document for filing solely because it is not presented in proper form as required by these rules or any local rule or practice.

Under Rule 8011(e), the party filing the document or, if represented, its counsel must sign all briefs and other submissions. If the document is filed electronically, an electronic signature must be provided in accordance with Rule 8011(e).

Changes Made After Publication. In subdivision (f), "or order in a particular case" was deleted as unnecessary. The discussion in the Committee Note about brief lengths was revised, and the discussion of subdivision (f) was expanded.

2018 Amendments

The rule is amended to conform to recent amendments to F.R.App.P. 32, which reduced the word limits generally allowed for briefs. When Rule 32(a)(7)(B)'s type-volume limits for briefs were adopted in 1998, the word limits were based on an estimate of 280 words per page. Amended F.R.App.P. 32 applies a conversion ratio of 260 words per page and reduces the word limits accordingly. Rule 8015(a)(7) adopts the same reduced word limits for briefs prepared by computer.

In a complex case, a party may need to file a brief that exceeds the type-volume limitations specified in these rules, such as to include unusually voluminous information explaining relevant background or legal provisions or to respond to multiple briefs by opposing parties or amici. The Committee expects that courts will accommodate those situations by granting leave to exceed the type-volume limitations as appropriate.

Subdivision (f) is amended to make clear a court's ability (by local rule or order in a case) to increase the length limits for briefs and other documents. Subdivision (f) already established this authority as to the length limits in Rule 8015(a)(7); the amendment makes clear that this authority extends to all length limits in Part VIII of the Bankruptcy Rules.

A new subdivision (g) is added to set out a global list of items excluded from length computations, and the list of exclusions in former subdivision (a)(7)(B)(iii) is deleted. The certificate-of-compliance provision formerly in subdivision (a)(7)(C) is relocated to a new subdivision (h) and now applies to filings under all type-volume limits (other than Rule 8014(f)'s word limit)—including the new word limits in Rules 8013, 8016, 8017, and 8022. Conforming amendments are made to Official Form 417C.

Rule 8016.   Cross–Appeals

(a) Applicability

This rule applies to a case in which a cross-appeal is filed. Rules 8014(a)–(c), 8015(a)(7)(A)–(B), and 8018(a)(1)–(3) do not apply to such a case, except as otherwise provided in this rule.

(b) Designation of appellant

The party who files a notice of appeal first is the appellant for purposes of this rule and Rule 8018(a)(4) and (b) and Rule 8019. If notices are filed on the same day, the plaintiff, petitioner, applicant, or movant in the proceeding below is the appellant. These designations may be modified by the parties' agreement or by court order.

(c) Briefs

In a case involving a cross-appeal:

(1) Appellant's principal brief

The appellant must file a principal brief in the appeal. That brief must comply with Rule 8014(a).

(2) Appellee's principal and response brief

The appellee must file a principal brief in the cross-appeal and must, in the same brief, respond to the principal brief in the appeal. That brief must comply with Rule 8014(a), except that the brief need not include a statement of the case unless the appellee is dissatisfied with the appellant's statement.

(3) Appellant's response and reply brief

The appellant must file a brief that responds to the principal brief in the cross-appeal and may, in the same brief, reply to the response in the appeal. That brief must comply with Rule 8014(a)(2)–(8) and (10), except that none of the following need appear unless the appellant is dissatisfied with the appellee's statement in the cross-appeal:

    (A) the jurisdictional statement;

    (B) the statement of the issues and the applicable standard of appellate review; and

    (C) the statement of the case.

(4) Appellee's reply brief

The appellee may file a brief in reply to the response in the cross-appeal. That brief must comply with Rule 8014(a)(2)–(3) and (10) and must be limited to the issues presented by the cross-appeal.

(d) Length

(1) Page limitation

Unless it complies with paragraph (2), the appellant's principal brief must not exceed 30 pages; the appellee's principal and response brief, 35 pages; the appellant's response and reply brief, 30 pages; and the appellee's reply brief, 15 pages.

(2) Type-volume limitation

    (A) The appellant's principal brief or the appellant's response and reply brief is acceptable if it includes a certificate under Rule 8015(h) and:

        (i) contains no more than 13,000 words; or

        (ii) uses a monospaced face and contains no more than 1,300 lines of text.

    (B) The appellee's principal and response brief is acceptable if it includes a certificate under Rule 8015(h) and:

        (i) contains no more than 15,300 words; or

(ii) uses a monospaced face and contains no more than 1,500 lines of text.

(C) The appellee's reply brief is acceptable if it includes a certificate under Rule 8015(h) and contains no more than half of the type volume specified in subparagraph (A).

(e) Time to serve and file a brief

Briefs must be served and filed as follows, unless the district court or BAP by order in a particular case excuses the filing of briefs or specifies different time limits:

(1) the appellant's principal brief, within 30 days after the docketing of notice that the record has been transmitted or is available electronically;

(2) the appellee's principal and response brief, within 30 days after the appellant's principal brief is served;

(3) the appellant's response and reply brief, within 30 days after the appellee's principal and response brief is served; and

(4) the appellee's reply brief, within 14 days after the appellant's response and reply brief is served, but at least 7 days before scheduled argument unless the district court or BAP, for good cause, allows a later filing.

(As amended Mar. 30, 1987, eff. Aug. 1, 1987; Apr. 30, 1991, eff. Aug. 1, 1991; Apr. 25, 2014, eff. Dec. 1, 2014; Apr. 26, 2018, eff. Dec. 1, 2018.)

ADVISORY COMMITTEE NOTES

Subdivision (a) of this rule is adapted from Rule 36 F.R.App.P. Subdivision (b) is similar to subdivisions (c) and (d) of Rule 45 F.R.App.P.

1991 Amendment

Subdivision (b) is amended to enable the United States trustee to monitor the progress of the case. The requirements of this subdivision apply to an order of the district court or bankruptcy appellate panel staying its judgment pending appeal to the court of appeals pursuant to Rule 8017(b).

2014 Amendments

This rule is derived from F.R.App.P. 28.1. It governs the timing, content, length, filing, and service of briefs in bankruptcy appeals in which there is a cross-appeal. The former Part VIII rules did not separately address the topic of cross-appeals.

Subdivision (b) prescribes which party is designated the appellant when there is a cross-appeal. Generally, the first to file a notice of appeal will be the appellant.

Subdivision (c) specifies the briefs that the appellant and the appellee may file. Because of the dual role of the parties to the appeal and cross-appeal, each party is permitted to file a principal brief and a response to the opposing party's brief, as well as a reply brief. For the appellee, the principal brief in the cross-appeal and the response in the appeal are combined into a single brief. The appellant, on the other hand, initially files a principal brief in the appeal and later files a response to the appellee's principal brief in the cross-appeal, along with a reply brief in the appeal. The final brief that may be filed is the appellee's reply brief in the cross-appeal.

Subdivision (d), which prescribes page limits for briefs, is adopted from F.R.App.P. 28.1(e). It applies to briefs that are filed electronically, as well as to those filed in paper form. Like Rule 8015(a)(7), it imposes limits measured by either the number of pages or the number of words or lines of text.

Subdivision (e) governs the time for filing briefs in cases in which there is a cross-appeal. It adapts the provisions of F.R.App.P. 28.1(f).

Changes Made After Publication. Subdivision (d)(2)(D) was added, and subdivision (f) was deleted. In subdivision (a), the statement that Rule 8018(a) does not apply was changed to refer to Rule 8018(a)(1)–(3). In subdivision (b), Rule 8018(a)(4) was added to the list of rules. Conforming changes were made to the Committee Note.

2018 Amendments

The rule is amended to conform to recent amendments to F.R.App.P. 28.1, which reduced the word limits generally allowed for briefs in cross-appeals. When Rule 28.1 was adopted in 2005, it modeled its type-volume limits on those set forth in F.R.App.P. 32(a)(7) for briefs in cases that did not involve a cross-appeal. At that time, Rule 32(a)(7)(B) set word limits based on an estimate of 280 words per page. Amended F.R.App.P. 32 and 28.1 apply a conversion ratio of 260 words per page and reduce the word limits accordingly. Rule 8016(d)(2) adopts the same reduced word limits.

In a complex case, a party may need to file a brief that exceeds the type-volume limitations specified in these rules, such as to include unusually voluminous information explaining relevant background or legal provisions or to respond to multiple briefs by opposing parties or amici. The Committee expects that courts will accommodate those situations by granting leave to exceed the type-volume limitations as appropriate.

Subdivision (d) is amended to refer to new Rule 8015(h) (which now contains the certificate-of-compliance provision formerly in Rule 8015(a)(7)(C)).

Rule 8017. Brief of an Amicus Curiae

(a) During initial consideration of a case on the merits

(1) Applicability

This Rule 8017(a) governs amicus filings during a court's initial consideration of a case on the merits.

(2) When permitted

The United States or its officer or agency or a state may file an amicus brief without the consent of the parties or leave of court. Any other amicus curiae may file a brief only by leave of court or if the brief states that all parties have consented to its filing, but a district court or BAP may prohibit the filing of or may strike an amicus brief that would result in a judge's disqualification. On its own motion, and with notice to all parties to an appeal, the district court or BAP may request a brief by an amicus curiae.

(3) Motion for leave to file

The motion must be accompanied by the proposed brief and state:

    (A) the movant's interest; and

    (B) the reason why an amicus brief is desirable and why the matters asserted are relevant to the disposition of the appeal.

(4) Contents and form

An amicus brief must comply with Rule 8015. In addition to the requirements of Rule 8015, the cover must identify the party or parties supported and indicate whether the brief supports affirmance or reversal. If an amicus curiae is a corporation, the brief must include a disclosure statement like that required of parties by Rule 8012. An amicus brief need not comply with Rule 8014, but must include the following:

    (A) a table of contents, with page references;

    (B) a table of authorities—cases (alphabetically arranged), statutes, and other authorities—with references to the pages of the brief where they are cited;

    (C) a concise statement of the identity of the amicus curiae, its interest in the case, and the source of its authority to file;

    (D) unless the amicus curiae is one listed in the first sentence of subdivision (a)(2), a statement that indicates whether:

      (i) a party's counsel authored the brief in whole or in part;

      (ii) a party or a party's counsel contributed money that was intended to fund preparing or submitting the brief; and

      (iii) a person—other than the amicus curiae, its members, or its counsel—contributed money that was intended to fund preparing or submitting the brief and, if so, identifies each such person;

    (E) an argument, which may be preceded by a summary and need not include a statement of the applicable standard of review; and

    (F) a certificate of compliance, if required by Rule 8015(h).

(5) Length

Except by the district court's or BAP's permission, an amicus brief must be no more than one-half the maximum length authorized by these rules for a party's principal brief. If the court grants a party permission to file a longer brief, that extension does not affect the length of an amicus brief.

(6) Time for filing

An amicus curiae must file its brief, accompanied by a motion for filing when necessary, no later than 7 days after the principal brief of the party being supported is filed. An amicus curiae that does not support either party must file its brief no later than 7 days after the appellant's principal brief is filed. The district court or BAP may grant leave for later filing, specifying the time within which an opposing party may answer.

(7) Reply brief

Except by the district court's or BAP's permission, an amicus curiae may not file a reply brief.

(8) Oral argument

An amicus curiae may participate in oral argument only with the district court's or BAP's permission.

(b) During consideration of whether to grant rehearing

(1) Applicability

This Rule 8017(b) governs amicus filings during a district court's or BAP's consideration of whether to grant rehearing, unless a local rule or order in a case provides otherwise.

(2) When permitted

The United States or its officer or agency or a state may file an amicus brief without the consent of the parties or leave of court. Any other amicus curiae may file a brief only by leave of court.

(3) Motion for leave to file

Rule 8017(a)(3) applies to a motion for leave.

(4) Contents, form, and length

Rule 8017(a)(4) applies to the amicus brief. The brief must include a certificate under Rule 8015(h) and not exceed 2,600 words.

(5) Time for filing

An amicus curiae supporting the motion for rehearing or supporting neither party must file its brief, accompanied by a motion for filing when necessary, no later than 7 days after the motion is filed. An amicus curiae opposing the motion for rehearing must file its brief, accompanied by a motion for filing when necessary, no later than the date set by the court for the response.

(As amended Mar. 26, 2009, eff. Dec. 1, 2009; Apr. 25, 2014, eff. Dec. 1, 2014; Apr. 26, 2018, eff. Dec. 1, 2018.)

ADVISORY COMMITTEE NOTES

This rule is derived from Rule 62 F.R.Civ.P. and Rule 41 F.R.App.P.

Subdivision (a) accords to the parties to an appeal 10 days within which to decide whether to pursue an appeal to the court of appeals. In ordinary civil litigation there is a similar opportunity. Rule 62(a) F.R.Civ.P. automatically stays enforcement of a district court's judgment in a civil action and Rule 41(a) F.R.App.P. provides that the mandate of the court of appeals shall not issue for 21 days, unless the court otherwise directs. The district court or bankruptcy appellate panel may reduce the 10 day period of this subdivision.

Subdivision (b) vests in the district courts and the bankruptcy appellate panels the same authority the courts of appeals have under Rule 41(b) F.R.App.P. to stay their judgments pending appeal. Perfection of an appeal to the court of appeals while a stay entered by the district court or bankruptcy appellate panel is in effect results in the automatic continuation of that stay during the course of the appeal in the court of appeals.

Subdivision (c) is the same as Rule 62(g) F.R.Civ.P.

2009 Amendments

The rule is amended to implement changes in connection with the amendment to Rule 9006(a) and the manner by which time is computed under the rules. The deadline in the rule is amended to substitute a deadline that is a multiple of seven days. Throughout the rules, deadlines are amended in the following manner:

- 5–day periods become 7–day periods
- 10–day periods become 14–day periods
- 15–day periods become 14–day periods
- 20–day periods become 21–day periods
- 25–day periods become 28–day periods

2014 Amendments

This rule is derived from F.R.App.P. 29. The former Part VIII rules did not address the participation by an amicus curiae in a bankruptcy appeal.

Subdivision (a) adopts the provisions of F.R.App.P. 29(a). In addition, it authorizes the district court or BAP on its own motion—with notice to the parties—to request the filing of a brief by an amicus curiae.

Subdivisions (b)–(g) adopt F.R.App.P. 29(b)–(g).

Changes Made After Publication. No changes were made after publication.

2018 Amendments

Rule 8017 is amended to conform to the recent amendment to F.R.App.P. 29, which now addresses amicus filings in connection with petitions for rehearing. Former Rule 8017 is renumbered Rule 8017(a), and language is added to that subdivision (a) to state that its provisions apply to amicus filings during the district court's or BAP's initial consideration of a case on the merits. New subdivision (b) is added to address amicus filings in connection with a motion for rehearing. Subdivision (b) sets default rules that apply when a district court or BAP does not provide otherwise by local rule or by order in a case. A court remains free to adopt different rules governing whether amicus filings are permitted in connection with motions for rehearing and the procedures when such filings are permitted.

The amendment to subdivision (a)(2) authorizes orders or local rules that prohibit the filing of or permit the striking of an amicus brief by party consent if the brief would result in a judge's disqualification. The amendment does not alter or address the standards for when an amicus brief requires a judge's disqualification. It is modeled on an amendment to

F.R.App.P. 29(a). A comparable amendment to subdivision (b) is not necessary. Subdivision (b)(1) authorizes local rules and orders governing filings during a court's consideration of whether to grant rehearing. These local rules or orders may prohibit the filing of or permit the striking of an amicus brief that would result in a judge's disqualification. In addition, under subdivision (b)(2), a court may deny leave to file an amicus brief that would result in a judge's disqualification.

Rule 8018. Serving and Filing Briefs; Appendices

(a) Time to serve and file a brief

The following rules apply unless the district court or BAP by order in a particular case excuses the filing of briefs or specifies different time limits:

(1) The appellant must serve and file a brief within 30 days after the docketing of notice that the record has been transmitted or is available electronically.

(2) The appellee must serve and file a brief within 30 days after service of the appellant's brief.

(3) The appellant may serve and file a reply brief within 14 days after service of the appellee's brief, but a reply brief must be filed at least 7 days before scheduled argument unless the district court or BAP, for good cause, allows a later filing.

(4) If an appellant fails to file a brief on time or within an extended time authorized by the district court or BAP, an appellee may move to dismiss the appeal—or the district court or BAP, after notice, may dismiss the appeal on its own motion. An appellee who fails to file a brief will not be heard at oral argument unless the district court or BAP grants permission.

(b) Duty to serve and file an appendix to the brief

(1) Appellant

Subject to subdivision (e) and Rule 8009(d), the appellant must serve and file with its principal brief excerpts of the record as an appendix. It must contain the following:

   (A) the relevant entries in the bankruptcy docket;

   (B) the complaint and answer, or other equivalent filings;

   (C) the judgment, order, or decree from which the appeal is taken;

   (D) any other orders, pleadings, jury instructions, findings, conclusions, or opinions relevant to the appeal;

   (E) the notice of appeal; and

   (F) any relevant transcript or portion of it.

(2) Appellee

The appellee may also serve and file with its brief an appendix that contains material required to be included by the appellant or relevant to the appeal or cross-appeal, but omitted by the appellant.

(3) Cross-appellee

The appellant as cross-appellee may also serve and file with its response an appendix that contains material relevant to matters raised initially by the principal brief in the cross-appeal, but omitted by the cross-appellant.

(c) Format of the appendix

The appendix must begin with a table of contents identifying the page at which each part begins. The relevant docket entries must follow the table of contents. Other parts of the record must follow chronologically. When pages from the transcript of proceedings are placed in the appendix, the transcript page numbers must be shown in brackets immediately before the included pages. Omissions in the text of documents or of the transcript must be indicated by asterisks. Immaterial formal matters (captions, subscriptions, acknowledgments, and the like) should be omitted.

(d) Exhibits

Exhibits designated for inclusion in the appendix may be reproduced in a separate volume or volumes, suitably indexed.

(e) Appeal on the original record without an appendix

The district court or BAP may, either by rule for all cases or classes of cases or by order in a particular case, dispense with the appendix and permit an appeal to proceed on the original record, with the submission of any relevant parts of the record that the district court or BAP orders the parties to file.

(As amended Mar. 30, 1987, eff. Aug. 1, 1987; Apr. 27, 1995, eff. Dec. 1, 1995; Apr. 25, 2014, eff. Dec. 1, 2014.)

ADVISORY COMMITTEE NOTES

This rule is similar to Rule 47 F.R.App.P. and Rule 83 F.R.Civ.P. Local rules governing procedure before the bankruptcy courts may be promulgated under Rule 9028.

1987 Amendment

Rule 83 F.R.Civ.P. was amended in August 1985 to require greater participation by the public in the rule making process. The amendment to Rule 8018 incorporates Rule 83 F.R.Civ.P. Under 28 U.S.C. § 158(b)(2), appeals may be taken to a bankruptcy appellate panel only if the district court so authorizes. If a district court does not authorize appeals to the bankruptcy appellate panel, appeals will be to the district court. This rule is amended to authorize district courts to promulgate rules for appeals.

1995 Amendments

The amendments to this rule conform to the amendments to Rule 9029. See Committee Note to the amendments to Rule 9029.

2014 Amendments

This rule is derived from former Rule 8009 and F.R.App.P. 30 and 31. Like former Rule 8009, it addresses the timing of serving and filing briefs and appendices, as well as the content and format of appendices. Rule 8011 governs the methods of filing and serving briefs and appendices.

The rule retains the bankruptcy practice of permitting the appellee to file its own appendix, rather than requiring the appellant to include in its appendix matters designated by the appellee. Rule 8016 governs the timing of serving and filing briefs when a cross-appeal is taken. This rule's provisions about appendices apply to all appeals, including cross-appeals.

Subdivision (a) retains former Rule 8009's provision that allows the district court or BAP to dispense with briefing or to provide different time periods than this rule specifies. It increases some of the time periods for filing briefs from the periods prescribed by the former rule, while still retaining shorter time periods than some provided by F.R.App.P. 31(a). The time for filing the appellant's brief is increased from 14 to 30 days after the docketing of the notice of the transmission of the record or notice of the availability of the record. That triggering event is equivalent to docketing the appeal under former Rule 8007. Appellate Rule 31(a)(1), by contrast, provides the appellant 40 days after the record is filed to file its brief. The shorter time period for bankruptcy appeals reflects the frequent need for greater expedition in the resolution of bankruptcy appeals, while still providing the appellant more time to prepare its brief than the former rule provided.

Subdivision (a)(2) similarly expands the time period for filing the appellee's brief from 14 to 30 days after the service of the appellant's brief. This period is the same as F.R.App. 31(a)(1) provides.

Subdivision (a)(3) retains the 14–day time period for filing a reply brief that the former rule prescribed, but it qualifies that period to ensure that the final brief is filed at least 7 days before oral argument.

If a district court or BAP has a mediation procedure for bankruptcy appeals, that procedure could affect when briefs must be filed. See Rule 8027.

Subdivision (a)(4) is new. Based on F.R.App.P. 31(c), it provides for actions that may be taken—dismissal of the appeal or denial of participation in oral argument—if the appellant or appellee fails to file its brief.

Subdivisions (b) and **(c)** govern the content and format of the appendix to a brief. Subdivision (b) is similar to former Rule 8009(b), and subdivision (c) is derived from F.R.App.P. 30(d).

Subdivision (d), which addresses the inclusion of exhibits in the appendix, is derived from F.R.App.P. 30(e).

Changes Made After Publication. Subdivision (a)(4) was revised to provide more detail about the procedure for dismissing an appeal due to appellant's failure to timely file a brief.

Rule 8018.1. District–Court Review of a Judgment that the Bankruptcy Court Lacked the Constitutional Authority to Enter

If, on appeal, a district court determines that the bankruptcy court did not have the power under Article III of the Constitution to enter the judgment, order, or

decree appealed from, the district court may treat it as proposed findings of fact and conclusions of law.
(Added Apr. 26, 2018, eff. Dec. 1, 2018.)

ADVISORY COMMITTEE NOTES
2018 Amendments

This rule is new. It is added to prevent a district court from having to remand an appeal whenever it determines that the bankruptcy court lacked constitutional authority to enter the judgment, order, or decree appealed from. Consistent with the Supreme Court's decision in *Executive Benefits Insurance Agency v. Arkison*, 134 S. Ct. 2165 (2014), the district court in that situation may treat the bankruptcy court's judgment as proposed findings of fact and conclusions of law. Upon making the determination to proceed in that manner, the district court may choose to allow the parties to file written objections to specific proposed findings and conclusions and to respond to another party's objections, *see* Rule 9033; treat the parties' briefs as objections and responses; or prescribe other procedures for the review of the proposed findings of fact and conclusions of law.

Rule 8019. Oral Argument

(a) Party's statement

Any party may file, or a district court or BAP may require, a statement explaining why oral argument should, or need not, be permitted.

(b) Presumption of oral argument and exceptions

Oral argument must be allowed in every case unless the district judge—or all the BAP judges assigned to hear the appeal—examine the briefs and record and determine that oral argument is unnecessary because

(1) the appeal is frivolous;

(2) the dispositive issue or issues have been authoritatively decided; or

(3) the facts and legal arguments are adequately presented in the briefs and record, and the decisional process would not be significantly aided by oral argument.

(c) Notice of argument; postponement

The district court or BAP must advise all parties of the date, time, and place for oral argument, and the time allowed for each side. A motion to postpone the argument or to allow longer argument must be filed reasonably in advance of the hearing date.

(d) Order and contents of argument

The appellant opens and concludes the argument. Counsel must not read at length from briefs, the record, or authorities.

(e) Cross-appeals and separate appeals

If there is a cross-appeal, Rule 8016(b) determines which party is the appellant and which is the appellee for the purposes of oral argument. Unless the district court or BAP directs otherwise, a cross-appeal or separate appeal must be argued when the initial appeal is argued. Separate parties should avoid duplicative argument.

(f) Nonappearance of a party

If the appellee fails to appear for argument, the district court or BAP may hear the appellant's argument. If the appellant fails to appear for argument, the district court or BAP may hear the appellee's argument. If neither party appears, the case will be decided on the briefs unless the district court or BAP orders otherwise.

(g) Submission on briefs

The parties may agree to submit a case for decision on the briefs, but the district court or BAP may direct that the case be argued.

(h) Use of physical exhibits at argument; removal

Counsel intending to use physical exhibits other than documents at the argument must arrange to place them in the courtroom on the day of the argument before the court convenes. After the argument, counsel must remove the exhibits from the courtroom unless the district court or BAP directs otherwise. The clerk may destroy or dispose of the exhibits if counsel does not reclaim them within a reasonable time after the clerk gives notice to remove them.
(As amended Mar. 30, 1987, eff. Aug. 1, 1987; Apr. 25, 2014, eff. Dec. 1, 2014.)

ADVISORY COMMITTEE NOTES

This rule is derived from Rule 2 F.R.App.P.

2014 Amendments

This rule generally retains the provisions of former Rule 8012 and adds much of the additional detail of F.R.App.P. 34. By incorporating the more detailed provisions of the appellate rule, Rule 8019 promotes national uniformity regarding oral argument in bankruptcy appeals.

Subdivision (a), like F.R.App.P. 34(a)(1), now allows a party to submit a statement explaining why oral argument is or is not needed. It also authorizes a court to require this statement. Former Rule 8012 only authorized statements explaining why oral argument should be allowed.

Subdivision (b) retains the reasons set forth in former Rule 8012 for the district court or BAP to conclude that oral argument is not needed.

The remainder of this rule adopts the provisions of F.R.App.P. 34(b)–(g), with one exception. Rather than requiring the district court or BAP to hear appellant's argument if the appellee does not appear, subdivision (f) authorizes the district court or BAP to go forward with the argument in the appellee's absence. Should the court decide, however, to postpone the oral argument in that situation, it would be authorized to do so.

Changes Made After Publication. No changes were made after publication.

Rule 8020.   Frivolous Appeal and Other Misconduct

(a) Frivolous appeal—damages and costs

If the district court or BAP determines that an appeal is frivolous, it may, after a separately filed motion or notice from the court and reasonable opportunity to respond, award just damages and single or double costs to the appellee.

(b) Other misconduct

The district court or BAP may discipline or sanction an attorney or party appearing before it for other misconduct, including failure to comply with any court order. First, however, the court must afford the attorney or party reasonable notice, an opportunity to show cause to the contrary, and, if requested, a hearing.
(Added Apr. 11, 1997, eff. Dec. 1, 1997; Apr. 25, 2014, eff. Dec. 1, 2014.)

ADVISORY COMMITTEE NOTES

1997 Amendment

This rule is added to clarify that a district court hearing an appeal, or a bankruptcy appellate panel, has the authority to award damages and costs to an appellee if it finds that the appeal is frivolous. By conforming to the language of Rule 38 F.R.App.P., this rule recognizes that the authority to award damages and costs in connection with frivolous appeals is the same for district courts sitting as appellate courts, bankruptcy appellate panels, and courts of appeals.

GAP Report on Rule 8020. No changes to the published draft.

2014 Amendments

This rule is derived from former Rule 8020 and F.R.App.P. 38 and 46(c). Subdivision (a) permits an award of damages and costs to an appellee for a frivolous appeal. Subdivision (b) permits the district court or BAP to impose on parties as well as their counsel sanctions for misconduct other than taking a frivolous appeal. Failure to comply with a court order, for which sanctions may be imposed, may include a failure to comply with a local court rule.

Changes Made After Publication. No changes were made after publication.

Rule 8021.   Costs

(a) Against whom assessed

The following rules apply unless the law provides or the district court or BAP orders otherwise:

    (1) if an appeal is dismissed, costs are taxed against the appellant, unless the parties agree otherwise;

    (2) if a judgment, order, or decree is affirmed, costs are taxed against the appellant;

    (3) if a judgment, order, or decree is reversed, costs are taxed against the appellee;

    (4) if a judgment, order, or decree is affirmed or reversed in part, modified, or vacated, costs are taxed only as the district court or BAP orders.

(b) Costs for and against the United States

Costs for or against the United States, its agency, or its officer may be assessed under subdivision (a) only if authorized by law.

(c) Costs on appeal taxable in the bankruptcy court

The following costs on appeal are taxable in the bankruptcy court for the benefit of the party entitled to costs under this rule:

    (1) the production of any required copies of a brief, appendix, exhibit, or the record;

    (2) the preparation and transmission of the record;

    (3) the reporter's transcript, if needed to determine the appeal;

    (4) premiums paid for a bond or other security to preserve rights pending appeal; and

    (5) the fee for filing the notice of appeal.

(d) Bill of costs; objections

A party who wants costs taxed must, within 14 days after entry of judgment on appeal, file with the bankruptcy clerk, with proof of service, an itemized and verified bill of costs. Objections must be filed within 14 days after service of the bill of costs, unless the bankruptcy court extends the time.
(Added Apr. 25, 2014, eff. Dec. 1, 2014; as amended Apr. 26, 2018, eff. Dec. 1, 2018.)

ADVISORY COMMITTEE NOTES

2014 Amendments

This rule is derived from former Rule 8014 and F.R.App.P. 39. It retains the former rule's authorization for taxing appellate costs against the losing party and its specification of the costs that may be taxed. The rule also incorporates some of the additional details regarding the taxing of costs contained in F.R.App.P. 39. Consistent with former Rule 8014, the bankruptcy clerk has the responsibility for taxing all costs. Subdivision (b), derived from F.R.App.P. 39(b), clarifies that additional authority is required for the taxation of costs by or against federal governmental parties.

Changes Made After Publication. No changes were made after publication.

2018 Amendments

The amendment of subdivision (c) conforms this rule with the amendment of Rule 62 F.R.Civ.P., which is made applicable in adversary proceedings by Rule 7062. Rule 62 formerly required a party to provide a "supersedeas bond" to obtain a stay of the judgment and proceedings to enforce the judgment. As amended, Rule 62(b) allows a party to obtain a stay by providing a "bond or other security."

Rule 8022.   Motion for Rehearing

(a) Time to file; contents; response; action by the district court or BAP if granted

(1) Time

Unless the time is shortened or extended by order or local rule, any motion for rehearing by the district court or BAP must be filed within 14 days after entry of judgment on appeal.

(2) Contents

The motion must state with particularity each point of law or fact that the movant believes the district court or BAP has overlooked or misapprehended and must argue in support of the motion. Oral argument is not permitted.

(3) Response

Unless the district court or BAP requests, no response to a motion for rehearing is permitted. But ordinarily, rehearing will not be granted in the absence of such a request.

(4) Action by the district court or BAP

If a motion for rehearing is granted, the district court or BAP may do any of the following:

(A) make a final disposition of the appeal without reargument;

(B) restore the case to the calendar for reargument or resubmission; or

(C) issue any other appropriate order.

(b) Form of the motion; length

The motion must comply in form with Rule 8013(f)(1) and (2). Copies must be served and filed as provided by Rule 8011. Except by the district court's or BAP's permission:

(1) a motion for rehearing produced using a computer must include a certificate under Rule 8015(h) and not exceed 3,900 words; and

(2) a handwritten or typewritten motion must not exceed 15 pages.

(Added Apr. 25, 2014, eff. Dec. 1, 2014; as amended Apr. 26, 2018, eff. Dec. 1, 2018.)

ADVISORY COMMITTEE NOTES

2014 Amendments

This rule is derived from former Rule 8015 and F.R.App.P. 40. It deletes the provision of former Rule 8015 regarding the time for appeal to the court of appeals because the matter is addressed by F.R.App.P. 6(b)(2)(A).

Changes Made After Publication. In subdivision (b), the reference to local rule was deleted as unnecessary.

2018 Amendments

Subdivision (b) is amended to conform to the recent amendment to F.R.App.P. 40(b), which was one of several appellate rules in which word limits were substituted for page limits for documents prepared by computer. The word limits were derived from the previous page limits using the assumption that one page is equivalent to 260 words. Documents produced using a computer must include the certificate of compliance required by Rule 8015(h); completion of Official Form 417C suffices to meet that requirement.

Page limits are retained for papers prepared without the aid of a computer (i.e., handwritten or typewritten papers). For both the word limit and the page limit, the calculation excludes any items listed in Rule 8015(g).

Rule 8023.   Voluntary Dismissal

The clerk of the district court or BAP must dismiss an appeal if the parties file a signed dismissal agreement specifying how costs are to be paid and pay any fees that are due. An appeal may be dismissed on the appellant's motion on terms agreed to by the parties or fixed by the district court or BAP.

(Added Apr. 25, 2014, eff. Dec. 1, 2014.)

ADVISORY COMMITTEE NOTES

2014 Amendments

This rule is derived from former Rule 8001(c) and F.R.App.P. 42. The provision of the former rule regarding dismissal of appeals in the bankruptcy court prior to docketing of the appeal has been deleted. Now that docketing occurs promptly after a notice of appeal is filed, see Rules 8003(d) and 8004(c), an appeal likely will not be voluntarily dismissed before docketing.

The rule retains the provision of the former rule that the district or BAP clerk must dismiss an appeal upon the parties' agreement. District courts and BAPs continue to have discretion to dismiss an appeal on an appellant's motion. Nothing in the rule prohibits a district court or BAP from dismissing an appeal for other reasons authorized by law, such as the failure to prosecute an appeal.

Changes Made After Publication. No changes were made after publication.

Rule 8024.   Clerk's Duties on Disposition of the Appeal

(a) Judgment on appeal

The district or BAP clerk must prepare, sign, and enter the judgment after receiving the court's opinion or, if there is no opinion, as the court instructs. Noting the judgment on the docket constitutes entry of judgment.

(b) Notice of a judgment

Immediately upon the entry of a judgment, the district or BAP clerk must:

(1) transmit a notice of the entry to each party to the appeal, to the United States trustee, and to the bankruptcy clerk, together with a copy of any opinion; and

(2) note the date of the transmission on the docket.

(c) Returning physical items

If any physical items were transmitted as the record on appeal, they must be returned to the bankruptcy clerk on disposition of the appeal.

(Added Apr. 25, 2014, eff. Dec. 1, 2014.)

ADVISORY COMMITTEE NOTES
2014 Amendments

This rule is derived from former Rule 8016, which was adapted from F.R.App.P. 36 and 45(c) and (d). The rule is reworded to reflect that only items in the record that are physically, as opposed to electronically, transmitted to the district court or BAP need to be returned to the bankruptcy clerk. Other changes to the former rule are stylistic.

Changes Made After Publication. Stylistic changes were made to subdivision (c) and the Committee Note.

Rule 8025.   Stay of a District Court or BAP Judgment

(a) Automatic stay of judgment on appeal

Unless the district court or BAP orders otherwise, its judgment is stayed for 14 days after entry.

(b) Stay pending appeal to the court of appeals
(1) In general

On a party's motion and notice to all other parties to the appeal, the district court or BAP may stay its judgment pending an appeal to the court of appeals.

(2) Time limit

The stay must not exceed 30 days after the judgment is entered, except for cause shown.

(3) Stay continued

If, before a stay expires, the party who obtained the stay appeals to the court of appeals, the stay continues until final disposition by the court of appeals.

(4) Bond or other security

A bond or other security may be required as a condition for granting or continuing a stay of the judgment. A bond or other security may be required if a trustee obtains a stay, but not if a stay is obtained by the United States or its officer or agency or at the direction of any department of the United States government.

(c) Automatic stay of an order, judgment, or decree of a bankruptcy court

If the district court or BAP enters a judgment affirming an order, judgment, or decree of the bankruptcy court, a stay of the district court's or BAP's judgment automatically stays the bankruptcy court's order, judgment, or decree for the duration of the appellate stay.

(d) Power of a court of appeals not limited

This rule does not limit the power of a court of appeals or any of its judges to do the following:

(1) stay a judgment pending appeal;

(2) stay proceedings while an appeal is pending;

(3) suspend, modify, restore, vacate, or grant a stay or an injunction while an appeal is pending; or

(4) issue any order appropriate to preserve the status quo or the effectiveness of any judgment to be entered.

(Added Apr. 25, 2014, eff. Dec. 1, 2014.)

ADVISORY COMMITTEE NOTES
2014 Amendments

This rule is derived from former Rule 8017. Most of the changes to the former rule are stylistic. Subdivision (c) is new. It provides that if a district court or BAP affirms the bankruptcy court ruling and the appellate judgment is stayed, the bankruptcy court's order, judgment, or decree that is affirmed on appeal is automatically stayed to the same extent as the stay of the appellate judgment.

Changes Made After Publication. No changes were made after publication.

Rule 8026.   Rules by Circuit Councils and District Courts; Procedure When There Is No Controlling Law

(a) Local rules by circuit councils and district courts
(1) Adopting local rules

A circuit council that has authorized a BAP under 28 U.S.C. § 158(b) may make and amend rules governing the practice and procedure on appeal from a judgment, order, or decree of a bankruptcy court to the BAP. A district court may make and amend rules governing the practice and procedure on appeal from a judgment, order, or decree of a bankruptcy court to the district court. Local rules must be consistent with, but not duplicative of, Acts of Congress and these Part VIII rules. Rule 83 F.R.Civ.P. governs the procedure for making and amending rules to govern appeals.

(2) Numbering

Local rules must conform to any uniform numbering system prescribed by the Judicial Conference of the United States.

(3) Limitation on imposing requirements of form

A local rule imposing a requirement of form must not be enforced in a way that causes a party to lose any right because of a nonwillful failure to comply.

(b) Procedure when there is no controlling law
(1) In general

A district court or BAP may regulate practice in any manner consistent with federal law, applicable federal rules, the Official Forms, and local rules.

(2) Limitation on sanctions

No sanction or other disadvantage may be imposed for noncompliance with any requirement not in federal law, applicable federal rules, the Official Forms, or local rules unless the alleged violator has been furnished in the particular case with actual notice of the requirement.

(Added Apr. 25, 2014, eff. Dec. 1, 2014.)

ADVISORY COMMITTEE NOTES

2014 Amendments

This rule is derived from former Rule 8018. The changes to the former rule are stylistic.

Changes Made After Publication. No changes were made after publication.

Rule 8027. Notice of a Mediation Procedure

If the district court or BAP has a mediation procedure applicable to bankruptcy appeals, the clerk must notify the parties promptly after docketing the appeal of: (a) the requirements of the mediation procedure; and (b) any effect the mediation procedure has on the time to file briefs.

(Added Apr. 25, 2014, eff. Dec. 1, 2014.)

ADVISORY COMMITTEE NOTES

2014 Amendments

This rule is new. It requires the district or BAP clerk to advise the parties promptly after an appeal is docketed of any court mediation procedure that is applicable to bankruptcy appeals. The notice must state what the mediation requirements are and how the procedure affects the time for filing briefs.

Changes Made After Publication. No changes were made after publication.

Rule 8028. Suspension of Rules in Part VIII

In the interest of expediting decision or for other cause in a particular case, the district court or BAP, or where appropriate the court of appeals, may suspend the requirements or provisions of the rules in Part VIII, except Rules 8001, 8002, 8003, 8004, 8005, 8006, 8007, 8012, 8020, 8024, 8025, 8026, and 8028.

(Added Apr. 25, 2014, eff. Dec. 1, 2014.)

ADVISORY COMMITTEE NOTES

2014 Amendments

This rule is derived from former Rule 8019 and F.R.App.P. 2. To promote uniformity of practice and compliance with statutory authority, the rule includes a more extensive list of requirements that may not be suspended than either the former rule or the Federal Rules of Appellate Procedure provide. Rules governing the following matters may not be suspended:

- scope of the rules; definition of "BAP"; method of transmission;
- time for filing a notice of appeal;
- taking an appeal as of right;
- taking an appeal by leave;
- election to have an appeal heard by a district court instead of a BAP;
- certification of direct appeal to a court of appeals;
- stay pending appeal;
- corporate disclosure statement;
- sanctions for frivolous appeals and other misconduct;
- clerk's duties on disposition of an appeal;
- stay of a district court's or BAP's judgment;
- local rules; and
- suspension of the Part VIII rules.

Changes Made After Publication. No changes were made after publication.

Appendix: Length Limits Stated in Part VIII of the Federal Rules of Bankruptcy Procedure

This chart shows the length limits stated in Part VIII of the Federal Rules of Bankruptcy Procedure. Please bear in mind the following:

- In computing these limits, you can exclude the items listed in Rule 8015(g).
- If you are using a word limit or line limit (other than the word limit in Rule 8014(f)), you must include the certificate required by Rule 8015(h).
- If you are using a line limit, your document must be in monospaced typeface. A typeface is monospaced when each character occupies the same amount of horizontal space.
- For the limits in Rules 8013 and 8022:
  - You must use the word limit if you produce your document on a computer; and
  - You must use the page limit if you handwrite your document or type it on a typewriter.

Rule	Document Type	Word Limit	Page Limit	Line Limit
Motions				
8013(f)(3)	• Motion • Response to a motion	5,200	20	Not applicable
8013(f)(3)	• Reply to a response to a motion	2,600	10	Not applicable

	Rule	Document Type	Word Limit	Page Limit	Line Limit
Parties' briefs (where no cross-appeal)	8015(a)(7)	• Principal brief	13,000	30	1,300
	8015(a)(7)	• Reply brief	6,500	15	650
Parties' briefs (where cross-appeal)	8016(d)	• Appellant's principal brief • Appellant's response and reply brief	13,000	30	1,300
	8016(d)	• Appellee's principal and response brief	15,300	35	1,500
	8016(d)	• Appellee's reply brief	6,500	15	650
Party's supplemental letter	8014(f)	• Letter citing supplemental authorities	350	Not applicable	Not applicable
Amicus briefs	8017(a)(5)	• Amicus brief during initial consideration of case on merits	One-half the length set by the Part VIII Rules for a party's principal brief	One-half the length set by the Part VIII Rules for a party's principal brief	One-half the length set by the Part VIII Rules for a party's principal brief
	8017(b)(4)	• Amicus brief during consideration of whether to grant rehearing	2,600	Not applicable	Not applicable
Motion for rehearing	8022(b)	• Motion for rehearing	3,900	15	Not applicable

(Added Apr. 26, 2018, eff. Dec. 1, 2018.)

Rule 9001. General Definitions

The definitions of words and phrases in §§ 101, 902, 1101, and 1502 of the Code, and the rules of construction in § 102, govern their use in these rules. In addition, the following words and phrases used in these rules have the meanings indicated:

(1) "Bankruptcy clerk" means a clerk appointed pursuant to 28 U.S.C. § 156(b).

(2) "Bankruptcy Code" or "Code" means title 11 of the United States Code.

(3) "Clerk" means bankruptcy clerk, if one has been appointed, otherwise clerk of the district court.

(4) "Court" or "judge" means the judicial officer before whom a case or proceeding is pending.

(5) "Debtor." When any act is required by these rules to be performed by a debtor or when it is necessary to compel attendance of a debtor for examination and the debtor is not a natural person: (A) if the debtor is a corporation, "debtor" includes, if designated by the court, any or all of its officers, members of its board of directors or trustees or of a similar controlling body, a controlling stockholder or member, or any other person in control; (B) if the debtor is a partnership, "debtor" includes any or all of its general partners or, if designated by the court, any other person in control.

(6) "Firm" includes a partnership or professional corporation of attorneys or accountants.

(7) "Judgment" means any appealable order.

(8) "Mail" means first class, postage prepaid.

(9) "Notice provider" means any entity approved by the Administrative Office of the United States Courts to give notice to creditors under Rule 2002(g)(4).

(10) "Regular associate" means any attorney regularly employed by, associated with, or counsel to an individual or firm.

(11) "Trustee" includes a debtor in possession in a chapter 11 case.

(12) "United States trustee" includes an assistant United States trustee and any designee of the United States trustee.

(As amended Mar. 30, 1987, eff. Aug. 1, 1987; Apr. 30, 1991, eff. Aug. 1, 1991; Apr. 25, 2005, eff. Dec. 1, 2005; Apr. 28, 2010, eff. Dec. 1, 2010.)

ADVISORY COMMITTEE NOTES
1987 Amendment

The terms "bankruptcy clerk" and "clerk" have been defined to reflect that unless otherwise stated, for the purpose of these rules, the terms are meant to identify the court officer for the bankruptcy records. If a bankruptcy clerk is appointed, all filings are made with the bankruptcy clerk. If one has not been appointed, all filings are with the clerk of the district court. Rule 5005.

The rule is also amended to include a definition of "court or judge." Since a case or proceeding may be before a bankruptcy judge or a judge of the district court, "court or judge" is defined to mean the judicial officer before whom the case or proceeding is pending.

1991 Amendment

Section 582 of title 28 provides that the Attorney General may appoint one or more assistant United States trustees in any region when the public interest so requires. This rule is amended to clarify that an assistant United States trustee, as well as any designee of the United States trustee, is included within the meaning of "United States trustee" in the rules.

2005 Amendments

The rule is amended to add the definition of a notice provider and to renumber the final three definitions in the rule. A notice provider is an entity approved by the Administrative Office of the United States Courts to enter into agreements with entities to give notice to those entities in the form and manner agreed to by those parties. The new definition supports the amendment to Rule 2002(g)(4) that authorizes a notice provider to give notices under Rule 2002.

Many entities conduct business on a national scale and receive vast numbers of notices in bankruptcy cases throughout the country. Those entities can agree with a notice provider to receive their notices in a form and at an address or addresses that the creditor and notice provider agree upon. There are processes currently in use that provide substantial assurance that notices are not misdirected. Any notice provider would have to demonstrate to the Administrative Office of the United States Courts that it could provide the service in a manner that ensures the proper delivery of notice to creditors. Once the Administrative Office of the United States Courts approves the notice provider to enter into agreements with creditors, the notice provider and other entities can establish the relationship that will govern the delivery of notices in cases as provided in Rule 2002(g)(4).

2010 Amendments

The rule is amended to add § 1502 of the Code to the list of definitional provisions that are applicable to the Rules. That section was added to the Code by the 2005 amendments.

CROSS REFERENCES

"Clerk" defined, see Fed.Rules Bankr.Proc. Rule 9002, 11 USCA.

"Judgment" defined, see Fed.Rules Bankr.Proc. Rule 7054 and Rule 9002, 11 USCA.

Rule 9002. Meanings of Words in the Federal Rules of Civil Procedure When Applicable to Cases Under the Code

The following words and phrases used in the Federal Rules of Civil Procedure made applicable to cases under the Code by these rules have the meanings indicated unless they are inconsistent with the context:

(1) "Action" or "civil action" means an adversary proceeding or, when appropriate, a contested petition, or proceedings to vacate an order for relief or to determine any other contested matter.

(2) "Appeal" means an appeal as provided by 28 U.S.C. § 158.

(3) "Clerk" or "clerk of the district court" means the court officer responsible for the bankruptcy records in the district.

(4) "District court," "trial court," "court," "district judge," or "judge" means bankruptcy judge if the case or proceeding is pending before a bankruptcy judge.

(5) "Judgment" includes any order appealable to an appellate court.

(As amended Mar. 30, 1987, eff. Aug. 1, 1987; Apr. 22, 1993, eff. Aug. 1, 1993.)

ADVISORY COMMITTEE NOTES
1993 Amendments

This rule is revised to include the words "district judge" in anticipation of amendments to the Federal Rules of Civil Procedure.

CROSS REFERENCES

Contested matters, see Fed.Rules Bankr.Proc. Rule 9014, 11 USCA.

"Judgment" defined, see Fed.Rules Civ.Proc. Rule 54, 28 USCA.

One form of action, see Fed.Rules Civ.Proc. Rule 2, 28 USCA.

Procedural rules which govern adversary proceedings, see Fed.Rules Bankr.Proc. Rule 7001 et seq., 11 USCA.

Rule 9003. Prohibition of Ex Parte Contacts

(a) General prohibition

Except as otherwise permitted by applicable law, any examiner, any party in interest, and any attorney, accountant, or employee of a party in interest shall refrain from ex parte meetings and communications with the court concerning matters affecting a particular case or proceeding.

(b) United States trustee

Except as otherwise permitted by applicable law, the United States trustee and assistants to and employees or agents of the United States trustee shall refrain from ex parte meetings and communications with the court concerning matters affecting a particular case or proceeding. This rule does not preclude communications with the court to discuss general problems of administration and improvement of bankruptcy administration, including the operation of the United States trustee system.

(As amended Mar. 30, 1987, eff. Aug. 1, 1987; Apr. 30, 1991, eff. Aug. 1, 1991.)

ADVISORY COMMITTEE NOTES

This rule regulates the actions of parties in interest and their attorneys or others employed by parties in interest. This regulation of the conduct of parties in interest and their representative is designed to insure that the bankruptcy system operates fairly and that no appearance of unfairness is created. See H.Rep. No. 95–595, 95th Cong., 1st Sess. 95 et seq. (1977).

This rule is not a substitute for or limitation of any applicable canon of professional responsibility or judicial conduct. See, e.g., Canon 7, EC7–35, Disciplinary Rule 7–110(B) of the Code of Professional Responsibility: "Generally, in adversary proceedings a lawyer should not communicate with a judge relative to a matter pending before, or which is to be brought before, a tribunal over which he presides in circumstances which might have the effect or give the appearance of granting undue advantage to one party;" and Canon 3A(4) of the Code of Judicial Conduct: "A judge should . . . neither initiate nor consider ex parte or other communications concerning a pending or impending proceeding."

1987 Amendments

This rule is amended to apply to both the bankruptcy judges and the district judges of the district.

1991 Amendments

Subdivision (a) is amended to extend to examiners the prohibition on ex parte meetings and communications with the court.

Subdivision (b) is derived from Rule X–1010.

CROSS REFERENCES

Disqualification of judge, see Fed.Rules Bankr.Proc. Rule 5004, 11 USCA.

Rule 9004. General Requirements of Form

(a) Legibility; abbreviations

All petitions, pleadings, schedules and other papers shall be clearly legible. Abbreviations in common use in the English language may be used.

(b) Caption

Each paper filed shall contain a caption setting forth the name of the court, the title of the case, the bankruptcy docket number, and a brief designation of the character of the paper.

ADVISORY COMMITTEE NOTES

Subdivision (b). Additional requirements applicable to the caption for a petition are found in Rule 1005, to the caption for notices to creditors in Rule 2002(m), and to the caption for a pleading or other paper filed in an adversary proceeding in Rule 7010. Failure to comply with this or any other rule imposing a merely formal requirement does not ordinarily result in the loss of rights. See Rule 9005.

Rule 9005. Harmless Error

Rule 61 F.R.Civ.P. applies in cases under the Code. When appropriate, the court may order the correction of any error or defect or the cure of any omission which does not affect substantial rights.

Rule 9005.1. Constitutional Challenge to a Statute—Notice, Certification, and Intervention

Rule 5.1 F.R.Civ.P. applies in cases under the Code. (Added Apr. 30, 2007, eff. Dec. 1, 2007.)

ADVISORY COMMITTEE NOTES
2007 Adoption

The rule is added to adopt the new rule added to the Federal Rules of Civil Procedure. The new Civil Rule replaces Rule 24(c) F. R. Civ. P., so the cross reference to Civil Rule 24 contained in Rule 7024 is no longer sufficient to bring the provisions of new Civil Rule 5.1 into adversary proceedings. This rule also makes Civil Rule 5.1 applicable to all contested matters and other proceedings within the bankruptcy case.

Rule 9006. Computing and Extending Time; Time for Motion Papers

(a) Computing time

The following rules apply in computing any time period specified in these rules, in the Federal Rules of Civil Procedure, in any local rule or court order, or in any statute that does not specify a method of computing time.

(1) Period stated in days or a longer unit

When the period is stated in days or a longer unit of time:

  (A) exclude the day of the event that triggers the period;

  (B) count every day, including intermediate Saturdays, Sundays, and legal holidays; and

  (C) include the last day of the period, but if the last day is a Saturday, Sunday, or legal holiday, the period continues to run until the end of the next day that is not a Saturday, Sunday, or legal holiday.

(2) Period stated in hours

When the period is stated in hours:

  (A) begin counting immediately on the occurrence of the event that triggers the period;

  (B) count every hour, including hours during intermediate Saturdays, Sundays, and legal holidays; and

  (C) if the period would end on a Saturday, Sunday, or legal holiday, then continue the period until the same time on the next day that is not a Saturday, Sunday, or legal holiday.

(3) Inaccessibility of clerk's office

Unless the court orders otherwise, if the clerk's office is inaccessible:

  (A) on the last day for filing under Rule 9006(a)(1), then the time for filing is extended to the first accessible day that is not a Saturday, Sunday, or legal holiday; or

(B) during the last hour for filing under Rule 9006(a)(2), then the time for filing is extended to the same time on the first accessible day that is not a Saturday, Sunday, or legal holiday.

(4) "Last day" defined

Unless a different time is set by a statute, local rule, or order in the case, the last day ends:

(A) for electronic filing, at midnight in the court's time zone; and

(B) for filing by other means, when the clerk's office is scheduled to close.

(5) "Next day" defined

The "next day" is determined by continuing to count forward when the period is measured after an event and backward when measured before an event.

(6) "Legal holiday" defined

"Legal holiday" means:

(A) the day set aside by statute for observing New Year's Day, Martin Luther King Jr.'s Birthday, Washington's Birthday, Memorial Day, Independence Day, Labor Day, Columbus Day, Veterans' Day, Thanksgiving Day, or Christmas Day;

(B) any day declared a holiday by the President or Congress; and

(C) for periods that are measured after an event, any other day declared a holiday by the state where the district court is located. (In this rule, "state" includes the District of Columbia and any United States commonwealth or territory.)

(b) Enlargement

(1) In general

Except as provided in paragraphs (2) and (3) of this subdivision, when an act is required or allowed to be done at or within a specified period by these rules or by a notice given thereunder or by order of court, the court for cause shown may at any time in its discretion (1) with or without motion or notice order the period enlarged if the request therefor is made before the expiration of the period originally prescribed or as extended by a previous order or (2) on motion made after the expiration of the specified period permit the act to be done where the failure to act was the result of excusable neglect.

(2) Enlargement not permitted

The court may not enlarge the time for taking action under Rules 1007(d), 2003(a) and (d), 7052, 9023, and 9024.

(3) Enlargement governed by other rules

The court may enlarge the time for taking action under Rules 1006(b)(2), 1017(e), 3002(c), 4003(b), 4004(a), 4007(c), 4008(a), 8002, and 9033, only to the extent and under the conditions stated in those rules. In addition, the court may enlarge the time to file the statement required under Rule 1007(b)(7), and to file schedules and statements in a small business case under § 1116(3) of the Code, only to the extent and under the conditions stated in Rule 1007(c).

(c) Reduction

(1) In general

Except as provided in paragraph (2) of this subdivision, when an act is required or allowed to be done at or within a specified time by these rules or by a notice given thereunder or by order of court, the court for cause shown may in its discretion with or without motion or notice order the period reduced.

(2) Reduction not permitted

The court may not reduce the time for taking action under Rules 2002(a)(7), 2003(a), 3002(c), 3014, 3015, 4001(b)(2), (c)(2), 4003(a), 4004(a), 4007(c), 4008(a), 8002, and 9033(b). In addition, the court may not reduce the time under Rule 1007(c) to file the statement required by Rule 1007(b)(7).

(d) Motion papers

A written motion, other than one which may be heard ex parte, and notice of any hearing shall be served not later than seven days before the time specified for such hearing, unless a different period is fixed by these rules or by order of the court. Such an order may for cause shown be made on ex parte application. When a motion is supported by affidavit, the affidavit shall be served with the motion. Except as otherwise provided in Rule 9023, any written response shall be served not later than one day before the hearing, unless the court permits otherwise.

(e) Time of service

Service of process and service of any paper other than process or of notice by mail is complete on mailing.

(f) Additional time after service by mail or under Rule 5(b)(2)(D) or (F) F.R.Civ.P.

When there is a right or requirement to act or undertake some proceedings within a prescribed period after being served and that service is by mail or under Rule 5(b)(2)(D) (leaving with the clerk) or (F) (other means consented to) F.R.Civ.P., three days are added after the prescribed period would otherwise expire under Rule 9006(a).

(g) Grain storage facility cases

This rule shall not limit the court's authority under § 557 of the Code to enter orders governing procedures in cases in which the debtor is an owner or operator of a grain storage facility.

(As amended Mar. 30, 1987, eff. Aug. 1, 1987; Apr. 25, 1989, eff. Aug. 1, 1989; Apr. 30, 1991, eff. Aug. 1, 1991; Apr. 23, 1996, eff. Dec. 1, 1996; Apr. 26, 1999, eff. Dec. 1, 1999; Apr. 23, 2001, eff. Dec. 1, 2001; Apr. 25, 2005, eff. Dec. 1, 2005;

Apr. 23, 2008, eff. Dec. 1, 2008; Mar. 26, 2009, eff. Dec. 1, 2009; Apr. 16, 2013, eff. Dec. 1, 2013; Apr. 28, 2016, eff. Dec. 1, 2016.)

ADVISORY COMMITTEE NOTES

Subdivision (a). This rule is an adaptation of Rule 6 F.R.Civ.P. It governs the time for acts to be done and proceedings to be had in cases under the Code and any litigation arising therein.

Subdivision (b) is patterned after Rule 6(b) F.R.Civ.P. and Rule 26(b) F.R.App.P.

Paragraph (1) of this subdivision confers on the court discretion generally to authorize extensions of time for doing acts required or allowed by these rules or orders of court. The exceptions to this general authority to extend the time are contained in paragraphs (2) and (3).

In the interest of prompt administration of bankruptcy cases certain time periods may not be extended. Paragraph (2) lists the rules which establish time periods which may not be extended: Rule 1007(d), time for filing a list of 20 largest creditors; Rule 1017(b)(3), 30 day period for sending notice of dismissal for failure to pay the filing fee; Rule 1019(2), 20 day period for notice of conversion to a chapter 7 case; Rule 2003(a), meeting of creditors not more than 40 days after order for relief; Rule 2003(d), 10 days for filing a motion for resolution of an election dispute; Rule 3014, time for the § 1111(b)(2) election; Rule 4001(b), expiration of stay 30 days following the commencement of final hearing; Rule 7052(b), 10 day period to move to amend findings of fact; Rule 9015(f), 20 day period to move for judgment notwithstanding the verdict; Rule 9023, 10 day period to move for a new trial; and Rule 9024, time to move for relief from judgment.

Many rules which establish a time for doing an act also contain a specific authorization and standard for granting an extension of time and, in some cases, limit the length of an extension. In some instances it would be inconsistent with the objective of the rule and sound administration of the case to permit extension under Rule 9006(b)(1), but with respect to the other rules it is appropriate that the power to extend time be supplemented by Rule 9006(b)(1). Unless a rule which contains a specific authorization to extend time is listed in paragraph (3) of this subdivision, an extension of the time may be granted under paragraph (1) of this subdivision. If a rule is included in paragraph (3) an extension may not be granted under paragraph (1). The following rules are listed in paragraph (3): Rule 1006(b)(2), time for paying the filing fee in installments; Rule 3002(c), 90 day period for filing a claim in a chapter 7 or 13 case; Rule 4003(b), 30 days for filing objections to a claim of exemptions; Rule 4004(a), 60 day period to object to a discharge; Rule 4007(b), 60 day period to file a dischargeability complaint; and Rule 8002, 10 days for filing a notice of appeal.

Subdivision (c). Paragraph (1) of this subdivision authorizes the reduction of the time periods established by these rules or an order of the court. Excluded from this general authority are the time periods established by the rules referred to in paragraph (2) of the subdivision: Rule 2002(a) and (b), 20 day and 25 day notices of certain hearings and actions in the case; Rule 2003(a), meeting of creditors to be not less than 20 days after the order for relief; Rule 3002(c), 90 days for filing a claim in a chapter 7 or 13 case; Rule 3014, time for § 1111(b)(2) election; Rule 3015, 10 day period after filing of petition to file a chapter 13 plan; Rule 4003(a), 15 days for a dependent to claim exemptions; Rule 4004(a), 60

day period to object to a discharge; Rule 4007(c), 60 day period to file a dischargeability complaint; and Rule 8002, 10 days for filing a notice of appeal. Reduction of the time periods fixed in the rules referred to in this subdivision would be inconsistent with the purposes of those rules and would cause harmful uncertainty.

[The Advisory Committee Note for subd. (c) above states that Rule 2002(a) and (b) are excluded from the general authority for the reduction of time periods while the text of subd. (c)(2) specifies that only Rule 2002(a)(4) and (a)(8) are excluded.]

Subdivision (d) is derived from Rule 6(d) F.R.Civ.P. The reference is to Rule 9023 instead of to Rule 59(c) F.R.Civ.P. because Rule 9023 incorporates Rule 59 F.R.Civ.P. but excepts therefrom motions to reconsider orders allowing and disallowing claims.

Subdivision (f) is new and is the same as Rule 6(e) F.R.Civ.P.

1987 Amendment

Subdivision (a) is amended to conform to the 1984 amendments to Rule 6 F.R.Civ.P.

Subdivision (b). The reference to Rule 4001(b) in paragraph (3) is deleted because of the amendments made to Rule 4001. Rule 9033, which is new, contains specific provisions governing the extension of time to file objections to proposed findings of fact and conclusions of law. Rule 9033 is added to the rules referred to in paragraph (3).

Subdivision (c). Rule 4001(b)(2) and (c)(2) provide that a final hearing on a motion to use cash collateral or a motion for authority to obtain credit may be held no earlier than 15 days after the filing of the motion. These two rules are added to paragraph (2) to make it clear that the 15 day period may not be reduced. Rule 9033 is also added to paragraph (2).

Subdivision (g) is new. Under § 557 of the Code, as enacted by the 1984 amendments, the court is directed to expedite grain storage facility cases. This subdivision makes it clear this rule does not limit the court's authority under § 557.

The original Advisory Committee Note to this rule included the 25 day notice period of Rule 2002(b) as a time period which may not be reduced under Rule 9006(C)(2). This was an error.

1989 Amendment

Prior to 1987, subdivision (a) provided that intermediate weekends and legal holidays would not be counted in the computation of a time period if the prescribed or allowed time was less than 7 days. This rule was amended in 1987 to conform to Fed. R. Civ. P. 6(a) which provides for the exclusion of intermediate weekends and legal holidays if the time prescribed or allowed is less than 11 days. An undesirable result of the 1987 amendment was that 10-day time periods prescribed in the interest of prompt administration of bankruptcy cases were extended to at least 14 calendar days.

As a result of the present amendment, 10-day time periods prescribed or allowed will no longer be extended to at least 14 calendar days because of intermediate weekends and legal holidays.

1991 Amendment

As a result of the 1989 amendment to this rule, the method of computing time under subdivision (a) is not the same as the method of computing time under Rule 6(a) F.R.Civ.P. Subdivision (a) is amended to provide that it governs the computation of time periods prescribed by the Federal Rules of Civil Procedure when the Bankruptcy Rules make a civil rule applicable to a bankruptcy case or proceeding.

Subdivision (b)(2) is amended because of the deletion of Rule 1019(2). Reference to Rule 9015(f) is deleted because of the abrogation of Rule 9015 in 1987.

Subdivision (b)(3) is amended to limit the enlargement of time regarding dismissal of a chapter 7 case for substantial abuse in accordance with Rule 1017(e).

1996 Amendment

Subdivision (c)(2) is amended to conform to the abrogation of Rule 2002(a)(4) and the renumbering of Rule 2002(a)(8) to Rule 2002(a)(7).

GAP Report on Rule 9006. No changes since publication, except for a stylistic change.

1999 Amendments

Rule 9006(b)(2) is amended to conform to the abrogation of Rule 1017(b)(3).

GAP Report on Rule 9006. The proposed amendment to Rule 9006(b)(2) has been added as a technical change to conform to the abrogation of Rule 1017(b)(3). The proposed amendment to Rule 9006(c)(2), providing that the time under Rule 1019(6) to file a request for payment of an administrative expense after a case is converted to chapter 7 could not be reduced by the court, was deleted. The proposed amendments to Rule 1019(6) have been changed so that the court will fix the time for filing the request for payment. Since the court will fix the time limit, the court should have the power to reduce it. See GAP Report to Rule 1019(6).

2001 Amendments

Rule 5(b) F.R.Civ.P., which is made applicable in adversary proceedings by Rule 7005, is being restyled and amended to authorize service by electronic means—or any other means not otherwise authorized under Rule 5(b)—if consent is obtained from the person served. The amendment to Rule 9006(f) is intended to extend the three-day "mail rule" to service under Rule 5(b)(2)(D), including service by electronic means. The three-day rule also will apply to service under Rule 5(b)(2)(C) F.R.Civ.P. when the person served has no known address and the paper is served by leaving a copy with the clerk of the court.

Changes Made After Publication and Comments. No changes were made.

2005 Amendments

Rule 9006(f) is amended, consistent with a corresponding amendment to Rule 6(e) of the F.R. Civ. P, to clarify the method of counting the number of days to respond after service either by mail or under Civil Rule 5(b)(2)(C) or (D). Three days are added after the prescribed period expires. If, before the application of Rule 9006(f), the prescribed period is less than 8 days, intervening Saturdays, Sundays, and legal holidays are excluded from the calculation under Rule 9006(a). Some illustrations may be helpful.

Under existing Rule 9006(a), assuming that there are no legal holidays and that a response is due in seven days, if a paper is filed on a Monday, the seven day response period commences on Tuesday and concludes on Wednesday of the next week. Adding three days to the end of the period would extend it to Saturday, but because the response period ends on a weekend, the response day would be the following Monday, two weeks after the filing of the initial paper. If the paper is filed on a Tuesday, the seven-day response period would end on the following Thursday, and the response time would also be the following Monday. If the paper is mailed on a Wednesday, the initial seven-day period would expire nine days later on a Friday, but the response would again be due on the following Monday because of Rule 9006(f). If the paper is mailed on a Thursday, however, the seven day period ends on Monday, eleven days after the mailing of the service because of the exclusion of the two intervening Saturdays and Sundays. The response is due three days later on the following Thursday. If the paper is mailed on a Friday, the seven day period would conclude on a Tuesday, and the response is due three days later on a Friday.

No other change in the system of counting time is intended.

Other changes are stylistic.

2008 Amendments

Subdivision (b)(3) is amended to implement § 1116(3) of the Code, as amended by the 2005 amendments, which places specific limits on the extension of time for filing schedules and statements of financial affairs in a small business case.

Subdivisions (b)(3) and (c)(2) are amended to provide that enlargement or reduction of the time to file the statement of completion of a personal financial management course required by Rule 1007(b)(7) are governed by Rule 1007(c). Likewise, the amendments to subdivisions (b)(3) and (c)(2) recognize that the enlargement of time to file a reaffirmation agreement is governed by Rule 4008(a), and that reduction of the time provided under that rule is not permitted.

Other amendments are stylistic.

2009 Amendments

Subdivision (a). Subdivision (a) has been amended to simplify and clarify the provisions that describe how deadlines are computed. Subdivision (a) governs the computation of any time period found in a Federal Rule of Bankruptcy Procedure, a Federal Rule of Civil Procedure, a statute, a local rule, or a court order. In accordance with Bankruptcy Rule 9029(a), a local rule may not direct that a deadline be computed in a manner inconsistent with subdivision (a).

The time-computation provisions of subdivision (a) apply only when a time period must be computed. They do not apply when a fixed time to act is set. The amendments thus carry forward the approach taken in *Violette v. P.A. Days, Inc.*, 427 F.3d 1015, 1016 (6th Cir. 2005) (holding that Civil Rule 6(a) "does not apply to situations where the court has established a specific calendar day as a deadline"), and reject the contrary holding of *In re American Healthcare Management, Inc.*, 900 F.2d 827, 832 (5th Cir. 1990) (holding that Bankruptcy Rule 9006(a) governs treatment of date-certain deadline set by court order). If, for example, the date for filing is "no later than November 1, 2007," subdivision (a) does not govern. But if a filing is required to be made "within 10 days" or "within 72 hours," subdivision (a) describes how that deadline is computed.

Subdivision (a) does not apply when computing a time period set by a statute if the statute specifies a method of computing time. *See, e.g.*, 11 U.S.C. § 527(a)(2) (debt relief agencies must provide a written notice to an assisted person "not later than 3 business days" after providing bankruptcy assistance services).

Subdivision (a)(1). New subdivision (a)(1) addresses the computation of time periods that are stated in days. It also applies to time periods that are stated in weeks, months, or years. *See, e.g.*, Federal Rule of Civil Procedure 60(c)(1) made applicable to bankruptcy cases under Rule 9024. Subdivision (a)(1)(B)'s directive to "count every day" is relevant only if the period is stated in days (not weeks, months, or years).

Under former Rule 9006(a), a period of eight days or more was computed differently than a period of less than eight days. Intermediate Saturdays, Sundays, and legal holidays were included in computing the longer periods, but excluded in computing the shorter periods. Former Rule 9006(a) thus made computing deadlines unnecessarily complicated and led to counterintuitive results.

Under new subdivision (a)(1), all deadlines stated in days (no matter the length) are computed in the same way. The day of the event that triggers the deadline is not counted. All other days—including intermediate Saturdays, Sundays, and legal holidays—are counted, with only one exception: If the period ends on a Saturday, Sunday, or legal holiday, then the deadline falls on the next day that is not a Saturday, Sunday, or legal holiday. An illustration is provided below in the discussion of subdivision (a)(5). Subdivision (a)(3) addresses filing deadlines that expire on a day when the clerk's office is inaccessible.

Where subdivision (a) formerly referred to the "act, event, or default" that triggers the deadline, new subdivision (a) refers simply to the "event" that triggers the deadline; this change in terminology is adopted for brevity and simplicity, and is not intended to change meaning.

Periods previously expressed as less than eight days will be shortened as a practical matter by the decision to count intermediate Saturdays, Sundays, and legal holidays in computing all periods. Many of those periods have been lengthened to compensate for the change. *See, e.g.*, Rules 2008 (trustee's duty to notify court of acceptance of the appointment within five days is extended to seven days); 6004(b) (time for filing and service of objection to proposed use, sale or lease of property extended from five days prior to the hearing to seven days prior to the hearing); and 9006(d) (time for giving notice of a hearing extended from five days prior to the hearing to seven days).

Most of the 10–day periods were adjusted to meet the change in computation method by setting 14 days as the new period. *See, e.g.*, Rules 1007(h) (10–day period to file supplemental schedule for property debtor becomes entitled to acquire after the commencement of the case is extended to 14 days); 3020(e) (10–day stay of order confirming a chapter 11 plan extended to 14 days); 8002(a) (10–day period in which to file notice of appeal extended to 14 days). A 14–day period also has the advantage that the final day falls on the same day of the week as the event that triggered the period—the 14th day after a Monday, for example, is a Monday. This advantage of using week-long periods led to adopting seven-day periods to replace some of the periods set at less than 10

days, 21–day periods to replace 20–day periods, and 28–day periods to replace 25–day periods. Thirty-day and longer periods, however, were generally retained without change.

Subdivision (a)(2). New subdivision (a)(2) addresses the computation of time periods that are stated in hours. No such deadline currently appears in the Federal Rules of Bankruptcy Procedure. But some statutes contain deadlines stated in hours, as do some court orders issued in expedited proceedings.

Under subdivision (a)(2), a deadline stated in hours starts to run immediately on the occurrence of the event that triggers the deadline. The deadline generally ends when the time expires. If, however, the time period expires at a specific time (say, 2:17 p.m.) on a Saturday, Sunday, or legal holiday, then the deadline is extended to the same time (2:17 p.m.) on the next day that is not a Saturday, Sunday, or legal holiday. Periods stated in hours are not to be "rounded up" to the next whole hour. Subdivision (a)(3) addresses situations when the clerk's office is inaccessible during the last hour before a filing deadline expires.

Subdivision (a)(2)(B) directs that every hour be counted. Thus, for example, a 72–hour period that commences at 10:23 a.m. on Friday, November 2, 2007, will run until 9:23 a.m. on Monday, November 5; the discrepancy in start and end times in this example results from the intervening shift from daylight saving time to standard time.

Subdivision (a)(3). When determining the last day of a filing period stated in days or a longer unit of time, a day on which the clerk's office is not accessible because of the weather or another reason is treated like a Saturday, Sunday, or legal holiday. When determining the end of a filing period stated in hours, if the clerk's office is inaccessible during the last hour of the filing period computed under subdivision (a)(2) then the period is extended to the same time on the next day that is not a weekend, holiday, or day when the clerk's office is inaccessible.

Subdivision (a)(3)'s extensions apply "[u]nless the court orders otherwise." In some circumstances, the court might not wish a period of inaccessibility to trigger a full 24–hour extension; in those instances, the court can specify a briefer extension.

The text of the rule no longer refers to "weather or other conditions" as the reason for the inaccessibility of the clerk's office. The reference to "weather" was deleted from the text to underscore that inaccessibility can occur for reasons unrelated to weather, such as an outage of the electronic filing system. Weather can still be a reason for inaccessibility of the clerk's office. The rule does not attempt to define inaccessibility. Rather, the concept will continue to develop through caselaw. *See, e.g.*, William G. Phelps, *When Is Office of Clerk of Court Inaccessible Due to Weather or Other Conditions for Purpose of Computing Time Period for Filing Papers under Rule 6(a) of Federal Rules of Civil Procedure*, 135 A.L.R. Fed. 259 (1996) (collecting cases). In addition, many local provisions address inaccessibility for purposes of electronic filing. *See, e.g.*, D. Kan. Rule 5.4.11 ("A Filing User whose filing is made untimely as the result of a technical failure may seek appropriate relief from the court.").

Subdivision (a)(4). New subdivision (a)(4) defines the end of the last day of a period for purposes of subdivision (a)(1). Subdivision (a)(4) does not apply in computing periods stated in hours under subdivision (a)(2), and does not apply if a different time is set by a statute, local rule, or order in the case. A local rule may provide, for example, that papers filed in a drop box after the normal hours of the clerk's office are filed as of the day that is date-stamped on the papers by a device in the drop box.

28 U.S.C. § 452 provides that "[a]ll courts of the United States shall be deemed always open for the purpose of filing proper papers, issuing and returning process, and making motions and orders." A corresponding provision exists in Rule 5001(a). Some courts have held that these provisions permit an after-hours filing by handing the papers to an appropriate official. See, e.g., Casalduc v. Diaz, 117 F.2d 915, 917 (1st Cir. 1941). Subdivision (a)(4) does not address the effect of the statute on the question of after-hours filing; instead, the rule is designed to deal with filings in the ordinary course without regard to Section 452.

Subdivision (a)(5). New subdivision (a)(5) defines the "next" day for purposes of subdivisions (a)(1)(C) and (a)(2)(C). The Federal Rules of Bankruptcy Procedure contain both forward-looking time periods and backward-looking time periods. A forward-looking time period requires something to be done within a period of time *after* an event. See, e.g., Rules 1007(c) (the schedules, statements, and other documents shall be filed by the debtor within 14 days of the entry of the order for relief"); 1019(5)(B)(ii) ("the trustee, not later than 30 days after conversion of the case, shall file and transmit to the United States trustee a final report and account"); and 7012(a) ("If a complaint is duly served, the defendant shall serve an answer within 30 days after the issuance of the summons, except when a different time is prescribed by the court.").

A backward-looking time period requires something to be done within a period of time *before* an event. See, e.g., Rules 6004(b) ("an objection to a proposed use, sale, or lease of property shall be filed and served not less than seven days before the date set for the proposed action"); 9006(d) ("A written motion, other than one which may be heard ex parte, and notice of any hearing shall be served not later than seven days before the time specified for such hearing"). In determining what is the "next" day for purposes of subdivisions (a)(1)(C) and (a)(2)(C), one should continue counting in the same direction—that is, forward when computing a forward-looking period and backward when computing a backward-looking period. If, for example, a filing is due within 10 days *after* an event, and the tenth day falls on Saturday, September 1, 2007, then the filing is due on Tuesday, September 4, 2007 (Monday, September 3, is Labor Day). But if a filing is due 10 days *before* an event, and the tenth day falls on Saturday, September 1, then the filing is due on Friday, August 31.

Subdivision (a)(6). New subdivision (a)(6) defines "legal holiday" for purposes of the Federal Rules of Bankruptcy Procedure, including the time-computation provisions of subdivision (a). Subdivision (a)(6) continues to include within the definition of "legal holiday" days that are declared a holiday by the President or Congress.

For forward-counted periods—*i.e.*, periods that are measured after an event—subdivision (a)(6)(C) includes certain state holidays within the definition of legal holidays, and defines the term "state"—for purposes of subdivision (a)(6)— to include the District of Columbia and any commonwealth or territory of the United States. Thus, for purposes of subdivision (a)(6)'s definition of "legal holiday," "state" includes the District of Columbia, Guam, American Samoa, the U.S. Virgin Islands, the Commonwealth of Puerto Rico, and the Commonwealth of the Northern Mariana Islands.

However, state legal holidays are not recognized in computing backward-counted periods. For both forward- and backward-counted periods, the rule thus protects those who may be unsure of the effect of state holidays. For forward-counted deadlines, treating state holidays the same as federal holidays extends the deadline. Thus, someone who thought that the federal courts might be closed on a state holiday would be safeguarded against an inadvertent late filing. In contrast, for backward-counted deadlines, not giving state holidays the treatment of federal holidays allows filing on the state holiday itself rather than the day before. Take, for example, Monday, April 21, 2008 (Patriot's Day, a legal holiday in the relevant state). If a filing is due 14 days after an event, and the fourteenth day is April 21, then the filing is due on Tuesday, April 22 because Monday, April 21 counts as a legal holiday. But if a filing is due 14 days before an event, and the fourteenth day is April 21, the filing is due on Monday, April 21; the fact that April 21 is a state holiday does not make April 21 a legal holiday for purposes of computing this backward-counted deadline. But note that if the clerk's office is inaccessible on Monday, April 21, then subdivision (a)(3) extends the April 21 filing deadline forward to the next accessible day that is not a Saturday, Sunday or legal holiday—no earlier than Tuesday, April 22.

The rule is amended [this Committee note relates to subdivision (d)] to implement changes in connection with the amendment to Rule 9006(a) and the manner by which time is computed under the rules. The deadline in the rule is amended to substitute a deadline that is a multiple of seven days. Throughout the rules, deadlines are amended in the following manner:

- 5–day periods become 7–day periods
- 10–day periods become 14–day periods
- 15–day periods become 14–day periods
- 20–day periods become 21–day periods
- 25–day periods become 28–day periods

Subdivision (f) is amended to conform to the changes made to Rule 5(b)(2) of the Federal Rules of Civil Procedure as a part of the Civil Rules Restyling Project. As a part of that project, subparagraphs (b)(2)(C) and (D) of that rule were rewritten as subparagraphs (b)(2)(D), (E), and (F). The cross reference to those rules contained in subdivision (f) of this rule is corrected by this amendment.

2013 Amendments

The title of this rule is amended to draw attention to the fact that it prescribes time limits for the service of motion papers. These time periods apply unless another Bankruptcy Rule or a court order, including a local rule, prescribes different time periods. Rules 9013 and 9014 should also be consulted regarding motion practice. Rule 9013 governs the form of motions and the parties who must be served. Rule 9014 prescribes the procedures applicable to contested matters, including the method of serving motions commencing contested matters and subsequent papers. Subdivision (d) is amended to apply to any written response to a motion, rather than just to opposing affidavits. The caption of the subdivision is amended to reflect this change. Other changes are stylistic.

Changes Made After Publication and Comments. No changes were made.

2016 Amendments

Subdivision (f) is amended to remove service by electronic means under Civil Rule 5(b)(2)(E) from the modes of service that allow three added days to act after being served.

Rule 9006(f) and Civil Rule 6(d) contain similar provisions providing additional time for actions after being served by mail or by certain modes of service that are identified by reference to Civil Rule 5(b)(2). Rule 9006(f)—like Civil Rule 6(d)—is amended to remove the reference to service by electronic means under Rule 5(b)(2)(E). The amendment also adds clarifying parentheticals identifying the forms of service under Rule 5(b)(2) for which three days will still be added.

Civil Rule 5(b)—made applicable in bankruptcy proceedings by Rules 7005 and 9014(b)—was amended in 2001 to allow service by electronic means with the consent of the person served. Although electronic transmission seemed virtually instantaneous even then, electronic service was included in the modes of service that allow three added days to act after being served. There were concerns that the transmission might be delayed for some time, and particular concerns that incompatible systems might make it difficult or impossible to open attachments. Those concerns have been substantially alleviated by advances in technology and widespread skill in using electronic transmission.

A parallel reason for allowing the three added days was that electronic service was authorized only with the consent of the person to be served. Concerns about the reliability of electronic transmission might have led to refusals of consent; the three added days were calculated to alleviate these concerns.

Diminution of the concerns that prompted the decision to allow the three added days for electronic transmission is not the only reason for discarding this indulgence. Many rules have been changed to ease the task of computing time by adopting 7–, 14–, 21–, and 28–day periods that allow "day-of-the-week" counting. Adding three days at the end complicated the counting, and increased the occasions for further complication by invoking the provisions that apply when the last day is a Saturday, Sunday, or legal holiday.

Electronic service after business hours, or just before or during a weekend or holiday, may result in a practical reduction in the time available to respond. Extensions of time may be warranted to prevent prejudice.

Eliminating Rule 5(b) subparagraph (2)(E) from the modes of service that allow three added days means that the three added days cannot be retained by consenting to service by electronic means. Consent to electronic service in registering for electronic case filing, for example, does not count as consent to service "by any other means" of delivery under subparagraph (F).

Subdivision (f) is also amended to conform to a corresponding amendment of Civil Rule 6(d). The amendment clarifies that only the party that is served by mail or under the specified provisions of Civil Rule 5—and not the party making service—is permitted to add three days to any prescribed period for taking action after service is made.

CROSS REFERENCES

Completion of service by mail upon mailing, see Fed.Rules Civ.Proc. Rule 5, 28 USCA.

Computation and extension of time, see Federal Rules of Appellate Procedure Rule 26, 28 USCA.

Motions,

> Form and service, see Fed.Rules Bankr.Proc. Rule 9013, 11 USCA.
>
> On appeal to district court or bankruptcy appellate panel acted upon without hearing at any time, see Fed.Rules Bankr.Proc. Rule 8013, 11 USCA.

Time, see Fed.Rules Civ.Proc. Rule 6, 28 USCA.

Rule 9007. General Authority to Regulate Notices

When notice is to be given under these rules, the court shall designate, if not otherwise specified herein, the time within which, the entities to whom, and the form and manner in which the notice shall be given. When feasible, the court may order any notices under these rules to be combined.

(As amended Mar. 30, 1987, eff. Aug. 1, 1987.)

CROSS REFERENCES

Construction of phrase "after notice and a hearing", see 11 USCA § 102.

Notice as is appropriate of order for relief, see 11 USCA § 342.

Rule 9008. Service or Notice by Publication

Whenever these rules require or authorize service or notice by publication, the court shall, to the extent not otherwise specified in these rules, determine the form and manner thereof, including the newspaper or other medium to be used and the number of publications.

CROSS REFERENCES

Construction of phrase "after notice and a hearing", see 11 USCA § 102.

Notice as is appropriate of order for relief, see 11 USCA § 342.

Rule 9009. Forms

(a) Official forms

The Official Forms prescribed by the Judicial Conference of the United States shall be used without alteration, except as otherwise provided in these rules, in a particular Official Form, or in the national instructions for a particular Official Form. Official Forms may be modified to permit minor changes not affecting wording or the order of presenting information, including changes that:

(1) expand the prescribed areas for responses in order to permit complete responses;

(2) delete space not needed for responses; or

(3) delete items requiring detail in a question or category if the filer indicates—either by checking "no" or "none" or by stating in words—that there is nothing to report on that question or category.

(b) Director's forms

The Director of the Administrative Office of the United States Courts may issue additional forms for use under the Code.

(c) Construction

The forms shall be construed to be consistent with these rules and the Code.

(As amended Apr. 30, 1991, eff. Aug. 1, 1991; Apr. 23, 2008, eff. Dec. 1, 2008; Apr. 27, 2017, eff. Dec. 1, 2017.)

ADVISORY COMMITTEE NOTES

The rule continues the obligatory character of the Official Forms in the interest of facilitating the processing of the paperwork of bankruptcy administration, but provides that Official Forms will be prescribed by the Judicial Conference of the United States. The Supreme Court and the Congress will thus be relieved of the burden of considering the large number of complex forms used in bankruptcy practice. The use of the Official Forms has generally been held subject to a "rule of substantial compliance" and some of these rules, for example Rule 1002, specifically state that the filed document need only "conform substantially" to the Official Form. See also Rule 9005. The second sentence recognizes the propriety of combining and rearranging Official Forms to take advantage of technological developments and resulting economies.

The Director of the Administrative Office is authorized to issue additional forms for the guidance of the bar.

1991 Amendment

Rule 9029 is amended to clarify that local court rules may not prohibit or limit the use of the Official Forms.

2008 Amendments

The rule is amended to provide that a plan proponent in a small business chapter 11 case need not use an Official Form of a plan of reorganization and disclosure statement. The use of those forms is optional, and under Rule 3016(d) the proponent may submit a plan and disclosure statement in those cases that does not conform to the Official Forms.

2017 Amendments

This rule is amended and reorganized into separate subdivisions.

Subdivision (a) addresses permissible modifications to Official Forms. It requires that an Official Form be used without alteration, except when another rule, the Official Form itself, or the national instructions applicable to an Official Form permit alteration. The former language generally permitting alterations has been deleted, but the rule preserves the ability to make minor modifications to an Official Form that do not affect the wording or the order in which information is presented on a form. Permissible changes include those that merely expand or delete the space for responses as appropriate or delete inapplicable items so long as the filer indicates that no response is intended. For example, when more space will be necessary to completely answer a question on an Official Form without an attachment, the answer space may be expanded. Similarly, varying the width or orientation of columnar data on a form for clarity of presentation would be a permissible minor change. On the other hand, many Official Forms indicate on their face that certain changes are not

appropriate. Any changes that contravene the directions on an Official Form would be prohibited by this rule.

The creation of subdivision (b) and subdivision (c) is stylistic.

CROSS REFERENCES

Correction of harmless errors or cure of harmless omissions, see Fed.Rules Bankr.Proc. Rule 9005, 11 USCA.

Rule 9010. Representation and Appearances; Powers of Attorney

(a) Authority to act personally or by attorney

A debtor, creditor, equity security holder, indenture trustee, committee or other party may (1) appear in a case under the Code and act either in the entity's own behalf or by an attorney authorized to practice in the court, and (2) perform any act not constituting the practice of law, by an authorized agent, attorney in fact, or proxy.

(b) Notice of appearance

An attorney appearing for a party in a case under the Code shall file a notice of appearance with the attorney's name, office address and telephone number, unless the attorney's appearance is otherwise noted in the record.

(c) Power of attorney

The authority of any agent, attorney in fact, or proxy to represent a creditor for any purpose other than the execution and filing of a proof of claim or the acceptance or rejection of a plan shall be evidenced by a power of attorney conforming substantially to the appropriate Official Form. The execution of any such power of attorney shall be acknowledged before one of the officers enumerated in 28 U.S.C. § 459, § 953, Rule 9012, or a person authorized to administer oaths under the laws of the state where the oath is administered.

(As amended Mar. 30, 1987, eff. Aug. 1, 1987; Apr. 30, 1991, eff. Aug. 1, 1991.)

ADVISORY COMMITTEE NOTES

This rule is substantially the same as former Bankruptcy Rule 910 and does not purport to change prior holdings prohibiting a corporation from appearing pro se. See In re Las Colinas Development Corp., 585 F.2d 7 (1st Cir.1978).

1987 Amendment

Subdivision (c) is amended to include a reference to Rule 9012 which is amended to authorize a bankruptcy judge or clerk to administer oaths.

1991 Amendment

References to Official Form numbers in subdivision (c) are deleted in anticipation of future revision and renumbering of the Official Forms.

Ex parte relief from automatic stay, see Fed.Rules Bankr. Proc. Rule 4001, 11 USCA.

Payment of dividends to persons authorized to receive them by power of attorney executed and filed in accordance with this rule, see Fed.Rules Bankr.Proc. Rule 3009, 11 USCA.

Rule 9011. Signing of Papers; Representations to the Court; Sanctions; Verification and Copies of Papers

(a) Signature

Every petition, pleading, written motion, and other paper, except a list, schedule, or statement, or amendments thereto, shall be signed by at least one attorney of record in the attorney's individual name. A party who is not represented by an attorney shall sign all papers. Each paper shall state the signer's address and telephone number, if any. An unsigned paper shall be stricken unless omission of the signature is corrected promptly after being called to the attention of the attorney or party.

(b) Representations to the court

By presenting to the court (whether by signing, filing, submitting, or later advocating) a petition, pleading, written motion, or other paper, an attorney or unrepresented party is certifying that to the best of the person's knowledge, information, and belief, formed after an inquiry reasonable under the circumstances,[1]
—

(1) it is not being presented for any improper purpose, such as to harass or to cause unnecessary delay or needless increase in the cost of litigation;

(2) the claims, defenses, and other legal contentions therein are warranted by existing law or by a nonfrivolous argument for the extension, modification, or reversal of existing law or the establishment of new law;

(3) the allegations and other factual contentions have evidentiary support or, if specifically so identified, are likely to have evidentiary support after a reasonable opportunity for further investigation or discovery; and

(4) the denials of factual contentions are warranted on the evidence or, if specifically so identified, are reasonably based on a lack of information or belief.

(c) Sanctions

If, after notice and a reasonable opportunity to respond, the court determines that subdivision (b) has been violated, the court may, subject to the conditions stated below, impose an appropriate sanction upon the attorneys, law firms, or parties that have violated subdivision (b) or are responsible for the violation.

(1) How initiated

(A) By motion

A motion for sanctions under this rule shall be made separately from other motions or requests and shall describe the specific conduct alleged to violate subdivision (b). It shall be served as provided in Rule 7004. The motion for sanctions may not be filed with or presented to the court unless, within 21 days after service of the motion (or such other period as the court may prescribe), the challenged paper, claim, defense, contention, allegation, or denial is not withdrawn or appropriately corrected, except that this limitation shall not apply if the conduct alleged is the filing of a petition in violation of subdivision (b). If warranted, the court may award to the party prevailing on the motion the reasonable expenses and attorney's fees incurred in presenting or opposing the motion. Absent exceptional circumstances, a law firm shall be held jointly responsible for violations committed by its partners, associates, and employees.

(B) On court's initiative

On its own initiative, the court may enter an order describing the specific conduct that appears to violate subdivision (b) and directing an attorney, law firm, or party to show cause why it has not violated subdivision (b) with respect thereto.

(2) Nature of sanction; limitations

A sanction imposed for violation of this rule shall be limited to what is sufficient to deter repetition of such conduct or comparable conduct by others similarly situated. Subject to the limitations in subparagraphs (A) and (B), the sanction may consist of, or include, directives of a nonmonetary nature, an order to pay a penalty into court, or, if imposed on motion and warranted for effective deterrence, an order directing payment to the movant of some or all of the reasonable attorneys' fees and other expenses incurred as a direct result of the violation.

(A) Monetary sanctions may not be awarded against a represented party for a violation of subdivision (b)(2).

(B) Monetary sanctions may not be awarded on the court's initiative unless the court issues its order to show cause before a voluntary dismissal or settlement of the claims made by or against the party which is, or whose attorneys are, to be sanctioned.

(3) Order

When imposing sanctions, the court shall describe the conduct determined to constitute a violation of this rule and explain the basis for the sanction imposed.

(d) Inapplicability to discovery

Subdivisions (a) through (c) of this rule do not apply to disclosures and discovery requests, responses, objections, and motions that are subject to the provisions of Rules 7026 through 7037.

(e) Verification

Except as otherwise specifically provided by these rules, papers filed in a case under the Code need not be verified. Whenever verification is required by these rules, an unsworn declaration as provided in 28 U.S.C. § 1746 satisfies the requirement of verification.

(f) Copies of signed or verified papers

When these rules require copies of a signed or verified paper, it shall suffice if the original is signed or verified and the copies are conformed to the original. (As amended Mar. 30, 1987, eff. Aug. 1, 1987; Apr. 30, 1991, eff. Aug. 1, 1991; Apr. 11, 1997, eff. Dec. 1, 1997.)

1 So in original. The comma probably should not appear.

ADVISORY COMMITTEE NOTES

Subdivision (a). Excepted from the papers which an attorney for a debtor must sign are lists, schedules, statements of financial affairs, statements of executory contracts, Chapter 13 Statements and amendments thereto. Rule 1008 requires that these documents be verified by the debtor. Although the petition must also be verified, counsel for the debtor must sign the petition. See Official Form No. 1. An unrepresented party must sign all papers.

The last sentence of this subdivision authorizes a broad range of sanctions.

The word "document" is used in this subdivision to refer to all papers which the attorney or party is required to sign.

Subdivision (b) extends to all papers filed in cases under the Code the policy of minimizing reliance on the formalities of verification which is reflected in the third sentence of Rule 11 F.R.Civ.P. The second sentence of subdivision (b) permits the substitution of an unsworn declaration for the verification. See 28 U.S.C. § 1746. Rules requiring verification or an affidavit are as follows: Rule 1008, petitions, schedules, statements of financial affairs, Chapter 13 Statements and amendments; Rule 2006(e), list of multiple proxies and statement of facts and circumstances regarding their acquisition; Rule 4001(c), motion for ex parte relief from stay; Rule 7065, incorporating Rule 65(b) F.R.Civ.P. governing issuance of temporary restraining order; Rule 8011(d), affidavit in support of emergency motion on appeal.

1987 Amendment

The statement of intention of the debtor under § 521(2) of the Code is added to the documents which counsel is not required to sign.

1991 Amendment

Subdivision (a) is amended to conform to Rule 11 F.R.Civ.P. where appropriate, but also to clarify that it applies to the unnecessary delay or needless increase in the cost of the administration of the case. Deletion of the references to specific statements that are excluded from the scope of this subdivision is stylistic. As used in subdivision (a) of this rule, "statement" is limited to the statement of financial affairs and the statement of intention required to be filed under Rule 1007. Deletion of the reference to the Chapter 13 Statement is consistent with the amendment to Rule 1007(b).

1997 Amendment

This rule is amended to conform to the 1993 changes to F.R.Civ.P. 11. For an explanation of these amendments, see the advisory committee note to the 1993 amendments to F.R.Civ.P. 11.

The "safe harbor" provision contained in subdivision (c)(1)(A), which prohibits the filing of a motion for sanctions unless the challenged paper is not withdrawn or corrected within a prescribed time after service of the motion, does not apply if the challenged paper is a petition. The filing of a petition has immediate serious consequences, including the imposition of the automatic stay under § 362 of the Code, which may not be avoided by the subsequent withdrawal of the petition. In addition, a petition for relief under chapter 7 or chapter 11 may not be withdrawn unless the court orders dismissal of the case for cause after notice and a hearing.

GAP Report on Rule 9011. The proposed amendments to subdivision (a) were revised to clarify that a party not represented by an attorney must sign lists, schedules, and statements, as well as other papers that are filed.

CROSS REFERENCES

Affidavit in support of,

    Complaint seeking temporary restraining order, see Fed. Rules Bankr.Proc. Rule 7065, 11 USCA.

    Emergency motion on appeal, see Fed.Rules Bankr.Proc. Rule 8013, 11 USCA.

    Motion for ex parte relief from stay, see Fed.Rules Bankr.Proc. Rule 4001, 11 USCA.

Pleadings allowed, form of motions, see Fed.Rules Civ.Proc. Rule 7, 28 USCA.

Signing of pleadings, see Fed.Rules Civ.Proc. Rule 11, 28 USCA.

Statements in pleadings subject to obligations set forth in Rule 11, see Fed.Rules Civ.Proc. Rule 8, 28 USCA.

Verification of,

    Complaint seeking temporary restraining order, see Fed. Rules Bankr.Proc. Rule 7065, 11 USCA.

    List of multiple proxies and acquisition statement, see Fed.Rules Bankr.Proc. Rule 2006, 11 USCA.

    Motions for ex parte relief from stay, see Fed.Rules Bankr.Proc. Rule 4001, 11 USCA.

    Petitions and accompanying papers, see Fed.Rules Bankr.Proc. Rule 1008, 11 USCA.

Rule 9012.   Oaths and Affirmations

(a) Persons authorized to administer oaths

The following persons may administer oaths and affirmations and take acknowledgments: a bankruptcy judge, clerk, deputy clerk, United States trustee, officer authorized to administer oaths in proceedings before the courts of the United States or under the laws of the state where the oath is to be taken, or a diplomatic or consular officer of the United States in any foreign country.

(b) Affirmation in lieu of oath

When in a case under the Code an oath is required to be taken, a solemn affirmation may be accepted in lieu thereof.

(As amended Mar. 30, 1987, eff. Aug. 1, 1987; Apr. 30, 1991, eff. Aug. 1, 1991.)

ADVISORY COMMITTEE NOTES

This rule is derived from Rule 43(d) F.R.Civ.P.

The provisions of former Bankruptcy Rule 912(a) relating to who may administer oaths have been deleted as unnecessary. Bankruptcy judges and the clerks and deputy clerks of bankruptcy courts are authorized by statute to administer oaths and affirmations and to take acknowledgments. 28 U.S.C. §§ 459, 953. A person designated to preside at the meeting of creditors has authority under Rule 2003(b)(1) to administer the oath. Administration of the oath at a deposition is governed by Rule 7028.

1987 Amendment

Subdivision (a) has been added to the rule to authorize bankruptcy judges and clerks to administer oaths.

1991 Amendment

This rule is amended to conform to the 1986 amendment to § 343 which provides that the United States trustee may administer the oath to the debtor at the § 341 meeting. This rule also allows the United States trustee to administer oaths and affirmations and to take acknowledgments in other situations. This amendment also affects Rule 9010(c) relating to the acknowledgment of a power of attorney. The words "United States trustee" include a designee of the United States trustee pursuant to Rule 9001 and § 102(9) of the Code.

CROSS REFERENCES

Acknowledgment of power of attorney, see Fed.Rules Bankr.Proc. Rule 9010, 11 USCA.

Administration of oaths and acknowledgments by,

Clerks of court, see 28 USCA § 953.

Justices or judges, see 28 USCA § 459.

Affirmation in lieu of oath, see Fed.Rules Civ.Proc. Rule 43, 28 USCA.

"Oath" defined to include affirmation, see 1 USCA § 1.

Oath or affirmation of witnesses, see Fed.Rules Evid. Rule 603, 28 USCA.

Rule 9013. Motions: Form and Service

A request for an order, except when an application is authorized by the rules, shall be by written motion, unless made during a hearing. The motion shall state with particularity the grounds therefor, and shall set forth the relief or order sought. Every written motion, other than one which may be considered ex parte, shall be served by the moving party within the time determined under Rule 9006(d). The moving party shall serve the motion on:

(a) the trustee or debtor in possession and on those entities specified by these rules; or

(b) the entities the court directs if these rules do not require service or specify the entities to be served.

(As amended Mar. 30, 1987, eff. Aug. 1, 1987; Apr. 16, 2013, eff. Dec. 1, 2013.)

ADVISORY COMMITTEE NOTES

This rule is derived from Rule 5(a) and Rule 7(b)(1) F.R.Civ.P. Except when an application is specifically authorized by these rules, for example an application under Rule 2014 for approval of the employment of a professional, all requests for court action must be made by motion.

2013 Amendments

A cross-reference to Rule 9006(d) is added to this rule to call attention to the time limits for the service of motions, supporting affidavits, and written responses to motions. Rule 9006(d) prescribes time limits that apply unless other limits are fixed by these rules, a court order, or a local rule. The other changes are stylistic.

Changes Made After Publication and Comments. No changes were made.

Rule 9014. Contested Matters

(a) Motion. In a contested matter not otherwise governed by these rules, relief shall be requested by motion, and reasonable notice and opportunity for hearing shall be afforded the party against whom relief is sought. No response is required under this rule unless the court directs otherwise.

(b) Service. The motion shall be served in the manner provided for service of a summons and complaint by Rule 7004 and within the time determined under Rule 9006(d). Any written response to the motion shall be served within the time determined under Rule 9006(d). Any paper served after the motion shall be served in the manner provided by Rule 5(b) F. R. Civ. P.

(c) Application of Part VII rules. Except as otherwise provided in this rule, and unless the court directs otherwise, the following rules shall apply: 7009, 7017, 7021, 7025, 7026, 7028–7037, 7041, 7042, 7052, 7054–7056, 7064, 7069, and 7071. The following subdivisions of Fed. R. Civ. P. 26, as incorporated by Rule 7026, shall not apply in a contested matter unless the court directs otherwise: 26(a)(1) (mandatory disclosure), 26(a)(2) (disclosures regarding expert testimony) and 26(a)(3) (additional pre-trial disclosure), and 26(f) (mandatory meeting before scheduling conference/discovery plan). An entity that desires to perpetuate testimony may proceed in the same manner as provided in Rule 7027 for the taking of a deposition before an adversary proceeding. The court may at any stage in a particular matter direct that one or more of the other rules in Part VII shall apply. The court shall give the parties notice of any order issued under this paragraph to afford them a reasonable opportunity to comply with the procedures prescribed by the order.

(d) Testimony of witnesses. Testimony of witnesses with respect to disputed material factual issues shall be taken in the same manner as testimony in an adversary proceeding.

(e) Attendance of witnesses. The court shall provide procedures that enable parties to ascertain at a reasonable time before any scheduled hearing whether the hearing will be an evidentiary hearing at which witnesses may testify.

(As amended Mar. 30, 1987, eff. Aug. 1, 1987; Apr. 26, 1999, eff. Dec. 1, 1999; Apr. 29, 2002, eff. Dec. 1, 2002; Apr. 26, 2004, eff. Dec. 1, 2004; Apr. 16, 2013, eff. Dec. 1, 2013.)

ADVISORY COMMITTEE NOTES

Rules 1017(d), 3020(b)(1), 4001(a), 4003(d), and 6006(a), which govern respectively dismissal or conversion of a case, objections to confirmation of a plan, relief from the automatic stay and the use of cash collateral, avoidance of a lien under § 522(f) of the Code, and the assumption or rejection of executory contracts or unexpired leases, specifically provide that litigation under those rules shall be as provided in Rule 9014. This rule also governs litigation in other contested matters.

Whenever there is an actual dispute, other than an adversary proceeding, before the bankruptcy court, the litigation to resolve that dispute is a contested matter. For example, the filing of an objection to a proof of claim, to a claim of exemption, or to a disclosure statement creates a dispute which is a contested matter. Even when an objection is not formally required, there may be a dispute. If a party in interest opposes the amount of compensation sought by a professional, there is a dispute which is a contested matter.

When the rules of Part VII are applicable to a contested matter, reference in the Part VII rules to adversary proceedings is to be read as a reference to a contested matter. See Rule 9002(1).

1999 Amendments

This rule is amended to delete Rule 7062 from the list of Part VII rules that automatically apply in a contested matter.

Rule 7062 provides that Rule 62 F.R.Civ.P., which governs stays of proceedings to enforce a judgment, is applicable in adversary proceedings. The provisions of Rule 62, including the ten-day automatic stay of the enforcement of a judgment provided by Rule 62(a) and the stay as a matter of right by posting a supersedeas bond provided in Rule 62(d), are not appropriate for most orders granting or denying motions governed by Rule 9014.

Although Rule 7062 will not apply automatically in contested matters, the amended rule permits the court, in its discretion, to order that Rule 7062 apply in a particular matter, and Rule 8005 gives the court discretion to issue a stay or any other appropriate order during the pendency of an appeal on such terms as will protect the rights of all parties in interest. In addition, amendments to Rules 3020, 4001, 6004, and 6006 automatically stay certain types of orders for a period of ten days, unless the court orders otherwise.

GAP Report on Rule 9014. No changes since publication.

2002 Amendments

The list of Part VII rules that are applicable in a contested matter is extended to include Rule 7009 on pleading special matters, and Rule 7017 on real parties in interest, infants and incompetent persons, and capacity. The discovery rules made applicable in adversary proceedings apply in contested matters unless the court directs otherwise.

Subdivision (b) is amended to permit parties to serve papers, other than the original motion, in the manner provided in Rule 5(b) F.R. Civ.P. When the court requires a response to the motion, this amendment will permit service of the response in the same manner as an answer is served in an adversary proceeding.

Subdivision (d) is added to clarify that if the motion cannot be decided without resolving a disputed material issue of fact, an evidentiary hearing must be held at which testimony of witnesses is taken in the same manner as testimony is taken in an adversary proceeding or at a trial in a district court civil case. Rule 43(a), rather than Rule 43(e), F.R. Civ.P. would govern the evidentiary hearing on the factual dispute. Under Rule 9017, the Federal Rules of Evidence also apply in a contested matter. Nothing in the rule prohibits a court from resolving any matter that is submitted on affidavits by agreement of the parties.

Subdivision (e). Local procedures for hearings and other court appearances in a contested matter vary from district to district. In some bankruptcy courts, an evidentiary hearing at which witnesses may testify usually is held at the first court appearance in the contested matter. In other courts, it is customary for the court to delay the evidentiary hearing on disputed factual issues until some time after the initial hearing date. In order to avoid unnecessary expense and inconvenience, it is important for attorneys to know whether they should bring witnesses to a court appearance. The purpose of the final sentence of this rule is to require that the court provide a mechanism that will enable attorneys to know at a reasonable time before a scheduled hearing whether it will be necessary for witnesses to appear in court on that particular date.

Other amendments to this rule are stylistic.

Changes Made After Publication and Comments. The Advisory Committee made two changes to subdivision (d) after considering the comments received addressing the proposed rule. First, the word "material" is inserted to make explicit that which was implied in the published version of the proposed rule. Second, the reference to F.R.Civ.P. 43(a) was removed. The purpose of proposed subdivision (d) was to recognize that testimony should be taken in the same manner in both contested matters and adversary proceedings. The revision to the published rule states this more directly.

The Committee Note was amended to reflect the changes made in the text of the rule.

2004 Amendments

The rule is amended to provide that the mandatory disclosure requirements of Fed. R. Civ. P. 26, as incorporated by Rule 7026, do not apply in contested matters. The typically short time between the commencement and resolution of most contested matters makes the mandatory disclosure provisions of Rule 26 ineffective. Nevertheless, the court may by local rule or by order in a particular case provide that these provisions of the rule apply in a contested matter.

2013 Amendments

A cross-reference to Rule 9006(d) is added to subdivision (b) to call attention to the time limits for the service of motions, supporting affidavits, and written responses to motions. Rule 9006(d) prescribes time limits that apply unless other limits are fixed by these rules, a court order, or a local rule.

Changes Made After Publication and Comments. No changes were made.

HISTORICAL NOTES

References in Text

The Federal Rules of Civil Procedure, referred to in subds. (b) and (c), are set out in the Appendix to Title 28.

CROSS REFERENCES

Contested matters,

Assumption, rejection, or assignment of executory contract or unexpired lease, or proceeding to require trustee to act, see Fed.Rules Bankr.Proc. Rule 6006, 11 USCA.

Avoidance by debtor of transfers of exempt property, see Fed.Rules Bankr.Proc. Rule 4003, 11 USCA.

Dismissal or conversion to another chapter, see Fed. Rules Bankr.Proc. Rule 1017, 11 USCA.

Objection to confirmation of plan, see Fed.Rules Bankr. Proc. Rule 3020, 11 USCA.

Relief from automatic stay, see Fed.Rules Bankr.Proc. Rule 4001, 11 USCA.

Request for use of cash collateral, see Fed.Rules Bankr. Proc. Rule 4001, 11 USCA.

Effect of amendment of Federal Rules of Civil Procedure, see Fed.Rules Bankr.Proc. Rule 9032, 11 USCA.

Meanings of words in Federal Rules of Civil Procedure when applicable, see Fed.Rules Bankr.Proc. Rule 9002, 11 USCA.

Motions, form and service, see Fed.Rules Bankr.Proc. Rule 9013, 11 USCA.

Rule 9015.   Jury Trials

(a) Applicability of certain Federal Rules of Civil Procedure

Rules 38, 39, 47–49, and 51, F.R.Civ.P., and Rule 81(c) F.R.Civ.P. insofar as it applies to jury trials, apply in cases and proceedings, except that a demand made under Rule 38(b) F.R.Civ.P. shall be filed in accordance with Rule 5005.

(b) Consent to have trial conducted by bankruptcy judge

If the right to a jury trial applies, a timely demand has been filed pursuant to Rule 38(b) F.R.Civ.P., and the bankruptcy judge has been specially designated to conduct the jury trial, the parties may consent to have a jury trial conducted by a bankruptcy judge under 28 U.S.C. § 157(e) by jointly or separately filing a statement of consent within any applicable time limits specified by local rule.

(c) Applicability of Rule 50 F.R.Civ.P.

Rule 50 F.R.Civ.P. applies in cases and proceedings, except that any renewed motion for judgment or request for a new trial shall be filed no later than 14 days after the entry of judgment.

(Added Apr. 11, 1997, eff. Dec. 1, 1997; amended Mar. 26, 2009, eff. Dec. 1, 2009.)

ADVISORY COMMITTEE NOTES

1987 Abrogation

Former section 1480 of title 28 preserved a right to trial by jury in any case or proceeding under title 11 in which jury trial was provided by statute. Rule 9015 provided the procedure for jury trials in bankruptcy courts. Section 1480 was repealed. Section 1411 added by the 1984 amendments affords a jury trial only for personal injury or wrongful death claims, which 28 U.S.C. § 157(b)(5) requires be tried in the district court. Nevertheless, Rule 9015 has been cited as conferring a right to jury trial in other matters before bankruptcy judges. In light of the clear mandate of 28 U.S.C. § 2075 that the "rules shall not abridge, enlarge, or modify any substantive right," Rule 9015 is abrogated. In the event the courts of appeals or the Supreme Court define a right to jury trial in any bankruptcy matters, a local rule in substantially the form of Rule 9015 can be adopted pending amendment of these rules.

1997 Amendment

This rule provides procedures relating to jury trials. This rule is not intended to expand or create any right to trial by jury where such right does not otherwise exist.

GAP Report on Rule 9015. No changes to the published draft.

2009 Amendments

The rule is amended by deleting Rule 50 F.R.Civ.P. from the list in subdivision (a) of rules made applicable in cases and proceedings. However, subdivision (c) is added to make Rule 50 applicable in cases and proceedings, but it limits the time for filing certain post judgment motions to 14 days after the entry of judgment. The amendment is necessary because Rule 50 F.R.Civ.P. was amended in 2009 to extend the deadline for the filing of these post judgment motions to 28 days. That deadline corresponds to the 30–day deadline for filing a notice of appeal in a civil case under Rule 4(a)(1)(A) F. R. App. P. In a bankruptcy case, the deadline for filing a notice of appeal is 14 days. Therefore, the 28–day deadline for filing these post judgment motions would effectively override the notice of appeal deadline under Rule 8002(a) but for this amendment.

Other amendments are stylistic.

Rule 9016.   Subpoena

Rule 45 F.R.Civ.P. applies in cases under the Code.

(As amended Mar. 30, 1987, eff. Aug. 1, 1987.)

ADVISORY COMMITTEE NOTES

Although Rule 7004(d) authorizes nationwide service of process, Rule 45 F.R.Civ.P. limits the subpoena power to the judicial district and places outside the district which are within 100 miles of the place of trial or hearing.

Compelling attendance of witnesses by use of subpoena,

Deposition upon oral examination, see Fed.Rules Bankr. Proc. Rule 7030, 11 USCA.

Deposition upon written questions, see Fed.Rules Bankr. Proc. Rule 7031, 11 USCA.

Examination of debtor,

Apprehension and removal of debtor to compel attendance, see Fed.Rules Bankr.Proc. Rule 2005, 11 USCA.

Compelling attendance for examination and production of documentary evidence, see Fed.Rules Bankr.Proc. Rule 2004, 11 USCA.

Rule 9017.   Evidence

The Federal Rules of Evidence and Rules 43, 44 and 44.1 F.R.Civ.P. apply in cases under the Code.

ADVISORY COMMITTEE NOTES

Sections 251 and 252 of Public Law 95–598, amended Rule 1101 of the Federal Rules of Evidence to provide that the Federal Rules of Evidence apply in bankruptcy courts and to any case or proceeding under the Code. Rules 43, 44 and 44.1 of the F.R.Civ.P., which supplement the Federal Rules of Evidence, are by this rule made applicable to cases under the Code.

Examples of bankruptcy rules containing matters of an evidentiary nature are: Rule 2011, evidence of debtor retained in possession; Rule 3001(f), proof of claim constitutes prima facie evidence of the amount and validity of a claim; and Rule 5007(c), sound recording of court proceedings constitutes the record of the proceedings.

CROSS REFERENCES

Applicability of rules to proceedings and cases under this title, see Fed.Rules Evid. Rule 1101, 28 USCA.

Rule 9018.   Secret, Confidential, Scandalous, or Defamatory Matter

On motion or on its own initiative, with or without notice, the court may make any order which justice requires (1) to protect the estate or any entity in respect of a trade secret or other confidential research, development, or commercial information, (2) to protect any entity against scandalous or defamatory matter contained in any paper filed in a case under the Code, or (3) to protect governmental matters that are made confidential by statute or regulation. If an order is entered under this rule without notice, any entity affected thereby may move to vacate or modify the order, and after a hearing on notice the court shall determine the motion.

(As amended Mar. 30, 1987, eff. Aug. 1, 1987.)

ADVISORY COMMITTEE NOTES

This rule provides the procedure for invoking the court's power under § 107 of the Code.

CROSS REFERENCES

Motion to strike scandalous matter, see Fed.Rules Civ.Proc. Rule 12, 28 USCA.

Motions, form and service, see Fed.Rules Bankr.Proc. Rule 9013, 11 USCA.

Protective orders, see Fed.Rules Civ.Proc. Rule 26, 28 USCA.

Rule 9019.   Compromise and Arbitration

(a) Compromise

On motion by the trustee and after notice and a hearing, the court may approve a compromise or settlement. Notice shall be given to creditors, the United States trustee, the debtor, and indenture trustees as provided in Rule 2002 and to any other entity as the court may direct.

(b) Authority to compromise or settle controversies within classes

After a hearing on such notice as the court may direct, the court may fix a class or classes of controversies and authorize the trustee to compromise or settle controversies within such class or classes without further hearing or notice.

(c) Arbitration

On stipulation of the parties to any controversy affecting the estate the court may authorize the matter to be submitted to final and binding arbitration.

(As amended Mar. 30, 1987, eff. Aug. 1, 1987; Apr. 30, 1991, eff. Aug. 1, 1991; Apr. 22, 1993, eff. Aug. 1, 1993.)

ADVISORY COMMITTEE NOTES

Subdivisions (a) and (c) of this rule are essentially the same as the provisions of former Bankruptcy Rule 919 and subdivision (b) is the same as former Rule 8–514(b), which was applicable to railroad reorganizations. Subdivision (b) permits the court to deal efficiently with a case in which there may be a large number of settlements.

1991 Amendment

This rule is amended to enable the United States trustee to object or otherwise be heard in connection with a proposed compromise or settlement and otherwise to monitor the progress of the case.

1993 Amendments

Subdivision (a) is amended to conform to the language of § 102(1) of the Code. Other amendments are stylistic and make no substantive change.

CROSS REFERENCES

Motions, form and service, see Fed.Rules Bankr.Proc. Rule 9013, 11 USCA.

Rule 9020.   Contempt Proceedings

Rule 9014 governs a motion for an order of contempt made by the United States trustee or a party in interest.

(As amended Mar. 30, 1987, eff. Aug. 1, 1987; Apr. 30, 1991, eff. Aug. 1, 1991; Apr. 23, 2001, eff. Dec. 1, 2001.)

ADVISORY COMMITTEE NOTES

Section 1481 of Title 28 provides that a bankruptcy court "may not . . . punish a criminal contempt not committed in the presence of the judge of the court or warranting a punishment of imprisonment." Rule 9020 does not enlarge the power of bankruptcy courts.

Subdivision (a) is adapted from former Bankruptcy Rule 920 and Rule 42 F.R.Crim.P. Paragraph (1) of the subdivision permits summary imposition of punishment for contempt if the conduct is in the presence of the court and is of such nature that the conduct "obstruct[s] the administration of justice." See 18 U.S.C. § 401(a). Cases interpreting Rule 42(a) F.R.Crim.P. have held that when criminal contempt is in question summary disposition should be the exception: summary disposition should be reserved for situations where it is necessary to protect the judicial institution. 3 Wright, Federal Practice & Procedure—Criminal § 707 (1969). Those cases are equally pertinent to the application of this rule and, therefore, contemptuous conduct in the presence of the judge may often be punished only after the notice and hearing requirements of subdivision (b) are satisfied.

If the bankruptcy court concludes it is without power to punish or to impose the proper punishment for conduct which constitutes contempt, subdivision (a)(3) authorizes the bankruptcy court to certify the matter to the district court.

Subdivision (b) makes clear that when a person has a constitutional or statutory right to a jury trial in a criminal contempt matter this rule in no way affects that right. See Frank v. United States, 395 U.S. 147 (1969).

The Federal Rules of Civil Procedure do not specifically provide the procedure for the imposition of civil contempt sanctions. The decisional law governing the procedure for imposition of civil sanctions by the district courts will be equally applicable to the bankruptcy courts.

1987 Amendment

The United States Bankruptcy Courts, as constituted under the Bankruptcy Reform Act of 1978, were courts of law, equity, and admiralty with an inherent contempt power, but former 28 U.S.C. § 1481 restricted the criminal contempt power of bankruptcy judges. Under the 1984 amendments, bankruptcy judges are judicial officers of the district court, 28 U.S.C. §§ 151, 152(a)(1). There are no decisions by the courts of appeals concerning the authority of bankruptcy judges to punish for either civil or criminal contempt under the 1984 amendments. This rule, as amended, recognizes that bankruptcy judges may not have the power to punish for contempt.

Sound judicial administration requires that the initial determination of whether contempt has been committed should be made by the bankruptcy judge. If timely objections are not filed to the bankruptcy judge's order, the order has the same force and effect as an order of the district court. If objections are filed within 10 days of service of the order, the district court conducts a de novo review pursuant to Rule 9033 and any order of contempt is entered by the district court on completion of the court's review of the bankruptcy judge's order.

1991 Amendments

The words "with the clerk" in subdivision (c) are deleted as unnecessary. See Rules 5005(a) and 9001(3).

2001 Amendments

The amendments to this rule cover a motion for an order of contempt filed by the United States trustee or a party in interest. This rule, as amended, does not address a contempt proceeding initiated by the court sua sponte.

Whether the court is acting on motion under this rule or is acting sua sponte, these amendments are not intended to extend, limit, or otherwise affect either the contempt power of a bankruptcy judge or the role of the district judge regarding contempt orders. Issues relating to the contempt power of bankruptcy judges are substantive and are left to statutory and judicial development, rather than procedural rules.

This rule, as amended in 1987, delayed for ten days from service the effectiveness of a bankruptcy judge's order of contempt and rendered the order subject to de novo review by the district court. These limitations on contempt orders were added to the rule in response to the Bankruptcy Amendments and Federal Judgeship Act of 1984, Pub. L. No. 98–353, 98 Stat. 333, which provides that bankruptcy judges are judicial officers of the district court, but does not specifically mention contempt power. See 28 U.S.C. § 151. As explained in the committee note to the 1987 amendments to this rule, no decisions of the courts of appeals existed concerning the authority of a bankruptcy judge to punish for either civil or criminal contempt under the 1984 Act and, therefore, the rule as amended in 1987 "recognizes that bankruptcy judges may not have the power to punish for contempt." Committee Note to 1987 Amendments to Rule 9020.

Since 1987, several courts of appeals have held that bankruptcy judges have the power to issue civil contempt orders. See, e.g., Matter of Terrebonne Fuel and Lube, Inc., 108 F.3d 609 (5th Cir. 1997); In re Rainbow Magazine, Inc., 77 F.3d 278 (9th Cir. 1996). Several courts have distinguished between a bankruptcy judge's civil contempt power and criminal contempt power. See, e.g., Matter of Terrebonne Fuel and Lube, Inc., 108 F.3d at 613, n. 3 ("[a]lthough we find that bankruptcy judge's [sic] can find a party in civil contempt, we must point out that bankruptcy courts lack the power to hold persons in criminal contempt."). For other decisions regarding criminal contempt power, see, e.g., In re Ragar, 3 F.3d 1174 (8th Cir. 1993); Matter of Hipp, Inc., 895 F.2d 1503 (5th Cir. 1990). To the extent that Rule 9020, as amended in 1987, delayed the effectiveness of civil contempt orders and required de novo review by the district court, the rule may have been unnecessarily restrictive in view of judicial decisions recognizing that bankruptcy judges have the power to hold parties in civil contempt.

Subdivision (d), which provides that the rule shall not be construed to impair the right to trial by jury, is deleted as unnecessary and is not intended to deprive any party of the right to a jury trial when it otherwise exists.

Changes Made After Publication and Comments. No changes were made in the text of the proposed amendments. Stylistic changes were made to the Committee Note.

CROSS REFERENCES

Contempts, see 18 USCA §§ 401 et seq. and 3691 et seq.

Criminal contempt, see Fed.Rules Cr.Proc. Rule 42, 18 USCA.

Power of court to punish persons for contempts, see 11 USCA § 105.

Rule 9021. Entry of Judgment

A judgment or order is effective when entered under Rule 5003.

(As amended Mar. 30, 1987, eff. Aug. 1, 1987; Mar. 26, 2009, eff. Dec. 1, 2009.)

ADVISORY COMMITTEE NOTES

Subdivision (a). This rule is derived from Rule 58 F.R.Civ.P. The requirement that a judgment entered in an adversary proceeding or contested matter be set forth on a separate document is to eliminate uncertainty as to whether an opinion or memorandum of the court is a judgment. There is no sound reason to require that every order in a case under the Code be evidenced by a separate document.

Subdivision (b) establishes a procedure for entering a judgment of a bankruptcy court for the recovery of money or property in an index of judgments kept by the clerk of the district court. It clarifies the availability of the same remedies for the enforcement of a bankruptcy court judgment as those provided for the enforcement of a district court judgment. See 28 U.S.C. §§ 1961–63. When indexed in accordance with subdivision (b) of this rule a judgment of the bankruptcy court may be found by anyone searching for liens of record in the judgment records of the district court. Certification of a copy of the judgment to the clerk of the district court provides a basis for registration of the judgment pursuant to 28 U.S.C. § 1963 in any other district. When so registered, the judgment may be enforced by issuance of execution and orders for supplementary proceedings that may be served anywhere within the state where the registering court sits. See 7 Moore, Federal Practice 2409–11 (2d ed. 1971). The procedures available in the district court are not exclusive, however, and the holder of a judgment entered by the bankruptcy court may use the remedies under Rules 7069 and 7070 even if the judgment is indexed by the clerk of the district court.

Subdivision (c) makes it clear that when a district court hears a matter reserved to it by 28 U.S.C. §§ 1471, 1481, its judgments are entered in the district court's civil docket and in the docket of the bankruptcy court. When the district court acts as an appellate court, Rule 8016(a) governs the entry of judgments on appeal.

1987 Amendment

Former subdivision (a) was derived from Rule 58 F.R.Civ.P. As amended, Rule 9021 adopts Rule 58. The reference in Rule 58 to Rule 79(a) F.R.Civ.P. is to be read as a reference to Rule 5003.

2009 Amendments

The rule is amended in connection with the amendment that adds Rule 7058. The entry of judgment in adversary proceedings is governed by Rule 7058, and the entry of a judgment or order in all other proceedings is governed by this rule.

CROSS REFERENCES

Entry of judgment, see Fed.Rules Civ.Proc. Rule 58, 28 USCA.

Entry of judgment on appeal, see Fed.Rules Bankr.Proc. Rule 8024, 11 USCA.

Findings by court, see Fed.Rules Bankr.Proc. Rule 7052, 11 USCA.

Judgments rendered by district court,

Effect as lien on local property, see 28 USCA § 1962.

Interest allowed on money judgment, see 28 USCA § 1961.

Registration of final judgments in other districts, see 28 USCA § 1963.

Rule 9022. Notice of Judgment or Order

(a) Judgment or order of bankruptcy judge

Immediately on the entry of a judgment or order the clerk shall serve a notice of entry in the manner provided in Rule 5(b) F.R.Civ.P. on the contesting parties and on other entities as the court directs. Unless the case is a chapter 9 municipality case, the clerk shall forthwith transmit to the United States trustee a copy of the judgment or order. Service of the notice shall be noted in the docket. Lack of notice of the entry does not affect the time to appeal or relieve or authorize the court to relieve a party for failure to appeal within the time allowed, except as permitted in Rule 8002.

(b) Judgment or order of district judge

Notice of a judgment or order entered by a district judge is governed by Rule 77(d) F.R.Civ.P. Unless the case is a chapter 9 municipality case, the clerk shall forthwith transmit to the United States trustee a copy of a judgment or order entered by a district judge.

(As amended Mar. 30, 1987, eff. Aug. 1, 1987; Apr. 30, 1991, eff. Aug. 1, 1991; Apr. 23, 2001, eff. Dec. 1, 2001.)

ADVISORY COMMITTEE NOTES

Subdivision (a) of this rule is an adaptation of Rule 77(d) F.R.Civ.P.

Subdivision (b) complements Rule 9021(b). When a district court acts as an appellate court, Rule 8016(b) requires the clerk to give notice of the judgment on appeal.

1991 Amendments

This rule is amended to enable the United States trustee to be informed of all developments in the case so that administrative and supervisory functions provided in 28 U.S.C. § 586(a) may be performed.

2001 Amendments

Rule 5(b) F.R.Civ.P., which is made applicable in adversary proceedings by Rule 7005, is being restyled and amended to authorize service by electronic means—or any other means not otherwise authorized under Rule 5(b)—if consent is obtained from the person served. The amendment to Rule 9022(a) authorizes the clerk to serve notice of entry of a judgment or order by electronic means if the person served consents, or to use any other means of service authorized under Rule 5(b), including service by mail. This amendment conforms to the amendments made to Rule 77(d) F.R. Civ. P.

Changes Made After Publication and Comments. No changes were made.

Entry of judgment, district court record of judgment, see Fed.Rules Bankr.Proc. Rule 9021, 11 USCA.

Notice of judgment on appeal, see Fed.Rules Bankr.Proc. Rule 8024, 11 USCA.

Rule 9023. New Trials; Amendment of Judgments

Except as provided in this rule and Rule 3008, Rule 59 F.R.Civ.P. applies in cases under the Code. A motion for a new trial or to alter or amend a judgment shall be filed, and a court may on its own order a new trial, no later than 14 days after entry of judgment. In some circumstances, Rule 8008 governs post-judgment motion practice after an appeal has been docketed and is pending.

(As amended Mar. 26, 2009, eff. Dec. 1, 2009; Apr. 25, 2014, eff. Dec. 1, 2014.)

ADVISORY COMMITTEE NOTES

Rule 59 F.R.Civ.P. regulates motions for a new trial and amendment of judgment. Those motions must be served within 10 days of the entry of judgment. No similar time limit is contained in Rule 3008 which governs reconsideration of claims.

2009 Amendments

The rule is amended to limit to 14 days the time for a party to file a post judgment motion for a new trial and for the court to order sua sponte a new trial. In 2009, Rule 59 F.R.Civ.P. was amended to extend the deadline for these actions to 28 days after the entry of judgment. That deadline corresponds to the 30–day deadline for filing a notice of appeal in a civil case under Rule 4(a)(1)(A) F.R.App.P. In a bankruptcy case, however, the deadline for filing a notice of appeal is 14 days. Therefore, the 28–day deadline for filing a motion for a new trial or a motion to alter or amend a judgment would effectively override the notice of appeal deadline under Rule 8002(a) but for this amendment.

2014 Amendments

This rule is amended to include a cross-reference to Rule 8008. That rule governs the issuance of an indicative ruling when relief is sought that the court lacks authority to grant because of an appeal that has been docketed and is pending.

Changes Made After Publication

No changes were made after publication and comment.

CROSS REFERENCES

Amendment of findings by court, see Fed.Rules Bankr. Proc. Rule 7052, 11 USCA.

Effect of motion under this rule on time for appeal, see Fed.Rules Bankr.Proc. Rule 8002, 11 USCA.

Enlargement of ten-day period for motion for new trial not permitted, see Fed.Rules Bankr.Proc. Rule 9006, 11 USCA.

Time for service of opposing affidavits to motion for new trial, see Fed.Rules Bankr.Proc. Rule 9006, 11 USCA.

Rule 9024. Relief From Judgment or Order

Rule 60 F.R.Civ.P. applies in cases under the Code except that (1) a motion to reopen a case under the Code or for the reconsideration of an order allowing or disallowing a claim against the estate entered without a contest is not subject to the one-year limitation prescribed in Rule 60(c), (2) a complaint to revoke a discharge in a chapter 7 liquidation case may be filed only within the time allowed by § 727(e) of the Code, and (3) a complaint to revoke an order confirming a plan may be filed only within the time allowed by § 1144, § 1230, or § 1330. In some circumstances, Rule 8008 governs post-judgment motion practice after an appeal has been docketed and is pending.

(As amended Apr. 30, 1991, eff. Aug. 1, 1991; Apr. 23, 2008, eff. Dec. 1, 2008; Apr. 25, 2014, eff. Dec. 1, 2014.)

ADVISORY COMMITTEE NOTES

Motions to reopen cases are governed by Rule 5010. Reconsideration of orders allowing and disallowing claims is governed by Rule 3008. For the purpose of this rule all orders of the bankruptcy court are subject to Rule 60 F.R.Civ.P.

Pursuant to § 727(e) of the Code a complaint to revoke a discharge must be filed within one year of the entry of the discharge or, when certain grounds of revocation are asserted, the later of one year after the entry of the discharge or the date the case is closed. Under § 1144 and § 1330 of the Code a party must file a complaint to revoke an order confirming a chapter 11 or 13 plan within 180 days of its entry. Clauses (2) and (3) of this rule make it clear that the time periods established by §§ 727(e), 1144 and 1330 of the Code may not be circumvented by the invocation of F.R.Civ.P. 60(b).

1991 Amendment

Clause (3) is amended to include a reference to § 1230 of the Code which contains time limitations relating to revocation of confirmation of a chapter 12 plan. The time periods prescribed by § 1230 may not be circumvented by the invocation of F.R.Civ.P. 60(b).

2008 Amendments

The rule is amended to conform to the changes made to the Federal Rules of Civil Procedure through the restyling of those rules effective on December 1, 2007.

2014 Amendments

This rule is amended to include a cross-reference to Rule 8008. That rule governs the issuance of an indicative ruling when relief is sought that the court lacks authority to grant because of an appeal that has been docketed and is pending.

Changes Made After Publication. No changes were made after publication.

CROSS REFERENCES

Enlargement of time for motion for relief from judgment or order not permitted, see Fed.Rules Bankr.Proc. Rule 9006, 11 USCA.

Motions, form and service, see Fed.Rules Bankr.Proc. Rule 9013, 11 USCA.

Rule 9024

Reconsideration of allowance or disallowance of claims, see Fed.Rules Bankr.Proc. Rule 3008, 11 USCA.

Reopening cases, see Fed.Rules Bankr.Proc. Rule 5010, 11 USCA.

Revocation of discharges under individual debt adjustment plan, see 11 USCA § 1328.

Setting aside judgment by default, see Fed.Rules Bankr. Proc. Rule 7055, 11 USCA.

Rule 9025. Security: Proceedings Against Security Providers

Whenever the Code or these rules require or permit a party to give security, and security is given with one or more security providers, each provider submits to the jurisdiction of the court, and liability may be determined in an adversary proceeding governed by the rules in Part VII.

(As amended Apr. 26, 2018, eff. Dec. 1, 2018.)

ADVISORY COMMITTEE NOTES

This rule is an adaptation of Rule 65.1 F.R.Civ.P. and applies to any surety on a bond given pursuant to § 303(e) of the Code, Rules 2001, 2010, 5008, 7062, 7065, 8005, or any other rule authorizing the giving of such security.

2018 Amendments

This rule is amended to reflect the amendment of Rule 62 F.R.Civ.P., which is made applicable to adversary proceedings by Rule 7062. Rule 62 allows a party to obtain a stay of a judgment "by providing a bond or other security." Limiting this rule's enforcement procedures to sureties might exclude use of those procedures against a security provider that is not a surety. All security providers are brought into the rule by these amendments.

CROSS REFERENCES

Bonds,

Deposit or investment by trustee of money of estates, see 11 USCA § 345.

Indemnification bond in involuntary cases, see 11 USCA § 303.

Qualification to serve as trustee, see 11 USCA § 322.

Enforcement of bond or undertaking on injunction against surety, see Fed.Rules Bankr.Proc. Rule 7065, 11 USCA.

"Security" defined, see 11 USCA § 101.

Security, proceedings against sureties, see Fed.Rules Civ. Proc. Rule 65.1, 28 USCA.

Rule 9026. Exceptions Unnecessary

Rule 46 F.R.Civ.P. applies in cases under the Code.

Rule 9027. Removal

(a) Notice of removal

(1) Where filed; form and content

A notice of removal shall be filed with the clerk for the district and division within which is located the state or federal court where the civil action is pending. The notice shall be signed pursuant to Rule

9011 and contain a short and plain statement of the facts which entitle the party filing the notice to remove, contain a statement that upon removal of the claim or cause of action, the party filing the notice does or does not consent to entry of final orders or judgment by the bankruptcy court, and be accompanied by a copy of all process and pleadings.

(2) Time for filing; civil action initiated before commencement of the case under the Code

If the claim or cause of action in a civil action is pending when a case under the Code is commenced, a notice of removal may be filed only within the longest of (A) 90 days after the order for relief in the case under the Code, (B) 30 days after entry of an order terminating a stay, if the claim or cause of action in a civil action has been stayed under § 362 of the Code, or (C) 30 days after a trustee qualifies in a chapter 11 reorganization case but not later than 180 days after the order for relief.

(3) Time for filing; civil action initiated after commencement of the case under the Code

If a claim or cause of action is asserted in another court after the commencement of a case under the Code, a notice of removal may be filed with the clerk only within the shorter of (A) 30 days after receipt, through service or otherwise, of a copy of the initial pleading setting forth the claim or cause of action sought to be removed, or (B) 30 days after receipt of the summons if the initial pleading has been filed with the court but not served with the summons.

(b) Notice

Promptly after filing the notice of removal, the party filing the notice shall serve a copy of it on all parties to the removed claim or cause of action.

(c) Filing in non-bankruptcy court

Promptly after filing the notice of removal, the party filing the notice shall file a copy of it with the clerk of the court from which the claim or cause of action is removed. Removal of the claim or cause of action is effected on such filing of a copy of the notice of removal. The parties shall proceed no further in that court unless and until the claim or cause of action is remanded.

(d) Remand

A motion for remand of the removed claim or cause of action shall be governed by Rule 9014 and served on the parties to the removed claim or cause of action.

(e) Procedure after removal

(1) After removal of a claim or cause of action to a district court the district court or, if the case under the Code has been referred to a bankruptcy judge of the district, the bankruptcy judge, may issue all necessary orders and process to bring before it all

proper parties whether served by process issued by the court from which the claim or cause of action was removed or otherwise.

(2) The district court or, if the case under the Code has been referred to a bankruptcy judge of the district, the bankruptcy judge, may require the party filing the notice of removal to file with the clerk copies of all records and proceedings relating to the claim or cause of action in the court from which the claim or cause of action was removed.

(3) Any party who has filed a pleading in connection with the removed claim or cause of action, other than the party filing the notice of removal, shall file a statement that the party does or does not consent to entry of final orders or judgment by the bankruptcy court. A statement required by this paragraph shall be signed pursuant to Rule 9011 and shall be filed not later than 14 days after the filing of the notice of removal. Any party who files a statement pursuant to this paragraph shall mail a copy to every other party to the removed claim or cause of action.

(f) Process after removal

If one or more of the defendants has not been served with process, the service has not been perfected prior to removal, or the process served proves to be defective, such process or service may be completed or new process issued pursuant to Part VII of these rules. This subdivision shall not deprive any defendant on whom process is served after removal of the defendant's right to move to remand the case.

(g) Applicability of Part VII

The rules of Part VII apply to a claim or cause of action removed to a district court from a federal or state court and govern procedure after removal. Repleading is not necessary unless the court so orders. In a removed action in which the defendant has not answered, the defendant shall answer or present the other defenses or objections available under the rules of Part VII within 21 days following the receipt through service or otherwise of a copy of the initial pleading setting forth the claim for relief on which the action or proceeding is based, or within 21 days following the service of summons on such initial pleading, or within seven days following the filing of the notice of removal, whichever period is longest.

(h) Record supplied

When a party is entitled to copies of the records and proceedings in any civil action or proceeding in a federal or a state court, to be used in the removed civil action or proceeding, and the clerk of the federal or state court, on demand accompanied by payment or tender of the lawful fees, fails to deliver certified copies, the court may, on affidavit reciting the facts, direct such record to be supplied by affidavit or otherwise. Thereupon the proceedings, trial and judgment may be had in the court, and all process awarded, as if certified copies had been filed.

(i) Attachment or sequestration; securities

When a claim or cause of action is removed to a district court, any attachment or sequestration of property in the court from which the claim or cause of action was removed shall hold the property to answer the final judgment or decree in the same manner as the property would have been held to answer final judgment or decree had it been rendered by the court from which the claim or cause of action was removed. All bonds, undertakings, or security given by either party to the claim or cause of action prior to its removal shall remain valid and effectual notwithstanding such removal. All injunctions issued, orders entered and other proceedings had prior to removal shall remain in full force and effect until dissolved or modified by the court.

(As amended Mar. 30, 1987, eff. Aug. 1, 1987; Apr. 30, 1991, eff. Aug. 1, 1991; Apr. 29, 2002, eff. Dec. 1, 2002; Mar. 26, 2009, eff. Dec. 1, 2009; Apr. 28, 2016, eff. Dec. 1, 2016.)

ADVISORY COMMITTEE NOTES

Under 28 U.S.C. § 1478(a) "any claim or cause of action in a civil action, other than a proceeding before the United States Tax Court or a civil action by a Government unit to enforce [a] . . . regulatory or police power" may be removed "if the bankruptcy courts have jurisdiction over such claim or cause of action." This rule specifies how removal is accomplished, the procedure thereafter, and the procedure to request remand of the removed claim or cause of action. If the claim or cause of action which is removed to the bankruptcy court is subject to the automatic stay of § 362 of the Code, the litigation may not proceed in the bankruptcy court until relief from the stay is granted.

The subdivisions of this rule conform substantially to 28 U.S.C. §§ 1446–1450 and Rule 81(a) F.R.Civ.P. pertaining to removal to the district courts.

Subdivision (a)(1) is derived from 28 U.S.C. § 1446(a).

Subdivisions (a)(2) and (a)(3) are derived from paragraphs one and two of 28 U.S.C. § 1446(b). Timely exercise of the right to remove is as important in bankruptcy cases as in removals from a state court to a district court.

Subdivision (a)(2) governs the situation in which there is litigation pending and a party to the litigation becomes a debtor under the Code. Frequently, removal would be of little utility in such cases because the pending litigation will be stayed by § 362(a) on commencement of the case under the Code. As long as the stay remains in effect there is no reason to impose a time limit for removal to the bankruptcy court and, therefore, clause (B) of subdivision (a)(2) provides that a removal application may be filed within 30 days of entry of an order terminating the stay. Parties to stayed litigation will not be required to act immediately on commencement of a case under the Code to protect their right to remove. If the pending litigation is not stayed by § 362(a) of the Code, the removal application must ordinarily be filed within 90 days of the order for relief. Clause (C) contains an alternative period for a chapter 11 case. If a trustee is appointed, the removal application may be filed within 30 days of the trustee's qualification, provided that the removal application is filed not more than 180 days after the order for relief.

The removal application must be filed within the longest of the three possible periods. For example, in a chapter 11 case if the 90 day period expires but a trustee is appointed shortly thereafter, the removal application may be filed within 30 days of the trustee's qualification but not later than 180 days after the order for relief. Nevertheless, if the claim or cause of action in the civil action is stayed under § 362, the application may be filed after the 180 day period expires, provided the application is filed within 30 days of an order terminating the stay.

Subdivision (a)(3) applies to the situation in which the case under the Code is pending when the removable claim or cause of action is asserted in a civil action initiated in other than the bankruptcy court. The time for filing the application for removal begins to run on receipt of the first pleading containing the removable claim or cause of action. Only litigation not stayed by the code or by court order may properly be initiated after the case under the Code is commenced. See e.g., § 362(a).

Subdivision (b). With one exception, this subdivision is the same as 28 U.S.C. § 1446(d). The exemption from the bond requirement is enlarged to include a trustee or debtor in possession. Complete exemption from the bond requirement for removal is appropriate because of the limited resources which may be available at the beginning of a case and the small probability that an action will be improperly removed.

Recovery on the bond is permitted only when the removal was improper. If the removal is proper but the bankruptcy court orders the action remanded on equitable grounds, 28 U.S.C. § 1478(b), there is no recovery on the bond.

Subdivisions (c) and (d) are patterned on 28 U.S.C. § 1446(e).

Subdivision (e). There is no provision in the Federal Rules of Civil Procedure for seeking remand. The first sentence of this subdivision requires that a request for remand be by motion and that the moving party serve all other parties; however, no hearing is required. In recognition of the intrusion of the removal practice on the state and federal courts from which claims or causes of action are removed, the subdivision directs the bankruptcy court to decide remand motions as soon as practicable. The last sentence of this subdivision is derived from 28 U.S.C. § 1446(c).

Subdivisions (f) and (g), with appropriate changes to conform them to the bankruptcy context, are the same as 28 U.S.C. § 1447(a) and (b) and 28 U.S.C. § 1448, respectively.

Subdivisions (h) and (i) are taken from Rule 81(c) F.R.Civ.P.

Subdivisions (j) and (k) are derived from 28 U.S.C. § 1449 and § 1450, respectively.

Remand orders of bankruptcy judges are not appealable. 28 U.S.C. § 1478(b).

This rule does not deal with the question whether a single plaintiff or defendant may remove a claim or cause of action if there are two or more plaintiffs or defendants. See 28 U.S.C. § 1478.

1987 Amendment

Section 1452 of title 28, with certain exceptions, provides for removal of claims or causes of action in civil actions pending in state or federal courts when the claim or cause of action is within the jurisdiction conferred by 28 U.S.C. § 1334. An order granting or denying a motion for remand is not appealable. 28 U.S.C. § 1452(b). Under subdivision (e), as amended, the district court must enter the order on the remand motion; however, the bankruptcy judge conducts the initial hearing on the motion and files a report and recommendation. The parties may file objections. Review of the report and recommendation is pursuant to Rule 9033.

Subdivision (f) has been amended to provide that if there has been a referral pursuant to 28 U.S.C. § 157(a) the bankruptcy judge will preside over the removed civil action.

Subdivision (i) has been abrogated consistent with the abrogation of Rule 9015.

1991 Amendment

The abrogation of subdivision (b) is consistent with the repeal of 28 U.S.C. § 1446(d). The changes substituting the notice of removal for the application for removal conform to the 1988 amendments to 28 U.S.C. § 1446.

Rules 7008(a) and 7012(b) were amended in 1987 to require parties to allege in pleadings whether a proceeding is core or non-core and, if non-core, whether the parties consent to the entry of final orders or judgment by the bankruptcy judge. Subdivision (a)(1) is amended and subdivision (f)(3) is added to require parties to a removed claim or cause of action to make the same allegations. The party filing the notice of removal must include the allegation in the notice and the other parties who have filed pleadings must respond to the allegation in a separate statement filed within 10 days after removal. However, if a party to the removed claim or cause of action has not filed a pleading prior to removal, there is no need to file a separate statement under subdivision (f)(3) because the allegation must be included in the responsive pleading filed pursuant to Rule 7012(b).

Subdivision (e), redesignated as subdivision (d), is amended to delete the restriction that limits the role of the bankruptcy court to the filing of a report and recommendation for disposition of a motion for remand under 28 U.S.C. § 1452(b). This amendment is consistent with § 309(c) of the Judicial Improvements Act of 1990, which amended § 1452(b) so that it allows an appeal to the district court of a bankruptcy court's order determining a motion for remand. This subdivision is also amended to clarify that the motion is a contested matter governed by Rule 9014. The words "filed with the clerk" are deleted as unnecessary. See Rules 5005(a) and 9001(3).

2002 Amendments

Subdivision (a)(3) is amended to clarify that if a claim or cause of action is initiated after the commencement of a bankruptcy case, the time limits for filing a notice of removal of the claim or cause of action apply whether the case is still pending or has been suspended, dismissed, or closed.

Changes Made After Publication and Comments. No changes were made.

2009 Amendments

The rule is amended to implement changes in connection with the amendment to Rule 9006(a) and the manner by which time is computed under the rules. The deadlines in the rule are amended to substitute a deadline that is a multiple of

---

seven days. Throughout the rules, deadlines are amended in the following manner:

- 5–day periods become 7–day periods
- 10–day periods become 14–day periods
- 15–day periods become 14–day periods
- 20–day periods become 21–day periods
- 25–day periods become 28–day periods

2016 Amendments

Subdivisions (a)(1) and (e)(3) are amended to delete the requirement for a statement that the proceeding is core or non-core and to require in all removed actions a statement that the party does or does not consent to the entry of final orders or judgment by the bankruptcy court. Some proceedings that satisfy the statutory definition of core proceedings, 28 U.S.C. § 157(b)(2), may remain beyond the constitutional power of a bankruptcy judge to adjudicate finally. The amended rule calls for a statement regarding consent at the time of removal, whether or not a proceeding is termed non-core.

The party filing the notice of removal must include a statement regarding consent in the notice, and the other parties who have filed pleadings must respond in a separate statement filed within 14 days after removal. If a party to the removed claim or cause of action has not filed a pleading prior to removal, however, there is no need to file a separate statement under subdivision (e)(3), because a statement regarding consent must be included in a responsive pleading filed pursuant to Rule 7012(b). Rule 7016 governs the bankruptcy court's decision whether to hear and determine the proceeding, issue proposed findings of fact and conclusions of law, or take some other action in the proceeding.

CROSS REFERENCES

Removal of actions, see 28 USCA § 1446 et seq.

Removed actions, see Fed.Rules Civ.Proc. Rule 81, 28 USCA.

Rule 9028. Disability of a Judge

Rule 63 F.R.Civ.P. applies in cases under the Code.
(As amended Mar. 30, 1987, eff. Aug. 1, 1987.)

ADVISORY COMMITTEE NOTES

This rule is an adaptation of Rule 63 F.R.Civ.P.

1987 Amendment

Rule 9028 has been changed to adopt the procedures contained in Rule 63 of the Federal Rules of Civil Procedure for substituting a judge in the event of disability.

CROSS REFERENCES

Disability of judge, see Fed.Rules Civ.Proc. Rule 63, 28 USCA.

Rule 9029. Local Bankruptcy Rules; Procedure When There Is No Controlling Law

(a) Local bankruptcy rules

(1) Each district court acting by a majority of its district judges may make and amend rules governing practice and procedure in all cases and proceedings within the district court's bankruptcy jurisdiction which are consistent with—but not duplicative of— Acts of Congress and these rules and which do not prohibit or limit the use of the Official Forms. Rule 83 F.R.Civ.P. governs the procedure for making local rules. A district court may authorize the bankruptcy judges of the district, subject to any limitation or condition it may prescribe and the requirements of 83 F.R.Civ.P., to make and amend rules of practice and procedure which are consistent with— but not duplicative of—Acts of Congress and these rules and which do not prohibit or limit the use of the Official Forms. Local rules shall conform to any uniform numbering system prescribed by the Judicial Conference of the United States.

(2) A local rule imposing a requirement of form shall not be enforced in a manner that causes a party to lose rights because of a nonwillful failure to comply with the requirement.

(b) Procedure when there is no controlling law. A judge may regulate practice in any manner consistent with federal law, these rules, Official Forms, and local rules of the district. No sanction or other disadvantage may be imposed for noncompliance with any requirement not in federal law, federal rules, Official Forms, or the local rules of the district unless the alleged violator has been furnished in the particular case with actual notice of the requirement.
(As amended Mar. 30, 1987, eff. Aug. 1, 1987; Apr. 30, 1991, eff. Aug. 1, 1991; Apr. 27, 1995, eff. Dec. 1, 1995.)

ADVISORY COMMITTEE NOTES

This rule is an adaptation of Rule 83 F.R.Civ.P. and Rule 57(a) F.R.Crim.P. Under this rule bankruptcy courts may make local rules which govern practice before those courts. Circuit councils and district courts are authorized by Rule 8018 to make local rules governing appellate practice.

1987 Amendment

Rule 9029 is amended to authorize the district court to promulgate local rules governing bankruptcy practice. This rule, as amended, permits the district court to authorize the bankruptcy judges to promulgate or recommend local rules for adoption by the district court.

Effective August 1, 1985, Rule 83 F.R.Civ.P., governing adoption of local rules, was amended to achieve greater participation by the bar, scholars, and the public in the rule making process; to authorize the judicial council to abrogate local rules; and to make certain that single-judge standing orders are not inconsistent with these rules or local rules. Rule 9029 has been amended to incorporate Rule 83. The term "court" in the last sentence of the rule includes judges of the district court and the bankruptcy judges of the district. Rule 9001(4).

1991 Amendments

This rule is amended to make it clear that the Official Forms must be accepted in every bankruptcy court.

1995 Amendments

Subdivision (a). This rule is amended to reflect the requirement that local rules be consistent not only with applicable national rules but also with Acts of Congress. The amendment also states that local rules should not repeat applicable national rules and Acts of Congress.

The amendment also requires that the numbering of local rules conform with any uniform numbering system that may be prescribed by the Judicial Conference. Lack of uniform numbering might create unnecessary traps for counsel and litigants. A uniform numbering system would make it easier for an increasingly national bar and for litigants to locate a local rule that applies to a particular procedural issue.

Paragraph (2) of subdivision (a) is new. Its aim is to protect against loss of rights in the enforcement of local rules relating to matters of form. For example, a party should not be deprived of a right to a jury trial because its attorney, unaware of—or forgetting—a local rule directing that jury demands be noted in the caption of the case, includes a jury demand only in the body of the pleading. The proscription of paragraph (2) is narrowly drawn—covering only violations that are not willful and only those involving local rules directed to matters of form. It does not limit the court's power to impose substantive penalties upon a party if it or its attorney stubbornly or repeatedly violates a local rule, even one involving merely a matter of form. Nor does it affect the court's power to enforce local rules that involve more than mere matters of form—for example, a local rule requiring that a party demand a jury trial within a specified time period to avoid waiver of the right to a trial by jury.

Subdivision (b). This rule provides flexibility to the court in regulating practice when there is no controlling law. Specifically, it permits the court to regulate practice in any manner consistent with federal law, with rules adopted under 28 U.S.C. § 2075, with Official Forms, and with the district's local rules.

This rule recognizes that courts rely on multiple directives to control practice. Some courts regulate practice through the published Federal Rules and the local rules of the court. Some courts also have used internal operating procedures, standing orders, and other internal directives. Although such directives continue to be authorized, they can lead to problems. Counsel or litigants may be unaware of various directives. In addition, the sheer volume of directives may impose an unreasonable barrier. For example, it may be difficult to obtain copies of the directives. Finally, counsel or litigants may be unfairly sanctioned for failing to comply with a directive. For these reasons, the amendment to this rule disapproves imposing any sanction or other disadvantage on a person for noncompliance with such an internal directive, unless the alleged violator has been furnished in a particular case with actual notice of the requirement.

There should be no adverse consequence to a party or attorney for violating special requirements relating to practice before a particular judge unless the party or attorney has actual notice of those requirements. Furnishing litigants with a copy outlining the judge's practices—or attaching instructions to a notice setting a case for conference or trial—would suffice to give actual notice, as would an order in a case specifically adopting by reference a judge's standing order and indicating how copies can be obtained.

CROSS REFERENCES

Local rules to govern appellate practice, see Fed.Rules Bankr.Proc. Rule 8026, 11 USCA.

Rules by district courts, see Fed.Rules Civ.Proc. Rule 83, 28 USCA and Fed.Rules Cr.Proc. Rule 57, 18 USCA.

Rule 9030. Jurisdiction and Venue Unaffected

These rules shall not be construed to extend or limit the jurisdiction of the courts or the venue of any matters therein.

(As amended Mar. 30, 1987, eff. Aug. 1, 1987.)

ADVISORY COMMITTEE NOTES

The rule is an adaptation of Rule 82 F.R.Civ.P.

CROSS REFERENCES

Jurisdiction and venue unaffected, see Fed.Rules Civ.Proc. Rule 82, 28 USCA.

Power of Supreme Court to prescribe bankruptcy rules, see 28 USCA § 2075.

Rule 9031. Masters Not Authorized

Rule 53 F.R.Civ.P. does not apply in cases under the Code.

ADVISORY COMMITTEE NOTES

This rule precludes the appointment of masters in cases and proceedings under the Code.

Rule 9032. Effect of Amendment of Federal Rules of Civil Procedure

The Federal Rules of Civil Procedure which are incorporated by reference and made applicable by these rules shall be the Federal Rules of Civil Procedure in effect on the effective date of these rules and as thereafter amended, unless otherwise provided by such amendment or by these rules.

(As amended Apr. 30, 1991, eff. Aug. 1, 1991.)

ADVISORY COMMITTEE NOTES

1991 Amendment

This rule is amended to provide flexibility so that the Bankruptcy Rules may provide that subsequent amendments to a Federal Rule of Civil Procedure made applicable by these rules are not effective with regard to Bankruptcy Code cases or proceedings. For example, in view of the anticipated amendments to, and restructuring of, Rule 4 F.R.Civ.P., Rule 7004(g) will prevent such changes from affecting Bankruptcy Code cases until the Advisory Committee on Bankruptcy Rules has an opportunity to consider such amendments and to make appropriate recommendations for incorporating such amendments into the Bankruptcy Rules.

Rule 9033. Proposed Findings of Fact and Conclusions of Law

(a) Service

In a proceeding in which the bankruptcy court has issued proposed findings of fact and conclusions of law, the clerk shall serve forthwith copies on all parties by mail and note the date of mailing on the docket.

(b) Objections: time for filing

Within 14 days after being served with a copy of the proposed findings of fact and conclusions of law a party may serve and file with the clerk written objections which identify the specific proposed findings or conclusions objected to and state the grounds for such objection. A party may respond to another party's objections within 14 days after being served with a copy thereof. A party objecting to the bankruptcy judge's proposed findings or conclusions shall arrange promptly for the transcription of the record, or such portions of it as all parties may agree upon or the bankruptcy judge deems sufficient, unless the district judge otherwise directs.

(c) Extension of time

The bankruptcy judge may for cause extend the time for filing objections by any party for a period not to exceed 21 days from the expiration of the time otherwise prescribed by this rule. A request to extend the time for filing objections must be made before the time for filing objections has expired, except that a request made no more than 21 days after the expiration of the time for filing objections may be granted upon a showing of excusable neglect.

(d) Standard of review

The district judge shall make a de novo review upon the record or, after additional evidence, of any portion of the bankruptcy judge's findings of fact or conclusions of law to which specific written objection has been made in accordance with this rule. The district judge may accept, reject, or modify the proposed findings of fact or conclusions of law, receive further evidence, or recommit the matter to the bankruptcy judge with instructions.

(Added Mar. 30, 1987, eff. Aug. 1, 1987; amended Mar. 26, 2009, eff. Dec. 1, 2009; Apr. 28, 2016, eff. Dec. 1, 2016.)

ADVISORY COMMITTEE NOTES

Section 157(c)(1) of title 28 requires a bankruptcy judge to submit proposed findings of fact and conclusions of law to the district court when the bankruptcy judge has heard a non-core proceeding. This rule, which is modeled on Rule 72 F.R.Civ.P., provides the procedure for objecting to, and for review by, the district court of specific findings and conclusions.

Subdivision (a) requires the clerk to serve a copy of the proposed findings and conclusions on the parties. The bankruptcy clerk, or the district court clerk if there is no bankruptcy clerk in the district, shall serve a copy of the proposed findings and conclusions on all parties.

Subdivision (b) is derived from Rule 72(b) F.R.Civ.P. which governs objections to a recommended disposition by a magistrate.

Subdivision (c) is similar to Rule 8002(c) of the Bankruptcy Rules and provides for granting of extensions of time to file objections to proposed findings and conclusions.

Subdivision (d) adopts the de novo review provisions of Rule 72(b) F.R.Civ.P.

2009 Amendments

The rule is amended to implement changes in connection with the amendment to Rule 9006(a) and the manner by which time is computed under the rules. The deadlines in the rule are amended to substitute a deadline that is a multiple of seven days. Throughout the rules, deadlines are amended in the following manner:

- 5–day periods become 7–day periods
- 10–day periods become 14–day periods
- 15–day periods become 14–day periods
- 20–day periods become 21–day periods
- 25–day periods become 28–day periods

2016 Amendments

Subdivision (a) is amended to delete language limiting this provision to non-core proceedings. Some proceedings that satisfy the statutory definition of core proceedings, 28 U.S.C. § 157(b)(2), may remain beyond the constitutional power of a bankruptcy judge to adjudicate finally. If the bankruptcy court decides, pursuant to Rule 7016, that it is appropriate to issue proposed findings of fact and conclusions of law in a proceeding, this rule governs the subsequent procedures.

Rule 9034. Transmittal of Pleadings, Motion Papers, Objections, and Other Papers to the United States Trustee

Unless the United States trustee requests otherwise or the case is a chapter 9 municipality case, any entity that files a pleading, motion, objection, or similar paper relating to any of the following matters shall transmit a copy thereof to the United States trustee within the time required by these rules for service of the paper:

(a) a proposed use, sale, or lease of property of the estate other than in the ordinary course of business;

(b) the approval of a compromise or settlement of a controversy;

(c) the dismissal or conversion of a case to another chapter;

(d) the employment of professional persons;

(e) an application for compensation or reimbursement of expenses;

(f) a motion for, or approval of an agreement relating to, the use of cash collateral or authority to obtain credit;

(g) the appointment of a trustee or examiner in a chapter 11 reorganization case;

(h) the approval of a disclosure statement;

(i) the confirmation of a plan;

(j) an objection to, or waiver or revocation of, the debtor's discharge;

(k) any other matter in which the United States trustee requests copies of filed papers or the court orders copies transmitted to the United States trustee.

(Added Apr. 30, 1991, eff. Aug. 1, 1991.)

ADVISORY COMMITTEE NOTES

Section 307 of the Code gives the United States trustee the right to appear and be heard on issues in cases and proceedings under the Code. This rule is intended to keep the United States trustee informed of certain developments and disputes in which the United States may wish to be heard. This rule, which derives from Rule X–1008, also enables the United States trustee to monitor the progress of the case in accordance with 28 U.S.C. § 586(a). The requirement to transmit copies of certain pleadings, motion papers and other documents is intended to be flexible in that the United States trustee in a particular judicial district may request copies of papers in certain categories, and may request not to receive copies of documents in other categories, when the practice in that district makes that desirable. When the rules require that a paper be served on particular parties, the time period in which service is required is also applicable to transmittal to the United States trustee.

Although other rules require that certain notices be transmitted to the United States trustee, this rule goes further in that it requires the transmittal to the United States trustee of other papers filed in connection with these matters. This rule is not an exhaustive list of the matters of which the United States trustee may be entitled to receive notice.

Rule 9035. Applicability of Rules in Judicial Districts in Alabama and North Carolina

In any case under the Code that is filed in or transferred to a district in the State of Alabama or the State of North Carolina and in which a United States trustee is not authorized to act, these rules apply to the extent that they are not inconsistent with any federal statute effective in the case.

(Added Apr. 30, 1991, eff. Aug. 1, 1991; amended Apr. 11, 1997, eff. Dec. 1, 1997.)

ADVISORY COMMITTEE NOTES

Section 302(d)(3) of the Bankruptcy Judges, United States Trustees, and Family Farmer Bankruptcy Act of 1986 provides that amendments to the Code relating to United States trustees and quarterly fees required under 28 U.S.C. § 1930(a)(6) do not become effective in any judicial district in the States of Alabama and North Carolina until the district elects to be included in the United States trustee system, or October 1, 1992, whichever occurs first, unless Congress extends the deadline. If the United States trustee system becomes effective in these districts, the transition provisions in the 1986 Act will govern the application of the United States trustee amendments to cases that are pending at that time. See § 302(d)(3)(F). The statute, and not the bankruptcy court, determines whether a United States trustee is authorized to act in a particular case.

Section 302(d)(3)(I) of the 1986 Act authorizes the Judicial Conference of the United States to promulgate regulations governing the appointment of bankruptcy administrators to supervise the administration of estates and trustees in cases in the districts in Alabama and North Carolina until the provisions of the Act relating to the United States trustee take effect in these districts. Pursuant to this authority, in September 1987, the Judicial Conference promulgated regulations governing the selection and appointment of bankruptcy administrators and regulations governing the establishment, duties, and functions of bankruptcy administrators. Guidelines relating to the bankruptcy administrator program have been prescribed by the Director of the Administrative Office of the United States Courts.

Many of these rules were amended to implement the United States trustee system in accordance with the 1986 Act. Since the provisions of the 1986 Act relating to the United States trustee system are not effective in cases in Alabama and North Carolina in which a bankruptcy administrator is serving, rules referring to United States trustees are at least partially inconsistent with the provisions of the Bankruptcy Code and title 28 of the United States Code effective in such cases.

In determining the applicability of these rules in cases in Alabama and North Carolina in which a United States trustee is not authorized to act, the following guidelines should be followed:

(1) The following rules do not apply because they are inconsistent with the provisions of the Code or title 28 in these cases: 1002(b), 1007(1), 1009(c), 2002(k), 2007.1(b), 2015(a)(6), 2020, 3015(b), 5005(b), 7004(b)(10), 9003(b), and 9034.

(2) The following rules are partially inconsistent with the provisions of the Code effective in these cases and, therefore, are applicable with the following modifications:

(a) **Rule 2001(a) and (c)**—The court, rather than the United States trustee, appoints the interim trustee.

(b) **Rule 2003**—The duties of the United States trustee relating to the meeting of creditors or equity security holders are performed by the officer determined in accordance with regulations of the Judicial Conference, guidelines of the Director of the Administrative Office, local rules or court orders.

(c) **Rule 2007**—The court, rather than the United States trustee, appoints committees in chapter 9 and chapter 11 cases.

(d) **Rule 2008**—The bankruptcy administrator, rather than the United States trustee, informs the trustee of how to qualify.

(e) **Rule 2009(c) and (d)**—The court, rather than the United States trustee, appoints interim trustees in chapter 7 cases and trustees in chapter 11, 12 and 13 cases.

(f) **Rule 2010**—The court, rather than the United States trustee, determines the amount and sufficiency of the trustee's bond.

(g) **Rule 5010**—The court, rather than the United States trustee, appoints the trustee when a case is reopened.

(3) All other rules are applicable because they are consistent with the provisions of the Code and title 28 effective in these cases, except that any reference to the United States trustee is not applicable and should be disregarded.

Many of the amendments to the rules are designed to give the United States trustee, a member of the Executive Branch, notice of certain developments and copies of petitions, schedules, pleadings, and other papers. In contrast, the bankruptcy administrator is an officer in the Judicial Branch and matters relating to notice of developments and access to documents filed in the clerk's office are governed by regulations of the Judicial Conference of the United States, guidelines of the Administrative Office of the United States Courts, local rules, and court orders. Also, requirements for disclosure of connections with the bankruptcy administrator in applications for employment of professional persons, restrictions on appointments of relatives of bankruptcy administrators, effects of erroneously filing papers with the bankruptcy administrator, and other matters not covered by these rules may be governed by regulations of the Judicial Conference, guidelines of the Director of the Administrative Office, local rules, and court orders.

This rule will cease to have effect if a United States trustee is authorized in every case in the districts in Alabama and North Carolina.

1997 Amendment

Certain statutes that are not codified in title 11 or title 28 of the United States Code, such as § 105 of the Bankruptcy Reform Act of 1994, Pub.L. 103–394, 108 Stat. 4106, relate to bankruptcy administrators in the judicial districts of North Carolina and Alabama. This amendment makes it clear that the Bankruptcy Rules do not apply to the extent that they are inconsistent with these federal statutes.

GAP Report on Rule 9035. No changes to the published draft.

Rule 9036. Notice by Electronic Transmission

Whenever the clerk or some other person as directed by the court is required to send notice by mail and the entity entitled to receive the notice requests in writing that, instead of notice by mail, all or part of the information required to be contained in the notice be sent by a specified type of electronic transmission, the court may direct the clerk or other person to send the information by such electronic transmission. Notice by electronic means is complete on transmission.

(Added Apr. 22, 1993, eff. Aug. 1, 1993; amended Apr. 25, 2005, eff. Dec. 1, 2005.)

ADVISORY COMMITTEE NOTES

1993 Amendments

This rule is added to provide flexibility for banks, credit card companies, taxing authorities, and other entities that ordinarily receive notices by mail in a large volume of bankruptcy cases, to arrange to receive by electronic transmission all or part of the information required to be contained in such notices.

The use of electronic technology instead of mail to send information to creditors and interested parties will be more convenient and less costly for the sender and the receiver. For example, a bank that receives by mail, at different locations, notices of meetings of creditors pursuant to Rule 2002(a) in thousands of cases each year may prefer to receive only the vital information ordinarily contained in such notices by electronic transmission to one computer terminal.

The specific means of transmission must be compatible with technology available to the sender and the receiver. Therefore, electronic transmission of notices is permitted only upon request of the entity entitled to receive the notice, specifying the type of electronic transmission, and only if approved by the court.

Electronic transmission pursuant to the rule completes the notice requirements. The creditor or interested party is not thereafter entitled to receive the relevant notice by mail.

2005 Amendments

The rule is amended to delete the requirement that the sender of an electronic notice must obtain electronic confirmation that the notice was received. The amendment provides that notice is complete upon transmission. When the rule was first promulgated, confirmation of receipt of electronic notices was commonplace. In the current electronic environment, very few internet service providers offer the confirmation of receipt service. Consequently, compliance with the rule may be impossible, and the rule could discourage the use of electronic noticing.

Confidence in the delivery of email text messages now rivals or exceeds confidence in the delivery of printed materials. Therefore, there is no need for confirmation of receipt of electronic messages just as there is no such requirement for paper notices.

Rule 9037. Privacy Protection for Filings Made With the Court

(a) Redacted filings

Unless the court orders otherwise, in an electronic or paper filing made with the court that contains an individual's social-security number, taxpayer-identification number, or birth date, the name of an individual, other than the debtor, known to be and identified as a minor, or a financial-account number, a party or non-party making the filing may include only:

(1) the last four digits of the social-security number and taxpayer-identification number;

(2) the year of the individual's birth;

(3) the minor's initials; and

(4) the last four digits of the financial-account number.

(b) Exemptions from the redaction requirement

The redaction requirement does not apply to the following:

(1) a financial-account number that identifies the property allegedly subject to forfeiture in a forfeiture proceeding;

(2) the record of an administrative or agency proceeding unless filed with a proof of claim;

(3) the official record of a state-court proceeding;

(4) the record of a court or tribunal, if that record was not subject to the redaction requirement when originally filed;

(5) a filing covered by subdivision (c) of this rule; and

(6) a filing that is subject to § 110 of the Code.

(c) Filings made under seal

The court may order that a filing be made under seal without redaction. The court may later unseal the filing or order the entity that made the filing to file a redacted version for the public record.

(d) Protective orders

For cause, the court may by order in a case under the Code:

(1) require redaction of additional information; or

(2) limit or prohibit a nonparty's remote electronic access to a document filed with the court.

(e) Option for additional unredacted filing under seal

An entity making a redacted filing may also file an unredacted copy under seal. The court must retain the unredacted copy as part of the record.

(f) Option for filing a reference list

A filing that contains redacted information may be filed together with a reference list that identifies each item of redacted information and specifies an appropriate identifier that uniquely corresponds to each item listed. The list must be filed under seal and may be amended as of right. Any reference in the case to a listed identifier will be construed to refer to the corresponding item of information.

(g) Waiver of protection of identifiers

An entity waives the protection of subdivision (a) as to the entity's own information by filing it without redaction and not under seal.
(Added Apr. 30, 2007, eff. Dec. 1, 2007.)

ADVISORY COMMITTEE NOTES

2007 Adoption

The rule is adopted in compliance with section 205(c)(3) of the E–Government Act of 2002, Public Law No. 107–347. Section 205(c)(3) requires the Supreme Court to prescribe rules "to protect privacy and security concerns relating to electronic filing of documents and the public availability . . . of documents filed electronically." The rule goes further than the E–Government Act in regulating paper filings even when they are not converted to electronic form, but the number of filings that remain in paper form is certain to diminish over time. Most districts scan paper filings into the electronic case file, where they become available to the public in the same way as documents initially filed in electronic form. It is electronic availability, not the form of the initial filing, that raises the privacy and security concerns addressed in the E–Government Act.

The rule is derived from and implements the policy adopted by the Judicial Conference in September 2001 to address the privacy concerns resulting from public access to electronic case files. *See* http://www.privacy.uscourts.gov/Policy.htm. The Judicial Conference policy is that documents in case files generally should be made available electronically to the same extent they are available at the courthouse, provided that certain "personal data identifiers" are not included in the public file.

While providing for the public filing of some information, such as the last four digits of an account number, the rule does not intend to establish a presumption that this information never could or should be protected. For example, it may well be necessary in individual cases to prevent remote access by nonparties to any part of an account number or social-security number. It may also be necessary to protect information not covered by the redaction requirement—such as driver's license numbers and alien registration numbers—in a particular case. In such cases, protection may be sought under subdivision (c) or (d). Moreover, the rule does not affect the protection available under other rules, such as Rules 16 and 26(c) of the Federal Rules of Civil Procedure, or under other sources of protective authority.

Any personal information not otherwise protected by sealing or redaction will be made available over the internet. Counsel should therefore notify clients of this fact so that an informed decision may be made on what information is to be included in a document filed with the court.

An individual debtor's full social-security number or taxpayer-identification number is included on the notice of the § 341 meeting of creditors sent to creditors. Of course, that is not filed with the court, see Rule 1007(f) (the debtor "submits" this information), and the copy of the notice that is filed with the court does not include the full social-security number or taxpayer-identification number. Thus, since the full social-security number or taxpayer-identification number is not filed with the court, it is not available to a person searching that record.

The clerk is not required to review documents filed with the court for compliance with this rule. As subdivision (a) recognizes, the responsibility to redact filings rests with counsel, parties, and others who make filings with the court.

Subdivision (d) recognizes the court's inherent authority to issue a protective order to prevent remote access to private or sensitive information and to require redaction of material in addition to that which would be redacted under subdivision (a) of the rule. These orders may be issued whenever necessary either by the court on its own motion, or on motion of a party in interest.

Subdivision (e) allows an entity that makes a redacted filing to file an unredacted document under seal. This provision is derived from section 205(c)(3)(iv) of the E–Government Act. Subdivision (f) allows the option to file a reference list of redacted information. This provision is derived from section 205(c)(3)(v) of the E–Government Act, as amended in 2004.

In accordance with the E–Government Act, subdivision (f) of the rule refers to "redacted" information. The term "redacted" is intended to govern a filing that is prepared with abbreviated identifiers in the first instance, as well as a filing in which a personal identifier is edited after its preparation.

Subdivision (g) allows an entity to waive the protections of the rule as to that entity's own information by filing it in unredacted form. An entity may elect to waive the protection if, for example, it is determined that the costs of redaction outweigh the benefits to privacy. As to financial account numbers, the instructions to Schedules E and F of Official Form 6 note that the debtor may elect to include the complete account number on those schedules rather than limit the number to the final four digits. Including the complete number would operate as a waiver by the debtor under subdivision (g) as to the full information that the debtor set out on those schedules. The waiver operates only to the extent of the information that the entity filed without redaction. If an entity files an unredacted identifier by mistake, it may seek relief from the court.

Trial exhibits are subject to the redaction requirements of Rule 9037 to the extent they are filed with the court. Trial exhibits that are not initially filed with the court must be redacted in accordance with this rule if and when they are filed as part of an appeal or for other reasons.

PART X—UNITED STATES TRUSTEES [ABROGATED]

[Rules X–1001 to X–1010. Abrogated Apr. 30, 1991, eff. Aug. 1, 1991]

INTERIM AMENDMENTS TO THE FEDERAL BANKRUPTCY RULES

[In 2005, federal bankruptcy courts were encouraged to adopt, by general or standing order, certain Interim Bankruptcy Rules for implementing the Bankruptcy Abuse Prevention and Consumer Protection Act of 2005 (Pub. L. No. 109–08, 119 Stat. 23). The Interim Bankruptcy Rules were superseded by amendments to the Federal Rules of Bankruptcy Procedure that became effective on December 1, 2008. Thereafter, bankruptcy courts were encouraged to adopt a further interim rule, Interim Rule 1007–I, to implement the National Guard and Reservists Debt Relief Act of 2008 (Pub. L. 110–438, Oct. 20, 2008, 122 Stat. 5000). Interim Rule 1007–I is reproduced below.]

Rule 1007–I.[1] Lists, Schedules, Statements, and Other Documents; Time Limits; Expiration of Temporary Means Testing Exclusion

* * * * *

(b) SCHEDULES, STATEMENTS, AND OTHER DOCUMENTS REQUIRED.

* * * * *

(4) Unless either: (A) § 707(b)(2)(D)(i) applies, or (B) § 707(b)(2)(D)(ii) applies and the exclusion from means testing granted therein extends beyond the period specified by Rule 1017(e), an individual debtor in a chapter 7 case shall file a statement of current monthly income prepared as prescribed by the appropriate Official Form, and, if the current monthly income exceeds the median family income for the applicable state and household size, the information, including calculations, required by § 707(b), prepared as prescribed by the appropriate Official Form.

* * * * *

(c) TIME LIMITS. In a voluntary case, the schedules, statements, and other documents required by subdivision (b)(1), (4), (5), and (6) shall be filed with the petition or within 14 days thereafter, except as otherwise provided in subdivisions (d), (e), (f), (h), and (n) of this rule. In an involuntary case, the schedules, statements, and other documents required by subdivision (b)(1) shall be filed by the debtor within 14 days of the entry of the order for relief. In a voluntary case, the documents required by paragraphs (A), (C), and (D) of subdivision (b)(3) shall be filed with the petition. Unless the court orders otherwise, a debtor who has filed a statement under subdivision (b)(3)(B), shall file the documents required by subdivision (b)(3)(A) within 14 days of the order for relief. In a chapter 7 case, the debtor shall file the statement required by subdivision (b)(7) within 60 days after the first date set for the meeting of creditors under § 341 of the Code, and in a chapter 11 or 13 case no later than the date when the last payment was made by the debtor as required by the plan or the filing of a motion for a discharge under § 1141(d)(5)(B) or § 1328(b) of the Code. The court may, at any time and in its discretion, enlarge the time to file the statement required by subdivision (b)(7). The debtor shall file the statement required by subdivision (b)(8) no earlier than the date of the last payment made under the plan or the date of the filing of a motion for a discharge under §§ 1141(d)(5)(B), 1228(b), or 1328(b) of the Code. Lists, schedules, statements, and other documents filed prior to the conversion of a case to another chapter shall be deemed filed in the converted case unless the court directs otherwise. Except as provided in § 1116(3), any extension of time to file schedules, statements, and other documents required under this rule may be granted only on motion for cause shown and on notice to the United States trustee, any committee elected under § 705 or appointed under § 1102 of the Code, trustee, examiner, or other party as the court may direct. Notice of an extension shall be given to the United States trustee and to any committee, trustee, or other party as the court may direct.

* * * * *

(n) TIME LIMITS FOR, AND NOTICE TO, DEBTORS TEMPORARILY EXCLUDED FROM MEANS TESTING.

(1) An individual debtor who is temporarily excluded from means testing pursuant to § 707(b)(2)(D)(ii) of the Code shall file any statement and calculations required by subdivision (b)(4) no later than 14 days after the expiration of the temporary exclusion if the expiration occurs within the time specified by Rule 1017(e) for filing a motion pursuant to § 707(b)(2).

(2) If the temporary exclusion from means testing under § 707(b)(2)(D)(ii) terminates due to the cir-

---

1 Interim Rule 1007–I has been adopted by the bankruptcy courts to implement the National Guard and Reservists Debt Relief Act of 2008, Public Law No: 110–438, as amended by Public Law No. 112–64. The amended Act, which provides a temporary exclusion from the applica-tion of the means test for certain members of the National Guard and reserve components of the Armed Forces, applies to bankruptcy cases commenced in the seven-year period beginning December 19, 2008.

cumstances specified in subdivision (n)(1), and if the debtor has not previously filed a statement and calculations required by subdivision (b)(4), the clerk shall promptly notify the debtor that the required statement and calculations must be filed within the time specified in subdivision (n)(1).

OFFICIAL AND DIRECTOR'S BANKRUPTCY FORMS

Amendments received to December 1, 2018

OFFICIAL FORMS

For Complete Annotation Materials, see United States Code Annotated

OFFICIAL FORMS

Form B101. Voluntary Petition for Individuals Filing for Bankruptcy

Fill in this information to identify your case:

United States Bankruptcy Court for the:

_____ District of _____ .
(State)

Case number (if known): _____

Chapter you are filing under:
- ☐ Chapter 7
- ☐ Chapter 11
- ☐ Chapter 12
- ☐ Chapter 13

☐ Check if this is an amended filing

Official Form 101

Voluntary Petition for Individuals Filing for Bankruptcy   12/17

The bankruptcy forms use *you* and *Debtor 1* to refer to a debtor filing alone. A married couple may file a bankruptcy case together—called a *joint case*—and in joint cases, these forms use *you* to ask for information from both debtors. For example, if a form asks, "Do you own a car," the answer would be yes if either debtor owns a car. When information is needed about the spouses separately, the form uses *Debtor 1* and *Debtor 2* to distinguish between them. In joint cases, one of the spouses must report information as *Debtor 1* and the other as *Debtor 2*. The same person must be *Debtor 1* in all of the forms.

Be as complete and accurate as possible. If two married people are filing together, both are equally responsible for supplying correct information. If more space is needed, attach a separate sheet to this form. On the top of any additional pages, write your name and case number (if known). Answer every question.

Part 1: Identify Yourself

	About Debtor 1:	About Debtor 2 (Spouse Only in a Joint Case):
1. Your full name Write the name that is on your government-issued picture identification (for example, your driver's license or passport). Bring your picture identification to your meeting with the trustee.	First name _____ Middle name _____ Last name _____ Suffix (Sr., Jr., II, III) _____	First name _____ Middle name _____ Last name _____ Suffix (Sr., Jr., II, III) _____
2. All other names you have used in the last 8 years Include your married or maiden names.	First name _____ Middle name _____ Last name _____ First name _____ Middle name _____ Last name _____	First name _____ Middle name _____ Last name _____ First name _____ Middle name _____ Last name _____
3. Only the last 4 digits of your Social Security number or federal Individual Taxpayer Identification number (ITIN)	XXX – XX – ___ ___ ___ ___ OR 9 XX – XX – ___ ___ ___ ___	XXX – XX – ___ ___ ___ ___ OR 9 XX – XX – ___ ___ ___ ___

Official Form 101   Voluntary Petition for Individuals Filing for Bankruptcy   page 1

Form B101   OFFICIAL FORMS

Debtor 1 _____   Case number (if known) _____
          First Name   Middle Name   Last Name

About Debtor 1:	About Debtor 2 (Spouse Only in a Joint Case):

4. Any business names and Employer Identification Numbers (EIN) you have used in the last 8 years

Include trade names and *doing business as* names

☐ I have not used any business names or EINs.

Business name _____

Business name _____

EIN __ __ - __ __ __ __ __ __ __

EIN __ __ - __ __ __ __ __ __ __

☐ I have not used any business names or EINs.

Business name _____

Business name _____

EIN __ __ - __ __ __ __ __ __ __

EIN __ __ - __ __ __ __ __ __ __

5. Where you live

Number   Street _____

_____

City _____ State _____ ZIP Code _____

County _____

If your mailing address is different from the one above, fill it in here. Note that the court will send any notices to you at this mailing address.

Number   Street _____

P.O. Box _____

City _____ State _____ ZIP Code _____

If Debtor 2 lives at a different address:

Number   Street _____

_____

City _____ State _____ ZIP Code _____

County _____

If Debtor 2's mailing address is different from yours, fill it in here. Note that the court will send any notices to this mailing address.

Number   Street _____

P.O. Box _____

City _____ State _____ ZIP Code _____

6. Why you are choosing *this district* to file for bankruptcy

Check one:

☐ Over the last 180 days before filing this petition, I have lived in this district longer than in any other district.

☐ I have another reason. Explain. (See 28 U.S.C. § 1408.)

_____

_____

_____

Check one:

☐ Over the last 180 days before filing this petition, I have lived in this district longer than in any other district.

☐ I have another reason. Explain. (See 28 U.S.C. § 1408.)

_____

_____

_____

Official Form 101   Voluntary Petition for Individuals Filing for Bankruptcy   page 2

Debtor 1 _____   Case number (if known) _____
    First Name   Middle Name   Last Name

Part 2:   **Tell the Court About Your Bankruptcy Case**

7. The chapter of the Bankruptcy Code you are choosing to file under

Check one. (For a brief description of each, see *Notice Required by 11 U.S.C. § 342(b) for Individuals Filing for Bankruptcy* (Form 2010)). Also, go to the top of page 1 and check the appropriate box.

☐ Chapter 7

☐ Chapter 11

☐ Chapter 12

☐ Chapter 13

8. How you will pay the fee

☐ **I will pay the entire fee when I file my petition.** Please check with the clerk's office in your local court for more details about how you may pay. Typically, if you are paying the fee yourself, you may pay with cash, cashier's check, or money order. If your attorney is submitting your payment on your behalf, your attorney may pay with a credit card or check with a pre-printed address.

☐ **I need to pay the fee in installments.** If you choose this option, sign and attach the *Application for Individuals to Pay The Filing Fee in Installments* (Official Form 103A).

☐ **I request that my fee be waived** (You may request this option only if you are filing for Chapter 7. By law, a judge may, but is not required to, waive your fee, and may do so only if your income is less than 150% of the official poverty line that applies to your family size and you are unable to pay the fee in installments). If you choose this option, you must fill out the *Application to Have the Chapter 7 Filing Fee Waived* (Official Form 103B) and file it with your petition.

9. Have you filed for bankruptcy within the last 8 years?

☐ No

☐ Yes. District _____ When _____ / _____ / _____ Case number _____
                                    MM / DD / YYYY

       District _____ When _____ / _____ / _____ Case number _____
                                      MM / DD / YYYY

       District _____ When _____ / _____ / _____ Case number _____
                                      MM / DD / YYYY

10. Are any bankruptcy cases pending or being filed by a spouse who is not filing this case with you, or by a business partner, or by an affiliate?

☐ No

☐ Yes. Debtor _____ Relationship to you _____
       District _____ When _____ / _____ / _____ Case number, if known _____
                                      MM / DD / YYYY

       Debtor _____ Relationship to you _____

       District _____ When _____ / _____ / _____ Case number, if known _____
                                      MM / DD / YYYY

11. Do you rent your residence?

☐ No. Go to line 12.

☐ Yes. Has your landlord obtained an eviction judgment against you?

    ☐ No. Go to line 12.

    ☐ Yes. Fill out *Initial Statement About an Eviction Judgment Against You* (Form 101A) and file it as part of this bankruptcy petition.

Official Form 101   Voluntary Petition for Individuals Filing for Bankruptcy   page 3

Debtor 1 _____   Case number (if known) _____
     First Name   Middle Name   Last Name

Part 3:   **Report About Any Businesses You Own as a Sole Proprietor**

12. Are you a sole proprietor of any full- or part-time business?

A sole proprietorship is a business you operate as an individual, and is not a separate legal entity such as a corporation, partnership, or LLC.

If you have more than one sole proprietorship, use a separate sheet and attach it to this petition.

☐ No. Go to Part 4.

☐ Yes. Name and location of business

_____
Name of business, if any

_____
Number   Street

_____

_____
City   State   ZIP Code

Check the appropriate box to describe your business:

☐ Health Care Business (as defined in 11 U.S.C. § 101(27A))

☐ Single Asset Real Estate (as defined in 11 U.S.C. § 101(51B))

☐ Stockbroker (as defined in 11 U.S.C. § 101(53A))

☐ Commodity Broker (as defined in 11 U.S.C. § 101(6))

☐ None of the above

13. Are you filing under Chapter 11 of the Bankruptcy Code and are you a *small business debtor*?

For a definition of *small business debtor*, see 11 U.S.C. § 101(51D).

If you are filing under Chapter 11, the court must know whether you are a small business debtor so that it can set appropriate deadlines. If you indicate that you are a small business debtor, you must attach your most recent balance sheet, statement of operations, cash-flow statement, and federal income tax return or if any of these documents do not exist, follow the procedure in 11 U.S.C. § 1116(1)(B)

☐ No. I am not filing under Chapter 11

☐ No. I am filing under Chapter 11, but I am NOT a small business debtor according to the definition in the Bankruptcy Code.

☐ Yes. I am filing under Chapter 11 and I am a small business debtor according to the definition in the Bankruptcy Code.

Part 4:   **Report if You Own or Have Any Hazardous Property or Any Property That Needs Immediate Attention**

14. Do you own or have any property that poses or is alleged to pose a threat of imminent and identifiable hazard to public health or safety? Or do you own any property that needs immediate attention?

For example, do you own perishable goods, or livestock that must be fed, or a building that needs urgent repairs?

☐ No

☐ Yes. What is the hazard? _____

_____

If immediate attention is needed, why is it needed? _____

_____

Where is the property? _____
                Number   Street

_____

_____
City   State   ZIP Code

Official Form 101   **Voluntary Petition for Individuals Filing for Bankruptcy**   page 4

Debtor 1 _____   Case number *(if known)* _____
　　　　　First Name　　　Middle Name　　　Last Name

Part 5:	Explain Your Efforts to Receive a Briefing About Credit Counseling

15. Tell the court whether you have received a briefing about credit counseling.

The law requires that you receive a briefing about credit counseling before you file for bankruptcy. You must truthfully check one of the following choices. If you cannot do so, you are not eligible to file.

If you file anyway, the court can dismiss your case, you will lose whatever filing fee you paid, and your creditors can begin collection activities again.

About Debtor 1:

You must check one:

☐ **I received a briefing from an approved credit counseling agency within the 180 days before I filed this bankruptcy petition, and I received a certificate of completion.**
Attach a copy of the certificate and the payment plan, if any, that you developed with the agency.

☐ **I received a briefing from an approved credit counseling agency within the 180 days before I filed this bankruptcy petition, but I do not have a certificate of completion.**
Within 14 days after you file this bankruptcy petition, you MUST file a copy of the certificate and payment plan, if any.

☐ **I certify that I asked for credit counseling services from an approved agency, but was unable to obtain those services during the 7 days after I made my request, and exigent circumstances merit a 30-day temporary waiver of the requirement.**

To ask for a 30-day temporary waiver of the requirement, attach a separate sheet explaining what efforts you made to obtain the briefing, why you were unable to obtain it before you filed for bankruptcy, and what exigent circumstances required you to file this case.

Your case may be dismissed if the court is dissatisfied with your reasons for not receiving a briefing before you filed for bankruptcy.

If the court is satisfied with your reasons, you must still receive a briefing within 30 days after you file. You must file a certificate from the approved agency, along with a copy of the payment plan you developed, if any. If you do not do so, your case may be dismissed.

Any extension of the 30-day deadline is granted only for cause and is limited to a maximum of 15 days.

☐ **I am not required to receive a briefing about credit counseling because of:**

　☐ **Incapacity.**　I have a mental illness or a mental deficiency that makes me incapable of realizing or making rational decisions about finances.

　☐ **Disability.**　My physical disability causes me to be unable to participate in a briefing in person, by phone, or through the internet, even after I reasonably tried to do so.

　☐ **Active duty.**　I am currently on active military duty in a military combat zone.

If you believe you are not required to receive a briefing about credit counseling, you must file a motion for waiver of credit counseling with the court.

About Debtor 2 (Spouse Only in a Joint Case):

You must check one:

☐ **I received a briefing from an approved credit counseling agency within the 180 days before I filed this bankruptcy petition, and I received a certificate of completion.**
Attach a copy of the certificate and the payment plan, if any, that you developed with the agency.

☐ **I received a briefing from an approved credit counseling agency within the 180 days before I filed this bankruptcy petition, but I do not have a certificate of completion.**
Within 14 days after you file this bankruptcy petition, you MUST file a copy of the certificate and payment plan, if any.

☐ **I certify that I asked for credit counseling services from an approved agency, but was unable to obtain those services during the 7 days after I made my request, and exigent circumstances merit a 30-day temporary waiver of the requirement.**

To ask for a 30-day temporary waiver of the requirement, attach a separate sheet explaining what efforts you made to obtain the briefing, why you were unable to obtain it before you filed for bankruptcy, and what exigent circumstances required you to file this case.

Your case may be dismissed if the court is dissatisfied with your reasons for not receiving a briefing before you filed for bankruptcy.

If the court is satisfied with your reasons, you must still receive a briefing within 30 days after you file. You must file a certificate from the approved agency, along with a copy of the payment plan you developed, if any. If you do not do so, your case may be dismissed.

Any extension of the 30-day deadline is granted only for cause and is limited to a maximum of 15 days.

☐ **I am not required to receive a briefing about credit counseling because of:**

　☐ **Incapacity.**　I have a mental illness or a mental deficiency that makes me incapable of realizing or making rational decisions about finances.

　☐ **Disability.**　My physical disability causes me to be unable to participate in a briefing in person, by phone, or through the internet, even after I reasonably tried to do so.

　☐ **Active duty.**　I am currently on active military duty in a military combat zone.

If you believe you are not required to receive a briefing about credit counseling, you must file a motion for waiver of credit counseling with the court.

Official Form 101　　　　　Voluntary Petition for Individuals Filing for Bankruptcy　　　　　page 5

Form B101

Debtor 1 _____ Case number (if known) _____
      First Name   Middle Name   Last Name

Part 6: Answer These Questions for Reporting Purposes

16. What kind of debts do you have?

16a. **Are your debts primarily consumer debts?** *Consumer debts* are defined in 11 U.S.C. § 101(8) as "incurred by an individual primarily for a personal, family, or household purpose."

☐ No. Go to line 16b.
☐ Yes. Go to line 17.

16b. **Are your debts primarily business debts?** *Business debts* are debts that you incurred to obtain money for a business or investment or through the operation of the business or investment.

☐ No. Go to line 16c.
☐ Yes. Go to line 17.

16c. State the type of debts you owe that are not consumer debts or business debts.

_____

17. Are you filing under Chapter 7?

Do you estimate that after any exempt property is excluded and administrative expenses are paid that funds will be available for distribution to unsecured creditors?

☐ No. I am not filing under Chapter 7. Go to line 18.

☐ Yes. I am filing under Chapter 7. Do you estimate that after any exempt property is excluded and administrative expenses are paid that funds will be available to distribute to unsecured creditors?

    ☐ No
    ☐ Yes

18. How many creditors do you estimate that you owe?

☐ 1-49	☐ 1,000-5,000	☐ 25,001-50,000
☐ 50-99	☐ 5,001-10,000	☐ 50,001-100,000
☐ 100-199	☐ 10,001-25,000	☐ More than 100,000
☐ 200-999		

19. How much do you estimate your assets to be worth?

☐ $0-$50,000	☐ $1,000,001-$10 million	☐ $500,000,001-$1 billion
☐ $50,001-$100,000	☐ $10,000,001-$50 million	☐ $1,000,000,001-$10 billion
☐ $100,001-$500,000	☐ $50,000,001-$100 million	☐ $10,000,000,001-$50 billion
☐ $500,001-$1 million	☐ $100,000,001-$500 million	☐ More than $50 billion

20. How much do you estimate your liabilities to be?

☐ $0-$50,000	☐ $1,000,001-$10 million	☐ $500,000,001-$1 billion
☐ $50,001-$100,000	☐ $10,000,001-$50 million	☐ $1,000,000,001-$10 billion
☐ $100,001-$500,000	☐ $50,000,001-$100 million	☐ $10,000,000,001-$50 billion
☐ $500,001-$1 million	☐ $100,000,001-$500 million	☐ More than $50 billion

Part 7: Sign Below

For you

I have examined this petition, and I declare under penalty of perjury that the information provided is true and correct.

If I have chosen to file under Chapter 7, I am aware that I may proceed, if eligible, under Chapter 7, 11,12, or 13 of title 11, United States Code. I understand the relief available under each chapter, and I choose to proceed under Chapter 7.

If no attorney represents me and I did not pay or agree to pay someone who is not an attorney to help me fill out this document, I have obtained and read the notice required by 11 U.S.C. § 342(b).

I request relief in accordance with the chapter of title 11, United States Code, specified in this petition.

I understand making a false statement, concealing property, or obtaining money or property by fraud in connection with a bankruptcy case can result in fines up to $250,000, or imprisonment for up to 20 years, or both. 18 U.S.C. §§ 152, 1341, 1519, and 3571.

X _____ **X** _____
Signature of Debtor 1   Signature of Debtor 2

Executed on _____ Executed on _____
         MM / DD / YYYY   MM / DD / YYYY

Official Form 101   Voluntary Petition for Individuals Filing for Bankruptcy   page 6

Debtor 1 _____   Case number (if known) _____
          First Name   Middle Name   Last Name

For your attorney, if you are represented by one	I, the attorney for the debtor(s) named in this petition, declare that I have informed the debtor(s) about eligibility to proceed under Chapter 7, 11, 12, or 13 of title 11, United States Code, and have explained the relief available under each chapter for which the person is eligible. I also certify that I have delivered to the debtor(s) the notice required by 11 U.S.C. § 342(b) and, in a case in which § 707(b)(4)(D) applies, certify that I have no knowledge after an inquiry that the information in the schedules filed with the petition is incorrect.

If you are not represented by an attorney, you do not need to file this page.

X _____   Date _____
Signature of Attorney for Debtor   MM / DD / YYYY

Printed name _____

Firm name _____

Number   Street _____
_____

City _____   State _____   ZIP Code _____

Contact phone _____   Email address _____

Bar number _____   State _____

Debtor 1 _____ Case number (if known)_____
        First Name   Middle Name   Last Name

For you if you are filing this bankruptcy without an attorney **If you are represented by an attorney, you do not need to file this page.**	The law allows you, as an individual, to represent yourself in bankruptcy court, but **you should understand that many people find it extremely difficult to represent themselves successfully. Because bankruptcy has long-term financial and legal consequences, you are strongly urged to hire a qualified attorney.** To be successful, you must correctly file and handle your bankruptcy case. The rules are very technical, and a mistake or inaction may affect your rights. For example, your case may be dismissed because you did not file a required document, pay a fee on time, attend a meeting or hearing, or cooperate with the court, case trustee, U.S. trustee, bankruptcy administrator, or audit firm if your case is selected for audit. If that happens, you could lose your right to file another case, or you may lose protections, including the benefit of the automatic stay. You must list all your property and debts in the schedules that you are required to file with the court. Even if you plan to pay a particular debt outside of your bankruptcy, you must list that debt in your schedules. If you do not list a debt, the debt may not be discharged. If you do not list property or properly claim it as exempt, you may not be able to keep the property. The judge can also deny you a discharge of all your debts if you do something dishonest in your bankruptcy case, such as destroying or hiding property, falsifying records, or lying. Individual bankruptcy cases are randomly audited to determine if debtors have been accurate, truthful, and complete. **Bankruptcy fraud is a serious crime; you could be fined and imprisoned.** If you decide to file without an attorney, the court expects you to follow the rules as if you had hired an attorney. The court will not treat you differently because you are filing for yourself. To be successful, you must be familiar with the United States Bankruptcy Code, the Federal Rules of Bankruptcy Procedure, and the local rules of the court in which your case is filed. You must also be familiar with any state exemption laws that apply. Are you aware that filing for bankruptcy is a serious action with long-term financial and legal consequences? ❑ No ❑ Yes Are you aware that bankruptcy fraud is a serious crime and that if your bankruptcy forms are inaccurate or incomplete, you could be fined or imprisoned? ❑ No ❑ Yes Did you pay or agree to pay someone who is not an attorney to help you fill out your bankruptcy forms? ❑ No ❑ Yes. Name of Person_____ Attach *Bankruptcy Petition Preparer's Notice, Declaration, and Signature* (Official Form 119). By signing here, I acknowledge that I understand the risks involved in filing without an attorney. I have read and understood this notice, and I am aware that filing a bankruptcy case without an attorney may cause me to lose my rights or property if I do not properly handle the case. ✗ _____ ✗ _____ Signature of Debtor 1 Signature of Debtor 2 Date _____ MM / DD / YYYY Date _____ MM / DD / YYYY Contact phone _____ Contact phone _____ Cell phone _____ Cell phone _____ Email address _____ Email address _____

Official Form 101   Voluntary Petition for Individuals Filing for Bankruptcy   page 8

(Added Dec. 1, 2015; and amended Dec. 1, 2017.)

ADVISORY COMMITTEE NOTES

Official Form 101, *Voluntary Petition for Individuals Filing for Bankruptcy*, applies only in cases of individual debtors. Form 101 replaces Official Form 1, *Voluntary Petition*. It is renumbered to distinguish it from the forms used by non-individual debtors, such as corporations, and includes stylistic changes throughout the form. It is revised as part of the Forms Modernization Project, making it easier to read and, as a result, likely to generate more complete and accurate responses. Because the goals of the Forms Modernization Project include improving the interface between technology and the forms so as to increase efficiency and reduce the need to produce the same information in multiple formats, many of the open-ended questions and multiple-part instructions have been replaced with more specific questions.

Official Form 101 has been substantially reorganized. References to Exhibits A, B, C, and D, and the exhibits themselves, have been eliminated because the requested information is now asked in the form or is not applicable to individual debtors.

Part 1, *Identify Yourself*, line 6, replaces the venue box from page 2 of Official Form 1 and deletes venue questions that pertain only to non-individuals.

Part 2, *Tell the Court About Your Bankruptcy Case*, line 7, removes choices for chapters 9 and 15 filings because they do not pertain to individuals. The status of "being filed" is added to the question regarding bankruptcy cases pending or filed by a spouse, business partner, or affiliate (line 10). Lastly, the question "Do you rent your residence?" (line 11) and Official Forms 101A, *Initial Statement About an Eviction Judgment Against You*, and 101B, *Statement About Payment of an Eviction Judgment Against You*, replace "certification by a debtor who resides as a tenant of residential property," on page 2 of Official Form 1.

Part 3, *Report About Any Businesses You Own as a Sole Proprietor*, line 12, incorporates options from the "nature of business" box from page 1 of Official Form 1 that would apply to individual debtors, thus eliminating checkboxes for railroads and clearing banks. Part 3, line 13, also eliminates a

---

checkbox to report whether a plan was filed with the petition, or if plan acceptances were solicited prepetition. Additionally, line 13 rephrases the question relating to whether a debtor filing under Chapter 11 is a small business debtor.

Part 4, *Report if You Own or Have Any Hazardous Property or Any Property That Needs Immediate Attention*, line 14, replaces Exhibit C from Official Form 1 and adds the category of "property that needs immediate attention."

Part 5, *Explain Your Efforts to Receive a Briefing About Credit Counseling* (line 15), replaces Exhibit D from Official Form 1. Additionally, this part describes incapacity and disability using a simplified definition, tells the debtor of the ability to file a motion for a waiver, and eliminates statutory reference about districts where credit counseling does not apply because such districts are rare.

Part 6, *Answer These Questions for Reporting Purposes* (line 16c), provides a text field for the debtor to describe the type of debts owed if the debtor believes they are neither primarily consumer nor business debts.

Part 7, *Sign Below*, deletes from the debtor's declaration the phrase "to the best of my knowledge, information, and belief" in order to conform to the language of 28 U.S.C. § 1746. See Rule 1008. This part combines the two attorney signature blocks into one certification and eliminates signature lines for corporations/partnerships and chapter 15 Foreign Representative. The declaration and signature section for a non-attorney bankruptcy petition preparer (BPP) has also been removed as unnecessary. The same declaration, required under 11 U.S.C. § 110, is contained in Official 14 Form 119. That form must be completed and signed by the BPP and filed with each document prepared by a BPP.

2017 Amendment

Part 2, line 11, is amended to accurately reflect the requirements of § 362(*l*) of the Bankruptcy Code. All debtors against whom an eviction judgment has been entered with respect to their residence must fill out Official Form 101A (*Initial Statement About an Eviction Judgment Against You*), whether or not they desire to remain in their residence. Form 101A is deemed to be part of the petition.

Form B101A

Form B101A. Initial Statement About an Eviction Judgment Against You

---

Fill in this information to identify your case:

Debtor 1 _____
          First Name   Middle Name   Last Name

Debtor 2 _____
(Spouse, if filing) First Name   Middle Name   Last Name

United States Bankruptcy Court for the: _____ District of _____
                                                              (State)

Case number _____
(If known)

Official Form 101A

Initial Statement About an Eviction Judgment Against You   12/15

File this form with the court and serve a copy on your landlord when you first file bankruptcy only if:

■ you rent your residence; and

■ your landlord has obtained a judgment for possession in an eviction, unlawful detainer action, or
  similar proceeding (called *eviction judgment*) against you to possess your residence.

Landlord's name   _____

Landlord's address _____
                   Number   Street

                   _____ _____ _____
                   City   State   ZIP Code

If you want to stay in your rented residence after you file your case for bankruptcy, also complete the certification below.

Certification About Applicable Law and Deposit of Rent

I certify under penalty of perjury that:

☐ Under the state or other nonbankruptcy law that applies to the judgment for possession (*eviction judgment*),
   I have the right to stay in my residence by paying my landlord the entire delinquent amount.

☐ I have given the bankruptcy court clerk a deposit for the rent that would be due during the 30 days after I file
   the *Voluntary Petition for Individuals Filing for Bankruptcy* (Official Form 101).

X _____   X _____
  Signature of Debtor 1   Signature of Debtor 2

Date _____   Date _____
     MM / DD / YYYY   MM / DD / YYYY

Stay of Eviction: (a) **First 30 days after bankruptcy.** If you checked both boxes above, signed the form to certify that both apply,
                       and served your landlord with a copy of this statement, the automatic stay under 11 U.S.C. § 362(a)(3) will
                       apply to the continuation of the eviction against you for 30 days after you file your *Voluntary Petition for
                       Individual's Filing for Bankruptcy* (Official Form 101).

                  (b) **Stay after the initial 30 days.** If you wish to stay in your residence after that 30-day period and continue to
                       receive the protection of the automatic stay under 11 U.S.C. § 362(a)(3), you must pay the entire delinquent
                       amount to your landlord as stated in the eviction judgment before the 30-day period ends. You must also fill
                       out *Statement About Payment of an Eviction Judgment Against You* (Official Form 101B), file it with the
                       bankruptcy court, and serve your landlord a copy of it before the 30-day period ends.

Check the Bankruptcy Rules (http://www.uscourts.gov/rules-policies/current-rules-practice-procedure) and the local court's website (to find
your court's website go to http://www.uscourts.gov/court-locator) for any specific requirements that you might have to meet to serve this
statement. 11 U.S.C. §§ 362(b)(22) and 362(l).

Official Form 101A   Initial Statement About an Eviction Judgment Against You   16

(Added Dec. 1, 2015.)

ADVISORY COMMITTEE NOTES

Official Form 101A, *Initial Statement About an Eviction Judgment Against You*, and Official Form 101B, *Statement About Payment of an Eviction Judgment Against You*, are new forms promulgated as part of the Forms Modernization Project. They replace the *"Certification by a Debtor Who Resides as a Tenant of Residential Property"* section on Official Form 1, *Voluntary Petition*. The forms apply only in cases of individual debtors.

Official Form 101A explains that debtors need to complete and file the form only if their landlord has a judgment for possession or an eviction judgment against them and they rent their residence. The form further explains that if the debtor wishes to stay in their residence for 30 days after filing their bankruptcy petition, the certification must be completed. The form adds references to the provisions in the Bankruptcy Code that specify when debtor-tenants subject to eviction may remain in their residence after filing for bankruptcy.

The form eliminates the checkboxes that the debtor has served the landlord with the certification and paid the court the rent that would be due during the 30 days after the filing of the bankruptcy petition. Instead, debtors are required to certify under penalty of perjury that the rent has been paid to the court, and the instructions direct debtors to serve a copy of the statement on the landlord.

The form eliminates the checkbox that the debtor claims there are circumstances under applicable nonbankruptcy law under which the debtor would be permitted to cure the

For Complete Annotation Materials, see United States Code Annotated

710

monetary default that gave rise to the judgment for possession (or eviction judgment) and remain in residence. Instead, debtors are required to certify under penalty of perjury that they have the right to stay in their residence under state law or other nonbankruptcy law by paying their landlord the entire delinquent amount.

Form B101B. Statement About Payment of an Eviction Judgment Against You

Fill in this information to identify your case:

Debtor 1 _____
       First Name   Middle Name   Last Name

Debtor 2 _____
(Spouse, if filing) First Name   Middle Name   Last Name

United States Bankruptcy Court for the: _____ District of _____
                                        (State)

Case number _____
(If known)

Official Form 101B

Statement About Payment of an Eviction Judgment Against You   12/15

Fill out this form only if:

- you filed *Initial Statement About an Eviction Judgment Against You* (Official Form 101A); and
- you served a copy of Form 101A on your landlord; and
- you want to stay in your rented residence for more than 30 days after you file your *Voluntary Petition for Individuals Filing for Bankruptcy* (Official Form 101).

File this form within 30 days after you file your *Voluntary Petition for Individuals Filing for Bankruptcy* (Official Form 101). Also serve a copy on your landlord within that same time period.

Certification About Applicable Law and Payment of Eviction Judgment

I certify under penalty of perjury that (*Check all that apply*):

☐ Under the state or other nonbankruptcy law that applies to the judgment for possession (*eviction judgment*), I have the right to stay in my residence by paying my landlord the entire delinquent amount.

☐ Within 30 days after I filed my *Voluntary Petition for Individuals Filing for Bankruptcy* (Official Form 101), I have paid my landlord the entire amount I owe as stated in the judgment for possession (*eviction judgment*).

X _____   X _____
Signature of Debtor 1   Signature of Debtor 2

Date _____   Date _____
     MM / DD / YYYY   MM / DD / YYYY

You must serve your landlord with a copy of this form.

Check the Bankruptcy Rules (http://www.uscourts.gov/rules-policies/current-rules-practice-procedure) and the court's local website (go to http://www.uscourts.gov/court-locator to find your court's website) for any specific requirements that you might have to meet to serve this statement.

Official Form 101B   Statement About Payment of an Eviction Judgment Against You   17

(Added Dec. 1, 2015.)

ADVISORY COMMITTEE NOTES

Official Form 101A, *Initial Statement About an Eviction Judgment Against You*, and Official Form 101B, *Statement About Payment of an Eviction Judgment Against You*, are new forms promulgated as part of the Forms Modernization Project. They replace the "*Certification by a Debtor Who Resides as a Tenant of Residential Property*" section on Official Form 1, *Voluntary Petition*. The forms apply only in cases of individual debtors.

Official Form 101B is new. If debtors wish to stay in their residence for more than 30 days after filing the petition, they must complete, file, and serve the form within 30 days after the petition is filed. Under Official Form 101B, debtors certify under penalty of perjury that they have the right to stay in their residence under state law or other nonbankruptcy law by paying their landlord the entire delinquent amount and that they have paid their landlord the entire amount owed as stated in the judgment for possession or in the eviction judgment.

Form B103A. Application for Individuals to Pay the Filing Fee in Installments

---

Fill in this information to identify your case:

Debtor * _____
       First Name   Middle Name   Last Name

Debtor 2
(Spouse, if filing)   First Name   Middle Name   Last Name

United States Bankruptcy Court for the: _____ District of _____
       (State)

Case number _____
(If known)

☐ Check if this is an
amended filing

Official Form 103A

Application for Individuals to Pay the Filing Fee in Installments   12/15

Be as complete and accurate as possible. If two married people are filing together, both are equally responsible for supplying correct information.

Part 1:   Specify Your Proposed Payment Timetable

1. Which chapter of the Bankruptcy Code are you choosing to file under?

     ☐ Chapter 7
     ☐ Chapter 11
     ☐ Chapter 12
     ☐ Chapter 13

2. You may apply to pay the filing fee in up to four installments. Fill in the amounts you propose to pay and the dates you plan to pay them. Be sure all dates are business days. Then add the payments you propose to pay.

You must propose to pay the entire fee no later than 120 days after you file this bankruptcy case. If the court approves your application, the court will set your final payment timetable.

You propose to pay...

$ _____   ☐ With the filing of the petition

       ☐ On or before this date ...... MM / DD / YYYY

$ _____   On or before this date .... MM / DD / YYYY

$ _____   On or before this date .... MM / DD / YYYY

+ $ _____   On or before this date .... MM / DD / YYYY

Total $ _____ ◀ Your total must equal the entire fee for the chapter you checked in line 1.

Part 2:   Sign Below

By signing here, you state that you are unable to pay the full filing fee at once, that you want to pay the fee in installments, and that you understand that:

■ You must pay your entire filing fee before you make any more payments or transfer any more property to an attorney, bankruptcy petition preparer, or anyone else for services in connection with your bankruptcy case.

■ You must pay the entire fee no later than 120 days after you first file for bankruptcy, unless the court later extends your deadline. Your debts will not be discharged until your entire fee is paid.

■ If you do not make any payment when it is due, your bankruptcy case may be dismissed, and your rights in other bankruptcy proceedings may be affected.

X _____   X _____   X _____
Signature of Debtor 1   Signature of Debtor 2   Your attorney's name and signature, if you used one

Date _____   Date _____   Date _____
   MM / DD / YYYY   MM / DD / YYYY   MM / DD / YYYY

                                                    20

Official Form 103A   Application for Individuals to Pay the Filing Fee in Installments

---

Form B103A

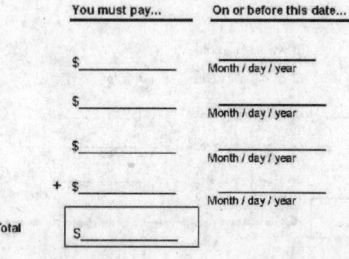

Fill in this information to identify the case:

Debtor 1 _____
      First Name   Middle Name   Last Name

Debtor 2
(Spouse, if filing) First Name   Middle Name   Last Name

United States Bankruptcy Court for the: _____   District of _____
                                                           (State)

Case number _____
  (If known)

Chapter filing under:

☐ Chapter 7
☐ Chapter 11
☐ Chapter 12
☐ Chapter 13

Order Approving Payment of Filing Fee in Installments

After considering the *Application for Individuals to Pay the Filing Fee in Installments* (Official Form 103A), the court orders that:

[ ] The debtor(s) may pay the filing fee in installments on the terms proposed in the application.

[ ] The debtor(s) must pay the filing fee according to the following terms:

You must pay...	On or before this date...
$_____	Month / day / year
$_____	Month / day / year
$_____	Month / day / year
+ $_____	Month / day / year
Total $_____	

Until the filing fee is paid in full, the debtor(s) must not make any additional payment or transfer any additional property to an attorney or to anyone else for services in connection with this case.

_____   By the court: _____
Month / day / year   United States Bankruptcy Judge

21

(Added Dec. 1, 2015.)

ADVISORY COMMITTEE NOTES

The form number is updated to comport with the form numbering style developed as part of the Forms Moderniza-tion Project. Other stylistic changes were made throughout the form.

Form B103B.   Application to Have the Chapter 7 Filing Fee Waived

Fill in this information to identify your case:

Debtor 1 _____
First Name   Middle Name   Last Name

Debtor 2 _____
(Spouse filing)   First Name   Middle Name   Last Name

United States Bankruptcy Court for the: _____   District of _____
(State)

Case number _____
(If known)

☐ Check if this is an amended filing

Official Form 103B

Application to Have the Chapter 7 Filing Fee Waived   12/15

Be as complete and accurate as possible. If two married people are filing together, both are equally responsible for supplying correct information. If more space is needed, attach a separate sheet to this form. On the top of any additional pages, write your name and case number (if known).

Part 1:   Tell the Court About Your Family and Your Family's Income

1. What is the size of your family?
Your *family* includes you, your spouse, and any dependents listed on *Schedule J: Your Expenses* (Official Form 106J).

Check all that apply:
☐ You
☐ Your spouse
☐ Your dependents

How many dependents? _____   Total number of people _____

2. Fill in your family's average monthly income.

Include your spouse's income if your spouse is living with you, even if your spouse is not filing.

Do not include your spouse's income if you are separated and your spouse is not filing with you.

Add your income and your spouse's income. Include the value (if known) of any non-cash governmental assistance that you receive, such as food stamps (benefits under the Supplemental Nutrition Assistance Program) or housing subsidies.

If you have already filled out *Schedule I: Your Income*, see line 10 of that schedule.

Subtract any non-cash governmental assistance that you included above.

Your family's average monthly net income

	That person's average monthly net income (take-home pay)
You	$_____
Your spouse +	$_____
Subtotal	$_____
−	$_____
Total	$_____

3. Do you receive non-cash governmental assistance?
☐ No
☐ Yes. Describe ....

Type of assistance
_____

4. Do you expect your family's average monthly net income to increase or decrease by more than 10% during the next 6 months?
☐ No
☐ Yes. Explain ....
_____

5. Tell the court why you are unable to pay the filing fee in installments within 120 days. If you have some additional circumstances that cause you to not be able to pay your filing fee in installments, explain them.
_____

Official Form 103B   Application to Have the Chapter 7 Filing Fee Waived   23   page 1

Form B103B   OFFICIAL FORMS

Debtor 1 _____   Case number (if known) _____
         First Name   Middle Name   Last Name

Part 2:   Tell the Court About Your Monthly Expenses

6. Estimate your average monthly expenses.

Include amounts paid by any government assistance that you $_____
reported on line 2.

If you have already filled out *Schedule J: Your Expenses,* copy
line 22 from that form.

7. Do these expenses cover anyone   ☐ No
who is not included in your family   ☐ Yes. Identify who ...... _____
as reported in line 1?

8. Does anyone other than you   ☐ No
regularly pay any of these
expenses?   ☐ Yes. How much do you regularly receive as contributions? $_____ monthly

If you have already filled out
Schedule I: Your Income, copy the
total from line 11.

9. Do you expect your average   ☐ No
monthly expenses to increase or
decrease by more than 10% during   ☐ Yes. Explain ...... _____
the next 6 months?

Part 3:   Tell the Court About Your Property

If you have already filled out *Schedule A/B: Property (Official Form 106A/B)* attach copies to this application and go to Part 4.

10. How much cash do you have?

Examples: Money you have in
your wallet, in your home, and on   Cash: $_____
hand when you file this application

11. Bank accounts and other deposits   Institution name: Amount:
of money?

Examples: Checking, savings,   Checking account: _____ $_____
money market, or other financial
accounts; certificates of deposit;   Savings account: _____ $_____
shares in banks, credit unions,
brokerage houses, and other   Other financial accounts: _____ $_____
similar institutions. If you have
more than one account with the   Other financial accounts: _____ $_____
same institution, list each. Do not
include 401(k) and IRA accounts.

12. Your home? (if you own it outright or
are purchasing it)   Number   Street _____ Current value: $_____

Examples: House, condominium   Amount you owe
manufactured home, or mobile home   City _____ State ____ ZIP Code ___ on mortgage and $_____
                                                                          liens:

13. Other real estate?

                                     Number   Street _____ Current value: $_____

                                                                          Amount you owe
                                     City _____ State ____ ZIP Code ___ on mortgage and $_____
                                                                          liens:

14. The vehicles you own?   Make: _____
                                     Model: _____   Current value: $_____
Examples: Cars, vans, trucks,
sports utility vehicles, motorcycles Year: _____   Amount you owe
tractors, boats   on lien: $_____
                                     Mileage _____

                                     Make: _____
                                     Model: _____   Current value: $_____
                                     Year: _____   Amount you owe
                                     Mileage _____   on lien: $_____

Official Form 103B   Application to Have the Chapter 7 Filing Fee Waived   page 2

Debtor 1 _____   Case number (if known) _____
     First Name   Middle Name   Last Name

15. Other assets?	**Describe the other assets:**	Current value: $ _____
Do not include household items and clothing.		Amount you owe on liens: $ _____

16. Money or property due you?
Examples: Tax refunds, past due or lump sum alimony, spousal support, child support, maintenance, divorce or property settlements, Social Security benefits, workers' compensation, personal injury recovery

Who owes you the money or property?	How much is owed?	Do you believe you will likely receive payment in the next 180 days?
_____	$ _____	☐ No
_____	$ _____	☐ Yes. Explain:

Part 4: Answer These Additional Questions

17. Have you paid anyone for services for this case, including filling out this application, the bankruptcy filing package, or the schedules?

☐ No
☐ Yes. Whom did you pay? *Check all that apply:*
   ☐ An attorney
   ☐ A bankruptcy petition preparer, paralegal, or typing service
   ☐ Someone else _____

How much did you pay?
$ _____

---

18. Have you promised to pay or do you expect to pay someone for services for your bankruptcy case?

☐ No
☐ Yes. Whom do you expect to pay? *Check all that apply:*
   ☐ An attorney
   ☐ A bankruptcy petition preparer, paralegal, or typing service
   ☐ Someone else _____

How much do you expect to pay?
$ _____

---

19. Has anyone paid someone on your behalf for services for this case?

☐ No
☐ Yes. Who was paid on your behalf? *Check all that apply:*
   ☐ An attorney
   ☐ A bankruptcy petition preparer, paralegal, or typing service
   ☐ Someone else _____

Who paid? *Check all that apply:*
   ☐ Parent
   ☐ Brother or sister
   ☐ Friend
   ☐ Pastor or clergy
   ☐ Someone else _____

How much did someone else pay?
$ _____

---

20. Have you filed for bankruptcy within the last 8 years?

☐ No
☐ Yes. District _____ When _____ Case number _____
                      MM/ DD/ YYYY
     District _____ When _____ Case number _____
                      MM/ DD/ YYYY
     District _____ When _____ Case number _____
                      MM/ DD/ YYYY

Part 5: Sign Below

By signing here under penalty of perjury, I declare that I cannot afford to pay the filing fee either in full or in installments. I also declare that the information I provided in this application is true and correct.

x _____   x _____
Signature of Debtor 1   Signature of Debtor 2

Date _____   Date _____
    MM / DD / YYYY   MM / DD / YYYY

Official Form 103B   Application to Have the Chapter 7 Filing Fee Waived   page 3

Fill in this information to identify the case:

Debtor 1 _____
              First Name   Middle Name   Last Name

Debtor 2 _____
(Spouse, if filing) First Name   Middle Name   Last Name

United States Bankruptcy Court for the: _____ District of _____
                                                            (State)

Case number _____
(If known)

Order on the Application to Have the Chapter 7 Filing Fee Waived

After considering the debtor's *Application to Have the Chapter 7 Filing Fee Waived* (Official Form 103B), the court orders that the application is:

[ ] **Granted.** However, the court may order the debtor to pay the fee in the future if developments in administering the bankruptcy case show that the waiver was unwarranted.

[ ] **Denied.** The debtor must pay the filing fee according to the following terms:

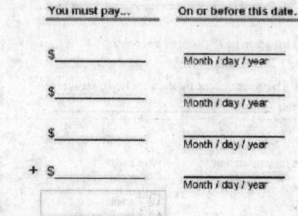

You must pay...	On or before this date...
$_____	Month / day / year
$_____	Month / day / year
$_____	Month / day / year
+ $_____	Month / day / year
Total $_____	

If the debtor would like to propose a different payment timetable, the debtor must file a motion promptly with a payment proposal. The debtor may use *Application for Individuals to Pay the Filing Fee in Installments* (Official Form 103A) for this purpose. The court will consider it.

The debtor must pay the entire filing fee before making any more payments or transferring any more property to an attorney, bankruptcy petition preparer, or anyone else in connection with the bankruptcy case. The debtor must also pay the entire filing fee to receive a discharge. If the debtor does not make any payment when it is due, the bankruptcy case may be dismissed and the debtor's rights in future bankruptcy cases may be affected.

[ ] **Scheduled for hearing.**

A hearing to consider the debtor's application will be held

on _____ at _____ AM / PM at _____.
    Month / day / year   Address of courthouse

If the debtor does not appear at this hearing, the court may deny the application.

_____   By the court: _____
Month / day / year   United States Bankruptcy Judge
                                                                          26

(Added Dec. 1, 2015.)

ADVISORY COMMITTEE NOTES

The form number is updated to comport with the form numbering style developed as part of the Forms Moderniza-tion Project. Other stylistic changes were made throughout the form.

Form B104.   For Individual Chapter 11 Cases: The List of Creditors Who Have the 20 Largest Unsecured Claims Against You Who Are Not Insiders (individuals)

Fill in this information to identify your case:

Debtor 1 _____
          First Name   Middle Name   Last Name

Debtor 2 _____
(Spouse, if filing) First Name   Middle Name   Last Name

United States Bankruptcy Court for the: _____ District of _____
                                                              (State)

Case number _____
(If known)

☐ Check if this is an
   amended filing

Official Form 104

For Individual Chapter 11 Cases: List of Creditors Who Have the 20 Largest Unsecured Claims Against You and Are Not Insiders
                                                                     12/15

If you are an individual filing for bankruptcy under Chapter 11, you must fill out this form. If you are filing under Chapter 7, Chapter 12, or Chapter 13, do not fill out this form. Do not include claims by anyone who is an *insider*. Insiders include your relatives; any general partners; relatives of any general partners; partnerships of which you are a general partner; corporations of which you are an officer, director, person in control, or owner of 20 percent or more of their voting securities; and any managing agent, including one for a business you operate as a sole proprietor. 11 U.S.C. § 101. Also, do not include claims by secured creditors unless the unsecured claim resulting from inadequate collateral value places the creditor among the holders of the 20 largest unsecured claims.

Be as complete and accurate as possible. If two married people are filing together, both are equally responsible for supplying correct information.

Part 1:   List the 20 Unsecured Claims in Order from Largest to Smallest. Do Not Include Claims by Insiders.

		Unsecured claim

1   What is the nature of the claim? _____ $ _____

Creditor's Name

Number   Street

As of the date you file, the claim is: Check all that apply.
☐ Contingent
☐ Unliquidated
☐ Disputed
☐ None of the above apply

City   State   ZIP Code

Contact

Contact phone

Does the creditor have a lien on your property?
☐ No
☐ Yes. Total claim (secured and unsecured): $ _____
        Value of security: – $ _____
        Unsecured claim $ _____

2   What is the nature of the claim? _____ $ _____

Creditor's Name

Number   Street

As of the date you file, the claim is: Check all that apply.
☐ Contingent
☐ Unliquidated
☐ Disputed
☐ None of the above apply

City   State   ZIP Code

Contact

Contact phone

Does the creditor have a lien on your property?
☐ No
☐ Yes. Total claim (secured and unsecured): $ _____
        Value of security: – $ _____
        Unsecured claim $ _____

Official Form 104   For Individual Chapter 11 Cases: List of Creditors Who Have the 20 Largest Unsecured Claims   page 1

28

Debtor 1 _____   Case number (if known) _____

First Name   Middle Name   Last Name

Unsecured claim

3

Creditor's Name

Number   Street

City   State   ZIP Code

Contact

Contact phone

What is the nature of the claim? _____ $ _____

As of the date you file, the claim is: Check all that apply.
- ☐ Contingent
- ☐ Unliquidated
- ☐ Disputed
- ☐ None of the above apply

Does the creditor have a lien on your property?
- ☐ No
- ☐ Yes. Total claim (secured and unsecured): $ _____
  - Value of security: – $ _____
  - Unsecured claim $ _____

4

Creditor's Name

Number   Street

City   State   ZIP Code

Contact

Contact phone

What is the nature of the claim? _____ $ _____

As of the date you file, the claim is: Check all that apply.
- ☐ Contingent
- ☐ Unliquidated
- ☐ Disputed
- ☐ None of the above apply

Does the creditor have a lien on your property?
- ☐ No
- ☐ Yes. Total claim (secured and unsecured): $ _____
  - Value of security: – $ _____
  - Unsecured claim $ _____

5

Creditor's Name

Number   Street

City   State   ZIP Code

Contact

Contact phone

What is the nature of the claim? _____ $ _____

As of the date you file, the claim is: Check all that apply.
- ☐ Contingent
- ☐ Unliquidated
- ☐ Disputed
- ☐ None of the above apply

Does the creditor have a lien on your property?
- ☐ No
- ☐ Yes. Total claim (secured and unsecured): $ _____
  - Value of security: – $ _____
  - Unsecured claim $ _____

6

Creditor's Name

Number   Street

City   State   ZIP Code

Contact

Contact phone

What is the nature of the claim? _____ $ _____

As of the date you file, the claim is: Check all that apply.
- ☐ Contingent
- ☐ Unliquidated
- ☐ Disputed
- ☐ None of the above apply

Does the creditor have a lien on your property?
- ☐ No
- ☐ Yes. Total claim (secured and unsecured): $ _____
  - Value of security: – $ _____
  - Unsecured claim $ _____

7

Creditor's Name

Number   Street

City   State   ZIP Code

Contact

Contact phone

What is the nature of the claim? _____ $ _____

As of the date you file, the claim is: Check all that apply.
- ☐ Contingent
- ☐ Unliquidated
- ☐ Disputed
- ☐ None of the above apply

Does the creditor have a lien on your property?
- ☐ No
- ☐ Yes. Total claim (secured and unsecured): $ _____
  - Value of security: – $ _____
  - Unsecured claim $ _____

Official Form 104   For Individual Chapter 11 Cases: List of Creditors Who Have the 20 Largest Unsecured Claims   29   page 2

Debtor 1 _____   Case number (if known) _____
     First Name   Middle Name   Last Name

		Unsecured claim

8

Creditor's name _____

What is the nature of the claim? _____ $ _____

As of the date you file, the claim is: Check all that apply.

Number   Street _____
- ☐ Contingent
- ☐ Unliquidated
- ☐ Disputed
- ☐ None of the above apply

City   State   ZIP Code

Does the creditor have a lien on your property?
- ☐ No
- ☐ Yes. Total claim (secured and unsecured): $ _____

Contact _____
    Value of security: – $ _____

Contact phone _____
    Unsecured claim $ _____

9

Creditor's name _____

What is the nature of the claim? _____ $ _____

As of the date you file, the claim is: Check all that apply.

Number   Street _____
- ☐ Contingent
- ☐ Unliquidated
- ☐ Disputed
- ☐ None of the above apply

City   State   ZIP Code

Does the creditor have a lien on your property?
- ☐ No
- ☐ Yes. Total claim (secured and unsecured): $ _____

Contact _____
    Value of security: – $ _____

Contact phone _____
    Unsecured claim $ _____

10

Creditor's name _____

What is the nature of the claim? _____ $ _____

As of the date you file, the claim is: Check all that apply.

Number   Street _____
- ☐ Contingent
- ☐ Unliquidated
- ☐ Disputed
- ☐ None of the above apply

City   State   ZIP Code

Does the creditor have a lien on your property?
- ☐ No
- ☐ Yes. Total claim (secured and unsecured): $ _____

Contact _____
    Value of security: – $ _____

Contact phone _____
    Unsecured claim $ _____

11

Creditor's name _____

What is the nature of the claim? _____ $ _____

As of the date you file, the claim is: Check all that apply.

Number   Street _____
- ☐ Contingent
- ☐ Unliquidated
- ☐ Disputed
- ☐ None of the above apply

City   State   ZIP Code

Does the creditor have a lien on your property?
- ☐ No
- ☐ Yes. Total claim (secured and unsecured): $ _____

Contact _____
    Value of security: – $ _____

Contact phone _____
    Unsecured claim $ _____

12

Creditor's name _____

What is the nature of the claim? _____ $ _____

As of the date you file, the claim is: Check all that apply.

Number   Street _____
- ☐ Contingent
- ☐ Unliquidated
- ☐ Disputed
- ☐ None of the above apply

City   State   ZIP Code

Does the creditor have a lien on your property?
- ☐ No
- ☐ Yes. Total claim (secured and unsecured): $ _____
    Value of security: – $ _____

Contact _____
    Unsecured claim $ _____

Contact phone _____

Form B104

OFFICIAL FORMS

Debtor 1 _____ _____ _____   Case number (if known) _____
        First Name   Middle Name   Last Name

		Unsecured claim

13

Creditor's name _____

Number   Street _____

_____

City   State   ZIP Code _____

Contact _____

Contact phone _____

What is the nature of the claim? _____ $_____

As of the date you file, the claim is: Check all that apply
- ☐ Contingent
- ☐ Unliquidated
- ☐ Disputed
- ☐ None of the above apply

Does the creditor have a lien on your property?
- ☐ No
- ☐ Yes. Total claim (secured and unsecured): $_____
  - Value of security: – $_____
  - Unsecured claim $_____

14

Creditor's name _____

Number   Street _____

_____

City   State   ZIP Code _____

Contact _____

Contact phone _____

What is the nature of the claim? _____ $_____

As of the date you file, the claim is: Check all that apply
- ☐ Contingent
- ☐ Unliquidated
- ☐ Disputed
- ☐ None of the above apply

Does the creditor have a lien on your property?
- ☐ No
- ☐ Yes. Total claim (secured and unsecured): $_____
  - Value of security: – $_____
  - Unsecured claim $_____

15

Creditor's name _____

Number   Street _____

_____

City   State   ZIP Code _____

Contact _____

Contact phone _____

What is the nature of the claim? _____ $_____

As of the date you file, the claim is: Check all that apply
- ☐ Contingent
- ☐ Unliquidated
- ☐ Disputed
- ☐ None of the above apply

Does the creditor have a lien on your property?
- ☐ No
- ☐ Yes. Total claim (secured and unsecured): $_____
  - Value of security: – $_____
  - Unsecured claim $_____

16

Creditor's name _____

Number   Street _____

_____

City   State   ZIP Code _____

Contact _____

Contact phone _____

What is the nature of the claim? _____ $_____

As of the date you file, the claim is: Check all that apply
- ☐ Contingent
- ☐ Unliquidated
- ☐ Disputed
- ☐ None of the above apply

Does the creditor have a lien on your property?
- ☐ No
- ☐ Yes. Total claim (secured and unsecured): $_____
  - Value of security: – $_____
  - Unsecured claim $_____

17

Creditor's name _____

Number   Street _____

_____

City   State   ZIP Code _____

Contact _____

Contact phone _____

What is the nature of the claim? _____ $_____

As of the date you file, the claim is: Check all that apply
- ☐ Contingent
- ☐ Unliquidated
- ☐ Disputed
- ☐ None of the above apply

Does the creditor have a lien on your property?
- ☐ No
- ☐ Yes. Total claim (secured and unsecured): $_____
  - Value of security: – $_____
  - Unsecured claim $_____

Official Form 104   For Individual Chapter 11 Cases: List of Creditors Who Have the 20 Largest Unsecured Claims   page 4

31

Debtor 1 _____ First Name   Middle Name   Last Name   Case number *(if known)* _____

Unsecured claim

18 _____

Creditor's Name _____

Number   Street _____

City   State   ZIP Code _____

Contact _____

Contact phone _____

What is the nature of the claim? _____ $_____

As of the date you file, the claim is: Check all that apply.
- ☐ Contingent
- ☐ Unliquidated
- ☐ Disputed
- ☐ None of the above apply

Does the creditor have a lien on your property?
- ☐ No
- ☐ Yes. Total claim (secured and unsecured): $_____
  - Value of security: − $_____
  - Unsecured claim $_____

19 _____

Creditor's Name _____

Number   Street _____

City   State   ZIP Code _____

Contact _____

Contact phone _____

What is the nature of the claim? _____ $_____

As of the date you file, the claim is: Check all that apply.
- ☐ Contingent
- ☐ Unliquidated
- ☐ Disputed
- ☐ None of the above apply

Does the creditor have a lien on your property?
- ☐ No
- ☐ Yes. Total claim (secured and unsecured): $_____
  - Value of security: − $_____
  - Unsecured claim $_____

20 _____

Creditor's Name _____

Number   Street _____

City   State   ZIP Code _____

Contact _____

Contact phone _____

What is the nature of the claim? _____ $_____

As of the date you file, the claim is: Check all that apply.
- ☐ Contingent
- ☐ Unliquidated
- ☐ Disputed
- ☐ None of the above apply

Does the creditor have a lien on your property?
- ☐ No
- ☐ Yes. Total claim (secured and unsecured): $_____
  - Value of security: − $_____
  - Unsecured claim $_____

Part 2:   Sign Below

Under penalty of perjury, I declare that the information provided in this form is true and correct.

X _____   **X** _____

Signature of Debtor 1   Signature of Debtor 2

Date _____   Date _____
    MM / DD / YYYY   MM / DD / YYYY

Official Form 104   For Individual Chapter 11 Cases: List of Creditors Who Have the 20 Largest Unsecured Claims   page 5

(Added Dec. 1, 2015.)

ADVISORY COMMITTEE NOTES

Official Form 104, *For Individual Chapter 11 Cases: List of Creditors Who Have the 20 Largest Unsecured Claims Against You and Are Not Insiders*, is revised as part of the Forms Modernization Project. It replaces Official Form 4, *List of Creditors Holding 20 Largest Unsecured Claims in chapter 11 cases filed by individuals or joint debtors*. The form is renumbered to distinguish it from the version to be used in chapter 11 cases filed by non-individuals, such as corporations and partnerships, and in chapter 9 cases.

Form 104 is reformatted to make it easier to complete and understand and to be more visually appealing. Blanks and checkboxes are provided for specific information about each claim, replacing columns for listing information. A separate, numbered section is provided for each of the 20 claims.

The instruction not to include fully secured claims is restated in less technical terms. Debtors are instructed to include a secured creditor only if the creditor has an unsecured claim resulting from inadequate collateral value that is among the 20 largest unsecured claims. Blanks are provided to calculate the value of the unsecured portion of a partially secured claim.

Examples of "insiders" are provided in addition to the statutory reference. The form adds an explicit instruction not to file the form in a chapter 7, chapter 12, or chapter 13 case. An instruction to be as complete and accurate as possible is added, along with a warning that, if two married people are filing jointly, both are equally responsible for supplying correct information.

With respect to children who may be creditors, the direction to state only the initials of a minor child and the name and address of the child's parent or guardian, rather than the child's full name, is moved to the general instruction booklet for the forms because it applies to all of the forms.

For Complete Annotation Materials, see United States Code Annotated

**Form B105. Involuntary Petition
Against an Individual**

☐ Check if this is an
    amended filing

Official Form 105

Involuntary Petition Against an Individual   12/15

Use this form to begin a bankruptcy case against an individual you allege to be a debtor subject to an involuntary case. If you want to begin a case against a non-individual, use the *Involuntary Petition Against a Non-Individual* (Official Form 205). Be as complete and accurate as possible. If more space is needed, attach a separate sheet to this form. On the top of any additional pages, write name and case number (if known).

Part 1:   Identify the Chapter of the Bankruptcy Code Under Which Petition Is Filed

1. Chapter of the   *Check one:*
   Bankruptcy Code
                              ☐ Chapter 7
                              ☐ Chapter 11

Part 2:   Identify the Debtor

2. Debtor's full name

   First name _____

   Middle name _____

   Last name _____

   Suffix (Sr., Jr., II, III) _____

3. Other names you know   _____
   the debtor has used in
   the last 8 years   _____

   Include any assumed,   _____
   married maiden, or trade
   names, or *doing business as*
   names.

4. Only the last 4 digits of   ☐ Unknown
   debtor's Social Security
   Number or federal
   Individual Taxpayer   XXX – XX – ___ ___ ___ ___   OR   9 xx – xx – ___ ___ ___ ___
   Identification Number
   (ITIN)

5. Any Employer   ☐ Unknown
   Identification Numbers
   (EINs) used in the last 8
   years   EIN ___ ___ – ___ ___ ___ ___ ___ ___

                               EIN ___ ___ – ___ ___ ___ ___ ___ ___

Official Form 105   Involuntary Petition Against an Individual   page 1

Debtor _____   Case number *if known* _____

6. Debtor's address	**Principal residence**	**Mailing address, if different from residence**
	Number Street	Number Street
	City State ZIP Code	City State ZIP Code
	County	
	Principal place of business	
	Number Street	
	City State ZIP Code	
	County	

7. Type of business

❑ Debtor does not operate a business

Check one if the debtor operates a business:

❑ Health Care Business (as defined in 11 U.S.C. § 101(27A))
❑ Single Asset Real Estate (as defined in 11 U.S.C. § 101(51B))
❑ Stockbroker (as defined in 11 U.S.C. § 101(53A))
❑ Commodity Broker (as defined in 11 U.S.C. § 101(6))
❑ None of the above

8. Type of debt

Each petitioner believes:

❑ Debts are primarily consumer debts. *Consumer debts are defined in 11 U.S.C. § 101(8) as "incurred by an individual primarily for a personal, family, or household purpose."*

❑ Debts are primarily business debts. *Business debts are debts that were incurred to obtain money for a business or investment or through the operation of the business or investment.*

9. Do you know of any bankruptcy cases pending by or against any partner, spouse, or affiliate of this debtor?

❑ No

❑ Yes   Debtor _____   Relationship _____

District _____ Date filed _____   Case number, if known _____
                                    MM / DD / YYYY

Debtor _____   Relationship _____

District _____ Date filed _____   Case number, if known _____
                                    MM / DD / YYYY

Official Form 105   Involuntary Petition Against an Individual   page 2

Debtor _____   Case number _____

Part 3:	Report About the Case

10. Venue

Reason for filing in this court.

Check one:

❑ Over the last 180 days before the filing of this bankruptcy, the debtor has resided, had the principal place of business, or had principal assets in this district longer than in any other district.

❑ A bankruptcy case concerning debtor's affiliates, general partner, or partnership is pending in this district.

❑ Other reason. Explain. (See 28 U.S.C. § 1408.) _____

---

11. Allegations

Each petitioner is eligible to file this petition under 11 U.S.C. § 303(b).

The debtor may be the subject of an involuntary case under 11 U.S.C. § 303(a).

At least one box must be checked:

❑ The debtor is generally not paying such debtor's debts as they become due, unless they are the subject of a bona fide dispute as to liability or amount.

❑ Within 120 days before the filing of this petition, a custodian, other than a trustee, receiver, or agent appointed or authorized to take charge of less than substantially all of the property of the debtor for the purpose of enforcing a lien against such property, was appointed or took possession.

---

12. Has there been a transfer of any claim against the debtor by or to any petitioner?

❑ No

❑ Yes. Attach all documents that evidence the transfer and any statements required under Bankruptcy Rule 1003(a).

---

13. Each petitioner's claim

Name of petitioner	Nature of petitioner's claim	Amount of the claim above the value of any lien
		$
		$
		$
	Total	$

If more than 3 petitioners, attach additional sheets with the statement under penalty of perjury, each petitioner's (or representative's) signature under the statement, along with the signature of the petitioner's attorney, and the information on the petitioning creditor, the petitioner's claim, the petitioner's representative, and the attorney following the format on this form.

Official Form 105   Involuntary Petition Against an Individual   page 3

Debtor _____   Case number _____

Part 4:   Request for Relief

Petitioners request that an order for relief be entered against the debtor under the chapter specified in Part 1 of this petition. If a petitioning creditor is a corporation, attach the corporate ownership statement required by Bankruptcy Rule 1010(b). If any petitioner is a foreign representative appointed in a foreign proceeding, a certified copy of the order of the court granting recognition is attached.

Petitioners declare under penalty of perjury that the information provided in this petition is true and correct. Petitioners understand that if they make a false statement, they could be fined up to $250,000 or imprisoned for up to 5 years, or both.
18 U.S.C. §§ 152 and 3571. If relief is not ordered, the court may award attorneys' fees, costs, damages, and punitive damages. 11 U.S.C. § 303(i).

Petitioners or Petitioners' Representative	Attorneys
✗ _____	✗ _____
Signature of petitioner or representative, including representative's title	Signature of attorney
_____	_____
Printed name of petitioner	Printed name
Date signed _____	_____
MM / DD / YYYY	Firm name, if any
	_____
Mailing address of petitioner	Number Street
	_____
_____	City State ZIP Code
Number Street	Date signed _____
_____	MM / DD / YYYY
City State ZIP Code	Contact phone _____ Email _____
If petitioner is an individual and is not represented by an attorney:	
Contact phone _____	
Email _____	
Name and mailing address of petitioner's representative, if any	
_____	
Name	
_____	
Number Street	
_____	
City State ZIP Code	

Official Form 105   Involuntary Petition Against an Individual   page 4

Debtor _____   Case number _if known_ _____

✗ _____
Signature of petitioner or representative, including representative's title

Printed name of petitioner _____

Date signed _____
     MM / DD /YYYY

Mailing address of petitioner

Number   Street _____

City _____ State _____ ZIP Code _____

Name and mailing address of petitioner's representative, if any

Name _____

Number   Street _____

City _____ State Z P Code _____

✗ _____
Signature of Attorney

Printed name _____

Firm name, if any _____

Number   Street _____

City _____ State _____ ZIP Code _____

Date signed _____
     MM / DD /YYYY

Contact phone _____ Email _____

✗ _____
Signature of petitioner or representative, including representative's title

Printed name of petitioner _____

Date signed _____
     MM / DD /YYYY

Mailing address of petitioner

Number   Street _____

City _____ State _____ ZIP Code _____

Name and mailing address of petitioner's representative, if any

Name _____

Number   Street _____

City _____ State Z P Code _____

✗ _____
Signature of Attorney

Printed name _____

Firm name, if any _____

Number   Street _____

City _____ State _____ ZIP Code _____

Date signed _____
     MM / DD /YYYY

Contact phone _____ Email _____

Official Form 105   Involuntary Petition Against an Individual   page 5

(Added Dec. 1, 2015.)

ADVISORY COMMITTEE NOTES

Official Form 105, _Involuntary Petition Against an Individual_, which is used only in cases of individual debtors, is revised in its entirety as part of the Forms Modernization Project, making it easier to read and, as a result, likely to generate more complete and accurate responses. In addition, the form is renumbered to distinguish it from the version to be used in non-individual cases, and stylistic changes were made throughout the form.

The form is derived from Official Form 5, _Involuntary Petition_. The new form separates questions into four parts likely to be more familiar to non-lawyers, groups questions of a similar nature together, and eliminates questions unrelated to individual debtors.

Part 1, _Identify the Chapter of the Bankruptcy Code Under Which Petition is Filed_, moves to the beginning of the form the question regarding the chapter of the Bankruptcy Code under which the petition is filed.

Part 2, _Identify the Debtor_, includes the questions regarding the debtor's name, prior names, Social Security Number, Individual Taxpayer Identification Number, and Employer Identification Number. Petitioners must list the address for the debtor's principal residence, mailing address (if different), and principal place of business. Petitioners must indicate whether the debtor operates a business, and, if so, use checkboxes to indicate whether the business falls into certain categories. The statutory definition of "consumer debts" is provided, as well as a definition of "business debts."

Part 3, _Report About the Case_, amends the question regarding venue to advise that venue is "the reason for filing in this court" and amends the choices for venue. The first option is revised to read: "Over the last 180 days before the filing of this bankruptcy, the debtor has resided, had the principal place of business, or had principal assets in this district longer than in any other district." Also, the form adds an option for "Other reason. Explain," with a statutory reference. In the question for Allegations, the exact citation to the Bankruptcy Code is provided for the second allegation, and checkboxes are provided for the last allegation. Petitioners must check "yes" or "no" to answer whether there has been a transfer of any claim against the debtor by or to a petitioner. The information regarding the petitioner's claims is moved to this part of the form, and the portion listing the amount of the claim is amended to ask about the amount of the claim that exceeds the value of the lien, if any.

Part 4, *Request for Relief*, amends the instructions to include a warning about making a false statement, and adds a separate requirement for each petitioner's mailing address. Also, petitioners' attorneys must provide their email addresses, or if a petitioner is an individual and not represented by an attorney, the contact phone and email address of that petitioner must be provided.

**Form B106Dec. Declaration About an
Individual Debtor's Schedules**

Fill in this information to identify your case:

Debtor 1 _____ _____ _____
      First Name   Middle Name   Last Name

Debtor 2 _____ _____ _____
(Spouse, if filing) First Name   Middle Name   Last Name

United States Bankruptcy Court for the: _____ District of _____
                                                     (State)

Case number _____
(If known)

☐ Check if this is an
   amended filing

Official Form 106Dec

Declaration About an Individual Debtor's Schedules   12/15

If two married people are filing together, both are equally responsible for supplying correct information.

You must file this form whenever you file bankruptcy schedules or amended schedules. Making a false statement, concealing property, or obtaining money or property by fraud in connection with a bankruptcy case can result in fines up to $250,000, or imprisonment for up to 20 years, or both. 18 U.S.C. §§ 152, 1341, 1519, and 3571.

Sign Below

Did you pay or agree to pay someone who is NOT an attorney to help you fill out bankruptcy forms?

☐ No

☐ Yes. Name of person_____ Attach Bankruptcy Petition Preparer's Notice, Declaration, and Signature (Official Form 119).

Under penalty of perjury, I declare that I have read the summary and schedules filed with this declaration and that they are true and correct.

✗ _____ ✗ _____
Signature of Debtor 1   Signature of Debtor 2

Date _____ Date _____
    MM / DD / YYYY   MM / DD / YYYY

Official Form 106Dec   Declaration About an Individual Debtor's Schedules   77

(Added Dec. 1, 2015.)

ADVISORY COMMITTEE NOTES

Official Form 106Dec, *Declaration About an Individual Debtor's Schedules*, replaces Official Form 6, *Declaration Concerning Debtor's Schedules*, in cases of individual debtors.

The form, which is to be signed by the debtor and filed with the debtor's schedules, deletes the Declaration and Signature of Bankruptcy Petition Preparer (BPP). Instead, the debtor is directed to complete and file Official Form 119, *Bankruptcy Petition Preparer's Notice, Declaration, and Signature*, if a BPP helped fill out the bankruptcy forms.

Because the form applies only to individual debtors, it no longer contains the Declaration Under Penalty of Perjury on Behalf of a Corporation or Partnership. It also deletes from the declaration the phrase "to the best of my knowledge, information, and belief" in order to conform to the language of 28 U.S.C. § 1746. See Rule 1008.

Form B106Sum.   A Summary of Your Assets and Liabilities and Certain Statistical Information (individuals)

Official Form 106Sum

Summary of Your Assets and Liabilities and Certain Statistical Information   12/15

Be as complete and accurate as possible. If two married people are filing together, both are equally responsible for supplying correct information. Fill out all of your schedules first; then complete the information on this form. If you are filing amended schedules after you file your original forms, you must fill out a new *Summary* and check the box at the top of this page.

Part 1: Summarize Your Assets

Your assets
Value of what you own

1. *Schedule A/B: Property* (Official Form 106A/B)

   1a. Copy line 55, Total real estate, from *Schedule A/B* .... $ _____

   1b. Copy line 62, Total personal property, from *Schedule A/B* .... $ _____

   1c. Copy line 63, Total of all property on *Schedule A/B* .... $ _____

Part 2: Summarize Your Liabilities

Your liabilities
Amount you owe

2. *Schedule D: Creditors Who Have Claims Secured by Property* (Official Form 106D)

   2a. Copy the total you listed in Column A, *Amount of claim* at the bottom of the last page of Part 1 of *Schedule D* .... $ _____

3. *Schedule E/F: Creditors Who Have Unsecured Claims* (Official Form 106E/F)

   3a. Copy the total claims from Part 1 (priority unsecured claims) from line 6e of *Schedule E/F* .... $ _____

   3b. Copy the total claims from Part 2 (nonpriority unsecured claims) from line 6j of *Schedule E/F* .... + $ _____

   Your total liabilities $ _____

Part 3: Summarize Your Income and Expenses

4. *Schedule I: Your Income* (Official Form 106I)

   Copy your combined monthly income from line 12 of *Schedule I* .... $ _____

5. *Schedule J: Your Expenses* (Official Form 106J)

   Copy your monthly expenses from line 22c of *Schedule J* .... $ _____

Form B106Sum   OFFICIAL FORMS

Debtor 1 _____ _____ _____   Case number (if known) _____

Part 4: Answer These Questions for Administrative and Statistical Records

6. Are you filing for bankruptcy under Chapters 7, 11, or 13?

☐ No. You have nothing to report on this part of the form. Check this box and submit this form to the court with your other schedules.
☐ Yes

7. What kind of debt do you have?

☐ Your debts are primarily consumer debts. *Consumer debts are those "incurred by an individual primarily for a personal family, or household purpose.* 11 U.S.C. § 101(8). Fill out lines 8-9g for statistical purposes. 28 U.S.C. § 159.

☐ Your debts are not primarily consumer debts. You have nothing to report on this part of the form. Check this box and submit this form to the court with your other schedules.

8. From the *Statement of Your Current Monthly Income:* Copy your total current monthly income from Official Form 122A-1 Line 11; OR, Form 122B Line 11; OR, Form 122C-1 Line 14. $ _____

9. Copy the following special categories of claims from Part 4, line 6 of *Schedule E/F:*

From Part 4 on *Schedule E/F,* copy the following:	Total claim
9a. Domestic support obligations (Copy line 6a.)	$ _____
9b. Taxes and certain other debts you owe the government. (Copy line 6b.)	$ _____
9c. Claims for death or personal injury while you were intoxicated. (Copy line 6c.)	$ _____
9d. Student loans. (Copy line 6f.)	$ _____
9e. Obligations arising out of a separation agreement or divorce that you did not report as priority claims. (Copy line 6g.)	$ _____
9f. Debts to pension or profit-sharing plans, and other similar debts. (Copy line 6h.)	+ $ _____
9g. Total. Add lines 9a through 9f.	$ _____

Official Form 106Sum   Summary of Your Assets and Liabilities and Certain Statistical Information   page 2 of 2
76

(Added Dec. 1, 2015.)

ADVISORY COMMITTEE NOTES

The schedules to be used in cases of individual debtors are revised as part of the Forms Modernization Project, making them easier to read and, as a result, likely to generate more complete and accurate responses. The goals of the Forms Modernization Project include improving the interface between technology and the forms so as to increase efficiency and reduce the need to produce the same information in multiple formats. Therefore, many of the open-ended questions and multiple-part instructions have been replaced with more specific questions. The individual debtor schedules are also renumbered, starting with the number 106 and followed by the letter or name of the schedule to distinguish them from the versions to be used in non-individual cases.

Official Form 106Sum, *Summary of Your Assets and Liabilities and Certain Statistical Information*, replaces Official Form 6, *Summary of Schedules and Statistical Summary of Certain Liability and Related Data (28 U.S.C. § 159)*, in cases of individual debtors.

The form is reformatted and updated with cross-references indicating the line numbers of specific schedules from which the summary information is to be gathered. In addition, because most filings are now done electronically, the form no longer requires the debtor to indicate which schedules are attached or to state the number of sheets of paper used for the schedules.

For Complete Annotation Materials, see United States Code Annotated

Form B106A/B. Schedule A/B: Property
(combines real and personal
property, individuals)

Fill in this information to identify your case and this filing:

Debtor 1 _____
First Name   Middle Name   Last Name

Debtor 2
(Spouse, if filing) First Name   Middle Name   Last Name

United States Bankruptcy Court for the: _____   District of _____
(State)

Case number _____

☐ Check if this is an
amended filing

Official Form 106A/B

Schedule A/B: Property   12/15

In each category, separately list and describe items. List an asset only once. If an asset fits in more than one category, list the asset in the category where you think it fits best. Be as complete and accurate as possible. If two married people are filing together, both are equally responsible for supplying correct information. If more space is needed, attach a separate sheet to this form. On the top of any additional pages, write your name and case number (if known). Answer every question.

Part 1:   Describe Each Residence, Building, Land, or Other Real Estate You Own or Have an Interest In

1. Do you own or have any legal or equitable interest in any residence, building, land, or similar property?

☐ No. Go to Part 2.
☐ Yes. Where is the property?

1.1. _____
Street address, if available, or other description

_____

_____
City   State   ZIP Code

_____
County

What is the property? Check all that apply
☐ Single-family home
☐ Duplex or multi-unit building
☐ Condominium or cooperative
☐ Manufactured or mobile home
☐ Land
☐ Investment property
☐ Timeshare
☐ Other _____

Who has an interest in the property? Check one.
☐ Debtor 1 only
☐ Debtor 2 only
☐ Debtor 1 and Debtor 2 only
☐ At least one of the debtors and another

Other information you wish to add about this item, such as local property identification number: _____

Do not deduct secured claims or exemptions. Put the amount of any secured claims on Schedule D: Creditors Who Have Claims Secured by Property.

Current value of the   Current value of the
entire property?   portion you own?

$_____ $_____

Describe the nature of your ownership interest (such as fee simple, tenancy by the entireties, or a life estate), if known.

_____

☐ Check if this is community property
(see instructions)

If you own or have more than one, list here:

1.2. _____
Street address, if available, or other description

_____

_____
City   State   ZIP Code

_____
County

What is the property? Check all that apply.
☐ Single-family home
☐ Duplex or multi-unit building
☐ Condominium or cooperative
☐ Manufactured or mobile home
☐ Land
☐ Investment property
☐ Timeshare
☐ Other _____

Who has an interest in the property? Check one.
☐ Debtor 1 only
☐ Debtor 2 only
☐ Debtor 1 and Debtor 2 only
☐ At least one of the debtors and another

Other information you wish to add about this item, such as local property identification number: _____

Do not deduct secured claims or exemptions. Put the amount of any secured claims on Schedule D: Creditors Who Have Claims Secured by Property.

Current value of the   Current value of the
entire property?   portion you own?

$_____ $_____

Describe the nature of your ownership interest (such as fee simple, tenancy by the entireties, or a life estate), if known.

_____

☐ Check if this is community property
(see instructions)

Official Form 106A/B   Schedule A/B: Property   42
                                                                            page 1

Form B106A/B

Debtor 1 _____
First Name   Middle Name   Last Name

Case number (if known) _____

1.3.	**What is the property?** Check all that apply.	Do not deduct secured claims or exemptions. Put the amount of any secured claims on *Schedule D: Creditors Who Have Claims Secured by Property.*

Street address, if available, or other description

☐ Single-family home
☐ Duplex or multi-unit building
☐ Condominium or cooperative
☐ Manufactured or mobile home
☐ Land
☐ Investment property
☐ Timeshare
☐ Other _____

Current value of the entire property?   **Current value of the portion you own?**

$_____ $_____

Describe the nature of your ownership interest (such as fee simple, tenancy by the entireties, or a life estate), if known.

_____

City   State   ZIP Code

Who has an interest in the property? Check one.

☐ Debtor 1 only
☐ Debtor 2 only
☐ Debtor 1 and Debtor 2 only
☐ At least one of the debtors and another

County

☐ Check if this is community property (see instructions)

Other information you wish to add about this item, such as local property identification number: _____

2. Add the dollar value of the portion you own for all of your entries from Part 1, including any entries for pages you have attached for Part 1. Write that number here. ➔ $_____

Part 2: Describe Your Vehicles

Do you own, lease, or have legal or equitable interest in any vehicles, whether they are registered or not? Include any vehicles you own that someone else drives. If you lease a vehicle, also report it on *Schedule G: Executory Contracts and Unexpired Leases.*

3. Cars, vans, trucks, tractors, sport utility vehicles, motorcycles

☐ No
☐ Yes

3.1. Make: _____
     Model: _____
     Year: _____
     Approximate mileage: _____
     Other information:

Who has an interest in the property? Check one.

☐ Debtor 1 only
☐ Debtor 2 only
☐ Debtor 1 and Debtor 2 only
☐ At least one of the debtors and another

☐ Check if this is community property (see instructions)

Do not deduct secured claims or exemptions. Put the amount of any secured claims on *Schedule D: Creditors Who Have Claims Secured by Property.*

Current value of the entire property?   **Current value of the portion you own?**

$_____ $_____

If you own or have more than one, describe here:

3.2. Make: _____
     Model: _____
     Year: _____
     Approximate mileage: _____
     Other information:

Who has an interest in the property? Check one.

☐ Debtor 1 only
☐ Debtor 2 only
☐ Debtor 1 and Debtor 2 only
☐ At least one of the debtors and another

☐ Check if this is community property (see instructions)

Do not deduct secured claims or exemptions. Put the amount of any secured claims on *Schedule D: Creditors Who Have Claims Secured by Property.*

Current value of the entire property?   **Current value of the portion you own?**

$_____ $_____

Official Form 106A/B   Schedule A/B: Property   43
                                                          page 2

Debtor 1 _____   Case number (if known) _____
          First Name   Middle Name   Last Name

3.3 Make: _____

Model: _____

Year: _____

Approximate mileage: _____

Other information:

[   ]

Who has an interest in the property? Check one.

☐ Debtor 1 only
☐ Debtor 2 only
☐ Debtor 1 and Debtor 2 only
☐ At least one of the debtors and another

☐ Check if this is community property (see instructions)

Do not deduct secured claims or exemptions. Put the amount of any secured claims on *Schedule D: Creditors Who Have Claims Secured by Property.*

Current value of the entire property?   Current value of the portion you own?

$_____ $_____

3.4 Make: _____

Model: _____

Year: _____

Approximate mileage: _____

Other information:

[   ]

Who has an interest in the property? Check one.

☐ Debtor 1 only
☐ Debtor 2 only
☐ Debtor 1 and Debtor 2 only
☐ At least one of the debtors and another

☐ Check if this is community property (see instructions)

Do not deduct secured claims or exemptions. Put the amount of any secured claims on *Schedule D: Creditors Who Have Claims Secured by Property.*

Current value of the entire property?   Current value of the portion you own?

$_____ $_____

4. Watercraft, aircraft, motor homes, ATVs and other recreational vehicles, other vehicles, and accessories

Examples: Boats, trailers, motors, personal watercraft, fishing vessels, snowmobiles, motorcycle accessories

☐ No
☐ Yes

4.1 Make: _____

Model: _____

Year: _____

Other information:

[   ]

Who has an interest in the property? Check one.

☐ Debtor 1 only
☐ Debtor 2 only
☐ Debtor 1 and Debtor 2 only
☐ At least one of the debtors and another

☐ Check if this is community property (see instructions)

Do not deduct secured claims or exemptions. Put the amount of any secured claims on *Schedule D: Creditors Who Have Claims Secured by Property.*

Current value of the entire property?   Current value of the portion you own?

$_____ $_____

If you own or have more than one, list here:

4.2 Make: _____

Model: _____

Year: _____

Other information:

[   ]

Who has an interest in the property? Check one.

☐ Debtor 1 only
☐ Debtor 2 only
☐ Debtor 1 and Debtor 2 only
☐ At least one of the debtors and another

☐ Check if this is community property (see instructions)

Do not deduct secured claims or exemptions. Put the amount of any secured claims on *Schedule D: Creditors Who Have Claims Secured by Property.*

Current value of the entire property?   Current value of the portion you own?

$_____ $_____

5. Add the dollar value of the portion you own for all of your entries from Part 2, including any entries for pages you have attached for Part 2. Write that number here ....➔ $[   ]

Form B106A/B

Debtor 1 _____ Case number (if known)_____

First Name   Middle Name   Last Name

Part 3: Describe Your Personal and Household Items

Do you own or have any legal or equitable interest in any of the following items?

Current value of the portion you own?
Do not deduct secured claims or exemptions.

6. Household goods and furnishings
   Examples: Major appliances, furniture, linens, china, kitchenware
   ☐ No
   ☐ Yes. Describe........ [_____] $_____

7. Electronics
   Examples: Televisions and radios; audio, video, stereo, and digital equipment; computers, printers, scanners; music collections; electronic devices including cell phones, cameras, media players, games
   ☐ No
   ☐ Yes. Describe........ [_____] $_____

8. Collectibles of value
   Examples: Antiques and figurines; paintings, prints, or other artwork; books, pictures, or other art objects; stamp, coin, or baseball card collections; other collections, memorabilia, collectibles
   ☐ No
   ☐ Yes. Describe........ [_____] $_____

9. Equipment for sports and hobbies
   Examples: Sports, photographic, exercise, and other hobby equipment; bicycles, pool tables, golf clubs, skis; canoes and kayaks; carpentry tools; musical instruments
   ☐ No
   ☐ Yes. Describe........ [_____] $_____

10. Firearms
   Examples: Pistols, rifles, shotguns, ammunition, and related equipment
   ☐ No
   ☐ Yes. Describe........ [_____] $_____

11. Clothes
   Examples: Everyday clothes, furs, leather coats, designer wear, shoes, accessories
   ☐ No
   ☐ Yes. Describe........ [_____] $_____

12. Jewelry
   Examples: Everyday jewelry, costume jewelry, engagement rings, wedding rings, heirloom jewelry, watches, gems, gold, silver
   ☐ No
   ☐ Yes. Describe........ [_____] $_____

13. Non-farm animals
   Examples: Dogs, cats, birds, horses
   ☐ No
   ☐ Yes. Describe........ [_____] $_____

14. Any other personal and household items you did not already list, including any health aids you did not list
   ☐ No
   ☐ Yes. Give specific information [_____] $_____

15. Add the dollar value of all of your entries from Part 3, including any entries for pages you have attached for Part 3. Write that number here ....→ $_____

Official Form 106A/B   Schedule A/B: Property   45 / page 4

For Complete Annotation Materials, see United States Code Annotated

736

Debtor 1 _____   Case number (if known) _____
    First Name   Middle Name   Last Name

Part 4:   **Describe Your Financial Assets**

Do you own or have any legal or equitable interest in any of the following?   **Current value of the portion you own?**
Do not deduct secured claims or exemptions.

16. Cash

Examples: Money you have in your wallet, in your home, in a safe deposit box, and on hand when you file your petition

☐ No
☐ Yes .... Cash: .... $ _____

17. Deposits of money

Examples: Checking, savings, or other financial accounts; certificates of deposit; shares in credit unions, brokerage houses, and other similar institutions. If you have multiple accounts with the same institution, list each.

☐ No
☐ Yes ....   Institution name:

17.1. Checking account:	_____	$ _____
17.2. Checking account:	_____	$ _____
17.3. Savings account:	_____	$ _____
17.4. Savings account:	_____	$ _____
17.5. Certificates of deposit:	_____	$ _____
17.6. Other financial account:	_____	$ _____
17.7. Other financial account:	_____	$ _____
17.8. Other financial account:	_____	$ _____
17.9. Other financial account:	_____	$ _____

18. Bonds, mutual funds, or publicly traded stocks

Examples: Bond funds, investment accounts with brokerage firms, money market accounts

☐ No
☐ Yes ....   Institution or issuer name:

       _____ $ _____
       _____ $ _____
       _____ $ _____

19. Non-publicly traded stock and interests in incorporated and unincorporated businesses, including an interest in an LLC, partnership, and joint venture

☐ No   Name of entity: % of ownership:
☐ Yes. Give specific information about them. ....

	_____	_____ %	$ _____
	_____	_____ %	$ _____
	_____	_____ %	$ _____

Official Form 106A/B   Schedule A/B: Property   46 / page 5

Form B106A/B   OFFICIAL FORMS

Debtor 1 _____   Case number _____

20. Government and corporate bonds and other negotiable and non-negotiable instruments

Negotiable instruments include personal checks, cashiers' checks, promissory notes, and money orders.
Non-negotiable instruments are those you cannot transfer to someone by signing or delivering them.

☐ No
☐ Yes. Give specific   Issuer name:
information about
them: ....   _____ $_____
                           _____ $_____
                           _____ $_____

21. Retirement or pension accounts
Examples: Interests in IRA, ERISA, Keogh, 401(k), 403(b), thrift savings accounts, or other pension or profit-sharing plans

☐ No
☐ Yes. List each
account separately.   Type of account: Institution name:

401(k) or similar plan: _____ $_____

Pension plan: _____ $_____

IRA: _____ $_____

Retirement account: _____ $_____

Keogh: _____ $_____

Additional account: _____ $_____

Additional account: _____ $_____

22. Security deposits and prepayments
Your share of all unused deposits you have made so that you may continue service or use from a company
Examples: Agreements with landlords, prepaid rent, public utilities (electric, gas, water), telecommunications
companies, or others

☐ No
☐ Yes ....   Institution name or individual:

Electric: _____ $_____

Gas: _____ $_____

Heating oil: _____ $_____

Security deposit on rental unit: _____ $_____

Prepaid rent: _____ $_____

Telephone: _____ $_____

Water: _____ $_____

Rented furniture: _____ $_____

Other: _____ $_____

23. Annuities (A contract for a periodic payment of money to you, either for life or for a number of years)

☐ No
☐ Yes ....   Issuer name and description:

                           _____ $_____
                           _____ $_____
                           _____ $_____

Official Form 106A/B   Schedule A/B: Property   47
                                                                            page 6

For Complete Annotation Materials, see United States Code Annotated

738

Debtor 1 _____   Case number *(if known)* _____
     First Name   Middle Name   Last Name

24. Interests in an education IRA, in an account in a qualified ABLE program, or under a qualified state tuition program.
26 U.S.C. §§ 530(b)(1), 529A(b), and 529(b)(1).

☐ No

☐ Yes _____   Institution name and description. Separately file the records of any interests.11 U.S.C. § 521(c):

	$
_____	$_____
_____	$_____
_____	$_____

25. Trusts, equitable or future interests in property (other than anything listed in line 1), and rights or powers exercisable for your benefit

☐ No

☐ Yes. Give specific information about them. | | $_____ |

26. Patents, copyrights, trademarks, trade secrets, and other intellectual property
Examples: Internet domain names, websites, proceeds from royalties and licensing agreements

☐ No

☐ Yes. Give specific information about them. | | $_____ |

27. Licenses, franchises, and other general intangibles
Examples: Building permits, exclusive licenses, cooperative association holdings, liquor licenses, professional licenses

☐ No

☐ Yes. Give specific information about them. | | $_____ |

Money or property owed to you?   **Current value of the portion you own?**
Do not deduct secured claims or exemptions.

28. Tax refunds owed to you

☐ No

☐ Yes. Give specific information about them, including whether you already filed the returns and the tax years. | | Federal: $_____ |
| | State: $_____ |
| | Local: $_____ |

29. Family support
Examples: Past due or lump sum alimony, spousal support, child support, maintenance, divorce settlement, property settlement

☐ No

☐ Yes. Give specific information.

	Alimony: $_____
	Maintenance: $_____
	Support: $_____
	Divorce settlement: $_____
	Property settlement: $_____

30. Other amounts someone owes you
Examples: Unpaid wages, disability insurance payments, disability benefits, sick pay, vacation pay, workers' compensation, Social Security benefits; unpaid loans you made to someone else

☐ No

☐ Yes. Give specific information. | | $_____ |

Debtor 1 _____ Case number (if known) _____
       First Name   Middle Name   Last Name

31. Interests in insurance policies

Examples: Health, disability, or life insurance; health savings account (HSA); credit, homeowner's, or renter's insurance

☐ No

☐ Yes. Name the insurance company   Company name: Beneficiary: Surrender or refund value:
       of each policy and list its value.

                                                                 $_____

                                                                 $_____

                                                                  $_____

32. Any interest in property that is due you from someone who has died

If you are the beneficiary of a living trust, expect proceeds from a life insurance policy, or are currently entitled to receive property because someone has died.

☐ No

☐ Yes. Give specific information............ $_____

33. Claims against third parties, whether or not you have filed a lawsuit or made a demand for payment

Examples: Accidents, employment disputes, insurance claims, or rights to sue

☐ No

☐ Yes. Describe each claim............ $_____

34. Other contingent and unliquidated claims of every nature, including counterclaims of the debtor and rights to set off claims

☐ No

☐ Yes. Describe each claim............ $_____

35. Any financial assets you did not already list

☐ No

☐ Yes. Give specific information.......... $_____

36. Add the dollar value of all of your entries from Part 4, including any entries for pages you have attached for Part 4. Write that number here .... → $_____

Part 5:   **Describe Any Business-Related Property You Own or Have an Interest In. List any real estate in Part 1.**

37. Do you own or have any legal or equitable interest in any business-related property?

☐ No. Go to Part 6.

☐ Yes. Go to line 38.

                                                      Current value of the portion you own?

                                                      Do not deduct secured claims or exemptions

38. Accounts receivable or commissions you already earned

☐ No

☐ Yes. Describe ..... $_____

39. Office equipment, furnishings, and supplies

Examples: Business-related computers, software, modems, printers, copiers, fax machines, rugs, telephones, desks, chairs, electronic devices

☐ No

☐ Yes. Describe...... $_____

Debtor 1 _____   Case number (if known) _____
First Name   Middle Name   Last Name

40. Machinery, fixtures, equipment, supplies you use in business, and tools of your trade

☐ No
☐ Yes. Describe..... [   ] $_____

41. Inventory

☐ No
☐ Yes. Describe..... [   ] $_____

42. Interests in partnerships or joint ventures

☐ No
☐ Yes. Describe.....   Name of entity: % of ownership:

_____   _____ % $_____
_____   _____ % $_____
_____   _____ % $_____

43. Customer lists, mailing lists, or other compilations

☐ No
☐ Yes. Do your lists include personally identifiable information (as defined in 11 U.S.C. § 101(41A))?

   ☐ No
   ☐ Yes. Describe..... [   ] $_____

44. Any business-related property you did not already list

☐ No
☐ Yes. Give specific   _____ $_____
   information ....   _____ $_____
             _____ $_____
             _____ $_____
             _____ $_____
             _____ $_____

45. Add the dollar value of all of your entries from Part 5, including any entries for pages you have attached
for Part 5. Write that number here .... → $_____

Part 6:   Describe Any Farm- and Commercial Fishing-Related Property You Own or Have an Interest In.
If you own or have an interest in farmland, list it in Part 1.

46. Do you own or have any legal or equitable interest in any farm- or commercial fishing-related property?

☐ No. Go to Part 7.
☐ Yes. Go to line 47.

Current value of the
portion you own?
Do not deduct secured claims
or exemptions.

47. Farm animals
Examples: Livestock, poultry, farm-raised fish

☐ No
☐ Yes..................... [   ] $_____

Debtor 1 _____ Case number (if known) _____

48. Crops—either growing or harvested

  ❏ No
  ❏ Yes. Give specific
    information......... $_____

49. Farm and fishing equipment, implements, machinery, fixtures, and tools of trade

  ❏ No
  ❏ Yes $_____

50. Farm and fishing supplies, chemicals, and feed

  ❏ No
  ❏ Yes $_____

51. Any farm- and commercial fishing-related property you did not already list

  ❏ No
  ❏ Yes. Give specific
    information......... $_____

52. Add the dollar value of all of your entries from Part 6, including any entries for pages you have attached
   for Part 6. Write that number here   ➔ $_____

Part 7:   Describe All Property You Own or Have an Interest in That You Did Not List Above

53. Do you have other property of any kind you did not already list?
  Examples: Season tickets, country club membership

  ❏ No
  ❏ Yes. Give specific
    information......... $_____
                                      $_____
                                      $_____

54. Add the dollar value of all of your entries from Part 7. Write that number here .... ➔ $_____

Part 8:   List the Totals of Each Part of this Form

55. Part 1: Total real estate, line 2 .... ➔ $_____

56. Part 2: Total vehicles, line 5 $_____

57. Part 3: Total personal and household items, line 15 $_____

58. Part 4: Total financial assets, line 36 $_____

59. Part 5: Total business-related property, line 45 $_____

60. Part 6: Total farm- and fishing-related property, line 52 $_____

61. Part 7: Total other property not listed, line 54   + $_____

62. Total personal property. Add lines 56 through 61. .... $_____   Copy personal property total ➔ + $_____

63. Total of all property on Schedule A/B. Add line 55 + line 62. .... $_____

(Added Dec. 1, 2015.)

ADVISORY COMMITTEE NOTES

Official Form 106A/B, *Schedule A/B: Property,* consolidates information about an individual debtor's real and personal property into a single form. It replaces Official Form 6A, *Real Property,* and Official Form 6B, *Personal Property,* in cases of individual debtors. In addition to specific questions about the assets, the form also includes open text fields for providing additional information regarding particular assets when appropriate.

The layout and categories of property on Official Form 106A/B have changed. Instead of dividing property interests into two categories (real or personal property), the new form uses seven categories likely to be more familiar to nonlawyers: real estate, vehicles, personal household items, financial assets, business-related property, farm- and commercial fishing-related property, and a catch-all category for property that was not listed elsewhere in the form. The new form categories and the examples provided in many of the categories are designed to prompt debtors to be thorough and list all of their interests in property. The debtor may describe generally items of minimal value (such as children's clothes) by adding the value of the items and reporting the total.

Although a particular item of property may fit into more than one category, the instructions for the form explain that it should be listed only once.

In addition, because property that falls within a particular category may not be specifically elicited by the particular line items on the form, the debtor is asked in Parts 3–6 (lines 14, 35, 44, and 51) to specifically identify and value any other property in the category.

In Part 1, *Describe Each Residence, Building, Land, or Other Real Estate You Own or Have an Interest In,* the debtor is asked to state the "current value of the portion you own," and to also state who has an interest in the property. In addition, the debtor is asked for the nature of the ownership interest, if known by the debtor. Furthermore, instead of asking for an open-ended description of the property, the form guides the debtor in answering the description question by providing eight options from which to choose: single-family home, duplex or multi-unit building, condominium or cooperative, manufactured or mobile home, land, investment property, timeshare, and other.

Part 2, *Describe Your Vehicles*, also guides the debtor in answering the question, asking for the make, model, year, and mileage of the car or other vehicle. Because mileage is just a general indication of vehicle value, the debtor is not required to list the exact mileage, but instead is prompted to provide the approximate mileage.

Part 3, *Describe Your Personal and Household Items*, simplifies wording, updates categories, and uses more common terms. For example, "Wearing apparel" is changed to "Clothes" and examples include furs, which were previously grouped with jewelry. Firearms, on the other hand, which were previously grouped with sports and other hobbies, are now set out as a separate category. Additionally, because a new Part 6 has been added to separately describe farm-related property, Part 3 includes a category for "Non-farm animals."

Part 4, *Describe Your Financial Assets*, prompts a listing of the debtor's financial assets through several questions providing separate space, after each listed type of account or deposit, for the institution or issuer name and the value of the debtor's interest in the asset. Two new categories of financial assets are added: "Bonds, mutual funds, or publicly traded stocks" and "Claims against third parties, whether or not you have filed a lawsuit or made a demand for payment." In

addition, qualified ABLE accounts, as defined in 26 U.S.C. § 529A(b), are added to the list of accounts in question 24. This change is made in response to the Tax Increase Prevention Act of 2014, Pub. Law No. 113–295, which excludes ABLE account contributions meeting the specified requirements from property of the estate.

Part 5, *Describe Any Business–Related Property You Own or Have an Interest In*, provides prompts for listing business-related property, such as accounts receivable, inventory, and machinery, and includes a direction to list business-related real estate in Part 1, to avoid listing real estate twice.

Part 6, *Describe Any Farm– and Commercial Fishing–Related Property You Own or Have an Interest In*, provides prompts for listing farm- or commercial fishing-related property, such as farm animals, crops, and feed. It also includes a direction to list any farm- or commercial fishing-related real estate in Part 1.

Part 7, *Describe All Property You Own or Have an Interest in That You Did Not List Above*, is a catch-all provision that allows the debtor to report property that is difficult to categorize.

Part 8, *List the Totals of Each Part of this Form*, tabulates the total value of the debtor's interest in the listed property. The tabulation includes two subtotals, one for real estate, which corresponds to the real property total that was reported on former Official Form 6A. The second subtotal is of Parts 2–7, which corresponds to the personal property total that was reported on former Official Form 6B.

Form B106C. Schedule C: The Property You Claim as Exempt (individuals)

Fill in this information to identify your case:

Debtor 1 _____ First Name _____ Middle Name _____ Last Name

Debtor 2
(Spouse, if filing) First Name _____ Middle Name _____ Last Name

United States Bankruptcy Court for the: _____ District of _____

Case number
(if known) _____

☐ Check if this is an amended filing

Official Form 106C

Schedule C: The Property You Claim as Exempt   04/16

Be as complete and accurate as possible. If two married people are filing together, both are equally responsible for supplying correct information. Using the property you listed on *Schedule A/B: Property* (Official Form 106A/B) as your source, list the property that you claim as exempt. If more space is needed, fill out and attach to this page as many copies of *Part 2: Additional Page* as necessary. On the top of any additional pages, write your name and case number (if known).

For each item of property you claim as exempt, you must specify the amount of the exemption you claim. One way of doing so is to state a specific dollar amount as exempt. Alternatively, you may claim the full fair market value of the property being exempted up to the amount of any applicable statutory limit. Some exemptions—such as those for health aids, rights to receive certain benefits, and tax-exempt retirement funds—may be unlimited in dollar amount. However, if you claim an exemption of 100% of fair market value under a law that limits the exemption to a particular dollar amount and the value of the property is determined to exceed that amount, your exemption would be limited to the applicable statutory amount.

Part 1:   Identify the Property You Claim as Exempt

1. **Which set of exemptions are you claiming?** *Check one only, even if your spouse is filing with you.*

   ☐ You are claiming state and federal nonbankruptcy exemptions. 11 U.S.C. § 522(b)(3)

   ☐ You are claiming federal exemptions. 11 U.S.C. § 522(b)(2)

2. **For any property you list on *Schedule A/B* that you claim as exempt, fill in the information below.**

Brief description of the property and line on *Schedule A/B* that lists this property	Current value of the portion you own	Amount of the exemption you claim	Specific laws that allow exemption
	Copy the value from *Schedule A/B*	*Check only one box for each exemption*	
Brief description: _____	$_____	☐ $_____	
Line from *Schedule A/B*: _____		☐ 100% of fair market value, up to any applicable statutory limit	_____
Brief description: _____	$_____	☐ $_____	
Line from *Schedule A/B*: _____		☐ 100% of fair market value, up to any applicable statutory limit	_____
Brief description: _____	$_____	☐ $_____	
Line from *Schedule A/B*: _____		☐ 100% of fair market value, up to any applicable statutory limit	_____

3. **Are you claiming a homestead exemption of more than $160,375?**

   (Subject to adjustment on 4/01/19 and every 3 years after that for cases filed on or after the date of adjustment.)

   ☐ No

   ☐ Yes. Did you acquire the property covered by the exemption within 1,215 days before you filed this case?

       ☐ No

       ☐ Yes

Official Form 106C   Schedule C: The Property You Claim as Exempt   page 1 of __

Debtor 1 _____   Case number _____
     First Name   Middle Name   Last Name

Part 2:   **Additional Page**

Brief description of the property and line on *Schedule A/B* that lists this property	Current value of the portion you own Copy the value from *Schedule A/B*	Amount of the exemption you claim *Check only one box for each exemption*	Specific laws that allow exemption
Brief description: _____ Line from *Schedule A/B*: ___	$_____	☐ $_____ ☐ 100% of fair market value, up to any applicable statutory limit	_____
Brief description: _____ Line from *Schedule A/B*: ___	$_____	☐ $_____ ☐ 100% of fair market value, up to any applicable statutory limit	_____
Brief description: _____ Line from *Schedule A/B*: ___	$_____	☐ $_____ ☐ 100% of fair market value, up to any applicable statutory limit	_____
Brief description: _____ Line from *Schedule A/B*: ___	$_____	☐ $_____ ☐ 100% of fair market value, up to any applicable statutory limit	_____
Brief description: _____ Line from *Schedule A/B*: ___	$_____	☐ $_____ ☐ 100% of fair market value, up to any applicable statutory limit	_____
Brief description: _____ Line from *Schedule A/B*: ___	$_____	☐ $_____ ☐ 100% of fair market value, up to any applicable statutory limit	_____
Brief description: _____ Line from *Schedule A/B*: ___	$_____	☐ $_____ ☐ 100% of fair market value, up to any applicable statutory limit	_____
Brief description: _____ Line from *Schedule A/B*: ___	$_____	☐ $_____ ☐ 100% of fair market value, up to any applicable statutory limit	_____
Brief description: _____ Line from *Schedule A/B*: ___	$_____	☐ $_____ ☐ 100% of fair market value, up to any applicable statutory limit	_____
Brief description: _____ Line from *Schedule A/B*: ___	$_____	☐ $_____ ☐ 100% of fair market value, up to any applicable statutory limit	_____
Brief description: _____ Line from *Schedule A/B*: ___	$_____	☐ $_____ ☐ 100% of fair market value, up to any applicable statutory limit	_____
Brief description: _____ Line from *Schedule A/B*: ___	$_____	☐ $_____ ☐ 100% of fair market value, up to any applicable statutory limit	_____

Official Form 106C   Schedule C: The Property You Claim as Exempt   page 2 of __

(Added Dec. 1, 2015; and amended Apr. 1, 2016.)

ADVISORY COMMITTEE NOTES

Official Form 106C, *Schedule C: The Property You Claim as Exempt*, replaces Official Form 6C, *Property Claimed as Exempt*, in cases of individual debtors.

Part 1, *Identify the Property You Claim as Exempt*, includes a table to list the property the debtor seeks to exempt, the value of the property owned by the debtor, the amount of the claimed exemption, and the law that allows the exemption. The first column asks for a brief description of the exempt property, and it also asks for the line number where the property is listed on Schedule A/B. The second column asks for the value of the portion of the asset owned by the debtor, rather than the entire asset. The third column asks for the amount, rather than the value, of the exemption claim.

The form has also been changed in light of the Supreme Court's ruling in *Schwab v. Reilly*, 560 U.S. 770 (2010). Entries in the "amount of the exemption you claim" column may now be listed as either a dollar limited amount or as 100% of fair market value, up to any applicable statutory limit. For example, a debtor might claim 100% of fair market value for a home covered by an exemption capped at $15,000, and that limit would be applicable. This choice would impose no dollar limit where the exemption is unlimited in dollar amount, such as some exemptions for health aids, certain governmental benefits, and tax-exempt retirement funds.

Form B106D. Schedule D: Creditors Who Hold Claims Secured by Property (against individuals)

Fill in this information to identify your case:

Debtor 1 _____ _____ _____
First Name · Middle Name · Last Name

Debtor 2 _____ _____ _____
(Spouse, if filing) First Name · Middle Name · Last Name

United States Bankruptcy Court for the: _____ District of _____
(State)

Case number _____
(If known)

☐ Check if this is an amended filing

Official Form 106D

Schedule D: Creditors Who Have Claims Secured by Property   12/15

Be as complete and accurate as possible. If two married people are filing together, both are equally responsible for supplying correct information. If more space is needed, copy the Additional Page, fill it out, number the entries, and attach it to this form. On the top of any additional pages, write your name and case number (if known).

1. Do any creditors have claims secured by your property?
   ☐ No. Check this box and submit this form to the court with your other schedules. You have nothing else to report on this form.
   ☐ Yes. Fill in all of the information below.

Part 1: List All Secured Claims

2. List all secured claims. If a creditor has more than one secured claim, list the creditor separately for each claim. If more than one creditor has a particular claim, list the other creditors in Part 2. As much as possible, list the claims in alphabetical order according to the creditor's name.

		Column A Amount of claim Do not deduct the value of collateral.	Column B Value of collateral that supports this claim	Column C Unsecured portion if any

2.1

Creditor's Name

Number   Street

_____

City   State   ZIP Code

Who owes the debt? Check one.
☐ Debtor 1 only
☐ Debtor 2 only
☐ Debtor 1 and Debtor 2 only
☐ At least one of the debtors and another

☐ Check if this claim relates to a community debt

Date debt was incurred _____

Describe the property that secures the claim: $_____ $_____ $_____

_____

As of the date you file, the claim is: Check all that apply.
☐ Contingent
☐ Unliquidated
☐ Disputed

Nature of lien. Check all that apply.
☐ An agreement you made (such as mortgage or secured car loan)
☐ Statutory lien (such as tax lien, mechanic's lien)
☐ Judgment lien from a lawsuit
☐ Other (including a right to offset) _____

Last 4 digits of account number __ __ __ __

2.2

Creditor's Name

Number   Street

_____

City   State   ZIP Code

Who owes the debt? Check one.
☐ Debtor 1 only
☐ Debtor 2 only
☐ Debtor 1 and Debtor 2 only
☐ At least one of the debtors and another

☐ Check if this claim relates to a community debt

Date debt was incurred _____

Describe the property that secures the claim: $_____ $_____ $_____

_____

As of the date you file, the claim is: Check all that apply.
☐ Contingent
☐ Unliquidated
☐ Disputed

Nature of lien. Check all that apply.
☐ An agreement you made (such as mortgage or secured car loan)
☐ Statutory lien (such as tax lien, mechanic's lien)
☐ Judgment lien from a lawsuit
☐ Other (including a right to offset) _____

Last 4 digits of account number __ __ __ __

Add the dollar value of your entries in Column A on this page. Write that number here: $_____

Official Form 106D   Schedule D: Creditors Who Have Claims Secured by Property   page 1 of ___

54

Debtor 1 _____   Case number _____

		Column A Amount of claim Do not deduct the value of collateral	Column B Value of collateral that supports this claim	Column C Unsecured portion if any
Part 1:	**Additional Page** After listing any entries on this page, number them beginning with 2.3, followed by 2.4, and so forth.			

☐

Creditor's Name

Number   Street

City   State   ZIP Code

Who owes the debt? Check one.
- ☐ Debtor 1 only
- ☐ Debtor 2 only
- ☐ Debtor 1 and Debtor 2 only
- ☐ At least one of the debtors and another

☐ Check if this claim relates to a community debt

Date debt was incurred _____

Describe the property that secures the claim: $_____ $_____ $_____

As of the date you file, the claim is: Check all that apply.
- ☐ Contingent
- ☐ Unliquidated
- ☐ Disputed

Nature of lien. Check all that apply.
- ☐ An agreement you made (such as mortgage or secured car loan)
- ☐ Statutory lien (such as tax lien, mechanic's lien)
- ☐ Judgment lien from a lawsuit
- ☐ Other (including a right to offset) _____

Last 4 digits of account number __ __ __ __

☐

Creditor's Name

Number   Street

City   State   ZIP Code

Who owes the debt? Check one.
- ☐ Debtor 1 only
- ☐ Debtor 2 only
- ☐ Debtor 1 and Debtor 2 only
- ☐ At least one of the debtors and another

☐ Check if this claim relates to a community debt

Date debt was incurred _____

Describe the property that secures the claim: $_____ $_____ $_____

As of the date you file, the claim is: Check all that apply.
- ☐ Contingent
- ☐ Unliquidated
- ☐ Disputed

Nature of lien. Check all that apply.
- ☐ An agreement you made (such as mortgage or secured car loan)
- ☐ Statutory lien (such as tax lien, mechanic's lien)
- ☐ Judgment lien from a lawsuit
- ☐ Other (including a right to offset) _____

Last 4 digits of account number __ __ __ __

☐

Creditor's Name

Number   Street

City   State   ZIP Code

Who owes the debt? Check one.
- ☐ Debtor 1 only
- ☐ Debtor 2 only
- ☐ Debtor 1 and Debtor 2 only
- ☐ At least one of the debtors and another

☐ Check if this claim relates to a community debt

Date debt was incurred _____

Describe the property that secures the claim: $_____ $_____ $_____

As of the date you file, the claim is: Check all that apply.
- ☐ Contingent
- ☐ Unliquidated
- ☐ Disputed

Nature of lien. Check all that apply.
- ☐ An agreement you made (such as mortgage or secured car loan)
- ☐ Statutory lien (such as tax lien, mechanic's lien)
- ☐ Judgment lien from a lawsuit
- ☐ Other (including a right to offset) _____

Last 4 digits of account number __ __ __ __

Add the dollar value of your entries in Column A on this page. Write that number here: $_____

If this is the last page of your form, add the dollar value totals from all pages. Write that number here: $_____

55

Debtor 1 _____ Case number (if known) _____
    First Name   Middle Name   Last Name

Part 2:   **List Others to Be Notified for a Debt That You Already Listed**

Use this page only if you have others to be notified about your bankruptcy for a debt that you already listed in Part 1. For example, if a collection agency is trying to collect from you for a debt you owe to someone else, list the creditor in Part 1, and then list the collection agency here. Similarly, if you have more than one creditor for any of the debts that you listed in Part 1, list the additional creditors here. If you do not have additional persons to be notified for any debts in Part 1, do not fill out or submit this page.

☐

Name _____

Number   Street

_____

City   State   ZIP Code

On which line in Part 1 did you enter the creditor? ____

Last 4 digits of account number __ __ __ __

☐

Name _____

Number   Street

_____

City   State   ZIP Code

On which line in Part 1 did you enter the creditor? ____

Last 4 digits of account number __ __ __ __

☐

Name _____

Number   Street

_____

City   State   ZIP Code

On which line in Part 1 did you enter the creditor? ____

Last 4 digits of account number __ __ __ __

☐

Name _____

Number   Street

_____

City   State   ZIP Code

On which line in Part 1 did you enter the creditor? ____

Last 4 digits of account number __ __ __ __

☐

Name _____

Number   Street

_____

City   State   ZIP Code

On which line in Part 1 did you enter the creditor?

Last 4 digits of account number __ __ __ __

☐

Name _____

Number   Street

_____

City   State   ZIP Code

On which line in Part 1 did you enter the creditor? ____

Last 4 digits of account number __ __ __ __

Official Form 106D   Part 2 of Schedule D: Creditors Who Have Claims Secured by Property   page ___ of ___

56

(Added Dec. 1, 2015.)

ADVISORY COMMITTEE NOTES

Official Form 106D, *Schedule D: Creditors Who Have Claims Secured by Property*, replaces Official Form 6D, *Creditors Holding Secured Claims*, in cases of individual debtors.

Part 1, *List All Secured Claims*, now directs the debtor to list only the last four digits of the account number. Part 1 also adds four checkboxes with which to describe the nature of the lien: an agreement the debtor made (such as mortgage or secured car loan); statutory lien (such as tax lien, mechanic's lien); judgment lien from a lawsuit; and other.

The form adds Part 2, *List Others to Be Notified for a Debt That You Already Listed*. The debtor is instructed to use Part 2 if there is a need to notify someone about the bankruptcy filing other than the creditor for a debt listed in Part 1. For example, if a collection agency is trying to collect for a creditor listed in Part 1, the collection agency would be listed in Part 2.

Form B106E/F. Schedule E/F: Creditors Who Have Unsecured Claims (against individuals, combines priority and non-priority)

Fill in this information to identify your case:

Debtor 1 _____
　　　　　First Name　　　　Middle Name　　　　Last Name

Debtor 2 _____
(Spouse, filing) First Name　Middle Name　　　Last Name

United States Bankruptcy Court for the: _____ District of _____
　　　　　　　　　　　　　　　　　　　　　　　　　　　(State)

Case number _____
(if known)

☐ Check if this is an amended filing

Official Form 106E/F

Schedule E/F: Creditors Who Have Unsecured Claims　　　12/15

Be as complete and accurate as possible. Use Part 1 for creditors with PRIORITY claims and Part 2 for creditors with NONPRIORITY claims. List the other party to any executory contracts or unexpired leases that could result in a claim. Also list executory contracts on *Schedule A/B: Property* (Official Form 106A/B) and on *Schedule G: Executory Contracts and Unexpired Leases* (Official Form 106G). Do not include any creditors with partially secured claims that are listed in *Schedule D: Creditors Who Have Claims Secured by Property.* If more space is needed, copy the Part you need, fill it out, number the entries in the boxes on the left. Attach the Continuation Page to this page. On the top of any additional pages, write your name and case number (if known).

Part 1:　List All of Your PRIORITY Unsecured Claims

1. Do any creditors have priority unsecured claims against you?
   ☐ No. Go to Part 2.
   ☐ Yes.

2. List all of your priority unsecured claims. If a creditor has more than one priority unsecured claim, list the creditor separately for each claim. For each claim listed, identify what type of claim it is. If a claim has both priority and nonpriority amounts, list that claim here and show both priority and nonpriority amounts. As much as possible, list the claims in alphabetical order according to the creditor's name. If you have more than two priority unsecured claims, fill out the Continuation Page of Part 1. If more than one creditor holds a particular claim, list the other creditors in Part 3.

   (For an explanation of each type of claim, see the instructions for this form in the instruction booklet.)

		Total claim	Priority amount	Nonpriority amount

2.1 _____
Priority Creditor's Name
_____
Number　　Street
_____
City　　　　State　　ZIP Code

Who incurred the debt? Check one.
☐ Debtor 1 only
☐ Debtor 2 only
☐ Debtor 1 and Debtor 2 only
☐ At least one of the debtors and another
☐ Check if this claim is for a community debt

Is the claim subject to offset?
☐ No
☐ Yes

Last 4 digits of account number ___ ___ ___ ___　$_____　$_____　$_____

When was the debt incurred? _____

As of the date you file, the claim is: Check all that apply
☐ Contingent
☐ Unliquidated
☐ Disputed

Type of PRIORITY unsecured claim:
☐ Domestic support obligations
☐ Taxes and certain other debts you owe the government
☐ Claims for death or personal injury while you were intoxicated
☐ Other. Specify _____

2.2 _____
Priority Creditor's Name
_____
Number　　Street
_____
City　　　　State　　ZIP Code

Who incurred the debt? Check one.
☐ Debtor 1 only
☐ Debtor 2 only
☐ Debtor 1 and Debtor 2 only
☐ At least one of the debtors and another
☐ Check if this claim is for a community debt

Is the claim subject to offset?
☐ No
☐ Yes

Last 4 digits of account number ___ ___ ___ ___　$_____　$_____　$_____

When was the debt incurred? _____

As of the date you file, the claim is: Check all that apply
☐ Contingent
☐ Unliquidated
☐ Disputed

Type of PRIORITY unsecured claim:
☐ Domestic support obligations
☐ Taxes and certain other debts you owe the government
☐ Claims for death or personal injury while you were intoxicated
☐ Other. Specify _____

Official Form 106E/F　　　　Schedule E/F: Creditors Who Have Unsecured Claims　　　　page 1 of ___

57

Debtor 1 _____ _____ _____
        First Name   Middle Name   Last Name

Case number _(if known)_ _____

Part 1: Your PRIORITY Unsecured Claims — Continuation Page

After listing any entries on this page, number them beginning with 2.3, followed by 2.4, and so forth.

		Total claim	Priority amount	Nonpriority amount

Entry 1

Priority Creditor's Name

Number   Street

City   State   ZIP Code

Who incurred the debt? Check one.
☐ Debtor 1 only
☐ Debtor 2 only
☐ Debtor 1 and Debtor 2 only
☐ At least one of the debtors and another
☐ Check if this claim is for a community debt

Is the claim subject to offset?
☐ No
☐ Yes

Last 4 digits of account number __ __ __ __ $_____ $_____ $_____

When was the debt incurred? _____

As of the date you file, the claim is: Check all that apply.
☐ Contingent
☐ Unliquidated
☐ Disputed

Type of PRIORITY unsecured claim:
☐ Domestic support obligations
☐ Taxes and certain other debts you owe the government
☐ Claims for death or personal injury while you were intoxicated
☐ Other. Specify _____

Entry 2

Priority Creditor's Name

Number   Street

City   State   ZIP Code

Who incurred the debt? Check one.
☐ Debtor 1 only
☐ Debtor 2 only
☐ Debtor 1 and Debtor 2 only
☐ At least one of the debtors and another
☐ Check if this claim is for a community debt

Is the claim subject to offset?
☐ No
☐ Yes

Last 4 digits of account number __ __ __ __ $_____ $_____ $_____

When was the debt incurred? _____

As of the date you file, the claim is: Check all that apply.
☐ Contingent
☐ Unliquidated
☐ Disputed

Type of PRIORITY unsecured claim:
☐ Domestic support obligations
☐ Taxes and certain other debts you owe the government
☐ Claims for death or personal injury while you were intoxicated
☐ Other. Specify _____

Entry 3

Priority Creditor's Name

Number   Street

City   State   ZIP Code

Who incurred the debt? Check one.
☐ Debtor 1 only
☐ Debtor 2 only
☐ Debtor 1 and Debtor 2 only
☐ At least one of the debtors and another
☐ Check if this claim is for a community debt

Is the claim subject to offset?
☐ No
☐ Yes

Last 4 digits of account number __ __ __ __ $_____ $_____ $_____

When was the debt incurred? _____

As of the date you file, the claim is: Check all that apply.
☐ Contingent
☐ Unliquidated
☐ Disputed

Type of PRIORITY unsecured claim:
☐ Domestic support obligations
☐ Taxes and certain other debts you owe the government
☐ Claims for death or personal injury while you were intoxicated
☐ Other. Specify _____

58

Official Form 106E/F   Schedule E/F: Creditors Who Have Unsecured Claims   page __ of __

Debtor 1 _____   Case number _____
      First Name   Middle Name   Last Name

Part 2:   List All of Your NONPRIORITY Unsecured Claims

3. **Do any creditors have nonpriority unsecured claims against you?**

☐ No. You have nothing to report in this part. Submit this form to the court with your other schedules.
☐ Yes

4. **List all of your nonpriority unsecured claims in the alphabetical order of the creditor who holds each claim.** If a creditor has more than one nonpriority unsecured claim, list the creditor separately for each claim. For each claim listed, identify what type of claim it is. Do not list claims already included in Part 1. If more than one creditor holds a particular claim, list the other creditors in Part 3. If you have more than three nonpriority unsecured claims fill out the Continuation Page of Part 2.

		Total claim

4.1

Nonpriority Creditor's Name

Number   Street

City   State   ZIP Code

Who incurred the debt? Check one.
☐ Debtor 1 only
☐ Debtor 2 only
☐ Debtor 1 and Debtor 2 only
☐ At least one of the debtors and another

☐ Check if this claim is for a community debt

Is the claim subject to offset?
☐ No
☐ Yes

Last 4 digits of account number __ __ __ __ $_____

When was the debt incurred? _____

As of the date you file, the claim is: Check all that apply.
☐ Contingent
☐ Unliquidated
☐ Disputed

Type of NONPRIORITY unsecured claim:
☐ Student loans
☐ Obligations arising out of a separation agreement or divorce that you did not report as priority claims
☐ Debts to pension or profit-sharing plans, and other similar debts
☐ Other. Specify _____

4.2

Nonpriority Creditor's Name

Number   Street

City   State   ZIP Code

Who incurred the debt? Check one.
☐ Debtor 1 only
☐ Debtor 2 only
☐ Debtor 1 and Debtor 2 only
☐ At least one of the debtors and another

☐ Check if this claim is for a community debt

Is the claim subject to offset?
☐ No
☐ Yes

Last 4 digits of account number __ __ __ __ $_____

When was the debt incurred? _____

As of the date you file, the claim is: Check all that apply.
☐ Contingent
☐ Unliquidated
☐ Disputed

Type of NONPRIORITY unsecured claim:
☐ Student loans
☐ Obligations arising out of a separation agreement or divorce that you did not report as priority claims
☐ Debts to pension or profit-sharing plans, and other similar debts
☐ Other. Specify _____

4.3

Nonpriority Creditor's Name

Number   Street

City   State   ZIP Code

Who incurred the debt? Check one.
☐ Debtor 1 only
☐ Debtor 2 only
☐ Debtor 1 and Debtor 2 only
☐ At least one of the debtors and another

☐ Check if this claim is for a community debt

Is the claim subject to offset?
☐ No
☐ Yes

Last 4 digits of account number __ __ __ __ $_____

When was the debt incurred? _____

As of the date you file, the claim is: Check all that apply.
☐ Contingent
☐ Unliquidated
☐ Disputed

Type of NONPRIORITY unsecured claim:
☐ Student loans
☐ Obligations arising out of a separation agreement or divorce that you did not report as priority claims
☐ Debts to pension or profit-sharing plans, and other similar debts
☐ Other. Specify _____

59

Official Form 106E/F   Schedule E/F: Creditors Who Have Unsecured Claims   page __ of __

Form B106E/F

Debtor 1 _____ Case number _____

Part 2:   Your NONPRIORITY Unsecured Claims   Continuation Page

After listing any entries on this page, number them beginning with 4.5, followed by 4.6, and so forth.

Total claim

___

Nonpriority Creditor's Name _____

Number   Street _____

City   State   ZIP Code

Who incurred the debt? Check one.

☐ Debtor 1 only
☐ Debtor 2 only
☐ Debtor 1 and Debtor 2 only
☐ At least one of the debtors and another

☐ Check if this claim is for a community debt

Is the claim subject to offset?

☐ No
☐ Yes

Last 4 digits of account number __ __ __ __ $_____

When was the debt incurred? _____

As of the date you file, the claim is: Check all that apply.

☐ Contingent
☐ Unliquidated
☐ Disputed

Type of NONPRIORITY unsecured claim:

☐ Student loans
☐ Obligations arising out of a separation agreement or divorce that you did not report as priority claims
☐ Debts to pension or profit-sharing plans, and other similar debts
☐ Other. Specify_____

___

Nonpriority Creditor's Name _____

Number   Street _____

City   State   ZIP Code

Who incurred the debt? Check one.

☐ Debtor 1 only
☐ Debtor 2 only
☐ Debtor 1 and Debtor 2 only
☐ At least one of the debtors and another

☐ Check if this claim is for a community debt

Is the claim subject to offset?

☐ No
☐ Yes

Last 4 digits of account number __ __ __ __ $_____

When was the debt incurred? _____

As of the date you file, the claim is: Check all that apply.

☐ Contingent
☐ Unliquidated
☐ Disputed

Type of NONPRIORITY unsecured claim:

☐ Student loans
☐ Obligations arising out of a separation agreement or divorce that you did not report as priority claims
☐ Debts to pension or profit-sharing plans, and other similar debts
☐ Other. Specify_____

___

Nonpriority Creditor's Name _____

Number   Street _____

City   State   ZIP Code

Who incurred the debt? Check one.

☐ Debtor 1 only
☐ Debtor 2 only
☐ Debtor 1 and Debtor 2 only
☐ At least one of the debtors and another

☐ Check if this claim is for a community debt

Is the claim subject to offset?

☐ No
☐ Yes

Last 4 digits of account number __ __ __ __ $_____

When was the debt incurred? _____

As of the date you file, the claim is: Check all that apply.

☐ Contingent
☐ Unliquidated
☐ Disputed

Type of NONPRIORITY unsecured claim:

☐ Student loans
☐ Obligations arising out of a separation agreement or divorce that you did not report as priority claims
☐ Debts to pension or profit-sharing plans, and other similar debts
☐ Other. Specify_____

60

Official Form 106E/F   Schedule E/F: Creditors Who Have Unsecured Claims   page __ of __

Debtor 1 _____   Case number _____
First Name   Middle Name   Last Name

Part 3:   List Others to Be Notified About a Debt That You Already Listed

6. Use this page only if you have others to be notified about your bankruptcy, for a debt that you already listed in Parts 1 or 2. For example, if a collection agency is trying to collect from you for a debt you owe to someone else, list the original creditor in Parts 1 or 2, then list the collection agency here. Similarly, if you have more than one creditor for any of the debts that you listed in Parts 1 or 2, list the additional creditors here. If you do not have additional persons to be notified for any debts in Parts 1 or 2, do not fill out or submit this page.

_____
Name

_____
Number   Street

_____

_____
City   State   ZIP Code

On which entry in Part 1 or Part 2 did you list the original creditor?

Line _____ of (Check one): ❑ Part 1: Creditors with Priority Unsecured Claims
                             ❑ Part 2: Creditors with Nonpriority Unsecured Claims

Last 4 digits of account number __ __ __ __

_____
Name

_____
Number   Street

_____

_____
City   State   ZIP Code

On which entry in Part 1 or Part 2 did you list the original creditor?

Line _____ of (Check one): ❑ Part 1: Creditors with Priority Unsecured Claims
                             ❑ Part 2: Creditors with Nonpriority Unsecured Claims

Last 4 digits of account number __ __ __ __

_____
Name

_____
Number   Street

_____

_____
City   State   ZIP Code

On which entry in Part 1 or Part 2 did you list the original creditor?

Line _____ of (Check one): ❑ Part 1: Creditors with Priority Unsecured Claims
                             ❑ Part 2: Creditors with Nonpriority Unsecured Claims

Last 4 digits of account number

_____
Name

_____
Number   Street

_____

_____
City   State   ZIP Code

On which entry in Part 1 or Part 2 did you list the original creditor?

Line _____ of (Check one): ❑ Part 1: Creditors with Priority Unsecured Claims
                             ❑ Part 2: Creditors with Nonpriority Unsecured Claims

Last 4 digits of account number __ __ __ __

_____
Name

_____
Number   Street

_____

_____
City   State   ZIP Code

On which entry in Part 1 or Part 2 did you list the original creditor?

Line _____ of (Check one): ❑ Part 1: Creditors with Priority Unsecured Claims
                             ❑ Part 2: Creditors with Nonpriority Unsecured Claims

Last 4 digits of account number __ __ __ __

_____
Name

_____
Number   Street

_____

_____
City   State   ZIP Code

On which entry in Part 1 or Part 2 did you list the original creditor?

Line _____ of (Check one): ❑ Part 1: Creditors with Priority Unsecured Claims
                             ❑ Part 2: Creditors with Nonpriority Unsecured Claims

Last 4 digits of account number __ __ __ __

_____
Name

_____
Number   Street

_____

_____
City   State   ZIP Code

On which entry in Part 1 or Part 2 did you list the original creditor?

Line _____ of (Check one): ❑ Part 1: Creditors with Priority Unsecured Claims
                             ❑ Part 2: Creditors with Nonpriority Unsecured Claims

Last 4 digits of account number __ __ __ __

61

Official Form 106E/F   Schedule E/F: Creditors Who Have Unsecured Claims   page __ of __

Debtor 1 _____ Case number _____
     First Name   Middle Name   Last Name

Part 4:   **Add the Amounts for Each Type of Unsecured Claim**

6. Total the amounts of certain types of unsecured claims. This information is for statistical reporting purposes only. 28 U.S.C. § 159.
   Add the amounts for each type of unsecured claim.

			Total claim
Total claims from Part 1	6a. Domestic support obligations	6a.	$ _____
	6b. Taxes and certain other debts you owe the government	6b.	$ _____
	6c. Claims for death or personal injury while you were intoxicated	6c.	$ _____
	6d. Other. Add all other priority unsecured claims. Write that amount here.	6d. +	$ _____
	6e. Total. Add lines 6a through 6d.	6e.	$ _____

			Total claim
Total claims from Part 2	6f. Student loans	6f.	$ _____
	6g. Obligations arising out of a separation agreement or divorce that you did not report as priority claims	6g.	$ _____
	6h. Debts to pension or profit-sharing plans, and other similar debts	6h.	$ _____
	6i. Other. Add all other nonpriority unsecured claims. Write that amount here.	6i. +	$ _____
	6j. Total. Add lines 6f through 6i.	6j.	$ _____

(Added Dec. 1, 2015.)

ADVISORY COMMITTEE NOTES

Official Form 106E/F, *Schedule E/F: Creditors Who Have Unsecured Claims*, consolidates information about priority and nonpriority unsecured claims into a single form. It replaces Official Form 6E, *Creditors Holding Unsecured Priority Claims*, and Official Form 6F, *Creditors Holding Unsecured Nonpriority Claims*, in cases of individual debtors.

Although both priority and nonpriority unsecured claims are reported in Official Form 106E/F, the two types of claims are separately grouped so that the total for each type can be reported for case administration and statistical purposes. The form eliminates the question "consideration for claim" and instructs debtors to list claims in the alphabetical order of creditors as much as possible.

Part 1, *List All of Your PRIORITY Unsecured Claims*, includes four checkboxes for identifying the type of priority that applies to the claim: domestic support obligations; taxes and certain other debts owed to the government; claims for death or personal injury while intoxicated; and "other." The first three categories are required to be separately reported for statistical purposes. If the debtor selects "other," the debtor must specify the basis of the priority, *e.g.*, wages or employee benefit plan contribution.

Part 2, *List All of Your NONPRIORITY Unsecured Claims*, contains four checkboxes, including three for types of claims that must be separately reported for statistical purposes: student loans; obligations arising out of a separation agreement or divorce not listed as priority claims; and debts to pension or profit-sharing plans and other similar debts. The remaining "other" checkbox treats claims not subject to separate reporting. If the debtor selects "other," the debtor must specify the basis of the claim.

Part 3, *List Others to Be Notified About a Debt That You Already Listed*, is new. The debtor is instructed to use Part 3 only if there is a need to give notice of the bankruptcy to someone other than a creditor listed in Parts 1 and 2. For example, if a collection agency is trying to collect for a creditor listed in Part 1, the collection agency would be listed in Part 3.

Finally, Part 4, *Add the Amounts for Each Type of Unsecured Claim*, requires the debtor to provide the total amounts of particular types of unsecured claims for statistical reporting purposes and the overall totals of the priority and nonpriority unsecured claims reported in this form.

Form B106G

Form B106G. Schedule G: Executory Contracts and Unexpired Leases (individuals)

Fill in this information to identify your case:

Debtor _____
First Name   Middle Name   Last Name

Debtor 2 _____
(Spouse if filing) First Name   Middle Name   Last Name

United States Bankruptcy Court for the: _____ District of _____
(State)

Case number _____
(If known)

☐ Check if this is an amended filing

Official Form 106G

Schedule G: Executory Contracts and Unexpired Leases

12/15

Be as complete and accurate as possible. If two married people are filing together, both are equally responsible for supplying correct information. If more space is needed, copy the additional page, fill it out, number the entries, and attach it to this page. On the top of any additional pages, write your name and case number (if known).

1. Do you have any executory contracts or unexpired leases?
    ☐ No. Check this box and file this form with the court with your other schedules. You have nothing else to report on this form.
    ☐ Yes. Fill in all of the information below even if the contracts or leases are listed on *Schedule A/B: Property* (Official Form 106A/B).

2. List separately each person or company with whom you have the contract or lease. Then state what each contract or lease is for (for example, rent, vehicle lease, cell phone). See the instructions for this form in the instruction booklet for more examples of executory contracts and unexpired leases.

Person or company with whom you have the contract or lease	State what the contract or lease is for
2.1 Name	
Number Street	
City State ZIP Code	
2.2 Name	
Number Street	
City State ZIP Code	
2.3 Name	
Number Street	
City State ZIP Code	
2.4 Name	
Number Street	
City State ZIP Code	
2.5 Name	
Number Street	
City State ZIP Code	

63

Official Form 106G   Schedule G: Executory Contracts and Unexpired Leases   page 1 of ___

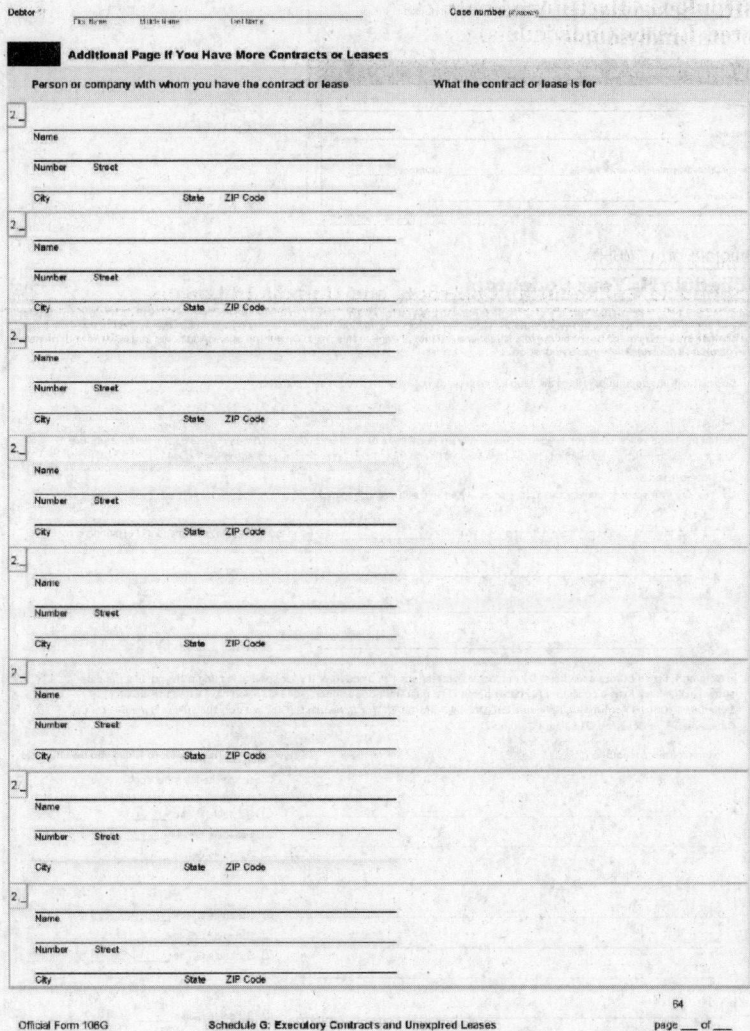

Debtor _____   Case number (if known)_____
        First Name   Middle Name   Last Name

Additional Page If You Have More Contracts or Leases

Person or company with whom you have the contract or lease	What the contract or lease is for

2.__

Name

Number   Street

City   State   ZIP Code

2.__

Name

Number   Street

City   State   ZIP Code

2.__

Name

Number   Street

City   State   ZIP Code

2.__

Name

Number   Street

City   State   ZIP Code

2.__

Name

Number   Street

City   State   ZIP Code

2.__

Name

Number   Street

City   State   ZIP Code

2.__

Name

Number   Street

City   State   ZIP Code

2.__

Name

Number   Street

City   State   ZIP Code

Official Form 106G   Schedule G: Executory Contracts and Unexpired Leases   page ___ of ___

(Added Dec. 1, 2015.)

ADVISORY COMMITTEE NOTES

Official Form 106G, *Schedule G: Executory Contracts and Unexpired Leases,* replaces Official Form 6G, *Executory Contracts and Unexpired Leases,* in cases of individual debtors.

The form is simplified. Instead of requiring the debtor to make multiple assertions about each potential executory contract or unexpired lease, the form simply requires the debtor to identify the name and address of the other party to the contract or lease, and to state what the contract or lease deals with. Definitions and examples of executory contracts and unexpired leases are included in the separate instructions for the form.

An additional page is provided in case the debtor has so many executory contracts and unexpired leases that the available page is not adequate. If the debtor needs to use the additional page, the debtor is required to fill in the entry number.

Form B106H. Schedule H: Your Codebtors (individuals)

Fill in this information to identify your case:

Debtor 1 _____
          First Name   Middle Name   Last Name

Debtor 2 _____
(Spouse if filing) First Name   Middle Name   Last Name

United States Bankruptcy Court for the: _____ District of _____
                                                                     (State)

Case number _____
(if known)

☐ Check if this is an amended filing

Official Form 106H

Schedule H: Your Codebtors   12/15

Codebtors are people or entities who are also liable for any debts you may have. Be as complete and accurate as possible. If two married people are filing together, both are equally responsible for supplying correct information. If more space is needed, copy the Additional Page, fill it out, and number the entries in the boxes on the left. Attach the Additional Page to this page. On the top of any Additional Pages, write your name and case number (if known). Answer every question.

1. Do you have any codebtors? (If you are filing a joint case, do not list either spouse as a codebtor.)

   ☐ No

   ☐ Yes

2. Within the last 8 years, have you lived in a community property state or territory? (*Community property states and territories include* Arizona, California, Idaho, Louisiana, Nevada, New Mexico, Puerto Rico, Texas, Washington, and Wisconsin.)

   ☐ No. Go to line 3

   ☐ Yes. Did your spouse, former spouse, or legal equivalent live with you at the time?

      ☐ No

      ☐ Yes. In which community state or territory did you live? _____ Fill in the name and current address of that person.

       _____
       Name of your spouse, former spouse, or legal equivalent

       Number   Street

       City   State   ZIP Code

3. In Column 1, list all of your codebtors. Do not include your spouse as a codebtor if your spouse is filing with you. List the person shown in line 2 again as a codebtor only if that person is a guarantor or cosigner. Make sure you have listed the creditor on *Schedule D* (Official Form 106D), *Schedule E/F* (Official Form 106E/F), or *Schedule G* (Official Form 106G). Use *Schedule D, Schedule E/F, or Schedule G* to fill out Column 2.

Column 1: Your codebtor	Column 2: The creditor to whom you owe the debt
	Check all schedules that apply:
3.1 Name _____	☐ Schedule D, line _____
Number Street	☐ Schedule E/F, line _____
City State ZIP Code	☐ Schedule G, line _____
3.2 Name _____	☐ Schedule D, line _____
Number Street	☐ Schedule E/F, line _____
City State ZIP Code	☐ Schedule G, line _____
3.3 Name _____	☐ Schedule D, line _____
Number Street	☐ Schedule E/F, line _____
City State ZIP Code	☐ Schedule G, line _____

65

Official Form 106H   Schedule H: Your Codebtors   page 1 of __

Debtor 1 _____   Case number _____
          First Name   Middle Name   Last Name

Additional Page to List More Codebtors

Column 1: Your codebtor	Column 2. The creditor to whom you owe the debt
	Check all schedules that apply:

Name _____
- ☐ Schedule D, line _____
- ☐ Schedule E/F, line _____
- ☐ Schedule G, line _____

Number   Street _____

City _____ **State** _____ **ZIP Code** _____

Name _____
- ☐ Schedule D, line _____
- ☐ Schedule E/F, line _____
- ☐ Schedule G, line _____

Number   Street _____

City _____ **State** _____ **ZIP Code** _____

Name _____
- ☐ Schedule D, line _____
- ☐ Schedule E/F, line _____
- ☐ Schedule G, line _____

Number   Street _____

City _____ **State** _____ **ZIP Code** _____

Name _____
- ☐ Schedule D, line _____
- ☐ Schedule E/F, line _____
- ☐ Schedule G, line _____

Number   Street _____

City _____ **State** _____ **ZIP Code** _____

Name _____
- ☐ Schedule D, line _____
- ☐ Schedule E/F, line _____
- ☐ Schedule G, line _____

Number   Street _____

City _____ **State** _____ **ZIP Code** _____

Name _____
- ☐ Schedule D, line _____
- ☐ Schedule E/F, line _____
- ☐ Schedule G, line _____

Number   Street _____

City _____ **State** _____ **ZIP Code** _____

Name _____
- ☐ Schedule D, line _____
- ☐ Schedule E/F, line _____
- ☐ Schedule G, line _____

Number   Street _____

City _____ **State** _____ **ZIP Code** _____

Name _____
- ☐ Schedule D, line _____
- ☐ Schedule E/F, line _____
- ☐ Schedule G, line _____

Number   Street _____

City _____ **State** _____ **ZIP Code** _____

Official Form 106H   Schedule H: Your Codebtors   page ___ of ___

(Added Dec. 1, 2015.)

ADVISORY COMMITTEE NOTES

Official Form 106H, *Schedule H: Your Codebtors*, replaces Official Form 6H, *Codebtors*, in cases of individual debtors.

The form breaks out the questions about whether there are any codebtors, and whether the debtor has lived with a spouse, former spouse, or legal equivalent in a community property state in the prior eight years. It also removes Alaska from the listed community property states. Finally, it asks the debtor to indicate where the debt is listed on Schedule D, Schedule E/F, or Schedule G, thereby eliminating the need to list the name and address of the creditor.

Form B106I   OFFICIAL FORMS

Form B106I. Schedule I: Your
  Income (individuals)

Fill in this information to identify your case:

Debtor 1 _____
              First Name   Middle Name   Last Name

Debtor 2 _____
(Spouse, if filing) First Name   Middle Name   Last Name

United States Bankruptcy Court for the: _____ District of _____
                                                                    (State)

Case number _____
  (If known)

Check if this is:
☐ An amended filing
☐ A supplement showing postpetition chapter 13
   income as of the following date:
   _____
   MM / DD / YYYY

Official Form 106I

Schedule I: Your Income   12/15

Be as complete and accurate as possible. If two married people are filing together (Debtor 1 and Debtor 2), both are equally responsible for supplying correct information. If you are married and not filing jointly, and your spouse is living with you, include information about your spouse. If you are separated and your spouse is not filing with you, do not include information about your spouse. If more space is needed, attach a separate sheet to this form. On the top of any additional pages, write your name and case number (if known). Answer every question.

Part 1:   Describe Employment

1. Fill in your employment information.		Debtor 1	Debtor 2 or non-filing spouse
If you have more than one job, attach a separate page with information about additional employers. Include part-time, seasonal, or self-employed work. Occupation may include student or homemaker, if it applies.	Employment status	☐ Employed ☐ Not employed	☐ Employed ☐ Not employed
	Occupation	_____	_____
	Employer's name	_____	_____
	Employer's address	_____ Number Street	_____ Number Street
		_____	_____
		City State ZIP Code	City State ZIP Code
	How long employed there?	_____	_____

Part 2:   Give Details About Monthly Income

Estimate monthly income as of the date you file this form. If you have nothing to report for any line, write $0 in the space. Include your non-filing spouse unless you are separated.

If you or your non-filing spouse have more than one employer, combine the information for all employers for that person on the lines below. If you need more space, attach a separate sheet to this form.

		For Debtor 1	For Debtor 2 or non-filing spouse
2. List monthly gross wages, salary, and commissions (before all payroll deductions). If not paid monthly, calculate what the monthly wage would be.	2.	$_____	$_____
3. Estimate and list monthly overtime pay.	3.	+ $_____	+ $_____
4. Calculate gross income. Add line 2 + line 3.	4.	$_____	$_____

Official Form 106I   Schedule I: Your Income   page 1
                                                                                     87

Official Form 106I   Schedule I: Your Income   page 2

(Added Dec. 1, 2015.)

ADVISORY COMMITTEE NOTES

Official Form 106I, *Schedule I: Your Income*, replaces Official Form 6I, *Your Income*, in cases of individual debtors.

The form is one of an initial set of forms that were published as part of the Forms Modernization Project in 2012. It is renumbered and internal cross references are updated to conform to the new numbering system now being introduced by the Forms Modernization Project.

Form B106J. Schedule J: Your Expenses

Official Form 106J

Schedule J: Your Expenses   12/15

Be as complete and accurate as possible. If two married people are filing together, both are equally responsible for supplying correct information. If more space is needed, attach another sheet to this form. On the top of any additional pages, write your name and case number (if known). Answer every question.

Part 1: Describe Your Household

1. Is this a joint case?

☐ No. Go to line 2.
☐ Yes. Does Debtor 2 live in a separate household?

   ☐ No
   ☐ Yes. Debtor 2 must file Official Form 106J-2, *Expenses for Separate Household of Debtor 2*.

2. Do you have dependents?   ☐ No

Do not list Debtor 1 and   ☐ Yes. Fill out this information for
Debtor 2.   each dependent ....

Do not state the dependents'
names.

Dependent's relationship to Debtor 1 or Debtor 2	Dependent's age	Does dependent live with you?
_____	_____	☐ No ☐ Yes
_____	_____	☐ No ☐ Yes
_____	_____	☐ No ☐ Yes
_____	_____	☐ No ☐ Yes
_____	_____	☐ No ☐ Yes

3. Do your expenses include   ☐ No
   expenses of people other than   ☐ Yes
   yourself and your dependents?

Part 2: Estimate Your Ongoing Monthly Expenses

Estimate your expenses as of your bankruptcy filing date unless you are using this form as a supplement in a Chapter 13 case to report expenses as of a date after the bankruptcy is filed. If this is a supplemental *Schedule J*, check the box at the top of the form and fill in the applicable date.

Include expenses paid for with non-cash government assistance if you know the value of
such assistance and have included it on *Schedule I: Your Income* (Official Form 106I).

		Your expenses
4. The rental or home ownership expenses for your residence. Include first mortgage payments and any rent for the ground or lot.	4.	$_____
If not included in line 4:		
4a. Real estate taxes	4a.	$_____
4b. Property, homeowner's, or renter's insurance	4b.	$_____
4c. Home maintenance, repair, and upkeep expenses	4c.	$_____
4d. Homeowner's association or condominium dues	4d.	$_____

Debtor 1 _____
        First Name   Middle Name   Last Name

Case number _____
           (if known)

	Your expenses

5. Additional mortgage payments for your residence, such as home equity loans   5. $_____

6. Utilities:

   6a. Electricity, heat, natural gas   6a. $_____

   6b. Water, sewer, garbage collection   6b. $_____

   6c. Telephone, cell phone, Internet, satellite, and cable services   6c. $_____

   6c. Other. Specify: _____   6d. $_____

7. Food and housekeeping supplies   7. $_____

8. Childcare and children's education costs   8. $_____

9. Clothing, laundry, and dry cleaning   9. $_____

10. Personal care products and services   10. $_____

11. Medical and dental expenses   11. $_____

12. Transportation. Include gas, maintenance, bus or train fare.
Do not include car payments.   12. $_____

13. Entertainment, clubs, recreation, newspapers, magazines, and books   13. $_____

14. Charitable contributions and religious donations   14. $_____

15. Insurance.
Do not include insurance deducted from your pay or included in lines 4 or 20.

   15a. Life insurance   15a. $_____

   15b. Health insurance   15b. $_____

   15c. Vehicle insurance   15c. $_____

   15d. Other insurance. Specify: _____   15d. $_____

16. Taxes. Do not include taxes deducted from your pay or included in lines 4 or 20.
Specify: _____   16. $_____

17. Installment or lease payments:

   17a. Car payments for Vehicle 1   17a. $_____

   17b. Car payments for Vehicle 2   17b. $_____

   17c. Other. Specify: _____   17c. $_____

   17d. Other. Specify: _____   17d. $_____

18. Your payments of alimony, maintenance, and support that you did not report as deducted from
your pay on line 5, Schedule I, Your Income (Official Form 106I).   18. $_____

19. Other payments you make to support others who do not live with you.
Specify: _____   19. $_____

20. Other real property expenses not included in lines 4 or 5 of this form or on Schedule I: Your Income.

   20a. Mortgages on other property   20a. $_____

   20b. Real estate taxes   20b. $_____

   20c. Property, homeowner's, or renter's insurance   20c. $_____

   20d. Maintenance, repair, and upkeep expenses   20d. $_____

   20e. Homeowner's association or condominium dues   20e. $_____

Official Form 106J   Schedule J: Your Expenses   page 2

Debtor 1 _____   Case number _____

First Name   Middle Name   Last Name

21. Other. Specify: _____   21.   +$ _____

22. **Calculate your monthly expenses.**

    22a. Add lines 4 through 21.   22a. $ _____

    22b. Copy line 22 (monthly expenses for Debtor 2), if any, from Official Form 106J-2   22b. $ _____

    22c. Add line 22a and 22b. The result is your monthly expenses.   22c. $ _____

23. **Calculate your monthly net income.**

    23a. Copy line 12 (your combined monthly income) from Schedule I.   23a. $ _____

    23b. Copy your monthly expenses from line 22c above.   23b.   –$ _____

    23c. Subtract your monthly expenses from your monthly income.
        The result is your monthly net income.   23c. $ _____

24. **Do you expect an increase or decrease in your expenses within the year after you file this form?**

    For example, do you expect to finish paying for your car loan within the year or do you expect your
    mortgage payment to increase or decrease because of a modification to the terms of your mortgage?

    ☐ No.

    ☐ Yes   Explain here:

Official Form 106J   Schedule J: Your Expenses   page 3

(Added Dec. 1, 2015.)

ADVISORY COMMITTEE NOTES

Official Form 106J, *Schedule J: Your Expenses*, replaces Official Form 6J, *Your Expenses*, in cases of individual debtors.

The form is one of an initial set of forms that were published as part of the Forms Modernization Project in 2012. It is renumbered and internal cross references are updated to conform to the new numbering system now being introduced by the Forms Modernization Project.

The form has been revised to include references to new *Schedule J–2: Expenses for Separate Household of Debtor 2* (Official Form 106J–2) at line 1 and new line 22b. The revisions clarify how to calculate monthly net income in joint cases where Debtor 1 and Debtor 2 maintain separate households. Line 22b is added so Schedule J and Schedule J–2 are easily coordinated.

**Form B106J-2. Schedule J-2: Expenses
for Separate Household of Debtor 2**

Fill in this information to identify your case:

Debtor 1 _____ First Name _____ Middle Name _____ Last Name	
Debtor 2 (Spouse, if filing) First Name _____ Middle Name _____ Last Name	
United States Bankruptcy Court for the: _____ District of _____ (State)	
Case number (If known) _____	

Check if this is:

☐ An amended filing

☐ A supplement showing postpetition chapter 13
expenses as of the following date:

_____
MM / DD / YYYY

Official Form 106J-2

Schedule J-2: Expenses for Separate Household of Debtor 2   12/15

Use this form for Debtor 2's separate household expenses ONLY IF Debtor 1 and Debtor 2 maintain separate households. *If Debtor 1 and Debtor 2 have one or more dependents in common, list the dependents on both Schedule J and this form. Answer the questions on this form only with respect to expenses for Debtor 2 that are not reported on Schedule J.* Be as complete and accurate as possible. If more space is needed, attach another sheet to this form. On the top of any additional pages, write your name and case number (if known). Answer every question.

Part 1:   Describe Your Household

1. Do you and Debtor 1 maintain separate households?

   ☐ No. Do not complete this form.
   ☐ Yes.

2. Do you have dependents?

   Do not list Debtor 1 but list all other dependents of Debtor 2 regardless of whether listed as a dependent of Debtor 1 on Schedule J.

   Do not state the dependents' names.

	Dependent's relationship to Debtor 2:	Dependent's age	Does dependent live with you?
☐ No			
☐ Yes. Fill out this information for each dependent.	_____	_____	☐ No ☐ Yes
	_____	_____	☐ No ☐ Yes
	_____	_____	☐ No ☐ Yes
	_____	_____	☐ No ☐ Yes
	_____	_____	☐ No ☐ Yes

3. Do your expenses include expenses of people other than yourself, your dependents, and Debtor 1?

   ☐ No
   ☐ Yes

Part 2:   Estimate Your Ongoing Monthly Expenses

Estimate your expenses as of your bankruptcy filing date unless you are using this form as a supplement in a Chapter 13 case to report expenses as of a date after the bankruptcy is filed.

Include expenses paid for with non-cash government assistance if you know the value of such assistance and have included it on *Schedule I: Your Income* (Official Form 106I.)

		Your expenses
4. The rental or home ownership expenses for your residence. Include first mortgage payments and any rent for the ground or lot.	4.	$_____
If not included in line 4:		
4a. Real estate taxes	4a.	$_____
4b. Property, homeowner's, or renter's insurance	4b.	$_____
4c. Home maintenance, repair, and upkeep expenses	4c.	$_____
4d. Homeowner's association or condominium dues	4d.	$_____

Official Form 106J-2   Schedule J-2: Expenses for Separate Household of Debtor 2   page 1

Form B106J-2

Debtor _____ Case number _____

First Name   Middle Name   Last Name

		Your expenses

5. Additional mortgage payments for your residence, such as home equity loans   5. $_____

6. **Utilities:**

   6a.   Electricity, heat, natural gas   6a. $_____

   6b.   Water, sewer, garbage collection   6b. $_____

   6c.   Telephone, cell phone, Internet, satellite, and cable services   6c. $_____

   6d.   Other. Specify: _____   6d. $_____

7. Food and housekeeping supplies   7. $_____

8. Childcare and children's education costs   8. $_____

9. Clothing, laundry, and dry cleaning   9. $_____

10. Personal care products and services   10. $_____

11. Medical and dental expenses   11. $_____

12. Transportation. Include gas, maintenance, bus or train fare.
Do not include car payments.   12. $_____

13. Entertainment, clubs, recreation, newspapers, magazines, and books   13. $_____

14. Charitable contributions and religious donations   14. $_____

15. Insurance.
Do not include insurance deducted from your pay or included in lines 4 or 20.

   15a.   Life insurance   15a. $_____

   15b.   Health insurance   15b. $_____

   15c.   Vehicle insurance   15c. $_____

   15d.   Other insurance. Specify: _____   15d. $_____

16. Taxes. Do not include taxes deducted from your pay or included in lines 4 or 20.
Specify: _____   16. $_____

17. Installment or lease payments:

   17a.   Car payments for Vehicle 1   17a. $_____

   17b.   Car payments for Vehicle 2   17b. $_____

   17c.   Other. Specify: _____   17c. $_____

   17d.   Other. Specify: _____   17d. $_____

18. Your payments of alimony, maintenance, and support that you did not report as deducted from
your pay on line 5, *Schedule I, Your Income* (Official Form 106I).   18. $_____

19. Other payments you make to support others who do not live with you.
Specify: _____   19. $_____

20. Other real property expenses not included in lines 4 or 5 of this form or on *Schedule I: Your Income.*

   20a.   Mortgages on other property   20a. $_____

   20b.   Real estate taxes   20b. $_____

   20c.   Property, homeowner's, or renter's insurance   20c. $_____

   20d.   Maintenance, repair, and upkeep expenses   20d. $_____

   20e.   Homeowner's association or condominium dues   20e. $_____

Official Form 106J-2   Schedule J-2: Expenses for Separate Household of Debtor 2   page 2

Debtor _____   Case number _____
     First Name   Middle Name   Last Name

21. Other. Specify: _____   21.   +$ _____

22. **Your monthly expenses.** Add lines 5 through 21.
    The result is the monthly expenses of Debtor 2. Copy the result to line 22b of Schedule J to calculate the
    total expenses for Debtor 1 and Debtor 2.   22. $ _____

23. Line not used on this form.

24. **Do you expect an increase or decrease in your expenses within the year after you file this form?**

    For example, do you expect to finish paying for your car loan within the year or do you expect your
    mortgage payment to increase or decrease because of a modification to the terms of your mortgage?

    ☐ No.
    ☐ Yes.   Explain here:

Official Form 106J-2   Schedule J-2: Expenses for Separate Household of Debtor 2   74
                                                                 page 3

(Added Dec. 1, 2015.)

ADVISORY COMMITTEE NOTES

    Official Form 106J–2 is new. It is used to report the monthly expenses of Debtor 2 in a joint debtor case only if Debtor 1 and Debtor 2 maintain separate households.

**Form B107. Your Statement of Financial Affairs
for Individuals Filing for Bankruptcy**

Fill in this information to identify your case:

Debtor 1 _____
        First Name   Middle Name   Last Name

Debtor 2
(Spouse, if filing)   First Name   Middle Name   Last Name

United States Bankruptcy Court for the: _____ District of _____

Case number _____
(if known)

☐ Check if this is an
amended filing

Official Form 107

Statement of Financial Affairs for Individuals Filing for Bankruptcy   04/16

Be as complete and accurate as possible. If two married people are filing together, both are equally responsible for supplying correct information. If more space is needed, attach a separate sheet to this form. On the top of any additional pages, write your name and case number (if known). Answer every question.

Part 1:   **Give Details About Your Marital Status and Where You Lived Before**

1. What is your current marital status?

☐ Married
☐ Not married

2. During the last 3 years, have you lived anywhere other than where you live now?

☐ No
☐ Yes. List all of the places you lived in the last 3 years. Do not include where you live now.

Debtor 1:	Dates Debtor 1 lived there	Debtor 2:	Dates Debtor 2 lived there
		☐ Same as Debtor 1	☐ Same as Debtor 1
Number Street	From _____ To _____	Number Street	From _____ To _____
City State ZIP Code		City State ZIP Code	
		☐ Same as Debtor 1	☐ Same as Debtor 1
Number Street	From _____ To _____	Number Street	From _____ To _____
City State ZIP Code		City State ZIP Code	

3. Within the last 8 years, did you ever live with a spouse or legal equivalent in a community property state or territory? (*Community property states and territories* include Arizona, California, Idaho, Louisiana, Nevada, New Mexico, Puerto Rico, Texas, Washington, and Wisconsin.)

☐ No
☐ Yes. Make sure you fill out *Schedule H: Your Codebtors* (Official Form 106H).

Part 2:   **Explain the Sources of Your Income**

Official Form 107   Statement of Financial Affairs for Individuals Filing for Bankruptcy   page 1

Debtor 1 _____   Case number _____
        First Name   Middle Name   Last Name

4. Did you have any income from employment or from operating a business during this year or the two previous calendar years?

Fill in the total amount of income you received from all jobs and all businesses, including part-time activities.

If you are filing a joint case and you have income that you receive together, list it only once under Debtor 1.

☐ No

☐ Yes. Fill in the details.

	Debtor 1		Debtor 2	
	Sources of income Check all that apply.	Gross income (before deductions and exclusions)	Sources of income Check all that apply.	Gross income (before deductions and exclusions)
From January 1 of current year until the date you filed for bankruptcy:	☐ Wages, commissions, bonuses, tips ☐ Operating a business	$_____	☐ Wages, commissions, bonuses, tips ☐ Operating a business	$_____
For last calendar year: (January 1 to December 31, _____) YYYY	☐ Wages, commissions, bonuses, tips ☐ Operating a business	$_____	☐ Wages, commissions, bonuses, tips ☐ Operating a business	$_____
For the calendar year before that: (January 1 to December 31, _____) YYYY	☐ Wages, commissions, bonuses, tips ☐ Operating a business	$_____	☐ Wages, commissions, bonuses, tips ☐ Operating a business	$_____

5. Did you receive any other income during this year or the two previous calendar years?

Include income regardless of whether that income is taxable. Examples of *other income* are alimony; child support; Social Security, unemployment, and other public benefit payments; pensions; rental income; interest; dividends; money collected from lawsuits; royalties; and gambling and lottery winnings. If you are filing a joint case and you have income that you received together, list it only once under Debtor 1.

List each source and the gross income from each source separately. Do not include income that you listed in line 4.

☐ No

☐ Yes. Fill in the details.

	Debtor 1		Debtor 2	
	Sources of income Describe below.	Gross income from each source (before deductions and exclusions)	Sources of income Describe below.	Gross income from each source (before deductions and exclusions)
From January 1 of current year until the date you filed for bankruptcy:	_____ _____ _____	$_____ $_____ $_____	_____ _____ _____	$_____ $_____ $_____
For last calendar year: (January 1 to December 31, _____) YYYY	_____ _____ _____	$_____ $_____ $_____	_____ _____ _____	$_____ $_____ $_____
For the calendar year before that: (January 1 to December 31, _____) YYYY	_____ _____ _____	$_____ $_____ $_____	_____ _____ _____	$_____ $_____ $_____

Debtor 1 _____ _____ _____   Case number _____
         First Name   Middle Name   Last Name

| Part 3: | List Certain Payments You Made Before You Filed for Bankruptcy |

6. Are either Debtor 1's or Debtor 2's debts primarily consumer debts?

☐ No. Neither Debtor 1 nor Debtor 2 has primarily consumer debts. *Consumer debts* are defined in 11 U.S.C. § 101(8) as
"incurred by an individual primarily for a personal, family, or household purpose."

During the 90 days before you filed for bankruptcy, did you pay any creditor a total of $6,425* or more?

☐ No. Go to line 7.

☐ Yes. List below each creditor to whom you paid a total of $6,425* or more in one or more payments and the
total amount you paid that creditor. Do not include payments for domestic support obligations, such as
child support and alimony. Also, do not include payments to an attorney for this bankruptcy case.

* Subject to adjustment on 4/01/19 and every 3 years after that for cases filed on or after the date of adjustment.

☐ Yes. Debtor 1 or Debtor 2 or both have primarily consumer debts.

During the 90 days before you filed for bankruptcy, did you pay any creditor a total of $600 or more?

☐ No. Go to line 7.

☐ Yes. List below each creditor to whom you paid a total of $600 or more and the total amount you paid that
creditor. Do not include payments for domestic support obligations, such as child support and
alimony. Also, do not include payments to an attorney for this bankruptcy case.

	Dates of payment	Total amount paid	Amount you still owe	Was this payment for...
Creditor's Name _____ Number Street _____ _____ City State ZIP Code	_____ _____ _____	$_____	$_____	☐ Mortgage ☐ Car ☐ Credit card ☐ Loan repayment ☐ Suppliers or vendors ☐ Other _____
Creditor's Name _____ Number Street _____ _____ City State ZIP Code	_____ _____ _____	$_____	$_____	☐ Mortgage ☐ Car ☐ Credit card ☐ Loan repayment ☐ Suppliers or vendors ☐ Other
Creditor's Name _____ Number Street _____ _____ City State ZIP Code	_____ _____ _____	$_____	$_____	☐ Mortgage ☐ Car ☐ Credit card ☐ Loan repayment ☐ Suppliers or vendors ☐ Other _____

For Complete Annotation Materials, see United States Code Annotated

Debtor 1 _____   Case number (if known)_____
      First Name   Middle Name   Last Name

7. Within 1 year before you filed for bankruptcy, did you make a payment on a debt you owed anyone who was an insider?

Insiders include your relatives; any general partners; relatives of any general partners; partnerships of which you are a general partner; corporations of which you are an officer, director, person in control, or owner of 20% or more of their voting securities; and any managing agent, including one for a business you operate as a sole proprietor. 11 U.S.C. § 101. Include payments for domestic support obligations, such as child support and alimony.

☐ No
☐ Yes. List all payments to an insider.

	Dates of payment	Total amount paid	Amount you still owe	Reason for this payment
Insider's Name _____	_____	$_____	$_____	
Number Street _____	_____			
_____	_____			
City State ZIP Code				
Insider's Name _____		$_____	$_____	
Number Street _____	_____			
_____	_____			
City State ZIP Code				

8. Within 1 year before you filed for bankruptcy, did you make any payments or transfer any property on account of a debt that benefited an insider?

Include payments on debts guaranteed or cosigned by an insider.

☐ No
☐ Yes. List all payments that benefited an insider.

	Dates of payment	Total amount paid	Amount you still owe	Reason for this payment Include creditor's name
Insider's Name _____	_____	$_____	$_____	
Number Street _____	_____			
_____	_____			
City State ZIP Code				
Insider's Name _____	_____	$_____	$_____	
Number Street _____	_____			
_____				
City State ZIP Code				

Official Form 107   Statement of Financial Affairs for Individuals Filing for Bankruptcy   page 4

Debtor 1 _____ Case number (if known) _____
First Name   Middle Name   Last Name

9. Within 1 year before you filed for bankruptcy, were you a party in any lawsuit, court action, or administrative proceeding?
List all such matters, including personal injury cases, small claims actions, divorces, collection suits, paternity actions, support or custody modifications, and contract disputes.

☐ No
☐ Yes. Fill in the details.

	Nature of the case	Court or agency	Status of the case
Case title _____		Court Name _____	☐ Pending
			☐ On appeal
_____		Number Street	☐ Concluded
Case number _____		City State ZIP Code	
Case title _____		Court Name _____	☐ Pending
			☐ On appeal
_____		Number Street	☐ Concluded
Case number _____		City State ZIP Code	

10. Within 1 year before you filed for bankruptcy, was any of your property repossessed, foreclosed, garnished, attached, seized, or levied?
Check all that apply and fill in the details below.

☐ No. Go to line 11.
☐ Yes. Fill in the information below.

	Describe the property	Date	Value of the property
Creditor's Name		_____	$_____
Number Street	**Explain what happened**		
	☐ Property was repossessed.		
_____	☐ Property was foreclosed.		
	☐ Property was garnished.		
City State ZIP Code	☐ Property was attached, seized, or levied.		

	Describe the property	Date	Value of the property
Creditor's Name		_____	$_____
Number Street	**Explain what happened**		
	☐ Property was repossessed.		
_____	☐ Property was foreclosed.		
	☐ Property was garnished.		
City State ZIP Code	☐ Property was attached, seized, or levied.		

Official Form 107   Statement of Financial Affairs for Individuals Filing for Bankruptcy   page 5

Debtor 1 _____   Case number (if known)_____
              First Name   Middle Name   Last Name

11. Within 90 days before you filed for bankruptcy, did any creditor, including a bank or financial institution, set off any amounts from your accounts or refuse to make a payment because you owed a debt?

☐ No

☐ Yes. Fill in the details

	Describe the action the creditor took	Date action was taken	Amount
Creditor's Name			
			$_____
Number Street			
City State ZIP Code	Last 4 digits of account number: XXXX–___ ___ ___ ___		

12. Within 1 year before you filed for bankruptcy, was any of your property in the possession of an assignee for the benefit of creditors, a court-appointed receiver, a custodian, or another official?

☐ No

☐ Yes

Part 5:   List Certain Gifts and Contributions

13. Within 2 years before you filed for bankruptcy, did you give any gifts with a total value of more than $600 per person?

☐ No

☐ Yes. Fill in the details for each gift.

Gifts with a total value of more than $600 per person	Describe the gifts	Dates you gave the gifts	Value
Person to Whom You Gave the Gift		_____	$_____
		_____	$_____
Number Street			
City State ZIP Code			
Person's relationship to you			

Gifts with a total value of more than $600 per person	Describe the gifts	Dates you gave the gifts	Value
Person to Whom You Gave the Gift		_____	$_____
		_____	$_____
Number Street			
City State ZIP Code			
Person's relationship to you _____			

Form B107

Debtor 1 _____   Case number (if known)_____
     First Name   Middle Name   Last Name

14. Within 2 years before you filed for bankruptcy, did you give any gifts or contributions with a total value of more than $600 to any charity?

☐ No
☐ Yes. Fill in the details for each gift or contribution.

Gifts or contributions to charities that total more than $600	Describe what you contributed	Date you contributed	Value
Charity's Name _____		_____	$_____
_____		_____	$_____
Number Street			
City State ZIP Code			

Part 6: List Certain Losses

15. Within 1 year before you filed for bankruptcy or since you filed for bankruptcy, did you lose anything because of theft, fire, other disaster, or gambling?

☐ No
☐ Yes. Fill in the details.

Describe the property you lost and how the loss occurred	Describe any insurance coverage for the loss Include the amount that insurance has paid. List pending insurance claims on line 33 of Schedule A/B: Property.	Date of your loss	Value of property lost
		_____	$_____

Part 7: List Certain Payments or Transfers

16. Within 1 year before you filed for bankruptcy, did you or anyone else acting on your behalf pay or transfer any property to anyone you consulted about seeking bankruptcy or preparing a bankruptcy petition?
Include any attorneys, bankruptcy petition preparers, or credit counseling agencies for services required in your bankruptcy.

☐ No
☐ Yes. Fill in the details.

	Description and value of any property transferred	Date payment or transfer was made	Amount of payment
Person Who Was Paid _____		_____	$_____
Number Street _____		_____	$_____
_____			
City State ZIP Code			
Email or website address _____			
Person Who Made the Payment, if Not You			

Official Form 107   Statement of Financial Affairs for Individuals Filing for Bankruptcy   page 7

Debtor 1 _____ Case number _(if known)_____

   First Name   Middle Name   Last Name

	Description and value of any property transferred	Date payment or transfer was made	Amount of payment
Person Who Was Paid _____			
Number Street		_____	$_____
_____			
_____		_____	$_____
City State ZIP Code			
Email or website address			
Person Who Made the Payment, if Not You			

17. Within 1 year before you filed for bankruptcy, did you or anyone else acting on your behalf pay or transfer any property to anyone who promised to help you deal with your creditors or to make payments to your creditors?
Do not include any payment or transfer that you listed on line 16.

☐ No
☐ Yes. Fill in the details.

	Description and value of any property transferred	Date payment or transfer was made	Amount of payment
Person Who Was Paid			
Number Street		_____	$_____
_____			
City State ZIP Code			$_____

18. Within 2 years before you filed for bankruptcy, did you sell, trade, or otherwise transfer any property to anyone, other than property transferred in the ordinary course of your business or financial affairs?
Include both outright transfers and transfers made as security (such as the granting of a security interest or mortgage on your property).
Do not include gifts and transfers that you have already listed on this statement.

☐ No
☐ Yes. Fill in the details.

	Description and value of property transferred	Describe any property or payments received or debts paid in exchange	Date transfer was made
Person Who Received Transfer			
Number Street			_____
_____			
City State ZIP Code			
Person's relationship to you			
Person Who Received Transfer			
Number Street			_____
_____			
City State ZIP Code			
Person's relationship to you			

Form B107

Debtor 1 _____   Case number (if known)_____
        First Name   Middle Name   Last Name

19. Within 10 years before you filed for bankruptcy, did you transfer any property to a self-settled trust or similar device of which you are a beneficiary? (These are often called *asset-protection devices*.)

☐ No
☐ Yes. Fill in the details.

	Description and value of the property transferred	Date transfer was made
Name of trust _____		
_____		

Part 8: List Certain Financial Accounts, Instruments, Safe Deposit Boxes, and Storage Units

20. Within 1 year before you filed for bankruptcy, were any financial accounts or instruments held in your name, or for your benefit, closed, sold, moved, or transferred?
Include checking, savings, money market, or other financial accounts; certificates of deposit; shares in banks, credit unions, brokerage houses, pension funds, cooperatives, associations, and other financial institutions.

☐ No
☐ Yes. Fill in the details.

	Last 4 digits of account number	Type of account or instrument	Date account was closed, sold, moved, or transferred	Last balance before closing or transfer
Name of Financial Institution _____	XXXX-__ __ __ __	☐ Checking ☐ Savings ☐ Money market ☐ Brokerage ☐ Other	_____	$_____
Number Street _____				
City ____ State ____ ZIP Code ____				
Name of Financial Institution _____	XXXX-__ __ __ __	☐ Checking ☐ Savings ☐ Money market ☐ Brokerage ☐ Other_____	_____	$_____
Number Street _____				
City ____ State ____ ZIP Code ____				

21. Do you now have, or did you have within 1 year before you filed for bankruptcy, any safe deposit box or other depository for securities, cash, or other valuables?

☐ No
☐ Yes. Fill in the details.

	Who else had access to it?	Describe the contents	Do you still have it?
Name of Financial Institution _____	Name _____		☐ No ☐ Yes
Number Street _____	Number Street _____		
City ____ State ____ ZIP Code ____	City ____ State ____ ZIP Code ____		

For Complete Annotation Materials, see United States Code Annotated

Debtor 1 _____   Case number (if known) _____
             First Name   Middle Name   Last Name

22. Have you stored property in a storage unit or place other than your home within 1 year before you filed for bankruptcy?

☐ No
☐ Yes. Fill in the details.

	Who else has or had access to it?	Describe the contents	Do you still have it?
			☐ No
Name of Storage Facility	Name		☐ Yes
Number Street	Number Street		
	City State ZIP Code		
City State ZIP Code			

Part 9:   Identify Property You Hold or Control for Someone Else

23. Do you hold or control any property that someone else owns? Include any property you borrowed from, are storing for, or hold in trust for someone.

☐ No
☐ Yes. Fill in the details.

	Where is the property?	Describe the property	Value
Owner's Name			$_____
Number Street	Number Street		
	City State ZIP Code		
City State ZIP Code			

Part 10:   Give Details About Environmental Information

For the purpose of Part 10, the following definitions apply:

- *Environmental law* means any federal, state, or local statute or regulation concerning pollution, contamination, releases of hazardous or toxic substances, wastes, or material into the air, land, soil, surface water, groundwater, or other medium, including statutes or regulations controlling the cleanup of these substances, wastes, or material.

- *Site* means any location, facility, or property as defined under any environmental law, whether you now own, operate, or utilize it or used to own, operate, or utilize it, including disposal sites.

- *Hazardous material* means anything an environmental law defines as a hazardous waste, hazardous substance, toxic substance, hazardous material, pollutant, contaminant, or similar term.

Report all notices, releases, and proceedings that you know about, regardless of when they occurred.

24. Has any governmental unit notified you that you may be liable or potentially liable under or in violation of an environmental law?

☐ No
☐ Yes. Fill in the details.

	Governmental unit	Environmental law, if you know it	Date of notice
Name of site	Governmental unit		_____
Number Street	Number Street		
	City State ZIP Code		
City State ZIP Code			

Official Form 107   Statement of Financial Affairs for Individuals Filing for Bankruptcy   page 10

For Complete Annotation Materials, see United States Code Annotated

Debtor 1 _____   Case number (if known) _____
     First Name   Middle Name   Last Name

25. Have you notified any governmental unit of any release of hazardous material?

❑ No

❑ Yes. Fill in the details.

	Governmental unit	Environmental law, if you know it	Date of notice
Name of site	Governmental unit		
Number Street	Number Street		
City State ZIP Code	City State ZIP Code		

26. Have you been a party in any judicial or administrative proceeding under any environmental law? Include settlements and orders.

❑ No

❑ Yes. Fill in the details.

	Court or agency	Nature of the case	Status of the case
Case title _____	Court Name		❑ Pending
	Number Street		❑ On appeal
Case number	City State ZIP Code		❑ Concluded

Part 11: Give Details About Your Business or Connections to Any Business

27. Within 4 years before you filed for bankruptcy, did you own a business or have any of the following connections to any business?

❑ A sole proprietor or self-employed in a trade, profession, or other activity, either full-time or part-time

❑ A member of a limited liability company (LLC) or limited liability partnership (LLP)

❑ A partner in a partnership

❑ An officer, director, or managing executive of a corporation

❑ An owner of at least 5% of the voting or equity securities of a corporation

❑ No. None of the above applies. Go to Part 12.

❑ Yes. Check all that apply above and fill in the details below for each business.

	Describe the nature of the business	Employer Identification number Do not include Social Security number or ITIN.
Business Name		EIN: __ __ - __ __ __ __ __ __ __
Number Street	Name of accountant or bookkeeper	Dates business existed
City State ZIP Code		From _____ To _____
	Describe the nature of the business	Employer Identification number Do not include Social Security number or ITIN.
Business Name		EIN: __ __ - __ __ __ __ __ __ __
Number Street	Name of accountant or bookkeeper	Dates business existed
City State ZIP Code		From _____ To _____

Debtor 1 _____ Case number (if known)_____
     First Name   Middle Name   Last Name

	Describe the nature of the business	Employer Identification number
Business Name		Do not include Social Security number or ITIN.
		EIN: __ __ – __ __ __ __ __ __ __
Number Street	Name of accountant or bookkeeper	Dates business existed
City State ZIP Code		From _____ To _____

28. Within 2 years before you filed for bankruptcy, did you give a financial statement to anyone about your business? Include all financial institutions, creditors, or other parties.

❑ No
❑ Yes. Fill in the details below.

Date issued

Name

MM / DD / YYYY

Number Street

City   State   ZIP Code

Part 12:   Sign Below

I have read the answers on this *Statement of Financial Affairs* and any attachments, and I declare under penalty of perjury that the answers are true and correct. I understand that making a false statement, concealing property, or obtaining money or property by fraud in connection with a bankruptcy case can result in fines up to $250,000, or imprisonment for up to 20 years, or both.
18 U.S.C. §§ 152, 1341, 1519, and 3571.

✗ _____   ✗ _____
Signature of Debtor 1   Signature of Debtor 2

Date _____   Date _____

Did you attach additional pages to *Your Statement of Financial Affairs for Individuals Filing for Bankruptcy* (Official Form 107)?

❑ No
❑ Yes

Did you pay or agree to pay someone who is not an attorney to help you fill out bankruptcy forms?

❑ No
❑ Yes. Name of person_____   Attach the *Bankruptcy Petition Preparer's Notice, Declaration, and Signature* (Official Form 119).

(Added Dec. 1, 2015; and amended Apr. 1, 2016.)

ADVISORY COMMITTEE NOTES

Official Form 107, *Statement of Financial Affairs for Individuals Filing for Bankruptcy*, which applies only in cases of individual debtors, is revised in its entirety as part of the Forms Modernization Project, making it easier to read and, as a result, likely to generate more complete and accurate responses. The goals of the Forms Modernization Project include improving the interface between technology and the forms so as to increase efficiency and reduce the need to produce the same information in multiple formats. Therefore, many of the open-ended questions and multiple-part instructions have been replaced with more specific questions. In addition, the form is renumbered to distinguish it from the version to be used in non-individual cases, and stylistic changes were made throughout the form.

The form is derived from former Official Form 7, *Statement of Financial Affairs*. The new form uses eleven sections likely to be more understandable to non-lawyers, groups questions of a similar nature together, and eliminates questions unrelated to individual debtors. The new form deletes the instruction, previously found in many questions, that married debtors filing under chapter 12 or chapter 13 must include information applicable to their spouse, even if their spouse is not filing with them, unless the spouses are separated. This change was made because a non-filing spouse's general financial affairs are not relevant to the debtor's bankruptcy case.

Part 1, *Give Details About Your Marital Status and Where You Lived Before*, moves the questions regarding the debtor's prior addresses, as well as residences in a community property state, to the beginning of the form. The form eliminates the "name used" question in reference to prior addresses. Also, the debtor is no longer required to list the name of a spouse or former spouse who lived with the debtor in a community property state since that information will be provided in Official Form 106H.

Part 2, *Explain the Sources of Your Income*, consolidates the questions regarding income, adding "wages, commissions, bonuses, tips" as a category for sources of income, and it eliminates the option to report income on a fiscal year basis. In addition, the form provides examples of types of "other income." The time period is clarified to indicate that the prior two years means two calendar years, plus the portion of the calendar year in which the bankruptcy is filed.

Part 3, *List Certain Payments You Made Before You Filed for Bankruptcy*, includes questions related to payments made in the 90 days prior to bankruptcy, with a separate question for payments made to insiders within one year before filing for bankruptcy. The statutory definition of consumer debt is provided. The question regarding the nature of the debtor's debts requires the debtor to use checkboxes to indicate whether or not they are primarily consumer debts. The form instructs debtors not to include payments for domestic support obligations in the section regarding insider payments. The form provides a separate question regarding payments or transfers on account of a debt that benefited an insider. For both questions regarding payments to insiders, the debtor is required to provide a reason for the payment. Partnerships of which the debtor is a general partner have been added to the examples of "insiders."

Part 4, *Identify Legal Actions, Repossessions, and Foreclosures*, consolidates questions regarding actions against the debtor's property. The form provides examples of types of legal actions, and requires the debtor to indicate the status of any action. The form adds the requirements that a debtor include any property levied on within a year of filing for bankruptcy and that the debtor provide the last four digits of any account number for any setoffs. Also, a debtor must list any assignment for the benefit of creditors made within one year of filing for bankruptcy.

Part 5, *List Certain Gifts and Contributions*, changes the reporting threshold to $600 per person or charity and increases the look-back period from one to two years.

Part 6, *List Certain Losses*, clarifies how to report insurance coverage for losses. It provides that the debtor must include on this form amounts of insurance that have been paid, but must list pending insurance claims on Official Form 106A/B.

Part 7, *List Certain Payments or Transfers*, includes questions regarding payments or transfers of property by the debtor. The question regarding payments or transfers to anyone who was consulted about seeking bankruptcy or preparing a bankruptcy petition requires the email or website address of the person who was paid, as well as the name of the person who made the payment if it was not the debtor. There is a separate question asked about payments or transfers to anyone who promised to help the debtor deal with creditors or make payments to creditors, reminding the debtor not to include any payments or transfers already listed. Also, the debtor must list any transfers of property, outright or for security purposes, made within two years of filing for bankruptcy, unless the transfer was made in the ordinary course of the debtor's business. There is a reminder not to list gifts or other transfers already included elsewhere on the form. The question regarding self-settled trusts adds an explanation that such trusts are often referred to as asset-protection devices.

Part 8, *List Certain Financial Accounts, Safe Deposit Boxes, and Storage Units*, adds money market accounts to the examples provided for the question regarding financial accounts or instruments and removes "other instruments" from the examples. Also, the form adds a question about whether the debtor has or had property stored in a storage unit within one year of filing for bankruptcy. The debtor must provide the name and address of the storage facility and anyone who has or had access to the unit, as well as a description of the contents and whether the debtor still has access to the storage unit. Storage units that are part of the building in which the debtor resides are excluded.

Part 9, *Identify Property You Hold or Control for Someone Else*, instructs that the debtor should include any property that the debtor borrowed from, is storing for, or is holding in trust for someone.

Part 10, *Give Details About Environmental Information*, requires the debtor to list the case title and nature of the case for any judicial or administrative proceeding under any environmental law and to indicate the status of the case.

Part 11, *Give Details About Your Business or Connections to Any Business*, eliminates instructions that apply only to corporations and partnerships. The debtor must indicate if, within four years (previously six years) before filing for bankruptcy, the debtor owned a business or had certain connections to a business, with five categories of businesses provided as checkboxes. If the debtor has a connection to a business, the debtor must list the name, address, nature, and Employer Identification number of the business, the dates the business existed, and the name of an accountant or bookkeeper for the business. Accounting information requested is truncated; the debtor is simply required to provide the name of the business bookkeeper or accountant.

Part 12, *Sign Below*, eliminates the signature boxes for a partnership or corporation and a non-attorney bankruptcy petition preparer. Also, the debtor is asked to indicate through checkboxes whether additional pages are attached to the form.

Form B108. Statement of Intention for Individuals Filing Under Chapter 7

Fill in this information to identify your case:

Debtor 1 _____

Debtor 2 _____
(Spouse, if filing) First name   Middle name   Last name

United States Bankruptcy Court for the: _____ District of _____

Case number _____
(if known)

☐ Check if this is an amended filing

Official Form 108

Statement of Intention for Individuals Filing Under Chapter 7   12/15

If you are an individual filing under chapter 7, you must fill out this form if:
■ creditors have claims secured by your property, or
■ you have leased personal property and the lease has not expired.

You must file this form with the court within 30 days after you file your bankruptcy petition or by the date set for the meeting of creditors, whichever is earlier, unless the court extends the time for cause. You must also send copies to the creditors and lessors you list on the form.

If two married people are filing together in a joint case, both are equally responsible for supplying correct information.
Both debtors must sign and date the form.

Be as complete and accurate as possible. If more space is needed, attach a separate sheet to this form. On the top of any additional pages, write your name and case number (if known).

Part 1: List Your Creditors Who Have Secured Claims

1. For any creditors that you listed in Part 1 of Schedule D: Creditors Who Have Claims Secured by Property (Official Form 106D), fill in the information below.

Identify the creditor and the property that is collateral	What do you intend to do with the property that secures a debt?	Did you claim the property as exempt on Schedule C?
Creditor's name: Description of property securing debt:	☐ Surrender the property. ☐ Retain the property and redeem it. ☐ Retain the property and enter into a Reaffirmation Agreement. ☐ Retain the property and [explain]: _____	☐ No ☐ Yes
Creditor's name: Description of property securing debt:	☐ Surrender the property. ☐ Retain the property and redeem it. ☐ Retain the property and enter into a Reaffirmation Agreement. ☐ Retain the property and [explain]: _____	☐ No ☐ Yes
Creditor's name: Description of property securing debt:	☐ Surrender the property. ☐ Retain the property and redeem it. ☐ Retain the property and enter into a Reaffirmation Agreement. ☐ Retain the property and [explain]: _____	☐ No ☐ Yes
Creditor's name: Description of property securing debt:	☐ Surrender the property. ☐ Retain the property and redeem it. ☐ Retain the property and enter into a Reaffirmation Agreement. ☐ Retain the property and [explain]: _____	☐ No ☐ Yes

102

Official Form 108   Statement of Intention for Individuals Filing Under Chapter 7   page 1

Debtor 1 _____ Case number _____

Part 2:   **List Your Unexpired Personal Property Leases**

For any unexpired personal property lease that you listed in *Schedule G: Executory Contracts and Unexpired Leases* (Official Form 106G), fill in the information below. Do not list real estate leases. *Unexpired leases* are leases that are still in effect; the lease period has not yet ended. You may assume an unexpired personal property lease if the trustee does not assume it. 11 U.S.C. § 365(p)(2).

Describe your unexpired personal property leases	Will the lease be assumed?
Lessor's name: _____ Description of leased property:	☐ No ☐ Yes
Lessor's name: _____ Description of leased property:	☐ No ☐ Yes
Lessor's name: _____ Description of leased property:	☐ No ☐ Yes
Lessor's name: _____ Description of leased property:	☐ No ☐ Yes
Lessor's name: _____ Description of leased property:	☐ No ☐ Yes
Lessor's name: _____ Description of leased property:	☐ No ☐ Yes
Lessor's name: _____ Description of leased property:	☐ No ☐ Yes

Part 3:   **Sign Below**

Under penalty of perjury, I declare that I have indicated my intention about any property of my estate that secures a debt and any personal property that is subject to an unexpired lease.

X _____   **X** _____
Signature of Debtor 1   Signature of Debtor 2

Date _____   Date _____
MM / DD / YYYY   MM / DD / YYYY

Official Form 108   Statement of Intention for Individuals Filing Under Chapter 7   103 page 2

(Added Dec. 1, 2015.)

ADVISORY COMMITTEE NOTES

Official Form 108, *Statement of Intention for Individuals Filing Under Chapter 7*, is revised in its entirety as part of the Forms Modernization Project, making it easier to read and, as a result, likely to generate more complete and accurate responses. In addition, the form is renumbered, and stylistic changes are made throughout the form.

The form is derived from former Official Form 8, *Chapter 7—Individual Debtor's Statement of Intention.* The new form uses language likely to be understandable to non-lawyers. In addition, the instructions are more extensive, advising an individual Chapter 7 debtor that the form must be completed and filed within 30 days and that the debtor must deliver copies of the form to creditors and lessors listed on the form.

Part 1, *List Your Creditors Who Have Secured Claims*, refers to entering into a "Reaffirmation Agreement" rather than asking whether the debtor intends to "reaffirm the debt." In addition, the debtor is asked if the property is claimed as exempt on Schedule C (Official Form 106C).

Part 2, *List Your Unexpired Personal Property Leases*, defines unexpired leases and explains that a debtor may assume an unexpired personal property lease if the trustee does not assume it.

Form B113.   Chapter 13 Plan

Fill in this information to identify your case:

Debtor 1 _____
          First Name   Middle Name   Last Name

Debtor 2 _____
(Spouse, if filing) First Name   Middle Name   Last Name

United States Bankruptcy Court for the: _____ District of _____
                                                      (State)

Case number _____
(if known)

☐ Check if this is an amended plan, and list below the sections of the plan that have been changed.

_____

_____

Official Form 113
Chapter 13 Plan   12/17

Part 1:   **Notices**

To Debtors: This form sets out options that may be appropriate in some cases, but the presence of an option on the form does not indicate that the option is appropriate in your circumstances or that it is permissible in your judicial district. Plans that do not comply with local rules and judicial rulings may not be confirmable.

In the following notice to creditors, you must check each box that applies.

To Creditors: Your rights may be affected by this plan. **Your claim may be reduced, modified, or eliminated.**

You should read this plan carefully and discuss it with your attorney if you have one in this bankruptcy case. If you do not have an attorney, you may wish to consult one.

If you oppose the plan's treatment of your claim or any provision of this plan, you or your attorney must file an objection to confirmation at least 7 days before the date set for the hearing on confirmation, unless otherwise ordered by the Bankruptcy Court. The Bankruptcy Court may confirm this plan without further notice if no objection to confirmation is filed. See Bankruptcy Rule 3015. In addition, you may need to file a timely proof of claim in order to be paid under any plan.

The following matters may be of particular importance. *Debtors must check one box on each line to state whether or not the plan includes each of the following items. If an item is checked as "Not included" or if both boxes are checked, the provision will be ineffective if set out later in the plan.*

1.1	A limit on the amount of a secured claim, set out in Section 3.2, which may result in a partial payment or no payment at all to the secured creditor	☐ Included	☐ Not included
1.2	Avoidance of a judicial lien or nonpossessory, nonpurchase-money security interest, set out in Section 3.4	☐ Included	☐ Not included
1.3	Nonstandard provisions, set out in Part 8	☐ Included	☐ Not included

Part 2:   **Plan Payments and Length of Plan**

2.1   Debtor(s) will make regular payments to the trustee as follows:

$ _____   per_____   for _____ months

[and $ _____   per_____   for _____ months.] *Insert additional lines if needed.*

If fewer than 60 months of payments are specified, additional monthly payments will be made to the extent necessary to make the payments to creditors specified in this plan.

Form B113

Debtor _____   Case number _____

2.2 Regular payments to the trustee will be made from future income in the following manner:

Check all that apply.

❑ Debtor(s) will make payments pursuant to a payroll deduction order.

❑ Debtor(s) will make payments directly to the trustee.

❑ Other (specify method of payment) _____

2.3 Income tax refunds.

Check one.

❑ Debtor(s) will retain any income tax refunds received during the plan term.

❑ Debtor(s) will supply the trustee with a copy of each income tax return filed during the plan term within 14 days of filing the return and will turn over to the trustee all income tax refunds received during the plan term.

❑ Debtor(s) will treat income tax refunds as follows:

_____

_____

2.4 Additional payments.

Check one.

❑ **None.** *If "None" is checked, the rest of § 2.4 need not be completed or reproduced.*

❑ Debtor(s) will make additional payment(s) to the trustee from other sources, as specified below. Describe the source, estimated amount, and date of each anticipated payment.

_____

_____

2.5 The total amount of estimated payments to the trustee provided for in §§ 2.1 and 2.4 is $ _____.

Part 3:   Treatment of Secured Claims

3.1 Maintenance of payments and cure of default, if any.

Check one.

❑ **None.** *If "None" is checked, the rest of § 3.1 need not be completed or reproduced.*

❑ The debtor(s) will maintain the current contractual installment payments on the secured claims listed below, with any changes required by the applicable contract and noticed in conformity with any applicable rules. These payments will be disbursed either by the trustee or directly by the debtor(s), as specified below. Any existing arrearage on a listed claim will be paid in full through disbursements by the trustee, with interest, if any, at the rate stated. Unless otherwise ordered by the court, the amounts listed on a proof of claim filed before the filing deadline under Bankruptcy Rule 3002(c) control over any contrary amounts listed below as to the current installment payment and arrearage. In the absence of a contrary timely filed proof of claim, the amounts stated below are controlling. If relief from the automatic stay is ordered as to any item of collateral listed in this paragraph, then, unless otherwise ordered by the court, all payments under this paragraph as to that collateral will cease, and all secured claims based on that collateral will no longer be treated by the plan. The final column includes only payments disbursed by the trustee rather than by the debtor(s).

Name of creditor	Collateral	Current installment payment (including escrow)	Amount of arrearage (if any)	Interest rate on arrearage (if applicable)	Monthly plan payment on arrearage	Estimated total payments by trustee
_____	_____	$_____ Disbursed by: ❑ Trustee ❑ Debtor(s)	$_____	____%	$_____	$_____
_____	_____	$_____ Disbursed by: ❑ Trustee ❑ Debtor(s)	$_____	____%	$_____	$_____

Insert additional claims as needed.

Official Form 113   Chapter 13 Plan   Page 2

Debtor _____   Case number _____

3.2 Request for valuation of security, payment of fully secured claims, and modification of undersecured claims. *Check one.*

☐ **None.** *If "None" is checked, the rest of § 3.2 need not be completed or reproduced.*

The remainder of this paragraph will be effective only if the applicable box in Part 1 of this plan is checked.

☐ The debtor(s) request that the court determine the value of the secured claims listed below. For each non-governmental secured claim listed below, the debtor(s) state that the value of the secured claim should be as set out in the column headed *Amount of secured claim.* For secured claims of governmental units, unless otherwise ordered by the court, the value of a secured claim listed in a proof of claim filed in accordance with the Bankruptcy Rules controls over any contrary amount listed below. For each listed claim, the value of the secured claim will be paid in full with interest at the rate stated below.

The portion of any allowed claim that exceeds the amount of the secured claim will be treated as an unsecured claim under Part 5 of this plan. If the amount of a creditor's secured claim is listed below as having no value, the creditor's allowed claim will be treated in its entirety as an unsecured claim under Part 5 of this plan. Unless otherwise ordered by the court, the amount of the creditor's total claim listed on the proof of claim controls over any contrary amounts listed in this paragraph.

The holder of any claim listed below as having value in the column headed *Amount of secured claim* will retain the lien on the property interest of the debtor(s) or the estate(s) until the earlier of:

(a)   payment of the underlying debt determined under nonbankruptcy law, or

(b)   discharge of the underlying debt under 11 U.S.C. § 1328, at which time the lien will terminate and be released by the creditor.

Name of creditor	Estimated amount of creditor's total claim	Collateral	Value of collateral	Amount of claims senior to creditor's claim	Amount of secured claim	Interest rate	Monthly payment to creditor	Estimated total of monthly payments
_____	$_____	_____	$____	$_____	$_____	___%	$_____	$_____
_____	$_____	_____	$____	$_____	$_____	___%	$_____	$_____

Insert additional claims as needed.

3.3 Secured claims excluded from 11 U.S.C. § 506.

Check one.

☐ **None.** *If "None" is checked, the rest of § 3.3 need not be completed or reproduced.*

☐ The claims listed below were either:

(1)   incurred within 910 days before the petition date and secured by a purchase money security interest in a motor vehicle acquired for the personal use of the debtor(s), or

(2)   incurred within 1 year of the petition date and secured by a purchase money security interest in any other thing of value.

These claims will be paid in full under the plan with interest at the rate stated below. These payments will be disbursed either by the trustee or directly by the debtor(s), as specified below. Unless otherwise ordered by the court, the claim value stated on a proof of claim filed before the filing deadline under Bankruptcy Rule 3002(c) controls over any contrary amount listed below. In the absence of a contrary timely filed proof of claim, the amounts stated below are controlling. The final column includes only payments disbursed by the trustee rather than by the debtor(s).

Name of creditor	Collateral	Amount of claim	Interest rate	Monthly plan payment	Estimated total payments by trustee
_____	_____	$_____	___%	$_____ Disbursed by: ☐ Trustee ☐ Debtor(s)	$_____
_____	_____	$_____	___%	$_____ Disbursed by: ☐ Trustee ☐ Debtor(s)	$_____

Insert additional claims as needed.

For Complete Annotation Materials, see United States Code Annotated

Form B113

Debtor _____ Case number _____

3.4 Lien avoidance.

Check one.

☐ **None.** *If "None" is checked, the rest of § 3.4 need not be completed or reproduced.*
The remainder of this paragraph will be effective only if the applicable box in Part 1 of this plan is checked.

☐ The judicial liens or nonpossessory, nonpurchase money security interests securing the claims listed below impair exemptions to which the debtor(s) would have been entitled under 11 U.S.C. § 522(b). Unless otherwise ordered by the court, a judicial lien or security interest securing a claim listed below will be avoided to the extent that it impairs such exemptions upon entry of the order confirming the plan. The amount of the judicial lien or security interest that is avoided will be treated as an unsecured claim in Part 5 to the extent allowed. The amount, if any, of the judicial lien or security interest that is not avoided will be paid in full as a secured claim under the plan. See 11 U.S.C. § 522(f) and Bankruptcy Rule 4003(d). *If more than one lien is to be avoided, provide the information separately for each lien.*

Information regarding judicial lien or security interest	Calculation of lien avoidance		Treatment of remaining secured claim
Name of creditor _____	a. Amount of lien	$_____	**Amount of secured claim after avoidance (line a minus line f)** $_____
	b. Amount of all other liens	$_____	
Collateral _____	c. Value of claimed exemptions	+ $_____	**Interest rate (if applicable)**
	d. Total of adding lines a, b, and c	$_____	_____ %
Lien identification (such as judgment date, date of lien recording, book and page number) _____ _____	e. Value of debtor(s)' interest in property	– $_____	**Monthly payment on secured claim** $_____
	f. Subtract line e from line d.	$_____	**Estimated total payments on secured claim** $_____

Extent of exemption impairment
(Check applicable box):

☐ **Line f is equal to or greater than line a.**

The entire lien is avoided. *(Do not complete the next column.)*

☐ **Line f is less than line a.**

A portion of the lien is avoided. *(Complete the next column.)*

Insert additional claims as needed.

3.5 Surrender of collateral.

Check one.

☐ **None.** *If "None" is checked, the rest of § 3.5 need not be completed or reproduced.*

☐ The debtor(s) elect to surrender to each creditor listed below the collateral that secures the creditor's claim. The debtor(s) request that upon confirmation of this plan the stay under 11 U.S.C. § 362(a) be terminated as to the collateral only and that the stay under § 1301 be terminated in all respects. Any allowed unsecured claim resulting from the disposition of the collateral will be treated in Part 5 below.

Name of creditor	Collateral
_____	_____
_____	_____

Insert additional claims as needed.

Debtor _____   Case number _____

Part 4:   Treatment of Fees and Priority Claims

4.1 General

Trustee's fees and all allowed priority claims, including domestic support obligations other than those treated in § 4.5, will be paid in full without postpetition interest.

4.2 Trustee's fees

Trustee's fees are governed by statute and may change during the course of the case but are estimated to be _____% of plan payments; and during the plan term, they are estimated to total $_____.

4.3 Attorney's fees

The balance of the fees owed to the attorney for the debtor(s) is estimated to be $_____.

4.4 Priority claims other than attorney's fees and those treated in § 4.5.

Check one.

☐ **None.** *If "None" is checked, the rest of § 4.4 need not be completed or reproduced.*

☐ The debtor(s) estimate the total amount of other priority claims to be _____

4.5 Domestic support obligations assigned or owed to a governmental unit and paid less than full amount.

Check one.

☐ **None.** *If "None" is checked, the rest of § 4.5 need not be completed or reproduced.*

☐ The allowed priority claims listed below are based on a domestic support obligation that has been assigned to or is owed to a governmental unit and will be paid less than the full amount of the claim under 11 U.S.C. § 1322(a)(4). *This plan provision requires that payments in § 2.1 be for a term of 60 months; see 11 U.S.C. § 1322(a)(4).*

Name of creditor	Amount of claim to be paid
_____	$_____
_____	$_____

Insert additional claims as needed.

Part 5:   Treatment of Nonpriority Unsecured Claims

5.1 Nonpriority unsecured claims not separately classified.

Allowed nonpriority unsecured claims that are not separately classified will be paid, pro rata. If more than one option is checked, the option providing the largest payment will be effective. *Check all that apply.*

☐ The sum of $_____.

☐ _____% of the total amount of these claims, an estimated payment of $_____.

☐ The funds remaining after disbursements have been made to all other creditors provided for in this plan.

If the estate of the debtor(s) were liquidated under chapter 7, nonpriority unsecured claims would be paid approximately $_____. Regardless of the options checked above, payments on allowed nonpriority unsecured claims will be made in at least this amount.

Form B113

OFFICIAL FORMS

Debtor _____ Case number _____

5.2 Maintenance of payments and cure of any default on nonpriority unsecured claims. *Check one.*

☐ **None.** *If "None" is checked, the rest of § 5.2 need not be completed or reproduced.*

☐ The debtor(s) will maintain the contractual installment payments and cure any default in payments on the unsecured claims listed below on which the last payment is due after the final plan payment. These payments will be disbursed either by the trustee or directly by the debtor(s), as specified below. The claim for the arrearage amount will be paid in full as specified below and disbursed by the trustee. The final column includes only payments disbursed by the trustee rather than by the debtor(s).

Name of creditor	Current installment payment	Amount of arrearage to be paid	Estimated total payments by trustee
_____	$_____ Disbursed by: ☐ Trustee ☐ Debtor(s)	$_____	$_____
_____	$_____ Disbursed by: ☐ Trustee ☐ Debtor(s)	$_____	$_____

Insert additional claims as needed.

5.3 Other separately classified nonpriority unsecured claims. *Check one.*

☐ **None.** *If "None" is checked, the rest of § 5.3 need not be completed or reproduced.*

☐ The nonpriority unsecured allowed claims listed below are separately classified and will be treated as follows.

Name of creditor	Basis for separate classification and treatment	Amount to be paid on the claim	Interest rate (if applicable)	Estimated total amount of payments
_____	_____	$_____	_____%	$_____
_____	_____	$_____	_____%	$_____

Insert additional claims as needed.

Part 6: Executory Contracts and Unexpired Leases

6.1 The executory contracts and unexpired leases listed below are assumed and will be treated as specified. All other executory contracts and unexpired leases are rejected. *Check one.*

☐ **None.** *If "None" is checked, the rest of § 6.1 need not be completed or reproduced.*

☐ **Assumed Items.** Current installment payments will be disbursed either by the trustee or directly by the debtor(s), as specified below, subject to any contrary court order or rule. Arrearage payments will be disbursed by the trustee. The final column includes only payments disbursed by the trustee rather than by the debtor(s).

Debtor _____   Case number _____

Name of creditor	Description of leased property or executory contract	Current installment payment	Amount of arrearage to be paid	Treatment of arrearage (Refer to other plan section if applicable)	Estimated total payments by trustee
_____	_____	$ _____ Disbursed by: ☐ Trustee ☐ Debtor(s)	$ _____	_____ _____	$ _____
_____	_____	$ _____ Disbursed by: ☐ Trustee ☐ Debtor(s)	$ _____	_____ _____	$ _____

Insert additional contracts or leases as needed.

Part 7:   Vesting of Property of the Estate

7.1 Property of the estate will vest in the debtor(s) upon

Check the applicable box:

☐ plan confirmation.

☐ entry of discharge.

☐ other: _____

Part 8:   Nonstandard Plan Provisions

8.1 Check "None" or List Nonstandard Plan Provisions

☐ **None.** *If "None" is checked, the rest of Part 8 need not be completed or reproduced.*

Under Bankruptcy Rule 3015(c), nonstandard provisions must be set forth below. A nonstandard provision is a provision not otherwise included in the Official Form or deviating from it. Nonstandard provisions set out elsewhere in this plan are ineffective.

The following plan provisions will be effective only if there is a check in the box "Included" in § 1.3.

_____

_____

_____

_____

_____

_____

Form B113

OFFICIAL FORMS

Debtor _____ Case number _____

Part 9: Signature(s):

9.1 Signatures of Debtor(s) and Debtor(s)' Attorney

If the Debtor(s) do not have an attorney, the Debtor(s) must sign below; otherwise the Debtor(s) signatures are optional. The attorney for the Debtor(s), if any, must sign below.

✗ _____   **✗** _____
　　Signature of Debtor 1　　　　　　　　　　　　　Signature of Debtor 2

　　Executed on _____　　　　　　　　Executed on _____
　　　　　　　　MM / DD / YYYY　　　　　　　　　　　　　　MM / DD / YYYY

✗ _____   Date _____
　　Signature of Attorney for Debtor(s)　　　　　　　　　MM / DD / YYYY

By filing this document, the Debtor(s), if not represented by an attorney, or the Attorney for Debtor(s) also certify(ies) that the wording and order of the provisions in this Chapter 13 plan are identical to those contained in Official Form 113, other than any nonstandard provisions included in Part 8.

Exhibit: Total Amount of Estimated Trustee Payments

The following are the estimated payments that the plan requires the trustee to disburse. If there is any difference between the amounts set out below and the actual plan terms, the plan terms control.

a. **Maintenance and cure payments on secured claims** *(Part 3, Section 3.1 total)* $_____

b. **Modified secured claims** *(Part 3, Section 3.2 total)* $_____

c. **Secured claims excluded from 11 U.S.C. § 506** *(Part 3, Section 3.3 total)* $_____

d. **Judicial liens or security interests partially avoided** *(Part 3, Section 3.4 total)* $_____

e. **Fees and priority claims** *(Part 4 total)* $_____

f. **Nonpriority unsecured claims** *(Part 5, Section 5.1, highest stated amount)* $_____

g. **Maintenance and cure payments on unsecured claims** *(Part 5, Section 5.2 total)* $_____

h. **Separately classified unsecured claims** *(Part 5, Section 5.3 total)* $_____

i. **Trustee payments on executory contracts and unexpired leases** *(Part 6, Section 6.1 total)* $_____

j. **Nonstandard payments** *(Part 8, total)*   + $_____

Total of lines a through J $_____

Official Form 113   Chapter 13 Plan – Exhibit   Page 1

(Added Dec. 1, 2017.)

ADVISORY COMMITTEE NOTES

Official Form 113 is new and is the required plan form in all chapter 13 cases, except to the extent that Rule 3015(c) permits the use of a Local Form. Except as permitted by Rule 9009, alterations to the Official Form are not permitted. As the form explains, spaces for responses may be expanded or collapsed as appropriate, and sections that are inapplicable do not need to be reproduced. Portions of the form provide multiple options for provisions of a debtor's plan, but some of those options may not be appropriate in a given debtor's situation or may not be allowed in the court presiding over the case. Debtors are advised to refer to applicable local rulings. Nothing in the Official Form requires confirmation of a plan containing provisions inconsistent with applicable law.

Part 1. This part sets out warnings to both debtors and creditors. For creditors, if the plan includes one or more of the provisions listed in this part, the appropriate boxes must be checked. For example, if Part 8 of the plan proposes a provision not included in, or contrary to, the Official Form, that nonstandard provision will be ineffective if the appropriate check box in Part 1 is not selected.

Part 2. This part states the proposed periodic plan payments, the estimated total plan payments, and sources of funding for the plan. Section 2.1 allows the debtor or debtors to propose periodic payments in other than monthly intervals. For example, if the debtor receives a paycheck every week and wishes to make plan payments from each check, that should be indicated in § 2.1. If the debtor proposes to make payments according to different "steps," the amounts and intervals of those payments should also be indicated in § 2.1. Section 2.2 provides for the manner in which the debtor will make regular payments to the trustee. If the debtor selects the option of making payments pursuant to a payroll deduction order, that selection serves as a request by the debtor for entry of the order. Whether to enter a payroll deduction order is determined by the court. See Code § 1325(c). If the debtor selects the option of making payments other than by direct payments to the trustee or by a payroll deduction order, the alternative method (e.g., a designated third party electronic funds transfer program) must be specified. Section 2.3 provides for the treatment of any income tax refunds received during the plan term.

Part 3. This part provides for the treatment of secured claims.

The Official Form contains no provision for proposing pre-confirmation adequate protection payments to secured creditors, leaving that subject to local rules, orders, forms, custom, and practice. A Director's Form for notice of and order on proposed adequate protection payments has been created and may be used for that purpose.

Section 3.1 provides for the treatment of claims under Code § 1322(b)(5) (maintaining current payments and curing any arrearage). For the claim of a secured creditor listed in § 3.1, an estimated arrearage amount should be given. A contrary arrearage or current installment payment amount listed on the creditor's timely filed proof of claim, unless contested by objection or motion, will control over the amount given in the plan.

In § 3.2, the plan may propose to determine under Code § 506(a) the value of a secured claim. For example, the plan could seek to reduce the secured portion of a creditor's claim to the value of the collateral securing it. For the secured claim of a non-governmental creditor, that determination would be binding upon confirmation of the plan. For the secured claim of a governmental unit, however, a contrary valuation listed on the creditor's proof of claim, unless contested by objection or motion, would control over the valuation given in the plan. *See* Bankruptcy Rule 3012. Bankruptcy Rule 3002 contemplates that a debtor, the trustee, or another entity may file a proof of claim if the creditor does not do so in a timely manner. *See* Bankruptcy Rules 3004 and 3005. Section 3.2 will not be effective unless the appropriate check box in Part 1 is selected.

Section 3.3 deals with secured claims that under the so-called "hanging paragraph" of § 1325(a)(5) may not be bifurcated into secured and unsecured portions under Code § 506(a), but it allows for the proposal of an interest rate other than the contract rate to be applied to payments on such a claim. A contrary claim amount listed on the creditor's timely filed proof of claim, unless contested by objection or motion, will control over the amount given in the plan. If appropriate, a claim may be treated under § 3.1 instead of § 3.3.

In § 3.4, the plan may propose to avoid certain judicial liens or security interests encumbering exempt property in accordance with Code § 522(f). This section includes space for the calculation of the amount of the judicial lien or security interest that is avoided. A plan proposing avoidance in § 3.4 must be served in the manner provided by Bankruptcy Rule 7004 for service of a summons and complaint. *See* Bankruptcy Rule 4003. Section 3.4 will not be effective unless the appropriate check box in Part 1 is selected.

Section 3.5 provides for elections to surrender collateral and requests for termination of the stay under § 362(a) and § 1301 with respect to the collateral surrendered. Termination will be effective upon confirmation of the plan.

Part 4. This part provides for the treatment of trustee's fees and claims entitled to priority status. Section 4.1 provides that trustee's fees and all allowed priority claims (other than those domestic support obligations treated in § 4.5) will be paid in full. In § 4.2, the plan lists an estimate of the trustee's

fees. Although the estimate may indicate whether the plan will be feasible, it does not affect the trustee's entitlement to fees as determined by statute. In § 4.3, the form requests a statement of the balance of attorney's fees owed. Additional details about payments of attorney's fees, including information about their timing and approval, are left to the requirements of local practice. In § 4.4, the plan calls for an estimated amount of other priority claims. A contrary amount listed on the creditor's proof of claim, unless changed by court order in response to an objection or motion, will control over the amount given in § 4.4. In § 4.5, the plan may propose to pay less than the full amount of a domestic support obligation that has been assigned to, or is owed to, a governmental unit, but not less than the amount that claim would have received in a chapter 7 liquidation. *See* §§ 1322(a)(4) and 1325(a)(4) of the Code. This plan provision requires that the plan payments be for a term of 60 months. *See* § 1322(a)(4).

Part 5. This part provides for the treatment of unsecured claims that are not entitled to priority status. In § 5.1, the plan may propose to pay nonpriority unsecured claims in accordance with several options. One or more options may be selected. For example, the plan could propose simply to pay unsecured creditors any funds remaining after disbursements to other creditors, or it could also provide that a defined percentage of the total amount of unsecured claims will be paid. In § 5.2, the plan may propose to cure any arrearages and maintain periodic payments on long-term, nonpriority unsecured debts pursuant to § 1322(b)(5) of the Code. In § 5.3, the plan may provide for the separate classification of nonpriority unsecured claims (such as co-debtor claims) as permitted under Code § 1322(b)(1).

Part 6. This part provides for executory contracts and unexpired leases. An executory contract or unexpired lease is rejected unless it is listed in this part. If the plan proposes neither to assume nor reject an executory contract or unexpired lease, that treatment would have to be set forth as a nonstandard provision in Part 8.

The Official Form contains no provision on the order of distribution of payments under the plan, leaving that to local rules, orders, custom, and practice. If the debtor desires to propose a specific order of distribution, it must be contained in Part 8.

Part 7. This part defines when property of the estate will revest in the debtor or debtors. One choice must be selected— upon plan confirmation, upon entry of discharge the case, or upon some other specified event. This plan provision is subject to a contrary court order under Code § 1327(b).

Part 8. This part gives the debtor or debtors the opportunity to propose provisions that are not otherwise in, or that deviate from, the Official Form. All such nonstandard provisions must be set forth in this part and nowhere else in the plan. This part will not be effective unless the appropriate check box in Part 1 is selected. *See* Bankruptcy Rule 3015(c).

Part 9. The plan must be signed by the attorney for the debtor or debtors. If the debtor or debtors are not represented by an attorney, they must sign the plan, but the signature of represented debtors is optional. In addition to the certifications set forth in Rule 9011(b), the signature constitutes a certification that the wording and order of Official Form 113 have not been altered, other than by including any nonstandard provision in Part 8.

Form B119. Bankruptcy Petition Preparer's Notice, Declaration, and Signature

Official Form 119

Bankruptcy Petition Preparer's Notice, Declaration, and Signature   12/15

Bankruptcy petition preparers as defined in 11 U.S.C. § 110 must fill out this form every time they help prepare documents that are filed in the case. If more than one bankruptcy petition preparer helps with the documents, each must sign in Part 2. A bankruptcy petition preparer who does not comply with the provisions of title 11 of the United States Code and the Federal Rules of Bankruptcy Procedure may be fined, imprisoned, or both. 11 U.S.C. § 110; 18 U.S.C. § 156.

Part 1:   Notice to Debtor

Bankruptcy petition preparers must give the debtor a copy of this form and have the debtor sign it before they prepare any documents for filing or accept any compensation. A signed copy of this form must be filed with any document prepared.

Bankruptcy petition preparers are not attorneys and may not practice law or give you legal advice, including the following:

- whether to file a petition under the Bankruptcy Code (11 U.S.C. § 101 et seq.);
- whether filing a case under chapter 7, 11, 12, or 13 is appropriate;
- whether your debts will be eliminated or discharged in a case under the Bankruptcy Code;
- whether you will be able to keep your home, car, or other property after filing a case under the Bankruptcy Code;
- what tax consequences may arise because a case is filed under the Bankruptcy Code;
- whether any tax claims may be discharged;
- whether you may or should promise to repay debts to a creditor or enter into a reaffirmation agreement;
- how to characterize the nature of your interests in property or your debts; or
- what procedures and rights apply in a bankruptcy case.

The bankruptcy petition preparer _____ has notified me of
                                                         Name
any maximum allowable fee before preparing any document for filing or accepting any fee.

_____   Date _____
Signature of Debtor 1 acknowledging receipt of this notice   MM / DD / YYYY

_____   Date _____
Signature of Debtor 2 acknowledging receipt of this notice   MM / DD / YYYY

Debtor 1 _____   Case number (if known) _____
          First Name   Middle Name   Last Name

Part 2:   Declaration and Signature of the Bankruptcy Petition Preparer

Under penalty of perjury, I declare that:

- I am a bankruptcy petition preparer or the officer, principal, responsible person, or partner of a bankruptcy petition preparer;

- I or my firm prepared the documents listed below and gave the debtor a copy of them and the *Notice to Debtor by Bankruptcy Petition Preparer* as required by 11 U.S.C. §§ 110(b), 110(h), and 342(b); and

- if rules or guidelines are established according to 11 U.S.C. § 110(h) setting a maximum fee for services that bankruptcy petition preparers may charge, I or my firm notified the debtor of the maximum amount before preparing any document for filing or before accepting any fee from the debtor.

Printed name _____   Title, if any _____   Firm name, if it applies _____

Number _____ Street _____

City _____   State _____ ZIP Code _____   Contact phone _____

I or my firm prepared the documents checked below and the completed declaration is made a part of each document that I check:
(Check all that apply.)

☐ Voluntary Petition (Form 101)
☐ Statement About Your Social Security Numbers (Form 121)
☐ Summary of Your Assets and Liabilities and Certain Statistical Information (Form 106Sum)
☐ Schedule A/B (Form 106A/B)
☐ Schedule C (Form 106C)
☐ Schedule D (Form 106D)
☐ Schedule E/F (Form 106E/F)
☐ Schedule G (Form 106G)
☐ Schedule H (Form 106H)

☐ Schedule I (Form 106I)
☐ Schedule J (Form 106J)
☐ Declaration About an Individual Debtor's Schedules (Form 106Dec)
☐ Statement of Financial Affairs (Form 107)
☐ Statement of Intention for Individuals Filing Under Chapter 7 (Form 108)
☐ Chapter 7 Statement of Your Current Monthly Income (Form 122A-1)
☐ Statement of Exemption from Presumption of Abuse Under § 707(b)(2) (Form 122A-1Supp)
☐ Chapter 7 Means Test Calculation (Form 122A-2)

☐ Chapter 11 Statement of Your Current Monthly Income (Form 122B)
☐ Chapter 13 Statement of Your Current Monthly Income and Calculation of Commitment Period (Form 122C-1)
☐ Chapter 13 Calculation of Your Disposable Income (Form 122C-2)
☐ Application to Pay Filing Fee in Installments (Form 103A)
☐ Application to Have Chapter 7 Filing Fee Waived (Form 103B)
☐ A list of names and addresses of all creditors (creditor or mailing matrix)
☐ Other _____

Bankruptcy petition preparers must sign and give their Social Security numbers. If more than one bankruptcy petition preparer prepared the documents to which this declaration applies, the signature and Social Security number of each preparer must be provided. 11 U.S.C. § 110.

_____   _____   Date _____
Signature of bankruptcy petition preparer or officer, principal, responsible   Social Security number of person who signed   MM / DD / YYYY
person, or partner

_____
Printed name

_____   _____   Date _____
Signature of bankruptcy petition preparer or officer, principal, responsible   Social Security number of person who signed   MM / DD / YYYY
person, or partner

_____
Printed name

(Added Dec. 1, 2015.)

ADVISORY COMMITTEE NOTES

Official Form 119, *Bankruptcy Petition Preparer's Notice, Declaration, and Signature*, applies only in cases of individual debtors. It is revised as part of the Forms Modernization Project, making it easier to read and, as a result, likely to generate more complete and accurate responses. In addition, the form is renumbered, and stylistic changes are made throughout the form.

The form is derived from former Official Form 19, *Declaration and Signature of Non-Attorney Bankruptcy Petition Preparer*. An instruction is added to the form that provides statutory citations. Filers are advised that if more than one bankruptcy petition preparer helped with the documents, each must sign the form.

Part 1, *Notice to Debtor*, is moved to the beginning of the form and revised. An instruction is added that bankruptcy petition preparers must give the debtor a copy of the form and have the debtor sign it before they prepare any documents for filing or accept compensation, and that the form must be filed with any document prepared. It warns the debtor that bankruptcy petition preparers are not attorneys and may not practice law or give legal advice, with a list of examples of advice that may not be provided by a bankruptcy petition preparer. The signature line of this part includes a statement that the debtor acknowledges receipt of the notice.

Part 2, *Declaration and Signature of the Bankruptcy Petition Preparer*, revises the declaration by the bankruptcy petition preparer to include an officer, principal, responsible person, or partner of a bankruptcy petition preparer. The bankruptcy petition preparer must provide a firm name, if applicable, as well as a contact phone, and must indicate which documents the bankruptcy petition preparer prepared from a list of documents. An "other" option is provided for any additional documents. The signature line includes spaces for the bankruptcy petition preparer to enter a social security number, and language regarding an officer, principal, responsible person, or partner of the bankruptcy petition preparer.

Form B121. Your Statement About Your Social Security Numbers

Official Form 121

Statement About Your Social Security Numbers   12/15

Use this form to tell the court about any Social Security or federal Individual Taxpayer Identification numbers you have used. Do not file this form as part of the public case file. This form must be submitted separately and must not be included in the court's public electronic records. Please consult local court procedures for submission requirements.

To protect your privacy, the court will not make this form available to the public. You should not include a full Social Security Number or Individual Taxpayer Number on any other document filed with the court. The court will make only the last four digits of your numbers known to the public. However, the full numbers will be available to your creditors, the U.S. Trustee or bankruptcy administrator, and the trustee assigned to your case.

Making a false statement, concealing property, or obtaining money or property by fraud in connection with a bankruptcy case can result in fines up to $250,000, or imprisonment for up to 20 years, or both. 18 U.S.C. §§ 152, 1341, 1519, and 3571.

Part 1: Tell the Court About Yourself and Your spouse if Your Spouse is Filing With You

	For Debtor 1:	For Debtor 2 (Only if Spouse is Filing):
1. Your name	First name	First name
	Middle name	Middle name
	Last name	Last name

Part 2: Tell the Court About all of Your Social Security or Federal Individual Taxpayer Identification Numbers

2. All Social Security Numbers you have used

_ _ _ - _ _ - _ _ _ _   _ _ _ - _ _ - _ _ _ _

_ _ _ - _ _ - _ _ _ _   _ _ _ - _ _ - _ _ _ _

☐ You do not have a Social Security number.   ☐ You do not have a Social Security number.

3. All federal Individual Taxpayer Identification Numbers (ITIN) you have used

9 _ _ - _ _ - _ _ _ _   9 _ _ - _ _ - _ _ _ _

9 _ _ - _ _ - _ _ _ _   9 _ _ - _ _ - _ _ _ _

☐ You do not have an ITIN.   ☐ You do not have an ITIN.

Part 3: Sign Below

Under penalty of perjury, I declare that the information I have provided in this form is true and correct.

Under penalty of perjury, I declare that the information I have provided in this form is true and correct.

X _____   X _____
Signature of Debtor 1   Signature of Debtor 2

Date _____   Date _____
MM / DD / YYYY   MM / DD / YYYY

Official Form 121   Statement About Your Social Security Numbers   109

(Added Dec. 1, 2015.)

ADVISORY COMMITTEE NOTES

Official Form 121, *Statement About Your Social Security Numbers*, is revised as part of the Forms Modernization Project. The form, which applies only in cases of individual debtors, replaces former Official Form 21, *Statement of Social Security Number(s)*. It is renumbered to distinguish it from the forms used by non-individual debtors, such as corporations and partnerships.

To make Form 121 easier to understand and complete, the form is divided into three sections, and directions on the form are simplified. The debtor's Employer Tax–Identification number (EIN) is eliminated from the form, and the debtor's name is moved from the caption to the body of the form.

Form B122A–1   OFFICIAL FORMS

Form B122A–1. Chapter 7 Statement of Your Current Monthly Income and Means–Test Calculation

Official Form 122A–1

Chapter 7 Statement of Your Current Monthly Income   12/15

Be as complete and accurate as possible. If two married people are filing together, both are equally responsible for being accurate. If more space is needed, attach a separate sheet to this form. Include the line number to which the additional information applies. On the top of any additional pages, write your name and case number (if known). If you believe that you are exempted from a presumption of abuse because you do not have primarily consumer debts or because of qualifying military service, complete and file *Statement of Exemption from Presumption of Abuse Under § 707(b)(2)* (Official Form 122A-1Supp) with this form.

Part 1:   Calculate Your Current Monthly Income

1. What is your marital and filing status? Check one only.

   ☐ Not married. Fill out Column A, lines 2-11.

   ☐ Married and your spouse is filing with you. Fill out both Columns A and B, lines 2-11.

   ☐ Married and your spouse is NOT filing with you. You and your spouse are:

       ☐ Living in the same household and are not legally separated. Fill out both Columns A and B, lines 2-11.

       ☐ Living separately or are legally separated. Fill out Column A, lines 2-11; do not fill out Column B. By checking this box, you declare under penalty of perjury that you and your spouse are legally separated under nonbankruptcy law that applies or that you and your spouse are living apart for reasons that do not include evading the Means Test requirements. 11 U.S.C. § 707(b)(7)(B).

   Fill in the average monthly income that you received from all sources, derived during the 6 full months before you file this bankruptcy case. 11 U.S.C. § 101(10A). For example, if you are filing on September 15, the 6-month period would be March 1 through August 31. If the amount of your monthly income varied during the 6 months, add the income for all 6 months and divide the total by 6. Fill in the result. Do not include any income amount more than once. For example, if both spouses own the same rental property, put the income from that property in one column only. If you have nothing to report for any line, write $0 in the space.

	Column A Debtor 1	Column B Debtor 2 or non-filing spouse
2. Your gross wages, salary, tips, bonuses, overtime, and commissions (before all payroll deductions).	$_____	$_____
3. Alimony and maintenance payments. Do not include payments from a spouse if Column B is filled in.	$_____	$_____
4. All amounts from any source which are regularly paid for household expenses of you or your dependents, including child support. Include regular contributions from an unmarried partner, members of your household, your dependents, parents, and roommates. Include regular contributions from a spouse only if Column B is not filled in. Do not include payments you listed on line 3.	$_____	$_____

5. Net income from operating a business, profession, or farm

	Debtor 1	Debtor 2			
Gross receipts (before all deductions)	$_____	$_____			
Ordinary and necessary operating expenses	– $_____	– $_____			
Net monthly income from a business, profession, or farm	$_____	$_____	Copy here →	$_____	$_____

6. Net income from rental and other real property

	Debtor 1	Debtor 2			
Gross receipts (before all deductions)	$_____	$_____			
Ordinary and necessary operating expenses	– $_____	– $_____			
Net monthly income from rental or other real property	$_____	$_____	Copy here →	$_____	$_____

| 7. Interest, dividends, and royalties | | | | $_____ | $_____ |

For Complete Annotation Materials, see United States Code Annotated

796

Debtor 1 _____

First Name   Middle Name   Last Name

Case number (if known) _____

	Column A Debtor 1	Column B Debtor 2 or non-filing spouse
8. Unemployment compensation	$_____	$_____

Do not enter the amount if you contend that the amount received was a benefit under the Social Security Act. Instead, list it here: .... ↓

For you.. $_____

For your spouse.. $_____

9. Pension or retirement income. Do not include any amount received that was a benefit under the Social Security Act. $_____ $_____

10. Income from all other sources not listed above. Specify the source and amount. Do not include any benefits received under the Social Security Act or payments received as a victim of a war crime, a crime against humanity, or international or domestic terrorism. If necessary, list other sources on a separate page and put the total below.

    _____ $_____ $_____

    _____ $_____ $_____

Total amounts from separate pages, if any.   + $_____   + $_____

11. Calculate your total current monthly income. Add lines 2 through 10 for each column. Then add the total for Column A to the total for Column B.

    $_____   + $_____   = $_____

                                Total current monthly income

Part 2:   **Determine Whether the Means Test Applies to You**

12. Calculate your current monthly income for the year. Follow these steps:

12a. Copy your total current monthly income from line 11. .... Copy line 11 here→ $_____

      Multiply by 12 (the number of months in a year).   x 12

12b. The result is your annual income for this part of the form.   12b. $_____

13. Calculate the median family income that applies to you. Follow these steps:

Fill in the state in which you live.   [_____]

Fill in the number of people in your household.   [_____]

Fill in the median family income for your state and size of household. .... 13. $_____

To find a list of applicable median income amounts, go online using the link specified in the separate instructions for this form. This list may also be available at the bankruptcy clerk's office.

14. How do the lines compare?

14a. ☐ Line 12b is less than or equal to line 13. On the top of page 1, check box 1, *There is no presumption of abuse.* Go to Part 3.

14b. ☐ Line 12b is more than line 13. On the top of page 1, check box 2, *The presumption of abuse is determined by Form 122A-2.* Go to Part 3 and fill out Form 122A-2.

Part 3:   **Sign Below**

By signing here, I declare under penalty of perjury that the information on this statement and in any attachments is true and correct.

X _____   X _____

Signature of Debtor 1   Signature of Debtor 2

Date _____   Date _____

     MM / DD / YYYY   MM / DD / YYYY

If you checked line 14a, do NOT fill out or file Form 122A-2.

If you checked line 14b, fill out Form 122A-2 and file it with this form.

Official Form 122A-1   Chapter 7 Statement of Your Current Monthly Income   page 2

(Added Dec. 1, 2015.)

ADVISORY COMMITTEE NOTES

Official Forms 122A-1, 122A-1Supp, 122A-2, 122B, 122C-1, and 122C-2 are updated to comport with the form numbering style developed as part of the Forms Modernization Project. The forms are derived from Official Forms 22A-1, 22A-1Supp, 22A-2, 22B, 122C-1, and 22C-2.

A statement is added to line 26 of Forms 122A-2 and 122C-2 explaining that contributions to qualified ABLE accounts, as defined in 26 U.S.C. § 529A(b), may be included in the deduction for contributions to the care of household or family members. Authorization of the deduction of such contributions was added to Bankruptcy Code § 707(b)(2)(A)(ii)(II) by the Tax Increase Prevention Act of 2014, Pub. Law No. 113-295.

Official Forms 122A-1, 122B, and 122C-1 are revised to add a workspace column for debtor 2 at questions 5 and 6 on the forms.

Official Form 122B is also revised to remove former Part 2. This portion of the form provided for the exclusion of certain income of a debtor's non-filing spouse; since that income is not required to be reported, its exclusion is unnecessary.

Other stylistic changes were made throughout the forms.

Form B122A–1Supp.   Chapter 7 Means Test Exemption Attachment

Fill in this information to identify your case:

Debtor 1 _____
     First Name   Middle Name   Last Name

Debtor 2 _____
(Spouse, if filing) First Name   Middle Name   Last Name

United States Bankruptcy Court for the: _____ District of _____

Case number _____
(If known)

☐ Check if this is an amended filing

Official Form 122A–1Supp

Statement of Exemption from Presumption of Abuse Under § 707(b)(2)   12/15

File this supplement together with *Chapter 7 Statement of Your Current Monthly Income* (Official Form 122A-1), if you believe that you are exempted from a presumption of abuse. Be as complete and accurate as possible. If two married people are filing together, and any of the exclusions in this statement applies to only one of you, the other person should complete a separate Form 122A-1 if you believe that this is required by 11 U.S.C. § 707(b)(2)(C).

Part 1:   Identify the Kind of Debts You Have

1. Are your debts primarily consumer debts? *Consumer debts are defined in 11 U.S.C. § 101(8) as "incurred by an individual primarily for a personal, family, or household purpose."* Make sure that your answer is consistent with the answer you gave at line 16 of the *Voluntary Petition for Individuals Filing for Bankruptcy* (Official Form 101).

   ☐ No. Go to Form 122A-1, or the top of page 1 of that form, check box 1. *There is no presumption of abuse*, and sign Part 3. Then submit this supplement with the signed Form 122A-1.

   ☐ Yes. Go to Part 2.

Part 2:   Determine Whether Military Service Provisions Apply to You

2. Are you a disabled veteran (as defined in 38 U.S.C. § 3741(1))?

   ☐ No. Go to line 3.

   ☐ Yes. Did you incur debts mostly while you were on active duty or while you were performing a homeland defense activity? 10 U.S.C. § 101(d)(1); 32 U.S.C. § 901(1).

     ☐ No. Go to line 3.

     ☐ Yes. Go to Form 122A-1, on the top of page 1 of that form, check box 1. *There is no presumption of abuse*, and sign Part 3. Then submit this supplement with the signed Form 122A-1.

3. Are you or have you been a Reservist or member of the National Guard?

   ☐ No. Complete Form 122A-1. Do not submit this supplement.

   ☐ Yes. Were you called to active duty or did you perform a homeland defense activity? 10 U.S.C. § 101(d)(1); 32 U.S.C. § 901(1).

     ☐ No. Complete Form 122A-1. Do not submit this supplement.

     ☐ Yes. Check any one of the following categories that applies:

       ☐ I was called to active duty after September 11, 2001, for at least 90 days and remain on active duty.

       ☐ I was called to active duty after September 11, 2001, for at least 90 days and was released from active duty on _____ which is fewer than 540 days before I file this bankruptcy case.

       ☐ I am performing a homeland defense activity for at least 90 days.

       ☐ I performed a homeland defense activity for at least 90 days, ending on _____ which is fewer than 540 days before I file this bankruptcy case.

> If you checked one of the categories to the left, go to Form 122A-1. On the top of page 1 of Form 122A-1, check box 3. *The Means Test does not apply now*, and sign Part 3. Then submit this supplement with the signed Form 122A-1. You are not required to fill out the rest of Official Form 122A-1 during the exclusion period. The *exclusion period* means the time you are on active duty or are performing a homeland defense activity, and for 540 days afterward. 11 U.S.C. § 707(b)(2)(D)(ii).
>
> If your exclusion period ends before your case is closed, you may have to file an amended form later.

Official Form 122A-1Supp   Statement of Exemption from Presumption of Abuse Under § 707(b)(2)   113

(Added Dec. 1, 2015.)

ADVISORY COMMITTEE NOTES

Official Forms 122A–1, 122A–1Supp, 122A–2, 122B, 122C–1, and 122C–2 are updated to comport with the form numbering style developed as part of the Forms Modernization Project. The forms are derived from Official Forms 22A–1, 22A–1Supp, 22A–2, 22B, 122C–1, and 22C–2.

A statement is added to line 26 of Forms 122A–2 and 122C–2 explaining that contributions to qualified ABLE accounts, as defined in 26 U.S.C. § 529A(b), may be included in the deduction for contributions to the care of household or family members. Authorization of the deduction of such contributions was added to Bankruptcy Code § 707(b)(2)(A)(ii)(II) by the Tax Increase Prevention Act of 2014, Pub. Law No. 113–295.

Official Forms 122A–1, 122B, and 122C–1 are revised to add a workspace column for debtor 2 at questions 5 and 6 on the forms.

Official Form 122B is also revised to remove former Part 2. This portion of the form provided for the exclusion of certain income of a debtor's non-filing spouse; since that income is not required to be reported, its exclusion is unnecessary.

Other stylistic changes were made throughout the forms.

Form B122A–2. Chapter 7 Means Test Calculation

Fill in this information to identify your case:

Debtor 1 _____
    First Name   Middle Name   Last Name

Debtor 2
(Spouse, if filing)   First Name   Middle Name   Last Name

United States Bankruptcy Court for the: _____ District of _____

Case number _____
(If known)

Check the appropriate box as directed in lines 40 or 42:

According to the calculations required by this Statement:

☐ 1. There is no presumption of abuse.

☐ 2. There is a presumption of abuse.

☐ Check if this is an amended filing

Official Form 122A–2

Chapter 7 Means Test Calculation   04/16

To fill out this form, you will need your completed copy of *Chapter 7 Statement of Your Current Monthly Income* (Official Form 122A-1).

Be as complete and accurate as possible. If two married people are filing together, both are equally responsible for being accurate. If more space is needed, attach a separate sheet to this form. Include the line number to which the additional information applies. On the top of any additional pages, write your name and case number (if known).

Part 1:   **Determine Your Adjusted Income**

1. Copy your total current monthly income. .... Copy line 11 from Official Form 122A-1 here ➔ .... $_____

2. Did you fill out Column B in Part 1 of Form 122A-1?

    ☐ No. Fill in $0 for the total on line 3.

    ☐ Yes. Is your spouse filing with you?

        ☐ No. Go to line 3.

        ☐ Yes. Fill in $0 for the total on line 3.

3. Adjust your current monthly income by subtracting any part of your spouse's income not used to pay for the household expenses of you or your dependents. Follow these steps:

    On line 11, Column B of Form 122A-1, was any amount of the income you reported for your spouse NOT regularly used for the household expenses of you or your dependents?

    ☐ No. Fill in 0 for the total on line 3.

    ☐ Yes. Fill in the information below.

State each purpose for which the income was used For example, the income is used to pay your spouse's tax debt or to support people other than you or your dependents	Fill in the amount you are subtracting from your spouse's income
_____	$_____
_____	$_____
_____	+$_____
Total.	$_____ Copy total here .... ➔ –$_____

4. Adjust your current monthly income. Subtract the total on line 3 from line 1. $_____

Form B122A–2

Debtor 1 _____

First Name   Middle Name   Last Name

Case number (if known) _____

Part 2:   Calculate Your Deductions from Your Income

The Internal Revenue Service (IRS) issues National and Local Standards for certain expense amounts. Use these amounts to answer the questions in lines 6-15. To find the IRS standards, go online using the link specified in the separate instructions for this form. This information may also be available at the bankruptcy clerk's office.

Deduct the expense amounts set out in lines 6-15 regardless of your actual expense. In later parts of the form, you will use some of your actual expenses if they are higher than the standards. Do not deduct any amounts that you subtracted from your spouse's income in line 3 and do not deduct any operating expenses that you subtracted from income in lines 5 and 6 of Form 122A–1.

If your expenses differ from month to month, enter the average expense.

Whenever this part of the form refers to you, it means both you and your spouse if Column B of Form 122A–1 is filled in.

---

5. **The number of people used in determining your deductions from income**

   Fill in the number of people who could be claimed as exemptions on your federal income tax return, plus the number of any additional dependents whom you support. This number may be different from the number of people in your household.

   [   ]

National Standards   You must use the IRS National Standards to answer the questions in lines 6-7.

---

6. **Food, clothing, and other items:** Using the number of people you entered in line 5 and the IRS National Standards, fill in the dollar amount for food, clothing, and other items. $_____

7. **Out-of-pocket health care allowance:** Using the number of people you entered in line 5 and the IRS National Standards, fill in the dollar amount for out-of-pocket health care. The number of people is split into two categories—people who are under 65 and people who are 65 or older—because older people have a higher IRS allowance for health care costs. If your actual expenses are higher than this IRS amount, you may deduct the additional amount on line 22.

   People who are under 65 years of age

   7a. Out-of-pocket health care allowance per person $_____

   7b. Number of people who are under 65   X _____

   7c. Subtotal. Multiply line 7a by line 7b. $_____   Copy here➔ $_____

   People who are 65 years of age or older

   7d. Out-of-pocket health care allowance per person $_____

   7e. Number of people who are 65 or older   X _____

   7f. Subtotal. Multiply line 7d by line 7e. $_____   Copy here➔ + $_____

   7g. Total. Add lines 7c and 7f .... $_____   Copy total here➔ $_____

Official Form 122A–2   Chapter 7 Means Test Calculation   page 2

Debtor 1 _____   Case number (if known)_____
            First Name   Middle Name   Last Name

| Local Standards | You must use the IRS Local Standards to answer the questions in lines 8-15. |

Based on information from the IRS, the U.S. Trustee Program has divided the IRS Local Standard for housing for bankruptcy purposes into two parts:

- Housing and utilities – Insurance and operating expenses
- Housing and utilities – Mortgage or rent expenses

To answer the questions in lines 8-9, use the U.S. Trustee Program chart.

To find the chart, go online using the link specified in the separate instructions for this form. This chart may also be available at the bankruptcy clerk's office.

8. Housing and utilities – Insurance and operating expenses: Using the number of people you entered in line 5, fill in the dollar amount listed for your county for insurance and operating expenses. .... $_____

9. Housing and utilities – Mortgage or rent expenses:

9a. Using the number of people you entered in line 5, fill in the dollar amount listed for your county for mortgage or rent expenses.. $_____

9b. Total average monthly payment for all mortgages and other debts secured by your home.

To calculate the total average monthly payment, add all amounts that are contractually due to each secured creditor in the 60 months after you file for bankruptcy. Then divide by 60.

Name of the creditor	Average monthly payment
_____	$_____
_____	$_____
_____	+ $_____

Total average monthly payment $_____ Copy here➡   – $_____   Repeat this amount on line 33a.

9c. Net mortgage or rent expense.
Subtract line 9b (total average monthly payment) from line 9a (mortgage or rent expense). If this amount is less than $0, enter $0 .... $_____ Copy here➡ $_____

10. If you claim that the U.S. Trustee Program's division of the IRS Local Standard for housing is incorrect and affects the calculation of your monthly expenses, fill in any additional amount you claim. $_____

Explain why.   _____

11. Local transportation expenses: Check the number of vehicles for which you claim an ownership or operating expense.

☐ 0. Go to line 14.
☐ 1. Go to line 12.
☐ 2 or more. Go to line 12.

12. Vehicle operation expense: Using the IRS Local Standards and the number of vehicles for which you claim the operating expenses, fill in the Operating Costs that apply for your Census region or metropolitan statistical area. $_____

Form B122A-2   OFFICIAL FORMS

Debtor 1 _____   Case number (if known)_____
        First Name   Middle Name   Last Name

13. **Vehicle ownership or lease expense:** Using the IRS Local Standards, calculate the net ownership or lease expense for each vehicle below. You may not claim the expense if you do not make any loan or lease payments on the vehicle. In addition, you may not claim the expense for more than two vehicles.

Vehicle 1   Describe Vehicle 1: _____

13a. Ownership or leasing costs using IRS Local Standard. .... $_____

13b. Average monthly payment for all debts secured by Vehicle 1.
      Do not include costs for leased vehicles.

      To calculate the average monthly payment here and on line 13e, add all amounts that are contractually due to each secured creditor in the 60 months after you filed for bankruptcy. Then divide by 60.

Name of each creditor for Vehicle 1	Average monthly payment
_____	$_____
_____	+ $_____

      Total average monthly payment $_____   Copy here➔   – $_____   Repeat this amount on line 33b.

13c. Net Vehicle 1 ownership or lease expense
      Subtract line 13b from line 13a. If this amount is less than $0, enter $0. ...... $_____   Copy net Vehicle 1 expense here ....➔ $_____

Vehicle 2   Describe Vehicle 2: _____

13d. Ownership or leasing costs using IRS Local Standard. .... $_____

13e. Average monthly payment for all debts secured by Vehicle 2.
      Do not include costs for leased vehicles.

Name of each creditor for Vehicle 2	Average monthly payment
_____	$_____
_____	+ $_____

      Total average monthly payment $_____   Copy here➔   – $_____   Repeat this amount on line 33c.

13f. Net Vehicle 2 ownership or lease expense
      Subtract line 13e from 13d. If this amount is less than $0, enter $0. ...... $_____   Copy net Vehicle 2 expense here ➔ $_____

14. **Public transportation expense:** If you claimed 0 vehicles in line 11, using the IRS Local Standards, fill in the *Public Transportation* expense allowance regardless of whether you use public transportation. $_____

15. **Additional public transportation expense:** If you claimed 1 or more vehicles in line 11 and if you claim that you may also deduct a public transportation expense, you may fill in what you believe is the appropriate expense, but you may not claim more than the IRS Local Standard for *Public Transportation*. $_____

Official Form 122A-2   Chapter 7 Means Test Calculation   page 4

Debtor 1 _____   Case number (if known) _____
            First Name   Middle Name   Last Name

Other Necessary Expenses	In addition to the expense deductions listed above, you are allowed your monthly expenses for the following IRS categories.

16. **Taxes:** The total monthly amount that you will actually owe for federal, state and local taxes, such as income taxes, self-employment taxes, Social Security taxes, and Medicare taxes. You may include the monthly amount withheld from your pay for these taxes. However, if you expect to receive a tax refund, you must divide the expected refund by 12 and subtract that number from the total monthly amount that is withheld to pay for taxes.

Do not include real estate, sales, or use taxes. $_____

17. **Involuntary deductions:** The total monthly payroll deductions that your job requires, such as retirement contributions, union dues, and uniform costs.

Do not include amounts that are not required by your job, such as voluntary 401(k) contributions or payroll savings. $_____

18. **Life insurance:** The total monthly premiums that you pay for your own term life insurance. If two married people are filing together, include payments that you make for your spouse's term life insurance. Do not include premiums for life insurance on your dependents, for a non-filing spouse's life insurance, or for any form of life insurance other than term. $_____

19. **Court-ordered payments:** The total monthly amount that you pay as required by the order of a court or administrative agency, such as spousal or child support payments.

Do not include payments on past due obligations for spousal or child support. You will list these obligations in line 35. $_____

20. **Education:** The total monthly amount that you pay for education that is either required:
   - as a condition for your job, or
   - for your physically or mentally challenged dependent child if no public education is available for similar services. $_____

21. **Childcare:** The total monthly amount that you pay for childcare, such as babysitting, daycare, nursery, and preschool.

Do not include payments for any elementary or secondary school education. $_____

22. **Additional health care expenses, excluding insurance costs:** The monthly amount that you pay for health care that is required for the health and welfare of you or your dependents and that is not reimbursed by insurance or paid by a health savings account. Include only the amount that is more than the total entered in line 7.
Payments for health insurance or health savings accounts should be listed only in line 25. $_____

23. **Optional telephones and telephone services:** The total monthly amount that you pay for telecommunication services for you and your dependents, such as pagers, call waiting, caller identification, special long distance, or business cell phone service, to the extent necessary for your health and welfare or that of your dependents or for the production of income, if it is not reimbursed by your employer.   + $_____

Do not include payments for basic home telephone, internet and cell phone service. Do not include self-employment expenses, such as those reported on line 5 of Official Form 122A-1, or any amount you previously deducted.

24. **Add all of the expenses allowed under the IRS expense allowances.**
Add lines 6 through 23 $_____

Form B122A–2

OFFICIAL FORMS

Debtor 1 _____ First Name   Middle Name   Last Name   Case number (if known) _____

Additional Expense Deductions	These are additional deductions allowed by the Means Test

Note: Do not include any expense allowances listed in lines 6-24

25. **Health insurance, disability insurance, and health savings account expenses.** The monthly expenses for health insurance, disability insurance, and health savings accounts that are reasonably necessary for yourself, your spouse, or your dependents.

Health insurance $_____

Disability insurance $_____

Health savings account   + $_____

Total $_____   Copy total here ➔ .... $_____

Do you actually spend this total amount?

☐ No. How much do you actually spend? $_____
☐ Yes

26. **Continuing contributions to the care of household or family members.** The actual monthly expenses that you will continue to pay for the reasonable and necessary care and support of an elderly, chronically ill, or disabled member of your household or member of your immediate family who is unable to pay for such expenses. These expenses may include contributions to an account of a qualified ABLE program. 26 U.S.C. § 529A(b). $_____

27. **Protection against family violence.** The reasonably necessary monthly expenses that you incur to maintain the safety of you and your family under the Family Violence Prevention and Services Act or other federal laws that apply. $_____

By law, the court must keep the nature of these expenses confidential.

28. **Additional home energy costs.** Your home energy costs are included in your insurance and operating expenses on line 8.

If you believe that you have home energy costs that are more than the home energy costs included in expenses on line 8, then fill in the excess amount of home energy costs. $_____

You must give your case trustee documentation of your actual expenses, and you must show that the additional amount claimed is reasonable and necessary.

29. **Education expenses for dependent children who are younger than 18.** The monthly expenses (not more than $160.42* per child) that you pay for your dependent children who are younger than 18 years old to attend a private or public elementary or secondary school. $_____

You must give your case trustee documentation of your actual expenses, and you must explain why the amount claimed is reasonable and necessary and not already accounted for in lines 6-23.

* Subject to adjustment on 4/01/19, and every 3 years after that for cases begun on or after the date of adjustment.

30. **Additional food and clothing expense.** The monthly amount by which your actual food and clothing expenses are higher than the combined food and clothing allowances in the IRS National Standards. That amount cannot be more than 5% of the food and clothing allowances in the IRS National Standards. $_____

To find a chart showing the maximum additional allowance, go online using the link specified in the separate instructions for this form. This chart may also be available at the bankruptcy clerk's office.

You must show that the additional amount claimed is reasonable and necessary.

31. **Continuing charitable contributions.** The amount that you will continue to contribute in the form of cash or financial instruments to a religious or charitable organization. 26 U.S.C. § 170(c)(1) (2).   + $_____

32. **Add all of the additional expense deductions.**
Add lines 25 through 31. $_____

Debtor 1 _____   Case number (if known)_____
          First Name   Middle Name   Last Name

Deductions for Debt Payment

33. For debts that are secured by an interest in property that you own, including home mortgages, vehicle loans, and other secured debt, fill in lines 33a through 33e.

To calculate the total average monthly payment, add all amounts that are contractually due to each secured creditor in the 60 months after you file for bankruptcy. Then divide by 60.

		Average monthly payment
Mortgages on your home:		
33a. Copy line 9b here ....→	$	
Loans on your first two vehicles:		
33b. Copy line 13b here ....→	$	
33c. Copy line 13e here ....→	$_____	

33d. List other secured debts:

Name of each creditor for other secured debt	Identify property that secures the debt	Does payment include taxes or insurance?	
_____	_____	☐ No ☐ Yes	$_____
_____	_____	☐ No ☐ Yes	$_____
_____	_____	☐ No ☐ Yes	+ $_____

33e. Total average monthly payment. Add lines 33a through 33d........................ $_____   Copy total here→ $_____

34. Are any debts that you listed in line 33 secured by your primary residence, a vehicle, or other property necessary for your support or the support of your dependents?

☐ No. Go to line 35.
☐ Yes. State any amount that you must pay to a creditor, in addition to the payments listed in line 33, to keep possession of your property (called the *cure amount*). Next, divide by 60 and fill in the information below.

Name of the creditor	Identify property that secures the debt	Total cure amount		Monthly cure amount
_____	_____	$_____	÷ 60 =	$_____
_____	_____	$_____	÷ 60 =	$_____
_____	_____	$_____	÷ 60 =	+ $_____
		Total	$_____	Copy total here→ $_____

35. Do you owe any priority claims such as a priority tax, child support, or alimony — that are past due as of the filing date of your bankruptcy case? 11 U.S.C. § 507.

☐ No. Go to line 36.
☐ Yes. Fill in the total amount of all of these priority claims. Do not include current or ongoing priority claims, such as those you listed in line 19.

Total amount of all past-due priority claims .... $_____ ÷ 60 = $_____

Form B122A–2

Debtor 1 _____ First Name   Middle Name   Last Name   Case number (if known)_____

36. Are you eligible to file a case under Chapter 13? 11 U.S.C. § 109(e).
For more information, go online using the link for *Bankruptcy Basics* specified in the separate instructions for this form. *Bankruptcy Basics* may also be available at the bankruptcy clerk's office.

☐ No. Go to line 37.

☐ Yes. Fill in the following information.

Projected monthly plan payment if you were filing under Chapter 13. $_____

Current multiplier for your district as stated on the list issued by the Administrative Office of the United States Courts (for districts in Alabama and North Carolina) or by the Executive Office for United States Trustees (for all other districts).   x _____

To find a list of district multipliers that includes your district, go online using the link specified in the separate instructions for this form. This list may also be available at the bankruptcy clerk's office.

Average monthly administrative expense if you were filing under Chapter 13 $_____   Copy total here ➡ $_____

37. **Add all of the deductions for debt payment.**
Add lines 33e through 36 $_____

Total Deductions from Income

38. **Add all of the allowed deductions.**

Copy line 24, *All of the expenses allowed under IRS expense allowances*....................... $_____

Copy line 32, *All of the additional expense deductions*......... $_____

Copy line 37, *All of the deductions for debt payment*...........   + $_____

Total deductions $_____   Copy total here ....➡ $_____

<table>
<tr><td>Part 3:</td><td>Determine Whether There Is a Presumption of Abuse</td></tr>
</table>

39. Calculate monthly disposable income for 60 months.

39a. Copy line 4, *adjusted current monthly income*..... $_____

39b. Copy line 38, *Total deductions*. ....   – $_____

39c. Monthly disposable income. 11 U.S.C. § 707(b)(2). Subtract line 39b from line 39a. $_____   Copy here➡ $_____

For the next 60 months (5 years) ....   x 60

39d. Total. Multiply line 39c by 60 .... $_____   Copy here➡ $_____

40. Find out whether there is a presumption of abuse. Check the box that applies:

☐ The line 39d is less than $7,700*. On the top of page 1 of this form, check box 1, *There is no presumption of abuse*. Go to Part 5.

☐ The line 39d is more than $12,850*. On the top of page 1 of this form, check box 2, *There is a presumption of abuse*. You may fill out Part 4 if you claim special circumstances. Then go to Part 5.

☐ The line 39d is at least $7,700*, but not more than $12,850*. Go to line 41.

* Subject to adjustment on 4/01/19, and every 3 years after that for cases filed on or after the date of adjustment.

Debtor 1 _____   Case number *(if known)* _____
First Name   Middle Name   Last Name

41. 41a. **Fill in the amount of your total nonpriority unsecured debt.** If you filled out A
Summary of Your Assets and Liabilities and Certain Statistical Information Schedules
(Official Form 106Sum), you may refer to line 3b on that form .... $ _____

x .25

41b. **25% of your total nonpriority unsecured debt.** 11 U.S.C. § 707(b)(2)(A)(i)(I).
Multiply line 41a by 0.25. .... $ _____   Copy
here ➔ $ _____

42. **Determine whether the income you have left over after subtracting all allowed deductions
is enough to pay 25% of your unsecured, nonpriority debt.**
Check the box that applies:

☐ **Line 39d is less than line 41b.** On the top of page 1 of this form, check box 1, *There is no presumption of abuse*.
Go to Part 5.

☐ **Line 39d is equal to or more than line 41b.** On the top of page 1 of this form, check box 2, *There is a presumption
of abuse*. You may fill out Part 4 if you claim special circumstances. Then go to Part 5.

Part 4:   Give Details About Special Circumstances

43. **Do you have any special circumstances that justify additional expenses or adjustments of current monthly income for which there is no
reasonable alternative?** 11 U.S.C. § 707(b)(2)(B).

☐ **No** Go to Part 5.
☐ **Yes** Fill in the following information. All figures should reflect your average monthly expense or income adjustment
for each item. You may include expenses you listed in line 25.

You must give a detailed explanation of the special circumstances that make the expenses or income
adjustments necessary and reasonable. You must also give your case trustee documentation of your actual
expenses or income adjustments.

Give a detailed explanation of the special circumstances	Average monthly expense or income adjustment
_____	$ _____
_____	$ _____
_____	$ _____
_____	$ _____

Part 5:   Sign Below

By signing here, I declare under penalty of perjury that the information on this statement and in any attachments is true and correct.

X _____   **X** _____
Signature of Debtor 1   Signature of Debtor 2

Date _____   Date _____
MM / DD / YYYY   MM / DD / YYYY

Official Form 122A–2   Chapter 7 Means Test Calculation   page 9

(Added Dec. 1, 2015; and amended Apr. 1, 2016.)

ADVISORY COMMITTEE NOTES

Official Forms 122A–1, 122A–1Supp, 122A–2, 122B, 122C–1, and 122C–2 are updated to comport with the form numbering style developed as part of the Forms Modernization Project. The forms are derived from Official Forms 22A–1, 22A–1Supp, 22A–2, 22B, 122C–1, and 22C–2.

A statement is added to line 26 of Forms 122A–2 and 122C–2 explaining that contributions to qualified ABLE accounts, as defined in 26 U.S.C. § 529A(b), may be included in the deduction for contributions to the care of household or family members. Authorization of the deduction of such contributions was added to Bankruptcy Code § 707(b)(2)(A)(ii)(II) by the Tax Increase Prevention Act of 2014, Pub. Law No. 113–295.

Official Forms 122A–1, 122B, and 122C–1 are revised to add a workspace column for debtor 2 at questions 5 and 6 on the forms.

Official Form 122B is also revised to remove former Part 2. This portion of the form provided for the exclusion of certain income of a debtor's non-filing spouse; since that income is not required to be reported, its exclusion is unnecessary.

Other stylistic changes were made throughout the forms.

Form B122B

Form B122B. Chapter 11 Statement of Your Current Monthly Income

---

Fill in this information to identify your case:

Debtor 1 _____
FIRST NAME   MIDDLE NAME   LAST NAME

Debtor 2 _____
(Spouse, if filing) First Name   Middle Name   Last Name

United States Bankruptcy Court for the: _____ District of _____
(State)

Case number _____
(If known)

☐ Check if this is an amended filing

Official Form 122B

Chapter 11 Statement of Your Current Monthly Income   12/15

You must file this form if you are an individual and are filing for bankruptcy under Chapter 11. If more space is needed, attach a separate sheet to this form. Include the line number to which the additional information applies. On the top of any additional pages, write your name and case number (if known).

Part 1:   Calculate Your Current Monthly Income

1. What is your marital and filing status? Check one only.

   ☐ Not married. Fill out Column A, lines 2-11.
   ☐ Married and your spouse is filing with you. Fill out both Columns A and B, lines 2-11.
   ☐ Married and your spouse is NOT filing with you. Fill out Column A, lines 2-11.

   Fill in the average monthly income that you received from all sources, derived during the 6 full months before you file this bankruptcy case. 11 U.S.C. § 101(10A). For example, if you are filing on September 15, the 6-month period would be March 1 through August 31. If the amount of your monthly income varied during the 6 months, add the income for all 6 months and divide the total by 6. Fill in the result.
   Do not include any income amount more than once. For example, if both spouses own the same rental property, put the income from that property in one column only. If you have nothing to report for any line, write $0 in the space.

	Column A Debtor 1	Column B Debtor 2
2. Your gross wages, salary, tips, bonuses, overtime, and commissions (before all payroll deductions).	$_____	$_____
3. Alimony and maintenance payments. Do not include payments from a spouse if Column B is filled in.	$_____	$_____
4. All amounts from any source which are regularly paid for household expenses of you or your dependents, including child support. Include regular contributions from an unmarried partner, members of your household, your dependents, parents, and roommates. Include regular contributions from a spouse only if Column B is not filled in. Do not include payments you listed on line 3.	$_____	$_____

5. Net income from operating a business, profession, or farm

	Debtor 1	Debtor 2			
Gross receipts (before all deductions)	$____	$____			
Ordinary and necessary operating expenses	– $____	– $____			
Net monthly income from a business, profession, or farm	$____	$____	Copy here →	$_____	$_____

6. Net income from rental and other real property

	Debtor 1	Debtor 2			
Gross receipts (before all deductions)	$____	$____			
Ordinary and necessary operating expenses	– $____	– $____			
Net monthly income from rental or other real property	$____	$____	Copy here →	$_____	$_____

Debtor 1 _____ _____ _____   Case number (if known) _____

	Column A Debtor 1	Column B Debtor 2

7. Interest, dividends, and royalties $_____ $_____

8. Unemployment compensation $_____ $_____

Do not enter the amount if you contend that the amount received was a benefit
under the Social Security Act. Instead, list it here: ....↓

For you .... $_____

For your spouse .... $_____

9. Pension or retirement income. Do not include any amount received that was a
benefit under the Social Security Act $_____ $_____

10. Income from all other sources not listed above. Specify the source and amount.
Do not include any benefits received under the Social Security Act or payments
received as a victim of a war crime, a crime against humanity, or international or
domestic terrorism.

If necessary, list other sources on a separate page and put the total below.

_____ $_____ $_____

_____ $_____ $_____

Total amounts from separate pages, if any   + $_____ + $_____

11. Calculate your total current monthly income.
Add lines 2 through 10 for each column.
Then add the total for Column A to the total for Column B. $_____ + $_____ = $_____

Total current
monthly income

Part 2:   Sign Below

By signing here, under penalty of perjury I declare that the information on this statement and in any attachments is true and correct.

X _____   X _____
Signature of Debtor 1   Signature of Debtor 2

Date _____   Date _____
MM / DD / YYYY   MM / DD / YYYY

(Added Dec. 1, 2015.)

ADVISORY COMMITTEE NOTES

Official Forms 122A–1, 122A–1Supp, 122A–2, 122B, 122C–1, and 122C–2 are updated to comport with the form numbering style developed as part of the Forms Modernization Project. The forms are derived from Official Forms 22A–1, 22A–1Supp, 22A–2, 22B, 22C–1, and 22C–2.

A statement is added to line 26 of Forms 122A–2 and 122C–2 explaining that contributions to qualified ABLE accounts, as defined in 26 U.S.C. § 529A(b), may be included in the deduction for contributions to the care of household or family members. Authorization of the deduction of such contributions was added to Bankruptcy Code § 707(b)(2)(A)(ii)(II) by the Tax Increase Prevention Act of 2014, Pub. Law No. 113–295.

Official Forms 122A–1, 122B, and 122C–1 are revised to add a workspace column for debtor 2 at questions 5 and 6 on the forms.

Official Form 122B is also revised to remove former Part 2. This portion of the form provided for the exclusion of certain income of a debtor's non-filing spouse; since that income is not required to be reported, its exclusion is unnecessary.

Other stylistic changes were made throughout the forms.

Form B122C–1. Chapter 13 Statement of Your Current Monthly Income and Calculation of Commitment Period

Fill in this information to identify your case:

Debtor 1 _____
First Name   Middle Name   Last Name

Debtor 2 _____
(Spouse if filing) First Name   Middle Name   Last Name

United States Bankruptcy Court for the: _____ District of _____
(State)

Case number _____
(If known)

Check as directed in lines 17 and 21:

According to the calculations required by this Statement:

☐ 1. Disposable income is not determined under 11 U.S.C. § 1325(b)(3).

☐ 2. Disposable income is determined under 11 U.S.C. § 1325(b)(3).

☐ 3. The commitment period is 3 years.

☐ 4. The commitment period is 5 years.

☐ Check if this is an amended filing

Official Form 122C–1

Chapter 13 Statement of Your Current Monthly Income and Calculation of Commitment Period   12/15

Be as complete and accurate as possible. If two married people are filing together, both are equally responsible for being accurate. If more space is needed, attach a separate sheet to this form. Include the line number to which the additional information applies. On the top of any additional pages, write your name and case number (if known).

Part 1: Calculate Your Average Monthly Income

1. What is your marital and filing status? Check one only.

☐ Not married. Fill out Column A, lines 2-11.

☐ Married. Fill out both Columns A and B, lines 2-11.

Fill in the average monthly income that you received from all sources, derived during the 6 full months before you file this bankruptcy case. 11 U.S.C. § 101(10A). For example, if you are filing on September 15, the 6-month period would be March 1 through August 31. If the amount of your monthly income varied during the 6 months, add the income for all 6 months and divide the total by 6. Fill in the result. Do not include any income amount more than once. For example, if both spouses own the same rental property, put the income from that property in one column only. If you have nothing to report for any line, write $0 in the space.

	Column A Debtor 1	Column B Debtor 2 or non-filing spouse
2. Your gross wages, salary, tips, bonuses, overtime, and commissions (before all payroll deductions).	$_____	$_____
3. Alimony and maintenance payments. Do not include payments from a spouse.	$_____	$_____
4. All amounts from any source which are regularly paid for household expenses of you or your dependents, including child support. Include regular contributions from an unmarried partner, members of your household, your dependents, parents, and roommates. Do not include payments from a spouse. Do not include payments you listed on line 3.	$_____	$_____

5. Net income from operating a business, profession, or farm

	Debtor 1	Debtor 2			
Gross receipts (before all deductions)	$_____	$_____			
Ordinary and necessary operating expenses	– $_____	– $_____			
Net monthly income from a business, profession, or farm	$_____	$_____	Copy here →	$_____	$_____

6. Net income from rental and other real property

	Debtor 1	Debtor 2			
Gross receipts (before all deductions)	$_____	$_____			
Ordinary and necessary operating expenses	– $_____	– $_____			
Net monthly income from rental or other real property	$_____	$_____	Copy here →	$_____	$_____

OFFICIAL FORMS

Form B122C-1

Debtor 1 _____
First Name   Middle Name   Last Name

Case number _____

	Column A Debtor 1	Column B Debtor 2 or non-filing spouse
7. Interest, dividends, and royalties	$_____	$_____
8. Unemployment compensation		

Do not enter the amount if you contend that the amount received was a benefit under the Social Security Act. Instead, list it here: _____ ↓

For you .... $_____
For your spouse .... $_____

9. Pension or retirement income. Do not include any amount received that was a benefit under the Social Security Act. $_____ $_____

10. Income from all other sources not listed above. Specify the source and amount. Do not include any benefits received under the Social Security Act or payments received as a victim of a war crime, a crime against humanity, or international or domestic terrorism. If necessary, list other sources on a separate page and put the total below.

$_____ $_____
$_____ $_____

Total amounts from separate pages, if any.   +$_____   +$_____

11. Calculate your total average monthly income. Add lines 2 through 10 for each column. Then add the total for Column A to the total for Column B.

$_____ + $_____ = $_____ Total average monthly income

Part 2: Determine How to Measure Your Deductions from Income

12. Copy your total average monthly income from line 11. .... $_____

13. Calculate the marital adjustment. Check one:

☐ You are not married. Fill in 0 below.
☐ You are married and your spouse is filing with you. Fill in 0 below.
☐ You are married and your spouse is not filing with you.

Fill in the amount of the income listed in line 11, Column B, that was NOT regularly paid for the household expenses of you or your dependents, such as payment of the spouse's tax liability or the spouse's support of someone other than you or your dependents.

Below, specify the basis for excluding this income and the amount of income devoted to each purpose. If necessary, list additional adjustments on a separate page.

If this adjustment does not apply, enter 0 below.

_____ $_____
_____ $_____
_____ +$_____

Total .... $_____ Copy here → – _____

14. Your current monthly income. Subtract the total in line 13 from line 12. $_____

15. Calculate your current monthly income for the year. Follow these steps:

15a. Copy line 14 here → .... $_____
Multiply line 15a by 12 (the number of months in a year).   x 12

15b. The result is your current monthly income for the year for this part of the form. .... $_____

Official Form 122C-1   Chapter 13 Statement of Your Current Monthly Income and Calculation of Commitment Period   126   page 2

Form B122C–1

Debtor 1 _____ Case number _____
First Name   Middle Name   Last Name

16. Calculate the median family income that applies to you. Follow these steps:

16a. Fill in the state in which you live. _____

16b. Fill in the number of people in your household. _____

16c. Fill in the median family income for your state and size of household. .... $_____
To find a list of applicable median income amounts, go online using the link specified in the separate instructions for this form. This list may also be available at the bankruptcy clerk's office.

17. How do the lines compare?

17a. ☐ Line 15b is less than or equal to line 16c. On the top of page 1 of this form, check box 1, *Disposable income is not determined under 11 U.S.C. § 1325(b)(3)*. Go to Part 3. Do NOT fill out *Calculation of Your Disposable Income* (Official Form 122C–2).

17b. ☐ Line 15b is more than line 16c. On the top of page 1 of this form, check box 2, *Disposable income is determined under 11 U.S.C. § 1325(b)(3)*. Go to Part 3 and fill out *Calculation of Your Disposable Income* (Official Form 122C–2). On line 39 of that form, copy your current monthly income from line 14 above.

Part 3: Calculate Your Commitment Period Under 11 U.S.C. § 1325(b)(4)

18. Copy your total average monthly income from line 11. .... $_____

19. Deduct the marital adjustment if it applies. If you are married, your spouse is not filing with you, and you contend that calculating the commitment period under 11 U.S.C. § 1325(b)(4) allows you to deduct part of your spouse's income, copy the amount from line 13.

19a. If the marital adjustment does not apply, fill in 0 on line 19a. .... – $_____

19b. Subtract line 19a from line 18. $_____

20. Calculate your current monthly income for the year. Follow these steps:

20a. Copy line 19b. .... $_____

Multiply by 12 (the number of months in a year). x 12

20b. The result is your current monthly income for the year for this part of the form. $_____

20c. Copy the median family income for your state and size of household from line 16c. .... $_____

21. How do the lines compare?

☐ Line 20b is less than line 20c. Unless otherwise ordered by the court, on the top of page 1 of this form, check box 3. *The commitment period is 3 years.* Go to Part 4.

☐ Line 20b is more than or equal to line 20c. Unless otherwise ordered by the court, on the top of page 1 of this form, check box 4, *The commitment period is 5 years.* Go to Part 4.

Part 4: Sign Below

By signing here, under penalty of perjury I declare that the information on this statement and in any attachments is true and correct.

✗ _____   ✗ _____
Signature of Debtor 1   Signature of Debtor 2

Date _____   Date _____
MM / DD / YYYY   MM / DD / YYYY

If you checked 17a, do NOT fill out or file Form 122C–2.
If you checked 17b, fill out Form 122C–2 and file it with this form. On line 39 of that form, copy your current monthly income from line 14 above.

Official Form 122C–1   Chapter 13 Statement of Your Current Monthly Income and Calculation of Commitment Period   127   page 3

(Added Dec. 1, 2015.)

ADVISORY COMMITTEE NOTES

Official Forms 122A–1, 122A–1Supp, 122A–2, 122B, 122C–1, and 122C–2 are updated to comport with the form numbering style developed as part of the Forms Modernization Project. The forms are derived from Official Forms 22A–1, 22A–1Supp, 22A–2, 22B, 122C–1, and 22C–2.

A statement is added to line 26 of Forms 122A–2 and 122C–2 explaining that contributions to qualified ABLE accounts, as defined in 26 U.S.C. § 529A(b), may be included in the deduction for contributions to the care of household or family members. Authorization of the deduction of such contributions was added to Bankruptcy Code § 707(b)(2)(A)(ii)(II) by the Tax Increase Prevention Act of 2014, Pub. Law No. 113–295.

Official Forms 122A–1, 122B, and 122C–1 are revised to add a workspace column for debtor 2 at questions 5 and 6 on the forms.

Official Form 122B is also revised to remove former Part 2. This portion of the form provided for the exclusion of certain income of a debtor's non-filing spouse; since that income is not required to be reported, its exclusion is unnecessary.

Other stylistic changes were made throughout the forms.

Form B122C–2. Chapter 13 Calculation of Your Disposable Income

Fill in this information to identify your case:

Debtor 1 _____
         First Name   Middle Name   Last Name

Debtor 2 _____
(Spouse, if filing) First Name   Middle Name   Last Name

United States Bankruptcy Court for the: _____ District of _____

Case number _____
(If known)

☐ Check if this is an amended filing

Official Form 122C-2

Chapter 13 Calculation of Your Disposable Income

04/16

To fill out this form, you will need your completed copy of *Chapter 13 Statement of Your Current Monthly Income and Calculation of Commitment Period* (Official Form 122C–1).

Be as complete and accurate as possible. If two married people are filing together, both are equally responsible for being accurate. If more space is needed, attach a separate sheet to this form. Include the line number to which the additional information applies. On the top of any additional pages, write your name and case number (if known).

Part 1:   Calculate Your Deductions from Your Income

The Internal Revenue Service (IRS) issues National and Local Standards for certain expense amounts. Use these amounts to answer the questions in lines 6-15. To find the IRS standards, go online using the link specified in the separate instructions for this form. This information may also be available at the bankruptcy clerk's office.

Deduct the expense amounts set out in lines 6-15 regardless of your actual expense. In later parts of the form, you will use some of your actual expenses if they are higher than the standards. Do not include any operating expenses that you subtracted from income in lines 5 and 6 of Form 122C–1, and do not deduct any amounts that you subtracted from your spouse's income in line 13 of Form 122C–1.

If your expenses differ from month to month, enter the average expense.

Note: Line numbers 1-4 are not used in this form. These numbers apply to information required by a similar form used in chapter 7 cases.

5. **The number of people used in determining your deductions from income**
    Fill in the number of people who could be claimed as exemptions on your federal income tax return, plus the number of any additional dependents whom you support. This number may be different from the number of people in your household.

    ☐

National Standards   You must use the IRS National Standards to answer the questions in lines 6-7.

6. **Food, clothing, and other items:** Using the number of people you entered in line 5 and the IRS National Standards, fill in the dollar amount for food, clothing, and other items. $_____

7. **Out-of-pocket health care allowance:** Using the number of people you entered in line 5 and the IRS National Standards, fill in the dollar amount for out-of-pocket health care. The number of people is split into two categories—people who are under 65 and people who are 65 or older—because older people have a higher IRS allowance for health care costs. If your actual expenses are higher than this IRS amount, you may deduct the additional amount on line 22.

Official Form 122C-2   Chapter 13 Calculation of Your Disposable Income   page 1

Form B122C–2

Debtor 1 _____ _____ _____   Case number _____
      First Name   Middle Name   Last Name

People who are under 65 years of age

7a. Out-of-pocket health care allowance per person $_____

7b. Number of people who are under 65 X_____

7c. Subtotal. Multiply line 7a by line 7b. $_____ Copy here ➔ $_____

People who are 65 years of age or older

7d. Out-of-pocket health care allowance per person $_____

7e. Number of people who are 65 or older X_____

7f. Subtotal. Multiply line 7d by line 7e. $_____ Copy here ➔ + $_____

7g. **Total.** Add lines 7c and 7f. .... $_____ Copy here ➔ $_____

Local Standards   You must use the IRS Local Standards to answer the questions in lines 8-15.

Based on information from the IRS, the U.S. Trustee Program has divided the IRS Local Standard for housing for bankruptcy purposes into two parts:

■ Housing and utilities – Insurance and operating expenses
■ Housing and utilities – Mortgage or rent expenses

To answer the questions in lines 8-9, use the U.S. Trustee Program chart. To find the chart, go online using the link specified in the separate instructions for this form. This chart may also be available at the bankruptcy clerk's office.

8. **Housing and utilities – Insurance and operating expenses:** Using the number of people you entered in line 5, fill in the dollar amount listed for your county for insurance and operating expenses. $_____

9. **Housing and utilities – Mortgage or rent expenses:**

    9a. Using the number of people you entered in line 5, fill in the dollar amount listed for your county for mortgage or rent expenses. $_____

    9b. Total average monthly payment for all mortgages and other debts secured by your home.

      To calculate the total average monthly payment, add all amounts that are contractually due to each secured creditor in the 60 months after you file for bankruptcy. Next divide by 60.

Name of the creditor	Average monthly payment
_____	$_____
_____	$_____
_____	+ $_____

    9b. Total average monthly payment $_____ Copy here ➔ – $_____ Repeat this amount on line 33a.

    9c. Net mortgage or rent expense.

      Subtract line 9b (*total average monthly payment*) from line 9a (*mortgage or rent expense*). If this number is less than $0, enter $0. $_____ Copy here ➔ .... $_____

10. If you claim that the U.S. Trustee Program's division of the IRS Local Standard for housing is incorrect and affects the calculation of your monthly expenses, fill in any additional amount you claim. $_____

    Explain why: _____

Official Form 122C-2   Chapter 13 Calculation of Your Disposable Income   page 2

Debtor 1   _____   _____   _____   Case number *(if known)* _____
          First Name   Middle Name   Last Name

11. **Local transportation expenses:** Check the number of vehicles for which you claim an ownership or operating expense.

     ☐ 0. Go to line 14.
     ☐ 1. Go to line 12.
     ☐ 2 or more. Go to line 12.

12. **Vehicle operation expense:** Using the IRS Local Standards and the number of vehicles for which you claim the operating expenses, fill in the *Operating Costs* that apply for your Census region or metropolitan statistical area. $_____

13. **Vehicle ownership or lease expense:** Using the IRS Local Standards, calculate the net ownership or lease expense for each vehicle below. You may not claim the expense if you do not make any loan or lease payments on the vehicle. In addition, you may not claim the expense for more than two vehicles.

     Vehicle 1   **Describe Vehicle 1:** _____

13a. Ownership or leasing costs using IRS Local Standard .... $_____

13b. Average monthly payment for all debts secured by Vehicle 1.
     Do not include costs for leased vehicles.

     To calculate the average monthly payment here and on line 13e, add all amounts that are contractually due to each secured creditor in the 60 months after you file for bankruptcy. Then divide by 60.

Name of each creditor for Vehicle 1	Average monthly payment
	$
_____	+ $
Total average monthly payment	$_____

     Copy here →   – $_____   Repeat this amount on line 33b.

13c. Net Vehicle 1 ownership or lease expense
     Subtract line 13b from line 13a. If this number is less than $0, enter $0. .... $_____   Copy net Vehicle 1 expense here → $_____

     Vehicle 2   **Describe Vehicle 2:** _____

13d. Ownership or leasing costs using IRS Local Standard .... $_____

13e. Average monthly payment for all debts secured by Vehicle 2.
     Do not include costs for leased vehicles.

Name of each creditor for Vehicle 2	Average monthly payment
	$
_____	+ $
Total average monthly payment	$_____

     Copy here →   – $_____   Repeat this amount on line 33c.

13f. Net Vehicle 2 ownership or lease expense
     Subtract line 13e from 13d. If this number is less than $0, enter $0. .... $_____   Copy net Vehicle 2 expense here → $_____

14. **Public transportation expense:** If you claimed 0 vehicles in line 11, using the IRS Local Standards, fill in the *Public Transportation* expense allowance regardless of whether you use public transportation. $_____

15. **Additional public transportation expense:** If you claimed 1 or more vehicles in line 11 and if you claim that you may also deduct a public transportation expense, you may fill in what you believe is the appropriate expense, but you may not claim more than the IRS Local Standard for *Public Transportation.* $_____

Form B122C-2

Debtor 1 _____ Case number _____
        First Name   Middle Name   Last Name

Other Necessary Expenses   In addition to the expense deductions listed above, you are allowed your monthly expenses for the following IRS categories.

16. **Taxes:** The total monthly amount that you actually pay for federal, state and local taxes, such as income taxes, self-employment taxes, social security taxes, and Medicare taxes. You may include the monthly amount withheld from your pay for these taxes. However, if you expect to receive a tax refund, you must divide the expected refund by 12 and subtract that number from the total monthly amount that is withheld to pay for taxes. Do not include real estate, sales, or use taxes. $_____

17. **Involuntary deductions:** The total monthly payroll deductions that your job requires, such as retirement contributions, union dues, and uniform costs.
Do not include amounts that are not required by your job, such as voluntary 401(k) contributions or payroll savings. $_____

18. **Life insurance:** The total monthly premiums that you pay for your own term life insurance. If two married people are filing together, include payments that you make for your spouse's term life insurance.
Do not include premiums for life insurance on your dependents, for a non-filing spouse's life insurance, or for any form of life insurance other than term. $_____

19. **Court-ordered payments:** The total monthly amount that you pay as required by the order of a court or administrative agency, such as spousal or child support payments.
Do not include payments on past due obligations for spousal or child support. You will list these obligations in line 35. $_____

20. **Education:** The total monthly amount that you pay for education that is either required:
   ■ as a condition for your job, or
   ■ for your physically or mentally challenged dependent child if no public education is available for similar services. $_____

21. **Childcare:** The total monthly amount that you pay for childcare, such as babysitting, daycare, nursery, and preschool.
Do not include payments for any elementary or secondary school education. $_____

22. **Additional health care expenses, excluding insurance costs:** The monthly amount that you pay for health care that is required for the health and welfare of you or your dependents and that is not reimbursed by insurance or paid by a health savings account. Include only the amount that is more than the total entered in line 7.
Payments for health insurance or health savings accounts should be listed only in line 25. $_____

23. **Optional telephones and telephone services:** The total monthly amount that you pay for telecommunication services for you and your dependents, such as pagers, call waiting, caller identification, special long distance, or business cell phone service, to the extent necessary for your health and welfare or that of your dependents or for the production of income, if it is not reimbursed by your employer.
Do not include payments for basic home telephone, internet or cell phone service. Do not include self-employment expenses, such as those reported on line 5 of Form 122C-1, or any amount you previously deducted.   + $_____

24. Add all of the expenses allowed under the IRS expense allowances.
Add lines 6 through 23. $_____

Additional Expense Deductions   These are additional deductions allowed by the Means Test.
Note: Do not include any expense allowances listed in lines 6-24.

25. **Health insurance, disability insurance, and health savings account expenses.** The monthly expenses for health insurance, disability insurance and health savings accounts that are reasonably necessary for yourself, your spouse, or your dependents.

   Health insurance $_____

   Disability insurance $_____

   Health savings account   + $_____

   Total $_____   Copy total here➡ .... $_____

   Do you actually spend this total amount?
   ☐ No. How much do you actually spend? $_____
   ☐ Yes

26. **Continuing contributions to the care of household or family members.** The actual monthly expenses that you will continue to pay for the reasonable and necessary care and support of an elderly, chronically ill, or disabled member of your household or member of your immediate family who is unable to pay for such expenses. These expenses may include contributions to an account of a qualified ABLE program. 26 U.S.C. § 529A(b). $_____

27. **Protection against family violence.** The reasonably necessary monthly expenses that you incur to maintain the safety of you and your family under the Family Violence Prevention and Services Act or other federal laws that apply.
By law, the court must keep the nature of these expenses confidential. $_____

For Complete Annotation Materials, see United States Code Annotated

Debtor 1 _____ Case number _____
        First Name   Middle Name   Last Name

28. **Additional home energy costs.** Your home energy costs are included in your insurance and operating expenses on line 8.

If you believe that you have home energy costs that are more than the home energy costs included in expenses on line 8, then fill in the excess amount of home energy costs.

$_____

You must give your case trustee documentation of your actual expenses, and you must show that the additional amount claimed is reasonable and necessary.

29. **Education expenses for dependent children who are younger than 18.** The monthly expenses (not more than $160.42* per child) that you pay for your dependent children who are younger than 18 years old to attend a private or public elementary or secondary school.

$_____

You must give your case trustee documentation of your actual expenses, and you must explain why the amount claimed is reasonable and necessary and not already accounted for in lines 6-23.

  *   Subject to adjustment on 4/01/19, and every 3 years after that for cases begun on or after the date of adjustment.

30. **Additional food and clothing expense.** The monthly amount by which your actual food and clothing expenses are higher than the combined food and clothing allowances in the IRS National Standards. That amount cannot be more than 5% of the food and clothing allowances in the IRS National Standards.

$_____

To find a chart showing the maximum additional allowance, go online using the link specified in the separate instructions for this form. This chart may also be available at the bankruptcy clerk's office.

You must show that the additional amount claimed is reasonable and necessary.

31. **Continuing charitable contributions.** The amount that you will continue to contribute in the form of cash or financial instruments to a religious or charitable organization. 11 U.S.C. § 548(d)(3) and (4).

+ $_____

Do not include any amount more than 15% of your gross monthly income.

32. **Add all of the additional expense deductions.**

Add lines 25 through 31.

$_____

Deductions for Debt Payment

33. **For debts that are secured by an interest in property that you own, including home mortgages, vehicle loans, and other secured debt, fill in lines 33a through 33e.**

To calculate the total average monthly payment, add all amounts that are contractually due to each secured creditor in the 60 months after you file for bankruptcy. Then divide by 60.

	Average monthly payment
Mortgages on your home	
33a. Copy line 9b here .... →	$_____
Loans on your first two vehicles	
33b. Copy line 13b here .... →	$_____
33c. Copy line 13e here. .... →	$_____

33d. List other secured debts:

Name of each creditor for other secured debt	Identify property that secures the debt	Does payment include taxes or insurance?	
_____	_____	☐ No ☐ Yes	$_____
_____	_____	☐ No ☐ Yes	$_____
_____	_____	☐ No ☐ Yes	+ $_____

33e. Total average monthly payment. Add lines 33a through 33d. .... $_____   Copy total here→ $_____

Official Form 122C-2   Chapter 13 Calculation of Your Disposable Income   page 6

Form B122C-2

Debtor 1 _____   Case number _____
   First Name   Middle Name   Last Name

34. Are any debts that you listed in line 33 secured by your primary residence, a vehicle, or other property necessary for your support or the support of your dependents?

☐ No. Go to line 35.

☐ Yes. State any amount that you must pay to a creditor, in addition to the payments listed in line 33, to keep possession of your property (called the *cure amount*). Next, divide by 60 and fill in the information below.

Name of the creditor	Identify property that secures the debt	Total cure amount		Monthly cure amount
_____	_____	$_____	÷ 60 =	$_____
_____	_____	$_____	÷ 60 =	$_____
_____	_____	$_____	÷ 60 =	+ $_____
		Total	$_____	Copy total here ➔ $_____

35. Do you owe any priority claims—such as a priority tax, child support, or alimony—that are past due as of the filing date of your bankruptcy case? 11 U.S.C. § 507

☐ No. Go to line 36.

☐ Yes. Fill in the total amount of all of these priority claims. Do not include current or ongoing priority claims, such as those you listed in line 19.

   Total amount of all past-due priority claims. .... $_____ ÷ 60 $_____

36. Projected monthly Chapter 13 plan payment $_____

Current multiplier for your district as stated on the list issued by the Administrative Office of the United States Courts (for districts in Alabama and North Carolina) or by the Executive Office for United States Trustees (for all other districts).

To find a list of district multipliers that includes your district, go online using the link specified in the separate instructions for this form. This list may also be available at the bankruptcy clerk's office.   X _____

Average monthly administrative expense $_____   Copy total here ➔ $_____

37. Add all of the deductions for debt payment. Add lines 33e through 36. $_____

Total Deductions from Income

38. Add all of the allowed deductions.

Copy line 24 *All of the expenses allowed under IRS expense allowances*. .... $_____

Copy line 32 *All of the additional expense deductions*.......................... $_____

Copy line 37 *All of the deductions for debt payment*........................... + $_____

Total deductions.. $_____   Copy total here ➔ $_____

Debtor 1 _____ Case number *(if known)* _____
     First Name   Middle Name   Last Name

Part 2: Determine Your Disposable Income Under 11 U.S.C. § 1325(b)(2)

39. Copy your total current monthly income from line 14 of Form 122C-1, *Chapter 13 Statement of Your Current Monthly Income and Calculation of Commitment Period.* $ _____

40. **Fill in any reasonably necessary income you receive for support for dependent children.** The monthly average of any child support payments, foster care payments, or disability payments for a dependent child, reported in Part I of Form 122C-1, that you received in accordance with applicable nonbankruptcy law to the extent reasonably necessary to be expended for such child. $ _____

41. **Fill in all qualified retirement deductions.** The monthly total of all amounts that your employer withheld from wages as contributions for qualified retirement plans, as specified in 11 U.S.C. § 541(b)(7) plus all required repayments of loans from retirement plans, as specified in 11 U.S.C. § 362(b)(19). $ _____

42. **Total of all deductions allowed under 11 U.S.C. § 707(b)(2)(A).** Copy line 38 here ➔ $ _____

43. **Deduction for special circumstances.** If special circumstances justify additional expenses and you have no reasonable alternative, describe the special circumstances and their expenses. You must give your case trustee a detailed explanation of the special circumstances and documentation for the expenses.

Describe the special circumstances	Amount of expense
	$ _____
_____	$ _____
_____	+ $ _____
Total	$ _____ ➔ *Copy here* + $ _____

44. **Total adjustments.** Add lines 40 through 43. .... $ _____ *Copy here* ➔   − $ _____

45. **Calculate your monthly disposable income under § 1325(b)(2).** Subtract line 44 from line 39. $ _____

Part 3: Change in Income or Expenses

46. **Change in income or expenses.** If the income in Form 122C-1 or the expenses you reported in this form have changed or are virtually certain to change after the date you filed your bankruptcy petition and during the time your case will be open, fill in the information below. For example, if the wages reported increased after you filed your petition, check 122C-1 in the first column, enter line 2 in the second column, explain why the wages increased, fill in when the increase occurred, and fill in the amount of the increase.

Form	Line	Reason for change	Date of change	Increase or decrease?	Amount of change
☐ 122C-1 ☐ 122C-2	___	_____	_____	☐ Increase ☐ Decrease	$ _____
☐ 122C-1 ☐ 122C-2	___	_____	_____	☐ Increase ☐ Decrease	$ _____
☐ 122C-1 ☐ 122C-2	___	_____	_____	☐ Increase ☐ Decrease	$ _____
☐ 122C-1 ☐ 122C-2	___	_____	_____	☐ Increase ☐ Decrease	$ _____

Form B122C–2

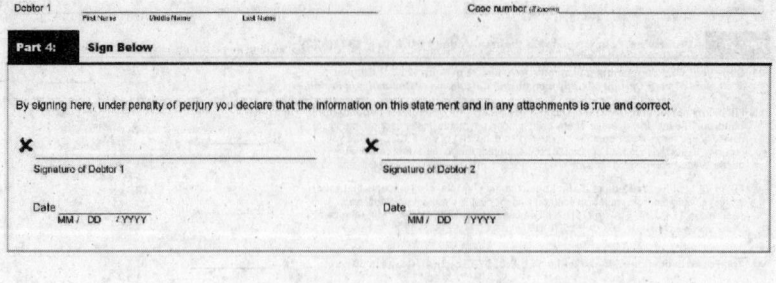

(Added Dec. 1, 2015; and amended Apr. 1, 2016.)

ADVISORY COMMITTEE NOTES

Official Forms 122A–1, 122A–1Supp, 122A–2, 122B, 122C–1, and 122C–2 are updated to comport with the form numbering style developed as part of the Forms Modernization Project. The forms are derived from Official Forms 22A–1, 22A–1Supp, 22A–2, 22B, 122C–1, and 22C–2.

A statement is added to line 26 of Forms 122A–2 and 122C–2 explaining that contributions to qualified ABLE accounts, as defined in 26 U.S.C. § 529A(b), may be included in the deduction for contributions to the care of household or family members. Authorization of the deduction of such contributions was added to Bankruptcy Code § 707(b)(2)(A)(ii)(II) by the Tax Increase Prevention Act of 2014, Pub. Law No. 113–295.

Official Forms 122A–1, 122B, and 122C–1 are revised to add a workspace column for debtor 2 at questions 5 and 6 on the forms.

Official Form 122B is also revised to remove former Part 2. This portion of the form provided for the exclusion of certain income of a debtor's non-filing spouse; since that income is not required to be reported, its exclusion is unnecessary.

Other stylistic changes were made throughout the forms.

Form B201. Voluntary Petition for Non-Individuals Filing for Bankruptcy

Fill in this information to identify the case:

United States Bankruptcy Court for the:

_____ District of _____
(State)

Case number (if known): _____ Chapter _____

☐ Check if this is an
amended filing

Official Form 201

Voluntary Petition for Non-Individuals Filing for Bankruptcy   04/16

If more space is needed, attach a separate sheet to this form. On the top of any additional pages, write the debtor's name and the case number (if known). For more information, a separate document, *Instructions for Bankruptcy Forms for Non-Individuals*, is available.

1. Debtor's name
_____

2. All other names debtor used
   in the last 8 years
   Include any assumed names,
   trade names, and *doing business
   as* names
_____
_____
_____

3. Debtor's federal Employer
   Identification Number (EIN)
   _ _ - _ _ _ _ _ _ _

4. Debtor's address

   Principal place of business

   Number   Street
   _____

   City   State   ZIP Code

   County

   Mailing address, if different from principal place of business

   Number   Street

   P.O. Box

   City   State   ZIP Code

   Location of principal assets, if different from principal place of business

   Number   Street

   City   State   ZIP Code

5. Debtor's website (URL) _____

6. Type of debtor
   ☐ Corporation (including Limited Liability Company (LLC) and Limited Liability Partnership (LLP))
   ☐ Partnership (excluding LLP)
   ☐ Other. Specify: _____

Official Form 201   Voluntary Petition for Non-Individuals Filing for Bankruptcy   page 1

Form B201

Debtor _____   Case number (if known) _____
Name

7. Describe debtor's business

A. *Check one:*

☐ Health Care Business (as defined in 11 U.S.C. § 101(27A))

☐ Single Asset Real Estate (as defined in 11 U.S.C. § 101(51B))

☐ Railroad (as defined in 11 U.S.C. § 101(44))

☐ Stockbroker (as defined in 11 U.S.C. § 101(53A))

☐ Commodity Broker (as defined in 11 U.S.C. § 101(6))

☐ Clearing Bank (as defined in 11 U.S.C. § 781(3))

☐ None of the above

B. *Check all that apply:*

☐ Tax-exempt entity (as described in 26 U.S.C. § 501)

☐ Investment company, including hedge fund or pooled investment vehicle (as defined in 15 U.S.C. § 80a-3)

☐ Investment advisor (as defined in 15 U.S.C. § 80b-2(a)(11))

C. NAICS (North American Industry Classification System) 4-digit code that best describes debtor. See http://www.uscourts.gov/four-digit-national-association-naics-codes .

_____ _____ _____ _____

8. Under which chapter of the Bankruptcy Code is the debtor filing?

Check one:

☐ Chapter 7

☐ Chapter 9

☐ Chapter 11. *Check all that apply:*

    ☐ Debtor's aggregate noncontingent liquidated debts (excluding debts owed to insiders or affiliates) are less than $2,566,050 (amount subject to adjustment on 4/01/19 and every 3 years after that).

    ☐ The debtor is a small business debtor as defined in 11 U.S.C. § 101(51D). If the debtor is a small business debtor, attach the most recent balance sheet, statement of operations, cash-flow statement, and federal income tax return or if all of these documents do not exist, follow the procedure in 11 U.S.C. § 1116(1)(B).

    ☐ A plan is being filed with this petition.

    ☐ Acceptances of the plan were solicited prepetition from one or more classes of creditors, in accordance with 11 U.S.C. § 1126(b).

    ☐ The debtor is required to file periodic reports (for example, 10K and 10Q) with the Securities and Exchange Commission according to § 13 or 15(d) of the Securities Exchange Act of 1934. File the *Attachment to Voluntary Petition for Non-Individuals Filing for Bankruptcy under Chapter 11* (Official Form 201A) with this form.

    ☐ The debtor is a shell company as defined in the Securities Exchange Act of 1934 Rule 12b-2.

☐ Chapter 12

9. Were prior bankruptcy cases filed by or against the debtor within the last 8 years?

If more than 2 cases, attach a separate list.

☐ No

☐ Yes.   District _____   When _____   Case number _____
                                          MM / DD / YYYY

                 District _____   When _____   Case number _____
                                          MM / DD / YYYY

10. Are any bankruptcy cases pending or being filed by a business partner or an affiliate of the debtor?

List all cases. If more than 1, attach a separate list.

☐ No

☐ Yes.   Debtor _____   Relationship _____

        District _____   When _____
                                           MM / DD / YYYY

        Case number if known _____

Official Form 201   Voluntary Petition for Non-Individuals Filing for Bankruptcy   page 2

For Complete Annotation Materials, see United States Code Annotated

822

Debtor _____   Case number (if known)_____
     Name

11. Why is the case filed in *this* district?

Check all that apply:

☐ Debtor has had its domicile, principal place of business, or principal assets in this district for 180 days immediately preceding the date of this petition or for a longer part of such 180 days than in any other district

☐ A bankruptcy case concerning debtor's affiliate, general partner, or partnership is pending in this district.

12. Does the debtor own or have possession of any real property or personal property that needs immediate attention?

☐ No

☐ Yes. Answer below for each property that needs immediate attention. Attach additional sheets if needed.

Why does the property need immediate attention? *(Check all that apply.)*

☐ It poses or is alleged to pose a threat of imminent and identifiable hazard to public health or safety.

What is the hazard?_____

☐ It needs to be physically secured or protected from the weather.

☐ It includes perishable goods or assets that could quickly deteriorate or lose value without attention (for example, livestock, seasonal goods, meat, dairy, produce, or securities-related assets or other options).

☐ Other _____

Where is the property?

    Number   Street

_____

    City   State   ZIP Code

Is the property insured?

☐ No

☐ Yes. Insurance agency _____

    Contact name _____

    Phone _____

Statistical and administrative information

13. Debtor's estimation of available funds

Check one:

☐ Funds will be available for distribution to unsecured creditors.

☐ After any administrative expenses are paid, no funds will be available for distribution to unsecured creditors.

14. Estimated number of creditors

☐ 1-49	☐ 1,000-5,000	☐ 25,001-50,000
☐ 50-99	☐ 5,001-10,000	☐ 50,001-100,000
☐ 100-199	☐ 10,001-25,000	☐ More than 100,000
☐ 200-999		

15. Estimated assets

☐ $0-$50,000	☐ $1,000,001-$10 million	☐ $500,000,001-$1 billion
☐ $50,001-$100,000	☐ $10,000,001-$50 million	☐ $1,000,000,001-$10 billion
☐ $100,001-$500,000	☐ $50,000,001-$100 million	☐ $10,000,000,001-$50 billion
☐ $500,001-$1 million	☐ $100,000,001-$500 million	☐ More than $50 billion

---

Official Form 201   Voluntary Petition for Non-Individuals Filing for Bankruptcy   page 3

For Complete Annotation Materials, see United States Code Annotated

Form B201

Debtor _____ Case number _(If known)_ _____
Name

16. Estimated liabilities

- ☐ $0-$50,000
- ☐ $50,001-$100,000
- ☐ $100,001-$500,000
- ☐ $500,001-$1 million

- ☐ $1,000,001-$10 million
- ☐ $10,000,001-$50 million
- ☐ $50,000,001-$100 million
- ☐ $100,000,001-$500 million

- ☐ $500,000,001-$1 billion
- ☐ $1,000,000,001-$10 billion
- ☐ $10,000,000,001-$50 billion
- ☐ More than $50 billion

Request for Relief, Declaration, and Signatures

WARNING -- Bankruptcy fraud is a serious crime. Making a false statement in connection with a bankruptcy case can result in fines up to $500,000 or imprisonment for up to 20 years, or both. 18 U.S.C. §§ 152, 1341, 1519, and 3571.

17. Declaration and signature of authorized representative of debtor

- The debtor requests relief in accordance with the chapter of title 11, United States Code, specified in this petition.

- I have been authorized to file this petition on behalf of the debtor.

- I have examined the information in this petition and have a reasonable belief that the information is true and correct.

declare under penalty of perjury that the foregoing is true and correct.

Executed on _____
MM / DD / YYYY

✗ _____   _____
Signature of authorized representative of debtor   Printed name

Title _____

18. Signature of attorney

✗ _____   Date _____
Signature of attorney for debtor   MM / DD / YYYY

Printed name _____

Firm name _____

Number   Street _____

City _____   State _____ ZIP Code _____

Contact phone _____   Email address _____

Bar number _____   State _____

Official Form 201   Voluntary Petition for Non-Individuals Filing for Bankruptcy   page 4

(Added Dec. 1, 2015; and amended Apr. 1, 2016.)

ADVISORY COMMITTEE NOTES

Official Form 201, _Voluntary Petition for Non–Individuals Filing for Bankruptcy_, replaces Official Form 1, _Voluntary Petition_, for non-individual debtors. It is renumbered to distinguish it from the forms used by individual debtors and includes formatting and stylistic changes throughout the form.

Official Form 201 is revised as part of the Forms Modernization Project, making it easier to read and, as a result, likely to generate more complete and accurate responses. The goals of the Forms Modernization Project include improving the interface between technology and the forms so as to increase efficiency and reducing the need to produce the same information in multiple formats.

The Forms Modernization Project made a preliminary decision that separate forms should be created for individual debtors and for non-individual debtors because separate areas of inquiry apply to each group. The forms for non-individuals do not include questions that pertain only to individuals and use a more open-ended response format. Also, where possible, the forms for non-individuals parallel how businesses commonly keep their financial records.

Official Form 201 has been substantially reformatted and reorganized. References to Exhibits B, C, and D, and the exhibits themselves, have been eliminated because the requested information is now asked in the form or is not applicable to non-individual debtors. Official Form 201A, _Attachment to Voluntary Petition for Non-Individuals Filing for Bankruptcy Under Chapter 11_, has replaced Exhibit A. The debtor is instructed to file Official Form 201A if the debtor is filing under chapter 11 and is required to file periodic reports with the Securities and Exchange Commission. A checkbox has been added to the form to indicate whether it is an amended filing.

In Question 2, _All other names debtor used in the last 8 years_, instructions pertaining only to individuals have been deleted, and an instruction to include doing business as names and assumed names has been added. In Question 3, _Debtor's federal Employee Identification Number (EIN)_, references to social security numbers and individual taxpayer I.D. numbers

---

For Complete Annotation Materials, see United States Code Annotated

have been deleted. In Question 4, *Debtor's address*, the order of listing the various addresses for the debtor has been rearranged, and an address for the location of principal assets is required if different from the principal place of business. Also, the form has been revised to include a space for listing the debtor's website in Question 5.

In Question 6, *Type of Debtor*, options pertaining only to individual debtors have been deleted, and an instruction that the "partnership" option does not include LLPs has been added. Question 7, *Describe debtor's business*, is revised to include a statutory citation for each business type, to add an option for "none of the above," and to delete the option for "other." A new instruction requires the debtor to indicate if the debtor is an investment company, including a hedge fund or pooled investment vehicle; an investment advisor; or a tax exempt entity. The definition of "tax exempt entity" has been removed and replaced with a statutory citation. Additionally, an instruction has been added to require the debtor to list its North American Industry Classification System 4-digit code. A hyperlink is provided for information on finding the correct code.

In Question 8, *Under which chapter of the Bankruptcy Code is the debtor filing*, several separate boxes have been combined, and the options for Chapter 13 and Chapter 15 have been deleted. More detailed options have been added for Chapter 11. The question regarding the nature of the debtor's debts has been removed.

Question 9, *Were prior bankruptcy cases filed by or against the debtor within the last 8 years*, has been revised to instruct the debtor to include prior bankruptcy cases filed against the debtor and to list the district rather than location of the prior filings. In Question 10, *Are any bankruptcy cases pending or being filed by a business partner or an affiliate of the debtor*, the reference to spouse and the requirement to list the judge in any other cases have been removed.

Question 11, *Why is this case filed in this district*, has been revised to delete references that pertain only to individuals.

Question 12, *Does the debtor own or have possession of any real property or personal property that needs immediate attention*, replaces Exhibit C from Official Form 1. The category of "property that needs immediate attention" has been added, as well as options to indicate why the property needs immediate attention. Additionally, the form has been revised to require the debtor to list the location of the property and whether or not the property is insured and, if so, the insurance details.

Statistical and administrative information has been moved to immediately above the signature line, and the reference to exempt property has been removed. The maximum values for "Estimated Assets" and "Estimated Liabilities" have been increased from "more than $1 billion" to "more than $50 billion." *Request for Relief, Declaration, and Signatures* has been reformatted and the signature lines for individual debtors and non-attorney bankruptcy petition preparers have been removed.

Form B201A

Form B201A. Attachment to Voluntary Petition for Non–Individuals Filing for Bankruptcy Under Chapter 11

Official Form 201A (12/15)

[If debtor is required to file periodic reports (e.g., forms 10K and 10Q) with the Securities and Exchange Commission pursuant to Section 13 or 15(d) of the Securities Exchange Act of 1934 and is requesting relief under chapter 11 of the Bankruptcy Code, this Exhibit "A" shall be completed and attached to the petition.]

[Caption as in Form 416B]

Attachment to Voluntary Petition for Non-Individuals Filing for Bankruptcy under Chapter 11

1. If any of the debtor's securities are registered under Section 12 of the Securities Exchange Act of 1934, the SEC file number is _____.

2. The following financial data is the latest available information and refers to the debtor's condition on _____

   a. Total assets $_____

   b. Total debts (including debts listed in 2.c., below) $_____

   c. Debt securities held by more than 500 holders

Approximate number of holders:

secured ☐	unsecured ☐	subordinated ☐	$ _____	_____
secured ☐	unsecured ☐	subordinated ☐	$ _____	_____
secured ☐	unsecured ☐	subordinated ☐	$ _____	_____
secured ☐	unsecured ☐	subordinated ☐	$ _____	_____
secured ☐	unsecured ☐	subordinated ☐	$ _____	_____

   d. Number of shares of preferred stock   _____

   e. Number of shares common stock   _____

Comments, if any: _____

_____

_____

3. Brief description of debtor's business: _____

_____

_____

4. List the names of any person who directly or indirectly owns, controls, or holds, with power to vote, 5% or more of the voting securities of debtor:

_____

_____

_____

Official Form 201A   Attachment to Voluntary Petition for Non-Individuals Filing for Bankruptcy under Chapter 11   144

(Added Dec. 1, 2015.)

Form B202. Declaration Under Penalty of Perjury for Non–Individual Debtors (for petition, schedules, SOFA, etc.)

Fill in this information to identify the case and this filing:

Debtor Name _____

United States Bankruptcy Court for the: _____ District of _____
(State)

Case number (If known) _____

Official Form 202

Declaration Under Penalty of Perjury for Non-Individual Debtors   12/15

An individual who is authorized to act on behalf of a non-individual debtor, such as a corporation or partnership, must sign and submit this form for the schedules of assets and liabilities, any other document that requires a declaration that is not included in the document, and any amendments of those documents. This form must state the individual's position or relationship to the debtor, the identity of the document, and the date. Bankruptcy Rules 1008 and 9011.

WARNING -- Bankruptcy fraud is a serious crime. Making a false statement, concealing property, or obtaining money or property by fraud in connection with a bankruptcy case can result in fines up to $500,000 or imprisonment for up to 20 years, or both. 18 U.S.C. §§ 152, 1341, 1519, and 3571.

Declaration and signature

I am the president, another officer, or an authorized agent of the corporation; a member or an authorized agent of the partnership; or another individual serving as a representative of the debtor in this case.

I have examined the information in the documents checked below and I have a reasonable belief that the information is true and correct:

☐ Schedule A/B: Assets–Real and Personal Property (Official Form 206A/B)

☐ Schedule D: Creditors Who Have Claims Secured by Property (Official Form 206D)

☐ Schedule E/F: Creditors Who Have Unsecured Claims (Official Form 206E/F)

☐ Schedule G: Executory Contracts and Unexpired Leases (Official Form 206G)

☐ Schedule H: Codebtors (Official Form 206H)

☐ Summary of Assets and Liabilities for Non-Individuals (Official Form 206Sum)

☐ Amended Schedule _____

☐ Chapter 11 or Chapter 9 Cases: List of Creditors Who Have the 20 Largest Unsecured Claims and Are Not Insiders (Official Form 204)

☐ Other document that requires a declaration_____

I declare under penalty of perjury that the foregoing is true and correct.

Executed on _____   ✗ _____
MM / DD / YYYY   Signature of individual signing on behalf of debtor

_____
Printed name

_____
Position or relationship to debtor

Official Form 202   Declaration Under Penalty of Perjury for Non-Individual Debtors   145

(Added Dec. 1, 2015.)

ADVISORY COMMITTEE NOTES

Official Form 202, *Declaration Under Penalty of Perjury for Non–Individual Debtors*, replaces Official Form 2, Declaration Under Penalty of Perjury on Behalf of a Corporation or Partnership, and the section of Official Form 6 Declaration, *Declaration Concerning Debtor's Schedules* containing a corporation's or partnership's declaration. It is renumbered to distinguish it from the forms used by individual debtors and includes formatting and stylistic changes throughout the form.

Official Form 202 is revised as part of the Forms Modernization Project, making it easier to read and, as a result, likely to generate more complete and accurate responses. The goals of the Forms Modernization Project include improving the interface between technology and the forms so as to increase efficiency and reducing the need to produce the same information in multiple formats.

Official Form 202 has been substantially reformatted and reorganized with elements from both Official Form 2 and the section of Official Form 6 for a corporation or partnership. Instructions have been added, along with warning language regarding bankruptcy fraud. Checkboxes are provided so the declaration will indicate the documents included with the declaration, including the schedules and Official Form 204, *Chapter 11 or Chapter 9 Cases: List of Creditors Who Have the 20 Largest Unsecured Claims and Are Not Insiders*. If the declaration accompanies another document, a space is provided to include a description of the attached document. The phrase "to the best of my information and belief" has been deleted from the declaration in order to conform to the language of 28 U.S.C. § 1746. See Rule 1008. The form, however, includes a statement that the person signing the declaration has examined the information in the documents subject to the declaration and has "a reasonable belief that the information is true and correct." Finally, the person signing the declaration must indicate his or her position or relationship to the debtor.

Form B204. For Chapter 11 Cases: The List of Creditors Who Have the 20 Largest Unsecured Claims Against You Who Are Not Insiders (non-individuals)

Fill in this information to identify the case:

Debtor name _____

United States Bankruptcy Court for the _____ District of _____
(State)

Case number (if known) _____

☐ Check if this is an amended filing

Official Form 204

Chapter 11 or Chapter 9 Cases: List of Creditors Who Have the 20 Largest Unsecured Claims and Are Not Insiders   12/15

A list of creditors holding the 20 largest unsecured claims must be filed in a Chapter 11 or Chapter 9 case. Include claims which the debtor disputes. Do not include claims by any person or entity who is an *insider*, as defined in 11 U.S.C. § 101(31). Also, do not include claims by secured creditors, unless the unsecured claim resulting from inadequate collateral value places the creditor among the holders of the 20 largest unsecured claims.

	Name of creditor and complete mailing address, including zip code	Name, telephone number, and email address of creditor contact	Nature of the claim (for example, trade debts, bank loans, professional services, and government contracts)	Indicate if claim is contingent, unliquidated, or disputed	Amount of unsecured claim If the claim is fully unsecured, fill in only unsecured claim amount. If claim is partially secured, fill in total claim amount and deduction for value of collateral or setoff to calculate unsecured claim		
					Total claim, if partially secured	Deduction for value of collateral or setoff	Unsecured claim
1							
2							
3							
4							
5							
6							
7							
8							

Official Form 204   Chapter 11 or Chapter 9 Cases: List of Creditors Who Have the 20 Largest Unsecured Claims   '47   page 1

Debtor _____   Case number _____

Name of creditor and complete mailing address, including zip code	Name, telephone number, and email address of creditor contact	Nature of the claim (for example, trade debts, bank loans, professional services, and government contracts)	Indicate if claim is contingent, unliquidated, or disputed	Amount of unsecured claim If the claim is fully unsecured, fill in only unsecured claim amount. If claim is partially secured, fill in total claim amount and deduction for value of collateral or setoff to calculate unsecured claim.		
				Total claim, if partially secured	Deduction for value of collateral or setoff	Unsecured claim
9						
10						
11						
12						
13						
14						
15						
16						
17						
18						
19						
20						

Official Form 204   Chapter 11 or Chapter 9 Cases: List of Creditors Who Have the 20 Largest Unsecured Claims   145   page 2

(Added Dec. 1, 2015.)

ADVISORY COMMITTEE NOTES

Official Form 204, *Chapter 11 or Chapter 9 Cases: List of Creditors Who Have the 20 Largest Unsecured Claims and Are Not Insiders*, replaces Official Form 4, *List of Creditors Holding 20 Largest Unsecured Claims*, for non-individual debtors. It is renumbered to distinguish it from the forms used by individual debtors and includes formatting and stylistic changes throughout the form.

Official Form 204 is revised as part of the Forms Modernization Project, making it easier to read and, as a result, likely to generate more complete and accurate responses. The goals of the Forms Modernization Project include improving the interface between technology and the forms so as to increase efficiency and reducing the need to produce the same information in multiple formats.

The Forms Modernization Project made a preliminary decision that separate forms should be created for individual debtors and for non-individual debtors because separate areas of inquiry apply to each group. The forms for non-individuals do not include questions that pertain only to individuals and use a more open-ended response format. Also, where possible, the forms for non-individuals parallel how businesses commonly keep their financial records.

Official Form 204 has been reformatted and reorganized. The instructions have been shortened and revised to include a full cite to the definition of "insider" and a revised explanation of when to include a secured creditor's unsecured claim. The warning regarding the disclosure of a minor child's name has been deleted as a caution has been added to the general instructions for all forms regarding listing a minor child's name.

The heading of the second column of the form has been revised to require the "name, telephone number, and email address of creditor contact," eliminating the need to provide a complete mailing address for the creditor contact. Additional examples of "nature of claim" have been provided in the third column. In the fourth column, "subject to setoff" has been removed as an option.

The fifth column has been revised to include three separate potential entries to be used to list the value of the unsecured claim: the total claim, if partially secured; the deduction for value of collateral or setoff; and unsecured claim. The new instructions for the fifth column contain an explanation that if a claim is a fully unsecured claim, only the final sub-column needs to be completed, and that all of the columns must be completed if a claim is partially secured.

The signature line and the instruction to include a declaration have been deleted from the form.

Form B205. Involuntary Petition Against a Non–Individual

Official Form 205

Involuntary Petition Against a Non-Individual

12/15

Use this form to begin a bankruptcy case against a non-individual you allege to be a debtor subject to an involuntary case. If you want to begin a case against an individual, use the *Involuntary Petition Against an Individual* (Official Form 105). Be as complete and accurate as possible. If more space is needed, attach any additional sheets to this form. On the top of any additional pages, write debtor's name and case number (if known).

Part 1:   Identify the Chapter of the Bankruptcy Code Under Which Petition Is Filed

1. Chapter of the Bankruptcy Code	Check one: ☐ Chapter 7 ☐ Chapter 11

Part 2:   Identify the Debtor

2. Debtor's name	
3. Other names you know the debtor has used in the last 8 years Include any assumed names, trade names, or *doing business as* names.	
4. Debtor's federal Employer Identification Number (EIN)	☐ Unknown EIN __ _ _____

5. Debtor's address

Principal place of business		Mailing address, if different	
Number Street		Number Street	
		P.O. Box	
City State ZIP Code		City State ZIP Code	
		Location of principal assets, if different from principal place of business	
County		Number Street	
		City State ZIP Code	

Debtor _____ Case number (if known)_____

6. Debtor's website (URL)	_____

7. Type of debtor

☐ Corporation (including Limited Liability Company (LLC) and Limited Liability Partnership (LLP))

☐ Partnership (excluding LLP)

☐ Other type of debtor. Specify: _____

8. Type of debtor's business

Check one:

☐ Health Care Business (as defined in 11 U.S.C. § 101(27A))

☐ Single Asset Real Estate (as defined in 11 U.S.C. § 101(51B))

☐ Railroad (as defined in 11 U.S.C. § 101(44))

☐ Stockbroker (as defined in 11 U.S.C. § 101(53A))

☐ Commodity Broker (as defined in 11 U.S.C. § 101(6))

☐ Clearing Bank (as defined in 11 U.S.C. § 781(3))

☐ None of the types of business listed.

☐ Unknown type of business.

9. To the best of your knowledge, are any bankruptcy cases pending by or against any partner or affiliate of this debtor?

☐ No

☐ Yes. Debtor _____ Relationship _____

District _____ Date filed _____ Case number, if known_____

MM / DD / YYYY

Debtor _____ Relationship _____

District _____ Date filed _____ Case number, if known_____

MM / DD / YYYY

Part 3: Report About the Case

10. Venue

Check one:

☐ Over the last 180 days before the filing of this bankruptcy, the debtor had a domicile, principal place of business, or principal assets in this district longer than in any other district.

☐ A bankruptcy case concerning debtor's affiliates, general partner, or partnership is pending in this district.

11. Allegations

Each petitioner is eligible to file this petition under 11 U.S.C. § 303(b).

The debtor may be the subject of an involuntary case under 11 U.S.C. § 303(a).

At least one box must be checked:

☐ The debtor is generally not paying its debts as they become due, unless they are the subject of a bona fide dispute as to liability or amount.

☐ Within 120 days before the filing of this petition, a custodian, other than a trustee, receiver, or an agent appointed or authorized to take charge of less than substantially all of the property of the debtor for the purpose of enforcing a lien against such property, was appointed or took possession.

12. Has there been a transfer of any claim against the debtor by or to any petitioner?

☐ No

☐ Yes. Attach all documents that evidence the transfer and any statements required under Bankruptcy Rule 1003(a).

Official Form 205   Involuntary Petition Against a Non-Individual   page 2

Debtor _____   Case number (if known) _____

13. Each petitioner's claim

Name of petitioner	Nature of petitioner's claim	Amount of the claim above the value of any lien
_____	_____	$ _____
_____	_____	$ _____
_____	_____	$ _____
	Total of petitioners' claims	$ _____

If more space is needed to list petitioners, attach additional sheets. Write the alleged debtor's name and the case number, if known, at the top of each sheet. Following the format of this form, set out the information required in Parts 3 and 4 of the form for each additional petitioning creditor, the petitioner's claim, the petitioner's representative, and the petitioner's attorney. Include the statement under penalty of perjury set out in Part 4 of the form, followed by each additional petitioner's (or representative's) signature, along with the signature of the petitioner's attorney.

Part 4:   Request for Relief

WARNING -- Bankruptcy fraud is a serious crime. Making a false statement in connection with a bankruptcy case can result in fines up to $500,000 or imprisonment for up to 20 years, or both. 18 U.S.C. §§ 152, 1341, 1519, and 3571.

Petitioners request that an order for relief be entered against the debtor under the chapter of 11 U.S.C. specified in this petition. If a petitioning creditor is a corporation, attach the corporate ownership statement required by Bankruptcy Rule 1010(b). If any petitioner is a foreign representative appointed in a foreign proceeding, attach a certified copy of the order of the court granting recognition.

I have examined the information in this document and have a reasonable belief that the information is true and correct.

Petitioners or Petitioners' Representative

Name and mailing address of petitioner

Name _____

Number   Street _____

City _____ State _____ ZIP Code _____

Name and mailing address of petitioner's representative, if any

Name _____

Number   Street _____

City _____ State _____ ZIP Code _____

I declare under penalty of perjury that the foregoing is true and correct.

Executed on _____
MM / DD / YYYY

✗ _____
Signature of petitioner or representative, including representative's title

Attorneys

Printed name _____

Firm name, if any _____

Number   Street _____

City _____ State _____ ZIP Code _____

Contact phone _____ Email _____

Bar number _____

State _____

✗ _____
Signature of attorney

Date signed _____
MM / DD / YYYY

Official Form 205   Involuntary Petition Against a Non-Individual   page 3

Debtor _____   Case number _____

Name and mailing address of petitioner

Name _____

Number   Street _____

City _____ State ____ ZIP Code ____

Name and mailing address of petitioner's representative, if any

Name _____

Number   Street _____

City _____ State ____ ZIP Code ____

I declare under penalty of perjury that the foregoing is true and correct.

Executed on ____ / ____ / _____
             MM / DD / YYYY

✗ _____
Signature of petitioner or representative, including representative's title

Printed name _____

Firm name, if any _____

Number   Street _____

City _____ State ____ ZIP Code ____

Contact phone _____ Email _____

Bar number _____

State _____

✗ _____
Signature of attorney

Date signed ____ / ____ / _____
            MM / DD / YYYY

Name and mailing address of petitioner

Name _____

Number   Street _____

City _____ State ____ ZIP Code ____

Name and mailing address of petitioner's representative, if any

Name _____

Number   Street _____

City _____ State ____ ZIP Code ____

I declare under penalty of perjury that the foregoing is true and correct.

Executed on ____ / ____ / _____
             MM / DD / YYYY

✗ _____
Signature of petitioner or representative, including representative's title

Printed name _____

Firm name, if any _____

Number   Street _____

City _____ State ____ ZIP Code ____

Contact phone _____ Email _____

Bar number _____

State _____

✗ _____
Signature of attorney

Date signed ____ / ____ / _____
            MM / DD / YYYY

Official Form 205   Involuntary Petition Against a Non-Individual   page 4

(Added Dec. 1, 2015.)

ADVISORY COMMITTEE NOTES

Official Form 205, *Involuntary Petition Against a Non–Individual*, replaces Official Form 5, Involuntary Petition, for non-individual debtors. It is renumbered to distinguish it from the forms used by individual debtors and includes formatting and stylistic changes throughout the form.

Official Form 205 is revised as part of the Forms Modernization Project, making it easier to read and, as a result, likely to generate more complete and accurate responses. The goals of the Forms Modernization Project include improving the interface between technology and the forms so as to increase efficiency and reducing the need to produce the same information in multiple formats.

The Forms Modernization Project made a preliminary decision that separate forms should be created for individual debtors and for non-individual debtors because separate areas of inquiry apply to each group. The forms for non-individuals do not include questions that pertain only to individuals and use a more open-ended response format. Also, where possible, the forms for non-individuals parallel how businesses commonly keep their financial records.

Part 1, *Identify the Chapter of the Bankruptcy Code Under Which Petition is Filed*, has been moved to the beginning of the form.

In Part 2, *Identify the Debtor*, instructions pertaining only to individuals have been deleted, and an instruction to include doing-business-as names and assumed names has been added. The references to social security numbers and individual taxpayer I.D. numbers have been deleted. The order of listing the various addresses for the debtor have been rearranged in Line 5, and an address for the location of principal assets is required if different from the principal place of business. The form has been revised to include a space for listing the debtor's website in Line 6.

Also in Part 2, the options for type of debtor that pertained only to individuals have been deleted, and an instruction that the "partnership" option does not include LLPs has been added. The options regarding the type of debtor's business have been revised to include a statutory citation for each business type, to add an option for "none of the above," and to delete the option for "other." The question regarding pending

Form B205

bankruptcy cases has been revised to remove the reference to spouse and the requirement to list the judge in any other cases.

In Part 3, *Report About the Case*, the question regarding venue has been revised in Line 10 to read "[o]ver the last 180 days before the filing of this bankruptcy, the debtor had a domicile, principal place or business, or principal assets in this district longer than in any other district." In the question for Allegations, "each" has been added to the first allegation, the exact citation to the Bankruptcy Code has been provided for the second allegation, and checkboxes have been provided for the last allegation. Also, in Line 12, petitioners must check "yes" or "no" to answer whether there has been any transfer of any claim against the debtor by or to a petitioner.

The information regarding the petitioner's claims has been moved to Part 3, and the portion listing the amount of the claim is amended to ask about the amount of the claim that exceeds the value of the lien, if any.

Part 4, *Request for Relief*, has been amended to include a warning about making a false statement, and the declaration under penalty of perjury has been revised in order to conform to the language of 28 U.S.C. § 1746. See Rule 1008. A statement has been added that each petitioner, or the petitioner's representative, has reviewed the information in the petition and has "a reasonable belief that the information is true and correct." A requirement has been added for each petitioner's mailing address. Also, petitioners' attorneys must provide their email addresses, bar number, and state of bar membership.

Form B206Sum. A Summary of Your Assets and Liabilities (non-individuals)

Fill in this information to identify the case:

Debtor name _____

United States Bankruptcy Court for the: _____ District of _____
(State)

Case number (if known) _____

☐ Check if this is an
amended filing

Official Form 206Sum

Summary of Assets and Liabilities for Non-Individuals   12/15

Part 1: Summary of Assets

1. *Schedule A/B: Assets–Real and Personal Property* (Official Form 206A/B)

   1a. Real property:
     Copy line 88 from *Schedule A/B* .... $ _____

   1b. Total personal property:
     Copy line 91A from *Schedule A/B* .... $ _____

   1c. Total of all property:
     Copy line 92 from *Schedule A/B* .... $ _____

Part 2: Summary of Liabilities

2. *Schedule D: Creditors Who Have Claims Secured by Property* (Official Form 206D)
   Copy the total dollar amount listed in Column A, *Amount of claim*, from line 3 of *Schedule D* .... $ _____

3. *Schedule E/F: Creditors Who Have Unsecured Claims* (Official Form 206E/F)

   3a. Total claim amounts of priority unsecured claims:
     Copy the total claims from Part 1 from line 6a of *Schedule E/F* .... $ _____

   3b. Total amount of claims of nonpriority amount of unsecured claims:
     Copy the total of the amount of claims from Part 2 from line 6b of *Schedule E/F* .... + $ _____

4. Total liabilities ....
   Lines 2 + 3a + 3b $ _____

180

Official Form 206Sum   Summary of Assets and Liabilities for Non-Individuals   page 1

(Added Dec. 1, 2015.)

ADVISORY COMMITTEE NOTES

The schedules to be used in cases of non-individual debtors have been revised as part of the Forms Modernization Project, making them easier to read and, as a result, likely to generate more complete and accurate responses. The goals of the Forms Modernization Project include improving the interface between technology and the forms so as to increase efficiency and reduce the need to produce the same information in multiple formats.

The Forms Modernization Project made a preliminary decision that separate forms should be created for individual debtors and for non-individual debtors because separate areas of inquiry apply to each group. The forms for non-individuals eliminate questions that pertain only to individuals and use a more open-ended response format. Also, where possible, the forms for non-individuals parallel how businesses commonly keep their financial records. The non-individual debtor schedules are also renumbered, starting with the number 206 and followed by the letter or name of the schedule to distinguish them from the versions to be used in individual cases. Each form includes a checkbox to indicate whether it is an amended filing.

Official Form 206Sum, *Summary of Assets and Liabilities for Non–Individuals*, replaces Official Form 6, *Summary of Schedules and Statistical Summary of Certain Liability and Related Data (28 U.S.C. § 159)*, in cases of non-individual debtors. The form is reformatted and updated with cross-references indicating the line numbers from specific schedules from which the summary information is to be gathered, and the Statistical Summary is deleted because it only applies to individual debtors. In addition, because most filings are now done electronically, the form no longer requires the debtor to

---

For Complete Annotation Materials, see United States Code Annotated indicate which schedules are attached or to state the number of sheets of paper used for the schedules.

Schedules C, Exemptions, I, Income and J, Expenses. There are no Official Forms for Schedules C, I, and J in non-individual debtor cases. There is no need for an Official Form 206C for non-individual debtors because exemptions are inapplicable to non-individual debtors. And, although section 521(a) of the Bankruptcy Code requires all debtors, including non-individual debtors, to provide schedules of income and expenses, uncertainty about the state of the debtor's business on the petition date—whether it is operating or not, for example—makes it difficult to create standard income and expense forms for non-individual debtors. Some bankruptcy courts have adopted local rules and forms for reporting the income and expenses of non-individual debtors, and Director's Procedural Forms 2060I and 2060J, can be used and modified as appropriate if there are no applicable local rules and forms.

Declaration. There is no Official Form 206, Declaration. The portion of Official Form 6 Declaration for a declaration on behalf of a corporation or partnership has been replaced by Official Form 202, *Declaration Under Penalty of Perjury for Non–Individual Debtors*. Official Form 202 includes checkboxes for the schedules included in Official Form 206.

Form B206A/B. Schedule A/B: Property
(combines real and personal property,
non-individuals)

Fill in this information to identify the case:

Debtor name _____

United States Bankruptcy Court for the:_____ District of _____
                                                    (State)

Case number (if known): _____

☐ Check if this is an
   amended filing

Official Form 206A/B

Schedule A/B: Assets — Real and Personal Property   12/15

Disclose all property, real and personal, which the debtor owns or in which the debtor has any other legal, equitable, or future interest. Include all property in which the debtor holds rights and powers exercisable for the debtor's own benefit. Also include assets and properties which have no book value, such as fully depreciated assets or assets that were not capitalized. In Schedule A/B, list any executory contracts or unexpired leases. Also list them on *Schedule G: Executory Contracts and Unexpired Leases* (Official Form 206G).

Be as complete and accurate as possible. If more space is needed, attach a separate sheet to this form. At the top of any pages added, write the debtor's name and case number (if known). Also identify the form and line number to which the additional information applies. If an additional sheet is attached, include the amounts from the attachment in the total for the pertinent part.

For Part 1 through Part 11, list each asset under the appropriate category or attach separate supporting schedules, such as a fixed asset schedule or depreciation schedule, that gives the details for each asset in a particular category. List each asset only once. In valuing the debtor's interest, do not deduct the value of secured claims. See the instructions to understand the terms used in this form.

Part 1: Cash and cash equivalents

1. Does the debtor have any cash or cash equivalents?

   ☐ No. Go to Part 2.
   ☐ Yes. Fill in the information below.

All cash or cash equivalents owned or controlled by the debtor	Current value of debtor's interest

2. Cash on hand $_____

3. Checking, savings, money market, or financial brokerage accounts *(Identify all)*

   Name of institution (bank or brokerage firm)   Type of account   Last 4 digits of account number
   3.1 _____   _____   ____ ____ ____ ____ $_____
   3.2 _____   _____   ____ ____ ____ ____ $_____

4. Other cash equivalents *(Identify all)*

   4.1 _____ $_____
   4.2 _____ $_____

5. Total of Part 1 $_____
   Add lines 2 through 4 (including amounts on any additional sheets). Copy the total to line 80.

Part 2: Deposits and prepayments

6. Does the debtor have any deposits or prepayments?

   ☐ No. Go to Part 3.
   ☐ Yes. Fill in the information below.

                                                               Current value of
                                                               debtor's interest

7. Deposits, including security deposits and utility deposits

   Description, including name of holder of deposit
   7.1 _____ $_____
   7.2 _____ $_____

Debtor _____   Case number _____

8. Prepayments, including prepayments on executory contracts, leases, insurance, taxes, and rent

Description, including name of holder of prepayment

8.1. _____ $_____

8.2. _____ $_____

9. Total of Part 2.

Add lines 7 through 8. Copy the total to line 81. $_____

Part 3:   **Accounts receivable**

10. Does the debtor have any accounts receivable?

☐ No. Go to Part 4.

☐ Yes. Fill in the information below.

                                               Current value of debtor's interest

11. Accounts receivable

11a. 90 days old or less: _____ – _____ = ... → $_____

                 face amount   doubtful or uncollectible accounts

11b. Over 90 days old: _____ – _____ = ... → $_____

                 face amount   doubtful or uncollectible accounts

12. Total of Part 3

Current value on lines 11a + 11b = line 12. Copy the total to line 82. $_____

Part 4:   **Investments**

13. Does the debtor own any investments?

☐ No. Go to Part 5.

☐ Yes. Fill in the information below.

                                   Valuation method used for current value   Current value of debtor's interest

14. Mutual funds or publicly traded stocks not included in Part 1

Name of fund or stock:

14.1. _____ _____ $_____

14.2. _____ _____ $_____

15. Non-publicly traded stock and interests in incorporated and unincorporated businesses, including any interest in an LLC, partnership, or joint venture

Name of entity: % of ownership:

15.1. _____ _____% _____ $_____

15.2. _____ _____% _____ $_____

16. Government bonds, corporate bonds, and other negotiable and non-negotiable instruments not included in Part 1

Describe:

16.1. _____ _____ $_____

16.2. _____ _____ $_____

17. Total of Part 4

Add lines 14 through 16. Copy the total to line 83. $_____

Debtor _____   Case number _____

Part 5: Inventory, excluding agriculture assets

18. Does the debtor own any inventory (excluding agriculture assets)?
- ☐ No. Go to Part 6.
- ☐ Yes. Fill in the information below.

General description	Date of the last physical inventory	Net book value of debtor's interest (Where available)	Valuation method used for current value	Current value of debtor's interest
19. Raw materials				
_____	MM / DD / YYYY	$_____	_____	$_____
20. Work in progress				
_____	MM / DD / YYYY	$_____	_____	$_____
21. Finished goods, including goods held for resale				
_____	MM / DD / YYYY	$_____	_____	$_____
22. Other inventory or supplies				
_____	MM / DD / YYYY	$_____	_____	$_____

23. Total of Part 5 $_____
    Add lines 19 through 22. Copy the total to line 84.

24. Is any of the property listed in Part 5 perishable?
- ☐ No
- ☐ Yes

25. Has any of the property listed in Part 5 been purchased within 20 days before the bankruptcy was filed?
- ☐ No
- ☐ Yes. Book value _____ Valuation method _____ Current value _____

26. Has any of the property listed in Part 5 been appraised by a professional within the last year?
- ☐ No
- ☐ Yes

Part 6: Farming and fishing-related assets (other than titled motor vehicles and land)

27. Does the debtor own or lease any farming and fishing-related assets (other than titled motor vehicles and land)?
- ☐ No. Go to Part 7.
- ☐ Yes. Fill in the information below.

General description	Net book value of debtor's interest (Where available)	Valuation method used for current value	Current value of debtor's interest
28. Crops—either planted or harvested			
_____	$_____	_____	$_____
29. Farm animals Examples: Livestock, poultry, farm-raised fish			
_____	$_____	_____	$_____
30. Farm machinery and equipment (Other than titled motor vehicles)			
_____	$_____	_____	$_____
31. Farm and fishing supplies, chemicals, and feed			
_____	$_____	_____	$_____
32. Other farming and fishing-related property not already listed in Part 6			
_____	$_____	_____	$_____

Official Form 206A/B   Schedule A/B: Assets — Real and Personal Property   160
                                                                                                page 3

Form B206A/B OFFICIAL FORMS

Debtor _____ Case number (if known)_____

33. **Total of Part 6.**
    Add lines 28 through 32. Copy the total to line 85. $ |_____|

34. Is the debtor a member of an agricultural cooperative?
    ☐ No
    ☐ Yes. Is any of the debtor's property stored at the cooperative?
       ☐ No
       ☐ Yes

35. Has any of the property listed in Part 6 been purchased within 20 days before the bankruptcy was filed?
    ☐ No
    ☐ Yes. Book value $_____ Valuation method _____ Current value $_____

36. Is a depreciation schedule available for any of the property listed in Part 6?
    ☐ No
    ☐ Yes

37. Has any of the property listed in Part 6 been appraised by a professional within the last year?
    ☐ No
    ☐ Yes

Part 7:	Office furniture, fixtures, and equipment; and collectibles

38. Does the debtor own or lease any office furniture, fixtures, equipment, or collectibles?
    ☐ No. Go to Part 8.
    ☐ Yes. Fill in the information below.

General description	Net book value of debtor's interest (Where available)	Valuation method used for current value	Current value of debtor's interest
39. Office furniture	$_____	_____	$_____
40. Office fixtures	$_____	_____	$_____
41. Office equipment, including all computer equipment and communication systems equipment and software	$_____	_____	$_____

42. **Collectibles** Examples: Antiques and figurines; paintings, prints, or other artwork; books, pictures, or other art objects; china and crystal; stamp, coin, or baseball card collections; other collections, memorabilia, or collectibles

42.1 _____	$_____	_____	$_____
42.2 _____	$_____	_____	$_____
42.3 _____	$_____	_____	$_____

43. **Total of Part 7.**
    Add lines 39 through 42. Copy the total to line 86. $ |_____|

44. Is a depreciation schedule available for any of the property listed in Part 7?
    ☐ No
    ☐ Yes

45. Has any of the property listed in Part 7 been appraised by a professional within the last year?
    ☐ No
    ☐ Yes

Debtor _____   Case number (if known)_____
         Name

Part 8:   Machinery, equipment, and vehicles

46. Does the debtor own or lease any machinery, equipment, or vehicles?

☐ No. Go to Part 9.

☐ Yes. Fill in the information below.

General description Include year, make, model, and identification numbers (i.e., VIN, HIN, or N-number)	Net book value of debtor's interest (Where available)	Valuation method used for current value	Current value of debtor's interest

47. Automobiles, vans, trucks, motorcycles, trailers, and titled farm vehicles

47.1 _____ $_____   _____ $_____

47.2 _____ $_____   _____ $_____

47.3 _____ $_____   _____ $_____

47.4 _____ $_____   _____ $_____

48. Watercraft, trailers, motors, and related accessories Examples: Boats, trailers, motors, floating homes, personal watercraft, and fishing vessels

48.1 _____ $_____   _____ $_____

48.2 _____ $_____   _____ $_____

49. Aircraft and accessories

49.1 _____ $_____   _____ $_____

49.2 _____ $_____   _____ $_____

50. Other machinery, fixtures, and equipment (excluding farm machinery and equipment)

_____ $_____   _____ $_____

51. Total of Part 8.

Add lines 47 through 50. Copy the total to line 87. $_____

52. Is a depreciation schedule available for any of the property listed in Part 8?

☐ No

☐ Yes

53. Has any of the property listed in Part 8 been appraised by a professional within the last year?

☐ No

☐ Yes

Official Form 206A/B   Schedule A/B: Assets — Real and Personal Property   162
                                                                                         page 5

Form B206A/B   OFFICIAL FORMS

Part 9:   Real property

54. Does the debtor own or lease any real property?
    ☐ No. Go to Part 10.
    ☐ Yes. Fill in the information below.

55. Any building, other improved real estate, or land which the debtor owns or in which the debtor has an interest

Description and location of property Include street address or other description such as Assessor Parcel Number (APN), and type of property (for example, acreage, factory, warehouse, apartment or office building), if available	Nature and extent of debtor's interest in property	Net book value of debtor's interest (Where available)	Valuation method used for current value	Current value of debtor's interest
55.1 _____	_____	$ _____	_____	$ _____
55.2 _____	_____	$ _____	_____	$ _____
55.3 _____	_____	$ _____	_____	$ _____
55.4 _____	_____	$ _____	_____	$ _____
55.5 _____	_____	$ _____	_____	$ _____
55.6 _____	_____	$ _____	_____	$ _____

56. Total of Part 9.
    Add the current value on lines 55.1 through 55.6 and entries from any additional sheets. Copy the total to line 88. $ _____

57. Is a depreciation schedule available for any of the property listed in Part 9?
    ☐ No
    ☐ Yes

58. Has any of the property listed in Part 9 been appraised by a professional within the last year?
    ☐ No
    ☐ Yes

Part 10:   Intangibles and intellectual property

59. Does the debtor have any interests in intangibles or intellectual property?
    ☐ No. Go to Part 11.
    ☐ Yes. Fill in the information below.

General description	Net book value of debtor's interest (Where available)	Valuation method used for current value	Current value of debtor's interest
60. Patents, copyrights, trademarks, and trade secrets _____	$ _____	_____	$ _____
61. Internet domain names and websites _____	$ _____	_____	$ _____
62. Licenses, franchises, and royalties _____	$ _____	_____	$ _____
63. Customer lists, mailing lists, or other compilations _____	$ _____	_____	$ _____
64. Other intangibles, or intellectual property _____	$ _____	_____	$ _____
65. Goodwill _____	$ _____	_____	$ _____

66. Total of Part 10.
    Add lines 60 through 65. Copy the total to line 89. $ _____

For Complete Annotation Materials, see United States Code Annotated

844

Debtor _____   Case number _____

67. Do your lists or records include personally identifiable information of customers (as defined in 11 U.S.C. §§ 101(41A) and 107)?

☐ No
☐ Yes

68. Is there an amortization or other similar schedule available for any of the property listed in Part 10?

☐ No
☐ Yes

69. Has any of the property listed in Part 10 been appraised by a professional within the last year?

☐ No
☐ Yes

Part 11:   All other assets

70. Does the debtor own any other assets that have not yet been reported on this form?

Include all interests in executory contracts and unexpired leases not previously reported on this form.

☐ No. Go to Part 12.
☐ Yes. Fill in the information below.

Current value of debtor's interest

71. Notes receivable

Description (include name of obligor)

_____   Total face amount – doubtful or uncollectible amount = → $_____

72. Tax refunds and unused net operating losses (NOLs)

Description (for example, federal, state, local)

_____   Tax year _____ $_____
_____   Tax year _____ $_____
_____   Tax year _____ $_____

73. Interests in insurance policies or annuities

_____ $_____

74. Causes of action against third parties (whether or not a lawsuit has been filed)

_____ $_____

Nature of claim   _____
Amount requested $_____

75. Other contingent and unliquidated claims or causes of action of every nature, including counterclaims of the debtor and rights to set off claims

_____ $_____

Nature of claim   _____
Amount requested $_____

76. Trusts, equitable or future interests in property

_____ $_____

77. Other property of any kind not already listed Examples: Season tickets, country club membership

_____ $_____
_____ $_____

78. Total of Part 11.

Add lines 71 through 77. Copy the total to line 90. $_____

79. Has any of the property listed in Part 11 been appraised by a professional within the last year?

☐ No
☐ Yes

Official Form 206A/B   Schedule A/B: Assets — Real and Personal Property   164
                                                                                    page 7

Form B206A/B

OFFICIAL FORMS

Debtor _____

Case number (if known) _____

Part 12: Summary

In Part 12 copy all of the totals from the earlier parts of the form.

Type of property	Current value of personal property	Current value of real property
80. Cash, cash equivalents, and financial assets. *Copy line 5, Part 1.*	$_____	
81. Deposits and prepayments. *Copy line 9, Part 2.*	$_____	
82. Accounts receivable. *Copy line 12, Part 3.*	$_____	
83. Investments. *Copy line 17, Part 4*	$_____	
84. Inventory. *Copy line 23, Part 5.*	$_____	
85. Farming and fishing-related assets. *Copy line 33, Part 6.*	$_____	
86. Office furniture, fixtures, and equipment; and collectibles. *Copy line 43, Part 7.*	$_____	
87. Machinery, equipment, and vehicles. *Copy line 51, Part 8.*	$_____	
88. Real property. *Copy line 56, Part 9.* ....→		$_____
89. Intangibles and intellectual property. *Copy line 66, Part 10.*	$_____	
90. All other assets. *Copy line 78, Part 11.*	+ $_____	
91. Total. Add lines 80 through 90 for each column. .... 91a.	$_____	+ 91b. $_____

92. Total of all property on Schedule A/B. Lines 91a + 91b = 92 .... $_____

Official Form 206A/B   Schedule A/B: Assets — Real and Personal Property   165 page 8

(Added Dec. 1, 2015.)

ADVISORY COMMITTEE NOTES

Official Form 206A/B, *Schedule A/B: Assets—Real and Personal Property*, consolidates information about a non-individual debtor's real and personal property into a single form and replaces Official Form 6A—*Real Property* and Official Form 6B—*Personal Property*, in cases of non-individual debtors. The layout and categories of property on Official Form 206A/B have changed. Instead of dividing property interests into two categories (real or personal property), the new form uses eleven categories of property types. For each part, the specific items are broken out and debtors are instructed to total the part and list the total on a specific line later in the form.

Part 1: *Cash and cash equivalents*, includes cash and cash equivalents and a shortened list of examples. All financial assets other than cash or cash equivalents are moved to Part 4: Investments. In the section to list checking, savings, money market, or financial brokerage accounts, debtors are instruct-

ed to include the name of the institution and the last 4-digits of any account number.

In Part 2: *Deposits and prepayments*, adds prepayments and examples. A requirement has been added to include the name of the holder of any deposit.

Part 3: *Accounts receivable*, has been revised to divide accounts receivable into two categories depending on age and asks for separate values for the two categories.

Part 4: *Investments*, has been expanded and includes more detail.

Part 5: *Inventory*, excluding agricultural assets, has been amended to separate non-agricultural from agricultural assets, and has been expanded to include more detail. Categories of inventory are listed, and debtors must include the last date of physical inventory, the net book value of debtor's interest (if available), the valuation method used for current value, and the current value of debtor's interest. The form has been further amended to require the debtor to indicate whether the properties listed are perishable, whether any of the property was purchased within 20 days of the bankruptcy filing, and whether any of the property was appraised by a professional within the year prior to the bankruptcy filing.

In Part 6: *Farming- and Fishing-Related Assets (other than titled motor vehicles and land)*, the form has been amended to require more detailed responses and to require the debtor to indicate the net book value of the debtor's interest, the valuation method used for current value, and the current value of debtor's interest. A requirement to list fishing supplies has been added. The form has been further amended to require the debtor to indicate whether the properties listed are perishable, whether any of the property was purchased within 20 days of the bankruptcy filing, whether a depreciation schedule is available for any of the property listed, and whether any of the property was appraised by a professional within the year prior to the bankruptcy filing.

Part 7: *Office furniture, fixtures, and equipment; and collectibles*, has been amended to combine several categories of assets and to require more detail, including requiring the debtor to indicate the net book value of the debtor's interest, the valuation method used for current value, and the current value of debtor's interest. Examples of collectibles are provided. The form has been further amended to require the debtor to indicate whether a depreciation schedule is available for any property listed and whether any of the property listed was appraised by a professional within the year prior to the bankruptcy filing.

Part 8: *Machinery, equipment, and vehicles*, has been amended to combine several categories of property and to require more detail, including requiring the debtor to indicate the net book value of the debtor's interest, the valuation method used for current value, and the current value of debtor's interest. More examples are provided for each property type. The form has been further amended to indicate whether a depreciation schedule is available for any property listed and whether any of the property listed was appraised by a professional within the year prior to the bankruptcy filing.

Part 9: *Real property*, includes the elements of Official Form 6A, *Real Property*, and has been amended to expand the required information to include the net book value of the debtor's interest and the valuation method used for current value. Also, an instruction has been added for the description and location of the property. The form has been further amended to indicate whether a depreciation schedule is available for any property listed and whether any of the property listed was appraised by a professional within the year prior to the bankruptcy filing.

Part 10: *Intangibles and intellectual property*, includes amendments to combine several categories of property and to include more property types. The debtor is required to list the net book value of the debtor's interest and the valuation method used for current value. The question regarding personally identifiable information has been revised, and the form has been amended to require the debtor to indicate if there is an amortization schedule or similar schedule available for any property listed and whether any of the property listed was appraised by a professional within the year prior to the bankruptcy filing.

Part 11: *All other assets*, includes a new category for notes receivable, which requires a description, including the name of the obligor, the face amount, and any uncollectible amount. In addition, the form has been amended to combine tax refunds and net operating losses into a single question and to require more detail, to delete the requirement to list the insurance company name for any interests in insurance policies, to expand the question regarding contingent and unliquidated claims, and to include examples of other property. The form has been further amended to include a question regarding whether the property listed was appraised by a professional within the year prior to the bankruptcy filing.

Part 12, *Summary*, has been amended to list relevant line numbers for each type of property.

Form B206D. Schedule D: Creditors Who Hold Claims Secured by Property (against non-individuals)

Fill in this information to identify the case:

Debtor name _____

United States Bankruptcy Court for the: _____ District of _____
State

Case number (if known): _____

☐ Check if this is an amended filing

Official Form 206D

Schedule D: Creditors Who Have Claims Secured by Property   12/15

Be as complete and accurate as possible.

1. Do any creditors have claims secured by debtor's property?
   ☐ No. Check this box and submit page 1 of this form to the court with debtor's other schedules. Debtor has nothing else to report on this form.
   ☐ Yes. Fill in all of the information below.

Part 1:   List Creditors Who Have Secured Claims

2. List in alphabetical order all creditors who have secured claims. If a creditor has more than one secured claim, list the creditor separately for each claim.

		Column A Amount of claim Do not deduct the value of collateral.	Column B Value of collateral that supports this claim

2.1 Creditor's name _____

Describe debtor's property that is subject to a lien _____

$_____ $_____

Creditor's mailing address _____

_____

_____

Describe the lien _____

Creditor's email address, if known _____

Is the creditor an insider or related party?
☐ No
☐ Yes

Date debt was incurred _____

Is anyone else liable on this claim?
☐ No
☐ Yes. Fill out *Schedule H: Codebtors* (Official Form 206H)

Last 4 digits of account number _____

Do multiple creditors have an interest in the same property?
☐ No
☐ Yes. Specify each creditor, including this creditor, and its relative priority.

As of the petition filing date, the claim is:
Check all that apply.
☐ Contingent
☐ Unliquidated
☐ Disputed

2.2 Creditor's name _____

Describe debtor's property that is subject to a lien _____

$_____ $_____

Creditor's mailing address _____

_____

Describe the lien _____

Creditor's email address, if known _____

Is the creditor an insider or related party?
☐ No
☐ Yes

Date debt was incurred _____

Is anyone else liable on this claim?
☐ No
☐ Yes. Fill out *Schedule H: Codebtors* (Official Form 206H)

Last 4 digits of account number _____

Do multiple creditors have an interest in the same property?
☐ No
☐ Yes. Have you already specified the relative priority?
   ☐ No. Specify each creditor, including this creditor, and its relative priority.

   _____

   ☐ Yes. The relative priority of creditors is specified on lines _____

As of the petition filing date, the claim is:
Check all that apply.
☐ Contingent
☐ Unliquidated
☐ Disputed

3. Total of the dollar amounts from Part 1, Column A, including the amounts from the Additional Page, if any. $_____

166

Official Form 206D   Schedule D: Creditors Who Have Claims Secured by Property   page 1 of ___

Debtor _____ Case number _____
Name

Part 1:	Additional Page	Column A	Column B
		Amount of claim	Value of collateral
		Do net deduct the value of collateral.	that supports this claim

Copy this page only if more space is needed. Continue numbering the lines sequentially from the previous page.

2. Creditor's name

Describe debtor's property that is subject to a lien

_____ $_____ $_____

Creditor's mailing address

Describe the lien

Creditor's email address, if known

Is the creditor an insider or related party?
☐ No
☐ Yes

Date debt was incurred _____

Is anyone else liable on this claim?
☐ No
☐ Yes. Fill out Schedule H: Codebtors (Official Form 206H).

Last 4 digits of account number ____ ____ ____ ____

Do multiple creditors have an interest in the same property?
☐ No
☐ Yes. Have you already specified the relative priority?

As of the petition filing date, the claim is:
Check all that apply.
☐ Contingent
☐ Unliquidated
☐ Disputed

 ☐ No. Specify each creditor, including this creditor, and its relative priority.

 ☐ Yes. The relative priority of creditors is specified on lines _____

---

2. Creditor's name

Describe debtor's property that is subject to a lien

_____ $_____ $_____

Creditor's mailing address

Describe the lien

Creditor's email address, if known

Is the creditor an insider or related party?
☐ No
☐ Yes

Date debt was incurred _____

Is anyone else liable on this claim?
☐ No
☐ Yes. Fill out Schedule H: Codebtors (Official Form 206H).

Last 4 digits of account number ____ ____ ____ ____

Do multiple creditors have an interest in the same property?
☐ No
☐ Yes. Have you already specified the relative priority?

As of the petition filing date, the claim is:
Check all that apply.
☐ Contingent
☐ Unliquidated
☐ Disputed

 ☐ No. Specify each creditor, including this creditor, and its relative priority.

 ☐ Yes. The relative priority of creditors is specified on lines _____

Official Form 206D   Additional Page of Schedule D: Creditors Who Have Claims Secured by Property   107 page ___ of ___

Debtor 1 _____   Case number _____

Part 2:   **List Others to Be Notified for a Debt Already Listed in Part 1**

List in alphabetical order any others who must be notified for a debt already listed in Part 1. Examples of entities that may be listed are collection agencies, assignees of claims listed above, and attorneys for secured creditors.

If no others need to be notified for the debts listed in Part 1, do not fill out or submit this page. If additional pages are needed, copy this page.

Name and address	On which line in Part 1 did you enter the related creditor?	Last 4 digits of account number for this entity
_____	Line 2 __	__ __ __ __
_____	Line 2 __	__ __ __ __
_____	Line 2 __	__ __ __ __
_____	Line 2 __	__ __ __ __
_____	Line 2 __	__ __ __ __
_____	Line 2 __	__ __ __ __
_____	Line 2 __	__ __ __ __
_____	Line 2 __	__ __ __ __
_____	Line 2 __	__ __ __ __
_____	Line 2	
_____	Line 2 __	__ __ __ __
_____	Line 2 __	__ __ __ __
_____	Line 2 __	__ __ __ __
_____	Line 2 __	__ __ __ __

Form 206D   Official Part 2 of Schedule D: Creditors Who Have Claims Secured by Property   page ___ of ___

(Added Dec. 1, 2015.)

ADVISORY COMMITTEE NOTES

Official Form 206D, *Schedule D: Creditors Who Have Claims Secured by Property,* replaces Official Form 6D, *Creditors Holding Secured Claims,* for non-individual debtors and has been revised to eliminate instructions that pertain only to individuals. The form has been further amended to instruct debtors that if a creditor has more than one secured claim, to list the creditor separately for each claim; to list the creditor's email address, if known; to indicate if multiple creditors have an interest in the same collateral; to list the order of each creditor's priority interest in the collateral; and to indicate whether the creditor is an insider or related party.

The debtor is also instructed to describe the lien and to fill out Schedule H: Codebtors, if anyone else is liable on the claim. Finally, the form has been amended to require the debtor to list the value of the debtor's property that secures the claim.

A new Part 2: *List Others to be Notified for a Debt Already Listed in Part 1* has been added, with instructions to list any others who must be notified about the bankruptcy for a debt listed in Part 1 of the form. Examples are provided. The debtor must include the relevant line from Part 1 and the last 4 digits of the account number for the entity.

A new Part 3: *Total Amounts of Claims and the Unsecured Portion of Claims,* has been added.

Form B206E/F. Schedule E/F: Creditors Who Have Unsecured Claims (against non-individuals, combines priority and non-priority)

Fill in this information to identify the case:

Debtor _____

United States Bankruptcy Court for the: _____ District of _____
(State)

Case number _____
(If known)

☐ Check if this is an amended filing

Official Form 206E/F

Schedule E/F: Creditors Who Have Unsecured Claims

12/15

Be as complete and accurate as possible. Use Part 1 for creditors with PRIORITY unsecured claims and Part 2 for creditors with NONPRIORITY unsecured claims. List the other party to any executory contracts or unexpired leases that could result in a claim. Also list executory contracts on *Schedule A/B: Assets - Real and Personal Property* (Official Form 206A/B) and on *Schedule G: Executory Contracts and Unexpired Leases* (Official Form 206G). Number the entries in Parts 1 and 2 in the boxes on the left. If more space is needed for Part 1 or Part 2, fill out and attach the Additional Page of that Part included in this form.

Part 1:   List All Creditors with PRIORITY Unsecured Claims

1. Do any creditors have priority unsecured claims? (See 11 U.S.C. § 507).
   ☐ No. Go to Part 2.
   ☐ Yes. Go to line 2.

2. List in alphabetical order all creditors who have unsecured claims that are entitled to priority in whole or in part. If the debtor has more than 3 creditors with priority unsecured claims, fill out and attach the Additional Page of Part 1.

		Total claim	Priority amount

2.1 Priority creditor's name and mailing address
_____
_____
_____

As of the petition filing date, the claim is: $_____ $_____
Check all that apply.
☐ Contingent
☐ Unliquidated
☐ Disputed

Date or dates debt was incurred
_____

Basis for the claim:
_____

Last 4 digits of account number ___ ___ ___ ___

Is the claim subject to offset?
☐ No
☐ Yes

Specify Code subsection of PRIORITY unsecured claim: 11 U.S.C. § 507(a) (____)

2.2 Priority creditor's name and mailing address
_____
_____

As of the petition filing date, the claim is: $_____ $_____
Check all that apply.
☐ Contingent
☐ Unliquidated
☐ Disputed

Date or dates debt was incurred
_____

Basis for the claim:
_____

Last 4 digits of account number ___ ___ ___ ___

Is the claim subject to offset?
☐ No
☐ Yes

Specify Code subsection of PRIORITY unsecured claim: 11 U.S.C. § 507(a) (____)

2.3 Priority creditor's name and mailing address
_____
_____

As of the petition filing date, the claim is: $_____ $_____
Check all that apply.
☐ Contingent
☐ Unliquidated
☐ Disputed

Date or dates debt was incurred
_____

Basis for the claim:
_____

Last 4 digits of account number ___ ___ ___ ___

Is the claim subject to offset?
☐ No
☐ Yes

Specify Code subsection of PRIORITY unsecured claim: 11 U.S.C. § 507(a) (____)

169

Official Form 206E/F   Schedule E/F: Creditors Who Have Unsecured Claims   page 1 of ___

Form B206E/F

Debtor _____ Name

Case number (if known) _____

Part 1. Additional Page

Copy this page if more space is needed. Continue numbering the lines sequentially from the previous page. If no additional PRIORITY creditors exist, do not fill out or submit this page.

	Total claim	Priority amount

2_ Priority creditor's name and mailing address

_____

_____

_____

As of the petition filing date, the claim is:
Check all that apply.
❏ Contingent
❏ Unliquidated
❏ Disputed

$_____ $_____

Date or dates debt was incurred

_____

Basis for the claim:

_____

Last 4 digits of account number ___ ___ ___ ___

Specify Code subsection of PRIORITY unsecured claim: 11 U.S.C. § 507(a) (____)

Is the claim subject to offset?
❏ No
❏ Yes

2_ Priority creditor's name and mailing address

_____

_____

_____

As of the petition filing date, the claim is:
Check all that apply.
❏ Contingent
❏ Unliquidated
❏ Disputed

$_____ $_____

Date or dates debt was incurred

_____

Basis for the claim:

_____

Last 4 digits of account number ___ ___ ___ ___

Specify Code subsection of PRIORITY unsecured claim: 11 U.S.C. § 507(a) (____)

Is the claim subject to offset?
❏ No
❏ Yes

2_ Priority creditor's name and mailing address

_____

_____

_____

As of the petition filing date, the claim is:
Check all that apply.
❏ Contingent
❏ Unliquidated
❏ Disputed

$_____ $_____

Date or dates debt was incurred

_____

Basis for the claim:

_____

Last 4 digits of account number ___ ___ ___ ___

Specify Code subsection of PRIORITY unsecured claim: 11 U.S.C. § 507(a) (____)

Is the claim subject to offset?
❏ No
❏ Yes

2_ Priority creditor's name and mailing address

_____

_____

_____

As of the petition filing date, the claim is:
Check all that apply.
❏ Contingent
❏ Unliquidated
❏ Disputed

$_____ $_____

Date or dates debt was incurred

_____

Basis for the claim:

_____

Last 4 digits of account number ___ ___ ___ ___

Specify Code subsection of PRIORITY unsecured claim: 11 U.S.C. § 507(a) (____)

Is the claim subject to offset?
❏ No
❏ Yes

17C

Official Form 206E/F

Schedule E/F: Creditors Who Have Unsecured Claims

page ___ of ___

Debtor _____   Case number _____

Part 2:   List All Creditors with NONPRIORITY Unsecured Claims

3. List in alphabetical order all of the creditors with nonpriority unsecured claims. If the debtor has more than 6 creditors with nonpriority unsecured claims, fill out and attach the Additional Page of Part 2.

		Amount of claim

3.1 Nonpriority creditor's name and mailing address

_____

_____

_____

As of the petition filing date, the claim is:
Check all that apply.
☐ Contingent
☐ Unliquidated
☐ Disputed

Basis for the claim: _____

Date or dates debt was incurred   _____

Last 4 digits of account number   __ __ __ __

Is the claim subject to offset?
☐ No
☐ Yes

$ _____

3.2 Nonpriority creditor's name and mailing address

_____

_____

_____

As of the petition filing date, the claim is:
Check all that apply.
☐ Contingent
☐ Unliquidated
☐ Disputed

Basis for the claim: _____

Date or dates debt was incurred   _____

Last 4 digits of account number   __ __ __ __

Is the claim subject to offset?
☐ No
☐ Yes

$ _____

3.3 Nonpriority creditor's name and mailing address

_____

_____

_____

As of the petition filing date, the claim is:
Check all that apply.
☐ Contingent
☐ Unliquidated
☐ Disputed

Basis for the claim: _____

Date or dates debt was incurred   _____

Last 4 digits of account number   __ __ __ __

Is the claim subject to offset?
☐ No
☐ Yes

$ _____

3.4 Nonpriority creditor's name and mailing address

_____

_____

_____

As of the petition filing date, the claim is:
Check all that apply.
☐ Contingent
☐ Unliquidated
☐ Disputed

Basis for the claim: _____

Date or dates debt was incurred   _____

Last 4 digits of account number   __ __ __ __

Is the claim subject to offset?
☐ No
☐ Yes

$ _____

3.5 Nonpriority creditor's name and mailing address

_____

_____

_____

As of the petition filing date, the claim is:
Check all that apply.
☐ Contingent
☐ Unliquidated
☐ Disputed

Basis for the claim: _____

Date or dates debt was incurred   _____

Last 4 digits of account number   __ __ __ __

Is the claim subject to offset?
☐ No
☐ Yes

$ _____

3.6 Nonpriority creditor's name and mailing address

_____

_____

_____

As of the petition filing date, the claim is:
Check all that apply.
☐ Contingent
☐ Unliquidated
☐ Disputed

Basis for the claim: _____

Date or dates debt was incurred   _____

Last 4 digits of account number   __ __ __ __

Is the claim subject to offset?
☐ No
☐ Yes

$ _____

171

Official Form 206E/F   Schedule E/F: Creditors Who Have Unsecured Claims   page __ of __

Form B206E/F

Debtor _____   Case number _____

Part 2:   Additional Page

Copy this page only if more space is needed. Continue numbering the lines sequentially from the previous page. If no additional NONPRIORITY creditors exist, do not fill out or submit this page.

Amount of claim

3.___ Nonpriority creditor's name and mailing address

As of the petition filing date, the claim is:
Check all that apply.
❏ Contingent
❏ Unliquidated
❏ Disputed
❏ Liquidated and neither contingent nor disputed

$_____

Basis for the claim: _____

Date or dates debt was incurred _____

Is the claim subject to offset?
❏ No
❏ Yes

Last 4 digits of account number ____ ____ ____ ____

3.___ Nonpriority creditor's name and mailing address

As of the petition filing date, the claim is:
Check all that apply.
❏ Contingent
❏ Unliquidated
❏ Disputed

$_____

Basis for the claim: _____

Date or dates debt was incurred _____

Is the claim subject to offset?
❏ No
❏ Yes

Last 4 digits of account number ____ ____ ____ ____

3.___ Nonpriority creditor's name and mailing address

As of the petition filing date, the claim is:
Check all that apply.
❏ Contingent
❏ Unliquidated
❏ Disputed

$_____

Basis for the claim: _____

Date or dates debt was incurred _____

Is the claim subject to offset?
❏ No
❏ Yes

Last 4 digits of account number ____ ____ ____ ____

3.___ Nonpriority creditor's name and mailing address

As of the petition filing date, the claim is:
Check all that apply.
❏ Contingent
❏ Unliquidated
❏ Disputed

$_____

Basis for the claim: _____

Date or dates debt was incurred _____

Is the claim subject to offset?
❏ No
❏ Yes

Last 4 digits of account number ____ ____ ____ ____

3.___ Nonpriority creditor's name and mailing address

As of the petition filing date, the claim is:
Check all that apply.
❏ Contingent
❏ Unliquidated
❏ Disputed

$_____

Basis for the claim: _____

Date or dates debt was incurred _____

Is the claim subject to offset?
❏ No
❏ Yes

Last 4 digits of account number ____ ____ ____ ____

172

Official Form 206E/F   Schedule E/F: Creditors Who Have Unsecured Claims   page ___ of ___

Debtor _____   Case number _____
                  Name

Part 3:   List Others to Be Notified About Unsecured Claims

4.   List in alphabetical order any others who must be notified for claims listed in Parts 1 and 2. Examples of entities that may be listed are collection agencies, assignees of claims listed above, and attorneys for unsecured creditors.

     If no others need to be notified for the debts listed in Parts 1 and 2, do not fill out or submit this page. If additional pages are needed, copy the next page.

Name and mailing address	On which line in Part 1 or Part 2 is the related creditor (if any) listed?	Last 4 digits of account number, if any
4.1. _____	Line ____ ☐ Not listed. Explain _____	____
4.2. _____	Line ____ ☐ Not listed. Explain _____	____
4.3. _____	Line ____ ☐ Not listed. Explain _____	____
4.4. _____	Line ____ ☐ Not listed. Explain _____	____
4.1. _____	Line ____ ☐ Not listed. Explain _____	____
4.5. _____	Line ____ ☐ Not listed. Explain _____	____
4.6. _____	Line ____ ☐ Not listed. Explain _____	____
4.7. _____	Line ____ ☐ Not listed. Explain _____	____
4.8. _____	Line ____ ☐ Not listed. Explain _____	____
4.9. _____	Line ____ ☐ Not listed. Explain _____	____
4.10. _____	Line ____ ☐ Not listed. Explain _____	____
4.11. _____	Line ____ ☐ Not listed. Explain _____	____

Official Form 206E/F   Schedule E/F: Creditors Who Have Unsecured Claims   page ___ of ___

173

Debtor _____   Case number _____
       Name

Part 3:   **Additional Page for Others to Be Notified About Unsecured Claims**

Name and mailing address	On which line in Part 1 or Part 2 is the related creditor (if any) listed?	Last 4 digits of account number, if any
4.__	Line ____ ☐ Not listed. Explain _____	____ ____ ____ ____
4.__	Line ____ ☐ Not listed. Explain _____	____ ____ ____ ____
4.__	Line ____ ☐ Not listed. Explain _____	____ ____ ____ ____
4.__	Line ____ ☐ Not listed. Explain _____	____ ____ ____ ____
4.__	Line ____ ☐ Not listed. Explain _____	____ ____ ____ ____
4.__	Line ____ ☐ Not listed. Explain _____	____ ____ ____ ____
4.__	Line ____ ☐ Not listed. Explain _____	____ ____ ____ ____
4.__	Line ____ ☐ Not listed. Explain _____	____ ____ ____ ____
4.__	Line ____ ☐ Not listed. Explain _____	____ ____ ____ ____
4.__	Line ____ ☐ Not listed. Explain _____	____ ____ ____ ____
4.__	Line ____ ☐ Not listed. Explain _____	____ ____ ____ ____
4.__	Line ____ ☐ Not listed. Explain _____	____ ____ ____ ____
4.__	Line ____ ☐ Not listed. Explain _____	____ ____ ____ ____
4.__	Line ____ ☐ Not listed. Explain _____	____ ____ ____ ____

174

Official Form 206E/F   Schedule E/F: Creditors Who Have Unsecured Claims   page __ of __

Debtor _____   Case number _____

Part 4:   Total Amounts of the Priority and Nonpriority Unsecured Claims

5. Add the amounts of priority and nonpriority unsecured claims.

		Total of claim amounts
5a. Total claims from Part 1	5a.	$_____
5b. Total claims from Part 2	5b. +	$_____
5c. Total of Parts 1 and 2 Lines 5a + 5b = 5c.	5c.	$_____

Official Form 206E/F   Schedule E/F: Creditors Who Have Unsecured Claims   page ___ of ___

(Added Dec. 1, 2015.)

ADVISORY COMMITTEE NOTES

Official Form 206E/F, *Schedule E/F: Creditors Who Have Unsecured Claims,* has been amended to combine Official Form 6E, *Schedule E – Creditors Holding Unsecured Priority Claims* and Official Form 6F, *Schedule F – Creditors Holding Unsecured Nonpriority Claims* for non-individual debtors. Priority unsecured claims are listed in Part 1, and nonpriority unsecured claims are listed in Part 2. The instructions have been revised to require the debtor to list the other party to any executory contract or unexpired lease on this schedule and on *Schedule A/B Real and Personal Property* and *Schedule G: Executory Contracts and Unexpired Leases* (Official Forms 206A/B and 206G).

Part 1, *List All Creditors with PRIORITY Unsecured Claims,* has been revised to delete the requirement to list the amount not entitled to priority and to add requirements to specify the Code section for the priority unsecured claim and whether the claim is subject to offset. A new requirement was added to Part 2, *List All Creditor's with NONPRIORITY Unsecured Claims,* to indicate if the claim is subject to offset. The instructions have also been significantly shortened. Part 3, *List Others to be Notified About Unsecured Claims,* has been added, with instructions to list any others who must be notified for claims listed in Parts 1 and 2. Examples are given. The debtor must include the relevant line from Part 1 or 2 and the last 4 digits of the account number for the entity. A new Part 4: *Total Amounts of the Priority and Nonpriority Unsecured Claims* has been added.

Form B206G

Form B206G. Schedule G: Executory Contracts and Unexpired Leases (non-individuals)

Fill in this information to identify the case:

Debtor name _____

United States Bankruptcy Court for the:_____ District of _____
(State)

Case number (if known): _____ Chapter ____

☐ Check if this is an amended filing

Official Form 206G

Schedule G: Executory Contracts and Unexpired Leases   12/15

Be as complete and accurate as possible. If more space is needed, copy and attach the additional page, numbering the entries consecutively.

1. Does the debtor have any executory contracts or unexpired leases?

   ☐ No. Check this box and file this form with the court with the debtor's other schedules. There is nothing else to report on this form.

   ☐ Yes. Fill in all of the information below even if the contracts or leases are listed on *Schedule A/B: Assets - Real and Personal Property* (Official Form 206A/B).

2. List all contracts and unexpired leases | State the name and mailing address for all other parties with whom the debtor has an executory contract or unexpired lease

2.1 State what the contract or lease is for and the nature of the debtor's interest _____

State the term remaining _____

List the contract number of any government contract _____

2.2 State what the contract or lease is for and the nature of the debtor's interest _____

State the term remaining _____

List the contract number of any government contract _____

2.3 State what the contract or lease is for and the nature of the debtor's interest _____

State the term remaining _____

List the contract number of any government contract _____

2.4 State what the contract or lease is for and the nature of the debtor's interest _____

State the term remaining _____

List the contract number of any government contract _____

2.5 State what the contract or lease is for and the nature of the debtor's interest _____

State the term remaining _____

List the contract number of any government contract _____

Official Form 206G   Schedule G: Executory Contracts and Unexpired Leases   176   page 1 of ___

Debtor _____ Case number _____

Additional Page if Debtor Has More Executory Contracts or Unexpired Leases

Copy this page only if more space is needed. Continue numbering the lines sequentially from the previous page.

List all contracts and unexpired leases	State the name and mailing address for all other parties with whom the debtor has an executory contract or unexpired lease

2._ State what the contract or lease is for and the nature of the debtor's interest
State the term remaining
List the contract number of any government contract

2._ State what the contract or lease is for and the nature of the debtor's interest
State the term remaining
List the contract number of any government contract

2._ State what the contract or lease is for and the nature of the debtor's interest
State the term remaining
List the contract number of any government contract

2._ State what the contract or lease is for and the nature of the debtor's interest
State the term remaining
List the contract number of any government contract

2._ State what the contract or lease is for and the nature of the debtor's interest
State the term remaining
List the contract number of any government contract

2._ State what the contract or lease is for and the nature of the debtor's interest
State the term remaining
List the contract number of any government contract

2._ State what the contract or lease is for and the nature of the debtor's interest
State the term remaining
List the contract number of any government contract

177

Official Form 206G   Schedule G: Executory Contracts and Unexpired Leases   page ___ of ___

(Added Dec. 1, 2015.)

ADVISORY COMMITTEE NOTES

Official Form 206G, *Schedule G: Executory Contracts and Unexpired Leases*, replaces Official Form 6G—*Executory Contracts and Unexpired Leases* for non-individual debtors.

The form has been amended to delete the instruction regarding the listing of a minor child's name from the form as a caution is included in the general instructions for all forms regarding listing a minor child's name. A new requirement has been added to state the remaining term for any contract or lease listed.

Form B206H. Schedule H: Your Codebtors (non-individuals)

☐ Check if this is an
amended filing

Official Form 206H

Schedule H: Codebtors   12/15

Be as complete and accurate as possible. If more space is needed, copy the Additional Page, numbering the entries consecutively. Attach the Additional Page to this page.

1. Does the debtor have any codebtors?
   ☐ No. Check this box and submit this form to the court with the debtor's other schedules. Nothing else needs to be reported on this form.
   ☐ Yes

2. In Column 1, list as codebtors all of the people or entities who are also liable for any debts listed by the debtor in the schedules of creditors. *Schedules D-G.* Include all guarantors and co-obligors. In Column 2, identify the creditor to whom the debt is owed and each schedule on which the creditor is listed. If the codebtor is liable on a debt to more than one creditor, list each creditor separately in Column 2.

Column 1: Codebtor		Column 2: Creditor	
Name	Mailing address	Name	Check all schedules that apply:
2.1 _____	Street _____ _____ City State ZIP Code	_____	☐ D ☐ E/F ☐ G
2.2 _____	Street _____ _____ City State ZIP Code	_____	☐ D ☐ E/F ☐ G
2.3 _____	Street _____ _____ City State ZIP Code	_____	☐ D ☐ E/F ☐ G
2.4 _____	Street _____ _____ City State ZIP Code	_____	☐ D ☐ E/F ☐ G
2.5 _____	Street _____ _____ City State ZIP Code	_____	☐ D ☐ E/F ☐ G
2.6 _____	Street _____ _____ City State ZIP Code	_____	☐ D ☐ E/F ☐ G

178

Official Form 206H   Schedule H: Codebtors   page 1 of ___

Debtor _____

Case number _____

Additional Page if Debtor Has More Codebtors

Copy this page only if more space is needed. Continue numbering the lines sequentially from the previous page.

Column 1: Codebtor

Column 2: Creditor

Name	Mailing address	Name	Check all schedules that apply:
2.__	Street / City / State / ZIP Code		☐ D ☐ E/F ☐ G
2.__	Street / City / State / ZIP Code		☐ D ☐ E/F ☐ G
2.__	Street / City / State / ZIP Code		☐ D ☐ E/F ☐ G
2.__	Street / City / State / ZIP Code		☐ D ☐ E/F ☐ G
2.__	Street / City / State / ZIP Code		☐ D ☐ E/F ☐ G
2.__	Street / City / State / ZIP Code		☐ D ☐ E/F ☐ G
2.__	Street / City / State / ZIP Code		☐ D ☐ E/F ☐ G
2.__	Street / City / State / ZIP Code		☐ D ☐ E/F ☐ G

Official Form 206H   Schedule H: Codebtors   179   page ___ of ___

(Added Dec. 1, 2015.)

ADVISORY COMMITTEE NOTES

Official Form 206H, *Schedule H: Codebtors*, replaces Official Form 6H—*Codebtors* for non-individual debtors. The form has been amended to delete the instruction regarding the listing of a minor child's name from the form as a caution is included in the general instructions for all forms regarding listing a minor child's name. A new requirement is added to indicate by checkbox what schedule applies to each codebtor.

Form B207. Statement of Your Financial Affairs (Non–Individuals)

Fill in this information to identify the case:

Debtor name _____

United States Bankruptcy Court for the: _____ District of _____
(State)

Case number (if known): _____

☐ Check if this is an amended filing

Official Form 207

Statement of Financial Affairs for Non-Individuals Filing for Bankruptcy   04/16

The debtor must answer every question. If more space is needed, attach a separate sheet to this form. On the top of any additional pages, write the debtor's name and case number (if known).

Part 1:   Income

1. Gross revenue from business

☐ None

Identify the beginning and ending dates of the debtor's fiscal year, which may be a calendar year	Sources of revenue Check all that apply	Gross revenue (before deductions and exclusions)
From the beginning of the fiscal year to filing date: From ___ MM/DD/YYYY to Filing date	☐ Operating a business ☐ Other _____	$_____
For prior year: From ___ MM/DD/YYYY to ___ MM/DD/YYYY	☐ Operating a business ☐ Other _____	$_____
For the year before that: From ___ MM/DD/YYYY to ___ MM/DD/YYYY	☐ Operating a business ☐ Other _____	$_____

2. Non-business revenue

Include revenue regardless of whether that revenue is taxable. Non-business income may include interest, dividends, money collected from lawsuits, and royalties. List each source and the gross revenue for each separately. Do not include revenue listed in line 1

☐ None

	Description of sources of revenue	Gross revenue from each source (before deductions and exclusions)
From the beginning of the fiscal year to filing date: From ___ MM/DD/YYYY to Filing date	_____	$_____
For prior year: From ___ MM/DD/YYYY to ___ MM/DD/YYYY	_____	$_____
For the year before that: From ___ MM/DD/YYYY to ___ MM/DD/YYYY	_____	$_____

Debtor _____   Case number (if known) _____
Name

Part 2: List Certain Transfers Made Before Filing for Bankruptcy

3. Certain payments or transfers to creditors within 90 days before filing this case

List payments or transfers—including expense reimbursements—to any creditor, other than regular employee compensation, within 90 days before filing this case unless the aggregate value of all property transferred to that creditor is less than $6,425. (This amount may be adjusted on 4/01/19 and every 3 years after that with respect to cases filed on or after the date of adjustment.)

☐ None

Creditor's name and address	Dates	Total amount or value	Reasons for payment or transfer Check all that apply
3.1. Creditor's name Street City State ZIP Code	____	$ ____	☐ Secured debt ☐ Unsecured loan repayments ☐ Suppliers or vendors ☐ Services ☐ Other _____
3.2. Creditor's name Street City State ZIP Code	____	$ ____	☐ Secured debt ☐ Unsecured loan repayments ☐ Suppliers or vendors ☐ Services ☐ Other _____

4. Payments or other transfers of property made within 1 year before filing this case that benefited any insider

List payments or transfers, including expense reimbursements, made within 1 year before filing this case on debts owed to an insider or guaranteed or cosigned by an insider unless the aggregate value of all property transferred to or for the benefit of the insider is less than $6,425. (This amount may be adjusted on 4/01/19 and every 3 years after that with respect to cases filed on or after the date of adjustment.) Do not include any payments listed in line 3. Insiders include officers, directors, and anyone in control of a corporate debtor and their relatives; general partners of a partnership debtor and their relatives; affiliates of the debtor and insiders of such affiliates; and any managing agent of the debtor. 11 U.S.C. § 101(31).

☐ None

Insider's name and address	Dates	Total amount or value	Reasons for payment or transfer
4.1. Insider's name Street City State ZIP Code Relationship to debtor	____	$ ____	
4.2. Insider's name Street City State ZIP Code Relationship to debtor	____	$ ____	

Official Form 207   Statement of Financial Affairs for Non-Individuals Filing for Bankruptcy   page 2

Debtor _____   Case number (if known) _____
         Name

5. Repossessions, foreclosures, and returns

List all property of the debtor that was obtained by a creditor within 1 year before filing this case, including property repossessed by a creditor, sold at a foreclosure sale, transferred by a deed in lieu of foreclosure, or returned to the seller. Do not include property listed in line 6.

❏ None

Creditor's name and address	Description of the property	Date	Value of property
5.1.			$_____
Creditor's name			
Street			
City State ZIP Code			
5.2.			$_____
Creditor's name			
Street			
City State ZIP Code			

6. Setoffs

List any creditor, including a bank or financial institution, that within 90 days before filing this case set off or otherwise took anything from an account of the debtor without permission or refused to make a payment at the debtor's direction from an account of the debtor because the debtor owed a debt.

❏ None

Creditor's name and address	Description of the action creditor took	Date action was taken	Amount
Creditor's name			$_____
Street			
City State ZIP Code	Last 4 digits of account number: XXXX–__ __ __ __		

Part 3:   Legal Actions or Assignments

7. Legal actions, administrative proceedings, court actions, executions, attachments, or governmental audits

List the legal actions, proceedings, investigations, arbitrations, mediations, and audits by federal or state agencies in which the debtor was involved in any capacity—within 1 year before filing this case.

❏ None

Case title	Nature of case	Court or agency's name and address	Status of case
7.1.			❏ Pending
		Name	❏ On appeal
Case number		Street	❏ Concluded
		City State ZIP Code	
7.2. Case title		Court or agency's name and address	❏ Pending
		Name	❏ On appeal
Case number		Street	❏ Concluded
		City State ZIP Code	

Official Form 207   Statement of Financial Affairs for Non-Individuals Filing for Bankruptcy   page 3

For Complete Annotation Materials, see United States Code Annotated

Debtor _____   Case number (if known)_____
              Name

6. Assignments and receivership

List any property in the hands of an assignee for the benefit of creditors during the 120 days before filing this case and any property in the hands of a receiver, custodian, or other court-appointed officer within 1 year before filing this case.

☐ None

Custodian's name and address	Description of the property	Value
Custodian's name		$_____
	Case title	Court name and address
Street		
	Case number	Name
City State ZIP Code		Street
	Date of order or assignment	City State ZIP Code

Part 4:   Certain Gifts and Charitable Contributions

9. List all gifts or charitable contributions the debtor gave to a recipient within 2 years before filing this case unless the aggregate value of the gifts to that recipient is less than $1,000

☐ None

Recipient's name and address	Description of the gifts or contributions	Dates given	Value
9.1 Recipient's name			$_____
Street			
City State ZIP Code			
Recipient's relationship to debtor			
9.2 Recipient's name			$_____
Street			
City State ZIP Code			
Recipient's relationship to debtor			

Part 5:   Certain Losses

10. All losses from fire, theft, or other casualty within 1 year before filing this case.

☐ None

Description of the property lost and how the loss occurred	Amount of payments received for the loss	Date of loss	Value of property lost
	If you have received payments to cover the loss, for example, from insurance, government compensation, or tort liability, list the total received. List unpaid claims on Official Form 106A/B (Schedule A/B: Assets – Real and Personal Property).		
			$_____

Official Form 207   Statement of Financial Affairs for Non-Individuals Filing for Bankruptcy   page 4

Debtor _____   Case number (if known) _____
                Name

Part 6:   Certain Payments or Transfers

11. Payments related to bankruptcy

List any payments of money or other transfers of property made by the debtor or person acting on behalf of the debtor within 1 year before the filing of this case to another person or entity, including attorneys, that the debtor consulted about debt consolidation or restructuring, seeking bankruptcy relief, or filing a bankruptcy case.

☐ None

Who was paid or who received the transfer?	If not money, describe any property transferred	Dates	Total amount or value

11.1 _____   _____   _____ $ _____

Address

Street _____

_____

City   State   ZIP Code

Email or website address
_____

Who made the payment, if not debtor?

_____

Who was paid or who received the transfer?	If not money, describe any property transferred	Dates	Total amount or value

11.2 _____   _____   _____ $ _____

Address

Street _____

City   State   ZIP Code

Email or website address
_____

Who made the payment, if not debtor?

_____

12. Self-settled trusts of which the debtor is a beneficiary

List any payments or transfers of property made by the debtor or a person acting on behalf of the debtor within 10 years before the filing of this case to a self-settled trust or similar device.
Do not include transfers already listed on this statement.

☐ None

Name of trust or device	Describe any property transferred	Dates transfers were made	Total amount or value
_____	_____	_____	$ _____
Trustee	_____		

Debtor _____   Case number (if known) _____
       Name

13. Transfers not already listed on this statement

List any transfers of money or other property—by sale, trade, or any other means—made by the debtor or a person acting on behalf of the debtor within 2 years before the filing of this case to another person, other than property transferred in the ordinary course of business or financial affairs. Include both outright transfers and transfers made as security. Do not include gifts or transfers previously listed on this statement.

☐ None

Who received transfer?	Description of property transferred or payments received or debts paid in exchange	Date transfer was made	Total amount or value

13.1 _____   _____ $_____

    Address

    Street

    City   State   ZIP Code

    Relationship to debtor

Who received transfer?   _____ $_____

13.2 _____

    Address

    Street

    City   State   ZIP Code

    Relationship to debtor

Part 7:   Previous Locations

14. Previous addresses

List all previous addresses used by the debtor within 3 years before filing this case and the dates the addresses were used.

☐ Does not apply

Address	Dates of occupancy

14.1 _____   From _____ To _____
    Street

    City   State ZIP Code

14.2 _____   From _____ To _____
    Street

    City   State ZIP Code

Official Form 207   Statement of Financial Affairs for Non-Individuals Filing for Bankruptcy   page 6

Form B207

Debtor _____   Case number (if known)_____
　　　　　Name

Part 8: Health Care Bankruptcies

15. Health Care bankruptcies

Is the debtor primarily engaged in offering services and facilities for:
- diagnosing or treating injury, deformity, or disease, or
- providing any surgical, psychiatric, drug treatment, or obstetric care?

☐ No. Go to Part 9.
☐ Yes. Fill in the information below.

Facility name and address	Nature of the business operation, including type of services the debtor provides	If debtor provides meals and housing, number of patients in debtor's care
15.1 Facility name		
Street	Location where patient records are maintained (if different from facility address). If electronic, identify any service provider.	How are records kept?
		Check all that apply:
City State ZIP Code		☐ Electronically ☐ Paper

Facility name and address	Nature of the business operation, including type of services the debtor provides	If debtor provides meals and housing, number of patients in debtor's care
15.2 Facility name		
Street	Location where patient records are maintained (if different from facility address). If electronic, identify any service provider.	How are records kept?
		Check all that apply:
City State ZIP Code		☐ Electronically ☐ Paper

Part 9: Personally Identifiable Information

16. Does the debtor collect and retain personally identifiable information of customers?

☐ No.
☐ Yes. State the nature of the information collected and retained. _____

　　　Does the debtor have a privacy policy about that information?
　　　☐ No
　　　☐ Yes

17. Within 6 years before filing this case, have any employees of the debtor been participants in any ERISA, 401(k), 403(b), or other pension or profit-sharing plan made available by the debtor as an employee benefit?

☐ No. Go to Part 10.
　　Yes. Does the debtor serve as plan administrator?
　　☐ No. Go to Part 10.
　　☐ Yes. Fill in below:

Name of plan	Employer identification number of the plan
_____	EIN: __ __ – __ __ __ __ __ __ __

　　Has the plan been terminated?
　　☐ No
　　☐ Yes

Debtor _____ Case number (if known) _____
　　　　Name

Part 10: Certain Financial Accounts, Safe Deposit Boxes, and Storage Units

18. **Closed financial accounts**

Within 1 year before filing this case, were any financial accounts or instruments held in the debtor's name, or for the debtor's benefit, closed, sold, moved, or transferred?

Include checking, savings, money market, or other financial accounts; certificates of deposit; and shares in banks, credit unions, brokerage houses, cooperatives, associations, and other financial institutions.

❏ None

Financial institution name and address	Last 4 digits of account number	Type of account	Date account was closed, sold, moved, or transferred	Last balance before closing or transfer
18.1 Name _____ Street _____ City　State　ZIP Code	XXXX-_ _ _ _	❏ Checking ❏ Savings ❏ Money market ❏ Brokerage ❏ Other_____	_____	$_____
18.2 Name _____ Street _____ City　State　ZIP Code	XXXX-_ _ _ _	❏ Checking ❏ Savings ❏ Money market ❏ Brokerage ❏ Other_____		$_____

19. **Safe deposit boxes**

List any safe deposit box or other depository for securities, cash, or other valuables the debtor now has or did have within 1 year before filing this case.

❏ None

Depository institution name and address	Names of anyone with access to it	Description of the contents	Does debtor still have it?
Name _____ Street _____ City　State　ZIP Code	_____ _____ Address _____	_____	❏ No ❏ Yes

20. **Off-premises storage**

List any property kept in storage units or warehouses within 1 year before filing this case. Do not include facilities that are in a part of a building in which the debtor does business.

❏ None

Facility name and address	Names of anyone with access to it	Description of the contents	Does debtor still have it?
Name _____ Street _____ City　State　ZIP Code	_____ _____ Address _____	_____	❏ No ❏ Yes

Official Form 207　　　Statement of Financial Affairs for Non-Individuals Filing for Bankruptcy　　　page 8

Form B207

Debtor _____ Case number (if known) _____

Name

Part 11: Property the Debtor Holds or Controls That the Debtor Does Not Own

21. **Property held for another**

List any property that the debtor holds or controls that another entity owns. Include any property borrowed from, being stored for, or held in trust. Do not list leased or rented property.

☐ None

Owner's name and address	Location of the property	Description of the property	Value
			$_____
Name			
Street			
City State ZIP Code			

Part 12: Details About Environmental Information

For the purpose of Part 12, the following definitions apply:

■ *Environmental law* means any statute or governmental regulation that concerns pollution, contamination, or hazardous material regardless of the medium affected (air, land, water, or any other medium).

■ *Site* means any location, facility, or property, including disposal sites, that the debtor now owns, operates, or utilizes or that the debtor formerly owned, operated, or utilized.

■ *Hazardous material* means anything that an environmental law defines as hazardous or toxic, or describes as a pollutant, contaminant, or a similarly harmful substance.

Report all notices, releases, and proceedings known, regardless of when they occurred.

22. **Has the debtor been a party in any judicial or administrative proceeding under any environmental law?** Include settlements and orders.

☐ No
☐ Yes. Provide details below.

Case title	Court or agency name and address	Nature of the case	Status of case
			☐ Pending
Case number	Name		☐ On appeal
	Street		☐ Concluded
	City State ZIP Code		

23. **Has any governmental unit otherwise notified the debtor that the debtor may be liable or potentially liable under or in violation of an environmental law?**

☐ No
☐ Yes. Provide details below.

Site name and address	Governmental unit name and address	Environmental law, if known	Date of notice
Name	Name		
Street	Street		
City State ZIP Code	City State ZIP Code		

Official Form 207   Statement of Financial Affairs for Non-Individuals Filing for Bankruptcy   page 9

Debtor _____   Case number (if known)_____
                Name

24. Has the debtor notified any governmental unit of any release of hazardous material?

❏ No

❏ Yes. Provide details below.

Site name and address	Governmental unit name and address	Environmental law, if known	Date of notice
Name _____	Name _____	_____	_____
Street _____	Street _____	_____	
City State ZIP Code	City State ZIP Code		

Part 13:   Details About the Debtor's Business or Connections to Any Business

25. Other businesses in which the debtor has or has had an interest

List any business for which the debtor was an owner, partner, member, or otherwise a person in control within 6 years before filing this case. Include this information even if already listed in the Schedules.

❏ None

Business name and address	Describe the nature of the business	Employer identification number Do not include Social Security number or ITIN.
25.1. Name _____ Street _____ City State ZIP Code	_____	EIN: __ __ - __ __ __ __ __ __ __ Dates business existed From _____ To _____
25.2. Name _____ Street _____ City State ZIP Code	_____	EIN: __ __ - __ __ __ __ __ __ __ Dates business existed From _____ To _____
25.3. Name _____ Street _____ City State ZIP Code	_____	EIN: __ __ - __ __ __ __ __ __ __ Dates business existed From _____ To _____

Debtor _____   Case number *(if known)* _____
       Name

26. Books, records, and financial statements

26a. List all accountants and bookkeepers who maintained the debtor's books and records within 2 years before filing this case.

☐ None

Name and address	Dates of service

26a.1.
Name _____   From _____ To _____

Street _____

City _____ State _____ ZIP Code _____

Name and address	Dates of service

26a.2.
Name _____   From _____ To _____

Street _____

City _____ State _____ ZIP Code _____

26b. List all firms or individuals who have audited, compiled, or reviewed debtor's books of account and records or prepared a financial statement within 2 years before filing this case.

☐ None

Name and address	Dates of service

26b.1.
Name _____   From _____ To _____

Street _____

City _____ State _____ ZIP Code _____

Name and address	Dates of service

26b.2.
Name _____   From _____ To _____

Street _____

City _____ State _____ ZIP Code _____

26c. List all firms or individuals who were in possession of the debtor's books of account and records when this case is filed.

☐ None

Name and address	If any books of account and records are unavailable, explain why

26c.1.
Name _____   _____

Street _____   _____

City _____ State _____ ZIP Code _____

Debtor _____   Case number _____
          Name

Name and address	If any books of account and records are unavailable, explain why

26c.2
Name _____
Street _____
_____
City   State   ZIP Code

26d. List all financial institutions, creditors, and other parties, including mercantile and trade agencies, to whom the debtor issued a financial statement within 2 years before filing this case.

☐ None

Name and address

26d.1
Name _____
Street _____
_____
City   State   ZIP Code

Name and address

26d.2
Name _____
Street _____
_____
City   State   ZIP Code

27. Inventories

Have any inventories of the debtor's property been taken within 2 years before filing this case?

☐ No
☐ Yes. Give the details about the two most recent inventories.

Name of the person who supervised the taking of the inventory	Date of inventory	The dollar amount and basis (cost, market, or other basis) of each inventory
_____	_____	$_____

Name and address of the person who has possession of inventory records

27.1
Name _____
State _____
City   State   ZIP Code

Official Form 207   Statement of Financial Affairs for Non-Individuals Filing for Bankruptcy   page 12

Form B207   OFFICIAL FORMS

Debtor _____   Case number _____
        Name

Name of the person who supervised the taking of the inventory	Date of inventory	The dollar amount and basis (cost, market, or other basis) of each inventory
_____	____	$ _____

Name and address of the person who has possession of inventory records

27.2
Name _____
Street _____
City _____ State _____ ZIP Code

28. List the debtor's officers, directors, managing members, general partners, members in control, controlling shareholders, or other people in control of the debtor at the time of the filing of this case.

Name	Address	Position and nature of any interest	% of interest, if any
_____	_____	_____	_____
_____	_____	_____	_____
_____	_____	_____	_____
_____	_____	_____	_____

29. Within 1 year before the filing of this case, did the debtor have officers, directors, managing members, general partners, members in control of the debtor, or shareholders in control of the debtor who no longer hold these positions?
☐ No
☐ Yes. Identify below.

Name	Address	Position and nature of any interest	Period during which position or interest was held
_____	_____	_____	From ___ To ___
_____	_____	_____	From ___ To ___
_____	_____	_____	From ___ To ___
_____	_____	_____	From ___ To ___

30. Payments, distributions, or withdrawals credited or given to insiders

Within 1 year before filing this case, did the debtor provide an insider with value in any form, including salary, other compensation, draws, bonuses, loans, credits on loans, stock redemptions, and options exercised?
☐ No
☐ Yes. Identify below.

Name and address of recipient	Amount of money or description and value of property	Dates	Reason for providing the value

30.1
Name _____
Street _____
City _____ State _____ ZIP Code
Relationship to debtor

Official Form 207   Statement of Financial Affairs for Non-Individuals Filing for Bankruptcy   page 13

Debtor _____   Case number (if known) _____
          Name

Name and address of recipient

30.2

Name _____

Street _____

City _____ State _____ ZIP Code _____

Relationship to debtor

_____

31. Within 6 years before filing this case, has the debtor been a member of any consolidated group for tax purposes?

☐ No
☐ Yes. Identify below.

Name of the parent corporation	Employer identification number of the parent corporation
	EIN: __ __ – __ __ __ __ __ __ __

32. Within 6 years before filing this case, has the debtor as an employer been responsible for contributing to a pension fund?

☐ No
☐ Yes. Identify below.

Name of the pension fund	Employer identification number of the pension fund
	EIN: __ __ – __ __ __ __ __ __ __

Part 14:   Signature and Declaration

WARNING — Bankruptcy fraud is a serious crime. Making a false statement, concealing property, or obtaining money or property by fraud in connection with a bankruptcy case can result in fines up to $500,000 or imprisonment for up to 20 years, or both.
18 U.S.C. §§ 152, 1341, 1519, and 3571.

I have examined the information in this *Statement of Financial Affairs* and any attachments and have a reasonable belief that the information is true and correct.

I declare under penalty of perjury that the foregoing is true and correct.

Executed on _____
                MM / DD / YYYY

✗ _____   Printed name _____
Signature of individual signing on behalf of the debtor

Position or relationship to debtor _____

Are additional pages to *Statement of Financial Affairs for Non-Individuals Filing for Bankruptcy* (Official Form 207) attached?
☐ No
☐ Yes

Official Form 207   Statement of Financial Affairs for Non-Individuals Filing for Bankruptcy   page 14

(Added Dec. 1, 2015; and amended Apr. 1, 2016.)

ADVISORY COMMITTEE NOTES

Official Form 207, *Statement of Financial Affairs for Non–Individuals Filing for Bankruptcy*, replaces Official Form 7, *Statement of Financial Affairs*, for non-individual debtors. It is renumbered to distinguish it from the forms used by individual debtors and includes formatting and stylistic changes throughout the form.

Official Form 207 is revised as part of the Forms Modernization Project, making it easier to read and, as a result, likely to generate more complete and accurate responses. The goals of the Forms Modernization Project include improving the interface between technology and the forms so as to increase efficiency and reducing the need to produce the same information in multiple formats.

The Forms Modernization Project made a preliminary decision that separate forms should be created for individual debtors and for non-individual debtors because separate areas of inquiry apply to each group. The forms for non-individuals do not include questions that pertain only to individuals and

use a more open-ended response format. Also, where possible, the forms for non-individuals parallel how businesses commonly keep their financial records.

The form is derived from Official Form 7, *Statement of Financial Affairs*, and has been substantially reorganized. The form is divided into 14 sections grouping similar questions together. Many of the instructions have been shortened, and questions and instructions pertaining to individual debtors have been deleted. The instructions at the beginning of the form have been shortened, and the definitions deleted or moved to other parts of the form.

In Part 1, *Income*, the questions regarding gross revenue from business and non-business revenue have been consolidated, and checkboxes have been added to indicate the source of revenue. Also, the debtor is instructed to include revenue only once.

In Part 2, *List Certain Transfers Made Before Filing for Bankruptcy*, information that pertains only to individuals has been eliminated, and the questions related to payments made in the 90 days prior to bankruptcy, payments made to insiders

---

For Complete Annotation Materials, see United States Code Annotated

within one year prior to bankruptcy, repossessions, and set-offs have been consolidated. Instructions have been added to include expense reimbursements in answer to the questions regarding payments and to exclude regular employee compensation from the question regarding payments within 90 days. A dollar limitation has been added to the instructions for the question regarding payments to insiders. Checkboxes have been added to both questions to provide a reason for the payment, and the explanation that the dollar limitation changes every three years has been moved to the instructions from the footnotes. "Amount still owing" has been removed, and a definition of "insider" has been added along with a statutory citation to the question regarding insiders. Partnerships have been added to examples of "insiders." The question regarding setoffs includes a revised definition and has been revised to require that the debtor provide a description of the creditor's actions and the last four digits of any account number.

In Part 3, *Legal Actions or Assignments*, several questions have been consolidated, instructions pertaining only to individuals have been removed, and additional examples have been added. Checkboxes have been added to indicate the status of the legal action. The requirement to list the terms of any assignment or settlement has been removed.

In Part 4, *Certain Gifts and Charitable Contributions*, instructions pertaining only to individuals have been removed, and the reporting threshold has been changed to $1,000 per recipient. The look-back period has been increased from one to two years.

Part 5, *Certain Losses*, has been revised to expand the types of payments for losses, and an instruction has been added to list unpaid claims on Official Form 206A/B (*Schedule A/B: Assets—Real and Personal Property*). Portions of the instructions that pertain only to individuals have been removed. Losses due to gambling have been excluded from this part.

In Part 6, *Certain Payments or Transfers*, the questions regarding payments related to bankruptcy, payments to self-settled trusts, and other payments or transfers have been consolidated. Instructions and questions that relate only to individuals have been eliminated. An instruction has been added to include payments related to restructuring, and the email or website of the person who received the money or transfer is added as a requirement. In response to the question regarding self-settled trusts and other transfers not already listed, debtors are instructed to include payments or transfers of property made by a person acting on behalf of the debtor. A requirement has been added to the question regarding self-settled trusts to list the name of the trustee. The relationship to the debtor must be included for all transfers not already listed, as well as any debts paid in exchange. There is a reminder added not to include transfers already listed.

Part 7, *Previous Locations*, has been revised in the instructions, and information pertaining only to individuals has been deleted.

Part 8, *Health Care Bankruptcies*, is new. Part 8 requires additional information if the debtor is primarily engaged in offering services and facilities for diagnosing or treating injury, deformity, or disease or providing any surgical, psychiatric, drug treatment, or obstetric care. This part has been added to comply with the special requirements imposed by the Bankruptcy Abuse Prevention and Consumer Protection Act of 2005.

Part 9, *Personally Identifiable Information*, is also new and includes questions about pension and profit sharing plans and adds a question about whether the debtor collects and retains personally identifiable information of customers. Questions are added about whether the debtor is the plan administrator of any pension or profit sharing plan and if any such plan is terminated. Similar to Part 8, this part has been added to comply with the special requirements imposed by the Bankruptcy Abuse Prevention and Consumer Protection Act of 2005.

In Part 10, *Certain Financial Accounts, Safe Deposit Boxes, and Storage Units*, money market accounts have been added to the examples provided for the question regarding financial accounts, and checkboxes have been added to indicate the type of account. The requirement of the date of surrender of any safe deposit box has been removed. A question has been added about whether the debtor has property kept in storage units or warehouses within one year of filing, and the debtor must provide the facility name and address, the name and address of anyone with access to the facility, the description of the contents, and whether the debtor still has the storage unit or warehouse. Facilities that are in a part of a building in which the debtor does business are excluded.

In Part 11, *Property the Debtor Holds or Controls That the Debtor Does Not Own*, an instruction has been added to include any property borrowed from, being stored for, or held in trust, and to exclude leased or rented property.

Part 12, *Details About Environmental Information*, has been revised to include new definitions of "Environmental law," "Site," and "Hazardous materials." An instruction to report all notices, releases, and proceedings known, regardless of when they occurred, has been added.

In Part 13, *Details About the Debtor's Business or Connections to Any Business*, questions regarding various business issues have been consolidated, and instructions that pertain only to individuals have been eliminated. The five-percent ownership limitation has been eliminated. The phrase "kept or supervised the keeping of books or account and records" has been replaced with "maintained the debtor's books and records." The instructions for the question regarding auditing or preparation of financial records have been revised to add compiling and reviewing the debtor's books of account and records. A requirement has been added to explain if the debtor's books of account and records are unavailable. The questions regarding current and former officers, directors, managing members, general partners, members in control, or controlling shareholders have combined the formerly separate corporate and partnership questions. The question regarding former officers and partners has been changed to add the requirement of indicating the start and end dates for each listing. The instruction for withdrawals from a partnership or distribution by a corporation has been changed to add salary, other compensation, and draws to the list of examples.

In Part 14, *Signature and Declaration*, the declaration under penalty of perjury has been revised in order to conform to the language of 28 U.S.C. § 1746. See Rule 1008. A statement has been added that the individual signing on behalf of the debtor has reviewed the information in the Statement of Financial Affairs and any attachments and has "a reasonable belief that the information is true and correct."

The signature boxes for bankruptcy petition preparers have been eliminated, and checkboxes for the debtor to indicate whether additional pages are attached to the form have been added.

Form B309A. (For Individuals or Joint Debtors)
Notice of Chapter 7 Bankruptcy Case—No Proof of Claim Deadline

Information to identify the case:

Debtor 1 _____ First Name _____ Middle Name _____ Last Name	Last 4 digits of Social Security number or ITIN ____ ____ EIN
Debtor 2 (Spouse filing) _____ First Name _____ Middle Name _____ Last Name	Last 4 digits of Social Security number or ITIN ____ ____ EIN
United States Bankruptcy Court for the: _____ District of _____ (State)	[Date case filed for chapter 7 ____ MM / DD / YYYY OR
Case number: _____	[Date case filed in chapter ____ MM / DD / YYYY Date case converted to chapter 7 ____ MM / DD / YYYY]

Official Form 309A (For Individuals or Joint Debtors)

Notice of Chapter 7 Bankruptcy Case — No Proof of Claim Deadline 12/15

For the debtors listed above, a case has been filed under chapter 7 of the Bankruptcy Code. An order for relief has been entered.

This notice has important information about the case for creditors, debtors, and trustees, including information about the meeting of creditors and deadlines. Read both pages carefully.

The filing of the case imposed an automatic stay against most collection activities. This means that creditors generally may not take action to collect debts from the debtors or the debtors' property. For example, while the stay is in effect, creditors cannot sue, garnish wages, assert a deficiency, repossess property, or otherwise try to collect from the debtors. Creditors cannot demand repayment from debtors by mail, phone, or otherwise. Creditors who violate the stay can be required to pay actual and punitive damages and attorney's fees. Under certain circumstances, the stay may be limited to 30 days or not exist at all, although debtors can ask the court to extend or impose a stay.

The debtors are seeking a discharge. Creditors who assert that the debtors are not entitled to a discharge of any debts or who want to have a particular debt excepted from discharge may be required to file a complaint in the bankruptcy clerk's office within the deadlines specified in this notice. (See line 9 for more information.)

To protect your rights, consult an attorney. All documents filed in the case may be inspected at the bankruptcy clerk's office at the address listed below or through PACER (Public Access to Court Electronic Records at www.pacer.gov).

The staff of the bankruptcy clerk's office cannot give legal advice.

To help creditors correctly identify debtors, debtors submit full Social Security or Individual Taxpayer Identification Numbers, which may appear on a version of this notice. However, the full numbers must not appear on any document filed with the court.

Do not file this notice with any proof of claim or other filing in the case. Do not include more than the last four digits of a Social Security or Individual Taxpayer Identification Number in any document, including attachments, that you file with the court.

	About Debtor 1:	About Debtor 2:
1. Debtor's full name		
2. All other names used in the last 8 years		
3. Address		If Debtor 2 lives at a different address:
4. Debtor's attorney Name and address		Contact phone _____ Email _____
5. Bankruptcy trustee Name and address		Contact phone _____ Email _____

For more information, see page 2 ▶

Official Form 309A (For Individuals or Joint Debtors)   Notice of Chapter 7 Bankruptcy Case — No Proof of Claim Deadline   page 1

Debtor _____   Case number _____
             Name

6. Bankruptcy clerk's office Documents in this case may be filed at this address. You may inspect all records filed in this case at this office or online at www.pacer.gov.	Hours open _____ Contact phone _____

7. Meeting of creditors Debtors must attend the meeting to be questioned under oath. In a joint case, both spouses must attend. Creditors may attend, but are not required to do so.	_____ at _____ Date Time The meeting may be continued or adjourned to a later date. If so, the date will be on the court docket.	Location:

8. Presumption of abuse If the presumption of abuse arises, you may have the right to file a motion to dismiss the case under 11 U.S.C. § 707(b). Debtors may rebut the presumption by showing special circumstances.	[The presumption of abuse does not arise.] [The presumption of abuse arises.] [Insufficient information has been filed to permit the clerk to determine whether the presumption of abuse arises. If more complete information is filed and shows that the presumption has arisen, the clerk will notify creditors.]

9. Deadlines
The bankruptcy clerk's office must receive these documents and any required filing fee by the following deadlines.
	File by the deadline to object to discharge or to challenge whether certain debts are dischargeable:
	
	You must file a complaint:
	  if you assert that the debtor is not entitled to receive a discharge of any debts under any of the subdivisions of 11 U.S.C. § 727(a)(2) through (7).
	  or
	  if you want to have a debt excepted from discharge under 11 U.S.C. § 523(a)(2), (4), or (6).
	
	You must file a motion if you assert that the discharge should be denied under § 727(a)(8) or (9).
		Filing deadline: _____

	Deadline to object to exemptions: The law permits debtors to keep certain property as exempt. If you believe that the law does not authorize an exemption claimed, you may file an objection.	**Filing deadline:** 30 days after the conclusion of the meeting of creditors

10. Proof of claim Please do not file a proof of claim unless you receive a notice to do so.	No property appears to be available to pay creditors. Therefore, please do not file a proof of claim now. If it later appears that assets are available to pay creditors, the clerk will send you another notice telling you that you may file a proof of claim and stating the deadline.

11. Creditors with a foreign address	If you are a creditor receiving a notice mailed to a foreign address, you may file a motion asking the court to extend the deadlines in this notice. Consult an attorney familiar with United States bankruptcy law if you have any questions about your rights in this case.

12. Exempt property	The law allows debtors to keep certain property as exempt. Fully exempt property will not be sold and distributed to creditors. Debtors must file a list of property claimed as exempt. You may inspect that list at the bankruptcy clerk's office or online at www.pacer.gov. If you believe that the law does not authorize an exemption that the debtors claim, you may file an objection. The bankruptcy clerk's office must receive the objection by the deadline to object to exemptions in line 9.

Official Form 309A (For Individuals or Joint Debtors)   Notice of Chapter 7 Bankruptcy Case — No Proof of Claim Deadline   page 2

(Added Dec. 1, 2015.)

ADVISORY COMMITTEE NOTES

Official Forms 309A–I, collectively the Bankruptcy Case Commencement Notices, have been revised as part of the Forms Modernization Project to make them easier to read and understand. The notices, derived from Official Forms 9A–I are renumbered and stylistic changes have been made.

References to the limitations on the automatic stay imposed by 11 U.S.C. § 362(c)(3) and (4) in some repeat bankruptcy filings by individuals have been deleted from the three versions of the notice for cases filed by corporations and partnerships. Email addresses for the debtor's attorney and the trustee have been added to the form.

The parties are informed that they may review papers filed in the case through the judiciary's PACER system (Public Access to Court Electronic Records) as well as at the bankruptcy clerk's office.

The lettering scheme for the versions of Official Form 309 track the versions of Official Form 9 used in different types of bankruptcy cases with following exceptions. Official Forms 9E(Alt.) and 9F(Alt.) have been eliminated by including alternative language in Official Forms 309E and 309F to be used if the court sets a deadline for filing claims at the start of the chapter 11 case. In addition, the B and C versions have been reversed in order. That is, Official Form 9C has been designated 309B and Official Form 9B as 309C. This groups together the notices for chapter 7 individual debtors and for non-individual debtors. Finally, as a result of the reformatting, Official Form 309C has been reduced to a single page.

The four versions of the form for chapter 7 cases have been renamed to state whether the notice specifies a deadline for filing proofs of claim, rather than whether the case is an "asset" or "no-asset" case.

For Complete Annotation Materials, see United States Code Annotated

Form B309B. (For Individuals or Joint Debtors)
Notice of Chapter 7 Bankruptcy Case—
Proof of Claim Deadline Set

Information to identify the case:

Debtor 1 _____
First Name   Middle Name   Last Name

Last 4 digits of Social Security number or ITIN __ __ __ __

EIN __ __ - __ __ __ __ __ __ __

Debtor 2
(Spouse, if filing) First Name   Middle Name   Last Name

Last 4 digits of Social Security number or ITIN __ __ __ __

EIN __ __ - __ __ __ __ __ __ __

United States Bankruptcy Court for the _____ District of _____
(State)

|Date case filed for chapter 7 _____   MM / DD / YYYY   OR

Case number: _____

Date case filed in chapter _____   MM / DD / YYYY

Date case converted to chapter 7 _____   MM / DD / YYYY

Official Form 309B (For Individuals or Joint Debtors)

Notice of Chapter 7 Bankruptcy Case — Proof of Claim Deadline Set   12/15

For the debtors listed above, a case has been filed under chapter 7 of the Bankruptcy Code. An order for relief has been entered.

This notice has important information about the case for creditors, debtors, and trustees, including information about the meeting of creditors and deadlines. Read both pages carefully.

The filing of the case imposed an automatic stay against most collection activities. This means that creditors generally may not take action to collect debts from the debtors or the debtors' property. For example, while the stay is in effect, creditors cannot sue, garnish wages, assert a deficiency, repossess property, or otherwise try to collect from the debtors. Creditors cannot demand repayment from debtors by mail, phone, or otherwise. Creditors who violate the stay can be required to pay actual and punitive damages and attorney's fees. Under certain circumstances, the stay may be limited to 30 days or not exist at all, although debtors can ask the court to extend or impose a stay.

The debtors are seeking a discharge. Creditors who assert that the debtors are not entitled to a discharge of any debts or who want to have a particular debt excepted from discharge may be required to file a complaint in the bankruptcy clerk's office within the deadlines specified in this notice. (See line 9 for more information.)

To protect your rights, consult an attorney. All documents filed in the case may be inspected at the bankruptcy clerk's office at the address listed below or through PACER (Public Access to Court Electronic Records at www.pacer.gov).

The staff of the bankruptcy clerk's office cannot give legal advice.

To help creditors correctly identify debtors, debtors submit full Social Security or Individual Taxpayer Identification Numbers, which may appear on a version of this notice. However, the full numbers must not appear on any document filed with the court.

Do not file this notice with any proof of claim or other filing in the case. Do not include more than the last four digits of a Social Security or Individual Taxpayer Identification Number in any document, including attachments, that you file with the court.

	About Debtor 1:	About Debtor 2:
1. Debtor's full name		
2. All other names used in the last 8 years		
3. Address		If Debtor 2 lives at a different address:
4. Debtor's attorney Name and address		Contact phone _____ Email _____
5. Bankruptcy trustee Name and address		Contact phone _____ Email _____

For more information, see page 2 ▶

Official Form 309B (For Individuals or Joint Debtors) Notice of Chapter 7 Bankruptcy Case — Proof of Claim Deadline Set   page 1

Debtor _____   Case number _____

6. Bankruptcy clerk's office Documents in this case may be filed at this address. You may inspect all records filed in this case at this office or online at www.pacer.gov.	Hours open _____ Contact phone _____
7. Meeting of creditors Debtors must attend the meeting to be questioned under oath. In a joint case, both spouses must attend. Creditors may attend, but are not required to do so.	Date _____ at _____ Location: Time The meeting may be continued or adjourned to a later date. If so, the date will be on the court docket.
8. Presumption of abuse If the presumption of abuse arises, you may have the right to file a motion to dismiss the case under 11 U.S.C. § 707(b). Debtors may rebut the presumption by showing special circumstances.	[The presumption of abuse does not arise.] [The presumption of abuse arises.] [Insufficient information has been filed to permit the clerk to determine whether the presumption of abuse arises. If more complete information is filed and shows that the presumption has arisen, the clerk will notify creditors.]
9. Deadlines The bankruptcy clerk's office must receive these documents and any required filing fee by the following deadlines.	**File by the deadline to object to discharge or to challenge whether certain debts are dischargeable:** Filing deadline: _____ **You must file a complaint:** ■ if you assert that the debtor is not entitled to receive a discharge of any debts under any of the subdivisions of 11 U.S.C. § 727(a)(2) through (7), or ■ if you want to have a debt excepted from discharge under 11 U.S.C. § 523(a)(2), (4), or (6). **You must file a motion:** ■ if you assert that the discharge should be denied under § 727(a)(8) or (9). **Deadline for all creditors to file a proof of claim (except governmental units):** Filing deadline: _____ **Deadline for governmental units to file a proof of claim:** Filing deadline: _____ **Deadlines for filing proof of claim:** A proof of claim is a signed statement describing a creditor's claim. A proof of claim form may be obtained at www.uscourts.gov or any bankruptcy clerk's office. If you do not file a proof of claim by the deadline, you might not be paid on your claim. To be paid, you must file a proof of claim even if your claim is listed in the schedules that the debtor filed. Secured creditors retain rights in their collateral regardless of whether they file a proof of claim. Filing a proof of claim submits the creditor to the jurisdiction of the bankruptcy court, with consequences a lawyer can explain. For example, a secured creditor who files a proof of claim may surrender important nonmonetary rights, including the right to a jury trial. **Deadline to object to exemptions:** Filing deadline: 30 days after the conclusion of the meeting of creditors The law permits debtors to keep certain property as exempt. If you believe that the law does not authorize an exemption claimed, you may file an objection.
10. Creditors with a foreign address	If you are a creditor receiving a notice mailed to a foreign address, you may file a motion asking the court to extend the deadlines in this notice. Consult an attorney familiar with United States bankruptcy law if you have any questions about your rights in this case.
11. Liquidation of the debtor's property and payment of creditors' claims	The bankruptcy trustee listed on the front of this notice will collect and sell the debtor's property that is not exempt. If the trustee can collect enough money, creditors may be paid some or all of the debts owed to them in the order specified by the Bankruptcy Code. To ensure you receive any share of that money, you must file a proof of claim as described above.
12. Exempt property	The law allows debtors to keep certain property as exempt. Fully exempt property will not be sold and distributed to creditors. Debtors must file a list of property claimed as exempt. You may inspect that list at the bankruptcy clerk's office or online at www.pacer.gov. If you believe that the law does not authorize an exemption that the debtors claim, you may file an objection. The bankruptcy clerk's office must receive the objection by the deadline to object to exemptions in line 9.

Official Form 309B (For Individuals or Joint Debtors) Notice of Chapter 7 Bankruptcy Case — Proof of Claim Deadline Set   page 2

(Added Dec. 1, 2015.)

ADVISORY COMMITTEE NOTES

Official Forms 309A–I, collectively the Bankruptcy Case Commencement Notices, have been revised as part of the Forms Modernization Project to make them easier to read and understand. The notices, derived from Official Forms 9A–I are renumbered and stylistic changes have been made.

References to the limitations on the automatic stay imposed by 11 U.S.C. § 362(c)(3) and (4) in some repeat bankruptcy filings by individuals have been deleted from the three versions of the notice for cases filed by corporations and partnerships. Email addresses for the debtor's attorney and the trustee have been added to the form.

The parties are informed that they may review papers filed in the case through the judiciary's PACER system (Public Access to Court Electronic Records) as well as at the bankruptcy clerk's office.

The lettering scheme for the versions of Official Form 309 track the versions of Official Form 9 used in different types of bankruptcy cases with following exceptions. Official Forms 9E(Alt.) and 9F(Alt.) have been eliminated by including alternative language in Official Forms 309E and 309F to be used if the court sets a deadline for filing claims at the start of the chapter 11 case. In addition, the B and C versions have been reversed in order. That is, Official Form 9C has been designated 309B and Official Form 9B as 309C. This groups together the notices for chapter 7 individual debtors and for non-individual debtors. Finally, as a result of the reformatting, Official Form 309C has been reduced to a single page.

The four versions of the form for chapter 7 cases have been renamed to state whether the notice specifies a deadline for filing proofs of claim, rather than whether the case is an "asset" or "no-asset" case.

Form B309C

Form B309C. (For Corporations or Partnerships)
 Notice of Chapter 7 Bankruptcy Case—No
 Proof of Claim Deadline Set

Information to identify the case:

Debtor _____

EIN _____

United States Bankruptcy Court for the: _____ District of _____
(State)

Case number: _____

Date case filed for chapter 7 _____ MM /DD/YYYY or

Date case filed in chapter _____ MM /DD/YYYY

Date case converted to chapter 7 _____ MM /DD/YYYY

Official Form 309C (For Corporations or Partnerships)

Notice of Chapter 7 Bankruptcy Case — No Proof of Claim Deadline   12/15

For the debtor listed above, a case has been filed under chapter 7 of the Bankruptcy Code. An order for relief has been entered.

This notice has important information about the case for creditors, debtors, and trustees, including information about the meeting of creditors and deadlines.

The filing of the case imposed an automatic stay against most collection activities. This means that creditors generally may not take action to collect debts from the debtor or the debtor's property. For example, while the stay is in effect, creditors cannot sue, assert a deficiency, repossess property, or otherwise try to collect from the debtor. Creditors cannot demand repayment from debtors by mail, phone, or otherwise. Creditors who violate the stay can be required to pay actual and punitive damages and attorney's fees.

To protect your rights, consult an attorney. All documents filed in the case may be inspected at the bankruptcy clerk's office at the address listed below or through PACER (Public Access to Court Electronic Records at www.pacer.gov).

The staff of the bankruptcy clerk's office cannot give legal advice.

Do not file this notice with any proof of claim or other filing in the case.

1. **Debtor's full name**	
2. **All other names used in the last 8 years**	
3. **Address**	
4. **Debtor's attorney** Name and address	Contact phone _____ Email _____
5. **Bankruptcy trustee** Name and address	Contact phone _____ Email _____
6. **Bankruptcy clerk's office** Documents in this case may be filed at this address You may inspect all records filed in this case at this office or online at www.pacer.gov	Hours open _____ Contact phone _____
7. **Meeting of creditors** The debtor's representative must attend the meeting to be questioned under oath. Creditors may attend, but are not required to do so.	Date _____ at _____ Time The meeting may be continued or adjourned to a later date. If so, the date will be on the court docket. Location:
8. **Proof of claim** Please do not file a proof of claim unless you receive a notice to do so.	No property appears to be available to pay creditors. Therefore, please do not file a proof of claim now. If it later appears that assets are available to pay creditors, the clerk will send you another notice telling you that you may file a proof of claim and stating the deadline.
9. **Creditors with a foreign address**	If you are a creditor receiving a notice mailed to a foreign address, you may file a motion asking the court to extend the deadlines in this notice. Consult an attorney familiar with United States bankruptcy law if you have any questions about your rights in this case.

Official Form 309C (For Corporations or Partnerships) Notice of Chapter 7 Bankruptcy Case — No Proof of Claim Deadline   211

(Added Dec. 1, 2015.)

ADVISORY COMMITTEE NOTES

Official Forms 309A–I, collectively the Bankruptcy Case Commencement Notices, have been revised as part of the Forms Modernization Project to make them easier to read and understand. The notices, derived from Official Forms 9A–I are renumbered and stylistic changes have been made.

References to the limitations on the automatic stay imposed by 11 U.S.C. § 362(c)(3) and (4) in some repeat bankruptcy filings by individuals have been deleted from the three versions of the notice for cases filed by corporations and partnerships. Email addresses for the debtor's attorney and the trustee have been added to the form.

The parties are informed that they may review papers filed in the case through the judiciary's PACER system (Public Access to Court Electronic Records) as well as at the bankruptcy clerk's office.

The lettering scheme for the versions of Official Form 309 track the versions of Official Form 9 used in different types of bankruptcy cases with following exceptions. Official Forms 9E(Alt.) and 9F(Alt.) have been eliminated by including alternative language in Official Forms 309E and 309F to be used if the court sets a deadline for filing claims at the start of the chapter 11 case. In addition, the B and C versions have been reversed in order. That is, Official Form 9C has been designated 309B and Official Form 9B as 309C. This groups together the notices for chapter 7 individual debtors and for

---

For Complete Annotation Materials, see United States Code Annotated

882

non-individual debtors. Finally, as a result of the reformatting, Official Form 309C has been reduced to a single page.

The four versions of the form for chapter 7 cases have been renamed to state whether the notice specifies a deadline for filing proofs of claim, rather than whether the case is an "asset" or "no-asset" case.

Form B309D

Form B309D. (For Corporations or Partnerships)
Notice of Chapter 7 Bankruptcy Case—Proof of Claim Deadline Set

---

Information to identify the case:

Debtor _____   EIN ___-_____

United States Bankruptcy Court for the: _____ District of _____

Case number: _____

Date case filed for chapter 7 ____ MM/DD/YYYY

Date case filed in chapter ____ MM/DD/YYYY

Date case converted to chapter 7 ____ MM/DD/YYYY

Official Form 309D (For Corporations or Partnerships)

Notice of Chapter 7 Bankruptcy Case — Proof of Claim Deadline Set 12/15

For the debtor listed above, a case has been filed under chapter 7 of the Bankruptcy Code. An order for relief has been entered.

This notice has important information about the case for creditors, debtors, and trustees, including information about the meeting of creditors and deadlines. Read both pages carefully.

The filing of the case imposed an automatic stay against most collection activities. This means that creditors generally may not take action to collect debts from the debtor or the debtor's property. For example, while the stay is in effect, creditors cannot sue, assert a deficiency, repossess property, or otherwise try to collect from the debtor. Creditors cannot demand repayment from debtors by mail, phone, or otherwise. Creditors who violate the stay can be required to pay actual and punitive damages and attorney's fees.

To protect your rights, consult an attorney. All documents filed in the case may be inspected at the bankruptcy clerk's office at the address listed below or through PACER (Public Access to Court Electronic Records at www.pacer.gov).

The staff of the bankruptcy clerk's office cannot give legal advice.

Do not file this notice with any proof of claim or other filing in the case.

---

1. Debtor's full name	
2. All other names used in the last 8 years	
3. Address	
4. Debtor's attorney Name and address	Contact phone _____ Email _____
5. Bankruptcy trustee Name and address	Contact phone _____ Email _____
6. Bankruptcy clerk's office Documents in this case may be filed at this address. You may inspect all records filed in this case at this office or online at www.pacer.gov.	Hours open _____ Contact phone _____
7. Meeting of creditors The debtor's representative must attend the meeting to be questioned under oath. Creditors may attend, but are not required to do so.	_____ at _____ Date Time Location: The meeting may be continued or adjourned to a later date. If so, the date will be on the court docket.

For more information, see page 2 ▶

Official Form 309D (For Corporations or Partnerships)   Notice of Chapter 7 Bankruptcy Case   Proof of Claim Deadline Set   page 1

Debtor _____   Case number (if known) _____
Name

8. Deadlines The bankruptcy clerk's office must receive proofs of claim by the following deadlines.	Deadline for all creditors to file a proof of claim (except governmental units):	Filing deadline: _____
	Deadline for governmental units to file a proof of claim:	Filing deadline: _____

A proof of claim is a signed statement describing a creditor's claim. A proof of claim form may be obtained at www.uscourts.gov or any bankruptcy clerk's office. If you do not file a proof of claim by the deadline, you might not be paid on your claim. To be paid, you must file a proof of claim even if your claim is listed in the schedules that the debtor filed.

Secured creditors retain rights in their collateral regardless of whether they file a proof of claim. Filing a proof of claim submits the creditor to the jurisdiction of the bankruptcy court, with consequences a lawyer can explain. For example, a secured creditor who files a proof of claim may surrender important nonmonetary rights, including the right to a jury trial.

9. Creditors with a foreign address	If you are a creditor receiving a notice mailed to a foreign address, you may file a motion asking the court to extend the deadlines in this notice. Consult an attorney familiar with United States bankruptcy law if you have any questions about your rights in this case.
10. Liquidation of the debtor's property and payment of creditors' claims	The bankruptcy trustee listed on the front of this notice will collect and sell the debtor's property. If the trustee can collect enough money, creditors may be paid some or all of the debts owed to them, in the order specified by the Bankruptcy Code. To ensure you receive any share of that money, you must file a proof of claim, as described above.

(Added Dec. 1, 2015.)

ADVISORY COMMITTEE NOTES

Official Forms 309A–I, collectively the Bankruptcy Case Commencement Notices, have been revised as part of the Forms Modernization Project to make them easier to read and understand. The notices, derived from Official Forms 9A–I are renumbered and stylistic changes have been made.

References to the limitations on the automatic stay imposed by 11 U.S.C. § 362(c)(3) and (4) in some repeat bankruptcy filings by individuals have been deleted from the three versions of the notice for cases filed by corporations and partnerships. Email addresses for the debtor's attorney and the trustee have been added to the form.

The parties are informed that they may review papers filed in the case through the judiciary's PACER system (Public Access to Court Electronic Records) as well as at the bankruptcy clerk's office.

The lettering scheme for the versions of Official Form 309 track the versions of Official Form 9 used in different types of bankruptcy cases with following exceptions. Official Forms 9E(Alt.) and 9F(Alt.) have been eliminated by including alternative language in Official Forms 309E and 309F to be used if the court sets a deadline for filing claims at the start of the chapter 11 case. In addition, the B and C versions have been reversed in order. That is, Official Form 9C has been designated 309B and Official Form 9B as 309C. This groups together the notices for chapter 7 individual debtors and for non-individual debtors. Finally, as a result of the reformatting, Official Form 309C has been reduced to a single page.

The four versions of the form for chapter 7 cases have been renamed to state whether the notice specifies a deadline for filing proofs of claim, rather than whether the case is an "asset" or "no-asset" case.

Form B309E

Form B309E. (For Individuals or Joint Debtors)
Notice of Chapter 11 Bankruptcy Case

Information to identify the case:

Debtor 1 _____ First Name Middle Name Last Name	Last 4 digits of Social Security number or ITIN EIN _ _ _ – _ _ – _ _ _ _
Debtor 2 _____ (Spouse, if filing) First Name Middle Name Last Name	Last 4 digits of Social Security number or ITIN EIN _ _ _ – _ _ – _ _ _ _
United States Bankruptcy Court for the _____ District of _____ (State)	Date case filed for chapter 11 ____ MM / DD / YYYY OR Date case filed in chapter ____ MM / DD / YYYY Date case converted to chapter 11 ____ MM / DD / YYYY

Official Form 309E (For Individuals or Joint Debtors)

Notice of Chapter 11 Bankruptcy Case

12/15

For the debtors listed above, a case has been filed under chapter 11 of the Bankruptcy Code. An order for relief has been entered.

This notice has important information about the case for creditors and debtors, including information about the meeting of creditors and deadlines. Read both pages carefully.

The filing of the case imposed an automatic stay against most collection activities. This means that creditors generally may not take action to collect debts from the debtors or the debtors' property. For example, while the stay is in effect, creditors cannot sue, garnish wages, assert a deficiency, repossess property, or otherwise try to collect from the debtors. Creditors cannot demand repayment from debtors by mail, phone, or otherwise. Creditors who violate the stay can be required to pay actual and punitive damages and attorney's fees. Under certain circumstances, the stay may be limited to 30 days or not exist at all, although debtors can ask the court to extend or impose a stay.

Confirmation of a chapter 11 plan may result in a discharge of debt. Creditors who assert that the debtors are not entitled to a discharge of any debts or who want to have a particular debt excepted from discharge may be required to file a complaint in the bankruptcy clerk's office within the deadlines specified in this notice. (See line 10 below for more information.)

To protect your rights, consult an attorney. All documents filed in the case may be inspected at the bankruptcy clerk's office at the address listed below or through PACER (Public Access to Court Electronic Records at www.pacer.gov).

The staff of the bankruptcy clerk's office cannot give legal advice.

To help creditors correctly identify debtors, debtors submit full Social Security or Individual Taxpayer Identification Numbers, which may appear on a version of this notice. However, the full numbers must not appear on any document filed with the court.

Do not file this notice with any proof of claim or other filing in the case. Do not include more than the last four digits of a Social Security or Individual Taxpayer Identification Number in any document, including attachments, that you file with the court.

	About Debtor 1:	About Debtor 2:
1. Debtor's full name		
2. All other names used in the last 8 years		
3. Address		If Debtor 2 lives at a different address:
4. Debtor's attorney Name and address		Contact phone _____ Email _____
5. Bankruptcy clerk's office Documents in this case may be filed at this address. You may inspect all records filed in this case at this office or online at www.pacer.gov.		Hours open _____ Contact phone _____

For more information, see page 2 ▶

Official Form 309E (For Individuals or Joint Debtors)   Notice of Chapter 11 Bankruptcy Case   page 1

6. Meeting of creditors Debtors must attend the meeting to be questioned under oath. In a joint case, both spouses must attend. Creditors may attend, but are not required to do so.	_____ at _____ Date Time The meeting may be continued or adjourned to a later date. If so, the date will be on the court docket.	Location:

7. Deadlines The bankruptcy clerk's office must receive these documents and any required filing fee by the following deadlines.	**File by the deadline to object to discharge or to challenge whether certain debts are dischargeable:** **You must file a complaint:** ■ if you assert that the debtor is not entitled to receive a discharge of any debts under 11 U.S.C. § 1141(d)(3); or ■ if you want to have a debt excepted from discharge under 11 U.S.C. § 523(a)(2), (4), or (6).	First date set for hearing on confirmation of plan. The court will send you a notice of that date later. **Filing deadline for dischargeability complaints:** _____
	Deadline for filing proof of claim:	[Not yet set. If a deadline is set, the court will send you another notice.] or [date, if set by the court]
	A proof of claim is a signed statement describing a creditor's claim. A proof of claim form may be obtained at www.uscourts.gov or any bankruptcy clerk's office. Your claim will be allowed in the amount scheduled unless: ■ your claim is designated as *disputed, contingent,* or *unliquidated;* ■ you file a proof of claim in a different amount; or ■ you receive another notice. If your claim is not scheduled or if your claim is designated as *disputed, contingent,* or *unliquidated,* you must file a proof of claim or you might not be paid on your claim and you might be unable to vote on a plan. You may file a proof of claim even if your claim is scheduled. You may review the schedules at the bankruptcy clerk's office or online at www.pacer.gov. Secured creditors retain rights in their collateral regardless of whether they file a proof of claim. Filing a proof of claim submits a creditor to the jurisdiction of the bankruptcy court, with consequences a lawyer can explain. For example, a secured creditor who files a proof of claim may surrender important nonmonetary rights, including the right to a jury trial.	
	Deadline to object to exemptions: The law permits debtors to keep certain property as exempt. If you believe that the law does not authorize an exemption claimed, you may file an objection.	**Filing deadline:** 30 days after the *conclusion* of the meeting of creditors

8. Creditors with a foreign address	If you are a creditor receiving mailed notice at a foreign address, you may file a motion asking the court to extend the deadlines in this notice. Consult an attorney familiar with United States bankruptcy law if you have any questions about your rights in this case.
9. Filing a Chapter 11 bankruptcy case	Chapter 11 allows debtors to reorganize or liquidate according to a plan. A plan is not effective unless the court confirms it. You may receive a copy of the plan and a disclosure statement telling you about the plan, and you may have the opportunity to vote on the plan. You will receive notice of the date of the confirmation hearing, and you may object to confirmation of the plan and attend the confirmation hearing. Unless a trustee is serving, the debtor will remain in possession of the property and may continue to operate the debtor's business.
10. Discharge of debts	Confirmation of a chapter 11 plan may result in a discharge of debts, which may include all or part of a debt. See 11 U.S.C. § 1141(d). However, unless the court orders otherwise, the debts will not be discharged until all payments under the plan are made. A discharge means that creditors may never try to collect the debt from the debtors personally except as provided in the plan. If you believe that a particular debt owed to you should be excepted from the discharge under 11 U.S.C. § 523 (a)(2), (4), or (6), you must file a complaint and pay the filing fee in the bankruptcy clerk's office by the deadline. If you believe that the debtors are not entitled to a discharge of any of their debts under 11 U.S.C. § 1141 (d)(3), you must file a complaint and pay the filing fee in the clerk's office by the first date set for the hearing on confirmation of the plan. The court will send you another notice telling you of that date.
11. Exempt property	The law allows debtors to keep certain property as exempt. Fully exempt property will not be sold and distributed to creditors, even if the case is converted to chapter 7. Debtors must file a list of property claimed as exempt. You may inspect that list at the bankruptcy clerk's office or online at www.pacer.gov. If you believe that the law does not authorize an exemption that the debtors claim, you may file an objection. The bankruptcy clerk's office must receive the objection by the deadline to object to exemptions in line 7.

(Added Dec. 1, 2015.)

ADVISORY COMMITTEE NOTES

Official Forms 309A–I, collectively the Bankruptcy Case Commencement Notices, have been revised as part of the Forms Modernization Project to make them easier to read and understand. The notices, derived from Official Forms 9A–I are renumbered and stylistic changes have been made.

References to the limitations on the automatic stay imposed by 11 U.S.C. § 362(c)(3) and (4) in some repeat bankruptcy filings by individuals have been deleted from the three versions of the notice for cases filed by corporations and partnerships. Email addresses for the debtor's attorney and the trustee have been added to the form.

The parties are informed that they may review papers filed in the case through the judiciary's PACER system (Public Access to Court Electronic Records) as well as at the bankruptcy clerk's office.

The lettering scheme for the versions of Official Form 309 track the versions of Official Form 9 used in different types of bankruptcy cases with following exceptions. Official Forms 9E(Alt.) and 9F(Alt.) have been eliminated by including alternative language in Official Forms 309E and 309F to be used if the court sets a deadline for filing claims at the start of the chapter 11 case. In addition, the B and C versions have been reversed in order. That is, Official Form 9C has been designated 309B and Official Form 9B as 309C. This groups together the notices for chapter 7 individual debtors and for non-individual debtors. Finally, as a result of the reformatting, Official Form 309C has been reduced to a single page.

The four versions of the form for chapter 7 cases have been renamed to state whether the notice specifies a deadline for filing proofs of claim, rather than whether the case is an "asset" or "no-asset" case.

Form B309F

Form B309F. (For Corporations or Partnerships)
Notice of Chapter 11 Bankruptcy Case

Information to identify the case:

Debtor _____
Name

United States Bankruptcy Court for the: _____ District of _____
(State)

Case number: _____

EIN __ __ – __ __ __ __ __ __ __

[Date case filed for chapter 11 _____
MM / DD / YYYY OR

[Date case filed in chapter _____ _____
MM / DD / YYYY

Date case converted to chapter 11 _____
MM / DD / YYYY]

Official Form 309F (For Corporations or Partnerships)

Notice of Chapter 11 Bankruptcy Case
12/17

For the debtor listed above, a case has been filed under chapter 11 of the Bankruptcy Code. An order for relief has been entered.

This notice has important information about the case for creditors, debtors, and trustees, including information about the meeting of creditors and deadlines. Read both pages carefully.

The filing of the case imposed an automatic stay against most collection activities. This means that creditors generally may not take action to collect debts from the debtor or the debtor's property. For example, while the stay is in effect, creditors cannot sue, assert a deficiency, repossess property, or otherwise try to collect from the debtor. Creditors cannot demand repayment from the debtor by mail, phone, or otherwise. Creditors who violate the stay can be required to pay actual and punitive damages and attorney's fees.

Confirmation of a chapter 11 plan may result in a discharge of debt. A creditor who wants to have a particular debt excepted from discharge may be required to file a complaint in the bankruptcy clerk's office within the deadline specified in this notice. (See line 11 below for more information.)

To protect your rights, consult an attorney. All documents filed in the case may be inspected at the bankruptcy clerk's office at the address listed below or through PACER (Public Access to Court Electronic Records at www.pacer.gov).

The staff of the bankruptcy clerk's office cannot give legal advice.

Do not file this notice with any proof of claim or other filing in the case.

---

1. **Debtor's full name**

2. **All other names used in the last 8 years**

3. **Address**

4. **Debtor's attorney**
   Name and address

   Contact phone _____
   Email _____

5. **Bankruptcy clerk's office**
   Documents in this case may be filed at this address.
   You may inspect all records filed in this case at this office or online at www.pacer.gov.

   Hours open _____
   Contact phone _____

6. **Meeting of creditors**
   The debtor's representative must attend the meeting to be questioned under oath.
   Creditors may attend, but are not required to do so.

   _____ at _____
   Date   Time

   The meeting may be continued or adjourned to a later date. If so, the date will be on the court docket.

   Location: _____

For more information, see page 2 ▶

Debtor _____   Case number (if known) _____
　　　　Name

7. Proof of claim deadline	**Deadline for filing proof of claim:**	[Not yet set. If a deadline is set, the court will send you another notice.] or
		[date, if set by the court)]
	A proof of claim is a signed statement describing a creditor's claim. A proof of claim form may be obtained at www.uscourts.gov or any bankruptcy clerk's office.	
	Your claim will be allowed in the amount scheduled unless:	
	▪ your claim is designated as *disputed, contingent,* or *unliquidated,*	
	▪ you file a proof of claim in a different amount; or	
	▪ you receive another notice.	
	If your claim is not scheduled or if your claim is designated as *disputed, contingent,* or *unliquidated,* you must file a proof of claim or you might not be paid on your claim and you might be unable to vote on a plan. You may file a proof of claim even if your claim is scheduled.	
	You may review the schedules at the bankruptcy clerk's office or online at www.pacer.gov.	
	Secured creditors retain rights in their collateral regardless of whether they file a proof of claim. Filing a proof of claim submits a creditor to the jurisdiction of the bankruptcy court, with consequences a lawyer can explain. For example, a secured creditor who files a proof of claim may surrender important nonmonetary rights, including the right to a jury trial.	
8. Exception to discharge deadline The bankruptcy clerk's office must receive a complaint and any required filing fee by the following deadline.	If § 523(c) applies to your claim and you seek to have it excepted from discharge, you must start a judicial proceeding by filing a complaint by the deadline stated below. **Deadline for filing the complaint:** _____	
9. Creditors with a foreign address	If you are a creditor receiving notice mailed to a foreign address, you may file a motion asking the court to extend the deadlines in this notice. Consult an attorney familiar with United States bankruptcy law if you have any questions about your rights in this case.	
10. Filing a Chapter 11 bankruptcy case	Chapter 11 allows debtors to reorganize or liquidate according to a plan. A plan is not effective unless the court confirms it. You may receive a copy of the plan and a disclosure statement telling you about the plan, and you may have the opportunity to vote on the plan. You will receive notice of the date of the confirmation hearing, and you may object to confirmation of the plan and attend the confirmation hearing. Unless a trustee is serving, the debtor will remain in possession of the property and may continue to operate its business.	
11. Discharge of debts	Confirmation of a chapter 11 plan may result in a discharge of debts, which may include all or part of your debt. See 11 U.S.C. § 1141(d). A discharge means that creditors may never try to collect the debt from the debtor except as provided in the plan. If you want to have a particular debt owed to you excepted from the discharge and § 523(c) applies to your claim, you must start a judicial proceeding by filing a complaint and paying the filing fee in the bankruptcy clerk's office by the deadline.	

Official Form 309F (For Corporations or Partnerships)　　Notice of Chapter 11 Bankruptcy Case　　　　　　　　page 2

(Added Dec. 1, 2015; and amended Dec. 1, 2017.)

ADVISORY COMMITTEE NOTES

Official Forms 309A–I, collectively the Bankruptcy Case Commencement Notices, have been revised as part of the Forms Modernization Project to make them easier to read and understand. The notices, derived from Official Forms 9A–I are renumbered and stylistic changes have been made.

References to the limitations on the automatic stay imposed by 11 U.S.C. § 362(c)(3) and (4) in some repeat bankruptcy filings by individuals have been deleted from the three versions of the notice for cases filed by corporations and partnerships. Email addresses for the debtor's attorney and the trustee have been added to the form.

The parties are informed that they may review papers filed in the case through the judiciary's PACER system (Public Access to Court Electronic Records) as well as at the bankruptcy clerk's office.

The lettering scheme for the versions of Official Form 309 track the versions of Official Form 9 used in different types of bankruptcy cases with following exceptions. Official Forms 9E(Alt.) and 9F(Alt.) have been eliminated by including alternative language in Official Forms 309E and 309F to be used if the court sets a deadline for filing claims at the start of the chapter 11 case. In addition, the B and C versions have been reversed in order. That is, Official Form 9C has been designated 309B and Official Form 9B as 309C. This groups together the notices for chapter 7 individual debtors and for non-individual debtors. Finally, as a result of the reformatting, Official Form 309C has been reduced to a single page.

The four versions of the form for chapter 7 cases have been renamed to state whether the notice specifies a deadline for filing proofs of claim, rather than whether the case is an "asset" or "no-asset" case.

2017 Amendment

Official Form 309F (For Corporations or Partnerships), *Notice of Chapter 11 Bankruptcy Case,* is amended at Lines 8

For Complete Annotation Materials, see United States Code Annotated

and 11. Both lines previously stated that a creditor seeking to have a debt excepted from discharge under § 1141(d)(6)(A) must file a complaint by the stated deadline. That statement has been revised in light of ambiguities in § 1141(d)(6)(A) regarding its relationship with § 523. Specifically, the provision is unclear about whether not only a debt "owed to a domestic governmental unit" but also a debt "owed to a person as the result of an action filed under subchapter III of chapter 37 of title 31 or any similar State statute" must be of the type described by § 523(a)(2)(A) and (B). The provision is also unclear about whether the procedural requirements of § 523(c)(1) apply, given that § 1141(d)(6)(A) specifically refers to § 523(a) but not to § 523(c). Rather than take a position on the proper interpretation of § 1141(d)(6)(A), the form leaves to creditors the determination of whether § 523(c) applies to their claims, in which case they must commence a dischargeability proceeding by the Rule 4007(c) deadline that is stated on the form.

Official Forms 309G, (For Individual Debtors), *Notice of Chapter 12 Bankruptcy Case*, 309H, (For Corporations and Partnerships), *Notice of Chapter 12 Bankruptcy Case*, and 309I, *Notice of Chapter 13 Bankruptcy Case*, are each amended at Line 9 to remove references to "plan summaries" in conformance with amendments to Rule 3015(d) made in 2017.

Form B309G. (For Individuals or Joint Debtors)
Notice of Chapter 12 Bankruptcy Case

Information to identify the case:

Debtor 1			Last 4 digits of Social Security number or ITIN ___ ___ ___ ___
First Name	Middle Name	Last Name	EIN ___ ___ – ___ ___ ___ ___ ___ ___ ___
Debtor 2			Last 4 digits of Social Security number or ITIN ___ ___ ___ ___
(Spouse, if filing) First Name	Middle Name	Last Name	EIN ___ ___ – ___ ___ ___ ___ ___ ___ ___

United States Bankruptcy Court for the: _____ District of _____ (State)

[Date case filed for chapter 12 ____ MM / DD / YYYY OR

Case number: _____

[Date case filed in chapter ____ MM / DD / YYYY

Date case converted to chapter 12 ____ MM / DD / YYYY

Official Form 309G (For Individuals or Joint Debtors)

Notice of Chapter 12 Bankruptcy Case   12/17

For the debtors listed above, a case has been filed under chapter 12 of the Bankruptcy Code. An order for relief has been entered.

This notice has important information about the case for creditors, debtors, and trustees, including information about the meeting of creditors and deadlines. Read both pages carefully.

The filing of the case imposed an automatic stay against most collection activities. This means that creditors generally may not take action to collect debts from the debtors, from the debtors' property, or from certain codebtors. For example, while the stay is in effect, creditors cannot sue, garnish wages, assert a deficiency, repossess property, or otherwise try to collect from the debtors. Creditors cannot demand repayment from debtors by mail, phone, or otherwise. Creditors who violate the stay can be required to pay actual and punitive damages and attorney's fees.

Confirmation of a chapter 12 plan may result in a discharge of debt. Creditors who want to have a particular debt excepted from discharge may be required to file a complaint in the bankruptcy clerk's office within the deadline specified in this notice. (See line 13 below for more information.)

To protect your rights, consult an attorney. All documents filed in the case may be inspected at the bankruptcy clerk's office at the address listed below or through PACER (Public Access to Court Electronic Records at www.pacer.gov).

The staff of the bankruptcy clerk's office cannot give legal advice.

To help creditors correctly identify debtors, debtors submit full Social Security or Individual Taxpayer Identification Numbers, which may appear on a version of this notice. However, the full numbers must not appear on any document filed with the court.

Do not file this notice with any proof of claim or other filing in the case. Do not include more than the last four digits of a Social Security or Individual Taxpayer Identification Number in any document, including attachments, that you file with the court.

	About Debtor 1:	About Debtor 2:
1. **Debtor's full name**		
2. **All other names used in the last 8 years**		
3. **Address**		If Debtor 2 lives at a different address:
4. **Debtor's attorney** Name and address		Contact phone _____ Email _____
5. **Bankruptcy trustee** Name and address		Contact phone _____ Email _____
6. **Bankruptcy clerk's office** Documents in this case may be filed at this address. You may inspect all records filed in this case at this office or online at www.pacer.gov.		Hours open _____ Contact phone _____

For more information, see page 2 ▶

Official Form 309G (For Individuals or Joint Debtors)   Notice of Chapter 12 Bankruptcy Case   page 1

Form B309G

Debtor _____ Case number (if known) _____
Name

7. Meeting of creditors Debtors must attend the meeting to be questioned under oath. In a joint case, both spouses must attend. Creditors may attend, but are not required to do so.	_____ at _____ Date Time Location: The meeting may be continued or adjourned to a later date. If so, the date will be on the court docket.

8. Deadlines
The bankruptcy clerk's office must receive these documents and any required filing fee by the following deadlines.

Deadline to file a complaint to challenge dischargeability of certain debts: Filing deadline: _____

You must start a judicial proceeding by filing a complaint if you want to have a debt excepted from discharge under 11 U.S.C. § 523(a)(2), (4), or (6).

Deadline for all creditors to file a proof of claim (except governmental units):   Filing deadline: _____

Deadline for governmental units to file a proof of claim: Filing deadline: _____

Deadlines for filing proof of claim:

A proof of claim is a signed statement describing a creditor's claim. A proof of claim form may be obtained at www.uscourts.gov or any bankruptcy clerk's office.

If you do not file a proof of claim by the deadline, you might not be paid on your claim. To be paid, you must file a proof of claim even if your claim is listed in the schedules that the debtor filed.

Secured creditors retain rights in their collateral regardless of whether they file a proof of claim. Filing a proof of claim submits the creditor to the jurisdiction of the bankruptcy court, with consequences a lawyer can explain. For example, a secured creditor who files a proof of claim may surrender important nonmonetary rights, including the right to a jury trial.

Deadline to object to exemptions: Filing deadline: 30 days after the *conclusion* of the meeting of creditors

The law permits debtors to keep certain property as exempt.

If you believe that the law does not authorize an exemption claimed, you may file an objection.

9. Filing of plan

[The debtor has filed a plan, which is attached. The hearing on confirmation will be held on: _____ at _____
Location: _____
_____   _____
Date   Time]

Or [The debtor has filed a plan. The plan and notice of confirmation hearing will be sent separately.]

Or [The debtor has not filed a plan as of this date. A copy of the plan and a notice of the hearing on confirmation will be sent separately.]

10. Creditors with a foreign address

If you are a creditor receiving a notice mailed to a foreign address, you may file a motion asking the court to extend the deadlines in this notice. Consult an attorney familiar with United States bankruptcy law if you have any questions about your rights in this case.

11. Filing a Chapter 12 bankruptcy case

Chapter 12 allows family farmers and family fishermen to reorganize according to a plan. A plan is not effective unless the court confirms it. You may receive a copy of the plan. You may object to confirmation of the plan and attend the confirmation hearing. The debtor will remain in possession of the property and may continue to operate the business unless the court orders otherwise.

12. Discharge of debts

Confirmation of a chapter 12 plan may result in a discharge of debts, which may include all or part of your debt. Unless the court orders otherwise, the discharge will not be effective until all payments under the plan are made. A discharge means that you may never try to collect the debt from the debtor except as provided in the plan. If you want to have a particular debt excepted under 11 U.S.C. § 523(a)(2), (4), or (6), you must start a judicial proceeding by filing a complaint and paying the filing fee in the clerk's office by the deadline.

13. Exempt property

The law allows debtors to keep certain property as exempt. Fully exempt property will not be sold and distributed to creditors, even if the case is converted to chapter 7. Debtors must file a list of property claimed as exempt. You may inspect that list at the bankruptcy clerk's office. If you believe that the law does not authorize an exemption that the debtors claim, you may file an objection. The bankruptcy clerk's office must receive the objection by the deadline to object to exemptions in line 8.

Official Form 309G (For Individuals or Joint Debtors)   Notice of Chapter 12 Bankruptcy Case   page 2

(Added Dec. 1, 2015; and amended Dec. 1, 2017.)

ADVISORY COMMITTEE NOTES

Official Forms 309A–I, collectively the Bankruptcy Case Commencement Notices, have been revised as part of the Forms Modernization Project to make them easier to read and understand. The notices, derived from Official Forms 9A–I are renumbered and stylistic changes have been made.

References to the limitations on the automatic stay imposed by 11 U.S.C. § 362(c)(3) and (4) in some repeat bankruptcy filings by individuals have been deleted from the three versions of the notice for cases filed by corporations and partnerships. Email addresses for the debtor's attorney and the trustee have been added to the form.

The parties are informed that they may review papers filed in the case through the judiciary's PACER system (Public Access to Court Electronic Records) as well as at the bankruptcy clerk's office.

The lettering scheme for the versions of Official Form 309 track the versions of Official Form 9 used in different types of bankruptcy cases with following exceptions. Official Forms 9E(Alt.) and 9F(Alt.) have been eliminated by including alternative language in Official Forms 309E and 309F to be used if the court sets a deadline for filing claims at the start of the chapter 11 case. In addition, the B and C versions have been reversed in order. That is, Official Form 9C has been designated 309B and Official Form 9B as 309C. This groups together the notices for chapter 7 individual debtors and for non-individual debtors. Finally, as a result of the reformatting, Official Form 309C has been reduced to a single page.

The four versions of the form for chapter 7 cases have been renamed to state whether the notice specifies a deadline for filing proofs of claim, rather than whether the case is an "asset" or "no-asset" case.

2017 Amendment

Official Form 309F (For Corporations or Partnerships), *Notice of Chapter 11 Bankruptcy Case*, is amended at Lines 8

and 11. Both lines previously stated that a creditor seeking to have a debt excepted from discharge under § 1141(d)(6)(A) must file a complaint by the stated deadline. That statement has been revised in light of ambiguities in § 1141(d)(6)(A) regarding its relationship with § 523. Specifically, the provision is unclear about whether not only a debt "owed to a domestic governmental unit" but also a debt "owed to a person as the result of an action filed under subchapter III of chapter 37 of title 31 or any similar State statute" must be of the type described by § 523(a)(2)(A) and (B). The provision is also unclear about whether the procedural requirements of § 523(c)(1) apply, given that § 1141(d)(6)(A) specifically refers to § 523(a) but not to § 523(c). Rather than take a position on the proper interpretation of § 1141(d)(6)(A), the form leaves to creditors the determination of whether § 523(c) applies to their claims, in which case they must commence a dischargeability proceeding by the Rule 4007(c) deadline that is stated on the form.

Official Forms 309G, (For Individual Debtors), *Notice of Chapter 12 Bankruptcy Case*, 309H, (For Corporations and Partnerships), *Notice of Chapter 12 Bankruptcy Case*, and 309I, *Notice of Chapter 13 Bankruptcy Case*, are each amended at Line 9 to remove references to "plan summaries" in conformance with amendments to Rule 3015(d) made in 2017.

Form B309H. (For Corporations or Partnerships)
Notice of Chapter 12 Bankruptcy Case

Information to identify the case:

Debtor _____
Name

EIN __ __ - __ __ __ __ __ __ __

United States Bankruptcy Court for the: _____ District of _____
(State)

Case number: _____

[Date case filed for chapter 12 _____ MM / DD / YYYY OR

[Date case filed in chapter _____ MM / DD / YYYY

Date case converted to chapter 12 _____ MM / DD / YYYY]

Official Form 309H (For Corporations or Partnerships)

Notice of Chapter 12 Bankruptcy Case   12/17

For the debtor listed above, a case has been filed under chapter 12 of the Bankruptcy Code. An order for relief has been entered.

This notice has important information about the case for creditors, debtors, and trustees, including information about the meeting of creditors and deadlines. Read both pages carefully.

The filing of the case imposed an automatic stay against most collection activities. This means that creditors generally may not take action to collect debts from the debtor, the debtor's property, or certain codebtors. For example, while the stay is in effect, creditors cannot sue, assert a deficiency, repossess property, or otherwise try to collect from the debtor. Creditors cannot demand repayment from the debtor by mail, phone, or otherwise. Creditors who violate the stay can be required to pay actual and punitive damages and attorney's fees.

Confirmation of a chapter 12 plan may result in the discharge of debt. Creditors who want to have a particular debt excepted from discharge may be required to file a complaint in the bankruptcy clerk's office within the deadline specified in this notice. (See line 13 below for more information.)

To protect your rights, consult an attorney. All documents filed in the case may be inspected at the bankruptcy clerk's office at the address listed below or through PACER (Public Access to Court Electronic Records at www.pacer.gov)

The staff of the bankruptcy clerk's office cannot give legal advice.

Do not file this notice with any proof of claim or other filing in the case.

1. Debtor's full name	
2. All other names used in the last 8 years	
3. Address	
4. Debtor's attorney Name and address	Contact phone _____ Email _____
5. Bankruptcy clerk's office Documents in this case may be filed at this address. You may inspect all records filed in this case at this office or online at www.pacer.gov.	Hours open _____ Contact phone _____
6. Bankruptcy trustee Name and address	Contact phone _____ Email _____

For more information, see page 2 ▶

Official Form 309H (For Corporations or Partnerships)   **Notice of Chapter 12 Bankruptcy Case**   page 1

Debtor _____   Case number (if known) _____
                Name

7. Meeting of creditors The debtor's representative must attend the meeting to be questioned under oath. Creditors may attend, but are not required to do so.	_____ at _____ Date Time The meeting may be continued or adjourned to a later date. If so, the date will be on the court docket.	Location:
8. Exception to discharge deadline The bankruptcy clerk's office must receive a complaint and any required filing fee by the following deadline.	You must start a judicial proceeding by filing a complaint if you want to have a debt excepted from discharge under 11 U.S.C. § 523(a)(2), (4), or (6)	Deadline for filing the complaint: _____
9. Filing of plan	[The debtor has filed a plan, which is attached. The hearing on confirmation will be held on: _____ at _____ Location:_____ Date Time] Or [The debtor has filed a plan. The plan and notice of confirmation hearing will be sent separately.] Or [The debtor has not filed a plan as of this date. A copy of the plan and a notice of the hearing on confirmation will be sent separately.]	
10. Deadlines	**Deadline for all creditors to file a proof of claim (except governmental units):** **Deadline for governmental units to file a proof of claim:** A proof of claim is a signed statement describing a creditor's claim. A proof of claim form may be obtained at www.uscourts.gov or any bankruptcy clerk's office. If you do not file a proof of claim by the deadline, you might not be paid on your claim. To be paid, you must file a proof of claim even if your claim is listed in the schedules that the debtor filed. Secured creditors retain rights in their collateral regardless of whether they file a proof of claim. Filing a proof of claim submits the creditor to the jurisdiction of the bankruptcy court, with consequences a lawyer can explain. For example, a secured creditor who files a proof of claim may surrender important nonmonetary rights, including the right to a jury trial.	Filing deadline: _____ Filing deadline: _____
11. Creditors with a foreign address	If you are a creditor receiving a notice mailed to a foreign address, you may file a motion asking the court to extend the deadlines in this notice. Consult an attorney familiar with United States bankruptcy law if you have any questions about your rights in this case.	
12. Filing a chapter 12 bankruptcy case	Chapter 12 allows family farmers and family fishermen to reorganize according to a plan. A plan is not effective unless the court confirms it. You may receive a copy of the plan. You may object to confirmation of the plan and attend the confirmation hearing. The debtor will remain in possession of the property and may continue to operate the business.	
13. Discharge of debts	Confirmation of a chapter 12 plan may result in a discharge of debts, which may include all or part of your debt. Unless the court orders otherwise, the discharge will not be effective until all payments under the plan are made. A discharge means that you may never try to collect the debt from the debtor except as provided in the plan. If you want to have a particular debt excepted from discharge under 11 U.S.C. § 523(a)(2), (4), or (6), you must start a judicial proceeding by filing a complaint and paying the filing fee in the bankruptcy clerk's office by the deadline.	

Official Form 309H (For Corporations or Partnerships)   Notice of Chapter 12 Bankruptcy Case   page 2

(Added Dec. 1, 2015; and amended Dec. 1, 2017.)

ADVISORY COMMITTEE NOTES

Official Forms 309A–I, collectively the Bankruptcy Case Commencement Notices, have been revised as part of the Forms Modernization Project to make them easier to read and understand. The notices, derived from Official Forms 9A–I are renumbered and stylistic changes have been made.

References to the limitations on the automatic stay imposed by 11 U.S.C. § 362(c)(3) and (4) in some repeat bankruptcy filings by individuals have been deleted from the three versions of the notice for cases filed by corporations and partnerships. Email addresses for the debtor's attorney and the trustee have been added to the form.

The parties are informed that they may review papers filed in the case through the judiciary's PACER system (Public Access to Court Electronic Records) as well as at the bankruptcy clerk's office.

The lettering scheme for the versions of Official Form 309 track the versions of Official Form 9 used in different types of bankruptcy cases with following exceptions. Official Forms 9E(Alt.) and 9F(Alt.) have been eliminated by including alternative language in Official Forms 309E and 309F to be used if the court sets a deadline for filing claims at the start of the chapter 11 case. In addition, the B and C versions have been reversed in order. That is, Official Form 9C has been designated 309B and Official Form 9B as 309C. This groups together the notices for chapter 7 individual debtors and for non-individual debtors. Finally, as a result of the reformatting, Official Form 309C has been reduced to a single page.

The four versions of the form for chapter 7 cases have been renamed to state whether the notice specifies a deadline for filing proofs of claim, rather than whether the case is an "asset" or "no-asset" case.

2017 Amendment

Official Form 309F (For Corporations or Partnerships), *Notice of Chapter 11 Bankruptcy Case*, is amended at Lines 8

and 11. Both lines previously stated that a creditor seeking to have a debt excepted from discharge under § 1141(d)(6)(A) must file a complaint by the stated deadline. That statement has been revised in light of ambiguities in § 1141(d)(6)(A) regarding its relationship with § 523. Specifically, the provision is unclear about whether not only a debt "owed to a domestic governmental unit" but also a debt "owed to a person as the result of an action filed under subchapter III of chapter 37 of title 31 or any similar State statute" must be of the type described by § 523(a)(2)(A) and (B). The provision is also unclear about whether the procedural requirements of § 523(c)(1) apply, given that § 1141(d)(6)(A) specifically refers to § 523(a) but not to § 523(c). Rather than take a position on the proper interpretation of § 1141(d)(6)(A), the form leaves to creditors the determination of whether § 523(c) applies to their claims, in which case they must commence a dischargeability proceeding by the Rule 4007(c) deadline that is stated on the form.

Official Forms 309G, (For Individual Debtors), *Notice of Chapter 12 Bankruptcy Case*, 309H, (For Corporations and Partnerships), *Notice of Chapter 12 Bankruptcy Case*, and 309I, *Notice of Chapter 13 Bankruptcy Case*, are each amended at Line 9 to remove references to "plan summaries" in conformance with amendments to Rule 3015(d) made in 2017.

Form B309I. Notice of Chapter 13 Bankruptcy Case

Information to identify the case:

Debtor 1	First Name	Middle Name	Last Name	Last 4 digits of Social Security number or ITIN ___ ___ ___ ___
				EIN ___ ___ – ___ ___ ___ ___ ___ ___ ___
Debtor 2 (Spouse, if filing)	First Name	Middle Name	Last Name	Last 4 digits of Social Security number or ITIN ___ ___ ___ ___
				EIN ___ ___ – ___ ___ ___ ___ ___ ___ ___
United States Bankruptcy Court for the: _____		District of _____ (State)		[Date case filed for chapter 13 _____ MM / DD / YYYY OR
Case number: _____				[Date case filed in chapter _____ MM / DD / YYYY
				Date case converted to chapter 13 _____ MM / DD / YYYY]

Official Form 309I

Notice of Chapter 13 Bankruptcy Case   12/17

For the debtors listed above, a case has been filed under chapter 13 of the Bankruptcy Code. An order for relief has been entered.

This notice has important information about the case for creditors, debtors, and trustees, including information about the meeting of creditors and deadlines. Read both pages carefully.

The filing of the case imposed an automatic stay against most collection activities. This means that creditors generally may not take action to collect debts from the debtors, the debtors' property, and certain codebtors. For example, while the stay is in effect, creditors cannot sue, garnish wages, assert a deficiency, repossess property, or otherwise try to collect from the debtors. Creditors cannot demand repayment from debtors by mail, phone, or otherwise. Creditors who violate the stay can be required to pay actual and punitive damages and attorney's fees. Under certain circumstances, the stay may be limited to 30 days or not exist at all, although debtors can ask the court to extend or impose a stay.

Confirmation of a chapter 13 plan may result in a discharge. Creditors who assert that the debtors are not entitled to a discharge under 11 U.S.C. § 1328(f) must file a motion objecting to discharge in the bankruptcy clerk's office within the deadline specified in this notice. Creditors who want to have their debt excepted from discharge may be required to file a complaint in the bankruptcy clerk's office by the same deadline. (See line 13 below for more information.)

To protect your rights, consult an attorney. All documents filed in the case may be inspected at the bankruptcy clerk's office at the address listed below or through PACER (Public Access to Court Electronic Records at www.pacer.gov).

The staff of the bankruptcy clerk's office cannot give legal advice.

To help creditors correctly identify debtors, debtors submit full Social Security or Individual Taxpayer Identification Numbers, which may appear on a version of this notice. However, the full numbers must not appear on any document filed with the court.

Do not file this notice with any proof of claim or other filing in the case. Do not include more than the last four digits of a Social Security or Individual Taxpayer Identification Number in any document, including attachments, that you file with the court.

	About Debtor 1:	About Debtor 2:
1.	Debtor's full name	
2.	All other names used in the last 8 years	
3.	Address	If Debtor 2 lives at a different address:
4.	Debtor's attorney Name and address	Contact phone _____ Email _____
5.	Bankruptcy trustee Name and address	Contact phone _____ Email _____
6.	Bankruptcy clerk's office Documents in this case may be filed at this address. You may inspect all records filed in this case at this office or online at www.pacer.gov.	Hours open _____ Contact phone _____

For more information, see page 2 ▶

Official Form 309I   Notice of Chapter 13 Bankruptcy Case   page 1

Debtor _____ Case number (if known) _____
Name

7. Meeting of creditors Debtors must attend the meeting to be questioned under oath. In a joint case, both spouses must attend. Creditors may attend, but are not required to do so.	_____ at _____ Date Time The meeting may be continued or adjourned to a later date. If so, the date will be on the court docket.	Location:

8. Deadlines
The bankruptcy clerk's office must receive these documents and any required filing fee by the following deadlines.
	Deadline to file a complaint to challenge dischargeability of certain debts:
	You must file:
	    a motion if you assert that the debtors are not entitled to receive a discharge under U.S.C. § 1328(f), or
	    a complaint if you want to have a particular debt excepted from discharge under 11 U.S.C. § 523(a)(2) or (4).
		Filing deadline: _____

	Deadline for all creditors to file a proof of claim (except governmental units):	Filing deadline: _____
	Deadline for governmental units to file a proof of claim:	Filing deadline: _____
	Deadlines for filing proof of claim: A proof of claim is a signed statement describing a creditor's claim. A proof of claim form may be obtained at www.uscourts.gov or any bankruptcy clerk's office. If you do not file a proof of claim by the deadline, you might not be paid on your claim. To be paid, you must file a proof of claim even if your claim is listed in the schedules that the debtor filed. Secured creditors retain rights in their collateral regardless of whether they file a proof of claim. Filing a proof of claim submits the creditor to the jurisdiction of the bankruptcy court, with consequences a lawyer can explain. For example, a secured creditor who files a proof of claim may surrender important nonmonetary rights, including the right to a jury trial.	
	Deadline to object to exemptions: The law permits debtors to keep certain property as exempt. If you believe that the law does not authorize an exemption claimed, you may file an objection.	Filing deadline: 30 days after the *conclusion* of the meeting of creditors
9. Filing of plan	[The debtor has filed a plan, which is attached. The hearing on confirmation will be held on: _____ at _____ Location: _____ Date Time] Or [The debtor has filed a plan. The plan and notice of confirmation hearing will be sent separately.] Or [The debtor has not filed a plan as of this date. A copy of the plan and a notice of the hearing on confirmation will be sent separately.]	
10. Creditors with a foreign address	If you are a creditor receiving a notice mailed to a foreign address, you may file a motion asking the court to extend the deadline in this notice. Consult an attorney familiar with United States bankruptcy law if you have any questions about your rights in this case.	
11. Filing a chapter 13 bankruptcy case	Chapter 13 allows an individual with regular income and debts below a specified amount to adjust debts according to a plan. A plan is not effective unless the court confirms it. You may object to confirmation of the plan and appear at the confirmation hearing. A copy of the plan [is included with this notice] or [will be sent to you later], and [the confirmation hearing will be held on the date shown in line 9 of this notice] or [the court will send you a notice of the confirmation hearing]. The debtor will remain in possession of the property and may continue to operate the business, if any, unless the court orders otherwise.	
12. Exempt property	The law allows debtors to keep certain property as exempt. Fully exempt property will not be sold and distributed to creditors, even if the case is converted to chapter 7. Debtors must file a list of property claimed as exempt. You may inspect that list at the bankruptcy clerk's office or online at www.pacer.gov. If you believe that the law does not authorize an exemption that debtors claimed, you may file an objection by the deadline.	
13. Discharge of debts	Confirmation of a chapter 13 plan may result in a discharge of debts, which may include all or part of a debt. However, unless the court orders otherwise, the debts will not be discharged until all payments under the plan are made. A discharge means that creditors may never try to collect the debt from the debtors personally except as provided in the plan. If you want to have a particular debt excepted from discharge under 11 U.S.C. § 523(a)(2) or (4), you must file a complaint and pay the filing fee in the bankruptcy clerk's office by the deadline. If you believe that the debtors are not entitled to a discharge of any of their debts under 11 U.S.C. § 1328(f), you must file a motion. The bankruptcy clerk's office must receive the objection by the deadline to object to exemptions in line 8.	

Official Form 309I   Notice of Chapter 13 Bankruptcy Case   page 2

(Added Dec. 1, 2015; and amended Dec. 1, 2017.)

ADVISORY COMMITTEE NOTES

Official Forms 309A–I, collectively the Bankruptcy Case Commencement Notices, have been revised as part of the Forms Modernization Project to make them easier to read and understand. The notices, derived from Official Forms 9A–I are renumbered and stylistic changes have been made.

References to the limitations on the automatic stay imposed by 11 U.S.C. § 362(c)(3) and (4) in some repeat bankruptcy filings by individuals have been deleted from the three versions of the notice for cases filed by corporations and partnerships. Email addresses for the debtor's attorney and the trustee have been added to the form.

The parties are informed that they may review papers filed in the case through the judiciary's PACER system (Public Access to Court Electronic Records) as well as at the bankruptcy clerk's office.

The lettering scheme for the versions of Official Form 309 track the versions of Official Form 9 used in different types of bankruptcy cases with following exceptions. Official Forms 9E(Alt.) and 9F(Alt.) have been eliminated by including alternative language in Official Forms 309E and 309F to be used if the court sets a deadline for filing claims at the start of the chapter 11 case. In addition, the B and C versions have been reversed in order. That is, Official Form 9C has been designated 309B and Official Form 9B as 309C. This groups together the notices for chapter 7 individual debtors and for non-individual debtors. Finally, as a result of the reformatting, Official Form 309C has been reduced to a single page.

The four versions of the form for chapter 7 cases have been renamed to state whether the notice specifies a deadline for filing proofs of claim, rather than whether the case is an "asset" or "no-asset" case.

2017 Amendment

Official Form 309F (For Corporations or Partnerships), *Notice of Chapter 11 Bankruptcy Case*, is amended at Lines 8

and 11. Both lines previously stated that a creditor seeking to have a debt excepted from discharge under § 1141(d)(6)(A) must file a complaint by the stated deadline. That statement has been revised in light of ambiguities in § 1141(d)(6)(A) regarding its relationship with § 523. Specifically, the provision is unclear about whether not only a debt "owed to a domestic governmental unit" but also a debt "owed to a person as the result of an action filed under subchapter III of chapter 37 of title 31 or any similar State statute" must be of the type described by § 523(a)(2)(A) and (B). The provision is also unclear about whether the procedural requirements of § 523(c)(1) apply, given that § 1141(d)(6)(A) specifically refers to § 523(a) but not to § 523(c). Rather than take a position on the proper interpretation of § 1141(d)(6)(A), the form leaves to creditors the determination of whether § 523(c) applies to their claims, in which case they must commence a dischargeability proceeding by the Rule 4007(c) deadline that is stated on the form.

Official Forms 309G, (For Individual Debtors), *Notice of Chapter 12 Bankruptcy Case*, 309H, (For Corporations and Partnerships), *Notice of Chapter 12 Bankruptcy Case*, and 309I, *Notice of Chapter 13 Bankruptcy Case*, are each amended at Line 9 to remove references to "plan summaries" in conformance with amendments to Rule 3015(d) made in 2017.

**Form B312.　Order and Notice for Hearing
on Disclosure Statement**

Official Form 312 (12/15)

[Caption as in 416A]

Order and Notice for Hearing on Disclosure Statement

To the debtor, its creditors, and other parties in interest:

A disclosure statement and a plan under chapter 11 [or chapter 9] of the Bankruptcy Code having been filed by
_____ on _____,

IT IS ORDERED and notice is hereby given, that:

1.　The hearing to consider the approval of the disclosure statement shall be held at:

_____

on _____ at _____ o'clock ___.m.

2.　_____ is fixed as the last day for filing and serving in
accordance with Fed. R. Bankr. P. 3017(a) written objections to the disclosure statement.

3.　Within _____ days after entry of this order, the disclosure statement and plan shall be
distributed in accordance with Fed. R. Bankr. P. 3017(a).

4.　Requests for copies of the disclosure statement and plan shall be mailed to the debtor in
possession [or trustee or debtor or _____] at the following mailing
address:

[_____].

_____　　　　　　　　**By the court:** _____
MM / DD / YYYY　　　　　　　　　　　　　　　　　United States Bankruptcy Judge

225

(Added Dec. 1, 2015.)

ADVISORY COMMITTEE NOTES

Official Form 312, *Order and Notice for Hearing on Disclosure Statement* replaces Official Form 12, *Order and Notice*

for Hearing on Disclosure Statement. It is renumbered as part of the Forms Modernization Project, and includes stylistic changes throughout the form.

Form B313. Order Approving Disclosure State-ment and Fixing Time for Filing Acceptances or Rejections of Plan, Combined With Notice Thereof

Official Form 313 (12/15)

[Caption as in 416A]

Order Approving Disclosure Statement and Fixing Time for Filing Acceptances or Rejections of Plan, Combined with Notice Thereof

A disclosure statement under chapter 11 of the Bankruptcy Code having been filed by
_____ on _____ [if
appropriate, and by _____, on _____], referring to a plan under
chapter 11 of the Code filed by _____ on _____ [if appropriate, and by
_____ on _____ respectively] [if appropriate, as modified by a
modification filed on _____]; and

It having been determined after hearing on notice that the disclosure statement [or statements] contain[s] adequate information:

IT IS ORDERED, and notice is hereby given, that:

A. The disclosure statement filed by _____ dated _____ [if appropriate, and by _____ dated _____] is [are] approved.

B. _____ is fixed as the last day for filing written acceptances or rejections of the plan [or plans] referred to above.

C. Within _____ days after the entry of this order, the plan [or plans] or a summary or summaries thereof approved by the court, [and [if appropriate] a summary approved by the court of its opinion, if any, dated _____, approving the disclosure statement [or statements]], the disclosure statement [or statements], and a ballot conforming to *Ballot for Accepting or Rejecting Plan of Reorganization* (Official Form 314) shall be mailed to creditors, equity security holders, and other parties in interest, and shall be transmitted to the United States trustee, as provided in Fed. R. Bankr. P. 3017(d).

D. If acceptances are filed for more than one plan, preferences among the plans so accepted may be indicated.

E. [If appropriate] _____ is fixed for the hearing on confirmation of the plan [or plans].

F. [If appropriate] _____ is fixed as the last day for filing and serving pursuant to Fed. R. Bankr. P. 3020(b)(*) written objections to confirmation of the plan.

_____
MM / DD / YYYY

By the court: _____
United States Bankruptcy Judge

[If the court directs that a copy of the opinion should be transmitted in lieu of or in addition to the summary thereof, the appropriate change should be made in paragraph C of this order.]

227

(Added Dec. 1, 2015.)

ADVISORY COMMITTEE NOTES

Official Form 313, *Order Approving Disclosure Statement and Fixing Time for Filing Acceptances or Rejections of Plan, Combined with Notice Thereof* replaces Official Form 13, *Order Approving Disclosure Statement and Fixing Time for Filing Acceptances or Rejections of Plan, Combined with Notice Thereof*. It is renumbered as part of the Forms Modernization Project, and includes stylistic changes throughout the form.

Form B314. Ballot for Accepting or Rejecting Plan

Official Form 314 (12/15)

[Caption as in 416A]

Class [ ] Ballot for Accepting or Rejecting Plan of Reorganization

[Proponent] filed a plan of reorganization dated [Date] (the *Plan*) for the Debtor in this case. The Court has [conditionally] approved a disclosure statement with respect to the Plan (the *Disclosure Statement*). The Disclosure Statement provides information to assist you in deciding how to vote your ballot. If you do not have a Disclosure Statement, you may obtain a copy from [name, address, telephone number and telecopy number of proponent/proponent's attorney.]

Court approval of the disclosure statement does not indicate approval of the Plan by the Court.

You should review the Disclosure Statement and the Plan before you vote. You may wish to seek legal advice concerning the Plan and your classification and treatment under the Plan. Your [claim] [equity interest] has been placed in class [ ] under the Plan. If you hold claims or equity interests in more than one class, you will receive a ballot for each class in which you are entitled to vote.

If your ballot is not received by [name and address of proponent's attorney or other appropriate address] on or before [date], and such deadline is not extended, your vote will not count as either an acceptance or rejection of the Plan.

If the Plan is confirmed by the Bankruptcy Court, it will be binding on you whether or not you vote.

Acceptance or Rejection of the Plan

[At this point the ballot should provide for voting by the particular class of creditors or equity holders receiving the ballot using one of the following alternatives:]

[If the voter is the holder of a secured, priority, or unsecured nonpriority claim:]

The undersigned, the holder of a Class [ ] claim against the Debtor in the unpaid amount of Dollars ($)

[or, if the voter is the holder of a bond, debenture, or other debt security:]

The undersigned, the holder of a Class [ ] claim against the Debtor, consisting of Dollars (S   ) principal amount of [describe bond, debenture, or other debt security] of the Debtor (For purposes of this Ballot, it is not necessary and you should not adjust the principal amount for any accrued or unmatured interest.)

[or, if the voter is the holder of an equity interest:]

The undersigned, the holder of Class [ ] equity interest in the Debtor, consisting of _____ shares or other interests of [describe equity interest] in the Debtor

229

Official Form 314 (12/15)   page 2

[In each case, the following language should be included:]

Check one box only

❑ **Accepts the plan**

❑ **Rejects the plan**

Dated: _____

Print or type name: _____

Signature: _____ Title (if corporation or partnership) _____

Address: _____

_____

_____

Return this ballot to:

[Name and address of proponent's attorney or other appropriate address]

230

(Added Dec. 1, 2015.)

ADVISORY COMMITTEE NOTES

Official Form 314, *Ballot for Accepting or Rejecting Plan* replaces Official Form 14, *Ballot for Accepting or Rejecting Plan*. It is renumbered as part of the Forms Modernization Project, and includes stylistic changes throughout the form.

Form B315. Order Confirming Plan

Official Form 315 (12/15)

[Caption as in 416A]

Order Confirming Plan

The plan under chapter 11 of the Bankruptcy Code filed by _____, on
_____ [*if applicable*, as modified by a modification filed on _____,] or a
summary thereof, having been transmitted to creditors and equity security holders; and

It having been determined after hearing on notice that the requirements for confirmation set forth in
11 U.S.C. § 1129(a) [or, *if appropriate*, 11 U.S.C. § 1129(b)] have been satisfied;

IT IS ORDERED that:

The plan filed by _____, on _____.

[*If appropriate*, include dates and any other pertinent details of modifications to the plan] is confirmed. [*If
the plan provides for an injunction against conduct not otherwise enjoined under the Code, include the
information required by Rule 3020.*]

A copy of the confirmed plan is attached.

_____   **By the court:** _____
MM / DD / YYYY   United States Bankruptcy Judge

232

(Added Dec. 1, 2015.)

ADVISORY COMMITTEE NOTES

Official Form 315, *Order Confirming Plan* replaces Official Form 15, *Order Confirming Plan*. It is renumbered as part of the Forms Modernization Project, and includes stylistic changes throughout the form.

Form B318.   Discharge of Debtor in a Chapter 7 Case

Information to identify the case:

Debtor 1 _____

First Name   Middle Name   Last Name

Last 4 digits of Social Security number or ITIN ____

EIN __ - _____

Debtor 2 _____

(Spouse, if filing) First Name   Middle Name   Last Name

Last 4 digits of Social Security number or ITIN ____

EIN __ - _____

United States Bankruptcy Court for the: _____ District of _____

(State)

Case number: _____

Order of Discharge

IT IS ORDERED: A discharge under 11 U.S.C. § 727 is granted to:

_____   [   ]

[include all names used by each debtor, including trade names, within the 8 years prior to the filing of the petition]

_____   By the court: _____

MM / DD / YYYY   United States Bankruptcy Judge

Explanation of Bankruptcy Discharge in a Chapter 7 Case

This order does not close or dismiss the case, and it does not determine how much money, if any, the trustee will pay creditors.

Creditors cannot collect discharged debts

This order means that no one may make any attempt to collect a discharged debt from the debtors personally. For example, creditors cannot sue, garnish wages, assert a deficiency, or otherwise try to collect from the debtors personally on discharged debts. Creditors cannot contact the debtors by mail, phone, or otherwise in any attempt to collect the debt personally. Creditors who violate this order can be required to pay debtors damages and attorney's fees.

However, a creditor with a lien may enforce a claim against the debtors' property subject to that lien unless the lien was avoided or eliminated. For example, a creditor may have the right to foreclose a home mortgage or repossess an automobile.

This order does not prevent debtors from paying any debt voluntarily or from paying reaffirmed debts according to the reaffirmation agreement. 11 U.S.C. § 524(c), (f).

Most debts are discharged

Most debts are covered by the discharge, but not all. Generally, a discharge removes the debtors' personal liability for debts owed before the debtors' bankruptcy case was filed.

Also, if this case began under a different chapter of the Bankruptcy Code and was later converted to chapter 7, debts owed before the conversion are discharged.

In a case involving community property: Special rules protect certain community property owned by the debtor's spouse, even if that spouse did not file a bankruptcy case.

For more information, see page 2 ▶

Some debts are not discharged

Examples of debts that are not discharged are:

debts that are domestic support obligations;

debts for most student loans;

debts for most taxes;

debts that the bankruptcy court has decided or will decide are not discharged in this bankruptcy case;

debts for most fines, penalties, forfeitures, or criminal restitution obligations;

some debts which the debtors did not properly list;

debts for certain types of loans owed to pension, profit sharing, stock bonus, or retirement plans, and

debts for death or personal injury caused by operating a vehicle while intoxicated.

Also, debts covered by a valid reaffirmation agreement are not discharged.

In addition, this discharge does not stop creditors from collecting from anyone else who is also liable on the debt, such as an insurance company or a person who cosigned or guaranteed a loan.

> **This information is only a general summary of the bankruptcy discharge; some exceptions exist. Because the law is complicated, you should consult an attorney to determine the exact effect of the discharge in this case.**

(Added Dec. 1, 2015.)

ADVISORY COMMITTEE NOTES

Official Form 318, *Order of Discharge*, is revised and renumbered as part of the Forms Modernization Project. The form is used to issue a discharge in chapter 7 cases filed by individuals or joint debtors. It replaces former Official Form 18, *Discharge of Debtor*, Director's Procedural Form 18J, *Discharge of Joint Debtors*, and Director's Procedural Form 18JO, *Discharge of One Joint Debtor*.

To make the discharge order and the explanation of it easier to read and understand, legal terms are explained more fully or replaced with commonly understood terms, and the form is reformatted.

Reaffirmed debts are explained more fully, and readers are informed that a discharge will not stop creditors from collecting debts from any property in which they have a valid lien. In addition, readers are advised that the discharge does not stop creditors from collecting from anyone else who is liable on the debt, such as a cosigner on the loan or an insurance company.

Director's Procedural Forms 18J and 18JO are no longer needed because Form 318 specifies the names of the debtors, or debtor, to whom the discharge is issued. Any alternate names of the debtor or debtors appear in the order not in the information box at the top of the form.

Form B401. Petition for Recognition
of Foreign Proceeding

Fill in this information to identify the case:

United States Bankruptcy Court for the:

District of _____

Case number (if known): _____ Chapter 15

☐ Check if this is an
amended filing

Official Form 401

Chapter 15 Petition for Recognition of a Foreign Proceeding   12/15

If more space is needed, attach a separate sheet to this form. On the top of any additional pages, write debtor's name and case number (if known).

1. **Debtor's name**   _____

2. **Debtor's unique identifier**   For non-individual debtors:

   ☐ Federal Employer Identification Number (EIN) __ __ – __ __ __ __ __ __ __

   ☐ Other _____ Describe identifier _____

   For individual debtors:

   ☐ Social Security number   xxx – xx– __ __ __ __

   ☐ Individual Taxpayer Identification number (ITIN) 9 xx – xx – __ __ __ __

   ☐ Other _____ Describe identifier _____

3. **Name of foreign representative(s)**   _____

4. **Foreign proceeding in which appointment of the foreign representative(s) occurred**   _____

5. **Nature of the foreign proceeding**

   Check one:

   ☐ Foreign main proceeding
   ☐ Foreign nonmain proceeding
   ☐ Foreign main proceeding, or in the alternative foreign nonmain proceeding

6. **Evidence of the foreign proceeding**

   ☐ A certified copy, translated into English, of the decision commencing the foreign proceeding and appointing the foreign representative is attached.

   ☐ A certificate, translated into English, from the foreign court, affirming the existence of the foreign proceeding and of the appointment of the foreign representative, is attached.

   ☐ Other evidence of the existence of the foreign proceeding and of the appointment of the foreign representative is described below, and relevant documentation, translated into English, is attached.

   _____

7. **Is this the only foreign proceeding with respect to the debtor known to the foreign representative(s)?**

   ☐ No. (Attach a statement identifying each country in which a foreign proceeding by, regarding, or against the debtor is pending.)

   ☐ Yes

Official Form 401   Chapter 15 Petition for Recognition of a Foreign Proceeding   page 1

Form B401   OFFICIAL FORMS

Debtor _____   Case number (if known) _____

8. Others entitled to notice   Attach a list containing the names and addresses of:

    (i)   all persons or bodies authorized to administer foreign proceedings of the debtor,

    (ii) all parties to litigation pending in the United States in which the debtor is a party at the time of filing of this petition, and

    (iii) all entities against whom provisional relief is being sought under § 1519 of the Bankruptcy Code.

9. Addresses   Country where the debtor has the center of its main interests:

_____

Debtor's registered office:

Number	Street

P.O. Box _____

City	State/Province/Region	ZIP/Postal Code

Country _____

Individual debtor's habitual residence:

Number	Street

P.O. Box _____

City	State/Province/Region	ZIP/Postal Code

Country _____

Address of foreign representative(s):

Number	Street

P.O. Box _____

City	State/Province/Region	ZIP/Postal Code

Country _____

10. Debtor's website (URL)   _____

11. Type of debtor   Check one:

☐ Non-individual (check one):

    ☐ Corporation. Attach a corporate ownership statement containing the information described in Fed. R. Bankr. P. 7007.1.

    ☐ Partnership

    ☐ Other. Specify: _____

☐ Individual

Debtor _____   Case number (if known) _____

12. Why is venue proper in this district?

Check one:

☐ Debtor's principal place of business or principal assets in the United States are in this district.

☐ Debtor does not have a place of business or assets in the United States, but the following action or proceeding in a federal or state court is pending against the debtor in this district:

☐ If neither box is checked, venue is consistent with the interests of justice and the convenience of the parties, having regard to the relief sought by the foreign representative, because:

13. Signature of foreign representative(s)

I request relief in accordance with chapter 15 of title 11, United States Code.

I am the foreign representative of a debtor in a foreign proceeding, the debtor is eligible for the relief sought in this petition, and I am authorized to file this petition.

I have examined the information in this petition and have a reasonable belief that the information is true and correct.

I declare under penalty of perjury that the foregoing is true and correct.

✗ _____   _____
  Signature of foreign representative   Printed name

Executed on _____
            MM / DD / YYYY

✗ _____   _____
  Signature of foreign representative   Printed name

Executed on _____
            MM / DD / YYYY

14. Signature of attorney

✗ _____   Date _____
  Signature of Attorney for foreign representative   MM / DD / YYYY

Printed name _____

Firm name _____

Number   Street _____

City _____ State _____ ZIP Code _____

Contact phone _____ Email address _____

Bar number _____ State _____

(Added Dec. 1, 2015.)

ADVISORY COMMITTEE NOTES

Official Form 401 is required for any petition seeking recognition of a foreign proceeding under chapter 15 of the Bankruptcy Code. The form, which applies to foreign proceedings involving individual and non-individual debtors, consolidates information formerly included on Official Form 1 (*Voluntary Petition*). The petition must be signed by the foreign representative, under penalty of perjury, and by the foreign representative's attorney.

The petition requires disclosure of the foreign proceeding in which the foreign representative has been appointed (Line 4) and whether it is a foreign main proceeding or foreign nonmain proceeding (Line 5). If the foreign representative seeks recognition of the foreign proceeding as a foreign main proceeding or, in the alternative, a foreign nonmain proceeding, that request should be indicated in Line 5. Each country where any additional foreign proceeding known to the foreign representative is pending must be disclosed on Line 7. See Bankruptcy Rule 1004.2. Evidence of the foreign proceeding and of the foreign representative's appointment must accompany the petition. See 11 U.S.C. § 1515(b). These documents must be translated into English in accordance with 11 U.S.C. § 1515(d). The foreign representative must also attach a list of persons or bodies entitled to notice. See Bankruptcy Rule 2002(q).

The petition calls for information about the debtor, including the debtor's name (Line 1), other unique identifying information, if available (Line 2), and center of main interest (Line 9). The type of debtor is also requested (Line 11).

The foreign representative must indicate the basis for venue in the district by selecting an appropriate checkbox and, if necessary, providing additional information, such as a statement explaining why venue in the district is appropriate (Line 12). See 28 U.S.C. § 1410.

Form B410. Proof of Claim

Fill in this information to identify the case:

Debtor 1 _____

Debtor 2
(Spouse, if filing) _____

United States Bankruptcy Court for the: District of _____

Case number _____

Official Form 410

Proof of Claim   04/16

Read the instructions before filling out this form. This form is for making a claim for payment in a bankruptcy case. Do not use this form to make a request for payment of an administrative expense. Make such a request according to 11 U.S.C. § 503.

Filers must leave out or redact information that is entitled to privacy on this form or on any attached documents. Attach redacted copies of any documents that support the claim, such as promissory notes, purchase orders, invoices, itemized statements of running accounts, contracts, judgments, mortgages, and security agreements. Do not send original documents; they may be destroyed after scanning. If the documents are not available, explain in an attachment.

A person who files a fraudulent claim could be fined up to $500,000, imprisoned for up to 5 years, or both. 18 U.S.C. §§ 152, 157, and 3571.

Fill in all the information about the claim as of the date the case was filed. That date is on the notice of bankruptcy (Form 309) that you received.

Part 1:	Identify the Claim

1. Who is the current creditor?

Name of the current creditor (the person or entity to be paid for this claim) _____

Other names the creditor used with the debtor _____

2. Has this claim been acquired from someone else?

☐ No
☐ Yes. From whom? _____

3. Where should notices and payments to the creditor be sent?

Federal Rule of Bankruptcy Procedure (FRBP) 2002(g)

Where should notices to the creditor be sent?	Where should payments to the creditor be sent? (if different)
Name _____	Name _____
Number Street _____	Number Street _____
City _____ State _____ ZIP Code _____	City _____ State _____ ZIP Code _____
Contact phone _____	Contact phone _____
Contact email _____	Contact email _____

Uniform claim identifier for electronic payments in chapter 13 (if you use one)

_ _

4. Does this claim amend one already filed?

☐ No
☐ Yes. Claim number on court claims registry (if known) _____   Filed on _____ MM / DD / YYYY

5. Do you know if anyone else has filed a proof of claim for this claim?

☐ No
☐ Yes. Who made the earlier filing? _____

Part 2: Give Information About the Claim as of the Date the Case Was Filed

6. Do you have any number you use to identify the debtor?

☐ No

☐ Yes. Last 4 digits of the debtor's account or any number you use to identify the debtor: ___ ___ ___ ___

7. How much is the claim? $_____ . Does this amount include interest or other charges?

☐ No

☐ Yes. Attach statement itemizing interest, fees, expenses, or other charges required by Bankruptcy Rule 3001(c)(2)(A).

8. What is the basis of the claim?

Examples: Goods sold, money loaned, lease, services performed, personal injury or wrongful death, or credit card.

Attach redacted copies of any documents supporting the claim required by Bankruptcy Rule 3001(c).

Limit disclosing information that is entitled to privacy, such as health care information.

_____

9. Is all or part of the claim secured?

☐ No

☐ Yes. The claim is secured by a lien on property.

Nature of property:

☐ Real estate. If the claim is secured by the debtor's principal residence, file a *Mortgage Proof of Claim Attachment* (Official Form 410-A) with this *Proof of Claim.*

☐ Motor vehicle

☐ Other. Describe: _____

Basis for perfection: _____

Attach redacted copies of documents, if any, that show evidence of perfection of a security interest (for example, a mortgage, lien, certificate of title, financing statement, or other document that shows the lien has been filed or recorded.)

Value of property: $_____

Amount of the claim that is secured: $_____

Amount of the claim that is unsecured: $_____ (The sum of the secured and unsecured amounts should match the amount in line 7.)

Amount necessary to cure any default as of the date of the petition: $_____

Annual Interest Rate (when case was filed)_____%

☐ Fixed

☐ Variable

10. Is this claim based on a lease?

☐ No

☐ Yes. Amount necessary to cure any default as of the date of the petition. $_____

11. Is this claim subject to a right of setoff?

☐ No

☐ Yes. Identify the property: _____

Official Form 410   Proof of Claim   page 2

12. Is all or part of the claim entitled to priority under 11 U.S.C. § 507(a)?

A claim may be partly priority and partly nonpriority. For example, in some categories, the law limits the amount entitled to priority.

☐ No

☐ Yes. *Check one:*

	Amount entitled to priority
☐ Domestic support obligations (including alimony and child support) under 11 U.S.C. § 507(a)(1)(A) or (a)(1)(B).	$_____
☐ Up to $2,850* of deposits toward purchase, lease, or rental of property or services for personal, family, or household use. 11 U.S.C. § 507(a)(7).	$_____
☐ Wages, salaries, or commissions (up to $12,850*) earned within 180 days before the bankruptcy petition is filed or the debtor's business ends, whichever is earlier. 11 U.S.C. § 507(a)(4).	$_____
☐ Taxes or penalties owed to governmental units. 11 U.S.C. § 507(a)(8).	$_____
☐ Contributions to an employee benefit plan. 11 U.S.C. § 507(a)(5).	$_____
☐ Other. Specify subsection of 11 U.S.C. § 507(a)(__) that applies.	$_____

* Amounts are subject to adjustment on 4/01/19 and every 3 years after that for cases begun on or after the date of adjustment.

Part 3:   **Sign Below**

The person completing this proof of claim must sign and date it. FRBP 9011(b).

If you file this claim electronically, FRBP 5005(a)(2) authorizes courts to establish local rules specifying what a signature is.

A person who files a fraudulent claim could be fined up to $500,000, imprisoned for up to 5 years, or both. 18 U.S.C. §§ 152, 157, and 3571.

Check the appropriate box:

☐ I am the creditor.

☐ I am the creditor's attorney or authorized agent.

☐ I am the trustee, or the debtor, or their authorized agent. Bankruptcy Rule 3004.

☐ I am a guarantor, surety, endorser, or other codebtor. Bankruptcy Rule 3005.

I understand that an authorized signature on this *Proof of Claim* serves as an acknowledgment that when calculating the amount of the claim, the creditor gave the debtor credit for any payments received toward the debt.

I have examined the information in this *Proof of Claim* and have a reasonable belief that the information is true and correct.

I declare under penalty of perjury that the foregoing is true and correct.

Executed on date _____
      MM / DD / YYYY

_____

Signature

Print the name of the person who is completing and signing this claim:

Name _____
      First name   Middle name   Last name

Title _____

Company _____
      Identify the corporate servicer as the company if the authorized agent is a servicer.

Address _____
      Number   Street

_____
City   State   ZIP Code

Contact phone _____   Email _____

(Added Dec. 1, 2015; and amended Apr. 1, 2016.)

ADVISORY COMMITTEE NOTES

Official Form 410, *Proof of Claim*, applies in all cases. Form 410 replaces Official Form 10, *Proof of Claim*. It is renumbered to distinguish it from the forms used by debtors for case opening, and includes stylistic changes throughout the form. It is revised as part of the Forms Modernization Project, making it easier to read and, as a result, likely to generate more complete and accurate responses. Because the goals of the Forms Modernization Project include improving the interface between technology and the forms so as to increase efficiency and reduce the need to produce the same information in multiple formats, many of the open-ended questions and multiple-part instructions have been replaced with more specific questions.

Official Form 410 has been substantially reorganized. A new question has been added at line 10 that solicits information about claims based on leases.

Form B410A. Proof of Claim, Attachment A

Mortgage Proof of Claim Attachment

(12/15)

If you file a claim secured by a security interest in the debtor's principal residence, you must use this form as an attachment to your proof of claim. See separate instructions.

Part 1: Mortgage and Case Information

Case number:

Debtor 1:

Debtor 2:

Last 4 digits to identify:

Creditor:

Servicer:

Fixed accrual/daily simple interest/other:

Part 2: Total Debt Calculation

Principal balance:

Interest due:

Fees, costs due:

Escrow deficiency for funds advanced:

Less total funds on hand: —

Total debt:

Part 3: Arrearage as of Date of the Petition

Principal & interest due:

Prepetition fees due:

Escrow deficiency for funds advanced:

Projected escrow shortage:

Less funds on hand: —

Total prepetition arrearage:

Part 4: Monthly Mortgage Payment

Principal & interest:

Monthly escrow:

Private mortgage insurance:

Total monthly payment:

Part 5: Loan Payment History from First Date of Default

	Account Activity						How Funds Were Applied/Amount Incurred					Balance After Amount Received or Incurred			
A.	B.	C.	D.	E.	F.	G.	H.	I.	J.	K.	L.	M.	N.	O.	P.	Q.
Date	Contractual payment amount	Funds received	Amount incurred	Description	Contractual due date	Prin. int & esc past due balance	Amount to principal	Amount to interest	Amount to escrow	Unapplied funds	Amount to fees or charges	Principal balance	Accrued interest balance	Escrow balance	Fees/ Charges balance	Unapplied funds balance

Official Form 410A   Mortgage Proof of Claim Attachment   page 1 of __

Form B410A

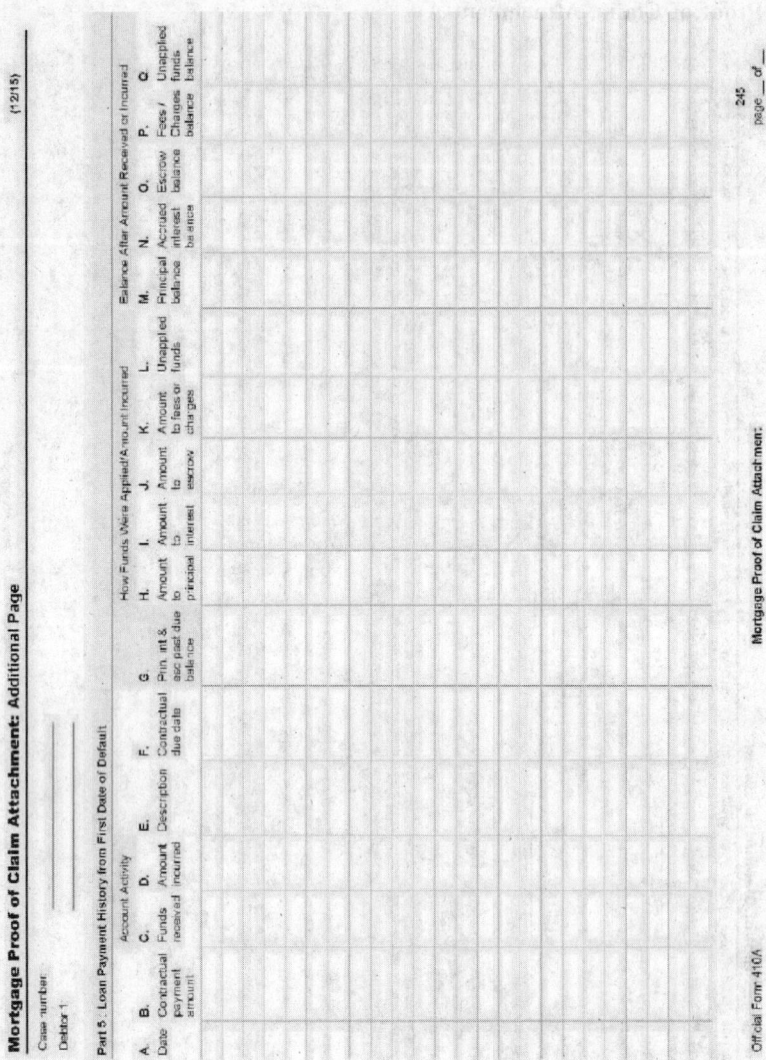

Mortgage Proof of Claim Attachment: Additional Page (12/15)

Case number:

Debtor 1

Part 5: Loan Payment History from First Date of Default

	Account Activity					How Funds Were Applied/Amount Incurred					Balance After Amount Received or Incurred				
A. Date	B. Contractual payment amount	C. Funds received	D. Amount incurred	E. Description	F. Contractual due date	G. Prin. int & esc past due balance	H. Amount to principal	I. Amount to interest	J. Amount to escrow	K. Amount to fees or charges	L. Unapplied funds	M. Principal balance	N. Accrued interest balance	O. Escrow balance	P. Fees / Charges balance	Q. Unapplied funds balance

Official Form 410A   Mortgage Proof of Claim Attachment   245   page ___ of ___

(Added Dec. 1, 2015.)

ADVISORY COMMITTEE NOTES

Official Form 410A, *Mortgage Proof of Claim Attachment*, is revised in its content and format. Rather than requiring a home mortgage claimant to fill in blanks with itemized information about the principal, interest, and fees due as of the petition date and the amount necessary to cure a prepetition default, the form now requires the claimant to provide a loan history that reveals when payments were received, how they were applied, when fees and charges were incurred, and when escrow charges were satisfied. Because completion of the revised form can be automated, it will permit claimants to comply with Rule 3001(c)(2)(C) with efficiency and accuracy. Attachment of a loan history with a home mortgage proof of claim will also provide transparency about the basis for the claimant's calculation of the claim and arrearage amount.

The loan history should begin with the first date on which the borrower failed to make a payment in accordance with the terms of the note and mortgage, unless the note was subsequently brought current with no principal, interest, fees, escrow payments, or other charges immediately payable.

Form B410S–1. Proof of Claim, Supplement 1

Fill In this Information to Identify the case:

Debtor 1 _____

Debtor 2 _____
(Spouse, filing)

United States Bankruptcy Court for the _____ District of _____

Case number _____

Official Form 410S1

Notice of Mortgage Payment Change

12/15

If the debtor's plan provides for payment of postpetition contractual installments on your claim secured by a security interest in the debtor's principal residence, you must use this form to give notice of any changes in the installment payment amount. File this form as a supplement to your proof of claim at least 21 days before the new payment amount is due. See Bankruptcy Rule 3002.1.

Name of creditor: _____   Court claim no. (if known): _____

Last 4 digits of any number you use to identify the debtor's account: _____

Date of payment change:
Must be at least 21 days after date of this notice   __/__/__

New total payment: $ _____
Principal, interest, and escrow, if any

Part 1:   Escrow Account Payment Adjustment

1. Will there be a change in the debtor's escrow account payment?

☐ No
☐ Yes. Attach a copy of the escrow account statement prepared in a form consistent with applicable nonbankruptcy law. Describe the basis for the change. If a statement is not attached, explain why: _____

Current escrow payment: $ _____   New escrow payment: $ _____

Part 2:   Mortgage Payment Adjustment

2. Will the debtor's principal and interest payment change based on an adjustment to the interest rate on the debtor's variable-rate account?

☐ No
☐ Yes. Attach a copy of the rate change notice prepared in a form consistent with applicable nonbankruptcy law. If a notice is not attached, explain why: _____

Current interest rate: _____%   New interest rate: _____%

Current principal and interest payment: $ _____   New principal and interest payment: $ _____

Part 3:   Other Payment Change

3. Will there be a change in the debtor's mortgage payment for a reason not listed above?

☐ No
☐ Yes. Attach a copy of any documents describing the basis for the change, such as a repayment plan or loan modification agreement. (Court approval may be required before the payment change can take effect.)

Reason for change: _____

Current mortgage payment: $ _____   New mortgage payment: $ _____

Official Form 410S1   Notice of Mortgage Payment Change   page 1
246

Form B410S-1 OFFICIAL FORMS

Debtor 1 _____ Case number _____

Part 4:   Sign Here

The person completing this Notice must sign it. Sign and print your name and your title, if any, and state your address and telephone number.

Check the appropriate box.

☐ I am the creditor.

☐ I am the creditor's authorized agent.

I declare under penalty of perjury that the information provided in this claim is true and correct to the best of my knowledge, information, and reasonable belief.

✗ _____   Date ___/___/___
  Signature

Print: _____   Title _____
       First Name   Middle Name   Last Name

Company _____

Address _____
       Number   Street

       _____
       City   State   ZIP Code

Contact phone (_____) _____-_____   Email _____

(Added Dec. 1, 2015.)

ADVISORY COMMITTEE NOTES

Official Forms 410S1 and 410S2, *Notice of Mortgage Payment Change and Notice of Postpetition Mortgage Fees, Expenses, and Charges,* are revised as part of the Forms Modernization Project. There are formatting changes throughout the forms.

Form B410S–2. Proof of Claim, Supplement 2

Fill in this information to identify the case:

Debtor 1 _____

Debtor 2 _____
(Spouse, if filing)

United States Bankruptcy Court for the: _____ District of _____
(State)

Case number _____

Official Form 410S2

Notice of Postpetition Mortgage Fees, Expenses, and Charges   12/16

If the debtor's plan provides for payment of postpetition contractual installments on your claim secured by a security interest in the debtor's principal residence, you must use this form to give notice of any fees, expenses, and charges incurred after the bankruptcy filing that you assert are recoverable against the debtor or against the debtor's principal residence.

File this form as a supplement to your proof of claim. See Bankruptcy Rule 3002.1.

Name of creditor: _____   Court claim no. (if known): _____

Last 4 digits of any number you use to
identify the debtor's account: ___ ___ ___ ___

Does this notice supplement a prior notice of postpetition fees, expenses, and charges?

☐ No

☐ Yes. Date of the last notice: ____ / ____ / ____

Part 1:   **Itemize Postpetition Fees, Expenses, and Charges**

Itemize the fees, expenses, and charges incurred on the debtor's mortgage account after the petition was filed. Do not include any escrow account disbursements or any amounts previously itemized in a notice filed in this case. If the court has previously approved an amount, indicate that approval in parentheses after the date the amount was incurred.

Description	Dates incurred		Amount
1. Late charges	_____	(1)	$ _____
2. Non-sufficient funds (NSF) fees	_____	(2)	$ _____
3. Attorney fees	_____	(3)	$ _____
4. Filing fees and court costs	_____	(4)	$ _____
5. Bankruptcy/Proof of claim fees	_____	(5)	$ _____
6. Appraisal/Broker's price opinion fees	_____	(6)	$ _____
7. Property inspection fees	_____	(7)	$ _____
8. Tax advances (non-escrow)	_____	(8)	$ _____
9. Insurance advances (non-escrow)	_____	(9)	$ _____
10. Property preservation expenses. Specify:_____	_____	(10)	$ _____
11. Other. Specify:_____	_____	(11)	$ _____
12. Other. Specify:_____	_____	(12)	$ _____
13. Other. Specify:_____	_____	(13)	$ _____
14. Other. Specify:_____	_____	(14)	$ _____

The debtor or trustee may challenge whether the fees, expenses, and charges you listed are required to be paid.
See 11 U.S.C. § 1322(b)(5) and Bankruptcy Rule 3002.1.

Official Form 410S2   **Notice of Postpetition Mortgage Fees, Expenses, and Charges**   page 1

Form B410S–2

Debtor 1 _____ Case number (if known) _____
First Name   Middle Name   Last Name

Part 2:   Sign Here

The person completing this Notice must sign it. Sign and print your name and your title, if any, and state your address and telephone number.

Check the appropriate box.

❑ I am the creditor.

❑ I am the creditor's authorized agent.

I declare under penalty of perjury that the information provided in this claim is true and correct to the best of my knowledge, information, and reasonable belief.

✗ _____   Date ___/___/___
Signature

Print: _____   Title _____
First Name   Middle Name   Last Name

Company _____

Address _____
Number   Street

_____
City   State   ZIP Code

Contact phone (_____) _____–_____   Email _____

(Added Dec. 1, 2015; and amended Dec. 1, 2016.)

ADVISORY COMMITTEE NOTES

Official Forms 410S1 and 410S2, *Notice of Mortgage Payment Change and Notice of Postpetition Mortgage Fees, Expenses, and Charges*, are revised as part of the Forms Modernization Project. There are formatting changes throughout the forms.

2016 Amendment

Form 410S2, *Notice of Postpetition Mortgage Fees, Expenses, and Charges*, is amended in the instructions in Part 1 to clarify how to report previously approved fees, expenses, or charges. The following language is added: "If the court has previously approved an amount, indicate that approval in parentheses after the date the amount was incurred." This amended language replaces the prior instruction not to report any amounts previously ruled on by the bankruptcy court.

Form B411A.   General Power of Attorney

Official Form 411A (12/18)

United States Bankruptcy Court

_____ District Of _____

In re _____   Case No. _____
                Debtor

                                           Chapter _____

GENERAL POWER OF ATTORNEY

To _____ of * _____ , and

_____ of * _____

        The undersigned claimant hereby authorizes you, or any one of you, as attorney in fact for the undersigned and with full power of substitution, to vote on any question that may be lawfully submitted to creditors of the debtor in the above-entitled case; [if appropriate] to vote for a trustee of the estate of the debtor and for a committee of creditors; to receive dividends, and in general to perform any act not constituting the practice of law for the undersigned in all matters arising in this case.

Dated: _____

        Signed: _____

        By: _____

        as _____

        Address: _____

        _____

[_If executed by an individual_] Acknowledged before me on _____

[_If executed on behalf of a partnership_] Acknowledged before me on _____
by _____ who says that he [_or_ she] is a member of the partnership
named above and is authorized to execute this power of attorney in its behalf.

[_If executed on behalf of a corporation_] Acknowledged before me on _____ ,
by _____ who says that he [_or_ she] is _____
of the corporation named above and is authorized to execute this power of attorney in its behalf.

_____

_____

[_Official character._]

* State mailing address.

(Added Dec. 1, 2018.)

ADVISORY COMMITTEE NOTES

This form replaces Director's Bankruptcy Form 4011A, which, in turn, was derived from former Official Form 11A in 2015 as part of the Bankruptcy Forms Modernization project.

Parties routinely modify the General Power of Attorney form to conform to state law, the needs of the case, or local practice. Because the exact language of the form is not needed, and Rule 9009, as amended on December 1, 2017, generally restricts alteration of the Official Forms, the form was abrogated as an Official Bankruptcy Form and reissued as a Director's Bankruptcy Form.

Bankruptcy Rule 9010(c), however, requires that "[t]he authority of any agent, attorney in fact, or proxy to represent a creditor for any purpose...shall be evidenced by a power of attorney conforming substantially to the appropriate Official Form" (emphasis added). The form is therefore reissued as an Official Form. Because only substantial conformity to the Official Form is required by Rule 9010(c), parties will be able to continue modifying the form as needed to conform to state law, the needs of the case, or local practice.

Form 411B

OFFICIAL FORMS

Form B411B. Special Power of Attorney

Official Form 411B (12/18)

United States Bankruptcy Court

_____ District Of _____

In re _____   Case No. _____
                    Debtor
                                           Chapter _____

SPECIAL POWER OF ATTORNEY

To _____ of * _____ , and

_____ of * _____

  The undersigned claimant hereby authorizes you, or any one of you, as attorney in fact for the undersigned |*if desired*: and with full power of substitution,| to attend the meeting of creditors of the debtor or any adjournment thereof, and to vote in my behalf on any question that may be lawfully submitted to creditors at such meeting or adjourned meeting, and for a trustee or trustees of the estate of the debtor.

Dated: _____

            Signed: _____

              By: _____

              as _____

            Address: _____

               _____

[*If executed by an individual*] Acknowledged before me on _____

[*If executed on behalf of a partnership*] Acknowledged before me on
by _____ who says that he |*or she*| is a member of the partnership named above and is authorized to execute this power of attorney in its behalf.

[*If executed on behalf of a corporation*] Acknowledged before me on
by _____ who says that he |*or she*| is _____ of the corporation named above and is authorized to execute this power of attorney in its behalf.

           _____

            [*Official character.*]

* State mailing address.

(Added Dec. 1, 2018.)

ADVISORY COMMITTEE NOTES

This form replaces Director's Bankruptcy Form 4011B, which, in turn, was derived from former Official Form 11B in 2015 as part of the Bankruptcy Forms Modernization project.

Parties routinely modify the Special Power of Attorney form to conform to state law, the needs of the case, or local practice. Because the exact language of the form is not needed, and Rule 9009, as amended on December 1, 2017, generally restricts alteration of the Official Forms, the form was abrogated as an Official Bankruptcy Form and reissued as a Director's Bankruptcy Form.

Bankruptcy Rule 9010(c), however, requires that "[t]he authority of any agent, attorney in fact, or proxy to represent a creditor for any purpose...shall be evidenced by a power of attorney conforming substantially to the appropriate Official Form" (emphasis added). The form is therefore reissued as an Official Form. Because only substantial conformity to the Official Form is required by Rule 9010(c), parties will be able to continue modifying the form as needed to conform to state law, the needs of the case, or local practice.

Form B416A. Caption

Official Form 416A (12/15)

Form 416A. CAPTION (FULL)

United States Bankruptcy Court

_____ District Of _____

In re _____,

[Set forth here all names including married, maiden, and trade names used by debtor within the last 8 years.]

Debtor

Case No. _____

Address _____

_____

Last four digits of Social-Security or Individual Tax- Payer-Identification (ITIN) No(s)., (if any): _____

Chapter _____

Employer's Tax Identification No(s). (if any): _____

_____

[Designation of Character of Paper]

(Added Dec. 1, 2015.)

ADVISORY COMMITTEE NOTES

Official Form 416A, *Caption*, applies on all forms where prescribed. Form 416A replaces Official Form 16A, *Caption*. It is renumbered as part of the Forms Modernization Project.

Form B416B.   Caption (Short Title)

Official Form 416B (12/15)

Form 416B CAPTION (Short Title)

(May be used if 11 U.S.C. § 342(c) is not applicable)

United States Bankruptcy Court

_____ District Of _____

In re _____,

                        Debtor

Case No.

_____

Chapter

_____

[Designation of Character of Paper]

254

(Added Dec. 1, 2015.)

ADVISORY COMMITTEE NOTES

Official Form 416B, *Caption*, applies on all forms where prescribed. Form 416B replaces Official Form 16B, *Caption*. It is renumbered as part of the Forms Modernization Project.

Form B416D. Caption for Use in Adversary Proceeding Other Than for a Complaint Filed by a Debtor

Official Form 416D (12/15)

Form 416D Caption for Use in Adversary Proceeding

United States Bankruptcy Court

_____ District Of _____

In re _____,   Case No.
                                                _____
        Debtor

        _____,   Chapter
                                                _____
        Plaintiff

        _____,   Adv. Proc. No.
                                                _____
        Defendant

COMPLAINT [*or other designation*]

[If in a Notice of Appeal and Statement of Election (see Form 417A) or other notice filed and served by the debtor, the caption must be altered to include the debtor's address and Employer's Tax Identification Numbers(s) or last four digits of Social Security Number(s) as in Form 416A]

256

(Added Dec. 1, 2015.)

ADVISORY COMMITTEE NOTES

Official Form 416D, *Caption for Use in Adversary Proceeding Other Than for a Complaint Filed by a Debtor*, applies on all forms where prescribed. Form 416D replaces Official Form 16D, *Caption for Use in Adversary Proceeding Other Than for a Complaint Filed by a Debtor*. It is renumbered as part of the Forms Modernization Project.

**Form B417A. Notice of Appeal
and Statement of Election**
Official Form 417A (12/18)

[Caption as in Form 416A, 416B, or 416D, as appropriate]

NOTICE OF APPEAL AND STATEMENT OF ELECTION

Part 1: Identify the appellant(s)

1. Name(s) of appellant(s): _____
_____

2. Position of appellant(s) in the adversary proceeding or bankruptcy case that is the subject of this appeal:

For appeals in an adversary proceeding.

❏ Plaintiff
❏ Defendant
❏ Other (describe) _____

For appeals in a bankruptcy case and not in an adversary proceeding.

❏ Debtor
❏ Creditor
❏ Trustee
❏ Other (describe) _____

Part 2: Identify the subject of this appeal

1. Describe the judgment, order, or decree appealed from: _____

2. State the date on which the judgment, order, or decree was entered: _____

Part 3: Identify the other parties to the appeal

List the names of all parties to the judgment, order, or decree appealed from and the names, addresses, and telephone numbers of their attorneys (attach additional pages if necessary):

1. Party: _____ Attorney: _____
                                          _____
                                          _____
                                          _____

2. Party: _____ Attorney: _____
                                          _____
                                          _____
                                          _____

Official Form 417A   Notice of Appeal and Statement of Election   page 1

Part 4: Optional election to have appeal heard by District Court (applicable only in certain districts)

If a Bankruptcy Appellate Panel is available in this judicial district, the Bankruptcy Appellate Panel will hear this appeal unless, pursuant to 28 U.S.C. § 158(c)(1), a party elects to have the appeal heard by the United States District Court. If an appellant filing this notice wishes to have the appeal heard by the United States District Court, check below. Do not check the box if the appellant wishes the Bankruptcy Appellate Panel to hear the appeal.

❑ Appellant(s) elect to have the appeal heard by the United States District Court rather than by the Bankruptcy Appellate Panel.

Part 5: Sign below

_____   Date: _____
Signature of attorney for appellant(s) (or appellant(s)
if not represented by an attorney)

Name, address, and telephone number of attorney
(or appellant(s) if not represented by an attorney):
_____
_____
_____
_____

Fee waiver notice: If appellant is a child support creditor or its representative and appellant has filed the form specified in § 304(g) of the Bankruptcy Reform Act of 1994, no fee is required.

[**Note to inmate filers:** If you are an inmate filer in an institution and you seek the timing benefit of Fed. R. Bankr. P. 8002(c)(1), complete Director's Form 4170 (Declaration of Inmate Filing) and file that declaration along with the Notice of Appeal.]

Official Form 417A   Notice of Appeal and Statement of Election   page 2

(Added Dec. 1, 2015; and amended Dec. 1, 2018.)

ADVISORY COMMITTEE NOTES

The form is amended to include a notice to inmate filers that Director's Form 4170 may be used to provide a declaration under Rule 8002(c)(1) regarding the mailing of a notice of appeal using an institution's legal mail system.

Form B417B

Form B417B. Optional Appellee Statement of Election to Proceed in District Court

Official Form 417B (12/15)

[Caption as in Form 416A, 416B, or 416D, as appropriate]

OPTIONAL APPELLEE STATEMENT OF ELECTION TO PROCEED IN DISTRICT COURT

This form should be filed only if all of the following are true:

- this appeal is pending in a district served by a Bankruptcy Appellate Panel,
- the appellant(s) did not elect in the Notice of Appeal to proceed in the District Court rather than in the Bankruptcy Appellate Panel,
- no other appellee has filed a statement of election to proceed in the district court, and
- you elect to proceed in the District Court.

Part 1: Identify the appellee(s) electing to proceed in the District Court

1. Name(s) of appellee(s): _____

    _____

2. Position of appellee(s) in the adversary proceeding or bankruptcy case that is the subject of this appeal:

    For appeals in an adversary proceeding.
    - ☐ Plaintiff
    - ☐ Defendant
    - ☐ Other (describe) _____

    For appeals in a bankruptcy case and not in an adversary proceeding.
    - ☐ Debtor
    - ☐ Creditor
    - ☐ Trustee
    - ☐ Other (describe) _____

Part 2: Election to have this appeal heard by the District Court (applicable only in certain districts)

I (we) elect to have the appeal heard by the United States District Court rather than by the Bankruptcy Appellate Panel.

Part 3: Sign below

_____   Date: _____
Signature of attorney for appellee(s) (or appellee(s)
if not represented by an attorney)

Name, address, and telephone number of attorney
(or appellee(s) if not represented by an attorney):
_____
_____
_____

Official Form 417B   Optional Appellee Statement of Election to Proceed in District Court

261

(Added Dec. 1, 2015.)

ADVISORY COMMITTEE NOTES

The form number is updated to comport with the form numbering style developed as part of the Forms Moderniza-tion Project. Other stylistic changes were made throughout the form.

For Complete Annotation Materials, see United States Code Annotated

Form B417C. Certificate of Compliance With
Rule 8015(a)(7)(B) or 8016(d)(2)

Official Form 417C (12/18)

[This certification must be appended to your document if its length is calculated by maximum number of words or lines of text rather than number of pages.]

Certificate of Compliance with Type-Volume Limit, Typeface Requirements, and Type-Style Requirements

1. This document complies with [the type-volume limit of Fed. R. Bankr. P. [*insert Rule citation; e.g.,8015(a)(7)(B)*]] [the word limit of Fed. R. Bankr. P. [*insert Rule citation; e.g., 8013(f)(3)(A)*]] because, excluding the parts of the document exempted by Fed. R. Bankr. P. 8015(g) [and [*insert applicable Rule citation, if any*]]:

❏ this document contains [*state the number of*] words, or

❏ this brief uses a monospaced typeface and contains [*state the number of*] lines of text.

2. This document complies with the typeface requirements of Fed. R. Bankr. P. 8015(a)(5) and the type-style requirements of Fed. R. Bankr. P. 8015(a)(6) because:

❏ this document has been prepared in a proportionally spaced typeface using [*state name and version of word-processing program*] in [*state font size and name of type style*], or

❏ this brief has been prepared in a monospaced typeface using [*state name and version of word-processing program*] with [*state number of characters per inch and name of type style*].

_____   Date: _____
Signature

Print name of person signing certificate of compliance:

_____

Official Form 417C   Certificate of Compliance With Type-Volume Limit, Typeface Requirements, and Type-Style Requirements

(Added Dec. 1, 2015; and amended Dec. 1, 2018.)

ADVISORY COMMITTEE NOTES

The form is amended to reflect changes in the length limits specified by Part VIII of the Bankruptcy Rules for appellate documents and the broadened requirement for a certificate of compliance under Rule 8015(h). The rule now requires certification of compliance with the type-volume or word limits for briefs filed under Rule 8015(a)(7)(b), 8016(d)(2), or 8017(b)(4), and documents filed under Rule 8013(f)(3)(A), 8013(f)(3)(C), or 8022(b)(1).

Form B420A

Form B420A. Notice of [Motion to] [Objection to]

Official Form 420A (Notice of Motion or Objection) (12/16)

United States Bankruptcy Court

_____ District of _____

In re

[Set forth here all names including married, maiden, and trade names used by debtor within last 8 years.]

       Debtor

Address _____

_____

Last four digits of Social Security or Individual Tax-payer Identification (ITIN) No(s).,(if any): _____

Employer's Tax Identification (EIN) No(s).(if any): _____

)
)
)
)
)
) Case No.
) _____
)
) Chapter
) _____
)
)
)
)
)

NOTICE OF [MOTION TO] [OBJECTION TO]

_____has filed papers with the court to [relief sought in motion or objection].

Your rights may be affected. You should read these papers carefully and discuss them with your attorney, if you have one in this bankruptcy case. (If you do not have an attorney, you may wish to consult one.)

If you do not want the court to [relief sought in motion or objection], or if you want the court to consider your views on the [motion] [objection], then on or before (date), you or your attorney must:

[File with the court a written request for a hearing {or, _if the court requires a written response_, an answer, explaining your position} at:

  {address of the bankruptcy clerk's office}

If you mail your {request}{response} to the court for filing, you must mail it early enough so the court will **receive** it on or before the date stated above.

You must also send a copy to:

  {movant's attorney's name and address}

  {names and addresses of others to be served}]

[Attend the hearing scheduled to be held on (date), (year) , at ____ a.m./p.m. in Courtroom____, United States Bankruptcy Court, {address}.]

[Other steps required to oppose a motion or objection under local rule or court order.]

If you or your attorney do not take these steps, the court may decide that you do not oppose the relief sought in the motion or objection and may enter an order granting that relief.

Date: _____

Signature: _____
Name: _____
Address: _____

(Added Dec. 1, 2016.)

ADVISORY COMMITTEE NOTES

The form numbers are updated to comport with the form numbering style developed as part of the Forms Moderniza-tion project. The forms are also amended to change the phrase "mail" to "send" to reflect the fact that there are various methods of providing documents to other parties.

Form B420B. Notice of Objection to Claim

Official Form 420B (Notice of Objection to Claim) (12/16)

United States Bankruptcy Court

_____ District of _____

In re
*[Set forth here all names including married, maiden,
and trade names used by debtor within last 8 years.]*

)
)
)
)
)
Debtor   )   Case No. _____
)
Address _____   )
_____   )
)   Chapter _____
Last four digits of Social Security or Individual Tax-payer   )
Identification (ITIN) No(s).,(if any):   )
)
_____   )
Employer's Tax Identification (EIN) No(s).(if any): _____   )

NOTICE OF OBJECTION TO CLAIM

_____ has filed an objection to your claim in this bankruptcy case.

Your claim may be reduced, modified, or eliminated. You should read these papers carefully and discuss them with your attorney, if you have one.

If you do not want the court to eliminate or change your claim, then on or before _(date)_, you or your lawyer must:

{If required by local rule or court order.}

[File with the court a written response to the objection, explaining your position, at:

{address of the bankruptcy clerk's office}

If you mail your response to the court for filing, you must mail it early enough so that the court will **receive** it on or before the date stated above.

You must also send a copy to:

{objector's attorney's name and address}

{names and addresses of others to be served}]

Attend the hearing on the objection, scheduled to be held on _(date)_, _(year)_ , at ___ a.m./p.m. in Courtroom____, United States Bankruptcy Court, {address}.

If you or your attorney do not take these steps, the court may decide that you do not oppose the objection to your claim.

Date: _____   Signature: _____
Name: _____
Address: _____

(Added Dec. 1, 2016.)

ADVISORY COMMITTEE NOTES

The form numbers are updated to comport with the form numbering style developed as part of the Forms Moderniza-tion project. The forms are also amended to change the phrase "mail" to "send" to reflect the fact that there are various methods of providing documents to other parties.

**Form B423.   Certification About a Financial
Management Course**

Fill in this information to identify the case:

Debtor 1 _____
          First Name   Middle Name   Last Name

Debtor 2
(Spouse, if filing) First Name   Middle Name   Last Name

United States Bankruptcy Court for the: _____ District of _____

Case number _____
(If known)

Official Form 423

Certification About a Financial Management Course   12/15

If you are an individual, you must take an approved course about personal financial management if:

■ you filed for bankruptcy under chapter 7 or 13, or

■ you filed for bankruptcy under chapter 11 and § 1141 (d)(3) applies.

In a joint case, each debtor must take the course. 11 U.S.C. §§ 727(a)(11) and 1328(g).

After you finish the course, the provider will give you a certificate. The provider may notify the court that you have completed the course. If the provider does notify the court, you need not file this form. If the provider does not notify the court, then Debtor 1 and Debtor 2 must each file this form with the certificate number before your debts will be discharged.

■ If you filed under chapter 7 and you need to file this form, file it within 60 days after the first date set for the meeting of creditors under § 341 of the Bankruptcy Code.

■ If you filed under chapter 11 or 13 and you need to file this form, file it before you make the last payment that your plan requires or before you file a motion for a discharge under § 1141(d)(5)(B) or § 1328(b) of the Bankruptcy Code. Fed. R. Bankr. P. 1007(c).

In some cases, the court can waive the requirement to take the financial management course. To have the requirement waived, you must file a motion with the court and obtain a court order.

Part 1:   Tell the Court About the Required Course

You must check one:

❏ I completed an approved course in personal financial management:

Date I took the course _____ / _____ / _____
                        MM / DD / YYYY

Name of approved provider _____

Certificate number _____

❏ I am not required to complete a course in personal financial management because the court has granted my motion for a waiver of the requirement based on (check one):

❏ **Incapacity.** I have a mental illness or a mental deficiency that makes me incapable of realizing or making rational decisions about finances.

❏ **Disability.** My physical disability causes me to be unable to complete a course in personal financial management in person, by phone, or through the internet, even after I reasonably tried to do so.

❏ **Active duty.** I am currently on active military duty in a military combat zone.

❏ **Residence.** I live in a district in which the United States trustee (or bankruptcy administrator) has determined that the approved instructional courses cannot adequately meet my needs.

Part 2:   Sign Here

I certify that the information I have provided is true and correct.

_____   _____   Date
Signature of debtor named on certificate   Printed name of debtor   MM / DD / YYYY

(Added Dec. 1, 2015.)

ADVISORY COMMITTEE NOTES

Official Form 423, *Certification About a Financial Management Course*, is revised as part of the Forms Modernization Project. The form replaces former Official Form 23, *Debtor's Certification of Completion of Postpetition Instructional Course Concerning Personal Financial Management.* Form 423 is renumbered to distinguish it from the forms used by non-individual debtors, such as corporations and partnerships.

To make Form 423 easier to understand, legal terms are explained more fully or replaced with commonly understood terms, and the form is reformatted. Part 1, *Tell the Court About the Required Course*, provides definitions for "incapacity" and "disability," rather than providing statutory citations.

A statement is added that, in some cases, the court can waive the requirement to complete the financial management course. To have the requirement waived, the debtor must file a motion with the court and obtain a court order.

Form B424.   Certification to Court of Appeals

Official Form 424 (12/15)

[Caption as described in Fed. R. Bankr. P. 7010 or 9004(b), as applicable]

Certification to Court of Appeals by All Parties

A notice of appeal having been filed in the above-styled matter on _____[Date], _____,
_____, and _____, [names of all the appellants and all the
appellees, if any], who are all the appellants [and all the appellees] hereby certify to the court under 28 U.S.C.
§ 158(d)(2)(A) that a circumstance specified in 28 U.S.C. § 158(d)(2) exists as stated below.

Leave to appeal in this matter:

❏ is required under 28 U.S.C. § 158(a)

❏ is not required under 28 U.S.C. § 158(a).

[If from a final judgment, order, or decree] This certification arises in an appeal from a final judgment,
order, or decree of the United States Bankruptcy Court for the _____ District of _____
entered on _____[Date].

[If from an interlocutory order or decree] This certification arises in an appeal from an interlocutory
order or decree, and the parties hereby request leave to appeal as required by 28 U.S.C. § 158(a).

*[The certification shall contain one or more of the following statements, as is appropriate to the
circumstances.]*

The judgment, order, or decree involves a question of law as to which there is no controlling decision
of the court of appeals for this circuit or of the Supreme Court of the United States, or involves a
matter of public importance.

Or

The judgment, order, or decree involves a question of law requiring resolution of conflicting decisions.

Or

An immediate appeal from the judgment, order, or decree may materially advance the progress of the case or
proceeding in which the appeal is taken.

Official Form 424 continued
(12/15)

[The parties may include or attach the information specified in Rule 8006.]

Signed: *[If there are more than two signatories, all must sign and provide the information requested below. Attach*
           additional signed sheets if needed.]

Attorneys for Appellant and
Appellee (or Appellant and
Appellee, if not represented   _____   _____
by an attorney):

Printed names of signers: _____   _____

Addresses: _____   _____

                                 _____   _____

                                 _____   _____

Telephone numbers: (____)____-_____   (____)____-_____

Date: ____/____/_____   ____/____/_____
                                 MM / DD / YYYY   MM / DD / YYYY

(Added Dec. 1, 2015.)

ADVISORY COMMITTEE NOTES

Official Form 424, *Certification to Court of Appeal by All Parties* replaces Official Form 24, *Certification to Court of Appeal by All Parties*. It is revised as part of the Forms Modernization Project, and includes stylistic changes throughout the form.

Form B425A. Plan of Reorganization for Small Business Under Chapter 11

Fill in this information to identify the case:

Debtor Name _____

United States Bankruptcy Court for the: _____   District of _____
                                                              (State)

Case number: _____

☐ Check if this is an amended filing

Official Form 425A _____

Plan of Reorganization for Small Business Under Chapter 11   12/17

[Name of Proponent]_____['s Plan of Reorganization, Dated [Insert Date]

Article 1: Summary

This Plan of Reorganization (the *Plan*) under chapter 11 of the Bankruptcy Code (the *Code*) proposes to pay creditors of [insert the name of the Debtor] (the *Debtor*) from [Specify sources of payment, such as an infusion of capital, loan proceeds, sale of assets, cash flow from operations, or future income].

This Plan provides for:
☐ classes of priority claims;
☐ classes of secured claims;
☐ classes of non-priority unsecured claims; and
☐ classes of equity security holders.

Non-priority unsecured creditors holding allowed claims will receive distributions, which the proponent of this Plan has valued at approximately ☐ cents on the dollar. This Plan also provides for the payment of administrative and priority claims.

All creditors and equity security holders should refer to Articles 3 through 6 of this Plan for information regarding the precise treatment of their claim. A disclosure statement that provides more detailed information regarding this Plan and the rights of creditors and equity security holders has been circulated with this Plan. **Your rights may be affected. You should read these papers carefully and discuss them with your attorney, if you have one. (If you do not have an attorney, you may wish to consult one.)**

Article 2: Classification of Claims and Interests

2.01 **Class 1** .... All allowed claims entitled to priority under § 507(a) of the Code (except administrative expense claims under § 507(a)(2), ["gap" period claims in an involuntary case under § 507(a)(3).] and priority tax claims under § 507(a)(8)).

[Add classes of priority claims, if applicable]

2.02 **Class 2** .... The claim of [_____], to the extent allowed as a secured claim under § 506 of the Code.

[Add other classes of secured creditors, if any. *Note:* Section 1129(a)(9)(D) of the Code provides that a secured tax claim which would otherwise meet the description of a priority tax claim under § 507(a)(8) of the Code is to be paid in the same manner and over the same period as prescribed in § 507(a)(8).]

2.03 **Class 3** .... All non-priority unsecured claims allowed under § 502 of the Code.

[Add other classes of unsecured claims, if any.]

Official Form 425A   Plan of Reorganization for Small Business Under Chapter 11   page 1

Debtor Name _____ Case number _____

2.04	Class 4	Equity interests of the Debtor. [If the Debtor is an individual, change this heading to *The interests of the individual Debtor in property of the estate.*]

Article 3: Treatment of Administrative Expense Claims, Priority Tax Claims, and Quarterly and Court Fees

3.01	Unclassified claims	Under section § 1123(a)(1), administrative expense claims, ["gap" period claims in an involuntary case allowed under § 502(f) of the Code.] and priority tax claims are not in classes.
3.02	Administrative expense claims	Each holder of an administrative expense claim allowed under § 503 of the Code, [and a "gap" claim in an involuntary case allowed under § 502(f) of the Code,] will be paid in full on the effective date of this Plan, in cash, or upon such other terms as may be agreed upon by the holder of the claim and the Debtor.
3.03	Priority tax claims	Each holder of a priority tax claim will be paid [Specify terms of treatment consistent with § 1129(a)(9)(C) of the Code].
3.04	Statutory fees	All fees required to be paid under 28 U.S.C. § 1930 that are owed on or before the effective date of this Plan have been paid or will be paid on the effective date.
3.05	Prospective quarterly fees	All quarterly fees required to be paid under 28 U.S.C. § 1930(a)(6) or (a)(7) will accrue and be timely paid until the case is closed, dismissed, or converted to another chapter of the Code.

Article 4: Treatment of Claims and Interests Under the Plan

4.01 Claims and interests shall be treated as follows under this Plan:

Class	Impairment	Treatment
Class 1 – Priority claims excluding those in Article 3	☐ Impaired ☐ Unimpaired	[Insert treatment of priority claims in this Class, including the form, amount and timing of distribution, if any. For example: "Class 1 is unimpaired by this Plan, and each holder of a Class 1 Priority Claim will be paid in full, in cash, upon the later of the effective date of this Plan, or the date on which such claim is allowed by a final non-appealable order. Except: _____ ."] [Add classes of priority claims if applicable]
Class 2 – Secured claim of [Insert name of secured creditor.]	☐ Impaired ☐ Unimpaired	[Insert treatment of secured claim in this Class, including the form, amount and timing of distribution, if any.] [Add classes of secured claims if applicable]
Class 3 – Non-priority unsecured creditors	☐ Impaired ☐ Unimpaired	[Insert treatment of unsecured creditors in this Class, including the form, amount and timing of distribution, if any.] [Add administrative convenience class if applicable]
Class 4 - Equity security holders of the Debtor	☐ Impaired ☐ Unimpaired	[Insert treatment of equity security holders in this Class, including the form, amount and timing of distribution, if any.]

Article 5: Allowance and Disallowance of Claims

5.01	Disputed claim	A *disputed claim* is a claim that has not been allowed or disallowed [by a final non-appealable order], and as to which either: (i) a proof of claim has been filed or deemed filed, and the Debtor or another party in interest has filed an objection; or (ii) no proof of claim has been filed, and the Debtor has scheduled such claim as disputed, contingent, or unliquidated.
5.02	Delay of distribution on a disputed claim	No distribution will be made on account of a disputed claim unless such claim is allowed [by a final non-appealable order].

Official Form 425A   Plan of Reorganization for Small Business Under Chapter 11   page 2

Debtor Name _____   Case number:_____

5.03	Settlement of disputed claims	The Debtor will have the power and authority to settle and compromise a disputed claim with court approval and compliance with Rule 9019 of the Federal Rules of Bankruptcy Procedure.

Article 6: Provisions for Executory Contracts and Unexpired Leases

6.01	Assumed executory contracts and unexpired leases	(a) The Debtor assumes, and if applicable assigns, the following executory contracts and unexpired leases as of the effective date: [List assumed, or if applicable assigned, executory contracts and unexpired leases.]
		(b) Except for executory contracts and unexpired leases that have been assumed, and if applicable assigned, before the effective date or under section 6.01(a) of this Plan, or that are the subject of a pending motion to assume, and if applicable assign, the Debtor will be conclusively deemed to have rejected all executory contracts and unexpired leases as of the effective date. A proof of a claim arising from the rejection of an executory contract or unexpired lease under this section must be filed no later than [_____] days after the date of the order confirming this Plan.

Article 7: Means for Implementation of the Plan

[Insert here provisions regarding how the plan will be implemented as required under § 1123(a)(5) of the Code. For example, provisions may include those that set out how the plan will be funded, including any claims reserve to be established in connection with the plan, as well as who will be serving as directors, officers or voting trustees of the reorganized Debtor.]

Article 8: General Provisions

8.01	Definitions and rules of construction	The definitions and rules of construction set forth in §§ 101 and 102 of the Code shall apply when terms defined or construed in the Code are used in this Plan, and they are supplemented by the following definitions: [Insert additional definitions if necessary].
8.02	Effective date	The effective date of this Plan is the first business day following the date that is 14 days after the entry of the confirmation order. If, however, a stay of the confirmation order is in effect on that date, the effective date will be the first business day after the date on which the stay expires or is otherwise terminated.
8.03	Severability	If any provision in this Plan is determined to be unenforceable, the determination will in no way limit or affect the enforceability and operative effect of any other provision of this Plan.
8.04	Binding effect	The rights and obligations of any entity named or referred to in this Plan will be binding upon, and will inure to the benefit of the successors or assigns of such entity.
8.05	Captions	The headings contained in this Plan are for convenience of reference only and do not affect the meaning or interpretation of this Plan.

Form B425A   OFFICIAL FORMS

Debtor Name _____   Case number _____

|8.06 **Controlling effect**   Unless a rule of law or procedure is supplied by federal law (including the Code or the Federal Rules of Bankruptcy Procedure), the laws of the State of _____ govern this Plan and any agreements, documents, and instruments executed in connection with this Plan, except as otherwise provided in this Plan.]

|8.07 **Corporate governance**   [If the Debtor is a corporation include provisions required by § 1123(a)(6) of the Code.]

|8.08 **Retention of Jurisdiction**   Language addressing the extent and the scope of the bankruptcy court's jurisdiction after the effective date of the plan.]

Article 9: Discharge

Check one box.

9.01 ☐   **Discharge if the Debtor is an individual and § 1141(d)(3) is not applicable.** Confirmation of this Plan does not discharge any debt provided for in this Plan until the court grants a discharge on completion of all payments under this Plan, or as otherwise provided in § 1141(d)(5) of the Code. The Debtor will not be discharged from any debt excepted from discharge under § 523 of the Code, except as provided in Rule 4007(c) of the Federal Rules of Bankruptcy Procedure.

☐   **Discharge if the Debtor is a partnership and § 1141(d)(3) is not applicable.** On the effective date of this Plan, the Debtor will be discharged from any debt that arose before confirmation of this Plan, to the extent specified in § 1141(d)(1)(A) of the Code. The Debtor will not be discharged from any debt imposed by this Plan.

☐   **Discharge if the Debtor is a corporation and § 1141(d)(3) is not applicable.** On the effective date of this Plan, the Debtor will be discharged from any debt that arose before confirmation of this Plan, to the extent specified in § 1141(d)(1)(A) of the Code, except that the Debtor will not be discharged of any debt:

   (i)   imposed by this Plan; or

   (ii) to the extent provided in § 1141(d)(6).

☐   **No discharge if § 1141(d)(3) is applicable.** In accordance with § 1141(d)(3) of the Code, the Debtor will not receive any discharge of debt in this bankruptcy case.

Article 10: Other Provisions

[Insert other provisions, as applicable.]

Respectfully submitted,

✗ _____
[Signature of the Plan Proponent]   [Printed Name]

✗ _____
[Signature of the Attorney for the Plan Proponent]   [Printed Name]

Official Form 425A   Plan of Reorganization for Small Business Under Chapter 11   page 5

(Added Dec. 1, 2017.)

ADVISORY COMMITTEE NOTES

Official Form 425A, *Plan of Reorganization for Small Business Under Chapter 11*, replaces Official Form 25A, *Plan of Reorganization in Small Business Case Under Chapter 11*. It is revised as part of the Forms Modernization Project, making it easier to read, and includes formatting and stylistic changes throughout the form. It is intended to provide an illustrative format, rather than a specific prescription for the form's language or content of a plan in any particular case.

In Article 1, *Summary*, a category is added for priority claims that are required to be classified and provided for under the plan, and the category for "unsecured claims" is revised to provide for only "non-priority unsecured claims." Also, the value that the proponent estimates to be distributed to unsecured claims is revised to clarify that the estimate is limited to non-priority claims. The instruction to identify and briefly summarize priority and administrative claims that will not be paid on the effective date of the plan, to the extent permitted by the Bankruptcy Code, is eliminated because it is duplicative of the information requested in Articles 3 and 4.

In Article 2, *Classification of Claims and Interests*, section 2.01 is revised to clarify that the priority of claims is determined under section 507(a) of the Bankruptcy Code and to provide for the classification of priority claims where necessary and appropriate. See 11 U.S.C. § 1129(a)(9)(B). Section 2.03 is revised to clarify that Class 3 "unsecured claims" are limited to "non-priority unsecured claims."

In Article 3, *Treatment of Administrative Expense Claims, Priority Tax Claims, and Quarterly and Court Fees*, the title and categories of claims have been revised to include all unclassified administrative and priority claims and all fees payable under 28 U.S.C. § 1930 for which the Bankruptcy Code specifies the treatment under the plan. See 11 U.S.C. § 1129(a)(9), (12). In the title, the reference to "United States Trustee fees" is changed to "Quarterly and Court Fees" to include all of the fees payable under 28 U.S.C. § 1930. Also, section 3.04 is revised to include all statutory fees under 28 U.S.C. § 1930(a), and quarterly fees payable under 28 U.S.C.

§ 1930(a)(6) and (7) after the effective date of the plan are moved to a new section 3.05.

Article 4, *Treatment of Claims and Interests Under the Plan,* is revised to conform to the changes made in sections 2.01 and 2.03 of the plan to classify priority claims, if applicable, and to distinguish the non-priority unsecured claims.

In Article 6, *Provisions for Executory Contracts and Unexpired Leases,* references to the assumption of executory contracts and unexpired leases are expanded to include assignment, if applicable. Section 6.01 is revised to clarify that executory contracts and unexpired leases are assumed, and if applicable assigned, under section 6.01(a) and rejected under section 6.01(b) as of the effective date of the plan. Section 6.01(b) is revised to clarify that all executory contracts and unexpired leases that have been previously assumed, and if applicable assigned, or are the subject of a pending motion to assume, and if applicable assign, as of plan confirmation are also excluded from presumed rejection under the plan.

In Article 9, *Discharge,* the third option is revised to delete the reference to Rule 4007(c) and to clarify that corporations will not be discharged of debts to the extent specified in section 1141(d)(6) of the Bankruptcy Code.

The caption block for the plan is formatted for a non-individual debtor. An individual chapter 11 debtor should use the caption block formatted for individual debtors, including a joint case involving more than one individual debtor, such as the caption found in Official Form B309I.

Form B425B. Disclosure Statement for Small Business Under Chapter 11

Fill in this information to identify the case:

Debtor Name _____

United States Bankruptcy Court for the: _____ District of _____
(State)

Case number: _____

☐ Check if this is an amended filing

Official Form 425B

Disclosure Statement for Small Business Under Chapter 11

12/17

[Name of Proponent]'s Disclosure Statement, Dated [Insert Date]

Table of Contents. See instructions about how to modify the table of contents if you do not have all of the sections below.

[Insert when text is finalized]

Form B425B

OFFICIAL FORMS

Debtor Name _____   Case number_____

For Complete Annotation Materials, see United States Code Annotated

940

Debtor Name _____   Case number_____

I. Introduction

This is the disclosure statement (the *Disclosure Statement*) in the small business chapter 11 case of _____ (the *Debtor*). This Disclosure Statement provides information about the Debtor and the Plan filed on [insert date] (the *Plan*) to help you decide how to vote.

A copy of the Plan is attached as *Exhibit A*. **Your rights may be affected**. You should read the Plan and this Disclosure Statement carefully. You may wish to consult an attorney about your rights and your treatment under the Plan.

The proposed distributions under the Plan are discussed at pages [-] of this Disclosure Statement. [General unsecured creditors are classified in Class [ ] and will receive a distribution of [ ] % of their allowed claims, to be distributed as follows [_____].

A. Purpose of This Document

This Disclosure Statement describes:

- The Debtor and significant events during the bankruptcy case,

- How the Plan proposes to treat claims or equity interests of the type you hold (*i.e.*, what you will receive on your claim or equity interest if the plan is confirmed),

- Who can vote on or object to the Plan,

- What factors the Bankruptcy Court (the *Court*) will consider when deciding whether to confirm the Plan,

- Why [the proponent] believes the Plan is feasible, and how the treatment of your claim or equity interest under the Plan compares to what you would receive on your claim or equity interest in liquidation, and

- The effect of confirmation of the Plan.

Be sure to read the Plan as well as the Disclosure Statement. This Disclosure Statement describes the Plan, but it is the Plan itself that will, if confirmed, establish your rights.

B. Deadlines for Voting and Objecting; Date of Plan Confirmation Hearing

The Court has not yet confirmed the Plan described in this Disclosure Statement. A separate order has been entered setting the following information:

- Time and place of the hearing to [finally approve this disclosure statement and] confirm the plan,

- Deadline for voting to accept or reject the plan, and

- Deadline for objecting to the [**adequacy of disclosure and**] confirmation of the plan.

If you want additional information about the Plan or the voting procedure, you should contact [insert name and address of representative of plan proponent].

Debtor Name _____   Case number_____

C. Disclaimer

The Court has [conditionally] approved this Disclosure Statement as containing adequate information to enable parties affected by the Plan to make an informed judgment about its terms. The Court has not yet determined whether the Plan meets the legal requirements for confirmation, and the fact that the Court has approved this Disclosure Statement does not constitute an endorsement of the Plan by the Court, or a recommendation that it be accepted.

II. Background

A. Description and History of the Debtor's Business

The Debtor is a [corporation, partnership, etc.]. Since [insert year operations commenced], the Debtor has been in the business of [_____]. [Describe the Debtor's business].

B. Insiders of the Debtor

[Insert a detailed list of the names of Debtor's insiders as defined in § 101(31) of the United States Bankruptcy Code (the Code) and their relationship to the Debtor.

For each insider, list all compensation paid by the Debtor or its affiliates to that person or entity during the 2 years prior to the commencement of the Debtor's bankruptcy case, as well as compensation paid during the pendency of this chapter 11 case.]

C. Management of the Debtor During the Bankruptcy

List the name and position of all current officers, directors, managing members, or other persons in control (collectively the *Management*) who will not have a position post-confirmation that you list in III D 2.

Name	Position

D. Events Leading to Chapter 11 Filing

[Describe the events that led to the commencement of the Debtor's bankruptcy case.]

Debtor Name _____　　　Case number_____

E. Significant Events During the Bankruptcy Case

[Describe significant events during the Debtor's bankruptcy case:

- Describe any asset sales outside the ordinary course of business, Debtor in Possession financing, or cash collateral orders.
- Identify the professionals approved by the court.
- Describe any adversary proceedings that have been filed or other significant litigation that has occurred (including contested claim disallowance proceedings), and any other significant legal or administrative proceedings that are pending or have been pending during the case in a forum other than the Court.
- Describe any steps taken to improve operations and profitability of the Debtor.
- Describe other events as appropriate.]

F. Projected Recovery of Avoidable Transfers

Check one box.

☐　The Debtor does not intend to pursue preference, fraudulent conveyance, or other avoidance actions.

☐　The Debtor estimates that up to $[   ] may be realized from the recovery of fraudulent, preferential or other avoidable transfers. While the results of litigation cannot be predicted with certainty and it is possible that other causes of action may be identified, the following is a summary of the preference, fraudulent conveyance and other avoidance actions filed or expected to be filed in this case:

Transaction	Defendant	Amount Claimed

☐　The Debtor has not yet completed its investigation with regard to prepetition transactions. If you received a payment or other transfer within 90 days of the bankruptcy, or other transfer avoidable under the Code, the Debtor may seek to avoid such transfer.

G. Claims Objections

Except to the extent that a claim is already allowed pursuant to a final non-appealable order, the Debtor reserves the right to object to claims. Therefore, even if your claim is allowed for voting purposes, you may not be entitled to a distribution if an objection to your claim is later upheld. Disputed claims are treated in Article 5 of the Plan.

Debtor Name _____   Case number_____

H. Current and Historical Financial Conditions

The identity and fair market value of the estate's assets are listed in *Exhibit B*. [Identify source and basis of valuation.]

The Debtor's most recent financial statements [if any] issued before bankruptcy, each of which was filed with the Court, are set forth in *Exhibit C*.

[The most recent post-petition operating report filed since the commencement of the Debtor's bankruptcy case is set forth in *Exhibit D*.]

[A summary of the Debtor's periodic operating reports filed since the commencement of the Debtor's bankruptcy case is set forth in *Exhibit D*.]

III. Summary of the Plan of Reorganization and Treatment of Claims and Equity Interests

A. What Is the Purpose of the Plan of Reorganization?

As required by the Code, the Plan places claims and equity interests in various classes and describes the treatment each class will receive. The Plan also states whether each class of claims or equity interests is impaired or unimpaired. If the Plan is confirmed, your recovery will be limited to the amount provided by the Plan.

B. Unclassified Claims

Certain types of claims are automatically entitled to specific treatment under the Code. They are not considered impaired, and holders of such claims do not vote on the Plan. They may, however, object if, in their view, their treatment under the Plan does not comply with that required by the Code. Therefore, the Plan Proponent has *not* placed the following claims in any class:

1. Administrative expenses, involuntary gap claims, and quarterly and Court fees

Administrative expenses are costs or expenses of administering the Debtor's chapter 11 case which are allowed under § 503(b) of the Code. Administrative expenses include the value of any goods sold to the Debtor in the ordinary course of business and received within 20 days before the date of the bankruptcy petition, and compensation for services and reimbursement of expenses awarded by the court under § 330(a) of the Code. The Code requires that all administrative expenses be paid on the effective date of the Plan, unless a particular claimant agrees to a different treatment. Involuntary gap claims allowed under § 502(f) of the Code are entitled to the same treatment as administrative expense claims. The Code also requires that fees owed under section 1930 of title 28, including quarterly and court fees, have been paid or will be paid on the effective date of the Plan.

The following chart lists the Debtor's estimated administrative expenses, and quarterly and court fees, and their proposed treatment under the Plan:

Type	Estimated Amount Owed	Proposed Treatment
Administrative expenses		Paid in full on the effective date of the Plan, unless the holder of a particular claim has agreed to different treatment
Involuntary gap claims		Paid in full on the effective date of the Plan, unless the holder of a particular claim has agreed to different treatment
Statutory Court fees		Paid in full on the effective date of the Plan

Debtor Name _____   Case number_____

_____

_____

| Statutory quarterly fees | Paid in full on the effective date of the Plan |

| Total | | |

2. Priority tax claims

Priority tax claims are unsecured income, employment, and other taxes described by § 507(a)(8) of the Code. Unless the holder of such a § 507(a)(8) priority tax claim agrees otherwise, it must receive the present value of such claim pursuant to 11 U.S.C. § 511, in regular installments paid over a period not exceeding 5 years from the order of relief.

The following chart lists the Debtor's estimated § 507(a)(8) priority tax claims and their proposed treatment under the Plan:

Description (Name and type of tax)	Estimated Amount Owed	Date of Assessment	Treatment	
	$		Payment interval	
			[Monthly] payment	$
			Begin date	
			End date	
			Interest rate	%
			Total payout amount	$
	$		Payment interval	
			[Monthly] payment	$
			Begin date	
			End date	
			Interest rate	%
			Total payout amount	$

C. Classes of Claims and Equity Interests

The following are the classes set forth in the Plan, and the proposed treatment that they will receive under the Plan:

1. Classes of secured claims

Allowed Secured Claims are claims secured by property of the Debtor's bankruptcy estate (or that are subject to setoff) to the extent allowed as secured claims under § 506 of the Code. If the value of the collateral or setoffs securing the creditor's claim is less than the amount of the creditor's allowed claim, the deficiency will [be classified as a general unsecured claim].

Form B425B   OFFICIAL FORMS

The following chart lists all classes containing Debtor's secured prepetition claims and their proposed treatment under the Plan:

Class #	Description	Impairment?	Treatment	
	Secured claim of: Name	☐ Impaired ☐ Unimpaired	[Monthly] payment	$
	Collateral description		Payments begin	
	Allowed secured amount $		Payments end	
	Priority of lien		[Balloon payment]	
	Principal owed		Interest rate	%
	Pre-pet. arrearage		Treatment of lien	
	Total claim $		[Additional payment required to cure defaults]	$
	Secured claim of: Name	☐ Impaired ☐ Unimpaired	[Monthly] payment	$
	Collateral description		Payment begin	
	Allowed secured amount $		Payments end	
	Priority of lien		[Balloon payment]	
	Principal owed		Interest rate	%
	Pre-pet. arrearage		Treatment of lien	
	Total claim $		[Additional payment required to cure defaults]	$

2. Classes of priority unsecured claims

The Code requires that, with respect to a class of claims of a kind referred to in §§ 507(a)(1), (4), (5), (6), and (7), each holder of such a claim receive cash on the effective date of the Plan equal to the allowed amount of such claim, unless a particular claimant agrees to a different treatment or the class agrees to deferred cash payments.

Debtor Name _____   Case number_____

The following chart lists all classes containing claims under §§ 507(a)(1), (4), (5), (6), and (7) of
the Code and their proposed treatment under the Plan:

Class #	Description	Impairment?	Treatment
	Priority unsecured claim pursuant to section [insert]	☐ Impaired ☐ Unimpaired	
	Total amount of claims $		
	Priority unsecured claim pursuant to section [insert]	☐ Impaired ☐ Unimpaired	
	Total amount of claims $		

3. Classes of general unsecured claims

General unsecured claims are not secured by property of the estate and are not entitled to
priority under § 507(a) of the Code. [Insert description of § 1122(b) convenience class if applicable.]

The following chart identifies the Plan's proposed treatment of classes ☐ through ☐, which
contain general unsecured claims against the Debtor:

Class #	Description	Impairment?	Treatment
	[1122(b) Convenience Class]	☐ Impaired ☐ Unimpaired	[Insert proposed treatment, such as "Paid in full in cash on effective date of the Plan or when due under contract or applicable nonbankruptcy law"]
	General unsecured class	☐ Impaired ☐ Unimpaired	[Monthly] payment $
			Payments begin
			Payments end
			[Balloon payment] $
			Interest rate from [date] %
			Estimated percent of claim paid %

Debtor Name _____   Case number_____

4. Classes of equity interest holders

Equity interest holders are parties who hold an ownership interest (*i.e.*, equity interest) in the Debtor. In a corporation, entities holding preferred or common stock are equity interest holders. In a partnership, equity interest holders include both general and limited partners. In a limited liability company (*LLC*), the equity interest holders are the members. Finally, with respect to an individual who is a debtor, the Debtor is the equity interest holder.

The following chart sets forth the Plan's proposed treatment of the classes of equity interest holders: [There may be more than one class of equity interests in, for example, a partnership case, or a case where the prepetition Debtor had issued multiple classes of stock.]

Class #	Description	Impairment?	Treatment
	Equity interest holders	☐ Impaired ☐ Unimpaired	

D. Means of Implementing the Plan

1. Source of payments

Payments and distributions under the Plan will be funded by the following:

[Describe the source of funds for payments under the Plan.]

2. Post-confirmation Management

The Post-Confirmation Management of the Debtor (including officers, directors, managing members, and other persons in control), and their compensation, shall be as follows:

Name	Position	Compensation

E. Risk Factors

The proposed Plan has the following risks:

[List all risk factors that might affect the Debtor's ability to make payments and other distributions required under the Plan.]

Debtor Name _____   Case number_____

F. Executory Contracts and Unexpired Leases

The Plan in Article 6 lists all executory contracts and unexpired leases that the Debtor will assume, and if applicable assign, under the Plan. *Assumption* means that the Debtor has elected to continue to perform the obligations under such contracts and unexpired leases, and to cure defaults of the type that must be cured under the Code, if any. Article 6 also lists how the Debtor will cure and compensate the other party to such contract or lease for any such defaults.

If you object to the assumption, and if applicable the assignment, of your unexpired lease or executory contract under the Plan, the proposed cure of any defaults, the adequacy of assurance of performance, you must file and serve your objection to the Plan within the deadline for objecting to the confirmation of the Plan, unless the Court has set an earlier time.

All executory contracts and unexpired leases that are not listed in Article 6 or have not previously been assumed, and if applicable assigned, or are not the subject of a pending motion to assume, and if applicable assign, will be rejected under the Plan. Consult your adviser or attorney for more specific information about particular contracts or leases.

If you object to the rejection of your contract or lease, you must file and serve your objection to the Plan within the deadline for objecting to the confirmation of the Plan.

[The deadline for filing a Proof of Claim based on a claim arising from the rejection of a lease or contract is _____].

Any claim based on the rejection of a contract or lease will be barred if the proof of claim is not timely filed, unless the Court orders otherwise.]

G. Tax Consequences of Plan

Creditors and equity interest holders concerned with how the plan may affect their tax liability should consult with their own accountants, attorneys, and/or advisors.

The following are the anticipated tax consequences of the Plan: [List the following general consequences as a minimum:

(1) Tax consequences to the Debtor of the Plan;

(2) General tax consequences on creditors of any discharge, and the general tax consequences of receipt of plan consideration after confirmation.]

For Complete Annotation Materials, see United States Code Annotated

Debtor Name _____   Case number_____

IV. Confirmation Requirements and Procedures

To be confirmable, the Plan must meet the requirements listed in §1129 of the Code. These include the requirements that:

— the Plan must be proposed in good faith;

— if a class of claims is impaired under the Plan, at least one impaired class of claims must accept the Plan, without counting votes of insiders;

— the Plan must distribute to each creditor and equity interest holder at least as much as the creditor or equity interest holder would receive in a chapter 7 liquidation case, unless the creditor or equity interest holder votes to accept the Plan; and

— the Plan must be feasible.

These requirements are not the only requirements listed in § 1129, and they are not the only requirements for confirmation.

A. Who May Vote or Object

Any party in interest may object to the confirmation of the Plan if the party believes that the requirements for confirmation are not met.

Many parties in interest, however, are not entitled to vote to accept or reject the Plan. Except as stated in Part IV.A.3 below, a creditor or equity interest holder has a right to vote for or against the Plan only if that creditor or equity interest holder has a claim or equity interest that is both

(1) allowed or allowed for voting purposes and

(2) impaired.

In this case, the Plan Proponent believes that classes [____] are impaired and that holders of claims in each of these classes are therefore entitled to vote to accept or reject the Plan. The Plan Proponent believes that classes [____] are unimpaired and that holders of claims in each of these classes, therefore, do not have the right to vote to accept or reject the Plan.

1. What is an allowed claim or an allowed equity interest?

Only a creditor or equity interest holder with an allowed claim or an allowed equity interest has the right to vote on the Plan. Generally, a claim or equity interest is allowed if either

(1) the Debtor has scheduled the claim on the Debtor's schedules, unless the claim has been scheduled as disputed, contingent, or unliquidated, or

(2) the creditor has filed a proof of claim or equity interest, unless an objection has been filed to such proof of claim or equity interest.

When a claim or equity interest is not allowed, the creditor or equity interest holder holding the claim or equity interest cannot vote unless the Court, after notice and hearing, either overrules the objection or allows the claim or equity interest for voting purposes pursuant to Rule 3018(a) of the Federal Rules of Bankruptcy Procedure.

The deadline for filing a proof of claim in this case was [_____].

[If applicable – The deadline for filing objections to claims is [_____].]

2. What is an impaired claim or impaired equity interest?

As noted above, the holder of an allowed claim or equity interest has the right to vote only if it

Debtor Name _____   Case number_____

is in a class that is *impaired* under the Plan. As provided in § 1124 of the Code, a class is considered *impaired* if the Plan alters the legal, equitable, or contractual rights of the members of that class.

3. Who is not entitled to vote

The holders of the following five types of claims and equity interests are *not* entitled to vote:

- holders of claims and equity interests that have been disallowed by an order of the Court;
- holders of other claims or equity interests that are not "allowed claims" or "allowed equity interests" (as discussed above), unless they have been "allowed" for voting purposes;
- holders of claims or equity interests in unimpaired classes;
- holders of claims entitled to priority pursuant to §§ 507(a)(2), (a)(3), and (a)(8) of the Code;
- holders of claims or equity interests in classes that do not receive or retain any value under the Plan; and
- administrative expenses.

Even if you are not entitled to vote on the plan, you have a right to object to the confirmation of the Plan [and to the adequacy of the Disclosure Statement].

4. Who can vote in more than one class

A creditor whose claim has been allowed in part as a secured claim and in part as an unsecured claim, or who otherwise hold claims in multiple classes, is entitled to accept or reject a Plan in each capacity, and should cast one ballot for each claim.

B. Votes Necessary to Confirm the Plan

If impaired classes exist, the Court cannot confirm the Plan unless:

(1) all impaired classes have voted to accept the Plan; or

(2) at least one impaired class of creditors has accepted the Plan without counting the votes of any insiders within that class, and the Plan is eligible to be confirmed by "cram down" of the non-accepting classes, as discussed later in Section B.2.

1. Votes necessary for a class to accept the plan

A class of claims accepts the Plan if both of the following occur:

(1) the holders of more than ½ of the allowed claims in the class, who vote, cast their votes to accept the Plan; and

(2) the holders of at least ⅔ in dollar amount of the allowed claims in the class, who vote, cast their votes to accept the Plan.

A class of equity interests accepts the Plan if the holders of at least ⅔ in amount of the allowed equity interests in the class, who vote, cast their votes to accept the Plan.

2. Treatment of non-accepting classes of secured claims, general unsecured claims, and interests

Even if one or more impaired classes reject the Plan, the Court may nonetheless confirm the Plan upon the request of the Plan proponent if the non-accepting classes are treated in the manner prescribed by § 1129(b) of the Code. A plan that binds non-accepting classes is commonly referred to as a *cram down* plan. The Code allows the Plan to bind non-accepting classes of claims or equity interests if it meets all the requirements for consensual confirmation except the voting requirements of § 1129(a)(8) of the Code, does not *discriminate unfairly*, and

Official Form 425B   Disclosure Statement for Small Business Under Chapter 11   page **13**

Debtor Name _____   Case number_____

is *fair and equitable* toward each impaired class that has not voted to accept the Plan.

You should consult your own attorney if a *cram down* confirmation will affect your claim or equity interest, as the variations on this general rule are numerous and complex.

C. Liquidation Analysis

To confirm the Plan, the Court must find that all creditors and equity interest holders who do not accept the Plan will receive at least as much under the Plan as such claim and equity interest holders would receive in a chapter 7 liquidation. A liquidation analysis is attached to this Disclosure Statement as *Exhibit E*.

D. Feasibility

The Court must find that confirmation of the Plan is not likely to be followed by the liquidation, or the need for further financial reorganization, of the Debtor or any successor to the Debtor, unless such liquidation or reorganization is proposed in the Plan.

1. Ability to initially fund plan

The Plan Proponent believes that the Debtor will have enough cash on hand on the effective date of the Plan to pay all the claims and expenses that are entitled to be paid on that date. Tables showing the amount of cash on hand on the effective date of the Plan, and the sources of that cash are attached to this disclosure statement as *Exhibit F*.

2. Ability to make future plan payments and operate without further reorganization

The Plan Proponent must also show that it will have enough cash over the life of the Plan to make the required Plan payments and operate the debtor's business.
The Plan Proponent has provided projected financial information. Those projections are listed in *Exhibit G*.
The Plan Proponent's financial projections show that the Debtor will have an aggregate annual average cash flow, after paying operating expenses and post-confirmation taxes, of $ _____.
The final Plan payment is expected to be paid on _____.
[Summarize the numerical projections, and highlight any assumptions that are not in accord with past experience. Explain why such assumptions should now be made.]
You should consult with your accountant or other financial advisor if you have any questions pertaining to these projections.

Debtor Name _____   Case number_____

V. Effect of Confirmation of Plan

A.   Discharge of Debtor

Check one box:

☐   **Discharge if the Debtor is an individual and 11 U.S.C. § 1141(d)(3) is not applicable.** Confirmation of the Plan does not discharge any debt provided for in the Plan until the court grants a discharge on completion of all payments under the Plan, or as otherwise provided in § 1141(d)(5) of the Code. Debtor will not be discharged from any debt excepted from discharge under § 523 of the Code, except as provided in Rule 4007(c) of the Federal Rules of Bankruptcy Procedure.

☐   **Discharge if the Debtor is a partnership and § 1141(d)(3) of the Code is not applicable.** On the effective date of the Plan, the Debtor shall be discharged from any debt that arose before confirmation of the Plan, subject to the occurrence of the effective date, to the extent specified in § 1141(d)(1)(A) of the Code. However, the Debtor shall not be discharged from any debt imposed by the Plan. After the effective date of the Plan your claims against the Debtor will be limited to the debts imposed by the Plan.

☐   **Discharge if the Debtor is a corporation and § 1141(d)(3) is not applicable.** On the effective date of the Plan, the Debtor shall be discharged from any debt that arose before confirmation of the Plan, subject to the occurrence of the effective date, to the extent specified in § 1141(d)(1)(A) of the Code, except that the Debtor shall not be discharged of any debt:

    (i)   imposed by the Plan, or

    (ii)   to the extent provided in 11 U.S.C. § 1141(d)(6).

☐   **No Discharge if § 1141(d)(3) is applicable.** In accordance with § 1141(d)(3) of the Code, the Debtor will not receive any discharge of debt in this bankruptcy case.

B. Modification of Plan

The Plan Proponent may modify the Plan at any time before confirmation of the Plan. However, the Court may require a new disclosure statement and/or re-voting on the Plan.

[If the Debtor is not an individual, add the following:

The Plan Proponent may also seek to modify the Plan at any time after confirmation only if

(1) the Plan has not been substantially consummated and

(2) the Court authorizes the proposed modifications after notice and a hearing.]

[If the Debtor is an individual, add the following:

Upon request of the Debtor, the United States trustee, or the holder of an allowed unsecured claim, the Plan may be modified at any time after confirmation of the Plan but before the completion of payments under the Plan, to

(1)   increase or reduce the amount of payments under the Plan on claims of a particular class,

(2)   extend or reduce the time period for such payments, or

(3)   alter the amount of distribution to a creditor whose claim is provided for by the Plan to the extent necessary to take account of any payment of the claim made other than under the Plan.]

For Complete Annotation Materials, see United States Code Annotated

953

Debtor Name _____   Case number_____

C. Final Decree

Once the estate has been fully administered, as provided in Rule 3022 of the Federal Rules of Bankruptcy Procedure, the Plan Proponent, or such other party as the Court shall designate in the Plan Confirmation Order, shall file a motion with the Court to obtain a final decree to close the case. Alternatively, the Court may enter such a final decree on its own motion.

VI. Other Plan Provisions

[Insert other provisions here, as necessary and appropriate.]

✗ _____   _____
[Signature of the Plan Proponent]   [Printed Name]

✗ _____   _____
[Signature of the Attorney for the Plan Proponent]   [Printed Name]

Debtor Name _____   Case number_____

Exhibits

Exhibit A: Copy of Proposed Plan of Reorganization

Form B425B   OFFICIAL FORMS

Debtor Name _____   Case number_____

    Exhibit B: Identity and Value of Material Assets of Debtor

Debtor Name _____   Case number_____

Exhibit C: Prepetition Financial Statements
(to be taken from those filed with the court)

Debtor Name _____   Case number_____

Exhibit D: [Most Recently Filed Postpetition Operating Report]
[Summary of Postpetition Operating Reports]

Debtor Name _____   ·   Case number_____

Exhibit E: Liquidation Analysis

Plan Proponent's Estimated Liquidation Value of Assets

Assets	
a. Cash on hand	$
b. Accounts receivable	$
c. Inventory	$
d. Office furniture and equipment	$
e. Machinery and equipment	$
f. Automobiles	$
g. Building and land	$
h. Customer list	$
i. Investment property (such as stocks, bonds or other financial assets)	$
j. Lawsuits or other claims against third-parties	$
K. Other intangibles (such as avoiding powers actions)	$

Total Assets at Liquidation Value		
		$
Less: Secured creditors' recoveries	–	$
Less: Chapter 7 trustee fees and expenses	–	$
Less: Chapter 11 administrative expenses	–	$
Less: Priority claims, excluding administrative expense claims	–	$
[Less: Debtor's claimed exemptions]	–	$

(1) Balance for unsecured claims	$
(2) Total dollar amount of unsecured claims	$

Percentage of claims which unsecured creditors would receive or retain in a chapter 7 liquidation:	%	
Percentage of claims which unsecured creditors will receive or retain under the Plan:	%	[Divide (1) by (2)]

Form B425B

Debtor Name _____   Case number_____

Exhibit F: Cash on hand on the effective date of the Plan

Cash on hand on effective date of plan		$
Less:	Amount of administrative expenses payable on effective date of the Plan	− $
Less:	Amount of statutory costs and charges	− $
Less:	Amount of cure payments for executory contracts	− $
Less:	Other Plan payments due on effective date of the Plan	− $
Balance after paying these amounts		$

The sources of the cash Debtor will have on hand by the effective date of the Plan are estimated as follows:

Cash in Debtor's bank account now	$
Net earnings between now and effective date of the Plan [State the basis for such projections]	$
Borrowing [Separately state terms of repayment]	$
Capital contributions	$
Other	$
Total (This number should match "cash on hand" figure noted above)	$

Official Form 425B   Disclosure Statement for Small Business Under Chapter 11   page 22

For Complete Annotation Materials, see United States Code Annotated
960

Debtor Name _____   Case number_____

Exhibit G: Projections of Cash Flow for Post-Confirmation Period

(Added Dec. 1, 2017.)

ADVISORY COMMITTEE NOTES

Official Form 425B, *Disclosure Statement for Small Business Under Chapter 11*, replaces Official Form 25B, *Disclosure Statement in Small Business Case Under Chapter 11*. It is revised as part of the Forms Modernization Project, making it easier to read, and includes formatting and stylistic changes throughout the form. Where possible, the form parallels how businesses commonly keep their financial records. It is intended to provide an illustrative format for disclosure, rather than a specific prescription for the form's language or content.

Part I, *Introduction*, is revised to clarify that the disclosure statement is being provided for purposes of voting on the plan. The instructions that the recipient discuss the plan and disclosure statement with an attorney are revised to clarify

that, if the recipient has an attorney, the recipient is not required to consult with the attorney, but may wish to consult with an attorney regardless of whether it has one.

Part I.B., *Deadlines for Voting and Objecting; Date of Plan Confirmation Hearing*, is revised to provide for the court's entry of a separate order setting time frames for hearings and deadlines, see Official Form 313, and to delete those dates from the form as redundant. Also, this part is revised to clarify that requests for additional information about the voting procedure, in addition to the plan, should be directed to the plan proponent's representative.

In Part I.C., *Disclaimer*, the instruction to provide the date by which an objection to final approval of the disclosure statement must be filed is eliminated as duplicative of the court's order required under Part I.B. Repetitive language indicating that the court's approval of the disclosure statement is not final is eliminated.

For Complete Annotation Materials, see United States Code Annotated

961

Form B425B

In Part II.C., *Management of the Debtor During the Bankruptcy*, the title is revised to eliminate the reference to the debtor's management before the bankruptcy, and the instruction is revised to limit the required disclosure to those current officers, directors, managing members, and other persons in control who will not retain a position after confirmation. The instruction to provide information regarding the debtor's pre-petition management is deleted because similar information is required in the *Statement of Financial Affairs of Non-Individuals Filing for Bankruptcy*, Official Form 207. The instruction to provide information regarding the debtor's post-confirmation management is incorporated in Part III.D.2, *Post-confirmation Management*, of the form.

In Part III.B.1, *Administrative expenses, involuntary gap claims, and quarterly and Court fees*, the title and form are revised to clarify that the debtor must provide for the treatment of all fees and expenses owed under 28 U.S.C. § 1930, including quarterly fees and court fees. See 11 U.S.C. § 1129(a)(12). Also, the title and form are revised to include involuntary "gap" period claims in an involuntary case under section 502(f) of the Bankruptcy Code. See 11 U.S.C. §§ 507(a)(3), 1129(a)(9)(A). The reference to the provision governing the allowance of administrative expenses is corrected and changed from section 507(a) to 503(b) of the Bankruptcy Code. The example is revised to include compensation for services and reimbursement of expenses awarded by the court under section 330(a) of the Bankruptcy Code. The requirement that any agreement to pay professional fees and expenses and other unclassified administrative expenses on a date other than the effective date be in writing is deleted. See 11 U.S.C. § 1129(a)(9). The list is revised to include a single category of administrative expenses allowed under section 503(b) of the Bankruptcy Code, deleting as redundant the specific categories for reclamation claims under section 503(b)(9) and approved professional fees and expenses under section 503(b)(2), and to clarify that any holder of an allowed administrative expense claim may agree to payment other than in full on the effective date. Id.

Part III.B.2, *Priority tax claims*, is revised to include a reference to section 511 of the Bankruptcy Code governing the rate of interest on tax claims.

Part III.C.2, *Classes of priority unsecured claims*, is revised to comply with section 1129(a)(9)(B), including the addition that any particular claimant may agree to treatment other than cash payment in full on the effective date and to clarify that any class may agree to deferred cash payments. See 11 U.S.C. § 1129(a)(9)(B).

Part III.D.2, *Post-confirmation Management*, is revised to comply with section 1129(a)(5) of the Bankruptcy Code.

Part III.F., *Executory Contracts and Unexpired Leases*, is revised to incorporate changes to Official Form 425A, Plan of Reorganization for Small Business Under Chapter 11. "Exhibit 5.1" is changed to "Article 6" of the plan. References to the assumption of executory contracts and unexpired leases are expanded to include assignment, if applicable, including the requirement that a party objecting to the assignment of an executory contract or unexpired lease under the plan must timely file and serve an objection to the plan. The form is revised to clarify that executory contracts and unexpired leases that have been previously assumed, and if applicable assigned, or are the subject of a pending motion to assume, and if applicable assign, as of plan confirmation are also excluded from presumed rejection under the plan.

In Part IV, *Confirmation Requirements and Procedures*, the introduction is revised to delete references to subsections (a) and (b) to clarify that a plan must satisfy all of the requirements of section 1129 of the Bankruptcy Code. Also, the form is revised to clarify that the requirement to obtain the acceptance of at least one impaired accepting class of claims, excluding any acceptance by an insider, applies only if the plan proposes to impair at least one class of claims. See 11 U.S.C. § 1129(a)(10).

In Part IV.B.1, *Votes necessary for a class to accept the plan*, the standards for confirmation in the event the plan has impaired classes have been corrected. See 11 U.S.C. § 1129(a)(8)(A), (10) and (b).

The title to Part IV.B.2, *Treatment of non-accepting classes of secured claims, general unsecured claims, and interests*, is revised for clarity to exclude priority claimants. See 11 U.S.C. § 1129(b). Also, the requirement that the proponent must request confirmation pursuant to section 1129(b) of the Bankruptcy Code is added.

In Part IV.D.2, *Ability to make future plan payments and operate without further reorganization*, the requirement that the plan proponent show that the business will have sufficient cash flow to operate the business, in addition to making the required plan payments, is new. See 11 U.S.C. § 1129(a)(11).

In Part V.A., *Discharge of Debtor*, the third option is revised to delete the reference to Rule 4007(c) and to clarify that corporations will not be discharged of debts to the extent specified in section 1141(d)(6) of the Bankruptcy Code.

In the title to Exhibit G, *Projections of Cash Flow for Post–Confirmation Period*, the reference to "and Earnings" is deleted to ensure consistency given the disparate ways in which "earnings" can be interpreted.

The caption block for the disclosure statement is formatted for a non-individual debtor. An individual chapter 11 debtor should use the caption block formatted for individual debtors, including a joint case involving more than one individual debtor, such as the caption found in Official Form B309I.

Form B425C. Monthly Operating Report for Small Business Under Chapter 11

Debtor Name _____

United States Bankruptcy Court for the: _____ District of _____
(State)

Case number: _____

☐ Check if this is an
amended filing

Official Form 425C

Monthly Operating Report for Small Business Under Chapter 11   12/17

Month: _____   Date report filed: _____
                                                                MM / DD / YYYY

Line of business: _____   NAISC code: _____

In accordance with title 28, section 1746, of the United States Code, I declare under penalty of perjury that I have examined the following small business monthly operating report and the accompanying attachments and, to the best of my knowledge, these documents are true, correct, and complete.

Responsible party: _____

Original signature of responsible party _____

Printed name of responsible party _____

1. Questionnaire

Answer all questions on behalf of the debtor for the period covered by this report, unless otherwise indicated.

		Yes	No	N/A
	If you answer *No* to any of the questions in lines 1-9, attach an explanation and label it *Exhibit A*.			
1.	Did the business operate during the entire reporting period?	☐	☐	☐
2.	Do you plan to continue to operate the business next month?	☐	☐	☐
3.	Have you paid all of your bills on time?	☐	☐	☐
4.	Did you pay your employees on time?	☐	☐	☐
5.	Have you deposited all the receipts for your business into debtor in possession (DIP) accounts?	☐	☐	☐
6.	Have you timely filed your tax returns and paid all of your taxes?	☐	☐	☐
7.	Have you timely filed all other required government filings?	☐	☐	☐
8.	Are you current on your quarterly fee payments to the U.S. Trustee or Bankruptcy Administrator?	☐	☐	☐
9.	Have you timely paid all of your insurance premiums?	☐	☐	☐
	If you answer *Yes* to any of the questions in lines 10-18, attach an explanation and label it *Exhibit B*.			
10.	Do you have any bank accounts open other than the DIP accounts?	☐	☐	☐
11.	Have you sold any assets other than inventory?	☐	☐	☐
12.	Have you sold or transferred any assets or provided services to anyone related to the DIP in any way?	☐	☐	☐
13.	Did any insurance company cancel your policy?	☐	☐	☐
14.	Did you have any unusual or significant unanticipated expenses?	☐	☐	☐
15.	Have you borrowed money from anyone or has anyone made any payments on your behalf?	☐	☐	☐
16.	Has anyone made an investment in your business?	☐	☐	☐

Form B425C

Debtor Name _____   Case number_____

17. Have you paid any bills you owed before you filed bankruptcy?   ☐ ☐ ☐

18. Have you allowed any checks to clear the bank that were issued before you filed bankruptcy?   ☐ ☐ ☐

2. Summary of Cash Activity for All Accounts

19. **Total opening balance of all accounts**

    This amount must equal what you reported as the cash on hand at the end of the month in the previous month. If this is your first report, report the total cash on hand as of the date of the filing of this case. $ _____

20. **Total cash receipts**

    Attach a listing of all cash received for the month and label it *Exhibit C*. Include all cash received even if you have not deposited it at the bank, collections on receivables, credit card deposits, cash received from other parties, or loans, gifts, or payments made by other parties on your behalf. Do not attach bank statements in lieu of *Exhibit C*.

    Report the total from *Exhibit C* here. $ _____

21. **Total cash disbursements**

    Attach a listing of all payments you made in the month and label it *Exhibit D*. List the date paid, payee, purpose, and amount. Include all cash payments, debit card transactions, checks issued even if they have not cleared the bank, outstanding checks issued before the bankruptcy was filed that were allowed to clear this month, and payments made by other parties on your behalf. Do not attach bank statements in lieu of *Exhibit D*.

    Report the total from *Exhibit D* here.   − $ _____

22. **Net cash flow**

    Subtract line 21 from line 20 and report the result here.
    This amount may be different from what you may have calculated as *net profit*.   + $ _____

23. **Cash on hand at the end of the month**

    Add line 22 + line 19. Report the result here.

    Report this figure as the *cash on hand at the beginning of the month* on your next operating report.   = $ _____

    This amount may not match your bank account balance because you may have outstanding checks that have not cleared the bank or deposits in transit.

3. Unpaid Bills

Attach a list of all debts (including taxes) which you have incurred since the date you filed bankruptcy but have not paid. Label it *Exhibit E*. Include the date the debt was incurred, who is owed the money, the purpose of the debt, and when the debt is due. Report the total from *Exhibit E* here.

24. **Total payables** $ _____

    (Exhibit E)

Debtor Name _____   Case number_____

4. Money Owed to You

Attach a list of all amounts owed to you by your customers for work you have done or merchandise you
have sold. Include amounts owed to you both before, and after you filed bankruptcy. Label it *Exhibit F*.
Identify who owes you money, how much is owed, and when payment is due. Report the total from
Exhibit F here.

25. **Total receivables** $ _____

    (Exhibit F)

5. Employees

26. What was the number of employees when the case was filed?   _____

27. What is the number of employees as of the date of this monthly report?   _____

6. Professional Fees

28. How much have you paid this month in professional fees related to this bankruptcy case? $ _____

29. How much have you paid in professional fees related to this bankruptcy case since the case was filed? $ _____

30. How much have you paid this month in other professional fees? $ _____

31. How much have you paid in total other professional fees since filing the case? $ _____

7. Projections

Compare your actual cash receipts and disbursements to what you projected in the previous month.
Projected figures in the first month should match those provided at the initial debtor interview, if any.

	Column A		Column B		Column C
	Projected	−	**Actual**	=	**Difference**
	Copy lines 35-37 from the previous month's report.		Copy lines 20-22 of this report.		Subtract Column B from Column A.
32. **Cash receipts**	$ _____	−	$ _____	=	$ _____
33. **Cash disbursements**	$ _____	−	$ _____	=	$ _____
34. **Net cash flow**	$ _____	−	$ _____	=	$ _____

35. Total projected cash receipts for the next month: $ _____

36. Total projected cash disbursements for the next month: − $ _____

37. Total projected net cash flow for the next month: = $ _____

Form B425C

OFFICIAL FORMS

Debtor Name _____   Case number_____

8. Additional Information

If available, check the box to the left and attach copies of the following documents.

☐ 38. Bank statements for each open account (redact all but the last 4 digits of account numbers).

☐ 39. Bank reconciliation reports for each account.

☐ 40. Financial reports such as an income statement (profit & loss) and/or balance sheet.

☐ 41. Budget, projection, or forecast reports.

☐ 42. Project, job costing, or work-in-progress reports.

Official Form 425C   Monthly Operating Report for Small Business Under Chapter 11   page 4

(Added Dec. 1, 2017.)

ADVISORY COMMITTEE NOTES

Official Form 425C, *Monthly Operating Report for Small Business Under Chapter 11*, replaces Official Form 25C, *Small Business Monthly Operating Report*. It is revised as part of the Forms Modernization Project, which was designed so that persons completing the forms would do so accurately and completely. To facilitate this, Official Form 425C is renumbered and includes formatting and stylistic changes throughout the form. The form requires basic financial information that the Internal Revenue Service recommends that businesses maintain.

The form is revised to add a checkbox to indicate if the report is an amended filing. It also clarifies that persons completing the form on behalf of the debtor should answer all questions for the period covered by the report, unless otherwise indicated. All instructions indicating that the U.S. Trustee may waive the attachments to the form are eliminated.

The form is reorganized. The previous sections for Tax and Banking Information are eliminated as redundant of informa-

tion requested elsewhere within the form. The previous sections for *Income, Summary of Cash on Hand, Expenses, and Cash Profit* are revised and incorporated into Section 2, *Summary of Cash Activity for All Accounts.*

In Part 1, *Questionnaire*, a third checkbox column option, "N/A," has been added to indicate if the question is not applicable. New exhibits to be attached provide explanations for any negative responses to questions 1 through 9 (Exhibit A) and any affirmative answers to questions 10 through 18 (Exhibit B). The questions are reorganized and renumbered, and several are revised. Question 1 is revised to ask whether the business operated during the period. Question 8, regarding the payment of quarterly fees under 28 U.S.C. § 1930(a)(6), is revised to include payments to the bankruptcy administrator. Question 15 is expanded to include payments made on the debtor's behalf. The question whether the debtor has paid anything to an attorney or other professionals is eliminated, as redundant of information disclosed in Part 6. A new question 17 is added inquiring whether the debtor has allowed any checks to clear the bank that were issued before the bankruptcy case.

Part 2, *Summary of Cash Activity for All Accounts*, clarifies and simplifies the reporting of the debtor's cash on hand during the period, and the letters of the attached exhibits are revised. References to "income," "expenses," and "cash profit" are eliminated. Line 19 clarifies that the cash on hand at the beginning of the month is the same as the cash on hand reported at the end of the previous month (or the commencement of the case if no prior report has been submitted). Net cash flow during the month, calculated in line 22, is equal to total cash receipts in line 20 (as itemized in Exhibit C) less total cash disbursements in line 21 (as itemized in Exhibit D). Net cash flow is added to the beginning balance to calculate the cash on hand at the end of the month in line 23. The form is revised to add explanations of the receipts and disbursements to be included in Exhibits C and D, as well as an instruction to clarify that bank statements should not be submitted in lieu of the exhibits.

In Part 3, *Unpaid Bills*, the exhibit letter is revised to Exhibit E.

In Part 4, *Money Owed to You*, the exhibit letter is revised to Exhibit F.

In Part 6, *Professional Fees*, the subheadings "Bankruptcy Related" and "Non–Bankruptcy Related" are eliminated.

Part 7, *Projections*, is revised to compare the debtor's actual cash receipts, cash disbursements, and net cash flow for the month to the projections in the previous month's report (or if the case is new, that the debtor reported at the initial debtor interview). See 11 U.S.C. § 308(b)(2) and (3). References to "income," "expenses," "cash profit," and the 180 day look-back period are eliminated.

Part 8, *Additional Information*, is revised to clarify which documents should be attached, if available and regardless of whether the debtor prepares them internally. These documents are: (1) redacted bank statements for each open account; (2) bank reconciliation reports for each account; (3) financial reports such as an income statement (profit & loss) or balance sheet; (4) budget, projection, or forecast reports; and (5) project, job casting, or work-in-progress reports.

The caption block for this form is formatted for a non-individual debtor. An individual chapter 11 debtor should use the caption block formatted for individual debtors, including a joint case involving more than one individual debtor, such as the caption found in Official Form B309I.

Form B426. Periodic Report Regarding Value, Operations and Profitability of Entities in Which the Debtor's Estate Holds a Substantial or Controlling Interest

Fill in this information to identify the case:
Debtor Name _____
United States Bankruptcy Court for the:_____ District of _____   (State)
Case number: _____

Official Form 426

Periodic Report Regarding Value, Operations, and Profitability of Entities in Which the Debtor's Estate Holds a Substantial or Controlling Interest
12/17

This is the *Periodic Report* as of [＿＿＿＿] on the value, operations, and profitability of those entities in which a Debtor holds, or two or more Debtors collectively hold, a substantial or controlling interest (a "Controlled Non-Debtor Entity"), as required by Bankruptcy Rule 2015.3. For purposes of this form, "Debtor" shall include the estate of such Debtor.

[Name of Debtor] holds a substantial or controlling interest in the following entities:

Name of Controlled Non-Debtor Entity	Interest of the Debtor	Tab #

This *Periodic Report* contains separate reports (*Entity Reports*) on the value, operations, and profitability of each Controlled Non-Debtor Entity.

Each *Entity Report* consists of five exhibits.

Exhibit A contains the most recently available: balance sheet, statement of income (*loss*), statement of cash flows, and a statement of changes in shareholders' or partners' equity (*deficit*) for the period covered by the *Entity Report*, along with summarized footnotes.

Exhibit B describes the Controlled Non-Debtor Entity's business operations.

Exhibit C describes claims between the Controlled Non-Debtor Entity and any other Controlled Non-Debtor Entity.

Exhibit D describes how federal, state or local taxes, and any tax attributes, refunds, or other benefits, have been allocated between or among the Controlled Non-Debtor Entity and any Debtor or any other Controlled Non-Debtor Entity and includes a copy of each tax sharing or tax allocation agreement to which the Controlled Non-Debtor Entity is a party with any other Controlled Non-Debtor Entity.

Exhibit E describes any payment, by the Controlled Non-Debtor Entity, of any claims, administrative expenses or professional fees that have been or could be asserted against any Debtor, or the incurrence of any obligation to make such payments, together with the reason for the entity's payment thereof or incurrence of any obligation with respect thereto.

This *Periodic Report* must be signed by a representative of the trustee or debtor in possession.

Official Form 426   Periodic Report About Controlled Non-Debtor Entities' Value, Operations, and Profitability   page 1

Debtor Name _____   Case number_____

The undersigned, having reviewed the *Entity Reports* for each Controlled Non-Debtor Entity, and being familiar with the Debtor's financial affairs, verifies under the penalty of perjury that to the best of his or her knowledge, (I) this *Periodic Report* and the attached *Entity Reports* are complete, accurate, and truthful to the best of his or her knowledge, and (II) the Debtor did not cause the creation of any entity with actual deliberate intent to evade the requirements of Bankruptcy Rule 2015.3

For non-Individual Debtors:	✗ _____
	Signature of Authorized Individual
	_____
	Printed name of Authorized Individual
	Date _____
	MM / DD /YYYY

For Individual Debtors:	✗ _____	✗ _____
	Signature of Debtor 1	Signature of Debtor 2
	_____	_____
	Printed name of Debtor 1	Printed name of Debtor 2
	Date _____	Date _____
	MM / DD /YYYY	MM / DD /YYYY

Official Form 426   Periodic Report About Controlled Non-Debtor Entity's Value, Operations, and Profitability   page **2**

Debtor Name _____   Case number_____

Exhibit A: Financial Statements for [Name of Controlled Non-Debtor Entity]

Debtor Name _____   Case number_____

Exhibit A-1: Balance Sheet for [Name of Controlled Non-Debtor Entity] **as of** [date]

[Provide a balance sheet dated as of the end of the most recent 3-month period of the current fiscal year and as of the end of the preceding fiscal year.

Describe the source of this information.]

Form B426

OFFICIAL FORMS

Debtor Name _____   Case number_____

Exhibit A-2: Statement of Income (*Loss*) for [Name of Controlled Non-Debtor Entity] for period ending [date]

[Provide a statement of income (*loss*) for the following periods:

(i) For the initial report:

  a. the period between the end of the preceding fiscal year and the end of the most recent 3-month period of the current fiscal year; and

  b. the prior fiscal year.

(ii) For subsequent reports, since the closing date of the last report.

Describe the source of this information.]

Debtor Name _____   Case number_____

Exhibit A-3: Statement of Cash Flows for [Name of Controlled Non-Debtor Entity] **for period ending** [date]

[Provide a statement of changes in cash position for the following periods:

(i) For the initial report:

    a. the period between the end of the preceding fiscal year and the end of the most recent 3-month period of the current fiscal year; and

    b. the prior fiscal year.

(ii) For subsequent reports, since the closing date of the last report.

Describe the source of this information.]

Form B426

Debtor Name _____   Case number_____

Exhibit A-4: Statement of Changes in Shareholders'/Partners' Equity (*Deficit*) for [Name of Controlled Non-Debtor Entity]
for period ending [date]

[Provide a statement of changes in shareholders'/partners equity (*deficit*) for the following periods:

(i) For the initial report:

    a. the period between the end of the preceding fiscal year and the end of the most recent 3-month period of
      the current fiscal year; and

    b. the prior fiscal year.

(ii) For subsequent reports, since the closing date of the last report.

Describe the source of this information.]

Debtor Name _____   Case number_____

Exhibit B: Description of Operations for [Name of Controlled Non-Debtor Entity]

[Describe the nature and extent of the Debtor's interest in the Controlled Non-Debtor Entity.

Describe the business conducted and intended to be conducted by the Controlled Non-Debtor Entity, focusing on the entity's dominant business segments.

Describe the source of this information.]

Form B426

Debtor Name _____   Case number_____

Exhibit C: Description of Intercompany Claims

[List and describe the Controlled Non-Debtor Entity's claims against any other Controlled Non-Debtor Entity, together with the basis for such claims and whether each claim is contingent, unliquidated or disputed.

Describe the source of this information.]

Debtor Name _____   Case number_____

Exhibit D: Allocation of Tax Liabilities and Assets

[Describe how income, losses, tax payments, tax refunds, or other tax attributes relating to federal, state, or local taxes have been allocated between or among the Controlled Non-Debtor Entity and one or more other Controlled Non-Debtor Entities.

Include a copy of each tax sharing or tax allocation agreement to which the entity is a party with any other Controlled Non-Debtor Entity.

Describe the source of this information.]

Form B426

Debtor Name _____   Case number_____

Exhibit E: Description of Controlled Non-Debtor Entity's payments of Administrative Expenses, or Professional Fees otherwise payable by a Debtor

[Describe any payment made, or obligations incurred (or claims purchased), by the Controlled Non-Debtor Entity in connection with any claims, administrative expenses, or professional fees that have been or could be asserted against any Debtor.

Describe the source of this information.]

(Added Dec. 1, 2017.)

ADVISORY COMMITTEE NOTES

Official Form 426, *Periodic Report Regarding Value, Operations, and Profitability of Entities in Which the Debtor's Estate Holds a Substantial or Controlling Interest*, is revised and renumbered as part of the Forms Modernization Project. It implements section 419 of the Bankruptcy Abuse Prevention and Consumer Protection Act of 2005 ("BAPCPA"), Pub. L. No. 109–8, 119 Stat. 23 (April 20, 2005), which requires a chapter 11 debtor to file periodic reports on the profitability of any entities in which the estate holds a substantial or controlling interest. The form is to be used when required by Rule 2015.3, with such variations as may be approved by the court pursuant to subdivisions (d) and (e) of that rule.

In addition to formatting revisions, certain aspects of Official Form 426 are changed to make the form easier for the debtor to complete and to better identify the kinds of information that a debtor must disclose in accordance with section 419 of BAPCPA and Rule 2015.3.

Official Form 426 limits its application to entities in which the debtor has a substantial or controlling interest, which the rule defines as a "Controlled Non–Debtor Entity." The scope of this defined term is guided by subdivisions (a) and (c) of Rule 2015.3.

Official Form 426 eliminates the requirement to file a valuation of the Controlled Non–Debtor Entity. Exhibit A to Official Form 426 requires only periodic filings of the Controlled Non–Debtor Entity's most recently available balance sheet, statement of income (loss), statement of cash flows, and statement of changes in shareholders' or partners' equity (*deficit*), together with summarized footnotes for such financial statements. If any of these financial statements are not available, the debtor can seek relief under Rule 2015.3(d).

Exhibit B to Official Form 426 requires a description of the Controlled Non–Debtor Entity's business, which was required by Exhibit C of former Rule 26.

Exhibits C, D, and E to Official Form 426 are new. Exhibit C requires a description of claims between a Controlled Non–Debtor Entity and any other Controlled Non–Debtor Entity. Exhibit D requires disclosure of information relating to the

---

allocation of taxable income, losses, and other attributes among Controlled Non–Debtor Entities. Exhibit E requires disclosure about a Controlled Non–Debtor Entity's payment of claims or administrative expenses that would otherwise have been payable by a debtor.

The caption block for this form is formatted for a non-individual debtor. An individual chapter 11 debtor should use the caption block formatted for individual debtors, including a joint case involving more than one individual debtor, such as the caption found in Official Form 309I.

Form B427

Form B427. **Cover Sheet for Reaffirmation Agreement**

Fill in this information to identify your case:

Debtor 1 _____
         First Name   Middle Name   Last Name

Debtor 2 _____
(Spouse, if filing) First Name   Middle Name   Last Name

United States Bankruptcy Court for the: _____ District of _____
                                                        (State)

Case number _____
(If known)

Official Form 427

Cover Sheet for Reaffirmation Agreement   12/15

Anyone who is a party to a reaffirmation agreement may fill out and file this form. Fill it out completely, attach it to the reaffirmation agreement, and file the documents within the time set under Bankruptcy Rule 4008.

Part 1:	Explain the Repayment Terms of the Reaffirmation Agreement

1. Who is the creditor?

   _____
   Name of the creditor

2. How much is the debt?

   On the date that the bankruptcy case is filed $_____

   To be paid under the reaffirmation agreement $_____

   $_____ per month for _____ months (if fixed interest rate)

3. What is the Annual Percentage Rate (APR) of interest? (See Bankruptcy Code § 524(k)(3)(E).)

   Before the bankruptcy case was filed _____ %

   Under the reaffirmation agreement _____ % ☐ Fixed rate
                                                         ☐ Adjustable rate

4. Does collateral secure the debt?

   ☐ No
   ☐ Yes. Describe the collateral. _____

          Current market value $_____

5. Does the creditor assert that the debt is nondischargeable?

   ☐ No
   ☐ Yes. Attach an explanation of the nature of the debt and the basis for contending that the debt is nondischargeable.

6. Using information from *Schedule I: Your Income* (Official Form 106I) and *Schedule J: Your Expenses* (Official Form 106J), fill in the amounts.

   Income and expenses reported on Schedules I and J

   6a. Combined monthly income from line 12 of Schedule I $_____

   6b. Monthly expenses from line 22c of Schedule J   – $_____

   6c. Monthly payments on all reaffirmed debts not listed on Schedule J   – $_____

   6d. Scheduled net monthly income $_____
   Subtract lines 6b and 6c from 6a.
   If the total is less than 0, put the number in brackets.

   Income and expenses stated on the reaffirmation agreement

   6e. Monthly income from all sources after payroll deductions $_____

   6f. Monthly expenses   – $_____

   6g. Monthly payments on all reaffirmed debts not included in monthly expenses   – $_____

   6h. Present net monthly income $_____
   Subtract lines 6f and 6g from 6e.
   If the total is less than 0, put the number in brackets.

Official Form 427   Cover Sheet for Reaffirmation Agreement   270
                                                                          page 1

Debtor 1 _____ Case number (if known) _____

7. Are the income amounts on lines 6a and 6e different?
- ☐ No
- ☐ Yes. Explain why they are different and complete line 10. _____

8. Are the expense amounts on lines 6b and 6f different?
- ☐ No
- ☐ Yes. Explain why they are different and complete line 10. _____

9. Is the net monthly income in line 6h less than 0?
- ☐ No
- ☐ Yes. A presumption of hardship arises (unless the creditor is a credit union).
  Explain how the debtor will make monthly payments on the reaffirmed debt and pay other living expenses. Complete line 10.

10. Debtor's certification about lines 7-9

If any answer on lines 7-9 is Yes, the debtor must sign here.

If all the answers on lines 7-9 are No, go to line 11.

I certify that each explanation on lines 7-9 is true and correct.

✗ _____ ✗ _____
Signature of Debtor 1   Signature of Debtor 2 (Spouse Only in a Joint Case)

11. Did an attorney represent the debtor in negotiating the reaffirmation agreement?
- ☐ No
- ☐ Yes. Has the attorney executed a declaration or an affidavit to support the reaffirmation agreement?
  - ☐ No
  - ☐ Yes

Part 2: Sign Here

Whoever fills out this form must sign here.

I certify that the attached agreement is a true and correct copy of the reaffirmation agreement between the parties identified on this Cover Sheet for Reaffirmation Agreement.

✗ _____ Date _____
Signature   MM / DD / YYYY

Printed Name

Check one:
- ☐ Debtor or Debtor's Attorney
- ☐ Creditor or Creditor's Attorney

Official Form 427   Cover Sheet for Reaffirmation Agreement   page 2

(Added Dec. 1, 2015.)

ADVISORY COMMITTEE NOTES

Official Form 427, *Cover Sheet for Reaffirmation Agreement*, is revised and renumbered as part of the Forms Modernization Project. The form replaces former Official Form 27, *Reaffirmation Agreement Cover Sheet*. To make it easier to understand, the form is reformatted, and legal terms are explained more fully or replaced with commonly understood terms.

The calculation of the debtor's net monthly income is expanded to include the debtor's net monthly income at the time the bankruptcy petition is filed, as well as the debtor's net monthly income at the time of the reaffirmation agreement. Rather than requiring filers to state their relationship to the case, checkboxes are provided for the debtor or the debtor's attorney and for the creditor or the creditor's attorney.

Line 3 of the form has been changed to clarify the requirement to disclose an annual percentage rate of interest. Section 524(k)(3)(E) of the Bankruptcy Code defines the "Annual Percentage Rate" to be disclosed in connection with a reaffirmation agreement. Line 3 of the form now includes a reference to that Code provision, which in appropriate circumstances permits disclosure of the simple interest rate as the Annual Percentage Rate.

DIRECTOR'S FORMS

Form B1040. Adversary Proceeding Cover Sheet

B1040 (FORM 1040) (12/15)

ADVERSARY PROCEEDING COVER SHEET (Instructions on Reverse)	ADVERSARY PROCEEDING NUMBER (Court Use Only)

PLAINTIFFS	DEFENDANTS

ATTORNEYS (Firm Name, Address, and Telephone No.)	ATTORNEYS (If Known)

PARTY (Check One Box Only)
- ☐ Debtor
- ☐ U.S. Trustee/Bankruptcy Admin
- ☐ Creditor
- ☐ Other
- ☐ Trustee

PARTY (Check One Box Only)
- ☐ Debtor
- ☐ U.S. Trustee/Bankruptcy Admin
- ☐ Creditor
- ☐ Other
- ☐ Trustee

CAUSE OF ACTION (WRITE A BRIEF STATEMENT OF CAUSE OF ACTION, INCLUDING ALL U.S. STATUTES INVOLVED)

NATURE OF SUIT

(Number up to five (5) boxes starting with lead cause of action as 1, first alternative cause as 2, second alternative cause as 3, etc.)

FRBP 7001(1) – Recovery of Money/Property
- ☐ 11-Recovery of money/property - §542 turnover of property
- ☐ 12-Recovery of money/property - §547 preference
- ☐ 13-Recovery of money/property - §548 fraudulent transfer
- ☐ 14-Recovery of money/property - other

FRBP 7001(2) – Validity, Priority or Extent of Lien
- ☐ 21-Validity, priority or extent of lien or other interest in property

FRBP 7001(3) – Approval of Sale of Property
- ☐ 31-Approval of sale of property of estate and of a co-owner - §363(h)

FRBP 7001(4) – Objection/Revocation of Discharge
- ☐ 41-Objection / revocation of discharge - §727(c),(d),(e)

FRBP 7001(5) – Revocation of Confirmation
- ☐ 51-Revocation of confirmation

FRBP 7001(6) – Dischargeability
- ☐ 66-Dischargeability - §523(a)(1),(14),(14A) priority tax claims
- ☐ 62-Dischargeability - §523(a)(2), false pretenses, false representation, actual fraud
- ☐ 67-Dischargeability - §523(a)(4), fraud as fiduciary, embezzlement, larceny

(continued next column)

FRBP 7001(6) – Dischargeability (continued)
- ☐ 61-Dischargeability - §523(a)(5), domestic support
- ☐ 68-Dischargeability - §523(a)(6), willful and malicious injury
- ☐ 63-Dischargeability - §523(a)(8), student loan
- ☐ 64-Dischargeability - §523(a)(15), divorce or separation obligation (other than domestic support)
- ☐ 65-Dischargeability - other

FRBP 7001(7) – Injunctive Relief
- ☐ 71-Injunctive relief – imposition of stay
- ☐ 72-Injunctive relief – other

FRBP 7001(8) Subordination of Claim or Interest
- ☐ 81-Subordination of claim or interest

FRBP 7001(9) Declaratory Judgment
- ☐ 91-Declaratory judgment

FRBP 7001(10) Determination of Removed Action
- ☐ 01-Determination of removed claim or cause

Other
- ☐ SS-SIPA Case - 15 U.S.C. §§78aaa et.seq.
- ☐ 02-Other (e.g. other actions that would have been brought in state court if unrelated to bankruptcy case)

☐ Check if this case involves a substantive issue of state law	☐ Check if this is asserted to be a class action under FRCP 23
☐ Check if a jury trial is demanded in complaint	Demand $
Other Relief Sought	

Form B1040

B1040 (FORM 1040) (12/15)

BANKRUPTCY CASE IN WHICH THIS ADVERSARY PROCEEDING ARISES		
NAME OF DEBTOR	BANKRUPTCY CASE NO.	
DISTRICT IN WHICH CASE IS PENDING	DIVISION OFFICE	NAME OF JUDGE
RELATED ADVERSARY PROCEEDING (IF ANY)		
PLAINTIFF	DEFENDANT	ADVERSARY PROCEEDING NO.
DISTRICT IN WHICH ADVERSARY IS PENDING	DIVISION OFFICE	NAME OF JUDGE
SIGNATURE OF ATTORNEY (OR PLAINTIFF)		
DATE	PRINT NAME OF ATTORNEY (OR PLAINTIFF)	

INSTRUCTIONS

The filing of a bankruptcy case creates an "estate" under the jurisdiction of the bankruptcy court which consists of all of the property of the debtor, wherever that property is located. Because the bankruptcy estate is so extensive and the jurisdiction of the court so broad, there may be lawsuits over the property or property rights of the estate. There also may be lawsuits concerning the debtor's discharge. If such a lawsuit is filed in a bankruptcy court, it is called an adversary proceeding.

A party filing an adversary proceeding must also must complete and file Form 1040, the Adversary Proceeding Cover Sheet, unless the party files the adversary proceeding electronically through the court's Case Management/Electronic Case Filing system (CM/ECF). (CM/ECF captures the information on Form 1040 as part of the filing process.) When completed, the cover sheet summarizes basic information on the adversary proceeding. The clerk of court needs the information to process the adversary proceeding and prepare required statistical reports on court activity.

The cover sheet and the information contained on it do not replace or supplement the filing and service of pleadings or other papers as required by law, the Bankruptcy Rules, or the local rules of court. The cover sheet, which is largely self-explanatory, must be completed by the plaintiff's attorney (or by the plaintiff if the plaintiff is not represented by an attorney). A separate cover sheet must be submitted to the clerk for each complaint filed.

Plaintiffs and Defendants. Give the names of the plaintiffs and defendants exactly as they appear on the complaint.

Attorneys. Give the names and addresses of the attorneys, if known.

Party Check the most appropriate box in the first column for the plaintiffs and the second column for the defendants.

Demand. Enter the dollar amount being demanded in the complaint.

Signature. This cover sheet must be signed by the attorney of record in the box on the second page of the form. If the plaintiff is represented by a law firm, a member of the firm must sign. If the plaintiff is pro se, that is, not represented by an attorney, the plaintiff must sign.

(Added Dec. 1, 2015.)

**Form B1130.   Motion, Notice and Order
for Adequate Protection Payments
and Opportunity to Object**

B1130 (Form 1130) (12/17)

United States Bankruptcy Court

_____ District of _____

In re _____, Debtor   Case No. _____

                                                Chapter   13

**Motion, Notice and Order for Adequate Protection Payments
and Opportunity to Object**

The Debtor, states as follows:

1. On _____, the Debtor(s) filed a petition under Title 11 commencing a Chapter 13 case.

2. The debtor proposes to make adequate protection payments, pursuant to §1326 (a) (1) (c) beginning no later than 30 days after the petition date, to the holders of the allowed secured claims and in the amounts specified below:

Secured Creditor	Collateral Description	Adequate Protection Payment

3. The Debtor will make the adequate protection payments, until the debtor's plan is confirmed, in the following manner:

□ (a) The Trustee will disburse the payments monthly from the plan payments received from the debtor.

□ (b) The debtor will disburse the payments monthly, and will (1) reduce the plan payments made to the Trustee and (2) provide evidence of such payment to the Trustee, such as a copy of a check or money order, that includes the date and amount of the payment.

□ (c) Other: _____.

Dated:_____   _____
                                              Debtor

                                 By:_____
                                              Counsel

                                 Approved:_____
                                    Chapter 13 Trustee

DIRECTOR'S FORMS

B1130 (Form 1130) (12/17)

United States Bankruptcy Court

_____ District of _____

In re _____, Debtor   Case No. _____

                                              Chapter   13

Order for Adequate Protection Payments and Opportunity to Object

This case coming before the Court on the Debtor's notice of Proposed Adequate Protection Payments, It is hereby ordered that the Debtor or Trustee is authorized to make the Adequate Protection Payment as set forth therein.

       IF A CREDITOR OR OTHER PARTY IN INTEREST HAS ANY OBJECTION TO THE ADEQUATE PROTECTION PAYMENTS DETAILED IN THIS ORDER, A WRITTEN OBJECTION MUST BE FILED WITH THE U.S. BANKRUPTCY COURT CLERK WITHIN 21 DAYS OF THE DATE THIS ORDER IS ENTERED.

Dated:_____

                                             _____
                                           United States Bankruptcy Judge

I, _____, Counsel for the Debtor, hereby certify that I have today, the ____ day of _____, _____, mailed a copy of (this) (the foregoing) Notice of Adequate Protection and Order _____ to the following Creditor(s) in the following manner: (Name and address of creditors served)

(Added Dec. 1, 2017.)

Form B1310. Exemplification Certificate

B1310 (Form 1310) (12/15)

United States Bankruptcy Court

_____ District Of _____

In re

Case No. _____

Debtor

EXEMPLIFICATION CERTIFICATE

I, _____, clerk of the bankruptcy court for this district and keeper of the records and seal of the court, certify that the documents attached are true copies of

now remaining among the records of the court. In testimony of this statement, I sign my name, and affix the seal of this court at _____, in the State of _____, this _____.

[Seal of Court]

_____
Clerk of the Bankruptcy Court

I, _____, bankruptcy judge for this district certify that _____ is and was at the date of the above certificate clerk of the bankruptcy court for this district, duly appointed and sworn, and keeper of the records and seal of the court, and that the above certificate of the clerk and the clerk's attestation are in due form of law.

_____
Date

_____
Bankruptcy Judge

I, _____, clerk of the bankruptcy court for this district and keeper of the seal of the court, certify that the Honorable _____ is and was on the date of the above certificate a judge of this court, duly appointed and sworn; and that I am well acquainted with this handwriting and official signature and know and certify the signature written above to be that of the judge.

In testimony of this statement, I sign my name, and affix the seal of the court at _____, in the State of _____, this _____

[Seal of Court]

_____
Clerk of the Bankruptcy Court

Form B1310

Instructions Form B1310 (12/15)

EXEMPLIFICATION CERTIFICATE

This form is required by some states when a document is certified by a federal court for filing with a state or local authority. It is only necessary for the clerk to execute the form when a person requests that the form be completed. It is suggested, however, that the clerk keep a record of the situations in which a request is made, so that the clerk can anticipate the need for the form in the future.

At its September 1997 meeting, the Judicial Conference fixed the fee for preparation of an Exemplification Certificate at twice the fee for certifying a document. As of December 1, 2014, the current fee for certification is $21. Bankruptcy Court Miscellaneous Fee Schedule, Item 2.

Remember that the exemplification is for use with state courts. Pursuant to treaty, for certification of documents to be filed in a foreign country an apostille must be employed. Only a district court clerk can issue an apostille.

(Added Dec. 1, 2015.)

**Form B1320.   Application for Search
of Bankruptcy Records**

B1320 (Form 1320) (12/16)

UNITED STATES BANKRUPTCY COURT
_____ **District Of** _____

APPLICATION FOR SEARCH OF BANKRUPTCY RECORDS *

Name of individual or business that is the subject of the search:	Social-Security No. or Individual Taxpayer-Identification No. (TIN) of Subject:
	Employer Tax-Identification No. (EIN) (if any) of Subject:

Please search your records for the following information regarding the individual or business named above:
- ◻ pending or closed bankruptcy cases in this district;
- ◻ pending or closed adversary proceedings;
- ◻ judgments/evidence of satisfaction of judgments; and
- ◻ other [describe briefly]

Please search for the period from _____ to _____.

A fee of $31.00 is charged for each name or item searched. Payment by check or money order must be enclosed. Please do not send cash through the mail.

Name, address, and phone number of the person requesting the search:

CERTIFICATE OF SEARCH

The undersigned clerk hereby certifies the following results of a diligent search of the records of the court:
[Check only the items for which a search was requested and a fee paid.]

A. Bankruptcy Cases:
- ◻ None found.
- ◻ Case filed on _____ *(date)*.
  - ◻ Voluntary   ◻ Involuntary
  - ◻ Pending   ◻ Closed on _____ *(date)*.
  - ◻ Discharge granted on _____ *(date)*.

B. Adversary Proceedings:
- ◻ None found.
- ◻ Subject is a party to the following proceeding:

_____ *(Plaintiff)* v. _____ *(Defendant)*
Adversary Proceeding No._____, filed on _____ *(date)*.
◻ Pending   ◻ Closed on_____ *(date)*.
Disposition: ◻ Dismissed on _____ *(date)*.
◻ Final Judgment entered on _____ *(date)*.
Case Number of Related Bankruptcy Case _____

_____ Clerk of the Bankruptcy Court

Date: _____   By: _____ Deputy Clerk

* This form may contain complete social-security numbers. It should not be filed electronically.

(Added Dec. 1, 2015; and amended Dec. 1, 2016.)

Form B1330.   Claims Register

B1330 (Form 1330) (12/15)

CLAIMS REGISTER   Page No. _____

NAME OF DEBTOR			CASE NUMBER
	NAME AND ADDRESS OF CLAIMANT (AND NAME AND ADDRESS OF ATTORNEY, IF ANY)	AMOUNT OF CLAIMS FILED AND ALLOWED	REMARKS
CLAIM NO.		FILED $	
DATE FILED		ALLOWED $	
CLAIM NO.		FILED $	
DATE FILED		ALLOWED $	
CLAIM NO.		FILED $	
DATE FILED		ALLOWED $	
CLAIM NO.		FILED $	
DATE FILED		ALLOWED $	
CLAIM NO.		FILED $	
DATE FILED		ALLOWED $	
CLAIM NO.		FILED $	
DATE FILED		ALLOWED $	
CLAIM NO.		FILED $	
DATE FILED		ALLOWED $	
CLAIM NO.		FILED $	
DATE FILED		ALLOWED $	

(Added Dec. 1, 2015.)

Form B2000. Required Lists, Schedules, Statements, and Fees

B2000 (Form 2000) (12/18)

UNITED STATES BANKRUPTCY COURT
REQUIRED LISTS, SCHEDULES, STATEMENTS, AND FEES
Voluntary Chapter 7 Case

☐ **Filing Fee of $245.** If the fee is to be paid in installments or the debtor requests a waiver of the fee, the debtor must be an individual and must file a signed application for court approval. Official Form 103A or 103B and Fed.R.Bankr.P. 1006(b), (c).

☐ **Administrative fee of $75 and trustee surcharge of $15.** If the debtor is an individual and the court grants the debtor's request, these fees are payable in installments or may be waived.

☐ **Voluntary Petition for Individuals Filing for Bankruptcy** (Official Form 101) or **Voluntary Petition for Non-Individuals Filing for Bankruptcy** (Official Form 201); **Names and addresses of all creditors** of the debtor. Must be filed WITH the petition. Fed.R.Bankr.P. 1007(a)(1).

☐ **Notice to Individual Debtor with Primarily Consumer Debts** under 11 U.S.C. § 342(b) (Director's Form 2010), if applicable. Required if the debtor is an individual with primarily consumer debts. The notice must be GIVEN to the debtor before the petition is filed. Certification that the notice has been given must be FILED with the petition or within 15 days. 11 U.S.C. §§ 342(b), 521(a)(1)(B)(iii), 707(a)(3). Official Form 101 contains spaces for the certification.

☐ **Bankruptcy Petition Preparer's Notice, Declaration, and Signature** (Official Form 119). Required if a "bankruptcy petition preparer" prepares the petition. Must be submitted WITH the petition. 11 U.S.C. § 110(h)(2).

☐ **Statement About Your Social Security Numbers** (Official Form 121). Required if the debtor is an individual. Must be submitted WITH the petition. Fed.R.Bankr.P. 1007(f).

☐ **Credit Counseling Requirement** (Official Form 101); **Certificate of Credit Counseling and Debt Repayment Plan**, if applicable; **Section 109(h)(3) certification or § 109(h)(4) request**, if applicable. If applicable, the Certificate of Credit Counseling and Debt Repayment Plan must be filed with the petition or within 14 days. If applicable, the § 109(h)(3) certification or the § 109(h)(4) request must be filed WITH the petition. Fed.R.Bankr.P. 1007(b)(3), (c).

☐ **Statement disclosing compensation paid or to be paid to a "bankruptcy petition preparer"** (Director's Form 2800). Required if a "bankruptcy petition preparer" prepares the petition. Must be submitted WITH the petition. 11 U.S.C. §110(h)(2).

☐ **Statement of Your Current Monthly Income** (Official Form 122A). Required if the debtor is an individual. Must be filed with the petition or within 14 days. Fed.R.Bankr.P. 1007(b), (c).

☐ **Schedules of assets and liabilities** (Official Forms 106 or 206). Must be filed with the petition or within 14 days. Fed.R.Bankr.P. 1007(b),(c).

☐ **Schedule of Executory Contracts and Unexpired Leases** (Schedule G of Official Form 106 or 206). Must be filed with the petition or within 14 days. Fed.R.Bankr.P. 1007(b), (c).

☐ **Schedules of Your Income and Your Expenses** (Schedules I and J of Official Form 106). If the debtor is an individual, Schedules I and J of Official Form 106 must be filed with the petition or within 14 days. 11 U.S.C. § 521(1) and Fed.R.Bankr.P. 1007(b), (c).

☐ **Statement of financial affairs** (Official Form 107 or 207). Must be filed with the petition or within 14 days. Fed.R.Bankr.P. 1007(b), (c).

☐ **Copies of all payment advices or other evidence of payment** received by the debtor from any employer within 60 days before the filing of the petition. Required if the debtor is an individual. Must be filed with the petition or within 14 days. Fed.R.Bankr.P. 1007(b), (c).

☐ **Statement of Intention for Individuals Filing Under Chapter 7** (Official Form 108). Required ONLY if the debtor is an individual and the schedules of assets and liabilities contain debts secured by property of the estate or personal property subject to an unexpired lease. Must be filed within 30 days or by the date set for the Section 341 meeting of creditors, whichever is earlier. 11 U.S.C. §§ 362(h) and 521(a)(2).

☐ **Statement disclosing compensation paid or to be paid to the attorney** for the debtor (Director's Form 2030). Required if the debtor is represented by an attorney. Must be filed within 14 days or any other date set by the court. 11 U.S.C. § 329 and Fed.R.Bankr.P. 2016(b).

☐ **Certification About a Financial Management Course** (Official Form 423), if applicable. Required if the debtor is an individual, unless the course provider has notified the court that the debtor has completed the course. Must be filed within 60 days of the first date set for the meeting of creditors. 11 U.S.C. § 727(a)(11) and Fed.R.Bankr.P. 1007(b)(7), (c).

Form B2000

DIRECTOR'S FORMS

B2000 (Form 2000) (12/18)

REQUIRED LISTS, SCHEDULES, STATEMENTS, AND FEES
Voluntary Chapter 11 Case

☐ **Filing fee of $1,167.** If the fee is to be paid in installments, the debtor must be an individual and must file a signed application for court approval. Official Form 103A and Fed.R.Bankr.P. 1006(b).

☐ **Administrative fee of $550.** If the debtor is an individual and the court grants the debtor's request, this fee is payable in installments.

☐ **United States Trustee quarterly fee.** The debtor, or trustee if one is appointed, is required also to pay a fee to the United States trustee at the conclusion of each calendar quarter until the case is dismissed or converted to another chapter. The calculation of the amount to be paid is set out in 28 U.S.C. § 1930(a)(6). As authorized by 28 U.S.C. § 1930(a)(7), the quarterly fee is paid to the clerk of court in chapter 11 cases in Alabama and North Carolina.

☐ **Voluntary Petition for Individuals Filing for Bankruptcy (Official Form 101)** or **Voluntary Petition for Non-Individuals Filing for Bankruptcy** (Official Form 201). **Names and addresses of all creditors** of the debtor. Must be filed WITH the petition. Fed.R.Bankr.P. 1007(a)(1).

☐ **Notice to Individual Debtor with Primarily Consumer Debts** under 11 U.S.C. § 342(b) (Director's Form 2010), if applicable. Required if the debtor is an individual with primarily consumer debts. The notice must be GIVEN to the debtor before the petition is filed. Certification that the notice has been given must be FILED with the petition or within 15 days. 11 U.S.C. §§ 342(b), 521(a)(1)(B)(iii), 1112(e). Official Form 101 contains spaces for the certification.

☐ **Bankruptcy Petition Preparer's Notice, Declaration, and Signature (Official Form 119).** Required if a "bankruptcy petition preparer" prepares the petition. Must be submitted WITH the petition. 11 U.S.C. § 110(b)(2).

☐ **Statement About Your Social Security Numbers (Official Form 121).** Required if the debtor is an individual. Must be submitted WITH the petition. Fed.R.Bankr.P. 1007(f).

☐ **Credit Counseling Requirement (Official Form 101); Certificate of Credit Counseling and Debt Repayment Plan,** if applicable; **Section 109(h)(3) certification or § 109(h)(4) request,** if applicable. If applicable, the Certificate of Credit Counseling and Debt Repayment Plan must be filed with the petition or within 14 days. If applicable, the § 109(h)(3) certification or the § 109(h)(4) request must be filed WITH the petition. Fed.R.Bankr.P. 1007(b)(3), (c).

☐ **Statement disclosing compensation paid or to be paid to a "bankruptcy petition preparer"** (Director's Form 2800). Required if a "bankruptcy petition preparer" prepares the petition. Must be submitted WITH the petition. 11 U.S.C. §110(h)(2).

☐ **Statement of Your Current Monthly Income (Official Form 122B).** Required if the debtor is an individual. Must be filed with the petition or within 14 days. Fed.R.Bankr.P. 1007(b), (c).

☐ **For Individual Chapter 11 Cases: List of Creditors Who Have the 20 Largest Unsecured Claims Against You and Are Not Insiders** (Official Form 104) or **Chapter 11 or Chapter 9 Cases: List of Creditors Who Have the 20 Largest Unsecured Claims and Are Not Insiders** (Official Form 204). Must be filed WITH the petition. Fed.R.Bankr.P. 1007(d).

☐ **Names and addresses of equity security holders of the debtor.** Must be filed with the petition or within 14 days, unless the court orders otherwise. Fed.R.Bankr.P. 1007(a)(3).

☐ **Schedules of Assets and Liabilities (Official Form 106 or 206).** Must be filed with the petition or within 14 days. Fed.R.Bankr.P. 1007(b), (c).

☐ **Schedule of Executory Contracts and Unexpired Leases (Schedule G of Official Form 106 or 206).** Must be filed with the petition or within 14 days. Fed.R.Bankr.P. 1007(b), (c).

☐ **Schedules of Current Income and Expenditures.** If the debtor is an individual, Schedules I and J of Official Form 106 must be used for this purpose. Must be filed with the petition or within 14 days. 11 U.S.C. § 521(1) and Fed.R.Bankr.P. 1007(b), (c).

☐ **Statement of Financial Affairs (Official Form 107 or 207).** Must be filed with the petition or within 14 days. Fed.R.Bankr.P. 1007(b), (c).

☐ **Copies of all payment advices or other evidence of payment** received by debtor from any employer within 60 days before the filing of the petition. Required if the debtor is an individual. Must be filed WITH the petition or within 14 days. Fed.R.Bankr.P. 1007(b), (c).

☐ **Statement disclosing compensation paid or to be paid to the attorney** for the debtor (Director's Form 2030), if applicable. Required if the debtor is represented by an attorney. Must be filed within 14 days or any other date set by the court. 11 U.S.C. § 329 and Fed.R.Bankr.P. 2016(b).

☐ **Certification About a Financial Management Course (Official Form 423),** if applicable. Required if the debtor is an individual and § 1141(d)(3) applies, unless the course provider has notified the court that the debtor has completed the course. Must be filed no later than the date of the last payment under the plan or the filing of a motion for a discharge under § 1141(d)(5)(B). 11 U.S.C. § 1141(d)(3) and Fed.R.Bankr.P. 1007(b)(7), (c).

☐ **Statement concerning pending proceedings of the kind described in § 522(q)(1),** if applicable. Required if the debtor is an individual and has claimed exemptions under state or local law as described in § 522(b)(3) in excess of $160,375*. Must be filed no later than the date of the last payment made under the plan or the date of the filing of a motion for a discharge under § 1141(d)(5)(B). 11 U.S.C. § 1141(d)(5)(C) and Fed.R.Bankr.P. 1007(b)(8), (c).

* Amount subject to adjustment on 4/01/19, and every three years thereafter with respect to cases commenced on or after the date of adjustment.

B2000 (Form 2000) (12/18)

REQUIRED LISTS, SCHEDULES, STATEMENTS, AND FEES
Chapter 12 Case

☐ **Filing Fee of $200.** If the fee is to be paid in installments, the debtor must be an individual and must file a signed application for court approval. Official Form 103A and Fed.R.Bankr.P. 1006(b).

☐ **Administrative fee of $75.** If the debtor is an individual and the court grants the debtor's request, this fee is payable in installments.

☐ **Voluntary Petition for Individuals Filing for Bankruptcy** (Official Form 101) or **Voluntary Petition for Non-Individuals Filing for Bankruptcy** (Official Form 201). **Names and addresses of all creditors** of the debtor. Must be filed WITH the petition. Fed.R.Bankr.P. 1007(a)(1).

☐ **Notice to Individual Debtor with Primarily Consumer Debts** under 11 U.S.C. § 342(b) (Director's Form 2010), if applicable. Required if the debtor is an individual with primarily consumer debts. The notice must be GIVEN to the debtor before the petition is filed. Certification that the notice has been given must be FILED with the court in a timely manner. 11 U.S.C. §§ 342(b), 521(a)(1)(B)(iii). Official Form 101 contains spaces for the certification.

☐ **Bankruptcy Petition Preparer's Notice, Declaration, and Signature** (Official Form 119). Required if a "bankruptcy petition preparer" prepares the petition. Must be submitted WITH the petition. 11 U.S.C. § 110(b)(2).

☐ **Statement of Your Social Security Numbers** (Official Form 121). Required if the debtor is an individual. Must be submitted WITH the petition. Fed.R.Bankr.P. 1007(f).

☐ **Credit Counseling Requirement** (Official Form 101); **Certificate of Credit Counseling and Debt Repayment Plan**, if applicable; **Section 109(h)(3) certification or § 109(h)(4) request**, if applicable. If applicable, the Certificate of Credit Counseling and Debt Repayment Plan must be filed with the petition or within 14 days. If applicable, the § 109(h)(3) certification or the § 109(h)(4) request must be filed WITH the petition. Fed.R.Bankr.P. 1007(b)(3), (c).

☐ **Statement disclosing compensation paid or to be paid to a "bankruptcy petition preparer"** (Director's Form 2800). Required if a "bankruptcy petition preparer" prepares the petition. Must be submitted WITH the petition. 11 U.S.C. §110(h)(2).

☐ **Schedules of Assets and Liabilities** (Official Form 106 or 206). Must be filed with the petition or within 14 days. Fed.R.Bankr.P. 1007(b), (c).

☐ **Schedule of Executory Contracts and Unexpired Leases** (Schedule G of Official Form 106 or 206). Must be filed with the petition or within 14 days. Fed.R.Bankr.P. 1007(b), (c).

☐ **Schedules of Current Income and Expenditures.** If the debtor is an individual, Schedule I and J of Official Form 106 must be used for this purpose. Must be filed with the petition or within 14 days. 11 U.S.C. § 521(1) and Fed.R.Bankr.P. 1007(b), (c).

☐ **Statement of Financial Affairs** (Official Form 107 or 207). Must be filed with the petition or within 14 days. Fed.R.Bankr.P. 1007(b), (c).

☐ **Copies of all payment advices** or other evidence of payment received by the debtor from any employer within 60 days before the filing of the petition if the debtor is an individual. Must be filed with the petition or within 14 days. Fed.R.Bankr.P. 1007(b), (c).

☐ **Statement disclosing compensation paid or to be paid to the attorney** for the debtor (Director's Form 2030), if applicable. Must be filed within 14 days or any other date set by the court. 11 U.S.C. § 329 and Fed.R.Bankr.P. 2016(b).

☐ **Chapter 12 Plan.** Must be filed within 90 days. 11 U.S.C. § 1221.

☐ **Statement concerning pending proceedings of the kind described in § 522(q)(1)**, if applicable. Required if the debtor is an individual and has claimed exemptions under state or local law as described in §522(b)(3) in excess of $160,375*. Must be filed no later than the date of the last payment made under the plan or the date of the filing of a motion for a discharge under § 1228(b). 11 U.S.C. § 1228(f) and Fed.R.Bankr.P. 1007(b)(8), (c).

* Amount subject to adjustment on 4/01/19, and every three years thereafter with respect to cases commenced on or after the date of adjustment.

Form B2000

B2000 (Form 2000) (12/18)

REQUIRED LISTS, SCHEDULES, STATEMENTS, AND FEES
Chapter 13 Case

☐   **Filing fee of $235.** If the fee is to be paid in installments, the debtor must file a signed application for court approval. Official Form 103A and Fed.R.Bankr.P. 1006(b).

☐   **Administrative fee of $75.** If the court grants the debtor's request, this fee is payable in installments.

☐   **Voluntary Petition for Individuals Filing for Bankruptcy** (Official Form 101). **Names and addresses of all creditors** of the debtor. Must be filed WITH the petition. Fed.R.Bankr.P. 1007(a)(1).

☐   **Notice to Individual Debtor with Primarily Consumer Debts** under 11 U.S.C. § 342(b) (Director's Form 2010), if applicable. Required if the debtor is an individual with primarily consumer debts. The notice must be GIVEN to the debtor before the petition is filed. Certification that the notice has been given must be FILED with the petition or within 15 days. 11 U.S.C. §§ 342(b), 521(a)(1)(B)(iii), 1307(c)(9). Official Form 101 contains spaces for the certification.

☐   **Bankruptcy Petition Preparer's Notice, Declaration, and Signature** (Official Form 119). Required if a "bankruptcy petition preparer" prepares the petition. Must be submitted WITH the petition. 11 U.S.C. § 110(h)(2).

☐   **Statement of Social Security Number** (Official Form 121). Must be submitted WITH the petition. Fed.R.Bankr.P. 1007(f).

☐   **Credit Counseling Requirement** (Official Form 101); **Certificate of Credit Counseling and Debt Repayment Plan,** if applicable; **Section 109(h)(3) certification or § 109(h)(4) request,** if applicable. If applicable, the Certificate of Credit Counseling and Debt Repayment Plan must be filed with the petition or within 14 days. If applicable, the § 109(h)(3) certification or the § 109(h)(4) request must be filed WITH the petition. Fed.R.Bankr.P. 1007(b)(3), (c).

☐   **Statement disclosing compensation paid or to be paid to a "bankruptcy petition preparer"** (Director's Form 2800). Required if a "bankruptcy petition preparer" prepares the petition. Must be submitted WITH the petition. 11 U.S.C. §110(h)(2).

☐   **Statement of Your Current Monthly Income** (Official Form 122C). Must be filed with the petition or within 14 days. Fed.R.Bankr.P. 1007.

☐   **Schedules of Assets and Liabilities** (Official Form 106). Must be filed with the petition or within 14 days. Fed.R.Bankr.P. 1007(b), (c).

☐   **Schedule of Executory Contracts and Unexpired Leases** (Schedule G of Official Form 106). Must be filed with the petition or within 14 days. Fed.R.Bankr.P. 1007(b), (c).

☐   **Schedules of Current Income and Expenditures** (Schedules I and J of Official Form 106). Must be filed with the petition or within 14 days. 11 U.S.C. § 521(1) and Fed.R.Bankr.P. 1007(b), (c).

☐   **Statement of Financial Affairs** (Official Form 107). Must be filed with the petition or within 14 days. Fed.R.Bankr.P. 1007(b), (c).

☐   **Copies of all payment advices or other evidence of payment** received by the debtor from any employer within 60 days before the filing of the petition. Must be filed with the petition or within 14 days. Fed.R.Bankr.P. 1007(b), (c).

☐   **Chapter 13 Plan.** (Official Form 113), or local form plan (check with your local court for required plan version). Fed.R.Bankr.P 3015.1. Must be filed with the petition or within 14 days. Fed.R.Bankr.P. 3015.

☐   **Statement disclosing compensation paid or to be paid to the attorney** for the debtor (Director's Form 2030), if applicable. Must be filed within 14 days or any other date set by the court. 11 U.S.C. § 329 and Fed.R.Bankr.P. 2016(b).

☐   **Certification About a Financial Management Course** (Official Form 423), if applicable. Must be filed no later than the date of the last payment made under the plan or the date of the filing of a motion for a discharge under § 1328(b), unless the course provider has notified the court that the debtor has completed the course. 11 U.S.C. § 1328(g)(1) and Fed.R.Bankr.P. 1007(b)(7), (c).

☐   **Statement concerning pending proceedings of the kind described in § 522(q)(1),** if applicable. Required if the debtor has claimed exemptions under state or local law as described in §522(b)(3) in excess of $160,375*. Must be filed no later than the date of the last payment made under the plan or the date of the filing of a motion for a discharge under § 1328(b). 11 U.S.C. § 1328(h) and Fed.R.Bankr.P. 1007(b)(8), (c).

* Amount subject to adjustment on 4/01/19, and every three years thereafter with respect to cases commenced on or after the date of adjustment.

(Added Dec. 1, 2015; and amended Apr. 1, 2016; Dec. 1, 2018.)

Form B2010. Notice Required by 11
U.S.C. § 342(b) for Individuals
Filing for Bankruptcy

Notice Required by 11 U.S.C. § 342(b) for
Individuals Filing for Bankruptcy (Form 2010)

This notice is for you if:

- You are an individual filing for bankruptcy, and

- Your debts are primarily consumer debts. *Consumer debts* are defined in 11 U.S.C. § 101(8) as "incurred by an individual primarily for a personal, family, or household purpose."

The types of bankruptcy that are available to individuals

Individuals who meet the qualifications may file under one of four different chapters of the Bankruptcy Code:

- Chapter 7   Liquidation

- Chapter 11—   Reorganization

- Chapter 12—   Voluntary repayment plan for family farmers or fishermen

- Chapter 13   Voluntary repayment plan for individuals with regular income

You should have an attorney review your decision to file for bankruptcy and the choice of chapter.

Chapter 7:   Liquidation

	$245	filing fee
	$75	administrative fee
+	$15	trustee surcharge
	$335	total fee

Chapter 7 is for individuals who have financial difficulty preventing them from paying their debts and who are willing to allow their non-exempt property to be used to pay their creditors. The primary purpose of filing under chapter 7 is to have your debts discharged. The bankruptcy discharge relieves you after bankruptcy from having to pay many of your pre-bankruptcy debts. Exceptions exist for particular debts, and liens on property may still be enforced after discharge. For example, a creditor may have the right to foreclose a home mortgage or repossess an automobile.

However, if the court finds that you have committed certain kinds of improper conduct described in the Bankruptcy Code, the court may deny your discharge.

You should know that even if you file chapter 7 and you receive a discharge, some debts are not discharged under the law. Therefore, you may still be responsible to pay:

- most taxes;

- most student loans;

- domestic support and property settlement obligations;

- most fines, penalties, forfeitures, and criminal restitution obligations; and

- certain debts that are not listed in your bankruptcy papers.

You may also be required to pay debts arising from:

- fraud or theft;

- fraud or defalcation while acting in breach of fiduciary capacity;

- intentional injuries that you inflicted; and

- death or personal injury caused by operating a motor vehicle, vessel, or aircraft while intoxicated from alcohol or drugs.

If your debts are primarily consumer debts, the court can dismiss your chapter 7 case if it finds that you have enough income to repay creditors a certain amount. You must file *Chapter 7 Statement of Your Current Monthly Income* (Official Form 122A–1) if you are an individual filing for bankruptcy under chapter 7. This form will determine your current monthly income and compare whether your income is more than the median income that applies in your state.

If your income is not above the median for your state, you will not have to complete the other chapter 7 form, the *Chapter 7 Means Test Calculation* (Official Form 122A-2).

If your income is above the median for your state, you must file a second form —the *Chapter 7 Means Test Calculation* (Official Form 122A–2). The calculations on the form— sometimes called the *Means Test*—deduct from your income living expenses and payments on certain debts to determine any amount available to pay unsecured creditors. If your income is more than the median income for your state of residence and family size, depending on the results of the *Means Test,* the U.S. trustee, bankruptcy administrator, or creditors can file a motion to dismiss your case under § 707(b) of the Bankruptcy Code. If a motion is filed, the court will decide if your case should be dismissed. To avoid dismissal, you may choose to proceed under another chapter of the Bankruptcy Code.

If you are an individual filing for chapter 7 bankruptcy, the trustee may sell your property to pay your debts, subject to your right to exempt the property or a portion of the proceeds from the sale of the property. The property, and the proceeds from property that your bankruptcy trustee sells or liquidates that you are entitled to, is called *exempt property*. Exemptions may enable you to keep your home, a car, clothing, and household items or to receive some of the proceeds if the property is sold.

Exemptions are not automatic. To exempt property, you must list it on *Schedule C: The Property You Claim as Exempt* (Official Form 106C). If you do not list the property, the trustee may sell it and pay all of the proceeds to your creditors.

Chapter 11: Reorganization

	$1,167	filing fee
+	$550	administrative fee
	$1,717	total fee

Chapter 11 is often used for reorganizing a business, but is also available to individuals. The provisions of chapter 11 are too complicated to summarize briefly.

Read These Important Warnings

Because bankruptcy can have serious long-term financial and legal consequences, including loss of your property, you should hire an attorney and carefully consider all of your options before you file. Only an attorney can give you legal advice about what can happen as a result of filing for bankruptcy and what your options are. If you do file for bankruptcy, an attorney can help you fill out the forms properly and protect you, your family, your home, and your possessions.

Although the law allows you to represent yourself in bankruptcy court, you should understand that many people find it difficult to represent themselves successfully. The rules are technical, and a mistake or inaction may harm you. If you file without an attorney, you are still responsible for knowing and following all of the legal requirements.

You should not file for bankruptcy if you are not eligible to file or if you do not intend to file the necessary documents.

Bankruptcy fraud is a serious crime; you could be fined and imprisoned if you commit fraud in your bankruptcy case. Making a false statement, concealing property, or obtaining money or property by fraud in connection with a bankruptcy case can result in fines up to $250,000, or imprisonment for up to 20 years, or both. 18 U.S.C. §§ 152, 1341, 1519, and 3571.

Chapter 12: Repayment plan for family farmers or fishermen

	$200	filing fee
+	$75	administrative fee
	$275	total fee

Similar to chapter 13, chapter 12 permits family farmers and fishermen to repay their debts over a period of time using future earnings and to discharge some debts that are not paid.

Chapter 13: Repayment plan for individuals with regular income

	$235	filing fee
+	$75	administrative fee
	$310	total fee

Chapter 13 is for individuals who have regular income and would like to pay all or part of their debts in installments over a period of time and to discharge some debts that are not paid. You are eligible for chapter 13 only if your debts are not more than certain dollar amounts set forth in 11 U.S.C. § 109.

Under chapter 13, you must file with the court a plan to repay your creditors all or part of the money that you owe them, usually using your future earnings. If the court approves your plan, the court will allow you to repay your debts, as adjusted by the plan, within 3 years or 5 years, depending on your income and other factors.

After you make all the payments under your plan, many of your debts are discharged. The debts that are not discharged and that you may still be responsible to pay include:

- domestic support obligations,
- most student loans,
- certain taxes,
- debts for fraud or theft,
- debts for fraud or defalcation while acting in a fiduciary capacity,
- most criminal fines and restitution obligations,
- certain debts that are not listed in your bankruptcy papers,
- certain debts for acts that caused death or personal injury, and
- certain long-term secured debts.

Notice Required by 11 U.S.C. U.S.C. § 342(b) for Individuals Filing for Bankruptcy (Form 2010)   page 3

Warning: File Your Forms on Time

Section 521(a)(1) of the Bankruptcy Code requires that you promptly file detailed information about your creditors, assets, liabilities, income, expenses and general financial condition. The court may dismiss your bankruptcy case if you do not file this information within the deadlines set by the Bankruptcy Code, the Bankruptcy Rules, and the local rules of the court.

For more information about the documents and their deadlines, go to:
http://www.uscourts.gov/bkforms/bankruptcy_forms.html#procedure.

Bankruptcy crimes have serious consequences

- If you knowingly and fraudulently conceal assets or make a false oath or statement under penalty of perjury—either orally or in writing—in connection with a bankruptcy case, you may be fined, imprisoned, or both.

- All information you supply in connection with a bankruptcy case is subject to examination by the Attorney General acting through the Office of the U.S. Trustee, the Office of the U.S. Attorney, and other offices and employees of the U.S. Department of Justice.

Make sure the court has your mailing address

The bankruptcy court sends notices to the mailing address you list on *Voluntary Petition for Individuals Filing for Bankruptcy* (Official Form 101). To ensure that you receive information about your case, Bankruptcy Rule 4002 requires that you notify the court of any changes in your address.

A married couple may file a bankruptcy case together—called a *joint case*. If you file a joint case and each spouse lists the same mailing address on the bankruptcy petition, the bankruptcy court generally will mail you and your spouse one copy of each notice, unless you file a statement with the court asking that each spouse receive separate copies.

Understand which services you could receive from credit counseling agencies

The law generally requires that you receive a credit counseling briefing from an approved credit counseling agency. 11 U.S.C. § 109(h). If you are filing a joint case, both spouses must receive the briefing. With limited exceptions, you must receive it within the 180 days *before* you file your bankruptcy petition. This briefing is usually conducted by telephone or on the Internet.

In addition, after filing a bankruptcy case, you generally must complete a financial management instructional course before you can receive a discharge. If you are filing a joint case, both spouses must complete the course.

You can obtain the list of agencies approved to provide both the briefing and the instructional course from:
http://justice.gov/ust/eo/hapcpa/ccde/cc_approved.html.

In Alabama and North Carolina, go to:
http://www.uscourts.gov/FederalCourts/Bankruptcy/BankruptcyResources/ApprovedCredit AndDebtCounselors.aspx.

If you do not have access to a computer, the clerk of the bankruptcy court may be able to help you obtain the list.

Notice Required by 11 U.S.C. U.S.C. § 342(b) for Individuals Filing for Bankruptcy (Form 2010)   page **4**

(Added Dec. 1, 2015.)

Form B2020. Statement of Military Service

B2020 (Form 2020) (12/15)

United States Bankruptcy Court

_____ **District of** _____

In re _____   Case Number _____

Chapter _____

STATEMENT OF MILITARY SERVICE

The Servicemembers' Civil Relief Act of 2003, Pub. L. No. 108-189, provides for the temporary suspension of certain judicial proceedings or transactions that may adversely affect military servicemembers, their dependents, and others. Each party to a bankruptcy case who might be eligible for relief under the act should complete this form and file it with the Bankruptcy Court.

IDENTIFICATION OF SERVICEMEMBER

❑   Self (Debtor, Codebtor, Creditor, Other)

❑   Non-Filing Spouse of Debtor (name)_____

❑   Other   (Name of servicemember)_____

            (Relationship of filer to servicemember)_____

            (Type of liability) _____

TYPE OF MILITARY SERVICE

U.S. Armed Forces (Army, Navy, Air Force, Marine Corps, or Coast Guard) or commissioned officer of the Public Health Service or the National Oceanic and Atmospheric Administration (specify type of service) _____

❑   Active Service since   _____   (date)

❑   Inductee - ordered to report on   _____   (date)

❑   Retired / Discharged   _____   (date)

U.S. Military Reserves and National Guard

❑   Active Service since   _____   (date)

❑   Impending Active Service -orders postmarked   _____   (date)

            Ordered to report on   _____   (date)

❑   Retired /Discharged   _____   (date)

U.S. Citizen Serving with U.S. ally in war or military action (specify ally and war or action)

_____

❑   Active Service since   _____   (date)

❑   Retired/Discharged   _____   (date)

DEPLOYMENT

❑   Servicemember deployed overseas on _____   (date)

        Anticipated completion of overseas tour-of-duty _____   (date)

SIGNATURE

_____

_____   Date _____

(print name)

_Of_   _This statement is for information use only. Filing this statement with the Bankruptcy Court does not constitute an application for or invoke the benefits and relief available under the Servicemembers' Civil Relief Act of 2003._

(Added Dec. 1, 2015.)

Form B2030

**Form B2030. Attorney's Disclosure
of Compensation**

B2030 (Form 2030) (12/15)

United States Bankruptcy Court

_____ District Of _____

In re

Case No. _____

Debtor

Chapter _____

DISCLOSURE OF COMPENSATION OF ATTORNEY FOR DEBTOR

1. Pursuant to 11 U.S.C. § 329(a) and Fed. Bankr. P. 2016(b), I certify that I am the attorney for the above
    named debtor(s) and that compensation paid to me within one year before the filing of the petition in
    bankruptcy, or agreed to be paid to me, for services rendered or to be rendered on behalf of the debtor(s) in
    contemplation of or in connection with the bankruptcy case is as follows:

    For legal services, I have agreed to accept . . . . $_____

    Prior to the filing of this statement I have received . . . . $_____

    Balance Due . . . . $_____

2. The source of the compensation paid to me was:

    ☐ Debtor   ☐ Other (specify)

3. The source of compensation to be paid to me is:

    ☐ Debtor   ☐ Other (specify)

4. ☐ I have not agreed to share the above-disclosed compensation with any other person unless they are
       members and associates of my law firm.

    ☐ I have agreed to share the above-disclosed compensation with a other person or persons who are not
       members or associates of my law firm. A copy of the agreement, together with a list of the names of the
       people sharing in the compensation, is attached.

5. In return for the above-disclosed fee, I have agreed to render legal service for all aspects of the bankruptcy
    case, including:

    a. Analysis of the debtor's financial situation, and rendering advice to the debtor in determining whether to
        file a petition in bankruptcy;

    b. Preparation and filing of any petition, schedules, statements of affairs and plan which may be required;

    c. Representation of the debtor at the meeting of creditors and confirmation hearing, and any adjourned
        hearings thereof;

B2030 (Form 2030) (12/15)

    d.   Representation of the debtor in adversary proceedings and other contested bankruptcy matters;

    e.   [Other provisions as needed]

6.   By agreement with the debtor(s), the above-disclosed fee does not include the following services:

CERTIFICATION

    I certify that the foregoing is a complete statement of any agreement or arrangement for payment to me for representation of the debtor(s) in this bankruptcy proceeding.

Date	_Signature of Attorney_
	Name of law firm

(Added Dec. 1, 2015.)

Form B2040

Form B2040. Notice of Need to File Proof of Claim Due to Recovery of Assets

B2040 (Form 2040) (12/15)

United States Bankruptcy Court
_____ District Of _____

In re _____   Case No. _____

                Debtor*

Address:

                                                Chapter _____

Last four digits of Social-Security or Individual Taxpayer-
Identification (ITIN) No(s).,(if any): _____
Employer Tax-Identification (EIN) No(s).(if any): _____

NOTICE OF NEED TO FILE PROOF OF CLAIM
DUE TO RECOVERY OF ASSETS

NOTICE IS GIVEN THAT:

      The initial notice in this case instructed creditors that it was not necessary to file a proof of claim. Since that notice was sent, assets have been recovered by the trustee.

      Creditors who wish to share in any distribution of funds must file a proof of claim with the clerk of the bankruptcy court at the address below on or before:

> Date:

      Creditors who do not file a proof of claim on or before this date might not share in any distribution from the debtor's estate.

      A proof of claim form may be obtained at www.uscourts.gov or any bankruptcy clerk's office. It may be filed by regular mail. To receive acknowledgment of your filing, you may either enclose a stamped self-addressed envelope and a copy of this proof of claim or you may access the court's PACER system (www.pacer.psc.uscourts.gov) to view your filed proof of claim.

      There is no fee for filing the proof of claim.

      Any creditor who has filed a proof of claim already need not file another proof of claim.

Address of the Bankruptcy Court

Clerk of the Bankruptcy Court

By:_____
                Deputy Clerk
Date:_____

* Set forth all names, including trade names, used by the debtor(s) within the last 8 years. For joint debtors, set forth the last four digits of both social-security numbers or individual taxpayer-identification numbers.

(Added Dec. 1, 2015.)

**Form B2050. Notice to Creditors
and Other Parties in Interest**

B2050 (Form 2050) (12/15)

United States Bankruptcy Court
_____ District Of _____

In re

      Debtor*   Case No. _____

Address:

                                             Chapter _____

Last four digits of Social-Security or Individual Taxpayer-
Identification (ITIN) No(s).,(if any):
Employer Tax-Identification (EIN) No(s).(if any):

NOTICE TO CREDITORS AND OTHER PARTIES IN INTEREST

Notice is given that:

_____
Clerk of the Bankruptcy Court

By:
_____
Deputy Clerk

Date: _____

_____
* _Set forth all names, including trade names, used by the debtor(s) within
the last 8 years. For joint debtors, set forth the last four digits of both
social-security numbers or individual taxpayer-identification numbers._

(Added Dec. 1, 2015.)

Form B2060

**Form B2060. Certificate of Commencement
of Case**

B2060 (Form 2060) (12/15)

United States Bankruptcy Court
_____ District Of _____

In re

     Debtor*

Case No. _____

Address:

Chapter _____

Last four digits of Social-Security or Individual Taxpayer-
Identification (ITIN) No(s).,(if any):
Employer Tax-Identification (EIN) No(s).(if any):

CERTIFICATE OF COMMENCEMENT OF CASE

I certify that on _____ (date),

☐   the above named debtor filed a petition requesting relief
     under chapter _____ of the Bankruptcy Code (title 11
     of the United States Code), or

☐   a petition was filed against the above named debtor under
     chapter _____ of the Bankruptcy Code (title 11 of the
     United States Code), and

☐   that as of the date below the case has not been dismissed.

                           _____
                           Clerk of the Bankruptcy Court

                           By:

                           Deputy Clerk

                           Date: _____

_* Set forth all names, including trade names, used by the debtor(s) within
the last 8 years. For joint debtors, set forth the last four digits of both
social-security numbers or individual taxpayer-identification numbers._

(Added Dec. 1, 2015.)

Form B2070. Certificate of Retention of Debtor in Possession

B2070 (Form 2070) (12/15)

United States Bankruptcy Court
_____ District Of _____

In re
                                                    Case No. _____

    Debtor*

Address:
                                                    Chapter _____

Last four digits of Social-Security or Individual Taxpayer-
Identification (ITIN) No(s).,(if any):
Employer Tax-Identification (EIN) No(s).(if any):

CERTIFICATE OF RETENTION OF DEBTOR IN POSSESSION

    I hereby certify that the above-named debtor continues in possession of its estate as debtor in possession, no trustee having been appointed.

                                         _____
                                       Clerk of the Bankruptcy Court

Date: _____   By:
                                       _____
                                       Deputy Clerk

_____
* Set forth all names, including trade names, used by the debtor(s) within the last 8 years. For joint debtors, set forth the last four digits of both social-security numbers or individual taxpayer-identification numbers.

(Added Dec. 1, 2015.)

Form B2100A

Form B2100A. Transfer of Claim Other Than for Security

B2100A (Form 2100A) (12/15)

United States Bankruptcy Court

_____ District Of _____

In re _____,   Case No. _____

TRANSFER OF CLAIM OTHER THAN FOR SECURITY

A CLAIM HAS BEEN FILED IN THIS CASE or deemed filed under 11 U.S.C. § 1111(a). Transferee hereby gives evidence and notice pursuant to Rule 3001(e)(2), Fed. R. Bankr. P., of the transfer, other than for security, of the claim referenced in this evidence and notice.

_____   _____
Name of Transferee   Name of Transferor

Name and Address where notices to transferee   Court Claim # (if known):
should be sent: Amount of Claim:
                                                 Date Claim Filed:

Phone: _____   Phone: _____
Last Four Digits of Acct #: _____   Last Four Digits of Acct. #: _____

Name and Address where transferee payments
should be sent (if different from above):

Phone: _____
Last Four Digits of Acct #: _____

I declare under penalty of perjury that the information provided in this notice is true and correct to the best of my knowledge and belief.

By:_____   Date:_____
     Transferee/Transferee's Agent

Penalty for making a false statement: Fine of up to $500,000 or imprisonment for up to 5 years, or both. 18 U.S.C. §§ 152 & 3571.

(Added Dec. 1, 2015.)

**Form B2100B. Notice of Transfer
of Claim of Than for Security**

B2100B (Form 2100B) (12/15)

United States Bankruptcy Court

_____ District Of _____

In re _____,   Case No. _____

NOTICE OF TRANSFER OF CLAIM OTHER THAN FOR SECURITY

Claim No. _____ (if known) was filed or deemed filed under 11 U.S.C. § 1111(a) in this case by the alleged transferor. As evidence of the transfer of that claim, the transferee filed a Transfer of Claim Other than for Security in the clerk's office of this court on _____ (date).

Name of Alleged Transferor   Name of Transferee

Address of Alleged Transferor: Address of Transferee:

~~DEADLINE TO OBJECT TO TRANSFER~~

The alleged transferor of the claim is hereby notified that objections must be filed with the court within twenty-one (21) days of the mailing of this notice. If no objection is timely received by the court, the transferee will be substituted as the original claimant without further order of the court.

Date: _____

_____
CLERK OF THE COURT

(Added Dec. 1, 2015.)

Form B2300A

Form B2300A.   Order Confirming Chapter 12 Plan

B2300A (Form 2300A) (12/15)

United States Bankruptcy Court
_____ District Of _____

In re _____   Case No. _____
              Debtor*

Address: _____   Chapter 12

Last four digits of Social-Security or Individual Taxpayer-
Identification (ITIN) No(s).,(if any):
Employer Tax-Identification (EIN) No(s).(if any):

ORDER CONFIRMING CHAPTER 12 PLAN

      The debtor's plan was filed on _____ (date), and was modified on _____ (date). The plan or a summary of the plan was transmitted to creditors pursuant to Bankruptcy Rule 3015. The court finds that the plan meets the requirements of 11 U.S.C. § 1225.

IT IS ORDERED THAT:

The debtor's chapter 12 plan is confirmed, with the following provisions:

    1. Payments:
    Amount of each payment: $_____

    Due date of each payment: the   ☐ _____ day of each month, or
                                   ☐ _____

    Period of payments: ☐ _____ months,
                                ☐ until a _____ % dividend is paid to creditors holding
            allowed unsecured claims, or
                                ☐ _____

    Payable to:
    _____ Standing Trustee
    _____
    _____

    2. Attorney's Fees:
    The debtor's attorney is awarded a fee in the amount of $_____, of which
    $_____ is due and payable from the estate.

    3. [Other provisions as needed] _____

_____   _____
        Date   _Bankruptcy Judge_

* _Set forth all names, including trade names, used by the debtor(s) within the last 8 years. For joint debtors, set forth the last four digits of both social-security numbers or individual taxpayer-identification numbers._

(Added Dec. 1, 2015.)

Form B2300B.   Order Confirming Chapter 13 Plan

B2300B (Form 2300B) (12/15)

United States Bankruptcy Court
_____ District Of _____

In re _____   Case No. _____
                    Debtor*

Address: _____   Chapter 13

Last four digits of Social-Security or Individual Taxpayer-
Identification (ITIN) No(s).,(if any):
Employer Tax-Identification (EIN) No(s).(if any):

ORDER CONFIRMING CHAPTER 13 PLAN

The debtor's plan was filed on _____ (date), and was modified on _____ (date).
The plan or a summary of the plan was transmitted to creditors pursuant to Bankruptcy Rule 3015. The court finds
that the plan meets the requirements of 11 U.S.C. § 1325.

IT IS ORDERED THAT:

The debtor's chapter 13 plan is confirmed, with the following provisions:

1. Payments:
Amount of each payment: $ _____

Due date of each payment: the   ☐ _____ day of each month, or
                                 ☐ _____

Period of payments: ☐ _____ months,
                       ☐ until a _____ % dividend is paid to creditors holding
                       allowed unsecured claims, or
                       ☐ _____

Payable to:
_____ Standing Trustee
_____
_____

2. Attorney's Fees:
The debtor's attorney is awarded a fee in the amount of $_____, of which $_____ is
due and payable from the estate.

3. [Other provisions as needed] _____

_____   _____
        Date   Bankruptcy Judge

*Set forth all names, including trade names, used by the debtor(s) within the last 8 years. For joint debtors, set
forth the last four digits of both social-security numbers or individual taxpayer-identification numbers.*

(Added Dec. 1, 2015.)

Form B2310A. Order Fixing Time to Object to Proposed Modification of Confirmed Chapter 12 Plan

B2310A (Form 2310A) (12/15)

United States Bankruptcy Court
_____ District Of _____

In re

      Debtor*

Case No. _____

Address:

Chapter _____

Last four digits of Social-Security or Individual Taxpayer-
Identification (ITIN) No(s).,(if any):
Employer Tax-Identification (EIN) No(s).(if any):

ORDER FIXING TIME TO OBJECT TO PROPOSED MODIFICATION
OF CONFIRMED CHAPTER 12 PLAN

To the debtor, trustee, and creditors:

_____ filed a proposed modification of the confirmed plan on _____ (date). A copy of the proposed modification is attached.

IT IS ORDERED AND NOTICE IS GIVEN THAT:

1.   The last day for filing a written objection to the proposed modification is:

> Date:

2.   The proponent of the proposed modification is directed to serve a copy or summary of the proposed modification of the plan, together with a copy of this order, on the debtor, the trustee, the United States trustee, and all creditors no later than 21 days before the date set forth above.

3.   Any objection to the proposed modification shall be filed and served on the debtor, the trustee, the United States trustee, and all creditors.

4.   If an objection is filed, a hearing to consider the proposed modification will be held at:

Address	Room
	Date and Time

If no objection is filed, the court may not hold a hearing.

Date: _____   BY THE COURT

_____
United States Bankruptcy Judge

* Set forth all names, including trade names, used by the debtor(s) within the last 8 years. For joint debtors, set forth the last four digits of both social-security numbers or individual taxpayer-identification numbers.

(Added Dec. 1, 2015.)

**Form B2310B. Order Fixing Time to Object
to Proposed Modification of Confirmed
Chapter 13 Plan**

B2310B (Form 2310B) (12/15)

United States Bankruptcy Court
_____ District Of _____

In re

        Debtor*

                                  Case No. _____

Address:

                                    Chapter _____

Last four digits of Social-Security or Individual Taxpayer-
Identification (ITIN) No(s).,(if any):
Employer Tax-Identification (EIN) No(s).(if any):

ORDER FIXING TIME TO OBJECT TO PROPOSED MODIFICATION
OF CONFIRMED CHAPTER 13 PLAN

To the debtor, trustee, and creditors:

               _____filed a proposed modification of the confirmed
plan on _____ (date). A copy of the proposed modification is
attached.

IT IS ORDERED AND NOTICE IS GIVEN THAT:

    1.   The last day for filing a written objection to the proposed
          modification is:

          | Date: |

    2.   The proponent of the proposed modification is directed to
          serve a copy or summary of the proposed modification of the
          plan, together with a copy of this order, on the debtor, the
          trustee, the United States trustee, and all creditors no
          later than 21 days before the date set forth above.

    3.   Any objection to the proposed modification shall be filed
          and served on the debtor, the trustee, the United States
          trustee, and all creditors.

4. If an objection is filed, a hearing to consider the proposed
    modification will be held at:

Address	Room
	Date and Time

If no objection is filed, the court may not hold a hearing.

Date: _____   BY THE COURT

                                    _____
                                    United States Bankruptcy Judge

** Set forth all names, including trade names, used by the debtor(s) within the
last 8 years. For joint debtors, set forth the last four digits of both
social-security numbers or individual taxpayer-identification numbers.*

(Added Dec. 1, 2015.)

Form B2400A.   Reaffirmation Documents

B2400A (Form 2400A) (12/15)

> Check one.
> ☐ Presumption of Undue Hardship
> ☐ No Presumption of Undue Hardship
> *See Debtor's Statement in Support of
> Reaffirmation, Part II below, to determine
> which box to check.*

UNITED STATES BANKRUPTCY COURT
_____ **District of** _____

In re _____,   Case No. _____
　　　　　Debtor

　　　　　　　　　　　　　　　　　　　　　　　　Chapter _____

REAFFIRMATION DOCUMENTS

Name of Creditor: _____

☐ Check this box if Creditor is a Credit Union

I. REAFFIRMATION AGREEMENT

Reaffirming a debt is a serious financial decision. Before entering into this Reaffirmation Agreement, you must review the important disclosures, instructions, and definitions found in Part V of this Reaffirmation Documents packet.

1. Brief description of the original agreement being reaffirmed: _____

　　　　　　　　　　　　　　　　　　　　　　　　　For example, auto loan

2. *AMOUNT REAFFIRMED*:　　　$_____

　　　The Amount Reaffirmed is the entire amount that you are agreeing to pay. This
　　　may include unpaid principal, interest, and fees and costs (if any) arising on or
　　　before the date you sign this Reaffirmation Agreement.

　　　See the definition of "Amount Reaffirmed" in Part V.C below.

3. The *ANNUAL PERCENTAGE RATE* applicable to the Amount Reaffirmed is _____%.

　　　See definition of "Annual Percentage Rate" in Part V.C below.

　　　This is a *(check one)* ☐ Fixed rate　　　　☐ Variable rate

If the loan has a variable rate, the future interest rate may increase or decrease from the Annual Percentage Rate disclosed here.

4. Reaffirmation Agreement Repayment Terms:

    ❐ If fixed term, $_____ per month for _____ months starting on_____ .

    ❐ If not fixed term, describe repayment terms: _____ .

5. Describe the collateral, if any, securing the debt:

       Description: _____
       Current Market Value $_____

6. Did the debt that is being reaffirming arise from the purchase of the collateral described above?

    ❐ Yes   ❐ No

    If yes, what was the purchase price for the collateral? $_____
    If no, what was the amount of the original loan? $_____

7. Detail the changes made by this Reaffirmation Agreement to the most recent credit terms on the reaffirmed debt and any related agreement:

	Terms as of the Date of Bankruptcy	Terms After Reaffirmation
Balance due *(including fees and costs)*	$_____	$_____
Annual Percentage Rate	_____%	_____%
Monthly Payment	$_____	$_____

8. ❐ Check this box if the creditor is agreeing to provide you with additional future credit in connection with this Reaffirmation Agreement. Describe the credit limit, the Annual Percentage Rate that applies to future credit and any other terms on future purchases and advances using such credit: _____
_____

II. DEBTOR'S STATEMENT IN SUPPORT
OF REAFFIRMATION AGREEMENT

1. Were you represented by an attorney during the course of negotiating this agreement?

    Check one.   ❐ Yes   ❐ No

2. Is the creditor a credit union?

    Check one.   ❐ Yes   ❐ No

Form B2400A   DIRECTOR'S FORMS

B2400A (Form 2400A) (12/15)   Page 3

3. If your answer to EITHER question 1. or 2. above is "No" complete a. and b. below.

    a.. My present monthly income and expenses are:

        i. Monthly income from all sources after payroll deductions
        (take-home pay plus any other income) $_____

        ii. Monthly expenses (including all reaffirmed debts except
        this one) $_____

        iii. Amount available to pay this reaffirmed debt (subtract ii. from i.) $_____

        iv. Amount of monthly payment required for this reaffirmed debt $_____

*If the monthly payment on this reaffirmed debt (line iv.) **is greater than** the amount you have available to pay this reaffirmed debt (line iii.), you must check the box at the top of page one that says "Presumption of Undue Hardship." Otherwise, you must check the box at the top of page one that says "No Presumption of Undue Hardship."*

    b. I believe this reaffirmation agreement will not impose an undue hardship on my dependents or on me because:

        Check one of the two statements below, if applicable:

        ❐ I can afford to make the payments on the reaffirmed debt because my monthly income is greater than my monthly expenses even after I include in my expenses the monthly payments on all debts I am reaffirming, including this one.

        ❐ I can afford to make the payments on the reaffirmed debt even though my monthly income is less than my monthly expenses after I include in my expenses the monthly payments on all debts I am reaffirming, including this one, because: _____
_____

        Use an additional page if needed for a full explanation.

4. If your answers to BOTH questions 1. and 2. above were "Yes," check the following statement, if applicable:

        ❐ I believe this reaffirmation agreement is in my financial interest and I can afford to make the payments on the reaffirmed debt.

Also, check the box at the top of page one that says "No Presumption of Undue Hardship."

III. CERTIFICATION BY DEBTOR(S) AND SIGNATURES OF PARTIES

I (We) hereby certify that:

i. I (We) agree to reaffirm the debt described above.

ii. Before signing this reaffirmation agreement, I (we) read the terms disclosed in this Reaffirmation Agreement (Part I) and the Disclosure Statement, Instructions and Definitions included in Part V below;

iii. The Debtor's Statement in Support of Reaffirmation Agreement (Part II above) is true and complete;

iv. I am (We are) entering into this agreement voluntarily and fully informed of my (our) rights and responsibilities; and

v. I (We) have received a copy of this completed and signed Reaffirmation Documents packet.

SIGNATURE(S):

Date _____   Signature _____

                                              Debtor

Date _____   Signature _____

                                          Joint Debtor, if any

If a joint reaffirmation agreement, both debtors must sign.

Reaffirmation Agreement Terms Accepted by Creditor:

Creditor _____   _____

            Print Name   *Address*

_____   _____   _____

Print Name of Representative   *Signature*   *Date*

IV. CERTIFICATION BY DEBTOR'S ATTORNEY (IF ANY)

To be filed only if the attorney represented the debtor during the course of negotiating this agreement.

I hereby certify that: (1) this agreement represents a fully informed and voluntary agreement by the debtor; (2) this agreement does not impose an undue hardship on the debtor or any dependent of the debtor; and (3) I have fully advised the debtor of the legal effect and consequences of this agreement and any default under this agreement.

❑ A presumption of undue hardship has been established with respect to this agreement. In my opinion, however, the debtor is able to make the required payment.

Check box, if the presumption of undue hardship box is checked on page 1 and the creditor is not a Credit Union.

Date _____   Signature of Debtor's Attorney_____

                  Print Name of Debtor's Attorney _____

Form B2400A

V. DISCLOSURE STATEMENT AND INSTRUCTIONS TO DEBTOR(S)

Before agreeing to reaffirm a debt, review the terms disclosed in the Reaffirmation Agreement (Part I) and these additional important disclosures and instructions.

Reaffirming a debt is a serious financial decision. The law requires you to take certain steps to make sure the decision is in your best interest. If these steps, detailed in Part B below, are not completed, the reaffirmation agreement is not effective, even though you have signed it.

A.   DISCLOSURE STATEMENT

1. **What are your obligations if you reaffirm a debt?** A reaffirmed debt remains your personal legal obligation. Your reaffirmed debt is not discharged in your bankruptcy case. That means that if you default on your reaffirmed debt after your bankruptcy case is over, your creditor may be able to take your property or your wages. Your obligations will be determined by the reaffirmation agreement, which may have changed the terms of the original agreement. If you are reaffirming an open end credit agreement, that agreement or applicable law may permit the creditor to change the terms of that agreement in the future under certain conditions.

2. **Are you required to enter into a reaffirmation agreement by any law?** No, you are not required to reaffirm a debt by any law. Only agree to reaffirm a debt if it is in your best interest. Be sure you can afford the payments that you agree to make.

3. **What if your creditor has a security interest or lien?** Your bankruptcy discharge does not eliminate any lien on your property. A "lien" is often referred to as a security interest, deed of trust, mortgage, or security deed. The property subject to a lien is often referred to as collateral. Even if you do not reaffirm and your personal liability on the debt is discharged, your creditor may still have a right under the lien to take the collateral if you do not pay or default on the debt. If the collateral is personal property that is exempt or that the trustee has abandoned, you may be able to redeem the item rather than reaffirm the debt. To redeem, you make a single payment to the creditor equal to the current value of the collateral, as the parties agree or the court determines.

4. **How soon do you need to enter into and file a reaffirmation agreement?** If you decide to enter into a reaffirmation agreement, you must do so before you receive your discharge. After you have entered into a reaffirmation agreement and all parts of this Reaffirmation Documents packet requiring signature have been signed, either you or the creditor should file it as soon as possible. The signed agreement must be filed with the court no later than 60 days after the first date set for the meeting of creditors, so that the court will have time to schedule a hearing to approve the agreement if approval is required.

5. **Can you cancel the agreement?** You may rescind (cancel) your reaffirmation agreement at any time before the bankruptcy court enters your discharge, or during the 60-day period that begins on the date your reaffirmation agreement is filed with the court, whichever occurs later. To rescind (cancel) your reaffirmation agreement, you must notify the creditor that your reaffirmation agreement is rescinded (or canceled). Remember that you can rescind the agreement, even if the court approves it, as long as you rescind within the time allowed.

6. **When will this reaffirmation agreement be effective?**

   a. **If you *were represented* by an attorney during the negotiation of your reaffirmation agreement**

   i. **if the creditor is not a Credit Union**, your reaffirmation agreement becomes effective upon filing with the court unless the reaffirmation is presumed to be an undue hardship in which case the agreement becomes effective only after the court approves it;

   ii. **if the creditor is a Credit Union**, your reaffirmation agreement becomes effective when it is filed with the court.

   b. **If you *were not represented* by an attorney during the negotiation of your reaffirmation agreement**, the reaffirmation agreement will not be effective unless the court approves it. To have the court approve your agreement, you must file a motion. See Instruction 5, below. The court will notify you and the creditor of the hearing on your reaffirmation agreement. You must attend this hearing, at which time the judge will review your reaffirmation agreement. If the judge decides that the reaffirmation agreement is in your best interest, the agreement will be approved and will become effective. However, if your reaffirmation agreement is for a consumer debt secured by a mortgage, deed of trust, security deed, or other lien on your real property, like your home, you do not need to file a motion or get court approval of your reaffirmation agreement.

7. **What if you have questions about what a creditor can do?** If you have questions about reaffirming a debt or what the law requires, consult with the attorney who helped you negotiate this agreement. If you do not have an attorney helping you, you may ask the judge to explain the effect of this agreement to you at the hearing to approve the reaffirmation agreement. When this disclosure refers to what a creditor "may" do, it is not giving any creditor permission to do anything. The word "may" is used to tell you what might occur if the law permits the creditor to take the action.

B. INSTRUCTIONS

1. Review these Disclosures and carefully consider the decision to reaffirm. If you want to reaffirm, review and complete the information contained in the Reaffirmation Agreement (Part I above). If your case is a joint case, both spouses must sign the agreement if both are reaffirming the debt.

2. Complete the Debtor's Statement in Support of Reaffirmation Agreement (Part II above). Be sure that you can afford to make the payments that you are agreeing to make and that you have received a copy of the Disclosure Statement and a completed and signed Reaffirmation Agreement.

3. If you were represented by an attorney during the negotiation of your Reaffirmation Agreement, your attorney must sign and date the Certification By Debtor's Attorney section (Part IV above).

4. You or your creditor must file with the court the original of this Reaffirmation Documents packet and a completed Reaffirmation Agreement Cover Sheet (Official Bankruptcy Form 427).

5. *If you are not represented by an attorney, you must also complete and file with the court a separate document entitled "Motion for Court Approval of Reaffirmation Agreement unless your reaffirmation agreement is for a consumer debt secured by a lien on your real property, such as your home.* You can use Form B2400B to do this.

Form B2400A

C.   **DEFINITIONS**

1.   **"Amount Reaffirmed"** means the total amount of debt that you are agreeing to pay (reaffirm) by entering into this agreement. The amount of debt includes any unpaid fees and costs arising on or before the date you sign this agreement that you are agreeing to pay. Your credit agreement may obligate you to pay additional amounts that arise after the date you sign this agreement. You should consult your credit agreement to determine whether you are obligated to pay additional amounts that may arise after the date of this agreement.

2.   **"Annual Percentage Rate"** means the interest rate on a loan expressed under the rules required by federal law. The annual percentage Rate (as opposed to the "stated interest rate") tells you the full cost of your credit including many of the creditor's fees and charges. You will find the annual percentage rate for your original agreement on the disclosure statement that was given to you when the loan papers were signed or on the monthly statements sent to you for an open end credit account such as a credit card.

3.   **"Credit Union"** means a financial institution as defined in 12 U.S.C. § 461(b)(1)(A)(iv). It is owned and controlled by and provides financial services to its members and typically uses words like "Credit Union" or initials like "C.U." or "F.C.U." in its name.

(Added Dec. 1, 2015.)

Form B2400A/B Alt.   Reaffirmation Agreement

B2400A/B ALT (Form 2400A/B ALT) (12/15)

☐ **Presumption of Undue Hardship**
☐ **No Presumption of Undue Hardship**
(Check box as directed in Part D: Debtor's Statement
in Support of Reaffirmation Agreement.)

UNITED STATES BANKRUPTCY COURT
_____ **District of** _____

In re _____,   Case No. _____
           Debtor   Chapter _____

REAFFIRMATION AGREEMENT
[Indicate all documents included in this filing by checking each applicable box.]

☐ Part A: Disclosures, Instructions, and   ☐ Part D: Debtor's Statement in
    Notice to Debtor (pages 1 - 5)   Support of Reaffirmation Agreement

☐ Part B: Reaffirmation Agreement   ☐ Part E: Motion for Court Approval

☐ Part C: Certification by Debtor's Attorney

*[**Note:** Complete Part E only if debtor was not represented by an attorney during
the course of negotiating this agreement. **Note also:** If you complete Part E, you must
prepare and file Form 2400C ALT - Order on Reaffirmation Agreement.]*

Name of Creditor: _____

☐ *[Check this box if]* Creditor is a Credit Union as defined in §19(b)(1)(a)(iv) of the
    Federal Reserve Act

PART A: DISCLOSURE STATEMENT, INSTRUCTIONS AND NOTICE TO DEBTOR

1.   **DISCLOSURE STATEMENT**

Before Agreeing to Reaffirm a Debt, Review These Important Disclosures:

SUMMARY OF REAFFIRMATION AGREEMENT
This Summary is made pursuant to the requirements of the Bankruptcy Code.

AMOUNT REAFFIRMED

The amount of debt you have agreed to reaffirm: $_____

*The amount of debt you have agreed to reaffirm includes all fees and costs (if any) that have
accrued as of the date of this disclosure. Your credit agreement may obligate you to pay additional
amounts which may come due after the date of this disclosure. Consult your credit agreement.*

Form B2400A/B Alt   DIRECTOR'S FORMS

ANNUAL PERCENTAGE RATE

[The annual percentage rate can be disclosed in different ways, depending on the type of debt.]

a. If the debt is an extension of "credit" under an "open end credit plan," as those terms are defined in § 103 of the Truth in Lending Act, such as a credit card, the creditor may disclose the annual percentage rate shown in (i) below or, to the extent this rate is not readily available or not applicable, the simple interest rate shown in (ii) below, or both.

(i) The Annual Percentage Rate disclosed, or that would have been disclosed, to the debtor in the most recent periodic statement prior to entering into the reaffirmation agreement described in Part B below or, if no such periodic statement was given to the debtor during the prior six months, the annual percentage rate as it would have been so disclosed at the time of the disclosure statement: _____%.

--- And/Or ---

(ii) The simple interest rate applicable to the amount reaffirmed as of the date this disclosure statement is given to the debtor: _____%. If different simple interest rates apply to different balances included in the amount reaffirmed, the amount of each balance and the rate applicable to it are:

$_____ @ _____%;
$_____ @ _____%;
$_____ @ _____%.

b. If the debt is an extension of credit other than under than an open end credit plan, the creditor may disclose the annual percentage rate shown in (I) below, or, to the extent this rate is not readily available or not applicable, the simple interest rate shown in (ii) below, or both.

(i) The Annual Percentage Rate under §128(a)(4) of the Truth in Lending Act, as disclosed to the debtor in the most recent disclosure statement given to the debtor prior to entering into the reaffirmation agreement with respect to the debt or, if no such disclosure statement was given to the debtor, the annual percentage rate as it would have been so disclosed: _____%.

--- And/Or ---

(ii) The simple interest rate applicable to the amount reaffirmed as of the date this disclosure statement is given to the debtor: _____%. If different simple interest rates apply to different balances included in the amount reaffirmed, the amount of each balance and the rate applicable to it are:

$ _____ @ _____ %;
$ _____ @ _____ %;
$ _____ @ _____ %.

c. If the underlying debt transaction was disclosed as a variable rate transaction on the most recent disclosure given under the Truth in Lending Act:

The interest rate on your loan may be a variable interest rate which changes from time to time, so that the annual percentage rate disclosed here may be higher or lower.

d. If the reaffirmed debt is secured by a security interest or lien, which has not been waived or determined to be void by a final order of the court, the following items or types of items of the debtor's goods or property remain subject to such security interest or lien in connection with the debt or debts being reaffirmed in the reaffirmation agreement described in Part B.

<u>Item or Type of Item</u>   <u>Original Purchase Price or Original Amount of Loan</u>

Optional---*At the election of the creditor, a repayment schedule using one or a combination of the following may be provided:*

Repayment Schedule:

Your first payment in the amount of $_____ is due on _____ (date), but the future payment amount may be different. Consult your reaffirmation agreement or credit agreement, as applicable.

— *Or* —

Your payment schedule will be: _____ (number) payments in the amount of $_____ each, payable (monthly, annually, weekly, etc.) on the _____ (day) of each _____ (week, month, etc.), unless altered later by mutual agreement in writing.

— *Or* —

A reasonably specific description of the debtor's repayment obligations to the extent known by the creditor or creditor's representative.

2. INSTRUCTIONS AND NOTICE TO DEBTOR

B2400A/B ALT (Form 2400A/B ALT) (12/15)   4

Reaffirming a debt is a serious financial decision. The law requires you to take certain steps to make sure the decision is in your best interest. If these steps are not completed, the reaffirmation agreement is not effective, even though you have signed it.

1. Read the disclosures in this Part A carefully. Consider the decision to reaffirm carefully. Then, if you want to reaffirm, sign the reaffirmation agreement in Part B (or you may use a separate agreement you and your creditor agree on).

2. Complete and sign Part D and be sure you can afford to make the payments you are agreeing to make and have received a copy of the disclosure statement and a completed and signed reaffirmation agreement.

3. If you were represented by an attorney during the negotiation of your reaffirmation agreement, the attorney must have signed the certification in Part C.

4. If you were not represented by an attorney during the negotiation of your reaffirmation agreement, you must have completed and signed Part E.

5. The original of this disclosure must be filed with the court by you or your creditor. If a separate reaffirmation agreement (other than the one in Part B) has been signed, it must be attached.

6. If the creditor is not a Credit Union and you were represented by an attorney during the negotiation of your reaffirmation agreement, your reaffirmation agreement becomes effective upon filing with the court unless the reaffirmation is presumed to be an undue hardship as explained in Part D. If the creditor is a Credit Union and you were represented by an attorney during the negotiation of your reaffirmation agreement, your reaffirmation agreement becomes effective upon filing with the court.

7. If you were not represented by an attorney during the negotiation of your reaffirmation agreement, it will not be effective unless the court approves it. The court will notify you and the creditor of the hearing on your reaffirmation agreement. You must attend this hearing in bankruptcy court where the judge will review your reaffirmation agreement. The bankruptcy court must approve your reaffirmation agreement as consistent with your best interests, except that no court approval is required if your reaffirmation agreement is for a consumer debt secured by a mortgage, deed of trust, security deed, or other lien on your real property, like your home.

YOUR RIGHT TO RESCIND (CANCEL) YOUR REAFFIRMATION AGREEMENT

You may rescind (cancel) your reaffirmation agreement at any time before the bankruptcy court enters a discharge order, or before the expiration of the 60-day period that begins on the date your reaffirmation agreement is filed with the court, whichever occurs later. To rescind (cancel) your reaffirmation agreement, you must notify the creditor that your reaffirmation agreement is rescinded (or canceled).

Frequently Asked Questions:

What are your obligations if you reaffirm the debt? A reaffirmed debt remains your personal legal obligation. It is not discharged in your bankruptcy case. That means that if you default on your reaffirmed debt after your bankruptcy case is over, your creditor may be able to take your property or your wages. Otherwise, your obligations will be determined by the reaffirmation agreement which may have changed the terms of the original agreement. For example, if you are reaffirming an open end credit agreement, the creditor may be permitted by that agreement or applicable law to change the terms of that agreement in the future under certain conditions.

Are you required to enter into a reaffirmation agreement by any law? No, you are not required to reaffirm a debt by any law. Only agree to reaffirm a debt if it is in your best interest. Be sure you can afford the payments you agree to make.

What if your creditor has a security interest or lien? Your bankruptcy discharge does not eliminate any lien on your property. A "lien" is often referred to as a security interest, deed of trust, mortgage or security deed. Even if you do not reaffirm and your personal liability on the debt is discharged, because of the lien your creditor may still have the right to take the property securing the lien if you do not pay the debt or default on it. If the lien is on an item of personal property that is exempt under your State's law or that the trustee has abandoned, you may be able to redeem the item rather than reaffirm the debt. To redeem, you must make a single payment to the creditor equal to the amount of the allowed secured claim, as agreed by the parties or determined by the court.

NOTE: When this disclosure refers to what a creditor "may" do, it does not use the word "may" to give the creditor specific permission. The word "may" is used to tell you what might occur if the law permits the creditor to take the action. If you have questions about your reaffirming a debt or what the law requires, consult with the attorney who helped you negotiate this agreement reaffirming a debt. If you don't have an attorney helping you, the judge will explain the effect of your reaffirming a debt when the hearing on the reaffirmation agreement is held.

B2400A/B ALT (Form 2400A/B ALT) (12/15)   6

PART B: REAFFIRMATION AGREEMENT.

I (we) agree to reaffirm the debts arising under the credit agreement described below.

1. Brief description of credit agreement:

2. Description of any changes to the credit agreement made as part of this reaffirmation agreement:

SIGNATURE(S):

Borrower: Accepted by creditor:

_____   _____
(Print Name)   (Printed Name of Creditor)

_____   _____
(Signature)   (Address of Creditor)

Date: _____   _____
                                                           (Signature)

Co-borrower, if also reaffirming these debts: _____

_____   (Printed Name and Title of Individual
(Print Name)   Signing for Creditor)

_____   Date of creditor acceptance:
(Signature)

Date: _____   _____

PART C: CERTIFICATION BY DEBTOR'S ATTORNEY (IF ANY).

[To be filed only if the attorney represented the debtor during the course of negotiating this agreement.]

I hereby certify that (1) this agreement represents a fully informed and voluntary agreement by the debtor; (2) this agreement does not impose an undue hardship on the debtor or any dependent of the debtor; and (3) I have fully advised the debtor of the legal effect and consequences of this agreement and any default under this agreement.

☐ *[Check box, if applicable and the creditor is not a Credit Union.]* A presumption of undue hardship has been established with respect to this agreement. In my opinion, however, the debtor is able to make the required payment.

Printed Name of Debtor's Attorney: _____

Signature of Debtor's Attorney: _____

Date: _____

Form B2400A/B Alt

DIRECTOR'S FORMS

PART D: DEBTOR'S STATEMENT IN SUPPORT OF REAFFIRMATION AGREEMENT

*[Read and complete sections 1 and 2, **OR**, if the creditor is a Credit Union and the debtor is represented by an attorney, read section 3. Sign the appropriate signature line(s) and date your signature. If you complete sections 1 and 2 **and** your income less monthly expenses does not leave enough to make the payments under this reaffirmation agreement, check the box at the top of page 1 indicating "Presumption of Undue Hardship." Otherwise, check the box at the top of page 1 indicating "No Presumption of Undue Hardship"]*

1. I believe this reaffirmation agreement will not impose an undue hardship on my dependents or me. I can afford to make the payments on the reaffirmed debt because my monthly income (take home pay plus any other income received) is $_____, and my actual current monthly expenses including monthly payments on post-bankruptcy debt and other reaffirmation agreements total $_____, leaving $_____ to make the required payments on this reaffirmed debt.

I understand that if my income less my monthly expenses does not leave enough to make the payments, this reaffirmation agreement is presumed to be an undue hardship on me and must be reviewed by the court. However, this presumption may be overcome if I explain to the satisfaction of the court how I can afford to make the payments here: _____

_____

_____

(Use an additional page if needed for a full explanation.)

2. I received a copy of the Reaffirmation Disclosure Statement in Part A and a completed and signed reaffirmation agreement.

Signed: _____
    (Debtor)

    _____
    (Joint Debtor, if any)

Date: _____

— Or —

[If the creditor is a Credit Union and the debtor is represented by an attorney]

3. I believe this reaffirmation agreement is in my financial interest. I can afford to make the payments on the reaffirmed debt. I received a copy of the Reaffirmation Disclosure Statement in Part A and a completed and signed reaffirmation agreement.

Signed: _____
    (Debtor)

    _____
    (Joint Debtor, if any)

Date: _____

PART E: MOTION FOR COURT APPROVAL
[To be completed and filed only if the debtor is not represented by an attorney during the course of negotiating this agreement.]

MOTION FOR COURT APPROVAL OF REAFFIRMATION AGREEMENT

I (we), the debtor(s), affirm the following to be true and correct:

I am not represented by an attorney in connection with this reaffirmation agreement.

I believe this reaffirmation agreement is in my best interest based on the income and expenses I have disclosed in my Statement in Support of this reaffirmation agreement, and because (provide any additional relevant reasons the court should consider):

Therefore, I ask the court for an order approving this reaffirmation agreement under the following provisions (*check all applicable boxes*):

□ 11 U.S.C. § 524(c)(6) (debtor is not represented by an attorney during the course of the negotiation of the reaffirmation agreement)

□ 11 U.S.C. § 524(m) (presumption of undue hardship has arisen because monthly expenses exceed monthly income)

Signed: _____
     (Debtor)

     _____
     (Joint Debtor, if any)

Date: _____

(Added Dec. 1, 2015.)

Form B2400B

Form B2400B. Motion for Approval
of Reaffirmation Agreement

B2400B (Form B2400B) (12/15)

UNITED STATES BANKRUPTCY COURT
District of _____

In re _____,   Case No._____
          Debtor

                                           Chapter_____

MOTION FOR APPROVAL OF REAFFIRMATION AGREEMENT

I (we), the debtor(s), affirm the following to be true and correct:

I am not represented by an attorney in connection with this reaffirmation agreement.

I believe this reaffirmation agreement is in my best interest based on the income and expenses I have disclosed in my Statement in Support of Reaffirmation Agreement, and because *(provide any additional relevant reasons the court should consider)*:

Therefore, I ask the court for an order approving this reaffirmation agreement under the following provisions *(check all applicable boxes)*:

☐ 11 U.S.C. § 524(c)(6) (debtor is not represented by an attorney during the course of the negotiation of the reaffirmation agreement)

☐ 11 U.S.C. § 524(m) (presumption of undue hardship has arisen because monthly expenses exceed monthly income, as explained in Part II of Form B2400A, Reaffirmation Documents)

Signed: _____
          (Debtor)

          _____
          (Joint Debtor, if any)

Date: _____

(Added Dec. 1, 2015.)

Form B2400C. Order on Reaffirmation Agreement

B2400C (Form B2400C) (12/15)

United States Bankruptcy Court
_____ District of _____

In re _____,   Case No._____
                        Debtor   Chapter _____

ORDER ON REAFFIRMATION AGREEMENT

The debtor(s) _____ has (have) filed a motion for approval of the reaffirmation agreement dated _____ made between the debtor(s) and creditor _____. The court held the hearing required by 11 U.S.C. § 524(d) on notice to the debtor(s) and the creditor on _____ (date).

COURT ORDER: □ The court grants the debtor's motion under 11 U.S.C. § 524(c)(6)(A) and approves the reaffirmation agreement described above as not imposing an undue hardship on the debtor(s) or a dependent of the debtor(s) and as being in the best interest of the debtor(s).

□ The court grants the debtor's motion under 11 U.S.C. § 524(k)(8) and approves the reaffirmation agreement described above.

□ The court does not disapprove the reaffirmation agreement under 11 U.S.C. § 524(m).

□ The court disapproves the reaffirmation agreement under 11 U.S.C. § 524(m).

□ The court does not approve the reaffirmation agreement.

BY THE COURT

Date: _____   _____
                                      United States Bankruptcy Judge

(Added Dec. 1, 2015.)

Form B2400C Alt

Form B2400C Alt. Order on Reaffirmation Agreement

B2400C ALT (Form 2400C ALT) (12/15)

United States Bankruptcy Court
_____District of _____

In re _____,   Case No._____
            Debtor   Chapter _____

ORDER ON REAFFIRMATION AGREEMENT

The debtor(s) _____ has (have) filed a motion for approval of
            (Name(s) of debtor(s))
the reaffirmation agreement dated _____ made between the debtor(s) and
            (Date of agreement)
_____. The court held the hearing required by 11 U.S.C. § 524(d)
    (Name of creditor)
on notice to the debtor(s) and the creditor on _____.
                                        (Date)

COURT ORDER: ☐ The court grants the debtor's motion under 11 U.S.C. § 524(c)(6)(A)
                  and approves the reaffirmation agreement described above as not
                  imposing an undue hardship on the debtor(s) or a dependent of the
                  debtor(s) and as being in the best interest of the debtor(s).

                ☐ The court grants the debtor's motion under 11 U.S.C. § 524(k)(8)
                  and approves the reaffirmation agreement described above.

                ☐ The court does not disapprove the reaffirmation agreement under
                  11 U.S.C. § 524(m).

                ☐ The court disapproves the reaffirmation agreement under
                  11 U.S.C. § 524(m).

                ☐ The court does not approve the reaffirmation agreement.

                        BY THE COURT

Date: _____   _____
                                United States Bankruptcy Judge

(Added Dec. 1, 2015.)

**Form B2500A. Summons in an
Adversary Proceeding**

Instructions, Form B2500A
12.01.05

SUMMONS IN AN ADVERSARY PROCEEDING

<u>Purpose of the Form</u>

Certain categories of relief may be granted in a bankruptcy court only through an adversary proceeding. The usual focus of the adversary proceeding is a trial of the allegations made by the plaintiff against the defendant.

The first step in commencing an adversary proceeding is the filing of a complaint, setting forth the facts and allegations which the plaintiff believes justify the granting of relief against the defendant, and stating the relief which the plaintiff seeks. As each complaint is unique, there is no specific form provided by the court.

The summons is the notice which accompanies the complaint, advising of the names of the parties, the court in which the adversary proceeding was filed, and the time limits for responding to the complaint.

The summons should be prepared by the plaintiff's attorney and signed and issued by the clerk. The plaintiff's attorney is responsible for serving the summons and a copy of the complaint. If the plaintiff does not have an attorney, the plaintiff is responsible for preparing the summons and serving the summons and complaint.

<u>Applicable Law and Rules</u>

1. In general, Fed. R. Bankr. P. 7001 requires that an adversary proceeding be commenced 1) to recover money or property; 2) to determine the validity, priority, or extent of a lien or other interest in property; 3) to obtain court approval for the sale of both the interest of the estate and of a co-owner of property; 4) to object to or revoke a discharge; 5) to revoke an order of confirmation of a plan; 6) to determine the dischargeability of a debt; 7) to obtain an injunction; 8) to subordinate an allowed claim or interest; 9) to obtain a declaratory judgment relating to any of the foregoing; or 10) to determine a claim or cause of action removed from a state court pursuant to section 1452 of title 28 (28 U.S.C. § 1452).

2. Fed. R. Bankr. P. 7004 adopts portions of Rule 4 of the Federal Rules of Civil Procedure, and sets forth other provisions for the issuance and service of a summons. These rules are detailed and complex, and should be read in their entirety.

3. Rule 4(a) specifies the information that the plaintiff's attorney (or the plaintiff) must provide on the summons form. Rule 4(b) provides that, upon or after the filing of the complaint, the clerk shall issue the summons to the plaintiff's attorney (or the plaintiff). It is then the responsibility of the plaintiff's attorney (or the plaintiff) to serve the summons on the defendant.

4. If the debtor is the plaintiff, section 342(c) of the Bankruptcy Code (11 U.S.C. §

342(c)) requires that the caption of the complaint include the debtor's name and address, and the last four digits of the debtor's taxpayer identification number. An individual debtor's social security number is the debtor's taxpayer identification number. In order to satisfy this requirement, the portion of Official Form 416A which sets out the last four digits of the debtor's taxpayer identification number can be inserted in the caption of Form 2500A.

5. A copy of the complaint must be served with the summons. Rule 4(c).

6. It is a good idea to submit several copies of the summons to the clerk with the original complaint, so that each copy may be signed by the clerk. It is recommended that at least four copies be submitted: one for the court records, one for service on the defendant, one for the plaintiff's attorney's records (or the plaintiff's records), and one to be returned to the court after the certificate of service has been completed. Of course, if there is more than one defendant, each must be served with a separate copy of the summons, so additional copies should be submitted to the clerk for issuance.

7. The summons and complaint may be served in a variety of ways which are set forth in Rules 7004 and 4. When the defendant is an individual, other than an infant or incompetent person, the easiest method is for the summons and complaint to be mailed by first class mail postage prepaid to the individual's dwelling house or usual place of abode or to the place where the individual regularly conducts a business or profession. Rule 7004(b)(1).

8. When the debtor is a defendant and the debtor is represented by an attorney, the summons and complaint must be served on both the debtor and the debtor's attorney. Rule 7004(g). Service on the debtor may be made by mailing the summons and complaint to the debtor at the address shown on the petition or to any other address designated by the debtor in a document filed with the court. Rule 7004(b)(9). Service on the debtor's attorney may be made by any means authorized by Federal Rule of Civil Procedure 5(b), including service by electronic means if the attorney has consented in writing to electronic service. Rule 7004(g).

9. Rule 7004(h) provides that service on a bank, savings and loan, or other insured depository institution in a contested matter or adversary proceeding must be made by certified mail addressed to an officer of the institution unless one of three exceptions applies. Those exceptions are 1) the attorney for the depository institution has filed a paper in the matter or has otherwise entered his or her appearance, 2) the court, following the procedure set out in the rule, orders otherwise, and 3) the depository institution has waived the requirement in writing by designating an officer to receive service. (Insured depository institutions are defined in section 3 of the Federal Deposit Insurance Act (12 U.S.C. § 1813).)

10. Because of the exceptions and the placement of the certified mail requirement in Rule 7004 rather than Fed. R. Bankr. P. 2002, the requirement applies in an adversary

proceeding only to the service of the summons and complaint or the service of the third-party summons and third-party complaint and only if the depository institution is a defendant or third-party defendant.

11.   If service was made by personal service, by residence service, or pursuant to state law, the service must be made by someone who is not a party, and who is at least 18 years of age. Rule 7004(a).

12.   The summons and complaint may be served anywhere in the United States. Rule 7004(d).

13.   The summons and complaint must be served 7 days after the summons is issued. Service is complete upon mailing, not upon delivery by the Postal Service. If more than 7 days pass before service is completed, a new summons will be issued for service. Rule 7004(e) and Fed. R. Bankr. P. 9006(e).

14.   If the summons and complaint are not served within 120 days of the filing of the complaint, the court may dismiss the action. Rule 4(m).

15.   On the back of the summons is a certificate of service of the summons. After service has been made, this certificate should be completed, and filed with the court.

16.   Fed. R. Bankr. P. 7012(a) provides that once a complaint is served, the defendant has 30 days after the issuance of the summons to file an answer or make one of the motions specified in Fed. R. Civ. P. 12 (made applicable by Rule 7012(b)). If the United States or one of its agencies or officers is the defendant, the time to file an answer or make a motion is 35 days. The court can order these time limits shortened or extended. If such an order is entered, the new time limit must be stated in the summons.

Instructions

Caption

1.   Identify the Judicial District in which the bankruptcy case was filed.
Example: "Eastern District of California."

2.   "In re": Insert the name of the debtor as it appears in the bankruptcy petition. Then insert the names of the plaintiff(s) and defendant(s) as they appear on the original complaint.

3.   If the debtor is the plaintiff, include the debtor's name and address, and the last four digits of the debtor's taxpayer identification number in the caption. The portion of Official Form 416A which includes the last four digits of the debtor's taxpayer identification number can be inserted in the caption of the summons for this purpose.

DIRECTOR'S FORMS

4. "Case No.": Insert the bankruptcy case number assigned by the court at the time of filing.

5. "Adv. Proc. No.": Insert the number assigned by the court to the adversary proceeding at the time of the filing of the complaint.

Address of Clerk:

Be sure to indicate the proper address for the clerk's office.

Name and Address of Plaintiff's Attorney:

The complete mailing address of the plaintiff's attorney must be set forth in the space provided, including zip code. If the street address is different, that must also be stated, including room number. If the plaintiff is not represented by an attorney, the plaintiff's mailing and street address should be placed in the space.

Certificate of Service

1. Line 1 (name) is to be completed with the full name of the person who served the summons and complaint.

2. Line 2 (date) is to be completed with the month, day and year service was perfected.

3. The appropriate box should be checked to show how service was made.

   If mail service, state the mailing address, city, state and zip code of the place to which the summons and complaint were mailed.

   If personal service, state both the name of the person to whom the summons and complaint were given, and the address at which this occurred.

   If residence service, state both the name of the adult to whom the summons and complaint were given, and the address at which this occurred.

   If certified mail service on an insured depository institution, state both the name of the officer to whom the summons and complaint were mailed and the mailing address, city, state, and zip code to which service was mailed.

   If service by publication, describe the steps take to perfect service.

   If service was made pursuant to state law, fill in the blank with the name of state under whose laws the summons and complaint were served, and describe briefly the method of service, including the name of the person served and the address at which the person was served.

4.　　　Date: Insert on this line the month, day, and year the certificate is signed.

5.　　　Signature: - The person who completed service of the summons and complaint must sign. This must be an ORIGINAL signature.

6.　　　In the space directly below the Date and Signature lines, print or type the name and business address of the person who signed the certificate.

General Information for the Clerk

There are three basic summons forms, this one and Forms B 2500B and B 2500C. This form does not set a time for either the pretrial conference or the trial, Form B 2500B fixes a time and place for a pretrial conference, and Form B 2500C fixes a trial date. Each court should decide which form or forms is to be used in that district, and make that form or forms available to the bar and parties.

Fed. R. Bankr. P. 7004 incorporates by reference Rule 4(b) of the Federal Rules of Civil Procedure, which provides that the clerk is to issue the summons to the plaintiff's attorney (or the plaintiff) upon or after the filing of the complaint. If requested, more than one copy can be issued. In the instructions to the public, it is recommended that the plaintiff seek the issuance of at least four copies of the summons: one for the court to file with the original complaint; one for service on the defendant, one for the plaintiff's attorney's records (or the plaintiff's records), and one to be returned to the court after the certificate of service has been completed. Of course, if there is more than one defendant, each must be served with a separate copy of the summons, so additional copies are recommended to be submitted to the court for issuance.

The plaintiff's attorney (or the plaintiff) is responsible for serving the summons and complaint, not the clerk.

There is no charge for the issuance of a summons, beyond the fee for commencing the adversary proceeding.

The plaintiff's attorney should have filled in his or her address in the appropriate space on the form. As the defendant may choose to serve an answer or motion on the plaintiff by mail or in person, the space should contain both the street and mailing address of the plaintiff's attorney, if the addresses are different. If the plaintiff is not represented by an attorney, the plaintiff's address(es) should be filled in.

The clerk may wish to fill in the space marked "Address of Clerk" before providing the form to the public.

As is set out in detail in the instructions to the public, there are a series of deadlines for actions to be taken in the adversary proceeding. The most important of these are:

1.　　　If the summons is not served within 7 days, a new summons must be issued. Rule 7004(e).

2.　　　If no summons is served within 120 days, the court is authorized by Rule 4(m) to dismiss the adversary proceeding on its own motion, after notice to the plaintiff.

3.　　　If the defendant does not answer or make a motion pursuant to Fed. R. Bankr. P. 7012 within 30 days, or such time as court may fix, the plaintiff may seek the entry of a default. (See form B 2600). The United States, its agencies, and its officers have 35 days to answer or make a motion.

If the court enters an order changing the last day by which the defendant must answer the complaint or make a motion, that date MUST be stated on the summons, and the superseded information regarding the deadline must be deleted.

Form B2500A

B2500A (Form 2500A) (12/15)

United States Bankruptcy Court

_____District Of _____

In re _____,)   Case No. _____
        Debtor   )
)   Chapter _____
)
_____)
        Plaintiff   )
)
        v.   )   Adv. Proc. No. _____
)
_____)
        Defendant   )

SUMMONS IN AN ADVERSARY PROCEEDING

YOU ARE SUMMONED and required to file a motion or answer to the complaint which is attached to this summons with the clerk of the bankruptcy court within 30 days after the date of issuance of this summons, except that the United States and its offices and agencies shall file a motion or answer to the complaint within 35 days.

          Address of the clerk:

At the same time, you must also serve a copy of the motion or answer upon the plaintiff's attorney.

          Name and Address of Plaintiff's Attorney:

If you make a motion, your time to answer is governed by Fed. R. Bankr. P. 7012.

IF YOU FAIL TO RESPOND TO THIS SUMMONS, YOUR FAILURE WILL BE DEEMED TO BE YOUR CONSENT TO ENTRY OF A JUDGMENT BY THE BANKRUPTCY COURT AND JUDGMENT BY DEFAULT MAY BE TAKEN AGAINST YOU FOR THE RELIEF DEMANDED IN THE COMPLAINT.

                        _____ (Clerk of the Bankruptcy Court)

Date: _____   By: _____(Deputy Clerk)

B2500A (Form 2500A) (12/15)

CERTIFICATE OF SERVICE

I, _____(name), certify that service of this summons and a copy of
the complaint was made _____(date) by:

❑   Mail service: Regular, first class United States mail, postage fully pre-paid, addressed
     to:

❑   Personal Service: By leaving the process with the defendant or with an officer or agent
     of defendant at:

❑   Residence Service: By leaving the process with the following adult at:

❑   Certified Mail Service on an Insured Depository Institution: By sending the process by
     certified mail addressed to the following officer of the defendant at:

❑   Publication: The defendant was served as follows: [Describe briefly]

❑   State Law: The defendant was served pursuant to the laws of the State of _____, as
     follows: [Describe briefly]

If service was made by personal service, by residence service, or pursuant to state law, I further
certify that I am, and at all times during the service of process was, not less than 18 years of age and
not a party to the matter concerning which service of process was made.

Under penalty of perjury, I declare that the foregoing is true and correct.

Date _____   Signature _____

              Print Name: _____

              Business Address: _____

                                 _____

(Added Dec. 1, 2015.)

**Form B2500B. Summons and Notice of Pretrial
Conference in an Adversary Proceeding**

Instructions, Form B2500B
12.01.05

SUMMONS AND NOTICE OF PRETRIAL CONFERENCE
IN AN ADVERSARY PROCEEDING

Purpose of the Form

   Certain categories of relief may be granted in a bankruptcy court only through an
adversary proceeding. The usual focus of the adversary proceeding is a trial of the
allegations made by the plaintiff against the defendant.

   The first step in commencing an adversary proceeding is the filing of a complaint,
setting forth the facts and allegations which the plaintiff believes justify the granting of relief
against the defendant, and stating the relief which the plaintiff seeks. As each complaint is
unique, there is no specific form provided by the court.

   The summons is the notice which accompanies the complaint, advising of the names
of the parties, the court in which the adversary proceeding was filed, and the time limits for
responding to the complaint.

   The summons also may set the time and place of a pretrial conference between the
parties and the judge. At this conference, the court may determine whether there is any
possibility of settlement of the case, and will issue a scheduling order for pretrial activities.

   The summons should be prepared by the plaintiff's attorney and signed and issued by the
clerk. The plaintiff's attorney is responsible for serving the summons and a copy of the
complaint. If the plaintiff does not have an attorney, the plaintiff is responsible for preparing
the summons and serving the summons and complaint.

Applicable Law and Rules

1.   In general, Fed. R. Bankr. P. 7001 requires that an adversary proceeding be commenced:
     1) to recover property; 2) to determine the validity, priority, or extent of a lien or other
     interest in property; 3) to obtain court approval for the sale of both the interest of the
     estate and of a co-owner of property; 4) to object to or revoke a discharge; 5) to revoke an
     order of confirmation of a plan; 6) to determine the dischargeability of a debt; 7) to obtain
     an injunction; 8) to subordinate an allowed claim or interest; 9) to obtain a declaratory
     judgment relating to any of the foregoing; or 10) to determine a claim or cause of action
     removed from a state or federal court pursuant to section 1452 of title 28 (28 U.S.C. §
     1452).

2.   Fed. R. Bankr. P. 7004 adopts portions of Rule 4 of the Federal Rules of Civil
     Procedure, and sets forth other provisions for the issuance and service of a summons.
     These rules are detailed and complex, and should be read in their entirety.

3.   Rule 4(a) specifies the information that the plaintiff's attorney (or the plaintiff) must
     provide on the summons form. Rule 4(b) provides that, upon or after the filing of the

complaint, the clerk shall issue the summons to the plaintiff's attorney (or the plaintiff). It is then the responsibility of the plaintiff's attorney (or the plaintiff) to serve the summons on the defendant.

4. If the debtor is the plaintiff, section 342(c) of the Bankruptcy Code (11 U.S.C. § 342(c)) requires that the caption of the complaint include the debtor's name and address, and the last four digits of the debtor's taxpayer identification number. An individual debtor's social security number is the debtor's taxpayer identification number. In order to satisfy this requirement, the portion of Official Form 416A which sets out the last four digits of the debtor's taxpayer identification number can be inserted in the caption of Form 2500B.

5. A copy of the complaint must be served with the summons. Rule 4(c).

6. It is a good idea to submit several copies of the summons to the clerk with the original complaint, so that each copy may be signed by the clerk. It is recommended that at least four copies be submitted: one for the court records, one for service on the defendant, one for the plaintiff's attorney's records (or the plaintiff's records), and one to be returned to the court after the certificate of service has been completed. Of course, if there is more than one defendant, each must be served with a separate copy of the summons, so additional copies should be submitted to the clerk for issuance.

7. The summons and complaint may be served in a variety of ways which are set forth in Rules 7004 and 4. When the defendant is an individual, other than an infant or incompetent person, the easiest method is for the summons and complaint to be mailed by first class mail postage prepaid to the individual's dwelling house or usual place of abode or to the place where the individual regularly conducts a business or profession. Rule 7004(b)(1).

8. When the debtor is a defendant and the debtor is represented by an attorney, the summons and complaint must be served on both the debtor and the debtor's attorney. Rule 7004(g). Service on the debtor may be made by mailing the summons and complaint to the debtor at the address shown on the petition or to any other address designated by the debtor in a document filed with the court. Rule 7004(b)(9). Service on the debtor's attorney may be made by any means authorized by Federal Rule of Civil Procedure 5(b), including service by electronic means if the attorney has consented in writing to electronic service. Rule 7004(g).

9. Rule 7004(h) provides that service on a bank, savings and loan, or other insured depository institution in a contested matter or adversary proceeding must be made by certified mail addressed to an officer of the institution unless one of three exceptions paper in the matter or has otherwise entered his or her appearance, 2) the court, following the procedure set out in the rule, orders otherwise, and 3) the depository institution has waived the requirement in writing by designating an officer to receive service. (Insured depository institutions are defined in section 3

of the Federal Deposit Insurance Act (12 U.S.C. § 1813).)

10.   Because of the exceptions and the placement of the certified mail requirement in Rule 7004 rather than Fed. R. Bankr. P. 2002, the requirement applies in an adversary proceeding only to the service of the summons and complaint or the service of the third-party summons and third-party complaint and only if the depository institution is a defendant or third-party defendant.

11.   If service was made by personal service, by residence service, or pursuant to state law, the service must be made by someone who is not a party, and who is at least 18 years of age. Rule 7004(a).

12.   The summons and complaint may be served anywhere in the United States. Rule 7004(d).

13.   The summons and complaint must be served 7 days after the summons is issued. Service is complete upon mailing, not upon delivery by the Postal Service. If more than 7 days pass before service is completed, a new summons will be issued for service. Rule 7004(e) and Fed. R. Bankr. P. 9006(e).

14.   If the summons and complaint are not served within 120 days of the filing of the complaint, the court may dismiss the action. Rule 4(m).

15.   On the back of the summons is a certificate of service of the summons. After service has been made, this certificate should be completed, and filed with the court.

16.   Fed. R. Bankr. P. 7012(a) provides that once a complaint is served, the defendant has 30 days after the issuance of summons to file an answer or make one of the motions specified in Fed. R. Civ. P. 12 (made applicable by Rule 7012). If the United States or one of its agencies or officers is the defendant, the time to file an answer or make a motion is 35 days. The court can order these time limits shortened or extended. If such an order is entered, the new time limit must be stated in the summons.

17.   Fed. R. Bankr. P. 7016 adopts Rule 16 of the Federal Rules of Civil Procedure for the purpose of establishing pretrial conferences. This rule provides that:

> In any action, the court may order the attorneys and any unrepresented parties to appear for one or more pretrial conferences for such purposes as:
>
> (1) expediting disposition of the action;
>
> (2) establishing early and continuing control so that the case will not be protracted because of lack of management;
>
> (3) discouraging wasteful pretrial activities;

(4) improving the quality of the trial through more thorough preparation; and

(5) facilitating settlement.

18.   Rule 16(b) provides that after the pretrial conference, the court may enter a scheduling order that limits the time to join other parties, amend the pleadings, complete discovery, and file motions.

19.   The scheduling order also may set a trial date, fix dates for further pretrial conferences, modify the disclosures required by Fed. R. Civ. P. 26(a),(e)(1), as incorporated by Fed. R. Bankr. P. 7026, modify the extent of discovery, provide for disclosure or discovery of electronically stored information, include any agreements the parties reach for asserting claims of privilege or of protection of trial-preparation material after information is produced, and other appropriate matters.

20.   Rule 16(c)(1) provides that a party represented by an attorney must authorize at least one of its attorneys to make stipulations and admissions about all matters than can be reasonably anticipated for discussion at the pretrial conference. If appropriate, the court may require that a party or its representative be present or reasonably available by other means to consider possible settlement.

21.   Some of the matters which may be discussed at pretrial conferences are listed in Rule 16(c)(2).

22.   Pursuant to Rule 16(f), if no appearance is made at the pretrial conference, if a party is not prepared, if a party fails to participate in good faith, or if a party fails to obey a pretrial scheduling order, the judge may impose sanctions, including reasonable expenses and attorney's fees.

Instructions

Caption

1.   Identify the Judicial District in which the bankruptcy case was filed. Example: "Eastern District of California."

2.   "In re": Insert the name of the debtor as it appears in the bankruptcy petition. Then insert the names of the plaintiff(s) and defendant(s) as they appear on the original complaint.

3.   If the debtor is the plaintiff, include the debtor's name and address, and the last four digits of the debtor's taxpayer identification number in the caption. The portion of Official Form 416A which includes the last four digits of the debtor's taxpayer identification number can be inserted in the caption of the summons for

Form B2500B

this purpose.

4. "Case No.": Insert the bankruptcy case number assigned by the court at the time of filing.

5. "Adv. Proc. No.": Insert the number assigned by the court to the adversary proceeding at the time of the filing of the complaint.

Address of Clerk:

Be sure to indicate the proper address for the clerk's office.

Name and Address of Plaintiff's Attorney:

The complete mailing address of the plaintiff's attorney must be set forth in the space provided, including zip code. If the street address is different, that must also be stated, including room number. If the plaintiff is not represented by an attorney, the plaintiff's mailing and street address should be placed in the space.

Certificate of Service

1. Line 1 (name) is to be completed with the full name of the person who served the summons and complaint.

2. Line 2 (date) is to be completed with the month, day and year service was perfected.

3. The appropriate box should be checked to show how service was made.

If mail service, state the mailing address, city, state and zip code of the place to which the summons and complaint were mailed.

If personal service, state both the name of the person to whom the summons and complaint were given, and the address at which this occurred.

If residence service, state both the name of the adult to whom the summons and complaint were given, and the address at which this occurred.

If certified mail service on an insured depository institution, state both the name of the officer to whom the summons and complaint were mailed and the mailing address, city, state, and zip code to which service was mailed.

If service by publication, describe the steps take to perfect service.

If service was made pursuant to state law, fill in the blank with the name of state under whose laws the summons and complaint were served, and describe briefly the method of service, including the name of the person served and the address at which the person was served.

4.   Date: - Insert on this line the month, day, and year the certificate is signed.

5.   Signature: - The person who completed service of the summons and complaint must sign. This must be an ORIGINAL signature.

6.   In the space directly below the Date and Signature lines, print or type the name and business address of the person who signed the certificate.

General Information for the Clerk

There are three basic summons forms, this one and Forms B 2500A and B 2500C. Form B2500A does not set a time for either the pretrial conference or the trial, this form fixes a time and place for a pretrial conference, and Form B 2500C fixes a trial date. Each court should decide which form or forms is to be used in that district, and make that form or forms available to the bar and parties.

Fed. R. Bankr. P. 7004 incorporates by reference Rule 4(b) of the Federal Rules of Civil Procedure, which provides that the clerk is to issue the summons to the plaintiff's attorney (or the plaintiff) upon or after the filing of the complaint. If requested, more than one copy can be issued. In the instructions to the public, it is recommended that the plaintiff's attorney (or the plaintiff) seek the issuance of at least four copies of the summons: one for the court to file with the original complaint; one for service on the defendant; one for the plaintiff's attorney's records (or the plaintiff's records), and one to be returned to the court after the certificate of service has been completed. Of course, if there is more than one defendant, each must be served with a separate copy of the summons, so additional copies are recommended to be submitted to the court for issuance.

The plaintiff's attorney (or the plaintiff) is responsible for serving the summons and complaint, not the clerk.

There is no charge for the issuance of a summons, beyond the fee for commencing the adversary proceeding.

The plaintiff's attorney should have filled in his or her address in the appropriate space on the form. As the defendant may choose to serve an answer or motion on the plaintiff by mail or in person, the space should contain both the street and mailing address of the plaintiff's attorney, if the addresses are different. If the plaintiff is not represented by an attorney, the plaintiff's address(es) should be filled in.

The clerk may wish to fill in the space marked "Address of Clerk" before providing the form to the public.

As is set out in detail in the instructions to the public, there are a series of deadlines for actions to be taken in the adversary proceeding. The most important of these are:

1. If the summons is not served within 7 days, a new summons must be issued. Rule 7004(e).

2. If no summons is served within 120 days, the court is authorized by Rule 4(m) to dismiss the adversary proceeding on its own motion, after notice to the plaintiff.

3. If the defendant does not answer or make a motion pursuant to Fed. R. Bankr. P. 7012 within 30 days, or such time as the court may fix, the plaintiff may seek the entry of a default. (See Form B2600). The United States, its agencies, and its officers have 35 days to answer or make a motion.

If the court enters an order changing the last day by which the defendant must answer the complaint or make a motion, that date MUST be stated on the summons, and the superseded information regarding the deadline must be deleted.

Pretrial conferences are successful in easing a court's calendar only if they are scheduled early in the case. In recognition of this fact, Rule 16(b) imposes a tight schedule on pretrial conferences, restricting the issuance of a scheduling order to within 120 days after the filing of the complaint.

B 2500B (Form 2500B) (12/15)

United States Bankruptcy Court

_____District Of _____

In re _____,	)	Case No. _____
Debtor	)	
	)	Chapter _____
	)	
_____	)	
Plaintiff	)	
	)	
v.	)	Adv. Proc. No. _____
	)	
_____	)	
Defendant	)	

SUMMONS AND NOTICE OF PRETRIAL CONFERENCE
IN AN ADVERSARY PROCEEDING

YOU ARE SUMMONED and required to file a motion or answer to the complaint which is attached to this summons with the clerk of the bankruptcy court within 30 days after the date of issuance of this summons, except that the United States and its offices and agencies shall file a motion or answer to the complaint within 35 days.

Address of the clerk:

At the same time, you must also serve a copy of the motion or answer upon the plaintiff's attorney.

Name and Address of Plaintiff's Attorney:

If you make a motion, your time to answer is governed by Fed. R. Bankr. P. 7012.

YOU ARE NOTIFIED that a pretrial conference of the proceeding commenced by the filing of the complaint will be held at the following time and place:

Address: Room:
                                                  Date and Time:

IF YOU FAIL TO RESPOND TO THIS SUMMONS, YOUR FAILURE WILL BE DEEMED TO BE YOUR CONSENT TO ENTRY OF A JUDGMENT BY THE BANKRUPTCY COURT AND JUDGMENT BY DEFAULT MAY BE TAKEN AGAINST YOU FOR THE RELIEF DEMANDED IN THE COMPLAINT.

_____(Clerk of the Bankruptcy Court)

Date: _____   By: _____(Deputy Clerk)

Form B2500B   DIRECTOR'S FORMS

B 2500B (Form 2500B) (12/15)

CERTIFICATE OF SERVICE

I, _____(name), certify that service of this summons and a copy of the complaint was made _____(date) by:

❑   Mail service: Regular, first class United States mail, postage fully pre-paid, addressed to:

❑   Personal Service: By leaving the process with the defendant or with an officer or agent of defendant at:

❑   Residence Service: By leaving the process with the following adult at:

❑   Certified Mail Service on an Insured Depository Institution: By sending the process by certified mail addressed to the following officer of the defendant at:

❑   Publication: The defendant was served as follows: [Describe briefly]

❑   State Law: The defendant was served pursuant to the laws of the State of _____, as follows: [Describe briefly]

If service was made by personal service, by residence service, or pursuant to state law, I further certify that I am, and at all times during the service of process was, not less than 18 years of age and not a party to the matter concerning which service of process was made.

Under penalty of perjury, I declare that the foregoing is true and correct.

Date _____   Signature _____

Print Name: _____

Business Address: _____

                      _____

(Added Dec. 1, 2015.)

Form B2500C.   Summons and Notice of Trial in an Adversary Proceeding

Instructions, Form B2500C
12.01.15

SUMMONS AND NOTICE OF TRIAL IN AN ADVERSARY PROCEEDING

Purpose of the Form

Certain categories of relief may be granted in a bankruptcy court only through an adversary proceeding. The usual focus of the adversary proceeding is a trial of the allegations made by the plaintiff against the defendant.

The first step in commencing an adversary proceeding is the filing of a complaint, setting forth the facts and allegations which the plaintiff believes justify the granting of relief against the defendant, and stating the relief which the plaintiff seeks. As each complaint is unique, there is no specific form provided by the court.

The summons is the notice which accompanies the complaint, advising of the names of the parties, the court in which the adversary proceeding was filed, the time limits for responding to the complaint, and the date, time, and place for the trial.

The summons also may set the time and place of a pretrial conference between the parties and the judge. At this conference, the court may determine whether there is any possibility of settlement of the case, and will issue a scheduling order for pretrial activities.

The summons should be prepared by the plaintiff's attorney and signed and issued by the clerk. The plaintiff's attorney is responsible for serving the summons and a copy of the complaint. If the plaintiff does not have an attorney, the plaintiff is responsible for preparing the summons and serving the summons and complaint.

Applicable Law and Rules

1.   In general, Fed. R. Bankr. P. 7001 requires that an adversary proceeding be commenced 1) to recover property; 2) to determine the validity, priority, or extent of a lien or other interest in property; 3) to obtain court approval for the sale of both the interest of the estate and of a co-owner of property; 4) to object to or revoke a discharge; 5) to revoke an order of confirmation of a plan; 6) to determine the dischargeability of a debt; 7) to obtain an injunction; 8) to subordinate an allowed claim or interest; 9) to obtain a declaratory judgment relating to any of the foregoing; or 10) to determine a claim or cause of action removed from a state or federal court pursuant to section 1452 of title 28 (28 U.S.C. § 1452).

2.   Fed. R. Bankr. P. 7004 adopts portions of Rule 4 of the Federal Rules of Civil Procedure, and sets forth other provisions for the issuance and service of a summons. These rules are detailed and complex, and should be read in their entirety.

Form B2500C
Page 2

3.   Rule 4(a) specifies the information that the plaintiff's attorney (or the plaintiff) must provide on the summons form. Rule 4(b) provides that, upon or after the filing of the complaint, the clerk shall issue the summons to the plaintiff's attorney (or the plaintiff). It is then the responsibility of the plaintiff's attorney (or the plaintiff) to serve the summons on the defendant.

4.   If the debtor is the plaintiff, section 342(c) of the Bankruptcy Code (11 U.S.C. § 342(c)) requires that the caption of the complaint include the debtor's name and address, and the last four digits of the debtor's taxpayer identification number. An individual debtor's social security number is the debtor's taxpayer identification number. In order to satisfy this requirement, the portion of Official Form 416A which sets out the last four digits of the debtor's taxpayer identification number can be inserted in the caption of Form 2500C.

5.   A copy of the complaint must be served with the summons. Rule 4(c).

6.   It is a good idea to submit several copies of the summons to the clerk with the original complaint, so that each copy may be signed by the clerk. It is recommended that at least four copies be submitted: one for the court records, one for service on the defendant, one for the plaintiff's attorney's records (or the plaintiff's records), and one to be returned to the court after the certificate of service has been completed. Of course, if there is more than one defendant, each must be served with a separate copy of the summons, so additional copies should be submitted to the clerk for issuance.

7.   The summons and complaint may be served in a variety of ways which are set forth in Rules 7004 and 4. When the defendant is an individual, other than an infant or incompetent person, the easiest method is for the summons and complaint to be mailed by first class mail postage prepaid to the individual's dwelling house or usual place of abode or to the place where the individual regularly conducts a business or profession. Rule 7004(b)(1).

8.   When the debtor is a defendant and the debtor is represented by an attorney, the summons and complaint must be served on both the debtor and the debtor's attorney. Rule 7004(g). Service on the debtor may be made by mailing the summons and complaint to the debtor at the address shown on the petition or to any other address designated by the debtor in a document filed with the court. Rule 7004(b)(9). Service on the debtor's attorney may be made by any means authorized by Federal Rule of Civil Procedure 5(b), including service by electronic means if the attorney has consented in writing to electronic service. Rule 7004(g).

9.   Rule 7004(h) provides that service on a bank, savings and loan, or other insured depository institution in a contested matter or adversary proceeding must be made by certified mail addressed to an officer of the institution unless one of three exceptions

Form B2500C
Page 3

3.   Rule 4(a) specifies the information that the plaintiff's attorney (or the plaintiff) must
      paper in the matter or has otherwise entered his or her appearance, 2) the court, following
      the procedure set out in the rule, orders otherwise, and 3) the depository institution has
      waived the requirement in writing by designating an officer to receive service. (Insured
      depository institutions are defined in section 3 of the Federal Deposit Insurance Act (12
      U.S.C. § 1813).)

10.   Because of the exceptions and the placement of the certified mail requirement in Rule
      7004 rather than Fed. R. Bankr. P. 2002, the requirement applies in an adversary
      proceeding only to the service of the summons and complaint or the service of the third-
      party summons and third-party complaint and only if the depository institution is a
      defendant or third-party defendant.

11.   If service was made by personal service, by residence service, or pursuant to state law, the
      service must be made by someone who is not a party, and who is at least 18 years of age.
      Rule 7004(a).

12.   The summons and complaint may be served anywhere in the United States. Rule
      7004(d).

13.   The summons and complaint must be served 7 days after the summons is issued. Service
      is complete upon mailing, not upon delivery by the Postal Service. If more than 7 days
      pass before service is completed, a new summons will be issued for service. Rule
      7004(e) and Fed. R. Bankr. P. 9006(e).

14.   If the summons and complaint are not served within 120 days of the filing of the
      complaint, the court may dismiss the action. Rule 4(m).

15.   On the back of the summons is a certificate of service of the summons. After service has
      been made, this certificate should be completed, and filed with the court.

16.   Fed. R. Bankr. P. 7012(a) provides that once a complaint is served, the defendant has 30
      days after the issuance of summons to file an answer or make one of the motions
      specified in Fed. R. Civ. P. 12 (made applicable by Rule 7012). If the United States or
      one of its agencies or officers is the defendant, the time to file an answer or make a
      motion is 35 days. The court can order these time limits shortened or extended. If such
      an order is entered, the new time limit must be stated in the summons.

Form B2500C

Form B2500C
Page 4

Instructions

Caption

1. Identify the Judicial District in which the bankruptcy case was filed. Example: "Eastern District of California."

2. "In re": Insert the name of the debtor as it appears in the bankruptcy petition. Then insert the names of the plaintiff(s) and defendant(s) as they appear on the original complaint.

3. If the debtor is the plaintiff, include the debtor's name and address, and the last four digits of the debtor's taxpayer identification number in the caption. The portion of Official Form 416A which includes the last four digits of the debtor's taxpayer identification number can be inserted in the caption of the summons for this purpose.

4. "Case No.": Insert the bankruptcy case number assigned by the court at the time of filing.

5. "Adv. Proc. No.": Insert the number assigned by the court to the adversary proceeding at the time of the filing of the complaint.

Address of Clerk:

Be sure to indicate the proper address for the clerk's office.

Name and Address of Plaintiff's Attorney:

The complete mailing address of the plaintiff's attorney must be set forth in the space provided, including zip code. If the street address is different, that must also be stated, including room number. If the plaintiff is not represented by an attorney, the plaintiff's mailing and street address should be placed in the space.

Location, Date, and Time of Trial

This information should be set forth with the full street address of the court and room number where the trial will take place.

Certificate of Service

1. Line 1 (name) is to be completed with the full name of the person who served the summons and complaint.

Form B2500C
Page 5

2.   Line 2 (date) is to be completed with the month, day and year service was perfected.

3.   The appropriate box should be checked to show how service was made.

        If mail service, state the mailing address, city, state and zip code of the place to
        which the summons and complaint were mailed.

        If personal service, state both the name of the person to whom the summons and
        complaint were given, and the address at which this occurred.

        If residence service, state both the name of the adult to whom the summons and
        complaint were given, and the address at which this occurred.

        If certified mail service on an insured depository institution, state both the name
        of the officer to whom the summons and complaint were mailed and the mailing
        address, city, state, and zip code to which service was mailed.

        If service by publication, describe the steps take to perfect service.

        If service was made pursuant to state law, fill in the blank with the name of state
        under whose laws the summons and complaint were served, and describe briefly
        the method of service, including the name of the person served and the address at
        which the person was served.

4.   Date: - Insert on this line the month, day, and year the certificate is signed.

5.   Signature: - The person who completed service of the summons and complaint must sign.
        This must be an ORIGINAL signature.

6.   In the space directly below the Date and Signature lines, print or type the name and
        business address of the person who signed the certificate.

General Information for the Clerk

        There are three basic summons forms, this one and Forms B 2500A and B 2500B. Form
B 2500A does not set a time for either the pretrial conference or the trial, Form B 2500B sets a
time and place for a pretrial conference, and this form fixes a trial date. Each court should decide
which form or forms is to be used in that district, and make that form or forms available to the
bar and parties.

        Fed. R. Bankr. P. 7004 incorporates by reference Rule 4(b) of the Federal Rules of Civil
Procedure, which provides that the clerk is to issue the summons to the plaintiff's attorney (or the
plaintiff) upon or after the filing of the complaint. If requested, more than one copy can be

Form B2500C
Page 6

issued. In the instructions to the public, it is recommended that the plaintiff's attorney (or the plaintiff) seek the issuance of at least four copies of the summons: one for the court to file with the original complaint; one for service on the defendant, one for the plaintiff's attorney's records (or the plaintiff's records), and one to be returned to the court after the certificate of service has been completed. Of course, if there is more than one defendant, each must be served with a separate copy of the summons, so additional copies are recommended to be submitted to the court for issuance.

The plaintiff's attorney (or the plaintiff) is responsible for serving the summons and complaint, not the clerk.

There is no charge for the issuance of a summons, beyond the fee for commencing the adversary proceeding.

The plaintiff's attorney should have filled in his or her address in the appropriate space on the form. As the defendant may choose to serve an answer or motion on the plaintiff by mail or in person, the space should contain both the street and mailing address of the plaintiff's attorney, if the addresses are different. If the plaintiff is not represented by an attorney, the plaintiff's address(es) should be filled in.

The clerk may wish to fill in the space marked "Address of Clerk" before providing the form to the public.

As is set out in detail in the instructions to the public, there are a series of deadlines for actions to be taken in the adversary proceeding. The most important of these are:

1.   If the summons is not served within 7 days, a new summons must be issued. Rule 7004(e).

2.   If no summons is served within 120 days, the court is authorized by Rule 4(m) to dismiss the adversary proceeding on its own motion, after notice to the plaintiff.

3.   If the defendant does not answer or make a motion pursuant to Fed. R. Bankr. P. 7012 within 30 days, or such time as the court may fix, the plaintiff may seek the entry of a default. (See Form B 2600). The United States, its agencies, and its officers have 35 days to answer or make a motion.

If the court enters an order changing the last day by which the defendant must answer the complaint or make a motion, that date MUST be stated on the summons, and the superseded information regarding the deadline must be deleted.

B 2500C (Form 2500C) (12/15)

United States Bankruptcy Court

_____ District Of _____

In re _____,	)	Case No. _____
Debtor	)	
	)	Chapter _____
	)	
_____	)	
Plaintiff	)	
	)	
v.	)	Adv. Proc. No. _____
	)	
_____	)	
Defendant	)	

SUMMONS AND NOTICE OF TRIAL IN AN ADVERSARY PROCEEDING

YOU ARE SUMMONED and required to file a motion or answer to the complaint which is attached to this summons with the clerk of the bankruptcy court within 30 days after the date of issuance of this summons, except that the United States and its offices and agencies shall file a motion or answer to the complaint within 35 days.

        Address of the clerk:

At the same time, you must also serve a copy of the motion or answer upon the plaintiff's attorney.

        Name and Address of Plaintiff's Attorney:

If you make a motion, your time to answer is governed by Fed. R. Bankr. P. 7012.

YOU ARE NOTIFIED that a trial of the proceeding commenced by the filing of the complaint will be held at the following time and place:

        Address: Room:

                                      Date and Time:

IF YOU FAIL TO RESPOND TO THIS SUMMONS, YOUR FAILURE WILL BE DEEMED TO BE YOUR CONSENT TO ENTRY OF A JUDGMENT BY THE BANKRUPTCY COURT AND JUDGMENT BY DEFAULT MAY BE TAKEN AGAINST YOU FOR THE RELIEF DEMANDED IN THE COMPLAINT.

                            _____(Clerk of the Bankruptcy Court)

Date: _____ By: _____(Deputy Clerk)

Form B2500C

B 2500C (Form 2500C) (12/15)

CERTIFICATE OF SERVICE

I, _____ (name), certify that service of this summons and a copy of
the complaint was made _____ (date) by:

❑ Mail service: Regular, first class United States mail, postage fully pre-paid, addressed
to:

❑ Personal Service: By leaving the process with the defendant or with an officer or agent
of defendant at:

❑ Residence Service: By leaving the process with the following adult at:

❑ Certified Mail Service on an Insured Depository Institution: By sending the process by
certified mail addressed to the following officer of the defendant at:

❑ Publication: The defendant was served as follows: [Describe briefly]

❑ State Law: The defendant was served pursuant to the laws of the State of _____, as
follows: [Describe briefly]

If service was made by personal service, by residence service, or pursuant to state law, I further
certify that I am, and at all times during the service of process was, not less than 18 years of age and
not a party to the matter concerning which service of process was made.

Under penalty of perjury, I declare that the foregoing is true and correct.

Date _____   Signature _____

Print Name: _____

Business Address: _____

_____

(Added Dec. 1, 2015.)

Form B2500D.   Third–Party Summons

Instructions, Form B2500D
12.01.15

THIRD-PARTY SUMMONS

Purpose of the Form

Certain categories of relief may be granted in a bankruptcy court only through an adversary proceeding. The usual focus of the adversary proceeding is a trial of the allegations made by the plaintiff against the defendant.

The first step in commencing an adversary proceeding is the filing of a complaint, setting forth the facts and allegations which the plaintiff believes justify the granting of relief against the defendant, and stating the relief which the plaintiff seeks. As each complaint is unique, there is no specific form provided by the court.

The summons is the notice which accompanies the complaint, advising of the names of the parties, the court in which the adversary proceeding was filed, and the time limits for responding to the complaint.

The third-party summons is used when the defendant commences a third-party action. This occurs when the defendant seeks to include in the litigation an entity not already a party who may be liable to the defendant for all or part of the plaintiff's claims against the defendant. An easy example is the case of a car accident. The passenger in car A commences an adversary proceeding against the driver of car B. The driver of car B then files a third-party complaint against the driver of car A, to bring driver B's claims against driver A into the adversary proceeding.

In a third-party action, the defendant from the original lawsuit is known as the first-party defendant and the third-party plaintiff. The defendant in the third-party action is known as the third-party defendant.

As with a regular complaint, the filing of a third-party complaint triggers the issuance of a summons, using this form.

The third-party summons should be prepared by the third-party plaintiff's attorney and signed and issued by the clerk. The third-party plaintiff's attorney is responsible for serving the summons and a copy of the complaint. If the third-party plaintiff does not have an attorney, the third-party plaintiff is responsible for preparing the summons and serving the summons and complaint.

Applicable Law and Rules

1.   Fed. R. Bankr. P. 7014 incorporates by reference Rule 14 of the Federal Rules of Civil
        Procedure, concerning the conduct of third-party litigation. This rule provides that if the

Form B2500D
Page 2

third-party complaint is filed more than 14 days after the defendant serves an answer to the primary complaint, the defendant must obtain court approval prior to service. This approval must be obtained through a motion on notice to all of the parties of the original adversary proceeding.

2.   Fed. R. Bankr. P. 7004 adopts portions of Rule 4 of the Federal Rules of Civil Procedure, and sets forth other provisions for the issuance and service of a summons, including a third-party summons. These rules are detailed and complex, and should be read in their entirety.

3.   Rule 4(a) specifies the information that the third-party plaintiff's attorney (or the third-party plaintiff) must provide on the summons form. Rule 4(b) provides that, upon or after the filing of the third-party complaint, the clerk shall issue the summons to the third-party plaintiff's attorney (or the third-party plaintiff). It is then the responsibility of the third-party plaintiff's attorney (or the third-party plaintiff) to serve the summons on the third-party defendant and on the first-party plaintiff.

4.   If the debtor is the third-party plaintiff, section 342(c) of the Bankruptcy Code (11 U.S.C. § 342(c)) requires that the caption of the third-party complaint include the debtor's name and address, and the last four digits of the debtor's taxpayer identification number. An individual debtor's social security number is the debtor's taxpayer identification number. In order to satisfy this requirement, the portion of Official Form 416A which sets out the last four digits of the debtor's taxpayer identification number can be inserted in the caption of Form 2500D.

5.   A copy of the third-party complaint must be served with the third-party summons. Rule 4(c).

6.   It is a good idea to submit several copies of the summons with the original complaint, so that each copy may be signed by the court. It is recommended that at least five copies be submitted: one for the court records, one for service on the third-party defendant, one for service on the first-party plaintiff, one for the third-party plaintiff's attorney's records (or the plaintiff's records), and one to be returned to the court after the certificate of service has been completed. Of course, if there is more than one third-party defendant, each must be served with a separate copy of the summons, so additional copies should be submitted to the court for issuance.

7.   The summons and third-party complaint may be served in a variety of ways which are set forth in Rules 7004 and 4. When the third-party defendant is an individual, other than an infant or incompetent person, the easiest method is for the summons and complaint to be mailed by first class mail postage prepaid to the individual's dwelling house or usual place of abode or to the place where the individual regularly conducts a business or

Form B2500D
Page 3

profession. Rule 7004(b)(1).

8. Rule 7004(h) provides that service on a bank, savings and loan, or other insured depository institution in a contested matter or adversary proceeding must be made by certified mail addressed to an officer of the institution unless one of three exceptions applies. Those exceptions are 1) the attorney for the depository institution has filed a paper in the matter or has otherwise the procedure set out in the rule, 2) the court, following the procedure set out in the rule, orders otherwise, and 3) the depository institution has waived the requirement in writing by designating an officer to receive service. (Insured depository institutions are defined in section 3 of the Federal Deposit Insurance Act (12 U.S.C. § 1813).)

9. Because of the exceptions and the placement of the certified mail requirement in Rule 7004 rather than Fed. R. Bankr. P. 2002, the requirement applies in an adversary proceeding only to the service of the summons and complaint or the service of the third-party summons and third-party complaint and only if the depository institution is a defendant or third-party defendant.

10. If service was made by personal service, by residence service, or pursuant to state law, the service must be made by someone who is not a party, and who is at least 18 years of age. Rule 7004(a).

11. The summons and third-party complaint may be served anywhere in the United States. Rule 7004(d).

12. The summons and third-party complaint must be served 7 days after the summons is issued. Service is complete upon mailing, not upon delivery by the Postal Service. If more than 7 days pass before service is completed, a new summons will be issued for service. Rule 7004(e) and Fed. R. Bankr. P. 9006(e).

13. If the summons and third-party complaint are not served within 120 days of the filing of the third-party complaint, the court may dismiss the third-party action. Rule 4(m).

14. On the back of the summons is a certificate of service of the summons. After service has been made, this certificate should be completed, and filed with the court.

15. Fed. R. Bankr. P. 7012(a) provides that once a complaint is served, the third-party defendant has 30 days after the issuance of summons to file an answer or make one of the motions specified in Fed. R. Civ. P. 12 (made applicable by Rule 7012). If the United States or one of its agencies or officers is the third-party defendant, the time to file an answer or make a motion is 35 days. The court can order these time limits shortened or extended. If such an order is entered, the new time limit must be stated in the summons.

Form B2500D
Page 4

16.   Rule 14(a) provides that while the third-party defendant must file an answer or motion to
the third-party complaint, the third-party defendant has the option of whether to file an
answer or motion to the original complaint, unless the action is grounded in admiralty or
maritime law. In that event, the third-party defendant must file an answer or motion to
the first-party complaint.

Instructions

Caption

1.   Identify the Judicial District in which the bankruptcy case was filed. Example:
"Eastern District of California."

2.   "In re": Insert the name of the debtor as it appears in the bankruptcy petition.
Then insert the names of the plaintiff(s) and defendant(s) as they appear on the
original complaint. The name of the third party defendant as it appears on the
third party complaint should then be inserted.

3.   If the debtor is the third-party plaintiff, include the debtor's name, address, and the
last four digits of the debtor's taxpayer identification number in the caption. The
portion of Official Form 416A which includes the last four digits of the debtor's
taxpayer identification number can be inserted in the caption of the summons for
this purpose.

4.   "Case No." Insert the bankruptcy case number assigned by the court at the time of
filing.

5.   "Adv. Proc. No.": Insert the number assigned by the court to the adversary
proceeding at the time of the filing of the complaint.

Address of Clerk:

Be sure to indicate the proper address for the clerk's office.

Name and Address of Defendant's Attorney:

The complete mailing address of the defendant's attorney must be set forth in the space
provided, including zip code. If the street address is different, that must also be stated, including
room number. If the defendant (the third-party plaintiff) is not represented by an attorney, the
defendant's mailing and street address should be placed in the space.

Form B2500D
Page 5

<u>Name and Address of Plaintiff's Attorney:</u>

The complete mailing address of the first-party plaintiff's attorney must be set forth in the space provided, including zip code. If the street address is different, that must also be stated, including room number. If the plaintiff is not represented by an attorney, the plaintiff's mailing and street address should be placed in the space.

<u>Certificate of Service</u>

1.   Line 1 (name) is to be completed with the full name of the person who served the summons and complaint.

2.   Line 2 (date) is to be completed with the month, day and year service was perfected.

3.   The appropriate box should be checked to show how service was made.

        If mail service, state the mailing address, city, state and zip code of the place to which the summons and complaint were mailed.

        If personal service, state both the name of the person to whom the summons and complaint were given, and the address at which this occurred.

        If residence service, state both the name of the adult to whom the summons and complaint were given, and the address at which this occurred.

        If certified mail service on an insured depository institution, state both the name of the officer to whom the summons and complaint were mailed and the mailing address, city, state, and zip code to which service was mailed.

        If service by publication, describe the steps take to perfect service.

        If service was made pursuant to state law, fill in the blank with the name of state under whose laws the summons and complaint were served, and describe briefly the method of service, including the name of the person served and the address at which they were served.

4.   Date: Insert on this line the month, day, and year the certificate is signed.

5.   Signature: The person who completed service of the summons and complaint must sign. This must be an ORIGINAL signature.

6.   In the space directly below the Date and Signature lines, print or type the name and

Form B2500D
Page 6

    business address of the person who signed the certificate.

General Information for the Clerk

    The third-party summons is used when the defendant commences a third-party action. This occurs when the defendant seeks to include in the litigation an entity not already a party who may be liable to the defendant for all or part of the plaintiff's claims against the defendant. An easy example is the case of a car accident. The passenger in car A commences an adversary proceeding against the driver of car B. The driver of car B then files a third-party complaint against the driver of car A, to bring driver B's claims against driver A into the adversary proceeding.

    The third-party complaint does not commence a new action. No new file or docket should be created. Instead, when a third-party complaint is filed, the clerk should simply amend the caption of the pending adversary proceeding.

    Fed. R. Bankr. P. 7014 incorporates by reference Rule 14 of the Federal Rules of Civil Procedure regarding the conduct of third-party actions. Although Rule 14 requires the defendant to obtain court approval prior to commencement of a third-party action, if that action is commenced more than 14 days after the defendant serves an answer on the plaintiff, this a jurisdictional issue for the parties to resolve. The clerk should neither refuse to accept a third-party complaint for filing due to the failure of the third-party plaintiff to obtain the necessary court order, nor should the clerk advise any of the parties of the specific requirements of Rule 14 for court authorization for commencing a third-party action.

    Fed. R. Bankr. P. 7004 incorporates by reference Rule 4(b) of the Federal Rules of Civil Procedure, which provides that the clerk is to issue the third-party summons to the third-party plaintiff attorney (or the third-party plaintiff) upon or after the filing of the complaint. If requested, more than one copy can be issued. In the instructions to the public, it is recommended that the plaintiff seek the issuance of at least five summons: one for the court to file with the original complaint; one for service on the third-party defendant, one for service on the first-party plaintiff, one for the third-party plaintiff's records (or the third-party plaintiff's attorney's records), and one to be returned to the court after the certificate of service has been completed. Of course, if there is more than one third-party defendant, each must be served with a separate copy of the summons, so additional copies are recommended to be submitted to the court for issuance.

    The third-party plaintiff's attorney (or the third-party plaintiff) is responsible for serving the summons and third-party complaint, not the clerk.

    There is no fee for the filing of the third-party complaint, or for the issuance of any third-party summons.

Form B2500D
Page 7

The attorney for the third-party plaintiff (defendant) should have filled in his or her address and the address of the attorney for the first-party plaintiff (plaintiff) in the appropriate spaces on the form. As the third-party defendant may choose to serve an answer or motion on the parties by mail or in person, the spaces should contain both the street and mailing address of the attorneys if the addresses are different. If any of the parties are not represented by an attorney, that party's own name and address(es) should be entered in the appropriate space.

The clerk may wish to fill in the space marked "Address of Clerk" before providing the form to the public.

As is set out in detail in the instructions to the public, there are a series of deadlines for actions to be taken in the adversary proceeding. The most important of these are:

1.   If the summons is not served within 7 days, a new summons must be issued. Rule 7004(e).

2.   If no summons is served within 120 days, the court is authorized by Rule 4(m) to dismiss the adversary proceeding on its own motion, after notice to the plaintiff.

3.   If the defendant does not answer or make a motion pursuant to Fed. R. Bankr. P. 7012 within 30 days, or such time as the court may fix, the plaintiff may seek the entry of a default. (See form B 2600). The United States, its agencies, and its officers have 35 days to answer or make a motion.

If the court enters an order changing the last day by which the defendant must answer the complaint or make a motion, that date MUST be stated on the summons, and the superseded information regarding the deadline must be deleted.

The third-party summons does not include any place for notice of a pretrial conference or trial date. Such notice, if required, should be given by the third-party plaintiff in a separate document.

Form B2500D

DIRECTOR'S FORMS

B2500D (Form 2500D) (12/15)

United States Bankruptcy Court
_____ District Of _____

In re _____,) Case No. _____
   Debtor)
_____) Chapter _____
   Plaintiff)
    v.) Adv. Proc. No. _____
_____)
Defendant, Third-party plaintiff)
    v.)
_____)
  Third-party defendant)

THIRD-PARTY SUMMONS

YOU ARE SUMMONED and required to file a motion or answer to the third-party complaint which is attached to this summons with the clerk of the bankruptcy court within 30 days after the date of issuance of this summons, except that the United States and its offices and agencies shall file a motion or answer to the third-party complaint within 35 days.

   Address of the clerk:

At the same time, you must also serve a copy of the motion or answer upon the defendant's attorney.

   Name and Address of Defendant's Attorney:

At the same time, you must also serve a copy of the motion or answer upon the plaintiff's attorney.

   Name and Address of Plaintiff's Attorney:

If you make a motion, your time to answer is governed by Fed. R. Bankr. P. 7012. If you are also being served with a copy of the complaint of the plaintiff, you have the option of not answering the plaintiff's complaint **unless** this is an admiralty or maritime action subject to the provisions of Fed. R. Civ. P. 9(h) and 14(c), in which case you are required to file a motion or an answer to both the plaintiff's complaint and the third-party complaint, and to serve a copy of your motion or answer upon the appropriate parties.

IF YOU FAIL TO RESPOND TO THIS SUMMONS, YOUR FAILURE WILL BE DEEMED TO BE YOUR CONSENT TO ENTRY OF A JUDGMENT BY THE BANKRUPTCY COURT AND JUDGMENT BY DEFAULT MAY BE TAKEN AGAINST YOU FOR THE RELIEF DEMANDED IN THE THIRD-PARTY COMPLAINT.

        _____ (Clerk of the Bankruptcy Court)

Date: _____ By: _____ (Deputy Clerk)

B2500D (Form 2500D) (12/15)

CERTIFICATE OF SERVICE

I, _____(name), certify that service of this summons and a copy of
the third-party complaint was made _____(date) by:

☐   Mail service: Regular, first class United States mail, postage fully pre-paid, addressed
      to:

☐   Personal Service: By leaving the process with the third-party defendant or with an
      officer or agent of third-party defendant at:

☐   Residence Service: By leaving the process with the following adult at:

☐   Certified Mail Service on an Insured Depository Institution: By sending the process by
      certified mail addressed to the following officer of the third-party defendant at:

☐   Publication: The third-party defendant was served as follows: [Describe briefly]

☐   State Law: The third-party defendant was served pursuant to the laws of the State of
      _____, as follows: [Describe briefly]

   If service was made by personal service, by residence service, or pursuant to state law, I
further certify that I am, and at all times during the service of process was, not less than 18 years of age
and not a party to the matter concerning which service of process was made.

   Under penalty of perjury, I declare that the foregoing is true and correct.

   Date _____   Signature _____

      Print Name: _____

      Business Address: _____

                             _____

(Added Dec. 1, 2015.)

Form B2500E.   Summons to Debtor
in Involuntary Case

Instructions, Form 2500E
04/16

SUMMONS TO DEBTOR IN INVOLUNTARY CASE

Purpose of the Form

Bankruptcy cases can arise in two ways: An individual or business or municipality may file a voluntary petition, or creditors may file an involuntary petition against an individual or business.

The first step in commencing an involuntary bankruptcy proceeding is the filing of a petition by a creditor or creditors, using Official Form 5. The summons is the notice which accompanies the petition, advising of the names of the debtor and the attorney for the petitioning creditor(s), the court in which the proceeding was filed, and the time limits for responding to the petition.

Applicable Law and Rules

1. The primary statutory provisions for an involuntary bankruptcy proceeding are found in Section 303 of the Bankruptcy Code (11 U.S.C. § 303). These provisions are complex, and there are substantial penalties for filing an improper involuntary petition. Section 303 should therefore be read in its entirety prior to the filing of an involuntary petition.

2. Section 303(a) limits an involuntary petition to chapters 7 and 11. It further provides that the involuntary debtor may not be a farmer, family farmer, or a corporation which not is a moneyed, business, or commercial corporation.

3. Section 303(b) provides that each of the petitioning creditors must hold claims against the debtor which are not contingent as to liability and which are not the subject of a bona fide dispute. Although there are several complex criteria, the two basic ones are: 1) if the debtor has fewer than 12 creditors, only one creditor need file the involuntary petition, whereas if the debtor has 12 or more creditors, at least three of the creditors must join in the petition; and 2) the claims of the petitioning creditor or creditors must total at least $15,775.[1]

4. Fed. Bankr. P. 1010 states:

    On the filing of an involuntary petition . . . the clerk shall forthwith issue a summons for service. When an involuntary petition is filed, service shall be made on the debtor . . . . The summons shall be served with a copy of the petition in the manner provided for service of a summons and complaint by Rule 7004(a) or (b).

---

[1] The amount is subject to adjustment in 4/01/19, and every three years thereafter with respect to cases commenced on or after the date of adjustment.

Form 2500E
Page 2

If service cannot be so made, the court may order that the summons and petition to be served by mailing copies to the party's last known address, and by at least one publication in a manner and form directed by the court. The summons and petition may be served on the party anywhere. Rule 7004(e) and Rule 4(l) [of the Federal Rules of Civil Procedure] apply when service is made or attempted under this rule.

5.   Fed. R. Bankr. P. 7004(a) adopts portions of Fed. R. Civ. P. 4 and sets forth other provisions for the issuance and service of a summons. These rules are detailed and complex, and should be read in their entirety.

6.   Rule 4(a) specifies the information that the plaintiff's attorney (or the plaintiff) must provide on the summons form. Rule 4(b), provides that the clerk shall issue the summons to the petitioning creditor or its attorney. It is then the responsibility of the petitioning creditor (i.e., the "plaintiff") or the attorney to serve the summons on the debtor. On a summons to a debtor in an involuntary case, the petitioning creditor's attorney (or petitioning creditor) must fulfill the responsibilities of the plaintiff's attorney (or the plaintiff) described in Rule 4.

7.   A copy of the petition must be served with the summons. Rule 4(b).

8.   It is a good idea to submit several copies of the summons to the court with the petition, so that each copy may be signed by the court: one for the court records, one for service on the debtor, one for each of petitioning creditor's records (or the creditor's attorney's records), and one to be returned to the court after the certificate of service has been completed.

9.   The summons and petition may be served in a variety of ways which are set forth in Rules 1010, 7004, and 4. When the debtor is an individual, other than an infant or incompetent person, the easiest method is for the summons and petition to be mailed by first class mail postage prepaid to the individual's dwelling house or usual place of abode or to the place where the individual regularly conducts a business or profession. Rule 7004(b)(1).

10.   If service is made by personal service, by residence service, or pursuant to state law, the service must be made by someone who is not a party, and who is at least 18 years of age. Rule 7004(a).

11.   The summons and petition must be served 7 days after the summons is issued. Service is complete upon mailing, not upon delivery by the Postal Service. If more than 7 days pass before service is completed, a new summons will be issued for service. Rule 7004(e) and Fed. R. Bankr. P. 9006(e).

Form B2500E

DIRECTOR'S FORMS

Form 2500E
Page 3

12. If the summons and petition are not served within 90 days of the filing of the complaint, the court may dismiss the action. Rule 4(m).

13. On the back of the summons is a certificate of service of the summons. After service has been made, this certificate should be completed, and filed with the court.

14. Rule 1011 grants the debtor 21 days from the service of the summons to reply to the petition. Under the provisions of Section 303(h), if the debtor fails to timely reply to the involuntary petition, the court will enter an order for relief under the appropriate chapter of the Bankruptcy Code. See Form B 2530. If the debtor timely files an answer, the court will conduct a trial and will only enter the order for relief if the debtor is not generally paying its undisputed debts as they become due, or if within 120 days before the date of the filing of the petition, a custodian, other than a trustee, receiver, or agent authorized to take charge of less than substantially all of the property of the debtor for the purpose of enforcing a lien against such property, was appointed or took possession. Fed. R. Bankr. P. 1018 sets forth the procedures to be followed in the event of a contested involuntary petition.

15. Section 303(i) authorizes the court to order creditors that file improper involuntary petitions to pay the costs and attorney's fees of the debtor. If the court finds that the involuntary petition was brought in bad faith, it can also order the petitioning creditors to pay for all damages proximately caused by the filing, and may assess punitive damages.

Instructions

Caption

1. Identify the Judicial District in which the bankruptcy case was filed. Example: "Eastern District of California."

2. "In re": Insert the name of the debtor as it appears in the bankruptcy petition including all names, including trade names, used by the debtor within the last eight years.

3. "Case No.": Insert the bankruptcy case number assigned by the court at the time of filing.

4. "Chapter No.": Insert the chapter of the Bankruptcy Code under which the case was filed.

Address of Clerk:

Be sure to indicate the proper address for the clerk's office.

Form 2500E
Page 4

Name and Address of Petitioner's Attorney:

The complete mailing address of the attorney for the petitioning creditor must be set forth in the space provided, including zip code. If the street address is different, that must also be stated, including room number. If the petitioning creditor is not represented by an attorney, the petitioning creditor's mailing and street address should be placed in the space.

Certificate of Service

1.   Line 1 (name) is to be completed with the full name of the person who served the summons and petition.

2.   Line 1 (date) is to be completed with the month, day and year service was perfected.

3.   Describe the mode of service and the address at which the debtor was served in the space provided.

     If personal service was made, also include the name of the person to whom the summons and petition were given. If residence service was made, also include the name of the adult to whom the summons and petition were given. If service was made by publication, also describe the steps take to perfect service. If service was made pursuant to state law, also include the name of state under whose laws the summons and petition were served and a brief description of the method of service, including the name of the person served.

4.   Date: Insert on this line the month, day and year the certificate is signed.

5.   Signature: The person who completed service of the summons and petition must sign. This must be an ORIGINAL signature.

6.   In the space directly the Signature line, print or type the name and business address of the person who signed the certificate.

General Information for the Clerk

Fed. R. Bankr. P. 1010 requires a summons to be issued every time an involuntary petition is filed. The procedure is the same as in an adversary proceeding except that the petitioning creditor stands in for the "plaintiff" and debtor for the "defendant".

Fed. R. Bankr. P. 7004 incorporates by reference Rule 4(b) of the Federal Rules of Civil Procedure, which in combination with Rule 1010, provide that the clerk is to issue the summons to the petitioning creditor or the petitioning creditor's attorney upon or after the filing of the petition. If requested, more than one copy can be issued. In the instructions to the public, it is

Form 2500E
Page 5

recommended that the petitioning creditor seek the issuance of several copies of the summons: one for the court to file with the original petition; one for service on the debtor; one for each petitioning creditor's records (or the creditor's attorney's records), and one to be returned to the court after the certificate of service has been completed. The attorney representing the petitioning creditor or creditors is responsible for serving the summons and involuntary petition, not the clerk.

There is no charge for the issuance of a summons, beyond the fee for commencing the involuntary proceeding.

The petitioning creditor should have filled in the attorney's address in the appropriate space on the form. As the debtor may choose to serve an answer by mail or in person, the space should contain both the street and mailing address of the attorney, if the addresses are different. If the petitioning creditor is not represented by an attorney, the address of each petitioning creditor should be supplied.

The clerk may wish to fill in the space marked "Address of Clerk" before providing the form to the petitioning creditors.

As is set out in detail in the instructions to the public, there are a series of deadlines for actions to be taken in the involuntary proceeding. The most important of these are:

1. If the summons is not served within 7 days, a new summons must be issued. Rule 7004(e).

2. If no summons is served within 90 days, the court is authorized by Rule 4(m) to dismiss the proceeding on its own motion, after notice to the plaintiff.

3. If the defendant does not answer or make a motion pursuant to Fed. R. Bankr. P. 1011 within 21 days, or such time as court may fix, section 303(h) provides that the court shall enter an order for relief.

4. If the debtor timely files an answer or a motion pursuant to Rule 1011, section 303(h) requires that a trial be held to determine whether an order for relief is warranted. Bankruptcy Rule 1013 provides that "the court shall determine the issues of a contested petition at the earliest practicable time and forthwith enter an order for relief, dismiss the petition, or enter any other appropriate order."

B2500E (Form 2500E) (12/15)

United States Bankruptcy Court
_____District Of _____

In re _____,   )   Case No. _____
                 Debtor*   )
)   Chapter _____
)
)

SUMMONS TO DEBTOR IN INVOLUNTARY CASE

To the above named debtor:

A petition under title 11, United States Code was filed against you in this bankruptcy court on
_____ (date), requesting an order for relief under chapter _____ of the Bankruptcy
Code (title 11 of the United States Code).

YOU ARE SUMMONED and required to file with the clerk of the bankruptcy court a motion
or answer to the petition within 21 days after the service of this summons. A copy of the petition is
attached.

Address of the clerk:

At the same time, you must also serve a copy of your motion or answer on petitioner's attorney.

Name and Address of Petitioner's Attorney:

If you make a motion, your time to answer is governed by Fed. R. Bankr. P. 1011(c).

If you fail to respond to this summons, the order for relief will be entered.

_____ (Clerk of the Bankruptcy Court)

Date: _____   By: _____(Deputy Clerk)

* Set forth all names, including trade names, used by the debtor within the last 8 years. (Fed. R .Bankr. P. 1005).

Form B2500E

B2500E (Form 2500E) (12/15)

CERTIFICATE OF SERVICE

I, _____(name), certify that on _____
(date), I served this summons and a copy of the involuntary petition on _____
(name), the debtor in this case, by *[describe the mode of service and the address at which the debtor was served]*:

If service was made by personal service, by residence service, or pursuant to state law, I further certify that I am, and at all times during the service of process was, not less than 18 years of age and not a party to the matter concerning which service of process was made.

Under penalty of perjury, I declare that the foregoing is true and correct.

Date _____   Signature _____

Print Name: _____

Business Address: _____

_____

(Added Dec. 1, 2015. Amended April 1, 2016.)

Form B2500F. Summons in a Chapter 15 Case
Seeking Recognition of a Foreign
Nonmain Proceeding

B2500F (Form 2500F) (12/15)

United States Bankruptcy Court
_____District Of _____

In re _____,   Case No. _____

       Debtor   Chapter 15

SUMMONS IN A CHAPTER 15 CASE SEEKING RECOGNITION
OF A FOREIGN NONMAIN PROCEEDING

To _____:

     A petition for recognition of a foreign nonmain proceeding under chapter 15 of the United States Bankruptcy Code was filed in this bankruptcy court on _____by a representative of the debtor named above. A copy of the petition is attached to this summons .

     YOU ARE SUMMONED and required to file a motion or answer to the petition for recognition with the clerk of the bankruptcy court within __ days after the date of issuance of this summons.

         Address of the clerk:

At the same time, you must also serve a copy of the motion or answer upon the foreign representative's attorney.

         Name and address of foreign representative's attorney:

If you make a motion, your time to answer is governed by Fed. R. Bankr. P. 7012.

IF YOU FAIL TO RESPOND TO THIS SUMMONS, YOUR FAILURE WILL BE DEEMED TO BE YOUR CONSENT TO ENTRY OF AN ORDER RECOGNIZING THE FOREIGN NONMAIN PROCEEDING.

                         _____ (Clerk)

    Date: _____   By: _____ (Deputy Clerk)

Pursuant to Fed. R. Bankr. P. 1010, service shall be made on the debtor, any entity against whom provisional relief is sought under section 1519 of the Bankruptcy Code, and on any other parties as the court may direct.

Fed. R. Bankr. P. 1011(b) provides that a motion or answer to the petition shall be filed within 21 days after service of the summons unless the court prescribes a different time.

For Complete Annotation Materials, see United States Code Annotated

Form B2500F

B2500F (Form 2500F) (12/15)

CERTIFICATE OF SERVICE

I, _____(name), certify that service of this summons and a copy of the petition for recognition was made on _____(date) by:

❑   Mail service: Regular, first class United States mail, postage fully pre-paid, addressed to:

❑   Personal Service: By leaving the summons and petition with the party in interest to the petition or with an officer or agent of the party in interest at:

❑   Residence Service: By leaving the summons and petition with the following adult at:

❑   Certified Mail Service on an Insured Depository Institution: By sending the process by certified mail addressed to the following officer of the depository institution at:

❑   State Law: The summons and petition were served pursuant to the laws of the State of _____, as follows: [Describe briefly]

❑   Service in a Foreign Country: The summons and petition were served in a foreign country on an individual as provided by Fed. R. Civ. Proc 4(f), as incorporated by Fed. R. Bankr. P. 7004(a), or on a corporation as provided by Fed. R. Civ. P. 4(h), also incorporated by Fed. R. Bankr. P. 7004(a), as follows: [Describe briefly]

If service was made by personal service, by residence service, pursuant to state law, or in a foreign country, I further certify that I am, and at all times during the service of process was, not less than 18 years of age and not a party to the matter concerning which service of process was made.

Under penalty of perjury under the laws of the United States, I declare that the foregoing is true and correct.

Date _____   Signature _____

       Print Name: _____

       Business Address: _____

                           _____

If service is made in a foreign country pursuant to Fed. R. Civ. P. 4(f)(2),(3), attach a receipt signed by the addressee or other evidence that the summons and petition were delivered to the addressee. Fed. R. Civ. P. 4(l)(2), as incorporated by Fed. R. Bankr. P. 7004(a).

(Added Dec. 1, 2015.)

**Form B2530. Order for Relief
in an Involuntary Case**

B2530 (Form 2530 12/15)

United States Bankruptcy Court
_____ District Of _____

In re _____ Case No. _____
                           Debtor*

Address: _____ Chapter _____

Last four digits of Social-Security or Individual Taxpayer-
Identification (ITIN) No(s).(if any): _____
Employer Tax-Identification (EIN) No(s).(if any): _____

ORDER FOR RELIEF IN
AN INVOLUNTARY CASE

On consideration of the petition filed on _____ against
                                                  (date)
the above-named debtor, an order for relief under chapter ____of the Bankruptcy Code (title 11

of the United States Code) is granted.

_____   _____
      Date   Bankruptcy Judge

*Set forth all names, including trade names, used by the debtor within the last 8 years. (Fed. R. Bankr. P. 1005).

(Added Dec. 1, 2015.)

Form B2540

Form B2540. Subpoena for
Rule 2004 Examination

B2540 (Form 2540 – Subpoena for Rule 2004 Examination) (12/15)

UNITED STATES BANKRUPTCY COURT

_____ District of _____

In re _____   Case No. _____

_____ Debtor

Chapter _____

SUBPOENA FOR RULE 2004 EXAMINATION

To: _____

(Name of person to whom the subpoena is directed)

☐ _Testimony:_ YOU ARE COMMANDED to appear at the time, date, and place set forth below to testify at an examination under Rule 2004, Federal Rules of Bankruptcy Procedure. A copy of the court order authorizing the examination is attached.

PLACE	DATE AND TIME

The examination will be recorded by this method: _____

☐ _Production:_ You, or your representatives, must also bring with you to the examination the following documents, electronically stored information, or objects, and must permit inspection, copying, testing, or sampling of the material:

_____

The following provisions of Fed. R. Civ. P. 45, made applicable in bankruptcy cases by Fed. R. Bankr. P. 9016, are attached – Rule 45(c), relating to the place of compliance; Rule 45(d), relating to your protection as a person subject to a subpoena; and Rule 45(e) and 45(g), relating to your duty to respond to this subpoena and the potential consequences of not doing so.

Date: _____

CLERK OF COURT

OR

_____   _____
Signature of Clerk or Deputy Clerk   _Attorney's signature_

The name, address, email address, and telephone number of the attorney representing _(name of party)_
_____ , who issues or requests this subpoena, are:

_____

Notice to the person who issues or requests this subpoena

If this subpoena commands the production of documents, electronically stored information, or tangible things, or the inspection of premises before trial, a notice and a copy of this subpoena must be served on each party before it is served on the person to whom it is directed. Fed. R. Civ. P. 45(a)(4).

B2540 (Form 2540 – Subpoena for Rule 2004 Examination) (Page 2)

PROOF OF SERVICE
(This section should not be filed with the court unless required by Fed. R. Civ. P. 45.)

I received this subpoena for *(name of individual and title, if any):* _____
on *(date)* _____ .

☐ I served the subpoena by delivering a copy to the named person as follows:
_____
_____ on *(date)* _____ ; or

☐ I returned the subpoena unexecuted because:
_____

Unless the subpoena was issued on behalf of the United States, or one of its officers or agents, I have also tendered to the witness the fees for one day's attendance, and the mileage allowed by law, in the amount of $ _____ .

My fees are $ _____ for travel and $ _____ for services, for a total of $ _____ .

      I declare under penalty of perjury that this information is true and correct.

Date: _____

                    _____
                          Server's signature

                    _____
                          Printed name and title

                    _____
                          Server's address

Additional information concerning attempted service, etc.:

Form B2540

B2540 (Form 2540 – Subpoena for Rule 2004 Examination) (Page 3)

Federal Rule of Civil Procedure 45(c), (d), (e), and (g) (Effective 12/1/13)
(made applicable in bankruptcy cases by Rule 9016, Federal Rules of Bankruptcy Procedure)

(c) Place of compliance.

(1) For a Trial, Hearing, or Deposition. A subpoena may command a person to attend a trial, hearing, or deposition only as follows:
(A) within 100 miles of where the person resides, is employed, or regularly transacts business in person; or
(B) within the state where the person resides, is employed, or regularly transacts business in person, if the person
(i) is a party or a party's officer; or
(ii) is commanded to attend a trial and would not incur substantial expense.

(2) For Other Discovery. A subpoena may command:
(A) production of documents, or electronically stored information, or things at a place within 100 miles of where the person resides, is employed, or regularly transacts business in person; and
(B) inspection of premises, at the premises to be inspected.

(d) Protecting a Person Subject to a Subpoena; Enforcement.

(1) Avoiding Undue Burden or Expense; Sanctions. A party or attorney responsible for issuing and serving a subpoena must take reasonable steps to avoid imposing undue burden or expense on a person subject to the subpoena. The court for the district where compliance is required must enforce this duty and impose an appropriate sanction — which may include lost earnings and reasonable attorney's fees — on a party or attorney who fails to comply.

(2) Command to Produce Materials or Permit Inspection.
(A) *Appearance Not Required.* A person commanded to produce documents, electronically stored information, or tangible things, or to permit the inspection of premises, need not appear in person at the place of production or inspection unless also commanded to appear for a deposition, hearing, or trial.
(B) *Objections.* A person commanded to produce documents or tangible things or to permit inspection may serve on the party or attorney designated in the subpoena a written objection to inspecting, copying, testing or sampling any or all of the materials or to inspecting the premises — or to producing electronically stored information in the form or forms requested. The objection must be served before the earlier of the time specified for compliance or 14 days after the subpoena is served. If an objection is made, the following rules apply:
(i) At any time, on notice to the commanded person, the serving party may move the court for the district where compliance is required for an order compelling production or inspection.
(ii) These acts may be required only as directed in the order, and the order must protect a person who is neither a party nor a party's officer from significant expense resulting from compliance.

(3) Quashing or Modifying a Subpoena.
(A) *When Required.* On timely motion, the court for the district where compliance is required must quash or modify a subpoena that:
(i) fails to allow a reasonable time to comply;
(ii) requires a person to comply beyond the geographical limits specified in Rule 45(c);
(iii) requires disclosure of privileged or other protected matter, if no exception or waiver applies; or
(iv) subjects a person to undue burden.
(B) *When Permitted.* To protect a person subject to or affected by a subpoena, the court for the district where compliance is required may, on motion, quash or modify the subpoena if it requires:
(i) disclosing a trade secret or other confidential research, development, or commercial information; or

(ii) disclosing an unretained expert's opinion or information that does not describe specific occurrences in dispute and results from the expert's study that was not requested by a party.
(C) *Specifying Conditions as an Alternative.* In the circumstances described in Rule 45(d)(3)(B), the court may, instead of quashing or modifying a subpoena, order appearance or production under specified conditions if the serving party:
(i) shows a substantial need for the testimony or material that cannot be otherwise met without undue hardship; and
(ii) ensures that the subpoenaed person will be reasonably compensated.

(e) Duties in Responding to a Subpoena.

(1) Producing Documents or Electronically Stored Information. These procedures apply to producing documents or electronically stored information:
(A) *Documents.* A person responding to a subpoena to produce documents must produce them as they are kept in the ordinary course of business or must organize and label them to correspond to the categories in the demand.
(B) *Form for Producing Electronically Stored Information Not Specified.* If a subpoena does not specify a form for producing electronically stored information, the person responding must produce it in a form or forms in which it is ordinarily maintained or in a reasonably usable form or forms.
(C) *Electronically Stored Information Produced in Only One Form.* The person responding need not produce the same electronically stored information in more than one form.
(D) *Inaccessible Electronically Stored Information.* The person responding need not provide discovery of electronically stored information from sources that the person identifies as not reasonably accessible because of undue burden or cost. On motion to compel discovery or for a protective order, the person responding must show that the information is not reasonably accessible because of undue burden or cost. If that showing is made, the court may nonetheless order discovery from such sources if the requesting party shows good cause, considering the limitations of Rule 26(b)(2)(C). The court may specify conditions for the discovery.

(2) Claiming Privilege or Protection.
(A) *Information Withheld.* A person withholding subpoenaed information under a claim that it is privileged or subject to protection as trial-preparation material must:
(i) expressly make the claim; and
(ii) describe the nature of the withheld documents, communications, or tangible things in a manner that, without revealing information itself privileged or protected, will enable the parties to assess the claim.
(B) *Information Produced.* If information produced in response to a subpoena is subject to a claim of privilege or of protection as trial-preparation material, the person making the claim may notify any party that received the information of the claim and the basis for it. After being notified, a party must promptly return, sequester, or destroy the specified information and any copies it has, must not use or disclose the information until the claim is resolved, must take reasonable steps to retrieve the information if the party disclosed it before being notified, and may promptly present the information under seal to the court for the district where compliance is required for a determination of the claim. The person who produced the information must preserve the information until the claim is resolved.

(g) Contempt. The court for the district where compliance is required – and also, after a motion is transferred, the issuing court – may hold in contempt a person who, having been served, fails without adequate excuse to obey the subpoena or an order related to it.

For access to subpoena materials, see Fed. R. Civ. P. 45(a) Committee Note (2013)

(Added Dec. 1, 2015.)

Form B2550. Subpoena in an Adversary Proceeding

B2550 (Form 2550 Subpoena to Appear and Testify at a Hearing or Trial in a Bankruptcy Case or Adversary Proceeding) (12/15)

UNITED STATES BANKRUPTCY COURT

_____ District of _____

In re _____
                  Debtor

     (Complete if issued in an adversary proceeding)

Case No. _____

Chapter _____

_____
              Plaintiff
              v.

Adv. Proc. No. _____

_____
            Defendant

SUBPOENA TO APPEAR AND TESTIFY
AT A HEARING OR TRIAL IN A BANKRUPTCY CASE (OR ADVERSARY PROCEEDING)

To: _____
         (Name of person to whom the subpoena is directed)

☐ **YOU ARE COMMANDED** to appear in the United States Bankruptcy Court at the time, date, and place set forth below to testify at a hearing or trial in this bankruptcy case (or adversary proceeding). When you arrive, you must remain at the court until the judge or a court official allows you to leave.

PLACE	COURTROOM
	DATE AND TIME

You must also bring with you the following documents, electronically stored information, or objects *(leave blank if not applicable)*:

     The following provisions of Fed. R. Civ. P. 45, made applicable in bankruptcy cases by Fed. R. Bankr. P. 9016, are attached – Rule 45(c), relating to the place of compliance; Rule 45(d), relating to your protection as a person subject to a subpoena; and Rule 45(e) and 45(g), relating to your duty to respond to this subpoena and the potential consequences of not doing so.

Date: _____

CLERK OF COURT

                    OR

Signature of Clerk or Deputy Clerk   *Attorney's signature*

The name, address, email address, and telephone number of the attorney representing *(name of party)* _____ , who issues or requests this subpoena, are:

_____

Notice to the person who issues or requests this subpoena

If this subpoena commands the production of documents, electronically stored information, or tangible things, or the inspection of premises before trial, a notice and a copy of this subpoena must be served on each party before it is served on the person to whom it is directed. Fed. R. Civ. P. 45(a)(4).

B2550 (Form 2550 – Subpoena to Appear and Testify at a Hearing or Trial in a Bankruptcy Case or Adversary Proceeding) (Page 2)

PROOF OF SERVICE
(This section should not be filed with the court unless required by Fed. R. Civ. P. 45.)

I received this subpoena for *(name of individual and title, if any)*: _____
on *(date)* _____ .

☐ I served the subpoena by delivering a copy to the named person as follows: _____

_____ on *(date)* _____ ; or

☐ I returned the subpoena unexecuted because: _____

Unless the subpoena was issued on behalf of the United States, or one of its officers or agents, I have also tendered to the witness the fees for one day's attendance, and the mileage allowed by law, in the amount of $ _____ .

My fees are $ _____ for travel and $ _____ for services, for a total of $ _____ .

I declare under penalty of perjury that this information is true and correct.

Date: _____

_____
Server's signature

_____
Printed name and title

_____
Server's address

Additional information concerning attempted service, etc.:

B2550 (Form 2550 – Subpoena to Appear and Testify at a Hearing or Trial in a Bankruptcy Case or Adversary Proceeding) (Page 3)

Federal Rule of Civil Procedure 45(c), (d), (e), and (g) (Effective 12/1/13)
(made applicable in bankruptcy cases by Rule 9016, Federal Rules of Bankruptcy Procedure)

(c) Place of compliance.

(1) For a Trial, Hearing, or Deposition. A subpoena may command a person to attend a trial, hearing, or deposition only as follows:
(A) within 100 miles of where the person resides, is employed, or regularly transacts business in person; or
(B) within the state where the person resides, is employed, or regularly transacts business in person, if the person
(i) is a party or a party's officer; or
(ii) is commanded to attend a trial and would not incur substantial expense.

(2) For Other Discovery. A subpoena may command:
(A) production of documents, or electronically stored information, or things at a place within 100 miles of where the person resides, is employed, or regularly transacts business in person; and
(B) inspection of premises, at the premises to be inspected.

(d) Protecting a Person Subject to a Subpoena; Enforcement.

(1) Avoiding Undue Burden or Expense; Sanctions. A party or attorney responsible for issuing and serving a subpoena must take reasonable steps to avoid imposing undue burden or expense on a person subject to the subpoena. The court for the district where compliance is required must enforce this duty and impose an appropriate sanction — which may include lost earnings and reasonable attorney's fees — on a party or attorney who fails to comply.

(2) Command to Produce Materials or Permit Inspection.
(A) *Appearance Not Required.* A person commanded to produce documents, electronically stored information, or tangible things, or to permit the inspection of premises, need not appear in person at the place of production or inspection unless also commanded to appear for a deposition, hearing, or trial.
(B) *Objections.* A person commanded to produce documents or tangible things or to permit inspection may serve on the party or attorney designated in the subpoena a written objection to inspecting, copying, testing or sampling any or all of the materials or to inspecting the premises — or to producing electronically stored information in the form or forms requested. The objection must be served before the earlier of the time specified for compliance or 14 days after the subpoena is served. If an objection is made, the following rules apply:
(i) At any time, on notice to the commanded person, the serving party may move the court for the district where compliance is required for an order compelling production or inspection.
(ii) These acts may be required only as directed in the order, and the order must protect a person who is neither a party nor a party's officer from significant expense resulting from compliance.

(3) Quashing or Modifying a Subpoena.
(A) *When Required.* On timely motion, the court for the district where compliance is required must quash or modify a subpoena that:
(i) fails to allow a reasonable time to comply;
(ii) requires a person to comply beyond the geographical limits specified in Rule 45(c);
(iii) requires disclosure of privileged or other protected matter, if no exception or waiver applies; or
(iv) subjects a person to undue burden.
(B) *When Permitted.* To protect a person subject to or affected by a subpoena, the court for the district where compliance is required may, on motion, quash or modify the subpoena if it requires:
(i) disclosing a trade secret or other confidential research, development, or commercial information; or

(ii) disclosing an unretained expert's opinion or information that does not describe specific occurrences in dispute and results from the expert's study that was not requested by a party.
(C) *Specifying Conditions as an Alternative.* In the circumstances described in Rule 45(d)(3)(B), the court may, instead of quashing or modifying a subpoena, order appearance or production under specified conditions if the serving party:
(i) shows a substantial need for the testimony or material that cannot be otherwise met without undue hardship; and
(ii) ensures that the subpoenaed person will be reasonably compensated.

(e) Duties in Responding to a Subpoena.

(1) Producing Documents or Electronically Stored Information. These procedures apply to producing documents or electronically stored information:
(A) *Documents.* A person responding to a subpoena to produce documents must produce them as they are kept in the ordinary course of business or must organize and label them to correspond to the categories in the demand.
(B) *Form for Producing Electronically Stored Information Not Specified.* If a subpoena does not specify a form for producing electronically stored information, the person responding must produce it in a form or forms in which it is ordinarily maintained or in a reasonably usable form or forms.
(C) *Electronically Stored Information Produced in Only One Form.* The person responding need not produce the same electronically stored information in more than one form.
(D) *Inaccessible Electronically Stored Information.* The person responding need not provide discovery of electronically stored information from sources that the person identifies as not reasonably accessible because of undue burden or cost. On motion to compel discovery or for a protective order, the person responding must show that the information is not reasonably accessible because of undue burden or cost. If that showing is made, the court may nonetheless order discovery from such sources if the requesting party shows good cause, considering the limitations of Rule 26(b)(2)(C). The court may specify conditions for the discovery.

(2) Claiming Privilege or Protection.
(A) *Information Withheld.* A person withholding subpoenaed information under a claim that it is privileged or subject to protection as trial-preparation material must:
(i) expressly make the claim; and
(ii) describe the nature of the withheld documents, communications, or tangible things in a manner that, without revealing information itself privileged or protected, will enable the parties to assess the claim.
(B) *Information Produced.* If information produced in response to a subpoena is subject to a claim of privilege or of protection as trial-preparation material, the person making the claim may notify any party that received the information of the claim and the basis for it. After being notified, a party must promptly return, sequester, or destroy the specified information and any copies it has; must not use or disclose the information until the claim is resolved; must take reasonable steps to retrieve the information if the party disclosed it before being notified; and may promptly present the information under seal to the court for the district where compliance is required for a determination of the claim. The person who produced the information must preserve the information until the claim is resolved.

(g) Contempt. The court for the district where compliance is required — and also, after a motion is transferred, the issuing court — may hold in contempt a person who, having been served, fails without adequate excuse to obey the subpoena or an order related to it.

For access to subpoena materials, see Fed. R. Civ. P. 45(a) Committee Note (2013)

(Added Dec. 1, 2015.)

Form B2560

Form B2560.   Subpoena in a Case
Under the Bankruptcy Code

B2560 (Form 2560 – Subpoena to Testify at a Deposition in a Bankruptcy Case or Adversary Proceeding) (12/15)

UNITED STATES BANKRUPTCY COURT

_____ District of _____

In re _____
          Debtor

(Complete if issued in an adversary proceeding)

Case No. _____

Chapter _____

_____
          Plaintiff
              v.
_____
          Defendant

Adv. Proc. No. _____

SUBPOENA TO TESTIFY AT A DEPOSITION
IN A BANKRUPTCY CASE (OR ADVERSARY PROCEEDING)

To: _____

(Name of person to whom the subpoena is directed)

☐ _Testimony:_ YOU ARE COMMANDED to appear at the time, date, and place set forth below to testify at a deposition to be taken in this bankruptcy case (or adversary proceeding). If you are an organization, you must designate one or more officers, directors, or managing agents, or designate other persons who consent to testify on your behalf about the following matters, or those set forth in an attachment:

PLACE	DATE AND TIME

The deposition will be recorded by this method: _____

☐ _Production:_ You, or your representatives, must also bring with you to the deposition the following documents, electronically stored information, or objects, and must permit inspection, copying, testing, or sampling of the material:

The following provisions of Fed. R. Civ. P. 45, made applicable in bankruptcy cases by Fed. R. Bankr. P. 9016, are attached – Rule 45(c), relating to the place of compliance; Rule 45(d), relating to your protection as a person subject to a subpoena; and Rule 45(e) and 45(g), relating to your duty to respond to this subpoena and the potential consequences of not doing so.

Date: _____

          CLERK OF COURT

                                        OR

_____   _____
Signature of Clerk or Deputy Clerk   _Attorney's signature_

The name, address, email address, and telephone number of the attorney representing _(name of party)_ _____ , who issues or requests this subpoena, are:

Notice to the person who issues or requests this subpoena

B2560 (Form 2560 – Subpoena to Testify at a Deposition in a Bankruptcy Case or Adversary Proceeding) (Page 2)

If this subpoena commands the production of documents, electronically stored information, or tangible things, or the inspection of premises before trial, a notice and a copy of this subpoena must be served on each party before it is served on the person to whom it is directed. Fed. R. Civ. P. 45(a)(4).

PROOF OF SERVICE
(This section should not be filed with the court unless required by Fed. R. Civ. P. 45.)

I received this subpoena for *(name of individual and title, if any):* _____

on *(date)* _____ .

☐ I served the subpoena by delivering a copy to the named person as follows: _____

_____ on *(date)* _____ ; or

☐ I returned the subpoena unexecuted because: _____

_____

Unless the subpoena was issued on behalf of the United States, or one of its officers or agents, I have also tendered to the witness the fees for one day's attendance, and the mileage allowed by law, in the amount of $ _____

My fees are $ _____ for travel and $ _____ for services, for a total of $ _____ .

I declare under penalty of perjury that this information is true and correct.

Date: _____

_____
Server's signature

_____
Printed name and title

_____
Server's address

Additional information concerning attempted service, etc.:

B2560 (Form 2560 – Subpoena to Testify at a Deposition in a Bankruptcy Case or Adversary Proceeding) (Page 3)

Federal Rule of Civil Procedure 45(c), (d), (e), and (g) (Effective 12/1/13)
(made applicable in bankruptcy cases by Rule 9016, Federal Rules of Bankruptcy Procedure)

(c) Place of compliance.

(1) For a Trial, Hearing, or Deposition. A subpoena may command a person to attend a trial, hearing, or deposition only as follows:
(A) within 100 miles of where the person resides, is employed, or regularly transacts business in person; or
(B) within the state where the person resides, is employed, or regularly transacts business in person, if the person
(i) is a party or a party's officer; or
(ii) is commanded to attend a trial and would not incur substantial expense.

(2) For Other Discovery. A subpoena may command:
(A) production of documents, or electronically stored information, or things at a place within 100 miles of where the person resides, is employed, or regularly transacts business in person; and
(B) inspection of premises, at the premises to be inspected.

(d) Protecting a Person Subject to a Subpoena; Enforcement.

(1) Avoiding Undue Burden or Expense; Sanctions. A party or attorney responsible for issuing and serving a subpoena must take reasonable steps to avoid imposing undue burden or expense on a person subject to the subpoena. The court for the district where compliance is required must enforce this duty and impose an appropriate sanction — which may include lost earnings and reasonable attorney's fees — on a party or attorney who fails to comply.

(2) Command to Produce Materials or Permit Inspection.
(A) *Appearance Not Required.* A person commanded to produce documents, electronically stored information, or tangible things, or to permit the inspection of premises, need not appear in person at the place of production or inspection unless also commanded to appear for a deposition, hearing, or trial.
(B) *Objections.* A person commanded to produce documents or tangible things or to permit inspection may serve on the party or attorney designated in the subpoena a written objection to inspecting, copying, testing or sampling any or all of the materials or to inspecting the premises — or to producing electronically stored information in the form or forms requested. The objection must be served before the earlier of the time specified for compliance or 14 days after the subpoena is served. If an objection is made, the following rules apply:
(i) At any time, on notice to the commanded person, the serving party may move the court for the district where compliance is required for an order compelling production or inspection.
(ii) These acts may be required only as directed in the order, and the order must protect a person who is neither a party nor a party's officer from significant expense resulting from compliance.

(3) Quashing or Modifying a Subpoena.
(A) *When Required.* On timely motion, the court for the district where compliance is required must quash or modify a subpoena that:
(i) fails to allow a reasonable time to comply;
(ii) requires a person to comply beyond the geographical limits specified in Rule 45(c);
(iii) requires disclosure of privileged or other protected matter, if no exception or waiver applies; or
(iv) subjects a person to undue burden.
(B) *When Permitted.* To protect a person subject to or affected by a subpoena, the court for the district where compliance is required may, on motion, quash or modify the subpoena if it requires:
(i) disclosing a trade secret or other confidential research, development, or commercial information; or

(ii) disclosing an unretained expert's opinion or information that does not describe specific occurrences in dispute and results from the expert's study that was not requested by a party.
(C) *Specifying Conditions as an Alternative.* In the circumstances described in Rule 45(d)(3)(B), the court may, instead of quashing or modifying a subpoena, order appearance or production under specified conditions if the serving party:
(i) shows a substantial need for the testimony or material that cannot be otherwise met without undue hardship; and
(ii) ensures that the subpoenaed person will be reasonably compensated.

(e) Duties in Responding to a Subpoena.

(1) Producing Documents or Electronically Stored Information. These procedures apply to producing documents or electronically stored information:
(A) *Documents.* A person responding to a subpoena to produce documents must produce them as they are kept in the ordinary course of business or must organize and label them to correspond to the categories in the demand.
(B) *Form for Producing Electronically Stored Information Not Specified.* If a subpoena does not specify a form for producing electronically stored information, the person responding must produce it in a form or forms in which it is ordinarily maintained or in a reasonably usable form or forms.
(C) *Electronically Stored Information Produced in Only One Form.* The person responding need not produce the same electronically stored information in more than one form.
(D) *Inaccessible Electronically Stored Information.* The person responding need not provide discovery of electronically stored information from sources that the person identifies as not reasonably accessible because of undue burden or cost. On motion to compel discovery or for a protective order, the person responding must show that the information is not reasonably accessible because of undue burden or cost. If that showing is made, the court may nonetheless order discovery from such sources if the requesting party shows good cause, considering the limitations of Rule 26(b)(2)(C). The court may specify conditions for the discovery.

(2) Claiming Privilege or Protection.
(A) *Information Withheld.* A person withholding subpoenaed information under a claim that it is privileged or subject to protection as trial-preparation material must:
(i) expressly make the claim; and
(ii) describe the nature of the withheld documents, communications, or tangible things in a manner that, without revealing information itself privileged or protected, will enable the parties to assess the claim.
(B) *Information Produced.* If information produced in response to a subpoena is subject to a claim of privilege or of protection as trial-preparation material, the person making the claim may notify any party that received the information of the claim and the basis for it. After being notified, a party must promptly return, sequester, or destroy the specified information and any copies it has; must not use or disclose the information until the claim is resolved; must take reasonable steps to retrieve the information if the party disclosed it before being notified; and may promptly present the information under seal to the court for the district where compliance is required for a determination of the claim. The person who produced the information must preserve the information until the claim is resolved.

(g) Contempt. The court for the district where compliance is required – and also, after a motion is transferred, the issuing court – may hold in contempt a person who, having been served, fails without adequate excuse to obey the subpoena or an order related to it.

For access to subpoena materials, see Fed. R. Civ. P. 45(a) Committee Note (2013)

(Added Dec. 1, 2015.)

Form B2570. Subpoena to Produce Documents, Information, or Objects or to Permit Inspection in a Bankruptcy Case (or Adversary Proceeding)

B2570 (Form 2570 – Subpoena to Produce Documents, Information, or Objects or To Permit Inspection in a Bankruptcy Case or Adversary Proceeding) (12/15)

UNITED STATES BANKRUPTCY COURT

_____ District of _____

In re _____
             Debtor

(Complete if issued in an adversary proceeding)

Case No. _____

_____

            Plaintiff

Chapter

            v.

Adv. Proc. No. _____

_____

            Defendant

SUBPOENA TO PRODUCE DOCUMENTS, INFORMATION, OR OBJECTS OR TO PERMIT INSPECTION OF PREMISES IN A BANKRUPTCY CASE (OR ADVERSARY PROCEEDING)

To: _____

(Name of person to whom the subpoena is directed)

☐ *Production*: **YOU ARE COMMANDED** to produce at the time, date, and place set forth below the following documents, electronically stored information, or objects, and to permit inspection, copying, testing, or sampling of the material:

PLACE	DATE AND TIME

☐ *Inspection of Premises*: **YOU ARE COMMANDED** to permit entry onto the designated premises, land, or other property possessed or controlled by you at the time, date, and location set forth below, so that the requesting party may inspect, measure, survey, photograph, test, or sample the property or any designated object or operation on it.

PLACE	DATE AND TIME

      The following provisions of Fed. R. Civ. P. 45, made applicable in bankruptcy cases by Fed. R. Bankr. P. 9016, are attached Rule 45(c), relating to the place of compliance; Rule 45(d), relating to your protection as a person subject to a subpoena; and Rule 45(e) and 45(g), relating to your duty to respond to this subpoena and the potential consequences of not doing so.

Date: _____

         CLERK OF COURT

                   OR

    _____   _____
    Signature of Clerk or Deputy Clerk   *Attorney's signature*

The name, address, email address, and telephone number of the attorney representing *(name of party)* _____, who issues or requests this subpoena, are:

_____

Notice to the person who issues or requests this subpoena

B2570 (Form 2570 – Subpoena to Produce Documents, Information, or Objects or To Permit Inspection in a Bankruptcy Case or Adversary Proceeding) (Page 2)

If this subpoena commands the production of documents, electronically stored information, or tangible things, or the inspection of premises before trial, a notice and a copy of this subpoena must be served on each party before it is served on the person to whom it is directed. Fed. R. Civ. P. 45(a)(4).

PROOF OF SERVICE
(This section should not be filed with the court unless required by Fed. R. Civ. P. 45.)

I received this subpoena for *(name of individual and title, if any)*: _____

on *(date)* _____ .

☐ I served the subpoena by delivering a copy to the named person as follows: _____

_____ on *(date)* _____ ; or

☐ I returned the subpoena unexecuted because: _____

_____

Unless the subpoena was issued on behalf of the United States, or one of its officers or agents, I have also tendered to the witness the fees for one day's attendance, and the mileage allowed by law, in the amount of $ _____ .

My fees are $ _____ for travel and $ _____ for services, for a total of $ _____ .

I declare under penalty of perjury that this information is true and correct.

Date: _____

_____
Server's signature

_____
Printed name and title

_____
Server's address

Additional information concerning attempted service, etc.:

B2570 (Form 2570 – Subpoena to Produce Documents, Information, or Objects or To Permit Inspection in a Bankruptcy Case or Adversary Proceeding) (Page 3)

Federal Rule of Civil Procedure 45(c), (d), (e), and (g) (Effective 12/1/13)
(made applicable in bankruptcy cases by Rule 9016, Federal Rules of Bankruptcy Procedure)

(c) Place of compliance.

(1) For a Trial, Hearing, or Deposition. A subpoena may command a person to attend a trial, hearing, or deposition only as follows:
(A) within 100 miles of where the person resides, is employed, or regularly transacts business in person; or
(B) within the state where the person resides, is employed, or regularly transacts business in person, if the person
(i) is a party or a party's officer; or
(ii) is commanded to attend a trial and would not incur substantial expense.

(2) For Other Discovery. A subpoena may command:
(A) production of documents, or electronically stored information, or things at a place within 100 miles of where the person resides, is employed, or regularly transacts business in person; and
(B) inspection of premises, at the premises to be inspected.

(d) Protecting a Person Subject to a Subpoena; Enforcement.

(1) Avoiding Undue Burden or Expense; Sanctions. A party or attorney responsible for issuing and serving a subpoena must take reasonable steps to avoid imposing undue burden or expense on a person subject to the subpoena. The court for the district where compliance is required must enforce this duty and impose an appropriate sanction — which may include lost earnings and reasonable attorney's fees — on a party or attorney who fails to comply.

(2) Command to Produce Materials or Permit Inspection.
(A) *Appearance Not Required.* A person commanded to produce documents, electronically stored information, or tangible things, or to permit the inspection of premises, need not appear in person at the place of production or inspection unless also commanded to appear for a deposition, hearing, or trial.
(B) *Objections.* A person commanded to produce documents or tangible things or to permit inspection may serve on the party or attorney designated in the subpoena a written objection to inspecting, copying, testing or sampling any or all of the materials or to inspecting the premises — or to producing electronically stored information in the form or forms requested. The objection must be served before the earlier of the time specified for compliance or 14 days after the subpoena is served. If an objection is made, the following rules apply:
(i) At any time, on notice to the commanded person, the serving party may move the court for the district where compliance is required for an order compelling production or inspection.
(ii) These acts may be required only as directed in the order, and the order must protect a person who is neither a party nor a party's officer from significant expense resulting from compliance.

(3) Quashing or Modifying a Subpoena.
(A) *When Required.* On timely motion, the court for the district where compliance is required must quash or modify a subpoena that:
(i) fails to allow a reasonable time to comply;
(ii) requires a person to comply beyond the geographical limits specified in Rule 45(c);
(iii) requires disclosure of privileged or other protected matter, if no exception or waiver applies; or
(iv) subjects a person to undue burden.
(B) *When Permitted.* To protect a person subject to or affected by a subpoena, the court for the district where compliance is required may, on motion, quash or modify the subpoena if it requires:
(i) disclosing a trade secret or other confidential research, development, or commercial information; or

(ii) disclosing an unretained expert's opinion or information that does not describe specific occurrences in dispute and results from the expert's study that was not requested by a party.
(C) *Specifying Conditions as an Alternative.* In the circumstances described in Rule 45(d)(3)(B), the court may, instead of quashing or modifying a subpoena, order appearance or production under specified conditions if the serving party:
(i) shows a substantial need for the testimony or material that cannot be otherwise met without undue hardship; and
(ii) ensures that the subpoenaed person will be reasonably compensated.

(e) Duties in Responding to a Subpoena.

(1) Producing Documents or Electronically Stored Information. These procedures apply to producing documents or electronically stored information:
(A) *Documents.* A person responding to a subpoena to produce documents must produce them as they are kept in the ordinary course of business or must organize and label them to correspond to the categories in the demand.
(B) *Form for Producing Electronically Stored Information Not Specified.* If a subpoena does not specify a form for producing electronically stored information, the person responding must produce it in a form or forms in which it is ordinarily maintained or in a reasonably usable form or forms.
(C) *Electronically Stored Information Produced in Only One Form.* The person responding need not produce the same electronically stored information in more than one form.
(D) *Inaccessible Electronically Stored Information.* The person responding need not provide discovery of electronically stored information from sources that the person identifies as not reasonably accessible because of undue burden or cost. On motion to compel discovery or for a protective order, the person responding must show that the information is not reasonably accessible because of undue burden or cost. If that showing is made, the court may nonetheless order discovery from such sources if the requesting party shows good cause, considering the limitations of Rule 26(b)(2)(C). The court may specify conditions for the discovery.

(2) Claiming Privilege or Protection.
(A) *Information Withheld.* A person withholding subpoenaed information under a claim that it is privileged or subject to protection as trial-preparation material must:
(i) expressly make the claim; and
(ii) describe the nature of the withheld documents, communications, or tangible things in a manner that, without revealing information itself privileged or protected, will enable the parties to assess the claim.
(B) *Information Produced.* If information produced in response to a subpoena is subject to a claim of privilege or of protection as trial-preparation material, the person making the claim may notify any party that received the information of the claim and the basis for it. After being notified, a party must promptly return, sequester, or destroy the specified information and any copies it has; must not use or disclose the information until the claim is resolved; must take reasonable steps to retrieve the information if the party disclosed it before being notified; and may promptly present the information under seal to the court for the district where compliance is required for a determination of the claim. The person who produced the information must preserve the information until the claim is resolved.

...

(g) Contempt. The court for the district where compliance is required – and also, after a motion is transferred, the issuing court – may hold in contempt a person who, having been served, fails without adequate excuse to obey the subpoena or an order related to it.

For access to subpoena materials, see Fed. R. Civ. P. 45(a) Committee Note (2013)

(Added Dec. 1, 2015.)

Form B2600.   Entry of Default

B2600 (Form 2600) (12/15)

United States Bankruptcy Court

_____District Of_____

In re _____ ,   )
                  Debtor   )   Case No. _____

)

_____ ,   )   Chapter _____

              Plaintiff   )

)

          v.   )

_____ ,   )   Adv. Proc. No. _____

             Defendant   )

ENTRY OF DEFAULT

It appears from the record that the following defendant failed to plead or otherwise defend in this case as required by law.

Name:

Therefore, default is entered against the defendant as authorized by Federal Rule of Bankruptcy Procedure 7055.

_____
Clerk of the Bankruptcy Court

_____   By:_____
     Date   Deputy Clerk

(Added Dec. 1, 2015.)

Form B2610A. Judgment by Default

B2610A (Form 2610A) (12/15)

United States Bankruptcy Court

_____ District Of _____

In re _____,)
              Debtor   )
)
)
_____,)
              Plaintiff   )
)
          v.   )
)
_____,)
              Defendant   )
	Case No. _____
	
	Chapter _____
	
	Adv. Proc. No. _____

JUDGMENT BY DEFAULT

Default was entered against defendant _____
                                                                                          (name)

on _____. The plaintiff has requested entry of judgment by default and has filed an
          (date)

affidavit of the amount due and stating that this defendant is not in the military service.

Furthermore, it appears from the record that this defendant is not an infant or incompetent person.

Therefore, pursuant to Fed. R. Civ. P. 55(b)(1), as incorporated by Fed. R. Bankr. P. 7055, judgment

is entered against this defendant in favor of the plaintiff as follows:

_____   _____
      (Date)   (Clerk of the Bankruptcy Court)

(Added Dec. 1, 2015.)

Form B2610B.   Judgment by Default

B2160B (Form 2160B) (12/15)

United States Bankruptcy Court

_____ District Of _____

In re _____ ,   )
                    Debtor   )   Case No. _____
)
)   Chapter _____
_____ ,   )
          Plaintiff   )
)
        v.   )
)
_____ ,   )   Adv. Proc. No. _____
          Defendant   )

JUDGMENT BY DEFAULT

Default was entered against defendant _____
                                                    (name)
on _____. Therefore, on motion of the plaintiff, judgment is entered against that
      (date)
defendant in favor of the plaintiff as follows.

IT IS ORDERED THAT:

_____   _____
       Date   Bankruptcy Judge

(Added Dec. 1, 2015.)

Form B2610C. Judgment in an Adversary Proceeding

B 2610C (Form 2610C) (12/15)

UNITED STATES BANKRUPTCY COURT
for the
_____ District of _____

In re _____)   Case No. _____
        Debtor   )
)   Chapter _____
_____)
        Plaintiff   )   Adv. Proc. No. _____
        v.   )
_____)
        Defendant   )

JUDGMENT IN AN ADVERSARY PROCEEDING

The court has ordered that *(check one)*:

❑ The plaintiff *(name)* _____, recover from the defendant *(name)* _____, the

amount of _____ dollars ($ _____), which includes prejudgment interest at the

rate of _____ %, and postjudgment interest at the rate of _____ %, along with costs.

❑ The plaintiff *(name)* _____, recover nothing, the action be dismissed on the merits, and the

defendant *(name)* _____, recover costs from the plaintiff.

Date: *CLERK OF COURT*

                                  _____
                                    Signature of Clerk or Deputy Clerk

(Added Dec. 1, 2015.)

Form B2620

Form B2620. Notice of Entry of Judgment

B2620 (Form 2620) (12/15)

United States Bankruptcy Court

_____ District Of _____

In re _____,)
            Debtor) Case No. _____
)
) Chapter _____
_____,)
            Plaintiff)
)
         v.)
_____,) Adv. Proc. No. _____
           Defendant)

NOTICE OF ENTRY OF JUDGMENT

On _____, the following order (judgment) was entered on the docket:
      (date)

I certify that on this date a copy of this notice was mailed to the following:

_____
Clerk of the Bankruptcy Court

_____   By: _____
      Date   Deputy Clerk

(Added Dec. 1, 2015.)

Form B2630. Bill of Costs

B 2630

BILL OF COSTS

Applicable Law and Rules

1. Fed. R. Bankr. P. 7054(b) authorizes the court to allow costs to the prevailing party in an adversary proceeding. The text of this rule and of other relevant provisions of the law and rules is printed on the second page of the form.

2. The prevailing party must submit the bill of costs to the clerk on notice to the other parties to the adversary proceeding.

3. The length of time required for notice is often fixed by local rule. Some local rules also limit the time in which costs may be sought. In addition, the local rules may include specific filing procedures. A copy of the local rules may be obtained from the clerk of court.

4. The clerk will not tax costs unless the judgment signed by the court specifically awards costs to the prevailing party. Rule 7054(b). The Bankruptcy Rule is different from Fed. R. Civ. P. 54(d), where costs are allowed unless the court orders otherwise.

5. It is not necessary to have the bill of costs issued simultaneously with the entry of the judgment. Fed. R. Civ. P. 58, which is incorporated by reference by Fed. R. Bankr. P. 7058.

Instructions

Caption

1. Identify the Judicial District in which the bankruptcy case was filed. Example: "Eastern District of California."

2. "In re": Insert the name of the debtor as it appears in the bankruptcy petition. Then insert the names of the plaintiff(s) and defendant(s) as they appear on the original complaint.

3. "Case No.": Insert the bankruptcy case number assigned by the court at the time of filing.

4. "Adv. Proc. No.": Insert the number assigned to the adversary case by the court at the time of the filing of the complaint.

Fees: The fees necessarily incurred during the proceeding should be itemized in the space provided. The list is intended as a guide. It is not expected that every cost will be on the list. Therefore, several lines have been provided at the bottom of the list for additional costs to be itemized.

B 2630
continued

Declaration: The declaration serves as both an affirmation that the costs sought were actually incurred, were necessary, and have been calculated in good faith, and as an affidavit of service of the bill of costs on the judgment debtor.

Service: A copy of the proposed bill of costs must be served on the judgment debtor within one business day of the submission of the bill to the clerk, unless otherwise provided by local rule.

Objections: Either party may move for court review of the bill, on seven days notice. Rule 7054(b).

General Information for the Clerk

Prior to issuing the bill of costs, the clerk should ensure that:

1. A judgment was entered in the adversary proceeding.

2. The judgment specifically states that costs are awarded to the party seeking the bill of costs. NOTE: This is different from federal civil practice where Fed. R. Civ. P. 54 automatically permits costs. Fed. R. Bankr. P. 7054 specifically declines to follow this part of Rule 54.

3. The attorney's declaration has been executed, and that the name and address of the judgment debtor have been filled in. This declaration is both an affirmation that the costs sought in the bill are correctly calculated, and that the judgment debtor has been served with a copy of the proposed bill.

Rule 7054(b) permits either party to move for review of the clerk's action in fixing the costs, or in refusing to fix costs. The clerk will almost certainly be called upon to testify at such a hearing. Thus, the clerk should keep specific notes of the basis for any decision to amend or deny the bill of costs.

Some courts have adopted a local rule fixing the length of time for notice of the submission of the bill of costs. Several courts have also adopted a local rule limiting the time in which costs may be sought after the judgment is entered. In addition, some courts have adopted a local rule establishing specific procedures for the filing of the bill of costs and of objections to such bill prior to the clerk taxing costs. Clerks may wish to consider whether such rules should be adopted in their districts.

B2630 (Form 2630) (12/15)

United States Bankruptcy Court

_____ District Of _____

In re

Debtor _____

Plaintiff _____

v.

Defendant _____

Case No. _____

Chapter ____

Adv. Proc. No. _____

BILL OF COSTS

Judgment was entered in the above entitled action on _____ against _____ .
date

The clerk of the bankruptcy court is requested to tax the following as costs:

Fees of the clerk...	$ _____
Fees for service of summons and complaint	$ _____
Fees of the court reporter for any and all part of the transcript necessarily obtained for use in the case.....	$ _____
Fees and disbursements for printing	$ _____
Fees for witnesses (Itemized on reverse).....................	$ _____
Fees for exemplifications and copies of papers necessarily obtained for use in this case	$ _____
Docket fees under 28 U.S.C. § 1923..........................	$ _____
Costs incident to taking of depositions......................	$ _____
Costs as shown on Mandate of appellate court..............	$ _____
Other costs [Itemized on reverse]	$ _____
TOTAL	$ _____

DECLARATION

I, attorney for _____ declare under penalties of perjury that the
(name of party)

foregoing costs are correct and were necessarily incurred in this action, that the services for which fees have been charged were actually and necessarily performed, and that a copy of this Bill of Costs was mailed this day with postage fully prepaid to:

Name of Judgment
Debtor _____

Address _____

_____

_____

_____

Date _____ Signature of Attorney _____

COSTS ARE TAXED IN THE FOLLOWING AMOUNT AND INCLUDED IN THE JUDGMENT: $ _____

Clerk of the
Bankruptcy Court _____

Date _____ By Deputy Clerk: _____

Form B2630

B2630 (Form 2630)(12/15)   page 2

Witness Fees (computation, cf. 28 U.S.C. § 1821 for statutory fees)

Name and Residence	Attendance		Subsistence				Total Cost **Each** Witness
	Days	Total Cost	Days	Total Cost	Miles	Total Cost	
_____	___	$_____	___	$_____	___	$_____	$_____
_____	___	$_____	___	$_____	___	$_____	$_____
_____	___	$_____	___	$_____	___	$_____	$_____
_____	___	$_____	___	$_____	___	$_____	$_____
_____	___	$_____	___	$_____	___	$_____	$_____
_____	___	$_____	___	$_____	___	$_____	$_____
_____	___	$_____	___	$_____	___	$_____	$_____
_____	___	$_____	___	$_____	___	$_____	$_____
_____	___	$_____	___	$_____	___	$_____	$_____
_____	___	$_____	___	$_____	___	$_____	$_____
_____	___	$_____	___	$_____	___	$_____	$_____
_____	___	$_____	___	$_____	___	$_____	$_____
_____	___	$_____	___	$_____	___	$_____	$_____
_____	___	$_____	___	$_____	___	$_____	$_____
_____	___	$_____	___	$_____	___	$_____	$_____
_____	___	$_____	___	$_____	___	$_____	$_____
_____	___	$_____	___	$_____	___	$_____	$_____
_____	___	$_____	___	$_____	___	$_____	$_____
_____	___	$_____	___	$_____	___	$_____	$_____
_____	___	$_____	___	$_____	___	$_____	$_____
_____	___	$_____	___	$_____	___	$_____	$_____
_____	___	$_____	___	$_____	___	$_____	$_____
_____	___	$_____	___	$_____	___	$_____	$_____
_____	___	$_____	___	$_____	___	$_____	$_____
_____	___	$_____	___	$_____	___	$_____	$_____
						TOTAL	$_____

NOTICE

Section 1924, Title 28, U.S. Code provides:
"Before any bill of costs is taxed, the party claiming any item of cost or disbursement shall attach thereto an affidavit, made by himself or by his duly authorized attorney or agent having knowledge of the facts, that such item is correct and has been necessarily incurred in the case and that the services for which fees have been charged were actually and necessarily performed."

Section 1920 of Title 28 reads in part as follows:
"A bill of costs shall be filed in the case and, upon allowance, included in the judgment or decree."

The Federal Rules of Bankruptcy Procedure contain the following provisions:
Rule 7054(b)(1)
"(1) Costs *Other Than Attorney's Fees*. The court may allow costs to the prevailing party except when a statute of the United States or these rules otherwise provides. Costs against the United States, its officers and agencies shall be imposed only to the extent permitted by law. Costs may be taxed by the clerk on 14 days' notice; on motion served within seven days thereafter, the action of the clerk may be reviewed by the court."

Rule 9006(f)
"ADDITIONAL TIME AFTER SERVICE BY MAIL OR UNDER RULE 5(b)(2)(D), (E), OR (F) F.R.Civ.P. When there is a right or requirement to act or undertake some proceedings within a prescribed period after service and that service is by mail or under Rule 5(b)(2)(D), (E), or (F) F.R.Civ.P., three days are added after the prescribed period would otherwise expire under Rule 9006(a)."

Rule 7058
This rule incorporates Rule 58 F.R.Civ.P. Rule 58(e) provides, in part, "Ordinarily, the entry of judgment may not be delayed, nor the time for appeal extended, in order to tax costs or award fees."

(Added Dec. 1, 2015.)

**Form B2640. Writ of Execution to
the United States Marshal**

B2640 (Form 2640) (12/15)

United States Bankruptcy Court
_____ District Of _____

In re _____,   )
                                        Debtor   )   Case No. _____
)
)   Chapter _____
_____,   )
                        Plaintiff   )
)
                  v.   )
_____,   )   Adv. Proc. No. _____
                       Defendant   )

WRIT OF EXECUTION TO THE UNITED STATES MARSHAL

Name and Address of Judgment Creditor	Amount of Judgment: $_____ Other Costs: $
vs. Name and Address of Judgment Debtor	Date of Entry of Judgment: _____

TO THE UNITED STATES MARSHAL FOR THE _____ DISTRICT OF _____;
    You are directed to levy upon the property of the above named judgment debtor to satisfy a money judgment in accordance with the attached instructions.

TO THE JUDGMENT DEBTOR:
    You are notified that federal and state exemptions may be available to you and that you have a right to seek a court order releasing as exempt any property specified in the marshal's schedule from the levy.

_____   _____
            Date   Clerk of the Bankruptcy Court

(Added Dec. 1, 2015.)

Form B2650. Certification of Judgment for Registration in Another District

B2650 (Form 2650) (12/15)

United States Bankruptcy Court
_____ District Of _____

In re _____,   )
           Debtor   )   Case No. _____
)
)   Chapter _____
_____   )
          Plaintiff   )
)
     v.   )
_____,   )   Adv. Proc. No. _____
         Defendant   )

CERTIFICATION OF JUDGMENT FOR
REGISTRATION IN ANOTHER DISTRICT

I, clerk of the United States Bankruptcy Court, do certify that the attached judgment is a true and correct copy of the original judgment entered in this proceeding on _____ as it appears in the records of this court, and that:
                                                           (date)

☐   No notice of appeal from this judgment has been filed, and no motion of the kind set forth in Federal Rule of Civil Procedure 60, as made applicable by Federal Rule of Bankruptcy Procedure 9024, has been filed.

☐   No notice of appeal from this judgment has been filed, and any motions of the kind set forth in Federal Rule of Civil Procedure 60, as made applicable by Federal Rule of Bankruptcy Procedure 9024, have been disposed of, the latest order disposing of such a motion having been entered on _____.
                        (date)

☐   An appeal was taken from this judgment, and the judgment was affirmed by mandate of the _____ issued on _____.
              (name of court)   (date)

☐   An appeal was taken from this judgment, and the appeal was dismissed by order entered on _____.
       (date)

_____
Clerk of the Bankruptcy Court

_____   By: _____
Date   Deputy Clerk

(Added Dec. 1, 2015.)

Form B2700. Notice of Filing of Final Report of Trustee, of Hearing on Applications for Compensation [and of Hearing on Abandonment of Property by the Trustee]

B2700 (Form 2700) (12/15)

United States Bankruptcy Court
_____ District Of _____

In re _____
Debtor*

Address: _____

Case No. _____

Chapter _____

Last four digits of Social-Security or Individual Taxpayer-
Identification (ITIN) No(s).,(if any): _____
Employer Tax-Identification (EIN) No(s).(if any): _____

NOTICE OF FILING OF FINAL REPORT OF TRUSTEE, OF HEARING ON APPLICATIONS FOR COMPENSATION [AND OF HEARING ON ABANDONMENT OF PROPERTY BY THE TRUSTEE]

TO THE CREDITORS:

    1. NOTICE IS GIVEN that the final report of the trustee in this case has been filed and a hearing will be held by the court at the following place and time.

Address	Room
	Date and Time

    2. The hearing will be held for the purpose of examining the final report of the trustee, acting on applications for compensation, and transacting such other business as may properly come before the court. ATTENDANCE BY THE DEBTOR AND THE CREDITORS IS WELCOMED BUT IS NOT REQUIRED.

    3. The following applications for compensation have been filed:

Applicants	Commissions or Fees	Expenses
_____ Trustee	$_____	$_____
_____ Attorney for Trustee	$_____	$_____
_____	$_____	$_____
_____	$_____	$_____
_____	$_____	$_____
_____	$_____	$_____

---

* Set forth all names, including trade names, used by the debtor(s) within the last 8 years. For joint debtors, set forth the last four digits of both social-security numbers or individual taxpayer-identification numbers.

B2700 (Form 2700) (12/15) – Cont., page 2

4. The trustee's account shows total receipt of $\qquad$
and total disbursements of $\qquad$
for a balance on hand of $\qquad$

5. In addition to the commissions and fees that may be allowed by the court, liens and priority claims which must be paid in advance of general creditors have been allowed in the total amounts of

$\qquad$

General unsecured claims have been allowed in the amount of

$\qquad$

6. ☐ The debtor has been discharged.
   ☐ The debtor has not been discharged.

7. ☐ The trustee's application to abandon the following property will be heard and acted upon.

_____
Clerk of the Bankruptcy Court

By: _____

_____
Deputy Clerk

Date: _____

(Added Dec. 1, 2015.)

Form B2710. Final Decree

B2710 (Form 2710) (12/15)

United States Bankruptcy Court

_____ District Of _____

In re
_____ Case No. _____

Debtor

Last four digits of Social-Security or Individual Taxpayer-
Identification (ITIN) No(s).,(if any):   Chapter _____
Employer Tax-Identification (EIN) No(s).(if any):

FINAL DECREE

The estate of the above named debtor has been fully administered.

☐ The deposit required by the plan has been distributed.

IT IS ORDERED THAT:

☐ _____
                          (name of trustee)

is discharged as trustee of the estate of the above-named debtor and the bond is cancelled.

☐   the chapter _____case of the above named debtor is closed; and

☐   [other provisions as needed]

_____   _____
        Date   Bankruptcy Judge

*Set forth all names, including trade names, used by the debtor within the last 8 years. (Fed. R. Bankr. P. 1005). For joint debtors set forth both social security numbers.

(Added Dec. 1, 2015.)

Form B2800

Form B2800. Disclosure of Compensation of Bankruptcy Petition Preparer

B2800 (Form 2800) (12/15)

United States Bankruptcy Court
_____ District Of _____

In re _____   Case No. _____
  Debtor

                                            Chapter _____

DISCLOSURE OF COMPENSATION OF BANKRUPTCY PETITION PREPARER
[Must be filed with the petition if a bankruptcy petition preparer prepares the petition. 11 U.S.C. § 110(h)(2).]

1. Under 11 U.S.C. § 110(h), I declare under penalty of perjury that I am not an attorney or employee of an attorney, that I prepared or caused to be prepared one or more documents for filing by the above-named debtor(s) in connection with this bankruptcy case, and that compensation paid to me within one year before the filing of the bankruptcy petition, or agreed to be paid to me, for services rendered on behalf of the debtor(s) in contemplation of or in connection with the bankruptcy case is as follows:

For document preparation services I have agreed to accept............................ $_____

Prior to the filing of this statement I have received.............................. $_____

Balance Due.. $_____

2. I have prepared or caused to be prepared the following documents (itemize):

and provided the following services (itemize):

3. The source of the compensation paid to me was:
   Debtor   Other (specify)

4. The source of compensation to be paid to me is:
   Debtor   Other (specify)

5. The foregoing is a complete statement of any agreement or arrangement for payment to me for preparation of the petition filed by the debtor(s) in this bankruptcy case.

6. To my knowledge no other person has prepared for compensation a document for filing in connection with this bankruptcy case except as listed below:

NAME   SOCIAL SECURITY NUMBER

_____   _____   _____
      Signature   Social Security number of bankruptcy   Date
                            petition preparer*

_____   _____
Printed name and title, if any, of   Address
Bankruptcy Petition Preparer

* If the bankruptcy petition preparer is not an individual, state the Social Security number of the officer, principal, responsible person or partner of the bankruptcy petition preparer. (Required by 11 U.S.C. § 110).

A bankruptcy petition preparer's failure to comply with the provisions of title 11 and the Federal Rules of Bankruptcy Procedure may result in fines or imprisonment or both. 11 U.S.C. § 110; 18 U.S.C. § 156.

(Added Dec. 1, 2015.)

**Form B2810.   Appearance of Child Support
   Creditor or Representative**

B2810 (Form 2810) (12/15)

United States Bankruptcy Court

_____ District Of _____

In re _____,   Case No. _____
             Debtor(s)

APPEARANCE OF CHILD SUPPORT CREDITOR*
OR REPRESENTATIVE

I certify under penalty of perjury that I am a child support creditor* of the above-named debtor, or the authorized representative of such child support creditor, with respect to the child support obligation which is set out below.

Name:
Organization:
Address:

Telephone Number:

_____   X _____
      Date   Child Support Creditor* or Authorized Representative

---

Summary of Child Support Obligation

Amount in arrears: If Child Support has been assigned:

$ _____   Amount of Support which is owed
                                             under assignments:

Amount currently due per week or per month:
on a continuing basis: $ _____

$ _____   Amount owed primary child support
     (per week) (per month)   creditor (balance not assigned):

                                             $ _____

**Attach an itemized statement of account. Do not disclose the name of a minor child. See 11 U.S.C.
§ 112. If a social security number or a taxpayer identification number is included, set out only the
last four digits of the number. Judicial Conference Privacy Policy (09/01).**

---

* Child support creditor includes both creditor to whom the debtor has a primary obligation to pay child support as well as any entity to whom such support has been assigned, if pursuant to Section 402(a)(26) of the Social Security Act or if such debt has been assigned to the Federal Government or to any State or political subdivision of a State.

(Added Dec. 1, 2015.)

**Form B2830.   Chapter 13 Debtor's Certifications
Regarding Domestic Support Obligations
and Section 522(q)**

Instructions, Form B2830
12.01.15

CHAPTER 13 DEBTOR'S CERTIFICATIONS REGARDING
DOMESTIC SUPPORT OBLIGATIONS AND SECTION 522(q)

Form B2830 may be used by debtors to certify that they have complied with two of the requirements set out in 11 U.S.C. § 1328(a), for a discharge in chapter 13. The certifications must be made after the debtor has completed the plan payments.

Before completing this optional form, the debtor should determine whether the court has adopted a local form for making these certifications. If the court has adopted a local form, the debtor should use that form instead of Form B2830. Information on the court's local rules and forms is available on the court's website. Links to local court websites are posted at http://www.uscourts.gov/courtlinks/.

<u>Applicable Law and Rules</u>

Section 1328(a) of the Bankruptcy Code requires that any debtor who is required by a judicial or administrative order, or by statute, to pay a domestic support obligation, as defined by section 101(14A) of the Code, certify that all amounts payable under the order or statute that are due on or before the date of the certification have been paid. This certification requirement includes amounts due before the petition was filed, but only to the extent provided for by the plan. The debtor cannot receive a discharge until the certification has been filed.

Section 1302(d)(1)(C) requires the trustee to inform holders of domestic support obligation claims and State child support enforcement agencies of the granting of the debtor's discharge and, among other things, of the debtor's last recent known address and the last recent known name and address of the debtor's employer. Part II is included in Form B283 to provide these addresses to the trustee for the notification.

Section 1328(h) of the Code provides that the court may not grant a discharge in a chapter 13 case unless the court, after notice and a hearing held not more than 10 days before the date of the entry of the order granting the discharge, finds that there is no reasonable cause to believe that --

• section 522(q)(1) may be applicable to the debtor (or either of the joint debtors); and

• there is pending a proceeding in which the debtor (or either of the joint debtors) may be found guilty of a felony of the kind described in § 522(q)(1)(A) or liable for a debt of the kind described in § 522(q)(1)(B).

In order for § 522(q)(1) to be applicable, the debtor must have claimed an exemption in a homestead, residence, or burial plot pursuant to § 522(b)(3) and state or local law above a certain amount. The debtor's certification in Part III will enable the court to determine whether §1328(h) has any possible application to the case.

Instructions

Caption

1.   Identify the Judicial District in which the bankruptcy case was filed. Example: "Eastern District of California."

2.   "In re": Insert the name of the debtor as it appears in the bankruptcy petition.

3.   "Case No.": Insert the bankruptcy case number assigned by the court at the time of filing.

The instructions to the rest of the form are self-evident.

General Information for the Clerk

In a joint case, each debtor must file a § 1328(a) certification and a § 1328(h) certification, as described above. The certifications must be made after the plan payments have been completed.

DIRECTOR'S FORMS

B2830 (Form 2830) (04/16)

UNITED STATES BANKRUPTCY COURT

_____District Of_____

In re _____   Case No. _____
            Debtor

CHAPTER 13 DEBTOR'S CERTIFICATIONS REGARDING
DOMESTIC SUPPORT OBLIGATIONS AND SECTION 522(q)

Part I. Certification Regarding Domestic Support Obligations (check no more than one)

Pursuant to 11 U.S.C. Section 1328(a), I certify that:

❏   I owed no domestic support obligation when I filed my bankruptcy petition, and I have not been required to pay any such obligation since then.

❏   I am or have been required to pay a domestic support obligation. I have paid all such amounts that my chapter 13 plan required me to pay. I have also paid all such amounts that became due between the filing of my bankruptcy petition and today.

Part II. If you checked the second box, you must provide the information below.

My current address: _____

My current employer and my employer's address:_____

_____

Part III. Certification Regarding Section 522(q) (check no more than one)

Pursuant to 11 U.S.C. Section 1328(h), I certify that:

❏   I have not claimed an exemption pursuant to § 522(b)(3) and state or local law (1) in property that I or a dependent of mine uses as a residence, claims as a homestead, or acquired as a burial plot, as specified in § 522(p)(1), and (2) that exceeds $160,375* in value in the aggregate.

❏   I have claimed an exemption in property pursuant to § 522(b)(3) and state or local law (1) that I or a dependent of mine uses as a residence, claims as a homestead, or acquired as a burial plot, as specified in § 522(p)(1), and (2) that exceeds $160,375* in value in the aggregate.

*   Amounts are subject to adjustment on 4/01/19, and every 3 years thereafter with respect to cases commenced on or after the date of adjustment.

For Complete Annotation Materials, see United States Code Annotated

B2830 (Form 2830) (page 2)

Part IV. Debtor's Signature

I certify under penalty of perjury that the information provided in these
certifications is true and correct to the best of my knowledge and belief.

Executed on _____   _____
               Date   Debtor

(Added Dec. 1, 2015; and amended Apr. 1, 2016.)

Form B3130S. Order and Notice Conditionally Approving Disclosure Statement; Fixing Time for Filing Acceptances or Rejections of Plan; Fixing Time for Filing Objections to Disclosure Statement and Objections to Confirmation of Plan; and Fixing Time for Hearing on Final Approval of Disclosure Statement and Hearing on Confirmation of Plan

Form 3130S (12/15)

[Caption as in Official Form 416A]

Order and Notice Conditionally Approving Disclosure Statement; Fixing Time for Filing Acceptances or Rejections of Plan; Fixing Time for Filing Objections to Disclosure Statement and Objections to Confirmation of Plan; and Fixing Time for Hearing on Final Approval of Disclosure Statement and Hearing on Confirmation of Plan

A disclosure statement under chapter 11 of the Bankruptcy Code having been filed by
_____, on _____ with respect to a plan under chapter 11 of the Code filed by _____, on _____; and the debtor being, and having elected to be considered, a small business:

IT IS ORDERED, and notice is hereby given, that:

A. The disclosure statement filed by _____ is conditionally approved.

B. _____ is fixed as the last day for filing written acceptances or rejections of the plan referred to above.

C. Within _____ days after the entry of this order, the plan, the disclosure statement and a ballot conforming to Ballot for Accepting or Rejecting Plan of Reorganization (Official Form 314) shall be mailed to creditors, equity security holders, and other parties in interest, and shall be transmitted to the United States trustee.

D. _____ is fixed for the hearing on final approval of the disclosure statement (if a written objection has been timely filed) and for the hearing on confirmation of the plan.

E. _____ is fixed as the last day for filing and serving written objections to the disclosure statement and confirmation of the plan.

By the court:

_____
MM / DD / YYYY

_____
United States Bankruptcy Judge

(Added Dec. 1, 2015.)

**Form B3150S.   Order Approving Disclosure
Statement and Confirming Plan**

Form 3150S (12/15)

[Caption as in 416A]

Order Approving Disclosure Statement and Confirming Plan

The plan under chapter 11 of the Bankruptcy Code filed by _____, on
_____ having been transmitted to creditors and equity security holders together with a copy of the
disclosure statement conditionally approved by court on _____; and

 It having been determined after notice and a hearing that the requirements for final approval of the disclosure
statement have been satisfied, and it having been determined after a hearing on notice that the requirements for
confirmation of the plan under 11 U.S.C. § 1129 have been satisfied;

IT IS ORDERED that:

The disclosure statement filed by _____ on _____ is finally approved, and
The plan filed by _____, on _____, [If
appropriate, include dates and any other pertinent details of modifications to the plan] is confirmed.

A copy of the confirmed plan is attached.

	By the court: _____
_____ MM / DD / YYYY	United States Bankruptcy Judge

(Added Dec. 1, 2015.)

Form B3180F.   Chapter 12 Discharge

```
Information to identify the case:

Debtor 1 _____        Last 4 digits of Social Security number or ITIN _ _ _ _
              First Name    Middle Name    Last Name
                                                         EIN  _ _ - _ _ _ _ _ _ _
Debtor 2 _____        Last 4 digits of Social Security number or ITIN _ _ _ _
(Spouse, if filing) First Name  Middle Name  Last Name
                                                         EIN  _ _ - _ _ _ _ _ _ _

United States Bankruptcy Court for the: _____ District of _____
                                                              (State)

Case number: _____
```

Order of Discharge

IT IS ORDERED: A discharge under 11 U.S.C. § 1228(a) is granted to:

_____   [_____]
[include all names used by each debtor, including trade names, within the 8 years prior to the filing of the petition]

_____   By the court: _____
MM / DD / YYYY   United States Bankruptcy Judge

Explanation of Bankruptcy Discharge in a Chapter 12 Case

This order does not close or dismiss the case.

Creditors cannot collect discharged debts

This order means that no one may make any attempt to collect a discharged debt from the debtors personally. For example, creditors cannot sue, garnish wages, assert a deficiency, or otherwise try to collect from the debtors personally on discharged debts. Creditors cannot contact the debtors by mail, phone, or otherwise in any attempt to collect the debt personally. Creditors who violate this order can be required to pay debtors damages and attorney's fees.

However, a creditor with a lien may enforce a claim against the debtors' property subject to that lien unless the lien was avoided or eliminated. For example, a creditor may have the right to foreclose a home mortgage or repossess an automobile.

This order does not prevent debtors from paying any debt voluntarily. 11 U.S.C. § 524(f).

Most debts are discharged

Most debts are covered by the discharge, but not all. Generally, a discharge removes the debtors' personal liability for debts provided for by the chapter 12 plan.

In a case involving community property: Special rules protect certain community property owned by the debtor's spouse, even if that spouse did not file a bankruptcy case.

Some debts are not discharged

Examples of debts that are not discharged are:

- debts that are domestic support obligations;

- debts for most student loans;

- debts for most taxes;

- debts that the bankruptcy court has decided or will decide are not discharged in this bankruptcy case;

For more information, see page 2 ▶

Form 3180F   **Chapter 12 Discharge**   page **1**

- debts for most fines, penalties, forfeitures, or criminal restitution obligations;

- some debts which the debtors did not properly list;

- debts for certain types of loans owed to pension, profit sharing, stock bonus, or retirement plans;

- debts provided for under 11 U.S.C. § 1222(b)(5) or (b)(9) and on which the last payment or other transfer is due after the date on which the final payment under the plan was due; and

- debts for death or personal injury caused by operating a vehicle while intoxicated.

In addition, this discharge does not stop creditors from collecting from anyone else who is also liable on the debt, such as an insurance company or a person who cosigned or guaranteed a loan.

This information is only a general summary of a chapter 12 discharge; some exceptions exist. Because the law is complicated, you should consult an attorney to determine the exact effect of the discharge in this case.

Form 3180F   **Chapter 12 Discharge**   page **2**

(Added Dec. 1, 2015.)

Form B3180FH.   Chapter 12 Hardship Discharge

Information to identify the case:

Debtor 1 _____   Last 4 digits of Social Security number or ITIN _ _ _ _
            First Name   Middle Name   Last Name
                                                      EIN _ _ - _ _ _ _ _ _ _

Debtor 2 _____   Last 4 digits of Social Security number or ITIN _ _ _ _
(Spouse, if filing) First Name   Middle Name   Last Name
                                                      EIN _ _ - _ _ _ _ _ _ _

United States Bankruptcy Court for the: _____ District of _____
                                                    (State)

Case number: _____

Order of Discharge

IT IS ORDERED: A discharge under 11 U.S.C. § 1228(b) is granted to:

_____   [_____]

[include all names used by each debtor, including trade names, within the 8 years prior to the filing of the petition]

_____   By the court: _____
MM / DD / YYYY   United States Bankruptcy Judge

Explanation of Bankruptcy Discharge Before Completion of a Chapter 12 Plan

The court has determined that the debtors are entitled to a discharge pursuant to 11 U.S.C. § 1228(b) without completing all of the requirements under the chapter 12 plan. A discharge pursuant to § 1228(b) is referred to as a "hardship discharge."

This order does not close or dismiss the case.

Creditors cannot collect discharged debts

This order means that no one may make any attempt to collect a discharged debt from the debtors personally. For example, creditors cannot sue, garnish wages, assert a deficiency, or otherwise try to collect from the debtors personally on discharged debts. Creditors cannot contact the debtors by mail, phone, or otherwise in any attempt to collect the debt personally. Creditors who violate this order can be required to pay debtors damages and attorney's fees.

However, a creditor with a lien may enforce a claim against the debtors' property subject to that lien unless the lien was avoided or eliminated. For example, a creditor may have the right to foreclose a home mortgage or repossess an automobile.

This order does not prevent debtors from paying any debt voluntarily. 11 U.S.C. § 524(f).

Most debts are discharged

Most debts are covered by the discharge, but not all. Generally, a discharge removes the debtors' personal liability for debts provided for by the chapter 12 plan.

In a case involving community property: Special rules protect certain community property owned by the debtor's spouse, even if that spouse did not file a bankruptcy case.

Some debts are not discharged

Examples of debts that are not discharged are:

■ debts that are domestic support obligations;

■ debts for most student loans;

■ debts for most taxes;

For more information, see page 2 ▶

Form 3180FH   Chapter 12 Hardship Discharge   page 1

- debts that the bankruptcy court has decided or will decide are not discharged in this bankruptcy case;

- debts for most fines, penalties, forfeitures, or criminal restitution obligations;

- some debts which the debtors did not properly list;

- debts for certain types of loans owed to pension, profit sharing, stock bonus, or retirement plans;

- debts provided for under 11 U.S.C. § 1222(b)(5) or (b)(9) and on which the last payment or other transfer is due after the date on which the final payment under the plan was due; and

- debts for death or personal injury caused by operating a vehicle while intoxicated.

In addition, this discharge does not stop creditors from collecting from anyone else who is also liable on the debt, such as an insurance company or a person who cosigned or guaranteed a loan.

> **This information is only a general summary of a chapter 12 hardship discharge; some exceptions exist. Because the law is complicated, you should consult an attorney to determine the exact effect of the discharge in this case.**

Form 3180FH   **Chapter 12 Hardship Discharge**   page **2**

(Added Dec. 1, 2015.)

Form B3180RI. Individual Chapter 11 Discharge

Debtor 1 _____
First Name   Middle Name   Last Name

Last 4 digits of Social Security number or ITIN _ _ _ _

EIN _ _ – _ _ _ _ _ _ _

Debtor 2
(Spouse, if filing) First Name   Middle Name   Last Name

Last 4 digits of Social Security number or ITIN _ _ _ _

EIN _ _ – _ _ _ _ _ _ _

United States Bankruptcy Court for the: _____ District of _____
                                                    (State)

Case number: _____

Order of Discharge

IT IS ORDERED: A discharge under 11 U.S.C. § 1141(d)(5) is granted to:

_____ |_____|

[include all names used by each debtor, including trade names, within the 8 years prior to the filing of the petition]

_____
MM / DD / YYYY

By the court: _____
United States Bankruptcy Judge

Explanation of Bankruptcy Discharge in an Individual Chapter 11 Case

This order does not close or dismiss the case.

Creditors cannot collect discharged debts

This order means that no one may make any attempt to collect a discharged debt from the debtors personally. For example, creditors cannot sue, garnish wages, assert a deficiency, or otherwise try to collect from the debtors personally on discharged debts. Creditors cannot contact the debtors by mail, phone, or otherwise in any attempt to collect the debt personally. Creditors who violate this order can be required to pay debtors damages and attorney's fees.

However, a creditor with a lien may enforce a claim against the debtors' property subject to that lien unless the lien was avoided or eliminated. For example, a creditor may have the right to foreclose a home mortgage or repossess an automobile.

This order does not prevent debtors from paying any debt voluntarily. 11 U.S.C. § 524(f).

Most debts are discharged

Most debts are covered by the discharge, but not all. Generally, a discharge removes the debtors' personal liability for debts provided for by the chapter 11 plan.

In a case involving community property: Special rules protect certain community property owned by the debtor's spouse, even if that spouse did not file a bankruptcy case.

Some debts are not discharged

Examples of debts that are not discharged are:

■ debts that are domestic support obligations;

■ debts for most student loans;

■ debts for most taxes;

■ debts that the bankruptcy court has decided or will decide are not discharged in this bankruptcy case;

For more information, see page 2 ▶

Form 3180RI   **Individual Chapter 11 Discharge**   page **1**

- debts for most fines, penalties, forfeitures, or criminal restitution obligations;

- some debts which the debtors did not properly list;

- debts for certain types of loans owed to pension, profit sharing, stock bonus, or retirement plans; and

- debts for death or personal injury caused by operating a vehicle while intoxicated.

In addition, this discharge does not stop creditors from collecting from anyone else who is also liable on the debt, such as an insurance company or a person who cosigned or guaranteed a loan.

> **This information is only a general summary of an individual chapter 11 discharge; some exceptions exist. Because the law is complicated, you should consult an attorney to determine the exact effect of the discharge in this case.**

Form 3180RI   **Individual Chapter 11 Discharge**   page **2**

(Added Dec. 1, 2015.)

Form B3180W.   Chapter 13 Discharge

Information to identify the case:

Debtor 1 _____   Last 4 digits of Social Security number or ITIN _ _ _ _
First Name   Middle Name   Last Name
                                                        EIN   _ _ - _ _ _ _ _ _ _

Debtor 2 _____   Last 4 digits of Social Security number or ITIN _ _ _ _
(Spouse, if filing) First Name   Middle Name   Last Name
                                                        EIN   _ _ - _ _ _ _ _ _ _

United States Bankruptcy Court for the: _____ District of _____
                                                     (State)

Case number: _____

Order of Discharge   12/18

IT IS ORDERED: A discharge under 11 U.S.C. § 1328(a) is granted to:

_____   [_____]

[include all names used by each debtor, including trade names, within the 8 years prior to the filing of the petition]

_____   By the court: _____
MM / DD / YYYY   United States Bankruptcy Judge

Explanation of Bankruptcy Discharge in a Chapter 13 Case

This order does not close or dismiss the case.

Creditors cannot collect discharged debts

This order means that no one may make any attempt to collect a discharged debt from the debtors personally. For example, creditors cannot sue, garnish wages, assert a deficiency, or otherwise try to collect from the debtors personally on discharged debts. Creditors cannot contact the debtors by mail, phone, or otherwise in any attempt to collect the debt personally. Creditors who violate this order can be required to pay debtors damages and attorney's fees.

However, a creditor with a lien may enforce a claim against the debtors' property subject to that lien unless the lien was avoided or eliminated. For example, a creditor may have the right to foreclose a home mortgage or repossess an automobile.

This order does not prevent debtors from paying any debt voluntarily. 11 U.S.C. § 524(f).

Most debts are discharged

Most debts are covered by the discharge, but not all. Generally, a discharge removes the debtors' personal liability for debts provided for by the chapter 13 plan.

In a case involving community property: Special rules protect certain community property owned by the debtor's spouse, even if that spouse did not file a bankruptcy case.

Some debts are not discharged

Examples of debts that are not discharged are:

- debts that are domestic support obligations;

- debts for most student loans;

- debts for certain types of taxes specified in 11 U.S.C. §§ 507(a)(8)(C), 523(a)(1)(B), or 523(a)(1)(C) to the extent not paid in full under the plan;

For more information, see page 2 ▶

Form 3180W   Chapter 13 Discharge   page 1

* debts that the bankruptcy court has decided or will decide are not discharged in this bankruptcy case;

* debts for restitution, or a criminal fine, included in a sentence on debtor's criminal conviction;

* some debts which the debtors did not properly list;

* debts provided for under 11 U.S.C. § 1322(b)(5) and on which the last payment or other transfer is due after the date on which the final payment under the plan was due;

* debts for certain consumer purchases made after the bankruptcy case was filed if obtaining the trustee's prior approval of incurring the debt was practicable but was not obtained;

* debts for restitution, or damages, awarded in a civil action against the debtor as a result of malicious or willful injury by the debtor that caused personal injury to an individual or the death of an individual; and

* debts for death or personal injury caused by operating a vehicle while intoxicated.

In addition, this discharge does not stop creditors from collecting from anyone else who is also liable on the debt, such as an insurance company or a person who cosigned or guaranteed a loan.

This information is only a general summary of a chapter 13 discharge; some exceptions exist. Because the law is complicated, you should consult an attorney to determine the exact effect of the discharge in this case.

Form 3180W   **Chapter 13 Discharge**   page **2**

(Added Dec. 1, 2015; and amended Dec. 1, 2018.)

Form B3180WH.   Chapter 13 Hardship Discharge

Information to identify the case:

Debtor 1 _____
First Name   Middle Name   Last Name

Last 4 digits of Social Security number or ITIN _ _ _ _

EIN _ _ - _ _ _ _ _ _ _ _

Debtor 2
(Spouse, if filing) First Name   Middle Name   Last Name

Last 4 digits of Social Security number or ITIN _ _ _ _

EIN _ _ - _ _ _ _ _ _ _ _

United States Bankruptcy Court for the: _____ District of _____
(State)

Case number: _____

Order of Discharge

IT IS ORDERED: A discharge under 11 U.S.C. § 1328(b) is granted to:

_____   [_____]

[include all names used by each debtor, including trade names, within the 8 years prior to the filing of the petition]

_____
MM / DD / YYYY

By the court: _____
United States Bankruptcy Judge

Explanation of Bankruptcy Discharge Before Completion of a Chapter 13 Plan

The court has determined that the debtors are entitled to a discharge pursuant to 11 U.S.C. § 1328(b) without completing all of the requirements under the chapter 13 plan. A discharge pursuant to § 1328(b) is referred to as a "hardship discharge."

This order does not close or dismiss the case.

Creditors cannot collect discharged debts

This order means that no one may make any attempt to collect a discharged debt from the debtors personally. For example, creditors cannot sue, garnish wages, assert a deficiency, or otherwise try to collect from the debtors personally on discharged debts. Creditors cannot contact the debtors by mail, phone, or otherwise in any attempt to collect the debt personally. Creditors who violate this order can be required to pay debtors damages and attorney's fees.

However, a creditor with a lien may enforce a claim against the debtors' property subject to that lien unless the lien was avoided or eliminated. For example, a creditor may have the right to foreclose a home mortgage or repossess an automobile.

This order does not prevent debtors from paying any debt voluntarily. 11 U.S.C. § 524(f).

Most debts are discharged

Most debts are covered by the discharge, but not all. Generally, a discharge removes the debtors' personal liability for debts provided for by the chapter 13 plan.

In a case involving community property: Special rules protect certain community property owned by the debtor's spouse, even if that spouse did not file a bankruptcy case.

Some debts are not discharged

Examples of debts that are not discharged are:

■ debts that are domestic support obligations;

■ debts for most student loans;

For more information, see page 2 ▶

Form 3180WH   Chapter 13 Hardship Discharge   page **1**

- debts for most taxes;

- debts that the bankruptcy court has decided or will decide are not discharged in this bankruptcy case;

- debts for most fines, penalties, forfeitures, or criminal restitution obligations;

- some debts which the debtors did not properly list;

- debts for certain types of loans owed to pension, profit sharing, stock bonus, or retirement plans;

- debts provided for under 11 U.S.C. § 1322(b)(5) and on which the last payment or other transfer is due after the date on which the final payment under the plan was due;

- debts for certain consumer purchases made after the bankruptcy case was filed if obtaining the trustee's prior approval of incurring the debt was practicable but was not obtained; and

- debts for death or personal injury caused by operating a vehicle while intoxicated.

In addition, this discharge does not stop creditors from collecting from anyone else who is also liable on the debt, such as an insurance company or a person who cosigned or guaranteed a loan.

This information is only a general summary of a chapter 13 hardship discharge; some exceptions exist. Because the law is complicated, you should consult an attorney to determine the exact effect of the discharge in this case.

Form 3180WH   **Chapter 13 Hardship Discharge**   page **1**

(Added Dec. 1, 2015.)

Form B4100N. Notice of Final Cure Payment

Form 4100N

Notice of Final Cure Payment

10/15

File a separate notice for each creditor.

According to Bankruptcy Rule 3002.1(f), the trustee gives notice that the amount required to cure the prepetition default in the claim below has been paid in full and the debtor(s) have completed all payments under the plan.

Part 1:   Mortgage Information

Name of creditor: _____

Court claim no. (if known): _____

Last 4 digits of any number you use to identify the debtor's account: ___ ___ ___ ___

Property address:

Number	Street	

City   State   ZIP Code

Part 2:   Cure Amount

Total cure disbursements made by the trustee:		Amount
a. Allowed prepetition arrearage:	(a)	$ _____
b. Prepetition arrearage paid by the trustee.	(b)	$ _____
c. Amount of postpetition fees, expenses, and charges recoverable under Bankruptcy Rule 3002.1(c):	(c)	$ _____
d. Amount of postpetition fees, expenses, and charges recoverable under Bankruptcy Rule 3002.1(c) and paid by the trustee:	(d)	$ _____
e. Allowed postpetition arrearage:	(e)	$ _____
f. Postpetition arrearage paid by the trustee.	+ (f)	$ _____
g. **Total.** Add lines b, d, and f.	(g)	$ _____

Part 3:   Postpetition Mortgage Payment

Check one:

☐ Mortgage is paid through the trustee.

Current monthly mortgage payment: $ _____

The next postpetition payment is due on: ___/___/_____
                                                          MM / DD /YYYY

☐ Mortgage is paid directly by the debtor(s).

Form 4100N   Notice of Final Cure Payment   page 1

Debtor 1 _____   Case number _____
          First Name   Middle Name   Last Name

Part 4: A Response Is Required By Bankruptcy Rule 3002.1(g)

Under Bankruptcy Rule 3002.1(g), the creditor must file and serve on the debtor(s), their counsel, and the trustee, within 21 days after service of this notice, a statement indicating whether the creditor agrees that the debtor(s) have paid in full the amount required to cure the default and stating whether the debtor(s) have (i) paid all outstanding postpetition fees, costs, and escrow amounts due, and (ii) consistent with § 1322(b)(5) of the Bankruptcy Code, are current or all postpetition payments as of the date of the response. Failure to file and serve the statement may subject the creditor to further action of the court, including possible sanctions.

To assist in reconciling the claim, a history of payments made by the trustee is attached to copies of this notice sent to the debtor(s) and the creditor.

X _____   Date ____/____/_____
      Signature

Trustee _____
          First Name   Middle Name   Last Name

Address _____
          Number   Street

         _____
          City   State   ZIP Code

Contact phone (_____) _____ - _____   Email _____

(Added Oct. 1, 2015.)

Form B4100R

**Form B4100R. Response to Notice
of Final Cure Payment**

Form 4100R

Response to Notice of Final Cure Payment   10/15

According to Bankruptcy Rule 3002.1(g), the creditor responds to the trustee's notice of final cure payment.

Part 1: Mortgage Information

Name of creditor: _____   Court claim no. (if known):
                                                        _____

Last 4 digits of any number you use to identify the debtor's account: ___ — ___ — ___ — ___

Property address: _____
                 Number   Street

                 _____

                 _____
                 City   State   ZIP Code

Part 2: Prepetition Default Payments

Check one:

❑ Creditor agrees that the debtor(s) have paid in full the amount required to cure the prepetition default
  on the creditor's claim.

❑ Creditor disagrees that the debtor(s) have paid in full the amount required to cure the prepetition default
  on the creditor's claim. Creditor asserts that the total prepetition amount remaining unpaid as of the date $ _____
  of this response is.

Part 3: Postpetition Mortgage Payment

Check one:

❑ Creditor states that the debtor(s) are current with all postpetition payments consistent with § 1322(b)(5) of
  the Bankruptcy Code, including all fees, charges, expenses, escrow, and costs.

  The next postpetition payment from the debtor(s) is due on: __ / __ / ____
                                                              MM / DD / YYYY

❑ Creditor states that the debtor(s) are not current on all postpetition payments consistent with § 1322(b)(5)
  of the Bankruptcy Code, including all fees, charges, expenses, escrow, and costs.

  Creditor asserts that the total amount remaining unpaid as of the date of this response is:

  a. Total postpetition ongoing payments due: (a) $ _____

  b. Total fees, charges, expenses, escrow, and costs outstanding   + (b) $ _____

  c. Total. Add lines a and b.   (c) $ _____

  Creditor asserts that the debtor(s) are contractually
  obligated for the postpetition payment(s) that first became
  due on: __ / __ / ____
                                                             MM / DD / YYYY

Form 4100R   Response to Notice of Final Cure Payment   page 1

Debtor 1 _____   Case number (if known) _____
          First Name   Middle Name   Last Name

Part 4:   Itemized Payment History

If the creditor disagrees in Part 2 that the prepetition arrearage has been paid in full or states in Part 3 that the debtor(s) are not current with all postpetition payments, including all fees, charges, expenses, escrow, and costs, the creditor must attach an itemized payment history disclosing the following amounts from the date of the bankruptcy filing through the date of this response:

- all payments received;
- all fees, costs, escrow, and expenses assessed to the mortgage; and
- all amounts the creditor contends remain unpaid.

Part 5:   Sign Here

The person completing this response must sign it. The response must be filed as a supplement to the creditor's proof of claim.

Check the appropriate box.:

☐ I am the creditor.

☐ I am the creditor's authorized agent.

I declare under penalty of perjury that the information provided in this response is true and correct to the best of my knowledge, information, and reasonable belief.

Sign and print your name and your title, if any, and state your address and telephone number if different from the notice address listed on the proof of claim to which this response applies.

X _____   Date ____/____/_____
      Signature

Print _____   Title _____
      First Name   Middle Name   Last Name

Company _____

If different from the notice address listed on the proof of claim to which this response applies:

Address _____
        Number   Street

_____
        City   State   ZIP Code

Contact phone (_____) _____-_____   Email _____

Form 4100R   Response to Notice of Final Cure Payment   page 2

(Added Oct. 1, 2015.)

Form B4170

Form B4170. Declaration of Inmate Filing

Form 4170 (12/18)

Declaration of Inmate Filing

_____

[insert name of court; for example,
United States District Court for the District of Minnesota]

In re _____ *[insert debtor name]*

_____, Plaintiff

v.   Case No. _____

_____, Defendant

I am an inmate confined in an institution. Today, _____ *[insert date]*, I am depositing the _____ *[insert title of document; for example, "notice of appeal"]* in this case in the institution's internal mail system. First-class postage is being prepaid either by me or by the institution on my behalf.

I declare under penalty of perjury that the foregoing is true and correct (see 28 U.S.C. § 1746; 18 U.S.C. § 1621).

Sign your name here_____

Signed on _____ *[insert date]*

[Note to inmate filers: If your institution has a system designed for legal mail, you must use that system in order to receive the timing benefit of Fed. R. Bankr. P. 8002(c)(1) or Fed. R. Bankr. P. 8011(a)(2)(C).]

(Added Dec. 1, 2018.)

FEDERAL
RULES OF CIVIL PROCEDURE
FOR THE
UNITED STATES DISTRICT COURTS

Amendments received to December 1, 2018

RULES OF CIVIL PROCEDURE

RULES OF CIVIL PROCEDURE

TIME TABLE FOR LAWYERS IN FEDERAL CIVIL CASES
Amended to December 1, 2018

This table, prepared by the Publisher's editorial staff as a guide to the user, indicates the time for each of the steps of a civil action as provided by the Federal Rules of Civil Procedure and the Federal Rules of Appellate Procedure. Certain steps governed by statute and by the Rules of the Supreme Court are also listed. *The user should always consult the actual text of the rule or statute.* Usually the periods permitted for each of these steps may be enlarged by the court in its discretion. In some cases no enlargement is permitted. Citations to supporting authority are in the form "Civ.R. ——" for the Rules of Civil Procedure; "App.R. ——" for the Rules of Appellate Procedure; "28 U.S.C.A. § ——" for statutes; and "Supreme Court Rule ——".

ADMISSIONS

Requests for admissions, service of	On any other party a written request, for purposes of the pending action only. Civ.R. 36(a)(1).
Response to requested admissions	
	Written answers or objections must be served within 30 days after service of the request, or a shorter or longer time as may be stipulated to under Civ.R. 29 or be ordered by the court. Civ.R. 36(a).
ALTERNATE jurors	The institution of the alternate juror has been abolished. Civ.R. 47, 1991 Advisory Committee note, subd. (b).
ANSWER	See, also, "Responsive Pleadings", this table.
To complaint	
	Service within 21 days after being served with summons and complaint unless another time is specified by Civ.R. 12 or a federal statute. Civ.R. 12(a)(1)(A)(i).
	Service within 60 days after request is sent for waiver of service of summons or within 90 days after it was sent to defendant outside any judicial district of the United States unless another time is specified by Civ.R. 12 or a federal statute. Civ.R. 12(a)(1)(A)(ii).
	Service within 60 days after service on the United States attorney, in action against the United States, a United States agency, or a United States officer or employee sued only in an official capacity. Civ.R. 12(a)(2).
	Service within 60 days after service on the officer or employee or service on the United States attorney, whichever is later, in an action against a United States officer or employee sued in an individual capacity in connection with duties performed on the United States' behalf. Civ.R. 12(a)(3).
	The time for responsive pleading is altered by service of Civ.R. 12 motions. See "Responsive Pleadings", this table.
To counterclaim or cross-claim	
	Service within 21 days after being served with the pleading that states the counterclaim or cross-claim. Civ.R. 12(a)(1)(B).

ANSWER	**See, also, "Responsive Pleadings", this table.**
	60 days for United States, United States agency, or United States officer or employee. Civ.R. 12(a)(2), (3).
	The time for responsive pleading is altered by service of Civ.R. 12(a) motions, see "Responsive Pleadings", this table.
To notice of condemnation	Service within 21 days after being served with the notice. Civ.R. 71.1(e).
Removed actions	21 days after receipt of copy of initial pleading stating the claim for relief, or 21 days after service of summons for an initial pleading on file at time of service, or 7 days after filing of notice of removal, whichever is longest. Civ.R. 81(c).
Proceedings to cancel certificates of citizenship under 8 U.S.C.A. § 1451	60 days after service of petition. Civ.R. 81(a)(3).
ANSWERS (or objections) to interrogatories to party	
	Service within 30 days after service of the interrogatories. A shorter or longer time may be stipulated to under Civ.R. 29 or be ordered by the court. Civ.R. 33(b)(2).
APPEAL	
As of right	Except as provided in App.R. 4(a)(1)(B), 4(a)(4), and 4(c), notice must be filed with district clerk within 30 days after entry of judgment or order appealed from. App.R. 4(a)(1)(A).
	Notice may be filed by any party within 60 days after entry of judgment or order appealed from if one of the parties is the United States or its officers, employees, or agencies. App.R. 4(a)(1)(B).
	Entry of a judgment or order in the civil docket under Civ.R. 79(a) is entry for purposes of App.R. 4, unless Civ.R. 58(a) requires a separate document, in which case entry occurs when the judgment or order is entered under Civ.R. 79(a) and when the earlier of either the judgment or order is set forth on a separate document, or 150 days have run from entry of the judgment or order in the civil docket. App.R. 4(a)(7)(A).
	If a party files in the district court any of the following motions under the Federal Rules of Civil Procedure — and does so within the time allowed by those rules — the time to file an appeal runs for all parties from the entry of the order disposing of the last such remaining motion:

(i) for judgment under Civ.R. 50(b);

(ii) to amend or make additional factual findings under Civ.R. 52(b), whether or not granting the motion would alter the judgment;

(iii) for attorney's fees under Civ.R. 54 if the district court extends the time to appeal under Civ.R. 58;

(iv) to alter or amend the judgment under Civ.R. 59;

RULES OF CIVIL PROCEDURE

APPEAL

(v) for a new trial under Civ.R. 59;

(vi) for relief under Civ.R. 60 if the motion is filed no later than 28 days after the judgment is entered.

App.R. 4(a)(4)(A).

District court may extend for excusable neglect or good cause upon motion filed no later than 30 days after the time prescribed by App.R. 4(a) expires; no extension may exceed 30 days after the prescribed time or 14 days after the date when the order granting the motion is entered, whichever is later. App.R. 4(a)(5).

By other parties, within 14 days of filing of first notice of appeal, or within the time otherwise prescribed by App.R. 4(a), whichever period ends later. App.R. 4(a)(3).

By permission

Petition filed with circuit clerk with proof of service within time specified by statute or rule authorizing the appeal, or, if no such time is specified, within the time provided by App.R. 4(a) for filing a notice of appeal. App.R. 5(a).

Bankruptcy

If a motion for rehearing under Bankruptcy Rule 8022 is filed in a district court or in a bankruptcy appellate panel, time for appeal to court of appeals runs from entry of order disposing of motion. App.R. 6(b)(2)(A).

Class actions

A court of appeals may permit an appeal from an order granting or denying class-action certification under Civ.R. 23, but not from an order under Civ.R. 23(e)(1). A party must file a petition for permission to appeal with the circuit clerk within 14 days after the order is entered, or within 45 days after the order is entered if any party is the United States, a United States agency, or a United States officer or employee sued for an act or omission occurring in connection with duties performed on the United States' behalf. Civ.R. 23(f).

Inmates

If institution has a system designed for legal mail, an inmate must use that system to receive benefit of App.R. (4)(c)(1). A notice of appeal is timely filed if deposited in the institution's internal mail system on or before the last day for filing and (A) it is accompanied by (i) a declaration in compliance with 28 U.S.C. § 1746—or a notarized statement—setting out date of deposit and stating that first-class postage is being prepaid; or (ii) evidence showing that the notice was so deposited and postage was prepaid; or (B) the court of appeals exercises its discretion to permit the later filing of a declaration or notarized statement that satisfies App.R. 4(c)(1)(A)(i). App.R. 4(c)(1), see also App.R. 25(a)(2)(A)(iii).

Representation statement

Within 14 days after filing notice of appeal unless court of appeals designates another time, attorney who filed notice must file with the circuit clerk a statement naming the parties represented on appeal by that attorney. App.R. 12(b).

RULES OF CIVIL PROCEDURE

APPEAL

Entry of judgment or order, notice of	Lack of notice of entry by clerk does not affect time for appeal or relieve or authorize court to relieve party for failure to appeal within time allowed, except as allowed by App.R. 4(a). Civ.R. 77(d)(2).
Record (Appellant)	Within 14 days after filing notice of appeal or entry of an order disposing of last timely remaining motion specified in App.R. 4(a)(4)(A), whichever is later: Appellant to place written order for transcript and file copy of order with clerk; if none to be ordered, file a certificate to that effect; unless entire transcript to be included, within the 14 days provided in App.R. 10(b)(1) file a statement of issues and serve appellee a copy of order or certificate and of statement. App.R. 10(b)(1), (3)(A).
Record (Appellee)	Within 14 days after service of appellant's order or certificate and statement of issues, appellee to file and serve on appellant a designation of additional parts of transcript to be ordered. Unless within 14 days after service of that designation appellant has ordered all such parts and so notified appellee, appellee may within the following 14 days either order the parts or move in district court for order requiring appellant to do so. App.R. 10(b)(3)(B), (C).
Record (costs)	At time of ordering, party must make satisfactory arrangements with reporter for paying the cost of the transcript. App.R. 10(b)(4).
Record (Reporter)	If transcript cannot be completed within 30 days of receipt of order, reporter may request extension of time from circuit clerk. App.R. 11(b)(1)(B).
Stay of execution on a judgment and proceedings to enforce it	Effective when bond or other security is approved by court and remains in effect for the time specified in the bond or other security. Civ.R. 62(b).

At any time after judgment is entered, a party may obtain a stay by providing a bond or other security. Civ.R. 62(b). |
Briefs	Appellant must serve and file a brief within 40 days after the record is filed. Appellee must serve and file a brief within 30 days after service of the appellant's brief. A reply brief may be served and filed within 21 days after service of appellee's brief but, except for good cause, reply brief must be filed at least 7 days before argument. A court of appeals that routinely considers cases on the merits promptly after the briefs are filed may shorten the time to serve and file briefs, either by local rule or by order in a particular case. App.R. 31(a).
Transcripts	See "RECORD", ante, this heading.
Tax Court decisions	Review is commenced by filing a notice of appeal with the Tax Court clerk within 90 days after entry of decision. If a timely notice of appeal is filed by one party, any other party may file a notice of appeal within 120 days after entry of decision by the Tax Court. If timely motion to vacate or revise

RULES OF CIVIL PROCEDURE

APPEAL

decision is made, time to file notice of appeal runs from entry of order disposing of motion or from entry of new decision, whichever is later. App.R. 13(a)(1).

APPEAL from magistrate judge to court of appeals under 28 U.S.C.A. § 636(c)(3) and Civ.R. 73(c)

Appeal from judgment entered at a magistrate judge's direction may be taken to the court of appeals as would any other appeal from a district court judgment. Civ.R. 73(c); 28 U.S.C.A. § 636(c)(3).

APPEAL to Supreme Court

Direct appeals

30 days after entry of interlocutory or final order, judgment or decree holding Act of Congress unconstitutional in whole or in part under circumstances provided by 28 U.S.C.A. § 1253. 28 U.S.C.A. § 2101(a).

30 days from interlocutory judgment, order, or decree in any other direct appeal authorized by law from decision of district court. 28 U.S.C.A. § 2101(b).

60 days from final judgment, order, or decree in any other direct appeal authorized by law from decision of district court. 28 U.S.C.A. § 2101(b).

Other appeals and certiorari

90 days after entry of judgment or decree; justice of Supreme Court for good cause shown may extend time for applying for writ of certiorari for period not exceeding 60 days. 28 U.S.C.A. § 2101(c).

Briefs supporting certiorari

No separate brief in support of a petition for a writ of certiorari may be filed; see Supreme Court Rule 14.2.

Brief opposing certiorari

30 days after case is placed on the docket unless time is extended by Court or a Justice or by the Clerk under Supreme Court Rule 30.4; see Supreme Court Rule 15.3.

Brief on merits on appeal or certiorari

By petitioner or appellant, filed within 45 days of the order granting the writ of certiorari, noting probable jurisdiction or postponing consideration of jurisdiction; see Supreme Court Rule 25.1.

By respondent or appellee, filed within 30 days after the brief for the petitioner or appellant is filed; see Supreme Court Rule 25.2.

Reply brief, if any, filed within 30 days after the brief for respondent or appellee is filed, but any reply brief must actually be received by Clerk not later than 2 p.m. one week before the date of oral argument. See Supreme Court Rule 25.3.

Stay of mandate pending petition for certiorari

A stay of mandate pending filing a petition to the Supreme Court for certiorari must not exceed 90 days unless the period is extended for good cause, or within the period of stay, the party who obtained the stay notifies the circuit clerk in writing that the time for filing a petition has been extended, or that the petition has been filed. The court of appeals must issue the mandate immediately on receiving a

RULES OF CIVIL PROCEDURE

APPEAL to Supreme Court

copy of the Supreme Court order denying the petition, unless extraordinary circumstances exist. App.R. 41(d).

ATTORNEY'S fees

See "Costs", this table.

CLASS actions

Certification

At an early practicable time after a person sues or is sued as a class representative, the court must determine by order whether to certify the action as a class action. Civ.R. 23(c)(1)(A).

Settlement, voluntary dismissal, or compromise

Approval by court of settlement, voluntary dismissal, or compromise that would bind class members only after hearing and only on finding that it is fair, reasonable, and adequate after making certain listed considerations. Civ.R. 23(e)(2).

Attorney's fees

Claim for award of attorney's fees and nontaxable costs must be made by motion under Civ.R. 54(d)(2) subject to Civ.R. 23(h) at a time the court sets. Notice of motion must be served on all parties and, for motions by class counsel, directed to class members in a reasonable manner. Civ.R. 23(h)(1).

CLERICAL mistakes and mistakes of oversight or omission in judgments, orders, or record

May be corrected whenever found, on motion or on court's own, with or without notice; but after appeal docketed and while pending, may be corrected only with appellate court's leave. Civ.R. 60(a).

COMPLAINT

Filing commences action—must be served with summons. Civ.R. 3, 4(c)(1).

Service of summons and complaint within 90 days after filing. Civ.R. 4(m).

COMPUTATION of time

When the time period is stated in days or a longer unit of time: (1) exclude day of the event that triggers the period; (2) count every day, including intermediate Saturdays, Sundays, and legal holidays; and (3) include the last day of the period, but if the last day is a Saturday, Sunday, or legal holiday, the period continues to run until the end of the next day that is not a Saturday, Sunday, or legal holiday. Civ.R. 6(a)(1); App.R. 26(a)(1).

When the time period is stated in hours: (1) begin counting immediately on the occurrence of the event that triggers the period; (2) count every hour, including hours during intermediate Saturdays, Sundays, and legal holidays; and (3) if the period would end on a Saturday, Sunday, or legal holiday, the period continues to run until the same time on the next day that is not a Saturday, Sunday, or legal holiday. Civ.R. 6(a)(2); App.R. 26(a)(2).

If clerk's office is inaccessible: (1) on the last day for filing under Civ.R. 6(a)(1) or App.R. 26(a)(1), then the time for filing is extended to the first accessible day that is not a Saturday, Sunday, or legal holiday; or (2) during the last hour for filing under Civ.R. 6(a)(2) or App.R. 26(a)(2), then the

RULES OF CIVIL PROCEDURE

COMPUTATION of time

time for filing is extended to the same time on the first accessible day that is not a Saturday, Sunday, or legal holiday. Civ.R. 6(a)(3); App.R. 26(a)(3).

When a party may or must act within a specified time after being served and service is made under Civ.R. 5(b)(2)(C) (mail), (D) (leaving with the clerk), or (F) (other means consented to), 3 days are added after the period would otherwise expire under Civ.R. 6(a). Civ.R. 6(d).

Service by mail to the person's last known address is complete upon mailing. Civ.R. 5(b)(2)(C).

When a party may or must act within a specified time after being served, 3 days are added after the period would otherwise expire under App.R. 26(a), unless the paper is delivered on the date of service stated in the proof of service. For purposes of App.R. 26(c), a paper served electronically is treated as delivered on the date of service stated in the proof of service. App.R. 26(c).

Legal holidays are defined by Civ.R. 6(a)(6) and App.R. 26(a)(6).

Supreme Court matters—See Supreme Court Rule 30.

CONDEMNATION of property

    Answer to notice of condemnation

21 days after service of notice. Civ.R. 71.1(e)(2).

CORPORATE DISCLOSURE

Nongovernmental corporate parties must file, with first appearance, pleading, petition, motion, response, or other request addressed to the court, statement identifying any parent corporation and any publicly held corporation owning 10% or more of its stock or stating that there is no such corporation. Party must promptly file supplemental statement if any required information changes. Civ.R. 7.1.

COSTS

Taxation on 14 day's notice. Review taxation of costs on motion served within the next 7 days. Civ.R. 54(d)(1).

Failure of defendant located within the United States, without good cause, to sign and return requested waiver of service of summons requested by a plaintiff located within the United States incurs imposition of certain expenses. Defendant who, before being served with process, timely returns waiver need not serve an answer to the complaint until 60 days after request is sent or until 90 days if sent to the defendant outside any judicial district of the United States. Civ.R. 4(d)(2), (3).

    Attorney's fees and related nontaxable expenses

Motion filed no later than 14 days after entry of judgment. Civ.R. 54(d)(2)(B)(i).

RULES OF CIVIL PROCEDURE

CROSS APPEAL

Appellate rules — Within 14 days of filing of first notice of appeal or within the time otherwise prescribed by App.R. 4(a), whichever period ends later. App.R. 4(a)(3).

Inmates — Within 14 days after date when first notice of appeal was filed, or within the time otherwise prescribed by App.R. 4(a), whichever period ends later. The 14 day period runs from date district court dockets first notice of appeal. App.R. 4(a)(3), (c)(2).

DEFAULT

Entry by clerk — On the plaintiff's request; no time stated. Civ.R. 55(b)(1).

Entry by court — If party against whom default judgment is sought has appeared personally or by representative, that party or its representative must be served with written notice of application for default judgment at least 7 days before the hearing on such application. Civ.R. 55(b)(2).

DEFENSES and objections, presentation of

By pleading — See "Answer", this table.

By motion — Motion must be made before pleading if responsive pleading is allowed. Civ.R. 12(b).

At trial — Opposing party may assert at trial any defense to claim for relief to which such party is not required to serve responsive pleading. Civ.R. 12(b).

Motion affects time for responsive pleading — Service of motion under Civ.R. 12 alters times for responsive pleading. Civ.R. 12(a)(4). See "Responsive Pleadings", this table.

DEMURRERS — Abolished. Civ.R. 7, 2007 Advisory Committee note, relating to Civ.R. 7(c).

DEPOSITIONS — See, also, "Interrogatories to parties", "Depositions on written questions", this table.

Notice of filing — Promptly. Civ.R. 30(f)(4) and Civ.R. 31(c)(2).

Notice of taking — Reasonable written notice to every other party. Civ.R. 30(b)(1).

Objections — As to admissibility, objection may be made at hearing or trial to the admission of any deposition testimony that would be inadmissible if the witness were present and testifying, but subject to Civ.R. 28(b) and 32(d)(3). Civ.R. 32(b).

As to errors or irregularities in the notice, service promptly in writing. Civ.R. 32(d)(1).

As to disqualification of officer, objection made before deposition begins or promptly after the basis for disqualification becomes known or could have been known with reasonable diligence. Civ.R. 32(d)(2).

As to competence of deponent or competence, relevance, or materiality of testimony, not waived by failure to make the objection before or during deposition, unless the ground might have been corrected at that time. Civ.R. 32(d)(3)(A).

As to errors and irregularities at oral examination in manner of taking deposition, in the form of questions or answers, in the oath or affirmation, or in conduct of parties, and other matters that might have been corrected at that time, objection timely made during deposition. Civ.R. 32(d)(3)(B).

As to form of written questions under Civ.R. 31—service in writing within time allowed for serving responsive questions or, if recross-question, within 7 days after being served with it. Civ.R. 32(d)(3)(C).

As to completion and return (transcription, preparation, signing, certification, sealing, endorsing, sending, or otherwise)—motion to suppress made promptly after error or irregularity becomes known or, with reasonable diligence, could have been known. Civ.R. 32(d)(4).

Protective orders

Subsequent to certification that movant has in good faith conferred or attempted to confer with other affected parties to resolve dispute without court action. Civ.R. 26(c)(1).

Motion to terminate or limit examination

Any time during a deposition. Civ.R. 30(d)(3).

Perpetuate testimony pending appeal

Motion in court where judgment was rendered on same notice and service as if action was pending in district court. Civ.R. 27(b).

Perpetuate testimony before action

Service of notice and petition at least 21 days before date of hearing. Civ.R. 27(a)(2).

Taking

Time specified in the notice of taking. Civ. R. 30(b)(1).
Prior notice by a party to deponent and other parties to designate another method for recording deponent's testimony in addition to method specified in original notice. Civ.R. 30(b)(3)(B).

Review of transcript or recording

Request by a party or deponent before completion of deposition. Deponent has 30 days after notice of availability of transcript or recording to review and to sign statement listing changes and reasons for making them. Civ.R. 30(e)(1).

When taken

After parties have conferred as required by Civ.R. 26(f), except in proceeding exempted from initial disclosure under Civ.R. 26(a)(1)(B), or when authorized by rules, stipulation, or court order. Civ.R. 26(d)(1).

DEPOSITIONS on written questions

See, also, "Depositions", "Interrogatories to parties", this table.

When taken

After parties have conferred as required by Civ.R. 26(f), except in proceeding exempted from initial disclosure under Civ.R. 26(a)(1)(B), or when authorized by rules, stipulation, or court order. Civ.R. 26(d)(1).

Cross questions

Service within 14 days after service of the notice and direct questions. Court may extend or shorten time. Civ.R. 31(a)(5).

Redirect questions

Service within 7 days after being served with cross questions. Court may for good cause extend or shorten time. Civ.R. 31(a)(5).

Recross questions

Service within 7 days after service with redirect questions. Court may for good cause extend or shorten time. Civ.R. 31(a)(5).

Notice of filing of deposition

Promptly. Civ.R. 31(c).

Objections to form

Service within the time for serving responsive questions or, if question is a recross-question, within 7 days after being served with it. Civ.R. 32(d)(3)(C).

DISCOVERY

See, also, "Admissions", "Depositions", "Depositions on written questions", "Interrogatories to parties", "Production of documents", this Table.

Discovery Conference

Except in proceedings exempted from initial disclosure under Civ.R. 26(a)(1)(B) or when court orders otherwise, as soon as practicable and at least 21 days before a scheduling conference is to be held or a scheduling order is due under Civ.R. 16(b), the parties must confer to consider the nature and basis of their claims, defenses, and possibilities for promptly settling or resolving the case, to make or arrange for disclosures required by Civ.R. 26(a)(1), to discuss any issues about preserving discoverable information, and to develop a proposed discovery plan. A written report outlining the plan is to be submitted to the court within 14 days after the conference. Civ.R. 26(f)(1), (2); See, also, Civ.R. 26(d).

Without awaiting a discovery request and at or within 14 days after the parties' Civ.R. 26(f) conference, a party must provide information specified in Civ.R. 26(a)(1)(A). Civ.R. 26(a)(1)(A), (C). Disclosure of expert testimony under Civ.R. 26(a)(2), in absence of court order or stipulation, is to be made at least 90 days before trial date or date case is to be ready for trial or if evidence intended solely to contradict or rebut evidence on same subject matter identified by another party under Civ.R.

DISCOVERY

26(a)(2)(B) or (C), within 30 days after the other party's disclosure. Civ.R. 26(a)(2)(A), (D).

Disclosures under Civ.R. 26(a)(1) or (2), depositions, interrogatories, requests for documents or tangible things or to permit entry onto land, and requests for admission must not be filed until used in the proceeding or court orders filing. Civ.R. 5(d)(1)(A).

Identification of witnesses, documents, exhibits, including summaries of other evidence, and designation of witnesses whose testimony is expected to be presented by deposition with a transcript of pertinent testimony if deposition is not taken stenographically to be provided to other parties at least 30 days before trial unless otherwise ordered by court. Within 14 days thereafter, unless court sets different time, a party may serve and promptly file objections. Civ.R. 26(a)(3).

DISMISSAL for lack of subject-matter jurisdiction

Any time. Civ.R. 12(h)(3).

DISMISSAL by plaintiff voluntarily without court order

By filing notice of dismissal before service of answer or motion for summary judgment. Civ.R. 41(a)(1)(A).

DISMISSAL of counterclaim, crossclaim or third-party claim, voluntary

Before service of responsive pleading, or if none, before introduction of evidence at trial or hearing. Civ.R. 41(c).

DISMISSAL without prejudice

Service of summons and complaint not made within 90 days after filing of complaint, unless good cause for failure is shown. Civ.R. 4(m).

DOCUMENTS, Production of

See "Production of documents", this Table.

ENLARGEMENT of time generally

Act may or must be done within specified time

Court may for good cause extend time (1) with or without motion or notice if court acts, or if request is made, before the original time or its extension expires, or (2) on motion made after the time has expired if party failed to act because of excusable neglect; but court must not extend time to act under Civ.R. 50(b) and (d), 52(b), 59(b), (d) and (e), and 60(b). Civ.R. 6(b).

Affidavits in opposition, service

At least 7 days before the hearing, unless court permits service at another time, except as Civ.R. 59(c) provides otherwise. Civ.R. 6(c)(2).

Hearing of motions and defenses

Heard and decided before trial unless court orders deferral until trial. Civ.R. 12(i).

Service under Rule 5(b)(2)(C), (D), or (F)

Three days are added after the period would otherwise expire under Civ.R. 6(a). Civ.R. 6(d).

When a party may or must act within a specified time after being served, three days are added after the period would otherwise expire under Civ.R. 26(a), unless the paper is delivered on the date of service stated in the proof of service. A paper served electronically is treated as delivered on the

ENLARGEMENT of time generally

date of service stated in the proof of service. App.R. 26(c).

Injunction—temporary restraining order

May be extended 14 days by court for good cause or for a longer extension by consent of adverse party. Civ.R. 65(b)(2).

Response to request for admissions

A matter is admitted unless, within 30 days after being served, party serves on requesting party a written answer or objection. Time for responding may be lengthened or shortened by court or as the parties may stipulate to under Civ.R. 29. Civ.R. 36(a)(3).

Motion for judgment as a matter of law

No extension of the 28 day period under Civ.R. 50(b). Civ.R. 6(b).

Findings by the court, amendment of or make additional findings

No extension of the 28 day period under Civ.R. 52(b). Civ.R. 6(b).

Motion for new trial

No extension of the 28 day period under Civ.R. 50(d), 59(b), (d), and (e). Civ.R. 6(b).

Motion for relief from judgment or order

No extension of the 1 year period under Civ.R. 60(b). Civ.R. 6(b).

Appellate rules

Court for good cause may extend time prescribed by App.Rules or by its order to perform any act or may permit act to be done after expiration of such time; but court may not extend time for filing notice of appeal (except as authorized in App.R. 4), or petition for permission to appeal, or a notice of appeal from or a petition to enjoin, set aside, suspend, modify, enforce or otherwise review an order of an administrative agency, board, commission, or officer of the United States, unless specifically authorized by law. App.R. 26(b).

Supreme Court matters, depositions

See Supreme Court Rule 30.

EXCEPTIONS for insufficiency of pleadings
EXECUTION

Stay

Abolished. Civ.R. 7, 2007 Advisory Committee note, relating to Civ.R. 7(c).

Except as provided in Civ.R. 62(c) and (d), execution on a judgment and proceedings to enforce it are stayed for 30 days after its entry, unless the court orders otherwise. Civ.R. 62(a).

When judgment is lien on property under law of state where court is located, same stay of execution state court would give. Civ.R. 62(f).

Unless court orders otherwise, an interlocutory or final judgment in an action for an injunction or receivership, or a judgment or order that directs an accounting in an action for patent infringement, are not stayed after being entered, even if an appeal is taken. Civ.R. 62(c).

Stay in favor of government. Civ.R. 62(e).

EXECUTION

Stay of judgment as to multiple claims or multiple parties. Civ.R. 62(h).

FILING papers

Filing complaint commences civil action. Civ.R. 3.

Constitutional challenge to a statute. Civ.R. 5.1.

Service of summons and complaint within 90 days after filing of complaint. Civ.R. 4(m).

Any paper after complaint that is required to be served must be filed no later than a reasonable time after service. Civ.R. 5(d)(1)(A).
Any paper after complaint that is required to be served and is not filed electronically is filed by delivering it to the clerk or to a judge who agrees to accept it for filing. Civ.R. 5(d)(1), (2).
Electronic filing by persons represented or unrepresented by attorney, see Civ.R. 5(d)(3).

No certificate of service is required when a paper is served by filing it with the court's electronic-filing system. When a paper that is required to be served is served by other means: (i) if the paper is filed, a certificate of service must be filed with it or within a reasonable time after service; and (ii) if the paper is not filed, a certificate of service need not be filed unless filing is required by court order or by local rule. Civ.R. 5(d)(1)(B).

FINDINGS
Motion to amend

28 days after entry of judgment. Civ.R. 52(b). Exception from general rule relating to enlargement. Civ.R. 6(b)(2).

FOREIGN law

Notice by pleading or other writing required of party intending to raise an issue about a foreign country's law. Civ.R. 44.1.

HEARING of motions

A court may establish regular times and places for oral hearings on motions; by rule or order, court may provide for submitting and determining motions on briefs, without oral hearings. Civ.R. 78.

Service of notice at least 14 days before time specified for hearing unless motion may be heard ex parte, or otherwise these rules or a court order set a different time. Civ.R. 6(c).

Hearing of certain motions and defenses before trial on motion of party unless court orders deferral until trial. Civ.R. 12(i).

HOLIDAYS

New Year's Day, Martin Luther King, Jr.'s Birthday, Washington's Birthday, Memorial Day, Independence Day, Labor Day, Columbus Day, Veterans' Day, Thanksgiving Day, Christmas Day, and any day declared a holiday by the President or Congress and, for periods that are measured after an event, any other day declared a holiday by the state where the district court is located. Civ.R. 6(a)(6); App.R. 26(a)(6).

HOLIDAYS

Exclusion in computation of time. Civ.R. 6(a); App.R. 26(a).

INJUNCTION (Temporary restraining order granted without notice)

Order must state date and hour of issuance, promptly filed in clerk's office, and entered in the record. Civ.R. 65(b)(2).

Expiration at the time after entry, not to exceed 14 days, that court sets, unless before that time the court for good cause extends the order for like period or adverse party consents to a longer extension. Civ.R. 65(b)(2).

Motion for preliminary injunction must be set for hearing at earliest possible time, taking precedence over all other matters except hearings on older matters of same character. Civ.R. 65(b)(3).

Motion for dissolution or modification on 2 days' notice, or shorter notice set by the court; court must then hear and decide motion as promptly as justice requires. Civ.R. 65(b)(4).

INSTRUCTIONS

Requests

At close of evidence or at any earlier reasonable time that the court orders. After close of evidence for issues that could not reasonably have been anticipated by an earlier time that the court set for requests, and untimely requests for instructions on any issue with the court's permission. Civ.R. 51(a).

Proposed

Court must inform parties before instructing jury and before final jury arguments, and give parties opportunity to object before instructions and arguments are delivered. Civ.R. 51(b)(1), (2).

Time of

Court may instruct jury at any time before jury is discharged. Civ.R. 51(b)(3).

Objections

For parties informed of instructions or actions on requests before the jury is instructed and before final jury arguments, at the opportunity for objection provided under Civ.R. 51(b)(2). For parties not informed of instructions or actions on requests before time for objection under Civ.R. 51(b)(2), promptly after learning that instruction or request will be, or has been, given or refused. Civ.R. 51(c).

INTERROGATORIES

to parties

See, also, "Depositions", "Depositions on written questions", this table.

Service after parties have conferred as required by Civ.R. 26(f), except in a proceeding exempted from initial disclosure under Civ.R. 26(a)(1)(B), or when authorized by Rules of Civil Procedure, by stipulation, or by court order. Civ.R. 26(d)(1).

Answers or objections

INTERROGATORIES
to parties

Service within 30 days after service of the interrogatories. A shorter or longer time may be stipulated to under Civ.R. 29 or ordered by the court. Civ.R. 33(b)(2).

INTERVENTION

On timely motion. Civ.R. 24(a), (b).

Motion to intervene must be served on the parties as provided in Civ.R. 5. Civ.R. 24(c).

JUDGMENT or order

Alter or amend judgment, motion to

Must be filed no later than 28 days after entry of judgment. Civ.R. 59(e).

Exception to general rule, relating to extension of time. Civ.R. 6(b)(2).

Clerical mistakes, or from oversight or omission

May be corrected whenever found; but after an appeal has been docketed in appellate court and while appeal pending may be corrected only with leave of appellate court. Civ.R. 60(a).

Default

See "Default", this table.

Renewal of motion for judgment after trial

Not later than 28 days after entry of judgment. Exception from general rule relating to enlargement. Civ.R. 6(b)(2).

Entry of judgment

Subject to Civ.R. 54(b) and unless court orders otherwise, promptly by clerk without awaiting the court's direction, when the jury returns general verdict, court awards only costs or a sum certain, or court denies all relief. Promptly approved form of judgment by court and promptly entered by clerk, when jury returns special verdict or general verdict with answers to written questions, or when court grants other relief not described in Civ.R. 58(b). Entry may not be delayed in order to tax costs or award fees. Civ.R. 58(b), (e).

Time of entry—Entry of a judgment if separate document is not required when judgment is entered in the civil docket under Civ.R. 79(a). If separate document is required, when the judgment is entered in the civil docket under Civ.R. 79(a) and either the judgment is set out in a separate document, or 150 days have run from entry of the judgment in the civil docket, whichever is earlier. Civ.R. 58(c).

Entry, notice of

Immediately after entry, clerk must serve notice thereof as provided in Civ.R. 5(b) and record service on the docket. Party may also serve notice of entry provided in Civ.R. 5(b). Civ.R. 77(d)(1).

Lack of notice of entry does not affect time for appeal or relieve or authorize court to relieve party for failing to appeal within time allowed, except as allowed by App.R. 4(a). Civ.R. 77(d)(2).

Offer of judgment

Service at least 14 days before the date set for trial. Civ.R. 68(a).

Acceptance, written notice of—service within 14 days after service of offer. Civ.R. 68(a).

RULES OF CIVIL PROCEDURE

JUDGMENT or order

On pleadings, motion for judgment	After pleadings are closed but early enough not to delay the trial. Civ.R. 12(c).
Relief from, on grounds stated in Rule 60(b)	Motion within a reasonable time and no more than 1 year after entry of judgment or order or the date of the proceeding, for following grounds: (1) mistake, inadvertence, surprise, or excusable neglect; (2) newly discovered evidence; (3) fraud, misrepresentation, or misconduct by an opposing party. Civ.R. 60(b), (c). Exception from general rule relating to enlargement. Civ.R. 6(b)(2).
	Motion within a reasonable time, for following grounds: (1) judgment void, (2) judgment satisfied, released, or discharged, (3) prior underlying judgment reversed or vacated, (4) no longer equitable that judgment have prospective application, (5) any other reason justifying relief. Civ.R. 60(b). Exception from general rule relating to enlargement. Civ.R. 6(b)(2).
Stay	See "Execution", this table.
Summary judgment	See "Summary Judgment", this table.

JURY trial

Demand	Service of written demand — which may be included in a pleading — no later than 14 days after service of last pleading directed to the triable issue. Civ.R. 38(b).
	Adverse party may serve demand for jury trial within 14 days after service of first demand or within a shorter time ordered by the court. Civ.R. 38(c).
Removed actions	If at the time of removal all necessary pleadings have been served, a party entitled to a jury trial under Civ.R. 38 must be given one if party serves demand within 14 days after:
	(i) it files a notice of removal; or
	(ii) it is served with a notice of removal filed by another party. Civ.R. 81(c)(3)(B).
	Demand after removal not necessary in either of two instances: (1) before removal, party expressly demanded a jury trial in accordance with state law; (2) if state law did not require express demands for a jury trial and court does not order parties to do so within a specified time. Civ.R. 81(c)(3)(A).

LEGAL HOLIDAY — See "Holidays", this table.

MAGISTRATE JUDGES

Trial by consent	Consent of parties to magistrate judge's authority to be signified by filing statement consenting to the referral. Civ.R. 73(b)(1).
Pretrial matters	Objections of parties to order disposing of matter not dispositive of claim or defense to be served and filed within 14 days after being served with copy of order. Civ.R. 72(a).

MAGISTRATE JUDGES

| | Clerk must promptly mail copies to all parties of recommendation of magistrate judge for disposition of matter dispositive of claim or defense of a party or a prisoner petition. Specific written objections to recommended disposition may be served and filed within 14 days after service. Response to objections may be made within 14 days after being served with copy. Civ.R. 72(b)(1), (2). |

MAIL

| | Service under Civ.R. 5(b)(2)(C) (mail), (D) (leaving with the clerk), or (F) (other means consented to) adds 3 days after a prescribed period after service would otherwise expire under Civ.R. 6(a). Civ.R. 6(d).

When a party may or must act within a specified time after being served, 3 days are added after the period would otherwise expire under App.R. 26(a), unless the paper is delivered on the date of service stated in the proof of service. For purposes of App.R. 26(c), a paper served electronically is treated as delivered on the date of service stated in the proof of service. App.R. 26(c).

A brief or appendix not filed electronically is timely filed if on or before the last day for filing it is mailed to the clerk by first-class mail, or other class of mail that is at least as expeditious, postage prepaid; or dispatched to a third-party commercial carrier for delivery to the clerk within three days. App.R. 25(a)(2)(A)(ii). |

MASTERS

Order appointing master	Court may issue only after master files affidavit disclosing whether there is any ground for disqualification under 28 U.S.C. § 455 and, if ground is disclosed, the parties with court's approval waive the disqualification. Civ.R. 53(b)(3).
Amendment of order appointing	Order appointing master may be amended at any time after notice to parties and opportunity to be heard. Civ.R. 53(b)(4).
Order of master	A master who issues an order must file the order and promptly serve a copy on each party. The clerk must enter the order on the docket. Civ.R. 53(d).
Report of master	Master must report to court as required by appointing order. The master must file the report and promptly serve a copy on each party unless the court orders otherwise. Civ.R. 53(e).

In acting on, the court must give parties notice and an opportunity to be heard. Civ.R. 53(f)(1).

A party may file objections or motion to adopt or modify no later than 21 days after a copy of the master's order, report, or recommendations is served, unless the court sets a different time. Civ.R. 53(f)(2). |
| Compensation of master | The court must fix the master's compensation before or after judgment on the basis and terms stated in the appointing order, but the court may |

MASTERS

set a new basis and terms after giving notice and opportunity to be heard. Civ.R. 53(g)(1).

MORE DEFINITE STATEMENT

Furnished

Must be furnished within 14 days after notice of order or within the time the court sets, or court may strike pleading or issue any other appropriate order. Civ.R. 12(e).

Motion for

Must be made before responsive pleading is filed. Civ.R. 12(e).

MOTIONS, notices, and affidavits

See, also, specific headings, this table.

In general

A written motion, supporting affidavits, and notice of hearing thereof—service at least 14 days before time specified for hearing unless motion may be heard ex parte, or a different time is set by Rules of Civil Procedure or by order of court. Civ.R. 6(c).

Except as Civ.R. 59(c) provides otherwise, opposing affidavits must be served at least 7 days before hearing, unless court permits otherwise. Civ.R. 6(c).

Pleading, written motion, or other paper not signed by attorney or party must be stricken unless omission of signature is corrected promptly after being called to attention of attorney or party. Civ.R. 11(a).

NEW TRIAL

Motion and affidavits

Motion must be filed no later than 28 days after entry of judgment. Civ.R. 59(b). Exception from general rule relating to extending time. Civ.R. 6(b)(2). If motion based on affidavits, they must be filed with motion. Civ.R. 59(c).

Opposing affidavits

Opposing party has 14 days after being served to file. Civ.R. 59(c).

Initiative of court

Not later than 28 days after entry of judgment, court on its own may order new trial for any reason that would justify granting one on a party's motion. Civ.R. 59(d). Exception to general rule relating to extending time. Civ.R. 6(b)(2).

After giving parties notice and opportunity to be heard, court may grant a timely motion for new trial, for reason not stated in the motion. Civ.R. 59(d). Exception to general rule relating to extending time. Civ.R. 6(b)(2).

Judgment as a matter of law

Party against whom judgment as a matter of law is rendered must file a motion for a new trial under Civ.R. 59 no later than 28 days after entry of the judgment. Civ.R. 50(d).

OBJECTIONS to orders or rulings of court

At time ruling or order of court is requested or made; if party has no opportunity to object to ruling or order at time it is made, failing to object does not prejudice the party. Civ.R. 46.

Pretrial matters referred to magistrate judge

Objections of parties to order deciding pretrial matter not dispositive of claim or defense to be served and filed within 14 days after being served with copy of order. Civ.R. 72(a).

Specific written objections to recommended disposition of pretrial matter dispositive of claim or defense of a party may be served and filed within 14 days after service. Response to objections may be made within 14 days after being served with copy. Civ.R. 72(b)(1), (2).

OFFER of judgment

Must be served at least 14 days before the date set for trial. Civ.R. 68(a).

Acceptance must be served within 14 days after service of offer. Civ.R. 68(a).

ORDERS

See Judgment or order.

PLEADINGS

Amendment of

Once as matter of course within 21 days after serving its pleading, or if pleading is one to which a responsive pleading is required, 21 days after service of a responsive pleading or 21 days after service of a motion under Civ.R. 12(b), (e), or (f), whichever is earlier. Civ.R. 15(a)(1).

In all other cases, only with leave of court or written consent of opposing party. Civ.R. 15(a)(2).

During trial or after judgment to conform to evidence or to raise an unpleaded issue, but tried by express or implied consent of parties. Civ.R. 15(b).

Supplemental

On motion and reasonable notice, court may, on just terms, permit service of supplemental pleading setting out transactions, etc., that happened after the date of pleading to be supplemented. Civ.R. 15(d).

Opposing party plead to supplemental pleading—court may so order, within a specified time. Civ.R. 15(d).

Allegations of time

Such allegations are material when testing the sufficiency of a pleading. Civ.R. 9(f).

Judgment on, motion for

After pleadings are closed, but early enough not to delay trial. Civ.R. 12(c).

Striking of matter from

Motion made before responding to a pleading or, if no responsive pleading allowed, within 21 days after service of pleading. Civ.R. 12(f).

On court's own initiative at any time. Civ.R. 12(f).

RULES OF CIVIL PROCEDURE

PLEADINGS
Signing of

Pleading, written motion, or other paper not signed by attorney or party must be stricken unless omission of signature is corrected promptly after being called to attention of attorney or party. Civ.R. 11(a).

PLEAS

Abolished. Civ.R. 7, 2007 Advisory Committee note, relating to Civ.R. 7(c).

PRETRIAL conferences

Scheduling order to issue as soon as practicable but unless good cause for delay is found must issue within the earlier of 90 days after complaint served on defendant or 60 days after appearance of any defendant. Civ.R. 16(b).

PROCESS

See "Summons", this Table.

PRODUCTION of documents
Request for, service of

Within the scope of Civ.R. 26(b). Civ.R. 34(a).

Response to request

Within 30 days after service of the request or - if request was delivered under Civ.R. 26(d)(2) - within 30 days after the parties' first Civ.R. 26(f) conference. A shorter or longer time may be stipulated to under Civ.R. 29 or ordered by court. Civ.R. 34(b)(2)(A).

Time of inspection

The request must specify a reasonable time. Civ.R. 34(b)(1)(B).

Subpoena

See "Subpoena", this table.

REHEARING
Petition for panel rehearing

Petitions for panel rehearings may be filed within 14 days after entry of judgment unless the time is shortened or extended by order or local rule. In all civil cases in which the United States or its officer, employee, or agency is a party, the time within which any party may seek rehearing is 45 days after entry of judgment unless the time is shortened or extended by order. App.R. 40(a).

Issuance of mandate

The court's mandate must issue 7 days after the time to file a petition for rehearing expires, or 7 days after entry of an order denying a timely petition for panel rehearing, petition for rehearing en banc, or motion for stay of mandate, whichever is later. The court may shorten or extend the time by order. A party may move to stay the mandate pending the filing of a petition for a writ of certiorari in the Supreme Court. The stay must not exceed 90 days, unless the period is extended for good cause; or the party who obtained the stay notifies the circuit court in writing within the period of the stay that the time for filing a petition has been extended (in which case the stay continues for the extended period), or that the petition has been filed (in which case the stay continues until the Supreme Court's final disposition. App.R. 41(b), (d).

REMOVED actions

Answers, defenses, or objections

Within 21 days after receiving, through service or otherwise, a copy of the initial pleading stating the claim for relief, or within 21 days after being served with the summons for an initial pleading on file at the time of service, or within 7 days after the notice of removal is filed, whichever period is the longest. Civ.R. 81(c)(2).

Demand for jury trial

Demand after removal not necessary in either of two instances: (1) before removal, party expressly demanded a jury trial in accordance with state law; (2) if state law did not require express demands for a jury trial and court does not order parties to do so within a specified time. Civ.R. 81(c)(3)(A).

Notice of removal

Filing shall be within 30 days after receipt through service or otherwise of a copy of the initial pleading setting forth the claim for relief upon which the action or proceeding is based, or within 30 days after service of summons if such initial pleading has then been filed in court and is not required to be served on defendant, whichever period is shorter. 28 U.S.C.A. § 1446(b)(1).

Except as provided in 28 U.S.C.A. § 1446(c), if the case stated by the initial pleading is not removable, a notice of removal may be filed within 30 days after receipt by the defendant, through service or otherwise, of a copy of an amended pleading, motion, order or other paper from which it may first be ascertained that the case is one which is or has become removable. 28 U.S.C.A. § 1446(b)(3).

A case may not be removed on the basis of jurisdiction conferred by 28 U.S.C.A. § 1332 more than one year after commencement of the action, unless found that plaintiff has acted in bad faith in order to prevent a defendant from removing the action. 28 U.S.C.A. § 1446(c)(1).

REPLY

See, also, "Responsive pleadings", this table.

To answer

If ordered by court. Civ.R. 7(a)(7). Service within 21 days after being served with an order to reply, unless order specifies a different time. Civ.R. 12(a)(1)(C).

To counterclaim or crossclaim

Service of answer within 21 days after being served with the pleading that states the counterclaim or crossclaim. Civ.R. 12(a)(1)(B).

United States or agency or officer or employee thereof sued only in an official capacity must serve answer within 60 days after service on United States attorney. Civ.R. 12(a)(2).

United States officer or employee sued in an individual capacity in connection with duties performed on the United States' behalf must serve answer within 60 days after service on officer or employee or service on the United States attorney, whichever is later. Civ.R. 12(a)(3).

REPLY

Alteration of time by service of Civ.R. 12 motion | See "Responsive pleadings", this table.

RESPONSIVE PLEADINGS

See, also, "Answer", "Reply", this table.

To amend pleading | Within time remaining to respond to original pleading, or within 14 days after service of amended pleading, whichever is later, unless court orders otherwise. Civ.R. 15(a)(3).

To supplemental pleading | As ordered by court. Civ.R. 15(d).

Alteration of time by service of Civ.R. 12 motion | Service of motion permitted under Civ.R. 12 alters times for responsive pleadings as follows unless different time set by court:
(1) if court denies motion or postpones its disposition until trial, service of responsive pleading within 14 days after notice of the court's action; or
(2) if court grants motion for more definite statement, service of responsive pleading within 14 days after service of the more definite statement. Civ.R. 12(a)(4).

RESTRAINING order, temporary, without notice | See "Injunction", this table.

RETURN

The court may allow a summons or proof of service to be amended. Civ.R. 4(a)(2), (*l*)(3).

Proof of service must be made to the court by server's affidavit, except for service by United States marshal or deputy marshal. Civ.R. 4(*l*).

SANCTIONS | Presenting to court a pleading, written motion, or other paper is a certification under Civ.R. 11(b). If after notice and reasonable opportunity to respond, court determines that Civ.R. 11(b) was violated, sanctions may be imposed by a motion for sanctions which must not be filed or presented to court unless, within 21 days after service of the motion or another time period set by the court, the challenged matter is not withdrawn or appropriately corrected. Civ.R. 11(c)(1), (2). Sanctions are inapplicable to disclosures and discovery. Civ.R. 11(d).

SATURDAYS AND SUNDAYS, LEGAL HOLIDAYS | See "Computation of time", this table.

STAY or supersedeas | See "Appeal", "Execution", this table.

SUBPOENA

Objection | Before the earlier of the time specified for compliance or 14 days after service of the subpoena, service on the party or attorney designated in the subpoena of written objection to inspecting, copying, testing or sampling of any or all of the materials, or to inspecting the premises, or to producing electronically stored information in the form or forms requested. Civ.R. 45(d)(2)(B).

Motion to compel production | If objection has been made, the party serving the subpoena may at any time, on notice to the com-

SUBPOENA

manded person, move for an order compelling production or inspection. Civ.R. 45(d)(2)(B).

Motion to quash

The court for the district where compliance is required must quash or modify the subpoena on timely motion under certain circumstances. Civ.R. 45(d)(3)(A).

Witnesses, documentary evidence, etc.

Subpoena specifies time and place to: attend and give testimony; or produce designated documents, electronically stored information, or tangible things in the possession, custody or control of that person; or permit inspection of premises. Civ.R. 45(a)(1)(A)(iii), (C).

SUBSTITUTION of parties

In cases of death, incompetency, or transfer of interest—motion to substitute, together with notice of hearing, must be served on parties as provided in Civ.R. 5 and on nonparties as provided in Civ.R. 4. Civ.R. 25(a)(3), (b), (c).

Dismissal as to deceased party unless motion for substitution is made within 90 days after service of a statement noting the death. Civ.R. 25(a)(1).

Successor of public officer who is a party in an official capacity and who dies, resigns, or otherwise ceases to hold office while action is pending substituted automatically. Court may order substitution at any time, but absence of order does not affect substitution. Civ.R. 25(d).

SUMMARY JUDGMENT
Motion for

May move at any time until 30 days after the close of all discovery unless a different time is set by local rule or the court orders otherwise. Civ.R. 56(b).

SUMMONS

Served with a copy of complaint. Civ.R. 4(c)(1). If not served within 90 days after filing complaint, court must dismiss action without prejudice, order service be made within a specified time, or for good cause shown extend time for service for an appropriate period. Civ.R. 4(m).

Proof of service must be made to the court by server's affidavit, except for service by United States marshal or deputy marshal, unless waived. Civ.R. 4(l)(1).

Service within time allowed by Civ.R. 4(m) by any nonparty at least 18 years old, or at plaintiff's request a United States marshal, deputy marshal, or other person specially appointed by the court. Civ.R. 4(c)(2), (3).

SUPPLEMENTAL pleadings

See "Pleadings", this table.

SUPERSEDEAS or stay

See "Appeal", "Execution", this table.

TERM

Every district court considered always open for filing any paper, issuing and returning process, making a motion, or entering an order. Civ.R. 77(a).

THIRD–PARTY practice	Third-party plaintiff must, by motion, obtain the court's leave if it files the third-party complaint more than 14 days after serving its original answer. Civ.R. 14(a)(1).
VERDICT	
Renewal of motion for judgment after trial	Movant may renew motion for judgment as a matter of law by filing a motion no later than 28 days after the entry of judgment or — if the motion addresses a jury issue not decided by a verdict — no later than 28 days after the jury was discharged. Civ.R. 50(b). Exception from general rule relating to extension. Civ.R. 6(b)(2).
New trial where judgment as a matter of law rendered	Party against whom judgment as a matter of law is rendered must file a motion for a new trial under Civ.R. 59 no later than 28 days after entry of the judgment. Civ.R. 50(d).

EQUITY RULES REFERENCE TABLE

The Federal Rules of Civil Procedure supplant the Equity Rules since in general they cover the field now covered by the Equity Rules and the Conformity Act (former section 724 of this title).

This table shows the Equity Rules to which references are made in the notes to the Federal Rules of Civil Procedure.

Equity Rules	Federal Rules of Civil Procedure
1	77
2	77
3	79
4	77
5	77
6	78
7	4, 70
8	6, 70
9	70
10	18, 54
11	71
12	3, 4, 5, 12, 55
13	4
14	4
15	4, 45
16	6, 55
17	55
18	7, 8
19	1, 15, 61
20	12
21	11, 12
22	1
23	1, 39
24	11
25	8, 9, 10, 19
26	18, 20, 82
27	23
28	15
29	7, 12, 42, 55
30	8, 13, 82
31	7, 8, 12, 55
32	15
33	7, 12

Equity Rules	Federal Rules of Civil Procedure
34	15
35	15
36	11
37	17, 19, 20, 24
38	23
39	19
40	20
41	17
42	19, 20
43	12, 21
44	12, 21
45	25
46	43, 61
47	26
48	43
49	53
50	30, 80
51	30, 53
52	45, 53
53	53
54	26
55	30
56	40
57	40
58	26, 33, 34, 36
59	53
60	53
61	53
61½	53
62	53
63	53
64	26
65	53
66	53
67	53
68	53
69	59
70	17
70½	52
71	54
72	60, 61
73	65
74	62
75	75

Equity Rules	Federal Rules of Civil Procedure
76	75
77	76
78	43
79	83
80	6
81	86

ORDERS OF THE SUPREME COURT OF THE UNITED STATES ADOPTING AND AMENDING RULES

ORDER OF DECEMBER 20, 1937

It is ordered that Rules of Procedure for the District Courts of the United States be adopted pursuant to Section 2 of the Act of June 19, 1934, Chapter 651 (48 Stat. 1064), and the Chief Justice is authorized and directed to transmit the Rules as adopted to the Attorney General and to request him, as provided in that section, to report these Rules to the Congress at the beginning of the regular session in January next. MR. JUSTICE BRANDEIS states that he does not approve of the adoption of the Rules.

ORDER OF DECEMBER 28, 1939

1. That the first sentence of Rule 81(a)(6) of the Rules of Civil Procedure be amended so as to read as follows:

"(6) These rules do not apply to proceedings under the Act of September 13, 1888, c. 1015, § 13 (25 Stat. 479) as amended, U.S.C., Title 8, § 282, 8 U.S.C.A. § 282, relating to deportation of Chinese; they apply to proceedings for enforcement or review of compensation orders under the Longshoremen's and Harbor Workers' Compensation Act, Act of March 4, 1927, c. 509, §§ 18, 21 (44 Stat. 1434, 1436), U.S.C., Title 33, §§ 918, 921, 33 U.S.C.A. §§ 918, 921, except to the extent that matters of procedure are provided for in that Act".

2. **Effective Date.** That the foregoing amendment take effect on the day which is three months subsequent to the adjournment of the second regular session of the 76th Congress, but if that day is prior to September 1, 1940, then this amendment shall take effect on September 1, 1940. This amendment governs all proceedings in actions brought after it takes effect and also all further proceedings in actions then pending, except to the extent that in the opinion of the Court its application in a particular action pending when the amendment takes effect would not be feasible or would work injustice, in which event the former procedure applies.

3. That THE CHIEF JUSTICE be authorized to transmit this amendment to the Attorney General with the request that he report it to the Congress at the beginning of the regular session in January, 1940.

MR. JUSTICE BLACK does not approve of the adoption of this amendment.

ORDER OF DECEMBER 27, 1946

1. That subdivisions (a) and (b) of Rule 80 of the Rules of Civil Procedure be, and they hereby are, abrogated.

2. That Rules 6, 7, 12, 13, 14, 17, 24, 26, 27, 28, 33, 34, 36, 41, 45, 52, 54, 56, 58, 59, 60, 62, 65, 66, 68, 73, 75, 77, 79, 81, 84, and 86 of the Rules of Civil Procedure and Forms Nos. 17, 20, 22, and 25, be, and they hereby are, amended as hereinafter set forth.

[See the amendments made thereby under the respective rules and forms, post.]

3. That THE CHIEF JUSTICE be authorized to transmit these amendments to the Attorney General with the request that he report them to the Congress at the beginning of the regular session in January, 1947.

MR. JUSTICE FRANKFURTER joins in approval of the proposed amendments essentially because of his confidence in the informed judgment of the Advisory Committee on Rules of Civil Procedure.

ORDER OF DECEMBER 29, 1948

1. That the title "Rules of Civil Procedure for the District Courts of the United States" be amended to read "Rules of Civil Procedure for the United States District Courts".

2. That Rules 1, 17, 22, 24, 25, 27, 37, 45, 57, 60, 62, 65, 66, 67, 69, 72, 73, 74, 75, 76, 79, 81, 82, and 86 of the Rules of Civil Procedure and Forms Nos. 1, 19, 22, 23, and 27, be, and they hereby are, amended as hereinafter set forth.

[See the amendments made thereby under the respective rules and forms, post.]

3. That THE CHIEF JUSTICE be authorized to transmit these amendments to the Attorney General with the request that he report them to the Congress at the beginning of the regular session in January, 1949.

ORDER OF APRIL 30, 1951

1. That paragraph (7) of Rule 81(a) of the Rules of Civil Procedure, be, and it hereby is, abrogated.

2. That the Rules of Civil Procedure be, and they hereby are, amended by including therein a rule to govern condemnation cases in the United States District Courts, numbered 71A, as follows:

[See text of Rule 71A, post.]

3. Effective Date. That this Rule 71A and the amendment to Rule 81(a) will take effect on August 1, 1951. Rule 71A governs all proceedings in actions brought after it takes effect and also all further proceedings in actions then pending, except to the extent that in the opinion of the court its application in a particular action pending when the rule takes effect would not be feasible or would work injustice, in which event the former procedure applies.

4. That Forms Nos. 28 and 29 be, and they hereby are, approved and added to the Appendix of Forms to the Rules of Civil Procedure. The forms read respectively as follows:

[See text of Forms 28 and 29, post.]

5. That THE CHIEF JUSTICE be authorized to transmit these amendments to the Congress on or before May 1, 1951.

ORDER OF APRIL 17, 1961

1. That Rules 25, 54, 62 and 86 of the Rules of Civil Procedure and Forms Nos. 2 and 19, be, and they hereby are, amended as hereinafter set forth:

[See the amendments made thereby under the respective rules and forms, post.]

2. That THE CHIEF JUSTICE be authorized to transmit these amendments to Congress in accordance with the provisions of Title 28, U.S.C., Sec. 2072.

For Complete Annotation Materials, see United States Code Annotated

3. MR. JUSTICE BLACK does not join in approval of the Rules because he believes that it would be better for Congress to act directly by legislation on the matters treated by the Rules.

4. MR. JUSTICE DOUGLAS filed the following statement:

"Most of the proposed changes in the Rules of Civil Procedure are picayune and harmless, yet hardly worth making apart from any overall revision of the Rules. The change in Rule 25 of the Rules of Civil Procedure is, however, a major one; and it seems to me unwise. The policy that a cabinet officer under one administration pursues is often not the policy of the next administration. I would not make the contrary assumption, as does the proposed change. I think the ends served by *Snyder v. Buck*, 340 U.S. 15, 71 S.Ct. 93, 95 L.Ed. 15, are proper ones. The Rule in its present form leaves the burden on the claimant who challenges a particular government policy to re-establish that the controversy he had with a predecessor is a live one as respects the successor. The burden should rest there, not with the newcomer to office.

"The critical language in Rule 25(d) that is changed by the proposed amendment derived from 28 U.S.C. § 780 which the Revised Code dropped in 1949 because it had been incorporated in Rule 25(d). See 28 U.S.C., p. XXIX. The history of § 780 is reviewed in *Snyder v. Buck*, supra, pp. 18–19.

"Congress dealt with the matter beginning with the Act of February 8, 1899, 30 Stat. 822. The care with which it approached the problem is shown in H.R.Rep. No. 960, 55th Cong., 2d Sess., p. 2, where it is said:

" 'A mandamus proceeding against an officer is based upon the claim that he is personally refusing to perform some duty which the law requires of him in his official character, and if decided against him he is properly liable, personally, for all cost of the proceeding, but if he vacates the office before a decision, it might seem harsh to compel his successor to become a party to the suit and to the costs already accrued without having been guilty of any personal neglect of the official duty involved in the proceeding; but to provide against this seeming harshness your committee propose to amend the bill so as to give the succeeding official an opportunity to perform the official act involved in the proceeding and thereby prevent the survival of the action against himself, and if he fails to do so, he can not then complain of being mulct in costs accruing against his predecessor.'

"The provision of § 780 that the action might be continued against the successor in office on the requisite showing within the stated period was added by § 11 of the Judiciary Act of 1925. 43 Stat. 936, 941. The last word Congress spoke on the matter reflected the views in a Report submitted by Chief Justice Taft dated March 11, 1922, which explained § 11 in the following words:

" 'It will be noted . . . . . that the provision is not mandatory, but leaves it to the sound discretion of the court to determine whether there is a substantial need for continuing the cause and obtaining an adjudication of the questions involved. This will tend to restrict the exercise of the right to cases which have a sound basis.' This language was repeated in the Senate Committee Print, 68th Cong., 1st Sess., of A General Review of H.R. 10479, 67th Cong., p. 16. The language so carefully tailored by Congress is now rejected by the professional group who constitute our advisors in these matters. I do not think we should allow a known and established congressional policy to be so readily abrogated.

"We said in *Snyder v. Buck*, supra, p. 20, that if Rule 25(d) is to be amended in the manner then urged and now adopted 'the amending process is available.' Where we have a matter so heavily encrusted with legislative policy, I think any change should be left to Congress.

"I, therefore, dissent from the submission to Congress of the proposed amendments to Rule 25 of the Rules of Civil Procedure under 28 U.S.C. § 2072. For under that Act the Rules submitted become effective at the expiration of a 90–day period, unless Congress takes contrary action. This machinery seems therefore, inappropriate to me for effecting such a basic change in congressional policy as the proposed Rule 25(d) achieves."

ORDER OF JANUARY 21, 1963

1. That the Rules of Civil Procedure be, and they hereby are, amended by including therein Forms Number 30, 31 and 32, and the amendments to Rules 4, 5, 6, 7, 12, 13, 14, 15, 24, 25, 26, 28, 30, 41, 49, 50, 52, 56, 58, 71A, 77, 79, 81, and 86 and to Forms Number 3, 4, 5, 6, 7, 8, 9, 10, 11, 12, 13, 16, 18, 21, 22–A and 22–B, as hereinafter set forth:

[See additions and amendments made thereby under the respective rules and forms, post.]

2. That THE CHIEF JUSTICE be authorized to transmit these amendments to Congress in accordance with the provisions of Title 28, U.S.C., Sec. 2072.

MR. JUSTICE BLACK and MR. JUSTICE DOUGLAS are opposed to the submission of these rules [1] to the Congress under a statute which permits them to "take effect" and to repeal "all laws in conflict with such rules" without requiring any affirmative consideration, action, or approval of the rules by Congress or by the President.[2] We believe that while some of the Rules of Civil Procedure are simply housekeeping details,[3] many determine matters so substantially affecting the rights of litigants in law suits that in practical effect they are the equivalent of new legislation which, in our judgment, the Constitution requires to be initiated in and enacted by the Congress [4] and approved by the President.[5] The Constitution, as we read it, provides that all laws shall be enacted by the House, the Senate, and the President, not by the mere failure of Congress to reject proposals of an outside agency. Even were there not this constitutional limitation, the authorizing statute itself qualifies this Court's power by imposing upon it a solemn responsibility not to submit rules that "abridge, enlarge or modify any substantive right" and by specifically charging the Court with the duty to "preserve the right to trial by jury as at common law and as declared by the Seventh Amendment to the Constitution." [6] Our chief objections to the rules relate essentially to the fact that many of their provisions do "abridge, enlarge or modify" substantive rights and do not "preserve the right to trial by jury" but actually encroach upon it.

(1)(a) Rule 50(a) is amended by making the order of a judge granting a motion for a directed verdict effective without submitting the question to the jury at all. It was pointed out in *Galloway v. United States*, 319 U.S. 372, 396, 401–407, 63 S.Ct. 1077, 87 L.Ed. 1458 (dissenting opinion), how judges have whittled away or denied the right of trial by jury through the devices of directed verdicts and judgments notwithstanding verdicts. Although the amendment here is not itself a momentous one, it gives formal sanction to the process by which the courts have been wresting from juries the power to render verdicts. Since we do not approve of this sapping of the Seventh Amendment's guarantee of a jury trial, we cannot join even this technical *coup de grace*.

(b) The proposed amendment to 50(c) in practical effect vests appellate courts with more power than they have had to grant or deny new trials. The Court in *Cone v. West Virginia Pulp & Paper Co.,* 330 U.S. 212, 217–218, 67 S.Ct. 752, 91 L.Ed. 849, and *Globe Liquor Co. v. San Roman,* 332 U.S. 571, 68 S.Ct. 246, 92 L.Ed. 177, refused to construe the federal rules then existing to allow Courts of Appeals to interfere with trial judges' discretion to grant new trials. To the extent that jury verdicts are to be set aside and new trials granted, we believe that those who hear the evidence, the trial judges, are the ones who should primarily exercise such discretion.

(c) The proposed amendment to Rule 56(e) imposes additional burdens upon litigants to protect against summary judgments rendered without hearing evidence on the part of witnesses who are confronted by the persons against whom they testify so that these persons can subject the witnesses to cross-examination. The summary judgment procedure, while justified in some cases, is made a handy instrument to let judges rather than juries try law suits and to let those judges try cases not on evidence of witnesses subjected to cross-examination but on ex parte affidavits obtained by parties. Most trial lawyers would agree, we think, that a litigant can frequently obtain in an actual trial favorable testimony which could not have been secured by affidavits or even by depositions.

(d) If there are to be amendments, Rule 49 should be repealed. That rule authorizes judges to require juries to return "only a special verdict in the form of a special written finding upon each issue of fact" or to answer "written interrogatories upon one or more issues of fact the decision of which is necessary to a verdict" in addition to rendering the general verdict. Such devices are used to impair or wholly take away the power of a jury to render a general verdict. One of the ancient, fundamental reasons for having general jury verdicts was to preserve the right of trial by jury as an indispensable part of a free government. Many of the most famous constitutional controversies in England revolved around litigants' insistence, particularly in seditious libel cases, that a jury had the right to render a general verdict without being compelled to return a number of subsidiary findings to support its general verdict. Some English jurors had to go to jail because they insisted upon their right to render general verdicts over the repeated commands of tyrannical judges not to do so. Rule 49 is but another means utilized by courts to weaken the constitutional power of juries and to vest judges with more power to decide cases according to their own judgments. A scrutiny of the special verdict and written interrogatory cases in appellate courts will show the confusion that necessarily results from the employment of these devices and the ease with which judges can use them to take away the right to trial by jury. We believe that Rule 49 be repealed, not amplified.

(2) There is a proposal to amend Rule 41, which provides for dismissal of actions. We believe that, if the Rules are to be changed, a major amendment to this rule is required in the interest of justice. Before dismissing a plaintiff's action for failure of his lawyer to prosecute, the trial judge should be required to have notice served on the plaintiff himself. The hardship that can result from the absence of such requirement is shown by *Link v. Wabash R. Co.,* 370 U.S. 626, 82 S.Ct. 1386, 8 L.Ed.2d 734. Link's lawyer failed to appear in response to a judge's order for a pre-trial conference, and the judge dismissed the case. As pointed out in the dissent, plaintiff had been severely injured, and a fair system of justice should not have penalized him because his lawyer, through neglect or any other reason, failed to appear when ordered. It would do a defendant no injury for the court to refuse to dismiss any apparently bona fide case until the plaintiff has actually had notice that some failure of his lawyer has irked the judge.

(3) MR. JUSTICE BLACK and MR. JUSTICE DOUGLAS object to the changes in Rule 4, which for the first time permit a Federal District Court to obtain jurisdiction over a defendant by service of process outside the state or over his property by garnishment or attachment, under the circumstances and in the manner prescribed by state law. Those changes will apparently have little effect insofar as "federal question" litigation is concerned, since 28 U.S.C. § 1391(b) requires such suits to be brought "only in the judicial district where all defendants reside...." Diversity actions, however, may be greatly increased, for the effect of proposed 4(e) is not limited to suits authorized by such statutes as the Federal Interpleader Act, 28 U.S.C. § 1335. See Advisory Committee Rept., 5–8; 28 U.S.C. § 1391(a); Fed.Rules Civ.Proc. 1. We see no justification for an increase in the number of diversity cases. We also see no reason why the extent of a Federal District Court's personal jurisdiction should depend upon the existence or nonexistence of a state "long-arm" statute. Moreover, at present a state court action commenced by attachment or garnishment can get into a District Court only if a nonresident defendant chooses to appear and remove the case, see 28 U.S.C. § 1441, and there is no good reason, absent a congressional finding, why this should be changed.

Instead of recommending changes to the present Rules, we recommend that the statute authorizing this Court to prescribe Rules of Civil Procedure, if it is to remain a law, be amended to place the responsibility upon the Judicial Conference rather than upon this Court. Since the statute was first enacted in 1934, 48 Stat. 1064, the Judicial Conference has been enlarged and improved and is now very active in its surveillance of the work of the federal courts and in recommending appropriate legislation to Congress. The present Rules produced under 28 U.S.C. § 2072 are not prepared by us but by Committees of the Judicial Conference designated by the Chief Justice, and before coming to us they are approved by the Judicial Conference pursuant to 28 U.S.C. § 331.[7] The Committees and the Conference are composed of able and distinguished members and they render a high public service. It is they, however, who do the work, not we, and the rules have only our imprimatur. The only contribution that we actually make is an occasional exercise of a veto power. If the rule-making for Federal District Courts is to continue under the present plan, we believe that the Supreme Court should not have any part in the task; rather, the statute should be amended to substitute the Judicial Conference. The Judicial Conference can participate more actively in fashioning the rules and affirmatively contribute to their content and design better than we can. Transfer of the function to the Judicial Conference would relieve us of the embarrassment of having to sit in judgment on the constitutionality of rules which we have approved and which as applied in given situations might have to be declared invalid.

[1] See our earlier statements in 368 U.S. 1012–1014 and 346 U.S. 946–947.

2 28 U.S.C. § 2072 gives this Court the power to prescribe rules of practice and procedure for Federal District Courts and further provides that such rules

"shall not take effect until they have been reported to Congress by THE CHIEF JUSTICE at or after the beginning of a regular session thereof but not later than the first day of May, and until the expiration of ninety days after they have been thus reported.

"All laws in conflict with such rules shall be of no further force or effect after such rules have taken effect."

3 See 368 U.S. 1012.

4 "All legislative Powers herein granted shall be vested in a Congress of the United States, which shall consist of a Senate and House of Representatives." U.S. Const., Art. I, § 1.

5 Every Bill which shall have passed the House of Representatives and the Senate, shall, before it becomes a Law, be presented to the President of the United States; ...." U.S. Const., Art. I, § 7.

6 28 U.S.C. § 2072.

7 "The Conference shall also carry on a continuous study of the operation and effect of the general rules of practice and procedure now or hereafter in use as prescribed by the Supreme Court for the other courts of the United States pursuant to law. Such changes in and additions to those rules as the Conference may deem desirable to promote simplicity in procedure, fairness in administration, the just determination of litigation, and the elimination of unjustifiable expense and delay shall be recommended by the Conference from time to time to the Supreme Court for its consideration and adoption, modification or rejection, in accordance with law."

ORDER OF FEBRUARY 28, 1966

1. That the Rules of Civil Procedure for the United States District Courts be, and they hereby are, amended by including therein Rules 23.1, 23.2, 44.1 and 65.1, Supplemental Rules A, B, C, D, E and F for Certain Admiralty and Maritime Claims, and amendments to Rules 1, 4, 8, 9, 12, 13, 14, 15, 17, 18, 19, 20, 23, 24, 26, 38, 41, 42, 43, 44, 47, 53, 59, 65, 68, 73, 74, 75, 81 and 82, and to Forms 2 and 15, as hereinafter set forth:

[See added, amended and supplemental Rules and Forms, post.]

2. That the foregoing amendments and additions to the Rules of Civil Procedure shall take effect on July 1, 1966, and shall govern all proceedings in actions brought thereafter and also in all further proceedings in actions then pending, except to the extent that in the opinion of the court their application in a particular action then pending would not be feasible or would work injustice, in which event the former procedure applies.

3. That THE CHIEF JUSTICE be, and he hereby is, authorized to transmit to the Congress the foregoing amendments and additions to the Rules of Civil Procedure in accordance with the provisions of Title 28, U.S.C., §§ 2072 and 2073.

4. That: (a) subdivision (c) of Rule 6 of the Rules of Civil Procedure for the United States District Courts promulgated by this court on December 20, 1937, effective September 16, 1938; (b) Rule 2 of the Rules for Practice and Procedure under section 25 of An Act to amend and consolidate the Acts respecting copyright, approved March 4, 1909, promulgated by this court on June 1, 1909, effective July 1, 1909; and (c) the Rules of Practice in Admiralty and Maritime Cases, promulgated by this court on December 6, 1920, effective March 7, 1921, as revised, amended and supplemented, be, and they hereby are, rescinded, effective July 1, 1966.

MR. JUSTICE BLACK, dissenting.

The Amendments to the Federal Rules of Civil and Criminal Procedure today transmitted to the Congress are the work of very capable advisory committees. Those committees, not the Court, wrote the rules. Whether by this transmittal the individual members of the Court who voted to transmit the rules intended to express approval of the varied policy decisions the rules embody I am not sure. I am reasonably certain, however, that the Court's transmittal does not carry with it a decision that the amended rules are all constitutional. For such a decision would be the equivalent of an advisory opinion which, I assume the Court would unanimously agree, we are without constitutional power to give. And I agree with my Brother DOUGLAS that some of the proposed criminal rules go to the very border line if they do not actually transgress the constitutional right of a defendant not to be compelled to be a witness against himself. This phase of the criminal rules in itself so infects the whole collection of proposals that, without mentioning other objections, I am opposed to transmittal of the proposed amendments to the criminal rules.

I am likewise opposed to transmittal of the proposed revision of the civil rules. In the first place I think the provisions of 28 U.S.C. § 2072 (1964 ed.), under which these rules are transmitted and the corresponding section, 18 U.S.C. § 3771 (1964 ed.), relating to the criminal rules, both of which provide for giving transmitted rules the effect of law as though they had been properly enacted by Congress are unconstitutional for reasons I have previously stated.[1] And in prior dissents I have stated some of the basic reasons for my objections to repeated rules revisions[2] that tend to upset established meanings and need not repeat those grounds of objection here. The confusion created by the adoption of the present rules, over my objection, has been partially dispelled by judicial interpretations of them by this Court and others. New rules and extensive amendments to present rules will mean renewed confusion resulting in new challenges and new reversals and prejudicial "pretrial" dismissals of cases before a trial on the merits for failure of lawyers to understand and comply with new rules of uncertain meaning. Despite my continuing objection to the old rules, it seems to me that since they have at least gained some degree of certainty it would be wiser to "bear those ills we have than fly to others we know not of," unless, of course, we are reasonably sure that the proposed reforms of the old rules are badly needed. But I am not. The new proposals, at least some of them, have, as I view them, objectionable possibilities that cause me to believe our judicial system could get along much better without them.

The momentum given the proposed revision of the old rules by this Court's transmittal makes it practically certain that Congress, just as has this Court, will permit the rules to take effect exactly as they were written by the Advisory Committee on Rules. Nevertheless, I am including here a memorandum I submitted to the Court expressing objections to the Committee's proposals and suggesting changes should they be transmitted. These suggestions chiefly center around rules that grant broad discretion to trial judges with reference to class suits, pretrial procedures, and dismissal of cases with prejudice. Cases coming before the federal courts over the years now filling nearly 40 volumes of Federal Rules Decisions show an accumulation of grievances by lawyers and litigants about the way many trial judges exercise their almost unlimited discretionary powers to use pretrial procedures to dismiss cases without trials. In fact, many of these cases indicate a belief of many judges and legal commentators that the cause of justice is best served in the long run not by trials on the merits but by summary dismissals based on out of court affidavits, pretrial depositions, and other pretrial techniques. My belief is that open court trials on the merits where litigants have the right to prove their case or defense best comports with due process of law.

The proposed rules revisions, instead of introducing changes designed to prevent the continued abuse of pretrial power to dismiss cases summarily without trials, move in the opposite direction. Of course, each such dismissal results in removal of one more case from our congested court dockets, but that factor should not weigh more heavily in our system of justice than assuring a full-fledged due process trial of every bona fide lawsuit brought to vindicate an honest, substantial claim. It is to protect this ancient right of a person to have his case tried rather than summarily thrown out of court that I suggested to the Court that it recommend changes in the Committee's proposals of the nature set out in the following memorandum.

"Dear Brethren:

"I have gone over all the proposed amendments carefully and while there are probably some good suggestions, it is my belief that the bad results that can come from the adoption of these amendments predominate over any good they can bring about. I particularly think that every member of the Court should examine with great care the amendments relating to class suits. It seems to me that they place too much power in the hands of the trial judges and that the rules might almost as well simply provide that 'class suits can be maintained either for or against particular groups whenever in the discretion of a judge he thinks it is wise.' The power given to the judge to dismiss such suits or to divide them up into groups at will subjects members of classes to dangers that could not follow from carefully prescribed legal standards enacted to control class suits.

"In addition, the rules as amended, in my judgment, greatly aggravate the evil of vesting judges with practically uncontrolled power to dismiss with prejudice cases brought by plaintiffs or defenses interposed by defendants. The power to dismiss a plaintiff's case or to render judgments by default against defendants can work great harm to both parties. There are many inherent urges in existence which may subconsciously incline a judge towards disposing of the cases before him without having to go through the burden of a trial. Mr. Chief Justice White, before he became Chief Justice, wrote an opinion in the case of *Hovey v. Elliott,* 167 U.S. 409 [17 S.Ct. 841, 42 L.Ed. 215], which pointed out grave constitutional questions raised by attempting to punish the parties by depriving them of the right to try their law suits or to defend against law suits brought against them by others.

"Rule 41 entitled 'Dismissal of Actions' points up the great power of judges to dismiss actions and provides an automatic method under which a dismissal must be construed as a dismissal 'with prejudice' unless the judge specifically states otherwise. For that reason I suggest to the Conference that if the Rules are accepted, including that one, the last sentence of Rule 41(b) be amended so as to provide that a simple order of dismissal by a judge instead of operating 'as an adjudication upon the merits,' as the amended rule reads, shall provide that such a dismissal 'does not operate as an adjudication upon the merits.'

"As a further guarantee against oppressive dismissals I suggest the addition of the following as subdivision (c) of Rule 41.

" 'No plaintiff's case shall be dismissed or defendant's right to defend be cut off because of the neglect, misfeasance,

malfeasance, or failure of their counsel to obey any order of the court, until and unless such plaintiff or defendant shall have been personally served with notice of their counsel's delinquency, and not then unless the parties themselves do or fail to do something on their own part that can legally justify dismissal of the plaintiff's case or of the defendant's defense.'

"This proposed amendment is suggested in order to protect litigants, both plaintiffs and defendants, against being thrown out of court as a penalty for their lawyer's neglect or misconduct. The necessity for such a rule is shown, I think, by the dismissal in the plaintiff's case in *Link v. Wabash R. Co.,* 370 U.S. 626 [82 S.Ct. 1386, 8 L.Ed.2d 734]. The usual argument against this suggestion is that a party to a law suit hires his lawyer and should therefore be responsible for everything his lawyer does in the conduct of his case. This may be a good argument with reference to affluent litigants who not only know the best lawyers but are able to hire them. It is a wholly unrealistic argument, however, to make with reference to individual persons who do not know the ability of various lawyers or who are not financially able to hire those at the top of the bar and who are compelled to rely on the assumption that a lawyer licensed by the State is competent. It seems to me to be an uncivilized practice to punish clients by throwing their cases out of court because of their lawyers' conduct. It may be supportable by good, sound, formal logic but I think has no support whatever in a procedural system supposed to work as far as humanly possible to the end of obtaining equal and exact justice.

"For all the reasons stated above and in my previous objections to the transmittals of rules I dissent from the transmittals here."

[1] In a statement accompanying a previous transmittal of the civil rules, MR. JUSTICE DOUGLAS and I said:

"MR. JUSTICE BLACK and MR. JUSTICE DOUGLAS are opposed to the submission of these rules to the Congress under a statute which permits them to 'take effect' and to repeal 'all laws in conflict with such rules' without requiring any affirmative consideration, action, or approval of the rules by Congress or by the President. We believe that while some of the Rules of Civil Procedure are simply housekeeping details, many determine matters so substantially affecting the rights of litigants in lawsuits that in practical effect they are the equivalent of new legislation which, in our judgment, the Constitution requires to be initiated in and enacted by the Congress and approved by the President. The Constitution, as we read it, provides that all laws shall be enacted by the House, the Senate, and the President, not by the mere failure of Congress to reject proposals of an outside agency. * * * " (Footnotes omitted.) 374 U.S. 865–866.

[2] 346 U.S. 946, 374 U.S. 865. And see 368 U.S. 1011 and 1012.

MR. JUSTICE DOUGLAS, dissenting in part.

I reiterate today what I stated on an earlier occasion (374 U.S. 865, 869–870) (statement of Black and Douglas, JJ.), that the responsibility for promulgating Rules of the kind we send to Congress today should rest with the Judicial Conference and not the Court. It is the Judicial Conference, not the Court, which appoints the Advisory Committee on Criminal Rules which makes the actual recommendations.[1] Members of the Judicial Conference, being in large part judges of the lower courts and attorneys who are using the Rules day in and day out, are in a far better position to make a practical judgment upon their utility or inutility than we.

But since under the statute[2] the Rules go to Congress only on the initiative of the Court, I cannot be only a conduit. I think that placing our imprimatur on the amendments to the Rules entails a large degree of responsibility of judgment concerning them. Some of the criminal Rules which we forward to Congress today are very bothersome—not in the sense that they may be unwieldy or unworkable—but in the sense that they may entrench on important constitutional rights of defendants.

In my judgment, the amendments to Rule 16 dealing with discovery require further reflection. To the extent that they expand the defendant's opportunities for discovery, they accord with the views of a great many commentators who have concluded that a civilized society ought not to tolerate the conduct of a criminal prosecution as a "game." [3] But the proposed changes in the Rule go further. Rule 16(c) would permit a trial judge to condition granting the defendant discovery on the defendant's willingness to permit the prosecution to discover "scientific or medical reports, books, papers, documents, tangible objects, or copies or portions thereof" which (1) are in the defendant's possession; (2) he intends to produce at trial; and (3) are shown to be material to the preparation of the prosecution's case.[4]

The extent to which a court may compel the defendant to disclose information or evidence pertaining to his case without infringing the privilege against self-incrimination is a source of current controversy among judges, prosecutors, defense lawyers, and other legal commentators. A distinguished state court has concluded—although not without a strong dissent—that the privilege is not violated by discovery of the names of expert medical witnesses whose appearance at trial is contemplated by the defense.[5] I mean to imply no views on the point, except to note that a serious constitutional question lurks here.

The prosecution's opportunity to discover evidence in the possession of the defense is somewhat limited in the proposal with which we deal in that it is tied to the exercise by the defense of the right to discover from the prosecution. But *if* discovery, by itself, of information in the possession of the defendant would violate the privilege against self-incrimination, is it any less a violation if conditioned on the defendant's exercise of the opportunity to discover evidence? May benefits be conditioned on the abandonment of constitutional rights? See, e.g., *Sherbert v. Verner*, 374 U.S. 398, 403–406, 83 S.Ct. 1790, 1793–1795, 10 L.Ed.2d 965. To deny a defendant the opportunity to discovery—an opportunity not withheld from defendants who agree to prosecutorial discovery or from whom discovery is not sought—merely because the defendant chooses to exercise the constitutional right to refrain from self-incrimination arguably imposes a penalty upon the exercise of that fundamental privilege. It is said, however, that fairness may require disclosure by a defendant who obtains information from the prosecution.

Perhaps—but the proposed rule establishes no such standards. Its application is mechanical: if the defendant is allowed discovery, so, too, is the prosecution. No requirement is imposed, for example, that the subject matter of the material sought to be discovered by the prosecution be limited to that relating to the subject of the defendant's discovery.

The proposed addition of Rule 17.1 also suggests difficulties, perhaps of constitutional dimension. This rule would establish a pretrial conference procedure. The language of the rule and the Advisory Committee's comments suggest that under some circumstances, the conference might even take place in the absence of the defendant! Cf. *Lewis v. United States*, 146 U.S. 370, 13 S.Ct. 136, 36 L.Ed. 1011; Fed.Rules Crim.Proc. Rule 43.

The proposed amendment to Rule 32(c)(2) states that the trial judge "may" disclose to the defendant or his counsel the contents of a presentence report on which he is relying in fixing sentence. The imposition of sentence is of critical importance to a man convicted of crime. Trial judges need presentence reports so that they may have at their disposal the fullest possible information. See *Williams v. People of State of New York*, 337 U.S. 241, 69 S.Ct. 1079, 93 L.Ed. 1337. But while the formal rules of evidence do not apply to restrict the factors which the sentencing judge may consider, fairness would, in my opinion, require that the defendant be advised of the facts—perhaps very damaging to him—on which the judge intends to rely. The presentence report may be inaccurate, a flaw which may be of constitutional dimension. Cf. *Townsend v. Burke*, 334 U.S. 736, 68 S.Ct. 1252, 92 L.Ed. 1690. It may exaggerate the gravity of the defendant's prior offenses. The investigator may have made an incomplete investigation. See Tappan, Crime, Justice and Correction 556 (1960). There may be countervailing factors not disclosed by the probation report. In many areas we can rely on the sound exercise of discretion by the trial judge; but how can a judge know whether or not the presentence report calls for a reply by the defendant? Its faults may not appear on the face of the document.

Some States require full disclosure of the report to the defense.[6] The proposed Model Penal Code takes the middle-ground and requires the sentencing judge to disclose to the defense the factual contents of the report so that there is an opportunity to reply.[7] Whatever should be the rule for the federal courts, it ought not to be one which permits a judge to impose sentence on the basis of information of which the defendant may be unaware and to which he has not been afforded an opportunity to reply.

I do not think we should approve Rule 16, 17.1, and 32(c)(2). Instead, we should refer them back to the Judicial Conference and the Advisory Committee for further consideration and reflection, where I believe they were approved only by the narrowest majority.

WILLIAM O. DOUGLAS.

[1] 28 U.S.C. § 331 (1964 ed.) which establishes the Judicial Conference of the United States, provides that the Conference shall "carry on a continuous study of the operation and effect of the general rules of practice and procedure * * * prescribed by the Supreme Court * * *." The Conference has resolved that a standing Committee on Rules of Practice and Procedure be appointed by the Chief Justice and that, in addition, five advisory committees be established to recommend to the Judicial Conference changes in the rules of practice and procedure for the federal courts. See Annual Report of the Proceedings of the Judicial Conference of the United States 6–7 (1958).

[2] 18 U.S.C. § 3771 (1964 ed.).

[3] See, e.g., Brennan, The Criminal Prosecution: Sporting Event or Quest for Truth?, 1963 Wash.U.L.Q. 279; Louisell, Criminal Discovery: Dilemma Real or Apparent?, 49 Calif.L.Rev. 56 (1961); Traynor, Ground Lost and Found in Criminal Discovery, 39 N.Y.U.L.Rev. 228 (1964).

[4] The proposed rule explicitly provides that the prosecution may not discover nonmedical documents or reports "made by the defendant, or his attorneys or agents in connection with the investigation or defense of the case, or of statements made by the defendant, or by government or defense witnesses, or by prospective government or defense witnesses, to the defendant, his agents or attorneys."

[5] *Jones v. Superior Court of Nevada County*, 58 Cal.2d 56, 22 Cal.Rptr. 879, 372 P.2d 919, 96 A.L.R.2d 1213. See Comment, 51 Calif.L.Rev. 135; Note, 76 Harv.L.Rev. 838 (1963). The case is more extensively treated in Louisell, Criminal Discovery and Self–Incrimination, 53 Calif.L.Rev. 89 (1965).

6 E.g., Calif.Penal Code § 1203.

7 Model Penal Code § 7.07(5) (Proposed Official Draft, 1962). The Code provides that the sources of confidential information need not be disclosed. "Less disclosure than this hardly comports with elementary fairness." Comment to § 7.07 (Tent.Draft No. 2, 1954), at 55. A discarded draft of the amendment to Fed.Rules Crim.Proc.Rule 32 would have allowed disclosure to defense counsel of the report, from which the confidential sources would be removed. A defendant not represented by counsel would be told of the "essential facts" in the report. See 8 Moore's Federal Practice ¶¶ 32.03[4], 32.09 (1965).

ORDER OF DECEMBER 4, 1967

1. That the following rules, to be known as the Federal Rules of Appellate Procedure, be, and they hereby are, prescribed, pursuant to sections 3771 and 3772 of Title 18, United States Code, and sections 2072 and 2075 of Title 28, United States Code, to govern the procedure in appeals to United States courts of appeals from the United States district courts, in the review by United States courts of appeals of decisions of the Tax Court of the United States, in proceedings in the United States courts of appeals for the review or enforcement of orders of administrative agencies, boards, commissions and officers, and in applications for writs or other relief which a United States court of appeals or judge thereof is competent to give:

[See text of Rules of Appellate Procedure, post.]

2. That the foregoing rules shall take effect on July 1, 1968, and shall govern all proceedings in appeals and petitions for review or enforcement of orders thereafter brought and in all such proceedings then pending, except to the extent that in the opinion of the court of appeals their application in a particular proceeding then pending would not be feasible or would work injustice, in which case the former procedure may be followed.

3. That Rules 6, 9, 41, 77 and 81 of the Rules of Civil Procedure for the United States District Courts be, and they hereby are, amended, effective July 1, 1968, as hereinafter set forth:

[See the amendments made thereby under the respective rules, post.]

4. That the chapter heading "IX. APPEALS", all of Rules 72, 73, 74, 75 and 76 of the Rules of Civil Procedure for the United States District Courts, and Form 27 annexed to the said rules, be, and they hereby are, abrogated, effective July 1, 1968.

[Paragraphs 5 and 6 of the order pertain to certain Rules of Criminal Procedure for the United States District Courts and to certain Forms annexed to the said rules. For text, see Pamphlet containing Federal Rules of Criminal Procedure.]

7. That THE CHIEF JUSTICE be, and he hereby is, authorized to transmit to the Congress the foregoing new rules and amendments to and abrogation of existing rules, in accordance with the provisions of Title 18, U.S.C., § 3771, and Title 28, U.S.C., §§ 2072 and 2075.

ORDER OF MARCH 30, 1970

1. That subdivision (a) of Rule 5, subdivision (h) of Rule 9 and Rules 26, 29, 30, 31, 32, 33, 34, 35, 36 and 37, and subdivision (d) of Rule 45, subdivision (a) of Rule 69, and Form 24 of the Rules of Civil Procedure for the United States

District Courts be, and they hereby are, amended to read as follows:

[See the amendments made thereby under the respective rules and forms, post.]

2. That the foregoing amendments to the Rules of Civil Procedure shall take effect on July 1, 1970, and shall govern all proceedings in actions brought thereafter and also in all further proceedings in actions then pending, except to the extent that in the opinion of the court their application in a particular action then pending would not be feasible or would work injustice, in which event the former procedure applies.

3. That THE CHIEF JUSTICE be, and he hereby is, authorized to transmit to the Congress the foregoing amendments to the Rules of Civil Procedure in accordance with the provisions of Title 28, U.S.C. § 2072.

MR. JUSTICE BLACK and MR. JUSTICE DOUGLAS disapprove of the Amendments to the Federal Rules of Civil Procedure relating to Discovery, and dissent from the action of the Court in transmitting them to the Congress.

ORDER OF MARCH 1, 1971

1. That subdivision (a) of Rule 6, paragraph (4) of subdivision (a) of Rule 27, paragraph (6) of subdivision (b) of Rule 30, subdivision (c) of Rule 77, and paragraph (2) of subdivision (a) of Rule 81 of the Federal Rules of Civil Procedure be, and they hereby are, amended, effective July 1, 1971, to read as follows:

[See amendments made thereby under the respective rules, post.]

2. *[Certain Rules of Criminal Procedure for the United States District Courts amended].*

3. That subdivision (a) of Rule 26 and subdivision (a) of Rule 45 of the Federal Rules of Appellate Procedure be, and they hereby are, amended, effective July 1, 1971, to read as follows:

[See amendments made thereby under the respective Rules of Appellate Procedure, post.]

4. That THE CHIEF JUSTICE be, and he hereby is, authorized to transmit to the Congress the foregoing amendments to the Rules of Civil, Criminal and Appellate Procedure, in accordance with the provisions of Title 18 U.S.C. § 3771, and Title 28 U.S.C. §§ 2072 and 2075.

MR. JUSTICE BLACK and MR. JUSTICE DOUGLAS dissent.

ORDER OF NOVEMBER 20, 1972

1. That the rules hereinafter set forth, to be known as the Federal Rules of Evidence, be, and they hereby are, prescribed pursuant to Sections 3402, 3771, and 3772, Title 18, United States Code, and Sections 2072 and 2075, Title 28, United States Code, to govern procedure, in the proceedings and to the extent set forth therein, in the United States courts of appeals, the United States district courts, the District Court for the District of the Canal Zone and the district courts of Guam and the Virgin Islands, and before United States magistrates.

2. That the aforementioned Federal Rules of Evidence shall take effect on July 1, 1973, and shall be applicable to actions and proceedings brought thereafter and also to further procedure in actions and proceedings then pending,

except to the extent that in the opinion of the court their application in a particular action or proceeding then pending would not be feasible or would work injustice in which event the former procedure applies.

3. That subdivision (c) of Rule 30 and Rules 43 and 44.1 of the Federal Rules of Civil Procedure be, and they hereby are, amended, effective July 1, 1973, to read as hereinafter set forth:

*[See amendments made thereby under
the respective rules, post.]*

4. That subdivision (c) of Rule 32 of the Federal Rules of Civil Procedure be, and it hereby is, abrogated, effective July 1, 1973.

5. *[Certain Rules of Criminal Procedure for the United States District Courts amended].*

6. That THE CHIEF JUSTICE be, and he hereby is, authorized to transmit the foregoing new rules and amendments to and abrogation of existing rules to the Congress at the beginning of its next regular session, in accordance with the provisions of Title 18 U.S.C. § 3771 and Title 28 U.S.C. §§ 2072 and 2075.

ORDER OF DECEMBER 18, 1972

1. That Rule 43 of the Federal Rules of Civil Procedure, as amended by Order of this Court entered November 20, 1972, be, and it hereby is, further amended, effective July 1, 1973, to read as follows:

[See amendment made thereby under Rule 43 post.]

2. That THE CHIEF JUSTICE be, and he hereby is, authorized to transmit the foregoing amendment of Rule 43 of the Federal Rules of Civil Procedure to the Congress at the beginning of its next regular session in accordance with the provisions of Title 28, U.S.C. § 2072.

CONGRESSIONAL ACTION ON PROPOSED RULES OF EVIDENCE AND 1972 AMENDMENTS TO FEDERAL RULES OF CIVIL PROCEDURE AND FEDERAL RULES OF CRIMINAL PROCEDURE

Pub.L. 93–12, Mar. 30, 1973, 87 Stat. 9, provided: "That notwithstanding any other provisions of law, the Rules of Evidence for United States Courts and Magistrates, the Amendments to the Federal Rules of Civil Procedure, and the Amendments to the Federal Rules of Criminal Procedure, which are embraced by the orders entered by the Supreme Court of the United States on Monday, November 20, 1972, and Monday, December 18, 1972, shall have no force or effect except to the extent, and with such amendments, as they may be expressly approved by Act of Congress."

Pub.L. 93–595, § 3, Jan. 2, 1975, 88 Stat. 1959, provided that: "The Congress expressly approves the amendments to the Federal Rules of Civil Procedure, and the amendments to the Federal Rules of Criminal Procedure, which are embraced by the orders entered by the Supreme Court of the United States on November 20, 1972, and December 18, 1972, and such amendments shall take effect on the one hundred and eightieth day beginning after the date of the enactment of this Act [Jan. 2, 1975]."

ORDER OF APRIL 26, 1976

1. That the rules and forms governing proceedings in the United States District Courts under Section 2254 and Section 2255 of Title 28, United States Code, as approved by the Judicial Conference of the United States be, and they hereby are, prescribed pursuant to Section 2072 of Title 28, United States Code and Sections 3771 and 3772 of Title 18, United States Code.

2. That the aforementioned rules and forms shall take effect August 1, 1976, and shall be applicable to all proceedings then pending except to the extent that in the opinion of the court their application in a particular proceeding would not be feasible or would work injustice.

3. That THE CHIEF JUSTICE be, and he hereby is, authorized to transmit the aforementioned rules and forms governing Section 2254 and Section 2255 proceedings to the Congress in accordance with the provisions of Section 2072 of Title 28 and Sections 3771 and 3772 of Title 18, United States Code.

CONGRESSIONAL ACTION ON PROPOSED RULES AND FORMS GOVERNING PROCEEDINGS UNDER 28 U.S.C. §§ 2254 AND 2255

Pub.L. 94–349, § 2, July 8, 1976, 90 Stat. 822, provided: "That, notwithstanding the provisions of section 2072 of title 28 of the United States Code, the rules and forms governing section 2254 cases in the United States district courts and the rules and forms governing section 2255 proceedings in the United States district courts which are embraced by the order entered by the United States Supreme Court on April 26, 1976, and which were transmitted to the Congress on or about April 26, 1976, shall not take effect until thirty days after the adjournment sine die of the 94th Congress, or until and to the extent approved by Act of Congress, whichever is earlier."

Pub.L. 94–426, § 1, Sept. 28, 1976, 90 Stat. 1334, provided: "That the rules governing section 2254 cases in the United States district courts and the rules governing section 2255 proceedings for the United States district courts, as proposed by the United States Supreme Court, which were delayed by the Act entitled 'An Act to delay the effective date of certain proposed amendments to the Federal Rules of Criminal Procedure and certain other rules promulgated by the United States Supreme Court' (Public Law 94–349), are approved with the amendments set forth in section 2 of this Act and shall take effect as so amended, with respect to petitions under section 2254 and motions under section 2255 of title 28 of the United States Code filed on or after February 1, 1977."

ORDER OF APRIL 29, 1980

1. That the Federal Rules of Civil Procedure be, and they hereby are, amended by including therein amendments to Rules 4, 5, 26, 28, 30, 32, 33, 34, 37 and 45 as hereinafter set forth:

*[See amendments made thereby under
respective rules, post.]*

2. That the foregoing amendments to the Federal Rules of Civil Procedure shall take effect on August 1, 1980, and shall govern all civil proceedings thereafter commenced and, insofar as just and practicable, all proceedings then pending.

3. That subsection (e) of Rule 37 of the Federal Rules of Civil Procedure is hereby abrogated, effective August 1, 1980.

4. That THE CHIEF JUSTICE be, and he hereby is, authorized to transmit to the Congress the foregoing amendments to the Federal Rules of Civil Procedure in accordance with the provisions of Section 2072 of Title 28, United States Code.

MR. JUSTICE POWELL, with whom MR. JUSTICE STEWART and MR. JUSTICE REHNQUIST join, filed a dissenting statement.

I dissent from the Court's adoption of the amendments to Federal Rules of Civil Procedure 26, 33, 34, and 37—the cluster of Rules authorizing and regulating discovery generally, interrogatories, production of documents, and sanctions for failure to make discovery. These amendments are not inherently objectionable. Indeed, they represent the culmination of several years' work by the Judicial Conference's distinguished and conscientious Standing Committee on Rules of Practice and Procedure and Advisory Committee on Civil Rules.[1] But the changes embodied in the amendments fall short of those needed to accomplish reforms in civil litigation that are long overdue.

The American Bar Association proposed significant and substantial reforms.[2] Although the Standing Committee initially favored most of these proposals, it ultimately rejected them in large part. The ABA now accedes to the Standing Committee's amendments because they make some improvements, but the most recent report of the ABA Section of Litigation makes clear that the "serious and widespread abuse of discovery" will remain largely uncontrolled.[3] There are wide differences of opinion within the profession as to the need for reform. The bench and the bar are familiar with the existing Rules, and it often is said that the bar has a vested interest in maintaining the status quo. I imply no criticism of the bar or the Standing Committee when I suggest that the present recommendations reflect a compromise as well as the difficulty of framing satisfactory discovery Rules. But whatever considerations may have prompted the Committee's final decision, I doubt that many judges or lawyers familiar with the proposed amendments believe they will have an appreciable effect on the acute problems associated with discovery. The Court's adoption of these inadequate changes could postpone effective reform for another decade.

When the Federal Rules first appeared in 1938, the discovery provisions properly were viewed as a constructive improvement. But experience under the discovery Rules demonstrates that "not infrequently [they have been] exploited to the disadvantage of justice." *Herbert v. Lando,* 441 U.S. 153, 179 (1979) (POWELL, J., concurring). Properly limited and controlled discovery is necessary in most civil litigation. The present Rules, however, invite discovery of such scope and duration that district judges often cannot keep the practice within reasonable bounds.[4] Even in a relatively simple case, discovery through depositions, interrogatories, and demands for documents may take weeks. In complex litigation, discovery can continue for years. One must doubt whether empirical evidence would demonstrate that untrammeled discovery actually contributes to the just resolution of disputes. If there is disagreement about that, there is none whatever about the effect of discovery practices upon the average citizen's ability to afford legal remedies.

Delay and excessive expense now characterize a large percentage of all civil litigation. The problems arise in significant part, as every judge and litigator knows, from abuse of the discovery procedures available under the Rules.[5] Indeed, the National Conference on the Causes of Popular Dissatisfaction with the Administration of Justice, led by THE CHIEF JUSTICE,[6] identified "Abuse in the use of discovery [as] a major concern" within our legal system.[7] Lawyers devote an enormous number of "chargeable hours" to the practice of discovery. We may assume that discovery usually is conducted in good faith. Yet all too often discovery practices enable the party with greater financial resources to prevail by exhausting the resources of a weaker opponent. The mere threat of delay or unbearable expense denies justice to many actual or prospective litigants. Persons or businesses of comparatively limited means settle unjust claims and relinquish just claims simply because they cannot afford to litigate.[8] Litigation costs have become intolerable, and they cast a lengthening shadow over the basic fairness of our legal system.

I reiterate that I do not dissent because the modest amendments recommended by the Judicial Conference are undesirable. I simply believe that Congress' acceptance of these tinkering changes will delay for years the adoption of genuinely effective reforms. The process of change, as experience teaches, is tortuous and contentious. Favorable congressional action on these amendments will create complacency and encourage inertia. Meanwhile, the discovery Rules will continue to deny justice to those least able to bear the burdens of delay, escalating legal fees, and rising court costs.

The amendments to Rules 26, 33, 34, and 37 recommended by the Judicial Conference should be rejected, and the Conference should be directed to initiate a thorough re-examination of the discovery Rules that have become so central to the conduct of modern civil litigation.

[1] This Court's role in the rulemaking process is largely formalistic. Standing and advisory committees of the Judicial Conference make the initial studies, invite comments on their drafts, and prepare the Rules. Both the Judicial Conference and this Court necessarily rely upon the careful work of these committees. Congress should bear in mind that our approval of proposed Rules is more a certification that they are the products of proper procedures than a considered judgment on the merits of the proposals themselves. See generally 409 U.S. 1132, 1133 (1973) (DOUGLAS, J., dissenting from adoption of Federal Rules of Evidence); 383 U.S. 1032 (1966) (BLACK, J., dissenting from adoption of amendment to civil rules); 374 U.S. 865, 869–870 (1963) (statement of BLACK and DOUGLAS, JJ., upon adoption of amendments to Federal Rules of Civil Procedure).

[2] American Bar Association, Report of the Section of Litigation Special Committee for the Study of Discovery Abuse (App.Draft 1977).

[3] ABA Section of Litigation, Second Report of the Special Committee for the Study of Discovery Abuse, 5 (1980).

[4] MR. JUSTICE WHITE, writing for the Court, recently reminded the federal courts that "the discovery provisions . . . are subject to the injunction of Rule 1 that they be 'construed to secure the just, *speedy,* and *inexpensive* determination of every action.'" *Herbert v. Lando,* 441 U.S. 153, 177 (1979).

In his most recent Annual Report on the State of the Judiciary, THE CHIEF JUSTICE declared that "[t]he responsibility for control [of pretrial process] rests on both judges and lawyers. Where existing rules and statutes permit abuse, they must be changed. Where the power lies with judges to prevent or correct abuse and misuse of the system, judges must act." Address to American Bar Association Mid–Year Meeting, 6 (Feb. 3, 1980).

[5] Writing from his wide experience as a judge, practicing lawyer, and Attorney General, Griffin B. Bell advised the Standing Committee that "the scope of discovery is far too broad and that excessive discovery has significantly contributed to the delays, complexity and high cost of civil litigation in the federal courts." Letter to The Honorable Roszel C. Thomsen, Chairman of the Committee on Rules of Practice and Procedure of the Judicial Conference, 1 (June 27, 1978).

[6] THE CHIEF JUSTICE'S keynote address to this distinguished assembly, popularly known as the Pound Conference, recognized that discovery processes "are being misused and abused." See Burger, Agenda for 2000 A.D.—A Need for Systematic Anticipation, 70 F.R.D. 83, 95–96 (1976).

[7] See Erickson, The Pound Conference Recommendations: A Blueprint for the Justice System in the Twenty-first Century, 76 F.R.D. 277,

288 (1978); ABA, Report of Pound Conference Follow-up Task Force, 74 F.R.D. 159, 171–192 (1976).

8 "The principal function of procedural rules," as MR. JUSTICE BLACK observed in another context, "should be to serve as useful guides to help, not hinder, persons who have a legal right to bring their problems before the courts." 346 U.S. 946 (1954) (separate statement upon adoption of revised Supreme Court Rules).

ORDER OF APRIL 28, 1983

1. That the Federal Rules of Civil Procedure be, and they hereby are, amended by including therein new Rules 26(g), 53(f), 72 through 76 and new Official Forms 33 and 34, and amendments to Rules 6(b), 7(b), 11, 16, 26(a) and (b), 52(a), 53(a), (b) and (c) and 67, as hereinafter set forth:

[See additions and amendments made thereby under respective rules and forms, post.]

2. That the foregoing additions and amendments to the Federal Rules of Civil Procedure shall take effect on August 1, 1983 and shall govern all civil proceedings thereafter commenced and, insofar as just and practicable, in proceedings then pending.

3. That THE CHIEF JUSTICE be, and he hereby is, authorized to transmit to the Congress the foregoing additions to and changes in the Federal Rules of Civil Procedure in accordance with the provisions of Section 2072 of Title 28, United States Code.

ORDER OF APRIL 29, 1985

1. That the Federal Rules of Civil Procedure for the United States District Courts be, and they hereby are, amended by including therein a new Rule E(4)(f) to the Supplemental Rules for Certain Admiralty and Maritime Claims; amendments to Rules 6(a), 45(d)(2), 52(a), 71A(h) and 83; amendments to Supplemental Admiralty Rules B(1) and C(3); and amendments to Official Form 18–A, as hereinafter set forth:

[See additions and amendments made thereby under respective rules and forms, post.]

2. That the foregoing addition to and changes in the Federal Rules of Civil Procedure, the Supplemental Rules for Certain Admiralty and Maritime Claims, and the Official Form shall take effect on August 1, 1985 and shall govern all proceedings in civil actions thereafter commenced and, insofar as just and practicable, all proceedings in civil actions then pending.

3. That THE CHIEF JUSTICE be, and he hereby is, authorized to transmit to the Congress the foregoing addition to and changes in the rules of civil procedure in accordance with the provisions of Section 2072 of Title 28, United States Code.

ORDER OF MARCH 2, 1987

1. That the Federal Rules of Civil Procedure and the Supplemental Rules for Certain Admiralty and Maritime Claims be, and they hereby are, amended by including therein amendments to Civil Rules 4, 5, 6, 8, 9, 11, 12, 13, 14, 15, 16, 17, 18, 19, 20, 22, 23, 23.1, 24, 25, 26, 27, 28, 30, 31, 32, 34, 35, 36, 37 38, 41, 43, 44, 44.1, 45, 46, 49, 50, 51, 53, 54, 55, 56, 60, 62, 63, 65, 65.1, 68, 69, 71, 71A, 73, 75, 77, 78, 81, and to the Supplemental Rules for Certain Admiralty and Maritime Claims, Rules B, C, E, and F, as hereinafter set forth:

[See amendments made thereby under respective rules, post.]

2. That the foregoing amendments to the Federal Rules of Civil Procedure and the Supplemental Rules for Certain Admiralty and Maritime Claims shall take effect on August 1, 1987.

3. That THE CHIEF JUSTICE be, and he hereby is, authorized to transmit to the Congress the foregoing amendments in accordance with the provisions of Section 2072 of Title 28, United States Code.

ORDER OF APRIL 25, 1988

1. That the Federal Rules of Civil Procedure be, and they hereby are, amended by including therein amendments to Civil Rules 17 and 71, as hereinafter set forth:

[See amendments made thereby under respective rules, post.]

2. That the foregoing amendments to the Federal Rules of Civil Procedure shall take effect on August 1, 1988.

3. That THE CHIEF JUSTICE be, and he hereby is, authorized to transmit to the Congress the foregoing amendments in accordance with the provisions of Section 2072 of Title 28, United States Code.

ORDER OF APRIL 30, 1991

1. That the Federal Rules of Civil Procedure for the United States District Courts be, and they hereby are, amended by including therein new chapter headings VIII and IX, amendments to Rules C and E of the Supplemental Rules for Certain Admiralty and Maritime Claims, new Forms 1A and 1B to the Appendix of Forms, the abrogation of Form 18A, and amendments to Civil Rules 5, 15, 24, 34, 35, 41, 44, 45, 47, 48, 50, 52, 53, 63, 72, and 77, as hereinafter set forth.

[See additions and amendments made thereby under respective rules and forms, post.]

2. That the foregoing additions to and changes in the Federal Rules of Civil Procedure, the Supplemental Rules for Certain Admiralty and Maritime Claims, and the Civil Forms shall take effect on December 1, 1991, and shall govern all proceedings in civil actions thereafter commenced and, insofar as just and practicable, all proceedings in civil actions then pending.

3. That THE CHIEF JUSTICE be, and hereby is, authorized to transmit to the Congress the foregoing addition to and changes in the Rules of Civil Procedure in accordance with the provisions of Section 2072 of Title 28, United States Code.

[Congress may postpone the proposed rule and form additions and amendments effective December 1, 1991, may decline to approve such additions and amendments, or may make changes to the additions and amendments.]

ORDER OF APRIL 22, 1993

1. That the Federal Rules of Civil Procedure for the United States District Courts be, and they hereby are, amended by including therein amendments to Civil Rules 1, 4, 5, 11, 12, 15, 16, 26, 28, 29, 30, 31, 32, 33, 34, 36, 37, 38, 50, 52, 53, 54, 58, 71A, 72, 73, 74, 75, and 76, and new Rule 4.1, and abrogation of Form 18–A, and amendments to Forms 2, 33, 34, and 34A, and new Forms 1A, 1B, and 35.

[See amendments made thereby under respective rules and forms, post.]

2. That the foregoing amendments to the Federal Rules of Civil Procedure shall take effect on December 1, 1993, and shall govern all proceedings in civil cases thereafter commenced and, insofar as just and practicable, all proceedings in civil cases then pending.

3. That THE CHIEF JUSTICE be, and he hereby is, authorized to transmit to the Congress the foregoing amendments to the Federal Rules of Civil Procedure in accordance with the provisions of Section 2072 of Title 23, United States Code.

ORDER OF APRIL 27, 1995

1. That the Federal Rules of Civil Procedure for the United States District Courts be, and they hereby are, amended by including therein amendments to Civil Rules 50, 52, 59, and 83.

[See amendments made thereby under respective rules, post.]

2. That the foregoing amendments to the Federal Rules of Civil Procedure shall take effect on December 1, 1995, and shall govern all proceedings in civil cases thereafter commenced and, insofar as just and practicable, all proceedings in civil cases then pending.

3. That THE CHIEF JUSTICE be, and hereby is, authorized to transmit to the Congress the foregoing amendments to the Federal Rules of Civil Procedure in accordance with the provisions of Section 2072 of Title 28, United States Code.

ORDER OF APRIL 23, 1996

1. That the Federal Rules of Civil Procedure for the United States District Courts be, and they hereby are, amended by including therein amendments to Civil Rules 5 and 43.

[See amendments made thereby under respective rules, post]

2. That the foregoing amendments to the Federal Rules of Civil Procedure shall take effect on December 1, 1996, and shall govern all proceedings in civil cases thereafter commenced and, insofar as just and practicable, all proceedings in civil cases then pending.

3. That THE CHIEF JUSTICE be, and hereby is, authorized to transmit to the Congress the foregoing amendments to the Federal Rules of Civil Procedure in accordance with the provisions of Section 2072 of Title 28, United States Code.

ORDER OF APRIL 11, 1997

1. That the Federal Rules of Civil Procedure for the United States District Courts be, and they hereby are, amended by including therein amendments to Civil Rules 9 and 73, and abrogation of Rules 74, 75, and 76, and amendments to Forms 33 and 34.

[See amendments made thereby under respective rules, post]

2. That the foregoing amendments to the Federal Rules of Civil Procedure shall take effect on December 1, 1997, and shall govern all proceedings in civil cases thereafter com-

menced and, insofar as just and practicable, all proceedings in civil cases then pending.

3. That THE CHIEF JUSTICE be, and hereby is, authorized to transmit to the Congress the foregoing amendments to the Federal Rules of Civil Procedure in accordance with the provisions of Section 2072 of Title 28, United States Code.

ORDER OF APRIL 24, 1998

1. That the Federal Rules of Civil Procedure for the United States District Courts be, and they hereby are, amended by including therein a new Civil Rule 23(f).

[See amendments made thereby under respective rules, post]

2. That the foregoing amendments to the Federal Rules of Civil Procedure shall take effect on December 1, 1998, and shall govern all proceedings in civil cases thereafter commenced and, insofar as just and practicable, all proceedings in civil cases then pending.

3. That THE CHIEF JUSTICE be, and hereby is, authorized to transmit to the Congress the foregoing amendments to the Federal Rules of Civil Procedure in accordance with the provisions of Section 2072 of Title 28, United States Code.

ORDER OF APRIL 26, 1999

1. That the Federal Rules of Civil Procedure for the United States District Courts be, and they hereby are, amended by including therein amendments to Civil Rule 6(b) and Form 2.

[See amendments made thereby under respective rules, post.]

2. That the foregoing amendments to the Federal Rules of Civil Procedure shall take effect on December 1, 1999, and shall govern all proceedings in civil cases thereafter commenced and, insofar as just and practicable, all proceedings in civil cases then pending.

3. That THE CHIEF JUSTICE be, and hereby is, authorized to transmit to the Congress the foregoing amendments to the Federal Rules of Civil Procedure in accordance with the provisions of Section 2072 of Title 28, United States Code.

ORDER OF APRIL 17, 2000

1. That the Federal Rules of Civil Procedure for the United States District Courts be, and they hereby are, amended by including therein amendments to Civil Rules 4, 5, 12, 14, 26, 30, and 37 and to Rules B, C, and E of the Supplemental Rules for Certain Admiralty and Maritime Claims.

[See amendments made thereby under respective rules, post.]

2. That the foregoing amendments to the Federal Rules of Civil Procedure and the Supplemental Rules for Certain Admiralty and Maritime Claims shall take effect on December 1, 2000, and shall govern all proceedings in civil cases thereafter commenced and, insofar as just and practicable, all proceedings in civil cases then pending.

3. That THE CHIEF JUSTICE be, and hereby is, authorized to transmit to the Congress the foregoing amendments to the Federal Rules of Civil Procedure in accordance

with the provisions of Section 2072 of Title 28, United States Code.

ORDER OF APRIL 23, 2001

1. That the Federal Rules of Civil Procedure be, and they hereby are, amended by including therein amendments to Civil Rules 5, 6, 65, 77, 81, and 82.

[See amendments made thereby under respective rules, post.]

2. That the foregoing amendments to the Federal Rules of Civil Procedure shall take effect on December 1, 2001, and shall govern in all proceedings in civil cases thereafter commenced and, insofar as just and practicable, all proceedings then pending.

3. That THE CHIEF JUSTICE be, and hereby is, authorized to transmit to the Congress the foregoing amendments to the Federal Rules of Civil Procedure in accordance with the provisions of Section 2072 of Title 28, United States Code.

4. That the Rules for Practice and Procedure under section 25 of An Act To Amend and Consolidate the Acts Respecting Copyright, approved March 4, 1909, promulgated by this Court on June 1, 1909, effective July 1, 1909, as revised, be, and they hereby are, abrogated, effective December 1, 2001.

ORDER OF APRIL 29, 2002

1. That the Federal Rules of Civil Procedure be, and they hereby are, amended by including therein amendments to Civil Rules 54, 58, and 81, and a new Rule 7.1, and Rule C of Supplemental Rules for Certain Admiralty and Maritime Claims.

[See amendments made thereby under respective rules, post.]

2. That the foregoing amendments to the Federal Rules of Civil Procedure shall take effect on December 1, 2002, and shall govern in all proceedings in civil cases thereafter commenced and, insofar as just and practicable, all proceedings then pending.

3. That the CHIEF JUSTICE be, and hereby is, authorized to transmit to the Congress the foregoing amendments to the Federal Rules of Civil Procedure in accordance with the provisions of Section 2072 of Title 28, United States Code.

ORDER OF MARCH 27, 2003

1. That the Federal Rules of Civil Procedure be, and they hereby are, amended by including therein amendments to Civil Rules 23, 51, 53, 54, and 71A.

[See amendments made thereby under respective rules and forms, post.]

2. That Forms 19, 31, and 32 in the Appendix to the Federal Rules of Civil Procedure be, and they hereby are, amended by replacing all references to "19___" with references to "20___."

3. That the foregoing amendments to the Federal Rules of Civil Procedure shall take effect on December 1, 2003, and shall govern in all proceedings in civil cases thereafter commenced and, insofar as just and practicable, all proceedings then pending.

4. That the CHIEF JUSTICE be, and hereby is, authorized to transmit to the Congress the foregoing amendments to

the Federal Rules of Civil Procedure in accordance with the provisions of Section 2072 of Title 28, United States Code.

ORDER OF APRIL 25, 2005

1. That the Federal Rules of Civil Procedure be, and they hereby are, amended by including therein the amendments to Civil Rules 6, 27, and 45, and to Rules B and C of the Supplemental Rules for Certain Admiralty and Maritime Claims.

[See amendments made thereby under respective rules and forms, post.]

2. That the foregoing amendments to the Federal Rules of Civil Procedure and the Supplemental Rules for Certain Admiralty and Maritime Claims shall take effect on December 1, 2005, and shall govern in all proceedings thereafter commenced and, insofar as just and practicable, all proceedings then pending.

3. That the CHIEF JUSTICE be, and hereby is, authorized to transmit to the Congress the foregoing amendments to the Federal Rules of Civil Procedure in accordance with the provisions of Section 2072 of Title 28, United States Code.

ORDER OF APRIL 12, 2006

1. That the Federal Rules of Civil Procedure be, and they hereby are, amended by including therein the amendments to Civil Rules 5, 9, 14, 16, 24, 26, 33, 34, 37, 45, 50, and 65.1; Form 35; and new Rule 5.1.

2. That the Supplemental Rules for Admiralty or Maritime Claims and Asset Forfeiture Actions be, and they hereby are, amended by including therein the amendments to Rules A, C, and E, and new Rule G.

[See amendments made thereby under respective rules and forms, post.]

3. That the foregoing amendments to the Federal Rules of Civil Procedure and the Supplemental Rules for Admiralty or Maritime Claims and Asset Forfeiture Actions shall take effect on December 1, 2006, and shall govern in all proceedings thereafter commenced and, insofar as just and practicable, all proceedings then pending.

4. That THE CHIEF JUSTICE be, and hereby is, authorized to transmit to the Congress the foregoing amendments to the Federal Rules of Civil Procedure in accordance with the provisions of Section 2072 of Title 28, United States Code.

ORDER OF APRIL 30, 2007

1. That the Federal Rules of Civil Procedure be, and they hereby are, amended by including therein the amendments to Civil Rules 1 through 86 and new Rule 5.2.

2. That Forms 1 through 35 in the Appendix to the Federal Rules of Civil Procedure be, and they hereby are, amended to become restyled Forms 1 through 82.

[See amendments made thereby under respective rules and forms, post.]

3. That the foregoing amendments to the Federal Rules of Civil Procedure shall take effect on December 1, 2007, and shall govern in all proceedings thereafter commenced and, insofar as just and practicable, all proceedings then pending.

4. That THE CHIEF JUSTICE be, and hereby is, authorized to transmit to the Congress the foregoing amend-

ments to the Federal Rules of Civil Procedure in accordance with the provisions of Section 2072 of Title 28, United States Code.

ORDER OF APRIL 23, 2008

1. That the Supplemental Rules for Admiralty or Maritime Claims and Asset Forfeiture Actions be, and they hereby are, amended by including therein the amendment to Rule C.

[See amendment made thereby under Rule C post.]

2. That the foregoing amendment to the Supplemental Rules for Admiralty or Maritime Claims and Asset Forfeiture Actions shall take effect on December 1, 2008, and shall govern in all proceedings thereafter commenced and, insofar as just and practicable, all proceedings then pending.

3. That THE CHIEF JUSTICE be, and hereby is, authorized to transmit to the Congress the foregoing amendment to the Supplemental Rules for Admiralty or Maritime Claims and Asset Forfeiture Actions in accordance with the provisions of Section 2072 of Title 28, United States Code.

ORDER OF MARCH 26, 2009

1. That the Federal Rules of Civil Procedure be, and they hereby are, amended by including therein amendments to Civil Rules 6, 12, 13, 14, 15, 23, 27, 32, 38, 48, 50, 52, 53, 54, 55, 56, 59, 62, 65, 68, 71.1, 72, and 81, and new Rule 62.1, and Supplemental Rules B, C, and G, and Illustrative Civil Forms 3, 4, and 60.

[See amendments made thereby under respective rules and forms, post.]

2. That the foregoing amendments to the Federal Rules of Civil Procedure shall take effect on December 1, 2009, and shall govern in all proceedings thereafter commenced and, insofar as just and practicable, all proceedings then pending.

3. That THE CHIEF JUSTICE be, and hereby is, authorized to transmit to the Congress the foregoing amendments to the Federal Rules of Civil Procedure in accordance with the provisions of Section 2072 of Title 28, United States Code.

ORDER OF APRIL 28, 2010

1. That the Federal Rules of Civil Procedure be, and they hereby are, amended by including therein amendments to Civil Rules 8, 26, and 56, and Illustrative Civil Form 52.

[See amendments made thereby under respective rules and forms, post.]

2. That the foregoing amendments to the Federal Rules of Civil Procedure shall take effect on December 1, 2010, and shall govern in all proceedings thereafter commenced and, insofar as just and practicable, all proceedings then pending.

3. That THE CHIEF JUSTICE be, and hereby is, authorized to transmit to the Congress the foregoing amendments to the Federal Rules of Civil Procedure in accordance with the provisions of Section 2072 of Title 28, United States Code.

ORDER OF APRIL 16, 2013

1. That the Federal Rules of Civil Procedure be, and they hereby are, amended by including therein amendments to Civil Rules 37 and 45.

[See amendments made thereby under respective rules, post.]

2. That the foregoing amendments to the Federal Rules of Civil Procedure shall take effect on December 1, 2013, and shall govern in all proceedings in civil cases thereafter commenced and, insofar as just and practicable, all proceedings then pending.

3. That THE CHIEF JUSTICE be, and hereby is, authorized to transmit to the Congress the foregoing amendments to the Federal Rules of Civil Procedure in accordance with the provisions of Section 2072 of Title 28, United States Code.

ORDER OF APRIL 25, 2014

1. That the Federal Rules of Civil Procedure be, and they hereby are, amended by including therein an amendment to Civil Rule 77.

[See amendments made thereby under Rule 77, post.]

2. That the foregoing amendment to the Federal Rules of Civil Procedure shall take effect on December 1, 2014, and shall govern in all proceedings in civil cases thereafter commenced and, insofar as just and practicable, all proceedings then pending.

3. That THE CHIEF JUSTICE be, and hereby is, authorized to transmit to the Congress the foregoing amendment to the Federal Rules of Civil Procedure in accordance with the provisions of Section 2072 of Title 28, United States Code.

ORDER OF APRIL 29, 2015

1. That the Federal Rules of Civil Procedure be, and they hereby are, amended by including therein amendments to Civil Rules 1, 4, 16, 26, 30, 31, 33, 34, 37, 55, and 84, and the Appendix of Forms.

[See amendments made thereby under respective rules and forms, post.]

2. That the foregoing amendments to the Federal Rules of Civil Procedure shall take effect on December 1, 2015, and shall govern in all proceedings in civil cases thereafter commenced and, insofar as just and practicable, all proceedings then pending.

3. That THE CHIEF JUSTICE be, and hereby is, authorized to transmit to the Congress the foregoing amendments to the Federal Rules of Civil Procedure in accordance with the provisions of Section 2072 of Title 28, United States Code.

ORDER OF APRIL 28, 2016

1. That the Federal Rules of Civil Procedure be, and they hereby are, amended by including therein amendments to Civil Rules 4, 6, and 82.

[See amendments made thereby under respective rules, post.]

2. That the foregoing amendments to the Federal Rules of Civil Procedure shall take effect on December 1, 2016, and

---

shall govern in all proceedings in civil cases thereafter commenced and, insofar as just and practicable, all proceedings then pending.

3. That THE CHIEF JUSTICE be, and hereby is, authorized to transmit to the Congress the foregoing amendments to the Federal Rules of Civil Procedure in accordance with the provisions of Section 2072 of Title 28, United States Code.

ORDER OF APRIL 27, 2017

1. That the Federal Rules of Civil Procedure be, and they hereby are, amended by including therein amendments to Civil Rule 4.

[See amendments made thereby under respective rules, post.]

2. That the foregoing amendments to the Federal Rules of Civil Procedure shall take effect on December 1, 2017, and shall govern in all proceedings in civil cases thereafter commenced and, insofar as just and practicable, all proceedings then pending.

3. That THE CHIEF JUSTICE be, and hereby is, authorized to transmit to the Congress the foregoing amendment to the Federal Rules of Civil Procedure in accordance with the provisions of Section 2074 of Title 28, United States Code.

ORDER OF APRIL 26, 2018

1. That the Federal Rules of Civil Procedure be, and they hereby are, amended by including therein amendments to Civil Rules 5, 23, 62, and 65.1.

[See amendments made thereby under respective rules, post.]

2. That the foregoing amendments to the Federal Rules of Civil Procedure shall take effect on December 1, 2018, and shall govern in all proceedings in civil cases thereafter commenced and, insofar as just and practicable, all proceedings then pending.

3. That THE CHIEF JUSTICE be, and hereby is, authorized to transmit to the Congress the foregoing amendments to the Federal Rules of Civil Procedure in accordance with the provisions of Section 2074 of Title 28, United States Code.

HISTORICAL NOTES

The original Rules of Civil Procedure for the District Courts were adopted by order of the Supreme Court on Dec. 20, 1937, transmitted to Congress by the Attorney General on Jan. 3, 1938, and became effective on Sept. 16, 1938.

The Rules have been amended Dec. 28, 1939, eff. Apr. 3, 1941; Dec. 27, 1946, eff. Mar. 19, 1948; Dec. 29, 1948, eff. Oct. 20, 1949; Apr. 30, 1951, eff. Aug. 1, 1951; Apr. 17, 1961, eff. July 19, 1961; Jan. 21, 1963, eff. July 1, 1963; Feb. 28, 1966, eff. July 1, 1966; Dec. 4, 1967, eff. July 1, 1968; Mar. 30, 1970, eff. July 1, 1970; Mar. 1, 1971, eff. July 1, 1971; Nov. 20, 1972, and Dec. 18, 1972, eff. July 1, 1975; Apr. 29, 1980, eff. Aug. 1, 1980; Oct. 21, 1980, Pub.L. 96–481, Title II, § 205(a), (b), 94 Stat. 2330; Jan. 12, 1983, Pub.L. 97–462, §§ 2–4, 96 Stat. 2527–2530, eff. Feb. 26, 1983; Apr. 28, 1983, eff. Aug. 1, 1983; Apr. 29, 1985, eff. Aug. 1, 1985; Mar. 2, 1987, eff. Aug. 1, 1987; Apr. 25, 1988, eff. Aug. 1, 1988; Nov. 18, 1988, Pub.L. 100–690, Title VII, §§ 7047(b), 7049, 7050, 102 Stat. 4401; Apr. 30, 1991, eff. Dec. 1, 1991; Dec. 9, 1991, Pub.L. 102–198, § 11, 105 Stat. 1626; Apr. 22, 1993, eff. Dec. 1, 1993; Apr. 27, 1995, eff. Dec. 1, 1995; Apr. 23, 1996, eff. Dec. 1, 1996; Apr. 11, 1997, eff. Dec. 1, 1997 Apr. 24, 1998, eff. Dec. 1, 1998; Apr. 26, 1999, eff. Dec. 1, 1999; Apr. 17, 2000, eff. Dec. 1, 2000; Apr. 23, 2001, eff. Dec. 1, 2001; Apr. 29, 2002, eff. Dec. 1, 2002; Mar. 27, 2003, eff. Dec. 1, 2003; Apr. 25, 2005, eff. Dec. 1, 2005; Apr. 12, 2006, eff. Dec. 1, 2006; Apr. 30, 2007, eff. Dec. 1, 2007; Apr. 23, 2008, eff. Dec. 1, 2008; Mar. 26, 2009, eff. Dec. 1, 2009; Apr. 28, 2010, eff. Dec. 1, 2010; Apr. 16, 2013, eff. Dec. 1, 2013; Apr. 25, 2014, eff. Dec. 1, 2014; Apr. 29, 2015, eff. Dec. 1, 2015; Apr. 28, 2016, eff. Dec. 1, 2016; Apr. 27, 2017, eff. Dec. 1, 2017; Apr. 26, 2018, eff. Dec. 1, 2018.

CROSS REFERENCES

Procedure in original actions in Supreme Court of United States, see U.S.Sup.Ct. Rule 17, 28 USCA.

TITLE I. SCOPE OF RULES; FORM OF ACTION

Rule 1. Scope and Purpose

These rules govern the procedure in all civil actions and proceedings in the United States district courts, except as stated in Rule 81. They should be construed, administered, and employed by the court and the parties to secure the just, speedy, and inexpensive determination of every action and proceeding.
(Amended December 29, 1948, effective October 20, 1949; February 28, 1966, effective July 1, 1966; April 22, 1993, effective December 1, 1993; April 30, 2007, effective December 1, 2007; April 29, 2015, effective December 1, 2015.)

ADVISORY COMMITTEE NOTES
1937 Adoption

1. Rule 81 states certain limitations in the application of these rules to enumerated special proceedings.

2. The expression "district courts of the United States" appearing in the statute authorizing the Supreme Court of the United States to promulgate rules of civil procedure does not include the district courts held in the territories and insular possessions. See *Mookini et al. v. United States*, 1938, 58 S.Ct. 543, 303 U.S. 201, 82 L.Ed. 748.

3. These rules are drawn under the authority of the Act of June 19, 1934, U.S.C., Title 28, § 723b [see 2072] (Rules in actions at law; Supreme Court authorized to make), and § 723c [see 2072] (Union of equity and action at law rules; power of Supreme Court) and also other grants of rule making power to the Court. See Clark and Moore, *A New Federal Civil Procedure—I. The Background*, 44 Yale L.J. 387, 391 (1935). Under § 723b after the rules have taken effect all laws in conflict therewith are of no further force or effect. In accordance with § 723c the Court has united the general rules prescribed for cases in equity with those in

actions at law so as to secure one form of civil action and procedure for both. See Rule 2 (One Form of Action). For the former practice in equity and at law see U.S.C.A., Title 28, §§ 723 and 730 [see 2071 et seq.] (conferring power on the Supreme Court to make rules of practice in equity) and the [former] Equity Rules promulgated thereunder; U.S.C., Title 28, [former] § 724 (Conformity act); [former] Equity Rule 22 (Action at Law Erroneously Begun as Suit in Equity—Transfer); [former] Equity Rule 23 (Matters Ordinarily Determinable at Law When Arising in Suit in Equity to be Disposed of Therein); U.S.C., Title 28, [former] §§ 397 (Amendments to pleadings when case brought to wrong side of court), and 398 (Equitable defenses and equitable relief in actions at law).

4. With the second sentence compare U.S.C., Title 28, [former] §§ 777 (Defects of form; amendments), [former] 767 (Amendment of process); [former] Equity Rule 19 (Amendments Generally).

1948 Amendment

The amendment effective Oct. 20, 1949, substituted the words "United States district courts" for the words "district courts of the United States."

1966 Amendment

This is the fundamental change necessary to effect unification of the civil and admiralty procedure. Just as the 1938 rules abolished the distinction between actions at law and suits in equity, this change would abolish the distinction between civil actions and suits in admiralty. See also Rule 81.

1993 Amendment

The purpose of this revision, adding the words "and administered" to the second sentence, is to recognize the affirmative duty of the court to exercise the authority conferred by these rules to ensure that civil litigation is resolved not only fairly, but also without undue cost or delay. As officers of the court, attorneys share this responsibility with the judge to whom the case is assigned.

2007 Amendment

The language of Rule 1 has been amended as part of the general restyling of the Civil Rules to make them more easily understood and to make style and terminology consistent throughout the rules. These changes are intended to be stylistic only.

The merger of law, equity, and admiralty practice is complete. There is no need to carry forward the phrases that initially accomplished the merger.

The former reference to "suits of a civil nature" is changed to the more modern "civil actions and proceedings." This change does not affect such questions as whether the Civil Rules apply to summary proceedings created by statute. See SEC v. McCarthy, 322 F.3d 650 (9th Cir. 2003); see also New Hampshire Fire Ins. Co. v. Scanlon, 362 U.S. 404 (1960).

The Style Project

The Civil Rules are the third set of the rules to be restyled. The restyled Rules of Appellate Procedure took effect in 1998. The restyled Rules of Criminal Procedure took effect in 2002. The restyled Rules of Civil Procedure apply the same general drafting guidelines and principles used in restyling the Appellate and Criminal Rules.

1. General Guidelines

Guidance in drafting, usage, and style was provided by Bryan Garner, *Guidelines for Drafting and Editing Court Rules*, Administrative Office of the United States Courts (1996) and Bryan Garner, *Dictionary of Modern Legal Usage* (2d ed. 1995). *See also* Joseph Kimble, *Guiding Principles for Restyling the Civil Rules*, in *Preliminary Draft of Proposed Style Revision of the Federal Rules of Civil Procedure*, at x (Feb. 2005) (available at http://www.uscourts.gov/rules/Prelim_draft_proposed_pt1.pdf).

2. Formatting Changes

Many of the changes in the restyled Civil Rules result from using format to achieve clearer presentation. The rules are broken down into constituent parts, using progressively indented subparagraphs with headings and substituting vertical for horizontal lists. "Hanging indents" are used throughout. These formatting changes make the structure of the rules graphic and make the restyled rules easier to read and understand even when the words are not changed. Rule 14(a) illustrates the benefits of formatting changes.

3. Changes to Reduce Inconsistent, Ambiguous, Redundant, Repetitive, or Archaic Words

The restyled rules reduce the use of inconsistent terms that say the same thing in different ways. Because different words are presumed to have different meanings, such inconsistencies can result in confusion. The restyled rules reduce inconsistencies by using the same words to express the same meaning. For example, consistent expression is achieved without affecting meaning by the changes from "infant" in many rules to "minor" in all rules; from "upon motion or on its own initiative" in Rule 4(m) and variations in many other rules to "on motion or on its own"; and from "deemed" to "considered" in Rules 5(c), 12(e), and elsewhere. Some variations of expression have been carried forward when the context made that appropriate. As an example, "stipulate," "agree," and "consent" appear throughout the rules, and "written" qualifies these words in some places but not others. The number of variations has been reduced, but at times the former words were carried forward. None of the changes, when made, alters the rule's meaning.

The restyled rules minimize the use of inherently ambiguous words. For example, the word "shall" can mean "must," "may," or something else, depending on context. The potential for confusion is exacerbated by the fact that "shall" is no longer generally used in spoken or clearly written English. The restyled rules replace "shall" with "must," "may," or "should," depending on which one the context and established interpretation make correct in each rule.

The restyled rules minimize the use of redundant "intensifiers." These are expressions that attempt to add emphasis, but instead state the obvious and create negative implications for other rules. "The court in its discretion may" becomes "the court may"; "unless the order expressly directs otherwise" becomes "unless the court orders otherwise." The absence of intensifiers in the restyled rules does not change their substantive meaning. For example, the absence of the word "reasonable" to describe the written notice of foreign law required in Rule 44.1 does not mean that "unreasonable" notice is permitted.

The restyled rules also remove words and concepts that are outdated or redundant. The reference to "at law or in equity" in Rule 1 has become redundant with the merger of law and equity. Outdated words and concepts include the reference to "demurrers, pleas, and exceptions" in Rule 7(c); the reference to "mesne" process in Rule 77(c); and the reference in Rule 81(f) to a now-abolished official position.

The restyled rules remove a number of redundant cross-references. For example, Rule 8(b) states that a general denial is subject to the obligations of Rule 11, but all pleadings are subject to Rule 11. Removing such cross-references does not defeat application of the formerly cross-referenced rule.

4. Rule Numbers

The restyled rules keep the same rule numbers to minimize the effect on research. Subdivisions have been rearranged within some rules to achieve greater clarity and simplicity. The only change that moves one part of a rule to another is the transfer of former Rule 25(d)(2) to Rule 17(d). The restyled rules include a comparison chart to make it easy to identify transfers of provisions between subdivisions and re-designations of some subdivisions.

5. Other Changes

The style changes to the rules are intended to make no changes in substantive meaning. A very small number of minor technical amendments that arguably do change meaning were approved separately from the restyled rules, but become effective at the same time. An example is adding "e-mail address" to the information that must be included in pleadings. These minor changes occur in Rules 4(k), 9(h), 11(a), 14(b), 16(c)(1), 26(g)(1), 30(b), 31, 40, 71.1, and 78.

2015 Amendment

Rule 1 is amended to emphasize that just as the court should construe and administer these rules to secure the just, speedy, and inexpensive determination of every action, so the parties share the responsibility to employ the rules in the same way. Most lawyers and parties cooperate to achieve these ends. But discussions of ways to improve the administration of civil justice regularly include pleas to discourage over-use, misuse, and abuse of procedural tools that increase cost and result in delay. Effective advocacy is consistent with — and indeed depends upon — cooperative and proportional use of procedure.

This amendment does not create a new or independent source of sanctions. Neither does it abridge the scope of any other of these rules.

CROSS REFERENCES

Jurisdiction and venue as unaffected by these rules, see Fed.Rules Civ.Proc. Rule 82, 28 USCA.

Puerto Rico, governed by the rules as District Courts, see 28 USCA § 119.

Rule 2.   One Form of Action

There is one form of action—the civil action.
(Amended April 30, 2007, effective December 1, 2007.)

ADVISORY COMMITTEE NOTES
1937 Adoption

1. This rule modifies U.S.C., Title 28, [former] § 384 (Suits in equity, when not sustainable). U.S.C., Title 28, §§ 723 and 730 [sec. 2071, et seq.] (conferring power on the Supreme Court to make rules of practice in equity), are unaffected in so far as they relate to the rule making power in admiralty. These sections, together with § 723b [sec. 2072] (Rules in actions at law; Supreme Court authorized to make) are continued in so far as they are not inconsistent with § 2072, formerly § 723c (Union of equity and action at law rules; power of Supreme Court). See Note 3 to Rule 1. U.S.C., Title 28, [former] §§ 724 (Conformity act), 397 (Amendments to pleadings when case brought to wrong side of court) and 398 (Equitable defenses and equitable relief in actions at law) are superseded.

2. Reference to actions at law or suits in equity in all statutes should now be treated as referring to the civil action prescribed in these rules.

3. This rule follows in substance the usual introductory statements to code practices which provide for a single action and mode of procedure, with abolition of forms of action and procedural distinctions. Representative statutes are N.Y. Code 1848 (Laws 1848, ch. 379) § 62; N.Y.C.P.A. (1937) § 8; Calif.Code Civ.Proc. (Deering, 1937) § 307; 2 Minn.Stat.Ann. 1945 § 540.01; 2 Wash.Rev.Stat.Ann. (Remington, 1932) §§ 153, 255.

2007 Amendment

The language of Rule 2 has been amended as part of the general restyling of the Civil Rules to make them more easily understood and to make style and terminology consistent throughout the rules. These changes are intended to be stylistic only.

CROSS REFERENCES

Injunctions, see Fed.Rules Civ.Proc. Rule 65, 28 USCA.

Joinder of claims and remedies, see Fed.Rules Civ.Proc. Rule 18, 28 USCA.

Receivers, see Fed.Rules Civ.Proc. Rule 66, 28 USCA.

TITLE II.   COMMENCING AN ACTION; SERVICE OF PROCESS, PLEADINGS, MOTIONS, AND ORDERS

Rule 3.   Commencing an Action

A civil action is commenced by filing a complaint with the court.
(Amended April 30, 2007, effective December 1, 2007.)

ADVISORY COMMITTEE NOTES
1937 Adoption

1. Rule 5(e) defines what constitutes filing with the court.

2. This rule governs the commencement of all actions, including those brought by or against the United States or an officer or agency thereof, regardless of whether service is to be made personally pursuant to Rule 4(d), or otherwise pursuant to Rule 4(e).

3. With this rule compare [former] Equity Rule 12 (Issue of Subpoena—Time for Answer) and the following statutes (and other similar statutes) which provide a similar method for commencing an action:

U.S.C., Title 28:

§ 45 [former] (District courts; practice and procedure in certain cases under interstate commerce laws).

§ 762 [see 1402] (Petition in suit against United States).

§ 766 [see 2409] (Partition suits where United States is tenant in common or joint tenant).

4. This rule provides that the first step in an action is the filing of the complaint. Under Rule 4(a) this is to be followed forthwith by issuance of a summons and its delivery to an officer for service. Other rules providing for dismissal for failure to prosecute suggest a method available to attack unreasonable delay in prosecuting an action after it has been commenced. When a Federal or State statute of limitations is pleaded as a defense, a question may arise under this rule whether the mere filing of the complaint stops the running of the statute, or whether any further step is required, such as, service of the summons and complaint or their delivery to the marshal for service. The answer to this question may depend on whether it is competent for the Supreme Court, exercising the power to make rules of procedure without affecting substantive rights, to vary the operation of statutes of limitations. The requirement of rule 4(a) that the clerk shall forthwith issue the summons and deliver it to the marshal for service will reduce the chances of such a question arising.

2007 Amendment

The caption of Rule 3 has been amended as part of the general restyling of the Civil Rules to make them more easily understood and to make style and terminology consistent throughout the rules. These changes are intended to be stylistic only.

CROSS REFERENCES

Filing with the court defined, see Fed.Rules Civ.Proc. Rule 5, 28 USCA.

Rule 4.   Summons

(a) Contents; Amendments.

(1) *Contents.* A summons must:

(A) name the court and the parties;

(B) be directed to the defendant;

(C) state the name and address of the plaintiff's attorney or—if unrepresented—of the plaintiff;

(D) state the time within which the defendant must appear and defend;

(E) notify the defendant that a failure to appear and defend will result in a default judgment against the defendant for the relief demanded in the complaint;

(F) be signed by the clerk; and

(G) bear the court's seal.

(2) *Amendments.* The court may permit a summons to be amended.

(b) Issuance. On or after filing the complaint, the plaintiff may present a summons to the clerk for signature and seal. If the summons is properly completed, the clerk must sign, seal, and issue it to the plaintiff for service on the defendant. A summons—or a copy of a summons that is addressed to multiple defendants—must be issued for each defendant to be served.

(c) Service.

(1) *In General.* A summons must be served with a copy of the complaint. The plaintiff is responsible for having the summons and complaint served within the time allowed by Rule 4(m) and must furnish the necessary copies to the person who makes service.

(2) *By Whom.* Any person who is at least 18 years old and not a party may serve a summons and complaint.

(3) *By a Marshal or Someone Specially Appointed.* At the plaintiff's request, the court may order that service be made by a United States marshal or deputy marshal or by a person specially appointed by the court. The court must so order if the plaintiff is authorized to proceed in forma pauperis under 28 U.S.C. § 1915 or as a seaman under 28 U.S.C. § 1916.

(d) Waiving Service.

(1) *Requesting a Waiver.* An individual, corporation, or association that is subject to service under Rule 4(e), (f), or (h) has a duty to avoid unnecessary expenses of serving the summons. The plaintiff may notify such a defendant that an action has been commenced and request that the defendant waive service of a summons. The notice and request must:

(A) be in writing and be addressed:

(i) to the individual defendant; or

(ii) for a defendant subject to service under Rule 4(h), to an officer, a managing or general agent, or any other agent authorized by appointment or by law to receive service of process;

(B) name the court where the complaint was filed;

(C) be accompanied by a copy of the complaint, 2 copies of the waiver form appended to this Rule 4, and a prepaid means for returning the form;

(D) inform the defendant, using the form appended to this Rule 4, of the consequences of waiving and not waiving service;

(E) state the date when the request is sent;

(F) give the defendant a reasonable time of at least 30 days after the request was sent—or at least 60 days if sent to the defendant outside any judicial district of the United States—to return the waiver; and

(G) be sent by first-class mail or other reliable means.

(2) *Failure to Waive.* If a defendant located within the United States fails, without good cause, to sign and return a waiver requested by a plaintiff located within the United States, the court must impose on the defendant:

(A) the expenses later incurred in making service; and

(B) the reasonable expenses, including attorney's fees, of any motion required to collect those service expenses.

(3) *Time to Answer After a Waiver.* A defendant who, before being served with process, timely returns a waiver need not serve an answer to the complaint until 60 days after the request was sent—or until 90 days after it was sent to the defendant outside any judicial district of the United States.

(4) *Results of Filing a Waiver.* When the plaintiff files a waiver, proof of service is not required and these rules apply as if a summons and complaint had been served at the time of filing the waiver.

(5) *Jurisdiction and Venue Not Waived.* Waiving service of a summons does not waive any objection to personal jurisdiction or to venue.

(e) Serving an Individual Within a Judicial District of the United States. Unless federal law provides otherwise, an individual—other than a minor, an incompetent person, or a person whose waiver has been filed—may be served in a judicial district of the United States by:

(1) following state law for serving a summons in an action brought in courts of general jurisdiction in the state where the district court is located or where service is made; or

(2) doing any of the following:

(A) delivering a copy of the summons and of the complaint to the individual personally;

(B) leaving a copy of each at the individual's dwelling or usual place of abode with someone of suitable age and discretion who resides there; or

(C) delivering a copy of each to an agent authorized by appointment or by law to receive service of process.

(f) Serving an Individual in a Foreign Country. Unless federal law provides otherwise, an individual—other than a minor, an incompetent person, or a person whose waiver has been filed—may be served at a place not within any judicial district of the United States:

(1) by any internationally agreed means of service that is reasonably calculated to give notice, such as those authorized by the Hague Convention on the Service Abroad of Judicial and Extrajudicial Documents;

(2) if there is no internationally agreed means, or if an international agreement allows but does not specify other means, by a method that is reasonably calculated to give notice:

(A) as prescribed by the foreign country's law for service in that country in an action in its courts of general jurisdiction;

(B) as the foreign authority directs in response to a letter rogatory or letter of request; or

(C) unless prohibited by the foreign country's law, by:

(i) delivering a copy of the summons and of the complaint to the individual personally; or

(ii) using any form of mail that the clerk addresses and sends to the individual and that requires a signed receipt; or

(3) by other means not prohibited by international agreement, as the court orders.

(g) Serving a Minor or an Incompetent Person. A minor or an incompetent person in a judicial district of the United States must be served by following state law for serving a summons or like process on such a defendant in an action brought in the courts of general jurisdiction of the state where service is made. A minor or an incompetent person who is not within any judicial district of the United States must be served in the manner prescribed by Rule 4(f)(2)(A), (f)(2)(B), or (f)(3).

(h) Serving a Corporation, Partnership, or Association. Unless federal law provides otherwise or the defendant's waiver has been filed, a domestic or foreign corporation, or a partnership or other unincorporated association that is subject to suit under a common name, must be served:

(1) in a judicial district of the United States:

(A) in the manner prescribed by Rule 4(e)(1) for serving an individual; or

(B) by delivering a copy of the summons and of the complaint to an officer, a managing or general agent, or any other agent authorized by appointment or by law to receive service of process and—if the agent is one authorized by statute and the statute so requires—by also mailing a copy of each to the defendant; or

(2) at a place not within any judicial district of the United States, in any manner prescribed by Rule 4(f) for serving an individual, except personal delivery under (f)(2)(C)(i).

(i) Serving the United States and Its Agencies, Corporations, Officers, or Employees.

(1) *United States.* To serve the United States, a party must:

(A)(i) deliver a copy of the summons and of the complaint to the United States attorney for the district where the action is brought—or to an assistant United States attorney or clerical employee whom the United States attorney designates in a writing filed with the court clerk—or

(ii) send a copy of each by registered or certified mail to the civil-process clerk at the United States attorney's office;

(B) send a copy of each by registered or certified mail to the Attorney General of the United States at Washington, D.C.; and

(C) if the action challenges an order of a nonparty agency or officer of the United States, send a copy of each by registered or certified mail to the agency or officer.

(2) *Agency; Corporation; Officer or Employee Sued in an Official Capacity.* To serve a United States agency or corporation, or a United States officer or employee sued only in an official capacity, a party must serve the United States and also send a copy of the summons and of the complaint by registered or certified mail to the agency, corporation, officer, or employee.

(3) *Officer or Employee Sued Individually.* To serve a United States officer or employee sued in an individual capacity for an act or omission occurring in connection with duties performed on the United States' behalf (whether or not the officer or employee is also sued in an official capacity), a party must serve the United States and also serve the officer or employee under Rule 4(e), (f), or (g).

(4) *Extending Time.* The court must allow a party a reasonable time to cure its failure to:

(A) serve a person required to be served under Rule 4(i)(2), if the party has served either the United States attorney or the Attorney General of the United States; or

(B) serve the United States under Rule 4(i)(3), if the party has served the United States officer or employee.

(j) Serving a Foreign, State, or Local Government.

(1) *Foreign State.* A foreign state or its political subdivision, agency, or instrumentality must be served in accordance with 28 U.S.C. § 1608.

(2) *State or Local Government.* A state, a municipal corporation, or any other state-created governmental organization that is subject to suit must be served by:

(A) delivering a copy of the summons and of the complaint to its chief executive officer; or

(B) serving a copy of each in the manner prescribed by that state's law for serving a summons or like process on such a defendant.

(k) Territorial Limits of Effective Service.

(1) *In General.* Serving a summons or filing a waiver of service establishes personal jurisdiction over a defendant:

(A) who is subject to the jurisdiction of a court of general jurisdiction in the state where the district court is located;

(B) who is a party joined under Rule 14 or 19 and is served within a judicial district of the United States and not more than 100 miles from where the summons was issued; or

(C) when authorized by a federal statute.

(2) *Federal Claim Outside State–Court Jurisdiction.* For a claim that arises under federal law, serving a summons or filing a waiver of service establishes personal jurisdiction over a defendant if:

(A) the defendant is not subject to jurisdiction in any state's courts of general jurisdiction; and

(B) exercising jurisdiction is consistent with the United States Constitution and laws.

(*l***) Proving Service.**

(1) *Affidavit Required.* Unless service is waived, proof of service must be made to the court. Except for service by a United States marshal or deputy marshal, proof must be by the server's affidavit.

(2) *Service Outside the United States.* Service not within any judicial district of the United States must be proved as follows:

(A) if made under Rule 4(f)(1), as provided in the applicable treaty or convention; or

(B) if made under Rule 4(f)(2) or (f)(3), by a receipt signed by the addressee, or by other evidence satisfying the court that the summons and complaint were delivered to the addressee.

(3) *Validity of Service; Amending Proof.* Failure to prove service does not affect the validity of service. The court may permit proof of service to be amended.

(m) Time Limit for Service. If a defendant is not served within 90 days after the complaint is filed, the court—on motion or on its own after notice to the plaintiff—must dismiss the action without prejudice against that defendant or order that service be made within a specified time. But if the plaintiff shows good cause for the failure, the court must extend the time for service for an appropriate period. This subdivision (m) does not apply to service in a foreign country under Rule 4(f), 4(h)(2), or 4(j)(1), or to service of a notice under Rule 71.1(d)(3)(A).

(n) Asserting Jurisdiction over Property or Assets.

(1) *Federal Law.* The court may assert jurisdiction over property if authorized by a federal statute. Notice to claimants of the property must be given as provided in the statute or by serving a summons under this rule.

(2) *State Law.* On a showing that personal jurisdiction over a defendant cannot be obtained in the district where the action is brought by reasonable efforts to serve a summons under this rule, the court may assert jurisdiction over the defendant's assets found in the district. Jurisdiction is acquired by seizing the assets under the circumstances and in the manner provided by state law in that district.

Rule 4 Notice of a Lawsuit and Request to Waive Service of Summons.

(Caption)

To (*name the defendant or — if the defendant is a corporation, partnership, or association — name an officer or agent authorized to receive service*):

Why are you getting this?

A lawsuit has been filed against you, or the entity you represent, in this court under the number shown above. A copy of the complaint is attached.

This is not a summons, or an official notice from the court. It is a request that, to avoid expenses, you waive formal service of a summons by signing and returning the enclosed waiver. To avoid these expenses, you must return the signed waiver within (*give at least 30 days or at least 60 days if the defendant is outside any judicial district of the United States*) from the date shown below, which is the date this notice was sent. Two copies of the waiver form are enclosed, along with a stamped, self-addressed envelope or other prepaid means for returning one copy. You may keep the other copy.

What happens next?

If you return the signed waiver, I will file it with the court. The action will then proceed as if you had been served on the date the waiver is filed, but no summons will be served on you and you will have 60 days from the date this notice is sent (see the date below) to answer the complaint (or 90 days if this notice is sent to you outside any judicial district of the United States).

If you do not return the signed waiver within the time indicated, I will arrange to have the summons and complaint served on you. And I will ask the court to require you, or the entity you represent, to pay the expenses of making service.

Please read the enclosed statement about the duty to avoid unnecessary expenses.

I certify that this request is being sent to you on the date below.

Date: _____

_____
(Signature of the attorney
or unrepresented party)

_____
(Printed name)

_____
(Address)

_____
(E–mail address)

_____
(Telephone number)

Rule 4   Waiver of the Service of Summons.

(Caption)

To (*name the plaintiff's attorney or the unrepresented plaintiff*):

I have received your request to waive service of a summons in this action along with a copy of the complaint, two copies of this waiver form, and a prepaid means of returning one signed copy of the form to you.

I, or the entity I represent, agree to save the expense of serving a summons and complaint in this case.

I understand that I, or the entity I represent, will keep all defenses or objections to the lawsuit, the court's jurisdiction, and the venue of the action, but that I waive any objections to the absence of a summons or of service.

I also understand that I, or the entity I represent, must file and serve an answer or a motion under Rule 12 within 60 days from_____, the date when this request was sent (or 90 days if it was sent outside the United States). If I fail to do so, a default judgment will be entered against me or the entity I represent.

Date: _____

_____
(Signature of the attorney
or unrepresented party)

_____
(Printed name)

_____
(Address)

_____
(E–mail address)

_____
(Telephone number)

(Attach the following)

Duty to Avoid Unnecessary Expenses of Serving a Summons

Rule 4 of the Federal Rules of Civil Procedure requires certain defendants to cooperate in saving unnecessary expenses of serving a summons and complaint. A defendant who is located in the United States and who fails to return a signed waiver of service requested by a plaintiff located in the United States will be required to pay the expenses of service, unless the defendant shows good cause for the failure.

"Good cause" does not include a belief that the lawsuit is groundless, or that it has been brought in an improper venue, or that the court has no jurisdiction over this matter or over the defendant or the defendant's property.

If the waiver is signed and returned, you can still make these and all other defenses and objections, but you cannot object to the absence of a summons or of service.

If you waive service, then you must, within the time specified on the waiver form, serve an answer or a motion under Rule 12 on the plaintiff and file a copy with the court. By signing and returning the waiver form, you are allowed more time to respond than if a summons had been served.

(Amended January 21, 1963, effective July 1, 1963; February 28, 1966, effective July 1, 1966; April 29, 1980, effective

August 1, 1980; amended by Pub.L. 97-462, § 2, January 12, 1983, 96 Stat. 2527, effective 45 days after January 12, 1983; amended March 2, 1987, effective August 1, 1987; April 22, 1993, effective December 1, 1993; April 17, 2000, effective December 1, 2000; April 30, 2007, effective December 1, 2007; April 29, 2015, effective December 1, 2015; April 28, 2016, effective December 1, 2016; April 27, 2017, effective December 1, 2017.)

ADVISORY COMMITTEE NOTES

1937 Adoption

Note to Subdivision (a). With the provision permitting additional summons upon request of the plaintiff, compare former Equity Rule 14 (Alias Subpoena) and the last sentence of former Equity Rule 12 (Issue of Subpoena—Time for Answer).

Note to Subdivision (b). This rule prescribes a form of summons which follows substantially the requirements stated in former Equity Rules 12 (Issue of Subpoena—Time for Answer) and 7 (Process, Mesne and Final).

U.S.C., Title 28, § 721 [now 1691] (Sealing and testing of writs) is substantially continued insofar as it applies to a summons, but its requirements as to teste of process are superseded. U.S.C., Title 28, [former] § 722 (Teste of process, day of) is superseded.

See Rule 12(a) for a statement of the time within which the defendant is required to appear and defend.

Note to Subdivision (c). This rule does not affect U.S.C., Title 28, § 503 [see 566], as amended June 15, 1935 (Marshals; duties) and such statutes as the following insofar as they provide for service of process by a marshal, but modifies them in so far as they may imply service by a marshal only:

U.S.C., Title 15:

§ 5 (Bringing in additional parties) (Sherman Act)

§ 10 (Bringing in additional parties)

§ 25 (Restraining violations; procedure)

U.S.C., Title 28:

§ 45 [former] (Practice and procedure in certain cases under the interstate commerce laws)

Compare [former] Equity Rule 15 (Process, by Whom Served).

Note to Subdivision (d). Under this rule the complaint must always be served with the summons.

Paragraph (1). For an example of a statute providing for service upon an agent of an individual see U.S.C., Title 28, § 109 [now 1400, 1694] (Patent cases).

Paragraph (3). This enumerates the officers and agents of a corporation or of a partnership or other unincorporated association upon whom service of process may be made, and permits service of process only upon the officers, managing or general agents, or agents authorized by appointment or by law, of the corporation, partnership or unincorporated association against which the action is brought. See *Christian v. International Ass'n of Machinists*, 7 F.(2d) 481 (D.C.Ky.1925) and *Singleton v. Order of Railway Conductors of America*, 9 F.Supp. 417 (D.C.Ill.1935). Compare *Operative Plasterers' and Cement Finishers' International Ass'n of the United States and Canada v. Case*, 93 F.(2d) 56 (App.D.C.1937).

For a statute authorizing service upon a specified agent and requiring mailing to the defendant, see U.S.C., Title 6, § 7 (Surety companies as sureties; appointment of agents; service of process).

Paragraphs (4) and (5) provide a uniform and comprehensive method of service for all actions against the United States or an officer or agency thereof. For statutes providing for such service, see U.S.C., Title 7, §§ 217 (Proceedings for suspension of orders) 499k (Injunctions; application of injunction laws governing orders of Interstate Commerce Commission), 608c(15)(B) (Court review of ruling of Secretary of Agriculture), and 855 (making § 608c(15)(B) applicable to orders of the Secretary of Agriculture as to handlers of anti-hog-cholera serum and hog-cholera virus); U.S.C., Title 26, § 3679, (Bill in chancery to clear title to realty on which the United States has a lien for taxes); U.S.C., Title 28, former §§ 45, (District Courts; practice and procedure in certain cases under the interstate commerce laws), [former] 763 (Petition in suit against the United States; service; appearance by district attorney), 766 [now 2409] (Partition suits where United States is tenant in common or joint tenant), 902 [now 2410] (Foreclosure of mortgages or other liens on property in which the United States has an interest). These and similar statutes are modified in so far as they prescribe a different method of service or dispense with the service of a summons.

For the [former] Equity Rule on service, see [former] Equity Rule 13, Manner of Serving Subpoena.

Note to Subdivision (e). The provisions for the service of a summons or of notice or of an order in lieu of summons contained in U.S.C., Title 8, § 405 (Cancellation of certificates of citizenship fraudulently or illegally procured) (service by publication in accordance with State law); U.S.C., Title 28, § 118 [now 1655] (Absent defendants in suits to enforce liens); U.S.C., Title 35, § 72a [now 146, 291] (Jurisdiction of District Court of United States for the District of Columbia in certain equity suits where adverse parties reside elsewhere) (service by publication against parties residing in foreign countries); U.S.C., Title 38, § 445 [now 784] (Action against the United States on a veteran's contract of insurance) (parties not inhabitants of or not found within the district may be served with an order of the court, personally or by publication) and similar statutes are continued by this rule. Title 24, § 378 [now title 13, § 336] of the Code of the District of Columbia (Publication against non-resident; those absent for six months; unknown heirs or devisees; for divorce or in rem; actual service beyond District) is continued by this rule.

Note to Subdivision (f). This rule enlarges to some extent the present rule as to where service may be made. It does not, however, enlarge the jurisdiction of the district courts.

U.S.C., Title 28, §§ 113 [now 1392] (Suits in States containing more than one district) (where there are two or more defendants residing in different districts), [former] 115 (Suits of a local nature), 116 [now 1392] (Property in different districts in same state), [former] 838 (Executions run in all districts of state); U.S.C., Title 47, § 13 (Action for damages against a railroad or telegraph company whose officer or agent in control of a telegraph line refuses or fails to operate such line in a certain manner—"upon any agent of the company found in such state"); U.S.C., Title 49, § 321(c) [now 10330(b)] (Requiring designation of a process agent by interstate motor carriers and in case of failure so to do, service may be made upon any agent in the state) and similar statutes, allowing the running of process throughout a state, are substantially continued.

U.S.C., Title 15, §§ 5 (Bringing in additional parties) (Sherman Act), 25 (Restraining violations; procedure); U.S.C., Title 28, §§ 44 [now 2321] (Procedure in certain cases under interstate commerce laws; service of processes of court), 117 [now 754, 1692] (Property in different states in same circuit; jurisdiction of receiver), 839 [now 2413] (Executions; run in every State and Territory) and similar statutes, providing for the running of process beyond the territorial limits of a State, are expressly continued.

Note to Subdivision (g). With the second sentence compare [former] Equity Rule 15, (Process, by Whom Served).

Note to Subdivision (h). This rule substantially continues U.S.C., Title 28, [former] § 767 (Amendment of process).

1963 Amendment

Subdivision (b). Under amended subdivision (e) of this rule, an action may be commenced against a nonresident of the State in which the district court is held by complying with State procedures. Frequently the form of the summons or notice required in these cases by State law differs from the Federal form of summons described in present subdivision (b) and exemplified in Form 1. To avoid confusion, the amendment of subdivision (b) states that a form of summons or notice, corresponding "as nearly as may be" to the State form, shall be employed. See also a corresponding amendment of Rule 12(a) with regard to the time to answer.

Subdivision (d)(4). This paragraph, governing service upon the United States, is amended to allow the use of certified mail as an alternative to registered mail for sending copies of the papers to the Attorney General or to a United States officer or agency. Cf. N.J. Rule 4:5–2. See also the amendment of Rule 30(f)(1).

Subdivision (d)(7). Formerly a question was raised whether this paragraph, in the context of the rule as a whole, authorized service in original Federal actions pursuant to State statutes permitting service on a State official as a means of bringing a nonresident motorist defendant into court. It was argued in *McCoy v. Siler*, 205 F.2d 498, 501–2 (3d Cir.) (concurring opinion), cert. denied, 346 U.S. 872, 74 S.Ct. 120, 98 L.Ed. 380 (1953), that the effective service in those cases occurred not when the State official was served but when notice was given to the defendant outside the State, and that subdivision (f) (Territorial limits of effective service), as then worded, did not authorize out-of-State service. This contention found little support. A considerable number of cases held the service to be good, either by fixing upon the service on the official within the State as the effective service, thus satisfying the wording of subdivision (f) as it then stood, see *Holbrook v. Cafiero*, 18 F.R.D. 218 (D.Md.1955); *Pasternack v. Dalo*, 17 F.R.D. 420 (W.D.Pa.1955); *Super Prods. Corp. v. Parkin*, 20 F.R.D. 377 (S.D.N.Y.1957), or by reading paragraph (7) as not limited by subdivision (f). See *Giffin v. Ensign*, 234 F.2d 307 (3d Cir. 1956); 2 Moore's *Federal Practice*, ¶4.19 (2d ed. 1948); 1 Barron & Holtzoff, *Federal Practice & Procedure* § 182.1 (Wright ed. 1960); Comment, 27 U. of Chi.L.Rev. 751 (1960). See also *Olberding v. Illinois Central R.R.*, 201 F.2d 582 (6th Cir.), rev'd on other grounds, 346 U.S. 338, 74 S.Ct. 83, 98 L.Ed. 39 (1953); *Feinsinger v. Bard*, 195 F.2d 45 (7th Cir. 1952).

An important and growing class of State statutes base personal jurisdiction over nonresidents on the doing of acts or on other contacts within the State, and permit notice to be given the defendant outside the State without any requirement of service on a local State official. See, e.g., Ill.Ann.

Stat., c. 110, §§ 16, 17 (Smith–Hurd 1956); Wis.Stat. § 262.06 (1959). This service, employed in original Federal actions pursuant to paragraph (7), has also been held proper. See *Farr & Co. v. Cia. Intercontinental de Nav. de Cuba*, 243 F.2d 342 (2d Cir. 1957); *Kappus v. Western Hills Oil, Inc.*, 24 F.R.D. 123 (E.D.Wis.1959); *Star v. Rogalny*, 162 F.Supp. 181 (E.D.Ill.1957). It has also been held that the clause of paragraph (7) which permits service "in the manner prescribed by the law of the state," etc., is not limited by subdivision (c) requiring that service of all process be made by certain designated persons. See*Farr & Co. v. Cia. Intercontinental de Nav. de Cuba, supra.* But *cf. Sappia v. Lauro Lines*, 130 F.Supp. 810 (S.D.N.Y.1955).

The salutary results of these cases are intended to be preserved. See paragraph (7), with a clarified reference to State law, and amended subdivisions (e) and (f).

Subdivision (e). For the general relation between subdivisions (d) and (e), see 2 Moore, supra, ¶4.32.

The amendment of the first sentence inserting the word "thereunder" supports the original intention that the "order of court" must be authorized by a specific United States statute. See 1 Barron & Holtzoff, supra, at 731. The clause added at the end of the first sentence expressly adopts the view taken by commentators that, if no manner of service is prescribed in the statute or order, the service may be made in a manner stated in Rule 4. See 2 Moore, supra, ¶4.32, at 1004; Smit, *International Aspects of Federal Civil Procedure*, 61 Colum.L.Rev. 1031, 1036–39 (1961). But see Commentary, 5 Fed. Rules Serv. 791 (1942).

Examples of the statutes to which the first sentence relates are 28 U.S.C. § 2361 (Interpleader; process and procedure); 28 U.S.C. § 1655 (Lien enforcement; absent defendants).

The second sentence, added by amendment, expressly allows resort in original Federal actions to the procedures provided by State law for effecting service on nonresident parties (as well as on domiciliaries not found within the State). See, as illustrative, the discussion under amended subdivision (d)(7) of service pursuant to State nonresident motorist statutes and other comparable State statutes. Of particular interest is the change brought about by the reference in this sentence to State procedures for commencing actions against nonresidents by attachment and the like, accompanied by notice. Although an action commenced in a State court by attachment may be removed to the Federal court if ordinary conditions for removal are satisfied, see 28 U.S.C. § 1450; *Rorick v. Devon Syndicate, Ltd.*, 307 U.S. 299, 59 S.Ct. 877, 83 L.Ed. 1303 (1939); *Clark v. Wells*, 203 U.S. 164, 27 S.Ct. 43, 51 L.Ed. 138 (1906), there has heretofore been no provision recognized by the courts for commencing an original Federal civil action by attachment. See Currie,*Attachment and Garnishment in the Federal Courts*, 59 Mich.L.Rev. 337 (1961), arguing that this result came about through historical anomaly. Rule 64, which refers to attachment, garnishment, and similar procedures under State law, furnishes only provisional remedies in actions otherwise validly commenced. See *Big Vein Coal Co. v. Read*, 229 U.S. 31, 33 S.Ct. 694, 57 L.Ed. 1053 (1913); *Davis v. Ensign–Bickford Co.*, 139 F.2d 624 (8th Cir. 1944); 7 Moore's*Federal Practice* ¶64.05 (2d ed. 1954); 3 Barron & Holtzoff, *Federal Practice & Procedure* § 1423 (Wright ed. 1958); but *cf.* Note, 13 So.Calif.L.Rev. 361 (1940). The amendment will now permit the institution of original Federal actions against nonresidents through the use of familiar State procedures by which property of these defendants is brought within the custody of the court and some appropriate service is made upon them.

The necessity of satisfying subject-matter jurisdictional requirements and requirements of venue will limit the practical utilization of these methods of effecting service. Within those limits, however, there appears to be no reason for denying plaintiffs means of commencing actions in Federal courts which are generally available in the State courts. See 1 Barron & Holtzoff, supra, at 374–80; Nordbye, *Comments on Proposed Amendments to Rules of Civil Procedure for the United States District Courts,* 18 F.R.D. 105, 106 (1956); Note, 34 Corn.L.Q. 103 (1948); Note, 13 So.Calif.L.Rev. 361 (1940).

If the circumstances of a particular case satisfy the applicable Federal law (first sentence of Rule 4(e), as amended) and the applicable State law (second sentence), the party seeking to make the service may proceed under the Federal or the State law, at his option.

See also amended Rule 13(a), and the Advisory Committee's Note thereto.

Subdivision (f). The first sentence is amended to assure the effectiveness of service outside the territorial limits of the State in all the cases in which any of the rules authorize service beyond those boundaries. Besides the preceding provisions of Rule 4, see Rule 71A(d)(3). In addition, the new second sentence of the subdivision permits effective service within a limited area outside the State in certain special situations, namely, to bring in additional parties to a counterclaim or cross-claim (Rule 13 (h)), impleaded parties (Rule 14), and indispensable or conditionally necessary parties to a pending action (Rule 19); and to secure compliance with an order of commitment for civil contempt. In those situations effective service can be made at points not more than 100 miles distant from the courthouse in which the action is commenced, or to which it is assigned or transferred for trial.

The bringing in of parties under the 100-mile provision in the limited situations enumerated is designed to promote the objective of enabling the court to determine entire controversies. In the light of present-day facilities for communication and travel, the territorial range of the service allowed, analogous to that which applies to the service of a subpoena under Rule 45(e)(1), can hardly work hardship on the parties summoned. The provision will be especially useful in metropolitan areas spanning more than one State. Any requirements of subject-matter jurisdiction and venue will still have to be satisfied as to the parties brought in, although these requirements will be eased in some instances when the parties can be regarded as "ancillary." See *Pennsylvania R.R. v. Erie Avenue Warehouse Co.,* 5 F.R.Serv.2d 14a.62, Case 2 (3d Cir.1962); *Dery v. Wyer,* 265 F.2d 804 (2d Cir.1959); *United Artists Corp. v. Masterpiece Productions, Inc.,* 221 F.2d 213 (2d Cir.1955); *Lesnik v. Public Industrials Corp.,* 144 F.2d 968 (2d Cir.1944); *Vaughn v. Terminal Transp. Co.,* 162 F.Supp. 647 (E.D.Tenn.1957); and compare the fifth paragraph of the Advisory Committee's Note to Rule 4(e), as amended. The amendment is but a moderate extension of the territorial reach of Federal process and has ample practical justification. See 2 Moore, supra, § 4.01[13] (Supp.1960); 1 Barron & Holtzoff, supra, § 184; Note, 51 Nw.U.L.Rev. 354 (1956). But cf. Nordbye, *Comments on Proposed Amendments to Rules of Civil Procedure for the United States District Courts,* 18 F.R.D. 105, 106 (1956).

As to the need for enlarging the territorial area in which orders of commitment for civil contempt may be served,

see *Graber v. Graber,* 93 F.Supp. 281 (D.D.C.1950); *Teele Soap Mfg. Co. v. Pine Tree Products Co., Inc.,* 8 F.Supp. 546 (D.N.H.1934); *Mitchell v. Dexter,* 244 Fed. 926 (1st Cir.1917); *In re Graves,* 29 Fed. 60 (N.D.Iowa 1886).

As to the Court's power to amend subdivisions (e) and (f) as here set forth, see *Mississippi Pub. Corp. v. Murphree,* 326 U.S. 438, 66 S.Ct. 242, 90 L.Ed. 185 (1946).

Subdivision (i). The continual increase of civil litigation having international elements makes it advisable to consolidate, amplify, and clarify the provisions governing service upon parties in foreign countries. See generally Jones, *International Judicial Assistance: Procedural Chaos and a Program for Reform,* 62 Yale L.J. 515 (1953); Longley, *Serving Process, Subpoenas and Other Documents in Foreign Territory,* Proc.A.B.A., Sec.Int'l & Comp.L. 34 (1959); Smit, *International Aspects of Federal Civil Procedure,* 61 Colum.L.Rev. 1031 (1961).

As indicated in the opening lines of new subdivision (i), referring to the provisions of subdivision (e), the authority for effecting foreign service must be found in a statute of the United States or a statute or rule of court of the State in which the district court is held providing in terms or upon proper interpretation for service abroad upon persons not inhabitants of or found within the State. See the Advisory Committee's Note to amended Rule 4(d)(7) and Rule 4(e). For examples of Federal and State statutes expressly authorizing such service, see 8 U.S.C. § 1451(b); 35 U.S.C. §§ 146, 293; Me.Rev.Stat., ch. 22, § 70 (Supp.1961); Minn.Stat.Ann. § 303.13 (1947); N.Y.Veh. & Tfc.Law § 253. Several decisions have construed statutes to permit service in foreign countries, although the matter is not expressly mentioned in the statutes. See, e.g., *Chapman v. Superior Court,* 162 Cal. App.2d 421, 328 P.2d 23 (Dist.Ct.App.1958); *Sperry v. Fliegers,* 194 Misc. 438, 86 N.Y.S.2d 830 (Sup.Ct.1949); *Ewing v. Thompson,* 233 N.C. 564, 65 S.E.2d 17 (1951); *Rushing v. Bush,* 260 S.W.2d 900 (Tex.Ct.Civ.App.1953). Federal and State statutes authorizing service on nonresidents in such terms as to warrant the interpretation that service abroad is permissible include 15 U.S.C. §§ 77v(a), 78aa, 79y; 28 U.S.C. § 1655; 38 U.S.C. § 784(a); Ill.Ann.Stat., c. 110, §§ 16, 17 (Smith–Hurd 1956); Wis.Stat. § 262.06 (1959).

Under subdivisions (e) and (i), when authority to make foreign service is found in a Federal statute or statute or rule of court of a State, it is always sufficient to carry out the service in the manner indicated therein. Subdivision (i) introduces considerable further flexibility by permitting the foreign service and return thereof to be carried out in any of a number of other alternative ways that are also declared to be sufficient. Other aspects of foreign service continue to be governed by the other provisions of Rule 4. Thus, for example, subdivision (i) effects no change in the form of the summons, or the issuance of separate or additional summons, or the amendment of service.

Service of process beyond the territorial limits of the United States may involve difficulties not encountered in the case of domestic service. Service abroad may be considered by a foreign country to require the performance of judicial, and therefore, "sovereign," acts within its territory, which that country may conceive to be offensive to its policy or contrary to its law. See Jones, supra, at 537. For example, a person not qualified to serve process according to the law of the foreign country may find himself subject to sanctions if he attempts service therein. See Inter-American Juridical Committee, *Report on Uniformity of Legislation on International*

Cooperation in Judicial Procedures 20 (1952). The enforcement of a judgment in the foreign country in which the service was made may be embarrassed or prevented if the service did not comport with the law of that country. See ibid.

One of the purposes of subdivision (i) is to allow accommodation to the policies and procedures of the foreign country. It is emphasized, however, that the attitudes of foreign countries vary considerably and that the question of recognition of United States judgments abroad is complex. Accordingly, if enforcement is to be sought in the country of service, the foreign law should be examined before a choice is made among the methods of service allowed by subdivision (i).

Subdivision (i)(1). Subparagraph (a) of paragraph (1), permitting service by the method prescribed by the law of the foreign country for service on a person in that country in a civil action in any of its courts of general jurisdiction, provides an alternative that is likely to create least objection in the place of service and also is likely to enhance the possibilities of securing ultimate enforcement of the judgment abroad. See *Report on Uniformity of Legislation on International Cooperation in Judicial Procedures*, supra.

In certain foreign countries service in aid of litigation pending in other countries can lawfully be accomplished only upon request to the foreign courts, which in turn directs the service to be made. In many countries this has long been a customary way of accomplishing the service. See*In re Letters Rogatory out of First Civil Court of City of Mexico*, 261 Fed. 652 (S.D.N.Y.1919); Jones, supra, at 543; Comment, 44 Colum.L.Rev. 72 (1944); Note 58 Yale L.J. 1193 (1949). Subparagraph (B) of paragraph (1), referring to a letter rogatory, validates this method. A proviso, applicable to this subparagraph and the preceding one, requires, as a safeguard, that the service made shall be reasonably calculated to give actual notice of the proceedings to the party. See *Milliken v. Meyer*, 311 U.S. 457, 61 S.Ct. 339, 85 L.Ed. 278 (1940).

Subparagraph (C) of paragraph (1), permitting foreign service by personal delivery on individuals and corporations, partnerships, and associations, provides for a manner of service that is not only traditionally preferred, but also is most likely to lead to actual notice. Explicit provision for this manner of service was thought desirable because a number of Federal and State statutes permitting foreign service do not specifically provide for service by personal delivery abroad, see e.g., 35 U.S.C. §§ 146, 293; 46 U.S.C. § 1292; Calif.Ins.Code § 1612; N.Y.Veh. & Tfc. Law § 253, and it also may be unavailable under the law of the country in which the service is made.

Subparagraph (D) of paragraph (1), permitting service by certain types of mail, affords a manner of service that is inexpensive and expeditious, and requires a minimum of activity within the foreign country. Several statutes specifically provide for service in a foreign country by mail, e.g., Hawaii Rev.Laws §§ 230–31, 230–32 (1955); Minn.Stat.Ann. § 303.13 (1947); N.Y.Civ.Prac.Act, § 229–b; N.Y.Veh. & Tfc.Law § 253, and it has been sanctioned by the courts even in the absence of statutory provision specifying that form of service. *Zurini v. United States*, 189 F.2d 722 (8th Cir.1951); *United States v. Cardillo*, 135 F.Supp. 798 (W.D.Pa.1955); *Autogiro Co. v. Kay Gyroplanes, Ltd.*, 55 F.Supp. 919 (D.D.C.1944). Since the reliability of postal service may vary from country to country, service by mail is proper only when it is addressed to the party to be served and a form of mail requiring a signed receipt is used. An additional safeguard is provided by the requirement that the mailing be attended to by the clerk of the court. See also the provisions of paragraph (2) of this subdivision (i) regarding proof of service by mail.

Under the applicable law it may be necessary, when the defendant is an infant or incompetent person, to deliver the summons and complaint to a guardian, committee, or similar fiduciary. In such a case it would be advisable to make service under subparagraph (A), (B), or (E).

Subparagraph (E) of paragraph (1) adds flexibility by permitting the court by order to tailor the manner of service to fit the necessities of a particular case or the peculiar requirements of the law of the country in which the service is to be made. A similar provision appears in a number of statutes, e.g., 35 U.S.C. §§ 146, 293; 38 U.S.C. § 784(a); 46 U.S.C. § 1292.

The next-to-last sentence of paragraph (1) permits service under (C) and (E) to be made by any person who is not a party and is not less than 18 years of age or who is designated by court order or by the foreign court. Cf. Rule 45(c); N.Y.Civ.Prac.Act §§ 233, 235. This alternative increases the possibility that the plaintiff will be able to find a process server who can proceed unimpeded in the foreign country; it also may improve the changes of enforcing the judgment in the country of service. Especially is this alternative valuable when authority for the foreign service is found in a statute or rule of court that limits the group of eligible process servers to designated officials or special appointees who, because directly connected with another "sovereign," may be particularly offensive to the foreign country. See generally Smit, supra, at 1040–41. When recourse is had to subparagraph (A) or (B) the identity of the process server always will be determined by the law of the foreign country in which the service is made.

The last sentence of paragraph (1) sets forth an alternative manner for the issuance and transmission of the summons for service. After obtaining the summons from the clerk, the plaintiff must ascertain the best manner of delivering the summons and complaint to the person, court, or officer who will make the service. Thus the clerk is not burdened with the task of determining who is permitted to serve process under the law of a particular country or the appropriate governmental or nongovernmental channel for forwarding a letter rogatory. Under (D), however, the papers must always be posted by the clerk.

Subdivision (i)(2). When service is made in a foreign country, paragraph (2) permits methods for proof of service in addition to those prescribed by subdivision (g). Proof of service in accordance with the law of the foreign country is permitted because foreign process servers, unaccustomed to the form or the requirement of return of service prevalent in the United States, have on occasion been unwilling to execute the affidavit required by Rule 4(g). See Jones, supra, at 537; Longley, supra, at 35. As a corollary of the alternate manner of service in subdivision (i)(1)(E), proof of service as directed by order of the court is permitted. The special provision for proof of service by mail is intended as an additional safeguard when that method is used. On the type of evidence of delivery that may be satisfactory to a court in lieu of a signed receipt, see *Aero Associates, Inc. v. La Metropolitana*, 183 F.Supp. 357 (S.D.N.Y.1960).

1966 Amendment

The wording of Rule 4(f) is changed to accord with the amendment of Rule 13(h) referring to Rule 19 as amended.

1980 Amendment

Subdivision (a). This is a technical amendment to conform this subdivision with the amendment of subdivision (c).

Subdivision (c). The purpose of this amendment is to authorize service of process to be made by any person who is authorized to make service in actions in the courts of general jurisdiction of the state in which the district court is held or in which service is made.

There is a troublesome ambiguity in Rule 4. Rule 4(c) directs that all process is to be served by the marshal, by his deputy, or by a person specially appointed by the court. But Rule 4(d)(7) authorizes service in certain cases "in the manner prescribed by the law of the state in which the district court is held. . . ." And Rule 4(e), which authorizes service beyond the state and service in quasi in rem cases when state law permits such service, directs that "service may be made . . . under the circumstances and in the manner prescribed in the [state] statute or rule." State statutes and rules of the kind referred to in Rule 4(d)(7) and Rule 4(e) commonly designate the persons who are to make the service provided for, e.g., a sheriff or a plaintiff. When that is so, may the persons so designated by state law make service, or is service in all cases to be made by a marshal or by one specially appointed under present Rule 4(c)? The commentators have noted the ambiguity and have suggested the desirability of an amendment. See 2 Moore's *Federal Practice* ¶4.08 (1974); Wright & Miller, *Federal Practice and Procedure:* Civil § 1092 (1969). And the ambiguity has given rise to unfortunate results. See *United States for the use of Tanos v. St. Paul Mercury Ins. Co.,* 361 F.2d 838 (5th Cir. 1966); *Veeck v. Commodity Enterprises, Inc.,* 487 F.2d 423 (9th Cir.1973).

The ambiguity can be resolved by specific amendments to Rules 4(d)(7) and 4(e), but the Committee is of the view that there is no reason why Rule 4(c) should not generally authorize service of process in all cases by anyone authorized to make service in the courts of general jurisdiction of the state in which the district court is held or in which service is made. The marshal continues to be the obvious, always effective officer for service of process.

1987 Amendment

The amendments are technical. No substantive change is intended.

1993 Amendment

SPECIAL NOTE: Mindful of the constraints of the Rules Enabling Act, the Committee calls the attention of the Supreme Court and Congress to new subdivision (k)(2). Should this limited extension of service be disapproved, the Committee nevertheless recommends adoption of the balance of the rule, with subdivision (k)(1) becoming simply subdivision (k). The Committee Notes would be revised to eliminate references to subdivision (k)(2).

Purposes of Revision. The general purpose of this revision is to facilitate the service of the summons and complaint. The revised rule explicitly authorizes a means for service of the summons and complaint on any defendant. While the methods of service so authorized always provide appropriate notice to persons against whom claims are made, effective service under this rule does not assure that personal jurisdiction has been established over the defendant served.

First, the revised rule authorizes the use of any means of service provided by the law not only of the forum state, but also of the state in which a defendant is served, unless the defendant is a minor or incompetent.

Second, the revised rule clarifies and enhances the cost-saving practice of securing the assent of the defendant to dispense with actual service of the summons and complaint. This practice was introduced to the rule in 1983 by an act of Congress authorizing "service-by-mail," a procedure that effects economic service with cooperation of the defendant. Defendants that magnify costs of service by requiring expensive service not necessary to achieve full notice of an action brought against them are required to bear the wasteful costs. This provision is made available in actions against defendants who cannot be served in the districts in which the actions are brought.

Third, the revision reduces the hazard of commencing an action against the United States or its officers, agencies, and corporations. A party failing to effect service on all the offices of the United States as required by the rule is assured adequate time to cure defects in service.

Fourth, the revision calls attention to the important effect of the Hague Convention and other treaties bearing on service of documents in foreign countries and favors the use of internationally agreed means of service. In some respects, these treaties have facilitated service in foreign countries but are not fully known to the bar.

Finally, the revised rule extends the reach of federal courts to impose jurisdiction over the person of all defendant against whom federal law claims are made and who can be constitutionally subjected to the jurisdiction of the courts of the United States. The present territorial limits on the effectiveness of service to subject a defendant to the jurisdiction of the court over the defendant's person are retained for all actions in which there is a state in which personal jurisdiction can be asserted consistently with state law and the Fourteenth Amendment. A new provision enables district courts to exercise jurisdiction, if permissible under the Constitution and not precluded by statute, when a federal claim is made against a defendant not subject to the jurisdiction of any single state.

The revised rule is reorganized to make its provisions more accessible to those not familiar with all of them. Additional subdivisions in this rule allow for more captions; several overlaps among subdivisions are eliminated; and several disconnected provisions are removed, to be relocated in a new Rule 4.1.

The Caption of the Rule. Prior to this revision, Rule 4 was entitled "Process" and applied to the service of not only the summons but also other process as well, although these are not covered by the revised rule. Service of process in eminent domain proceedings is governed by Rule 71A. Service of a subpoena is governed by Rule 45, and service of papers such as orders, motions, notices, pleadings, and other documents is governed by Rule 5.

The revised rule is entitled "Summons" and applies only to that form of legal process. Unless service of the summons is waived, a summons must be served whenever a person is joined as a party against whom a claim is made. Those few provisions of the former rule which relate specifically to service of process other than a summons are relocated in Rule 4.1 in order to simplify the text of this rule.

Subdivision (a). Revised subdivision (a) contains most of the language of the former subdivision (b). The second sentence of the former subdivision (b) has been stricken, so that the federal court summons will be the same in all cases. Few states now employ, distinctive requirements of form for a summons and the applicability of such a requirement in federal court can only serve as a trap for an unwary party or attorney. A sentence is added to this subdivision authorizing an amendment of a summons. This sentence replaces the rarely used former subdivision 4(h). See 4A Wright & Miller, Federal Practice and Procedure § 1131 (2d ed. 1987).

Subdivision (b). Revised subdivision (b) replaces the former subdivision (a). The revised text makes clear that the responsibility for filling in the summons falls on the plaintiff, not the clerk of the court. If there are multiple defendants, the plaintiff may secure issuance of a summons for each defendant, or may serve copies of a single original bearing the names of multiple defendants if the addressee of the summons is effectively identified.

Subdivision (c). Paragraph (1) of revised subdivision (c) retains language from the former subdivision (d)(1). Paragraph (2) retains language from the former subdivision (a), and adds an appropriate caution regarding the time limit for service set forth in subdivision (m).

The 1983 revision of Rule 4 relieved the marshals' offices of much of the burden of serving the summons. Subdivision (c) eliminates the requirement for service by the marshal's office in actions in which the party seeking service is the United States. The United States, like other civil litigants, is now permitted to designate any person who is 18 years of age and not a party to serve its summons.

The court remains obligated to appoint a marshal, a deputy, or some other person to effect service of a summons in two classes of cases specified by statute: actions brought in forma pauperis or by a seaman. 28 U.S.C. §§ 1915, 1916. The court also retains discretion to appoint a process server on motion of a party. If a law enforcement presence appears to be necessary or advisable to keep the peace, the court should appoint a marshal or deputy or other official person to make the service. The Department of Justice may also call upon the Marshals Service to perform services in actions brought by the United States. 28 U.S.C. § 651.

Subdivision (d). This text is new, but is substantially derived from the former subdivisions (c)(2)(C) and (D), added to the rule by Congress in 1983. The aims of the provision are to eliminate the costs of service of a summons on many parties and to foster cooperation among adversaries and counsel. The rule operates to impose upon the defendant those costs that could have been avoided if the defendant had cooperated reasonably in the manner prescribed. This device is useful in dealing with defendants who are furtive, who reside in places not easily reached by process servers, or who are outside the United States and can be served only at substantial and unnecessary expense. Illustratively, there is no useful purpose achieved by requiring a plaintiff to comply with all the formalities of service in a foreign country, including costs of translation, when suing a defendant manufacturer, fluent in English, whose products are widely distributed in the United States. See Bankston v. Toyota Motor Corp., 889 F.2d 172 (8th Cir.1989).

The former text described this process as service-by-mail. This language misled some plaintiffs into thinking that service could be effected by mail without the affirmative cooperation of the defendant. E.g., Gulley v. Mayo Foundation, 886 F.2d

161 (8th Cir.1989). It is more accurate to describe the communication sent to the defendant as a request for a waiver of formal service.

The request for waiver of service may be sent only to defendants subject to service under subdivision (e), (f), or (h). The United States is not expected to waive service for the reason that its mail receiving facilities are inadequate to assure that the notice is actually received by the correct person in the Department of Justice. The same principle is applied to agencies, corporations, and officers of the United States and to other governments and entities subject to service under subdivision (j). Moreover, there are policy reasons why governmental entities should not be confronted with the potential for bearing costs of service in cases in which they ultimately prevail. Infants or incompetent persons likewise are not called upon to waive service because, due to their presumed inability to understand the request and its consequences, they must generally be served through fiduciaries.

It was unclear whether the former rule authorized, mailing of a request for "acknowledgement of service" to defendants outside the forum state. See 1 R. Casad, Jurisdiction in Civil Actions (2d Ed.) 5–29, 30 (1991) and cases cited. But, as Professor Casad observed, there was no reason not to employ this device in an effort to obtain service outside the state, and there are many instances in which it was in fact so used, with respect both to defendants within the United States and to defendants in other countries.

The opportunity for waiver has distinct advantages to a foreign defendant. By waiving service, the defendant can reduce the costs that may ultimately be taxed against it if unsuccessful in the lawsuit, including the sometimes substantial expense of translation that may be wholly unnecessary for defendants fluent in English. Moreover, a foreign defendant that waives service is afforded substantially more time to defend against the action than if it had been formally served: under Rule 12, a defendant ordinarily has only 20 days after service in which to file its answer or raise objections by motion, but by signing a waiver it is allowed 90 days after the date the request for waiver was mailed in which to submit its defenses. Because of the additional time needed for mailing and the unreliability of some foreign mail services, a period of 60 days (rather than the 30 days required for domestic transmissions) is provided for a return of a waiver sent to a foreign country.

It is hoped that, since transmission of the notice and waiver forms is a private nonjudicial act, does not purport to effect service, and is not accompanied by any summons or directive from a court, use of the procedure will not offend foreign sovereignties, even those that have withheld their assent to formal service by mail or have objected to the "service-by-mail" provisions of the former rule. Unless the addressee consents, receipt of the request under the revised rule does not give rise to any obligation to answer the lawsuit, does not provide a basis for default judgment, and does not suspend the statute of limitations in those states where the period continues to run until service. Nor are there any adverse consequences to a foreign defendant, since the provisions for shifting the expense of service to a defendant that declines to waive service apply only if the plaintiff and defendant are both located in the United States.

With respect to a defendant located in a foreign country like the United Kingdom, which accepts documents in English, whose Central Authority acts promptly in effecting service, and whose policies discourage its residents from waiving formal service, there will be little reason for a plaintiff to send the notice and request under subdivision (d) rather than use convention methods. On the other hand, the procedure offers significant potential benefits to a plaintiff when suing a defendant that, though fluent in English, is located in a country where, as a condition to formal service under a convention, documents must be translated into another language or where formal service will be otherwise costly or time-consuming.

Paragraph (1) is explicit that a timely waiver of service of a summons does not prejudice the right of a defendant to object by means of a motion authorized by Rule 12(b)(2) to the absence of jurisdiction over the defendant's person, or to assert other defenses that may be available. The only issues eliminated are those involving the sufficiency of the summons or the sufficiency of the method by which it is served.

Paragraph (2) states what the present rule implies: the defendant has a duty to avoid costs associated with the service of a summons not needed to inform the defendant regarding the commencement of an action. The text of the rule also sets forth the requirements for a Notice and Request for Waiver sufficient to put the cost-shifting provision in place. These requirements are illustrated in Forms 1A and 1B, which replace the former Form 18–A.

Paragraph (2)(A) is explicit that a request for waiver of service by a corporate defendant must be addressed to a person qualified to receive service. The general mail rooms of large organizations cannot be required to identify the appropriate individual recipient for an institutional summons.

Paragraph (2)(B) permits the use of alternatives to the United States mails in sending the Notice and Request. While private messenger services or electronic communications may be more expensive than the mail, they may be equally reliable and on occasion more convenient to the parties. Especially with respect to transmissions to foreign countries, alternative means may be desirable, for in some countries facsimile transmission is the most efficient and economical means of communication. If electronic means such as facsimile transmission are employed, the sender should maintain a record of the transmission to assure proof of transmission if receipt is denied, but a party receiving such a transmission has a duty to cooperate and cannot avoid liability for the resulting cost of formal service if the transmission is prevented at the point of receipt.

A defendant failing to comply with a request for waiver shall be given an opportunity to show good cause for the failure, but sufficient cause should be rare. It is not a good cause for failure to waive service that the claim is unjust or that the court lacks jurisdiction. Sufficient cause not to shift the cost of service would exist, however, if the defendant did not receive the request or was insufficiently literate in English to understand it. It should be noted that the provisions for shifting the cost of service apply only if the plaintiff and the defendant are both located in the United States, and accordingly a foreign defendant need not show "good cause" for its failure to waive service.

Paragraph (3) extends the time for answer if, before being served with process, the defendant waives formal service. The extension is intended to serve as an inducement to waive service and to assure that a defendant will not gain any delay be declining to waive service and thereby causing the additional time needed to effect service. By waiving service, a defendant is not called upon to respond to the complaint until

60 days from the date the notice was sent to it—90 days if the notice was sent to a foreign country—rather than within the 20 day period from date of service specified in Rule 12.

Paragraph (4) clarifies the effective date of service when service is waived; the provision is needed to resolve an issue arising when applicable law requires service of process to toll the statute of limitations. E.g., Morse v. Elmira Country Club, 752 F.2d 35 (2d Cir.1984). Cf. Walker v. Armco Steel Corp., 446 U.S. 740 (1980).

The provisions in former subdivision (c)(2)(C)(ii) of this rule may have been misleading to some parties. Some plaintiffs, not reading the rule carefully, supposed that receipt by the defendant of the mailed complaint had the effect both of establishing the jurisdiction of the court over the defendant's person and of tolling the statute of limitations in actions in which service of the summons is required to toll the limitations period. The revised rule is clear that, if the waiver is not returned and filed, the limitations period under such a law is not tolled and the action will not otherwise proceed until formal service of process is effected.

Some state limitations laws may toll an otherwise applicable statute at the time when the defendant receives notice of the action. Nevertheless, the device of requested waiver of service is not suitable if a limitations period which is about to expire is not tolled by filing the action. Unless there is ample time, the plaintiff should proceed directly to the formal methods for service identified in subdivisions (e), (f), or (h).

The procedure of requesting waiver of service should also not be used if the time for service under subdivision (m) will expire before the date on which the waiver must be returned. While a plaintiff has been allowed additional time for service in that situation, e.g., Prather v. Raymond Constr. Co., 570 F.Supp. 278 (N.D.Ga.1983), the court could refuse a request for additional time unless the defendant appears to have evaded service pursuant to subdivision (e) or (h). It may be noted that the presumptive time limit for service under subdivision (m) does not apply to service in a foreign country.

Paragraph (5) is a cost-shifting provision retained from the former rule. The costs that may be imposed on the defendant could include, for example, the cost of the time of a process server required to make contact with a defendant residing in a guarded apartment house or residential development. The paragraph is explicit that the costs of enforcing the cost-shifting provision are themselves recoverable from a defendant who fails to return the waiver. In the absence of such a provision, the purpose of the rule would be frustrated by the cost of its enforcement, which is likely to be high in relation to the small benefit secured by the plaintiff.

Some plaintiffs may send a notice and request for waiver and, without waiting for return of the waiver, also proceed with efforts to effect formal service on the defendant. To discourage this practice, the cost-shifting provisions in paragraphs (2) and (5) are limited to costs of effecting service incurred after the time expires for the defendant to return the waiver. Moreover, by returning the waiver within the time allowed and before being served with process, a defendant receives the benefit of the longer period for responding to the complaint afforded for waivers under paragraph (3).

Subdivision (e). This subdivision replaces former subdivisions (c)(2)(C)(i) and (d)(1). It provides a means for service of summons on individuals within a judicial district of the United States. Together with subdivision (f), it provides for service

---

on persons anywhere, subject to constitutional and statutory constraints.

Service of the summons under this subdivision does not conclusively establish the jurisdiction of the court over the person of the defendant. A defendant may assert the territorial limits of the court's reach set forth in subdivision (k), including the constitutional limitations that may be imposed by the Due Process Clause of the Fifth Amendment.

Paragraph (1) authorizes service in any judicial district in conformity with state law. This paragraph sets forth the language of former subdivision (c)(2)(C)(i), which authorized the use of the law of the state in which the district court sits, but adds as an alternative the use of the law of the state in which the service is effected.

Paragraph (2) retains the text of the former subdivision (d)(1) and authorizes the use of the familiar methods of personal or abode service or service on an authorized agent in any judicial district.

To conform to these provisions, the former subdivision (e) bearing on proceedings against parties not found within the state is stricken. Likewise stricken is the first sentence of the former subdivision (f), which had restricted the authority of the federal process server to the state in which the district court sits.

Subdivision (f). This subdivision provides for service on individuals who are in a foreign country, replacing the former subdivision (i) that was added to Rule 4 in 1963. Reflecting the pattern of Rule 4 in incorporating state law limitations on the exercise of jurisdiction over persons, the former subdivision (i) limited service outside the United States to cases in which extraterritorial service was authorized by state or federal law. The new rule eliminates the requirement of explicit authorization. On occasion, service in a foreign country was held to be improper for lack of statutory authority. E.g., Martens v. Winder, 341 F.2d 197 (9th Cir.), cert. denied, 382 U.S. 937 (1965). This authority, however, was found to exist by implication. E.g., SEC v. VTR, Inc., 39 F.R.D. 19 (S.D.N.Y.1966). Given the substantial increase in the number of international transactions and events that are the subject of litigation in federal courts, it is appropriate to infer a general legislative authority to effect service on defendants in a foreign country.

A secondary effect of this provision for foreign service of a federal summons is to facilitate the use of federal long-arm law in actions brought to enforce the federal law against defendants who cannot be served under any state law but who can be constitutionally subjected to the jurisdiction of the federal court. Such a provision is set forth in paragraph (2) of subdivision (k) of this rule, applicable only to persons not subject to the territorial jurisdiction of any particular state.

Paragraph (1) gives effect to the Hague Convention on the Service Abroad of Judicial and Extrajudicial Documents, which entered into force for the United States on February 10, 1969. See 28 U.S.C.A., Fed.R.Civ.P. 4 (Supp.1986). This Convention is an important means of dealing with problems of service in a foreign country. See generally 1 B. Ristau, International Judicial Assistance §§ 4–1–1 to 4–5–2 (1990). Use of the Convention procedures, when available, is mandatory if documents must be transmitted abroad to effect service. See Volkswagenwerk Aktiengesellschaft v. Schlunk, 486 U.S. 694 (1988) (noting that voluntary use of these procedures may be desirable even when service could constitutionally be effected in another manner); J. Weis, The Federal Rules and the Hague Conventions: Concerns of Conformity and Comity,

50 U.Pitt.L.Rev. 903 (1989). Therefore, this paragraph provides that, when service is to be effected outside a judicial district of the United States, the methods of service appropriate under an applicable treaty shall be employed if available and if the treaty so requires.

The Hague Convention furnishes safeguards against the abridgment of rights of parties through inadequate notice. Article 15 provides for verification of actual notice or a demonstration that process was served by a method prescribed by the internal laws of the foreign state before a default judgment may be entered. Article 16 of the Convention also enables the judge to extend the time for appeal after judgment if the defendant shows a lack of adequate notice either to defend or to appeal the judgment, or has disclosed a prima facie case on the merits.

The Hague Convention does not specify a time within which a foreign country's Central Authority must effect service, but Article 15 does provide that alternate methods may be used if a Central Authority does not respond within six months. Generally, a Central Authority can be expected to respond much more quickly than that limit might permit, but there have been occasions when the signatory state was dilatory or refused to cooperate for substantive reasons. In such cases, resort may be had to the provision set forth in subdivision (f)(3).

Two minor changes in the text reflect the Hague Convention. First, the term "letter of request" has been added. Although these words are synonymous with "letter rogatory," "letter of request" is preferred in modern usage. The provision should not be interpreted to authorize use of a letter of request when there is in fact no treaty obligation on the receiving country to honor such a request from this country or when the United States does not extend diplomatic recognition to the foreign nation. Second, the passage formerly found in subdivision (i)(1)(B), "when service in either case is reasonably calculated to give actual notice," has been relocated.

Paragraph (2) provides alternative methods for use when internationally agreed methods are not intended to be exclusive, or where there is no international agreement applicable. It contains most of the language formerly set forth in subdivision (i) of the rule. Service by methods that would violate foreign law is not generally authorized. Subparagraphs (A) and (B) prescribe the more appropriate methods for conforming to local practice or using a local authority. Subparagraph (C) prescribes other methods authorized by the former rule.

Paragraph (3) authorizes the court to approve other methods of service not prohibited by international agreements. The Hague Convention, for example, authorizes special forms of service in cases of urgency if convention methods will not permit service within the time required by the circumstances. Other circumstances that might justify the use of additional methods include the failure of the foreign country's Central Authority to effect service within the six-month period provided by the Convention, or the refusal of the Central Authority to serve a complaint seeking punitive damages or to enforce the antitrust laws of the United States. In such cases, the court may direct a special method of service not explicitly authorized by international agreement if not prohibited by the agreement. Inasmuch as our Constitution requires that reasonable notice be given, an earnest effort should be made to devise a method of communication that is consistent with due process and minimizes offense to foreign law. A court may in some instances specially authorize use of ordinary mail. Cf. Levin v. Ruby Trading Corp., 248 F.Supp. 537 (S.D.N.Y.1965).

Subdivision (g). This subdivision retains the text of former subdivision (d)(2). Provision is made for service upon an infant or incompetent person in a foreign country.

Subdivision (h). This subdivision retains the text of former subdivision (d)(3), with changes reflecting those made in subdivision (e). It also contains the provisions for service on a corporation or association in a foreign country, as formerly found in subdivision (i).

Frequent use should be made of the Notice and Request procedure set forth in subdivision (d) in actions against corporations. Care must be taken, however, to address the request to an individual officer or authorized agent of the corporation. It is not effective use of the Notice and Request procedure if the mail is sent undirected to the mail room of the organization.

Subdivision (i). This subdivision retains much of the text of former subdivisions (d)(4) and (d)(5). Paragraph (1) provides for service of a summons on the United States; it amends former subdivision (d)(4) to permit the United States attorney to be served by registered or certified mail. The rule does not authorize the use of the Notice and Request procedure of revised subdivision (d) when the United States is the defendant. To assure proper handling of mail in the United States attorney's office, the authorized mail service must be specifically addressed to the civil process clerk of the office of the United States attorney.

Paragraph (2) replaces former subdivision (d)(5). Paragraph (3) saves the plaintiff from the hazard of losing a substantive right because of failure to comply with the complex requirements of multiple service under this subdivision. That risk has proved to be more than nominal. E.g., Whale v. United States, 792 F.2d 951 (9th Cir.1986). This provision should be read in connection with the provisions of subdivision (c) of Rule 15 to preclude the loss of substantive rights against the United States or its agencies, corporations, or officers resulting from a plaintiff's failure to correctly identify and serve all the persons who should be named or served.

Subdivision (j). This subdivision retains the text of former subdivision (d)(6) without material change. The waiver-of-service provision is also inapplicable to actions against governments subject to service pursuant to this subdivision.

The revision adds a new paragraph (1) referring to the statute governing service of a summons on a foreign state and its political subdivisions, agencies, and instrumentalities, the Foreign Sovereign Immunities Act of 1976, 28 U.S.C. § 1608. The caption of the subdivision reflects that change.

Subdivision (k). This subdivision replaces the former subdivision (f), with no change in the title. Paragraph (1) retains the substance of the former rule in explicitly authorizing the exercise of personal jurisdiction over persons who can be reached under state long-arm law, the "100–mile bulge" provision added in 1963, or the federal interpleader act. Paragraph (1)(D) is new, but merely calls attention to federal legislation that may provide for nationwide or even worldwide service of process in cases arising under particular federal laws. Congress has provided for nationwide service of process and full exercise of territorial jurisdiction by all district courts with respect to specified federal actions. See 1 R. Casad, Jurisdiction in Civil Actions (2d Ed.) chap. 5 (1991).

Paragraph (2) is new. It authorizes the exercise of territorial jurisdiction over the person of any defendant against whom is made a claim arising under any federal law if that person is subject to personal jurisdiction in no state. This addition is a companion to the amendments made in revised subdivisions (e) and (f).

This paragraph corrects a gap in the enforcement of federal law. Under the former rule, a problem was presented when the defendant was a non-resident of the United States having contacts with the United States sufficient to justify the application of United States law and to satisfy federal standards of forum selection, but having insufficient contact with any single state to support jurisdiction under state long-arm legislation or meet the requirements of the Fourteenth Amendment limitation on state court territorial jurisdiction. In such cases, the defendant was shielded from the enforcement of federal law by the fortuity of a favorable limitation on the power of state courts, which was incorporated into the federal practice by the former rule. In this respect, the revision responds to the suggestion of the Supreme Court made in Omni Capital Int'l. v. Rudolf Wolff & Co., Ltd., 484 U.S. 97, 111 (1987).

There remain constitutional limitations on the exercise of territorial jurisdiction by federal courts over persons outside the United States. These restrictions arise from the Fifth Amendment rather than from the Fourteenth Amendment, which limits state-court reach and which was incorporated into federal practice by the reference to state law in the text of the former subdivision (e) that is deleted by this revision. The Fifth Amendment requires that any defendant have affiliating contacts with the United States sufficient to justify the exercise of personal jurisdiction over that party. Cf. Wells Fargo & Co. v. Wells Fargo Express Co., 556 F.2d 406, 418 (9th Cir.1977). There also may be a further Fifth Amendment constraint in that a plaintiff's forum selection might be so inconvenient to a defendant that it would be a denial of "fair play and substantial justice" required by the due process clause, even though the defendant had significant affiliating contacts with the United States. See DeJames v. Magnificent Carriers, 654 F.2d 280, 286 n. 3 (3rd Cir.), cert. denied, 454 U.S. 1085 (1981). Compare World–Wide Volkswagen Corp. v. Woodson, 444 U.S. 286, 293–294 (1980); Insurance Corp. of Ireland v. Compagnie des Bauxites de Guinee, 456 U.S. 694, 702–03 (1982); Burger King Corp. v. Rudzewicz, 471 U.S. 462, 476–78 (1985); Asahi Metal Indus. v. Superior Court of Cal., Solano County, 480 U.S. 102, 108–13 (1987). See generally R. Lusardi, Nationwide Service of Process: Due Process Limitations on the Power of the Sovereign, 33 Vill.L.Rev. 1 (1988).

This provision does not affect the operation of federal venue legislation. See generally 28 U.S.C. § 1391. Nor does it affect the operation of federal law providing for the change of venue. 28 U.S.C. §§ 1404, 1406. The availability of transfer for fairness and convenience under § 1404 should preclude most conflicts between the full exercise of territorial jurisdiction permitted by this rule and the Fifth Amendment requirement of "fair play and substantial justice."

The district court should be especially scrupulous to protect aliens who reside in a foreign country from forum selections so onerous that injustice could result. "[G]reat care and reserve should be exercised when extending our notions of personal jurisdiction into the international field." Asahi Metal Indus. v. Superior Court of Cal., Solano County, 480 U.S. 102, 115 (1987), quoting United States v. First Nat'l City Bank, 379 U.S. 378, 404 (1965) (Harlan, J., dissenting).

This narrow extension of the federal reach applies only if a claim is made against the defendant under federal law. It does not establish personal jurisdiction if the only claims are those arising under state law or the law of another country, even though there might be diversity or alienage subject matter jurisdiction as to such claims. If, however, personal jurisdiction is established under this paragraph with respect to a federal claim, then 28 U.S.C. § 1367(a) provides supplemental jurisdiction over related claims against that defendant, subject to the court's discretion to decline exercise of that jurisdiction under 28 U.S.C. § 1367(c).

Subdivision (l). This subdivision assembles in one place all the provisions of the present rule bearing on proof of service. No material change in the rule is effected. The provision that proof of service can be amended by leave of court is retained from the former subdivision (h). See generally 4A Wright & Miller, Federal Practice and Procedure § 1132 (2d ed. 1987).

Subdivision (m). This subdivision retains much of the language of the present subdivision (j).

The new subdivision explicitly provides that the court shall allow additional time if there is good cause for the plaintiff's failure to effect service in the prescribed 120 days, and authorizes the court to relieve a plaintiff of the consequences of an application of this subdivision even if there is no good cause shown. Such relief formerly was afforded in some cases, partly in reliance on Rule 6(b). Relief may be justified, for example, if the applicable statute of limitations would bar the refiled action, or if the defendant is evading service or conceals a defect in attempted service. E.g., Ditkof v. Owens–Illinois, Inc., 114 F.R.D. 104 (E.D.Mich.1987). A specific instance of good cause is set forth in paragraph (3) of this rule, which provides for extensions if necessary to correct oversights in compliance with the requirements of multiple service in actions against the United States or its officers, agencies, and corporations. The district court should also take care to protect pro se plaintiffs from consequences of confusion or delay attending the resolution of an in forma pauperis petition. Robinson v. America's Best Contacts & Eyeglasses, 876 F.2d 596 (7th Cir.1989).

The 1983 revision of this subdivision referred to the "party on whose behalf such service was required," rather than to the "plaintiff," a term used generically elsewhere in this rule to refer to any party initiating a claim against a person who is not a party to the action. To simplify the text, the revision returns to the usual practice in the rule of referring simply to the plaintiff even though its principles apply with equal force to defendants who may assert claims against non-parties under Rules 13(h), 14, 19, 20, or 21.

Subdivision (n). This subdivision provides for in rem and quasi-in-rem jurisdiction. Paragraph (1) incorporates any requirements of 28 U.S.C. § 1655 or similar provisions bearing on seizures or liens.

Paragraph (2) provides for other uses of quasi-in-rem jurisdiction but limits its use to exigent circumstances. Provisional remedies may be employed as a means to secure jurisdiction over the property of a defendant whose person is not within reach of the court, but occasions for the use of this provision should be rare, as where the defendant is a fugitive or assets are in imminent danger of disappearing. Until 1963, it was not possible under Rule 4 to assert jurisdiction in a federal court over the property of a defendant not personally served. The 1963 amendment to subdivision (e) authorized the use of state law procedures authorizing seizures of assets

as a basis for jurisdiction. Given the liberal availability of long-arm jurisdiction, the exercise of power quasi-in-rem has become almost an anachronism. Circumstances too spare to affiliate the defendant to the forum state sufficiently to support long-arm jurisdiction over the defendant's person are also inadequate to support seizure of the defendant's assets fortuitously found within the state. Shaffer v. Heitner, 433 U.S. 186 (1977).

2000 Amendment

Paragraph (2)(B) is added to Rule 4(i) to require service on the United States when a United States officer or employee is sued in an individual capacity for acts or omissions occurring in connection with duties performed on behalf of the United States. Decided cases provide uncertain guidance on the question whether the United States must be served in such actions. *See Vaccaro v. Dobre*, 81 F.3d 854, 856–857 (9th Cir.1996);*Armstrong v. Sears*, 33 F.3d 182, 185–187 (2d Cir.1994);*Ecclesiastical Order of the Ism of Am v. Chasin*, 845 F.2d 113, 116 (6th Cir.1988); *Light v. Wolf*, 816 F.2d 746 (D.C.Cir.1987); *see also Simpkins v. District of Columbia*, 108 F.3d 366, 368–369 (D.C.Cir.1997). Service on the United States will help to protect the interest of the individual defendant in securing representation by the United States, and will expedite the process of determining whether the United States will provide representation. It has been understood that the individual defendant must be served as an individual defendant, a requirement that is made explicit. Invocation of the individual service provisions of subdivisions (e), (f), and (g) invokes also the waiver-of-service provisions of subdivision (d).

Paragraph 2(B) reaches service when an officer or employee of the United States is sued in an individual capacity "for acts or omissions occurring in connection with the performance of duties on behalf of the United States." This phrase has been chosen as a functional phrase that can be applied without the occasionally distracting associations of such phrases as "scope of employment," "color of office," or "arising out of the employment." Many actions are brought against individual federal officers or employees of the United States for acts or omissions that have no connection whatever to their governmental roles. There is no reason to require service on the United States in these actions. The connection to federal employment that requires service on the United States must be determined as a practical matter, considering whether the individual defendant has reasonable grounds to look to the United States for assistance and whether the United States has reasonable grounds for demanding formal notice of the action.

An action against a former officer or employee of the United States is covered by paragraph (2)(B) in the same way as an action against a present officer or employee. Termination of the relationship between the individual defendant and the United States does not reduce the need to serve the United States.

Paragraph (3) is amended to ensure that failure to serve the United States in an action governed by paragraph 2(B) does not defeat an action. This protection is adopted because there will be cases in which the plaintiff reasonably fails to appreciate the need to serve the United States. There is no requirement, however, that the plaintiff show that the failure to serve the United States was reasonable. A reasonable time to effect service on the United States must be allowed after the failure is pointed out. An additional change ensures that if the United States or United States attorney is served in an action governed by paragraph 2(A), additional time is to be allowed even though no officer, employee, agency, or corporation of the United States was served.

GAP Report

The most important changes were made to ensure that no one would read the seemingly independent provisions of paragraphs 2(A) and 2(B) to mean that service must be made twice both on the United States and on the United States employee when the employee is sued in both official and individual capacities. The word "only" was added in subparagraph (A) and the new phrase "whether or not the officer or employee is sued also in an individual capacity" was inserted in subparagraph (B).

Minor changes were made to include "Employees" in the catch-line for subdivision (i), and to add "or employee" in paragraph 2(A). Although it may seem awkward to think of suit against an employee in an official capacity, there is no clear definition that separates "officers" from "employees" for this purpose. The published proposal to amend Rule 12(a)(3) referred to actions against an employee sued in an official capacity, and it seemed better to make the rules parallel by adding "employee" to Rule 4(i)(2)(A) than by deleting it from Rule 12(a)(3)(A).

2007 Amendment

The language of Rule 4 has been amended as part of the general restyling of the Civil Rules to make them more easily understood and to make style and terminology consistent throughout the rules. These changes are intended to be stylistic only.

Rule 4(d)(1)(C) corrects an inadvertent error in former Rule 4(d)(2)(G). The defendant needs two copies of the waiver form, not an extra copy of the notice and request.

Rule 4(g) changes "infant" to "minor." "Infant" in the present rule means "minor." Modern word usage suggests that "minor" will better maintain the intended meaning. The same change from "infant" to "minor" is made throughout the rules. In addition, subdivision (f)(3) is added to the description of methods of service that the court may order; the addition ensures the evident intent that the court not order service by means prohibited by international agreement.

Rule 4(i)(4) corrects a misleading reference to "the plaintiff" in former Rule 4(i)(3). A party other than a plaintiff may need a reasonable time to effect service. Rule 4(i)(4) properly covers any party.

Former Rule 4(j)(2) refers to service upon an "other governmental organization subject to suit." This is changed to "any other state-created governmental organization that is subject to suit." The change entrenches the meaning indicated by the caption ("Serving a Foreign, State, or Local Government"), and the invocation of state law. It excludes any risk that this rule might be read to govern service on a federal agency, or other entities not created by state law.

The former provision describing service on interpleader claimants [former (k)(1)(C)] is deleted as redundant in light of the general provision in (k)(1)(C) recognizing personal jurisdiction authorized by a federal statute.

2015 Amendment

Subdivision (d). Abrogation of Rule 84 and the other official forms requires that former Forms 5 and 6 be directly incorporated into Rule 4.

Subdivision (m). The presumptive time for serving a defendant is reduced from 120 days to 90 days. This change, together with the shortened times for issuing a scheduling order set by amended Rule 16(b)(2), will reduce delay at the beginning of litigation.

Shortening the presumptive time for service will increase the frequency of occasions to extend the time. More time may be needed, for example, when a request to waive service fails, a defendant is difficult to serve, or a marshal is to make service in an in forma pauperis action.

The final sentence is amended to make it clear that the reference to Rule 4 in Rule 71.1(d)(3)(A) does not include Rule 4(m). Dismissal under Rule 4(m) for failure to make timely service would be inconsistent with the limits on dismissal established by Rule 71.1(i)(1)(C).

Shortening the time to serve under Rule 4(m) means that the time of the notice required by Rule 15(c)(1)(C) for relation back is also shortened.

2016 Amendment

Rule 4(m) is amended to correct a possible ambiguity that appears to have generated some confusion in practice. Service in a foreign country often is accomplished by means that require more than the time set by Rule 4(m). This problem is recognized by the two clear exceptions for service on an individual in a foreign country under Rule 4(f) and for service on a foreign state under Rule 4(j)(1). The potential ambiguity arises from the lack of any explicit reference to service on a corporation, partnership, or other unincorporated association. Rule 4(h)(2) provides for service on such defendants at a place outside any judicial district of the United States "in any manner prescribed by Rule 4(f) for serving an individual, except personal delivery under (f)(2)(C)(i)." Invoking service "in the manner prescribed by Rule 4(f)" could easily be read to mean that service under Rule 4(h)(2) is also service "under" Rule 4(f). That interpretation is in keeping with the purpose to recognize the delays that often occur in effecting service in a foreign country. But it also is possible to read the words for what they seem to say— service is under Rule 4(h)(2), albeit in a manner borrowed from almost all, but not quite all, of Rule 4(f).

The amendment resolves this possible ambiguity.

2017 Amendment

This is a technical amendment that integrates the intended effect of the amendments adopted in 2015 and 2016.

HISTORICAL NOTES

Revision Notes and Legislative Reports

1983 Acts. Statement by a Member of the House Committee on the Judiciary, see 1982 U.S.Code Cong. and Adm. News, p. 4434.

Effective and Applicability Provisions

1983 Acts. Amendment by Pub.L. 97–462 effective 45 days after Jan. 12, 1983, see section 4 of Pub.L. 97–462, set out as a note under section 2071 of this title.

CROSS REFERENCES

Actions on war risk insurance claims, see 46 USCA § 53911.

Civil monetary penalties and assessments for Federal old-age survivors and disability insurance benefits and social security, see 42 USCA § 1320a-8.

Executions in favor of United States, see 28 USCA § 2413.

Motions to dismiss or quash for lack of jurisdiction over person, insufficiency of process or service of process, see Fed.Rules Civ.Proc. Rule 12, 28 USCA.

Process, generally, see 28 USCA § 1691 et seq.

Process in bankruptcy proceedings, see Fed.Rules Bankr. Proc. Rule 7004, 11 USCA.

Process to run outside State,

Actions under Security Act of 1933, see 15 USCA § 77v.

Actions under Security Act of 1934, see 15 USCA § 78aa.

Veterans' actions against United States on life insurance contracts, see 38 USCA § 1984.

Service of notice of application for leave to perpetuate testimony by taking deposition, see Fed.Rules Civ.Proc. Rule 27, 28 USCA.

Service on Government under this rule in civil action for false claims, see 31 USCA § 3730.

Venue of civil actions, see 28 USCA § 1391 et seq.

Rule 4.1.   Serving Other Process

(a) In General. Process—other than a summons under Rule 4 or a subpoena under Rule 45—must be served by a United States marshal or deputy marshal or by a person specially appointed for that purpose. It may be served anywhere within the territorial limits of the state where the district court is located and, if authorized by a federal statute, beyond those limits. Proof of service must be made under Rule 4(*l*).

(b) Enforcing Orders: Committing for Civil Contempt. An order committing a person for civil contempt of a decree or injunction issued to enforce federal law may be served and enforced in any district. Any other order in a civil-contempt proceeding may be served only in the state where the issuing court is located or elsewhere in the United States within 100 miles from where the order was issued.

(Adopted April 22, 1993, effective December 1, 1993; amended April 30, 2007, effective December 1, 2007.)

ADVISORY COMMITTEE NOTES

1993 Adoption

This is a new rule. Its purpose is to separate those few provisions of the former Rule 4 bearing on matters other than service of a summons to allow greater textual clarity in Rule 4. Subdivision (a) contains no new language.

Subdivision (b) replaces the final clause of the penultimate sentence of the former subdivision 4(f), a clause added to the rule in 1963. The new rule provides for nationwide service of orders of civil commitment enforcing decrees of injunctions issued to compel compliance with federal law. The rule makes no change in the practice with respect to the enforcement of injunctions or decrees not involving the enforcement of federally-created rights.

Service of process is not required to notify a party of a decree or injunction, or of an order that the party show cause why that party should not be held in contempt of such an order. With respect to a party who has once been served with a summons, the service of the decree or injunction itself or of an order to show cause can be made pursuant to Rule 5. Thus, for example, an injunction may be served on a party through that person's attorney. *Chagas v. United States*, 369 F.2d 643 (5th Cir.1966). The same is true for service of an order to show cause. *Waffenschmidt v. Mackay*, 763 F.2d 711 (5th Cir.1985).

The new rule does not affect the reach of the court to impose criminal contempt sanctions. Nationwide enforcement of federal decrees and injunctions is already available with respect to criminal contempt: a federal court may effect the arrest of a criminal contemnor anywhere in the United States, 28 U.S.C. § 3041, and a contemnor when arrested may be subject to removal to the district in which punishment may be imposed. Fed.R.Crim.P. 40. Thus, the present law permits criminal contempt enforcement against a contemnor wherever that person may be found.

The effect of the revision is to provide a choice of civil or criminal contempt sanctions in those situations to which it applies. Contempt proceedings, whether civil or criminal, must be brought in the court that was allegedly defied by a contumacious act. *Ex parte Bradley*, 74 U.S. 366 (1869). This is so even if the offensive conduct or inaction occurred outside the district of the court in which the enforcement proceeding must be conducted. *E.g., McCourtney v. United States*, 291 Fed. 497 (8th Cir.), *cert. denied*, 263 U.S. 714 (1923). For this purpose, the rule as before does not distinguish between parties and other persons subject to contempt sanctions by reason of their relation or connection to parties.

2007 Amendment

The language of Rule 4.1 has been amended as part of the general restyling of the Civil Rules to make them more easily understood and to make style and terminology consistent throughout the rules. These changes are intended to be stylistic only.

Rule 5.   Serving and Filing Pleadings and Other Papers

(a) Service: When Required.

(1) *In General.* Unless these rules provide otherwise, each of the following papers must be served on every party:

(A) an order stating that service is required;

(B) a pleading filed after the original complaint, unless the court orders otherwise under Rule 5(c) because there are numerous defendants;

(C) a discovery paper required to be served on a party, unless the court orders otherwise;

(D) a written motion, except one that may be heard ex parte; and

(E) a written notice, appearance, demand, or offer of judgment, or any similar paper.

(2) *If a Party Fails to Appear.* No service is required on a party who is in default for failing to appear. But a pleading that asserts a new claim for relief against such a party must be served on that party under Rule 4.

(3) *Seizing Property.* If an action is begun by seizing property and no person is or need be named as a defendant, any service required before the filing of an appearance, answer, or claim must be made on the person who had custody or possession of the property when it was seized.

(b) Service: How Made.

(1) *Serving an Attorney.* If a party is represented by an attorney, service under this rule must be made on the attorney unless the court orders service on the party.

(2) *Service in General.* A paper is served under this rule by:

(A) handing it to the person;

(B) leaving it:

(i) at the person's office with a clerk or other person in charge or, if no one is in charge, in a conspicuous place in the office; or

(ii) if the person has no office or the office is closed, at the person's dwelling or usual place of abode with someone of suitable age and discretion who resides there;

(C) mailing it to the person's last known address—in which event service is complete upon mailing;

(D) leaving it with the court clerk if the person has no known address;

(E) sending it to a registered user by filing it with the court's electronic-filing system or sending it by other electronic means that the person consented to in writing—in either of which events service is complete upon filing or sending, but is not effective if the filer or sender learns that it did not reach the person to be served; or

(F) delivering it by any other means that the person consented to in writing—in which event service is complete when the person making service delivers it to the agency designated to make delivery.

(3) *Using Court Facilities.* [Abrogated (Apr. 26, 2018, eff. Dec. 1, 2018.)]

(c) Serving Numerous Defendants.

(1) *In General.* If an action involves an unusually large number of defendants, the court may, on motion or on its own, order that:

(A) defendants' pleadings and replies to them need not be served on other defendants;

(B) any crossclaim, counterclaim, avoidance, or affirmative defense in those pleadings and replies to them will be treated as denied or avoided by all other parties; and

(C) filing any such pleading and serving it on the plaintiff constitutes notice of the pleading to all parties.

(2) *Notifying Parties.* A copy of every such order must be served on the parties as the court directs.

(d) Filing.

(1) *Required Filings; Certificate of Service.*

(A) *Papers after the Complaint.* Any paper after the complaint that is required to be served must be filed no later than a reasonable time after service. But disclosures under Rule 26(a)(1) or (2) and the following discovery requests and responses must not be filed until they are used in the proceeding or the court orders filing: depositions, interrogatories, requests for documents or tangible things or to permit entry onto land, and requests for admission.

(B) *Certificate of Service.* No certificate of service is required when a paper is served by filing it with the court's electronic-filing system. When a paper that is required to be served is served by other means:

(i) if the paper is filed, a certificate of service must be filed with it or within a reasonable time after service; and

(ii) if the paper is not filed, a certificate of service need not be filed unless filing is required by court order or by local rule.

(2) *Nonelectronic Filing.* A paper not filed electronically is filed by delivering it:

(A) to the clerk; or

(B) to a judge who agrees to accept it for filing, and who must then note the filing date on the paper and promptly send it to the clerk.

(3) *Electronic Filing and Signing.*

(A) *By a Represented Person—Generally Required; Exceptions.* A person represented by an attorney must file electronically, unless nonelectronic filing is allowed by the court for good cause or is allowed or required by local rule.

(B) *By an Unrepresented Person—When Allowed or Required.* A person not represented by an attorney:

(i) may file electronically only if allowed by court order or by local rule; and

(ii) may be required to file electronically only by court order, or by a local rule that includes reasonable exceptions.

(C) *Signing.* A filing made through a person's electronic-filing account and authorized by that person, together with that person's name on a signature block, constitutes the person's signature.

(D) *Same as a Written Paper.* A paper filed electronically is a written paper for purposes of these rules.

(4) *Acceptance by the Clerk.* The clerk must not refuse to file a paper solely because it is not in the form prescribed by these rules or by a local rule or practice.

(Amended January 21, 1963, effective July 1, 1963; March 30, 1970, effective July 1, 1970; April 29, 1980, effective August 1, 1980; March 2, 1987, effective August 1, 1987; April 30, 1991, effective December 1, 1991; April 22, 1993, effective December 1, 1993; April 23, 1996, effective December 1, 1996; April 17, 2000, effective December 1, 2000; April 23, 2001, effective December 1, 2001; April 12, 2006, effective December 1, 2006; April 30, 2007, effective December 1, 2007; April 26, 2018, effective December 1, 2018.)

ADVISORY COMMITTEE NOTES

1937 Adoption

Note to Subdivisions (a) and (b). Compare 2 Minn.Stat. (1927) §§ 9240, 9241, 9242; N.Y.C.P.A. (1937) §§ 163, 164 and N.Y.R.C.P. (1937) Rules 20, 21; 2 Wash.Rev.Stat.Ann. (Remington, 1932) §§ 244 to 249.

Note to Subdivision (d). Compare the present practice under former Equity Rule 12 (Issue of Subpoena—Time for Answer).

1963 Amendment

The words "affected thereby," stricken out by the amendment, introduced a problem of interpretation. See 1 Barron & Holtzoff, *Federal Practice & Procedure* 760–61 (Wright ed. 1960). The amendment eliminates this difficulty and promotes full exchange of information among the parties by requiring service of papers on all the parties to the action, except as otherwise provided in the rules. See also subdivision (c) of Rule 5. So, for example, a third-party defendant is required to serve his answer to the third-party complaint not only upon the defendant but also upon the plaintiff. See amended Form 22–A and the Advisory Committee's Note thereto.

As to the method of serving papers upon a party whose address is unknown, see Rule 5(b).

1970 Amendment

The amendment makes clear that all papers relating to discovery which are required to be served on any party must be served on all parties, unless the court orders otherwise. The present language expressly includes notices and demands, but it is not explicit as to answers or responses as provided in Rules 33, 34, and 36. Discovery papers may be voluminous or the parties numerous, and the court is empowered to vary the requirement if in a given case it proves needlessly onerous.

In actions begun by seizure of property, service will at times have to be made before the absent owner of the property has filed an appearance. For example, a prompt deposition may be needed in a maritime action in rem. See Rules 30(a) and 30(b)(2) and the related notes. A provision is added authorizing service on the person having custody or possession of the property at the time of its seizure.

1980 Amendment

Subdivision (d). By the terms of this rule and Rule 30(f)(1) discovery materials must be promptly filed, although it often happens that no use is made of the materials after they are filed. Because the copies required for filing are an added expense and the large volume of discovery filings presents serious problems of storage in some districts, the Committee in 1978 first proposed that discovery materials not be filed unless on order of the court or for use in the proceedings. But such materials are sometimes of interest to those who may have no access to them except by a requirement of filing, such as members of a class, litigants similarly

situated, or the public generally. Accordingly, this amendment and a change in Rule 30(f)(1) continue the requirement of filing but make it subject to an order of the court that discovery materials not be filed unless filing is requested by the court or is effected by parties who wish to use the materials in the proceeding.

1987 Amendment

The amendments are technical. No substantive change is intended.

1991 Amendment

Subdivision (d). This subdivision is amended to require that the person making service under the rule certify that service has been effected. Such a requirement has generally been imposed by local rule.

Having such information on file may be useful for many purposes, including proof of service if an issue arises concerning the effectiveness of the service. The certificate will generally specify the date as well as the manner of service, but parties employing private delivery services may sometimes be unable to specify the date of delivery. In the latter circumstance, a specification of the date of transmission of the paper to the delivery service may be sufficient for the purposes of this rule.

Subdivision (e). The words *"pleading and other"* are stricken as unnecessary. Pleadings are papers within the meaning of the rule. The revision also accommodates the development of the use of facsimile transmission for filing.

Several local district rules have directed the office of the clerk to refuse to accept for filing papers not conforming to certain requirements of form imposed by local rules or practice. This is not a suitable role for the office of the clerk, and the practice exposes litigants to the hazards of time bars; for these reasons, such rules are proscribed by this revision. The enforcement of these rules and of the local rules is a role for a judicial officer. A clerk may of course advise a party or counsel that a particular instrument is not in proper form, and may be directed to so inform the court.

1993 Amendment

This is a technical amendment, using the broader language of Rule 25 of the Federal Rules of Appellate Procedure. The district court—and the bankruptcy court by virtue of a cross-reference in Bankruptcy Rule 7005—can, by local rule, permit filing not only by facsimile transmissions but also by other electronic means, subject to standards approved by the Judicial Conference.

1996 Amendment

The present Rule 5(e) has authorized filing by facsimile or other electronic means on two conditions. The filing must be authorized by local rule. Use of this means of filing must be authorized by the Judicial Conference of the United States and must be consistent with standards established by the Judicial Conference. Attempts to develop Judicial Conference standards have demonstrated the value of several adjustments in the rule.

The most significant change discards the requirement that the Judicial Conference authorize local electronic filing rules. As before, each district may decide for itself whether it has the equipment and personnel required to establish electronic filing, but a district that wishes to establish electronic filing need no longer await Judicial Conference action.

The role of Judicial Conference standards is clarified by specifying that the standards are to govern technical matters. Technical standards can provide nationwide uniformity, enabling ready use of electronic filing without pausing to adjust for the otherwise inevitable variations among local rules. Judicial Conference adoption of technical standards should prove superior to specification in these rules. Electronic technology has advanced with great speed. The process of adopting Judicial Conference standards should prove speedier and more flexible in determining the time for the first uniform standards, in adjusting standards at appropriate intervals, and in sparing the Supreme Court and Congress the need to consider technological details. Until Judicial Conference standards are adopted, however, uniformity will occur only to the extent that local rules deliberately seek to copy other local rules.

It is anticipated that Judicial Conference standards will govern such technical specifications as data formatting, speed of transmission, means to transmit copies of supporting documents, and security of communication. Perhaps more important, standards must be established to assure proper maintenance and integrity of the record and to provide appropriate access and retrieval mechanisms. Local rules must address these issues until Judicial Conference standards are adopted.

The amended rule also makes clear the equality of filing by electronic means with written filings. An electronic filing that complies with the local rule satisfies all requirements for filing on paper, signature, or verification. An electronic filing that otherwise satisfies the requirements of 28 U.S.C. § 1746 need not be separately made in writing. Public access to electronic filings is governed by the same rules as govern written filings.

The separate reference to filing by facsimile transmission is deleted. Facsimile transmission continues to be included as an electronic means.

2000 Amendment

Subdivision (d). Rule 5(d) is amended to provide that disclosures under Rule 26(a)(1) and (2), and discovery requests and responses under Rules 30, 31, 33, 34, and 36 must not be filed until they are used in the action. "Discovery requests" includes deposition notices and "discovery responses" includes objections. The rule supersedes and invalidates local rules that forbid, permit, or require filing of these materials before they are used in the action. The former Rule 26(a)(4) requirement that disclosures under Rule 26(a)(1) and (2) be filed has been removed. Disclosures under Rule 26(a)(3), however, must be promptly filed as provided in Rule 26(a)(3). Filings in connection with Rule 35 examinations, which involve a motion proceeding when the parties do not agree, are unaffected by these amendments.

Recognizing the costs imposed on parties and courts by required filing of discovery materials that are never used in an action, Rule 5(d) was amended in 1980 to authorize court orders that excuse filing. Since then, many districts have adopted local rules that excuse or forbid filing. In 1989 the Judicial Conference Local Rules Project concluded that these local rules were inconsistent with Rule 5(d), but urged the Advisory Committee to consider amending the rule. *Local Rules Project* at 92 (1989). The Judicial Conference of the Ninth Circuit gave the Committee similar advice in 1997. The reality of nonfiling reflected in these local rules has even been assumed in drafting the national rules. In 1993, Rule 30(f)(1)

was amended to direct that the officer presiding at a deposition file it with the court or send it to the attorney who arranged for the transcript or recording. The Committee Note explained that this alternative to filing was designed for "courts which direct that depositions not be automatically filed." Rule 30(f)(1) has been amended to conform to this change in Rule 5(d).

Although this amendment is based on widespread experience with local rules, and confirms the results directed by these local rules, it is designed to supersede and invalidate local rules. There is no apparent reason to have different filing rules in different districts. Even if districts vary in present capacities to store filed materials that are not used in an action, there is little reason to continue expending court resources for this purpose. These costs and burdens would likely change as parties make increased use of audio- and videotaped depositions. Equipment to facilitate review and reproduction of such discovery materials may prove costly to acquire, maintain, and operate.

The amended rule provides that discovery materials and disclosures under Rule 26(a)(1) and (a)(2) must not be filed until they are "used in the proceeding." This phrase is meant to refer to proceedings in court. This filing requirement is not triggered by "use" of discovery materials in other discovery activities, such as depositions. In connection with proceedings in court, however, the rule is to be interpreted broadly; any use of discovery materials in court in connection with a motion, a pretrial conference under Rule 16, or otherwise, should be interpreted as use in the proceeding.

Once discovery or disclosure materials are used in the proceeding, the filing requirements of Rule 5(d) should apply to them. But because the filing requirement applies only with regard to materials that are used, only those parts of voluminous materials that are actually used need be filed. Any party would be free to file other pertinent portions of materials that are so used. *See* Fed. R. Evid. 106; *cf.* Rule 32(a)(4). If the parties are unduly sparing in their submissions, the court may order further filings. By local rule, a court could provide appropriate direction regarding the filing of discovery materials, such as depositions, that are used in proceedings.

"Shall" is replaced by "must" under the program to conform amended rules to current style conventions when there is no ambiguity.

GAP Report

The Advisory Committee recommends no changes to either the amendments to Rule 5(d) or the Committee Note as published.

2001 Amendment

Rule 5(b) is restyled.

Rule 5(b)(1) makes it clear that the provision for service on a party's attorney applies only to service made under Rules 5(a) and 77(d). Service under Rules 4, 4.1, 45(b), and 71A(d)(3)—as well as rules that invoke those rules—must be made as provided in those rules.

Subparagraphs (A), (B), and (C) of Rule 5(b)(2) carry forward the method-of-service provisions of former Rule 5(b).

Subparagraph (D) of Rule 5(b)(2) is new. It authorizes service by electronic means or any other means, but only if consent is obtained from the person served. The consent must be express, and cannot be implied from conduct. Early experience with electronic filing as authorized by Rule 5(d) is positive, supporting service by electronic means as well. Consent is required, however, because it is not yet possible to assume universal entry into the world of electronic communication. Subparagraph (D) also authorizes service by nonelectronic means. The Rule 5(b)(2)(B) provision making mail service complete on mailing is extended in subparagraph (D) to make service by electronic means complete on transmission; transmission is effected when the sender does the last act that must be performed by the sender. Service by other agencies is complete on delivery to the designated agency.

Finally, subparagraph (D) authorizes adoption of local rules providing for service through the court. Electronic case filing systems will come to include the capacity to make service by using the court's facilities to transmit all documents filed in the case. It may prove most efficient to establish an environment in which a party can file with the court, making use of the court's transmission facilities to serve the filed paper on all other parties. Transmission might be by such means as direct transmission of the paper, or by transmission of a notice of filing that includes an electronic link for direct access to the paper. Because service is under subparagraph (D), consent must be obtained from the persons served.

Consent to service under Rule 5(b)(2)(D) must be in writing, which can be provided by electronic means. Parties are encouraged to specify the scope and duration of the consent. The specification should include at least the persons to whom service should be made, the appropriate address or location for such service—such as the e-mail address or facsimile machine number, and the format to be used for attachments. A district court may establish a registry or other facility that allows advance consent to service by specified means for future actions.

Rule 6(e) is amended to allow additional time to respond when service is made under Rule 5(b)(2)(D). The additional time does not relieve a party who consents to service under Rule 5(b)(2)(D) of the responsibilities to monitor the facility designated for receiving service and to provide prompt notice of any address change.

Paragraph (3) addresses a question that may arise from a literal reading of the provision that service by electronic means is complete on transmission. Electronic communication is rapidly improving, but lawyers report continuing failures of transmission, particularly with respect to attachments. Ordinarily the risk of non-receipt falls on the person being served, who has consented to this form of service. But the risk should not extend to situations in which the person attempting service learns that the attempted service in fact did not reach the person to be served. Given actual knowledge that the attempt failed, service is not effected. The person attempting service must either try again or show circumstances that justify dispensing with service.

Paragraph (3) does not address the similar questions that may arise when a person attempting service learns that service by means other than electronic means in fact did not reach the person to be served. Case law provides few illustrations of circumstances in which a person attempting service actually knows that the attempt failed but seeks to act as if service had been made. This negative history suggests there is no need to address these problems in Rule 5(b)(3). This silence does not imply any view on these issues, nor on the circumstances that justify various forms of judicial action even though service has not been made.

Changes Made After Publication and Comments

Rule 5(b)(2)(D) was changed to require that consent be "in writing."

Rule 5(b)(3) is new. The published proposal did not address the question of failed service in the text of the rule. Instead, the Committee Note included this statement: "As with other modes of service, however, actual notice that the transmission was not received defeats the presumption of receipt that arises from the provision that service is complete on transmission. The sender must take additional steps to effect service. Service by other agencies is complete on delivery to the designated agency." The addition of paragraph (3) was prompted by consideration of the draft Appellate Rule 25(c) that was prepared for the meeting of the Appellate Rules Advisory Committee. This draft provided: "Service by electronic means is complete on transmission, unless the party making service is notified that the paper was not received." Although Appellate Rule 25(c) is being prepared for publication and comment, while Civil Rule 5(b) has been published and otherwise is ready to recommend for adoption, it seemed desirable to achieve some parallel between the two rules.

The draft Rule 5(b)(3) submitted for consideration by the Advisory Committee covered all means of service except for leaving a copy with the clerk of the court when the person to be served has no known address. It was not limited to electronic service for fear that a provision limited to electronic service might generate unintended negative implications as to service by other means, particularly mail. This concern was strengthened by a small number of opinions that say that service by mail is effective, because complete on mailing, even when the person making service has prompt actual notice that the mail was not delivered. The Advisory Committee voted to limit Rule 5(b)(3) to service by electronic means because this means of service is relatively new, and seems likely to miscarry more frequently than service by post. It was suggested during the Advisory Committee meeting that the question of negative implication could be addressed in the Committee Note. There was little discussion of this possibility. The Committee Note submitted above includes a "no negative implications" paragraph prepared by the Reporter for consideration by the Standing Committee.

The Advisory Committee did not consider at all a question that was framed during the later meeting of the Appellate Rules Advisory Committee. As approved by the Advisory Committee, Rule 5(b)(3) defeats service by electronic means "if the party making service learns that the attempted service did not reach the person to be served." It says nothing about the time relevant to learning of the failure. The omission may seem glaring. Curing the omission, however, requires selection of a time. As revised, proposed Appellate Rule 25(c) requires that the party making service learn of the failure within three calendar days. The Appellate Rules Advisory Committee will have the luxury of public comment and another year to consider the desirability of this short period. If Civil Rule 5(b) is to be recommended for adoption now, no such luxury is available. This issue deserves careful consideration by the Standing Committee.

Several changes are made in the Committee Note. (1) It requires that consent "be express, and cannot be implied from conduct." This addition reflects a more general concern stimulated by a reported ruling that an e-mail address on a firm's letterhead implied consent to e-mail service. (2) The paragraph discussing service through the court's facilities is expanded by describing alternative methods, including an "electronic link." (3) There is a new paragraph that states that the requirement of written consent can be satisfied by electronic means, and that suggests matters that should be addressed by the consent. (4) A paragraph is added to note the additional response time provided by amended Rule 6(e). (5) The final two paragraphs address newly added Rule 5(b)(3). The first explains the rule that electronic service is not effective if the person making service learns that it did not reach the person to be served. The second paragraph seeks to defeat any negative implications that might arise from limiting Rule 5(b)(3) to electronic service, not mail, not other means consented to such as commercial express service, and not service on another person on behalf of the person to be served.

Rule 6(e)

The Advisory Committee recommended that no change be made in Civil Rule 6(e) to reflect the provisions of Civil Rule 5(b)(2)(D) that, with the consent of the person to be served, would allow service by electronic or other means. Absent change, service by these means would not affect the time for acting in response to the paper served. Comment was requested, however, on the alternative that would allow an additional 3 days to respond. The alternative Rule 6(e) amendments are cast in a form that permits ready incorporation in the Bankruptcy Rules. Several of the comments suggest that the added three days should be provided. Electronic transmission is not always instantaneous, and may fail for any of a number of reasons. It may take three days to arrange for transmission in readable form. Providing added time to respond will not discourage people from asking for consent to electronic transmission, and may encourage people to give consent. The more who consent, the quicker will come the improvements that will make electronic service ever more attractive. Consistency with the Bankruptcy Rules will be a good thing, and the Bankruptcy Rules Advisory Committee believes the additional three days should be allowed.

2006 Amendment

Amended Rule 5(e) acknowledges that many courts have required electronic filing by means of a standing order, procedures manual, or local rule. These local practices reflect the advantages that courts and most litigants realize from electronic filing. Courts that mandate electronic filing recognize the need to make exceptions when requiring electronic filing imposes a hardship on a party. Under amended Rule 5(e), a local rule that requires electronic filing must include reasonable exceptions, but Rule 5(e) does not define the scope of those exceptions. Experience with the local rules that have been adopted and that will emerge will aid in drafting new local rules and will facilitate gradual convergence on uniform exceptions, whether in local rules or in an amended Rule 5(e).

2007 Amendment

The language of Rule 5 has been amended as part of the general restyling of the Civil Rules to make them more easily understood and to make style and terminology consistent throughout the rules. These changes are intended to be stylistic only.

Rule 5(a)(1)(E) omits the former reference to a designation of record on appeal. Appellate Rule 10 is a self-contained provision for the record on appeal, and provides for service.

Former Rule 5(b)(2)(D) literally provided that a local rule may authorize use of the court's transmission facilities to make service by non-electronic means agreed to by the parties. That was not intended. Rule 5(b)(3) restores the intended

meaning—court transmission facilities can be used only for service by electronic means.

Rule 5(d)(2)(B) provides that "a" judge may accept a paper for filing, replacing the reference in former Rule 5(e) to "the" judge. Some courts do not assign a designated judge to each case, and it may be important to have another judge accept a paper for filing even when a case is on the individual docket of a particular judge. The ministerial acts of accepting the paper, noting the time, and transmitting the paper to the court clerk do not interfere with the assigned judge's authority over the action.

2018 Amendments

Subdivision (b). Rule 5(b) is amended to revise the provisions for electronic service. Provision for electronic service was first made when electronic communication was not as widespread or as fully reliable as it is now. Consent of the person served to receive service by electronic means was required as a safeguard. Those concerns have substantially diminished, but have not disappeared entirely, particularly as to persons proceeding without an attorney.

The amended rule recognizes electronic service through the court's transmission facilities as to any registered user. A court may choose to allow registration only with the court's permission. But a party who registers will be subject to service through the court's facilities unless the court provides otherwise. With the consent of the person served, electronic service also may be made by means that do not utilize the court's facilities. Consent can be limited to service at a prescribed address or in a specified form, and may be limited by other conditions.

Service is complete when a person files the paper with the court's electronic-filing system for transmission to a registered user, or when one person sends it to another person by other electronic means that the other person has consented to in writing. But service is not effective if the person who filed with the court or the person who sent by other agreed-upon electronic means learns that the paper did not reach the person to be served. The rule does not make the court responsible for notifying a person who filed the paper with the court's electronic-filing system that an attempted transmission by the court's system failed. But a filer who learns that the transmission failed is responsible for making effective service.

Because Rule 5(b)(2)(E) now authorizes service through the court's facilities as a uniform national practice, Rule 5(b)(3) is abrogated. It is no longer necessary to rely on local rules to authorize such service.

Subdivision (d). Rule 5(d)(1) has provided that any paper after the complaint that is required to be served "must be filed within a reasonable time after service." Because "within" might be read as barring filing before the paper is served, "no later than" is substituted to ensure that it is proper to file a paper before it is served.

Under amended Rule 5(d)(1)(B), a certificate of service is not required when a paper is served by filing it with the court's electronic-filing system. When service is not made by filing with the court's electronic-filing system, a certificate of service must be filed with the paper or within a reasonable time after service, and should specify the date as well as the manner of service. For papers that are required to be served but must not be filed until they are used in the proceeding or the court orders filing, the certificate need not be filed until

---

the paper is filed, unless filing is required by local rule or court order.

Amended Rule 5(d)(3) recognizes increased reliance on electronic filing. Most districts have adopted local rules that require electronic filing, and allow reasonable exceptions as required by the former rule. The time has come to seize the advantages of electronic filing by making it generally mandatory in all districts for a person represented by an attorney. But exceptions continue to be available. Nonelectronic filing must be allowed for good cause. And a local rule may allow or require nonelectronic filing for other reasons.

Filings by a person proceeding without an attorney are treated separately. It is not yet possible to rely on an assumption that pro se litigants are generally able to seize the advantages of electronic filing. Encounters with the court's system may prove overwhelming to some. Attempts to work within the system may generate substantial burdens on a pro se party, on other parties, and on the court. Rather than mandate electronic filing, filing by pro se litigants is left for governing by local rules or court order. Efficiently handled electronic filing works to the advantage of all parties and the court. Many courts now allow electronic filing by pro se litigants with the court's permission. Such approaches may expand with growing experience in the courts, along with the greater availability of the systems required for electronic filing and the increasing familiarity of most people with electronic communication. Room is also left for a court to require electronic filing by a pro se litigant by court order or by local rule. Care should be taken to ensure that an order to file electronically does not impede access to the court, and reasonable exceptions must be included in a local rule that requires electronic filing by a pro se litigant. In the beginning, this authority is likely to be exercised only to support special programs, such as one requiring e-filing in collateral proceedings by state prisoners.

A filing made through a person's electronic-filing account and authorized by that person, together with that person's name on a signature block, constitutes the person's signature.

CROSS REFERENCES

Additional time for service by mail, see Fed.Rules Civ.Proc. Rule 6, 28 USCA.

Jury trial, waiver by failing to file demand, see Fed.Rules Civ.Proc. Rule 38, 28 USCA.

Rule 5.1. Constitutional Challenge to a Statute—Notice, Certification, and Intervention

(a) Notice by a Party. A party that files a pleading, written motion, or other paper drawing into question the constitutionality of a federal or state statute must promptly:

(1) file a notice of constitutional question stating the question and identifying the paper that raises it, if:

(A) a federal statute is questioned and the parties do not include the United States, one of its agencies, or one of its officers or employees in an official capacity; or

(B) a state statute is questioned and the parties do not include the state, one of its agencies, or one

of its officers or employees in an official capacity; and

(2) serve the notice and paper on the Attorney General of the United States if a federal statute is questioned—or on the state attorney general if a state statute is questioned—either by certified or registered mail or by sending it to an electronic address designated by the attorney general for this purpose.

(b) Certification by the Court. The court must, under 28 U.S.C. § 2403, certify to the appropriate attorney general that a statute has been questioned.

(c) Intervention; Final Decision on the Merits. Unless the court sets a later time, the attorney general may intervene within 60 days after the notice is filed or after the court certifies the challenge, whichever is earlier. Before the time to intervene expires, the court may reject the constitutional challenge, but may not enter a final judgment holding the statute unconstitutional.

(d) No Forfeiture. A party's failure to file and serve the notice, or the court's failure to certify, does not forfeit a constitutional claim or defense that is otherwise timely asserted.

(Adopted April 12, 2006, effective December 1, 2006; amended April 30, 2007, effective December 1, 2007.)

ADVISORY COMMITTEE NOTES
2006 Adoption

Rule 5.1 implements 28 U.S.C. § 2403, replacing the final three sentences of Rule 24(c). New Rule 5.1 requires a party that files a pleading, written motion, or other paper drawing in question the constitutionality of a federal or state statute to file a notice of constitutional question and serve it on the United States Attorney General or state attorney general. The party must promptly file and serve the notice of constitutional question. This notice requirement supplements the court's duty to certify a constitutional challenge to the United States Attorney General or state attorney general. The notice of constitutional question will ensure that the attorney general is notified of constitutional challenges and has an opportunity to exercise the statutory right to intervene at the earliest possible point in the litigation. The court's certification obligation remains, and is the only notice when the constitutionality of a federal or state statute is drawn in question by means other than a party's pleading, written motion, or other paper.

Moving the notice and certification provisions from Rule 24(c) to a new rule is designed to attract the parties' attention to these provisions by locating them in the vicinity of the rules that require notice by service and pleading.

Rule 5.1 goes beyond the requirements of § 2403 and the former Rule 24(c) provisions by requiring notice and certification of a constitutional challenge to any federal or state statute, not only those "affecting the public interest." It is better to assure, through notice, that the attorney general is able to determine whether to seek intervention on the ground that the act or statute affects a public interest. Rule 5.1 refers to a "federal statute," rather than the § 2403 reference to an "Act of Congress," to maintain consistency in the Civil

Rules vocabulary. In Rule 5.1 "statute" means any congressional enactment that would qualify as an "Act of Congress."

Unless the court sets a later time, the 60–day period for intervention runs from the time a party files a notice of constitutional question or from the time the court certifies a constitutional challenge, whichever is earlier. Rule 5.1(a) directs that a party promptly serve the notice of constitutional question. The court may extend the 60–period [So in original. Probably should read "60-day period".] on its own or on motion. One occasion for extension may arise if the court certifies a challenge under § 2403 after a party files a notice of constitutional question. Pretrial activities may continue without interruption during the intervention period, and the court retains authority to grant interlocutory relief. The court may reject a constitutional challenge to a statute at any time. But the court may not enter a final judgment holding a statute unconstitutional before the attorney general has responded or the intervention period has expired without response. This rule does not displace any of the statutory or rule procedures that permit dismissal of all or part of an action — including a constitutional challenge — at any time, even before service of process.

2007 Amendment

The language of Rule 5.1 has been amended as part of the general restyling of the Civil Rules to make them more easily understood and to make style and terminology consistent throughout the rules. These changes are intended to be stylistic only.

Rule 5.2. Privacy Protection For Filings Made With the Court

(a) Redacted Filings. Unless the court orders otherwise, in an electronic or paper filing with the court that contains an individual's social-security number, taxpayer-identification number, or birth date, the name of an individual known to be a minor, or a financial-account number, a party or nonparty making the filing may include only:

(1) the last four digits of the social-security number and taxpayer-identification number;

(2) the year of the individual's birth;

(3) the minor's initials; and

(4) the last four digits of the financial-account number.

(b) Exemptions from the Redaction Requirement. The redaction requirement does not apply to the following:

(1) a financial-account number that identifies the property allegedly subject to forfeiture in a forfeiture proceeding;

(2) the record of an administrative or agency proceeding;

(3) the official record of a state-court proceeding;

(4) the record of a court or tribunal, if that record was not subject to the redaction requirement when originally filed;

(5) a filing covered by Rule 5.2(c) or (d); and

(6) a pro se filing in an action brought under 28 U.S.C. §§ 2241, 2254, or 2255.

(c) Limitations on Remote Access to Electronic Files; Social–Security Appeals and Immigration Cases. Unless the court orders otherwise, in an action for benefits under the Social Security Act, and in an action or proceeding relating to an order of removal, to relief from removal, or to immigration benefits or detention, access to an electronic file is authorized as follows:

(1) the parties and their attorneys may have remote electronic access to any part of the case file, including the administrative record;

(2) any other person may have electronic access to the full record at the courthouse, but may have remote electronic access only to:

(A) the docket maintained by the court; and

(B) an opinion, order, judgment, or other disposition of the court, but not any other part of the case file or the administrative record.

(d) Filings Made Under Seal. The court may order that a filing be made under seal without redaction. The court may later unseal the filing or order the person who made the filing to file a redacted version for the public record.

(e) Protective Orders. For good cause, the court may by order in a case:

(1) require redaction of additional information; or

(2) limit or prohibit a nonparty's remote electronic access to a document filed with the court.

(f) Option for Additional Unredacted Filing Under Seal. A person making a redacted filing may also file an unredacted copy under seal. The court must retain the unredacted copy as part of the record.

(g) Option for Filing a Reference List. A filing that contains redacted information may be filed together with a reference list that identifies each item of redacted information and specifies an appropriate identifier that uniquely corresponds to each item listed. The list must be filed under seal and may be amended as of right. Any reference in the case to a listed identifier will be construed to refer to the corresponding item of information.

(h) Waiver of Protection of Identifiers. A person waives the protection of Rule 5.2(a) as to the person's own information by filing it without redaction and not under seal.

(Adopted April 30, 2007, effective December 1, 2007.)

ADVISORY COMMITTEE NOTES
2007 Adoption

The rule is adopted in compliance with section 205(c)(3) of the E–Government Act of 2002, Public Law 107–347. Section 205(c)(3) requires the Supreme Court to prescribe rules "to protect privacy and security concerns relating to electronic filing of documents and the public availability ... of documents filed electronically." The rule goes further than the E–Government Act in regulating paper filings even when they are not converted to electronic form. But the number of filings that remain in paper form is certain to diminish over time. Most districts scan paper filings into the electronic case file, where they become available to the public in the same way as documents initially filed in electronic form. It is electronic availability, not the form of the initial filing, that raises the privacy and security concerns addressed in the E–Government Act.

The rule is derived from and implements the policy adopted by the Judicial Conference in September 2001 to address the privacy concerns resulting from public access to electronic case files. See http://www.privacy.uscourts.gov/Policy.htm. The Judicial Conference policy is that documents in case files generally should be made available electronically to the same extent they are available at the courthouse, provided that certain "personal data identifiers" are not included in the public file.

While providing for the public filing of some information, such as the last four digits of an account number, the rule does not intend to establish a presumption that this information never could or should be protected. For example, it may well be necessary in individual cases to prevent remote access by nonparties to any part of an account number or social security number. It may also be necessary to protect information not covered by the redaction requirement—such as driver's license numbers and alien registration numbers—in a particular case. In such cases, protection may be sought under subdivision (d) or (e). Moreover, the Rule does not affect the protection available under other rules, such as Civil Rules 16 and 26(c), or under other sources of protective authority.

Parties must remember that any personal information not otherwise protected by sealing or redaction will be made available over the internet. Counsel should notify clients of this fact so that an informed decision may be made on what information is to be included in a document filed with the court.

The clerk is not required to review documents filed with the court for compliance with this rule. The responsibility to redact filings rests with counsel and the party or non-party making the filing.

Subdivision (c) provides for limited public access in Social Security cases and immigration cases. Those actions are entitled to special treatment due to the prevalence of sensitive information and the volume of filings. Remote electronic access by nonparties is limited to the docket and the written dispositions of the court unless the court orders otherwise. The rule contemplates, however, that nonparties can obtain full access to the case file at the courthouse, including access through the court's public computer terminal.

Subdivision (d) reflects the interplay between redaction and filing under seal. It does not limit or expand the judicially developed rules that govern sealing. But it does reflect the possibility that redaction may provide an alternative to sealing.

Subdivision (e) provides that the court can by order in a particular case for good cause require more extensive redaction than otherwise required by the Rule. Nothing in this subdivision is intended to affect the limitations on sealing that are otherwise applicable to the court.

Subdivision (f) allows a person who makes a redacted filing to file an unredacted document under seal. This provision is derived from section 205(c)(3)(iv) of the E–Government Act.

Subdivision (g) allows the option to file a register of redacted information. This provision is derived from section 205(c)(3)(v) of the E–Government Act, as amended in 2004. In accordance with the E–Government Act, subdivision (g) refers to "redacted" information. The term "redacted" is intended to govern a filing that is prepared with abbreviated identifiers in the first instance, as well as a filing in which a personal identifier is edited after its preparation.

Subdivision (h) allows a person to waive the protections of the rule as to that person's own personal information by filing it unsealed and in unredacted form. One may wish to waive the protection if it is determined that the costs of redaction outweigh the benefits to privacy. If a person files an unredacted identifier by mistake, that person may seek relief from the court.

Trial exhibits are subject to the redaction requirements of Rule 5.2 to the extent they are filed with the court. Trial exhibits that are not initially filed with the court must be redacted in accordance with the rule if and when they are filed as part of an appeal or for other reasons.

Rule 6.   Computing and Extending Time; Time for Motion Papers

(a) Computing Time. The following rules apply in computing any time period specified in these rules, in any local rule or court order, or in any statute that does not specify a method of computing time.

(1) *Period Stated in Days or a Longer Unit.* When the period is stated in days or a longer unit of time:

  (A) exclude the day of the event that triggers the period;

  (B) count every day, including intermediate Saturdays, Sundays, and legal holidays; and

  (C) include the last day of the period, but if the last day is a Saturday, Sunday, or legal holiday, the period continues to run until the end of the next day that is not a Saturday, Sunday, or legal holiday.

(2) *Period Stated in Hours.* When the period is stated in hours:

  (A) begin counting immediately on the occurrence of the event that triggers the period;

  (B) count every hour, including hours during intermediate Saturdays, Sundays, and legal holidays; and

  (C) if the period would end on a Saturday, Sunday, or legal holiday, the period continues to run until the same time on the next day that is not a Saturday, Sunday, or legal holiday.

(3) *Inaccessibility of the Clerk's Office.* Unless the court orders otherwise, if the clerk's office is inaccessible:

  (A) on the last day for filing under Rule 6(a)(1), then the time for filing is extended to the first accessible day that is not a Saturday, Sunday, or legal holiday; or

(B) during the last hour for filing under Rule 6(a)(2), then the time for filing is extended to the same time on the first accessible day that is not a Saturday, Sunday, or legal holiday.

(4) *"Last Day" Defined.* Unless a different time is set by a statute, local rule, or court order, the last day ends:

(A) for electronic filing, at midnight in the court's time zone; and

(B) for filing by other means, when the clerk's office is scheduled to close.

(5) *"Next Day" Defined.* The "next day" is determined by continuing to count forward when the period is measured after an event and backward when measured before an event.

(6) *"Legal Holiday" Defined.* "Legal holiday" means:

(A) the day set aside by statute for observing New Year's Day, Martin Luther King Jr.'s Birthday, Washington's Birthday, Memorial Day, Independence Day, Labor Day, Columbus Day, Veterans' Day, Thanksgiving Day, or Christmas Day;

(B) any day declared a holiday by the President or Congress; and

(C) for periods that are measured after an event, any other day declared a holiday by the state where the district court is located.

(b) Extending Time.

(1) *In General.* When an act may or must be done within a specified time, the court may, for good cause, extend the time:

(A) with or without motion or notice if the court acts, or if a request is made, before the original time or its extension expires; or

(B) on motion made after the time has expired if the party failed to act because of excusable neglect.

(2) *Exceptions.* A court must not extend the time to act under Rules 50(b) and (d), 52(b), 59(b), (d), and (e), and 60(b).

(c) Motions, Notices of Hearing, and Affidavits.

(1) *In General.* A written motion and notice of the hearing must be served at least 14 days before the time specified for the hearing, with the following exceptions:

(A) when the motion may be heard ex parte;

(B) when these rules set a different time; or

(C) when a court order—which a party may, for good cause, apply for ex parte—sets a different time.

(2) *Supporting Affidavit.* Any affidavit supporting a motion must be served with the motion. Except as Rule 59(c) provides otherwise, any opposing affidavit must be served at least 7 days before the

hearing, unless the court permits service at another time.

(d) Additional Time After Certain Kinds of Service. When a party may or must act within a specified time after being served and service is made under Rule 5(b)(2)(C) (mail), (D) (leaving with the clerk), or (F) (other means consented to), 3 days are added after the period would otherwise expire under Rule 6(a).

(Amended December 27, 1946, effective March 19, 1948; January 21, 1963, effective July 1, 1963; February 28, 1966, effective July 1, 1966; December 4, 1967, effective July 1, 1968; March 1, 1971, effective July 1, 1971; April 28, 1983, effective August 1, 1983; April 29, 1985, effective August 1, 1985; March 2, 1987, effective August 1, 1987; April 29, 1999, effective December 1, 1999; April 23, 2001, effective December 1, 2001; April 25, 2005, effective December 1, 2005; April 30, 2007, effective December 1, 2007; March 26, 2009, effective December 1, 2009; April 28, 2016, effective December 1, 2016.)

ADVISORY COMMITTEE NOTES
1937 Adoption

Note to Subdivisions (a) and (b). These are amplifications along lines common in state practices, of [former] Equity Rule 80 (Computation of Time—Sundays and Holidays) and of the provisions for enlargement of time found in [former] Equity Rules 8 (Enforcement of Final Decrees) and 16 (Defendant to Answer—Default—Decree Pro Confesso). See also Rule XIII, Rules and Forms in Criminal Cases, 1934, 292 U.S. 661, 666. Compare Ala.Code Ann. (Michie, 1928) § 13 and former Law Rule 8 of the Rules of the Supreme Court of the District of Columbia (1924), superseded in 1929 by Law Rule 8, Rules of the District Court of the United States for the District of Columbia (1937).

Note to Subdivision (c). This eliminates the difficulties caused by the expiration of terms of court. Such statutes as U.S.C., Title 28, [former] § 12 (Trials not discontinued by new term) are not affected. Compare Rules of the United States District Court of Minnesota, Rule 25 (Minn.Stat. (Mason, Supp.1936), p. 1089).

Note to Subdivision (d). Compare 2 Minn.Stat. (Mason, 1927) § 9246; N.Y.R.C.P. (1937) Rules 60 and 64.

1946 Amendment

Note to Subdivision (b). The purpose of the amendment is to clarify the finality of judgments. Prior to the advent of the Federal Rules of Civil Procedure, the general rule that a court loses jurisdiction to disturb its judgments, upon the expiration of the term at which they were entered, had long been the classic device which (together with the statutory limits on the time for appeal) gave finality to judgments. See note to rule 73(a). Rule 6(c) abrogates that limit on judicial power. That limit was open to many objections, one of them being inequality of operation because, under it, the time for vacating a judgment rendered early in a term was much longer than for a judgment rendered near the end of the term.

The question to be met under rule 6(b) is: how far should the desire to allow correction of judgments be allowed to postpone their finality? The rules contain a number of provisions permitting the vacation or modification of judgments on various grounds. Each of these rules contains express time limits on the motions for granting of relief. Rule 6(b) is a rule of general application giving wide discretion to the court to enlarge these time limits or revive them after they have expired, the only exceptions stated in the original rule being a prohibition against enlarging the time specified in Rule 59(b) and (d) for making motions for or granting new trials, and a prohibition against enlarging the time fixed by law for taking an appeal. It should also be noted that Rule 6(b) itself contains no limitation of time within which the court may exercise its discretion, and since the expiration of the term does not end its power, there is now no time limit on the exercise of its discretion under Rule 6(b).

Decisions of lower federal courts suggest that some of the rules containing time limits which may be set aside under Rule 6(b) are Rules 25, 50(b), 52(b), 60(b), and 73(g).

In a number of cases the effect of Rule 6(b) on the time limitations of these rules has been considered. Certainly the rule is susceptible of the interpretation that the court is given the power in its discretion to relieve a party from failure to act within the times specified in any of these other rules, with only the exceptions stated in Rule 6(b), and in some cases the rule has been so construed.

With regard to Rule 25(a) for substitution, it was held in *Anderson v. Brady*, Ky.1941, 1 F.R.D. 589, 4 Fed.Rules Service 25a.1, Case 1, and in *Anderson v. Yungkau*, C.C.A.6, 1946, 153 F.2d 685, certiorari granted 66 S.Ct. 1025, 328 U.S. 829, 90 L.Ed. 1606, that under Rule 6(b) the court had no authority to allow substitution of parties after the expiration of the limit fixed in Rule 25(a).

As to Rules 50(b) for judgments notwithstanding the verdict and 52(b) for amendment of findings and vacation of judgment, it was recognized in *Leishman v. Associated Wholesale Electric Co.*, 1943, 63 S.Ct. 543, 318 U.S. 203, 87 L.Ed. 714, that Rule 6(b) allowed the district court to enlarge the time to make a motion for amended findings and judgment beyond the limit expressly fixed in Rule 52(b). See *Coca-Cola v. Busch*, E.D.Pa.1943, 7 Fed.Rules Service, 59b.2, Case 4. Obviously, if the time limit in Rule 52(b) could be set aside under Rule 6(b), the time limit in Rule 50(b) for granting judgment notwithstanding the verdict (and thus vacating the judgment entered "forthwith" on the verdict) likewise could be set aside.

As to Rule 59 on motions for a new trial, it has been settled that the time limits in Rule 59(b) and (d) for making motions for or granting new trial could not be set aside under Rule 6(b), because Rule 6(b) expressly refers to Rule 59, and forbids it. See *Safeway Stores, Inc. v. Coe*, App.D.C.1943, 136 F.2d 771, 78 U.S.App.D.C. 19; *Jusino v. Morales & Tio*, C.C.A.1, 1944, 139 F.2d 946; *Coca-Cola Co. v. Busch*, E.D.Pa. 1943, 7 Fed.Rules Service 59b.2, Case 4; *Peterson v. Chicago Great Western Ry. Co.*, D.Neb.1943, 3 F.R.D. 346, 7 Fed. Rules Service 59b.2, Case 1; *Leishman v. Associated Wholesale Electric Co.*, 1943, 63 S.Ct. 543, 318 U.S. 203, 87 L.Ed. 714.

As to Rule 60(b) for relief from a judgment, it was held in *Schram v. O'Connor*, Mich.1941, 5 Fed.Rules Serv. 6b.31, Case 1, 2 F.R.D. 192, s.c. 5 Fed.Rules Serv. 6b.31, Case 2, 2 F.R.D. 192, that the six-months time limit in original rule 60(b) for making a motion for relief from a judgment for surprise, mistake, or excusable neglect could be set aside under Rule 6(b). The contrary result was reached in *Wallace v. United States*, C.C.A.2, 1944, 142 F.2d 240, certiorari denied 65 S.Ct. 37, 323 U.S. 712, 89 L.Ed. 573; *Reed v. South*

Atlantic Steamship Co. of Del., Del.1942, 2 F.R.D. 475, 6 Fed.Rules Serv. 60b.31, Case 1.

As to Rule 73(g), fixing the time for docketing an appeal, it was held in *Ainsworth v. Gill Glass & Fixture Co.*, C.C.A.3, 1939, 104 F.2d 83, that under Rule 6(b) the district court, upon motion made after the expiration of the forty-day period, stated in Rule 73(g), but before the expiration of the ninety-day period therein specified, could permit the docketing of the appeal on a showing of excusable neglect. The contrary was held in *Mutual Benefit Health & Accident Ass'n v. Snyder*, C.C.A.6, 1940, 109 F.2d 469 and in *Burke v. Canfield*, 1940, 111 F.2d 526, 72 App.D.C. 127.

The amendment of Rule 6(b) now proposed is based on the view that there should be a definite point where it can be said a judgment is final; that the right method of dealing with the problem is to list in Rule 6(b) the various other rules whose time limits may not be set aside, and then, if the time limit in any of those other rules is too short, to amend that other rule to give a longer time. The further argument is that Rule 6(c) abolished the long standing device to produce finality in judgments through expiration of the term, and since that limitation on the jurisdiction of courts to set aside their own judgments has been removed by Rule 6(c), some other limitation must be substituted or judgments never can be said to be final.

In this connection reference is made to the established rule that if a motion for new trial is seasonably made, the mere making or pendency of the motion destroys the finality of the judgment, and even though the motion is ultimately denied, the full time for appeal starts anew from the date of denial. Also, a motion to amend the findings under Rule 52(b) has the same effect on the time for appeal. *Leishman v. Associated Wholesale Electric Co.*, 1943, 63 S.Ct. 543, 318 U.S. 203, 87 L.Ed. 714. By the same reasoning a motion for judgment under Rule 50(b), involving as it does the vacation of a judgment entered "forthwith" on the verdict (Rule 58), operates to postpone, until an order is made, the running of the time for appeal. The Committee believes that the abolition by Rule 6(c) of the old rule that a court's power over its judgments ends with the term, requires a substitute limitation, and that unless Rule 6(b) is amended to prevent enlargement of the times specified in Rules 50(b), 52(b) and 60(b), and the limitation as to Rule 59(b) and (d) is retained, no one can say when a judgment is final. This is also true with regard to proposed Rule 59(e), which authorizes a motion to alter or amend a judgment, hence that rule is also included in the enumeration in amended Rule 6(b). In consideration of the amendment, however, it should be noted that Rule 60(b) is also to be amended so as to lengthen the six-months period originally prescribed in that rule to one year.

As to Rule 25 on substitution, while finality is not involved, the limit there fixed should be controlling. That rule, as amended, gives the court power, upon showing of a reasonable excuse, to permit substitution after the expiration of the two-year period.

As to Rule 73(g), it is believed that the conflict in decisions should be resolved and not left to further litigation, and that the rule should be listed as one whose limitation may not be set aside under Rule 6(b).

As to Rule 59(c), fixing the time for serving affidavits on motion for new trial, it is believed that the court should have authority under Rule 6(b) to enlarge the time, because, once the motion for new trial is made, the judgment no longer has

---

finality, and the extension of time for affidavits thus does not of itself disturb finality.

Other changes proposed in Rule 6(b) are merely clarifying and conforming. Thus "request" is substituted for "application" in clause (1) because an application is defined as a motion under Rule 7(b). The phrase "extend the time" is substituted for "enlarge the period" because the former is a more suitable expression and relates more clearly to both clauses (1) and (2). The final phrase in Rule 6(b), "or the period for taking an appeal as provided by law", is deleted and a reference to Rule 73(a) inserted, since it is proposed to state in that rule the time for appeal to a circuit court of appeals, which is the only appeal governed by the Federal Rules, and allows an extension of time. See Rule 72.

Subdivision (c). The purpose of this amendment is to prevent reliance upon the continued existence of a term as a source of power to disturb the finality of a judgment upon grounds other than those stated in these rules. See *Hill v. Hawes*, 1944, 64 S.Ct. 334, 320 U.S. 520, 88 L.Ed. 283; *Boaz v. Mutual Life Ins. Co. of New York*, C.C.A.8, 1944, 146 F.2d 321; *Bucy v. Nevada Construction Co.*, C.C.A.9, 1942, 125 F.2d 213.

1963 Amendment

Subdivision (a). This amendment is related to the amendment of Rule 77(c) changing the regulation of the days on which the clerk's office shall be open.

The wording of the first sentence of Rule 6(a) is clarified and the subdivision is made expressly applicable to computing periods of time set forth in local rules.

Saturday is to be treated in the same way as Sunday or a "legal holiday" in that it is not to be included when it falls on the last day of a computed period, nor counted as an intermediate day when the period is less than 7 days. "Legal holiday" is defined for purposes of this subdivision and amended Rule 77(c). Compare the definition of "holiday" in 11 U.S.C. § 1(18); also 5 U.S.C. § 86a; Executive Order No. 10358, *"Observance of Holidays,"* June 9, 1952, 17 Fed.Reg. 5269. In the light of these changes the last sentence of the present subdivision, dealing with half holidays, is eliminated.

With Saturdays and State holidays made "dies non" in certain cases by the amended subdivision, computation of the usual 5-day notice of motion or the 2-day notice to dissolve or modify a temporary restraining order may work out so as to cause embarrassing delay in urgent cases. The delay can be obviated by applying to the court to shorten the time, see Rules 6(d) and 65(b).

Subdivision (b). The prohibition against extending the time for taking action under Rule 25 (Substitution of parties) is eliminated. The only limitation of time provided for in amended Rule 25 is the 90-day period following a suggestion upon the record of the death of a party within which to make a motion to substitute the proper parties for the deceased party. See Rule 25(a)(1), as amended, and the Advisory Committee's Note thereto. It is intended that the court shall have discretion to enlarge that period.

1966 Amendment

P.L. 88–139, § 1, 77 Stat. 248, approved on October 16, 1963, amended 28 U.S.C. § 138 to read as follows: "The district court shall not hold formal terms." Thus Rule 6(c) is rendered unnecessary, and it is rescinded.

1967 Amendment

The amendment eliminates the references to Rule 73, which is to be abrogated.

1971 Amendment

The amendment adds Columbus Day to the list of legal holidays to conform the subdivision to the Act of June 28, 1968, 82 Stat. 250, which constituted Columbus Day a legal holiday effective after January 1, 1971.

The Act, which amended Title 5, U.S.C. § 6103(a), changes the day on which certain holidays are to be observed. Washington's Birthday, Memorial Day and Veterans Day are to be observed on the third Monday in February, the last Monday in May and the fourth Monday in October, respectively, rather than, as heretofore, on February 22, May 30, and November 11, respectively, Columbus Day is to be observed on the second Monday in October. New Year's Day, Independence Day, Thanksgiving Day and Christmas continue to be observed on the traditional days.

1983 Amendment

Subdivision (b). The amendment confers finality upon the judgments of magistrates by foreclosing enlargement of the time for appeal except as provided in new Rule 74(a) (20 day period for demonstration of excusable neglect).

1985 Amendment

Rule 6(a) is amended to acknowledge that weather conditions or other events may render the clerk's office inaccessible one or more days. Parties who are obliged to file something with the court during that period should not be penalized if they cannot do so. The amendment conforms to changes made in Federal Rule of Criminal Procedure 45(a), effective August 1, 1982.

The Rule also is amended to extend the exclusion of intermediate Saturdays, Sundays, and legal holidays to the computation of time periods less than 11 days. Under the current version of the Rule, parties bringing motions under rules with 10-day periods could have as few as 5 working days to prepare their motions. This hardship would be especially acute in the case of Rules 50(b) and (c)(2), 52(b), and 59(b), (d), and (e), which may not be enlarged at the discretion of the court. See Rule 6(b). If the exclusion of Saturdays, Sundays, and legal holidays will operate to cause excessive delay in urgent cases, the delay can be obviated by applying to the court to shorten the time. See Rule 6(b).

The Birthday of Martin Luther King, Jr., which becomes a legal holiday effective in 1986, has been added to the list of legal holidays enumerated in the Rule.

1987 Amendment

The amendments are technical. No substantive change is intended.

1999 Amendment

The reference to Rule 74(a) is stricken from the catalogue of time periods that cannot be extended by the district court. The change reflects the 1997 abrogation of Rule 74(a).

Rule 6 RULES OF CIVIL PROCEDURE

2001 Amendment

The additional three days provided by Rule 6(e) is extended to the means of service authorized by the new paragraph (D) added to Rule 5(b), including—with the consent of the person served—service by electronic or other means. The three-day addition is provided as well for service on a person with no known address by leaving a copy with the clerk of the court.

Changes Made After Publication and Comments

Proposed Rule 6(e) is the same as the "alternative proposal" that was published in August 1999.

2005 Amendment

Rule 6(e) is amended to remove any doubt as to the method for extending the time to respond after service by mail, leaving with the clerk of court, electronic means, or other means consented to by the party served. Three days are added after the prescribed period otherwise expires under Rule 6(a). Intermediate Saturdays, Sundays, and legal holidays are included in counting these added three days. If the third day is a Saturday, Sunday, or legal holiday, the last day to act is the next day that is not a Saturday, Sunday, or legal holiday. The effect of invoking the day when the prescribed period would otherwise expire under Rule 6(a) can be illustrated by assuming that the thirtieth day of a thirty-day period is a Saturday. Under Rule 6(a) the period expires on the next day that is not a Sunday or legal holiday. If the following Monday is a legal holiday, under Rule 6(a) the period expires on Tuesday. Three days are then added—Wednesday, Thursday, and Friday as the third and final day to act. If the period prescribed expires on a Friday, the three added days are Saturday, Sunday, and Monday, which is the third and final day to act unless it is a legal holiday. If Monday is a legal holiday, the next day that is not a legal holiday is the third and final day to act.

Application of Rule 6(e) to a period that is less than eleven days can be illustrated by a paper that is served by mailing on a Friday. If ten days are allowed to respond, intermediate Saturdays, Sundays, and legal holidays are excluded in determining when the period expires under Rule 6(a). If there is no legal holiday, the period expires on the Friday two weeks after the paper was mailed. The three added Rule 6(e) days are Saturday, Sunday, and Monday, which is the third and final day to act unless it is a legal holiday. If Monday is a legal holiday, the next day that is not a legal holiday is the final day to act.

2007 Amendment

The language of Rule 6 has been amended as part of the general restyling of the Civil Rules to make them more easily understood and to make style and terminology consistent throughout the rules. These changes are intended to be stylistic only.

2009 Amendment

Subdivision (a). Subdivision (a) has been amended to simplify and clarify the provisions that describe how deadlines are computed. Subdivision (a) governs the computation of any time period found in these rules, in any local rule or court order, or in any statute that does not specify a method of computing time. In accordance with Rule 83(a)(1), a local rule may not direct that a deadline be computed in a manner inconsistent with subdivision (a).

The time-computation provisions of subdivision (a) apply only when a time period must be computed. They do not apply when a fixed time to act is set. The amendments thus carry forward the approach taken in *Violette v. P.A. Days, Inc.*, 427 F.3d 1015, 1016 (6th Cir. 2005) (holding that Civil Rule 6(a) "does not apply to situations where the court has established a specific calendar day as a deadline"), and reject the contrary holding of *In re American Healthcare Management, Inc.*, 900 F.2d 827, 832 (5th Cir. 1990) (holding that Bankruptcy Rule 9006(a) governs treatment of date-certain deadline set by court order). If, for example, the date for filing is "no later than November 1, 2007," subdivision (a) does not govern. But if a filing is required to be made "within 10 days" or "within 72 hours," subdivision (a) describes how that deadline is computed.

Subdivision (a) does not apply when computing a time period set by a statute if the statute specifies a method of computing time. *See, e.g.*, 2 U.S.C. § 394 (specifying method for computing time periods prescribed by certain statutory provisions relating to contested elections to the House of Representatives).

Subdivision (a)(1). New subdivision (a)(1) addresses the computation of time periods that are stated in days. It also applies to time periods that are stated in weeks, months, or years. *See, e.g.*, Rule 60(c)(1). Subdivision (a)(1)(B)'s directive to "count every day" is relevant only if the period is stated in days (not weeks, months or years).

Under former Rule 6(a), a period of 11 days or more was computed differently than a period of less than 11 days. Intermediate Saturdays, Sundays, and legal holidays were included in computing the longer periods, but excluded in computing the shorter periods. Former Rule 6(a) thus made computing deadlines unnecessarily complicated and led to counterintuitive results. For example, a 10-day period and a 14-day period that started on the same day usually ended on the same day—and the 10-day period not infrequently ended later than the 14-day period. *See Miltimore Sales, Inc. v. Int'l Rectifier, Inc.*, 412 F.3d 685, 686 (6th Cir. 2005).

Under new subdivision (a)(1), all deadlines stated in days (no matter the length) are computed in the same way. The day of the event that triggers the deadline is not counted. All other days—including intermediate Saturdays, Sundays, and legal holidays—are counted, with only one exception: If the period ends on a Saturday, Sunday, or legal holiday, then the deadline falls on the next day that is not a Saturday, Sunday, or legal holiday. An illustration is provided below in the discussion of subdivision (a)(5). Subdivision (a)(3) addresses filing deadlines that expire on a day when the clerk's office is inaccessible.

Where subdivision (a) formerly referred to the "act, event, or default" that triggers the deadline, new subdivision (a) refers simply to the "event" that triggers the deadline; this change in terminology is adopted for brevity and simplicity, and is not intended to change meaning.

Periods previously expressed as less than 11 days will be shortened as a practical matter by the decision to count intermediate Saturdays, Sundays, and legal holidays in computing all periods. Many of those periods have been lengthened to compensate for the change. *See, e.g.*, Rule 14(a)(1).

Most of the 10-day periods were adjusted to meet the change in computation method by setting 14 days as the new period. A 14-day period corresponds to the most frequent result of a 10-day period under the former computation method—two Saturdays and two Sundays were excluded, giving 14 days in all. A 14–day period has an additional advantage. The final day falls on the same day of the week as the event that triggered the period—the 14th day after a Monday, for example, is a Monday. This advantage of using week-long periods led to adopting 7–day periods to replace some of the periods set at less than 10 days, and 21–day periods to replace 20–day periods. Thirty-day and longer periods, however, were generally retained without change.

Subdivision (a)(2). New subdivision (a)(2) addresses the computation of time periods that are stated in hours. No such deadline currently appears in the Federal Rules of Civil Procedure. But some statutes contain deadlines stated in hours, as do some court orders issued in expedited proceedings.

Under subdivision (a)(2), a deadline stated in hours starts to run immediately on the occurrence of the event that triggers the deadline. The deadline generally ends when the time expires. If, however, the time period expires at a specific time (say, 2:17 p.m.) on a Saturday, Sunday, or legal holiday, then the deadline is extended to the same time (2:17 p.m.) on the next day that is not a Saturday, Sunday, or legal holiday. Periods stated in hours are not to be "rounded up" to the next whole hour. Subdivision (a)(3) addresses situations when the clerk's office is inaccessible during the last hour before a filing deadline expires.

Subdivision (a)(2)(B) directs that every hour be counted. Thus, for example, a 72–hour period that commences at 10:23 a.m. on Friday, November 2, 2007, will run until 9:23 a.m. on Monday, November 5; the discrepancy in start and end times in this example results from the intervening shift from daylight saving time to standard time.

Subdivision (a)(3). When determining the last day of a filing period stated in days or a longer unit of time, a day on which the clerk's office is not accessible because of the weather or another reason is treated like a Saturday, Sunday, or legal holiday. When determining the end of a filing period stated in hours, if the clerk's office is inaccessible during the last hour of the filing period computed under subdivision (a)(2) then the period is extended to the same time on the next day that is not a weekend, holiday, or day when the clerk's office is inaccessible.

Subdivision (a)(3)'s extensions apply "[u]nless the court orders otherwise." In some circumstances, the court might not wish a period of inaccessibility to trigger a full 24–hour extension; in those instances, the court can specify a briefer extension.

The text of the rule no longer refers to "weather or other conditions" as the reason for the inaccessibility of the clerk's office. The reference to "weather" was deleted from the text to underscore that inaccessibility can occur for reasons unrelated to weather, such as an outage of the electronic filing system. Weather can still be a reason for inaccessibility of the clerk's office. The rule does not attempt to define inaccessibility. Rather, the concept will continue to develop through caselaw, *see, e.g.*, William G. Phelps, *When Is Office of Clerk of Court Inaccessible Due to Weather or Other Conditions for Purpose of Computing Time Period for Filing Papers under Rule 6(a) of Federal Rules of Civil Procedure*, 135 A.L.R. Fed. 259 (1996) (collecting cases). In addition, many local provisions address inaccessibility for purposes of electronic filing, *see, e.g.*, D. Kan. Rule 5.4.11 ("A Filing User whose filing is made untimely as the result of a technical failure may seek appropriate relief from the court.").

Subdivision (a)(4). New subdivision (a)(4) defines the end of the last day of a period for purposes of subdivision (a)(1). Subdivision (a)(4) does not apply in computing periods stated in hours under subdivision (a)(2), and does not apply if a different time is set by a statute, local rule, or order in the case. A local rule may, for example, address the problems that might arise if a single district has clerk's offices in different time zones, or provide that papers filed in a drop box after the normal hours of the clerk's office are filed as of the day that is date-stamped on the papers by a device in the drop box.

28 U.S.C. § 452 provides that "[a]ll courts of the United States shall be deemed always open for the purpose of filing proper papers, issuing and returning process, and making motions and orders." A corresponding provision exists in Rule 77(a). Some courts have held that these provisions permit an after-hours filing by handing the papers to an appropriate official. *See, e.g., Casalduc v. Diaz*, 117 F.2d 915, 917 (1st Cir. 1941). Subdivision (a)(4) does not address the effect of the statute on the question of after-hours filing; instead, the rule is designed to deal with filings in the ordinary course without regard to Section 452.

Subdivision (a)(5). New subdivision (a)(5) defines the "next" day for purposes of subdivisions (a)(1)(C) and (a)(2)(C). The Federal Rules of Civil Procedure contain both forward-looking time periods and backward-looking time periods. A forward-looking time period requires something to be done within a period of time *after* an event. *See, e.g.*, Rule 59(b) (motion for new trial "must be filed no later than 28 days after entry of the judgment"). A backward-looking time period requires something to be done within a period of time *before* an event. *See, e.g.*, Rule 26(f) (parties must hold Rule 26(f) conference "as soon as practicable and in any event at least 21 days before a scheduling conference is held or a scheduling order is due under Rule 16(b)"). In determining what is the "next" day for purposes of subdivisions (a)(1)(C) and (a)(2)(C), one should continue counting in the same direction—that is, forward when computing a forward-looking period and backward when computing a backward-looking period. If, for example, a filing is due within 30 days *after* an event, and the thirtieth day falls on Saturday, September 1, 2007, then the filing is due on Tuesday, September 4, 2007 (Monday, September 3, is Labor Day). But if a filing is due 21 days *before* an event, and the twenty-first day falls on Saturday, September 1, then the filing is due on Friday, August 31. If the clerk's office is inaccessible on August 31, then subdivision (a)(3) extends the filing deadline forward to the next accessible day that is not a Saturday, Sunday, or legal holiday—no later than Tuesday, September 4.

Subdivision (a)(6). New subdivision (a)(6) defines "legal holiday" for purposes of the Federal Rules of Civil Procedure, including the time-computation provisions of subdivision (a). Subdivision (a)(6) continues to include within the definition of "legal holiday" days that are declared a holiday by the President or Congress.

For forward-counted periods—*i.e.*, periods that are measured after an event—subdivision (a)(6)(C) includes certain state holidays within the definition of legal holidays. However, state legal holidays are not recognized in computing backward-counted periods. For both forward- and backward-counted periods, the rule thus protects those who may be unsure of the effect of state holidays. For forward-counted deadlines, treating state holidays the same as federal holidays extends the deadline. Thus, someone who thought that the federal courts might be closed on a state holiday would be safeguarded against an inadvertent late filing. In contrast, for backward-counted deadlines, not giving state holidays the treatment of federal holidays allows filing on the state holiday itself rather than the day before. Take, for example, Monday, April 21, 2008 (Patriot's Day, a legal holiday in the relevant state). If a filing is due 14 days after an event, and the fourteenth day is April 21, then the filing is due on Tuesday, April 22 because Monday, April 21 counts as a legal holiday. But if a filing is due 14 days before an event, and the fourteenth day is April 21, the filing is due on Monday, April 21; the fact that April 21 is a state holiday does not make April 21 a legal holiday for purposes of computing this backward-counted deadline. But note that if the clerk's office is inaccessible on Monday, April 21, then subdivision (a)(3) extends the April 21 filing deadline forward to the next accessible day that is not a Saturday, Sunday or legal holiday—no earlier than Tuesday, April 22.

[Subdivision (b)(2), (c)] The times set in the former rule at 1 or 5 days have been revised to 7 or 14 days. See the Note to Rule 6.

2016 Amendment

Rule 6(d) is amended to remove service by electronic means under Rule 5(b)(2)(E) from the modes of service that allow 3 added days to act after being served.

Rule 5(b)(2) was amended in 2001 to provide for service by electronic means. Although electronic transmission seemed virtually instantaneous even then, electronic service was included in the modes of service that allow 3 added days to act after being served. There were concerns that the transmission might be delayed for some time, and particular concerns that incompatible systems might make it difficult or impossible to open attachments. Those concerns have been substantially alleviated by advances in technology and in widespread skill in using electronic transmission.

A parallel reason for allowing the 3 added days was that electronic service was authorized only with the consent of the person to be served. Concerns about the reliability of electronic transmission might have led to refusals of consent; the 3 added days were calculated to alleviate these concerns.

Diminution of the concerns that prompted the decision to allow the 3 added days for electronic transmission is not the only reason for discarding this indulgence. Many rules have been changed to ease the task of computing time by adopting 7-, 14-, 21-, and 28-day periods that allow "day-of-the-week" counting. Adding 3 days at the end complicated the counting, and increased the occasions for further complication by invoking the provisions that apply when the last day is a Saturday, Sunday, or legal holiday.

Electronic service after business hours, or just before or during a weekend or holiday, may result in a practical reduction in the time available to respond. Extensions of time may be warranted to prevent prejudice.

Eliminating Rule 5(b) subparagraph (2)(E) from the modes of service that allow 3 added days means that the 3 added days cannot be retained by consenting to service by electronic means. Consent to electronic service in registering for electronic case filing, for example, does not count as consent to

service "by any other means" of delivery under subparagraph (F).

What is now Rule 6(d) was amended in 2005 "to remove any doubt as to the method for calculating the time to respond after service by mail, leaving with the clerk of court, electronic means, or by other means consented to by the party served." A potential ambiguity was created by substituting "after service" for the earlier references to acting after service "upon the party" if a paper or notice "is served upon the party" by the specified means. "[A]fter service" could be read to refer not only to a party that has been served but also to a party that has made service. That reading would mean that a party who is allowed a specified time to act after making service can extend the time by choosing one of the means of service specified in the rule, something that was never intended by the original rule or the amendment. Rules setting a time to act after making service include Rules 14(a)(1), 15(a)(1)(A), and 38(b)(1). "[A]fter being served" is substituted for "after service" to dispel any possible misreading.

HISTORICAL NOTES

Effective and Applicability Provisions

1946 Amendments. Effective date of amendment to this rule, see rule 86(b).

CROSS REFERENCES

Answer to,

    Complaint, see Fed.Rules Civ.Proc. Rule 12, 28 USCA.

    Cross-claim, see Fed.Rules Civ.Proc. Rule 12, 28 USCA.

    Interrogatories, see Fed.Rules Civ.Proc. Rule 33, 28 USCA.

Answers and objections to admissions, see Fed.Rules Civ. Proc. Rule 36, 28 USCA.

Demand for jury trial, see Fed.Rules Civ.Proc. Rule 38, 28 USCA.

Motion for,

    Amendment of findings, see Fed.Rules Civ.Proc. Rule 52, 28 USCA.

    New trial, see Fed.Rules Civ.Proc. Rule 59, 28 USCA.

    Relief from judgment or order, see Fed.Rules Civ.Proc. Rule 60, 28 USCA.

Motion to,

    Alter or amend judgment, see Fed.Rules Civ.Proc. Rule 59, 28 USCA.

    Set aside verdict and enter judgment, see Fed.Rules Civ.Proc. Rule 50, 28 USCA.

Notice of appeal, see 28 USCA § 2107.

Objections to interrogatories, see Fed.Rules Civ.Proc. Rule 33, 28 USCA.

Reply to counterclaim, see Fed.Rules Civ.Proc. Rule 12, 28 USCA.

Service by mail complete upon mailing, see Fed.Rules Civ.Proc. Rule 5, 28 USCA.

Substitution of parties, see Fed.Rules Civ.Proc. Rule 25, 28 USCA.

TITLE III. PLEADINGS AND MOTIONS

Rule 7. Pleadings Allowed; Form of Motions and Other Papers

(a) **Pleadings.** Only these pleadings are allowed:

(1) a complaint;

(2) an answer to a complaint;

(3) an answer to a counterclaim designated as a counterclaim;

(4) an answer to a crossclaim;

(5) a third-party complaint;

(6) an answer to a third-party complaint; and

(7) if the court orders one, a reply to an answer.

(b) **Motions and Other Papers.**

(1) *In General.* A request for a court order must be made by motion. The motion must:

(A) be in writing unless made during a hearing or trial;

(B) state with particularity the grounds for seeking the order; and

(C) state the relief sought.

(2) *Form.* The rules governing captions and other matters of form in pleadings apply to motions and other papers.

(Amended December 27, 1946, effective March 19, 1948; January 21, 1963, effective July 1, 1963; April 28, 1983, effective August 1, 1983; April 30, 2007, effective December 1, 2007.)

ADVISORY COMMITTEE NOTES

1937 Adoption

1. A provision designating pleadings and defining a motion is common in the state practice acts. See Smith-Hurd Ill. Stats. ch. 110, § 156 (Designation and order of pleadings); 2 Minn.Stat. (Mason, 1927) § 9246 (Definition of motion); and N.Y.C.P.A. (1937) § 113 (Definition of motion). Former Equity Rules 18 (Pleadings—Technical Forms Abrogated), 29 (Defenses—How Presented), and 33 (Testing Sufficiency of Defense) abolished technical forms of pleading, demurrers and pleas, and exceptions for insufficiency of an answer.

2. **Note to Subdivision (a).** This preserves the substance of [former] Equity Rule 31 (Reply—When Required—When Cause at Issue). Compare the English practice, *English Rules under the Judicature Act* (The Annual Practice, 1937) O. 23, r.r. 1, 2 (Reply to counterclaim; amended, 1933, to be subject to the rules applicable to defenses, O. 21). See O. 21, r.r. 1–14; O. 27, r. 13 (When pleadings deemed denied and put in issue). Under the codes the pleadings are generally limited. A reply is sometimes required to an affirmative defense in the answer. 1 Colo.Stat.Ann. (1935) § 66; Ore.Code Ann. (1930) §§ 1–614, 1–616. In other jurisdictions no reply is necessary to an affirmative defense in the answer, but a reply may be ordered by the court. N.C.Code Ann. (1935) § 525; 1 S.D.Comp.Laws (1929) § 2357. A reply to a counterclaim is usually required. Ark.Civ.Code (Crawford, 1934) §§ 123 to 125; Wis.Stat. (1935) §§ 263.20, 263.21. U.S.C. Title 28, [former] § 45 (District courts; practice and procedure in certain cases) is modified insofar as it may dispense with a reply to a counterclaim.

For amendment of pleadings, see Rule 15 dealing with amended and supplemental pleadings.

3. All statutes which use the words "petition", "bill of complaint", "plea", "demurrer", and other such terminology are modified in form by this rule.

1946 Amendment

Note. This amendment eliminates any question as to whether the compulsory reply, where a counterclaim is pleaded, is a reply only to the counterclaim or is a general reply to the answer containing the counterclaim. The Commentary, *Scope of Reply where Defendant Has Pleaded Counterclaim,* 1939, 1 Fed.Rules Serv. 672; *Fort Chartres and Ivy Landing Drainage and Levee District No. Five v. Thompson,* Ill.1945, 8 Fed.Rules Serv. 13.32, Case 1.

1963 Amendment

Certain redundant words are eliminated and the subdivision is modified to reflect the amendment of Rule 14(a) which in certain cases eliminates the requirement of obtaining leave to bring in a third-party defendant.

1983 Amendment

One of the reasons sanctions against improper motion practice have been employed infrequently is the lack of clarity of Rule 7. That rule has stated only generally that the pleading requirements relating to captions, signing, and other matters of form also apply to motions and other papers. The addition of Rule 7(b)(3) makes explicit the applicability of the signing requirement and the sanctions of Rule 11, which have been amplified.

2007 Amendment

The language of Rule 7 has been amended as part of the general restyling of the Civil Rules to make them more easily understood and to make style and terminology consistent throughout the rules. These changes are intended to be stylistic only.

Former Rule 7(a) stated that "there shall be * * * an answer to a cross-claim, if the answer contains a cross-claim * * *." Former Rule 12(a)(2) provided more generally that "[a] party served with a pleading stating a cross-claim against that party shall serve an answer thereto * * *." New Rule 7(a) corrects this inconsistency by providing for an answer to a crossclaim.

For the first time, Rule 7(a)(7) expressly authorizes the court to order a reply to a counterclaim answer. A reply may be as useful in this setting as a reply to an answer, a third-party answer, or a crossclaim answer.

Former Rule 7(b)(1) stated that the writing requirement is fulfilled if the motion is stated in a written notice of hearing. This statement was deleted as redundant because a single written document can satisfy the writing requirements both for a motion and for a Rule 6(c)(1) notice.

The cross-reference to Rule 11 in former Rule 7(b)(3) is deleted as redundant. Rule 11 applies by its own terms. The force and application of Rule 11 are not diminished by the deletion.

Former Rule 7(c) is deleted because it has done its work. If a motion or pleading is described as a demurrer, plea, or exception for insufficiency, the court will treat the paper as if properly captioned.

HISTORICAL NOTES
Effective and Applicability Provisions

1946 Amendments. Effective date of amendment to this rule, see rule 86(b).

CROSS REFERENCES

Procedure for motions in local practice, see Fed.Rules Civ.Proc. Rule 83, 28 USCA.

Service and filing of pleadings and other papers, see Fed. Rules Civ.Proc. Rule 5, 28 USCA.

Third-party practice, generally, see Fed.Rules Civ.Proc. Rule 14, 28 USCA.

Time for service of,

    Answer or reply, see Fed.Rules Civ.Proc. Rule 12, 28 USCA.

    Motions and affidavits, see Fed.Rules Civ.Proc. Rule 6, 28 USCA.

Treating defenses as counterclaims, see Fed.Rules Civ. Proc. Rule 8, 28 USCA.

Rule 7.1.   Disclosure Statement

(a) Who Must File; Contents. A nongovernmental corporate party must file two copies of a disclosure statement that:

    (1) identifies any parent corporation and any publicly held corporation owning 10% or more of its stock; or

    (2) states that there is no such corporation.

(b) Time to File; Supplemental Filing. A party must:

    (1) file the disclosure statement with its first appearance, pleading, petition, motion, response, or other request addressed to the court; and

    (2) promptly file a supplemental statement if any required information changes.

(Adopted April 29, 2002, effective December 1, 2002; April 30, 2007, effective December 1, 2007.)

ADVISORY COMMITTEE NOTES
2002 Adoption

Rule 7.1 is drawn from Rule 26.1 of the Federal Rules of Appellate Procedure, with changes to adapt to the circumstances of district courts that dictate different provisions for the time of filing, number of copies, and the like. The information required by Rule 7.1(a) reflects the "financial interest" standard of Canon 3C(1)(c) of the Code of Conduct for United States Judges. This information will support properly informed disqualification decisions in situations that call for automatic disqualification under Canon 3C(1)(c). It does not cover all of the circumstances that may call for disqualification

under the financial interest standard, and does not deal at all with other circumstances that may call for disqualification.

Although the disclosures required by Rule 7.1(a) may seem limited, they are calculated to reach a majority of the circumstances that are likely to call for disqualification on the basis of financial information that a judge may not know or recollect. Framing a rule that calls for more detailed disclosure will be difficult. Unnecessary disclosure requirements place a burden on the parties and on courts. Unnecessary disclosure of volumes of information may create a risk that a judge will overlook the one bit of information that might require disqualification, and also may create a risk that unnecessary disqualifications will be made rather than attempt to unravel a potentially difficult question. It has not been feasible to dictate more detailed disclosure requirements in Rule 7.1(a).

Rule 7.1 does not prohibit local rules that require disclosures in addition to those required by Rule 7.1. Developing experience with local disclosure practices and advances in electronic technology may provide a foundation for adopting more detailed disclosure requirements by future amendments of Rule 7.1.

Changes Made After Publication and Comment. The provisions that would require disclosure of additional information that may be required by the Judicial Conference have been deleted.

2007 Amendment

The language of Rule 7.1 has been amended as part of the general restyling of the Civil Rules to make them more easily understood and to make style and terminology consistent throughout the rules. These changes are intended to be stylistic only.

Rule 8.   General Rules of Pleading

(a) Claim for Relief. A pleading that states a claim for relief must contain:

    (1) a short and plain statement of the grounds for the court's jurisdiction, unless the court already has jurisdiction and the claim needs no new jurisdictional support;

    (2) a short and plain statement of the claim showing that the pleader is entitled to relief; and

    (3) a demand for the relief sought, which may include relief in the alternative or different types of relief.

(b) Defenses; Admissions and Denials.

    (1) *In General.* In responding to a pleading, a party must:

        (A) state in short and plain terms its defenses to each claim asserted against it; and

        (B) admit or deny the allegations asserted against it by an opposing party.

    (2) *Denials—Responding to the Substance.* A denial must fairly respond to the substance of the allegation.

    (3) *General and Specific Denials.* A party that intends in good faith to deny all the allegations of a pleading—including the jurisdictional grounds—may do so by a general denial. A party that does not

intend to deny all the allegations must either specifically deny designated allegations or generally deny all except those specifically admitted.

(4) *Denying Part of an Allegation.* A party that intends in good faith to deny only part of an allegation must admit the part that is true and deny the rest.

(5) *Lacking Knowledge or Information.* A party that lacks knowledge or information sufficient to form a belief about the truth of an allegation must so state, and the statement has the effect of a denial.

(6) *Effect of Failing to Deny.* An allegation—other than one relating to the amount of damages—is admitted if a responsive pleading is required and the allegation is not denied. If a responsive pleading is not required, an allegation is considered denied or avoided.

(c) Affirmative Defenses.

(1) *In General.* In responding to a pleading, a party must affirmatively state any avoidance or affirmative defense, including:

- accord and satisfaction;
- arbitration and award;
- assumption of risk;
- contributory negligence;
- duress;
- estoppel;
- failure of consideration;
- fraud;
- illegality;
- injury by fellow servant;
- laches;
- license;
- payment;
- release;
- res judicata;
- statute of frauds;
- statute of limitations; and
- waiver.

(2) *Mistaken Designation.* If a party mistakenly designates a defense as a counterclaim, or a counterclaim as a defense, the court must, if justice requires, treat the pleading as though it were correctly designated, and may impose terms for doing so.

(d) Pleading to Be Concise and Direct; Alternative Statements; Inconsistency.

(1) *In General.* Each allegation must be simple, concise, and direct. No technical form is required.

(2) *Alternative Statements of a Claim or Defense.* A party may set out 2 or more statements of a claim or defense alternatively or hypothetically, either in a single count or defense or in separate ones. If a party makes alternative statements, the pleading is sufficient if any one of them is sufficient.

(3) *Inconsistent Claims or Defenses.* A party may state as many separate claims or defenses as it has, regardless of consistency.

(e) Construing Pleadings. Pleadings must be construed so as to do justice.

(Amended February 28, 1966, effective July 1, 1966; March 2, 1987, effective August 1, 1987; April 30, 2007, effective December 1, 2007; April 28, 2010, effective December 1, 2010.)

ADVISORY COMMITTEE NOTES

1937 Adoption

Note to Subdivision (a). See [former] Equity Rules 25 (Bill of Complaint—Contents), and 30 (Answer—Contents—Counterclaim). Compare 2 Ind.Stat.Ann. (Burns, 1933) §§ 2–1004, 2–1015; 2 Ohio Gen.Code Ann. (Page, 1926) §§ 11305, 11314; Utah Rev.Stat.Ann. (1933) §§ 104–7–2, 104–9–1.

See Rule 19(c) for the requirement of a statement in a claim for relief of the names of persons who ought to be parties and the reason for their omission.

See Rule 23(b) for particular requirements as to the complaint in a secondary action by shareholders.

Note to Subdivision (b). 1. This rule supersedes the methods of pleading prescribed in U.S.C., Title 19, § 508 (Persons making seizures pleading general issue and proving special matter); U.S.C. Title 35, [former] §§ 40d (Proving under general issue, upon notice, that a statement in application for an extended patent is not true), 69 [now 282] (Pleading and proof in actions for infringement) and similar statutes.

2. This rule is, in part, [former] Equity Rule 30 (Answer—Contents—Counterclaim), with the matter on denials largely from the Connecticut practice. See Conn. Practice Book (1934) §§ 107, 108, and 122; Conn.Gen.Stat. (1930) §§ 5508 to 5514. Compare the English practice, *English Rules Under the Judicature Act* (The Annual Practice, 1937) O. 19, r.r. 17–20.

Note to Subdivision (c). This follows substantially *English Rules Under the Judicature Act* (The Annual Practice, 1937) O. 19, r. 15 and N.Y.C.P.A. (1937) § 242, with "surprise" omitted in this rule.

Note to Subdivision (d). The first sentence is similar to former Equity Rule 30 (Answer—Contents—Counterclaim). For the second sentence see former Equity Rule 31 (Reply—When Required—When Cause at Issue). This is similar to *English Rules Under the Judicature Act* (The Annual Practice, 1937) O. 19, r.r. 13, 18; and to the practice of the States.

Note to Subdivision (e). This rule is an elaboration upon [former] Equity Rule 30 (Answer—Contents—Counterclaim), plus a statement of the actual practice under some codes. Compare also [former] Equity Rule 18 (Pleadings—Technical Forms Abrogated). See Clark, *Code Pleading* (1928), pp. 171–4, 432–5; Hankin, *Alternative and Hypothetical Pleading* (1924), 33 Yale L.J. 365.

Note to Subdivision (f). A provision of like import is of frequent occurrence in the codes. Smith-Hurd Ill.Stats. ch. 110, § 157(3); 2 Minn.Stat. (Mason, 1927) § 9266; N.Y.C.P.A. (1937) § 275; 2 N.D.Comp.Laws Ann. (1913) § 7458.

1966 Amendment

The change here is consistent with the broad purposes of unification.

1987 Amendment

The amendments are technical. No substantive change is intended.

2007 Amendment

The language of Rule 8 has been amended as part of the general restyling of the Civil Rules to make them more easily understood and to make style and terminology consistent throughout the rules. These changes are intended to be stylistic only.

The former Rule 8(b) and 8(e) cross-references to Rule 11 are deleted as redundant. Rule 11 applies by its own terms. The force and application of Rule 11 are not diminished by the deletion.

Former Rule 8(b) required a pleader denying part of an averment to "specify so much of it as is true and material and * * * deny only the remainder." "[A]nd material" is deleted to avoid the implication that it is proper to deny something that the pleader believes to be true but not material.

Deletion of former Rule 8(e)(2)'s "whether based on legal, equitable, or maritime grounds" reflects the parallel deletions in Rule 1 and elsewhere. Merger is now successfully accomplished.

2010 Amendment

Subdivision (c)(1). "[D]ischarge in bankruptcy" is deleted from the list of affirmative defenses. Under 11 U.S.C. § 524(a)(1) and (2) a discharge voids a judgment to the extent that it determines a personal liability of the debtor with respect to a discharged debt. The discharge also operates as an injunction against commencement or continuation of an action to collect, recover, or offset a discharged debt. For these reasons it is confusing to describe discharge as an affirmative defense. But § 524(a) applies only to a claim that was actually discharged. Several categories of debt set out in 11 U.S.C. § 523(a) are excepted from discharge. The issue whether a claim was excepted from discharge may be determined either in the court that entered the discharge or—in most instances—in another court with jurisdiction over the creditor's claim.

CROSS REFERENCES

Amendment of pleadings, generally, see Fed.Rules Civ. Proc. Rule 15, 28 USCA.

Defenses in law or fact, how presented, see Fed.Rules Civ.Proc. Rule 12, 28 USCA.

Joinder of claims, see Fed.Rules Civ.Proc. Rule 18, 28 USCA.

Relief granted in judgment even if not demanded, see Fed.Rules Civ.Proc. Rule 54, 28 USCA.

Reply to counterclaims denominated as such, see Fed.Rules Civ.Proc. Rule 7, 28 USCA.

Rule 9.   Pleading Special Matters

(a) Capacity or Authority to Sue; Legal Existence.

    (1) *In General.* Except when required to show that the court has jurisdiction, a pleading need not allege:

       (A) a party's capacity to sue or be sued;

       (B) a party's authority to sue or be sued in a representative capacity; or

       (C) the legal existence of an organized association of persons that is made a party.

    (2) *Raising Those Issues.* To raise any of those issues, a party must do so by a specific denial, which must state any supporting facts that are peculiarly within the party's knowledge.

(b) Fraud or Mistake; Conditions of Mind. In alleging fraud or mistake, a party must state with particularity the circumstances constituting fraud or mistake. Malice, intent, knowledge, and other conditions of a person's mind may be alleged generally.

(c) Conditions Precedent. In pleading conditions precedent, it suffices to allege generally that all conditions precedent have occurred or been performed. But when denying that a condition precedent has occurred or been performed, a party must do so with particularity.

(d) Official Document or Act. In pleading an official document or official act, it suffices to allege that the document was legally issued or the act legally done.

(e) Judgment. In pleading a judgment or decision of a domestic or foreign court, a judicial or quasi-judicial tribunal, or a board or officer, it suffices to plead the judgment or decision without showing jurisdiction to render it.

(f) Time and Place. An allegation of time or place is material when testing the sufficiency of a pleading.

(g) Special Damages. If an item of special damage is claimed, it must be specifically stated.

(h) Admiralty or Maritime Claim.

    (1) *How Designated.* If a claim for relief is within the admiralty or maritime jurisdiction and also within the court's subject-matter jurisdiction on some other ground, the pleading may designate the claim as an admiralty or maritime claim for purposes of Rules 14(c), 38(e), and 82 and the Supplemental Rules for Admiralty or Maritime Claims and Asset Forfeiture Actions. A claim cognizable only in the admiralty or maritime jurisdiction is an admiralty or maritime claim for those purposes, whether or not so designated.

    (2) *Designation for Appeal.* A case that includes an admiralty or maritime claim within this subdivision (h) is an admiralty case within 28 U.S.C. § 1292(a)(3).

(Amended February 28, 1966, effective July 1, 1966; December 4, 1967, effective July 1, 1968; March 30, 1970, effective July 1, 1970; March 2, 1987, effective August 1, 1987; April 11, 1997, effective December 1, 1997; April 12, 2006, effective December 1, 2006; April 30, 2007, effective December 1, 2007.)

ADVISORY COMMITTEE NOTES

1937 Adoption

Note to Subdivision (a). Compare [former] Equity Rule 25 (Bill of Complaint—Contents) requiring disability to be stated; Utah Rev.Stat.Ann. (1933) § 104–13–15, enumerating a number of situations where a general averment of capacity is sufficient. For provisions governing averment of incorporation, see 2 Minn.Stat. (Mason, 1927) § 9271; N.Y.R.C.P. (1937) Rule 93; 2 N.D.Comp.Laws Ann. (1913) § 7981 et seq.

Note to Subdivision (b). See *English Rules Under the Judicature Act* (The Annual Practice, 1937) O. 19, r. 22.

Note to Subdivision (c). The codes generally have this or a similar provision. See *English Rules Under the Judicature Act* (The Annual Practice, 1937) O. 19, r. 14; 2 Minn.Stat. (Mason, 1927) § 9273; N.Y.R.C.P. (1937) Rule 92; 2 N.D.Comp.Laws Ann. (1913) § 7461; 2 Wash.Rev.Stat.Ann. (Remington, 1932) § 288.

Note to Subdivision (e). The rule expands the usual code provisions on pleading a judgment by including judgments or decisions of administrative tribunals and foreign courts. Compare Ark.Civ.Code (Crawford, 1934) § 141; 2 Minn.Stat. (Mason, 1927) § 9269; N.Y.R.C.P. (1937) Rule 95; 2 Wash. Rev.Stat.Ann. (Remington, 1932) § 287.

1966 Amendment

Certain distinctive features of the admiralty practice must be preserved for what are now suits in admiralty. This raises the question: After unification, when a single form of action is established, how will the counterpart of the present suit in admiralty be identifiable? In part the question is easily answered. Some claims for relief can only be suits in admiralty, either because the admiralty jurisdiction is exclusive or because no nonmaritime ground of federal jurisdiction exists. Many claims, however, are cognizable by the district courts whether asserted in admiralty or in a civil action, assuming the existence of a nonmaritime ground of jurisdiction. Thus at present the pleader has power to determine procedural consequences by the way in which he exercises the classic privilege given by the saving-to-suitors clause (28 U.S.C. § 1333) or by equivalent statutory provisions. For example, a longshoreman's claim for personal injuries suffered by reason of the unseaworthiness of a vessel may be asserted in a suit in admiralty or, if diversity of citizenship exists, in a civil action. One of the important procedural consequences is that in the civil action either party may demand a jury trial, while in the suit in admiralty there is no right to jury trial except as provided by statute.

It is no part of the purpose of unification to inject a right to jury trial into those admiralty cases in which that right is not provided by statute. Similarly as will be more specifically noted below, there is no disposition to change the present law as to interlocutory appeals in admiralty, or as to the venue of suits in admiralty; and, of course, there is no disposition to inject into the civil practice as it now is the distinctively maritime remedies (maritime attachment and garnishment, actions in rem, possessory, petitory and partition actions and limitation of liability). The unified rules must therefore provide some device for preserving the present power of the pleader to determine whether these historically maritime procedures shall be applicable to his claim or not; the pleader must be afforded some means of designating his claim as the counterpart of the present suit in admiralty, where its character as such is not clear.

The problem is different from the similar one concerning the identification of claims that were formerly suits in equity. While that problem is not free from complexities, it is broadly true that the modern counterpart of the suit in equity is distinguishable from the former action at law by the character of the relief sought. This mode of identification is possible in only a limited category of admiralty cases. In large numbers of cases the relief sought in admiralty is simple money damages, indistinguishable from the remedy afforded by the common law. This is true, for example, in the case of the longshoreman's action for personal injuries stated above. After unification has abolished the distinction between civil actions and suits in admiralty, the complaint in such an action would be almost completely ambiguous as to the pleader's intentions regarding the procedure invoked. The allegation of diversity of citizenship might be regarded as a clue indicating an intention to proceed as at present under the saving-to-suitors clause; but this, too, would be ambiguous if there were also reference to the admiralty jurisdiction, and the pleader ought not be required to forego mention of all available jurisdictional grounds.

Other methods of solving the problem were carefully explored, but the Advisory Committee concluded that the preferable solution is to allow the pleader who now has power to determine procedural consequences by filing a suit in admiralty to exercise that power under unification, for the limited instances in which procedural differences will remain, by a simple statement in his pleading to the effect that the claim is an admiralty or maritime claim.

The choice made by the pleader in identifying or in failing to identify his claim as an admiralty or maritime claim is not an irrevocable election. The rule provides that the amendment of a pleading to add or withdraw an identifying statement is subject to the principles of Rule 15.

1968 Amendment

The amendment eliminates the reference to Rule 73 which is to be abrogated and transfers to Rule 9(h) the substance of Subsection (h) of Rule 73 which preserved the right to an interlocutory appeal in admiralty cases which is provided by 28 U.S.C. § 1292(a)(3).

1970 Amendment

The reference to Rule 26(a) is deleted, in light of the transfer of that subdivision to Rule 30(a) and the elimination of the de bene esse procedure therefrom. See the Advisory Committee's note to Rule 30(a).

1987 Amendment

The amendment is technical. No substantive change is intended.

1997 Amendment

Section 1292(a)(3) of the Judicial Code provides for appeal from "[i]nterlocutory decrees of * * * district courts * * * determining the rights and liabilities of the parties to admiralty cases in which appeals from final decrees are allowed."

Rule 9(h) was added in 1966 with the unification of civil and admiralty procedure. Civil Rule 73(h) was amended at the same time to provide that the § 1292(a)(3) reference "to admiralty cases shall be construed to mean admiralty and maritime claims within the meaning of Rule 9(h)." This provision was transferred to Rule 9(h) when the Appellate Rules were adopted.

A single case can include both admiralty or maritime claims and nonadmiralty claims or parties. This combination reveals an ambiguity in the statement in present Rule 9(h) that an admiralty "claim" is an admiralty "case." An order "determining the rights and liabilities of the parties" within the meaning of § 1292(a)(3) may resolve only a nonadmiralty claim, or may simultaneously resolve interdependent admiralty and non-admiralty claims. Can appeal be taken as to the nonadmiralty matter, because it is part of a case that includes an admiralty claim, or is appeal limited to the admiralty claim?

The courts of appeals have not achieved full uniformity in applying the § 1292(a)(3) requirement that an order "determin[e] the rights and liabilities of the parties." It is common to assert that the statute should be construed narrowly, under the general policy that exceptions to the final judgment rule should be construed narrowly. This policy would suggest that the ambiguity should be resolved by limiting the interlocutory appeal right to orders that determine the rights and liabilities of the parties to an admiralty claim.

A broader view is chosen by this amendment for two reasons. The statute applies to admiralty "cases," and may itself provide for appeal from an order that disposes of a nonadmiralty claim that is joined in a single case with an admiralty claim. Although a rule of court may help to clarify and implement a statutory grant of jurisdiction, the line is not always clear between permissible implementation and impermissible withdrawal of jurisdiction. In addition, so long as an order truly disposes of the rights and liabilities of the parties within the meaning of § 1292(a)(3), it may prove important to permit appeal as to the non-admiralty claim. Disposition of the non-admiralty claim, for example, may make it unnecessary to consider the admiralty claim and have the same effect on the case and parties as disposition of the admiralty claim. Or the admiralty and non-admiralty claims may be interdependent. An illustration is provided by Roco Carriers, Ltd. v. M/V Nurnberg Express, 899 F.2d 1292 (2d Cir.1990). Claims for losses of ocean shipments were made against two defendants, one subject to admiralty jurisdiction and the other not. Summary judgment was granted in favor of the admiralty defendant and against the nonadmiralty defendant. The nonadmiralty defendant's appeal was accepted, with the explanation that the determination of its liability was "integrally linked with the determination of non-liability" of the admiralty defendant, and that "section 1292(a)(3) is not limited to admiralty claims; instead, it refers to admiralty cases." 899 F.2d at 1297. The advantages of permitting appeal by the nonadmiralty defendant would be particularly clear if the plaintiff had appealed the summary judgment in favor of the admiralty defendant.

It must be emphasized that this amendment does not rest on any particular assumptions as to the meaning of the § 1292(a)(3) provision that limits interlocutory appeal to orders that determine the rights and liabilities of the parties. It simply reflects the conclusion that so long as the case involves an admiralty claim and an order otherwise meets statutory requirements, the opportunity to appeal should not turn on the circumstance that the order does—or does not—dispose of an admiralty claim. No attempt is made to invoke the authority conferred by 28 U.S.C. § 1292(e) to provide by rule for appeal of an interlocutory decision that is not otherwise provided for by other subsections of § 1292.

GAP Report on Rule 9(h). No changes have been made in the published proposal.

2006 Amendment

Rule 9(h) is amended to conform to the changed title of the Supplemental Rules.

2007 Amendment

The language of Rule 9 has been amended as part of the general restyling of the Civil Rules to make them more easily understood and to make style and terminology consistent throughout the rules. These changes are intended to be stylistic only.

Rule 15 governs pleading amendments of its own force. The former redundant statement that Rule 15 governs an amendment that adds or withdraws a Rule 9(h) designation as an admiralty or maritime claim is deleted. The elimination of paragraph (2) means that "(3)" will be redesignated as "(2)" in Style Rule 9(h).

CROSS REFERENCES

Capacity to sue or be sued, see Fed.Rules Civ.Proc. Rule 17, 28 USCA.

Pleading affirmative defenses, see Fed.Rules Civ.Proc. Rule 8, 28 USCA.

Proof of official record, see Fed.Rules Civ.Proc. Rule 44, 28 USCA.

Rule 10.　Form of Pleadings

(a) Caption; Names of Parties. Every pleading must have a caption with the court's name, a title, a file number, and a Rule 7(a) designation. The title of the complaint must name all the parties; the title of other pleadings, after naming the first party on each side, may refer generally to other parties.

(b) Paragraphs; Separate Statements. A party must state its claims or defenses in numbered paragraphs, each limited as far as practicable to a single set of circumstances. A later pleading may refer by number to a paragraph in an earlier pleading. If doing so would promote clarity, each claim founded on a separate transaction or occurrence—and each defense other than a denial—must be stated in a separate count or defense.

(c) Adoption by Reference; Exhibits. A statement in a pleading may be adopted by reference elsewhere in the same pleading or in any other pleading or motion. A copy of a written instrument that is an exhibit to a pleading is a part of the pleading for all purposes.

(Amended April 30, 2007, effective December 1, 2007.)

ADVISORY COMMITTEE NOTES

1937 Adoption

The first sentence is derived in part from the opening statement of former Equity Rule 25 (Bill of Complaint—Contents). The remainder of the rule is an expansion in conformity with usual state provisions. For numbered paragraphs and separate statements, see Conn.Gen.Stat., 1930,

§ 5513; Smith-Hurd Ill.Stats. ch. 110, § 157(2); N.Y.R.C.P., (1937) Rule 90. For incorporation by reference, see N.Y.R.C.P., (1937) Rule 90. For written instruments as exhibits, see Smith-Hurd Ill.Stats. ch. 110, § 160.

2007 Amendment

The language of Rule 10 has been amended as part of the general restyling of the Civil Rules to make them more easily understood and to make style and terminology consistent throughout the rules. These changes are intended to be stylistic only.

CROSS REFERENCES

Captions in motions and other papers, see Fed.Rules Civ. Proc. Rule 7, 28 USCA.

Rule 11. Signing Pleadings, Motions, and Other Papers; Representations to the Court; Sanctions

(a) Signature. Every pleading, written motion, and other paper must be signed by at least one attorney of record in the attorney's name—or by a party personally if the party is unrepresented. The paper must state the signer's address, e-mail address, and telephone number. Unless a rule or statute specifically states otherwise, a pleading need not be verified or accompanied by an affidavit. The court must strike an unsigned paper unless the omission is promptly corrected after being called to the attorney's or party's attention.

(b) Representations to the Court. By presenting to the court a pleading, written motion, or other paper—whether by signing, filing, submitting, or later advocating it—an attorney or unrepresented party certifies that to the best of the person's knowledge, information, and belief, formed after an inquiry reasonable under the circumstances:

(1) it is not being presented for any improper purpose, such as to harass, cause unnecessary delay, or needlessly increase the cost of litigation;

(2) the claims, defenses, and other legal contentions are warranted by existing law or by a nonfrivolous argument for extending, modifying, or reversing existing law or for establishing new law;

(3) the factual contentions have evidentiary support or, if specifically so identified, will likely have evidentiary support after a reasonable opportunity for further investigation or discovery; and

(4) the denials of factual contentions are warranted on the evidence or, if specifically so identified, are reasonably based on belief or a lack of information.

(c) Sanctions.

(1) *In General.* If, after notice and a reasonable opportunity to respond, the court determines that Rule 11(b) has been violated, the court may impose an appropriate sanction on any attorney, law firm, or party that violated the rule or is responsible for the violation. Absent exceptional circumstances, a law firm must be held jointly responsible for a violation committed by its partner, associate, or employee.

(2) *Motion for Sanctions.* A motion for sanctions must be made separately from any other motion and must describe the specific conduct that allegedly violates Rule 11(b). The motion must be served under Rule 5, but it must not be filed or be presented to the court if the challenged paper, claim, defense, contention, or denial is withdrawn or appropriately corrected within 21 days after service or within another time the court sets. If warranted, the court may award to the prevailing party the reasonable expenses, including attorney's fees, incurred for the motion.

(3) *On the Court's Initiative.* On its own, the court may order an attorney, law firm, or party to show cause why conduct specifically described in the order has not violated Rule 11(b).

(4) *Nature of a Sanction.* A sanction imposed under this rule must be limited to what suffices to deter repetition of the conduct or comparable conduct by others similarly situated. The sanction may include nonmonetary directives; an order to pay a penalty into court; or, if imposed on motion and warranted for effective deterrence, an order directing payment to the movant of part or all of the reasonable attorney's fees and other expenses directly resulting from the violation.

(5) *Limitations on Monetary Sanctions.* The court must not impose a monetary sanction:

(A) against a represented party for violating Rule 11(b)(2); or

(B) on its own, unless it issued the show-cause order under Rule 11(c)(3) before voluntary dismissal or settlement of the claims made by or against the party that is, or whose attorneys are, to be sanctioned.

(6) *Requirements for an Order.* An order imposing a sanction must describe the sanctioned conduct and explain the basis for the sanction.

(d) Inapplicability to Discovery. This rule does not apply to disclosures and discovery requests, responses, objections, and motions under Rules 26 through 37. (Amended April 28, 1983, effective August 1, 1983; March 2, 1987, effective August 1, 1987; April 22, 1993, effective December 1, 1993; April 30, 2007, effective December 1, 2007.)

ADVISORY COMMITTEE NOTES

1937 Adoption

This is substantially the content of [former] Equity Rules 24 (Signature of Counsel) and 21 (Scandal and Impertinence) consolidated and unified. Compare former Equity Rule 36 (Officers Before Whom Pleadings Verified). Compare to similar purposes, *English Rules Under the Judicature Act* (The Annual Practice, 1937) O. 19, r. 4, and *Great Australian Gold Mining Co. v. Martin*, L.R. 5 Ch.Div. 1, 10 (1877). Subscription of pleadings is required in many codes. 2 Minn.

Stat. (Mason, 1927) § 9265; N.Y.R.C.P. (1937) Rule 91; 2 N.D.Comp.Laws Ann. (1913) § 7455.

This rule expressly continues any statute which requires a pleading to be verified or accompanied by an affidavit, such as: U.S.C., Title 28:

§ 381 [former] (Preliminary injunctions and temporary restraining orders)

§ 762 [now 1402] (Suit against the United States)

U.S.C., Title 28, § 829 [now 1927] (Costs; attorney liable for, when) is unaffected by this rule.

For complaints which must be verified under these rules, see Rules 23(b) (Secondary Action by Shareholders) and 65 (Injunctions).

For abolition of former rule in equity that the averments of an answer under oath must be overcome by the testimony of two witnesses or of one witness sustained by corroborating circumstances, see 12 P.S.Pa. § 1222; for the rule in equity itself, see *Greenfield v. Blumenthal,* C.C.A.3, 1934, 69 F.2d 294.

1983 Amendment

Since its original promulgation, Rule 11 has provided for the striking of pleadings and the imposition of disciplinary sanctions to check abuses in the signing of pleadings. Its provisions have always applied to motions and other papers by virtue of incorporation by reference in Rule 7(b)(2). The amendment and the addition of Rule 7(b)(3) expressly confirms this applicability.

Experience shows that in practice Rule 11 has not been effective in deterring abuses. See 6 Wright & Miller, *Federal Practice and Procedure: Civil* § 1334 (1971). There has been considerable confusion as to (1) the circumstances that should trigger striking a pleading or motion or taking disciplinary action, (2) the standard of conduct expected of attorneys who sign pleadings and motions, and (3) the range of available and appropriate sanctions. See Rodes, Ripple & Mooney, *Sanctions Imposable for Violations of the Federal Rules of Civil Procedure* 64–65, Federal Judicial Center (1981). The new language is intended to reduce the reluctance of courts to impose sanctions, see Moore, *Federal Practice* ¶ 7.05, at 1547, by emphasizing the responsibilities of the attorney and reenforcing those obligations by the imposition of sanctions.

The amended rule attempts to deal with the problem by building upon and expanding the equitable doctrine permitting the court to award expenses, including attorney's fees, to a litigant whose opponent acts in bad faith in instituting or conducting litigation. See, e.g., *Roadway Express, Inc. v. Piper,* 447 U.S. 752 (1980); *Hall v. Cole,* 412 U.S. 1, 5 (1973). Greater attention by the district courts to pleading and motion abuses and the imposition of sanctions when appropriate, should discourage dilatory or abusive tactics and help to streamline the litigation process by lessening frivolous claims or defenses.

The expanded nature of the lawyer's certification in the fifth sentence of amended Rule 11 recognizes that the litigation process may be abused for purposes other than delay. See, e.g., *Browning Debenture Holders' Committee v. DASA Corp.,* 560 F.2d 1078 (2d Cir.1977).

The words "good ground to support" the pleading in the original rule were interpreted to have both factual and legal elements. See, e.g., *Heart Disease Research Foundation v. General Motors Corp.,* 15 Fed.R.Serv.2d 1517, 1519 (S.D.N.Y.

1972). They have been replaced by a standard of conduct that is more focused.

The new language stresses the need for some prefiling inquiry into both the facts and the law to satisfy the affirmative duty imposed by the rule. The standard is one of reasonableness under the circumstances. See *Kinee v. Abraham Lincoln Fed. Sav. & Loan Ass'n,* 365 F.Supp. 975 (E.D.Pa.1973). This standard is more stringent than the original good-faith formula and thus it is expected that a greater range of circumstances will trigger its violation. See *Nemeroff v. Abelson,* 620 F.2d 339 (2d Cir.1980).

The rule is not intended to chill an attorney's enthusiasm or creativity in pursuing factual or legal theories. The court is expected to avoid using the wisdom of hindsight and should test the signer's conduct by inquiring what was reasonable to believe at the time the pleading, motion, or other paper was submitted. Thus, what constitutes a reasonable inquiry may depend on such factors as how much time for investigation was available to the signer; whether he had to rely on a client for information as to the facts underlying the pleading, motion, or other paper; whether the pleading, motion, or other paper was based on a plausible view of the law; or whether he depended on forwarding counsel or another member of the bar.

The rule does not require a party or an attorney to disclose privileged communications or work product in order to show that the signing of the pleading, motion, or other paper is substantially justified. The provisions of Rule 26(c), including appropriate orders after *in camera* inspection by the court, remain available to protect a party claiming privilege or work product protection.

Amended Rule 11 continues to apply to anyone who signs a pleading, motion, or other paper. Although the standard is the same for unrepresented parties, who are obliged themselves to sign the pleadings, the court has sufficient discretion to take account of the special circumstances that often arise in *pro se* situations. See *Haines v. Kerner,* 404 U.S. 519 (1972).

The provision in the original rule for striking pleadings and motions as sham and false has been deleted. The passage has rarely been utilized, and decisions thereunder have tended to confuse the issue of attorney honesty with the merits of the action. See generally Risinger, *Honesty in Pleading and its Enforcement: Some "Striking" Problems with Fed.R.Civ.P. 11,* 61 Minn.L.Rev. 1 (1976). Motions under this provision generally present issues better dealt with under Rules 8, 12, or 56. See *Murchison v. Kirby,* 27 F.R.D. 14 (S.D.N.Y.1961); 5 Wright & Miller, *Federal Practice and Procedure: Civil* § 1334 (1969).

The former reference to the inclusion of scandalous or indecent matter, which is itself strong indication that an improper purpose underlies the pleading, motion, or other paper, also has been deleted as unnecessary. Such matter may be stricken under Rule 12(f) as well as dealt with under the more general language of amended Rule 11.

The text of the amended rule seeks to dispel apprehensions that efforts to obtain enforcement will be fruitless by insuring that the rule will be applied when properly invoked. The word "sanctions" in the caption, for example, stresses a deterrent orientation in dealing with improper pleadings, motions or other papers. This corresponds to the approach in imposing sanctions for discovery abuses. See *National Hockey League v. Metropolitan Hockey Club,* 427 U.S. 639 (1976) (per curiam). And the words "shall impose" in the last sentence focus the court's attention on the need to impose sanctions for pleading and motion abuses. The court, however, retains the necessary flexibility to deal appropriately with violations of the rule. It has discretion to tailor sanctions to the particular facts of the case, with which it should be well acquainted.

The references in the former text to wilfulness as a prerequisite to disciplinary action has been deleted. However, in considering the nature and severity of the sanctions to be imposed, the court should take account of the state of the attorney's or party's actual or presumed knowledge when the pleading or other paper was signed. Thus, for example, when a party is not represented by counsel, the absence of legal advice is an appropriate factor to be considered.

Courts currently appear to believe they may impose sanctions on their own motion. See *North American Trading Corp. v. Zale Corp.,* 73 F.R.D. 293 (S.D.N.Y.1979). Authority to do so has been made explicit in order to overcome the traditional reluctance of courts to intervene unless requested by one of the parties. The detection and punishment of a violation of the signing requirement, encouraged by the amended rule, is part of the court's responsibility for securing the system's effective operation.

If the duty imposed by the rule is violated, the court should have the discretion to impose sanctions on either the attorney, the party the signing attorney represents, or both, or on an unrepresented party who signed the pleading, and the new rule so provides. Although Rule 11 has been silent on the point, courts have claimed the power to impose sanctions on an attorney personally, either by imposing costs or employing the contempt technique. See 5 Wright & Miller, *Federal Practice and Procedure: Civil* § 1334 (1969); 2A Moore, *Federal Practice* ¶ 11.02, at 2104 n. 8. This power has been used infrequently. The amended rule should eliminate any doubt as to the propriety of assessing sanctions against the attorney.

Even though it is the attorney whose signature violates the rule, it may be appropriate under the circumstances of the case to impose a sanction on the client. See *Browning Debenture Holders' Committee v. DASA Corp.,* supra. This modification brings Rule 11 in line with practice under Rule 37, which allows sanctions for abuses during discovery to be imposed upon the party, the attorney, or both.

A party seeking sanctions should give notice to the court and the offending party promptly upon discovering a basis for doing so. The time when sanctions are to be imposed rests in the discretion of the trial judge. However, it is anticipated that in the case of pleadings the sanctions issue under Rule 11 normally will be determined at the end of the litigation, and in the case of motions at the time when the motion is decided or shortly thereafter. The procedure obviously must comport with due process requirements. The particular format to be followed should depend on the circumstances of the situation and the severity of the sanction under consideration. In many situations the judge's participation in the proceedings provides him with full knowledge of the relevant facts and little further inquiry will be necessary.

To assure that the efficiencies achieved through more effective operation of the pleading regimen will not be offset by the cost of satellite litigation over the imposition of sanctions, the court must to the extent possible limit the scope of sanction proceedings to the record. Thus, discovery should be conducted only by leave of the court, and then only in extraordinary circumstances.

Although the encompassing reference to "other papers" in new Rule 11 literally includes discovery papers, the certification requirement in that context is governed by proposed new Rule 26(g). Discovery motions, however, fall within the ambit of Rule 11.

1987 Amendment

The amendments are technical. No substantive change is intended.

1993 Amendment

Purpose of revision. This revision is intended to remedy problems that have arisen in the interpretation and application of the 1983 revision of the rule. For empirical examination of experience under the 1983 rule, see, *e.g.,* New York State Bar Committee on Federal Courts, *Sanctions and Attorneys' Fees* (1987); T. Willging, *The Rule 11 Sanctioning Process* (1989); American Judicature Society, *Report of the Third Circuit Task Force on Federal Rule of Civil Procedure 11* (S. Burbank ed., 1989); E. Wiggins, T. Willging, and D. Stienstra, *Report on Rule 11* (Federal Judicial Center 1991). For book-length analyses of the case law, see G. Joseph, *Sanctions: The Federal Law of Litigation Abuse* (1989); J. Solovy, *The Federal Law of Sanctions* (1991); G. Vairo, *Rule 11 Sanctions: Case Law Perspectives and Preventive Measures* (1991).

The rule retains the principle that attorneys and pro se litigants have an obligation to the court to refrain from conduct that frustrates the aims of Rule 1. The revision broadens the scope of this obligation, but places greater constraints on the imposition of sanctions and should reduce the number of motions for sanctions presented to the court. New subdivision (d) removes from the ambit of this rule all discovery requests, responses, objections, and motions subject to the provisions of Rule 26 through 37.

Subdivision (a). Retained in this subdivision are the provisions requiring signatures on pleadings, written motions, and other papers. Unsigned papers are to be received by the Clerk, but then are to be stricken if the omission of the signature is not corrected promptly after being called to the attention of the attorney or pro se litigant. Correction can be made by signing the paper on file or by submitting a duplicate that contains the signature. A court may require by local rule that papers contain additional identifying information regarding the parties or attorneys, such as telephone numbers to facilitate facsimile transmissions, though, as for omission of a signature, the paper should not be rejected for failure to provide such information.

The sentence in the former rule relating to the effect of answers under oath is no longer needed and has been eliminated. The provision in the former rule that signing a paper constitutes a certificate that it has been read by the signer also has been eliminated as unnecessary. The obligations imposed under subdivision (b) obviously require that a pleading, written motion, or other paper be read before it is filed or submitted to the court.

Subdivisions (b) and (c). These subdivisions restate the provisions requiring attorneys and pro se litigants to conduct a reasonable inquiry into the law and facts before signing pleadings, written motions, and other documents, and prescribing sanctions for violation of these obligations. The revision in part expands the responsibilities of litigants to the court, while providing greater constraints and flexibility in dealing with infractions of the rule. The rule continues to require litigants to "stop-and-think" before initially making legal or factual contentions. It also, however, emphasizes the duty of candor by subjecting litigants to potential sanctions for insisting upon a position after it is no longer tenable and by generally providing protection against sanctions if they withdraw or correct contentions after a potential violation is called to their attention.

The rule applies only to assertions contained in papers filed with or submitted to the court. It does not cover matters arising for the first time during oral presentations to the court, when counsel may make statements that would not have been made if there had been more time for study and reflection. However, a litigant's obligations with respect to the contents of these papers are not measured solely as of the time they are filed with or submitted to the court, but include reaffirming to the court and advocating positions contained in those pleadings and motions after learning that they cease to have any merit. For example, an attorney who during a pretrial conference insists on a claim or defense should be viewed as "presenting to the court" that contention and would be subject to the obligations of subdivision (b) measured as of that time. Similarly, if after a notice of removal is filed, a party urges in federal court the allegations of a pleading filed in state court (whether as claims, defenses, or in disputes regarding removal or remand), it would be viewed as "presenting"—and hence certifying to the district court under Rule 11—those allegations.

The certification with respect to allegations and other factual contentions is revised in recognition that sometimes a litigant may have good reason to believe that a fact is true or false but may need discovery, formal or informal, from opposing parties or third persons to gather and confirm the evidentiary basis for the allegation. Tolerance of factual contentions in initial pleadings by plaintiffs or defendants when specifically identified as made on information and belief does not relieve litigants from the obligation to conduct an appropriate investigation into the facts that is reasonable under the circumstances; it is not a license to join parties, make claims, or present defenses without any factual basis or justification. Moreover, if evidentiary support is not obtained after a reasonable opportunity for further investigation or discovery, the party has a duty under the rule not to persist with that contention. Subdivision (b) does not require a formal amendment to pleadings for which evidentiary support is not obtained, but rather calls upon a litigant not thereafter to advocate such claims or defenses.

The certification is that there is (or likely will be) "evidentiary support" for the allegation, not that the party will prevail with respect to its contention regarding the fact. That summary judgment is rendered against a party does not necessarily mean, for purposes of this certification, that it had no evidentiary support for its position. On the other hand, if a party has evidence with respect to a contention that would suffice to defeat a motion for summary judgment based thereon, it would have sufficient "evidentiary support" for purposes of Rule 11.

Denials of factual contentions involve somewhat different considerations. Often, of course, a denial is premised upon the existence of evidence contradicting the alleged fact. At other times a denial is permissible because, after an appropriate investigation, a party has no information concerning the matter or, indeed, has a reasonable basis for doubting the credibility of the only evidence relevant to the matter. A party should not deny an allegation it knows to be true; but it is not required, simply because it lacks contradictory evidence, to admit an allegation that it believes is not true.

The changes in subdivisions (b)(3) and (b)(4) will serve to equalize the burden of the rule upon plaintiffs and defendants, who under Rule 8(b) are in effect allowed to deny allegations by stating that from their initial investigation they lack sufficient information to form a belief as to the truth of the allegation. If, after further investigation or discovery, a denial is no longer warranted, the defendant should not continue to insist on that denial. While sometimes helpful, formal amendment of the pleadings to withdraw an allegation or denial is not required by subdivision (b).

Arguments for extensions, modifications, or reversals of existing law or for creation of new law do not violate subdivision (b)(2) provided they are "nonfrivolous." This establishes an objective standard, intended to eliminate any "empty-head pure-heart" justification for patently frivolous arguments. However, the extent to which a litigant has researched the issues and found some support for its theories even in minority opinions, in law review articles, or through consultation with other attorneys should certainly be taken into account in determining whether paragraph (2) has been violated. Although arguments for a change of law are not required to be specifically so identified, a contention that is so identified should be viewed with greater tolerance under the rule.

The court has available a variety of possible sanctions to impose for violations, such as striking the offending paper; issuing an admonition, reprimand, or censure; requiring participation in seminars or other educational programs; ordering a fine payable to the court; referring the matter to disciplinary authorities (or, in the case of government attorneys, to the Attorney General, Inspector General, or agency head), etc. *See Manual for Complex Litigation, Second,* § 42.3. The rule does not attempt to enumerate the factors a court should consider in deciding whether to impose a sanction or what sanctions would be appropriate in the circumstances; but, for emphasis, it does specifically note that a sanction may be nonmonetary as well as monetary. Whether the improper conduct was willful, or negligent; whether it was part of a pattern of activity, or an isolated event; whether it infected the entire pleading, or only one particular count or defense; whether the person has engaged in similar conduct in other litigation; whether it was intended to injure; what effect it had on the litigation process in time or expense; whether the responsible person is trained in the law; what amount, given the financial resources of the responsible person, is needed to deter that person from repetition in the same case; what amount is needed to deter similar activity by other litigants: all of these may in a particular case be proper considerations. The court has significant discretion in determining what sanctions, if any, should be imposed for a violation, subject to the principle that the sanctions should not be more severe than reasonably necessary to deter repetition of the conduct by the offending person or comparable conduct by similarly situated persons.

Since the purpose of Rule 11 sanctions is to deter rather than to compensate, the rule provides that, if a monetary sanction is imposed, it should ordinarily be paid into court as a penalty. However, under unusual circumstances, particularly for (b)(1) violations, deterrence may be ineffective unless the sanction not only requires the person violating the rule to make a monetary payment, but also directs that some or all of this payment be made to those injured by the violation.

Accordingly, the rule authorizes the court, if requested in a motion and if so warranted, to award attorney's fees to another party. Any such award to another party, however, should not exceed the expenses and attorneys' fees for the services directly and unavoidably caused by the violation of the certification requirement. If, for example, a wholly unsupportable count were included in a multi-count complaint or counterclaim for the purpose of needlessly increasing the cost of litigation to an impecunious adversary, any award of expenses should be limited to those directly caused by inclusion of the improper count, and not those resulting from the filing of the complaint or answer itself. The award should not provide compensation for services that could have been avoided by an earlier disclosure of evidence or an earlier challenge to the groundless claims or defenses. Moreover, partial reimbursement of fees may constitute a sufficient deterrent with respect to violations by persons having modest financial resources. In cases brought under statutes providing for fees to be awarded to prevailing parties, the court should not employ cost-shifting under this rule in a manner that would be inconsistent with the standards that govern the statutory award of fees, such as stated in *Christiansburg Garment Co. v. EEOC*, 434 U.S. 412 (1978).

The sanction should be imposed on the persons—whether attorneys, law firms, or parties—who have violated the rule or who may be determined to be responsible for the violation. The person signing, filing, submitting, or advocating a document has a nondelegable responsibility to the court, and in most situations is the person to be sanctioned for a violation. Absent exceptional circumstances, a law firm is to be held also responsible when, as a result of a motion under subdivision (c)(1)(A), one of its partners, associates, or employees is determined to have violated the rule. Since such a motion may be filed only if the offending paper is not withdrawn or corrected within 21 days after service of the motion, it is appropriate that the law firm ordinarily be viewed as jointly responsible under established principles of agency. This provision is designed to remove the restrictions of the former rule. *Cf. Pavelic & LeFlore v. Marvel Entertainment Group*, 493 U.S. 120 (1989) (1983 version of Rule 11 does not permit sanctions against law firm of attorney signing groundless complaint).

The revision permits the court to consider whether other attorneys in the firm, co-counsel, other law firms, or the party itself should be held accountable for their part in causing a violation. When appropriate, the court can make an additional inquiry in order to determine whether the sanction should be imposed on such persons, firms, or parties either in addition to or, in unusual circumstances, instead of the person actually making the presentation to the court. For example, such an inquiry may be appropriate in cases involving governmental agencies or other institutional parties that frequently impose substantial restrictions on the discretion of individual attorneys employed by it.

Sanctions that involve monetary awards (such as a fine or an award of attorney's fees) may not be imposed on a represented party for causing a violation of subdivision (b)(2), involving frivolous contentions of law. Monetary responsibility for such violations is more properly placed solely on the party's attorneys. With this limitation, the rule should not be subject to attack under the Rules Enabling Act. See *Willy v. Coastal Corp.*, 503 U.S. 131 (1992); *Business Guides, Inc. v. Chromatic Communications Enter. Inc.*, 498 U.S. 533 (1991). This restriction does not limit the court's power to impose sanctions or remedial orders that may have collateral financial consequences upon a party, such as dismissal of a claim, preclusion of a defense, or preparation of amended pleadings.

Explicit provision is made for litigants to be provided notice of the alleged violation and an opportunity to respond before sanctions are imposed. Whether the matter should be decided solely on the basis of written submissions or should be scheduled for oral argument (or, indeed, for evidentiary presentation) will depend on the circumstances. If the court imposes a sanction, it must, unless waived, indicate its reasons in a written order or on the record; the court should not ordinarily have to explain its denial of a motion for sanctions. Whether a violation has occurred and what sanctions, if any, to impose for a violation are matters committed to the discretion of the trial court; accordingly, as under current law, the standard for appellate review of these decisions will be for abuse of discretion. *See Cooter & Gell v. Hartmarx Corp.*, 496 U.S. 384 (1990) (noting, however, that an abuse would be established if the court based its ruling on an erroneous view of the law or on a clearly erroneous assessment of the evidence).

The revision leaves for resolution on a case-by-case basis, considering the particular circumstances involved, the question as to when a motion for violation of Rule 11 should be served and when, if filed, it should be decided. Ordinarily the motion should be served promptly after the inappropriate paper is filed, and, if delayed too long, may be viewed as untimely. In other circumstances, it should not be served until the other party has had a reasonable opportunity for discovery. Given the "safe harbor" provisions discussed below, a party cannot delay serving its Rule 11 motion until conclusion of the case (or judicial rejection of the offending contention).

Rule 11 motions should not be made or threatened for minor, inconsequential violations of the standards prescribed by subdivision (b). They should not be employed as a discovery device or to test the legal sufficiency or efficacy of allegations in the pleadings; other motions are available for those purposes. Nor should Rule 11 motions be prepared to emphasize the merits of a party's position, to exact an unjust settlement, to intimidate an adversary into withdrawing contentions that are fairly debatable, to increase the costs of litigation, to create a conflict of interest between attorney and client, or to seek disclosure of matters otherwise protected by the attorney-client privilege or the work-product doctrine. As under the prior rule, the court may defer its ruling (or its decision as to the identity of the persons to be sanctioned) until final resolution of the case in order to avoid immediate conflicts of interest and to reduce the disruption created if a disclosure of attorney-client communications is needed to determine whether a violation occurred or to identify the person responsible for the violation.

The rule provides that requests for sanctions must be made as a separate motion, *i.e.*, not simply included as an additional prayer for relief contained in another motion. The motion for sanctions is not, however, to be filed until at least 21 days (or such other period as the court may set) after being served. If, during this period, the alleged violation is corrected, as by withdrawing (whether formally or informally) some allegation or contention, the motion should not be filed with the court. These provisions are intended to provide a type of "safe harbor" against motions under Rule 11 in that a party will not be subject to sanctions on the basis of another party's motion unless, after receiving the motion, it refuses to withdraw that position or to acknowledge candidly that it does not currently have evidence to support a specified allegation. Under the former rule, parties were sometimes reluctant to abandon a questionable contention lest that be viewed as evidence of a violation of Rule 11; under the revision, the timely withdrawal of a contention will protect a party against a motion for sanctions.

To stress the seriousness of a motion for sanctions and to define precisely the conduct claimed to violate the rule, the revision provides that the "safe harbor" period begins to run only upon service of the motion. In most cases, however, counsel should be expected to give informal notice to the other party, whether in person or by a telephone call or letter, of a potential violation before proceeding to prepare and serve a Rule 11 motion.

As under former Rule 11, the filing of a motion for sanctions is itself subject to the requirements of the rule and can lead to sanctions. However, service of a cross motion under Rule 11 should rarely be needed since under the revision the court may award to the person who prevails on a motion under Rule 11—whether the movant or the target of the motion—reasonable expenses, including attorney's fees, incurred in presenting or opposing the motion.

The power of the court to act on its own initiative is retained, but with the condition that this be done through a show cause order. This procedure provides the person with notice and an opportunity to respond. The revision provides that a monetary sanction imposed after a court-initiated show cause order be limited to a penalty payable to the court and that it be imposed only if the show cause order is issued before any voluntary dismissal or an agreement of the parties to settle the claims made by or against the litigant. Parties settling a case should not be subsequently faced with an unexpected order from the court leading to monetary sanctions that might have affected their willingness to settle or voluntarily dismiss a case. Since show cause orders will ordinarily be issued only in situations that are akin to a contempt of court, the rule does not provide a "safe harbor" to a litigant for withdrawing a claim, defense, etc., after a show cause order has been issued on the court's own initiative. Such corrective action, however, should be taken into account in deciding what—if any—sanction to impose if, after consideration of the litigant's response, the court concludes that a violation has occurred.

Subdivision (d). Rules 26(g) and 37 establish certification standards and sanctions that apply to discovery disclosures, requests, responses, objections, and motions. It is appropriate that Rules 26 through 37, which are specially designed for the discovery process, govern such documents and conduct rather than the more general provisions of Rule 11. Subdivision (d) has been added to accomplish this result.

Rule 11 is not the exclusive source for control of improper presentations of claims, defenses, or contentions. It does not supplant statutes permitting awards of attorney's fees to prevailing parties or alter the principles governing such awards. It does not inhibit the court in punishing for contempt, in exercising its inherent powers, or in imposing sanctions, awarding expenses, or directing remedial action authorized under other rules or under 28 U.S.C. § 1927. *See Chambers v. NASCO*, 501 U.S. 32 (1991). Chambers cautions, however, against reliance upon inherent powers if appropriate sanctions can be imposed under provisions such as Rule 11, and the procedures specified in Rule 11—notice, opportunity to respond, and findings—should ordinarily be employed when imposing a sanction under the court's inherent powers.

Finally, it should be noted that Rule 11 does not preclude a party from initiating an independent action for malicious prosecution or abuse of process.

2007 Amendment

The language of Rule 11 has been amended as part of the general restyling of the Civil Rules to make them more easily understood and to make style and terminology consistent throughout the rules. These changes are intended to be stylistic only.

Providing an e-mail address is useful, but does not of itself signify consent to filing or service by e-mail.

CROSS REFERENCES

Private securities litigation and sanctions for abusive litigation, see 15 USCA §§ 77z–1 and 78u–4.

Signing of motions and other papers, see Fed.Rules Civ. Proc. Rule 7, 28 USCA.

Rule 12.   Defenses and Objections: When and How Presented; Motion for Judgment on the Pleadings; Consolidating Motions; Waiving Defenses; Pretrial Hearing

(a) Time to Serve a Responsive Pleading.

(1) *In General.* Unless another time is specified by this rule or a federal statute, the time for serving a responsive pleading is as follows:

(A) A defendant must serve an answer:

(i) within 21 days after being served with the summons and complaint; or

(ii) if it has timely waived service under Rule 4(d), within 60 days after the request for a waiver was sent, or within 90 days after it was sent to the defendant outside any judicial district of the United States.

(B) A party must serve an answer to a counterclaim or crossclaim within 21 days after being served with the pleading that states the counterclaim or crossclaim.

(C) A party must serve a reply to an answer within 21 days after being served with an order to reply, unless the order specifies a different time.

(2) *United States and Its Agencies, Officers, or Employees Sued in an Official Capacity.* The United States, a United States agency, or a United States officer or employee sued only in an official capacity must serve an answer to a complaint, counterclaim, or crossclaim within 60 days after service on the United States attorney.

(3) *United States Officers or Employees Sued in an Individual Capacity.* A United States officer or employee sued in an individual capacity for an act or omission occurring in connection with duties performed on the United States' behalf must serve an answer to a complaint, counterclaim, or crossclaim within 60 days after service on the officer or employee or service on the United States attorney, whichever is later.

(4) *Effect of a Motion.* Unless the court sets a different time, serving a motion under this rule alters these periods as follows:

(A) if the court denies the motion or postpones its disposition until trial, the responsive pleading must be served within 14 days after notice of the court's action; or

(B) if the court grants a motion for a more definite statement, the responsive pleading must be served within 14 days after the more definite statement is served.

(b) How to Present Defenses. Every defense to a claim for relief in any pleading must be asserted in the responsive pleading if one is required. But a party may assert the following defenses by motion:

(1) lack of subject-matter jurisdiction;

(2) lack of personal jurisdiction;

(3) improper venue;

(4) insufficient process;

(5) insufficient service of process;

(6) failure to state a claim upon which relief can be granted; and

(7) failure to join a party under Rule 19.

A motion asserting any of these defenses must be made before pleading if a responsive pleading is allowed. If a pleading sets out a claim for relief that does not require a responsive pleading, an opposing party may assert at trial any defense to that claim. No defense or objection is waived by joining it with one or more other defenses or objections in a responsive pleading or in a motion.

(c) Motion for Judgment on the Pleadings. After the pleadings are closed—but early enough not to delay trial—a party may move for judgment on the pleadings.

(d) Result of Presenting Matters Outside the Pleadings. If, on a motion under Rule 12(b)(6) or 12(c), matters outside the pleadings are presented to and not excluded by the court, the motion must be treated as one for summary judgment under Rule 56. All parties must be given a reasonable opportunity to present all the material that is pertinent to the motion.

(e) Motion for a More Definite Statement. A party may move for a more definite statement of a pleading to which a responsive pleading is allowed but which is so vague or ambiguous that the party cannot reasonably prepare a response. The motion must be made before filing a responsive pleading and must point out the defects complained of and the details desired. If the court orders a more definite statement and the order is not obeyed within 14 days after notice of the order or within the time the court sets, the court

may strike the pleading or issue any other appropriate order.

(f) Motion to Strike. The court may strike from a pleading an insufficient defense or any redundant, immaterial, impertinent, or scandalous matter. The court may act:

(1) on its own; or

(2) on motion made by a party either before responding to the pleading or, if a response is not allowed, within 21 days after being served with the pleading.

(g) Joining Motions.

(1) *Right to Join.* A motion under this rule may be joined with any other motion allowed by this rule.

(2) *Limitation on Further Motions.* Except as provided in Rule 12(h)(2) or (3), a party that makes a motion under this rule must not make another motion under this rule raising a defense or objection that was available to the party but omitted from its earlier motion.

(h) Waiving and Preserving Certain Defenses.

(1) *When Some Are Waived.* A party waives any defense listed in Rule 12(b)(2)-(5) by:

(A) omitting it from a motion in the circumstances described in Rule 12(g)(2); or

(B) failing to either:

(i) make it by motion under this rule; or

(ii) include it in a responsive pleading or in an amendment allowed by Rule 15(a)(1) as a matter of course.

(2) *When to Raise Others.* Failure to state a claim upon which relief can be granted, to join a person required by Rule 19(b), or to state a legal defense to a claim may be raised:

(A) in any pleading allowed or ordered under Rule 7(a);

(B) by a motion under Rule 12(c); or

(C) at trial.

(3) *Lack of Subject–Matter Jurisdiction.* If the court determines at any time that it lacks subject-matter jurisdiction, the court must dismiss the action.

(i) Hearing Before Trial. If a party so moves, any defense listed in Rule 12(b)(1)-(7)—whether made in a pleading or by motion—and a motion under Rule 12(c) must be heard and decided before trial unless the court orders a deferral until trial.

(Amended December 27, 1946, effective March 19, 1948; January 21, 1963, effective July 1, 1963; February 28, 1966, effective July 1, 1966; March 2, 1987, effective August 1, 1987; April 22, 1993, effective December 1, 1993; April 17, 2000, effective December 1, 2000; April 30, 2007, effective December 1, 2007; March 26, 2009, effective December 1, 2009.)

ADVISORY COMMITTEE NOTES
1937 Adoption

Note to Subdivision (a). 1. Compare [former] Equity Rules 12 (Issue of Subpoena—Time for Answer) and 31 (Reply—When Required—When Cause at Issue); 4 Mont. Rev.Codes Ann. (1935) §§ 9107, 9158; N.Y.C. P.A. (1937) § 263; N.Y.R.C.P. (1937) Rules 109–111.

2. U.S.C., Title 28, § 763 (now § 547) (Petition in action against United States; service; appearance by district attorney) provides that the United States as a defendant shall have 60 days within which to answer or otherwise defend. This and other statutes which provide 60 days for the United States or an officer or agency thereof to answer or otherwise defend are continued by this rule. In so far as any statutes not excepted in rule 81 provide a different time for a defendant to defend, such statutes are modified. See U.S.C., Title 28, [former] § 45 (District courts; practice and procedure in certain cases under the interstate commerce laws) (30 days).

3. Compare the last sentence of [former] Equity Rule 29 (Defenses—How Presented) and N.Y.C.P.A. (1937) § 283. See Rule 15(a) for time within which to plead to an amended pleading.

Note to Subdivisions (b) and (d). 1. See generally [former] Equity Rules 29 (Defenses—How Presented), 33 (Testing Sufficiency of Defense), 43 (Defect of Parties—Resisting Objection), and 44 (Defect of Parties—Tardy Objection); N.Y.C.P.A. (1937) §§ 277–280; N.Y.R.C.P. (1937) Rules 106–112; *English Rules Under the Judicature Act* (The Annual Practice, 1937) O. 25, r.r. 1–4; Clark, *Code Pleading*, 1928, pp. 371–381.

2. For provisions authorizing defenses to be made in the answer or reply see *English Rules Under the Judicature Act*, (The Annual Practice, 1937) O. 25, r.r. 1–4; 1 Miss.Code Ann. (1930) §§ 378, 379. Compare Equity Rule 29 (Defenses—How Presented); U.S.C.A., Title 28, [former] § 45 (District Courts; practice and procedure in certain cases under the interstate commerce laws). U.S.C., Title 28, [former] § 45, substantially continued by this rule, provides: "No replication need be filed to the answer, and objections to the sufficiency of the petition or answer as not setting forth a cause of action or defense must be taken at the final hearing or by motion to dismiss the petition based on said grounds, which motion may be made at any time before answer is filed." Compare Calif.Code Civ.Proc., (Deering, 1937) § 433; 4 Nev.Comp. Laws (Hillyer, 1929) § 8600. For provisions that the defendant may demur and answer at the same time, see Calif.Code Civ.Proc. (Deering, 1937) § 431; 4 Nev.Comp.Laws (Hillyer, 1929) § 8598.

3. [Former] Equity Rule 29 (Defenses—How Presented) abolished demurrers and provided that defenses in point of law arising on the face of the bill should be made by motion to dismiss or in the answer, with further provision that every such point of law going to the whole or material part of the cause or causes stated might be called up and disposed of before final hearing "at the discretion of the court." Likewise many state practices have abolished the demurrer, or retain it only to attack substantial and not formal defects. See 6 Tenn.Code Ann. (Williams, 1934) § 8784; Ala.Code Ann. (Michie, 1928) § 9479; 2 Mass.Gen.Laws (Ter.Ed., 1932) ch. 231, §§ 15–18; Kansas Gen.Stat.Ann. (1935) §§ 60–705, 60–706.

Note to Subdivision (c). Compare [former] Equity Rule 33 (Testing Sufficiency of Defense); N.Y.R.C.P. (1937) Rules 111 and 112.

Note to Subdivisions (e) and (f). Compare [former] Equity Rules 20 (Further and Particular Statement in Pleading May be Required) and 21 (Scandal and Impertinence); *English Rules Under the Judicature Act* (The Annual Practice, 1937) O. 19, r.r. 7, 7a, 7b, 8; 4 Mont.Rev.Codes Ann. (1935) §§ 9166, 9167; N.Y.C.P.A. (1937) § 247; N.Y.C.P.A. (1937) Rules 103, 115, 116, 117; Wyo.Rev.Stat.Ann. (Courtright, 1931) §§ 89–1033, 89–1034.

Note to Subdivision (g). Compare Rules of the District Court of the United States for the District of Columbia (1937) Equity Rule 11; N.M. Rules of Pleading, Practice and Procedure, 38 N.M.Rep. vii. [105–408] (1934); Wash.Gen.Rules of the Superior Courts, 1 Wash.Rev.Stat.Ann. (Remington, 1932) p. 160, Rule VI(e) and (f).

Note to Subdivision (h). Compare Calif.Code Civ.Proc. (Deering, 1937) § 434; 2 Minn.Stat. (Mason, 1927) § 9252; N.Y.C.P.A. (1937) §§ 278 and 279; Wash.Gen.Rules of the Superior Courts, 1 Wash.Rev.Stat.Ann. (Remington, 1932) p. 160, Rule VI(e). This rule continues U.S.C.A., Title 28, former § 80 [now 1359, 1447, 1919] (Dismissal or remand) (of action over which district court lacks jurisdiction), while U.S.C.A., Title 28, § 399 (Amendments to show diverse citizenship) is continued by Rule 15.

1946 Amendment

Note. Subdivision (a). Various minor alterations in language have been made to improve the statement of the rule. All references to bills of particulars have been stricken in accordance with changes made in subdivision (e).

Subdivision (b). The addition of defense (7), "failure to join an indispensable party", cures an omission in the rules which are silent as to the mode of raising such failure. See Commentary, *Manner of Raising Objection of Non-Joinder of Indispensable Party*, 1940, 2 Fed.Rules Serv. 658, and, 1942, 5 Fed.Rules Serv. 820. In one case, *United States v. Metropolitan Life Ins. Co.*, E.D.Pa.1941, 36 F.Supp. 399, the failure to join an indispensable party was raised under Rule 12(c).

Rule 12(b)(6), permitting a motion to dismiss for failure of the complaint to state a claim on which relief can be granted, is substantially the same as the old demurrer for failure of a pleading to state a cause of action. Some courts have held that as the rule by its terms refers to statements in the complaint, extraneous matter on affidavits, depositions or otherwise, may not be introduced in support of the motion, or to resist it. On the other hand, in many cases the district courts have permitted the introduction of such material. When these cases have reached circuit courts of appeals in situations where the extraneous material so received shows that there is no genuine issue as to any material question of fact and that on the undisputed facts as disclosed by the affidavits or depositions, one party or the other is entitled to judgment as a matter of law, the circuit courts, properly enough, have been reluctant to dispose of the case merely on the face of the pleading, and in the interest of prompt disposition of the action have made a final disposition of it. In dealing with such situations the Second Circuit has made the sound suggestion that whatever its label or original basis, the motion may be treated as a motion for summary judgment and disposed of as such. *Samara v. United States*, C.C.A.2, 1942, 129 F.2d 594, certiorari denied 63 S.Ct. 258, 317 U.S. 686, 87 L.Ed. 549; *Boro Hall Corp. v. General Motors Corp.*, C.C.A.2, 1942, 124 F.2d 822, certiorari denied 63 S.Ct. 436, 317

U.S. 695, 87 L.Ed. 556. See, also, *Kithcart v. Metropolitan Life Ins. Co.*, C.C.A.8, 1945, 150 F.2d 997.

It has also been suggested that this practice could be justified on the ground that the federal rules permit "speaking" motions. The Committee entertains the view that on motion under Rule 12(b)(6) to dismiss for failure of the complaint to state a good claim, the trial court should have authority to permit the introduction of extraneous matter, such as may be offered on a motion for summary judgment, and if it does not exclude such matter the motion should then be treated as a motion for summary judgment and disposed of in the manner and on the conditions stated in Rule 56 relating to summary judgments, and, of course, in such a situation, when the case reaches the circuit court of appeals, that court should treat the motion in the same way. The Committee believes that such practice, however, should be tied to the summary judgment rule. The term "speaking motion" is not mentioned in the rules, and if there is such a thing its limitations are undefined. Where extraneous matter is received, by tying further proceedings to the summary judgment rule the courts have a definite basis in the rules for disposing of the motion.

The Committee emphasizes particularly the fact that the summary judgment rule does not permit a case to be disposed of by judgment on the merits on affidavits, which disclose a conflict on a material issue of fact, and unless this practice is tied to the summary judgment, rule, the extent to which a court, on the introduction of such extraneous matter, may resolve questions of fact on conflicting proof would be left uncertain.

The decisions dealing with this general situation may be generally grouped as follows: (1) cases dealing with the use of affidavits and other extraneous material on motions; (2) cases reversing judgments to prevent final determination on mere pleading allegations alone.

Under group (1) are: *Boro Hall Corp. v. General Motors Corp.*, C.C.A.2, 1942, 124 F.2d 822, certiorari denied 1943, 63 S.Ct. 436, 317 U.S. 695, 87 L.Ed. 556; *Gallup v. Caldwell*, C.C.A.3, 1941, 120 F.2d 90; *Central Mexico Light & Power Co. v. Munch*, C.C.A.2, 1940, 116 F.2d 85; *National Labor Relations Board v. Montgomery Ward & Co.*, 1944, 144 F.2d 528, 79 U.S.App.D.C. 200, certiorari denied 1944, 65 S.Ct. 134, 323 U.S. 774, 89 L.Ed. 619; *Urquhart v. American-La France Foamite Corp.*, 1944, 144 F.2d 542, 79 U.S.App.D.C. 219; *Samara v. United States*, C.C.A.2, 1942, 129 F.2d 594; *Cohen v. American Window Glass Co.*, C.C.A.2, 1942, 126 F.2d 111; *Sperry Products Inc. v. Association of American Railroads*, C.C.A.2, 1942, 132 F.2d 408; *Joint Council Dining Car Employees Local 370 v. Delaware, Lackawanna and Western R. Co.*, C.C.A.2, 1946, 157 F.2d 417; *Weeks v. Bareco Oil Co.*, C.C.A.7, 1941, 125 F.2d 84; *Carroll v. Morrison Hotel Corp.*, C.C.A.7, 1945, 149 F.2d 404; *Victory v. Manning*, C.C.A.3, 1942, 128 F.2d 415; *Locals No. 1470, No. 1469, and No. 1512 of International Longshoremen's Association v. Southern Pacific Co.*, C.C.A.5, 1942, 131 F.2d 605; *Lucking v. Delano*, C.C.A.6, 1942, 129 F.2d 283; *San Francisco Lodge No. 68 of International Association of Machinists v. Forrestal*, Cal. 1944, 58 F.Supp. 466; *Benson v. Export Equipment Corp.*, 1945, 164 P.2d 380, 49 N.M. 356, construing New Mexico rule identical with Rule 12(b)(6); *F. E. Myers & Bros. Co. v. Gould Pumps, Inc.*, W.D.N.Y.1946, 9 Fed.Rules Serv. 12b.33, Case 2, 5 F.R.D. 132. Cf. *Kohler v. Jacobs*, C.C.A.5, 1943, 138 F.2d 440; *Cohen v. United States*, C.C.A.8, 1942, 129 F.2d 733.

Under group (2) are: *Sparks v. England*, C.C.A.8, 1940, 113 F.2d 579; *Continental Collieries, Inc. v. Shober*, C.C.A.3, 1942, 130 F.2d 631; *Downey v. Palmer*, C.C.A.2, 1940, 114 F.2d 116; *DeLoach v. Crowley's Inc.*, C.C.A.5, 1942, 128 F.2d 378; *Leimer v. State Mutual Life Assurance Co. of Worcester, Mass.*, C.C.A.8, 1940, 108 F.2d 302; *Rossiter v. Vogel*, C.C.A.2, 1943, 134 F.2d 908, compare s.c., C.C.A.2, 1945, 148 F.2d 292; *Karl Kiefer Machine Co. v. United States Bottlers Machinery Co.*, C.C.A.7, 1940, 113 F.2d 356; *Chicago Metallic Mfg. Co. v. Edward Katzinger Co.*, C.C.A.7, 1941, 123 F.2d 518; *Louisiana Farmers' Protective Union, Inc. v. Great Atlantic & Pacific Tea Co. of America, Inc.*, C.C.A.8, 1942, 131 F.2d 419; *Publicity Bldg. Realty Corp. v. Hannegan*, C.C.A.8, 1943, 139 F.2d 583; *Dioguardi v. Durning*, C.C.A.2, 1944, 139 F.2d 774; *Package Closure Corp. v. Sealright Co., Inc.*, C.C.A.2, 1944, 141 F.2d 972; *Tahir Erk v. Glenn L. Martin Co.*, C.C.A.4, 1941, 116 F.2d 865; *Bell v. Preferred Life Assurance Society of Montgomery, Ala.*, 1943, 64 S.Ct. 5, 320 U.S. 238, 88 L.Ed. 15.

The addition at the end of subdivision (b) makes it clear that on a motion under Rule 12(b)(6) extraneous material may not be considered if the court excludes it, but that if the court does not exclude such material the motion shall be treated as a motion for summary judgment and disposed of as provided in Rule 56. It will also be observed that if a motion under Rule 12(b)(6) is thus converted into a summary judgment motion, the amendment insures that both parties shall be given a reasonable opportunity to submit affidavits and extraneous proofs to avoid taking a party by surprise through the conversion of the motion into a motion for summary judgment. In this manner and to this extent the amendment regularizes the practice above described. As the courts are already dealing with cases in this way, the effect of this amendment is really only to define the practice carefully and apply the requirements of the summary judgment rule in the disposition of the motion.

Subdivision (c). The sentence appended to subdivision (c) performs the same function and is grounded on the same reasons as the corresponding sentence added in subdivision (b).

Subdivision (d). The change here was made necessary because of the addition of defense (7) in subdivision (b).

Subdivision (e). References in this subdivision to a bill of particulars have been deleted, and the motion provided for is confined to one for more definite statement to be obtained only in cases where the movant cannot reasonably be required to frame an answer or other responsive pleading to the pleading in question. With respect to preparations for trial, the party is properly relegated to the various methods of examination and discovery provided in the rules for that purpose. *Slusher v. Jones*, E.D.Ky.1943, 7 Fed.Rules Serv. 12e.231, Case 5, 3 F.R.D. 168; *Best Foods, Inc. v. General Mills, Inc.*, D.Del.1943, 7 Fed.Rules Serv. 12e.231, Case 7, 3 F.R.D. 275; *Braden v. Callaway*, E.D.Tenn.1943, 8 Fed.Rules Serv. 12e.231, Case 1 (". . . most courts . . . conclude that the definiteness required is only such as will be sufficient for the party to prepare responsive pleadings"). Accordingly, the reference to the 20 day time limit has also been eliminated, since the purpose of this present provision is to state a time period where the motion for a bill is made for the purpose of preparing for trial.

Rule 12(e) as originally drawn has been the subject of more judicial rulings than any other part of the rules, and has been much criticized by commentators, judges and members of the

---

bar. See general discussion and cases cited in 1 Moore's *Federal Practice*, 1938, Cum.Supplement, § 12.07, under "Page 657"; also, Holtzoff, *New Federal Procedure and the Courts*, 1940, 35–41. And compare vote of Second Circuit Conference of Circuit and District Judges, June 1940, recommending the abolition of the bill of particulars; *Sun Valley Mfg. Co. v. Mylish*, E.D.Pa.1944, 8 Fed.Rules Serv. 12e.231, Case 6 ("Our experience . . . has demonstrated not only that 'the office of the bill of particulars is fast becoming obsolete' . . . but that in view of the adequate discovery procedure available under the Rules, motions for bills of particulars should be abolished altogether."); *Walling v. American Steamship Co.*, W.D.N.Y.1945, 4 F.R.D. 355, 8 Fed.Rules Serv. 12e.244, Case 8 (". . . the adoption of the rule was ill advised. It has led to confusion, duplication and delay.") The tendency of some courts freely to grant extended bills of particulars has served to neutralize any helpful benefits derived from rule 8, and has overlooked the intended use of the rules on depositions and discovery. The words "or to prepare for trial"—eliminated by the proposed amendment—have sometimes been seized upon as grounds for compulsory statement in the opposing pleading of all the details which the movant would have to meet at the trial. On the other hand, many courts have in effect read these words out of the rule. See *Walling v. Alabama Pipe Co.*, W.D.Mo.1942, 3 F.R.D. 159, 6 Fed.Rules Serv. 12e.244, Case 7; *Fleming v. Mason & Dixon Lines, Inc.*, E.D.Tenn.1941, 42 F.Supp. 230; *Kellogg Co. v. National Biscuit Co.*, D.N.J.1941, 38 F.Supp. 643; *Brown v. H. L. Green Co.*, S.D.N.Y.1943, 7 Fed.Rules Serv. 12e.231, Case 6; *Pedersen v. Standard Accident Ins. Co.*, W.D.Mo.1945, 8 Fed.Rules Serv. 12e.231, Case 8; *Bowles v. Ohse*, D.Neb.1945, 4 F.R.D. 403, 9 Fed.Rules Serv. 12e.231, Case 1; *Klages v. Cohen*, E.D.N.Y.1945, 9 Fed.Rules Serv. 8a.25, Case 4; *Bowles v. Lawrence*, D.Mass.1945, 8 Fed.Rules Serv. 12e.231, Case 19; *McKinney Tool & Mfg. Co. v. Hoyt*, N.D.Ohio 1945, 9 Fed.Rules Serv. 12e.235, Case 1; *Bowles v. Jack*, D.Minn.1945, 5 F.R.D. 1, 9 Fed.Rules Serv. 12e.244, Case 9. And it has been urged from the bench that the phrase be stricken, *Poole v. White*, N.D.W.Va.1941, 5 Fed. Rules Serv. 12e.231, Case 4, 2 F.R.D. 40. See also *Bowles v. Gabel*, W.D.Mo.1946, 9 Fed.Rules Serv. 12e.244, Case 10. ("The courts have never favored that portion of the rules which undertook to justify a motion of this kind for the purpose of aiding counsel in preparing his case for trial.").

Subdivision (f). This amendment affords a specific method of raising the insufficiency of a defense, a matter which has troubled some courts, although attack has been permitted in one way or another. See *Dysart v. Remington-Rand, Inc.*, D.Conn.1939, 31 F.Supp. 296; *Eastman Kodak Co. v. McAuley*, S.D.N.Y.1941, 4 Fed.Rules Serv., 12f.21, Case 8, 2 F.R.D. 21; *Schenley Distillers Corp. v. Renken*, E.D.S.C.1940, 34 F.Supp. 678; *Yale Transport Corp. v. Yellow Truck & Coach Mfg. Co.*, S.D.N.Y.1944, 3 F.R.D. 440; *United States v. Turner Milk Co.*, N.D.Ill.1941, 4 Fed.Rules Serv. 12b.51, Case 3, 1 F.R.D. 643; *Teiger v. Stephan Oderwald, Inc.*, S.D.N.Y.1940, 31 F.Supp. 626; *Teplitsky v. Pennsylvania R. Co.*, N.D.Ill. 1941, 38 F.Supp. 535; *Callagher v. Carroll*, E.D.N.Y.1939, 27 F.Supp. 568; *United States v. Palmer*, S.D.N.Y.1939, 28 F.Supp. 936. And see *Indemnity Ins. Co. of North America v. Pan American Airways, Inc.*, S.D.N.Y.1944, 58 F.Supp. 338; Commentary, *Modes of Attacking Insufficient Defenses in the Answer*, 901, 1939, 1 Fed.Rules Serv. 669, 1940, 2 Fed.Rules Serv. 640.

Subdivision (g). The change in title conforms with the companion provision in subdivision (h).

The alteration of the "except" clause requires that other than provided in subdivision (h) a party who resorts to a motion to raise defenses specified in the rule, must include in one motion all that are then available to him. Under the original rule defenses which could be raised by motion were divided into two groups which could be the subjects of two successive motions.

Subdivision (h). The addition of the phrase relating to indispensable parties is one of necessity.

1963 Amendment

This amendment conforms to the amendment of Rule 4(e). See also the Advisory Committee's Note to amended Rule 4(b).

1966 Amendment

Subdivision (b)(7). The terminology of this subdivision is changed to accord with the amendment of Rule 19. See the Advisory Committee's Note to Rule 19, as amended, especially the third paragraph therein before the caption "Subdivision (c)."

Subdivision (g). Subdivision (g) has forbidden a defendant who makes a preanswer motion under this rule from making a further motion presenting any defense or objection which was available to him at the time he made the first motion and which he could have included, but did not in fact include therein. Thus if the defendant moves before answer to dismiss the complaint for failure to state a claim, he is barred from making a further motion presenting the defense of improper venue, if that defense was available to him when he made his original motion. Amended subdivision (g) is to the same effect. This required consolidation of defenses and objections in a Rule 12 motion is salutary in that it works against piecemeal consideration of a case. For exceptions to the requirement of consolidation, see the last clause of subdivision (g), referring to new subdivision (h)(2).

Subdivision (h). The question has arisen whether an omitted defense which cannot be made the basis of a second motion may nevertheless be pleaded in the answer. Subdivision (h) called for waiver of "* * * defenses and objections which he [defendant] does not present * * * by motion * * * or, if he has made no motion, in his answer * * *." If the clause "if he has made no motion," was read literally, it seemed that the omitted defense was waived and could not be pleaded in the answer. On the other hand, the clause might be read as adding nothing of substance to the preceding words; in that event it appeared that a defense was not waived by reason of being omitted from the motion and might be set up in the answer. The decisions were divided. Favoring waiver, see *Keef v. Derounian*, 6 F.R.D. 11 (N.D.Ill.1946); *Elbinger v. Precision Metal Workers Corp.*, 18 F.R.D. 467 (E.D.Wis.1956); see also *Rensing v. Turner Aviation Corp.*, 166 F.Supp. 790 (N.D.Ill.1958); *P. Beiersdorf & Co. v. Duke Laboratories, Inc.*, 10 F.R.D. 282 (S.D.N.Y.1950); *Neset v. Christensen*, 92 F.Supp. 78 (E.D.N.Y.1950). Opposing waiver, see *Phillips v. Baker*, 121 F.2d 752 (9th Cir.1941); *Crum v. Graham*, 32 F.R.D. 173 (D.Mont.1963) (regretfully following the Phillips case); see also *Birnbaum v. Birrell*, 9 F.R.D. 72 (S.D.N.Y.1948); *Johnson v. Joseph Schlitz Brewing Co.*, 33 F.Supp. 176 (E.D.Tenn.1940); cf. *Carter v. American Bus Lines, Inc.*, 22 F.R.D. 323 (D.Neb.1958).

Amended subdivision (h)(1)(A) eliminates the ambiguity and states that certain specified defenses which were available to a party when he made a preanswer motion, but which he omitted from the motion, are waived. The specified defenses are lack of jurisdiction over the person, improper venue, insufficiency of process, and insufficiency of service of process (see Rule 12(b)(2)–(5)). A party who by motion invites the court to pass upon a threshold defense should bring forward all the specified defenses he then has and thus allow the court to do a reasonably complete job. The waiver reinforces the policy of subdivision (g) forbidding successive motions.

By amended subdivision (h)(1)(B), the specified defenses, even if not waived by the operation of (A), are waived by the failure to raise them by a motion under Rule 12 or in the responsive pleading or any amendment thereof to which the party is entitled as a matter of course. The specified defenses are of such a character that they should not be delayed and brought up for the first time by means of an application to the court to amend the responsive pleading.

Since the language of the subdivisions is made clear, the party is put on fair notice of the effect of his actions and omissions and can guard himself against unintended waiver. It is to be noted that while the defenses specified in subdivision (h)(1) are subject to waiver as there provided, the more substantial defenses of failure to state a claim upon which relief can be granted, failure to join a party indispensable under Rule 19, and failure to state a legal defense to a claim (see Rule 12(b)(6), (7), (f)), as well as the defense of lack of jurisdiction over the subject matter (see Rule 12(b)(1)), are expressly preserved against waiver by amended subdivision (h)(2) and (3).

1987 Amendment

The amendments are technical. No substantive change is intended.

1993 Amendment

Subdivision (a) is divided into paragraphs for greater clarity, and paragraph (1)(B) is added to reflect amendments to Rule 4. Consistent with Rule 4(d)(3), a defendant that timely waives service is allowed 60 days from the date the request was mailed in which to respond to the complaint, with an additional 30 days afforded if the request was sent out of the country. Service is timely waived if the waiver is returned within the time specified in the request (30 days after the request was mailed, or 60 days if mailed out of the country) and before being formally served with process. Sometimes a plaintiff may attempt to serve a defendant with process while also sending the defendant a request for waiver of service; if the defendant executes the waiver of service within the time specified and before being served with process, it should have the longer time to respond afforded by waiving service.

The date of sending the request is to be inserted by the plaintiff on the face of the request for waiver and on the waiver itself. This date is used to measure the return day for the waiver form, so that the plaintiff can know on a day certain whether formal service of process will be necessary; it is also a useful date to measure the time for answer when service is waived. The defendant who returns the waiver is given additional time for answer in order to assure that it loses nothing by waiving service of process.

2000 Amendment

Rule 12(a)(3)(B) is added to complement the addition of Rule 4(i)(2)(B). The purposes that underlie the requirement that service be made on the United States in an action that asserts individual liability of a United States officer or employee for acts occurring in connection with the performance of duties on behalf of the United States also require that the time to answer be extended to 60 days. Time is needed for the United States to determine whether to provide representation to the defendant officer or employee. If the United States provides representation, the need for an extended answer period is the same as in actions against the United States, a United States agency, or a United States officer sued in an official capacity.

An action against a former officer or employee of the United States is covered by subparagraph (3)(B) in the same way as an action against a present officer or employee. Termination of the relationship between the individual defendant and the United States does not reduce the need for additional time to answer.

GAP Report

No changes are recommended for Rule 12 as published.

2007 Amendment

The language of Rule 12 has been amended as part of the general restyling of the Civil Rules to make them more easily understood and to make style and terminology consistent throughout the rules. These changes are intended to be stylistic only.

Former Rule 12(a)(4)(A) referred to an order that postpones disposition of a motion "until the trial on the merits." Rule 12(a)(4) now refers to postponing disposition "until trial." The new expression avoids the ambiguity that inheres in "trial on the merits," which may become confusing when there is a separate trial of a single issue or another event different from a single all-encompassing trial.

2009 Amendment

The times set in the former rule at 10 or 20 days have been revised to 14 or 21 days. See the Note to Rule 6.

CROSS REFERENCES

Bill of particulars, see Fed.Rules Cr.Proc. Rule 7, 18 USCA.

Demurrers abolished, see Fed.Rules Civ.Proc. Rule 7, 28 USCA.

Demurrers abolished, see Fed.Rules Cr.Proc. Rule 12, 18 USCA.

Dismissal of actions,

Claims of opposing party, judgment on counterclaim or cross-claim, see Fed.Rules Civ.Proc. Rule 13, 28 USCA.

Class actions, see Fed.Rules Civ.Proc. Rule 23, 28 USCA.

Costs of previously-dismissed action, see Fed.Rules Civ. Proc. Rule 41, 28 USCA.

Depositions, right to use in former action, see Fed.Rules Civ.Proc. Rule 26, 28 USCA.

Failure to serve answers to interrogatories, see Fed. Rules Civ.Proc. Rule 37, 28 USCA.

Findings of fact and conclusions of law, necessity, see Fed.Rules Civ.Proc. Rule 52, 28 USCA.

Voluntary and involuntary dismissal, see Fed.Rules Civ. Proc. Rule 41, 28 USCA.

Districts courts,

Jurisdiction, see 28 USCA § 1331 et seq.

Trials, hearings, and orders in chambers, see Fed.Rules Civ.Proc. Rule 77, 28 USCA.

Venue, see 28 USCA § 1391 et seq.

Evidence on motions, see Fed.Rules Civ.Proc. Rule 43, 28 USCA.

Findings of fact and conclusions of law unnecessary, see Fed.Rules Civ.Proc. Rule 52, 28 USCA.

"Judgment", definition of, see Fed.Rules Civ.Proc. Rule 54, 28 USCA.

Motions,

Adoption of statement by reference, see Fed.Rules Civ. Proc. Rule 10, 28 USCA.

Courts always open for making, see 28 USCA § 452.

Evidence on, see Fed.Rules Civ.Proc. Rule 43, 28 USCA.

Extension of time, see Fed.Rules Civ.Proc. Rule 6, 28 USCA.

Form of, see Fed.Rules Civ.Proc. Rule 7, 28 USCA.

Motion day and oral hearings, see Fed.Rules Civ.Proc. Rule 78, 28 USCA.

Technical forms not required, see Fed.Rules Civ.Proc. Rule 8, 28 USCA.

Time for motions, generally, see Fed.Rules Civ.Proc. Rule 6, 28 USCA.

Parties,

Necessary joinder, see Fed.Rules Civ.Proc. Rule 19, 28 USCA.

Third-party defendant, defenses to third-party plaintiff and plaintiff's claims, see Fed.Rules Civ.Proc. Rule 14, 28 USCA.

Pleadings,

Affirmative defenses, see Fed.Rules Civ.Proc. Rule 8, 28 USCA.

Form of, see Fed.Rules Civ.Proc. Rule 10, 28 USCA.

Pleadings allowed, see Fed.Rules Civ.Proc. Rule 7, 28 USCA.

Striking for failure to serve answer to interrogatory, see Fed.Rules Civ.Proc. Rule 37, 28 USCA.

Waiver of objections to venue, see 28 USCA § 1406.

Rule 13.   Counterclaim and Crossclaim

(a) Compulsory Counterclaim.

(1) *In General.* A pleading must state as a counterclaim any claim that—at the time of its service—the pleader has against an opposing party if the claim:

(A) arises out of the transaction or occurrence that is the subject matter of the opposing party's claim; and

(B) does not require adding another party over whom the court cannot acquire jurisdiction.

(2) *Exceptions.* The pleader need not state the claim if:

(A) when the action was commenced, the claim was the subject of another pending action; or

(B) the opposing party sued on its claim by attachment or other process that did not establish personal jurisdiction over the pleader on that claim, and the pleader does not assert any counterclaim under this rule.

(b) Permissive Counterclaim. A pleading may state as a counterclaim against an opposing party any claim that is not compulsory.

(c) Relief Sought in a Counterclaim. A counterclaim need not diminish or defeat the recovery sought by the opposing party. It may request relief that exceeds in amount or differs in kind from the relief sought by the opposing party.

(d) Counterclaim Against the United States. These rules do not expand the right to assert a counterclaim—or to claim a credit—against the United States or a United States officer or agency.

(e) Counterclaim Maturing or Acquired After Pleading. The court may permit a party to file a supplemental pleading asserting a counterclaim that matured or was acquired by the party after serving an earlier pleading.

(f) [Abrogated]

(g) Crossclaim Against a Coparty. A pleading may state as a crossclaim any claim by one party against a coparty if the claim arises out of the transaction or occurrence that is the subject matter of the original action or of a counterclaim, or if the claim relates to any property that is the subject matter of the original action. The crossclaim may include a claim that the coparty is or may be liable to the cross-claimant for all or part of a claim asserted in the action against the cross-claimant.

(h) Joining Additional Parties. Rules 19 and 20 govern the addition of a person as a party to a counterclaim or crossclaim.

(i) Separate Trials; Separate Judgments. If the court orders separate trials under Rule 42(b), it may enter judgment on a counterclaim or crossclaim under Rule 54(b) when it has jurisdiction to do so, even if the opposing party's claims have been dismissed or otherwise resolved.

(Amended December 27, 1946, effective March 19, 1948; January 21, 1963, effective July 1, 1963; February 28, 1966, effective July 1, 1966; March 2, 1987, effective August 1, 1987; April 30, 2007, effective December 1, 2007; March 26, 2009, effective December 1, 2009.)

ADVISORY COMMITTEE NOTES

1937 Adoption

1. This is substantially [former] Equity Rule 30 (Answer—Contents—Counterclaim), broadened to include legal as well as equitable counterclaims.

2. Compare the English practice, *English Rules Under the Judicature Act* (The Annual Practice, 1937) O. 19, r.r. 2 and 3, and O. 21, r.r. 10–17; *Beddall v. Maitland*, L.R. 17 Ch.Div. 174, 181, 182 (1881).

3. Certain States have also adopted almost unrestricted provisions concerning both the subject matter of and the parties to a counterclaim. This seems to be the modern tendency. Ark.Civ.Code (Crawford, 1934) §§ 117 (as amended) and 118; N.J.Comp.Stat. (2 Cum.Supp. 1911–1924); N.Y.C.P.A. (1937) §§ 262, 266, 267 (all as amended, Laws of 1936, ch. 324), 268, 269, and 271; Wis.Stat. (1935) § 263.14(1)(c).

4. Most codes do not expressly provide for a counterclaim in the reply. Clark, *Code Pleading* (1928), p. 486. Ky.Codes (Carroll, 1932) Civ.Pract. § 98 does provide, however, for such counterclaim.

5. The provisions of this rule respecting counterclaims are subject to Rule 82 (Jurisdiction and Venue Unaffected). For a discussion of Federal jurisdiction and venue in regard to counterclaims and cross-claims, see Shulman and Jaegerman, *Some Jurisdictional Limitations in Federal Procedure* (1936), 45 Yale L.J. 393, 410 et seq.

6. This rule does not affect such statutes of the United States as U.S.C., Title 28, § 41(1) (now §§ 1332, 1345, 1359) (United States as plaintiff; civil suits at common law and in equity), relating to assigned claims in actions based on diversity of citizenship.

7. If the action proceeds to judgment without the interposition of a counterclaim as required by subdivision (a) of this rule, the counterclaim is barred. See *American Mills Co. v. American Surety Co.*, 260 U.S. 360, 43 S.Ct. 149, 67 L.Ed. 306 (1922); *Marconi Wireless Telegraph Co. v. National Electric Signalling Co.*, 206 Fed. 295 (E.D.N.Y., 1913); Hopkins, *Federal Equity Rules* (8th ed., 1933), p. 213; Simkins, *Federal Practice* (1934), p. 663.

8. For allowance of credits against the United States see U.S.C., Title 26, §§ 1672–1673 [sec. 7442] (Suits for refunds of internal revenue taxes—limitations); U.S.C., Title 28, § 774 (now § 2406) (Suits by United States against individuals; credits), [former] § 775 (Suits under postal laws; credits); U.S.C., Title 31, § 227 [now 3728] (Offsets against judgments and claims against United States).

1946 Amendment

Note. Subdivision (a). The use of the word "filing" was inadvertent. The word "serving" conforms with subdivision (e) and with usage generally throughout the rules.

The removal of the phrase "not the subject of a pending action" and the addition of the new clause at the end of the subdivision is designed to eliminate the ambiguity noted in *Prudential Insurance Co. of America v. Saxe*, App.D.C.1943, 77 U.S.App.D.C. 144, 134 F.2d 16, 33–34, cert. den., 1943, 319 U.S. 745, 63 S.Ct. 1033. The rewording of the subdivision in this respect insures against an undesirable possibility presented under the original rule whereby a party having a claim which would be the subject of a compulsory counterclaim could avoid stating it as such by bringing an independent action in another court after the commencement of the federal action but before serving his pleading in the federal action.

Subdivision (g). The amendment is to care for a situation such as where a second mortgagee is made defendant in a foreclosure proceeding and wishes to file a cross-complaint against the mortgagor in order to secure a personal judgment for the indebtedness and foreclose his lien. A claim of this sort by the second mortgagee may not necessarily arise out of the transaction or occurrence that is the subject matter of the original action under the terms of Rule 13(g).

Subdivision (h). The change clarifies the interdependence of Rules 13(i) and 54(b).

1963 Amendment

When a defendant, if he desires to defend his interest in property, is obliged to come in and litigate in a court to whose jurisdiction he could not ordinarily be subjected, fairness suggests that he should not be required to assert counterclaims, but should rather be permitted to do so at his election. If, however, he does elect to assert a counterclaim, it seems fair to require him to assert any other which is compulsory within the meaning of Rule 13(a). Clause (2), added by amendment to Rule 13(a), carries out this idea. It will apply to various cases described in Rule 4(e), as amended, where service is effected through attachment or other process by which the court does not acquire jurisdiction to render a personal judgment against the defendant. Clause (2) will also apply to actions commenced in State courts jurisdictionally grounded on attachment or the like, and removed to the Federal courts.

1966 Amendment

Rule 13(h), dealing with the joinder of additional parties to a counterclaim or cross-claim, has partaken of some of the textual difficulties of Rule 19 on necessary joinder of parties. See Advisory Committee's Note to Rule 19, as amended; cf. 3 *Moore's Federal Practice*, par. 13.39 (2d ed. 1963), and Supp. thereto; 1A Barron & Holtzoff, *Federal Practice and Procedure* § 399 (Wright ed. 1960). Rule 13(h) has also been inadequate in failing to call attention to the fact that a party pleading a counterclaim or cross-claim may join additional persons when the conditions for permissive joinder of parties under Rule 20 are satisfied.

The amendment of Rule 13(h) supplies the latter omission by expressly referring to Rule 20, as amended, and also incorporates by direct reference the revised criteria and procedures of Rule 19, as amended. Hereafter, for the purpose of determining who must or may be joined as additional parties to a counterclaim or cross-claim, the party pleading the claim is to be regarded as a plaintiff and the additional parties as plaintiffs or defendants as the case may be, and amended Rules 19 and 20 are to be applied in the usual fashion. See also Rules 13(a) (compulsory counterclaims) and 22 (interpleader).

The amendment of Rule 13(h), like the amendment of Rule 19, does not attempt to regulate Federal jurisdiction or venue. See Rule 82. It should be noted, however, that in some situations the decisional law has recognized "ancillary" Federal jurisdiction over counterclaims and cross-claims and "ancillary" venue as to parties to these claims.

1987 Amendment

The amendments are technical. No substantive change is intended.

2007 Amendment

The language of Rule 13 has been amended as part of the general restyling of the Civil Rules to make them more easily understood and to make style and terminology consistent throughout the rules. These changes are intended to be stylistic only.

The meaning of former Rule 13(b) is better expressed by deleting "not arising out of the transaction or occurrence that is the subject matter of the opposing party's claim." Both as a matter of intended meaning and current practice, a party may state as a permissive counterclaim a claim that does grow out of the same transaction or occurrence as an opposing party's claim even though one of the exceptions in Rule 13(a) means the claim is not a compulsory counterclaim.

2009 Amendment

Rule 13(f) is deleted as largely redundant and potentially misleading. An amendment to add a counterclaim will be governed by Rule 15. Rule 15(a)(1) permits some amendments to be made as a matter of course or with the opposing party's written consent. When the court's leave is required, the reasons described in Rule 13(f) for permitting amendment of a pleading to add an omitted counterclaim sound different from the general amendment standard in Rule 15(a)(2), but seem to be administered—as they should be—according to the same standard directing that leave should be freely given when justice so requires. The independent existence of Rule 13(f) has, however, created some uncertainty as to the availability of relation back of the amendment under Rule 15(c). *See 6 C. Wright, A. Miller & M. Kane, Federal Practice & Procedure: Civil 2d, § 1430 (1990).* Deletion of Rule 13(f) ensures that relation back is governed by the tests that apply to all other pleading amendments.

CROSS REFERENCES

Counterclaim,

Default judgment against counter-claimants, see Fed. Rules Civ.Proc. Rule 55, 28 USCA.

Dismissal, see Fed.Rules Civ.Proc. Rule 41, 28 USCA.

Mistake in designation of defense, see Fed.Rules Civ. Proc. Rule 8, 28 USCA.

Reply, see Fed.Rules Civ.Proc. Rule 7, 28 USCA.

Requisites of pleading, see Fed.Rules Civ.Proc. Rule 8, 28 USCA.

Service of pleadings, numerous defendants, see Fed. Rules Civ.Proc. Rule 5, 28 USCA.

Summary judgment, see Fed.Rules Civ.Proc. Rule 56, 28 USCA.

Third-party practice, see Fed.Rules Civ.Proc. Rule 14, 28 USCA.

Time for reply by United States, see Fed.Rules Civ.Proc. Rule 12, 28 USCA.

Cross-claim,

Answer to, if answer contains a cross-claim, see Fed. Rules Civ.Proc. Rule 7, 28 USCA.

Default judgment, see Fed.Rules Civ.Proc. Rule 55, 28 USCA.

Dismissal, see Fed.Rules Civ.Proc. Rule 41, 28 USCA.

Joinder, see Fed.Rules Civ.Proc. Rule 18, 28 USCA.

Requisites of pleading, see Fed.Rules Civ.Proc. Rule 8, 28 USCA.

Service of pleadings, numerous defendants, see Fed. Rules Civ.Proc. Rule 5, 28 USCA.

Summary judgment, see Fed.Rules Civ.Proc. Rule 56, 28 USCA.

Third-party practice, see Fed.Rules Civ.Proc. Rule 14, 28 USCA.

Time for answer by United States, see Fed.Rules Civ. Proc. Rule 12, 28 USCA.

Time of service of reply, see Fed.Rules Civ.Proc. Rule 12, 28 USCA.

Voluntary dismissal, see Fed.Rules Civ.Proc. Rule 41, 28 USCA.

Rule 14. Third–Party Practice

(a) When a Defending Party May Bring in a Third Party.

(1) *Timing of the Summons and Complaint.* A defending party may, as third-party plaintiff, serve a summons and complaint on a nonparty who is or may be liable to it for all or part of the claim against it. But the third-party plaintiff must, by motion, obtain the court's leave if it files the third-party complaint more than 14 days after serving its original answer.

(2) *Third–Party Defendant's Claims and Defenses.* The person served with the summons and third-party complaint—the "third-party defendant":

(A) must assert any defense against the third-party plaintiff's claim under Rule 12;

(B) must assert any counterclaim against the third-party plaintiff under Rule 13(a), and may assert any counterclaim against the third-party plaintiff under Rule 13(b) or any crossclaim against another third-party defendant under Rule 13(g);

(C) may assert against the plaintiff any defense that the third-party plaintiff has to the plaintiff's claim; and

(D) may also assert against the plaintiff any claim arising out of the transaction or occurrence that is the subject matter of the plaintiff's claim against the third-party plaintiff.

(3) *Plaintiff's Claims Against a Third–Party Defendant.* The plaintiff may assert against the third-party defendant any claim arising out of the transaction or occurrence that is the subject matter of the plaintiff's claim against the third-party plaintiff. The third-party defendant must then assert any defense under Rule 12 and any counterclaim under Rule 13(a), and may assert any counterclaim under Rule 13(b) or any crossclaim under Rule 13(g).

(4) *Motion to Strike, Sever, or Try Separately.* Any party may move to strike the third-party claim, to sever it, or to try it separately.

(5) *Third–Party Defendant's Claim Against a Nonparty.* A third-party defendant may proceed under this rule against a nonparty who is or may be liable to the third-party defendant for all or part of any claim against it.

(6) *Third–Party Complaint In Rem.* If it is within the admiralty or maritime jurisdiction, a third-party complaint may be in rem. In that event, a

reference in this rule to the "summons" includes the warrant of arrest, and a reference to the defendant or third-party plaintiff includes, when appropriate, a person who asserts a right under Supplemental Rule C(6)(a)(i) in the property arrested.

(b) When a Plaintiff May Bring in a Third Party. When a claim is asserted against a plaintiff, the plaintiff may bring in a third party if this rule would allow a defendant to do so.

(c) Admiralty or Maritime Claim.

(1) *Scope of Impleader.* If a plaintiff asserts an admiralty or maritime claim under Rule 9(h), the defendant or a person who asserts a right under Supplemental Rule C(6)(a)(i) may, as a third-party plaintiff, bring in a third-party defendant who may be wholly or partly liable—either to the plaintiff or to the third-party plaintiff—for remedy over, contribution, or otherwise on account of the same transaction, occurrence, or series of transactions or occurrences.

(2) *Defending Against a Demand for Judgment for the Plaintiff.* The third-party plaintiff may demand judgment in the plaintiff's favor against the third-party defendant. In that event, the third-party defendant must defend under Rule 12 against the plaintiff's claim as well as the third-party plaintiff's claim; and the action proceeds as if the plaintiff had sued both the third-party defendant and the third-party plaintiff.

(Amended December 27, 1946, effective March 19, 1948; January 21, 1963, effective July 1, 1963; February 28, 1966, effective July 1, 1966; March 2, 1987, effective August 1, 1987; April 17, 2000, effective December 1, 2000; April 12, 2006, effective December 1, 2006; April 30, 2007, effective December 1, 2007; March 26, 2009, effective December 1, 2009.)

ADVISORY COMMITTEE NOTES

1937 Adoption

Third-party impleader is in some aspects a modern innovation in law and equity although well known in admiralty. Because of its many advantages a liberal procedure with respect to it has developed in England, in the federal admiralty courts, and in some American state jurisdictions. See *English Rules Under the Judicature Act* (The Annual Practice, 1937) O. 16A, r.r. 1–13; United States Supreme Court Admiralty Rules (1920), Rule 56 (Right to Bring in Party Jointly Liable); 12 P.S.Pa. § 141; Wis.Stat. (1935) §§ 260.19, 260.20; N.Y.C.P.A. (1937) §§ 193(2), 211(a). Compare La. Code Pract. (Dart, 1932) §§ 378–388. For the practice in Texas as developed by judicial decision, see *Lottman v. Cuilla*, Tex.1926, 288 S.W. 123, 126. For a treatment of this subject see Gregory, *Legislative Loss Distribution in Negligence Actions* (1936); Shulman and Jaegerman, *Some Jurisdictional Limitations on Federal Procedure (1936)*, 45 Yale L.J. 393, 417 et seq.

Third-party impleader under the conformity act has been applied in actions at law in the Federal courts. *Lowry and Co., Inc. v. National City Bank of New York*, N.Y.1928, 28 F.2d 895; *Yellow Cab Co. of Philadelphia v. Rodgers*, C.C.A.3, 1932, 61 F.2d 729.

1946 Amendment

Note. The provisions in Rule 14(a) which relate to the impleading of a third party who is or may be liable to the plaintiff have been deleted by the proposed amendment. It has been held that under Rule 14(a) the plaintiff need not amend his complaint to state a claim against such third party if he does not wish to do so. *Satink v. Holland Township*, D.N.J.1940, 31 F.Supp. 229, noted, 1940, 88 U.Pa.L.Rev. 751; *Connelly v. Bender*, E.D.Mich.1941, 36 F.Supp. 368; *Whitmire v. Partin (Milton)*, E.D.Tenn.1941, 2 F.R.D. 83, 5 Fed. Rules Serv. 14a.513, Case 2; *Crim v. Lumbermen's Mutual Casualty Co.*, D.D.C.1939, 26 F.Supp. 715; *Carbola Chemical Co., Inc. v. Trundle*, S.D.N.Y.1943, 3 F.R.D. 502, 7 Fed.Rules Serv. 14a.224, Case 1; *Roadway Express, Inc. v. Automobile Ins. Co. of Hartford, Conn., (Providence Washington Ins. Co.)* N.D.Ohio 1945, 8 Fed.Rules Serv. 14a.513, Case 3. In *Delano v. Ives*, E.D.Pa.1941, 40 F.Supp. 672, the court said: ". . . the weight of authority is to the effect that a defendant cannot compel the plaintiff, who has sued him, to sue also a third party whom he does not wish to sue, by tendering in a third party complaint the third party as an additional defendant directly liable to the plaintiff." Thus impleader here amounts to no more than a mere offer of a party to the plaintiff, and if he rejects it, the attempt is a time-consuming futility. See *Satink v. Holland Township*, *supra*; *Malkin v. Arundel Corp.*, D.Md.1941, 36 F.Supp. 948; also Koenigsberger, *Suggestions for Changes in the Federal Rules of Civil Procedure*, 1941, 4 Fed.Rules Serv. 1010. But cf. *Atlantic Coast Line R. Co. v. United States Fidelity & Guaranty Co.*, Ga.1943, 52 F.Supp. 177. Moreover, in any case where the plaintiff could not have joined the third party originally because of jurisdictional limitations such as lack of diversity of citizenship, the majority view is that any attempt by the plaintiff to amend his complaint and assert a claim against the impleaded third party would be unavailing. *Hoskie v. Prudential Ins. Co. of America, (Lorrac Real Estate Corp.)*, E.D.N.Y.1941, 39 F.Supp. 305; *Johnson v. G. J. Sherrard Co., (New England Telephone & Telegraph Co.)*, D.Mass.1941, 5 Fed.Rules Serv. 14a.511, Case 1, 2 F.R.D. 164; *Thompson v. Cranston*, W.D.N.Y.1942, 6 Fed.Rules Serv. 14a.511, Case 1, 2 F.R.D. 270, affirmed CCA2d, 1942, 132 F.2d 631, certiorari denied 1945, 63 S.Ct. 1028, 319 U.S. 741, 87 L.Ed. 1698; *Friend v. Middle Atlantic Transportation Co.*, C.C.A.2, 1946, 153 F.2d 778, certiorari denied 1946, 66 S.Ct. 1370, 328 U.S. 865, 90 L.Ed. 1635; *Herrington v. Jones*, E.D.La.1941, 5 Fed.Rules Serv. 14a.511, Case 2, 2 F.R.D. 108; *Banks v. Employers' Liability Assurance Corp., (Central Surety & Ins. Corp.)* W.D.Mo.1943, 7 Fed.Rules Serv. 14a.11, Case 2; *Saunders v. Baltimore & Ohio R. Co.*, S.D.W.Va.1945, 9 Fed.Rules Serv. 14a.62, Case 2; *Hull v. United States Rubber Co. (Johnson Larsen and Co.)*, E.D.Mich.1945, 9 Fed.Rules Serv. 14a.62, Case 3. See also concurring opinion of Circuit Judge Minton in *People of State of Illinois for Use of Trust Co. of Chicago v. Maryland Casualty Co.*, C.C.A.7, 1942, 132 F.2d 850, 853. Contra: *Sklar v. Hayes (Singer)*, E.D.Pa.1941, 4 Fed.Rules Serv. 14a.511, Case 2, 1 F.R.D. 594. Discussion of the problem will be found in Commentary, *Amendment of Plaintiff's Pleading to Assert Claim Against Third-Party Defendant*, 1942, 5 Fed.Rules Serv. 811; Commentary, *Federal Jurisdiction in Third-Party Practice*, 1943, 6 Fed.Rules Serv. 766; Holtzoff, *Some Problems Under Federal Third-Party Practice*, 1941, 3 La.L.Rev. 408, 419–420; 1 Moore's *Federal Practice*, 1938, Cum.Supplement § 14.08. For these reasons

---

therefore, the words "or to the plaintiff" in the first sentence of subdivision (a) have been removed by the amendment; and in conformance therewith the words "the plaintiff" in the second sentence of the subdivision, and the words "or to the third-party plaintiff" in the concluding sentence thereof have likewise been eliminated.

The third sentence of rule 14(a) has been expanded to clarify the right of the third-party defendant to assert any defenses which the third-party plaintiff may have to the plaintiff's claim. This protects the impleaded third-party defendant where the third-party plaintiff fails or neglects to assert a proper defense to the plaintiff's action. A new sentence has also been inserted giving the third-party defendant the right to assert directly against the original plaintiff any claim arising out of the transaction or occurrence that is the subject matter of the plaintiff's claim against the third-party plaintiff. This permits all claims arising out of the same transaction or occurrence to be heard and determined in the same action. See *Atlantic Coast Line R. Co. v. United States Fidelity & Guaranty Co.*, Ga.1943, 52 F.Supp. 177. Accordingly, the next to the last sentence of subdivision (a) has also been revised to make clear that the plaintiff may, if he desires, assert directly against the third-party defendant either by amendment or by a new pleading any claim he may have against him arising out of the transaction or occurrence that is the subject matter of the plaintiff's claim against the third-party plaintiff. In such a case, the third-party defendant then is entitled to assert the defenses, counter-claims and cross-claims provided in Rules 12 and 13.

The sentence reading "The third-party defendant is bound by the adjudication of the third-party plaintiff's liability to the plaintiff, as well as of his own to the plaintiff, or to the third-party plaintiff" has been stricken from Rule 14(a), not to change the law, but because the sentence states a rule of substantive law which is not within the scope of a procedural rule. It is not the purpose of the rules to state the effect of a judgment.

The elimination of the words "the third-party plaintiff, or any other party" from the second sentence of rule 14(a), together with the insertion of the new phrases therein, are not changes of substance but are merely for the purpose of clarification.

1963 Amendment

Under the amendment of the initial sentences of the subdivision, a defendant as a third-party plaintiff may freely and without leave of court bring in a third-party defendant if he files the third-party complaint not later than 10 days after he serves his original answer. When the impleader comes so early in the case, there is little value in requiring a preliminary ruling by the court on the propriety of the impleader.

After the third-party defendant is brought in, the court has discretion to strike the third-party claim if it is obviously unmeritorious and can only delay or prejudice the disposition of the plaintiff's claim, or to sever the third-party claim or accord it separate trial if confusion or prejudice would otherwise result. This discretion, applicable not merely to the cases covered by the amendment where the third-party defendant is brought in without leave, but to all impleaders under the rule, is emphasized in the next-to-last sentence of the subdivision, added by amendment.

In dispensing with leave of court for an impleader filed not later than 10 days after serving the answer, but retaining the leave requirement for impleaders sought to be effected there-after, the amended subdivision takes a moderate position on the lines urged by some commentators, see Note, 43 Minn. L.Rev. 115 (1958); cf. Pa.R.Civ.P. 2252–53 (60 days after service on the defendant; Minn.R.Civ.P. 14.01 (45 days). Other commentators would dispense with the requirement of leave regardless of the time when impleader is effected, and would rely on subsequent action by the court to dismiss the impleader if it would unduly delay or complicate the litigation or would be otherwise objectionable. See 1A Barron & Holtzoff, *Federal Practice & Procedure* 649–50 (Wright ed. 1960); Comment, 58 Colum.L.Rev. 532, 546 (1958); cf. N.Y.Civ.Prac.Act § 193–a; Me.R.Civ.P. 14. The amended subdivision preserves the value of a preliminary screening, through the leave procedure, of impleaders attempted after the 10-day period.

The amendment applies also when an impleader is initiated by a third-party defendant against a person who may be liable to him, as provided in the last sentence of the subdivision.

1966 Amendment

Rule 14 was modeled on Admiralty Rule 56. An important feature of Admiralty Rule 56 was that it allowed impleader not only of a person who might be liable to the defendant by way of remedy over, but also of any person who might be liable to the plaintiff. The importance of this provision was that the defendant was entitled to insist that the plaintiff proceed to judgment against the third-party defendant. In certain cases this was a valuable implementation of a substantive right. For example, in a case of ship collision where a finding of mutual fault is possible, one shipowner, if sued alone, faces the prospect of an absolute judgment for the full amount of the damage suffered by an innocent third party; but if he can implead the owner of the other vessel, and if mutual fault is found, the judgment against the original defendant will be in the first instance only for a moiety of the damages; liability for the remainder will be conditioned on the plaintiff's inability to collect from the third-party defendant.

This feature was originally incorporated in Rule 14, but was eliminated by the amendment of 1946, so that under the amended rule a third party could not be impleaded on the basis that he might be liable to the plaintiff. One of the reasons for the amendment was that the Civil Rule, unlike the Admiralty Rule, did not require the plaintiff to go to judgment against the third-party defendant. Another reason was that where jurisdiction depended on diversity of citizenship the impleader of an adversary having the same citizenship as the plaintiff was not considered possible.

Retention of the admiralty practice in those cases that will be counterparts of a suit in admiralty is clearly desirable.

1987 Amendment

The amendments are technical. No substantive change is intended.

2000 Amendment

Subdivisions (a) and (c) are amended to reflect revisions in Supplemental Rule C(6).

GAP Report

Rule B(1)(a) was modified by moving "in an in personam action" out of paragraph (a) and into the first line of subdivision (1). This change makes it clear that all paragraphs of

---

subdivision (1) apply when attachment is sought in an in personam action. Rule B(1)(d) was modified by changing the requirement that the clerk deliver the summons and process to the person or organization authorized to serve it. The new form requires only that the summons and process be delivered, not that the clerk effect the delivery. This change conforms to present practice in some districts and will facilitate rapid service. It matches the spirit of Civil Rule 4(b), which directs the clerk to issue the summons "to the plaintiff for service on the defendant." A parallel change is made in Rule C(3)(b).

2006 Amendment

Rule 14 is amended to conform to changes in designating the paragraphs of Supplemental Rule C(6).

2007 Amendment

The language of Rule 14 has been amended as part of the general restyling of the Civil Rules to make them more easily understood and to make style and terminology consistent throughout the rules. These changes are intended to be stylistic only.

Former Rule 14 twice refers to counterclaims under Rule 13. In each case, the operation of Rule 13(a) depends on the state of the action at the time the pleading is filed. If plaintiff and third-party defendant have become opposing parties because one has made a claim for relief against the other, Rule 13(a) requires assertion of any counterclaim that grows out of the transaction or occurrence that is the subject matter of that claim. Rules 14(a)(2)(B) and (a)(3) reflect the distinction between compulsory and permissive counterclaims.

A plaintiff should be on equal footing with the defendant in making third-party claims, whether the claim against the plaintiff is asserted as a counterclaim or as another form of claim. The limit imposed by the former reference to "counterclaim" is deleted.

2009 Amendment

The time set in the former rule at 10 days has been revised to 14 days. See the Note to Rule 6.

CROSS REFERENCES

Third-party answer, service of third-party complaint, see Fed.Rules Civ.Proc. Rule 7, 28 USCA.

Third-party claim,

Dismissal of, see Fed.Rules Civ.Proc. Rule 41, 28 USCA.

Joinder, see Fed.Rules Civ.Proc. Rule 18, 28 USCA.

Judgment on less than all claims, see Fed.Rules Civ.Proc. Rule 54, 28 USCA.

Requisites, see Fed.Rules Civ.Proc. Rule 8, 28 USCA.

Separate trial, see Fed.Rules Civ.Proc. Rule 42, 28 USCA.

Third-party complaint, leave to summon person not an original party, see Fed.Rules Civ.Proc. Rule 7, 28 USCA.

Third-party plaintiff, default judgment against, see Fed. Rules Civ.Proc. Rule 55, 28 USCA.

Third-party tort liability to United States for hospital and medical care, see 42 USCA § 2651 et seq.

Rule 15.   Amended and Supplemental Pleadings

(a) Amendments Before Trial.

(1) *Amending as a Matter of Course.* A party may amend its pleading once as a matter of course within:

    (A) 21 days after serving it, or

    (B) if the pleading is one to which a responsive pleading is required, 21 days after service of a responsive pleading or 21 days after service of a motion under Rule 12(b), (e), or (f), whichever is earlier.

(2) *Other Amendments.* In all other cases, a party may amend its pleading only with the opposing party's written consent or the court's leave. The court should freely give leave when justice so requires.

(3) *Time to Respond.* Unless the court orders otherwise, any required response to an amended pleading must be made within the time remaining to respond to the original pleading or within 14 days after service of the amended pleading, whichever is later.

(b) Amendments During and After Trial.

(1) *Based on an Objection at Trial.* If, at trial, a party objects that evidence is not within the issues raised in the pleadings, the court may permit the pleadings to be amended. The court should freely permit an amendment when doing so will aid in presenting the merits and the objecting party fails to satisfy the court that the evidence would prejudice that party's action or defense on the merits. The court may grant a continuance to enable the objecting party to meet the evidence.

(2) *For Issues Tried by Consent.* When an issue not raised by the pleadings is tried by the parties' express or implied consent, it must be treated in all respects as if raised in the pleadings. A party may move—at any time, even after judgment—to amend the pleadings to conform them to the evidence and to raise an unpleaded issue. But failure to amend does not affect the result of the trial of that issue.

(c) Relation Back of Amendments.

(1) *When an Amendment Relates Back.* An amendment to a pleading relates back to the date of the original pleading when:

    (A) the law that provides the applicable statute of limitations allows relation back;

    (B) the amendment asserts a claim or defense that arose out of the conduct, transaction, or occurrence set out—or attempted to be set out—in the original pleading; or

    (C) the amendment changes the party or the naming of the party against whom a claim is asserted, if Rule 15(c)(1)(B) is satisfied and if, within the period provided by Rule 4(m) for serving the summons and complaint, the party to be brought in by amendment:

(i) received such notice of the action that it will not be prejudiced in defending on the merits; and

(ii) knew or should have known that the action would have been brought against it, but for a mistake concerning the proper party's identity.

(2) *Notice to the United States.* When the United States or a United States officer or agency is added as a defendant by amendment, the notice requirements of Rule 15(c)(1)(C)(i) and (ii) are satisfied if, during the stated period, process was delivered or mailed to the United States attorney or the United States attorney's designee, to the Attorney General of the United States, or to the officer or agency.

(d) Supplemental Pleadings. On motion and reasonable notice, the court may, on just terms, permit a party to serve a supplemental pleading setting out any transaction, occurrence, or event that happened after the date of the pleading to be supplemented. The court may permit supplementation even though the original pleading is defective in stating a claim or defense. The court may order that the opposing party plead to the supplemental pleading within a specified time.

(Amended January 21, 1963, effective July 1, 1963; February 28, 1966, effective July 1, 1966; March 2, 1987, effective August 1, 1987; April 30, 1991, effective December 1, 1991; amended by Pub.L. 102–198, § 11, December 9, 1991, 105 Stat. 1626; amended April 22, 1993, effective December 1, 1993; April 30, 2007, effective December 1, 2007; March 26, 2009, effective December 1, 2009.)

ADVISORY COMMITTEE NOTES

1937 Adoption

See generally for the present federal practice, [former] Equity Rules 19 (Amendments Generally), 28 (Amendment of Bill as of Course), 32 (Answer to Amended Bill), 34 (Supplemental Pleading), and 35 (Bills of Revivor and Supplemental Bills—Form); U.S.C. Title 28, § 399 [now 1653] (Amendments to show diverse citizenship) and [former] 777 (Defects of form; amendments). See *English Rules Under the Judicature Act* (The Annual Practice, 1937) O. 28, r. r. 1–13; O. 20, r. 4; O. 24, r. r. 1–3.

Note to Subdivision (a). The right to serve an amended pleading once as of course is common. 4 Mont.Rev.Codes Ann. (1935) § 9186; 1 Ore.Code Ann. (1930) § 1–904; 1 S.C.Code (Michie, 1932) § 493; *English Rules Under the Judicature Act* (The Annual Practice, 1937) O. 28, r. 2. Provision for amendment of pleading before trial, by leave of court, is in almost every code. If there is no statute the power of the court to grant leave is said to be inherent. Clark, *Code Pleading* (1928), pp. 498, 509.

Note to Subdivision (b). Compare [former] Equity Rule 19 (Amendments Generally) and code provisions which allow an amendment "at any time in furtherance of justice," (e.g., Ark.Civ.Code (Crawford, 1934) § 155) and which allow an amendment of pleadings to conform to the evidence, where

the adverse party has not been misled and prejudiced (e.g., N.M.Stat.Ann. (Courtright, 1929) §§ 105–601, 105–602).

Note to Subdivision (c). "Relation back" is a well recognized doctrine of recent and now more frequent application. Compare Ala.Code Ann. (Michie, 1928) § 9513; Smith-Hurd Ill.Stats. ch. 110, § 170(2); 2 Wash.Rev.Stat.Ann. (Remington, 1932) § 308–3(4). See U.S.C., Title 28, § 399 [now 1653] (Amendments to show diverse citizenship) for a provision for "relation back."

Note to Subdivision (d). This is an adaptation of former Equity Rule 34 (Supplemental Pleading).

1963 Amendment

Rule 15(d) is intended to give the court broad discretion in allowing a supplemental pleading. However, some cases, opposed by other cases and criticized by the commentators, have taken the rigid and formalistic view that where the original complaint fails to state a claim upon which relief can be granted, leave to serve a supplemental complaint must be denied. See *Bonner v. Elizabeth Arden, Inc.,* 177 F.2d 703 (2d Cir. 1949); *Bowles v. Senderowitz,* 65 F.Supp. 548 (E.D.Pa.), rev'd on other grounds, 158 F.2d 435 (3d Cir. 1946), cert. denied, *Senderowitz v. Fleming,* 330 U.S. 848, 67 S.Ct. 1091, 91 L.Ed. 1292 (1947); cf. *LaSalle Nat. Bank v. 222 East Chestnut St. Corp.,* 267 F.2d 247 (7th Cir.), cert. denied, 361 U.S. 836, 80 S.Ct. 88, 4 L.Ed.2d 77 (1959). But see *Camilla Cotton Oil Co. v. Spencer Kellogg & Sons,* 257 F.2d 162 (5th Cir. 1958); *Genuth v. National Biscuit Co.,* 81 F.Supp. 213 (S.D.N.Y.1948), app. dism., 177 F.2d 962 (2d Cir. 1949); 3 Moore's *Federal Practice* ¶ 15.01[5] (Supp.1960); 1A Barron & Holtzoff, *Federal Practice & Procedure* 820–21 (Wright ed. 1960). Thus plaintiffs have sometimes been needlessly remitted to the difficulties of commencing a new action even though events occurring after the commencement of the original action have made clear the right to relief.

Under the amendment the court has discretion to permit a supplemental pleading despite the fact that the original pleading is defective. As in other situations where a supplemental pleading is offered, the court is to determine in the light of the particular circumstances whether filing should be permitted, and if so, upon what terms. The amendment does not attempt to deal with such questions as the relation of the statute of limitations to supplemental pleadings, the operation of the doctrine of laches, or the availability of other defenses. All these questions are for decision in accordance with the principles applicable to supplemental pleadings generally. Cf. *Blau v. Lamb,* 191 F.Supp. 906 (S.D.N.Y.1961); *Lendonsol Amusement Corp. v. B. & Q. Assoc., Inc.,* 23 F.R.Serv. 15d.3, Case 1 (D.Mass.1957).

1966 Amendment

Rule 15(c) is amplified to state more clearly when an amendment of a pleading changing the party against whom a claim is asserted (including an amendment to correct a misnomer or misdescription of a defendant) shall "relate back" to the date of the original pleading.

The problem has arisen most acutely in certain actions by private parties against officers or agencies of the United States. Thus an individual denied social security benefits by the Secretary of Health, Education, and Welfare may secure review of the decision by bringing a civil action against that officer within sixty days. 42 U.S.C. § 405(g) (Supp. III, 1962). In several recent cases the claimants instituted timely action but mistakenly named as defendant the United States, the Department of HEW, the "Federal Security Administration" (a nonexistent agency), and a Secretary who had retired from the office nineteen days before. Discovering their mistakes, the claimants moved to amend their complaints to name the proper defendant; by this time the statutory sixty-day period had expired. The motions were denied on the ground that the amendment "would amount to the commencement of a new proceeding and would not relate back in time so as to avoid the statutory provision * * * that suit be brought within sixty days * * *" *Cohn v. Federal Security Adm.*, 199 F.Supp. 884, 885 (W.D.N.Y.1961); see also *Cunningham v. United States*, 199 F.Supp. 541 (W.D.Mo.1958); *Hall v. Department of HEW*, 199 F.Supp. 833 (S.D.Tex.1960); *Sandridge v. Folsom, Secretary of HEW*, 200 F.Supp. 25 (M.D.Tenn.1959). [The Secretary of Health, Education, and Welfare has approved certain ameliorative regulations under 42 U.S.C. § 405(g). See 29 Fed.Reg. 8209 (June 30, 1964); Jacoby, *The Effect of Recent Changes in the Law of "Nonstatutory" Judicial Review*, 53 Geo.L.J. 19, 42–43 (1964); see also *Simmons v. United States Dept. HEW*, 328 F.2d 86 (3d Cir. 1964).]

Analysis in terms of "new proceeding" is traceable to *Davis v. L. L. Cohen & Co.*, 268 U.S. 638 (1925), and *Mellon v. Arkansas Land & Lumber Co.*, 275 U.S. 460 (1928), but those cases antedate the adoption of the Rules which import different criteria for determining when an amendment is to "relate back". As lower courts have continued to rely on the *Davis* and *Mellon* cases despite the contrary intent of the Rules, clarification of Rule 15(c) is considered advisable.

Relation back is intimately connected with the policy of the statute of limitations. The policy of the statute limiting the time for suit against the Secretary of HEW would not have been offended by allowing relation back in the situations described above. For the government was put on notice of the claim within the stated period—in the particular instances, by means of the initial delivery of process to a responsible government official (see Rule 4(d)(4) and (5)). In these circumstances, characterization of the amendment as a new proceeding is not responsive to the realty [sic], but is merely question-begging; and to deny relation back is to defeat unjustly the claimant's opportunity to prove his case. See the full discussion by Byse, *Suing the "Wrong" Defendant in Judicial Review of Federal Administrative Action: Proposals for Reform,* 77 Harv.L.Rev. 40 (1963); see also Ill.Civ.P. Act § 46(4).

Much the same question arises in other types of actions against the government (see *Byse,* supra, at 45 n. 15). In actions between private parties, the problem of relation back of amendments changing defendants has generally been better handled by the courts, but incorrect criteria have sometimes been applied, leading sporadically to doubtful results. See 1A Barron & Holtzoff, *Federal Practice & Procedure* § 451 (Wright ed. 1960); 1 id. § 186 (1960); 2 id. § 543 (1961); 3 *Moore's Federal Practice,* par. 15.15 (Cum.Supp. 1962); Annot., *Change in Party After Statute of Limitations Has Run,* 8 A.L.R.2d 6 (1949). Rule 15(c) has been amplified to provide a general solution. An amendment changing the party against whom a claim is asserted relates back if the amendment satisfies the usual condition of Rule 15(c) of "arising out of the conduct * * * set forth * * * in the original pleading," and if, within the applicable limitations period, the party brought in by amendment, first, received such notice of the institution of the action—the notice need not be formal—that he would not be prejudiced in defending

the action, and, second, knew or should have known that the action would have been brought against him initially had there not been a mistake concerning the identity of the proper party. Revised Rule 15(c) goes on to provide specifically in the government cases that the first and second requirements are satisfied when the government has been notified in the manner there described (see Rule 4(d)(4) and (5)). As applied to the government cases, revised Rule 15(c) further advances the objectives of the 1961 amendment of Rule 25(d) (substitution of public officers).

The relation back of amendments changing plaintiffs is not expressly treated in revised Rule 15(c) since the problem is generally easier. Again the chief consideration of policy is that of the statute of limitations, and the attitude taken in revised Rule 15(c) toward change of defendants extends by analogy to amendments changing plaintiffs. Also relevant is the amendment of Rule 17(a) (real party in interest). To avoid forfeitures of just claims, revised Rule 17(a) would provide that no action shall be dismissed on the ground that it is not prosecuted in the name of the real party in interest until a reasonable time has been allowed for correction of the defect in the manner there stated.

1987 Amendment

The amendments are technical. No substantive change is intended.

1991 Amendment

The rule has been revised to prevent parties against whom claims are made from taking unjust advantage of otherwise inconsequential pleading errors to sustain a limitations defense.

Paragraph (c)(1). This provision is new. It is intended to make it clear that the rule does not apply to preclude any relation back that may be permitted under the applicable limitations law. Generally, the applicable limitations law will be state law. If federal jurisdiction is based on the citizenship of the parties, the primary reference is the law of the state in which the district court sits. *Walker v. Armco Steel Corp.,* 446 U.S. 740 (1980). If federal jurisdiction is based on a federal question, the reference may be to the law of the state governing relations between the parties. *E.g., Board of Regents v. Tomanio,* 446 U.S. 478 (1980). In some circumstances, the controlling limitations law may be federal law. *E.g., West v. Conrail, Inc.,* 107 S.Ct. 1538 (1987). Cf. *Burlington Northern R. Co. v. Woods,* 480 U.S. 1 (1987); *Stewart Organization v. Ricoh,* 108 S.Ct. 2239 (1988). Whatever may be the controlling body of limitations law, if that law affords a more forgiving principle of relation back than the one provided in this rule, it should be available to save the claim. Accord, *Marshall v. Mulrenin,* 508 F.2d 39 (1st Cir.1974). If *Schiavone v. Fortune,* 106 S.Ct. 2379 (1986) implies the contrary, this paragraph is intended to make a material change in the rule.

Paragraph (c)(3). This paragraph has been revised to change the result in *Schiavone v. Fortune, supra,* with respect to the problem of a misnamed defendant. An intended defendant who is notified of an action within the period allowed by Rule 4(m) [subdivision (m) in Rule 4 was a proposed subdivision which was withdrawn by the Supreme Court] for service of a summons and complaint may not under the revised rule defeat the action on account of a defect in the pleading with respect to the defendant's name, provided that the requirements of clauses (A) and (B) have been met. If the notice requirement is met within the Rule 4(m) [subdivision (m) in Rule 4 was a proposed subdivision which was withdrawn by the Supreme Court] period, a complaint may be amended at any time to correct a formal defect such as a misnomer or misidentification. On the basis of the text of the former rule, the Court reached a result in *Schiavone v. Fortune* that was inconsistent with the liberal pleading practices secured by Rule 8. See Bauer, *Schiavone: An Un-Fortune-ate Illustration of the Supreme Court's Role as Interpreter of the Federal Rules of Civil Procedure,* 63 Notre Dame L.Rev. 720 (1988); Brussack, *Outrageous Fortune: The Case for Amending Rule 15(c) Again,* 61 S.Cal.L.Rev. 671 (1988); Lewis, *The Excessive History of Federal Rule 15(c) and Its Lessons for Civil Rules Revision,* 86 Mich.L.Rev. 1507 (1987).

In allowing a name-correcting amendment within the time allowed by Rule 4(m), this rule allows not only the 120 days specified in that rule, but also any additional time resulting from any extension ordered by the court pursuant to that rule, as may be granted, for example, if the defendant is a fugitive from service of the summons.

This revision, together with the revision of Rule 4(i) with respect to the failure of a plaintiff in an action against the United States to effect timely service on all the appropriate officials, is intended to produce results contrary to those reached in *Gardner v. Gartman,* 880 F.2d 797 (4th Cir. 1989), *Rys v. U.S. Postal Service,* 886 F.2d 443 (1st Cir. 1989), *Martin's Food & Liquor, Inc. v. U.S. Dept. of Agriculture,* 14 F.R.D.3d 86 (N.D.Ill.1988). *But cf. Montgomery v. United States Postal Service,* 867 F.2d 900 (5th Cir. 1989), *Warren v. Department of the Army,* 867 F.2d 1156 (8th Cir. 1989); *Miles v. Department of the Army,* 881 F.2d 777 (9th Cir. 1989), *Barsten v. Department of the Interior,* 896 F.2d 422 (9th Cir. 1990); *Brown v. Georgia Dept. of Revenue,* 881 F.2d 1018 (11th Cir. 1989).

1993 Amendment

The amendment conforms the cross reference to Rule 4 to the revision of that rule.

2007 Amendment

The language of Rule 15 has been amended as part of the general restyling of the Civil Rules to make them more easily understood and to make style and terminology consistent throughout the rules. These changes are intended to be stylistic only.

Former Rule 15(c)(3)(A) called for notice of the "institution" of the action. Rule 15(c)(1)(C)(i) omits the reference to "institution" as potentially confusing. What counts is that the party to be brought in have notice of the existence of the action, whether or not the notice includes details as to its "institution."

2009 Amendment

Rule 15(a)(1) is amended to make three changes in the time allowed to make one amendment as a matter of course.

Former Rule 15(a) addressed amendment of a pleading to which a responsive pleading is required by distinguishing between the means used to challenge the pleading. Serving a responsive pleading terminated the right to amend. Serving a motion attacking the pleading did not terminate the right to amend, because a motion is not a "pleading" as defined in

Rule 7. The right to amend survived beyond decision of the motion unless the decision expressly cut off the right to amend.

The distinction drawn in former Rule 15(a) is changed in two ways. First, the right to amend once as a matter of course terminates 21 days after service of a motion under Rule 12(b), (e), or (f). This provision will force the pleader to consider carefully and promptly the wisdom of amending to meet the arguments in the motion. A responsive amendment may avoid the need to decide the motion or reduce the number of issues to be decided, and will expedite determination of issues that otherwise might be raised seriatim. It also should advance other pretrial proceedings.

Second, the right to amend once as a matter of course is no longer terminated by service of a responsive pleading. The responsive pleading may point out issues that the original pleader had not considered and persuade the pleader that amendment is wise. Just as amendment was permitted by former Rule 15(a) in response to a motion, so the amended rule permits one amendment as a matter of course in response to a responsive pleading. The right is subject to the same 21–day limit as the right to amend in response to a motion.

The 21–day periods to amend once as a matter of course after service of a responsive pleading or after service of a designated motion are not cumulative. If a responsive pleading is served after one of the designated motions is served, for example, there is no new 21–day period.

Finally, amended Rule 15(a)(1) extends from 20 to 21 days the period to amend a pleading to which no responsive pleading is allowed and omits the provision that cuts off the right if the action is on the trial calendar. Rule 40 no longer refers to a trial calendar, and many courts have abandoned formal trial calendars. It is more effective to rely on scheduling orders or other pretrial directions to establish time limits for amendment in the few situations that otherwise might allow one amendment as a matter of course at a time that would disrupt trial preparations. Leave to amend still can be sought under Rule 15(a)(2), or at and after trial under Rule 15(b).[1]

Abrogation of Rule 13(f) establishes Rule 15 as the sole rule governing amendment of a pleading to add a counterclaim.

The times set in the former rule at 10 or 20 days have been revised to 14 or 21 days. See the Note to Rule 6.

[1] If the proposed amendment to Rule 15(a)(3) ... changing the time period is approved by the Judicial Conference, the following additional sentence will be added to the Committee Note: "Amended Rule 15(a)(3) extends from 10 to 14 days the period to respond to an amended pleading."

HISTORICAL NOTES

Effective and Applicability Provisions

1991 Acts. Section 11(a) of Pub.L. 102–198 amended subd. (c)(3) of this rule, as transmitted to the Congress by the Supreme Court pursuant to section 2074 of title 28, United States Code, to become effective on December 1, 1991.

CROSS REFERENCES

Jurisdiction, amendment to show, see 28 USCA § 1653.

Recasting of pleadings on removal of cause, see 28 USCA § 1447.

Substitution of successor to public officer by supplemental pleading, see Fed.Rules Civ.Proc. Rule 25, 28 USCA.

Time for service of pleadings, see Fed.Rules Civ.Proc. Rule 12, 28 USCA.

Rule 16. Pretrial Conferences; Scheduling; Management

(a) **Purposes of a Pretrial Conference.** In any action, the court may order the attorneys and any unrepresented parties to appear for one or more pretrial conferences for such purposes as:

(1) expediting disposition of the action;

(2) establishing early and continuing control so that the case will not be protracted because of lack of management;

(3) discouraging wasteful pretrial activities;

(4) improving the quality of the trial through more thorough preparation; and

(5) facilitating settlement.

(b) **Scheduling.**

(1) *Scheduling Order.* Except in categories of actions exempted by local rule, the district judge—or a magistrate judge when authorized by local rule—must issue a scheduling order:

(A) after receiving the parties' report under Rule 26(f); or

(B) after consulting with the parties' attorneys and any unrepresented parties at a scheduling conference.

(2) *Time to Issue.* The judge must issue the scheduling order as soon as practicable, but unless the judge finds good cause for delay, the judge must issue it within the earlier of 90 days after any defendant has been served with the complaint or 60 days after any defendant has appeared.

(3) *Contents of the Order.*

(A) *Required Contents.* The scheduling order must limit the time to join other parties, amend the pleadings, complete discovery, and file motions.

(B) *Permitted Contents.* The scheduling order may:

(i) modify the timing of disclosures under Rules 26(a) and 26(e)(1);

(ii) modify the extent of discovery;

(iii) provide for disclosure, discovery, or preservation of electronically stored information;

(iv) include any agreements the parties reach for asserting claims of privilege or of protection as trial-preparation material after information is produced, including agreements reached under Federal Rule of Evidence 502;

(v) direct that before moving for an order relating to discovery, the movant must request a conference with the court;

(vi) set dates for pretrial conferences and for trial; and

(vii) include other appropriate matters.

(4) *Modifying a Schedule.* A schedule may be modified only for good cause and with the judge's consent.

(c) **Attendance and Matters for Consideration at a Pretrial Conference.**

(1) *Attendance.* A represented party must authorize at least one of its attorneys to make stipulations and admissions about all matters that can reasonably be anticipated for discussion at a pretrial conference. If appropriate, the court may require that a party or its representative be present or reasonably available by other means to consider possible settlement.

(2) *Matters for Consideration.* At any pretrial conference, the court may consider and take appropriate action on the following matters:

(A) formulating and simplifying the issues, and eliminating frivolous claims or defenses;

(B) amending the pleadings if necessary or desirable;

(C) obtaining admissions and stipulations about facts and documents to avoid unnecessary proof, and ruling in advance on the admissibility of evidence;

(D) avoiding unnecessary proof and cumulative evidence, and limiting the use of testimony under Federal Rule of Evidence 702;

(E) determining the appropriateness and timing of summary adjudication under Rule 56;

(F) controlling and scheduling discovery, including orders affecting disclosures and discovery under Rule 26 and Rules 29 through 37;

(G) identifying witnesses and documents, scheduling the filing and exchange of any pretrial briefs, and setting dates for further conferences and for trial;

(H) referring matters to a magistrate judge or a master;

(I) settling the case and using special procedures to assist in resolving the dispute when authorized by statute or local rule;

(J) determining the form and content of the pretrial order;

(K) disposing of pending motions;

(L) adopting special procedures for managing potentially difficult or protracted actions that may involve complex issues, multiple parties, difficult legal questions, or unusual proof problems;

(M) ordering a separate trial under Rule 42(b) of a claim, counterclaim, crossclaim, third-party claim, or particular issue;

(N) ordering the presentation of evidence early in the trial on a manageable issue that might, on the evidence, be the basis for a judgment as a matter of law under Rule 50(a) or a judgment on partial findings under Rule 52(c);

(O) establishing a reasonable limit on the time allowed to present evidence; and

(P) facilitating in other ways the just, speedy, and inexpensive disposition of the action.

(d) Pretrial Orders. After any conference under this rule, the court should issue an order reciting the action taken. This order controls the course of the action unless the court modifies it.

(e) Final Pretrial Conference and Orders. The court may hold a final pretrial conference to formulate a trial plan, including a plan to facilitate the admission of evidence. The conference must be held as close to the start of trial as is reasonable, and must be attended by at least one attorney who will conduct the trial for each party and by any unrepresented party. The court may modify the order issued after a final pretrial conference only to prevent manifest injustice.

(f) Sanctions.

(1) *In General.* On motion or on its own, the court may issue any just orders, including those authorized by Rule 37(b)(2)(A)(ii)-(vii), if a party or its attorney:

(A) fails to appear at a scheduling or other pretrial conference;

(B) is substantially unprepared to participate— or does not participate in good faith—in the conference; or

(C) fails to obey a scheduling or other pretrial order.

(2) *Imposing Fees and Costs.* Instead of or in addition to any other sanction, the court must order the party, its attorney, or both to pay the reasonable expenses—including attorney's fees—incurred because of any noncompliance with this rule, unless the noncompliance was substantially justified or other circumstances make an award of expenses unjust.

(Amended April 28, 1983, effective August 1, 1983; March 2, 1987, effective August 1, 1987; April 22, 1993, effective December 1, 1993; April 12, 2006, effective December 1, 2006; April 30, 2007, effective December 1, 2007; April 29, 2015, effective December 1, 2015.)

ADVISORY COMMITTEE NOTES

1937 Adoption

1. Similar rules of pre-trial procedure are now in force in Boston, Cleveland, Detroit, and Los Angeles, and a rule substantially like this one has been proposed for the urban centers of New York state. For a discussion of the successful operation of pre-trial procedure in relieving the congested condition of trial calendars of the courts in such cities and for the proposed New York plan, see *A Proposal for Minimizing Calendar Delay in Jury Cases* (Dec. 1936—published by the New York Law Society); *Pre-Trial Procedure and Administration*, Third Annual Report of the Judicial Council of the State of New York (1937), pages 207–243; *Report of the Commission on the Administration of Justice in New York State* (1934), pp. (288) to (290). See also *Pre-Trial Procedure in the Wayne Circuit Court*, Detroit, Michigan, Sixth Annual Report of the Judicial Council of Michigan (1936), pp. 63 to 75; and Sunderland, *The Theory and Practice of Pre-trial Proce-*

dure (Dec. 1937) 36 Mich.L.Rev. 215–226, 21 J.Am.Jud.Soc. 125. Compare the English procedure known as the "summons for directions," *English Rules Under the Judicature Act* (The Annual Practice, 1937) O. 38a; and a similar procedure in New Jersey, N.J.S.A. 2:27–135, 2:27–136, 2:27–160; N.J. Supreme Court Rules, 2 N.J.Misc.Rep. (1924) 1230, Rules 94, 92, 93, 95 (the last three as amended 1933, 11 N.J.Misc.Rep. (1933) 955).

2. Compare the similar procedure under Rule 56(d) (Summary Judgment—Case Not Fully Adjudicated on Motion). Rule 12(g) (Consolidation of Motions), by requiring to some extent the consolidation of motions dealing with matters preliminary to trial, is a step in the same direction. In connection with clause (5) of this rule, see Rules 53(b) (Masters; Reference) and 53(e)(3) (Master's Report; In Jury Actions).

1983 Amendment

Introduction

Rule 16 has not been amended since the Federal Rules were promulgated in 1938. In many respects, the rule has been a success. For example, there is evidence that pretrial conferences may improve the quality of justice rendered in the federal courts by sharpening the preparation and presentation of cases, tending to eliminate trial surprise, and improving, as well as facilitating, the settlement process. See 6 Wright & Miller, *Federal Practice and Procedure: Civil* § 1522 (1971). However, in other respects particularly with regard to case management, the rule has not always been as helpful as it might have been. Thus there has been a widespread feeling that amendment is necessary to encourage pretrial management that meets the needs of modern litigation. See *Report of the National Commission for the Review of Antitrust Laws and Procedures* (1979).

Major criticism of Rule 16 has centered on the fact that its application can result in over-regulation of some cases and under-regulation of others. In simple, run-of-the-mill cases, attorneys have found pretrial requirements burdensome. It is claimed that over-administration leads to a series of mini-trials that result in a waste of an attorney's time and needless expense to a client. Pollack, *Pretrial Procedures More Effectively Handled*, 65 F.R.D. 475 (1974). This is especially likely to be true when pretrial proceedings occur long before trial. At the other end of the spectrum, the discretionary character of Rule 16 and its orientation toward a single conference late in the pretrial process has led to under-administration of complex or protracted cases. Without judicial guidance beginning shortly after institution, these cases often become mired in discovery.

Four sources of criticism of pretrial have been identified. First, conferences often are seen as a mere exchange of legalistic contentions without any real analysis of the particular case. Second, the result frequently is nothing but a formal agreement on minutiae. Third, the conferences are seen as unnecessary and time-consuming in cases that will be settled before trial. Fourth, the meetings can be ceremonial and ritualistic, having little effect on the trial and being of minimal value, particularly when the attorneys attending the sessions are not the ones who will try the case or lack authority to enter into binding stipulations. See generally *McCargo v. Hedrick*, 545 F.2d 393 (4th Cir.1976); Pollack, *Pretrial Procedures More Effectively Handled*, 65 F.R.D. 475

(1974); Rosenberg, *The Pretrial Conference and Effective Justice* 45 (1964).

There also have been difficulties with the pretrial orders that issue following Rule 16 conferences. When an order is entered far in advance of trial, some issues may not be properly formulated. Counsel naturally are cautious and often try to preserve as many options as possible. If the judge who tries the case did not conduct the conference, he could find it difficult to determine exactly what was agreed to at the conference. But any insistence on a detailed order may be too burdensome, depending on the nature or posture of the case.

Given the significant changes in federal civil litigation since 1938 that are not reflected in Rule 16, it has been extensively rewritten and expanded to meet the challenges of modern litigation. Empirical studies reveal that when a trial judge intervenes personally at an early stage to assume judicial control over a case and to schedule dates for completion by the parties of the principal pretrial steps, the case is disposed of by settlement or trial more efficiently and with less cost and delay than when the parties are left to their own devices. Flanders, *Case Management and Court Management in United States District Courts* 17, Federal Judicial Center (1977). Thus, the rule mandates a pretrial scheduling order. However, although scheduling and pretrial conferences are encouraged in appropriate cases, they are not mandated.

Discussion

Subdivision (a); Pretrial Conferences; Objectives. The amended rule makes scheduling and case management an express goal of pretrial procedure. This is done in Rule 16(a) by shifting the emphasis away from a conference focused solely on the trial and toward a process of judicial management that embraces the entire pretrial phase, especially motions and discovery. In addition, the amendment explicitly recognizes some of the objectives of pretrial conferences and the powers that many courts already have assumed. Rule 16 thus will be a more accurate reflection of actual practice.

Subdivision (b); Scheduling and Planning. The most significant change in Rule 16 is the mandatory scheduling order described in Rule 16(b), which is based in part on Wisconsin Civil Procedure Rule 802.10. The idea of scheduling orders is not new. It has been used by many federal courts. See, *e.g.*, Southern District of Indiana, Local Rule 19.

Although a mandatory scheduling order encourages the court to become involved in case management early in the litigation, it represents a degree of judicial involvement that is not warranted in many cases. Thus, subdivision (b) permits each district court to promulgate a local rule under Rule 83 exempting certain categories of cases in which the burdens of scheduling orders exceed the administrative efficiencies that would be gained. See Eastern District of Virginia, Local Rule 12(1). Logical candidates for this treatment include social security disability matters, habeas corpus petitions, forfeitures, and reviews of certain administrative actions.

A scheduling conference may be requested either by the judge, a magistrate when authorized by district court rule, or a party within 120 days after the summons and complaint are filed. If a scheduling conference is not arranged within that time and the case is not exempted by local rule, a scheduling order must be issued under Rule 16(b), after some communication with the parties, which may be by telephone or mail rather than in person. The use of the term "judge" in subdivision (b) reflects the Advisory Committee's judgment that it is preferable that this task should be handled by a district judge rather than a magistrate, except when the magistrate is acting under 28 U.S.C. § 636(c). While personal supervision by the trial judge is preferred, the rule, in recognition of the impracticality or difficulty of complying with such a requirement in some districts, authorizes a district by local rule to delegate the duties to a magistrate. In order to formulate a practicable scheduling order, the judge, or a magistrate when authorized by district court rule, and attorneys are required to develop a timetable for the matters listed in Rule 16(b)(1)–(3). As indicated in Rule 16(b)(4)–(5), the order may also deal with a wide range of other matters. The rule is phrased permissively as to clauses (4) and (5), however, because scheduling these items at an early point may not be feasible or appropriate. Even though subdivision (b) relates only to scheduling, there is no reason why some of the procedural matters listed in Rule 16(c) cannot be addressed at the same time, at least when a scheduling conference is held.

Item (1) assures that at some point both the parties and the pleadings will be fixed, by setting a time within which joinder of parties shall be completed and the pleadings amended.

Item (2) requires setting time limits for interposing various motions that otherwise might be used as stalling techniques.

Item (3) deals with the problem of procrastination and delay by attorneys in a context in which scheduling is especially important-discovery. Scheduling the completion of discovery can serve some of the same functions as the conference described in Rule 26(f).

Item (4) refers to setting dates for conferences and for trial. Scheduling multiple pretrial conferences may well be desirable if the case is complex and the court believes that a more elaborate pretrial structure, such as that described in the *Manual for Complex Litigation*, should be employed. On the other hand, only one pretrial conference may be necessary in an uncomplicated case.

As long as the case is not exempted by local rule, the court must issue a written scheduling order even if no scheduling conference is called. The order, like pretrial orders under the former rule and those under new Rule 16(c), normally will "control the subsequent course of the action." See Rule 16(e). After consultation with the attorneys for the parties and any unrepresented parties-a formal motion is not necessary-the court may modify the schedule on a showing of good cause if it cannot reasonably be met despite the diligence of the party seeking the extension. Since the scheduling order is entered early in the litigation, this standard seems more appropriate than a "manifest injustice" or "substantial hardship" test. Otherwise, a fear that extensions will not be granted may encourage counsel to request the longest possible periods for completing pleading, joinder, and discovery. Moreover, changes in the court's calendar sometimes will oblige the judge or magistrate when authorized by district court rule to modify the scheduling order.

The district courts undoubtedly will develop several prototype scheduling orders for different types of cases. In addition, when no formal conference is held, the court may obtain scheduling information by telephone, mail, or otherwise. In many instances this will result in a scheduling order better suited to the individual case than a standard order, without taking the time that would be required by a formal conference.

Rule 16(b) assures that the judge will take some early control over the litigation, even when its character does not warrant holding a scheduling conference. Despite the fact that the process of preparing a scheduling order does not always bring the attorneys and judge together, the fixing of time limits serves

> to stimulate litigants to narrow the areas of inquiry and advocacy to those they believe are truly relevant and material. Time limits not only compress the amount of time for litigation, they should also reduce the amount of resources invested in litigation. Litigants are forced to establish discovery priorities and thus to do the most important work first.

Report of the National Commission for the Review of Antitrust Laws and Procedures 28 (1979).

Thus, except in exempted cases, the judge or a magistrate when authorized by district court rule will have taken some action in every case within 120 days after the complaint is filed that notifies the attorneys that the case will be moving toward trial. Subdivision (b) is reenforced by subdivision (f), which makes it clear that the sanctions for violating a scheduling order are the same as those for violating a pretrial order.

Subdivision (c); Subjects to be Discussed at Pretrial Conferences. This subdivision expands upon the list of things that may be discussed at a pretrial conference that appeared in original Rule 16. The intention is to encourage better planning and management of litigation. Increased judicial control during the pretrial process accelerates the processing and termination of cases. Flanders, *Case Management and Court Management in United States District Courts*, 39 Federal Judicial Center (1977). See also *Report of the National Commission for the Review of Antitrust Laws and Procedures* (1979).

The reference in Rule 16(c)(1) to "formulation" is intended to clarify and confirm the court's power to identify the litigable issues. It has been added in the hope of promoting efficiency and conserving judicial resources by identifying the real issues prior to trial, thereby saving time and expense for everyone. See generally *Meadow Gold Prods. Co. v. Wright*, 278 F.2d 867 (D.C.Cir.1960). The notion is emphasized by expressly authorizing the elimination of frivolous claims or defenses at a pretrial conference. There is no reason to require that this await a formal motion for summary judgment. Nor is there any reason for the court to wait for the parties to initiate the process called for in Rule 16(c)(1).

The timing of any attempt at issue formulation is a matter of judicial discretion. In relatively simple cases it may not be necessary or may take the form of a stipulation between counsel or a request by the court that counsel work together to draft a proposed order.

Counsel bear a substantial responsibility for assisting the court in identifying the factual issues worthy of trial. If counsel fail to identify an issue for the court, the right to have the issue tried is waived. Although an order specifying the issues is intended to be binding, it may be amended at trial to avoid manifest injustice. See Rule 16(e). However, the rule's effectiveness depends on the court employing its discretion sparingly.

Clause (6) acknowledges the widespread availability and use of magistrates. The corresponding provision in the original rule referred only to masters and limited the function of the reference to the making of "findings to be used as evidence" in a case to be tried to a jury. The new text is not limited and broadens the potential use of a magistrate to that permitted by the Magistrate's Act.

Clause (7) explicitly recognizes that it has become commonplace to discuss settlement at pretrial conferences. Since it obviously eases crowded court dockets and results in savings to the litigants and the judicial system, settlement should be facilitated at as early a stage of the litigation as possible. Although it is not the purpose of Rule 16(b)(7) to impose settlement negotiations on unwilling litigants, it is believed that providing a neutral forum for discussing the subject might foster it. See Moore's *Federal Practice* ¶ 16.17; 6 Wright & Miller, *Federal Practice and Procedure: Civil* § 1522 (1971). For instance, a judge to whom a case has been assigned may arrange, on his own motion or at a party's request, to have settlement conferences handled by another member of the court or by a magistrate. The rule does not make settlement conferences mandatory because they would be a waste of time in many cases. See Flanders, *Case Management and Court Management in the United States District Courts*, 39 Federal Judicial Center (1977). Requests for a conference from a party indicating a willingness to talk settlement normally should be honored, unless thought to be frivolous or dilatory.

A settlement conference is appropriate at any time. It may be held in conjunction with a pretrial or discovery conference, although various objectives of pretrial management, such as moving the case toward trial, may not always be compatible with settlement negotiations, and thus a separate settlement conference may be desirable. See 6 Wright & Miller, *Federal Practice and Procedure: Civil* § 1522, at p. 571 (1971).

In addition to settlement, Rule 16(c)(7) refers to exploring the use of procedures other than litigation to resolve the dispute. This includes urging the litigants to employ adjudicatory techniques outside the courthouse. See, for example, the experiment described in *Green, Marks & Olson, Settling Large Case Litigation: An Alternative Approach*, 11 Loyola of L.A.L.Rev. 493 (1978).

Rule 16(c)(10) authorizes the use of special pretrial procedures to expedite the adjudication of potentially difficult or protracted cases. Some district courts obviously have done so for many years. See Rubin, *The Managed Calendar: Some Pragmatic Suggestions About Achieving the Just, Speedy and Inexpensive Determination of Civil Cases in Federal Courts*, 4 Just.Sys.J. 135 (1976). Clause 10 provides an explicit authorization for such procedures and encourages their use. No particular techniques have been described; the Committee felt that flexibility and experience are the keys to efficient management of complex cases. Extensive guidance is offered in such documents as the *Manual for Complex Litigation*.

The rule simply identifies characteristics that make a case a strong candidate for special treatment. The four mentioned are illustrative, not exhaustive, and overlap to some degree. But experience has shown that one or more of them will be present in every protracted or difficult case and it seems desirable to set them out. See Kendig, *Procedures for Management of Non-Routine Cases*, 3 Hofstra L.Rev. 701 (1975).

The last sentence of subdivision (c) is new. See Wisconsin Civil Procedure Rule 802.11(2). It has been added to meet one of the criticisms of the present practice described earlier and insure proper preconference preparation so that the meeting is more than a ceremonial or ritualistic event. The reference to "authority" is not intended to insist upon the ability to settle the litigation. Nor should the rule be read to encourage the judge conducting the conference to compel attorneys to enter into stipulations or to make admissions that they consider to be unreasonable, that touch on matters that could not normally have been anticipated to arise at the conference, or on subjects of a dimension that normally require prior consultation with and approval from the client.

Subdivision (d); Final Pretrial Conference. This provision has been added to make it clear that the time between any final pretrial conference (which in a simple case may be the **only** pretrial conference) and trial should be as short as possible to be certain that the litigants make substantial progress with the case and avoid the inefficiency of having that preparation repeated when there is a delay between the last pretrial conference and trial. An optimum time of 10 days to two weeks has been suggested by one federal judge. Rubin, *The Managed Calendar: Some Pragmatic Suggestions About Achieving the Just, Speedy and Inexpensive Determination of Civil Cases in Federal Courts*, 4 Just.Sys.J. 135, 141 (1976). The Committee, however, concluded that it would be inappropriate to fix a precise time in the rule, given the numerous variables that could bear on the matter. Thus the timing has been left to the court's discretion.

At least one of the attorneys who will conduct the trial for each party must be present at the final pretrial conference. At this late date there should be no doubt as to which attorney or attorneys this will be. Since the agreements and stipulations made at this final conference will control the trial, the presence of lawyers who will be involved in it is especially useful to assist the judge in structuring the case, and to lead to a more effective trial.

Subdivision (e); Pretrial Orders. Rule 16(e) does not substantially change the portion of the original rule dealing with pretrial orders. The purpose of an order is to guide the course of the litigation and the language of the original rule making that clear has been retained. No compelling reason has been found for major revision, especially since this portion of the rule has been interpreted and clarified by over forty years of judicial decisions with comparatively little difficulty. See 6 Wright & Miller, *Federal Practice and Procedure: Civil* §§ 1521–30 (1971). Changes in language therefore have been kept to a minimum to avoid confusion.

Since the amended rule encourages more extensive pretrial management than did the original, two or more conferences may be held in many cases. The language of Rule 16(e) recognizes this possibility and the corresponding need to issue more than one pretrial order in a single case.

Once formulated, pretrial orders should not be changed lightly; but total inflexibility is undesirable. See, *e.g.*, *Clark v. Pennsylvania R.R. Co.*, 328 F.2d 591 (2d Cir.1964). The exact words used to describe the standard for amending the pretrial order probably are less important than the meaning given them in practice. By not imposing any limitation on the ability to modify a pretrial order, the rule reflects the reality that in any process of continuous management, what is done at one conference may have to be altered at the next. In the case of the final pretrial order, however, a more stringent standard is called for and the words "to prevent manifest injustice," which appeared in the original rule, have been retained. They have the virtue of familiarity and adequately describe the restraint the trial judge should exercise.

Many local rules make the plaintiff's attorney responsible for drafting a proposed pretrial order, either before or after the conference. Others allow the court to appoint any of the attorneys to perform the task, and others leave it to the court. See Note, *Pretrial Conference: A Critical Examination of Local Rules Adopted by Federal District Courts*, 64 Va.L.Rev. 467 (1978). Rule 16 has never addressed this matter. Since there is no consensus about which method of drafting the order works best and there is no reason to believe that nationwide uniformity is needed, the rule has been left silent on the point. See *Handbook for Effective Pretrial Procedure*, 37 F.R.D. 225 (1964).

Subdivision (f); Sanctions. Original Rule 16 did not mention the sanctions that might be imposed for failing to comply with the rule. However, courts have not hesitated to enforce it by appropriate measures. See, e.g., *Link v. Wabash R. Co.*, 370 U.S. 628 (1962) (district court's dismissal under Rule 41(b) after plaintiff's attorney failed to appear at a pretrial conference upheld); *Admiral Theatre Corp. v. Douglas Theatre*, 585 F.2d 877 (8th Cir.1978) (district court has discretion to exclude exhibits or refuse to permit the testimony of a witness not listed prior to trial in contravention of its pretrial order).

To reflect that existing practice, and to obviate dependence upon Rule 41(b) or the court's inherent power to regulate litigation, cf. *Societe Internationale Pour Participations Industrielles et Commerciales, S.A. v. Rogers*, 357 U.S. 197 (1958), Rule 16(f) expressly provides for imposing sanctions on disobedient or recalcitrant parties, their attorneys, or both in four types of situations. Rodes, Ripple & Mooney, *Sanctions Imposable for Violations of the Federal Rules of Civil Procedure* 65–67, 80–84, Federal Judicial Center (1981). Furthermore, explicit reference to sanctions reenforces the rule's intention to encourage forceful judicial management.

Rule 16(f) incorporates portions of Rule 37(b)(2), which prescribes sanctions for failing to make discovery. This should facilitate application of Rule 16(f), since courts and lawyers already are familiar with the Rule 37 standards. Among the sanctions authorized by the new subdivision are: preclusion order, striking a pleading, staying the proceeding, default judgment, contempt, and charging a party, his attorney, or both with the expenses, including attorney's fees, caused by noncompliance. The contempt sanction, however, is only available for a violation of a court order. The references in Rule 16(f) are not exhaustive.

As is true under Rule 37(b)(2), the imposition of sanctions may be sought by either the court or a party. In addition, the court has discretion to impose whichever sanction it feels is appropriate under the circumstances. Its action is reviewable under the abuse-of-discretion standard. See *National Hockey League v. Metropolitan Hockey Club, Inc.*, 427 U.S. 639 (1976).

1987 Amendment

The amendments are technical. No substantive change is intended.

1993 Amendment

Subdivision (b). One purpose of this amendment is to provide a more appropriate deadline for the initial scheduling order required by the rule. The former rule directed that the order be entered within 120 days from the filing of the complaint. This requirement has created problems because Rule 4(m) allows 120 days for service and ordinarily at least one defendant should be available to participate in the process of formulating the scheduling order. The revision provides that the order is to be entered within 90 days after the date a defendant first appears (whether by answer or by a motion under Rule 12) or, if earlier (as may occur in some actions against the United States or if service is waived under Rule 4), within 120 days after service of the complaint on a defendant. The longer time provided by the revision is not intended to encourage unnecessary delays in entering the scheduling order. Indeed, in most cases the order can and should be entered at a much earlier date. Rather, the additional time is intended to alleviate problems in multi-defendant cases and should ordinarily be adequate to enable participation by all defendants initially named in the action.

In many cases the scheduling order can and should be entered before this deadline. However, when setting a scheduling conference, the court should take into account the effect this setting will have in establishing deadlines for the parties to meet under revised Rule 26(f) and to exchange information under revised Rule 26(a)(1). While the parties are expected to stipulate to additional time for making their disclosures when warranted by the circumstances, a scheduling conference held before defendants have had time to learn much about the case may result in diminishing the value of the Rule 26(f) meeting, the parties' proposed discovery plan, and indeed the conference itself.

New paragraph (4) has been added to highlight that it will frequently be desirable for the scheduling order to include provisions relating to the timing of disclosures under Rule 26(a). While the initial disclosures required by Rule 26(a)(1) will ordinarily have been made before entry of the scheduling order, the timing and sequence for disclosure of expert testimony and of the witnesses and exhibits to be used at trial should be tailored to the circumstances of the case and is a matter that should be considered at the initial scheduling conference. Similarly, the scheduling order might contain provisions modifying the extent of discovery (*e.g.*, number and length of depositions) otherwise permitted under these rules or by a local rule.

The report from the attorneys concerning their meeting and proposed discovery plan, as required by revised Rule 26(f), should be submitted to the court before the scheduling order is entered. Their proposals, particularly regarding matters on which they agree, should be of substantial value to the court in setting the timing and limitations on discovery and should reduce the time of the court needed to conduct a meaningful conference under Rule 16(b). As under the prior rule, while a scheduling order is mandated, a scheduling conference is not. However, in view of the benefits to be derived from the litigants and a judicial officer meeting in person, a Rule 16(b) conference should, to the extent practicable, be held in all cases that will involve discovery.

This subdivision, as well as subdivision (c)(8), also is revised to reflect the new title of United States Magistrate Judges pursuant to the Judicial Improvements Act of 1990.

Subdivision (c). The primary purposes of the changes in subdivision (c) are to call attention to the opportunities for structuring of trial under Rules 42, 50, and 52 and to eliminate questions that have occasionally been raised regarding the authority of the court to make appropriate orders designed either to facilitate settlement or to provide for an efficient and economical trial. The prefatory language of this subdivision is revised to clarify the court's power to enter appropriate orders at a conference notwithstanding the objection of a party. Of course settlement is dependent upon agreement by the parties and, indeed, a conference is most effective and productive when the parties participate in a spirit of cooperation and mindful of their responsibilities under Rule 1.

Paragraph (4) is revised to clarify that in advance of trial the court may address the need for, and possible limitations on, the use of expert testimony under Rule 702 of the Federal Rules of Evidence. Even when proposed expert testimony might be admissible under the standards of Rules 403 and 702 of the evidence rules, the court may preclude or limit such testimony if the cost to the litigants—which may include the cost to adversaries of securing testimony on the same subjects by other experts—would be unduly expensive given the needs of the case and the other evidence available at trial.

Paragraph (5) is added (and the remaining paragraphs renumbered) in recognition that use of Rule 56 to avoid or reduce the scope of trial is a topic that can, and often should, be considered at a pretrial conference. Renumbered paragraph (11) enables the court to rule on pending motions for summary adjudication that are ripe for decision at the time of the conference. Often, however, the potential use of Rule 56 is a matter that arises from discussions during a conference. The court may then call for motions to be filed.

Paragraph (6) is added to emphasize that a major objective of pretrial conferences should be to consider appropriate controls on the extent and timing of discovery. In many cases the court should also specify the times and sequence for disclosure of written reports from experts under revised Rule 26(a)(2)(B) and perhaps direct changes in the types of experts from whom written reports are required. Consideration should also be given to possible changes in the timing or form of the disclosure of trial witnesses and documents under Rule 26(a)(3).

Paragraph (9) is revised to describe more accurately the various procedures that, in addition to traditional settlement conferences, may be helpful in settling litigation. Even if a case cannot immediately be settled, the judge and attorneys can explore possible use of alternative procedures such as mini-trials, summary jury trials, mediation, neutral evaluation, and nonbinding arbitration that can lead to consensual resolution of the dispute without a full trial on the merits. The rule acknowledges the presence of statutes and local rules or plans that may authorize use of some of these procedures even when not agreed to by the parties. See 28 U.S.C. §§ 473(a)(6), 473(b)(4), 651–58; Section 104(b)(2), Pub.L. 101–650. The rule does not attempt to resolve questions as to the extent a court would be authorized to require such proceedings as an exercise of its inherent powers.

The amendment of paragraph (9) should be read in conjunction with the sentence added to the end of subdivision (c), authorizing the court to direct that, in appropriate cases, a responsible representative of the parties be present or available by telephone during a conference in order to discuss possible settlement of the case. The sentence refers to participation by a party or its representative. Whether this would be the individual party, an officer of a corporate party, a representative from an insurance carrier, or someone else would depend on the circumstances. Particularly in litigation in which governmental agencies or large amounts of money are involved, there may be no one with on-the-spot settlement authority, and the most that should be expected is access to a person who would have a major role in submitting a recommendation to the body or board with ultimate decision-making responsibility. The selection of the appropriate representative should ordinarily be left to the party and its counsel. Finally, it should be noted that the unwillingness of a party to be available, even by telephone, for a settlement conference may be a clear signal that the time and expense involved in pursuing settlement is likely to be unproductive and that personal participation by the parties should not be required.

The explicit authorization in the rule to require personal participation in the manner stated is not intended to limit the reasonable exercise of the court's inherent powers, *e.g., G. Heileman Brewing Co. v. Joseph Oat Corp.,* 871 F.2d 648 (7th Cir.1989), or its power to require party participation under the Civil Justice Reform Act of 1990. See 28 U.S.C. § 473(b)(5) (civil justice expense and delay reduction plans adopted by district courts may include requirement that representatives "with authority to bind [parties] in settlement discussions" be available during settlement conferences).

New paragraphs (13) and (14) are added to call attention to the opportunities for structuring of trial under Rule 42 and under revised Rules 50 and 52.

Paragraph (15) is also new. It supplements the power of the court to limit the extent of evidence under Rules 403 and 611(a) of the Federal Rules of Evidence, which typically would be invoked as a result of developments during trial. Limits on the length of trial established at a conference in advance of trial can provide the parties with a better opportunity to determine priorities and exercise selectivity in presenting evidence than when limits are imposed during trial. Any such limits must be reasonable under the circumstances, and ordinarily the court should impose them only after receiving appropriate submissions from the parties outlining the nature of the testimony expected to be presented through various witnesses, and the expected duration of direct and cross-examination.

2006 Amendment

The amendment to Rule 16(b) is designed to alert the court to the possible need to address the handling of discovery of electronically stored information early in the litigation if such discovery is expected to occur. Rule 26(f) is amended to direct the parties to discuss discovery of electronically stored information if such discovery is contemplated in the action. Form 35 is amended to call for a report to the court about the results of this discussion. In many instances, the court's involvement early in the litigation will help avoid difficulties that might otherwise arise.

Rule 16(b) is also amended to include among the topics that may be addressed in the scheduling order any agreements that the parties reach to facilitate discovery by minimizing the risk of waiver of privilege or work-product protection. Rule 26(f) is amended to add to the discovery plan the parties' proposal for the court to enter a case-management or other order adopting such an agreement. The parties may agree to various arrangements. For example, they may agree to initial provision of requested materials without waiver of privilege or protection to enable the party seeking production to designate the materials desired or protection for actual production, with the privilege review of only those materials to follow. Alternatively, they may agree that if privileged or protected information is inadvertently produced, the producing party may by timely notice assert the privilege or protection and obtain return of the materials without waiver. Other arrangements are possible. In most circumstances, a party who receives information under such an arrangement cannot assert that production of the information waived a claim of privilege or of protection as trial-preparation material.

An order that includes the parties' agreement may be helpful in avoiding delay and excessive cost in discovery. *See Manual for Complex Litigation* (4th) § 11.446. Rule 16(b)(6) recognizes the propriety of including such agreements in the court's order. The rule does not provide the court with authority to enter such a case-management or other order without party agreement, or limit the court's authority to act on motion.

2007 Amendment

The language of Rule 16 has been amended as part of the general restyling of the Civil Rules to make them more easily understood and to make style and terminology consistent throughout the rules. These changes are intended to be stylistic only.

When a party or its representative is not present, it is enough to be reasonably available by any suitable means, whether telephone or other communication device.

2015 Amendment

The provision for consulting at a scheduling conference by "telephone, mail, or other means" is deleted. A scheduling conference is more effective if the court and parties engage in direct simultaneous communication. The conference may be held in person, by telephone, or by more sophisticated electronic means.

The time to issue the scheduling order is reduced to the earlier of 90 days (not 120 days) after any defendant has been served, or 60 days (not 90 days) after any defendant has appeared. This change, together with the shortened time for making service under Rule 4(m), will reduce delay at the beginning of litigation. At the same time, a new provision recognizes that the court may find good cause to extend the time to issue the scheduling order. In some cases it may be that the parties cannot prepare adequately for a meaningful Rule 26(f) conference and then a scheduling conference in the time allowed. Litigation involving complex issues, multiple parties, and large organizations, public or private, may be more likely to need extra time to establish meaningful collaboration between counsel and the people who can supply the information needed to participate in a useful way. Because the time for the Rule 26(f) conference is geared to the time for the scheduling conference or order, an order extending the time for the scheduling conference will also extend the time for the Rule 26(f) conference. But in most cases it will be desirable to hold at least a first scheduling conference in the time set by the rule.

Three items are added to the list of permitted contents in Rule 16(b)(3)(B).

The order may provide for preservation of electronically stored information, a topic also added to the provisions of a discovery plan under Rule 26(f)(3)(C). Parallel amendments of Rule 37(e) recognize that a duty to preserve discoverable information may arise before an action is filed.

The order also may include agreements incorporated in a court order under Evidence Rule 502 controlling the effects of disclosure of information covered by attorney-client privilege or work-product protection, a topic also added to the provisions of a discovery plan under Rule 26(f)(3)(D).

Finally, the order may direct that before filing a motion for an order relating to discovery the movant must request a conference with the court. Many judges who hold such conferences find them an efficient way to resolve most discovery disputes without the delay and burdens attending a formal motion, but the decision whether to require such conferences is left to the discretion of the judge in each case.

Change of Name

Reference to United States magistrate or to magistrate deemed to refer to United States magistrate judge pursuant to section 321 of Pub.L. 101–650, set out as a note under section 631 of this title.

TITLE IV. PARTIES

Rule 17. Plaintiff and Defendant; Capacity; Public Officers

(a) Real Party in Interest.

(1) *Designation in General.* An action must be prosecuted in the name of the real party in interest. The following may sue in their own names without joining the person for whose benefit the action is brought:

    (A) an executor;

    (B) an administrator;

    (C) a guardian;

    (D) a bailee;

    (E) a trustee of an express trust;

    (F) a party with whom or in whose name a contract has been made for another's benefit; and

    (G) a party authorized by statute.

(2) *Action in the Name of the United States for Another's Use or Benefit.* When a federal statute so provides, an action for another's use or benefit must be brought in the name of the United States.

(3) *Joinder of the Real Party in Interest.* The court may not dismiss an action for failure to prosecute in the name of the real party in interest until, after an objection, a reasonable time has been allowed for the real party in interest to ratify, join, or be substituted into the action. After ratification, joinder, or substitution, the action proceeds as if it had been originally commenced by the real party in interest.

(b) Capacity to Sue or Be Sued. Capacity to sue or be sued is determined as follows:

(1) for an individual who is not acting in a representative capacity, by the law of the individual's domicile;

(2) for a corporation, by the law under which it was organized; and

(3) for all other parties, by the law of the state where the court is located, except that:

    (A) a partnership or other unincorporated association with no such capacity under that state's law may sue or be sued in its common name to enforce a substantive right existing under the United States Constitution or laws; and

    (B) 28 U.S.C. §§ 754 and 959(a) govern the capacity of a receiver appointed by a United States court to sue or be sued in a United States court.

(c) Minor or Incompetent Person.

(1) *With a Representative.* The following representatives may sue or defend on behalf of a minor or an incompetent person:

    (A) a general guardian;

    (B) a committee;

    (C) a conservator; or

    (D) a like fiduciary.

(2) *Without a Representative.* A minor or an incompetent person who does not have a duly appointed representative may sue by a next friend or by a guardian ad litem. The court must appoint a guardian ad litem—or issue another appropriate order—to protect a minor or incompetent person who is unrepresented in an action.

(d) Public Officer's Title and Name. A public officer who sues or is sued in an official capacity may be designated by official title rather than by name, but the court may order that the officer's name be added. (Amended December 27, 1946, effective March 19, 1948; December 29, 1948, effective October 20, 1949; February 28, 1966, effective July 1, 1966; March 2, 1987, effective August 1, 1987; April 25, 1988, effective August 1, 1988; amended by Pub.L. 100–690, Title VII, § 7049, November 18, 1988, 102 Stat. 4401 (although amendment by Pub.L. 100–690 could not be executed due to prior amendment by Court order which made the same change effective August 1, 1988); April 30, 2007, effective December 1, 2007.)

ADVISORY COMMITTEE NOTES

1937 Adoption

Note to Subdivision (a). The real party in interest provision, except for the last clause which is new, is taken verbatim from [former] Equity Rule 37 (Parties Generally—Intervention), except that the word "expressly" has been omitted. For similar provisions see N.Y.C.P.A., (1937) § 210; Wyo. Rev.Stat.Ann. (1931) §§ 89–501, 89–502, 89–503; *English Rules Under the Judicature Act* (The Annual Practice, 1937) O. 16, r. 8. See, also Equity Rule 41 (Suit to Execute Trusts of Will—Heir as Party). For examples of statutes of the United States providing particularly for an action for the use or benefit of another in the name of the United States, see U.S.C., Title 40, § 270b [see now 40 U.S.C.A. § 3133(b)] (Suit by persons furnishing labor and material for work on public building contracts * * * may sue on a payment bond, "in the name of the United States for the use of the person suing"); and U.S.C., Title 25, § 201 (Penalties under laws relating to Indians—how recovered). Compare U.S.C., Title 26, Int.Rev. Code [1939], § 3745(c) [former § 1645(c)] (Suits for penalties, fines, and forfeitures, under this title, where not otherwise provided for, to be in name of United States).

Note to Subdivision (b). For capacity see generally Clark and Moore, *New Federal Civil Procedure*—II. Pleadings and Parties, 44 Yale L.J. 1291, 1312–1317 (1935) and specifically *Coppedge v. Clinton*, 72 F.2d 531 (C.C.A.10th, 1934) (natural person); *David Lupton's Sons Co. v. Automobile Club of America*, 225 U.S. 489, 32 S.Ct. 711, 56 L.Ed. 1177, Ann.Cas. 1914A, 699 (1912) (corporation); *Puerto Rico v. Russell & Co.*, 288 U.S. 476, 53 S.Ct. 447, 77 L.Ed. 903 (1933) (unincorporated assn.); *United Mine Workers of America v. Coronado Coal Co.*, 259 U.S. 344, 42 S.Ct. 570, 66 L.Ed. 975, 27 A.L.R. 762 (1922) (federal substantive right enforced against unincorporated association by suit against the association in its common name without naming all its members as parties). This rule follows the existing law as to such associations, as declared in the case last cited above. Compare *Moffat Tunnel League v. United States*, 289 U.S. 113, 53 S.Ct. 543, 77 L.Ed. 1069 (1933). See note to Rule 23, clause (1).

Note to Subdivision (c). The provision for infants and incompetent persons is substantially former Equity Rule 70 (Suits by or Against Incompetents) with slight additions. Compare the more detailed English provisions, *English Rules Under the Judicature Act* (The Annual Practice, 1937) O. 16, r.r. 16–21.

1946 Amendment

Note. The new matter [in subdivision (b)] makes clear the controlling character of Rule 66 regarding suits by or against a federal receiver in a federal court.

1948 Amendment

The amendment effective October 20, 1949, deleted the words "Rule 66" at the end of subdivision (b) and substituted the words "Title 28, U.S.C., §§ 754 and 959(a)".

1966 Amendment

The minor change in the text of the rule is designed to make it clear that the specific instances enumerated are not exceptions to, but illustrations of, the rule. These illustrations, of course, carry no negative implication to the effect that there are not other instances of recognition as the real party in interest of one whose standing as such may be in doubt. The enumeration is simply of cases in which there might be substantial doubt as to the issue but for the specific enumeration. There are other potentially arguable cases that are not excluded by the enumeration. For example, the enumeration states that the promisee in a contract for the benefit of a third party may sue as real party in interest; it does not say, because it is obvious, that the third-party beneficiary may sue (when the applicable law gives him that right.)

The rule adds to the illustrative list of real parties in interest a bailee—meaning, of course, a bailee suing on behalf of the bailor with respect to the property bailed. (When the possessor of property other than the owner sues for an invasion of the possessory interest he is the real party in interest.) The word "bailee" is added primarily to preserve the admiralty practice whereby the owner of a vessel as bailee of the cargo, or the master of the vessel as bailee of both vessel and cargo, sues for damage to either property interest or both. But there is no reason to limit such a provision to maritime situations. The owner of a warehouse in which household furniture is stored is equally entitled to sue on behalf of the numerous owners of the furniture stored. Cf. *Gulf Oil Corp. v. Gilbert*, 330 U.S. 501 (1947).

The provision that no action shall be dismissed on the ground that it is not prosecuted in the name of the real party in interest until a reasonable time has been allowed, after the objection has been raised, for ratification, substitution, etc., is added simply in the interests of justice. In its origin the rule concerning the real party in interest was permissive in purpose: it was designed to allow an assignee to sue in his own name. That having been accomplished, the modern function of the rule in its negative aspect is simply to protect the defendant against a subsequent action by the party actually entitled to recover, and to insure generally that the judgment will have its proper effect as res judicata.

This provision keeps pace with the law as it is actually developing. Modern decisions are inclined to be lenient when an honest mistake has been made in choosing the party in whose name the action is to be filed—in both maritime and nonmaritime cases. See *Levinson v. Deupree*, 345 U.S. 648 (1953); *Link Aviation, Inc. v. Downs*, 325 F.2d 613 (D.C.Cir. 1963). The provision should not be misunderstood or distorted. It is intended to prevent forfeiture when determination of the proper party to sue is difficult or when an understandable mistake has been made. It does not mean, for example, that, following an airplane crash in which all aboard were killed, an action may be filed in the name of John Doe (a fictitious person), as personal representative of Richard Roe (another fictitious person), in the hope that at a later time the attorney filing the action may substitute the real name of the real personal representative of a real victim, and have the benefit of suspension of the limitation period. It does not even mean, when an action is filed by the personal representative of John Smith, of Buffalo, in the good faith belief that he was aboard the flight, that upon discovery that Smith is alive and well, having missed the fatal flight, the representative of James Brown, of San Francisco, an actual victim, can be substituted to take advantage of the suspension of the limitation period. It is, in cases of this sort, intended to insure against forfeiture and injustice—in short, to codify in broad terms the salutary principle of *Levinson v. Deupree*, 345 U.S. 648 (1953), and *Link Aviation, Inc. v. Downs*, 325 F.2d 613 (D.C.Cir. 1963).

1987 Amendment

The amendments are technical. No substantive change is intended.

1988 Amendment

The amendment is technical. No substantive change is intended.

2007 Amendment

The language of Rule 17 has been amended as part of the general restyling of the Civil Rules to make them more easily understood and to make style and terminology consistent throughout the rules. These changes are intended to be stylistic only.

Rule 17(d) incorporates the provisions of former Rule 25(d)(2), which fit better with Rule 17.

HISTORICAL NOTES
Revision Notes and Legislative Reports

1988 Acts. For Related Reports, see 1988 U.S. Code Cong. and Adm.News, p. 5937.

Rule 18.   Joinder of Claims

(a) In General. A party asserting a claim, counterclaim, crossclaim, or third-party claim may join, as independent or alternative claims, as many claims as it has against an opposing party.

(b) Joinder of Contingent Claims. A party may join two claims even though one of them is contingent on the disposition of the other; but the court may grant relief only in accordance with the parties' relative substantive rights. In particular, a plaintiff may state a claim for money and a claim to set aside a conveyance that is fraudulent as to that plaintiff, without first obtaining a judgment for the money.

(Amended February 28, 1966, effective July 1, 1966; March 2, 1987, effective August 1, 1987; April 30, 2007, effective December 1, 2007.)

ADVISORY COMMITTEE NOTES

1937 Adoption

Note to Subdivision (a). 1. Recent development, both in code and common law states, has been toward unlimited joinder of actions. See Ill.Rev.Stat. (1937) ch. 110, § 168; N.J.S.A. 2:27–37, as modified by N.J.Sup.Ct.Rules, Rule 21, 2 N.J.Misc. 1208 (1924); N.Y.C.P.A. (1937) § 258 as amended by Laws of 1935, ch. 339.

2. This provision for joinder of actions has been patterned upon [former] Equity Rule 26 (Joinder of Causes of Action) and broadened to include multiple parties. Compare the English practice, *English Rules Under the Judicature Act* (The Annual Practice, 1937) O. 18, r.r. 1–9 (noting rules 1 and 6). The earlier American codes set forth classes of joinder, following the now abandoned New York rule. See N.Y.C.P.A. § 258 before amended in 1935; Compare Kan.Gen.Stat.Ann. (1935) § 60–601; Wis.Stat.(1935) § 263.04 for the more liberal practice.

3. The provisions of this rule for the joinder of claims are subject to Rule 82 (Jurisdiction and Venue Unaffected). For the jurisdictional aspects of joinder of claims, see Shulman and Jaegerman, *Some Jurisdictional Limitations on Federal Procedure* (1936), 45 Yale L.J. 393, 397–410. For separate trials of joined claims, see Rule 42(b).

Note to Subdivision (b). This rule is inserted to make it clear that in a single action a party should be accorded all the relief to which he is entitled regardless of whether it is legal or equitable or both. This necessarily includes a deficiency judgment in foreclosure actions formerly provided for in [former] Equity Rule 10 (Decree for Deficiency in Foreclosures, Etc.). In respect to fraudulent conveyances the rule changes the former rule requiring a prior judgment against the owner (*Braun v. American Laundry Mach. Co.*, 56 F.2d 197 (S.D.N.Y. 1932)) to conform to the provisions of the

Uniform Fraudulent Conveyance Act, §§ 9 and 10. See McLaughlin, *Application of the Uniform Fraudulent Conveyance Act*, 46 Harv.L.Rev. 404, 444 (1933).

1966 Amendment

The Rules "proceed upon the theory that no inconvenience can result from the joinder of any two or more matters in the pleadings, but only from trying two or more matters together which have little or nothing in common." Sunderland, *The New Federal Rules*, 45 W.Va.L.Q. 5, 13 (1938); see Clark, Code Pleading 58 (2d ed. 1947). Accordingly, Rule 18(a) has permitted a party to plead multiple claims of all types against an opposing party, subject to the court's power to direct an appropriate procedure for trying the claims. See Rules 42(b), 20(b), 21.

The liberal policy regarding joinder of claims in the pleadings extends to cases with multiple parties. However, the language used in the second sentence of Rule 18(a)—"if the requirements of Rules 19 [necessary joinder of parties], 20 [permissive joinder of parties], and 22 [interpleader] are satisfied"—has led some courts to infer that the rules regulating joinder of parties are intended to carry back to Rule 18(a) and to impose some special limits on joinder of claims in multiparty cases. In particular, Rule 20(a) has been read as restricting the operation of Rule 18(a) in certain situations in which a number of parties have been permissively joined in an action. In *Federal Housing Admr. v. Christianson*, 26 F.Supp. 419 (D.Conn.1939), the indorsee of two notes sued the three comakers of one note, and sought to join in the action a count on a second note which had been made by two of the three defendants. There was no doubt about the propriety of the joinder of the three parties defendant, for a right to relief was being asserted against all three defendants which arose out of a single "transaction" (the first note) and a question of fact or law "common" to all three defendants would arise in the action. See the text of Rule 20(a). The court, however, refused to allow the joinder of the count on the second note, on the ground that this right to relief, assumed to arise from a distinct transaction, did not involve a question common to all the defendants but only two of them. For analysis of the *Christianson* case and other authorities, see 2 Barron & Holtzoff, *Federal Practice & Procedure*, § 533.1 (Wright ed. 1961); 3 Moore's *Federal Practice*, par. 18.04[3] (2d ed. 1963).

If the court's view is followed, it becomes necessary to enter at the pleading stage into speculations about the exact relation between the claim sought to be joined against fewer than all the defendants properly joined in the action, and the claims asserted against all the defendants. Cf. Wright, *Joinder of Claims and Parties Under Modern Pleading Rules*, 36 Minn.L.Rev. 580, 605–06 (1952). Thus if it could be found in the Christianson situation that the claim on the second note arose out of the same transaction as the claim on the first or out of a transaction forming part of a "series," and that any question of fact or law with respect to the second note also arose with regard to the first, it would be held that the claim on the second note could be joined in the complaint. See 2 Barron & Holtzoff, supra, at 109; see also id. at 198 n. 60.4; cf. 3 Moore's *Federal Practice*, supra, at 1811. Such pleading niceties provide a basis for delaying and wasteful maneuver. It is more compatible with the design of the Rules to allow the claim to be joined in the pleading, leaving the question of possible separate trial of that claim to be later decided. See 2 Barron & Holtzoff, supra, § 533.1; Wright, supra, 36 Minn. L.Rev. at 604–11; *Developments in the Law—Multiparty*

Litigation in the Federal Courts, 71 Harv. 874, 970–71 (1958); Commentary, *Relation Between Joinder of Parties and Joinder of Claims,* 5 F.R.Serv. 822 (1942). It is instructive to note that the court in the *Christianson* case, while holding that the claim on the second note could not be joined as a matter of pleading, held open the possibility that both claims would later be consolidated for trial under Rule 42(a). See 26 F.Supp. 419.

Rule 18(a) is now amended not only to overcome the *Christianson* decision and similar authority, but also to state clearly as a comprehensive proposition, that a party asserting a claim (an original claim, counterclaim, cross-claim, or third-party claim) may join as many claims as he has against an opposing party. See *Noland Co., Inc. v. Graver Tank & Mfg. Co.,* 301 F.2d 43, 49–51 (4th Cir.1962); but cf. *C. W. Humphrey Co. v. Security Alum. Co.,* 31 F.R.D. 41 (E.D.Mich. 1962). This permitted joinder of claims is not affected by the fact that there are multiple parties in the action. The joinder of parties is governed by other rules operating independently.

It is emphasized that amended Rule 18(a) deals only with pleading. As already indicated, a claim properly joined as a matter of pleading need not be proceeded with together with the other claims if fairness or convenience justifies separate treatment.

Amended Rule 18(a), like the rule prior to amendment, does not purport to deal with questions of jurisdiction or venue which may arise with respect to claims properly joined as a matter of pleading. See Rule 82.

See also the amendment of Rule 20(a) and the Advisory Committee's Note thereto.

Free joinder of claims and remedies is one of the basic purposes of unification of the admiralty and civil procedure. The amendment accordingly provides for the inclusion in the rule of maritime claims as well as those which are legal and equitable in character.

1987 Amendment

The amendments are technical. No substantive change is intended.

2007 Amendment

The language of Rule 18 has been amended as part of the general restyling of the Civil Rules to make them more easily understood and to make style and terminology consistent throughout the rules. These changes are intended to be stylistic only.

Modification of the obscure former reference to a claim "heretofore cognizable only after another claim has been prosecuted to a conclusion" avoids any uncertainty whether Rule 18(b)'s meaning is fixed by retrospective inquiry from some particular date.

CROSS REFERENCES

Counterclaims and cross-claims, see Fed.Rules Civ.Proc. Rule 13, 28 USCA.

General rules of pleading, see Fed.Rules Civ.Proc. Rule 8, 28 USCA.

One form of action, see Fed.Rules Civ.Proc. Rule 2, 28 USCA.

Separate trials of claims, see Fed.Rules Civ.Proc. Rules 20 and 42, 28 USCA.

Severance of claim against party, see Fed.Rules Civ.Proc. Rule 20, 28 USCA.

Rule 19. Required Joinder of Parties

(a) Persons Required to Be Joined if Feasible.

(1) *Required Party.* A person who is subject to service of process and whose joinder will not deprive the court of subject-matter jurisdiction must be joined as a party if:

(A) in that person's absence, the court cannot accord complete relief among existing parties; or

(B) that person claims an interest relating to the subject of the action and is so situated that disposing of the action in the person's absence may:

(i) as a practical matter impair or impede the person's ability to protect the interest; or

(ii) leave an existing party subject to a substantial risk of incurring double, multiple, or otherwise inconsistent obligations because of the interest.

(2) *Joinder by Court Order.* If a person has not been joined as required, the court must order that the person be made a party. A person who refuses to join as a plaintiff may be made either a defendant or, in a proper case, an involuntary plaintiff.

(3) *Venue.* If a joined party objects to venue and the joinder would make venue improper, the court must dismiss that party.

(b) When Joinder Is Not Feasible. If a person who is required to be joined if feasible cannot be joined, the court must determine whether, in equity and good conscience, the action should proceed among the existing parties or should be dismissed. The factors for the court to consider include:

(1) the extent to which a judgment rendered in the person's absence might prejudice that person or the existing parties;

(2) the extent to which any prejudice could be lessened or avoided by:

(A) protective provisions in the judgment;

(B) shaping the relief; or

(C) other measures;

(3) whether a judgment rendered in the person's absence would be adequate; and

(4) whether the plaintiff would have an adequate remedy if the action were dismissed for nonjoinder.

(c) Pleading the Reasons for Nonjoinder. When asserting a claim for relief, a party must state:

(1) the name, if known, of any person who is required to be joined if feasible but is not joined; and

(2) the reasons for not joining that person.

(d) Exception for Class Actions. This rule is subject to Rule 23.

(Amended February 28, 1966, effective July 1, 1966; March 2, 1987, effective August 1, 1987; April 30, 2007, effective December 1, 2007.)

ADVISORY COMMITTEE NOTES

1937 Adoption

Note to Subdivision (a). The first sentence with verbal differences (e.g., "united" interest for "joint" interest) is to be found in [former] Equity Rule 37 (Parties Generally—Intervention). Such compulsory joinder provisions are common. Compare Alaska Comp.Laws (1933) § 3392 (containing in same sentence a "class suit" provision); Wyo.Rev.Stat.Ann. (Courtright, 1931) § 89–515 (immediately followed by "class suit" provisions, § 89–516). See also former Equity Rule 42 (Joint and Several Demands). For example of a proper case for involuntary plaintiff, see *Independent Wireless Telegraph Co. v. Radio Corp. of America*, 269 U.S. 459, 46 S.Ct. 166, 70 L.Ed. 357 (1926).

The joinder provisions of this rule are subject to Rule 82 (Jurisdiction and Venue Unaffected).

Note to Subdivision (b). For the substance of this rule see [former] Equity Rule 39 (Absence of Persons Who Would be Proper Parties) and U.S.C., Title 28, § 111 [now § 1391] (When part of several defendants cannot be served); *Camp v. Gress*, 250 U.S. 308, 39 S.Ct. 478, 63 L.Ed. 997 (1919). See also the second and third sentences of [former] Equity Rule 37 (Parties Generally—Intervention).

Note to Subdivision (c). For the substance of this rule see the fourth subdivision of [former] Equity Rule 25 (Bill of Complaint—Contents).

1966 Amendment

General Considerations

Whenever feasible, the persons materially interested in the subject of an action—see the more detailed description of these persons in the discussion of new subdivision (a) below—should be joined as parties so that they may be heard and a complete disposition made. When this comprehensive joinder cannot be accomplished—a situation which may be encountered in Federal courts because of limitations on service of process, subject matter jurisdiction, and venue—the case should be examined pragmatically and a choice made between the alternatives of proceeding with the action in the absence of particular interested persons, and dismissing the action.

Even if the court is mistaken in its decision to proceed in the absence of an interested person, it does not by that token deprive itself of the power to adjudicate as between the parties already before it through proper service of process. But the court can make a legally binding adjudication only between the parties actually joined in the action. It is true that an adjudication between the parties before the court may on occasion adversely affect the absent person as a practical matter, or leave a party exposed to a later inconsistent recovery by the absent person. These are factors which should be considered in deciding whether the action should proceed, or should rather be dismissed; but they do not themselves negate the court's power to adjudicate as between the parties who have been joined.

Defects in the Original Rule

The foregoing propositions were well understood in the older equity practice, see Hazard, *Indispensable Party: The Historical Origin of a Procedural Phantom*, 61 Colum.L.Rev. 1254 (1961), and Rule 19 could be and often was applied in consonance with them. But experience showed that the rule was defective in its phrasing and did not point clearly to the proper basis of decision.

Textual defects.—(1) The expression "persons * * * who ought to be parties if complete relief is to be accorded between those already parties," appearing in original subdivision (b), was apparently intended as a description of the persons whom it would be desirable to join in the action, all questions of feasibility of joinder being put to one side; but it was not adequately descriptive of those persons.

(2) The word "indispensable," appearing in original subdivision (b), was apparently intended as an inclusive reference to the interested persons in whose absence it would be advisable, all factors having been considered, to dismiss the action. Yet the sentence implied that there might be interested persons, not "indispensable," in whose absence the action ought also to be dismissed. Further, it seemed at least superficially plausible to equate the word "indispensable" with the expression "having a joint interest," appearing in subdivision (a). See *United States v. Washington Inst. of Tech., Inc.*, 138 F.2d 25, 26 (3d Cir. 1943); cf. *Chidester v. City of Newark*, 162 F.2d 598 (3d Cir. 1947). But persons holding an interest technically "joint" are not always so related to an action that it would be unwise to proceed without joining all of them, whereas persons holding an interest not technically "joint" may have this relation to an action. See Reed, *Compulsory Joinder of Parties in Civil Actions*, 55 Mich.L.Rev. 327, 356 ff., 483 (1957).

(3) The use of "indispensable" and "joint interest" in the context of original Rule 19 directed attention to the technical or abstract character of the rights or obligations of the persons whose joinder was in question, and correspondingly distracted attention from the pragmatic considerations which should be controlling.

(4) The original rule, in dealing with the feasibility of joining a person as a party to the action, besides referring to whether the person was "subject to the jurisdiction of the court as to both service of process and venue," spoke of whether the person could be made a party "without depriving the court of jurisdiction of the parties before it." The second quoted expression used "jurisdiction" in the sense of the competence of the court over the subject matter of the action, and in this sense the expression was apt. However, by a familiar confusion, the expression seems to have suggested to some that the absence from the lawsuit of a person who was "indispensable" or "who ought to be [a] part[y]" itself deprived the court of the power to adjudicate as between the parties already joined. See *Samuel Goldwyn, Inc. v. United Artists Corp.*, 113 F.2d 703, 707 (3d Cir. 1940); *McArthur v. Rosenbaum Co. of Pittsburgh*, 180 F.2d 617, 621 (3d Cir. 1949); cf. *Calcote v. Texas Pac. Coal & Oil Co.*, 157 F.2d 216 (5th Cir. 1946), cert. denied, 329 U.S. 782 (1946), noted in 56 Yale L.J. 1088 (1947); Reed, supra, 55 Mich.L.Rev. at 332–34.

Failure to point to correct basis of decision. The original rule did not state affirmatively what factors were relevant in deciding whether the action should proceed or be dismissed when joinder of interested persons was infeasible. In some instances courts did not undertake the relevant inquiry or were misled by the "jurisdiction" fallacy. In other instances there was undue preoccupation with abstract classifications of rights or obligations, as against consideration of the particular consequences of proceeding with the action and the ways by which these consequences might be ameliorated by the shaping of final relief or other precautions.

Although these difficulties cannot be said to have been general analysis of the cases showed that there was good reason for attempting to strengthen the rule. The literature also indicated how the rule should be reformed. See Reed, supra (discussion of the important case of *Shields v. Barrow,* 17 How. (58 U.S.) 130 (1854), appears at 55 Mich.L.Rev., p. 340 ff.); Hazard, supra; N.Y. Temporary Comm. on Courts, First Preliminary Report, Legis.Doc.1957, No. 6(b), pp. 28, 233; N.Y. Judicial Council, Twelfth Ann.Rep., Legis.Doc.1946, No. 17, p. 163; Joint Comm. on Michigan Procedural Revision, Final Report, Pt. III, p. 69 (1960); Note, *Indispensable Parties in the Federal Courts,* 65 Harv.L.Rev. 1050 (1952); *Developments in the Law—Multiparty Litigation in the Federal Courts,* 71 Harv.L.Rev. 874, 879 (1958); Mich.Gen.Court Rules, R. 205 (effective Jan. 1, 1963); N.Y.Civ.Prac.Law & Rules, § 1001 (effective Sept. 1, 1963).

The Amended Rule

New subdivision (a) defines the persons whose joinder in the action is desirable. Clause (1) stresses the desirability of joining those persons in whose absence the court would be obliged to grant partial or "hollow" rather than complete relief to the parties before the court. The interests that are being furthered here are not only those of the parties, but also that of the public in avoiding repeated lawsuits on the same essential subject matter. Clause (2)(i) recognizes the importance of protecting the person whose joinder is in question against the practical prejudice to him which may arise through a disposition of the action in his absence. Clause (2)(ii) recognizes the need for considering whether a party may be left, after the adjudication, in a position where a person not joined can subject him to a double or otherwise inconsistent liability. See Reed, supra, 55 Mich.L.Rev. at 330, 338; Note, supra, 65 Harv.L.Rev. at 1052–57; *Developments in the Law,* supra, 71 Harv.L.Rev. at 881–85.

The subdivision (a) definition of persons to be joined is not couched in terms of the abstract nature of their interests— "joint," "united," "separable," or the like. See N.Y. Temporary Comm. on Courts, First Preliminary Report, supra; Developments in the Law, supra, at 880. It should be noted particularly, however, that the description is not at variance with the settled authorities holding that a tortfeasor with the usual "joint-and-several" liability is merely a permissive party to an action against another with like liability. See 3 Moore's *Federal Practice* 2153 (2d ed. 1963); 2 Barron & Holtzoff, *Federal Practice & Procedure* § 513.8 (Wright ed. 1961). Joinder of these tortfeasors continues to be regulated by Rule 20; compare Rule 14 on third-party practice.

If a person as described in subdivision (a)(1)(2) is amenable to service of process and his joinder would not deprive the court of jurisdiction in the sense of competence over the action, he should be joined as a party; and if he has not been joined, the court should order him to be brought into the action. If a party joined has a valid objection to the venue and chooses to assert it, he will be dismissed from the action.

Subdivision (b).—When a person as described in subdivision (a)(1)–(2) cannot be made a party, the court is to determine whether in equity and good conscience the action should proceed among the parties already before it, or should be dismissed. That this decision is to be made in the light of pragmatic considerations has often been acknowledged by the courts. See *Roos v. Texas Co.,* 23 F.2d 171 (2d Cir. 1927),

cert. denied 277 U.S. 587 (1928); *Niles-Bement-Pond Co. v. Iron Moulders' Union,* 254 U.S. 77, 80 (1920). The subdivision sets out four relevant considerations drawn from the experience revealed in the decided cases. The factors are to a certain extent overlapping, and they are not intended to exclude other considerations which may be applicable in particular situations.

The first factor brings in a consideration of what a judgment in the action would mean to the absentee. Would the absentee be adversely affected in a practical sense, and if so, would the prejudice be immediate and serious, or remote and minor? The possible collateral consequences of the judgment upon the parties already joined are also to be appraised. Would any party be exposed to a fresh action by the absentee, and if so, how serious is the threat? See the elaborate discussion in Reed, supra; cf. *A. L. Smith Iron Co. v. Dickson,* 141 F.2d 3 (2d Cir. 1944); *Caldwell Mfg. Co. v. Unique Balance Co.,* 18 F.R.D. 258 (S.D.N.Y.1955).

The second factor calls attention to the measures by which prejudice may be averted or lessened. The "shaping of relief" is a familiar expedient to this end. See, e.g., the award of money damages in lieu of specific relief where the latter might affect an absentee adversely. *Ward v. Deavers,* 203 F.2d 72 (D.C.Cir.1953); *Miller & Lux, Inc. v. Nickel,* 141 F.Supp. 41 (N.D.Calif.1956). On the use of "protective provisions," see *Roos v. Texas Co.,* supra; *Atwood v. Rhode Island Hosp. Trust Co.,* 275 Fed. 513, 519 (1st Cir. 1921), cert. denied, 257 U.S. 661 (1922); cf. *Stumpf v. Fidelity Gas Co.,* 294 F.2d 886 (9th Cir. 1961); and the general statement in *National Licorice Co. v. Labor Board,* 309 U.S. 350, 363 (1940).

Sometimes the party is himself able to take measures to avoid prejudice. Thus a defendant faced with a prospect of a second suit by an absentee may be in a position to bring the latter into the action by defensive interpleader. See *Hudson v. Newell,* 172 F.2d 848, 852 mod., 176 F.2d 546 (5th Cir. 1949); *Gauss v. Kirk,* 198 F.2d 83, 86 (D.C.Cir. 1952); *Abel v. Brayton Flying Service, Inc.,* 248 F.2d 713, 716 (5th Cir. 1957) (suggestion of possibility of counter-claim under Rule 13(h)); cf. *Parker Rust-Proof Co. v. Western Union Tel. Co.,* 105 F.2d 976 (2d Cir. 1939), cert. denied, 308 U.S. 597 (1939). So also the absentee may sometimes be able to avert prejudice to himself by voluntarily appearing in the action or intervening on an ancillary basis. See *Developments in the Law,* supra, 71 Harv.L.Rev. at 882; Annot., *Intervention or Subsequent Joinder of Parties as Affecting Jurisdiction of Federal Court Based on Diversity of Citizenship,* 134 A.L.R. 335 (1941); *Johnson v. Middleton,* 175 F.2d 535 (7th Cir. 1949); *Kentucky Nat. Gas Corp. v. Duggins,* 165 F.2d 1011 (6th Cir. 1948); *McComb v. McCormack,* 159 F.2d 219 (5th Cir. 1947). The court should consider whether this, in turn, would impose undue hardship on the absentee. (For the possibility of the court's informing an absentee of the pendency of the action, see comment under subdivision (c) below.)

The third factor—whether an "adequate" judgment can be rendered in the absence of a given person—calls attention to the extent of the relief that can be accorded among the parties joined. It meshes with the other factors, especially the "shaping of relief" mentioned under the second factor. Cf. *Kroese v. General Steel Castings Corp.,* 179 F.2d 760 (3d Cir. 1949), cert. denied, 339 U.S. 983 (1950).

The fourth factor, looking to the practical effects of a dismissal, indicates that the court should consider whether there is any assurance that the plaintiff, if dismissed, could sue effectively in another forum where better joinder would be possible. See *Fitzgerald v. Haynes,* 241 F.2d 417, 420 (3d Cir. 1957); *Fouke v. Schenewerk,* 197 F.2d 234, 236 (5th Cir. 1952); cf. *Warfield v. Marks,* 190 F.2d 178 (5th Cir. 1951).

The subdivision uses the word "indispensable" only in a conclusory sense, that is, a person is "regarded as indispensable" when he cannot be made a party and, upon consideration of the factors above mentioned, it is determined that in his absence it would be preferable to dismiss the action, rather than to retain it.

A person may be added as a party at any stage of the action on motion or on the court's initiative (see Rule 21); and a motion to dismiss, on the ground that a person has not been joined and justice requires that the action should not proceed in his absence, may be made as late as the trial on the merits (see Rule 12(h)(2), as amended; cf. Rule 12(b)(7), as amended). However, when the moving party is seeking dismissal in order to protect himself against a later suit by the absent person (subdivision (a)(2)(ii)), and is not seeking vicariously to protect the absent person against a prejudicial judgment (subdivision (a)(2)(i)), his undue delay in making the motion can properly be counted against him as a reason for denying the motion. A joinder question should be decided with reasonable promptness, but decision may properly be deferred if adequate information is not available at the time. Thus the relationship of an absent person to the action, and the practical effects of an adjudication upon him and others, may not be sufficiently revealed at the pleading stage; in such a case it would be appropriate to defer decision until the action was further advanced. Cf. Rule 12(d).

The amended rule makes no special provision for the problem arising in suits against subordinate Federal officials where it has often been set up as a defense that some superior officer must be joined. Frequently this defense has been accompanied by or intermingled with defenses of sovereign community or lack of consent of the United States to suit. So far as the issue of joinder can be isolated from the rest, the new subdivision seems better adapted to handle it than the predecessor provision. See the discussion in *Johnson v. Kirkland,* 290 F.2d 440, 446–47 (5th Cir. 1961) (stressing the practical orientation of the decisions); *Shaughnessy v. Pedreiro,* 349 U.S. 48, 54 (1955). Recent legislation, P.L. 87–748, 76 Stat. 744, approved October 5, 1962, adding §§ 1361, 1391(e) to Title 28, U.S.C., vests original jurisdiction in the District Courts over actions in the nature of mandamus to compel officials of the United States to perform their legal duties, and extends the range of service of process and liberalizes venue in these actions. If, then, it is found that a particular official should be joined in the action, the legislation will make it easy to bring him in.

Subdivision (c) parallels the predecessor subdivision (c) of Rule 19. In some situations it may be desirable to advise a person who has not been joined of the fact that the action is pending, and in particular cases the court in its discretion may itself convey this information by directing a letter or other informal notice to the absentee.

Subdivision (d) repeats the exception contained in the first clause of the predecessor subdivision (a).

1987 Amendment

The amendments are technical. No substantive change is intended.

2007 Amendment

The language of Rule 19 has been amended as part of the general restyling of the Civil Rules to make them more easily understood and to make style and terminology consistent throughout the rules. These changes are intended to be stylistic only.

Former Rule 19(b) described the conclusion that an action should be dismissed for inability to join a Rule 19(a) party by carrying forward traditional terminology: "the absent person being thus regarded as indispensable." "Indispensable" was used only to express a conclusion reached by applying the tests of Rule 19(b). It has been discarded as redundant.

CROSS REFERENCES

Class actions, see Fed.Rules Civ.Proc. Rule 23, 28 USCA.

Indispensable party, defense of failure to join, see Fed. Rules Civ.Proc. Rule 12, 28 USCA.

Interpleader, see Fed.Rules Civ.Proc. Rule 22, 28 USCA.

Intervention, see Fed.Rules Civ.Proc. Rule 24, 28 USCA.

Jurisdiction and venue unaffected by these rules, see Fed. Rules Civ.Proc. Rule 82, 28 USCA.

Lien enforcement, ordering absent defendant to appear or plead, see 28 USCA § 1655.

Misjoinder and non-joinder of parties, see Fed.Rules Civ. Proc. Rule 21, 28 USCA.

Permissive joinder of parties, see Fed.Rules Civ.Proc. Rule 20, 28 USCA.

Substitution of parties, see Fed.Rules Civ.Proc. Rule 25, 28 USCA.

Rule 20.   Permissive Joinder of Parties

(a) Persons Who May Join or Be Joined.

(1) *Plaintiffs.* Persons may join in one action as plaintiffs if:

(A) they assert any right to relief jointly, severally, or in the alternative with respect to or arising out of the same transaction, occurrence, or series of transactions or occurrences; and

(B) any question of law or fact common to all plaintiffs will arise in the action.

(2) *Defendants.* Persons—as well as a vessel, cargo, or other property subject to admiralty process in rem—may be joined in one action as defendants if:

(A) any right to relief is asserted against them jointly, severally, or in the alternative with respect to or arising out of the same transaction, occurrence, or series of transactions or occurrences; and

(B) any question of law or fact common to all defendants will arise in the action.

(3) *Extent of Relief.* Neither a plaintiff nor a defendant need be interested in obtaining or defending against all the relief demanded. The court may grant judgment to one or more plaintiffs according to their rights, and against one or more defendants according to their liabilities.

(b) **Protective Measures.** The court may issue orders—including an order for separate trials—to protect a party against embarrassment, delay, expense, or other prejudice that arises from including a person against whom the party asserts no claim and who asserts no claim against the party.

(Amended February 28, 1966, effective July 1, 1966; March 2, 1987, effective August 1, 1987; April 30, 2007, effective December 1, 2007.)

ADVISORY COMMITTEE NOTES

1937 Adoption

The provisions for joinder here stated are in substance the provisions found in England, California, Illinois, New Jersey, and New York. They represent only a moderate expansion of the present federal equity practice to cover both law and equity actions.

With this rule compare also [former] Equity Rules 26 (Joinder of Causes of Action), 37 (Parties Generally—Intervention), 40 (Nominal Parties), and 42 (Joint and Several Demands).

The provisions of this rule for the joinder of parties are subject to Rule 82 (Jurisdiction and Venue Unaffected).

Note to Subdivision (a). The first sentence is derived from *English Rules Under the Judicature Act* (The Annual Practice, 1937) O. 16, r. 1. Compare Calif.Code Civ.Proc. (Deering, 1937) §§ 378, 379a; Ill.Rev.Stat. (1937) ch. 110, § 147–148; N.J.Comp.Stat. (2 Cum.Supp., 1911–1924), N.Y.C.P.A. (1937) §§ 209, 211. The second sentence is derived from *English Rules Under the Judicature Act* (The Annual Practice, 1937) O. 16, r. 4. The third sentence is derived from O. 16, r. 5, and the fourth from O. 16, r.r. 1 and 4.

Note to Subdivision (b). This is derived from *English Rules Under the Judicature Act* (The Annual Practice, 1937) O. 16, r.r. 1 and 5.

1966 Amendment

See the amendment of Rule 18(a) and the Advisory Committee's Note thereto. It has been thought that a lack of clarity in the antecedent of the word "them," as it appeared in two places in Rule 20(a), contributed to the view, taken by some courts, that this rule limited the joinder of claims in certain situations of permissive party joinder. Although the amendment of Rule 18(a) should make clear that this view is untenable, it has been considered advisable to amend Rule 20(a) to eliminate any ambiguity. See 2 Barron & Holtzoff, *Federal Practice & Procedure* 202 (Wright Ed. 1961).

A basic purpose of unification of admiralty and civil procedure is to reduce barriers to joinder; hence the reference to "any vessel," etc.

1987 Amendment

The amendments are technical. No substantive change is intended.

2007 Amendment

The language of Rule 20 has been amended as part of the general restyling of the Civil Rules to make them more easily understood and to make style and terminology consistent throughout the rules. These changes are intended to be stylistic only.

CROSS REFERENCES

Collusive or improper joinder of parties, jurisdiction of district courts, see 28 USCA § 1359.

Interpleader, see Fed.Rules Civ.Proc. Rule 22, 28 USCA.

Intervention, see Fed.Rules Civ.Proc. Rule 24, 28 USCA.

Joinder of persons needed for just adjudication, see Fed. Rules Civ.Proc. Rule 19, 28 USCA.

Misjoinder and non-joinder of parties, see Fed.Rules Civ. Proc. Rule 21, 28 USCA.

Substitution of parties, see Fed.Rules Civ.Proc. Rule 25, 28 USCA.

Rule 21. Misjoinder and Nonjoinder of Parties

Misjoinder of parties is not a ground for dismissing an action. On motion or on its own, the court may at any time, on just terms, add or drop a party. The court may also sever any claim against a party.

(Amended April 30, 2007, effective December 1, 2007.)

ADVISORY COMMITTEE NOTES

1937 Adoption

See *English Rules Under the Judicature Act* (The Annual Practice, 1937) O. 16, r. 11. See also [former] Equity Rules 43 (Defect of Parties—Resisting Objection) and 44 (Defect of Parties—Tardy Objection).

For separate trials see Rules 13(i) (Counterclaims and Cross-Claims: Separate Trials; Separate Judgments), 20(b) (Permissive Joinder of Parties: Separate Trials), and 42(b) (Separate Trials, generally) and the note to the latter rule.

2007 Amendment

The language of Rule 21 has been amended as part of the general restyling of the Civil Rules to make them more easily understood and to make style and terminology consistent throughout the rules. These changes are intended to be stylistic only.

CROSS REFERENCES

Collusive or improper joinder of parties, jurisdiction of district courts, see 28 USCA § 1359.

Intervention of parties, see Fed.Rules Civ.Proc. Rule 24, 28 USCA.

Joinder of persons needed for just adjudication, see Fed. Rules Civ.Proc. Rule 19, 28 USCA.

Permissive joinder of parties, see Fed.Rules Civ.Proc. Rule 20, 28 USCA.

Procedure after removal, generally, see 28 USCA § 1447.

Rule 22. Interpleader

(a) Grounds.

(1) *By a Plaintiff.* Persons with claims that may expose a plaintiff to double or multiple liability may be joined as defendants and required to interplead. Joinder for interpleader is proper even though:

(A) the claims of the several claimants, or the titles on which their claims depend, lack a common origin or are adverse and independent rather than identical; or

(B) the plaintiff denies liability in whole or in part to any or all of the claimants.

(2) *By a Defendant.* A defendant exposed to similar liability may seek interpleader through a cross-claim or counterclaim.

(b) Relation to Other Rules and Statutes. This rule supplements—and does not limit—the joinder of parties allowed by Rule 20. The remedy this rule provides is in addition to—and does not supersede or limit—the remedy provided by 28 U.S.C. §§ 1335, 1397, and 2361. An action under those statutes must be conducted under these rules.

(Amended December 29, 1948, effective October 20, 1949; March 2, 1987, effective August 1, 1987; April 30, 2007, effective December 1, 2007.)

ADVISORY COMMITTEE NOTES

1937 Adoption

The first paragraph provides for interpleader relief along the newer and more liberal lines of joinder in the alternative. It avoids the confusion and restrictions that developed around actions of strict interpleader and actions in the nature of interpleader. Compare *John Hancock Mutual Life Insurance Co. v. Kegan et al.*, 22 F.Supp. 326 (D.C.Md.1938). It does not change the rules on service of process, jurisdiction, and venue, as established by judicial decision.

The second paragraph allows an action to be brought under the recent interpleader statute when applicable. By this paragraph all remedies under the statute are continued, but the manner of obtaining them is in accordance with these rules. For temporary restraining orders and preliminary injunctions under this statute, see Rule 65(e).

This rule substantially continues such statutory provisions as U.S.C., Title 38, § 445 [now 784] (Actions on claims; jurisdiction; parties; procedure; limitation; witnesses; definitions) (actions upon veterans' contracts of insurance with the United States), providing for interpleader by the United States where it acknowledges indebtedness under a contract of insurance with the United States; U.S.C., Title 49, § 97 (Interpleader of conflicting claimants) (by carrier which has issued bill of lading). See Chaffee, *The Federal Interpleader Act of 1936: I and II* (1936), 45 Yale L.J. 963, 1161.

1948 Amendment

The amendment effective October 20, 1949, substituted the reference to "Title 28, U.S.C., §§ 1335, 1397, and 2361," at the end of the first sentence of paragraph (2), for the reference to "Section 24(26) of the Judicial Code, as amended, U.S.C., Title 28, § 41(26)." The amendment also substituted the words "those provisions" in the second sentence of paragraph (2) for the words "that section."

1987 Amendment

The amendment is technical. No substantive change is intended.

2007 Amendment

The language of Rule 22 has been amended as part of the general restyling of the Civil Rules to make them more easily understood and to make style and terminology consistent throughout the rules. These changes are intended to be stylistic only.

CROSS REFERENCES

Jurisdiction of district courts of interpleader action, see 28 USCA § 1335.

Permissive joinder of parties, see Fed.Rules Civ.Proc. Rule 20, 28 USCA.

Process and procedure in interpleader action, see 28 USCA § 2361.

Venue of interpleader action, see 28 USCA § 1397.

Rule 23.   Class Actions

(a) Prerequisites. One or more members of a class may sue or be sued as representative parties on behalf of all members only if:

(1) the class is so numerous that joinder of all members is impracticable;

(2) there are questions of law or fact common to the class;

(3) the claims or defenses of the representative parties are typical of the claims or defenses of the class; and

(4) the representative parties will fairly and adequately protect the interests of the class.

(b) Types of Class Actions. A class action may be maintained if Rule 23(a) is satisfied and if:

(1) prosecuting separate actions by or against individual class members would create a risk of:

(A) inconsistent or varying adjudications with respect to individual class members that would establish incompatible standards of conduct for the party opposing the class; or

(B) adjudications with respect to individual class members that, as a practical matter, would be dispositive of the interests of the other members not parties to the individual adjudications or would substantially impair or impede their ability to protect their interests;

(2) the party opposing the class has acted or refused to act on grounds that apply generally to the class, so that final injunctive relief or corresponding declaratory relief is appropriate respecting the class as a whole; or

(3) the court finds that the questions of law or fact common to class members predominate over any questions affecting only individual members, and that a class action is superior to other available methods for fairly and efficiently adjudicating the controversy. The matters pertinent to these findings include:

(A) the class members' interests in individually controlling the prosecution or defense of separate actions;

(B) the extent and nature of any litigation concerning the controversy already begun by or against class members;

(C) the desirability or undesirability of concentrating the litigation of the claims in the particular forum; and

(D) the likely difficulties in managing a class action.

(c) Certification Order; Notice to Class Members; Judgment; Issues Classes; Subclasses.

(1) *Certification Order.*

(A) *Time to Issue.* At an early practicable time after a person sues or is sued as a class representative, the court must determine by order whether to certify the action as a class action.

(B) *Defining the Class; Appointing Class Counsel.* An order that certifies a class action must define the class and the class claims, issues, or defenses, and must appoint class counsel under Rule 23(g).

(C) *Altering or Amending the Order.* An order that grants or denies class certification may be altered or amended before final judgment.

(2) *Notice.*

(A) *For (b)(1) or (b)(2) Classes.* For any class certified under Rule 23(b)(1) or (b)(2), the court may direct appropriate notice to the class.

(B) *For (b)(3) Classes.* For any class certified under Rule 23(b)(3)—or upon ordering notice under Rule 23(e)(1) to a class proposed to be certified for purposes of settlement under Rule 23(b)(3)—the court must direct to class members the best notice that is practicable under the circumstances, including individual notice to all members who can be identified through reasonable effort. The notice may be by one or more of the following: United States mail, electronic means, or other appropriate means. The notice must clearly and concisely state in plain, easily understood language:

(i) the nature of the action;

(ii) the definition of the class certified;

(iii) the class claims, issues, or defenses;

(iv) that a class member may enter an appearance through an attorney if the member so desires;

(v) that the court will exclude from the class any member who requests exclusion;

(vi) the time and manner for requesting exclusion; and

(vii) the binding effect of a class judgment on members under Rule 23(c)(3).

(3) *Judgment.* Whether or not favorable to the class, the judgment in a class action must:

(A) for any class certified under Rule 23(b)(1) or (b)(2), include and describe those whom the court finds to be class members; and

(B) for any class certified under Rule 23(b)(3), include and specify or describe those to whom the Rule 23(c)(2) notice was directed, who have not requested exclusion, and whom the court finds to be class members.

(4) *Particular Issues.* When appropriate, an action may be brought or maintained as a class action with respect to particular issues.

(5) *Subclasses.* When appropriate, a class may be divided into subclasses that are each treated as a class under this rule.

(d) Conducting the Action.

(1) *In General.* In conducting an action under this rule, the court may issue orders that:

(A) determine the course of proceedings or prescribe measures to prevent undue repetition or complication in presenting evidence or argument;

(B) require—to protect class members and fairly conduct the action—giving appropriate notice to some or all class members of:

(i) any step in the action;

(ii) the proposed extent of the judgment; or

(iii) the members' opportunity to signify whether they consider the representation fair and adequate, to intervene and present claims or defenses, or to otherwise come into the action;

(C) impose conditions on the representative parties or on intervenors;

(D) require that the pleadings be amended to eliminate allegations about representation of absent persons and that the action proceed accordingly; or

(E) deal with similar procedural matters.

(2) *Combining and Amending Orders.* An order under Rule 23(d)(1) may be altered or amended from time to time and may be combined with an order under Rule 16.

(e) Settlement, Voluntary Dismissal, or Compromise. The claims, issues, or defenses of a certified class—or a class proposed to be certified for purposes of settlement—may be settled, voluntarily dismissed, or compromised only with the court's approval. The following procedures apply to a proposed settlement, voluntary dismissal, or compromise:

(1) *Notice to the Class.*

(A) *Information That Parties Must Provide to the Court.* The parties must provide the court with information sufficient to enable it to determine whether to give notice of the proposal to the class.

(B) *Grounds for a Decision to Give Notice.* The court must direct notice in a reasonable manner to all class members who would be bound by the proposal if giving notice is justified by the parties' showing that the court will likely be able to:

(i) approve the proposal under Rule 23(e)(2); and

(ii) certify the class for purposes of judgment on the proposal.

(2) *Approval of the Proposal.* If the proposal would bind class members, the court may approve it only after a hearing and only on finding that it is fair, reasonable, and adequate after considering whether:

(A) the class representatives and class counsel have adequately represented the class;

(B) the proposal was negotiated at arm's length;

(C) the relief provided for the class is adequate, taking into account:

(i) the costs, risks, and delay of trial and appeal;

(ii) the effectiveness of any proposed method of distributing relief to the class, including the method of processing class-member claims;

(iii) the terms of any proposed award of attorney's fees, including timing of payment; and

(iv) any agreement required to be identified under Rule 23(e)(3); and

(D) the proposal treats class members equitably relative to each other.

(3) *Identifying Agreements.* The parties seeking approval must file a statement identifying any agreement made in connection with the proposal.

(4) *New Opportunity to be Excluded.* If the class action was previously certified under Rule 23(b)(3), the court may refuse to approve a settlement unless it affords a new opportunity to request exclusion to individual class members who had an earlier opportunity to request exclusion but did not do so.

(5) *Class–Member Objections.*

(A) *In General.* Any class member may object to the proposal if it requires court approval under this subdivision (e). The objection must state whether it applies only to the objector, to a specific subset of the class, or to the entire class, and also state with specificity the grounds for the objection.

(B) *Court Approval Required for Payment in Connection with an Objection.* Unless approved by the court after a hearing, no payment or other consideration may be provided in connection with:

(i) forgoing or withdrawing an objection, or

(ii) forgoing, dismissing, or abandoning an appeal from a judgment approving the proposal.

(C) *Procedure for Approval After an Appeal.* If approval under Rule 23(e)(5)(B) has not been obtained before an appeal is docketed in the court of appeals, the procedure of Rule 62.1 applies while the appeal remains pending.

(f) Appeals. A court of appeals may permit an appeal from an order granting or denying class-action certification under this rule, but not from an order under Rule 23(e)(1). A party must file a petition for permission to appeal with the circuit clerk within 14 days after the order is entered, or within 45 days after the order is entered if any party is the United States, a United States agency, or a United States officer or employee sued for an act or omission occurring in connection with duties performed on the United States' behalf. An appeal does not stay proceedings in the district court unless the district judge or the court of appeals so orders.

(g) Class Counsel.

(1) *Appointing Class Counsel.* Unless a statute provides otherwise, a court that certifies a class must appoint class counsel. In appointing class counsel, the court:

(A) must consider:

(i) the work counsel has done in identifying or investigating potential claims in the action;

(ii) counsel's experience in handling class actions, other complex litigation, and the types of claims asserted in the action;

(iii) counsel's knowledge of the applicable law; and

(iv) the resources that counsel will commit to representing the class;

(B) may consider any other matter pertinent to counsel's ability to fairly and adequately represent the interests of the class;

(C) may order potential class counsel to provide information on any subject pertinent to the appointment and to propose terms for attorney's fees and nontaxable costs;

(D) may include in the appointing order provisions about the award of attorney's fees or nontaxable costs under Rule 23(h); and

(E) may make further orders in connection with the appointment.

(2) *Standard for Appointing Class Counsel.* When one applicant seeks appointment as class counsel, the court may appoint that applicant only if the applicant is adequate under Rule 23(g)(1) and (4). If more than one adequate applicant seeks appointment, the court must appoint the applicant best able to represent the interests of the class.

(3) *Interim Counsel.* The court may designate interim counsel to act on behalf of a putative class before determining whether to certify the action as a class action.

(4) *Duty of Class Counsel.* Class counsel must fairly and adequately represent the interests of the class.

(h) Attorney's Fees and Nontaxable Costs. In a certified class action, the court may award reasonable attorney's fees and nontaxable costs that are authorized by law or by the parties' agreement. The following procedures apply:

(1) A claim for an award must be made by motion under Rule 54(d)(2), subject to the provisions of this subdivision (h), at a time the court sets. Notice of the motion must be served on all parties and, for motions by class counsel, directed to class members in a reasonable manner.

(2) A class member, or a party from whom payment is sought, may object to the motion.

(3) The court may hold a hearing and must find the facts and state its legal conclusions under Rule 52(a).

(4) The court may refer issues related to the amount of the award to a special master or a magistrate judge, as provided in Rule 54(d)(2)(D).

(Amended February 28, 1966, effective July 1, 1966; March 2, 1987, effective August 1, 1987; April 24, 1998, effective December 1, 1998; March 27, 2003, effective December 1, 2003; April 30, 2007, effective December 1, 2007; March 26, 2009, effective December 1, 2009; April 26, 2018, effective December 1, 2018.)

ADVISORY COMMITTEE NOTES

1937 Adoption

Note to Subdivision (a). This is a substantial restatement of [former] Equity Rule 38 (Representatives of Class) as that rule has been construed. It applies to all actions, whether formerly denominated legal or equitable. For a general analysis of class actions, effect of judgment, and requisites of jurisdiction see Moore, *Federal Rules of Civil Procedure: Some Problems Raised by the Preliminary Draft*, 25 Georgetown L.J. 551, 570 et seq. (1937); Moore and Cohn, *Federal Class Actions*, 32 Ill.L.Rev. 307 (1937); Moore and Cohn, *Federal Class Actions—Jurisdiction and Effect of Judgment*, 32 Ill.L.Rev. 555–567 (1938); Lesar, *Class Suits and the Federal Rules*, 22 Minn.L.Rev. 34 (1937); cf. Arnold and James, *Cases on Trials, Judgments and Appeals* (1936) 175; and see Blume, *Jurisdictional Amount in Representative Suits*, 15 Minn.L.Rev. 501 (1931).

The general test of [former] Equity Rule 38 (Representatives of Class) that the question should be "one of common or general interest to many persons constituting a class so numerous as to make it impracticable to bring them all before the court," is a common test. For states which require the two elements of a common or general interest and numerous persons, as provided for in [former] Equity Rule 38, see Del.Ch. Rule 113; Fla.Comp.Gen.Laws Ann. (Supp., 1936) § 4918(7); Georgia Code (1933) § 37–1002, and see *English Rules Under the Judicature Act* (The Annual Practice, 1937) O. 16, r. 9. For statutory provisions providing for class actions when the question is one of common or general interest or when the parties are numerous, see Ala.Code Ann. (Michie, 1928) § 5701; 2 Ind.Stat.Ann. (Burns, 1933) § 2–220; N.Y.C.P.A. (1937) 195; Wis.Stat. (1935) § 260.12. These statutes have, however, been uniformly construed as though phrased in the conjunctive. See *Garfein v. Stiglitz*, 260 Ky. 430, 86 S.W.2d 155 (1935). The rule adopts the test of [former] Equity Rule 38, but defines what constitutes a "common or general interest". Compare with code provisions which make the action dependent upon the propriety of joinder of the parties. See Blume, *The "Common Questions" Principle in the Code Provision for Representative Suits*, 30 Mich.L.Rev. 878 (1932). For discussion of what constitutes "numerous persons" see Wheaton, *Representative Suits Involving Numerous Litigants*, 19 Corn.L.Q. 399 (1934); Note, 36 Harv.L.Rev. 89 (1922).

Clause (1), Joint, Common, or Secondary Right. This clause is illustrated in actions brought by or against representatives of an unincorporated association. See *Oster v. Brotherhood of Locomotive Firemen and Enginemen*, 271 Pa. 419, 114 Atl. 377 (1921); *Pickett v. Walsh*, 192 Mass. 572, 78 N.E. 753, 6 L.R.A., N.S., 1067 (1906); *Colt v. Hicks*, 97 Ind.App. 177, 179 N.E. 335 (1932). Compare Rule 17(b) as to when an unincorporated association has capacity to sue or be sued in its common name; *United Mine Workers of America v. Coronado Coal Co.*, 42 S.Ct. 570, 259 U.S. 344, 66 L.Ed. 975, 27 A.L.R. 762 (1922) (an unincorporated association was sued as an entity for the purpose of enforcing against it a federal substantive right); Moore, *Federal Rules of Civil Procedure: Some Problems Raised by the Preliminary Draft*, 25 Georgetown L.J. 551, 566 (for discussion of jurisdictional requisites when an unincorporated association sues or is sued in its common name and jurisdiction is founded upon diversity of citizenship). For an action brought by representatives of one group against representatives of another group for distribution of a fund held by an unincorporated association, see *Smith v. Swormstedt*, 16 How. 288, 14 L.Ed. 942 (U.S. 1853). Compare *Christopher, et al. v. Brusselback*, 1938, 58 S.Ct. 350, 302 U.S. 500, 82 L.Ed. 388.

For an action to enforce rights held in common by policyholders against the corporate issuer of the policies, see *Supreme Tribe of Ben Hur v. Cauble*, 255 U.S. 356, 41 S.Ct. 338, 65 L.Ed. 673 (1921). See also *Terry v. Little*, 101 U.S. 216, 25 L.Ed. 864 (1880); *John A. Roebling's Sons Co. v. Kinnicutt*, 248 Fed. 596 (D.C.N.Y., 1917) dealing with the right held in common by creditors to enforce the statutory liability of stockholders.

Typical of a secondary action is a suit by stockholders to enforce a corporate right. For discussion of the general nature of these actions see *Ashwander v. Tennessee Valley Authority*, 297 U.S. 288, 56 S.Ct. 466, 80 L.Ed. 688 (1936); Glenn, *The Stockholder's Suit—Corporate and Individual Grievances*, 33 Yale L.J. 580 (1924); McLaughlin, *Capacity of Plaintiff-Stockholder to Terminate a Stockholder's Suit*, 46 Yale L.J. 421 (1937). See also Subdivision (b) of this rule which deals with Shareholder's Action; Note, 15 Minn.L.Rev. 453 (1931).

Clause (2). A creditor's action for liquidation or reorganization of a corporation is illustrative of this clause. An action by a stockholder against certain named defendants as representatives of numerous claimants presents a situation converse to the creditor's action.

Clause (3). See *Everglades Drainage League v. Napoleon Broward Drainage Dist.*, 253 Fed. 246 (D.C.Fla., 1918); *Gramling v. Maxwell*, 52 F.2d 256 (D.C.N.C., 1931), approved in 30 Mich.L.Rev. 624 (1932); *Skinner v. Mitchell*, 108 Kan. 861, 197 Pac. 569 (1921); *Duke of Bedford v. Ellis* (1901) A.C. 1, for class actions when there were numerous persons and there was only a question of law or fact common to them; and see Blume, *The "Common Questions" Principle in the Code Provision for Representative Suits*, 30 Mich.L.Rev. 878 (1932).

Note to Subdivision (b). This is [former] Equity Rule 27 (Stockholder's Bill) with verbal changes. See also *Hawes v.*

Oakland, 104 U.S. 450, 26 L.Ed. 827 (1882) and former Equity Rule 94, promulgated January 23, 1882, 104 U.S. IX.

Note to Subdivision (c). See McLaughlin, Capacity of Plaintiff-Stockholder to Terminate a Stockholder's Suit, 46 Yale L.J. 421 (1937).

Supplementary Note

Note. Subdivision (b), relating to secondary actions by shareholders, provides among other things, that in such an action the complainant "shall aver (1) that the plaintiff was a shareholder at the time of the transaction of which he complains or that his share thereafter devolved on him by operation of law * * *."

As a result of the decision in *Erie R. Co. v. Tompkins*, 1938, 304 U.S. 64, 58 S.Ct. 817 (decided April 25, 1938, after this rule was promulgated by the Supreme Court, though before it took effect) a question has arisen as to whether the provision above quoted deals with a matter of substantive right or is a matter of procedure. If it is a matter of substantive law or right, then under *Erie R. Co. v. Tompkins* clause (1) may not be validly applied in cases pending in states whose local law permits a shareholder to maintain such actions, although not a shareholder at the time of the transactions complained of. The Advisory Committee, believing the question should be settled in the courts, proposes no change in Rule 23 but thinks rather that the situation should be explained in an appropriate note.

The rule has a long history. In *Hawes v. Oakland*, 1882, 104 U.S. 450, the Court held that a shareholder could not maintain such an action unless he owned shares at the time of the transactions complained of, or unless they devolved on him by operation of law. At that time the decision in *Swift v. Tyson*, 1842, 16 Peters 1, was the law, and the federal courts considered themselves free to establish their own principles of equity jurisprudence, so the Court was not in 1882 and has not been, until *Erie R. Co. v. Tompkins* in 1938, concerned with the question whether *Hawes v. Oakland* dealt with substantive right or procedure.

Following the decision in *Hawes v. Oakland*, and at the same term, the Court, to implement its decision, adopted [former] Equity Rule 94, which contained the same provision above quoted from Rule 23 F.R.C.P. The provision in [former] Equity Rule 94 was later embodied in [former] Equity Rule 27, of which the present Rule 23 is substantially a copy.

In *City of Quincy v. Steel*, 1887, 120 U.S. 241, 245, 7 S.Ct. 520, the Court referring to *Hawes v. Oakland* said: "In order to give effect to the principles there laid down, this Court at that term adopted Rule 94 of the rules of practice for courts of equity of the United States."

Some other cases dealing with [former] Equity Rules 94 or 27 prior to the decision in *Erie R. Co. v. Tompkins* are *Dimpfel v. Ohio & Miss. R.R.*, 1884, 3 S.Ct. 573, 110 U.S. 209, 28 L.Ed. 121; *Illinois Central R. Co. v. Adams*, 1901, 21 S.Ct. 251, 180 U.S. 28, 34, 45 L.Ed. 410; *Venner v. Great Northern Ry.*, 1908, 28 S.Ct. 328, 209 U.S. 24, 30, 52 L.Ed. 666; *Jacobson v. General Motors Corp.*, S.D.N.Y.1938, 22 F.Supp. 255, 257. These cases generally treat *Hawes v. Oakland* as establishing a "principle" of equity, or as dealing not with jurisdiction but with the "right" to maintain an action, or have said that the defense under the equity rule is analogous to the defense that the plaintiff has no "title" and results in a dismissal "for want of equity."

Those state decisions which held that a shareholder acquiring stock after the event may maintain a derivative action are founded on the view that it is a right belonging to the shareholder at the time of the transaction and which passes as a right to the subsequent purchaser. See *Pollitz v. Gould*, 1911, 202 N.Y. 11, 94 N.E. 1088.

The first case arising after the decision in *Erie R. Co. v. Tompkins*, in which this problem was involved, was *Summers v. Hearst*, S.D.N.Y.1938, 23 F.Supp. 986. It concerned [former] Equity Rule 27, as Federal Rule 23 was not then in effect. In a well considered opinion Judge Leibell reviewed the decisions and said: "The federal cases that discuss this section of [former] Rule 27 support the view that it states a principle of substantive law." He quoted *Pollitz v. Gould*, 1911, 202 N.Y. 11, 94 N.E. 1088, as saying that the United States Supreme Court "seems to have been more concerned with establishing this rule as one of practice than of substantive law" but that "whether it be regarded as establishing a principle of law or a rule of practice, this authority has been subsequently followed in the United States courts."

He then concluded that, although the federal decisions treat the equity rule as "stating a principle of substantive law", if "[former] Equity Rule 27 is to be modified or revoked in view of *Erie R. Co. v. Tompkins*, it is not the province of this Court to suggest it, much less impliedly to follow that course by disregarding the mandatory provisions of the Rule."

In *Piccard v. Sperry Corporation*, S.D.N.Y.1941, 36 F.Supp. 1006, 1009–10, affirmed without opinion, C.C.A.2d 1941, 120 F.2d 328, a shareholder, not such at the time of the transactions complained of, sought to intervene. The court held an intervenor was as much subject to Rule 23 as an original plaintiff; and that the requirement of Rule 23(b) was "a matter of practice," not substance, and applied in New York where the state law was otherwise, despite *Erie R. Co. v. Tompkins*. In *New York v. Guaranty Trust Co. of New York*, C.C.A.2, 1944, 143 F.2d 503, rev'd on other grounds, 1945, 65 S.Ct. 1464, the court said: "Restrictions on the bringing of stockholders' actions, such as those imposed by F.R.C.P. 23(b) or other state statutes are procedural," citing the *Piccard* and other cases.

Some other federal decisions since 1938 touch the question.

In *Gallup v. Caldwell*, C.C.A.3, 1941, 120 F.2d 90, 95 arising in New Jersey, the point was raised but not decided, the court saying that it was not satisfied that the then New Jersey rule differed from Rule 23(b), and that "under the circumstances the proper course was to follow Rule 23(b)."

In *Mullins v. DeSoto Securities Co.*, W.D.La.1942, 45 F.Supp. 871, 878, the point was not decided, because the court found the Louisiana rule to be the same as that stated in Rule 23(b).

In *Toebelman v. Missouri-Kansas Pipe Line Co.*, D.Del. 1941, 41 F.Supp. 334, 340, the court dealt only with another part of Rule 23(b), relating to prior demands on the stockholders and did not discuss *Erie R. Co. v. Tompkins*, or its effect on the rule.

In *Perrott v. United States Banking Corp.*, D.Del.1944, 53 F.Supp. 953, it appeared that the Delaware law does not require the plaintiff to have owned shares at the time of the transaction complained of. The court sustained Rule 23(b), after discussion of the authorities, saying:

"It seems to me the rule does not go beyond procedure. * * * Simply because a particular plaintiff cannot qualify as a proper party to maintain such an action does not destroy or even whittle at the cause of action. The cause of action exists until a qualified plaintiff can get it started in a federal court."

In *Bankers Nat. Corp. v. Barr*, S.D.N.Y.1945, 9 Fed.Rules Serv. 23b.11, Case 1, the court held Rule 23(b) to be one of procedure, but that whether the plaintiff was a stockholder was a substantive question to be settled by state law.

The New York rule, as stated in *Pollitz v. Gould*, supra, has been altered by an act of the New York Legislature, Chapter 667, Laws of 1944, effective April 9, 1944, General Corporation Law, § 61, which provides that "in any action brought by a shareholder in the right of a * * * corporation, it must appear that the plaintiff was a stockholder at the time of the transaction of which he complains, or that his stock thereafter devolved upon him by operation of law." At the same time a further and separate provision was enacted, requiring under certain circumstances the giving of security for reasonable expenses and attorney's fees, to which security the corporation in whose right the action is brought and the defendants therein may have recourse. (Chapter 668, Laws of 1944, effective April 9, 1944, General Corporation Law, § 61-b.) These provisions are aimed at so-called "strike" stockholders' suits and their attendant abuses. *Shielcrawt v. Moffett*, Ct. App.1945, 294 N.Y. 180, 61 N.E.2d 435, rev'g 51 N.Y.S.2d 188, aff'g 49 N.Y.S.2d 64; *Noel Associates, Inc. v. Merrill*, Sup.Ct. 1944, 184 Misc. 646, 63 N.Y.S.2d 143.

Insofar as § 61 is concerned, it has been held that the section is procedural in nature. *Klum v. Clinton Trust Co.*, Sup.Ct.1944, 183 Misc. 340, 48 N.Y.S.2d 267; *Noel Associates, Inc. v. Merrill*, supra. In the latter case the court pointed out that "The 1944 amendment to Section 61 rejected the rule laid down in the Pollitz case and substituted, in place thereof, in its precise language, the rule which has long prevailed in the Federal Courts and which is now Rule 23(b) * * *." There is, nevertheless, a difference of opinion regarding the application of the statute to pending actions. See *Klum v. Clinton Trust Co.*, supra (applicable); *Noel Associates, Inc. v. Merrill*, supra (inapplicable).

With respect to § 61-b, which may be regarded as a separate problem, *Noel Associates, Inc. v. Merrill*, supra, it has been held that even though the statute is procedural in nature—a matter not definitely decided—the Legislature evinced no intent that the provisions should apply to actions pending when it became effective. *Shielcrawt v. Moffett*, supra. As to actions instituted after the effective date of the legislation, the constitutionality of § 61-b is in dispute. See *Wolf v. Atkinson*, Sup.Ct.1944, 182 Misc. 675, 49 N.Y.S.2d 703 (constitutional); *Citron v. Mangel Stores Corp.*, Sup.Ct.1944, 50 N.Y.S.2d 416 (unconstitutional); Zlinkoff, *The American Investor and the Constitutionality of § 61-b of the New York General Corporation Law*, 1945, 54 Yale L.J. 352.

New Jersey also enacted a statute, similar to Chapters 667 and 668 of the New York law. See P.L.1945, Ch. 131, R.S.Cum.Supp. 14:3-15. The New Jersey provision similar to Chapter 668, § 61-b, differs, however, in that it specifically applies retroactively. It has been held that this provision is procedural and hence will not govern a pending action brought against a New Jersey corporation in the New York courts. *Shielcrawt v. Moffett*, Sup.Ct.N.Y.1945, 184 Misc. 1074, 56 N.Y.S.2d 134.

See, also generally, 2 Moore's *Federal Practice*, 1938, 2250-2253, and Cum.Supplement § 23.05.

The decisions here discussed show that the question is a debatable one, and that there is respectable authority for either view, with a recent trend towards the view that Rule 23(b)(1) is procedural. There is reason to say that the question is one which should not be decided by the Supreme Court ex parte, but left to await a judicial decision in a litigated case, and that in the light of the material in this note, the only inference to be drawn from a failure to amend Rule 23(b) would be that the question is postponed to await a litigated case.

The Advisory Committee is unanimously of the opinion that this course should be followed.

If, however, the final conclusion is that the rule deals with a matter of substantive right, then the rule should be amended by adding a provision that Rule 23(b)(1) does not apply in jurisdictions where state law permits a shareholder to maintain a secondary action, although he was not a shareholder at the time of the transactions of which he complains.

1966 Amendment

Difficulties with the original rule. The categories of class actions in the original rule were defined in terms of the abstract nature of the rights involved: the so-called "true" category was defined as involving "joint, common, or secondary rights"; the "hybrid" category, as involving "several" rights related to "specific property"; the "spurious" category, as involving "several" rights affected by a common question and related to common relief. It was thought that the definitions accurately described the situations amenable to the class-suit device, and also would indicate the proper extent of the judgment in each category, which would in turn help to determine the res judicata effect of the judgment if questioned in a later action. Thus the judgments in "true" and "hybrid" class actions would extend to the class (although in somewhat different ways); the judgment in a "spurious" class action would extend only to the parties including intervenors. See Moore, *Federal Rules of Civil Procedure: Some Problems Raised by the Preliminary Draft*, 25 Geo.L.J. 551, 570-76 (1937).

In practice the terms "joint," "common," etc., which were used as the basis of the Rule 23 classification proved obscure and uncertain. See Chafee, *Some Problems of Equity* 245-46, 256-57 (1950); Kalven & Rosenfield, *The Contemporary Function of the Class Suit*, 8 U. of Chi.L.Rev. 684, 707 & n. 73 (1941); Keeffe, Levy & Donovan, *Lee Defeats Ben Hur*, 33 Corn.L.Q. 327, 329-36 (1948); *Developments in the Law: Multiparty Litigation in the Federal Courts*, 71 Harv. L.Rev. 874, 931 (1958); Advisory Committee's Note to Rule 19, as amended. The courts had considerable difficulty with these terms. See, e.g., *Gullo v. Veterans' Coop. H. Assn.*, 13 F.R.D. 11 (D.D.C.1952); *Shipley v. Pittsburgh & L.E.R. Co.*, 70 F.Supp. 870 (W.D.Pa.1947); *Deckert v. Independence Shares Corp.*, 27 F.Supp. 763 (E.D.Pa.1939), rev'd 108 F.2d 51 (3d Cir. 1939), rev'd, 311 U.S. 282 (1940), on remand, 39 F.Supp. 592 (E.D.Pa.1941), rev'd sub nom. *Pennsylvania Co. for Ins. on Lives v. Deckert*, 123 F.2d 979 (3d Cir.1941) (see Chafee, supra, at 264-65).

Nor did the rule provide an adequate guide to the proper extent of the judgments in class actions. First, we find instances of the courts classifying actions as "true" or intimating that the judgments would be decisive for the class where these results seemed appropriate but were reached by dint of depriving the word "several" of coherent meaning. See, e.g., *System Federation No. 91 v. Reed*, 180 F.2d 991 (6th Cir. 1950); *Wilson v. City of Paducah*, 100 F.Supp. 116 (W.D.Ky. 1951); *Citizens Banking Co. v. Monticello State Bank*, 143

F.2d 261 (8th Cir.1944); *Redmond v. Commerce Trust Co.*, 144 F.2d 140 (8th Cir.1944), cert. denied, 323 U.S. 776 (1944); *United States v. American Optical Co.*, 97 F.Supp. 66 (N.D.Ill.1951); *National Hairdressers' & C. Assn. v. Philad Co.*, 34 F.Supp. 264 (D.Del.1940); 41 F.Supp. 701 (D.Del. 1940), aff'd mem., 129 F.2d 1020 (3d Cir.1942). Second, we find cases classified by the courts as "spurious" in which, on a realistic view, it would seem fitting for the judgments to extend to the class. See, e.g., *Knapp v. Bankers Sec. Corp.*, 17 F.R.D. 245 (E.D.Pa.1954), aff'd 230 F.2d 717 (3d Cir.1956); *Giesecke v. Denver Tramway Corp.*, 81 F.Supp. 957 (D.Del. 1949); *York v. Guaranty Trust Co.*, 143 F.2d 503 (2d Cir. 1944), rev'd on grounds not here relevant, 326 U.S. 99 (1945) (see Chafee, supra, at 208); cf. *Webster Eisenlohr, Inc. v. Kalodner*, 145 F.2d 316, 320 (3d Cir.1944), cert. denied, 325 U.S. 867 (1945). But cf. the early decisions, *Duke of Bedford v. Ellis*, [1901] A.C. 1; *Sheffield Waterworks v. Yeomans*, L.R. 2 Ch.App. 8 (1866); *Brown v. Vermuden*, 1 Ch.Cas. 272, 22 Eng.Rep. 796 (1676).

The "spurious" action envisaged by original Rule 23 was in any event an anomaly because, although denominated a "class" action and pleaded as such, it was supposed not to adjudicate the rights or liabilities of any person not a party. It was believed to be an advantage of the "spurious" category that it would invite decisions that a member of the "class" could, like a member of the class in a "true" or "hybrid" action, intervene on an ancillary basis without being required to show an independent basis of Federal jurisdiction, and have the benefit of the date of the commencement of the action for purposes of the statute of limitations. See 3 Moore's *Federal Practice*, pars. 23.10[1], 23.12 (2d ed.1963). These results were attained in some instances but not in others. On the statute of limitations, see *Union Carbide & Carbon Corp. v. Nisley*, 300 F.2d 561 (10th Cir.1961), pet. cert. dism., 371 U.S. 801 (1963); but cf. *P. W. Husserl, Inc. v. Newman*, 25 F.R.D. 264 (S.D.N.Y.1960); *Athas v. Day*, 161 F.Supp. 916 (D.Colo. 1958). On ancillary intervention, see *Amen v. Black*, 234 F.2d 12 (10th Cir.1956), cert. granted, 352 U.S. 888 (1956), dism. on stip., 355 U.S. 600 (1958); but cf. *Wagner v. Kemper*, 13 F.R.D. 128 (W.D.Mo.1952). The results, however, can hardly depend upon the mere appearance of a "spurious" category in the rule; they should turn on more basic considerations. See discussion of subdivision (c)(1) below.

Finally, the original rule did not squarely address itself to the question of the measures that might be taken during the course of the action to assure procedural fairness, particularly giving notice to members of the class, which may in turn be related in some instances to the extension of the judgment to the class. See Chafee, supra, at 230–31; Keeffe, Levy & Donovan, supra; *Developments in the law*, supra, 71 Harv. L.Rev. at 937–38; Note, *Binding Effect of Class Actions*, 67 Harv.L.Rev. 1059, 1062–65 (1954); Note, *Federal Class Actions: A Suggested Revision of Rule 23*, 46 Colum.L.Rev. 818, 833–36 (1946); Mich.Gen.Court R. 208.4 (effective Jan. 1, 1963); Idaho R.Civ.P. 23(d); Minn.R.Civ.P. 23.04; N.Dak.R.Civ.P. 23(d).

The amended rule describes in more practical terms the occasions for maintaining class actions; provides that all class actions maintained to the end as such will result in judgments including those whom the court finds to be members of the class, whether or not the judgment is favorable to the class; and refers to the measures which can be taken to assure the fair conduct of these actions.

Subdivision (a) states the prerequisites for maintaining any class action in terms of the numerousness of the class making joinder of the members impracticable, the existence of questions common to the class, and the desired qualifications of the representative parties. See Weinstein, *Revision of Procedure: Some Problems in Class Actions*, 9 Buffalo L.Rev. 433, 458–59 (1960); 2 Barron & Holtzoff, *Federal Practice & Procedure* § 562, at 265, § 572, at 351–52 (Wright ed. 1961). These are necessary but not sufficient conditions for a class action. See, e.g., *Giordano v. Radio Corp. of Am.*, 183 F.2d 558, 560 (3d Cir.1950); *Zachman v. Erwin*, 186 F.Supp. 681 (S.D.Tex.1959); *Baim & Blank, Inc. v. Warren-Connelly Co., Inc.*, 19 F.R.D. 108 (S.D.N.Y.1956). Subdivision (b) describes the additional elements which in varying situations justify the use of a class action.

Subdivision (b)(1). The difficulties which would be likely to arise if resort were had to separate actions by or against the individual members of the class here furnish the reasons for, and the principal key to, the propriety and value of utilizing the class-action device. The considerations stated under clauses (A) and (B) are comparable to certain of the elements which define the persons whose joinder in an action is desirable as stated in Rule 19(a), as amended. See amended Rule 19(a)(2)(i) and (ii), and the Advisory Committee's Note thereto; Hazard, *Indispensable Party: The Historical Origin of a Procedural Phantom*, 61 Colum.L.Rev. 1254, 1259–60 (1961); cf. 3 Moore, supra, par. 23.08, at 3435.

Clause (A): One person may have rights against, or be under duties toward, numerous persons constituting a class, and be so positioned that conflicting or varying adjudications in lawsuits with individual members of the class might establish incompatible standards to govern his conduct. The class action device can be used effectively to obviate the actual or virtual dilemma which would thus confront the party opposing the class. The matter has been stated thus: "The felt necessity for a class action is greatest when the courts are called upon to order or sanction the alteration of the status quo in circumstances such that a large number of persons are in a position to call on a single person to alter the status quo, or to complain if it is altered, and the possibility exists that [the] actor might be called upon to act in inconsistent ways." Louisell & Hazard, *Pleading and Procedure: State and Federal* 719 (1962); see *Supreme Tribe of Ben-Hur v. Cauble*, 255 U.S. 356, 366–67 (1921). To illustrate: Separate actions by individuals against a municipality to declare a bond issue invalid or condition or limit it, to prevent or limit the making of a particular appropriation or to compel or invalidate an assessment, might create a risk of inconsistent or varying determinations. In the same way, individual litigations of the rights and duties of riparian owners, or of landowners' rights and duties respecting a claimed nuisance, could create a possibility of incompatible adjudications. Actions by or against a class provide a ready and fair means of achieving unitary adjudication. See *Maricopa County Mun. Water Con. Dist. v. Looney*, 219 F.2d 529 (9th Cir.1955); *Rank v. Krug*, 142 F.Supp. 1, 154–59 (S.D.Calif.1956), on app., *State of California v. Rank*, 293 F.2d 340, 348 (9th Cir.1961); *Gart v. Cole*, 263 F.2d 244 (2d Cir.1959), cert. denied 359 U.S. 978 (1959); cf. *Martinez v. Maverick Cty. Water Con. & Imp. Dist.*, 219 F.2d 666 (5th Cir.1955); 3 Moore, supra, par. 23.11[2], at 3458–59.

Clause (B): This clause takes in situations where the judgment in a nonclass action by or against an individual member of the class, while not technically concluding the other members, might do so as a practical matter. The vice of an individual action would lie in the fact that the other members of the class, thus practically concluded, would have had no representation in the lawsuit. In an action by policy holders against a fraternal benefit association attacking a financial reorganization of the society, it would hardly have been practical, if indeed it would have been possible, to confine the effects of a validation of the reorganization to the individual plaintiffs. Consequently a class action was called for with adequate representation of all members of the class. See *Supreme Tribe of Ben-Hur v. Cauble*, 255 U.S. 356 (1921); *Waybright v. Columbian Mut. Life Ins. Co.*, 30 F.Supp. 885 (W.D.Tenn.1939); cf. *Smith v. Swormstedt*, 16 How. (57 U.S.) 288 (1853). For much the same reason actions by shareholders to compel the declaration of a dividend[,] the proper recognition and handling of redemption or pre-emption rights, or the like (or actions by the corporation for corresponding declarations of rights), should ordinarily be conducted as class actions, although the matter has been much obscured by the insistence that each shareholder has an individual claim. See *Knapp v. Bankers Securities Corp.*, 17 F.R.D. 245 (E.D.Pa. 1954), aff'd, 230 F.2d 717 (3d Cir.1956); *Giesecke v. Denver Tramway Corp.*, 81 F.Supp. 957 (D.Del.1949); *Zahn v. Transamerica Corp.*, 162 F.2d 36 (3d Cir.1947); *Speed v. Transamerica Corp.*, 100 F.Supp. 461 (D.Del.1951); *Sobel v. Whittier Corp.*, 95 F.Supp. 643 (E.D.Mich.1951), app. dism., 195 F.2d 361 (6th Cir.1952); *Goldberg v. Whittier Corp.*, 111 F.Supp. 382 (E.D.Mich.1953); *Dann v. Studebaker-Packard Corp.*, 288 F.2d 201 (6th Cir.1961); *Edgerton v. Armour & Co.*, 94 F.Supp. 549 (S.D.Calif.1950); *Ames v. Mengel Co.*, 190 F.2d 344 (2d Cir.1951). (These shareholders' actions are to be distinguished from derivative actions by shareholders dealt with in new Rule 23.1). The same reasoning applies to an action which charges a breach of trust by an indenture trustee or other fiduciary similarly affecting the members of a large class of security holders or other beneficiaries, and which requires an accounting or like measures to restore the subject of the trust. See *Boesenberg v. Chicago T. & T. Co.*, 128 F.2d 245 (7th Cir.1942); *Citizens Banking Co. v. Monticello State Bank*, 143 F.2d 261 (8th Cir.1944); *Redmond v. Commerce Trust Co.*, 144 F.2d 140 (8th Cir.1944), cert. denied, 323 U.S. 776 (1944); cf. *York v. Guaranty Trust Co.*, 143 F.2d 503 (2d Cir.1944), rev'd on grounds not here relevant, 326 U.S. 99 (1945).

In various situations an adjudication as to one or more members of the class will necessarily or probably have an adverse practical effect on the interests of other members who should therefore be represented in the lawsuit. This is plainly the case when claims are made by numerous persons against a fund insufficient to satisfy all claims. A class action by or against representative members to settle the validity of the claims as a whole, or in groups, followed by separate proof of the amount of each valid claim and proportionate distribution of the fund, meets the problem. Cf. *Dickinson v. Burnham*, 197 F.2d 973 (2d Cir.1952), cert. denied, 344 U.S. 875 (1952); 3 Moore, supra, at par. 23.09. The same reasoning applies to an action by a creditor to set aside a fraudulent conveyance by the debtor and to appropriate the property to his claim, when the debtor's assets are insufficient to pay all creditors' claims. See *Heffernan v. Bennett & Armour*, 110 Cal.App.2d 564, 243 P.2d 846 (1952); cf. *City & County of San Francisco v. Market Street Ry.*, 95 Cal.App.2d 648, 213 P.2d 780 (1950). Similar problems, however, can arise in the absence of a fund either present or potential. A negative or mandatory injunction secured by one of a numerous class may disable the opposing party from performing claimed duties toward the other members of the class or materially affect his ability to do so. An adjudication as to movie "clearances and runs" nominally affecting only one exhibitor would often have practical effects on all the exhibitors in the same territorial area. Cf. *United States v. Paramount Pictures, Inc.*, 66 F.Supp. 323, 341–46 (S.D.N.Y.1946); 334 U.S. 131, 144–48 (1948). Assuming a sufficiently numerous class of exhibitors, a class action would be advisable. (Here representation of subclasses of exhibitors could become necessary; see subdivision (c)(3)(B).)

Subdivision (b)(2). This subdivision is intended to reach situations where a party has taken action or refused to take action with respect to a class, and final relief of an injunctive nature or of a corresponding declaratory nature, settling the legality of the behavior with respect to the class as a whole, is appropriate. Declaratory relief "corresponds" to injunctive relief when as a practical matter it affords injunctive relief or serves as a basis for later injunctive relief. The subdivision does not extend to cases in which the appropriate final relief relates exclusively or predominantly to money damages. Action or inaction is directed to a class within the meaning of this subdivision even if it has taken effect or is threatened only as to one or a few members of the class, provided it is based on grounds which have general application to the class.

Illustrative are various actions in the civil-rights field where a party is charged with discriminating unlawfully against a class, usually one whose members are incapable of specific enumeration. See *Potts v. Flax*, 313 F.2d 284 (5th Cir. 1963); *Bailey v. Patterson*, 323 F.2d 201 (5th Cir. 1963), cert. denied, 376 U.S. 910, (1964); *Brunson v. Board of Trustees of School District No. 1, Clarendon Cty., S.C.*, 311 F.2d 107 (4th Cir. 1962), cert. denied, 373 U.S. 933 (1963); *Green v. School Bd. of Roanoke, Va.*, 304 F.2d 118 (4th Cir. 1962); *Orleans Parish School Bd. v. Bush*, 242 F.2d 156 (5th Cir. 1957), cert. denied, 354 U.S. 921 (1957); *Mannings v. Board of Public Inst. of Hillsborough County, Fla.*, 277 F.2d 370 (5th Cir. 1960); *Northcross v. Board of Ed. of City of Memphis*, 302 F.2d 818 (6th Cir. 1962), cert. denied, 370 U.S. 944 (1962); *Frasier v. Board of Trustees of Univ. of N.C.*, 134 F.Supp. 589 (M.D.N.C.1955, 3-judge court), aff'd 350 U.S. 979 (1956). Subdivision (b)(2) is not limited to civil-rights cases. Thus an action looking to specific or declaratory relief could be brought by a numerous class of purchasers, say retailers of a given description, against a seller alleged to have undertaken to sell to that class at prices higher than those set for other purchasers, say retailers of another description, when the applicable law forbids such a pricing differential. So also a patentee of a machine, charged with selling or licensing the machine on condition that purchasers or licensees also purchase or obtain licenses to use an ancillary unpatented machine, could be sued on a class basis by a numerous group of purchasers or licensees, or by a numerous group of competing sellers or licensors of the unpatented machine, to test the legality of the "tying" condition.

Subdivision (b)(3). In the situations to which this subdivision relates, class-action treatment is not as clearly called for as in those described above, but it may nevertheless be convenient and desirable depending upon the particular facts. Subdivision (b)(3) encompasses those cases in which a class action would achieve economies of time, effort, and expense, and promote uniformity of decision as to persons similarly situated, without sacrificing procedural fairness or bringing about other undesirable results. Cf. Chafee, supra, at 201.

The court is required to find, as a condition of holding that a class action may be maintained under this subdivision, that the questions common to the class predominate over the questions affecting individual members. It is only where this predominance exists that economies can be achieved by means of the class-action device. In this view, a fraud perpetrated on numerous persons by the use of similar misrepresentations may be an appealing situation for a class action, and it may remain so despite the need, if liability is found, for separate determination of the damages suffered by individuals within the class. On the other hand, although having some common core, a fraud case may be unsuited for treatment as a class action if there was material variation in the representations made or in the kinds or degrees of reliance by the persons to whom they were addressed. See *Oppenheimer v. F. J. Young & Co., Inc.*, 144 F.2d 387 (2d Cir. 1944); *Miller v. National City Bank of N.Y.*, 166 F.2d 723 (2d Cir. 1948); and for like problems in other contexts, see *Hughes v. Encyclopaedia Britannica*, 199 F.2d 295 (7th Cir. 1952); *Sturgeon v. Great Lakes Steel Corp.*, 143 F.2d 819 (6th Cir. 1944). A "mass accident" resulting in injuries to numerous persons is ordinarily not appropriate for a class action because of the likelihood that significant questions, not only of damages but of liability and defenses of liability, would be present, affecting the individuals in different ways. In these circumstances an action conducted nominally as a class action would degenerate in practice into multiple lawsuits separately tried. See *Pennsylvania R.R. v. United States*, 111 F.Supp. 80 (D.N.J. 1953); cf. Weinstein, supra, 9 Buffalo L.Rev. at 469. Private damage claims by numerous individuals arising out of concerted antitrust violations may or may not involve predominating common questions. See *Union Carbide & Carbon Corp. v. Nisley*, 300 F.2d 561 (10th Cir. 1961), pet. cert. dism., 371 U.S. 801 (1963); cf. *Weeks v. Bareco Oil Co.*, 125 F.2d 84 (7th Cir. 1941); *Kainz v. Anheuser-Busch, Inc.*, 194 F.2d 737 (7th Cir. 1952); *Hess v. Anderson, Clayton & Co.*, 20 F.R.D. 466 (S.D.Calif.1957).

That common questions predominate is not itself sufficient to justify a class action under subdivision (b)(3), for another method of handling the litigious situation may be available which has greater practical advantages. Thus one or more actions agreed to by the parties as test or model actions may be preferable to a class action; or it may prove feasible and preferable to consolidate actions. Cf. Weinstein, supra, 9 Buffalo L.Rev. at 438–54. Even when a number of separate actions are proceeding simultaneously, experience shows that the burdens on the parties and the courts can sometimes be reduced by arrangements for avoiding repetitious discovery or the like. Currently the Coordinating Committee on Multiple Litigation in the United States District Courts (a subcommittee of the Committee on Trial Practice and Technique of the Judicial Conference of the United States) is charged with developing methods for expediting such massive litigation. To reinforce the point that the court with the aid of the parties ought to assess the relative advantages of alternative procedures for handling the total controversy, subdivision (b)(3) requires, as a further condition of maintaining the class action, that the court shall find that that procedure is "superior" to the others in the particular circumstances.

Factors (A)–(D) are listed, non-exhaustively, as pertinent to the findings. The court is to consider the interests of individual members of the class in controlling their own litigations and carrying them on as they see fit. See *Weeks v. Bareco Oil Co.*, 125 F.2d 84, 88–90, 93–94 (7th Cir. 1941) (anti-trust action); see also *Pentland v. Dravo Corp.*, 152 F.2d 851 (3d

Cir. 1945), and Chafee, supra, at 273–75, regarding policy of Fair Labor Standards Act of 1938, § 16(b), 29 U.S.C. § 216(b), prior to amendment by Portal-to-Portal Act of 1947, § 5(a). [The present provisions of 29 U.S.C. § 216(b) are not intended to be affected by Rule 23, as amended.]

In this connection the court should inform itself of any litigation actually pending by or against the individuals. The interests of individuals in conducting separate lawsuits may be so strong as to call for denial of a class action. On the other hand, these interests may be theoretic rather than practical; the class may have a high degree of cohesion and prosecution of the action through representatives would be quite unobjectionable, or the amounts at stake for individuals may be so small that separate suits would be impracticable. The burden that separate suits would impose on the party opposing the class, or upon the court calendars, may also fairly be considered. (See the discussion, under subdivision (c)(2) below, of the right of members to be excluded from the class upon their request.)

Also pertinent is the question of the desirability of concentrating the trial of the claims in the particular forum by means of a class action, in contrast to allowing the claims to be litigated separately in forums to which they would ordinarily be brought. Finally, the court should consider the problems of management which are likely to arise in the conduct of a class action.

Subdivision (c)(1). In order to give clear definition to the action, this provision requires the court to determine, as early in the proceedings as may be practicable, whether an action brought as a class action is to be so maintained. The determination depends in each case on satisfaction of the terms of subdivision (a) and the relevant provisions of subdivision (b).

An order embodying a determination can be conditional; the court may rule, for example, that a class action may be maintained only if the representation is improved through intervention of additional parties of a stated type. A determination once made can be altered or amended before the decision on the merits if, upon fuller development of the facts, the original determination appears unsound. A negative determination means that the action should be stripped of its character as a class action. See subdivision (d)(4). Although an action thus becomes a nonclass action, the court may still be receptive to interventions before the decision on the merits so that the litigation may cover as many interests as can be conveniently handled; the questions whether the intervenors in the nonclass action shall be permitted to claim "ancillary" jurisdiction or the benefit of the date of the commencement of the action for purposes of the statute of limitations are to be decided by reference to the laws governing jurisdiction and limitations as they apply in particular contexts.

Whether the court should require notice to be given to members of the class of its intention to make a determination, or of the order embodying it, is left to the court's discretion under subdivision (d)(2).

Subdivision (c)(2) makes special provision for class actions maintained under subdivision (b)(3). As noted in the discussion of the latter subdivision, the interests of the individuals in pursing their own litigations may be so strong here as to warrant denial of a class action altogether. Even when a class action is maintained under subdivision (b)(3), this individual interest is respected. Thus the court is required to direct notice to the members of the class of the right of each member to be excluded from the class upon his request. A member who does not request exclusion may, if he wishes, enter an appearance in the action through his counsel; whether or not he does so, the judgment in the action will embrace him.

The notice[,] setting forth the alternatives open to the members of the class, is to be the best practicable under the circumstances, and shall include individual notice to the members who can be identified through reasonable effort. (For further discussion of this notice, see the statement under subdivision (d)(2) below.)

Subdivision (c)(3). The judgment in a class action maintained as such to the end will embrace the class, that is, in a class action under subdivision (b)(1) or (b)(2), those found by the court to be class members; in a class action under subdivision (b)(3), those to whom the notice prescribed by subdivision (c)(2) was directed, excepting those who requested exclusion or who are ultimately found by the court not to be members of the class. The judgment has this scope whether it is favorable or unfavorable to the class. In a (b)(1) or (b)(2) action the judgment "describes" the members of the class, but need not specify the individual members; in a (b)(3) action the judgment "specifies" the individual members who have been identified and described the others.

Compare subdivision (c)(4) as to actions conducted as class actions only with respect to particular issues. Where the class-action character of the lawsuit is based solely on the existence of a "limited fund," the judgment, while extending to all claims of class members against the fund, has ordinarily left unaffected the personal claims of nonappearing members against the debtor. See 3 Moore, supra, par. 23.11[4].

Hitherto, in a few actions conducted as "spurious" class actions and thus nominally designed to extend only to parties and others intervening before the determination of liability, courts have held or intimated that class members might be permitted to intervene after a decision on the merits favorable to their interests, in order to secure the benefits of the decision for themselves, although they would presumably be unaffected by an unfavorable decision. See, as to the propriety of this so-called "one-way" intervention in "spurious" actions, the conflicting views expressed in *Union Carbide & Carbon Corp. v. Nisley*, 300 F.2d 561 (10th Cir. 1961), pet. cert. dism., 371 U.S. 801 (1963); *York v. Guaranty Trust Co.*, 143 F.2d 503, 529 (2d Cir. 1944), rev'd on grounds not here relevant, 326 U.S. 99 (1945); *Pentland v. Dravo Corp.*, 152 F.2d 851, 856 (3d Cir. 1945); *Speed v. Transamerica Corp.*, 100 F.Supp. 461, 463 (D.Del.1951); *State Wholesale Grocers v. Great Atl. & Pac. Tea Co.*, 24 F.R.D. 510 (N.D.Ill.1959); *Alabama Ind. Serv. Stat. Assn. v. Shell Pet. Corp.*, 28 F.Supp. 386, 390 (N.D.Ala.1939); *Tolliver v. Cudahy Packing Co.*, 39 F.Supp. 337, 339 (E.D.Tenn.1941); Kalven & Rosenfield, supra, 8 U. of Chi.L.Rev. 684 (1941); Comment, 53 Nw.U.L.Rev. 627, 632–33 (1958); *Developments in the Law*, supra, 71 Harv.L.Rev. at 935; 2 Barron & Holtzoff, supra, § 568; but cf. *Lockwood v. Hercules Powder Co.*, 7 F.R.D. 24, 28–29 (W.D.Mo.1947); *Abram v. San Joaquin Cotton Oil Co.*, 46 F.Supp. 969, 976–77 (S.D.Calif.1942); Chafee, supra, at 280, 285; 3 Moore, supra, par. 23.12, at 3476. Under proposed subdivision (c)(3), one-way intervention is excluded; the action will have been early determined to be a class or nonclass action, and in the former case the judgment, whether or not favorable, will include the class, as above stated.

Although thus declaring that the judgment in a class action includes the class, as defined, subdivision (c)(3) does not disturb the recognized principle that the court conducting the action cannot predetermine the *res judicata* effect of the judgment; this can be tested only in a subsequent action. See Restatement, Judgments § 86, comment (h), § 116 (1942). The court, however, in framing the judgment in any suit brought as a class action, must decide what its extent or coverage shall be, and if the matter is carefully considered, questions of *res judicata* are less likely to be raised at a later time and if raised will be more satisfactorily answered. See Chafee, supra, at 294; Weinstein, supra, 9 Buffalo L.Rev. at 460.

Subdivision (c)(4). This provision recognizes that an action may be maintained as a class action as to particular issues only. For example, in a fraud or similar case the action may retain its "class" character only through the adjudication of liability to the class; the members of the class may thereafter be required to come in individually and prove the amounts of their respective claims.

Two or more classes may be represented in a single action. Where a class is found to include subclasses divergent in interest, the class may be divided correspondingly, and each subclass treated as a class.

Subdivision (d) is concerned with the fair and efficient conduct of the action and lists some types of orders which may be appropriate.

The court should consider how the proceedings are to be arranged in sequence, and what measures should be taken to simplify the proof and argument. See subdivision (d)(1). The orders resulting from this consideration, like the others referred to in subdivision (d), may be combined with a pretrial order under Rule 16, and are subject to modification as the case proceeds.

Subdivision (d)(2) sets out a non-exhaustive list of possible occasions for orders requiring notice to the class. Such notice is not a novel conception. For example, in "limited fund" cases, members of the class have been notified to present individual claims after the basic class decision. Notice has gone to members of a class so that they might express any opposition to the representation, see *United States v. American Optical Co.*, 97 F.Supp. 66 (N.D.Ill.1951), and 1950–51 CCH Trade Cases 64573–74 (par. 62869); cf. *Weeks v. Bareco Oil Co.*, 125 F.2d 84, 94 (7th Cir. 1941), and notice may encourage interventions to improve the representation of the class. Cf. *Oppenheimer v. F. J. Young & Co.*, 144 F.2d 387 (2d Cir. 1944). Notice has been used to poll members on a proposed modification of a consent decree. See record in *Sam Fox Publishing Co. v. United States*, 366 U.S. 683 (1961).

Subdivision (d)(2) does not require notice at any stage, but rather calls attention to its availability and invokes the court's discretion. In the degree that there is cohesiveness or unity in the class and the representation is effective, the need for notice to the class will tend toward a minimum. These indicators suggest that notice under subdivision (d)(2) may be particularly useful and advisable in certain class actions maintained under subdivision (b)(3), for example, to permit members of the class to object to the representation. Indeed, under subdivision (c)(2), notice must be ordered, and is not merely discretionary, to give the members in a subdivision (b)(3) class action an opportunity to secure exclusion from the class. This mandatory notice pursuant to subdivision (c)(2), together with any discretionary notice which the court may find it advisable to give under subdivision (d)(2), is designed to fulfill requirements of due process to which the class action procedure is of course subject. See *Hansberry v. Lee*, 311

U.S. 32 (1940); *Mullane v. Central Hanover Bank & Trust Co.*, 339 U.S. 306 (1950); cf. *Dickinson v. Burnham*, 197 F.2d 973, 979 (2d Cir. 1952), and studies cited at 979 in 4; see also *All American Airways, Inc. v. Elderd*, 209 F.2d 247, 249 (2d Cir. 1954); *Gart v. Cole*, 263 F.2d 244, 248–49 (2d Cir. 1959), cert. denied, 359 U.S. 978 (1959).

Notice to members of the class, whenever employed under amended Rule 23, should be accommodated to the particular purpose but need not comply with the formalities for service of process. See Chafee, supra, at 230–31; *Brendle v. Smith*, 7 F.R.D. 119 (S.D.N.Y.1946). The fact that notice is given at one stage of the action does not mean that it must be given at subsequent stages. Notice is available fundamentally "for the protection of the members of the class or otherwise for the fair conduct of the action" and should not be used merely as a device for the undesirable solicitation of claims. See the discussion in *Cherner v. Transitron Electronic Corp.*, 201 F.Supp. 934 (D.Mass.1962); *Hormel v. United States*, 17 F.R.D. 303 (S.D.N.Y.1955).

In appropriate cases the court should notify interested government agencies of the pendency of the action or of particular steps therein.

Subdivision (d)(3) reflects the possibility of conditioning the maintenance of a class action, e.g., on the strengthening of the representation, see subdivision (c)(1) above; and recognizes that the imposition of conditions on intervenors may be required for the proper and efficient conduct of the action.

As to orders under subdivision (d)(4), see subdivision (c)(1) above.

Subdivision (e) requires approval of the court, after notice, for the dismissal or compromise of any class action.

1987 Amendment

The amendments are technical. No substantive change is intended.

1998 Amendment

Subdivision (f). This permissive interlocutory appeal provision is adopted under the power conferred by 28 U.S.C. § 1292(e). Appeal from an order granting or denying class certification is permitted in the sole discretion of the court of appeals. No other type of Rule 23 order is covered by this provision. The court of appeals is given unfettered discretion whether to permit the appeal, akin to the discretion exercised by the Supreme Court in acting on a petition for certiorari. This discretion suggests an analogy to the provision in 28 U.S.C. § 1292(b) for permissive appeal on certification by a district court. Subdivision (f), however, departs from the § 1291(b) model in two significant ways. It does not require that the district court certify the certification ruling for appeal, although the district court often can assist the parties and court of appeals by offering advice on the desirability of appeal. And it does not include the potentially limiting requirements of § 1292(b) that the district court order "involve[] a controlling question of law as to which there is substantial ground for difference of opinion and that an immediate appeal from the order may materially advance the ultimate termination of the litigation."

The courts of appeals will develop standards for granting review that reflect the changing areas of uncertainty in class litigation. The Federal Judicial Center study supports the view that many suits with class-action allegations present familiar and almost routine issues that are no more worthy of immediate appeal than many other interlocutory rulings. Yet several concerns justify expansion of present opportunities to appeal. An order denying certification may confront the plaintiff with a situation in which the only sure path to appellate review is by proceeding to final judgment on the merits of an individual claim that, standing alone, is far smaller than the costs of litigation. An order granting certification, on the other hand, may force a defendant to settle rather than incur the costs of defending a class action and run the risk of potentially ruinous liability. These concerns can be met at low cost by establishing in the court of appeals a discretionary power to grant interlocutory review in cases that show appeal-worthy certification issues.

Permission to appeal may be granted or denied on the basis of any consideration that the court of appeals finds persuasive. Permission is most likely to be granted when the certification decision turns on a novel or unsettled question of law, or when, as a practical matter, the decision on certification is likely dispositive of the litigation.

The district court, having worked through the certification decision, often will be able to provide cogent advice on the factors that bear on the decision whether to permit appeal. This advice can be particularly valuable if the certification decision is tentative. Even as to a firm certification decision, a statement of reasons bearing on the probably benefits and costs of immediate appeal can help focus the court of appeals decision, and may persuade the disappointed party that an attempt to appeal would be fruitless.

The 10–day period for seeking permission to appeal is designed to reduce the risk that attempted appeals will disrupt continuing proceedings. It is expected that the courts of appeals will act quickly in making the preliminary determination whether to permit appeal. Permission to appeal does not stay trial court proceedings. A stay should be sought first from the trial court. If the trial court refuses a stay, its action and any explanation of its views should weigh heavily with the court of appeals.

Appellate Rule 5 has been modified to establish the procedure for petitioning for leave to appeal under subdivision (f).

2003 Amendment

Subdivision (c). Subdivision (c) is amended in several respects. The requirement that the court determine whether to certify a class "as soon as practicable after commencement of an action" is replaced by requiring determination "at an early practicable time." The notice provisions are substantially revised.

Paragraph (1). Subdivision (c)(1)(A) is changed to require that the determination whether to certify a class be made "at an early practicable time." The "as soon as practicable" exaction neither reflects prevailing practice nor captures the many valid reasons that may justify deferring the initial certification decision. See Willging, Hooper & Niemic, *Empirical Study of Class Actions in Four Federal District Courts: Final Report to the Advisory Committee on Civil Rules 26–36* (Federal Judicial Center 1996).

Time may be needed to gather information necessary to make the certification decision. Although an evaluation of the probable outcome on the merits is not properly part of the certification decision, discovery in aid of the certification decision often includes information required to identify the nature of the issues that actually will be presented at trial. In this sense it is appropriate to conduct controlled discovery into the "merits," limited to those aspects relevant to making the certification decision on an informed basis. Active judicial supervision may be required to achieve the most effective balance that expedites an informed certification determination without forcing an artificial and ultimately wasteful division between "certification discovery" and "merits discovery." A critical need is to determine how the case will be tried. An increasing number of courts require a party requesting class certification to present a "trial plan" that describes the issues likely to be presented at trial and tests whether they are susceptible of class-wide proof. See Manual For Complex Litigation Third, § 21.213, p. 44; § 30.11, p. 214; § 30.12, p. 215.

Other considerations may affect the timing of the certification decision. The party opposing the class may prefer to win dismissal or summary judgment as to the individual plaintiffs without certification and without binding the class that might have been certified. Time may be needed to explore designation of class counsel under Rule 23(g), recognizing that in many cases the need to progress toward the certification determination may require designation of interim counsel under Rule 23(g)(2)(A).

Although many circumstances may justify deferring the certification decision, active management may be necessary to ensure that the certification decision is not unjustifiably delayed.

Subdivision (c)(1)(C) reflects two amendments. The provision that a class certification "may be conditional" is deleted. A court that is not satisfied that the requirements of Rule 23 have been met should refuse certification until they have been met. The provision that permits alteration or amendment of an order granting or denying class certification is amended to set the cut-off point at final judgment rather than "the decision on the merits." This change avoids the possible ambiguity in referring to "the decision on the merits." Following a determination of liability, for example, proceedings to define the remedy may demonstrate the need to amend the class definition or subdivide the class. In this setting the final judgment concept is pragmatic. It is not the same as the concept used for appeal purposes, but it should be flexible, particularly in protracted litigation.

The authority to amend an order under Rule 23(c)(1) before final judgment does not restore the practice of "one-way intervention" that was rejected by the 1966 revision of Rule 23. A determination of liability after certification, however, may show a need to amend the class definition. Decertification may be warranted after further proceedings.

If the definition of a class certified under Rule 23(b)(3) is altered to include members who have not been afforded notice and an opportunity to request exclusion, notice—including an opportunity to request exclusion—must be directed to the new class members under Rule 23(c)(2)(B).

Paragraph (2). The first change made in Rule 23(c)(2) is to call attention to the court's authority—already established in part by Rule 23(d)(2)—to direct notice of certification to a Rule 23(b)(1) or (b)(2) class. The present rule expressly requires notice only in actions certified under Rule 23(b)(3). Members of classes certified under Rules 23(b)(1) or (b)(2) have interests that may deserve protection by notice.

The authority to direct notice to class members in a (b)(1) or (b)(2) class action should be exercised with care. For several reasons, there may be less need for notice than in a (b)(3) class action. There is no right to request exclusion from a (b)(1) or (b)(2) class. The characteristics of the class may reduce the need for formal notice. The cost of providing notice, moreover, could easily cripple actions that do not seek damages. The court may decide not to direct notice after balancing the risk that notice costs may deter the pursuit of class relief against the benefits of notice.

When the court does direct certification notice in a (b)(1) or (b)(2) class action, the discretion and flexibility established by subdivision (c)(2)(A) extend to the method of giving notice. Notice facilitates the opportunity to participate. Notice calculated to reach a significant number of class members often will protect the interests of all. Informal methods may prove effective. A simple posting in a place visited by many class members, directing attention to a source of more detailed information, may suffice. The court should consider the costs of notice in relation to the probable reach of inexpensive methods.

If a Rule 23(b)(3) class is certified in conjunction with a (b)(2) class, the (c)(2)(B) notice requirements must be satisfied as to the (b)(3) class.

The direction that class-certification notice be couched in plain, easily understood language is a reminder of the need to work unremittingly at the difficult task of communicating with class members. It is difficult to provide information about most class actions that is both accurate and easily understood by class members who are not themselves lawyers. Factual uncertainty, legal complexity, and the complication of class-action procedure raise the barriers high. The Federal Judicial Center has created illustrative clear-notice forms that provide a helpful starting point for actions similar to those described in the forms.

Subdivision (e). Subdivision (e) is amended to strengthen the process of reviewing proposed class-action settlements. Settlement may be a desirable means of resolving a class action. But court review and approval are essential to assure adequate representation of class members who have not participated in shaping the settlement.

Paragraph (1). Subdivision (e)(1)(A) expressly recognizes the power of a class representative to settle class claims, issues, or defenses.

Rule 23(e)(1)(A) resolves the ambiguity in former Rule 23(e)'s reference to dismissal or compromise of "a class action." That language could be—and at times was—read to require court approval of settlements with putative class representatives that resolved only individual claims. See Manual for Complex Litigation Third, § 30.41. The new rule requires approval only if the claims, issues, or defenses of a certified class are resolved by a settlement, voluntary dismissal, or compromise.

Subdivision (e)(1)(B) carries forward the notice requirement of present Rule 23(e) when the settlement binds the class through claim or issue preclusion; notice is not required when the settlement binds only the individual class representatives. Notice of a settlement binding on the class is required either when the settlement follows class certification or when the decisions on certification and settlement proceed simultaneously.

Reasonable settlement notice may require individual notice in the manner required by Rule 23(c)(2)(B) for certification notice to a Rule 23(b)(3) class. Individual notice is appropriate, for example, if class members are required to take action—such as filing claims—to participate in the judgment, or if the court orders a settlement opt-out opportunity under Rule 23(e)(3).

Subdivision (e)(1)(C) confirms and mandates the already common practice of holding hearings as part of the process of approving settlement, voluntary dismissal, or compromise that would bind members of a class.

Subdivision (e)(1)(C) states the standard for approving a proposed settlement that would bind class members. The settlement must be fair, reasonable, and adequate. A helpful review of many factors that may deserve consideration is provided by *In re: Prudential Ins. Co. America Sales Practice Litigation Agent Actions*, 148 F.3d 283, 316–324 (3d Cir. 1998). Further guidance can be found in the Manual for Complex Litigation.

The court must make findings that support the conclusion that the settlement is fair, reasonable, and adequate. The findings must be set out in sufficient detail to explain to class members and the appellate court the factors that bear on applying the standard.

Settlement review also may provide an occasion to review the cogency of the initial class definition. The terms of the settlement themselves, or objections, may reveal divergent interests of class members and demonstrate the need to redefine the class or to designate subclasses. Redefinition of a class certified under Rule 23(b)(3) may require notice to new class members under Rule 23(c)(2)(B). See Rule 23(c)(1)(C).

Paragraph (2). Subdivision (e)(2) requires parties seeking approval of a settlement, voluntary dismissal, or compromise under Rule 23(e)(1) to file a statement identifying any agreement made in connection with the settlement. This provision does not change the basic requirement that the parties disclose all terms of the settlement or compromise that the court must approve under Rule 23(e)(1). It aims instead at related undertakings that, although seemingly separate, may have influenced the terms of the settlement by trading away possible advantages for the class in return for advantages for others. Doubts should be resolved in favor of identification.

Further inquiry into the agreements identified by the parties should not become the occasion for discovery by the parties or objectors. The court may direct the parties to provide to the court or other parties a summary or copy of the full terms of any agreement identified by the parties. The court also may direct the parties to provide a summary or copy of any agreement not identified by the parties that the court considers relevant to its review of a proposed settlement. In exercising discretion under this rule, the court may act in steps, calling first for a summary of any agreement that may have affected the settlement and then for a complete version if the summary does not provide an adequate basis for review. A direction to disclose a summary or copy of an agreement may raise concerns of confidentiality. Some agreements may include information that merits protection against general disclosure. And the court must provide an opportunity to claim work-product or other protections.

Paragraph (3). Subdivision (e)(3) authorizes the court to refuse to approve a settlement unless the settlement affords class members a new opportunity to request exclusion from a class certified under Rule 23(b)(3) after settlement terms are known. An agreement by the parties themselves to permit class members to elect exclusion at this point by the settlement agreement may be one factor supporting approval of the settlement. Often there is an opportunity to opt out at this point because the class is certified and settlement is reached in circumstances that lead to simultaneous notice of certification and notice of settlement. In these cases, the basic opportunity to elect exclusion applies without further complication.

In some cases, particularly if settlement appears imminent at the time of certification, it may be possible to achieve equivalent protection by deferring notice and the opportunity to elect exclusion until actual settlement terms are known. This approach avoids the cost and potential confusion of providing two notices and makes the single notice more meaningful. But notice should not be delayed unduly after certification in the hope of settlement.

Rule 23(e)(3) authorizes the court to refuse to approve a settlement unless the settlement affords a new opportunity to elect exclusion in a case that settles after a certification decision if the earlier opportunity to elect exclusion provided with the certification notice has expired by the time of the settlement notice. A decision to remain in the class is likely to be more carefully considered and is better informed when settlement terms are known.

The opportunity to request exclusion from a proposed settlement is limited to members of a (b)(3) class. Exclusion may be requested only by individual class members; no class member may purport to opt out other class members by way of another class action.

The decision whether to approve a settlement that does not allow a new opportunity to elect exclusion is confided to the court's discretion. The court may make this decision before directing notice to the class under Rule 23(e)(1)(B) or after the Rule 23(e)(1)(C) hearing. Many factors may influence the court's decision. Among these are changes in the information available to class members since expiration of the first opportunity to request exclusion, and the nature of the individual class members' claims.

The terms set for permitting a new opportunity to elect exclusion from the proposed settlement of a Rule 23(b)(3) class action may address concerns of potential misuse. The court might direct, for example, that class members who elect exclusion are bound by rulings on the merits made before the settlement was proposed for approval. Still other terms or conditions may be appropriate.

Paragraph (4). Subdivision (e)(4) confirms the right of class members to object to a proposed settlement, voluntary dismissal, or compromise. The right is defined in relation to a disposition that, because it would bind the class, requires court approval under subdivision (e)(1)(C).

Subdivision (e)(4)(B) requires court approval for withdrawal of objections made under subdivision (e)(4)(A). Review follows automatically if the objections are withdrawn on terms that lead to modification of the settlement with the class. Review also is required if the objector formally withdraws the objections. If the objector simply abandons pursuit of the objection, the court may inquire into the circumstances.

Approval under paragraph (4)(B) may be given or denied with little need for further inquiry if the objection and the disposition go only to a protest that the individual treatment afforded the objector under the proposed settlement is unfair because of factors that distinguish the objector from other class members. Different considerations may apply if the objector has protested that the proposed settlement is not fair, reasonable, or adequate on grounds that apply generally to a class or subclass. Such objections, which purport to represent class-wide interests, may augment the opportunity for obstruction or delay. If such objections are surrendered on terms that do not affect the class settlement or the objector's participation in the class settlement, the court often can approve withdrawal of the objections without elaborate inquiry.

Once an objector appeals, control of the proceeding lies in the court of appeals. The court of appeals may undertake review and approval of a settlement with the objector, perhaps as part of appeal settlement procedures, or may remand to the district court to take advantage of the district court's familiarity with the action and settlement.

Subdivision (g). Subdivision (g) is new. It responds to the reality that the selection and activity of class counsel are often critically important to the successful handling of a class action. Until now, courts have scrutinized proposed class counsel as well as the class representative under Rule 23(a)(4). This experience has recognized the importance of judicial evaluation of the proposed lawyer for the class, and this new subdivision builds on that experience rather than introducing an entirely new element into the class certification process. Rule 23(a)(4) will continue to call for scrutiny of the proposed class representative, while this subdivision will guide the court in assessing proposed class counsel as part of the certification decision. This subdivision recognizes the importance of class counsel, states the obligation to represent the interests of the class, and provides a framework for selection of class counsel. The procedure and standards for appointment vary depending on whether there are multiple applicants to be class counsel. The new subdivision also provides a method by which the court may make directions from the outset about the potential fee award to class counsel in the event the action is successful.

Paragraph (1) sets out the basic requirement that class counsel be appointed if a class is certified and articulates the obligation of class counsel to represent the interests of the class, as opposed to the potentially conflicting interests of individual class members. It also sets out the factors the court should consider in assessing proposed class counsel.

Paragraph (1)(A) requires that the court appoint class counsel to represent the class. Class counsel must be appointed for all classes, including each subclass that the court certifies to represent divergent interests.

Paragraph (1)(A) does not apply if "a statute provides otherwise." This recognizes that provisions of the Private Securities Litigation Reform Act of 1995, Pub. L. No. 104–67, 109 Stat. 737 (1995) (codified in various sections of 15 U.S.C.), contain directives that bear on selection of a lead plaintiff and the retention of counsel. This subdivision does not purport to supersede or to affect the interpretation of those provisions, or any similar provisions of other legislation.

Paragraph 1(B) recognizes that the primary responsibility of class counsel, resulting from appointment as class counsel, is to represent the best interests of the class. The rule thus establishes the obligation of class counsel, an obligation that may be different from the customary obligations of counsel to individual clients. Appointment as class counsel means that the primary obligation of counsel is to the class rather than to any individual members of it. The class representatives do not have an unfettered right to "fire" class counsel. In the same vein, the class representatives cannot command class counsel to accept or reject a settlement proposal. To the contrary, class counsel must determine whether seeking the court's approval of a settlement would be in the best interests of the class as a whole.

Paragraph (1)(C) articulates the basic responsibility of the court to appoint class counsel who will provide the adequate representation called for by paragraph (1)(B). It identifies criteria that must be considered and invites the court to consider any other pertinent matters. Although couched in terms of the court's duty, the listing also informs counsel seeking appointment about the topics that should be addressed in an application for appointment or in the motion for class certification.

The court may direct potential class counsel to provide additional information about the topics mentioned in paragraph (1)(C) or about any other relevant topic. For example, the court may direct applicants to inform the court concerning any agreements about a prospective award of attorney fees or nontaxable costs, as such agreements may sometimes be significant in the selection of class counsel. The court might also direct that potential class counsel indicate how parallel litigation might be coordinated or consolidated with the action before the court.

The court may also direct counsel to propose terms for a potential award of attorney fees and nontaxable costs. Attorney fee awards are an important feature of class action practice, and attention to this subject from the outset may often be a productive technique. Paragraph (2)(C) therefore authorizes the court to provide directions about attorney fees and costs when appointing class counsel. Because there will be numerous class actions in which this information is not likely to be useful, the court need not consider it in all class actions.

Some information relevant to class counsel appointment may involve matters that include adversary preparation in a way that should be shielded from disclosure to other parties. An appropriate protective order may be necessary to preserve confidentiality.

In evaluating prospective class counsel, the court should weigh all pertinent factors. No single factor should necessarily be determinative in a given case. For example, the resources counsel will commit to the case must be appropriate to its needs, but the court should be careful not to limit consideration to lawyers with the greatest resources.

If, after review of all applicants, the court concludes that none would be satisfactory class counsel, it may deny class certification, reject all applications, recommend that an application be modified, invite new applications, or make any other appropriate order regarding selection and appointment of class counsel.

Paragraph (2). This paragraph sets out the procedure that should be followed in appointing class counsel. Although it affords substantial flexibility, it provides the framework for appointment of class counsel in all class actions. For counsel who filed the action, the materials submitted in support of the motion for class certification may suffice to justify appointment so long as the information described in paragraph (g)(1)(C) is included. If there are other applicants, they ordinarily would file a formal application detailing their suitability for the position.

In a plaintiff class action the court usually would appoint as class counsel only an attorney or attorneys who have sought appointment. Different considerations may apply in defendant class actions.

The rule states that the court should appoint "class counsel." In many instances, the applicant will be an individual attorney. In other cases, however, an entire firm, or perhaps numerous attorneys who are not otherwise affiliated but are collaborating on the action will apply. No rule of thumb exists to determine when such arrangements are appropriate; the court should be alert to the need for adequate staffing of the case, but also to the risk of overstaffing or an ungainly counsel structure.

Paragraph (2)(A) authorizes the court to designate interim counsel during the pre-certification period if necessary to protect the interests of the putative class. Rule 23(c)(1)(B) directs that the order certifying the class include appointment of class counsel. Before class certification, however, it will usually be important for an attorney to take action to prepare for the certification decision. The amendment to Rule 23(c)(1) recognizes that some discovery is often necessary for that determination. It also may be important to make or respond to motions before certification. Settlement may be discussed before certification. Ordinarily, such work is handled by the lawyer who filed the action. In some cases, however, there may be rivalry or uncertainty that makes formal designation of interim counsel appropriate. Rule 23(g)(2)(A) authorizes the court to designate interim counsel to act on behalf of the putative class before the certification decision is made. Failure to make the formal designation does not prevent the attorney who filed the action from proceeding in it. Whether or not formally designated interim counsel, an attorney who acts on behalf of the class before certification must act in the best interests of the class as a whole. For example, an attorney who negotiates a pre-certification settlement must seek a settlement that is fair, reasonable, and adequate for the class.

Rule 23(c)(1) provides that the court should decide whether to certify the class "at an early practicable time," and directs that class counsel should be appointed in the order certifying the class. In some cases, it may be appropriate for the court to allow a reasonable period after commencement of the action for filing applications to serve as class counsel. The primary ground for deferring appointment would be that there is reason to anticipate competing applications to serve as class counsel. Examples might include instances in which more than one class action has been filed, or in which other attorneys have filed individual actions on behalf of putative class members. The purpose of facilitating competing applications in such a case is to afford the best possible representation for the class. Another possible reason for deferring appointment would be that the initial applicant was found inadequate, but it seems appropriate to permit additional applications rather than deny class certification.

Paragraph (2)(B) states the basic standard the court should use in deciding whether to certify the class and appoint class counsel in the single applicant situation—that the applicant be able to provide the representation called for by paragraph (1)(B) in light of the factors identified in paragraph (1)(C).

If there are multiple adequate applicants, paragraph (2)(B) directs the court to select the class counsel best able to represent the interests of the class. This decision should also be made using the factors outlined in paragraph (1)(C), but in the multiple applicant situation the court is to go beyond scrutinizing the adequacy of counsel and make a comparison of the strengths of the various applicants. As with the decision whether to appoint the sole applicant for the position, no single factor should be dispositive in selecting class counsel in cases in which there are multiple applicants. The fact that a given attorney filed the instant action, for example, might not weigh heavily in the decision if that lawyer had not done significant work identifying or investigating claims. Depending on the nature of the case, one important consideration might be the applicant's existing attorney-client relationship with the proposed class representative.

Paragraph (2)(C) builds on the appointment process by authorizing the court to include provisions regarding attorney fees in the order appointing class counsel. Courts may find it desirable to adopt guidelines for fees or nontaxable costs, or to direct class counsel to report to the court at regular intervals on the efforts undertaken in the action, to facilitate the court's later determination of a reasonable attorney fee.

Subdivision (h). Subdivision (h) is new. Fee awards are a powerful influence on the way attorneys initiate, develop, and conclude class actions. Class action attorney fee awards have heretofore been handled, along with all other attorney fee awards, under Rule 54(d)(2), but that rule is not addressed to the particular concerns of class actions. This subdivision is designed to work in tandem with new subdivision (g) on appointment of class counsel, which may afford an opportunity for the court to provide an early framework for an eventual fee award, or for monitoring the work of class counsel during the pendency of the action.

Subdivision (h) applies to "an action certified as a class action." This includes cases in which there is a simultaneous proposal for class certification and settlement even though technically the class may not be certified unless the court approves the settlement pursuant to review under Rule 23(e). When a settlement is proposed for Rule 23(e) approval, either after certification or with a request for certification, notice to class members about class counsel's fee motion would ordinarily accompany the notice to the class about the settlement proposal itself.

This subdivision does not undertake to create new grounds for an award of attorney fees or nontaxable costs. Instead, it applies when such awards are authorized by law or by agreement of the parties. Against that background, it provides a format for all awards of attorney fees and nontaxable costs in connection with a class action, not only the award to class counsel. In some situations, there may be a basis for making an award to other counsel whose work produced a beneficial result for the class, such as attorneys who acted for the class before certification but were not appointed class counsel, or attorneys who represented objectors to a proposed settlement under Rule 23(e) or to the fee motion of class counsel. Other situations in which fee awards are authorized by law or by agreement of the parties may exist.

This subdivision authorizes an award of "reasonable" attorney fees and nontaxable costs. This is the customary term for measurement of fee awards in cases in which counsel may obtain an award of fees under the "common fund" theory that applies in many class actions, and is used in many fee-shifting statutes. Depending on the circumstances, courts have approached the determination of what is reasonable in different ways. In particular, there is some variation among courts about whether in "common fund" cases the court should use the lodestar or a percentage method of determining what fee is reasonable. The rule does not attempt to resolve the question whether the lodestar or percentage approach should be viewed as preferable.

Active judicial involvement in measuring fee awards is singularly important to the proper operation of the class-action process. Continued reliance on caselaw development of fee-award measures does not diminish the court's responsibility. In a class action, the district court must ensure that the amount and mode of payment of attorney fees are fair and proper whether the fees come from a common fund or are otherwise paid. Even in the absence of objections, the court bears this responsibility.

Courts discharging this responsibility have looked to a variety of factors. One fundamental focus is the result actually achieved for class members, a basic consideration in any case in which fees are sought on the basis of a benefit achieved for class members. The Private Securities Litigation Reform Act of 1995 explicitly makes this factor a cap for a fee award in actions to which it applies. See 15 U.S.C. §§ 77z–1(a)(6); 78u–4(a)(6) (fee award should not exceed a "reasonable percentage of the amount of any damages and prejudgment interest actually paid to the class"). For a percentage approach to fee measurement, results achieved is the basic starting point.

In many instances, the court may need to proceed with care in assessing the value conferred on class members. Settlement regimes that provide for future payments, for example, may not result in significant actual payments to class members. In this connection, the court may need to scrutinize the manner and operation of any applicable claims procedure. In some cases, it may be appropriate to defer some portion of the fee award until actual payouts to class members are known. Settlements involving nonmonetary provisions for class members also deserve careful scrutiny to ensure that these provisions have actual value to the class. On occasion the court's Rule 23(e) review will provide a solid basis for this sort of evaluation, but in any event it is also important to assessing the fee award for the class.

At the same time, it is important to recognize that in some class actions the monetary relief obtained is not the sole determinant of an appropriate attorney fees award. Cf. *Blanchard v. Bergeron*, 489 U.S. 87, 95 (1989) (cautioning in an individual case against an "undesirable emphasis" on "the importance of the recovery of damages in civil rights litigation" that might "shortchange efforts to seek effective injunctive or declaratory relief").

Any directions or orders made by the court in connection with appointing class counsel under Rule 23(g) should weigh heavily in making a fee award under this subdivision.

Courts have also given weight to agreements among the parties regarding the fee motion, and to agreements between class counsel and others about the fees claimed by the motion. Rule 54(d)(2)(B) provides: "If directed by the court, the motion shall also disclose the terms of any agreement with respect to fees to be paid for the services for which claim is made." The agreement by a settling party not to oppose a fee application up to a certain amount, for example, is worthy of consideration, but the court remains responsible to determine a reasonable fee. "Side agreements" regarding fees provide at least perspective pertinent to an appropriate fee award.

In addition, courts may take account of the fees charged by class counsel or other attorneys for representing individual claimants or objectors in the case. In determining a fee for class counsel, the court's objective is to ensure an overall fee that is fair for counsel and equitable within the class. In some circumstances individual fee agreements between class counsel and class members might have provisions inconsistent with those goals, and the court might determine that adjustments in the class fee award were necessary as a result.

Finally, it is important to scrutinize separately the application for an award covering nontaxable costs. If costs were addressed in the order appointing class counsel, those directives should be a presumptive starting point in determining what is an appropriate award.

Paragraph (1). Any claim for an award of attorney fees must be sought by motion under Rule 54(d)(2), which invokes the provisions for timing of appeal in Rule 58 and Appellate Rule 4. Owing to the distinctive features of class action fee motions, however, the provisions of this subdivision control disposition of fee motions in class actions, while Rule 54(d)(2) applies to matters not addressed in this subdivision.

The court should direct when the fee motion must be filed. For motions by class counsel in cases subject to court review of a proposed settlement under Rule 23(e), it would be important to require the filing of at least the initial motion in time for inclusion of information about the motion in the notice to the class about the proposed settlement that is required by Rule 23(e). In cases litigated to judgment, the court might also order class counsel's motion to be filed promptly so that notice to the class under this subdivision (h) can be given.

Besides service of the motion on all parties, notice of class counsel's motion for attorney fees must be "directed to the class in a reasonable manner." Because members of the class have an interest in the arrangements for payment of class counsel whether that payment comes from the class fund or is made directly by another party, notice is required in all instances. In cases in which settlement approval is contemplated under Rule 23(e), notice of class counsel's fee motion should be combined with notice of the proposed settlement, and the provision regarding notice to the class is parallel to the requirements for notice under Rule 23(e). In adjudicated class actions, the court may calibrate the notice to avoid undue expense.

Paragraph (2). A class member and any party from whom payment is sought may object to the fee motion. Other parties—for example, nonsettling defendants—may not object because they lack a sufficient interest in the amount the court awards. The rule does not specify a time limit for making an objection. In setting the date objections are due, the court should provide sufficient time after the full fee motion is on file to enable potential objectors to examine the motion.

The court may allow an objector discovery relevant to the objections. In determining whether to allow discovery, the court should weigh the need for the information against the cost and delay that would attend discovery. See Rule 26(b)(2). One factor in determining whether to authorize discovery is the completeness of the material submitted in support of the fee motion, which depends in part on the fee measurement standard applicable to the case. If the motion provides thorough information, the burden should be on the objector to justify discovery to obtain further information.

Paragraph (3). Whether or not there are formal objections, the court must determine whether a fee award is justified and, if so, set a reasonable fee. The rule does not require a formal hearing in all cases. The form and extent of a hearing depend on the circumstances of the case. The rule does require findings and conclusions under Rule 52(a).

Paragraph (4). By incorporating Rule 54(d)(2), this provision gives the court broad authority to obtain assistance in determining the appropriate amount to award. In deciding whether to direct submission of such questions to a special master or magistrate judge, the court should give appropriate consideration to the cost and delay that such a process might entail.

2007 Amendment

The language of Rule 23 has been amended as part of the general restyling of the Civil Rules to make them more easily understood and to make style and terminology consistent throughout the rules. These changes are intended to be stylistic only.

Amended Rule 23(d)(2) carries forward the provisions of former Rule 23(d) that recognize two separate propositions. First, a Rule 23(d) order may be combined with a pretrial order under Rule 16. Second, the standard for amending the Rule 23(d) order continues to be the more open-ended standard for amending Rule 23(d) orders, not the more exacting standard for amending Rule 16 orders.

As part of the general restyling, intensifiers that provide emphasis but add no meaning are consistently deleted. Amended Rule 23(f) omits as redundant the explicit reference to court of appeals discretion in deciding whether to permit an interlocutory appeal. The omission does not in any way limit the unfettered discretion established by the original rule.

2009 Amendment

The time set in the former rule at 10 days has been revised to 14 days. See the Note to Rule 6.

2018 Amendments

Rule 23 is amended mainly to address issues related to settlement, and also to take account of issues that have emerged since the rule was last amended in 2003.

Subdivision (c)(2). As amended, Rule 23(e)(1) provides that the court must direct notice to the class regarding a proposed class-action settlement only after determining that the prospect of class certification and approval of the proposed settlement justifies giving notice. This decision has been called "preliminary approval" of the proposed class certification in Rule 23(b)(3) actions. It is common to send notice to the class simultaneously under both Rule 23(e)(1) and Rule 23(c)(2)(B), including a provision for class members to decide by a certain date whether to opt out. This amendment recognizes the propriety of this combined notice practice.

Subdivision (c)(2) is also amended to recognize contemporary methods of giving notice to class members. Since *Eisen v. Carlisle & Jacquelin*, 417 U.S. 156 (1974), interpreted the individual notice requirement for class members in Rule 23(b)(3) class actions, many courts have read the rule to require notice by first class mail in every case. But technological change since 1974 has introduced other means of communication that may sometimes provide a reliable additional or alternative method for giving notice. Although first class mail may often be the preferred primary method of giving notice, courts and counsel have begun to employ new technology to make notice more effective. Because there is no reason to expect that technological change will cease, when selecting a method or methods of giving notice courts should consider the capacity and limits of current technology, including class members' likely access to such technology.

Rule 23(c)(2)(B) is amended to take account of these changes. The rule continues to call for giving class members "the best notice that is practicable." It does not specify any particular means as preferred. Although it may sometimes be true that electronic methods of notice, for example email, are the most promising, it is important to keep in mind that a significant portion of class members in certain cases may have limited or no access to email or the Internet.

Instead of preferring any one means of notice, therefore, the amended rule relies on courts and counsel to focus on the means or combination of means most likely to be effective in the case before the court. The court should exercise its discretion to select appropriate means of giving notice. In providing the court with sufficient information to enable it to decide whether to give notice to the class of a proposed class-action settlement under Rule 23(e)(1), it would ordinarily be important to include details about the proposed method of giving notice and to provide the court with a copy of each notice the parties propose to use.

In determining whether the proposed means of giving notice is appropriate, the court should also give careful attention to the content and format of the notice and, if notice is given under both Rule 23(e)(1) and Rule 23(c)(2)(B), any claim form class members must submit to obtain relief.

Counsel should consider which method or methods of giving notice will be most effective; simply assuming that the "traditional" methods are best may disregard contemporary communication realities. The ultimate goal of giving notice is to enable class members to make informed decisions about whether to opt out or, in instances where a proposed settlement is involved, to object or to make claims. Rule 23(c)(2)(B) directs that the notice be "in plain, easily understood language." Means, format, and content that would be appropriate for class members likely to be sophisticated, for example in a securities fraud class action, might not be appropriate for a class having many members likely to be less sophisticated. The court and counsel may wish to consider the use of class notice experts or professional claims administrators.

Attention should focus also on the method of opting out provided in the notice. The proposed method should be as convenient as possible, while protecting against unauthorized opt-out notices.

Subdivision (e). The introductory paragraph of Rule 23(e) is amended to make explicit that its procedural requirements apply in instances in which the court has not certified a class at the time that a proposed settlement is presented to the court. The notice required under Rule 23(e)(1) then should also satisfy the notice requirements of amended Rule 23(c)(2)(B) for a class to be certified under Rule 23(b)(3), and trigger the class members' time to request exclusion. Information about the opt-out rate could then be available to the court when it considers final approval of the proposed settlement.

Subdivision (e)(1). The decision to give notice of a proposed settlement to the class is an important event. It should be based on a solid record supporting the conclusion that the proposed settlement will likely earn final approval after notice and an opportunity to object. The parties must provide the court with information sufficient to determine whether notice should be sent. At the time they seek notice to the class, the proponents of the settlement should ordinarily provide the court with all available materials they intend to submit to support approval under Rule 23(e)(2) and that they intend to make available to class members. The amended rule also specifies the standard the court should use in deciding whether to send notice—that it likely will be able both to approve the settlement proposal under Rule 23(e)(2) and, if it has not previously certified a class, to certify the class for purposes of judgment on the proposal.

The subjects to be addressed depend on the specifics of the particular class action and proposed settlement. But some general observations can be made.

One key element is class certification. If the court has already certified a class, the only information ordinarily necessary is whether the proposed settlement calls for any change in the class certified, or of the claims, defenses, or issues regarding which certification was granted. But if a class has not been certified, the parties must ensure that the court has a basis for concluding that it likely will be able, after the final hearing, to certify the class. Although the standards for certification differ for settlement and litigation purposes, the court cannot make the decision regarding the prospects for certification without a suitable basis in the record. The ultimate decision to certify the class for purposes of settlement cannot be made until the hearing on final approval of the proposed settlement. If the settlement is not approved, the parties' positions regarding certification for settlement should not be considered if certification is later sought for purposes of litigation.

Regarding the proposed settlement, many types of information might appropriately be provided to the court. A basic focus is the extent and type of benefits that the settlement will confer on the members of the class. Depending on the nature of the proposed relief, that showing may include details of the contemplated claims process and the anticipated rate of claims by class members. Because some funds are frequently left unclaimed, the settlement agreement ordinarily should address the distribution of those funds.

The parties should also supply the court with information about the likely range of litigated outcomes, and about the risks that might attend full litigation. Information about the extent of discovery completed in the litigation or in parallel actions may often be important. In addition, as suggested by Rule 23(b)(3)(B), the parties should provide information about the existence of other pending or anticipated litigation on behalf of class members involving claims that would be released under the proposal.

The proposed handling of an award of attorney's fees under Rule 23(h) ordinarily should be addressed in the parties' submission to the court. In some cases, it will be important to relate the amount of an award of attorney's fees to the expected benefits to the class. One way to address this issue is to defer some or all of the award of attorney's fees until the court is advised of the actual claims rate and results.

Another topic that normally should be considered is any agreement that must be identified under Rule 23(e)(3).

The parties may supply information to the court on any other topic that they regard as pertinent to the determination whether the proposal is fair, reasonable, and adequate. The court may direct the parties to supply further information about the topics they do address, or to supply information on topics they do not address. The court should not direct notice to the class until the parties' submissions show it is likely that the court will be able to approve the proposal after notice to the class and a final approval hearing.

Subdivision (e)(2). The central concern in reviewing a proposed class-action settlement is that it be fair, reasonable, and adequate. Courts have generated lists of factors to shed light on this concern. Overall, these factors focus on comparable considerations, but each circuit has developed its own vocabulary for expressing these concerns. In some circuits, these lists have remained essentially unchanged for thirty or forty years. The goal of this amendment is not to displace any factor, but rather to focus the court and the lawyers on the core concerns of procedure and substance that should guide the decision whether to approve the proposal.

A lengthy list of factors can take on an independent life, potentially distracting attention from the central concerns that inform the settlement-review process. A circuit's list might include a dozen or more separately articulated factors. Some of those factors—perhaps many—may not be relevant to a particular case or settlement proposal. Those that are relevant may be more or less important to the particular case. Yet counsel and courts may feel it necessary to address every factor on a given circuit's list in every case. The sheer number of factors can distract both the court and the parties from the central concerns that bear on review under Rule 23(e)(2).

This amendment therefore directs the parties to present the settlement to the court in terms of a shorter list of core concerns, by focusing on the primary procedural considerations and substantive qualities that should always matter to the decision whether to approve the proposal.

Approval under Rule 23(e)(2) is required only when class members would be bound under Rule 23(c)(3). Accordingly, in addition to evaluating the proposal itself, the court must determine whether it can certify the class under the standards of Rule 23(a) and (b) for purposes of judgment based on the proposal.

Paragraphs (A) and (B). These paragraphs identify matters that might be described as "procedural" concerns, looking to the conduct of the litigation and of the negotiations leading up to the proposed settlement. Attention to these matters is an important foundation for scrutinizing the substance of the proposed settlement. If the court has appointed class counsel or interim class counsel, it will have made an initial evaluation of counsel's capacities and experience. But the focus at this point is on the actual performance of counsel acting on behalf of the class.

The information submitted under Rule 23(e)(1) may provide a useful starting point in assessing these topics. For example, the nature and amount of discovery in this or other cases, or the actual outcomes of other cases, may indicate whether counsel negotiating on behalf of the class had an adequate information base. The pendency of other litigation about the same general subject on behalf of class members may also be pertinent. The conduct of the negotiations may be important as well. For example, the involvement of a neutral or court-affiliated mediator or facilitator in those negotiations may bear on whether they were conducted in a manner that would protect and further the class interests. Particular attention might focus on the treatment of any award of attorney's fees, with respect to both the manner of negotiating the fee award and its terms.

Paragraphs (C) and (D). These paragraphs focus on what might be called a "substantive" review of the terms of the proposed settlement. The relief that the settlement is expected to provide to class members is a central concern. Measuring the proposed relief may require evaluation of any proposed claims process; directing that the parties report back to the court about actual claims experience may be important. The contents of any agreement identified under Rule 23(e)(3) may also bear on the adequacy of the proposed relief, particularly regarding the equitable treatment of all members of the class.

Another central concern will relate to the cost and risk involved in pursuing a litigated outcome. Often, courts may need to forecast the likely range of possible classwide recoveries and the likelihood of success in obtaining such results.

That forecast cannot be done with arithmetic accuracy, but it can provide a benchmark for comparison with the settlement figure.

If the class has not yet been certified for trial, the court may consider whether certification for litigation would be granted were the settlement not approved.

Examination of the attorney-fee provisions may also be valuable in assessing the fairness of the proposed settlement. Ultimately, any award of attorney's fees must be evaluated under Rule 23(h), and no rigid limits exist for such awards. Nonetheless, the relief actually delivered to the class can be a significant factor in determining the appropriate fee award.

Often it will be important for the court to scrutinize the method of claims processing to ensure that it facilitates filing legitimate claims. A claims processing method should deter or defeat unjustified claims, but the court should be alert to whether the claims process is unduly demanding.

Paragraph (D) calls attention to a concern that may apply to some class action settlements—inequitable treatment of some class members vis-a-vis others. Matters of concern could include whether the apportionment of relief among class members takes appropriate account of differences among their claims, and whether the scope of the release may affect class members in different ways that bear on the apportionment of relief.

Subdivisions (e)(3) and (e)(4). Headings are added to subdivisions (e)(3) and (e)(4) in accord with style conventions. These additions are intended to be stylistic only.

Subdivision (e)(5). The submissions required by Rule 23(e)(1) may provide information critical to decisions whether to object or opt out. Objections by class members can provide the court with important information bearing on its determination under Rule 23(e)(2) whether to approve the proposal.

Subdivision (e)(5)(A). The rule is amended to remove the requirement of court approval for every withdrawal of an objection. An objector should be free to withdraw on concluding that an objection is not justified. But Rule 23(e)(5)(B)(i) requires court approval of any payment or other consideration in connection with withdrawing the objection.

The rule is also amended to clarify that objections must provide sufficient specifics to enable the parties to respond to them and the court to evaluate them. One feature required of objections is specification whether the objection asserts interests of only the objector, or of some subset of the class, or of all class members. Beyond that, the rule directs that the objection state its grounds "with specificity." Failure to provide needed specificity may be a basis for rejecting an objection. Courts should take care, however, to avoid unduly burdening class members who wish to object, and to recognize that a class member who is not represented by counsel may present objections that do not adhere to technical legal standards.

Subdivision (e)(5)(B). Good-faith objections can assist the court in evaluating a proposal under Rule 23(e)(2). It is legitimate for an objector to seek payment for providing such assistance under Rule 23(h).

But some objectors may be seeking only personal gain, and using objections to obtain benefits for themselves rather than assisting in the settlement-review process. At least in some instances, it seems that objectors—or their counsel—have sought to obtain consideration for withdrawing their objections or dismissing appeals from judgments approving class settlements. And class counsel sometimes may feel that avoiding the delay produced by an appeal justifies providing payment or other consideration to these objectors. Although the payment may advance class interests in a particular case, allowing payment perpetuates a system that can encourage objections advanced for improper purposes.

The court-approval requirement currently in Rule 23(e)(5) partly addresses this concern. Because the concern only applies when consideration is given in connection with withdrawal of an objection, however, the amendment requires approval under Rule 23(e)(5)(B)(i) only when consideration is involved. Although such payment is usually made to objectors or their counsel, the rule also requires court approval if a payment in connection with forgoing or withdrawing an objection or appeal is instead to another recipient. The term "consideration" should be broadly interpreted, particularly when the withdrawal includes some arrangements beneficial to objector counsel. If the consideration involves a payment to counsel for an objector, the proper procedure is by motion under Rule 23(h) for an award of fees.

Rule 23(e)(5)(B)(ii) applies to consideration in connection with forgoing, dismissing, or abandoning an appeal from a judgment approving the proposal. Because an appeal by a class-action objector may produce much longer delay than an objection before the district court, it is important to extend the court-approval requirement to apply in the appellate context. The district court is best positioned to determine whether to approve such arrangements; hence, the rule requires that the motion seeking approval be made to the district court.

Until the appeal is docketed by the circuit clerk, the district court may dismiss the appeal on stipulation of the parties or on the appellant's motion. See Fed. R. App. P. 42(a). Thereafter, the court of appeals has authority to decide whether to dismiss the appeal. This rule's requirement of district court approval of any consideration in connection with such dismissal by the court of appeals has no effect on the authority of the court of appeals to decide whether to dismiss the appeal. It is, instead, a requirement that applies only to providing consideration in connection with forgoing, dismissing, or abandoning an appeal.

Subdivision (e)(5)(C). Because the court of appeals has jurisdiction over an objector's appeal from the time that it is docketed in the court of appeals, the procedure of Rule 62.1 applies. That procedure does not apply after the court of appeals' mandate returns the case to the district court.

Subdivision (f). As amended, Rule 23(e)(1) provides that the court must direct notice to the class regarding a proposed class-action settlement only after determining that the prospect of eventual class certification justifies giving notice. But this decision does not grant or deny class certification, and review under Rule 23(f) would be premature. This amendment makes it clear that an appeal under this rule is not permitted until the district court decides whether to certify the class.

The rule is also amended to extend the time to file a petition for review of a class-action certification order to 45 days whenever a party is the United States, one of its agencies, or a United States officer or employee sued for an act or omission occurring in connection with duties performed on the United States' behalf. In such a case, the extension applies to a petition for permission to appeal by any party. The extension recognizes—as under Rules 4(i) and 12(a) and Appellate Rules 4(a)(1)(B) and 40(a)(1)—that the United

States has a special need for additional time in regard to these matters. It applies whether the officer or employee is sued in an official capacity or an individual capacity. An action against a former officer or employee of the United States is covered by this provision in the same way as an action against a present officer or employee. Termination of the relationship between the individual defendant and the United States does not reduce the need for additional time.

CROSS REFERENCES

Actions relating to unincorporated associations, see Fed. Rules Civ.Proc. Rule 23.2, 28 USCA.

Capacity of unincorporated association to sue or be sued, see Fed.Rules Civ.Proc. Rule 17, 28 USCA.

Coupon settlements, class actions, attorney fees, see 28 USCA § 1712.

Derivative actions by shareholders, see Fed.Rules Civ.Proc. Rule 23.1, 28 USCA.

Private securities litigation rebuttable presumption, see 15 USCA § 78u–4.

Procedure for class action settlements, protections and notice, generally, see 28 USCA § 1711 et seq.

Reduction of abusive litigation and rebuttable presumption, see 15 USCA § 77z–1.

Removal of interstate class actions to Federal district court, review of remand orders, exceptions, see 28 USCA § 1453.

Service of process on corporations in stockholder's derivative action, see 28 USCA § 1695.

Venue in stockholder's derivative action, see 28 USCA § 1401.

Rule 23.1. Derivative Actions

(a) **Prerequisites.** This rule applies when one or more shareholders or members of a corporation or an unincorporated association bring a derivative action to enforce a right that the corporation or association may properly assert but has failed to enforce. The derivative action may not be maintained if it appears that the plaintiff does not fairly and adequately represent the interests of shareholders or members who are similarly situated in enforcing the right of the corporation or association.

(b) **Pleading Requirements.** The complaint must be verified and must:

(1) allege that the plaintiff was a shareholder or member at the time of the transaction complained of, or that the plaintiff's share or membership later devolved on it by operation of law;

(2) allege that the action is not a collusive one to confer jurisdiction that the court would otherwise lack; and

(3) state with particularity:

(A) any effort by the plaintiff to obtain the desired action from the directors or comparable authority and, if necessary, from the shareholders or members; and

(B) the reasons for not obtaining the action or not making the effort.

(c) **Settlement, Dismissal, and Compromise.** A derivative action may be settled, voluntarily dismissed, or compromised only with the court's approval. Notice of a proposed settlement, voluntary dismissal, or compromise must be given to shareholders or members in the manner that the court orders.

(Adopted February 28, 1966, effective July 1, 1966; amended March 2, 1987, effective August 1, 1987; April 30, 2007, effective December 1, 2007.)

ADVISORY COMMITTEE NOTES

1966 Addition

A derivative action by a shareholder of a corporation or by a member of an unincorporated association has distinctive aspects which require the special provisions set forth in the new rule. The next-to-the-last sentence recognizes that the question of adequacy of representation may arise when the plaintiff is one of a group of shareholders or members. Cf. 3 Moore's *Federal Practice*, par. 23.08 (2d ed. 1963).

The court has inherent power to provide for the conduct of the proceedings in a derivative action, including the power to determine the course of the proceedings and require that any appropriate notice be given to shareholders or members.

1987 Amendment

The amendments are technical. No substantive change is intended.

2007 Amendment

The language of Rule 23.1 has been amended as part of the general restyling of the Civil Rules to make them more easily understood and to make style and terminology consistent throughout the rules. These changes are intended to be stylistic only.

CROSS REFERENCES

Actions relating to unincorporated associations, see Fed. Rules Civ.Proc. Rule 23.2, 28 USCA.

Capacity of unincorporated association to sue or to be sued, see Fed.Rules Civ.Proc. Rule 17, 28 USCA.

Class actions, see Fed.Rules Civ.Proc. Rule 23, 28 USCA.

Service of process on corporations in stockholder's derivative action, see 28 USCA § 1695.

Venue in stockholder's derivative action, see 28 USCA § 1401.

Rule 23.2. Actions Relating to Unincorporated Associations

This rule applies to an action brought by or against the members of an unincorporated association as a class by naming certain members as representative parties. The action may be maintained only if it appears that those parties will fairly and adequately protect the interests of the association and its members. In conducting the action, the court may issue any appropriate orders corresponding with those in Rule 23(d), and the procedure for settlement, voluntary dismissal, or compromise must correspond with the procedure in Rule 23(e).

(Adopted February 28, 1966, effective July 1, 1966; amended April 30, 2007, effective December 1, 2007.)

ADVISORY COMMITTEE NOTES
1966 Addition

Although an action by or against representatives of the membership of an unincorporated association has often been viewed as a class action, the real or main purpose of this characterization has been to give "entity treatment" to the association when for formal reasons it cannot sue or be sued as a jural person under Rule 17(b). See Louisell & Hazard, *Pleading and Procedure: State and Federal* 718 (1962); 3 Moore's *Federal Practice*, par. 23.08 (2d ed. 1963); Story, J. in *West v. Randall*, 29 Fed.Cas. 718, 722–23, No. 17,424 (C.C.D.R.I.1820); and, for examples, *Gibbs v. Buck*, 307 U.S. 66 (1939); *Tunstall v. Brotherhood of Locomotive F. & E.*, 148 F.2d 403 (4th Cir. 1945); *Oskoian v. Canuel*, 269 F.2d 311 (1st Cir. 1959). Rule 23.2 deals separately with these actions, referring where appropriate to Rule 23.

2007 Amendment

The language of Rule 23.2 has been amended as part of the general restyling of the Civil Rules to make them more easily understood and to make style and terminology consistent throughout the rules. These changes are intended to be stylistic only.

CROSS REFERENCES

Capacity of unincorporated association to sue or be sued, see Fed.Rules Civ.Proc. Rule 17, 28 USCA.

Class actions, see Fed.Rules Civ.Proc. Rule 23, 28 USCA.

Derivative actions by shareholders, see Fed.Rules Civ.Proc. Rule 23.1, 28 USCA.

Rule 24. Intervention

(a) Intervention of Right. On timely motion, the court must permit anyone to intervene who:

(1) is given an unconditional right to intervene by a federal statute; or

(2) claims an interest relating to the property or transaction that is the subject of the action, and is so situated that disposing of the action may as a practical matter impair or impede the movant's ability to protect its interest, unless existing parties adequately represent that interest.

(b) Permissive Intervention.

(1) *In General.* On timely motion, the court may permit anyone to intervene who:

(A) is given a conditional right to intervene by a federal statute; or

(B) has a claim or defense that shares with the main action a common question of law or fact.

(2) *By a Government Officer or Agency.* On timely motion, the court may permit a federal or state governmental officer or agency to intervene if a party's claim or defense is based on:

(A) a statute or executive order administered by the officer or agency; or

(B) any regulation, order, requirement, or agreement issued or made under the statute or executive order.

(3) *Delay or Prejudice.* In exercising its discretion, the court must consider whether the intervention will unduly delay or prejudice the adjudication of the original parties' rights.

(c) Notice and Pleading Required. A motion to intervene must be served on the parties as provided in Rule 5. The motion must state the grounds for intervention and be accompanied by a pleading that sets out the claim or defense for which intervention is sought.

(Amended December 27, 1946, effective March 19, 1948; December 29, 1948, effective October 20, 1949; January 21, 1963, effective July 1, 1963; February 28, 1966, effective July 1, 1966; March 2, 1987, effective August 1, 1987; April 30, 1991, effective December 1, 1991; April 12, 2006, effective December 1, 2006; April 30, 2007, effective December 1, 2007.)

ADVISORY COMMITTEE NOTES
1937 Adoption

The right to intervene given by the following and similar statutes is preserved, but the procedure for its assertion is governed by this rule:

U.S.C., Title 28 former sections:

45a [now 2323] (Special attorneys; participation by Interstate Commerce Commission; intervention) (in certain cases under interstate commerce laws)

48 [now 2322] (Suits to be against United States; intervention by United States)

401 [now 2403] (Intervention by United States; constitutionality of Federal statute)

U.S.C., Title 40:

276a–2(b) [now 3162(a)(2)] (Bonds of contractors for public buildings or works; rights of persons furnishing labor and materials).

Compare with the last sentence of [former] Equity Rule 37 (Parties Generally—Intervention). This rule amplifies and restates the present federal practice at law and in equity. For the practice in admiralty see Admiralty Rules 34 (How Third Party May Intervene) and 42 (Claims Against Proceeds in Registry). See generally Moore and Levi, *Federal Intervention: I The Right to Intervene and Reorganization* (1936), 45 Yale L.J. 565. Under the codes two types of intervention are provided, one for the recovery of specific real or personal property (2 Ohio Gen.Code Ann. (Page, 1926) § 11263; Wyo. Rev.Stat.Ann. (Courtright, 1931) § 89–522), and the other allowing intervention generally when the applicant has an interest in the matter in litigation (1 Colo.Stat.Ann. (1935) Code Civ.Proc. § 22; La.Code Pract. (Dart, 1932) Arts. 389–394; Utah Rev.Stat.Ann. (1933) § 104–3–24). The English intervention practice is based upon various rules and decisions and falls into the two categories of absolute right and discretionary right. For the absolute right see *English Rules Under the Judicature Act* (The Annual Practice, 1937) O. 12, r. 24 (admiralty), r. 25 (land), r. 23 (probate); O. 57, r. 12 (execution); J.A. (1925) §§ 181, 182, 183(2) (divorce); *In re Metropolitan Amalgamated Estates, Ltd.*, (1912) 2 Ch. 497 (receivership); *Wilson v. Church*, 9 Ch.D. 552 (1878) (representative action). For the discretionary right see O. 16, r. 11 (non-joinder) and *Re Fowler*, 142 L.T.Jo. 94 (Ch.1916), *Va-*

vasseur v. Krupp, 9 Ch.D. 351 (1878) (persons out of the jurisdiction).

1946 Amendment

Note. Subdivision (a). The addition to subdivision (a)(3) covers the situation where property may be in the actual custody of some other officer or agency—such as the Secretary of the Treasury—but the control and disposition of the property is lodged in the court wherein the action is pending.

Subdivision (b). The addition in subdivision (b) permits the intervention of governmental officers or agencies in proper cases and thus avoids exclusionary constructions of the rule. For an example of the latter, see *Matter of Bender Body Co.,* Ref. Ohio 1941, 47 F.Supp. 224, holding that the Administrator of the Office of Price Administration, then acting under the authority of an Executive Order of the President, could not intervene in a bankruptcy proceeding to protest the sale of assets above ceiling prices. Compare, however, *Securities and Exchange Commission v. United States Realty & Improvement Co.,* 1940, 310 U.S. 434, 60 S.Ct. 1044, where permissive intervention of the Commission to protect the public interest in an arrangement proceeding under Chapter XI of the Bankruptcy Act was upheld. See also dissenting opinion in *Securities and Exchange Commission v. Long Island Lighting Co.,* C.C.A.2d 1945, 148 F.2d 252, judgment vacated as moot and case remanded with direction to dismiss complaint, 1945, 325 U.S. 833, 65 S.Ct. 1085. For discussion see Commentary, *Nature of Permissive Intervention Under Rule 24b,* 1940, 3 Fed.Rules Serv. 704; Berger, *Intervention by Public Agencies in Private Litigation in the Federal Courts,* 1940, 50 Yale L.J. 65.

Regarding the construction of subdivision (b)(2), see *Allen Calculators, Inc. v. National Cash Register Co.,* 1944, 64 S.Ct. 905, 322 U.S. 137, 88 L.Ed. 1188.

1948 Amendment

The amendment effective Oct. 20, 1949, substituted the reference to "Title 28, U.S.C.A. § 2403" at the end of subdivision (c) for the reference to "the Act of August 24, 1937, c. 754, § 1."

1963 Amendment

This amendment conforms to the amendment of Rule 5(a). See the Advisory Committee's Note to that amendment.

1966 Amendment

In attempting to overcome certain difficulties which have arisen in the application of present Rule 24(a)(2) and (3), this amendment draws upon the revision of the related Rules 19 (joinder of persons needed for just adjudication) and 23 (class actions), and the reasoning underlying that revision.

Rule 24(a)(3) as amended in 1948 provided for intervention of right where the applicant established that he would be adversely affected by the distribution or disposition of property involved in an action to which he had not been made a party. Significantly, some decided cases virtually disregarded the language of this provision. Thus Professor Moore states: "The concept of a fund has been applied so loosely that it is possible for a court to find a fund in almost any in personam action." 4 Moore's *Federal Practice,* par. 24.09[3], at 55 (2d ed. 1962), and see, e.g., *Formulabs, Inc. v. Hartley Pen Co.,* 275 F.2d 52 (9th Cir.1960). This development was quite

natural, for Rule 24(a)(3) was unduly restricted. If an absentee would be substantially affected in a practical sense by the determination made in an action, he should, as a general rule, be entitled to intervene, and his right to do so should not depend on whether there is a fund to be distributed or otherwise disposed of. Intervention of right is here seen to be a kind of counterpart to Rule 19(a)(2)(i) on joinder of persons needed for a just adjudication: where, upon motion of a party in an action, an absentee should be joined so that he may protect his interest which as a practical matter may be substantially impaired by the disposition of the action, he ought to have a right to intervene in the action on his own motion. See Louisell & Hazard, *Pleading and Procedure: State and Federal* 749–50 (1962).

The general purpose of original Rule 24(a)(2) was to entitle an absentee, purportedly represented by a party, to intervene in the action if he could establish with fair probability that the representation was inadequate. Thus, where an action is being prosecuted or defended by a trustee, a beneficiary of the trust should have a right to intervene if he can show that the trustee's representation of his interest probably is inadequate; similarly a member of a class should have the right to intervene in a class action if he can show the inadequacy of the representation of his interest by the representative parties before the court.

Original Rule 24(a)(2), however, made it a condition of intervention that "the applicant is or may be bound by a judgment in the action," and this created difficulties with intervention in class actions. If the "bound" language was read literally in the sense of res judicata, it could defeat intervention in some meritorious cases. A member of a class to whom a judgment in a class action extended by its terms (see Rule 23(c)(3), as amended) might be entitled to show in a later action, when the judgment in the class action was claimed to operate as res judicata against him, that the "representative" in the class action had not in fact adequately represented him. If he could make this showing, the class-action judgment might be held not to bind him. See *Hansberry v. Lee,* 311 U.S. 32 (1940). If a class member sought to intervene in the class action proper, while it was still pending, on grounds of inadequacy of representation, he could be met with the argument: if the representation was in fact inadequate, he would not be "bound" by the judgment when it was subsequently asserted against him as res judicata, hence he was not entitled to intervene; if the representation was in fact adequate, there was no occasion or ground for intervention. See *Sam Fox Publishing Co. v. United States,* 366 U.S. 683 (1961); cf. *Sutphen Estates, Inc. v. United States,* 342 U.S. 19 (1951). This reasoning might be linguistically justified by original Rule 24(a)(2); but it could lead to poor results. Compare the discussion in *International M. & I. Corp. v. Von Clemm,* 301 F.2d 857 (2d Cir.1962); *Atlantic Refining Co. v. Standard Oil Co.,* 304 F.2d 387 (D.C.Cir.1962). A class member who claims that his "representative" does not adequately represent him, and is able to establish that proposition with sufficient probability, should not be put to the risk of having a judgment entered in the action which by its terms extends to him, and be obliged to test the validity of the judgment as applied to his interest by a later collateral attack. Rather he should, as a general rule, be entitled to intervene in the action.

The amendment provides that an applicant is entitled to intervene in an action when his position is comparable to that of a person under Rule 19(a)(2)(i), as amended, unless his interest is already adequately represented in the action by existing parties. The Rule 19(a)(2)(i) criterion imports practical considerations, and the deletion of the "bound" language similarly frees the rule from undue preoccupation with strict considerations of res judicata.

The representation whose adequacy comes into question under the amended rule is not confined to formal representation like that provided by a trustee for his beneficiary or a representative party in a class action for a member of the class. A party to an action may provide practical representation to the absentee seeking intervention although no such formal relationship exists between them, and the adequacy of this practical representation will then have to be weighed. See *International M. & I. Crop. v. Von Clemm*, and *Atlantic Refining Co. v. Standard Oil Co.*, both supra; *Wolpe v. Poretsky*, 144 F.2d 505 (D.C.Cir.1944), cert. denied, 323 U.S. 777 (1944); cf. *Ford Motor Co. v. Bisanz Bros.*, 249 F.2d 22 (8th Cir.1957); and generally, Annot., 84 A.L.R.2d 1412 (1961).

An intervention of right under the amended rule may be subject to appropriate conditions or restrictions responsive among other things to the requirements of efficient conduct of the proceedings.

1987 Amendment

The amendments are technical. No substantive change is intended.

1991 Amendment

Language is added to bring Rule 24(c) into conformity with the statute cited, resolving some confusion reflected in district court rules. As the text provides, counsel challenging the constitutionality of legislation in an action in which the appropriate government is not a party should call the attention of the court to its duty to notify the appropriate governmental officers. The statute imposes the burden of notification on the court, not the party making the constitutional challenge, partly in order to protect against any possible waiver of constitutional rights by parties inattentive to the need for notice. For this reason, the failure of a party to call the court's attention to the matter cannot be treated as a waiver.

2006 Amendment

New Rule 5.1 replaces the final three sentences of Rule 24(c), implementing the provisions of 28 U.S.C. § 2403. Section 2403 requires notification to the Attorney General of the United States when the constitutionality of an Act of Congress is called in question, and to the state attorney general when the constitutionality of a state statute is drawn into question.

2007 Amendment

The language of Rule 24 has been amended as part of the general restyling of the Civil Rules to make them more easily understood and to make style and terminology consistent throughout the rules. These changes are intended to be stylistic only.

The former rule stated that the same procedure is followed when a United States statute gives a right to intervene. This statement is deleted because it added nothing.

CROSS REFERENCES

Intervention of,

Parties interested in action to enforce, suspend or annul orders of the Surface Transportation Board, see 28 USCA § 2323.

United States where constitutionality of Federal statute is questioned, see 28 USCA § 2403.

Rule 25. Substitution of Parties

(a) Death.

(1) *Substitution if the Claim Is Not Extinguished.* If a party dies and the claim is not extinguished, the court may order substitution of the proper party. A motion for substitution may be made by any party or by the decedent's successor or representative. If the motion is not made within 90 days after service of a statement noting the death, the action by or against the decedent must be dismissed.

(2) *Continuation Among the Remaining Parties.* After a party's death, if the right sought to be enforced survives only to or against the remaining parties, the action does not abate, but proceeds in favor of or against the remaining parties. The death should be noted on the record.

(3) *Service.* A motion to substitute, together with a notice of hearing, must be served on the parties as provided in Rule 5 and on nonparties as provided in Rule 4. A statement noting death must be served in the same manner. Service may be made in any judicial district.

(b) Incompetency. If a party becomes incompetent, the court may, on motion, permit the action to be continued by or against the party's representative. The motion must be served as provided in Rule 25(a)(3).

(c) Transfer of Interest. If an interest is transferred, the action may be continued by or against the original party unless the court, on motion, orders the transferee to be substituted in the action or joined with the original party. The motion must be served as provided in Rule 25(a)(3).

(d) Public Officers; Death or Separation from Office. An action does not abate when a public officer who is a party in an official capacity dies, resigns, or otherwise ceases to hold office while the action is pending. The officer's successor is automatically substituted as a party. Later proceedings should be in the substituted party's name, but any misnomer not affecting the parties' substantial rights must be disregarded. The court may order substitution at any time, but the absence of such an order does not affect the substitution.

(Amended December 29, 1948, effective October 20, 1949; April 17, 1961, effective July 19, 1961; January 21, 1963, effective July 1, 1963; March 2, 1987, effective August 1, 1987; April 30, 2007, effective December 1, 2007.)

ADVISORY COMMITTEE NOTES

1937 Adoption

Note to Subdivision (a). 1. The first paragraph of this rule is based upon [former] Equity Rule 45 (Death of Party—Revivor) and U.S.C., Title 28, former § 778 (Death of parties; substitution of executor or administrator). The *scire facias* procedure provided for in the statute cited is superseded and the writ is abolished by Rule 81(b). Paragraph two states the content of U.S.C., Title 28, former § 779 (Death of one of several plaintiffs or defendants). With these two paragraphs compare generally *English Rules Under the Judicature Act* (The Annual Practice, 1937) O. 17, r.r. 1–10.

2. This rule modifies U.S.C., Title 28, [former] §§ 778 (Death of parties; substitution of executor or administrator), 779 (Death of one of several plaintiffs or defendants), and 780 (Survival of actions, suits, or proceedings, etc.), in so far as they differ from it.

Note to Subdivisions (b) and (c). These are a combination and adaptation of N.Y.C.P.A. (1937) § 83 and Calif.Code Civ.Proc. (1937) § 385; see also 4 Nev.Comp.Laws (Hillyer, 1929) § 8561.

Note to Subdivision (d). With the first and last sentences compare U.S.C.A., Title 28, former § 780 (Survival of actions, suits, or proceedings, etc.). With the second sentence of this subdivision compare *Ex parte La Prade*, 1933, 53 S.Ct. 682, 289 U.S. 444, 77 L.Ed. 1311.

1948 Amendment

The amendment effective October 19, 1949, inserted the words, "the Canal Zone, a territory, an insular possession," in the first sentence of subdivision (d), and, in the same sentence, after the phrase "or other governmental agency," deleted the words, "or any other officer specified in the Act of February 13, 1925, c. 229, § 11 (43 Stat. 941), formerly section 780 of this title."

1961 Amendment

Subdivision (d)(1). Present Rule 25(d) is generally considered to be unsatisfactory. 4 Moore's *Federal Practice* ¶25.01[7] (2d ed. 1950); Wright, *Amendments to the Federal Rules: The Function of a Continuing Rules Committee*, 7 Vand.L.Rev. 521, 529 (1954); *Developments in the Law—Remedies Against the United States and Its Officials*, 70 Harv.L.Rev. 827, 931–34 (1957). To require, as a condition of substituting a successor public officer as a party to a pending action, that an application be made with a showing that there is substantial need for continuing the litigation, can rarely serve any useful purpose and fosters a burdensome formality. And to prescribe a short, fixed time period for substitution which cannot be extended even by agreement, see *Snyder v. Buck*, 340 U.S. 15, 19 (1950), with the penalty of dismissal of the action, "makes a trap for unsuspecting litigants which seems unworthy of a great government." *Vibra Brush Corp. v. Schaffer*, 256 F.2d 681, 684 (2d Cir.1958). Although courts have on occasion found means of undercutting the rule, e.g. *Acheson v. Furusho*, 212 F.2d 284 (9th Cir.1954) (substitution of defendant officer unnecessary on theory that only a declaration of status was sought), it has operated harshly in many instances, e.g. *Snyder v. Buck*, supra; *Poindexter v. Folsom*, 242 F.2d 516 (3d Cir.1957).

Under the amendment, the successor is automatically substituted as a party without an application or showing of need to continue the action. An order of substitution is not required, but may be entered at any time if a party desires or the court thinks fit.

The general term "public officer" is used in preference to the enumeration which appears in the present rule. It comprises Federal, State, and local officers.

The expression "in his official capacity" is to be interpreted in its context as part of a simple procedural rule for substitution; care should be taken not to distort its meaning by mistaken analogies to the doctrine of sovereign immunity from suit or the Eleventh Amendment. The amended rule will apply to all actions brought by public officers for the government, and to any action brought in form against a named officer, but intrinsically against the government or the office or the incumbent thereof whoever he may be from time to time during the action. Thus the amended rule will apply to actions against officers to compel performance of official duties or to obtain judicial review of their orders. It will also apply to actions to prevent officers from acting in excess of their authority or under authority not validly conferred, cf. *Philadelphia Co. v. Stimson*, 223 U.S. 605 (1912), or from enforcing unconstitutional enactments, cf. *Ex parte Young*, 209 U.S. 123 (1908); *Ex parte La Prade*, 289 U.S. 444 (1933). In general it will apply whenever effective relief would call for corrective behavior by the one then having official status and power, rather than one who has lost that status and power through ceasing to hold office. Cf. *Land v. Dollar*, 330 U.S. 731 (1947); *Larson v. Domestic & Foreign Commerce Corp.*, 337 U.S. 682 (1949). Excluded from the operation of the amended rule will be the relatively infrequent actions which are directed to securing money judgments against the named officers enforceable against their personal assets; in these cases Rule 25(a)(1), not Rule 25(d), applies to the question of substitution. Examples are actions against officers seeking to make them pay damages out of their own pockets for defamatory utterances or other misconduct in some way related to the office, see *Barr v. Matteo*, 360 U.S. 564 (1959); *Howard v. Lyons*, 360 U.S. 593 (1959); *Gregoire v. Biddle*, 177 F.2d 579 (2d Cir.1949), cert. denied, 339 U.S. 949 (1950). Another example is the anomalous action for a tax refund against a collector of internal revenue, see *Ignelzi v. Granger*, 16 F.R.D. 517 (W.D.Pa.1955), 28 U.S.C. § 2006, 4 Moore, supra, ¶25.05, p. 531; but see 28 U.S.C. § 1346(a)(1), authorizing the bringing of such suits against the United States rather than the officer.

Automatic substitution under the amended rule, being merely a procedural device for substituting a successor for a past officeholder as a party, is distinct from and does not affect any substantive issues which may be involved in the action. Thus a defense of immunity from suit will remain in the case despite a substitution.

Where the successor does not intend to pursue the policy of his predecessor which gave rise to the lawsuit, it will be open to him, after substitution, as plaintiff to seek voluntary dismissal of the action, or as defendant to seek to have the action dismissed as moot or to take other appropriate steps to avert a judgment or decree. Contrast *Ex parte La Prade*, supra; *Allen v. Regents of the University System*, 304 U.S. 439 (1938); *McGrath v. National Assn. of Mfgrs.*, 344 U.S. 804 (1952); *Danenberg v. Cohen*, 213 F.2d 944 (7th Cir.1954).

As the present amendment of Rule 25(d)(1) eliminates a specified time period to secure substitution of public officers, the reference in Rule 6(b) (regarding enlargement of time) to

---

Rule 25 will no longer apply to these public-officer substitutions.

As to substitution on appeal, the rules of the appellate courts should be consulted.

Subdivision (d)(2). This provision, applicable in "official capacity" cases as described above, will encourage the use of the official title without any mention of the officer individually, thereby recognizing the intrinsic character of the action and helping to eliminate concern with the problem of substitution. If for any reason it seems desirable to add the individual's name, this may be done upon motion or on the court's initiative; thereafter the procedure of amended Rule 25(d)(1) will apply if the individual named ceases to hold office.

For examples of naming the officer or title rather than the officeholder, see *Annot.,* 102 A.L.R. 943, 948–52; *Comment,* 50 Mich.L.Rev. 443, 450 (1952); cf. 26 U.S.C. § 7484. Where an action is brought by or against a board or agency with continuity of existence, it has been often decided that there is no need to name the individual members and substitution is unnecessary when the personnel changes. 4 Moore, supra, ¶25.09, p. 536. The practice encouraged by amended Rule 25(d)(2) is similar.

1963 Amendment

Present Rule 25(a)(1), together with present Rule 6(b), results in an inflexible requirement that an action be dismissed as to a deceased party if substitution is not carried out within a fixed period measured from the time of the death. The hardships and inequities of this unyielding requirement plainly appear from the cases. See, e.g., *Anderson v. Yungkau,* 329 U.S. 482, 67 S.Ct. 428, 91 L.Ed. 436 (1947); *Iovino v. Waterson,* 274 F.2d 41 (1959), cert. denied, *Carlin v. Sovino,* 362 U.S. 949, 80 S.Ct. 860, 4 L.Ed.2d 867 (1960); *Perry v. Allen,* 239 F.2d 107 (5th Cir.1956); *Starnes v. Pennsylvania R.R.,* 26 F.R.D. 625 (E.D.N.Y.), aff'd per curiam, 295 F.2d 704 (2d Cir.1961), cert. denied, 369 U.S. 813, 82 S.Ct. 688, 7 L.Ed.2d 612 (1962); *Zdanok v. Glidden Co.,* 28 F.R.D. 346 (S.D.N.Y.1961). See also 4 Moore's *Federal Practice* ¶25.01[9] (Supp.1960); 2 Barron & Holtzoff, *Federal Practice & Procedure* § 621, at 420–21 (Wright ed.1961).

The amended rule establishes a time limit for the motion to substitute based not upon the time of the death, but rather upon the time information of the death is provided by means of a suggestion of death upon the record, i.e. service of a statement of the fact of the death. Cf. Ill.Ann.Stat., c. 110, § 54(2) (Smith-Hurd 1956). The motion may not be made later than 90 days after the service of the statement unless the period is extended pursuant to Rule 6(b), as amended. See the Advisory Committee's Note to amended Rule 6(b). See also the new Official Form 30.

A motion to substitute may be made by any party or by the representative of the deceased party without awaiting the suggestion of death. Indeed, the motion will usually be so made. If a party or the representative of the deceased party desires to limit the time within which another may make the motion, he may do so by suggesting the death upon the record.

A motion to substitute made within the prescribed time will ordinarily be granted, but under the permissive language of the first sentence of the amended rule ("the court may order") it may be denied by the court in the exercise of a sound discretion if made long after the death—as can occur if the suggestion of death is not made or is delayed—and circumstances have arisen rendering it unfair to allow substitution. Cf. *Anderson v. Yungkau,* supra, 329 U.S. at 485, 486, 67 S.Ct. at 430, 431, 91 L.Ed. 436, where it was noted under the present rule that settlement and distribution of the estate of a deceased defendant might be so far advanced as to warrant denial of a motion for substitution even though made within the time limit prescribed by that rule. Accordingly, a party interested in securing substitution under the amended rule should not assume that he can rest indefinitely awaiting the suggestion of death before he makes his motion to substitute.

1987 Amendment

The amendments are technical. No substantive change is intended.

2007 Amendment

The language of Rule 25 has been amended as part of the general restyling of the Civil Rules to make them more easily understood and to make style and terminology consistent throughout the rules. These changes are intended to be stylistic only.

Former Rule 25(d)(2) is transferred to become Rule 17(d) because it deals with designation of a public officer, not substitution.

HISTORICAL NOTES

Effective and Applicability Provisions

1961 Amendments. Amendment adopted on Apr. 17, 1961, effective July 19, 1961, see rule 86(d).

CROSS REFERENCES

Depositions, right to use after substitution, see Fed.Rules Civ.Proc. Rule 32, 28 USCA.

Extensions of time, see Fed.Rules Civ.Proc. Rule 6, 28 USCA.

TITLE V.   DISCLOSURES AND DISCOVERY

ADVISORY COMMITTEE'S EXPLANATORY STATEMENT CONCERNING 1970 AMENDMENTS TO DISCOVERY RULES

This statement is intended to serve as a general introduction to the amendments of Rules 26–37, concerning discovery, as well as related amendments of other rules. A separate note of customary scope is appended to amendments proposed for each rule. This statement provides a framework for the consideration of individual rule changes.

Changes in the Discovery Rules

The discovery rules, as adopted in 1938, were a striking and imaginative departure from tradition. It was expected from the outset that they would be important, but experience has shown them to play an even larger role than was initially foreseen. Although the discovery rules have been amended since 1938, the changes were relatively few and narrowly focused, made in order to remedy specific defects. The amendments now proposed reflect the first comprehensive review of the discovery rules undertaken since 1938. These amendments make substantial changes in the discovery rules. Those summarized here are among the more important changes.

Scope of Discovery. New provisions are made and existing provisions changed affecting the scope of discovery: (1) The contents of insurance policies are made discoverable (Rule 26(b)(2)). (2) A showing of good cause is no longer required for discovery of documents and things and entry upon land (Rule 34). However, a showing of need is required for discovery of "trial preparation" materials other than a party's discovery of his own statement and a witness' discovery of his own statement; and protection is afforded against disclosure in such documents of mental impressions, conclusions, opinions, or legal theories concerning the litigation. (Rule 26(b)(3)). (3) Provision is made for discovery with respect to experts retained for trial preparation, and particularly those experts who will be called to testify at trial (Rule 26(b)(4)). (4) It is provided that interrogatories and requests for admission are not objectionable simply because they relate to matters of opinion or contention, subject of course to the supervisory power of the court (Rules 33(b), 36(a)). (5) Medical examination is made available as to certain nonparties. (Rule 35(a)).

Mechanics of Discovery. A variety of changes are made in the mechanics of the discovery process, affecting the sequence and timing of discovery, the respective obligations of the parties with respect to requests, responses, and motions for court orders, and the related powers of the court to enforce discovery requests and to protect against their abusive use. A new provision eliminates the automatic grant of priority in discovery to one side (Rule 26(d)). Another provides that a party is not under a duty to supplement his responses to requests for discovery, except as specified (Rule 26(e)).

Other changes in the mechanics of discovery are designed to encourage extrajudicial discovery with a minimum of court intervention. Among these are the following: (1) The requirement that a plaintiff seek leave of court for early discovery requests is eliminated or reduced, and motions for a court order under Rule 34 are made unnecessary. Motions under Rule 35 are continued. (2) Answers and objections are to be served together and an enlargement of the time for response is provided. (3) The party seeking discovery, rather than the objecting party, is made responsible for invoking judicial determination of discovery disputes not resolved by the parties. (4) Judicial sanctions are tightened with respect to unjustified insistence upon or objection to discovery. These changes bring Rules 33, 34, and 36 substantially into line with the procedure now provided for depositions.

Failure to amend Rule 35 in the same way is based upon two considerations. First, the Columbia Survey (described below) finds that only about 5 percent of medical examinations require court motions, of which about half result in court orders. Second and of greater importance, the interest of the person to be examined in the privacy of his person was recently stressed by the Supreme Court in *Schlagenhauf v. Holder*, 379 U.S. 104 (1964). The court emphasized the trial judge's responsibility to assure that the medical examination was justified, particularly as to its scope.

Rearrangement of Rules. A limited rearrangement of the discovery rules has been made, whereby certain provisions are transferred from one rule to another. The reasons for this rearrangement are discussed below in a separate section of this statement and the details are set out in a table at the end of this statement.

Optional Procedures. In two instances, new optional procedures have been made available. A new procedure is provided to a party seeking to take the deposition of a corporation or other organization (Rule 30(b)(6)). A party on whom interrogatories have been served requesting information derivable from his business records may under specified circumstances produce the records rather than give answers (Rule 33(c)).

Other Changes. This summary of changes is by no means exhaustive. Various changes have been made in order to improve, tighten, or clarify particular provisions, to resolve conflicts in the case law, and to improve language. All changes, whether mentioned here or not, are discussed in the appropriate note for each rule.

A Field Survey of Discovery Practice

Despite widespread acceptance of discovery as an essential part of litigation, disputes have inevitably arisen concerning the values claimed for discovery and abuses alleged to exist. Many disputes about discovery relate to particular rule provisions or court decisions and can be studied in traditional fashion with a view to specific amendment. Since discovery is in large measure extra-judicial, however, even these disputes may be enlightened by a study of discovery "in the field." And some of the larger questions concerning discovery can be pursued only by a study of its operation at the law office level and in unreported cases.

The Committee, therefore, invited the Project for Effective Justice of Columbia Law School to conduct a field survey of discovery. Funds were obtained from the Ford Foundation and the Walter E. Meyer Research Institute of Law, Inc. The survey was carried on under the direction of Prof. Maurice Rosenberg of Columbia Law School. The Project for Effective Justice has submitted a report to the Committee entitled "Field Survey of Federal Pretrial Discovery" (hereafter referred to as the Columbia Survey). The Committee is deeply grateful for the benefit of this extensive undertaking and is most appreciative of the cooperation of the Project and the funding organizations. The Committee is particularly grateful to Professor Rosenberg who not only directed the survey but has given much time in order to assist the Committee in assessing the results.

The Columbia Survey concludes, in general, that there is no empirical evidence to warrant a fundamental change in the philosophy of the discovery rules. No widespread or profound failings are disclosed in the scope or availability of discovery. The costs of discovery do not appear to be oppressive, as a general matter, either in relation to ability to pay or to the stakes of the litigation. Discovery frequently provides evidence that would not otherwise be available to the parties and thereby makes for a fairer trial or settlement. On the other hand, no positive evidence is found that discovery promotes settlement.

More specific findings of the Columbia Survey are described in other Committee notes, in relation to particular rule provisions and amendments. Those interested in more detailed information may obtain it from the Project for Effective Justice.

Rearrangement of the Discovery Rules

The present discovery rules are structured entirely in terms of individual discovery devices, except for Rule 27 which deals with perpetuation of testimony, and Rule 37 which provides sanctions to enforce discovery. Thus, Rules 26 and 28 to 32 are in terms addressed only to the taking of a deposition of a party or third person. Rules 33 to 36 then deal in succession with four additional discovery devices: Written interrogatories to parties, production for inspection of documents and things, physical or mental examination and requests for admission.

Under the rules as promulgated in 1938, therefore, each of the discovery devices was separate and self-contained. A defect of this arrangement is that there is no natural location in the discovery rules for provisions generally applicable to all discovery or to several discovery devices. From 1938 until the present, a few amendments have applied a discovery provision to several rules. For example, in 1948, the scope of deposition discovery in Rule 26(b) and the provision for protective orders in Rule 30(b) were incorporated by reference in Rules 33 and 34. The arrangement was adequate so long as there were few provisions governing discovery generally and these provisions were relatively simple.

As will be seen, however, a series of amendments are now proposed which govern most or all of the discovery devices. Proposals of a similar nature will probably be made in the future. Under these circumstances, it is very desirable, even necessary, that the discovery rules contain one rule addressing itself to discovery generally.

Rule 26 is obviously the most appropriate rule for this purpose. One of its subdivisions, Rule 26(b), in terms governs only scope of deposition discovery, but it has been expressly incorporated by reference in Rules 33 and 34 and is treated by courts as setting a general standard. By means of a transfer to Rule 26 of the provisions for protective orders now contained in Rule 30(b), and a transfer from Rule 26 of provisions addressed exclusively to depositions, Rule 26 is converted into a rule concerned with discovery generally. It becomes a convenient vehicle for the inclusion of new provisions dealing with the scope, timing, and regulation of discovery. Few additional transfers are needed. See table showing rearrangement of rules, set out following this statement.

There are, to be sure, disadvantages in transferring any provision from one rule to another. Familiarity with the present pattern, reinforced by the references made by prior court decisions and the various secondary writings about the rules, is not lightly to be sacrificed. Revision of treatises and other reference works is burdensome and costly. Moreover, many States have adopted the existing pattern as a model for their rules.

On the other hand, the amendments now proposed will in any event require revision of texts and reference works as well as reconsideration by States following the Federal model. If these amendments are to be incorporated in an understandable way, a rule with general discovery provisions is needed. As will be seen, the proposed rearrangement produces a more coherent and intelligible pattern for the discovery rules taken as a whole. The difficulties described are those encountered whenever statutes are reexamined and revised. Failure to rearrange the discovery rules now would freeze the present scheme, making future change even more difficult.

Table Showing Rearrangement of Rules

Existing Rule No.	New Rule No.
26(a)	30(a), 31(a)
26(c)	30(c)
26(d)	32(a)
26(e)	32(b)
26(f)	32(c)
30(a)	30(b)
30(b)	26(c)
32	32(d)

Rule 26. Duty to Disclose; General Provisions Governing Discovery

(a) Required Disclosures.

(1) *Initial Disclosure.*

(A) *In General.* Except as exempted by Rule 26(a)(1)(B) or as otherwise stipulated or ordered by the court, a party must, without awaiting a discovery request, provide to the other parties:

(i) the name and, if known, the address and telephone number of each individual likely to have discoverable information—along with the subjects of that information—that the disclosing party may use to support its claims or defenses, unless the use would be solely for impeachment;

(ii) a copy—or a description by category and location—of all documents, electronically stored information, and tangible things that the disclosing party has in its possession, custody, or control and may use to support its claims or defenses, unless the use would be solely for impeachment;

(iii) a computation of each category of damages claimed by the disclosing party—who must also make available for inspection and copying as under Rule 34 the documents or other evidentiary material, unless privileged or protected from disclosure, on which each computation is based, including materials bearing on the nature and extent of injuries suffered; and

(iv) for inspection and copying as under Rule 34, any insurance agreement under which an insurance business may be liable to satisfy all or part of a possible judgment in the action or to indemnify or reimburse for payments made to satisfy the judgment.

(B) *Proceedings Exempt from Initial Disclosure.* The following proceedings are exempt from initial disclosure:

(i) an action for review on an administrative record;

(ii) a forfeiture action in rem arising from a federal statute;

(iii) a petition for habeas corpus or any other proceeding to challenge a criminal conviction or sentence;

(iv) an action brought without an attorney by a person in the custody of the United States, a state, or a state subdivision;

(v) an action to enforce or quash an administrative summons or subpoena;

(vi) an action by the United States to recover benefit payments;

(vii) an action by the United States to collect on a student loan guaranteed by the United States;

(viii) a proceeding ancillary to a proceeding in another court; and

(ix) an action to enforce an arbitration award.

(C) *Time for Initial Disclosures—In General.* A party must make the initial disclosures at or within 14 days after the parties' Rule 26(f) conference unless a different time is set by stipulation or court order, or unless a party objects during the conference that initial disclosures are not appropriate in this action and states the objection in the proposed discovery plan. In ruling on the objection, the court must determine what disclosures, if any, are to be made and must set the time for disclosure.

(D) *Time for Initial Disclosures—For Parties Served or Joined Later.* A party that is first served or otherwise joined after the Rule 26(f) conference must make the initial disclosures within 30 days after being served or joined, unless a different time is set by stipulation or court order.

(E) *Basis for Initial Disclosure; Unacceptable Excuses.* A party must make its initial disclosures based on the information then reasonably available to it. A party is not excused from making its disclosures because it has not fully investigated the case or because it challenges the sufficiency of another party's disclosures or because another party has not made its disclosures.

(2) *Disclosure of Expert Testimony.*

(A) *In General.* In addition to the disclosures required by Rule 26(a)(1), a party must disclose to the other parties the identity of any witness it may use at trial to present evidence under Federal Rule of Evidence 702, 703, or 705.

(B) *Witnesses Who Must Provide a Written Report.* Unless otherwise stipulated or ordered by the court, this disclosure must be accompanied by a written report—prepared and signed by the witness—if the witness is one retained or specially employed to provide expert testimony in the case or one whose duties as the party's employee regularly involve giving expert testimony. The report must contain:

(i) a complete statement of all opinions the witness will express and the basis and reasons for them;

(ii) the facts or data considered by the witness in forming them;

(iii) any exhibits that will be used to summarize or support them;

(iv) the witness's qualifications, including a list of all publications authored in the previous 10 years;

(v) a list of all other cases in which, during the previous 4 years, the witness testified as an expert at trial or by deposition; and

(vi) a statement of the compensation to be paid for the study and testimony in the case.

(C) *Witnesses Who Do Not Provide a Written Report.* Unless otherwise stipulated or ordered by the court, if the witness is not required to provide a written report, this disclosure must state:

(i) the subject matter on which the witness is expected to present evidence under Federal Rule of Evidence 702, 703, or 705; and

(ii) a summary of the facts and opinions to which the witness is expected to testify.

(D) *Time to Disclose Expert Testimony.* A party must make these disclosures at the times and in the sequence that the court orders. Absent a stipulation or a court order, the disclosures must be made:

(i) at least 90 days before the date set for trial or for the case to be ready for trial; or

(ii) if the evidence is intended solely to contradict or rebut evidence on the same subject matter identified by another party under Rule 26(a)(2)(B) or (C), within 30 days after the other party's disclosure.

(E) *Supplementing the Disclosure.* The parties must supplement these disclosures when required under Rule 26(e).

(3) *Pretrial Disclosures.*

(A) *In General.* In addition to the disclosures required by Rule 26(a)(1) and (2), a party must provide to the other parties and promptly file the following information about the evidence that it may present at trial other than solely for impeachment:

(i) the name and, if not previously provided, the address and telephone number of each witness—separately identifying those the party expects to present and those it may call if the need arises;

(ii) the designation of those witnesses whose testimony the party expects to present by deposition and, if not taken stenographically, a transcript of the pertinent parts of the deposition; and

(iii) an identification of each document or other exhibit, including summaries of other evidence—separately identifying those items the party expects to offer and those it may offer if the need arises.

(B) *Time for Pretrial Disclosures; Objections.* Unless the court orders otherwise, these disclosures must be made at least 30 days before trial. Within 14 days after they are made, unless the court sets a different time, a party may serve and promptly file a list of the following objections: any objections to the use under Rule 32(a) of a deposition designated by another party under Rule 26(a)(3)(A)(ii); and any objection, together with the grounds for it, that may be made to the admissibility of materials identified under Rule 26(a)(3)(A)(iii). An objection not so made—except for one under Federal Rule of Evidence 402 or 403—is waived unless excused by the court for good cause.

(4) *Form of Disclosures.* Unless the court orders otherwise, all disclosures under Rule 26(a) must be in writing, signed, and served.

(b) Discovery Scope and Limits.

(1) *Scope in General.* Unless otherwise limited by court order, the scope of discovery is as follows: Parties may obtain discovery regarding any nonprivileged matter that is relevant to any party's claim or defense and proportional to the needs of the case, considering the importance of the issues at stake in the action, the amount in controversy, the parties' relative access to relevant information, the parties' resources, the importance of the discovery in resolving the issues, and whether the burden or expense of the proposed discovery outweighs its likely benefit. Information within this scope of discovery need not be admissible in evidence to be discoverable.

(2) *Limitations on Frequency and Extent.*

(A) *When Permitted.* By order, the court may alter the limits in these rules on the number of depositions and interrogatories or on the length of depositions under Rule 30. By order or local rule, the court may also limit the number of requests under Rule 36.

(B) *Specific Limitations on Electronically Stored Information.* A party need not provide discovery of electronically stored information from sources that the party identifies as not reasonably accessible because of undue burden or cost. On motion to compel discovery or for a protective order, the party from whom discovery is sought must show that the information is not reasonably accessible because of undue burden or cost. If that showing is made, the court may nonetheless order discovery from such sources if the requesting party shows good cause, considering the limitations of Rule 26(b)(2)(C). The court may specify conditions for the discovery.

(C) *When Required.* On motion or on its own, the court must limit the frequency or extent of discovery otherwise allowed by these rules or by local rule if it determines that:

(i) the discovery sought is unreasonably cumulative or duplicative, or can be obtained from some other source that is more convenient, less burdensome, or less expensive;

(ii) the party seeking discovery has had ample opportunity to obtain the information by discovery in the action; or

(iii) the proposed discovery is outside the scope permitted by Rule 26(b)(1).

(3) *Trial Preparation: Materials.*

(A) *Documents and Tangible Things.* Ordinarily, a party may not discover documents and tangible things that are prepared in anticipation of litigation or for trial by or for another party or its representative (including the other party's attorney, consultant, surety, indemnitor, insurer, or agent). But, subject to Rule 26(b)(4), those materials may be discovered if:

(i) they are otherwise discoverable under Rule 26(b)(1); and

(ii) the party shows that it has substantial need for the materials to prepare its case and cannot, without undue hardship, obtain their substantial equivalent by other means.

(B) *Protection Against Disclosure.* If the court orders discovery of those materials, it must protect against disclosure of the mental impressions, conclusions, opinions, or legal theories of a party's attorney or other representative concerning the litigation.

(C) *Previous Statement.* Any party or other person may, on request and without the required showing, obtain the person's own previous statement about the action or its subject matter. If the request is refused, the person may move for a court order, and Rule 37(a)(5) applies to the award of expenses. A previous statement is either:

(i) a written statement that the person has signed or otherwise adopted or approved; or

(ii) a contemporaneous stenographic, mechanical, electrical, or other recording—or a transcription of it—that recites substantially verbatim the person's oral statement.

(4) *Trial Preparation: Experts.*

(A) *Deposition of an Expert Who May Testify.* A party may depose any person who has been identified as an expert whose opinions may be presented at trial. If Rule 26(a)(2)(B) requires a report from the expert, the deposition may be conducted only after the report is provided.

(B) *Trial–Preparation Protection for Draft Reports or Disclosures.* Rules 26(b)(3)(A) and (B) protect drafts of any report or disclosure required under Rule 26(a)(2), regardless of the form in which the draft is recorded.

(C) *Trial–Preparation Protection for Communications Between a Party's Attorney and Expert Witnesses.* Rules 26(b)(3)(A) and (B) protect communications between the party's attorney and any witness required to provide a report under Rule 26(a)(2)(B), regardless of the form of the communications, except to the extent that the communications:

(i) relate to compensation for the expert's study or testimony;

(ii) identify facts or data that the party's attorney provided and that the expert considered in forming the opinions to be expressed; or

(iii) identify assumptions that the party's attorney provided and that the expert relied on in forming the opinions to be expressed.

(D) *Expert Employed Only for Trial Preparation.* Ordinarily, a party may not, by interrogatories or deposition, discover facts known or opinions held by an expert who has been retained or specially employed by another party in anticipation of litigation or to prepare for trial and who is not expected to be called as a witness at trial. But a party may do so only:

(i) as provided in Rule 35(b); or

(ii) on showing exceptional circumstances under which it is impracticable for the party to obtain facts or opinions on the same subject by other means.

(E) *Payment.* Unless manifest injustice would result, the court must require that the party seeking discovery:

(i) pay the expert a reasonable fee for time spent in responding to discovery under Rule 26(b)(4)(A) or (D); and

(ii) for discovery under (D), also pay the other party a fair portion of the fees and expenses it reasonably incurred in obtaining the expert's facts and opinions.

(5) *Claiming Privilege or Protecting Trial-Preparation Materials.*

(A) *Information Withheld.* When a party withholds information otherwise discoverable by claiming that the information is privileged or subject to protection as trial-preparation material, the party must:

(i) expressly make the claim; and

(ii) describe the nature of the documents, communications, or tangible things not produced or disclosed—and do so in a manner that, without revealing information itself privileged or protected, will enable other parties to assess the claim.

(B) *Information Produced.* If information produced in discovery is subject to a claim of privilege or of protection as trial-preparation material, the party making the claim may notify any party that received the information of the claim and the basis for it. After being notified, a party must promptly return, sequester, or destroy the specified information and any copies it has; must not use or disclose the information until the claim is resolved; must take reasonable steps to retrieve the information if the party disclosed it before being notified; and may promptly present the information to the court under seal for a determination of the claim. The producing party must preserve the information until the claim is resolved.

(c) Protective Orders.

(1) *In General.* A party or any person from whom discovery is sought may move for a protective order in the court where the action is pending — or as an alternative on matters relating to a deposition, in the court for the district where the deposition will be taken. The motion must include a certification that the movant has in good faith conferred or attempted to confer with other affected parties in an effort to resolve the dispute without court action. The court may, for good cause, issue an order to protect a party or person from annoyance, embarrassment, oppression, or undue burden or expense, including one or more of the following:

(A) forbidding the disclosure or discovery;

(B) specifying terms, including time and place or the allocation of expenses, for the disclosure or discovery;

(C) prescribing a discovery method other than the one selected by the party seeking discovery;

(D) forbidding inquiry into certain matters, or limiting the scope of disclosure or discovery to certain matters;

(E) designating the persons who may be present while the discovery is conducted;

(F) requiring that a deposition be sealed and opened only on court order;

(G) requiring that a trade secret or other confidential research, development, or commercial information not be revealed or be revealed only in a specified way; and

(H) requiring that the parties simultaneously file specified documents or information in sealed envelopes, to be opened as the court directs.

(2) *Ordering Discovery.* If a motion for a protective order is wholly or partly denied, the court may, on just terms, order that any party or person provide or permit discovery.

(3) *Awarding Expenses.* Rule 37(a)(5) applies to the award of expenses.

(d) Timing and Sequence of Discovery.

(1) *Timing.* A party may not seek discovery from any source before the parties have conferred as required by Rule 26(f), except in a proceeding exempted from initial disclosure under Rule 26(a)(1)(B), or when authorized by these rules, by stipulation, or by court order.

(2) *Early Rule 34 Requests.*

(A) **Time to Deliver.** More than 21 days after the summons and complaint are served on a party, a request under Rule 34 may be delivered:

(i) to that party by any other party, and

(ii) by that party to any plaintiff or to any other party that has been served.

(B) *When Considered Served.* The request is considered to have been served at the first Rule 26(f) conference.

(3) *Sequence.* Unless the parties stipulate or the court orders otherwise for the parties' and witnesses' convenience and in the interests of justice:

(A) methods of discovery may be used in any sequence; and

(B) discovery by one party does not require any other party to delay its discovery.

(e) Supplementing Disclosures and Responses.

(1) *In General.* A party who has made a disclosure under Rule 26(a)—or who has responded to an interrogatory, request for production, or request for admission—must supplement or correct its disclosure or response:

(A) in a timely manner if the party learns that in some material respect the disclosure or response is incomplete or incorrect, and if the additional or corrective information has not otherwise been made known to the other parties during the discovery process or in writing; or

(B) as ordered by the court.

(2) *Expert Witness.* For an expert whose report must be disclosed under Rule 26(a)(2)(B), the party's duty to supplement extends both to information included in the report and to information given during the expert's deposition. Any additions or changes to this information must be disclosed by the time the party's pretrial disclosures under Rule 26(a)(3) are due.

(f) Conference of the Parties; Planning for Discovery.

(1) *Conference Timing.* Except in a proceeding exempted from initial disclosure under Rule 26(a)(1)(B) or when the court orders otherwise, the parties must confer as soon as practicable—and in any event at least 21 days before a scheduling conference is to be held or a scheduling order is due under Rule 16(b).

(2) *Conference Content; Parties' Responsibilities.* In conferring, the parties must consider the nature and basis of their claims and defenses and the possibilities for promptly settling or resolving the case; make or arrange for the disclosures required by Rule 26(a)(1); discuss any issues about preserving discoverable information; and develop a proposed discovery plan. The attorneys of record and all unrepresented parties that have appeared in the case are jointly responsible for arranging the conference, for attempting in good faith to agree on the proposed discovery plan, and for submitting to the court within 14 days after the conference a written report outlining the plan. The court may order the parties or attorneys to attend the conference in person.

(3) *Discovery Plan.* A discovery plan must state the parties' views and proposals on:

(A) what changes should be made in the timing, form, or requirement for disclosures under Rule 26(a), including a statement of when initial disclosures were made or will be made;

(B) the subjects on which discovery may be needed, when discovery should be completed, and whether discovery should be conducted in phases or be limited to or focused on particular issues;

(C) any issues about disclosure, discovery, or preservation of electronically stored information, including the form or forms in which it should be produced;

(D) any issues about claims of privilege or of protection as trial-preparation materials, including — if the parties agree on a procedure to assert these claims after production — whether to ask the court to include their agreement in an order under Federal Rule of Evidence 502;

(E) what changes should be made in the limitations on discovery imposed under these rules or by local rule, and what other limitations should be imposed; and

(F) any other orders that the court should issue under Rule 26(c) or under Rule 16(b) and (c).

(4) *Expedited Schedule.* If necessary to comply with its expedited schedule for Rule 16(b) conferences, a court may by local rule:

(A) require the parties' conference to occur less than 21 days before the scheduling conference is held or a scheduling order is due under Rule 16(b); and

(B) require the written report outlining the discovery plan to be filed less than 14 days after the parties' conference, or excuse the parties from submitting a written report and permit them to report orally on their discovery plan at the Rule 16(b) conference.

(g) Signing Disclosures and Discovery Requests, Responses, and Objections.

(1) *Signature Required; Effect of Signature.* Every disclosure under Rule 26(a)(1) or (a)(3) and every discovery request, response, or objection must be signed by at least one attorney of record in the attorney's own name—or by the party personally, if unrepresented—and must state the signer's address, e-mail address, and telephone number. By signing, an attorney or party certifies that to the best of the person's knowledge, information, and belief formed after a reasonable inquiry:

(A) with respect to a disclosure, it is complete and correct as of the time it is made; and

(B) with respect to a discovery request, response, or objection, it is:

(i) consistent with these rules and warranted by existing law or by a nonfrivolous argument for extending, modifying, or reversing existing law, or for establishing new law;

(ii) not interposed for any improper purpose, such as to harass, cause unnecessary delay, or needlessly increase the cost of litigation; and

(iii) neither unreasonable nor unduly burdensome or expensive, considering the needs of the case, prior discovery in the case, the amount in controversy, and the importance of the issues at stake in the action.

(2) *Failure to Sign.* Other parties have no duty to act on an unsigned disclosure, request, response, or objection until it is signed, and the court must strike it unless a signature is promptly supplied after the omission is called to the attorney's or party's attention.

(3) *Sanction for Improper Certification.* If a certification violates this rule without substantial justification, the court, on motion or on its own, must impose an appropriate sanction on the signer, the party on whose behalf the signer was acting, or both. The sanction may include an order to pay the reasonable expenses, including attorney's fees, caused by the violation.

(Amended December 27, 1946, effective March 19, 1948; January 21, 1963, effective July 1, 1963; February 28, 1966, effective July 1, 1966; March 30, 1970, effective July 1, 1970; April 29, 1980, effective August 1, 1980; April 28, 1983, effective August 1, 1983; March 2, 1987, effective August 1, 1987; April 22, 1993, effective December 1, 1993; April 17, 2000, effective December 1, 2000; April 12, 2006, effective December 1, 2006; April 30, 2007, effective December 1, 2007; April 28, 2010, effective December 1, 2010; April 29, 2015, effective December 1, 2015.)

ADVISORY COMMITTEE NOTES

1937 Adoption

Note to Subdivision (a). This rule freely authorizes the taking of depositions under the same circumstances and by the same methods whether for the purpose of discovery or for the purpose of obtaining evidence. Many states have adopted this practice on account of its simplicity and effectiveness, safeguarding it by imposing such restrictions upon the subsequent use of the deposition at the trial or hearing as are deemed advisable. See Ark.Civ.Code (Crawford, 1934) §§ 606 to 607; Calif.Code Civ.Proc. (Deering, 1937) § 2021; 1 Colo.Stat.Ann. (1935) Code Civ.Proc. § 376; Idaho Code Ann. (1932) § 16–906; Ill.Rules of Pract.Rule 19 (Smith-Hurd Ill. Stats. c. 110, § 259.19); Smith-Hurd Ill.Stats. c. 51, § 24; 2 Ind.Stat.Ann. (Burns, 1933) §§ 2–1501, 2–1506; Ky.Codes (Carroll, 1932) Civ.Pract. § 557; 1 Mo.Rev.Stat. (1929) § 1753; 4 Mont.Rev.Codes Ann. (1935) § 10645; Neb.Comp. Stat. (1929) ch. 20, §§ 1246–7; 4 Nev.Comp.Laws (Hillyer, 1929) § 9001; 2 N.H.Pub.Laws (1926) ch. 337, § 1; N.C.Code Ann. (1935) § 1809; 2 N.D.Comp.Laws Ann. (1913) §§ 7889 to 7897; 2 Ohio Gen.Code Ann. (Page, 1926) §§ 11525–6; 1 Ore.Code Ann. (1930) Tit. 9, § 1503; 1 S.D.Comp.Laws (1929) §§ 2713–16; Vernon's Ann.Civ.Stats.Tex. arts. 3738, 3752, 3769; Utah Rev.Stat.Ann. (1933) § 104–51–7; Wash.Rules of Practice adopted by the Supreme Ct., Rule 8, 2 Wash.Rev. Stat.Ann. (Remington, 1932) § 308–8; W.Va.Code (1931) ch.

57, art. 4, § 1. Compare [former] Equity Rules 47 (Depositions—To be Taken in Exceptional Instances); 54 (Depositions Under Revised Statutes, §§ 863, 865, 866, 867—Cross Examination); 58 (Discovery—Interrogatories—Inspection and Production of Documents—Admission of Execution or Genuineness).

This and subsequent rules incorporate, modify, and broaden the provisions for depositions under U.S.C., Title 28, [former] §§ 639 (Depositions *de bene esse;* when and where taken; notice), 640 (Same; mode of taking), 641 (Same; transmission to court), 644 (Depositions under *dedimus potestatem* and *in perpetuam*), 646 (Deposition under *dedimus potestatem;* how taken). These statutes are superseded in so far as they differ from this and subsequent rules. U.S.C. Title 28, [former] § 643 (Depositions; taken in mode prescribed by State laws) is superseded by the third sentence of Subdivision (a).

While a number of states permit discovery only from parties or their agents, others either make no distinction between parties or agents of parties and ordinary witnesses, or authorize the taking of ordinary depositions, without restriction, from any persons who have knowledge of relevant facts. See Ark.Civ.Code (Crawford, 1934) §§ 606 to 607; 1 Idaho Code Ann. (1932) § 16–906; Ill.Rules of Pract., Rule 19 (Smith-Hurd Ill.Stats. c. 110, § 259.19); Smith-Hurd Ill.Stats. c. 51, § 24; 2 Ind.Stat.Ann. (Burns, 1933) § 2–1501; Ky.Codes (Carroll, 1932) Civ.Pract. §§ 554 to 558; 2 Md.Ann.Code (Bagby, 1924) Art. 35, § 21; 2 Minn.Stat. (Mason, 1927) § 9820; Mo.St.Ann. §§ 1753, 1759, pp. 4023, 4026; Neb. Comp.Stat. (1929) ch. 20, §§ 1246–7; 2 N.H.Pub.Laws (1926) ch. 337, § 1; 2 N.D.Comp.Laws Ann. (1913) § 7897; 2 Ohio Gen.Code Ann. (Page, 1926) §§ 11525–6; 1 S.D.Comp.Laws (1929) §§ 2713–16; Vernon's Ann.Civil Stats.Tex. arts. 3738, 3752, 3769; Utah Rev.Stat.Ann. (1933) § 104–51–7; Wash. Rules of Practice adopted by Supreme Ct., Rule 8, 2 Wash. Rev.Stat.Ann. (Remington, 1932) § 308–8; W.Va.Code (1931) ch. 57, art. 4, § 1.

The more common practice in the United States is to take depositions on notice by the party desiring them, without any order from the court, and this has been followed in these rules. See Calif.Code Civ.Proc. (Deering, 1937) § 2031; 2 Fla.Comp.Gen.Laws Ann. (1927) §§ 4405–7; 1 Idaho Code Ann. (1932) § 16–902; Ill.Rules of Pract., Rule 19 (Smith-Hurd Ill.Stats. c. 110, § 259.19); Smith-Hurd Ill.Stats. c. 51, § 24; 2 Ind.Stat.Ann. (Burns, 1933) § 2–1502; Kan.Gen.Stat. Ann. (1935) § 60–2827; Ky.Codes (Carroll, 1932) Civ.Pract. § 565; 2 Minn.Stat. (Mason, 1927) § 9820; Mo.St.Ann. § 1761, p. 4029; 4 Mont.Rev.Codes Ann. (1935) § 10651; Nev.Comp.Laws (Hillyer, 1929) § 9002; N.C.Code Ann. (1935) § 1809; 2 N.D.Comp.Laws Ann. (1913) § 7895; Utah Rev.Stat.Ann. (1933) § 104–51–8.

Note to Subdivision (b). While the old chancery practice limited discovery to facts supporting the case of the party seeking it, this limitation has been largely abandoned by modern legislation. See Ala.Code Ann. (Michie, 1928) §§ 7764 to 7773; 2 Ind.Stat.Ann. (Burns, 1933) §§ 2–1028, 2–1506, 2–1728–2–1732; Iowa Code (1935) § 11185; Ky.Codes (Carroll, 1932) Civ.Pract. §§ 557, 606(8); La.Code Pract. (Dart, 1932) arts. 347–356; 2 Mass.Gen.Laws (Ter.Ed., 1932) ch. 231, §§ 61 to 67; Mo.St.Ann. §§ 1753, 1759, pp. 4023, 4026; Neb.Comp.Stat. (1929) §§ 20–1246, 20–1247; 2 N.H.Pub.Laws (1926) ch. 337, § 1; 2 Ohio Gen.Code Ann. (Page, 1926) §§ 11497, 11526; Vernon's Ann.Civ.Stats.Tex. arts. 3738, 3753, 3769; Wis.Stat. (1935) § 326.12; Ontario

Consol.Rules of Pract. (1928) Rules 237–347; Quebec Code of Civ.Proc. (Curran, 1922) §§ 286 to 290.

Note to Subdivisions (d), (e), and (f). The restrictions here placed upon the use of depositions at the trial or hearing are substantially the same as those provided in U.S.C., Title 28, [former] § 641, for depositions taken, *de bene esse*, with the additional provision that any deposition may be used when the court finds the existence of exceptional circumstances. Compare English Rules Under the Judicature Act (The Annual Practice, 1937) O. 37, r. 18 (with additional provision permitting use of deposition by consent of the parties). See also [former] Equity Rule 64 (Former Depositions, Etc. May be Used Before Master); and 2 Minn.Stat. (Mason, 1927) § 9835 (Use in a subsequent action of a deposition filed in a previously dismissed action between the same parties and involving the same subject matter).

1946 Amendment

Note. Subdivision (a). The amendment eliminates the requirement of leave of court for the taking of a deposition except where a plaintiff seeks to take a deposition within 20 days after the commencement of the action. The retention of the requirement where a deposition is sought by a plaintiff within 20 days of the commencement of the action protects a defendant who has not had an opportunity to retain counsel and inform himself as to the nature of the suit; the plaintiff, of course, needs no such protection. The present rule forbids the plaintiff to take a deposition, without leave of court, before the answer is served. Sometimes the defendant delays the serving of an answer for more than 20 days, but as 20 days are sufficient time for him to obtain a lawyer, there is no reason to forbid the plaintiff to take a deposition without leave merely because the answer has not been served. In all cases, Rule 30(a) empowers the court, for cause shown, to alter the time of the taking of a deposition, and Rule 30(b) contains provisions giving ample protection to persons who are unreasonably pressed. The modified practice here adopted is along the line of that followed in various states. See e.g., 8 Mo.Rev. Stat.Ann.1939, § 1917; 2 Burns' Ind.Stat.Ann.1933, § 2–1506.

Subdivision (b). The amendments to subdivision (b) make clear the broad scope of examination and that it may cover not only evidence for use at the trial but also inquiry into matters in themselves inadmissible as evidence but which will lead to the discovery of such evidence. The purpose of discovery is to allow a broad search for facts, the names of witnesses, or any other matters which may aid a party in the preparation or presentation of his case. *Engl v. Aetna Life Ins. Co.,* C.C.A.2, 1943, 139 F.2d 469; *Mahler v. Pennsylvania R. Co.,* E.D.N.Y.1945, 8 Fed.Rules Serv. 33.351, Case 1. In such a preliminary inquiry admissibility at trial should not be the test as to whether the information sought is within the scope of proper examination. Such a standard unnecessarily curtails the utility of discovery practice. Of course, matters entirely without bearing either as direct evidence or as leads to evidence are not within the scope of inquiry, but to the extent that the examination develops useful information, it functions successfully as an instrument of discovery, even if it produces no testimony directly admissible. *Lewis v. United Air Lines Transportation Corp.,* D.Conn.1939, 27 F.Supp. 946; *Engl v. Aetna Life Ins. Co.,* supra; *Mahler v. Pennsylvania R. Co.,* supra; *Bloomer v. Sirian Lamp Co.,* D.Del. 1944, 8 Fed.Rules Serv. 26b.31, Case 3; *Rosseau v. Langley,* N.Y.1945, 9 Fed.Rules Serv. 34.41, Case 1 (Rule 26 contemplates "examinations not merely for the narrow purpose of adducing testimony which may be offered in evidence but also for the broad discovery of information which may be useful in preparation for trial."); *Olson Transportation Co. v. Socony-Vacuum Co.,* E.D.Wis.1944, 8 Fed.Rules Serv. 34.41, Case 2 (". . . the Rules . . . permit 'fishing' for evidence as they should."); Note, 1945, 45 Col.L.Rev. 482. Thus hearsay, while inadmissible itself, may suggest testimony which properly may be proved. Under Rule 26(b) several cases, however, have erroneously limited discovery on the basis of admissibility, holding that the word "relevant" in effect meant "material and competent under the rules of evidence". *Poppino v. Jones Store Co.,* W.D.Mo.1940, 1 F.R.D. 215, 3 Fed.Rules Serv. 26b.5, Case 1; *Benevento v. A. & P. Food Stores, Inc.,* E.D.N.Y.1939, 26 F.Supp. 424. Thus it has been said that inquiry might not be made into statements or other matters which, when disclosed, amounted only to hearsay. *See Maryland for use of Montvila v. Pan-American Bus Lines, Inc.,* D.Md.1940, 1 F.R.D. 213, 3 Fed. Rules Serv. 26b.211, Case 3; *Gitto v. "Italia," Societa Anonima Di Navigazione,* E.D.N.Y.1940, 31 F.Supp. 567; *Rose Silk Mills, Inc. v. Insurance Co. of North America,* S.D.N.Y. 1939, 29 F.Supp. 504; *Colpak v. Hetterick,* E.D.N.Y.1941, 40 F.Supp. 350; *Matthies v. Peter F. Connolly Co.,* E.D.N.Y. 1941, 6 Fed.Rules Serv. 30a.22, Case 1, 2 F.R.D. 277; *Matter of Examination of Citizens Casualty Co. of New York,* S.D.N.Y.1942, 3 F.R.D. 171, 7 Fed.Rules Serv. 26b.211, Case 1; *United States v. Silliman,* D.C.N.J.1944, 8 Fed.Rules Serv. 26b.52, Case 1. The contrary and better view, however, has often been stated. See, e.g., *Engl v. Aetna Life Ins. Co.,* supra; *Stevenson v. Melady,* S.D.N.Y.1940, 3 Fed.Rules Serv. 26b.31, Case 1, 1 F.R.D. 329; *Lewis v. United Air Lines Transport Corp.,* supra; *Application of Zenith Radio Corp.,* E.D.Pa.1941, 4 Fed.Rules Serv. 30b.21, Case 1, 1 F.R.D. 627; *Steingut v. Guaranty Trust Co. of New York,* S.D.N.Y.1941, 1 F.R.D. 723, 4 Fed.Rules Serv. 26b.5, Case 2; *DeSeversky v. Republic Aviation Corp.,* E.D.N.Y.1941, 2 F.R.D. 183, 5 Fed.Rules Serv. 26b.31, Case 5; *Moore v. George A. Hormel & Co.,* S.D.N.Y.1942, 6 Fed.Rules Serv. 30b.41, Case 1, 2 F.R.D. 340; *Hercules Powder Co. v. Rohm & Haas Co.,* D.Del.1943, 7 Fed.Rules Serv. 45b.311, Case 2, 3 F.R.D. 302; *Bloomer v. Sirian Lamp Co.,* supra; *Crosby Steam Gage & Valve Co. v. Manning, Maxwell & Moore, Inc.,* D.Mass.1944, 8 Fed.Rules Serv. 26b.31, Case 1; *Patterson Oil Terminals, Inc. v. Charles Kurz & Co., Inc.,* E.D.Pa. 1945, 9 Fed.Rules Serv. 33.321, Case 2; *Pueblo Trading Co. v. Reclamation Dist. No. 1500,* N.D.Cal.1945, 9 Fed.Rules Serv. 33.321, Case 4, 4 F.R.D. 471. See also discussion as to the broad scope of discovery in *Hoffman v. Palmer,* C.C.A.2, 1942, 129 F.2d 976, 995–997, affirmed 63 S.Ct. 477, 318 U.S. 109, 87 L.Ed. 645; Note, 1945, 45 Col.L.Rev. 482.

1963 Amendment

This amendment conforms to the amendment of Rule 28(b). See the next-to-last paragraph of the Advisory Committee's Note to that amendment.

1966 Amendment

The requirement that the plaintiff obtain leave of court in order to serve notice of taking of a deposition within 20 days after commencement of the action gives rise to difficulties when the prospective deponent is about to become unavailable for examination. The problem is not confined to admiralty, but has been of special concern in that context because of the mobility of vessels and their personnel. When Rule 26 was adopted as Admiralty Rule 30A in 1961, the problem was alleviated by permitting depositions *de bene esse,* for which leave of court is not required. See Advisory Committee's Note to Admiralty Rule 30A (1961).

A continuing study is being made in the effort to devise a modification of the 20-day rule appropriate to both the civil and admiralty practice to the end that Rule 26(a) shall state a uniform rule applicable alike to what are now civil actions and suits in admiralty. Meanwhile, the exigencies of maritime litigation require preservation, for the time being at least, of the traditional *de bene esse* procedure for the post-unification counterpart of the present suit in admiralty. Accordingly, the amendment provides for continued availability of that procedure in admiralty and maritime claims within the meaning of Rule 9(h).

1970 Amendment

A limited rearrangement of the discovery rules is made, whereby certain rule provisions are transferred, as follows: Existing Rule 26(a) is transferred to Rules 30(a) and 31(a). Existing Rule 26(c) is transferred to Rule 30(c). Existing Rules 26(d), (e), and (f) are transferred to Rule 32. Revisions of the transferred provisions, if any, are discussed in the notes appended to Rules 30, 31, and 32. In addition, Rule 30(b) is transferred to Rule 26(c). The purpose of this rearrangement is to establish Rule 26 as a rule governing discovery in general. (The reasons are set out in the Advisory Committee's explanatory statement.)

Subdivision (a)—Discovery Devices. This is a new subdivision listing all of the discovery devices provided in the discovery rules and establishing the relationship between the general provisions of Rule 26 and the specific rules for particular discovery devices. The provision that the frequency of use of these methods is not limited confirms existing law. It incorporates in general form a provision now found in Rule 33.

Subdivision (b)—Scope of Discovery. This subdivision is recast to cover the scope of discovery generally. It regulates the discovery obtainable through any of the discovery devices listed in Rule 26(a).

All provisions as to scope of discovery are subject to the initial qualification that the court may limit discovery in accordance with these rules. Rule 26(c) (transferred from 30(b)) confers broad powers on the courts to regulate or prevent discovery even though the materials sought are within the scope of 26(b), and these powers have always been freely exercised. For example, a party's income tax return is generally held not privileged, 2A Barron & Holtzoff, *Federal Practice and Procedure,* § 651.2 (Wright ed. 1961), and yet courts have recognized that interests in privacy may call for a measure of extra protection. E.g., *Wiesenberger v. W. E. Hutton & Co.,* 35 F.R.D. 556 (S.D.N.Y.1964). Similarly, the courts have in appropriate circumstances protected materials that are primarily of an impeaching character. These two types of materials merely illustrate the many situations, not capable of governance by precise rule, in which courts must exercise judgment. The new subsections in Rule 26(b) do not change existing law with respect to such situations.

Subdivision (b)(1)—In General. The language is changed to provide for the scope of discovery in general terms. The existing subdivision, although in terms applicable only to depositions, is incorporated by reference in existing Rules 33 and 34. Since decisions as to relevance to the subject matter of the action are made for discovery purposes well in advance

of trial, a flexible treatment of relevance is required and the making of discovery, whether voluntary or under court order, is not a concession or determination of relevance for purposes of trial. *Cf.* 4 *Moore's Federal Practice* ¶26–16[1] (2d ed. 1966).

Subdivision (b)(2)—Insurance Policies. Both the cases and commentators are sharply in conflict on the question whether defendant's liability insurance coverage is subject to discovery in the usual situation when the insurance coverage is not itself admissible and does not bear on another issue in the case. Examples of Federal cases requiring disclosure and supporting comments: *Cook v. Welty,* 253 F.Supp. 875 (D.D.C.1966) (cases cited); *Johanek v. Aberle,* 27 F.R.D. 272 (D.Mont.1961); Williams, *Discovery of Dollar Limits in Liability Policies in Automobile Tort Cases,* 10 Ala.L.Rev. 355 (1958); Thode, *Some Reflections on the 1957 Amendments to the Texas Rules,* 37 Tex.L.Rev. 33, 40–42 (1958). Examples of Federal cases refusing disclosure and supporting comments: *Bisserier v. Manning,* 207 F.Supp. 476 (D.N.J.1962); *Cooper v. Stender,* 30 F.R.D. 389 (E.D.Tenn.1962); Frank, *Discovery and Insurance, Coverage,* 1959 Ins.L.J. 281; Fournier, *Pre-trial Discovery of Insurance Coverage and Limits,* 28 Ford.L.Rev. 215 (1959).

The division in reported cases is close. State decisions based on provisions similar to the federal rules are similarly divided. See cases collected in 2A Barron & Holtzoff, *Federal Practice and Procedure* § 647.1, nn. 45.5, 45.6 (Wright ed. 1961). It appears to be difficult if not impossible to obtain appellate review of the issue. Resolution by rule amendment is indicated. The question is essentially procedural in that it bears upon preparation for trial and settlement before trial, and courts confronting the question, however they have decided it, have generally treated it as procedural and governed by the rules.

The amendment resolves this issue in favor of disclosure. Most of the decisions denying discovery, some explicitly, reason from the text of Rule 26(b) that it permits discovery only of matters which will be admissible in evidence or appear reasonably calculated to lead to such evidence; they avoid considerations of policy, regarding them as foreclosed. See *Bisserier v. Manning, supra.* Some note also that facts about a defendant's financial status are not discoverable as such, prior to judgment with execution unsatisfied, and fear that, if courts hold insurance coverage discoverable, they must extend the principle to other aspects of the defendant's financial status. The cases favoring disclosure rely heavily on the practical significance of insurance in the decisions lawyers make about settlement and trial preparation. In *Clauss v. Danker,* 264 F.Supp. 246 (S.D.N.Y.1967), the court held that the rules forbid disclosure but called for an amendment to permit it.

Disclosure of insurance coverage will enable counsel for both sides to make the same realistic appraisal of the case, so that settlement and litigation strategy are based on knowledge and not speculation. It will conduce to settlement and avoid protracted litigation in some cases, though in others it may have an opposite effect. The amendment is limited to insurance coverage, which should be distinguished from any other facts concerning defendant's financial status (1) because insurance is an asset created specifically to satisfy the claim; (2) because the insurance company ordinarily controls the litigation; (3) because information about coverage is available only from defendant or his insurer; and (4) because disclosure does not involve a significant invasion of privacy.

Disclosure is required when the insurer "may be liable" on part or all of the judgment. Thus, an insurance company must disclose even when it contests liability under the policy, and such disclosure does not constitute a waiver of its claim. It is immaterial whether the liability is to satisfy the judgment directly or merely to indemnify or reimburse another after he pays the judgment.

The provision applies only to persons "carrying on an insurance business" and thus covers insurance companies and not the ordinary business concern that enters into a contract of indemnification. *Cf.* N.Y.Ins.Law § 41. Thus, the provision makes no change in existing law on discovery of indemnity agreements other than insurance agreements by persons carrying on an insurance business. Similarly, the provision does not cover the business concern that creates a reserve fund for purposes of self-insurance.

For some purposes other than discovery, an application for insurance is treated as a part of the insurance agreement. The provision makes clear that, for discovery purposes, the application is not to be so treated. The insurance application may contain personal and financial information concerning the insured, discovery of which is beyond the purpose of this provision.

In no instance does disclosure make the facts concerning insurance coverage admissible in evidence.

Subdivision (b)(3)—Trial Preparation: Materials. Some of the most controversial and vexing problems to emerge from the discovery rules have arisen out of requests for the production of documents or things prepared in anticipation of litigation or for trial. The existing rules make no explicit provision for such materials. Yet, two verbally distinct doctrines have developed, each conferring a qualified immunity on these materials—the "good cause" requirement in Rule 34 (now generally held applicable to discovery of documents via deposition under Rule 45 and interrogatories under Rule 33) and the work-product doctrine of *Hickman v. Taylor,* 329 U.S. 495 (1947). Both demand a showing of justification before production can be had, the one of "good cause" and the other variously described in the *Hickman* case: "necessity or justification," "denial * * * would unduly prejudice the preparation of petitioner's case," or "cause hardship or injustice" 329 U.S. at 509–510.

In deciding the *Hickman* case, the Supreme Court appears to have expressed a preference in 1947 for an approach to the problem of trial preparation materials by judicial decision rather than by rule. Sufficient experience has accumulated, however, with lower court applications of the *Hickman* decision to warrant a reappraisal.

The major difficulties visible in the existing case law are (1) confusion and disagreement as to whether "good cause" is made out by a showing of relevance and lack of privilege, or requires an additional showing of necessity, (2) confusion and disagreement as to the scope of the *Hickman* work-product doctrine, particularly whether it extends beyond work actually performed by lawyers, and (3) the resulting difficulty of relating the "good cause" required by Rule 34 and the "necessity or justification" of the work-product doctrine, so that their respective roles and the distinctions between them are understood.

Basic Standard.—Since Rule 34 in terms requires a showing of "good cause" for the production of all documents and things, whether or not trial preparation is involved, courts have felt that a single formula is called for and have differed over whether a showing of relevance and lack of privilege is enough or whether more must be shown. When the facts of the cases are studied, however, a distinction emerges based upon the type of materials. With respect to documents not obtained or prepared with an eye to litigation, the decisions, while not uniform, reflect a strong and increasing tendency to relate "good cause" to a showing that the documents are relevant to the subject matter of the action. *E.g., Connecticut Mutual Life Ins. Co. v. Shields,* 17 F.R.D. 273 (S.D.N.Y.1959), with cases cited; *Houdry Process Corp. v. Commonwealth Oil Refining Co.,* 24 F.R.D. 58 (S.D.N.Y.1955); see *Bell v. Commercial Ins. Co.,* 280 F.2d 514, 517 (3d Cir. 1960). When the party whose documents are sought shows that the request for production is unduly burdensome or oppressive, courts have denied discovery for lack of "good cause", although they might just as easily have based their decision on the protective provisions of existing Rule 30(b) (new Rule 26(c)). *E.g., Lauer v. Tankrederi,* 39 F.R.D. 334 (E.D.Pa.1966).

As to trial-preparation materials, however, the courts are increasingly interpreting "good cause" as requiring more than relevance. When lawyers have prepared or obtained the materials for trial, all courts require more than relevance; so much is clearly commanded by *Hickman.* But even as to the preparatory work of nonlawyers, while some courts ignore work-product and equate "good cause" with relevance, *e.g., Brown v. New York, N.H. & H.R.R.,* 17 F.R.D. 324 (S.D.N.Y. 1955), the more recent trend is to read "good cause" as requiring inquiry into the importance of and need for the materials as well as into alternative sources for securing the same information. In *Guilford Nat'l Bank v. Southern Ry.,* 297 F.2d 921 (4th Cir. 1962), statements of witnesses obtained by claim agents were held not discoverable because both parties had had equal access to the witnesses at about the same time, shortly after the collision in question. The decision was based solely on Rule 34 and "good cause"; the court declined to rule on whether the statements were work-products. The court's treatment of "good cause" is quoted at length and with approval in *Schlagenhauf v. Holder,* 379 U.S. 104, 117–118 (1964). See also *Mitchell v. Bass,* 252 F.2d 513 (8th Cir. 1958); *Hauger v. Chicago, R.I. & Pac. R.R.,* 216 F.2d 501 (7th Cir. 1954); *Burke v. United States,* 32 F.R.D. 213 (E.D.N.Y.1963). While the opinions dealing with "good cause" do not often draw an explicit distinction between trial preparation materials and other materials, in fact an overwhelming proportion of the cases in which a special showing is required are cases involving trial preparation materials.

The rules are amended by eliminating the general requirement of "good cause" from Rule 34 but retaining a requirement of a special showing for trial preparation materials in this subdivision. The required showing is expressed, not in terms of "good cause" whose generality has tended to encourage confusion and controversy, but in terms of the elements of the special showing to be made: substantial need of the materials in the preparation of the case and inability without undue hardship to obtain the substantial equivalent of the materials by other means.

These changes conform to the holdings of the cases, when viewed in light of their facts. Apart from trial preparation, the fact that the materials sought are documentary does not in and of itself require a special showing beyond relevance and absence of privilege. The protective provisions are of course available, and if the party from whom production is sought raises a special issue of privacy (as with respect to income tax returns or grand jury minutes) or points to evidence primarily impeaching, or can show serious burden or expense, the court will exercise its traditional power to decide whether to issue a protective order. On the other hand, the requirement of a special showing for discovery of trial preparation materials reflects the view that each side's informal evaluation of its case should be protected, that each side should be encouraged to prepare independently, and that one side should not automatically have the benefit of the detailed preparatory work of the other side. See Field and McKusick, *Maine Civil Practice* 264 (1959).

Elimination of a "good cause" requirement from Rule 34 and the establishment of a requirement of a special showing in this subdivision will eliminate the confusion caused by having two verbally distinct requirements of justification that the courts have been unable to distinguish clearly. Moreover, the language of the subdivision suggests the factors which the courts should consider in determining whether the requisite showing has been made. The importance of the materials sought to the party seeking them in preparation of his case and the difficulty he will have obtaining them by other means are factors noted in the *Hickman* case. The courts should also consider the likelihood that the party, even if he obtains the information by independent means, will not have the substantial equivalent of the documents the production of which he seeks.

Consideration of these factors may well lead the court to distinguish between witness statements taken by an investigator, on the one hand, and other parts of the investigative file, on the other. The court in *Southern Ry. v. Lanham*, 403 F.2d 119 (5th Cir. 1968), while it naturally addressed itself to the "good cause" requirements of Rule 34, set forth as controlling considerations the factors contained in the language of this subdivision. The analysis of the court suggests circumstances under which witness statements will be discoverable. The witness may have given a fresh and contemporaneous account in a written statement while he is available to the party seeking discovery only a substantial time thereafter. *Lanham, supra* at 127–128; *Guilford, supra* at 926. Or he may be reluctant or hostile. *Lanham, supra* at 128–129; *Brookshire v. Pennsylvania RR*, 14 F.R.D. 154 (N.D.Ohio 1953); *Diamond v. Mohawk Rubber Co.*, 33 F.R.D. 264 (D.Colo.1963). Or he may have a lapse of memory. *Tannenbaum v. Walker*, 16 F.R.D. 570 (E.D.Pa.1954). Or he may probably be deviating from his prior statement. *Cf. Hauger v. Chicago, R.I. & Pac. RR*, 216 F.2d 501 (7th Cir. 1954). On the other hand, a much stronger showing is needed to obtain evaluative materials in an investigator's reports. *Lanham, supra* at 131–133; *Pickett v. L. R. Ryan, Inc.*, 237 F.Supp. 198 (E.D.S.C.1965).

Materials assembled in the ordinary course of business, or pursuant to public requirements unrelated to litigation, or for other nonlitigation purposes are not under the qualified immunity provided by this subdivision. *Goosman v. A. Duie Pyle, Inc.*, 320 F.2d 45 (4th Cir. 1963); cf. *United States v. New York Foreign Trade Zone Operators, Inc.*, 304 F.2d 792 (2d Cir. 1962). No change is made in the existing doctrine, noted in the *Hickman* case, that one party may discover relevant facts known or available to the other party, even though such facts are contained in a document which is not itself discoverable.

Treatment of Lawyers; Special Protection of Mental Impressions, Conclusions, Opinions, and Legal Theories Concerning the Litigation.—The courts are divided as to whether the work-product doctrine extends to the preparatory work only of lawyers. The *Hickman* case left this issue open since the statements in that case were taken by a lawyer. As to courts of appeals compare *Alltmont v. United States*, 177 F.2d 971, 976 (3d Cir. 1949), cert. denied, 339 U.S. 967 (1950) (*Hickman* applied to statements obtained by FBI agents on theory it should apply to "all statements of prospective witnesses which a party has obtained for his trial counsel's use"), with *Southern Ry. v. Campbell*, 309 F.2d 569 (5th Cir. 1962) (Statements taken by claim agents not work-product), and *Guilford Nat'l Bank v. Southern Ry.*, 297 F.2d 921 (4th Cir. 1962) (avoiding issue of work-product as to claim agents, deciding case instead under Rule 34 "good cause"). Similarly, the district courts are divided on statements obtained by claim agents, compare, e.g., *Brown v. New York, N.H. & H.R.R.*, 17 F.R.D. 324 (S.D.N.Y.1955) with *Hanke v. Milwaukee Electric Ry. & Transp. Co.*, 7 F.R.D. 540 (E.D.Wis.1947); investigators, compare *Burke v. United States*, 32 F.R.D. 213 (E.D.N.Y.1963) with *Snyder v. United States*, 20 F.R.D. 7 (E.D.N.Y.1956); and insurers, compare *Gottlieb v. Bresler*, 24 F.R.D. 371 (D.D.C.1959) with *Burns v. Mulder*, 20 F.R.D. 605 (E.D.Pa.1957). See 4 Moore's *Federal Practice* ¶26.23[8.1] (2d ed. 1966); 2A Barron & Holtzoff, *Federal Practice and Procedure* § 652.2 (Wright ed. 1961).

A complication is introduced by the use made by courts of the "good cause" requirement of Rule 34, as described above. A court may conclude that trial preparation materials are not work-product because not the result of lawyer's work and yet hold that they are not producible because "good cause" has not been shown. Cf. *Guilford Nat'l Bank v. Southern Ry.*, 297 F.2d 921 (4th Cir. 1962), cited and described above. When the decisions on "good cause" are taken into account, the weight of authority affords protection of the preparatory work of both lawyers and nonlawyers (though not necessarily to the same extent) by requiring more than a showing of relevance to secure production.

Subdivision (b)(3) reflects the trend of the cases by requiring a special showing, not merely as to materials prepared by an attorney, but also as to materials prepared in anticipation of litigation or preparation for trial by or for a party or any representative acting on his behalf. The subdivision then goes on to protect against disclosure the mental impressions, conclusions, opinions, or legal theories concerning the litigation of an attorney or other representative of a party. The *Hickman* opinion drew special attention to the need for protecting an attorney against discovery of memoranda prepared from recollection of oral interviews. The courts have steadfastly safeguarded against disclosure of lawyers' mental impressions and legal theories, as well as mental impressions and subjective evaluations of investigators and claim-agents. In enforcing this provision of the subdivision, the courts will sometimes find it necessary to order disclosure of a document but with portions deleted.

Rules 33 and 36 have been revised in order to permit discovery calling for opinions, contentions, and admissions relating not only to fact but also to the application of law to fact. Under those rules, a party and his attorney or other representative may be required to disclose, to some extent, mental impressions, opinions, or conclusions. But documents or parts of documents containing these matters are protected against discovery by this subdivision. Even though a party may ultimately have to disclose in response to interrogatories or requests to admit, he is entitled to keep confidential documents containing such matters prepared for internal use.

Party's Right to Own Statement—An exception to the requirement of this subdivision enables a party to secure production of his own statement without any special showing. The cases are divided. Compare, *e.g., Safeway Stores, Inc. v. Reynolds,* 176 F.2d 476 (D.C. Cir.1949); *Shupe v. Pennsylvania R.R.,* 19 F.R.D. 144 (W.D.Pa.1956); with *e.g., New York Central R.R. v. Carr,* 251 F.2d 433 (4th Cir. 1957); *Belback v. Wilson Freight Forwarding Co.,* 40 F.R.D. 16 (W.D.Pa.1966).

Courts which treat a party's statement as though it were that of any witness overlook the fact that the party's statement is, without more, admissible in evidence. Ordinarily, a party gives a statement without insisting on a copy because he does not yet have a lawyer and does not understand the legal consequences of his actions. Thus, the statement is given at a time when he functions at a disadvantage. Discrepancies between his trial testimony and earlier statement may result from lapse of memory or ordinary inaccuracy; a written statement produced for the first time at trial may give such discrepancies a prominence which they do not deserve. In appropriate cases the court may order a party to be deposed before his statement is produced. *E.g., Smith v. Central Linen Service Co.,* 39 F.R.D. 15 (D.Md.1966); *McCoy v. General Motors Corp.,* 33 F.R.D. 354 (W.D.Pa.1963).

Commentators strongly support the view that a party be able to secure his statement without a showing. 4 *Moore's Federal Practice* ¶26.23[8.4] (2d ed. 1966); 2A Barron & Holtzoff, *Federal Practice and Procedure* § 652.3 (Wright ed. 1961); see also Note, *Developments in the Law—Discovery,* 74 Harv.L.Rev. 940, 1039 (1961). The following states have by statute or rule taken the same position: *Statutes:* Fla.Stat. Ann. § 92.33; Ga.Code Ann. § 38–2109(b); La.Stat.Ann.R.S. 13:3732; Mass.Gen.Laws Ann. c. 271, § 44; Minn.Stat.Ann. § 602.01; N.Y.C.P.L.R. § 3101(e); *Rules:* Mo.R.C.P. 56.01(a); N.Dak.R.C.P. 34(b); Wyo.R.C.P. 34(b); *cf.* Mich.G.C.R. 306.2.

In order to clarify and tighten the provision on statements by a party, the term "statement" is defined. The definition is adapted from 18 U.S.C. § 3500(e) (Jencks Act). The statement of a party may of course be that of plaintiff or defendant, and it may be that of an individual or of a corporation or other organization.

Witness' Right to Own Statement.—A second exception to the requirement of this subdivision permits a non-party witness to obtain a copy of his own statement without any special showing. Many, though not all, of the considerations supporting a party's right to obtain his statement apply also to the non-party witness. Insurance companies are increasingly recognizing that a witness is entitled to a copy of his statement and are modifying their regular practice accordingly.

Subdivision (b)(4)—Trial Preparation: Experts. This is a new provision dealing with discovery of information (including facts and opinions) obtained by a party from an expert retained by that party in relation to litigation or obtained by the expert and not yet transmitted to the party. The subdivision deals separately with those experts whom the party expects to call as trial witnesses and with those experts who have been retained or specially employed by the party but who are not expected to be witnesses. It should be noted that the subdivision does not address itself to the expert whose information was not acquired in preparation for trial but rather because he was an actor or viewer with respect to transactions or occurrences that are part of the subject matter of the lawsuit. Such an expert should be treated as an ordinary witness.

Subsection (b)(4)(A) deals with discovery of information obtained by or through experts who will be called as wit-

nesses at trial. The provision is responsive to problems suggested by a relatively recent line of authorities. Many of these cases present intricate and difficult issues as to which expert testimony is likely to be determinative. Prominent among them are food and drug, patent, and condemnation cases. See, *e.g., United States v. Nysco Laboratories, Inc.,* 26 F.R.D. 159, 162 (E.D.N.Y.1960) (food and drug); *E. I. du Pont de Nemours & Co. v. Phillips Petroleum Co.,* 24 F.R.D. 416, 421 (D.Del.1959) (patent); *Cold Metal Process Co. v. Aluminum Co. of America,* 7 F.R.D. 425 (N.D.Ohio 1947), aff'd, *Sachs v. Aluminum Co. of America,* 167 F.2d 570 (6th Cir. 1948) (same); *United States v. 50.34 Acres of Land,* 13 F.R.D. 19 (E.D.N.Y.1952) (condemnation).

In cases of this character, a prohibition against discovery of information held by expert witnesses produces in acute form the very evils that discovery has been created to prevent. Effective cross-examination of an expert witness requires advance preparation. The lawyer even with the help of his own experts frequently cannot anticipate the particular approach his adversary's expert will take or the data on which he will base his judgment on the stand. McGlothlin, *Some Practical Problems in Proof of Economic, Scientific, and Technical Facts,* 23 F.R.D. 467, 478 (1958). A California study of discovery and pretrial in condemnation cases notes that the only substitute for discovery of experts' valuation materials is "lengthy—and often fruitless—cross-examination during trial," and recommends pretrial exchange of such material. Calif.Law Rev.Comm'n, Discovery in Eminent Domain Proceedings 707–710 (Jan. 1963). Similarly, effective rebuttal requires advance knowledge of the line of testimony of the other side. If the latter is foreclosed by a rule against discovery, then the narrowing of issues and elimination of surprise which discovery normally produces are frustrated.

These considerations appear to account for the broadening of discovery against experts in the cases cited where expert testimony was central to the case. In some instances, the opinions are explicit in relating expanded discovery to improved cross-examination and rebuttal at trial. *Franks v. National Dairy Products Corp.,* 41 F.R.D. 234 (W.D.Tex. 1966); *United States v. 23.76 Acres,* 32 F.R.D. 593 (D.Md. 1963); see also an unpublished opinion of Judge Hincks, quoted in *United States v. 48 Jars, etc.,* 23 F.R.D. 192, 198 (D.D.C.1958). On the other hand, the need for a new provision is shown by the many cases in which discovery of expert trial witnesses is needed for effective cross-examination and rebuttal, and yet courts apply the traditional doctrine and refuse disclosure. *E.g., United States v. Certain Parcels of Land,* 25 F.R.D. 192 (N.D.Cal.1959); *United States v. Certain Acres,* 18 F.R.D. 98 (M.D.Ga.1955).

Although the trial problems flowing from lack of discovery of expert witnesses are most acute and noteworthy when the case turns largely on experts, the same problems are encountered when a single expert testifies. Thus, subdivision (b)(4)(A) draws no line between complex and simple cases, or between cases with many experts and those with but one. It establishes by rule substantially the procedure adopted by decision of the court in *Knighton v. Villian & Fassio,* 39 F.R.D. 11 (D.Md.1965). For a full analysis of the problem and strong recommendations to the same effect, see Friedenthal, *Discovery and Use of an Adverse Party's Expert Information,* 14 Stan.L.Rev. 455, 485–488 (1962); Long, *Discovery and Experts under the Federal Rules of Civil Procedure,* 38 F.R.D. 111 (1965).

Past judicial restrictions on discovery of an adversary's expert, particularly as to his opinions, reflect the fear that one side will benefit unduly from the other's better preparation. The procedure established in subsection (b)(4)(A) holds the risk to a minimum. Discovery is limited to trial witnesses, and may be obtained only at a time when the parties know who their expert witnesses will be. A party must as a practical matter prepare his own case in advance of that time, for he can hardly hope to build his case out of his opponent's experts.

Subdivision (b)(4)(A) provides for discovery of an expert who is to testify at the trial. A party can require one who intends to use the expert to state the substance of the testimony that the expert is expected to give. The court may order further discovery, and it has ample power to regulate its timing and scope and to prevent abuse. Ordinarily, the order for further discovery shall compensate the expert for his time, and may compensate the party who intends to use the expert for past expenses reasonably incurred in obtaining facts or opinions from the expert. Those provisions are likely to discourage abusive practices.

Subdivision (b)(4)(B) deals with an expert who has been retained or specially employed by the party in anticipation of litigation or preparation for trial (thus excluding an expert who is simply a general employee of the party not specially employed on the case), but who is not expected to be called as a witness. Under its provisions, a party may discover facts known or opinions held by such an expert only on a showing of exceptional circumstances under which it is impracticable for the party seeking discovery to obtain facts or opinions on the same subject by other means.

Subdivision (b)(4)(B) is concerned only with experts retained or specially consulted in relation to trial preparation. Thus the subdivision precludes discovery against experts who were informally consulted in preparation for trial, but not retained or specially employed. As an ancillary procedure, a party may on a proper showing require the other party to name experts retained or specially employed, but not those informally consulted.

These new provisions of subdivision (b)(4) repudiate the few decisions that have held an expert's information privileged simply because of his status as an expert, *e.g.*, *American Oil Co. v. Pennsylvania Petroleum Products Co.*, 23 F.R.D. 680, 685–686 (D.R.I.1959). See *Louisell, Modern California Discovery* 315–316 (1963). They also reject as ill-considered the decisions which have sought to bring expert information within the work-product doctrine. See *United States v. McKay*, 372 F.2d 174, 176–177 (5th Cir. 1967). The provisions adopt a form of the more recently developed doctrine of "unfairness". See *e.g.*, *United States v. 23.76 Acres of Land*, 32 F.R.D. 593, 597 (D.Md.1963); Louisell, *supra*, at 317–318; 4 *Moore's Federal Practice* 26.24 (2d ed. 1966).

Under subdivision (b)(4)(C), the court is directed or authorized to issue protective orders, including an order that the expert be paid a reasonable fee for time spent in responding to discovery, and that the party whose expert is made subject to discovery be paid a fair portion of the fees and expenses that the party incurred in obtaining information from the expert. The court may issue the latter order as a condition of discovery, or it may delay the order until after discovery is completed. These provisions for fees and expenses meet the objection that it is unfair to permit one side to obtain without cost the benefit of an expert's work for which the other side has paid, often a substantial sum. E.g., *Lewis v. United Air Lines Transp. Corp.*, 32 F.Supp. 21 (W.D.Pa.1940); *Walsh v. Reynolds Metal Co.*, 15 F.R.D. 376 (D.N.J.1954). On the other hand, a party may not obtain discovery simply by offering to pay fees and expenses. Cf. *Boynton v. R. J. Reynolds Tobacco Co.*, 36 F.Supp. 593 (D.Mass.1941).

In instances of discovery under subdivision (b)(4)(B), the court is directed to award fees and expenses to the other party, since the information is of direct value to the discovering party's preparation of his case. In ordering discovery under (b)(4)(A)(ii), the court has discretion whether to award fees and expenses to the other party; its decision should depend upon whether the discovering party is simply learning about the other party's case or is going beyond this to develop his own case. Even in cases where the court is directed to issue a protective order, it may decline to do so if it finds that manifest injustice would result. Thus, the court can protect, when necessary and appropriate, the interests of an indigent party.

Subdivision (c)—Protective Orders. The provisions of existing Rule 30(b) are transferred to this subdivision (c), as part of the rearrangement of Rule 26. The language has been changed to give it application to discovery generally. The subdivision recognizes the power of the court in the district where a deposition is being taken to make protective orders. Such power is needed when the deposition is being taken far from the court where the action is pending. The court in the district where the deposition is being taken may, and frequently will, remit the deponent or party to the court where the action is pending.

In addition, drafting changes are made to carry out and clarify the sense of the rule. Insertions are made to avoid any possible implication that a protective order does not extend to "time" as well as to "place" or may not safeguard against "undue burden or expense."

The new reference to trade secrets and other confidential commercial information reflects existing law. The courts have not given trade secrets automatic and complete immunity against disclosure, but have in each case weighed their claim to privacy against the need for disclosure. Frequently, they have been afforded a limited protection. See, *e.g.*, *Covey Oil Co. v. Continental Oil Co.*, 340 F.2d 993 (10th Cir. 1965); *Julius M. Ames Co. v. Bostitch, Inc.*, 235 F.Supp. 856 (S.D.N.Y.1964).

The subdivision contains new matter relating to sanctions. When a motion for a protective order is made and the court is disposed to deny it, the court may go a step further and issue an order to provide or permit discovery. This will bring the sanctions of Rule 37(b) directly into play. Since the court has heard the contentions of all interested persons, an affirmative order is justified. See *Rosenberg, Sanctions to Effectuate Pretrial Discovery*, 58 Col.L.Rev. 480, 492–493 (1958). In addition, the court may require the payment of expenses incurred in relation to the motion.

Subdivision (d)—Sequence and Priority. This new provision is concerned with the sequence in which parties may proceed with discovery and with related problems of timing. The principal effects of the new provision are first, to eliminate any fixed priority in the sequence of discovery, and second, to make clear and explicit the court's power to establish priority by an order issued in a particular case.

A priority rule developed by some courts, which confers priority on the party who first serves notice of taking a deposition, is unsatisfactory in several important respects:

First, this priority rule permits a party to establish a priority running to all depositions as to which he has given earlier notice. Since he can on a given day serve notice of taking many depositions he is in a position to delay his adversary's taking of depositions for an inordinate time. Some courts have ruled that deposition priority also permits a party to delay his answers to interrogatories and production of documents. *E.g., E. I. du Pont de Nemours & Co. v. Phillips Petroleum Co.*, 23 F.R.D. 237 (D.Del.1959); *but cf. Sturdevant v. Sears, Roebuck & Co.*, 32 F.R.D. 426 (W.D.Mo. 1963).

Second, since notice is the key to priority, if both parties wish to take depositions first a race results. See *Caldwell-Clements, Inc. v. McGraw-Hill Pub. Co.*, 11 F.R.D. 156 (S.D.N.Y.1951) (description of tactics used by parties). But the existing rules on notice of deposition create a race with runners starting from different positions. The plaintiff may not give notice without leave of court until 20 days after commencement of the action, whereas the defendant may serve notice at any time after commencement. Thus, a careful and prompt defendant can almost always secure priority. This advantage of defendants is fortuitous, because the purpose of requiring plaintiff to wait 20 days is to afford defendant an opportunity to obtain counsel, not to confer priority.

Third, although courts have ordered a change in the normal sequence of discovery on a number of occasions, *e.g., Kaeppler v. James H. Matthews & Co.*, 200 F.Supp. 229 (E.D.Pa.1961); *Park & Tilford Distillers Corp. v. Distillers Co.*, 19 F.R.D. 169 (S.D.N.Y.1956), and have at all times avowed discretion to vary the usual priority, most commentators are agreed that courts in fact grant relief only for "the most obviously compelling reasons." 2A Barron & Holtzoff, *Federal Practice and Procedure* 44–47 (Wright ed. 1961); see also Younger, *Priority of Pretrial Examination in the Federal Courts—A Comment*, 34 N.Y.U.L.Rev. 1271 (1959); Freund, *The Pleading and Pretrial of an Antitrust Claim*, 46 Corn.L.Q. 555, 564 (1964). Discontent with the fairness of actual practice has been evinced by other observers. Comments, 59 Yale L.J. 117, 134–136 (1949); Yudkin, *Some Refinements in Federal Discovery Procedure*, 11 Fed.B.J. 289, 296–297 (1951); *Developments in the Law-Discovery*, 74 Harv.L.Rev. 940, 954–958 (1961).

Despite these difficulties, some courts have adhered to the priority rule, presumably because it provides a test which is easily understood and applied by the parties without much court intervention. It thus permits deposition discovery to function extrajudicially, which the rules provide for and the courts desire. For these same reasons, courts are reluctant to make numerous exceptions to the rule.

The Columbia Survey makes clear that the problem of priority does not affect litigants generally. It found that most litigants do not move quickly to obtain discovery. In over half of the cases, both parties waited at least 50 days. During the first 20 days after commencement of the action—the period when defendant might assure his priority by noticing depositions—16 percent of the defendants acted to obtain discovery. A race could not have occurred in more than 16 percent of the cases and it undoubtedly occurred in fewer. On the other hand, five times as many defendants as plaintiffs served notice of deposition during the first 19 days. To the same effect, see Comment, *Tactical Use and Abuse of Depositions Under the Federal Rules*, 59 Yale L.J. 117, 134 (1949).

These findings do not mean, however, that the priority rule is satisfactory or that a problem of priority does not exist. The court decisions show that parties do battle on this issue and carry their disputes to court. The statistics show that these court cases are not typical. By the same token, they reveal that more extensive exercise of judicial discretion to vary the priority will not bring a flood of litigation, and that a change in the priority rule will in fact affect only a small fraction of the cases.

It is contended by some that there is no need to alter the existing priority practice. In support, it is urged that there is no evidence that injustices in fact result from present practice and that, in any event, the courts can and do promulgate local rules, as in New York, to deal with local situations and issue orders to avoid possible injustice in particular cases.

Subdivision (d) is based on the contrary view that the rule of priority based on notice is unsatisfactory and unfair in its operation. Subdivision (d) follows an approach adapted from Civil Rule 4 of the District Court for the Southern District of New York. That rule provides that starting 40 days after commencement of the action, unless otherwise ordered by the court, the fact that one party is taking a deposition shall not prevent another party from doing so "concurrently." In practice, the depositions are not usually taken simultaneously; rather, the parties work out arrangements for alternation in the taking of depositions. One party may take a complete deposition and then the other, or, if the depositions are extensive, one party deposes for a set time, and then the other. See *Caldwell-Clements, Inc. v. McCraw-Hill Pub. Co.*, 11 F.R.D. 156 (S.D.N.Y.1951).

In principle, one party's initiation of discovery should not wait upon the other's completion, unless delay is dictated by special considerations. Clearly the principle is feasible with respect to all methods of discovery other than depositions. And the experience of the Southern District of New York shows that the principle can be applied to depositions as well. The courts have not had an increase in motion business on this matter. Once it is clear to lawyers that they bargain on an equal footing, they are usually able to arrange for an orderly succession of depositions without judicial intervention. Professor Moore has called attention to Civil Rule 4 and suggested that it may usefully be extended to other areas. 4 *Moore's Federal Practice* 1154 (2d ed. 1966).

The court may upon motion and by order grant priority in a particular case. But a local court rule purporting to confer priority in certain classes of cases would be inconsistent with this subdivision and thus void.

Subdivision (e)—Supplementation of Responses. The rules do not now state whether interrogatories (and questions at deposition as well as requests for inspection and admissions) impose a "continuing burden" on the responding party to supplement his answers if he obtains new information. The issue is acute when new information renders substantially incomplete or inaccurate an answer which was complete and accurate when made. It is essential that the rules provide an answer to this question. The parties can adjust to a rule either way, once they know what it is. See 4 *Moore's Federal Practice* ¶33.25[4] (2d ed. 1966).

Arguments can be made both ways. Imposition of a continuing burden reduces the proliferation of additional sets of interrogatories. Some courts have adopted local rules establishing such a burden. *E.g.*, E.D.Pa.R. 20(f), quoted in *Taggart v. Vermont Transp. Co.*, 32 F.R.D. 587 (E.D.Pa.1963); D.Me.R. 15(c). Others have imposed the burden by decision.

E.g., Chenault v. Nebraska Farm Products, Inc., 9 F.R.D. 529, 533 (D.Nebr.1949). On the other hand, there are serious objections to the burden, especially in protracted cases. Although the party signs the answers, it is his lawyer who understands their significance and bears the responsibility to bring answers up to date. In a complex case all sorts of information reaches the party, who little understands its bearing on answers previously given to interrogatories. In practice, therefore, the lawyer under a continuing burden must periodically recheck all interrogatories and canvass all new information. But a full set of new answers may no longer be needed by the interrogating party. Some issues will have been dropped from the case, some questions are now seen as unimportant, and other questions must in any event be reformulated. See *Novick v. Pennsylvania R.R.,* 18 F.R.D. 296, 298 (W.D.Pa.1955).

Subdivision (e) provides that a party is not under a continuing burden except as expressly provided. Cf. Note, 68 Harv. L.Rev. 673, 677 (1955). An exception is made as to the identity of persons having knowledge of discoverable matters, because of the obvious importance to each side of knowing all witnesses and because information about witnesses routinely comes to each lawyer's attention. Many of the decisions on the issue of a continuing burden have in fact concerned the identity of witnesses. An exception is also made as to expert trial witnesses in order to carry out the provisions of Rule 26(b)(4). See *Diversified Products Corp. v. Sports Center Co.,* 42 F.R.D. 3 (D.Md.1967).

Another exception is made for the situation in which a party, or more frequently his lawyer, obtains actual knowledge that a prior response is incorrect. This exception does not impose a duty to check the accuracy of prior responses, but it prevents knowing concealment by a party or attorney. Finally, a duty to supplement may be imposed by order of the court in a particular case (including an order resulting from a pretrial conference) or by agreement of the parties. A party may of course make a new discovery request which requires supplementation of prior responses.

The duty will normally be enforced, in those limited instances where it is imposed, through sanctions imposed by the trial court, including exclusion of evidence, continuance, or other action, as the court may deem appropriate.

1980 Amendment

Subdivision (f). This subdivision is new. There has been widespread criticism of abuse of discovery. The Committee has considered a number of proposals to eliminate abuse, including a change in Rule 26(b)(1) with respect to the scope of discovery and a change in Rule 33(a) to limit the number of questions that can be asked by interrogatories to parties.

The Committee believes that abuse of discovery, while very serious in certain cases, is not so general as to require such basic changes in the rules that govern discovery in all cases. A very recent study of discovery in selected metropolitan districts tends to support its belief. P. Connolly, E. Holleman, & M. Kuhlman, *Judicial Controls and the Civil Litigative Process: Discovery* (Federal Judicial Center, 1978). In the judgment of the Committee abuse can best be prevented by intervention by the court as soon as abuse is threatened.

To this end this subdivision provides that counsel who has attempted without success to effect with opposing counsel a reasonable program or plan for discovery is entitled to the assistance of the court.

It is not contemplated that requests for discovery conferences will be made routinely. A relatively narrow discovery dispute should be resolved by resort to Rules 26(c) or 37(a), and if it appears that a request for a conference is in fact grounded in such a dispute, the court may refer counsel to those rules. If the court is persuaded that a request is frivolous or vexatious, it can strike it. See Rules 11 and 7(b)(2).

A number of courts routinely consider discovery matters in preliminary pretrial conferences held shortly after the pleadings are closed. This subdivision does not interfere with such a practice. It authorizes the court to combine a discovery conference with a pretrial conference under Rule 16 if a pretrial conference is held sufficiently early to prevent or curb abuse.

1983 Amendment

Excessive discovery and evasion or resistance to reasonable discovery requests pose significant problems. Recent studies have made some attempt to determine the sources and extent of the difficulties. See Brazil, *Civil Discovery: Lawyers' Views of its Effectiveness, Principal Problems and Abuses,* American Bar Foundation (1980); Connolly, Holleman & Kuhlman, *Judicial Controls and the Civil Litigative Process: Discovery,* Federal Judicial Center (1978); Ellington, *A Study of Sanctions for Discovery Abuse,* Department of Justice (1979); Schroeder & Frank, *The Proposed Changes in the Discovery Rules,* 1978 Ariz.St.L.J. 475.

The purpose of discovery is to provide a mechanism for making relevant information available to the litigants. "Mutual knowledge of all the relevant facts gathered by both parties is essential to proper litigation." *Hickman v. Taylor,* 329 U.S. 495, 507 (1947). Thus the spirit of the rules is violated when advocates attempt to use discovery tools as tactical weapons rather than to expose the facts and illuminate the issues by overuse of discovery or unnecessary use of defensive weapons or evasive responses. All of this results in excessively costly and time-consuming activities that are disproportionate to the nature of the case, the amount involved, or the issues or values at stake.

Given our adversary tradition and the current discovery rules, it is not surprising that there are many opportunities, if not incentives, for attorneys to engage in discovery that, although authorized by the broad, permissive terms of the rules, nevertheless results in delay. See Brazil, *The Adversary Character of Civil Discovery: A Critique and Proposals for Change,* 31 Vand.L.Rev. 1259 (1978). As a result, it has been said that the rules have "not infrequently [been] exploited to the disadvantage of justice." *Herbert v. Lando,* 441 U.S. 153, 179 (1979) (Powell, J., concurring). These practices impose costs on an already overburdened system and impede the fundamental goal of the "just, speedy, and inexpensive determination of every action." Fed.R.Civ.P. 1.

Subdivision (a); Discovery Methods. The deletion of the last sentence of Rule 26(a)(1), which provided that unless the court ordered otherwise under Rule 26(c) "the frequency of use" of the various discovery methods was not to be limited, is an attempt to address the problem of duplicative, redundant, and excessive discovery and to reduce it. The amendment, in conjunction with the changes in Rule 26(b)(1), is designed to encourage district judges to identify instances of needless discovery and to limit the use of the various discovery devices accordingly. The question may be raised by one of the parties, typically on a motion for a protective order, or by the

---

court on its own initiative. It is entirely appropriate to consider a limitation on the frequency of use of discovery at a discovery conference under Rule 26(f) or at any other pretrial conference authorized by these rules. In considering the discovery needs of a particular case, the court should consider the factors described in Rule 26(b)(1).

Subdivision (b); Discovery Scope and Limits. Rule 26(b)(1) has been amended to add a sentence to deal with the problem of over-discovery. The objective is to guard against redundant or disproportionate discovery by giving the court authority to reduce the amount of discovery that may be directed to matters that are otherwise proper subjects of inquiry. The new sentence is intended to encourage judges to be more aggressive in identifying and discouraging discovery overuse. The grounds mentioned in the amended rule for limiting discovery reflect the existing practice of many courts in issuing protective orders under Rule 26(c). See, e.g., *Carlson Cos. v. Sperry & Hutchinson Co.*, 374 F.Supp. 1080 (D.Minn.1974); *Dolgow v. Anderson*, 53 F.R.D. 661 (E.D.N.Y. 1971); *Mitchell v. American Tobacco Co.*, 33 F.R.D. 262 (M.D.Pa.1963); *Welty v. Clute*, 1 F.R.D. 446 (W.D.N.Y.1941). On the whole, however, district judges have been reluctant to limit the use of the discovery devices. See, *e.g., Apco Oil Co. v. Certified Transp., Inc.*, 46 F.R.D. 428 (W.D.Mo.1969). See generally 8 Wright & Miller, *Federal Practice and Procedure: Civil* §§ 2036, 2037, 2039, 2040 (1970).

The first element of the standard, Rule 26(b)(1)(i), is designed to minimize redundancy in discovery and encourage attorneys to be sensitive to the comparative costs of different methods of securing information. Subdivision (b)(1)(ii) also seeks to reduce repetitiveness and to oblige lawyers to think through their discovery activities in advance so that full utilization is made of each deposition, document request, or set of interrogatories. The elements of Rule 26(b)(1)(iii) address the problem of discovery that is disproportionate to the individual lawsuit as measured by such matters as its nature and complexity, the importance of the issues at stake in a case seeking damages, the limitations on a financially weak litigant to withstand extensive opposition to a discovery program or to respond to discovery requests, and the significance of the substantive issues, as measured in philosophic, social, or institutional terms. Thus the rule recognizes that many cases in public policy spheres, such as employment practices, free speech, and other matters, may have importance far beyond the monetary amount involved. The court must apply the standards in an even-handed manner that will prevent use of discovery to wage a war of attrition or as a device to coerce a party, whether financially weak or affluent.

The rule contemplates greater judicial involvement in the discovery process and thus acknowledges the reality that it cannot always operate on a self-regulating basis. See Connolly, Holleman & Kuhlman, *Judicial Controls and the Civil Litigative Process: Discovery* 77, Federal Judicial Center (1978). In an appropriate case the court could restrict the number of depositions, interrogatories, or the scope of a production request. But the court must be careful not to deprive a party of discovery that is reasonably necessary to afford a fair opportunity to develop and prepare the case.

The court may act on motion, or its own initiative. It is entirely appropriate to resort to the amended rule in conjunction with a discovery conference under Rule 26(f) or one of the other pretrial conferences authorized by the rules.

Subdivision (g); Signing of Discovery Requests, Responses, and Objections. Rule 26(g) imposes an affirmative duty to engage in pretrial discovery in a responsible manner that is consistent with the spirit and purposes of Rules 26 through 37. In addition, Rule 26(g) is designed to curb discovery abuse by explicitly encouraging the imposition of sanctions. The subdivision provides a deterrent to both excessive discovery and evasion by imposing a certification requirement that obliges each attorney to stop and think about the legitimacy of a discovery request, a response thereto, or an objection. The term "response" includes answers to interrogatories and to requests to admit as well as responses to production requests.

If primary responsibility for conducting discovery is to continue to rest with the litigants, they must be obliged to act responsibly and avoid abuse. With this in mind, Rule 26(g), which parallels the amendments to Rule 11, requires an attorney or unrepresented party to sign each discovery request, response, or objection. Motions relating to discovery are governed by Rule 11. However, since a discovery request, response, or objection usually deals with more specific subject matter than motions or papers, the elements that must be certified in connection with the former are spelled out more completely. The signature is a certification of the elements set forth in Rule 26(g).

Although the certification duty requires the lawyer to pause and consider the reasonableness of his request, response, or objection, it is not meant to discourage or restrict necessary and legitimate discovery. The rule simply requires that the attorney make a reasonable inquiry into the factual basis of his response, request, or objection.

The duty to make a "reasonable inquiry" is satisfied if the investigation undertaken by the attorney and the conclusions drawn therefrom are reasonable under the circumstances. It is an objective standard similar to the one imposed by Rule 11. See the Advisory Committee Note to Rule 11. See also *Kinee v. Abraham Lincoln Fed. Sav. & Loan Ass'n*, 365 F.Supp. 975 (E.D.Pa.1973). In making the inquiry, the attorney may rely on assertions by the client and on communications with other counsel in the case as long as that reliance is appropriate under the circumstances. Ultimately, what is reasonable is a matter for the court to decide on the totality of the circumstances.

Rule 26(g) does not require the signing attorney to certify the truthfulness of the client's factual responses to a discovery request. Rather, the signature certifies that the lawyer has made a reasonable effort to assure that the client has provided all the information and documents available to him that are responsive to the discovery demand. Thus, the lawyer's certification under Rule 26(g) should be distinguished from other signature requirements in the rules, such as those in Rules 30(e) and 33.

Nor does the rule require a party or an attorney to disclose privileged communications or work product in order to show that a discovery request, response, or objection is substantially justified. The provisions of Rule 26(c), including appropriate orders after *in camera* inspection by the court, remain available to protect a party claiming privilege or work product protection.

The signing requirement means that every discovery request, response, or objection should be grounded on a theory that is reasonable under the precedents or a good faith belief as to what should be the law. This standard is heavily dependent on the circumstances of each case. The certification speaks as of the time it is made. The duty to supplement discovery responses continues to be governed by Rule 26(e).

Concern about discovery abuse has led to widespread recognition that there is a need for more aggressive judicial control and supervision. *ACF Industries, Inc. v. EEOC*, 439 U.S. 1081 (1979) (certiorari denied) (Powell, J., dissenting). Sanctions to deter discovery abuse would be more effective if they were diligently applied "not merely to penalize those whose conduct may be deemed to warrant such a sanction, but to deter those who might be tempted to such conduct in the absence of such a deterrent." *National Hockey League v. Metropolitan Hockey Club*, 427 U.S. 639, 643 (1976). See also Note, *The Emerging Deterrence Orientation in the Imposition of Discovery Sanctions*, 91 Harv.L.Rev. 1033 (1978). Thus the premise of Rule 26(g) is that imposing sanctions on attorneys who fail to meet the rule's standards will significantly reduce abuse by imposing disadvantages therefor.

Because of the asserted reluctance to impose sanctions on attorneys who abuse the discovery rules, see Brazil, *Civil Discovery: Lawyers' Views of its Effectiveness, Principal Problems and Abuses*, American Bar Foundation (1980); Ellington, *A Study of Sanctions for Discovery Abuse*, Department of Justice (1979), Rule 26(g) makes explicit the authority judges now have to impose appropriate sanctions and requires them to use it. This authority derives from Rule 37, 28 U.S.C. § 1927, and the court's inherent power. See *Roadway Express, Inc. v. Piper*, 447 U.S. 752 (1980); *Martin v. Bell Helicopter Co.*, 85 F.R.D. 654, 661–62 (D.Col.1980); Note, *Sanctions Imposed by Courts on Attorneys Who Abuse the Judicial Process*, 44 U.Chi.L.Rev. 619 (1977). The new rule mandates that sanctions be imposed on attorneys who fail to meet the standards established in the first portion of Rule 26(g). The nature of the sanction is a matter of judicial discretion to be exercised in light of the particular circumstances. The court may take into account any failure by the party seeking sanctions to invoke protection under Rule 26(c) at an early stage in the litigation.

The sanctioning process must comport with due process requirements. The kind of notice and hearing required will depend on the facts of the case and the severity of the sanction being considered. To prevent the proliferation of the sanction procedure and to avoid multiple hearings, discovery in any sanction proceeding normally should be permitted only when it is clearly required by the interests of justice. In most cases the court will be aware of the circumstances and only a brief hearing should be necessary.

1987 Amendment

The amendments are technical. No substantive change is intended.

1993 Amendment

Subdivision (a). Through the addition of paragraphs (1)–(4), this subdivision imposes on parties a duty to disclose, without awaiting formal discovery requests, certain basic information that is needed in most cases to prepare for trial or make an informed decision about settlement. The rule requires all parties (1) early in the case to exchange information regarding potential witnesses, documentary evidence, damages, and insurance, (2) at an appropriate time during the discovery period to identify expert witnesses and provide a detailed written statement of the testimony that may be offered at trial through specially retained experts, and (3) as the trial date approaches to identify the particular evidence that may be offered at trial. The enumeration in Rule 26(a) of items to be disclosed does not prevent a court from requiring by order or local rule that the parties disclose additional information without a discovery request. Nor are parties precluded from using traditional discovery methods to obtain further information regarding these matters, as for example asking an expert during a deposition about testimony given in other litigation beyond the four-year period specified in Rule 26(a)(2)(B).

A major purpose of the revision is to accelerate the exchange of basic information about the case and to eliminate the paper work involved in requesting such information, and the rule should be applied in a manner to achieve those objectives. The concepts of imposing a duty of disclosure were set forth in Brazil, *The Adversary Character of Civil Discovery: A Critique and Proposals for Change*, 31 *Vand. L.Rev.* 1348 (1978), and Schwarzer, *The Federal Rules, the Adversary Process, and Discovery Reform*, 50 *U.Pitt.L.Rev. 703, 721–23 (1989)*.

The rule is based upon the experience of district courts that have required disclosure of some of this information through local rules, court-approved standard interrogatories, and standing orders. Most have required pretrial disclosure of the kind of information described in Rule 26(a)(3). Many have required written reports from experts containing information like that specified in Rule 26(a)(2)(B). While far more limited, the experience of the few state and federal courts that have required pre-discovery exchange of core information such as is contemplated in Rule 26(a)(1) indicates that savings in time and expense can be achieved, particularly if the litigants meet and discuss the issues in the case as a predicate for this exchange and if a judge supports the process, as by using the results to guide further proceedings in the case. Courts in Canada and the United Kingdom have for many years required disclosure of certain information without awaiting a request from an adversary.

Paragraph (1). As the functional equivalent of court-ordered interrogatories, this paragraph requires early disclosure, without need for any request, of four types of information that have been customarily secured early in litigation through formal discovery. The introductory clause permits the court, by local rule, to exempt all or particular types of cases from these disclosure requirement [*sic*] or to modify the nature of the information to be disclosed. It is expected that courts would, for example, exempt cases like Social Security reviews and government collection cases in which discovery would not be appropriate or would be unlikely. By order the court may eliminate or modify the disclosure requirements in a particular case, and similarly the parties, unless precluded by order or local rule, can stipulate to elimination or modification of the requirements for that case. The disclosure obligations specified in paragraph (1) will not be appropriate for all cases, and it is expected that changes in these obligations will be made by the court or parties when the circumstances warrant.

Authorization of these local variations is, in large measure, included in order to accommodate the Civil Justice Reform Act of 1990, which implicitly directs districts to experiment during the study period with differing procedures to reduce the time and expense of civil litigation. The civil justice delay and expense reduction plans adopted by the courts under the Act differ as to the type, form, and timing of disclosures required. Section 105(c)(1) of the Act calls for a report by the Judicial Conference to Congress by December 31, 1995, comparing experience in twenty of these courts; and section 105(c)(2)(B) contemplates that some changes in the Rules may then be needed. While these studies may indicate the desirability of further changes in Rule 26(a)(1), these changes probably could not become effective before December 1998 at the earliest. In the meantime, the present revision puts in place a series of disclosure obligations that, unless a court acts affirmatively to impose other requirements or indeed to reject all such requirements for the present, are designed to eliminate certain discovery, help focus the discovery that is needed, and facilitate preparation for trial or settlement.

Subparagraph (A) requires identification of all persons who, based on the investigation conducted thus far, are likely to have discoverable information relevant to the factual disputes between the parties. All persons with such information should be disclosed, whether or not their testimony will be supportive of the position of the disclosing party. As officers of the court, counsel are expected to disclose the identity of those persons who may be used by them as witnesses or who, if their potential testimony were known, might reasonably be expected to be deposed or called as a witness by any of the other parties. Indicating briefly the general topics on which such persons have information should not be burdensome, and will assist other parties in deciding which depositions will actually be needed.

Subparagraph (B) is included as a substitute for the inquiries routinely made about the existence and location of documents and other tangible things in the possession, custody, or control of the disclosing party. Although, unlike subdivision (a)(3)(C), an itemized listing of each exhibit is not required, the disclosure should describe and categorize, to the extent identified during the initial investigation, the nature and location of potentially relevant documents and records, including computerized data and other electronically-recorded information, sufficiently to enable opposing parties (1) to make an informed decision concerning which documents might need to be examined, at least initially, and (2) to frame their document requests in a manner likely to avoid squabbles resulting from the wording of the requests. As with potential witnesses, the requirement for disclosure of documents applies to all potentially relevant items then known to the party, whether or not supportive of its contentions in the case.

Unlike subparagraphs (C) and (D), subparagraph (B) does not require production of any documents. Of course, in cases involving few documents a disclosing party may prefer to provide copies of the documents rather than describe them, and the rule is written to afford this option to the disclosing party. If, as will be more typical, only the description is provided, the other parties are expected to obtain the documents desired by proceeding under Rule 34 or through informal requests. The disclosing party does not, by describing documents under subparagraph (B), waive its right to object to production on the basis of privilege or work product protection, or to assert that the documents are not sufficiently relevant to justify the burden or expense of production.

The initial disclosure requirements of subparagraphs (A) and (B) are limited to identification of potential evidence "relevant to disputed facts alleged with particularity in the pleadings." There is no need for a party to identify potential evidence with respect to allegations that are admitted. Broad, vague, and conclusory allegations sometimes tolerated in notice pleading—for example, the assertion that a product with many component parts is defective in some unspecified manner—should not impose upon responding parties the obligation at that point to search for and identify all persons possibly involved in, or all documents affecting, the design,

manufacture, and assembly of the product. The greater the specificity and clarity of the allegations in the pleadings, the more complete should be the listing of potential witnesses and types of documentary evidence. Although paragraphs (1)(A) and (1)(B) by their terms refer to the factual disputes defined in the pleadings, the rule contemplates that these issues would be informally refined and clarified during the meeting of the parties under subdivision (f) and that the disclosure obligations would be adjusted in the light of these discussions. The disclosure requirements should, in short, be applied with common sense in light of the principles of Rule 1, keeping in mind the salutary purposes that the rule is intended to accomplish. The litigants should not indulge in gamesmanship with respect to the disclosure obligations.

Subparagraph (C) imposes a burden of disclosure that includes the functional equivalent of a standing Request for Production under Rule 34. A party claiming damages or other monetary relief must, in addition to disclosing the calculation of such damages, make available the supporting documents for inspection and copying as if a request for such materials had been made under Rule 34. This obligation applies only with respect to documents then reasonably available to it and not privileged or protected as work product. Likewise, a party would not be expected to provide a calculation of damages which, as in many patent infringement actions, depends on information in the possession of another party or person.

Subparagraph (D) replaces subdivision (b)(2) of Rule 26, and provides that liability insurance policies be made available for inspection and copying. The last two sentences of that subdivision have been omitted as unnecessary, not to signify any change of law. The disclosure of insurance information does not thereby render such information admissible in evidence. See Rule 411, Federal Rules of Evidence. Nor does subparagraph (D) require disclosure of applications for insurance, though in particular cases such information may be discoverable in accordance with revised subdivision (a)(5).

Unless the court directs a different time, the disclosures required by subdivision (a)(1) are to be made at or within 10 days after the meeting of the parties under subdivision (f). One of the purposes of this meeting is to refine the factual disputes with respect to which disclosures should be made under paragraphs (1)(A) and (1)(B), particularly if an answer has not been filed by a defendant, or, indeed, to afford the parties an opportunity to modify by stipulation the timing or scope of these obligations. The time of this meeting is generally left to the parties provided it is held at least 14 days before a scheduling conference is held or before a scheduling order is due under Rule 16(b). In cases in which no scheduling conference is held, this will mean that the meeting must ordinarily be held within 75 days after a defendant has first appeared in the case and hence that the initial disclosures would be due no later than 85 days after the first appearance of a defendant.

Before making its disclosures, a party has the obligation under subdivision (g)(1) to make a reasonable inquiry into the facts of the case. The rule does not demand an exhaustive investigation at this stage of the case, but one that is reasonable under the circumstances, focusing on the facts that are alleged with particularity in the pleadings. The type of investigation that can be expected at this point will vary based upon such factors as the number and complexity of the issues; the location, nature, number, and availability of potentially relevant witnesses and documents; the extent of past working relationships between the attorney and the client, particularly in handling related or similar litigation; and of course how long the party has to conduct an investigation, either before or after filing of the case. As provided in the last sentence of subdivision (a)(1), a party is not excused from the duty of disclosure merely because its investigation is incomplete. The party should make its initial disclosures based on the pleadings and the information then reasonably available to it. As its investigation continues and as the issues in the pleadings are clarified, it should supplement its disclosures as required by subdivision (e)(1). A party is not relieved from its obligation of disclosure merely because another party has not made its disclosures or has made an inadequate disclosure.

It will often be desirable, particularly if the claims made in the complaint are broadly stated, for the parties to have their Rule 26(f) meeting early in the case, perhaps before a defendant has answered the complaint or had time to conduct other than a cursory investigation. In such circumstances, in order to facilitate more meaningful and useful initial disclosures, they can and should stipulate to a period of more than 10 days after the meeting in which to make these disclosures, at least for defendants who had no advance notice of the potential litigation. A stipulation at an early meeting affording such a defendant at least 60 days after receiving the complaint in which to make its disclosures under subdivision (a)(1)—a period that is two weeks longer than the time formerly specified for responding to interrogatories served with a complaint—should be adequate and appropriate in most cases.

Paragraph (2). This paragraph imposes an additional duty to disclose information regarding expert testimony sufficiently in advance of trial that opposing parties have a reasonable opportunity to prepare for effective cross examination and perhaps arrange for expert testimony from other witnesses. Normally the court should prescribe a time for these disclosures in a scheduling order under Rule 16(b), and in most cases the party with the burden of proof on an issue should disclose its expert testimony on that issue before other parties are required to make their disclosures with respect to that issue. In the absence of such a direction, the disclosures are to be made by all parties at least 90 days before the trial date or the date by which the case is to be ready for trial, except that an additional 30 days is allowed (unless the court specifies another time) for disclosure of expert testimony to be used solely to contradict or rebut the testimony that may be presented by another party's expert. For a discussion of procedures that have been used to enhance the reliability of expert testimony, see M. Graham, *Expert Witness Testimony and the Federal Rules of Evidence: Insuring Adequate Assurance of Trustworthiness*, 1986 U.Ill.L.Rev. 90.

Paragraph (2)(B) requires that persons retained or specially employed to provide expert testimony, or whose duties as an employee of the party regularly involve the giving of expert testimony, must prepare a detailed and complete written report, stating the testimony the witness is expected to present during direct examination, together with the reasons therefor. The information disclosed under the former rule in answering interrogatories about the "substance" of expert testimony was frequently so sketchy and vague that it rarely dispensed with the need to depose the expert and often was even of little help in preparing for a deposition of the witness. Revised Rule 37(c)(1) provides an incentive for full disclosure; namely, that a party will not ordinarily be permitted to use on direct examination any expert testimony not so disclosed. Rule 26(a)(2)(B) does not preclude counsel from providing assistance to experts in preparing the reports, and indeed, with experts such as automobile mechanics, this assistance may be needed. Nevertheless, the report, which is intended to set forth the substance of the direct examination, should be written in a manner that reflects the testimony to be given by the witness and it must be signed by the witness.

The report is to disclose the data and other information considered by the expert and any exhibits or charts that summarize or support the expert's opinions. Given this obligation of disclosure, litigants should no longer be able to argue that materials furnished to their experts to be used in forming their opinions—whether or not ultimately relied upon by the expert—are privileged or otherwise protected from disclosure when such persons are testifying or being deposed.

Revised subdivision (b)(4)(A) authorizes the deposition of expert witnesses. Since depositions of experts required to prepare a written report may be taken only after the report has been served, the length of the deposition of such experts should be reduced, and in many cases the report may eliminate the need for a deposition. Revised subdivision (e)(1) requires disclosure of any material changes made in the opinions of an expert from whom a report is required, whether the changes are in the written report or in testimony given at a deposition.

For convenience, this rule and revised Rule 30 continue to use the term "expert" to refer to those persons who will testify under Rule 702 of the Federal Rules of Evidence with respect to scientific, technical, and other specialized matters. The requirement of a written report in paragraph (2)(B), however, applies only to those experts who are retained or specially employed to provide such testimony in the case or whose duties as an employee of a party regularly involve the giving of such testimony. A treating physician, for example, can be deposed or called to testify at trial without any requirement for a written report. By local rule, order, or written stipulation, the requirement of a written report may be waived for particular experts or imposed upon additional persons who will provide opinions under Rule 702.

Paragraph (3). This paragraph imposes an additional duty to disclose, without any request, information customarily needed in final preparation for trial. These disclosures are to be made in accordance with schedules adopted by the court under Rule 16(b) or by special order. If no such schedule is directed by the court, the disclosures are to be made at least 30 days before commencement of the trial. By its terms, rule 26(a)(3) does not require disclosure of evidence to be used solely for impeachment purposes; however, disclosure of such evidence—as well as other items relating to conduct of trial—may be required by local rule or a pretrial order.

Subparagraph (A) requires the parties to designate the persons whose testimony they may present as substantive evidence at trial, whether in person or by deposition. Those who will probably be called as witnesses should be listed separately from those who are not likely to be called but who are being listed in order to preserve the right to do so if needed because of developments during trial. Revised Rule 37(c)(1) provides that only persons so listed may be used at trial to present substantive evidence. This restriction does not apply unless the omission was "without substantial justification" and hence would not bar an unlisted witness if the need for such testimony is based upon developments during trial that could not reasonably have been anticipated—*e.g.*, a change of testimony.

Listing a witness does not obligate the party to secure the attendance of the person at trial, but should preclude the party from objecting if the person is called to testify by another party who did not list the person as a witness.

Subparagraph (B) requires the party to indicate which of these potential witnesses will be presented by deposition at trial. A party expecting to use at trial a deposition not recorded by stenographic means is required by revised Rule 32 to provide the court with a transcript of the pertinent portions of such depositions. This rule requires that copies of the transcript of a nonstenographic deposition be provided to other parties in advance of trial for verification, an obvious concern since counsel often utilize their own personnel to prepare transcripts from audio or video tapes. By order or local rule, the court may require that parties designate the particular portions of stenographic depositions to be used at trial.

Subparagraph (C) requires disclosure of exhibits, including summaries (whether to be offered in lieu of other documentary evidence or to be used as an aid in understanding such evidence), that may be offered as substantive evidence. The rule requires a separate listing of each such exhibit, though it should permit voluminous items of a similar or standardized character to be described by meaningful categories. For example, unless the court has otherwise directed, a series of vouchers might be shown collectively as a single exhibit with their starting and ending dates. As with witnesses, the exhibits that will probably be offered are to be listed separately from those which are unlikely to be offered but which are listed in order to preserve the right to do so if needed because of developments during trial. Under revised Rule 37(c)(1) the court can permit use of unlisted documents the need for which could not reasonably have been anticipated in advance of trial.

Upon receipt of these final pretrial disclosures, other parties have 14 days (unless a different time is specified by the court) to disclose any objections they wish to preserve to the usability of the deposition testimony or to the admissibility of the documentary evidence (other than under Rules 402 and 403 of the Federal Rules of Evidence). Similar provisions have become commonplace either in pretrial orders or by local rules, and significantly expedite the presentation of evidence at trial, as well as eliminate the need to have available witnesses to provide "foundation" testimony for most items of documentary evidence. The listing of a potential objection does not constitute the making of that objection or require the court to rule on the objection; rather, it preserves the right of the party to make the objection when and as appropriate during trial. The court may, however, elect to treat the listing as a motion "in limine" and rule upon the objections in advance of trial to the extent appropriate.

The time specified in the rule for the final pretrial disclosures is relatively close to the trial date. The objective is to eliminate the time and expense in making these disclosures of evidence and objections in those cases that settle shortly before trial, while affording a reasonable time for final preparation for trial in those cases that do not settle. In many cases, it will be desirable for the court in a scheduling or pretrial order to set an earlier time for disclosures of evidence and provide more time for disclosing potential objections.

Paragraph (4). This paragraph prescribes the form of disclosures. A signed written statement is required, reminding the parties and counsel of the solemnity of the obligations imposed; and the signature on the initial or pretrial disclosure is a certification under subdivision (g)(1) that it is complete and correct as of the time when made. Consistent with Rule 5(d), these disclosures are to be filed with the court unless otherwise directed. It is anticipated that many courts will direct that expert reports required under paragraph (2)(B) not be filed until needed in connection with a motion or for trial.

Paragraph (5). This paragraph is revised to take note of the availability of revised Rule 45 for inspection from non-parties of documents and premises without the need for a deposition.

Subdivision (b). This subdivision is revised in several respects. First, former paragraph (1) is subdivided into two paragraphs for ease of reference and to avoid renumbering of paragraphs (3) and (4). Textual changes are then made in new paragraph (2) to enable the court to keep tighter rein on the extent of discovery. The information explosion of recent decades has greatly increased both the potential cost of wide-ranging discovery and the potential for discovery to be used as an instrument for delay or oppression. Amendments to Rules 30, 31, and 33 place presumptive limits on the number of depositions and interrogatories, subject to leave of court to pursue additional discovery. The revisions in Rule 26(b)(2) are intended to provide the court with broader discretion to impose additional restrictions on the scope and extent of discovery and to authorize courts that develop case tracking systems based on the complexity of cases to increase or decrease by local rule the presumptive number of depositions and interrogatories allowed in particular types or classifications of cases. The revision also dispels any doubt as to the power of the court to impose limitations on the length of depositions under Rule 30 or on the number of requests for admission under Rule 36.

Second, former paragraph (2), relating to insurance, has been relocated as part of the required initial disclosures under subdivision (a)(1)(D), and revised to provide for disclosure of the policy itself.

Third, paragraph (4)(A) is revised to provide that experts who are expected to be witnesses will be subject to deposition prior to trial, conforming the norm stated in the rule to the actual practice followed in most courts, in which depositions of experts have become standard. Concerns regarding the expense of such depositions should be mitigated by the fact that the expert's fees for the deposition will ordinarily be borne by the party taking the deposition. The requirement under subdivision (a)(2)(B) of a complete and detailed report of the expected testimony of certain forensic experts may, moreover, eliminate the need for some such depositions or at least reduce the length of the depositions. Accordingly, the deposition of an expert required by subdivision (a)(2)(B) to provide a written report may be taken only after the report has been served.

Paragraph (4)(C), bearing on compensation of experts, is revised to take account of the changes in paragraph (4)(A).

Paragraph (5) is a new provision. A party must notify other parties if it is withholding materials otherwise subject to disclosure under the rule or pursuant to a discovery request because it is asserting a claim of privilege or work product protection. To withhold materials without such notice is contrary to the rule, subjects the party to sanctions under Rule 37(b)(2), and may be viewed as a waiver of the privilege or protection.

The party must also provide sufficient information to enable other parties to evaluate the applicability of the claimed privilege or protection. Although the person from whom the discovery is sought decides whether to claim a privilege or protection, the court ultimately decides whether, if this claim is challenged, the privilege or protection applies. Providing information pertinent to the applicability of the privilege or protection should reduce the need for in camera examination of the documents.

The rule does not attempt to define for each case what information must be provided when a party asserts a claim of privilege or work product protection. Details concerning time, persons, general subject matter, etc., may be appropriate if only a few items are withheld, but may be unduly burdensome when voluminous documents are claimed to be privileged or protected, particularly if the items can be described by categories. A party can seek relief through a protective order under subdivision (c) if compliance with the requirement for providing this information would be an unreasonable burden. In rare circumstances some of the pertinent information affecting applicability of the claim, such as the identity of the client, may itself be privileged; the rule provides that such information need not be disclosed.

The obligation to provide pertinent information concerning withheld privileged materials applies only to items "otherwise discoverable." If a broad discovery request is made—for example, for all documents of a particular type during a twenty year period—and the responding party believes in good faith that production of documents for more than the past three years would be unduly burdensome, it should make its objection to the breadth of the request and, with respect to the documents generated in that three year period, produce the unprivileged documents and describe those withheld under the claim of privilege. If the court later rules that documents for a seven year period are properly discoverable, the documents for the additional four years should then be either produced (if not privileged) or described (if claimed to be privileged).

Subdivision (c). The revision requires that before filing a motion for a protective order the movant must confer—either in person or by telephone—with the other affected parties in a good faith effort to resolve the discovery dispute without the need for court intervention. If the movant is unable to get opposing parties even to discuss the matter, the efforts in attempting to arrange such a conference should be indicated in the certificate.

Subdivision (d). This subdivision is revised to provide that formal discovery—as distinguished from interviews of potential witnesses and other informal discovery—not commence until the parties have met and conferred as required by subdivision (f). Discovery can begin earlier if authorized under Rule 30(a)(2)(C) (deposition of person about to leave the country) or by local rule, order, or stipulation. This will be appropriate in some cases, such as those involving requests for a preliminary injunction or motions challenging personal jurisdiction. If a local rule exempts any types of cases in which discovery may be needed from the requirement of a meeting under Rule 26(f), it should specify when discovery may commence in those cases.

The meeting of counsel is to take place as soon as practicable and in any event at least 14 days before the date of the scheduling conference under Rule 16(b) or the date a scheduling order is due under Rule 16(b). The court can assure that discovery is not unduly delayed either by entering a special order or by setting the case for a scheduling conference.

Subdivision (e). This subdivision is revised to provide that the requirement for supplementation applies to all disclosures required by subdivisions (a)(1)–(3). Like the former rule, the duty, while imposed on a "party," applies whether the corrective information is learned by the client or by the attorney. Supplementations need not be made as each new item of information is learned but should be made at appropriate intervals during the discovery period, and with special promptness as the trial date approaches. It may be useful for the scheduling order to specify the time or times when supplementations should be made.

The revision also clarifies that the obligation to supplement responses to formal discovery requests applies to interrogatories, requests for production, and requests for admissions, but not ordinarily to deposition testimony. However, with respect to experts from whom a written report is required under subdivision (a)(2)(B), changes in the opinions expressed by the expert whether in the report or at a subsequent deposition are subject to a duty of supplemental disclosure under subdivision (e)(1).

The obligation to supplement disclosures and discovery responses applies whenever a party learns that its prior disclosures or responses are in some material respect incomplete or incorrect. There is, however, no obligation to provide supplemental or corrective information that has been otherwise made known to the parties in writing or during the discovery process, as when a witness not previously disclosed is identified during the taking of a deposition or when an expert during a deposition corrects information contained in an earlier report.

Subdivision (f). This subdivision was added in 1980 to provide a party threatened with abusive discovery with a special means for obtaining judicial intervention other than through discrete motions under Rules 26(c) and 37(a). The amendment envisioned a two-step process: first, the parties would attempt to frame a mutually agreeable plan; second, the court would hold a "discovery conference" and then enter an order establishing a schedule and limitations for the conduct of discovery. It was contemplated that the procedure, an elective one triggered on request of a party, would be used in special cases rather than as a routine matter. As expected, the device has been used only sparingly in most courts, and judicial controls over the discovery process have ordinarily been imposed through scheduling orders under Rule 16(b) or through rulings on discovery motions.

The provisions relating to a conference with the court are removed from subdivision (f). This change does not signal any lessening of the importance of judicial supervision. Indeed, there is a greater need for early judicial involvement to consider the scope and timing of the disclosure requirements of Rule 26(a) and the presumptive limits on discovery imposed under these rules or by local rules. Rather, the change is made because the provisions addressing the use of conferences with the court to control discovery are more properly included in Rule 16, which is being revised to highlight the court's powers regarding the discovery process.

The desirability of some judicial control of discovery can hardly be doubted. Rule 16, as revised, requires that the court set a time for completion of discovery and authorizes various other orders affecting the scope, timing, and extent of discovery and disclosures. Before entering such orders, the court should consider the views of the parties, preferably by means of a conference, but at the least through written submissions. Moreover, it is desirable that the parties' proposals regarding discovery be developed through a process where they meet in person, informally explore the nature and basis of the issues, and discuss how discovery can be conducted most efficiently and economically.

As noted above, former subdivision (f) envisioned the development of proposed discovery plans as an optional procedure to be used in relatively few cases. The revised rule directs that in all cases not exempted by local rule or special order the litigants must meet in person and plan for discovery. Following this meeting, the parties submit to the court their proposals for a discovery plan and can begin formal discovery. Their report will assist the court in seeing that the timing and scope of disclosures under revised Rule 26(a) and the limitations on the extent of discovery under these rules and local rules are tailored to the circumstances of the particular case.

To assure that the court has the litigants' proposals before deciding on a scheduling order and that the commencement of discovery is not delayed unduly, the rule provides that the meeting of the parties take place as soon as practicable and in any event at least 14 days before a scheduling conference is held or before a scheduling order is due under Rule 16(b). (Rule 16(b) requires that a scheduling order be entered within 90 days after the first appearance of a defendant or, if earlier, within 120 days after the complaint has been served on any defendant.) The obligation to participate in the planning process is imposed on all parties that have appeared in the case, including defendants who, because of a pending Rule 12 motion, may not have yet filed an answer in the case. Each such party should attend the meeting, either through one of its attorneys or in person if unrepresented. If more parties are joined or appear after the initial meeting, an additional meeting may be desirable.

Subdivision (f) describes certain matters that should be accomplished at the meeting and included in the proposed discovery plan. This listing does not exclude consideration of other subjects, such as the time when any dispositive motions should be filed and when the case should be ready for trial.

The parties are directed under subdivision (a)(1) to make the disclosures required by that subdivision at or within 10 days after this meeting. In many cases the parties should use the meeting to exchange, discuss, and clarify their respective disclosures. In other cases, it may be more useful if the disclosures are delayed until after the parties have discussed at the meeting the claims and defenses in order to define the issues with respect to which the initial disclosures should be made. As discussed in the Notes to subdivision (a)(1), the parties may also need to consider whether a stipulation extending this 10–day period would be appropriate, as when a defendant would otherwise have less than 60 days after being served in which to make its initial disclosure. The parties should also discuss at the meeting what additional information, although not subject to the disclosure requirements, can be made available informally without the necessity for formal discovery requests.

The report is to be submitted to the court within 10 days after the meeting and should not be difficult to prepare. In most cases counsel should be able to agree that one of them will be responsible for its preparation and submission to the court. Form 35 has been added in the Appendix to the Rules, both to illustrate the type of report that is contemplated and to serve as a checklist for the meeting.

The litigants are expected to attempt in good faith to agree on the contents of the proposed discovery plan. If they cannot agree on all aspects of the plan, their report to the court should indicate the competing proposals of the parties on those items, as well as the matters on which they agree. Unfortunately, there may be cases in which, because of disagreements about time or place or for other reasons, the meeting is not attended by all parties or, indeed, no meeting takes place. In such situations, the report—or reports—should describe the circumstances and the court may need to consider sanctions under Rule 37(g).

By local rule or special order, the court can exempt particular cases or types of cases from the meet-and-confer requirement of subdivision (f). In general this should include any types of cases which are exempted by local rule from the requirement for a scheduling order under Rule 16(b), such as cases in which there will be no discovery (e.g., bankruptcy appeals and reviews of social security determinations). In addition, the court may want to exempt cases in which discovery is rarely needed (e.g., government collection cases and proceedings to enforce administrative summonses) or in which a meeting of the parties might be impracticable (e.g., actions by unrepresented prisoners). Note that if a court exempts from the requirements for a meeting any types of cases in which discovery may be needed, it should indicate when discovery may commence in those cases.

Subdivision (g). Paragraph (1) is added to require signatures on disclosures, a requirement that parallels the provisions of paragraph (2) with respect to discovery requests, responses, and objections. The provisions of paragraph (3) have been modified to be consistent with Rules 37(a)(4) and 37(c)(1); in combination, these rules establish sanctions for violation of the rules regarding disclosures and discovery matters. Amended Rule 11 no longer applies to such violations.

2000 Amendment

Purposes of amendments. The Rule 26(a)(1) initial disclosure provisions are amended to establish a nationally uniform practice. The scope of the disclosure obligation is narrowed to cover only information that the disclosing party may use to support its position. In addition, the rule exempts specified categories of proceedings from initial disclosure, and permits a party who contends that disclosure is not appropriate in the circumstances of the case to present its objections to the court, which must then determine whether disclosure should be made. Related changes are made in Rules 26(d) and (f).

The initial disclosure requirements added by the 1993 amendments permitted local rules directing that disclosure would not be required or altering its operation. The inclusion of the "opt out" provision reflected the strong opposition to initial disclosure felt in some districts, and permitted experimentation with differing disclosure rules in those districts that were favorable to disclosure. The local option also recognized that—partly in response to the first publication in 1991 of a proposed disclosure rule—many districts had adopted a variety of disclosure programs under the aegis of the Civil Justice Reform Act. It was hoped that developing experience under a variety of disclosure systems would support eventual refinement of a uniform national disclosure practice. In addition, there was hope that local experience could identify categories of actions in which disclosure is not useful.

A striking array of local regimes in fact emerged for disclosure and related features introduced in 1993. *See* D. Stienstra, *Implementation of Disclosure in United States District Courts, With Specific Attention to Courts' Responses to Selected Amendments to Federal Rule of Civil Procedure 26* (Federal Judicial Center, March 30, 1998) (describing and categorizing local regimes). In its final report to Congress on the CJRA experience, the Judicial Conference recommended reexamination of the need for national uniformity, particularly in regard to initial disclosure. Judicial Conference, *Alternative Proposals for Reduction of Cost and Delay: Assessment of Principles, Guidelines and Techniques*, 175 F.R.D. 62, 98 (1997).

At the Committee's request, the Federal Judicial Center undertook a survey in 1997 to develop information on current disclosure and discovery practices. *See* T. Willging, J. Shapard, D. Stienstra & D. Miletich, *Discovery and Disclosure Practice, Problems, and Proposals for Change* (Federal Judicial Center, 1997). In addition, the Committee convened two conferences on discovery involving lawyers from around the country and received reports and recommendations on possible discovery amendments from a number of bar groups. Papers and other proceedings from the second conference are published in 39 Boston Col. L. Rev. 517–840 (1998).

The Committee has discerned widespread support for national uniformity. Many lawyers have experienced difficulty in coping with divergent disclosure and other practices as they move from one district to another. Lawyers surveyed by the Federal Judicial Center ranked adoption of a uniform national disclosure rule second among proposed rule changes (behind increased availability of judges to resolve discovery disputes) as a means to reduce litigation expenses without interfering with fair outcomes. *Discovery and Disclosure Practice, supra*, at 44–45. National uniformity is also a central purpose of the Rules Enabling Act of 1934, as amended, 28 U.S.C. §§ 2072–2077.

These amendments restore national uniformity to disclosure practice. Uniformity is also restored to other aspects of discovery by deleting most of the provisions authorizing local rules that vary the number of permitted discovery events or the length of depositions. Local rule options are also deleted from Rules 26(d) and (f).

Subdivision (a)(1). The amendments remove the authority to alter or opt out of the national disclosure requirements by local rule, invalidating not only formal local rules but also informal "standing" orders of an individual judge or court that purport to create exemptions from—or limit or expand—the disclosure provided under the national rule. *See* Rule 83. Case-specific orders remain proper, however, and are expressly required if a party objects that initial disclosure is not appropriate in the circumstances of the action. Specified categories of proceedings are excluded from initial disclosure under subdivision (a)(1)(E). In addition, the parties can stipulate to forgo disclosure, as was true before. But even in a case excluded by subdivision (a)(1)(E) or in which the parties stipulate to bypass disclosure, the court can order exchange of similar information in managing the action under Rule 16.

The initial disclosure obligation of subdivisions (a)(1)(A) and (B) has been narrowed to identification of witnesses and documents that the disclosing party may use to support its claims or defenses. "Use" includes any use at a pretrial conference, to support a motion, or at trial. The disclosure obligation is also triggered by intended use in discovery, apart from use to respond to a discovery request; use of a document to question a witness during a deposition is a common example. The disclosure obligation attaches both to witnesses and documents a party intends to use and also to witnesses and to documents the party intends to use if—in the language of Rule 26(a)(3)—"the need arises."

A party is no longer obligated to disclose witnesses or documents, whether favorable or unfavorable, that it does not intend to use. The obligation to disclose information the party may use connects directly to the exclusion sanction of Rule 37(c)(1). Because the disclosure obligation is limited to material that the party may use, it is no longer tied to particularized allegations in the pleadings. Subdivision (e)(1), which is unchanged, requires supplementation if information later acquired would have been subject to the disclosure requirement. As case preparation continues, a party must supplement its disclosures when it determines that it may use a witness or document that it did not previously intend to use.

The disclosure obligation applies to "claims and defenses," and therefore requires a party to disclose information it may use to support its denial or rebuttal of the allegations, claim, or defense of another party. It thereby bolsters the requirements of Rule 11(b)(4), which authorizes denials "warranted on the evidence," and disclosure should include the identity of any witness or document that the disclosing party may use to support such denials.

Subdivision (a)(3) presently excuses pretrial disclosure of information solely for impeachment. Impeachment information is similarly excluded from the initial disclosure requirement.

Subdivisions (a)(1)(C) and (D) are not changed. Should a case be exempted from initial disclosure by Rule 26(a)(1)(E) or by agreement or order, the insurance information described by subparagraph (D) should be subject to discovery, as it would have been under the principles of former Rule 26(b)(2), which was added in 1970 and deleted in 1993 as redundant in light of the new initial disclosure obligation.

New subdivision (a)(1)(E) excludes eight specified categories of proceedings from initial disclosure. The objective of this listing is to identify cases in which there is likely to be little or no discovery, or in which initial disclosure appears unlikely to contribute to the effective development of the case. The list was developed after a review of the categories excluded by local rules in various districts from the operation of Rule 16(b) and the conference requirements of subdivision (f). Subdivision (a)(1)(E) refers to categories of "proceedings" rather than categories of "actions" because some might not properly be labeled "actions." Case designations made by the parties or the clerk's office at the time of filing do not control application of the exemptions. The descriptions in the rule are generic and are intended to be administered by the parties—and, when needed, the courts—with the flexibility needed to adapt to gradual evolution in the types of proceedings that fall within these general categories. The exclusion of an action for review on an administrative record, for example, is intended to reach a proceeding that is framed as an "appeal" based solely on an administrative record. The exclusion should not apply to a proceeding in a form that commonly permits admission of new evidence to supplement the record. Item (vii), excluding a proceeding ancillary to proceedings in other courts, does not refer to bankruptcy proceedings; application of the Civil Rules to bankruptcy proceedings is determined by the Bankruptcy Rules.

Subdivision (a)(1)(E) is likely to exempt a substantial proportion of the cases in most districts from the initial disclosure requirement. Based on 1996 and 1997 case filing statistics, Federal Judicial Center staff estimate that, nationwide, these categories total approximately one-third of all civil filings.

The categories of proceedings listed in subdivision (a)(1)(E) are also exempted from the subdivision (f) conference requirement and from the subdivision (d) moratorium on discovery. Although there is no restriction on commencement of discovery in these cases, it is not expected that this opportunity will often lead to abuse since there is likely to be little or no discovery in most such cases. Should a defendant need more time to respond to discovery requests filed at the beginning of an exempted action, it can seek relief by motion under Rule 26(c) if the plaintiff is unwilling to defer the due date by agreement.

Subdivision (a)(1)(E)'s enumeration of exempt categories is exclusive. Although a case-specific order can alter or excuse initial disclosure, local rules or "standing" orders that purport to create general exemptions are invalid. *See* Rule 83.

The time for initial disclosure is extended to 14 days after the subdivision (f) conference unless the court orders otherwise. This change is integrated with corresponding changes requiring that the subdivision (f) conference be held 21 days before the Rule 16(b) scheduling conference or scheduling order, and that the report on the subdivision (f) conference be submitted to the court 14 days after the meeting. These changes provide a more orderly opportunity for the parties to review the disclosures, and for the court to consider the report. In many instances, the subdivision (f) conference and the effective preparation of the case would benefit from disclosure before the conference, and earlier disclosure is encouraged.

The presumptive disclosure date does not apply if a party objects to initial disclosure during the subdivision (f) conference and states its objection in the subdivision (f) discovery plan. The right to object to initial disclosure is not intended to afford parties an opportunity to "opt out" of disclosure unilaterally. It does provide an opportunity for an objecting party to present to the court its position that disclosure would be "inappropriate in the circumstances of the action." Making the objection permits the objecting party to present the question to the judge before any party is required to make disclosure. The court must then rule on the objection and determine what disclosures—if any—should be made. Ordinarily, this determination would be included in the Rule 16(b) scheduling order, but the court could handle the matter in a different fashion. Even when circumstances warrant suspending some disclosure obligations, others—such as the damages and insurance information called for by subdivisions (a)(1)(C) and (D)—may continue to be appropriate.

The presumptive disclosure date is also inapplicable to a party who is "first served or otherwise joined" after the subdivision (f) conference. This phrase refers to the date of service of a claim on a party in a defensive posture (such as a defendant or third-party defendant), and the date of joinder of a party added as a claimant or an intervenor. Absent court order or stipulation, a new party has 30 days in which to make its initial disclosures. But it is expected that later-added parties will ordinarily be treated the same as the original parties when the original parties have stipulated to forgo initial disclosure, or the court has ordered disclosure in a modified form.

Subdivision (a)(3). The amendment to Rule 5(d) forbids filing disclosures under subdivisions (a)(1) and (a)(2) until they are used in the proceeding, and this change is reflected in an amendment to subdivision (a)(4). Disclosures under subdivi-

sion (a)(3), however, may be important to the court in connection with the final pretrial conference or otherwise in preparing for trial. The requirement that objections to certain matters be filed points up the court's need to be provided with these materials. Accordingly, the requirement that subdivision (a)(3) materials be filed has been moved from subdivision (a)(4) to subdivision (a)(3), and it has also been made clear that they—and any objections—should be filed "promptly."

Subdivision (a)(4). The filing requirement has been removed from this subdivision. Rule 5(d) has been amended to provide that disclosures under subdivisions (a)(1) and (a)(2) must not be filed until used in the proceeding. Subdivision (a)(3) has been amended to require that the disclosures it directs, and objections to them, be filed promptly. Subdivision (a)(4) continues to require that all disclosures under subdivisions (a)(1), (a)(2), and (a)(3) be in writing, signed, and served.

"Shall" is replaced by "must" under the program to conform amended rules to current style conventions when there is no ambiguity.

GAP Report

The Advisory Committee recommends that the amendments to Rules 26(a)(1)(A) and (B) be changed so that initial disclosure applies to information the disclosing party "may use to support" its claims or defenses. It also recommends changes in the Committee Note to explain that disclosure requirement. In addition, it recommends inclusion in the Note of further explanatory matter regarding the exclusion from initial disclosure provided in new Rule 26(a)(1)(E) for actions for review on an administrative record and the impact of these exclusions on bankruptcy proceedings. Minor wording improvements in the Note are also proposed.

Subdivision (b)(1). In 1978, the Committee published for comment a proposed amendment, suggested by the Section of Litigation of the American Bar Association, to refine the scope of discovery by deleting the "subject matter" language. This proposal was withdrawn, and the Committee has since then made other changes in the discovery rules to address concerns about overbroad discovery. Concerns about costs and delay of discovery have persisted nonetheless, and other bar groups have repeatedly renewed similar proposals for amendment to this subdivision to delete the "subject matter" language. Nearly one-third of the lawyers surveyed in 1997 by the Federal Judicial Center endorsed narrowing the scope of discovery as a means of reducing litigation expense without interfering with fair case resolutions. *Discovery and Disclosure Practice, supra,* at 44–45 (1997). The Committee has heard that in some instances, particularly cases involving large quantities of discovery, parties seek to justify discovery requests that sweep far beyond the claims and defenses of the parties on the ground that they nevertheless have a bearing on the "subject matter" involved in the action.

The amendments proposed for subdivision (b)(1) include one element of these earlier proposals but also differ from these proposals in significant ways. The similarity is that the amendments describe the scope of party-controlled discovery in terms of matter relevant to the claim or defense of any party. The court, however, retains authority to order discovery of any matter relevant to the subject matter involved in the action for good cause. The amendment is designed to involve the court more actively in regulating the breadth of sweeping or contentious discovery. The Committee has been informed repeatedly by lawyers that involvement of the court in managing discovery is an important method of controlling problems of inappropriately broad discovery. Increasing the availability of judicial officers to resolve discovery disputes and increasing court management of discovery were both strongly endorsed by the attorneys surveyed by the Federal Judicial Center. *See Discovery and Disclosure Practice, supra,* at 44. Under the amended provisions, if there is an objection that discovery goes beyond material relevant to the parties' claims or defenses, the court would become involved to determine whether the discovery is relevant to the claims or defenses and, if not, whether good cause exists for authorizing it so long as it is relevant to the subject matter of the action. The good-cause standard warranting broader discovery is meant to be flexible.

The Committee intends that the parties and the court focus on the actual claims and defenses involved in the action. The dividing line between information relevant to the claims and defenses and that relevant only to the subject matter of the action cannot be defined with precision. A variety of types of information not directly pertinent to the incident in suit could be relevant to the claims or defenses raised in a given action. For example, other incidents of the same type, or involving the same product, could be properly discoverable under the revised standard. Information about organizational arrangements or filing systems of a party could be discoverable if likely to yield or lead to the discovery of admissible information. Similarly, information that could be used to impeach a likely witness, although not otherwise relevant to the claims or defenses, might be properly discoverable. In each instance, the determination whether such information is discoverable because it is relevant to the claims or defenses depends on the circumstances of the pending action.

The rule change signals to the court that it has the authority to confine discovery to the claims and defenses asserted in the pleadings, and signals to the parties that they have no entitlement to discovery to develop new claims or defenses that are not already identified in the pleadings. In general, it is hoped that reasonable lawyers can cooperate to manage discovery without the need for judicial intervention. When judicial intervention is invoked, the actual scope of discovery should be determined according to the reasonable needs of the action. The court may permit broader discovery in a particular case depending on the circumstances of the case, the nature of the claims and defenses, and the scope of the discovery requested.

The amendments also modify the provision regarding discovery of information not admissible in evidence. As added in 1946, this sentence was designed to make clear that otherwise relevant material could not be withheld because it was hearsay or otherwise inadmissible. The Committee was concerned that the "reasonably calculated to lead to the discovery of admissible evidence" standard set forth in this sentence might swallow any other limitation on the scope of discovery. Accordingly, this sentence has been amended to clarify that information must be relevant to be discoverable, even though inadmissible, and that discovery of such material is permitted if reasonably calculated to lead to the discovery of admissible evidence. As used here, "relevant" means within the scope of discovery as defined in this subdivision, and it would include information relevant to the subject matter involved in the action if the court has ordered discovery to that limit based on a showing of good cause.

Finally, a sentence has been added calling attention to the limitations of subdivision (b)(2)(i), (ii), and (iii). These limitations apply to discovery that is otherwise within the scope of subdivision (b)(1). The Committee has been told repeatedly that courts have not implemented these limitations with the vigor that was contemplated. *See 8 Federal Practice & Procedure* § 2008.1 at 121. This otherwise redundant cross-reference has been added to emphasize the need for active judicial use of subdivision (b)(2) to control excessive discovery. *Cf. Crawford-El v. Britton,* 118 S.Ct. 1584, 1597 (1998) (quoting Rule 26(b)(2)(iii) and stating that "Rule 26 vests the trial judge with broad discretion to tailor discovery narrowly").

GAP Report

The Advisory Committee recommends changing the rule to authorize the court to expand discovery to any "matter"—not "information"—relevant to the subject matter involved in the action. In addition, it recommends additional clarifying material in the Committee Note about the impact of the change on some commonly disputed discovery topics, the relationship between cost-bearing under Rule 26(b)(2) and expansion of the scope of discovery on a showing of good cause, and the meaning of "relevant" in the revision to the last sentence of current subdivision (b)(1). In addition, some minor clarifications of language changes have been proposed for the Committee Note.

Subdivision (b)(2). Rules 30, 31, and 33 establish presumptive national limits on the numbers of depositions and interrogatories. New Rule 30(d)(2) establishes a presumptive limit on the length of depositions. Subdivision (b)(2) is amended to remove the previous permission for local rules that establish different presumptive limits on these discovery activities. There is no reason to believe that unique circumstances justify varying these nationally-applicable presumptive limits in certain districts. The limits can be modified by court order or agreement in an individual action, but "standing" orders imposing different presumptive limits are not authorized. Because there is no national rule limiting the number of Rule 36 requests for admissions, the rule continues to authorize local rules that impose numerical limits on them. This change is not intended to interfere with differentiated case management in districts that use this technique by case-specific order as part of their Rule 16 process.

Subdivision (d). The amendments remove the prior authority to exempt cases by local rule from the moratorium on discovery before the subdivision (f) conference, but the categories of proceedings exempted from initial disclosure under subdivision (a)(1)(E) are excluded from subdivision (d). The parties may agree to disregard the moratorium where it applies, and the court may so order in a case, but "standing" orders altering the moratorium are not authorized.

Subdivision (f). As in subdivision (d), the amendments remove the prior authority to exempt cases by local rule from the conference requirement. The Committee has been informed that the addition of the conference was one of the most successful changes made in the 1993 amendments, and it therefore has determined to apply the conference requirement nationwide. The categories of proceedings exempted from initial disclosure under subdivision (a)(1)(E) are exempted from the conference requirement for the reasons that warrant exclusion from initial disclosure. The court may order that the conference need not occur in a case where otherwise required, or that it occur in a case otherwise exempted by subdivision (a)(1)(E). "Standing" orders altering the conference requirement for categories of cases are not authorized.

The rule is amended to require only a "conference" of the parties, rather than a "meeting." There are important benefits to face-to-face discussion of the topics to be covered in the conference, and those benefits may be lost if other means of conferring were routinely used when face-to-face meetings would not impose burdens. Nevertheless, geographic conditions in some districts may exact costs far out of proportion to these benefits. The amendment allows the court by case-specific order to require a face-to-face meeting, but "standing" orders so requiring are not authorized.

As noted concerning the amendments to subdivision (a)(1), the time for the conference has been changed to at least 21 days before the Rule 16 scheduling conference, and the time for the report is changed to no more than 14 days after the Rule 26(f) conference. This should ensure that the court will have the report well in advance of the scheduling conference or the entry of the scheduling order.

Since Rule 16 was amended in 1983 to mandate some case management activities in all courts, it has included deadlines for completing these tasks to ensure that all courts do so within a reasonable time. Rule 26(f) was fit into this scheme when it was adopted in 1993. It was never intended, however, that the national requirements that certain activities be completed by a certain time should delay case management in districts that move much faster than the national rules direct, and the rule is therefore amended to permit such a court to adopt a local rule that shortens the period specified for the completion of these tasks.

"Shall" is replaced by "must," "does," or an active verb under the program to conform amended rules to current style conventions when there is no ambiguity.

GAP Report

The Advisory Committee recommends adding a sentence to the published amendments to Rule 26(f) authorizing local rules shortening the time between the attorney conference and the court's action under Rule 16(b), and addition to the Committee Note of explanatory material about this change to the rule. This addition can be made without republication in response to public comments.

2006 Amendment

Subdivision (a). Rule 26(a)(1)(B) is amended to parallel Rule 34(a) by recognizing that a party must disclose electronically stored information as well as documents that it may use to support its claims or defenses. The term "electronically stored information" has the same broad meaning in Rule 26(a)(1) as in Rule 34(a). This amendment is consistent with the 1993 addition of Rule 26(a)(1)(B). The term "data compilations" is deleted as unnecessary because it is a subset of both documents and electronically stored information.

[Subdivision (a)(1)(E).] Civil forfeiture actions are added to the list of exemptions from Rule 26(a)(1) disclosure requirements. These actions are governed by new Supplemental Rule G. Disclosure is not likely to be useful.

Subdivision (b)(2). The amendment to Rule 26(b)(2) is designed to address issues raised by difficulties in locating, retrieving, and providing discovery of some electronically stored information. Electronic storage systems often make it easier to locate and retrieve information. These advantages are properly taken into account in determining the reasonable scope of discovery in a particular case. But some sources of electronically stored information can be accessed only with substantial burden and cost. In a particular case, these burdens and costs may make the information on such sources not reasonably accessible.

It is not possible to define in a rule the different types of technological features that may affect the burdens and costs of accessing electronically stored information. Information systems are designed to provide ready access to information used in regular ongoing activities. They also may be designed so as to provide ready access to information that is not regularly used. But a system may retain information on sources that are accessible only by incurring substantial burdens or costs. Subparagraph (B) is added to regulate discovery from such sources.

Under this rule, a responding party should produce electronically stored information that is relevant, not privileged, and reasonably accessible, subject to the (b)(2)(C) limitations that apply to all discovery. The responding party must also identify, by category or type, the sources containing potentially responsive information that it is neither searching nor producing. The identification should, to the extent possible, provide enough detail to enable the requesting party to evaluate the burdens and costs of providing the discovery and the likelihood of finding responsive information on the identified sources.

A party's identification of sources of electronically stored information as not reasonably accessible does not relieve the party of its common-law or statutory duties to preserve evidence. Whether a responding party is required to preserve unsearched sources of potentially responsive information that it believes are not reasonably accessible depends on the circumstances of each case. It is often useful for the parties to discuss this issue early in discovery.

The volume of — and the ability to search — much electronically stored information means that in many cases the responding party will be able to produce information from reasonably accessible sources that will fully satisfy the parties' discovery needs. In many circumstances the requesting party should obtain and evaluate the information from such sources before insisting that the responding party search and produce information contained on sources that are not reasonably accessible. If the requesting party continues to seek discovery of information from sources identified as not reasonably accessible, the parties should discuss the burdens and costs of accessing and retrieving the information, the needs that may establish good cause for requiring all or part of the requested discovery even if the information sought is not reasonably accessible, and conditions on obtaining and producing the information that may be appropriate.

If the parties cannot agree whether, or on what terms, sources identified as not reasonably accessible should be searched and discoverable information produced, the issue may be raised either by a motion to compel discovery or by a motion for a protective order. The parties must confer before bringing either motion. If the parties do not resolve the issue and the court must decide, the responding party must show that the identified sources of information are not reasonably accessible because of undue burden or cost. The requesting party may need discovery to test this assertion. Such discovery might take the form of requiring the responding party to conduct a sampling of information contained on the sources identified as not reasonably accessible; allowing some form of inspection of such sources; or taking depositions of witnesses knowledgeable about the responding party's information systems.

Once it is shown that a source of electronically stored information is not reasonably accessible, the requesting party may still obtain discovery by showing good cause, considering the limitations of Rule 26(b)(2)(C) that balance the costs and potential benefits of discovery. The decision whether to require a responding party to search for and produce information that is not reasonably accessible depends not only on the burdens and costs of doing so, but also on whether those burdens and costs can be justified in the circumstances of the case. Appropriate considerations may include: (1) the specificity of the discovery request; (2) the quantity of information available from other and more easily accessed sources; (3) the failure to produce relevant information that seems likely to have existed but is no longer available on more easily accessed sources; (4) the likelihood of finding relevant, responsive information that cannot be obtained from other, more easily accessed sources; (5) predictions as to the importance and usefulness of the further information; (6) the importance of the issues at stake in the litigation; and (7) the parties' resources.

The responding party has the burden as to one aspect of the inquiry — whether the identified sources are not reasonably accessible in light of the burdens and costs required to search for, retrieve, and produce whatever responsive information may be found. The requesting party has the burden of showing that its need for the discovery outweighs the burdens and costs of locating, retrieving, and producing the information. In some cases, the court will be able to determine whether the identified sources are not reasonably accessible and whether the requesting party has shown good cause for some or all of the discovery, consistent with the limitations of Rule 26(b)(2)(C), through a single proceeding or presentation. The good-cause determination, however, may be complicated because the court and parties may know little about what information the sources identified as not reasonably accessible might contain, whether it is relevant, or how valuable it may be to the litigation. In such cases, the parties may need some focused discovery, which may include sampling of the sources, to learn more about what burdens and costs are involved in accessing the information, what the information consists of, and how valuable it is for the litigation in light of information that can be obtained by exhausting other opportunities for discovery.

The good-cause inquiry and consideration of the Rule 26(b)(2)(C) limitations are coupled with the authority to set conditions for discovery. The conditions may take the form of limits on the amount, type, or sources of information required to be accessed and produced. The conditions may also include payment by the requesting party of part or all of the reasonable costs of obtaining information from sources that are not reasonably accessible. A requesting party's willingness to share or bear the access costs may be weighed by the court in determining whether there is good cause. But the producing party's burdens in reviewing the information for relevance and privilege may weigh against permitting the requested discovery.

The limitations of Rule 26(b)(2)(C) continue to apply to all discovery of electronically stored information, including that stored on reasonably accessible electronic sources.

Subdivision (b)(5). The Committee has repeatedly been advised that the risk of privilege waiver, and the work necessary to avoid it, add to the costs and delay of discovery. When the review is of electronically stored information, the risk of waiver, and the time and effort required to avoid it, can increase substantially because of the volume of electronically stored information and the difficulty in ensuring that all information to be produced has in fact been reviewed. Rule 26(b)(5)(A) provides a procedure for a party that has withheld information on the basis of privilege or protection as trial-

preparation material to make the claim so that the requesting party can decide whether to contest the claim and the court can resolve the dispute. Rule 26(b)(5)(B) is added to provide a procedure for a party to assert a claim of privilege or trial-preparation material protection after information is produced in discovery in the action and, if the claim is contested, permit any party that received the information to present the matter to the court for resolution.

Rule 26(b)(5)(B) does not address whether the privilege or protection that is asserted after production was waived by the production. The courts have developed principles to determine whether, and under what circumstances, waiver results from inadvertent production of privileged or protected information. Rule 26(b)(5)(B) provides a procedure for presenting and addressing these issues. Rule 26(b)(5)(B) works in tandem with Rule 26(f), which is amended to direct the parties to discuss privilege issues in preparing their discovery plan, and which, with amended Rule 16(b), allows the parties to ask the court to include in an order any agreements the parties reach regarding issues of privilege or trial-preparation material protection. Agreements reached under Rule 26(f)(4) and orders including such agreements entered under Rule 16(b)(6) may be considered when a court determines whether a waiver has occurred. Such agreements and orders ordinarily control if they adopt procedures different from those in Rule 26(b)(5)(B).

A party asserting a claim of privilege or protection after production must give notice to the receiving party. That notice should be in writing unless the circumstances preclude it. Such circumstances could include the assertion of the claim during a deposition. The notice should be as specific as possible in identifying the information and stating the basis for the claim. Because the receiving party must decide whether to challenge the claim and may sequester the information and submit it to the court for a ruling on whether the claimed privilege or protection applies and whether it has been waived, the notice should be sufficiently detailed so as to enable the receiving party and the court to understand the basis for the claim and to determine whether waiver has occurred. Courts will continue to examine whether a claim of privilege or protection was made at a reasonable time when delay is part of the waiver determination under the governing law.

After receiving notice, each party that received the information must promptly return, sequester, or destroy the information and any copies it has. The option of sequestering or destroying the information is included in part because the receiving party may have incorporated the information in protected trial-preparation materials. No receiving party may use or disclose the information pending resolution of the privilege claim. The receiving party may present to the court the questions whether the information is privileged or protected as trial-preparation material, and whether the privilege or protection has been waived. If it does so, it must provide the court with the grounds for the privilege or protection specified in the producing party's notice, and serve all parties. In presenting the question, the party may use the content of the information only to the extent permitted by the applicable law of privilege, protection for trial-preparation material, and professional responsibility.

If a party disclosed the information to nonparties before receiving notice of a claim of privilege or protection as trial-preparation material, it must take reasonable steps to retrieve the information and to return it, sequester it until the claim is resolved, or destroy it.

Whether the information is returned or not, the producing party must preserve the information pending the court's ruling on whether the claim of privilege or of protection is properly asserted and whether it was waived. As with claims made under Rule 26(b)(5)(A), there may be no ruling if the other parties do not contest the claim.

Subdivision (f). Rule 26(f) is amended to direct the parties to discuss discovery of electronically stored information during their discovery-planning conference. The rule focuses on "issues relating to disclosure or discovery of electronically stored information"; the discussion is not required in cases not involving electronic discovery, and the amendment imposes no additional requirements in those cases. When the parties do anticipate disclosure or discovery of electronically stored information, discussion at the outset may avoid later difficulties or ease their resolution.

When a case involves discovery of electronically stored information, the issues to be addressed during the Rule 26(f) conference depend on the nature and extent of the contemplated discovery and of the parties' information systems. It may be important for the parties to discuss those systems, and accordingly important for counsel to become familiar with those systems before the conference. With that information, the parties can develop a discovery plan that takes into account the capabilities of their computer systems. In appropriate cases identification of, and early discovery from, individuals with special knowledge of a party's computer systems may be helpful.

The particular issues regarding electronically stored information that deserve attention during the discovery planning stage depend on the specifics of the given case. *See Manual for Complex Litigation* (4th) § 40.25(2) (listing topics for discussion in a proposed order regarding meet-and-confer sessions). For example, the parties may specify the topics for such discovery and the time period for which discovery will be sought. They may identify the various sources of such information within a party's control that should be searched for electronically stored information. They may discuss whether the information is reasonably accessible to the party that has it, including the burden or cost of retrieving and reviewing the information. *See* Rule 26(b)(2)(B). Rule 26(f)(3) explicitly directs the parties to discuss the form or forms in which electronically stored information might be produced. The parties may be able to reach agreement on the forms of production, making discovery more efficient. Rule 34(b) is amended to permit a requesting party to specify the form or forms in which it wants electronically stored information produced. If the requesting party does not specify a form, Rule 34(b) directs the responding party to state the forms it intends to use in the production. Early discussion of the forms of production may facilitate the application of Rule 34(b) by allowing the parties to determine what forms of production will meet both parties' needs. Early identification of disputes over the forms of production may help avoid the expense and delay of searches or productions using inappropriate forms.

Rule 26(f) is also amended to direct the parties to discuss any issues regarding preservation of discoverable information during their conference as they develop a discovery plan. This provision applies to all sorts of discoverable information, but can be particularly important with regard to electronically stored information. The volume and dynamic nature of elec-

tronically stored information may complicate preservation obligations. The ordinary operation of computers involves both the automatic creation and the automatic deletion or overwriting of certain information. Failure to address preservation issues early in the litigation increases uncertainty and raises a risk of disputes.

The parties' discussion should pay particular attention to the balance between the competing needs to preserve relevant evidence and to continue routine operations critical to ongoing activities. Complete or broad cessation of a party's routine computer operations could paralyze the party's activities. *Cf. Manual for Complex Litigation* (4th) § 11.422 ("A blanket preservation order may be prohibitively expensive and unduly burdensome for parties dependent on computer systems for their day-to-day operations.") The parties should take account of these considerations in their discussions, with the goal of agreeing on reasonable preservation steps.

The requirement that the parties discuss preservation does not imply that courts should routinely enter preservation orders. A preservation order entered over objections should be narrowly tailored. Ex parte preservation orders should issue only in exceptional circumstances.

Rule 26(f) is also amended to provide that the parties should discuss any issues relating to assertions of privilege or of protection as trial-preparation materials, including whether the parties can facilitate discovery by agreeing on procedures for asserting claims of privilege or protection after production and whether to ask the court to enter an order that includes any agreement the parties reach. The Committee has repeatedly been advised about the discovery difficulties that can result from efforts to guard against waiver of privilege and work-product protection. Frequently parties find it necessary to spend large amounts of time reviewing materials requested through discovery to avoid waiving privilege. These efforts are necessary because materials subject to a claim of privilege or protection are often difficult to identify. A failure to withhold even one such item may result in an argument that there has been a waiver of privilege as to all other privileged materials on that subject matter. Efforts to avoid the risk of waiver can impose substantial costs on the party producing the material and the time required for the privilege review can substantially delay access for the party seeking discovery.

These problems often become more acute when discovery of electronically stored information is sought. The volume of such data, and the informality that attends use of e-mail and some other types of electronically stored information, may make privilege determinations more difficult, and privilege review correspondingly more expensive and time consuming. Other aspects of electronically stored information pose particular difficulties for privilege review. For example, production may be sought of information automatically included in electronic files but not apparent to the creator or to readers. Computer programs may retain draft language, editorial comments, and other deleted matter (sometimes referred to as "embedded data" or "embedded edits") in an electronic file but not make them apparent to the reader. Information describing the history, tracking, or management of an electronic file (sometimes called "metadata") is usually not apparent to the reader viewing a hard copy or a screen image. Whether this information should be produced may be among the topics discussed in the Rule 26(f) conference. If it is, it may need to be reviewed to ensure that no privileged information is included, further complicating the task of privilege review.

Parties may attempt to minimize these costs and delays by agreeing to protocols that minimize the risk of waiver. They may agree that the responding party will provide certain requested materials for initial examination without waiving any privilege or protection — sometimes known as a "quick peek." The requesting party then designates the documents it wishes to have actually produced. This designation is the Rule 34 request. The responding party then responds in the usual course, screening only those documents actually requested for formal production and asserting privilege claims as provided in Rule 26(b)(5)(A). On other occasions, parties enter agreements — sometimes called "clawback agreements"— that production without intent to waive privilege or protection should not be a waiver so long as the responding party identifies the documents mistakenly produced, and that the documents should be returned under those circumstances. Other voluntary arrangements may be appropriate depending on the circumstances of each litigation. In most circumstances, a party who receives information under such an arrangement cannot assert that production of the information waived a claim of privilege or of protection as trial-preparation material.

Although these agreements may not be appropriate for all cases, in certain cases they can facilitate prompt and economical discovery by reducing delay before the discovering party obtains access to documents, and by reducing the cost and burden of review by the producing party. A case-management or other order including such agreements may further facilitate the discovery process. Form 35 is amended to include a report to the court about any agreement regarding protections against inadvertent forfeiture or waiver of privilege or protection that the parties have reached, and Rule 16(b) is amended to recognize that the court may include such an agreement in a case-management or other order. If the parties agree to entry of such an order, their proposal should be included in the report to the court.

Rule 26(b)(5)(B) is added to establish a parallel procedure to assert privilege or protection as trial-preparation material after production, leaving the question of waiver to later determination by the court.

2007 Amendment

The language of Rule 26 has been amended as part of the general restyling of the Civil Rules to make them more easily understood and to make style and terminology consistent throughout the rules. These changes are intended to be stylistic only.

Former Rule 26(a)(5) served as an index of the discovery methods provided by later rules. It was deleted as redundant. Deletion does not affect the right to pursue discovery in addition to disclosure.

Former Rule 26(b)(1) began with a general statement of the scope of discovery that appeared to function as a preface to each of the five numbered paragraphs that followed. This preface has been shifted to the text of paragraph (1) because it does not accurately reflect the limits embodied in paragraphs (2), (3), or (4), and because paragraph (5) does not address the scope of discovery.

The reference to discovery of "books" in former Rule 26(b)(1) was deleted to achieve consistent expression through-

out the discovery rules. Books remain a proper subject of discovery.

Amended Rule 26(b)(3) states that a party may obtain a copy of the party's own previous statement "on request." Former Rule 26(b)(3) expressly made the request procedure available to a nonparty witness, but did not describe the procedure to be used by a party. This apparent gap is closed by adopting the request procedure, which ensures that a party need not invoke Rule 34 to obtain a copy of the party's own statement.

Rule 26(e) stated the duty to supplement or correct a disclosure or discovery response "to include information thereafter acquired." This apparent limit is not reflected in practice; parties recognize the duty to supplement or correct by providing information that was not originally provided although it was available at the time of the initial disclosure or response. These words are deleted to reflect the actual meaning of the present rule.

Former Rule 26(e) used different phrases to describe the time to supplement or correct a disclosure or discovery response. Disclosures were to be supplemented "at appropriate intervals." A prior discovery response must be "seasonably * * * amend[ed]." The fine distinction between these phrases has not been observed in practice. Amended Rule 26(e)(1)(A) uses the same phrase for disclosures and discovery responses. The party must supplement or correct "in a timely manner."

Former Rule 26(g)(1) did not call for striking an unsigned disclosure. The omission was an obvious drafting oversight. Amended Rule 26(g)(2) includes disclosures in the list of matters that the court must strike unless a signature is provided "promptly * * * after being called to the attorney's or party's attention."

Former Rule 26(b)(2)(A) referred to a "good faith" argument to extend existing law. Amended Rule 26(b)(1)(B)(i) changes this reference to a "nonfrivolous" argument to achieve consistency with Rule 11(b)(2).

As with the Rule 11 signature on a pleading, written motion, or other paper, disclosure and discovery signatures should include not only a postal address but also a telephone number and electronic-mail address. A signer who lacks one or more of those addresses need not supply a nonexistent item.

Rule 11(b)(2) recognizes that it is legitimate to argue for establishing new law. An argument to establish new law is equally legitimate in conducting discovery.

2010 Amendment

Rule 26. Rules 26(a)(2) and (b)(4) are amended to address concerns about expert discovery. The amendments to Rule 26(a)(2) require disclosure regarding expected expert testimony of those expert witnesses not required to provide expert reports and limit the expert report to facts or data (rather than "data or other information," as in the current rule) considered by the witness. Rule 26(b)(4) is amended to provide work-product protection against discovery regarding draft expert disclosures or reports and—with three specific exceptions—communications between expert witnesses and counsel.

In 1993, Rule 26(b)(4)(A) was revised to authorize expert depositions and Rule 26(a)(2) was added to provide disclosure, including—for many experts—an extensive report. Many courts read the disclosure provision to authorize discovery of all communications between counsel and expert witnesses and all draft reports. The Committee has been told repeatedly that routine discovery into attorney-expert communications and draft reports has had undesirable effects. Costs have risen. Attorneys may employ two sets of experts—one for purposes of consultation and another to testify at trial—because disclosure of their collaborative interactions with expert consultants would reveal their most sensitive and confidential case analyses. At the same time, attorneys often feel compelled to adopt a guarded attitude toward their interaction with testifying experts that impedes effective communication, and experts adopt strategies that protect against discovery but also interfere with their work.

Subdivision (a)(2)(B). Rule 26(a)(2)(B)(ii) is amended to provide that disclosure include all "facts or data considered by the witness in forming" the opinions to be offered, rather than the "data or other information" disclosure prescribed in 1993. This amendment is intended to alter the outcome in cases that have relied on the 1993 formulation in requiring disclosure of all attorney-expert communications and draft reports. The amendments to Rule 26(b)(4) make this change explicit by providing work-product protection against discovery regarding draft reports and disclosures or attorney-expert communications.

The refocus of disclosure on "facts or data" is meant to limit disclosure to material of a factual nature by excluding theories or mental impressions of counsel. At the same time, the intention is that "facts or data" be interpreted broadly to require disclosure of any material considered by the expert, from whatever source, that contains factual ingredients. The disclosure obligation extends to any facts or data "considered" by the expert in forming the opinions to be expressed, not only those relied upon by the expert.

Subdivision (a)(2)(C). Rule 26(a)(2)(C) is added to mandate summary disclosures of the opinions to be offered by expert witnesses who are not required to provide reports under Rule 26(a)(2)(B) and of the facts supporting those opinions. This disclosure is considerably less extensive than the report required by Rule 26(a)(2)(B). Courts must take care against requiring undue detail, keeping in mind that these witnesses have not been specially retained and may not be as responsive to counsel as those who have.

This amendment resolves a tension that has sometimes prompted courts to require reports under Rule 26(a)(2)(B) even from witnesses exempted from the report requirement. An (a)(2)(B) report is required only from an expert described in (a)(2)(B).

A witness who is not required to provide a report under Rule 26(a)(2)(B) may both testify as a fact witness and also provide expert testimony under Evidence Rule 702, 703, or 705. Frequent examples include physicians or other health care professionals and employees of a party who do not regularly provide expert testimony. Parties must identify such witnesses under Rule 26(a)(2)(A) and provide the disclosure required under Rule 26(a)(2)(C). The (a)(2)(C) disclosure obligation does not include facts unrelated to the expert opinions the witness will present.

Subdivision (a)(2)(D). This provision (formerly Rule 26(a)(2)(C)) is amended slightly to specify that the time limits for disclosure of contradictory or rebuttal evidence apply with regard to disclosures under new Rule 26(a)(2)(C), just as they do with regard to reports under Rule 26(a)(2)(B).

Subdivision (b)(4). Rule 26(b)(4)(B) is added to provide work-product protection under Rule 26(b)(3)(A) and (B) for drafts of expert reports or disclosures. This protection applies to all witnesses identified under Rule 26(a)(2)(A), whether they are required to provide reports under Rule 26(a)(2)(B) or are the subject of disclosure under Rule 26(a)(2)(C). It applies regardless of the form in which the draft is recorded, whether written, electronic, or otherwise. It also applies to drafts of any supplementation under Rule 26(e); *see* Rule 26(a)(2)(E).

Rule 26(b)(4)(C) is added to provide work-product protection for attorney-expert communications regardless of the form of the communications, whether oral, written, electronic, or otherwise. The addition of Rule 26(b)(4)(C) is designed to protect counsel's work product and ensure that lawyers may interact with retained experts without fear of exposing those communications to searching discovery. The protection is limited to communications between an expert witness required to provide a report under Rule 26(a)(2)(B) and the attorney for the party on whose behalf the witness will be testifying, including any "preliminary" expert opinions. Protected "communications" include those between the party's attorney and assistants of the expert witness. The rule does not itself protect communications between counsel and other expert witnesses, such as those for whom disclosure is required under Rule 26(a)(2)(C). The rule does not exclude protection under other doctrines, such as privilege or independent development of the work-product doctrine.

The most frequent method for discovering the work of expert witnesses is by deposition, but Rules 26(b)(4)(B) and (C) apply to all forms of discovery.

Rules 26(b)(4)(B) and (C) do not impede discovery about the opinions to be offered by the expert or the development, foundation, or basis of those opinions. For example, the expert's testing of material involved in litigation, and notes of any such testing, would not be exempted from discovery by this rule. Similarly, inquiry about communications the expert had with anyone other than the party's counsel about the opinions expressed is unaffected by the rule. Counsel are also free to question expert witnesses about alternative analyses, testing methods, or approaches to the issues on which they are testifying, whether or not the expert considered them in forming the opinions expressed. These discovery changes therefore do not affect the gatekeeping functions called for by *Daubert v. Merrell Dow Pharmaceuticals, Inc.,* 509 U.S. 579 (1993), and related cases.

The protection for communications between the retained expert and "the party's attorney" should be applied in a realistic manner, and often would not be limited to communications with a single lawyer or a single law firm. For example, a party may be involved in a number of suits about a given product or service, and may retain a particular expert witness to testify on that party's behalf in several of the cases. In such a situation, the protection applies to communications between the expert witness and the attorneys representing the party in any of those cases. Similarly, communications with in-house counsel for the party would often be regarded as protected even if the in-house attorney is not counsel of record in the action. Other situations may also justify a pragmatic application of the "party's attorney" concept.

Although attorney-expert communications are generally protected by Rule 26(b)(4)(C), the protection does not apply to the extent the lawyer and the expert communicate about matters that fall within three exceptions. But the discovery authorized by the exceptions does not extend beyond those specific topics. Lawyer-expert communications may cover many topics and, even when the excepted topics are included among those involved in a given communication, the protection applies to all other aspects of the communication beyond the excepted topics.

First, under Rule 26(b)(4)(C)(i) attorney-expert communications regarding compensation for the expert's study or testimony may be the subject of discovery. In some cases, this discovery may go beyond the disclosure requirement in Rule 26(a)(2)(B)(vi). It is not limited to compensation for work forming the opinions to be expressed, but extends to all compensation for the study and testimony provided in relation to the action. Any communications about additional benefits to the expert, such as further work in the event of a successful result in the present case, would be included. This exception includes compensation for work done by a person or organization associated with the expert. The objective is to permit full inquiry into such potential sources of bias.

Second, under Rule 26(b)(4)(C)(ii) discovery is permitted to identify facts or data the party's attorney provided to the expert and that the expert considered in forming the opinions to be expressed. The exception applies only to communications "identifying" the facts or data provided by counsel; further communications about the potential relevance of the facts or data are protected.

Third, under Rule 26(b)(4)(C)(iii) discovery regarding attorney-expert communications is permitted to identify any assumptions that counsel provided to the expert and that the expert relied upon in forming the opinions to be expressed. For example, the party's attorney may tell the expert to assume the truth of certain testimony or evidence, or the correctness of another expert's conclusions. This exception is limited to those assumptions that the expert actually did rely on in forming the opinions to be expressed. More general attorney-expert discussions about hypotheticals, or exploring possibilities based on hypothetical facts, are outside this exception.

Under the amended rule, discovery regarding attorney-expert communications on subjects outside the three exceptions in Rule 26(b)(4)(C), or regarding draft expert reports or disclosures, is permitted only in limited circumstances and by court order. A party seeking such discovery must make the showing specified in Rule 26(b)(3)(A)(ii)—that the party has a substantial need for the discovery and cannot obtain the substantial equivalent without undue hardship. It will be rare for a party to be able to make such a showing given the broad disclosure and discovery otherwise allowed regarding the expert's testimony. A party's failure to provide required disclosure or discovery does not show the need and hardship required by Rule 26(b)(3)(A); remedies are provided by Rule 37.

In the rare case in which a party does make this showing, the court must protect against disclosure of the attorney's mental impressions, conclusions, opinions, or legal theories under Rule 26(b)(3)(B). But this protection does not extend to the expert's own development of the opinions to be presented; those are subject to probing in deposition or at trial.

Former Rules 26(b)(4)(B) and (C) have been renumbered (D) and (E), and a slight revision has been made in (E) to take account of the renumbering of former (B).

2015 Amendment

Rule 26(b)(1) is changed in several ways.

Information is discoverable under revised Rule 26(b)(1) if it is relevant to any party's claim or defense and is proportional to the needs of the case. The considerations that bear on proportionality are moved from present Rule 26(b)(2)(C)(iii), slightly rearranged and with one addition.

Most of what now appears in Rule 26(b)(2)(C)(iii) was first adopted in 1983. The 1983 provision was explicitly adopted as part of the scope of discovery defined by Rule 26(b)(1). Rule 26(b)(1) directed the court to limit the frequency or extent of use of discovery if it determined that "the discovery is unduly burdensome or expensive, taking into account the needs of the case, the amount in controversy, limitations on the parties' resources, and the importance of the issues at stake in the litigation." At the same time, Rule 26(g) was added. Rule 26(g) provided that signing a discovery request, response, or objection certified that the request, response, or objection was "not unreasonable or unduly burdensome or expensive, given the needs of the case, the discovery already had in the case, the amount in controversy, and the importance of the issues at stake in the litigation." The parties thus shared the responsibility to honor these limits on the scope of discovery.

The 1983 Committee Note stated that the new provisions were added "to deal with the problem of over-discovery. The objective is to guard against redundant or disproportionate discovery by giving the court authority to reduce the amount of discovery that may be directed to matters that are otherwise proper subjects of inquiry. The new sentence is intended to encourage judges to be more aggressive in identifying and discouraging discovery overuse. The grounds mentioned in the amended rule for limiting discovery reflect the existing practice of many courts in issuing protective orders under Rule 26(c) ... On the whole, however, district judges have been reluctant to limit the use of the discovery devices."

The clear focus of the 1983 provisions may have been softened, although inadvertently, by the amendments made in 1993. The 1993 Committee Note explained: "[F]ormer paragraph (b)(1) [was] subdivided into two paragraphs for ease of reference and to avoid renumbering of paragraphs (3) and (4)." Subdividing the paragraphs, however, was done in a way that could be read to separate the proportionality provisions as "limitations," no longer an integral part of the (b)(1) scope provisions. That appearance was immediately offset by the next statement in the Note: "Textual changes are then made in new paragraph (2) to enable the court to keep tighter rein on the extent of discovery."

The 1993 amendments added two factors to the considerations that bear on limiting discovery: whether "the burden or expense of the proposed discovery outweighs its likely benefit," and "the importance of the proposed discovery in resolving the issues." Addressing these and other limitations added by the 1993 discovery amendments, the Committee Note stated that [t]he revisions in Rule 26(b)(2) are intended to provide the court with broader discretion to impose additional restrictions on the scope and extent of discovery ...'

The relationship between Rule 26(b)(1) and (2) was further addressed by an amendment made in 2000 that added a new sentence at the end of (b)(1): "All discovery is subject to the limitations imposed by Rule 26(b)(2)(i), (ii), and (iii)[now Rule 26(b)(2)(C)]." The Committee Note recognized that "[t]hese limitations apply to discovery that is otherwise within the scope of subdivision (b)(1)." It explained that the Committee had been told repeatedly that courts were not using these limitations as originally intended. "This otherwise redundant cross-reference has been added to emphasize the need for active judicial use of subdivision (b)(2) to control excessive discovery."

The present amendment restores the proportionality factors to their original place in defining the scope of discovery. This change reinforces the Rule 26(g) obligation of the parties to consider these factors in making discovery requests, responses, or objections.

Restoring the proportionality calculation to Rule 26(b)(1) does not change the existing responsibilities of the court and the parties to consider proportionality, and the change does not place on the party seeking discovery the burden of addressing all proportionality considerations.

Nor is the change intended to permit the opposing party to refuse discovery simply by making a boilerplate objection that it is not proportional. The parties and the court have a collective responsibility to consider the proportionality of all discovery and consider it in resolving discovery disputes.

The parties may begin discovery without a full appreciation of the factors that bear on proportionality. A party requesting discovery, for example, may have little information about the burden or expense of responding. A party requested to provide discovery may have little information about the importance of the discovery in resolving the issues as understood by the requesting party. Many of these uncertainties should be addressed and reduced in the parties' Rule 26(f) conference and in scheduling and pretrial conferences with the court. But if the parties continue to disagree, the discovery dispute could be brought before the court and the parties' responsibilities would remain as they have been since 1983. A party claiming undue burden or expense ordinarily has far better information — perhaps the only information — with respect to that part of the determination. A party claiming that a request is important to resolve the issues should be able to explain the ways in which the underlying information bears on the issues as that party understands them. The court's responsibility, using all the information provided by the parties, is to consider these and all the other factors in reaching a case-specific determination of the appropriate scope of discovery.

The direction to consider the parties' relative access to relevant information adds new text to provide explicit focus on considerations already implicit in present Rule 26(b)(2)(C)(iii). Some cases involve what often is called "information asymmetry." One party — often an individual plaintiff — may have very little discoverable information. The other party may have vast amounts of information, including information that can be readily retrieved and information that is more difficult to retrieve. In practice these circumstances often mean that the burden of responding to discovery lies heavier on the party who has more information, and properly so.

Restoring proportionality as an express component of the scope of discovery warrants repetition of parts of the 1983 and 1993 Committee Notes that must not be lost from sight. The 1983 Committee Note explained that "[t]he rule contemplates greater judicial involvement in the discovery process and thus acknowledges the reality that it cannot always operate on a self-regulating basis." The 1993 Committee Note further observed that "[t]he information explosion of recent decades has greatly increased both the potential cost of wide-ranging discovery and the potential for discovery to be used as an instrument for delay or oppression." What seemed an explosion in 1993 has been exacerbated by the advent of e-discovery. The present amendment again reflects the need for continuing and close judicial involvement in the cases that do not yield readily to the ideal of effective party management. It is expected that discovery will be effectively managed by the parties in many cases. But there will be important occasions for judicial management, both when the parties are legitimately unable to resolve important differences and when the parties fall short of effective, cooperative management on their own.

It also is important to repeat the caution that the monetary stakes are only one factor, to be balanced against other factors. The 1983 Committee Note recognized "the significance of the substantive issues, as measured in philosophic, social, or institutional terms. Thus the rule recognizes that many cases in public policy spheres, such as employment practices, free speech, and other matters, may have importance far beyond the monetary amount involved." Many other substantive areas also may involve litigation that seeks relatively small amounts of money, or no money at all, but that seeks to vindicate vitally important personal or public values.

So too, consideration of the parties' resources does not foreclose discovery requests addressed to an impecunious party, nor justify unlimited discovery requests addressed to a wealthy party. The 1983 Committee Note cautioned that "[t]he court must apply the standards in an even-handed manner that will prevent use of discovery to wage a war of attrition or as a device to coerce a party, whether financially weak or affluent."

The burden or expense of proposed discovery should be determined in a realistic way. This includes the burden or expense of producing electronically stored information. Computer-based methods of searching such information continue to develop, particularly for cases involving large volumes of electronically stored information. Courts and parties should be willing to consider the opportunities for reducing the burden or expense of discovery as reliable means of searching electronically stored information become available.

A portion of present Rule 26(b)(1) is omitted from the proposed revision. After allowing discovery of any matter relevant to any party's claim or defense, the present rule adds: "including the existence, description, nature, custody, condition, and location of any documents or other tangible things and the identity and location of persons who know of any discoverable matter." Discovery of such matters is so deeply entrenched in practice that it is no longer necessary to clutter the long text of Rule 26 with these examples. The discovery identified in these examples should still be permitted under the revised rule when relevant and proportional to the needs of the case. Framing intelligent requests for electronically stored information, for example, may require detailed information about another party's information systems and other information resources.

The amendment deletes the former provision authorizing the court, for good cause, to order discovery of any matter relevant to the subject matter involved in the action. The Committee has been informed that this language is rarely invoked. Proportional discovery relevant to any party's claim or defense suffices, given a proper understanding of what is relevant to a claim or defense. The distinction between matter relevant to a claim or defense and matter relevant to the subject matter was introduced in 2000. The 2000 Note offered three examples of information that, suitably focused, would be relevant to the parties' claims or defenses. The examples were "other incidents of the same type, or involving the same product"; "information about organizational arrangements or filing systems"; and "information that could be used to impeach a likely witness." Such discovery is not foreclosed by the amendments. Discovery that is relevant to the parties' claims or defenses may also support amendment of the pleadings to add a new claim or defense that affects the scope of discovery.

The former provision for discovery of relevant but inadmissible information that appears "reasonably calculated to lead to the discovery of admissible evidence" is also deleted. The phrase has been used by some, incorrectly, to define the scope of discovery. As the Committee Note to the 2000 amendments observed, use of the "reasonably calculated" phrase to define the scope of discovery "might swallow any other limitation on the scope of discovery." The 2000 amendments sought to prevent such misuse by adding the word "Relevant" at the beginning of the sentence, making clear that "'relevant' means within the scope of discovery as defined in this subdivision ..." The "reasonably calculated" phrase has continued to create problems, however, and is removed by these amendments. It is replaced by the direct statement that "Information within this scope of discovery need not be admissible in evidence to be discoverable." Discovery of nonprivileged information not admissible in evidence remains available so long as it is otherwise within the scope of discovery.

Rule 26(b)(2)(C)(iii) is amended to reflect the transfer of the considerations that bear on proportionality to Rule 26(b)(1). The court still must limit the frequency or extent of proposed discovery, on motion or on its own, if it is outside the scope permitted by Rule 26(b)(1).

Rule 26(c)(1)(B) is amended to include an express recognition of protective orders that allocate expenses for disclosure or discovery. Authority to enter such orders is included in the present rule, and courts already exercise this authority. Explicit recognition will forestall the temptation some parties may feel to contest this authority. Recognizing the authority does not imply that cost-shifting should become a common practice. Courts and parties should continue to assume that a responding party ordinarily bears the costs of responding.

Rule 26(d)(2) is added to allow a party to deliver Rule 34 requests to another party more than 21 days after that party has been served even though the parties have not yet had a required Rule 26(f) conference. Delivery may be made by any party to the party that has been served, and by that party to any plaintiff and any other party that has been served. Delivery does not count as service; the requests are considered to be served at the first Rule 26(f) conference. Under Rule 34(b)(2)(A) the time to respond runs from service. This relaxation of the discovery moratorium is designed to facilitate focused discussion during the Rule 26(f) conference. Discussion at the conference may produce changes in the requests. The opportunity for advance scrutiny of requests delivered before the Rule 26(f) conference should not affect a decision whether to allow additional time to respond.

Rule 26(d)(3) is renumbered and amended to recognize that the parties may stipulate to case-specific sequences of discovery.

Rule 26(f)(3) is amended in parallel with Rule 16(b)(3) to add two items to the discovery plan — issues about preserving electronically stored information and court orders under Evidence Rule 502.

CROSS REFERENCES

Depositions,

    Before action or pending appeal, see Fed.Rules Civ.Proc. Rule 27, 28 USCA.

    Of witnesses upon written questions, see Fed.Rules Civ. Proc. Rule 31, 28 USCA.

Depositions upon oral examination, requirements of, see Fed.Rules Civ.Proc. Rule 30, 28 USCA.

Persons before whom depositions may be taken, see Fed. Rules Civ.Proc. Rule 28, 28 USCA.

Sanctions for failure to make or cooperate in discovery, see Fed.Rules Civ.Proc. Rule 37, 28 USCA.

Stipulations regarding taking depositions, see Fed.Rules Civ.Proc. Rule 29, 28 USCA.

Subpoena for taking depositions, time and place of examination, see Fed.Rules Civ.Proc. Rule 45, 28 USCA.

Summary judgment, opposing motion, see Fed.Rules Civ. Proc. Rule 56, 28 USCA.

Use of deposition in court proceedings, effect of errors, irregularities, objections to admissibility, see Fed.Rules Civ. Proc. Rule 32, 28 USCA.

Written interrogatories of party, see Fed.Rules Civ.Proc. Rule 33, 28 USCA.

Rule 27.   Depositions to Perpetuate Testimony

(a) Before an Action Is Filed.

(1) *Petition.* A person who wants to perpetuate testimony about any matter cognizable in a United States court may file a verified petition in the district court for the district where any expected adverse party resides. The petition must ask for an order authorizing the petitioner to depose the named persons in order to perpetuate their testimony. The petition must be titled in the petitioner's name and must show:

    (A) that the petitioner expects to be a party to an action cognizable in a United States court but cannot presently bring it or cause it to be brought;

    (B) the subject matter of the expected action and the petitioner's interest;

    (C) the facts that the petitioner wants to establish by the proposed testimony and the reasons to perpetuate it;

    (D) the names or a description of the persons whom the petitioner expects to be adverse parties and their addresses, so far as known; and

    (E) the name, address, and expected substance of the testimony of each deponent.

(2) *Notice and Service.* At least 21 days before the hearing date, the petitioner must serve each expected adverse party with a copy of the petition and a notice stating the time and place of the hearing. The notice may be served either inside or outside the district or state in the manner provided in Rule 4. If that service cannot be made with reasonable diligence on an expected adverse party, the court may order service by publication or otherwise. The court must appoint an attorney to represent persons not served in the manner provided in Rule 4 and to cross-examine the deponent if an unserved person is not otherwise represented. If any expected adverse party is a minor or is incompetent, Rule 17(c) applies.

(3) Order and Examination. If satisfied that perpetuating the testimony may prevent a failure or delay of justice, the court must issue an order that designates or describes the persons whose depositions may be taken, specifies the subject matter of the examinations, and states whether the depositions will be taken orally or by written interrogatories. The depositions may then be taken under these rules, and the court may issue orders like those authorized by Rules 34 and 35. A reference in these rules to the court where an action is pending means, for purposes of this rule, the court where the petition for the deposition was filed.

(4) Using the Deposition. A deposition to perpetuate testimony may be used under Rule 32(a) in any later-filed district-court action involving the same subject matter if the deposition either was taken under these rules or, although not so taken, would be admissible in evidence in the courts of the state where it was taken.

(b) Pending Appeal.

(1) In General. The court where a judgment has been rendered may, if an appeal has been taken or may still be taken, permit a party to depose witnesses to perpetuate their testimony for use in the event of further proceedings in that court.

(2) Motion. The party who wants to perpetuate testimony may move for leave to take the depositions, on the same notice and service as if the action were pending in the district court. The motion must show:

(A) the name, address, and expected substance of the testimony of each deponent; and

(B) the reasons for perpetuating the testimony.

(3) Court Order. If the court finds that perpetuating the testimony may prevent a failure or delay of justice, the court may permit the depositions to be taken and may issue orders like those authorized by Rules 34 and 35. The depositions may be taken and used as any other deposition taken in a pending district-court action.

(c) Perpetuation by an Action. This rule does not limit a court's power to entertain an action to perpetuate testimony.

(Amended December 27, 1946, effective March 19, 1948; December 29, 1948, effective October 20, 1949; March 1, 1971, effective July 1, 1971; March 2, 1987, effective August 1, 1987; April 25, 2005, effective December 1, 2005; April 30, 2007, effective December 1, 2007; March 26, 2009, effective December 1, 2009.)

ADVISORY COMMITTEE NOTES
1937 Adoption

Note to Subdivision (a). This rule offers a simple method of perpetuating testimony in cases where it is usually allowed under equity practice or under modern statutes. See *Arizona v. California*, 1934, 54 S.Ct. 735, 292 U.S. 341, 78 L.Ed. 1298; *Todd Engineering Dry Dock and Repair Co. v. United States*, C.C.A.5, 1929, 32 F.2d 734; *Hall v. Stout*, 4 Del.Ch. 269 (1871). For comparable state statutes see Ark.Civ.Code (Crawford, 1934) §§ 666 to 670; Calif.Code Civ.Proc. (Deering, 1937) 2083–2089; Smith-Hurd Ill.Stats. c. 51, §§ 39 to 46; Iowa Code (1935) §§ 11400 to 11407; 2 Mass.Gen.Laws (Ter. Ed., 1932) ch. 233, §§ 46 to 63; N.Y.C.P.A. (1937) § 295; Ohio Gen.Code Ann. (Throckmorton, 1936) §§ 12216 to 12222; Va. Code Ann. (Michie, 1936) § 6235; Wis.Stat. (1935) §§ 326.27 to 326.29. The appointment of an attorney to represent absent parties or parties not personally notified, or a guardian ad litem to represent minors and incompetents, is provided for in several of the above statutes.

Note to Subdivision (b). This follows the practice approved in *Richter v. Union Trust Co.*, 1885, 5 S.Ct. 1162, 115 U.S. 55, 29 L.Ed. 345, by extending the right to perpetuate testimony to cases pending an appeal.

Note to Subdivision (c). This preserves the right to employ a separate action to perpetuate testimony under U.S.C., Title 28, [former] § 644 (Depositions under *dedimus potestatem* and *in perpetuam*) as an alternate method.

1946 Amendment

Note. Since the second sentence in subdivision (a)(3) refers only to depositions, it is arguable that Rules 34 and 35 are inapplicable in proceedings to perpetuate testimony. The new matter [in subdivisions (a)(3) and (b)] clarifies. A conforming change is also made in subdivision (b).

1948 Amendment

The amendment effective October 1949, substituted the words "United States district court" in subdivision (a)(1) and (4) for "district court of the United States."

1971 Amendment

The reference intended in this subdivision is to the rule governing the use of depositions in court proceedings. Formerly Rule 26(d), that rule is now Rule 32(a). The subdivision is amended accordingly.

1987 Amendment

The amendments are technical. No substantive change is intended.

2005 Amendment

The outdated cross-reference to former Rule 4(d) is corrected to incorporate all Rule 4 methods of service. Former Rule 4(d) has been allocated to many different subdivisions of Rule 4. Former Rule 4(d) did not cover all categories of defendants or modes of service, and present Rule 4 reaches further than all of former Rule 4. But there is no reason to distinguish between the different categories of defendants and modes of service encompassed by Rule 4. Rule 4 service provides effective notice. Notice by such means should be provided to any expected adverse party that comes within Rule 4.

Other changes are made to conform Rule 27(a)(2) to current style conventions.

2007 Amendment

The language of Rule 27 has been amended as part of the general restyling of the Civil Rules to make them more easily understood and to make style and terminology consistent throughout the rules. These changes are intended to be stylistic only.

2009 Amendment

The time set in the former rule at 20 days has been revised to 21 days. See the Note to Rule 6.

CROSS REFERENCES

Persons before whom depositions may be taken, see Fed. Rules Civ.Proc. Rule 28, 28 USCA.

Rule 28. Persons Before Whom Depositions May Be Taken

(a) Within the United States.

(1) *In General.* Within the United States or a territory or insular possession subject to United States jurisdiction, a deposition must be taken before:

(A) an officer authorized to administer oaths either by federal law or by the law in the place of examination; or

(B) a person appointed by the court where the action is pending to administer oaths and take testimony.

(2) *Definition of "Officer."* The term "officer" in Rules 30, 31, and 32 includes a person appointed by the court under this rule or designated by the parties under Rule 29(a).

(b) In a Foreign Country.

(1) *In General.* A deposition may be taken in a foreign country:

(A) under an applicable treaty or convention;

(B) under a letter of request, whether or not captioned a "letter rogatory";

(C) on notice, before a person authorized to administer oaths either by federal law or by the law in the place of examination; or

(D) before a person commissioned by the court to administer any necessary oath and take testimony.

(2) *Issuing a Letter of Request or a Commission.* A letter of request, a commission, or both may be issued:

(A) on appropriate terms after an application and notice of it; and

(B) without a showing that taking the deposition in another manner is impracticable or inconvenient.

(3) *Form of a Request, Notice, or Commission.* When a letter of request or any other device is used according to a treaty or convention, it must be captioned in the form prescribed by that treaty or convention. A letter of request may be addressed "To the Appropriate Authority in [name of country]." A deposition notice or a commission must designate by name or descriptive title the person before whom the deposition is to be taken.

(4) *Letter of Request—Admitting Evidence.* Evidence obtained in response to a letter of request need not be excluded merely because it is not a verbatim transcript, because the testimony was not taken under oath, or because of any similar departure from the requirements for depositions taken within the United States.

(c) Disqualification. A deposition must not be taken before a person who is any party's relative, employee, or attorney; who is related to or employed by any party's attorney; or who is financially interested in the action.

(Amended December 27, 1946, effective March 19, 1948; January 21, 1963, effective July 1, 1963; April 29, 1980, effective August 1, 1980; March 2, 1987, effective August 1, 1987; April 22, 1993, effective December 1, 1993; April 30, 2007, effective December 1, 2007.)

ADVISORY COMMITTEE NOTES

1937 Adoption

In effect this rule is substantially the same as U.S.C., Title 28, [former] § 639 (Depositions *de bene esse*; when and where taken; notice). U.S.C., Title 28, [former] § 642 (Depositions, acknowledgments, and affidavits taken by notaries public) does not conflict with subdivision (a).

1946 Amendment

Note. The added language [in subdivision (a)] provides for the situation, occasionally arising, when depositions must be taken in an isolated place where there is no one readily available who has the power to administer oaths and take testimony according to the terms of the rule as originally stated. In addition, the amendment affords a more convenient method of securing depositions in the case where state lines intervene between the location of various witnesses otherwise rather closely grouped. The amendment insures that the person appointed shall have adequate power to perform his duties. It has been held that a person authorized to act in the premises, as, for example, a master, may take testimony outside the district of his appointment. *Consolidated Fastener Co. v. Columbian Button & Fastener Co.,* C.C.N.D.N.Y.1898, 85 Fed. 54; *Mathieson Alkali Works v. Arnold, Hoffman & Co.,* C.C.A.1, 1929, 31 F.2d 1.

1963 Amendment

The amendment of clause (1) is designed to facilitate depositions in foreign countries by enlarging the class of persons before whom the depositions may be taken on notice. The class is no longer confined, as at present, to a secretary of embassy or legation, consul general, consul, vice consul, or consular agent of the United States. In a country that regards the taking of testimony by a foreign official in aid of litigation pending in a court of another country as an infringement upon its sovereignty, it will be expedient to notice depositions before officers of the country in which the examination is taken. See generally *Symposium, Letters Rogatory* (Grossman ed. 1956); Doyle, *Taking Evidence by Deposition and Letters Rogatory and Obtaining Documents in Foreign Territory,* Proc.A.B.A., Sec.Int'l & Comp.L. 37 (1959); Heilpern, *Procuring Evidence Abroad,* 14 Tul.L.Rev. 29 (1939); Jones, *International Judicial Assistance: Procedural Chaos and a Program for Reform,* 62 Yale L.J. 515, 526–29 (1953); Smit, *International Aspects of Federal Civil Procedure,* 61 Colum.L.Rev. 1031, 1056–58 (1961).

Clause (2) of amended subdivision (b), like the corresponding provision of subdivision (a) dealing with depositions taken in the United States, makes it clear that the appointment of a person by commission in itself confers power upon him to administer any necessary oath.

It has been held that a letter rogatory will not be issued unless the use of a notice or commission is shown to be impossible or impractical. See, e.g., *United States v. Matles,* 154 F.Supp. 574 (E.D.N.Y.1957); *The Edmund Fanning,* 89 F.Supp. 282 (E.D.N.Y.1950); *Branyan v. Koninklijke Luchtvaart Maatschappij,* 13 F.R.D. 425 (S.D.N.Y.1953). See also *Ali Akber Kiachif v. Philco International Corp.,* 10 F.R.D. 277 (S.D.N.Y.1950). The intent of the fourth sentence of the amended subdivision is to overcome this judicial antipathy and to permit a sound choice between depositions under a letter rogatory and on notice or by commission in the light of all the circumstances. In a case in which the foreign country will compel a witness to attend or testify in aid of a letter rogatory but not in aid of a commission, a letter rogatory may be preferred on the ground that it is less expensive to execute, even if there is plainly no need for compulsive process. A letter rogatory may also be preferred when it cannot be demonstrated that a witness will be recalcitrant or when the witness states that he is willing to testify voluntarily, but the contingency exists that he will change his mind at the last moment. In the latter case, it may be advisable to issue both a commission and a letter rogatory, the latter to be executed if the former fails. The choice between a letter rogatory and a commission may be conditioned by other factors, including the nature and extent of the assistance that the foreign country will give to the execution of either.

In executing a letter rogatory the courts of other countries may be expected to follow their customary procedure for taking testimony. See *United States v. Paraffin Wax,* 2255 Bags, 23 F.R.D. 289 (E.D.N.Y.1959). In many noncommon-law countries the judge questions the witness, sometimes without first administering an oath, the attorneys put any supplemental questions either to the witness or through the judge, and the judge dictates a summary of the testimony, which the witness acknowledges as correct. See *Jones, supra,* at 530–32; *Doyle, supra,* at 39–41. The last sentence of the amended subdivision provides, contrary to the implications of some authority, that evidence recorded in such a fashion need not be excluded on that account. See *The Mandu,* 11 F.Supp. 845 (E.D.N.Y.1935). But *cf. Nelson v. United States,* 17 Fed.Cas. 1340 (No. 10,116) (C.C.D.Pa.1816); *Winthrop v. Union Ins. Co.,* 30 Fed.Cas. 376 (No. 17901) (C.C.D.Pa.1807). The specific reference to the lack of an oath or a verbatim transcript is intended to be illustrative. Whether or to what degree the value or weight of the evidence may be affected by the method of taking or recording the testimony is left for determination according to the circumstances of the particular case, *cf. Uebersee Finanz-Korporation, A.G. v. Brownell,* 121 F.Supp. 420 (D.D.C.1954); *Danisch v. Guardian Life Ins. Co.,* 19 F.R.D. 235 (S.D.N.Y. 1956); the testimony may indeed be so devoid of substance or probative value as to warrant its exclusion altogether.

Some foreign countries are hostile to allowing a deposition to be taken in their country, especially by notice or commission, or to lending assistance in the taking of a deposition. Thus compliance with the terms of amended subdivision (b) may not in all cases ensure completion of a deposition abroad. Examination of the law and policy of the particular foreign country in advance of attempting a deposition is therefore advisable. See 4 *Moore's Federal Practice* ¶¶28.05–28.08 (2d ed. 1950).

1980 Amendment

The amendments are clarifying.

1987 Amendment

The amendment is technical. No substantive change is intended.

1993 Amendment

This revision is intended to make effective use of the Hague Convention on the Taking of Evidence Abroad in Civil or Commercial Matters, and of any similar treaties that the United States may enter into in the future which provide procedures for taking depositions abroad. The party taking the deposition is ordinarily obliged to conform to an applicable treaty or convention if an effective deposition can be taken by such internationally approved means, even though a verbatim transcript is not available or testimony cannot be taken under oath. For a discussion of the impact of such treaties upon the discovery process, and of the application of principles of comity upon discovery in countries not signatories to a convention, see *Société Nationale Industrielle Aérospatiale v. United States District Court,* 482 U.S. 522 (1987).

The term "letter of request" has been substituted in the rule for the term "letter rogatory" because it is the primary method provided by the Hague Convention. A letter rogatory is essentially a form of letter of request. There are several other minor changes that are designed merely to carry out the intent of the other alterations.

2007 Amendment

The language of Rule 28 has been amended as part of the general restyling of the Civil Rules to make them more easily understood and to make style and terminology consistent throughout the rules. These changes are intended to be stylistic only.

HISTORICAL NOTES

Treaties and Conventions; Taking of Evidence Abroad in Civil or Commercial Matters; Observance On and After Oct. 7, 1972, by United States and Citizens and Persons Subject to Jurisdiction of United States

For text of Convention, see provisions set out as a note under section 1781 of this title.

CROSS REFERENCES

Certification and filing of depositions by officer, see Fed. Rules Civ.Proc. Rule 30, 28 USCA.

Objections to admissibility of depositions, see Fed.Rules Civ.Proc. Rule 32, 28 USCA.

Procedures for taking of depositions, evidence abroad in civil or commercial matters, see 28 USCA § 1781.

Taking responses to written interrogatories and preparation of record, see Fed.Rules Civ.Proc. Rule 31, 28 USCA.

Rule 29. Stipulations About Discovery Procedure

Unless the court orders otherwise, the parties may stipulate that:

(a) a deposition may be taken before any person, at any time or place, on any notice, and in the manner specified—in which event it may be used in the same way as any other deposition; and

(b) other procedures governing or limiting discovery be modified—but a stipulation extending the time for any form of discovery must have court approval if it would interfere with the time set for completing discovery, for hearing a motion, or for trial.

(Amended March 30, 1970, effective July 1, 1970; April 22, 1993, effective December 1, 1993; April 30, 2007, effective December 1, 2007.)

ADVISORY COMMITTEE NOTES

1970 Amendment

There is no provision for stipulations varying the procedures by which methods of discovery other than depositions are governed. It is common practice for parties to agree on such variations, and the amendment recognizes such agreements and provides a formal mechanism in the rules for giving them effect. Any stipulation varying the procedures may be superseded by court order, and stipulations extending the time for response to discovery under Rules 33, 34, and 36 require court approval.

1993 Amendment

This rule is revised to give greater opportunity for litigants to agree upon modifications to the procedures governing discovery or to limitations upon discovery. Counsel are encouraged to agree on less expensive and time-consuming methods to obtain information, as through voluntary exchange of documents, use of interviews in lieu of depositions, etc. Likewise, when more depositions or interrogatories are needed than allowed under these rules or when more time is needed to complete a deposition than allowed under a local rule, they can, by agreeing to the additional discovery, eliminate the need for a special motion addressed to the court.

Under the revised rule, the litigants ordinarily are not required to obtain the court's approval of these stipulations. By order or local rule, the court can, however, direct that its approval be obtained for particular types of stipulations; and, in any event, approval must be obtained if a stipulation to extend the 30–day period for responding to interrogatories, requests for production, or requests for admissions would interfere with dates set by the court for completing discovery, for hearing of a motion, or for trial.

2007 Amendment

The language of Rule 29 has been amended as part of the general restyling of the Civil Rules to make them more easily understood and to make style and terminology consistent throughout the rules. These changes are intended to be stylistic only.

Rule 30. Depositions by Oral Examination

(a) When a Deposition May Be Taken.

(1) *Without Leave.* A party may, by oral questions, depose any person, including a party, without leave of court except as provided in Rule 30(a)(2). The deponent's attendance may be compelled by subpoena under Rule 45.

(2) *With Leave.* A party must obtain leave of court, and the court must grant leave to the extent consistent with Rule 26(b)(1) and (2):

(A) if the parties have not stipulated to the deposition and:

(i) the deposition would result in more than 10 depositions being taken under this rule or Rule 31 by the plaintiffs, or by the defendants, or by the third-party defendants;

(ii) the deponent has already been deposed in the case; or

(iii) the party seeks to take the deposition before the time specified in Rule 26(d), unless the party certifies in the notice, with supporting facts, that the deponent is expected to leave the United States and be unavailable for examination in this country after that time; or

(B) if the deponent is confined in prison.

(b) Notice of the Deposition; Other Formal Requirements.

(1) *Notice in General.* A party who wants to depose a person by oral questions must give reasonable written notice to every other party. The notice must state the time and place of the deposition and, if known, the deponent's name and address. If the name is unknown, the notice must provide a general description sufficient to identify the person or the particular class or group to which the person belongs.

(2) *Producing Documents.* If a subpoena duces tecum is to be served on the deponent, the materials designated for production, as set out in the subpoena, must be listed in the notice or in an attachment. The notice to a party deponent may be accompanied by a request under Rule 34 to produce documents and tangible things at the deposition.

(3) *Method of Recording.*

(A) *Method Stated in the Notice.* The party who notices the deposition must state in the notice the method for recording the testimony. Unless the court orders otherwise, testimony may be recorded by audio, audiovisual, or stenographic means. The noticing party bears the recording costs. Any party may arrange to transcribe a deposition.

(B) *Additional Method.* With prior notice to the deponent and other parties, any party may designate another method for recording the testimony in addition to that specified in the original notice. That party bears the expense of the additional record or transcript unless the court orders otherwise.

(4) *By Remote Means.* The parties may stipulate—or the court may on motion order—that a deposition be taken by telephone or other remote means. For the purpose of this rule and Rules 28(a), 37(a)(2), and 37(b)(1), the deposition takes place where the deponent answers the questions.

(5) *Officer's Duties.*

(A) *Before the Deposition.* Unless the parties stipulate otherwise, a deposition must be conducted before an officer appointed or designated under Rule 28. The officer must begin the deposition with an on-the-record statement that includes:

(i) the officer's name and business address;

(ii) the date, time, and place of the deposition;

(iii) the deponent's name;

(iv) the officer's administration of the oath or affirmation to the deponent; and

(v) the identity of all persons present.

(B) *Conducting the Deposition; Avoiding Distortion.* If the deposition is recorded non-stenographically, the officer must repeat the items in Rule 30(b)(5)(A)(i)-(iii) at the beginning of each unit of the recording medium. The deponent's and attorneys' appearance or demeanor must not be distorted through recording techniques.

(C) *After the Deposition.* At the end of a deposition, the officer must state on the record that the deposition is complete and must set out any stipulations made by the attorneys about custody of the transcript or recording and of the exhibits, or about any other pertinent matters.

(6) *Notice or Subpoena Directed to an Organization.* In its notice or subpoena, a party may name as the deponent a public or private corporation, a partnership, an association, a governmental agency, or other entity and must describe with reasonable particularity the matters for examination. The named organization must then designate one or more officers, directors, or managing agents, or designate other persons who consent to testify on its behalf; and it may set out the matters on which each person designated will testify. A subpoena must advise a nonparty organization of its duty to make this designation. The persons designated must testify about information known or reasonably available to the organization. This paragraph (6) does not preclude a deposition by any other procedure allowed by these rules.

(c) Examination and Cross–Examination; Record of the Examination; Objections; Written Questions.

(1) *Examination and Cross–Examination.* The examination and cross-examination of a deponent proceed as they would at trial under the Federal Rules of Evidence, except Rules 103 and 615. After putting the deponent under oath or affirmation, the officer must record the testimony by the method designated under Rule 30(b)(3)(A). The testimony must be recorded by the officer personally or by a person acting in the presence and under the direction of the officer.

(2) *Objections.* An objection at the time of the examination—whether to evidence, to a party's conduct, to the officer's qualifications, to the manner of taking the deposition, or to any other aspect of the deposition—must be noted on the record, but the examination still proceeds; the testimony is taken subject to any objection. An objection must be stated concisely in a nonargumentative and nonsuggestive manner. A person may instruct a deponent not to answer only when necessary to preserve a privilege, to enforce a limitation ordered by the court, or to present a motion under Rule 30(d)(3).

(3) *Participating Through Written Questions.* Instead of participating in the oral examination, a party may serve written questions in a sealed envelope on the party noticing the deposition, who must deliver them to the officer. The officer must ask the deponent those questions and record the answers verbatim.

(d) Duration; Sanction; Motion to Terminate or Limit.

(1) *Duration.* Unless otherwise stipulated or ordered by the court, a deposition is limited to one day of 7 hours. The court must allow additional time consistent with Rule 26(b)(1) and (2) if needed to fairly examine the deponent or if the deponent, another person, or any other circumstance impedes or delays the examination.

(2) *Sanction.* The court may impose an appropriate sanction—including the reasonable expenses and attorney's fees incurred by any party—on a person who impedes, delays, or frustrates the fair examination of the deponent.

(3) *Motion to Terminate or Limit.*

(A) *Grounds.* At any time during a deposition, the deponent or a party may move to terminate or limit it on the ground that it is being conducted in bad faith or in a manner that unreasonably annoys, embarrasses, or oppresses the deponent or party. The motion may be filed in the court where the action is pending or the deposition is being taken. If the objecting deponent or party so demands, the deposition must be suspended for the time necessary to obtain an order.

(B) *Order.* The court may order that the deposition be terminated or may limit its scope and manner as provided in Rule 26(c). If terminated, the deposition may be resumed only by order of the court where the action is pending.

(C) *Award of Expenses.* Rule 37(a)(5) applies to the award of expenses.

(e) Review by the Witness; Changes.

(1) *Review; Statement of Changes.* On request by the deponent or a party before the deposition is completed, the deponent must be allowed 30 days after being notified by the officer that the transcript or recording is available in which:

(A) to review the transcript or recording; and

(B) if there are changes in form or substance, to sign a statement listing the changes and the reasons for making them.

(2) *Changes Indicated in the Officer's Certificate.* The officer must note in the certificate prescribed by Rule 30(f)(1) whether a review was requested and, if so, must attach any changes the deponent makes during the 30–day period.

(f) Certification and Delivery; Exhibits; Copies of the Transcript or Recording; Filing.

(1) *Certification and Delivery.* The officer must certify in writing that the witness was duly sworn and that the deposition accurately records the witness's testimony. The certificate must accompany the record of the deposition. Unless the court orders otherwise, the officer must seal the deposition in an envelope or package bearing the title of the action and marked "Deposition of [witness's name]" and must promptly send it to the attorney who arranged for the transcript or recording. The attorney must store it under conditions that will protect it against loss, destruction, tampering, or deterioration.

(2) *Documents and Tangible Things.*

(A) *Originals and Copies.* Documents and tangible things produced for inspection during a deposition must, on a party's request, be marked for identification and attached to the deposition. Any party may inspect and copy them. But if the person who produced them wants to keep the originals, the person may:

(i) offer copies to be marked, attached to the deposition, and then used as originals—after giving all parties a fair opportunity to verify the copies by comparing them with the originals; or

(ii) give all parties a fair opportunity to inspect and copy the originals after they are marked—in which event the originals may be used as if attached to the deposition.

(B) *Order Regarding the Originals.* Any party may move for an order that the originals be attached to the deposition pending final disposition of the case.

(3) *Copies of the Transcript or Recording.* Unless otherwise stipulated or ordered by the court, the officer must retain the stenographic notes of a deposition taken stenographically or a copy of the recording of a deposition taken by another method. When paid reasonable charges, the officer must furnish a copy of the transcript or recording to any party or the deponent.

(4) *Notice of Filing.* A party who files the deposition must promptly notify all other parties of the filing.

(g) Failure to Attend a Deposition or Serve a Subpoena; Expenses. A party who, expecting a deposition to be taken, attends in person or by an attorney may recover reasonable expenses for attending, including attorney's fees, if the noticing party failed to:

(1) attend and proceed with the deposition; or

(2) serve a subpoena on a nonparty deponent, who consequently did not attend.

(Amended January 21, 1963, effective July 1, 1963; March 30, 1970, effective July 1, 1970; March 1, 1971, effective July 1, 1971; November 20, 1972, effective July 1, 1975; April 29, 1980, effective August 1, 1980; March 2, 1987, effective August 1, 1987; April 22, 1993, effective December 1, 1993; April 17, 2000, effective December 1, 2000; April 30, 2007, effective December 1, 2007; April 29, 2015, effective December 1, 2015.)

ADVISORY COMMITTEE NOTES

1937 Adoption

Note to Subdivision (a). This is in accordance with common practice. See U.S.C., Title 28, [former] § 639 (Depositions *de bene esse*; when and where taken; notice), the relevant provisions of which are incorporated in this rule; West's Ann.Code Civ.Proc. § 2031; and statutes cited in respect to notice in the Note to Rule 26(a). The provision for enlarging or shortening the time of notice has been added to give flexibility to the rule.

Note to Subdivisions (b) and (d). These are introduced as a safeguard for the protection of parties and deponents on account of the unlimited right of discovery given by Rule 26.

Note to Subdivisions (c) and (e). These follow the general plan of [former] Equity Rule 51 (Evidence Taken Before Examiners, Etc.) and U.S.C., Title 28, [former] §§ 640 (Depositions *de bene esse*; mode of taking), and [former] 641 (Same; transmission to court), but are more specific. They also permit the deponent to require the officer to make changes in the deposition if the deponent is not satisfied with it. See also [former] Equity Rule 50 (Stenographer—Appointment—Fees.)

Note to Subdivision (f). Compare [former] Equity Rule 55 (Depositions Deemed Published When Filed.)

Note to Subdivision (g). This is similar to 2 Minn.Stat. (Mason, 1927) § 9833, but is more extensive.

1963 Amendment

This amendment corresponds to the change in Rule 4(d)(4). See Advisory Committee's Note to that amendment.

1970 Amendment

Subdivision (a). This subdivision contains the provisions of existing Rule 26(a), transferred here as part of the rearrangement relating to Rule 26. Existing Rule 30(a) is transferred to 30(b). Changes in language have been made to conform to the new arrangement.

This subdivision is further revised in regard to the requirement of leave of court for taking a deposition. The present procedure, requiring a plaintiff to obtain leave of court if he serves notice of taking a deposition within 20 days after commencement of the action, is changed in several respects. First, leave is required by reference to the time the deposition is to be taken rather than the date of serving notice of taking. Second, the 20-day period is extended to 30 days and runs from the service of summons and complaint on any defendant, rather than the commencement of the action. *Cf.* Ill.S.Ct.R. 19–1 S–H Ill.Ann.Stat. § 101.19–1. Third, leave is not required beyond the time that defendant initiates discovery, thus showing that he has retained counsel. As under the present practice, a party not afforded a reasonable opportunity to appear at a deposition, because he has not yet been served with process, is protected against use of the deposition at trial against him. See Rule 32(a), transferred from 26(d). Moreover, he can later redepose the witness if he so desires.

The purpose of requiring the plaintiff to obtain leave of court is, as stated by the Advisory Committee that proposed the present language of Rule 26(a), to protect "a defendant who has not had an opportunity to retain counsel and inform himself as to the nature of the suit." Note to 1948 amendment of Rule 26(a), quoted in 3A Barron & Holtzoff, *Federal Practice and Procedure* 455–456 (Wright ed. 1958). In order to assure defendant of this opportunity, the period is lengthened to 30 days. This protection, however, is relevant to the time of taking the deposition, not to the time that notice is served. Similarly, the protective period should run from the service of process rather than the filing of the complaint with the court. As stated in the note to Rule 26(d), the courts have used the service of notice as a convenient reference point for assigning priority in taking depositions, but with the elimination of priority in new Rule 26(d) the reference point is no longer needed. The new procedure is consistent in principle with the provisions of Rules 33, 34, and 36 as revised.

Plaintiff is excused from obtaining leave even during the initial 30-day period if he gives the special notice provided in subdivision (b)(2). The required notice must state that the person to be examined is about to go out of the district where the action is pending and more than 100 miles from the place of trial, or out of the United States, or on a voyage to sea, and will be unavailable for examination unless deposed within the 30-day period. These events occur most often in maritime litigation, when seamen are transferred from one port to another or are about to go to sea. Yet, there are analogous situations in nonmaritime litigation, and although the maritime problems are more common, a rule limited to claims in the admiralty and maritime jurisdiction is not justified.

In the recent unification of the civil and admiralty rules, this problem was temporarily met through addition in Rule 26(a) of a provision that depositions *de bene esse* may continue to be taken as to admiralty and maritime claims within the meaning of Rule 9(h). It was recognized at the time that "a uniform rule applicable alike to what are now civil actions and suits in admiralty" was clearly preferable, but the de bene esse procedure was adopted "for the time being at least." See Advisory Committee's Note in Report of the Judicial Conference: Proposed Amendments to Rules of Civil Procedure 43–44 (1966).

The changes in Rule 30(a) and the new Rule 30(b)(2) provide a formula applicable to ordinary civil as well as maritime claims. They replace the provision for depositions *de bene esse*. They authorize an early deposition without leave of court where the witness is about to depart and, unless his deposition is promptly taken, (1) it will be impossible or very difficult to depose him before trial or (2) his deposition can later be taken but only with substantially increased effort and expense. *Cf. S.S. Hai Chang*, 1966 A.M.C. 2239 (S.D.N.Y.1966), in which the deposing party is required to prepay expenses and counsel fees of the other party's lawyer when the action is pending in New York and depositions are to be taken on the West Coast. Defendant is protected by a provision that the deposition cannot be used against him if he was unable through exercise of diligence to obtain counsel to represent him.

The distance of 100 miles from place of trial is derived from the *de bene esse* provision and also conforms to the reach of a subpoena of the trial court, as provided in Rule 45(e). See also S.D.N.Y. Civ.R. 5(a). Some parts of the *de bene esse* provision are omitted from Rule 30(b)(2). Modern deposition practice adequately covers the witness who lives more than 100 miles away from place of trial. If a witness is aged or infirm, leave of court can be obtained.

Subdivision (b). Existing Rule 30(b) on protective orders has been transferred to Rule 26(c), and existing Rule 30(a) relating to the notice of taking deposition has been transferred to this subdivision. Because new material has been added, subsection numbers have been inserted.

Subdivision (b)(1). If a subpoena duces tecum is to be served, a copy thereof or a designation of the materials to be produced must accompany the notice. Each party is thereby enabled to prepare for the deposition more effectively.

Subdivision (b)(2). This subdivision is discussed in the note to subdivision (a), to which it relates.

Subdivision (b)(3). This provision is derived from existing Rule 30(a), with a minor change of language.

Subdivision (b)(4). In order to facilitate less expensive procedures, provision is made for the recording of testimony by other than stenographic means—*e.g.*, by mechanical, electronic, or photographic means. Because these methods give rise to problems of accuracy and trustworthiness, the party taking the deposition is required to apply for a court order. The order is to specify how the testimony is to be recorded, preserved, and filed, and it may contain whatever additional safeguards the court deems necessary.

Subdivision (b)(5). A provision is added to enable a party, through service of notice, to require another party to produce documents or things at the taking of his deposition. This may now be done as to a nonparty deponent through use of a subpoena duces tecum as authorized by Rule 45, but some courts have held that documents may be secured from a party only under Rule 34. See 2A Barron & Holtzoff, *Federal Practice and Procedure* § 644.1 n. 83.2, § 792 n. 16 (Wright ed. 1961). With the elimination of "good cause" from Rule 34, the reason for this restrictive doctrine has disappeared. *Cf.* N.Y.C.P.L.R. § 3111.

Whether production of documents or things should be obtained directly under Rule 34 or at the deposition under this rule will depend on the nature and volume of the documents or things. Both methods are made available. When the documents are few and simple, and closely related to the oral examination, ability to proceed via this rule will facilitate discovery. If the discovering party insists on examining many and complex documents at the taking of the deposition, thereby causing undue burdens on others, the latter may, under Rules 26(c) or 30(d), apply for a court order that the examining party proceed via Rule 34 alone.

Subdivision (b)(6). A new provision is added, whereby a party may name a corporation, partnership, association, or governmental agency as the deponent and designate the matters on which he requests examination, and the organization shall then name one or more of its officers, directors, or managing agents, or other persons consenting to appear and testify on its behalf with respect to matters known or reasonably available to the organization. *Cf.* Alberta Sup.Ct.R. 255. The organization may designate persons other than officers, directors, and managing agents, but only with their consent. Thus, an employee or agent who has an independent or conflicting interest in the litigation—for example, in a personal injury case—can refuse to testify on behalf of the organization.

This procedure supplements the existing practice whereby the examining party designates the corporate official to be deposed. Thus, if the examining party believes that certain officials who have not testified pursuant to this subdivision have added information, he may depose them. On the other hand, a court's decision whether to issue a protective order may take account of the availability and use made of the procedures provided in this subdivision.

The new procedure should be viewed as an added facility for discovery, one which may be advantageous to both sides as well as an improvement in the deposition process. It will reduce the difficulties now encountered in determining, prior to the taking of a deposition, whether a particular employee or agent is a "managing agent." See Note, *Discovery Against Corporations Under the Federal Rules*, 47 Iowa L.Rev. 1006–1016 (1962). It will curb the "bandying" by which officers or managing agents of a corporation are deposed in turn but each disclaims knowledge of facts that are clearly known to persons in the organization and thereby to it. *Cf. Haney v. Woodward & Lothrop, Inc.*, 330 F.2d 940, 944 (4th Cir. 1964). The provision should also assist organizations which find that an unnecessarily large number of their officers and agents are being deposed by a party uncertain of who in the organization has knowledge. Some courts have held that under the existing rules a corporation should not be burdened with choosing which person is to appear for it. E.g., *United States v. Gahagan Dredging Corp.*, 24 F.R.D. 328, 329 (S.D.N.Y.1958). This burden is not essentially different from that of answering interrogatories under Rule 33, and is in any case lighter than that of an examining party ignorant of who in the corporation has knowledge.

Subdivision (c). A new sentence is inserted at the beginning, representing the transfer of existing Rule 26(c) to this subdivision. Another addition conforms to the new provision in subdivision (b)(4).

The present rule provides that transcription shall be carried out unless all parties waive it. In view of the many depositions taken from which nothing useful is discovered, the revised language provides that transcription is to be performed if any party requests it. The fact of the request is relevant to the exercise of the court's discretion in determining who shall pay for transcription.

Parties choosing to serve written questions rather than participate personally in an oral deposition are directed to serve their questions on the party taking the deposition, since the officer is often not identified in advance. Confidentiality is preserved, since the questions may be served in a sealed envelope.

Subdivision (d). The assessment of expenses incurred in relation to motions made under this subdivision (d) is made subject to the provisions of Rule 37(a). The standards for assessment of expenses are more fully set out in Rule 37(a), and these standards should apply to the essentially similar motions of this subdivision.

Subdivision (e). The provision relating to the refusal of a witness to sign his deposition is tightened through insertion of a 30-day time period.

Subdivision (f)(1). A provision is added which codifies in a flexible way the procedure for handling exhibits related to the deposition and at the same time assures each party that he may inspect and copy documents and things produced by a nonparty witness in response to a subpoena duces tecum. As a general rule and in the absence of agreement to the contrary or order of the court, exhibits produced without objection are to be annexed to and returned with the deposition, but a witness may substitute copies for purposes of marking and he may obtain return of the exhibits. The right of the parties to inspect exhibits for identification and to make copies is assured. *Cf.* N.Y.C.P.L.R. § 3116(c).

1971 Amendment

The subdivision permits a party to name a corporation or other form of organization as a deponent in the notice of examination and to describe in the notice the matters about which discovery is desired. The organization is then obliged to designate natural persons to testify on its behalf. The amendment clarifies the procedure to be followed if a party desires to examine a non-party organization through persons designated by the organization. Under the rules, a subpoena rather than a notice of examination is served on a non-party to compel attendance at the taking of a deposition. The amendment provides that a subpoena may name a non-party organization as the deponent and may indicate the matters about which discovery is desired. In that event, the non-party organization must respond by designating natural persons, who are then obliged to testify as to matters known or reasonably available to the organization. To insure that a non-party organization that is not represented by counsel has knowledge of its duty to designate, the amendment directs the party seeking discovery to advise of the duty in the body of the subpoena.

1972 Amendment

Subdivision (c). Existing Rule 43(b), which is to be abrogated, deals with the use of leading questions, the calling, interrogation, impeachment, and scope of cross-examination of adverse parties, officers, etc. These topics are dealt with in many places in the Rules of Evidence. Moreover, many pertinent topics included in the Rules of Evidence are not mentioned in Rule 43(b), e.g. privilege. A reference to the Rules of Evidence generally is therefore made in subdivision (c) of Rule 30.

1980 Amendment

Subdivision (b)(4). It has been proposed that electronic recording of depositions be authorized as a matter of course, subject to the right of a party to seek an order that a deposition be recorded by stenographic means. The Committee is not satisfied that a case has been made for a reversal of present practice. The amendment is made to encourage parties to agree to the use of electronic recording of depositions so that conflicting claims with respect to the potential of electronic recording for reducing costs of depositions can be appraised in the light of greater experience. The provision that the parties may stipulate that depositions may be recorded by other than stenographic means seems implicit in Rule 29. The amendment makes it explicit. The provision that the stipulation or order shall designate the person before whom the deposition is to be taken is added to encourage the naming of the recording technician as that person, eliminating the necessity of the presence of one whose only function is to administer the oath. See Rules 28(a) and 29.

Subdivision (b)(7). Depositions by telephone are now authorized by Rule 29 upon stipulation of the parties. The amendment authorizes that method by order of the court. The final sentence is added to make it clear that when a deposition is taken by telephone it is taken in the district and at the place where the witness is to answer the questions rather than that where the questions are propounded.

Subdivision (f)(1). For the reasons set out in the Note following the amendment of Rule 5(d), the court may wish to permit the parties to retain depositions unless they are to be used in the action. The amendment of the first paragraph permits the court to so order.

The amendment of the second paragraph is clarifying. The purpose of the paragraph is to permit a person who produces materials at a deposition to offer copies for marking and annexation to the deposition. Such copies are a "substitute" for the originals, which are not to be marked and which can thereafter be used or even disposed of by the person who produces them. In the light of that purpose, the former language of the paragraph had been justly termed "opaque." Wright & Miller, *Federal Practice and Procedure: Civil* § 2114.

1987 Amendment

The amendments are technical. No substantive change is intended.

1993 Amendment

Subdivision (a). Paragraph (1) retains the first and third sentences from the former subdivision (a) without significant modification. The second and fourth sentences are relocated.

Paragraph (2) collects all provisions bearing on requirements of leave of court to take a deposition.

Paragraph (2)(A) is new. It provides a limit on the number of depositions the parties may take, absent leave of court or stipulation with the other parties. One aim of this revision is to assure judicial review under the standards stated in Rule 26(b)(2) before any side will be allowed to take more than ten depositions in a case without agreement of the other parties. A second objective is to emphasize that counsel have a professional obligation to develop a mutual cost-effective plan for discovery in the case. Leave to take additional depositions should be granted when consistent with the principles of Rule 26(b)(2), and in some cases the ten-per-side limit should be reduced in accordance with those same principles. Consideration should ordinarily be given at the planning meeting of the parties under Rule 26(f) and at the time of a scheduling conference under Rule 16(b) as to enlargements or reductions in the number of depositions, eliminating the need for special motions.

A deposition under Rule 30(b)(6) should, for purposes of this limit, be treated as a single deposition even though more than one person may be designated to testify.

In multi-party cases, the parties on any side are expected to confer and agree as to which depositions are most needed, given the presumptive limit on the number of depositions they can take without leave of court. If these disputes cannot be amicably resolved, the court can be requested to resolve the dispute or permit additional depositions.

Paragraph (2)(B) is new. It requires leave of court if any witness is to be deposed in the action more than once. This requirement does not apply when a deposition is temporarily recessed for convenience of counsel or the deponent or to enable additional materials to be gathered before resuming the deposition. If significant travel costs would be incurred to resume the deposition, the parties should consider the feasibility of conducting the balance of the examination by telephonic means.

Paragraph (2)(C) revises the second sentence of the former subdivision (a) as to when depositions may be taken. Consistent with the changes made in Rule 26(d), providing that formal discovery ordinarily not commence until after the litigants have met and conferred as directed in revised Rule 26(f), the rule requires leave of court or agreement of the parties if a deposition is to be taken before that time (except when a witness is about to leave the country).

Subdivision (b). The primary change in subdivision (b) is that parties will be authorized to record deposition testimony by nonstenographic means without first having to obtain permission of the court or agreement from other counsel.

Former subdivision (b)(2) is partly relocated in subdivision (a)(2)(C) of this rule. The latter two sentences of the first paragraph are deleted, in part because they are redundant to Rule 26(g) and in part because Rule 11 no longer applies to discovery requests. The second paragraph of the former subdivision (b)(2), relating to use of depositions at trial where a party was unable to obtain counsel in time for an accelerated deposition, is relocated in Rule 32.

New paragraph (2) confers on the party taking the deposition the choice of the method of recording, without the need to obtain prior court approval for one taken other than stenographically. A party choosing to record a deposition only by videotape or audiotape should understand that a transcript will be required by Rule 26(a)(3)(B) and Rule 32(c) if the deposition is later to be offered as evidence at trial or on a dispositive motion under Rule 56. Objections to the non-stenographic recording of a deposition, when warranted by the circumstances, can be presented to the court under Rule 26(c).

Paragraph (3) provides that other parties may arrange, at their own expense, for the recording of a deposition by a means (stenographic, visual, or sound) in addition to the method designated by the person noticing the deposition. The former provisions of this paragraph, relating to the court's power to change the date of a deposition, have been eliminated as redundant in view of Rule 26(c)(2).

Revised paragraph (4) requires that all depositions be recorded by an officer designated or appointed under Rule 28 and contains special provisions designed to provide basic safeguards to assure the utility and integrity of recordings taken other than stenographically.

Paragraph (7) is revised to authorize the taking of a deposition not only by telephone but also by other remote electronic means, such as satellite television, when agreed to by the parties or authorized by the court.

Subdivision (c). Minor changes are made in this subdivision to reflect those made in subdivision (b) and to complement the new provisions of subdivision (d)(1), aimed at reducing the number of interruptions during depositions.

In addition, the revision addresses a recurring problem as to whether other potential deponents can attend a deposition. Courts have disagreed, some holding that witnesses should be excluded through invocation of Rule 615 of the evidence rules, and others holding that witnesses may attend unless excluded by an order under Rule 26(c)(5). The revision provides that other witnesses are not automatically excluded from a deposition simply by the request of a party. Exclusion, however, can be ordered under Rule 26(c)(5) when appropriate; and, if exclusion is ordered, consideration should be given as to whether the excluded witnesses likewise should be precluded from reading, or being otherwise informed about, the testimony given in the earlier depositions. The revision addresses only the matter of attendance by potential deponents, and does not attempt to resolve issues concerning attendance by others, such as members of the public or press.

Subdivision (d). The first sentence of new paragraph (1) provides that any objections during a deposition must be made concisely and in a non-argumentative and non-suggestive manner. Depositions frequently have been unduly prolonged, if not unfairly frustrated, by lengthy objections and colloquy, often suggesting how the deponent should respond. While objections may, under the revised rule, be made during a deposition, they ordinarily should be limited to those that under Rule 32(d)(3) might be waived if not made at that time, *i.e.*, objections on grounds that might be immediately obviated, removed, or cured, such as to the form of a question or the responsiveness of an answer. Under Rule 32(b), other objections can, even without the so-called "usual stipulation" preserving objections, be raised for the first time at trial and therefore should be kept to a minimum during a deposition.

Directions to a deponent not to answer a question can be even more disruptive than objections. The second sentence of new paragraph (1) prohibits such directions except in the three circumstances indicated: to claim a privilege or protection against disclosure (*e.g.*, as work product), to enforce a court directive limiting the scope or length of permissible discovery, or to suspend a deposition to enable presentation of a motion under paragraph (3).

Paragraph (2) is added to this subdivision to dispel any doubts regarding the power of the court by order or local rule to establish limits on the length of depositions. The rule also explicitly authorizes the court to impose the cost resulting from obstructive tactics that unreasonably prolong a deposition on the person engaged in such obstruction. This sanction may be imposed on a non-party witness as well as a party or attorney, but is otherwise congruent with Rule 26(g).

It is anticipated that limits on the length of depositions prescribed by local rules would be presumptive only, subject to modification by the court or by agreement of the parties. Such modifications typically should be discussed by the parties in their meeting under Rule 26(f) and included in the scheduling order required by Rule 16(b). Additional time, moreover, should be allowed under the revised rule when justified under the principles stated in Rule 26(b)(2). To reduce the number of special motions, local rules should ordinarily permit—and indeed encourage—the parties to agree to additional time, as when, during the taking of a deposition, it becomes clear that some additional examination is needed.

Paragraph (3) authorizes appropriate sanctions not only when a deposition is unreasonably prolonged, but also when an attorney engages in other practices that improperly frustrate the fair examination of the deponent, such as making improper objections or giving directions not to answer prohibited by paragraph (1). In general, counsel should not engage in any conduct during a deposition that would not be allowed in the presence of a judicial officer. The making of an excessive number of unnecessary objections may itself constitute sanctionable conduct, as may the refusal of an attorney to agree with other counsel on a fair apportionment of the time allowed for examination of a deponent or a refusal to agree to a reasonable request for some additional time to complete a deposition, when that is permitted by the local rule or order.

Subdivision (e). Various changes are made in this subdivision to reduce problems sometimes encountered when depositions are taken stenographically. Reporters frequently have difficulties obtaining signatures—and the return of depositions—from deponents. Under the revision pre-filing review by the deponent is required only if requested before the deposition is completed. If review is requested, the deponent will be allowed 30 days to review the transcript or recording and to indicate any changes in form or substance. Signature of the deponent will be required only if review is requested and changes are made.

Subdivision (f). Minor changes are made in this subdivision to reflect those made in subdivision (b). In courts which direct that depositions not be automatically filed, the reporter can transmit the transcript or recording to the attorney taking the deposition (or ordering the transcript or record), who then becomes custodian for the court of the original record of the deposition. Pursuant to subdivision (f)(2), as under the prior rule, any other party is entitled to secure a copy of the deposition from the officer designated to take the deposition; accordingly, unless ordered or agreed, the officer must retain a copy of the recording or the stenographic notes.

2000 Amendment

Subdivision (d). Paragraph (1) has been amended to clarify the terms regarding behavior during depositions. The references to objections " to evidence" and limitations "on evidence" have been removed to avoid disputes about what is "evidence" and whether an objection is to, or a limitation is on, discovery instead. It is intended that the rule apply to any objection to a question or other issue arising during a deposition, and to any limitation imposed by the court in connection with a deposition, which might relate to duration or other matters.

The current rule places limitations on instructions that a witness not answer only when the instruction is made by a "party." Similar limitations should apply with regard to anyone who might purport to instruct a witness not to answer a question. Accordingly, the rule is amended to apply the limitation to instructions by any person. The amendment is not intended to confer new authority on nonparties to instruct witnesses to refuse to answer deposition questions. The amendment makes it clear that, whatever the legitimacy of giving such instructions, the nonparty is subject to the same limitations as parties.

Paragraph (2) imposes a presumptive durational limitation of one day of seven hours for any deposition. The Committee has been informed that overlong depositions can result in undue costs and delays in some circumstances. This limitation contemplates that there will be reasonable breaks during the day for lunch and other reasons, and that the only time to be counted is the time occupied by the actual deposition. For purposes of this durational limit, the deposition of each person designated under Rule 30(b)(6) should be considered a separate deposition. The presumptive duration may be extended, or otherwise altered, by agreement. Absent agreement, a court order is needed. The party seeking a court order to extend the examination, or otherwise alter the limitations, is expected to show good cause to justify such an order.

Parties considering extending the time for a deposition—and courts asked to order an extension—might consider a variety of factors. For example, if the witness needs an interpreter, that may prolong the examination. If the examination will cover events occurring over a long period of time, that may justify allowing additional time. In cases in which the witness will be questioned about numerous or lengthy documents, it is often desirable for the interrogating party to send copies of the documents to the witness sufficiently in advance of the deposition so that the witness can become familiar with them. Should the witness nevertheless not read the documents in advance, thereby prolonging the deposition, a court could consider that a reason for extending the time limit. If the examination reveals that documents have been requested but not produced, that may justify further examination once production has occurred. In multi-party cases, the need for each party to examine the witness may warrant additional time, although duplicative questioning should be avoided and parties with similar interests should strive to designate one lawyer to question about areas of common interest. Similarly, should the lawyer for the witness want to examine the witness, that may require additional time. Finally, with regard to expert witnesses, there may more often be a need for additional time—even after the submission of the report required by Rule 26(a)(2)—for full exploration of the theories upon which the witness relies.

It is expected that in most instances the parties and the witness will make reasonable accommodations to avoid the need for resort to the court. The limitation is phrased in terms of a single day on the assumption that ordinarily a single day would be preferable to a deposition extending over multiple days; if alternative arrangements would better suit the parties, they may agree to them. It is also assumed that there will be reasonable breaks during the day. Preoccupation with timing is to be avoided.

The rule directs the court to allow additional time where consistent with Rule 26(b)(2) if needed for a fair examination of the deponent. In addition, if the deponent or another person impedes or delays the examination, the court must authorize extra time. The amendment makes clear that additional time should also be allowed where the examination is impeded by an "other circumstance," which might include a power outage, a health emergency, or other event.

In keeping with the amendment to Rule 26(b)(2), the provision added in 1993 granting authority to adopt a local rule limiting the time permitted for depositions has been removed. The court may enter a case-specific order directing shorter depositions for all depositions in a case or with regard to a specific witness. The court may also order that a deposition be taken for limited periods on several days.

Paragraph (3) includes sanctions provisions formerly included in paragraph (2). It authorizes the court to impose an appropriate sanction on any person responsible for an impediment that frustrated the fair examination of the deponent.

This could include the deponent, any party, or any other person involved in the deposition. If the impediment or delay results from an "other circumstance" under paragraph (2), ordinarily no sanction would be appropriate.

Former paragraph (3) has been renumbered (4) but is otherwise unchanged.

Subdivision (f)(1): This subdivision is amended because Rule 5(d) has been amended to direct that discovery materials, including depositions, ordinarily should not be filed. The rule already has provisions directing that the lawyer who arranged for the transcript or recording preserve the deposition. Rule 5(d) provides that, once the deposition is used in the proceeding, the attorney must file it with the court.

"Shall" is replaced by "must" or "may" under the program to conform amended rules to current style conventions when there is no ambiguity.

GAP Report

The Advisory Committee recommends deleting the requirement in the published proposed amendments that the deponent consent to extending a deposition beyond one day, and adding an amendment to Rule 30(f)(1) to conform to the published amendment to Rule 5(d) regarding filing of depositions. It also recommends conforming the Committee Note with regard to the deponent veto, and adding material to the Note to provide direction on computation of the durational limitation on depositions, to provide examples of situations in which the parties might agree—or the court order—that a deposition be extended, and to make clear that no new authority to instruct a witness is conferred by the amendment. One minor wording improvement in the Note is also suggested.

2007 Amendment

The language of Rule 30 has been amended as part of the general restyling of the Civil Rules to make them more easily understood and to make style and terminology consistent throughout the rules. These changes are intended to be stylistic only.

The right to arrange a deposition transcription should be open to any party, regardless of the means of recording and regardless of who noticed the deposition.

"[O]ther entity" is added to the list of organizations that may be named as deponent. The purpose is to ensure that the deposition process can be used to reach information known or reasonably available to an organization no matter what abstract fictive concept is used to describe the organization. Nothing is gained by wrangling over the place to fit into current rule language such entities as limited liability companies, limited partnerships, business trusts, more exotic common-law creations, or forms developed in other countries.

2015 Amendment

Rule 30 is amended in parallel with Rules 31 and 33 to reflect the recognition of proportionality in Rule 26(b)(1).

HISTORICAL NOTES

Effective Date of Amendment Proposed November 20, 1972

Amendment of this rule embraced by the order entered by the Supreme Court of the United States on November 20, 1972, effective on the 180th day beginning after January 2, 1975, see section 3 of Pub.L. 93–595, Jan. 2, 1975, 88 Stat. 1959, set out as a note under section 2071 of Title 28.

Discovery and production of documents and things for inspection, copying, or photographing, see Fed.Rules Civ. Proc. Rule 34, 28 USCA.

Interrogatories to parties, scope and use at trial, see Fed. Rules Civ.Proc. Rule 33, 28 USCA.

Persons before whom deposition may be taken, see Fed. Rules Civ.Proc. Rule 28, 28 USCA.

Stipulations regarding discovery procedure, see Fed.Rules Civ.Proc. Rule 29, 28 USCA.

Subpoena for taking depositions, place of examination, see Fed.Rules Civ.Proc. Rule 45, 28 USCA.

United States magistrate judges, power to administer oaths and take depositions, see 28 USCA § 636.

Use of depositions in court proceedings, motion to suppress, effect of errors or irregularities, objections to admissibility, waiver of objections, see Fed.Rules Civ.Proc. Rule 32, 28 USCA.

Rule 31. Depositions by Written Questions

(a) When a Deposition May Be Taken.

(1) *Without Leave.* A party may, by written questions, depose any person, including a party, without leave of court except as provided in Rule 31(a)(2). The deponent's attendance may be compelled by subpoena under Rule 45.

(2) *With Leave.* A party must obtain leave of court, and the court must grant leave to the extent consistent with Rule 26(b)(1) and (2):

(A) if the parties have not stipulated to the deposition and:

(i) the deposition would result in more than 10 depositions being taken under this rule or Rule 30 by the plaintiffs, or by the defendants, or by the third-party defendants;

(ii) the deponent has already been deposed in the case; or

(iii) the party seeks to take a deposition before the time specified in Rule 26(d); or

(B) if the deponent is confined in prison.

(3) *Service; Required Notice.* A party who wants to depose a person by written questions must serve them on every other party, with a notice stating, if known, the deponent's name and address. If the name is unknown, the notice must provide a general description sufficient to identify the person or the particular class or group to which the person belongs. The notice must also state the name or descriptive title and the address of the officer before whom the deposition will be taken.

(4) *Questions Directed to an Organization.* A public or private corporation, a partnership, an association, or a governmental agency may be deposed by written questions in accordance with Rule 30(b)(6).

(5) *Questions from Other Parties.* Any questions to the deponent from other parties must be served

on all parties as follows: cross-questions, within 14 days after being served with the notice and direct questions; redirect questions, within 7 days after being served with cross-questions; and recross-questions, within 7 days after being served with redirect questions. The court may, for good cause, extend or shorten these times.

(b) Delivery to the Officer; Officer's Duties. The party who noticed the deposition must deliver to the officer a copy of all the questions served and of the notice. The officer must promptly proceed in the manner provided in Rule 30(c), (e), and (f) to:

(1) take the deponent's testimony in response to the questions;

(2) prepare and certify the deposition; and

(3) send it to the party, attaching a copy of the questions and of the notice.

(c) Notice of Completion or Filing.

(1) *Completion.* The party who noticed the deposition must notify all other parties when it is completed.

(2) *Filing.* A party who files the deposition must promptly notify all other parties of the filing.

(Amended March 30, 1970, effective July 1, 1970; March 2, 1987, effective August 1, 1987; April 22, 1993, effective December 1, 1993; April 30, 2007, effective December 1, 2007; April 29, 2015, effective December 1, 2015.)

ADVISORY COMMITTEE NOTES

1937 Adoption

This rule is in accordance with common practice. In most of the states listed in the Note to Rule 26(a), provisions similar to this rule will be found in the statutes which in their respective statutory compilations follow those cited in the Note to Rule 26(a).

1970 Amendment

Confusion is created by the use of the same terminology to describe both the taking of a deposition upon "written interrogatories" pursuant to this rule and the serving of "written interrogatories" upon parties pursuant to Rule 33. The distinction between these two modes of discovery will be more readily and clearly grasped through substitution of the word "questions" for "interrogatories" throughout this rule.

Subdivision (a). A new paragraph is inserted at the beginning of this subdivision to conform to the rearrangement of provisions in Rules 26(a), 30(a), and 30(b).

The revised subdivision permits designation of the deponent by general description or by class or group. This conforms to the practice for depositions on oral examination.

The new procedure provided in Rule 30(b)(6) for taking the deposition of a corporation or other organization through persons designated by the organization is incorporated by reference.

The service of all questions, including cross, redirect, and recross, is to be made on all parties. This will inform the parties and enable them to participate fully in the procedure.

The time allowed for service of cross, redirect, and recross questions has been extended. Experience with the existing time limits shows them to be unrealistically short. No special restriction is placed on the time for serving the notice of taking the deposition and the first set of questions. Since no party is required to serve cross questions less than 30 days after the notice and questions are served, the defendant has sufficient time to obtain counsel. The court may for cause shown enlarge or shorten the time.

Subdivision (d). Since new Rule 26(c) provides for protective orders with respect to all discovery, and expressly provides that the court may order that one discovery device be used in place of another, subdivision (d) is eliminated as unnecessary.

1987 Amendment

The amendments are technical. No substantive change is intended.

1993 Amendments

Subdivision (a). The first paragraph of subdivision (a) is divided into two subparagraphs, with provisions comparable to those made in the revision of Rule 30. Changes are made in the former third paragraph, numbered in the revision as paragraph (4), to reduce the total time for developing cross-examination, redirect, and recross questions from 50 days to 28 days.

2007 Amendment

The language of Rule 31 has been amended as part of the general restyling of the Civil Rules to make them more easily understood and to make style and terminology consistent throughout the rules. These changes are intended to be stylistic only.

The party who noticed a deposition on written questions must notify all other parties when the deposition is completed, so that they may make use of the deposition. A deposition is completed when it is recorded and the deponent has either waived or exercised the right of review under Rule 30(e)(1).

2015 Amendment

Rule 31 is amended in parallel with Rules 30 and 33 to reflect the recognition of proportionality in Rule 26(b)(1).

CROSS REFERENCES

Written interrogatories of a party, see Fed.Rules Civ.Proc. Rule 33, 28 USCA.

Rule 32. Using Depositions in Court Proceedings

(a) Using Depositions.

(1) *In General.* At a hearing or trial, all or part of a deposition may be used against a party on these conditions:

(A) the party was present or represented at the taking of the deposition or had reasonable notice of it;

(B) it is used to the extent it would be admissible under the Federal Rules of Evidence if the deponent were present and testifying; and

(C) the use is allowed by Rule 32(a)(2) through (8).

(2) *Impeachment and Other Uses.* Any party may use a deposition to contradict or impeach the testimony given by the deponent as a witness, or for any other purpose allowed by the Federal Rules of Evidence.

(3) *Deposition of Party, Agent, or Designee.* An adverse party may use for any purpose the deposition of a party or anyone who, when deposed, was the party's officer, director, managing agent, or designee under Rule 30(b)(6) or 31(a)(4).

(4) *Unavailable Witness.* A party may use for any purpose the deposition of a witness, whether or not a party, if the court finds:

(A) that the witness is dead;

(B) that the witness is more than 100 miles from the place of hearing or trial or is outside the United States, unless it appears that the witness's absence was procured by the party offering the deposition;

(C) that the witness cannot attend or testify because of age, illness, infirmity, or imprisonment;

(D) that the party offering the deposition could not procure the witness's attendance by subpoena; or

(E) on motion and notice, that exceptional circumstances make it desirable—in the interest of justice and with due regard to the importance of live testimony in open court—to permit the deposition to be used.

(5) *Limitations on Use.*

(A) *Deposition Taken on Short Notice.* A deposition must not be used against a party who, having received less than 14 days' notice of the deposition, promptly moved for a protective order under Rule 26(c)(1)(B) requesting that it not be taken or be taken at a different time or place—and this motion was still pending when the deposition was taken.

(B) *Unavailable Deponent; Party Could Not Obtain an Attorney.* A deposition taken without leave of court under the unavailability provision of Rule 30(a)(2)(A)(iii) must not be used against a party who shows that, when served with the notice, it could not, despite diligent efforts, obtain an attorney to represent it at the deposition.

(6) *Using Part of a Deposition.* If a party offers in evidence only part of a deposition, an adverse party may require the offeror to introduce other parts that in fairness should be considered with the part introduced, and any party may itself introduce any other parts.

(7) *Substituting a Party.* Substituting a party under Rule 25 does not affect the right to use a deposition previously taken.

(8) *Deposition Taken in an Earlier Action.* A deposition lawfully taken and, if required, filed in any federal- or state-court action may be used in a later action involving the same subject matter between the same parties, or their representatives or successors in interest, to the same extent as if taken in the later action. A deposition previously taken may also be used as allowed by the Federal Rules of Evidence.

(b) Objections to Admissibility. Subject to Rules 28(b) and 32(d)(3), an objection may be made at a hearing or trial to the admission of any deposition testimony that would be inadmissible if the witness were present and testifying.

(c) Form of Presentation. Unless the court orders otherwise, a party must provide a transcript of any deposition testimony the party offers, but may provide the court with the testimony in nontranscript form as well. On any party's request, deposition testimony offered in a jury trial for any purpose other than impeachment must be presented in nontranscript form, if available, unless the court for good cause orders otherwise.

(d) Waiver of Objections.

(1) *To the Notice.* An objection to an error or irregularity in a deposition notice is waived unless promptly served in writing on the party giving the notice.

(2) *To the Officer's Qualification.* An objection based on disqualification of the officer before whom a deposition is to be taken is waived if not made:

(A) before the deposition begins; or

(B) promptly after the basis for disqualification becomes known or, with reasonable diligence, could have been known.

(3) *To the Taking of the Deposition.*

(A) *Objection to Competence, Relevance, or Materiality.* An objection to a deponent's competence—or to the competence, relevance, or materiality of testimony—is not waived by a failure to make the objection before or during the deposition, unless the ground for it might have been corrected at that time.

(B) *Objection to an Error or Irregularity.* An objection to an error or irregularity at an oral examination is waived if:

(i) it relates to the manner of taking the deposition, the form of a question or answer, the oath or affirmation, a party's conduct, or other matters that might have been corrected at that time; and

(ii) it is not timely made during the deposition.

(C) *Objection to a Written Question.* An objection to the form of a written question under Rule 31 is waived if not served in writing on the party submitting the question within the time for serving responsive questions or, if the question is a recross-question, within 7 days after being served with it.

(4) *To Completing and Returning the Deposition.* An objection to how the officer transcribed the testimony—or prepared, signed, certified, sealed, endorsed, sent, or otherwise dealt with the deposition—is waived unless a motion to suppress is made promptly after the error or irregularity becomes known or, with reasonable diligence, could have been known.

(Amended March 30, 1970, effective July 1, 1970; November 20, 1972, effective July 1, 1975; April 29, 1980, effective August 1, 1980; March 2, 1987, effective August 1, 1987; April 22, 1993, effective December 1, 1993; April 30, 2007, effective December 1, 2007; March 26, 2009, effective December 1, 2009.)

ADVISORY COMMITTEE NOTES

1937 Adoption

This rule is in accordance with common practice. In most of the states listed in the note to rule 26, provisions similar to this rule will be found in the statutes which in their respective statutory compilations follow those cited in the Note to Rule 26.

1970 Amendment

As part of the rearrangement of the discovery rules, existing subdivisions (d), (e), and (f) of Rule 26 are transferred to Rule 32 as new subdivisions (a), (b), and (c). The provisions of Rule 32 are retained as subdivision (d) of Rule 32 with appropriate changes in the lettering and numbering of subheadings. The new rule is given a suitable new title. A beneficial byproduct of the rearrangement is that provisions which are naturally related to one another are placed in one rule.

A change is made in new Rule 32(a), whereby it is made clear that the rules of evidence are to be applied to depositions offered at trial as though the deponent were then present and testifying at trial. This eliminates the possibility of certain technical hearsay objections which are based, not on the contents of deponent's testimony, but on his absence from court. The language of present Rule 26(d) does not appear to authorize these technical objections, but it is not entirely clear. Note present Rule 26(e), transferred to Rule 32(b); see 2A Barron & Holtzoff, *Federal Practice and Procedure* 164–166 (Wright ed. 1961).

An addition in Rule 32(a)(2) provides for use of a deposition of a person designated by a corporation or other organization, which is a party, to testify on its behalf. This complements the new procedure for taking the deposition of a corporation or other organization provided in Rules 30(b)(6) and 31(a). The addition is appropriate, since the deposition is in substance and effect that of the corporation or other organization which is a party.

A change is made in the standard under which a party offering part of a deposition in evidence may be required to introduce additional parts of the deposition. The new standard is contained in a proposal made by the Advisory Committee on Rules of Evidence. See Rule 1–07 and accompanying Note, *Preliminary Draft of Proposed Rules of Evidence for the United States District Courts and Magistrates* 21–22 (March, 1969).

References to other rules are changed to conform to the rearrangement, and minor verbal changes have been made for clarification. The time for objecting to written questions served under Rule 31 is slightly extended.

1972 Amendment

Subdivision (c). The concept of "making a person one's own witness" appears to have had significance principally in two respects: impeachment and waiver of incompetency. Neither retains any vitality under the Rules of Evidence. The old prohibition against impeaching one's own witness is eliminated by Evidence Rule 607. The lack of recognition in the Rules of Evidence of state rules of incompetency in the Dead Man's area renders it unnecessary to consider aspects of waiver arising from calling the incompetent party-witness. Subdivision (c) is deleted because it appears to be no longer necessary in the light of the Rules of Evidence.

1980 Amendment

Subdivision (a)(1). Rule 801(d) of the Federal Rules of Evidence permits a prior inconsistent statement of a witness in a deposition to be used as substantive evidence. And Rule 801(d)(2) makes the statement of an agent or servant admissible against the principal under the circumstances described in the Rule. The language of the present subdivision is, therefore, too narrow.

Subdivision (a)(4). The requirement that a prior action must have been dismissed before depositions taken for use in it can be used in a subsequent action was doubtless an oversight, and the courts have ignored it. See Wright & Miller, *Federal Practice and Procedure: Civil* § 2150. The final sentence is added to reflect the fact that the Federal Rules of Evidence permit a broader use of depositions previously taken under certain circumstances. For example, Rule 804(b)(1) of the Federal Rules of Evidence provides that if a witness is unavailable, as that term is defined by the rule, his deposition in any earlier proceeding can be used against a party to the prior proceeding who had an opportunity and similar motive to develop the testimony of the witness.

1987 Amendment

The amendment is technical. No substantive change is intended.

1993 Amendment

Subdivision (a). The last sentence of revised subdivision (a) not only includes the substance of the provisions formerly contained in the second paragraph of Rule 30(b)(2), but adds a provision to deal with the situation when a party, receiving minimal notice of a proposed deposition, is unable to obtain a court ruling on its motion for a protective order seeking to delay or change the place of the deposition. Ordinarily a party does not obtain protection merely by the filing of a motion for a protective order under Rule 26(c); any protection is dependent upon the court's ruling. Under the revision, a party receiving less than 11 days notice of a deposition can, provided its motion for a protective order is filed promptly, be spared the risks resulting from nonattendance at the deposition held before its motion is ruled upon. Although the revision of Rule 32(a) covers only the risk that the deposition could be used against the non-appearing movant, it should also follow that, when the proposed deponent is the movant, the deponent would have "just cause" for failing to appear for purposes of Rule 37(d)(1). Inclusion of this provision is not intended to signify that 11 days' notice is the minimum advance notice for all depositions or that greater than 10 days should necessarily be deemed sufficient in all situations.

Subdivision (c). This new subdivision, inserted at the location of a subdivision previously abrogated, is included in view of the increased opportunities for video-recording and audio-recording of depositions under revised Rule 30(b). Under this rule a party may offer deposition testimony in any of the forms authorized under Rule 30(b) but, if offering it in a nonstenographic form, must provide the court with a transcript of the portions so offered. On request of any party in a jury trial, deposition testimony offered other than for impeachment purposes is to be presented in a nonstenographic form if available, unless the court directs otherwise. Note that under Rule 26(a)(3)(B) a party expecting to use nonstenographic deposition testimony as substantive evidence is required to provide other parties with a transcript in advance of trial.

2007 Amendment

The language of Rule 32 has been amended as part of the general restyling of the Civil Rules to make them more easily understood and to make style and terminology consistent throughout the rules. These changes are intended to be stylistic only.

Former Rule 32(a) applied "[a]t the trial or upon the hearing of a motion or an interlocutory proceeding." The amended rule describes the same events as "a hearing or trial."

The final paragraph of former Rule 32(a) allowed use in a later action of a deposition "lawfully taken and duly filed in the former action." Because of the 2000 amendment of Rule 5(d), many depositions are not filed. Amended Rule 32(a)(8) reflects this change by excluding use of an unfiled deposition only if filing was required in the former action.

2009 Amendment

The times set in the former rule at less than 11 days and within 5 days have been revised to 14 days and 7 days. See the Note to Rule 6.

HISTORICAL NOTES

References in Text

The Federal Rules of Evidence, referred to in subd. (a)(1), (2) and (8), are set out in this title.

Effective Date of Amendment Proposed November 20, 1972

Amendment of this rule embraced by the order entered by the Supreme Court of the United States on November 20, 1972, effective on the 180th day beginning after January 2, 1975, see section 3 of Pub.L. 93–595, Jan. 2, 1975, 88 Stat. 1959, set out as a note under section 2071 of Title 28.

CROSS REFERENCES

Presentence reports for guilty defendant of offense punishable by death notwithstanding this section, see 18 USCA § 3593.

Rejection of deposition by court after refusal to sign, see Fed.Rules Civ.Proc. Rule 30, 28 USCA.

For Complete Annotation Materials, see United States Code Annotated

Rule 33. Interrogatories to Parties

(a) In General.

(1) *Number.* Unless otherwise stipulated or ordered by the court, a party may serve on any other party no more than 25 written interrogatories, including all discrete subparts. Leave to serve additional interrogatories may be granted to the extent consistent with Rule 26(b)(1) and (2).

(2) *Scope.* An interrogatory may relate to any matter that may be inquired into under Rule 26(b). An interrogatory is not objectionable merely because it asks for an opinion or contention that relates to fact or the application of law to fáct, but the court may order that the interrogatory need not be answered until designated discovery is complete, or until a pretrial conference or some other time.

(b) Answers and Objections.

(1) *Responding Party.* The interrogatories must be answered:

    (A) by the party to whom they are directed; or

    (B) if that party is a public or private corporation, a partnership, an association, or a governmental agency, by any officer or agent, who must furnish the information available to the party.

(2) *Time to Respond.* The responding party must serve its answers and any objections within 30 days after being served with the interrogatories. A shorter or longer time may be stipulated to under Rule 29 or be ordered by the court.

(3) *Answering Each Interrogatory.* Each interrogatory must, to the extent it is not objected to, be answered separately and fully in writing under oath.

(4) *Objections.* The grounds for objecting to an interrogatory must be stated with specificity. Any ground not stated in a timely objection is waived unless the court, for good cause, excuses the failure.

(5) *Signature.* The person who makes the answers must sign them, and the attorney who objects must sign any objections.

(c) Use. An answer to an interrogatory may be used to the extent allowed by the Federal Rules of Evidence.

(d) Option to Produce Business Records. If the answer to an interrogatory may be determined by examining, auditing, compiling, abstracting, or summarizing a party's business records (including electronically stored information), and if the burden of deriving or ascertaining the answer will be substantially the same for either party, the responding party may answer by:

(1) specifying the records that must be reviewed, in sufficient detail to enable the interrogating party to locate and identify them as readily as the responding party could; and

(2) giving the interrogating party a reasonable opportunity to examine and audit the records and to make copies, compilations, abstracts, or summaries.

(Amended December 27, 1946, effective March 19, 1948; March 30, 1970, effective July 1, 1970; April 29, 1980, effective August 1, 1980; April 22, 1993, effective December 1, 1993; April 12, 2006, effective December 1, 2006; April 30, 2007, effective December 1, 2007; April 29, 2015, effective December 1, 2015.)

ADVISORY COMMITTEE NOTES

1937 Adoption

This rule restates the substance of [former] Equity Rule 58 (Discovery—Interrogatories—Inspection and Production of Documents—Admission of Execution or Genuineness), with modifications to conform to these rules.

1946 Amendment

Note. The added second sentence in the first paragraph of Rule 33 conforms with a similar change in Rule 26(a) and will avoid litigation as to when the interrogatories may be served. Original Rule 33 does not state the times at which parties may serve written interrogatories upon each other. It has been the accepted view, however, that the times were the same in Rule 33 as those stated in Rule 26(a). *United States v. American Solvents & Chemical Corp. of California*, D.Del. 1939, 30 F.Supp. 107; *Sheldon v. Great Lakes Transit Corp.*, W.D.N.Y.1942, 2 F.R.D. 272, 5 Fed.Rules Serv. 33.11, Case 3; *Musher Foundation, Inc., v. Alba Trading Co.*, S.D.N.Y.1941, 42 F.Supp. 281; 2 *Moore's Federal Practice*, 1938, 2621. The time within which leave of court must be secured by a plaintiff has been fixed at 10 days, in view of the fact that a defendant has 10 days within which to make objections in any case, which should give him ample time to engage counsel and prepare.

Further in the first paragraph of Rule 33, the word "service" is substituted for "delivery" in conformance with the use of the word "serve" elsewhere in the rule and generally throughout the rules. See also Note to Rule 13(a) herein. The portion of the rule dealing with practice on objections has been revised so as to afford a clearer statement of the procedure. The addition of the words "to interrogatories to which objection is made" insures that only the answers to the objectionable interrogatories may be deferred, and that the answers to interrogatories not objectionable shall be forthcoming within the time prescribed in the rule. Under the original wording, answers to all interrogatories may be withheld until objections, sometimes to but a few interrogatories, are determined. The amendment expedites the procedure of the rule and serves to eliminate the strike value of objections to minor interrogatories. The elimination of the last sentence of the original rule is in line with the policy stated subsequently in this note.

The added second paragraph in Rule 33 contributes clarity and specificity as to the use and scope of interrogatories to the parties. The field of inquiry will be as broad as the scope of examination under Rule 26(b). There is no reason why interrogatories should be more limited than depositions, particularly when the former represent an inexpensive means of securing useful information. See *Hoffman v. Wilson Line, Inc.*, E.D.Pa.1946, 9 Fed.Rules Serv. 33.514, Case 2; *Brewster v. Technicolor, Inc.*, N.Y.1941, 2 F.R.D. 186, 5 Fed.Rules Serv. 33.319, Case 3; *Kingsway Press, Inc. v. Farrell Pub-*

lishing Corp., S.D.N.Y.1939, 30 F.Supp. 775. Under present Rule 33 some courts have unnecessarily restricted the breadth of inquiry on various grounds. See *Auer v. Hershey Creamery Co.,* D.N.J.1939, 2 Fed.Rules Serv. 33.31, Case 2, 1 F.R.D. 14; *Tudor v. Leslie,* D.Mass.1940, 1 F.R.D. 448, 4 Fed.Rules Serv. 33.324, Case 1. Other courts have read into the rule the requirement that interrogation should be directed only towards "important facts", and have tended to fix a more or less arbitrary limit as to the number of interrogatories which could be asked in any case. See *Knox v. Alter,* W.D.Pa.1942, 2 F.R.D. 337, 6 Fed.Rules Serv. 33.352, Case 1; *Byers Theaters, Inc. v. Murphy,* W.D.Va.1940, 3 Fed.Rules Serv. 33.31, Case 3, 1 F.R.D. 286; *Coca-Cola Co. v. Dixi-Cola Laboratories, Inc.,* D.Md.1939, 30 F.Supp. 275. See also comment on these restrictions in Holtzoff, *Instruments of Discovery under Federal Rules of Civil Procedure,* 1942, 41 Mich.L.Rev. 205, 216–217. Under amended Rule 33, the party interrogated is given the right to invoke such protective orders under Rule 30(b) as are appropriate to the situation. At the same time, it is provided that the number of or number of sets of interrogatories to be served may not be limited arbitrarily or as a general policy to any particular number, but that a limit may be fixed only as justice requires to avoid annoyance, expense, embarrassment or oppression in individual cases. The party interrogated, therefore, must show the necessity for limitation on that basis. It will be noted that in accord with this change the last sentence of the present rule, restricting the sets of interrogatories to be served, has been stricken. In *J. Schoeneman, Inc. v. Brauer,* W.D.Mo.1940, 1 F.R.D. 292, 3 Fed.Rules Serv. 33.31, Case 2, the court said: "Rule 33 * * * has been interpreted * * * as being just as broad in its implications as in the case of depositions * * * It makes no difference therefore, how many interrogatories are propounded. If the inquiries are pertinent the opposing party cannot complain." To the same effect, see *Canuso v. City of Niagara Falls,* W.D.N.Y.1945, 8 Fed.Rules Serv. 33.352, Case 1; *Hoffman v. Wilson Line, Inc.,* supra.

By virtue of express language in the added second paragraph of Rule 33, as amended, any uncertainty as to the use of the answers to interrogatories is removed. The omission of a provision on this score in the original rule has caused some difficulty. See, e.g., *Bailey v. New England Mutual Life Ins. Co.,* S.D.Cal.1940, 1 F.R.D. 494, 4 Fed.Rules Serv. 33.46, Case 1.

The second sentence of the second paragraph in Rule 33, as amended, concerns the situation where a party wishes to serve interrogatories on a party after having taken his deposition, or vice versa. It has been held that an oral examination of a party, after the submission to him and answer of interrogatories, would be permitted. *Howard v. State Marine Corp.,* S.D.N.Y.1940, 4 Fed.Rules Serv. 33.62, Case 1, 1 F.R.D. 499; *Stevens v. Minder Construction Co.,* S.D.N.Y. 1943, 3 F.R.D. 498, 7 Fed.Rules Serv. 30b.31, Case 2. But objections have been sustained to interrogatories served after the oral deposition of a party had been taken. *McNally v. Simons,* S.D.N.Y.1940, 3 Fed.Rules Serv. 33.61, Case 1, 1 F.R.D. 254; *Currier v. Currier,* S.D.N.Y.1942, 3 F.R.D. 21, 6 Fed.Rules Serv. 33.61, Case 1. Rule 33, as amended, permits either interrogatories after a deposition or a deposition after interrogatories. It may be quite desirable or necessary to elicit additional information by the inexpensive method of interrogatories where a deposition has already been taken. The party to be interrogated, however, may seek a protective order from the court under Rule 30(b) where the additional deposition or interrogation works a hardship or injustice on the party from whom it is sought.

1970 Amendment

Subdivision (a). The mechanics of the operation of Rule 33 are substantially revised by the proposed amendment, with a view to reducing court intervention. There is general agreement that interrogatories spawn a greater percentage of objections and motions than any other discovery device. The Columbia Survey shows that, although half of the litigants resorted to depositions and about one-third used interrogatories, about 65 percent of the objections were made with respect to interrogatories and 26 percent related to depositions. See also Speck, *The Use of Discovery in United States District Courts,* 60 Yale L.J. 1132, 1144, 1151 (1951); Note, 36 Minn.L.Rev. 364, 379 (1952).

The procedures now provided in Rule 33 seem calculated to encourage objections and court motions. The time periods now allowed for responding to interrogatories—15 days for answers and 10 days for objections—are too short. The Columbia Survey shows that tardy response to interrogatories is common, virtually expected. The same was reported in Speck, *supra,* 60 Yale L.J. 1132, 1144. The time pressures tend to encourage objections as a means of gaining time to answer.

The time for objections is even shorter than for answers, and the party runs the risk that if he fails to object in time he may have waived his objections. *E.g., Cleminshaw v. Beech Aircraft Corp.,* 21 F.R.D. 300 (D.Del.1957); See 4 *Moore's Federal Practice,* ¶33.27 (2d ed. 1966); 2A Barron & Holtzoff, *Federal Practice and Procedure* 372–373 (Wright ed. 1961). It often seems easier to object than to seek an extension of time. Unlike Rules 30(d) and 37(a), Rule 33 imposes no sanction of expenses on a party whose objections are clearly unjustified.

Rule 33 assures that the objections will lead directly to court, through its requirement that they be served with a notice of hearing. Although this procedure does not preclude an out-of-court resolution of the dispute, the procedure tends to discourage informal negotiations. If answers are served and they are thought inadequate, the interrogating party may move under Rule 37(a) for an order compelling adequate answers. There is no assurance that the hearing on objections and that on inadequate answers will be heard together.

The amendment improves the procedure of Rule 33 in the following respects:

(1) The time allowed for response is increased to 30 days and this time period applies to both answers and objections, but a defendant need not respond in less than 45 days after service of the summons and complaint upon him. As is true under existing law, the responding party who believes that some parts or all of the interrogatories are objectionable may choose to seek a protective order under new Rule 26(c) or may serve objections under this rule. Unless he applies for a protective order, he is required to serve answers or objections in response to the interrogatories, subject to the sanctions provided in Rule 37(d). Answers and objections are served together, so that a response to each interrogatory is encouraged, and any failure to respond is easily noted.

(2) In view of the enlarged time permitted for response, it is no longer necessary to require leave of court for service of interrogatories. The purpose of this requirement—that defendant have time to obtain counsel before a response must be

made—is adequately fulfilled by the requirement that interrogatories be served upon a party with or after service of the summons and complaint upon him.

Some would urge that the plaintiff nevertheless not be permitted to serve interrogatories with the complaint. They fear that a routine practice might be invited, whereby form interrogatories would accompany most complaints. More fundamentally, they feel that, since very general complaints are permitted in present-day pleading, it is fair that the defendant have a right to take the lead in serving interrogatories. (These views apply also to Rule 36.) The amendment of Rule 33 rejects these views, in favor of allowing both parties to go forward with discovery, each free to obtain the information he needs respecting the case.

(3) If objections are made, the burden is on the interrogating party to move under Rule 37(a) for a court order compelling answers, in the course of which the court will pass on the objections. The change in the burden of going forward does not alter the existing obligation of an objecting party to justify his objections. *E.g., Pressley v. Bochlke,* 33 F.R.D. 316 (W.D.N.C. 1963). If the discovering party asserts that an answer is incomplete or evasive, again he may look to Rule 37(a) for relief, and he should add this assertion to his motion to overrule objections. There is no requirement that the parties consult informally concerning their differences, but the new procedure should encourage consultation, and the court may by local rule require it.

The proposed changes are similar in approach to those adopted by California in 1961. See Calif.Code Civ.Proc. § 2030(a). The experience of the Los Angeles Superior Court is informally reported as showing that the California amendment resulted in a significant reduction in court motions concerning interrogatories. Rhode Island takes a similar approach. See R. 33, *R.I.R. Civ.Proc. Official Draft,* p. 74 (Boston Law Book Co.).

A change is made in subdivision (a) which is not related to the sequence of procedures. The restriction to "adverse" parties is eliminated. The courts have generally construed this restriction as precluding interrogatories unless an issue between the parties is disclosed by the pleadings—even though the parties may have conflicting interests. E.g., *Mozeika v. Kaufman Construction Co.,* 25 F.R.D. 233 (E.D.Pa. 1960) (plaintiff and third-party defendant); *Biddle v. Hutchinson,* 24 F.R.D. 256 (M.D.Pa.1959) (codefendants). The resulting distinctions have often been highly technical. In *Schlagenhauf v. Holder,* 379 U.S. 104 (1964), the Supreme Court rejected a contention that examination under Rule 35 could be had only against an "opposing" party, as not in keeping "with the aims of a liberal, nontechnical application of the Federal Rules." 379 U.S. at 116. Eliminating the requirement of "adverse" parties from Rule 33 brings it into line with all other discovery rules.

A second change in subdivision (a) is the addition of the term "governmental agency" to the listing of organizations whose answers are to be made by any officer or agent of the organization. This does not involve any change in existing law. Compare the similar listing in Rule 30(b)(6).

The duty of a party to supplement his answers to interrogatories is governed by a new provision in Rule 26(e).

Subdivision (b). There are numerous and conflicting decisions on the question whether and to what extent interrogatories are limited to matters "of fact," or may elicit opinions, contentions, and legal conclusions. Compare, e.g., *Payer, Hewitt & Co. v. Bellanca Corp.,* 26 F.R.D. 219 (D.Del.1960)

(opinions bad); *Zinsky v. New York Central R.R.,* 36 F.R.D. 680 (N.D.Ohio 1964) (factual opinion or contention good, but legal theory bad); *United States v. Carter Products, Inc.,* 28 F.R.D. 373 (S.D.N.Y.1961) (factual contentions and legal theories bad) with *Taylor v. Sound Steamship Lines, Inc.,* 100 F.Supp. 388 (D.Conn.1951) (opinions good); *Bynum v. United States,* 36 F.R.D. 14 (E.D.La.1964) (contentions as to facts constituting negligence good). For lists of the many conflicting authorities, see 4 *Moore's Federal Practice* ¶33.17 (2d ed. 1966); 2A Barron & Holtzoff, *Federal Practice and Procedure* § 768 (Wright ed. 1961).

Rule 33 is amended to provide that an interrogatory is not objectionable merely because it calls for an opinion or contention that relates to fact or the application of law to fact. Efforts to draw sharp lines between facts and opinions have invariably been unsuccessful, and the clear trend of the cases is to permit "factual" opinions. As to requests for opinions or contentions that call for the application of law to fact, they can be most useful in narrowing and sharpening the issues, which is a major purpose of discovery. See *Diversified Products Corp. v. Sports Center Co.,* 42 F.R.D. 3 (D.Md.1967); Moore, *supra;* Field & McKusick, *Maine Civil Practice* § 26.18 (1959). On the other hand, under the new language interrogatories may not extend to issues of "pure law," i.e., legal issues unrelated to the facts of the case. *Cf. United States v. Maryland & Va. Milk Producers Assn., Inc.,* 22 F.R.D. 300 (D.D.C.1958).

Since interrogatories involving mixed questions of law and fact may create disputes between the parties which are best resolved after much or all of the other discovery has been completed, the court is expressly authorized to defer an answer. Likewise, the court may delay determination until pretrial conference, if it believes that the dispute is best resolved in the presence of the judge.

The principal question raised with respect to the cases permitting such interrogatories is whether they reintroduce undesirable aspects of the prior pleading practice, whereby parties were chained to misconceived contentions or theories, and ultimate determination on the merits was frustrated. See James, *The Revival of Bills of Particulars under the Federal Rules,* 71 Harv.L.Rev. 1473 (1958). But there are few if any instances in the recorded cases demonstrating that such frustration has occurred. The general rule governing the use of answers to interrogatories is that under ordinary circumstances they do not limit proof. See, *e.g., McElroy v. United Air Lines, Inc.,* 21 F.R.D. 100 (W.D.Mo.1967); *Pressley v. Boehlke,* 33 F.R.D. 316, 317 (W.D.N.C.1963). Although in exceptional circumstances reliance on an answer may cause such prejudice that the court will hold the answering party bound to his answer, *e.g., Zielinski v. Philadelphia Piers, Inc.,* 139 F.Supp. 408 (E.D.Pa.1956), the interrogating party will ordinarily not be entitled to rely on the unchanging character of the answers he receives and cannot base prejudice on such reliance. The rule does not affect the power of a court to permit withdrawal or amendment of answers to interrogatories.

The use of answers to interrogatories at trial is made subject to the rules of evidence. The provisions governing use of depositions, to which Rule 33 presently refers, are not entirely apposite to answers to interrogatories, since deposition practice contemplates that all parties will ordinarily participate through cross-examination. See 4 *Moore's Federal Practice* ¶33.29[1] (2d ed. 1966).

Certain provisions are deleted from subdivision (b) because they are fully covered by new Rule 26(c) providing for protective orders and Rules 26(a) and 26(d). The language of the subdivision is thus simplified without any change of substance.

Subdivision (c). This is a new subdivision, adapted from Calif.Code Civ.Proc. § 2030(c), relating especially to interrogatories which require a party to engage in burdensome or expensive research into his own business records in order to give an answer. The subdivision gives the party an option to make the records available and place the burden of research of the party who seeks the information. "This provision, without undermining the liberal scope of interrogatory discovery, places the burden of discovery upon its potential benefittee," Louisell, *Modern California Discovery,* 124–125 (1963), and alleviates a problem which in the past has troubled Federal courts. See Speck, *The Use of Discovery in United States District Courts,* 60 Yale L.J. 1132, 1142–1144 (1951). The interrogating party is protected against abusive use of this provision through the requirement that the burden of ascertaining the answer be substantially the same for both sides. A respondent may not impose on an interrogating party a mass of records as to which research is feasible only for one familiar with the records. At the same time, the respondent unable to invoke this subdivision does not on that account lose the protection available to him under new Rule 26(c) against oppressive or unduly burdensome or expensive interrogatories. And even when the respondent successfully invokes the subdivision, the court is not deprived of its usual power, in appropriate cases, to require that the interrogating party reimburse the respondent for the expense of assembling his records and making them intelligible.

1980 Amendment

Subdivision (c). The Committee is advised that parties upon whom interrogatories are served have occasionally responded by directing the interrogating party to a mass of business records or by offering to make all of their records available, justifying the response by the option provided by this subdivision. Such practices are an abuse of the option. A party who is permitted by the terms of this subdivision to offer records for inspection in lieu of answering an interrogatory should offer them in a manner than permits the same direct and economical access that is available to the party. If the information sought exists in the form of compilations, abstracts or summaries then available to the responding party, those should be made available to the interrogating party. The final sentence is added to make it clear that a responding party has the duty to specify, by category and location, the records from which answers to interrogatories can be derived.

1993 Amendment

Purpose of Revision. The purpose of this revision is to reduce the frequency and increase the efficiency of interrogatory practice. The revision is based on experience with local rules. For ease of reference, subdivision (a) is divided into two subdivisions and the remaining subdivisions renumbered.

Subdivision (a). Revision of this subdivision limits interrogatory practice. Because Rule 26(a)(1)–(3) requires disclosure of much of the information previously obtained by this form of discovery, there should be less occasion to use it. Experience in over half of the district courts has confirmed that limitations on the number of interrogatories are useful and manageable. Moreover, because the device can be costly and may be used as a means of harassment, it is desirable to subject its use to the control of the court consistent with the principles stated in Rule 26(b)(2), particularly in multi-party cases where it has not been unusual for the same interrogatory to be propounded to a party by more than one of its adversaries.

Each party is allowed to serve 25 interrogatories upon any other party, but must secure leave of court (or a stipulation from the opposing party) to serve a larger number. Parties cannot evade this presumptive limitation through the device of joining as "subparts" questions that seek information about discrete separate subjects. However, a question asking about communications of a particular type should be treated as a single interrogatory even though it requests that the time, place, persons present, and contents be stated separately for each such communication.

As with the number of depositions authorized by Rule 30, leave to serve additional interrogatories is to be allowed when consistent with Rule 26(b)(2). The aim is not to prevent needed discovery, but to provide judicial scrutiny before parties make potentially excessive use of this discovery device. In many cases it will be appropriate for the court to permit a larger number of interrogatories in the scheduling order entered under Rule 16(b).

Unless leave of court is obtained, interrogatories may not be served prior to the meeting of the parties under Rule 26(f).

When a case with outstanding interrogatories exceeding the number permitted by this rule is removed to federal court, the interrogating party must seek leave allowing the additional interrogatories, specify which twenty-five are to be answered, or resubmit interrogatories that comply with the rule. Moreover, under Rule 26(d), the time for response would be measured from the date of the parties' meeting under Rule 26(f). See Rule 81(c), providing that these rules govern procedures after removal.

Subdivision (b). A separate subdivision is made of the former second paragraph of subdivision (a). Language is added to paragraph (1) of this subdivision to emphasize the duty of the responding party to provide full answers to the extent not objectionable. If, for example, an interrogatory seeking information about numerous facilities or products is deemed objectionable, but an interrogatory seeking information about a lesser number of facilities or products would not have been objectionable, the interrogatory should be answered with respect to the latter even though an objection is raised as to the balance of the facilities or products. Similarly, the fact that additional time may be needed to respond to some questions (or to some aspects of questions) should not justify a delay in responding to those questions (or other aspects of questions) that can be answered within the prescribed time.

Paragraph (4) is added to make clear that objections must be specifically justified, and that unstated or untimely grounds for objection ordinarily are waived. Note also the provisions of revised Rule 26(b)(5), which require a responding party to indicate when it is withholding information under a claim of privilege or as trial preparation materials.

These provisions should be read in light of Rule 26(g), authorizing the court to impose sanctions on a party and attorney making an unfounded objection to an interrogatory.

Subdivisions (c) and (d). The provisions of former subdivisions (b) and (c) are renumbered.

2006 Amendment

Rule 33(d) is amended to parallel Rule 34(a) by recognizing the importance of electronically stored information. The term "electronically stored information" has the same broad meaning in Rule 33(d) as in Rule 34(a). Much business information is stored only in electronic form; the Rule 33(d) option should be available with respect to such records as well.

Special difficulties may arise in using electronically stored information, either due to its form or because it is dependent on a particular computer system. Rule 33(d) allows a responding party to substitute access to documents or electronically stored information for an answer only if the burden of deriving the answer will be substantially the same for either party. Rule 33(d) states that a party electing to respond to an interrogatory by providing electronically stored information must ensure that the interrogating party can locate and identify it "as readily as can the party served," and that the responding party must give the interrogating party a "reasonable opportunity to examine, audit, or inspect" the information. Depending on the circumstances, satisfying these provisions with regard to electronically stored information may require the responding party to provide some combination of technical support, information on application software, or other assistance. The key question is whether such support enables the interrogating party to derive or ascertain the answer from the electronically stored information as readily as the responding party. A party that wishes to invoke Rule 33(d) by specifying electronically stored information may be required to provide direct access to its electronic information system, but only if that is necessary to afford the requesting party an adequate opportunity to derive or ascertain the answer to the interrogatory. In that situation, the responding party's need to protect sensitive interests of confidentiality or privacy may mean that it must derive or ascertain and provide the answer itself rather than invoke Rule 33(d).

2007 Amendment

The language of Rule 33 has been amended as part of the general restyling of the Civil Rules to make them more easily understood and to make style and terminology consistent throughout the rules. These changes are intended to be stylistic only.

The final sentence of former Rule 33(a) was a redundant cross-reference to the discovery moratorium provisions of Rule 26(d). Rule 26(d) is now familiar, obviating any need to carry forward the redundant cross-reference.

Former Rule 33(b)(5) was a redundant reminder of Rule 37(a) procedure and is omitted as no longer useful.

Former Rule 33(c) stated that an interrogatory "is not necessarily objectionable merely because an answer * * * involves an opinion or contention * * * ." "[I]s not necessarily" seemed to imply that the interrogatory might be objectionable merely for this reason. This implication has been ignored in practice. Opinion and contention interrogatories are used routinely. Amended Rule 33(a)(2) embodies the current meaning of Rule 33 by omitting "necessarily."

2015 Amendment

Rule 33 is amended in parallel with Rules 30 and 31 to reflect the recognition of proportionality in Rule 26(b)(1).

Rule 34. Producing Documents, Electronically Stored Information, and Tangible Things, or Entering Onto Land, for Inspection and Other Purposes

(a) In General. A party may serve on any other party a request within the scope of Rule 26(b):

(1) to produce and permit the requesting party or its representative to inspect, copy, test, or sample the following items in the responding party's possession, custody, or control:

(A) any designated documents or electronically stored information—including writings, drawings, graphs, charts, photographs, sound recordings, images, and other data or data compilations—stored in any medium from which information can be obtained either directly or, if necessary, after translation by the responding party into a reasonably usable form; or

(B) any designated tangible things; or

(2) to permit entry onto designated land or other property possessed or controlled by the responding party, so that the requesting party may inspect, measure, survey, photograph, test, or sample the property or any designated object or operation on it.

(b) Procedure.

(1) *Contents of the Request.* The request:

(A) must describe with reasonable particularity each item or category of items to be inspected;

(B) must specify a reasonable time, place, and manner for the inspection and for performing the related acts; and

(C) may specify the form or forms in which electronically stored information is to be produced.

(2) *Responses and Objections.*

(A) *Time to Respond.* The party to whom the request is directed must respond in writing within 30 days after being served or — if the request was delivered under Rule 26(d)(2) — within 30 days after the parties' first Rule 26(f) conference. A shorter or longer time may be stipulated to under Rule 29 or be ordered by the court.

(B) *Responding to Each Item.* For each item or category, the response must either state that inspection and related activities will be permitted as requested or state with specificity the grounds for objecting to the request, including the reasons. The responding party may state that it will produce copies of documents or of electronically stored information instead of permitting inspection. The production must then be completed no later than the time for inspection specified in the request or another reasonable time specified in the response.

(C) *Objections.* An objection must state whether any responsive materials are being withheld on the basis of that objection. An objection to part of a request must specify the part and permit inspection of the rest.

(D) *Responding to a Request for Production of Electronically Stored Information.* The response may state an objection to a requested form for producing electronically stored information. If the responding party objects to a requested form—or if no form was specified in the request—the party must state the form or forms it intends to use.

(E) *Producing the Documents or Electronically Stored Information.* Unless otherwise stipulated or ordered by the court, these procedures apply to producing documents or electronically stored information:

(i) A party must produce documents as they are kept in the usual course of business or must organize and label them to correspond to the categories in the request;

(ii) If a request does not specify a form for producing electronically stored information, a party must produce it in a form or forms in which it is ordinarily maintained or in a reasonably usable form or forms; and

(iii) A party need not produce the same electronically stored information in more than one form.

(c) Nonparties. As provided in Rule 45, a nonparty may be compelled to produce documents and tangible things or to permit an inspection.

(Amended December 27, 1946, effective March 19, 1948; March 30, 1970, effective July 1, 1970; April 29, 1980, effective August 1, 1980; March 2, 1987, effective August 1, 1987; April 30, 1991, effective December 1, 1991; April 22, 1993, effective December 1, 1993; April 12, 2006, effective December 1, 2006; April 30, 2007, effective December 1, 2007; April 29, 2015, effective December 1, 2015.)

ADVISORY COMMITTEE NOTES

1937 Adoption

In England orders are made for the inspection of documents, *English Rules Under the Judicature Act (The Annual Practice,* 1937) O. 31, r.r. 14, et seq., or for the inspection of tangible property or for entry upon land, O. 50, r. 3. Michigan provides for inspection of damaged property when such damage is the ground of the action. Mich.Court Rules Ann. (Searl, 1933) Rule 41, § 2.

Practically all states have statutes authorizing the court to order parties in possession or control of documents to permit other parties to inspect and copy them before trial. See Ragland, *Discovery Before Trial* (1932) Appendix, p. 267, setting out the statutes.

Compare [former] Equity Rule 58 (Discovery—Interrogatories—Inspection and Production of Documents—Admission of Execution or Genuineness) (fifth paragraph).

1946 Amendment

Note. The changes in clauses (1) and (2) correlate the scope of inquiry permitted under Rule 34 with that provided in Rule 26(b), and thus remove any ambiguity created by the former differences in language. As stated in *Olson Transpor-tation Co. v. Socony-Vacuum Oil Co.,* E.D.Wis.1944, 8 Fed. Rules Serv. 34.41, Case 2, "* * * Rule 34 is a direct and simple method of discovery." At the same time the addition of the words following the term "parties" makes certain that the person in whose custody, possession, or control the evidence reposes may have the benefit of the applicable protective orders stated in Rule 30(b). This change should be considered in the light of the proposed expansion of Rule 30(b).

An objection has been made that the word "designated" in Rule 34 has been construed with undue strictness in some district court cases so as to require great and impracticable specificity in the description of documents, papers, books, etc., sought to be inspected. The Committee, however, believes that no amendment is needed, and that the proper meaning of "designated" as requiring specificity has already been delineated by the Supreme Court. *See Brown v. United States,* 1928, 48 S.Ct. 288, 276 U.S. 134, 143, 72 L.Ed. 500 ("The subpoena * * * specifies * * * with reasonable particularity the subjects to which the documents called for related."); *Consolidated Rendering Co. v. Vermont,* 1908, 28 S.Ct. 178, 207 U.S. 541, 543–544, 52 L.Ed. 327 ("We see no reason why all such books, papers and correspondence which related to the subject of inquiry, and were described with reasonable detail, should not be called for and the company directed to produce them. Otherwise, the State would be compelled to designate each particular paper which it desired, which presupposes an accurate knowledge of such papers, which the tribunal desiring the papers would probably rarely, if ever, have.").

1970 Amendment

Rule 34 is revised to accomplish the following major changes in the existing rule: (1) to eliminate the requirement of good cause; (2) to have the rule operate extrajudicially; (3) to include testing and sampling as well as inspecting or photographing tangible things; and (4) to make clear that the rule does not preclude an independent action for analogous discovery against persons not parties.

Subdivision (a). Good cause is eliminated because it has furnished an uncertain and erratic protection to the parties from whom production is sought and is now rendered unnecessary by virtue of the more specific provisions added to Rule 26(b) relating to materials assembled in preparation for trial and to experts retained or consulted by parties.

The good cause requirement was originally inserted in Rule 34 as a general protective provision in the absence of experience with the specific problems that would arise thereunder. As the note to Rule 26(b)(3) on trial preparation materials makes clear, good cause has been applied differently to varying classes of documents, though not without confusion. It has often been said in court opinions that good cause requires a consideration of need for the materials and of alternative means of obtaining them, i.e., something more than relevance and lack of privilege. But the overwhelming proportion of the cases in which the formula of good cause has been applied to require a special showing are those involving trial preparation. In practice, the courts have not treated documents as having a special immunity to discovery simply because of their being documents. Protection may be afforded to claims of privacy or secrecy or of undue burden or expense under what is now Rule 26(c) (previously Rule 30(b)). To be sure, an appraisal of "undue" burden inevitably entails consideration of the needs of the party seeking discovery.

With special provisions added to govern trial preparation materials and experts, there is no longer any occasion to retain the requirement of good cause.

The revision of Rule 34 to have it operate extrajudicially, rather than by court order, is to a large extent a reflection of existing law office practice. The Columbia Survey shows that of the litigants seeking inspection of documents or things, only about 25 percent filed motions for court orders. This minor fraction nevertheless accounted for a significant number of motions. About half of these motions were uncontested and in almost all instances the party seeking production ultimately prevailed. Although an extrajudicial procedure will not drastically alter existing practice under Rule 34—it will conform to it in most cases—it has the potential of saving court time in a substantial though proportionately small number of cases tried annually.

The inclusion of testing and sampling of tangible things and objects or operations on land reflects a need frequently encountered by parties in preparation for trial. If the operation of a particular machine is the basis of a claim for negligent injury, it will often be necessary to test its operating parts or to sample and test the products it is producing. *Cf.* Mich.Gen.Ct.R. 310.1(1) (1963) (testing authorized).

The inclusive description of "documents" is revised to accord with changing technology. It makes clear that Rule 34 applies to electronics data compilations from which information can be obtained only with the use of detection devices, and that when the data can as a practical matter be made usable by the discovering party only through respondent's devices, respondent may be required to use his devices to translate the data into usable form. In many instances, this means that respondent will have to supply a print-out of computer data. The burden thus placed on respondent will vary from case to case, and the courts have ample power under Rule 26(c) to protect respondent against undue burden or expense, either by restricting discovery or requiring that the discovering party pay costs. Similarly, if the discovering party needs to check the electronic source itself, the court may protect respondent with respect to preservation of his records, confidentiality of nondiscoverable matters, and costs.

Subdivision (b). The procedure provided in Rule 34 is essentially the same as that in Rule 33, as amended, and the discussion in the note appended to that rule is relevant to Rule 34 as well. Problems peculiar to Rule 34 relate to the specific arrangements that must be worked out for inspection and related acts of copying, photographing, testing, or sampling. The rule provides that a request for inspection shall set forth the items to be inspected either by item or category, describing each with reasonable particularity, and shall specify a reasonable time, place, and manner of making the inspection.

Subdivision (c). Rule 34 as revised continues to apply only to parties. Comments from the bar make clear that in the preparation of cases for trial it is occasionally necessary to enter land or inspect large tangible things in the possession of a person not a party, and that some courts have dismissed independent actions in the nature of bills in equity for such discovery on the ground that Rule 34 is preemptive. While an ideal solution to this problem is to provide for discovery against persons not parties in Rule 34, both the jurisdictional and procedural problems are very complex. For the present, this subdivision makes clear that Rule 34 does not preclude independent actions for discovery against persons not parties.

1980 Amendment

Subdivision (b). The Committee is advised that, "It is apparently not rare for parties deliberately to mix critical documents with others in the hope of obscuring significance." *Report of the Special Committee for the Study of Discovery Abuse, Section of Litigation of the American Bar Association* (1977) 22. The sentence added by this subdivision follows the recommendation of the *Report*.

1987 Amendment

The amendment is technical. No substantive change is intended.

1991 Amendment

This amendment reflects the change effected by revision of Rule 45 to provide for subpoenas to compel non-parties to produce documents and things and to submit to inspections of premises. The deletion of the text of the former paragraph is not intended to preclude an independent action for production of documents or things or for permission to enter upon land, but such actions may no longer be necessary in light of this revision.

1993 Amendment

The rule is revised to reflect the change made by Rule 26(d), preventing a party from seeking formal discovery prior to the meeting of the parties required by Rule 26(f). Also, like a change made in Rule 33, the rule is modified to make clear that, if a request for production is objectionable only in part, production should be afforded with respect to the unobjectionable portions.

When a case with outstanding requests for production is removed to federal court, the time for response would be measured from the date of the parties' meeting. See Rule 81(c), providing that these rules govern procedures after removal.

2006 Amendment

Subdivision (a). As originally adopted, Rule 34 focused on discovery of "documents" and "things." In 1970, Rule 34(a) was amended to include discovery of data compilations, anticipating that the use of computerized information would increase. Since then, the growth in electronically stored information and in the variety of systems for creating and storing such information has been dramatic. Lawyers and judges interpreted the term "documents" to include electronically stored information because it was obviously improper to allow a party to evade discovery obligations on the basis that the label had not kept pace with changes in information technology. But it has become increasingly difficult to say that all forms of electronically stored information, many dynamic in nature, fit within the traditional concept of a "document." Electronically stored information may exist in dynamic databases and other forms far different from fixed expression on paper. Rule 34(a) is amended to confirm that discovery of electronically stored information stands on equal footing with discovery of paper documents. The change clarifies that Rule 34 applies to information that is fixed in a tangible form and to information that is stored in a medium from which it can be retrieved and examined. At the same time, a Rule 34 request for production of "documents" should be understood to encompass, and the response should include, electronically stored information unless discovery in the action has clearly distinguished between electronically stored information and "documents."

Discoverable information often exists in both paper and electronic form, and the same or similar information might exist in both. The items listed in Rule 34(a) show different ways in which information may be recorded or stored. Images, for example, might be hard-copy documents or electronically stored information. The wide variety of computer systems currently in use, and the rapidity of technological change, counsel against a limiting or precise definition of electronically stored information. Rule 34(a)(1) is expansive and includes any type of information that is stored electronically. A common example often sought in discovery is electronic communications, such as e-mail. The rule covers — either as documents or as electronically stored information — information "stored in any medium," to encompass future developments in computer technology. Rule 34(a)(1) is intended to be broad enough to cover all current types of computer-based information, and flexible enough to encompass future changes and developments.

References elsewhere in the rules to "electronically stored information" should be understood to invoke this expansive approach. A companion change is made to Rule 33(d), making it explicit that parties choosing to respond to an interrogatory by permitting access to responsive records may do so by providing access to electronically stored information. More generally, the term used in Rule 34(a)(1) appears in a number of other amendments, such as those to Rules 26(a)(1), 26(b)(2), 26(b)(5)(B), 26(f), 34(b), 37(f), and 45. In each of these rules, electronically stored information has the same broad meaning it has under Rule 34(a)(1). References to "documents" appear in discovery rules that are not amended, including Rules 30(f), 36(a), and 37(c)(2). These references should be interpreted to include electronically stored information as circumstances warrant.

The term "electronically stored information" is broad, but whether material that falls within this term should be produced, and in what form, are separate questions that must be addressed under Rules 26(b), 26(c), and 34(b).

The Rule 34(a) requirement that, if necessary, a party producing electronically stored information translate it into reasonably usable form does not address the issue of translating from one human language to another. *See In re Puerto Rico Elect. Power Auth.*, 687 F.2d 501, 504–510 (1st Cir. 1989).

Rule 34(a)(1) is also amended to make clear that parties may request an opportunity to test or sample materials sought under the rule in addition to inspecting and copying them. That opportunity may be important for both electronically stored information and hard-copy materials. The current rule is not clear that such testing or sampling is authorized; the amendment expressly permits it. As with any other form of discovery, issues of burden and intrusiveness raised by requests to test or sample can be addressed under Rules 26(b)(2) and 26(c). Inspection or testing of certain types of electronically stored information or of a responding party's electronic information system may raise issues of confidentiality or privacy. The addition of testing and sampling to Rule 34(a) with regard to documents and electronically stored information is not meant to create a routine right of direct access to a party's electronic information system, although such access might be justified in some circumstances. Courts

should guard against undue intrusiveness resulting from inspecting or testing such systems.

Rule 34(a)(1) is further amended to make clear that tangible things must — like documents and land sought to be examined — be designated in the request.

Subdivision (b). Rule 34(b) provides that a party must produce documents as they are kept in the usual course of business or must organize and label them to correspond with the categories in the discovery request. The production of electronically stored information should be subject to comparable requirements to protect against deliberate or inadvertent production in ways that raise unnecessary obstacles for the requesting party. Rule 34(b) is amended to ensure similar protection for electronically stored information.

The amendment to Rule 34(b) permits the requesting party to designate the form or forms in which it wants electronically stored information produced. The form of production is more important to the exchange of electronically stored information than of hard-copy materials, although a party might specify hard copy as the requested form. Specification of the desired form or forms may facilitate the orderly, efficient, and cost-effective discovery of electronically stored information. The rule recognizes that different forms of production may be appropriate for different types of electronically stored information. Using current technology, for example, a party might be called upon to produce word processing documents, e-mail messages, electronic spreadsheets, different image or sound files, and material from databases. Requiring that such diverse types of electronically stored information all be produced in the same form could prove impossible, and even if possible could increase the cost and burdens of producing and using the information. The rule therefore provides that the requesting party may ask for different forms of production for different types of electronically stored information.

The rule does not require that the requesting party choose a form or forms of production. The requesting party may not have a preference. In some cases, the requesting party may not know what form the producing party uses to maintain its electronically stored information, although Rule 26(f)(3) is amended to call for discussion of the form of production in the parties' prediscovery conference.

The responding party also is involved in determining the form of production. In the written response to the production request that Rule 34 requires, the responding party must state the form it intends to use for producing electronically stored information if the requesting party does not specify a form or if the responding party objects to a form that the requesting party specifies. Stating the intended form before the production occurs may permit the parties to identify and seek to resolve disputes before the expense and work of the production occurs. A party that responds to a discovery request by simply producing electronically stored information in a form of its choice, without identifying that form in advance of the production in the response required by Rule 34(b), runs a risk that the requesting party can show that the produced form is not reasonably usable and that it is entitled to production of some or all of the information in an additional form. Additional time might be required to permit a responding party to assess the appropriate form or forms of production.

If the requesting party is not satisfied with the form stated by the responding party, or if the responding party has objected to the form specified by the requesting party, the parties must meet and confer under Rule 37(a)(2)(B) in an effort to resolve the matter before the requesting party can file a motion to compel. If they cannot agree and the court resolves the dispute, the court is not limited to the forms initially chosen by the requesting party, stated by the responding party, or specified in this rule for situations in which there is no court order or party agreement.

If the form of production is not specified by party agreement or court order, the responding party must produce electronically stored information either in a form or forms in which it is ordinarily maintained or in a form or forms that are reasonably usable. Rule 34(a) requires that, if necessary, a responding party "translate" information it produces into a "reasonably usable" form. Under some circumstances, the responding party may need to provide some reasonable amount of technical support, information on application software, or other reasonable assistance to enable the requesting party to use the information. The rule does not require a party to produce electronically stored information in the form it which it is ordinarily maintained, as long as it is produced in a reasonably usable form. But the option to produce in a reasonably usable form does not mean that a responding party is free to convert electronically stored information from the form in which it is ordinarily maintained to a different form that makes it more difficult or burdensome for the requesting party to use the information efficiently in the litigation. If the responding party ordinarily maintains the information it is producing in a way that makes it searchable by electronic means, the information should not be produced in a form that removes or significantly degrades this feature.

Some electronically stored information may be ordinarily maintained in a form that is not reasonably usable by any party. One example is "legacy" data that can be used only by superseded systems. The questions whether a producing party should be required to convert such information to a more usable form, or should be required to produce it at all, should be addressed under Rule 26(b)(2)(B).

Whether or not the requesting party specified the form of production, Rule 34(b) provides that the same electronically stored information ordinarily need be produced in only one form.

2007 Amendment

The language of Rule 34 has been amended as part of the general restyling of the Civil Rules to make them more easily understood and to make style and terminology consistent throughout the rules. These changes are intended to be stylistic only.

The final sentence in the first paragraph of former Rule 34(b) was a redundant cross-reference to the discovery moratorium provisions of Rule 26(d). Rule 26(d) is now familiar, obviating any need to carry forward the redundant cross-reference.

The redundant reminder of Rule 37(a) procedure in the second paragraph of former Rule 34(b) is omitted as no longer useful.

2015 Amendment

Several amendments are made in Rule 34, aimed at reducing the potential to impose unreasonable burdens by objections to requests to produce.

Rule 34(b)(2)(A) is amended to fit with new Rule 26(d)(2). The time to respond to a Rule 34 request delivered before the parties' Rule 26(f) conference is 30 days after the first Rule 26(f) conference.

Rule 34(b)(2)(B) is amended to require that objections to Rule 34 requests be stated with specificity. This provision adopts the language of Rule 33(b)(4), eliminating any doubt that less specific objections might be suitable under Rule 34. The specificity of the objection ties to the new provision in Rule 34(b)(2)(C) directing that an objection must state whether any responsive materials are being withheld on the basis of that objection. An objection may state that a request is overbroad, but if the objection recognizes that some part of the request is appropriate the objection should state the scope that is not overbroad. Examples would be a statement that the responding party will limit the search to documents or electronically stored information created within a given period of time prior to the events in suit, or to specified sources. When there is such an objection, the statement of what has been withheld can properly identify as matters "withheld" anything beyond the scope of the search specified in the objection.

Rule 34(b)(2)(B) is further amended to reflect the common practice of producing copies of documents or electronically stored information rather than simply permitting inspection. The response to the request must state that copies will be produced. The production must be completed either by the time for inspection specified in the request or by another reasonable time specifically identified in the response. When it is necessary to make the production in stages the response should specify the beginning and end dates of the production.

Rule 34(b)(2)(C) is amended to provide that an objection to a Rule 34 request must state whether anything is being withheld on the basis of the objection. This amendment should end the confusion that frequently arises when a producing party states several objections and still produces information, leaving the requesting party uncertain whether any relevant and responsive information has been withheld on the basis of the objections. The producing party does not need to provide a detailed description or log of all documents withheld, but does need to alert other parties to the fact that documents have been withheld and thereby facilitate an informed discussion of the objection. An objection that states the limits that have controlled the search for responsive and relevant materials qualifies as a statement that the materials have been "withheld."

CROSS REFERENCES

Consequences of failure to comply with discovery order, see Fed.Rules Civ.Proc. Rule 37, 28 USCA.

Perpetuation of testimony, order and examination, see Fed. Rules Civ.Proc. Rule 27, 28 USCA.

Subpoena for production of documentary evidence, see Fed. Rules Civ.Proc. Rule 45, 28 USCA.

Summary judgment, continuance to procure discovery opposing, see Fed.Rules Civ.Proc. Rule 56, 28 USCA.

Rule 35. Physical and Mental Examinations
(a) Order for an Examination.

(1) *In General.* The court where the action is pending may order a party whose mental or physical condition—including blood group—is in controversy to submit to a physical or mental examination by a suitably licensed or certified examiner. The court has

the same authority to order a party to produce for examination a person who is in its custody or under its legal control.

(2) *Motion and Notice; Contents of the Order.* The order:

(A) may be made only on motion for good cause and on notice to all parties and the person to be examined; and

(B) must specify the time, place, manner, conditions, and scope of the examination, as well as the person or persons who will perform it.

(b) Examiner's Report.

(1) *Request by the Party or Person Examined.* The party who moved for the examination must, on request, deliver to the requester a copy of the examiner's report, together with like reports of all earlier examinations of the same condition. The request may be made by the party against whom the examination order was issued or by the person examined.

(2) *Contents.* The examiner's report must be in writing and must set out in detail the examiner's findings, including diagnoses, conclusions, and the results of any tests.

(3) *Request by the Moving Party.* After delivering the reports, the party who moved for the examination may request—and is entitled to receive—from the party against whom the examination order was issued like reports of all earlier or later examinations of the same condition. But those reports need not be delivered by the party with custody or control of the person examined if the party shows that it could not obtain them.

(4) *Waiver of Privilege.* By requesting and obtaining the examiner's report, or by deposing the examiner, the party examined waives any privilege it may have—in that action or any other action involving the same controversy—concerning testimony about all examinations of the same condition.

(5) *Failure to Deliver a Report.* The court on motion may order—on just terms—that a party deliver the report of an examination. If the report is not provided, the court may exclude the examiner's testimony at trial.

(6) *Scope.* This subdivision (b) applies also to an examination made by the parties' agreement, unless the agreement states otherwise. This subdivision does not preclude obtaining an examiner's report or deposing an examiner under other rules.

(Amended March 30, 1970, effective July 1, 1970; March 2, 1987, effective August 1, 1987; amended by Pub.L. 100–690, Title VII, § 7047(b), November 18, 1988, 102 Stat. 4401; amended April 30, 1991, effective December 1, 1991; April 30, 2007, effective December 1, 2007.)

ADVISORY COMMITTEE NOTES

1937 Adoption

Physical examination of parties before trial is authorized by statute or rule in a number of states. See Ariz.Rev. Code Ann. (Struckmeyer, 1928) § 4468; Mich. Court Rules Ann. (Searl, 1933) Rule 41, § 2; 2 N.J.Comp.Stat. (1910); N.Y.C.P.A. (1937) § 306; 1 S.D.Comp.Laws (1929) § 2716A; 3 Wash.Rev.Stat.Ann. (Remington, 1932) § 1230–1.

Mental examination of parties is authorized in Iowa. Iowa Code (1935) ch. 491–F1. See McCash, *The Evolution of the Doctrine of Discovery and Its Present Status in Iowa*, 20 Ia.L.Rev. 68 (1934).

The constitutionality of legislation providing for physical examination of parties was sustained in *Lyon v. Manhattan Railway Co.*, 1894, 37 N.E. 113, 142 N.Y. 298, and *McGovern v. Hope*, 1899, 42 A. 830, 63 N.J.L. 76. In *Union Pacific Ry. Co. v. Botsford*, 1891, 11 S.Ct. 1000, 141 U.S. 250, 35 L.Ed. 734, it was held that the court could not order the physical examination of a party in the absence of statutory authority. But in *Camden and Suburban Ry. Co. v. Stetson*, 1900, 20 S.Ct. 617, 177 U.S. 172, 44 L.Ed. 721 where there was statutory authority for such examination, derived from a state statute made operative by the conformity act, the practice was sustained. Such authority is now found in the present rule made operative by the Act of June 19, 1934, c. 651, U.S.C., Title 28, § 2072, formerly §§ 723b (Rules in actions at law; Supreme Court authorized to make) and 723c (Union of equity and action at law rules; power of Supreme Court).

1970 Amendment

Subdivision (a). Rule 35(a) has hitherto provided only for an order requiring a party to submit to an examination. It is desirable to extend the rule to provide for an order against the party for examination of a person in his custody or under his legal control. As appears from the provisions of amended Rule 37(b)(2) and the comment under that rule, an order to "produce" the third person imposes only an obligation to use good faith efforts to produce the person.

The amendment will settle beyond doubt that a parent or guardian suing to recover for injuries to a minor may be ordered to produce the minor for examination. Further, the amendment expressly includes blood examination within the kinds of examinations that can be ordered under the rule. See *Beach v. Beach*, 114 F.2d 479 (D.C. Cir. 1940). Provisions similar to the amendment have been adopted in at least 10 States: Calif. Code Civ.Proc. § 2032; Ida.R.Civ.P. 35; Ill. S–H Ann. c. 110A, § 215; Md.R.P. 420; Mich.Gen.Ct.R. 311; Minn.R.Civ.P. 35; Mo.Vern.Ann.R.Civ.p. 60.01; N.Dak.R.Civ.P. 35; N.Y.C.P.L. § 3121; Wyo.R.Civ.P. 35.

The amendment makes no change in the requirements of Rule 35 that, before a court order may issue, the relevant physical or mental condition must be shown to be "in controversy" and "good cause" must be shown for the examination. Thus, the amendment has no effect on the recent decision of the Supreme Court in *Schlagenhauf v. Holder*, 379 U.S. 104 (1964), stressing the importance of these requirements and applying them to the facts of the case. The amendment makes no reference to employees of a party. Provisions relating to employees in the State statutes and rules cited above appear to have been virtually unused.

Subdivision (b)(1). This subdivision is amended to correct an imbalance in Rule 35(b)(1) as heretofore written. Under that text, a party causing a Rule 35(a) examination to be made is required to furnish to the party examined, on request, a copy of the examining physician's report. If he delivers this copy, he is in turn entitled to receive from the party examined reports of all examinations of the same condition previously or later made. But the rule has not in terms entitled the examined party to receive from the party causing the Rule 35(a) examination any reports of earlier examinations of the same condition to which the latter may have access. The amendment cures this defect. See La.Stat.Ann., Civ.Proc. art 1495 (1960); Utah R.Civ.P. 35(c).

The amendment specifies that the written report of the examining physician includes results of all tests made, such as results of X-rays and cardiograms. It also embodies changes required by the broadening of Rule 35(a) to take in persons who are not parties.

Subdivision (b)(3). This new subdivision removes any possible doubt that reports of examination may be obtained although no order for examination has been made under Rule 35(a). Examinations are very frequently made by agreement, and sometimes before the party examined has an attorney. The courts have uniformly ordered that reports be supplied, see 4 *Moore's Federal Practice* ¶35.06, n. 1 (2d ed. 1966); 2A Barron & Holtzoff, *Federal Practice and Procedure* § 823, n. 22 (Wright ed. 1961), and it appears best to fill the technical gap in the present rule.

The subdivision also makes clear that reports of examining physicians are discoverable not only under Rule 35(b), but under other rules as well. To be sure, if the report is privileged, then discovery is not permissible under any rule other than Rule 35(b) and it is permissible under Rule 35(b) only if the party requests a copy of the report of examination made by the other party's doctor. *Sher v. De Haven,* 199 F.2d 777 (D.C. Cir. 1952), *cert. denied* 345 U.S. 936 (1953). But if the report is unprivileged and is subject to discovery under the provisions of rules other than Rule 35(b)—such as Rules 34 or 26(b)(3) or (4)—discovery should not depend upon whether the person examined demands a copy of the report. Although a few cases have suggested the contrary, *e.g., Galloway v. National Dairy Products Corp.,* 24 F.R.D. 362 (E.D.Pa.1959), the better considered district court decisions hold that Rule 35(b) is not preemptive. *E.g., Leszynski v. Russ,* 29 F.R.D. 10, 12 (D.Md.1961) and cases cited. The question was recently given full consideration in *Buffington v. Wood,* 351 F.2d 292 (3d Cir. 1965), holding that Rule 35(b) is not preemptive.

1987 Amendment

The amendments are technical. No substantive change is intended.

1991 Amendment

The revision authorizes the court to require physical or mental examinations conducted by any person who is suitably licensed or certified.

The rule was revised in 1988 by Congressional enactment to authorize mental examinations by licensed clinical psychologists. This revision extends that amendment to include other certified or licensed professionals, such as dentists or occupational therapists, who are not physicians or clinical psychologists, but who may be well-qualified to give valuable testimony about the physical or mental condition that is the subject of dispute.

The requirement that the examiner be *suitably* licensed or certified is a new requirement. The court is thus expressly authorized to assess the credentials of the examiner to assure that no person is subjected to a court-ordered examination by an examiner whose testimony would be of such limited value that it would be unjust to require the person to undergo the invasion of privacy associated with the examination. This authority is not wholly new, for under the former rule, the court retained discretion to refuse to order an examination, or to restrict an examination. 8 WRIGHT & MILLER, FEDERAL PRACTICE & PROCEDURE § 2234 (1986 Supp.). The revision is intended to encourage the exercise of this discretion, especially with respect to examinations by persons having narrow qualifications.

The court's responsibility to determine the suitability of the examiner's qualifications applies even to a proposed examination by a physician. If the proposed examination and testimony calls for an expertise that the proposed examiner does not have, it should not be ordered, even if the proposed examiner is a physician. The rule does not, however, require that the license or certificate be conferred by the jurisdiction in which the examination is conducted.

2007 Amendment

The language of Rule 35 has been amended as part of the general restyling of the Civil Rules to make them more easily understood and to make style and terminology consistent throughout the rules. These changes are intended to be stylistic only.

HISTORICAL NOTES

Revision Notes and Legislative Reports

1988 Acts. For Related Reports, see 1988 U.S.Code Cong. and Adm.News, p. 5937.

CROSS REFERENCES

Consequences of failure to submit to examination, see Fed. Rules Civ.Proc. Rule 37, 28 USCA.

Perpetuation of testimony, order and examination, see Fed. Rules Civ.Proc. Rule 27, 28 USCA.

Rule 36. Requests for Admission

(a) Scope and Procedure.

(1) *Scope.* A party may serve on any other party a written request to admit, for purposes of the pending action only, the truth of any matters within the scope of Rule 26(b)(1) relating to:

(A) facts, the application of law to fact, or opinions about either; and

(B) the genuineness of any described documents.

(2) *Form; Copy of a Document.* Each matter must be separately stated. A request to admit the genuineness of a document must be accompanied by a copy of the document unless it is, or has been, otherwise furnished or made available for inspection and copying.

(3) *Time to Respond; Effect of Not Responding.* A matter is admitted unless, within 30 days after being served, the party to whom the request is directed serves on the requesting party a written answer or objection addressed to the matter and signed by the party or its attorney. A shorter or longer time for responding may be stipulated to under Rule 29 or be ordered by the court.

(4) *Answer.* If a matter is not admitted, the answer must specifically deny it or state in detail why the answering party cannot truthfully admit or deny it. A denial must fairly respond to the substance of the matter; and when good faith requires that a party qualify an answer or deny only a part of a matter, the answer must specify the part admitted and qualify or deny the rest. The answering party may assert lack of knowledge or information as a reason for failing to admit or deny only if the party states that it has made reasonable inquiry and that the information it knows or can readily obtain is insufficient to enable it to admit or deny.

(5) *Objections.* The grounds for objecting to a request must be stated. A party must not object solely on the ground that the request presents a genuine issue for trial.

(6) *Motion Regarding the Sufficiency of an Answer or Objection.* The requesting party may move to determine the sufficiency of an answer or objection. Unless the court finds an objection justified, it must order that an answer be served. On finding that an answer does not comply with this rule, the court may order either that the matter is admitted or that an amended answer be served. The court may defer its final decision until a pretrial conference or a specified time before trial. Rule 37(a)(5) applies to an award of expenses.

(b) Effect of an Admission; Withdrawing or Amending It. A matter admitted under this rule is conclusively established unless the court, on motion, permits the admission to be withdrawn or amended. Subject to Rule 16(e), the court may permit withdrawal or amendment if it would promote the presentation of the merits of the action and if the court is not persuaded that it would prejudice the requesting party in maintaining or defending the action on the merits. An admission under this rule is not an admission for any other purpose and cannot be used against the party in any other proceeding.

(Amended December 27, 1946, effective March 19, 1948; March 30, 1970, effective July 1, 1970; March 2, 1987, effective August 1, 1987; April 22, 1993, effective December 1, 1993; April 30, 2007, effective December 1, 2007.)

ADVISORY COMMITTEE NOTES

1937 Adoption

Compare similar rules: [Former] Equity Rule 58 (last paragraph, which provides for the admission of the execution and genuineness of documents); *English Rules Under the Judicature Act* (The Annual Practice, 1937) O. 32; Ill.Rev. Stat. (1937) ch. 110, § 182 and Rule 18 (Ill.Rev.Stat. (1937) ch. 110, § 259.18); 2 Mass.Gen.Laws (Ter.Ed., 1932) ch. 231,

§ 69; Mich. Court Rules Ann. (Searl, 1933) Rule 42; N.J. Comp.Stat. (2 Cum.Supp. 1911–1924); N.Y.C.P.A. (1937) §§ 322, 323; Wis.Stat. (1935) § 327.22.

1946 Amendment

Note. The first change in the first sentence of Rule 36(a) and the addition of the new second sentence, specifying when requests for admissions may be served, bring Rule 36 in line with amended Rules 26(a) and 33. There is no reason why these rules should not be treated alike. Other provisions of Rule 36(a) give the party whose admissions are requested adequate protection.

The second change in the first sentence of the rule [subdivision (a)] removes any uncertainty as to whether a party can be called upon to admit matters of fact other than those set forth in relevant documents described in and exhibited with the request. In *Smyth v. Kaufman*, C.C.A.2, 1940, 114 F.2d 40, it was held that the word "therein", now stricken from the rule [said subdivision] referred to the request and that a matter of fact not related to any document could be presented to the other party for admission or denial. The rule of this case is now clearly stated.

The substitution of the word "served" for "delivered" in the third sentence of the amended rule [said subdivision] is in conformance with the use of the word "serve" elsewhere in the rule and generally throughout the rules. See also Notes to Rules 13(a) and 33 herein. The substitution [in said subdivision] of "shorter or longer" for "further" will enable a court to designate a lesser period than 10 days for answer. This conforms with a similar provision already contained in Rule 33.

The addition of clause (1) [in said subdivision] specifies the method by which a party may challenge the propriety of a request to admit. There has been considerable difference of judicial opinion as to the correct method, if any, available to secure relief from an allegedly improper request. See Commentary, *Methods of Objecting to Notice to Admit*, 1942, 5 Fed.Rules Serv. 835; *International Carbonic Engineering Co. v. Natural Carbonic Products, Inc.*, S.D.Cal.1944, 57 F.Supp. 248. The changes in clause (1) are merely of a clarifying and conforming nature.

The first of the added last two sentences [in said subdivision] prevents an objection to a part of a request from holding up the answer, if any, to the remainder. See similar proposed change in Rule 33. The last sentence strengthens the rule by making the denial accurately reflect the party's position. It is taken, with necessary changes, from Rule 8(b).

1970 Amendment

Rule 36 serves two vital purposes, both of which are designed to reduce trial time. Admissions are sought, first to facilitate proof with respect to issues that cannot be eliminated from the case, and secondly, to narrow the issues by eliminating those that can be. The changes made in the rule are designed to serve these purposes more effectively. Certain disagreements in the courts about the proper scope of the rule are resolved. In addition, the procedural operation of the rule is brought into line with other discovery procedures, and the binding effect of an admission is clarified. See generally Finman, *The Request for Admissions in Federal Civil Procedure*, 71 Yale L.J. 371 (1962).

Subdivision (a). As revised, the subdivision provides that a request may be made to admit any matters within the scope of Rule 26(b) that relate to statements or opinions of fact or of the application of law to fact. It thereby eliminates the requirement that the matters be "of fact." This change resolves conflicts in the court decisions as to whether a request to admit matters of "opinion" and matters involving "mixed law and fact" is proper under the rule. As to "opinion," compare, e.g., *Jackson Buff Corp. v. Marcelle*, 20 F.R.D. 139 (E.D.N.Y.1957); *California v. The S. S. Jules Fribourg*, 19 F.R.D. 432 (N.D.Calif.1955), with e.g., *Photon, Inc. v. Harris Intertype, Inc.*, 28 F.R.D. 327 (D.Mass.1961); *Hise v. Lockwood Grader Corp.*, 153 F.Supp. 276 (D.Nebr.1957). As to "mixed law and fact" the majority of courts sustain objections, e.g., *Minnesota Mining and Mfg. Co. v. Norton Co.*, 36 F.R.D. 1 (N.D.Ohio 1964), but *McSparran v. Hanigan*, 225 F.Supp. 628 (E.D.Pa.1963) is to the contrary.

Not only is it difficult as a practical matter to separate "fact" from "opinion," see 4 *Moore's Federal Practice* ¶36.04 (2d ed. 1966); cf. 2A Barron & Holtzoff, *Federal Practice and Procedure* 317 (Wright ed. 1961), but an admission on a matter of opinion may facilitate proof or narrow the issues or both. An admission of a matter involving the application of law to fact may, in a given case, even more clearly narrow the issues. For example, an admission that an employee acted in the scope of his employment may remove a major issue from the trial. In *McSparran v. Hanigan, supra*, plaintiff admitted that "the premises on which said accident occurred, were occupied or under the control" of one of the defendants, 225 F.Supp. at 636. This admission, involving law as well as fact, removed one of the issues from the lawsuit and thereby reduced the proof required at trial. The amended provision does not authorize requests for admissions of law unrelated to the facts of the case.

Requests for admission involving the application of law to fact may create disputes between the parties which are best resolved in the presence of the judge after much or all of the other discovery has been completed. Power is therefore expressly conferred upon the court to defer decision until a pretrial conference is held or until a designated time prior to trial. On the other hand, the court should not automatically defer decision; in many instances, the importance of the admission lies in enabling the requesting party to avoid the burdensome accumulation of proof prior to the pretrial conference.

Courts have also divided on whether an answering party may properly object to request for admission as to matters which that party regards as "in dispute." Compare, e.g., *Syracuse Broadcasting Corp. v. Newhouse*, 271 F.2d 910, 917 (2d Cir. 1959); *Driver v. Gindy Mfg. Corp.*, 24 F.R.D. 473 (E.D.Pa.1959); with, e.g., *McGonigle v. Baxter*, 27 F.R.D. 504 (E.D.Pa.1961); *United States v. Ehbauer*, 13 F.R.D. 462 (W.D.Mo.1952). The proper response in such cases is an answer. The very purpose of the request is to ascertain whether the answering party is prepared to admit or regards the matter as presenting a genuine issue for trial. In his answer, the party may deny, or he may give as his reason for inability to admit or deny the existence of a genuine issue. The party runs no risk of sanctions if the matter is genuinely in issue, since Rule 37(c) provides a sanction of costs only when there are no good reasons for a failure to admit.

On the other hand, requests to admit may be so voluminous and so framed that the answering party finds the task of identifying what is in dispute and what is not unduly burdensome. If so, the responding party may obtain a protective order under Rule 26(c). Some of the decisions sustaining objections on "disputability" grounds could have been justified by the burdensome character of the requests. See, e.g., *Syracuse Broadcasting Corp. v. Newhouse, supra*.

Another sharp split of authority exists on the question whether a party may base his answer on lack of information or knowledge without seeking out additional information. One line of cases has held that a party may answer on the basis of such knowledge as he has at the time he answers. E.g., *Jackson Buff Corp. v. Marcelle*, 20 F.R.D. 139 (E.D.N.Y. 1957); *Sladek v. General Motors Corp.*, 16 F.R.D. 104 (S.D.Iowa 1954). A larger group of cases, supported by commentators, has taken the view that if the responding party lacks knowledge, he must inform himself in reasonable fashion. E.g., *Hise v. Lockwood Grader Corp.*, 153 F.Supp. 276 (D.Nebr. 1957); *E. H. Tate Co. v. Jiffy Enterprises, Inc.*, 16 F.R.D. 571 (E.D.Pa.1954); Finman, *supra*, 71 Yale L.J. 371, 404–409; 4 *Moore's Federal Practice* ¶36.04 (2d ed. 1966); 2A Barron & Holtzoff, *Federal Practice and Procedure* 509 (Wright ed. 1961).

The rule as revised adopts the majority view, as in keeping with a basic principle of the discovery rules that a reasonable burden may be imposed on the parties when its discharge will facilitate preparation for trial and ease the trial process. It has been argued against this view that one side should not have the burden of "proving" the other side's case. The revised rule requires only that the answering party make reasonable inquiry and secure such knowledge and information as are readily obtainable by him. In most instances, the investigation will be necessary either to his own case or to preparation for rebuttal. Even when it is not, the information may be close enough at hand to be "readily obtainable." Rule 36 requires only that the party state that he has taken these steps. The sanction for failure of a party to inform himself before he answers lies in the award of costs after trial, as provided in Rule 37(c).

The requirement that the answer to a request for admission be sworn is deleted, in favor of a provision that the answer be signed by the party or by his attorney. The provisions of Rule 36 make it clear that admissions function very much as pleadings do. Thus, when a party admits in part and denies in part, his admission is for purposes of the pending action only and may not be used against him in any other proceeding. The broadening of the rule to encompass mixed questions of law and fact reinforces this feature. Rule 36 does not lack a sanction for false answers; Rule 37(c) furnishes an appropriate deterrent.

The existing language describing the available grounds for objection to a request for admission is eliminated as neither necessary nor helpful. The statement that objection may be made to any request which is "improper" adds nothing to the provisions that the party serve an answer or objection addressed to each matter and that he state his reasons for any objection. None of the other discovery rules sets forth grounds for objection, except so far as all are subject to the general provisions of Rule 26.

Changes are made in the sequence of procedures in Rule 36 so that they conform to the new procedures in Rules 33 and 34. The major changes are as follows:

(1) The normal time for response to a request for admissions is lengthened from 10 to 30 days, conforming more closely to prevailing practice. A defendant need not respond, however, in less than 45 days after service of the summons and complaint upon him. The court may lengthen or shorten the time when special situations require it.

(2) The present requirement that the plaintiff wait 10 days to serve requests without leave of court is eliminated. The revised provision accords with those in Rules 33 and 34.

(3) The requirement that the objecting party move automatically for a hearing on his objection is eliminated, and the burden is on the requesting party to move for an order. The change in the burden of going forward does not modify present law on burden of persuasion. The award of expenses incurred in relation to the motion is made subject to the comprehensive provisions of Rule 37(a)(4).

(4) A problem peculiar to Rule 36 arises if the responding party serves answers that are not in conformity with the requirements of the rule—for example, a denial is not "specific," or the explanation of inability to admit or deny is not "in detail." Rule 36 now makes no provision for court scrutiny of such answers before trial, and it seems to contemplate that defective answers bring about admissions just as effectively as if no answer had been served. Some cases have so held. E.g., *Southern Ry. Co. v. Crosby*, 201 F.2d 878 (4th Cir. 1953); *United States v. Laney*, 96 F.Supp. 482 (E.D.S.C.1951).

Giving a defective answer the automatic effect of an admission may cause unfair surprise. A responding party who purported to deny or to be unable to admit or deny will for the first time at trial confront the contention that he has made a binding admission. Since it is not always easy to know whether a denial is "specific" or an explanation is "in detail," neither party can know how the court will rule at trial and whether proof must be prepared. Some courts, therefore, have entertained motions to rule on defective answers. They have at times ordered that amended answers be served, when the defects were technical, and at other times have declared that the matter was admitted. E.g., *Woods v. Stewart*, 171 F.2d 544 (5th Cir. 1948); *SEC v. Kaye, Real & Co.*, 122 F.Supp. 639 (S.D.N.Y.1954); *Sieb's Hatcheries, Inc. v. Lindley*, 13 F.R.D. 113 (W.D.Ark.1952). The rule as revised conforms to the latter practice.

Subdivision (b). The rule does not how indicate the extent to which a party is bound by his admission. Some courts view admissions as the equivalent of sworn testimony. E.g., *Ark–Tenn Distributing Corp. v. Breidt*, 209 F.2d 359 (3d Cir. 1954); *United States v. Lemons*, 125 F.Supp. 686 (W.D.Ark. 1954); 4 *Moore's Federal Practice* ¶36.08 (2d ed. 1966 Supp.). At least in some jurisdictions a party may rebut his own testimony, e.g., *Alamo v. Del Rosario*, 98 F.2d 328 (D.C.Cir. 1938), and by analogy an admission made pursuant to Rule 36 may likewise be thought rebuttable. The courts in *Ark–Tenn* and *Lemons, supra*, reasoned in this way, although the results reached may be supported on different grounds. In *McSparran v. Hanigan*, 225 F.Supp. 628, 636–637 (E.D.Pa.1963), the court held that an admission is conclusively binding, though noting the confusion created by prior decisions.

The new provisions give an admission a conclusively binding effect, for purposes only of the pending action, unless the admission is withdrawn or amended. In form and substance a Rule 36 admission is comparable to an admission in pleadings or a stipulation drafted by counsel for use at trial, rather than to an evidentiary admission of a party. Louisell, *Modern California Discovery* § 8.07 (1963); 2A Barron & Holtzoff, *Federal Practice and Procedure* § 838 (Wright ed. 1961). Unless the party securing an admission can depend on its binding effect, he cannot safely avoid the expense of preparing to prove the very matters on which he has secured the admission, and the purpose of the rule is defeated. Field v. McKusick, *Maine Civil Practice* § 36.4 (1959); Finman, *supra*, 71 Yale L.J. 371, 418–426; Comment, 56 Nw.U.L.Rev. 679, 682–683 (1961).

Provision is made for withdrawal or amendment of an admission. This provision emphasizes the importance of having the action resolved on the merits, while at the same time assuring each party that justified reliance on an admission in preparation for trial will not operate to his prejudice. Cf. *Moosman v. Joseph P. Blitz, Inc.*, 358 F.2d 686 (2d Cir. 1966).

1987 Amendment

The amendments are technical. No substantive change is intended.

1993 Amendment

The rule is revised to reflect the change made by Rule 26(d), preventing a party from seeking formal discovery until after the meeting of the parties required by Rule 26(f).

2007 Amendment

The language of Rule 36 has been amended as part of the general restyling of the Civil Rules to make them more easily understood and to make style and terminology consistent throughout the rules. These changes are intended to be stylistic only.

The final sentence of the first paragraph of former Rule 36(a) was a redundant cross-reference to the discovery moratorium provisions of Rule 26(d). Rule 26(d) is now familiar, obviating any need to carry forward the redundant cross-reference. The redundant reminder of Rule 37(c) in the second paragraph was likewise omitted.

CROSS REFERENCES

Expenses on refusal to admit, see Fed.Rules Civ.Proc. Rule 37, 28 USCA.

Pretrial conferences, sanctions for failure to obey scheduling or order, see Fed.Rules Civ.Proc. Rule 16, 28 USCA.

Use of admissions on motions for summary judgment, see Fed.Rules Civ.Proc. Rule 56, 28 USCA.

Rule 37. Failure to Make Disclosures or to Cooperate in Discovery; Sanctions

(a) Motion for an Order Compelling Disclosure or Discovery.

(1) *In General.* On notice to other parties and all affected persons, a party may move for an order compelling disclosure or discovery. The motion must include a certification that the movant has in good faith conferred or attempted to confer with the person or party failing to make disclosure or discovery in an effort to obtain it without court action.

(2) *Appropriate Court.* A motion for an order to a party must be made in the court where the action is pending. A motion for an order to a nonparty must be made in the court where the discovery is or will be taken.

(3) *Specific Motions.*

(A) *To Compel Disclosure.* If a party fails to make a disclosure required by Rule 26(a), any other party may move to compel disclosure and for appropriate sanctions.

(B) *To Compel a Discovery Response.* A party seeking discovery may move for an order compelling an answer, designation, production, or inspection. This motion may be made if:

(**i**) a deponent fails to answer a question asked under Rule 30 or 31;

(**ii**) a corporation or other entity fails to make a designation under Rule 30(b)(6) or 31(a)(4);

(**iii**) a party fails to answer an interrogatory submitted under Rule 33; or

(**iv**) a party fails to produce documents or fails to respond that inspection will be permitted — or fails to permit inspection — as requested under Rule 34.

(C) *Related to a Deposition.* When taking an oral deposition, the party asking a question may complete or adjourn the examination before moving for an order.

(4) *Evasive or Incomplete Disclosure, Answer, or Response.* For purposes of this subdivision (a), an evasive or incomplete disclosure, answer, or response must be treated as a failure to disclose, answer, or respond.

(5) *Payment of Expenses; Protective Orders.*

(A) *If the Motion Is Granted (or Disclosure or Discovery Is Provided After Filing).* If the motion is granted—or if the disclosure or requested discovery is provided after the motion was filed—the court must, after giving an opportunity to be heard, require the party or deponent whose conduct necessitated the motion, the party or attorney advising that conduct, or both to pay the movant's reasonable expenses incurred in making the motion, including attorney's fees. But the court must not order this payment if:

(**i**) the movant filed the motion before attempting in good faith to obtain the disclosure or discovery without court action;

(**ii**) the opposing party's nondisclosure, response, or objection was substantially justified; or

(**iii**) other circumstances make an award of expenses unjust.

(B) *If the Motion Is Denied.* If the motion is denied, the court may issue any protective order authorized under Rule 26(c) and must, after giving an opportunity to be heard, require the movant, the attorney filing the motion, or both to pay the party or deponent who opposed the motion its reasonable expenses incurred in opposing the motion, including attorney's fees. But the court must not order this payment if the motion was substantially justified or other circumstances make an award of expenses unjust.

(C) *If the Motion Is Granted in Part and Denied in Part.* If the motion is granted in part and denied in part, the court may issue any protective order authorized under Rule 26(c) and may, after giving an opportunity to be heard, apportion the reasonable expenses for the motion.

(b) Failure to Comply with a Court Order.

(1) *Sanctions Sought in the District Where the Deposition Is Taken.* If the court where the discovery is taken orders a deponent to be sworn or to answer a question and the deponent fails to obey, the failure may be treated as contempt of court. If a deposition-related motion is transferred to the court where the action is pending, and that court orders a deponent to be sworn or to answer a question and the deponent fails to obey, the failure may be treated as contempt of either the court where the discovery is taken or the court where the action is pending.

(2) *Sanctions Sought in the District Where the Action Is Pending.*

(A) *For Not Obeying a Discovery Order.* If a party or a party's officer, director, or managing agent—or a witness designated under Rule 30(b)(6) or 31(a)(4)—fails to obey an order to provide or permit discovery, including an order under Rule 26(f), 35, or 37(a), the court where the action is pending may issue further just orders. They may include the following:

(**i**) directing that the matters embraced in the order or other designated facts be taken as established for purposes of the action, as the prevailing party claims;

(**ii**) prohibiting the disobedient party from supporting or opposing designated claims or defenses, or from introducing designated matters in evidence;

(**iii**) striking pleadings in whole or in part;

(**iv**) staying further proceedings until the order is obeyed;

(**v**) dismissing the action or proceeding in whole or in part;

(**vi**) rendering a default judgment against the disobedient party; or

(**vii**) treating as contempt of court the failure to obey any order except an order to submit to a physical or mental examination.

(B) *For Not Producing a Person for Examination.* If a party fails to comply with an order under Rule 35(a) requiring it to produce another person for examination, the court may issue any of the orders listed in Rule 37(b)(2)(A)(i)-(vi), unless the disobedient party shows that it cannot produce the other person.

(C) *Payment of Expenses.* Instead of or in addition to the orders above, the court must order the disobedient party, the attorney advising that party, or both to pay the reasonable expenses, including attorney's fees, caused by the failure, unless the failure was substantially justified or other circumstances make an award of expenses unjust.

(c) Failure to Disclose, to Supplement an Earlier Response, or to Admit.

(1) *Failure to Disclose or Supplement.* If a party fails to provide information or identify a witness as required by Rule 26(a) or (e), the party is not allowed to use that information or witness to supply evidence on a motion, at a hearing, or at a trial, unless the failure was substantially justified or is harmless. In addition to or instead of this sanction, the court, on motion and after giving an opportunity to be heard:

(A) may order payment of the reasonable expenses, including attorney's fees, caused by the failure;

(B) may inform the jury of the party's failure; and

(C) may impose other appropriate sanctions, including any of the orders listed in Rule 37(b)(2)(A)(i)-(vi).

(2) *Failure to Admit.* If a party fails to admit what is requested under Rule 36 and if the requesting party later proves a document to be genuine or the matter true, the requesting party may move that the party who failed to admit pay the reasonable expenses, including attorney's fees, incurred in making that proof. The court must so order unless:

(A) the request was held objectionable under Rule 36(a);

(B) the admission sought was of no substantial importance;

(C) the party failing to admit had a reasonable ground to believe that it might prevail on the matter; or

(D) there was other good reason for the failure to admit.

(d) Party's Failure to Attend Its Own Deposition, Serve Answers to Interrogatories, or Respond to a Request for Inspection.

(1) *In General.*

(A) *Motion; Grounds for Sanctions.* The court where the action is pending may, on motion, order sanctions if:

(i) a party or a party's officer, director, or managing agent—or a person designated under Rule 30(b)(6) or 31(a)(4)—fails, after being served with proper notice, to appear for that person's deposition; or

(ii) a party, after being properly served with interrogatories under Rule 33 or a request for inspection under Rule 34, fails to serve its answers, objections, or written response.

(B) *Certification.* A motion for sanctions for failing to answer or respond must include a certification that the movant has in good faith conferred or attempted to confer with the party failing to act in an effort to obtain the answer or response without court action.

(2) *Unacceptable Excuse for Failing to Act.* A failure described in Rule 37(d)(1)(A) is not excused on the ground that the discovery sought was objectionable, unless the party failing to act has a pending motion for a protective order under Rule 26(c).

(3) *Types of Sanctions.* Sanctions may include any of the orders listed in Rule 37(b)(2)(A)(i)-(vi). Instead of or in addition to these sanctions, the court must require the party failing to act, the attorney advising that party, or both to pay the reasonable expenses, including attorney's fees, caused by the failure, unless the failure was substantially justified or other circumstances make an award of expenses unjust.

(e) Failure to Preserve Electronically Stored Information. If electronically stored information that should have been preserved in the anticipation or conduct of litigation is lost because a party failed to take reasonable steps to preserve it, and it cannot be restored or replaced through additional discovery, the court:

(1) upon finding prejudice to another party from loss of the information, may order measures no greater than necessary to cure the prejudice; or

(2) only upon finding that the party acted with the intent to deprive another party of the information's use in the litigation may:

(A) presume that the lost information was unfavorable to the party;

(B) instruct the jury that it may or must presume the information was unfavorable to the party; or

(C) dismiss the action or enter a default judgment.

(f) Failure to Participate in Framing a Discovery Plan. If a party or its attorney fails to participate in good faith in developing and submitting a proposed discovery plan as required by Rule 26(f), the court may, after giving an opportunity to be heard, require that party or attorney to pay to any other party the reasonable expenses, including attorney's fees, caused by the failure.

(Amended December 29, 1948, effective October 20, 1949; March 30, 1970, effective July 1, 1970; April 29, 1980, effective August 1, 1980; amended by Pub.L. 96–481, Title II, § 205(a), October 21, 1980, 94 Stat. 2330, effective October 1, 1981; amended March 2, 1987, effective August 1, 1987; April 22, 1993, effective December 1, 1993; April 17, 2000, effective December 1, 2000; April 12, 2006, effective December 1, 2006; April 30, 2007, effective December 1, 2007; April 16, 2013, effective December 1, 2013; April 29, 2015, effective December 1, 2015.)

ADVISORY COMMITTEE NOTES
1937 Adoption

The provisions of this rule authorizing orders establishing facts or excluding evidence or striking pleadings, or authorizing judgments of dismissal or default, for refusal to answer questions or permit inspection or otherwise make discovery, are in accord with *Hammond Packing Co. v. Arkansas*, 1909, 29 S.Ct. 370, 212 U.S. 322, 53 L.Ed. 530, 15 Ann.Cas. 645, which distinguishes between the justifiable use of such measures as a means of compelling the production of evidence, and their unjustifiable use, as in *Hovey v. Elliott*, 1897, 17 S.Ct. 841, 167 U.S. 409, 42 L.Ed. 215, for the mere purpose of punishing for contempt.

1948 Amendment

The amendment effective October 1949, substituted the reference to "Title 28, U.S.C., § 1783" in subdivision (e) for the reference to "the Act of July 3, 1926, c. 762, § 1 (44 Stat. 835), U.S.C., Title 28, § 711."

1970 Amendment

Rule 37 provides generally for sanctions against parties or persons unjustifiably resisting discovery. Experience has brought to light a number of defects in the language of the rule as well as instances in which it is not serving the purposes for which it was designed. See Rosenberg, *Sanctions to Effectuate Pretrial Discovery*, 58 Col.L.Rev. 480 (1958). In addition, changes being made in other discovery rules require conforming amendments to Rule 37.

Rule 37 sometimes refers to a "failure" to afford discovery and at other times to a "refusal" to do so. Taking note of this dual terminology, courts have imported into "refusal" a requirement of "wilfullness." See *Roth v. Paramount Pictures Corp.*, 8 F.R.D. 31 (W.D.Pa.1948); *Campbell v. Johnson*, 101 F.Supp. 705, 707 (S.D.N.Y.1951). In *Societe Internationale v. Rogers*, 357 U.S. 197 (1958), the Supreme Court concluded that the rather random use of these two terms in Rule 37 showed no design to use them with consistently distinctive meanings, that "refused" in Rule 37(b)(2) meant simply a failure to comply, and that wilfullness was relevant only to the selection of sanctions, if any, to be imposed. Nevertheless, after the decision in *Societe*, the court in *Hinson v. Michigan Mutual Liability Co.*, 275 F.2d 537 (5th Cir. 1960) once again ruled that "refusal" required wilfullness. Substitution of "failure" for "refusal" throughout Rule 37 should eliminate this confusion and bring the rule into harmony with the *Societe Internationale* decision. See Rosenberg, *supra*, 58 Col. L.Rev. 480, 489–490 (1958).

Subdivision (a). Rule 37(a) provides relief to a party seeking discovery against one who, with or without stated objections, fails to afford the discovery sought. It has always fully served this function in relation to depositions, but the amendments being made to Rules 33 and 34 give Rule 37(a) added scope and importance. Under existing Rule 33, a party objecting to interrogatories must make a motion for court hearing on his objections. The changes now made in Rules 33 and 37(a) make it clear that the interrogating party must move to compel answers, and the motion is provided for in Rule 37(a). Existing Rule 34, since it requires a court order prior to production of documents or things or permission to enter on land, has no relation to Rule 37(a). Amendments of Rules 34 and 37(a) create a procedure similar to that provided for Rule 33.

Subdivision (a)(1). This is a new provision making clear to which court a party may apply for an order compelling discovery. Existing Rule 37(a) refers only to the court in which the deposition is being taken; nevertheless, it has been held that the court where the action is pending has "inherent power" to compel a party deponent to answer. *Lincoln Laboratories, Inc. v. Savage Laboratories, Inc.*, 27 F.R.D. 476 (D.Del.1961). In relation to Rule 33 interrogatories and Rule 34 requests for inspection, the court where the action is pending is the appropriate enforcing tribunal. The new provision eliminates the need to resort to inherent power by spelling out the respective roles of the court where the action is pending and the court where the deposition is taken. In some instances, two courts are available to a party seeking to compel answers from a party deponent. The party seeking discovery may choose the court to which he will apply, but the court has power to remit the party to the other court as a more appropriate forum.

Subdivision (a)(2). This subdivision contains the substance of existing provisions of Rule 37(a) authorizing motions to compel answers to questions put at depositions and to interrogatories. New provisions authorize motions for orders compelling designation under Rules 30(b)(6) and 31(a) and compelling inspection in accordance with a request made under Rule 34. If the court denies a motion, in whole or part, it may accompany the denial with issuance of a protective order. Compare the converse provision in Rule 26(c).

Subdivision (a)(3). This new provision makes clear that an evasive or incomplete answer is to be considered, for purposes of subdivision (a), a failure to answer. The courts have consistently held that they have the power to compel adequate answers. *E.g., Cone Mills Corp. v. Joseph Bancroft & Sons Co.*, 33 F.R.D. 318 (D.Del.1963). This power is recognized and incorporated into the rule.

Subdivision (a)(4). This subdivision amends the provisions for award of expenses, including reasonable attorney's fees, to the prevailing party or person when a motion is made for an order compelling discovery. At present, an award of expenses is made only if the losing party or person is found to have acted without substantial justification. The change requires that expenses be awarded unless the conduct of the losing party or person is found to have been substantially justified. The test of "substantial justification" remains, but the change in language is intended to encourage judges to be more alert to abuses occurring in the discovery process.

On many occasions, to be sure, the dispute over discovery between the parties is genuine, though ultimately resolved one way or the other by the court. In such cases, the losing party is substantially justified in carrying the matter to court. But the rules should deter the abuse implicit in carrying or forcing a discovery dispute to court when no genuine dispute exists. And the potential or actual imposition of expenses is virtually the sole formal sanction in the rules to deter a party from pressing to a court hearing frivolous requests for or objections to discovery.

The present provision of Rule 37(a) that the court shall require payment if it finds that the defeated party acted without "substantial justification" may appear adequate, but in fact it has been little used. Only a handful of reported cases include an award of expenses, and the Columbia Survey found that in only one instance out of about 50 motions decided under Rule 37(a) did the court award expenses. It appears that the courts do not utilize the most important available sanction to deter abusive resort to the judiciary.

The proposed change provides in effect that expenses should ordinarily be awarded unless a court finds that the losing party acted justifiably in carrying his point to court. At the same time, a necessary flexibility is maintained, since the court retains the power to find that other circumstances make an award of expenses unjust—as where the prevailing party also acted unjustifiably. The amendment does not significantly narrow the discretion of the court, but rather presses the court to address itself to abusive practices. The present provision that expenses may be imposed upon either the party or his attorney or both is unchanged. But it is not contemplated that expenses will be imposed upon the attorney merely because the party is indigent.

Subdivision (b). This subdivision deals with sanctions for failure to comply with a court order. The present captions for subsections (1) and (2) entitled, "Contempt" and "Other Consequences," respectively, are confusing. One of the consequences listed in (2) is the arrest of the party, representing the exercise of the contempt power. The contents of the subsections show that the first authorizes the sanction of contempt (and no other) by the court in which the deposition is taken, whereas the second subsection authorizes a variety of sanctions, including contempt, which may be imposed by the court in which the action is pending. The captions of the subsections are changed to reflect their contents.

The scope of Rule 37(b)(2) is broadened by extending it to include any order "to provide or permit discovery," including orders issued under Rules 37(a) and 35. Various rules authorize orders for discovery—*e.g.*, Rule 35(b)(1), Rule 26(c) as revised, Rule 37(d). See Rosenberg, *supra*, 58 Col.L.Rev. 480, 484–486. Rule 37(b)(2) should provide comprehensively for enforcement of all these orders. *Cf. Societe Internationale v. Rogers*, 357 U.S. 197, 207 (1958). On the other hand, the reference to Rule 34 is deleted to conform to the changed procedure in that rule.

A new subsection (E) provides that sanctions which have been available against a party for failure to comply with an order under Rule 35(a) to submit to examination will now be available against him for his failure to comply with a Rule 35(a) order to produce a third person for examination, unless he shows that he is unable to produce the person. In this context, "unable" means in effect "unable in good faith." See *Societe Internationale v. Rogers*, 357 U.S. 197 (1958).

Subdivision (b)(2) is amplified to provide for payment of reasonable expenses caused by the failure to obey the order. Although Rules 37(b)(2) and 37(d) have been silent as to award of expenses, courts have nevertheless ordered them on occasion. *E.g., United Sheeplined Clothing Co. v. Arctic Fur Cap Corp.*, 165 F.Supp. 193 (S.D.N.Y.1958); *Austin Theatre, Inc. v. Warner Bros. Pictures, Inc.*, 22 F.R.D. 302 (S.D.N.Y. 1958). The provision places the burden on the disobedient party to avoid expenses by showing that his failure is justified or that special circumstances make an award of expenses unjust. Allocating the burden in this way conforms to the changed provisions as to expenses in Rule 37(a), and is particularly appropriate when a court order is disobeyed.

An added reference to directors of a party is similar to a change made in subdivision (d) and is explained in the note to that subdivision. The added reference to persons designated by a party under Rules 30(b)(6) or 31(a) to testify on behalf of the party carries out the new procedure in those rules for taking a deposition of a corporation or other organization.

Subdivision (c). Rule 37(c) provides a sanction for the enforcement of Rule 36 dealing with requests for admission. Rule 36 provides the mechanism whereby a party may obtain from another party in appropriate instances either (1) an admission, or (2) a sworn and specific denial or (3) a sworn statement "setting forth in detail the reasons why he cannot truthfully admit or deny." If the party obtains the second or third of these responses, in proper form, Rule 36 does not provide for a pretrial hearing on whether the response is warranted by the evidence thus far accumulated. Instead, Rule 37(c) is intended to provide posttrial relief in the form of a requirement that the party improperly refusing the admission pay the expenses of the other side in making the necessary proof at trial.

Rule 37(c), as now written, addresses itself in terms only to the sworn denial and is silent with respect to the statement of reasons for an inability to admit or deny. There is no apparent basis for this distinction, since the sanction provided in Rule 37(c) should deter all unjustified failures to admit. This omission in the rule has caused confused and diverse treatment in the courts. One court has held that if a party give inadequate reasons, he should be treated before trial as having denied the request, so that Rule 37(c) may apply. *Bertha Bldg. Corp. v. National Theatres Corp.*, 15 F.R.D. 339 (E.D.N.Y.1954). Another has held that the party should be treated as having admitted the request. *Heng Hsin Co. v. Stern, Morgenthau & Co.*, 20 Fed.Rules Serv. 36a.52, Case 1 (S.D.N.Y. Dec. 10, 1954). Still another has ordered a new response, without indicating what the outcome should be if the new response were inadequate. *United States Plywood Corp. v. Hudson Lumber Co.*, 127 F.Supp. 489, 497–498 (S.D.N.Y. 1954). See generally Finman, *The Request for Admissions in Federal Civil Procedure*, 71 Yale L.J. 371, 426–430 (1962). The amendment eliminates this defect in Rule 37(c) by bringing within its scope all failures to admit.

Additional provisions in Rule 37(c) protect a party from having to pay expenses if the request for admission was held objectionable under Rule 36(a) or if the party failing to admit had reasonable ground to believe that he might prevail on the matter. The latter provision emphasizes that the true test under Rule 37(c) is not whether a party prevailed at trial but whether he acted reasonably in believing that he might prevail.

Subdivision (d). The scope of subdivision (d) is broadened to include responses to requests for inspection under Rule 34, thereby conforming to the new procedures of Rule 34.

Two related changes are made in subdivision (d): the permissible sanctions are broadened to include such orders "as are just"; and the requirement that the failure to appear or respond be "wilful" is eliminated. Although Rule 37(d) in terms provides for only three sanctions, all rather severe, the courts have interpreted it as permitting softer sanctions than those which it sets forth. E.g., *Gill v. Stolow*, 240 F.2d 669 (2d Cir.1957); *Saltzman v. Birrell*, 156 F.Supp. 538 (S.D.N.Y. 1957); 2A Barron & Holtzoff, *Federal Practice and Procedure* 554–557 (Wright ed. 1961). The rule is changed to provide the greater flexibility as to sanctions which the cases show is needed.

The resulting flexibility as to sanctions eliminates any need to retain the requirement that the failure to appear or respond be "wilful." The concept of "wilful failure" is at best subtle and difficult, and the cases do not supply a bright line. Many courts have imposed sanctions without referring to wilfullness. E.g., *Milewski v. Schneider Transportation Co.*, 238 F.2d 397 (6th Cir.1956); *Dictograph Products, Inc. v. Kentworth Corp.*, 7 F.R.D. 543 (W.D.Ky.1947). In addition, in view of the possibility of light sanctions, even a negligent failure should come within Rule 37(d). If default is caused by counsel's ignorance of Federal practice, cf. *Dunn v. Pa. R.R.*,

96 F.Supp. 597 (N.D.Ohio 1951), or by his preoccupation with another aspect of the case, *cf. Maurer–Neuer, Inc. v. United Packinghouse Workers,* 26 F.R.D. 139 (D.Kans.1960), dismissal of the action and default judgment are not justified, but the imposition of expenses and fees may well be. "Wilfullness" continues to play a role, along with various other factors, in the choice of sanctions. Thus, the scheme conforms to Rule 37(b) as construed by the Supreme Court in *Societe Internationale v. Rogers,* 357 U.S. 197, 208 (1958).

A provision is added to make clear that a party may not properly remain completely silent even when he regards a notice to take his deposition or a set of interrogatories or requests to inspect as improper and objectionable. If he desires not to appear or not to respond, he must apply for a protective order. The cases are divided on whether a protective order must be sought. Compare *Collins v. Wayland,* 139 F.2d 677 (9th Cir. 1944), *cert. den.* 322 U.S. 744; *Bourgeois v. El Paso Natural Gas Co.,* 20 F.R.D. 358 (S.D.N.Y.1957); *Loosley v. Stone,* 15 F.R.D. 373 (S.D.Ill.1954), with *Scarlatos v. Kulukundis,* 21 F.R.D. 185 (S.D.N.Y.1957); *Ross v. True Temper Corp.,* 11 F.R.D. 307 (N.D.Ohio 1951). Compare also Rosenberg, *supra,* 58 Col.L.Rev. 480, 496 (1958) with 2A Barron & Holtzoff, *Federal Practice and Procedure* 530–531 (Wright ed. 1961). The party from whom discovery is sought is afforded, through Rule 26(c), a fair and effective procedure whereby he can challenge the request made. At the same time, the total noncompliance with which Rule 37(d) is concerned may impose severe inconvenience or hardship on the discovering party and substantially delay the discovery process. Cf. 2B Barron & Holtzoff, *Federal Practice and Procedure* 306–307 (Wright ed. 1961) (response to a subpoena).

The failure of an officer or managing agent of a party to make discovery as required by present Rule 37(d) is treated as the failure of the party. The rule as revised provides similar treatment for a director of a party. There is slight warrant for the present distinction between officers and managing agents on the one hand and directors on the other. Although the legal power over a director to compel his making discovery may not be as great as over officers or managing agents, *Campbell v. General Motors Corp.,* 13 F.R.D. 331 (S.D.N.Y.1952), the practical differences are negligible. That a director's interests are normally aligned with those of his corporation is shown by the provisions of old Rule 26(d)(2), transferred to 32(a)(2) (deposition of director of party may be used at trial by an adverse party for any purpose) and of Rule 43(b) (director of party may be treated at trial as a hostile witness on direct examination by any adverse party). Moreover, in those rare instances when a corporation is unable through good faith efforts to compel a director to make discovery, it is unlikely that the court will impose sanctions. Cf. *Societe Internationale v. Rogers,* 357 U.S. 197 (1958).

Subdivision (e). The change in the caption conforms to the language of 28 U.S.C. § 1783, as amended in 1964.

Subdivision (f). Until recently, costs of a civil action could be awarded against the United States only when expressly provided by Act of Congress, and such provision was rarely made. See H.R.Rep.No. 1535, 89th Cong., 2d Sess., 2–3 (1966). To avoid any conflict with this doctrine, Rule 37(f) has provided that expenses and attorney's fees may not be imposed upon the United States under Rule 37. See 2A Barron & Holtzoff, *Federal Practice and Procedure* 857 (Wright ed. 1961).

A major change in the law was made in 1966, 80 Stat. 308, 28 U.S.C. § 2412 (1966), whereby a judgment for costs may ordinarily be awarded to the prevailing party in any civil action brought by or against the United States. Costs are not to include the fees and expenses of attorneys. In light of this legislative development, Rule 37(f) is amended to permit the award of expenses and fees against the United States under Rule 37, but only to the extent permitted by statute. The amendment brings Rule 37(f) into line with present and future statutory provisions.

1980 Amendment

Subdivision (b)(2). New Rule 26(f) provides that if a discovery conference is held, at its close the court shall enter an order respecting the subsequent conduct of discovery. The amendment provides that the sanctions available for violation of other court orders respecting discovery are available for violation of the discovery conference order.

Subdivision (e). Subdivision (e) is stricken. Title 28, U.S.C. § 1783 no longer refers to sanctions. The subdivision otherwise duplicates Rule 45(e)(2).

Subdivision (g). New Rule 26(f) imposes a duty on parties to participate in good faith in the framing of a discovery plan by agreement upon the request of any party. This subdivision authorizes the court to award to parties who participate in good faith in an attempt to frame a discovery plan the expenses incurred in the attempt if any party or his attorney fails to participate in good faith and thereby causes additional expense.

Failure of United States to Participate in Good Faith in Discovery. Rule 37 authorizes the court to direct that parties or attorneys who fail to participate in good faith in the discovery process pay the expenses, including attorneys' fees, incurred by other parties as a result of that failure. Since attorneys' fees cannot ordinarily be awarded against the United States (28 U.S.C. § 2412), there is often no practical remedy for the misconduct of its officers and attorneys. However, in the case of a government attorney who fails to participate in good faith in discovery, nothing prevents a court in an appropriate case from giving written notification of that fact to the Attorney General of the United States and other appropriate heads of offices or agencies thereof.

1987 Amendment

The amendments are technical. No substantive change is intended.

1993 Amendment

Subdivision (a). This subdivision is revised to reflect the revision of Rule 26(a), requiring disclosure of matters without a discovery request.

Pursuant to new subdivision (a)(2)(A), a party dissatisfied with the disclosure made by an opposing party may under this rule move for an order to compel disclosure. In providing for such a motion, the revised rule parallels the provisions of the former rule dealing with failures to answer particular interrogatories. Such a motion may be needed when the information to be disclosed might be helpful to the party seeking the disclosure but not to the party required to make the disclosure. If the party required to make the disclosure would need the material to support its own contentions, the more effective enforcement of the disclosure requirement will be to exclude the evidence not disclosed, as provided in subdivision (c)(1) of this revised rule.

Language is included in the new paragraph and added to the subparagraph (B) that requires litigants to seek to resolve discovery disputes by informal means before filing a motion with the court. This requirement is based on successful experience with similar local rules of court promulgated pursuant to Rule 83.

The last sentence of paragraph (2) is moved into paragraph (4).

Under revised paragraph (3), evasive or incomplete disclosures and responses to interrogatories and production requests are treated as failures to disclose or respond. Interrogatories and requests for production should not be read or interpreted in an artificially restrictive or hypertechnical manner to avoid disclosure of information fairly covered by the discovery request, and to do so is subject to appropriate sanctions under subdivision (a).

Revised paragraph (4) is divided into three subparagraphs for ease of reference, and in each the phrase "after opportunity for hearing" is changed to "after affording an opportunity to be heard" to make clear that the court can consider such questions on written submissions as well as on oral hearings.

Subparagraph (A) is revised to cover the situation where information that should have been produced without a motion to compel is produced after the motion is filed but before it is brought on for hearing. The rule also is revised to provide that a party should not be awarded its expenses for filing a motion that could have been avoided by conferring with opposing counsel.

Subparagraph (C) is revised to include the provision that formerly was contained in subdivision (a)(2) and to include the same requirement of an opportunity to be heard that is specified in subparagraphs (A) and (B).

Subdivision (c). The revision provides a self-executing sanction for failure to make a disclosure required by Rule 26(a), without need for a motion under subdivision (a)(2)(A).

Paragraph (1) prevents a party from using as evidence any witnesses or information that, without substantial justification, has not been disclosed as required by Rules 26(a) and 26(e)(1). This automatic sanction provides a strong inducement for disclosure of material that the disclosing party would expect to use as evidence, whether at a trial, at a hearing, or on a motion, such as one under Rule 56. As disclosure of evidence offered solely for impeachment purposes is not required under those rules, this preclusion sanction likewise does not apply to that evidence.

Limiting the automatic sanction to violations "without substantial justification," coupled with the exception for violations that are "harmless," is needed to avoid unduly harsh penalties in a variety of situations: e.g., the inadvertent omission from a Rule 26(a)(1)(A) disclosure of the name of a potential witness known to all parties; the failure to list as a trial witness a person so listed by another party; or the lack of knowledge of a pro se litigant of the requirement to make disclosures. In the latter situation, however, exclusion would be proper if the requirement for disclosure had been called to the litigant's attention by either the court or another party.

Preclusion of evidence is not an effective incentive to compel disclosure of information that, being supportive of the position of the opposing party, might advantageously be concealed by the disclosing party. However, the rule provides the court with a wide range of other sanctions—such as declaring specified facts to be established, preventing contradictory evidence, or, like spoliation of evidence, allowing the

jury to be informed of the fact of nondisclosure—that, though not self-executing, can be imposed when found to be warranted after a hearing. The failure to identify a witness or document in a disclosure statement would be admissible under the Federal Rules of Evidence under the same principles that allow a party's interrogatory answers to be offered against it.

Subdivision (d). This subdivision is revised to require that, where a party fails to file any response to interrogatories or a Rule 34 request, the discovering party should informally seek to obtain such responses before filing a motion for sanctions.

The last sentence of this subdivision is revised to clarify that it is the pendency of a motion for protective order that may be urged as an excuse for a violation of subdivision (d). If a party's motion has been denied, the party cannot argue that its subsequent failure to comply would be justified. In this connection, it should be noted that the filing of a motion under Rule 26(c) is not self-executing—the relief authorized under that rule depends on obtaining the court's order to that effect.

Subdivision (g). This subdivision is modified to conform to the revision of Rule 26(f).

2000 Amendment

Subdivision (c)(1). When this subdivision was added in 1993 to direct exclusion of materials not disclosed as required, the duty to supplement discovery responses pursuant to Rule 26(e)(2) was omitted. In the face of this omission, courts may rely on inherent power to sanction for failure to supplement as required by Rule 26(e)(2), see 8 Federal Practice & Procedure § 2050 at 607–09, but that is an uncertain and unregulated ground for imposing sanctions. There is no obvious occasion for a Rule 37(a) motion in connection with failure to supplement, and ordinarily only Rule 37(c)(1) exists as rule-based authority for sanctions if this supplementation obligation is violated.

The amendment explicitly adds failure to comply with Rule 26(e)(2) as a ground for sanctions under Rule 37(c)(1), including exclusion of withheld materials. The rule provides that this sanction power only applies when the failure to supplement was "without substantial justification." Even if the failure was not substantially justified, a party should be allowed to use the material that was not disclosed if the lack of earlier notice was harmless.

"Shall" is replaced by "is" under the program to conform amended rules to current style conventions when there is no ambiguity.

GAP Report

The Advisory Committee recommends that the published amendment proposal be modified to state that the exclusion sanction can apply to failure "to amend a prior response to discovery as required by Rule 26(e)(2)." In addition, one minor phrasing change is recommended for the Committee Note.

2006 Amendment

Subdivision (f). Subdivision (f) is new. It focuses on a distinctive feature of computer operations, the routine alteration and deletion of information that attends ordinary use. Many steps essential to computer operation may alter or destroy information, for reasons that have nothing to do with how that information might relate to litigation. As a result, the ordinary operation of computer systems creates a risk that a party may lose potentially discoverable information without culpable conduct on its part. Under Rule 37(f), absent exceptional circumstances, sanctions cannot be imposed for loss of electronically stored information resulting from the routine, good-faith operation of an electronic information system.

Rule 37(f) applies only to information lost due to the "routine operation of an electronic information system" — the ways in which such systems are generally designed, programmed, and implemented to meet the party's technical and business needs. The "routine operation" of computer systems includes the alteration and overwriting of information, often without the operator's specific direction or awareness, a feature with no direct counterpart in hard-copy documents. Such features are essential to the operation of electronic information systems.

Rule 37(f) applies to information lost due to the routine operation of an information system only if the operation was in good faith. Good faith in the routine operation of an information system may involve a party's intervention to modify or suspend certain features of that routine operation to prevent the loss of information, if that information is subject to a preservation obligation. A preservation obligation may arise from many sources, including common law, statutes, regulations, or a court order in the case. The good faith requirement of Rule 37(f) means that a party is not permitted to exploit the routine operation of an information system to thwart discovery obligations by allowing that operation to continue in order to destroy specific stored information that it is required to preserve. When a party is under a duty to preserve information because of pending or reasonably anticipated litigation, intervention in the routine operation of an information system is one aspect of what is often called a "litigation hold." Among the factors that bear on a party's good faith in the routine operation of an information system are the steps the party took to comply with a court order in the case or party agreement requiring preservation of specific electronically stored information.

Whether good faith would call for steps to prevent the loss of information on sources that the party believes are not reasonably accessible under Rule 26(b)(2) depends on the circumstances of each case. One factor is whether the party reasonably believes that the information on such sources is likely to be discoverable and not available from reasonably accessible sources.

The protection provided by Rule 37(f) applies only to sanctions "under these rules." It does not affect other sources of authority to impose sanctions or rules of professional responsibility.

This rule restricts the imposition of "sanctions." It does not prevent a court from making the kinds of adjustments frequently used in managing discovery if a party is unable to provide relevant responsive information. For example, a court could order the responding party to produce an additional witness for deposition, respond to additional interrogatories, or make similar attempts to provide substitutes or alternatives for some or all of the lost information.

2007 Amendment

The language of Rule 37 has been amended as part of the general restyling of the Civil Rules to make them more easily understood and to make style and terminology consistent throughout the rules. These changes are intended to be stylistic only.

2013 Amendment

Rule 37(b) is amended to conform to amendments made to Rule 45, particularly the addition of Rule 45(f) providing for transfer of a subpoena-related motion to the court where the action is pending. A second sentence is added to Rule 37(b)(1) to deal with contempt of orders entered after such a transfer. The Rule 45(f) transfer provision is explained in the Committee Note to Rule 45.

Changes Made After Publication and Comment

No changes were made after publication and comment.

2015 Amendment

Subdivision (a). Rule 37(a)(3)(B)(iv) is amended to reflect the common practice of producing copies of documents or electronically stored information rather than simply permitting inspection. This change brings item (iv) into line with paragraph (B), which provides a motion for an order compelling "production, or inspection."

Subdivision (e). Present Rule 37(e), adopted in 2006, provides: "Absent exceptional circumstances, a court may not impose sanctions under these rules on a party for failing to provide electronically stored information lost as a result of the routine, good-faith operation of an electronic information system." This limited rule has not adequately addressed the serious problems resulting from the continued exponential growth in the volume of such information. Federal circuits have established significantly different standards for imposing sanctions or curative measures on parties who fail to preserve electronically stored information. These developments have caused litigants to expend excessive effort and money on preservation in order to avoid the risk of severe sanctions if a court finds they did not do enough.

New Rule 37(e) replaces the 2006 rule. It authorizes and specifies measures a court may employ if information that should have been preserved is lost, and specifies the findings necessary to justify these measures. It therefore forecloses reliance on inherent authority or state law to determine when certain measures should be used. The rule does not affect the validity of an independent tort claim for spoliation if state law applies in a case and authorizes the claim.

The new rule applies only to electronically stored information, also the focus of the 2006 rule. It applies only when such information is lost. Because electronically stored information often exists in multiple locations, loss from one source may often be harmless when substitute information can be found elsewhere.

The new rule applies only if the lost information should have been preserved in the anticipation or conduct of litigation and the party failed to take reasonable steps to preserve it. Many court decisions hold that potential litigants have a duty to preserve relevant information when litigation is reasonably foreseeable. Rule 37(e) is based on this common-law duty; it does not attempt to create a new duty to preserve. The rule does not apply when information is lost before a duty to preserve arises.

In applying the rule, a court may need to decide whether and when a duty to preserve arose. Courts should consider the extent to which a party was on notice that litigation was likely and that the information would be relevant. A variety of events may alert a party to the prospect of litigation. Often these events provide only limited information about that prospective litigation, however, so that the scope of information that should be preserved may remain uncertain. It is important not to be blinded to this reality by hindsight arising from familiarity with an action as it is actually filed.

Although the rule focuses on the common-law obligation to preserve in the anticipation or conduct of litigation, courts may sometimes consider whether there was an independent requirement that the lost information be preserved. Such requirements arise from many sources — statutes, administrative regulations, an order in another case, or a party's own information-retention protocols. The court should be sensitive, however, to the fact that such independent preservation requirements may be addressed to a wide variety of concerns unrelated to the current litigation. The fact that a party had an independent obligation to preserve information does not necessarily mean that it had such a duty with respect to the litigation, and the fact that the party failed to observe some other preservation obligation does not itself prove that its efforts to preserve were not reasonable with respect to a particular case.

The duty to preserve may in some instances be triggered or clarified by a court order in the case. Preservation orders may become more common, in part because Rules 16(b)(3)(B)(iii) and 26(f)(3)(C) are amended to encourage discovery plans and orders that address preservation. Once litigation has commenced, if the parties cannot reach agreement about preservation issues, promptly seeking judicial guidance about the extent of reasonable preservation may be important.

The rule applies only if the information was lost because the party failed to take reasonable steps to preserve the information. Due to the ever-increasing volume of electronically stored information and the multitude of devices that generate such information, perfection in preserving all relevant electronically stored information is often impossible. As under the current rule, the routine, good-faith operation of an electronic information system would be a relevant factor for the court to consider in evaluating whether a party failed to take reasonable steps to preserve lost information, although the prospect of litigation may call for reasonable steps to preserve information by intervening in that routine operation. This rule recognizes that "reasonable steps" to preserve suffice; it does not call for perfection. The court should be sensitive to the party's sophistication with regard to litigation in evaluating preservation efforts; some litigants, particularly individual litigants, may be less familiar with preservation obligations than others who have considerable experience in litigation.

Because the rule calls only for reasonable steps to preserve, it is inapplicable when the loss of information occurs despite the party's reasonable steps to preserve. For example, the information may not be in the party's control. Or information the party has preserved may be destroyed by events outside the party's control — the computer room may be flooded, a "cloud" service may fail, a malign software attack may disrupt a storage system, and so on. Courts may, however, need to assess the extent to which a party knew of and protected against such risks.

Another factor in evaluating the reasonableness of preservation efforts is proportionality. The court should be sensitive to party resources; aggressive preservation efforts can be extremely costly, and parties (including governmental parties) may have limited staff and resources to devote to those efforts. A party may act reasonably by choosing a less costly

form of information preservation, if it is substantially as effective as more costly forms. It is important that counsel become familiar with their clients' information systems and digital data — including social media — to address these issues. A party urging that preservation requests are disproportionate may need to provide specifics about these matters in order to enable meaningful discussion of the appropriate preservation regime.

When a party fails to take reasonable steps to preserve electronically stored information that should have been preserved in the anticipation or conduct of litigation, and the information is lost as a result, Rule 37(e) directs that the initial focus should be on whether the lost information can be restored or replaced through additional discovery. Nothing in the rule limits the court's powers under Rules 16 and 26 to authorize additional discovery. Orders under Rule 26(b)(2)(B) regarding discovery from sources that would ordinarily be considered inaccessible or under Rule 26(c)(1)(B) on allocation of expenses may be pertinent to solving such problems. If the information is restored or replaced, no further measures should be taken. At the same time, it is important to emphasize that efforts to restore or replace lost information through discovery should be proportional to the apparent importance of the lost information to claims or defenses in the litigation. For example, substantial measures should not be employed to restore or replace information that is marginally relevant or duplicative.

Subdivision (e)(1). This subdivision applies only if information should have been preserved in the anticipation or conduct of litigation, a party failed to take reasonable steps to preserve the information, information was lost as a result, and the information could not be restored or replaced by additional discovery. In addition, a court may resort to (e)(1) measures only "upon finding prejudice to another party from loss of the information." An evaluation of prejudice from the loss of information necessarily includes an evaluation of the information's importance in the litigation.

The rule does not place a burden of proving or disproving prejudice on one party or the other. Determining the content of lost information may be a difficult task in some cases, and placing the burden of proving prejudice on the party that did not lose the information may be unfair. In other situations, however, the content of the lost information may be fairly evident, the information may appear to be unimportant, or the abundance of preserved information may appear sufficient to meet the needs of all parties. Requiring the party seeking curative measures to prove prejudice may be reasonable in such situations. The rule leaves judges with discretion to determine how best to assess prejudice in particular cases.

Once a finding of prejudice is made, the court is authorized to employ measures "no greater than necessary to cure the prejudice." The range of such measures is quite broad if they are necessary for this purpose. There is no all-purpose hierarchy of the severity of various measures; the severity of given measures must be calibrated in terms of their effect on the particular case. But authority to order measures no greater than necessary to cure prejudice does not require the court to adopt measures to cure every possible prejudicial effect. Much is entrusted to the court's discretion.

In an appropriate case, it may be that serious measures are necessary to cure prejudice found by the court, such as forbidding the party that failed to preserve information from putting on certain evidence, permitting the parties to present evidence and argument to the jury regarding the loss of information, or giving the jury instructions to assist in its evaluation of such evidence or argument, other than instructions to which subdivision (e)(2) applies. Care must be taken, however, to ensure that curative measures under subdivision (e)(1) do not have the effect of measures that are permitted under subdivision (e)(2) only on a finding of intent to deprive another party of the lost information's use in the litigation. An example of an inappropriate (e)(1) measure might be an order striking pleadings related to, or precluding a party from offering any evidence in support of, the central or only claim or defense in the case. On the other hand, it may be appropriate to exclude a specific item of evidence to offset prejudice caused by failure to preserve other evidence that might contradict the excluded item of evidence.

Subdivision (e)(2). This subdivision authorizes courts to use specified and very severe measures to address or deter failures to preserve electronically stored information, but only on finding that the party that lost the information acted with the intent to deprive another party of the information's use in the litigation. It is designed to provide a uniform standard in federal court for use of these serious measures when addressing failure to preserve electronically stored information. It rejects cases such as *Residential Funding Corp. v. DeGeorge Financial Corp.*, 306 F.3d 99 (2d Cir. 2002), that authorize the giving of adverse-inference instructions on a finding of negligence or gross negligence.

Adverse-inference instructions were developed on the premise that a party's intentional loss or destruction of evidence to prevent its use in litigation gives rise to a reasonable inference that the evidence was unfavorable to the party responsible for loss or destruction of the evidence. Negligent or even grossly negligent behavior does not logically support that inference. Information lost through negligence may have been favorable to either party, including the party that lost it, and inferring that it was unfavorable to that party may tip the balance at trial in ways the lost information never would have. The better rule for the negligent or grossly negligent loss of electronically stored information is to preserve a broad range of measures to cure prejudice caused by its loss, but to limit the most severe measures to instances of intentional loss or destruction.

Similar reasons apply to limiting the court's authority to presume or infer that the lost information was unfavorable to the party who lost it when ruling on a pretrial motion or presiding at a bench trial. Subdivision (e)(2) limits the ability of courts to draw adverse inferences based on the loss of information in these circumstances, permitting them only when a court finds that the information was lost with the intent to prevent its use in litigation.

Subdivision (e)(2) applies to jury instructions that permit or require the jury to presume or infer that lost information was unfavorable to the party that lost it. Thus, it covers any instruction that directs or permits the jury to infer from the loss of information that it was in fact unfavorable to the party that lost it. The subdivision does not apply to jury instructions that do not involve such an inference. For example, subdivision (e)(2) would not prohibit a court from allowing the parties to present evidence to the jury concerning the loss and likely relevance of information and instructing the jury that it may consider that evidence, along with all the other evidence in the case, in making its decision. These measures, which would not involve instructing a jury it may draw an adverse

inference from loss of information, would be available under subdivision (e)(1) if no greater than necessary to cure prejudice. In addition, subdivision (e)(2) does not limit the discretion of courts to give traditional missing evidence instructions based on a party's failure to present evidence it has in its possession at the time of trial.

Subdivision (e)(2) requires a finding that the party acted with the intent to deprive another party of the information's use in the litigation. This finding may be made by the court when ruling on a pretrial motion, when presiding at a bench trial, or when deciding whether to give an adverse inference instruction at trial. If a court were to conclude that the intent finding should be made by a jury, the court's instruction should make clear that the jury may infer from the loss of the information that it was unfavorable to the party that lost it only if the jury first finds that the party acted with the intent to deprive another party of the information's use in the litigation. If the jury does not make this finding, it may not infer from the loss that the information was unfavorable to the party that lost it.

Subdivision (e)(2) does not include a requirement that the court find prejudice to the party deprived of the information. This is because the finding of intent required by the subdivision can support not only an inference that the lost information was unfavorable to the party that intentionally destroyed it, but also an inference that the opposing party was prejudiced by the loss of information that would have favored its position. Subdivision (e)(2) does not require any further finding of prejudice.

Courts should exercise caution, however, in using the measures specified in (e)(2). Finding an intent to deprive another party of the lost information's use in the litigation does not require a court to adopt any of the measures listed in subdivision (e)(2). The remedy should fit the wrong, and the severe measures authorized by this subdivision should not be used when the information lost was relatively unimportant or lesser measures such as those specified in subdivision (e)(1) would be sufficient to redress the loss.

HISTORICAL NOTES

Revision Notes and Legislative Reports

1980 Acts. Senate Report No. 96–974, Related House Report, and House Conference Report No. 96–1434, see 1980 U.S.Code Cong. and Adm.News, p. 4953.

Effective and Applicability Provisions

1980 Acts. Amendment by Pub.L. 96–481 effective Oct. 1, 1981, and applicable to adversary adjudication defined in section 504(b)(1)(C) of Title 5, and to civil actions and adversary adjudications described in section 2412 of Title 28, Judiciary and Judicial Procedure, which are pending on, or commenced on or after Oct. 1, 1981, see section 208 of Pub.L. 96–481, set out as an Effective Date note under section 504 of Title 5, Government Organization and Employees.

CROSS REFERENCES

Failure to attend taking of a deposition or to serve subpoena, payment of expenses, see Fed.Rules Civ.Proc. Rule 30, 28 USCA.

TITLE VI. TRIALS

Rule 38.   Right to a Jury Trial; Demand

(a) Right Preserved. The right of trial by jury as declared by the Seventh Amendment to the Constitution—or as provided by a federal statute—is preserved to the parties inviolate.

(b) Demand. On any issue triable of right by a jury, a party may demand a jury trial by:

(1) serving the other parties with a written demand—which may be included in a pleading—no later than 14 days after the last pleading directed to the issue is served; and

(2) filing the demand in accordance with Rule 5(d).

(c) Specifying Issues. In its demand, a party may specify the issues that it wishes to have tried by a jury; otherwise, it is considered to have demanded a jury trial on all the issues so triable. If the party has demanded a jury trial on only some issues, any other party may—within 14 days after being served with the demand or within a shorter time ordered by the court—serve a demand for a jury trial on any other or all factual issues triable by jury.

(d) Waiver; Withdrawal. A party waives a jury trial unless its demand is properly served and filed. A proper demand may be withdrawn only if the parties consent.

(e) Admiralty and Maritime Claims. These rules do not create a right to a jury trial on issues in a claim that is an admiralty or maritime claim under Rule 9(h). (Amended February 28, 1966, effective July 1, 1966; March 2, 1987, effective August 1, 1987; April 22, 1993, effective December 1, 1993; April 30, 2007, effective December 1, 2007; March 26, 2009, effective December 1, 2009.)

ADVISORY COMMITTEE NOTES

1937 Adoption

This rule provides for the preservation of the constitutional right of trial by jury as directed in the enabling act (act of June 19, 1934, 48 Stat. 1064, U.S.C., Title 28, § 723c [sec. 2072]), and it and the next rule make definite provision for claim and waiver of jury trial, following the method used in many American states and in England and the British Dominions. Thus the claim must be made at once on initial pleading or appearance under Ill.Rev.Stat. (1937) ch. 110, § 188; 6 Tenn.Code Ann. (Williams, 1934) § 8734; compare Wyo.Rev. Stat.Ann. (1931) § 89–1320 (with answer or reply); within 10 days after the pleadings are completed or the case is at issue under 2 Conn.Gen.Stat. (1930) § 5624; Hawaii Rev.Laws (1935) § 4101; 2 Mass.Gen.Laws (Ter.Ed.1932) ch.·231, § 60; 3 Mich.Comp.Laws (1929) § 14263; Mich. Court Rules Ann. (Searl, 1933) Rule 33 (15 days); England (until 1933) O. 36, r.r. 2 and 6; and Ontario Jud. Act (1927) § 57(1) (4 days, or, where prior notice of trial, 2 days from such notice); or at a definite time varying under different codes, from 10 days before notice of trial to 10 days after notice, or, as in many, when the case is called for assignment, Ariz.Rev.Code Ann.

(Struckmeyer, 1928) § 3802; Calif. Code Civ.Proc. (Deering, 1937) § 631, par. 4; Iowa Code (1935) § 10724; 4 Nev.Comp. Laws (Hillyer, 1929) § 8782; N.M. Stat.Ann. (Courtright, 1929) § 105–814; N.Y.C.P.A. (1937) § 426, subdivision 5 (applying to New York, Bronx, Richmond, Kings, and Queens Counties); R.I. Pub. Laws (1929), ch. 1327, amending R.I. Gen.Laws (1923) ch. 337, § 6; Utah Rev.Stat.Ann. (1933) § 104–23–6; 2 Wash.Rev.Stat.Ann. (Remington, 1932) § 316; England (4 days after notice of trial), Administration of Justice Act (1933) § 6 and amended rule under the Judicature Act (The Annual Practice, 1937), O. 36, r. 1; Australia High Court Procedure Act (1921) § 12, Rules, O. 33, r. 2; Alberta Rules of Ct. (1914) 172, 183, 184; British Columbia Sup.Ct. Rules (1925) O. 36, r.r. 2, 6, 11, and 16; New Brunswick Jud. Act (1927) O. 36, r.r. 2 and 5. See James, Trial by Jury and the New Federal Rules of Procedure (1936), 45 Yale L.J. 1022.

Rule 81(c) provides for claim for jury trial in removed actions.

The right to trial by jury as declared in U.S.C., Title 28, § 770 (Trial of issues of fact; by jury; exceptions), and similar statutes, is unaffected by this rule. This rule modifies U.S.C., Title 28, [former] § 773 (Trial of issues of fact; by court).

1966 Amendment

See Note to Rule 9(h), supra.

1987 Amendment

The amendments are technical. No substantive change is intended.

1993 Amendment

Language requiring the filing of a jury demand as provided in subdivision (d) is added to subdivision (b) to eliminate an apparent ambiguity between the two subdivisions. For proper scheduling of cases, it is important that jury demands not only be served on other parties, but also be filed with the court.

2007 Amendment

The language of Rule 38 has been amended as part of the general restyling of the Civil Rules to make them more easily understood and to make style and terminology consistent throughout the rules. These changes are intended to be stylistic only.

2009 Amendment

The times set in the former rule at 10 days have been revised to 14 days. See the Note to Rule 6.

CROSS REFERENCES

Admiralty and maritime case, trial of issues of fact by jury, see 28 USCA § 1873.

Calendar to designate cases as jury actions, see Fed.Rules Civ.Proc. Rule 79, 28 USCA.

Declaratory judgment actions, right to jury trial, see Fed. Rules Civ.Proc. Rule 57, 28 USCA.

Default judgment, right of trial by jury, see Fed.Rules Civ.Proc. Rule 55, 28 USCA.

Directed verdict, motion for which is not granted, not a waiver of trial by jury, see Fed.Rules Civ.Proc. Rule 50, 28 USCA.

Juries, generally, see 28 USCA § 1861 et seq.

Recovery of forfeitures in actions on bonds and specialties, jury assessment of amount due, see 28 USCA § 1874.

Removed actions, time for service of jury demand, see Fed.Rules Civ.Proc. Rule 81, 28 USCA.

Supreme Court, jury trial in original actions at law, see 28 USCA § 1872.

Trial by jury or by the court, see Fed.Rules Civ.Proc. Rule 39, 28 USCA.

Trustee and receivers, right to jury trial in actions against, see 28 USCA § 959.

United States, jury trial denied in actions against, see 28 USCA § 2402.

Rule 39. Trial by Jury or by the Court

(a) When a Demand Is Made. When a jury trial has been demanded under Rule 38, the action must be designated on the docket as a jury action. The trial on all issues so demanded must be by jury unless:

(1) the parties or their attorneys file a stipulation to a nonjury trial or so stipulate on the record; or

(2) the court, on motion or on its own, finds that on some or all of those issues there is no federal right to a jury trial.

(b) When No Demand Is Made. Issues on which a jury trial is not properly demanded are to be tried by the court. But the court may, on motion, order a jury trial on any issue for which a jury might have been demanded.

(c) Advisory Jury; Jury Trial by Consent. In an action not triable of right by a jury, the court, on motion or on its own:

(1) may try any issue with an advisory jury; or

(2) may, with the parties' consent, try any issue by a jury whose verdict has the same effect as if a jury trial had been a matter of right, unless the action is against the United States and a federal statute provides for a nonjury trial.

(Amended April 30, 2007, effective December 1, 2007.)

ADVISORY COMMITTEE NOTES

1937 Adoption

The provisions for express waiver of jury trial found in U.S.C., Title 28, [former] § 773 (Trial of issues of fact; by court) are incorporated in this rule. See Rule 38, however, which extends the provisions for waiver of jury. U.S.C., Title 28, [former] § 772 (Trial of issues of fact; in equity in patent causes) is unaffected by this rule. When certain of the issues are to be tried by jury and others by the court, the court may determine the sequence in which such issues shall be tried.

See Liberty Oil Co. v. Condon Nat. Bank, 260 U.S. 235, 43 S.Ct. 118, 67 L.Ed. 232 (1922).

A discretionary power in the courts to send issues of fact to the jury is common in state procedure. Compare Calif. Code Civ.Proc. (Deering, 1937) § 592; 1 Colo.Stat.Ann. (1935) Code Civ.Proc., ch. 12, § 191; Conn.Gen.Stat. (1930) § 5625; 2 Minn.Stat. (Mason, 1927) § 9288; 4 Mont.Rev.Codes Ann. (1935) § 9327; N.Y.C.P.A. (1937) § 430; 2 Ohio Gen.Code Ann. (Page, 1926) § 11380; 1 Okla.Stat.Ann. (Harlow, 1931) § 351 [12 Okl.St.Ann. § 557]; Utah Rev.Stat.Ann. (1933) § 104–23–5; 2 Wash.Rev.Stat.Ann. (Remington, 1932) § 315; Wis.Stat. (1935) § 270.07. See [former] Equity Rule 23 (Matters Ordinarily Determinable at Law When Arising in Suit in Equity to be Disposed of Therein) and U.S.C., Title 28 [former] § 772 (Trial of issues of fact; in equity in patent causes); *Colleton Merc. Mfg. Co. v. Savannah River Lumber Co.*, C.C.A.4, 1922, 280 F. 358; *Fed. Res. Bk. of San Francisco v. Idaho Grimm Alfalfa Seed Growers' Ass'n*, C.C.A.9, 1925, 8 F.2d 922, certiorari denied 46 S.Ct. 347, 270 U.S. 646, 70 L.Ed. 778 (1926); *Watt v. Starke*, 1879, 101 U.S. 247, 25 L.Ed. 826.

2007 Amendment

The language of Rule 39 has been amended as part of the general restyling of the Civil Rules to make them more easily understood and to make style and terminology consistent throughout the rules. These changes are intended to be stylistic only.

CROSS REFERENCES

Demand for jury trial, see Fed.Rules Civ.Proc. Rule 38, 28 USCA.

Enlargement of time after expiration of period prescribed, see Fed.Rules Civ.Proc. Rule 6, 28 USCA.

Findings of fact required in actions tried with an advisory jury, see Fed.Rules Civ.Proc. Rule 52, 28 USCA.

Report of masters in jury actions, see Fed.Rules Civ.Proc. Rule 53, 28 USCA.

Rule 40. Scheduling Cases for Trial

Each court must provide by rule for scheduling trials. The court must give priority to actions entitled to priority by a federal statute.

(Amended April 30, 2007, effective December 1, 2007.)

ADVISORY COMMITTEE NOTES

1937 Adoption

U.S.C., Title 28, [former] § 769 (Notice of case for trial) is modified. See former Equity Rule 56 (On Expiration of Time for Depositions, Case Goes on Trial Calendar). See also [former] Equity Rule 57 (Continuances).

For examples of statutes giving precedence, see U.S.C., Title 28, § 47 (now §§ 1253, 2101, 2325) (Injunctions as to orders of Interstate Commerce Commission); § 380 (now §§ 1253, 2101, 2284) (Injunctions; alleged unconstitutionality of state statutes); § 380a (now §§ 1253, 2101, 2284) (Same; Constitutionality of federal statute); [former] § 768 (Priority of cases where a state is party); Title 15, § 28 (Antitrust laws; suits against monopolies expedited); Title 22, § 240 (Petition for restoration of property seized as munitions of war, etc.); and Title 49, [former] § 44 (Proceedings in equity under interstate commerce laws; expedition of suits).

2007 Amendment

The language of Rule 40 has been amended as part of the general restyling of the Civil Rules to make them more easily understood and to make style and terminology consistent throughout the rules. These changes are intended to be stylistic only.

The best methods for scheduling trials depend on local conditions. It is useful to ensure that each district adopts an explicit rule for scheduling trials. It is not useful to limit or dictate the provisions of local rules.

CROSS REFERENCES

Adaption of local rules not inconsistent with these rules, see Fed.Rules Civ.Proc. Rule 83, 28 USCA.

Rule 41. Dismissal of Actions

(a) Voluntary Dismissal.

(1) *By the Plaintiff.*

(A) *Without a Court Order.* Subject to Rules 23(e), 23.1(c), 23.2, and 66 and any applicable federal statute, the plaintiff may dismiss an action without a court order by filing:

(i) a notice of dismissal before the opposing party serves either an answer or a motion for summary judgment; or

(ii) a stipulation of dismissal signed by all parties who have appeared.

(B) *Effect.* Unless the notice or stipulation states otherwise, the dismissal is without prejudice. But if the plaintiff previously dismissed any federal- or state-court action based on or including the same claim, a notice of dismissal operates as an adjudication on the merits.

(2) *By Court Order; Effect.* Except as provided in Rule 41(a)(1), an action may be dismissed at the plaintiff's request only by court order, on terms that the court considers proper. If a defendant has pleaded a counterclaim before being served with the plaintiff's motion to dismiss, the action may be dismissed over the defendant's objection only if the counterclaim can remain pending for independent adjudication. Unless the order states otherwise, a dismissal under this paragraph (2) is without prejudice.

(b) Involuntary Dismissal; Effect. If the plaintiff fails to prosecute or to comply with these rules or a court order, a defendant may move to dismiss the action or any claim against it. Unless the dismissal order states otherwise, a dismissal under this subdivision (b) and any dismissal not under this rule—except one for lack of jurisdiction, improper venue, or failure to join a party under Rule 19—operates as an adjudication on the merits.

(c) Dismissing a Counterclaim, Crossclaim, or Third-Party Claim. This rule applies to a dismissal of any counterclaim, crossclaim, or third-party claim. A claimant's voluntary dismissal under Rule 41(a)(1)(A)(i) must be made:

(1) before a responsive pleading is served; or

(2) if there is no responsive pleading, before evidence is introduced at a hearing or trial.

(d) Costs of a Previously Dismissed Action. If a plaintiff who previously dismissed an action in any court files an action based on or including the same claim against the same defendant, the court:

(1) may order the plaintiff to pay all or part of the costs of that previous action; and

(2) may stay the proceedings until the plaintiff has complied.

(Amended December 27, 1946, effective March 19, 1948; January 21, 1963, effective July 1, 1963; February 28, 1966, effective July 1, 1966; December 4, 1967, effective July 1, 1968; March 2, 1987, effective August 1, 1987; April 30, 1991, effective December 1, 1991; April 30, 2007, effective December 1, 2007.)

ADVISORY COMMITTEE NOTES

1937 Adoption

Note to Subdivision (a). Compare Ill.Rev.Stat. (1937) c. 110, § 176, and *English Rules Under the Judicature Act* (The Annual Practice, 1937) O. 26.

Provisions regarding dismissal in such statutes as U.S.C., Title 8, § 164 [see 1329] (Jurisdiction of district courts in immigration cases) and U.S.C., Title 31, § 232 [now 3730] (Liability of persons making false claims against United States; suits) are preserved by paragraph (1).

Note to Subdivision (b). This provides for the equivalent of a nonsuit on motion by the defendant after the completion of the presentation of evidence by the plaintiff. Also, for actions tried without a jury, it provides the equivalent of the directed verdict practice for jury actions which is regulated by Rule 50.

1946 Amendment

Note. Subdivision (a). The insertion of the reference to Rule 66 correlates Rule 41(a)(1) with the express provisions concerning dismissal set forth in amended Rule 66 on receivers.

The change in Rule 41(a)(1)(i) gives the service of a motion for summary judgment by the adverse party the same effect in preventing unlimited dismissal as was originally given only to the service of an answer. The omission of reference to a motion for summary judgment in the original rule was subject to criticism. 3 *Moore's Federal Practice*, 1938, 3037–3038, n. 12. A motion for summary judgment may be forthcoming prior to answer, and if well taken will eliminate the necessity for an answer. Since such a motion may require even more research and preparation than the answer itself, there is good reason why the service of the motion, like that of the answer, should prevent a voluntary dismissal by the adversary without court approval.

The word "generally" has been stricken from Rule 41(a)(1)(ii) in order to avoid confusion and to conform with the elimination of the necessity for special appearance by original Rule 12(b).

Subdivision (b). In some cases tried without a jury, where at the close of plaintiff's evidence the defendant moves for dismissal under Rule 41(b) on the ground that plaintiff's evidence is insufficient for recovery, the plaintiff's own evidence may be conflicting or present questions of credibility. In ruling on the defendant's motion, questions arise as to the function of the judge in evaluating the testimony and whether findings should be made if the motion is sustained. Three circuits hold that as the judge is the trier of the facts in such a situation his function is not the same as on a motion to direct a verdict, where the jury is the trier of the facts, and that the judge in deciding such a motion in a non-jury case may pass on conflicts of evidence and credibility, and if he performs that function of evaluating the testimony and grants the motion on the merits, findings are required. *Young v. United States,* C.C.A.9, 1940, 111 F.2d 823; *Gary Theatre Co. v. Columbia Pictures Corporation,* C.C.A.7, 1941, 120 F.2d 891; *Bach v. Friden Calculating Machine Co., Inc.,* C.C.A.6, 1945, 148 F.2d 407. Cf. *Mateas v. Fred Harvey, a Corporation,* C.C.A.9, 1945, 146 F.2d 989. The Third Circuit has held that on such a motion the function of the court is the same as on a motion to direct in a jury case, and that the court should only decide whether there is evidence which would support a judgment for the plaintiff, and therefore, findings are not required by Rule 52. *Federal Deposit Insurance Corp. v. Mason,* C.C.A.3, 1940, 115 F.2d 548; *Schad v. Twentieth Century-Fox Film Corp.,* C.C.A.3, 1943, 136 F.2d 991. The added sentence in Rule 41(b) incorporates the view of the Sixth, Seventh and Ninth Circuits. See also 3 *Moore's Federal Practice,* 1938, Cum.Supplement § 41.03, under "Page 3045"; Commentary, *The Motion to Dismiss in Non-Jury Cases,* 1946, 9 Fed.Rules Serv., Comm.Pg. 41b.14.

1963 Amendment

Under the present text of the second sentence of this subdivision, the motion for dismissal at the close of the plaintiff's evidence may be made in a case tried to a jury as well as in a case tried without a jury. But, when made in a jury-tried case, this motion overlaps the motion for a directed verdict under Rule 50(a), which is also available in the same situation. It has been held that the standard to be applied in deciding the Rule 41(b) motion at the close of the plaintiff's evidence in a jury-tried case is the same as that used upon a motion for a directed verdict made at the same stage; and, just as the court need not make findings pursuant to Rule 52(a) when it directs a verdict, so in a jury-tried case it may omit these findings in granting the Rule 41(b) motion. See generally *O'Brien v. Westinghouse Electric Corp.,* 293 F.2d 1, 5–10 (3d Cir. 1961).

As indicated by the discussion in the *O'Brien* case, the overlap has caused confusion. Accordingly, the second and third sentences of Rule 41(b) are amended to provide that the motion for dismissal at the close of the plaintiff's evidence shall apply only to nonjury cases (including cases tried with an advisory jury). Hereafter the correct motion in jury-tried cases will be the motion for a directed verdict. This involves no change of substance. It should be noted that the court upon a motion for a directed verdict may in appropriate circumstances deny that motion and grant instead a new trial, or a voluntary dismissal without prejudice under Rule 41(a)(2). See 6 *Moore's Federal Practice* ¶59.08[5] (2d ed.

1954); *cf. Cone v. West Virginia Pulp & Paper Co.,* 330 U.S. 212, 217, 67 S.Ct. 752, 91 L.Ed. 849 (1947).

The first sentence of Rule 41(b), providing for dismissal for failure to prosecute or to comply with the Rules or any order of court, and the general provisions of the last sentence remain applicable in jury as well as nonjury cases.

The amendment of the last sentence of Rule 41(b) indicates that a dismissal for lack of an indispensable party does not operate as an adjudication on the merits. Such a dismissal does not bar a new action, for it is based merely "on a plaintiff's failure to comply with a precondition requisite to the Court's going forward to determine the merits of his substantive claim." See *Costello v. United States,* 365 U.S. 265, 284–288, 81 S.Ct. 534, 5 L.Ed.2d 551 & n. 5 (1961); *Mallow v. Hinde,* 12 Wheat. (25 U.S.) 193, 6 L.Ed. 599 (1827); Clark, *Code Pleading* 602 (2d ed. 1947); *Restatement of Judgments* § 49, comm. a, b (1942). This amendment corrects an omission from the rule and is consistent with an earlier amendment, effective in 1948, adding "the defense of failure to join an indispensable party" to clause (1) of Rule 12(h).

1966 Amendment

The terminology is changed to accord with the amendment of Rule 19. See that amended rule and the Advisory Committee's Note thereto.

1968 Amendment

The amendment corrects an inadvertent error in the reference to amended Rule 23.

1987 Amendment

The amendment is technical. No substantive change is intended.

1991 Amendment

Language is deleted that authorized the use of this rule as a means of terminating a non-jury action on the merits when the plaintiff has failed to carry a burden of proof in presenting the plaintiff's case. The device is replaced by the new provisions of Rule 52(c), which authorize entry of judgment against the defendant as well as the plaintiff, and earlier than the close of the case of the party against whom judgment is rendered. A motion to dismiss under Rule 41 on the ground that a plaintiff's evidence is legally insufficient should now be treated as a motion for judgment on partial findings as provided in Rule 52(c).

2007 Amendment

The language of Rule 41 has been amended as part of the general restyling of the Civil Rules to make them more easily understood and to make style and terminology consistent throughout the rules. These changes are intended to be stylistic only.

When Rule 23 was amended in 1966, Rules 23.1 and 23.2 were separated from Rule 23. Rule 41(a)(1) was not then amended to reflect the Rule 23 changes. In 1968 Rule 41(a)(1) was amended to correct the cross-reference to what had become Rule 23(e), but Rules 23.1 and 23.2 were inadvertently overlooked. Rules 23.1 and 23.2 are now added to the list of exceptions in Rule 41(a)(1)(A). This change does not affect established meaning. Rule 23.2 explicitly incorporates Rule

23(e), and thus was already absorbed directly into the exceptions in Rule 41(a)(1). Rule 23.1 requires court approval of a compromise or dismissal in language parallel to Rule 23(e) and thus supersedes the apparent right to dismiss by notice of dismissal.

CROSS REFERENCES

Approval of court for dismissal of class action, see Fed. Rules Civ.Proc. Rule 23, 28 USCA.

Costs, see Fed.Rules Civ.Proc. Rule 54, 28 USCA.

Counterclaim, crossclaim or third-party claim, see Fed. Rules Civ.Proc. Rules 13 and 14, 28 USCA.

Discontinuance of civil actions arising under immigration laws, see 8 USCA § 1329.

Findings of fact in non-jury action, see Fed.Rules Civ.Proc. Rule 52, 28 USCA.

Motion for directed verdict at close of evidence offered by an opponent, see Fed.Rules Civ.Proc. Rule 50, 28 USCA.

Motion to dismiss, generally, see Fed.Rules Civ.Proc. Rule 12, 28 USCA.

Order of court for dismissal of action wherein receiver has been appointed, see Fed.Rules Civ.Proc. Rule 66, 28 USCA.

Production of documents, dismissal for failure of, see Fed. Rules Civ.Proc. Rule 37, 28 USCA.

Taxation of costs, see 28 USCA § 1920.

Withdrawal or discontinuance of false claim actions against United States, see 31 USCA § 3730.

Rule 42.   Consolidation; Separate Trials

(a) Consolidation. If actions before the court involve a common question of law or fact, the court may:

(1) join for hearing or trial any or all matters at issue in the actions;

(2) consolidate the actions; or

(3) issue any other orders to avoid unnecessary cost or delay.

(b) Separate Trials. For convenience, to avoid prejudice, or to expedite and economize, the court may order a separate trial of one or more separate issues, claims, crossclaims, counterclaims, or third-party claims. When ordering a separate trial, the court must preserve any federal right to a jury trial.

(Amended February 28, 1966, effective July 1, 1966; April 30, 2007, effective December 1, 2007.)

ADVISORY COMMITTEE NOTES

1937 Adoption

Subdivision (a) is based upon U.S.C., Title 28, [former] § 734 (Orders to save costs; consolidation of causes of like nature) but in so far as the statute differs from this rule, it is modified.

For comparable statutes dealing with consolidation see Ark.Dig.Stat. (Crawford & Moses, 1921) § 1081; Calif.Code Civ.Proc. (Deering, 1937) § 1048; N.M.Stat.Ann. (Courtright, 1929) § 105–828; N.Y.C.P.A. (1937) §§ 96, 96a, and 97; American Judicature Society, Bulletin XIV, (1919) Art. 26.

For severance or separate trials see Calif.Code Civ.Proc. (Deering, 1937) § 1048; N.Y.C.P.A. (1937) § 96; American

Judicature Society, Bulletin XIV (1919) Art. 3, § 2 and Art. 10, § 10. See also the third sentence of Equity Rule 29 (Defenses—How Presented) providing for discretionary separate hearing and disposition before trial of pleas in bar or abatement, and see also Rule 12(d) of these rules for preliminary hearings of defenses and objections.

For the entry of separate judgments, see Rule 54(b) (Judgment at Various Stages).

1966 Amendment

In certain suits in admiralty separation for trial of the issues of liability and damages (or of the extent of liability other than damages, such as salvage and general average) has been conducive to expedition and economy, especially because of the statutory right to interlocutory appeal in admiralty cases (which is of course preserved by these Rules). While separation of issues for trial is not to be routinely ordered, it is important that it be encouraged where experience has demonstrated its worth. Cf. Weinstein, *Routine Bifurcation of Negligence Trials*, 14 Vand.L.Rev. 831 (1961).

In cases (including some cases within the admiralty and maritime jurisdiction) in which the parties have a constitutional or statutory right of trial by jury, separation of issues may give rise to problems. See *e.g., United Air Lines, Inc. v. Wiener*, 286 F.2d 302 (9th Cir.1961). Accordingly, the proposed change in Rule 42 reiterates the mandate of Rule 38 respecting preservation of the right to jury trial.

2007 Amendment

The language of Rule 42 has been amended as part of the general restyling of the Civil Rules to make them more easily understood and to make style and terminology consistent throughout the rules. These changes are intended to be stylistic only.

CROSS REFERENCES

Preliminary hearings of defenses and objections, see Fed. Rules Civ.Proc. Rule 12, 28 USCA.

Separate,

    Judgments, see Fed.Rules Civ.Proc. Rule 54, 28 USCA.

    Trial for parties, see Fed.Rules Civ.Proc. Rule 20, 28 USCA.

    Trials of counterclaims or crossclaims, see Fed.Rules Civ.Proc. Rule 13, 28 USCA.

Third-party claims, see Fed.Rules Civ.Proc. Rule 14, 28 USCA.

Rule 43.   Taking Testimony

(a) In Open Court. At trial, the witnesses' testimony must be taken in open court unless a federal statute, the Federal Rules of Evidence, these rules, or other rules adopted by the Supreme Court provide otherwise. For good cause in compelling circumstances and with appropriate safeguards, the court may permit testimony in open court by contemporaneous transmission from a different location.

(b) Affirmation Instead of an Oath. When these rules require an oath, a solemn affirmation suffices.

(c) Evidence on a Motion. When a motion relies on facts outside the record, the court may hear the matter on affidavits or may hear it wholly or partly on oral testimony or on depositions.

(d) Interpreter. The court may appoint an interpreter of its choosing; fix reasonable compensation to be paid from funds provided by law or by one or more parties; and tax the compensation as costs.

(Amended February 28, 1966, effective July 1, 1966; November 20, 1972, and December 18, 1972, effective July 1, 1975; March 2, 1987, effective August 1, 1987; April 23, 1996, effective December 1, 1996; April 30, 2007, effective December 1, 2007.)

ADVISORY COMMITTEE NOTES

1937 Adoption

Note to Subdivision (a). The first sentence is a restatement of the substance of U.S.C., Title 28, § 635 (Proof in common-law actions), [former] § 637 (see §§ 2072, 2073) (Proof in equity and admiralty), and [former] Equity Rule 46 (Trial—Testimony Usually Taken in Open Court—Rulings on Objections to Evidence). This rule abolishes in patent and trademark actions, the practice under [former] Equity Rule 48 of setting forth in affidavits the testimony in chief of expert witnesses whose testimony is directed to matters of opinion. The second and third sentences on admissibility of evidence and Subdivision (b) on contradiction and cross-examination modify U.S.C., Title 28, § 725 (now 1652) (Laws of states as rules of decision) insofar as that statute has been construed to prescribe conformity to state rules of evidence. Compare Callahan and Ferguson, *Evidence and the New Federal Rules of Civil Procedure*, 45 Yale L.J. 622 (1936), and *Same: 2*, 47 Yale L.J. 195 (1937). The last sentence modifies to the extent indicated U.S.C., Title 28, [former] § 631 (Competency of witnesses governed by State laws).

Note to Subdivision (b). See 4 *Wigmore on Evidence* (2d ed., 1923) § 1885 et seq.

Note to Subdivision (c). See [former] Equity Rule 46 (Trial—Testimony Usually Taken in Open Court-Rulings on Objections to Evidence). With the last sentence compare *Dowagiac v. Lochren*, 143 Fed. 211 (C.C.A. 8th, 1906). See also *Blease v. Garlington*, 92 U.S. 1, 23 L.Ed. 521 (1876); *Nelson v. United States*, 201 U.S. 92, 114, 26 S.Ct. 358, 50 L.Ed. 673 (1906); *Unkle v. Wills*, 281 Fed. 29 (C.C.A. 8th, 1922).

See Rule 61 for harmless error in either the admission or exclusion of evidence.

Note to Subdivision (d). See [former] Equity Rule 78 (Affirmation in Lieu of Oath) and U.S.C., Title 1, § 1 (Words importing singular number, masculine gender, etc.; extended application), providing for affirmation in lieu of oath.

Supplementary Note on Advisory Committee Regarding Rules 43 and 44

Note. These rules have been criticized and suggested improvements offered by commentators. 1 *Wigmore on Evidence*, 3d ed. 1940, 200–204; Green, *The Admissibility of Evidence Under the Federal Rules*, 1941, 55 Harv.L.Rev. 197. Cases indicate, however, that the rule is working better than these commentators had expected. *Boerner v. United States*, C.C.A.2d, 1941, 117 F.2d 387, cert. den., 1941, 313 U.S. 587, 61 S.Ct. 1120; *Mosson v. Liberty Fast Freight Co.*, C.C.A.2d, 1942, 124 F.2d, 448; *Hartford Accident & Indemnity Co. v. Olivier*, C.C.A. 5th, 1941, 123 F.2d 709; *Anzano v. Metropoli-*

tan Life Ins. Co. of New York, C.C.A.3d, 1941, 118 F.2d 430; *Franzen v. E. I. DuPont De Nemours & Co.*, C.C.A.3d, 1944, 146 F.2d 837; *Fakouri v. Cadais*, C.C.A. 5th, 1945, 147 F.2d 667; *In re C. & P. Co.*, S.D.Cal.1945, 63 F.Supp. 400, 408. But cf. *United States v. Aluminum Co. of America*, S.D.N.Y. 1938, 1 Fed.Rules Serv. 43a.3, Case 1; Note, 1946, 46 Col. L.Rev. 267. While consideration of a comprehensive and detailed set of rules of evidence seems very desirable, it has not been feasible for the Committee so far to undertake this important task. Such consideration should include the adaptability to federal practice of all or parts of the proposed Code of Evidence of the American Law Institute. See Armstrong, *Proposed Amendments to Federal Rules of Civil Procedure*, 4 F.R.D. 124, 137–138.

1966 Amendment

Note to Subdivision (f). This new subdivision [subdivision (f)] authorizes the court to appoint interpreters (including interpreters for the deaf), to provide for their compensation, and to tax the compensation as costs. Compare proposed subdivision (b) of Rule 28 of the Federal Rules of Criminal Procedure.

1972 Amendment

Rule 43, entitled Evidence, has heretofore served as the basic rule of evidence for civil cases in federal courts. Its very general provisions are superseded by the detailed provisions of the new Rules of Evidence. The original title and many of the provisions of the rule are, therefore, no longer appropriate.

Subdivision (a). The provision for taking testimony in open court is not duplicated in the Rules of Evidence and is retained. Those dealing with admissibility of evidence and competency of witnesses, however, are no longer needed or appropriate since those topics are covered at large in the Rules of Evidence. They are accordingly deleted. The language is broadened, however, to take account of acts of Congress dealing with the taking of testimony, as well as of the Rules of Evidence and any other rules adopted by the Supreme Court.

Subdivision (b). The subdivision is no longer needed or appropriate since the matters with which it deals are treated in the Rules of Evidence. The use of leading questions, both generally and in the interrogation of an adverse party or witness identified with him, is the subject of Evidence Rule 611(c). Who may impeach is treated in Evidence Rule 601 [sic; probably means 607], and scope of cross-examination is covered in Evidence Rule 611(b). The subdivision is accordingly deleted.

Subdivision (c). Offers of proof and making a record of excluded evidence are treated in Evidence Rule 103. The subdivision is no longer needed or appropriate and is deleted.

1987 Amendment

The amendment is technical. No substantive change is intended.

1996 Amendment

Rule 43(a) is revised to conform to the style conventions adopted for simplifying the present Civil Rules. The only intended changes of meaning are described below.

The requirement that testimony be taken "orally" is deleted. The deletion makes it clear that testimony of a witness may be given in open court by other means if the witness is not able to communicate orally. Writing or sign language are common examples. The development of advanced technology may enable testimony to be given by other means. A witness unable to sign or write by hand may be able to communicate through a computer or similar device.

Contemporaneous transmission of testimony from a different location is permitted only on showing good cause in compelling circumstances. The importance of presenting live testimony in court cannot be forgotten. The very ceremony of trial and the presence of the factfinder may exert a powerful force for truthtelling. The opportunity to judge the demeanor of a witness face-to-face is accorded great value in our tradition. Transmission cannot be justified merely by showing that it is inconvenient for the witness to attend the trial.

The most persuasive showings of good cause and compelling circumstances are likely to arise when a witness is unable to attend trial for unexpected reasons, such as accident or illness, but remains able to testify from a different place. Contemporaneous transmission may be better than an attempt to reschedule the trial, particularly if there is a risk that other—and perhaps more important—witnesses might not be available at a later time.

Other possible justifications for remote transmission must be approached cautiously. Ordinarily depositions, including video depositions, provide a superior means of securing the testimony of a witness who is beyond the reach of a trial subpoena, or of resolving difficulties in scheduling a trial that can be attended by all witnesses. Deposition procedures ensure the opportunity of all parties to be represented while the witness is testifying. An unforeseen need for the testimony of a remote witness that arises during trial, however, may establish good cause and compelling circumstances. Justification is particularly likely if the need arises from the interjection of new issues during trial or from the unexpected inability to present testimony as planned from a different witness.

Good cause and compelling circumstances may be established with relative ease if all parties agree that testimony should be presented by transmission. The court is not bound by a stipulation, however, and can insist on live testimony. Rejection of the parties' agreement will be influenced, among other factors, by the apparent importance of the testimony in the full context of the trial.

A party who could reasonably foresee the circumstances offered to justify transmission of testimony will have special difficulty in showing good cause and the compelling nature of the circumstances. Notice of a desire to transmit testimony from a different location should be given as soon as the reasons are known, to enable other parties to arrange a deposition, or to secure an advance ruling on transmission so as to know whether to prepare to be present with the witness while testifying.

No attempt is made to specify the means of transmission that may be used. Audio transmission without video images may be sufficient in some circumstances, particularly as to less important testimony. Video transmission ordinarily should be preferred when the cost is reasonable in relation to the matters in dispute, the means of the parties, and the circumstances that justify transmission. Transmission that merely produces the equivalent of a written statement ordinarily should not be used.

Safeguards must be adopted that ensure accurate identification of the witness and that protect against influence by persons present with the witness. Accurate transmission likewise must be assured.

Other safeguards should be employed to ensure that advance notice is given to all parties of foreseeable circumstances that may lead the proponent to offer testimony by transmission. Advance notice is important to protect the opportunity to argue for attendance of the witness at trial. Advance notice also ensures an opportunity to depose the witness, perhaps by video record, as a means of supplementing transmitted testimony.

2007 Amendment

The language of Rule 43 has been amended as part of the general restyling of the Civil Rules to make them more easily understood and to make style and terminology consistent throughout the rules. These changes are intended to be stylistic only.

HISTORICAL NOTES

References in Text

The Federal Rules of Evidence, referred to in subd. (a), are set out in this title.

CROSS REFERENCES

Amendment of pleading to conform to evidence, see Fed. Rules Civ.Proc. Rule 15, 28 USCA.

Compelling giving of testimony, application of rules, see Fed.Rules Civ.Proc. Rule 81, 28 USCA.

Depositions of witnesses in foreign country, see 28 USCA § 1781.

Evidence,

    Generally, see 28 USCA § 1731 et seq.

    Hearing before master, see Fed.Rules Civ.Proc. Rule 53, 28 USCA.

Exceptions to rulings unnecessary, see Fed.Rules Civ.Proc. Rule 46, 28 USCA.

Foreign law, determination of, see Fed.Rules Civ.Proc. Rule 44.1, 28 USCA.

Harmless error in admitting or excluding evidence, see Fed.Rules Civ.Proc. Rule 61, 28 USCA.

Interested persons, competency, see 28 USCA § 1822.

Offer of judgment, see Fed.Rules Civ.Proc. Rule 68, 28 USCA.

Perpetuation of testimony by action, see Fed.Rules Civ. Proc. Rule 27, 28 USCA.

Pretrial procedure, see Fed.Rules Civ.Proc. Rule 16, 28 USCA.

Proof of official record, see Fed.Rules Civ.Proc. Rule 44, 28 USCA.

Record made in regular course of business, see 28 USCA § 1732.

Record on appeal, form of testimony included in, see Federal Rules of Appellate Procedure Rule 10, 28 USCA.

Subpoena for attendance of witnesses and obtaining evidence, see Fed.Rules Civ.Proc. Rule 45, 28 USCA.

United States, evidence to establish claim on default, see Fed.Rules Civ.Proc. Rule 55, 28 USCA.

Witnesses, generally, see 28 USCA § 1821 et seq.

Rule 44. Proving an Official Record

(a) Means of Proving.

(1) *Domestic Record.* Each of the following evidences an official record—or an entry in it—that is otherwise admissible and is kept within the United States, any state, district, or commonwealth, or any territory subject to the administrative or judicial jurisdiction of the United States:

(A) an official publication of the record; or

(B) a copy attested by the officer with legal custody of the record—or by the officer's deputy—and accompanied by a certificate that the officer has custody. The certificate must be made under seal:

(i) by a judge of a court of record in the district or political subdivision where the record is kept; or

(ii) by any public officer with a seal of office and with official duties in the district or political subdivision where the record is kept.

(2) *Foreign Record.*

(A) *In General.* Each of the following evidences a foreign official record—or an entry in it—that is otherwise admissible:

(i) an official publication of the record; or

(ii) the record—or a copy—that is attested by an authorized person and is accompanied either by a final certification of genuineness or by a certification under a treaty or convention to which the United States and the country where the record is located are parties.

(B) *Final Certification of Genuineness.* A final certification must certify the genuineness of the signature and official position of the attester or of any foreign official whose certificate of genuineness relates to the attestation or is in a chain of certificates of genuineness relating to the attestation. A final certification may be made by a secretary of a United States embassy or legation; by a consul general, vice consul, or consular agent of the United States; or by a diplomatic or consular official of the foreign country assigned or accredited to the United States.

(C) *Other Means of Proof.* If all parties have had a reasonable opportunity to investigate a foreign record's authenticity and accuracy, the court may, for good cause, either:

(i) admit an attested copy without final certification; or

(ii) permit the record to be evidenced by an attested summary with or without a final certification.

(b) Lack of a Record. A written statement that a diligent search of designated records revealed no record or entry of a specified tenor is admissible as evidence that the records contain no such record or entry. For domestic records, the statement must be authenticated under Rule 44(a)(1). For foreign records, the statement must comply with (a)(2)(C)(ii).

(c) Other Proof. A party may prove an official record—or an entry or lack of an entry in it—by any other method authorized by law.

(Amended February 28, 1966, effective July 1, 1966; March 2, 1987, effective August 1, 1987; April 30, 1991, effective December 1, 1991; April 30, 2007, effective December 1, 2007.)

ADVISORY COMMITTEE NOTES

1937 Adoption

This rule provides a simple and uniform method of proving public records, and entry or lack of entry therein, in all cases including those specifically provided for by statutes of the United States. Such statutes are not superseded, however, and proof may also be made according to their provisions whenever they differ from this rule. Some of those statutes are:

U.S.C., Title 28 [former sections]:

§ 661[now 1733] (Copies of department or corporation records and papers; admissibility; seal)

§ 662[now 1733] (Same; in office of General Counsel of the Treasury)

§ 663[now 1733] (Instruments and papers of Comptroller of Currency; admissibility)

§ 664[now 1733] (Organization certificates of national banks; admissibility)

§ 665[now 1733] (Transcripts from books of Treasury in suits against delinquents; admissibility)

§ 666[now 1733] (Same; certificate by Secretary or Assistant Secretary)

§ 670[now 1743] (Admissibility of copies of statements of demands by Post Office Department)

§ 671[now 1733] (Admissibility of copies of post office records and statement of accounts)

§ 672[former] (Admissibility of copies of records in General Land Office)

§ 673[now 1744] (Admissibility of copies of records, and so forth, of Patent Office)

§ 674[now 1745] (Copies of foreign letters patent as prima facie evidence)

§ 675[former] (Copies of specifications and drawings of patents admissible)

§ 676[now 1736] (Extracts from Journals of Congress admissible when injunction of secrecy removed)

§ 677[now 1740] (Copies of records in offices of United States consuls admissible)

§ 678[former] (Books and papers in certain district courts)

§ 679[former] (Records in clerks' offices, Western District of North Carolina)

§ 680[former] (Records in clerks' offices of former district of California)

§ 681[now 1734] (Original records lost or destroyed; certified copy admissible)

§ 682[now 1734] (Same; when certified copy not obtainable)

§ 685[now 1735] (Same; certified copy of official papers)

§ 687[now 1738] (Authentication of legislative acts; proof of judicial proceedings of State)

§ 688[now 1739] (Proofs of records in offices not pertaining to courts)

§ 689[now 1742] (Copies of foreign records relating to land titles)

§ 695[now 1732] (Writings and records made in regular course of business; admissibility)

§ 695e[now 1741] (Foreign documents on record in public offices; certification)

U.S.C., Title 1:

§ 30[now 112] (Statutes at large; contents; admissibility in evidence)

§ 30a[now 113] ("Little and Brown's" edition of laws and treaties competent evidence of Acts of Congress)

§ 54[now 204] (Codes and supplements as establishing prima facie the laws of United States and District of Columbia, etc.)

§ 55[now 208] (Copies of supplements to Code of Laws of United States and of District of Columbia Code and supplements; conclusive evidence of original)

U.S.C., Title 5:

§ 490[former] (Records of Department of Interior; authenticated copies as evidence)

U.S.C., Title 6:

§ 7[now Title 31, § 9306] (Surety Companies as sureties; appointment of agents; service of process)

U.S.C., Title 8:

§ 9a[see 1435(c)] (Citizenship of children of persons naturalized under certain laws; repatriation of native-born women married to aliens prior to September 22, 1922; copies of proceedings)

§ 356[see 1443] (Regulations for execution of naturalization laws; certified copies of papers as evidence)

§ 399b(d)[see 1443] (Certifications of naturalization records; authorization; admissibility as evidence)

U.S.C., Title 11:

§ 44(d), (e), (f), (g)[former] (Bankruptcy court proceedings and orders as evidence)

§ 204[former] (Extensions extended, etc.; evidence of confirmation)

§ 207(j)[former] (Corporate reorganizations; certified copy of decree as evidence)

U.S.C., Title 15:

§ 127 (Trade-mark records in Patent Office; copies as evidence)

U.S.C., Title 20:

§ 52 (Smithsonian Institution; evidence of title to site and buildings)

U.S.C., Title 25:

§ 6 (Bureau of Indian Affairs; seal; authenticated and certified documents; evidence)

U.S.C., Title 31:

§ 46[now 704] (Laws governing General Accounting Office; copies of books, records, etc., thereof as evidence)

U.S.C., Title 38:

§ 11g[see 202] (Seal of Veterans' Administration; authentication of copies of records)

U.S.C., Title 40:

§ 238 [former 44 U.S.C.A. § 300h] (National Archives; seal; reproduction of archives; fee; admissibility in evidence of reproductions)

§ 270c [see now 40 U.S.C.A. § 3133(a)] (Bonds of contractors for public works; right of person furnishing labor or material to copy of bond)

U.S.C., Title 43:

§§ 57–59 (Copies of land surveys, etc., in certain states and districts admissible as evidence)

§ 83 (General Land Office registers and receivers; transcripts of records as evidence)

U.S.C., Title 46:

§ 823 (Records of Maritime Commission; copies; publication of reports; evidence)

U.S.C., Title 47:

§ 154(m) (Federal Communications Commission; copies of reports and decisions as evidence)

§ 412 (Documents filed with Federal Communications Commission as public records; prima facie evidence; confidential records)

U.S.C., Title 49:

§ 14(3)[now 10310] (Interstate Commerce Commission reports and decisions; printing and distribution of copies)

§ 16(13)[now 10303(b)] (Copies of schedules, tariffs, etc. filed with Interstate Commerce Commission as evidence)

§ 19a(i)[now 10785(c)] (Valuation of property of carriers by Interstate Commerce Commission; final published valuations as evidence)

Supplementary Note of Advisory Committee Regarding Rules 43 and 44.

For supplementary note of Advisory Committee on this rule, see note under Rule 43.

1966 Amendment

Note to Subdivision (a)(1). These provisions on proof of official records kept within the United States are similar in substance to those heretofore appearing in Rule 44. There is a more exact description of the geographical areas covered. An official record kept in one of the areas enumerated qualifies for proof under subdivision (a)(1) even though it is not a United States official record. For example, an official record kept in one of these areas by a government in exile falls within subdivision (a)(1). It also falls within subdivision (a)(2) which may be availed of alternatively. Cf. *Banco de Espana v. Federal Reserve Bank,* 114 F.2d 438 (2d Cir. 1940).

Note to Subdivision (a)(2). Foreign official records may be proved, as heretofore, by means of official publications thereof. See *United States v. Aluminum Co. of America,* 1 F.R.D. 71 (S.D.N.Y.1939). Under this rule, a document that, on its face, appears to be an official publication, is admissible, unless a party opposing its admission into evidence shows that it lacks that character.

The rest of subdivision (a)(2) aims to provide greater clarity, efficiency, and flexibility in the procedure for authenticating copies of foreign official records.

The reference to attestation by "the officer having the legal custody of the record," hitherto appearing in Rule 44, has been found inappropriate for official records kept in foreign countries where the assumed relation between custody and the authority to attest does not obtain. See 2B Barron & Holtzoff, Federal Practice & Procedure § 992 (Wright ed. 1961). Accordingly it is provided that an attested copy may be obtained from any person authorized by the law of the foreign country to make the attestation without regard to whether he is charged with responsibility for maintaining the record or keeping it in his custody.

Under Rule 44 a United States foreign service officer has been called on to certify to the authority of the foreign official attesting the copy as well as the genuineness of his signature and his official position. See Schlesinger, *Comparative Law 57* (2d ed. 1959); Smit, *International Aspects of Federal Civil Procedure,* 61 Colum.L.Rev. 1031, 1063 (1961); 22 C.F.R. § 92.41(a), (e) (1958). This has created practical difficulties. For example, the question of the authority of the foreign officer might raise issues of foreign law which were beyond the knowledge of the United States officer. The difficulties are met under the amended rule by eliminating the element of the authority of the attesting foreign official from the scope of the certifying process, and by specifically permitting use of the chain-certificate method. Under this method, it is sufficient if the original attestation purports to have been issued by an authorized person and is accompanied by a certificate of another foreign official whose certificate may in turn be followed by that of a foreign official of higher rank. The process continues until a foreign official is reached as to whom the United States foreign service official (or a diplomatic or consular officer of the foreign country assigned or accredited to the United States) has adequate information upon which to base a "final certification." See *New York Life Ins. Co. v. Aronson,* 38 F.Supp. 687 (W.D.Pa.1941); 22 C.F.R. § 92.37 (1958).

The final certification (a term used in contradistinction to the certificates prepared by the foreign officials in a chain) relates to the incumbency and genuineness of signature of the foreign official who attested the copy of the record or, where the chain-certificate method is used, of a foreign official whose certificate appears in the chain, whether that certificate is the last in the chain or not. A final certification may be prepared on the basis of material on file in the consulate or any other satisfactory information.

Although the amended rule will generally facilitate proof of foreign official records, it is recognized that in some situations it may be difficult or even impossible to satisfy the basic requirements of the rule. There may be no United States consul in a particular foreign country; the foreign officials may not cooperate, peculiarities may exist or arise hereafter in the law or practice of a foreign country. See *United States v. Grabina,* 119 F.2d 863 (2d Cir. 1941); and, generally, Jones, *International Judicial Assistance: Procedural Chaos and a Program for Reform,* 62 Yale L.J. 515, 548–49 (1953). Therefore the final sentence of subdivision (a)(2) provides the court with discretion to admit an attested copy of a record without a final certification, or an attested summary of a record with or without a final certification. See Rep. of Comm. on Comparative Civ.Proc. & Prac., Proc. A.B.A., Sec. Int'l & Comp.L. 123, 130–31 (1952); Model Code of Evidence §§ 517, 519 (1942). This relaxation should be permitted only when it is shown that the party has been unable to satisfy the basic requirements of the amended rule despite his reasonable efforts. Moreover it is specially provided that the parties must be given a reasonable opportunity in these cases to examine into the authenticity and accuracy of the copy or summary.

Note to Subdivision (b). This provision relating to proof of lack of record is accommodated to the changes made in subdivision (a).

Note to Subdivision (c). The amendment insures that international agreements of the United States are unaffected by the rule. Several consular conventions contain provisions for reception of copies or summaries of foreign official records. See, e.g., Consular Conv. with Italy, May 8, 1878, art. X, 20 Stat. 725, T.S. No. 178 (Dept. State 1878). See also 28 U.S.C. §§ 1740–42, 1745; *Fakouri v. Cadais,* 149 F.2d 321 (5th Cir.1945), cert. denied 326 U.S. 742 (1945); 5 *Moore's Federal Practice,* par. 44.05 (2d ed. 1951).

1987 Amendment

The amendments are technical. No substantive change is intended.

1991 Amendment

The amendment to paragraph (a)(1) strikes the references to specific territories, two of which are no longer subject to the jurisdiction of the United States, and adds a generic term to describe governments having a relationship with the United States such that their official records should be treated as domestic records.

The amendment to paragraph (a)(2) adds a sentence to dispense with the final certification by diplomatic officers when the United States and the foreign country where the record is located are parties to a treaty or convention that abolishes or displaces the requirement. In that event the treaty or convention is to be followed. This changes the former procedure for authenticating foreign official records only with respect to records from countries that are parties to the Hague Convention Abolishing the Requirement of Legalization for Foreign Public Documents. Moreover, it does not affect the former practice of attesting the records, but only changes the method of certifying the attestation.

The Hague Public Documents Convention provides that the requirement of a final certification is abolished and replaced with a model *apostille,* which is to be issued by officials of the country where the records are located. See Hague Public Documents Convention, Arts. 2–4. The *apostille* certifies the signature, official position, and seal of the attesting officer. The authority who issues the *apostille* must maintain a register or card index showing the serial number of the *apostille* and other relevant information recorded on it. A foreign court can then check the serial number and information on the *apostille* with the issuing authority in order to guard against the use of fraudulent *apostilles.* This system provides a reliable method for maintaining the integrity of the authentication process, and the *apostille* can be accorded greater weight than the normal authentication procedure because foreign officials are more likely to know the precise capacity under their law of the attesting officer than would an American official. See generally Comment, *The United States and the Hague Convention Abolishing the Requirement of Legalization for Foreign Public Documents,* 11 HARV. INT'L L.J. 476, 482, 488 (1970).

2007 Amendment

The language of Rule 44 has been amended as part of the general restyling of the Civil Rules to make them more easily understood and to make style and terminology consistent throughout the rules. These changes are intended to be stylistic only.

CROSS REFERENCES

Authenticated and certified copy of government record by archivist admissible on evidence, see 44 USCA § 2116.

Rule 44.1.　Determining Foreign Law

A party who intends to raise an issue about a foreign country's law must give notice by a pleading or other writing. In determining foreign law, the court may consider any relevant material or source, including testimony, whether or not submitted by a party or admissible under the Federal Rules of Evidence. The court's determination must be treated as a ruling on a question of law.

(Adopted February 28, 1966, effective July 1, 1966; amended November 20, 1972, effective July 1, 1975; March 2, 1987, effective August 1, 1987; April 30, 2007, effective December 1, 2007.)

ADVISORY COMMITTEE NOTES

1966 Adoption

Rule 44.1 is added by amendment to furnish Federal courts with a uniform and effective procedure for raising and determining an issue concerning the law of a foreign country.

To avoid unfair surprise, the *first sentence* of the new rule requires that a party who intends to raise an issue of foreign law shall give notice thereof. The uncertainty under Rule 8(a) about whether foreign law must be pleaded—compare *Siegelman v. Cunard White Star, Ltd.*, 221 F.2d 189 (2d Cir.1955), and *Pedersen v. United States*, 191 F.Supp. 95 (D. Guam 1961), with *Harrison v. United Fruit Co.*, 143 F.Supp. 598 (S.D.N.Y.1956)—is eliminated by the provision that the notice shall be "written" and "reasonable." It may, but need not be, incorporated in the pleadings. In some situations the pertinence of foreign law is apparent from the outset; accordingly the necessary investigation of that law will have been accomplished by the party at the pleading stage, and the notice can be given conveniently in the pleadings. In other situations the pertinence of foreign law may remain doubtful until the case is further developed. A requirement that notice of foreign law be given only through the medium of the pleadings would tend in the latter instances to force the party to engage in a peculiarly burdensome type of investigation which might turn out to be unnecessary; and correspondingly the adversary would be forced into a possible wasteful investigation. The liberal provisions for amendment of the pleadings afford help if the pleadings are used as the medium of giving notice of the foreign law; but it seems best to permit a written notice to be given outside of and later than the pleadings, provided the notice is reasonable.

The new rule does not attempt to set any definite limit on the party's time for giving the notice of an issue of foreign law; in some cases the issue may not become apparent until the trial and notice then given may still be reasonable. The stage which the case had reached at the time of the notice, the reason proffered by the party for his failure to give earlier notice, and the importance to the case as a whole of the issue of foreign law sought to be raised, are among the factors which the court should consider in deciding a question of the reasonableness of a notice. If notice is given by one party it need not be repeated by any other and serves as a basis for presentation of material on the foreign law by all parties.

The *second sentence* of the new rule describes the materials to which the court may resort in determining an issue of foreign law. Heretofore the district courts, applying Rule 43(a), have looked in certain cases to State law to find the rules of evidence by which the content of foreign-country law is to be established. The State laws vary; some embody

procedures which are inefficient, time consuming and expensive. See, generally, Nussbaum, *Proving the Law of Foreign Countries*, 3 Am. J. Comp. L. 60 (1954). In all events the ordinary rules of evidence are often inapposite to the problem of determining foreign law and have in the past prevented examination of material which could have provided a proper basis for the determination. The new rule permits consideration by the court of any relevant material, including testimony, without regard to its admissibility under Rule 43. Cf. N.Y. Civ. Prac. Law & Rules, R. 4511 (effective Sept. 1, 1963); 2 Va. Code Ann. tit. 8, § 8–273; 2 W. Va. Code Ann. § 5711.

In further recognition of the peculiar nature of the issue of foreign law, the new rule provides that in determining this law the court is not limited by material presented by the parties; it may engage in its own research and consider any relevant material thus found. The court may have at its disposal better foreign law materials than counsel have presented, or may wish to reexamine and amplify material that has been presented by counsel in partisan fashion or in insufficient detail. On the other hand, the court is free to insist on a complete presentation by counsel.

There is no requirement that the court give formal notice to the parties of its intention to engage in its own research on an issue of foreign law which has been raised by them, or of its intention to raise and determine independently an issue not raised by them. Ordinarily the court should inform the parties of material it has found diverging substantially from the material which they have presented; and in general the court should give the parties an opportunity to analyze and counter new points upon which it proposes to rely. See Schlesinger, *Comparative Law* 142 (2d ed. 1959); Wyzanski, *A Trial Judge's Freedom and Responsibility*, 65 Harv.L.Rev. 1281, 1296 (1952); cf. *Siegelman v. Cunard White Star, Ltd.*, supra, 221 F.2d at 197. To require, however, that the court give formal notice from time to time as it proceeds with its study of the foreign law would add an element of undesirable rigidity to the procedure for determining issues of foreign law.

The new rule refrains from imposing an obligation on the court to take "judicial notice" of foreign law because this would put an extreme burden on the court in many cases; and it avoids use of the concept of "judicial notice" in any form because of the uncertain meaning of that concept as applied to foreign law. See, e.g., Stern, *Foreign Law in the Courts: Judicial Notice and Proof*, 45 Calif.L.Rev. 23, 43 (1957). Rather the rule provides flexible procedures for presenting and utilizing material on issues of foreign law by which a sound result can be achieved with fairness to the parties.

Under the *third sentence*, the court's determination of an issue of foreign law is to be treated as a ruling on a question of "law," not "fact," so that appellate review will not be narrowly confined by the "clearly erroneous" standard of Rule 52(a). Cf. *Uniform Judicial Notice of Foreign Law Act* § 3; Note, 72 Harv.L.Rev. 318 (1958).

The new rule parallels Article IV of the Uniform Interstate and International Procedure Act, approved by the Commissioners on Uniform State Laws in 1962, except that § 4.03 of Article IV states that "[t]he court, not the jury" shall determine foreign law. The new rule does not address itself to this problem, since the Rules refrain from allocating functions as between the court and the jury. See Rule 38(a). It has long been thought, however, that the jury is not the appropriate body to determine issues of foreign law. See, e.g., Story,

Conflict of Laws, § 638 (1st ed. 1834, 8th ed. 1883); 1 Greenleaf, *Evidence,* § 486 (1st ed. 1842, 16th ed. 1899); 4 Wigmore, *Evidence* § 2558 (1st ed. 1905); 9 id. § 2558 (3d ed. 1940). The majority of the States have committed such issues to determination by the court. See Article 5 of the Uniform Judicial Notice of Foreign Law Act, adopted by twenty-six states, 9A U.L.A. 318 (1957) (Suppl.1961, at 134); N.Y.Civ. Prac.Law & Rules, R. 4511 (effective Sept. 1, 1963); Wigmore, loc. cit. And Federal courts that have considered the problem in recent years have reached the same conclusion without reliance on statute. See *Jansson v. Swedish American Line,* 185 F.2d 212, 216 (1st Cir.1950); *Bank of Nova Scotia v. San Miguel,* 196 F.2d 950, 957, n. 6 (1st Cir.1952); *Liechti v. Roche,* 198 F.2d 174 (5th Cir.1952); *Daniel Lumber Co. v. Empresas Hondurenas, S.A.,* 215 F.2d 465 (5th Cir. 1954).

1972 Amendment

Since the purpose of the provision is to free the judge, in determining foreign law, from any restrictions imposed by evidence rules, a general reference to the Rules of Evidence is appropriate and is made.

1987 Amendment

The amendment is technical. No substantive change is intended.

2007 Amendment

The language of Rule 44.1 has been amended as part of the general restyling of the Civil Rules to make them more easily understood and to make style and terminology consistent throughout the rules. These changes are intended to be stylistic only.

HISTORICAL NOTES

References in Text

The Federal Rules of Evidence, referred to in text, are set out in this title.

Effective Date of Amendment Proposed November 20, 1972

Amendment of this rule embraced by the order entered by the Supreme Court of the United States on November 20, 1972, effective on the 180th day beginning after January 2, 1975, see section 3 of Pub.L. 93–595, Jan. 2, 1975, 88 Stat. 1959, set out as a note under section 2071 of Title 28.

Rule 45. Subpoena

(a) In General.

(1) *Form and Contents.*

(A) *Requirements—In General.* Every subpoena must:

(i) state the court from which it issued;

(ii) state the title of the action and its civil-action number;

(iii) command each person to whom it is directed to do the following at a specified time and place: attend and testify; produce designated documents, electronically stored information, or tangible things in that person's possession, custody, or control; or permit the inspection of premises; and

(iv) set out the text of Rule 45(d) and (e).

(B) *Command to Attend a Deposition—Notice of the Recording Method.* A subpoena commanding attendance at a deposition must state the method for recording the testimony.

(C) *Combining or Separating a Command to Produce or to Permit Inspection; Specifying the Form for Electronically Stored Information.* A command to produce documents, electronically stored information, or tangible things or to permit the inspection of premises may be included in a subpoena commanding attendance at a deposition, hearing, or trial, or may be set out in a separate subpoena. A subpoena may specify the form or forms in which electronically stored information is to be produced.

(D) *Command to Produce; Included Obligations.* A command in a subpoena to produce documents, electronically stored information, or tangible things requires the responding person to permit inspection, copying, testing, or sampling of the materials.

(2) *Issuing Court.* A subpoena must issue from the court where the action is pending.

(3) *Issued by Whom.* The clerk must issue a subpoena, signed but otherwise in blank, to a party who requests it. That party must complete it before service. An attorney also may issue and sign a subpoena if the attorney is authorized to practice in the issuing court.

(4) *Notice to Other Parties Before Service.* If the subpoena commands the production of documents, electronically stored information, or tangible things or the inspection of premises before trial, then before it is served on the person to whom it is directed, a notice and a copy of the subpoena must be served on each party.

(b) Service.

(1) *By Whom and How; Tendering Fees.* Any person who is at least 18 years old and not a party may serve a subpoena. Serving a subpoena requires delivering a copy to the named person and, if the subpoena requires that person's attendance, tendering the fees for 1 day's attendance and the mileage allowed by law. Fees and mileage need not be tendered when the subpoena issues on behalf of the United States or any of its officers or agencies.

(2) *Service in the United States.* A subpoena may be served at any place within the United States.

(3) *Service in a Foreign Country.* 28 U.S.C. § 1783 governs issuing and serving a subpoena directed to a United States national or resident who is in a foreign country.

(4) *Proof of Service.* Proving service, when necessary, requires filing with the issuing court a statement showing the date and manner of service and the names of the persons served. The statement must be certified by the server.

(c) Place of Compliance.

(1) *For a Trial, Hearing, or Deposition.* A subpoena may command a person to attend a trial, hearing, or deposition only as follows:

(A) within 100 miles of where the person resides, is employed, or regularly transacts business in person; or

(B) within the state where the person resides, is employed, or regularly transacts business in person, if the person

(i) is a party or a party's officer; or

(ii) is commanded to attend a trial and would not incur substantial expense.

(2) *For Other Discovery.* A subpoena may command:

(A) production of documents, electronically stored information, or tangible things at a place within 100 miles of where the person resides, is employed, or regularly transacts business in person; and

(B) inspection of premises at the premises to be inspected.

(d) Protecting a Person Subject to a Subpoena; Enforcement.

(1) *Avoiding Undue Burden or Expense; Sanctions.* A party or attorney responsible for issuing and serving a subpoena must take reasonable steps to avoid imposing undue burden or expense on a person subject to the subpoena. The court for the district where compliance is required must enforce this duty and impose an appropriate sanction—which may include lost earnings and reasonable attorney's fees—on a party or attorney who fails to comply.

(2) *Command to Produce Materials or Permit Inspection.*

(A) *Appearance Not Required.* A person commanded to produce documents, electronically stored information, or tangible things, or to permit the inspection of premises, need not appear in person at the place of production or inspection unless also commanded to appear for a deposition, hearing, or trial.

(B) *Objections.* A person commanded to produce documents or tangible things or to permit inspection may serve on the party or attorney designated in the subpoena a written objection to inspecting, copying, testing, or sampling any or all of the materials or to inspecting the premises—or to producing electronically stored information in the form or forms requested. The objection must be served before the earlier of the time specified for compliance or 14 days after the subpoena is served. If an objection is made, the following rules apply:

(i) At any time, on notice to the commanded person, the serving party may move the court for the district where compliance is required for an order compelling production or inspection.

(ii) These acts may be required only as directed in the order, and the order must protect a person who is neither a party nor a party's officer from significant expense resulting from compliance.

(3) *Quashing or Modifying a Subpoena.*

(A) *When Required.* On timely motion, the court for the district where compliance is required must quash or modify a subpoena that:

(i) fails to allow a reasonable time to comply;

(ii) requires a person to comply beyond the geographical limits specified in Rule 45(c);

(iii) requires disclosure of privileged or other protected matter, if no exception or waiver applies; or

(iv) subjects a person to undue burden.

(B) *When Permitted.* To protect a person subject to or affected by a subpoena, the court for the district where compliance is required may, on motion, quash or modify the subpoena if it requires:

(i) disclosing a trade secret or other confidential research, development, or commercial information; or

(ii) disclosing an unretained expert's opinion or information that does not describe specific occurrences in dispute and results from the expert's study that was not requested by a party.

(C) *Specifying Conditions as an Alternative.* In the circumstances described in Rule 45(d)(3)(B), the court may, instead of quashing or modifying a subpoena, order appearance or production under specified conditions if the serving party:

(i) shows a substantial need for the testimony or material that cannot be otherwise met without undue hardship; and

(ii) ensures that the subpoenaed person will be reasonably compensated.

(e) Duties in Responding to a Subpoena.

(1) *Producing Documents or Electronically Stored Information.* These procedures apply to producing documents or electronically stored information:

(A) *Documents.* A person responding to a subpoena to produce documents must produce them as they are kept in the ordinary course of business or must organize and label them to correspond to the categories in the demand.

(B) *Form for Producing Electronically Stored Information Not Specified.* If a subpoena does not specify a form for producing electronically stored information, the person responding must produce it in a form or forms in which it is ordinarily maintained or in a reasonably usable form or forms.

(C) *Electronically Stored Information Produced in Only One Form.* The person responding need not produce the same electronically stored information in more than one form.

(D) *Inaccessible Electronically Stored Information.* The person responding need not provide discovery of electronically stored information from sources that the person identifies as not reasonably accessible because of undue burden or cost. On motion to compel discovery or for a protective order, the person responding must show that the information is not reasonably accessible because of undue burden or cost. If that showing is made, the court may nonetheless order discovery from such sources if the requesting party shows good cause, considering the limitations of Rule 26(b)(2)(C). The court may specify conditions for the discovery.

(2) *Claiming Privilege or Protection.*

(A) *Information Withheld.* A person withholding subpoenaed information under a claim that it is privileged or subject to protection as trial-preparation material must:

   (i) expressly make the claim; and

   (ii) describe the nature of the withheld documents, communications, or tangible things in a manner that, without revealing information itself privileged or protected, will enable the parties to assess the claim.

(B) *Information Produced.* If information produced in response to a subpoena is subject to a claim of privilege or of protection as trial-preparation material, the person making the claim may notify any party that received the information of the claim and the basis for it. After being notified, a party must promptly return, sequester, or destroy the specified information and any copies it has; must not use or disclose the information until the claim is resolved; must take reasonable steps to retrieve the information if the party disclosed it before being notified; and may promptly present the information under seal to the court for the district where compliance is required for a determination of the claim. The person who produced the information must preserve the information until the claim is resolved.

(f) Transferring a Subpoena–Related Motion. When the court where compliance is required did not issue the subpoena, it may transfer a motion under this rule to the issuing court if the person subject to the subpoena consents or if the court finds exceptional circumstances. Then, if the attorney for a person subject to a subpoena is authorized to practice in the court where the motion was made, the attorney may file papers and appear on the motion as an officer of the issuing court. To enforce its order, the issuing court may transfer the order to the court where the motion was made.

(g) Contempt. The court for the district where compliance is required—and also, after a motion is transferred, the issuing court—may hold in contempt a person who, having been served, fails without adequate excuse to obey the subpoena or an order related to it. (Amended December 27, 1946, effective March 19, 1948; December 29, 1948, effective October 20, 1949; March 30, 1970, effective July 1, 1970; April 29, 1980, effective August 1, 1980; April 29, 1985, effective August 1, 1985; March 2, 1987, effective August 1, 1987; April 30, 1991, effective December 1, 1991; April 25, 2005, effective December 1, 2005; April 12, 2006, effective December 1, 2006; April 30, 2007, effective December 1, 2007; April 16, 2013, effective December 1, 2013.)

ADVISORY COMMITTEE NOTES

1937 Adoption

This rule applies to subpoenas ad testificandum and duces tecum issued by the district courts for attendance at a hearing or a trial, or to take depositions. It does not apply to the enforcement of subpoenas issued by administrative officers and commissions pursuant to statutory authority. The enforcement of such subpoenas by the district courts is regulated by appropriate statutes. Many of these statutes do not place any territorial limits on the validity of subpoenas so issued, but provide that they may be served anywhere within the United States. Among such statutes are the following:

U.S.C., Title 7, §§ 222 and 511n (Secretary of Agriculture)

U.S.C., Title 15, § 49 (Federal Trade Commission)

U.S.C., Title 15, §§ 77v(b), 78u(c), 79r(d) (Securities and Exchange Commission)

U.S.C., Title 16, §§ 797(g) and 825f (Federal Power Commission)

U.S.C., Title 19, § 1333(b) (Tariff Commission)

U.S.C., Title 22, §§ 268, 270d and 270e (International Commissions, etc.)

U.S.C., Title 26, §§ 614, 619(b) [see 7456] (Board of Tax Appeals)

U.S.C., Title 26, § 1523(a) [see 7608] (Internal Revenue Officers)

U.S.C., Title 29, § 161 (Labor Relations Board)

U.S.C., Title 33, § 506 (Secretary of Army)

U.S.C., Title 35, §§ 54 to 56 [now 24] (Patent Office proceedings)

U.S.C., Title 38, [former] § 133 (Veterans' Administration)

U.S.C., Title 41, § 6507 (Secretary of Labor)

U.S.C., Title 45, § 157 Third. (h) (Board of Arbitration under Railway Labor Act)

U.S.C., Title 45, § 222(b) (Investigation Commission under Railroad Retirement Act of 1935)

U.S.C., Title 46, § 1124(b) (Maritime Commission)

U.S.C., Title 47, § 409(c) and (d) (Federal Communications Commission)

U.S.C., Title 49, § 12(2) and (3) [now 10321] (Interstate Commerce Commission)

U.S.C., Title 49, § 173a [see 1484] (Secretary of Commerce)

Note to Subdivisions (a) and (b). These simplify the form of subpoena as provided in U.S.C., Title 28, [former] § 655 (Witnesses; subpoena; form; attendance under); and broaden U.S.C, Title 28, [former] § 636 (Production for books and writings) to include all actions, and to extend to any person. With the provision for relief from an oppressive or unreasonable subpoena duces tecum, compare N.Y.C.P.A. (1937) § 411.

Note to Subdivision (c). This provides for the simple and convenient method of service permitted under many state codes; e.g., N.Y.C.P.A. (1937) §§ 220, 404, J.Ct.Act, § 191; 3 Wash.Rev.Stat.Ann. (Remington, 1932) § 1218. Compare former Equity Rule 15 (Process, by Whom Served).

For statutes governing fees and mileage of witnesses see:

U.S.C., Title 28 former sections:

    600a[now 1871] (Per diem; mileage)

    600c[now 1821, 1823] (Amount per diem and mileage for witnesses; subsistence)

    600d[former] (Fees and mileage in certain states)

    601[former] (Witnesses' fees; enumeration)

    602[now 1824] (Fees and mileage of jurors and witnesses)

    603[see Title 5, §§ 5515, 5537] (No officer of court to have witness fees)

Note to Subdivision (d). The method provided in paragraph (1) for the authorization of the issuance of subpoenas has been employed in some districts. See *Henning v. Boyle*, S.D.N.Y.1901, 112 F. 397. The requirement of an order for the issuance of a subpoena duces tecum is in accordance with U.S.C., Title 28, [former] § 647 (Deposition under dedimus potestatem; subpoena duces tecum). The provisions of paragraph (2) are in accordance with common practice. See U.S.C., Title 28, former § 648 (Deposition under dedimus potestatem; witnesses, when required to attend); N.Y.C.P.A. (1937) § 300; 1 N.J.Rev.Stat. (1937) 2:27–174.

Note to Subdivision (e). The first paragraph continues the substance of U.S.C., Title 28, [former] § 654 (Witnesses; subpoenas; may run into another district). Compare U.S.C., Title 11, [former] § 69 (Referees in bankruptcy; contempts before) (production of books and writings) which is not affected by this rule. For examples of statutes which allow the court, upon proper application and cause shown, to authorize the clerk of the court to issue a subpoena for a witness who lives in another district and at a greater distance than 100 miles from the place of the hearing or trial, see:

U.S.C., Title 15:

    § 23 (Suits by United States; subpoenas for witnesses) (under antitrust laws).

U.S.C., Title 38:

    § 445[now 784] (Actions on claims; jurisdiction; parties; procedure; limitation; witnesses; definitions) (Veterans' insurance contracts).

The second paragraph continues the present procedure applicable to certain witnesses who are in foreign countries. See U.S.C., Title 28, §§ 711 [now 1783] (Letters rogatory to take testimony of witness, addressed to court of foreign country; failure of witness to appear; subpoena) and 713 [now 1783] (Service of Subpoena on witness in foreign country).

Note to Subdivision (f). Compare [former] Equity Rule 52 (Attendance of Witnesses Before Commissioner, Master, or Examiner).

1946 Amendment

Note to Subdivision (b). The added words, "or tangible things" in subdivision (b) merely make the rule for the subpoena duces tecum at the trial conform to that of subdivision (d) for the subpoena at the taking of depositions. The insertion of the words "or modify" in clause (1) affords desirable flexibility.

Subdivision (d). The added last sentence of amended subdivision (d)(1) properly gives the subpoena for documents or tangible things the same scope as provided in Rule 26(b), thus promoting uniformity. The requirement in the last sentence of original Rule 45(d)(1)—to the effect that leave of court should be obtained for the issuance of such a subpoena—has been omitted. This requirement is unnecessary and oppressive on both counsel and court, and it had been criticized by district judges. There is no satisfactory reason for a differentiation between a subpoena for the production of documentary evidence by a witness at a trial (Rule 45(a)) and for the production of the same evidence at the taking of a deposition. Under this amendment, the person subpoenaed may obtain the protection afforded by any of the orders permitted under Rule 30(b) or Rule 45(b). See *Application of Zenith Radio Corp.*, E.D.Pa.1941, 4 F.Rules Serv. 30b.21. Case 1, 1 F.R.D. 627; *Fox v. House*, Okla.1939, 29 F.Supp. 673; *United States of America for the Use of Tilo Roofing Co., Inc. v. J. Slotnik Co.*, Conn.1944, 3 F.R.D. 408.

The changes in subdivisions (d)(2) give the court the same power in the case of residents of the district as is conferred in the case of non-residents, and permit the court to fix a place for attendance which may be more convenient and accessible for the parties than that specified in the rule.

1948 Amendment

The amendment effective October 1949, substituted the reference to "Title 28, U.S.C., § 1783" at the end of subdivision (e)(2) for the reference to "the Act of July 3, 1926, c. 762, §§ 1, 3 (44 Stat. 835), U.S.C., Title 28, § 713."

1970 Amendment

At present, when a subpoena duces tecum is issued to a deponent, he is required to produce the listed materials at the deposition, but is under no clear compulsion to permit their inspection and copying. This results in confusion and uncertainty before the time the deposition is taken, with no mechanism provided whereby the court can resolve the matter. Rule 45(d)(1), as revised, makes clear that the subpoena authorizes inspection and copying of the materials produced. The deponent is afforded full protection since he can object, thereby forcing the party serving the subpoena to obtain a court order if he wishes to inspect and copy. The procedure is thus analogous to that provided in Rule 34.

The changed references to other rules conform to changes made in those rules. The deletion of words in the clause describing the proper scope of the subpoena conforms to a change made in the language of Rule 34. The reference to Rule 26(b) is unchanged but encompasses new matter in that subdivision. The changes make it clear that the scope of discovery through a subpoena is the same as that applicable to Rule 34 and the other discovery rules.

1980 Amendment

Subdivision (d)(1). The amendment defines the term "proof of service" as used in the first sentence of the present subdivision. For want of a definition, the district court clerks have been obliged to fashion their own, with results that vary from district to district. All that seems required is a simple certification on a copy of the notice to take a deposition that the notice has been served on every other party to the action. That is the proof of service required by Rule 25(d) of both the Federal Rules of Appellate Procedure and the Supreme Court Rules.

Subdivision (e)(1). The amendment makes the reach of a subpoena of a district court at least as extensive as that of the state courts of general jurisdiction in the state in which the district court is held. Under the present rule the reach of a district court subpoena is often greater, since it extends throughout the district. No reason appears why it should be less, as it sometimes is because of the accident of district lines. Restrictions upon the reach of subpoenas are imposed to prevent undue inconvenience to witnesses. State statutes and rules of court are quite likely to reflect the varying degrees of difficulty and expense attendant upon local travel.

1985 Amendment

Present Rule 45(d)(2) has two sentences setting forth the territorial scope of deposition subpoenas. The first sentence is directed to depositions taken in the judicial district in which the deponent resides; the second sentence addresses situations in which the deponent is not a resident of the district in which the deposition is to take place. The Rule, as currently constituted, creates anomalous situations that often cause logistical problems in conducting litigation.

The first sentence of the present Rule states that a deponent may be required to attend only in the *county* wherein that person resides or is employed or transacts business in person, that is, where the person lives or works. Under this provision a deponent can be compelled, without court order, to travel from one end of that person's home county to the other, no matter how far that may be. The second sentence of the Rule is somewhat more flexible, stating that someone who does not reside in the district in which the deposition is to be taken can be required to attend in the county where the person is served with the subpoena, *or* within 40 miles from the place of service.

Under today's conditions there is no sound reason for distinguishing between residents of the district or county in which a deposition is to be taken and nonresidents, and the Rule is amended to provide that any person may be subpoenaed to attend a deposition within a specified radius from that person's residence, place of business, or where the person was served. The 40-mile radius has been increased to 100 miles.

1987 Amendment

The amendments are technical. No substantive change is intended.

1991 Amendment

Purposes of Revision. The purposes of this revision are (1) to clarify and enlarge the protections afforded persons who are required to assist the court by giving information or evidence; (2) to facilitate access outside the deposition procedure provided by Rule 30 to documents and other information in the possession of persons who are not parties; (3) to facilitate service of subpoenas for depositions or productions of evidence at places distant from the district in which an action is proceeding; (4) to enable the court to compel a witness found within the state in which the court sits to attend trial; (5) to clarify the organization of the text of the rule.

Subdivision (a). This subdivision is amended in seven significant respects.

First, Paragraph (a)(3) modifies the requirement that a subpoena be issued by the clerk of court. Provision is made for the issuance of subpoenas by attorneys as officers of the court. This revision perhaps culminates an evolution. Subpoenas were long issued by specific order of the court. As this became a burden to the court, general orders were made authorizing clerks to issue subpoenas on request. Since 1948, they have been issued in blank by the clerk of any federal court to any lawyer, the clerk serving as stationer to the bar. In allowing counsel to issue the subpoena, the rule is merely a recognition of present reality.

Although the subpoena is in a sense the command of the attorney who completes the form, defiance of a subpoena is nevertheless an act in defiance of a court order and exposes the defiant witness to contempt sanctions. In *ICC v. Brimson*, 154 U.S. 447 (1894), the Court upheld a statute directing federal courts to issue subpoenas to compel testimony before the ICC. In *CAB v. Hermann*, 353 U.S. 322 (1957), the Court approved as established practice the issuance of administrative subpoenas as a matter of absolute agency right. And in *NLRB v. Warren Co.*, 350 U.S. 107 (1955), the Court held that the lower court had no discretion to withhold sanctions against a contemnor who violated such subpoenas. The 1948 revision of Rule 45 put the attorney in a position similar to that of the administrative agency, as a public officer entitled to use the court's contempt power to investigate facts in dispute. Two courts of appeals have touched on the issue and have described lawyer-issued subpoenas as mandates of the court. *Waste Conversion, Inc. v. Rollins Environmental Services (NJ), Inc.*, 893 F.2d 605 (3d Cir., 1990); *Fisher v. Marubent Cotton Corp.*, 526 F.2d 1338, 1340 (8th Cir., 1975). Cf. *Young v. United States ex rel Vuitton et Fils S.A.*, 481 U.S. 787, 821 (1987) (Scalia, J., concurring). This revision makes the rule explicit that the attorney acts as an officer of the court in issuing and signing subpoenas.

Necessarily accompanying the evolution of this power of the lawyer as officer of the court is the development of increased responsibility and liability for the misuse of this power. The latter development is reflected in the provisions of subdivision (c) of this rule, and also in the requirement imposed by paragraph (3) of this subdivision that the attorney issuing a subpoena must sign it.

Second, Paragraph (a)(3) authorizes attorneys in distant districts to serve as officers authorized to issue commands in the name of the court. Any attorney permitted to represent a client in a federal court, even one admitted pro haec vice, has the same authority as a clerk to issue a subpoena from any federal court for the district in which the subpoena is served and enforced. In authorizing attorneys to issue subpoenas from distant courts, the amended rule effectively authorizes service of a subpoena anywhere in the United States by an attorney representing any party. This change is intended to ease the administrative burdens of inter-district law practice. The former rule resulted in delay and expense caused by the need to secure forms from clerks' offices some distance from the place at which the action proceeds. This change does not enlarge the burden on the witness.

Pursuant to Paragraph (a)(2), a subpoena for a deposition must still issue from the court in which the deposition or production would be compelled. Accordingly, a motion to quash such a subpoena if it overbears the limits of the subpoena power must, as under the previous rule, be presented to the court for the district in which the deposition would occur. Likewise, the court in whose name the subpoena is issued is responsible for its enforcement.

Third, in order to relieve attorneys of the need to secure an appropriate seal to affix to a subpoena issued as an officer of a distant court, the requirement that a subpoena be under seal is abolished by the provisions of Paragraph (a)(1).

Fourth, Paragraph (a)(1) authorizes the issuance of a subpoena to compel a non-party to produce evidence independent of any deposition. This revision spares the necessity of a deposition of the custodian of evidentiary material required to be produced. A party seeking additional production from a person subject to such a subpoena may serve an additional subpoena requiring additional production at the same time and place.

Fifth, Paragraph (a)(2) makes clear that the person subject to the subpoena is required to produce materials in that person's control whether or not the materials are located within the district or within the territory within which the subpoena can be served. The non-party witness is subject to the same scope of discovery under this rule as that person would be as a party to whom a request is addressed pursuant to Rule 34.

Sixth, Paragraph (a)(1) requires that the subpoena include a statement of the rights and duties of witnesses by setting forth in full the text of the new subdivisions (c) and (d).

Seventh, the revised rule authorizes the issuance of a subpoena to compel the inspection of premises in the possession of a non-party. Rule 34 has authorized such inspections of premises in the possession of a party as discovery compelled under Rule 37, but prior practice required an independent proceeding to secure such relief ancillary to the federal proceeding when the premises were not in the possession of a party. Practice in some states has long authorized such use of a subpoena for this purpose without apparent adverse consequence.

Subdivision (b). Paragraph (b)(1) retains the text of the former subdivision (c) with minor changes.

The reference to the United States marshal and deputy marshal is deleted because of the infrequency of the use of these officers for this purpose. Inasmuch as these officers meet the age requirement, they may still be used if available.

A provision requiring service of prior notice pursuant to Rule 5 of compulsory pretrial production or inspection has been added to paragraph (b)(1). The purpose of such notice is to afford other parties an opportunity to object to the production or inspection, or to serve a demand for additional documents or things. Such additional notice is not needed with respect to a deposition because of the requirement of notice imposed by Rule 30 or 31. But when production or inspection is sought independently of a deposition, other parties may need notice in order to monitor the discovery and in order to pursue access to any information that may or should be produced.

Paragraph (b)(2) retains language formerly set forth in subdivision (e) and extends its application to subpoenas for depositions or production.

Paragraph (b)(3) retains language formerly set forth in paragraph (d)(1) and extends its applications to subpoenas for trial or hearing or production.

Subdivision (c). This provision is new and states the rights of witnesses. It is not intended to diminish rights conferred by Rules 26–37 or any other authority.

Paragraph (c)(1) gives specific application to the principle stated in Rule 26(g) and specifies liability for earnings lost by a non-party witness as a result of a misuse of the subpoena. No change in existing law is thereby effected. Abuse of a subpoena is an actionable tort, *Board of Ed. v. Farmingdale Classroom Teach. Ass'n*, 38 N.Y.2d 397, 380 N.Y.S.2d 635, 343 N.E.2d 278 (1975), and the duty of the attorney to the non-party is also embodied in Model Rule of Professional Conduct 4.4. The liability of the attorney is correlative to the expanded power of the attorney to issue subpoenas. The liability may include the cost of fees to collect attorneys' fees owed as a result of a breach of this duty.

Paragraph (c)(2) retains language from the former subdivision (b) and paragraph (d)(1). The 10–day period for response to a subpoena is extended to 14 days to avoid the complex calculations associated with short time periods under Rule 6 and to allow a bit more time for such objections to be made.

A non-party required to produce documents or materials is protected against significant expense resulting from involuntary assistance to the court. This provision applies, for example, to a non-party required to provide a list of class members. The court is not required to fix the costs in advance of production, although this will often be the most satisfactory accommodation to protect the party seeking discovery from excessive costs. In some instances, it may be preferable to leave uncertain costs to be determined after the materials have been produced, provided that the risk of uncertainty is fully disclosed to the discovering party. See, *e.g.*, *United States v. Columbia Broadcasting Systems, Inc.*, 666 F.2d 364 (9th Cir.1982).

Paragraph (c)(3) explicitly authorizes the quashing of a subpoena as a means of protecting a witness from misuse of the subpoena power. It replaces and enlarges on the former subdivision (b) of this rule and tracks the provisions of Rule 26(c). While largely repetitious, this rule is addressed to the witness who may read it on the subpoena, where it is required to be printed by the revised paragraph (a)(1) of this rule.

Subparagraph (c)(3)(A) identifies those circumstances in which a subpoena must be quashed or modified. It restates the former provisions with respect to the limits of mandatory travel that are set forth in the former paragraphs (d)(2) and (e)(1), with one important change. Under the revised rule, a federal court can compel a witness to come from any place in the state to attend trial, whether or not the local state law so provides. This extension is subject to the qualification provided in the next paragraph, which authorizes the court to condition enforcement of a subpoena compelling a non-party witness to bear substantial expense to attend trial. The traveling non-party witness may be entitled to reasonable compensation for the time and effort entailed.

Clause (c)(3)(A)(iv) requires the court to protect all persons from undue burden imposed by the use of the subpoena power. Illustratively, it might be unduly burdensome to compel an adversary to attend trial as a witness if the adversary is known to have no personal knowledge of matters in dispute, especially so if the adversary would be required to incur substantial travel burdens.

Subparagraph (c)(3)(B) identifies circumstances in which a subpoena should be quashed unless the party serving the subpoena shows a substantial need and the court can devise an appropriate accommodation to protect the interests of the witness. An additional circumstance in which such action is required is a request for costly production of documents; that situation is expressly governed by subparagraph (b)(2)(B)[1].

Clause (c)(3)(B)(i) authorizes the court to quash, modify, or condition a subpoena to protect the person subject to or affected by the subpoena from unnecessary or unduly harmful disclosures of confidential information. It corresponds to Rule 26(c)(7).

Clause (c)(3)(B)(ii) provides appropriate protection for the intellectual property of the non-party witness; it does not apply to the expert retained by a party, whose information is subject to the provisions of Rule 26(b)(4). A growing problem has been the use of subpoenas to compel the giving of evidence and information by unretained experts. Experts are not exempt from the duty to give evidence, even if they cannot be compelled to prepare themselves to give effective testimony, *e.g., Carter–Wallace, Inc. v. Otte*, 474 F.2d 529 (2d Cir.1972), but compulsion to give evidence may threaten the intellectual property of experts denied the opportunity to bargain for the value of their services. See generally Maurer, *Compelling the Expert Witness: Fairness and Utility Under the Federal Rules of Civil Procedure*, 19 GA.L.REV. 71 (1984); Note, *Discovery and Testimony of Unretained Experts*, 1987 DUKE L.J. 140. Arguably the compulsion to testify can be regarded as a "taking" of intellectual property. The rule establishes the right of such persons to withhold their expertise, at least unless the party seeking it makes the kind of showing required for a conditional denial of a motion to quash as provided in the final sentence of subparagraph (c)(3)(B); that requirement is the same as that necessary to secure work product under Rule 26(b)(3) and gives assurance of reasonable compensation. The Rule thus approves the accommodation of competing interests exemplified in *United States v. Columbia Broadcasting Systems Inc.*, 666 F.2d 364 (9th Cir.1982). See also *Wright v. Jeep Corporation*, 547 F.Supp. 871 (E.D.Mich.1982).

As stated in *Kaufman v. Edelstein*, 539 F.2d 811, 822 (2d Cir.1976), the district court's discretion in these matters should be informed by "the degree to which the expert is being called because of his knowledge of facts relevant to the case rather than in order to give opinion testimony; the difference between testifying to a previously formed or expressed opinion and forming a new one; the possibility that, for other reasons, the witness is a unique expert; the extent to which the calling party is able to show the unlikelihood that any comparable witness will willingly testify; and the degree to which the witness is able to show that he has been oppressed by having continually to testify. . . ."

Clause (c)(3)(B)(iii) protects non-party witnesses who may be burdened to perform the duty to travel in order to provide testimony at trial. The provision requires the court to condition a subpoena requiring travel of more than 100 miles on reasonable compensation.

Subdivision (d). This provision is new. Paragraph (d)(1) extends to non-parties the duty imposed on parties by the last paragraph of Rule 34(b), which was added in 1980.

Paragraph (d)(2) is new and corresponds to the new Rule 26(b)(5) [paragraph (5) in Rule 26(b) was a proposed paragraph which was withdrawn by the Supreme Court]. Its purpose is to provide a party whose discovery is constrained by a claim of privilege or work product protection with information sufficient to evaluate such a claim and to resist if it seems unjustified. The person claiming a privilege or protection cannot decide the limits of that party's own entitlement.

A party receiving a discovery request who asserts a privilege or protection but fails to disclose that claim is at risk of waiving the privilege or protection. A person claiming a privilege or protection who fails to provide adequate information about the privilege or protection claim to the party seeking the information is subject to an order to show cause why the person should not be held in contempt under subdivision (e). Motions for such orders and responses to motions are subject to the sanctions provisions of Rules 7 and 11.

A person served a subpoena that is too broad may be faced with a burdensome task to provide full information regarding all that person's claims to privilege or work product protection. Such a person is entitled to protection that may be secured through an objection made pursuant to paragraph (c)(2).

Subdivision (e). This provision retains most of the language of the former subdivision (f).

"Adequate cause" for a failure to obey a subpoena remains undefined. In at least some circumstances, a non-party might be guilty of contempt for refusing to obey a subpoena even though the subpoena manifestly overreaches the appropriate limits of the subpoena power. *E.g., Walker v. City of Birmingham*, 388 U.S. 307 (1967). But, because the command of the subpoena is not in fact one uttered by a judicial officer, contempt should be very sparingly applied when the non-party witness has been overborne by a party or attorney. The language added to subdivision (f) is intended to assure that result where a non-party has been commanded, on the signature of an attorney, to travel greater distances than can be compelled pursuant to this rule.

[1] So in original. Probably should be "subparagraph (c)(2)(B)".

2005 Amendment

This amendment closes a small gap in regard to notifying witnesses of the manner for recording a deposition. A deposition subpoena must state the method for recording the testimony.

Rule 30(b)(2) directs that the party noticing a deposition state in the notice the manner for recording the testimony, but the notice need not be served on the deponent. The deponent learns of the recording method only if the deponent is a party or is informed by a party. Rule 30(b)(3) permits another party to designate an additional method of recording with prior notice to the deponent and the other parties. The deponent thus has notice of the recording method when an additional method is designated. This amendment completes the notice provisions to ensure that a nonparty deponent has notice of the recording method when the recording method is described only in the deposition notice.

A subpoenaed witness does not have a right to refuse to proceed with a deposition due to objections to the manner of recording. But under rare circumstances, a nonparty witness might have a ground for seeking a protective order under Rule 26(c) with regard to the manner of recording or the use of the deposition if recorded in a certain manner. Should such a witness not learn of the manner of recording until the deposition begins, undesirable delay or complication might result. Advance notice of the recording method affords an opportunity to raise such protective issues.

Other changes are made to conform Rule 45(a)(2) to current style conventions.

2006 Amendment

Rule 45 is amended to conform the provisions for subpoenas to changes in other discovery rules, largely related to discovery of electronically stored information. Rule 34 is amended to provide in greater detail for the production of electronically stored information. Rule 45(a)(1)(C) is amended to recognize that electronically stored information, as defined in Rule 34(a), can also be sought by subpoena. Like Rule 34(b), Rule 45(a)(1) is amended to provide that the subpoena can designate a form or forms for production of electronic data. Rule 45(c)(2) is amended, like Rule 34(b), to authorize the person served with a subpoena to object to the requested form or forms. In addition, as under Rule 34(b), Rule 45(d)(1)(B) is amended to provide that if the subpoena does not specify the form or forms for electronically stored information, the person served with the subpoena must produce electronically stored information in a form or forms in which it is usually maintained or in a form or forms that are reasonably usable. Rule 45(d)(1)(C) is added to provide that the person producing electronically stored information should not have to produce the same information in more than one form unless so ordered by the court for good cause.

As with discovery of electronically stored information from parties, complying with a subpoena for such information may impose burdens on the responding person. Rule 45(c) provides protection against undue impositions on nonparties. For example, Rule 45(c)(1) directs that a party serving a subpoena "shall take reasonable steps to avoid imposing undue burden or expense on a person subject to the subpoena," and Rule 45(c)(2)(B) permits the person served with the subpoena to object to it and directs that an order requiring compliance "shall protect a person who is neither a party nor a party's officer from significant expense resulting from" compliance. Rule 45(d)(1)(D) is added to provide that the responding person need not provide discovery of electronically stored information from sources the party identifies as not reasonably accessible, unless the court orders such discovery for good cause, considering the limitations of Rule 26(b)(2)(C), on terms that protect a nonparty against significant expense. A parallel provision is added to Rule 26(b)(2).

Rule 45(a)(1)(B) is also amended, as is Rule 34(a), to provide that a subpoena is available to permit testing and sampling as well as inspection and copying. As in Rule 34, this change recognizes that on occasion the opportunity to perform testing or sampling may be important, both for documents and for electronically stored information. Because testing or sampling may present particular issues of burden or intrusion for the person served with the subpoena, however, the protective provisions of Rule 45(c) should be enforced with vigilance when such demands are made. Inspection or testing of certain types of electronically stored information or of a person's electronic information system may raise issues of confidentiality or privacy. The addition of sampling and testing to Rule 45(a) with regard to documents and electronically stored information is not meant to create a routine right of direct access to a person's electronic information system,

although such access might be justified in some circumstances. Courts should guard against undue intrusiveness resulting from inspecting or testing such systems.

Rule 45(d)(2) is amended, as is Rule 26(b)(5), to add a procedure for assertion of privilege or of protection as trial-preparation materials after production. The receiving party may submit the information to the court for resolution of the privilege claim, as under Rule 26(b)(5)(B).

Other minor amendments are made to conform the rule to the changes described above.

2007 Amendment

The language of Rule 45 has been amended as part of the general restyling of the Civil Rules to make them more easily understood and to make style and terminology consistent throughout the rules. These changes are intended to be stylistic only.

The reference to discovery of "books" in former Rule 45(a)(1)(C) was deleted to achieve consistent expression throughout the discovery rules. Books remain a proper subject of discovery.

Former Rule 45(b)(1) required "prior notice" to each party of any commanded production of documents and things or inspection of premises. Courts have agreed that notice must be given "prior" to the return date, and have tended to converge on an interpretation that requires notice to the parties before the subpoena is served on the person commanded to produce or permit inspection. That interpretation is adopted in amended Rule 45(b)(1) to give clear notice of general present practice.

The language of former Rule 45(d)(2) addressing the manner of asserting privilege is replaced by adopting the wording of Rule 26(b)(5). The same meaning is better expressed in the same words.

2013 Amendment

Rule 45 was extensively amended in 1991. The goal of the present amendments is to clarify and simplify the rule. The amendments recognize the court where the action is pending as the issuing court, permit nationwide service of a subpoena, and collect in a new subdivision (c) the previously scattered provisions regarding place of compliance. These changes resolve a conflict that arose after the 1991 amendment about a court's authority to compel a party or party officer to travel long distances to testify at trial; such testimony may now be required only as specified in new Rule 45(c). In addition, the amendments introduce authority in new Rule 45(f) for the court where compliance is required to transfer a subpoena-related motion to the court where the action is pending on consent of the person subject to the subpoena or in exceptional circumstances.

Subdivision (a). This subdivision is amended to provide that a subpoena issues from the court where the action is pending. Subdivision (a)(3) specifies that an attorney authorized to practice in that court may issue a subpoena, which is consistent with current practice.

In Rule 45(a)(1)(D), "person" is substituted for "party" because the subpoena may be directed to a nonparty.

Rule 45(a)(4) is added to highlight and slightly modify a notice requirement first included in the rule in 1991. Under the 1991 amendments, Rule 45(b)(1) required prior notice of the service of a "documents only" subpoena to the other parties. Rule 45(b)(1) was clarified in 2007 to specify that this notice must be served before the subpoena is served on the witness.

The Committee has been informed that parties serving subpoenas frequently fail to give the required notice to the other parties. The amendment moves the notice requirement to a new provision in Rule 45(a) and requires that the notice include a copy of the subpoena. The amendments are intended to achieve the original purpose of enabling the other parties to object or to serve a subpoena for additional materials.

Parties desiring access to information produced in response to the subpoena will need to follow up with the party serving it or the person served to obtain such access. The rule does not limit the court's authority to order notice of receipt of produced materials or access to them. The party serving the subpoena should in any event make reasonable provision for prompt access.

Subdivision (b). The former notice requirement in Rule 45(b)(1) has been moved to new Rule 45(a)(4).

Rule 45(b)(2) is amended to provide that a subpoena may be served at any place within the United States, removing the complexities prescribed in prior versions.

Subdivision (c). Subdivision (c) is new. It collects the various provisions on where compliance can be required and simplifies them. Unlike the prior rule, place of service is not critical to place of compliance. Although Rule 45(a)(1)(A)(iii) permits the subpoena to direct a place of compliance, that place must be selected under Rule 45(c).

Rule 45(c)(1) addresses a subpoena to testify at a trial, hearing, or deposition. Rule 45(c)(1)(A) provides that compliance may be required within 100 miles of where the person subject to the subpoena resides, is employed, or regularly conducts business in person. For parties and party officers, Rule 45(c)(1)(B)(i) provides that compliance may be required anywhere in the state where the person resides, is employed, or regularly conducts business in person. When an order under Rule 43(a) authorizes testimony from a remote location, the witness can be commanded to testify from any place described in Rule 45(c)(1).

Under Rule 45(c)(1)(B)(ii), nonparty witnesses can be required to travel more than 100 miles within the state where they reside, are employed, or regularly transact business in person only if they would not, as a result, incur "substantial expense." When travel over 100 miles could impose substantial expense on the witness, the party that served the subpoena may pay that expense and the court can condition enforcement of the subpoena on such payment.

Because Rule 45(c) directs that compliance may be commanded only as it provides, these amendments resolve a split in interpreting Rule 45's provisions for subpoenaing parties and party officers. *Compare In re Vioxx Products Liability Litigation*, 438 F.Supp. 2d 664 (E.D. La. 2006) (finding authority to compel a party officer from New Jersey to testify at trial in New Orleans), *with Johnson v. Big Lots Stores, Inc.*, 251 F.R.D. 213 (E.D. La. 2008) (holding that Rule 45 did not require attendance of plaintiffs at trial in New Orleans when they would have to travel more than 100 miles from outside the state). Rule 45(c)(1)(A) does not authorize a subpoena for trial to require a party or party officer to travel more than 100 miles unless the party or party officer resides, is employed, or regularly transacts business in person in the state.

Depositions of parties, and officers, directors, and managing agents of parties need not involve use of a subpoena. Under Rule 37(d)(1)(A)(i), failure of such a witness whose deposition was properly noticed to appear for the deposition can lead to Rule 37(b) sanctions (including dismissal or default but not contempt) without regard to service of a subpoena and without regard to the geographical limitations on compliance with a subpoena. These amendments do not change that existing law; the courts retain their authority to control the place of party depositions and impose sanctions for failure to appear under Rule 37(b).

For other discovery, Rule 45(c)(2) directs that inspection of premises occur at those premises, and that production of documents, tangible things, and electronically stored information may be commanded to occur at a place within 100 miles of where the person subject to the subpoena resides, is employed, or regularly conducts business in person. Under the current rule, parties often agree that production, particularly of electronically stored information, be transmitted by electronic means. Such arrangements facilitate discovery, and nothing in these amendments limits the ability of parties to make such arrangements.

Rule 45(d)(3)(A)(ii) directs the court to quash any subpoena that purports to compel compliance beyond the geographical limits specified in Rule 45(c).

Subdivision (d). Subdivision (d) contains the provisions formerly in subdivision (c). It is revised to recognize the court where the action is pending as the issuing court, and to take account of the addition of Rule 45(c) to specify where compliance with a subpoena is required.

Subdivision (f). Subdivision (f) is new. Under Rules 45(d)(2)(B), 45(d)(3), and 45(e)(2)(B), subpoena-related motions and applications are to be made to the court where compliance is required under Rule 45(c). Rule 45(f) provides authority for that court to transfer the motion to the court where the action is pending. It applies to all motions under this rule, including an application under Rule 45(e)(2)(B) for a privilege determination.

Subpoenas are essential to obtain discovery from nonparties. To protect local nonparties, local resolution of disputes about subpoenas is assured by the limitations of Rule 45(c) and the requirements in Rules 45(d) and (e) that motions be made in the court in which compliance is required under Rule 45(c). But transfer to the court where the action is pending is sometimes warranted. If the person subject to the subpoena consents to transfer, Rule 45(f) provides that the court where compliance is required may do so.

In the absence of consent, the court may transfer in exceptional circumstances, and the proponent of transfer bears the burden of showing that such circumstances are present. The prime concern should be avoiding burdens on local nonparties subject to subpoenas, and it should not be assumed that the issuing court is in a superior position to resolve subpoena-related motions. In some circumstances, however, transfer may be warranted in order to avoid disrupting the issuing court's management of the underlying litigation, as when that court has already ruled on issues presented by the motion or the same issues are likely to arise in discovery in many districts. Transfer is appropriate only if such interests outweigh the interests of the nonparty served with the subpoena in obtaining local resolution of the motion. Judges in compliance districts may find it helpful to consult with the judge in the issuing court presiding over the underlying case while addressing subpoena-related motions.

If the motion is transferred, judges are encouraged to permit telecommunications methods to minimize the burden a transfer imposes on nonparties, if it is necessary for attorneys admitted in the court where the motion is made to appear in the court in which the action is pending. The rule provides that if these attorneys are authorized to practice in the court where the motion is made, they may file papers and appear in the court in which the action is pending in relation to the motion as officers of that court.

After transfer, the court where the action is pending will decide the motion. If the court rules that discovery is not justified, that should end the matter. If the court orders further discovery, it is possible that retransfer may be important to enforce the order. One consequence of failure to obey such an order is contempt, addressed in Rule 45(g). Rule 45(g) and Rule 37(b)(1) are both amended to provide that disobedience of an order enforcing a subpoena after transfer is contempt of the issuing court and the court where compliance is required under Rule 45(c). In some instances, however, there may be a question about whether the issuing court can impose contempt sanctions on a distant nonparty. If such circumstances arise, or if it is better to supervise compliance in the court where compliance is required, the rule provides authority for retransfer for enforcement. Although changed circumstances may prompt a modification of such an order, it is not expected that the compliance court will reexamine the resolution of the underlying motion.

Subdivision (g). Subdivision (g) carries forward the authority of former subdivision (e) to punish disobedience of subpoenas as contempt. It is amended to make clear that, in the event of transfer of a subpoena-related motion, such disobedience constitutes contempt of both the court where compliance is required under Rule 45(c) and the court where the action is pending. If necessary for effective enforcement, Rule 45(f) authorizes the issuing court to transfer its order after the motion is resolved.

The rule is also amended to clarify that contempt sanctions may be applied to a person who disobeys a subpoena-related order, as well as one who fails entirely to obey a subpoena. In civil litigation, it would be rare for a court to use contempt sanctions without first ordering compliance with a subpoena, and the order might not require all the compliance sought by the subpoena. Often contempt proceedings will be initiated by an order to show cause, and an order to comply or be held in contempt may modify the subpoena's command. Disobedience of such an order may be treated as contempt.

The second sentence of former subdivision (e) is deleted as unnecessary.

Changes Made After Publication and Comment

As described in the Report, the published preliminary draft was modified in several ways after the public comment period. The words "before trial" were restored to the notice provision that was moved to new Rule 45(a)(4). The place of compliance in new Rule 45(c)(2)(A) was changed to a place "within 100 miles of where the person resides, is employed, or regularly conducts business." In new Rule 45(f), the party consent feature was removed, meaning consent of the person subject to the subpoena is sufficient to permit transfer to the issuing court. In addition, style changes were made after consultation with the Standing Committee's Style Consultant. In the Committee Note, clarifications were made in response to points raised during the public comment period.

HISTORICAL NOTES

Treaties and Conventions; Taking of Evidence Abroad in Civil or Commercial Matters; Observance On and After Oct. 7, 1972, by United States and Citizens and Persons Subject to Jurisdiction of United States

For text of Convention, see provisions set out as a note under section 1781 of this title.

CROSS REFERENCES

Motion for order for production of documents, see Fed. Rules Civ.Proc. Rule 34, 28 USCA.

Scope of deposition on oral examination, see Fed.Rules Civ.Proc. Rule 26, 28 USCA.

Subpoenas in civil cases brought by United States under antitrust laws, see 15 USCA § 23.

Rule 46.   Objecting to a Ruling or Order

A formal exception to a ruling or order is unnecessary. When the ruling or order is requested or made, a party need only state the action that it wants the court to take or objects to, along with the grounds for the request or objection. Failing to object does not prejudice a party who had no opportunity to do so when the ruling or order was made.

(Amended March 2, 1987, effective August 1, 1987; April 30, 2007, effective December 1, 2007.)

ADVISORY COMMITTEE NOTES

1937 Adoption

Abolition of formal exceptions is often provided by statute. See Ill.Rev.Stat. (1937), ch. 110, § 204; Neb.Comp.Stat. (1929) § 20–1139; N.M.Stat.Ann. (Courtright, 1929) § 105–830; 2 N.D.Comp.Laws Ann. (1913) § 7653; Ohio Code Ann. (Throckmorton, 1936) § 11560; 1 S.D.Comp.Laws (1929) § 2542; Utah Rev.Stat.Ann. (1933) §§ 104–39–2, 104–24–18; Va.Rules of Court, Rule 22, 163 Va. v. xii (1935); Wis.Stat. (1935) § 270.39. Compare N.Y.C.P.A. (1937) §§ 583, 445, and 446, all as amended by L.1936, ch. 915. Rule 51 deals with objections to the court's instructions to the jury.

U.S.C., Title 28, [former] § 776 (Bill of exceptions; authentication; signing of by judge) and [former] § 875 (Review of findings in cases tried without a jury) are superseded insofar as they provide for formal exceptions, and a bill of exceptions.

1987 Amendment

The amendments are technical. No substantive change is intended.

2007 Amendment

The language of Rule 46 has been amended as part of the general restyling of the Civil Rules to make them more easily understood and to make style and terminology consistent throughout the rules. These changes are intended to be stylistic only.

CROSS REFERENCES

Exceptions unnecessary, see Fed.Rules Cr.Proc. Rule 51, 18 USCA.

Harmless error, see Fed.Rules Civ.Proc. Rule 61, 28 USCA.

Objections to instructions, see Fed.Rules Civ.Proc. Rule 51, 28 USCA.

Rule 47.   Selecting Jurors

(a) Examining Jurors. The court may permit the parties or their attorneys to examine prospective jurors or may itself do so. If the court examines the jurors, it must permit the parties or their attorneys to make any further inquiry it considers proper, or must itself ask any of their additional questions it considers proper.

(b) Peremptory Challenges. The court must allow the number of peremptory challenges provided by 28 U.S.C. § 1870.

(c) Excusing a Juror. During trial or deliberation, the court may excuse a juror for good cause.
(Amended February 28, 1966, effective July 1, 1966; April 30, 1991, effective December 1, 1991; April 30, 2007, effective December 1, 2007.)

ADVISORY COMMITTEE NOTES

1937 Adoption

Note to Subdivision (a). This permits a practice found very useful by Federal trial judges. For an example of a state practice in which the examination by the court is supplemented by further inquiry by counsel, see Rule 27 of the Code of Rules for the District Courts of Minnesota, 186 Minn. xxxiii (1932), 3 Minn.Stat. (Mason, Supp.1936) Appendix 4, p. 1062.

Note to Subdivision (b). The provision for an alternate juror is one often found in modern state codes. See N.C.Code (1935) § 2330(a); Ohio Gen.Code Ann. (Page, Supp. 1926–1935) § 11419–47; Pa.Stat.Ann. (Purdon, Supp.1936) Title 17, § 1153; compare U.S.C., Title 28, [former] § 417a (Alternate jurors in criminal trials); 1 N.J.Rev.Stat. (1937) 2:91A–1, 2:91A–2, 2:91A–3.

Provisions for qualifying, drawing, and challenging of jurors are found in U.S.C., Title 28:

- § 411 [now 1861] (Qualifications and exemptions)
- § 412 [now 1864] (Manner of drawing)
- § 413 [now 1865] (Apportioned in district)
- § 415 [see 1862] (Not disqualified because of race or color)
- § 416 [now 1867] (Venire; service and return)
- § 417 [now 1866] (Talesmen for petit jurors)
- § 418 [now 1866] (Special juries)
- § 423 [now 1869] (Jurors not to serve more than once a year)
- § 424 [now 1870] (Challenges)

and D.C.Code (1930) Title 18, §§ 341 to 360 (Juries and Jury Commission) and Title 6, § 366 (Peremptory challenges).

1966 Amendment

The revision of this subdivision brings it into line with the amendment of Rule 24(c) of this Federal Rules of Criminal Procedure. That rule previously allowed four alternate jurors, as contrasted with the two allowed in civil cases, and the amendments increase the number to a maximum of six in all cases. The Advisory Committee's Note to amended Criminal Rule 24(c) points to experience demonstrating that four alter-

nates may not be enough in some lengthy criminal trials; and the same may be said of civil trials. The Note adds:

"The words 'or are found to be' are added to the second sentence to make clear that an alternate juror may be called in the situation where it is first discovered during the trial that a juror was unable or disqualified to perform his duties at the time he was sworn."

1991 Amendment

Subdivision (b). The former provision for alternate jurors is stricken and the institution of the alternate juror abolished.

The former rule reflected the long-standing assumption that a jury would consist of exactly twelve members. It provided for additional jurors to be used as substitutes for jurors who are for any reason excused or disqualified from service after the commencement of the trial. Additional jurors were traditionally designated at the outset of the trial, and excused at the close of the evidence if they had not been promoted to full service on account of the elimination of one of the original jurors.

The use of alternate jurors has been a source of dissatisfaction with the jury system because of the burden it places on alternates who are required to listen to the evidence but denied the satisfaction of participating in its evaluation.

Subdivision (c). This provision makes it clear that the court may in appropriate circumstances excuse a juror during the jury deliberations without causing a mistrial. Sickness, family emergency or juror misconduct that might occasion a mistrial are examples of appropriate grounds for excusing a juror. It is not grounds for the dismissal of a juror that the juror refuses to join with fellow jurors in reaching a unanimous verdict.

2007 Amendment

The language of Rule 47 has been amended as part of the general restyling of the Civil Rules to make them more easily understood and to make style and terminology consistent throughout the rules. These changes are intended to be stylistic only.

CROSS REFERENCES

Challenges of jurors, see 28 USCA § 1870.

Jury trial of right, see Fed.Rules Civ.Proc. Rule 38, 28 USCA.

Manner of drawing trial jurors, see 28 USCA § 1864.

Qualifications of jurors, see 28 USCA § 1861.

Trial jurors, see Fed.Rules Cr.Proc. Rule 24, 18 USCA.

Rule 48.   Number of Jurors; Verdict; Polling

(a) Number of Jurors. A jury must begin with at least 6 and no more than 12 members, and each juror must participate in the verdict unless excused under Rule 47(c).

(b) Verdict. Unless the parties stipulate otherwise, the verdict must be unanimous and must be returned by a jury of at least 6 members.

(c) Polling. After a verdict is returned but before the jury is discharged, the court must on a party's request, or may on its own, poll the jurors individually.

If the poll reveals a lack of unanimity or lack of assent by the number of jurors that the parties stipulated to, the court may direct the jury to deliberate further or may order a new trial.

(Amended April 30, 1991, effective December 1, 1991; April 30, 2007, effective December 1, 2007; March 26, 2009, effective December 1, 2009.)

ADVISORY COMMITTEE NOTES

1937 Adoption

For provisions in state codes, compare Utah Rev.Stat.Ann. (1933) § 48–0–5 (In civil cases parties may agree in open court on lesser number of jurors); 2 Wash.Rev.Stat.Ann. (Remington, 1932) § 323 (Parties may consent to any number of jurors not less than three).

1991 Amendment

The former rule was rendered obsolete by the adoption in many districts of local rules establishing six as the standard size for a civil jury.

It appears that the minimum size of a jury consistent with the Seventh Amendment is six. *Cf. Ballew v. Georgia*, 435 U.S. 223 (1978) (holding that a conviction based on a jury of less than six is a denial of due process of law). If the parties agree to trial before a smaller jury, a verdict can be taken, but the parties should not other than in exceptional circumstances be encouraged to waive the right to a jury of six, not only because of the constitutional stature of the right, but also because smaller juries are more erratic and less effective in serving to distribute responsibility for the exercise of judicial power.

Because the institution of the alternate juror has been abolished by the proposed revision of Rule 47, it will ordinarily be prudent and necessary, in order to provide for sickness or disability among jurors, to seat more than six jurors. The use of jurors in excess of six increases the representativeness of the jury and harms no interest of a party. *Ray v. Parkside Surgery Center*, 13 F.R.Serv. 585 (6th Cir.1989).

If the court takes the precaution of seating a jury larger than six, an illness occurring during the deliberation period will not result in a mistrial, as it did formerly, because all seated jurors will participate in the verdict and a sufficient number will remain to render a unanimous verdict of six or more.

In exceptional circumstances, as where a jury suffers depletions during trial and deliberation that are greater than can reasonably be expected, the parties may agree to be bound by a verdict rendered by fewer than six jurors. The court should not, however, rely upon the availability of such an agreement, for the use of juries smaller than six is problematic for reasons fully explained in *Ballew v. Georgia*, supra.

2007 Amendment

The language of Rule 48 has been amended as part of the general restyling of the Civil Rules to make them more easily understood and to make style and terminology consistent throughout the rules. These changes are intended to be stylistic only.

2009 Amendment

Jury polling is added as new subdivision (c), which is drawn from Criminal Rule 31(d) with minor revisions to reflect Civil Rules Style and the parties' opportunity to stipulate to a nonunanimous verdict.

CROSS REFERENCES

Advisory jury, see Fed.Rules Civ.Proc. Rule 39, 28 USCA.

Jury trial of right, see Fed.Rules Civ.Proc. Rule 38, 28 USCA.

Right to jury trial, see USCA Const. Amend. VII.

Rule 49.   Special Verdict; General Verdict and Questions

(a) Special Verdict.

(1) *In General.* The court may require a jury to return only a special verdict in the form of a special written finding on each issue of fact. The court may do so by:

  (A) submitting written questions susceptible of a categorical or other brief answer;

  (B) submitting written forms of the special findings that might properly be made under the pleadings and evidence; or

  (C) using any other method that the court considers appropriate.

(2) *Instructions.* The court must give the instructions and explanations necessary to enable the jury to make its findings on each submitted issue.

(3) *Issues Not Submitted.* A party waives the right to a jury trial on any issue of fact raised by the pleadings or evidence but not submitted to the jury unless, before the jury retires, the party demands its submission to the jury. If the party does not demand submission, the court may make a finding on the issue. If the court makes no finding, it is considered to have made a finding consistent with its judgment on the special verdict.

(b) General Verdict with Answers to Written Questions.

(1) *In General.* The court may submit to the jury forms for a general verdict, together with written questions on one or more issues of fact that the jury must decide. The court must give the instructions and explanations necessary to enable the jury to render a general verdict and answer the questions in writing, and must direct the jury to do both.

(2) *Verdict and Answers Consistent.* When the general verdict and the answers are consistent, the court must approve, for entry under Rule 58, an appropriate judgment on the verdict and answers.

(3) *Answers Inconsistent with the Verdict.* When the answers are consistent with each other but one or more is inconsistent with the general verdict, the court may:

(A) approve, for entry under Rule 58, an appropriate judgment according to the answers, notwithstanding the general verdict;

(B) direct the jury to further consider its answers and verdict; or

(C) order a new trial.

(4) *Answers Inconsistent with Each Other and the Verdict.* When the answers are inconsistent with each other and one or more is also inconsistent with the general verdict, judgment must not be entered; instead, the court must direct the jury to further consider its answers and verdict, or must order a new trial.

(Amended January 21, 1963, effective July 1, 1963; March 2, 1987, effective August 1, 1987; April 30, 2007, effective December 1, 2007.)

ADVISORY COMMITTEE NOTES

1937 Adoption

The Federal courts are not bound to follow state statutes authorizing or requiring the court to ask a jury to find a special verdict or to answer interrogatories. *Victor American Fuel Co. v. Peccarich,* 209 Fed. 568 (C.C.A.8th, 1913), cert. den. 232 U.S. 727, 34 S.Ct. 603, 58 L.Ed. 817 (1914); *Spokane and I.E.R. Co. v. Campbell,* 217 Fed. 518 (C.C.A.9th, 1914), affd. 241 U.S. 497, 36 S.Ct. 683, 60 L.Ed. 1125 (1916); Simkins, *Federal Practice* (1934) § 186. The power of a territory to adopt by statute the practice under Subdivision (b) has been sustained. *Walker v. New Mexico and Southern Pacific R.R.,* 165 U.S. 593, 17 S.Ct. 421, 41 L.Ed. 837 (1897); *Southwestern Brewery and Ice Co. v. Schmidt,* 226 U.S. 162, 33 S.Ct. 68, 57 L.Ed. 170 (1912).

Compare Wis.Stat. (1935) §§ 270.27, 270.28 and 270.30; Green, *A New Development in Jury Trial* (1927), 13 A.B.A.J. 715; *Morgan, A Brief History of Special Verdicts and Special Interrogatories,* 1923, 32 Yale L.J. 575.

The provisions of U.S.C., Title 28, [former] § 400(3) (now §§ 2201, 2202) (Declaratory judgments authorized; procedure) permitting the submission of issues of fact to a jury are covered by this rule.

1963 Amendment

This amendment conforms to the amendment of Rule 58. See the Advisory Committee's Note to Rule 58, as amended.

1987 Amendment

The amendments are technical. No substantive change is intended.

2007 Amendment

The language of Rule 49 has been amended as part of the general restyling of the Civil Rules to make them more easily understood and to make style and terminology consistent throughout the rules. These changes are intended to be stylistic only.

CROSS REFERENCES

Advisory jury, see Fed.Rules Civ.Proc. Rule 39, 28 USCA.

New trial, see Fed.Rules Civ.Proc. Rule 59, 28 USCA.

Rule 50. Judgment as a Matter of Law in a Jury Trial; Related Motion for a New Trial; Conditional Ruling

(a) Judgment as a Matter of Law.

(1) *In General.* If a party has been fully heard on an issue during a jury trial and the court finds that a reasonable jury would not have a legally sufficient evidentiary basis to find for the party on that issue, the court may:

(A) resolve the issue against the party; and

(B) grant a motion for judgment as a matter of law against the party on a claim or defense that, under the controlling law, can be maintained or defeated only with a favorable finding on that issue.

(2) *Motion.* A motion for judgment as a matter of law may be made at any time before the case is submitted to the jury. The motion must specify the judgment sought and the law and facts that entitle the movant to the judgment.

(b) Renewing the Motion After Trial; Alternative Motion for a New Trial. If the court does not grant a motion for judgment as a matter of law made under Rule 50(a), the court is considered to have submitted the action to the jury subject to the court's later deciding the legal questions raised by the motion. No later than 28 days after the entry of judgment—or if the motion addresses a jury issue not decided by a verdict, no later than 28 days after the jury was discharged—the movant may file a renewed motion for judgment as a matter of law and may include an alternative or joint request for a new trial under Rule 59. In ruling on the renewed motion, the court may:

(1) allow judgment on the verdict, if the jury returned a verdict;

(2) order a new trial; or

(3) direct the entry of judgment as a matter of law.

(c) Granting the Renewed Motion; Conditional Ruling on a Motion for a New Trial.

(1) *In General.* If the court grants a renewed motion for judgment as a matter of law, it must also conditionally rule on any motion for a new trial by determining whether a new trial should be granted if the judgment is later vacated or reversed. The court must state the grounds for conditionally granting or denying the motion for a new trial.

(2) *Effect of a Conditional Ruling.* Conditionally granting the motion for a new trial does not affect the judgment's finality; if the judgment is reversed, the new trial must proceed unless the appellate court orders otherwise. If the motion for a new trial is conditionally denied, the appellee may assert error in that denial; if the judgment is reversed, the case must proceed as the appellate court orders.

(d) Time for a Losing Party's New–Trial Motion. Any motion for a new trial under Rule 59 by a party against whom judgment as a matter of law is rendered must be filed no later than 28 days after the entry of the judgment.

(e) Denying the Motion for Judgment as a Matter of Law; Reversal on Appeal. If the court denies the motion for judgment as a matter of law, the prevailing party may, as appellee, assert grounds entitling it to a new trial should the appellate court conclude that the trial court erred in denying the motion. If the appellate court reverses the judgment, it may order a new trial, direct the trial court to determine whether a new trial should be granted, or direct the entry of judgment. (Amended January 21, 1963, effective July 1, 1963; March 2, 1987, effective August 1, 1987; April 30, 1991, effective December 1, 1991; April 22, 1993, effective December 1, 1993; April 27, 1995, effective December 1, 1995; April 12, 2006, effective December 1, 2006; April 30, 2007, effective December 1, 2007; March 26, 2009, effective December 1, 2009.)

ADVISORY COMMITTEE NOTES
1937 Adoption

Note to Subdivision (a). The present federal rule is changed to the extent that the formality of an express reservation of rights against waiver is no longer necessary. See *Sampliner v. Motion Picture Patents Co.*, 41 S.Ct. 79, 254 U.S. 233, 65 L.Ed. 240 (1920); *Union Indemnity Co. v. United States*, 74 F.2d 645 (C.C.A. 6th, 1935). The requirement that specific grounds for the motion for a directed verdict must be stated settles a conflict in the federal cases. See Simkins, *Federal Practice* (1934) § 189.

Note to Subdivision (b). For comparable state practice upheld under the conformity act, see *Baltimore and Carolina Line v. Redman*, 55 S.Ct. 890, 295 U.S. 654, 79 L.Ed. 1636 (1935); compare *Slocum v. New York Life Ins. Co.*, 33 S.Ct. 523, 228 U.S. 364, 57 L.Ed. 879, Ann.Cas.1914D, 1029 (1913).

See *Northern Ry. Co. v. Page*, 47 S.Ct. 491, 274 U.S. 65, 71 L.Ed. 929 (1927), following the Massachusetts practice of alternative verdicts, explained in Thorndike, *Trial by Jury in United States Courts*, 26 Harv.L.Rev. 732 (1913). See also Thayer, *Judicial Administration*, 63 U. of Pa.L.Rev. 585, 600–601, and note 32 (1915); Scott, *Trial by Jury and the Reform of Civil Procedure*, 31 Harv.L.Rev. 669, 685 (1918); Comment, 34 Mich.L.Rev. 93, 98 (1935).

1963 Amendment

Subdivision (a). The practice, after the court has granted a motion for a directed verdict, of requiring the jury to express assent to a verdict they did not reach by their own deliberations serves no useful purpose and may give offense to the members of the jury. See 2B Barron & Holtzoff, *Federal Practice & Procedure* § 1072, at 367 (Wright ed. 1961); Blume, *Origin and Development of the Directed Verdict*, 48 Mich.L.Rev. 555, 582–85, 589–90 (1950). The final sentence of the subdivision, added by amendment, provides that the court's order granting a motion for a directed verdict is effective in itself, and that no action need be taken by the foreman or other members of the jury. See Ariz.R.Civ.P. 50(c); cf. Fed.R.Crim.P. 29(a). No change is intended in the standard to be applied in deciding the motion. To assure this

interpretation, and in the interest of simplicity, the traditional term, "directed verdict," is retained.

Subdivision (b). A motion for judgment notwithstanding the verdict will not lie unless it was preceded by a motion for a directed verdict made at the close of all the evidence.

The amendment of the second sentence of this subdivision sets the time limit for making the motion for judgment n.o.v. at 10 days after the entry of judgment, rather than 10 days after the reception of the verdict. Thus the time provision is made consistent with that contained in Rule 59(b) (time for motion for new trial) and Rule 52(b) (time for motion to amend findings by the court).

Subdivision (c) deals with the situation where a party joins a motion for a new trial with his motion for judgment n.o.v., or prays for a new trial in the alternative, and the motion for judgment n.o.v. is granted. The procedure to be followed in making rulings on the motion for the new trial, and the consequences of the rulings thereon, were partly set out in *Montgomery Ward & Co. v. Duncan*, 311 U.S. 243, 253, 61 S.Ct. 189, 85 L.Ed. 147 (1940), and have been further elaborated in later cases. See *Cone v. West Virginia Pulp & Paper Co.*, 330 U.S. 212, 67 S.Ct. 752, 91 L.Ed. 849 (1947); *Globe Liquor Co., Inc. v. San Roman*, 332 U.S. 571, 68 S.Ct. 246, 92 L.Ed. 177 (1948); *Fountain v. Filson*, 336 U.S. 681, 69 S.Ct. 754, 93 L.Ed. 971 (1949); *Johnson v. New York, N.H. & H.R.R. Co.*, 344 U.S. 48, 73 S.Ct. 125, 97 L.Ed. 77 (1952). However, courts as well as counsel have often misunderstood the procedure, and it will be helpful to summarize the proper practice in the text of the rule. The amendments do not alter the effects of a jury verdict or the scope of appellate review.

In the situation mentioned, subdivision (c)(1) requires that the court make a "conditional" ruling on the new-trial motion, i.e., a ruling which goes on the assumption that the motion for judgment n.o.v. was erroneously granted and will be reversed or vacated; and the court is required to state its grounds for the conditional ruling. Subdivision (c)(1) then spells out the consequences of a reversal of the judgment in the light of the conditional ruling on the new-trial motion.

If the motion for new trial has been conditionally granted, and the judgment is reversed, "the new trial shall proceed unless the appellate court has otherwise ordered." The party against whom the judgment n.o.v. was entered below may, as appellant, besides seeking to overthrow that judgment, also attack the conditional grant of the new trial. And the appellate court, if it reverses the judgment n.o.v., may in an appropriate case also reverse the conditional grant of the new trial and direct that judgment be entered on the verdict. See *Bailey v. Slentz*, 189 F.2d 406 (10th Cir. 1951); *Moist Cold Refrigerator Co. v. Lou Johnson Co.*, 249 F.2d 246 (9th Cir. 1957), cert. denied, 356 U.S. 968, 78 S.Ct. 1008, 2 L.Ed.2d 1074 (1958); *Peters v. Smith*, 221 F.2d 721 (3d Cir. 1955); *Dailey v. Timmer*, 292 F.2d 824 (3d Cir. 1961), explaining *Lind v. Schenley Industries, Inc.*, 278 F.2d 79 (3d Cir.), cert. denied, 364 U.S. 835, 81 S.Ct. 58, 5 L.Ed.2d 60 (1960); *Cox v. Pennsylvania R.R.*, 120 A.2d 214 (D.C.Mun.Ct.App.1956); 3 Barron & Holtzoff, *Federal Practice & Procedure* § 1302.1 at 346–47 (Wright ed. 1958); 6 *Moore's Federal Practice* ¶59.16 at 3915 n. 8a (2d ed. 1954).

If the motion for a new trial has been conditionally denied, and the judgment is reversed, "subsequent proceedings shall be in accordance with the order of the appellate court." The party in whose favor judgment n.o.v. was entered below may, as appellee, besides seeking to uphold that judgment, also urge on the appellate court that the trial court committed error in conditionally denying the new trial. The appellee may assert this error in his brief, without taking a cross-appeal. Cf. *Patterson v. Pennsylvania R.R.*, 238 F.2d 645, 650 (6th Cir. 1956); *Hughes v. St. Louis Nat. L. Baseball Club, Inc.*, 359 Mo. 993, 997, 224 S.W.2d 989, 992 (1949). If the appellate court concludes that the judgment cannot stand, but accepts the appellee's contention that there was error in the conditional denial of the new trial, it may order a new trial in lieu of directing the entry of judgment upon the verdict.

Subdivision (c)(2), which also deals with the situation where the trial court has granted the motion for judgment n.o.v., states that the verdict-winner may apply to the trial court for a new trial pursuant to Rule 59 after the judgment n.o.v. has been entered against him. In arguing to the trial court in opposition to the motion for judgment n.o.v., the verdict-winner may, and often will, contend that he is entitled, at the least, to a new trial, and the court has a range of discretion to grant a new trial or (where plaintiff won the verdict) to order a dismissal of the action without prejudice instead of granting judgment n.o.v. See *Cone v. West Virginia Pulp & Paper Co.*, supra, 330 U.S. at 217, 218, 67 S.Ct. at 755, 756, 91 L.Ed. 849. Subdivision (c)(2) is a reminder that the verdict-winner is entitled, even after entry of judgment n.o.v. against him, to move for a new trial in the usual course. If in these circumstances the motion is granted, the judgment is superseded.

In some unusual circumstances, however, the grant of the new-trial motion may be only conditional, and the judgment will not be superseded. See the situation in *Tribble v. Bruin*, 279 F.2d 424 (4th Cir. 1960) (upon a verdict for plaintiff, defendant moves for and obtains judgment n.o.v.; plaintiff moves for a new trial on the ground of inadequate damages; trial court might properly have granted plaintiff's motion, conditional upon reversal of the judgment n.o.v.).

Even if the verdict-winner makes no motion for a new trial, he is entitled upon his appeal from the judgment n.o.v. not only to urge that that judgment should be reversed and judgment entered upon the verdict, but that errors were committed during the trial which at the least entitle him to a new trial.

Subdivision (d) deals with the situation where judgment has been entered on the jury verdict, the motion for judgment n.o.v. and any motion for a new trial having been denied by the trial court. The verdict-winner, as appellee, besides seeking to uphold the judgment may urge upon the appellate court that in case the trial court is found to have erred in entering judgment on the verdict, there are grounds for granting him a new trial instead of directing the entry of judgment for his opponent. In appropriate cases the appellate court is not precluded from itself directing that a new trial be had. See *Weade v. Dichmann, Wright & Pugh, Inc.*, 337 U.S. 801, 69 S.Ct. 1326, 93 L.Ed. 1704 (1949). Nor is it precluded in proper cases from remanding the case for a determination by the trial court as to whether a new trial should be granted. The latter course is advisable where the grounds urged are suitable for the exercise of trial court discretion.

Subdivision (d) does not attempt a regulation of all aspects of the procedure where the motion for judgment n.o.v. and any accompanying motion for a new trial are denied, since the problems have not been fully canvassed in the decisions and the procedure is in some respects still in a formative stage. It is, however, designed to give guidance on certain important features of the practice.

1987 Amendment

The amendments are technical. No substantive change is intended.

1991 Amendment

Subdivision (a). The revision of this subdivision aims to facilitate the exercise by the court of its responsibility to assure the fidelity of its judgment to the controlling law, a responsibility imposed by the Due Process Clause of the Fifth Amendment. Cf. *Galloway v. United States*, 319 U.S. 372 (1943).

The revision abandons the familiar terminology of *direction of verdict* for several reasons. The term is misleading as a description of the relationship between judge and jury. It is also freighted with anachronisms some of which are the subject of the text of former subdivision (a) of this rule that is deleted in this revision. Thus, it should not be necessary to state in the text of this rule that a motion made pursuant to it is not a waiver of the right to jury trial, and only the antiquities of directed verdict practice suggest that it might have been. The term "judgment as a matter of law" is an almost equally familiar term and appears in the text of Rule 56; its use in Rule 50 calls attention to the relationship between the two rules. Finally, the change enables the rule to refer to preverdict and post-verdict motions with a terminology that does not conceal the common identity of two motions made at different times in the proceeding.

If a motion is denominated a motion for directed verdict or for judgment notwithstanding the verdict, the party's error is merely formal. Such a motion should be treated as a motion for judgment as a matter of law in accordance with this rule.

Paragraph (a)(1) articulates the standard for the granting of a motion for judgment as a matter of law. It effects no change in the existing standard. That existing standard was not expressed in the former rule, but was articulated in long-standing case law. See generally Cooper, *Directions for Directed Verdicts: A Compass for Federal Courts*, 55 MINN. L.REV. 903 (1971). The expressed standard makes clear that action taken under the rule is a performance of the court's duty to assure enforcement of the controlling law and is not an intrusion on any responsibility for factual determinations conferred on the jury by the Seventh Amendment or any other provision of federal law. Because this standard is also used as a reference point for entry of summary judgment under 56(a), it serves to link the two related provisions.

The revision authorizes the court to perform its duty to enter judgment as a matter of law at any time during the trial, as soon as it is apparent that either party is unable to carry a burden of proof that is essential to that party's case. Thus, the second sentence of paragraph (a)(1) authorizes the court to consider a motion for judgment as a matter of law as soon as a party has completed a presentation on a fact essential to that party's case. Such early action is appropriate when economy and expedition will be served. In no event, however, should the court enter judgment against a party who has not been apprised of the materiality of the dispositive fact and been afforded an opportunity to present any available evidence bearing on that fact. In order further to facilitate the exercise of the authority provided by this rule, Rule 16 is also revised to encourage the court to schedule an order of trial that proceeds first with a presentation on an issue that is likely to be dispositive, if such an issue is identified in the course of pretrial. Such scheduling can be appropriate where the court is uncertain whether favorable action should be taken under Rule 56. Thus, the revision affords the court the alternative of denying a motion for summary judgment while scheduling a separate trial of the issue under Rule 42(b) or scheduling the trial to begin with a presentation on that essential fact which the opposing party seems unlikely to be able to maintain.

Paragraph (a)(2) retains the requirement that a motion for judgment be made prior to the close of the trial, subject to renewal after a jury verdict has been rendered. The purpose of this requirement is to assure the responding party an opportunity to cure any deficiency in that party's proof that may have been overlooked until called to the party's attention by a late motion for judgment. Cf. *Farley Transp. Co. v. Santa Fe Trail Transp. Co.,* 786 F.2d 1342 (9th Cir.1986) ("If the moving party is then permitted to make a later attack on the evidence through a motion for judgment notwithstanding the verdict or an appeal, the opposing party may be prejudiced by having lost the opportunity to present additional evidence before the case was submitted to the jury"); *Benson v. Allphin,* 786 F.2d 268 (7th Cir.1986) ("the motion for directed verdict at the close of all the evidence provides the nonmovant an opportunity to do what he can to remedy the deficiencies in his case . . ."); *McLaughlin v. The Fellows Gear Shaper Co.,* 4 F.R.Serv.3d 607 (3d Cir.1986) (per Adams, J., dissenting: "This Rule serves important practical purposes in ensuring that neither party is precluded from presenting the most persuasive case possible and in preventing unfair surprise after a matter has been submitted to the jury"). At one time, this requirement was held to be of constitutional stature, being compelled by the Seventh Amendment. Cf. *Slocum v. New York Insurance Co.,* 228 U.S. 364 (1913). But cf. *Baltimore & Carolina Line v. Redman,* 295 U.S. 654 (1935).

The second sentence of paragraph (a)(2) does impose a requirement that the moving party articulate the basis on which a judgment as a matter of law might be rendered. The articulation is necessary to achieve the purpose of the requirement that the motion be made before the case is submitted to the jury, so that the responding party may seek to correct any overlooked deficiencies in the proof. The revision thus alters the result in cases in which courts have used various techniques to avoid the requirement that a motion for a directed verdict be made as a predicate to a motion for judgment notwithstanding the verdict. E.g., *Benson v. Allphin,* 788 F.2d 268 (7th Cir.1986) ("this circuit has allowed something less than a formal motion for directed verdict to preserve a party's right to move for judgment notwithstanding the verdict"). *See generally* 9 WRIGHT & MILLER, FEDERAL PRACTICE AND PROCEDURE § 2537 (1971 and Supp.). The information required with the motion may be supplied by explicit reference to materials and argument previously supplied to the court.

This subdivision deals only with the entry of judgment and not with the resolution of particular factual issues as a matter of law. The court may, as before, properly refuse to instruct a jury to decide an issue if a reasonable jury could on the evidence presented decide that issue in only one way.

Subdivision (b). This provision retains the concept of the former rule that the post-verdict motion is a renewal of an earlier motion made at the close of the evidence. One purpose of this concept was to avoid any question arising under the Seventh Amendment. *Montgomery Ward & Co. v. Duncan,* 311 U.S. 243 (1940). It remains useful as a means of

defining the appropriate issue posed by the post-verdict motion. A post-trial motion for judgment can be granted only on grounds advanced in the pre-verdict motion. *E.g., Kutner Buick, Inc. v. American Motors Corp.,* 848 F.2d 614 (3d Cir.1989).

Often it appears to the court or to the moving party that a motion for judgment as a matter of law made at the close of the evidence should be reserved for a post-verdict decision. This is so because a jury verdict for the moving party moots the issue and because a preverdict ruling gambles that a reversal may result in a new trial that might have been avoided. For these reasons, the court may often wisely decline to rule on a motion for judgment as a matter of law made at the close of the evidence, and it is not inappropriate for the moving party to suggest such a postponement of the ruling until after the verdict has been rendered.

In ruling on such a motion, the court should disregard any jury determination for which there is no legally sufficient evidentiary basis enabling a reasonable jury to make it. The court may then decide such issues as a matter of law and enter judgment if all other material issues have been decided by the jury on the basis of legally sufficient evidence, or by the court as a matter of law.

The revised rule is intended for use in this manner with Rule 49. Thus, the court may combine facts established as a matter of law either before trial under Rule 56 or at trial on the basis of the evidence presented with other facts determined by the jury under instructions provided under Rule 49 to support a proper judgment under this rule.

This provision also retains the former requirement that a post-trial motion under the rule must be made within 10 days after entry of a contrary judgment. The renewed motion must be served and filed as provided by Rule 5. A purpose of this requirement is to meet the requirements of F.R.App.P. 4(a)(4).

Subdivision (c). Revision of this subdivision conforms the language to the change in diction set forth in subdivision (a) of this revised rule.

Subdivision (d). Revision of this subdivision conforms the language to that of the previous subdivisions.

1993 Amendment

This technical amendment corrects an ambiguity in the text of the 1991 revision of the rule, which, as indicated in the Notes, was not intended to change the existing standards under which "directed verdicts" could be granted. This amendment makes clear that judgments as a matter of law in jury trials may be entered against both plaintiffs and defendants and with respect to issues or defenses that may not be wholly dispositive of a claim or defense.

1995 Amendment

The only change, other than stylistic, intended by this revision is to prescribe a uniform explicit time for filing of post-judgment motions under this rule—no later than 10 days after entry of the judgment. Previously, there was an inconsistency in the wording of Rules 50, 52, and 59 with respect to whether certain post-judgment motions had to be filed, or merely served, during that period. This inconsistency caused special problems when motions for a new trial were joined with other post-judgment motions. These motions affect the finality of the judgment, a matter often of importance to third persons as well as the parties and the court. The Committee believes that each of these rules should be revised to require filing before end of the 10–day period. Filing is an event that can be determined with certainty from court records. The phrase "no later than" is used—rather than "within"—to include post-judgment motions that sometimes are filed before actual entry of the judgment by the clerk. It should be noted that under Rule 6(a) Saturdays, Sundays, and legal holidays are excluded in measuring the 10–day period, and that under Rule 5 the motions when filed are to contain a certificate of service on other parties.

2006 Amendment

The language of Rule 50(a) has been amended as part of the general restyling of the Civil Rules to make them more easily understood and to make style and terminology consistent throughout the rules. These changes are intended to be stylistic only.

Rule 50(b) is amended to permit renewal of any Rule 50(a) motion for judgment as a matter of law, deleting the requirement that a motion be made at the close of all the evidence. Because the Rule 50(b) motion is only a renewal of the preverdict motion, it can be granted only on grounds advanced in the preverdict motion. The earlier motion informs the opposing party of the challenge to the sufficiency of the evidence and affords a clear opportunity to provide additional evidence that may be available. The earlier motion also alerts the court to the opportunity to simplify the trial by resolving some issues, or even all issues, without submission to the jury. This fulfillment of the functional needs that underlie present Rule 50(b) also satisfies the Seventh Amendment. Automatic reservation of the legal questions raised by the motion conforms to the decision in *Baltimore & Carolina Line v. Redman*, 297 U.S. 654 (1935).

This change responds to many decisions that have begun to move away from requiring a motion for judgment as a matter of law at the literal close of all the evidence. Although the requirement has been clearly established for several decades, lawyers continue to overlook it. The courts are slowly working away from the formal requirement. The amendment establishes the functional approach that courts have been unable to reach under the present rule and makes practice more consistent and predictable.

Many judges expressly invite motions at the close of all the evidence. The amendment is not intended to discourage this useful practice.

Finally, an explicit time limit is added for making a posttrial motion when the trial ends without a verdict or with a verdict that does not dispose of all issues suitable for resolution by verdict. The motion must be made no later than 10 days after the jury was discharged.

2007 Amendment

The language of Rule 50 has been amended as part of the general restyling of the Civil Rules to make them more easily understood and to make style and terminology consistent throughout the rules. These changes are intended to be stylistic only.

Former Rule 50(b) stated that the court reserves ruling on a motion for judgment as a matter of law made at the close of all the evidence "[i]f, for any reason, the court does not grant" the motion. The words "for any reason" reflected the proposition that the reservation is automatic and inescapable. The ruling is reserved even if the court explicitly denies the

motion. The same result follows under the amended rule. If the motion is not granted, the ruling is reserved.

Amended Rule 50(e) identifies the appellate court's authority to direct the entry of judgment. This authority was not described in former Rule 50(d), but was recognized in *Weisgram v. Marley Co.*, 528 U.S. 440 (2000), and in *Neely v. Martin K. Eby Construction Company*, 386 U.S. 317 (1967). When Rule 50(d) was drafted in 1963, the Committee Note stated that "[s]ubdivision (d) does not attempt a regulation of all aspects of the procedure where the motion for judgment n.o.v. and any accompanying motion for a new trial are denied * * *." Express recognition of the authority to direct entry of judgment does not otherwise supersede this caution.

2009 Amendment

Former Rules 50, 52, and 59 adopted 10–day periods for their respective post-judgment motions. Rule 6(b) prohibits any expansion of those periods. Experience has proved that in many cases it is not possible to prepare a satisfactory post-judgment motion in 10 days, even under the former rule that excluded intermediate Saturdays, Sundays, and legal holidays. These time periods are particularly sensitive because Appellate Rule 4 integrates the time to appeal with a timely motion under these rules. Rather than introduce the prospect of uncertainty in appeal time by amending Rule 6(b) to permit additional time, the former 10–day periods are expanded to 28 days. Rule 6(b) continues to prohibit expansion of the 28–day period.

CROSS REFERENCES

Grounds for new trial, see Fed.Rules Civ.Proc. Rule 59, 28 USCA.

Involuntary dismissal at end of plaintiff's case, see Fed. Rules Civ.Proc. Rule 41, 28 USCA.

Motions for directed verdict abolished in criminal cases, see Fed.Rules Cr.Proc. Rule 29, 18 USCA.

Rule 51. Instructions to the Jury; Objections; Preserving a Claim of Error

(a) Requests.

(1) *Before or at the Close of the Evidence.* At the close of the evidence or at any earlier reasonable time that the court orders, a party may file and furnish to every other party written requests for the jury instructions it wants the court to give.

(2) *After the Close of the Evidence.* After the close of the evidence, a party may:

(A) file requests for instructions on issues that could not reasonably have been anticipated by an earlier time that the court set for requests; and

(B) with the court's permission, file untimely requests for instructions on any issue.

(b) Instructions. The court:

(1) must inform the parties of its proposed instructions and proposed action on the requests before instructing the jury and before final jury arguments;

(2) must give the parties an opportunity to object on the record and out of the jury's hearing before the instructions and arguments are delivered; and

(3) may instruct the jury at any time before the jury is discharged.

(c) Objections.

(1) *How to Make.* A party who objects to an instruction or the failure to give an instruction must do so on the record, stating distinctly the matter objected to and the grounds for the objection.

(2) *When to Make.* An objection is timely if:

(A) a party objects at the opportunity provided under Rule 51(b)(2); or

(B) a party was not informed of an instruction or action on a request before that opportunity to object, and the party objects promptly after learning that the instruction or request will be, or has been, given or refused.

(d) Assigning Error; Plain Error.

(1) *Assigning Error.* A party may assign as error:

(A) an error in an instruction actually given, if that party properly objected; or

(B) a failure to give an instruction, if that party properly requested it and—unless the court rejected the request in a definitive ruling on the record—also properly objected.

(2) *Plain Error.* A court may consider a plain error in the instructions that has not been preserved as required by Rule 51(d)(1) if the error affects substantial rights.

(Amended March 2, 1987, effective August 1, 1987; March 27, 2003, effective December 1, 2003; April 30, 2007, effective December 1, 2007.)

ADVISORY COMMITTEE NOTES

1937 Adoption

Supreme Court Rule 8 requires exceptions to the charge of the court to the jury which shall distinctly state the several matters of law in the charge to which exception is taken. Similar provisions appear in the rules of the various Circuit Courts of Appeals.

1987 Amendment

Although Rule 51 in its present form specifies that the court shall instruct the jury only after the arguments of the parties are completed, in some districts (typically those in states where the practice is otherwise) it is common for the parties to stipulate to instruction before the arguments. The purpose of the amendment is to give the court discretion to instruct the jury either before or after argument. Thus, the rule as revised will permit resort to the long-standing federal practice or to an alternative procedure, which has been praised because it gives counsel the opportunity to explain the instructions, argue their application to the facts and thereby give the jury the maximum assistance in determining the issues and arriving at a good verdict on the law and the evidence. As an ancillary benefit, this approach aids counsel

by supplying a natural outline so that arguments may be directed to the essential fact issues which the jury must decide. See generally Raymond, *Merits and Demerits of the Missouri System of Instructing Juries,* 5 St. Louis U.L.J. 317 (1959). Moreover, if the court instructs before an argument, counsel then know the precise words the court has chosen and need not speculate as to the words the court will later use in its instructions. Finally, by instructing ahead of argument the court has the attention of the jurors when they are fresh and can give their full attention to the court's instructions. It is more difficult to hold the attention of jurors after lengthy arguments.

2003 Amendment

Rule 51 is revised to capture many of the interpretations that have emerged in practice. The revisions in text will make uniform the conclusions reached by a majority of decisions on each point. Additions also are made to cover some practices that cannot now be anchored in the text of Rule 51.

Scope. Rule 51 governs instructions to the trial jury on the law that governs the verdict. A variety of other instructions cannot practicably be brought within Rule 51. Among these instructions are preliminary instructions to a venire, and cautionary or limiting instructions delivered in immediate response to events at trial.

Requests. Subdivision (a) governs requests. Apart from the plain error doctrine recognized in subdivision (d)(2), a court is not obliged to instruct the jury on issues raised by the evidence unless a party requests an instruction. The revised rule recognizes the court's authority to direct that requests be submitted before trial.

The close-of-the-evidence deadline may come before trial is completed on all potential issues. Trial may be formally bifurcated or may be sequenced in some less formal manner. The close of the evidence is measured by the occurrence of two events: completion of all intended evidence on an identified phase of the trial and impending submission to the jury with instructions.

The risk in directing a pretrial request deadline is that trial evidence may raise new issues or reshape issues the parties thought they had understood. Courts need not insist on pretrial requests in all cases. Even if the request time is set before trial or early in the trial, subdivision (a)(2)(A) permits requests after the close of the evidence to address issues that could not reasonably have been anticipated at the earlier time for requests set by the court.

Subdivision (a)(2)(B) expressly recognizes the court's discretion to act on an untimely request. The most important consideration in exercising the discretion confirmed by subdivision (a)(2)(B) is the importance of the issue to the case—the closer the issue lies to the "plain error" that would be recognized under subdivision (d)(2), the better the reason to give an instruction. The cogency of the reason for failing to make a timely request also should be considered. To be considered under subdivision (a)(2)(B) a request should be made before final instructions and before final jury arguments. What is a "final" instruction and argument depends on the sequence of submitting the case to the jury. If separate portions of the case are submitted to the jury in sequence, the final arguments and final instructions are those made on submitting to the jury the portion of the case addressed by the arguments and instructions.

Instructions. Subdivision (b)(1) requires the court to inform the parties, before instructing the jury and before final jury arguments related to the instruction, of the proposed instructions as well as the proposed action on instruction requests. The time limit is addressed to final jury arguments to reflect the practice that allows interim arguments during trial in complex cases; it may not be feasible to develop final instructions before such interim arguments. It is enough that counsel know of the intended instructions before making final arguments addressed to the issue. If the trial is sequenced or bifurcated, the final arguments addressed to an issue may occur before the close of the entire trial.

Subdivision (b)(2) complements subdivision (b)(1) by carrying forward the opportunity to object established by present Rule 51. It makes explicit the opportunity to object on the record, ensuring a clear memorial of the objection.

Subdivision (b)(3) reflects common practice by authorizing instructions at any time after trial begins and before the jury is discharged.

Objections. Subdivision (c) states the right to object to an instruction or the failure to give an instruction. It carries forward the formula of present Rule 51 requiring that the objection state distinctly the matter objected to and the grounds of the objection, and makes explicit the requirement that the objection be made on the record. The provisions on the time to object make clear that it is timely to object promptly after learning of an instruction or action on a request when the court has not provided advance information as required by subdivision (b)(1). The need to repeat a request by way of objection is continued by new subdivision (d)(1)(B) except where the court made a definitive ruling on the record.

Preserving a claim of error and plain error. Many cases hold that a proper request for a jury instruction is not alone enough to preserve the right to appeal failure to give the instruction. The request must be renewed by objection. This doctrine is appropriate when the court may not have sufficiently focused on the request, or may believe that the request has been granted in substance although in different words. But this doctrine may also prove a trap for the unwary who fail to add an objection after the court has made it clear that the request has been considered and rejected on the merits. Subdivision (d)(1)(B) establishes authority to review the failure to grant a timely request, despite a failure to add an objection, when the court has made a definitive ruling on the record rejecting the request.

Many circuits have recognized that an error not preserved under Rule 51 may be reviewed in exceptional circumstances. The language adopted to capture these decisions in subdivision (d)(2) is borrowed from Criminal Rule 52. Although the language is the same, the context of civil litigation often differs from the context of criminal prosecution; actual application of the plain-error standard takes account of the differences. The Supreme Court has summarized application of Criminal Rule 52 as involving four elements: (1) there must be an error; (2) the error must be plain; (3) the error must affect substantial rights; and (4) the error must seriously affect the fairness, integrity, or public reputation of judicial proceedings. Johnson v. U.S., 520 U.S. 461, 466–467, 469–470 (1997). (The Johnson case quoted the fourth element from its decision in a civil action, U.S. v. Atkinson, 297 U.S. 157, 160 (1936): "In exceptional circumstances, especially in criminal cases, appellate courts, in the public interest, may, of their own motion, notice errors to which no exception has been taken, if the errors are obvious, or if they otherwise substantially affect the fairness, integrity, or public reputation of judicial proceedings.")

The court's duty to give correct jury instructions in a civil action is shaped by at least four factors.

The factor most directly implied by a "plain" error rule is the obviousness of the mistake. The importance of the error is a second major factor. The costs of correcting an error reflect a third factor that is affected by a variety of circumstances. In a case that seems close to the fundamental error line, account also may be taken of the impact a verdict may have on nonparties.

2007 Amendment

The language of Rule 51 has been amended as part of the general restyling of the Civil Rules to make them more easily understood and to make style and terminology consistent throughout the rules. These changes are intended to be stylistic only.

CROSS REFERENCES

Formal exceptions unnecessary, see Fed.Rules Civ.Proc. Rule 46, 28 USCA.

Motion for directed verdict, see Fed.Rules Civ.Proc. Rule 50, 28 USCA.

Rule 52. Findings and Conclusions by the Court; Judgment on Partial Findings

(a) Findings and Conclusions.

(1) *In General.* In an action tried on the facts without a jury or with an advisory jury, the court must find the facts specially and state its conclusions of law separately. The findings and conclusions may be stated on the record after the close of the evidence or may appear in an opinion or a memorandum of decision filed by the court. Judgment must be entered under Rule 58.

(2) *For an Interlocutory Injunction.* In granting or refusing an interlocutory injunction, the court must similarly state the findings and conclusions that support its action.

(3) *For a Motion.* The court is not required to state findings or conclusions when ruling on a motion under Rule 12 or 56 or, unless these rules provide otherwise, on any other motion.

(4) *Effect of a Master's Findings.* A master's findings, to the extent adopted by the court, must be considered the court's findings.

(5) *Questioning the Evidentiary Support.* A party may later question the sufficiency of the evidence supporting the findings, whether or not the party requested findings, objected to them, moved to amend them, or moved for partial findings.

(6) *Setting Aside the Findings.* Findings of fact, whether based on oral or other evidence, must not be set aside unless clearly erroneous, and the reviewing court must give due regard to the trial

court's opportunity to judge the witnesses' credibility.

(b) Amended or Additional Findings. On a party's motion filed no later than 28 days after the entry of judgment, the court may amend its findings—or make additional findings—and may amend the judgment accordingly. The motion may accompany a motion for a new trial under Rule 59.

(c) Judgment on Partial Findings. If a party has been fully heard on an issue during a nonjury trial and the court finds against the party on that issue, the court may enter judgment against the party on a claim or defense that, under the controlling law, can be maintained or defeated only with a favorable finding on that issue. The court may, however, decline to render any judgment until the close of the evidence. A judgment on partial findings must be supported by findings of fact and conclusions of law as required by Rule 52(a).

(Amended December 27, 1946, effective March 19, 1948; January 21, 1963, effective July 1, 1963; April 28, 1983, effective August 1, 1983; April 29, 1985, effective August 1, 1985; April 30, 1991, effective December 1, 1991; April 22, 1993, effective December 1, 1993; April 27, 1995, effective December 1, 1995; April 30, 2007, effective December 1, 2007; March 26, 2009, effective December 1, 2009.)

ADVISORY COMMITTEE NOTES

1937 Adoption

See [former] Equity Rule 70½, as amended Nov. 25, 1935, (Findings of Fact and Conclusions of Law) and U.S.C., Title 28, [former] § 764 (Opinion, findings, and conclusions in action against United States) which are substantially continued in this rule. The provisions of U.S.C., Title 28, [former] §§ 773 (Trial of issues of fact; by court) and [former] 875 (Review in cases tried without a jury) are superseded in so far as they provide a different method of finding facts and a different method of appellate review. The rule stated in the third sentence of Subdivision (a) accords with the decisions on the scope of the review in modern federal equity practice. It is applicable to all classes of findings in cases tried without a jury whether the finding is of a fact concerning which there was conflict of testimony, or of a fact deduced or inferred from uncontradicted testimony. See *Silver King Coalition Mines Co. v. Silver King Consolidated Mining Co.*, C.C.A.8, 1913, 204 F. 166, certiorari denied 33 S.Ct. 1051, 229 U.S. 624, 57 L.Ed. 1356; *Warren v. Keep*, 1894, 15 S.Ct. 83, 155 U.S. 265, 39 L.Ed. 144; *Furrer v. Ferris*, 1892, 12 S.Ct. 821, 145 U.S. 132, 36 L.Ed. 649; *Tilghman v. Proctor*, 1888, 8 S.Ct. 894, 125 U.S. 136, 149, 31 L.Ed. 664; *Kimberly v. Arms*, 1889, 9 S.Ct. 355, 129 U.S. 512, 524, 32 L.Ed. 764. Compare *Kaeser & Blair Inc. v. Merchants' Ass'n*, C.C.A.6, 1933, 64 F.2d 575, 576; *Dunn v. Trefry*, C.C.A.1, 1919, 260 F. 147.

In the following states findings of fact are required in all cases tried without a jury (waiver by the parties being permitted as indicated at the end of the listing): Arkansas, Civ.Code (Crawford, 1934) § 364; California, Code Civ.Proc. (Deering, 1937) §§ 632, 634; Colorado, 1 Stat.Ann. (1935) Code Civ.Proc. §§ 232, 291 (in actions before referees or for possession of and damages to land); Connecticut, Gen.Stats. §§ 5660, 5664; Idaho, 1 Code Ann. (1932) §§ 7–302 through

7–305; Massachusetts (equity cases), 2 Gen.Laws (Ter.Ed., 1932) ch. 214, § 23; Minnesota, 2 Stat. (Mason, 1927) § 9311; Nevada, 4 Comp.Laws (Hillyer, 1929) §§ 8783–8784; New Jersey, Sup.Ct.Rule 113, 2 N.J.Misc. 1197, 1239 (1924); New Mexico, Stat.Ann. (Courtright, 1929) §§ 105–813; North Carolina, Code (1935) § 569; North Dakota, 2 Comp.Laws Ann. (1913) § 7641; Oregon, 2 Code Ann. (1930) §§ 2–502; South Carolina, Code (Michie, 1932) § 649; South Dakota, 1 Comp. Laws (1929) §§ 2525–2526; Utah, Rev.Stat.Ann. (1933) §§ 104–26–2, 104–26–3; Vermont (where jury trial waived), Pub.Laws (1933) § 2069; Washington, 2 Rev.Stat.Ann. (Remington, 1932) § 367; Wisconsin, Stat. (1935) § 270.33. The parties may waive this requirement for findings in California, Idaho, North Dakota, Nevada, New Mexico, Utah, and South Dakota.

In the following states the review of findings of fact in all non-jury cases, including jury waived cases, is assimilated to the equity review: Alabama, Code Ann. (Michie, 1928) §§ 9498, 8599; California, Code Civ.Proc. (Derring, 1937) § 956a; but see 20 Calif.Law Rev. 171 (1932); Colorado, *Johnson v. Kountze*, 1895, 43 P. 445, 21 Colo. 486, semble; Illinois, *Baker v. Hinricks*, 1934, 194 N.E. 284, 359 Ill. 138; *Weininger v. Metropolitan Fire Ins. Co.*, 1935, 195 N.E. 420, 359 Ill. 584, 98 A.L.R. 169; Minnesota, *State Bank of Gibbon v. Walter*, 1926, 208 N.W. 423, 167 Minn. 37; *Waldron v. Page*, 1934, 253 N.W. 894, 191 Minn. 302; New Jersey N.J.S.A. 2:27–241, 2:27–363, as interpreted in *Bussy v. Hatch*, 1920, 111 A. 546, 95 N.J.L. 56; New York, *York Mortgage Corporation v. Clotar Const. Corp.*, 1930, 172 N.E. 265, 254 N.Y. 128; North Dakota, Comp.Laws Ann. (1913) § 7846, as amended by N.D.Laws 1933, c. 208; *Milnor Holding Co. v. Holt*, 1933, 248 N.W. 315, 63 N.D. 362, 370; Oklahoma, *Wichita Mining and Improvement Co. v. Hale*, 1908, 94 P. 530, 20 Okl. 159; South Dakota, *Randall v. Burk Township*, 4 S.D. 337, 57 N.W. 4 (1893); Texas, *Custard v. Flowers*, 1929, 14 S.W.2d 109; Utah, Rev.Stat.Ann. (1933) § 104–41–5; Vermont, *Roberge v. Troy*, 1933, 163 A. 770, 105 Vt. 134; Washington, 2 Rev.Stat.Ann. (Remington, 1932) §§ 309–316; *McCullough v. Puget Sound Realty Associates*, 1913, 136 Pac. 1146, 76 Wash. 700, but see *Cornwall v. Anderson*, 1915, 148 P. 1, 85 Wash. 369; West Virginia, *Kinsey v. Carr*, 1906, 55 S.E. 1004, 60 W.Va. 449, semble; Wisconsin, Stat. (1935) § 251.09; *Campbell v. Sutliff*, 1927, 214 N.W. 374, 193 Wis. 370; *Gessler v. Erwin Co.*, 1924, 193 N.W. 303, 182 Wis. 315.

For examples of an assimilation of the review of findings of fact in cases tried without a jury to the review at law as made in several states, see Clark and Stone, *Review of Findings of Fact*, 4 U. of Chi.L.Rev. 190, 215 (1937).

1946 Amendment

Note to Subdivision (a). The amended rule makes clear that the requirement for findings of fact and conclusions of law thereon applies in a case with an advisory jury. This removes an ambiguity in the rule as originally stated, but carries into effect what has been considered its intent. 3 *Moore's Federal Practice*, 1938, 3119. *Hurwitz v. Hurwitz*, 1943, 136 F.2d 796, 78 U.S.App.D.C. 66.

The two sentences added at the end of Rule 52(a) eliminate certain difficulties which have arisen concerning findings and conclusions. The first of the two sentences permits findings of fact and conclusions of law to appear in an opinion or memorandum of decision. See, e.g., *United States v. One 1941 Ford Sedan*, S.D.Tex.1946, 65 F.Supp. 84. Under original Rule 52(a) some courts have expressed the view that findings and conclusions could not be incorporated in an opinion. *Detective Comics, Inc. v. Bruns Publications,* S.D.N.Y.1939, 28 F.Supp. 399; *Pennsylvania Co. for Insurance on Lives & Granting Annuities v. Cincinnati & L.E.R. Co.,* S.D.Ohio 1941, 43 F.Supp. 5; *United States v. Aluminum Co. of America,* S.D.N.Y.1941, 2 F.R.D. 224, 5 Fed. Rules Serv. 52a.11, Case 3; see also s.c., 44 F.Supp. 97. But, to the contrary, see *Wellman v. United States,* D.Mass.1938, 25 F.Supp. 868; *Cook v. United States,* D.Mass.1939, 26 F.Supp. 253; *Proctor v. White,* D.Mass.1939, 28 F.Supp. 161; *Green Valley Creamery, Inc. v. United States,* C.C.A.1, 1939, 108 F.2d 342. See also *Matton Oil Transfer Corp. v. The Dynamic,* C.C.A.2, 1941, 123 F.2d 999; *Carter Coal Co. v. Litz,* C.C.A.4, 1944, 140 F.2d 934; *Woodruff v. Heiser,* C.C.A.10, 1945, 150 F.2d 869; *Coca Cola Co. v. Busch,* Pa.1943, 7 Fed. Rules Serv. 59b.2, Case 4; Oglebay, *Some Developments in Bankruptcy Law,* 1944, 18 J. of Nat'l Ass'n of Ref. 68, 69. Findings of fact aid in the process of judgment and in defining for future cases the precise limitations of the issues and the determination thereon. Thus they not only aid the appellate court on review, *Hurwitz v. Hurwitz,* App.D.C.1943, 136 F.2d 796, 78 U.S.App.D.C. 66, but they are an important factor in the proper application of the doctrines of res judicata and estoppel by judgment. Nordbye, *Improvements in Statement of Findings of Fact and Conclusions of Law,* 1 F.R.D. 25, 26–27; *United States v. Forness,* C.C.A.2, 1942, 125 F.2d 928, certiorari denied 1942, 62 S.Ct. 1293, 316 U.S. 694, 86 L.Ed. 1764. These findings should represent the judge's own determination and not the long, often argumentative statements of successful counsel. *United States v. Forness,* supra; *United States v. Crescent Amusement Co.,* 1944, 1945, 65 S.Ct. 254, 323 U.S. 173, 89 L.Ed. 160. Consequently, they should be a part of the judge's opinion and decision, either stated therein or stated separately. *Matton Oil Transfer Corp. v. The Dynamic,* supra. But the judge need only make brief, definite, pertinent findings and conclusions upon the contested matters; there is no necessity for over-elaboration of detail or particularization of facts. *United States v. Forness,* supra; *United States v. Crescent Amusement Co.,* supra. See also *Petterson Lighterage & Towing Corp. v. New York Central R. Co.,* C.C.A.2, 1942, 126 F.2d 992; *Brown Paper Mill Co., Inc. v. Irwin,* C.C.A.8, 1943, 134 F.2d 337; *Allen Bradley Co. v. Local Union No. 3, I.B.E.W.,* C.C.A.2, 1944, 145 F.2d 215, reversed on other grounds 65 S.Ct. 1533, 325 U.S. 797; *Young v. Murphy,* Ohio 1946, 9 Fed.Rules Serv. 52a.11, Case 2.

The last sentence of Rule 52(a) as amended will remove any doubt that findings and conclusions are unnecessary upon decision of a motion, particularly one under Rule 12 or Rule 56, except as provided in amended Rule 41(b). As so holding, see *Thomas v. Peyser,* App.D.C.1941, 118 F.2d 369; *Schad v. Twentieth Century-Fox Corp.,* C.C.A.3, 1943, 136 F.2d 991; *Prudential Ins. Co. of America v. Goldstein,* N.Y.1942, 43 F.Supp. 767; *Somers Coal Co. v. United States,* N.D.Ohio 1942, 2 F.R.D. 532, 6 Fed.Rules Serv. 52a.1, Case 1; *Pen-Ken Oil & Gas Corp. v. Warfield Natural Gas Co.,* E.D.Ky.1942, 2 F.R.D. 355, 5 Fed. Rules Serv. 52a.1, Case 3; also Commentary, *Necessity of Findings of Fact,* 1941, 4 Fed. Rules Serv. 936.

1963 Amendment

This amendment conforms to the amendment of Rule 58. See the Advisory Committee's Note to Rule 58, as amended.

1983 Amendment

Rule 52(a) has been amended to revise its penultimate sentence to provide explicitly that the district judge may make the findings of fact and conclusions of law required in nonjury cases orally. Nothing in the prior text of the rule forbids this practice, which is widely utilized by district judges. See Christensen, *A Modest Proposal for Immeasurable Improvement,* 64 A.B.A.J. 693 (1978). The objective is to lighten the burden on the trial court in preparing findings in nonjury cases. In addition, the amendment should reduce the number of published district court opinions that embrace written findings.

1985 Amendment

Rule 52(a) has been amended (1) to avoid continued confusion and conflicts among the circuits as to the standard of appellate review of findings of fact by the court, (2) to eliminate the disparity between the standard of review as literally stated in Rule 52(a) and the practice of some courts of appeals, and (3) to promote nationwide uniformity. See Note, *Rule 52(a): Appellate Review of Findings of Fact Based on Documentary or Undisputed Evidence,* 49 Va. L.Rev. 506, 536 (1963).

Some courts of appeal have stated that when a trial court's findings do not rest on demeanor evidence and evaluation of a witness' credibility, there is no reason to defer to the trial court's findings and the appellate court more readily can find them to be clearly erroneous. See, e.g., *Marcum v. United States,* 621 F.2d 142, 144–45 (5th Cir.1980). Others go further, holding that appellate review may be had without application of the "clearly erroneous" test since the appellate court is in as good a position as the trial court to review a purely documentary record. See, *e.g., Atari, Inc. v. North American Philips Consumer Electronics Corp.,* 672 F.2d 607, 614 (7th Cir.), cert. denied, 459 U.S. 880 (1982); *Lydle v. United States,* 635 F.2d 763, 765 n. 1 (6th Cir.1981); *Swanson v. Baker Indus., Inc.,* 615 F.2d 479, 483 (8th Cir.1980); *Taylor v. Lombard,* 606 F.2d 371, 372 (2d Cir.1979), cert. denied, 445 U.S. 946 (1980); *Jack Kahn Music Co. v. Baldwin Piano & Organ Co.,* 604 F.2d 755, 758 (2d Cir.1979); *John R. Thompson Co. v. United States,* 477 F.2d 164, 167 (7th Cir.1973).

A third group has adopted the view that the "clearly erroneous" rule applies in all nonjury cases even when findings are based solely on documentary evidence or on inferences from undisputed facts. See, *e.g., Maxwell v. Sumner,* 673 F.2d 1031, 1036 (9th Cir.), *cert. denied,* 459 U.S. 976 (1982); *United States v. Texas Education Agency,* 647 F.2d 504, 506–07 (5th Cir.1981), *cert. denied,* 454 U.S. 1143 (1982); *Constructora Maza, Inc. v. Banco de Ponce,* 616 F.2d 573, 576 (1st Cir.1980); *In re Sierra Trading Corp.,* 482 F.2d 333, 337 (10th Cir.1973); *Case v. Morrisette,* 475 F.2d 1300, 1306–07 (D.C.Cir.1973).

The commentators also disagree as to the proper interpretation of the Rule. *Compare* Wright, *The Doubtful Omniscience of Appellate Courts,* 41 Minn.L.Rev. 751, 769–70 (1957) (language and intent of Rule support view that "clearly erroneous" test should apply to all forms of evidence), *and* 9 C. Wright & A. Miller, *Federal Practice and Procedure: Civil § 2587,* at 740 (1971) (language of the Rule is clear), *with* 5A J. Moore, *Federal Practice* ¶ 52.04, 2687–88 (2d ed. 1982) (Rule as written supports broader review of findings based on non-demeanor testimony).

The Supreme Court has not clearly resolved the issue. See, *Bose Corp. v. Consumers Union of United States, Inc.,* 466 U.S. 485, 104 S.Ct. 1949, 1958 (1984); *Pullman Standard v. Swint,* 456 U.S. 273, 293 (1982); *United States v. General Motors Corp.,* 384 U.S. 127, 141 n. 16 (1966); *United States v. United States Gypsum Co.,* 333 U.S. 364, 394–96 (1948).

The principal argument advanced in favor of a more searching appellate review of findings by the district court based solely on documentary evidence is that the rationale of Rule 52(a) does not apply when the findings do not rest on the trial court's assessment of credibility of the witnesses but on an evaluation of documentary proof and the drawing of inferences from it, thus eliminating the need for any special deference to the trial court's findings. These considerations are outweighed by the public interest in the stability and judicial economy that would be promoted by recognizing that the trial court, not the appellate tribunal, should be the finder of the facts. To permit courts of appeals to share more actively in the fact-finding function would tend to undermine the legitimacy of the district courts in the eyes of litigants, multiply appeals by encouraging appellate retrial of some factual issues, and needlessly reallocate judicial authority.

1991 Amendment

Subdivision (c) is added. It parallels the revised Rule 50(a), but is applicable to non-jury trials. It authorizes the court to enter judgment at any time that it can appropriately make a dispositive finding of fact on the evidence.

The new subdivision replaces part of Rule 41(b), which formerly authorized a dismissal at the close of the plaintiff's case if the plaintiff had failed to carry an essential burden of proof. Accordingly, the reference to Rule 41 formerly made in subdivision (a) of this rule is deleted.

As under the former Rule 41(b), the court retains discretion to enter no judgment prior to the close of the evidence.

Judgment entered under this rule differs from a summary judgment under Rule 56 in the nature of the evaluation made by the court. A judgment on partial findings is made after the court has heard all the evidence bearing on the crucial issue of fact, and the finding is reversible only if the appellate court finds it to be "clearly erroneous." A summary judgment, in contrast, is made on the basis of facts established on account of the absence of contrary evidence or presumptions; such establishments of fact are rulings on questions of law as provided in Rule 56(a) and are not shielded by the "clear error" standard of review.

1993 Amendment

This technical amendment corrects an ambiguity in the text of the 1991 revision of the rule, similar to the revision being made to Rule 50. This amendment makes clear that judgments as a matter of law in nonjury trials may be entered against both plaintiffs and defendants and with respect to issues or defenses that may not be wholly dispositive of a claim or defense.

1995 Amendment

The only change, other than stylistic, intended by this revision is to require that any motion to amend or add findings after a nonjury trial must be filed no later than 10 days after entry of the judgment. Previously, there was an inconsistency in the wording of Rules 50, 52, and 59 with respect to whether certain post-judgment motions had to be filed, or merely served, during that period. This inconsistency caused special problems when motions for a new trial were joined with other post-judgment motions. These motions affect the finality of the judgment, a matter often of importance to third persons as well as the parties and the court. The Committee believes that each of these rules should be revised to require filing before end of the 10-day period. Filing is an event that can be determined with certainty from court records. The phrase "no later than" is used—rather than "within"—to include post-judgment motions that sometimes are filed before actual entry of the judgment by the clerk. It should be noted that under Rule 6(a) Saturdays, Sundays, and legal holidays are excluded in measuring the 10-day period, and that under Rule 5 the motions when filed are to contain a certificate of service on other parties.

2007 Amendment

The language of Rule 52 has been amended as part of the general restyling of the Civil Rules to make them more easily understood and to make style and terminology consistent throughout the rules. These changes are intended to be stylistic only.

Former Rule 52(a) said that findings are unnecessary on decisions of motions "except as provided in subdivision (c) of this rule." Amended Rule 52(a)(3) says that findings are unnecessary "unless these rules provide otherwise." This change reflects provisions in other rules that require Rule 52 findings on deciding motions. Rules 23(e), 23(h), and 54(d)(2)(C) are examples.

Amended Rule 52(a)(5) includes provisions that appeared in former Rule 52(a) and 52(b). Rule 52(a) provided that requests for findings are not necessary for purposes of review. It applied both in an action tried to a court without a jury and also in granting or refusing an interlocutory injunction. Rule 52(b), applicable to findings "made in actions tried without a jury," provided that the sufficiency of the evidence might be "later questioned whether or not in the district court the party raising the question objected to the findings, moved to amend them, or moved for partial findings." Former Rule 52(b) did not explicitly apply to decisions granting or refusing an interlocutory injunction. Amended Rule 52(a)(5) makes explicit the application of this part of former Rule 52(b) to interlocutory injunction decisions.

Former Rule 52(c) provided for judgment on partial findings, and referred to it as "judgment as a matter of law." Amended Rule 52(c) refers only to "judgment," to avoid any confusion with a Rule 50 judgment as a matter of law in a jury case. The standards that govern judgment as a matter of law in a jury case have no bearing on a decision under Rule 52(c).

2009 Amendment

Former Rules 50, 52, and 59 adopted 10-day periods for their respective post-judgment motions. Rule 6(b) prohibits any expansion of those periods. Experience has proved that in many cases it is not possible to prepare a satisfactory post-judgment motion in 10 days, even under the former rule that excluded intermediate Saturdays, Sundays, and legal holidays. These time periods are particularly sensitive because Appellate Rule 4 integrates the time to appeal with a timely motion under these rules. Rather than introduce the prospect of uncertainty in appeal time by amending Rule 6(b) to permit additional time, the former 10-day periods are expanded to 28 days. Rule 6(b) continues to prohibit expansion of the 28–day period.

CROSS REFERENCES

Advisory jury, see Fed.Rules Civ.Proc. Rule 39, 28 USCA.

Extension of time to apply for amendment of findings, limitation on, see Fed.Rules Civ.Proc. Rule 6, 28 USCA.

Master's report, inclusion of findings of fact and conclusions of law, see Fed.Rules Civ.Proc. Rule 53, 28 USCA.

Motion for additional findings, termination of running of time for appeal to court of appeals, see Federal Rules of Appellate Procedure Rule 4, 28 USCA.

Motion for new trial, amendment of findings on, see Fed. Rules Civ.Proc. Rule 59, 28 USCA.

Record on appeal to include findings, see Federal Rules of Appellate Procedure Rule 10, 28 USCA.

Special verdicts, making of findings on, see Fed.Rules Civ.Proc. Rule 49, 28 USCA.

Stay of proceedings to enforce judgment pending disposition of motion to amend, see Fed.Rules Civ.Proc. Rule 62, 28 USCA.

Rule 53. Masters

(a) Appointment.

(1) *Scope.* Unless a statute provides otherwise, a court may appoint a master only to:

(A) perform duties consented to by the parties;

(B) hold trial proceedings and make or recommend findings of fact on issues to be decided without a jury if appointment is warranted by:

(i) some exceptional condition; or

(ii) the need to perform an accounting or resolve a difficult computation of damages; or

(C) address pretrial and posttrial matters that cannot be effectively and timely addressed by an available district judge or magistrate judge of the district.

(2) *Disqualification.* A master must not have a relationship to the parties, attorneys, action, or court that would require disqualification of a judge under 28 U.S.C. § 455, unless the parties, with the court's approval, consent to the appointment after the master discloses any potential grounds for disqualification.

(3) *Possible Expense or Delay.* In appointing a master, the court must consider the fairness of imposing the likely expenses on the parties and must protect against unreasonable expense or delay.

(b) Order Appointing a Master.

(1) *Notice.* Before appointing a master, the court must give the parties notice and an opportunity to be heard. Any party may suggest candidates for appointment.

(2) *Contents.* The appointing order must direct the master to proceed with all reasonable diligence and must state:

(A) the master's duties, including any investigation or enforcement duties, and any limits on the master's authority under Rule 53(c);

(B) the circumstances, if any, in which the master may communicate ex parte with the court or a party;

(C) the nature of the materials to be preserved and filed as the record of the master's activities;

(D) the time limits, method of filing the record, other procedures, and standards for reviewing the master's orders, findings, and recommendations; and

(E) the basis, terms, and procedure for fixing the master's compensation under Rule 53(g).

(3) *Issuing.* The court may issue the order only after:

(A) the master files an affidavit disclosing whether there is any ground for disqualification under 28 U.S.C. § 455; and

(B) if a ground is disclosed, the parties, with the court's approval, waive the disqualification.

(4) *Amending.* The order may be amended at any time after notice to the parties and an opportunity to be heard.

(c) Master's Authority.

(1) *In General.* Unless the appointing order directs otherwise, a master may:

(A) regulate all proceedings;

(B) take all appropriate measures to perform the assigned duties fairly and efficiently; and

(C) if conducting an evidentiary hearing, exercise the appointing court's power to compel, take, and record evidence.

(2) *Sanctions.* The master may by order impose on a party any noncontempt sanction provided by Rule 37 or 45, and may recommend a contempt sanction against a party and sanctions against a nonparty.

(d) Master's Orders.
A master who issues an order must file it and promptly serve a copy on each party. The clerk must enter the order on the docket.

(e) Master's Reports.
A master must report to the court as required by the appointing order. The master must file the report and promptly serve a copy on each party, unless the court orders otherwise.

(f) Action on the Master's Order, Report, or Recommendations.

(1) *Opportunity for a Hearing; Action in General.* In acting on a master's order, report, or recommendations, the court must give the parties notice and an opportunity to be heard; may receive evidence; and may adopt or affirm, modify, wholly or partly reject or reverse, or resubmit to the master with instructions.

(2) *Time to Object or Move to Adopt or Modify.* A party may file objections to—or a motion to adopt

or modify—the master's order, report, or recommendations no later than 21 days after a copy is served, unless the court sets a different time.

(3) Reviewing Factual Findings. The court must decide de novo all objections to findings of fact made or recommended by a master, unless the parties, with the court's approval, stipulate that:

    (A) the findings will be reviewed for clear error; or

    (B) the findings of a master appointed under Rule 53(a)(1)(A) or (C) will be final.

(4) Reviewing Legal Conclusions. The court must decide de novo all objections to conclusions of law made or recommended by a master.

(5) Reviewing Procedural Matters. Unless the appointing order establishes a different standard of review, the court may set aside a master's ruling on a procedural matter only for an abuse of discretion.

(g) Compensation.

(1) Fixing Compensation. Before or after judgment, the court must fix the master's compensation on the basis and terms stated in the appointing order, but the court may set a new basis and terms after giving notice and an opportunity to be heard.

(2) Payment. The compensation must be paid either:

    (A) by a party or parties; or

    (B) from a fund or subject matter of the action within the court's control.

(3) Allocating Payment. The court must allocate payment among the parties after considering the nature and amount of the controversy, the parties' means, and the extent to which any party is more responsible than other parties for the reference to a master. An interim allocation may be amended to reflect a decision on the merits.

(h) Appointing a Magistrate Judge. A magistrate judge is subject to this rule only when the order referring a matter to the magistrate judge states that the reference is made under this rule.

(Amended February 28, 1966, effective July 1, 1966; April 28, 1983, effective August 1, 1983; March 2, 1987, effective August 1, 1987; April 30, 1991, effective December 1, 1991; April 22, 1993, effective December 1, 1993; March 27, 2003, effective December 1, 2003; April 30, 2007, effective December 1, 2007; March 26, 2009, effective December 1, 2009.)

ADVISORY COMMITTEE NOTES

1937 Adoption

Note to Subdivision (a). This is a modification of former Equity Rule 68 (Appointment and Compensation of Masters).

Note to Subdivision (b). This is substantially the first sentence of [former] Equity Rule 59 (Reference to Master—Exceptional, Not Usual) extended to actions formerly legal. See *Ex parte Peterson,* 1920, 40 S.Ct. 543, 253 U.S. 300, 64 L.Ed. 919.

Note to Subdivision (c). This is [former] Equity Rules 62 (Powers of Master) and 65 (Claimants Before Master Examinable by Him) with slight modifications. Compare [former] Equity Rules 49 (Evidence Taken Before Examiners, Etc.) and 51 (Evidence Taken Before Examiners, Etc.).

Note to Subdivision (d). (1) This is substantially a combination of the second sentence of [former] Equity Rule 59 (Reference to Master—Exceptional, Not Usual) and [former] Equity Rule 60 (Proceedings Before Master). Compare [former] Equity Rule 53 (Notice of Taking Testimony Before Examiner, Etc.).

(2) This is substantially [former] Equity Rule 52 (Attendance of Witnesses Before Commissioner, Master, or Examiner).

(3) This is substantially [former] Equity Rule 63 (Form of Accounts Before Master).

Note to Subdivision (e). This contains the substance of [former] Equity Rules 61 (Master's Report—Documents Identified but not Set Forth), 61½ (Master's Report—Presumption as to Correctness—Review), and 66 (Return of Master's Report—Exceptions—Hearing), with modifications as to the form and effect of the report and for inclusion of reports by auditors, referees, and examiners, and references in actions formerly legal. Compare [former] Equity Rules 49 (Evidence Taken Before Examiners, Etc.) and 67 (Costs on Exceptions to Master's Report). See *Camden v. Stuart,* 144 U.S. 104, 12 S.Ct. 585, 36 L.Ed. 363 (1892); *Ex parte Peterson,* 253 U.S. 300, 40 S.Ct. 543, 64 L.Ed. 919 (1920).

1966 Amendment

These changes are designed to preserve the admiralty practice whereby difficult computations are referred to a commissioner or assessor, especially after an interlocutory judgment determining liability. As to separation of issues for trial see Rule 42(b).

1983 Amendment

Subdivision (a). The creation of full-time magistrates, who serve at government expense and have no nonjudicial duties competing for their time, eliminates the need to appoint standing masters. Thus the prior provision in Rule 53(a) authorizing the appointment of standing masters is deleted. Additionally, the definition of "master" in subdivision (a) now eliminates the superseded office of commissioner.

The term "special master" is retained in Rule 53 in order to maintain conformity with 28 U.S.C. § 636(b)(2), authorizing a judge to designate a magistrate "to serve as a special master pursuant to the applicable provisions of this title and the Federal Rules of Civil Procedure for the United States District Courts." Obviously, when a magistrate serves as a special master, the provisions for compensation of masters are inapplicable, and the amendment to subdivision (a) so provides.

Although the existence of magistrates may make the appointment of outside masters unnecessary in many instances, see, e.g., *Gautreaux v. Chicago Housing Authority,* 384 F.Supp. 37 (N.D.Ill.1974), mandamus denied *sub nom., Chicago Housing Authority v. Austin,* 511 F.2d 82 (7th Cir.1975); *Avco Corp. v. American Tel. & Tel. Co.,* 68 F.R.D. 532 (S.D.Ohio 1975), such masters may prove useful when some special expertise is desired or when a magistrate is unavailable for lengthy and detailed supervision of a case.

Subdivision (b). The provisions of 28 U.S.C. § 636(b)(2) not only permit magistrates to serve as masters under Rule 53(b) but also eliminate the exceptional condition requirement of Rule 53(b) when the reference is made with the consent of the parties. The amendment to subdivision (b) brings Rule 53 into harmony with the statute by exempting magistrates, appointed with the consent of the parties, from the general requirement that some exceptional condition requires the reference. It should be noted that subdivision (b) does not address the question, raised in recent decisional law and commentary, as to whether the exceptional condition requirement is applicable when *private masters* who are not magistrates are appointed with the consent of the parties. See Silberman, *Masters and Magistrates Part II: The American Analogue*, 50 N.Y.U.L.Rev. 1297, 1354 (1975).

Subdivision (c). The amendment recognizes the abrogation of Federal Rule 43(c) by the Federal Rules of Evidence.

Subdivision (f). The new subdivision responds to confusion flowing from the dual authority for references of pretrial matters to magistrates. Such references can be made, with or without the consent of the parties, pursuant to Rule 53 or under 28 U.S.C. § 636(b)(1)(A) and (b)(1)(B). There are a number of distinctions between references made under the statute and under the rule. For example, under the statute nondispositive pretrial matters may be referred to a magistrate, without consent, for final determination with reconsideration by the district judge if the magistrate's order is clearly erroneous or contrary to law. Under the rule, however, the appointment of a master, without consent of the parties, to supervise discovery would require some exceptional condition (Rule 53(b)) and would subject the proceedings to the report procedures of Rule 53(e). If an order of reference does not clearly articulate the source of the court's authority the resulting proceedings could be subject to attack on grounds of the magistrate's noncompliance with the provisions of Rule 53. This subdivision therefore establishes a presumption that the limitations of Rule 53 are not applicable unless the reference is specifically made subject to Rule 53.

A magistrate serving as a special master under 28 U.S.C. § 636(b)(2) is governed by the provisions of Rule 53, with the exceptional condition requirement lifted in the case of a consensual reference.

1987 Amendment

The amendments are technical. No substantive change is intended.

1991 Amendment

The purpose of the revision is to expedite proceedings before a master. The former rule required only a filing of the master's report, with the clerk then notifying the parties of the filing. To receive a copy, a party would then be required to secure it from the clerk. By transmitting directly to the parties, the master can save some efforts of counsel. Some local rules have previously required such action by the master.

1993 Amendment

This revision is made to conform the rule to changes made by the Judicial Improvements Act of 1990.

2003 Amendment

Rule 53 is revised extensively to reflect changing practices in using masters. From the beginning in 1938, Rule 53 focused primarily on special masters who perform trial functions. Since then, however, courts have gained experience with masters appointed to perform a variety of pretrial and post-trial functions. See Willging, Hooper, Leary, Miletich, Reagan, & Shapard, *Special Masters' Incidence and Activity* (Federal Judicial Center 2000). This revised Rule 53 recognizes that in appropriate circumstances masters may properly be appointed to perform these functions and regulates such appointments. Rule 53 continues to address trial masters as well, but permits appointment of a trial master in an action to be tried to a jury only if the parties consent. The new rule clarifies the provisions that govern the appointment and function of masters for all purposes. Rule 53(g) also changes the standard of review for findings of fact made or recommended by a master. The core of the original Rule 53 remains, including its prescription that appointment of a master must be the exception and not the rule.

Special masters are appointed in many circumstances outside the Civil Rules. Rule 53 applies only to proceedings that Rule 1 brings within its reach.

Subdivision (a)(1)

District judges bear primary responsibility for the work of their courts. A master should be appointed only in limited circumstances. Subdivision (a)(1) describes three different standards, relating to appointments by consent of the parties, appointments for trial duties, and appointments for pretrial or post-trial duties.

Consent Masters. Subparagraph (a)(1)(A) authorizes appointment of a master with the parties' consent. Party consent does not require that the court make the appointment; the court retains unfettered discretion to refuse appointment.

Trial Masters. Use of masters for the core functions of trial has been progressively limited. These limits are reflected in the provisions of subparagraph (a)(1)(B) that restrict appointments to exercise trial functions. The Supreme Court gave clear direction to this trend in *La Buy v. Howes Leather Co.*, 352 U.S. 249 (1957); earlier roots are sketched in *Los Angeles Brush Mfg. Corp. v. James*, 272 U.S. 701 (1927). As to nonjury trials, this trend has developed through elaboration of the "exceptional condition" requirement in present Rule 53(b). This phrase is retained, and will continue to have the same force as it has developed. Although the provision that a reference "shall be the exception and not the rule" is deleted, its meaning is embraced for this setting by the exceptional condition requirement.

Subparagraph (a)(1)(B)(ii) carries forward the approach of present Rule 53(b), which exempts from the "exceptional condition" requirement "matters of account and of difficult computation of damages." This approach is justified only as to essentially ministerial determinations that require mastery of much detailed information but that do not require extensive determinations of credibility. Evaluations of witness credibility should only be assigned to a trial master when justified by an exceptional condition.

The use of a trial master without party consent is abolished as to matters to be decided by a jury unless a statute provides for this practice.

Abolition of the direct power to appoint a trial master as to issues to be decided by a jury leaves the way free to appoint a trial master with the consent of all parties. A trial master should be appointed in a jury case, with consent of the parties and concurrence of the court, only if the parties waive jury trial with respect to the issues submitted to the master or if the master's findings are to be submitted to the jury as evidence in the manner provided by former Rule 53(e)(3). In no circumstance may a master be appointed to preside at a jury trial.

The central function of a trial master is to preside over an evidentiary hearing on the merits of the claims or defenses in the action. This function distinguishes the trial master from most functions of pretrial and post-trial masters. If any master is to be used for such matters as a preliminary injunction hearing or a determination of complex damages issues, for example, the master should be a trial master. The line, however, is not distinct. A pretrial master might well conduct an evidentiary hearing on a discovery dispute, and a post-trial master might conduct evidentiary hearings on questions of compliance.

Rule 53 has long provided authority to report the evidence without recommendations in nonjury trials. This authority is omitted from Rule 53(a)(1)(B). In some circumstances a master may be appointed under Rule 53(a)(1)(A) or (C) to take evidence and report without recommendations.

For nonjury cases, a master also may be appointed to assist the court in discharging trial duties other than conducting an evidentiary hearing.

Pretrial and Post–Trial Masters. Subparagraph (a)(1)(C) authorizes appointment of a master to address pretrial or post-trial matters. Appointment is limited to matters that cannot be addressed effectively and in a timely fashion by an available district judge or magistrate judge of the district. A master's pretrial or post-trial duties may include matters that could be addressed by a judge, such as reviewing discovery documents for privilege, or duties that might not be suitable for a judge. Some forms of settlement negotiations, investigations, or administration of an organization are familiar examples of duties that a judge might not feel free to undertake.

Magistrate Judges. Particular attention should be paid to the prospect that a magistrate judge may be available for special assignments. United States magistrate judges are authorized by statute to perform many pretrial functions in civil actions. 28 U.S.C. § 636(b)(1). Ordinarily a district judge who delegates these functions should refer them to a magistrate judge acting as magistrate judge.

There is statutory authority to appoint a magistrate judge as special master. 28 U.S.C. § 636(b)(2). In special circumstances, or when expressly authorized by a statute other than § 636(b)(2), it may be appropriate to appoint a magistrate judge as a master when needed to perform functions outside those listed in § 636(b)(1). There is no apparent reason to appoint a magistrate judge to perform as master duties that could be performed in the role of magistrate judge. Party consent is required for trial before a magistrate judge, moreover, and this requirement should not be undercut by resort to Rule 53 unless specifically authorized by statute; see 42 U.S.C. § 2000e–5(f)(5).

Pretrial Masters. The appointment of masters to participate in pretrial proceedings has developed extensively over the last two decades as some district courts have felt the need for additional help in managing complex litigation. This practice is not well regulated by present Rule 53, which focuses on masters as trial participants. Rule 53 is amended to confirm the authority to appoint—and to regulate the use of—pretrial masters.

A pretrial master should be appointed only when the need is clear. Direct judicial performance of judicial functions may be particularly important in cases that involve important public issues or many parties. At the extreme, a broad delegation of pretrial responsibility as well as a delegation of trial responsibilities can run afoul of Article III.

A master also may be appointed to address matters that blur the divide between pretrial and trial functions. The court's responsibility to interpret patent claims as a matter of law, for example, may be greatly assisted by appointing a master who has expert knowledge of the field in which the patent operates. Review of the master's findings will be de novo under Rule 53(g)(4), but the advantages of initial determination by a master may make the process more effective and timely than disposition by the judge acting alone. Determination of foreign law may present comparable difficulties. The decision whether to appoint a master to address such matters is governed by subdivision (a)(1)(C), not the trial-master provisions of subdivision (a)(1)(B).

Post–Trial Masters. Courts have come to rely on masters to assist in framing and enforcing complex decrees. Present Rule 53 does not directly address this practice. Amended Rule 53 authorizes appointment of post-trial masters for these and similar purposes. The constraint of subdivision (a)(1)(C) limits this practice to cases in which the master's duties cannot be performed effectively and in a timely fashion by an available district judge or magistrate judge of the district.

Reliance on a master is appropriate when a complex decree requires complex policing, particularly when a party has proved resistant or intransigent. This practice has been recognized by the Supreme Court, see *Local 28, Sheet Metal Workers' Internat. Assn. v. EEOC*, 478 U.S. 421, 481–482 (1986). The master's role in enforcement may extend to investigation in ways that are quite unlike the traditional role of judicial officers in an adversary system.

Expert Witness Overlap. This rule does not address the difficulties that arise when a single person is appointed to perform overlapping roles as master and as court-appointed expert witness under Evidence Rule 706. Whatever combination of functions is involved, the Rule 53(a)(1)(B) limit that confines trial masters to issues to be decided by the court does not apply to a person who also is appointed as an expert witness under Evidence Rule 706.

Subdivision (a)(2) and (3)

Masters are subject to the Code of Conduct for United States Judges, with exceptions spelled out in the Code. Special care must be taken to ensure that there is no actual or apparent conflict of interest involving a master. The standard of disqualification is established by 28 U.S.C. § 455. The affidavit required by Rule 53(b)(3) provides an important source of information about possible grounds for disqualification, but careful inquiry should be made at the time of making the initial appointment. The disqualification standards established by § 455 are strict. Because a master is not a public judicial officer, it may be appropriate to permit the parties to consent to appointment of a particular person as master in circumstances that would require disqualification of a judge. The judge must be careful to ensure that no party feels any pressure to consent, but with such assurances—and with the judge's own determination that there is no troubling conflict of interests or disquieting appearance of impropriety—consent may justify an otherwise barred appointment.

One potential disqualification issue is peculiar to the master's role. It may happen that a master who is an attorney represents a client whose litigation is assigned to the judge who appointed the attorney as master. Other parties to the litigation may fear that the attorney-master will gain special respect from the judge. A flat prohibition on appearance before the appointing judge during the time of service as master, however, might in some circumstances unduly limit the opportunity to make a desirable appointment. These matters may be regulated to some extent by state rules of professional responsibility. The question of present conflicts, and the possibility of future conflicts, can be considered at the time of appointment. Depending on the circumstances, the judge may consider it appropriate to impose a non-appearance condition on the lawyer-master, and perhaps on the master's firm as well.

Subdivision (b)

The order appointing a pretrial master is vitally important in informing the master and the parties about the nature and extent of the master's duties and authority. Care must be taken to make the order as precise as possible. The parties must be given notice and opportunity to be heard on the question whether a master should be appointed and on the terms of the appointment. To the extent possible, the notice should describe the master's proposed duties, time to complete the duties, standards of review, and compensation. Often it will be useful to engage the parties in the process of identifying the master, inviting nominations, and reviewing potential candidates. Party involvement may be particularly useful if a pretrial master is expected to promote settlement.

The hearing requirement of Rule 53(b)(1) can be satisfied by an opportunity to make written submissions unless the circumstances require live testimony.

Rule 53(b)(2) requires precise designation of the master's duties and authority. Clear identification of any investigating or enforcement duties is particularly important. Clear delineation of topics for any reports or recommendations is also an important part of this process. And it is important to protect against delay by establishing a time schedule for performing the assigned duties. Early designation of the procedure for fixing the master's compensation also may provide useful guidance to the parties.

Ex parte communications between a master and the court present troubling questions. Ordinarily the order should prohibit such communications, assuring that the parties know where authority is lodged at each step of the proceedings. Prohibiting ex parte communications between master and court also can enhance the role of a settlement master by assuring the parties that settlement can be fostered by confidential revelations that will not be shared with the court. Yet there may be circumstances in which the master's role is enhanced by the opportunity for ex parte communications with the court. A master assigned to help coordinate multiple proceedings, for example, may benefit from off-the-record exchanges with the court about logistical matters. The rule does not directly regulate these matters. It requires only that the court exercise its discretion and address the topic in the order of appointment.

Similarly difficult questions surround ex part e communications between a master and the parties. Ex parte communications may be essential in seeking to advance settlement. Ex parte communications also may prove useful in other settings, as with in camera review of documents to resolve privilege questions. In most settings, however, ex parte communica-

tions with the parties should be discouraged or prohibited. The rule requires that the court address the topic in the order of appointment.

Subdivision (b)(2)(C) provides that the appointment order must state the nature of the materials to be preserved and filed as the record of the master's activities, and (b)(2)(D) requires that the order state the method of filing the record. It is not feasible to prescribe the nature of the record without regard to the nature of the master's duties. The records appropriate to discovery duties may be different from those appropriate to encouraging settlement, investigating possible violations of a complex decree, or making recommendations for trial findings. A basic requirement, however, is that the master must make and file a complete record of the evidence considered in making or recommending findings of fact on the basis of evidence. The order of appointment should routinely include this requirement unless the nature of the appointment precludes any prospect that the master will make or recommend evidence-based findings of fact. In some circumstances it may be appropriate for a party to file materials directly with the court as provided by Rule 5(e), but in many circumstances filing with the court may be inappropriate. Confidentiality is important with respect to many materials that may properly be considered by a master. Materials in the record can be transmitted to the court, and filed, in connection with review of a master's order, report, or recommendations under subdivisions (f) and (g). Independently of review proceedings, the court may direct filing of any materials that it wishes to make part of the public record.

The provision in subdivision (b)(2)(D) that the order must state the standards for reviewing the master's orders, findings, or recommendations is a reminder of the provisions of subdivision (g)(3) that recognize stipulations for review less searching than the presumptive requirement of de novo decision by the court. Subdivision (b)(2)(D) does not authorize the court to supersede the limits of subdivision (g)(3).

In setting the procedure for fixing the master's compensation, it is useful at the outset to establish specific guidelines to control total expense. The court has power under subdivision (h) to change the basis and terms for determining compensation after notice to the parties.

Subdivision (b)(3) permits entry of the order appointing a master only after the master has filed an affidavit disclosing whether there is any ground for disqualification under 28 U.S.C. § 455. If the affidavit discloses a possible ground for disqualification, the order can enter only if the court determines that there is no ground for disqualification or if the parties, knowing of the ground for disqualification, consent with the court's approval to waive the disqualification.

The provision in Rule 53(b)(4) for amending the order of appointment is as import ant as the provisions for the initial order. Anything that could be done in the initial order can be done by amendment. The hearing requirement can be satisfied by an opportunity to make written submissions unless the circumstances require live testimony.

Subdivision (c)

Subdivision (c) is a simplification of the provisions scattered throughout present Rule 53. It is intended to provide the broad and flexible authority necessary to discharge the master's responsibilities. The most important delineation of a master's authority and duties is provided by the Rule 53(b) appointing order.

Subdivision (d)

` The subdivision (d) provisions for evidentiary hearings are reduced from the extensive provisions in current Rule 53. This simplification of the rule is not intended to diminish the authority that may be delegated to a master. Reliance is placed on the broad and general terms of subdivision (c).

Subdivision (e)

Subdivision (e) provides that a master's order must be filed and entered on the docket. It must be promptly served on the parties, a task ordinarily accomplished by mailing or other means as permitted by Rule 5(b). In some circumstances it may be appropriate to have the clerk's office assist the master in mailing the order to the parties.

Subdivision (f)

Subdivision (f) restates some of the provisions of present Rule 53(e)(1). The report is the master's primary means of communication with the court. The materials to be provided to support review of the report will depend on the nature of the report. The master should provide all portions of the record preserved under Rule 53(b)(2)(C) that the master deems relevant to the report. The parties may designate additional materials from the record, and may seek permission to supplement the record with evidence. The court may direct that additional materials from the record be provided and filed. Given the wide array of tasks that may be assigned to a pretrial master, there may be circumstances that justify sealing a report or review record against public access—a report on continuing or failed settlement efforts is the most likely example. A post-trial master may be assigned duties in formulating a decree that deserve similar protection. Such circumstances may even justify denying access to the report or review materials by the parties, although this step should be taken only for the most compelling reasons. Sealing is much less likely to be appropriate with respect to a trial master's report.

Before formally making an order, report, or recommendations, a master may find it helpful to circulate a draft to the parties for review and comment. The usefulness of this practice depends on the nature of the master's proposed action.

Subdivision (g)

The provisions of subdivision (g)(1), describing the court's powers to afford a hearing, take evidence, and act on a master's order, report, or recommendations are drawn from present Rule 53(e)(2), but are not limited, as present Rule 53(e)(2) is limited, to the report of a trial master in a nonjury action. The requirement that the court must afford an opportunity to be heard can be satisfied by taking written submissions when the court acts on the report without taking live testimony.

The subdivision (g)(2) time limits for objecting to—or seeking adoption or modification of—a master's order, report, or recommendations, are important. They are not jurisdictional. Although a court may properly refuse to entertain untimely review proceedings, the court may excuse the failure to seek timely review. The basic time period is lengthened to 20 days because the present 10-day period may be too short to permit thorough study and response to a complex report dealing with complex litigation. If no party asks the court to act on a master's report, the court is free to adopt the master's action or to disregard it at any relevant point in the proceedings.

Subdivision (g)(3) establishes the standards of review for a master's findings of fact or recommended findings of fact. The court must decide de novo all objections to findings of fact made or recommended by the master unless the parties stipulate, with the court's consent, that the findings will be reviewed for clear error or—with respect to a master appointed on the parties' consent or appointed to address pretrial or post-trial matters—that the findings will be final. Clear-error review is more likely to be appropriate with respect to findings that do not go to the merits of the underlying claims or defenses, such as findings of fact bearing on a privilege objection to a discovery request. Even if no objection is made, the court is free to decide the facts de novo; to review for clear error if an earlier approved stipulation provided clear-error review; or to withdraw its consent to a stipulation for clear-error review or finality, and then to decide de novo. If the court withdraws its consent to a stipulation for finality or clear-error review, it may reopen the opportunity to object.

Under Rule 53(g)(4), the court must decide de novo all objections to conclusions of law made or recommended by a master. As with findings of fact, the court also may decide conclusions of law de novo when no objection is made.

Apart from factual and legal questions, masters often make determinations that, when made by a trial court, would be treated as matters of procedural discretion. The court may set a standard for review of such matters in the order of appointment, and may amend the order to establish the standard. If no standard is set by the original or amended order appointing the master, review of procedural matters is for abuse of discretion. The subordinate role of the master means that the trial court's review for abuse of discretion may be more searching than the review that an appellate court makes of a trial court.

If a master makes a recommendation on any matter that does not fall within Rule 53(g)(3), (4), or (5), the court may act on the recommendation under Rule 53(g)(1).

Subdivision (h)

The need to pay compensation is a substantial reason for care in appointing private persons as masters.

Payment of the master's fees must be allocated among the parties and any property or subject-matter within the court's control. The amount in controversy and the means of the parties may provide some guidance in making the allocation. The nature of the dispute also may be important—parties pursuing matters of public interest, for example, may deserve special protection. A party whose unreasonable behavior has occasioned the need to appoint a master, on the other hand, may properly be charged all or a major portion of the master's fees. It may be proper to revise an interim allocation after decision on the merits. The revision need not await a decision that is final for purposes of appeal, but may be made to reflect disposition of a substantial portion of the case.

The basis and terms for fixing compensation should be stated in the order of appointment. The court retains power to alter the initial basis and terms, after notice and an opportunity to be heard, but should protect the parties against unfair surprise.

The provision of former Rule 53(a) that the "provision for compensation shall not apply when a United States Magistrate Judge is designated to serve as a master" is deleted as unnecessary. Other provisions of law preclude compensation.

Subdivision (i)

Rule 53(i) carries forward unchanged former Rule 53(f).

2007 Amendment

The language of Rule 53 has been amended as part of the general restyling of the Civil Rules to make them more easily understood and to make style and terminology consistent throughout the rules. These changes are intended to be stylistic only.

2009 Amendment

The time set in the former rule at 20 days has been revised to 21 days. See the Note to Rule 6.

HISTORICAL NOTES

Change of Name

United States magistrate appointed under section 631 of Title 28, Judiciary and Judicial Procedure, to be known as United States magistrate judge after Dec. 1, 1990, with any reference to United States magistrate or magistrate in Title 28, in any other Federal statute, etc., deemed a reference to United States magistrate judge appointed under section 631 of Title 28, see section 321 of Pub.L. 101–650, set out as a note under section 631 of Title 28.

CROSS REFERENCES

Adoption of master's findings by court, see Fed.Rules Civ. Proc. Rule 52, 28 USCA.

Clerks of courts, ineligible to appointment as master, see 28 USCA § 957.

Default judgment, reference to determine account or amount of damages, see Fed.Rules Civ.Proc. Rule 55, 28 USCA.

Pretrial determination as to preliminary reference, see Fed.Rules Civ.Proc. Rule 16, 28 USCA.

Report, judgment not required to recite, see Fed.Rules Civ.Proc. Rule 54, 28 USCA.

Three–judge court, appointment of master by single judge, see 28 USCA § 2284.

United States magistrate judges, fees for attending to any reference, see 28 USCA § 633.

TITLE VII. JUDGMENT

Rule 54. Judgment; Costs

(a) **Definition; Form.** "Judgment" as used in these rules includes a decree and any order from which an appeal lies. A judgment should not include recitals of pleadings, a master's report, or a record of prior proceedings.

(b) **Judgment on Multiple Claims or Involving Multiple Parties.** When an action presents more than one claim for relief—whether as a claim, counterclaim, crossclaim, or third-party claim—or when multiple parties are involved, the court may direct entry of a final judgment as to one or more, but fewer than all, claims or parties only if the court expressly determines that there is no just reason for delay. Otherwise, any order or other decision, however designated, that adjudicates fewer than all the claims or the rights and liabilities of fewer than all the parties does not end the action as to any of the claims or parties and may be revised at any time before the entry of a judgment adjudicating all the claims and all the parties' rights and liabilities.

(c) **Demand for Judgment; Relief to Be Granted.** A default judgment must not differ in kind from, or exceed in amount, what is demanded in the pleadings. Every other final judgment should grant the relief to which each party is entitled, even if the party has not demanded that relief in its pleadings.

(d) **Costs; Attorney's Fees.**

(1) *Costs Other Than Attorney's Fees.* Unless a federal statute, these rules, or a court order provides otherwise, costs—other than attorney's fees—should be allowed to the prevailing party. But costs against the United States, its officers, and its agencies may be imposed only to the extent allowed by law. The clerk may tax costs on 14 days' notice. On motion served within the next 7 days, the court may review the clerk's action.

(2) *Attorney's Fees.*

(A) *Claim to Be by Motion.* A claim for attorney's fees and related nontaxable expenses must be made by motion unless the substantive law requires those fees to be proved at trial as an element of damages.

(B) *Timing and Contents of the Motion.* Unless a statute or a court order provides otherwise, the motion must:

(i) be filed no later than 14 days after the entry of judgment;

(ii) specify the judgment and the statute, rule, or other grounds entitling the movant to the award;

(iii) state the amount sought or provide a fair estimate of it; and

(iv) disclose, if the court so orders, the terms of any agreement about fees for the services for which the claim is made.

(C) *Proceedings.* Subject to Rule 23(h), the court must, on a party's request, give an opportunity for adversary submissions on the motion in accordance with Rule 43(c) or 78. The court may decide issues of liability for fees before receiving submissions on the value of services. The court must find the facts and state its conclusions of law as provided in Rule 52(a).

(D) *Special Procedures by Local Rule; Reference to a Master or a Magistrate Judge.* By local rule, the court may establish special procedures to resolve fee-related issues without extensive evidentiary hearings. Also, the court may refer issues concerning the value of services to a special master under Rule 53 without regard to the limitations of Rule 53(a)(1), and may refer a motion for attorney's fees to a magistrate judge under Rule 72(b) as if it were a dispositive pretrial matter.

(E) *Exceptions.* Subparagraphs (A)-(D) do not apply to claims for fees and expenses as sanctions for violating these rules or as sanctions under 28 U.S.C. § 1927.

(Amended December 27, 1946, effective March 19, 1948; April 17, 1961, effective July 19, 1961; March 2, 1987, effective August 1, 1987; April 22, 1993, effective December 1, 1993; April 29, 2002, effective December 1, 2002; March 27, 2003, effective December 1, 2003; April 30, 2007, effective December 1, 2007; March 26, 2009, effective December 1, 2009.)

ADVISORY COMMITTEE NOTES

1937 Adoption

Note to Subdivision (a). The second sentence is derived substantially from [former] Equity Rule 71 (Form of Decree).

Note to Subdivision (b). This provides for the separate judgment of equity and code practice. See Wis.Stat. (1935) § 270.54; Compare N.Y.C.P.A. (1937) § 476.

Note to Subdivision (c). For the limitation on default contained in the first sentence, see 2 N.D.Comp.Laws Ann. (1913) § 7680; N.Y.C.P.A. (1937) § 479. Compare *English Rules Under the Judicature Act* (The Annual Practice, 1937) O. 13, r.r. 3–12. The remainder is a usual code provision. It makes clear that a judgment should give the relief to which a party is entitled, regardless of whether it is legal or equitable or both. This necessarily includes the deficiency judgment in foreclosure cases formerly provided for by Equity Rule 10 (Decree for Deficiency in Foreclosures, Etc.).

Note to Subdivision (d). For the present rule in common law actions, see *Ex parte Peterson,* 253 U.S. 300, 40 S.Ct. 543, 64 L.Ed. 919 (1920); Payne, *Costs in Common Law Actions in the Federal Courts* (1935), 21 Va.L.Rev. 397.

The provisions as to costs in actions in forma pauperis contained in U.S.C., Title 28, former §§ 832–836 [now 1915] are unaffected by this rule. Other sections of U.S.C., Title 28, which are unaffected by this rule are: [former] §§ 815 (Costs; plaintiff not entitled to, when), 821 [now 1928] (Costs; infringement of patent; disclaimer), 825 (Costs; several actions), 829 [now 1927] (Costs; attorney liable for, when), and 830 [now 1920] (Costs; bill of; taxation).

The provisions of the following and similar statutes as to costs against the United States and its officers and agencies are specifically continued:

U.S.C., Title 15, §§ 77v(a), 78aa, 79y (Securities and Exchange Commission)

U.S.C., Title 16, § 825p (Federal Power Commission)

U.S.C., Title 26, [former] §§ 3679(d) and 3745(d) (Internal revenue actions)

U.S.C., Title 26, [former] § 3770(b)(2) (Reimbursement of costs of recovery against revenue officers)

U.S.C., Title 28, [former] § 817 (Internal revenue actions)

U.S.C., Title 28, § 836 [now 1915] (United States—actions in *forma pauperis*)

U.S.C., Title 28, § 842 [now 2006] (Actions against revenue officers)

U.S.C., Title 28, § 870 [now 2408] (United States—in certain cases)

U.S.C., Title 28, [former] § 906 (United States—foreclosure actions)

U.S.C., Title 47, § 401 (Communications Commission)

The provisions of the following and similar statutes as to costs are unaffected:

U.S.C., Title 7, § 210(f) (Actions for damages based on an order of the Secretary of Agriculture under Stockyards Act)

U.S.C., Title 7, § 499g(c) (Appeals from reparations orders of Secretary of Agriculture under Perishable Commodities Act)

U.S.C., Title 8, [former] § 45 (Action against district attorneys in certain cases)

U.S.C., Title 15, § 15 (Actions for injuries due to violation of antitrust laws)

U.S.C., Title 15, § 72 (Actions for violation of law forbidding importation or sale of articles at less than market value or wholesale prices)

U.S.C., Title 15, § 77k (Actions by persons acquiring securities registered with untrue statements under Securities Act of 1933)

U.S.C., Title 15, § 78i(e) (Certain actions under the Securities Exchange Act of 1934)

U.S.C., Title 15, § 78r (Similar to 78i(e))

U.S.C., Title 15, § 96 (Infringement of trade-mark—damages)

U.S.C., Title 15, § 99 (Infringement of trade-mark—injunctions)

U.S.C., Title 15, § 124 (Infringement of trade-mark—damages)

U.S.C., Title 19, § 274 (Certain actions under customs law)

U.S.C., Title 30, § 32 (Action to determine right to possession of mineral lands in certain cases)

U.S.C., Title 31, §§ 232 [now 3730] and 234 [former] (Action for making false claims upon United States)

U.S.C., Title 33, § 926 (Actions under Harbor Workers' Compensation Act)

U.S.C., Title 35, § 67 [now 281, 284] (Infringement of patent—damages)

U.S.C., Title 35, § 69 [now 282] (Infringement of patent—pleading and proof)

U.S.C., Title 35, § 71 [now 288] (Infringement of patent—when specification too broad)

U.S.C., Title 45, § 153p (Actions for non-compliance with an order of National R.R. Adjustment Board for payment of money)

U.S.C., Title 46, [former] § 38 (Action for penalty for failure to register vessel)

U.S.C., Title 46, § 829 (Action based on non-compliance with an order of Maritime Commission for payment of money)

U.S.C., Title 46, § 941 (Certain actions under Ship Mortgage Act)

U.S.C., Title 46, § 1227 (Actions for damages for violation of certain provisions of the Merchant Marine Act, 1936)

U.S.C., Title 47, § 206 (Actions for certain violations of Communications Act of 1934)

U.S.C., Title 49, § 16(2) [now 11705] (Action based on non-compliance with an order of I.C.C. for payment of money)

1946 Amendment

Note. The historic rule in the federal courts has always prohibited piecemeal disposal of litigation and permitted appeals only from final judgments except in those special instances covered by statute. *Hohorst v. Hamburg—American Packet Co.*, 1893, 13 S.Ct. 590, 148 U.S. 262, 37 L.Ed. 443; *Rexford v. Brunswick-Balke-Collender Co.*, 1913, 33 S.Ct. 515, 228 U.S. 339, 57 L.Ed. 864; *Collins v. Miller*, 1920, 40 S.Ct. 347, 252 U.S. 364, 64 L.Ed. 616. Rule 54(b) was originally adopted in view of the wide scope and possible content of the newly created "civil action" in order to avoid the possible injustice of a delay in judgment of a distinctly separate claim to await adjudication of the entire case. It was not designed to overturn the settled federal rule stated above, which, indeed, has more recently been reiterated in *Catlin v. United States*, 1945, 65 S.Ct. 631, 324 U.S. 229, 89 L.Ed. 911. See also *United States v. Florian*, 1941, 61 S.Ct. 713, 312 U.S. 656, 85 L.Ed. 1105; *Reeves v. Beardall*, 1942, 62 S.Ct. 1085, 316 U.S. 283, 86 L.Ed. 1478.

Unfortunately, this was not always understood, and some confusion ensued. Hence situations arose where district courts made a piecemeal disposition of an action and entered what the parties thought amounted to a judgment, although a trial remained to be had on other claims similar or identical with those disposed of. In the interim the parties did not know their ultimate rights, and accordingly took an appeal, thus putting the finality of the partial judgment in question. While most appellate courts have reached a result generally in accord with the intent of the rule, yet there have been divergent precedents and division of views which have served to render the issues more clouded to the parties appellant. It hardly seems a case where multiplicity of precedents will tend to remove the problem from debate. The problem is presented and discussed in the following cases: *Atwater v. North American Coal Corp.*, C.C.A.2, 1940, 111 F.2d 125; *Rosenblum v. Dingfelder*, C.C.A.2, 1940, 111 F.2d 406; *Audi-Vision, Inc. v. RCA Mfg. Co., Inc.*, C.C.A.2, 1943, 136 F.2d 621; *Zalkind v. Scheinman*, C.C.A.2, 1943, 139 F.2d 895; *Oppenheimer v. F. J. Young & Co., Inc.*, C.C.A.2, 1944, 144 F.2d 387; *Libbey-Owens-Ford Glass Co. v. Sylvania Industrial Corp.*, C.C.A.2, 1946, 154 F.2d 814, certiorari denied 1946, 66 S.Ct. 1353, 328 U.S. 859, 90 L.Ed. 1630; *Zarati Steamship Co. v. Park Bridge Corp.*, C.C.A.2, 1946, 154 F.2d 377; *Baltimore and Ohio R. Co. v. United Fuel Gas Co.*, C.C.A.4, 1946, 154 F.2d 545; *Jefferson Electric Co. v. Sola Electric Co.*, C.C.A.7, 1941, 122 F.2d 124; *Leonard v. Socony-Vacuum Oil Co.*, C.C.A.7, 1942, 130 F.2d 535; *Markham v. Kasper*, C.C.A.7, 1945, 152 F.2d 270; *Hanney v. Franklin Fire Ins. Co. of Philadelphia*, C.C.A.9, 1944, 142 F.2d 864; *Toomey v. Toomey*, App.D.C.1945, 149 F.2d 19, 80 U.S.App.D.C. 77.

In view of the difficulty thus disclosed, the Advisory Committee in its two preliminary drafts of proposed amendments attempted to redefine the original rule with particular stress upon the interlocutory nature of partial judgments which did not adjudicate all claims arising out of a single transaction or occurrence. This attempt appeared to meet with almost universal approval from those of the profession commenting upon it, although there were, of course, helpful suggestions for additional changes in language or clarification of detail. But cf. Circuit Judge Frank's dissenting opinion in *Libbey-Owens-Ford Glass Co. v. Sylvania Industrial Corp.*, supra, n. 21 of the dissenting opinion. The Committee, however, became convinced on careful study of its own proposals that the seeds of ambiguity still remained, and that it had not completely solved the problem of piecemeal appeals. After extended consideration, it concluded that a retention of the older federal rule was desirable, and that this rule needed only the exercise of a discretionary power to afford a remedy in the infrequent harsh case to provide a simple, definite, workable rule. This is afforded by amended Rule 54(b). It re-establishes an ancient policy with clarity and precision. For the possibility of staying execution where not all claims are disposed of under Rule 54(b), see amended Rule 62(h).

1961 Amendment

This rule permitting appeal, upon the trial court's determination of "no just reason for delay," from a judgment upon one or more but less than all the claims in an action, has generally been given a sympathetic construction by the courts and its validity is settled. *Reeves v. Beardall*, 316 U.S. 283 (1942); *Sears, Roebuck & Co. v. Mackey*, 351 U.S. 427 (1956); *Cold Metal Process Co. v. United Engineering & Foundry Co.*, 351 U.S. 445 (1956).

A serious difficulty has, however, arisen because the rule speaks of claims but nowhere mentions parties. A line of cases has developed in the circuits consistently holding the rule to be inapplicable to the dismissal, even with the requisite trial court determination, of one or more but less than all defendants jointly charged in an action, i.e. charged with various forms of concerted or related wrongdoing or related liability. See *Mull v. Ackerman*, 279 F.2d 25 (2d Cir. 1960); *Richards v. Smith*, 276 F.2d 652 (5th Cir. 1960); *Hardy v. Bankers Life & Cas. Co.*, 222 F.2d 827 (7th Cir. 1955); *Steiner v. 20th Century-Fox Film Corp.*, 220 F.2d 105 (9th Cir. 1955). For purposes of Rule 54(b) it was arguable that there were as many "claims" as there were parties defendant and that the rule in its present text applied where less than all of the parties were dismissed, cf. *United Artists Corp. v. Masterpiece Productions, Inc.*, 221 F.2d 213, 215 (2d Cir. 1955); *Bowling Machines, Inc. v. First Nat. Bank*, 283 F.2d 39 (1st Cir. 1960); but the Courts of Appeals are now committed to an opposite view.

The danger of hardship through delay of appeal until the whole action is concluded may be at least as serious in the multiple-parties situations as in multiple-claims cases, see *Pabellon v. Grace Line, Inc.*, 191 F.2d 169, 179 (2d Cir. 1951), cert. denied, 342 U.S. 893 (1951), and courts and commentators have urged that Rule 54(b) be changed to take in the former. See *Reagan v. Traders & General Ins. Co.*, 255 F.2d 845 (5th Cir. 1958); *Meadows v. Greyhound Corp.*, 235 F.2d 233 (5th Cir. 1956); *Steiner v. 20th Century-Fox Film Corp.*, supra; 6 Moore's Federal Practice ¶54.34[2] (2d ed. 1953); 3 Barron & Holtzoff, *Federal Practice & Procedure* § 1193.2 (Wright ed. 1958); *Developments in the Law—Multiparty Litigation*, 71 Harv.L.Rev. 874, 981 (1958); Note, 62 Yale L.J. 263, 271 (1953); Ill.Ann.Stat. ch. 110, § 50(2) (Smith-Hurd 1956). The amendment accomplishes this purpose by referring explicitly to parties.

There has been some recent indication that interlocutory appeal under the provisions of 28 U.S.C. § 1292(b), added in 1958, may now be available for the multiple-parties cases here considered. See *Jaftex Corp. v. Randolph Mills, Inc.*, 282 F.2d 508 (2d Cir. 1960). The Rule 54(b) procedure seems preferable for those cases, and § 1292(b) should be held inapplicable to them when the rule is enlarged as here proposed. See *Luckenbach Steamship Co., Inc., v. H. Muehlstein & Co., Inc.*, 280 F.2d 755, 757 (2d Cir. 1960); 1 Barron & Holtzoff, supra, § 58.1, p. 321 (Wright ed. 1960).

1987 Amendment

The amendment is technical. No substantive change is intended.

1993 Amendment

Subdivision (d). This revision adds paragraph (2) to this subdivision to provide for a frequently recurring form of litigation not initially contemplated by the rules—disputes over the amount of attorneys' fees to be awarded in the large number of actions in which prevailing parties may be entitled to such awards or in which the court must determine the fees to be paid from a common fund. This revision seeks to harmonize and clarify procedures that have been developed through case law and local rules.

Paragraph (1). Former subdivision (d), providing for taxation of costs by the clerk, is renumbered as paragraph (1) and revised to exclude applications for attorneys' fees.

Paragraph (2). This new paragraph establishes a procedure for presenting claims for attorneys' fees, whether or not denominated as "costs." It applies also to requests for reimbursement of expenses, not taxable as costs, when recoverable under governing law incident to the award of fees. *Cf. West Virginia Univ. Hosp. v. Casey*, 499 U.S. 83 (1991), holding, prior to the Civil Rights Act of 1991, that expert witness fees were not recoverable under 42 U.S.C. § 1988. As noted in subparagraph (A), it does not, however, apply to fees recoverable as an element of damages, as when sought under the terms of a contract; such damages typically are to be claimed in a pleading and may involve issues to be resolved by a jury. Nor, as provided in subparagraph (E), does it apply to awards of fees as sanctions authorized or mandated under these rules or under 28 U.S.C. § 1927.

Subparagraph (B) provides a deadline for motions for attorneys' fees—14 days after final judgment unless the court or a statute specifies some other time. One purpose of this provision is to assure that the opposing party is informed of the claim before the time for appeal has elapsed. Prior law did not prescribe any specific time limit on claims for attorneys' fees. *White v. New Hampshire Dep't of Employment Sec.*, 455 U.S. 445 (1982). In many nonjury cases the court will want to consider attorneys' fee issues immediately after rendering its judgment on the merits of the case. Note that the time for making claims is specifically stated in some legislation, such as the Equal Access to Justice Act, 28 U.S.C. § 2412(d)(1)(B) (30-day filing period).

Prompt filing affords an opportunity for the court to resolve fee disputes shortly after trial, while the services performed are freshly in mind. It also enables the court in appropriate circumstances to make its ruling on a fee request in time for any appellate review of a dispute over fees to proceed at the same time as review on the merits of the case.

Filing a motion for fees under this subdivision does not affect the finality or the appealability of a judgment, though revised Rule 58 provides a mechanism by which prior to appeal the court can suspend the finality to resolve a motion for fees. If an appeal on the merits of the case is taken, the court may rule on the claim for fees, may defer its ruling on the motion, or may deny the motion without prejudice, directing under subdivision (d)(2)(B) a new period for filing after the appeal has been resolved. A notice of appeal does not extend the time for filing a fee claim based on the initial judgment, but the court under subdivision (d)(2)(B) may effectively extend the period by permitting claims to be filed after resolution of the appeal. A new period for filing will automatically begin if a new judgment is entered following a reversal or remand by the appellate court or the granting of a motion under Rule 59.

The rule does not require that the motion be supported at the time of filing with the evidentiary material bearing on the fees. This material must of course be submitted in due course, according to such schedule as the court may direct in light of the circumstances of the case. What is required is the filing of a motion sufficient to alert the adversary and the court that there is a claim for fees, and the amount of such fees (or a fair estimate).

If directed by the court, the moving party is also required to disclose any fee agreement, including those between attorney and client, between attorneys sharing a fee to be awarded, and between adversaries made in partial settlement of a dispute where the settlement must be implemented by court action as may be required by Rules 23(e) and 23.1 or other like provisions. With respect to the fee arrangements requiring court approval, the court may also by local rule require disclosure immediately after such arrangements are agreed to. *E.g.*, Rule 5 of United States District Court for the Eastern District of New York; *cf. In re "Agent Orange" Product Liability Litigation (MDL 381)*, 611 F.Supp. 1452, 1464 (E.D.N.Y.1985).

In the settlement of class actions resulting in a common fund from which fees will be sought, courts frequently have required that claims for fees be presented in advance of hearings to consider approval of the proposed settlement. The rule does not affect this practice, as it permits the court to require submissions of fee claims in advance of entry of judgment.

Subparagraph (C) assures the parties of an opportunity to make an appropriate presentation with respect to issues involving the evaluation of legal services. In some cases, an evidentiary hearing may be needed, but this is not required in every case. The amount of time to be allowed for the preparation of submissions both in support of and in opposition to awards should be tailored to the particular case.

The court is explicitly authorized to make a determination of the liability for fees before receiving submissions by the parties bearing on the amount of an award. This option may be appropriate in actions in which the liability issue is doubtful and the evaluation issues are numerous and complex.

The court may order disclosure of additional information, such as that bearing on prevailing local rates or on the appropriateness of particular services for which compensation is sought.

On rare occasion, the court may determine that discovery under Rules 26–37 would be useful to the parties. *Compare* Rules Governing Section 2254 Cases in the U.S. District Courts, Rule 6. *See* Note, *Determining the Reasonableness of Attorneys' Fees—the Discoverability of Billing Records*, 64 B.U.L.Rev. 241 (1984). In complex fee disputes, the court may use case management techniques to limit the scope of the dispute or to facilitate the settlement of fee award disputes.

Fee awards should be made in the form of a separate judgment under Rule 58 since such awards are subject to review in the court of appeals. To facilitate review, the paragraph provides that the court set forth its findings and conclusions as under Rule 52(a), though in most cases this explanation could be quite brief.

Subparagraph (D) explicitly authorizes the court to establish procedures facilitating the efficient and fair resolution of fee claims. A local rule, for example, might call for matters to be presented through affidavits, or might provide for issuance of proposed findings by the court, which would be treated as accepted by the parties unless objected to within a specified time. A court might also consider establishing a schedule reflecting customary fees or factors affecting fees within the community, as implicitly suggested by Justice O'Connor in *Pennsylvania v. Delaware Valley Citizens' Council*, 483 U.S. 711, 733 (1987) (O'Connor, J., concurring) (how particular markets compensate for contingency). *Cf. Thompson v. Kennickell*, 710 F.Supp. 1 (D.D.C.1989) (use of findings in other cases to promote consistency). The parties, of course, should be permitted to show that in the circumstances of the case such a schedule should not be applied or that different hourly rates would be appropriate.

The rule also explicitly permits, without need for a local rule, the court to refer issues regarding the amount of a fee award in a particular case to a master under Rule 53. The district judge may designate a magistrate judge to act as a master for this purpose or may refer a motion for attorneys' fees to a magistrate judge for proposed findings and recommendations under Rule 72(b). This authorization eliminates any controversy as to whether such references are permitted under Rule 53(b) as "matters of account and of difficult computation of damages" and whether motions for attorneys' fees can be treated as the equivalent of a dispositive pretrial matter that can be referred to a magistrate judge. For consistency and efficiency, all such matters might be referred to the same magistrate judge.

Subparagraph (E) excludes from this rule the award of fees as sanctions under these rules or under 28 U.S.C. § 1927.

2002 Amendment

Subdivision (d)(2)(C) is amended to delete the requirement that judgment on a motion for attorney fees be set forth in a separate document. This change complements the amendment of Rule 58(a)(1), which deletes the separate document requirement for an order disposing of a motion for attorney fees under Rule 54. These changes are made to support amendment of Rule 4 of the Federal Rules of Appellate Procedure. It continues to be important that a district court make clear its meaning when it intends an order to be the final disposition of a motion for attorney fees.

The requirement in subdivision (d)(2)(B) that a motion for attorney fees be not only filed but also served no later than 14 days after entry of judgment is changed to require filing only, to establish a parallel with Rules 50, 52, and 59. Service continues to be required under Rule 5(a).

2003 Amendment

Rule 54(d)(2)(D) is revised to reflect amendments to Rule 53.

2007 Amendment

The language of Rule 54 has been amended as part of the general restyling of the Civil Rules to make them more easily understood and to make style and terminology consistent throughout the rules. These changes are intended to be stylistic only.

The words "or class member" have been removed from Rule 54(d)(2)(C) because Rule 23(h)(2) now addresses objections by class members to attorney-fee motions. Rule 54(d)(2)(C) is amended to recognize that Rule 23(h) now controls those aspects of attorney-fee motions in class actions to which it is addressed.

2009 Amendment

Former Rule 54(d)(1) provided that the clerk may tax costs on 1 day's notice. That period was unrealistically short. The new 14–day period provides a better opportunity to prepare and present a response. The former 5–day period to serve a motion to review the clerk's action is extended to 7 days to reflect the change in the Rule 6(a) method for computing periods of less than 11 days.

HISTORICAL NOTES

Effective and Applicability Provisions

1961 Amendments. Amendment adopted on Apr. 17, 1961, effective July 19, 1961, see Rule 86(d).

CROSS REFERENCES

Appellate court directing entry of judgment, see 28 USCA § 2106.

Bond for costs on appeal, filing with notice of appeal, see Federal Rules of Appellate Procedure Rule 7, 28 USCA.

Books and records kept by the clerk, civil docket, index and correct copy of every final judgment, see Fed.Rules Civ.Proc. Rule 79, 28 USCA.

Claims Court judgment finding plaintiff indebted to United States as judgment of district court, see 28 USCA § 2508.

Costs,
  Absent defendant, setting aside judgment and pleading on payment of, see 28 USCA § 1655.
  Admissions on genuineness of documents or truth of factual matters, expenses on failure to make, see Fed. Rules Civ.Proc. Rule 37, 28 USCA.
  Claimant in proceedings to condemn or forfeit property seized, see 28 USCA § 2465.
  Clerk of court of appeals, payment into Treasury, see 28 USCA § 711.
  Contempt of witness in foreign country failing to respond to subpoena, see 28 USCA § 1784.
  Offer of judgment affecting, see Fed.Rules Civ.Proc. Rule 68, 28 USCA.
  Previously dismissed action, see Fed.Rules Civ.Proc. Rule 41, 28 USCA.
  Stay of execution and enforcement of judgment to obtain certiorari from Supreme Court, see 28 USCA § 2101.
  Summary judgment, affidavits presented in bad faith, see Fed.Rules Civ.Proc. Rule 56, 28 USCA.

Counterclaim or crossclaim, judgment on, see Fed.Rules Civ.Proc. Rule 13, 28 USCA.

Court record of judgment lost or destroyed, enforcement where United States is interested, see 28 USCA § 1735.

Declaratory judgment, see 28 USCA §§ 2201, 2202 and Fed.Rules Civ.Proc. Rule 57, 28 USCA.

Default judgment, parties entitled to, see Fed.Rules Civ. Proc. Rule 55, 28 USCA.

District Courts, removal of cases from State courts, see 28 USCA § 1441 et seq.

Fees and costs, see 28 USCA § 1911 et seq.

Judgment as a matter of law in actions tried by jury, alternative motion for new trial, conditional ruling, see Fed. Rules Civ.Proc. Rule 50, 28 USCA.

Judgment for specific act, vesting title, consequences of failure to comply, see Fed.Rules Civ.Proc. Rule 70, 28 USCA.

Jurisdiction of district court, diversity of citizenship, amount in controversy, see 28 USCA § 1332.

Modification or vacation of judgment, errors not affecting, substantial rights not ground for, see Fed.Rules Civ.Proc. Rule 61, 28 USCA.

Motion as termination of running of time for appeal, see Federal Rules of Appellate Procedure Rule 4, 28 USCA.

New trials, amendment of judgments, see Fed.Rules Civ. Proc. Rule 59, 28 USCA.

Pending actions and judgments, see 28 USCA § 1961 et seq.

Pleading judgment, see Fed.Rules Civ.Proc. Rule 9, 28 USCA.

Record on appeal, composition, see Federal Rules of Appellate Procedure Rule 10, 28 USCA.

Sales under judgment, see 28 USCA § 2001 et seq.

Single judge of three-judge court not to enter, see 28 USCA § 2284.

Stay of proceedings to enforce a judgment, generally, see Fed.Rules Civ.Proc. Rule 62, 28 USCA.

Stay or injunction pending appeal, proceedings against surety, see Federal Rules of Appellate Procedure Rule 8, 28 USCA.

Stipulation for stay of execution of process in rem issued in admiralty case, see 28 USCA § 2464.

Third party tort liability to United States for hospital and medical care, see 42 USCA § 2651 et seq.

Time,

    Entry of judgment, generally, see Fed.Rules Civ.Proc. Rule 58, 28 USCA.

    Extension of time for relief from judgment, motion to amend judgment, see Fed.Rules Civ.Proc. Rule 6, 28 USCA.

    Motion for relief from judgment or order, grounds for, finality of judgment unaffected, see Fed.Rules Civ. Proc. Rule 60, 28 USCA.

Tort claims against, judgment as bar to action against employee, see 28 USCA § 2676.

United States as party, generally, see 28 USCA § 2401 et seq.

Verdict submitted on written interrogatories to jury, judgment on, see Fed.Rules Civ.Proc. Rule 49, 28 USCA.

Rule 55. Default; Default Judgment

(a) Entering a Default. When a party against whom a judgment for affirmative relief is sought has failed to plead or otherwise defend, and that failure is shown by affidavit or otherwise, the clerk must enter the party's default.

(b) Entering a Default Judgment.

(1) *By the Clerk.* If the plaintiff's claim is for a sum certain or a sum that can be made certain by computation, the clerk—on the plaintiff's request, with an affidavit showing the amount due—must enter judgment for that amount and costs against a defendant who has been defaulted for not appearing and who is neither a minor nor an incompetent person.

(2) *By the Court.* In all other cases, the party must apply to the court for a default judgment. A default judgment may be entered against a minor or incompetent person only if represented by a general guardian, conservator, or other like fiduciary who has appeared. If the party against whom a default judgment is sought has appeared personally or by a representative, that party or its representative must be served with written notice of the application at least 7 days before the hearing. The court may conduct hearings or make referrals—preserving any federal statutory right to a jury trial—when, to enter or effectuate judgment, it needs to:

    (A) conduct an accounting;

    (B) determine the amount of damages;

    (C) establish the truth of any allegation by evidence; or

    (D) investigate any other matter.

(c) Setting Aside a Default or a Default Judgment. The court may set aside an entry of default for good cause, and it may set aside a final default judgment under Rule 60(b).

(d) Judgment Against the United States. A default judgment may be entered against the United States, its officers, or its agencies only if the claimant establishes a claim or right to relief by evidence that satisfies the court.

(Amended March 2, 1987, effective August 1, 1987; April 30, 2007, effective December 1, 2007; March 26, 2009, effective December 1, 2009; April 29, 2015, effective December 1, 2015.)

ADVISORY COMMITTEE NOTES

1937 Adoption

This represents the joining of the equity decree *pro confesso* (former Equity Rules 12 (Issue of Subpoena—Time for Answer), 16 (Defendant to Answer—Default—Decree *Pro Confesso*), 17 (Decree *Pro Confesso* to be Followed by Final Decree—Setting Aside Default), 29 (Defenses—How Presented), 31 (Reply—When Required—When Cause at Issue)) and the judgment by default now governed by U.S.C., Title 28, [former] § 724 (Conformity act). For dismissal of an action for failure to comply with these rules or any order of the court, see Rule 41(b).

Note to Subdivision (a). The provision for the entry of default comes from the Massachusetts practice, 2 Mass.Gen. Laws (Ter.Ed., 1932) ch. 231, § 57. For affidavit of default, see 2 Minn.Stat. (Mason, 1927) § 9256.

Note to Subdivision (b). The provision in paragraph (1) for the entry of judgment by the clerk when plaintiff claims a sum certain is found in the N.Y.C.P.A. (1937) § 485, in Calif.Code Civ.Proc. (Deering, 1937) § 585(1), and in Conn.Practice Book (1934) § 47. For provisions similar to paragraph (2), compare Calif.Code, *supra*, § 585(2);

N.Y.C.P.A. (1937) § 490; 2 Minn.Stat. (Mason, 1927) § 9256(3); 2 Wash.Rev.Stat.Ann. (Remington, 1932) § 411(2). U.S.C., Title 28, § 1874, formerly § 785 (Action to recover forfeiture in bond) and similar statutes are preserved by the last clause of paragraph (2).

Note to Subdivision (e). This restates substantially the last clause of U.S.C., Title 28, [former] § 763 (Action against the United States under the Tucker Act). As this rule governs in all actions against the United States, U.S.C., Title 28, [former] § 45 (Practice and procedure in certain cases under the interstate commerce laws) and similar statutes are modified insofar as they contain anything inconsistent therewith.

Supplementary Note

Note. The operation of Rule 55(b) (Judgment) is directly affected by the Soldiers' and Sailors' Civil Relief Act of 1940 ([former] 50 U.S.C. [App.] § 501 *et seq.*) [now 50 U.S.C. 3901 et seq.]. Section 200 of the Act [former 50 U.S.C. Appendix, § 520] imposes specific requirements which must be fulfilled before a default judgment can be entered (*e.g., Ledwith v. Storkan* (D.Neb. 1942) 6 Fed.Rules Serv. 60b.24, Case 2, 2 F.R.D. 539, and also provides for the vacation of a judgment in certain circumstances. See discussion in Commentary, *Effect of Conscription Legislation on the Federal Rules* (1940) 3 Fed.Rules Serv. 725; 3 *Moore's Federal Practice* (1938) Cum.Supplement § 55.02.

1987 Amendment

The amendments are technical. No substantive change is intended.

2007 Amendment

The language of Rule 55 has been amended as part of the general restyling of the Civil Rules to make them more easily understood and to make style and terminology consistent throughout the rules. These changes are intended to be stylistic only.

Former Rule 55(a) directed the clerk to enter a default when a party failed to plead or otherwise defend "as provided by these rules." The implication from the reference to defending "as provided by these rules" seemed to be that the clerk should enter a default even if a party did something showing an intent to defend, but that act was not specifically described by the rules. Courts in fact have rejected that implication. Acts that show an intent to defend have frequently prevented a default even though not connected to any particular rule. "[A]s provided by these rules" is deleted to reflect Rule 55(a)'s actual meaning.

Amended Rule 55 omits former Rule 55(d), which included two provisions. The first recognized that Rule 55 applies to described claimants. The list was incomplete and unnecessary. Rule 55(a) applies Rule 55 to any party against whom a judgment for affirmative relief is requested. The second provision was a redundant reminder that Rule 54(c) limits the relief available by default judgment.

2009 Amendment

The time set in the former rule at 3 days has been revised to 7 days. See the Note to Rule 6.

2015 Amendment

Rule 55(c) is amended to make plain the interplay between Rules 54(b), 55(c), and 60(b). A default judgment that does not dispose of all of the claims among all parties is not a final judgment unless the court directs entry of final judgment under Rule 54(b). Until final judgment is entered, Rule 54(b) allows revision of the default judgment at any time. The demanding standards set by Rule 60(b) apply only in seeking relief from a final judgment.

CROSS REFERENCES

Failure to serve answers to interrogatories, entry of default judgment, see Fed.Rules Civ.Proc. Rule 37, 28 USCA.

Judgments, demand for, relief awarded on default, see Fed.Rules Civ.Proc. Rule 54, 28 USCA.

Summons as notice to defendant, judgment by default will be entered on failure to appear and defend, see Fed.Rules Civ.Proc. Rule 4, 28 USCA.

Rule 56. Summary Judgment

(a) Motion for Summary Judgment or Partial Summary Judgment. A party may move for summary judgment, identifying each claim or defense—or the part of each claim or defense—on which summary judgment is sought. The court shall grant summary judgment if the movant shows that there is no genuine dispute as to any material fact and the movant is entitled to judgment as a matter of law. The court should state on the record the reasons for granting or denying the motion.

(b) Time to File a Motion. Unless a different time is set by local rule or the court orders otherwise, a party may file a motion for summary judgment at any time until 30 days after the close of all discovery.

(c) Procedures.

(1) *Supporting Factual Positions.* A party asserting that a fact cannot be or is genuinely disputed must support the assertion by:

(A) citing to particular parts of materials in the record, including depositions, documents, electronically stored information, affidavits or declarations, stipulations (including those made for purposes of the motion only), admissions, interrogatory answers, or other materials; or

(B) showing that the materials cited do not establish the absence or presence of a genuine dispute, or that an adverse party cannot produce admissible evidence to support the fact.

(2) *Objection That a Fact Is Not Supported by Admissible Evidence.* A party may object that the material cited to support or dispute a fact cannot be presented in a form that would be admissible in evidence.

(3) *Materials Not Cited.* The court need consider only the cited materials, but it may consider other materials in the record.

(4) *Affidavits or Declarations.* An affidavit or declaration used to support or oppose a motion must

be made on personal knowledge, set out facts that would be admissible in evidence, and show that the affiant or declarant is competent to testify on the matters stated.

(d) When Facts Are Unavailable to the Nonmovant. If a nonmovant shows by affidavit or declaration that, for specified reasons, it cannot present facts essential to justify its opposition, the court may:

(1) defer considering the motion or deny it;

(2) allow time to obtain affidavits or declarations or to take discovery; or

(3) issue any other appropriate order.

(e) Failing to Properly Support or Address a Fact. If a party fails to properly support an assertion of fact or fails to properly address another party's assertion of fact as required by Rule 56(c), the court may:

(1) give an opportunity to properly support or address the fact;

(2) consider the fact undisputed for purposes of the motion;

(3) grant summary judgment if the motion and supporting materials—including the facts considered undisputed—show that the movant is entitled to it; or

(4) issue any other appropriate order.

(f) Judgment Independent of the Motion. After giving notice and a reasonable time to respond, the court may:

(1) grant summary judgment for a nonmovant;

(2) grant the motion on grounds not raised by a party; or

(3) consider summary judgment on its own after identifying for the parties material facts that may not be genuinely in dispute.

(g) Failing to Grant All the Requested Relief. If the court does not grant all the relief requested by the motion, it may enter an order stating any material fact—including an item of damages or other relief—that is not genuinely in dispute and treating the fact as established in the case.

(h) Affidavit or Declaration Submitted in Bad Faith. If satisfied that an affidavit or declaration under this rule is submitted in bad faith or solely for delay, the court—after notice and a reasonable time to respond—may order the submitting party to pay the other party the reasonable expenses, including attorney's fees, it incurred as a result. An offending party or attorney may also be held in contempt or subjected to other appropriate sanctions.

(Amended December 27, 1946, effective March 19, 1948; January 21, 1963, effective July 1, 1963; March 2, 1987, effective August 1, 1987; April 30, 2007, effective December 1, 2007; March 26, 2009, effective December 1, 2009; April 28, 2010, effective December 1, 2010.)

ADVISORY COMMITTEE NOTES

1937 Adoption

This rule is applicable to all actions, including those against the United States or an officer or agency thereof.

Summary judgment procedure is a method for promptly disposing of actions in which there is no genuine issue as to any material fact. It has been extensively used in England for more than 50 years and has been adopted in a number of American states. New York, for example, has made great use of it. During the first nine years after its adoption there, the records of New York county alone show 5,600 applications for summary judgments. Report of the Commission on the Administration of Justice in New York State (1934), p. 383. See also *Third Annual Report of the Judicial Council of the State of New York* (1937), p. 30.

In England it was first employed only in cases of liquidated claims, but there has been a steady enlargement of the scope of the remedy until it is now used in actions to recover land or chattels and in all other actions at law, for liquidated or unliquidated claims, except for a few designated torts and breach of promise of marriage. *English Rules Under the Judicature Act* (The Annual Practice, 1937) O. 3, r. 6; Orders 14, 14A, and 15; see also O. 32, r. 6, authorizing an application for judgment at any time upon admissions. In Michigan (3 Comp.Laws (1929) § 14260) and Illinois (Smith-Hurd Ill.Stats. c. 110, §§ 181, 259.15, 259.16), it is not limited to liquidated demands. New York (N.Y.R.C.P. (1937) Rule 113; see also Rule 107) has brought so many classes of actions under the operation of the rule that the Commission on Administration of Justice in New York State (1934) recommend that all restrictions be removed and that the remedy be available "in any action" (p. 287). For the history and nature of the summary judgment procedure and citations of state statutes, see Clark and Samenow, *The Summary Judgment* (1929), 38 Yale L.J. 423.

Note to Subdivision (d). See Rule 16 (Pre-Trial Procedure; Formulating Issues) and the Note thereto.

Note to Subdivisions (e) and (f). These are similar to rules in Michigan. Mich.Court Rules Ann. (Searl, 1933) Rule 30.

1946 Amendment

Note to Subdivision (a). The amendment allows a claimant to move for a summary judgment at any time after the expiration of 20 days from the commencement of the action or after service of a motion for summary judgment by the adverse party. This will normally operate to permit an earlier motion by the claimant than under the original rule, where the phrase "at any time after the pleading in answer thereto has been served" operates to prevent a claimant from moving for summary judgment, even in a case clearly proper for its exercise, until a formal answer has been filed. Thus in *Peoples Bank v. Federal Reserve Bank of San Francisco,* N.D.Cal.1944, 58 F.Supp. 25, the plaintiff's countermotion for a summary judgment was stricken as premature, because the defendant had not filed an answer. Since Rule 12(a) allows at least 20 days for an answer, that time plus the 10 days required in Rule 56(c) means that under original Rule 56(a) a minimum period of 30 days necessarily has to elapse in every case before the claimant can be heard on his right to a summary judgment. An extension of time by the court or the service of preliminary motions of any kind will prolong that period even further. In many cases this merely represents unnecessary delay. See *United States v. Adler's Creamery, Inc.*, C.C.A.2, 1939, 107 F.2d 987. The changes are in the interest of more expeditious litigation. The 20-day period, as provided, gives the defendant an opportunity to secure counsel and determine a course of action. But in a case where the defendant himself makes a motion for summary judgment within that time, there is no reason to restrict the plaintiff and the amended rule so provides.

Subdivision (c). The amendment of Rule 56(c), by the addition of the final sentence, resolves a doubt expressed in *Sartor v. Arkansas Natural Gas Corp.*, 1944, 64 S.Ct. 724, 321 U.S. 620, 88 L.Ed. 967. See also Commentary, Summary Judgment as to Damages, 1944, 7 Fed.Rules Serv. 974; *Madeirense Do Brasil S/A v. Stulman-Emrick Lumber Co.*, C.C.A.2d, 1945, 147 F.2d 399, certiorari denied 1945, 65 S.Ct. 1201, 325 U.S. 861, 89 L.Ed. 1982. It makes clear that although the question of recovery depends on the amount of damages, the summary judgment rule is applicable and summary judgment may be granted in a proper case. If the case is not fully adjudicated it may be dealt with as provided in subdivision (d) of Rule 56, and the right to summary recovery determined by a preliminary order, interlocutory in character, and the precise amount of recovery left for trial.

Subdivision (d). Rule 54(a) defines "judgment" as including a decree and "any order from which an appeal lies." Subdivision (d) of Rule 56 indicates clearly, however, that a partial summary "judgment" is not a final judgment, and, therefore, that it is not appealable, unless in the particular case some statute allows an appeal from the interlocutory order involved. The partial summary judgment is merely a pretrial adjudication that certain issues shall be deemed established for the trial of the case. This adjudication is more nearly akin to the preliminary order under Rule 16, and likewise serves the purpose of speeding up litigation by eliminating before trial matters wherein there is no genuine issue of fact. See *Leonard v. Socony-Vacuum Oil Co.*, C.C.A.7, 1942, 130 F.2d 535; *Biggins v. Oltmer Iron Works*, C.C.A.7, 1946, 154 F.2d 214; 3 *Moore's Federal Practice*, 1938, 3190–3192. Since interlocutory appeals are not allowed, except where specifically provided by statute, see 3 Moore, op. cit. supra, 3155–3156, this interpretation is in line with that policy, *Leonard v. Socony-Vacuum Oil Co.*, supra. See also *Audi Vision Inc. v. RCA Mfg. Co.*, C.C.A.2, 1943, 136 F.2d 621; *Toomey v. Toomey*, 1945, 149 F.2d 19, 80 U.S.App.D.C. 77; *Biggins v. Oltmer Iron Works*, supra; *Catlin v. United States*, 1945, 65 S.Ct. 631, 324 U.S. 229, 89 L.Ed. 911.

1963 Amendment

Subdivision (c). By the amendment "answers to interrogatories" are included among the materials which may be considered on motion for summary judgment. The phrase was inadvertently omitted from the rule, see 3 Barron & Holtzoff, *Federal Practice & Procedure* 159–60 (Wright ed. 1958), and the courts have generally reached by interpretation the result which will hereafter be required by the text of the amended rule. See Annot., 74 A.L.R.2d 984 (1960).

Subdivision (e). The words "answers to interrogatories" are added in the third sentence of this subdivision to conform to the amendment of subdivision (c).

The last two sentences are added to overcome a line of cases, chiefly in the Third Circuit, which has impaired the utility of the summary judgment device. A typical case is as follows: A party supports his motion for summary judgment by affidavits or other evidentiary matter sufficient to show that there is no genuine issue as to a material fact. The adverse party, in opposing the motion, does not produce any evidentiary matter, or produces some but not enough to establish that there is a genuine issue for trial. Instead, the adverse party rests on averments of his pleadings which on their face present an issue. In this situation Third Circuit cases have taken the view that summary judgment must be denied, at least if the averments are "well-pleaded," and not suppositious, conclusory, or ultimate. See *Frederick Hart & Co., Inc. v. Recordgraph Corp.*, 169 F.2d 580 (3d Cir. 1948); *United States ex rel. Kolton v. Halpern*, 260 F.2d 590 (3d Cir. 1958); *United States ex rel. Nobles v. Ivey Bros. Constr. Co., Inc.*, 191 F.Supp. 383 (D.Del.1961); *Jamison v. Pennsylvania Salt Mfg. Co.*, 22 F.R.D. 238 (W.D.Pa.1958); *Bunny Bear, Inc. v. Dennis Mitchell Industries*, 139 F.Supp. 542 (E.D.Pa. 1956); *Levy v. Equitable Life Assur. Society*, 18 F.R.D. 164 (E.D.Pa.1955).

The very mission of the summary judgment procedure is to pierce the pleadings and to assess the proof in order to see whether there is a genuine need for trial. The Third Circuit doctrine, which permits the pleadings themselves to stand in the way of granting an otherwise justified summary judgment, is incompatible with the basic purpose of the rule. See 6 *Moore's Federal Practice* 2069 (2d ed. 1953); 3 Barron & Holtzoff, supra, § 1235.1.

It is hoped that the amendment will contribute to the more effective utilization of the salutary device of summary judgment.

The amendment is not intended to derogate from the solemnity of the pleadings. Rather it recognizes that, despite the best efforts of counsel to make his pleadings accurate, they may be overwhelmingly contradicted by the proof available to his adversary.

Nor is the amendment designed to affect the ordinary standards applicable to the summary judgment motion. So, for example: Where an issue as to a material fact cannot be resolved without observation of the demeanor of witnesses in order to evaluate their credibility, summary judgment is not appropriate. Where the evidentiary matter in support of the motion does not establish the absence of a genuine issue, summary judgment must be denied even if no opposing evidentiary matter is presented. And summary judgment may be inappropriate where the party opposing it shows under subdivision (f) that he cannot at the time present facts essential to justify his opposition.

1987 Amendment

The amendments are technical. No substantive change is intended.

2007 Amendment

The language of Rule 56 has been amended as part of the general restyling of the Civil Rules to make them more easily understood and to make style and terminology consistent throughout the rules. These changes are intended to be stylistic only.

Former Rule 56(a) and (b) referred to summary-judgment motions on or against a claim, counterclaim, or crossclaim, or to obtain a declaratory judgment. The list was incomplete. Rule 56 applies to third-party claimants, intervenors, claimants in interpleader, and others. Amended Rule 56(a) and (b) carry forward the present meaning by referring to a party claiming relief and a party against whom relief is sought.

Former Rule 56(c), (d), and (e) stated circumstances in which summary judgment "shall be rendered," the court "shall if practicable" ascertain facts existing without substantial controversy, and "if appropriate, shall" enter summary judgment. In each place "shall" is changed to "should." It is established that although there is no discretion to enter summary judgment when there is a genuine issue as to any material fact, there is discretion to deny summary judgment when it appears that there is no genuine issue as to any material fact. *Kennedy v. Silas Mason Co.*, 334 U.S. 249, 256–257 (1948). Many lower court decisions are gathered in 10A Wright, Miller & Kane, Federal Practice & Procedure: Civil 3d, § 2728. "Should" in amended Rule 56(c) recognizes that courts will seldom exercise the discretion to deny summary judgment when there is no genuine issue as to any material fact. Similarly sparing exercise of this discretion is appropriate under Rule 56(e)(2). Rule 56(d)(1), on the other hand, reflects the more open-ended discretion to decide whether it is practicable to determine what material facts are not genuinely at issue.

Former Rule 56(d) used a variety of different phrases to express the Rule 56(c) standard for summary judgment—that there is no genuine issue as to any material fact. Amended Rule 56(d) adopts terms directly parallel to Rule 56(c).

2009 Amendment

The timing provisions for summary judgment are outmoded. They are consolidated and substantially revised in new subdivision (c)(1). The new rule allows a party to move for summary judgment at any time, even as early as the commencement of the action. If the motion seems premature both subdivision (c)(1) and Rule 6(b) allow the court to extend the time to respond. The rule does set a presumptive deadline at 30 days after the close of all discovery.

The presumptive timing rules are default provisions that may be altered by an order in the case or by local rule. Scheduling orders are likely to supersede the rule provisions in most cases, deferring summary-judgment motions until a stated time or establishing different deadlines. Scheduling orders tailored to the needs of the specific case, perhaps adjusted as it progresses, are likely to work better than default rules. A scheduling order may be adjusted to adopt the parties' agreement on timing, or may require that discovery and motions occur in stages—including separation of expert-witness discovery from other discovery.

Local rules may prove useful when local docket conditions or practices are incompatible with the general Rule 56 timing provisions.

If a motion for summary judgment is filed before a responsive pleading is due from a party affected by the motion, the time for responding to the motion is 21 days after the responsive pleading is due.

2010 Amendment

Rule 56 is revised to improve the procedures for presenting and deciding summary-judgment motions and to make the procedures more consistent with those already used in many courts. The standard for granting summary judgment remains unchanged. The language of subdivision (a) continues to require that there be no genuine dispute as to any material fact and that the movant be entitled to judgment as a matter of law. The amendments will not affect continuing development of the decisional law construing and applying these phrases.

Subdivision (a). Subdivision (a) carries forward the summary-judgment standard expressed in former subdivision (c), changing only one word—genuine "issue" becomes genuine "dispute." "Dispute" better reflects the focus of a summary-judgment determination. As explained below, "shall" also is restored to the place it held from 1938 to 2007.

The first sentence is added to make clear at the beginning that summary judgment may be requested not only as to an entire case but also as to a claim, defense, or part of a claim or defense. The subdivision caption adopts the common phrase "partial summary judgment" to describe disposition of less than the whole action, whether or not the order grants all the relief requested by the motion.

"Shall" is restored to express the direction to grant summary judgment. The word "shall" in Rule 56 acquired significance over many decades of use. Rule 56 was amended in 2007 to replace "shall" with "should" as part of the Style Project, acting under a convention that prohibited any use of "shall." Comments on proposals to amend Rule 56, as published in 2008, have shown that neither of the choices available under the Style Project conventions—"must" or "should"—is suitable in light of the case law on whether a district court has discretion to deny summary judgment when there appears to be no genuine dispute as to any material fact. Compare *Anderson v. Liberty Lobby, Inc.*, 477 U.S. 242, 255 (1986)("Neither do we suggest that the trial courts should act other than with caution in granting summary judgment or that the trial court may not deny summary judgment in a case in which there is reason to believe that the better course would be to proceed to a full trial. *Kennedy v. Silas Mason Co.*, 334 U.S. 249 * * * (1948)"), with *Celotex Corp. v. Catrett*, 477 U.S. 317, 322 (1986)("In our view, the plain language of Rule 56(c) mandates the entry of summary judgment, after adequate time for discovery and upon motion, against a party who fails to make a showing sufficient to establish the existence of an element essential to that party's case, and on which that party will bear the burden of proof at trial."). Eliminating "shall" created an unacceptable risk of changing the summary-judgment standard. Restoring "shall" avoids the unintended consequences of any other word.

Subdivision (a) also adds a new direction that the court should state on the record the reasons for granting or denying the motion. Most courts recognize this practice. Among other advantages, a statement of reasons can facilitate an appeal or subsequent trial-court proceedings. It is particularly important to state the reasons for granting summary judgment. The form and detail of the statement of reasons are left to the court's discretion.

The statement on denying summary judgment need not address every available reason. But identification of central issues may help the parties to focus further proceedings.

Subdivision (b). The timing provisions in former subdivisions (a) and (c) are superseded. Although the rule allows a motion for summary judgment to be filed at the commencement of an action, in many cases the motion will be premature until the nonmovant has had time to file a responsive pleading or other pretrial proceedings have been had. Scheduling orders or other pretrial orders can regulate timing to fit the needs of the case.

Subdivision (c). Subdivision (c) is new. It establishes a common procedure for several aspects of summary-judgment motions synthesized from similar elements developed in the cases or found in many local rules.

Subdivision (c)(1) addresses the ways to support an assertion that a fact can or cannot be genuinely disputed. It does not address the form for providing the required support. Different courts and judges have adopted different forms including, for example, directions that the support be included in the motion, made part of a separate statement of facts, interpolated in the body of a brief or memorandum, or provided in a separate statement of facts included in a brief or memorandum.

Subdivision (c)(1)(A) describes the familiar record materials commonly relied upon and requires that the movant cite the particular parts of the materials that support its fact positions. Materials that are not yet in the record—including materials referred to in an affidavit or declaration—must be placed in the record. Once materials are in the record, the court may, by order in the case, direct that the materials be gathered in an appendix, a party may voluntarily submit an appendix, or the parties may submit a joint appendix. The appendix procedure also may be established by local rule. Pointing to a specific location in an appendix satisfies the citation requirement. So too it may be convenient to direct that a party assist the court in locating materials buried in a voluminous record.

Subdivision (c)(1)(B) recognizes that a party need not always point to specific record materials. One party, without citing any other materials, may respond or reply that materials cited to dispute or support a fact do not establish the absence or presence of a genuine dispute. And a party who does not have the trial burden of production may rely on a showing that a party who does have the trial burden cannot produce admissible evidence to carry its burden as to the fact.

Subdivision (c)(2) provides that a party may object that material cited to support or dispute a fact cannot be presented in a form that would be admissible in evidence. The objection functions much as an objection at trial, adjusted for the pretrial setting. The burden is on the proponent to show that the material is admissible as presented or to explain the admissible form that is anticipated. There is no need to make a separate motion to strike. If the case goes to trial, failure to challenge admissibility at the summary-judgment stage does not forfeit the right to challenge admissibility at trial.

Subdivision (c)(3) reflects judicial opinions and local rules provisions stating that the court may decide a motion for summary judgment without undertaking an independent search of the record. Nonetheless, the rule also recognizes that a court may consider record materials not called to its attention by the parties.

Subdivision (c)(4) carries forward some of the provisions of former subdivision (e)(1). Other provisions are relocated or omitted. The requirement that a sworn or certified copy of a paper referred to in an affidavit or declaration be attached to the affidavit or declaration is omitted as unnecessary given the requirement in subdivision (c)(1)(A) that a statement or dispute of fact be supported by materials in the record.

A formal affidavit is no longer required. 28 U.S.C. § 1746 allows a written unsworn declaration, certificate, verification, or statement subscribed in proper form as true under penalty of perjury to substitute for an affidavit.

Subdivision (d). Subdivision (d) carries forward without substantial change the provisions of former subdivision (f).

A party who seeks relief under subdivision (d) may seek an order deferring the time to respond to the summary-judgment motion.

Subdivision (e). Subdivision (e) addresses questions that arise when a party fails to support an assertion of fact or fails to properly address another party's assertion of fact as required by Rule 56(c). As explained below, summary judgment cannot be granted by default even if there is a complete failure to respond to the motion, much less when an attempted response fails to comply with Rule 56(c) requirements. Nor should it be denied by default even if the movant completely fails to reply to a nonmovant's response. Before deciding on other possible action, subdivision (e)(1) recognizes that the court may afford an opportunity to properly support or address the fact. In many circumstances this opportunity will be the court's preferred first step.

Subdivision (e)(2) authorizes the court to consider a fact as undisputed for purposes of the motion when response or reply requirements are not satisfied. This approach reflects the "deemed admitted" provisions in many local rules. The fact is considered undisputed only for purposes of the motion; if summary judgment is denied, a party who failed to make a proper Rule 56 response or reply remains free to contest the fact in further proceedings. And the court may choose not to consider the fact as undisputed, particularly if the court knows of record materials that show grounds for genuine dispute.

Subdivision (e)(3) recognizes that the court may grant summary judgment only if the motion and supporting materials—including the facts considered undisputed under subdivision (e)(2)—show that the movant is entitled to it. Considering some facts undisputed does not of itself allow summary judgment. If there is a proper response or reply as to some facts, the court cannot grant summary judgment without determining whether those facts can be genuinely disputed. Once the court has determined the set of facts—both those it has chosen to consider undisputed for want of a proper response or reply and any that cannot be genuinely disputed despite a procedurally proper response or reply—it must determine the legal consequences of these facts and permissible inferences from them.

Subdivision (e)(4) recognizes that still other orders may be appropriate. The choice among possible orders should be designed to encourage proper presentation of the record. Many courts take extra care with pro se litigants, advising them of the need to respond and the risk of losing by summary judgment if an adequate response is not filed. And the court may seek to reassure itself by some examination of the record before granting summary judgment against a pro se litigant.

Subdivision (f). Subdivision (f) brings into Rule 56 text a number of related procedures that have grown up in practice. After giving notice and a reasonable time to respond the court may grant summary judgment for the nonmoving party; grant a motion on legal or factual grounds not raised by the parties; or consider summary judgment on its own. In many cases it may prove useful first to invite a motion; the invited motion will automatically trigger the regular procedure of subdivision (c).

Subdivision (g). Subdivision (g) applies when the court does not grant all the relief requested by a motion for summary judgment. It becomes relevant only after the court has applied the summary-judgment standard carried forward in subdivision (a) to each claim, defense, or part of a claim or defense, identified by the motion. Once that duty is discharged, the court may decide whether to apply the summary-judgment standard to dispose of a material fact that is not genuinely in dispute. The court must take care that this determination does not interfere with a party's ability to accept a fact for purposes of the motion only. A nonmovant, for example, may feel confident that a genuine dispute as to one or a few facts will defeat the motion, and prefer to avoid the cost of detailed response to all facts stated by the movant. This position should be available without running the risk that the fact will be taken as established under subdivision (g) or otherwise found to have been accepted for other purposes.

If it is readily apparent that the court cannot grant all the relief requested by the motion, it may properly decide that the cost of determining whether some potential fact disputes may be eliminated by summary disposition is greater than the cost of resolving those disputes by other means, including trial. Even if the court believes that a fact is not genuinely in dispute it may refrain from ordering that the fact be treated as established. The court may conclude that it is better to leave open for trial facts and issues that may be better illuminated by the trial of related facts that must be tried in any event.

Subdivision (h). Subdivision (h) carries forward former subdivision (g) with three changes. Sanctions are made discretionary, not mandatory, reflecting the experience that courts seldom invoke the independent Rule 56 authority to impose sanctions. See Cecil & Cort, Federal Judicial Center Memorandum on Federal Rule of Civil Procedure 56(g) Motions for Sanctions (April 2, 2007). In addition, the rule text is expanded to recognize the need to provide notice and a reasonable time to respond. Finally, authority to impose other appropriate sanctions also is recognized.

CROSS REFERENCES

Dismissal of action prior to service of motion for summary judgment, see Fed.Rules Civ.Proc. Rule 41, 28 USCA.

Findings of fact and conclusions of law unnecessary, see Fed.Rules Civ.Proc. Rule 52, 28 USCA.

Injunctions, single judge not to enter summary judgment, see 28 USCA § 2284.

Jurisdiction for lawsuits against terrorist states and bar on motions to dismiss, see 28 USCA § 1605.

Motion for judgment on pleadings, see Fed.Rules Civ.Proc. Rule 12, 28 USCA.

Rule 57. Declaratory Judgment

These rules govern the procedure for obtaining a declaratory judgment under 28 U.S.C. § 2201. Rules 38 and 39 govern a demand for a jury trial. The existence of another adequate remedy does not preclude a declaratory judgment that is otherwise appropriate. The court may order a speedy hearing of a declaratory-judgment action.

(Amended December 29, 1948, effective October 20, 1949; April 30, 2007, effective December 1, 2007.)

ADVISORY COMMITTEE NOTES

1937 Adoption

The fact that a declaratory judgment may be granted "whether or not further relief is or could be prayed" indicates that declaratory relief is alternative or cumulative and not exclusive or extraordinary. A declaratory judgment is appropriate when it will "terminate the controversy" giving rise on undisputed or relatively undisputed facts, it operates frequently as a summary proceeding, justifying docketing the case for early hearing as on a motion, as provided for in California (Code Civ.Proc. (Deering, 1937) § 1062a), Michigan (3 Comp.Laws (1929) § 13904), and Kentucky (Codes (Carroll, 1932) Civ.Pract. § 639a–3).

The "controversy" must necessarily be "of a justiciable nature, thus excluding an advisory decree upon a hypothetical state of facts." *Ashwander v. Tennessee Valley Authority*, 1936, 56 S.Ct. 466, 473, 297 U.S. 288, 80 L.Ed. 688. The existence or non-existence of any right, duty, power, liability, privilege, disability, or immunity or of any fact upon which such legal relations depend, or of a status, may be declared. The petitioner must have a practical interest in the declaration sought and all parties having an interest therein or adversely affected must be made parties or be cited. A declaration may not be rendered if a special statutory proceeding has been provided for the adjudication of some special type of case, but general ordinary or extraordinary legal remedies, whether regulated by statute or not, are not deemed special statutory proceedings.

When declaratory relief will not be effective in settling the controversy, the court may decline to grant it. But the fact that another remedy would be equally effective affords no ground for declining declaratory relief. The demand for relief shall state with precision the declaratory judgment relief, cumulatively or in the alternative; but when coercive relief only is sought but is deemed ungrantable, or inappropriate, the court may *sua sponte*, if it serves a useful purpose, grant instead a declaration of rights. *Hasselbring v. Koepke*, 1933, 248 N.W. 869, 263 Mich. 466, 93 A.L.R. 1170. Written instruments, including ordinances and statutes, may be construed before or after breach at the petition of a properly interested party, process being served on the private parties or public officials interested. In other respects the Uniform Declaratory Judgment Act affords a guide to the scope and function of the Federal act. Compare *Aetna Life Insurance Co. v. Haworth*, 1937, 57 S.Ct. 461, 300 U.S. 227, 81 L.Ed. 617, 108 A.L.R. 1000; *Nashville, Chattanooga & St. Louis Ry. v. Wallace*, 1933, 53 S.Ct. 345, 288 U.S. 249, 77 L.Ed. 730, 87 A.L.R. 1191; *Gully, Tax Collector v. Interstate Natural Gas Co.*, 82 F.2d 145 (C.C.A.5, 1936); *Ohio Casualty Ins. Co. v. Plummer*, Tex.1935, 13 F.Supp. 169; Borchard, Declaratory Judgments (1934), *passim*.

1948 Amendment

The amendment effective October 1949, substituted the reference to "Title 28, U.S.C., § 2201" in the first sentence for the reference to "Section 274(d) of the Judicial Code, as amended, U.S.C., Title 28, § 400".

2007 Amendment

The language of Rule 57 has been amended as part of the general restyling of the Civil Rules to make them more easily understood and to make style and terminology consistent throughout the rules. These changes are intended to be stylistic only.

Rule 58. Entering Judgment

(a) Separate Document. Every judgment and amended judgment must be set out in a separate document, but a separate document is not required for an order disposing of a motion:

(1) for judgment under Rule 50(b);

(2) to amend or make additional findings under Rule 52(b);

(3) for attorney's fees under Rule 54;

(4) for a new trial, or to alter or amend the judgment, under Rule 59; or

(5) for relief under Rule 60.

(b) Entering Judgment.

(1) *Without the Court's Direction.* Subject to Rule 54(b) and unless the court orders otherwise, the clerk must, without awaiting the court's direction, promptly prepare, sign, and enter the judgment when:

(A) the jury returns a general verdict;

(B) the court awards only costs or a sum certain; or

(C) the court denies all relief.

(2) *Court's Approval Required.* Subject to Rule 54(b), the court must promptly approve the form of the judgment, which the clerk must promptly enter, when:

(A) the jury returns a special verdict or a general verdict with answers to written questions; or

(B) the court grants other relief not described in this subdivision (b).

(c) Time of Entry. For purposes of these rules, judgment is entered at the following times:

(1) if a separate document is not required, when the judgment is entered in the civil docket under Rule 79(a); or

(2) if a separate document is required, when the judgment is entered in the civil docket under Rule 79(a) and the earlier of these events occurs:

(A) it is set out in a separate document; or

(B) 150 days have run from the entry in the civil docket.

(d) Request for Entry. A party may request that judgment be set out in a separate document as required by Rule 58(a).

(e) Cost or Fee Awards. Ordinarily, the entry of judgment may not be delayed, nor the time for appeal extended, in order to tax costs or award fees. But if a timely motion for attorney's fees is made under Rule 54(d)(2), the court may act before a notice of appeal has been filed and become effective to order that the motion have the same effect under Federal Rule of Appellate Procedure 4(a)(4) as a timely motion under Rule 59.

(Amended December 27, 1946, effective March 19, 1948; January 21, 1963, effective July 1, 1963; April 22, 1993, effective December 1, 1993; April 29, 2002, effective December 1, 2002; April 30, 2007, effective December 1, 2007.)

ADVISORY COMMITTEE NOTES

1937 Adoption

See Wis.Stat. (1935) § 270.31 (judgment entered forthwith on verdict of jury unless otherwise ordered), § 270.65 (where trial is by the court, entered by direction of the court), § 270.63 (entered by clerk on judgment on admitted claim for money). Compare 1 Idaho Code Ann. (1932) § 7–1101, and 4 Mont.Rev.Codes Ann. (1935) § 9403, which provide that judgment in jury cases be entered by clerk within 24 hours after verdict unless court otherwise directs. Conn.Practice Book (1934), § 200, provides that all judgments shall be entered within one week after rendition. In some States such as Washington, 2 Rev.Stat.Ann. (Remington, 1932), § 431, in jury cases the judgment is entered two days after the return of verdict to give time for making motion for new trial; § 435 (*ibid.*), provides that all judgments shall be entered by the clerk, subject to the court's direction.

1946 Amendment

Note. The reference to Rule 54(b) is made necessary by the amendment of that rule.

Two changes have been made in Rule 58 in order to clarify the practice. The substitution of the more inclusive phrase "all relief be denied" for the words "there be no recovery", makes it clear that the clerk shall enter the judgment forthwith in the situations specified without awaiting the filing of a formal judgment approved by the court. The phrase "all relief be denied" covers cases such as the denial of a bankrupt's discharge and similar situations where the relief sought is refused but there is literally no denial of a "recovery".

The addition of the last sentence in the rule emphasizes that judgments are to be entered promptly by the clerk without waiting for the taxing of costs. Certain district court rules, for example, Civil Rule 22 of the Southern District of New York—until its annulment Oct. 1, 1945, for conflict with this rule—and the like rule of the Eastern District of New York, are expressly in conflict with this provision, although the federal law is of long standing and well settled. *Fowler v. Hamill*, 1891, 11 S.Ct. 663, 139 U.S. 549, 35 L.Ed. 266; *Craig v. The Hartford*, C.C.Cal.1856, Fed.Cas. No. 3,333; *Tuttle v. Claflin*, C.C.A.2, 1895, 60 F. 7, certiorari denied 1897; 17 S.Ct. 992, 166 U.S. 721, 41 L.Ed. 1188; *Prescott & A.C. Ry. Co. v. Atchison, T. & S.F.R. Co.*, C.C.A.2, 1897, 84 F. 213; *Stallo v. Wagner*, C.C.A.2, 1917, 245 F. 636, 639–40; *Brown v. Parker*, C.C.A.8, 1899, 97 F. 446; *Allis-Chalmers v. United States*, C.C.A.7, 1908, 162 F. 679. And this applies even though state law is to the contrary. *United States v. Nordbye*, C.C.A.8, 1935, 75 F.2d 744, certiorari denied 56 S.Ct. 103,

296 U.S. 572, 80 L.Ed. 404. Inasmuch as it has been held that failure of the clerk thus to enter judgment is a "misprision" "not to be excused", *The Washington*, C.C.A.2, 1926, 16 F.2d 206, such a district court rule may have serious consequences for a district court clerk. Rules of this sort also provide for delay in entry of the judgment contrary to Rule 58. See *Commissioner of Internal Revenue v. Bedford's Estate*, 1945, 65 S.Ct. 1157, 325 U.S. 283, 91 L.Ed. 1611.

1963 Amendment

Under the present rule a distinction has sometimes been made between judgments on general jury verdicts, on the one hand, and, on the other, judgments upon decisions of the court that a party shall recover only money or costs or that all relief shall be denied. In the first situation, it is clear that the clerk should enter the judgment without awaiting a direction by the court unless the court otherwise orders. In the second situation it was intended that the clerk should similarly enter the judgment forthwith upon the court's decision; but because of the separate listing in the rule, and the use of the phrase "upon receipt . . . of the direction," the rule has sometimes been interpreted as requiring the clerk to await a separate direction of the court. All these judgments are usually uncomplicated, and should be handled in the same way. The amended rule accordingly deals with them as a single group in clause (1) (substituting the expression "only a sum certain" for the present expression "only money"), and requires the clerk to prepare, sign and enter them forthwith, without awaiting court direction, unless the court makes a contrary order. (The clerk's duty is ministerial and may be performed by a deputy clerk in the name of the clerk. See 28 U.S.C. § 956; cf. *Gilbertson v. United States*, 168 Fed. 672 (7th Cir. 1909).) The more complicated judgments described in clause (2) must be approved by the court before they are entered.

Rule 58 is designed to encourage all reasonable speed in formulating and entering the judgment when the case has been decided. Participation by the attorneys through the submission of forms of judgment involves needless expenditure of time and effort and promotes delay, except in special cases where counsel's assistance can be of real value. See *Matteson v. United States*, 240 F.2d 517, 518–19 (2d Cir. 1956). Accordingly, the amended rule provides that attorneys shall not submit forms of judgment unless directed to do so by the court. This applies to the judgments mentioned in clause (2) as well as clause (1).

Hitherto some difficulty has arisen, chiefly where the court has written an opinion or memorandum containing some apparently directive or dispositive words, e.g., "the plaintiff's motion [for summary judgment] is granted," see *United States v. F. & M. Schaefer Brewing Co.*, 356 U.S. 227, 229, 78 S.Ct. 674, 2 L.Ed.2d 721 (1958). Clerks on occasion have viewed these opinions or memoranda as being in themselves a sufficient basis for entering judgment in the civil docket as provided by Rule 79(a). However, where the opinion or memorandum has not contained all the elements of a judgment, or where the judge has later signed a formal judgment, it has become a matter of doubt whether the purported entry of judgment was effective, starting the time running for post-verdict motions and for the purpose of appeal. See id.; and compare *Blanchard v. Commonwealth Oil Co.*, 294 F.2d 834 (5th Cir. 1961); *United States v. Higginson*, 238 F.2d 439 (1st Cir. 1956); *Danzig v. Virgin Isle Hotel, Inc.*, 278 F.2d 580 (3d Cir. 1960); *Sears v. Austin*, 282 F.2d 340 (9th Cir. 1960), with *Matteson v. United States*, supra; *Erstling v. Southern Bell*

Tel. & Tel. Co., 255 F.2d 93 (5th Cir. 1958); *Barta v. Oglala Sioux Tribe*, 259 F.2d 553 (8th Cir. 1958) cert. denied, 358 U.S. 932, 79 S.Ct. 320, 3 L.Ed.2d 304 (1959); *Beacon Fed. S. & L. Assn. v. Federal Home L. Bank Bd.*, 266 F.2d 246 (7th Cir.), cert. denied, 361 U.S. 823, 80 S.Ct. 70, 4 L.Ed.2d 67 (1959); *Ram v. Paramount Film D. Corp.*, 278 F.2d 191 (4th Cir. 1960).

The amended rule eliminates these uncertainties by requiring that there be a judgment set out on a separate document—distinct from any opinion or memorandum—which provides the basis for the entry of judgment. That judgment shall be on separate documents is also indicated in Rule 79(b); and see General Rule 10 of the U.S. District Courts for the Eastern and Southern Districts of New York; *Ram v. Paramount Film D. Corp.*, supra, at 194.

See the amendment of Rule 79(a) and the new specimen forms of judgment, Forms 31 and 32.

See also Rule 55(b)(1) and (2) covering the subject of judgments by default.

1993 Amendment

Ordinarily the pendency or post-judgment filing of a claim for attorney's fees will not affect the time for appeal from the underlying judgment. See Budinich v. Becton Dickinson & Co., 486 U.S. 196 (1988). Particularly if the claim for fees involves substantial issues or is likely to be affected by the appellate decision, the district court may prefer to defer consideration of the claim for fees until after the appeal is resolved. However, in many cases it may be more efficient to decide fee questions before an appeal is taken so that appeals relating to the fee award can be heard at the same time as appeals relating to the merits of the case. This revision permits, but does not require, the court to delay the finality of the judgment for appellate purposes under revised Fed. R.App.P. 4(a) until the fee dispute is decided. To accomplish this result requires entry of an order by the district court before the time a notice of appeal becomes effective for appellate purposes. If the order is entered, the motion for attorney's fees is treated in the same manner as a timely motion under Rule 59.

2002 Amendment

Rule 58 has provided that a judgment is effective only when set forth on a separate document and entered as provided in Rule 79(a). This simple separate document requirement has been ignored in many cases. The result of failure to enter judgment on a separate document is that the time for making motions under Rules 50, 52, 54(d)(2)(B), 59, and some motions under Rule 60, never begins to run. The time to appeal under Appellate Rule 4(a) also does not begin to run. There have been few visible problems with respect to Rule 50, 52, 54(d)(2)(B), 59, or 60 motions, but there have been many and horridly confused problems under Appellate Rule 4(a). These amendments are designed to work in conjunction with Appellate Rule 4(a) to ensure that appeal time does not linger on indefinitely, and to maintain the integration of the time periods set for Rules 50, 52, 54(d)(2)(B), 59, and 60 with Appellate Rule 4(a).

Rule 58(a) preserves the core of the present separate document requirement, both for the initial judgment and for any amended judgment. No attempt is made to sort through the confusion that some courts have found in addressing the elements of a separate document. It is easy to prepare a separate document that recites the terms of the judgment without offering additional explanation or citation of authority. Forms 31 and 32 provide examples.

Rule 58 is amended, however, to address a problem that arises under Appellate Rule 4(a). Some courts treat such orders as those that deny a motion for new trial as a "judgment," so that appeal time does not start to run until the order is entered on a separate document. Without attempting to address the question whether such orders are appealable, and thus judgments as defined by Rule 54(a), the amendment provides that entry on a separate document is not required for an order disposing of the motions listed in Appellate Rule 4(a). The enumeration of motions drawn from the Appellate Rule 4(a) list is generalized by omitting details that are important for appeal time purposes but that would unnecessarily complicate the separate document requirement. As one example, it is not required that any of the enumerated motions be timely. Many of the enumerated motions are frequently made before judgment is entered. The exemption of the order disposing of the motion does not excuse the obligation to set forth the judgment itself on a separate document. And if disposition of the motion results in an amended judgment, the amended judgment must be set forth on a separate document.

Rule 58(b) discards the attempt to define the time when a judgment becomes "effective." Taken in conjunction with the Rule 54(a) definition of a judgment to include "any order from which an appeal lies," the former Rule 58 definition of effectiveness could cause strange difficulties in implementing pretrial orders that are appealable under interlocutory appeal provisions or under expansive theories of finality. Rule 58(b) replaces the definition of effectiveness with a new provision that defines the time when judgment is entered. If judgment is promptly set forth on a separate document, as should be done when required by Rule 58(a)(1), the new provision will not change the effect of Rule 58. But in the cases in which court and clerk fail to comply with this simple requirement, the motion time periods set by Rules 50, 52, 54, 59, and 60 begin to run after expiration of 150 days from entry of the judgment in the civil docket as required by Rule 79(a).

A companion amendment of Appellate Rule 4(a)(7) integrates these changes with the time to appeal.

The new all-purpose definition of the entry of judgment must be applied with common sense to other questions that may turn on the time when judgment is entered. If the 150–day provision in Rule 58(b)(2)(B)—designed to integrate the time for post-judgment motions with appeal time—serves no purpose, or would defeat the purpose of another rule, it should be disregarded. In theory, for example, the separate document requirement continues to apply to an interlocutory order that is appealable as a final decision under collateral-order doctrine. Appealability under collateral-order doctrine should not be complicated by failure to enter the order as a judgment on a separate document—there is little reason to force trial judges to speculate about the potential appealability of every order, and there is no means to ensure that the trial judge will always reach the same conclusion as the court of appeals. Appeal time should start to run when the collateral order is entered without regard to creation of a separate document and without awaiting expiration of the 150 days provided by Rule 58(b)(2). Drastic surgery on Rules 54(a) and 58 would be required to address this and related issues, however, and it is better to leave this conundrum to the pragmatic disregard that seems its present fate. The present amendments do not seem to make matters worse, apart from one false appearance. If a pretrial order is set forth on a separate document that meets the requirements of Rule 58(b), the time to move for reconsideration seems to begin to run, perhaps years before final judgment. And even if there is no separate document, the time to move for reconsideration seems to begin 150 days after entry in the civil docket. This apparent problem is resolved by Rule 54(b), which expressly permits revision of all orders not made final under Rule 54(b) "at any time before the entry of judgment adjudicating all the claims and the rights and liabilities of all the parties."

New Rule 58(d) replaces the provision that attorneys shall not submit forms of judgment except on direction of the court. This provision was added to Rule 58 to avoid the delays that were frequently encountered by the former practice of directing the attorneys for the prevailing party to prepare a form of judgment, and also to avoid the occasionally inept drafting that resulted from attorney-prepared judgments. See *11 Wright, Miller & Kane, Federal Practice & Procedure: Civil 2d, § 2786*. The express direction in Rule 58(a)(2) for prompt action by the clerk, and by the court if court action is required, addresses this concern. The new provision allowing any party to move for entry of judgment on a separate document will protect all needs for prompt commencement of the periods for motions, appeals, and execution or other enforcement.

Changes Made After Publication and Comment Minor style changes were made. The definition of the time of entering judgment in Rule 58(b) was extended to reach all Civil Rules, not only the Rules described in the published version—Rules 50, 52, 54(d)(2)(B), 59, 60, and 62. And the time of entry was extended from 60 days to 150 days after entry in the civil docket without a required separate document.

2007 Amendment

The language of Rule 58 has been amended as part of the general restyling of the Civil Rules to make them more easily understood and to make style and terminology consistent throughout the rules. These changes are intended to be stylistic only.

CROSS REFERENCES

General verdict accompanied by answers to interrogatories by jury, see Fed.Rules Civ.Proc. Rule 49, 28 USCA.

Judgment for particular claim or counterclaim, see Fed. Rules Civ.Proc. Rule 54, 28 USCA.

Notation of entry of judgment, see Fed.Rules Civ.Proc. Rule 79, 28 USCA.

Notice of entry of judgment, see Fed.Rules Civ.Proc. Rule 77, 28 USCA.

Record on appeal, see Federal Rules of Appellate Procedure Rule 10, 28 USCA.

Time for new trial, see Fed.Rules Civ.Proc. Rule 59, 28 USCA.

Time to appeal, see Federal Rules of Appellate Procedure Rule 4, 28 USCA.

Rule 59. New Trial; Altering or Amending a Judgment

(a) In General.

(1) Grounds for New Trial. The court may, on motion, grant a new trial on all or some of the issues—and to any party—as follows:

　　(A) after a jury trial, for any reason for which a new trial has heretofore been granted in an action at law in federal court; or

　　(B) after a nonjury trial, for any reason for which a rehearing has heretofore been granted in a suit in equity in federal court.

(2) Further Action After a Nonjury Trial. After a nonjury trial, the court may, on motion for a new trial, open the judgment if one has been entered, take additional testimony, amend findings of fact and conclusions of law or make new ones, and direct the entry of a new judgment.

(b) Time to File a Motion for a New Trial. A motion for a new trial must be filed no later than 28 days after the entry of judgment.

(c) Time to Serve Affidavits. When a motion for a new trial is based on affidavits, they must be filed with the motion. The opposing party has 14 days after being served to file opposing affidavits. The court may permit reply affidavits.

(d) New Trial on the Court's Initiative or for Reasons Not in the Motion. No later than 28 days after the entry of judgment, the court, on its own, may order a new trial for any reason that would justify granting one on a party's motion. After giving the parties notice and an opportunity to be heard, the court may grant a timely motion for a new trial for a reason not stated in the motion. In either event, the court must specify the reasons in its order.

(e) Motion to Alter or Amend a Judgment. A motion to alter or amend a judgment must be filed no later than 28 days after the entry of the judgment. (Amended December 27, 1946, effective March 19, 1948; February 28, 1966, effective July 1, 1966; April 27, 1995, effective December 1, 1995; April 30, 2007, effective December 1, 2007; March 26, 2009, effective December 1, 2009.)

ADVISORY COMMITTEE NOTES
1937 Adoption

This rule represents an amalgamation of the petition for rehearing of [former] Equity Rule 69 (Petition for Rehearing) and the motion for new trial of 28 U.S.C., § 2111, formerly § 391 (New trials; harmless error), made in the light of the experience and provision of the code States. Compare Calif.Code Civ.Proc., Deering, 1937, §§ 656 to 663a, 28 U.S.C., § 2111, formerly § 391 (New trials; harmless error) is thus substantially continued in this rule. U.S.C., Title 28, [former] § 840 (Executions; stay on conditions) is modified insofar as it contains time provisions inconsistent with Subdivision (b). For the effect of the motion for new trial upon the time for taking an appeal see *Morse v. United States*, 1926, 46 S.Ct. 241, 270 U.S. 151, 70 L.Ed. 518; *Aspen Mining and Smelting Co. v. Billings*, 1893, 14 S.Ct. 4, 150 U.S. 31, 37 L.Ed. 986.

For partial new trials which are permissible under Subdivision (a), see *Gasoline Products Co., Inc. v. Champlin Refining Co.*, 1931, 51 S.Ct. 513, 283 U.S. 494, 75 L.Ed. 1188;

Schuerholz v. Roach, C.C.A.4, 1932, 58 F.2d 32; *Simmons v. Fish*, 1912, 97 N.E. 102, 210 Mass. 563, Ann.Cas.1912D, 588 (sustaining and recommending the practice and citing federal cases and cases in accord from about sixteen States and contra from three States). The procedure in several States provides specifically for partial new trials. Ariz.Rev.Code Ann., Struckmeyer, 1928, § 3852; Calif.Code Civ.Proc., Deering, 1937, §§ 657, 662; Smith-Hurd Ill.Stats., 1937, c. 110, § 216 (Par. (f)); Md.Ann.Code, Bagby, 1924, Art. 5, §§ 25, 26; Mich.Court Rules Ann., Searl, 1933, Rule 47, § 2; Miss. Sup.Ct.Rule 12, 161 Miss. 903, 905, 1931; N.J.Sup.Ct.Rules 131, 132, 147, 2 N.J.Misc. 1197, 1246–1251, 1255, 1924; 2 N.D.Comp.Laws Ann., 1913, § 7844, as amended by N.D.Laws 1927, ch. 214.

1946 Amendment

Note. Subdivision (b). With the time for appeal to a circuit court of appeals reduced in general to 30 days by the proposed amendment of Rule 73(a), the utility of the original "except" clause, which permits a motion for a new trial on the ground of newly discovered evidence to be made before the expiration of the time for appeal, would have been seriously restricted. It was thought advisable, therefore, to take care of this matter in another way. By amendment of Rule 60(b), newly discovered evidence is made the basis for relief from a judgment, and the maximum time limit has been extended to one year. Accordingly the amendment of Rule 59(b) eliminates the "except" clause and its specific treatment of newly discovered evidence as a ground for a motion for new trial. This ground remains, however, as a basis for a motion for new trial served not later than 10 days after the entry of judgment. See also Rule 60(b).

As to the effect of a motion under subdivision (b) upon the running of appeal time, see amended Rule 73(a) and Note.

Note to Subdivision (e). This subdivision has been added to care for a situation such as that arising in *Boaz v. Mutual Life Ins. Co. of New York*, C.C.A.8, 1944, 146 F.2d 321, and makes clear that the district court possesses the power asserted in that case to alter or amend a judgment after its entry. The subdivision deals only with alteration or amendment of the original judgment in a case and does not relate to a judgment upon motion as provided in Rule 50(b). As to the effect of a motion under subdivision (e) upon the running of appeal time, see amended Rule 73(a) and Note.

The title of Rule 59 has been expanded to indicate the inclusion of this subdivision.

1966 Amendment

By narrow interpretation of Rule 59(b) and (d), it has been held that the trial court is without power to grant a motion for a new trial, timely served, by an order made more than 10 days after the entry of judgment, based upon a ground not stated in the motion but perceived and relied on by the trial court sua sponte. *Freid v. McGrath*, 133 F.2d 350 (D.C.Cir. 1942); *National Farmers Union Auto. & Cas. Co. v. Wood*, 207 F.2d 659 (10th Cir. 1953); *Bailey v. Slentz*, 189 F.2d 406 (10th Cir. 1951); *Marshall's U.S. Auto Supply, Inc. v. Cashman*, 111 F.2d 140 (10th Cir. 1940), cert. denied, 311 U.S. 667 (1940); but see *Steinberg v. Indemnity Ins. Co.*, 36 F.R.D. 253 (E.D.La.1964).

The result is undesirable. Just as the court has power under Rule 59(d) to grant a new trial of its own initiative within the 10 days, so it should have power, when an effective new trial motion has been made and is pending, to decide it on grounds thought meritorious by the court although not advanced in the motion. The second sentence added by amendment to Rule 59(d) confirms the court's power in the latter situation, with provision that the parties be afforded a hearing before the power is exercised. See 6 *Moore's Federal Practice,* par. 59.09[2] (2d ed. 1953).

In considering whether a given ground has or has not been advanced in the motion made by the party, it should be borne in mind that the particularity called for in stating the grounds for a new trial motion is the same as that required for all motions by Rule 7(b)(1). The latter rule does not require ritualistic detail but rather a fair indication to court and counsel of the substance of the grounds relied on. See *Lebeck v. William A. Jarvis Co.,* 250 F.2d 285 (3d Cir. 1957); *Tsai v. Rosenthal,* 297 F.2d 614 (8th Cir. 1961); *General Motors Corp. v. Perry,* 303 F.2d 544 (7th Cir. 1962); cf. *Grimm v. California Spray-Chemical Corp.,* 264 F.2d 145 (9th Cir. 1959); *Cooper v. Midwest Feed Products Co.,* 271 F.2d 177 (8th Cir. 1959).

1995 Amendment

The only change, other than stylistic, intended by this revision is to add explicit time limits for filing motions for a new trial, motions to alter or amend a judgment, and affidavits opposing a new trial motion. Previously, there was an inconsistency in the wording of Rules 50, 52, and 59 with respect to whether certain post-judgment motions had to be filed, or merely served, during the prescribed period. This inconsistency caused special problems when motions for a new trial were joined with other post-judgment motions. These motions affect the finality of the judgment, a matter often of importance to third persons as well as the parties and the court. The Committee believes that each of these rules should be revised to require filing before end of the 10–day period. Filing is an event that can be determined with certainty from court records. The phrase "no later than" is used—rather than "within"—to include post-judgment motions that sometimes are filed before actual entry of the judgment by the clerk. It should be noted that under Rule 5 the motions when filed are to contain a certificate of service on other parties. It also should be noted that under Rule 6(a) Saturdays, Sundays, and legal holidays are excluded in measuring the 10–day period, but that Bankruptcy Rule 9006(a) excludes intermediate Saturdays, Sundays, and legal holidays only in computing periods less than 8 days.

2007 Amendment

The language of Rule 59 has been amended as part of the general restyling of the Civil Rules to make them more easily understood and to make style and terminology consistent throughout the rules. These changes are intended to be stylistic only.

2009 Amendment

Former Rules 50, 52, and 59 adopted 10–day periods for their respective post-judgment motions. Rule 6(b) prohibits any expansion of those periods. Experience has proved that in many cases it is not possible to prepare a satisfactory post-judgment motion in 10 days, even under the former rule that excluded intermediate Saturdays, Sundays, and legal holidays. These time periods are particularly sensitive because Appellate Rule 4 integrates the time to appeal with a timely motion

under these rules. Rather than introduce the prospect of uncertainty in appeal time by amending Rule 6(b) to permit additional time, the former 10–day periods are expanded to 28 days. Rule 6(b) continues to prohibit expansion of the 28–day period.

Former Rule 59(c) set a 10–day period after being served with a motion for new trial to file opposing affidavits. It also provided that the period could be extended for up to 20 days for good cause or by stipulation. The apparent 20–day limit on extending the time to file opposing affidavits seemed to conflict with the Rule 6(b) authority to extend time without any specific limit. This tension between the two rules may have been inadvertent. It is resolved by deleting the former Rule 59(c) limit. Rule 6(b) governs. The underlying 10–day period was extended to 14 days to reflect the change in the Rule 6(a) method for computing periods of less than 11 days.

CROSS REFERENCES

Answers to written interrogatories inconsistent with general verdict as ground for ordering new trial, see Fed.Rules Civ.Proc. Rule 49, 28 USCA.

Claims Court, grounds for new trial, see 28 USCA § 2515.

Extension of time for motion, see Fed.Rules Civ.Proc. Rule 6, 28 USCA.

Harmless error not ground for new trial, see Fed.Rules Civ.Proc. Rule 61, 28 USCA.

Joinder of motion for new trial with renewal motion for judgment as a matter of law, see Fed.Rules Civ.Proc. Rule 50, 28 USCA.

Motion to amend findings or make additional findings, see Fed.Rules Civ.Proc. Rule 52, 28 USCA.

Stay of execution or proceedings to enforce judgment on motion for new trial, see Fed.Rules Civ.Proc. Rule 62, 28 USCA.

Termination of running of time for appeal to court of appeals, see Federal Rules of Appellate Procedure Rule 4, 28 USCA.

Rule 60. Relief From a Judgment or Order

(a) Corrections Based on Clerical Mistakes; Oversights and Omissions. The court may correct a clerical mistake or a mistake arising from oversight or omission whenever one is found in a judgment, order, or other part of the record. The court may do so on motion or on its own, with or without notice. But after an appeal has been docketed in the appellate court and while it is pending, such a mistake may be corrected only with the appellate court's leave.

(b) Grounds for Relief from a Final Judgment, Order, or Proceeding. On motion and just terms, the court may relieve a party or its legal representative from a final judgment, order, or proceeding for the following reasons:

(1) mistake, inadvertence, surprise, or excusable neglect;

(2) newly discovered evidence that, with reasonable diligence, could not have been discovered in time to move for a new trial under Rule 59(b);

(3) fraud (whether previously called intrinsic or extrinsic), misrepresentation, or misconduct by an opposing party;

(4) the judgment is void;

(5) the judgment has been satisfied, released, or discharged; it is based on an earlier judgment that has been reversed or vacated; or applying it prospectively is no longer equitable; or

(6) any other reason that justifies relief.

(c) Timing and Effect of the Motion.

(1) *Timing.* A motion under Rule 60(b) must be made within a reasonable time—and for reasons (1), (2), and (3) no more than a year after the entry of the judgment or order or the date of the proceeding.

(2) *Effect on Finality.* The motion does not affect the judgment's finality or suspend its operation.

(d) Other Powers to Grant Relief. This rule does not limit a court's power to:

(1) entertain an independent action to relieve a party from a judgment, order, or proceeding;

(2) grant relief under 28 U.S.C. § 1655 to a defendant who was not personally notified of the action; or

(3) set aside a judgment for fraud on the court.

(e) Bills and Writs Abolished. The following are abolished: bills of review, bills in the nature of bills of review, and writs of coram nobis, coram vobis, and audita querela.

(Amended December 27, 1946, effective March 19, 1948; December 29, 1948, effective October 20, 1949; March 2, 1987, effective August 1, 1987; April 30, 2007, effective December 1, 2007.)

ADVISORY COMMITTEE NOTES

1937 Adoption

Note to Subdivision (a). See [former] Equity Rule 72 (Correction of Clerical Mistakes in Orders and Decrees); Mich.Court Rules Ann. (Searl, 1933) Rule 48, § 3; 2 Wash. Rev.Stat.Ann. (Remington, 1932) § 464(3); Wyo.Rev.Stat. Ann. (Courtright, 1931) § 89–2301(3). For an example of a very liberal provision for the correction of clerical errors and for amendment after judgment, see Va.Code Ann. (Michie, 1936) §§ 6329, 6333.

Note to Subdivision (b). Application to the court under this subdivision does not extend the time for taking an appeal, as distinguished from the motion for new trial. This section is based upon Calif.Code Civ.Proc. (Deering, 1937) § 473. See also N.Y.C.P.A. (1937) § 108; 2 Minn.Stat. (Mason, 1927) § 9283.

For the independent action to relieve against mistake, etc., see Dobie, *Federal Procedure*, pages 760 to 765, compare 639; and Simkins, *Federal Practice*, ch. CXXI (pp. 820 to 830) and ch. CXXII (pp. 831 to 834), compare § 214.

1946 Amendment

Note. Subdivision (a). The amendment incorporates the view expressed in *Perlman v. 322 West Seventy-Second Street, Co., Inc.,* C.C.A.2d, 1942, 127 F.2d 716; 3 *Moore's*

Federal Practice, 1938, 3276, and further permits correction after docketing, with leave of the appellate court. Some courts have thought that upon the taking of an appeal the district court lost its power to act. See *Schram v. Safety Investment Co.,* E.D.Mich.1942, 45 F.Supp. 636; also *Miller v. United States,* C.C.A.7th, 1940, 114 F.2d 267.

Subdivision (b). When promulgated, the rules contained a number of provisions, including those found in Rule 60(b), describing the practice by a motion to obtain relief from judgments, and these rules, coupled with the reservation in Rule 60(b) of the right to entertain a new action to relieve a party from a judgment, were generally supposed to cover the field. Since the rules have been in force, decisions have been rendered that the use of bills of review, coram nobis, or audita querela, to obtain relief from final judgments is still proper, and that various remedies of this kind still exist although they are not mentioned in the rules and the practice is not prescribed in the rules. It is obvious that the rules should be complete in this respect and define the practice with respect to any existing rights or remedies to obtain relief from final judgments. For extended discussion of the old common law writs and equitable remedies, the interpretation of Rule 60, and proposals for change, see Moore and Rogers, *Federal Relief from Civil Judgments,* 1946, 55 Yale L.J. 623. See also 3 *Moore's Federal Practice,* 1938, 3254 et seq.; Commentary, *Effect of Rule 60b on Other Methods of Relief From Judgment,* 1941, 4 Fed.Rules Serv. 942, 945; *Wallace v. United States,* C.C.A.2d, 1944, 142 F.2d 240, certiorari denied 65 S.Ct. 37, 323 U.S. 712, 89 L.Ed. 573.

The reconstruction of Rule 60(b) has for one of its purposes a clarification of this situation. Two types of procedure to obtain relief from judgments are specified in the rules as it is proposed to amend them. One procedure is by motion in the court and in the action in which the judgment was rendered. The other procedure is by a new or independent action to obtain relief from a judgment, which action may or may not be begun in the court which rendered the judgment. Various rules, such as the one dealing with a motion for new trial and for amendment of judgments, Rule 59, one for amended findings, Rule 52, and one for judgment notwithstanding the verdict, Rule 50(b), and including the provisions of Rule 60(b) as amended, prescribe the various types of cases in which the practice by motion is permitted. In each case there is a limit upon the time within which resort to a motion is permitted, and this time limit may not be enlarged under Rule 6(b). If the right to make a motion is lost by the expiration of the time limits fixed in these rules, the only other procedural remedy is by a new or independent action to set aside a judgment upon those principles which have heretofore been applied in such an action. Where the independent action is resorted to, the limitations of time are those of laches or statutes of limitations. The Committee has endeavored to ascertain all the remedies and types of relief heretofore available by coram nobis, coram vobis, audita querela, bill of review, or bill in the nature of a bill of review. See Moore and Rogers, *Federal Relief from Civil Judgments,* 1946, 55 Yale L.J. 623, 659 to 682. It endeavored then to amend the rules to permit, either by motion or by independent action, the granting of various kinds of relief from judgments which were permitted in the federal courts prior to the adoption of these rules, and the amendment concludes with a provision abolishing the use of bills of review and the other common law writs referred to, and requiring the practice to be by motion or by independent action.

To illustrate the operation of the amendment, it will be noted that under Rule 59(b) as it now stands, without amendment, a motion for new trial on the ground of newly discovered evidence is permitted within ten days after the entry of the judgment, or after that time upon leave of the court. It is proposed to amend Rule 59(b) by providing that under that rule a motion for new trial shall be served not later than ten days after the entry of the judgment, whatever the ground be for the motion, whether error by the court or newly discovered evidence. On the other hand, one of the purposes of the bill of review in equity was to afford relief on the ground of newly discovered evidence long after the entry of the judgment. Therefore, to permit relief by a motion similar to that heretofore obtained on bill of review, Rule 60(b) as amended permits an application for relief to be made by motion, on the ground of newly discovered evidence, within one year after judgment. Such a motion under Rule 60(b) does not affect the finality of the judgment, but a motion under Rule 59, made within 10 days, does affect finality and the running of the time for appeal.

If these various amendments, including principally those to Rule 60(b), accomplish the purpose for which they are intended, the federal rules will deal with the practice in every sort of case in which relief from final judgments is asked, and prescribe the practice. With reference to the question whether, as the rules now exist, relief by coram nobis, bills of review, and so forth, is permissible, the generally accepted view is that the remedies are still available, although the precise relief obtained in a particular case by use of these ancillary remedies is shrouded in ancient lore and mystery. See *Wallace v. United States,* C.C.A.2d, 1944, 142 F.2d 240, certiorari denied 65 S.Ct. 37, 323 U.S. 712, 89 L.Ed. 573; *Fraser v. Doing,* App.D.C.1942, 130 F.2d 617; *Jones v. Watts,* C.C.A.5th, 1944, 142 F.2d 575; *Preveden v. Hahn,* S.D.N.Y. 1941, 36 F.Supp. 952; *Cavallo v. Agwilines, Inc.,* S.D.N.Y. 1942, 6 Fed.Rules Serv. 60b.31, Case 2, 2 F.R.D. 526; *McGinn v. United States,* D.C.Mass.1942, 6 Fed.Rules Serv. 60b.51, Case 3, 2 F.R.D. 562; *City of Shattuck, Oklahoma ex rel. Versluis v. Oliver,* W.D.Okl.1945, 8 Fed.Rules Serv. 60b.31, Case 3; Moore and Rogers, *Federal Relief from Civil Judgments,* 1946, 55 Yale L.J. 623, 631 to 653; 3 *Moore's Federal Practice,* 1938, 3254 et seq.; Commentary, *Effect of Rule 60b on Other Methods of Relief From Judgment,* op. cit. supra. Cf. *Norris v. Camp,* C.C.A.10th, 1944, 144 F.2d 1; *Reed v. South Atlantic Steamship Co. of Delaware,* D.Del. 1942, 2 F.R.D. 475, 6 Fed.Rules Serv. 60b.31, Case 1; *Laughlin v. Berens,* D.D.C.1945, 8 Fed.Rules Serv. 60b.51, Case 1, 73 W.L.R. 209.

The transposition of the words "the court" and the addition of the word "and" at the beginning of the first sentence are merely verbal changes. The addition of the qualifying word "final" emphasizes the character of the judgments, orders or proceedings from which Rule 60(b) affords relief; and hence interlocutory judgments are not brought within the restrictions of the rule, but rather they are left subject to the complete power of the court rendering them to afford such relief from them as justice requires.

The qualifying pronoun "his" has been eliminated on the basis that it is too restrictive, and that the subdivision should include the mistake or neglect of others which may be just as material and call just as much for supervisory jurisdiction as where the judgment is taken against the party through *his* mistake, inadvertence, etc.

Fraud, whether intrinsic or extrinsic, misrepresentation, or other misconduct of an adverse party are express grounds for relief by motion under amended subdivision (b). There is no sound reason for their exclusion. The incorporation of fraud and the like within the scope of the rule also removes confusion as to the proper procedure. It has been held that relief from a judgment obtained by extrinsic fraud could be secured by motion within a "reasonable time," which might be after the time stated in the rule had run. *Fiske v. Buder,* C.C.A.8th, 1942, 125 F.2d 841; see also inferentially *Bucy v. Nevada Construction Co.,* C.C.A.9th, 1942, 125 F.2d 213. On the other hand, it has been suggested that in view of the fact that fraud was omitted from original Rule 60(b) as a ground for relief, an independent action was the only proper remedy. Commentary, *Effect of Rule 60b on Other Methods of Relief From Judgment,* 1941, 4 Fed.Rules Serv. 942, 945. The amendment settles this problem by making fraud an express ground for relief by motion; and under the saving clause, fraud may be urged as a basis for relief by independent action insofar as established doctrine permits. See Moore and Rogers, *Federal Relief from Civil Judgments,* 1946, 55 Yale L.J. 623, 653 to 659; 3 Moore's Federal Practice, 1938, 3267 et seq. And the rule expressly does not limit the power of the court, when fraud has been perpetrated upon it, to give relief under the saving clause. As an illustration of this situation, see *Hazel-Atlas Glass Co. v. Hartford Empire Co.,* 1944, 64 S.Ct. 997, 322 U.S. 238, 88 L.Ed. 1250.

The time limit for relief by motion in the court and in the action in which the judgment was rendered has been enlarged from six months to one year.

It should be noted that Rule 60(b) does not assume to define the substantive law as to the grounds for vacating judgments, but merely prescribes the practice in proceedings to obtain relief. It should also be noted that under § 200(4) of the Soldiers' and Sailors' Civil Relief Act of 1940, § 501 et seq. [§ 520(4)] of the Appendix to Title 50, a judgment rendered in any action or proceeding governed by the section may be vacated under certain specified circumstances upon proper application to the court.

1948 Amendment

The amendment effective October, 1949 substituted the reference to "Title 28, U.S.C. § 1655," in the next to the last sentence of subdivision (b), for the reference to "Section 57 of the Judicial Code, U.S.C., Title 28, § 118".

1987 Amendment

The amendment is technical. No substantive change is intended.

2007 Amendment

The language of Rule 60 has been amended as part of the general restyling of the Civil Rules to make them more easily understood and to make style and terminology consistent throughout the rules. These changes are intended to be stylistic only.

The final sentence of former Rule 60(b) said that the procedure for obtaining any relief from a judgment was by motion as prescribed in the Civil Rules or by an independent action. That provision is deleted as unnecessary. Relief continues to be available only as provided in the Civil Rules or by independent action.

Enlargement of time under this rule prohibited, see Fed. Rules Civ.Proc. Rule 6, 28 USCA.

Formal terms of district court abolished, see 28 USCA § 138.

Stay of proceedings pending disposition of motion under this rule, see Fed.Rules Civ.Proc. Rule 62, 28 USCA.

Time for appeal, see 28 USCA § 2107.

Time for motion for new trial, see Fed.Rules Civ.Proc. Rule 59, 28 USCA.

Rule 61. Harmless Error

Unless justice requires otherwise, no error in admitting or excluding evidence—or any other error by the court or a party—is ground for granting a new trial, for setting aside a verdict, or for vacating, modifying, or otherwise disturbing a judgment or order. At every stage of the proceeding, the court must disregard all errors and defects that do not affect any party's substantial rights.
(Amended April 30, 2007, effective December 1, 2007.)

ADVISORY COMMITTEE NOTES

1937 Adoption

A combination of U.S.C., Title 28, § 2111, [former] § 391 (New trials; harmless error) and [former] § 777 (Defects of form; amendments) with modifications. See *McCandless v. United States*, 1936, 56 S.Ct. 764, 298 U.S. 342, 80 L.Ed. 1205. Compare [former] Equity Rule 72 (Correction of Clerical Mistakes in Orders and Decrees); and last sentence of [former] Equity Rule 46 (Trial—Testimony Usually Taken in Open Court—Rulings on Objections to Evidence). For the last sentence see the last sentence of [former] Equity Rule 19 (Amendments Generally).

2007 Amendment

The language of Rule 61 has been amended as part of the general restyling of the Civil Rules to make them more easily understood and to make style and terminology consistent throughout the rules. These changes are intended to be stylistic only.

Admissibility of evidence, generally, see Fed.Rules Civ. Proc. Rule 43, 28 USCA.

Formal exceptions unnecessary, see Fed.Rules Civ.Proc. Rule 46, 28 USCA.

Grounds for new trial, see Fed.Rules Civ.Proc. Rules 33 and 59, 28 USCA.

Harmless and plain error, see Fed.Rules Cr.Proc. Rule 52, 18 USCA.

Harmless error on appeal or certiorari, see 28 USCA § 2111.

Instructions to jury, see Fed.Rules Civ.Proc. Rule 51, 28 USCA.

Judgment as a matter of law in actions tried by jury, alternative motion for new trial, see Fed.Rules Civ.Proc. Rule 50, 28 USCA.

Motion to vacate judgment or order, see Fed.Rules Civ. Proc. Rule 60, 28 USCA.

Power of appellate court to affirm, modify, reverse, and remand case, see 28 USCA § 2106.

Rule 62. Stay of Proceedings to Enforce a Judgment

(a) Automatic Stay. Except as provided in Rule 62(c) and (d), execution on a judgment and proceedings to enforce it are stayed for 30 days after its entry, unless the court orders otherwise.

(b) Stay by Bond or Other Security. At any time after judgment is entered, a party may obtain a stay by providing a bond or other security. The stay takes effect when the court approves the bond or other security and remains in effect for the time specified in the bond or other security.

(c) Stay of an Injunction, Receivership, or Patent Accounting Order. Unless the court orders otherwise, the following are not stayed after being entered, even if an appeal is taken:

(1) an interlocutory or final judgment in an action for an injunction or receivership; or

(2) a judgment or order that directs an accounting in an action for patent infringement.

(d) Injunction Pending an Appeal. While an appeal is pending from an interlocutory order or final judgment that grants, continues, modifies, refuses, dissolves, or refuses to dissolve or modify an injunction, the court may suspend, modify, restore, or grant an injunction on terms for bond or other terms that secure the opposing party's rights. If the judgment appealed from is rendered by a statutory three-judge district court, the order must be made either:

(1) by that court sitting in open session; or

(2) by the assent of all its judges, as evidenced by their signatures.

(e) Stay Without Bond on an Appeal by the United States, Its Officers, or Its Agencies. The court must not require a bond, obligation, or other security from the appellant when granting a stay on an appeal by the United States, its officers, or its agencies or on an appeal directed by a department of the federal government.

(f) Stay in Favor of a Judgment Debtor Under State Law. If a judgment is a lien on the judgment debtor's property under the law of the state where the court is located, the judgment debtor is entitled to the same stay of execution the state court would give.

(g) Appellate Court's Power Not Limited. This rule does not limit the power of the appellate court or one of its judges or justices:

(1) to stay proceedings—or suspend, modify, restore, or grant an injunction—while an appeal is pending; or

(2) to issue an order to preserve the status quo or the effectiveness of the judgment to be entered.

(h) Stay with Multiple Claims or Parties. A court may stay the enforcement of a final judgment entered under Rule 54(b) until it enters a later judgment or judgments, and may prescribe terms necessary to secure the benefit of the stayed judgment for the party in whose favor it was entered.

(Amended December 27, 1946, effective March 19, 1948; December 29, 1948, effective October 20, 1949; April 17, 1961, effective July 19, 1961; March 2, 1987, effective August 1, 1987; April 30, 2007, effective December 1, 2007; March 26, 2009, effective December 1, 2009; April 26, 2018, effective December 1, 2018.)

ADVISORY COMMITTEE NOTES

1937 Adoption

Note to Subdivision (a). The first sentence states the substance of the last sentence of U.S.C., Title 28, [former] § 874 (Supersedeas). The remainder of the subdivision states the substance of the last clause of U.S.C., Title 28, § 1292, [formerly] § 227 (Appeals in proceedings for injunctions; receivers; and admiralty), and of §§ 1292, 2107, [formerly] § 227a (Appeals in suits in equity for infringement of letters patent for inventions; stay of proceedings for accounting), but extended to include final as well as interlocutory judgments.

Note to Subdivision (b). This modifies U.S.C., Title 28, [former] § 840 (Executions; stay on conditions).

Note to Subdivision (c). Compare [former] Equity Rule 74 (Injunction Pending Appeal); and *Cumberland Telephone and Telegraph Co. v. Louisiana Public Service Commission,* 1922, 43 S.Ct. 75, 260 U.S. 212, 67 L.Ed. 217. See Simkins, Federal Practice (1934), § 916, in regard to the effect of appeal on injunctions and the giving of bonds. See U.S.C., [former] Title 6 (Official and Penal Bonds) for bonds by surety companies. For statutes providing for a specially constituted district court of three judges, see:

U.S.C., Title 7:

§ 217 (Proceedings for suspension of orders of Secretary of Agriculture under Stockyards Act)—by reference.

§ 499k (Injunctions; application of injunction laws governing orders of Interstate Commerce Commission to orders of Secretary of Agriculture under Perishable Commodities Act)—by reference.

U.S.C., Title 15:

§ 28 (Antitrust laws; suits against monopolies expedited)

U.S.C., Title 28, former:

§ 47 [now 2325 (repealed)] (Injunctions as to orders of Interstate Commerce Commission, etc.)

§ 380 [now 2284] (Injunctions; alleged unconstitutionality of State statutes)

§ 380a [now 2284] (Same; constitutionality of federal statute)

U.S.C., Title 49:

§ 44 [former] (Suits in equity under interstate commerce laws; expedition of suits)

Note to Subdivision (d). This modifies U.S.C., Title 28, [former] § 874 (Supersedeas). See Rule 36(2), Rules of the Supreme Court of the United States, which governs supersedeas bonds on direct appeals to the Supreme Court, and Rule 73(d), of these rules, which governs supersedeas bonds on

appeals to a circuit court of appeals. The provisions governing supersedeas bonds in both kinds of appeals are substantially the same.

Note to Subdivision (e). This states the substance of U.S.C., Title 28, § 2408, formerly § 870 (Bond; not required of the United States).

Note to Subdivision (f). This states the substance of U.S.C., Title 28, [former] § 841 (Executions; stay of one term) with appropriate modification to conform to the provisions of Rule 6(c) as to terms of court.

1946 Amendment

Note. Subdivision (a). [This subdivision not amended]. Sections 203 and 204 of the Soldiers' and Sailors' Civil Relief Act of 1940, [former] 50 U.S.C., Appendix, § 501 et seq. [§§ 523, 524] [now 50 U.S.C. §§ 3933, 3934], provide under certain circumstances for the issuance and continuance of a stay of execution of any judgment or order entered against a person in military service. See *Bowsman v. Peterson,* D.Neb. 1942, 45 F.Supp. 741. Section 201 of the Act [50 U.S.C. § 3931] permits under certain circumstances the issuance of a stay of any action or proceeding at any stage thereof, where either the plaintiff or defendant is a person in military service. See also note to Rule 64 herein.

Subdivision (b). This change was necessary because of the proposed addition to Rule 59 of subdivision (e).

Subdivision (h). In proposing to revise Rule 54(b), the Committee thought it advisable to include a separate provision in Rule 62 for stay of enforcement of a final judgment in cases involving multiple claims.

1948 Amendment

The amendment effective October 1949 deleted at the end of subdivision (g) the following language which originally appeared after the word "entered": "and these rules do not supersede the provisions of Section 210 of the Judicial Code, as amended, U.S.C., Title 28, [former] § 47a, or of other statutes of the United States to the effect that stays pending appeals to the Supreme Court may be granted only by that court or a justice thereof."

1961 Amendment

The amendment adopted Apr. 17, 1961, effective July 19, 1961, eliminated words "on some but not all of the claims presented in the action" which followed "final judgment".

1987 Amendment

The amendment is technical. No substantive change is intended.

2007 Amendment

The language of Rule 62 has been amended as part of the general restyling of the Civil Rules to make them more easily understood and to make style and terminology consistent throughout the rules. These changes are intended to be stylistic only.

The final sentence of former Rule 62(a) referred to Rule 62(c). It is deleted as an unnecessary. Rule 62(c) governs of its own force.

2009 Amendment

The time set in the former rule at 10 days has been revised to 14 days. See the Note to Rule 6.

2018 Amendments

Subdivisions (a), (b), (c), and (d) of former Rule 62 are reorganized and the provisions for staying a judgment are revised.

The provisions for staying an injunction, receivership, or order for a patent accounting are reorganized by consolidating them in new subdivisions (c) and (d). There is no change in meaning. The language is revised to include all of the words used in 28 U.S.C. § 1292(a)(1) to describe the right to appeal from interlocutory actions with respect to an injunction, but subdivisions (c) and (d) apply both to interlocutory injunction orders and to final judgments that grant, refuse, or otherwise deal with an injunction.

New Rule 62(a) extends the period of the automatic stay to 30 days. Former Rule 62(a) set the period at 14 days, while former Rule 62(b) provided for a court-ordered stay "pending disposition of" motions under Rules 50, 52, 59, and 60. The time for making motions under Rules 50, 52, and 59, however, was later extended to 28 days, leaving an apparent gap between expiration of the automatic stay and any of those motions (or a Rule 60 motion) made more than 14 days after entry of judgment. The revised rule eliminates any need to rely on inherent power to issue a stay during this period. Setting the period at 30 days coincides with the time for filing most appeals in civil actions, providing a would-be appellant the full period of appeal time to arrange a stay by other means. A 30–day automatic stay also suffices in cases governed by a 60–day appeal period.

Amended Rule 62(a) expressly recognizes the court's authority to dissolve the automatic stay or supersede it by a court-ordered stay. One reason for dissolving the automatic stay may be a risk that the judgment debtor's assets will be dissipated. Similarly, it may be important to allow immediate enforcement of a judgment that does not involve a payment of money. The court may address the risks of immediate execution by ordering dissolution of the stay only on condition that security be posted by the judgment creditor. Rather than dissolve the stay, the court may choose to supersede it by ordering a stay that lasts longer or requires security.

Subdivision 62(b) carries forward in modified form the supersedeas bond provisions of former Rule 62(d). A stay may be obtained under subdivision (b) at any time after judgment is entered. Thus a stay may be obtained before the automatic stay has expired, or after the automatic stay has been lifted by the court. The new rule's text makes explicit the opportunity to post security in a form other than a bond. The stay takes effect when the court approves the bond or other security and remains in effect for the time specified in the bond or security—a party may find it convenient to arrange a single bond or other security that persists through completion of post-judgment proceedings in the trial court and on through completion of all proceedings on appeal by issuance of the appellate mandate. This provision does not supersede the opportunity for a stay under 28 U.S.C. § 2101(f) pending review by the Supreme Court on certiorari. Finally, subdivision (b) changes the provision in former subdivision (d) that "an appellant" may obtain a stay. Under new subdivision (b), "a party" may obtain a stay. For example, a party may wish to secure a stay pending disposition of post-judgment proceedings after expiration of the automatic stay, not yet knowing whether it will want to appeal.

CROSS REFERENCES

Deposit of bonds or notes of United States in lieu of surety, see 31 USCA § 9303.

Execution, see Fed.Rules Civ.Proc. Rule 69, 28 USCA.

Security not required of United States, see 28 USCA § 2408.

Stay of execution of judgment against person in military service, see 50 USCA § 3934.

Supersedeas bond for stay on appeal to court of appeals, see Federal Rules of Appellate Procedure Rule 8, 28 USCA.

Rule 62.1.   Indicative Ruling on a Motion for Relief That Is Barred by a Pending Appeal

(a) Relief Pending Appeal. If a timely motion is made for relief that the court lacks authority to grant because of an appeal that has been docketed and is pending, the court may:

    (1) defer considering the motion;

    (2) deny the motion; or

    (3) state either that it would grant the motion if the court of appeals remands for that purpose or that the motion raises a substantial issue.

(b) Notice to the Court of Appeals. The movant must promptly notify the circuit clerk under Federal Rule of Appellate Procedure 12.1 if the district court states that it would grant the motion or that the motion raises a substantial issue.

(c) Remand. The district court may decide the motion if the court of appeals remands for that purpose.

(Added March 26, 2009, effective December 1, 2009.)

ADVISORY COMMITTEE NOTES

2009 Adoption

This new rule adopts for any motion that the district court cannot grant because of a pending appeal the practice that most courts follow when a party makes a Rule 60(b) motion to vacate a judgment that is pending on appeal. After an appeal has been docketed and while it remains pending, the district court cannot grant a Rule 60(b) motion without a remand. But it can entertain the motion and deny it, defer consideration, or state that it would grant the motion if the court of appeals remands for that purpose or state that the motion raises a substantial issue. Experienced lawyers often refer to the suggestion for remand as an "indicative ruling." (Appellate Rule 4(a)(4) lists six motions that, if filed within the relevant time limit, suspend the effect of a notice of appeal filed before or after the motion is filed until the last such motion is disposed of. The district court has authority to grant the motion without resorting to the indicative ruling procedure.)

This clear procedure is helpful whenever relief is sought from an order that the court cannot reconsider because the order is the subject of a pending appeal. Rule 62.1 does not attempt to define the circumstances in which an appeal limits or defeats the district court's authority to act in the face of a pending appeal. The rules that govern the relationship between trial courts and appellate courts may be complex, depending in part on the nature of the order and the source of appeal jurisdiction. Rule 62.1 applies only when those rules deprive the district court of authority to grant relief without appellate permission. If the district court concludes that it has authority to grant relief without appellate permission, it can act without falling back on the indicative ruling procedure.

To ensure proper coordination of proceedings in the district court and in the appellate court, the movant must notify the circuit clerk under Federal Rule of Appellate Procedure 12.1 if the district court states that it would grant the motion or that the motion raises a substantial issue. Remand is in the court of appeals' discretion under Appellate Rule 12.1.

Often it will be wise for the district court to determine whether it in fact would grant the motion if the court of appeals remands for that purpose. But a motion may present complex issues that require extensive litigation and that may either be mooted or be presented in a different context by decision of the issues raised on appeal. In such circumstances the district court may prefer to state that the motion raises a substantial issue, and to state the reasons why it prefers to decide only if the court of appeals agrees that it would be useful to decide the motion before decision of the pending appeal. The district court is not bound to grant the motion after stating that the motion raises a substantial issue; further proceedings on remand may show that the motion ought not be granted.

Rule 63. Judge's Inability to Proceed

If a judge conducting a hearing or trial is unable to proceed, any other judge may proceed upon certifying familiarity with the record and determining that the case may be completed without prejudice to the parties. In a hearing or a nonjury trial, the successor judge must, at a party's request, recall any witness whose testimony is material and disputed and who is available to testify again without undue burden. The successor judge may also recall any other witness. (Amended March 2, 1987, effective August 1, 1987; April 30, 1991, effective December 1, 1991; April 30, 2007, effective December 1, 2007.)

ADVISORY COMMITTEE NOTES

1937 Adoption

This rule adapts and extends the provisions of U.S.C., Title 28, [former] § 776 (Bill of exceptions; authentication; signing of by judge) to include all duties to be performed by the judge after verdict or judgment. The statute is therefore superseded.

1987 Amendment

The amendments are technical. No substantive change is intended.

1991 Amendment

The revision substantially displaces the former rule. The former rule was limited to the disability of the judge, and made no provision for disqualification or possible other rea-

sons for the withdrawal of the judge during proceedings. In making provision for other circumstances, the revision is not intended to encourage judges to discontinue participation in a trial for any but compelling reasons. Cf. *United States v. Lane,* 708 F.2d 1394, 1395–1397 (9th Cir.1983). Manifestly, a substitution should not be made for the personal convenience of the court, and the reasons for a substitution should be stated on the record.

The former rule made no provision for the withdrawal of the judge during the trial, but was limited to disqualification after trial. Several courts concluded that the text of the former rule prohibited substitution of a new judge prior to the points described in the rule, thus requiring a new trial, whether or not a fair disposition was within reach of a substitute judge. *E.g., Whalen v. Ford Motor Credit Co.,* 684 F.2d 272 (4th Cir.1982, en banc) *cert. denied,* 459 U.S. 910 (1982) (jury trial); *Arrow–Hart, Inc. v. Philip Carey Co.,* 552 F.2d 711 (6th Cir.1977) (non-jury trial). *See generally* Comment, *The Case of the Dead Judge: Fed.R.Civ.P. 63: Whalen v. Ford Motor Credit Co.,* 67 MINN.L.REV. 827 (1983).

The increasing length of federal trials has made it likely that the number of trials interrupted by the disability of the judge will increase. An efficient mechanism for completing these cases without unfairness is needed to prevent unnecessary expense and delay. To avoid the injustice that may result if the substitute judge proceeds despite unfamiliarity with the action, the new Rule provides, in language similar to Federal Rule of Criminal Procedure 25(a), that the successor judge must certify familiarity with the record and determine that the case may be completed before that judge without prejudice to the parties. This will necessarily require that there be available a transcript or a videotape of the proceedings prior to substitution. If there has been a long but incomplete jury trial, the prompt availability of the transcript or videotape is crucial to the effective use of this rule, for the jury cannot long be held while an extensive transcript is prepared without prejudice to one or all parties.

The revised text authorizes the substitute judge to make a finding of fact at a bench trial based on evidence heard by a different judge. This may be appropriate in limited circumstances. First, if a witness has become unavailable, the testimony recorded at trial can be considered by the successor judge pursuant to Fed. R. Evid. 804, being equivalent to a recorded deposition available for use at trial pursuant to Rule 32. For this purpose, a witness who is no longer subject to a subpoena to compel testimony at trial is unavailable. Secondly, the successor judge may determine that particular testimony is not material or is not disputed, and so need not be reheard. The propriety of proceeding in this manner may be marginally affected by the availability of a videotape record; a judge who has reviewed a trial on videotape may be entitled to greater confidence in his or her ability to proceed.

The court would, however, risk error to determine the credibility of a witness not seen or heard who is available to be recalled. Cf. *Anderson v. City of Bessemer City NC,* 470 U.S. 564, 575 (1985); *Marshall v. Jerrico Inc.,* 446 U.S. 238, 242 (1980). See also *United States v. Radatz,* 447 U.S. 667 (1980).

2007 Amendment

The language of Rule 63 has been amended as part of the general restyling of the Civil Rules to make them more easily understood and to make style and terminology consistent throughout the rules. These changes are intended to be stylistic only.

CROSS REFERENCES

Disability of judge, successor judge, certification of familiarity with record in order to proceed, see Fed.Rules Cr.Proc. Rule 25, 18 USCA.

Findings of fact and conclusions of law, see Fed.Rules Civ.Proc. Rule 52, 28 USCA.

New trial, see Fed.Rules Civ.Proc. Rule 59, 28 USCA.

TITLE VIII.   PROVISIONAL AND FINAL REMEDIES

ADVISORY COMMITTEE NOTES

1991 Amendment

The purpose of the revision is to divide this chapter of the Rules into two. No substantive change is effected.

Rule 64.   Seizing a Person or Property

(a) Remedies Under State Law—In General. At the commencement of and throughout an action, every remedy is available that, under the law of the state where the court is located, provides for seizing a person or property to secure satisfaction of the potential judgment. But a federal statute governs to the extent it applies.

(b) Specific Kinds of Remedies. The remedies available under this rule include the following—however designated and regardless of whether state procedure requires an independent action:

- arrest;
- attachment;
- garnishment;
- replevin;
- sequestration; and
- other corresponding or equivalent remedies.

(Amended April 30, 2007, effective December 1, 2007.)

ADVISORY COMMITTEE NOTES

1937 Adoption

This rule adopts the existing Federal law, except that it specifies the applicable State law to be that of the time when the remedy is sought. Under U.S.C., Title 28, [former] § 726 (Attachments as provided by State laws) the plaintiff was entitled to remedies by attachment or other process which were on June 1, 1872, provided by the applicable State law, and the district courts might, from time to time, by general rules, adopt such State laws as might be in force. This statute is superseded as are district court rules which are rendered unnecessary by the rule.

Lis pendens. No rule concerning lis pendens is stated, for this would appear to be a matter of substantive law affecting State laws of property. It has been held that in the absence of a State statute expressly providing for the recordation of notice of the pendency of Federal actions, the commencement of a Federal action is notice to all persons affected. *King v. Davis*, 137 F. 198 (W.D.Va., 1903). It has been held, however, that when a state statute does so provide expressly, its provisions are binding. *United States v. Calcasieu Timber Co.*, 236 F. 196 (C.C.A.5th, 1916).

For statutes of the United States on attachment, see, e.g.:

U.S.C., Title 28 former:

§ 737 [now 2710] (Attachment in postal suits)

§ 738 [now 2711] (Attachment; application for warrant)

§ 739 [now 2712] (Attachment; issue of warrant)

§ 740 [now 2713] (Attachment; trial of ownership of property)

§ 741 [now 2714] (Attachment; investment of proceeds of attached property)

§ 742 [now 2715] (Attachment; publication of attachment)

§ 743 [now 2716] (Attachment; personal notice of attachment)

§ 744 [now 2717] (Attachment; discharge; bond)

§ 745 [former] (Attachment; accrued rights not affected)

§ 746 (Attachments dissolved in conformity with State laws)

For statutes of the United States on garnishment, see, e.g.:

U.S.C., Title 28, former:

§ 748 [now 2405] (Garnishees in suits by United States against a corporation)

§ 749 [now 2405] (Same; issue tendered on denial of indebtedness)

§ 750 [now 2405] (Same; garnishee failing to appear)

For statutes of the United States on arrest, see, e.g.:

U.S.C., Title 28 former:

§ 376 [now 1651] (Writs of ne exeat)

§ 755 [former] (Special bail in suits for duties and penalties)

§ 756 [former] (Defendant giving bail in one district and committed in another)

§ 757 [former] (Defendant giving bail in one district and committed in another; defendant held until judgment in first suit)

§ 758 [former] (Bail and affidavits; taking by commissioners)

§ 759 [former] (Calling of bail in Kentucky)

§ 760 [former] (Clerks may take bail de bene esse)

§ 843 [now 2007] (Imprisonment for debt)

§ 844 [now 2007] (Imprisonment for debt; discharge according to State laws)

§ 845 [now 2007] (Imprisonment for debt; jail limits)

For statutes of the United States on replevin, see, e.g.:

U.S.C., Title 28:

§ 2463, formerly § 747 (Replevy of property taken under revenue laws).

Supplementary Note

Note. Sections 203 and 204 of the Soldiers' and Sailors' Civil Relief Act of 1940, [former] 50 U.S.C.Appendix, § 501 et seq. [§§ 523 and 524] [now 50 U.S.C. §§ 3933, 3934], provide under certain circumstances for the issuance and continuance of a stay of the execution of any judgment entered against a person in military service, or the vacation or stay of any attachment or garnishment directed against such person's property, money, or debts in the hands of another. See also Note to Rule 62 herein.

2007 Amendment

The language of Rule 64 has been amended as part of the general restyling of the Civil Rules to make them more easily understood and to make style and terminology consistent throughout the rules. These changes are intended to be stylistic only.

Former Rule 64 stated that the Civil Rules govern an action in which any remedy available under Rule 64(a) is used. The Rules were said to govern from the time the action is commenced if filed in federal court, and from the time of removal if removed from state court. These provisions are deleted as redundant. Rule 1 establishes that the Civil Rules apply to all actions in a district court, and Rule 81(c)(1) adds reassurance that the Civil Rules apply to a removed action "after it is removed."

CROSS REFERENCES

Execution, see Fed.Rules Civ.Proc. Rule 69, 28 USCA.

Rule 65. Injunctions and Restraining Orders

(a) Preliminary Injunction.

(1) *Notice.* The court may issue a preliminary injunction only on notice to the adverse party.

(2) *Consolidating the Hearing with the Trial on the Merits.* Before or after beginning the hearing on a motion for a preliminary injunction, the court may advance the trial on the merits and consolidate it with the hearing. Even when consolidation is not ordered, evidence that is received on the motion and that would be admissible at trial becomes part of the trial record and need not be repeated at trial. But the court must preserve any party's right to a jury trial.

(b) Temporary Restraining Order.

(1) *Issuing Without Notice.* The court may issue a temporary restraining order without written or oral notice to the adverse party or its attorney only if:

(A) specific facts in an affidavit or a verified complaint clearly show that immediate and irreparable injury, loss, or damage will result to the movant before the adverse party can be heard in opposition; and

(B) the movant's attorney certifies in writing any efforts made to give notice and the reasons why it should not be required.

(2) *Contents; Expiration.* Every temporary restraining order issued without notice must state the date and hour it was issued; describe the injury and state why it is irreparable; state why the order was issued without notice; and be promptly filed in the clerk's office and entered in the record. The order expires at the time after entry—not to exceed 14 days—that the court sets, unless before that time the court, for good cause, extends it for a like period or the adverse party consents to a longer extension. The reasons for an extension must be entered in the record.

(3) *Expediting the Preliminary–Injunction Hearing.* If the order is issued without notice, the motion for a preliminary injunction must be set for hearing at the earliest possible time, taking precedence over all other matters except hearings on older matters of the same character. At the hearing, the party who obtained the order must proceed with the motion; if the party does not, the court must dissolve the order.

(4) *Motion to Dissolve.* On 2 days' notice to the party who obtained the order without notice—or on shorter notice set by the court—the adverse party may appear and move to dissolve or modify the order. The court must then hear and decide the motion as promptly as justice requires.

(c) Security. The court may issue a preliminary injunction or a temporary restraining order only if the movant gives security in an amount that the court considers proper to pay the costs and damages sustained by any party found to have been wrongfully enjoined or restrained. The United States, its officers, and its agencies are not required to give security.

(d) Contents and Scope of Every Injunction and Restraining Order.

(1) *Contents.* Every order granting an injunction and every restraining order must:

(A) state the reasons why it issued;

(B) state its terms specifically; and

(C) describe in reasonable detail—and not by referring to the complaint or other document—the act or acts restrained or required.

(2) *Persons Bound.* The order binds only the following who receive actual notice of it by personal service or otherwise:

(A) the parties;

(B) the parties' officers, agents, servants, employees, and attorneys; and

(C) other persons who are in active concert or participation with anyone described in Rule 65(d)(2)(A) or (B).

(e) Other Laws Not Modified. These rules do not modify the following:

(1) any federal statute relating to temporary restraining orders or preliminary injunctions in actions affecting employer and employee;

(2) 28 U.S.C. § 2361, which relates to preliminary injunctions in actions of interpleader or in the nature of interpleader; or

(3) 28 U.S.C. § 2284, which relates to actions that must be heard and decided by a three-judge district court.

(f) Copyright Impoundment. This rule applies to copyright-impoundment proceedings.

(Amended December 27, 1946, effective March 19, 1948; December 29, 1948, effective October 20, 1949; February 28, 1966, effective July 1, 1966; March 2, 1987, effective August 1, 1987; April 23, 2001, effective December 1, 2001; April 30, 2007, effective December 1, 2007; March 26, 2009, effective December 1, 2009.)

ADVISORY COMMITTEE NOTES

1937 Adoption

Note to Subdivisions (a) and (b). These are taken from U.S.C., Title 28, [former] § 381 (Injunctions; preliminary injunctions and temporary restraining orders).

Note to Subdivision (c). Except for the last sentence, this is substantially U.S.C., Title 28, [former] § 382 (Injunctions; security on issuance of). The last sentence continues the following and similar statutes which expressly except the United States or an officer or agency thereof from such security requirements: U.S.C. Title 15, §§ 77t(b), 78u(e), and 79r(f) (Securities and Exchange Commission). It also excepts the United States or an officer or agency thereof from such security requirements in any action in which a restraining order or interlocutory judgment of injunction issues in its favor whether there is an express statutory exception from such security requirements or not.

See U.S.C., [former] Title 6 (Official and Penal Bonds) for bonds by surety companies.

Note to Subdivision (d). This is substantially U.S.C., Title 28, [former] § 383 (Injunctions; requisites of order; binding effect).

Note to Subdivision (e). The words "relating to temporary restraining orders and preliminary injunctions in actions affecting employer and employee" are words of description and not of limitation.

Compare [former] Equity Rule 73 (Preliminary Injunctions and Temporary Restraining Orders) which is substantially equivalent to the statutes.

For other statutes dealing with injunctions which are continued, see e.g.:

U.S.C., Title 28 former:

§ 46 [now 2324] (Suits to enjoin orders of Interstate Commerce Commission to be against United States)

§ 47 [now 2325] (Injunctions as to orders of Interstate Commerce Commission; appeal to Supreme Court; time for taking)

§ 378 [former] (Injunctions; when granted)

§ 379 [now 2283] (Injunctions; stay in State courts)

§ 380 [now 1253, 2101, 2281, 2284] (Injunctions; alleged unconstitutionality of State statutes; appeal to Supreme Court)

§ 380a [now 1253, 2101, 2281, 2284] (Injunctions; constitutionality of Federal statute; application for hearing; appeal to Supreme Court)

U.S.C., Title 7:

§ 216 (Court proceedings to enforce orders; injunction)

§ 217 (Proceedings for suspension of orders)

U.S.C., Title 15:

§ 4 (Jurisdiction of courts; duty of district attorney; procedure)

§ 25 (Restraining violations; procedure)

§ 26 (Injunctive relief for private parties; exceptions)

§ 77t(b) (Injunctions and prosecution of offenses)

1946 Amendment

Note. It has been held that in actions on preliminary injunction bonds the district court has discretion to grant relief in the same proceeding or to require the institution of a new action on the bond. *Russell v. Farley*, 1881, 105 U.S. 433, 466. It is believed, however, that in all cases the litigant should have a right to proceed on the bond in the same proceeding, in the manner provided in Rule 73(f) for a similar situation. The paragraph added to Rule 65(c) insures this result and is in the interest of efficiency. There is no reason why Rules 65(c) and 73(f) should operate differently. Compare § 50, sub. n of the Bankruptcy Act, 11 U.S.C. § 78, sub. n, under which actions on all bonds furnished pursuant to the Act may be proceeded upon summarily in the bankruptcy court. See 2 *Collier on Bankruptcy*, 14th ed. by Moore and Oglebay, 1853–1854.

1948 Amendment

The amendment effective October 1949, changed subdivision (e) in the following respects: in the first clause the amendment substituted the words "any statute of the United States" for the words "the Act of October 15, 1914, c. 323, §§ 1 and 20 (38 Stat. 730), U.S.C., Title 29, §§ 52 and 53, or the Act of March 23, 1932, c. 90 (47 Stat. 70), U.S.C., Title 29, c. 6"; in the second clause of subdivision (e) the amendment substituted the reference to "Title 28, U.S.C., § 2361" for the reference to "Section 24(26) of the Judicial Code as amended, U.S.C., Title 28, § 41(26)"; and the third clause was amended to read "Title 28, U.S.C., § 2284," etc., as at present, instead of "the Act of August 24, 1937, c. 754, § 3, relating to actions to enjoin the enforcement of acts of Congress."

1966 Amendment

Subdivision (a)(2). This new subdivision provides express authority for consolidating the hearing of an application for a preliminary injunction with the trial on the merits. The authority can be exercised with particular profit when it appears that a substantial part of the evidence offered on the application will be relevant to the merits and will be presented in such form as to qualify for admission on the trial proper. Repetition of evidence is thereby avoided. The fact that the proceedings have been consolidated should cause no delay in the disposition of the application for the preliminary injunction, for the evidence will be directed in the first instance to that relief, and the preliminary injunction, if justified by the proof, may be issued in the course of the consolidated proceedings. Furthermore, to consolidate the proceedings will tend to expedite the final disposition of the action. It is believed that consolidation can be usefully availed of in many cases.

The subdivision further provides that even when consolidation is not ordered, evidence received in connection with an application for a preliminary injunction which would be admissible on the trial on the merits forms part of the trial record. This evidence need not be repeated on the trial. On the other hand, repetition is not altogether prohibited. That would be impractical and unwise. For example, a witness testifying comprehensively on the trial who has previously testified upon the application for a preliminary injunction might sometimes be hamstrung in telling his story if he could not go over some part of his prior testimony to connect it with his present testimony. So also, some repetition of testimony may be called for where the trial is conducted by a judge who did not hear the application for the preliminary injunction. In general, however, repetition can be avoided with an increase of efficiency in the conduct of the case and without any distortion of the presentation of evidence by the parties.

Since an application for a preliminary injunction may be made in an action in which, with respect to all or part of the merits, there is a right to trial by jury, it is appropriate to add the caution appearing in the last sentence of the subdivision. In such a case the jury will have to hear all the evidence bearing on its verdict, even if some part of the evidence has already been heard by the judge alone on the application for the preliminary injunction.

The subdivision is believed to reflect the substance of the best current practice and introduces no novel conception.

Subdivision (b). In view of the possibly drastic consequences of a temporary restraining order, the opposition should be heard, if feasible, before the order is granted. Many judges have properly insisted that, when time does not permit of formal notice of the application to the adverse party, some expedient, such as telephonic notice to the attorney for the adverse party, be resorted to if this can reasonably be done. On occasion, however, temporary restraining orders have been issued without any notice when it was feasible for some fair, although informal, notice to be given. See the emphatic criticisms in *Pennsylvania Rd. Co. v. Transport Workers Union*, 278 F.2d 693, 694 (3d Cir. 1960); *Arvida Corp. v. Sugarman*, 259 F.2d 428, 429 (2d Cir. 1958); *Lummus Co. v. Commonwealth Oil Ref. Co., Inc.*, 297 F.2d 80, 83 (2d Cir. 1961), cert. denied, 368 U.S. 986 (1962).

Heretofore the first sentence of subdivision (b), in referring to a notice "served" on the "adverse party" on which a "hearing" could be held, perhaps invited the interpretation that the order might be granted without notice if the circumstances did not permit of a formal hearing on the basis of a formal notice. The subdivision is amended to make it plain that informal notice, which may be communicated to the attorney rather than the adverse party, is to be preferred to no notice at all.

Before notice can be dispensed with, the applicant's counsel must give his certificate as to any efforts made to give notice and the reasons why notice should not be required. This certificate is in addition to the requirement of an affidavit or verified complaint setting forth the facts as to the irreparable injury which would result before the opposition could be heard.

The amended subdivision continues to recognize that a temporary restraining order may be issued without any notice when the circumstances warrant.

Subdivision (c). Original Rules 65 and 73 contained substantially identical provisions for summary proceedings against sureties on bonds required or permitted by the rules. There was fragmentary coverage of the same subject in the Admiralty Rules. Clearly, a single comprehensive rule is required, and is incorporated as Rule 65.1.

1987 Amendment

The amendments are technical. No substantive change is intended.

2001 Amendment

New subdivision (f) is added in conjunction with abrogation of the antiquated Copyright Rules of Practice adopted for proceedings under the 1909 Copyright Act. Courts have naturally turned to Rule 65 in response to the apparent inconsistency of the former Copyright Rules with the discretionary impoundment procedure adopted in 1976, 17 U.S.C. § 503(a). Rule 65 procedures also have assuaged well-founded doubts whether the Copyright Rules satisfy more contemporary requirements of due process. See, e.g., *Religious Technology Center v. Netcom On–Line Communications Servs., Inc.*, 923 F.Supp. 1231, 1260–1265 (N.D.Cal.1995); *Paramount Pictures Corp. v. Doe*, 821 F.Supp. 82 (E.D.N.Y.1993); *WPOW, Inc. v. MRLJ Enterprises*, 584 F.Supp. 132 (D.D.C.1984).

A common question has arisen from the experience that notice of a proposed impoundment may enable an infringer to defeat the court's capacity to grant effective relief. Impoundment may be ordered on an ex parte basis under subdivision (b) if the applicant makes a strong showing of the reasons why notice is likely to defeat effective relief. Such no-notice procedures are authorized in trademark infringement proceedings, see 15 U.S.C. § 1116(d), and courts have provided clear illustrations of the kinds of showings that support ex parte relief. See *Matter of Vuitton et Fils S.A.*, 606 F.2d 1 (2d Cir.1979); *Vuitton v. White*, 945 F.2d 569 (3d Cir.1991). In applying the tests for no-notice relief, the court should ask whether impoundment is necessary, or whether adequate protection can be had by a less intrusive form of no-notice relief shaped as a temporary restraining order.

This new subdivision (f) does not limit use of trademark procedures in cases that combine trademark and copyright claims. Some observers believe that trademark procedures should be adopted for all copyright cases, a proposal better considered by Congressional processes than by rulemaking processes.

2007 Amendment

The language of Rule 65 has been amended as part of the general restyling of the Civil Rules to make them more easily understood and to make style and terminology consistent throughout the rules. These changes are intended to be stylistic only.

The final sentence of former Rule 65(c) referred to Rule 65.1. It is deleted as unnecessary. Rule 65.1 governs of its own force.

Rule 65(d)(2) clarifies two ambiguities in former Rule 65(d). The former rule was adapted from former 28 U.S.C. § 363, but omitted a comma that made clear the common doctrine that a party must have actual notice of an injunction in order to be bound by it. Amended Rule 65(d) restores the meaning of the earlier statute, and also makes clear the proposition that an injunction can be enforced against a person who acts in concert with a party's officer, agent, servant, employee, or attorney.

2009 Amendment

The time set in the former rule at 10 days has been revised to 14 days. See the Note to Rule 6.

CROSS REFERENCES

Antitrust laws, restraining violation, see 15 USCA § 4.

Appeals,

Appellate court's power to suspend, modify or grant pending appeal, injunction pending, see Fed.Rules Civ. Proc. Rule 62, 28 USCA.

District courts to courts of appeals, interlocutory orders of district courts, see 28 USCA § 1292.

Atomic Energy Act, enjoining violation of Act or regulation, see 42 USCA § 2280.

Clayton Antitrust Act, violation of, see 15 USCA §§ 25 and 26.

Copyrights, injunction against infringement, see 17 USCA § 502.

Fair Labor Standards Act, restraint of violations of regulations, see 29 USCA § 217.

Federal Deposit Insurance Corporation termination of status as insured depository institution and applicability of rule, see 12 USCA § 1818.

Findings by the Court, judgment on partial findings, see Fed.Rules Civ.Proc. Rule 52, 28 USCA.

Internal revenue, prohibition of suits to restrain assessment or collection, see 26 USCA § 7421.

Labor-Management Relations Act,

Petition by Attorney General to enjoin strike or lockout, see 29 USCA § 178.

Restraining unfair labor practices, see 29 USCA §§ 160 and 161.

Patent infringement, see 35 USCA § 283.

Securities Act, actions to restrain violations, see 15 USCA § 77t.

Securities Exchange Act, restraint of violations, see 15 USCA § 78u.

Stay of State court proceedings, see 28 USCA § 2283.

Three-judge court, composition of, see 28 USCA § 2284.

Rule 65.1. Proceedings Against a Security Provider

Whenever these rules (including the Supplemental Rules for Admiralty or Maritime Claims and Asset Forfeiture Actions) require or allow a party to give security, and security is given with one or more security providers, each provider submits to the court's jurisdiction and irrevocably appoints the court clerk as its agent for receiving service of any papers that affect its liability on the security. The security provider's liability may be enforced on motion without an independent action. The motion and any notice that the court orders may be served on the court clerk, who must promptly send a copy of each to every security provider whose address is known.

(Adopted February 28, 1966, effective July 1, 1966; amended March 2, 1987, effective August 1, 1987; April 12, 2006, effective December 1, 2006; April 30, 2007, effective December 1, 2007; April 26, 2018, effective December 1, 2018.)

ADVISORY COMMITTEE NOTES
1966 Addition

See Note to Rule 65.

1987 Amendment

The amendments are technical. No substantive change is intended.

2006 Amendment

Rule 65.1 is amended to conform to the changed title of the Supplemental Rules.

2007 Amendment

The language of Rule 65.1 has been amended as part of the general restyling of the Civil Rules to make them more easily understood and to make style and terminology consistent throughout the rules. These changes are intended to be stylistic only.

2018 Amendments

Rule 65.1 is amended to reflect the amendments of Rule 62. Rule 62 allows a party to obtain a stay of a judgment "by providing a bond or other security." Limiting Rule 65.1 enforcement procedures to sureties might exclude use of those procedures against a security provider that is not a surety. All security providers, including sureties, are brought into Rule 65.1 by these amendments. But the reference to "bond" is retained in Rule 62 because it has a long history.

The word "mail" is changed to "send" to avoid restricting the method of serving security providers.

Rule 66. Receivers

These rules govern an action in which the appointment of a receiver is sought or a receiver sues or is sued. But the practice in administering an estate by a receiver or a similar court-appointed officer must accord with the historical practice in federal courts or with a local rule. An action in which a receiver has been appointed may be dismissed only by court order. (Amended December 27, 1946, effective March 19, 1948; December 29, 1948, effective October 20, 1949; April 30, 2007, effective December 1, 2007.)

ADVISORY COMMITTEE NOTES
1946 Amendment

Note. The title of Rule 66 has been expanded to make clear the subject of the rule, i.e., federal equity receivers.

The first sentence added to Rule 66 prevents a dismissal by any party, after a federal equity receiver has been appointed, except upon leave of court. A party should not be permitted to oust the court and its officer without the consent of that court. See Civil Rule 31(e), Eastern District of Washington.

The second sentence added at the beginning of the rule deals with suits by or against a federal equity receiver. The first clause thereof eliminates the formal ceremony of an ancillary appointment before suit can be brought by a receiver, and is in accord with the more modern state practice, and with more expeditious and less expensive judicial administration. 2 *Moore's Federal Practice*, 1938, 2088–2091. For the rule necessitating ancillary appointment, see *Sterrett v. Second Nat. Bank*, 1918, 39 S.Ct. 27, 248 U.S. 73, 63 L.Ed. 135; *Kelley v. Queeney*, W.D.N.Y.1941, 41 F.Supp. 1015; see also *McCandless v. Furlaud*, 1934, 55 S.Ct. 42, 293 U.S. 67, 79 L.Ed. 202. This rule has been extensively criticized. First,

Extraterritorial Powers of Receivers, 1932, 27 Ill.L.Rev. 271; Rose, *Extraterritorial Actions by Receivers,* 1933, 17 Minn. L.Rev. 704; Laughlin, *The Extraterritorial Powers of Receivers,* 1932, 45 Harv.L.Rev. 429; Clark and Moore, *A New Federal Civil Procedure—II, Pleadings and Parties,* 1935, 44 Yale L.J. 1291, 1312–1315; Note, 1932, 30 Mich.L.Rev. 1322. See also comment in *Bicknell v. Lloyd-Smith,* C.C.A.2d, 1940, 109 F.2d 527, certiorari denied 61 S.Ct. 15, 311 U.S. 650, 85 L.Ed. 416. The second clause of the sentence merely incorporates the well-known and general rule that, absent statutory authorization, a federal receiver cannot be sued without leave of the court which appointed him, applied in the federal courts since *Barton v. Barbour,* 1881, 104 U.S. 126. See also 1 *Clark on Receivers,* 2d ed., § 549. Under [§ 959 of this title, formerly] 28 U.S.C. § 125 leave of court is unnecessary when a receiver is sued "in respect of any act or transaction of his in carrying on the business" connected with the receivership property, but such suit is subject to the general equity jurisdiction of the court in which the receiver was appointed, so far as justice necessitates.

Capacity of a state court receiver to sue or be sued in Federal court is governed by Rule 17(b).

The last sentence added to Rule 66 assures the application of the rules in all matters except actual administration of the receivership estate itself. Since this implicitly carries with it the applicability of those rules relating to appellate procedure, the express reference thereto contained in Rule 66 has been stricken as superfluous. Under Rule 81(a)(1) the rules do not apply to bankruptcy proceedings except as they may be made applicable by order of the Supreme Court. Rule 66 is applicable to what is commonly known as a federal "chancery" or "equity" receiver, or similar type of court officer. It is not designed to regulate or affect receivers in bankruptcy, which are governed by the Bankruptcy Act and the General Orders. Since the Federal Rules are applicable in bankruptcy by virtue of General Orders in Bankruptcy 36 and 37 [see Appendix II following Rules of Bankruptcy Procedure, Title 11] only to the extent that they are not inconsistent with the Bankruptcy Act or the General Orders, Rule 66 is not applicable to bankruptcy receivers. See 1 *Collier on Bankruptcy,* 14th ed. by Moore and Oglebay, ¶¶2.23–2.36.

1948 Amendment

The amendment effective October 1949 deleted a sentence which formerly appeared immediately following the first sentence and which read as follows: "A receiver shall have the capacity to sue in any district court without ancillary appointment; but actions against a receiver may not be commenced without leave of the court appointing him except when authorized by a statute of the United States."

2007 Amendment

The language of Rule 66 has been amended as part of the general restyling of the Civil Rules to make them more easily understood and to make style and terminology consistent throughout the rules. These changes are intended to be stylistic only.

CROSS REFERENCES

Receiver suable without leave of court, see 28 USCA § 959.

Rule 67. Deposit Into Court

(a) Depositing Property. If any part of the relief sought is a money judgment or the disposition of a sum of money or some other deliverable thing, a party—on notice to every other party and by leave of court—may deposit with the court all or part of the money or thing, whether or not that party claims any of it. The depositing party must deliver to the clerk a copy of the order permitting deposit.

(b) Investing and Withdrawing Funds. Money paid into court under this rule must be deposited and withdrawn in accordance with 28 U.S.C. §§ 2041 and 2042 and any like statute. The money must be deposited in an interest-bearing account or invested in a court-approved, interest-bearing instrument.

(Amended December 29, 1948, effective October 20, 1949; April 28, 1983, effective August 1, 1983; April 30, 2007, effective December 1, 2007.)

ADVISORY COMMITTEE NOTES

1937 Adoption

This rule provides for deposit in court generally, continuing similar special provisions contained in such statutes as U.S.C., Title 28, [§§ 1335, 1397, 2361, formerly] § 41(26) (Original jurisdiction of bills of interpleader, and of bills in the nature of interpleader). See generally *Howard v. United States,* 1902, 22 S.Ct. 543, 184 U.S. 676, 46 L.Ed. 754; United States Supreme Court Admiralty Rules (1920), Rules 37 (Bringing Funds into Court), 41 (Funds in Court Registry), and 42 (Claims Against Proceeds in Registry). With the first sentence, compare *English Rules Under the Judicature Act* (The Annual Practice, 1937) O. 22, r. 1(1).

1948 Amendment

The amendment effective October 1949 substituted the reference to "Title 28, U.S.C.A., §§ 2041, and 2042" for the reference to "Sections 995 and 996, Revised Statutes, as amended, U.S.C.A., Title 28, §§ 851, 852." The amendment also added the words "as amended" following the citation of the Act of June 26, 1934, c. 756, § 23, and, in the parenthetical citation immediately following, added the reference to "58 Stat. 845".

1983 Amendment

Rule 67 has been amended in three ways. The first change is the addition of the clause in the first sentence. Some courts have construed the present rule to permit deposit only when the party making it claims no interest in the fund or thing deposited. E.g., *Blasin-Stern v. Beech-Nut Life Savers Corp.,* 429 F.Supp. 533 (D. Puerto Rico 1975); *Dinkins v. General Aniline & Film Corp.,* 214 F.Supp. 281 (S.D.N.Y. 1963). However, there are situations in which a litigant may wish to be relieved of responsibility for a sum or thing, but continue to claim an interest in all or part of it. In these cases the deposit-in-court procedure should be available; in addition to the advantages to the party making the deposit, the procedure gives other litigants assurance that any judgment will be collectable. The amendment is intended to accomplish that.

The second change is the addition of a requirement that the order of deposit be served on the clerk of the court in which the sum or thing is to be deposited. This is simply to assure that the clerk knows what is being deposited and what his responsibilities are with respect to the deposit. The latter point is particularly important since the rule as amended contemplates that deposits will be placed in interest-bearing accounts; the clerk must know what treatment has been ordered for the particular deposit.

The third change is to require that any money be deposited in an interest-bearing account or instrument approved by the court.

2007 Amendment

The language of Rule 67 has been amended as part of the general restyling of the Civil Rules to make them more easily understood and to make style and terminology consistent throughout the rules. These changes are intended to be stylistic only.

Rule 68. Offer of Judgment

(a) Making an Offer; Judgment on an Accepted Offer. At least 14 days before the date set for trial, a party defending against a claim may serve on an opposing party an offer to allow judgment on specified terms, with the costs then accrued. If, within 14 days after being served, the opposing party serves written notice accepting the offer, either party may then file the offer and notice of acceptance, plus proof of service. The clerk must then enter judgment.

(b) Unaccepted Offer. An unaccepted offer is considered withdrawn, but it does not preclude a later offer. Evidence of an unaccepted offer is not admissible except in a proceeding to determine costs.

(c) Offer After Liability is Determined. When one party's liability to another has been determined but the extent of liability remains to be determined by further proceedings, the party held liable may make an offer of judgment. It must be served within a reasonable time—but at least 14 days—before the date set for a hearing to determine the extent of liability.

(d) Paying Costs After an Unaccepted Offer. If the judgment that the offeree finally obtains is not more favorable than the unaccepted offer, the offeree must pay the costs incurred after the offer was made. (Amended December 27, 1946, effective March 19, 1948; February 28, 1966, effective July 1, 1966; March 2, 1987, effective August 1, 1987; April 30, 2007, effective December 1, 2007; March 26, 2009, effective December 1, 2009.)

ADVISORY COMMITTEE NOTES

1937 Adoption

See 2 Minn.Stat. (Mason, 1927) § 9323; 4 Mont.Rev.Codes Ann. (1935) § 9770; N.Y.C.P.A. (1937) § 177.

For the recovery of costs against the United States, see Rule 54(d).

1946 Amendment

Note. The third sentence of Rule 68 has been altered to make clear that evidence of an unaccepted offer is admissible in a proceeding to determine the costs of the action but is not otherwise admissible.

The two sentences substituted for the deleted last sentence of the rule assure a party the right to make a second offer where the situation permits—as, for example, where a prior offer was not accepted but the plaintiff's judgment is nullified and a new trial ordered, whereupon the defendant desires to make a second offer. It is implicit, however, that as long as the case continues—whether there be a first, second or third trial—and the defendant makes no further offer, his first and only offer will operate to save him the costs from the time of that offer if the plaintiff ultimately obtains a judgment less than the sum offered. In the case of successive offers not accepted, the offeror is saved the costs incurred after the making of the offer which was equal to or greater than the judgment ultimately obtained. These provisions should serve to encourage settlements and avoid protracted litigation.

The phrase "before the trial begins", in the first sentence of the rule, has been construed in *Cover v. Chicago Eye Shield Co.*, C.C.A.7th, 1943, 136 F.2d 374, certiorari denied 64 S.Ct. 53, 320 U.S. 749, 88 L.Ed. 445.

1966 Amendment

This logical extension of the concept of offer of judgment is suggested by the common admiralty practice of determining liability before the amount of liability is determined.

1987 Amendment

The amendments are technical. No substantive change is intended.

2007 Amendment

The language of Rule 68 has been amended as part of the general restyling of the Civil Rules to make them more easily understood and to make style and terminology consistent throughout the rules. These changes are intended to be stylistic only.

2009 Amendment

Former Rule 68 allowed service of an offer of judgment more than 10 days before the trial begins, or—if liability has been determined—at least 10 days before a hearing to determine the extent of liability. It may be difficult to know in advance when trial will begin or when a hearing will be held. The time is now measured from the date set for trial or hearing; resetting the date establishes a new time for serving the offer.

The former 10-day periods are extended to 14 days to reflect the change in the Rule 6(a) method for computing periods less than 11 days.

Rule 69. Execution

(a) In General.

(1) *Money Judgment; Applicable Procedure.* A money judgment is enforced by a writ of execution, unless the court directs otherwise. The procedure on execution—and in proceedings supplementary to and in aid of judgment or execution—must accord with the procedure of the state where the court is located, but a federal statute governs to the extent it applies.

(2) *Obtaining Discovery.* In aid of the judgment or execution, the judgment creditor or a successor in interest whose interest appears of record may obtain discovery from any person—including the judgment debtor—as provided in these rules or by the procedure of the state where the court is located.

(b) Against Certain Public Officers. When a judgment has been entered against a revenue officer in the circumstances stated in 28 U.S.C. § 2006, or against an officer of Congress in the circumstances stated in 2 U.S.C. § 118,[1] the judgment must be satisfied as those statutes provide.

(Amended December 29, 1948, effective October 20, 1949; March 30, 1970, effective July 1, 1970; March 2, 1987 effective August 1, 1987; April 30, 2007, effective December 1, 2007.)

1 Now editorially reclassified 2 U.S.C. § 5503.

ADVISORY COMMITTEE NOTES

1937 Adoption

Note to Subdivision (a). This follows in substance U.S.C. Title 28, [former] §§ 727 (Executions as provided by State laws) and [former 729] [now Title 42, § 1988] (Proceedings in vindication of civil rights), except that, as in the similar case of attachments (see note to Rule 64), the rule specifies the applicable state law to be that of the time when the remedy is sought, and thus renders unnecessary, as well as supersedeas, local district court rules.

Statutes of the United States on execution, when applicable, govern under this rule. Among these are:

U.S.C., Title 12:

§ 91 (Transfers by bank and other acts in contemplation of insolvency)

§ 632 (Jurisdiction of United States district courts in cases arising out of foreign banking jurisdiction where Federal reserve bank a party)

U.S.C., Title 19:

§ 199 (Judgments for customs duties, how payable)

U.S.C., Title 26 [I.R.C.1939]:

§ 1610(a) [former] (Surrender of property subject to distraint)

U.S.C., Title 28 former:

§ 122 [now 1656] (Creation of new district or transfer of territory; lien)

§ 350 [now 2101] (Time for making application for appeal or certiorari; stay pending application for certiorari)

§ 489 [now 547] (District Attorneys; reports to Department of Justice)

§ 574 [now 1921] (Marshals, fees enumerated)

§ 786 [former] (Judgments for duties; collected in coin)

§ 811 [now 1961] (Interest on judgments)

§ 838 [former] (Executions; run in all districts of State)

§ 839 [now 2413] (Executions; run in every State and Territory)

§ 840 [former] (Executions; stay on conditions), as modified by Rule 62(b)

§ 841 [former] (Executions; stay of one term), as modified by Rule 62(f)

§ 842 [now 2006] (Executions; against officers of revenue in cases of probable cause), as incorporated in Subdivision (b) of this rule

§ 843 [now 2007] (Imprisonment for debt)

§ 844 [now 2007] (Imprisonment for debt; discharge according to State laws)

§ 845 [now 2007] (Imprisonment for debt; jail limits)

§ 846 [now 2005] (Fieri Facias; appraisal of goods; appraisers)

§ 847 [now 2001] (Sales; real property under order or decree)

§ 848 [now 2004] (Sales; personal property under order or decree)

§ 849 [now 2002] (Sales; necessity of notice)

§ 850 [now 2003] (Sales; death of marshall after levy or after sale)

§ 869 [former] (Bond in former error and on appeal), as incorporated in Rule 73(c)

§ 874 [former] (Supersedeas), as modified by Rules 62(d) and 73(d)

U.S.C., Title 31:

§ 195 [now 3715] (Purchase on execution)

U.S.C., Title 33:

§ 918 (Collection of defaulted payments)

U.S.C., Title 49:

§ 74(g) [former] (Causes of action arising out of Federal control of railroads; execution and other process)

Special statutes of the United States on exemption from execution are also continued. Among these are:

U.S.C., Title 2:

§ 118 (Actions against officers of Congress for official acts)

U.S.C., Title 5 former:

§ 729 [see 8346, 8470] (Federal employees retirement annuities not subject to assignment, execution, levy or other legal process)

U.S.C., Title 10 former:

§ 610 [now 3690, 8690] (Exemption of enlisted men from arrest on civil process)

U.S.C., Title 22 former:

§ 21(h) [see 4060] (Foreign service retirement and disability system; establishment; rules and regulations; annuities; nonassignable; exemption from legal process)

U.S.C., Title 33:

§ 916 (Assignment and exemption from claims of creditors) (Longshoremen's and Harborworkers' Compensation Act)

U.S.C., Title 38 former:

§ 54 [see 3101] (Attachment, levy or seizure of moneys due pensioners prohibited)

§ 393 [former] (Army and Navy Medal of Honor Roll; pensions additional to other pensions; liability to attachment, etc.) Compare [former] Title 34, § 365(c) (Medal of Honor Roll; special pension to persons enrolled)

§ 618 [see 3101] (Benefits exempt from seizure under process and taxation; no deductions for indebtedness to United States)

U.S.C., Title 43:

§ 175 (Exemption from execution of homestead land)

U.S.C., Title 48 former:

§ 1371o (Panama canal and railroad retirement annuities, exemption from execution and so forth.)

Supplementary Note

Note. With respect to the provisions of the Soldiers' and Sailors' Civil Relief Act of 1940, [former] 50 U.S.C. Appendix, § 501 et seq. [now 50 U.S.C. § 3901 et seq.], see notes to Rules 62 and 64 herein.

1948 Amendment

The amendment effective October 1949, substituted the citation of "Title 28, U.S.C., § 2006" in subdivision (b) in place of the citation to "Section 989, Revised Statutes, U.S.C., Title 28, § 842".

1970 Amendment

The amendment assures that, in aid of execution on a judgment, all discovery procedures provided in the rules are available and not just discovery via the taking of a deposition. Under the present language, one court had held that Rule 34 discovery is unavailable to the judgment creditor. *M. Lowenstein & Sons, Inc. v. American Underwear Mfg. Co.*, 11 F.R.D. 172 (E.D.Pa.1951). Notwithstanding the language, and relying heavily on legislative history referring to Rule 33, the Fifth Circuit has held that a judgment creditor may invoke Rule 33 interrogatories. *United States v. McWhirter*, 376 F.2d 102 (5th Cir. 1967). But the court's reasoning does not extend to discovery except as provided in Rules 26–33. One commentator suggests that the existing language might properly be stretched to all discovery, 7 *Moore's Federal Practice* ¶69.05[1] (2d ed. 1966), but another believes that a rules amendment is needed. 3 Barron & Holtzoff, *Federal Practice and Procedure* 1484 (Wright ed. 1958). Both commentators and the court in *McWhirter* are clear that, as a matter of policy, Rule 69 should authorize the use of all discovery devices provided in the rules.

1987 Amendment

The amendments are technical. No substantive change is intended.

2007 Amendment

The language of Rule 69 has been amended as part of the general restyling of the Civil Rules to make them more easily understood and to make style and terminology consistent throughout the rules. These changes are intended to be stylistic only.

Amended Rule 69(b) incorporates directly the provisions of 2 U.S.C. § 118 and 28 U.S.C. § 2006, deleting the incomplete statement in former Rule 69(b) of the circumstances in which execution does not issue against an officer.

HISTORICAL AND STATUTORY NOTES

References in Text

2 U.S.C. § 118, referred to in subd. (b), was editorially reclassified as 2 U.S.C. 5503.

CROSS REFERENCES

Executions and judicial sales, see 28 USCA § 2001 et seq.

Executions in favor of United States, see 28 USCA § 2413.

Power to issue writ of execution, see 28 USCA § 1651.

Seizure of person or property for satisfaction of judgment, see Fed.Rules Civ.Proc. Rule 64, 28 USCA.

Stay of execution of judgment, see Fed.Rules Civ.Proc. Rule 62, 28 USCA.

Writ of execution for delivery of possession, see Fed.Rules Civ.Proc. Rule 70, 28 USCA.

Rule 70. Enforcing a Judgment for a Specific Act

(a) Party's Failure to Act; Ordering Another to Act. If a judgment requires a party to convey land, to deliver a deed or other document, or to perform any other specific act and the party fails to comply within the time specified, the court may order the act to be done—at the disobedient party's expense—by another person appointed by the court. When done, the act has the same effect as if done by the party.

(b) Vesting Title. If the real or personal property is within the district, the court—instead of ordering a conveyance—may enter a judgment divesting any party's title and vesting it in others. That judgment has the effect of a legally executed conveyance.

(c) Obtaining a Writ of Attachment or Sequestration. On application by a party entitled to performance of an act, the clerk must issue a writ of attachment or sequestration against the disobedient party's property to compel obedience.

(d) Obtaining a Writ of Execution or Assistance. On application by a party who obtains a judgment or order for possession, the clerk must issue a writ of execution or assistance.

(e) Holding in Contempt. The court may also hold the disobedient party in contempt.
(Amended April 30, 2007, effective December 1, 2007.)

ADVISORY COMMITTEE NOTES

1937 Adoption

Compare [former] Equity Rules 7 (Process, Mesne and Final), 8 (Enforcement of Final Decrees), and 9 (Writ of Assistance). To avoid possible confusion, both old and new denominations for attachment (sequestration) and execution (assistance) are used in this rule. Compare with the provision in this rule that the judgment may itself vest title, 6 Tenn. Ann.Code (Williams, 1934), § 10594; 2 Conn.Gen.Stat. (1930), § 5455; N.M.Stat.Ann. (Courtright, 1929), § 117–117; 2 Ohio Gen.Code Ann. (Page, 1926), § 11590; and England, Supreme Court of Judicature Act (1925), § 47.

2007 Amendment

The language of Rule 70 has been amended as part of the general restyling of the Civil Rules to make them more easily understood and to make style and terminology consistent throughout the rules. These changes are intended to be stylistic only.

CROSS REFERENCES

Contempts, power of court, see 18 USCA § 401.

Execution, see Fed.Rules Civ.Proc. Rule 69, 28 USCA.

Power to issue writs, see 28 USCA § 1651.

Remedies of attachment and sequestration, see Fed.Rules Civ.Proc. Rule 64, 28 USCA.

Rule 71. Enforcing Relief for or Against a Nonparty

When an order grants relief for a nonparty or may be enforced against a nonparty, the procedure for enforcing the order is the same as for a party.
(Amended March 2, 1987, effective August 1, 1987; April 30, 2007, effective December 1, 2007.)

ADVISORY COMMITTEE NOTES

1937 Adoption

Compare [former] Equity Rule 11 (Process in Behalf of and Against Persons Not Parties). Compare also *Terrell v. Allison*, 1875, 21 Wall. 289, 22 L.Ed. 634; *Farmers' Loan and Trust Co. v. Chicago and A. Ry. Co.*, C.C.Ind.1890, 44 F. 653; *Robert Findlay Mfg. Co. v. Hygrade Lighting Fixture Corp.*, E.D.N.Y.1923, 288 F. 80; *Thompson v. Smith*, C.C.Minn.1870, Fed.Cas. No. 13,977.

1987 Amendment

The amendments are technical. No substantive change is intended.

2007 Amendment

The language of Rule 71 has been amended as part of the general restyling of the Civil Rules to make them more easily understood and to make style and terminology consistent throughout the rules. These changes are intended to be stylistic only.

CROSS REFERENCES

Execution, see Fed.Rules Civ.Proc. Rule 69, 28 USCA.

Parties, generally, see Fed.Rules Civ.Proc. Rule 17 et seq., 28 USCA.

Power to issue writs, see 28 USCA § 1651.

Process, generally, see Fed.Rules Civ.Proc. Rule 4, 28 USCA.

Writs of attachment, sequestration and equivalent remedies, see Fed.Rules Civ.Proc. Rule 64, 28 USCA.

TITLE IX. SPECIAL PROCEEDINGS

Rule 71.1. Condemning Real or Personal Property

(a) **Applicability of Other Rules.** These rules govern proceedings to condemn real and personal property by eminent domain, except as this rule provides otherwise.

(b) **Joinder of Properties.** The plaintiff may join separate pieces of property in a single action, no matter whether they are owned by the same persons or sought for the same use.

(c) **Complaint.**

(1) *Caption.* The complaint must contain a caption as provided in Rule 10(a). The plaintiff must, however, name as defendants both the property—designated generally by kind, quantity, and location—and at least one owner of some part of or interest in the property.

(2) *Contents.* The complaint must contain a short and plain statement of the following:

(A) the authority for the taking;

(B) the uses for which the property is to be taken;

(C) a description sufficient to identify the property;

(D) the interests to be acquired; and

(E) for each piece of property, a designation of each defendant who has been joined as an owner or owner of an interest in it.

(3) *Parties.* When the action commences, the plaintiff need join as defendants only those persons who have or claim an interest in the property and whose names are then known. But before any hearing on compensation, the plaintiff must add as defendants all those persons who have or claim an interest and whose names have become known or can be found by a reasonably diligent search of the records, considering both the property's character and value and the interests to be acquired. All others may be made defendants under the designation "Unknown Owners."

(4) *Procedure.* Notice must be served on all defendants as provided in Rule 71.1(d), whether they were named as defendants when the action commenced or were added later. A defendant may answer as provided in Rule 71.1(e). The court, meanwhile, may order any distribution of a deposit that the facts warrant.

(5) *Filing; Additional Copies.* In addition to filing the complaint, the plaintiff must give the clerk at least one copy for the defendants' use and additional copies at the request of the clerk or a defendant.

(d) **Process.**

(1) *Delivering Notice to the Clerk.* On filing a complaint, the plaintiff must promptly deliver to the clerk joint or several notices directed to the named defendants. When adding defendants, the plaintiff must deliver to the clerk additional notices directed to the new defendants.

(2) *Contents of the Notice.*

(A) *Main Contents.* Each notice must name the court, the title of the action, and the defendant to whom it is directed. It must describe the property sufficiently to identify it, but need not describe any property other than that to be taken from the named defendant. The notice must also state:

(i) that the action is to condemn property;

(ii) the interest to be taken;

(iii) the authority for the taking;

(iv) the uses for which the property is to be taken;

(v) that the defendant may serve an answer on the plaintiff's attorney within 21 days after being served with the notice;

(vi) that the failure to so serve an answer constitutes consent to the taking and to the court's authority to proceed with the action and fix the compensation; and

(vii) that a defendant who does not serve an answer may file a notice of appearance.

(B) *Conclusion.* The notice must conclude with the name, telephone number, and e-mail address of the plaintiff's attorney and an address within the district in which the action is brought where the attorney may be served.

(3) *Serving the Notice.*

(A) *Personal Service.* When a defendant whose address is known resides within the United States or a territory subject to the administrative or judicial jurisdiction of the United States, personal service of the notice (without a copy of the complaint) must be made in accordance with Rule 4.

(B) *Service by Publication.*

(i) A defendant may be served by publication only when the plaintiff's attorney files a certificate stating that the attorney believes the defendant cannot be personally served, because after diligent inquiry within the state where the complaint is filed, the defendant's place of residence is still unknown or, if known, that it is beyond the territorial limits of personal service. Service is then made by publishing the notice—once a week for at least 3 successive weeks—in a newspaper published in the county where the property is located or, if there is no such newspaper, in a newspaper with general circulation where the property is located. Before the last publication, a copy of the notice must also be mailed to every defendant who cannot be personally served but whose place of residence is then known. Unknown owners may be served by publication in the same manner by a notice addressed to "Unknown Owners."

(ii) Service by publication is complete on the date of the last publication. The plaintiff's attorney must prove publication and mailing by a certificate, attach a printed copy of the published notice, and mark on the copy the newspaper's name and the dates of publication.

(4) *Effect of Delivery and Service.* Delivering the notice to the clerk and serving it have the same effect as serving a summons under Rule 4.

(5) *Amending the Notice; Proof of Service and Amending the Proof.* Rule 4(a)(2) governs amending the notice. Rule 4(l) governs proof of service and amending it.

(e) Appearance or Answer.

(1) *Notice of Appearance.* A defendant that has no objection or defense to the taking of its property may serve a notice of appearance designating the property in which it claims an interest. The defendant must then be given notice of all later proceedings affecting the defendant.

(2) *Answer.* A defendant that has an objection or defense to the taking must serve an answer within 21 days after being served with the notice. The answer must:

(A) identify the property in which the defendant claims an interest;

(B) state the nature and extent of the interest; and

(C) state all the defendant's objections and defenses to the taking.

(3) *Waiver of Other Objections and Defenses; Evidence on Compensation.* A defendant waives all objections and defenses not stated in its answer. No other pleading or motion asserting an additional objection or defense is allowed. But at the trial on compensation, a defendant—whether or not it has previously appeared or answered—may present evidence on the amount of compensation to be paid and may share in the award.

(f) Amending Pleadings. Without leave of court, the plaintiff may—as often as it wants—amend the complaint at any time before the trial on compensation. But no amendment may be made if it would result in a dismissal inconsistent with Rule 71.1(i)(1) or (2). The plaintiff need not serve a copy of an amendment, but must serve notice of the filing, as provided in Rule 5(b), on every affected party who has appeared and, as provided in Rule 71.1(d), on every affected party who has not appeared. In addition, the plaintiff must give the clerk at least one copy of each amendment for the defendants' use, and additional copies at the request of the clerk or a defendant. A defendant may appear or answer in the time and manner and with the same effect as provided in Rule 71.1(e).

(g) Substituting Parties. If a defendant dies, becomes incompetent, or transfers an interest after being joined, the court may, on motion and notice of hearing, order that the proper party be substituted. Service of the motion and notice on a nonparty must be made as provided in Rule 71.1(d)(3).

(h) Trial of the Issues.

(1) *Issues Other Than Compensation; Compensation.* In an action involving eminent domain under federal law, the court tries all issues, including compensation, except when compensation must be determined:

(A) by any tribunal specially constituted by a federal statute to determine compensation; or

(B) if there is no such tribunal, by a jury when a party demands one within the time to answer or within any additional time the court sets, unless the court appoints a commission.

(2) *Appointing a Commission; Commission's Powers and Report.*

(A) *Reasons for Appointing.* If a party has demanded a jury, the court may instead appoint a three-person commission to determine compensation because of the character, location, or quantity of the property to be condemned or for other just reasons.

(B) *Alternate Commissioners.* The court may appoint up to two additional persons to serve as alternate commissioners to hear the case and replace commissioners who, before a decision is filed, the court finds unable or disqualified to perform their duties. Once the commission renders its final decision, the court must discharge any alternate who has not replaced a commissioner.

(C) *Examining the Prospective Commissioners.* Before making its appointments, the court must advise the parties of the identity and qualifications of each prospective commissioner and alternate, and may permit the parties to examine them. The parties may not suggest appointees, but for good cause may object to a prospective commissioner or alternate.

(D) *Commission's Powers and Report.* A commission has the powers of a master under Rule 53(c). Its action and report are determined by a majority. Rule 53(d), (e), and (f) apply to its action and report.

(i) Dismissal of the Action or a Defendant.

(1) *Dismissing the Action.*

(A) *By the Plaintiff.* If no compensation hearing on a piece of property has begun, and if the plaintiff has not acquired title or a lesser interest or taken possession, the plaintiff may, without a court order, dismiss the action as to that property by filing a notice of dismissal briefly describing the property.

(B) *By Stipulation.* Before a judgment is entered vesting the plaintiff with title or a lesser interest in or possession of property, the plaintiff and affected defendants may, without a court order, dismiss the action in whole or in part by filing a stipulation of dismissal. And if the parties so stipulate, the court may vacate a judgment already entered.

(C) *By Court Order.* At any time before compensation has been determined and paid, the court may, after a motion and hearing, dismiss the action as to a piece of property. But if the plaintiff has already taken title, a lesser interest, or possession as to any part of it, the court must award compensation for the title, lesser interest, or possession taken.

(2) *Dismissing a Defendant.* The court may at any time dismiss a defendant who was unnecessarily or improperly joined.

(3) *Effect.* A dismissal is without prejudice unless otherwise stated in the notice, stipulation, or court order.

(j) Deposit and Its Distribution.

(1) *Deposit.* The plaintiff must deposit with the court any money required by law as a condition to the exercise of eminent domain and may make a deposit when allowed by statute.

(2) *Distribution; Adjusting Distribution.* After a deposit, the court and attorneys must expedite the proceedings so as to distribute the deposit and to determine and pay compensation. If the compensation finally awarded to a defendant exceeds the amount distributed to that defendant, the court must enter judgment against the plaintiff for the deficiency. If the compensation awarded to a defendant is less than the amount distributed to that defendant, the court must enter judgment against that defendant for the overpayment.

(k) Condemnation Under a State's Power of Eminent Domain. This rule governs an action involving eminent domain under state law. But if state law provides for trying an issue by jury—or for trying the issue of compensation by jury or commission or both—that law governs.

(*l*) Costs. Costs are not subject to Rule 54(d).

(Adopted April 30, 1951, effective August 1, 1951; amended January 21, 1963, effective July 1, 1963; April 29, 1985, effective August 1, 1985; March 2, 1987, effective August 1, 1987; April 25, 1988, effective August 1, 1988; amended by Pub.L. 100–690, Title VII, § 7050, November 18, 1988, 102 Stat. 4401 (although amendment by Pub.L. 100–690 could not be executed due to prior amendment by Court order which made the same change effective August 1, 1988); amended April 22, 1993, effective December 1, 1993; March 27, 2003, effective December 1, 2003; April 30, 2007, effective December 1, 2007; March 26, 2009, effective December 1, 2009.)

ADVISORY COMMITTEE NOTES

1951 Addition

Supplementary Report

The Court will remember that at its conference on December 2, 1948, the discussion was confined to subdivision (h) of the rule (* * *), the particular question being whether the tribunal to award compensation should be a commission or a jury in cases where the Congress has not made specific provision on the subject. The Advisory Committee was agreed from the outset that a rule should not be promulgated which would overturn the decision of the Congress as to the kind of tribunal to fix compensation, provided that the system established by Congress was found to be working well. We found two instances where the Congress had specified the kind of tribunal to fix compensation. One case was the

District of Columbia ([former] §§ 361 to 386 of Title 40 [now D.C. Code, Title 16, § 1301 et seq.]) where a rather unique system exists under which the court is required in all cases to order the selection of a "jury" of five from among not less than twenty names drawn from "the special box provided by law." They must have the usual qualifications of jurors and in addition must be freeholders of the District and not in the service of the United States or the District. That system has been in effect for many years, and our inquiry revealed that it works well under the conditions prevailing in the District, and is satisfactory to the courts of the District, the legal profession and to property owners.

The other instance is that of the Tennessee Valley Authority, where the act of Congress (section 831x of Title 16) provides that compensation is fixed by three disinterested commissioners appointed by the court, whose award goes before the District Court for confirmation or modification. The Advisory Committee made a thorough inquiry into the practical operation of the TVA commission system. We obtained from counsel for the TVA the results of their experience, which afforded convincing proof that the commission system is preferable under the conditions affecting TVA and that the jury system would not work satisfactorily. We then, under date of February 6, 1947, wrote every Federal judge who had ever sat in a TVA condemnation case, asking his views as to whether the commission system is satisfactory and whether a jury system should be preferred. Of 21 responses from the judges 17 approved the commission system and opposed the substitution of a jury system for the TVA. Many of the judges went further and opposed the use of juries in any condemnation cases. Three of the judges preferred the jury system, and one dealt only with the TVA provision for a three judge district court. The Advisory Committee has not considered abolition of the three judge requirement of the TVA Act, because it seemed to raise a question of jurisdiction, which cannot be altered by rule. Nevertheless the Department of Justice continued its advocacy of the jury system for its asserted expedition and economy; and others favored a uniform procedure. In consequence of these divided counsels the Advisory Committee was itself divided, but in its May 1948 Report to the Court recommended the following rule as approved by a majority (* * *):

(h) Trial. If the action involves the exercise of the power of eminent domain under the law of the United States, any tribunal especially constituted by an Act of Congress governing the case for the trial of the issue of just compensation shall be the tribunal for the determination of that issue; but if there is no such specially constituted tribunal any party may have a trial by jury of the issue of just compensation by filing a demand therefor within the time allowed for answer or within such further time as the court may fix. Trial of all issues shall otherwise be by the court.

The effect of this was to preserve the existing systems in the District of Columbia and in TVA cases, but to provide for a jury to fix compensation in all other cases.

Before the Court's conference of December 2, 1948, the Chief Justice informed the Committee that the Court was particularly interested in the views expressed by Judge John Paul, Judge of the United States District Court for the Western District of Virginia, in a letter from him to the chairman of the Advisory Committee, dated February 13, 1947. Copies of all the letters from judges who had sat in TVA cases had been made available to the Court, and this letter from Judge Paul is one of them. Judge Paul strongly opposed jury trials and recommended the commission system in large projects like the TVA, and his views seemed to have impressed the Court and to have been the occasion for the conference.

The reasons which convinced the Advisory Committee that the use of commissioners instead of juries is desirable in TVA cases were these:

1. The TVA condemns large areas of land of similar kind, involving many owners. Uniformity in awards is essential. The commission system tends to prevent discrimination and provide for uniformity in compensation. The jury system tends to lack of uniformity. Once a reasonable and uniform standard of values for the area has been settled by a commission, litigation ends and settlements result.

2. Where large areas are involved many small landowners reside at great distances from the place where a court sits. It is a great hardship on humble people to have to travel long distances to attend a jury trial. A commission may travel around and receive the evidence of the owner near his home.

3. It is impracticable to take juries long distances to view the premises.

4. If the cases are tried by juries the burden on the time of the courts is excessive.

These considerations are the very ones Judge Paul stressed in his letter. He pointed out that they applied not only to the TVA but to other large governmental projects, such as flood control, hydroelectric power, reclamation, national forests, and others. So when the representatives of the Advisory Committee appeared at the Court's conference December 2, 1948, they found it difficult to justify the proposed provision in subdivision (h) of the rule that a jury should be used to fix compensation in all cases where Congress had not specified the tribunal. If our reasons for preserving the TVA system were sound, provision for a jury in similar projects of like magnitude seemed unsound.

Aware of the apparent inconsistency between the acceptance of the TVA system and the provision for a jury in all other cases, the members of the Committee attending the conference of December 2, 1948, then suggested that in the other cases the choice of jury or commission be left to the discretion of the District Court, going back to a suggestion previously made by Committee members and reported at page 15 of the Preliminary Draft of June 1947. They called the attention of the Court to the fact that the entire Advisory Committee had not been consulted about this suggestion and proposed that the draft be returned to the Committee for further consideration, and that was done.

The proposal we now make for subdivision (h) is as follows:

(h) Trial. If the action involves the exercise of the power of eminent domain under the law of the United States, any tribunal specially constituted by an Act of Congress governing the case for the trial of the issue of just compensation shall be the tribunal for the determination of that issue; but if there is no such specially constituted tribunal any party may have a trial by jury of the issue of just compensation by filing a demand therefor within the time allowed for answer or within such further time as the court may fix, unless the court in its discretion orders that, because of the character, location, or quantity of the property to be condemned, or for other reasons in the interest of justice, the issue of compensation shall be determined by a commission of three persons appointed by it. If a commission is appointed it shall have the powers of a master provided in subdivision (c) of Rule 53 and proceedings before it shall be governed by the provisions of paragraphs (1) and (2) of subdivision (d) of Rule 53. Its action and report shall be determined by a majority and its findings and report shall have the effect, and be dealt with by the court in accordance with the practice, prescribed in paragraph (2) of subdivision (e) of Rule 53. Trial of all issues shall otherwise be by the court.

In the 1948 draft the Committee had been almost evenly divided as between jury or commission and that made it easy for us to agree on the present draft. It would be difficult to state in a rule the various conditions to control the District Court in its choice and we have merely stated generally the matters which should be considered by the District Court.

The rule as now drafted seems to meet Judge Paul's objection. In large projects like the TVA the court may decide to use a commission. In a great number of cases involving only sites for buildings or other small areas, where use of a jury is appropriate, a jury may be chosen. The District Court's discretion may also be influenced by local preference or habit, and the preference of the Department of Justice and the reasons for its preference will doubtless be given weight. The Committee is convinced that there are some types of cases in which use of a commission is preferable and others in which a jury may be appropriately used, and that it would be a mistake to provide that the same kind of tribunal should be used in all cases. We think the available evidence clearly leads to that conclusion.

When this suggestion was made at the conference of December 2, 1948, representatives of the Department of Justice opposed it, expressing opposition to the use of a commission in any case. Their principal ground for opposition to commissions was then based on the assertion that the commission system is too expensive because courts allow commissioners too large compensation. The obvious answer to that is that the compensation of commissioners ought to be fixed or limited by law, as was done in the TVA Act, and the agency dealing with appropriations—either the Administrative Office or some other interested department of the government—should correct that evil, if evil there be, by obtaining such legislation. Authority to promulgate rules of procedure does not include power to fix compensation of government employees. The Advisory Committee is not convinced that even without such legislation the commission system is more expensive than the jury system. The expense of jury trials includes not only the per diem and mileage of the jurors impaneled for a case but like items for the entire venire. In computing cost of jury trials, the salaries of court officials, judges, clerks, marshals and deputies must be considered. No figures have been given to the Committee to establish that the cost of the commission system is the greater.

We earnestly recommend the rule as now drafted for promulgation by the Court, in the public interest.

The Advisory Committee have given more time to this rule, including time required for conferences with the Department of Justice to hear statements of its representatives, than has been required by any other rule. The rule may not be perfect but if faults develop in practice they may be promptly cured. Certainly the present conformity system is atrocious.

Under state practices, just compensation is normally determined by one of three methods: by commissioners; by commissioners with a right of appeal to and trial de novo before a jury; and by a jury, without a commission. A trial to the court or to the court including a master are, however, other methods that are occasionally used. Approximately 5 states use only commissioners; 23 states use commissioners with a trial de novo before a jury; and 18 states use only the jury. This classification is advisedly stated in approximate terms, since the same state may utilize diverse methods, depending upon different types of condemnations or upon the locality of the property, and since the methods used in a few states do not permit of a categorical classification. To reject the proposed rule and leave the situation as it is would not satisfy the views of the Department of Justice. The Department and the Advisory Committee agree that the use of a commission, with appeal to a jury, is a wasteful system.

The Department of Justice has a voluminous "Manual on Federal Eminent Domain," the 1940 edition of which has 948 pages with an appendix of 73 more pages. The title page informs us the preparation of the manual was begun during the incumbency of Attorney General Cummings, was continued under Attorney General Murphy, and completed during the incumbency of Attorney General Jackson. The preface contains the following statement:

It should also be mentioned that the research incorporated in the manual would be of invaluable assistance in the drafting of a new uniform code, or rules of court, for federal condemnation proceedings, which are now greatly confused, not only by the existence of over seventy federal statutes governing condemnations for different purposes—statutes which sometimes conflict with one another—but also by the countless problems occasioned by the requirements of conformity to state law. Progress of the work has already demonstrated that the need for such reform exists.

It is not surprising that more than once Attorneys General have asked the Advisory Committee to prepare a federal rule and rescue the government from this morass.

The Department of Justice has twice tried and failed to persuade the Congress to provide that juries shall be used in all condemnation cases. The debates in Congress show that part of the opposition to the Department of Justice's bills came from representatives opposed to jury trials in all cases, and in part from a preference for the conformity system. Our present proposal opens the door for district judges to yield to local preferences on the subject. It does much for the Department's points of view. It is a great improvement over the present so-called conformity system. It does away with the wasteful "double" system prevailing in 23 states where awards by commissions are followed by jury trials.

Aside from the question as to the choice of a tribunal to award compensation, the proposed rule would afford a simple and improved procedure.

We turn now to an itemized explanation of the other changes we have made in the 1948 draft. Some of these result from recent amendments to the Judicial Code. Others result from a reconsideration by the Advisory Committee of provisions which we thought could be improved.

   1. In the amended Judicial Code, the district courts are designated as "United States District Courts" instead of "District Courts of the United States," and a corresponding change has been made in the rule.

   2. After the 1948 draft was referred back to the committee, the provision in subdivision (c)(2), relating to naming defendants, * * * which provided that the plaintiff shall add as defendants all persons having or claiming an interest in that property whose names can be ascertained by a

search of the records to the extent commonly made by competent searchers of title in the vicinity "in light of the type and value of the property involved," the phrase in quotation marks was changed to read "in the light of the character and value of the property involved and the interests to be acquired."

The Department of Justice made a counter proposal * * * that there be substituted the words "reasonably diligent search of the records, considering the type." When the American Bar Association thereafter considered the draft, it approved the Advisory Committee's draft of this subdivision, but said that it had no objection to the Department's suggestion. Thereafter, in an effort to eliminate controversy, the Advisory Committee accepted the Department's suggestion as to (c)(2), using the word "character" instead of the word "type."

The Department of Justice also suggested that in subdivision (d)(3)(ii) relating to service by publication, the search for a defendant's residence as a preliminary to publication be limited to the state in which the complaint is filed. Here again the American Bar Association's report expressed the view that the Department's suggestion was unobjectionable and the Advisory Committee thereupon adopted it.

3. Subdivision (k) of the 1948 draft is as follows:

(k) Condemnation Under a State's Power of Eminent Domain. If the action involves the exercise of the power of eminent domain under the law of a state, the practice herein prescribed may be altered to the extent necessary to observe and enforce any condition affecting the substantial rights of a litigant attached by the state law to the exercise of the state's power of eminent domain.

Occasionally condemnation cases under a state's power of eminent domain reach a United States District Court because of diversity of citizenship. Such cases are rare, but provision should be made for them.

The 1948 draft of (k) required a district court to decide whether a provision of state law specifying the tribunal to award compensation is or is not a "condition" attached to the exercise of the state's power. On reconsideration we concluded that it would be wise to redraft (k) so as to avoid that troublesome question. As to conditions in state laws which affect the substantial rights of a litigant, the district courts would be bound to give them effect without any rule on the subject. Accordingly we present two alternative revisions. One suggestion supported by a majority of the Advisory Committee is as follows:

(k) Condemnation Under a State's Power of Eminent Domain. The practice herein prescribed governs in actions involving the exercise of the power of eminent domain under the law of a state, provided that if the state law makes provision for trial of any issue by jury, or for trial of the issue of compensation by jury or commission or both, that provision shall be followed.

The other is as follows:

(k) Condemnation Under a State's Power of Eminent Domain. The practice herein prescribed governs in actions involving the exercise of the power of eminent domain under the law of a state, provided that if the state law gives a right to a trial by jury such a trial shall in any case be allowed to the party demanding it within the time permitted by these rules, and in that event no hearing before a commission shall be had.

The first proposal accepts the state law as to the tribunals to fix compensation, and in that respect leaves the parties in precisely the same situation as if the case were pending in a state court, including the use of a commission with appeal to a jury, if the state law so provides. It has the effect of avoiding any question as to whether the decisions in *Erie R. Co. v. Tompkins* and later cases have application to a situation of this kind.

The second proposal gives the parties a right to a jury trial if that is provided for by state law, but prevents the use of both commission and jury. Those members of the Committee who favor the second proposal do so because of the obvious objections to the double trial, with a commission and appeal to a jury. As the decisions in *Erie R. Co. v. Tompkins* and later cases may have a bearing on this point, and the Committee is divided, we think both proposals should be placed before the Court.

4. The provision * * * of the 1948 draft * * * prescribing the effective date of the rule was drafted before the recent amendment of the Judicial Code on that subject. On May 10, 1950, the President approved an act which amended section 2072 of Title 28, United States Code, to read as follows:

> Such rules shall not take effect until they have been reported to Congress by the Chief Justice at or after the beginning of a regular session thereof but not later than the first day of May, and until the expiration of ninety days after they have been thus reported.

To conform to the statute now in force, we suggest a provision as follows:

Effective Date. This Rule 71A and the amendment to Rule 81(a) will take effect on August 1, 1951. Rule 71A governs all proceedings in actions brought after it takes effect and also all further proceedings in actions then pending, except to the extent that in the opinion of the court its application in a particular action pending when the rule takes effect would not be feasible or would work injustice, in which event the former procedure applies.

If the rule is not reported to Congress by May 1, 1951, this provision must be altered.

[Par. 3 of Supreme Court Order adopted Apr. 30, 1951, setting out this rule and providing for the abrogation of par. (7) of Rule 81(a), and providing for the Effective Date, as stated herein, was transmitted to Congress on May 1, 1951 by the Chief Justice of the United States (House Document No. 121, May 1, 1951, 82nd Cong., 1st Sess.), in conformity with § 2072 of this title. As no action was taken by Congress within the 90-day period required by that section, this rule and the abrogation of par. (7) of Rule 81(a) took effect on Aug. 1, 1951, as provided in said order.]

5. We call attention to the fact that the proposed rule does not contain a provision for the procedure to be followed in order to exercise the right of the United States to take immediate possession or title, when the condemnation proceeding is begun. There are several statutes conferring such a right which are cited in the original notes to the May 1948 draft * * *. The existence of this right is taken into account in the rule. In subdivision (c)(2), * * * it is stated: "Upon the commencement of the action, the plaintiff need join as defendants only the persons having or claiming an interest in the property whose names are then known." That is to enable the United States to exercise the right to immediate title or possession without the delay involved in ascertaining the names of all interested parties. The right

is also taken into account in the provision relating to dismissal (paragraph (i), subdivisions (1), (2), and (3), * * *); also in paragraph (j) relating to deposits and their distribution.

The Advisory Committee considered whether the procedure for exercising the right should be specified in the rule and decided against it, as the procedure now being followed seems to be giving no trouble, and to draft a rule to fit all the statutes on the subject might create confusion.

The American Bar Association has taken an active interest in a rule for condemnation cases. In 1944 its House of Delegates adopted a resolution which among other things resolved:

That before adoption by the Supreme Court of the United States of any redraft of the proposed rule, time and opportunity should be afforded to the bar to consider and make recommendations concerning any such redraft.

Accordingly, in 1950 the revised draft was submitted to the American Bar Association and its section of real property, probate and trust law appointed a committee to consider it. That committee was supplied with copies of the written statement from the Department of Justice giving the reasons relied on by the Department for preferring a rule to use juries in all cases. The Advisory Committee's report was approved at a meeting of the section of real property law, and by the House of Delegates at the annual meeting of September 1950. The American Bar Association report gave particular attention to the question whether juries or commissions should be used to fix compensation, approved the Advisory Committee's solution appearing in their latest draft designed to allow use of commissions in projects comparable to the TVA, and rejected the proposal for use of juries in all cases.

In November 1950 a committee of the Federal Bar Association, the chairman of which was a Special Assistant to the Attorney General, made a report which reflected the attitude of the Department of Justice on the condemnation rule.

Aside from subdivision (h) about the tribunal to award compensation the final draft of the condemnation rule here presented has the approval of the American Bar Association and, we understand, the Department of Justice, and we do not know of any opposition to it. Subdivision (h) has the unanimous approval of the Advisory Committee and has been approved by the American Bar Association. The use of commissions in TVA cases, and, by fair inference, in cases comparable to the TVA, is supported by 17 out of 20 judges who up to 1947 had sat in TVA cases. The legal staff of the TVA has vigorously objected to the substitution of juries for commissions in TVA cases. We regret to report that the Department of Justice still asks that subdivision (h) be altered to provide for jury trials in an cases where Congress has not specified the tribunal. We understand that the Department approves the proposal that the system prevailing in 23 states for the "double" trial, by commission with appeal to and trial de novo before a jury, should be abolished, and also asks that on demand a jury should be substituted for a commission, in those states where use of a commission alone is now required. The Advisory Committee has no evidence that commissions do not operate satisfactorily in the case of projects comparable to the TVA.

Original Report

General Statement. 1. Background. When the Advisory Committee was formulating its recommendations to the Court concerning rules of procedure, which subsequently became the Federal Rules of 1938, the Committee concluded at an early stage not to fix the procedure in condemnation cases. This is a matter principally involving the exercise of the federal power of eminent domain, as very few condemnation cases involving the state's power reach the United States District Courts. The Committee's reasons at that time were that inasmuch as condemnation proceedings by the United States are governed by statutes of the United States, prescribing different procedure for various agencies and departments of the government, or, in the absence of such statutes, by local state practice under the Conformity Act (former § 258 of Title 40), it would be extremely difficult to draft a uniform rule satisfactory to the various agencies and departments of the government and to private parties; and that there was no general demand for a uniform rule. The Committee continued in that belief until shortly before the preparation of the April 1937 Draft of the Rules, when the officials of the Department of Justice having to do with condemnation cases urgently requested the Committee to propose rules on this subject. The Committee undertook the task and drafted a Condemnation Rule which appeared for the first time as Rule 74 of the April 1937 Draft. After the publication and distribution of this initial draft many objections were urged against it by counsel for various governmental agencies, whose procedure in condemnation cases was prescribed by federal statutes. Some of these agencies wanted to be excepted in whole or in part from the operation of the uniform rule proposed in April 1937. And the Department of Justice changed its position and stated that it preferred to have government condemnations conducted by local attorneys familiar with the state practice, which was applied under the Conformity Act where the Acts of Congress do not prescribe the practice; that it preferred to work under the Conformity Act without a uniform rule of procedure. The profession generally showed little interest in the proposed uniform rule. For these reasons the Advisory Committee in its Final Report to the Court in November 1937 proposed that all of Rule 74 be stricken and that the Federal Rules be made applicable only to appeals in condemnation cases. See note to Rule 74 of the Final Report.

Some of six or seven years later when the Advisory Committee was considering the subject of amendments to the Federal Rules both government officials and the profession generally urged the adoption of some uniform procedure. This demand grew out of the volume of condemnation proceedings instituted during the war, and the general feeling of dissatisfaction with the diverse condemnation procedures that were applicable in the federal courts. A strongly held belief was that both the sovereign's power to condemn and the property owner's right to compensation could be promoted by a simplified rule. As a consequence the Committee proposed a Rule 71A on the subject of condemnation in its Preliminary Draft of May 1944. In the Second Preliminary Draft of May 1945 this earlier proposed Rule 71A was, however, omitted. The Committee did not then feel that it had sufficient time to prepare a revised draft satisfactorily to it which would meet legitimate objections made to the draft of May 1944. To avoid unduly delaying the proposed amendments to existing rules the Committee concluded to proceed in the regular way with the preparation of the amendments to these rules and deal with the question of a condemnation rule as an independent matter. As a consequence it made no recommendations to the Court on condemnation in its Final Report of Proposed Amendments of June 1946; and the amendments which the

Court adopted in December 1946 did not deal with condemnation. After concluding its task relative to amendments, the Committee returned to a consideration of eminent domain, its proposed Rule 71A of May 1944, the suggestions and criticisms that had been presented in the interim, and in June 1947 prepared and distributed to the profession another draft of a proposed condemnation rule. This draft contained several alternative provisions, specifically called attention to and asked for opinion relative to these matters, and in particular as to the constitution of the tribunal to award compensation. The present draft was based on the June 1947 formulation, in light of the advice of the profession on both matters of substance and form.

2. Statutory Provisions. The need for a uniform condemnation rule in the federal courts arises from the fact that by various statutes Congress has prescribed diverse procedures for certain condemnation proceedings, and, in the absence of such statutes, has prescribed conformity to local state practice under former § 258 of Title 40. This general conformity adds to the diversity of procedure since in the United States there are multifarious methods of procedure in existence. Thus in 1931 it was said that there were 269 different methods of judicial procedure in different classes of condemnation cases and 56 methods of nonjudicial or administrative procedure. First Report of Judicial Council of Michigan, 1931, § 46, pp. 55 to 56. These numbers have not decreased. Consequently, the general requirement of conformity to state practice and procedure, particularly where the condemnor is the United States, leads to expense, delay and uncertainty. In advocacy of a uniform federal rule, see Armstrong, *Proposed Amendments to Federal Rules for Civil Procedure*, 1944, 4 F.R.D. 124, 134; id., *Report of the Advisory Committee on Federal Rules of Civil Procedure Recommending Amendments*, 1946, 5 F.R.D. 339, 357.

There are a great variety of Acts of Congress authorizing the exercise of the power of eminent domain by the United States and its officers and agencies. These statutes for the most part do not specify the exact procedure to be followed, but where procedure is prescribed, it is by no means uniform.

The following are instances of Acts which merely authorize the exercise of the power without specific declaration as to the procedure:

U.S.C., Title 16:

§ 404c–11 (Mammoth Cave National Park; acquisition of lands, interests in lands or other property for park by the Secretary of the Interior).

§ 426d (Stones River National Park; acquisition of land for parks by the Secretary of the Army).

§ 450aa (George Washington Carver National Monument; acquisition of land by the Secretary of the Interior).

§ 517 (National forest reservation; title to lands to be acquired by the Secretary of Agriculture).

U.S.C., Title 42:

§§ 1805(b)(5), 1813(b) [now §§ 2061 and 2112, and §§ 2221 to 2224, respectively, of Title 42] (Atomic Energy Act).

The following are instances of Acts which authorized condemnation and declare that the procedure is to conform what that of similar actions in state courts:

U.S.C., Title 16:

§ 423k (Richmond National Battlefield Park; acquisition of lands by the Secretary of the Interior).

§ 814 (Exercise by water power licensee of power of eminent domain).

U.S.C., Title 24:

§ 78 [Repealed] (Condemnation of land for the former National Home for Disabled Volunteer Soldiers).

U.S.C., Title 33:

§ 591 (Condemnation of lands and materials for river and harbor improvement by the Secretary of the Army).

U.S.C., Title 40:

§ 257 [now § 3113] (Condemnation of realty for sites for public building and for other public uses by the Secretary of the Treasury authorized).

§ 258 [Omitted as superseded by this rule] (Same procedure).

U.S.C., Title 50:

§ 171 [Repealed and is now covered by § 2663 of Title 10] (Acquisition of land by the Secretary of the Army for national defense).

§ 172 [Repealed and is now covered by §§ 2664 and 2665 of Title 10] (Acquisition of property by the Secretary of the Army, etc., for production of lumber).

§ 632 App. [Omitted as terminated by § 645 of the former Appendix to Title 50] (Second War Powers Act, 1942; acquisition of real property for war purposes by the Secretary of Army, the Secretary of the Navy and others).

The following are Acts in which a more or less complete code of procedure is set forth in connection with the taking:

U.S.C., Title 16:

§ 831x (Condemnation by Tennessee Valley Authority).

U.S.C., Title 40:

§ 361–386 [Repealed] [now D.C.Code, Title 16, § 1301 et seq.] (Acquisition of lands in District of Columbia for use of United States; condemnation).

3. Adjustment of Rule to Statutory Provisions. While it was apparent that the principle of uniformity should be the basis for a rule to replace the multiple diverse procedures set out above, there remained a serious question as to whether an exception could properly be made relative to the method of determining compensation. Where Congress had provided for conformity to state law the following were the general methods in use: an initial determination by commissioners, with appeal to a judge; an initial award, likewise made by commissioners, but with the appeal to a jury; and determination by a jury without a previous award by commissioners. In two situations Congress had specified the tribunal to determine the issue of compensation: condemnation by the Tennessee Valley Authority; and condemnation in the District of Columbia. Under the TVA procedure the initial determination of value is by three disinterested commissioners, appointed by the court, from a locality other than the one in which the land lies. Either party may except to the award of the commission; in that case the exceptions are to be heard by three district judges (unless the parties stipulate for a lesser number), with a right of appeal to the circuit court of appeals. The TVA is a regional agency. It is faced with the necessity of acquiring a very substantial acreage within a relatively small area, and charged with the task of carrying on within the Tennessee Valley and in cooperation with the local people a permanent program involving navigation and flood control, electric power, soil conservation, and general regional development. The success of this program is partially dependent upon the good will and cooperation of the people of the Tennessee Valley, and this in turn partially depends upon the land acquisition program. Disproportionate awards among landowners would create dissatisfaction and ill will. To secure uniformity in treatment Congress provided the rather unique procedure of the three-judge court to review de novo the initial award of the commissioners. This procedure has worked to the satisfaction of the property owners and the TVA. A full statement of the TVA position and experience is set forth in Preliminary Draft of Proposed Rule to Govern Condemnation Cases (June, 1947) 15–19. A large majority of the district judges with experience under this procedure approve it, subject to some objection to the requirement for a three-judge district court to review commissioners' awards. A statutory three-judge requirement is, however, jurisdictional and must be strictly followed. *Stratton v. St. Louis, Southwestern Ry. Co.*, 1930, 51 S.Ct. 8, 282 U.S. 10, 75 L.Ed. 135; *Ayrshire Collieries Corp. v. United States*, 1947, 67 S.Ct. 1168, 331 U.S. 132, 91 L.Ed. 1391. Hence except insofar as the TVA statute itself authorizes the parties to stipulate for a court of less than three judges, the requirement must be followed, and would seem to be beyond alteration by court rule even if change were thought desirable. Accordingly the TVA procedure is retained for the determination of compensation in TVA condemnation cases. It was also thought desirable to retain the specific method Congress had prescribed for the District of Columbia, which is a so-called jury of five appointed by the court. This is a local matter and the specific treatment accorded by Congress has given local satisfaction.

Aside from the foregoing limited exceptions dealing with the TVA and the District of Columbia, the question was whether a uniform method for determining compensation should be a commission with appeal to a district judge, or a commission with appeal to a jury, or a jury without a commission. Experience with the commission on a nationwide basis, and in particular with the utilization of a commission followed by an appeal to a jury, has been that the commission is time consuming and expensive. Furthermore, it is largely a futile procedure where it is preparatory to jury trial. Since in the bulk of states a land owner is entitled eventually to a jury trial, since the jury is a traditional tribunal for the determination of questions of value, and since experience with juries has proved satisfactory to both government and land owner, the right to jury trial is adopted as the general rule. Condemnation involving the TVA and the District of Columbia are the two exceptions. See Note to Subdivision (h), infra.

Note to Subdivision (a). As originally promulgated the Federal Rules governed appeals in condemnation proceedings but were not otherwise applicable. Rule 81(a)(7). Pre-appeal procedure, in the main, conformed to state procedure. See statutes and discussion, supra. The purpose of Rule 71A is to provide a uniform procedure for condemnation in the federal district courts, including the District of Columbia. To achieve this purpose Rule 71A prescribes such specialized procedure as is required by condemnation proceedings, otherwise it utilizes the general framework of the Federal Rules where specific detail is unnecessary. The adoption of Rule 71A, of course, renders paragraph (7) of Rule 81(a) unnecessary.

The promulgation of a rule for condemnation procedure is within the rulemaking power. The Enabling Act [Act of June 19, 1934, c. 651, §§ 1, 2 (48 Stat. 1064), former §§ 723b, 723c, now § 2072, of this title] gives the Supreme Court "the power to prescribe, by general rules * * * the forms of process, writs, pleadings, and motions, and the practice and procedure in civil actions at law." Such rules, however, must not abridge, enlarge, or modify substantive rights. In *Kohl v. United States*, 1875, 91 U.S. 367, 23 L.Ed. 449, a proceeding instituted by the United States to appropriate land for a postoffice site under a statute enacted for such purpose, the Supreme Court held that "a proceeding to take land in virtue of the government's eminent domain, and determining the compensation to be made for it, is * * * a suit at common law, when initiated in a court." See, also, *Madisonville Traction Co. v. Saint Bernard Mining Co.*, 1905, 25 S.Ct. 251, 196 U.S. 239, 49 L.Ed. 462, infra, under subdivision (k). And the Conformity Act [former § 258 of Title 40], which is superseded by Rule 71A, deals only with "practice, pleadings, forms and proceedings and not with matters of substantive laws." *United States v. 243.22 Acres of Land in Village of Farmingdale, Town of Babylon, Suffolk County, N.Y.*, D.C.N.Y.1942, 43 F.Supp. 561, affirmed 129 F.2d 678, certiorari denied 63 S.Ct. 441, 317 U.S. 698, 87 L.Ed. 558.

Rule 71A affords a uniform procedure for all cases of condemnation invoking the national power of eminent domain, and, to the extent stated in subdivision (k), for cases invoking a state's power of eminent domain; and supplants all statutes prescribing a different procedure. While the almost exclusive utility of the rule is for the condemnation of real property, it also applies to the condemnation of personal property, either as an incident to real property or as the sole object of the proceeding, when permitted or required by statute. See former § 438j [now § 5001] of Title 38 (World War Veterans' Relief Act); former §§ 1805, 1811, and 1813 of Title 42 (Atomic Energy Act); former § 79 [now § 100] of Title 50 (Nitrates Act); former §§ 161 to 165 and § 166, of Title 50 (Helium Gas Act). Requisitioning of personal property with the right in the owner to sue the United States, where the compensation cannot be agreed upon (see former § 1813 [now §§ 2221 to 2224] of Title 42, for example) will continue to be the normal method of acquiring personal property and Rule 71A in no way interferes with or restricts any such right. Only where the law requires or permits the formal procedure of condemnation to be utilized will the rule have any applicability to the acquisition of personal property.

Rule 71A is not intended to and does not supersede the Act of February 26, 1931, c. 307, §§ 1 to 5 (46 Stat. 1421), §§ 258a to 258e of Title 40, which is a supplementary condemnation statute, permissive in its nature and designed to permit the prompt acquisition of title by the United States, pending the condemnation proceeding, upon a deposit in court. See *United States v. 76,800 Acres, More or Less, of Land, in Bryan and Liberty Counties, Ga.*, D.C.Ga.1942, 44 F.Supp. 653; *United States v. 17,280 Acres of Land, More or Less, Situated in Saunders County, Neb.*, D.C.Neb.1942, 47 F.Supp. 267. The same is true insofar as the following or any other statutes authorize the acquisition of title or the taking of immediate possession:

U.S.C., Title 33:

§ 594 (When immediate possession of land may be taken; for a work of river and harbor improvements.)

U.S.C., Title 42:

§ 1813(b) [now §§ 2221 to 2224 of Title 42] (When immediate possession may be taken under Atomic Energy Act).

U.S.C., Title 50:

§ 171 [Repealed and is now covered by § 2663 of Title 10] (Acquisition of land by the Secretary of the Army for national defense).

§ 632 App. [Omitted as terminated by § 645 of the former Appendix to Title 50] (Second War Powers Act, 1942; acquisition of real property for war purposes by the

Secretary of the Army, the Secretary of the Navy, and others).

Note to Subdivision (b). This subdivision provides for broad joinder in accordance with the tenor of other rules such as Rule 18. To require separate condemnation proceedings for each piece of property separately owned would be unduly burdensome and would serve no useful purpose. And a restriction that only properties may be joined which are to be acquired for the same public use would also cause difficulty. For example, a unified project to widen a street, construct a bridge across a navigable river, and for the construction of approaches to the level of the bridge on both sides of the river might involve acquiring property for different public uses. Yet it is eminently desirable that the plaintiff may in one proceeding condemn all the property interests and rights necessary to carry out this project. Rule 21 which allows the court to sever and proceed separately with any claim against a party, and Rule 42(b) giving the court broad discretion to order separate trials give adequate protection to all defendants in condemnation proceedings.

Note to Subdivision (c). Since a condemnation proceeding is in rem and since a great many property owners are often involved, paragraph (1) requires the property to be named and only one of the owners. In other respects and caption will contain the name of the court, the title of the action, file number, and a designation of the pleading as a complaint in accordance with Rule 10(a).

Since the general standards of pleading are stated in other rules, paragraph (2) prescribes only the necessary detail for condemnation proceedings. Certain statutes allow the United States to acquire title or possession immediately upon commencement of an action. See the Act of February 26, 1931, c. 307, §§ 1 to 5 (46 Stat. 1421), §§ 258a to 258e of Title 40; and § 594 of Title 33, former § 1813(b) of Title 42, former § 171 of Title 50, former § 632 of the Appendix to Title 50, supra. To carry out the purpose of such statutes and to aid the condemnor in instituting the action even where title is not acquired at the outset, the plaintiff is initially required to join as defendants only the persons having or claiming an interest in the property whose names are then known. This is no way prejudices the property owner, who must eventually be joined as a defendant, served with process, and allowed to answer before there can be any hearing involving the compensation to be paid for his piece of property. The rule requires the plaintiff to name all persons having or claiming an interest in the property of whom the plaintiff has learned and, more importantly, those appearing of record. By charging the plaintiff with the necessity to make "a search of the records of the extent commonly made by competent searches of title in the vicinity in light of the type and value of the property involved" both the plaintiff and property owner are protected. Where a short term interest in property of little value is involved, as a two or three year easement over a vacant land for purposes of ingress and egress to other property, a search of the records covering a long period of time is not required. Where on the other hand fee simple title in valuable property is being condemned the search must necessarily cover a much longer period of time and be commensurate with the interests involved. But even here the search is related to the type made by competent title searchers in the vicinity. A search that extends back to the original patent may be feasible in some midwestern and western states and be proper under certain circumstances. In the Atlantic seaboard states such a search is normally not feasible nor desirable. There is a common sense business accommodation of what title search-

ers can and should do. For state statutes requiring persons appearing as owners or otherwise interested in the property to be named as defendants, see 3 Colo.Stat.Ann., 1935, c. 61, § 2; Ill.Ann.Stat. (Smith-Hurd) c. 47, § 2; 1 Iowa Code, 1946, § 472.3; Kans.Stat.Ann., 1935, § 26–101; 2 Mass.Laws Ann., 1932, c. 80A, § 4; 7 Mich.Stat.Ann., 1936, § 8.2; 2 Minn.Stat., Mason 1927, § 6541; 20 N.J.Stat.Ann., 1939, § 1–2; 3 Wash.Revised Stat., Remington, 1932, Title 6, § 891. For state provisions allowing persons whose names are not known to be designated under the descriptive term of "unknown owner", see Hawaii Revised Laws, 1945, c. 8, § 310 ("such [unknown] defendant may be joined in the petition under a fictitious name."); Ill.Ann.Stat. (Smith-Hurd) c. 47, § 2 ("Persons interested, whose names are unknown, may be made parties defendant by the description of the unknown owners; * * *"); Maryland Code Ann., 1939, Art. 33A, § 1 ("In case any owner or owners is or are not known, he or they may be described in such petition as the unknown owner or owners, or the unknown heir or heirs of a deceased owner."); 2 Mass.Laws Ann., 1932, c. 80A, § 4 ("Persons not in being, unascertained or unknown who may have an interest in any of such land shall be made parties respondent by such description as seems appropriate, * * *"); New Mex.Stat.Ann., 1941, § 25–901 ("the owners * * * shall be parties defendant, by name, if the names are known, and by description of the unknown owners of the land therein described, if their names are unknown."); Utah Code Ann., 1943, § 104–61–7 ("The names of all owners and claimants of the property, if known, or a statement that they are unknown, who must be styled defendants").

The last sentence of paragraph (2) enables the court to expedite the distribution of a deposit, in whole or in part, as soon as pertinent facts of ownership, value and the like are established. See also subdivision (j).

The signing of the complaint is governed by Rule 11.

Note to Subdivision (d). In lieu of a summons, which is the initial process in other civil actions under Rule 4(a), subdivision (d) provides for a notice which is to contain sufficient information so that the defendant in effect obtains the plaintiff's statement of his claim against the defendant to whom the notice is directed. Since the plaintiff's attorney is an officer of the court and to prevent unduly burdening the clerk of the court, paragraph (1) of subdivision (d) provides that plaintiff's attorney shall prepare and deliver a notice or notices to the clerk. Flexibility is provided by the provision for joint or several notices, and for additional notices. Where there are only a few defendants it may be convenient to prepare but one notice directed to all the defendants. In other cases where there are many defendants it will be more convenient to prepare two or more notices; but in any event a notice must be directed to each named defendant. Paragraph (2) provides that the notice is to be signed by the plaintiff's attorney. Since the notice is to be delivered to the clerk, the issuance of the notice will appear of record in the court. The clerk should forthwith deliver the notice or notices for service to the marshal or to a person specially appointed to serve the notice. Rule 4(a). The form of the notice is such that, in addition to informing the defendant of the plaintiff's statement of claim, it tells the defendant precisely what his rights are. Failure on the part of the defendant to serve an answer constitutes a consent to the taking and to the authority of the court to proceed to fix compensation therefor, but it does not preclude the defendant from presenting evidence as to the amount of compensation due him or in sharing the award of distribution. See subdivision (e); Form 28.

While under Rule 4(f) the territorial limits of a summons are normally the territorial limits of the state in which the district court is held, the territorial limits for personal service of a notice under Rule 71A(d)(3) are those of the nation. This extension of process is here proper since the aim of the condemnation proceeding is not to enforce any personal liability and the property owner is helped, not imposed upon, by the best type of service possible. If personal service cannot be made either because the defendant's whereabouts cannot be ascertained, or, if ascertained, the defendant cannot be personally served, as where he resides in a foreign country such as Canada or Mexico, then service by publication is proper. The provisions for this type of service are set forth in the rule and are in no way governed by § 118 [now § 1655] of this title.

Note to Subdivision (e). Departing from the scheme of Rule 12, subdivision (e) requires all defenses and objections to be presented in an answer and does not authorize a preliminary motion. There is little need for the latter in condemnation proceedings. The general standard of pleading is governed by other rules, particularly Rule 8, and this subdivision (e) merely prescribes what matters the answer should set forth. Merely by appearing in the action a defendant can receive notice of all proceedings affecting him. And without the necessity of answering a defendant may present evidence as to the amount of compensation due him, and he may share in the distribution of the award. See also subdivision (d)(2); Form 28.

Note to Subdivision (f). Due to the number of persons who may be interested in the property to be condemned, there is a likelihood that the plaintiff will need to amend his complaint, perhaps many times, to add new parties or state new issues. This subdivision recognizes that fact and does not burden the court with applications by the plaintiff for leave to amend. At the same time all defendants are adequately protected; and their need to amend the answer is adequately protected by Rule 15, which is applicable by virtue of subdivision (a) of this Rule 71A.

Note to Subdivision (g). A condemnation action is a proceeding in rem. Commencement of the action as against a defendant by virtue of his joinder pursuant to subdivision (c)(2) is the point of cut-off and there is no mandatory requirement for substitution because of a subsequent change of interest, although the court is given ample power to require substitution. Rule 25 is inconsistent with subdivision (g) and hence inapplicable. Accordingly, the time periods of Rule 25 do not govern to require dismissal nor to prevent substitution.

Note to Subdivision (h). This subdivision prescribes the method for determining the issue of just compensation in cases involving the federal power of eminent domain. The method of jury trial provided by subdivision (h) will normally apply in cases involving the state power by virtue of subdivision (k).

Congress has specially constituted a tribunal for the trial of the issue of just compensation in two instances: condemnation under the Tennessee Valley Authority Act; and condemnation in the District of Columbia. These tribunals are retained for reasons set forth in the General Statement: 3. Adjustment of Rule to Statutory Provisions, supra. Subdivision (h) also has prospective application so that if Congress should create another special tribunal, that tribunal will determine the issue of just compensation. Subject to these exceptions the general

method of trial of that issue is to be by jury if any party demands it, otherwise that issue, as well as all other issues, are to be tried by the court.

As to the TVA procedure that is continued, § 831x of Title 16 requires that three commissioners be appointed to fix the compensation; that exceptions to their award are to be heard by three district judges (unless the parties stipulate for a lesser number) and that the district judges try the question de novo; that an appeal to the circuit court of appeals may be taken within 30 days from the filing of the decision of the district judges; and that the circuit court of appeals shall on the record fix compensation "without regard to the awards or findings theretofore made by the commissioners or the district judges." The mode of fixing compensation in the District of Columbia, which is also continued, is prescribed in former §§ 361 to 386 of Title 40. Under former § 371 the court is required in all cases to order the selection of a jury of five from among not less than 20 names, drawn "from the special box provided by law." They must have the usual qualifications of jurors and in addition must be freeholders of the District, and not in the service of the United States or the District. A special oath is administered to the chosen jurors. The trial proceeds in the ordinary way, except that the jury is allowed to separate after they have begun to consider their verdict.

There is no constitutional right to jury trial in a condemnation proceeding. *Bauman v. Ross*, 1897, 17 S.Ct. 966, 167 U.S. 548, 42 L.Ed. 270. See, also, Hines, *Does the Seventh Amendment to the Constitution of the United States Require Jury Trials in all Condemnation Proceedings?*, 1925, 11 Va.L.Rev. 505; Blair, *Federal Condemnation Proceedings and the Seventh Amendment*, 1927, 41 Harv.L.Rev. 29; 3 *Moore's Federal Practice*, 1938, 3007. Prior to Rule 71A, jury trial in federal condemnation proceedings was, however, enjoyed under the general conformity statute, former § 258 of Title 40, in states which provided for jury trial. See generally, 2 Lewis, *Eminent Domain*, 3d ed. 1909, §§ 509, 510; 3 Moore, op. cit. supra. Since the general conformity statute is superseded by Rule 71A, see supra under subdivision (a), and since it was believed that the rule to be substituted should likewise give a right to jury trial, subdivision (h) establishes that method as the general one for determining the issue of just compensation.

Note to Subdivision (i). Both the right of the plaintiff to dismiss by filing a notice of dismissal and the right of the court to permit a dismissal are circumscribed to the extent that where the plaintiff has acquired the title or a lesser interest or possession, viz., any property interest for which just compensation should be paid, the action may not be dismissed, without the defendant's consent, and the property owner remitted to another court, such as the Court of Claims, to recover just compensation for the property right taken. Circuity of action is thus prevented without increasing the liability of the plaintiff to pay just compensation for any interest that is taken. Freedom of dismissal is accorded, where both the condemnor and condemnee agree, up to the time of the entry of judgment vesting plaintiff with title. And power is given to the court, where the parties agree, to vacate the judgment and thus revest title in the property owner. In line with Rule 21, the court may at any time drop a defendant who has been unnecessarily or improperly joined as where it develops that he has no interest.

Note to Subdivision (j). Whatever the substantive law is concerning the necessity of making a deposit will continue to govern. For statutory provisions concerning deposit in court in condemnation proceedings by the United States, see § 258a of [former] Title 40; § 594 of Title 33; acquisition of title and possession statutes referred to in note to subdivision (a), supra. If the plaintiff is invoking the state's power of eminent domain the necessity of deposit will be governed by the state law. For discussion of such law, see 1 Nichols, Eminent Domain, 2d ed. 1917, §§ 209 to 216. For discussion of the function of deposit and the power of the court to enter judgment in cases both of deficiency and overpayment, see *United States v. Miller*, 1943, 63 S.Ct. 276, 317 U.S. 369, 87 L.Ed. 336, 147 A.L.R. 55, rehearing denied 63 S.Ct. 557, 318 U.S. 798, 87 L.Ed. 1162 (judgment in favor of plaintiff for overpayment ordered).

The court is to make distribution of the deposit as promptly as the facts of the case warrant. See also subdivision (c)(2).

Note to Subdivision (k). While the overwhelming number of cases that will be brought in the federal courts under this rule will be actions involving the federal power of eminent domain, a small percentage of cases may be instituted in the federal court or removed thereto on the basis of diversity or alienage which will involve the power of eminent domain under the law of a state. See *Boom Co. v. Patterson*, 1878, 98 U.S. 403, 25 L.Ed. 206; *Searl v. School District No. 2*, 1888, 8 S.Ct. 460, 124 U.S. 197, 31 L.Ed. 415; *Madisonville Traction Co. v. Saint Bernard Mining Co.*, 1905, 25 S.Ct. 251, 196 U.S. 239, 49 L.Ed. 462. In the Madisonville case, and in cases cited therein, it has been held that condemnation actions brought by state corporations in the exercise of a power delegated by the state might be governed by procedure prescribed by the laws of the United States, whether the cases were begun in or removed to the federal court. See, also, *Franzen v. Chicago, M. & St. P. Ry. Co.*, C.C.A.7th, 1921, 278 F. 370, 372.

Any condition affecting the substantial right of a litigant attached by state law is to be observed and enforced, such as making a deposit in court where the power of eminent domain is conditioned upon so doing. (See also subdivision (j). Subject to this qualification, subdivision (k) provides that in cases involving the state power of eminent domain, the practice prescribed by other subdivisions of Rule 71A shall govern.

Note to Subdivision (*l*). Since the condemnor will normally be the prevailing party and since he should not recover his costs against the property owner, Rule 54(d), which provides generally that costs shall go to the prevailing party, is made inapplicable. Without attempting to state what the rule on costs is, the effect of subdivision (*l*) is that costs shall be awarded in accordance with the law that has developed in condemnation cases. This has been summarized as follows: "Costs of condemnation proceedings are not assessable against the condemnee, unless by stipulation he agrees to assume some or all of them. Such normal expenses of the proceeding as bills for publication of notice, commissioners' fees, the cost of transporting commissioners and jurors to take a view, fees for attorneys to represent defendants who have failed to answer, and witness' fees, are properly charged to the government, though not taxed as costs. Similarly, if it is necessary that a conveyance be executed by a commissioner, the United States pay his fees and those for recording the deed. However, the distribution of the award is a matter in which the United States has no legal interest. Expenses incurred in ascertaining the identity of distributees and deciding between conflicting claimants are properly chargeable against the award, not against the United States, although

United States attorneys are expected to aid the court in such matters as amici curiae." Lands Division Manual 861. For other discussion and citation, see *Grand River Dam Authority v. Jarvis*, C.C.A.10th, 1942, 124 F.2d 914. Costs may not be taxed against the United States except to the extent permitted by law. *United States v. 125.71 Acres of Land in Loyalhanna Tp., Westmoreland County, Pa.*, D.C.Pa.1944, 54 F.Supp. 193; Lands Division Manual 859. Even if it were thought desirable to allow the property owner's costs to be taxed against the United States, this is a matter for legislation and not court rule.

1963 Amendment

This amendment conforms to the amendment of Rule 4(f).

1985 Amendment

Rule 71A(h) provides that except when Congress has provided otherwise, the issue of just compensation in a condemnation case may be tried by a jury if one of the parties so demands, unless the court in its discretion orders the issue determined by a commission of three persons. In 1980, the Comptroller General of the United States in a Report to Congress recommended that use of the commission procedure should be encouraged in order to improve and expedite the trial of condemnation cases. The Report noted that long delays were being caused in many districts by such factors as crowded dockets, the precedence given criminal cases, the low priority accorded condemnation matters, and the high turnover of Assistant United States Attorneys. The Report concluded that revising Rule 71A to make the use of the commission procedure more attractive might alleviate the situation.

Accordingly, Rule 71A(h) is being amended in a number of respects designed to assure the quality and utility of a Rule 71A commission. First, the amended Rule will give the court discretion to appoint, in addition to the three members of a commission, up to two additional persons as alternate commissioners who would hear the case and be available, at any time up to the filing of the decision by the three-member commission, to replace any commissioner who becomes unable or disqualified to continue. The discretion to appoint alternate commissioners can be particularly useful in protracted cases, avoiding expensive retrials that have been required in some cases because of the death or disability of a commissioner. Prior to replacing a commissioner an alternate would not be present at, or participate in, the commission's deliberations.

Second, the amended Rule requires the court, before appointment, to advise the parties of the identity and qualifications of each prospective commissioner and alternate. The court then may authorize the examination of prospective appointees by the parties and each party has the right to challenge for cause. The objective is to insure that unbiased and competent commissioners are appointed.

The amended Rule does not prescribe a qualification standard for appointment to a commission, although it is understood that only persons possessing background and ability to appraise real estate valuation testimony and to award fair and just compensation on the basis thereof would be appointed. In most situations the chairperson should be a lawyer and all members should have some background qualifying them to weigh proof of value in the real estate field and, when possible, in the particular real estate market embracing the land in question.

The amended Rule should give litigants greater confidence in the commission procedure by affording them certain rights to participate in the appointment of commission members that are roughly comparable to the practice with regard to jury selection. This is accomplished by giving the court permission to allow the parties to examine prospective commissioners and by recognizing the right of each party to object to the appointment of any person for cause.

1987 Amendment

The amendments are technical. No substantive change is intended.

1988 Amendment

The amendment is technical. No substantive change is intended.

1993 Amendment

The references to the subdivisions of Rule 4 are deleted in light of the revision of that rule.

2003 Amendment

The references to specific subdivisions of Rule 53 are deleted or revised to reflect amendments of Rule 53.

2007 Amendment

The language of Rule 71A has been amended as part of the general restyling of the Civil Rules to make them more easily understood and to make style and terminology consistent throughout the rules. These changes are intended to be stylistic only.

Former Rule 71A has been redesignated as Rule 71.1 to conform to the designations used for all other rules added with the original numbering system.

Rule 71.1(e) allows a defendant to appear without answering. Former form 28 (now form 60) includes information about this right in the Rule 71.1(d)(2) notice. It is useful to confirm this practice in the rule.

The information that identifies the attorney is changed to include telephone number and electronic-mail address, in line with similar amendments to Rules 11(a) and 26(g)(1).

2009 Amendment

The times set in the former rule at 20 days have been revised to 21 days. See the Note to Rule 6.

CROSS REFERENCES

Jurisdiction and venue in condemnation proceedings, see 28 USCA §§ 1358 and 1403.

Reclamation projects, compensation for rights-of-way, see 43 USCA § 945b.

Tennessee Valley Authority, procedure in condemnation proceedings, see 16 USCA § 831x.

Rule 72. Magistrate Judges: Pretrial Order

(a) Nondispositive Matters. When a pretrial matter not dispositive of a party's claim or defense is referred to a magistrate judge to hear and decide, the magistrate judge must promptly conduct the required proceedings and, when appropriate, issue a written order stating the decision. A party may serve and file objections to the order within 14 days after being served with a copy. A party may not assign as error a defect in the order not timely objected to. The district judge in the case must consider timely objections and modify or set aside any part of the order that is clearly erroneous or is contrary to law.

(b) Dispositive Motions and Prisoner Petitions.

(1) *Findings and Recommendations.* A magistrate judge must promptly conduct the required proceedings when assigned, without the parties' consent, to hear a pretrial matter dispositive of a claim or defense or a prisoner petition challenging the conditions of confinement. A record must be made of all evidentiary proceedings and may, at the magistrate judge's discretion, be made of any other proceedings. The magistrate judge must enter a recommended disposition, including, if appropriate, proposed findings of fact. The clerk must promptly mail a copy to each party.

(2) *Objections.* Within 14 days after being served with a copy of the recommended disposition, a party may serve and file specific written objections to the proposed findings and recommendations. A party may respond to another party's objections within 14 days after being served with a copy. Unless the district judge orders otherwise, the objecting party must promptly arrange for transcribing the record, or whatever portions of it the parties agree to or the magistrate judge considers sufficient.

(3) *Resolving Objections.* The district judge must determine de novo any part of the magistrate judge's disposition that has been properly objected to. The district judge may accept, reject, or modify the recommended disposition; receive further evidence; or return the matter to the magistrate judge with instructions.

(Former Rule 72 abrogated December 4, 1967, effective July 1, 1968; new Rule 72 adopted April 28, 1983, effective August 1, 1983; amended April 30, 1991, effective December 1, 1991; April 22, 1993, effective December 1, 1993; April 30, 2007, effective December 1, 2007; March 26, 2009, effective December 1, 2009.)

ADVISORY COMMITTEE NOTES

1983 Addition

Subdivision (a). This subdivision addresses court-ordered referrals of nondispositive matters under 28 U.S.C. § 636(b)(1)(A). The rule calls for a written order of the magistrate's disposition to preserve the record and facilitate review. An oral order read into the record by the magistrate will satisfy this requirement.

No specific procedures or timetables for raising objections to the magistrate's rulings on nondispositive matters are set forth in the Magistrates Act. The rule fixes a 10-day period in order to avoid uncertainty and provide uniformity that will eliminate the confusion that might arise if different periods were prescribed by local rule in different districts. It also is contemplated that a party who is successful before the magistrate will be afforded an opportunity to respond to objections raised to the magistrate's ruling.

The last sentence of subdivision (a) specifies that reconsideration of a magistrate's order, as provided for in the Magistrates Act, shall be by the district judge to whom the case is assigned. This rule does not restrict experimentation by the district courts under 28 U.S.C. § 636(b)(3) involving references of matters other than pretrial matters, such as appointment of counsel, taking of default judgments, and acceptance of jury verdicts when the judge is unavailable.

Subdivision (b). This subdivision governs court-ordered referrals of dispositive pretrial matters and prisoner petitions challenging conditions of confinement, pursuant to statutory authorization in 28 U.S.C. § 636(b)(1)(B). This rule does not extend to habeas corpus petitions, which are covered by the specific rules relating to proceedings under Sections 2254 and 2255 of Title 28.

This rule implements the statutory procedures for making objections to the magistrate's proposed findings and recommendations. The 10-day period, as specified in the statute, is subject to Rule 6(e) which provides for an additional 3-day period when service is made by mail. Although no specific provision appears in the Magistrates Act, the rule specifies a 10-day period for a party to respond to objections to the magistrate's recommendation.

Implementing the statutory requirements, the rule requires the district judge to whom the case is assigned to make a de novo determination of those portions of the report, findings, or recommendations to which timely objection is made. The term "de novo" signifies that the magistrate's findings are not protected by the clearly erroneous doctrine, but does not indicate that a second evidentiary hearing is required. See *United States v. Raddatz*, 417 [447] U.S. 667 (1980). See also Silberman, *Masters and Magistrates Part II: The American Analogue*, 50 N.Y.U. L.Rev. 1297, 1367 (1975). When no timely objection is filed, the court need only satisfy itself that there is no clear error on the face of the record in order to accept the recommendation. See *Campbell v. United States Dist. Court*, 501 F.2d 196, 206 (9th Cir.1974), cert. denied, 419 U.S. 879, quoted in House Report No. 94–1609, 94th Cong.2d Sess. (1976) at 3. Compare *Park Motor Mart, Inc. v. Ford Motor Co.*, 616 F.2d 603 (1st Cir.1980). Failure to make timely objection to the magistrate's report prior to its adoption by the district judge may constitute a waiver of appellate review of the district judge's order. *See United States v. Walters*, 638 F.2d 947 (6th Cir.1981).

1991 Amendment

This amendment is intended to eliminate a discrepancy in measuring the 10 days for serving and filing objections to a magistrate's action under subdivisions (a) and (b) of this Rule. The rule as promulgated in 1983 required objections to the magistrate's handling of nondispositive matters to be served and filed within 10 days of entry of the order, but required objections to dispositive motions to be made within 10 days of being served with a copy of the recommended disposition. Subdivision (a) is here amended to conform to subdivision (b) to avoid any confusion or technical defaults, particularly in connection with magistrate orders that rule on both dispositive and nondispositive matters.

The amendment is also intended to assure that objections to magistrate's orders that are not timely made shall not be considered. *Compare* Rule 51.

1993 Amendment

This revision is made to conform the rule to changes made by the Judicial Improvements Act of 1990.

2007 Amendment

The language of Rule 72 has been amended as part of the general restyling of the Civil Rules to make them more easily understood and to make style and terminology consistent throughout the rules. These changes are intended to be stylistic only.

2009 Amendment

The times set in the former rule at 10 days have been revised to 14 days. See the Note to Rule 6.

HISTORICAL NOTES

Change of Name

Reference to United States magistrate or to magistrate deemed to refer to United States magistrate judge pursuant to section 321 of Pub.L. 101–650, set out as a note under section 631 of this title.

Rule 73.   Magistrate Judges: Trial by Consent; Appeal

(a) Trial by Consent. When authorized under 28 U.S.C. § 636(c), a magistrate judge may, if all parties consent, conduct a civil action or proceeding, including a jury or nonjury trial. A record must be made in accordance with 28 U.S.C. § 636(c)(5).

(b) Consent Procedure.

(1) *In General.* When a magistrate judge has been designated to conduct civil actions or proceedings, the clerk must give the parties written notice of their opportunity to consent under 28 U.S.C. § 636(c). To signify their consent, the parties must jointly or separately file a statement consenting to the referral. A district judge or magistrate judge may be informed of a party's response to the clerk's notice only if all parties have consented to the referral.

(2) *Reminding the Parties About Consenting.* A district judge, magistrate judge, or other court official may remind the parties of the magistrate judge's availability, but must also advise them that they are free to withhold consent without adverse substantive consequences.

(3) *Vacating a Referral.* On its own for good cause—or when a party shows extraordinary circumstances—the district judge may vacate a referral to a magistrate judge under this rule.

(c) Appealing a Judgment. In accordance with 28 U.S.C. § 636(c)(3), an appeal from a judgment entered at a magistrate judge's direction may be taken to the court of appeals as would any other appeal from a district-court judgment.

(Former Rule 73 abrogated December 4, 1967, effective July 1, 1968; new Rule 73 adopted April 28, 1983, effective August 1, 1983; amended March 2, 1987, effective August 1, 1987; April 22, 1993, effective December 1, 1993; April 11, 1997, effective December 1, 1997; April 30, 2007, effective December 1, 2007.)

ADVISORY COMMITTEE NOTES

1983 Addition

Subdivision (a). This subdivision implements the broad authority of the 1979 amendments to the Magistrates Act, 28 U.S.C. § 636(c), which permit a magistrate to sit in lieu of a district judge and exercise civil jurisdiction over a case, when the parties consent. See McCabe, *The Federal Magistrate Act of 1979*, 16 Harv.J.Legis. 343, 364–79 (1979). In order to exercise this jurisdiction, a magistrate must be specially designated under 28 U.S.C. § 636(c)(1) by the district court or courts he serves. The only exception to a magistrate's exercise of civil jurisdiction, which includes the power to conduct jury and nonjury trials and decide dispositive motions, is the contempt power. A hearing on contempt is to be conducted by the district judge upon certification of the facts and an order to show cause by the magistrate. See 28 U.S.C. § 639(e). In view of 28 U.S.C. § 636(c)(1) and this rule, it is unnecessary to amend Rule 58 to provide that the decision of a magistrate is a "decision by the court" for the purposes of that rule and a "final decision of the district court" for purposes of 28 U.S.C. § 1291 governing appeals.

Subdivision (b). This subdivision implements the blind consent provision of 28 U.S.C. § 636(c)(2) and is designed to ensure that neither the judge nor the magistrate attempts to induce a party to consent to reference of a civil matter under this rule to a magistrate. See House Rep. No. 96–444, 96th Cong. 1st Sess. 8 (1979).

The rule opts for a uniform approach in implementing the consent provision by directing the clerk to notify the parties of their opportunity to elect to proceed before a magistrate and by requiring the execution and filing of a consent form or forms setting forth the election. However, flexibility at the local level is preserved in that local rules will determine how notice shall be communicated to the parties, and local rules will specify the time period within which an election must be made.

The last paragraph of subdivision (b) reiterates the provision in 28 U.S.C. § 636(c)(6) for vacating a reference to the magistrate.

Subdivision (c). Under 28 U.S.C. § 636(c)(3), the normal route of appeal from the judgment of a magistrate—the only route that will be available unless the parties otherwise agree in advance—is an appeal by the aggrieved party "directly to the appropriate United States court of appeals from the judgment of the magistrate in the same manner as an appeal from any other judgment of a district court." The quoted statutory language indicates Congress' intent that the same procedures and standards of appealability that govern appeals from district court judgments govern appeals from magistrates' judgments.

Subdivision (d). 28 U.S.C. § 636(c)(4) offers parties who consent to the exercise of civil jurisdiction by a magistrate an alternative appeal route to that provided in subdivision (c) of this rule. This optional appellate route was provided by Congress in recognition of the fact that not all civil cases warrant the same appellate treatment. In cases where the amount in controversy is not great and there are no difficult questions of law to be resolved, the parties may desire to avoid the expense and delay of appeal to the court of appeals by electing an appeal to the district judge. See McCabe, *The Federal Magistrate Act of 1979*, 16 Harv.J.Legis. 343, 388 (1979). This subdivision provides that the parties may elect the optional appeal route at the time of reference to a magistrate. To this end, the notice by the clerk under subdivision (b) of this rule shall explain the appeal option and the corollary restriction on review by the court of appeals. This approach will avoid later claims of lack of consent to the avenue of appeal. The choice of the alternative appeal route to the judge of the district court should be made by the parties in their forms of consent. Special appellate rules to govern appeals from a magistrate to a district judge appear in new Rules 74 through 76.

1987 Amendment

The amendment is technical. No substantive change is intended.

1993 Amendment

This revision is made to conform the rule to changes made by the Judicial Improvements Act of 1990. The Act requires that, when being reminded of the availability of a magistrate judge, the parties be advised that withholding of consent will have no "adverse substantive consequences." They may, however, be advised if the withholding of consent will have the adverse procedural consequence of a potential delay in trial.

1997 Amendment

The Federal Courts Improvement Act of 1996 repealed the former provisions of 28 U.S.C. § 636(c)(4) and (5) that enabled parties that had agreed to trial before a magistrate judge to agree also that appeal should be taken to the district court. Rule 73 is amended to conform to this change. Rules 74, 75, and 76 are abrogated for the same reason. The portions of Form 33 and Form 34 that referred to appeals to the district court also are deleted.

2007 Amendment

The language of Rule 73 has been amended as part of the general restyling of the Civil Rules to make them more easily understood and to make style and terminology consistent throughout the rules. These changes are intended to be stylistic only.

HISTORICAL NOTES

Change of Name

Reference to United States magistrate or to magistrate deemed to refer to United States magistrate judge pursuant to section 321 of Pub.L. 101–650, set out as a note under section 631 of this title.

Rule 74. Method of Appeal From Magistrate Judge to District Judge Under Title 28, U.S.C. § 636(c)(4) and Rule 73(d) [Abrogated]

(Former Rule 74 abrogated December 4, 1967, effective July 1, 1968; new Rule 74 adopted April 28, 1983, effective August 1, 1983; amended April 22, 1993, effective December 1, 1993;

abrogated April 11, 1997, effective December 1, 1997; April 30, 2007, effective December 1, 2007.)

ADVISORY COMMITTEE NOTES
1997 Amendment

Rule 74 is abrogated for the reasons described in the Note to Rule 73.

2007 Amendment

Rule 74 was abrogated in 1997 to reflect repeal of the statute providing for appeal from a magistrate judge's judgment to the district court. The rule number is reserved for possible future use.

Rule 75. Proceedings on Appeal From Magistrate Judge to District Judge Under Rule 73(d) [Abrogated]

(Former Rule 75 abrogated December 4, 1967, effective July 1, 1968; new Rule 75 adopted April 28, 1983, effective August 1, 1983; amended March 2, 1987, effective August 1, 1987; April 22, 1993, effective December 1, 1993; abrogated April 11, 1997, effective December 1, 1997; April 30, 2007, effective December 1, 2007.)

ADVISORY COMMITTEE NOTES
1997 Amendment

Rule 75 is abrogated for the reasons described in the Note to Rule 73.

2007 Amendment

Rule 75 was abrogated in 1997 to reflect repeal of the statute providing for appeal from a magistrate judge's judgment to the district court. The rule number is reserved for possible future use.

Rule 76. Judgment of the District Judge on The Appeal Under Rule 73(d) and Costs [Abrogated]

(Former Rule 76 abrogated December 4, 1967, effective July 1, 1968; new Rule 76 adopted April 28, 1983, effective August 1, 1983; amended April 22, 1993, effective December 1, 1993; abrogated April 11, 1997, effective December 1, 1997; April 30, 2007, effective December 1, 2007.)

ADVISORY COMMITTEE NOTES
1997 Amendment

Rule 76 is abrogated for the reasons described in the Note to Rule 73.

2007 Amendment

Rule 76 was abrogated in 1997 to reflect repeal of the statute providing for appeal from a magistrate judge's judgment to the district court. The rule number is reserved for possible future use.

TITLE X. DISTRICT COURTS AND CLERKS: CONDUCTING BUSINESS; ISSUING ORDERS

Rule 77. Conducting Business; Clerk's Authority; Notice of an Order or Judgment

(a) When Court Is Open. Every district court is considered always open for filing any paper, issuing and returning process, making a motion, or entering an order.

(b) Place for Trial and Other Proceedings. Every trial on the merits must be conducted in open court and, so far as convenient, in a regular courtroom. Any other act or proceeding may be done or conducted by a judge in chambers, without the attendance of the clerk or other court official, and anywhere inside or outside the district. But no hearing—other than one ex parte—may be conducted outside the district unless all the affected parties consent.

(c) Clerk's Office Hours; Clerk's Orders.

(1) *Hours.* The clerk's office—with a clerk or deputy on duty—must be open during business hours every day except Saturdays, Sundays, and legal holidays. But a court may, by local rule or order, require that the office be open for specified hours on Saturday or a particular legal holiday other than one listed in Rule 6(a)(6)(A).

(2) *Orders.* Subject to the court's power to suspend, alter, or rescind the clerk's action for good cause, the clerk may:

(A) issue process;

(B) enter a default;

(C) enter a default judgment under Rule 55(b)(1); and

(D) act on any other matter that does not require the court's action.

(d) Serving Notice of an Order or Judgment.

(1) *Service.* Immediately after entering an order or judgment, the clerk must serve notice of the entry, as provided in Rule 5(b), on each party who is not in default for failing to appear. The clerk must record the service on the docket. A party also may serve notice of the entry as provided in Rule 5(b).

(2) *Time to Appeal Not Affected by Lack of Notice.* Lack of notice of the entry does not affect the time for appeal or relieve—or authorize the court to relieve—a party for failing to appeal within the time allowed, except as allowed by Federal Rule of Appellate Procedure (4)(a).

(Amended December 27, 1946, effective March 19, 1948; January 21, 1963, effective July 1, 1963; December 4, 1967, effective July 1, 1968; March 1, 1971, effective July 1, 1971; March 2, 1987, effective August 1, 1987; April 30, 1991, effective December 1, 1991; April 23, 2001, effective December 1, 2001; April 30, 2007, effective December 1, 2007; April 25, 2014, effective December 1, 2014.)

ADVISORY COMMITTEE NOTES
1937 Adoption

This rule states the substance of U.S.C., Title 28, § 452, formerly § 13 (Courts open as courts of admiralty and equity). Compare [former] Equity Rules 1 (District Court Always Open For Certain Purposes—Orders at Chambers), 2 (Clerk's Office Always Open, Except, Etc.), 4 (Notice of Orders), and 5 (Motions Grantable of Course by Clerk).

1946 Amendment

Note. Rule 77(d) has been amended to avoid such situations as the one arising in *Hill v. Hawes*, 1944, 64 S.Ct. 334, 320 U.S. 520, 88 L.Ed. 283. In that case, an action instituted in the District Court for the District of Columbia, the clerk failed to give notice of the entry of a judgment for defendant as required by Rule 77(d). The time for taking an appeal then was 20 days under Rule 10 of the Court of Appeals (later enlarged by amendment to thirty days), and due to lack of notice of the entry of judgment the plaintiff failed to file his notice of appeal within the prescribed time. On this basis the trial court vacated the original judgment and then re-entered it, whereupon notice of appeal was filed. The Court of Appeals dismissed the appeal as taken too late. The Supreme Court, however, held that although rule 77(d) did not purport to attach any consequence to the clerk's failure to give notice as specified, the terms of the rule were such that the appellant was entitled to rely on it, and the trial court in such a case, in the exercise of a sound discretion, could vacate the former judgment and enter a new one, so that the appeal would be within the allowed time.

Because of Rule 6(c), which abolished the old rule that the expiration of the term ends a court's power over its judgment, the effect of the decision in *Hill v. Hawes* is to give the district court power, in its discretion and without time limit, and long after the term may have expired, to vacate a judgment and reenter it for the purpose of reviving the right of appeal. This seriously affects the finality of judgments. See also proposed Rule 6(c) and Note; proposed Rule 60(b) and Note; and proposed Rule 73(a) and Note.

Rule 77(d) as amended makes it clear that notification by the clerk of the entry of a judgment has nothing to do with the starting of the time for appeal; that time starts to run from the date of entry of judgment and not from the date of notice of the entry. Notification by the clerk is merely for the convenience of litigants. And lack of such notification in itself has no effect upon the time for appeal; but in considering an application for extension of time for appeal as provided in Rule 73(a), the court may take into account, as one of the factors affecting its decision, whether the clerk failed to give notice as provided in Rule 77(d) or the party failed to receive the clerk's notice. It need not, however, extend the time for appeal merely because the clerk's notice was not sent or received. It would, therefore, be entirely unsafe for a party to rely on absence of notice from the clerk of the entry of a judgment, or to rely on the adverse party's failure to serve notice of the entry of a judgment. Any party may, of course, serve timely notice of the entry of a judgment upon the adverse party and thus preclude a successful application, under Rule 73(a), for the extension of the time for appeal.

1963 Amendment

Subdivision (c). The amendment authorizes closing of the clerk's office on Saturday as far as civil business is concerned. However, a district court may require its clerk's office to remain open for specified hours on Saturdays or "legal holidays" other than those enumerated ("Legal holiday" is defined in Rule 6(a), as amended.) The clerk's offices of many district courts have customarily remained open on some of the days appointed as holidays by State law. This practice could be continued by local rule or order.

Subdivision (d). This amendment conforms to the amendment of Rule 5(a). See the Advisory Committee's Note to that amendment.

1968 Amendment

The provisions of Rule 73(a) are incorporated in Rule 4(a) of the Federal Rules of Appellate Procedure.

1971 Amendment

The amendment adds Columbus Day to the list of legal holidays. See the Note accompanying the amendment of Rule 6(a).

1987 Amendment

The amendments are technical. No substantive change is intended. The Birthday of Martin Luther King, Jr. is added to the list of national holidays in Rule 77.

1991 Amendment

This revision is a companion to the concurrent amendment to Rule 4 of the Federal Rules of Appellate Procedure. The purpose of the revisions is to permit district courts to ease strict sanctions now imposed on appellants whose notices of appeal are filed late because of their failure to receive notice of entry of a judgment. See, e.g. *Tucker v. Commonwealth Land Title Ins. Co.*, 800 F.2d 1054 (11th Cir.1986); *Ashby Enterprises, Ltd. v. Weitzman, Dym & Associates*, 780 F.2d 1043 (D.C.Cir.1986); *In re OPM Leasing Services, Inc.*, 769 F.2d 911 (2d Cir.1985); *Spika v. Village of Lombard, Ill.*, 763 F.2d 282 (7th Cir.1985); *Hall v. Community Mental Health Center of Beaver County*, 772 F.2d 42 (3d Cir.1985); *Wilson v. Atwood v. Stark*, 725 F.2d 255 (5th Cir. en banc), cert. dismissed, 105 S.Ct. 17 (1984); *Case v. BASF Wyandotte*, 727 F.2d 1034 (Fed.Cir.1984), cert. denied, 105 S.Ct. 386 (1984); *Hensley v. Chesapeake & Ohio R.R. Co.*, 651 F.2d 226 (4th Cir.1981); *Buckeye Cellulose Corp. v. Electric Construction Co.*, 569 F.2d 1036 (8th Cir.1978).

Failure to receive notice may have increased in frequency with the growth in the caseload in the clerks' offices. The present strict rule imposes a duty on counsel to maintain contact with the court while a case is under submission. Such contact is more difficult to maintain if counsel is outside the district, as is increasingly common, and can be a burden to the court as well as counsel.

The effect of the revisions is to place a burden on prevailing parties who desire certainty that the time for appeal is running. Such parties can take the initiative to assure that their adversaries receive effective notice. An appropriate procedure for such notice is provided in Rule 5.

The revised rule lightens the responsibility but not the workload of the clerk's offices, for the duty of that office to give notice of entry of judgment must be maintained.

2001 Amendment

Rule 77(d) is amended to reflect changes in Rule 5(b). A few courts have experimented with serving Rule 77(d) notices by electronic means on parties who consent to this procedure. The success of these experiments warrants express authorization. Because service is made in the manner provided in Rule 5(b), party consent is required for service by electronic or other means described in Rule 5(b)(2)(D). The same provision is made for a party who wishes to ensure actual communication of the Rule 77(d) notice by also serving notice.

Changes Made After Publication and Comments

Rule 77(d) was amended to correct an oversight in the published version. The clerk is to note "service," not "mailing," on the docket.

2007 Amendment

The language of Rule 77 has been amended as part of the general restyling of the Civil Rules to make them more easily understood and to make style and terminology consistent throughout the rules. These changes are intended to be stylistic only.

2014 Amendment

The amendment corrects an inadvertent failure to revise the cross-reference to Rule 6(a) when what was Rule 6(a)(4)(A) became Rule 6(a)(6)(A).

HISTORICAL NOTES

References in Text

The Federal Rules of Appellate Procedure, referred to in subd. (d), are set out in Title 28, U.S.C.A., Federal Rules of Appellate Procedure.

CROSS REFERENCES

Books and records kept by clerk and entries therein, see Fed.Rules Civ.Proc. Rule 79, 28 USCA.

Courts always open, see Fed.Rules Cr.Proc. Rule 56, 18 USCA and 28 USCA § 452.

Entry of default judgment by clerk, see Fed.Rules Civ. Proc. Rule 55, 28 USCA.

Execution, see Fed.Rules Civ.Proc. Rule 69, 28 USCA.

Service of papers on attorney or party, see Fed.Rules Civ.Proc. Rule 5, 28 USCA.

Rule 78.   Hearing Motions; Submission on Briefs

(a) Providing a Regular Schedule for Oral Hearings. A court may establish regular times and places for oral hearings on motions.

(b) Providing for Submission on Briefs. By rule or order, the court may provide for submitting and determining motions on briefs, without oral hearings.
(Amended March 2, 1987, effective August 1, 1987; April 30, 2007, effective December 1, 2007.)

ADVISORY COMMITTEE NOTES

1937 Adoption

Compare [former] Equity Rule 6 (Motion Day) with the first paragraph of this rule. The second paragraph authorizes a procedure found helpful for the expedition of business in some of the Federal and State courts. See Rule 43(e) of these rules dealing with evidence on motions. Compare *Civil Practice Rules of the Municipal Court of Chicago* (1935), Rules 269, 270, 271.

1987 Amendment

The amendment is technical. No substantive change is intended.

2007 Amendment

The language of Rule 78 has been amended as part of the general restyling of the Civil Rules to make them more easily understood and to make style and terminology consistent throughout the rules. These changes are intended to be stylistic only.

Rule 16 has superseded any need for the provision in former Rule 78 for orders for the advancement, conduct, and hearing of actions.

CROSS REFERENCES

Local rules not to be inconsistent with these rules, see Fed.Rules Civ.Proc. Rule 83, 28 USCA.

Motions, see Fed.Rules Civ.Proc. Rule 45, 28 USCA.

Motions and other papers, see Fed.Rules Civ.Proc. Rule 7, 28 USCA.

Service of affidavits in support of and in opposition to motions, timing, see Fed.Rules Civ.Proc. Rule 6, 28 USCA.

Use of affidavits on motions, see Fed.Rules Civ.Proc. Rule 43, 28 USCA.

Rule 79.   Records Kept by the Clerk

(a) Civil Docket.

(1) *In General.* The clerk must keep a record known as the "civil docket" in the form and manner prescribed by the Director of the Administrative Office of the United States Courts with the approval of the Judicial Conference of the United States. The clerk must enter each civil action in the docket. Actions must be assigned consecutive file numbers, which must be noted in the docket where the first entry of the action is made.

(2) *Items to be Entered.* The following items must be marked with the file number and entered chronologically in the docket:

(A) papers filed with the clerk;

(B) process issued, and proofs of service or other returns showing execution; and

(C) appearances, orders, verdicts, and judgments.

(3) *Contents of Entries; Jury Trial Demanded.* Each entry must briefly show the nature of the paper filed or writ issued, the substance of each proof of service or other return, and the substance and date of entry of each order and judgment. When a jury trial has been properly demanded or ordered, the clerk must enter the word "jury" in the docket.

(b) Civil Judgments and Orders. The clerk must keep a copy of every final judgment and appealable order; of every order affecting title to or a lien on real or personal property; and of any other order that the court directs to be kept. The clerk must keep these in the form and manner prescribed by the Director of the Administrative Office of the United States Courts with the approval of the Judicial Conference of the United States.

(c) Indexes; Calendars. Under the court's direction, the clerk must:

(1) keep indexes of the docket and of the judgments and orders described in Rule 79(b); and

(2) prepare calendars of all actions ready for trial, distinguishing jury trials from nonjury trials.

(d) Other Records. The clerk must keep any other records required by the Director of the Administrative Office of the United States Courts with the approval of the Judicial Conference of the United States.

(Amended December 27, 1946, effective March 19, 1948; December 29, 1948, effective October 20, 1949; January 21, 1963, effective July 1, 1963; April 30, 2007, effective December 1, 2007.)

ADVISORY COMMITTEE NOTES

1937 Adoption

Compare [former] Equity Rule 3 (Books Kept by Clerk and Entries Therein). In connection with this rule, see also the following statutes of the United States:

U.S.C., Title 5 former:

§ 301 [See Title 28, § 526] (Officials for investigation of official acts, records and accounts of marshals, attorneys, clerks of courts, United States commissioners, referees and trustees)

§ 318 [former] (Accounts of district attorneys)

U.S.C., Title 28 former:

§ 556 [former] (Clerks of district courts; books open to inspection)

§ 567 [now 751] (Same; accounts)

§ 568 [now 751] (Same; reports and accounts of moneys received; dockets)

§ 813 [former] (Indices of judgment debtors to be kept by clerks)

And see "Instructions to United States Attorneys, Marshals, Clerks and Commissioners" issued by the Attorney General of the United States.

1946 Amendment

Note. Subdivision (a). The amendment substitutes the Director of the Administrative Office of the United States Courts, acting subject to the approval of the Judicial Conference of Senior Circuit Judges, in the place of the Attorney General as a consequence of and in accordance with the provisions of the act establishing the Administrative Office and transferring functions thereto. Act of August 7, 1939, c. 501, §§ 1 to 7, 53 Stat. 1223, 28 U.S.C.A. §§ 601 to 610, formerly §§ 444 to 450.

Subdivision (b). The change in this subdivision does not alter the nature of the judgments and orders to be recorded in permanent form but it does away with the express requirement that they be recorded in a book. This merely gives latitude for the preservation of court records in other than book form, if that shall seem advisable, and permits with the approval of the Judicial Conference the adoption of such modern, space-saving methods as microphotography. See *Proposed Improvements in the Administration of the Offices of Clerks of United States District Courts*, prepared by the Bureau of the Budget, 1941, 38–42. See also Rule 55, Federal Rules of Criminal Procedure.

Subdivision (c). The words "Separate and" have been deleted as unduly rigid. There is no sufficient reason for requiring that the indices in all cases be separate; on the contrary, the requirement frequently increases the labor of persons searching the records as well as the labor of the clerk's force preparing them. The matter should be left to administrative discretion.

The other changes in the subdivision merely conform with those made in subdivision (b) of the rule.

Subdivision (d). Subdivision (d) is a new provision enabling the Administrative Office, with the approval of the Judicial Conference, to carry out any improvements in clerical procedure with respect to books and records which may be deemed advisable. See report cited in Note to subdivision (b), supra.

1948 Amendment

The amendment effective October 1949, substituted the name, "Judicial Conference of the United States," for "Judicial Conference of Senior Circuit Judges," in the first sentence of subdivision (a), and in subdivisions (b) and (d).

1963 Amendment

The terminology is clarified without any change of the prescribed practice. See amended Rule 58, and the Advisory Committee's Note thereto.

2007 Amendment

The language of Rule 79 has been amended as part of the general restyling of the Civil Rules to make them more easily understood and to make style and terminology consistent throughout the rules. These changes are intended to be stylistic only.

CROSS REFERENCES

Entry of judgment, see Fed.Rules Civ.Proc. Rule 58, 28 USCA.

Examination of court dockets by Director of Administrative Office of the United States Court, see 28 USCA § 604.

Filing of pleading and other papers with clerk or judge, see Fed.Rules Civ.Proc. Rule 5, 28 USCA.

Lien of judgment, see 28 USCA § 1962.

Notice of entry of judgment or order, see Fed.Rules Civ. Proc. Rule 77, 28 USCA.

Notice of entry of orders by clerk, see Fed.Rules Cr.Proc. Rule 49, 18 USCA.

Obsolete papers disposed of in accordance with rules of Judicial Conference of the United States, see 28 USCA § 457.

Records, see Fed.Rules Cr.Proc. Rule 55, 18 USCA.

Registration of judgments for money or property in other districts, see 28 USCA § 1963.

Return of execution of process, see Fed.Rules Civ.Proc. Rule 4, 28 USCA.

Survey and recommendation of Judicial Conference of the United States, see 28 USCA § 331.

Time for serving demand for jury trial, see Fed.Rules Civ.Proc. Rule 38, 28 USCA.

Rule 80.   Stenographic Transcript as Evidence

If stenographically reported testimony at a hearing or trial is admissible in evidence at a later trial, the testimony may be proved by a transcript certified by the person who reported it.

(Amended December 27, 1946, effective March 19, 1948; April 30, 2007, effective December 1, 2007.)

ADVISORY COMMITTEE NOTES

1937 Adoption

Note to Subdivision (a). This follows substantially [former] Equity Rule 50 (Stenographer— Appointment— Fees). [This subdivision was abrogated. See amendment note of Advisory Committee below.]

Note to Subdivision (b). See *Reports of Conferences of Senior Circuit Judges with the Chief Justice of the United States* (1936), 22 A.B.A.J. 818, 819; (1937), 24 A.B.A.J. 75, 77. [This subdivision was abrogated. See amendment note of Advisory Committee below.]

Note to Subdivision (c). Compare Iowa Code (1935) § 11353.

1946 Amendment

Note. Subdivisions (a) and (b) of Rule 80 have been abrogated because of Public Law 222, 78th Cong., c. 3, 2d Sess., approved Jan. 20, 1944, 28 U.S.C. §§ 550, 604, 753, 1915, 1920, formerly § 9a, providing for the appointment of official stenographers for each district court, prescribing their duties, providing for the furnishing of transcripts, the taxation of the fees therefor as costs, and other related matters. This statute has now been implemented by Congressional appropriation available for the fiscal year beginning July 1, 1945.

Subdivision (c) of Rule 80 (Stenographic Report or Transcript as Evidence) has been retained unchanged.

2007 Amendment

The language of Rule 80 has been amended as part of the general restyling of the Civil Rules to make them more easily understood and to make style and terminology consistent throughout the rules. These changes are intended to be stylistic only.

CROSS REFERENCES

Appointment and compensation of court reporters, fees for transcripts, see 28 USCA § 753.

Fees of court reporter for stenographic transcript taxable as costs, see 28 USCA § 1920.

Payment by United States for fees for transcripts and printing record on appeal furnished persons proceeding in forma pauperis, see 28 USCA § 1915.

Proof of official record, see Fed.Rules Civ.Proc. Rule 44, 28 USCA.

TITLE XI.   GENERAL PROVISIONS

Rule 81.   Applicability of the Rules in General; Removed Actions

(a) Applicability to Particular Proceedings.

(1) *Prize Proceedings.* These rules do not apply to prize proceedings in admiralty governed by 10 U.S.C. §§ 7651–7681.

(2) *Bankruptcy.* These rules apply to bankruptcy proceedings to the extent provided by the Federal Rules of Bankruptcy Procedure.

(3) *Citizenship.* These rules apply to proceedings for admission to citizenship to the extent that the practice in those proceedings is not specified in federal statutes and has previously conformed to the practice in civil actions. The provisions of 8 U.S.C. § 1451 for service by publication and for answer apply in proceedings to cancel citizenship certificates.

(4) *Special Writs.* These rules apply to proceedings for habeas corpus and for quo warranto to the extent that the practice in those proceedings:

(A) is not specified in a federal statute, the Rules Governing Section 2254 Cases, or the Rules Governing Section 2255 Cases; and

(B) has previously conformed to the practice in civil actions.

(5) *Proceedings Involving a Subpoena.* These rules apply to proceedings to compel testimony or the production of documents through a subpoena issued by a United States officer or agency under a federal statute, except as otherwise provided by statute, by local rule, or by court order in the proceedings.

(6) *Other Proceedings.* These rules, to the extent applicable, govern proceedings under the following laws, except as these laws provide other procedures:

(A) 7 U.S.C. §§ 292, 499g(c), for reviewing an order of the Secretary of Agriculture;

(B) 9 U.S.C., relating to arbitration;

(C) 15 U.S.C. § 522, for reviewing an order of the Secretary of the Interior;

(D) 15 U.S.C. § 715d(c), for reviewing an order denying a certificate of clearance;

(E) 29 U.S.C. §§ 159, 160, for enforcing an order of the National Labor Relations Board;

(F) 33 U.S.C. §§ 918, 921, for enforcing or reviewing a compensation order under the Longshore and Harbor Workers' Compensation Act; and

(G) 45 U.S.C. § 159, for reviewing an arbitration award in a railway-labor dispute.

(b) Scire Facias and Mandamus. The writs of scire facias and mandamus are abolished. Relief previously available through them may be obtained by appropriate action or motion under these rules.

(c) Removed Actions.

(1) *Applicability.* These rules apply to a civil action after it is removed from a state court.

(2) *Further Pleading.* After removal, repleading is unnecessary unless the court orders it. A defendant who did not answer before removal must answer or present other defenses or objections under these rules within the longest of these periods:

(A) 21 days after receiving—through service or otherwise—a copy of the initial pleading stating the claim for relief;

(B) 21 days after being served with the summons for an initial pleading on file at the time of service; or

(C) 7 days after the notice of removal is filed.

(3) *Demand for a Jury Trial.*

(A) *As Affected by State Law.* A party who, before removal, expressly demanded a jury trial in accordance with state law need not renew the demand after removal. If the state law did not require an express demand for a jury trial, a party need not make one after removal unless the court orders the parties to do so within a specified time. The court must so order at a party's request and may so order on its own. A party who fails to make a demand when so ordered waives a jury trial.

(B) *Under Rule 38.* If all necessary pleadings have been served at the time of removal, a party entitled to a jury trial under Rule 38 must be given one if the party serves a demand within 14 days after:

(i) it files a notice of removal; or

(ii) it is served with a notice of removal filed by another party.

(d) Law Applicable.

(1) *"State Law" Defined.* When these rules refer to state law, the term "law" includes the state's statutes and the state's judicial decisions.

(2) *"State" Defined.* The term "state" includes, where appropriate, the District of Columbia and any United States commonwealth or territory.

(3) *"Federal Statute" Defined in the District of Columbia.* In the United States District Court for the District of Columbia, the term "federal statute" includes any Act of Congress that applies locally to the District.

(Amended December 28, 1939, effective April 3, 1941; December 27, 1946, effective March 19, 1948; December 29, 1948, effective October 20, 1949; April 30, 1951, effective August 1, 1951; January 21, 1963, effective July 1, 1963; February 28, 1966, effective July 1, 1966; December 4, 1967, effective July 1, 1968; March 1, 1971, effective July 1, 1971; March 2, 1987, effective August 1, 1987; April 23, 2001, effective December 1, 2001; April 29, 2002, effective December 1, 2002; April 30, 2007, effective December 1, 2007; March 26, 2009, effective December 1, 2009.)

ADVISORY COMMITTEE NOTES

1937 Adoption

Note to Subdivision (a). Paragraph (1): Compare the enabling act, Act of June 19, 1934, U.S.C., Title 28, § 2072, formerly § 723b (Rules in actions at law; Supreme Court authorized to make) and § 2072, formerly § 723c (Union of equity and action at law rules; power of Supreme Court). For the application of these rules in bankruptcy and copyright proceedings, see Orders xxxvi and xxxvii in Bankruptcy and Rule 1 of Rules of Practice and Procedure under § 25 of the copyright act, Act of March 4, 1909, U.S.C., Title 17, former § 25 [see 412, 501 et seq.] (Infringement and rules of procedure).

For examples of statutes which are preserved by paragraph (2) see: U.S.C., Title 8, [former] ch. 9 (Naturalization); Title 28, former ch. 14 [now 153] (Habeas corpus); Title 28, former §§ 377a to 377c [now D.C.Code, Title 16 § 3501 et seq.] (Quo warranto); and such forfeiture statutes as U.S.C., Title 7, former § 116 (Misbranded seeds, confiscation), and Title 21, § 334(b), formerly § 14 (Pure Food and Drug Act—condemnation of adulterated or misbranded Food; procedure). See also *443 Cans of Frozen Eggs Product v. U.S.*, 1912, 33 S.Ct. 50, 226 U.S. 172, 57 L.Ed. 174.

For examples of statutes which under paragraph (7) will continue to govern procedure in condemnation cases, see U.S.C. [former] Title 40, [former] § 258 (Condemnation of realty for sites for public building, etc., procedure); U.S.C., Title 16, § 831x (Condemnation by Tennessee Valley Authority); U.S.C., [former] Title 40, § 120 (Acquisition of lands for public use in District of Columbia); [former] Title 40, ch. 7 [now D.C.Code, Title 16, § 1301 et seq.] (Acquisition of lands in District of Columbia for use of United States; condemnation).

Note to Subdivision (b). Some statutes which will be affected by this subdivision are;

U.S.C., Title 7:

§ 222 (Federal Trade Commission powers adopted for enforcement of Stockyards Act) (By reference to Title 15, § 49)

U.S.C., Title 15:

§ 49 (Enforcement of Federal Trade Commission orders and antitrust laws)

§ 77t(c) (Enforcement of Securities and Exchange Commission orders and Securities Act of 1933)

§ 78u(f) (Same; Securities Exchange Act of 1934)

§ 79r(g) (Same; Public Utility Holding Company Act of 1935)

U.S.C., Title 16:

§ 820 (Proceedings in equity for revocation or to prevent violations of license of Federal Power Commission licensee)

§ 825m(b) (Mandamus to compel compliance with Federal Water Power Act, etc.)

U.S.C., Title 19:

§ 1333(c) (Mandamus to compel compliance with orders of Tariff Commission, etc.)

U.S.C., Title 28, former:

§ 377 [now 1651] (Power to issue writs)

§ 572 [now 1923] (Fees, attorneys, solicitors and proctors)

§ 778 [former] (Death of parties; substitution of executor or administrator). Compare Rule 25(a) (Substitution of parties; death), and the note thereto.

U.S.C., Title 33:

§ 495 (Removal of bridges over navigable waters)

U.S.C., Title 45:

§ 88 (Mandamus against Union Pacific Railroad Company)

§ 153(p) (Mandamus to enforce orders of Adjustment Board under Railway Labor Act)

§ 185 (Same; National Air Transport Adjustment Board) (By reference to § 153)

U.S.C., Title 47:

§ 11 (Powers of Federal Communications Commission)

§ 401(a) (Enforcement of Federal Communications Act and orders of Commission)

§ 406 (Same; Compelling furnishing of facilities; mandamus)

U.S.C., Title 49:

§ 19a(l) [now 11703] (Mandamus to compel compliance with Interstate Commerce Act)

§ 20(9) [now 11703] (Jurisdiction to compel compliance with interstate commerce laws by mandamus)

For comparable provisions in state practice see Smith-Hurd Ill.Stats.c. 110, § 179 (1937); Calif.Code Civ.Proc. (Deering, 1937) § 802.

Note to Subdivision (c). Such statutes as the following dealing with the removal of actions are substantially continued and made subject to these rules:

U.S.C., Title 28 former:

§ 71 [now 1441, 1445, 1447] (Removal of suits from state courts)

§ 72 [now 1446, 1447] (Same; procedure)

§ 73 [former] (Same; suits under grants of land from different states)

§ 74 [now 1443, 1446, 1447] (Same; causes against persons denied civil rights)

§ 75 [now 1446] (Same; petitioner in actual custody of state court)

§ 76 [now 1442, 1446, 1447] (Same; suits and prosecutions against revenue officers)

§ 77 [now 1442] (Same; suits by aliens)

§ 78 [now 1449] (Same; copies of records refused by clerk of state court)

§ 79 [now 1450] (Same; previous attachment bonds or orders)

§ 80 [now 1359, 1447, 1919] (Same; dismissal or remand)

§ 81 [now 1447] (Same; proceedings in suits removed)

§ 82 [former] (Same; record; filing and return)

§ 83 [now 1447, 1448] (Service of process after removal)

U.S.C., Title 28, §§ 1446, 1447, formerly § 72, supra, however, is modified by shortening the time for pleading in removed actions.

Note to Subdivision (e). The last sentence of this subdivision modifies U.S.C., Title 28, § 1652, formerly § 725 (Laws of States as rules of decision) in so far as that statute has been construed to govern matters of procedure and to exclude state judicial decisions relative thereto.

1946 Amendment

Note to Subdivision (a). Despite certain dicta to the contrary, *Lynn v. United States,* C.C.A.5th, 1940, 110 F.2d 586; *Mount Tivy Winery, Inc. v. Lewis,* N.D.Cal.1942, 42 F.Supp. 636, it is manifest that the rules apply to actions against the United States under the Tucker Act [28 U.S.C., §§ 41(20), 250, 251, 254, 257, 258, 287, 289, 292, 761–765 [now 791, 1346, 1401, 1402, 1491, 1493, 1496, 1501, 1503, 2071, 2072, 2411, 2412, 2501, 2506, 2509, 2510]]. See United States to use of *Foster Wheeler Corp. v. American Surety Co. of New York,* E.D.N.Y.1939, 25 F.Supp. 700; *Boerner v. United States,* E.D.N.Y.1939, 26 F.Supp. 769; *United States v. Gallagher,* C.C.A.9th, 1945, 151 F.2d 556. Rules 1 and 81 provide that the rules shall apply to all suits of a civil nature, whether cognizable as cases at law or in equity except those specifically excepted; and the character of the various proceedings excepted by express statement in Rule 81, as well as the language of the rules generally, shows that the term "civil action" [Rule 2] includes actions against the United States. Moreover, the rules in many places expressly make provision for the situation wherein the United States is a party as either plaintiff or defendant. See Rules 4(d)(4), 12(a), 13(d), 25(d), 37(f), 39(c), 45(c), 54(d), 55(e), 62(e), and 65(c). In *United States v. Sherwood,* 1941, 61 S.Ct. 767, 312 U.S. 584, 85 L.Ed. 1058, the Solicitor General expressly conceded in his brief for the United States that the rules apply to Tucker Act cases. The Solicitor General stated: "The Government, of course, recognizes that the Federal Rules of Civil Procedure apply to cases brought under the Tucker Act." (Brief for the United States, p. 31). Regarding *Lynn v. United States,* supra, the Solicitor General said: "In *Lynn v. United States* . . . the Circuit Court of Appeals for the Fifth Circuit went beyond the Government's contention there, and held that an action under the Tucker Act is neither an action at law nor a suit in equity and, seemingly, that the Federal Rules of Civil Procedure are, therefore, inapplicable. We think the suggestion is erroneous. Rules 4(d), 12(a), 39(c), and 55(e) expressly contemplate suits against the United States, and nothing in the enabling Act (48 Stat. 1064, 28 U.S.C. §§ 723b, 723c [see 2072]) suggests that the Rules are inapplicable to Tucker Act proceedings, which in terms are to accord with court rules and their subsequent modifications (Sec. 4, Act of March 3, 1887, 24 Stat. 505, 28 U.S.C. § 761 [see 2071, 2072])." (Brief for the United States, p. 31, n. 17.)

United States v. Sherwood, supra, emphasizes, however, that the application of the rules in Tucker Act cases affects only matters of procedure and does not operate to extend jurisdiction. See also Rule 82. In the Sherwood case, the New York Supreme Court, acting under § 795 of the New York Civil Practice Act, made an order, authorizing Sherwood, as a judgment creditor, to maintain a suit under the Tucker Act to recover damages from the United States for breach of its contract with the judgment debtor, Kaiser, for construction of a post office building. Sherwood brought suit against the United States and Kaiser in the District Court for the Eastern District of New York. The question before the United States Supreme Court was whether a United States District Court had jurisdiction to entertain a suit against the United States wherein private parties were joined as parties defendant. It was contended that either the Federal Rules of Civil Procedure or the Tucker Act, or both, embodied the consent of the United States to be sued in litigations in which issues between the plaintiff and third persons were to be adjudicated. Regarding the effect of the Federal Rules, the Court declared that nothing in the rules, so far as they may be applicable in Tucker Act cases, authorized the maintenance of any suit against the United States to which it had not otherwise consented. The matter involved was not one of procedure but of jurisdiction, the limits of which were marked by the consent of the United States to be sued. The jurisdiction thus limited is unaffected by the Federal Rules of Civil Procedure.

Subdivision (a)(2). The added sentence makes it clear that the rules have not superseded the requirements of U.S.C., Title 28, § 2253, formerly § 466. *Schenk v. Plummer*, C.C.A.9, 1940, 113 F.2d 726.

For correct application of the rules in proceedings for forfeiture of property for violation of a statute of the United States, such as under U.S.C., Title 22, § 405 (seizure of war materials intended for unlawful export) or U.S.C., Title 21, § 334(b) (Federal Food, Drug, and Cosmetic Act; formerly Title 21, U.S.C. § 14, Pure Food and Drug Act), see *Reynal v. United States*, C.C.A.5, 1945, 153 F.2d 929; *United States v. 108 Boxes of Cheddar Cheese*, S.D.Iowa 1943, 3 F.R.D. 40.

Subdivision (a)(3). The added sentence makes it clear that the rules apply to appeals from proceedings to enforce administrative subpoenas. See *Perkins v. Endicott Johnson Corp.*, C.C.A.2d 1942, 128 F.2d 208, affirmed on other grounds 63 S.Ct. 339, 317 U.S. 501, 87 L.Ed. 424; *Walling v. News Printing Inc.*, C.C.A.3, 1945, 148 F.2d 57; *McCrone v. United States*, 1939, 59 S.Ct. 685, 307 U.S. 61, 83 L.Ed. 1108. And, although the provision allows full recognition of the fact that the rigid application of the rules in the proceedings themselves may conflict with the summary determination desired, *Goodyear Tire & Rubber Co. v. National Relations Board*, C.C.A.6, 1941, 122 F.2d 450; *Cudahy Packing Co. v. National Labor Relations Board*, C.C.A.10, 1941, 117 F.2d 692, it is drawn so as to permit application of any of the rules in the proceedings whenever the district court deems them helpful. See, e.g., *Peoples Natural Gas Co. v. Federal Power Commission*, App.D.C.1942, 127 F.2d 153, certiorari denied 62 S.Ct. 1298, 316 U.S. 700, 86 L.Ed. 1769; *Martin v. Chandis Securities Co.*, C.C.A.9th, 1942, 128 F.2d 731. Compare the application of the rules in summary proceedings in bankruptcy under General Order 37. See 1 *Collier on Bankruptcy*, 14th ed. by Moore and Oglebay, 326–327; 2 Collier, op.cit.supra, 1401–1402; 3 Collier, op.cit.supra, 228–231; 4 Collier, op.cit.supra, 1199–1202.

Subdivision (a)(6). Section 405 of U.S.C., Title 8 originally referred to in the last sentence of paragraph (6), has been repealed and § 738 [now 1451], U.S.C., Title 8, has been enacted in its stead. The last sentence of paragraph (6) has, therefore, been amended in accordance with this change. The sentence has also been amended so as to refer directly to the statute regarding the provision of time for answer, thus avoiding any confusion attendant upon a change in the statute.

That portion of subdivision (a)(6) making the rules applicable to proceedings for enforcement or review of compensation orders under the Longshoremen's and Harbor Workers' Compensation Act [33 U.S.C. § 901 et seq.] was added by an amendment made pursuant to order of the Court, December 28, 1939, effective three months subsequent to the adjournment of the 76th Congress, January 3, 1941.

Subdivision (c). The change in subdivision (c) effects more speedy trials in removed actions. In some states many of the courts have only two terms a year. A case, if filed 20 days before a term, is returnable to that term, but if filed less than 20 days before a term, is returnable to the following term, which convenes six months later. Hence, under the original wording of Rule 81(c), where a case is filed less than 20 days before the term and is removed within a few days but before answer, it is possible for the defendant to delay interposing his answer or presenting his defenses by motion for six months or more. The rule as amended prevents this result.

Subdivision (f). The use of the phrase "the United States or an officer or agency thereof" in the rules (as e.g., in Rule 12(a) and amended Rule 73(a)) could raise the question of whether "officer" includes a collector of internal revenue, a former collector, or the personal representative of a deceased collector, against whom suits for tax refunds are frequently instituted. Difficulty might ensue for the reason that a suit against a collector or his representative has been held to be a personal action. *Sage v. United States*, 1919, 39 S.Ct. 415, 250 U.S. 33, 63 L.Ed. 828; *Smietanka v. Indiana Steel Co.*, 1921, 42 S.Ct. 1, 257 U.S. 1, 66 L.Ed. 99; *United States v. Nunnally Investment Co.*, 1942, 62 S.Ct. 1064, 316 U.S. 258, 86 L.Ed. 1455. The addition of subdivision (f) to Rule 81 dispels any doubts on the matter and avoids further litigation.

1948 Amendment

The amendment effective October 1949, substituted the words "United States District Court" for the words "District Court of the United States" in the last sentence of subdivision (a)(1) and in the first and third sentences of subdivision (e). The amendment substituted the words "United States district courts" in lieu of "district courts of the United States" in subdivision (a)(4) and (5) and in the first sentence of subdivision (c).

The amendment effective October 20, 1949, also made the following changes:

In subdivision (a)(1), the reference to "Title 17, U.S.C." was substituted for the reference to "the Act of March 4, 1909, c. 320, § 25 (35 Stat. 1081), as amended, U.S.C., Title 17, § 25."

In subdivision (a)(2), the reference to "Title 28, U.S.C., § 2253" was substituted for "U.S.C., Title 28, § 466."

In subdivision (a)(3), the reference in the first sentence to "Title 9, U.S.C.," was substituted for "the Act of February 12, 1925, c. 213 (43 Stat. 883), U.S.C., Title 9".

In subdivision (a)(5), the words "as amended" were inserted after the parenthetical citation of "(49 Stat. 453)," and after the citations of "Title 29, §§ 159 and 160," former references to subdivisions "(e), (g), and (i)" were deleted.

In subdivision (a)(6), after the words "These rules" at the beginning of the first sentence, the following words were deleted: "do not apply to proceedings under the Act of September 13, 1888, c. 1015, § 13 (25 Stat. 479), as amended, U.S.C., Title 8, [former] § 282, relating to deportation of Chinese; they". Also in the first sentence, after the parenthetical citation of "(44 Stat. 1434, 1436)," the words "as amended" were added. In the last sentence, the words "October 14, 1940, c. 876, § 338 (54 Stat. 1158)" were inserted in lieu of the words "June 29, 1906, c. 3592, § 15 (34 Stat. 601), as amended."

In subdivision (c), the word "all" originally appearing in the first sentence between the words "govern" and "procedure" was deleted. In the third sentence, the portion beginning with the words "20 days after the receipt" and including all the remainder of that sentence was substituted for the following language: "the time allowed for answer by the law of the state or within 5 days after the filing of the transcript of the record in the district court of the United States, whichever period is longer, but in any event within 20 days after the filing of the transcript". In the fourth or last sentence, after the words at the beginning of the sentence, "If at the time of removal all necessary pleadings have been," the word "served" was inserted in lieu of the word "filed," and the concluding words of the sentence, "petition for removal is filed if he is the petitioner," together with the final clause immediately following, were substituted for the words "record of the action is filed in the district court of the United States."

1963 Amendment

Subdivision (a)(4). This change reflects the transfer of functions from the Secretary of Commerce to the Secretary of the Interior made by 1939 Reorganization Plan No. II, § 4(e), 53 Stat. 1433.

Subdivision (a)(6). The proper current reference is to the 1952 statute superseding the 1940 statute.

Subdivision (c). Most of the cases have held that a party who has made a proper express demand for jury trial in the State court is not required to renew the demand after removal of the action. *Zakoscielny v. Waterman Steamship Corp.*, 16 F.R.D. 314 (D.Md.1954); *Talley v. American Bakeries Co.*, 15 F.R.D. 391 (E.D.Tenn.1954); *Rehrer v. Service Trucking Co.*, 15 F.R.D. 113 (D.Del.1953); 5 *Moore's Federal Practice* ¶38.39[3] (2d ed. 1951); 1 Barron & Holtzoff, *Federal Practice & Procedure* § 132 (Wright ed. 1960). But there is some authority to the contrary. *Petsel v. Chicago, B. & Q.R. Co.*, 101 F.Supp. 1006 (S.D.Iowa 1951); *Nelson v. American Nat. Bank & Trust Co.*, 9 F.R.D. 680 (E.D.Tenn.1950). The amendment adopts the preponderant view.

In order still further to avoid unintended waivers of jury trial, the amendment provides that where by State law applicable in the court from which the case is removed a party is entitled to jury trial without making an express demand, he need not make a demand after removal. However, the district court for calendar or other purposes may on its own motion direct the parties to state whether they demand a jury, and the court must make such a direction upon the request of any party. Under the amendment a district court may find it convenient to establish a routine practice of giving these directions to the parties in appropriate cases.

Subdivision (f). The amendment recognizes the change of nomenclature made by Treasury Dept. Order 150–26(2), 18 Fed.Reg. 3499 (1953).

As to a special problem arising under Rule 25 (Substitution of parties) in actions for refund of taxes, see the Advisory Committee's Note to the amendment of Rule 25(d), effective July 19, 1961; and 4 *Moore's Federal Practice* ¶25.09 at 531 (2d ed. 1950).

1966 Amendment

See Note to Rule 1, supra.

Statutory proceedings to forfeit property for violation of the laws of the United States, formerly governed by the admiralty rules, will be governed by the unified and supplemental rules. See Supplemental Rule A.

Upon the recommendation of the judges of the United States District Court for the District of Columbia, the Federal Rules of Civil Procedure are made applicable to probate proceedings in that court. The exception with regard to adoption proceedings is removed because the court no longer has jurisdiction of those matters; and the words "mental health" are substituted for "lunacy" to conform to the current characterization in the District.

The purpose of the amendment to paragraph (3) is to permit the deletion from Rule 73(a) of the clause "unless a shorter time is provided by law." The 10 day period fixed for an appeal under 45 U.S.C. § 159 is the only instance of a shorter time provided for appeals in civil cases. Apart from the unsettling effect of the clause, it is eliminated because its retention would preserve the 15 day period heretofore allowed by 28 U.S.C. § 2107 for appeals from interlocutory decrees in admiralty, it being one of the purposes of the amendment to make the time for appeals in civil and admiralty cases uniform under the unified rules. See Advisory Committee's Note to subdivision (a) of Rule 73.

1968 Amendment

The amendments eliminate inappropriate references to appellate procedure.

1971 Amendment

Title 28, U.S.C., § 2243 now requires that the custodian of a person detained must respond to an application for a writ of habeas corpus "within three days unless for good cause additional time, not exceeding twenty days, is allowed." The amendment increases to forty days the additional time that the district court may allow in habeas corpus proceedings involving persons in custody pursuant to a judgment of a state court. The substantial increase in the number of such proceedings in recent years has placed a considerable burden on state authorities. Twenty days has proved in practice too short a time in which to prepare and file the return in many such cases. Allowance of additional time should, of course, be granted only for good cause.

While the time allowed in such a case for the return of the writ may not exceed forty days, this does not mean that the state must necessarily be limited to that period of time to provide for the federal court the transcript of the proceedings of a state trial or plenary hearing if the transcript must be prepared after the habeas corpus proceeding has begun in the federal court.

1987 Amendment

The amendments are technical. No substantive change is intended.

2001 Amendment

Former Copyright Rule 1 made the Civil Rules applicable to copyright proceedings except to the extent the Civil Rules were inconsistent with Copyright Rules. Abrogation of the Copyright Rules leaves the Civil Rules fully applicable to copyright proceedings. Rule 81(a)(1) is amended to reflect this change.

The District of Columbia Court Reform and Criminal Procedure Act of 1970, Pub.L. 91–358, 84 Stat. 473, transferred mental health proceedings formerly held in the United States District Court for the District of Columbia to local District of Columbia courts. The provision that the Civil Rules do not apply to these proceedings is deleted as superfluous.

The reference to incorporation of the Civil Rules in the Federal Rules of Bankruptcy Procedure has been restyled.

Changes Made After Publication and Comments

The Committee Note was amended to correct the inadvertent omission of a negative. As revised, it correctly reflects the language that is stricken from the rule.

2002 Amendment

This amendment brings Rule 81(a)(2) into accord with the Rules Governing § 2254 and § 2255 proceedings. In its present form, Rule 81(a)(2) includes return-time provisions that are inconsistent with the provisions in the Rules Governing §§ 2254 and 2255. The inconsistency should be eliminated, and it is better that the time provisions continue to be set out in the other rules without duplication in Rule 81. Rule 81 also directs that the writ be directed to the person having custody of the person detained. Similar directions exist in the § 2254 and § 2255 rules, providing additional detail for applicants subject to future custody. There is no need for partial duplication in Rule 81.

The provision that the civil rules apply to the extent that practice is not set forth in the § 2254 and § 2255 rules dovetails with the provisions in Rule 11 of the § 2254 rules and Rule 12 of the § 2255 rules.

Changes Made After Publication and Comment The only change since publication is deletion of an inadvertent reference to § 2241 proceedings.

2007 Amendment

The language of Rule 81 has been amended as part of the general restyling of the Civil Rules to make them more easily understood and to make style and terminology consistent throughout the rules. These changes are intended to be stylistic only.

Rule 81(c) has been revised to reflect the amendment of 28 U.S.C. § 1446(a) that changed the procedure for removal from a petition for removal to a notice of removal.

Former Rule 81(e), drafted before the decision in *Erie R.R. v. Tompkins*, 304 U.S. 64 (1938), defined state law to include "the statutes of that state and the state judicial decisions construing them." The *Erie* decision reinterpreted the Rules of Decision Act, now 28 U.S.C. § 1652, recognizing that the "laws" of the states include the common law established by judicial decisions. Long-established practice reflects this understanding, looking to state common law as well as statutes and court rules when a Civil Rule directs use of state law. Amended Rule 81(d)(1) adheres to this practice, including all state judicial decisions, not only those that construe state statutes.

Former Rule 81(f) is deleted. The office of district director of internal revenue was abolished by restructuring under the Internal Revenue Service Restructuring and Reform Act of 1998, Pub.L. 105–206, July 22, 1998, 26 U.S.C. § 1 Note.

2009 Amendment

[Subdivision (c)] The times set in the former rule at 5, 10, and 20 days have been revised to 7, 14, and 21 days, respectively. See the Note to Rule 6.

[Subdivision (d)] Several Rules incorporate local state practice. Rule 81(d) now provides that "the term 'state' includes, where appropriate, the District of Columbia." The definition is expanded to include any commonwealth or territory of the United States. As before, these entities are included only "where appropriate." They are included for the reasons that counsel incorporation of state practice. For example, state holidays are recognized in computing time under Rule 6(a). Other, quite different, examples are Rules 64(a), invoking state law for prejudgment remedies, and 69(a)(1), relying on state law for the procedure on execution. Including commonwealths and territories in these and other rules avoids the gaps that otherwise would result when the federal rule relies on local practice rather than provide a uniform federal approach. Including them also establishes uniformity between federal courts and local courts in areas that may involve strong local interests, little need for uniformity among federal courts, or difficulty in defining a uniform federal practice that integrates effectively with local practice.

Adherence to a local practice may be refused as not "appropriate" when the local practice would impair a significant federal interest.

HISTORICAL NOTES

Effective Date of Abrogation

Abrogation of par. (7) of subdivision (a) of this rule as effective Aug. 1, 1951, see Effective Date note incorporated within the Supplementary Report set out under the heading 1951 Addition in the Advisory Committee Notes appearing under Rule 71.1 of these rules.

Pending Actions

For applicability of Supreme Court amendments to pending cases, see Orders of the Supreme Court of the United States Adopting and Amending Rules set out preceding Rule 1 of these rules.

CROSS REFERENCES

Antitrust Civil Process Act petitions, application of rules, see 15 USCA § 1314.

Demand for jury trial, see Fed.Rules Civ.Proc. Rule 38, 28 USCA.

Habeas corpus, see 28 USCA § 2241 et seq.

Power of court to issue writs, see 28 USCA § 1651.

Procedure before and after removal, generally, see 28 USCA §§ 1446 and 1447.

Scope of rules, see Fed.Rules Civ.Proc. Rule 1, 28 USCA.

Rule 82. Jurisdiction and Venue Unaffected

These rules do not extend or limit the jurisdiction of the district courts or the venue of actions in those courts. An admiralty or maritime claim under Rule 9(h) is governed by 28 U.S.C. § 1390.

(Amended December 29, 1948, effective October 20, 1949; February 28, 1966, effective July 1, 1966; April 23, 2001, effective December 1, 2001; April 30, 2007, effective December 1, 2007; April 28, 2016, effective December 1, 2016.)

ADVISORY COMMITTEE NOTES

1937 Adoption

These rules grant extensive power of joining claims and counterclaims in one action, but, as this rule states, such grant does not extend federal jurisdiction. The rule is declaratory of existing practice under the [former] Federal Equity Rules with regard to such provisions as [former] Equity Rule 26 on Joinder of Causes of Action and [former] Equity Rule 30 on Counterclaims. Compare Shulman and Jaegerman, *Some*

Jurisdictional Limitations on Federal Procedure, 45 Yale L.J. 393 (1936).

1948 Amendment

The amendment effective October 1949, substituted the words "United States district courts" for "district courts of the United States."

1966 Amendment

Title 28, U.S.C., § 1391(b) provides: "A civil action wherein jurisdiction is not founded solely on diversity of citizenship may be brought only in the judicial district where all defendants reside, except as otherwise provided by law." This provision cannot appropriately be applied to what were formerly suits in admiralty. The rationale of decisions holding it inapplicable rests largely on the use of the term "civil action": i.e., a suit in admiralty is not a "civil action" within the statute. By virtue of the amendment to Rule 1, the provisions of Rule 2 convert suits in admiralty into civil actions. The added sentence is necessary to avoid an undesirable change in existing law with respect to venue.

2001 Amendment

The final sentence of Rule 82 is amended to delete the reference to 28 U.S.C. § 1393, which has been repealed.

Style Comment

The recommendation that the change be made without publication carries with it a recommendation that style changes not be made. Styling would carry considerable risks. The first sentence of Rule 82, for example, states that the Civil Rules do not "extend or limit the jurisdiction of the United States district courts." That sentence is a flat lie if "jurisdiction" includes personal or quasi-in rem jurisdiction. The styling project on this rule requires publication and comment.

2007 Amendment

The language of Rule 82 has been amended as part of the general restyling of the Civil Rules to make them more easily understood and to make style and terminology consistent throughout the rules. These changes are intended to be stylistic only.

2016 Amendment

Rule 82 is amended to reflect the enactment of 28 U.S.C. § 1390 and the repeal of § 1392.

Rule 83. Rules by District Courts; Judge's Directives

(a) Local Rules.

(1) *In General.* After giving public notice and an opportunity for comment, a district court, acting by a majority of its district judges, may adopt and amend rules governing its practice. A local rule must be consistent with—but not duplicate—federal statutes and rules adopted under 28 U.S.C. §§ 2072 and 2075, and must conform to any uniform numbering system prescribed by the Judicial Conference of the United States. A local rule takes effect on the date specified by the district court and remains in effect unless amended by the court or abrogated by the judicial council of the circuit. Copies of rules and amendments must, on their adoption, be furnished to the judicial council and the Administrative Office of the United States Courts and be made available to the public.

(2) *Requirement of Form.* A local rule imposing a requirement of form must not be enforced in a way that causes a party to lose any right because of a nonwillful failure to comply.

(b) Procedure When There Is No Controlling Law. A judge may regulate practice in any manner consistent with federal law, rules adopted under 28 U.S.C. §§ 2072 and 2075, and the district's local rules. No sanction or other disadvantage may be imposed for noncompliance with any requirement not in federal law, federal rules, or the local rules unless the alleged violator has been furnished in the particular case with actual notice of the requirement.

(Amended April 29, 1985, effective August 1, 1985; April 27, 1995, effective December 1, 1995; April 30, 2007, effective December 1, 2007.)

ADVISORY COMMITTEE NOTES

1937 Adoption

This rule substantially continues U.S.C., Title 28, § 2071, formerly § 731 (Rules of practice in district courts) with the additional requirement that copies of such rules and amendments be furnished to the Supreme Court of the United States. See [former] Equity Rule 79 (Additional Rules by District Court). With the last sentence compare United States Supreme Court Admiralty Rules, 1920, Rule 44 (Right of Trial Courts to Make Rules of Practice) (originally promulgated in 1842).

1985 Amendment

Rule 83, which has not been amended since the Federal Rules were promulgated in 1938, permits each district to adopt local rules not inconsistent with the Federal Rules by a majority of the judges. The only other requirement is that copies be furnished to the Supreme Court.

The widespread adoption of local rules and the modest procedural prerequisites for their promulgation have led many commentators to question the soundness of the process as well as the validity of some rules. See 12 C. Wright & A. Miller, *Federal Practice and Procedure: Civil* § 3152, at 217 (1973); Caballero, *Is There an Over-Exercise of Local Rule-Making Powers by the United States District Courts?*, 24 Fed.Bar News 325 (1977). Although the desirability of local rules for promoting uniform practice within a district is widely accepted, several commentators also have suggested reforms to increase the quality, simplicity, and uniformity of the local rules. See Note, *Rule 83 and the Local Federal Rules*, 67 Colum.L.Rev. 1251 (1967), and Comment, *The Local Rules of Civil Procedure in the Federal District Courts—A Survey*, 1966 Duke L.J. 1011.

The amended Rule attempts, without impairing the procedural validity of existing local rules, to enhance the local rulemaking process by requiring appropriate public notice of proposed rules and an opportunity to comment on them.

Although some district courts apparently consult the local bar before promulgating rules, many do not, which has led to criticism of a process that has district judges consulting only with each other. See 12 C. Wright & A. Miller, *supra*, § 3152, at 217; Blair, *The New Local Rules for Federal Practice in Iowa*, 23 Drake L.Rev. 517 (1974). The new language subjects local rulemaking to scrutiny similar to that accompanying the Federal Rules, administrative rulemaking, and legislation. It attempts to assure that the expert advice of practitioners and scholars is made available to the district court before local rules are promulgated. See Weinstein, *Reform of Court Rule-Making Procedures* 84–87, 127–37, 151 (1977).

The amended Rule does not detail the procedure for giving notice and an opportunity to be heard since conditions vary from district to district. Thus, there is no explicit requirement for a public hearing, although a district may consider that procedure appropriate in all or some rulemaking situations. See generally, Weinstein, *supra*, at 117–37, 151. The new Rule does not foreclose any other form of consultation. For example, it can be accomplished through the mechanism of an "Advisory Committee" similar to that employed by the Supreme Court in connection with the Federal Rules themselves.

The amended Rule provides that a local rule will take effect upon the date specified by the district court and will remain in effect unless amended by the district court or abrogated by the judicial council. The effectiveness of a local rule should not be deferred until approved by the judicial council because that might unduly delay promulgation of a local rule that should become effective immediately, especially since some councils do not meet frequently. Similarly, it was thought that to delay a local rule's effectiveness for a fixed period of time would be arbitrary and that to require the judicial council to abrogate a local rule within a specified time would be inconsistent with its power under 28 U.S.C. § 332 (1976) to nullify a local rule at any time. The expectation is that the judicial council will examine all local rules, including those currently in effect, with an eye toward determining whether they are valid and consistent with the Federal Rules, promote inter-district uniformity and efficiency, and do not undermine the basic objectives of the Federal Rules.

The amended Rule requires copies of local rules to be sent upon their promulgation to the judicial council and the Administrative Office of the United States Courts rather than to the Supreme Court. The Supreme Court was the appropriate filing place in 1938, when Rule 83 originally was promulgated, but the establishment of the Administrative Office makes it a more logical place to develop a centralized file of local rules. This procedure is consistent with both the Criminal and the Appellate Rules. See Fed.R.Crim.P. 57(a); Fed.R.App.P. 47. The Administrative Office also will be able to provide improved utilization of the file because of its recent development of a Local Rules Index.

The practice pursued by some judges of issuing standing orders has been controversial, particularly among members of the practicing bar. The last sentence in Rule 83 has been amended to make certain that standing orders are not inconsistent with the Federal Rules or any local district court rules. Beyond that, it is hoped that each district will adopt procedures, perhaps by local rule, for promulgating and reviewing single-judge standing orders.

1995 Amendment

Subdivision (a). This rule is amended to reflect the requirement that local rules be consistent not only with the national rules but also with Acts of Congress. The amendment also states that local rules should not repeat Acts of Congress or national rules.

The amendment also requires that the numbering of local rules conform with any uniform numbering system that may be prescribed by the Judicial Conference. Lack of uniform numbering might create unnecessary traps for counsel and litigants. A uniform numbering system would make it easier for an increasingly national bar and for litigants to locate a local rule that applies to a particular procedural issue.

Paragraph (2) is new. Its aim is to protect against loss of rights in the enforcement of local rules relating to matters of form. For example, a party should not be deprived of a right to a jury trial because its attorney, unaware of—or forgetting—a local rule directing that jury demands be noted in the caption of the case, includes a jury demand only in the body of the pleading. The proscription of paragraph (2) is narrowly drawn—covering only violations attributable to nonwillful failure to comply and only those involving local rules directed to matters of form. It does not limit the court's power to impose substantive penalties upon a party if it or its attorney contumaciously or willfully violates a local rule, even one involving merely a matter of form. Nor does it affect the court's power to enforce local rules that involve more than mere matters of form—for example, a local rule requiring parties to identify evidentiary matters relied upon to support or oppose motions for summary judgment.

Subdivision (b). This rule provides flexibility to the court in regulating practice when there is no controlling law. Specifically, it permits the court to regulate practice in any manner consistent with Acts of Congress, with rules adopted under 28 U.S.C. §§ 2072 and 2075, and with the district local rules.

This rule recognizes that courts rely on multiple directives to control practice. Some courts regulate practice through the published Federal Rules and the local rules of the court. Some courts also have used internal operating procedures, standing orders, and other internal directives. Although such directives continue to be authorized, they can lead to problems. Counsel or litigants may be unaware of various directives. In addition, the sheer volume of directives may impose an unreasonable barrier. For example, it may be difficult to obtain copies of the directives. Finally, counsel or litigants may be unfairly sanctioned for failing to comply with a directive. For these reasons, the amendment to this rule disapproves imposing any sanction or other disadvantage on a person for noncompliance with such an internal directive, unless the alleged violator has been furnished actual notice of the requirement in a particular case.

There should be no adverse consequence to a party or attorney for violating special requirements relating to practice before a particular court unless the party or attorney has actual notice of those requirements. Furnishing litigants with a copy outlining the judge's practices—or attaching instructions to a notice setting a case for conference or trial—would suffice to give actual notice, as would an order in a case specifically adopting by reference a judge's standing order and indicating how copies can be obtained.

2007 Amendment

The language of Rule 83 has been amended as part of the general restyling of the Civil Rules to make them more easily understood and to make style and terminology consistent throughout the rules. These changes are intended to be stylistic only.

HISTORICAL NOTES

Change of Name

Reference to United States magistrate or to magistrate deemed to refer to United States magistrate judge pursuant to section 321 of Pub.L. 101–650, set out as a note under section 631 of this title.

CROSS REFERENCES

Local rules, see Fed.Rules Cr.Proc. Rule 57, 18 USCA.

Rule-making power, generally, see 28 USCA § 2071.

Rule 84.   Forms [Abrogated]

(Amended December 27, 1946, effective March 19, 1948; April 30, 2007, effective December 1, 2007; abrogated April 29, 2015, effective December 1, 2015.)

ADVISORY COMMITTEE NOTES

1937 Adoption

In accordance with the practice found useful in many codes, provision is here made for a limited number of official forms which may serve as guides in pleading. Compare 2 Mass. Gen.Laws (Ter.Ed., 1932) ch. 231, § 147, Forms 1–47; *English Annual Practice* (1937) Appendix A to M, inclusive; *Conn.Practice Book* (1934) Rules, 47–68, pp. 123 to 427.

1946 Amendment

Note. The amendment serves to emphasize that the forms contained in the Appendix of Forms are sufficient to withstand attack under the rules under which they are drawn, and that the practitioner using them may rely on them to that extent. The circuit courts of appeals generally have upheld the use of the forms as promoting desirable simplicity and brevity of statement. *Sierocinski v. E. I. DuPont DeNemours & Co.*, C.C.A.3, 1939, 103 F.2d 843; *Swift & Co. v. Young*, C.C.A.4, 1939, 107 F.2d 170; *Sparks v. England*, C.C.A.8, 1940, 113 F.2d 579; *Ramsouer v. Midland Valley R. Co.*, C.C.A.8, 1943, 135 F.2d 101. And the forms as a whole have met with widespread approval in the courts. See cases cited in 1 Moore's Federal Practice, 1938, Cum. Supplement § 8.07, under "Page 554"; see also Commentary, The Official Forms, 1941, 4 Fed.Rules Serv. 954. In Cook, "Facts" and "Statements of Fact", 1937, 4 U.Chi.L.Rev. 233, 245–246, it is said with reference to what is now Rule 84: ". . . pleaders in the federal courts are not to be left to guess as to the meaning of [the] language" in Rule 8(a) regarding the form of the complaint. "All of which is as it should be. In no other way can useless litigation be avoided." Ibid. The amended rule will operate to discourage isolated results such as those found in *Washburn v. Moorman Mfg. Co.*, S.D.Cal.1938, 25 F.Supp. 546; *Employers Mutual Liability Ins. Co. of Wisconsin v. Blue Line Transfer Co.*, W.D.Mo.1941, 2 F.R.D. 121, 5 Fed.Rules Serv. 12e.235, Case 2.

2007 Amendment

The language of Rule 84 has been amended as part of the general restyling of the Civil Rules to make them more easily understood and to make style and terminology consistent throughout the rules. These changes are intended to be stylistic only.

2015 Amendment

Rule 84 was adopted when the Civil Rules were established in 1938 "to indicate, subject to the provisions of these rules, the simplicity and brevity of statement which the rules contemplate." The purpose of providing illustrations for the rules, although useful when the rules were adopted, has been fulfilled. Accordingly, recognizing that there are many alternative sources for forms, including the website of the Administrative Office of the United States Courts, the websites of many district courts, and local law libraries that contain many commercially published forms, Rule 84 and the Appendix of Forms are no longer necessary and have been abrogated. The abrogation of Rule 84 does not alter existing pleading standards or otherwise change the requirements of Civil Rule 8.

Rule 85.   Title

These rules may be cited as the Federal Rules of Civil Procedure.

(Amended April 30, 2007, effective December 1, 2007.)

ADVISORY COMMITTEE NOTES

2007 Amendment

The language of Rule 85 has been amended as part of the general restyling of the Civil Rules to make them more easily understood and to make style and terminology consistent throughout the rules. These changes are intended to be stylistic only.

Rule 86.   Effective Dates

(a) In General. These rules and any amendments take effect at the time specified by the Supreme Court, subject to 28 U.S.C. § 2074. They govern:

(1) proceedings in an action commenced after their effective date; and

(2) proceedings after that date in an action then pending unless:

(A) the Supreme Court specifies otherwise; or

(B) the court determines that applying them in a particular action would be infeasible or work an injustice.

(b) December 1, 2007 Amendments. If any provision in Rules 1–5.1, 6–73, or 77–86 conflicts with another law, priority in time for the purpose of 28 U.S.C. § 2072(b) is not affected by the amendments taking effect on December 1, 2007.

(Amended December 27, 1946, effective March 19, 1948; December 29, 1948, effective October 20, 1949; April 17, 1961, effective July 19, 1961; January 21, 1963, and March 18, 1963, effective July 1, 1963; April 30, 2007, effective December 1, 2007.)

ADVISORY COMMITTEE NOTES

1937 Adoption

See former Equity Rule 81 (These Rules Effective February 1, 1913—Old Rules Abrogated).

2007 Amendment

The language of Rule 86 has been amended as part of the general restyling of the Civil Rules to make them more easily understood and to make style and terminology consistent throughout the rules. These changes are intended to be stylistic only.

The subdivisions that provided a list of the effective dates of the original Civil Rules and amendments made up to 1963 are deleted as no longer useful.

Rule 86(b) is added to clarify the relationship of amendments taking effect on December 1, 2007, to other laws for the purpose of applying the "supersession" clause in 28 U.S.C. § 2072(b). Section 2072(b) provides that a law in conflict with an Enabling Act Rule "shall be of no further force or effect after such rule[ ] ha[s] taken effect." The amendments that take effect on December 1, 2007, result from the general restyling of the Civil Rules and from a small number of technical revisions adopted on a parallel track. None of these amendments is intended to affect resolution of any conflict that might arise between a rule and another law. Rule 86(b) makes this intent explicit. Any conflict that arises should be resolved by looking to the date the specific conflicting rule provision first became effective.

HISTORICAL NOTES

Effective and Applicability Provisions

1948 Amendments. The first regular session of the 81st Congress adjourned sine die on Oct. 19, 1949, therefore the amendments to Rules 1, 17, 22, 24, 25, 27, 37, 45, 57, 60, 65, 66, 67, 69, 72–76, 79, 81, 82, and 86 and to forms 1, 19, 22, 23, and 27 became effective on Oct. 20, 1949, following the adjournment as provided for in subsection (c) of this rule.

1946 Amendments. The first regular session of the 80th Congress adjourned sine die on Friday, Dec. 19, 1947, therefore the amendments to Rules 6, 7, 12, 13, 14, 17, 24, 26, 27, 28, 33, 34, 36, 41, 45, 52, 54, 56, 58, 59, 60, 62, 65, 66, 68, 73, 75, 77, 79, 80, 81, 84, and 86, became effective Mar. 19, 1948 as provided for in subsection (b) of this rule.

Effective Date of 1966 Amendment; Transmission to Congress; Rescission

Sections 2 to 4 of the Order of the Supreme Court, dated Feb. 28, 1966, 383 U.S. 1031, provided:

"**2.** That the foregoing amendments and additions to the Rules of Civil Procedure shall take effect on July 1, 1966, and shall govern all proceedings in actions brought thereafter and also in all further proceedings in actions then pending, except to the extent that in the opinion of the court their application in a particular action then pending would not be feasible or would work injustice, in which event the former procedure applies.

"**3.** That the Chief Justice be, and he hereby is, authorized to transmit to the Congress the foregoing amendments and additions to the Rules of Civil Procedure in accordance with the provisions of Title 28, U.S.C., §§ 2072 and 2073.

"**4.** That: (a) subdivision (c) of Rule 6 of the Rules of Civil Procedure for the United States District Courts promulgated by this court on December 20, 1937, effective September 16, 1938; (b) Rule 2 of the Rules for Practice and Procedure under section 25 of An Act To amend and consolidate the Acts respecting copyright, approved March 4, 1909, promulgated by this court on June 1, 1909, effective July 1, 1909; and (c) the Rules of Practice in Admiralty and Maritime Cases, promulgated by this court on December 6, 1920, effective March 7, 1921, as revised, amended and supplemented, be, and they hereby are, rescinded, effective July 1, 1966."

CROSS REFERENCES

All laws in conflict with these rules to be of no further force and effect, see 28 USCA § 2072.

Effective date, see Fed.Rules Cr.Proc. Rule 59, 18 USCA.

APPENDIX OF FORMS [ABROGATED]

Form 1. Caption [Abrogated]

(Added Apr. 30, 2007, eff. Dec. 1, 2007. Abrogated eff. Dec. 1, 2015.)

Form 2. Date, Signature, Address, E–Mail Address, and Telephone Number [Abrogated]

(Added Apr. 30, 2007, eff. Dec. 1, 2007. Abrogated eff. Dec. 1, 2015.)

Form 3. Summons [Abrogated]

(Added Apr. 30, 2007, eff. Dec. 1, 2007; amended Mar. 26, 2009, eff. Dec. 1, 2009. Abrogated eff. Dec. 1, 2015.)

Form 4. Summons on a Third-Party Complaint [Abrogated]

(Added Apr. 30, 2007, eff. Dec. 1, 2007; amended Mar. 26, 2009, eff. Dec. 1, 2009. Abrogated eff. Dec. 1, 2015.)

Form 5. Notice of a Lawsuit and Request to Waive Service of a Summons [Abrogated]

(Added Apr. 30, 2007, eff. Dec. 1, 2007. Abrogated eff. Dec. 1, 2015.)

Form 6. Waiver of the Service of Summons [Abrogated]

(Added Apr. 30, 2007, eff. Dec. 1, 2007. Abrogated eff. Dec. 1, 2015.)

Form 7. Statement of Jurisdiction [Abrogated]

(Added Apr. 30, 2007, eff. Dec. 1, 2007. Abrogated eff. Dec. 1, 2015.)

Form 8. Statement of Reasons for Omitting a Party [Abrogated]

(Added Apr. 30, 2007, eff. Dec. 1, 2007. Abrogated eff. Dec. 1, 2015.)

Form 9. Statement Noting a Party's Death [Abrogated]

(Added Apr. 30, 2007, eff. Dec. 1, 2007. Abrogated eff. Dec. 1, 2015.)

Form 10. Complaint to Recover a Sum Certain [Abrogated]

(Added Apr. 30, 2007, eff. Dec. 1, 2007. Abrogated eff. Dec. 1, 2015.)

Form 11. Complaint for Negligence [Abrogated]

(Added Apr. 30, 2007, eff. Dec. 1, 2007. Abrogated eff. Dec. 1, 2015.)

Form 12. Complaint for Negligence When the Plaintiff Does Not Know Who Is Responsible [Abrogated]

(Added Apr. 30, 2007, eff. Dec. 1, 2007. Abrogated eff. Dec. 1, 2015.)

Form 13. Complaint for Negligence Under the Federal Employers' Liability Act [Abrogated]

(Added Apr. 30, 2007, eff. Dec. 1, 2007. Abrogated eff. Dec. 1, 2015.)

Form 14. Complaint for Damages Under the Merchant Marine Act [Abrogated]

(Added Apr. 30, 2007, eff. Dec. 1, 2007. Abrogated eff. Dec. 1, 2015.)

Form 15. Complaint for the Conversion of Property [Abrogated]

(Added Apr. 30, 2007, eff. Dec. 1, 2007. Abrogated eff. Dec. 1, 2015.)

Form 16. Third–Party Complaint [Abrogated]

(Added Apr. 30, 2007, eff. Dec. 1, 2007. Abrogated eff. Dec. 1, 2015.)

Form 17. Complaint for Specific Performance of a Contract to Convey Land [Abrogated]

(Added Apr. 30, 2007, eff. Dec. 1, 2007. Abrogated eff. Dec. 1, 2015.)

Form 18. Complaint for Patent Infringement [Abrogated]

(Added Apr. 30, 2007, eff. Dec. 1, 2007. Abrogated eff. Dec. 1, 2015.)

Form 19. Complaint for Copyright Infringement and Unfair Competition [Abrogated]

(Added Apr. 30, 2007, eff. Dec. 1, 2007. Abrogated eff. Dec. 1, 2015.)

Form 20. Complaint for Interpleader and Declaratory Relief [Abrogated]

(Added Apr. 30, 2007, eff. Dec. 1, 2007. Abrogated eff. Dec. 1, 2015.)

Form 21. Complaint on a Claim for a Debt and to Set Aside a Fraudulent Conveyance Under Rule 18(b) [Abrogated]

(Added Apr. 30, 2007, eff. Dec. 1, 2007. Abrogated eff. Dec. 1, 2015.)

Form 30. Answer Presenting Defenses Under Rule 12(b) [Abrogated]

(Added Apr. 30, 2007, eff. Dec. 1, 2007. Abrogated eff. Dec. 1, 2015.)

Form 31. Answer to a Complaint for Money Had and Received With a Counterclaim for Interpleader [Abrogated]

(Added Apr. 30, 2007, eff. Dec. 1, 2007. Abrogated eff. Dec. 1, 2015.)

Form 40. Motion to Dismiss Under Rule 12(b) for Lack of Jurisdiction, Improper Venue, Insufficient Service of Process, or Failure to State a Claim [Abrogated]

(Added Apr. 30, 2007, eff. Dec. 1, 2007. Abrogated eff. Dec. 1, 2015.)

Form 41. Motion to Bring in a Third–Party Defendant [Abrogated]

(Added Apr. 30, 2007, eff. Dec. 1, 2007. Abrogated eff. Dec. 1, 2015.)

Form 42. Motion to Intervene as a Defendant Under Rule 24 [Abrogated]

(Added Apr. 30, 2007, eff. Dec. 1, 2007. Abrogated eff. Dec. 1, 2015.)

Form 50. Request to Produce Documents and Tangible Things, or to Enter Onto Land Under Rule 34 [Abrogated]

(Added Apr. 30, 2007, eff. Dec. 1, 2007. Abrogated eff. Dec. 1, 2015.)

Form 51. Request for Admissions Under Rule 36 [Abrogated]

(Added Apr. 30, 2007, eff. Dec. 1, 2007. Abrogated eff. Dec. 1, 2015.)

Form 52. Report of the Parties' Planning Meeting [Abrogated]

(Added Apr. 30, 2007, eff. Dec. 1, 2007. As amended Apr. 28, 2010, eff. Dec. 1, 2010. Abrogated eff. Dec. 1, 2015.)

Form 60. Notice of Condemnation [Abrogated]

(Added Apr. 30, 2007, eff. Dec. 1, 2007; amended Mar. 26, 2009, eff. Dec. 1, 2009. Abrogated eff. Dec. 1, 2015.)

Form 61. Complaint for Condemnation [Abrogated]

(Added Apr. 30, 2007, eff. Dec. 1, 2007. Abrogated eff. Dec. 1, 2015.)

Form 70. Judgment on a Jury Verdict [Abrogated]

(Added Apr. 30, 2007, eff. Dec. 1, 2007. Abrogated eff. Dec. 1, 2015.)

Form 71. Judgment by the Court Without a Jury [Abrogated]

(Added Apr. 30, 2007, eff. Dec. 1, 2007. Abrogated eff. Dec. 1, 2015.)

Form 80. Notice of a Magistrate Judge's Availability [Abrogated]

(Added Apr. 30, 2007, eff. Dec. 1, 2007. Abrogated eff. Dec. 1, 2015.)

Form 81. Consent to an Assignment to a Magistrate Judge [Abrogated]

(Added Apr. 30, 2007, eff. Dec. 1, 2007. Abrogated eff. Dec. 1, 2015.)

Form 82. Order of Assignment to a Magistrate Judge [Abrogated]

(Added Apr. 30, 2007, eff. Dec. 1, 2007. Abrogated eff. Dec. 1, 2015.)

SUPPLEMENTAL RULES FOR ADMIRALTY OR MARITIME CLAIMS AND ASSET FORFEITURE ACTIONS

Amendments received to December 1, 2018

ADVISORY COMMITTEE NOTES
1966 Adoption

The amendments to the Federal Rules of Civil Procedure to unify the civil and admiralty procedure, together with the Supplemental Rules for Certain Admiralty and Maritime Claims, completely superseded the Admiralty Rules, effective July 1, 1966. Accordingly, the latter were rescinded.

1985 Amendment

Since their promulgation in 1966, the Supplemental Rules for Certain Admiralty and Maritime Claims have preserved the special procedures of arrest and attachment unique to admiralty law. In recent years, however, these Rules have been challenged as violating the principles of procedural due process enunciated in the United States Supreme Court's decision in *Sniadach v. Family Finance Corp.*, 395 U.S. 337 (1969), and later developed in *Fuentes v. Shevin*, 407 U.S. 67 (1972); *Mitchell v. W.T. Grant Co.*, 416 U.S. 600 (1974); and *North Georgia Finishing, Inc. v. Di–Chem, Inc.*, 419 U.S. 601 (1975). These Supreme Court decisions provide five basic criteria for a constitutional seizure of property: (1) effective notice to persons having interests in the property seized, (2) judicial review prior to attachment, (3) avoidance of conclusory allegations in the complaint, (4) security posted by the plaintiff to protect the owner of the property under attachment, and (5) a meaningful and timely hearing after attachment.

Several commentators have found the Supplemental Rules lacking on some or all five grounds. *E.g.*, Batiza & Partridge, *The Constitutional Challenge to Maritime Seizures*, 26 Loy. L.Rev. 203 (1980); Morse, *The Conflict Between the Supreme Court Admiralty Rules and Sniadach–Fuentes: A Collision Course?*, 3 Fla.St.U.L.Rev. 1 (1975). The federal courts have varied in their disposition of challenges to the Supplemental Rules. The Fourth and Fifth Circuits have affirmed the constitutionality of Rule C. *Amstar Corp. v. S/S Alexandros T.*, 664 F.2d 904 (4th Cir.1981); *Merchants National Bank of Mobile v. The Dredge General G.L. Gillespie*, 663 F.2d 1338 (5th Cir.1981), *cert. dismissed*, 456 U.S. 966 (1982). However, a district court in the Ninth Circuit found Rule C unconstitutional. *Alyeska Pipeline Service Co. v. The Vessel Bay Ridge*, 509 F.Supp. 1115 (D. Alaska 1981), *appeal dismissed*, 703 F.2d 381 (9th Cir.1983). Rule B(1) has received similar inconsistent treatment. The Ninth and Eleventh Circuits have upheld its constitutionality. *Polar Shipping, Ltd. v. Oriental Shipping Corp.*, 680 F.2d 627 (9th Cir.1982); *Schiffahartsgesellschaft Leonhardt & Co. v. A. Bottacchi S.A. de Navegacion*, 732 F.2d 1543 (11th Cir.1984). On the other hand, a Washington district court has found it to be constitutionally deficient. *Grand Bahama Petroleum Co. v. Canadian Transportation Agencies, Ltd.*, 450 F.Supp. 447 (W.D. Wash. 1978). The constitutionality of both rules was questioned in *Techem Chem Co. v. M/T Choyo Maru*, 416 F.Supp. 960 (D. Md. 1976). Thus, there is uncertainty as to whether the current rules prescribe constitutionally sound procedures for guidance of courts and counsel. See generally Note, *Due Process in Admiralty Arrest and Attachment*, 56 Tex.L.Rev. 1091 (1978).

Due to the controversy and uncertainty that have surrounded the Supplemental Rules, local admiralty bars and the Maritime Law Association of the United States have sought to strengthen the constitutionality of maritime arrest and attachment by encouraging promulgation of local admiralty rules providing for prompt post-seizure hearings. Some districts also adopted rules calling for judicial scrutiny of applications for arrest or attachment. Nonetheless, the result has been a lack of uniformity and continued concern over the constitutionality of the existing practice. The amendments that follow are intended to provide rules that meet the requirements prescribed by the Supreme Court and to develop uniformity in the admiralty practice.

Rule A. Scope of Rules

(1) These Supplemental Rules apply to:

(A) the procedure in admiralty and maritime claims within the meaning of Rule 9(h) with respect to the following remedies:

(i) maritime attachment and garnishment,

(ii) actions in rem,

(iii) possessory, petitory, and partition actions, and

(iv) actions for exoneration from or limitation of liability;

(B) forfeiture actions in rem arising from a federal statute; and

(C) the procedure in statutory condemnation proceedings analogous to maritime actions in rem, whether within the admiralty and maritime jurisdiction or not. Except as otherwise provided, references in these Supplemental Rules to actions in rem include such analogous statutory condemnation proceedings.

(2) The Federal Rules of Civil Procedure also apply to the foregoing proceedings except to the extent that they are inconsistent with these Supplemental Rules. (Added Feb. 28, 1966, eff. July 1, 1966; amended Apr. 12, 2006, eff. Dec. 1, 2006.)

ADVISORY COMMITTEE NOTES
1966 Adoption

Certain distinctively maritime remedies must be preserved in unified rules. The commencement of an action by attachment or garnishment has heretofore been practically unknown in federal jurisprudence except in admiralty, although the amendment of Rule 4(e) effective July 1, 1963, makes available that procedure in accordance with state law. The maritime proceeding in rem is unique, except as it has been emulated by statute, and is closely related to the substantive maritime law relating to liens. Arrest of the vessel or other maritime property is an historic remedy in controversies over title or right to possession, and in disputes among co-owners over the vessel's employment. The statutory right to limit liability is limited to owners of vessels, and has its own complexities. While the unified federal rules are generally applicable to these distinctive proceedings, certain special rules dealing with them are needed.

Arrest of the person and imprisonment for debt are not included because there remedies are not peculiarly maritime. The practice is not uniform but conforms to state law. See 2 Benedict § 286 [Note: reference is to the 6th Edition of Benedict on Admiralty and not to the current 7th Edition]; 28 U.S.C., § 2007; FRCP 64, 69. The relevant provisions of Admiralty Rules 2, 3, and 4 are unnecessary or obsolete.

No attempt is here made to compile a complete and self-contained code governing these distinctively maritime remedies. The more limited objective is to carry forward the relevant provisions of the former Rules of Practice for Admiralty and Maritime Cases, modernized and revised to some extent but still in the context of history and precedent. Accordingly, these Rules are not to be construed as limiting or impairing the traditional power of a district court, exercising the admiralty and maritime jurisdiction, to adapt its procedures and its remedies in the individual case, consistently with these rules, to secure the just, speedy, and inexpensive determination of every action. (See *Swift & Co., Packers v. Compania Columbiana Del Caribe, S/A,* 339 U.S. 684, (1950); Rule 1). In addition, of course, the district courts retain the power to make local rules not inconsistent with these rules. See Rule 83; cf. Admiralty Rule 44.

2006 Amendment

Rule A is amended to reflect the adoption of Rule G to govern procedure in civil forfeiture actions. Rule G(1) contemplates application of other Supplemental Rules to the extent that Rule G does not address an issue. One example is the Rule E(4)(c) provision for arresting intangible property.

Rule B. In Personam Actions: Attachment and Garnishment

(1) When Available; Complaint, Affidavit, Judicial Authorization, and Process. In an in personam action:

(a) If a defendant is not found within the district when a verified complaint praying for attachment and the affidavit required by Rule B(1)(b) are filed, a verified complaint may contain a prayer for process to attach the defendant's tangible or intangible personal property—up to the amount sued for—in the hands of garnishees named in the process.

(b) The plaintiff or the plaintiff's attorney must sign and file with the complaint an affidavit stating that, to the affiant's knowledge, or on information and belief, the defendant cannot be found within the district. The court must review the complaint and affidavit and, if the conditions of this Rule B appear to exist, enter an order so stating and authorizing process of attachment and garnishment. The clerk may issue supplemental process enforcing the court's order upon application without further court order.

(c) If the plaintiff or the plaintiff's attorney certifies that exigent circumstances make court review impracticable, the clerk must issue the summons and process of attachment and garnishment. The plaintiff has the burden in any post-attachment hearing under Rule E(4)(f) to show that exigent circumstances existed.

(d)(i) If the property is a vessel or tangible property on board a vessel, the summons, process, and any supplemental process must be delivered to the marshal for service.

(ii) If the property is other tangible or intangible property, the summons, process, and any supplemental process must be delivered to a person or organization authorized to serve it, who may be (A) a marshal; (B) someone under contract with the United States; (C) someone specially appointed by the court for that purpose; or, (D) in an action brought by the United States, any officer or employee of the United States.

(e) The plaintiff may invoke state-law remedies under Rule 64 for seizure of person or property for the purpose of securing satisfaction of the judgment.

(2) Notice to Defendant. No default judgment may be entered except upon proof—which may be by affidavit—that:

(a) the complaint, summons, and process of attachment or garnishment have been served on the defendant in a manner authorized by Rule 4;

(b) the plaintiff or the garnishee has mailed to the defendant the complaint, summons, and process of attachment or garnishment, using any form of mail requiring a return receipt; or

(c) the plaintiff or the garnishee has tried diligently to give notice of the action to the defendant but could not do so.

(3) Answer.

(a) By Garnishee. The garnishee shall serve an answer, together with answers to any interrogatories served with the complaint, within 21 days after service of process upon the garnishee. Interrogatories to the garnishee may be served with the complaint without leave of court. If the garnishee refuses or neglects to answer on oath as to the debts, credits, or effects of the defendant in the garnishee's hands, or any interrogatories concerning such debts, credits, and effects that may be propounded by the plaintiff, the court may award compulsory process against the garnishee. If the garnishee admits any debts, credits, or effects, they shall be held in the garnishee's hands or paid into the registry of the court, and shall be held in either case subject to the further order of the court.

(b) By Defendant. The defendant shall serve an answer within 30 days after process has been executed, whether by attachment of property or service on the garnishee.

(Added Feb. 28, 1966, eff. July 1, 1966; amended Apr. 29, 1985, eff. Aug. 1, 1985; Mar. 2, 1987, eff. Aug. 1, 1987; Apr. 17, 2000, eff. Dec. 1, 2000; Apr. 25, 2005, eff. Dec. 1, 2005; Mar. 26, 2009, eff. Dec. 1, 2009.)

ADVISORY COMMITTEE NOTES
1966 Adoption
Subdivision (1)

This preserves the traditional maritime remedy of attachment and garnishment, and carries forward the relevant substance of Admiralty Rule 2. In addition, or in the alternative, provision is made for the use of similar state remedies made available by the amendment of Rule 4(e) effective July 1, 1963. On the effect of appearance to defend against attachment see Rule E(8).

The rule follows closely the language of Admiralty Rule 2. No change is made with respect to the property subject to attachment. No change is made in the condition that makes the remedy available. The rules have never defined the clause, "if the defendant shall not be found within the district," and no definition is attempted here. The subject seems one best left for the time being to development on a case-by-case basis. The proposal does shift from the marshal (on whom it now rests in theory) to the plaintiff the burden of establishing that the defendant cannot be found in the district.

A change in the context of the practice is brought about by Rule 4(f), which will enable summons to be served throughout the state instead of, as heretofore, only within the district. The Advisory Committee considered whether the rule on attachment and garnishment should be correspondingly changed to permit those remedies only when the defendant cannot be found within the state and concluded that the remedy should not be so limited.

The effect is to enlarge the class of cases in which the plaintiff may proceed by attachment or garnishment although jurisdiction of the person of the defendant may be independently obtained. This is possible at the present time where, for example, a corporate defendant has appointed an agent within the district to accept service of process but is not carrying on activities there sufficient to subject it to jurisdiction. (*Seawind Compania, S.A. v. Crescent Line, Inc.,* 320 F.2d 580 (2d Cir.1963)), or where, though the foreign corporation's activities in the district are sufficient to subject it personally to the jurisdiction, there is in the district no officer on whom process can be served (*United States v. Cia. Naviera Continental, S.A.,* 178 F.Supp. 561, (S.D.N.Y.1959)).

Process of attachment or garnishment will be limited to the district. See Rule E(3)(a).

Subdivision (2)

The former Admiralty Rules did not provide for notice to the defendant in attachment and garnishment proceedings. None is required by the principles of due process, since it is assumed that the garnishee or custodian of the property attached will either notify the defendant or be deprived of the right to plead the judgment as a defense in an action against him by the defendant. *Harris v. Balk,* 198 U.S. 215 (1905); *Pennoyer v. Neff,* 95 U.S. 714 (1878). Modern conceptions of fairness, however, dictate that actual notice be given to persons known to claim an interest in the property that is the subject of the action where that is reasonably practicable. In attachment and garnishment proceedings the persons whose interests will be affected by the judgment are identified by the complaint. No substantial burden is imposed on the plaintiff by a simple requirement that he notify the defendant of the action by mail.

In the usual case the defendant is notified of the pendency of the proceedings by the garnishee or otherwise, and appears to claim the property and to make his answer. Hence notice by mail is not routinely required in all cases, but only in those in which the defendant has not appeared prior to the time when a default judgment is demanded. The rule therefore provides only that no default judgment shall be entered except upon proof of notice, or of inability to give notice despite diligent efforts to do so. Thus the burden of giving notice is further minimized.

In some cases the plaintiff may prefer to give notice by serving process in the usual way instead of simply by mail. (Rule 4(d).) In particular, if the defendant is in a foreign country the plaintiff may wish to utilize the modes of notice recently provided to facilitate compliance with foreign laws and procedures (Rule 4(i)). The rule provides for these alternatives.

The rule does not provide for notice by publication because there is no problem concerning unknown claimants, and publication has little utility in proportion to its expense where the identity of the defendant is known.

Subdivision (3)

Subdivision (a) incorporates the substance of Admiralty Rule 36.

The Admiralty Rules were silent as to when the garnishee and the defendant were to answer. See also 2 Benedict ch. XXIV [Reference is to the 6th Edition of Benedict on Admiralty and not to the current 7th Edition].

The rule proceeds on the assumption that uniform and definite periods of time for responsive pleadings should be substituted for return days (see the discussion under Rule C(6), below). Twenty days seems sufficient time for the garnishee to answer (cf. FRCP 12(a)), and an additional 10 days should suffice for the defendant. When allowance is made for the time required for notice to reach the defendant this gives the defendant in attachment and garnishment approximately the same time that defendants have to answer when personally served.

1985 Amendment

Rule B(1) has been amended to provide for judicial scrutiny before the issuance of any attachment or garnishment process. Its purpose is to eliminate doubts as to whether the Rule is consistent with the principles of procedural due process enunciated by the Supreme Court in *Sniadach v. Family Finance Corp.,* 395 U.S. 337 (1969); and later developed in *Fuentes v. Shevin,* 407 U.S. 67 (1972); *Mitchell v. W.T. Grant Co.,* 416 U.S. 600 (1974); and *North Georgia Finishing, Inc. v. Di-Chem, Inc.,* 419 U.S. 601 (1975). Such doubts were raised in *Grand Bahama Petroleum Co. v. Canadian Transportation Agencies, Ltd.,* 450 F.Supp. 447 (W.D.Wash.1978); and *Schiffahartsgesellschaft Leonhardt & Co. v. A. Bottacchi S.A. de Navegacion,* 552 F.Supp. 771 (S.D.Ga.1982), which was reversed, 732 F.2d 1543 (11th Cir.1984). But compare *Polar Shipping Ltd. v. Oriental Shipping Corp.,* 680 F.2d 627 (9th Cir.1982), in which a majority of the panel upheld the constitutionality of Rule B because of the unique commercial context in which it is invoked. The practice described in Rule B(1) has been adopted in some districts by local rule. E.g.,

N.D. Calif. Local Rule 603.3; W.D.Wash. Local Admiralty Rule 15(d).

The rule envisions that the order will issue when the plaintiff makes a prima facie showing that he has a maritime claim against the defendant in the amount sued for and the defendant is not present in the district. A simple order with conclusory findings is contemplated. The reference to review by the "court" is broad enough to embrace review by a magistrate as well as by a district judge.

The new provision recognizes that in some situations, such as when the judge is unavailable and the ship is about to depart from the jurisdiction, it will be impracticable, if not impossible, to secure the judicial review contemplated by Rule B(1). When "exigent circumstances" exist, the rule enables the plaintiff to secure the issuance of the summons and process of attachment and garnishment, subject to a later showing that the necessary circumstances actually existed. This provision is intended to provide a safety valve without undermining the requirement of preattachment scrutiny. Thus, every effort to secure judicial review, including conducting a hearing by telephone, should be pursued before resorting to the exigent-circumstances procedure.

Rule B(1) also has been amended so that the garnishee shall be named in the "process" rather than in the "complaint." This should solve the problem presented in *Filia Compania Naviera, S.A. v. Petroship, S.A.*, 1983 A.M.C. 1 (S.D.N.Y.1982), and eliminate any need for an additional judicial review of the complaint and affidavit when a garnishee is added.

1987 Amendment

The amendments are technical. No substantive change is intended.

2000 Amendment

Rule B(1) is amended in two ways, and style changes have been made.

The service provisions of Rule C(3) are adopted in paragraph (d), providing alternatives to service by a marshal if the property to be seized is not a vessel or tangible property on board a vessel.

The provision that allows the plaintiff to invoke state attachment and garnishment remedies is amended to reflect the 1993 amendments of Civil Rule 4. Former Civil Rule 4(e), incorporated in Rule B(1), allowed general use of state quasi-in-rem jurisdiction if the defendant was not an inhabitant of, or found within, the state. Rule 4(e) was replaced in 1993 by Rule 4(n)(2), which permits use of state law to seize a defendant's assets only if personal jurisdiction over the defendant cannot be obtained in the district where the action is brought. Little purpose would be served by incorporating Rule 4(n)(2) in Rule B, since maritime attachment and garnishment are available whenever the defendant is not found within the district, a concept that allows attachment or garnishment even in some circumstances in which personal jurisdiction also can be asserted. In order to protect against any possibility that elimination of the reference to state quasi-in-rem jurisdiction remedies might seem to defeat continued use of state security devices, paragraph (e) expressly incorporates Civil Rule 64. Because Rule 64 looks only to security, not jurisdiction, the former reference to Rule E(8) is deleted as no longer relevant.

Rule B(2)(a) is amended to reflect the 1993 redistribution of the service provisions once found in Civil Rule 4(d) and (i). These provisions are now found in many different subdivisions of Rule 4. The new reference simply incorporates Rule 4, without designating the new subdivisions, because the function of Rule B(2) is simply to describe the methods of notice that suffice to support a default judgment. Style changes also have been made.

2005 Amendment

Rule B(1) is amended to incorporate the decisions in *Heidmar, Inc. v. Anomina Ravennate Di Armamento Sp.A. of Ravenna*, 132 F.3d 264, 267–268 (5th Cir. 1998), and *Navieros InterAmericanos, S.A. v. M/V Vasilia Express*, 120 F.3d 304, 314–315 (1st Cir. 1997). The time for determining whether a defendant is "found" in the district is set at the time of filing the verified complaint that prays for attachment and the affidavit required by Rule B(1)(b). As provided by Rule B(1)(b), the affidavit must be filed with the complaint. A defendant cannot defeat the security purpose of attachment by appointing an agent for service of process after the complaint and affidavit are filed. The complaint praying for attachment need not be the initial complaint. So long as the defendant is not found in the district, the prayer for attachment may be made in an amended complaint; the affidavit that the defendant cannot be found must be filed with the amended complaint.

2009 Amendment

The time set in the former rule at 20 days has been revised to 21 days. See the Note to Rule 6.

Rule C.   In Rem Actions: Special Provisions

(1) When Available. An action in rem may be brought:

    (a) To enforce any maritime lien;

    (b) Whenever a statute of the United States provides for a maritime action in rem or a proceeding analogous thereto.

Except as otherwise provided by law a party who may proceed in rem may also, or in the alternative, proceed in personam against any person who may be liable.

Statutory provisions exempting vessels or other property owned or possessed by or operated by or for the United States from arrest or seizure are not affected by this rule. When a statute so provides, an action against the United States or an instrumentality thereof may proceed on in rem principles.

(2) Complaint. In an action in rem the complaint must:

    (a) be verified;

    (b) describe with reasonable particularity the property that is the subject of the action; and

    (c) state that the property is within the district or will be within the district while the action is pending.

(3) Judicial Authorization and Process.

    (a) Arrest Warrant.

(i) The court must review the complaint and any supporting papers. If the conditions for an in rem action appear to exist, the court must issue an order directing the clerk to issue a warrant for the arrest of the vessel or other property that is the subject of the action.

(ii) If the plaintiff or the plaintiff's attorney certifies that exigent circumstances make court review impracticable, the clerk must promptly issue a summons and a warrant for the arrest of the vessel or other property that is the subject of the action. The plaintiff has the burden in any post-arrest hearing under Rule E(4)(f) to show that exigent circumstances existed.

(b) Service.

(i) If the property that is the subject of the action is a vessel or tangible property on board a vessel, the warrant and any supplemental process must be delivered to the marshal for service.

(ii) If the property that is the subject of the action is other property, tangible or intangible, the warrant and any supplemental process must be delivered to a person or organization authorized to enforce it, who may be: (A) a marshal; (B) someone under contract with the United States; (C) someone specially appointed by the court for that purpose; or, (D) in an action brought by the United States, any officer or employee of the United States.

(c) Deposit in Court. If the property that is the subject of the action consists in whole or in part of freight, the proceeds of property sold, or other intangible property, the clerk must issue—in addition to the warrant—a summons directing any person controlling the property to show cause why it should not be deposited in court to abide the judgment.

(d) Supplemental Process. The clerk may upon application issue supplemental process to enforce the court's order without further court order.

(4) Notice. No notice other than execution of process is required when the property that is the subject of the action has been released under Rule E(5). If the property is not released within 14 days after execution, the plaintiff must promptly—or within the time that the court allows—give public notice of the action and arrest in a newspaper designated by court order and having general circulation in the district, but publication may be terminated if the property is released before publication is completed. The notice must specify the time under Rule C(6) to file a statement of interest in or right against the seized property and to answer. This rule does not affect the notice requirements in an action to foreclose a preferred ship mortgage under 46 U.S.C. §§ 31301 et seq., as amended.

(5) Ancillary Process. In any action in rem in which process has been served as provided by this rule, if any part of the property that is the subject of the action has not been brought within the control of the court because it has been removed or sold, or because it is intangible property in the hands of a person who has not been served with process, the court may, on motion, order any person having possession or control of such property or its proceeds to show cause why it should not be delivered into the custody of the marshal or other person or organization having a warrant for the arrest of the property, or paid into court to abide the judgment; and, after hearing, the court may enter such judgment as law and justice may require.

(6) Responsive Pleading; Interrogatories.

(a) Statement of Interest; Answer. In an action in rem:

(i) a person who asserts a right of possession or any ownership interest in the property that is the subject of the action must file a verified statement of right or interest:

(A) within 14 days after the execution of process, or

(B) within the time that the court allows;

(ii) the statement of right or interest must describe the interest in the property that supports the person's demand for its restitution or right to defend the action;

(iii) an agent, bailee, or attorney must state the authority to file a statement of right or interest on behalf of another; and

(iv) a person who asserts a right of possession or any ownership interest must serve an answer within 21 days after filing the statement of interest or right.

(b) Interrogatories. Interrogatories may be served with the complaint in an in rem action without leave of court. Answers to the interrogatories must be served with the answer to the complaint.

(Added Feb. 28, 1966, eff. July 1, 1966; amended Apr. 29, 1985, eff. Aug. 1, 1985; Mar. 2, 1987, eff. Aug. 1, 1987; Apr. 30, 1991, eff. Dec. 1, 1991; Apr. 17, 2000, eff. Dec. 1, 2000; Apr. 29, 2002, eff. Dec. 1, 2002; Apr. 25, 2005, eff. Dec. 1, 2005; Apr. 12, 2006, eff. Dec. 1, 2006; Apr. 23, 2008, eff. Dec. 1, 2008; Mar. 26, 2009, eff. Dec. 1, 2009.)

ADVISORY COMMITTEE NOTES

1966 Adoption

Subdivision (1).

This rule is designed not only to preserve the proceeding in rem as it now exists in admiralty cases, but to preserve the substance of Admiralty Rules 13–18. The general reference to enforcement of any maritime lien is believed to state the existing law, and is an improvement over the enumeration in the former Admiralty Rules, which is repetitious and incomplete (e.g., there was no reference to general average). The reference to any maritime lien is intended to include liens created by state law which are enforceable in admiralty.

The main concern of Admiralty Rules 13–18 was with the question whether certain actions might be brought in rem or also, or in the alternative, in personam. Essentially, therefore, these rules deal with questions of substantive law, for in general an action in rem may be brought to enforce any maritime lien, and no action in personam may be brought when the substantive law imposes no personal liability.

These rules may be summarized as follows:

1. Cases in which the plaintiff may proceed in rem and/or in personam:

    a. Suits for seamen's wages;

    b. Suits by materialmen for supplies, repairs, etc.;

    c. Suits for pilotage;

    d. Suits for collision damages;

    e. Suits founded on mere maritime hypothecation;

    f. Suits for salvage.

2. Cases in which the plaintiff may proceed only in personam:

    a. Suits for assault and beating.

3. Cases in which the plaintiff may proceed only in rem:

    a. Suits on bottomry bonds.

The coverage is incomplete, since the rules omit mention of many cases in which the plaintiff may proceed in rem or in personam. This revision proceeds on the principle that it is preferable to make a general statement as to the availability of the remedies, leaving out conclusions on matters of substantive law. Clearly it is not necessary to enumerate the cases listed under Item 1, above, nor to try to complete the list.

The rule eliminates the provision of Admiralty Rule 15 that actions for assault and beating may be brought only in personam. A preliminary study fails to disclose any reason for the rule. It is subject to so many exceptions that it is calculated to deceive rather than to inform. A seaman may sue in rem when he has been beaten by a fellow member of the crew so vicious as to render the vessel unseaworthy, *The Rolph*, 293 Fed. 269, aff'd 299 Fed. 52 (9th Cir. 1923), or where the theory of the action is that a beating by the master is a breach of the obligation under the shipping articles to treat the seaman with proper kindness, *The David Evans*, 187 Fed. 775 (D.Hawaii 1911); and a passenger may sue in rem on the theory that the assault is a breach of the contract of passage, *The Western States*, 159 Fed. 354 (2d Cir. 1908). To say that an action for money damages may be brought only in personam seems equivalent to saying that a maritime lien shall not exist; and that, in turn, seems equivalent to announcing a rule of substantive law rather than a rule of procedure. Dropping the rule will leave it to the courts to determine whether a lien exists as a matter of substantive law.

The specific reference to bottomry bonds is omitted because, as a matter of hornbook substantive law, there is no personal liability on such bonds.

Subdivision (2).

This incorporates the substance of Admiralty Rules 21 and 22.

Subdivision (3).

Derived from Admiralty Rules 10 and 37. The provision that the warrant is to be issued by the clerk is new, but is assumed to state existing law.

There is remarkably little authority bearing on Rule 37, although the subject would seem to be an important one. The rule appears on its face to have provided for a sort of ancillary process, and this may well be the case when tangible property, such as a vessel, is arrested, and intangible property such as freight is incidentally involved. It can easily happen, however, that the only property against which the action may be brought is intangible, as where the owner of a vessel under charter has a lien on subfreights. See 2 Benedict § 299 and cases cited. [Reference is to the 6th Edition of Benedict on Admiralty and not to the current 7th Edition]. In such cases it would seem that the order to the person holding the fund is equivalent to original process, taking the place of the warrant for arrest. That being so, it would also seem that (1) there should be some provision for notice, comparable to that given when tangible property is arrested, and (2) it should not be necessary, as Rule 37 provided, to petition the court for issuance of the process, but that it should issue as of course. Accordingly the substance of Rule 37 is included in the rule covering ordinary process, and notice will be required by Rule C(4). Presumably the rules omit any requirement of notice in these cases because the holder of the funds (e.g., the cargo owner) would be required on general principles (cf. *Harris v. Balk*, 198 U.S. 215 (1905)) to notify his obligee (e.g., the charterer); but in actions in rem such notice seems plainly inadequate because there may be adverse claims to the fund (e.g., there may be liens against the subfreights for seamen's wages, etc.). Compare Admiralty Rule 9.

Subdivision (4).

This carries forward the notice provision of Admiralty Rule 10, with one modification. Notice by publication is too expensive and ineffective a formality to be routinely required. When, as usually happens, the vessel or other property is released on bond or otherwise there is no point in publishing notice; the vessel is freed from the claim of the plaintiff and no other interest in the vessel can be affected by the proceedings. If, however, the vessel is not released, general notice is required in order that all persons, including unknown claimants, may appear and be heard, and in order that the judgment in rem shall be binding on all the world.

Subdivision (5).

This incorporates the substance of Admiralty Rule 9.

There are remarkably few cases dealing directly with the rule. In The *George Prescott*, 10 Fed.Cas. 222 (No. 5,339) (E.D.N.Y.1865), the master and crew of a vessel libeled her for wages, and other lienors also filed libels. One of the lienors suggested to the court that prior to the arrest of the vessel the master had removed the sails, and asked that he be ordered to produce them. He admitted removing the sails and selling them, justifying on the ground that he held a mortgage on the vessel. He was ordered to pay the proceeds into court. Cf. *United States v. The Zarko*, 187 F.Supp. 371 (S.D.Cal.1960), where an armature belonging to a vessel subject to a preferred ship mortgage was in possession of a repairman claiming a lien.

It is evident that, though the rule has had a limited career in the reported cases, it is a potentially important one. It is also evident that the rule is framed in terms narrower than the principle that supports it. There is no apparent reason for limiting it to ships and their appurtenances (2 Benedict § 299) [Reference is to the 6th Edition of Benedict on Admiralty and not to the current 7th Edition]. Also, the reference to "third parties" in the existing rule seems unfortunate. In *The George Prescott*, the person who removed and sold the sails was a plaintiff in the action, and relief against him was just as necessary as if he had been a stranger.

Another situation in which process of this kind would seem to be useful is that in which the principal property that is the subject of the action is a vessel, but her pending freight is

---

incidentally involved. The warrant of arrest, and notice of its service, should be all that is required by way of original process and notice; ancillary process without notice should suffice as to the incidental intangibles.

The distinction between Admiralty Rules 9 and 37 is not at once apparent, but seems to be this: Where the action was against property that could not be seized by the marshal because it was intangible, the original process was required to be similar to that issued against a garnishee, and general notice was required (though not provided for by the present rule; cf. Advisory Committee's Note to Rule C(3)). Under Admiralty Rule 9 property had been arrested and general notice had been given, but some of the property had been removed or for some other reason could not be arrested. Here no further notice was necessary.

The rule also makes provision for this kind of situation: The proceeding is against a vessel's pending freight only; summons has been served on the person supposedly holding the funds, and general notice has been given; it develops that another person holds all or part of the funds. Ancillary process should be available here without further notice.

Subdivision (6).

Adherence to the practice of return days seems unsatisfactory. The practice varies significantly from district to district. A uniform rule should be provided so that any claimant or defendant can readily determine when he is required to file or serve a claim or answer.

A virtue of the return-day practice is that it requires claimants to come forward and identify themselves at an early stage of the proceedings—before they could fairly be required to answer. The draft is designed to preserve this feature of the present practice by requiring early filing of the claim. The time schedule contemplated in the draft is closely comparable to the present practice in the Southern District of New York, where the claimant has a minimum of 8 days to claim and three weeks thereafter to answer.

This rule also incorporates the substance of Admiralty Rule 25. The present rule's emphasis on "the true and bona fide owner" is omitted, since anyone having the right to possession can claim (2 Benedict § 324) [Reference is to the 6th Edition of Benedict on Admiralty and not to the current 7th Edition].

1985 Amendment

Rule C(3) has been amended to provide for judicial scrutiny before the issuance of any warrant of arrest. Its purpose is to eliminate any doubt as to the rule's constitutionality under the *Sniadach* line of cases. *Sniadach v. Family Finance Corp.*, 395 U.S. 337 (1969); *Fuentes v. Shevin*, 407 U.S. 67 (1972); *Mitchell v. W.T. Grant Co.*, 416 U.S. 600 (1974); and *North Georgia Finishing, Inc. v. Di-Chem, Inc.*, 419 U.S. 601 (1975). This was thought desirable even though both the Fourth and the Fifth Circuits have upheld the existing rule. *Amstar Corp. v. S/S Alexandros T.*, 664 F.2d 904 (4th Cir. 1981); *Merchants National Bank of Mobile v. The Dredge General G.L. Gillespie*, 663 F.2d 1338 (5th Cir.1981), *cert. dismissed*, 456 U.S. 966 (1982). A contrary view was taken by Judge Tate in the *Merchants National Bank* case and by the district court in *Alyeska Pipeline Service Co. v. The Vessel Bay Ridge*, 509 F.Supp. 1115 (D.Alaska 1981), *appeal dismissed*, 703 F.2d 381 (9th Cir.1983).

The rule envisions that the order will issue upon a prima facie showing that the plaintiff has an action in rem against the defendant in the amount sued for and that the property is within the district. A simple order with conclusory findings is contemplated. The reference to review by the "court" is broad enough to embrace a magistrate as well as a district judge.

The new provision recognizes that in some situations, such as when a judge is unavailable and the vessel is about to depart from the jurisdiction, it will be impracticable, if not impossible, to secure the judicial review contemplated by Rule C(3). When "exigent circumstances" exist, the rule enables the plaintiff to secure the issuance of the summons and warrant of arrest, subject to a later showing that the necessary circumstances actually existed. This provision is intended to provide a safety valve without undermining the requirement of pre-arrest scrutiny. Thus, every effort to secure judicial review, including conducting a hearing by telephone, should be pursued before invoking the exigent-circumstances procedure.

The foregoing requirements for prior court review or proof of exigent circumstances do not apply to actions by the United States for forfeitures for federal statutory violations. In such actions a prompt hearing is not constitutionally required, *United States v. Eight Thousand Eight Hundred and Fifty Dollars*, 103 S.Ct. 2005 (1983); *Calero-Toledo v. Pearson Yacht Leasing Co.*, 416 U.S. 663 (1974), and could prejudice the government in its prosecution of the claimants as defendants in parallel criminal proceedings since the forfeiture hearing could be misused by the defendants to obtain by way of civil discovery information to which they would not otherwise be entitled and subject the government and the courts to the unnecessary burden and expense of two hearings rather than one.

1987 Amendment

The amendments are technical. No substantive change is intended.

1991 Amendment

These amendments are designed to conform the rule to Fed.R.Civ.P. 4, as amended. As with recent amendments to Rule 4, it is intended to relieve the Marshals Service of the burden of using its limited personnel and facilities for execution of process in routine circumstances. Doing so may involve a contractual arrangement with a person or organization retained by the government to perform these services, or the use of other government officers and employees, or the special appointment by the court of persons available to perform suitably.

The seizure of a vessel, with or without cargo, remains a task assigned to the Marshal. Successful arrest of a vessel frequently requires the enforcement presence of an armed government official and the cooperation of the United States Coast Guard and other governmental authorities. If the marshal is called upon to seize the vessel, it is expected that the same officer will also be responsible for the seizure of any property on board the vessel at the time of seizure that is to be the object of arrest or attachment.

2000 Amendment

Style changes have been made throughout the revised portions of Rule C. Several changes of meaning have been made as well.

Subdivision 2. In rem jurisdiction originally extended only to property within the judicial district. Since 1986, Congress released only by order of the court, on such terms and conditions and on the giving of such security as the court may require.

(6) Reduction or Impairment of Security. Whenever security is taken the court may, on motion and hearing, for good cause shown, reduce the amount of security given; and if the surety shall be or become insufficient, new or additional sureties may be required on motion and hearing.

(7) Security on Counterclaim.

(a) When a person who has given security for damages in the original action asserts a counterclaim that arises from the transaction or occurrence that is the subject of the original action, a plaintiff for whose benefit the security has been given must give security for damages demanded in the counterclaim unless the court, for cause shown, directs otherwise. Proceedings on the original claim must be stayed until this security is given unless the court directs otherwise.

(b) The plaintiff is required to give security under Rule E(7)(a) when the United States or its corporate instrumentality counterclaims and would have been required to give security to respond in damages if a private party but is relieved by law from giving security.

(8) Restricted Appearance. An appearance to defend against an admiralty and maritime claim with respect to which there has issued process in rem, or process of attachment and garnishment, may be expressly restricted to the defense of such claim, and in that event is not an appearance for the purposes of any other claim with respect to which such process is not available or has not been served.

(9) Disposition of Property; Sales.

(a) Interlocutory Sales; Delivery.

(i) On application of a party, the marshal, or other person having custody of the property, the court may order all or part of the property sold—with the sales proceeds, or as much of them as will satisfy the judgment, paid into court to await further orders of the court—if:

(A) the attached or arrested property is perishable, or liable to deterioration, decay, or injury by being detained in custody pending the action;

(B) the expense of keeping the property is excessive or disproportionate; or

(C) there is an unreasonable delay in securing release of the property.

(ii) In the circumstances described in Rule E(9)(a)(i), the court, on motion by a defendant or a person filing a statement of interest or right under Rule C(6), may order that the property, rather than being sold, be delivered to the movant upon giving security under these rules.

(b) Sales; Proceeds. All sales of property shall be made by the marshal or a deputy marshal, or by other person or organization having the warrant, or by any other person assigned by the court where the marshal or other person or organization having the warrant is a party in interest; and the proceeds of sale shall be forthwith paid into the registry of the court to be disposed of according to law.

(10) Preservation of Property. When the owner or another person remains in possession of property attached or arrested under the provisions of Rule E(4)(b) that permit execution of process without taking actual possession, the court, on a party's motion or on its own, may enter any order necessary to preserve the property and to prevent its removal.

(Added Feb. 28, 1966, eff. July 1, 1966; amended Apr. 29, 1985, eff. Aug. 1, 1985; Mar. 2, 1987, eff. Aug. 1, 1987; Apr. 30, 1991, eff. Dec. 1, 1991; Apr. 17, 2000, eff. Dec. 1, 2000; Apr. 12, 2006, eff. Dec. 1, 2006.)

2 Repealed by Pub. L. 98–89, § 4(b), Aug. 26, 1983, 97 Stat. 600, section 1 of which enacted Title 46, Shipping.

ADVISORY COMMITTEE NOTES
1966 Adoption

Subdivisions (1), (2).

Adapted from Admiralty Rule 24. The rule is based on the assumption that there is no more need for security for costs in maritime personal actions than in civil cases generally, but that there is reason to retain the requirement for actions in which property is seized. As to proceedings for limitation of liability see Rule F(1).

Subdivision (3).

The Advisory Committee has concluded for practical reasons that process requiring seizure of property should continue to be served only within the geographical limits of the district. Compare Rule B(1), continuing the condition that process of attachment and garnishment may be served only if the defendant is not found within the district.

The provisions of Admiralty Rule 1 concerning the persons by whom process is to be served will be superseded by FRCP 4(c).

Subdivision (4).

This rule is intended to preserve the provisions of Admiralty Rules 10 and 36 relating to execution of process, custody of property seized by the marshal, and the marshal's return. It is also designed to make express provision for matters not heretofore covered.

The provision relating to clearance in subdivision (b) is suggested by Admiralty Rule 44 of the District of Maryland.

Subdivision (d) is suggested by English Rule 12, Order 75.

28 U.S.C., § 1921 as amended in 1962 contains detailed provisions relating to the expenses of seizing and preserving property attached or arrested.

Subdivision (5).

In addition to Admiralty Rule 11 (see Rule E(9)), the release of property seized on process of attachment or in rem was dealt with by Admiralty Rules 5, 6, 12, and 57, and 28 U.S.C., § 2464 (formerly Rev.Stat. § 941). The rule consolidates these provisions and makes them uniformly applicable to attachment and garnishment and actions in rem.

---

has enacted a number of jurisdictional and venue statutes for forfeiture and criminal matters that in some circumstances permit a court to exercise authority over property outside the district. 28 U.S.C. § 1355(b)(1) allows a forfeiture action in the district where an act or omission giving rise to forfeiture occurred, or in any other district where venue is established by § 1395 or by any other statute. Section 1355(b)(2) allows an action to be brought as provided in (b)(1) or in the United States District Court for the District of Columbia when the forfeiture property is located in a foreign country or has been seized by authority of a foreign government. Section 1355(d) allows a court with jurisdiction under § 1355(b) to cause service in any other district of process required to bring the forfeiture property before the court. Section 1395 establishes venue of a civil proceeding for forfeiture in the district where the forfeiture accrues or the defendant is found; in any district where the property is found; in any district into which the property is brought, if the property initially is outside any judicial district; or in any district where the vessel is arrested if the proceeding is an admiralty proceeding to forfeit a vessel. Section 1395(e) deals with a vessel or cargo entering a port of entry closed by the President, and transportation to or from a state or section declared to be in insurrection. 18 U.S.C. § 981(h) creates expanded jurisdiction and venue over property located elsewhere that is related to a criminal prosecution pending in the district. These amendments, and related amendments of Rule E(3), bring these Rules into step with the new statutes. No change is made as to admiralty and maritime proceedings that do not involve a forfeiture governed by one of the new statutes.

Subdivision (2) has been separated into lettered paragraphs to facilitate understanding.

Subdivision (3). Subdivision (3) has been rearranged and divided into lettered paragraphs to facilitate understanding.

Paragraph (b)(i) is amended to make it clear that any supplemental process addressed to a vessel or tangible property on board a vessel, as well as the original warrant, is to be served by the marshal.

Subdivision (4). Subdivision (4) has required that public notice state the time for filing an answer, but has not required that the notice set out the earlier time for filing a statement of interest or claim. The amendment requires that both times be stated.

A new provision is added, allowing termination of publication if the property is released more than 10 days after execution but before publication is completed. Termination will save money, and also will reduce the risk of confusion as to the status of the property.

Subdivision (6). Subdivision (6) has applied a single set of undifferentiated provisions to civil forfeiture proceedings and to in rem admiralty proceedings. Because some differences in procedure are desirable, these proceedings are separated by adopting a new paragraph (a) for civil forfeiture proceedings and recasting the present rule as paragraph (b) for in rem admiralty proceedings. The provision for interrogatories and answers is carried forward as paragraph (c). Although this established procedure for serving interrogatories with the complaint departs from the general provisions of Civil Rule 26(d), the special needs of expedition that often arise in admiralty justify continuing the practice.

Both paragraphs (a) and (b) require a statement of interest or right rather than the "claim" formerly required. The new wording permits parallel drafting, and facilitates cross-references in other rules. The substantive nature of the statement

remains the same as the former claim. The requirements of (a) and (b) are, however, different in some respects.

In a forfeiture proceeding governed by paragraph (a), a statement must be filed by a person who asserts an interest in or a right against the property involved. This category includes every right against the property, such as a lien, whether or not it establishes ownership or a right to possession. In determining who has an interest in or a right against property, courts may continue to rely on precedents that have developed the meaning of "claims" or "claimants" for the purpose of civil forfeiture proceedings.

In an admiralty and maritime proceeding governed by paragraph (b), a statement is filed only by a person claiming a right of possession or ownership. Other claims against the property are advanced by intervention under Civil Rule 24, as it may be supplemented by local admiralty rules. The reference to ownership includes every interest that qualifies as ownership under domestic or foreign law. If an ownership interest is asserted, it makes no difference whether its character is legal, equitable, or something else.

Paragraph (a) provides more time than paragraph (b) for filing a statement. Admiralty and maritime in rem proceedings often present special needs for prompt action that do not commonly arise in forfeiture proceedings.

Paragraphs (a) and (b) do not limit the right to make a restricted appearance under Rule E(8).

2002 Amendment

Rule C(3) is amended to reflect the provisions of 18 U.S.C. § 985, enacted by the Civil Asset Forfeiture Reform Act of 2000, 114 Stat. 202, 214–215. Section 985 provides, subject to enumerated exceptions, that real property that is the subject of a civil forfeiture action is not to be seized until an order of forfeiture is entered. A civil forfeiture action is initiated by filing a complaint, posting notice, and serving notice on the property owner. The summons and arrest procedure is no longer appropriate.

Rule C(6)(a)(i)(A) is amended to adopt the provision enacted by 18 U.S.C. § 983(a)(4)(A), shortly before Rule C(6)(a)(i)(A) took effect, that sets the time for filing a verified statement as 30 days rather than 20 days, and that sets the first alternative event for measuring the 30 days as the date of service of the Government's complaint.

Rule C(6)(a)(iii) is amended to give notice of the provision enacted by 18 U.S.C. § 983(a)(4)(B) that requires that the answer in a forfeiture proceeding be filed within 20 days. Without this notice, unwary litigants might rely on the provision of Rule 5(d) that allows a reasonable time for filing after service.

Rule C(6)(b)(iv) is amended to change the requirement that an answer be filed within 20 days to a requirement that it be served within 20 days. Service is the ordinary requirement, as in Rule 12(a). Rule 5(d) requires filing within a reasonable time after service.

Changes Made After Publication and Comment No changes have been made since publication.

2005 Amendment

Rule C(6)(b)(i)(A) is amended to delete the reference to a time 10 days after completed publication under Rule C(4). This change corrects an oversight in the amendments made in 2000. Rule C(4) requires publication of notice only if the property that is the subject of the action is not released within 10 days after execution of process. Execution of process will always be earlier than publication.

2006 Amendment

Rule C is amended to reflect the adoption of Rule G to govern procedure in civil forfeiture actions.

2008 Amendment

Supplemental Rule C(6)(a)(i) is amended to correct an inadvertent omission in the 2006 amendment to Rule C. The amendment is technical and stylistic in nature. No substantive change is intended.

2009 Amendment

The times set in the former rule at 10 or 20 days have been revised to 14 or 21 days. See the Note to Rule 6.

Rule D.   Possessory, Petitory, and Partition Actions

In all actions for possession, partition, and to try title maintainable according to the course of the admiralty practice with respect to a vessel, in all actions so maintainable with respect to the possession of cargo or other maritime property, and in all actions by one or more part owners against the others to obtain security for the return of the vessel from any voyage undertaken without their consent, or by one or more part owners against the others to obtain possession of the vessel for any voyage on giving security for its safe return, the process shall be by a warrant of arrest of the vessel, cargo, or other property, and by notice in the manner provided by Rule B(2) to the adverse party or parties.

(Added Feb. 28, 1966, eff. July 1, 1966.)

ADVISORY COMMITTEE NOTES

1966 Adoption

This carries forward the substance of Admiralty Rule 19.

Rule 19 provided the remedy of arrest in controversies involving title and possession in general. See *The Tilton*, 23 Fed.Cas.1277 (No. 14,054) (C.C.D.Mass.1830). In addition it provided that remedy in controversies between co-owners respecting the employment of a vessel. It did not deal comprehensively with controversies between co-owners, omitting the remedy of partition. Presumably the omission is traceable to the fact that, when the rules were originally promulgated, concepts of substantive law (sometimes stated as concepts of jurisdiction) denied the remedy of partition except where the parties in disagreement were the owners of equal shares. See *The Steamboat Orleans*, 36 U.S. (11 Pet.) 175 (1837). The Supreme Court has now removed any doubt as to the jurisdiction of the district courts to partition a vessel, and has held in addition that no fixed principle of federal admiralty law limits the remedy to the case of equal shares. *Madruga v. Superior Court*, 346 U.S. 556 (1954). It is therefore appropriate to include a reference to partition in the rule.

Rule E.   Actions In Rem and Quasi In Rem: General Provisions

(1) Applicability. Except as otherwise provided, this rule applies to actions in personam with process of maritime attachment and garnishment, actions in rem, and petitory, possessory, and partition actions, supplementing Rules B, C, and D.

(2) Complaint; Security.

(a) Complaint. In actions to which this rule is applicable the complaint shall state the circumstances from which the claim arises with such particularity that the defendant or claimant will be able, without moving for a more definite statement, to commence an investigation of the facts and to frame a responsive pleading.

(b) Security for Costs. Subject to the provisions of Rule 54(d) and of relevant statutes, the court may, on the filing of the complaint or on the appearance of any defendant, claimant, or any other party, or at any later time, require the plaintiff, defendant, claimant, or other party to give security, or additional security, in such sum as the court shall direct to pay all costs and expenses that shall be awarded against the party by any interlocutory order or by the final judgment, or on appeal by any appellate court.

(3) Process.

(a) In admiralty and maritime proceedings process in rem or of maritime attachment and garnishment may be served only within the district.

(b) Issuance and Delivery. Issuance and delivery of process in rem, or of maritime attachment and garnishment, shall be held in abeyance if the plaintiff so requests.

(4) Execution of Process; Marshal's Return; Custody of Property; Procedures for Release.

(a) In General. Upon issuance and delivery of the process, or, in the case of summons with process of attachment and garnishment, when it appears that the defendant cannot be found within the district, the marshal or other person or organization having a warrant shall forthwith execute the process in accordance with this subdivision (4), making due and prompt return.

(b) Tangible Property. If tangible property is to be attached or arrested, the marshal or other person or organization having the warrant shall take it into the marshal's possession for safe custody. If the character or situation of the property is such that the taking of actual possession is impracticable, the marshal or other person executing the process shall affix a copy thereof to the property in a conspicuous place and leave a copy of the complaint and process with the person having possession or the person's agent. In furtherance of the marshal's custody of any vessel the marshal is authorized to make a

written request to the collector of customs not to grant clearance to such vessel until notified by the marshal or deputy marshal or by the clerk that the vessel has been released in accordance with these rules.

(c) Intangible Property. If intangible property is to be attached or arrested the marshal or other person or organization having the warrant shall execute the process by leaving with the garnishee or other obligor a copy of the complaint and process requiring the garnishee or other obligor to answer as provided in Rules B(3)(a) and C(6); or the marshal may accept for payment into the registry of the court the amount owed to the extent of the amount claimed by the plaintiff with interest and costs, in which event the garnishee or other obligor shall not be required to answer unless alias process shall be served.

(d) Directions With Respect to Property in Custody. The marshal or other person or organization having the warrant may at any time apply to the court for directions with respect to property that has been attached or arrested, and shall give notice of such application to any or all of the parties as the court may direct.

(e) Expenses of Seizing and Keeping Property; Deposit. These rules do not alter the provisions of Title 28, U.S.C., § 1921, as amended, relative to the expenses of seizing and keeping property attached or arrested and to the requirement of deposits to cover such expenses.

(f) Procedure for Release From Arrest or Attachment. Whenever property is arrested or attached, any person claiming an interest in it shall be entitled to a prompt hearing at which the plaintiff shall be required to show why the arrest or attachment should not be vacated or other relief granted consistent with these rules. This subdivision shall have no application to suits for seamen's wages when process is issued upon a certification of sufficient cause filed pursuant to Title 46, U.S.C. §§ 603 and 604 [2] or to actions by the United States for forfeitures for violation of any statute of the United States.

(5) Release of Property.

(a) Special Bond. Whenever process of maritime attachment and garnishment or process in rem is issued the execution of such process shall be stayed, or the property released, on the giving of security, to be approved by the court or clerk, or by stipulation of the parties, conditioned to answer the judgment of the court or of any appellate court. The parties may stipulate the amount and nature of such security. In the event of the inability or refusal of the parties so to stipulate the court shall fix the principal sum of the bond or stipulation at an amount sufficient to cover the amount of the plaintiff's claim

fairly stated with accrued interest and costs; but the principal sum shall in no event exceed (i) twice the amount of the plaintiff's claim or (ii) the value of the property on due appraisement, whichever is smaller. The bond or stipulation shall be conditioned for the payment of the principal sum and interest thereon at 6 per cent per annum.

(b) General Bond. The owner of any vessel may file a general bond or stipulation, with sufficient surety, to be approved by the court, conditioned to answer the judgment of such court in all or any actions that may be brought thereafter in such court in which the vessel is attached or arrested. Thereupon the execution of all such process against such vessel shall be stayed so long as the amount secured by such bond or stipulation is at least double the aggregate amount claimed by plaintiffs in all actions begun and pending in which such vessel has been attached or arrested. Judgments and remedies may be had on such bond or stipulation as if a special bond or stipulation had been filed in each of such actions. The district court may make necessary orders to carry this rule into effect, particularly as to the giving of proper notice of any action against or attachment of a vessel for which a general bond has been filed. Such bond or stipulation shall be indorsed by the clerk with a minute of the actions wherein process is so stayed. Further security may be required by the court at any time.

If a special bond or stipulation is given in a particular case, the liability on the general bond or stipulation shall cease as to that case.

(c) Release by Consent or Stipulation; Order of Court or Clerk; Costs. Any vessel, cargo, or other property in the custody of the marshal or other person or organization having the warrant may be released forthwith upon the marshal's acceptance and approval of a stipulation, bond, or other security, signed by the party on whose behalf the property is detained or the party's attorney and expressly authorizing such release, if all costs and charges of the court and its officers shall have first been paid. Otherwise no property in the custody of the marshal, other person or organization having the warrant, or other officer of the court shall be released without an order of the court; but such order may be entered as of course by the clerk, upon the giving of approved security as provided by law and these rules, or upon the dismissal or discontinuance of the action; but the marshal or other person or organization having the warrant shall not deliver any property so released until the costs and charges of the officers of the court shall first have been paid.

(d) Possessory, Petitory, and Partition Actions. The foregoing provisions of this subdivision (5) do not apply to petitory, possessory, and partition actions. In such cases the property arrested shall be has enacted a number of jurisdictional and venue statutes for forfeiture and criminal matters that in some circumstances permit a court to exercise authority over property outside the district. 28 U.S.C. § 1355(b)(1) allows a forfeiture action in the district where an act or omission giving rise to forfeiture occurred, or in any other district where venue is established by § 1395 or by any other statute. Section 1355(b)(2) allows an action to be brought as provided in (b)(1) or in the United States District Court for the District of Columbia when the forfeiture property is located in a foreign country or has been seized by authority of a foreign government. Section 1355(d) allows a court with jurisdiction under § 1355(b) to cause service in any other district of process required to bring the forfeiture property before the court. Section 1395 establishes venue of a civil proceeding for forfeiture in the district where the forfeiture accrues or the defendant is found; in any district where the property is found; in any district into which the property is brought, if the property initially is outside any judicial district; or in any district where the vessel is arrested if the proceeding is an admiralty proceeding to forfeit a vessel. Section 1395(e) deals with a vessel or cargo entering a port of entry closed by the President, and transportation to or from a state or section declared to be in insurrection. 18 U.S.C. § 981(h) creates expanded jurisdiction and venue over property located elsewhere that is related to a criminal prosecution pending in the district. These amendments, and related amendments of Rule E(3), bring these Rules into step with the new statutes. No change is made as to admiralty and maritime proceedings that do not involve a forfeiture governed by one of the new statutes.

Subdivision (2) has been separated into lettered paragraphs to facilitate understanding.

Subdivision (3). Subdivision (3) has been rearranged and divided into lettered paragraphs to facilitate understanding.

Paragraph (b)(i) is amended to make it clear that any supplemental process addressed to a vessel or tangible property on board a vessel, as well as the original warrant, is to be served by the marshal.

Subdivision (4). Subdivision (4) has required that public notice state the time for filing an answer, but has not required that the notice set out the earlier time for filing a statement of interest or claim. The amendment requires that both times be stated.

A new provision is added, allowing termination of publication if the property is released more than 10 days after execution but before publication is completed. Termination will save money, and also will reduce the risk of confusion as to the status of the property.

Subdivision (6). Subdivision (6) has applied a single set of undifferentiated provisions to civil forfeiture proceedings and to in rem admiralty proceedings. Because some differences in procedure are desirable, these proceedings are separated by adopting a new paragraph (a) for civil forfeiture proceedings and recasting the present rule as paragraph (b) for in rem admiralty proceedings. The provision for interrogatories and answers is carried forward as paragraph (c). Although this established procedure for serving interrogatories with the complaint departs from the general provisions of Civil Rule 26(d), the special needs of expedition that often arise in admiralty justify continuing the practice.

Both paragraphs (a) and (b) require a statement of interest or right rather than the "claim" formerly required. The new wording permits parallel drafting, and facilitates cross-references in other rules. The substantive nature of the statement

remains the same as the former claim. The requirements of (a) and (b) are, however, different in some respects.

In a forfeiture proceeding governed by paragraph (a), a statement must be filed by a person who asserts an interest in or a right against the property involved. This category includes every right against the property, such as a lien, whether or not it establishes ownership or a right to possession. In determining who has an interest in or a right against property, courts may continue to rely on precedents that have developed the meaning of "claims" or "claimants" for the purpose of civil forfeiture proceedings.

In an admiralty and maritime proceeding governed by paragraph (b), a statement is filed only by a person claiming a right of possession or ownership. Other claims against the property are advanced by intervention under Civil Rule 24, as it may be supplemented by local admiralty rules. The reference to ownership includes every interest that qualifies as ownership under domestic or foreign law. If an ownership interest is asserted, it makes no difference whether its character is legal, equitable, or something else.

Paragraph (a) provides more time than paragraph (b) for filing a statement. Admiralty and maritime in rem proceedings often present special needs for prompt action that do not commonly arise in forfeiture proceedings.

Paragraphs (a) and (b) do not limit the right to make a restricted appearance under Rule E(8).

2002 Amendment

Rule C(3) is amended to reflect the provisions of 18 U.S.C. § 985, enacted by the Civil Asset Forfeiture Reform Act of 2000, 114 Stat. 202, 214–215. Section 985 provides, subject to enumerated exceptions, that real property that is the subject of a civil forfeiture action is not to be seized until an order of forfeiture is entered. A civil forfeiture action is initiated by filing a complaint, posting notice, and serving notice on the property owner. The summons and arrest procedure is no longer appropriate.

Rule C(6)(a)(i)(A) is amended to adopt the provision enacted by 18 U.S.C. § 983(a)(4)(A), shortly before Rule C(6)(a)(i)(A) took effect, that sets the time for filing a verified statement as 30 days rather than 20 days, and that sets the first alternative event for measuring the 30 days as the date of service of the Government's complaint.

Rule C(6)(a)(iii) is amended to give notice of the provision enacted by 18 U.S.C. § 983(a)(4)(B) that requires that the answer in a forfeiture proceeding be filed within 20 days. Without this notice, unwary litigants might rely on the provision of Rule 5(d) that allows a reasonable time for filing after service.

Rule C(6)(b)(iv) is amended to change the requirement that an answer be filed within 20 days to a requirement that it be served within 20 days. Service is the ordinary requirement, as in Rule 12(a). Rule 5(d) requires filing within a reasonable time after service.

Changes Made After Publication and Comment No changes have been made since publication.

2005 Amendment

Rule C(6)(b)(i)(A) is amended to delete the reference to a time 10 days after completed publication under Rule C(4). This change corrects an oversight in the amendments made in 2000. Rule C(4) requires publication of notice only if the property that is the subject of the action is not released within 10 days after execution of process. Execution of process will always be earlier than publication.

2006 Amendment

Rule C is amended to reflect the adoption of Rule G to govern procedure in civil forfeiture actions.

2008 Amendment

Supplemental Rule C(6)(a)(i) is amended to correct an inadvertent omission in the 2006 amendment to Rule C. The amendment is technical and stylistic in nature. No substantive change is intended.

2009 Amendment

The times set in the former rule at 10 or 20 days have been revised to 14 or 21 days. See the Note to Rule 6.

Rule D.   Possessory, Petitory, and Partition Actions

In all actions for possession, partition, and to try title maintainable according to the course of the admiralty practice with respect to a vessel, in all actions so maintainable with respect to the possession of cargo or other maritime property, and in all actions by one or more part owners against the others to obtain security for the return of the vessel from any voyage undertaken without their consent, or by one or more part owners against the others to obtain possession of the vessel for any voyage on giving security for its safe return, the process shall be by a warrant of arrest of the vessel, cargo, or other property, and by notice in the manner provided by Rule B(2) to the adverse party or parties.

(Added Feb. 28, 1966, eff. July 1, 1966.)

ADVISORY COMMITTEE NOTES

1966 Adoption

This carries forward the substance of Admiralty Rule 19.

Rule 19 provided the remedy of arrest in controversies involving title and possession in general. See *The Tilton,* 23 Fed.Cas.1277 (No. 14,054) (C.C.D.Mass.1830). In addition it provided that remedy in controversies between co-owners respecting the employment of a vessel. It did not deal comprehensively with controversies between co-owners, omitting the remedy of partition. Presumably the omission is traceable to the fact that, when the rules were originally promulgated, concepts of substantive law (sometimes stated as concepts of jurisdiction) denied the remedy of partition except where the parties in disagreement were the owners of equal shares. See *The Steamboat Orleans,* 36 U.S. (11 Pet.) 175 (1837). The Supreme Court has now removed any doubt as to the jurisdiction of the district courts to partition a vessel, and has held in addition that no fixed principle of federal admiralty law limits the remedy to the case of equal shares. *Madruga v. Superior Court,* 346 U.S. 556 (1954). It is therefore appropriate to include a reference to partition in the rule.

Rule E.   Actions In Rem and Quasi In Rem: General Provisions

(1) Applicability. Except as otherwise provided, this rule applies to actions in personam with process of maritime attachment and garnishment, actions in rem, and petitory, possessory, and partition actions, supplementing Rules B, C, and D.

(2) Complaint; Security.

  (a) Complaint. In actions to which this rule is applicable the complaint shall state the circumstances from which the claim arises with such particularity that the defendant or claimant will be able, without moving for a more definite statement, to commence an investigation of the facts and to frame a responsive pleading.

  (b) Security for Costs. Subject to the provisions of Rule 54(d) and of relevant statutes, the court may, on the filing of the complaint or on the appearance of any defendant, claimant, or any other party, or at any later time, require the plaintiff, defendant, claimant, or other party to give security, or additional security, in such sum as the court shall direct to pay all costs and expenses that shall be awarded against the party by any interlocutory order or by the final judgment, or on appeal by any appellate court.

(3) Process.

  (a) In admiralty and maritime proceedings process in rem or of maritime attachment and garnishment may be served only within the district.

  (b) Issuance and Delivery. Issuance and delivery of process in rem, or of maritime attachment and garnishment, shall be held in abeyance if the plaintiff so requests.

(4) Execution of Process; Marshal's Return; Custody of Property; Procedures for Release.

  (a) In General. Upon issuance and delivery of the process, or, in the case of summons with process of attachment and garnishment, when it appears that the defendant cannot be found within the district, the marshal or other person or organization having a warrant shall forthwith execute the process in accordance with this subdivision (4), making due and prompt return.

  (b) Tangible Property. If tangible property is to be attached or arrested, the marshal or other person or organization having the warrant shall take it into the marshal's possession for safe custody. If the character or situation of the property is such that the taking of actual possession is impracticable, the marshal or other person executing the process shall affix a copy thereof to the property in a conspicuous place and leave a copy of the complaint and process with the person having possession or the person's agent. In furtherance of the marshal's custody of any vessel the marshal is authorized to make a written request to the collector of customs not to grant clearance to such vessel until notified by the marshal or deputy marshal or by the clerk that the vessel has been released in accordance with these rules.

(c) Intangible Property. If intangible property is to be attached or arrested the marshal or other person or organization having the warrant shall execute the process by leaving with the garnishee or other obligor a copy of the complaint and process requiring the garnishee or other obligor to answer as provided in Rules B(3)(a) and C(6); or the marshal may accept for payment into the registry of the court the amount owed to the extent of the amount claimed by the plaintiff with interest and costs, in which event the garnishee or other obligor shall not be required to answer unless alias process shall be served.

(d) Directions With Respect to Property in Custody. The marshal or other person or organization having the warrant may at any time apply to the court for directions with respect to property that has been attached or arrested, and shall give notice of such application to any or all of the parties as the court may direct.

(e) Expenses of Seizing and Keeping Property; Deposit. These rules do not alter the provisions of Title 28, U.S.C., § 1921, as amended, relative to the expenses of seizing and keeping property attached or arrested and to the requirement of deposits to cover such expenses.

(f) Procedure for Release From Arrest or Attachment. Whenever property is arrested or attached, any person claiming an interest in it shall be entitled to a prompt hearing at which the plaintiff shall be required to show why the arrest or attachment should not be vacated or other relief granted consistent with these rules. This subdivision shall have no application to suits for seamen's wages when process is issued upon a certification of sufficient cause filed pursuant to Title 46, U.S.C. §§ 603 and 604 [2] or to actions by the United States for forfeitures for violation of any statute of the United States.

(5) Release of Property.

(a) Special Bond. Whenever process of maritime attachment and garnishment or process in rem is issued the execution of such process shall be stayed, or the property released, on the giving of security, to be approved by the court or clerk, or by stipulation of the parties, conditioned to answer the judgment of the court or of any appellate court. The parties may stipulate the amount and nature of such security. In the event of the inability or refusal of the parties so to stipulate the court shall fix the principal sum of the bond or stipulation at an amount sufficient to cover the amount of the plaintiff's claim

fairly stated with accrued interest and costs; but the principal sum shall in no event exceed (i) twice the amount of the plaintiff's claim or (ii) the value of the property on due appraisement, whichever is smaller. The bond or stipulation shall be conditioned for the payment of the principal sum and interest thereon at 6 per cent per annum.

(b) General Bond. The owner of any vessel may file a general bond or stipulation, with sufficient surety, to be approved by the court, conditioned to answer the judgment of such court in all or any actions that may be brought thereafter in such court in which the vessel is attached or arrested. Thereupon the execution of all such process against such vessel shall be stayed so long as the amount secured by such bond or stipulation is at least double the aggregate amount claimed by plaintiffs in all actions begun and pending in which such vessel has been attached or arrested. Judgments and remedies may be had on such bond or stipulation as if a special bond or stipulation had been filed in each of such actions. The district court may make necessary orders to carry this rule into effect, particularly as to the giving of proper notice of any action against or attachment of a vessel for which a general bond has been filed. Such bond or stipulation shall be indorsed by the clerk with a minute of the actions wherein process is so stayed. Further security may be required by the court at any time.

If a special bond or stipulation is given in a particular case, the liability on the general bond or stipulation shall cease as to that case.

(c) Release by Consent or Stipulation; Order of Court or Clerk; Costs. Any vessel, cargo, or other property in the custody of the marshal or other person or organization having the warrant may be released forthwith upon the marshal's acceptance and approval of a stipulation, bond, or other security, signed by the party on whose behalf the property is detained or the party's attorney and expressly authorizing such release, if all costs and charges of the court and its officers shall have first been paid. Otherwise no property in the custody of the marshal, other person or organization having the warrant, or other officer of the court shall be released without an order of the court; but such order may be entered as of course by the clerk, upon the giving of approved security as provided by law and these rules, or upon the dismissal or discontinuance of the action; but the marshal or other person or organization having the warrant shall not deliver any property so released until the costs and charges of the officers of the court shall first have been paid.

(d) Possessory, Petitory, and Partition Actions. The foregoing provisions of this subdivision (5) do not apply to petitory, possessory, and partition actions. In such cases the property arrested shall be released only by order of the court, on such terms and conditions and on the giving of such security as the court may require.

(6) Reduction or Impairment of Security. Whenever security is taken the court may, on motion and hearing, for good cause shown, reduce the amount of security given; and if the surety shall be or become insufficient, new or additional sureties may be required on motion and hearing.

(7) Security on Counterclaim.

(a) When a person who has given security for damages in the original action asserts a counterclaim that arises from the transaction or occurrence that is the subject of the original action, a plaintiff for whose benefit the security has been given must give security for damages demanded in the counterclaim unless the court, for cause shown, directs otherwise. Proceedings on the original claim must be stayed until this security is given unless the court directs otherwise.

(b) The plaintiff is required to give security under Rule E(7)(a) when the United States or its corporate instrumentality counterclaims and would have been required to give security to respond in damages if a private party but is relieved by law from giving security.

(8) Restricted Appearance. An appearance to defend against an admiralty and maritime claim with respect to which there has issued process in rem, or process of attachment and garnishment, may be expressly restricted to the defense of such claim, and in that event is not an appearance for the purposes of any other claim with respect to which such process is not available or has not been served.

(9) Disposition of Property; Sales.

(a) Interlocutory Sales; Delivery.

(i) On application of a party, the marshal, or other person having custody of the property, the court may order all or part of the property sold— with the sales proceeds, or as much of them as will satisfy the judgment, paid into court to await further orders of the court—if:

(A) the attached or arrested property is perishable, or liable to deterioration, decay, or injury by being detained in custody pending the action;

(B) the expense of keeping the property is excessive or disproportionate; or

(C) there is an unreasonable delay in securing release of the property.

(ii) In the circumstances described in Rule E(9)(a)(i), the court, on motion by a defendant or a person filing a statement of interest or right under Rule C(6), may order that the property, rather than being sold, be delivered to the movant upon giving security under these rules.

(b) Sales; Proceeds. All sales of property shall be made by the marshal or a deputy marshal, or by other person or organization having the warrant, or by any other person assigned by the court where the marshal or other person or organization having the warrant is a party in interest; and the proceeds of sale shall be forthwith paid into the registry of the court to be disposed of according to law.

(10) Preservation of Property. When the owner or another person remains in possession of property attached or arrested under the provisions of Rule E(4)(b) that permit execution of process without taking actual possession, the court, on a party's motion or on its own, may enter any order necessary to preserve the property and to prevent its removal.

(Added Feb. 28, 1966, eff. July 1, 1966; amended Apr. 29, 1985, eff. Aug. 1, 1985; Mar. 2, 1987, eff. Aug. 1, 1987; Apr. 30, 1991, eff. Dec. 1, 1991; Apr. 17, 2000, eff. Dec. 1, 2000; Apr. 12, 2006, eff. Dec. 1, 2006.)

2 Repealed by Pub. L. 98–89, § 4(b), Aug. 26, 1983, 97 Stat. 600, section 1 of which enacted Title 46, Shipping.

ADVISORY COMMITTEE NOTES
1966 Adoption

Subdivisions (1), (2).

Adapted from Admiralty Rule 24. The rule is based on the assumption that there is no more need for security for costs in maritime personal actions than in civil cases generally, but that there is reason to retain the requirement for actions in which property is seized. As to proceedings for limitation of liability see Rule F(1).

Subdivision (3).

The Advisory Committee has concluded for practical reasons that process requiring seizure of property should continue to be served only within the geographical limits of the district. Compare Rule B(1), continuing the condition that process of attachment and garnishment may be served only if the defendant is not found within the district.

The provisions of Admiralty Rule 1 concerning the persons by whom process is to be served will be superseded by FRCP 4(c).

Subdivision (4).

This rule is intended to preserve the provisions of Admiralty Rules 10 and 36 relating to execution of process, custody of property seized by the marshal, and the marshal's return. It is also designed to make express provision for matters not heretofore covered.

The provision relating to clearance in subdivision (b) is suggested by Admiralty Rule 44 of the District of Maryland.

Subdivision (d) is suggested by English Rule 12, Order 75.

28 U.S.C., § 1921 as amended in 1962 contains detailed provisions relating to the expenses of seizing and preserving property attached or arrested.

Subdivision (5).

In addition to Admiralty Rule 11 (see Rule E(9)), the release of property seized on process of attachment or in rem was dealt with by Admiralty Rules 5, 6, 12, and 57, and 28 U.S.C., § 2464 (formerly Rev.Stat. § 941). The rule consolidates these provisions and makes them uniformly applicable to attachment and garnishment and actions in rem.

The rule restates the substance of Admiralty Rule 5. Admiralty Rule 12 dealt only with ships arrested on in rem process. Since the same ground appears to be covered more generally by 28 U.S.C., § 2464, the subject matter of Rule 12 is omitted. The substance of Admiralty Rule 57 is retained. 28 U.S.C., § 2464 is incorporated with changes of terminology, and with a substantial change as to the amount of the bond. See 2 Benedict 395 n. 1a [Reference is to the 6th Edition of Benedict on Admiralty and not to the current 7th Edition.] *The Lotosland*, 2 F.Supp. 42 (S.D.N.Y.1933). The provision for general bond is enlarged to include the contingency of attachment as well as arrest of the vessel.

Subdivision (6).

Adapted from Admiralty Rule 8.

Subdivision (7).

Derived from Admiralty Rule 50.

Title 46, U.S.C., § 783 extends the principle of Rule 50 to the Government when sued under the Public Vessels Act, presumably on the theory that the credit of the Government is the equivalent of the best security. The rule adopts this principle and extends it to all cases in which the Government is defendant although the Suits in Admiralty Act contains no parallel provisions.

Subdivision (8).

Under the liberal joinder provisions of unified rules the plaintiff will be enabled to join with maritime actions in rem, or maritime actions in personam with process of attachment and garnishment, claims with respect to which such process is not available, including nonmaritime claims. Unification should not, however, have the result that, in order to defend against an admiralty and maritime claim with respect to which process in rem or quasi in rem has been served, the claimant or defendant must subject himself personally to the jurisdiction of the court with reference to other claims with respect to which such process is not available or has not been served, especially when such other claims are nonmaritime. So far as attachment and garnishment are concerned this principle holds true whether process is issued according to admiralty tradition and the Supplemental Rules or according to Rule 4(e) as incorporated by Rule B(1).

A similar problem may arise with respect to civil actions other than admiralty and maritime claims within the meaning of Rule 9(h). That is to say, in an ordinary civil action, whether maritime or not, there may be joined in one action claims with respect to which process of attachment and garnishment is available under state law and Rule 4(e) and claims with respect to which such process is not available or has not been served. The general Rules of Civil Procedure do not specify whether an appearance in such cases to defend the claim with respect to which process of attachment and garnishment has issued is an appearance for the purposes of the other claims. In that context the question has been considered best left to case-by-case development. Where admiralty and maritime claims within the meaning of Rule 9(h) are concerned, however, it seems important to include a specific provision to avoid an unfortunate and unintended effect of unification. No inferences whatever as to the effect of such an appearance in an ordinary civil action should be drawn from the specific provision here and the absence of such a provision in the general Rules.

Subdivision (9).

Adapted from Admiralty Rules 11, 12, and 40. Subdivision (a) is necessary because of various provisions as to disposition of property in forfeiture proceedings. In addition to particular statutes, note the provisions of 28 U.S.C., §§ 2461–65.

The provision of Admiralty Rule 12 relating to unreasonable delay was limited to ships but should have broader application. See 2 Benedict 404 [Reference is to the 6th Edition of Benedict on Admiralty and not to the current 7th Edition]. Similarly, both Rules 11 and 12 were limited to actions in rem, but should equally apply to attached property.

1985 Amendment

Rule E(4)(f) makes available the type of prompt post-seizure hearing in proceedings under Supplemental Rules B and C that the Supreme Court has called for in a number of cases arising in other contexts. See *North Georgia Finishing, Inc. v. Di-Chem, Inc.*, 419 U.S. 601 (1975); *Mitchell v. W.T. Grant Co.*, 416 U.S. 600 (1974). Although post-attachment and post-arrest hearings always have been available on motion, an explicit statement emphasizing promptness and elaborating the procedure has been lacking in the Supplemental Rules. Rule E(4)(f) is designed to satisfy the constitutional requirement of due process by guaranteeing to the shipowner a prompt post-seizure hearing at which he can attack the complaint, the arrest, the security demanded, or any other alleged deficiency in the proceedings. The amendment also is intended to eliminate the previously disparate treatment under local rules of defendants whose property has been seized pursuant to Supplemental Rules B and C.

The new Rule E(4)(f) is based on a proposal by the Maritime Law Association of the United States and on local admiralty rules in the Eastern, Northern, and Southern Districts of New York. E.D.N.Y. Local Rule 13; N.D.N.Y. Local Rule 13; S.D.N.Y. Local Rule 12. Similar provisions have been adopted by other maritime districts. E.g., N.D.Calif. Local Rule 603.4; W.D.La. Local Admiralty Rule 21. Rule E(4)(f) will provide uniformity in practice and reduce constitutional uncertainties.

Rule E(4)(f) is triggered by the defendant or any other person with an interest in the property seized. Upon an oral or written application similar to that used in seeking a temporary restraining order, see Rule 65(b), the court is required to hold a hearing as promptly as possible to determine whether to allow the arrest or attachment to stand. The plaintiff has the burden of showing why the seizure should not be vacated. The hearing also may determine the amount of security to be granted or the propriety of imposing counter-security to protect the defendant from an improper seizure.

The foregoing requirements for prior court review or proof of exigent circumstances do not apply to actions by the United States for forfeitures for federal statutory violations. In such actions a prompt hearing is not constitutionally required, *United States v. Eight Thousand Eight Hundred and Fifty Dollars*, 103 S.Ct. 2005 (1983); *Calero-Toledo v. Pearson Yacht Leasing Co.*, 416 U.S. 663 (1974), and could prejudice the government in its prosecution of the claimants as defendants in parallel criminal proceedings since the forfeiture hearing could be misused by the defendants to obtain by way of civil discovery information to which they would not otherwise be entitled and subject the government and the courts to the unnecessary burden and expense of two hearings rather than one.

1987 Amendment

The amendments are technical. No substantive change is intended.

1991 Amendment

These amendments are designed to conform this rule to Fed.R.Civ.P. 4, as amended. They are intended to relieve the Marshals Service of the burden of using its limited personnel and facilities for execution of process in routine circumstances. Doing so may involve a contractual arrangement with a person or organization retained by the government to perform these services, or the use of other government officers and employees, or the special appointment by the court of persons available to perform suitably.

2000 Amendment

Style changes have been made throughout the revised portions of Rule E. Several changes of meaning have been made as well.

Subdivision (3). Subdivision (3) is amended to reflect the distinction drawn in Rule C(2)(c) and (d). Service in an admiralty or maritime proceeding still must be made within the district, as reflected in Rule C(2)(c), while service in forfeiture proceedings may be made outside the district when authorized by statute, as reflected in Rule C(2)(d).

Subdivision (7). Subdivision (7)(a) is amended to make it clear that a plaintiff need give security to meet a counterclaim only when the counterclaim is asserted by a person who has given security to respond in damages in the original action.

Subdivision (8). Subdivision (8) is amended to reflect the change in Rule B(1)(e) that deletes the former provision incorporating state quasi-in-rem jurisdiction. A restricted appearance is not appropriate when state law is invoked only for security under Civil Rule 64, not as a basis of quasi-in-rem jurisdiction. But if state law allows a special, limited, or restricted appearance as an incident of the remedy adopted from state law, the state practice applies through Rule 64 "in the manner provided by" state law.

Subdivision (9). Subdivision 9(b)(ii) is amended to reflect the change in Rule C(6) that substitutes a statement of interest or right for a claim.

Subdivision (10). Subdivision 10 is new. It makes clear the authority of the court to preserve and to prevent removal of attached or arrested property that remains in the possession of the owner or other person under Rule E(4)(b).

2006 Amendment

Rule E is amended to reflect the adoption of Rule G to govern procedure in civil forfeiture actions.

HISTORICAL NOTES

References in Text

Sections 603 and 604 of Title 46, referred to in subd. (4)(f), were repealed by Pub.L. 98–89, § 4(b), Aug. 26, 1983, 97 Stat. 600, section 1 of which enacted Title 46, Shipping.

Rule F. Limitation of Liability

(1) Time for Filing Complaint; Security. Not later than six months after receipt of a claim in writing, any vessel owner may file a complaint in the appropriate district court, as provided in subdivision (9) of this rule, for limitation of liability pursuant to statute. The owner (a) shall deposit with the court, for the benefit of claimants, a sum equal to the amount or value of the owner's interest in the vessel and pending freight, or approved security therefor, and in addition such sums, or approved security therefor, as the court may from time to time fix as necessary to carry out the provisions of the statutes as amended; or (b) at the owner's option shall transfer to a trustee to be appointed by the court, for the benefit of claimants, the owner's interest in the vessel and pending freight, together with such sums, or approved security therefor, as the court may from time to time fix as necessary to carry out the provisions of the statutes as amended. The plaintiff shall also give security for costs and, if the plaintiff elects to give security, for interest at the rate of 6 percent per annum from the date of the security.

(2) Complaint. The complaint shall set forth the facts on the basis of which the right to limit liability is asserted and all facts necessary to enable the court to determine the amount to which the owner's liability shall be limited. The complaint may demand exoneration from as well as limitation of liability. It shall state the voyage if any, on which the demands sought to be limited arose, with the date and place of its termination; the amount of all demands including all unsatisfied liens or claims of lien, in contract or in tort or otherwise, arising on that voyage, so far as known to the plaintiff, and what actions and proceedings, if any, are pending thereon; whether the vessel was damaged, lost, or abandoned, and, if so, when and where; the value of the vessel at the close of the voyage or, in case of wreck, the value of her wreckage, strippings, or proceeds, if any, and where and in whose possession they are; and the amount of any pending freight recovered or recoverable. If the plaintiff elects to transfer the plaintiff's interest in the vessel to a trustee, the complaint must further show any prior paramount liens thereon, and what voyages or trips, if any, she has made since the voyage or trip on which the claims sought to be limited arose, and any existing liens arising upon any such subsequent voyage or trip, with the amounts and causes thereof, and the names and addresses of the lienors, so far as known; and whether the vessel sustained any injury upon or by reason of such subsequent voyage or trip.

(3) Claims Against Owner; Injunction. Upon compliance by the owner with the requirements of subdivision (1) of this rule all claims and proceedings against the owner or the owner's property with respect to the matter in question shall cease. On application of the plaintiff the court shall enjoin the further prosecution of any action or proceeding against the plaintiff or the plaintiff's property with respect to any claim subject to limitation in the action.

(4) Notice to Claimants. Upon the owner's compliance with subdivision (1) of this rule the court shall issue a notice to all persons asserting claims with respect to which the complaint seeks limitation, admonishing them to file their respective claims with the clerk of the court and to serve on the attorneys for the plaintiff a copy thereof on or before a date to be named in the notice. The date so fixed shall not be less than 30 days after issuance of the notice. For cause shown, the court may enlarge the time within which claims may be filed. The notice shall be published in such newspaper or newspapers as the court may direct once a week for four successive weeks prior to the date fixed for the filing of claims. The plaintiff not later than the day of second publication shall also mail a copy of the notice to every person known to have made any claim against the vessel or the plaintiff arising out of the voyage or trip on which the claims sought to be limited arose. In cases involving death a copy of such notice shall be mailed to the decedent at the decedent's last known address, and also to any person who shall be known to have made any claim on account of such death.

(5) Claims and Answer. Claims shall be filed and served on or before the date specified in the notice provided for in subdivision (4) of this rule. Each claim shall specify the facts upon which the claimant relies in support of the claim, the items thereof, and the dates on which the same accrued. If a claimant desires to contest either the right to exoneration from or the right to limitation of liability the claimant shall file and serve an answer to the complaint unless the claim has included an answer.

(6) Information to be Given Claimants. Within 30 days after the date specified in the notice for filing claims, or within such time as the court thereafter may allow, the plaintiff shall mail to the attorney for each claimant (or if the claimant has no attorney to the claimant) a list setting forth (a) the name of each claimant, (b) the name and address of the claimant's attorney (if the claimant is known to have one), (c) the nature of the claim, i.e., whether property loss, property damage, death, personal injury etc., and (d) the amount thereof.

(7) Insufficiency of Fund or Security. Any claimant may by motion demand that the funds deposited in court or the security given by the plaintiff be increased on the ground that they are less than the value of the plaintiff's interest in the vessel and pending freight. Thereupon the court shall cause due appraisement to be made of the value of the plaintiff's interest in the vessel and pending freight; and if the court finds that the deposit or security is either insufficient or excessive it shall order its increase or reduction. In like manner any claimant may demand that the deposit or security be increased on the ground that it is insufficient to carry out the provisions of the statutes relating to claims in respect of loss of life or bodily injury; and, after notice and hearing, the court may similarly order that the deposit or security be increased or reduced.

(8) Objections to Claims: Distribution of Fund. Any interested party may question or controvert any claim without filing an objection thereto. Upon determination of liability the fund deposited or secured, or the proceeds of the vessel and pending freight, shall be divided pro rata, subject to all relevant provisions of law, among the several claimants in proportion to the amounts of their respective claims, duly proved, saving, however, to all parties any priority to which they may be legally entitled.

(9) Venue; Transfer. The complaint shall be filed in any district in which the vessel has been attached or arrested to answer for any claim with respect to which the plaintiff seeks to limit liability; or, if the vessel has not been attached or arrested, then in any district in which the owner has been sued with respect to any such claim. When the vessel has not been attached or arrested to answer the matters aforesaid, and suit has not been commenced against the owner, the proceedings may be had in the district in which the vessel may be, but if the vessel is not within any district and no suit has been commenced in any district, then the complaint may be filed in any district. For the convenience of parties and witnesses, in the interest of justice, the court may transfer the action to any district; if venue is wrongly laid the court shall dismiss or, if it be in the interest of justice, transfer the action to any district in which it could have been brought. If the vessel shall have been sold, the proceeds shall represent the vessel for the purposes of these rules.

(Added Feb. 28, 1966, eff. July 1, 1966; amended Mar. 2, 1987, eff. Aug. 1, 1987.)

ADVISORY COMMITTEE NOTES

1966 Adoption

Subdivision (1).

The amendments of 1936 to the Limitation Act superseded to some extent the provisions of Admiralty Rule 51, especially with respect to the time of filing the complaint and with respect to security. The rule here incorporates in substance the 1936 amendment of the Act (46 U.S.C., § 185) with a slight modification to make it clear that the complaint may be filed at any time not later than six months after a claim has been lodged with the owner.

Subdivision (2).

Derived from Admiralty Rules 51 and 53.

Subdivision (3).

This is derived from the last sentence of 46 U.S.C. § 185 and the last paragraph of Admiralty Rule 51.

Subdivision (4).

Derived from Admiralty Rule 51.

Subdivision (5).

Derived from Admiralty Rules 52 and 53.

Subdivision (6).

Derived from Admiralty Rule 52.

Subdivision (7).

Derived from Admiralty Rule 52 and 46 U.S.C., § 185. Subdivision (8).

Derived from Admiralty Rule 52. Subdivision (9).

Derived from Admiralty Rule 54. The provision for transfer is revised to conform closely to the language of 28 U.S.C. §§ 1404(a) and 1406(a), though it retains the existing rule's provision for transfer to any district for convenience. The revision also makes clear what has been doubted: that the court may transfer if venue is wrongly laid.

1987 Amendment

The amendments are technical. No substantive change is intended.

Rule G.   Forfeiture Actions In Rem

(1) Scope. This rule governs a forfeiture action in rem arising from a federal statute. To the extent that this rule does not address an issue, Supplemental Rules C and E and the Federal Rules of Civil Procedure also apply.

(2) Complaint. The complaint must:

(a) be verified;

(b) state the grounds for subject-matter jurisdiction, in rem jurisdiction over the defendant property, and venue;

(c) describe the property with reasonable particularity;

(d) if the property is tangible, state its location when any seizure occurred and—if different—its location when the action is filed;

(e) identify the statute under which the forfeiture action is brought; and

(f) state sufficiently detailed facts to support a reasonable belief that the government will be able to meet its burden of proof at trial.

(3) Judicial Authorization and Process.

(a) **Real Property.** If the defendant is real property, the government must proceed under 18 U.S.C. § 985.

(b) **Other Property; Arrest Warrant.** If the defendant is not real property:

(i) the clerk must issue a warrant to arrest the property if it is in the government's possession, custody, or control;

(ii) the court—on finding probable cause—must issue a warrant to arrest the property if it is not in the government's possession, custody, or control and is not subject to a judicial restraining order; and

(iii) a warrant is not necessary if the property is subject to a judicial restraining order.

(c) **Execution of Process.**

(i) The warrant and any supplemental process must be delivered to a person or organization authorized to execute it, who may be: (A) a marshal or any other United States officer or employee; (B) someone under contract with the United States; or (C) someone specially appointed by the court for that purpose.

(ii) The authorized person or organization must execute the warrant and any supplemental process on property in the United States as soon as practicable unless:

(A) the property is in the government's possession, custody, or control; or

(B) the court orders a different time when the complaint is under seal, the action is stayed before the warrant and supplemental process are executed, or the court finds other good cause.

(iii) The warrant and any supplemental process may be executed within the district or, when authorized by statute, outside the district.

(iv) If executing a warrant on property outside the United States is required, the warrant may be transmitted to an appropriate authority for serving process where the property is located.

(4) Notice.

(a) **Notice by Publication.**

(i) **When Publication Is Required.** A judgment of forfeiture may be entered only if the government has published notice of the action within a reasonable time after filing the complaint or at a time the court orders. But notice need not be published if:

(A) the defendant property is worth less than $1,000 and direct notice is sent under Rule G(4)(b) to every person the government can reasonably identify as a potential claimant; or

(B) the court finds that the cost of publication exceeds the property's value and that other means of notice would satisfy due process.

(ii) **Content of the Notice.** Unless the court orders otherwise, the notice must:

(A) describe the property with reasonable particularity;

(B) state the times under Rule G(5) to file a claim and to answer; and

(C) name the government attorney to be served with the claim and answer.

(iii) **Frequency of Publication.** Published notice must appear:

(A) once a week for three consecutive weeks; or

(B) only once if, before the action was filed, notice of nonjudicial forfeiture of the same property was published on an official internet government forfeiture site for at least 30 consecutive days, or in a newspaper of general circulation for three consecutive weeks in a district where publication is authorized under Rule G(4)(a)(iv).

(iv) Means of Publication. The government should select from the following options a means of publication reasonably calculated to notify potential claimants of the action:

(A) if the property is in the United States, publication in a newspaper generally circulated in the district where the action is filed, where the property was seized, or where property that was not seized is located;

(B) if the property is outside the United States, publication in a newspaper generally circulated in a district where the action is filed, in a newspaper generally circulated in the country where the property is located, or in legal notices published and generally circulated in the country where the property is located; or

(C) instead of (A) or (B), posting a notice on an official internet government forfeiture site for at least 30 consecutive days.

(b) Notice to Known Potential Claimants.

(i) Direct Notice Required. The government must send notice of the action and a copy of the complaint to any person who reasonably appears to be a potential claimant on the facts known to the government before the end of the time for filing a claim under Rule G(5)(a)(ii)(B).

(ii) Content of the Notice. The notice must state:

(A) the date when the notice is sent;

(B) a deadline for filing a claim, at least 35 days after the notice is sent;

(C) that an answer or a motion under Rule 12 must be filed no later than 21 days after filing the claim; and

(D) the name of the government attorney to be served with the claim and answer.

(iii) Sending Notice.

(A) The notice must be sent by means reasonably calculated to reach the potential claimant.

(B) Notice may be sent to the potential claimant or to the attorney representing the potential claimant with respect to the seizure of the property or in a related investigation, administrative forfeiture proceeding, or criminal case.

(C) Notice sent to a potential claimant who is incarcerated must be sent to the place of incarceration.

(D) Notice to a person arrested in connection with an offense giving rise to the forfeiture who is not incarcerated when notice is sent may be sent to the address that person last gave to the agency that arrested or released the person.

(E) Notice to a person from whom the property was seized who is not incarcerated when notice is sent may be sent to the last address that person gave to the agency that seized the property.

(iv) When Notice Is Sent. Notice by the following means is sent on the date when it is placed in the mail, delivered to a commercial carrier, or sent by electronic mail.

(v) Actual Notice. A potential claimant who had actual notice of a forfeiture action may not oppose or seek relief from forfeiture because of the government's failure to send the required notice.

(5) Responsive Pleadings.

(a) Filing a Claim.

(i) A person who asserts an interest in the defendant property may contest the forfeiture by filing a claim in the court where the action is pending. The claim must:

(A) identify the specific property claimed;

(B) identify the claimant and state the claimant's interest in the property;

(C) be signed by the claimant under penalty of perjury; and

(D) be served on the government attorney designated under Rule G(4)(a)(ii)(C) or (b)(ii)(D).

(ii) Unless the court for good cause sets a different time, the claim must be filed:

(A) by the time stated in a direct notice sent under Rule G(4)(b);

(B) if notice was published but direct notice was not sent to the claimant or the claimant's attorney, no later than 30 days after final publication of newspaper notice or legal notice under Rule G(4)(a) or no later than 60 days after the first day of publication on an official internet government forfeiture site; or

(C) if notice was not published and direct notice was not sent to the claimant or the claimant's attorney:

(1) if the property was in the government's possession, custody, or control when the complaint was filed, no later than 60 days after the filing, not counting any time when the complaint was under seal or when the action was stayed before execution of a warrant issued under Rule G(3)(b); or

(2) if the property was not in the government's possession, custody, or control when the complaint was filed, no later than 60 days after the government complied with 18 U.S.C. § 985(c) as to real property, or 60 days after process was executed on the property under Rule G(3).

(iii) A claim filed by a person asserting an interest as a bailee must identify the bailor, and if filed on the bailor's behalf must state the authority to do so.

(b) Answer. A claimant must serve and file an answer to the complaint or a motion under Rule 12 within 21 days after filing the claim. A claimant waives an objection to in rem jurisdiction or to venue if the objection is not made by motion or stated in the answer.

(6) Special Interrogatories.

(a) Time and Scope. The government may serve special interrogatories limited to the claimant's identity and relationship to the defendant property without the court's leave at any time after the claim is filed and before discovery is closed. But if the claimant serves a motion to dismiss the action, the government must serve the interrogatories within 21 days after the motion is served.

(b) Answers or Objections. Answers or objections to these interrogatories must be served within 21 days after the interrogatories are served.

(c) Government's Response Deferred. The government need not respond to a claimant's motion to dismiss the action under Rule G(8)(b) until 21 days after the claimant has answered these interrogatories.

(7) Preserving, Preventing Criminal Use, and Disposing of Property; Sales.

(a) Preserving and Preventing Criminal Use of Property. When the government does not have actual possession of the defendant property the court, on motion or on its own, may enter any order necessary to preserve the property, to prevent its removal or encumbrance, or to prevent its use in a criminal offense.

(b) Interlocutory Sale or Delivery.

(i) Order to Sell. On motion by a party or a person having custody of the property, the court may order all or part of the property sold if:

    (A) the property is perishable or at risk of deterioration, decay, or injury by being detained in custody pending the action;

    (B) the expense of keeping the property is excessive or is disproportionate to its fair market value;

    (C) the property is subject to a mortgage or to taxes on which the owner is in default; or

    (D) the court finds other good cause.

(ii) Who Makes the Sale. A sale must be made by a United States agency that has authority to sell the property, by the agency's contractor, or by any person the court designates.

(iii) Sale Procedures. The sale is governed by 28 U.S.C. §§ 2001, 2002, and 2004, unless all parties, with the court's approval, agree to the sale, aspects of the sale, or different procedures.

(iv) Sale Proceeds. Sale proceeds are a substitute res subject to forfeiture in place of the property that was sold. The proceeds must be held in an interest-bearing account maintained by the United States pending the conclusion of the forfeiture action.

(v) Delivery on a Claimant's Motion. The court may order that the property be delivered to the claimant pending the conclusion of the action if the claimant shows circumstances that would permit sale under Rule G(7)(b)(i) and gives security under these rules.

(c) Disposing of Forfeited Property. Upon entry of a forfeiture judgment, the property or proceeds from selling the property must be disposed of as provided by law.

(8) Motions.

(a) Motion To Suppress Use of the Property as Evidence. If the defendant property was seized, a party with standing to contest the lawfulness of the seizure may move to suppress use of the property as evidence. Suppression does not affect forfeiture of the property based on independently derived evidence.

(b) Motion To Dismiss the Action.

(i) A claimant who establishes standing to contest forfeiture may move to dismiss the action under Rule 12(b).

(ii) In an action governed by 18 U.S.C. § 983(a)(3)(D) the complaint may not be dismissed on the ground that the government did not have adequate evidence at the time the complaint was filed to establish the forfeitability of the property. The sufficiency of the complaint is governed by Rule G(2).

(c) Motion To Strike a Claim or Answer.

(i) At any time before trial, the government may move to strike a claim or answer:

    (A) for failing to comply with Rule G(5) or (6), or

    (B) because the claimant lacks standing.

(ii) The motion:

    (A) must be decided before any motion by the claimant to dismiss the action; and

    (B) may be presented as a motion for judgment on the pleadings or as a motion to determine after a hearing or by summary judgment whether the claimant can carry the burden of establishing standing by a preponderance of the evidence.

(d) Petition To Release Property.

(i) If a United States agency or an agency's contractor holds property for judicial or nonjudicial forfeiture under a statute governed by 18 U.S.C. § 983(f), a person who has filed a claim to the property may petition for its release under § 983(f).

(ii) If a petition for release is filed before a judicial forfeiture action is filed against the property, the petition may be filed either in the district where the property was seized or in the district where a warrant to seize the property issued. If a judicial forfeiture action against the property is later filed in another district—or if the government shows that the action will be filed in another district—the petition may be transferred to that district under 28 U.S.C. § 1404.

(e) Excessive Fines. A claimant may seek to mitigate a forfeiture under the Excessive Fines Clause of the Eighth Amendment by motion for summary judgment or by motion made after entry of a forfeiture judgment if:

(i) the claimant has pleaded the defense under Rule 8; and

(ii) the parties have had the opportunity to conduct civil discovery on the defense.

(9) Trial. Trial is to the court unless any party demands trial by jury under Rule 38.

(Added Apr. 12, 2006, eff. Dec. 1, 2006; amended Mar. 26, 2009, eff. Dec. 1, 2009.)

ADVISORY COMMITTEE NOTES

2006 Adoption

Rule G is added to bring together the central procedures that govern civil forfeiture actions. Civil forfeiture actions are in rem proceedings, as are many admiralty proceedings. As the number of civil forfeiture actions has increased, however, reasons have appeared to create sharper distinctions within the framework of the Supplemental Rules. Civil forfeiture practice will benefit from distinctive provisions that express and focus developments in statutory, constitutional, and decisional law. Admiralty practice will be freed from the pressures that arise when the needs of civil forfeiture proceedings counsel interpretations of common rules that may not be suitable for admiralty proceedings.

Rule G generally applies to actions governed by the Civil Asset Forfeiture Reform Act of 2000 (CAFRA) and also to actions excluded from it. The rule refers to some specific CAFRA provisions; if these statutes are amended, the rule should be adapted to the new provisions during the period required to amend the rule.

Rule G is not completely self-contained. Subdivision (1) recognizes the need to rely at times on other Supplemental Rules and the place of the Supplemental Rules within the basic framework of the Civil Rules.

Supplemental Rules A, C, and E are amended to reflect the adoption of Rule G.

Subdivision (1).

Rule G is designed to include the distinctive procedures that govern a civil forfeiture action. Some details, however, are better supplied by relying on Rules C and E. Subdivision (1) incorporates those rules for issues not addressed by Rule G. This general incorporation is at times made explicit — subdivision (7)(b)(v), for example, invokes the security provisions of Rule E. But Rules C and E are not to be invoked to create conflicts with Rule G. They are to be used only when Rule G, fairly construed, does not address the issue.

The Civil Rules continue to provide the procedural framework within which Rule G and the other Supplemental Rules operate. Both Rule G(1) and Rule A state this basic proposition. Rule G, for example, does not address pleadings amend-

ments. Civil Rule 15 applies, in light of the circumstances of a forfeiture action.

Subdivision (2).

Rule E(2)(a) requires that the complaint in an admiralty action "state the circumstances from which the claim arises with such particularity that the defendant or claimant will be able, without moving for a more definite statement, to commence an investigation of the facts and to frame a responsive pleading." Application of this standard to civil forfeiture actions has evolved to the standard stated in subdivision (2)(f). The complaint must state sufficiently detailed facts to support a reasonable belief that the government will be able to meet its burden of proof at trial. *See U. S. v. Mondragon*, 313 F.3d 862 (4th Cir. 2002). Subdivision (2)(f) carries this forfeiture case law forward without change.

Subdivision (3).

Subdivision (3) governs in rem process in a civil forfeiture action.

Paragraph (a). Paragraph (a) reflects the provisions of 18 U.S.C. § 985.

Paragraph (b). Paragraph (b) addresses arrest warrants when the defendant is not real property. Subparagraph (i) directs the clerk to issue a warrant if the property is in the government's possession, custody, or control. If the property is not in the government's possession, custody, or control and is not subject to a restraining order, subparagraph (ii) provides that a warrant issues only if the court finds probable cause to arrest the property. This provision departs from former Rule C(3)(a)(i), which authorized issuance of summons and warrant by the clerk without a probable-cause finding. The probable-cause finding better protects the interests of persons interested in the property. Subparagraph (iii) recognizes that a warrant is not necessary if the property is subject to a judicial restraining order. The government remains free, however, to seek a warrant if it anticipates that the restraining order may be modified or vacated.

Paragraph (c). Subparagraph (ii) requires that the warrant and any supplemental process be served as soon as practicable unless the property is already in the government's possession, custody, or control. But it authorizes the court to order a different time. The authority to order a different time recognizes that the government may have secured orders sealing the complaint in a civil forfeiture action or have won a stay after filing. The seal or stay may be ordered for reasons, such as protection of an ongoing criminal investigation, that would be defeated by prompt service of the warrant. Subparagraph (ii) does not reflect any independent ground for ordering a seal or stay, but merely reflects the consequences for execution when sealing or a stay is ordered. A court also may order a different time for service if good cause is shown for reasons unrelated to a seal or stay. Subparagraph (iv) reflects the uncertainty surrounding service of an arrest warrant on property not in the United States. It is not possible to identify in the rule the appropriate authority for serving process in all other countries. Transmission of the warrant to an appropriate authority, moreover, does not ensure that the warrant will be executed. The rule requires only that the warrant be transmitted to an appropriate authority.

Subdivision (4).

Paragraph (a). Paragraph (a) reflects the traditional practice of publishing notice of an in rem action.

Subparagraph (i) recognizes two exceptions to the general publication requirement. Publication is not required if the defendant property is worth less than $1,000 and direct notice is sent to all reasonably identifiable potential claimants as required by subdivision (4)(b). Publication also is not required if the cost would exceed the property's value and the court finds that other means of notice would satisfy due process. Publication on a government-established internet forfeiture site, as contemplated by subparagraph (iv), would be at a low marginal publication cost, which would likely be the cost to compare to the property value.

Subparagraph (iv) states the basic criterion for selecting the means and method of publication. The purpose is to adopt a means reasonably calculated to reach potential claimants. The government should choose from among these means a method that is reasonably likely to reach potential claimants at a cost reasonable in the circumstances.

If the property is in the United States and newspaper notice is chosen, publication may be where the action is filed, where the property was seized, or — if the property was not seized — where the property is located. Choice among these places is influenced by the probable location of potential claimants.

If the property is not in the United States, account must be taken of the sensitivities that surround publication of legal notices in other countries. A foreign country may forbid local publication. If potential claimants are likely to be in the United States, publication in the district where the action is filed may be the best choice. If potential claimants are likely to be located abroad, the better choice may be publication by means generally circulated in the country where the property is located.

Newspaper publication is not a particularly effective means of notice for most potential claimants. Its traditional use is best defended by want of affordable alternatives. Paragraph (iv)(C) contemplates a government-created internet forfeiture site that would provide a single easily identified means of notice. Such a site could allow much more direct access to notice as to any specific property than publication provides.

Paragraph (b). Paragraph (b) is entirely new. For the first time, Rule G expressly recognizes the due process obligation to send notice to any person who reasonably appears to be a potential claimant.

Subparagraph (i) states the obligation to send notice. Many potential claimants will be known to the government because they have filed claims during the administrative forfeiture stage. Notice must be sent, however, no matter what source of information makes it reasonably appear that a person is a potential claimant. The duty to send notice terminates when the time for filing a claim expires.

Notice of the action does not require formal service of summons in the manner required by Rule 4 to initiate a personal action. The process that begins an in rem forfeiture action is addressed by subdivision (3). This process commonly gives notice to potential claimants. Publication of notice is required in addition to this process. Due process requirements have moved beyond these traditional means of notice, but are satisfied by practical means that are reasonably calculated to accomplish actual notice.

Subparagraph (ii)(B) directs that the notice state a deadline for filing a claim that is at least 35 days after the notice is sent. This provision applies both in actions that fall within 18 U.S.C. § 983(a)(4)(A) and in other actions. Section 983(a)(4)(A) states that a claim should be filed no later than 30 days after service of the complaint. The variation introduced by subparagraph (ii)(B) reflects the procedure of § 983(a)(2)(B) for nonjudicial forfeiture proceedings. The nonjudicial procedure requires that a claim be filed "not later than the deadline set forth in a personal notice letter (which may be not earlier than 35 days after the date the letter is sent) * * *." This procedure is as suitable in a civil forfeiture action as in a nonjudicial forfeiture proceeding. Thirty–five days after notice is sent ordinarily will extend the claim time by no more than a brief period; a claimant anxious to expedite proceedings can file the claim before the deadline; and the government has flexibility to set a still longer period when circumstances make that desirable.

Subparagraph (iii) begins by stating the basic requirement that notice must be sent by means reasonably calculated to reach the potential claimant. No attempt is made to list the various means that may be reasonable in different circumstances. It may be reasonable, for example, to rely on means that have already been established for communication with a particular potential claimant. The government's interest in choosing a means likely to accomplish actual notice is bolstered by its desire to avoid post-forfeiture challenges based on arguments that a different method would have been more likely to accomplish actual notice. Flexible rule language accommodates the rapid evolution of communications technology.

Notice may be directed to a potential claimant through counsel, but only to counsel already representing the claimant with respect to the seizure of the property, or in a related investigation, administrative forfeiture proceeding, or criminal case.

Subparagraph (iii)(C) reflects the basic proposition that notice to a potential claimant who is incarcerated must be sent to the place of incarceration. Notice directed to some other place, such as a pre-incarceration residence, is less likely to reach the potential claimant. This provision does not address due process questions that may arise if a particular prison has deficient procedures for delivering notice to prisoners. *See Dusenbery v. U.S.*, 534 U.S. 161 (2002).

Items (D) and (E) of subparagraph (iii) authorize the government to rely on an address given by a person who is not incarcerated. The address may have been given to the agency that arrested or released the person, or to the agency that seized the property. The government is not obliged to undertake an independent investigation to verify the address.

Subparagraph (iv) identifies the date on which notice is considered to be sent for some common means, without addressing the circumstances for choosing among the identified means or other means. The date of sending should be determined by analogy for means not listed. Facsimile transmission, for example, is sent upon transmission. Notice by personal delivery is sent on delivery.

Subparagraph (v), finally, reflects the purpose to effect actual notice by providing that a potential claimant who had actual notice of a forfeiture proceeding cannot oppose or seek relief from forfeiture because the government failed to comply with subdivision (4)(b).

Subdivision (5).

Paragraph (a). Paragraph (a) establishes that the first step of contesting a civil forfeiture action is to file a claim. A claim is required by 18 U.S.C. § 983(a)(4)(A) for actions covered by § 983. Paragraph (a) applies this procedure as well to actions not covered by § 983. "Claim" is used to describe this first pleading because of the statutory references to claim and claimant. It functions in the same way as the statement of interest prescribed for an admiralty proceeding by Rule C(6), and is not related to the distinctive meaning of "claim" in admiralty practice.

If the claimant states its interest in the property to be as bailee, the bailor must be identified. A bailee who files a claim on behalf of a bailor must state the bailee's authority to do so.

The claim must be signed under penalty of perjury by the person making it. An artificial body that can act only through an agent may authorize an agent to sign for it. Excusable inability of counsel to obtain an appropriate signature may be grounds for an extension of time to file the claim.

Paragraph (a)(ii) sets the time for filing a claim. Item (C) applies in the relatively rare circumstance in which notice is not published and the government did not send direct notice to the claimant because it did not know of the claimant or did not have an address for the claimant.

Paragraph (b). Under 18 U.S.C. § 983(a)(4)(B), which governs many forfeiture proceedings, a person who asserts an interest by filing a claim "shall file an answer to the Government's complaint for forfeiture not later than 20 days after the date of the filing of the claim." Paragraph (b) recognizes that this statute works within the general procedures established by Civil Rule 12. Rule 12(a)(4) suspends the time to answer when a Rule 12 motion is served within the time allowed to answer. Continued application of this rule to proceedings governed by § 983(a)(4)(B) serves all of the purposes advanced by Rule 12(a)(4), see U. S. v. $8,221,877.16, 330 F.3d 141 (3d Cir. 2003); permits a uniform procedure for all civil forfeiture actions; and recognizes that a motion under Rule 12 can be made only after a claim is filed that provides background for the motion.

Failure to present an objection to in rem jurisdiction or to venue by timely motion or answer waives the objection. Waiver of such objections is familiar. An answer may be amended to assert an objection initially omitted. But Civil Rule 15 should be applied to an amendment that for the first time raises an objection to in rem jurisdiction by analogy to the personal jurisdiction objection provision in Civil Rule 12(h)(1)(B). The amendment should be permitted only if it is permitted as a matter of course under Rule 15(a).

A claimant's motion to dismiss the action is further governed by subdivisions (6)(c), (8)(b), and (8)(c).

Subdivision (6).

Subdivision (6) illustrates the adaptation of an admiralty procedure to the different needs of civil forfeiture. Rule C(6) permits interrogatories to be served with the complaint in an in rem action without limiting the subjects of inquiry. Civil forfeiture practice does not require such an extensive departure from ordinary civil practice. It remains useful, however, to permit the government to file limited interrogatories at any time after a claim is filed to gather information that bears on the claimant's standing. Subdivisions (8)(b) and (c) allow a claimant to move to dismiss only if the claimant has standing, and recognize the government's right to move to dismiss a claim for lack of standing. Subdivision (6) interrogatories are integrated with these provisions in that the interrogatories are limited to the claimant's identity and relationship to the defendant property. If the claimant asserts a relationship to the property as bailee, the interrogatories can inquire into the bailor's interest in the property and the bailee's relationship to the bailor. The claimant can accelerate the time to serve

subdivision (6) interrogatories by serving a motion to dismiss — the interrogatories must be served within 20 days after the motion is served. Integration is further accomplished by deferring the government's obligation to respond to a motion to dismiss until 20 days after the claimant moving to dismiss has answered the interrogatories.

Special interrogatories served under Rule G(6) do not count against the presumptive 25–interrogatory limit established by Rule 33(a). Rule 33 procedure otherwise applies to these interrogatories.

Subdivision (6) supersedes the discovery "moratorium" of Rule 26(d) and the broader interrogatories permitted for admiralty proceedings by Rule C(6).

Subdivision (7).

Paragraph (a). Paragraph (a) is adapted from Rule E(9)(b). It provides for preservation orders when the government does not have actual possession of the defendant property. It also goes beyond Rule E(9) by recognizing the need to prevent use of the defendant property in ongoing criminal offenses.

Paragraph (b). Paragraph (b)(i)(C) recognizes the authority, already exercised in some cases, to order sale of property subject to a defaulted mortgage or to defaulted taxes. The authority is narrowly confined to mortgages and tax liens; other lien interests may be addressed, if at all, only through the general good-cause provision. The court must carefully weigh the competing interests in each case.

Paragraph (b)(i)(D) establishes authority to order sale for good cause. Good cause may be shown when the property is subject to diminution in value. Care should be taken before ordering sale to avoid diminished value.

Paragraph (b)(iii) recognizes that if the court approves, the interests of all parties may be served by their agreement to sale, aspects of the sale, or sale procedures that depart from governing statutory procedures.

Paragraph (c) draws from Rule E(9)(a), (b), and (c). Disposition of the proceeds as provided by law may require resolution of disputed issues. A mortgagee's claim to the property or sale proceeds, for example, may be disputed on the ground that the mortgage is not genuine. An undisputed lien claim, on the other hand, may be recognized by payment after an interlocutory sale.

Subdivision (8).

Subdivision (8) addresses a number of issues that are unique to civil forfeiture actions.

Paragraph (a). Standing to suppress use of seized property as evidence is governed by principles distinct from the principles that govern claim standing. A claimant with standing to contest forfeiture may not have standing to seek suppression. Rule G does not of itself create a basis of suppression standing that does not otherwise exist.

Paragraph (b). Paragraph (b)(i) is one element of the system that integrates the procedures for determining a claimant's standing to claim and for deciding a claimant's motion to dismiss the action. Under paragraph (c)(ii), a motion to dismiss the action cannot be addressed until the court has decided any government motion to strike the claim or answer. This procedure is reflected in the (b)(i) reminder that a motion to dismiss the forfeiture action may be made only by a claimant who establishes claim standing. The government, moreover, need not respond to a claimant's motion to dismiss until 20 days after the claimant has answered any subdivision (6) interrogatories.

Paragraph (b)(ii) mirrors 18 U.S.C. § 983(a)(3)(D). It applies only to an action independently governed by § 983(a)(3)(D), implying nothing as to actions outside § 983(a)(3)(D). The adequacy of the complaint is measured against the pleading requirements of subdivision (2), not against the quality of the evidence available to the government when the complaint was filed.

Paragraph (c). As noted with paragraph (b), paragraph (c) governs the procedure for determining whether a claimant has standing. It does not address the principles that govern claim standing.

Paragraph (c)(i)(A) provides that the government may move to strike a claim or answer for failure to comply with the pleading requirements of subdivision (5) or to answer subdivision (6) interrogatories. As with other pleadings, the court should strike a claim or answer only if satisfied that an opportunity should not be afforded to cure the defects under Rule 15. Not every failure to respond to subdivision (6) interrogatories warrants an order striking the claim. But the special role that subdivision (6) plays in the scheme for determining claim standing may justify a somewhat more demanding approach than the general approach to discovery sanctions under Rule 37.

Paragraph (c)(ii) directs that a motion to strike a claim or answer be decided before any motion by the claimant to dismiss the action. A claimant who lacks standing is not entitled to challenge the forfeiture on the merits.

Paragraph (c)(ii) further identifies three procedures for addressing claim standing. If a claim fails on its face to show facts that support claim standing, the claim can be dismissed by judgment on the pleadings. If the claim shows facts that would support claim standing, those facts can be tested by a motion for summary judgment. If material facts are disputed, precluding a grant of summary judgment, the court may hold an evidentiary hearing. The evidentiary hearing is held by the court without a jury. The claimant has the burden to establish claim standing at a hearing; procedure on a government summary judgment motion reflects this allocation of the burden.

Paragraph (d). The hardship release provisions of 18 U.S.C. § 983(f) do not apply to a civil forfeiture action exempted from § 983 by § 983(i).

Paragraph (d)(ii) reflects the venue provisions of 18 U.S.C. § 983(f)(3)(A) as a guide to practitioners. In addition, it makes clear the status of a civil forfeiture action as a "civil action" eligible for transfer under 28 U.S.C. § 1404. A transfer decision must be made on the circumstances of the particular proceeding. The district where the forfeiture action is filed has the advantage of bringing all related proceedings together, avoiding the waste that flows from consideration of different parts of the same forfeiture proceeding in the court where the warrant issued or the court where the property was seized. Transfer to that court would serve consolidation, the purpose that underlies nationwide enforcement of a seizure warrant. But there may be offsetting advantages in retaining the petition where it was filed. The claimant may not be able to litigate, effectively or at all, in a distant court. Issues relevant to the petition may be better litigated where the property was seized or where the warrant issued. One element, for example, is whether the claimant has sufficient ties to the community to provide assurance that the property will be available at the time of trial. Another is whether continued government possession would prevent the claimant from working. Determining whether seizure of the claimant's automobile prevents work may turn on assessing the realities of local public transit facilities.

Paragraph (e). The Excessive Fines Clause of the Eighth Amendment forbids an excessive forfeiture. *U.S. v. Bajakajian*, 524 U.S. 321 (1998). 18 U.S.C. § 983(g) provides a "petition" "to determine whether the forfeiture was constitutionally excessive" based on finding "that the forfeiture is grossly disproportional to the offense." Paragraph (e) describes the procedure for § 983(g) mitigation petitions and adopts the same procedure for forfeiture actions that fall outside § 983(g). The procedure is by motion, either for summary judgment or for mitigation after a forfeiture judgment is entered. The claimant must give notice of this defense by pleading, but failure to raise the defense in the initial answer may be cured by amendment under Rule 15. The issues that bear on mitigation often are separate from the issues that determine forfeiture. For that reason it may be convenient to resolve the issue by summary judgment before trial on the forfeiture issues. Often, however, it will be more convenient to determine first whether the property is to be forfeited. Whichever time is chosen to address mitigation, the parties must have had the opportunity to conduct civil discovery on the defense. The extent and timing of discovery are governed by the ordinary rules.

Subdivision (9).

Subdivision (9) serves as a reminder of the need to demand jury trial under Rule 38. It does not expand the right to jury trial. *See U.S. v. One Parcel of Property Located at 32 Medley Lane*, 2005 WL 465421 (D.Conn.2005), ruling that the court, not the jury, determines whether a forfeiture is constitutionally excessive.

2009 Amendment

The times set in the former rule at 20 days have been revised to 21 days. See the Note to Rule 6.

FEDERAL RULES OF EVIDENCE

Pub.L. 93–595, § 1, January 2, 1975, 88 Stat. 1926
Amendments received to December 1, 2018

ORDERS OF THE SUPREME COURT OF THE UNITED STATES ADOPTING AND AMENDING RULES

ORDER OF NOVEMBER 20, 1972

1. That the rules hereinafter set forth, to be known as the Federal Rules of Evidence, be, and they hereby are, prescribed pursuant to Sections 3402, 3771, and 3772, Title 18, United States Code, and Sections 2072 and 2075, Title 28, United States Code, to govern procedure, in the proceedings and to the extent set forth therein, in the United States courts of appeals, the United States district courts, the District Court for the District of the Canal Zone and the district courts of Guam and the Virgin Islands, and before United States magistrates.

2. That the aforementioned Federal Rules of Evidence shall take effect on July 1, 1973, and shall be applicable to actions and proceedings brought thereafter and also to further procedure in actions and proceedings then pending, except to the extent that in the opinion of the court their application in a particular action or proceeding then pending would not be feasible or would work injustice in which event the former procedure applies.

3. That subdivision (c) of Rule 30 and Rules 43 and 44.1 of the Federal Rules of Civil Procedure be, and they hereby are, amended, effective July 1, 1973, to read as hereinafter set forth:

[See amendments made thereby under the respective Rules of Civil Procedure.]

4. That subdivision (c) of Rule 32 of the Federal Rules of Civil Procedure be, and it hereby is, abrogated, effective July 1, 1973.

5. That Rules 26, 26.1 and 28 of the Federal Rules of Criminal Procedure be, and they hereby are, amended effective July 1, 1973, to read as hereinafter set forth.

[See amendments made thereby under the respective Rules of Criminal Procedure.]

6. That the Chief Justice be, and he hereby is, authorized to transmit the foregoing new rules and amendments to and abrogation of existing rules to the Congress at the beginning of its next regular session, in accordance with the provisions of Title 18 U.S.C. § 3771 and Title 28 U.S.C. §§ 2072 and 2075.

CONGRESSIONAL ACTION ON PROPOSED RULES OF EVIDENCE AND 1972 AMENDMENTS TO FEDERAL RULES OF CIVIL PROCEDURE AND FEDERAL RULES OF CRIMINAL PROCEDURE

Pub.L. 93–12, Mar. 30, 1973, 87 Stat. 9, provided: "That notwithstanding any other provisions of law, the Rules of Evidence for United States Courts and Magistrates, the Amendments to the Federal Rules of Civil Procedure, and the Amendments to the Federal Rules of Criminal Procedure, which are embraced by the orders entered by the Supreme Court of the United States on Monday, November 20, 1972, and Monday, December 18, 1972, shall have no force or effect except to the extent, and with such amendments, as they may be expressly approved by Act of Congress."

Pub.L. 93–595, § 3, Jan. 2, 1975, 88 Stat. 1959, provided that: "The Congress expressly approves the amendments to the Federal Rules of Civil Procedure, and the amendments to the Federal Rules of Criminal Procedure, which are embraced by the orders entered by the Supreme Court of the United States on November 20, 1972, and December 18, 1972, and such amendments shall take effect on the one hundred and eightieth day beginning after the date of the enactment of this Act [Jan. 2, 1975]."

ORDER OF APRIL 30, 1979

1. That Rule 410 of the Federal Rules of Evidence be, and it hereby is, amended to read as follows:

[See amendment made thereby following Rule 410, post.]

2. That the foregoing amendment to the Federal Rules of Evidence shall take effect on November 1, 1979, and shall be applicable to all proceedings then pending except to the extent that in the opinion of the court the application of the amended rule in a particular proceeding would not be feasible or would work injustice.

3. That THE CHIEF JUSTICE be, and he hereby is, authorized to transmit to the Congress the foregoing amendment to the Federal Rules of Evidence in accordance with the provisions of 28 U.S.C. § 2076.

CONGRESSIONAL ACTION ON AMENDMENT PROPOSED APRIL 30, 1979

Pub.L. 96–42, July 31, 1979, 93 Stat. 326, provided that the amendment proposed and transmitted to the Federal Rules of Evidence affecting rule 410, shall not take effect until Dec. 1, 1980, or until and then only to the extent approved by Act of Congress, whichever is earlier.

ORDER OF MARCH 2, 1987

1. That the Federal Rules of Evidence be, and they hereby are, amended by including therein amendments to Rules 101, 104, 106, 404, 405, 411, 602, 603, 604, 606, 607, 608, 609, 610, 611, 612, 613, 615, 701, 703, 705, 706, 801, 803, 804, 806, 902, 1004, 1007 and 1101, as hereinafter set forth:

[See amendments made thereby under respective rules, post.]

2. That the foregoing changes in the Federal Rules of Evidence shall take effect on October 1, 1987.

3. That THE CHIEF JUSTICE be, and he hereby is, authorized to transmit to the Congress the foregoing changes

in the rules of evidence in accordance with the provisions of Section 2076 of Title 28, United States Code.

ORDER OF APRIL 25, 1988

1. That the Federal Rules of Evidence be, and they hereby are, amended by including therein amendments to Rules 101, 602, 608, 613, 615, 902, and 1101, as hereinafter set forth:

[See amendments made thereby under respective rules, post.]

2. That the foregoing changes in the Federal Rules of Evidence shall take effect on November 1, 1988.

3. That THE CHIEF JUSTICE be, and he hereby is, authorized to transmit to the Congress the foregoing changes in the rules of evidence in accordance with the provisions of Section 2076 of Title 28, United States Code.

ORDER OF JANUARY 26, 1990

1. That the Federal Rules of Evidence be, and they hereby are, amended by including therein amendments to Rule 609(a)(1) and (2), as hereinafter set forth:

[See amendment made thereby, post].

2. That the foregoing changes in the Federal Rules of Evidence shall take effect on December 1, 1990.

3. That THE CHIEF JUSTICE be, and he hereby is, authorized to transmit to the Congress the foregoing changes in the rules of evidence in accordance with the provisions of Section 2074 of Title 28, United States Code.

ORDER OF APRIL 30, 1991

1. That the Federal Rules of Evidence for the United States District Courts be, and they hereby are, amended by including therein amendments to Evidence Rules 404(b) and 1102.

[See amendments made thereby under respective rules, post.]

2. That the foregoing amendments to the Federal Rules of Evidence shall take effect on December 1, 1991, and shall govern in all proceedings thereafter commenced and, insofar as just and practicable, all proceedings then pending.

3. That THE CHIEF JUSTICE be, and he hereby is, authorized to transmit to the Congress the foregoing amendments to the Federal Rules of Evidence in accordance with the provisions of Section 2072 of Title 28, United States Code.

ORDER OF APRIL 22, 1993

1. That the Federal Rules of Evidence for the United States District Courts be, and they hereby are, amended by including therein amendments to Evidence Rules 101, 705, and 1101.

[See amendments made thereby under respective rules, post.]

2. That the foregoing amendments to the Federal Rules of Evidence shall take effect on December 1, 1993, and shall govern in all proceedings thereafter commenced and, insofar as just and practicable, all proceedings then pending.

3. That THE CHIEF JUSTICE be, and he hereby is, authorized to transmit to the Congress the foregoing amendments to the Federal Rules of Evidence in accordance with the provisions of Section 2072 of Title 28, United States Code.

ORDER OF APRIL 29, 1994

ORDERED:

1. That the Federal Rules of Evidence for the United States District Courts be, and they hereby are, amended by including therein an amendment to Evidence Rule 412.

[See amendment made hereby under Rule 412, post.]

2. That the foregoing amendment to the Federal Rules of Evidence shall take effect on December 1, 1994, and shall govern in all proceedings thereafter commenced and, insofar as just and practicable, all proceedings then pending.

3. That THE CHIEF JUSTICE be, and he hereby is, authorized to transmit to the Congress the foregoing amendment to the Federal Rules of Evidence in accordance with the provisions of Section 2072 of Title 28, United States Code.

ORDER OF APRIL 11, 1997

ORDERED:

1. That the Federal Rules of Evidence be, and they hereby are, amended by including therein amendments to Evidence Rules 407, 801, 803(24), 804(b)(5), and 806, and new Rules 804(b)(6) and 807.

[See amendments made thereby under respective rules, post.]

2. That the foregoing amendments to the Federal Rules of Evidence shall take effect on December 1, 1997, and shall govern in all proceedings thereafter commenced and, insofar as just and practicable, all proceedings then pending.

3. That THE CHIEF JUSTICE be, and hereby is, authorized to transmit to the Congress the foregoing amendments to the Federal Rules of Evidence in accordance with the provisions of Section 2072 of Title 28, United States Code.

ORDER OF APRIL 24, 1998

ORDERED:

1. That the Federal Rules of Evidence be, and they hereby are, amended by including therein amendments to Evidence Rule 615.

[See amendments made thereby under respective rules, post.]

2. That the foregoing amendments to the Federal Rules of Evidence shall take effect on December 1, 1998, and shall govern in all proceedings thereafter commenced and, insofar as just and practicable, all proceedings then pending.

3. That THE CHIEF JUSTICE be, and hereby is, authorized to transmit to the Congress the foregoing amendments to the Federal Rules of Evidence in accordance with the provisions of Section 2072 of Title 28, United States Code.

ORDER OF APRIL 17, 2000

ORDERED:

1. That the Federal Rules of Evidence for the United States District Courts be, and they hereby are, amended by including therein amendments to Evidence Rules 103, 404, 701, 702, 703, 803(6), and 902.

[See amendments made thereby under respective rules, post.]

2. That the foregoing amendments to the Federal Rules of Evidence shall take effect on December 1, 2000, and shall govern all proceedings thereafter commenced and, insofar as just and practicable, all proceedings then pending.

3. That THE CHIEF JUSTICE be, and hereby is, authorized to transmit to the Congress the foregoing amendments to the Federal Rules of Evidence in accordance with the provisions of Section 2072 of Title 28, United States Code.

ORDER OF MARCH 27, 2003

ORDERED:

1. That the Federal Rules of Evidence be, and they hereby are, amended by including therein the amendments to Evidence Rule 608(b).

[See amendments made thereby under respective rules, post.]

2. That the foregoing amendments to the Federal Rules of Evidence shall take effect on December 1, 2003, and shall govern in all proceedings thereafter commenced and, insofar as just and practicable, all proceedings then pending.

3. That THE CHIEF JUSTICE be, and hereby is, authorized to transmit to the Congress the foregoing amendments to the Federal Rules of Evidence in accordance with the provisions of Section 2072 of Title 28, United States Code.

ORDER OF APRIL 12, 2006

1. That the Federal Rules of Evidence be, and they hereby are, amended by including therein the amendments to Evidence Rules 404, 408, 606, and 609.

[See amendments made thereby under respective rules, post.]

2. That the foregoing amendments to the Federal Rules of Evidence shall take effect on December 1, 2006, and shall govern in all proceedings thereafter commenced and, insofar as just and practicable, all proceedings then pending.

3. That THE CHIEF JUSTICE be, and hereby is, authorized to transmit to the Congress the foregoing amendments to the Federal Rules of Evidence in accordance with the provisions of Section 2072 of Title 28, United States Code.

ORDER OF APRIL 28, 2010

1. That the Federal Rules of Evidence be, and they hereby are, amended by including therein an amendment to Evidence Rule 804.

[See amendments made hereby under Rule 804, post.]

2. That the foregoing amendment to the Federal Rules of Evidence shall take effect on December 1, 2010, and shall govern in all proceedings thereafter commenced and, insofar as just and practicable, all proceedings then pending.

3. That THE CHIEF JUSTICE be, and hereby is, authorized to transmit to the Congress the foregoing amendment to the Federal Rules of Evidence in accordance with the provisions of Section 2072 of Title 28, United States Code.

ORDER OF APRIL 26, 2011

1. That the Federal Rules of Evidence be, and they hereby are, amended by including therein the amendments to Evidence Rules 101–1103.

[See amendments made thereby under respective rules, post]

2. That the foregoing amendments to the Federal Rules of Evidence shall take effect on December 1, 2011, and shall govern in all proceedings thereafter commenced and, insofar as just and practicable, all proceedings then pending.

3. That THE CHIEF JUSTICE be, and hereby is, authorized to transmit to the Congress the foregoing amendments to the Federal Rules of Evidence in accordance with the provisions of Section 2072 of Title 28, United States Code.

ORDER OF APRIL 16, 2013

1. That the Federal Rules of Evidence be, and they hereby are, amended by including therein an amendment to Evidence Rule 803.

[See amendments made thereby under respective rules, post]

2. That the foregoing amendment to the Federal Rules of Evidence shall take effect on December 1, 2013, and shall govern in all proceedings thereafter commenced and, insofar as just and practicable, all proceedings then pending.

3. That the CHIEF JUSTICE be, and hereby is, authorized to transmit to the Congress the foregoing amendment to the Federal Rules of Evidence in accordance with the provisions of Section 2072 of Title 28, United States Code.

ORDER OF APRIL 25, 2014

1. That the Federal Rules of Evidence be, and they hereby are, amended by including therein amendments to Evidence Rules 801(d)(1)(B) and 803(6)–(8).

[See amendments made thereby under respective rules, post]

2. That the foregoing amendments to the Federal Rules of Evidence shall take effect on December 1, 2014, and shall govern in all proceedings thereafter commenced and, insofar as just and practicable, all proceedings then pending.

3. That the CHIEF JUSTICE be, and hereby is, authorized to transmit to the Congress the foregoing amendments to the Federal Rules of Evidence in accordance with the provisions of Section 2072 of Title 28, United States Code.

ORDER OF APRIL 27, 2017

1. That the Federal Rules of Evidence be, and they hereby are, amended by including therein amendments to Evidence Rules 803 and 902.

[See infra pp. ___ ___ ___.]

2. That the foregoing amendments to the Federal Rules of Evidence shall take effect on December 1, 2017, and shall govern in all proceedings thereafter commenced and, insofar as just and practicable, all proceedings then pending.

3. That THE CHIEF JUSTICE be, and hereby is, authorized to transmit to the Congress the foregoing amendments to the Federal Rules of Evidence in accordance with the provisions of Section 2074 of Title 28, United States Code.

HISTORICAL NOTES

Revision Notes and Legislative Reports

For legislative history and purpose of Pub.L. 93–595, see House, Senate and Conference Reports, set out following the text of these rules.

Effective Date and Application of Rules

The Federal Rules of Evidence were adopted by order of the Supreme Court on Nov. 20, 1972, transmitted to Congress by the Chief Justice on Feb. 5, 1973, and to have become effective on July 1, 1973. Pub.L. 93–12, Mar. 30, 1973, 87 Stat. 9, provided that the proposed rules "shall have no force or effect except to the extent, and with such amendments, as they may be expressly approved by Act of Congress". Pub.L. 93–595, Jan. 2, 1975, 88 Stat. 1926, enacted the Federal Rules of Evidence proposed by the Supreme Court, with amendments made by Congress, to take effect on July 1, 1975.

The Rules have been amended Oct. 16, 1975, Pub.L. 94–113, § 1, 89 Stat. 576, eff. Oct. 31, 1975; Dec. 12, 1975, Pub.L.

94–149, § 1, 89 Stat. 805; Oct. 28, 1978, Pub.L. 95–540, § 2, 92 Stat. 2046; Nov. 6, 1978, Pub.L. 95–598, Title II, § 251, 92 Stat. 2673, eff. Oct. 1, 1979; Apr. 30, 1979, eff. Dec. 1, 1980; Apr. 2, 1982, Pub.L. 97–164, Title I, § 142, Title IV, § 402, 96 Stat. 45, 57, eff. Oct. 1, 1982; Oct. 12, 1984, Pub.L. 98–473, Title IV, § 406, 98 Stat. 2067; Mar. 2, 1987, eff. Oct. 1, 1987; Apr. 25, 1988, eff. Nov. 1, 1988; Nov. 18, 1988, Pub.L. 100–690, Title VII, §§ 7046, 7075, 102 Stat. 4400, 4405; Jan. 26, 1990, eff. Dec. 1, 1990; Apr. 30, 1991, eff. Dec. 1, 1991; Apr. 22, 1993, eff. Dec. 1, 1993; Apr. 29, 1994, eff. Dec. 1, 1994; Sept. 13, 1994, Pub.L. 103–322, title IV, § 40141, title XXXII, § 320935, 108 Stat. 1918, 2135; Apr. 11, 1997, eff. Dec. 1, 1997; Apr. 24, 1998, eff. Dec. 1, 1998; Apr. 17, 2000, eff. Dec. 1, 2000; Mar. 27, 2003, eff. Dec. 1, 2003; Apr. 12, 2006, eff. Dec. 1, 2006; Sept. 19, 2008, Pub.L. 110–322, § 1(a), 122 Stat. 3537; Apr. 28, 2010, eff. Dec. 1, 2010; Apr. 26, 2011, eff. Dec. 1, 2011; Apr. 13, 2013, eff. Dec. 1, 2013; Apr. 25, 2014, eff. Dec. 1, 2014; Apr. 27, 2017, eff. Dec. 1, 2017.

ARTICLE I. GENERAL PROVISIONS

Rule
101. Scope; Definitions.
102. Purpose.
103. Rulings on Evidence.
104. Preliminary Questions.
105. Limiting Evidence That Is Not Admissible Against Other Parties or for Other Purposes.
106. Remainder of or Related Writings or Recorded Statements.

HISTORICAL NOTES

Change of Name

United States magistrate appointed under section 631 of Title 28, Judiciary and Judicial Procedure, to be known as United States magistrate judge after Dec. 1, 1990, with any reference to United States magistrate or magistrate in Title 28, in any other Federal statute, etc., deemed a reference to United States magistrate judge appointed under section 631 of Title 28, see section 321 of Pub.L. 101–650, set out as a note under section 631 of Title 28.

Rule 101. Scope; Definitions

(a) Scope. These rules apply to proceedings in United States courts. The specific courts and proceedings to which the rules apply, along with exceptions, are set out in Rule 1101.

(b) Definitions. In these rules:

(1) "civil case" means a civil action or proceeding;

(2) "criminal case" includes a criminal proceeding;

(3) "public office" includes a public agency;

(4) "record" includes a memorandum, report, or data compilation;

(5) a "rule prescribed by the Supreme Court" means a rule adopted by the Supreme Court under statutory authority; and

(6) a reference to any kind of written material or any other medium includes electronically stored information.

(Pub.L. 93–595, § 1, Jan. 2, 1975, 88 Stat. 1929; Mar. 2, 1987, eff. Oct. 1, 1987; Apr. 25, 1988, eff. Nov. 1, 1988; Apr. 22, 1993, eff. Dec. 1, 1993; Apr. 26, 2011, eff. Dec. 1, 2011.)

ADVISORY COMMITTEE NOTES

1972 Proposed Rules

Rule 1101 specifies in detail the courts, proceedings, questions, and stages of proceedings to which the rules apply in whole or in part.

1987 Amendments

United States bankruptcy judges are added to conform this rule with Rule 1101(b) and Bankruptcy Rule 9017.

1988 Amendments

The amendment is technical. No substantive change is intended.

1993 Amendments

This revision is made to conform the rule to changes made by the Judicial Improvements Act of 1990.

2011 Amendments

The language of Rule 101 has been amended, and definitions have been added, as part of the general restyling of the Evidence Rules to make them more easily understood and to make style and terminology consistent throughout the rules. These changes are intended to be stylistic only. There is no intent to change any result in any ruling on evidence admissibility.

The reference to electronically stored information is intended to track the language of Fed. R. Civ. P. 34.

The Style Project

The Evidence Rules are the fourth set of national procedural rules to be restyled. The restyled Rules of Appellate

Procedure took effect in 1998. The restyled Rules of Criminal Procedure took effect in 2002. The restyled Rules of Civil Procedure took effect in 2007. The restyled Rules of Evidence apply the same general drafting guidelines and principles used in restyling the Appellate, Criminal, and Civil Rules.

1. General Guidelines.

Guidance in drafting, usage, and style was provided by Bryan Garner, *Guidelines for Drafting and Editing Court Rules*, Administrative Office of the United States Courts (1969) and Bryan Garner, *Dictionary of Modern Legal Usage* (2d ed. 1995). *See also* Joseph Kimble, *Guiding Principles for Restyling the Civil Rules*, in *Preliminary Draft of Proposed Style Revision of the Federal Rules of Civil Procedure*, at page x (Feb. 2005) (available at http://www.uscourts.gov/ RulesAndPolicies/rules/Prelim_draft_proposed _ptl.pdf); Joseph Kimble, *Lessons in Drafting from the New Federal Rules of Civil Procedure*, 12 Scribes J. Legal Writing 25 (2008–2009). For specific commentary on the Evidence restyling project, see Joseph Kimble, *Drafting Examples from the Proposed New Federal Rules of Evidence*, 88 Mich. B.J. 52 (Aug. 2009); 88 Mich. B.J. 46 (Sept. 2009); 88 Mich. B.J. 54 (Oct. 2009); 88 Mich. B.J. 50 (Nov. 2009).

2. Formatting Changes.

Many of the changes in the restyled Evidence Rules result from using format to achieve clearer presentations. The rules are broken down into constituent parts, using progressively indented subparagraphs with headings and substituting vertical for horizontal lists. "Hanging indents" are used throughout. These formatting changes make the structure of the rules graphic and make the restyled rules easier to read and understand even when the words are not changed. Rules 103, 404(b), 606(b), and 612 illustrate the benefits of formatting changes.

3. Changes to Reduce Inconsistent, Ambiguous, Redundant, Repetitive, or Archaic Words.

The restyled rules reduce the use of inconsistent terms that say the same thing in different ways. Because different words are presumed to have different meanings, such inconsistencies can result in confusion. The restyled rules reduce inconsistencies by using the same words to express the same meaning. For example, consistent expression is achieved by not switching between "accused" and "defendant" or between "party opponent" and "opposing party" or between the various formulations of civil and criminal action/case/proceeding.

The restyled rules minimize the use of inherently ambiguous words. For example, the word "shall" can mean "must," "may," or something else, depending on context. The potential for confusion is exacerbated by the fact the word "shall" is no longer generally used in spoken or clearly written English. The restyled rules replace "shall" with "must," "may," or "should," depending on which one the context and established interpretation make correct in each rule.

The restyled rules minimize the use of redundant "intensifiers." These are expressions that attempt to add emphasis, but instead state the obvious and create negative implications for other rules. The absence of intensifiers in the restyled rules does not change their substantive meaning. *See, e.g.,* Rule 104(c) (omitting "in all cases"); Rule 602 (omitting "but need not"); Rule 611(b) (omitting "in the exercise of discretion").

The restyled rules also remove words and concepts that are outdated or redundant.

4. Rule Numbers.

The restyled rules keep the same numbers to minimize the effect on research. Subdivisions have been rearranged within some rules to achieve greater clarity and simplicity.

5. No Substantive Change.

The Committee made special efforts to reject any purported style improvement that might result in a substantive change in the application of a rule. The Committee considered a change to be "substantive" if any of the following conditions were met:

a. Under the existing practice in any circuit, the change could lead to a different result on a question of admissibility (e.g., a change that requires a court to provide either a less or more stringent standard in evaluating the admissibility of particular evidence);

b. Under the existing practice in any circuit, it could lead to a change in the procedure by which an admissibility decision is made (e.g., a change in the time in which an objection must be made, or a change in whether a court must hold a hearing on an admissibility question);

c. The change would restructure a rule in a way that would alter the approach that courts and litigants have used to think about, and argue about, questions of admissibility (e.g., merging Rules 104(a) and 104(b) into a single subdivision); or

d. It changes a "sacred phrase"—one that has become so familiar in practice that to alter it would be unduly disruptive to practice and expectations. Examples in the Evidence Rules include "unfair prejudice" and "truth of the matter asserted."

HISTORICAL NOTES

Change of Name

United States magistrate appointed under section 631 of Title 28, Judiciary and Judicial Procedure, to be known as United States magistrate judge after Dec. 1, 1990, with any reference to United States magistrate or magistrate in Title 28, in any other Federal statute, etc., deemed a reference to United States magistrate judge appointed under section 631 of Title 28, see section 321 of Pub.L. 101–650, set out as a note under section 631 of Title 28.

CROSS REFERENCES

Scope, see Fed.Rules Civ.Proc. Rule 1, 28 USCA.

Scope, see Fed.Rules Cr.Proc. Rule 1, 18 USCA.

Rule 102. Purpose

These rules should be construed so as to administer every proceeding fairly, eliminate unjustifiable expense and delay, and promote the development of evidence law, to the end of ascertaining the truth and securing a just determination.

(Pub.L. 93–595, § 1, Jan. 2, 1975, 88 Stat.1929; Apr. 26, 2011, eff. Dec. 1, 2011.)

ADVISORY COMMITTEE NOTES

1972 Proposed Rules

For similar provisions see Rule 2 of the Federal Rules of Criminal Procedure, Rule 1 of the Federal Rules of Civil Procedure, California Evidence Code § 2, and New Jersey Evidence Rule 5.

2011 Amendments

The language of Rule 102 has been amended as part of the restyling of the Evidence Rules to make them more easily understood and to make style and terminology consistent throughout the rules. These changes are intended to be stylistic only. There is no intent to change any result in any ruling on evidence admissibility.

CROSS REFERENCES

Construction, see Fed.Rules Civ.Proc. Rule 1, 28 USCA.

Purpose and construction, see Fed.Rules Cr.Proc. Rule 2, 18 USCA.

Rule 103. Rulings on Evidence

(a) Preserving a Claim of Error. A party may claim error in a ruling to admit or exclude evidence only if the error affects a substantial right of the party and:

>   **(1)** if the ruling admits evidence, a party, on the record:

>   >   **(A)** timely objects or moves to strike; and

>   >   **(B)** states the specific ground, unless it was apparent from the context; or

>   **(2)** if the ruling excludes evidence, a party informs the court of its substance by an offer of proof, unless the substance was apparent from the context.

(b) Not Needing to Renew an Objection or Offer of Proof. Once the court rules definitively on the record—either before or at trial—a party need not renew an objection or offer of proof to preserve a claim of error for appeal.

(c) Court's Statement About the Ruling; Directing an Offer of Proof. The court may make any statement about the character or form of the evidence, the objection made, and the ruling. The court may direct that an offer of proof be made in question-and-answer form.

(d) Preventing the Jury from Hearing Inadmissible Evidence. To the extent practicable, the court must conduct a jury trial so that inadmissible evidence is not suggested to the jury by any means.

(e) Taking Notice of Plain Error. A court may take notice of a plain error affecting a substantial right, even if the claim of error was not properly preserved.

(Pub.L. 93–595, § 1, Jan. 2, 1975, 88 Stat. 1929; Apr. 17, 2000, eff. Dec. 1, 2000; Apr. 26, 2011, eff. Dec. 1, 2011.)

ADVISORY COMMITTEE NOTES
1972 Proposed Rules

Note to Subdivision (a). Subdivision (a) states the law as generally accepted today. Rulings on evidence cannot be assigned as error unless (1) a substantial right is affected, and (2) the nature of the error was called to the attention of the judge, so as to alert him to the proper course of action and enable opposing counsel to take proper corrective measures. The objection and the offer of proof are the techniques for accomplishing these objectives. For similar provisions see

Uniform Rules 4 and 5; California Evidence Code §§ 353 and 354; Kansas Code of Civil Procedure §§ 60–404 and 60–405. The rule does not purport to change the law with respect to harmless error. See 28 USC § 2111, F.R.Civ.P. 61, F.R.Crim.P. 52, and decisions construing them. The status of constitutional error as harmless or not is treated in Chapman v. California, 386 U.S. 18, 87 S.Ct. 824, 17 L.Ed.2d 705 (1967), reh. denied id. 987, 87 S.Ct. 1283, 18 L.Ed.2d 241.

Note to Subdivision (b). The first sentence is the third sentence of Rule 43(c) of the Federal Rules of Civil Procedure virtually verbatim. Its purpose is to reproduce for an appellate court, insofar as possible, a true reflection of what occurred in the trial court. The second sentence is in part derived from the final sentence of Rule 43(c). It is designed to resolve doubts as to what testimony the witness would have in fact given, and, in nonjury cases, to provide the appellate court with material for a possible final disposition of the case in the event of reversal of a ruling which excluded evidence. See 5 Moore's Federal Practice § 43.11 (2d ed. 1968). Application is made discretionary in view of the practical impossibility of formulating a satisfactory rule in mandatory terms.

Note to Subdivision (c). This subdivision proceeds on the supposition that a ruling which excludes evidence in a jury case is likely to be a pointless procedure if the excluded evidence nevertheless comes to the attention of the jury. *Bruton v. United States,* 389 U.S. 818, 88 S.Ct. 126, 19 L.Ed.2d 70 (1968). Rule 43(c) of the Federal Rules of Civil Procedure provides: "The court may require the offer to be made out of the hearing of the jury." *In re McConnell,* 370 U.S. 230, 82 S.Ct. 1288, 8 L.Ed.2d 434 (1962), left some doubt whether questions on which an offer is based must first be asked in the presence of the jury. The subdivision answers in the negative. The judge can foreclose a particular line of testimony and counsel can protect his record without a series of questions before the jury, designed at best to waste time and at worst "to waft into the jury box" the very matter sought to be excluded.

Note to Subdivision (d). This wording of the plain error principle is from Rule 52(b) of the Federal Rules of Criminal Procedure. While judicial unwillingness to be constructed by mechanical breakdowns of the adversary system has been more pronounced in criminal cases, there is no scarcity of decisions to the same effect in civil cases. In general, see Campbell, Extent to Which Courts of Review Will Consider Questions Not Properly Raised and Preserved, 7 Wis.L.Rev. 91, 160 (1932); Vestal, Sua Sponte Consideration in Appellate Review, 27 Fordham L.Rev. 477 (1958–59); 64 Harv.L.Rev. 652 (1951). In the nature of things the application of the plain error rule will be more likely with respect to the admission of evidence than to exclusion, since failure to comply with normal requirements of offers of proof is likely to produce a record which simply does not disclose the error.

2000 Amendment

The amendment applies to all rulings on evidence whether they occur at or before trial, including so-called *"in limine"* rulings. One of the most difficult questions arising from *in limine* and other evidentiary rulings is whether a losing party must renew an objection or offer of proof when the evidence is or would be offered at trial, in order to preserve a claim of error on appeal. Courts have taken differing approaches to this question. Some courts have held that a renewal at the time the evidence is to be offered at trial is always required.

See, e.g., Collins v. Wayne Corp., 621 F.2d 777 (5th Cir. 1980). Some courts have taken a more flexible approach, holding that renewal is not required if the issue decided is one that (1) was fairly presented to the trial court for an initial ruling, (2) may be decided as a final matter before the evidence is actually offered, and (3) was ruled on definitively by the trial judge, *See, e.g., Rosenfeld v. Basquiat*, 78 F.3d 84 (2d Cir. 1996) (admissibility of former testimony under the Dead Man's Statute; renewal not required). Other courts have distinguished between objections to evidence, which must be renewed when evidence is offered, and offers of proof, which need not be renewed after a definitive determination is made that the evidence is inadmissible. *See, e.g., Fusco v. General Motors Corp.*, 11 F.3d 259 (1st Cir. 1993). Another court, aware of this Committee's proposed amendment, has adopted its approach. *Wilson v. Williams*, 182 F. 3d 562 (7th Cir.1999) (en banc). Differing views on this question create uncertainty for litigants and unnecessary work for the appellate courts.

The amendment provides that a claim of error with respect to a definitive ruling is preserved for review when the party has otherwise satisfied the objection or offer of proof requirements of Rule 103(a). When the ruling is definitive, a renewed objection or offer of proof at the time the evidence is to be offered is more a formalism than a necessity. *See* Fed.R.Civ.P. 46 (formal exceptions unnecessary); Fed.R.Cr.P. 51 (same); *United States v. Mejia–Alarcon*, 995 F.2d 982, 986 (10th Cir. 1993) ("Requiring a party to renew an objection when the district court has issued a definitive ruling on a matter that can be fairly decided before trial would be in the nature of a formal exception and therefore unnecessary."). On the other hand, when the trial court appears to have reserved its ruling or to have indicated that the ruling is provisional, it makes sense to require the party to bring the issue to the court's attention subsequently. *See, e.g., United States v. Vest*, 116 F.3d 1179, 1188 (7th Cir. 1997) (where the trial court ruled *n limine* that testimony from defense witnesses could not be admitted, but allowed the defendant to seek leave at trial to call the witnesses should their testimony turn out to be relevant, the defendant's failure to seek such leave at trial meant that it was "too late to reopen the issue now on appeal"); *United States v. Valenti*, 60 F.3d 941 (2d Cir. 1995) (failure to proffer evidence at trial waives any claim of error where the trial judge had stated that he would reserve judgment on the *in limine* motion until he had heard the trial evidence).

The amendment imposes the obligation on counsel to clarify whether an *in limine* or other evidentiary ruling is definitive when there is doubt on that point. *See, e.g., Walden v. Georgia–Pacific Corp.*, 126 F.3d 506, 520 (3d Cir. 1997) (although "the district court told plaintiffs' counsel not to reargue every ruling, it did not countermand its clear opening statement that all of its rulings were tentative, and counsel never requested clarification, as he might have done.").

Even where the court's ruling is definitive, nothing in the amendment prohibits the court from revisiting its decision when the evidence is to be offered. If the court changes its initial ruling, or if the opposing party violates the terms of the initial ruling, objection must be made when the evidence is offered to preserve the claim of error for appeal. The error, if any, in such a situation occurs only when the evidence is offered and admitted. *United States Aviation Underwriters, Inc. v. Olympia Wings, Inc.*, 896 F.2d 949, 956 (5th Cir. 1990) ("objection is required to preserve error when an opponent, or the court itself, violates a motion *in limine* that was granted"); *United States v. Roenigk*, 810 F.2d 809 (8th Cir. 1987)

(claim of error was not preserved where the defendant failed to object at trial to secure the benefit of a favorable advance ruling).

A definitive advance ruling is reviewed in light of the facts and circumstances before the trial court at the time of the ruling. If the relevant facts and circumstances change materially after the advance ruling has been made, those facts and circumstances cannot be relied upon on appeal unless they have been brought to the attention of the trial court by way of a renewed, and timely, objection, offer of proof, or motion to strike. *See Old Chief v. United States*, 519 U.S. 172, 182, n.6 (1997) ("It is important that a reviewing court evaluate the trial court's decision from its perspective when it had to rule and not indulge in review by hindsight."). Similarly, if the court decides in an advance ruling that proffered evidence is admissible subject to the eventual introduction by the proponent of a foundation for the evidence, and that foundation is never provided, the opponent cannot claim error based on the failure to establish the foundation unless the opponent calls that failure to the court's attention by a timely motion to strike or other suitable motion. *See Huddleston v. United States*, 485 U.S. 681, 690, n.7 (1988) ("It is, of course, not the responsibility of the judge *sua sponte* to ensure that the foundation evidence is offered; the objector must move to strike the evidence if at the close of the trial the offeror has failed to satisfy the condition.").

Nothing in the amendment is intended to affect the provisions of Fed.R.Civ.P. 72(a) or 28 U.S.C. § 636(b)(1) pertaining to nondispositive pretrial rulings by magistrate judges in proceedings that are not before a magistrate judge by consent of the parties. Fed.R.Civ.P. 72(a) provides that a party who fails to file a written objection to a magistrate judge's nondispositive order within ten days of receiving a copy "may not thereafter assign as error a defect" in the order. 28 U.S.C. § 636(b)(1) provides that any party "may serve and file written objections to such proposed findings and recommendations as provided by rules of court" within ten days of receiving a copy of the order. Several courts have held that a party must comply with this statutory provision in order to preserve a claim of error. *See, e.g., Wells v. Shriners Hospital*, 109 F.3d 198, 200 (4th Cir. 1997)("[i]n this circuit, as in others, a party 'may' file objections within ten days or he may not, as he chooses, but he 'shall' do so if he wishes further consideration."). When Fed.R.Civ.P. 72(a) or 28 U.S.C. § 636(b)(1) is operative, its requirement must be satisfied in order for a party to preserve a claim of error on appeal, even where Evidence Rule 103(a) would not require a subsequent objection or offer of proof.

Nothing in the amendment is intended to affect the rule set forth in *Luce v. United States*, 469 U.S. 38 (1984), and its progeny. The amendment provides that an objection or offer of proof need not be renewed to preserve a claim of error with respect to a definitive pretrial ruling. *Luce* answers affirmatively a separate question: whether a criminal defendant must testify at trial in order to preserve a claim of error predicated upon a trial court's decision to admit the defendant's prior convictions for impeachment. The *Luce* principle has been extended by many lower courts to other situations. *See United States v. DiMatteo*, 759 F.2d 831 (11th Cir. 1985) (applying *Luce* where the defendant's witness would be impeached with evidence offered under Rule 608). *See also United States v. Goldman*, 41 F.3d 785, 788 (1st Cir. 1994) ("Although *Luce* involved impeachment by conviction under Rule 609, the reasons given by the Supreme Court for requiring the defendant to testify apply with full force to the kind of Rule 403 and 404 objections that are advanced by Goldman in this case."); *Palmieri v. DeFaria*, 88 F.3d 136 (2d Cir. 1996) (where the plaintiff decided to take an adverse judgment rather than challenge an advance ruling by putting on evidence at trial, the *in limine* ruling would not be reviewed on appeal); *United States v. Ortiz*, 857 F.2d 900 (2d Cir. 1988) (where uncharged misconduct is ruled admissible if the defendant pursues a certain defense, the defendant must actually pursue that defense at trial in order to preserve a claim of error on appeal); *United States v. Bond*, 87 F.3d 695 (5th Cir. 1996) (where the trial court rules *in limine* that the defendant would waive his fifth amendment privilege were he to testify, the defendant must take the stand and testify in order to challenge that ruling on appeal).

The amendment does not purport to answer whether a party who objects to evidence that the court finds admissible in a definitive ruling, and who then offers the evidence to "remove the sting" of its anticipated prejudicial effect, thereby waives the right to appeal the trial court's ruling. *See, e.g., United States v. Fisher*, 106 F.3d 622 (5th Cir. 1997) (where the trial judge ruled *in limine* that the government could use a prior conviction to impeach the defendant if he testified, the defendant did not waive his right to appeal by introducing the conviction on direct examination); *Judd v. Rodman*, 105 F.3d 1339 (11th Cir. 1997) (an objection made *in limine* is sufficient to preserve a claim of error when the movant, as a matter of trial strategy, presents the objectionable evidence herself on direct examination to minimize its prejudicial effect); *Gill v. Thomas*, 83 F.3d 537, 540 (1st Cir. 1996) ("by offering the misdemeanor evidence himself, Gill waived his opportunity to object and thus did not preserve the issue for appeal"); *United States v. Williams*, 939 F.2d 721 (9th Cir. 1991) (objection to impeachment evidence was waived where the defendant was impeached on direct examination).

GAP Report—Proposed Amendment to Rule 103(a)

The Committee made the following changes to the published draft of the proposed amendment to Evidence Rule 103(a):

1. A minor stylistic change was made in the text, in accordance with the suggestion of the Style Subcommittee of the Standing Committee on Rules of Practice and Procedure.

2. The second sentence of the amended portion of the published draft was deleted, and the Committee Note was amended to reflect the fact that nothing in the amendment is intended to affect the rule of *Luce v. United States*.

3. The Committee Note was updated to include cases decided after the proposed amendment was issued for public comment.

4. The Committee Note was amended to include a reference to a Civil Rule and a statute requiring objections to certain Magistrate Judge rulings to be made to the District Court.

5. The Committee Note was revised to clarify that an advance ruling does not encompass subsequent developments at trial that might be the subject of an appeal.

2011 Amendments

The language of Rule 103 has been amended as part of the restyling of the Evidence Rules to make them more easily understood and to make style and terminology consistent throughout the rules. These changes are intended to be stylistic only. There is no intent to change any result in any ruling on evidence admissibility.

HISTORICAL NOTES

Conference Committee Notes, House Report No. 93–1597

The House bill contains the word "judge". The Senate amendment substitutes the word "court" in order to conform with usage elsewhere in the House bill.

The Conference adopts the Senate amendment.

CROSS REFERENCES

Fair and impartial trial and jury, right to, see USCA Const. Amend. VI.

Harmless error, see 28 USCA § 2111 and Fed.Rules Civ. Proc. Rule 61, 28 USCA.

Harmless error and plain error, see Fed.Rules Cr.Proc. Rule 52, 18 USCA.

Objections,

Absence of not prejudicial, see Fed.Rules Cr.Proc. Rule 51, 18 USCA.

Absence of on rulings not prejudicial, see Fed.Rules Civ.Proc. Rule 46, 28 USCA.

Admissibility of depositions, see Fed.Rules Cr.Proc. Rule 15, 18 USCA.

Suppression of evidence,

Motion for return of property involved in seizure, see Fed.Rules Cr.Proc. Rule 41, 18 USCA.

Motion to suppress evidence, see Fed.Rules Cr.Proc. Rule 12, 18 USCA.

Rule 104. Preliminary Questions

(a) In General. The court must decide any preliminary question about whether a witness is qualified, a privilege exists, or evidence is admissible. In so deciding, the court is not bound by evidence rules, except those on privilege.

(b) Relevance That Depends on a Fact. When the relevance of evidence depends on whether a fact exists, proof must be introduced sufficient to support a finding that the fact does exist. The court may admit the proposed evidence on the condition that the proof be introduced later.

(c) Conducting a Hearing So That the Jury Cannot Hear It. The court must conduct any hearing on a preliminary question so that the jury cannot hear it if:

(1) the hearing involves the admissibility of a confession;

(2) a defendant in a criminal case is a witness and so requests; or

(3) justice so requires.

(d) Cross–Examining a Defendant in a Criminal Case. By testifying on a preliminary question, a defendant in a criminal case does not become subject to cross-examination on other issues in the case.

(e) Evidence Relevant to Weight and Credibility. This rule does not limit a party's right to introduce before the jury evidence that is relevant to the weight or credibility of other evidence.

(Pub.L. 93–595, § 1, Jan. 2, 1975, 88 Stat.1930; Mar. 2, 1987, eff. Oct. 1, 1987; Apr. 26, 2011, eff. Dec. 1, 2011.)

ADVISORY COMMITTEE NOTES

1972 Proposed Rule

Note to Subdivision (a). The applicability of a particular rule of evidence often depends upon the existence of a condition. Is the alleged expert a qualified physician? Is a witness whose former testimony is offered unavailable? Was a stranger present during a conversation between attorney and client? In each instance the admissibility of evidence will turn upon the answer to the question of the existence of the condition. Accepted practice, incorporated in the rule, places on the judge the responsibility for these determinations. McCormick § 53; Morgan, Basic Problems of Evidence 45–50 (1962).

To the extent that these inquiries are factual, the judge acts as a trier of fact. Often, however, rulings on evidence call for an evaluation in terms of a legally set standard. Thus when a hearsay statement is offered as a declaration against interest, a decision must be made whether it possesses the required against-interest characteristics. These decisions, too, are made by the judge.

In view of these considerations, this subdivision refers to preliminary requirements generally by the broad term "questions," without attempt at specification.

This subdivision is of general application. It must, however, be read as subject to the special provisions for "conditional relevancy" in subdivision (b) and those for confessions in subdivision (d).

If the question is factual in nature, the judge will of necessity receive evidence pro and con on the issue. The rule provides that the rules of evidence in general do not apply to this process. McCormick § 53, p. 123, n. 8, points out that the authorities are "scattered and inconclusive," and observes:

"Should the exclusionary law of evidence, 'the child of the jury system' in Thayer's phrase, be applied to this hearing before the judge? Sound sense backs the view that it should not, and that the judge should be empowered to hear any relevant evidence, such as affidavits or other reliable hearsay."

This view is reinforced by practical necessity in certain situations. An item, offered and objected to, may itself be considered in ruling on admissibility, though not yet admitted in evidence. Thus, the content of an asserted declaration against interest must be considered in ruling whether it is against interest. Again, common practice calls for considering the testimony of a witness, particularly a child, in determining competency. Another example is the requirement of Rule 602 dealing with personal knowledge. In the case of hearsay, it is enough, if the declarant "so far as appears [has] had an opportunity to observe the fact declared." McCormick, § 10, p. 19.

If concern is felt over the use of affidavits by the judge in preliminary hearings on admissibility, attention is directed to the many important judicial determinations made on the basis of affidavits. Rule 47 of the Federal Rules of Criminal Procedure provides:

"An application to the court for an order shall be by motion. * * * It may be supported by affidavit."

The Rules of Civil Procedure are more detailed. Rule 43(e), dealing with motions generally, provides:

"When a motion is based on facts not appearing of record the court may hear the matter on affidavits presented by the respective parties, but the court may direct that the matter be heard wholly or partly on oral testimony or depositions." Rule 4(g) provides for proof of service by affidavit. Rule 56 provides in detail for the entry of summary judgment based on affidavits. Affidavits may supply the foundation for temporary restraining orders under Rule 65(b).

The study made for the California Law Revision Commission recommended an amendment to Uniform Rule 2 as follows:

"In the determination of the issue aforesaid [preliminary determination], exclusionary rules shall not apply, subject, however, to Rule 45 and any valid claim of privilege." Tentative Recommendation and a Study Relating to the Uniform Rules of Evidence (Article VIII, Hearsay), Cal.Law Revision Comm'n, Rep., Rec. & Studies, 470 (1962). The proposal was not adopted in the California Evidence Code. The Uniform Rules are likewise silent on the subject. However, New Jersey Evidence Rule 8(1), dealing with preliminary inquiry by the judge, provides:

"In his determination the rules of evidence shall not apply except for Rule 4 [exclusion on grounds of confusion, etc.] or a valid claim of privilege."

Note to Subdivision (b). In some situations, the relevancy of an item of evidence, in the large sense, depends upon the existence of a particular preliminary fact. Thus when a spoken statement is relied upon to prove notice to X, it is without probative value unless X heard it. Or if a letter purporting to be from Y is relied upon to establish an admission by him, it has no probative value unless Y wrote or authorized it. Relevance in this sense has been labelled "conditional relevancy." Morgan, Basic Problems of Evidence 45–46 (1962). Problems arising in connection with it are to be distinguished from problems of logical relevancy, e.g., evidence in a murder case that accused on the day before purchased a weapon of the kind used in the killing, treated in Rule 401.

If preliminary questions of conditional relevancy were determined solely by the judge, as provided in subdivision (a), the functioning of the jury as a trier of fact would be greatly restricted and in some cases virtually destroyed. These are appropriate questions for juries. Accepted treatment, as provided in the rule, is consistent with that given fact questions generally. The judge makes a preliminary determination whether the foundation evidence is sufficient to support a finding of fulfillment of the condition. If so, the item is admitted. If after all the evidence on the issue is in, pro and con, the jury could reasonably conclude that fulfillment of the condition is not established, the issue is for them. If the evidence is not such as to allow a finding, the judge withdraws the matter from their consideration. Morgan, *supra;* California Evidence Code § 403; New Jersey Rule 8(2). See also Uniform Rules 19 and 67.

The order of proof here, as generally, is subject to the control of the judge.

Note to Subdivision (c). Preliminary hearings on the admissibility of confessions must be conducted outside the hearing of the jury. See *Jackson v. Denno,* 378 U.S. 368, 84 S.Ct. 1774, 12 L.Ed.2d 908 (1964). Otherwise, detailed treatment of when preliminary matters should be heard outside the hearing of the jury is not feasible. The procedure is time consuming. Not infrequently the same evidence which is relevant to the issue of establishment of fulfillment of a condition precedent to admissibility is also relevant to weight or credibility, and time is saved by taking foundation proof in the presence of the jury. Much evidence on preliminary questions, though not relevant to jury issues, may be heard by the jury with no adverse effect. A great deal must be left to the discretion of the judge who will act as the interests of justice require.

Note to Subdivision (d). The limitation upon cross-examination is designed to encourage participation by the accused in the determination of preliminary matters. He may testify concerning them without exposing himself to cross-examination generally. The provision is necessary because of the breadth of cross-examination under Rule 611(b).

The rule does not address itself to questions of the subsequent use of testimony given by an accused at a hearing on a preliminary matter. See *Walder v. United States*, 347 U.S. 62 (1954); *Simmons v. United States*, 390 U.S. 377 (1968); *Harris v. New York*, 401 U.S. 222 (1971).

Note to Subdivision (e). For similar provisions see Uniform Rule 8; California Evidence Code § 406; Kansas Code of Civil Procedure § 60–408; New Jersey Evidence Rule 8(1).

1974 Enactment

Rule 104(c) as submitted to the Congress provided that hearings on the admissibility of confessions shall be conducted outside the presence of the jury and hearings on all other preliminary matters should be so conducted when the interests of justice require. The Committee amended the Rule to provide that where an accused is a witness as to a preliminary matter, he has the right, upon his request, to be heard outside the jury's presence. Although recognizing that in some cases duplication of evidence would occur and that the procedure could be subject to abuse, the Committee believed that a proper regard for the right of an accused not to testify generally in the case dictates that he be given an option to testify out of the presence of the jury on preliminary matters.

The Committee construes the second sentence of subdivision (c) as applying to civil actions and proceedings as well as to criminal cases, and on this assumption has left the sentence unamended. House Report No. 93–650.

Under rule 104(c) the hearing on a preliminary matter may at times be conducted in front of the jury. Should an accused testify in such a hearing, waiving his privilege against self-incrimination as to the preliminary issue, rule 104(d) provides that he will not generally be subject to cross-examination as to any other issue. This rule is not, however, intended to immunize the accused from cross-examination where, in testifying about a preliminary issue, he injects other issues into the hearing. If he could not be cross-examined about any issues gratuitously raised by him beyond the scope of the preliminary matters, injustice might result. Accordingly, in order to prevent any such unjust result, the committee intends the rule to be construed to provide that the accused may subject himself to cross-examination as to issues raised by his own testimony upon a preliminary matter before a jury. Senate Report No. 93–1277.

1987 Amendments

The amendments are technical. No substantive change is intended.

2011 Amendments

The language of Rule 104 has been amended as part of the restyling of the Evidence Rules to make them more easily understood and to make style and terminology consistent throughout the rules. These changes are intended to be stylistic only. There is no intent to change any result in any ruling on evidence admissibility.

CROSS REFERENCES

Cross-examination, scope of, see Fed.Rules Evid. Rule 611, 28 USCA.

Functions of court and jury, determination of admissibility, see Fed.Rules Evid. Rule 1008, 28 USCA.

Preliminary questions of fact, inapplicability of these rules to, see Fed.Rules Evid. Rule 1101, 28 USCA.

Privileges, see Fed.Rules Evid. Rule 501, 28 USCA.

Rape, relevancy of evidence conditioned upon fulfillment of fact, see Fed.Rules Evid. Rule 412, 28 USCA.

Relevancy and its limits, see Fed.Rules Evid. Rule 401 et seq., 28 USCA.

Self-incrimination, freedom from, see USCA Const. Amend. V.

Witnesses, see Fed.Rules Evid. Rule 601 et seq., 28 USCA.

Rule 105. Limiting Evidence That Is Not Admissible Against Other Parties or for Other Purposes

If the court admits evidence that is admissible against a party or for a purpose—but not against another party or for another purpose—the court, on timely request, must restrict the evidence to its proper scope and instruct the jury accordingly.

(Pub.L. 93–595, § 1, Jan. 2, 1975, 88 Stat. 1930; Apr. 26, 2011, eff. Dec. 1, 2011.)

ADVISORY COMMITTEE NOTES

1972 Proposed Rules

A close relationship exists between this rule and Rule 403 which requires exclusion when "probative value is substantially outweighed by the danger of unfair prejudice, confusion of the issues, or misleading the jury." The present rule recognizes the practice of admitting evidence for a limited purpose and instructing the jury accordingly. The availability and effectiveness of this practice must be taken into consideration in reaching a decision whether to exclude for unfair prejudice under Rule 403. In *Bruton v. United States*, 389 U.S. 818, 88 S.Ct. 126, 19 L.Ed.2d 70 (1968), the Court ruled that a limiting instruction did not effectively protect the accused against the prejudicial effect of admitting in evidence the confession of a codefendant which implicated him. The decision does not, however, bar the use of limited admissibility with an instruction where the risk of prejudice is less serious.

Similar provisions are found in Uniform Rule 6; California Evidence Code § 355; Kansas Code of Civil Procedure § 60–406; New Jersey Evidence Rule 6. The wording of the present rule differs, however, in repelling any implication that limiting or curative instructions are sufficient in all situations.

1974 Enactment

Rule 106 as submitted by the Supreme Court (now Rule 105 in the bill) dealt with the subject of evidence which is admissible as to one party or for one purpose but is not admissible against another party or for another purpose. The Committee adopted this Rule without change on the understanding that it does not affect the authority of a court to order a severance in a multi-defendant case. House Report No. 93–650.

2011 Amendments

The language of Rule 105 has been amended as part of the restyling of the Evidence Rules to make them more easily understood and to make style and terminology consistent throughout the rules. These changes are intended to be stylistic only. There is no intent to change any result in any ruling on evidence admissibility.

CROSS REFERENCES

Exclusion of evidence for prejudice, confusion, or waste of time, see Fed.Rules Evid. Rule 403, 28 USCA.

Rule 106. Remainder of or Related Writings or Recorded Statements

If a party introduces all or part of a writing or recorded statement, an adverse party may require the introduction, at that time, of any other part—or any other writing or recorded statement—that in fairness ought to be considered at the same time.

(Pub.L. 93–595, § 1, Jan. 2, 1975, 88 Stat. 1930; Mar. 2, 1987, eff. Oct. 1, 1987; Apr. 26, 2011, eff. Dec. 1, 2011.)

ADVISORY COMMITTEE NOTES
1972 Proposed Rules

The rule is an expression of the rule of completeness. McCormick § 56. It is manifested as to depositions in Rule 32(a)(4) of the Federal Rules of Civil Procedure, of which the proposed rule is substantially a restatement.

The rule is based on two considerations. The first is the misleading impression created by taking matters out of context. The second is the inadequacy of repair work when delayed to a point later in the trial. See McCormick § 56; California Evidence Code § 356. The rule does not in any way circumscribe the right of the adversary to develop the matter on cross-examination or as part of his own case.

For practical reasons, the rule is limited to writings and recorded statements and does not apply to conversations.

1987 Amendments

The amendments are technical. No substantive change is intended.

2011 Amendments

The language of Rule 106 has been amended as part of the restyling of the Evidence Rules to make them more easily understood and to make style and terminology consistent throughout the rules. These changes are intended to be stylistic only. There is no intent to change any result in any ruling on evidence admissibility.

CROSS REFERENCES

Depositions, admission of remainder of, see Fed.Rules Civ. Proc. Rule 32, 28 USCA.

Writings and recordings, admissibility of duplicates and other evidence of contents, see Fed.Rules Evid. Rule 1003 and Rule 1004, 28 USCA.

ARTICLE II. JUDICIAL NOTICE

Rule
201. Judicial Notice of Adjudicative Facts.

Rule 201. Judicial Notice of Adjudicative Facts

(a) **Scope.** This rule governs judicial notice of an adjudicative fact only, not a legislative fact.

(b) **Kinds of Facts That May Be Judicially Noticed.** The court may judicially notice a fact that is not subject to reasonable dispute because it:

(1) is generally known within the trial court's territorial jurisdiction; or

(2) can be accurately and readily determined from sources whose accuracy cannot reasonably be questioned.

(c) **Taking Notice.** The court:

(1) may take judicial notice on its own; or

(2) must take judicial notice if a party requests it and the court is supplied with the necessary information.

(d) **Timing.** The court may take judicial notice at any stage of the proceeding.

(e) **Opportunity to Be Heard.** On timely request, a party is entitled to be heard on the propriety of taking judicial notice and the nature of the fact to be noticed. If the court takes judicial notice before notifying a party, the party, on request, is still entitled to be heard.

(f) **Instructing the Jury.** In a civil case, the court must instruct the jury to accept the noticed fact as conclusive. In a criminal case, the court must instruct the jury that it may or may not accept the noticed fact as conclusive.

(Pub.L. 93–595, § 1, Jan. 2, 1975, 88 Stat. 1930; Apr. 26, 2011, eff. Dec. 1, 2011.)

ADVISORY COMMITTEE NOTES
1972 Proposed Rules

Note to Subdivision (a). This is the only evidence rule on the subject of judicial notice. It deals only with judicial notice of "adjudicative" facts. No rule deals with judicial notice of "legislative" facts. Judicial notice of matters of foreign law is treated in Rule 44.1 of the Federal Rules of Civil Procedure and Rule 26.1 of the Federal Rules of Criminal Procedure.

The omission of any treatment of legislative facts results from fundamental differences between adjudicative facts and legislative facts. Adjudicative facts are simply the facts of the particular case. Legislative facts, on the other hand, are those which have relevance to legal reasoning and the law-making process, whether in the formulation of a legal principle or ruling by a judge or court or in the enactment of a legislative body. The terminology was coined by Professor Kenneth Davis in his article An Approach to Problems of Evidence in the Administrative Process, 55 Harv.L.Rev. 364, 404–407 (1942). The following discussion draws extensively upon his writings. In addition, see the same author's Judicial Notice, 55 Colum.L.Rev. 945 (1955); Administrative Law Treatise, ch. 15 (1958); A System of Judicial Notice Based on Fairness and Convenience, in Perspectives of Law 69 (1964).

The usual method of establishing adjudicative facts is through the introduction of evidence, ordinarily consisting of the testimony of witnesses. If particular facts are outside the area of reasonable controversy, this process is dispensed with as unnecessary. A high degree of indisputability is the essential prerequisite.

Legislative facts are quite different. As Professor Davis says:

"My opinion is that judge-made law would stop growing if judges, in thinking about questions of law and policy, were forbidden to take into account the facts they believe, as distinguished from facts which are 'clearly * * * within the domain of the indisputable.' Facts most needed in thinking about difficult problems of law and policy have a way of being outside the domain of the clearly indisputable." A System of Judicial Notice Based on Fairness and Convenience, *supra*, at 82.

An illustration is *Hawkins v. United States*, 358 U.S. 74, 79 S.Ct. 136, 3 L.Ed.2d 125 (1958), in which the Court refused to discard the common law rule that one spouse could not testify against the other, saying, "Adverse testimony given in criminal proceedings would, we think, be likely to destroy almost any marriage." This conclusion has a large intermixture of fact, but the factual aspect is scarcely "indisputable." See Hutchins and Slesinger, Some Observations on the Law of Evidence—Family Relations, 13 Minn.L.Rev. 675 (1929). If the destructive effect of the giving of adverse testimony by a spouse is not indisputable, should the Court have refrained from considering it in the absence of supporting evidence?

"If the Model Code or the Uniform Rules had been applicable, the Court would have been barred from thinking about the essential factual ingredient of the problems before it, and such a result would be obviously intolerable. What the law needs at its growing points is more, not less, judicial thinking about the factual ingredients of problems of what the law ought to be, and the needed facts are seldom 'clearly' indisputable." Davis, *supra*, at 83.

Professor Morgan gave the following description of the methodology of determining domestic law:

"In determining the content or applicability of a rule of domestic law, the judge is unrestricted in his investigation and conclusion. He may reject the propositions of either party or of both parties. He may consult the sources of pertinent data to which they refer, or he may refuse to do so. He may make an independent search for persuasive data or rest content with what he has or what the parties present. * * * [T]he parties do no more than to assist; they control no part of the process." Morgan, Judicial Notice, 57 Harv.L.Rev. 269, 270–271 (1944).

This is the view which should govern judicial access to legislative facts. It renders inappropriate any limitation in the form of indisputability, any formal requirements of notice other than those already inherent in affording opportunity to hear and be heard and exchanging briefs, and any requirement of formal findings at any level. It should, however leave open the possibility of introducing evidence through regular channels in appropriate situations. See *Borden's Farm Products Co. v. Baldwin*, 293 U.S. 194, 55 S.Ct. 187, 79 L.Ed. 281 (1934), where the cause was remanded for the taking of evidence as to the economic conditions and trade practices underlying the New York Milk Control Law.

Similar considerations govern the judicial use of non-adjudicative facts in ways other than formulating laws and rules. Thayer described them as a part of the judicial reasoning process.

"In conducting a process of judicial reasoning, as of other reasoning, not a step can be taken without assuming something which has not been proved; and the capacity to do this with competent judgment and efficiency, is imputed to judges and juries as part of their necessary mental outfit." Thayer, Preliminary Treatise on Evidence 279–280 (1898).

As Professor Davis points out, A System of Judicial Notice Based on Fairness and Convenience, in Perspectives of Law 69, 73 (1964), every case involves the use of hundreds or thousands of non-evidence facts. When a witness in an automobile accident case says "car," everyone, judge and jury included, furnishes, from non-evidence sources within himself, the supplementing information that the "car" is an automobile, not a railroad car, that it is self-propelled, probably by an internal combustion engine, that it may be assumed to have four wheels with pneumatic rubber tires, and so on. The judicial process cannot construct every case from scratch, like Descartes creating a world based on the postulate *Cogito, ergo sum.* These items could not possibly be introduced into evidence, and no one suggests that they be. Nor are they appropriate subjects for any formalized treatment of judicial notice of facts. See Levin and Levy, Persuading the Jury with Facts Not in Evidence: The Fiction–Science Spectrum, 105 U.Pa.L.Rev. 139 (1956).

Another aspect of what Thayer had in mind is the use of non-evidence facts to appraise or assess the adjudicative facts of the case. Pairs of cases from two jurisdictions illustrate this use and also the difference between non-evidence facts thus used and adjudicative facts. In People v. Strook, 347 Ill. 460, 179 N.E. 821 (1932), venue in Cook County had been held not established by testimony that the crime was committed at 7956 South Chicago Avenue, since judicial notice would not be taken that the address was in Chicago. However, the same court subsequently ruled that venue in Cook County was established by testimony that a crime occurred at 8900 South Anthony Avenue, since notice would be taken of the common practice of omitting the name of the city when speaking of local addresses, and the witness was testifying in Chicago. *People v. Pride*, 16 Ill.2d 82, 156 N.E.2d 551 (1951). And in *Hughes v. Vestal*, 264 N.C. 500, 142 S.E.2d 361 (1965), the Supreme Court of North Carolina disapproved the trial judge's admission in evidence of a state-published table of automobile stopping distances on the basis of judicial notice, though the court itself had referred to the same table in an earlier case in a "rhetorical and illustrative" way in determining that the defendant could not have stopped her car in time to avoid striking a child who suddenly appeared in the highway and that a nonsuit was properly granted. *Ennis v.*

Dupree, 262 N.C. 224, 136 S.E.2d 702 (1964). See also *Brown v. Hale,* 263 N.C. 176, 139 S.E.2d 210 (1964); *Clayton v. Rimmer,* 262 N.C. 302, 136 S.E.2d 562 (1964). It is apparent that this use of non-evidence facts in evaluating the adjudicative facts of the case is not an appropriate subject for a formalized judicial notice treatment.

In view of these considerations, the regulation of judicial notice of facts by the present rule extends only to adjudicative facts.

What, then, are "adjudicative" facts? Davis refers to them as those "which relate to the parties," or more fully:

"When a court or an agency finds facts concerning the immediate parties—who did what, where, when, how, and with what motive or intent—the court or agency is performing an adjudicative function, and the facts are conveniently called adjudicative facts. * * *

"Stated in other terms, the adjudicative facts are those to which the law is applied in the process of adjudication. They are the facts that normally go to the jury in a jury case. They relate to the parties, their activities, their properties, their businesses." 2 Administrative Law Treatise 353.

Note to Subdivision (b). With respect to judicial notice of adjudicative facts, the tradition has been one of caution in requiring that the matter be beyond reasonable controversy. This tradition of circumspection appears to be soundly based, and no reason to depart from it is apparent. As Professor Davis says:

"The reason we use trial-type procedure, I think, is that we make the practical judgment, on the basis of experience, that taking evidence, subject to cross-examination and rebuttal, is the best way to resolve controversies involving disputes of adjudicative facts, that is, facts pertaining to the parties. The reason we require a determination on the record is that we think fair procedure in resolving disputes of adjudicative facts calls for giving each party a chance to meet in the appropriate fashion the facts that come to the tribunal's attention, and the appropriate fashion for meeting disputed adjudicative facts includes rebuttal evidence, cross-examination, usually confrontation, and argument (either written or oral or both). The key to a fair trial is opportunity to use the appropriate weapons (rebuttal evidence, cross-examination, and argument) to meet adverse materials that come to the tribunal's attention." A System of Judicial Notice Based on Fairness and Convenience, in Perspectives of Law 69, 93 (1964).

The rule proceeds upon the theory that these considerations call for dispensing with traditional methods of proof only in clear cases. Compare Professor Davis' conclusion that judicial notice should be a matter of convenience, subject to requirements of procedural fairness. *Id.,* 94.

This rule is consistent with Uniform Rule 9(1) and (2) which limit judicial notice of facts to those "so universally known that they cannot reasonably be the subject of dispute," those "so generally known or of such common notoriety within the territorial jurisdiction of the court that they cannot reasonably be the subject of dispute," and those "capable of immediate and accurate determination by resort to easily accessible sources of indisputable accuracy." The traditional textbook treatment has included these general categories (matters of common knowledge, facts capable of verification), McCormick §§ 324, 325, and then has passed on into detailed treatment of such specific topics as facts relating to the personnel and records of the court, *Id.* § 327, and other governmental facts, *Id.* § 328. The California draftsmen, with a background of detailed statutory regulation of judicial notice, followed a

somewhat similar pattern. California Evidence Code §§ 451, 452. The Uniform Rules, however, were drafted on the theory that these particular matters are included within the general categories and need no specific mention. This approach is followed in the present rule.

The phrase "propositions of generalized knowledge," found in Uniform Rule 9(1) and (2) is not included in the present rule. It was, it is believed, originally included in Model Code Rules 801 and 802 primarily in order to afford some minimum recognition to the right of the judge in his "legislative" capacity (not acting as the trier of fact) to take judicial notice of very limited categories of generalized knowledge. The limitations thus imposed have been discarded herein as undesirable, unworkable, and contrary to existing practice. What is left, then, to be considered, is the status of a "proposition of generalized knowledge" as an "adjudicative" fact to be noticed judicially and communicated by the judge to the jury. Thus viewed, it is considered to be lacking practical significance. While judges use judicial notice of "propositions of generalized knowledge" in a variety of situations: determining the validity and meaning of statutes, formulating common law rules, deciding whether evidence should be admitted, assessing the sufficiency and effect of evidence, all are essentially nonadjudicative in nature. When judicial notice is seen as a significant vehicle for progress in the law, these are the areas involved, particularly in developing fields of scientific knowledge. See McCormick 712. It is not believed that judges now instruct juries as to "propositions of generalized knowledge" derived from encyclopedias or other sources, or that they are likely to do so, or, indeed, that it is desirable that they do so. There is a vast difference between ruling on the basis of judicial notice that radar evidence of speed is admissible and explaining to the jury its principles and degree of accuracy, or between using a table of stopping distances of automobiles at various speeds in a judicial evaluation of testimony and telling the jury its precise application in the case. For cases raising doubt as to the propriety of the use of medical texts by lay triers of fact in passing on disability claims in administrative proceedings, see *Sayers v. Gardner,* 380 F.2d 940 (6th Cir.1967); *Ross v. Gardner,* 365 F.2d 554 (6th Cir.1966); *Sosna v. Celebrezze,* 234 F.Supp. 289 (E.D.Pa. 1964); *Glendenning v. Ribicoff,* 213 F.Supp. 301 (W.D.Mo. 1962).

Notes to Subdivisions (c) and (d). Under subdivision (c) the judge has a discretionary authority to take judicial notice, regardless of whether he is so requested by a party. The taking of judicial notice is mandatory, under subdivision (d), only when a party requests it and the necessary information is supplied. This scheme is believed to reflect existing practice. It is simple and workable. It avoids troublesome distinctions in the many situations in which the process of taking judicial notice is not recognized as such.

Compare Uniform Rule 9 making judicial notice of facts universally known mandatory without request, and making judicial notice of facts generally known in the jurisdiction or capable of determination by resort to accurate sources discretionary in the absence of request but mandatory if request is made and the information furnished. But see Uniform Rule 10(3), which directs the judge to decline to take judicial notice if available information fails to convince him that the matter falls clearly within Uniform Rule 9 or is insufficient to enable him to notice it judicially. Substantially the same approach is found in California Evidence Code §§ 451–453 and in New

---

Jersey Evidence Rule 9. In contrast, the present rule treats alike all adjudicative facts which are subject to judicial notice.

Note to Subdivision (e). Basic considerations of procedural fairness demand an opportunity to be heard on the propriety of taking judicial notice and the tenor of the matter noticed. The rule requires the granting of that opportunity upon request. No formal scheme of giving notice is provided. An adversely affected party may learn in advance that judicial notice is in contemplation, either by virtue of being served with a copy of a request by another party under subdivision (d) that judicial notice be taken, or through an advance indication by the judge. Or he may have no advance notice at all. The likelihood of the latter is enhanced by the frequent failure to recognize judicial notice as such. And in the absence of advance notice, a request made after the fact could not in fairness be considered untimely. See the provision for hearing on timely request in the Administrative Procedure Act, 5 U.S.C. § 556(e). See also Revised Model State Administrative Procedure Act (1961), 9C U.L.A. § 10(4) (Supp.1967).

Note to Subdivision (f). In accord with the usual view, judicial notice may be taken at any stage of the proceedings, whether in the trial court or on appeal. Uniform Rule 12; California Evidence Code § 459; Kansas Rules of Evidence § 60–412; New Jersey Evidence Rule 12; McCormick § 330, p. 712.

Note to Subdivision (g). Much of the controversy about judicial notice has centered upon the question whether evidence should be admitted in disproof of facts of which judicial notice is taken.

The writers have been divided. Favoring admissibility are Thayer, Preliminary Treatise on Evidence 308 (1898); 9 Wigmore § 2567; Davis, A System of Judicial Notice Based on Fairness and Convenience, in Perspectives of Law, 69, 76–77 (1964). Opposing admissibility are Keeffe, Landis and Shaad, Sense and Nonsense about Judicial Notice, 2 Stan.L.Rev. 664, 668 (1950); McNaughton, Judicial Notice—Excerpts Relating to the Morgan–Whitmore Controversy, 14 Vand.L.Rev. 779 (1961); Morgan, Judicial Notice, 57 Harv.L.Rev. 269, 279 (1944); McCormick 710–711. The Model Code and the Uniform Rules are predicated upon indisputability of judicially noticed facts.

The proponents of admitting evidence in disproof have concentrated largely upon legislative facts. Since the present rule deals only with judicial notice of adjudicative facts, arguments directed to legislative facts lose their relevancy.

Within its relatively narrow area of adjudicative facts, the rule contemplates there is to be no evidence before the jury in disproof. The judge instructs the jury to take judicially noticed facts as established. This position is justified by the undesirable effects of the opposite rule in limiting the rebutting party, though not his opponent, to admissible evidence, in defeating the reasons for judicial notice, and in affecting the substantive law to an extent and in ways largely unforeseeable. Ample protection and flexibility are afforded by the broad provision for opportunity to be heard on request, set forth in subdivision (e).

Authority upon the propriety of taking judicial notice against an accused in a criminal case with respect to matters other than venue is relatively meager. Proceeding upon the theory that the right of jury trial does not extend to matters which are beyond reasonable dispute, the rule does not distinguish between criminal and civil cases. *People v. Mayes*, 113 Cal. 618, 45 P. 860 (1896); *Ross v. United States*, 374 F.2d 97 (8th Cir.1967). Cf. *State v. Main*, 94 R.I. 338, 180 A.2d 814 (1962); *State v. Lawrence*, 120 Utah 323, 234 P.2d 600 (1951).

Note on Judicial Notice of Law. By rules effective July 1, 1966, the method of invoking the law of a foreign country is covered elsewhere. Rule 44.1 of the Federal Rules of Civil Procedure; Rule 26.1 of the Federal Rules of Criminal Procedure. These two new admirably designed rules are founded upon the assumption that the manner in which law is fed into the judicial process is never a proper concern of the rules of evidence but rather of the rules of procedure. The Advisory Committee on Evidence, believing that this assumption is entirely correct, proposes no evidence rule with respect to judicial notice of law, and suggests that those matters of law which, in addition to foreign-country law, have traditionally been treated as requiring pleading and proof and more recently as the subject of judicial notice be left to the Rules of Civil and Criminal Procedure.

1974 Enactment

Rule 201(g) as received from the Supreme Court provided that when judicial notice of a fact is taken, the court shall instruct the jury to accept that fact as established. Being of the view that mandatory instruction to a jury in a criminal case to accept as conclusive any fact judicially noticed is inappropriate because contrary to the spirit of the Sixth Amendment right to a jury trial, the Committee adopted the 1969 Advisory Committee draft of this subsection, allowing a mandatory instruction in civil actions and proceedings and a discretionary instruction in criminal cases. House Report No. 93–650.

2011 Amendments

The language of Rule 201 has been amended as part of the restyling of the Evidence Rules to make them more easily understood and to make style and terminology consistent throughout the rules. These changes are intended to be stylistic only. There is no intent to change any result in any ruling on evidence admissibility.

CROSS REFERENCES

Determination of foreign law, see Fed.Rules Civ.Proc. Rule 44.1, 28 USCA and Fed.Rules Cr.Proc. Rule 26.1, 18 USCA.

Due process right to notice and hearing, see USCA Const. Amend. XIV.

Instructions, see Fed.Rules Civ.Proc. Rule 51, 28 USCA and Fed.Rules Cr.Proc. Rule 30, 18 USCA.

ARTICLE III. PRESUMPTIONS IN CIVIL CASES

Rule

Rule 301.   **Presumptions in Civil Cases Generally**

In a civil case, unless a federal statute or these rules provide otherwise, the party against whom a presumption is directed has the burden of producing evidence to rebut the presumption. But this rule does not shift the burden of persuasion, which remains on the party who had it originally.

(Pub.L. 93–595, § 1, Jan. 2, 1975, 88 Stat. 1931; Apr. 26, 2011, eff. Dec. 1, 2011.)

ADVISORY COMMITTEE NOTES

1972 Proposed Rules

This rule governs presumptions generally. See Rule 302 for presumptions controlled by state law and Rule 303 [deleted] for those against an accused in a criminal case.

Presumptions governed by this rule are given the effect of placing upon the opposing party the burden of establishing the nonexistence of the presumed fact, once the party invoking the presumption establishes the basic facts giving rise to it. The same considerations of fairness, policy, and probability which dictate the allocation of the burden of the various elements of a case as between the prima facie case of a plaintiff and affirmative defenses also underlie the creation of presumptions. These considerations are not satisfied by giving a lesser effect to presumptions. Morgan and Maguire, Looking Backward and Forward at Evidence, 50 Harv.L.Rev. 909, 913 (1937); Morgan, Instructing the Jury upon Presumptions and Burden of Proof, 47 Harv.L.Rev. 59, 82 (1933); Cleary, Presuming and Pleading: An Essay on Juristic Immaturity, 12 Stan.L.Rev. 5 (1959).

The so-called "bursting bubble" theory, under which a presumption vanishes upon the introduction of evidence which would support a finding of the nonexistence of the presumed fact, even though not believed, is rejected as according presumptions too "slight and evanescent" an effect. Morgan and Maguire, *supra*, at p. 913.

In the opinion of the Advisory Committee, no constitutional infirmity attends this view of presumptions. In *Mobile, J. & K. C. R. Co. v. Turnipseed*, 219 U.S. 35, 31 S.Ct. 136, 55 L.Ed. 78 (1910), the Court upheld a Mississippi statute which provided that in actions against railroads proof of injury inflicted by the running of trains should be prima facie evidence of negligence by the railroad. The injury in the case had resulted from a derailment. The opinion made the points (1) that the only effect of the statute was to impose on the railroad the duty of producing some evidence to the contrary, (2) that an inference may be supplied by law if there is a rational connection between the fact proved and the fact presumed, as long as the opposite party is not precluded from presenting his evidence to the contrary, and (3) that considerations of public policy arising from the character of the business justified the application in question. Nineteen years later, in *Western & Atlantic R. Co. v. Henderson*, 279 U.S. 639, 49 S.Ct. 445, 73 L.Ed. 884 (1929), the Court overturned a Georgia statute making railroads liable for damages done by trains, unless the railroad made it appear that reasonable care had been used, the presumption being against the railroad. The declaration alleged the death of plaintiff's husband from a grade crossing collision, due to specified acts of negligence by defendant. The jury were instructed that proof of the injury raised a presumption of negligence; the burden shifted to the railroad to prove ordinary care; and unless it did so, they should find for plaintiff. The instruction was held erroneous in an opinion stating (1) that there was no rational connection between the mere fact of collision and negligence on the part of anyone, and (2) that the statute was different from that in

Turnipseed in imposing a burden upon the railroad. The reader is left in a state of some confusion. Is the difference between a derailment and a grade crossing collision of no significance? Would the *Turnipseed* presumption have been bad if it had imposed a burden of persuasion on defendant, although that would in nowise have impaired its "rational connection"? If *Henderson* forbids imposing a burden of persuasion on defendants, what happens to affirmative defenses?

Two factors serve to explain *Henderson*. The first was that it was common ground that negligence was indispensable to liability. Plaintiff thought so, drafted her complaint accordingly, and relied upon the presumption. But how in logic could the same presumption establish her alternative grounds of negligence that the engineer was so blind he could not see decedent's truck and that he failed to stop after he saw it? Second, take away the basic assumption of no liability without fault, as *Turnipseed* intimated might be done ("considerations of public policy arising out of the character of the business"), and the structure of the decision in *Henderson* fails. No question of logic would have arisen if the statute had simply said: a prima facie case of liability is made by proof of injury by a train; lack of negligence is an affirmative defense, to be pleaded and proved as other affirmative defenses. The problem would be one of economic due process only. While it seems likely that the Supreme Court of 1929 would have voted that due process was denied, that result today would be unlikely. See, for example, the shift in the direction of absolute liability in the consumer cases. Prosser, The Assault upon the Citadel (Strict Liability to the Consumer), 69 Yale L.J. 1099 (1960).

Any doubt as to the constitutional permissibility of a presumption imposing a burden of persuasion of the nonexistence of the presumed fact in civil cases is laid at rest by *Dick v. New York Life Ins. Co.*, 359 U.S. 437, 79 S.Ct. 921, 3 L.Ed.2d 935 (1959). The Court unhesitatingly applied the North Dakota rule that the presumption against suicide imposed on defendant the burden of proving that the death of insured, under an accidental death clause, was due to suicide.

"Proof of coverage and of death by gunshot wound shifts the burden to the insurer to establish that the death of the insured was due to his suicide." 359 U.S. at 443, 79 S.Ct. at 925.

"In a case like this one, North Dakota presumes that death was accidental and places on the insurer the burden of proving that death resulted from suicide." *Id.* at 446, 79 S.Ct. at 927.

The rational connection requirement survives in criminal cases, *Tot v. United States*, 319 U.S. 463, 63 S.Ct. 1241, 87 L.Ed. 1519 (1943), because the Court has been unwilling to extend into that area the greater-includes-the-lesser theory of *Ferry v. Ramsey*, 277 U.S. 88, 48 S.Ct. 443, 72 L.Ed. 796 (1928). In that case the Court sustained a Kansas statute under which bank directors were personally liable for deposits made with their assent and with knowledge of insolvency, and the fact of insolvency was prima facie evidence of assent and knowledge of insolvency. Mr. Justice Holmes pointed out that the state legislature could have made the directors personally liable to depositors in every case. Since the statute imposed a less stringent liability, "the thing to be considered is the result reached, not the possibly inartificial or clumsy way of reaching it." *Id.* at 94, 48 S.Ct. at 444. Mr. Justice Sutherland dissented: though the state could have created an absolute liability, it did not purport to do so; a rational connection was necessary, but lacking, between the liability created and the prima facie evidence of it; the result might be different if the basis of the presumption were being open for business.

The Sutherland view has prevailed in criminal cases by virtue of the higher standard of notice there required. The fiction that everyone is presumed to know the law is applied to the substantive law of crimes as an alternative to complete unenforceability. But the need does not extend to criminal evidence and procedure, and the fiction does not encompass them. "Rational connection" is not fictional or artificial, and so it is reasonable to suppose that Gainey should have known that his presence at the site of an illicit still could convict him of being connected with (carrying on) the business, *United States v. Gainey,* 380 U.S. 63, 85 S.Ct. 754, 13 L.Ed.2d 658 (1965), but not that Romano should have known that his presence at a still could convict him of possessing it, *United States v. Romano,* 382 U.S. 136, 86 S.Ct. 279, 15 L.Ed.2d 210 (1965).

In his dissent in Gainey, Mr. Justice Black put it more artistically:

"It might be argued, although the Court does not so argue or hold, that Congress if it wished could make presence at a still a crime in itself, and so Congress should be free to create crimes which are called 'possession' and 'carrying on an illegal distillery business' but which are defined in such a way that unexplained presence is sufficient and indisputable evidence in all cases to support conviction for those offenses. See *Ferry v. Ramsey,* 277 U.S. 88, 48 S.Ct. 443, 72 L.Ed. 796. Assuming for the sake of argument that Congress could make unexplained presence a criminal act, and ignoring also the refusal of this Court in other cases to uphold a statutory presumption on such a theory, see *Heiner v. Donnan,* 285 U.S. 312, 52 S.Ct. 358, 76 L.Ed. 772, there is no indication here that Congress intended to adopt such a misleading method of draftsmanship, nor in my judgment could the statutory provisions if so construed escape condemnation for vagueness, under the principles applied in *Lanzetta v. New Jersey,* 306 U.S. 451, 59 S.Ct. 618, 83 L.Ed. 888, and many other cases." 380 U.S. at 84, n. 12, 85 S.Ct. at 766.

And the majority opinion in *Romano* agreed with him:

"It may be, of course, that Congress has the power to make presence at an illegal still a punishable crime, but we find no clear indication that it intended to so exercise this power. The crime remains possession, not presence, and with all due deference to the judgment of Congress, the former may not constitutionally be inferred from the latter." 382 U.S. at 144, 86 S.Ct. at 284.

The rule does not spell out the procedural aspects of its application. Questions as to when the evidence warrants submission of a presumption and what instructions are proper under varying states of fact are believed to present no particular difficulties.

1974 Enactment

Rule 301 as submitted by the Supreme Court provided that in all cases a presumption imposes on the party against whom it is directed the burden of proving that the nonexistence of the presumed fact is more probable than its existence. The Committee limited the scope of Rule 301 to "civil actions and proceedings" to effectuate its decision not to deal with the question of presumptions in criminal cases. (See note on [proposed] Rule 303 in discussion of Rules deleted). With

respect to the weight to be given a presumption in a civil case, the Committee agreed with the judgment implicit in the Court's version that the so-called "bursting bubble" theory of presumptions, whereby a presumption vanishes upon the appearance of any contradicting evidence by the other party, gives to presumptions too slight an effect. On the other hand, the Committee believed that the Rule proposed by the Court, whereby a presumption permanently alters the burden of persuasion, no matter how much contradicting evidence is introduced—a view shared by only a few courts—lends too great a force to presumptions. Accordingly, the Committee amended the Rule to adopt an intermediate position under which a presumption does not vanish upon the introduction of contradicting evidence, and does not change the burden of persuasion; instead it is merely deemed sufficient evidence of the fact presumed, to be considered by the jury or other finder of fact. House Report No. 93–650.

The rule governs presumptions in civil cases generally. Rule 302 provides for presumptions in cases controlled by State law.

As submitted by the Supreme Court, presumptions governed by this rule were given the effect of placing upon the opposing party the burden of establishing the nonexistence of the presumed fact, once the party invoking the presumption established the basic facts giving rise to it.

Instead of imposing a burden of persuasion on the party against whom the presumption is directed, the House adopted a provision which shifted the burden of going forward with the evidence. They further provided that "even though met with contradicting evidence, a presumption is sufficient evidence of the fact presumed, to be considered by the trier of fact." The effect of the amendment is that presumptions are to be treated as evidence.

The committee feels the House amendment is ill-advised. As the joint committees (the Standing Committee on Practice and Procedure of the Judicial Conference and the Advisory Committee on the Rules of Evidence) stated: "Presumptions are not evidence, but ways of dealing with evidence." This treatment requires juries to perform the task of considering "as evidence" facts upon which they have no direct evidence and which may confuse them in performance of their duties. California had a rule much like that contained in the House amendment. It was sharply criticized by Justice Traynor in *Speck v. Sarver* [20 Cal.2d 585, 128 P.2d 16, 21 (1942)] and was repealed after 93 troublesome years [Cal.Ev.Code 1965 § 600].

Professor McCormick gives a concise and compelling critique of the presumption as evidence rule:

"Another solution, formerly more popular than now, is to instruct the jury that the presumption is 'evidence', to be weighed and considered with the testimony in the case. This avoids the danger that the jury may infer that the presumption is conclusive, but it probably means little to the jury, and certainly runs counter to accepted theories of the nature of evidence." [McCormick, Evidence, 669 (1954); *id.* 825 (2d ed. 1972)].

For these reasons the committee has deleted that provision of the House-passed rule that treats presumptions as evidence. The effect of the rule as adopted by the committee is to make clear that while evidence of facts giving rise to a presumption shifts the burden of coming forward with evidence to rebut or meet the presumption, it does not shift the burden of persuasion on the existence of the presumed facts. The burden of persuasion remains on the party to whom it is allocated under the rules governing the allocation in the first instance.

The court may instruct the jury that they may infer the existence of the presumed fact from proof of the basic facts giving rise to the presumption. However, it would be inappropriate under this rule to instruct the jury that the inference they are to draw is conclusive. Senate Report 93–1277.

The House bill provides that a presumption in civil actions and proceedings shifts to the party against whom it is directed the burden of going forward with evidence to meet or rebut it. Even though evidence contradicting the presumption is offered, a presumption is considered sufficient evidence of the presumed fact to be considered by the jury. The Senate amendment provides that a presumption shifts to the party against whom it is directed the burden of going forward with evidence to meet or rebut the presumption, but it does not shift to that party the burden of persuasion on the existence of the presumed fact.

Under the Senate amendment, a presumption is sufficient to get a party past an adverse party's motion to dismiss made at the end of his case-in-chief. If the adverse party offers no evidence contradicting the presumed fact, the court will instruct the jury that if it finds the basic facts, it may presume the existence of the presumed fact. If the adverse party does offer evidence contradicting the presumed fact, the court cannot instruct the jury that it may *presume* the existence of the presumed fact from proof of the basic facts. The court may, however, instruct the jury that it may infer the existence of the presumed fact from proof of the basic facts.

The conference adopts the Senate amendment. House Conference Report No. 93–1597.

2011 Amendments

The language of Rule 301 has been amended as part of the restyling of the Evidence Rules to make them more easily understood and to make style and terminology consistent throughout the rules. These changes are intended to be stylistic only. There is no intent to change any result in any ruling on evidence admissibility.

CROSS REFERENCES

Self-authentication,
Foreign public documents, see Fed.Rules Evid. Rule 902, 28 USCA.
Presumptions under Acts of Congress, see Fed.Rules Evid. Rule 902, 28 USCA.

Rule 302. Applying State Law to Presumptions in Civil Cases

In a civil case, state law governs the effect of a presumption regarding a claim or defense for which state law supplies the rule of decision.

(Pub.L. 93–595, § 1, Jan. 2, 1975, 88 Stat. 1931; Apr. 26, 2011, eff. Dec. 1, 2011.)

ADVISORY COMMITTEE NOTES

1972 Proposed Rules

A series of Supreme Court decisions in diversity cases leaves no doubt of the relevance of *Erie Railroad Co. v. Tompkins*, 304 U.S. 64, 58 S.Ct. 817, 82 L.Ed. 1188 (1938), to questions of burden of proof. These decisions are *Cities Service Oil Co. v. Dunlap*, 308 U.S. 208, 60 S.Ct. 201, 84 L.Ed. 196 (1939), *Palmer v. Hoffman*, 318 U.S. 109, 63 S.Ct. 477, 87 L.Ed. 645 (1943), and *Dick v. New York Life Ins. Co.*, 359 U.S. 437, 79 S.Ct. 921, 3 L.Ed.2d 935 (1959). They involved burden of proof, respectively, as to status as bona fide purchaser, contributory negligence, and nonaccidental death (suicide) of an insured. In each instance the state rule was held to be applicable. It does not follow, however, that all presumptions in diversity cases are governed by state law. In each case cited, the burden of proof question had to do with a substantive element of the claim or defense. Application of the state law is called for only when the presumption operates upon such an element. Accordingly the rule does not apply state law when the presumption operates upon a lesser aspect of the case, i.e. "tactical" presumptions.

The situations in which the state law is applied have been tagged for convenience in the preceding discussion as "diversity cases." The designation is not a completely accurate one since *Erie* applies to any claim or issue having its source in state law, regardless of the basis of federal jurisdiction, and does not apply to a federal claim or issue, even though jurisdiction is based on diversity. *Vestal, Erie R.R. v. Tompkins:* A Projection, 48 Iowa L.Rev. 248, 257 (1963); Hart and Wechsler, The Federal Courts and the Federal System, 697 (1953); 1A Moore, Federal Practice ¶ 0.305[3] (2d ed. 1965); Wright, Federal Courts, 217–218 (1963). Hence the rule employs, as appropriately descriptive, the phrase "as to which state law supplies the rule of decision." See A.L.I. Study of the Division of Jurisdiction Between State and Federal Courts, § 2344(c), p. 40, P.F.D. No. 1 (1965).

2011 Amendments

The language of Rule 302 has been amended as part of the restyling of the Evidence Rules to make them more easily understood and to make style and terminology consistent throughout the rules. These changes are intended to be stylistic only. There is no intent to change any result in any ruling on evidence admissibility.

CROSS REFERENCES

State laws as rules of decision, see 28 USCA § 1652.

ARTICLE IV. RELEVANCE AND ITS LIMITS

Rule 401. Test for Relevant Evidence

Evidence is relevant if:

(a) it has any tendency to make a fact more or less probable than it would be without the evidence; and

(b) the fact is of consequence in determining the action.

(Pub.L. 93–595, § 1, Jan. 2, 1975, 88 Stat.1931; Apr. 26, 2011, eff. Dec. 1, 2011.)

ADVISORY COMMITTEE NOTES

1972 Proposed Rules

Problems of relevancy call for an answer to the question whether an item of evidence, when tested by the processes of legal reasoning, possesses sufficient probative value to justify receiving it in evidence. Thus, assessment of the probative value of evidence that a person purchased a revolver shortly prior to a fatal shooting with which he is charged is a matter of analysis and reasoning.

The variety of relevancy problems is coextensive with the ingenuity of counsel in using circumstantial evidence as a means of proof. An enormous number of cases fall in no set pattern, and this rule is designed as a guide for handling them. On the other hand, some situations recur with sufficient frequency to create patterns susceptible of treatment by specific rules. Rule 404 and those following it are of that variety; they also serve as illustrations of the application of the present rule as limited by the exclusionary principles of Rule 403.

Passing mention should be made of so-called "conditional" relevancy. Morgan, Basic Problems of Evidence 45–46 (1962). In this situation, probative value depends not only upon satisfying the basic requirement of relevancy as described above but also upon the existence of some matter of fact. For example, if evidence of a spoken statement is relied upon to prove notice, probative value is lacking unless the person sought to be charged heard the statement. The problem is one of fact, and the only rules needed are for the purpose of determining the respective functions of judge and jury. See Rules 104(b) and 901. The discussion which follows in the present note is concerned with relevancy generally, not with any particular problem of conditional relevancy.

Relevancy is not an inherent characteristic of any item of evidence but exists only as a relation between an item of evidence and a matter properly provable in the case. Does the item of evidence tend to prove the matter sought to be proved? Whether the relationship exists depends upon principles evolved by experience or science, applied logically to the situation at hand. James, Relevancy, Probability and the Law, 29 Calif.L.Rev. 689, 696, n. 15 (1941), in Selected Writings on Evidence and Trial 610, 615, n. 15 (Fryer ed. 1957). The rule summarizes this relationship as a "tendency to make the existence" of the fact to be proved "more probable or less probable." Compare Uniform Rule 1(2) which states the crux of relevancy as "a tendency in reason," thus perhaps empha-

sizing unduly the logical process and ignoring the need to draw upon experience or science to validate the general principle upon which relevancy in a particular situation depends.

The standard of probability under the rule is "more * * * probable than it would be without the evidence." Any more stringent requirement is unworkable and unrealistic. As McCormick § 152, p. 317, says, "A brick is not a wall," or, as Falknor, Extrinsic Policies Affecting Admissibility, 10 Rutgers L.Rev. 574, 576 (1956), quotes Professor McBaine, " * * * [I]t is not to be supposed that every witness can make a home run." Dealing with probability in the language of the rule has the added virtue of avoiding confusion between questions of admissibility and questions of the sufficiency of the evidence.

The rule uses the phrase "fact that is of consequence to the determination of the action" to describe the kind of fact to which proof may properly be directed. The language is that of California Evidence Code § 210; it has the advantage of avoiding the loosely used and ambiguous word "material." Tentative Recommendation and a Study Relating to the Uniform Rules of Evidence (Art. I. General Provisions), Cal.Law Revision Comm'n, Rep., Rec. & Studies, 10–11 (1964). The fact to be proved may be ultimate, intermediate, or evidentiary; it matters not, so long as it is of consequence in the determination of the action. Cf. Uniform Rule 1(2) which requires that the evidence relate to a "material" fact.

The fact to which the evidence is directed need not be in dispute. While situations will arise which call for the exclusion of evidence offered to prove a point conceded by the opponent, the ruling should be made on the basis of such considerations as waste of time and undue prejudice (see Rule 403), rather than under any general requirement that evidence is admissible only if directed to matters in dispute. Evidence which is essentially background in nature can scarcely be said to involve disputed matter, yet it is universally offered and admitted as an aid to understanding. Charts, photographs, views of real estate, murder weapons, and many other items of evidence fall in this category. A rule limiting admissibility to evidence directed to a controversial point would invite the exclusion of this helpful evidence, or at least the raising of endless questions over its admission. Cf. California Evidence Code § 210, defining relevant evidence in terms of tendency to prove a disputed fact.

2011 Amendments

The language of Rule 401 has been amended as part of the restyling of the Evidence Rules to make them more easily understood and to make style and terminology consistent throughout the rules. These changes are intended to be stylistic only. There is no intent to change any result in any ruling on evidence admissibility.

CROSS REFERENCES

Eye witness testimony, see 18 USCA § 3502.

Relevancy conditioned on fact, admissibility of evidence, see Fed.Rules Evid. Rule 104, 28 USCA.

Rule 402. General Admissibility of Relevant Evidence

Relevant evidence is admissible unless any of the following provides otherwise:

- the United States Constitution;
- a federal statute;
- these rules; or
- other rules prescribed by the Supreme Court.

Irrelevant evidence is not admissible.
(Pub.L. 93–595, § 1, Jan. 2, 1975, 88 Stat. 1931; Apr. 26, 2011, eff. Dec. 1, 2011.)

ADVISORY COMMITTEE NOTES
1972 Proposed Rules

The provisions that all relevant evidence is admissible, with certain exceptions, and that evidence which is not relevant is not admissible are "a presupposition involved in the very conception of a rational system of evidence." Thayer, Preliminary Treatise on Evidence 264 (1898). They constitute the foundation upon which the structure of admission and exclusion rests. For similar provisions see California Evidence Code §§ 350, 351. Provisions that all relevant evidence is admissible are found in Uniform Rule 7(f); Kansas Code of Civil Procedure § 60–407(f); and New Jersey Evidence Rule 7(f); but the exclusion of evidence which is not relevant is left to implication.

Not all relevant evidence is admissible. The exclusion of relevant evidence occurs in a variety of situations and may be called for by these rules, by the Rules of Civil and Criminal Procedure, by Bankruptcy Rules, by Act of Congress, or by constitutional considerations.

Succeeding rules in the present article, in response to the demands of particular policies, require the exclusion of evidence despite its relevancy. In addition, Article V recognizes a number of privileges; Article VI imposes limitations upon witnesses and the manner of dealing with them; Article VII specifies requirements with respect to opinions and expert testimony; Article VIII excludes hearsay not falling within an exception; Article IX spells out the handling of authentication and identification; and Article X restricts the manner of proving the contents of writings and recordings.

The Rules of Civil and Criminal Procedure in some instances require the exclusion of relevant evidence. For example, Rules 30(b) and 32(a)(3) of the Rules of Civil Procedure, by imposing requirements of notice and unavailability of the deponent, place limits on the use of relevant depositions. Similarly, Rule 15 of the Rules of Criminal Procedure restricts the use of depositions in criminal cases, even though relevant. And the effective enforcement of the command, originally statutory and now found in Rule 5(a) of the Rules of Criminal Procedure, that an arrested person be taken without unnecessary delay before a commissioner or other similar officer is held to require the exclusion of statements elicited during detention in violation thereof. *Mallory v. United States*, 354 U.S. 449, 77 S.Ct. 1356, 1 L.Ed.2d 1479 (1957); 18 U.S.C. § 3501(c).

While congressional enactments in the field of evidence have generally tended to expand admissibility beyond the scope of the common law rules, in some particular situations they have restricted the admissibility of relevant evidence. Most of this legislation has consisted of the formulation of a privilege or of a prohibition against disclosure. 8 U.S.C. § 1202(f), records of refusal of visas or permits to enter United States confidential, subject to discretion of Secretary of State to make available to court upon certification of need; 10 U.S.C. § 3693, replacement certificate of honorable discharge from Army not admissible in evidence; 10 U.S.C. § 8693, same as to Air Force; 11 U.S.C. § 25(a)(10), testimony given by bankrupt on his examination not admissible in criminal proceedings against him, except that given in hearing upon objection to discharge; 11 U.S.C. § 205(a), railroad reorganization petition, if dismissed, not admissible in evidence; 11 U.S.C. § 403(a), list of creditors filed with municipal composition plan not an admission; 13 U.S.C. § 9(a), census information confidential, retained copies of reports privileged; 47 U.S.C. § 605, interception and divulgence of wire or radio communications prohibited unless authorized by sender. These statutory provisions would remain undisturbed by the rules.

The rule recognizes but makes no attempt to spell out the constitutional considerations which impose basic limitations upon the admissibility of relevant evidence. Examples are evidence obtained by unlawful search and seizure. *Weeks v. United States*, 232 U.S. 383, 34 S.Ct. 341, 58 L.Ed. 652 (1914); *Katz v. United States*, 389 U.S. 347, 88 S.Ct. 507, 19 L.Ed.2d 576 (1967); incriminating statement elicited from an accused in violation of right to counsel. *Massiah v. United States*, 377 U.S. 201, 84 S.Ct. 1199, 12 L.Ed.2d 246 (1964).

1974 Enactment

Rule 402 as submitted to the Congress contained the phrase "or by other rules adopted by the Supreme Court". To accommodate the view that the Congress should not appear to acquiesce in the Court's judgment that it has authority under the existing Rules Enabling Acts to promulgate Rules of Evidence, the Committee amended the above phrase to read "or by other rules prescribed by the Supreme Court pursuant to statutory authority" in this and other Rules where the reference appears. House Report No. 93–650.

2011 Amendments

The language of Rule 402 has been amended as part of the restyling of the Evidence Rules to make them more easily understood and to make style and terminology consistent throughout the rules. These changes are intended to be stylistic only. There is no intent to change any result in any ruling on evidence admissibility.

CROSS REFERENCES

Aliens, confidentiality of Department of State records of issuance or refusal of visas, see 8 USCA § 1202.

Census information, confidential nature of, see 13 USCA § 9.

Certificates of discharge, replacements as evidence, see 10 USCA § 1041.

Confession, delay in bringing detainee before magistrate affecting admissibility of, see 18 USCA § 3501.

Eye witness testimony, see 18 USCA § 3502.

Notice to and availability of deponent as determining admissibility of depositions, see Fed.Rules Civ.Proc. Rules 30, 32, 28 USCA and Fed.Rules Cr.Proc. Rule 15, 18 USCA.

Proceedings before magistrate, exclusion of evidence obtained in violation of rights, see Fed.Rules Cr.Proc. Rule 5, 18 USCA.

Relevancy conditioned on fact, see Fed.Rules Evid. Rule 104, 28 USCA.

Testimony of debtor and of persons examined,

Immunity from self-incrimination, see 11 USCA § 344.

Immunity of witnesses, see 18 USCA § 6001 et seq.

Wire or radio communications, unauthorized use or publication prohibited, see 47 USCA § 605.

Rule 403. Excluding Relevant Evidence for Prejudice, Confusion, Waste of Time, or Other Reasons

The court may exclude relevant evidence if its probative value is substantially outweighed by a danger of one or more of the following: unfair prejudice, confusing the issues, misleading the jury, undue delay, wasting time, or needlessly presenting cumulative evidence. (Pub.L. 93–595, § 1, Jan. 2, 1975, 88 Stat. 1932; Apr. 26, 2011, eff. Dec. 1, 2011.)

ADVISORY COMMITTEE NOTES

1972 Proposed Rules

The case law recognizes that certain circumstances call for the exclusion of evidence which is of unquestioned relevance. These circumstances entail risks which range all the way from inducing decision on a purely emotional basis, at one extreme, to nothing more harmful than merely wasting time, at the other extreme. Situations in this area call for balancing the probative value of and need for the evidence against the harm likely to result from its admission. Slough, Relevancy Unraveled, 5 Kan.L.Rev. 1, 12–15 (1956); Trautman, Logical or Legal Relevancy—A Conflict in Theory, 5 Van.L.Rev. 385, 392 (1952); McCormick § 152, pp. 319–321. The rules which follow in this Article are concrete applications evolved for particular situations. However, they reflect the policies underlying the present rule, which is designed as a guide for the handling of situations for which no specific rules have been formulated.

Exclusion for risk of unfair prejudice, confusion of issues, misleading the jury, or waste of time, all find ample support in the authorities. "Unfair prejudice" within its context means an undue tendency to suggest decision on an improper basis, commonly, though not necessarily, an emotional one.

The rule does not enumerate surprise as a ground for exclusion, in this respect following Wigmore's view of the common law. 6 Wigmore § 1849. Cf. McCormick § 152, p. 320, n. 29, listing unfair surprise as a ground for exclusion but stating that it is usually "coupled with the danger of prejudice and confusion of issues." While Uniform Rule 45 incorporates surprise as a ground and is followed in Kansas Code of Civil Procedure § 60–445, surprise is not included in California Evidence Code § 352 or New Jersey Rule 4, though both the latter otherwise substantially embody Uniform Rule 45. While it can scarcely be doubted that claims of unfair surprise may still be justified despite procedural requirements of notice and instrumentalities of discovery, the granting of a continuance is a more appropriate remedy than exclusion of the evidence. Tentative Recommendation and a Study Relating to the Uniform Rules of Evidence (Art. VI. Extrinsic Policies Affecting Admissibility), Cal.Law Revision Comm'n, Rep., Rec. & Studies, 612 (1964). Moreover, the impact of a rule excluding evidence on the ground of surprise would be difficult to estimate.

In reaching a decision whether to exclude on grounds of unfair prejudice, consideration should be given to the proba-ble effectiveness or lack of effectiveness of a limiting instruction. See Rule 106 [now 105] and Advisory Committee's Note thereunder. The availability of other means of proof may also be an appropriate factor.

2011 Amendments

The language of Rule 403 has been amended as part of the restyling of the Evidence Rules to make them more easily understood and to make style and terminology consistent throughout the rules. These changes are intended to be stylistic only. There is no intent to change any result in any ruling on evidence admissibility.

CROSS REFERENCES

Eye witness testimony, see 18 USCA § 3502.

Limiting admissibility of evidence to proper scope and parties, see Fed.Rules Evid. Rule 105, 28 USCA.

Rule 404. Character Evidence; Crimes or Other Acts

(a) Character Evidence.

(1) Prohibited Uses. Evidence of a person's character or character trait is not admissible to prove that on a particular occasion the person acted in accordance with the character or trait.

(2) Exceptions for a Defendant or Victim in a Criminal Case. The following exceptions apply in a criminal case:

(A) a defendant may offer evidence of the defendant's pertinent trait, and if the evidence is admitted, the prosecutor may offer evidence to rebut it;

(B) subject to the limitations in Rule 412, a defendant may offer evidence of an alleged victim's pertinent trait, and if the evidence is admitted, the prosecutor may:

(i) offer evidence to rebut it; and

(ii) offer evidence of the defendant's same trait; and

(C) in a homicide case, the prosecutor may offer evidence of the alleged victim's trait of peacefulness to rebut evidence that the victim was the first aggressor.

(3) Exceptions for a Witness. Evidence of a witness's character may be admitted under Rules 607, 608, and 609.

(b) Crimes, Wrongs, or Other Acts.

(1) Prohibited Uses. Evidence of a crime, wrong, or other act is not admissible to prove a person's character in order to show that on a particular occasion the person acted in accordance with the character.

(2) Permitted Uses; Notice in a Criminal Case. This evidence may be admissible for another purpose, such as proving motive, opportunity, intent, preparation, plan, knowledge, identity, absence of mistake, or lack of accident. On request by a defendant in a criminal case, the prosecutor must:

(A) provide reasonable notice of the general nature of any such evidence that the prosecutor intends to offer at trial; and

(B) do so before trial—or during trial if the court, for good cause, excuses lack of pretrial notice.

(Pub.L. 93–595, § 1, Jan. 2, 1975, 88 Stat.1932; Mar. 2, 1987, eff. Oct. 1, 1987; Apr. 30, 1991, eff. Dec. 1, 1991; Apr. 17, 2000, eff. Dec. 1, 2000; Apr. 12, 2006, eff. Dec. 1, 2006; Apr. 26, 2011, eff. Dec. 1, 2011.)

ADVISORY COMMITTEE NOTES
1972 Proposed Rules

Note to Subdivision (a). This subdivision deals with the basic question whether character evidence should be admitted. Once the admissibility of character evidence in some form is established under this rule, reference must then be made to Rule 405, which follows, in order to determine the appropriate method of proof. If the character is that of a witness, see Rules 608 and 610 for methods of proof.

Character questions arise in two fundamentally different ways. (1) Character may itself be an element of a crime, claim, or defense. A situation of this kind is commonly referred to as "character in issue." Illustrations are: the chastity of the victim under a statute specifying her chastity as an element of the crime of seduction, or the competency of the driver in an action for negligently entrusting a motor vehicle to an incompetent driver. No problem of the general relevancy of character evidence is involved, and the present rule therefore has no provision on the subject. The only question relates to allowable methods of proof, as to which see Rule 405, immediately following. (2) Character evidence is susceptible of being used for the purpose of suggesting an inference that the person acted on the occasion in question consistently with his character. This use of character is often described as "circumstantial." Illustrations are: evidence of a violent disposition to prove that the person was the aggressor in an affray, or evidence of honesty in disproof of a charge of theft. This circumstantial use of character evidence raises questions of relevancy as well as questions of allowable methods of proof.

In most jurisdictions today, the circumstantial use of character is rejected but with important exceptions: (1) an accused may introduce pertinent evidence of good character (often misleadingly described as "putting his character in issue"), in which event the prosecution may rebut with evidence of bad character; (2) an accused may introduce pertinent evidence of the character of the victim, as in support of a claim of self-defense to a charge of homicide or consent in a case of rape, and the prosecution may introduce similar evidence in rebuttal of the character evidence, or, in a homicide case, to rebut a claim that deceased was the first aggressor, however proved; and (3) the character of a witness may be gone into as bearing on his credibility. McCormick §§ 155–161. This pattern is incorporated in the rule. While its basis lies more in history and experience than in logic an underlying justification can fairly be found in terms of the relative presence and absence of prejudice in the various situations. Falknor, Extrinsic Policies Affecting Admissibility, 10 Rutgers L.Rev. 574, 584 (1956); McCormick § 157. In any event, the criminal rule is so deeply imbedded in our jurisprudence as to assume almost constitutional proportions and to override doubts of the basic relevancy of the evidence.

The limitation to pertinent traits of character, rather than character generally, in paragraphs (1) and (2) is in accordance with the prevailing view. McCormick § 158, p. 334. A similar provision in Rule 608, to which reference is made in paragraph (3), limits character evidence respecting witnesses to the trait of truthfulness or untruthfulness.

The argument is made that circumstantial use of character ought to be allowed in civil cases to the same extent as in criminal cases, i.e. evidence of good (nonprejudicial) character would be admissible in the first instance, subject to rebuttal by evidence of bad character. Falknor, Extrinsic Policies Affecting Admissibility, 10 Rutgers L.Rev. 574, 581–583 (1956); Tentative Recommendation and a Study Relating to the Uniform Rules of Evidence (Art. VI. Extrinsic Policies Affecting Admissibility), Cal.Law Revision Comm'n, Rep., Rec. & Studies, 657–658 (1964). Uniform Rule 47 goes farther, in that it assumes that character evidence in general satisfies the conditions of relevancy, except as provided in Uniform Rule 48. The difficulty with expanding the use of character evidence in civil cases is set forth by the California Law Revision Commission in its ultimate rejection of Uniform Rule 47, *id.*, 615:

"Character evidence is of slight probative value and may be very prejudicial. It tends to distract the trier of fact from the main question of what actually happened on the particular occasion. It subtly permits the trier of fact to reward the good man and to punish the bad man because of their respective characters despite what the evidence in the case shows actually happened."

Much of the force of the position of those favoring greater use of character evidence in civil cases is dissipated by their support of Uniform Rule 48 which excludes the evidence in negligence cases, where it could be expected to achieve its maximum usefulness. Moreover, expanding concepts of "character," which seem of necessity to extend into such areas as psychiatric evaluation and psychological testing, coupled with expanded admissibility, would open up such vistas of mental examinations as caused the Court concern in *Schlagenhauf v. Holder*, 379 U.S. 104, 85 S.Ct. 234, 13 L.Ed.2d 152 (1964). It is believed that those espousing change have not met the burden of persuasion.

Note to Subdivision (b). Subdivision (b) deals with a specialized but important application of the general rule excluding circumstantial use of character evidence. Consistently with that rule, evidence of other crimes, wrongs, or acts is not admissible to prove character as a basis for suggesting the inference that conduct on a particular occasion was in conformity with it. However, the evidence may be offered for another purpose, such as proof of motive, opportunity, and so on, which does not fall within the prohibition. In this situation the rule does not require that the evidence be excluded. No mechanical solution is offered. The determination must be made whether the danger of undue prejudice outweighs the probative value of the evidence in view of the availability of other means of proof and other facts appropriate for making decision of this kind under Rule 403. Slough and Knightly, Other Vices, Other Crimes, 41 Iowa L.Rev. 325 (1956).

Note to Subdivision (b). The second sentence of Rule 404(b) as submitted to the Congress began with the words "This subdivision does not exclude the evidence when offered". The Committee amended this language to read "It may, however, be admissible", the words used in the 1971 Advisory Committee draft, on the ground that this formulation properly placed greater emphasis on admissibility than did the final Court version. House Report No. 93–650.

Note to Subdivision (b). This rule provides that evidence of other crimes, wrongs, or acts is not admissible to prove character but may be admissible for other specified purposes such as proof of motive.

Although your committee sees no necessity in amending the rule itself, it anticipates that the use of the discretionary word "may" with respect to the admissibility of evidence of crimes, wrongs, or acts is not intended to confer any arbitrary discretion on the trial judge. Rather, it is anticipated that with respect to permissible uses for such evidence, the trial judge may exclude it only on the basis of those considerations set forth in Rule 403, i.e., prejudice, confusion or waste of time. Senate Report No. 93–1277.

1987 Amendments

The amendments are technical. No substantive change is intended.

1991 Amendments

Rule 404(b) has emerged as one of the most cited Rules in the Rules of Evidence. And in many criminal cases evidence of an accused's extrinsic acts is viewed as an important asset in the prosecution's case against an accused. Although there are a few reported decisions on use of such evidence by the defense, *see, e.g., United States v. McClure*, 546 F.2d 670 (5th Cir.1990) (acts of informant offered in entrapment defense), the overwhelming number of cases involve introduction of that evidence by the prosecution.

The amendment to Rule 404(b) adds a pretrial notice requirement in criminal cases and is intended to reduce surprise and promote early resolution on the issue of admissibility. The notice requirement thus places Rule 404(b) in the mainstream with notice and disclosure provisions in other rules of evidence. *See, e.g.,* Rule 412 (written motion of intent to offer evidence under rule), Rule 609 (written notice of intent to offer conviction older than 10 years), Rule 803(24) and 804(b)(5) (notice of intent to use residual hearsay exceptions).

The Rule expects that counsel for both the defense and the prosecution will submit the necessary request and information in a reasonable and timely fashion. Other than requiring pretrial notice, no specific time limits are stated in recognition that what constitutes a reasonable request or disclosure will depend largely on the circumstances of each case. *Compare* Fla.Stat.Ann. § 90.404(2)(b) (notice must be given at least 10 days before trial) *with* Tex.R.Evid. 404(b) (no time limit).

Likewise, no specific form of notice is required. The Committee considered and rejected a requirement that the notice satisfy the particularity requirements normally required of language used in a charging instrument. *Cf.* Fla. Stat.Ann. § 90.404(2)(b) (written disclosure must describe uncharged misconduct with particularity required of an indictment or information). Instead, the Committee opted for a generalized notice provision which requires the prosecution to

apprise the defense of the general nature of the evidence of extrinsic acts. The Committee does not intend that the amendment will supercede other rules of admissibility or disclosure, such as the Jencks Act, 18 U.S.C. § 3500, et seq. nor require the prosecution to disclose directly or indirectly the names and addresses of its witnesses, something it is currently not required to do under Federal Rule of Criminal Procedure 16.

The amendment requires the prosecution to provide notice, regardless of how it intends to use the extrinsic act evidence at trial, i.e., during its case-in-chief, for impeachment, or for possible rebuttal. The court in its discretion may, under the facts, decide that the particular request or notice was not reasonable, either because of the lack of timeliness or completeness. Because the notice requirement serves as condition precedent to admissibility of 404(b) evidence, the offered evidence is inadmissible if the court decides that the notice requirement has not been met.

Nothing in the amendment precludes the court from requiring the government to provide it with an opportunity to rule *in limine* on 404(b) evidence before it is offered or even mentioned during trial. When ruling *in limine*, the court may require the government to disclose to it the specifics of such evidence which the court must consider in determining admissibility.

The amendment does not extend to evidence of acts which are "intrinsic" to the charged offense, *see United States v. Williams*, 900 F.2d 823 (5th Cir.1990) (noting distinction between 404(b) evidence and intrinsic offense evidence). Nor is the amendment intended to redefine what evidence would otherwise be admissible under Rule 404(b). Finally, the Committee does not intend through the amendment to affect the role of the court and the jury in considering such evidence. *See United States v. Huddleston*, 485 U.S. 681, 108 S.Ct. 1496 (1988).

2000 Amendments

Rule 404(a)(1) has been amended to provide that when the accused attacks the character of an alleged victim under subdivision (a)(2) of this Rule, the door is opened to an attack on the same character trait of the accused. Current law does not allow the government to introduce negative character evidence as to the accused unless the accused introduces evidence of good character. *See, e.g., United States v. Fountain*, 768 F.2d 790 (7th Cir. 1985) (when the accused offers proof of self-defense, this permits proof of the alleged victim's character trait for peacefulness, but it does not permit proof of the accused's character trait for violence).

The amendment makes clear that the accused cannot attack the alleged victim's character and yet remain shielded from the disclosure of equally relevant evidence concerning the same character trait of the accused. For example, in a murder case with a claim of self-defense, the accused, to bolster this defense, might offer evidence of the alleged victim's violent disposition. If the government has evidence that the accused has a violent character, but is not allowed to offer this evidence as part of its rebuttal, the jury has only part of the information it needs for an informed assessment of the probabilities as to who was the initial aggressor. This may be the case even if evidence of the accused's prior violent acts is admitted under Rule 404(b), because such evidence can be admitted only for limited purposes and not to show action in conformity with the accused's character on a specific occasion.

Thus, the amendment is designed to permit a more balanced presentation of character evidence when an accused chooses to attack the character of the alleged victim.

The amendment does not affect the admissibility of evidence of specific acts of uncharged misconduct offered for a purpose other than proving character under Rule 404(b). Nor does it affect the standards for proof of character by evidence of other sexual behavior or sexual offenses under Rules 412–415. By its placement in Rule 404(a)(1), the amendment covers only proof of character by way of reputation or opinion.

The amendment does not permit proof of the accused's character if the accused merely uses character evidence for a purpose other than to prove the alleged victim's propensity to act in a certain way. *See United States v. Burks*, 470 F.2d 432, 434–5 (D.C.Cir. 1972) (evidence of the alleged victim's violent character, when known by the accused, was admissible "on the issue of whether or not the defendant reasonably feared he was in danger of imminent great bodily harm"). Finally, the amendment does not permit proof of the accused's character when the accused attacks the alleged victim's character as a witness under Rule 608 or 609.

The term "alleged" is inserted before each reference to "victim" in the Rule, in order to provide consistency with Evidence Rule 412.

GAP Report—Proposed Amendment to Rule 404(a)

The Committee made the following changes to the published draft of the proposed amendment to Evidence Rule 404(a):

1. The term "a pertinent trait of character" was changed to "the same trait of character," in order to limit the scope of the government's rebuttal. The Committee Note was revised to accord with this change in the text.

2. The word "alleged" was added before each reference in the Rule to a "victim" in order to provide consistency with Evidence Rule 412. The Committee Note was amended to accord with this change in the text.

3. The Committee Note was amended to clarify that rebuttal is not permitted under this Rule if the accused proffers evidence of the alleged victim's character for a purpose other than to prove the alleged victim's propensity to act in a certain manner.

2006 Amendments

The Rule has been amended to clarify that in a civil case evidence of a person's character is never admissible to prove that the person acted in conformity with the character trait. The amendment resolves the dispute in the case law over whether the exceptions in subdivisions (a)(1) and (2) permit the circumstantial use of character evidence in civil cases. *Compare Carson v. Polley*, 689 F.2d 562, 576 (5th Cir. 1982) ("when a central issue in a case is close to one of a criminal nature, the exceptions to the Rule 404(a) ban on character evidence may be invoked"), *with SEC v. Towers Financial Corp.*, 966 F.Supp. 203 (S.D.N.Y. 1997) (relying on the terms "accused" and "prosecution" in Rule 404(a) to conclude that the exceptions in subdivisions (a)(1) and (2) are inapplicable in civil cases). The amendment is consistent with the original intent of the Rule, which was to prohibit the circumstantial use of character evidence in civil cases, even where closely related to criminal charges. *See Ginter v. Northwestern Mut. Life Ins. Co.*, 576 F.Supp. 627, 629–30 (D. Ky.1984) ("It seems beyond peradventure of doubt that the drafters of F.R.Evi. 404(a) explicitly intended that all character evidence, except where 'character is at issue' was to be excluded" in civil cases).

The circumstantial use of character evidence is generally discouraged because it carries serious risks of prejudice, confusion and delay. *See Michelson v. United States*, 335 U.S. 469, 476 (1948) ("The overriding policy of excluding such evidence, despite its admitted probative value, is the practical experience that its disallowance tends to prevent confusion of issues, unfair surprise and undue prejudice."). In criminal cases, the so-called "mercy rule" permits a criminal defendant to introduce evidence of pertinent character traits of the defendant and the victim. But that is because the accused, whose liberty is at stake, may need "a counterweight against the strong investigative and prosecutorial resources of the government." C. Mueller & L. Kirkpatrick, *Evidence: Practice Under the Rules*, pp. 264–5 (2d ed. 1999). See also Richard Uviller, *Evidence of Character to Prove Conduct: Illusion, Illogic, and Injustice in the Courtroom*, 130 U.Pa. L.Rev. 845, 855 (1982) (the rule prohibiting circumstantial use of character evidence "was relaxed to allow the criminal defendant with so much at stake and so little available in the way of conventional proof to have special dispensation to tell the factfinder just what sort of person he really is"). Those concerns do not apply to parties in civil cases.

The amendment also clarifies that evidence otherwise admissible under Rule 404(a)(2) may nonetheless be excluded in a criminal case involving sexual misconduct. In such a case, the admissibility of evidence of the victim's sexual behavior and predisposition is governed by the more stringent provisions of Rule 412.

Nothing in the amendment is intended to affect the scope of Rule 404(b). While Rule 404(b) refers to the "accused," the "prosecution," and a "criminal case," it does so only in the context of a notice requirement. The admissibility standards of Rule 404(b) remain fully applicable to both civil and criminal cases.

2011 Amendments

The language of Rule 404 has been amended as part of the restyling of the Evidence Rules to make them more easily understood and to make style and terminology consistent throughout the rules. These changes are intended to be stylistic only. There is no intent to change any result in any ruling on evidence admissibility.

CROSS REFERENCES

Extortionate credit transactions, admissibility of evidence to show,

> Reputation as to collection practices, see 18 USCA § 892.
>
> Reputation of defendant within community, see 18 USCA § 894.
>
> Threat as means of collection, see 18 USCA § 894.

Witnesses, evidence of religious beliefs or opinions, see Fed.Rules Evid. Rule 610, 28 USCA.

Rule 405. Methods of Proving Character

(a) By Reputation or Opinion. When evidence of a person's character or character trait is admissible, it may be proved by testimony about the person's reputation or by testimony in the form of an opinion. On cross-examination of the character witness, the court may allow an inquiry into relevant specific instances of the person's conduct.

(b) By Specific Instances of Conduct. When a person's character or character trait is an essential element of a charge, claim, or defense, the character or trait may also be proved by relevant specific instances of the person's conduct.

(Pub.L. 93–595, § 1, Jan. 2, 1975, 88 Stat. 1932; Mar. 2, 1987, eff. Oct. 1, 1987; Apr. 26, 2011, eff. Dec. 1, 2011.)

ADVISORY COMMITTEE NOTES

1972 Proposed Rules

The rule deals only with allowable methods of proving character, not with the admissibility of character evidence, which is covered in Rule 404.

Of the three methods of proving character provided by the rule, evidence of specific instances of conduct is the most convincing. At the same time it possesses the greatest capacity to arouse prejudice, to confuse, to surprise, and to consume time. Consequently the rule confines the use of evidence of this kind to cases in which character is, in the strict sense, in issue and hence deserving of a searching inquiry. When character is used circumstantially and hence occupies a lesser status in the case, proof may be only by reputation and opinion. These latter methods are also available when character is in issue. This treatment is, with respect to specific instances of conduct and reputation, conventional contemporary common law doctrine. McCormick § 153.

In recognizing opinion as a means of proving character, the rule departs from usual contemporary practice in favor of that of an earlier day. See 7 Wigmore § 1986, pointing out that the earlier practice permitted opinion and arguing strongly for evidence based on personal knowledge and belief as contrasted with "the secondhand, irresponsible product of multiplied guesses and gossip which we term 'reputation'." It seems likely that the persistence of reputation evidence is due to its largely being opinion in disguise. Traditionally character has been regarded primarily in moral overtones of good and bad: chaste, peaceable, truthful, honest. Nevertheless, on occasion nonmoral considerations crop up, as in the case of the incompetent driver, and this seems bound to happen increasingly. If character is defined as the kind of person one is, then account must be taken of varying ways of arriving at the estimate. These may range from the opinion of the employer who has found the man honest to the opinion of the psychiatrist based upon examination and testing. No effective dividing line exists between character and mental capacity, and the latter traditionally has been provable by opinion.

According to the great majority of cases, on cross-examination inquiry is allowable as to whether the reputation witness has heard of particular instances of conduct pertinent to the trait in question. *Michelson v. United States,* 335 U.S. 469, 69 S.Ct. 213, 93 L.Ed. 168 (1948); Annot., 47 A.L.R.2d 1258. The theory is that, since the reputation witness relates what he has heard, the inquiry tends to shed light on the accuracy of his hearing and reporting. Accordingly, the opinion witness would be asked whether he knew, as well as whether he had heard. The fact is, of course, that these distinctions are of slight if any practical significance, and the second sentence of subdivision (a) eliminates them as a factor in formulating questions. This recognition of the propriety of inquiring into specific instances of conduct does not circumscribe inquiry otherwise into the bases of opinion and reputation testimony.

The express allowance of inquiry into specific instances of conduct on cross-examination in subdivision (a) and the express allowance of it as part of a case in chief when character is actually in issue in subdivision (b) contemplate that testimony of specific instances is not generally permissible on the direct examination of an ordinary opinion witness to character. Similarly as to witnesses to the character of witnesses under Rule 608(b). Opinion testimony on direct in these situations ought in general to correspond to reputation testimony as now given, *i.e.,* be confined to the nature and extent of observation and acquaintance upon which the opinion is based. See Rule 701.

1974 Enactment

Note to Subdivision (a). Rule 405(a) as submitted proposed to change existing law by allowing evidence of character in the form of opinion as well as reputation testimony. Fearing, among other reasons, that wholesale allowance of opinion testimony might tend to turn a trial into a swearing contest between conflicting character witnesses, the Committee decided to delete from this Rule, as well as from Rule 608(a) which involves a related problem, reference to opinion testimony. House Report No. 93–650.

The Senate makes two language changes in the nature of conforming amendments. The Conference adopts the Senate amendments. House Report No. 93–1597.

1987 Amendments

The amendment is technical. No substantive change is intended.

2011 Amendments

The language of Rule 405 has been amended as part of the restyling of the Evidence Rules to make them more easily understood and to make style and terminology consistent throughout the rules. These changes are intended to be stylistic only. There is no intent to change any result in any ruling on evidence admissibility.

CROSS REFERENCES

Extortionate credit transactions, admissibility of evidence to show,

> Reputation as to collection practices, see 18 USCA § 892.
>
> Reputation of defendant within community, see 18 USCA § 894.
>
> Threat as means of collection, see 18 USCA § 894.

Witnesses,

> Character and conduct, see Fed.Rules Evid. Rule 608, 28 USCA.
>
> Impeachment by conviction of crime, see Fed.Rules Evid. Rule 609, 28 USCA.
>
> Opinion testimony, see Fed.Rules Evid. Rule 701, 28 USCA.
>
> Religious opinions or beliefs, see Fed.Rules Evid. Rule 610, 28 USCA.

Rule 406. Habit; Routine Practice

Evidence of a person's habit or an organization's routine practice may be admitted to prove that on a particular occasion the person or organization acted in accordance with the habit or routine practice. The court may admit this evidence regardless of whether it is corroborated or whether there was an eyewitness. (Pub.L. 93–595, § 1, Jan. 2, 1975, 88 Stat. 1932; Apr. 26, 2011, eff. Dec. 1, 2011.)

ADVISORY COMMITTEE NOTES
1972 Proposed Rules

An oft-quoted paragraph, McCormick, § 162, p. 340, describes habit in terms effectively contrasting it with character:

"Character and habit are close akin. Character is a generalized description of one's disposition, or of one's disposition in respect to a general trait, such as honesty, temperance, or peacefulness. 'Habit,' in modern usage, both lay and psychological, is more specific. It describes one's regular response to a repeated specific situation. If we speak of character for care, we think of the person's tendency to act prudently in all the varying situations of life, in business, family life, in handling automobiles and in walking across the street. A habit, on the other hand, is the person's regular practice of meeting a particular kind of situation with a specific type of conduct, such as the habit of going down a particular stairway two stairs at a time, or of giving the hand-signal for a left turn, or of alighting from railway cars while they are moving. The doing of the habitual acts may become semi-automatic."

Equivalent behavior on the part of a group is designated "routine practice of an organization" in the rule.

Agreement is general that habit evidence is highly persuasive as proof of conduct on a particular occasion. Again quoting McCormick § 162, p. 341:

"Character may be thought of as the sum of one's habits though doubtless it is more than this. But unquestionably the uniformity of one's response to habit is far greater than the consistency with which one's conduct conforms to character or disposition. Even though character comes in only exceptionally as evidence of an act, surely any sensible man in investigating whether X did a particular act would be greatly helped in his inquiry by evidence as to whether he was in the habit of doing it."

When disagreement has appeared, its focus has been upon the question what constitutes habit, and the reason for this is readily apparent. The extent to which instances must be multiplied and consistency of behavior maintained in order to rise to the status of habit inevitably gives rise to differences of opinion. Lewan, Rationale of Habit Evidence, 16 Syracuse L.Rev. 39, 49 (1964). While adequacy of sampling and uniformity of response are key factors, precise standards for measuring their sufficiency for evidence purposes cannot be formulated.

The rule is consistent with prevailing views. Much evidence is excluded simply because of failure to achieve the status of habit. Thus, evidence of intemperate "habits" is generally excluded when offered as proof of drunkenness in accident cases, Annot., 46 A.L.R.2d 103, and evidence of other assaults is inadmissible to prove the instant one in a civil assault action, Annot., 66 A.L.R.2d 806. In *Levin v. United States*, 119 U.S.App.D.C. 156, 338 F.2d 265 (1964), testimony as to the religious "habits" of the accused, offered as tending to prove that he was at home observing the Sabbath rather than out obtaining money through larceny by trick, was held properly excluded:

"It seems apparent to us that an individual's religious practices would not be the type of activities which would lend themselves to the characterization of 'invariable regularity.'

[1 Wigmore 520.] Certainly the very volitional basis of the activity raises serious questions as to its invariable nature, and hence its probative value." *Id.* at 272.

These rulings are not inconsistent with the trend towards admitting evidence of business transactions between one of the parties and a third person as tending to prove that he made the same bargain or proposal in the litigated situation. Slough, Relevancy Unraveled, 6 Kan.L.Rev. 38–41 (1957). Nor are they inconsistent with such cases as *Whittemore v. Lockheed Aircraft Corp.*, 65 Cal.App.2d 737, 151 P.2d 670 (1944), upholding the admission of evidence that plaintiff's intestate had on four other occasions flown planes from defendant's factory for delivery to his employer airline, offered to prove that he was piloting rather than a guest on a plane which crashed and killed all on board while en route for delivery.

A considerable body of authority has required that evidence of the routine practice of an organization be corroborated as a condition precedent to its admission in evidence. Slough, Relevancy Unraveled, 5 Kan.L.Rev. 404, 449 (1957). This requirement is specifically rejected by the rule on the ground that it relates to the sufficiency of the evidence rather than admissibility. A similar position is taken in New Jersey Rule 49. The rule also rejects the requirement of the absence of eyewitnesses, sometimes encountered with respect to admitting habit evidence to prove freedom from contributory negligence in wrongful death cases. For comment critical of the requirements see Frank, J., in *Cereste v. New York*, N.H. & H.R. Co., 231 F.2d 50 (2d Cir.1956), cert. denied 351 U.S. 951, 76 S.Ct. 848, 100 L.Ed. 1475, 10 Vand.L.Rev. 447 (1957); McCormick § 162, p. 342. The omission of the requirement from the California Evidence Code is said to have effected its elimination. Comment, Cal.Ev.Code § 1105.

2011 Amendments

The language of Rule 406 has been amended as part of the restyling of the Evidence Rules to make them more easily understood and to make style and terminology consistent throughout the rules. These changes are intended to be stylistic only. There is no intent to change any result in any ruling on evidence admissibility.

CROSS REFERENCES

Opinion testimony by lay witnesses, see Fed.Rules Evid. Rule 701, 28 USCA.

Rule 407. Subsequent Remedial Measures

When measures are taken that would have made an earlier injury or harm less likely to occur, evidence of the subsequent measures is not admissible to prove:

- negligence;
- culpable conduct;
- a defect in a product or its design; or
- a need for a warning or instruction.

But the court may admit this evidence for another purpose, such as impeachment or—if disputed—proving ownership, control, or the feasibility of precautionary measures.

(Pub.L. 93–595, § 1, Jan. 2, 1975, 88 Stat. 1932; Apr. 11, 1997, eff. Dec. 1, 1997; Apr. 26, 2011, eff. Dec. 1, 2011.)

ADVISORY COMMITTEE NOTES

1972 Proposed Rules

The rule incorporates conventional doctrine which excludes evidence of subsequent remedial measures as proof of an admission of fault. The rule rests on two grounds. (1) The conduct is not in fact an admission, since the conduct is equally consistent with injury by mere accident or through contributory negligence. Or, as Baron Bramwell put it, the rule rejects the notion that "because the world gets wiser as it gets older, therefore it was foolish before." *Hart v. Lancashire & Yorkshire Ry. Co.*, 21 L.T.R. N.S. 261, 263 (1869). Under a liberal theory of relevancy this ground alone would not support exclusion as the inference is still a possible one. (2) The other, and more impressive, ground for exclusion rests on a social policy of encouraging people to take, or at least not discouraging them from taking, steps in furtherance of added safety. The courts have applied this principle to exclude evidence of subsequent repairs, installation of safety devices, changes in company rules, and discharge of employees, and the language of the present rule is broad enough to encompass all of them. See Falknor, Extrinsic Policies Affecting Admissibility, 10 Rutgers L.Rev. 574, 590 (1956).

The second sentence of the rule directs attention to the limitations of the rule. Exclusion is called for only when the evidence of subsequent remedial measures is offered as proof of negligence or culpable conduct. In effect it rejects the suggested inference that fault is admitted. Other purposes are, however, allowable, including ownership or control, existence of duty, and feasibility of precautionary measures, if controverted, and impeachment. 2 Wigmore § 283; Annot., 64 A.L.R.2d 1296. Two recent federal cases are illustrative. *Boeing Airplane Co. v. Brown*, 291 F.2d 310 (9th Cir.1961), an action against an airplane manufacturer for using an allegedly defectively designed alternator shaft which caused a plane crash, upheld the admission of evidence of subsequent design modification for the purpose of showing that design changes and safeguards were feasible. And *Powers v. J.B. Michael & Co.*, 329 F.2d 674 (6th Cir.1964), an action against a road contractor for negligent failure to put out warning signs, sustained the admission of evidence that defendant subsequently put out signs to show that the portion of the road in question was under defendant's control. The requirement that the other purpose be controverted calls for automatic exclusion unless a genuine issue be present and allows the opposing party to lay the groundwork for exclusion by making an admission. Otherwise the factors of undue prejudice, confusion of issues, misleading the jury, and waste of time remain for consideration under Rule 403.

For comparable rules, see Uniform Rule 51; California Evidence Code § 1151; Kansas Code of Civil Procedure § 60–451; New Jersey Evidence Rule 51.

1997 Amendments

The amendment to Rule 407 makes two changes in the rule. First, the words "an injury or harm allegedly caused by" were added to clarify that the rule applies only to changes made after the occurrence that produced the damages giving rise to the action. Evidence of measures taken by the defendant prior to the "event" causing "injury or harm" do not fall within the exclusionary scope of Rule 407 even if they occurred after the manufacture or design of the product. See *Chase v. General Motors Corp.*, 856 F.2d 17, 21–22 (4th Cir. 1988).

Second, Rule 407 has been amended to provide that evidence of subsequent remedial measures may not be used to prove "a defect in a product or its design, or that a warning or instruction should have accompanied a product." This amendment adopts the view of a majority of the circuits that have interpreted Rule 407 to apply to products liability actions. See *Raymond v. Raymond Corp.*, 938 F.2d 1518, 1522 (1st Cir. 1991); *In re Joint Eastern District and Southern District Asbestos Litigation v. Armstrong World industries, Inc.*, 995 F.2d 343 (2d Cir. 1993); *Cann v. Ford Motor Co.*, 658 F.2d 54, 60 (2d Cir. 1981), *cert. denied*, 456 U.S. 960 (1982); *Kelly v. Crown Equipment Co.*, 970 F.2d 1273, 1275 (3d Cir. 1992); *Werner v. Upjohn, Inc.*, 628 F.2d 848 (4th Cir. 1980); *cert. denied*, 449 U.S. 1080 (1981); *Grenada Steel Industries, Inc. v. Alabama Oxygen Co., Inc.*, 695 F.2d 883 (5th Cir. 1983); *Bauman v. Volkswagenwerk Aktiengesellschaft*, 621 F.2d 230, 232 (6th Cir. 1980); *Flaminio v. Honda Motor Company, Ltd.*, 733 F.2d 463, 469 (7th Cir. 1984); *Gauthier v. AMF, Inc.*, 788 F.2d 634, 636–37 (9th Cir. 1986).

Although this amendment adopts a uniform federal rule, it should be noted that evidence of subsequent remedial measures may be admissible pursuant to the second sentence of Rule 407. Evidence of subsequent measures that is not barred by Rule 407 may still be subject to exclusion on Rule 403 grounds when the dangers of prejudice or confusion substantially outweigh the probative value of the evidence.

GAP Report on Rule 407. The words "injury or harm" were substituted for the word "event " in line 3. The stylization changes in the second sentence of the rule were eliminated. The words "causing 'injury or harm' " were added to the Committee Note.

2011 Amendments

The language of Rule 407 has been amended as part of the general restyling of the Evidence Rules to make them more easily understood and to make style and terminology consistent throughout the rules. These changes are intended to be stylistic only. There is no intent to change any result in any ruling on evidence admissibility.

Rule 407 previously provided that evidence was not excluded if offered for a purpose not explicitly prohibited by the Rule. To improve the language of the Rule, it now provides that the court may admit evidence if offered for a permissible purpose. There is no intent to change the process for admitting evidence covered by the Rule. It remains the case that if offered for an impermissible purpose, it must be excluded, and if offered for a purpose not barred by the Rule, its admissibility remains governed by the general principles of Rules 402, 403, 801, etc.

Rule 408.   Compromise Offers and Negotiations

(a) Prohibited Uses. Evidence of the following is not admissible—on behalf of any party—either to prove or disprove the validity or amount of a disputed claim or to impeach by a prior inconsistent statement or a contradiction:

(1) furnishing, promising, or offering—or accepting, promising to accept, or offering to accept—a valuable consideration in compromising or attempting to compromise the claim; and

(2) conduct or a statement made during compromise negotiations about the claim—except when offered in a criminal case and when the negotiations related to a claim by a public office in the exercise of its regulatory, investigative, or enforcement authority.

(b) Exceptions. The court may admit this evidence for another purpose, such as proving a witness's bias or prejudice, negating a contention of undue delay, or proving an effort to obstruct a criminal investigation or prosecution.

(Pub.L. 93–595, § 1, Jan. 2, 1975, 88 Stat. 1933; Apr. 12, 2006, eff. Dec. 1, 2006; Apr. 26, 2011, eff. Dec. 1, 2011.)

ADVISORY COMMITTEE NOTES

1972 Proposed Rules

As a matter of general agreement, evidence of an offer to compromise a claim is not receivable in evidence as an admission of, as the case may be, the validity or invalidity of the claim. As with evidence of subsequent remedial measures, dealt with in Rule 407, exclusion may be based on two grounds. (1) The evidence is irrelevant, since the offer may be motivated by a desire for peace rather than from any concession of weakness of position. The validity of this position will vary as the amount of the offer varies in relation to the size of the claim and may also be influenced by other circumstances. (2) A more consistently impressive ground is promotion of the public policy favoring the compromise and settlement of disputes. McCormick §§ 76, 251. While the rule is ordinarily phrased in terms of offers of compromise, it is apparent that a similar attitude must be taken with respect to completed compromises when offered against a party thereto. This latter situation will not, of course, ordinarily occur except when a party to the present litigation has compromised with a third person.

The same policy underlies the provision of Rule 68 of the Federal Rules of Civil Procedure that evidence of an unaccepted offer of judgment is not admissible except in a proceeding to determine costs.

The practical value of the common law rule has been greatly diminished by its inapplicability to admissions of fact, even though made in the course of compromise negotiations, unless hypothetical, stated to be "without prejudice," or so connected with the offer as to be inseparable from it. McCormick § 251, pp. 540–541. An inevitable effect is to inhibit freedom of communication with respect to compromise, even among lawyers. Another effect is the generation of controversy over whether a given statement falls within or without the protected area. These considerations account for the expansion of the rule herewith to include evidence of conduct or statements made in compromise negotiations, as well as the offer or completed compromise itself. For similar provisions see California Evidence Code §§ 1152, 1154.

The policy considerations which underlie the rule do not come into play when the effort is to induce a creditor to settle an admittedly due amount for a lesser sum. McCormick § 251, p. 540. Hence the rule requires that the claim be disputed as to either validity or amount.

The final sentence of the rule serves to point out some limitations upon its applicability. Since the rule excludes only when the purpose is proving the validity or invalidity of the claim or its amount, an offer for another purpose is not within

the rule. The illustrative situations mentioned in the rule are supported by the authorities. As to proving bias or prejudice of a witness, see Annot., 161 A.L.R. 395, *contra, Fenberg v. Rosenthal,* 348 Ill.App. 510, 109 N.E.2d 402 (1952), and negativing a contention of lack of due diligence in presenting a claim, 4 Wigmore § 1061. An effort to "buy off" the prosecution or a prosecuting witness in a criminal case is not within the policy of the rule of exclusion. McCormick § 251, p. 542.

For other rules of similar import, see Uniform Rules 52 and 53; California Evidence Code §§ 1152, 1154; Kansas Code of Civil Procedure §§ 60–452, 60–453; New Jersey Evidence Rules 52 and 53.

1974 Enactment

Under existing federal law evidence of conduct and statements made in compromise negotiations is admissible in subsequent litigation between the parties. The second sentence of Rule 408 as submitted by the Supreme Court proposed to reverse that doctrine in the interest of further promoting nonjudicial settlement of disputes. Some agencies of government expressed the view that the Court formulation was likely to impede rather than assist efforts to achieve settlement of disputes. For one thing, it is not always easy to tell when compromise negotiations begin, and informal dealings end. Also, parties dealing with government agencies would be reluctant to furnish factual information at preliminary meetings; they would wait until "compromise negotiations" began and thus hopefully effect an immunity for themselves with respect to the evidence supplied. In light of these considerations, the Committee recast the Rule so that admissions of liability or opinions given during compromise negotiations continue inadmissible, but evidence of unqualified factual assertions is admissible. The latter aspect of the Rule is drafted, however, so as to preserve other possible objections to the introduction of such evidence. The Committee intends no modification of current law whereby a party may protect himself from future use of his statements by couching them in hypothetical conditional form. House Report No. 93–650.

This rule as reported makes evidence of settlement or attempted settlement of a disputed claim inadmissible when offered as an admission of liability or the amount of liability. The purpose of this rule is to encourage settlements which would be discouraged if such evidence were admissible.

Under present law, in most jurisdictions, statements of fact made during settlement negotiations, however, are excepted from this ban and are admissible. The only escape from admissibility of statements of fact made in a settlement negotiation is if the declarant or his representative expressly states that the statement is hypothetical in nature or is made without prejudice. Rule 408 as submitted by the Court reversed the traditional rule. It would have brought statements of fact within the ban and made them, as well as an offer of settlement, inadmissible.

The House amended the rule and would continue to make evidence of facts disclosed during compromise negotiations admissible. It thus reverted to the traditional rule. The House committee report states that the committee intends to preserve current law under which a party may protect himself by couching his statements in hypothetical form [See House Report No. 93–650 above]. The real impact of this amendment, however, is to deprive the rule of much of its salutary effect. The exception for factual admissions was believed by the Advisory Committee to hamper free communication between parties and thus to constitute an unjustifiable restraint upon efforts to negotiate settlements—the encouragement of which is the purpose of the rule. Further, by protecting hypothetically phrased statements, it constituted a preference for the sophisticated, and a trap for the unwary.

Three States which had adopted rules of evidence patterned after the proposed rules prescribed by the Supreme Court opted for versions of rule 408 identical with the Supreme Court draft with respect to the inadmissibility of conduct or statements made in compromise negotiations [Nev.Rev.Stats. § 48.105; N.Mex.Stats.Anno. (1973 Supp.) § 20–4–408; West's Wis.Stats.Anno. (1973 Supp.) § 904.08].

For these reasons, the committee has deleted the House amendment and restored the rule to the version submitted by the Supreme Court with one additional amendment. This amendment adds a sentence to insure that evidence, such as documents, is not rendered inadmissible merely because it is presented in the course of compromise negotiations if the evidence is otherwise discoverable. A party should not be able to immunize from admissibility documents otherwise discoverable merely by offering them in a compromise negotiation. Senate Report No. 93–1277.

The House bill provides that evidence of admissions of liability or opinions given during compromise negotiations is not admissible, but that evidence of facts disclosed during compromise negotiations is not inadmissible by virtue of having been first disclosed in the compromise negotiations. The Senate amendment provides that evidence of conduct or statements made in compromise negotiations is not admissible. The Senate amendment also provides that the rule does not require the exclusion of any evidence otherwise discoverable merely because it is presented in the course of compromise negotiations.

The House bill was drafted to meet the objection of executive agencies that under the rule as proposed by the Supreme Court, a party could present a fact during compromise negotiations and thereby prevent an opposing party from offering evidence of that fact at trial even though such evidence was obtained from independent sources. The Senate amendment expressly precludes this result.

The Conference adopts the Senate amendment. House Report No. 93–1597.

2006 Amendment

Rule 408 has been amended to settle some questions in the courts about the scope of the Rule, and to make it easier to read. First, the amendment provides that Rule 408 does not prohibit the introduction in a criminal case of statements or conduct during compromise negotiations regarding a civil dispute by a government regulatory, investigative, or enforcement agency. *See, e.g., United States v. Prewitt*, 34 F.3d 436, 439 (7th Cir. 1994) (admissions of fault made in compromise of a civil securities enforcement action were admissible against the accused in a subsequent criminal action for mail fraud). Where an individual makes a statement in the presence of government agents, its subsequent admission in a criminal case should not be unexpected. The individual can seek to protect against subsequent disclosure through negotiation and agreement with the civil regulator or an attorney for the government.

Statements made in compromise negotiations of a claim by a government agency may be excluded in criminal cases where the circumstances so warrant under Rule 403. For example, if an individual was unrepresented at the time the statement was made in a civil enforcement proceeding, its probative value in a subsequent criminal case may be minimal. But there is no absolute exclusion imposed by Rule 408.

In contrast, statements made during compromise negotiations of other disputed claims are not admissible in subsequent criminal litigation, when offered to prove liability for, invalidity of, or amount of those claims. When private parties enter into compromise negotiations they cannot protect against the subsequent use of statements in criminal cases by way of private ordering. The inability to guarantee protection against subsequent use could lead to parties refusing to admit fault, even if by doing so they could favorably settle the private matter. Such a chill on settlement negotiations would be contrary to the policy of Rule 408.

The amendment distinguishes statements and conduct (such as a direct admission of fault) made in compromise negotiations of a civil claim by a government agency from an offer or acceptance of a compromise of such a claim. An offer or acceptance of a compromise of any civil claim is excluded under the Rule if offered against the defendant as an admission of fault. In that case, the predicate for the evidence would be that the defendant, by compromising with the government agency, has admitted the validity and amount of the civil claim, and that this admission has sufficient probative value to be considered as evidence of guilt. But unlike a direct statement of fault, an offer or acceptance of a compromise is not very probative of the defendant's guilt. Moreover, admitting such an offer or acceptance could deter a defendant from settling a civil regulatory action, for fear of evidentiary use in a subsequent criminal action. *See, e.g.*, Fishman, *Jones on Evidence, Civil and Criminal*, § 22:16 at 199, n.83 (7th ed. 2000) ("A target of a potential criminal investigation may be unwilling to settle civil claims against him if by doing so he increases the risk of prosecution and conviction.").

The amendment retains the language of the original rule that bars compromise evidence only when offered as evidence of the "validity," "invalidity," or "amount" of the disputed claim. The intent is to retain the extensive case law finding Rule 408 inapplicable when compromise evidence is offered for a purpose other than to prove the validity, invalidity, or amount of a disputed claim. *See, e.g., Athey v. Farmers Ins. Exchange*, 234 F.3d 357 (8th Cir. 2000) (evidence of settlement offer by insurer was properly admitted to prove insurer's bad faith); *Coakley & Williams v. Structural Concrete Equip.*, 973 F.2d 349 (4th Cir. 1992) (evidence of settlement is not precluded by Rule 408 where offered to prove a party's intent with respect to the scope of a release); *Cates v. Morgan Portable Bldg. Corp.*, 708 F.2d 683 [sic; probably should read 780 F.2d 683] (7th Cir. 1985) (Rule 408 does not bar evidence of a settlement when offered to prove a breach of the settlement agreement, as the purpose of the evidence is to prove the fact of settlement as opposed to the validity or amount of the underlying claim); *Uforma/Shelby Bus. Forms, Inc. v. NLRB*, 111 F.3d 1284 (6th Cir. 1997) (threats made in settlement negotiations were admissible; Rule 408 is inapplicable when the claim is based upon a wrong that is committed during the course of settlement negotiations). So for example, Rule 408 is inapplicable if offered to show that a party made fraudulent statements in order to settle a litigation.

The amendment does not affect the case law providing that Rule 408 is inapplicable when evidence of the compromise is offered to prove notice. *See, e.g., United States v. Austin*, 54 F.3d 394 (7th Cir. 1995) (no error to admit evidence of the

---

defendant's settlement with the FTC, because it was offered to prove that the defendant was on notice that subsequent similar conduct was wrongful); *Spell v. McDaniel*, 824 F.2d 1380 (4th Cir. 1987) (in a civil rights action alleging that an officer used excessive force, a prior settlement by the City of another brutality claim was properly admitted to prove that the City was on notice of aggressive behavior by police officers).

The amendment prohibits the use of statements made in settlement negotiations when offered to impeach by prior inconsistent statement or through contradiction. Such broad impeachment would tend to swallow the exclusionary rule and would impair the public policy of promoting settlements. *See McCormick on Evidence* at 186 (5th ed. 1999) ("Use of statements made in compromise negotiations to impeach the testimony of a party, which is not specifically treated in Rule 408, is fraught with danger of misuse of the statements to prove liability, threatens frank interchange of information during negotiations, and generally should not be permitted."). *See also EEOC v. Gear Petroleum, Inc.*, 948 F.2d 1542 (10th Cir.1991) (letter sent as part of settlement negotiation cannot be used to impeach defense witnesses by way of contradiction or prior inconsistent statement; such broad impeachment would undermine the policy of encouraging uninhibited settlement negotiations).

The amendment makes clear that Rule 408 excludes compromise evidence even when a party seeks to admit its own settlement offer or statements made in settlement negotiations. If a party were to reveal its own statement or offer, this could itself reveal the fact that the adversary entered into settlement negotiations. The protections of Rule 408 cannot be waived unilaterally because the Rule, by definition, protects both parties from having the fact of negotiation disclosed to the jury. Moreover, proof of statements and offers made in settlement would often have to be made through the testimony of attorneys, leading to the risks and costs of disqualification. *See generally Pierce v. F.R. Tripler & Co.*, 955 F.2d 820, 828 (2d Cir. 1992) (settlement offers are excluded under Rule 408 even if it is the offeror who seeks to admit them; noting that the "widespread admissibility of the substance of settlement offers could bring with it a rash of motions for disqualification of a party's chosen counsel who would likely become a witness at trial").

The sentence of the Rule referring to evidence "otherwise discoverable" has been deleted as superfluous. *See, e.g.*, Advisory Committee Note to Maine Rule of Evidence 408 (refusing to include the sentence in the Maine version of Rule 408 and noting that the sentence "seems to state what the law would be if it were omitted"); Advisory Committee Note to Wyoming Rule of Evidence 408 (refusing to include the sentence in Wyoming Rule 408 on the ground that it was "superfluous"). The intent of the sentence was to prevent a party from trying to immunize admissible information, such as a pre-existing document, through the pretense of disclosing it during compromise negotiations. *See Ramada Development Co. v. Rauch*, 644 F.2d 1097 (5th Cir. 1981). But even without the sentence, the Rule cannot be read to protect pre-existing information simply because it was presented to the adversary in compromise negotiations.

2011 Amendments

The language of Rule 408 has been amended as part of the general restyling of the Evidence Rules to make them more easily understood and to make style and terminology consis-

tent throughout the rules. These changes are intended to be stylistic only. There is no intent to change any result in any ruling on evidence admissibility.

Rule 408 previously provided that evidence was not excluded if offered for a purpose not explicitly prohibited by the Rule. To improve the language of the Rule, it now provides that the court may admit evidence if offered for a permissible purpose. There is no intent to change the process for admitting evidence covered by the Rule. It remains the case that if offered for an impermissible purpose, it must be excluded, and if offered for a purpose not barred by the Rule, its admissibility remains governed by the general principles of Rules 402, 403, 801, etc.

The Committee deleted the reference to "liability" on the ground that the deletion makes the Rule flow better and easier to read, and because "liability" is covered by the broader term "validity." Courts have not made substantive decisions on the basis of any distinction between validity and liability. No change in current practice or in the coverage of the Rule is intended.

CROSS REFERENCES

Offer of judgment inadmissible as evidence, exception, see Fed.Rules Civ.Proc. Rule 68, 28 USCA.

Rule 409. Offers to Pay Medical and Similar Expenses

Evidence of furnishing, promising to pay, or offering to pay medical, hospital, or similar expenses resulting from an injury is not admissible to prove liability for the injury.
(Pub.L. 93–595, § 1, Jan. 2, 1975, 88 Stat.1933; Apr. 26, 2011, eff. Dec. 1, 2011.)

ADVISORY COMMITTEE NOTES

1972 Proposed Rules

The considerations underlying this rule parallel those underlying Rules 407 and 408, which deal respectively with subsequent remedial measures and offers of compromise. As stated in Annot., 20 A.L.R.2d 291, 293:

"[G]enerally, evidence of payment of medical, hospital, or similar expenses of an injured party by the opposing party, is not admissible, the reason often given being that such payment or offer is usually made from humane impulses and not from an admission of liability, and that to hold otherwise would tend to discourage assistance to the injured person."

Contrary to Rule 408, dealing with offers of compromise, the present rule does not extend to conduct or statements not a part of the act of furnishing or offering or promising to pay. This difference in treatment arises from fundamental differences in nature. Communication is essential if compromises are to be effected, and consequently broad protection of statements is needed. This is not so in cases of payments or offers or promises to pay medical expenses, where factual statements may be expected to be incidental in nature.

For rules on the same subject, but phrased in terms of "humanitarian motives," see Uniform Rule 52; California Evidence Code § 1152; Kansas Code of Civil Procedure § 60–452; New Jersey Evidence Rule 52.

2011 Amendments

The language of Rule 409 has been amended as part of the restyling of the Evidence Rules to make them more easily understood and to make style and terminology consistent throughout the rules. These changes are intended to be stylistic only. There is no intent to change any result in any ruling on evidence admissibility.

Rule 410.   Pleas, Plea Discussions, and Related Statements

(a) Prohibited Uses. In a civil or criminal case, evidence of the following is not admissible against the defendant who made the plea or participated in the plea discussions:

(1) a guilty plea that was later withdrawn;

(2) a nolo contendere plea;

(3) a statement made during a proceeding on either of those pleas under Federal Rule of Criminal Procedure 11 or a comparable state procedure; or

(4) a statement made during plea discussions with an attorney for the prosecuting authority if the discussions did not result in a guilty plea or they resulted in a later-withdrawn guilty plea.

(b) Exceptions. The court may admit a statement described in Rule 410(a)(3) or (4):

(1) in any proceeding in which another statement made during the same plea or plea discussions has been introduced, if in fairness the statements ought to be considered together; or

(2) in a criminal proceeding for perjury or false statement, if the defendant made the statement under oath, on the record, and with counsel present.

(Pub.L. 93–595, § 1, Jan. 2, 1975, 88 Stat. 1933; Pub.L. 94–149, § 1(9), Dec. 12, 1975, 89 Stat. 805; Apr. 30, 1979, eff. Dec. 1, 1980; Apr. 26, 2011, eff. Dec. 1, 2011.)

ADVISORY COMMITTEE NOTES

1972 Proposed Rules

Withdrawn pleas of guilty were held inadmissible in federal prosecutions in *Kercheval v. United States,* 274 U.S. 220, 47 S.Ct. 582, 71 L.Ed. 1009 (1927). The Court pointed out that to admit the withdrawn plea would effectively set at naught the allowance of withdrawal and place the accused in a dilemma utterly inconsistent with the decision to award him a trial. The New York Court of Appeals, in *People v. Spitaleri,* 9 N.Y.2d 168, 212 N.Y.S.2d 53, 173 N.E.2d 35 (1961), reexamined and overturned its earlier decisions which had allowed admission. In addition to the reasons set forth in Kercheval, which was quoted at length, the court pointed out that the effect of admitting the plea was to compel defendant to take the stand by way of explanation and to open the way for the prosecution to call the lawyer who had represented him at the time of entering the plea. State court decisions for and against admissibility are collected in Annot., 86 A.L.R.2d 326.

Pleas of *nolo contendere* are recognized by Rule 11 of the Rules of Criminal Procedure, although the law of numerous States is to the contrary. The present rule gives effect to the principal traditional characteristic of the *nolo* plea, i.e. avoid-

ing the admission of guilt which is inherent in pleas of guilty. This position is consistent with the construction of Section 5 of the Clayton Act, 15 U.S.C. § 16(a), recognizing the inconclusive and compromise nature of judgments based on *nolo* pleas. *General Electric Co. v. City of San Antonio,* 334 F.2d 480 (5th Cir.1964); *Commonwealth Edison Co. v. Allis–Chalmers Mfg. Co.,* 323 F.2d 412 (7th Cir.1963), cert. denied 376 U.S. 939, 84 S.Ct. 794, 11 L.Ed.2d 659; *Armco Steel Corp. v. North Dakota,* 376 F.2d 206 (8th Cir.1967); *City of Burbank v. General Electric Co.,* 329 F.2d 825 (9th Cir.1964). See also state court decisions in Annot., 18 A.L.R.2d 1287, 1314.

Exclusion of offers to plead guilty or *nolo* has as its purpose the promotion of disposition of criminal cases by compromise. As pointed out in McCormick § 251, p. 543.

"Effective criminal law administration in many localities would hardly be possible if a large proportion of the charges were not disposed of by such compromises."

See also *People v. Hamilton,* 60 Cal.2d 105, 32 Cal.Rptr. 4, 383 P.2d 412 (1963), discussing legislation designed to achieve this result. As with compromise offers generally, Rule 408, free communication is needed, and security against having an offer of compromise or related statement admitted in evidence effectively encourages it.

Limiting the exclusionary rule to use against the accused is consistent with the purpose of the rule, since the possibility of use for or against other persons will not impair the effectiveness of withdrawing pleas or the freedom of discussion which the rule is designed to foster. See A.B.A. Standards Relating to Pleas of Guilty § 2.2 (1968). See also the narrower provisions of New Jersey Evidence Rule 52(2) and the unlimited exclusion provided in California Evidence Code § 1153.

1974 Enactment

The Committee added the phrase "Except as otherwise provided by Act of Congress" to Rule 410 as submitted by the Court in order to preserve particular congressional policy judgments as to the effect of a plea of guilty or of nolo contendere. See 15 U.S.C. 16(a). The Committee intends that its amendment refers to both present statutes and statutes subsequently enacted. House Report No. 93–650.

As adopted by the House, rule 410 would make inadmissible pleas of guilty or nolo contendere subsequently withdrawn as well as offers to make such pleas. Such a rule is clearly justified as a means of encouraging pleading. However, the House rule would then go on to render inadmissible for any purpose statements made in connection with these pleas or offers as well.

The committee finds this aspect of the House rule unjustified. Of course, in certain circumstances such statements should be excluded. If, for example, a plea is vitiated because of coercion, statements made in connection with the plea may also have been coerced and should be inadmissible on that basis. In other cases, however, voluntary statements of an accused made in court on the record, in connection with a plea, and determined by a court to be reliable should be admissible even though the plea is subsequently withdrawn. This is particularly true in those cases where, if the House rule were in effect, a defendant would be able to contradict his previous statements and thereby lie with impunity [See *Harris v. New York,* 401 U.S. 222 (1971)]. To prevent such an injustice, the rule has been modified to permit the use of such statements for the limited purposes of impeachment and in subsequent perjury or false statement prosecutions. Senate Report No. 93–1277.

The House bill provides that evidence of a guilty or nolo contendere plea, of an offer of either plea, or of statements made in connection with such pleas or offers of such pleas, is inadmissible in any civil or criminal action, case or proceeding against the person making such plea or offer. The Senate amendment makes the rule inapplicable to a voluntary and reliable statement made in court on the record where the statement is offered in a subsequent prosecution of the declarant for perjury or false statement.

The issues raised by Rule 410 are also raised by proposed Rule 11(e)(6) of the Federal Rules of Criminal Procedure presently pending before Congress. This proposed rule, which deals with the admissibility of pleas of guilty or nolo contendere, offers to make such pleas, and statements made in connection with such pleas, was promulgated by the Supreme Court on April 22, 1974, and in the absence of congressional action will become effective on August 1, 1975. The conferees intend to make no change in the presently-existing case law until that date, leaving the courts free to develop rules in this area on a case-by-case basis.

The Conferees further determined that the issues presented by the use of guilty and nolo contendere pleas, offers of such pleas, and statements made in connection with such pleas or offers, can be explored in greater detail during Congressional consideration of Rule 11(e)(6) of the Federal Rules of Criminal Procedure. The Conferees believe, therefore, that it is best to defer its effective date until August 1, 1975. The Conferees intend that Rule 410 would be superseded by any subsequent Federal Rule of Criminal Procedure or act of Congress with which it is inconsistent, if the Federal Rule of Criminal Procedure or Act of Congress takes effect or becomes law after the date of the enactment of the act establishing the rules of evidence.

The conference adopts the Senate amendment with an amendment that expresses the above intentions. House Report No. 93–1597.

1979 Amendments

Present rule 410 conforms to rule 11(e)(6) of the Federal Rules of Criminal Procedure. A proposed amendment to rule 11(e)(6) would clarify the circumstances in which pleas, plea discussions and related statements are inadmissible in evidence: see Advisory Committee Note thereto. The amendment proposed above would make comparable changes in rule 410.

2011 Amendments

The language of Rule 410 has been amended as part of the restyling of the Evidence Rules to make them more easily understood and to make style and terminology consistent throughout the rules. These changes are intended to be stylistic only. There is no intent to change any result in any ruling on evidence admissibility.

HISTORICAL NOTES

Revision Notes and Legislative Reports

1975 Acts. House Report No. 94–599, see 1975 U.S. Code Cong. and Adm. News, p. 1585.

References in Text

Rule 11 of the Federal Rules of Criminal Procedure, referred to in par. (3), is classified to Title 18, Federal Rules of Criminal Procedure.

CROSS REFERENCES

Antitrust actions, final judgments or decrees in favor of government as prima facie evidence, see 15 USCA § 16.

Arrest of judgment motion, time, see Fed.Rules Cr.Proc. Rule 34, 18 USCA.

Motion attacking sentence, see 28 USCA § 2255.

Withdrawal of plea of guilty or nolo contendere, see Fed. Rules Cr.Proc. Rule 32, 18 USCA.

Rule 411. Liability Insurance

Evidence that a person was or was not insured against liability is not admissible to prove whether the person acted negligently or otherwise wrongfully. But the court may admit this evidence for another purpose, such as proving a witness's bias or prejudice or proving agency, ownership, or control.

(Pub.L. 93–595, § 1, Jan. 2, 1975, 88 Stat.1933; Mar. 2, 1987, eff. Oct. 1, 1987; Apr. 26, 2011, eff. Dec. 1, 2011.)

ADVISORY COMMITTEE NOTES

1972 Proposed Rules

The courts have with substantial unanimity rejected evidence of liability insurance for the purpose of proving fault, and absence of liability insurance as proof of lack of fault. At best the inference of fault from the fact of insurance coverage is a tenuous one, as is its converse. More important, no doubt, has been the feeling that knowledge of the presence or absence of liability insurance would induce juries to decide cases on improper grounds. McCormick § 168; Annot., 4 A.L.R.2d 761. The rule is drafted in broad terms so as to include contributory negligence or other fault of a plaintiff as well as fault of a defendant.

The second sentence points out the limits of the rule, using well established illustrations. *Id.*

For similar rules see Uniform Rule 54; California Evidence Code § 1155; Kansas Code of Civil Procedure § 60–454; New Jersey Evidence Rule 54.

1987 Amendments

The amendment is technical. No substantive change is intended.

2011 Amendments

The language of Rule 411 has been amended as part of the general restyling of the Evidence Rules to make them more easily understood and to make style and terminology consistent throughout the rules. These changes are intended to be stylistic only. There is no intent to change any result in any ruling on evidence admissibility.

Rule 411 previously provided that evidence was not excluded if offered for a purpose not explicitly prohibited by the Rule. To improve the language of the Rule, it now provides that the court may admit evidence if offered for a permissible purpose. There is no intent to change the process for admitting evidence covered by the Rule. It remains the case that if offered for an impermissible purpose, it must be excluded, and if offered for a purpose not barred by the Rule, its admissibility remains governed by the general principles of Rules 402, 403, 801, etc.

CROSS REFERENCES

Discovery of insurance agreements, see Fed.Rules Civ.Proc. Rule 26, 28 USCA.

Rule 412. Sex–Offense Cases: The Victim's Sexual Behavior or Predisposition

(a) Prohibited Uses. The following evidence is not admissible in a civil or criminal proceeding involving alleged sexual misconduct:

(1) evidence offered to prove that a victim engaged in other sexual behavior; or

(2) evidence offered to prove a victim's sexual predisposition.

(b) Exceptions.

(1) **Criminal Cases.** The court may admit the following evidence in a criminal case:

(A) evidence of specific instances of a victim's sexual behavior, if offered to prove that someone other than the defendant was the source of semen, injury, or other physical evidence;

(B) evidence of specific instances of a victim's sexual behavior with respect to the person accused of the sexual misconduct, if offered by the defendant to prove consent or if offered by the prosecutor; and

(C) evidence whose exclusion would violate the defendant's constitutional rights.

(2) **Civil Cases.** In a civil case, the court may admit evidence offered to prove a victim's sexual behavior or sexual predisposition if its probative value substantially outweighs the danger of harm to any victim and of unfair prejudice to any party. The court may admit evidence of a victim's reputation only if the victim has placed it in controversy.

(c) Procedure to Determine Admissibility.

(1) **Motion.** If a party intends to offer evidence under Rule 412(b), the party must:

(A) file a motion that specifically describes the evidence and states the purpose for which it is to be offered;

(B) do so at least 14 days before trial unless the court, for good cause, sets a different time;

(C) serve the motion on all parties; and

(D) notify the victim or, when appropriate, the victim's guardian or representative.

(2) **Hearing.** Before admitting evidence under this rule, the court must conduct an in camera hearing and give the victim and parties a right to attend and be heard. Unless the court orders otherwise, the motion, related materials, and the record of the hearing must be and remain sealed.

(d) Definition of "Victim." In this rule, "victim" includes an alleged victim.

(Added Pub.L. 95–540, § 2(a), Oct. 28, 1978, 92 Stat. 2046; amended Pub.L. 100–690, Title VII, § 7046(a), Nov. 18, 1988, 102 Stat. 4400; Apr. 29, 1994, eff. Dec. 1, 1994; Pub.L. 103–322, Title IV, § 40141(b), Sept. 13, 1994, 108 Stat. 1919; Apr. 26, 2011, eff. Dec. 1, 2011.)

ADVISORY COMMITTEE NOTES

1994 Amendments

Rule 412 has been revised to diminish some of the confusion engendered by the original rule and to expand the protection afforded alleged victims of sexual misconduct. Rule 412 applies to both civil and criminal proceedings. The rule aims to safeguard the alleged victim against the invasion of privacy, potential embarrassment and sexual stereotyping that is associated with public disclosure of intimate sexual details and the infusion of sexual innuendo into the factfinding process. By affording victims protection in most instances, the rule also encourages victims of sexual misconduct to institute and to participate in legal proceedings against alleged offenders

Rule 412 seeks to achieve these objectives by barring evidence relating to the alleged victim's sexual behavior or alleged sexual predisposition, whether offered as substantive evidence of for impeachment, except in designated circumstances in which the probative value of the evidence significantly outweighs possible harm to the victim.

The revised rule applies in all cases involving sexual misconduct without regard to whether the alleged victim or person accused is a party to the litigation. Rule 412 extends to "pattern" witnesses in both criminal and civil cases whose testimony about other instances of sexual misconduct by the person accused is otherwise admissible. When the case does not involve alleged sexual misconduct, evidence relating to a third-party witness' alleged sexual activities is not within the ambit of Rule 412. The witness will, however, be protected by other rules such as Rules 404 and 608, as well as Rule 403.

The terminology "alleged victim" is used because there will frequently be a factual dispute as to whether sexual misconduct occurred. It does not connote any requirement that the misconduct be alleged in the pleadings. Rule 412 does not, however, apply unless the person against whom the evidence is offered can reasonably be characterized as a "victim of alleged sexual misconduct." When this is not the case, as for instance in a defamation action involving statements concerning sexual misconduct in which the evidence is offered to show that the alleged defamatory statements were true or did not damage the plaintiff's reputation, neither Rule 404 nor this rule will operate to bar the evidence; Rule 401 and 403 will continue to control. Rule 412 will, however, apply in a Title VII action in which the plaintiff has alleged sexual harassment.

The reference to a person "accused" is also used in a non-technical sense. There is no requirement that there be a criminal charge pending against the person or even that the misconduct would constitute a criminal offense. Evidence offered to prove allegedly false prior claims by the victim is not barred by Rule 412. However, the evidence is subject to the requirements of Rule 404.

Subdivision (a). As amended, Rule 412 bars evidence offered to prove the victim's sexual behavior and alleged sexual predisposition. Evidence, which might otherwise be admissible under Rules 402, 404(b), 405, 607, 608, 609 of some other evidence rule, must be excluded if Rule 412 so requires. The word "other" is used to suggest some flexibility in admitting evidence "intrinsic" to the alleged sexual misconduct. *Cf.* Committee Note to 1991 amendment to Rule 404(b)

Past sexual behavior connotes all activities that involve actual physical conduct, i.e. sexual intercourse or sexual contact. *See, e.g., United States v. Galloway*, 937 F.2d 542 (10th Cir. 1991), *cert. denied*, 113 S.Ct. 418 (1992) (use of contraceptives inadmissible since use implies sexual activity); *United States v. One Feather*, 702 F.2d 736 (8th Cir. 1983) (birth of an illegitimate child inadmissible); *State v. Carmichael*, 727 P.2d 918, 925 (Kan. 1986) (evidence of venereal disease inadmissible). In addition, the word "behavior" should be construed to include activities of the mind, such as fantasies or dreams. *See* 23 C. Wright and K. Graham, Jr., *Federal Practice and Procedure*, § 5384 at p. 548 (1980) ("While there may be some doubt under statutes that require 'conduct,' it would seem that the language of Rule 412 is broad enough to encompass the behavior of the mind.").

The rule has been amended to also exclude all other evidence relating to an alleged victim of sexual misconduct that is offered to prove a sexual predisposition. This amendment is designed to exclude evidence that does not directly refer to sexual activities or thoughts but that the proponent believes may have a sexual connotation for the factfinder. Admission of such evidence would contravene Rule 412's objectives of shielding the alleged victim from potential embarrassment and safeguarding the victim against stereotypical thinking. Consequently, unless the (b)(2) exception is satisfied, evidence such as that relating to the alleged victim's mode of dress, speech, or life-style will not be admissible.

The introductory phrase in subdivision (a) was deleted because it lacked clarity and contained no explicit reference to the other provisions of the law that were intended to be overridden. The conditional clause, "except as provided in subdivisions (b) and (c)" is intended to make clear that evidence of the types described in subdivision (a) is admissible only under the strictures of those sections.

The reason for extending the rule to all criminal cases is obvious. The strong social policy of protecting a victim's privacy and encouraging victims to come forward to report criminal acts is not confined to cases that involve a charge of sexual assault. The need to protect the victim is equally great when a defendant is charged with kidnapping, and evidence is offered, either to prove motive or as background, that the defendant sexually assaulted the victim.

The reason for extending Rule 412 to civil cases is equally obvious. The need to protect alleged victims against invasions of privacy, potential embarrassment, and unwarranted sexual stereotyping, and the wish to encourage victims to come forward when they have been sexually molested do not disappear because the context has shifted from a criminal prosecution to a claim for damages or injunctive relief. There is a strong social policy in not only punishing those who engage in sexual misconduct, but in also providing relief to the victim. Thus, Rule 412 applies in any civil case in which a person claims to be the victim of sexual misconduct, such as actions for sexual battery or sexual harassment.

Subdivision (b). Subdivision (b) spells out the specific circumstances in which some evidence may be admissible that would otherwise be barred by the general rule expressed in subdivision (a). As amended, Rule 412 will be virtually unchanged in criminal cases, but will provide protection to any person alleged to be a victim of sexual misconduct

regardless of the charge actually brought against an accused. A new exception has been added for civil cases.

In a criminal case, evidence may be admitted under subdivision (b)(1) pursuant to three possible exceptions, provided the evidence also satisfies other requirements for admissibility specified in the Federal Rules of Evidence, including Rule 403. Subdivisions (b)(1)(A) and (b)(1)(B) require proof in the form of specific instances of sexual behavior in recognition of the limited probative value and dubious reliability of evidence of reputation or evidence in the form of an opinion.

Under subdivision (b)(1)(A), evidence of specific instances of sexual behavior with persons other than the person whose sexual misconduct is alleged may be admissible if it is offered to prove that another person was the source of semen, injury or other physical evidence. Where the prosecution has directly or indirectly asserted that the physical evidence originated with the accused, the defendant must be afforded an opportunity to prove that another person was responsible. See *United States v. Begay*, 937 F.2d 515, 523 n. 10 (10th Cir. 1991). Evidence offered for the specific purpose identified in this subdivision may still be excluded if it does not satisfy Rules 401 or 403. *See, e.g., United States v. Azure*, 845 F.2d 1503, 1505-06 (8th Cir. 1988) (10 year old victim's injuries indicated recent use of force; court excluded evidence of consensual sexual activities with witness who testified at in camera hearing that he had never hurt victim and failed to establish recent activities).

Under the exception in subdivision (b)(1)(B), evidence of specific instances of sexual behavior with respect to the person whose sexual misconduct is alleged is admissible if offered to prove consent, or offered by the prosecution. Admissible pursuant to this exception might be evidence of prior instances of sexual activities between the alleged victim and the accused, as well as statements in which the alleged victim expresses an intent to engage in sexual intercourse with the accused, or voiced sexual fantasies involving that specific accused. In a prosecution for child sexual abuse, for example, evidence of uncharged sexual activity between the accused and the alleged victim offered by the prosecution may be admissible pursuant to Rule 404(b) to show a pattern of behavior. Evidence relating to the victim's alleged sexual predisposition is not admissible pursuant to this exception.

Under subdivision (b)(1)(C), evidence of specific instances of conduct may not be excluded if the result would be to deny a criminal defendant the protections afforded by the Constitution. For example, statements in which the victim has expressed an intent to have sex with the first person encountered on a particular occasion might not be excluded without violating the due process right of a rape defendant seeking to prove consent. Recognition of this basic principle was expressed on subdivision (b)(1) of the original rule. The United States Supreme Court has recognized that in various circumstances a defendant may have a right to introduce evidence otherwise precluded by an evidence rule under the Confrontation Clause. *See, e.g., Olden v. Kentucky*, 488 U.S. 227 (1988) (defendant in rape cases had right to inquire into alleged victim's cohabitation with another man to show bias).

Subdivision (b)(2) governs the admissibility of otherwise proscribed evidence in civil cases. It employs a balancing test rather than the specific exceptions stated in subdivision (b)(1) in recognition of the difficulty of foreseeing future developments in the law. Greater flexibility is needed to accommodate evolving causes of action such as claims for sexual harassment.

The balancing test requires the proponent of the evidence, whether plaintiff or defendant, to convince the court that the probative value of the proffered evidence "substantially outweighs the danger of harm to any victim and of unfair prejudice of any party." This test for admitting evidence offered to prove sexual behavior or sexual propensity in civil cases differs in three respects from the general rule governing admissibility set forth in Rule 403. First, it Reverses that usual procedure spelled out in Rule 403 by shifting the burden to the proponent to demonstrate admissibility rather than making the opponent justify exclusion of the evidence. Second, the standard expressed in subdivision (b)(2) is more stringent than in the original rule; it raises the threshold for admission by requiring that the probative value of the evidence *substantially* outweigh the specified dangers. Finally, the Rule 412 test puts "harm to the victim" on the scale in addition to prejudice to the parties.

Evidence of reputation may be received in a civil case only if the alleged victim has put his or her reputation into controversy. The victim may do so without making a specific allegation in a pleading. *Cf.* Fed.R.Civ.P. 35(a).

Subdivision (c). Amended subdivision (c) is more concise and understandable than the subdivision it replaces. The requirement of a motion before trial is continued in the amended rule, as is the provision that a late motion may be permitted for good cause shown. In deciding whether to permit late filing, the court may take into account the conditions previously included in the rule: namely whether the evidence is newly discovered and could not have been obtained earlier through the existence of due diligence, and whether the issue to which such evidence relates has newly arisen in the case. The rule recognizes that in some instances the circumstances that justify an application to introduce evidence otherwise barred by Rule 412 will not become apparent until trial.

The amended rule provides that before admitting evidence that falls within that prohibition of Rule 412(a), the court must hold a hearing in camera at which the alleged victim and any party must be afforded the right to be present and an opportunity to be heard. All papers connected with the motion must be kept and remain under seal during the course of trial and appellate proceedings unless otherwise ordered. This is to assure that the privacy of the alleged victim is preserved in all cases in which the court rules that proffered evidence is not admissible, and in which the hearing refers to matters that are not received, or are received in another form.

The procedures set forth in subdivision (c) do not apply to discovery of a victim's past sexual conduct or predisposition in civil cases, which will be continued to be governed by Fed. R. Civ. P. 26. In order not to undermine the rationale of Rule 412, however, courts should enter appropriate orders pursuant to Fed. R. Civ. P. 26(c) to protect the victim against unwarranted inquiries and to ensure confidentiality. Courts should presumptively issue protective orders barring discovery unless the party seeking discovery makes a showing that the evidence sought to be discovered would be relevant under the facts and theories of the particular case, and cannot be obtained except through discovery. In an action for sexual harassment, for instance, while some evidence of the alleged victim's sexual behavior and/or predisposition in the workplace may perhaps be relevant, non-work place conduct will usually be irrelevant. *Cf. Burns v. McGregor Electronic Industries, Inc.,* 989 F.2d 959, 962-63 (8th Cir. 1993) (posing for a nude magazine outside work hours is irrelevant to issue of unwelcomeness of sexual advances at work). Confidentiality orders should be presumptively granted as well.

One substantive change made in subdivision (c) is the elimination of the following sentence: "Notwithstanding subdivision (b) of Rule 104, if the relevancy of the evidence which the accused seeks to offer in trial depends upon the fulfillment of a condition of fact, the court, at the hearing in chambers or at a subsequent hearing in chambers scheduled for such purpose, shall accept evidence on the issue of whether such condition of fact is fulfilled and shall determine such issue." On its face, this language would appear to authorize a trial judge to exclude evidence of past sexual conduct between alleged victim and an accused or a defendant in a civil case based upon the judge's belief that such past acts did not occur. Such an authorization raises questions of invasion of the right to a jury trial under the Sixth and Seventh Amendments. *See* 1 S. Saltzburg & M. Martin, *Federal Rules of Evidence Manual,* 396-97 (5th ed. 1990).

The Advisory Committee concluded that the amended rule provided adequate protection for all persons claiming to be the victims of sexual misconduct, and that it was inadvisable to continue to include a provision in the rule that has been confusing and that raises substantial constitutional issues. [Advisory Committee Note adopted by Congressional Conference Report accompanying Pub.L. 103–322. See H.R. Conf. Rep. No. 103–711, 103rd Cong., 2nd Sess., 383 (1994).]

Congressional Discussion

The following discussion in the House of Representatives of October 10, 1978, preceded passage of H.R. 4727, which enacted Rule 412. The discussion appears in 124 Cong.Record, at page H. 11944.

Mr. MANN. Mr. Speaker, I yield myself such time as I may consume.

Mr. Speaker, for many years in this country, evidentiary rules have permitted the introduction of evidence about a rape victim's prior sexual conduct. Defense lawyers were permitted great latitude in bringing out intimate details about a rape victim's life. Such evidence quite often serves no real purpose and only results in embarrassment to the rape victim and unwarranted public intrusion into her private life.

The evidentiary rules that permit such inquiry have in recent years come under question; and the States have taken the lead to change and modernize their evidentiary rules about evidence of a rape victim's prior sexual behavior. The bill before us similarly seeks to modernize the Federal Evidentiary rules.

The present Federal Rules of Evidence reflect the traditional approach. If a defendant in a rape case raises the defense of consent, that defendant may then offer evidence about the victim's prior sexual behavior. Such evidence may be in the form of opinion evidence, evidence of reputation, or evidence of specific instances of behavior. Rule 404(a)(2) of the Federal Rules of Evidence permits the introduction of evidence of a "pertinent character trait." The advisory committee note to that rule cites, as an example of what the rule covers, the character of a rape victim when the issue is consent. Rule 405 of the Federal Rules of Evidence permits the use of opinion or reputation evidence or the use of evidence of specific behavior to show a character trait.

Thus, Federal evidentiary rules permit a wide ranging inquiry into the private conduct of a rape victim, even though that conduct may have at best a tenuous connection to the offense for which the defendant is being tried.

H.R. 4727 amends the Federal Rules of Evidence to add a new rule, applicable only in criminal cases, to spell out when, and under what conditions, evidence of a rape victim's prior sexual behavior can be admitted. The new rule provides that reputation or opinion evidence about a rape victim's prior sexual behavior is not admissible. The new rule also provides that a court cannot admit evidence of specific instances of a rape victim's prior sexual conduct except in three circumstances.

The first circumstance is where the Constitution requires that the evidence be admitted. This exception is intended to cover those infrequent instances where, because of an unusual chain of circumstances, the general rule of inadmissibility, if followed, would result in denying the defendant a constitutional right.

The second circumstance in which the defendant can offer evidence of specific instances of a rape victim's prior sexual behavior is where the defendant raises the issue of consent and the evidence is of sexual behavior with the defendant. To admit such evidence, however, the court must find that the evidence is relevant and that its probative value outweighs the danger of unfair prejudice.

The third circumstance in which a court can admit evidence of specific instances of a rape victim's prior sexual behavior is where the evidence is of behavior with someone other than the defendant and is offered by the defendant on the issue of whether or not he was the source of semen or injury. Again, such evidence will be admitted only if the court finds that the evidence is relevant and that its probative value outweighs the danger of unfair prejudice.

The new rule further provides that before evidence is admitted under any of these exceptions, there must be an in camera hearing—that is, a proceeding that takes place in the judge's chambers out of the presence of the jury and the general public. At this hearing, the defendant will present the evidence he intends to offer and be able to argue why it should be admitted. The prosecution, of course, will be able to argue against that evidence being admitted.

The purpose of the in camera hearing is twofold. It gives the defendant an opportunity to demonstrate to the court why certain evidence is admissible and ought to be presented to the jury. At the same time, it protects the privacy of the rape victim in those instances when the court finds that evidence is inadmissible. Of course, if the court finds the evidence to be admissible, the evidence will be presented to the jury in open court.

The effect of this legislation, therefore, is to preclude the routine use of evidence of specific instances of a rape victim's prior sexual behavior. Such evidence will be admitted only in clearly and narrowly defined circumstances and only after an in camera hearing. In determining the admissibility of such evidence, the court will consider all of the facts and circumstances surrounding the evidence, such as the amount of time that lapsed between the alleged prior act and the rape charged in the prosecution. The greater the lapse of time, of course, the less likely it is that such evidence will be admitted.

Mr. Speaker, the principal purpose of this legislation is to protect rape victims from the degrading and embarrassing disclosure of intimate details about their private lives. It does so by narrowly circumscribing when such evidence may be admitted. It does not do so, however, by sacrificing any constitutional right possessed by the defendant. The bill before us fairly balances the interests involved—the rape victim's interest in protecting her private life from unwarranted public exposure; the defendant's interest in being able adequately to present a defense by offering relevant and probative evidence; and society's interest in a fair trial, one where unduly prejudicial evidence is not permitted to becloud the issues before the jury.

I urge support of the bill.

Mr. WIGGINS. Mr. Speaker, I yield myself such time as I may consume.

(Mr. WIGGINS asked and was given permission to revise and extend his remarks.)

Mr. WIGGINS. Mr. Speaker, this legislation addresses itself to a subject that is certainly a proper one for our consideration. Many of us have been troubled for years about the indiscriminate and prejudicial use of testimony with respect to a victim's prior sexual behavior in rape and similar cases. This bill deals with that problem. It is not, in my opinion, Mr. Speaker, a perfect bill in the manner in which it deals with the problem, but my objections are not so fundamental as would lead me to oppose the bill.

I think, Mr. Speaker, that it is unwise to adopt a per se rule absolutely excluding evidence of reputation and opinion with respect to the victim—and this bill does that—but it is difficult for me to foresee the specific case in which such evidence might be admissible. The trouble is this, Mr. Speaker: None of us can foresee perfectly all of the various circumstances under which the propriety of evidence might be before the court. If this bill has a defect, in my view it is because it adopts a per se rule with respect to opinion and reputation evidence.

Alternatively we might have permitted that evidence to be considered in camera as we do other evidence under the bill.

I should note, however, in fairness, having expressed minor reservations, that the bill before the House at this time does improve significantly upon the bill which was presented to our committee.

I will not detail all of those improvements but simply observe that the bill upon which we shall soon vote is a superior product to that which was initially considered by our subcommittee.

Mr. Speaker, I ask my colleagues to vote for this legislation as being, on balance, worthy of their support, and urge its adoption.

I reserve the balance of my time.

Mr. MANN. Mr. Speaker, this legislation has more than 100 cosponsors, but its principal sponsor, as well as its architect is the gentlewoman from New York (Ms. Holtzman). As the drafter of the legislation she will be able to provide additional information about the probable scope and effect of the legislation.

I yield such time as she may consume to the gentlewoman from New York (Ms. Holtzman).

(Ms. HOLTZMAN asked and was given permission to revise and extend her remarks.)

Ms. HOLTZMAN. Mr. Speaker, I would like to begin first by complimenting the distinguished gentleman from South Carolina (Mr. Mann), the chairman of the subcommittee, for his understanding of the need for corrective legislation in this area and for the fairness with which he has conducted the subcommittee hearings. I would like also to compliment the other members of the subcommittee, including the gentleman from California (Mr. Wiggins).

Too often in this country victims of rape are humiliated and harassed when they report and prosecute the rape. Bullied and cross-examined about their prior sexual experiences, many find the trial almost as degrading as the rape itself. Since rape trials become inquisitions into the victim's morality, not trials of the defendant's innocence or guilt, it is not surprising that it is the least reported crime. It is estimated that as few as one in ten rapes is ever reported.

Mr. Speaker, over 30 States have taken some action to limit the vulnerability of rape victims to such humiliating cross-examination of their past sexual experiences and intimate personal histories. In federal courts, however, it is permissible still to subject rape victims to brutal cross-examination about their past sexual histories. H.R. 4727 would rectify this problem in Federal courts and I hope, also serve as a model to suggest to the remaining states that reform of existing rape laws is important to the equity of our criminal justice system.

H.R. 4727 applies only to criminal rape cases in Federal courts. The bill provides that neither the prosecution nor the defense can introduce any reputation or opinion evidence about the victim's past sexual conduct. It does permit, however, the introduction of specific evidence about the victim's past sexual conduct in three very limited circumstances.

First, this evidence can be introduced if it deals with the victim's past sexual relations with the defendant and is relevant to the issue of whether she consented. Second, when the defendant claims he had no relations with the victim, he can use evidence of the victim's past sexual relations with others if the evidence rebuts the victim's claim that the rape caused certain physical consequences, such as semen or injury. Finally, the evidence can be introduced if it is constitutionally required. This last exception, added in subcommittee, will insure that the defendant's constitutional rights are protected.

Before any such evidence can be introduced, however, the court must determine at a hearing in chambers that the evidence falls within one of the exceptions.

Furthermore, unless constitutionally required, the evidence of specific instances of prior sexual conduct cannot be introduced at all it if would be more prejudicial and inflammatory that probative.

Mr. Speaker, I urge adoption of this bill. It will protect women from both injustice and indignity.

Mr. MANN. Mr. Speaker, I have no further requests for time, and I yield back the balance of my time.

Mr. WIGGINS. Mr. Speaker, I have no further requests for time, and yield back the balance of my time.

The SPEAKER pro tempore. The question is on the motion offered by the gentleman from South Carolina (Mr. Mann) that the House suspend the rules and pass the bill H.R. 4727, as amended.

The question was taken; and (two-thirds having voted in favor thereof) the rules were suspended and the bill, as amended, was passed.

A motion to reconsider was laid on the table.

2011 Amendments

The language of Rule 412 has been amended as part of the restyling of the Evidence Rules to make them more easily understood and to make style and terminology consistent

throughout the rules. These changes are intended to be stylistic only. There is no intent to change any result in any ruling on evidence admissibility.

HISTORICAL NOTES
Revision Notes and Legislative Reports
1988 Acts. For Related Reports, see 1988 U.S. Code Cong. and Adm. News, p. 5937.

Effective and Applicability Provisions
1978 Acts. Section 3 of Pub.L. 95–540 provided that: "The amendments made by this Act [enacting this rule] shall apply to trials which begin more than thirty days after the date of the enactment of this Act [Oct. 28, 1978]."

Rule 413. Similar Crimes in Sexual–Assault Cases

(a) Permitted Uses. In a criminal case in which a defendant is accused of a sexual assault, the court may admit evidence that the defendant committed any other sexual assault. The evidence may be considered on any matter to which it is relevant.

(b) Disclosure to the Defendant. If the prosecutor intends to offer this evidence, the prosecutor must disclose it to the defendant, including witnesses' statements or a summary of the expected testimony. The prosecutor must do so at least 15 days before trial or at a later time that the court allows for good cause.

(c) Effect on Other Rules. This rule does not limit the admission or consideration of evidence under any other rule.

(d) Definition of "Sexual Assault." In this rule and Rule 415, "sexual assault" means a crime under federal law or under state law (as "state" is defined in 18 U.S.C. § 513) involving:

(1) any conduct prohibited by 18 U.S.C. chapter 109A;

(2) contact, without consent, between any part of the defendant's body—or an object—and another person's genitals or anus;

(3) contact, without consent, between the defendant's genitals or anus and any part of another person's body;

(4) deriving sexual pleasure or gratification from inflicting death, bodily injury, or physical pain on another person; or

(5) an attempt or conspiracy to engage in conduct described in subparagraphs (1)–(4).

(Added Pub.L. 103–322, Title XXXII, § 320935(a), Sept. 13, 1994, 108 Stat. 2136; Apr. 26, 2011, eff. Dec. 1, 2011.)

ADVISORY COMMITTEE NOTES
2011 Amendments
The language of Rule 413 has been amended as part of the restyling of the Evidence Rules to make them more easily understood and to make style and terminology consistent throughout the rules. These changes are intended to be

stylistic only. There is no intent to change any result in any ruling on evidence admissibility.

HISTORICAL NOTES

Effective and Applicability Provisions

Section 320935(b) to (e) of Pub.L. 103–322, as amended Pub.L. 104–208, Div. A, Title I, § 101(a), [Title I, § 120], Sept. 30, 1996, 110 Stat. 3009–25, provided that:

"(b) **Implementation.**—The amendments made by subsection (a) [enacting Federal Rules of Evidence 413, 414, and 415] shall become effective pursuant to subsection (d).

"(c) **Recommendations by Judicial Conference.**—Not later than 150 days after the date of enactment of this Act [Sept. 13, 1994], the Judicial Conference of the United States shall transmit to Congress a report containing recommendations for amending the Federal Rules of Evidence as they affect the admission of evidence of a defendant's prior sexual assault or child molestation crimes in cases involving sexual assault and child molestation. The Rules Enabling Act [28 U.S.C.A. § 2072] shall not apply to the recommendations made by the Judicial Conference pursuant to this section.

"(d) **Congressional action.**—

"(1) If the recommendations described in subsection (c) are the same as the amendment made by subsection (a) [enacting Federal Rules of Evidence 413, 414, and 415], then the amendments made by subsection (a) shall become effective 30 days after the transmittal of the recommendations.

"(2) If the recommendations described in subsection (c) are different than the amendments made by subsection (a) [enacting Federal Rules of Evidence 413, 414, and 415], the amendments made by subsection (a) shall become effective 150 days after the transmittal of the recommendations unless otherwise provided by law.

"(3) If the Judicial Conference fails to comply with subsection (c), the amendments made by subsection (a) [enacting Federal of Evidence 413, 414, and 415] shall become effective 150 days after the date the recommendations were due under subsection (c) unless otherwise provided by law.

"(e) **Application.**—The amendments made by subsection (a) [enacting Federal Rules of Evidence 413, 414, and 415] shall apply to proceedings commenced on or after the effective date of such amendments, including all trials commenced on or after the effective date of such amendments."

[The Judicial Conference transmitted a report to Congress on Feb. 9, 1995, containing recommendations described in subsec. (c) different than the amendments made by section 320935(a) of Pub.L. 103–322. Congress did not follow the recommendations submitted or provide otherwise by law. Accordingly, Rules 413, 414, and 415, as added by section 320935(a) of Pub.L. 103–322, became effective on July 9, 1995.]

Submitted to the Congress in accordance with section 320935 of the Violent Crime Control and Law Enforcement Act of 1994 (Pub.L. No. 103–322)

I. INTRODUCTION

This report is transmitted to Congress in accordance with the Violent Crime Control and Law Enforcement Act of 1994, Pub.L. No. 103–322 (September 13, 1994). Section 320935 of the Act invited the Judicial Conference of the United States within 150 days (February 10, 1995) to submit "a report containing recommendations for amending the Federal Rules of Evidence as they affect the admission of evidence of a defendant's prior sexual assault or child molestation crimes in cases involving sexual assault or child molestation."

Under the Act, new Rules 413, 414, and 415 would be added to the Federal Rules of Evidence. These Rules would admit evidence of a defendant's past similar acts in criminal and civil cases involving a sexual assault or child molestation offense for its bearing on any matter to which it is relevant. The effective date of new Rules 413–415 is contingent in part upon the nature of the recommendations submitted by the Judicial Conference.

After careful study, the Judicial Conference urges Congress to reconsider its decision on the policy questions underlying the new rules for reasons set out in Part III below.

If Congress does not reconsider its decision on the underlying policy questions, the Judicial Conference recommends incorporation of the provisions of new Rules 413–415 as amendments to Rules 404 and 405 of the Federal Rules of Evidence. The amendments would not change the substance of the congressional enactment but would clarify drafting ambiguities and eliminate possible constitutional infirmities.

II. BACKGROUND

Under the Act, the Judicial Conference was provided 150 days within which to make and submit to Congress alternative recommendations to new Evidence Rules 413–415. Consideration of Rules 413–415 by the Judicial Conference was specifically excepted from the exacting review procedures set forth in the Rules Enabling Act (codified at 28 U.S.C. §§ 2071–2077). Although the Conference acted on these new rules on an expedited basis to meet the Act's deadlines, the review process was thorough.

The new rules would apply to both civil and criminal cases. Accordingly, the Judicial Conference's Advisory Committee on Criminal Rules and the Advisory Committee on Civil Rules reviewed the rules at separate meetings in October 1994. At the same time and in preparation for its consideration of the new rules, the Advisory Committee on Evidence Rules sent out a notice soliciting comment on new Evidence Rules 413, 414, and 415. The notice was sent to the courts, including all federal judges, about 900 evidence law professors, 40 women's rights organizations, and 1,000 other individuals and interested organizations.

III. DISCUSSION

On October 17–18, 1994, the Advisory Committee on Evidence Rules met in Washington, D.C. It considered the public responses, which included 84 written comments, representing 112 individuals, 8 local and 8 national legal organizations. The overwhelming majority of judges, lawyers, law professors, and legal organizations who responded opposed new Evidence Rules 413, 414, and 415. The principal objections expressed were that the rules would permit the admission of unfairly prejudicial evidence and contained numerous drafting problems not intended by their authors.

The Advisory Committee on Evidence Rules submitted its report to the Judicial Conference Committee on Rules of Practice and Procedure (Standing Committee) for review at its January 11–13, 1995 meeting. The committee's report was unanimous except for a dissenting vote by the representative of the Department of Justice. The advisory committee believed that the concerns expressed by Congress and embodied in new Evidence Rules 413, 414, and 415 are already adequately addressed in the existing Federal Rules of Evidence. In particular, Evidence Rule 404(b) now allows the admission of evidence against a criminal defendant of the commission of prior crimes, wrongs, or acts for specified purposes, including to show intent, plan, motive, preparation, identity, knowledge, or absence of mistake or accident.

Furthermore, the new rules, which are not supported by empirical evidence, could diminish significantly the protections that have safeguarded persons accused in criminal cases and parties in civil cases against undue prejudice. These protections form a fundamental part of American jurisprudence and have evolved under long-standing rules and case law. A significant concern identified by the committee was the danger of convicting a criminal defendant for past, as opposed to charged, behavior or for being a bad person.

In addition, the advisory committee concluded that, because prior bad acts would be admissible even though not the subject of a conviction, mini-trials within trials concerning those acts would result when a defendant seeks to rebut such evidence. The committee also noticed that many of the comments received had concluded that the Rules, as drafted, were mandatory—that is, such evidence had to be admitted regardless of other rules of evidence such as the hearsay rule or the Rule 403 balancing test. The committee believed that this position was arguable because Rules 413–415 declare without qualification that such evidence "is admissible." In contrast, the new Rule 412, passed as part of the same legislation, provided that certain evidence "is admissible if it is otherwise admissible under these Rules." Fed.R.Evid. 412(b)(2). If the critics are right, Rules 413–415 free the prosecution from rules that apply to the defendant—including the hearsay rule and Rule 403. If so, serious constitutional questions would arise.

The Advisory Committees on Criminal and Civil Rules unanimously, except for representatives of the Department of Justice, also opposed the new rules. Those committees also concluded that the new rules would permit the introduction of unreliable but highly prejudicial evidence and would complicate trials by causing mini-trials of other alleged wrongs. After the advisory committees reported, the Standing Committee unanimously, again except for the representative of the Department of Justice, agreed with the view of the advisory committees.

It is important to note the highly unusual unanimity of the members of the Standing and Advisory Committees, composed of over 40 judges, practicing lawyers, and academicians, in taking the view that Rules 413–415 are undesirable. Indeed, the only supporters of the Rules were representatives of the Department of Justice.

For these reasons, the Standing Committee recommended that Congress reconsider its decision on the policy questions embodied in new Evidence Rules 413, 414, and 415.

However, if Congress will not reconsider its decision on the policy questions, the Standing Committee recommended that Congress consider an alternative draft recommended by the Advisory Committee on Evidence Rules. That Committee drafted proposed amendments to existing Evidence Rules 404 and 405 that would both correct ambiguities and possible constitutional infirmities identified in new Evidence Rules 413, 414, and 415 yet still effectuate Congressional intent. In particular, the proposed amendments:

(1) expressly apply the other rules of evidence to evidence offered under the new rules;

(2) expressly allow the party against whom such evidence is offered to use similar evidence in rebuttal;

(3) expressly enumerate the factors to be weighed by a court in making its Rule 403 determination;

(4) render the notice provisions consistent with the provisions in existing Rule 404 regarding criminal cases;

(5) eliminate the special notice provisions of Rules 413–415 in civil cases so that notice will be required as provided in the Federal Rules of Civil Procedure; and

(6) permit reputation or opinion evidence after such evidence is offered by the accused or defendant.

The Standing Committee reviewed the new rules and the alternative recommendations. It concurred with the views of the Evidence Rules Committee and recommended that the Judicial Conference adopt them.

IV. RECOMMENDATIONS

The Judicial Conference concurs with the views of the Standing Committee and urges that Congress reconsider its policy determinations underlying Evidence Rules 413–415. In the alternative, the attached amendments to Evidence Rules 404 and 405 are recommended, in lieu of new Evidence Rules 413, 414, and 415. The alternative amendments to Evidence Rules 404 and 405 are accompanied by the Advisory Committee Notes, which explain them in detail.

RULE 404. CHARACTER EVIDENCE NOT ADMISSIBLE TO PROVE CONDUCT; EXCEPTIONS; OTHER CRIMES

* * * *

(4) Character in sexual misconduct cases. Evidence of another act of sexual assault or child molestation, or evidence to rebut such proof or an inference therefrom, if that evidence is otherwise admissible under these rules, in a criminal case in which the accused is charged with sexual assault or child molestation, or in a civil case in which a claim is predicated on a party's alleged commission of sexual assault or child molestation.

(A) In weighing the probative value of such evidence, the court may, as part of its rule 403 determination, consider:

(i) proximity in time to the charged or predicate misconduct;

(ii) similarity to the charged or predicate misconduct;

(iii) frequency of the other acts;

(iv) surrounding circumstances;

(v) relevant intervening events; and

(vi) other relevant similarities or differences.

(B) In a criminal case in which the prosecution intends to offer evidence under this subdivision, it must disclose the evidence, including statements of witnesses or a summary of the substance of any testimony, at a reasonable time in advance of trial, or during trial if the court excuses pretrial notice on good cause shown.

(C) For purposes of this subdivision.

(i) "sexual assault" means conduct—or an attempt or conspiracy to engage in conduct—of the type proscribed by chapter 109A of title 18, United States Code, or conduct that involved deriving sexual pleasure or gratification from inflicting death, bodily injury, or physical pain on another person irrespective of the age of the victim—regardless of whether that conduct would have subjected the actor to federal jurisdiction.

(ii) "child molestation" means conduct—or an attempt or conspiracy to engage in conduct—of the type proscribed by chapter 110 of title 18, United States Code, or conduct, committed in relation to a child below the age of

14 years, either of the type proscribed by chapter 109A of title 18, United States Code, or that involved deriving sexual pleasure or gratification from inflicting death, bodily injury, or physical pain on another person—regardless of whether that conduct would have subjected the actor to federal jurisdiction.

(b) Other crimes, wrongs, or acts. Evidence of other crimes, wrongs, or acts is not admissible to prove the character of a person in order to show action in conformity therewith except as provided in subdivision (a)....

Note to Rule 404(a)(4)

The Committee has redrafted Rules 413, 414 and 415 which the Violent Crime Control and Law Enforcement Act of 1994 conditionally added to the Federal Rules of Evidence.[1] These modifications do not change the substance of the congressional enactment. The changes were made in order to integrate the provisions both substantively and stylistically with the existing Rules of Evidence; to illuminate the intent expressed by the principal drafters of the measure; to clarify drafting ambiguities that might necessitate considerable judicial attention if they remained unresolved; and to eliminate possible constitutional infirmities.

The Committee placed the new provisions in Rule 404 because this rule governs the admissibility of character evidence. The congressional enactment constitutes a new exception to the general rule stated in subdivision (a). The Committee also combined the three separate rules proposed by Congress into one subdivision (a)(4) in accordance with the rules' customary practice of treating criminal and civil issues jointly. An amendment to Rule 405 has been added because the authorization of a new form of character evidence in this rule has an impact on methods of proving character that were not explicitly addressed by Congress. The stylistic changes are self-evident. They are particularly noticeable in the definition section in subdivision (a)(4)(C) in which the Committee eliminated, without any change in meaning, graphic details of sexual acts.

The Committee added language that explicitly provides that evidence under this subdivision must satisfy other rules of evidence such as the hearsay rules in Article VIII and the expert testimony rules in Article VII. Although principal sponsors of the legislation had stated that they intended other evidentiary rules to apply, the Committee believes that the opening phrase of the new subdivision 'if otherwise admissible under these rules' is needed to clarify the relationship between subdivision (a)(4) and other evidentiary provisions.

The Committee also expressly made subdivision (a)(4) subject to Rule 403 balancing in accordance with the repeatedly stated objectives of the legislation's sponsors with which representatives of the Justice Department expressed agreement. Many commentators on Rules 413–415 had objected that Rule 403's applicability was obscured by the actual language employed.

In addition to clarifying the drafters' intent, an explicit reference to Rule 403 may be essential to insulate the rule against constitutional challenge. Constitutional concerns also led the Committee to acknowledge specifically the opposing party's right to offer in rebuttal character evidence that the rules would otherwise bar, including evidence of a third person's prior acts of sexual misconduct offered to prove that the third person rather than the party committed the acts in issue.

In order to minimize the need for extensive and time-consuming judicial interpretation, the Committee listed factors that a court may consider in discharging Rule 403 balancing. Proximity in time is taken into account in a related rule. See Rule 609(b). Similarity, frequency and surrounding circumstances have long been considered by courts in handling other crimes evidence pursuant to Rule 404(b). Relevant intervening events, such as extensive medical treatment of the accused between the time of the prior proffered act and the charged act, may affect the strength of the propensity inference for which the evidence is offered. The final factor—'other relevant similarities or differences'—is added in recognition of the endless variety of circumstances that confront a trial court in rulings on admissibility. Although subdivision (4)(A) explicitly refers to factors that bear on probative value, this enumeration does not eliminate a judge's responsibility to take into account the other factors mentioned in Rule 403 itself—'the danger of unfair prejudice, confusion of the issues, ... misleading the jury, ... undue delay, waste of time, or needless presentation of cumulative evidence.' In addition, the Advisory Committee Note to Rule 403 reminds judges that 'The availability of other means of proof may also be an appropriate factor.'

The Committee altered slightly the notice provision in criminal cases. Providing the trial court with some discretion to excuse pretrial notice was thought preferable to the inflexible 15–day rule provided in Rules 414 and 415. Furthermore, the formulation is identical to that contained in the 1991 amendment to Rule 404(b) so that no confusion will result from having two somewhat different notice provisions in the same rule. The Committee eliminated the notice provision for civil cases stated in Rule 415 because it did not believe that Congress intended to alter the usual time table for disclosure and discovery provided by the Federal Rules of Civil Procedure.

The definition section was simplified with no change in meaning. The reference to 'the law of a State' was eliminated as unnecessarily confusing and restrictive. Conduct committed outside the United States ought equally to be eligible for admission. Evidence offered pursuant to subdivision (a)(4) must relate to a form of conduct proscribed by either chapter 109A or 110 of title 18, United States Code, regardless of whether the actor was subject to federal jurisdiction.

RULE 405. METHODS OF PROVING CHARACTER

(a) Reputation or opinion. In all cases in which evidence of character or a trait of character of a person is admissible, proof may be made by testimony as to reputation or by testimony in the form of an opinion except as provided in subdivision (c) of this rule. On cross-examination, inquiry is allowable into relevant specific instances of conduct.

* * * *

(c) Proof in sexual misconduct cases. In a case in which evidence is offered under rule 404(a)(4), proof may be made by specific instances of conduct, testimony as to reputation, or testimony in the form of an opinion, except that the prosecution or claimant may offer reputation or opinion testimony only after the opposing party has offered such testimony.

Note to Rule 405(c)

The addition of a new subdivision (a)(4) to Rule 404 necessitates adding a new subdivision (c) to Rule 405 to govern methods of proof. Congress clearly intended no change in the preexisting law that precludes the prosecution or a claimant from offering reputation or opinion testimony in its case

---

in chief to prove that the opposing party acted in conformity with character. When evidence is admissible pursuant to Rule 404(a)(4), the proponents proof must consist of specific instances of conduct. The opposing party, however, is free to respond with reputation or opinion testimony (including expert testimony if otherwise admissible) as well as evidence of specific instances. In a criminal case, the admissibility of reputation or opinion testimony would, in any event, be authorized by Rule 404(a)(1). The extension to civil cases is essential in order to provide the opponent with an adequate opportunity to refute allegations about a character for sexual misconduct. Once the opposing party offers reputation or opinion testimony, however, the prosecution or claimant may counter using such methods of proof.

[1] Congress provided that the rules would take effect unless within a specified time period the Judicial Conference made recommendations to amend the rules that Congress enacted.

Congressional Discussion

Floor Statement of the Principal House Sponsor, Representative Susan Molinari, Concerning the Prior Crimes Evidence Rules for Sexual Assault and Child Molestation Cases (Cong.Rec. H8991–92, Aug. 21, 1994):

Mr. Speaker, the revised conference bill contains a critical reform that I have long sought to protect the public from crimes of sexual violence—general rules of admissibility in sexual assault and child molestation cases for evidence that the defendant has committed offenses of the same type on other occasions. The enactment of this reform is first and foremost a triumph for the public—for the women who will not be raped and the children who will not be molested because we have strengthened the legal system's tools for bringing the perpetrators of these atrocious crimes to justice.

Senator Dole and I initially proposed this reform in February of 1991 in the Women's Equal Opportunity Act bill, and we later re-introduced it in the Sexual Assault Prevention Act bills of the 102d and 103d Congresses. The proposal also enjoyed the strong support of the Administration in the 102d Congress, and was included in President Bush's violent crime bill of that Congress, S. 635. The Senate passed the proposed rules on Nov. 5, 1993, by a vote of 75 to 19, in a crime bill amendment offered by Senate Dole. This Chamber endorsed the same rules on June 29, 1994, by a vote of 348 to 62, through a motion to instruct conferees that I offered.

The rules in the revised conference bill are substantially identical to our earlier proposals. We have agreed to a temporary deferral of the effective date of the new rules, pending a report by the Judicial Conference, in order to accommodate procedural objections raised by opponents of the reform. However, regardless of what the Judicial Conference may recommend, the new rules will take effect within at most 300 days of the enactment of this legislation, unless repealed or modified by subsequent legislation.

The need for these rules, their precedential support, their interpretation, and the issues and policy questions they raise have been analyzed at length in the legislative history of this proposal. I would direct the Members' attention particularly to two earlier statements:

The first is the portion of the section-by-section analysis accompanying these rules in section 801 of S. 635, which President Bush transmitted to Congress in 1991. That statement appears on pages S 3238 [to] S 3242 of the daily edition of the Congressional Record for March 13, 1991.

The second is the prepared text of an address—entitled "Evidence of Propensity and Probability in Sex Offense Cases and Other Cases"—by Senior Counsel David J. Karp of the Office of Policy Development of the U.S. Department of Justice. Mr. Karp, who is the author of the new evidence rules, presented this statement on behalf of the Justice Department to the Evidence Section of the Association of American Law Schools on January 9, 1993. The statement provided a detailed account of the views of the legislative sponsors and the Administration concerning the proposed reform, and should also be considered an authoritative part of its legislative history.

These earlier statements address the issues raised by this reform in considerable detail. In my present remarks, I will simply emphasize the following essential points:

The new rules will supersede in sex offense cases the restrictive aspects of Federal Rule of Evidence 404(b). In contrast to Rule 404(b)'s general prohibition of evidence of character or propensity, the new rules for sex offense cases authorize admission and consideration of evidence of an uncharged offense for its bearing "on any matter to which it is relevant." This includes the defendant's propensity to commit sexual assault or child molestation offenses, and assessment of the probability or improbability that the defendant has been falsely or mistakenly accused of such an offense.

In other respects, the general standards of the rules of evidence will continue to apply, including the restrictions on hearsay evidence and the court's authority under Evidence Rule 403 to exclude evidence whose probative value is substantially outweighed by its prejudicial effect. Also, the government (or the plaintiff in a civil case) will generally have to disclose to the defendant any evidence that is to be offered under the new rules at least 15 days before trial.

The proposed reform is critical to the protection of the public from rapists and child molesters, and is justified by the distinctive characteristics of the cases it will affect. In child molestation cases, for example, a history of similar acts tends to be exceptionally probative because it shows an unusual disposition of the defendant—a sexual or sadosexual interest in children—that simply does not exist in ordinary people. Moreover, such cases require reliance on child victims whose credibility can readily be attacked in the absence of substantial corroboration. In such cases, there is a compelling public interest in admitting all significant evidence that will illumine the credibility of the charge and any denial by the defense.

Similarly, adult-victim sexual assault cases are distinctive, and often turn on difficult credibility determinations. Alleged consent by the victim is rarely an issue in prosecutions for other violent crimes—the accused mugger does not claim that the victim freely handed over [his] wallet as a gift—but the defendant in a rape case often contends that the victim engaged in consensual sex and then falsely accused him. Knowledge that the defendant has committed rapes on other occasions is frequently critical in assessing the relative plausibility of these claims and accurately deciding cases that would otherwise become unresolvable swearing matches.

The practical effect of the new rules is to put evidence of uncharged offenses in sexual assault and child molestation cases on the same footing as other types of relevant evidence that are not subject to a special exclusionary rule. The presumption is in favor of admission. The underlying legislative judgment is that the evidence admissible pursuant to the proposed rules is typically relevant and probative, and that its probative value is normally not outweighed by any risk of prejudice or other adverse effects.

In line with this judgment, the rules do not impose arbitrary or artificial restrictions on the admissibility of evidence. Evidence of offenses for which the defendant has not previously been prosecuted or convicted will be admissible, as well as evidence of prior convictions. No time limit is imposed on the uncharged offenses for which evidence may be admitted; as a practical matter, evidence of other sex offenses by the defendant is often probative and properly admitted, notwithstanding very substantial lapses of time in relation to the charged offense or offenses. *See, e.g., United States v. Hadley,* 918 F.2d 848, 850–51 (9th Cir. 1990), *cert. dismissed,* 113 S.Ct. 486 (1992) (evidence of offenses occurring up to 15 years earlier admitted); *State v. Plymate,* 345 N.W.2d 327 (Neb. 1984) (evidence of defendant's commission of other child molestations more than 20 years earlier admitted).

Finally, the practical efficacy of these rules will depend on faithful execution by judges of the will of Congress in adopting this critical reform. To implement the legislative intent, the courts must liberally construe these rules to provide the basis for a fully informed decision of sexual assault and child molestation cases, including assessment of the defendant's propensities and questions of probability in light of the defendant's past conduct.

Rule 414. Similar Crimes in Child–Molestation Cases

(a) Permitted Uses. In a criminal case in which a defendant is accused of child molestation, the court may admit evidence that the defendant committed any other child molestation. The evidence may be considered on any matter to which it is relevant.

(b) Disclosure to the Defendant. If the prosecutor intends to offer this evidence, the prosecutor must disclose it to the defendant, including witnesses' statements or a summary of the expected testimony. The prosecutor must do so at least 15 days before trial or at a later time that the court allows for good cause.

(c) Effect on Other Rules. This rule does not limit the admission or consideration of evidence under any other rule.

(d) Definition of "Child" and "Child Molestation." In this rule and Rule 415:

(1) "child" means a person below the age of 14; and

(2) "child molestation" means a crime under federal law or under state law (as "state" is defined in 18 U.S.C. § 513) involving:

(A) any conduct prohibited by 18 U.S.C. chapter 109A and committed with a child;

(B) any conduct prohibited by 18 U.S.C. chapter 110;

(C) contact between any part of the defendant's body—or an object—and a child's genitals or anus;

(D) contact between the defendant's genitals or anus and any part of a child's body;

(E) deriving sexual pleasure or gratification from inflicting death, bodily injury, or physical pain on a child; or

(F) an attempt or conspiracy to engage in conduct described in subparagraphs (A)–(E).

(Added Pub.L. 103–322, Title XXXII, § 320935(a), Sept. 13, 1994, 108 Stat. 2136; Apr. 26, 2011, eff. Dec. 1, 2011.)

ADVISORY COMMITTEE NOTES

2011 Amendments

The language of Rule 414 has been amended as part of the restyling of the Evidence Rules to make them more easily understood and to make style and terminology consistent throughout the rules. These changes are intended to be stylistic only. There is no intent to change any result in any ruling on evidence admissibility.

HISTORICAL NOTES

Effective and Applicability Provisions

1995 Acts. Rule effective July 9, 1995, see section 320935(b) to (e) of Pub.L. 103–322, set out as a note under rule 413 of these rules.

Congressional Discussion

See Floor Statement following Rule 413.

Rule 415. Similar Acts in Civil Cases Involving Sexual Assault or Child Molestation

(a) Permitted Uses. In a civil case involving a claim for relief based on a party's alleged sexual assault or child molestation, the court may admit evidence that the party committed any other sexual assault or child molestation. The evidence may be considered as provided in Rules 413 and 414.

(b) Disclosure to the Opponent. If a party intends to offer this evidence, the party must disclose it to the party against whom it will be offered, including witnesses' statements or a summary of the expected testimony. The party must do so at least 15 days before trial or at a later time that the court allows for good cause.

(c) Effect on Other Rules. This rule does not limit the admission or consideration of evidence under any other rule.

(Added Pub.L. 103–322, Title XXXII, § 320935(a), Sept. 13, 1994, 108 Stat. 2137; Apr. 26, 2011, eff. Dec. 1, 2011.)

ADVISORY COMMITTEE NOTES

2011 Amendments

The language of Rule 415 has been amended as part of the restyling of the Evidence Rules to make them more easily understood and to make style and terminology consistent throughout the rules. These changes are intended to be stylistic only. There is no intent to change any result in any ruling on evidence admissibility.

HISTORICAL NOTES
Effective and Applicability Provisions
1995 Acts. Rule effective July 9, 1995, see section 320935(b) to (e) of Pub.L. 103–322, set out as a note under rule 413 of these rules.

Congressional Discussion
See Floor Statement following Rule 413.

ARTICLE V. PRIVILEGES

Rule 501. Privilege in General

The common law—as interpreted by United States courts in the light of reason and experience—governs a claim of privilege unless any of the following provides otherwise:

- the United States Constitution;
- a federal statute; or
- rules prescribed by the Supreme Court.

But in a civil case, state law governs privilege regarding a claim or defense for which state law supplies the rule of decision.

(Pub.L. 93–595, § 1, Jan. 2, 1975, 88 Stat. 1933; Apr. 26, 2011, eff. Dec. 1, 2011.)

ADVISORY COMMITTEE NOTES

1974 Enactment

Article V as submitted to Congress contained thirteen Rules. Nine of those Rules defined specific non-constitutional privileges which the federal courts must recognize (i.e. required reports, lawyer-client, psychotherapist-patient, husband-wife, communications to clergymen, political vote, trade secrets, secrets of state and other official information, and identity of informer.) Another Rule provided that only those privileges set forth in Article V or in some other Act of Congress could be recognized by the federal courts. The three remaining Rules addressed collateral problems as to waiver of privilege by voluntary disclosure, privileged matter disclosed under compulsion or without opportunity to claim privilege, comment upon or inference from a claim of privilege, and jury instruction with regard thereto.

The Committee amended Article V to eliminate all of the Court's specific Rules on privileges. Instead, the Committee, through a single Rule, 501, left the law of privileges in its present state and further provided that privileges shall continue to be developed by the courts of the United States under a uniform standard applicable both in civil and criminal cases. That standard, derived from Rule 26 of the Federal Rules of Criminal Procedure, mandates the application of the principles of the common law as interpreted by the courts of the United States in the light of reason and experience. The words "person, government, State, or political subdivision thereof" were added by the Committee to the lone term "witnesses" used in Rule 26 to make clear that, as under present law, not only witnesses may have privileges. The Committee also included in its amendment a proviso modeled after Rule 302 and similar to language added by the Commit-

tee to Rule 601 relating to the competency of witnesses. The proviso is designed to require the application of State privilege law in civil actions and proceedings governed by *Erie R. Co. v. Tompkins*, 304 U.S. 64 (1938), a result in accord with current federal court decisions. See *Republic Gear Co. v. Borg-Warner Corp.*, 381 F.2d 551, 555–556 n. 2 (2nd Cir. 1967). The Committee deemed the proviso to be necessary in the light of the Advisory Committee's view (see its note to Court [proposed] Rule 501) that this result is not mandated under *Erie*.

The rationale underlying the proviso is that federal law should not supersede that of the States in substantive areas such as privilege absent a compelling reason. The Committee believes that in civil cases in the federal courts where an element of a claim or defense is not grounded upon a federal question, there is no federal interest strong enough to justify departure from State policy. In addition, the Committee considered that the Court's proposed Article V would have promoted forum shopping in some civil actions, depending upon differences in the privilege law applied as among the State and federal courts. The Committee's proviso, on the other hand, under which the federal courts are bound to apply the State's privilege law in actions founded upon a State-created right or defense, removes the incentive to "shop". House Report No. 93–650.

Article V as submitted to Congress contained 13 rules. Nine of those rules defined specific nonconstitutional privileges which the Federal courts must recognize (i.e., required reports, lawyer-client, psychotherapist-patient, husband-wife, communications to clergymen, political vote, trade secrets, secrets of state and other official information, and identity of informer). Many of these rules contained controversial modifications or restrictions upon common law privileges. As noted supra, the House amended article V to eliminate all of the Court's specific rules on privileges. Through a single rule, 501, the House provided that privileges shall be governed by the principles of the common law as interpreted by the courts of the United States in the light of reason and experience (a standard derived from rule 26 of the Federal Rules of Criminal Procedure) except in the case of an element of a civil claim or defense as to which State law supplies the rule of decision, in which event state privilege law was to govern.

The committee agrees with the main thrust of the House amendment: that a federally developed common law based on modern reason and experience shall apply except where the State nature of the issues renders deference to State privilege law the wiser course, as in the usual diversity case. The committee understands that thrust of the House amendment to require that State privilege law be applied in "diversity" cases (actions on questions of State law between citizens of different States arising under 28 U.S.C. § 1332). The language of the House amendment, however, goes beyond this in some respects, and falls short of it in others: State privilege law applies even in nondiversity, Federal question civil cases, where an issue governed by State substantive law is the object of the evidence (such issues do sometimes arise in such cases); and, in all instances where State privilege law is to be applied, e.g., on proof of a State issue in a diversity case, a close reading reveals that State privilege law is not to be applied unless the matter to be proved is an element of that state claim or defense, as distinguished from a step along the way in the proof of it.

The committee is concerned that the language used in the House amendment could be difficult to apply. It provides that "in civil actions * * * with respect to an element of a claim or defense as to which State law supplies the rule of decision," State law on privilege applies. The question of what is an element of a claim or defense is likely to engender considerable litigation. If the matter in question constitutes an element of a claim, State law supplies the privilege rule; whereas if it is a mere item of proof with respect to a claim, then, even though State law might supply the rule of decision, Federal law on the privilege would apply. Further, disputes will arise as to how the rule should be applied in an antitrust action or in a tax case where the Federal statute is silent as to a particular aspect of the substantive law in question, but Federal cases had incorporated State law by reference to State law. [For a discussion of reference to State substantive law, see note on Federal Incorporation by Reference of State Law, Hart & Wechsler, The Federal Courts and the Federal System, pp. 491–494 (2d ed. 1973).] Is a claim (or defense) based on such a reference a claim or defense as to which federal or State law supplies the rule of decision?

Another problem not entirely avoidable is the complexity or difficulty the rule introduces into the trial of a Federal case containing a combination of Federal and State claims and defenses, e.g. an action involving Federal antitrust and State unfair competition claims. Two different bodies of privilege law would need to be consulted. It may even develop that the same witness-testimony might be relevant on both counts and privileged as to one but not the other. [The problems with the House formulation are discussed in Rothstein, The Proposed Amendments to the Federal Rules of Evidence, 62 Georgetown University Law Journal 125 (1973) at notes 25, 26 and 70–74 and accompanying text.]

The formulation adopted by the House is pregnant with litigious mischief. The committee has, therefore, adopted what we believe will be a clearer and more practical guideline for determining when courts should respect State rules of privilege. Basically, it provides that in criminal and Federal question civil cases, federally evolved rules on privilege should apply since it is Federal policy which is being enforced. [It is also intended that the Federal law of privileges should be applied with respect to pendent State law claims when they arise in a Federal question case.] Conversely, in diversity cases where the litigation in question turns on a substantive question of State law, and is brought in the Federal courts because the parties reside in different States, the committee believes it is clear that State rules of privilege should apply unless the proof is directed at a claim or defense for which Federal law supplies the rule of decision (a situation which would not commonly arise.) [While such a situation might require use of two bodies of privilege law, federal and state, in the same case, nevertheless the occasions on which this would be required are considerably reduced as compared with the House version, and confined to situations where the Federal and State interests are such as to justify application of neither privilege law to the case as a whole. If the rule proposed here results in two conflicting bodies of privilege law applying to the same piece of evidence in the same case, it is contem-

plated that the rule favoring reception of the evidence should be applied. This policy is based on the present rule 43(a) of the Federal Rules of Civil Procedure which provides: In any case, the statute or rule which favors the reception of the evidence governs and the evidence shall be presented according to the most convenient method prescribed in any of the statutes or rules to which reference is herein made.] It is intended that the State rules of privilege should apply equally in original diversity actions and diversity actions removed under 28 U.S.C. § 1441(b).

Two other comments on the privilege rule should be made. The committee has received a considerable volume of correspondence from psychiatric organizations and psychiatrists concerning the deletion of rule 504 of the rule submitted by the Supreme Court. It should be clearly understood that, in approving this general rule as to privileges, the action of Congress should not be understood as disapproving any recognition of a psychiatrist-patient, or husband-wife, or any other of the enumerated privileges contained in the Supreme Court rules. Rather, our action should be understood as reflecting the view that the recognition of a privilege based on a confidential relationship and other privileges should be determined on a case-by-case basis.

Further, we would understand that the prohibition against spouses testifying against each other is considered a rule of privilege and covered by this rule and not by rule 601 of the competency of witnesses. Senate Report No. 93–1277.

Rule 501 deals with the privilege of a witness not to testify. Both the House and Senate bills provide that federal privilege law applies in criminal cases. In civil actions and proceedings, the House bill provides that state privilege law applies "to an element of a claim or defense as to which State law supplies the rule of decision." The Senate bill provides that "in civil actions and proceedings arising under 28 U.S.C. § 1332 or 28 U.S.C. § 1335, or between citizens of different States and removed under 28 U.S.C. § 1441(b) the privilege of a witness, person, government, State or political subdivision thereof is determined in accordance with State law, unless with respect to the particular claim or defense, Federal law supplies the rule of decision."

The wording of the House and Senate bills differs in the treatment of civil actions and proceedings. The rule in the House bill applies to evidence that relates to "an element of a claim or defense." If an item of proof tends to support or defeat a claim or defense, or an element of a claim or defense, and if state law supplies the rule of decision for that claim or defense, then state privilege law applies to that item of proof.

Under the provision in the House bill, therefore, state privilege law will usually apply in diversity cases. There may be diversity cases, however, where a claim or defense is based upon federal law. In such instances, federal privilege law will apply to evidence relevant to the federal claim or defense. See *Sola Electric Co. v. Jefferson Electric Co.*, 317 U.S. 173 (1942).

In nondiversity jurisdiction civil cases, federal privilege law will generally apply. In those situations where a federal court adopts or incorporates state law to fill interstices or gaps in federal statutory phrases, the court generally will apply federal privilege law. As Justice Jackson has said:

A federal court sitting in a non-diversity case such as this does not sit as a local tribunal. In some cases it may see fit for special reasons to give the law of a particular state highly persuasive or even controlling effect, but in the last analysis its decision turns upon the law of the United States, not that of any state.

D'Oench, Duhme & Co. v. Federal Deposit Insurance Corp., 315 U.S. 447, 471 (1942) (Jackson, J., concurring). When a federal court chooses to absorb state law, it is applying the state law as a matter of federal common law. Thus, state law does not supply the rule of decision (even though the federal court may apply a rule derived from state decisions), and state privilege law would not apply. See C.A. Wright, Federal Courts 251–252 (2d ed. 1970); *Holmberg v. Armbrecht,* 327 U.S. 392 (1946); *DeSylva v. Ballentine,* 351 U.S. 570, 581 (1956); 9 Wright & Miller, Federal Rules and Procedure § 2408.

In civil actions and proceedings, where the rule of decision as to a claim or defense or as to an element of a claim or defense is supplied by state law, the House provision requires that state privilege law apply.

The Conference adopts the House provision. House Report No. 93–1597.

2011 Amendments

The language of Rule 501 has been amended as part of the restyling of the Evidence Rules to make them more easily understood and to make style and terminology consistent throughout the rules. These changes are intended to be stylistic only. There is no intent to change any result in any ruling on evidence admissibility.

CROSS REFERENCES

Aliens, confidentiality of Department of State records of issuance or refusal of visas, see 8 USCA § 1202.

Atomic energy, development and control of, licensee incident reports as evidence, see 42 USCA § 2240.

Census information as confidential, see 13 USCA § 9.

Certificates of discharge, replacements as evidence, see 10 USCA § 1041.

Competency of accused as witness on own request, see 18 USCA § 3481.

Depositions upon written questions, see Fed.Rules Civ. Proc. Rule 31, 28 USCA.

Discovery and inspection of statements, confessions, etc., in possession of government, see Fed.Rules Cr.Proc. Rule 16, 18 USCA.

Discovery, general provisions concerning, see Fed.Rules Civ.Proc. Rule 26, 28 USCA.

Equal employment opportunity conciliation proceedings, inadmissibility as evidence in subsequent proceedings, see 42 USCA § 2000e–5.

Government agencies, publication of public information, see 5 USCA § 552.

Government witnesses, statements and report of not subject to subpoena, discovery, or inspection, see 18 USCA § 3500.

Grand jury proceedings, secrecy of, see Fed.Rules Cr.Proc. Rule 6, 18 USCA.

Importation of alien for immoral purpose, testimony of spouse admissible, see 8 USCA § 1328.

Liability insurance, discovery proceedings, see Fed.Rules Civ.Proc. Rule 26, 28 USCA.

Physician-patient privilege, waiver of, see Fed.Rules Civ. Proc. Rule 35, 28 USCA.

Presentence investigation report, disclosure of contents, see Fed.Rules Cr.Proc. Rule 32, 18 USCA.

Public availability of information filed with Securities and Exchange Commission, see 15 USCA § 78x.

Safety appliances and railroad equipment, reports of and investigation of accidents, see 49 USCA §§ 20703 and 20903.

Self-incrimination, protection against, see USCA Const. Amend. V.

State laws as rules of decision, see 28 USCA § 1652.

Subpoena for taking depositions, see Fed.Rules Civ.Proc. Rule 45, 28 USCA.

Testimony of debtor and of persons examined,

    Immunity from self-incrimination, see 11 USCA § 344.

    Immunity of witnesses, see 18 USCA § 6001 et seq.

Wire or radio communications, unauthorized use or publication prohibited, see 47 USCA § 605.

Rule 502.   Attorney–Client Privilege and Work Product; Limitations on Waiver

The following provisions apply, in the circumstances set out, to disclosure of a communication or information covered by the attorney-client privilege or work-product protection.

(a) Disclosure Made in a Federal Proceeding or to a Federal Office or Agency; Scope of a Waiver. When the disclosure is made in a federal proceeding or to a federal office or agency and waives the attorney-client privilege or work-product protection, the waiver extends to an undisclosed communication or information in a federal or state proceeding only if:

    (1) the waiver is intentional;

    (2) the disclosed and undisclosed communications or information concern the same subject matter; and

    (3) they ought in fairness to be considered together.

(b) Inadvertent Disclosure. When made in a federal proceeding or to a federal office or agency, the disclosure does not operate as a waiver in a federal or state proceeding if:

    (1) the disclosure is inadvertent;

    (2) the holder of the privilege or protection took reasonable steps to prevent disclosure; and

    (3) the holder promptly took reasonable steps to rectify the error, including (if applicable) following Federal Rule of Civil Procedure 26(b)(5)(B).

(c) Disclosure Made in a State Proceeding. When the disclosure is made in a state proceeding and is not the subject of a state-court order concerning waiver, the disclosure does not operate as a waiver in a federal proceeding if the disclosure:

    (1) would not be a waiver under this rule if it had been made in a federal proceeding; or

    (2) is not a waiver under the law of the state where the disclosure occurred.

(d) Controlling Effect of a Court Order. A federal court may order that the privilege or protection is not waived by disclosure connected with the litigation pending before the court—in which event the disclosure is also not a waiver in any other federal or state proceeding.

(e) Controlling Effect of a Party Agreement. An agreement on the effect of disclosure in a federal proceeding is binding only on the parties to the agreement, unless it is incorporated into a court order.

(f) Controlling Effect of This Rule. Notwithstanding Rules 101 and 1101, this rule applies to state proceedings and to federal court-annexed and federal court-mandated arbitration proceedings, in the circumstances set out in the rule. And notwithstanding Rule 501, this rule applies even if state law provides the rule of decision.

(g) Definitions. In this rule:

(1) "attorney-client privilege" means the protection that applicable law provides for confidential attorney-client communications; and

(2) "work-product protection" means the protection that applicable law provides for tangible material (or its intangible equivalent) prepared in anticipation of litigation or for trial.

(Pub.L. 110–322, § 1(a), Sept. 19, 2008, 122 Stat. 3537; Apr. 26, 2011, eff. Dec. 1, 2011.)

ADVISORY COMMITTEE NOTES

2011 Amendments

Rule 502 has been amended by changing the initial letter of a few words from uppercase to lowercase as part of the restyling of the Evidence Rules to make style and terminology consistent throughout the rules. There is no intent to change any result in any ruling on evidence admissibility.

ADVISORY COMMITTEE NOTES

Explanatory Note (Revised 11/28/2007)

This new rule has two major purposes:

1) It resolves some longstanding disputes in the courts about the effect of certain disclosures of communications or information protected by the attorney-client privilege or as work product—specifically those disputes involving inadvertent disclosure and subject matter waiver.

2) It responds to the widespread complaint that litigation costs necessary to protect against waiver of attorney-client privilege or work product have become prohibitive due to the concern that any disclosure (however innocent or minimal) will operate as a subject matter waiver of all protected communications or information. This concern is especially troubling in cases involving electronic discovery. See, e.g., Hopson v. City of Baltimore, 232 F.R.D. 228, 244 (D.Md. 2005) (electronic discovery may encompass "millions of documents" and to insist upon "record-by-record pre-production privilege review, on pain of subject matter waiver, would impose upon parties costs of production that bear no proportionality to what is at stake in the litigation").

The rule seeks to provide a predictable, uniform set of standards under which parties can determine the consequences of a disclosure of a communication or information covered by the attorney-client privilege or work-product protection. Parties to litigation need to know, for example, that if they exchange privileged information pursuant to a confidentiality order, the court's order will be enforceable. Moreover, if a federal court's confidentiality order is not enforceable in a state court then the burdensome costs of privilege review and retention are unlikely to be reduced.

The rule makes no attempt to alter federal or state law on whether a communication or information is protected under the attorney-client privilege or work-product immunity as an initial matter. Moreover, while establishing some exceptions to waiver, the rule does not purport to supplant applicable waiver doctrine generally.

The rule governs only certain waivers by disclosure. Other common-law waiver doctrines may result in a finding of waiver even where there is no disclosure of privileged information or work product. See, e.g., Nguyen v. Excel Corp., 197 F.3d 200 (5th Cir. 1999) (reliance on an advice of counsel defense waives the privilege with respect to attorney-client communications pertinent to that defense); Ryers v. Burleson, 100 F.R.D. 436 (D.D.C. 1983) (allegation of lawyer malpractice constituted a waiver of confidential communications under the circumstances). The rule is not intended to displace or modify federal common law concerning waiver of privilege or work product where no disclosure has been made.

Subdivision (a). The rule provides that a voluntary disclosure in a federal proceeding or to a federal office or agency, if a waiver, generally results in a waiver only of the communication or information disclosed; a subject matter waiver (of either privilege or work product) is reserved for those unusual situations in which fairness requires a further disclosure of related, protected information, in order to prevent a selective and misleading presentation of evidence to the disadvantage of the adversary. See, e.g., In re United Mine Workers of America Employee Benefit Plans Litig., 159 F.R.D. 307, 312 (D.D.C. 1994) (waiver of work product limited to materials actually disclosed, because the party did not deliberately disclose documents in an attempt to gain a tactical advantage). Thus, subject matter waiver is limited to situations in which a party intentionally puts protected information into the litigation in a selective, misleading and unfair manner. It follows that an inadvertent disclosure of protected information can never result in a subject matter waiver. See Rule 502(b). The rule rejects the result in In re Sealed Case, 877 F.2d 976 (D.C.Cir. 1989), which held that inadvertent disclosure of documents during discovery automatically constituted a subject matter waiver.

The language concerning subject matter waiver—"ought in fairness"—is taken from Rule 106, because the animating principle is the same. Under both Rules, a party that makes a selective, misleading presentation that is unfair to the adversary opens itself to a more complete and accurate presentation.

To assure protection and predictability, the rule provides that if a disclosure is made at the federal level, the federal rule on subject matter waiver governs subsequent state court determinations on the scope of the waiver by that disclosure.

Subdivision (b). Courts are in conflict over whether an inadvertent disclosure of a communication or information protected as privileged or work product constitutes a waiver. A few courts find that a disclosure must be intentional to be a waiver. Most courts find a waiver only if the disclosing party acted carelessly in disclosing the communication or information and failed to request its return in a timely manner. And a few courts hold that any inadvertent disclosure of a communication or information protected under the attorney-client privilege or as work product constitutes a waiver without regard to the protections taken to avoid such a disclosure. *See generally Hopson v. City of Baltimore*, 232 F.R.D. 228 (D.Md. 2005), for a discussion of this case law.

The rule opts for the middle ground: inadvertent disclosure of protected communications or information in connection with a federal proceeding or to a federal office or agency does not constitute a waiver if the holder took reasonable steps to prevent disclosure and also promptly took reasonable steps to rectify the error. This position is in accord with the majority view on whether inadvertent disclosure is a waiver.

Cases such as *Lois Sportswear, U.S.A., Inc. v. Levi Strauss & Co.*, 104 F.R.D. 103, 105 (S.D.N.Y. 1985) and *Hartford Fire Ins. Co. v. Garvey*, 109 F.R.D. 323, 332 (N.D.Cal. 1985), set out a multi-factor test for determining whether inadvertent disclosure is a waiver. The stated factors (none of which is dispositive) are the reasonableness of precautions taken, the time taken to rectify the error, the scope of discovery, the extent of disclosure and the overriding issue of fairness. The rule does not explicitly codify that test, because it is really a set of non-determinative guidelines that vary from case to case. The rule is flexible enough to accommodate any of those listed factors. Other considerations bearing on the reasonableness of a producing party's efforts include the number of documents to be reviewed and the time constraints for production. Depending on the circumstances, a party that uses advanced analytical software applications and linguistic tools in screening for privilege and work product may be found to have taken "reasonable steps" to prevent inadvertent disclosure. The implementation of an efficient system of records management before litigation may also be relevant.

The rule does not require the producing party to engage in a post-production review to determine whether any protected communication or information has been produced by mistake. But the rule does require the producing party to follow up on any obvious indications that a protected communication or information has been produced inadvertently.

The rule applies to inadvertent disclosures made to a federal office or agency, including but not limited to an office or agency that is acting in the course of its regulatory, investigative or enforcement authority. The consequences of waiver, and the concomitant costs of pre-production privilege review, can be as great with respect to disclosures to offices and agencies as they are in litigation.

Subdivision (c). Difficult questions can arise when 1) a disclosure of a communication or information protected by the attorney-client privilege or as work product is made in a state proceeding, 2) the communication or information is offered in a subsequent federal proceeding on the ground that the disclosure waived the privilege or protection, and 3) the state and federal laws are in conflict on the question of waiver. The Committee determined that the proper solution for the federal court is to apply the law that is most protective of privilege and work product. If the state law is more protective (such as where the state law is that an inadvertent disclosure can never be a waiver), the holder of the privilege or protection may well have relied on that law when making the disclosure in the state proceeding. Moreover, applying a more restrictive federal law of waiver could impair the state objective of

preserving the privilege or work-product protection for disclosures made in state proceedings. On the other hand, if the federal law is more protective, applying the state law of waiver to determine admissibility in federal court is likely to undermine the federal objective of limiting the costs of production.

The rule does not address the enforceability of a state court confidentiality order in a federal proceeding, as that question is covered both by statutory law and principles of federalism and comity. *See* 28 U.S.C. § 1738 (providing that state judicial proceedings "shall have the same full faith and credit in every court within the United States . . . as they have by law or usage in the courts of such State . . . from which they are taken"). *See also Tucker v. Ohtsu Tire & Rubber Co.*, 191 F.R.D. 495, 499 (D.Md. 2000) (noting that a federal court considering the enforceability of a state confidentiality order is "constrained by principles of comity, courtesy, and . . . federalism"). Thus, a state court order finding no waiver in connection with a disclosure made in a state court proceeding is enforceable under existing law in subsequent federal proceedings.

Subdivision (d). Confidentiality orders are becoming increasingly important in limiting the costs of privilege review and retention, especially in cases involving electronic discovery. But the utility of a confidentiality order in reducing discovery costs is substantially diminished if it provides no protection outside the particular litigation in which the order is entered. Parties are unlikely to be able to reduce the costs of pre-production review for privilege and work product if the consequence of disclosure is that the communications or information could be used by non-parties to the litigation.

There is some dispute on whether a confidentiality order entered in one case is enforceable in other proceedings. *See generally Hopson v. City of Baltimore*, 232 F.R.D. 228 (D.Md. 2005), for a discussion of this case law. The rule provides that when a confidentiality order governing the consequences of disclosure in that case is entered in a federal proceeding, its terms are enforceable against non-parties in any federal or state proceeding. For example, the court order may provide for return of documents without waiver irrespective of the care taken by the disclosing party; the rule contemplates enforcement of "claw-back" and "quick peek" arrangements as a way to avoid the excessive costs of pre-production review for privilege and work product. *See Zubulake v. UBS Warburg LLC*, 216 F.R.D. 280, 290 (S.D.N.Y. 2003) (noting that parties may enter into "so-called 'claw-back' agreements that allow the parties to forego privilege review altogether in favor of an agreement to return inadvertently produced privilege documents"). The rule provides a party with a predictable protection from a court order—predictability that is needed to allow the party to plan in advance to limit the prohibitive costs of privilege and work product review and retention.

Under the rule, a confidentiality order is enforceable whether or not it memorializes an agreement among the parties to the litigation. Party agreement should not be a condition of enforceability of a federal court's order.

Under subdivision (d), a federal court may order that disclosure of privileged or protected information "in connection with" a federal proceeding does not result in waiver. But subdivision (d) does not allow the federal court to enter an order determining the waiver effects of a separate disclosure of the same information in other proceedings, state or federal. If a disclosure has been made in a state proceeding (and is not the subject of a state-court order on waiver), then subdivision

(d) is inapplicable. Subdivision (c) would govern the federal court's determination whether the state-court disclosure waived the privilege or protection in the federal proceeding.

Subdivision (e). Subdivision (e) codifies the well-established proposition that parties can enter an agreement to limit the effect of waiver by disclosure between or among them. Of course such an agreement can bind only the parties to the agreement. The rule makes clear that if parties want protection against non-parties from a finding of waiver by disclosure, the agreement must be made part of a court order.

Subdivision (f). The protections against waiver provided by Rule 502 must be applicable when protected communications or information disclosed in federal proceedings are subsequently offered in state proceedings. Otherwise the holders of protected communications and information, and their lawyers, could not rely on the protections provided by the Rule, and the goal of limiting costs in discovery would be substantially undermined. Rule 502(f) is intended to resolve any potential tension between the provisions of Rule 502 that apply to state proceedings and the possible limitations on the applicability of the Federal Rules of Evidence otherwise provided by Rules 101 and 1101.

The rule is intended to apply in all federal court proceedings, including court-annexed and court-ordered arbitrations, without regard to any possible limitations of Rules 101 and 1101. This provision is not intended to raise an inference about the applicability of any other rule of evidence in arbitration proceedings more generally.

The costs of discovery can be equally high for state and federal causes of action, and the rule seeks to limit those costs in all federal proceedings, regardless of whether the claim arises under state or federal law. Accordingly, the rule applies to state law causes of action brought in federal court.

Subdivision (g). The rule's coverage is limited to attorney-client privilege and work product. The operation of waiver by disclosure, as applied to other evidentiary privileges, remains a question of federal common law. Nor does the rule purport to apply to the Fifth Amendment privilege against compelled self-incrimination.

The definition of work product "materials" is intended to include both tangible and intangible information. *See In re Cendant Corp. Sec. Litig.*, 343 F.3d 658, 662 (3d Cir. 2003) ("work product protection extends to both tangible and intangible work product").

Committee Letter

The letter from the Committee on Rules of Practice and Procedure of the Judicial Conference of the United States to the Committee on the Judiciary of the U.S. Senate and House of Representatives, dated September 26, 2007, provided:

On behalf of the Judicial Conference of the United States, I respectfully submit a proposed addition to the Federal Rules of Evidence. The Conference recommends that Congress adopt this proposed rule as Federal Rule of Evidence 502.

The Rule provides for protections against waiver of the attorney-client privilege or work product immunity. The Conference submits this proposal directly to Congress because of the limitations on the rulemaking function of the federal courts in matters dealing with evidentiary privilege. Unlike all other federal rules of procedure prescribed under the Rules Enabling Act, those rules governing evidentiary privilege must by approved by an Act of Congress, 28 U.S.C. § 2074(b).

Description of the Process Leading to the Proposed Rule

The Judicial Conference Rules Committees have long been concerned about the rising costs of litigation, much of which has been caused by the review, required under current law, of every document produced in discovery, in order to determine whether the document contains privileged information. In 2006, the House Judiciary Committee Chair suggested that the Judicial Conference consider proposing a rule dealing with waiver of attorney-client privilege and work product, in order to limit these rising costs. The Judicial Conference was urged to proceed with rulemaking that would:

- protect against the forfeiture of privilege when a disclosure in discovery is the result of an innocent mistake; and

- permit parties, and courts, to protect against the consequences of waiver by permitting disclosures of privileged information between the parties to litigation.

The task of drafting a proposed rule was referred to the Advisory Committee on Evidence Rules (the "Advisory Committee"). The Advisory Committee prepared a draft Rule 502 and invited a select group of judges, lawyers, and academics to testify before the Advisory Committee about the need for the rule, and to suggest any improvements. The Advisory Committee considered all the testimony presented by these experts and redrafted the rule accordingly. At its Spring 2006 meeting, the Advisory Committee approved for release for public comment a proposed Rule 502 that would provide certain exceptions to the federal common law on waiver of privileges and work product. That rule was approved for release for public comment by the Committee on Rules of Practice and Procedure ("the Standing Committee"). The public comment period began in August 2006 and ended February 15, 2007. The Advisory Committee received more that [sic] 70 public comments, and also heard the testimony of more than 20 witnesses at two public hearings. The rule released for public comment was also carefully reviewed by the Standing Committee's Subcommittee on Style. In April 2007, the Advisory Committee issued a revised proposed Rule 502 taking into account the public comment, the views of the Subcommittee on Style, and its own judgment. The revised rule was approved by the Standing Committee and the Judicial Conference. It is enclosed with this letter.

In order to inform Congress of the legal issues involved in this rule, the proposed Rule 502 also includes a proposed Committee Note of the kind that accompanies all rules adopted through the Rules Enabling Act. This Committee Note may be incorporated as all or part of the legislative history of the rule if it is adopted by Congress. *See, e.g.,* House Conference Report 103–711 (stating that the "Conferees intend that the Advisory Committee Note on [Evidence] Rule 412, as transmitted by the Judicial Conference of the United States to the Supreme Court on October 25, 1993, applies to Rule 412 as enacted by this section" of the Violent Crime Control and Law Enforcement Act of 1994).

Problems Addressed by the Proposed Rule

In drafting the proposed Rule, the Advisory Committee concluded that the current law on waiver of privilege and work product is responsible in large part for the rising costs of discovery, especially discovery of electronic information. In complex litigation the lawyers spend significant amounts of time and effort to preserve the privilege and work product. The reason is that if a protected document is produced, there is a risk that a court will find a subject matter waiver that will apply not only to the instant case and document but to other cases and documents as well. Moreover, an enormous amount of expense is put into document production in order to protect against inadvertent disclosure of privileged information, because the producing party risks a ruling that even a mistaken disclosure can result in a subject matter waiver. Advisory Committee members also expressed the view that the fear of waiver leads to extravagant claims of privilege. Members concluded that if there were a way to produce documents in discovery without risking subject matter waiver, the discovery process could be made much less expensive. The Advisory Committee noted that the existing law on the effect of inadvertent disclosures and on the scope of waiver is far from consistent or certain. It also noted that agreements between parties with regard to the effect of disclosure on privilege are common, but are unlikely to decrease the costs of discovery due to the ineffectiveness of such agreements as to persons not party to them.

Proposed Rule 502 does not attempt to deal comprehensively with either attorney-client privilege or work-product protection. It also does not purport to cover all issues concerning waiver or forfeiture of either the attorney-client privilege or work-product protection. Rather, it deals primarily with issues involved in the disclosure of protected information in federal court proceedings or to a federal public office or agency. The rule binds state courts only with regard to disclosures made in federal proceedings. It deals with disclosures made in state proceedings only to the extent that the effect of those disclosures becomes an issue in federal litigation. The Rule covers issues of scope of waiver, inadvertent disclosure, and the controlling effect of court orders and agreements.

Rule 502 provides the following protections against waiver of privilege or work product:

●*Limitations on Scope of Waiver.* Subdivision (a) provides that if a waiver is found, it applies only to the information disclosed, unless a broader waiver is made necessary by the holder's intentional and misleading use of privileged or protected communications or information.

●*Protections Against Inadvertent Disclosure.* Subdivision (b) provides that an inadvertent disclosure of privileged or protected communications or information, when made at the federal level, does not operate as a waiver if the holder took reasonable steps to prevent such a disclosure and employed reasonably prompt measures to retrieve the mistakenly disclosed communications or information.

●*Effect on State Proceedings and Disclosures Made in State Courts.* Subdivision (c) provides that 1) if there is a disclosure of privileged or protected communications or information at the federal level, then state courts must honor Rule 502 in subsequent state proceedings; and 2) if there is a disclosure of privileged or protected communications or information in a state proceeding, then admissibility in a subsequent federal proceeding is determined by the law that is most protective against waiver.

●*Orders Protecting Privileged Communications Binding on Non-Parties.* Subdivision (d) provides that if a federal court enters an order providing that a disclosure of privileged or protected communications or information does not constitute a waiver, that order is enforceable against all persons and entities in any federal or state proceeding. This provision allows parties in an action in which such an order is entered to limit their costs of pre-production privilege review.

●*Agreements Protecting Privileged Communications Binding on Parties.* Subdivision (e) provides that parties in a federal proceeding can enter into a confidentiality agreement providing for mutual protection against waiver in that proceeding. While those agreements bind the signatory parties, they are not binding on non-parties unless incorporated into a court order.

Drafting Choices Made by the Advisory Committee

The Advisory Committee made a number of important drafting choices in Rule 502. This section explains those choices.

1) The effect in state proceedings of disclosures initially made in state proceedings. Rule 502 does not apply to a disclosure made in a state proceeding when the disclosed communication or information is subsequently offered in another state proceeding. The first draft of Rule 502 provided for uniform waiver rules in federal and state proceedings, regardless of where the initial disclosure was made. This draft raised the objections of the Conference of State Chief Justices. State judges argued that the Rule as drafted offended principles of federalism and comity, by superseding state law of privilege waiver, even for disclosures that are made initially in state proceedings—and even when the disclosed material is then offered in a state proceeding (the so-called "state-to-state" problem). In response to these objections, the Advisory Committee voted unanimously to scale back the Rule, so that it would not cover the "state-to-state" problem. Under the current proposal state courts are bound by the Federal Rule only when a disclosure is made at the federal level and the disclosed communication or information is later offered in a state proceeding (the so-called "federal-to-state" problem).

During the public comment period on the scaled-back rule, the Advisory Committee received many requests from lawyers and lawyer groups to return to the original draft and provide a uniform rule of privilege waiver that would bind both state and federal courts, for disclosures made in either state or federal proceedings. These comments expressed the concern that if states were not bound by a uniform federal rule on privilege waiver, the protections afforded by Rule 502 would be undermined; parties and their lawyers might not be able to rely on the protections of the Rule, for fear that a state law would find a waiver even though the Federal Rule would not.

The Advisory Committee determined that these comments raised a legitimate concern, but decided not to extend Rule 502 to govern a state court's determination of waiver with respect to disclosures made in state proceedings. The Committee relied on the following considerations:

●Rule 502 is located in the Federal Rules of Evidence, a body of rules determining the admissibility of evidence in federal proceedings. Parties in a state proceeding determining the effect of a disclosure made in that proceeding or in other state courts would be unlikely to look to the Federal Rules of Evidence for the answer.

●In the Advisory Committee's view, Rule 502, as proposed herein, does fulfill its primary goal of reducing the costs of discovery in *federal* proceedings. Rule 502 by its terms governs state courts with regard to the effect of disclosures initially made in federal proceedings or to federal offices or agencies. Parties and their lawyers in federal proceedings can therefore predict the consequences of disclosure by referring to Rule 502; there is no possibility that a state court could find a waiver when Rule 502 would not, when the disclosure is initially made at the federal level.

The Judicial Conference has no position on the merits of separate legislation to cover the problem of waiver of privilege and work product when the disclosure is made at the state level and the consequence is to be determined in a state court.

2) Other applications of Rule 502 to state court proceedings. Although disclosures made in state court proceedings and later offered in state proceedings would not be covered, Rule 502 would have an effect on state court proceedings where the disclosure is initially made in a federal proceeding or to a federal office or agency. Most importantly, state courts in such circumstances would be bound by federal protection orders. The other protections against waiver in Rule 502—against mistaken disclosure and subject matter waiver—would also bind state courts as to disclosures initially made at the federal level. The Rule, as submitted, specifically provides that it applies to state proceedings under the circumstances set out in the Rule. This protection is needed, otherwise parties could not rely on Rule 502 even as to federal disclosures, for fear that a state court would find waiver even when a federal court would not.

3) Disclosures made in state proceedings and offered in a subsequent federal proceeding. Earlier drafts of proposed Rule 502 did not determine the question of what rule would apply when a disclosure is made in state court and the waiver determination is to be made in a subsequent federal proceeding. Proposed Rule 502 as submitted herein provides that all of the provisions of Rule 502 apply unless the state law of privilege is more protective (less likely to find waiver) than the federal law. The Advisory Committee determined that this solution best preserved federal interests in protecting against waiver, and also provided appropriate respect for state attempts to give greater protection to communications and information covered by the attorney-client privilege or work-product doctrine.

4) Selective waiver. At the suggestion of the House Judiciary Committee Chair, the Advisory Committee considered a rule that would allow persons and entities to cooperate with government agencies without waiving all privileges as to other parties in subsequent litigation. Such a rule is known as a "selective waiver" rule, meaning that disclosure of protected communications or information to the government waives the protection only selectively—to the government—and not to any other person or entity.

The selective waiver provision proved to be very controversial. The Advisory Committee determined that it would not propose adoption of a selective waiver provision; but in light of the request from the House Judiciary Committee, the Advisory Committee did prepare language for a selective waiver provision should Congress decide to proceed. The draft language for a selective waiver provision is available on request.

Conclusion

Proposed Rule 502 is respectfully submitted for consideration by Congress as a rule that will effectively limit the skyrocketing costs of discovery. Members of the Standing Committee, the Advisory Committee, as well as their reporters and consultants, are ready to assist Congress in any way it sees fit.

Sincerely,

Lee H. Rosenthal
Chair, Committee on Rules of Practice and Procedure

Addendum to Advisory Committee Notes

STATEMENT OF CONGRESSIONAL INTENT REGARDING RULE 502 OF THE FEDERAL RULES OF EVIDENCE

During consideration of this rule in Congress, a number of questions were raised about the scope and contours of the effect of the proposed rule on current law regarding attorney-client privilege and work-product protection. These questions were ultimately answered satisfactorily, without need to revise the text of the rule as submitted to Congress by the Judicial Conference.

In general, these questions are answered by keeping in mind the limited though important purpose and focus of the rule. The rule addresses only the effect of disclosure, under specified circumstances, of a communication that is otherwise protected by attorney-client privilege, or of information that is protected by work-product protection, on whether the disclosure itself operates as a waiver of the privilege or protection for purposes of admissibility of evidence in a federal or state judicial or administrative proceeding. The rule does not alter the substantive law regarding attorney-client privilege or work-product protection in any other respect, including the burden on the party invoking the privilege (or protection) to prove that the particular information (or communication) qualifies for it. And it is not intended to alter the rules and practices governing use of information outside this evidentiary context.

Some of these questions are addressed more specifically below, in order to help further avoid uncertainty in the interpretation and application of the rule.

Subdivision (a)—Disclosure vs. Use

This subdivision does not alter the substantive law regarding when a party's strategic use in litigation of otherwise privileged information obliges that party to waive the privilege regarding other information concerning the same subject matter, so that the information being used can be fairly considered in context. One situation in which this issue arises, the assertion as a defense in patent-infringement litigation that a party was relying on advice of counsel, is discussed elsewhere in this Note. In this and similar situations, under subdivision (a)(1) the party using an attorney-client communication to its advantage in the litigation has, in so doing, intentionally waived the privilege as to other communications concerning the same subject matter, regardless of the circumstances in which the communication being so used was initially disclosed.

Subdivision (b)—Fairness Considerations

The standard set forth in this subdivision for determining whether a disclosure operates as a waiver of the privilege or protection is, as explained elsewhere in this Note, the majority rule in the federal courts. The majority rule has simply been distilled here into a standard designed to be predictable in its application. This distillation is not intended to foreclose notions of fairness from continuing to inform application of the standard in all aspects as appropriate in particular cases—for example, as to whether steps taken to rectify an erroneous inadvertent disclosure were sufficiently prompt under subdivision (b)(3) where the receiving party has relied on the information disclosed.

Subdivisions (a) and (b)—Disclosures to Federal Office or Agency

This rule, as a Federal Rule of Evidence, applies to admissibility of evidence. While subdivisions (a) and (b) are written broadly to apply as appropriate to disclosures of information to a federal office or agency, they do not apply to uses of information—such as routine use in government publications—that fall outside the evidentiary context. Nor do these subdivisions relieve the party seeking to protect the information as privileged from the burden of proving that the privilege applies in the first place.

Subdivision (d)—Court Orders

This subdivision authorizes a court to enter orders only in the context of litigation pending before the court. And it does not alter the law regarding waiver of privilege resulting from having acquiesced in the use of otherwise privileged information. Therefore, this subdivision does not provide a basis for a court to enable parties to agree to a selective waiver of the privilege, such as to a federal agency conducting an investigation, while preserving the privilege as against other parties seeking the information. This subdivision is designed to enable a court to enter an order, whether on motion of one or more parties or on its own motion, that will allow the parties to conduct and respond to discovery expeditiously, without the need for exhaustive pre-production privilege reviews, while still preserving each party's right to assert the privilege to preclude use in litigation of information disclosed in such discovery. While the benefits of a court order under this subdivision would be equally available in government enforcement actions as in private actions, acquiescence by the disclos-

ing party in use by the federal agency of information disclosed pursuant to such an order would still be treated as under current law for purposes of determining whether the acquiescence in use of the information, as opposed to its mere disclosure, effects a waiver of the privilege. The same applies to acquiescence in use by another private party.

Moreover, whether the order is entered on motion of one or more parties, or on the court's own motion, the court retains its authority to include the conditions it deems appropriate In the circumstances.

Subdivision (e)—Party Agreements

This subdivision simply makes clear that while parties to a case may agree among themselves regarding the effect of disclosures between each other in a federal proceeding, it is not binding on others unless it is incorporated into a court order. This subdivision does not confer any authority on a court to enter any order regarding the effect of disclosures. That authority must be found in subdivision (d), or elsewhere.

HISTORICAL NOTES

Revision Notes and Legislative Reports

2008 Acts. Senate Report No. 110–264, see 2008 U.S. Code Cong. and Adm. News, p. 1305.

Effective and Applicability Provisions

2008 Acts. Pub.L. 110–322, § 1(c), Sept. 19, 2008, 122 Stat. 3538, provided that: "The amendments made by this Act [enacting this rule] shall apply in all proceedings commenced after the date of enactment of this Act [Sept. 19, 2008] and, insofar as is just and practicable, in all proceedings pending on such date of enactment [Sept. 19, 2008]."

ARTICLE VI. WITNESSES

Rule

Rule 601.   Competency to Testify in General

Every person is competent to be a witness unless these rules provide otherwise. But in a civil case, state law governs the witness's competency regarding a claim or defense for which state law supplies the rule of decision.

(Pub.L. 93–595, § 1, Jan. 2, 1975, 88 Stat.1934; Apr. 26, 2011, eff. Dec. 1, 2011.)

ADVISORY COMMITTEE NOTES

1972 Proposed Rules

This general ground-clearing eliminates all grounds of incompetency not specifically recognized in the succeeding rules of this Article. Included among the grounds thus abolished are religious belief, conviction of crime, and connection with the litigation as a party or interested person or spouse of a party or interested person. With the exception of the so-called Dead Man's Acts, American jurisdictions generally have ceased to recognize these grounds.

The Dead Man's Acts are surviving traces of the common law disqualification of parties and interested persons. They exist in variety too great to convey conviction of their wisdom and effectiveness. These rules contain no provision of this kind. For the reasoning underlying the decision not to give effect to state statutes in diversity cases, see the Advisory Committee's Note to Rule 501.

No mental or moral qualifications for testifying as a witness are specified. Standards of mental capacity have proved elusive in actual application. A leading commentator observes that few witnesses are disqualified on that ground. Weihofen, Testimonial Competence and Credibility, 34 Geo. Wash.L.Rev. 53 (1965). Discretion is regularly exercised in favor of allowing the testimony. A witness wholly without capacity is difficult to imagine. The question is one particularly suited to the jury as one of weight and credibility, subject to judicial authority to review the sufficiency of the evidence. 2 Wigmore §§ 501, 509. Standards of moral qualification in practice consist essentially of evaluating a person's truthfulness in terms of his own answers about it. Their principal utility is in affording an opportunity on voir dire examination to impress upon the witness his moral duty. This result may, however, be accomplished more directly, and without haggling in terms of legal standards, by the manner of administering the oath or affirmation under Rule 603.

Admissibility of religious belief as a ground of impeachment is treated in Rule 610. Conviction of crime as a ground of impeachment is the subject of Rule 609. Marital relationship is the basis for privilege under Rule 505. Interest in the outcome of litigation and mental capacity are, of course, highly relevant to credibility and require no special treatment to render them admissible along with other matters bearing upon the perception, memory, and narration of witnesses.

1974 Enactment

Rule 601 as submitted to the Congress provided that "Every person is competent to be a witness except as otherwise provided in these rules." One effect of the Rule as proposed would have been to abolish age, mental capacity, and other grounds recognized in some State jurisdictions as making a person incompetent as a witness. The greatest controversy centered around the Rule's rendering inapplicable in the federal courts the so-called Dead Man's Statutes which exist in some States. Acknowledging that there is substantial disagreement as to the merit of Dead Man's Statutes, the Committee nevertheless believed that where such statutes have been enacted they represent State policy which should not be overturned in the absence of a compelling federal interest. The Committee therefore amended the Rule to make competency in civil actions determinable in accordance with State law with respect to elements of claims or defenses as to which State law supplies the rule of decision. Cf. *Courtland v. Walston & Co., Inc.,* 340 F.Supp. 1076, 1087–1092 (S.D.N.Y.1972). House Report No. 93–650.

The amendment to rule 601 parallels the treatment accorded Rule 501 discussed immediately above. Senate Report No. 93–1277.

Rule 601 deals with competency of witnesses. Both the House and Senate bills provide that federal competency law applies in criminal cases. In civil actions and proceedings, the House bill provides that state competency law applies "to an element of a claim or defense as to which State law supplies the rule of decision." The Senate bill provides that "in civil actions and proceedings arising under 28 U.S.C. § 1332 or 28 U.S.C. § 1335, or between citizens of different States and removed under 28 U.S.C. § 1441(b) the competency of a witness, person, government, State or political subdivision thereof is determined in accordance with State law, unless with respect to the particular claim or defense, Federal law supplies the rule of decision."

The wording of the House and Senate bills differs in the treatment of civil actions and proceedings. The rule in the House bill applies to evidence that relates to "an element of a claim or defense." If an item of proof tends to support or defeat a claim or defense, or an element of a claim or defense, and if state law supplies the rule of decision for that claim or defense, then state competency law applies to that item of proof.

For reasons similar to those underlying its action on Rule 501, the Conference adopts the House provision. House Report No. 93–1597.

2011 Amendments

The language of Rule 601 has been amended as part of the restyling of the Evidence Rules to make them more easily understood and to make style and terminology consistent throughout the rules. These changes are intended to be stylistic only. There is no intent to change any result in any ruling on evidence admissibility.

CROSS REFERENCES

Accused at own request as competent witness, see 18 USCA § 3481.

Competency of interested persons, share of penalties payable, see 28 USCA § 1822.

Oral testimony in open court, see Fed.Rules Civ.Proc. Rule 43, 28 USCA and Fed.Rules Cr.Proc. Rule 26, 18 USCA.

Privileges of witnesses, general rule, see Fed.Rules Evid. Rule 501, 28 USCA.

State laws as rules of decision, see 28 USCA § 1652.

Rule 602. Need for Personal Knowledge

A witness may testify to a matter only if evidence is introduced sufficient to support a finding that the witness has personal knowledge of the matter. Evidence to prove personal knowledge may consist of the witness's own testimony. This rule does not apply to a witness's expert testimony under Rule 703.

(Pub.L. 93–595, § 1, Jan. 2, 1975, 88 Stat. 1934; Mar. 2, 1987, eff. Oct. 1, 1987; Apr. 25, 1988, eff. Nov. 1, 1988; Apr. 26, 2011, eff. Dec. 1, 2011.)

ADVISORY COMMITTEE NOTES

1972 Proposed Rules

" * * * [T]he rule requiring that a witness who testifies to a fact which can be perceived by the senses must have had an opportunity to observe, and must have actually observed the fact" is a "most pervasive manifestation" of the common law insistence upon "the most reliable sources of information." McCormick § 10, p. 19. These foundation requirements may, of course, be furnished by the testimony of the witness himself; hence personal knowledge is not an absolute but may consist of what the witness thinks he knows from personal perception. 2 Wigmore § 650. It will be observed that the rule is in fact a specialized application of the provisions of Rule 104(b) on conditional relevancy.

This rule does not govern the situation of a witness who testifies to a hearsay statement as such, if he has personal knowledge of the making of the statement. Rules 801 and 805 would be applicable. This rule would, however, prevent him from testifying to the subject matter of the hearsay statement, as he has no personal knowledge of it.

The reference to Rule 703 is designed to avoid any question of conflict between the present rule and the provisions of that rule allowing an expert to express opinions based on facts of which he does not have personal knowledge.

1987 Amendments

The amendments are technical. No substantive change is intended.

1988 Amendments

The amendment is technical. No substantive change is intended.

2011 Amendments

The language of Rule 602 has been amended as part of the restyling of the Evidence Rules to make them more easily understood and to make style and terminology consistent throughout the rules. These changes are intended to be stylistic only. There is no intent to change any result in any ruling on evidence admissibility.

CROSS REFERENCES

Hearsay evidence, generally, see Fed.Rules Evid. Rule 801 et seq., 28 USCA.

Relevancy of evidence as conditional, see Fed.Rules Evid. Rule 104, 28 USCA.

Rule 603. Oath or Affirmation to Testify Truthfully

Before testifying, a witness must give an oath or affirmation to testify truthfully. It must be in a form designed to impress that duty on the witness's conscience.

(Pub.L. 93–595, § 1, Jan. 2, 1975, 88 Stat. 1934; Mar. 2, 1987, eff. Oct. 1, 1987; Apr. 26, 2011, eff. Dec. 1, 2011.)

ADVISORY COMMITTEE NOTES

1972 Proposed Rules

The rule is designed to afford the flexibility required in dealing with religious adults, atheists, conscientious objectors, mental defectives, and children. Affirmation is simply a solemn undertaking to tell the truth; no special verbal formula is required. As is true generally, affirmation is recognized by federal law. "Oath" includes affirmation, 1 U.S.C. § 1; judges and clerks may administer oaths and affirmations, 28 U.S.C. §§ 459, 953; and affirmations are acceptable in lieu of oaths under Rule 43(d) of the Federal Rules of Civil Procedure. Perjury by a witness is a crime, 18 U.S.C. § 1621.

1987 Amendments

The amendments are technical. No substantive change is intended.

2011 Amendments

The language of Rule 603 has been amended as part of the restyling of the Evidence Rules to make them more easily understood and to make style and terminology consistent throughout the rules. These changes are intended to be stylistic only. There is no intent to change any result in any ruling on evidence admissibility.

CROSS REFERENCES

Administration of oaths and affirmations,

Clerk of court and deputies, see 28 USCA § 953.

Justice or judge of United States, see 28 USCA § 459.

Affirmation in lieu of oath, see Fed.Rules Civ.Proc. Rule 43, 28 USCA.

Examination of debtor under oath, see 11 USCA § 343.

False declarations before grand jury or court, see 18 USCA § 1623.

"Oath" as including affirmation, see 1 USCA § 1 and Fed.Rules Cr.Proc. Rule 1, 18 USCA.

Perjury, generally, see 18 USCA § 1621.

Rule 604. Interpreter

An interpreter must be qualified and must give an oath or affirmation to make a true translation.

(Pub.L. 93–595, § 1, Jan. 2, 1975, 88 Stat. 1934; Mar. 2, 1987, eff. Oct. 1, 1987; Apr. 26, 2011, eff. Dec. 1, 2011.)

ADVISORY COMMITTEE NOTES

1972 Proposed Rules

The rule implements Rule 43(f) of the Federal Rules of Civil Procedure and Rule 28(b) of the Federal Rules of Criminal Procedure, both of which contain provisions for the appointment and compensation of interpreters.

1987 Amendments

The amendment is technical. No substantive change is intended.

2011 Amendments

The language of Rule 604 has been amended as part of the restyling of the Evidence Rules to make them more easily understood and to make style and terminology consistent throughout the rules. These changes are intended to be stylistic only. There is no intent to change any result in any ruling on evidence admissibility.

CROSS REFERENCES

Appointment and compensation of interpreters, see Fed. Rules Civ.Proc. Rule 43, 28 USCA and Fed.Rules Cr.Proc. Rule 28, 18 USCA.

Foreign documents, depositions to authenticate, see 18 USCA § 3493.

Opinions and expert testimony, see Fed.Rules Evid. Rule 701 et seq., 28 USCA.

Rule 605. Judge's Competency as a Witness

The presiding judge may not testify as a witness at the trial. A party need not object to preserve the issue.

(Pub.L. 93–595, § 1, Jan. 2, 1975, 88 Stat. 1934; Apr. 26, 2011, eff. Dec. 1, 2011.)

ADVISORY COMMITTEE NOTES

1972 Proposed Rules

In view of the mandate of 28 U.S.C. § 455 that a judge disqualify himself in "any case in which he * * * is or has been a material witness," the likelihood that the presiding judge in a federal court might be called to testify in the trial over which he is presiding is slight. Nevertheless the possibility is not totally eliminated.

The solution here presented is a broad rule of incompetency, rather than such alternatives as incompetency only as to material matters, leaving the matter to the discretion of the judge, or recognizing no incompetency. The choice is the result of inability to evolve satisfactory answers to questions which arise when the judge abandons the bench for the witness stand. Who rules on objections? Who compels him to answer? Can he rule impartially on the weight and admissibility of his own testimony? Can he be impeached or cross-examined effectively? Can he, in a jury trial, avoid conferring his seal of approval on one side in the eyes of the jury? Can he, in a bench trial, avoid an involvement destructive of impartiality? The rule of general incompetency has substantial support. See Report of the Special Committee on the Propriety of Judges Appearing as Witnesses, 36 A.B.A.J. 630 (1950); cases collected in Annot. 157 A.L.R. 311; McCormick § 68, p. 147; Uniform Rule 42; California Evidence Code § 703; Kansas Code of Civil Procedure § 60–442; New Jersey Evidence Rule 42. Cf. 6 Wigmore § 1909, which advocates leaving the matter to the discretion of the judge, and statutes to that effect collected in Annot. 157 A.L.R. 311.

The rule provides an "automatic" objection. To require an actual objection would confront the opponent with a choice between not objecting, with the result of allowing the testimony, and objecting, with the probable result of excluding the testimony but at the price of continuing the trial before a judge likely to feel that his integrity had been attacked by the objector.

2011 Amendments

The language of Rule 605 has been amended as part of the restyling of the Evidence Rules to make them more easily understood and to make style and terminology consistent throughout the rules. These changes are intended to be stylistic only. There is no intent to change any result in any ruling on evidence admissibility.

CROSS REFERENCES

Disqualification of judge to dispose of criminal contempt, see Fed.Rules Cr.Proc. Rule 42, 18 USCA.

Disqualification of justice, judge, or magistrate, see 28 USCA § 455.

Rule 606. Juror's Competency as a Witness

(a) At the Trial. A juror may not testify as a witness before the other jurors at the trial. If a juror is called to testify, the court must give a party an opportunity to object outside the jury's presence.

(b) During an Inquiry Into the Validity of a Verdict or Indictment.

(1) Prohibited Testimony or Other Evidence. During an inquiry into the validity of a verdict or indictment, a juror may not testify about any statement made or incident that occurred during the jury's deliberations; the effect of anything on that juror's or another juror's vote; or any juror's mental processes concerning the verdict or indictment. The

court may not receive a juror's affidavit or evidence of a juror's statement on these matters.

(2) Exceptions. A juror may testify about whether:

    (A) extraneous prejudicial information was improperly brought to the jury's attention;

    (B) an outside influence was improperly brought to bear on any juror; or

    (C) a mistake was made in entering the verdict on the verdict form.

(Pub.L. 93–595, § 1, Jan. 2, 1975, 88 Stat. 1934; Pub.L. 94–149, § 1(10), Dec. 12, 1975, 89 Stat. 805; Mar. 2, 1987, eff. Oct. 1, 1987; Apr. 12, 2006, eff. Dec. 1, 2006; Apr. 26, 2011, eff. Dec. 1, 2011.)

ADVISORY COMMITTEE NOTES
1972 Proposed Rules

Note to Subdivision (a). The considerations which bear upon the permissibility of testimony by a juror in the trial in which he is sitting as juror bear an obvious similarity to those evoked when the judge is called as a witness. See Advisory Committee's Note to Rule 605. The judge is not, however in this instance so involved as to call for departure from usual principles requiring objection to be made; hence the only provision on objection is that opportunity be afforded for its making out of the presence of the jury. Compare Rule 605.

Note to Subdivision (b). Whether testimony, affidavits, or statements of jurors should be received for the purpose of invalidating or supporting a verdict or indictment, and if so, under what circumstances, has given rise to substantial differences of opinion. The familiar rubric that a juror may not impeach his own verdict, dating from Lord Mansfield's time, is a gross oversimplification. The values sought to be promoted by excluding the evidence include freedom of deliberation, stability and finality of verdicts, and protection of jurors against annoyance and embarrassment. *McDonald v. Pless*, 238 U.S. 264, 35 S.Ct. 783, 59 L.Ed. 1300 (1915). On the other hand, simply putting verdicts beyond effective reach can only promote irregularity and injustice. The rule offers an accommodation between these competing considerations.

The mental operations and emotional reactions of jurors in arriving at a given result would, if allowed as a subject of inquiry, place every verdict at the mercy of jurors and invite tampering and harassment. See *Grenz v. Werre*, 129 N.W.2d 681 (N.D.1964). The authorities are in virtually complete accord in excluding the evidence. Fryer, Note on Disqualification of Witnesses, Selected Writings on Evidence and Trial 345, 347 (Fryer ed. 1957); Maguire, Weinstein, et al., Cases on Evidence 887 (5th ed. 1965); 8 Wigmore § 2349 (McNaughton Rev.1961). As to matters other than mental operations and emotional reactions of jurors, substantial authority refuses to allow a juror to disclose irregularities which occur in the jury room, but allows his testimony as to irregularities occurring outside and allows outsiders to testify as to occurrences both inside and out. 8 Wigmore § 2354 (McNaughton Rev.1961). However, the door of the jury room is not necessarily a satisfactory dividing point, and the Supreme Court has refused to accept it for every situation. *Mattox v. United States*, 146 U.S. 140, 13 S.Ct. 50, 36 L.Ed. 917 (1892).

Under the federal decisions the central focus has been upon insulation of the manner in which the jury reached its verdict, and this protection extends to each of the components of deliberation, including arguments, statements, discussions, mental and emotional reactions, votes, and any other feature of the process. Thus testimony or affidavits of jurors have been held incompetent to show a compromise verdict. *Hyde v. United States*, 225 U.S. 347, 382 (1912); a quotient verdict, *McDonald v. Pless*, 238 U.S. 264 (1915); speculation as to insurance coverage. *Holden v. Porter*, 405 F.2d 878 (10th Cir.1969); *Farmers Coop. Elev. Ass'n v. Strand*, 382 F.2d 224, 230 (8th Cir.1967), cert. denied 389 U.S. 1014; misinterpretation of instructions, *Farmers Coop. Elev. Ass'n v. Strand*, supra; mistake in returning verdict, *United States v. Chereton*, 309 F.2d 197 (6th Cir.1962); interpretation of guilty plea by one defendant as implicating others, *United States v. Crosby*, 294 F.2d 928, 949 (2d Cir.1961). The policy does not, however, foreclose testimony by jurors as to prejudicial extraneous information or influences injected into or brought to bear upon the deliberative process. Thus a juror is recognized as competent to testify to statements by the bailiff or the introduction of a prejudicial newspaper account into the jury room, *Mattox v. United States*, 146 U.S. 140 (1892). See also *Parker v. Gladden*, 385 U.S. 363 (1966).

This rule does not purport to specify the substantive grounds for setting aside verdicts for irregularity; it deals only with the competency of jurors to testify concerning those grounds. Allowing them to testify as to matters other than their own inner reactions involves no particular hazard to the values sought to be protected. The rule is based upon this conclusion. It makes no attempt to specify the substantive grounds for setting aside verdicts for irregularity.

See also Rule 6(e) of the Federal Rules of Criminal Procedure and 18 U.S.C. § 3500, governing the secrecy of grand jury proceedings. The present rule does not relate to secrecy and disclosure but to the competency of certain witnesses and evidence.

1974 Enactment

Note to Subdivision (b). As proposed by the Court, Rule 606(b) limited testimony by a juror in the course of an inquiry into the validity of a verdict or indictment. He could testify as to the influence of extraneous prejudicial information brought to the jury's attention (e.g. a radio newscast or a newspaper account) or an outside influence which improperly had been brought to bear upon a juror (e.g. a threat to the safety of a member of his family), but he could not testify as to other irregularities which occurred in the jury room. Under this formulation a quotient verdict could not be attacked through the testimony of a juror, nor could a juror testify to the drunken condition of a fellow juror which so disabled him that he could not participate in the jury's deliberations.

The 1969 and 1971 Advisory Committee drafts would have permitted a member of the jury to testify concerning these kinds of irregularities in the jury room. The Advisory Committee note in the 1971 draft stated that " * * * the door of the jury room is not a satisfactory dividing point, and the Supreme Court has refused to accept it." The Advisory Committee further commented that—

The trend has been to draw the dividing line between testimony as to mental processes, on the one hand, and as to the existence of conditions or occurrences of events calculated improperly to influence the verdict on the other hand, without regard to whether the happening is within or without the jury room. * * * The jurors are the persons who know what really happened. Allowing them to testify

as to matters other than their own reactions involves no particular hazard to the values sought to be protected. The rule is based upon this conclusion. It makes no attempt to specify the substantive grounds for setting aside verdicts for irregularity.

Objective jury misconduct may be testified to in California, Florida, Iowa, Kansas, Nebraska, New Jersey, North Dakota, Ohio, Oregon, Tennessee, Texas, and Washington.

Persuaded that the better practice is that provided for in the earlier drafts, the Committee amended subdivision (b) to read in the text of those drafts. House Report No. 93–650.

Note to Subdivision (b). As adopted by the House, this rule would permit the impeachment of verdicts by inquiry into, not the mental processes of the jurors, but what happened in terms of conduct in the jury room. This extension of the ability to impeach a verdict is felt to be unwarranted and ill-advised.

The rule passed by the House embodies a suggestion by the Advisory Committee of the Judicial Conference that is considerably broader than the final version adopted by the Supreme Court, which embodied long-accepted Federal law. Although forbidding the impeachment of verdicts by inquiry into the jurors' mental processes, it deletes from the Supreme Court version the proscription against testimony "as to any matter or statement occurring during the course of the jury's deliberations." This deletion would have the effect of opening verdicts up to challenge on the basis of what happened during the jury's internal deliberations, for example, where a juror alleged that the jury refused to follow the trial judge's instructions or that some of the jurors did not take part in deliberations.

Permitting an individual to attack a jury verdict based upon the jury's internal deliberations has long been recognized as unwise by the Supreme Court. In *McDonald v. Pless*, the Court stated:

* * * *

[L]et it once be established that verdicts solemnly made and publicly returned into court can be attacked and set aside on the testimony of those who took part in their publication and all verdicts could be, and many would be, followed by an inquiry in the hope of discovering something which might invalidate the finding. Jurors would be harassed and beset by the defeated party in an effort to secure from them evidence of facts which might establish misconduct sufficient to set aside a verdict. If evidence thus secured could be thus used, the result would be to make what was intended to be a private deliberation, the constant subject of public investigation—to the destruction of all frankness and freedom of discussion and conference [238 U.S. 264, at 267 (1914)].

* * * *

As it stands then, the rule would permit the harassment of former jurors by losing parties as well as the possible exploitation of disgruntled or otherwise badly-motivated ex-jurors.

Public policy requires a finality to litigation. And common fairness requires that absolute privacy be preserved for jurors to engage in the full and free debate necessary to the attainment of just verdicts. Jurors will not be able to function effectively if their deliberations are to be scrutinized in post-trial litigation. In the interest of protecting the jury system and the citizens who make it work, rule 606 should not permit any inquiry into the internal deliberations of the jurors. Senate Report No. 93–1277.

For Complete Annotation Materials, see United States Code Annotated

Note to Subdivision (b). Rule 606(b) deals with juror testimony in an inquiry into the validity of a verdict or indictment. The House bill provides that a juror cannot testify about his mental processes or about the effect of anything upon his or another juror's mind as influencing him to assent to or dissent from a verdict or indictment. Thus, the House bill allows a juror to testify about objective matters occurring during the jury's deliberation, such as the misconduct of another juror or the reaching of a quotient verdict. The Senate bill does not permit juror testimony about any matter or statement occurring during the course of the jury's deliberations. The Senate bill does provide, however, that a juror may testify on the question whether extraneous prejudicial information was improperly brought to the jury's attention and on the question whether any outside influence was improperly brought to bear on any juror.

The Conference adopts the Senate amendment. The Conferees believe that jurors should be encouraged to be conscientious in promptly reporting to the court misconduct that occurs during jury deliberations. House Report No. 93–1597.

1987 Amendments

The amendments are technical. No substantive change is intended.

2006 Amendments

Rule 606(b) has been amended to provide that juror testimony may be used to prove that the verdict reported was the result of a mistake in entering the verdict on the verdict form. The amendment responds to a divergence between the text of the Rule and the case law that has established an exception for proof of clerical errors. *See, e.g., Plummer v. Springfield Term. Ry.,* 5 F.3d 1, 3 (1st Cir. 1993) ("A number of circuits hold, and we agree, that juror testimony regarding an alleged clerical error, such as announcing a verdict different than that agreed upon, does not challenge the validity of the verdict or the deliberation of mental processes, and therefore is not subject to Rule 606(b)."); *Teevee Toons, Inc., v. MP3.Com, Inc.,* 148 F.Supp.2d 276, 278 (S.D.N.Y. 2001) (noting that Rule 606(b) has been silent regarding inquiries designed to confirm the accuracy of a verdict).

In adopting the exception for proof of mistakes in entering the verdict on the verdict form, the amendment specifically rejects the broader exception, adopted by some courts, permitting the use of juror testimony to prove that the jurors were operating under a misunderstanding about the consequences of the result that they agreed upon. *See, e.g., Attridge v. Cencorp Div. of Dover Techs. Int'l, Inc.,* 836 F.2d 113, 116 (2d Cir. 1987); *Eastridge Development Co., v. Halpert Associates, Inc.,* 853 F.2d 772 (10th Cir. 1988). The broader exception is rejected because an inquiry into whether the jury misunderstood or misapplied an instruction goes to the jurors' mental processes underlying the verdict, rather than the verdict's accuracy in capturing what the jurors had agreed upon. *See, e.g., Karl v. Burlington Northern R.R.,* 880 F.2d 68, 74 (8th Cir. 1989) (error to receive juror testimony on whether verdict was the result of jurors' misunderstanding of instructions: "The jurors did not state that the figure written by the foreman was different from that which they agreed upon, but indicated that the figure the foreman wrote down was intended to be a net figure, not a gross figure. Receiving such statements violates Rule 606(b) because the testimony relates to how the jury interpreted the court's instructions, and concerns the jurors' 'mental process-

es,' which is forbidden by the rule."); *Robles v. Exxon Corp.,* 862 F.2d 1201, 1208 (5th Cir. 1989) ("the alleged error here goes to the substance of what the jury was asked to decide, necessarily implicating the jury's mental processes insofar as it questions the jury's understanding of the court's instructions and application of those instructions to the facts of the case"). Thus, the exception established by the amendment is limited to cases such as "where the jury foreperson wrote down, in response to an interrogatory, a number different from that agreed upon by the jury, or mistakenly stated that the defendant was 'guilty' when the jury had actually agreed that the defendant was not guilty." *Id.*

It should be noted that the possibility of errors in the verdict form will be reduced substantially by polling the jury. Rule 606(b) does not, of course, prevent this precaution. *See* 8C. Wigmore, *Evidence,* § 2350 at 691 (McNaughten ed. 1961) (noting that the reasons for the rule barring juror testimony, "namely, the dangers of uncertainty and of tampering with the jurors to procure testimony, disappear in large part if such investigation as may be desired is *made by the judge* and takes place *before the jurors' discharge* and separation") (emphasis in original). Errors that come to light after polling the jury "may be corrected on the spot, or the jury may be sent out to continue deliberations, or, if necessary, a new trial may be ordered." C. Mueller & L. Kirkpatrick, *Evidence Under the Rules* at 671 (2d ed. 1999) (citing *Sincox v. United States,* 571 F.2d 876, 878–79 (5th Cir. 1978)).

2011 Amendments

The language of Rule 606 has been amended as part of the restyling of the Evidence Rules to make them more easily understood and to make style and terminology consistent throughout the rules. These changes are intended to be stylistic only. There is no intent to change any result in any ruling on evidence admissibility.

HISTORICAL NOTES

Revision Notes and Legislative Reports

1975 Acts. House Report No. 94–599, see 1975 U.S. Code Cong. and Adm. News, p. 1585.

CROSS REFERENCES

Grand jury, secrecy of proceedings and disclosure, see Fed.Rules Cr.Proc. Rule 6, 18 USCA.

Statements and reports of witnesses, demands for, see 18 USCA § 3500.

Rule 607. Who May Impeach a Witness

Any party, including the party that called the witness, may attack the witness's credibility.

(Pub.L. 93–595, § 1, Jan. 2, 1975, 88 Stat.1934; Mar. 2, 1987, eff. Oct. 1, 1987; Apr. 26, 2011, eff. Dec. 1, 2011.)

ADVISORY COMMITTEE NOTES

1972 Proposed Rules

The traditional rule against impeaching one's own witness is abandoned as based on false premises. A party does not hold out his witnesses as worthy of belief, since he rarely has a free choice in selecting them. Denial of the right leaves the party at the mercy of the witness and the adversary. If the impeachment is by a prior statement, it is free from hearsay dangers and is excluded from the category of hearsay under Rule 801(d)(1). Ladd, Impeachment of One's Own Witness— New Developments, 4 U.Chi.L.Rev. 69 (1936); McCormick § 38; 3 Wigmore §§ 896–918. The substantial inroads into the old rule made over the years by decisions, rules, and statutes are evidence of doubts as to its basic soundness and workability. Cases are collected in 3 Wigmore § 905. Revised Rule 32(a)(1) of the Federal Rules of Civil Procedure allows any party to impeach a witness by means of his deposition, and Rule 43(b) has allowed the calling and impeachment of an adverse party or person identified with him. Illustrative statutes allowing a party to impeach his own witness under varying circumstances are Ill.Rev.Stats.1967, c. 110, § 60; Mass.Laws Annot. 1959, c. 233, § 23; 20 N.M.Stats.Annot. 1953, § 20–2–4; N.Y. CPLR § 4514 (McKinney 1963); 12 Vt.Stats.Annot.1959, §§ 1641a, 1642. Complete judicial rejection of the old rule is found in *United States v. Freeman,* 302 F.2d 347 (2d Cir.1962). The same result is reached in Uniform Rule 20; California Evidence Code § 785; Kansas Code of Civil Procedure § 60–420. See also New Jersey Evidence Rule 20.

1987 Amendments

The amendment is technical. No substantive change is intended.

2011 Amendments

The language of Rule 607 has been amended as part of the restyling of the Evidence Rules to make them more easily understood and to make style and terminology consistent throughout the rules. These changes are intended to be stylistic only. There is no intent to change any result in any ruling on evidence admissibility.

CROSS REFERENCES

Character evidence, inadmissibility to prove conduct, see Fed.Rules Evid. Rule 404, 28 USCA.

Cross-examination, right of, see USCA Const. Amend. VI.

Depositions, use for impeachment of deponent, see Fed. Rules Civ.Proc. Rule 32, 28 USCA and Fed.Rules Cr.Proc. Rule 15, 18 USCA.

Prior statements of witnesses not hearsay where witness cross-examined, see Fed.Rules Evid. Rule 801, 28 USCA.

Relevant evidence excluded on grounds of prejudice, confusion, or cumulation, see Fed.Rules Evid. Rule 403, 28 USCA.

Rule 608. A Witness's Character for Truthfulness or Untruthfulness

(a) Reputation or Opinion Evidence. A witness's credibility may be attacked or supported by testimony about the witness's reputation for having a character for truthfulness or untruthfulness, or by testimony in the form of an opinion about that character. But evidence of truthful character is admissible only after the witness's character for truthfulness has been attacked.

(b) Specific Instances of Conduct. Except for a criminal conviction under Rule 609, extrinsic evidence is not admissible to prove specific instances of a witness's conduct in order to attack or support the witness's character for truthfulness. But the court may,

on cross-examination, allow them to be inquired into if they are probative of the character for truthfulness or untruthfulness of:

(1) the witness; or

(2) another witness whose character the witness being cross-examined has testified about.

By testifying on another matter, a witness does not waive any privilege against self-incrimination for testimony that relates only to the witness's character for truthfulness.

(Pub.L. 93–595, § 1, Jan. 2, 1975, 88 Stat.1935; Mar. 2, 1987, eff. Oct. 1, 1987; Apr. 25, 1988, eff. Nov. 1, 1988; Mar. 27, 2003, eff. Dec. 1, 2003; Apr. 26, 2011, eff. Dec. 1, 2011.)

ADVISORY COMMITTEE NOTES

1972 Proposed Rules

Note to Subdivision (a). In Rule 404(a) the general position is taken that character evidence is not admissible for the purpose of proving that the person acted in conformity therewith, subject, however, to several exceptions, one of which is character evidence of a witness as bearing upon his credibility. The present rule develops that exception.

In accordance with the bulk of judicial authority, the inquiry is strictly limited to character for veracity, rather than allowing evidence as to character generally. The result is to sharpen relevancy, to reduce surprise, waste of time, and confusion, and to make the lot of the witness somewhat less unattractive. McCormick § 44.

The use of opinion and reputation evidence as means of proving the character of witnesses is consistent with Rule 405(a). While the modern practice has purported to exclude opinion, witnesses who testify to reputation seem in fact often to be giving their opinions, disguised somewhat misleadingly as reputation. See McCormick § 44. And even under the modern practice, a common relaxation has allowed inquiry as to whether the witnesses would believe the principal witness under oath. *United States v. Walker,* 313 F.2d 236 (6th Cir.1963), and cases cited therein; McCormick § 44, pp. 94–95, n. 3.

Character evidence in support of credibility is admissible under the rule only after the witness' character has first been attacked, as has been the case at common law. Maguire, Weinstein, et al., Cases on Evidence 295 (5th ed. 1965); McCormick § 49, p. 105; 4 Wigmore § 1104. The enormous needless consumption of time which a contrary practice would entail justifies the limitation. Opinion or reputation that the witness is untruthful specifically qualifies as an attack under the rule, and evidence of misconduct, including conviction of crime, and of corruption also fall within this category. Evidence of bias or interest does not. McCormick § 49; 4 Wigmore §§ 1106, 1107. Whether evidence in the form of contradiction is an attack upon the character of the witness must depend upon the circumstances. McCormick § 49. Cf. 4 Wigmore §§ 1108, 1109.

As to the use of specific instances on direct by an opinion witness, see the Advisory Committee's Note to Rule 405, *supra.*

Note to Subdivision (b). In conformity with Rule 405, which forecloses use of evidence of specific incidents as proof in chief of character unless character is an issue in the case, the present rule generally bars evidence of specific instances of conduct of a witness for the purpose of attacking or supporting his credibility. There are, however, two exceptions: (1) specific instances are provable when they have been the subject of criminal conviction, and (2) specific instances may be inquired into on cross-examination of the principal witness or of a witness giving an opinion of his character for truthfulness.

(1) Conviction of crime as a technique of impeachment is treated in detail in Rule 609, and here is merely recognized as an exception to the general rule excluding evidence of specific incidents for impeachment purposes.

(2) Particular instances of conduct, though not the subject of criminal conviction, may be inquired into on cross-examination of the principal witness himself or of a witness who testifies concerning his character for truthfulness. Effective cross-examination demands that some allowance be made for going into matters of this kind, but the possibilities of abuse are substantial. Consequently safeguards are erected in the form of specific requirements that the instances inquired into be probative of truthfulness or its opposite and not remote in time. Also, the overriding protection of Rule 403 requires that probative value not be outweighed by danger of unfair prejudice, confusion of issues, or misleading the jury, and that of Rule 611 bars harassment and undue embarrassment.

The final sentence constitutes a rejection of the doctrine of such cases as *People v. Sorge,* 301 N.Y. 198, 93 N.E.2d 637 (1950), that any past criminal act relevant to credibility may be inquired into on cross-examination, in apparent disregard of the privilege against self-incrimination. While it is clear that an ordinary witness cannot make a partial disclosure of incriminating matter and then invoke the privilege on cross-examination, no tenable contention can be made that merely by testifying he waives his right to foreclose inquiry on cross-examination into criminal activities for the purpose of attacking his credibility. So to hold would reduce the privilege to a nullity. While it is true that an accused, unlike an ordinary witness, has an option whether to testify, if the option can be exercised only at the price of opening up inquiry as to any and all criminal acts committed during his lifetime, the right to testify could scarcely be said to possess much vitality. In *Griffin v. California,* 380 U.S. 609, 85 S.Ct. 1229, 14 L.Ed.2d 106 (1965), the Court held that allowing comment on the election of an accused not to testify exacted a constitutionally impermissible price, and so here. While no specific provision in terms confers constitutional status on the right of an accused to take the stand in his own defense, the existence of the right is so completely recognized that a denial of it or substantial infringement upon it would surely be of due process dimensions. See *Ferguson v. Georgia,* 365 U.S. 570, 81 S.Ct. 756, 5 L.Ed.2d 783 (1961); McCormick § 131; 8 Wigmore § 2276 (McNaughton Rev.1961). In any event, wholly aside from constitutional considerations, the provision represents a sound policy.

1974 Enactment

Note to Subdivision (a). Rule 608(a) as submitted by the Court permitted attack to be made upon the character for truthfulness or untruthfulness of a witness either by reputation or opinion testimony. For the same reason underlying its decision to eliminate the admissibility of opinion testimony in Rule 405(a), the Committee amended Rule 608(a) to delete the reference to opinion testimony.

Note to Subdivision (b). The second sentence of Rule 608(b) as submitted by the Court permitted specific instances of misconduct of a witness to be inquired into on cross-examination for the purpose of attacking his credibility, if probative of truthfulness or untruthfulness, "and not remote in time". Such cross-examination could be of the witness himself or of another witness who testifies as to "his" character for truthfulness or untruthfulness.

The Committee amended the Rule to emphasize the discretionary power of the court in permitting such testimony and deleted the reference to remoteness in time as being unnecessary and confusing (remoteness from time of trial or remoteness from the incident involved?). As recast, the Committee amendment also makes clear the antecedent of "his" in the original Court proposal. House Report No. 93–650.

The Senate amendment adds the words "opinion or" to conform the first sentence of the rule with the remainder of the rule.

The Conference adopts the Senate amendment. House Report No. 93–1597.

1987 Amendments

The amendments are technical. No substantive change is intended.

1988 Amendments

The amendment is technical. No substantive change is intended.

2003 Amendments

The Rule has been amended to clarify that the absolute prohibition on extrinsic evidence applies only when the sole reason for proffering that evidence is to attack or support the witness' character for truthfulness. See *United States v. Abel,* 469 U.S. 45 (1984); *United States v. Fusco,* 748 F.2d 996 (5th Cir. 1984) (Rule 608(b) limits the use of evidence "designed to show that the witness has done things, unrelated to the suit being tried, that make him more or less believable per se"); Ohio R.Evid. 608(b). On occasion the Rule's use of the overbroad term "credibility" has been read "to bar extrinsic evidence for bias, competency and contradiction impeachment since they too deal with credibility." American Bar Association Section of Litigation, *Emerging Problems Under the Federal Rules of Evidence* at 161 (3d ed. 1998). The amendment conforms the language of the Rule to its original intent, which was to impose an absolute bar on extrinsic evidence only if the sole purpose for offering the evidence was to prove the witness' character for veracity. See Advisory Committee Note to Rule 608(b) (stating that the Rule is "[i]n conformity with Rule 405, which forecloses use of evidence of specific incidents as proof in chief of character unless character is in issue in the case ... ").

By limiting the application of the Rule to proof of a witness' character for truthfulness, the amendment leaves the admissibility of extrinsic evidence offered for other grounds of impeachment (such as contradiction, prior inconsistent statement, bias and mental capacity) to Rules 402 and 403. See, e.g., *United States v. Winchenbach,* 197 F.3d 548 (1st Cir. 1999) (admissibility of a prior inconsistent statement offered for impeachment is governed by Rules 402 and 403, not Rule 608(b)); *United States v. Tarantino,* 846 F.2d 1384 (D.C. Cir. 1988) (admissibility of extrinsic evidence offered to contradict a witness is governed by Rules 402 and 403); *United States v.*

Lindemann, 85 F.3d 1232 (7th Cir. 1996) (admissibility of extrinsic evidence of bias is governed by Rules 402 and 403).

It should be noted that the extrinsic evidence prohibition of Rule 608(b) bars any reference to the consequences that a witness might have suffered as a result of an alleged bad act. For example, Rule 608(b) prohibits counsel from mentioning that a witness was suspended or disciplined for the conduct that is the subject of impeachment, when that conduct is offered only to prove the character of the witness. *See United States v. Davis*, 183 F.3d 231, 257 n.12 (3d Cir. 1999) (emphasizing that in attacking the defendant's character for truthfulness "the government cannot make reference to Davis's forty-four day suspension or that Internal Affairs found that he lied about" an incident because "[s]uch evidence would not only be hearsay to the extent it contains assertion of fact, it would be inadmissible extrinsic evidence under Rule 608(b)"). *See also* Stephen A. Saltzburg, *Impeaching the Witness: Prior Bad Acts and Extrinsic Evidence*, 7 Crim. Just. 28, 31 (Winter 1993) ("counsel should not be permitted to circumvent the no-extrinsic-evidence provision by tucking a third person's opinion about prior acts into a question asked of the witness who has denied the act").

For purposes of consistency the term "credibility" has been replaced by the term "character for truthfulness" in the last sentence of subdivision (b). The term "credibility" is also used in subdivision (a). But the Committee found it unnecessary to substitute "character for truthfulness" for "credibility" in Rule 608(a), because subdivision (a)(1) already serves to limit impeachment to proof of such character.

Rules 609(a) and 610 also use the term "credibility" when the intent of those Rules is to regulate impeachment of a witness' character for truthfulness. No inference should be derived from the fact that the Committee proposed an amendment to Rule 608(b) but not to Rules 609 and 610.

2011 Amendments

The language of Rule 608 has been amended as part of the general restyling of the Evidence Rules to make them more easily understood and to make style and terminology consistent throughout the rules. These changes are intended to be stylistic only. There is no intent to change any result in any ruling on evidence admissibility.

The Committee is aware that the Rule's limitation of bad-act impeachment to "cross-examination" is trumped by Rule 607, which allows a party to impeach witnesses on direct examination. Courts have not relied on the term "on cross-examination" to limit impeachment that would otherwise be permissible under Rules 607 and 608. The Committee therefore concluded that no change to the language of the Rule was necessary in the context of a restyling project.

CROSS REFERENCES

Character evidence,
> Inadmissible to prove conduct, exceptions, see Fed.Rules Evid. Rule 404, 28 USCA.
> Methods of proving character, see Fed.Rules Evid. Rule 405, 28 USCA.

Extortionate credit transactions, admissibility of evidence to show,
> Reputation as to collection practices, see 18 USCA § 892.
> Reputation of defendant within community, see 18 USCA § 894.
> Threat as means of collection, see 18 USCA § 894.

Immunity of witnesses, order compelling testimony, see 18 USCA §§ 6002 and 6003.

Opinion evidence, see Fed.Rules Evid. Rule 701 et seq., 28 USCA.

Prejudice, confusion, or waste of time, exclusion of evidence for, see Fed.Rules Evid. Rule 403, 28 USCA.

Self-incrimination, see USCA Const. Amend. V.

Rule 609.   Impeachment by Evidence of a Criminal Conviction

(a) In General. The following rules apply to attacking a witness's character for truthfulness by evidence of a criminal conviction:

> **(1)** for a crime that, in the convicting jurisdiction, was punishable by death or by imprisonment for more than one year, the evidence:
>> **(A)** must be admitted, subject to Rule 403, in a civil case or in a criminal case in which the witness is not a defendant; and
>> **(B)** must be admitted in a criminal case in which the witness is a defendant, if the probative value of the evidence outweighs its prejudicial effect to that defendant; and

> **(2)** for any crime regardless of the punishment, the evidence must be admitted if the court can readily determine that establishing the elements of the crime required proving—or the witness's admitting—a dishonest act or false statement.

(b) Limit on Using the Evidence After 10 Years. This subdivision (b) applies if more than 10 years have passed since the witness's conviction or release from confinement for it, whichever is later. Evidence of the conviction is admissible only if:

> **(1)** its probative value, supported by specific facts and circumstances, substantially outweighs its prejudicial effect; and

> **(2)** the proponent gives an adverse party reasonable written notice of the intent to use it so that the party has a fair opportunity to contest its use.

(c) Effect of a Pardon, Annulment, or Certificate of Rehabilitation. Evidence of a conviction is not admissible if:

> **(1)** the conviction has been the subject of a pardon, annulment, certificate of rehabilitation, or other equivalent procedure based on a finding that the person has been rehabilitated, and the person has not been convicted of a later crime punishable by death or by imprisonment for more than one year; or

> **(2)** the conviction has been the subject of a pardon, annulment, or other equivalent procedure based on a finding of innocence.

(d) Juvenile Adjudications. Evidence of a juvenile adjudication is admissible under this rule only if:

> **(1)** it is offered in a criminal case;

---

(2) the adjudication was of a witness other than the defendant;

(3) an adult's conviction for that offense would be admissible to attack the adult's credibility; and

(4) admitting the evidence is necessary to fairly determine guilt or innocence.

(e) Pendency of an Appeal. A conviction that satisfies this rule is admissible even if an appeal is pending. Evidence of the pendency is also admissible. (Pub.L. 93–595, § 1, Jan. 2, 1975, 88 Stat.1935; Mar. 2, 1987, eff. Oct. 1, 1987; Jan. 26, 1990, eff. Dec. 1, 1990; Apr. 12, 2006, eff. Dec. 1, 2006; Apr. 26, 2011, eff. Dec. 1, 2011.)

ADVISORY COMMITTEE NOTES
1972 Proposed Rules

As a means of impeachment, evidence of conviction of crime is significant only because it stands as proof of the commission of the underlying criminal act. There is little dissent from the general proposition that at least some crimes are relevant to credibility but much disagreement among the cases and commentators about which crimes are usable for this purpose. See McCormick § 43; 2 Wright, Federal Practice and Procedure: Criminal § 416 (1969). The weight of traditional authority has been to allow use of felonies generally, without regard to the nature of the particular offense, and of *crimen falsi* without regard to the grade of the offense. This is the view accepted by Congress in the 1970 amendment of § 14–305 of the District of Columbia Code, P.L. 91–358, 84 Stat. 473. Uniform Rule 21 and Model Code Rule 106 permit only crimes involving "dishonesty or false statement." Others have thought that the trial judge should have discretion to exclude convictions if the probative value of the evidence of the crime is substantially outweighed by the danger of unfair prejudice. *Luck v. United States,* 121 U.S.App.D.C. 151, 348 F.2d 763 (1965); McGowan, Impeachment of Criminal Defendants by Prior Convictions, 1970 Law & Soc.Order 1. Whatever may be the merits of those views, this rule is drafted to accord with the Congressional policy manifested in the 1970 legislation.

The proposed rule incorporates certain basic safeguards, in terms applicable to all witnesses but of particular significance to an accused who elects to testify. These protections include the imposition of definite time limitations, giving effect to demonstrated rehabilitation, and generally excluding juvenile adjudications.

Note to Subdivision (a). For purposes of impeachment, crimes are divided into two categories by the rule: (1) those of what is generally regarded as felony grade, without particular regard to the nature of the offense, and (2) those involving dishonesty or false statement, without regard to the grade of the offense. Probable convictions are not limited to violations of federal law. By reason of our constitutional structure, the federal catalog of crimes is far from being a complete one, and resort must be had to the laws of the states for the specification of many crimes. For example, simple theft as compared with theft from interstate commerce. Other instances of borrowing are the Assimilative Crimes Act, making the state law of crimes applicable to the special territorial and maritime jurisdiction of the United States, 18 U.S.C. § 13, and the provision of the Judicial Code disqualifying persons as jurors on the grounds of state as well as federal convictions, 28 U.S.C. § 1865. For evaluation of the crime in terms of seriousness, reference is made to the congressional measurement of felony (subject to imprisonment in excess of one year) rather than adopting state definitions which vary considerably. See 28 U.S.C. § 1865, *supra,* disqualifying jurors for conviction in state or federal court of crime punishable by imprisonment for more than one year.

Note to Subdivision (b). Few statutes recognize a time limit on impeachment by evidence of conviction. However, practical considerations of fairness and relevancy demand that some boundary be recognized. See Ladd, Credibility Tests—Current Trends, 89 U.Pa.L.Rev. 166, 176–177 (1940). This portion of the rule is derived from the proposal advanced in Recommendation Proposing in Evidence Code, § 788(5), p. 142, Cal.Law Rev.Comm'n (1965), though not adopted. See California Evidence Code § 788.

Note to Subdivision (c). A pardon or its equivalent granted solely for the purpose of restoring civil rights lost by virtue of a conviction has no relevance to an inquiry into character. If, however, the pardon or other proceeding is hinged upon a showing of rehabilitation the situation is otherwise. The result under the rule is to render the conviction inadmissible. The alternative of allowing in evidence both the conviction and the rehabilitation has not been adopted for reasons of policy, economy of time, and difficulties of evaluation.

A similar provision is contained in California Evidence Code § 788. Cf. A.L.I. Model Penal Code, Proposed Official Draft § 306.6(3)(e) (1962), and discussion in A.L.I. Proceedings 310 (1961).

Pardons based on innocence have the effect, of course, of nullifying the conviction *ab initio.*

Note to Subdivision (d). The prevailing view has been that a juvenile adjudication is not usable for impeachment. *Thomas v. United States,* 74 App.D.C. 167, 121 F.2d 905 (1941); *Cotton v. United States,* 355 F.2d 480 (10th Cir.1966). This conclusion was based upon a variety of circumstances. By virtue of its informality, frequently diminished quantum of required proof, and other departures from accepted standards for criminal trials under the theory of *parens patriae,* the juvenile adjudication was considered to lack the precision and general probative value of the criminal conviction. While *In re Gault,* 387 U.S. 1, 87 S.Ct. 1428, 18 L.Ed.2d 527 (1967), no doubt eliminates these characteristics insofar as objectionable, other obstacles remain. Practical problems of administration are raised by the common provisions in juvenile legislation that records be kept confidential and that they be destroyed after a short time. While *Gault* was skeptical as to the realities of confidentiality of juvenile records, it also saw no constitutional obstacles to improvement. 387 U.S. at 25, 87 S.Ct. 1428. See also Note, Rights and Rehabilitation in the Juvenile Courts, 67 Colum.L.Rev. 281, 289 (1967). In addition, policy considerations much akin to those which dictate exclusion of adult convictions after rehabilitation has been established strongly suggest a rule of excluding juvenile adjudications. Admittedly, however, the rehabilitative process may in a given case be a demonstrated failure, or the strategic importance of a given witness may be so great as to require the overriding of general policy in the interests of particular justice. See *Giles v. Maryland,* 386 U.S. 66, 87 S.Ct. 793, 17 L.Ed.2d 737 (1967). Wigmore was outspoken in his condemnation of the disallowance of juvenile adjudications to impeach, especially when the witness is the complainant in a case of molesting a minor. 1 Wigmore § 196; 3 *Id.* §§ 924a, 980. The rule recognizes discretion in the judge to effect an accommodation among these various factors by departing from the general principle of exclusion. In deference to the general pattern and policy of juvenile statutes, however, no discretion is accorded when the witness is the accused in a criminal case.

Note to Subdivision (e). The presumption of correctness which ought to attend judicial proceedings supports the position that pendency of an appeal does not preclude use of a conviction for impeachment. *United States v. Empire Packing Co.,* 174 F.2d 16 (7th Cir.1949), cert. denied 337 U.S. 959, 69 S.Ct. 1534, 93 L.Ed. 1758; *Bloch v. United States,* 226 F.2d 185 (9th Cir.1955), cert. denied 350 U.S. 948, 76 S.Ct. 323, 100 L.Ed. 826 and 353 U.S. 959, 77 S.Ct. 868, 1 L.Ed.2d 910; and see *Newman v. United States,* 331 F.2d 968 (8th Cir.1964). *Contra, Campbell v. United States,* 85 U.S.App.D.C. 133, 176 F.2d 45 (1949). The pendency of an appeal is, however, a qualifying circumstance properly considerable.

1974 Enactment

Note to Subdivision (a). Rule 609(a) as submitted by the Court was modeled after Section 133(a) of Public Law 91–358, 14 D.C.Code 305(b)(1), enacted in 1970. The Rule provided that:

> For the purpose of attacking the credibility of a witness, evidence that he has been convicted of a crime is admissible but only if the crime (1) was punishable by death or imprisonment in excess of one year under the law under which he was convicted or (2) involved dishonesty or false statement regardless of the punishment.

As reported to the Committee by the Subcommittee, Rule 609(a) was amended to read as follows:

> For the purpose of attacking the credibility of a witness, evidence that he has been convicted of a crime is admissible only if the crime (1) was punishable by death or imprisonment in excess of one year, unless the court determines that the danger of unfair prejudice outweighs the probative value of the evidence of the conviction, or (2) involved dishonesty or false statement.

In full committee, the provision was amended to permit attack upon the credibility of a witness by prior conviction only if the prior crime involved dishonesty or false statement. While recognizing that the prevailing doctrine in the federal courts and in most States allows a witness to be impeached by evidence of prior felony convictions without restriction as to type, the Committee was of the view that, because of the danger of unfair prejudice in such practice and the deterrent effect upon an accused who might wish to testify, and even upon a witness who was not the accused, cross-examination by evidence of prior conviction should be limited to those kinds of convictions bearing directly on credibility, *i.e.,* crimes involving dishonesty or false statement.

Note to Subdivision (b). Rule 609(b) as submitted by the Court was modeled after Section 133(a) of Public Law 91–358, 14 D.C.Code 305(b)(2)(B), enacted in 1970. The Rule provided:

> Evidence of a conviction under this rule is not admissible if a period of more than ten years has elapsed since the date of the release of the witness from confinement imposed for his most recent conviction, or the expiration of the period of his parole, probation, or sentence granted or imposed with respect to his most recent conviction, whichever is the later date.

Under this formulation, a witness' entire past record of criminal convictions could be used for impeachment (provided the conviction met the standard of subdivision (a)), if the witness had been most recently released from confinement, or the period of his parole or probation had expired, within ten years of the conviction.

The Committee amended the Rule to read in the text of the 1971 Advisory Committee version to provide that upon the expiration of ten years from the date of a conviction of a witness, or of his release from confinement for that offense, that conviction may no longer be used for impeachment. The Committee was of the view that after ten years following a person's release from confinement (or from the date of his conviction) the probative value of the conviction with respect to that person's credibility diminished to a point where it should no longer be admissible.

Note to Subdivision (c). Rule 609(c) as submitted by the Court provided in part that evidence of a witness' prior conviction is not admissible to attack his credibility if the conviction was the subject of a pardon, annulment, or other equivalent procedure, based on a showing of rehabilitation, and the witness has not been convicted of a subsequent crime. The Committee amended the Rule to provide that the "subsequent crime" must have been "punishable by death or imprisonment in excess of one year", on the ground that a subsequent conviction of an offense not a felony is insufficient to rebut the finding that the witness has been rehabilitated. The Committee also intends that the words "based on a finding of the rehabilitation of the person convicted" apply not only to "certificate of rehabilitation, or other equivalent procedure," but also to "pardon" and "annulment." House Report No. 93–650.

Note to Subdivision (a). As proposed by the Supreme Court, the rule would allow the use of prior convictions to impeach if the crime was a felony or a misdemeanor if the misdemeanor involved dishonesty or false statement. As modified by the House, the rule would admit prior convictions for impeachment purposes only if the offense, whether felony or misdemeanor, involved dishonesty or false statement.

The committee has adopted a modified version of the House-passed rule. In your committee's view, the danger of unfair prejudice is far greater when the accused, as opposed to other witnesses, testifies, because the jury may be prejudiced not merely on the question of credibility but also on the ultimate question of guilt or innocence. Therefore, with respect to defendants, the committee agreed with the House limitation that only offenses involved false statement or dishonesty may be used. By that phrase, the committee means crimes such as perjury or subornation of perjury, false statement, criminal fraud, embezzlement or false pretense, or any other offense, in the nature of *crimen falsi* the commission of which involves some element of untruthfulness, deceit or falsification bearing on the accused's propensity to testify truthfully.

With respect to other witnesses, in addition to any prior conviction involving false statement or dishonesty, any other felony may be used to impeach if, and only if, the court finds that the probative value of such evidence outweighs its prejudicial effect against the party offering that witness.

Notwithstanding this provision, proof of any prior offense otherwise admissible under Rule 404 could still be offered for the purposes sanctioned by that rule. Furthermore, the committee intends that notwithstanding this rule, a defendant's misrepresentation regarding the existence or nature of prior convictions may be met by rebuttal evidence, including the record of such prior convictions. Similarly, such records may be offered to rebut representations made by the defendant regarding his attitude toward or willingness to commit a general category of offense, although denials or other representations by the defendant regarding the specific conduct which forms the basis of the charge against him shall not make prior convictions admissible to rebut such statement.

In regard to either type of representation, of course, prior convictions may be offered in rebuttal only if the defendant's statement is made in response to defense counsel's questions or is made gratuitously in the course of cross-examination. Prior convictions may not be offered as rebuttal evidence if the prosecution has sought to circumvent the purpose of this rule by asking questions which elicit such representations from the defendant.

One other clarifying amendment has been added to this subsection, that is, to provide that the admissibility of evidence of a prior conviction is permitted only upon cross-examination of a witness. It is not admissible if a person does not testify. It is to be understood, however, that a court record of a prior conviction is admissible to prove that conviction if the witness has forgotten or denies its existence.

Note to Subdivision (b). Although convictions over ten years old generally do not have much probative value, there may be exceptional circumstances under which the conviction substantially bears on the credibility of the witness. Rather than exclude all convictions over 10 years old, the committee adopted an amendment in the form of a final clause to the section granting the court discretion to admit convictions over 10 years old, but only upon a determination by the court that the probative value of the conviction supported by specific facts and circumstances, substantially outweighs its prejudicial effect.

It is intended that convictions over 10 years old will be admitted very rarely and only in exceptional circumstances. The rules provide that the decision be supported by specific facts and circumstances thus requiring the court to make specific findings on the record as to the particular facts and circumstances it has considered in determining that the probative value of the conviction substantially outweighs its prejudicial impact. It is expected that, in fairness, the court will give the party against whom the conviction is introduced a full and adequate opportunity to contest its admission. Senate Report No. 93–1277.

Rule 609 defines when a party may use evidence of a prior conviction in order to impeach a witness. The Senate amendments make changes in two subsections of Rule 609.

Note to Subdivision (a). The House bill provides that the credibility of a witness can be attacked by proof of prior conviction of a crime only if the crime involves dishonesty or false statement. The Senate amendment provides that a witness' credibility may be attacked if the crime (1) was punishable by death or imprisonment in excess of one year under the law under which he was convicted or (2) involves dishonesty or false statement, regardless of the punishment.

The Conference adopts the Senate amendment with an amendment. The Conference amendment provides that the credibility of a witness, whether a defendant or someone else, may be attacked by proof of a prior conviction but only if the crime: (1) was punishable by death or imprisonment in excess of one year under the law under which he was convicted and the court determines that the probative value of the conviction outweighs its prejudicial effect to the defendant; or (2) in-

volved dishonesty or false statement regardless of the punishment.

By the phrase "dishonesty and false statement" the Conference means crimes such as perjury or subornation of perjury, false statement, criminal fraud, embezzlement, or false pretense, or any other offense in the nature of *crimen falsi*, the commission of which involves some element of deceit, untruthfulness, or falsification bearing on the accused's propensity to testify truthfully.

The admission of prior convictions involving dishonesty and false statement is not within the discretion of the Court. Such convictions are peculiarly probative of credibility and, under this rule, are always to be admitted. Thus, judicial discretion granted with respect to the admissibility of other prior convictions is not applicable to those involving dishonesty or false statement.

With regard to the discretionary standard established by paragraph (1) of Rule 609(a), the Conference determined that the prejudicial effect to be weighed against the probative value of the conviction is specifically the prejudicial effect *to the defendant*. The danger of prejudice to a witness other than the defendant (such as injury to the witness' reputation in his community) was considered and rejected by the Conference as an element to be weighed in determining admissibility. It was the judgment of the Conference that the danger of prejudice to a nondefendant witness is outweighed by the need for the trier of fact to have as much relevant evidence on the issue of credibility as possible. Such evidence should only be excluded where it presents a danger of improperly influencing the outcome of the trial by persuading the trier of fact to convict the defendant on the basis of his prior criminal record.

Note to Subdivision (b). The House bill provides in subsection (b) that evidence of conviction of a crime may not be used for impeachment purposes under subsection (a) if more than ten years have elapsed since the date of the conviction or the date the witness was released from confinement imposed for the conviction, whichever is later. The Senate amendment permits the use of convictions older than ten years, if the court determines, in the interests of justice, that the probative value of the conviction, supported by specific facts and circumstances, substantially outweighs its prejudicial effect.

The Conference adopts the Senate amendment with an amendment requiring notice by a party that he intends to request that the court allow him to use a conviction older than ten years. The Conferees anticipate that a written notice, in order to give the adversary a fair opportunity to contest the use of the evidence, will ordinarily include such information as the date of the conviction, the jurisdiction, and the offense or statute involved. In order to eliminate the possibility that the flexibility of this provision may impair the ability of a party-opponent to prepare for trial, the Conferees intend that the notice provision operate to avoid surprise. House Report No. 93–1597.

1987 Amendments

The amendments are technical. No substantive change is intended.

1990 Amendments

The amendment to Rule 609(a) makes two changes in the rule. The first change removes from the rule the limitation that the conviction may only be elicited during cross-examination, a limitation that virtually every circuit has found to be inapplicable. It is common for witnesses to reveal on direct examination their convictions to "remove the sting" of the impeachment. *See e.g., United States v. Bad Cob*, 560 F.2d 877 (8th Cir.1977). The amendment does not contemplate that a court will necessarily permit proof of prior convictions through testimony, which might be time-consuming and more prejudicial than proof through a written record. Rules 403 and 611(a) provide sufficient authority for the court to protect against unfair or disruptive methods of proof.

The second change effected by the amendment resolves an ambiguity as to the relationship of Rules 609 and 403 with respect to impeachment of witnesses other than the criminal defendant. *See, Green v. Bock Laundry Machine Co.*, 109 S.Ct. 1981, 490 U.S. 504 (1989). The amendment does not disturb the special balancing test for the criminal defendant who chooses to testify. Thus, the rule recognizes that, in virtually every case in which prior convictions are used to impeach the testifying defendant, the defendant faces a unique risk of prejudice—*i.e.*, the danger that convictions that would be excluded under Fed.R.Evid. 404 will be misused by a jury as propensity evidence despite their introduction solely for impeachment purposes. Although the rule does not forbid all use of convictions to impeach a defendant, it requires that the government show that the probative value of convictions as impeachment evidence outweighs their prejudicial effect.

Prior to the amendment, the rule appeared to give the defendant the benefit of the special balancing test when defense witnesses other than the defendant were called to testify. In practice, however, the concern about unfairness to the defendant is most acute when the defendant's own convictions are offered as evidence. Almost all of the decided cases concern this type of impeachment, and the amendment does not deprive the defendant of any meaningful protection, since Rule 403 now clearly protects against unfair impeachment of any defense witness other than the defendant. There are cases in which a defendant might be prejudiced when a defense witness is impeached. Such cases may arise, for example, when the witness bears a special relationship to the defendant such that the defendant is likely to suffer some spill-over effect from impeachment of the witness.

The amendment also protects other litigants from unfair impeachment of their witnesses. The danger of prejudice from the use of prior convictions is not confined to criminal defendants. Although the danger that prior convictions will be misused as character evidence is particularly acute when the defendant is impeached, the danger exists in other situations as well. The amendment reflects the view that it is desirable to protect all litigants from the unfair use of prior convictions, and that the ordinary balancing test of Rule 403, which provides that evidence shall not be excluded unless its prejudicial effect substantially outweighs its probative value, is appropriate for assessing the admissibility of prior convictions for impeachment of any witness other than a criminal defendant.

The amendment reflects a judgment that decisions interpreting Rule 609(a) as requiring a trial court to admit convictions in civil cases that have little, if anything, to do with credibility reach undesirable results. *See, e.g., Diggs v. Lyons*, 741 F.2d 577 (3d Cir.1984), *cert. denied*, 105 S.Ct. 2157 (1985). The amendment provides the same protection against unfair prejudice arising from prior convictions used for impeachment purposes as the rules provide for other evidence.

The amendment finds support in decided cases. *See, e.g., Petty v. Ideco*, 761 F.2d 1146 (5th Cir.1985); *Czaka v. Hickman*, 703 F.2d 317 (8th Cir.1983).

Fewer decided cases address the question whether Rule 609(a) provides any protection against unduly prejudicial prior convictions used to impeach government witnesses. Some courts have read Rule 609(a) as giving the government no protection for its witnesses. *See, e.g., United States v. Thorne*, 547 F.2d 56 (8th Cir.1976); *United States v. Nevitt*, 563 F.2d 406 (9th Cir.1977), *cert. denied*, 444 U.S. 847 (1979). This approach also is rejected by the amendment. There are cases in which impeachment of government witnesses with prior convictions that have little, if anything, to do with credibility may result in unfair prejudice to the government's interest in a fair trial and unnecessary embarrassment to a witness. Fed.R.Evid. 412 already recognizes this and excluded certain evidence of past sexual behavior in the context of prosecutions for sexual assaults.

The amendment applies the general balancing test of Rule 403 to protect all litigants against unfair impeachment of witnesses. The balancing test protects civil litigants, the government in criminal cases, and the defendant in a criminal case who calls other witnesses. The amendment addresses prior convictions offered under Rule 609, not for other purposes, and does not run afoul, therefore, of *Davis v. Alaska*, 415 U.S. 308 (1974). *Davis* involved the use of a prior juvenile adjudication not to prove a past law violation, but to prove bias. The defendant in a criminal case has the right to demonstrate the bias of a witness and to be assured a fair trial, but not to unduly prejudice a trier of fact. *See generally* Rule 412. In any case in which the trial court believes that confrontation rights require admission of impeachment evidence, obviously the Constitution would take precedence over the rule.

The probability that prior convictions of an ordinary government witness will be unduly prejudicial is low in most criminal cases. Since the behavior of the witness is not the issue in dispute in most cases, there is little chance that the trier of fact will misuse the convictions offered as impeachment evidence as propensity evidence. Thus, trial courts will be skeptical when the government objects to impeachment of its witnesses with prior convictions. Only when the government is able to point to a real danger of prejudice that is sufficient to outweigh substantially the probative value of the conviction for impeachment purposes will the conviction be excluded.

The amendment continues to divide subdivision (a) into subsections (1) and (2) thus facilitating retrieval under current computerized research programs which distinguish the two provisions. The Committee recommended no substantive change in subdivision (a)(2), even though some cases raise a concern about the proper interpretation of the words "dishonesty or false statement." These words were used but not explained in the original Advisory Committee Note accompanying Rule 609. Congress extensively debated the rule, and the Report of the House and Senate Conference Committee states that "[b]y the phrase 'dishonesty and false statement,' the Conference means crimes such as perjury, subornation of perjury, false statement, criminal fraud, embezzlement, or false pretense, or any other offense in the nature of *crimen falsi*, commission of which involves some element of deceit, untruthfulness, or falsification bearing on the accused's propensity to testify truthfully." The Advisory Committee concluded that the Conference Report provides sufficient guidance to trial courts and that no amendment is necessary, notwithstanding some decisions that take an unduly broad view of "dishonesty," admitting convictions such as for bank robbery or bank larceny. Subsection (a)(2) continues to apply to any witness, including a criminal defendant.

Finally, the Committee determined that it was unnecessary to add to the rule language stating that, when a prior conviction is offered under Rule 609, the trial court is to consider the probative value of the prior conviction *for impeachment*, not for other purposes. The Committee concluded that the title of the rule, its first sentence, and its placement among the impeachment rules clearly establish that evidence offered under Rule 609 is offered only for purposes of impeachment.

2006 Amendments

The amendment provides that Rule 609(a)(2) mandates the admission of evidence of a conviction only when the conviction required the proof of (or in the case of a guilty plea, the admission of) an act of dishonesty or false statement. Evidence of all other convictions is inadmissible under this subsection, irrespective of whether the witness exhibited dishonesty or made a false statement in the process of the commission of the crime of conviction. Thus, evidence that a witness was convicted for a crime of violence, such as murder, is not admissible under Rule 609(a)(2), even if the witness acted deceitfully in the course of committing the crime.

The amendment is meant to give effect to the legislative intent to limit the convictions that are to be automatically admitted under subdivision (a)(2). The Conference Committee provided that by "dishonesty and false statement" it meant "crimes such as perjury, subornation of perjury, false statement, criminal fraud, embezzlement, or false pretense, or any other offense in the nature of *crimen falsi*, the commission of which involves some element of deceit, untruthfulness, or falsification bearing on the [witness's] propensity to testify truthfully." Historically, offenses classified as *crimina falsi* have included only those crimes in which the ultimate criminal act was itself an act of deceit. *See* Green, *Deceit and the Classification of Crimes: Federal Rule of Evidence 609(a)(2) and the Origins of* Crimen Falsi, 90 J. Crim. L. & Criminology 1087 (2000).

Evidence of crimes in the nature of *crimina falsi* must be admitted under Rule 609(a)(2), regardless of how such crimes are specifically charged. For example, evidence that a witness was convicted of making a false claim to a federal agent is admissible under this subdivision regardless of whether the crime was charged under a section that expressly references deceit (e.g., 18 U.S.C. § 1001, Material Misrepresentation to the Federal Government) or a section that does not (*e.g.*, 18 U.S.C. § 1503, Obstruction of Justice).

The amendment requires that the proponent have ready proof that the conviction required the factfinder to find, or the defendant to admit, an act of dishonesty or false statement. Ordinarily, the statutory elements of the crime will indicate whether it is one of dishonesty or false statement. Where the deceitful nature of the crime is not apparent from the statute and the face of the judgment — as, for example, where the conviction simply records a finding of guilt for a statutory offense that does not reference deceit expressly — a proponent may offer information such as an indictment, a statement of admitted facts, or jury instructions to show that the factfinder had to find, or the defendant had to admit, an act of dishonesty or false statement in order for the witness to have been convicted. *Cf. Taylor v. United States*, 495 U.S. 575, 602 (1990) (providing that a trial court may look to a charging instrument or jury instructions to ascertain the nature of a prior offense where the statute is insufficiently clear on its face); *Shepard v. United States*, 125 S.Ct. 1254 (2005) (the inquiry to determine whether a guilty plea to a crime defined by a nongeneric statute necessarily admitted elements of the generic offense was limited to the charging document's terms, the terms of a plea agreement or transcript of colloquy between judge and defendant in which the factual basis for the plea was confirmed by the defendant, or a comparable judicial record). But the amendment does not contemplate a "mini-trial" in which the court plumbs the record of the previous proceeding to determine whether the crime was in the nature of *crimen falsi*.

The amendment also substitutes the term "character for truthfulness" for the term "credibility" in the first sentence of the Rule. The limitations of Rule 609 are not applicable if a conviction is admitted for a purpose other than to prove the witness's character for untruthfulness. *See, e.g., United States v. Lopez*, 979 F.2d 1024 (5th Cir. 1992) (Rule 609 was not applicable where the conviction was offered for purposes of contradiction). The use of the term "credibility" in subdivision (d) is retained, however, as that subdivision is intended to govern the use of a juvenile adjudication for any type of impeachment.

2011 Amendments

The language of Rule 609 has been amended as part of the restyling of the Evidence Rules to make them more easily understood and to make style and terminology consistent throughout the rules. These changes are intended to be stylistic only. There is no intent to change any result in any ruling on evidence admissibility.

CROSS REFERENCES

Character evidence, inadmissibility to prove conduct, see Fed.Rules Evid. Rule 404, 28 USCA.

Laws of states adopted for areas within Federal jurisdiction, see 18 USCA § 13.

Rule 610. Religious Beliefs or Opinions

Evidence of a witness's religious beliefs or opinions is not admissible to attack or support the witness's credibility.

(Pub.L. 93–595, § 1, Jan. 2, 1975, 88 Stat.1936; Mar. 2, 1987, eff. Oct. 1, 1987; Apr. 26, 2011, eff. Dec. 1, 2011.)

ADVISORY COMMITTEE NOTES

1972 Proposed Rules

While the rule forecloses inquiry into the religious beliefs or opinions of a witness for the purpose of showing that his character for truthfulness is affected by their nature, an inquiry for the purpose of showing interest or bias because of them is not within the prohibition. Thus disclosure of affiliation with a church which is a party to the litigation would be allowable under the rule. *Cf.* Tucker v. Reil, 51 Ariz. 357, 77 P.2d 203 (1938). To the same effect, though less specifically worded, is California Evidence Code § 789. See 3 Wigmore § 936.

1987 Amendments

The amendment is technical. No substantive change is intended.

2011 Amendments

The language of Rule 610 has been amended as part of the restyling of the Evidence Rules to make them more easily understood and to make style and terminology consistent throughout the rules. These changes are intended to be stylistic only. There is no intent to change any result in any ruling on evidence admissibility.

Rule 611. Mode and Order of Examining Witnesses and Presenting Evidence

(a) Control by the Court; Purposes. The court should exercise reasonable control over the mode and order of examining witnesses and presenting evidence so as to:

(1) make those procedures effective for determining the truth;

(2) avoid wasting time; and

(3) protect witnesses from harassment or undue embarrassment.

(b) Scope of Cross–Examination. Cross-examination should not go beyond the subject matter of the direct examination and matters affecting the witness's credibility. The court may allow inquiry into additional matters as if on direct examination.

(c) Leading Questions. Leading questions should not be used on direct examination except as necessary to develop the witness's testimony. Ordinarily, the court should allow leading questions:

(1) on cross-examination; and

(2) when a party calls a hostile witness, an adverse party, or a witness identified with an adverse party.

(Pub.L. 93–595, § 1, Jan. 2, 1975, 88 Stat. 1936; Mar. 2, 1987, eff. Oct. 1, 1987; Apr. 26, 2011, eff. Dec. 1, 2011.)

ADVISORY COMMITTEE NOTES

1972 Proposed Rules

Note to Subdivision (a). Spelling out detailed rules to govern the mode and order of interrogating witnesses and presenting evidence is neither desirable nor feasible. The ultimate responsibility for the effective working of the adversary system rests with the judge. The rule sets forth the objectives which he should seek to attain.

Item (1) restates in broad terms the power and obligation of the judge as developed under common law principles. It covers such concerns as whether testimony shall be in the form of a free narrative or responses to specific questions, McCormick § 5, the order of calling witnesses and presenting evidence, 6 Wigmore § 1867, the use of demonstrative evidence, McCormick § 179, and the many other questions arising during the course of a trial which can be solved only by the judge's common sense and fairness in view of the particular circumstances.

Item (2) is addressed to avoidance of needless consumption of time, a matter of daily concern in the disposition of cases. A companion piece is found in the discretion vested in the judge to exclude evidence as a waste of time in Rule 403(b).

Item (3) calls for a judgment under the particular circumstances whether interrogation tactics entail harassment or undue embarrassment. Pertinent circumstances include the importance of the testimony, the nature of the inquiry, its relevance to credibility, waste of time, and confusion. McCormick § 42. In *Alford v. United States*, 282 U.S. 687, 694, 51 S.Ct. 218, 75 L.Ed. 624 (1931), the Court pointed out that, while the trial judge should protect the witness from questions which "go beyond the bounds of proper cross-examination merely to harass, annoy or humiliate," this protection by no means forecloses efforts to discredit the witness. Reference to the transcript of the prosecutor's cross-examination in *Berger v. United States*, 295 U.S. 78, 55 S.Ct. 629, 79 L.Ed. 1314 (1935), serves to lay at rest any doubts as to the need for judicial control in this area.

The inquiry into specific instances of conduct of a witness allowed under Rule 608(b) is, of course, subject to this rule.

Note to Subdivision (b). The tradition in the federal courts and in numerous state courts has been to limit the scope of cross-examination to matters testified to on direct, plus matters bearing upon the credibility of the witness. Various reasons have been advanced to justify the rule of limited cross-examination. (1) A party vouches for his own witness but only to the extent of matters elicited on direct. *Resurrection Gold Mining Co. v. Fortune Gold Mining Co.*, 129 F. 668, 675 (8th Cir.1904), quoted in Maguire, Weinstein, et al., Cases on Evidence 277, n. 38 (5th ed. 1965). But the concept of vouching is discredited, and Rule 607 rejects it. (2) A party cannot ask his own witness leading questions. This is a problem properly solved in terms of what is necessary for a proper development of the testimony rather than by a mechanistic formula similar to the vouching concept. See discussion under subdivision (c). (3) A practice of limited cross-examination promotes orderly presentation of the case. *Finch v. Weiner*, 109 Conn. 616, 145 A. 31 (1929). While this latter reason has merit, the matter is essentially one of the order of presentation and not one in which involvement at the appellate level is likely to prove fruitful. See, for example, *Moyer v. Aetna Life Ins. Co.*, 126 F.2d 141 (3rd Cir.1942); *Butler v. New York Central R. Co.*, 253 F.2d 281 (7th Cir. 1958); *United States v. Johnson*, 285 F.2d 35 (9th Cir.1960); *Union Automobile Indemnity Ass'n v. Capitol Indemnity Ins. Co.*, 310 F.2d 318 (7th Cir.1962). In evaluating these considerations, McCormick says:

"The foregoing considerations favoring the wide-open or restrictive rules may well be thought to be fairly evenly balanced. There is another factor, however, which seems to swing the balance overwhelmingly in favor of the wide-open rule. This is the consideration of economy of time and energy. Obviously, the wide-open rule presents little or no opportunity for dispute in its application. The restrictive practice in all its forms, on the other hand, is productive in many court rooms, of continual bickering over the choice of the numerous variations of the 'scope of the direct' criterion, and of their application to particular cross-questions. These controversies are often reventilated on appeal, and reversals for error in their determination are frequent. Observance of these vague and ambiguous restrictions is a matter of constant and hampering concern to the cross-examiner. If these efforts, delays and misprisions were the necessary incidents to the guarding of substantive rights or the fundamentals of fair trial, they might be worth the cost. As the price of the choice of an obviously debatable regulation of the order of evidence, the sacrifice seems misguided. The American Bar Association's Committee for the Improvement of the Law of Evidence for the year 1937–38 said this:

'The rule limiting cross-examination to the precise subject of the direct examination is probably the most frequent rule (except the Opinion rule) leading in the trial practice today to refined and technical quibbles which obstruct the progress of the trial, confuse the jury, and give rise to appeal on technical grounds only. Some of the instances in which Supreme Courts have ordered new trials for the mere transgression of this rule about the order of evidence have been astounding.

'We recommend that the rule allowing questions upon any part of the issue known to the witness * * * be adopted. * * *' " McCormick, § 27, p. 51. See also 5 Moore's Federal Practice ¶ 43.10 (2nd ed. 1964).

The provision of the second sentence, that the judge may in the interests of justice limit inquiry into new matters on cross-examination, is designed for those situations in which the result otherwise would be confusion, complication, or protraction of the case, not as a matter of rule but as demonstrable in the actual development of the particular case.

The rule does not purport to determine the extent to which an accused who elects to testify thereby waives his privilege against self-incrimination. The question is a constitutional one, rather than a mere matter of administering the trial. Under *Simmons v. United States*, 390 U.S. 377, 88 S.Ct. 967, 19 L.Ed.2d 1247 (1968), no general waiver occurs when the accused testifies on such preliminary matters as the validity of a search and seizure or the admissibility of a confession. Rule 104(d), *supra*. When he testifies on the merits, however, can he foreclose inquiry into an aspect or element of the crime by avoiding it on direct? The affirmative answer given in *Tucker v. United States*, 5 F.2d 818 (8th Cir.1925), is inconsistent with the description of the waiver as extending to "all other relevant facts" in *Johnson v. United States*, 318 U.S. 189, 195, 63 S.Ct. 549, 87 L.Ed. 704 (1943). See also *Brown v. United States*, 356 U.S. 148, 78 S.Ct. 622, 2 L.Ed.2d 589 (1958). The situation of an accused who desires to testify on some but not all counts of a multiple-count indictment is one to be approached, in the first instance at least, as a problem of severance under Rule 14 of the Federal Rules of Criminal Procedure. *Cross v. United States*, 118 U.S.App.D.C. 324, 335 F.2d 987 (1964). Cf. *United States v. Baker*, 262 F.Supp. 657, 686 (D.D.C.1966). In all events, the extent of the waiver of the privilege against self-incrimination ought not to be determined as a by-product of a rule on scope of cross-examination.

Note to Subdivision (c). The rule continues the traditional view that the suggestive powers of the leading question are as a general proposition undesirable. Within this tradition, however, numerous exceptions have achieved recognition: The witness who is hostile, unwilling, or biased; the child witness or the adult with communication problems; the witness whose recollection is exhausted; and undisputed preliminary matters. 3 Wigmore §§ 774–778. An almost total unwillingness to reverse for infractions has been manifested by appellate courts. See cases cited in 3 Wigmore § 770. The matter clearly falls within the area of control by the judge over the mode and order of interrogation and presentation and accordingly is phrased in words of suggestion rather than command.

The rule also conforms to tradition in making the use of leading questions on cross-examination a matter of right. The purpose of the qualification "ordinarily" is to furnish a basis for denying the use of leading questions when the cross-examination is cross-examination in form only and not in fact, as for example the "cross-examination" of a party by his own counsel after being called by the opponent (savoring more of re-direct) or of an insured defendant who proves to be friendly to the plaintiff.

The final sentence deals with categories of witnesses automatically regarded and treated as hostile. Rule 43(b) of the Federal Rules of Civil Procedure has included only "an adverse party or an officer, director, or managing agent of a public or private corporation or of a partnership or association which is an adverse party." This limitation virtually to persons whose statements would stand as admissions is believed to be an unduly narrow concept of those who may safely be regarded as hostile without further demonstration. See, for example, *Maryland Casualty Co. v. Kador*, 225 F.2d 120 (5th Cir.1955), and *Degelos v. Fidelity and Casualty Co.*, 313 F.2d 809 (5th Cir.1963), holding despite the language of Rule 43(b) that an insured fell within it, though not a party in an action under the Louisiana direct action statute. The phrase of the rule, "witness identified with" an adverse party, is designed to enlarge the category of persons thus callable.

1974 Enactment

Note to Subdivision (b). As submitted by the Court, Rule 611(b) provided:

A witness may be cross-examined on any matter relevant to any issue in the case, including credibility. In the interests of justice, the judge may limit cross-examination with respect to matters not testified to on direct examination.

The Committee amended this provision to return to the rule which prevails in the federal courts and thirty-nine State jurisdictions. As amended, the Rule is in the text of the 1969 Advisory Committee draft. It limits cross-examination to credibility and to matters testified to on direct examination, unless the judge permits more, in which event the cross-examiner must proceed as if on direct examination. This traditional rule facilitates orderly presentation by each party at trial. Further, in light of existing discovery procedures, there appears to be no need to abandon the traditional rule.

Note to Subdivision (c). The third sentence of Rule 611(c) as submitted by the Court provided that:

In civil cases, a party is entitled to call an adverse party or witness identified with him and interrogate by leading questions.

The Committee amended this Rule to permit leading questions to be used with respect to any hostile witness, not only an adverse party or person identified with such adverse party. The Committee also substituted the word "When" for the phrase "In civil cases" to reflect the possibility that in criminal cases a defendant may be entitled to call witnesses identified with the government, in which event the Committee believed the defendant should be permitted to inquire with leading questions. House Report No. 93–650.

Note to Subdivision (b). Rule 611(b) as submitted by the Supreme Court permitted a broad scope of cross-examination: "cross-examination on any matter relevant to any issue in the case" unless the judge, in the interests of justice, limited the scope of cross-examination.

The House narrowed the Rule to the more traditional practice of limiting cross-examination to the subject matter of direct examination (and credibility), but with discretion in the judge to permit inquiry into additional matters in situations where that would aid in the development of the evidence or otherwise facilitate the conduct of the trial.

The committee agrees with the House amendment. Although there are good arguments in support of broad cross-examination from perspectives of developing all relevant evidence, we believe the factors of insuring an orderly and predictable development of the evidence weigh in favor of the narrower rule, especially when discretion is given to the trial judge to permit inquiry into additional matters. The committee expressly approves this discretion and believes it will permit sufficient flexibility allowing a broader scope of cross-examination whenever appropriate.

The House amendment providing broader discretionary cross-examination permitted inquiry into additional matters only as if on direct examination. As a general rule, we concur with this limitation, however, we would understand that this limitation would not preclude the utilization of leading questions if the conditions of subsection (c) of this rule were met, bearing in mind the judge's discretion in any case to limit the scope of cross-examination [see McCormick on Evidence, §§ 24–26 (especially 24) (2d ed. 1972)].

Further, the committee has received correspondence from Federal judges commenting on the applicability of this rule to section 1407 of title 28. It is the committee's judgment that this rule as reported by the House is flexible enough to provide sufficiently broad cross-examination in appropriate situations in multidistrict litigation.

Note to Subdivision (c). As submitted by the Supreme Court, the rule provided: "In civil cases, a party is entitled to call an adverse party or witness identified with him and interrogate by leading questions."

The final sentence of subsection (c) was amended by the House for the purpose of clarifying the fact that a "hostile witness"—that is a witness who is hostile in fact—could be subject to interrogation by leading questions. The rule as submitted by the Supreme Court declared certain witnesses hostile as a matter of law and thus subject to interrogation by leading questions without any showing of hostility in fact. These were adverse parties or witnesses identified with adverse parties. However, the wording of the first sentence of subsection (c) while generally prohibiting the use of leading questions on direct examination, also provides "except as may be necessary to develop his testimony." Further, the first paragraph of the Advisory Committee note explaining the subsection makes clear that they intended that leading questions could be asked of a hostile witness or a witness who was unwilling or biased and even though that witness was not associated with an adverse party. Thus, we question whether the House amendment was necessary.

However, concluding that it was not intended to affect the meaning of the first sentence of the subsection and was intended solely to clarify the fact that leading questions are permissible in the interrogation of a witness, who is hostile in fact, the committee accepts that House amendment.

The final sentence of this subsection was also amended by the House to cover criminal as well as civil cases. The committee accepts this amendment, but notes that it may be difficult in criminal cases to determine when a witness is "identified with an adverse party," and thus the rule should be applied with caution. Senate Report No. 93–1277.

1987 Amendments

The amendment is technical. No substantive change is intended.

2011 Amendments

The language of Rule 611 has been amended as part of the restyling of the Evidence Rules to make them more easily understood and to make style and terminology consistent throughout the rules. These changes are intended to be stylistic only. There is no intent to change any result in any ruling on evidence admissibility.

CROSS REFERENCES

Cross-examination, right of, see USCA Const. Amend. VI.

Indictment, jury list, and list of witnesses furnished prisoner in capital cases, see 18 USCA § 3432.

Prejudice, confusion, or waste of time, exclusion of evidence for, see Fed.Rules Evid. Rule 403, 28 USCA.

Self-incrimination, protection against, see USCA Const. Amend. V.

Testimony by accused on preliminary matter, scope of cross-examination, see Fed.Rules Evid. Rule 104, 28 USCA.

Rule 612.   Writing Used to Refresh a Witness's Memory

(a) Scope. This rule gives an adverse party certain options when a witness uses a writing to refresh memory:

    (1) while testifying; or

    (2) before testifying, if the court decides that justice requires the party to have those options.

(b) Adverse Party's Options; Deleting Unrelated Matter. Unless 18 U.S.C. § 3500 provides otherwise in a criminal case, an adverse party is entitled to have the writing produced at the hearing, to inspect it, to cross-examine the witness about it, and to introduce in evidence any portion that relates to the witness's testimony. If the producing party claims that the writing includes unrelated matter, the court must examine the writing in camera, delete any unrelated portion, and order that the rest be delivered to the adverse party. Any portion deleted over objection must be preserved for the record.

(c) Failure to Produce or Deliver the Writing. If a writing is not produced or is not delivered as ordered, the court may issue any appropriate order. But if the prosecution does not comply in a criminal case, the court must strike the witness's testimony or—if justice so requires—declare a mistrial.

(Pub.L. 93–595, § 1, Jan. 2, 1975, 88 Stat. 1936; Mar. 2, 1987, eff. Oct. 1, 1987; Apr. 26, 2011, eff. Dec. 1, 2011.)

ADVISORY COMMITTEE NOTES
1972 Proposed Rules

The treatment of writings used to refresh recollection while on the stand is in accord with settled doctrine. McCormick

§ 9, p. 15. The bulk of the case law has, however, denied the existence of any right to access by the opponent when the writing is used prior to taking the stand, though the judge may have discretion in the matter. *Goldman v. United States*, 316 U.S. 129, 62 S.Ct. 993, 86 L.Ed. 1322 (1942); *Needelman v. United States*, 261 F.2d 802 (5th Cir.1958), cert. dismissed 362 U.S. 600, 80 S.Ct. 960, 4 L.Ed.2d 980, rehearing denied 363 U.S. 858, 80 S.Ct. 1606, 4 L.Ed.2d 1739, Annot., 82 A.L.R.2d 473, 562 and 7 A.L.R.3d 181, 247. An increasing group of cases has repudiated the distinction. *People v. Scott*, 29 Ill.2d 97, 193 N.E.2d 814 (1963); *State v. Mucci*, 25 N.J. 423, 136 A.2d 761 (1957); *State v. Hunt*, 25 N.J. 514, 138 A.2d 1 (1958); *State v. Deslovers*, 40 R.I. 89, 100 A. 64 (1917), and this position is believed to be correct. As Wigmore put it, "the risk of imposition and the need of safeguard is just as great" in both situations. 3 Wigmore § 762, p. 111. To the same effect is McCormick, § 9, p. 17.

The purpose of the phrase "for the purpose of testifying" is to safeguard against using the rule as a pretext for wholesale exploration of an opposing party's files and to insure that access is limited only to those writings which may fairly be said in fact to have an impact upon the testimony of the witness.

The purpose of the rule is the same as that of the *Jencks* statute, 18 U.S.C. § 3500: to promote the search of credibility and memory. The same sensitivity to disclosure of government files may be involved; hence the rule is expressly made subject to the statute, subdivision (a) of which provides: "In any criminal prosecution brought by the United States, no statement or report in the possession of the United States which was made by a Government witness or prospective Government witness (other than the defendant) shall be the subject of subpena, discovery, or inspection until said witness has testified on direct examination in the trial of the case." Items falling within the purview of the statute are producible only as provided by its terms, *Palermo v. United States*, 360 U.S. 343, 351 (1959), and disclosure under the rule is limited similarly by the statutory conditions. With this limitation in mind, some differences of application may be noted. The *Jencks* statute applies only to statements of witnesses; the rule is not so limited. The statute applies only to criminal cases; the rule applies to all cases. The statute applies only to government witnesses; the rule applies to all witnesses. The statute contains no requirement that the statement be consulted for purposes of refreshment before or while testifying; the rule so requires. Since many writings would qualify under either statute or rule, a substantial overlap exists, but the identity of procedures makes this of no importance.

The consequences of nonproduction by the government in a criminal case are those of the *Jencks* statute, striking the testimony or in exceptional cases a mistrial. 18 U.S.C. § 3500(d). In other cases these alternatives are unduly limited, and such possibilities as contempt, dismissal, finding issues against the offender, and the like are available. See Rule 16(g) of the Federal Rules of Criminal Procedure and Rule 37(b) of the Federal Rules of Civil Procedure for appropriate sanctions.

1974 Enactment

As submitted to Congress, Rule 612 provided that except as set forth in 18 U.S.C. 3500, if a witness uses a writing to refresh his memory for the purpose of testifying, "either before or while testifying," an adverse party is entitled to have the writing produced at the hearing, to inspect it, to cross-examine the witness on it, and to introduce in evidence those portions relating to the witness' testimony. The Committee amended the Rule so as still to require the production of writings used by a witness while testifying, but to render the production of writings used by a witness to refresh his memory before testifying discretionary with the court in the interests of justice, as is the case under existing federal law. See Goldman v. United States, 316 U.S. 129 (1942). The Committee considered that permitting an adverse party to require the production of writings used before testifying could result in fishing expeditions among a multitude of papers which a witness may have used in preparing for trial.

The Committee intends that nothing in the Rule be construed as barring the assertion of a privilege with respect to writings used by a witness to refresh his memory. House Report No. 93–650.

1987 Amendments

The amendment is technical. No substantive change is intended.

2011 Amendments

The language of Rule 612 has been amended as part of the restyling of the Evidence Rules to make them more easily understood and to make style and terminology consistent throughout the rules. These changes are intended to be stylistic only. There is no intent to change any result in any ruling on evidence admissibility.

CROSS REFERENCES

Confrontation with, and cross-examination of, witnesses, see USCA Const. Amend. VI.

Discovery and inspection of statements and reports, failure to comply with order, see Fed.Rules Cr.Proc. Rule 16, 18 USCA.

Refusal to make discovery or comply with order, see Fed. Rules Civ.Proc. Rule 37, 28 USCA.

Rule 613. Witness's Prior Statement

(a) Showing or Disclosing the Statement During Examination. When examining a witness about the witness's prior statement, a party need not show it or disclose its contents to the witness. But the party must, on request, show it or disclose its contents to an adverse party's attorney.

(b) Extrinsic Evidence of a Prior Inconsistent Statement. Extrinsic evidence of a witness's prior inconsistent statement is admissible only if the witness is given an opportunity to explain or deny the statement and an adverse party is given an opportunity to examine the witness about it, or if justice so requires. This subdivision (b) does not apply to an opposing party's statement under Rule 801(d)(2).

(Pub.L. 93–595, § 1, Jan. 2, 1975, 88 Stat.1936; Mar. 2, 1987, eff. Oct. 1, 1987; Apr. 25, 1988, eff. Nov. 1, 1988; Apr. 26, 2011, eff. Dec. 1, 2011.)

ADVISORY COMMITTEE NOTES

1972 Proposed Rules

Note to Subdivision (a). The Queen's Case, 2 Br. & B. 284, 129 Eng.Rep. 976 (1820), laid down the requirement that a cross-examiner, prior to questioning the witness about his own prior statement in writing, must first show it to the witness. Abolished by statute in the country of its origin, the requirement nevertheless gained currency in the United States. The rule abolishes this useless impediment, to cross-examination. Ladd, Some Observations on Credibility: Impeachment of Witnesses, 52 Cornell L.Q. 239, 246–247 (1967); McCormick § 28; 4 Wigmore §§ 1259–1260. Both oral and written statements are included.

The provision for disclosure to counsel is designed to protect against unwarranted insinuations that a statement has been made when the fact is to the contrary.

The rule does not defeat the application of Rule 1002 relating to production of the original when the contents of a writing are sought to be proved. Nor does it defeat the application of Rule 26(b)(3) of the Rules of Civil Procedure, as revised, entitling a person on request to a copy of his own statement, though the operation of the latter may be suspended temporarily.

Note to Subdivision (b). The familiar foundation requirement that an impeaching statement first be shown to the witness before it can be proved by extrinsic evidence is preserved but with some modifications. See Ladd, Some Observations on Credibility: Impeachment of Witnesses, 52 Cornell L.Q. 239, 247 (1967). The traditional insistence that the attendance of the witness be directed to the statement on cross-examination is relaxed in favor of simply providing the witness an opportunity to explain and the opposite party an opportunity to examine on the statement, with no specification of any particular time or sequence. Under this procedure, several collusive witnesses can be examined before disclosure of a joint prior inconsistent statement. See Comment to California Evidence Code § 770. Also, dangers of oversight are reduced. See McCormick § 37, p. 68.

In order to allow for such eventualities as the witness becoming unavailable by the time the statement is discovered, a measure of discretion is conferred upon the judge. Similar provisions are found in California Evidence Code § 770 and New Jersey Evidence Rule 22(b).

Under principles of *expression unius* the rule does not apply to impeachment by evidence of prior inconsistent conduct. The use of inconsistent statements to impeach a hearsay declaration is treated in Rule 806.

1987 Amendments

The amendments are technical. No substantive change is intended.

1988 Amendments

The amendment is technical. No substantive change is intended.

2011 Amendments

The language of Rule 613 has been amended as part of the restyling of the Evidence Rules to make them more easily understood and to make style and terminology consistent throughout the rules. These changes are intended to be stylistic only. There is no intent to change any result in any ruling on evidence admissibility.

CROSS REFERENCES

Attacking and supporting credibility of declarant, see Fed. Rules Evid. Rule 806, 28 USCA.

Contents of writings, recordings, and photographs, original required to prove, see Fed.Rules Evid. Rule 1004, 28 USCA.

Depositions and discovery, trial preparation, see Fed.Rules Civ.Proc. Rule 26, 28 USCA.

Rule 614.   Court's Calling or Examining a Witness

(a) Calling. The court may call a witness on its own or at a party's request. Each party is entitled to cross-examine the witness.

(b) Examining. The court may examine a witness regardless of who calls the witness.

(c) Objections. A party may object to the court's calling or examining a witness either at that time or at the next opportunity when the jury is not present. (Pub.L. 93–595, § 1, Jan. 2, 1975, 88 Stat.1937; Apr. 26, 2011, eff. Dec. 1, 2011.)

ADVISORY COMMITTEE NOTES

1972 Proposed Rules

Note to Subdivision (a). While exercised more frequently in criminal than in civil cases, the authority of the judge to call witnesses is well established. McCormick § 8, p. 14; Maguire, Weinstein, et al., Cases on Evidence 303–304 (5th ed. 1965); 9 Wigmore § 2484. One reason for the practice, the old rule against impeaching one's own witness, no longer exists by virtue of Rule 607, *supra*. Other reasons remain, however, to justify the continuation of the practice of calling court's witnesses. The right to cross-examine, with all it implies, is assured. The tendency of juries to associate a witness with the party calling him, regardless of technical aspects of vouching, is avoided. And the judge is not imprisoned within the case as made by the parties.

Note to Subdivision (b). The authority of the judge to question witnesses is also well established. McCormick § 8, pp. 12–13; Maguire, Weinstein, et al., Cases on Evidence 737–739 (5th ed. 1965); 3 Wigmore § 784. The authority is, of course, abused when the judge abandons his proper role and assumes that of advocate, but the manner in which interrogation should be conducted and the proper extent of its exercise are not susceptible of formulation in a rule. The omission in no sense precludes courts of review from continuing to reverse for abuse.

Note to Subdivision (c). The provision relating to objections is designed to relieve counsel of the embarrassment attendant upon objecting to questions by the judge in the presence of the jury, while at the same time assuring that objections are made in apt time to afford the opportunity to take possible corrective measures. Compare the "automatic" objection feature of Rule 605 when the judge is called as a witness.

2011 Amendments

The language of Rule 614 has been amended as part of the restyling of the Evidence Rules to make them more easily understood and to make style and terminology consistent throughout the rules. These changes are intended to be stylistic only. There is no intent to change any result in any ruling on evidence admissibility.

CROSS REFERENCES

Confrontation with, and cross-examination of, witnesses, see USCA Const. Amend. VI.

Contempt for failure of subpoenaed foreigner to appear, see 28 USCA § 1784.

Subpoena of foreigners or foreign documents, see 28 USCA § 1783.

Rule 615. Excluding Witnesses

At a party's request, the court must order witnesses excluded so that they cannot hear other witnesses' testimony. Or the court may do so on its own. But this rule does not authorize excluding:

(a) a party who is a natural person;

(b) an officer or employee of a party that is not a natural person, after being designated as the party's representative by its attorney;

(c) a person whose presence a party shows to be essential to presenting the party's claim or defense; or

(d) a person authorized by statute to be present.
(Pub.L. 93–595, § 1, Jan. 2, 1975, 88 Stat.1937; Mar. 2, 1987, eff. Oct. 1, 1987; Apr. 25, 1988, eff. Nov. 1, 1988; Pub.L. 100–690, Nov. 18, 1988, Title VII, § 7075(a), 102 Stat. 4405; Apr. 24, 1998, eff. Dec. 1, 1998; Apr. 26, 2011, eff. Dec. 1, 2011.)

ADVISORY COMMITTEE NOTES

1972 Proposed Rules

The efficacy of excluding or sequestering witnesses has long been recognized as a means of discouraging and exposing fabrication, inaccuracy, and collusion. 6 Wigmore §§ 1837–1838. The authority of the judge is admitted, the only question being whether the matter is committed to his discretion or one of right. The rule takes the latter position. No time is specified for making the request.

Several categories of persons are excepted. (1) Exclusion of persons who are parties would raise serious problems of confrontation and due process. Under accepted practice they are not subject to exclusion. 6 Wigmore § 1841. (2) As the equivalent of the right of a natural-person party to be present, a party which is not a natural person is entitled to have a representative present. Most of the cases have involved allowing a police officer who has been in charge of an investigation to remain in court despite the fact that he will be a witness. United States v. Infanzon, 235 F.2d 318, (2d Cir. 1956); *Portomene v. United States,* 221 F.2d 582 (5th Cir. 1955); *Powell v. United States,* 208 F.2d 618 (6th Cir.1953); *Jones v. United States,* 252 F.Supp. 781 (W.D.Okl.1966). Designation of the representative by the attorney rather than by the client may at first glance appear to be an inversion of the attorney-client relationship, but it may be assumed that the attorney will follow the wishes of the client, and the

solution is simple and workable. See California Evidence Code § 777. (3) The category contemplates such persons as an agent who handled the transaction being litigated or an expert needed to advise counsel in the management of the litigation. See 6 Wigmore § 1841, n. 4.

1974 Enactment

Many district courts permit government counsel to have an investigative agent at counsel table throughout the trial although the agent is or may be a witness. The practice is permitted as an exception to the rule of exclusion and compares with the situation defense counsel finds himself in—he always has the client with him to consult during the trial. The investigative agent's presence may be extremely important to government counsel, especially when the case is complex or involves some specialized subject matter. The agent, too, having lived with the case for a long time, may be able to assist in meeting trial surprises where the best-prepared counsel would otherwise have difficulty. Yet, it would not seem the Government could often meet the burden under rule 615 of showing that the agent's presence is essential. Furthermore, it could be dangerous to use the agent as a witness as early in the case as possible, so that he might then help counsel as a nonwitness, since the agent's testimony could be needed in rebuttal. Using another, nonwitness agent from the same investigative agency would not generally meet government counsel's needs.

This problem is solved if it is clear that investigative agents are within the group specified under the second exception made in the rule, for "an officer or employee of a party which is not a natural person designated as its representative by its attorney." It is our understanding that this was the intention of the House committee. It is certainly this committee's construction of the rule. Senate Report No. 93–1277.

1987 Amendments

The amendment is technical. No substantive change is intended.

1988 Amendments

The amendment is technical. No substantive change is intended.

1998 Amendments

The amendment is in response to: (1) the Victim's Rights and Restitution Act of 1990, 42 U.S.C. § 10606, which guarantees, within certain limits, the right of a crime victim to attend the trial; and (2) the Victim Rights Clarification Act of 1997 (18 U.S.C. § 3510).

2011 Amendments

The language of Rule 615 has been amended as part of the restyling of the Evidence Rules to make them more easily understood and to make style and terminology consistent throughout the rules. These changes are intended to be stylistic only. There is no intent to change any result in any ruling on evidence admissibility.

HISTORICAL NOTES

Revision Notes and Legislative Reports

1988 Acts. For Related Reports, see 1988 U.S. Code Cong. and Adm. News, p. 5937.

1988 Amendments. Pub.L. 100–690 inserted "a" before "party which is not a natural person".

ARTICLE VII. OPINIONS AND EXPERT TESTIMONY

Rule

Rule 701.　Opinion Testimony by Lay Witnesses

If a witness is not testifying as an expert, testimony in the form of an opinion is limited to one that is:

(a) rationally based on the witness's perception;

(b) helpful to clearly understanding the witness's testimony or to determining a fact in issue; and

(c) not based on scientific, technical, or other specialized knowledge within the scope of Rule 702.
(Pub.L. 93–595, § 1, Jan. 2, 1975, 88 Stat.1937; Mar. 2, 1987, eff. Oct. 1, 1987; Apr. 17, 2000, eff. Dec. 1, 2000; Apr. 26, 2011, eff. Dec. 1, 2011.)

ADVISORY COMMITTEE NOTES

1972 Proposed Rules

The rule retains the traditional objective of putting the trier of fact in possession of an accurate reproduction of the event.

Limitation (a) is the familiar requirement of first-hand knowledge or observation.

Limitation (b) is phrased in terms of requiring testimony to be helpful in resolving issues. Witnesses often find difficulty in expressing themselves in language which is not that of an opinion or conclusion. While the courts have made concessions in certain recurring situations, necessity as a standard for permitting opinions and conclusions has proved too elusive and too unadaptable to particular situations for purposes of satisfactory judicial administration. McCormick § 11. Moreover, the practical impossibility of determining by rule what is a "fact," demonstrated by a century of litigation of the question of what is a fact for purposes of pleading under the Field Code, extends into evidence also. 7 Wigmore § 1919. The rule assumes that the natural characteristics of the adversary system will generally lead to an acceptable result, since the detailed account carries more conviction than the broad assertion, and a lawyer can be expected to display his witness to the best advantage. If he fails to do so, cross-examination and argument will point up the weakness. See Ladd, Expert Testimony, 5 Vand.L.Rev. 414, 415–417 (1952). If, despite these considerations, attempts are made to introduce meaningless assertions which amount to little more than choosing up sides, exclusion for lack of helpfulness is called for by the rule.

The language of the rule is substantially that of Uniform Rule 56(1). Similar provisions are California Evidence Code § 800; Kansas Code of Civil Procedure § 60–456(a); New Jersey Evidence Rule 56(1).

1987 Amendments

The amendments are technical. No substantive change is intended.

2000 Amendments

Rule 701 has been amended to eliminate the risk that the reliability requirements set forth in Rule 702 will be evaded through the simple expedient of proffering an expert in lay witness clothing. Under the amendment, a witness' testimony must be scrutinized under the rules regulating expert opinion to the extent that the witness is providing testimony based on scientific, technical, or other specialized knowledge within the scope of Rule 702. *See generally Asplundh Mfg. Div. v. Benton Harbor Eng'g*, 57 F.3d 1190 (3d Cir. 1995). By channeling testimony that is actually expert testimony to Rule 702, the amendment also ensures that a party will not evade the expert witness disclosure requirements set forth in Fed. R.Civ.P. 26 and Fed.R.Crim.P. 16 by simply calling an expert witness in the guise of a layperson. *See* Joseph, *Emerging Expert Issues Under the 1993 Disclosure Amendments to the Federal Rules of Civil Procedure*, 164 F.R.D. 97, 108 (1996) (noting that "there is no good reason to allow what is essentially surprise expert testimony." and that "the Court should be vigilant to preclude manipulative conduct designed to thwart the expert disclosure and discovery process"). *See also United States v. Figueroa–Lopez*, 125 F.3d 1241, 1246 (9th Cir. 1997) (law enforcement agents testifying that the defendant's conduct was consistent with that of a drug trafficker could not testify as lay witnesses; to permit such testimony under Rule 701 "subverts the requirements of Federal Rule of Criminal Procedure 16(a)(1)(E)").

The amendment does not distinguish between expert and lay *witnesses*, but rather between expert and lay *testimony*. Certainly it is possible for the same witness to provide both lay and expert testimony in a single case. *See, e.g, United States v. Figueroa–Lopez*, 125 F.3d 1241, 1246 (9th Cir. 1997) (law enforcement agents could testify that the defendant was acting suspiciously, without being qualified as experts; however, the rules on experts were applicable where the agents testified on the basis of extensive experience that the defendant was using code words to refer to drug quantities and prices). The amendment makes clear that any part of a witness' testimony that is based upon scientific, technical, or other specialized knowledge within the scope of Rule 702 is governed by the standards of Rule 702 and the corresponding disclosure requirements of the Civil and Criminal Rules.

The amendment is not intended to affect the "prototypical example[s] of the type of evidence contemplated by the adoption of Rule 701 relat[ing] to the appearance of persons or things, identity, the manner of conduct, competency of a person, degrees of light or darkness, sound, size, weight, distance, and an endless number of items that cannot be described factually in words apart from inferences." *Asplundh Mfg. Div. v. Benton Harbor Eng' g*, 57 F.3d 1190, 1196 (3d Cir. 1995).

For example, most courts have permitted the owner or officer of a business to testify to the value or projected profits of the business, without the necessity of qualifying the witness as an accountant, appraiser, or similar expert. *See, e.g., Lightning Lube, Inc. v. Witco Corp.* 4 F.3d 1153 (3d Cir. 1993) (no abuse of discretion in permitting the plaintiff's owner to give lay opinion testimony as to damages, as it was based on his knowledge and participation in the day-to-day affairs of the business). Such opinion testimony is admitted not because of experience, training or specialized knowledge within the realm of an expert, but because of the particularized knowledge that the witness has by virtue of his or her position in the business. The amendment does not purport to change this analysis. Similarly, courts have permitted lay witnesses to testify that a substance appeared to be a narcotic, so long as a foundation of familiarity with the substance is established. *See, e.g., United States v. Westbrook*, 896 F.2d 330 (8th Cir. 1990) (two lay witnesses who were heavy amphetamine users were properly permitted to testify that a substance was amphetamine; but it was error to permit another witness to make such an identification where she had no experience with amphetamines). Such testimony is not based on specialized knowledge within the scope of Rule 702, but rather is based upon a layperson's personal knowledge. If, however, that witness were to describe how a narcotic was manufactured, or to describe the intricate workings of a narcotic distribution network, then the witness would have to qualify as an expert under Rule 702. *United States v. Figueroa–Lopez, supra.*

The amendment incorporates the distinctions set forth in *State v. Brown*, 836 S.W.2d 530, 549 (1992), a case involving former Tennessee Rule of Evidence 701, a rule that precluded lay witness testimony based on "special knowledge." In *Brown*, the court declared that the distinction between lay and expert witness testimony is that lay testimony "results from a process of reasoning familiar in everyday life," while expert testimony "results from a process of reasoning which can be mastered only by specialists in the field." The court in *Brown* noted that a lay witness with experience could testify that a substance appeared to be blood, but that a witness would have to qualify as an expert before he could testify that bruising around the eyes is indicative of skull trauma. That is the kind of distinction made by the amendment to this Rule.

GAP Report—Proposed Amendment to Rule 701

The Committee made the following changes to the published draft of the proposed amendment to Evidence Rule 701:

1. The words "within the scope of Rule 702" were added at the end of the proposed amendment, to emphasize that the Rule does not require witnesses to qualify as experts unless their testimony is of the type traditionally considered within the purview of Rule 702. The Committee Note was amended to accord with this textual change.

2. The Committee Note was revised to provide further examples of the kind of testimony that could and could not be proffered under the limitation imposed by the proposed amendment.

2011 Amendments

The language of Rule 701 has been amended as part of the general restyling of the Evidence Rules to make them more easily understood and to make style and terminology consistent throughout the rules. These changes are intended to be stylistic only. There is no intent to change any result in any ruling on evidence admissibility.

The Committee deleted all reference to an "inference" on the grounds that the deletion made the Rule flow better and easier to read, and because any "inference" is covered by the broader term "opinion." Courts have not made substantive decisions on the basis of any distinction between an opinion and an inference. No change in current practice is intended.

Rule 702. Testimony by Expert Witnesses

A witness who is qualified as an expert by knowledge, skill, experience, training, or education may testify in the form of an opinion or otherwise if:

(a) the expert's scientific, technical, or other specialized knowledge will help the trier of fact to understand the evidence or to determine a fact in issue;

(b) the testimony is based on sufficient facts or data;

(c) the testimony is the product of reliable principles and methods; and

(d) the expert has reliably applied the principles and methods to the facts of the case.

(Pub.L. 93–595, § 1, Jan. 2, 1975, 88 Stat. 1937; Apr. 17, 2000, eff. Dec. 1, 2000; Apr. 26, 2011, eff. Dec. 1, 2011.)

ADVISORY COMMITTEE NOTES
1972 Proposed Rules

An intelligent evaluation of facts is often difficult or impossible without the application of some scientific, technical, or other specialized knowledge. The most common source of this knowledge is the expert witness, although there are other techniques for supplying it.

Most of the literature assumes that experts testify only in the form of opinions. The assumption is logically unfounded. The rule accordingly recognizes that an expert on the stand may give a dissertation or exposition of scientific or other principles relevant to the case, leaving the trier of fact to apply them to the facts. Since much of the criticism of expert testimony has centered upon the hypothetical question, it seems wise to recognize that opinions are not indispensable and to encourage the use of expert testimony in non-opinion form when counsel believes the trier can itself draw the requisite inference. The use of opinions is not abolished by the rule, however. It will continue to be permissible for the experts to take the further step of suggesting the inference which should be drawn from applying the specialized knowledge to the facts. See Rules 703 to 705.

Whether the situation is a proper one for the use of expert testimony is to be determined on the basis of assisting the trier. "There is no more certain test for determining when experts may be used than the common sense inquiry whether the untrained layman would be qualified to determine intelligently and to the best possible degree the particular issue without enlightenment from those having a specialized understanding of the subject involved in the dispute." Ladd, Expert Testimony, 5 Vand.L.Rev. 414, 418 (1952). When opinions are excluded, it is because they are unhelpful and therefore superfluous and a waste of time. 7 Wigmore § 1918.

The rule is broadly phrased. The fields of knowledge which may be drawn upon are not limited merely to the "scientific" and "technical" but extend to all "specialized" knowledge. Similarly, the expert is viewed, not in a narrow sense, but as a person qualified by "knowledge, skill, experience, training or education." Thus within the scope of the rule are not only experts in the strictest sense of the word, e.g., physicians, physicists, and architects, but also the large group sometimes called "skilled" witnesses, such as bankers or landowners testifying to land values.

2000 Amendments

Rule 702 has been amended in response to *Daubert v. Merrell Dow Pharmaceuticals, Inc.*, 509 U.S. 579 (1993), and to the many cases applying *Daubert*, including *Kumho Tire Co. v. Carmichael*, 119 S.Ct. 1167 (1999). In *Daubert* the Court charged trial judges with the responsibility of acting as gatekeepers to exclude unreliable expert testimony, and the Court in *Kumho* clarified that this gatekeeper function applies to all expert testimony, not just testimony based in science. *See also Kumho*, 119 S.Ct. at 1178 (citing the Committee Note to the proposed amendment to Rule 702, which had been released for public comment before the date of the *Kumho* decision). The amendment affirms the trial court's role as gatekeeper and provides some general standards that the trial court must use to assess the reliability and helpfulness of proffered expert testimony. Consistently with *Kumho*, the Rule as amended provides that all types of expert testimony present questions of admissibility for the trial court in deciding whether the evidence is reliable and helpful. Consequently, the admissibility of all expert testimony is governed by the principles of Rule 104(a). Under that Rule, the proponent has the burden of establishing that the pertinent admissibility requirements are met by a preponderance of the evidence. *See Bourjaily v. United States*, 483 U.S. 171 (1987).

Daubert set forth a non-exclusive checklist for trial courts to use in assessing the reliability of scientific expert testimony. The specific factors explicated by the *Daubert* Court are (1) whether the expert's technique or theory can be or has been tested—that is, whether the expert's theory can be challenged in some objective sense, or whether it is instead simply a subjective, conclusory approach that cannot reasonably be assessed for reliability; (2) whether the technique or theory has been subject to peer review and publication; (3) the known or potential rate of error of the technique or theory when applied; (4) the existence and maintenance of standards and controls; and (5) whether the technique or theory has been generally accepted in the scientific community. The Court in *Kumho* held that these factors might also be applicable in assessing the reliability of non-scientific expert testimony, depending upon "the particular circumstances of the particular case at issue." 119 S.Ct. at 1175.

No attempt has been made to "codify" these specific factors. *Daubert* itself emphasized that the factors were neither exclusive nor dispositive. Other cases have recognized that not all of the specific *Daubert* factors can apply to every type of expert testimony. In addition to *Kumho*, 119 S.Ct. at 1175, *see Tyus v. Urban Search Management*, 102 F.3d 256 (7th Cir. 1996) (noting that the factors mentioned by the Court in *Daubert* do not neatly apply to expert testimony from a sociologist). *See also Kannankeril v. Terminix Int'l, Inc.*, 128 F.3d 802, 809 (3d Cir. 1997) (holding that lack of peer review or publication was not dispositive where the expert's opinion was supported by "widely accepted scientific knowledge"). The standards set forth in the amendment are broad enough to require consideration of any or all of the specific *Daubert* factors where appropriate.

Courts both before and after *Daubert* have found other factors relevant in determining whether expert testimony is sufficiently reliable to be considered by the trier of fact. These factors include:

(1) Whether experts are "proposing to testify about matters growing naturally and directly out of research they have conducted independent of the litigation, or whether they have developed their opinions expressly for purposes of testifying." *Daubert v. Merrell Dow Pharmaceuticals, Inc.*, 43 F.3d 1311, 1317 (9th Cir. 1995).

(2) Whether the expert has unjustifiably extrapolated from an accepted premise to an unfounded conclusion. *See General Elec. Co. v. Joiner*, 522 U.S. 136, 146 (1997) (noting that in some cases a trial court "may conclude that there is simply too great an analytical gap between the data and the opinion proffered").

(3) Whether the expert has adequately accounted for obvious alternative explanations. *See Claar v. Burlington N.R.R.*, 29 F.3d 499 (9th Cir. 1994) (testimony excluded where the expert failed to consider other obvious causes for the plaintiff's condition). *Compare Ambrosini v. Labarraque*, 101 F.3d 129 (D.C. Cir. 1996) (the possibility of some uneliminated causes presents a question of weight, so long as the most obvious causes have been considered and reasonably ruled out by the expert).

(4) Whether the expert "is being as careful as he would be in his regular professional work outside his paid litigation consulting." *Sheehan v. Daily Racing Form, Inc.*, 104 F.3d 940, 942 (7th Cir. 1997). *See Kumho Tire Co. v. Carmichael*, 119 S.Ct. 1167, 1176 (1999) (*Daubert* requires the trial court to assure itself that the expert "employs in the courtroom the same level of intellectual rigor that characterizes the practice of an expert in the relevant field").

(5) Whether the field of expertise claimed by the expert is known to reach reliable results for the type of opinion the expert would give. *See Kumho Tire Co. v. Carmichael*, 119 S.Ct.1167, 1175 (1999) (*Daubert's* general acceptance factor does not "help show that an expert's testimony is reliable where the discipline itself lacks reliability, as for example, do theories grounded in any so-called generally accepted principles of astrology or necromancy."), *Moore v. Ashland Chemical, Inc.*, 151 F.3d 269 (5th Cir. 1998) (en banc) (clinical doctor was properly precluded from testifying to the toxicological cause of the plaintiff's respiratory problem, where the opinion was not sufficiently grounded in scientific methodology); *Sterling v. Velsicol Chem. Corp.*, 855 F.2d 1188 (6th Cir. 1988) (rejecting testimony based on "clinical ecology" as unfounded and unreliable).

All of these factors remain relevant to the determination of the reliability of expert testimony under the Rule as amended. Other factors may also be relevant. *See Kumho*, 119 S.Ct. 1167, 1176 ("[W]e conclude that the trial judge must have considerable leeway in deciding in a particular case how to go about determining whether particular expert testimony is reliable."). Yet no single factor is necessarily dispositive of the reliability of a particular expert's testimony. *See, e.g., Heller v. Shaw Industries, Inc.*, 167 F.3d 146, 155 (3d Cir. 1999) ("not only must each stage of the expert's testimony be reliable, but each stage must be evaluated practically and flexibly without bright-line exclusionary (or inclusionary) rules."); *Daubert v. Merrell Dow Pharmaceuticals, Inc.*, 43 F.3d 1311, 1317, n.5 (9th Cir. 1995) (noting that some expert disciplines "have the courtroom as a principal theatre of operations" and as to these disciplines "the fact that the expert has developed an expertise principally for purposes of litigation will obviously not be a substantial consideration.").

A review of the caselaw after *Daubert* shows that the rejection of expert testimony is the exception rather than the rule. *Daubert* did not work a "seachange over federal evidence law," and "the trial court's role as gatekeeper is not intended to serve as a replacement for the adversary system." *United States v. 14.38 Acres of Land Situated in Leflore County, Mississippi*, 80 F.3d 1074, 1078 (5th Cir. 1996). As the Court in *Daubert* stated: "Vigorous cross-examination, presentation of contrary evidence, and careful instruction on the burden of proof are the traditional and appropriate means of attacking shaky but admissible evidence." 509 U.S. at 595. Likewise, this amendment is not intended to provide an excuse for an automatic challenge to the testimony of every expert. *See Kumho Tire Co. v. Carmichael*, 119 S.Ct.1167, 1176 (1999) (noting that the trial judge has the discretion "both to avoid unnecessary 'reliability' proceedings in ordinary cases where the reliability of an expert's methods is properly taken for granted, and to require appropriate proceedings in the less usual or more complex cases where cause for questioning the expert's reliability arises.").

When a trial court, applying this amendment, rules that an expert's testimony is reliable, this does not necessarily mean that contradictory expert testimony is unreliable. The amendment is broad enough to permit testimony that is the product of competing principles or methods in the same field of expertise. *See, e.g., Heller v. Shaw Industries, Inc.*, 167 F.3d 146, 160 (3d Cir. 1999) (expert testimony cannot be excluded simply because the expert uses one test rather than another, when both tests are accepted in the field and both reach reliable results). As the court stated in *In re Paoli R.R. Yard PCB Litigation*, 35 F.3d 717, 744 (3d Cir. 1994), proponents "do not have to demonstrate to the judge by a preponderance of the evidence that the assessments of their experts are correct, they only have to demonstrate by a preponderance of evidence that their opinions are reliable.... The evidentiary requirement of reliability is lower than the merits standard of correctness." *See also Daubert v. Merrell Dow Pharmaceuticals, Inc.*, 43 F.3d 1311, 1318 (9th Cir. 1995) (scientific experts might be permitted to testify if they could show that the methods they used were also employed by "a recognized minority of scientists in their field."); *Ruiz-Troche v. Pepsi Cola*, 161 F.3d 77, 85 (1st Cir. 1998) ("*Daubert* neither requires nor empowers trial courts to determine which of several competing scientific theories has the best provenance.").

The Court in *Daubert* declared that the "focus, of course, must be solely on principles and methodology, not on the conclusions they generate." 509 U.S. at 595. Yet as the Court later recognized, "conclusions and methodology are not entirely distinct from one another." *General Elec. Co. v. Joiner*, 522 U.S. 136, 146 (1997). Under the amendment, as under *Daubert*, when an expert purports to apply principles and methods in accordance with professional standards, and yet reaches a conclusion that other experts in the field would not reach, the trial court may fairly suspect that the principles and methods have not been faithfully applied. *See Lust v. Merrell Dow Pharmaceuticals, Inc.*, 89 F.3d 594, 598 (9th Cir. 1996). The amendment specifically provides that the trial court must scrutinize not only the principles and methods used by the expert, but also whether those principles and methods have been properly applied to the facts of the case. As the court noted in *In re Paoli R.R. Yard PCB Litig.*, 35 F.3d 717, 745 (3d Cir. 1994), "*any* step that renders the analysis unreliable

... renders the expert's testimony inadmissible. *This is true whether the step completely changes a reliable methodology or merely misapplies that methodology.*"

If the expert purports to apply principles and methods to the facts of the case, it is important that this application be conducted reliably. Yet it might also be important in some cases for an expert to educate the factfinder about general principles, without ever attempting to apply these principles to the specific facts of the case. For example, experts might instruct the factfinder on the principles of thermodynamics, or bloodclotting, or on how financial markets respond to corporate reports, without ever knowing about or trying to tie their testimony into the facts of the case. The amendment does not alter the venerable practice of using expert testimony to educate the factfinder on general principles. For this kind of generalized testimony, Rule 702 simply requires that: (1) the expert be qualified; (2) the testimony address a subject matter on which the factfinder can be assisted by an expert; (3) the testimony be reliable; and (4) the testimony "fit" the facts of the case.

As stated earlier, the amendment does not distinguish between scientific and other forms of expert testimony. The trial court's gatekeeping function applies to testimony by any expert. *See Kumho Tire Co. v. Carmichael*, 119 S.Ct. 1167, 1171 (1999) ("We conclude that *Daubert's* general holding— setting forth the trial judge's general 'gatekeeping' obligation—applies not only to testimony based on 'scientific' knowledge, but also to testimony based on 'technical' and 'other specialized' knowledge."). While the relevant factors for determining reliability will vary from expertise to expertise, the amendment rejects the premise that an expert's testimony should be treated more permissively simply because it is outside the realm of science. An opinion from an expert who is not a scientist should receive the same degree of scrutiny for reliability as an opinion from an expert who purports to be a scientist. *See Watkins v. Telsmith, Inc.*, 121 F.3d 984, 991 (5th Cir. 1997) ("[I]t seems exactly backwards that experts who purport to rely on general engineering principles and practical experience might escape screening by the district court simply by stating that their conclusions were not reached by any particular method or technique."). Some types of expert testimony will be more objectively verifiable, and subject to the expectations of falsifiability, peer review, and publication, than others. Some types of expert testimony will not rely on anything like a scientific method, and so will have to be evaluated by reference to other standard principles attendant to the particular area of expertise. The trial judge in all cases of proffered expert testimony must find that it is properly grounded, well-reasoned, and not speculative before it can be admitted. The expert's testimony must be grounded in an accepted body of learning or experience in the expert's field, and the expert must explain how the conclusion is so grounded. *See, e.g.*, American College of Trial Lawyers, Standards and Procedures for Determining the Admissibility of Expert Testimony after *Daubert*, 157 F.R.D. 571, 579 (1994) ("[W]hether the testimony concerns economic principles, accounting standards, property valuation or other non-scientific subjects, it should be evaluated by reference to the 'knowledge and experience' of that particular field.").

The amendment requires that the testimony must be the product of reliable principles and methods that are reliably applied to the facts of the case. While the terms "principles" and "methods" may convey a certain impression when applied to scientific knowledge, they remain relevant when applied to testimony based on technical or other specialized knowledge. For example, when a law enforcement agent testifies regarding the use of code words in a drug transaction, the principle used by the agent is that participants in such transactions regularly use code words to conceal the nature of their activities. The method used by the agent is the application of extensive experience to analyze the meaning of the conversations. So long as the principles and methods are reliable and applied reliably to the facts of the case, this type of testimony should be admitted.

Nothing in this amendment is intended to suggest that experience alone—or experience in conjunction with other knowledge, skill, training or education—may not provide a sufficient foundation for expert testimony. To the contrary, the text of Rule 702 expressly contemplates that an expert may be qualified on the basis of experience. In certain fields, experience is the predominant, if not sole, basis for a great deal of reliable expert testimony. *See, e.g., United States v. Jones*, 107 F.3d 1147 (6th Cir. 1997) (no abuse of discretion in admitting the testimony of a handwriting examiner who had years of practical experience and extensive training, and who explained his methodology in detail); *Tassin v. Sears Roebuck*, 946 F.Supp. 1241, 1248 (M.D.La. 1996) (design engineer's testimony can be admissible when the expert's opinions "are based on facts, a reasonable investigation, and traditional technical/mechanical expertise, and he provides a reasonable link between the information and procedures he uses and the conclusions he reaches"). *See also Kumho Tire Co. v. Carmichael*, 119 S.Ct. 1167, 1178 (1999) (stating that "no one denies that an expert might draw a conclusion from a set of observations based on extensive and specialized experience.").

If the witness is relying solely or primarily on experience, then the witness must explain how that experience leads to the conclusion reached, why that experience is a sufficient basis for the opinion, and how that experience is reliably applied to the facts. The trial court's gatekeeping function requires more than simply "taking the expert's word for it." *See Daubert v. Merrell Dow Pharmaceuticals, Inc.*, 43 F.3d 1311, 1319 (9th Cir. 1995) ("We've been presented with only the experts' qualifications, their conclusions and their assurances of reliability. Under *Daubert*, that's not enough."). The more subjective and controversial the expert's inquiry, the more likely the testimony should be excluded as unreliable. *See O'Conner v. Commonwealth Edison Co.*, 13 F.3d 1090 (7th Cir. 1994) (expert testimony based on a completely subjective methodology held properly excluded). *See also Kumho Tire Co. v. Carmichael*, 119 S.Ct. 1167, 1176 (1999) ("[I]t will at times be useful to ask even of a witness whose expertise is based purely on experience, say, a perfume tester able to distinguish among 140 odors at a sniff, whether his preparation is of a kind that others in the field would recognize as acceptable.").

Subpart (1) of Rule 702 calls for a quantitative rather than qualitative analysis. The amendment requires that expert testimony be based on sufficient underlying "facts or data." The term "data" is intended to encompass the reliable opinions of other experts. See the original Advisory Committee Note to Rule 703. The language "facts or data" is broad enough to allow an expert to rely on hypothetical facts that are supported by the evidence. *Id.*

When facts are in dispute, experts sometimes reach different conclusions based on competing versions of the facts. The emphasis in the amendment on " sufficient facts or data" is not intended to authorize a trial court to exclude an expert's testimony on the ground that the court believes one version of the facts and not the other.

There has been some confusion over the relationship between Rules 702 and 703. The amendment makes clear that the sufficiency of the basis of an expert' s testimony is to be decided under Rule 702. Rule 702 sets forth the overarching requirement of reliability, and an analysis of the sufficiency of the expert's basis cannot be divorced from the ultimate reliability of the expert's opinion. In contrast, the "reasonable reliance" requirement of Rule 703 is a relatively narrow inquiry. When an expert relies on inadmissible information, Rule 703 requires the trial court to determine whether that information is of a type reasonably relied on by other experts in the field. If so, the expert can rely on the information in reaching an opinion. However, the question whether the expert is relying on a *sufficient* basis of information—whether admissible information or not—is governed by the requirements of Rule 702.

The amendment makes no attempt to set forth procedural requirements for exercising the trial court's gatekeeping function over expert testimony. *See* Daniel J. Capra, *The Daubert Puzzle*, 38 Ga.L.Rev. 699, 766 (1998) [*sic*, should be "32 Ga.L.Rev. 699, 766 (1998)"] ("Trial courts should be allowed substantial discretion in dealing with *Daubert* questions; any attempt to codify procedures will likely give rise to unnecessary changes in practice and create difficult questions for appellate review."). Courts have shown considerable ingenuity and flexibility in considering challenges to expert testimony under *Daubert*, and it is contemplated that this will continue under the amended Rule. *See, e.g., Cortes-Irizarry v. Corporacion Insular*, 111 F.3d 184 (1st Cir. 1997) (discussing the application of *Daubert* in ruling on a motion for summary judgment); *In re Paoli R.R. Yard PCB Litig.*, 35 F.3d 717, 736, 739 (3d Cir. 1994) (discussing the use of *in limine* hearings); *Claar v. Burlington N.R.R.*, 29 F.3d 499, 502–05 (9th Cir. 1994) (discussing the trial court's technique of ordering experts to submit serial affidavits explaining the reasoning and methods underlying their conclusions).

The amendment continues the practice of the original Rule in referring to a qualified witness as an "expert." This was done to provide continuity and to minimize change. The use of the term "expert" in the Rule does not, however, mean that a jury should actually be informed that a qualified witness is testifying as an "expert." Indeed, there is much to be said for a practice that prohibits the use of the term "expert" by both the parties and the court at trial. Such a practice "ensures that trial courts do not inadvertently put their stamp of authority" on a witness's opinion, and protects against the jury's being "overwhelmed by the so-called 'experts'." Hon. Charles Richey, *Proposals to Eliminate the Prejudicial Effect of the Use of the Word "Expert" Under the Federal Rules of Evidence in Criminal and Civil Jury Trials*, 154 F.R.D. 537, 559 (1994) (setting forth limiting instructions and a standing order employed to prohibit the use of the term " expert" injury trials).

GAP Report—Proposed Amendment to Rule 702

The Committee made the following changes to the published draft of the proposed amendment to Evidence Rule 702:

1. The word "reliable" was deleted from Subpart (1) of the proposed amendment, in order to avoid an overlap with Evidence Rule 703, and to clarify that an expert opinion need not be excluded simply because it is based on hypothetical facts. The Committee Note was amended to accord with this textual change.

2. The Committee Note was amended throughout to include pertinent references to the Supreme Court's decision in *Kumho Tire Co. v. Carmichael*, which was rendered after the proposed amendment was released for public comment. Other citations were updated as well.

3. The Committee Note was revised to emphasize that the amendment is not intended to limit the right to jury trial, nor to permit a challenge to the testimony of every expert, nor to preclude the testimony of experience-based experts, nor to prohibit testimony based on competing methodologies within a field of expertise.

4. Language was added to the Committee Note to clarify that no single factor is necessarily dispositive of the reliability inquiry mandated by Evidence Rule 702.

2011 Amendments

The language of Rule 702 has been amended as part of the restyling of the Evidence Rules to make them more easily understood and to make style and terminology consistent throughout the rules. These changes are intended to be stylistic only. There is no intent to change any result in any ruling on evidence admissibility.

Rule 703. Bases of an Expert's Opinion Testimony

An expert may base an opinion on facts or data in the case that the expert has been made aware of or personally observed. If experts in the particular field would reasonably rely on those kinds of facts or data in forming an opinion on the subject, they need not be admissible for the opinion to be admitted. But if the facts or data would otherwise be inadmissible, the proponent of the opinion may disclose them to the jury only if their probative value in helping the jury evaluate the opinion substantially outweighs their prejudicial effect.

(Pub.L. 93–595, § 1, Jan. 2, 1975, 88 Stat.1937; Mar. 2, 1987, eff. Oct. 1, 1987; Apr. 17, 2000, eff. Dec. 1, 2000; Apr. 26, 2011, eff. Dec. 1, 2011.)

ADVISORY COMMITTEE NOTES
1972 Proposed Rules

Facts or data upon which expert opinions are based may, under the rule, be derived from three possible sources. The first is the firsthand observation of the witness with opinions based thereon traditionally allowed. A treating physician affords an example. Rheingold, The Basis of Medical Testimony, 15 Vand.L.Rev. 473, 489 (1962). Whether he must first relate his observations is treated in Rule 705. The second source, presentation at the trial, also reflects existing practice. The technique may be the familiar hypothetical question or having the expert attend the trial and hear the testimony establishing the facts. Problems of determining what testimony the expert relied upon, when the latter technique is employed and the testimony is in conflict, may be resolved by resort to Rule 705. The third source contemplated by the rule consists of presentation of data to the expert outside of court and other than by his own perception. In this respect the rule is designed to broaden the basis for expert opinions beyond that current in many jurisdictions and to bring the judicial practice into line with the practice of the experts themselves when not in court. Thus a physician in his own

practice bases his diagnosis on information from numerous sources and of considerable variety, including statements by patients and relatives, reports and opinions from nurses, technicians and other doctors, hospital records, and X rays. Most of them are admissible in evidence, but only with the expenditure of substantial time in producing and examining various authenticating witnesses. The physician makes life-and-death decisions in reliance upon them. His validation, expertly performed and subject to cross-examination, ought to suffice for judicial purposes. Rheingold, *supra*, at 531; McCormick § 15. A similar provision is California Evidence Code § 801(b).

The rule also offers a more satisfactory basis for ruling upon the admissibility of public opinion poll evidence. Attention is directed to the validity of the techniques employed rather than to relatively fruitless inquiries whether hearsay is involved. See Judge Feinberg's careful analysis in Zippo Mfg. Co. v. Rogers Imports, Inc., 216 F.Supp. 670 (S.D.N.Y. 1963). See also Blum et al., The Art of Opinion Research: A Lawyer's Appraisal of an Emerging Service, 24 U.Chi.L.Rev. 1 (1956); Bonynge Trademark Surveys and Techniques and Their Use in Litigation, 48 A.B.A.J. 329 (1962); Zeisel, The Uniqueness of Survey Evidence, 45 Cornell L.Q. 322 (1960); Annot., 76 A.L.R.2d 919.

If it be feared that enlargement of permissible data may tend to break down the rules of exclusion unduly, notice should be taken that the rule requires that the facts or data "be of a type reasonably relied upon by experts in the particular field." The language would not warrant admitting in evidence the opinion of an "accidentologist" as to the point of impact in an automobile collision based on statements of bystanders since this requirement is not satisfied. See Comment, Cal.Law Rev.Comm'n, Recommendation Proposing an Evidence Code 148–150 (1965).

1987 Amendments

The amendment is technical. No substantive change is intended.

2000 Amendments

Rule 703 has been amended to emphasize that when an expert reasonably relies on inadmissible information to form an opinion or inference, the underlying information is not admissible simply because the opinion or inference is admitted. Courts have reached different results on how to treat inadmissible information when it is reasonably relied upon by an expert in forming an opinion or drawing an inference. *Compare United States v. Rollins*, 862 F.2d 1282 (7th Cir. 1988) (admitting, as part of the basis of an FBI agent's expert opinion on the meaning of code language, the hearsay statements of an informant), *with United States v. 0.59 Acres of Land*, 109 F.3d 1493 (9th Cir. 1997) (error to admit hearsay offered as the basis of an expert opinion, without a limiting instruction). Commentators have also taken differing views. *See e.g.*, Ronald Carlson, *Policing the Bases of Modern Expert Testimony*, 39 Vand.L.Rev. 577 (1986) (advocating limits on the jury's consideration of otherwise inadmissible evidence used as the basis for an expert opinion); Paul Rice, *Inadmissible Evidence as a Basis for Expert Testimony: A Response to Professor Carlson*, 40 Vand.L.Rev. 583 (1987) (advocating unrestricted use of information reasonably relied upon by an expert).

When information is reasonably relied upon by an expert and yet is admissible only for the purpose of assisting the jury in evaluating an expert's opinion, a trial court applying this Rule must consider the information's probative value in assisting the jury to weigh the expert's opinion on the one hand, and the risk of prejudice resulting from the jury's potential misuse of the information for substantive purposes on the other. The information may be disclosed to the jury, upon objection, only if the trial court finds that the probative value of the information in assisting the jury to evaluate the expert's opinion substantially outweighs its prejudicial effect. If the otherwise inadmissible information is admitted under this balancing test, the trial judge must give a limiting instruction upon request, informing the jury that the underlying information must not be used for substantive purposes. *See* Rule 105. In determining the appropriate course, the trial court should consider the probable effectiveness or lack of effectiveness of a limiting instruction under the particular circumstances.

The amendment governs only the disclosure to the jury of information that is reasonably relied on by an expert, when that information is not admissible for substantive purposes. It is not intended to affect the admissibility of an expert's testimony. Nor does the amendment prevent an expert from relying on information that is inadmissible for substantive purposes.

Nothing in this Rule restricts the presentation of underlying expert facts or data when offered by an adverse party. *See* Rule 705. Of course, an adversary's attack on an expert's basis will often open the door to a proponent's rebuttal with information that was reasonably relied upon by the expert, even if that information would not have been discloseable initially under the balancing test provided by this amendment. Moreover, in some circumstances the proponent might wish to disclose information that is relied upon by the expert in order to "remove the sting" from the opponent's anticipated attack, and thereby prevent the jury from drawing an unfair negative inference. The trial court should take this consideration into account in applying the balancing test provided by this amendment.

This amendment covers facts or data that cannot be admitted for any purpose other than to assist the jury to evaluate the expert's opinion. The balancing test provided in this amendment is not applicable to facts or data that are admissible for any other purpose but have not yet been offered for such a purpose at the time the expert testifies.

The amendment provides a presumption against disclosure to the jury of information used as the basis of an expert's opinion and not admissible for any substantive purpose, when that information is offered by the proponent of the expert. In a multi-party case, where one party proffers an expert whose testimony is also beneficial to other parties, each such party should be deemed a "proponent" within the meaning of the amendment.

GAP Report—Proposed Amendment to Rule 703

The Committee made the following changes to the published draft of the proposed amendment to Evidence Rule 703:

1. A minor stylistic change was made in the text, in accordance with the suggestion of the Style Subcommittee of the Standing Committee on Rules of Practice and Procedure.

2. The words "in assisting the jury to evaluate the expert's opinion" were added to the text, to specify the proper purpose for offering the otherwise inadmissible information relied on by an expert. The Committee Note was revised to accord with this change in the text.

3. Stylistic changes were made to the Committee Note.

4. The Committee Note was revised to emphasize that the balancing test set forth in the proposal should be used to determine whether an expert's basis may be disclosed to the jury either (1) in rebuttal or (2) on direct examination to "remove the sting" of an opponent's anticipated attack on an expert's basis.

2011 Amendments

The language of Rule 703 has been amended as part of the general restyling of the Evidence Rules to make them more easily understood and to make style and terminology consistent throughout the rules. These changes are intended to be stylistic only. There is no intent to change any result in any ruling on evidence admissibility.

The Committee deleted all reference to an "inference" on the grounds that the deletion made the Rule flow better and easier to read, and because any "inference" is covered by the broader term "opinion." Courts have not made substantive decisions on the basis of any distinction between an opinion and an inference. No change in current practice is intended.

CROSS REFERENCES

Personal knowledge evidence of as prerequisite to testimony by witness, see Fed.Rules Evid. Rule 602, 28 USCA.

Rule 704.   Opinion on an Ultimate Issue

(a) In General—Not Automatically Objectionable. An opinion is not objectionable just because it embraces an ultimate issue.

(b) Exception. In a criminal case, an expert witness must not state an opinion about whether the defendant did or did not have a mental state or condition that constitutes an element of the crime charged or of a defense. Those matters are for the trier of fact alone.

(Pub.L. 93–595, § 1, Jan. 2, 1975, 88 Stat. 1937; Pub.L. 98–473, Title II, § 406, Oct. 12, 1984, 98 Stat. 2067; Apr. 26, 2011, eff. Dec. 1, 2011.)

ADVISORY COMMITTEE NOTES

1972 Proposed Rules

The basic approach to opinions, lay and expert, in these rules is to admit them when helpful to the trier of fact. In order to render this approach fully effective and to allay any doubt on the subject, the so-called "ultimate issue" rule is specifically abolished by the instant rule.

The older cases often contained strictures against allowing witnesses to express opinions upon ultimate issues, as a particular aspect of the rule against opinions. The rule was unduly restrictive, difficult of application, and generally served only to deprive the trier of fact of useful information. 7 Wigmore §§ 1920, 1921; McCormick § 12. The basis usually assigned for the rule, to prevent the witness from "usurping the province of the jury," is aptly characterized as "empty rhetoric." 7 Wigmore § 1920, p. 17. Efforts to meet the felt needs of particular situations led to odd verbal circumlocutions which were said not to violate the rule. Thus a witness could express his estimate of the criminal responsibility of an accused in terms of sanity or insanity, but not in terms of ability to tell right from wrong or other more modern standard. And in cases of medical causation, witnesses were sometimes required to couch their opinions in cautious phrases of "might or could," rather than "did," though the result was to deprive many opinions of the positiveness to which they were entitled, accompanied by the hazard of a ruling of insufficiency to support a verdict. In other instances the rule was simply disregarded, and, as concessions to need, opinions were allowed upon such matters as intoxication, speed, handwriting, and value, although more precise coincidence with an ultimate issue would scarcely be possible.

Many modern decisions illustrate the trend to abandon the rule completely. People v. Wilson, 25 Cal.2d 341, 153 P.2d 720 (1944), whether abortion necessary to save life of patient; *Clifford–Jacobs Forging Co. v. Industrial Comm.*, 19 Ill.2d 236, 166 N.E.2d 582 (1960), medical causation; *Dowling v. L. H. Shattuck*, Inc., 91 N.H. 234, 17 A.2d 529 (1941), proper method of shoring ditch; *Schweiger v. Solbeck*, 191 Or. 454, 230 P.2d 195 (1951), cause of landslide. In each instance the opinion was allowed.

The abolition of the ultimate issue rule does not lower the bars so as to admit all opinions. Under Rules 701 and 702, opinions must be helpful to the trier of fact, and Rule 403 provides for exclusion of evidence which wastes time. These provisions afford ample assurances against the admission of opinions which would merely tell the jury what result to reach, somewhat in the manner of the oath-helpers of an earlier day. They also stand ready to exclude opinions phrased in terms of inadequately explored legal criteria. Thus the question, "Did T have capacity to make a will?" would be excluded, while the question, "Did T have sufficient mental capacity to know the nature and extent of his property and the natural objects of his bounty and to formulate a rational scheme of distribution?" would be allowed. McCormick § 12.

For similar provisions see Uniform Rule 56(4); California Evidence Code § 805; Kansas Code of Civil Procedure § 60–456(d); New Jersey Evidence Rule 56(3).

2011 Amendments

The language of Rule 704 has been amended as part of the general restyling of the Evidence Rules to make them more easily understood and to make style and terminology consistent throughout the rules. These changes are intended to be stylistic only. There is no intent to change any result in any ruling on evidence admissibility.

The Committee deleted all reference to an "inference" on the grounds that the deletion made the Rule flow better and easier to read, and because any "inference" is covered by the broader term "opinion." Courts have not made substantive decisions on the basis of any distinction between an opinion and an inference. No change in current practice is intended.

CROSS REFERENCES

Relevancy of evidence and its limits, see Fed.Rules Evid. Rule 401 et seq., 28 USCA.

Rule 705. Disclosing the Facts or Data Underlying an Expert's Opinion

Unless the court orders otherwise, an expert may state an opinion—and give the reasons for it—without first testifying to the underlying facts or data. But the expert may be required to disclose those facts or data on cross-examination.

(Pub.L. 93–595, § 1, Jan. 2, 1975, 88 Stat. 1938; Mar. 2, 1987, eff. Oct. 1, 1987; Apr. 22, 1993, eff. Dec. 1, 1993; Apr. 26, 2011, eff. Dec. 1, 2011.)

ADVISORY COMMITTEE NOTES

1972 Proposed Rules

The hypothetical question has been the target of a great deal of criticism as encouraging partisan bias, affording an opportunity for summing up in the middle of the case, and as complex and time consuming. Ladd, Expert Testimony, 5 Vand.L.Rev. 414, 426–427 (1952). While the rule allows counsel to make disclosure of the underlying facts or data as a preliminary to the giving of an expert opinion, if he chooses, the instances in which he is required to do so are reduced. This is true whether the expert bases his opinion on data furnished him at secondhand or observed by him at firsthand.

The elimination of the requirement of preliminary disclosure at the trial of underlying facts or data has a long background of support. In 1937 the Commissioners on Uniform State Laws incorporated a provision to this effect in their Model Expert Testimony Act, which furnished the basis for Uniform Rules 57 and 58. Rule 4515, N.Y. CPLR (McKinney 1963), provides:

"Unless the court orders otherwise, questions calling for the opinion of an expert witness need not be hypothetical in form, and the witness may state his opinion and reasons without first specifying the data upon which it is based. Upon cross-examination, he may be required to specify the data * * *."

See also California Evidence Code § 802; Kansas Code of Civil Procedure §§ 60–456, 60–457; New Jersey Evidence Rules 57, 58.

If the objection is made that leaving it to the cross-examiner to bring out the supporting data is essentially unfair, the answer is that he is under no compulsion to bring out any facts or data except those unfavorable to the opinion. The answer assumes that the cross-examiner has the advance knowledge which is essential for effective cross-examination. This advance knowledge has been afforded, though imperfectly, by the traditional foundation requirement. Rule 26(b)(4) of the Rules of Civil Procedure, as revised, provides for substantial discovery in this area, obviating in large measure the obstacles which have been raised in some instances to discovery of findings, underlying data, and even the identity of the experts. Friedenthal Discovery and Use of an Adverse Party's Expert Information, 14 Stan.L.Rev. 455 (1962).

These safeguards are reinforced by the discretionary power of the judge to require preliminary disclosure in any event.

1987 Amendment

The amendment is technical. No substantive change is intended.

1993 Amendment

This rule, which relates to the manner of presenting testimony at trial, is revised to avoid an arguable conflict with revised Rules 26(a)(2)(B) and 26(e)(1) of the Federal Rules of Civil Procedure or with revised Rule 16 of the Federal Rules of Criminal Procedure, which require disclosure in advance of trial of the basis and reasons for an expert's opinions.

If a serious question is raised under Rule 702 or 703 as to the admissibility of expert testimony, disclosure of the underlying facts or data on which opinions are based may, of course, be needed by the court before deciding whether, and to what extent, the person should be allowed to testify. This rule does not preclude such an inquiry.

2011 Amendments

The language of Rule 705 has been amended as part of the general restyling of the Evidence Rules to make them more easily understood and to make style and terminology consistent throughout the rules. These changes are intended to be stylistic only. There is no intent to change any result in any ruling on evidence admissibility.

The Committee deleted all reference to an "inference" on the grounds that the deletion made the Rule flow better and easier to read, and because any "inference" is covered by the broader term "opinion." Courts have not made substantive decisions on the basis of any distinction between an opinion and an inference. No change in current practice is intended.

CROSS REFERENCES

Scope of discovery, see Fed.Rules Civ.Proc. Rule 26, 28 USCA.

Rule 706.   Court–Appointed Expert Witnesses

(a) **Appointment Process.** On a party's motion or on its own, the court may order the parties to show cause why expert witnesses should not be appointed and may ask the parties to submit nominations. The court may appoint any expert that the parties agree on and any of its own choosing. But the court may only appoint someone who consents to act.

(b) **Expert's Role.** The court must inform the expert of the expert's duties. The court may do so in writing and have a copy filed with the clerk or may do so orally at a conference in which the parties have an opportunity to participate. The expert:

(1) must advise the parties of any findings the expert makes;

(2) may be deposed by any party;

(3) may be called to testify by the court or any party; and

(4) may be cross-examined by any party, including the party that called the expert.

(c) **Compensation.** The expert is entitled to a reasonable compensation, as set by the court. The compensation is payable as follows:

(1) in a criminal case or in a civil case involving just compensation under the Fifth Amendment, from any funds that are provided by law; and

(2) in any other civil case, by the parties in the proportion and at the time that the court directs— and the compensation is then charged like other costs.

(d) **Disclosing the Appointment to the Jury.** The court may authorize disclosure to the jury that the court appointed the expert.

(e) **Parties' Choice of Their Own Experts.** This rule does not limit a party in calling its own experts. (Pub.L. 93–595, § 1, Jan. 2, 1975, 88 Stat.1938; Mar. 2, 1987, eff. Oct. 1, 1987; Apr. 26, 2011, eff. Dec. 1, 2011.)

ADVISORY COMMITTEE NOTES
1972 Proposed Rules

The practice of shopping for experts, the venality of some experts, and the reluctance of many reputable experts to involve themselves in litigation, have been matters of deep concern. Though the contention is made that court appointed experts acquire an aura of infallibility to which they are not entitled, Levy, Impartial Medical Testimony—Revisited, 34 Temple L.Q. 416 (1961), the trend is increasingly to provide for their use. While experience indicates that actual appointment is a relatively infrequent occurrence, the assumption may be made that the availability of the procedure in itself decreases the need for resorting to it. The ever-present possibility that the judge may appoint an expert in a given case must inevitably exert a sobering effect on the expert witness of a party and upon the person utilizing his services.

The inherent power of a trial judge to appoint an expert of his own choosing is virtually unquestioned. *Scott v. Spanjer Bros., Inc.,* 298 F.2d 928 (2d Cir.1962); *Danville Tobacco Assn. v. Bryant–Buckner Associates,* Inc., 333 F.2d 202 (4th Cir.1964); Sink, The Unused Power of a Federal Judge to Call His Own Expert Witnesses, 29 S.Cal.L.Rev. 195 (1956); 2 Wigmore § 563, 9 *id.* § 2484; Annot., 95 A.L.R.2d 383. Hence the problem becomes largely one of detail.

The New York plan is well known and is described in Report by Special Committee of the Association of the Bar of the City of New York: Impartial Medical Testimony (1956). On recommendation of the Section of Judicial Administration, local adoption of an impartial medical plan was endorsed by the American Bar Association. 82 A.B.A.Rep. 184–185 (1957). Descriptions and analyses of plans in effect in various parts of the country are found in Van Dusen, A United States District Judge's View of the Impartial Medical Expert System, 32 F.R.D. 498 (1963); Wick and Kightlinger, Impartial Medical Testimony Under the Federal Civil Rules: A Tale of Three Doctors, 34 Ins. Counsel J. 115 (1967); and numerous articles collected in Klein, Judicial Administration and the Legal Profession 393 (1963). Statutes and rules include California Evidence Code §§ 730–733; Illinois Supreme Court Rule 215(d), Ill.Rev.Stat.1969, c. 110A, § 215(d); Burns Indiana Stats.1956, § 9–1702; Wisconsin Stats.Annot.1958, § 957.27.

In the federal practice, a comprehensive scheme for court appointed experts was initiated with the adoption of Rule 28 of the Federal Rules of Criminal Procedure in 1946. The Judicial Conference of the United States in 1953 considered court appointed experts in civil cases, but only with respect to whether they should be compensated from public funds, a proposal which was rejected. Report of the Judicial Conference of the United States 23 (1953). The present rule expands the practice to include civil cases.

Note to Subdivision (a). Subdivision (a) is based on Rule 28 of the Federal Rules of Criminal Procedure, with a few changes, mainly in the interest of clarity. Language has been added to provide specifically for the appointment either on motion of a party or on the judge's own motion. A provision subjecting the court appointed expert to deposition procedures has been incorporated. The rule has been revised to make definite the right of any party, including the party calling him, to cross-examine.

Note to Subdivision (b). Subdivision (b) combines the present provision for compensation in criminal cases with what seems to be a fair and feasible handling of civil cases, originally found in the Model Act and carried from there into Uniform Rule 60. See also California Evidence Code §§ 730–731. The special provision for Fifth Amendment compensation cases is designed to guard against reducing constitutionally guaranteed just compensation by requiring the recipient to pay costs. See Rule 71A(*l*) of the Rules of Civil Procedure.

Note to Subdivision (c). Subdivision (c) seems to be essential if the use of court appointed experts is to be fully effective. Uniform Rule 61 so provides.

Note to Subdivision (d). Subdivision (d) is in essence the last sentence of Rule 28(a) of the Federal Rules of Criminal Procedure.

1987 Amendment

The amendments are technical. No substantive change is intended.

2011 Amendments

The language of Rule 706 has been amended as part of the restyling of the Evidence Rules to make them more easily understood and to make style and terminology consistent throughout the rules. These changes are intended to be stylistic only. There is no intent to change any result in any ruling on evidence admissibility.

CROSS REFERENCES

Appointment of interpreters, see Fed.Rules Cr.Proc. Rule 28, 18 USCA.

ARTICLE VIII. HEARSAY

Rule

801. Definitions That Apply to This Article; Exclusions From Hearsay.
802. The Rule Against Hearsay.
803. Exceptions to the Rule Against Hearsay—Regardless of Whether the Declarant Is Available as a Witness.
804. Exceptions to the Rule Against Hearsay—When the Declarant Is Unavailable as a Witness.
805. Hearsay Within Hearsay.
806. Attacking and Supporting the Declarant's Credibility.
807. Residual Exception.

ADVISORY COMMITTEE NOTES

1972 Proposed Rules

Introductory Note; The Hearsay Problem. The factors to be considered in evaluating the testimony of a witness are perception, memory, and narration. Morgan, Hearsay Dangers and the Application of the Hearsay Concept, 62 Harv. L.Rev. 177 (1948), Selected Writings on Evidence and Trial 764, 765 (Fryer ed. 1957); Shientag, Cross–Examination—A Judge's Viewpoint, 3 Record 12 (1948); Strahorn, A Reconsideration of the Hearsay Rule and Admissions, 85 U.Pa.L.Rev. 484, 485 (1937), Selected Writings, *supra*, 756, 757; Weinstein, Probative Force of Hearsay, 46 Iowa L.Rev. 331 (1961). Sometimes a fourth is added, sincerity, but in fact it seems merely to be an aspect of the three already mentioned.

In order to encourage the witness to do his best with respect to each of these factors, and to expose any inaccuracies which may enter in, the Anglo–American tradition has evolved three conditions under which witnesses will ideally be required to testify: (1) under oath, (2) in the personal presence of the trier of fact, (3) subject to cross-examination.

(1) Standard procedure calls for the swearing of witnesses. While the practice is perhaps less effective than in an earlier time, no disposition to relax the requirement is apparent, other than to allow affirmation by persons with scruples against taking oaths.

(2) The demeanor of the witness traditionally has been believed to furnish trier and opponent with valuable clues. *Universal Camera Corp. v. N.L.R.B.*, 340 U.S. 474, 495–496, 71 S.Ct. 456, 95 L.Ed. 456 (1951); Sahm, Demeanor Evidence: Elusive and Intangible Imponderables, 47 A.B.A.J. 580 (1961), quoting numerous authorities. The witness himself will probably be impressed with the solemnity of the occasion and the possibility of public disgrace. Willingness to falsify may reasonably become more difficult in the presence of the person against whom directed. Rules 26 and 43(a) of the Federal Rules of Criminal and Civil Procedure, respectively, include the general requirement that testimony be taken orally in open court. The Sixth Amendment right of confrontation is a manifestation of these beliefs and attitudes.

(3) Emphasis on the basis of the hearsay rule today tends to center upon the condition of cross-examination. All may not agree with Wigmore that cross-examination is "beyond doubt the greatest legal engine ever invented for the discovery of truth," but all will agree with his statement that it has become a "vital feature" of the Anglo–American system. 5 Wigmore § 1367, p. 29. The belief, or perhaps hope, that cross-examination is effective in exposing imperfections of perception, memory, and narration is fundamental. Morgan, Foreword to Model Code of Evidence 37 (1942).

The logic of the preceding discussion might suggest that no testimony be received unless in full compliance with the three ideal conditions. No one advocates this position. Common sense tells that much evidence which is not given under the three conditions may be inherently superior to much that is. Moreover, when the choice is between evidence which is less than best and no evidence at all, only clear folly would dictate an across-the-board policy of doing without. The problem thus resolves itself into effecting a sensible accommodation between these considerations and the desirability of giving testimony under the ideal conditions.

The solution evolved by the common law has been a general rule excluding hearsay but subject to numerous exceptions under circumstances supposed to furnish guarantees of trustworthiness. Criticisms of this scheme are that it is bulky and complex, fails to screen good from bad hearsay realistically, and inhibits the growth of the law of evidence.

For Complete Annotation Materials, see United States Code Annotated

Since no one advocates excluding all hearsay, three possible solutions may be considered: (1) abolish the rule against hearsay and admit all hearsay; (2) admit hearsay possessing sufficient probative force, but with procedural safeguards; (3) revise the present system of class exceptions.

(1) Abolition of the hearsay rule would be the simplest solution. The effect would not be automatically to abolish the giving of testimony under ideal conditions. If the declarant were available, compliance with the ideal conditions would be optional with either party. Thus the proponent could call the declarant as a witness as a form of presentation more impressive than his hearsay statement. Or the opponent could call the declarant to be cross-examined upon his statement. This is the tenor of Uniform Rule 63(1), admitting the hearsay declaration of a person "who is present at the hearing and available for cross-examination." Compare the treatment of declarations of available declarants in Rule 801(d)(1) of the instant rules. If the declarant were unavailable, a rule of free admissibility would make no distinctions in terms of degrees of noncompliance with the ideal conditions and would exact no quid pro quo in the form of assurances of trustworthiness. Rule 503 of the Model Code did exactly that, providing for the admissibility of any hearsay declaration by an unavailable declarant, finding support in the Massachusetts act of 1898, enacted at the instance of Thayer, Mass.Gen.L.1932, c. 233, § 65, and in the English act of 1938, St.1938, c. 28, Evidence. Both are limited to civil cases. The draftsmen of the Uniform Rules chose a less advanced and more conventional position. Comment, Uniform Rule 63. The present Advisory Committee has been unconvinced of the wisdom of abandoning the traditional requirement of some particular assurance of credibility as a condition precedent to admitting the hearsay declaration of an unavailable declarant.

In criminal cases, the Sixth Amendment requirement of confrontation would no doubt move into a large part of the area presently occupied by the hearsay rule in the event of the abolition of the latter. The resultant split between civil and criminal evidence is regarded as an undesirable development.

(2) Abandonment of the system of class exceptions in favor of individual treatment in the setting of the particular case, accompanied by procedural safeguards, has been impressively advocated. Weinstein, The Probative Force of Hearsay, 46 Iowa L.Rev. 331 (1961). Admissibility would be determined by weighing the probative force of the evidence against the possibility of prejudice, waste of time, and the availability of more satisfactory evidence. The bases of the traditional hearsay exceptions would be helpful in assessing probative force. Ladd, The Relationship of the Principles of Exclusionary Rules of Evidence to the Problem of Proof, 18 Minn. L.Rev. 506 (1934). Procedural safeguards would consist of notice of intention to use hearsay, free comment by the judge on the weight of the evidence, and a greater measure of authority in both trial and appellate judges to deal with evidence on the basis of weight. The Advisory Committee has rejected this approach to hearsay as involving too great a measure of judicial discretion, minimizing the predictability of rulings, enhancing the difficulties of preparation for trial, adding a further element to the already over-complicated congeries of pretrial procedures, and requiring substantially different rules for civil and criminal cases. The only way in which the probative force of hearsay differs from the probative force of other testimony is in the absence of oath, demeanor, and cross-examination as aids in determining credibility. For a judge to exclude evidence because he does not believe it has been described as "altogether atypical, extraordinary. * * *" Chadbourn, Bentham and the Hearsay Rule—A Benthamic View of Rule 63(4)(c) of the Uniform Rules of Evidence, 75 Harv.L.Rev. 932, 947 (1962).

(3) The approach to hearsay in these rules is that of the common law, i.e., a general rule excluding hearsay, with exceptions under which evidence is not required to be excluded even though hearsay. The traditional hearsay exceptions are drawn upon for the exceptions, collected under two rules, one dealing with situations where availability of the declarant is regarded as immaterial and the other with those where unavailability is made a condition to the admission of the hearsay statement. Each of the two rules concludes with a provision for hearsay statements not within one of the specified exceptions "but having comparable circumstantial guarantees of trustworthiness." Rules 803(24) and 804(b)(6). This plan is submitted as calculated to encourage growth and development in this area of the law, while conserving the values and experience of the past as a guide to the future.

Confrontation and Due Process. Until very recently, decisions invoking the confrontation clause of the Sixth Amendment were surprisingly few, a fact probably explainable by the former inapplicability of the clause to the states and by the hearsay rule's occupancy of much the same ground. The pattern which emerges from the earlier cases invoking the clause is substantially that of the hearsay rule, applied to criminal cases: an accused is entitled to have the witnesses against him testify under oath, in the presence of himself and trier, subject to cross-examination; yet considerations of public policy and necessity require the recognition of such exceptions as dying declarations and former testimony of unavailable witnesses. *Mattox v. United States*, 156 U.S. 237, 15 S.Ct. 337, 39 L.Ed. 409 (1895); *Motes v. United States*, 178 U.S. 458, 20 S.Ct. 993, 44 L.Ed. 1150 (1900); *Delaney v. United States*, 263 U.S. 586, 44 S.Ct. 206, 68 L.Ed. 462 (1924). Beginning with *Snyder v. Massachusetts*, 291 U.S. 97, 54 S.Ct. 330, 78 L.Ed. 674 (1934), the Court began to speak of confrontation as an aspect of procedural due process, thus extending its applicability to state cases and to federal cases other than criminal. The language of *Snyder* was that of an elastic concept of hearsay. The deportation case of *Bridges v. Wixon*, 326 U.S. 135, 65 S.Ct. 1443, 89 L.Ed. 2103 (1945), may be read broadly as imposing a strictly construed right of confrontation in all kinds of cases or narrowly as the product of a failure of the Immigration and Naturalization Service to follow its own rules. *In re Oliver*, 333 U.S. 257, 68 S.Ct. 499, 92 L.Ed. 682 (1948), ruled that cross-examination was essential to due process in a state contempt proceeding, but in *United States v. Nugent*, 346 U.S. 1, 73 S.Ct. 991, 97 L.Ed. 1417 (1953), the court held that it was not an essential aspect of a "hearing" for a conscientious objector under the Selective Service Act. *Stein v. New York*, 346 U.S. 156, 196, 73 S.Ct. 1077, 97 L.Ed. 1522 (1953), disclaimed any purpose to read the hearsay rule into the Fourteenth Amendment, but in *Greene v. McElroy*, 360 U.S. 474, 79 S.Ct. 1400, 3 L.Ed.2d 1377 (1959), revocation of security clearance without confrontation and cross-examination was held unauthorized, and a similar result was reached in *Willner v. Committee on Character*, 373 U.S. 96, 83 S.Ct. 1175, 10 L.Ed.2d 224 (1963). Ascertaining the constitutional dimensions of the confrontation-hearsay aggregate against the background of these cases is a matter of some difficulty, yet the general pattern is at least not inconsistent with that of the hearsay rule.

In 1965 the confrontation clause was held applicable to the states. *Pointer v. Texas,* 380 U.S. 400, 85 S.Ct. 1065, 13 L.Ed.2d 923 (1965). Prosecution use of former testimony given at a preliminary hearing where petitioner was not represented by counsel was a violation of the clause. The same result would have followed under conventional hearsay doctrine read in the light of a constitutional right to counsel, and nothing in the opinion suggests any difference in essential outline between the hearsay rule and the right of confrontation. In the companion case of *Douglas v. Alabama,* 380 U.S. 415, 85 S.Ct. 1074, 13 L.Ed.2d 934 (1965), however, the result reached by applying the confrontation clause is one reached less readily via the hearsay rule. A confession implicating petitioner was put before the jury by reading it to the witness in portions and asking if he made that statement. The witness refused to answer on grounds of self-incrimination. The result, said the Court, was to deny cross-examination, and hence confrontation. True, it could broadly be said that the confession was a hearsay statement which for all practical purposes was put in evidence. Yet a more easily accepted explanation of the opinion is that its real thrust was in the direction of curbing undesirable prosecutorial behavior, rather than merely applying rules of exclusion, and that the confrontation clause was the means selected to achieve this end. Comparable facts and a like result appeared in *Brookhart v. Janis,* 384 U.S. 1, 86 S.Ct. 1245, 16 L.Ed.2d 314 (1966).

The pattern suggested in *Douglas* was developed further and more distinctly in a pair of cases at the end of the 1966 term. *United States v. Wade,* 388 U.S. 218, 87 S.Ct. 1926, 18 L.Ed.2d 1149 (1967), and *Gilbert v. California,* 388 U.S. 263, 87 S.Ct. 1951, 18 L.Ed.2d 1178 (1967), hinged upon practices followed in identifying accused persons before trial. This pretrial identification was said to be so decisive an aspect of the case that accused was entitled to have counsel present; a pretrial identification made in the absence of counsel was not itself receivable in evidence and, in addition, might fatally infect a courtroom identification. The presence of counsel at the earlier identification was described as a necessary prerequisite for "a meaningful confrontation at trial." *United States v. Wade, supra,* 388 U.S. at p. 236, 87 S.Ct. at p. 1937. *Wade* involved no evidence of the fact of a prior identification and hence was not susceptible of being decided on hearsay grounds. In *Gilbert,* witnesses did testify to an earlier identification, readily classifiable as hearsay under a fairly strict view of what constitutes hearsay. The Court, however, carefully avoided basing the decision on the hearsay ground, choosing confrontation instead. 388 U.S. 263, 272, n. 3, 87 S.Ct. 1951. See also *Parker v. Gladden,* 385 U.S. 363, 87 S.Ct. 468, 17 L.Ed.2d 420 (1966), holding that the right of confrontation was violated when the bailiff made prejudicial statements to jurors, and Note, 75 Yale L.J. 1434 (1966).

Under the earlier cases, the confrontation clause may have been little more than a constitutional embodiment of the hearsay rule, even including traditional exceptions but with some room for expanding them along similar lines. But under the recent cases the impact of the clause clearly extends beyond the confines of the hearsay rule. These considerations have led the Advisory Committee to conclude that a hearsay rule can function usefully as an adjunct to the confrontation right in constitutional areas and independently in nonconstitutional areas. In recognition of the separateness of the confrontation clause and the hearsay rule, and to avoid inviting collisions between them or between the hearsay rule and other exclusionary principles, the exceptions set forth in Rules 803 and 804 are stated in terms of exemption from the general exclusionary mandate of the hearsay rule, rather than in positive terms of admissibility. See Uniform Rule 63(1) to (31) and California Evidence Code §§ 1200–1340.

Rule 801. Definitions That Apply to This Article; Exclusions From Hearsay

(a) Statement. "Statement" means a person's oral assertion, written assertion, or nonverbal conduct, if the person intended it as an assertion.

(b) Declarant. "Declarant" means the person who made the statement.

(c) Hearsay. "Hearsay" means a statement that:

(1) the declarant does not make while testifying at the current trial or hearing; and

(2) a party offers in evidence to prove the truth of the matter asserted in the statement.

(d) Statements That Are Not Hearsay. A statement that meets the following conditions is not hearsay:

(1) **A Declarant–Witness's Prior Statement.** The declarant testifies and is subject to cross-examination about a prior statement, and the statement:

(A) is inconsistent with the declarant's testimony and was given under penalty of perjury at a trial, hearing, or other proceeding or in a deposition;

(B) is consistent with the declarant's testimony and is offered:

(i) to rebut an express or implied charge that the declarant recently fabricated it or acted from a recent improper influence or motive in so testifying; or

(ii) to rehabilitate the declarant's credibility as a witness when attacked on another ground; or

(C) identifies a person as someone the declarant perceived earlier.

(2) **An Opposing Party's Statement.** The statement is offered against an opposing party and:

(A) was made by the party in an individual or representative capacity;

(B) is one the party manifested that it adopted or believed to be true;

(C) was made by a person whom the party authorized to make a statement on the subject;

(D) was made by the party's agent or employee on a matter within the scope of that relationship and while it existed; or

(E) was made by the party's coconspirator during and in furtherance of the conspiracy.

The statement must be considered but does not by itself establish the declarant's authority under (C); the existence or scope of the relationship under (D); or the existence of the conspiracy or participation in it under (E).

(Pub.L. 93–595, § 1, Jan. 2, 1975, 88 Stat.1938; Pub.L. 94–113, § 1, Oct. 16, 1975, 89 Stat. 576; Mar. 2, 1987, eff. Oct. 1, 1987; Apr. 11, 1997, eff. Dec. 1, 1997; Apr. 26, 2011, eff. Dec. 1, 2011; Apr. 25, 2014, eff. Dec. 1, 2014.)

ADVISORY COMMITTEE NOTES

1972 Proposed Rules

Note to Subdivision (a). The definition of "statement" assumes importance because the term is used in the definition of hearsay in subdivision (c). The effect of the definition of "statement" is to exclude from the operation of the hearsay rule all evidence of conduct, verbal or nonverbal, not intended as an assertion. The key to the definition is that nothing is an assertion unless intended to be one.

It can scarcely be doubted that an assertion made in words is intended by the declarant to be an assertion. Hence verbal assertions readily fall into the category of "statement." Whether nonverbal conduct should be regarded as a statement for purposes of defining hearsay requires further consideration. Some nonverbal conduct, such as the act of pointing to identify a suspect in a lineup, is clearly the equivalent of words, assertive in nature, and to be regarded as a statement. Other nonverbal conduct, however, may be offered as evidence that the person acted as he did because of his belief in the existence of the condition sought to be proved, from which belief the existence of the condition may be inferred. This sequence is, arguably, in effect an assertion of the existence of the condition and hence properly includable within the hearsay concept. See Morgan, Hearsay Dangers and the Application of the Hearsay Concept, 62 Harv.L.Rev. 177, 214, 217 (1948), and the elaboration in Finman, Implied Assertions as Hearsay: Some Criticisms of the Uniform Rules of Evidence, 14 Stan.L.Rev. 682 (1962). Admittedly evidence of this character is untested with respect to the perception, memory, and narration (or their equivalents) of the actor, but the Advisory Committee is of the view that these dangers are minimal in the absence of an intent to assert and do not justify the loss of the evidence on hearsay grounds. No class of evidence is free of the possibility of fabrication, but the likelihood is less with nonverbal than with assertive verbal conduct. The situations giving rise to the nonverbal conduct are such as virtually to eliminate questions of sincerity. Motivation, the nature of the conduct, and the presence or absence of reliance will bear heavily upon the weight to be given the evidence. Falknor, The "Hear–Say" Rule as a "See–Do" Rule: Evidence of Conduct, 33 Rocky Mt.L.Rev. 133 (1961). Similar considerations govern nonassertive verbal conduct and verbal conduct which is assertive but offered as a basis for inferring something other than the matter asserted, also excluded from the definition of hearsay by the language of subdivision (c).

When evidence of conduct is offered on the theory that it is not a statement, and hence not hearsay, a preliminary determination will be required to determine whether an assertion is intended. The rule is so worded as to place the burden upon the party claiming that the intention existed; ambiguous and doubtful cases will be resolved against him and in favor of admissibility. The determination involves no greater difficulty than many other preliminary questions of fact. Maguire, The Hearsay System: Around and Through the Thicket, 14 Vand.L.Rev. 741, 765–767 (1961).

For similar approaches, see Uniform Rule 62(1); California Evidence Code §§ 225, 1200; Kansas Code of Civil Procedure § 60–459(a); New Jersey Evidence Rule 62(1).

Note to Subdivision (c). The definition follows along familiar lines in including only statements offered to prove the truth of the matter asserted. McCormick § 225; 5 Wigmore § 1361, 6 *id.* § 1766. If the significance of an offered statement lies solely in the fact that it was made, no issue is raised as to the truth of anything asserted, and the statement is not hearsay. *Emich Motors Corp. v. General Motors Corp.*, 181 F.2d 70 (7th Cir.1950), rev'd on other grounds 340 U.S. 558, 71 S.Ct. 408, 95 L.Ed. 534, letters of complaint from customers offered as a reason for cancellation of dealer's franchise, to rebut contention that franchise was revoked for refusal to finance sales through affiliated finance company. The effect is to exclude from hearsay the entire category of "verbal acts" and "verbal parts of an act," in which the statement itself affects the legal rights of the parties or is a circumstance bearing on conduct affecting their rights.

The definition of hearsay must, of course, be read with reference to the definition of statement set forth in subdivision (a).

Testimony given by a witness in the course of court proceedings is excluded since there is compliance with all the ideal conditions for testifying.

Note to Subdivision (d). Several types of statements which would otherwise literally fall within the definition are expressly excluded from it:

(1) *Prior statement by witness.* Considerable controversy has attended the question whether a prior out-of-court statement by a person now available for cross-examination concerning it, under oath and in the presence of the trier of fact, should be classed as hearsay. If the witness admits on the stand that he made the statement and that it was true, he adopts the statement and there is no hearsay problem. The hearsay problem arises when the witness on the stand denies having made the statement or admits having made it but denies its truth. The argument in favor of treating these latter statements as hearsay is based upon the ground that the conditions of oath, cross-examination, and demeanor observation did not prevail at the time the statement was made and cannot adequately be supplied by the later examination. The logic of the situation is troublesome. So far as concerns the oath, its mere presence has never been regarded as sufficient to remove a statement from the hearsay category, and it receives much less emphasis than cross-examination as a truth-compelling device. While strong expressions are found to the effect that no conviction can be had or important right taken away on the basis of statements not made under fear of prosecution for perjury, *Bridges v. Wixon*, 326 U.S. 135, 65 S.Ct. 1443, 89 L.Ed. 2103 (1945), the fact is that, of the many common law exceptions to the hearsay rule, only that for reported testimony has required the statement to have been made under oath. Nor is it satisfactorily explained why cross-examination cannot be conducted subsequently with success. The decisions contending most vigorously for its inadequacy in fact demonstrate quite thorough exploration of the weaknesses and doubts attending the earlier statement. *State v. Saporen*, 205 Minn. 358, 285 N.W. 898 (1939); *Ruhala v. Roby*, 379 Mich. 102, 150 N.W.2d 146 (1967); *People v. Johnson*, 68 Cal.2d 646, 68 Cal.Rptr. 599, 441 P.2d 111 (1968). In respect to demeanor, as Judge Learned Hand observed in *Di Carlo v. United States*, 6 F.2d 364 (2d Cir.1925), when the jury decides that the truth is not what the witness says now, but what he said before, they are still deciding from what they see and hear in court. The bulk of the case law nevertheless has been against allowing prior statements of witnesses to be

used generally as substantive evidence. Most of the writers and Uniform Rule 63(1) have taken the opposite position.

The position taken by the Advisory Committee in formulating this part of the rule is funded upon an unwillingness to countenance the general use of prior prepared statements as substantive evidence, but with a recognition that particular circumstances call for a contrary result. The judgment is one more of experience than of logic. The rule requires in each instance, as a general safeguard, that the declarant actually testify as a witness, and it then enumerates three situations in which the statement is excepted from the category of hearsay. Compare Uniform Rule 63(1) which allows any out-of-court statement of a declarant who is present at the trial and available for cross-examination.

(A) Prior inconsistent statements traditionally have been admissible to impeach but not as substantive evidence. Under the rule they are substantive evidence. As has been said by the California Law Revision Commission with respect to a similar provision:

"Section 1235 admits inconsistent statements of witnesses because the dangers against which the hearsay rule is designed to protect are largely nonexistent. The declarant is in court and may be examined and cross-examined in regard to his statements and their subject matter. In many cases, the inconsistent statement is more likely to be true than the testimony of the witness at the trial because it was made nearer in time to the matter to which it relates and is less likely to be influenced by the controversy that gave rise to the litigation. The trier of fact has the declarant before it and can observe his demeanor and the nature of his testimony as he denies or tries to explain away the inconsistency. Hence, it is in as good a position to determine the truth or falsity of the prior statement as it is to determine the truth or falsity of the inconsistent testimony given in court. Moreover, Section 1235 will provide a party with desirable protection against the 'turncoat' witness who changes his story on the stand and deprives the party calling him of evidence essential to his case." Comment, California Evidence Code § 1235. See also McCormick § 39. The Advisory Committee finds these views more convincing than those expressed in *People v. Johnson,* 68 Cal.2d 646, 68 Cal.Rptr. 599, 441 P.2d 111 (1968). The constitutionality of the Advisory Committee's view was upheld in *California v. Green,* 399 U.S. 149, 90 S.Ct. 1930, 26 L.Ed.2d 489 (1970). Moreover, the requirement that the statement be inconsistent with the testimony given assures a thorough exploration of both versions while the witness is on the stand and bars any general and indiscriminate use of previously prepared statements.

(B) Prior consistent statements traditionally have been admissible to rebut charges of recent fabrication or improper influence or motive but not as substantive evidence. Under the rule they are substantive evidence. The prior statement is consistent with the testimony given on the stand, and, if the opposite party wishes to open the door for its admission in evidence, no sound reason is apparent why it should not be received generally.

(C) The admission of evidence of identification finds substantial support, although it falls beyond a doubt in the category of prior out-of-court statements. Illustrative are *People v. Gould,* 54 Cal.2d 621, 7 Cal.Rptr. 273, 354 P.2d 865 (1960); *Judy v. State,* 218 Md. 168, 146 A.2d 29 (1958); *State v. Simmons,* 63 Wash.2d 17, 385 P.2d 389 (1963); California Evidence Code § 1238; New Jersey Evidence Rule 63(1)(c); N.Y.Code of Criminal Procedure § 393–b. Further cases are found in 4 Wigmore § 1130. The basis is the generally unsatisfactory and inconclusive nature of courtroom identifications as compared with those made at an earlier time under less suggestive conditions. The Supreme Court considered the admissibility of evidence of prior identification in *Gilbert v. California,* 388 U.S. 263, 87 S.Ct. 1951, 18 L.Ed.2d 1178 (1967). Exclusion of lineup identification was held to be required because the accused did not then have the assistance of counsel. Significantly, the Court carefully refrained from placing its decision on the ground that testimony as to the making of a prior out-of-court identification ("That's the man") violated either the hearsay rule or the right of confrontation because not made under oath, subject to immediate cross-examination, in the presence of the trier. Instead the Court observed:

"There is a split among the States concerning the admissibility of prior extra-judicial identifications, as independent evidence of identity, both by the witness and third parties present at the prior identification. See 71 ALR2d 449. It has been held that the prior identification is hearsay, and, when admitted through the testimony of the identifier, is merely a prior consistent statement. The recent trend, however, is to admit the prior identification under the exception that admits as substantive evidence a prior communication by a witness who is available for cross-examination at the trial. See 5 ALR2d Later Case Service 1225–1228. * * *" 388 U.S. at 272, n. 3, 87 S.Ct. at 1956.

(2) *Admissions.* Admissions by a party-opponent are excluded from the category of hearsay on the theory that their admissibility in evidence is the result of the adversary system rather than satisfaction of the conditions of the hearsay rule. Strahorn, A Reconsideration of the Hearsay Rule and Admissions, 85 U.Pa.L.Rev. 484, 564 (1937); Morgan, Basic Problems of Evidence 265 (1962); 4 Wigmore § 1048. No guarantee of trustworthiness is required in the case of an admission. The freedom which admissions have enjoyed from technical demands of searching for an assurance of truthworthiness in some against-interest circumstance, and from the restrictive influences of the opinion rule and the rule requiring firsthand knowledge, when taken with the apparently prevalent satisfaction with the results, calls for generous treatment of this avenue to admissibility.

The rule specifies five categories of statements for which the responsibility of a party is considered sufficient to justify reception in evidence against him:

(A) A party's own statement is the classic example of an admission. If he has a representative capacity and the statement is offered against him in that capacity, no inquiry whether he was acting in the representative capacity in making the statement is required; the statement need only be relevant to represent affairs. To the same effect in California Evidence Code § 1220. Compare Uniform Rule 63(7), requiring a statement to be made in a representative capacity to be admissible against a party in a representative capacity.

(B) Under established principles an admission may be made by adopting or acquiescing in the statement of another. While knowledge of contents would ordinarily be essential, this is not inevitably so: "X is a reliable person and knows what he is talking about." See McCormick § 246, p. 527, n. 15. Adoption or acquiescence may be manifested in any appropriate manner. When silence is relied upon, the theory is that the person would, under the circumstances, protest the statement made in his presence, if untrue. The decision in each case calls for an evaluation in terms of probable human behavior. In civil cases, the results have generally been satisfactory. In criminal cases, however, troublesome questions have been raised by decisions holding that failure to deny is an admission: the inference is a fairly weak one, to begin with; silence may be motivated by advice of counsel or realization that "anything you say may be used against you"; unusual opportunity is afforded to manufacture evidence; and encroachment upon the privilege against self-incrimination seems inescapably to be involved. However, recent decisions of the Supreme Court relating to custodial interrogation and the right to counsel appear to resolve these difficulties. Hence the rule contains no special provisions concerning failure to deny in criminal cases.

(C) No authority is required for the general proposition that a statement authorized by a party to be made should have the status of an admission by the party. However, the question arises whether only statements to third persons should be so regarded, to the exclusion of statements by the agent to the principal. The rule is phrased broadly so as to encompass both. While it may be argued that the agent authorized to make statements to his principal does not speak for him, Morgan, Basic Problems of Evidence 273 (1962), communication to an outsider has not generally been thought to be an essential characteristic of an admission. Thus a party's books or records are usable against him, without regard to any intent to disclose to third persons. 5 Wigmore § 1557. See also McCormick § 78, pp. 159–161. In accord is New Jersey Evidence Rule 63(8)(a). Cf. Uniform Rule 63(8)(a) and California Evidence Code § 1222 which limit status as an admission in this regard to statements authorized by the party to be made "for" him, which is perhaps an ambiguous limitation to statements to third persons. Falknor, Vicarious Admissions and the Uniform Rules, 14 Vand. L.Rev. 855, 860–861 (1961).

(D) The tradition has been to test the admissibility of statements by agents, as admissions, by applying the usual test of agency. Was the admission made by the agent acting in the scope of his employment? Since few principals employ agents for the purpose of making damaging statements, the usual result was exclusion of the statement. Dissatisfaction with this loss of valuable and helpful evidence has been increasing. A substantial trend favors admitting statements related to a matter within the scope of the agency or employment. *Grayson v. Williams,* 256 F.2d 61 (10th Cir.1958); *Koninklijke Luchtvaart Maatschappij N.V. KLM Royal Dutch Airlines v. Tuller,* 110 U.S.App.D.C. 282, 292 F.2d 775, 784 (1961); *Martin v. Savage Truck Lines,* Inc., 121 F.Supp. 417 (D.D.C.1954), and numerous state court decisions collected in 4 Wigmore, 1964 Supp. pp. 66–73, with comments by the editor that the statements should have been excluded as not within scope of agency. For the traditional view see *Northern Oil Co. v. Socony Mobil Oil Co.,* 347 F.2d 81, 85 (2d Cir.1965) and cases cited therein. Similar provisions are found in Uniform Rule 63(9)(a), Kansas Code of Civil Procedure § 60–460(i)(1), and New Jersey Evidence Rule 63(9)(a).

(E) The limitation upon the admissibility of statements of co-conspirators to those made "during the course and in furtherance of the conspiracy" is in the accepted pattern. While the broadened view of agency taken in item (iv) might suggest wider admissibility of statements of co-conspirators, the agency theory of conspiracy is at best a fiction and ought not to serve as a basis for admissibility beyond that already established. See Levie, Hearsay and Conspiracy, 52 Mich. L.Rev. 1159 (1954); Comment, 25 U.Chi.L.Rev. 530 (1958). The rule is consistent with the position of the Supreme Court

in denying admissibility to statements made after the objectives of the conspiracy have either failed or been achieved. *Krulewitch v. United States,* 336 U.S. 440, 69 S.Ct. 716, 93 L.Ed. 790 (1949); *Wong Sun v. United States,* 371 U.S. 471, 490, 83 S.Ct. 407, 9 L.Ed.2d 441 (1963). For similarly limited provisions see California Evidence Code § 1223 and New Jersey Rule 63(9)(b). Cf. Uniform Rule 63(9)(b).

1974 Enactment

Note to Subdivision (d)(1). Present federal law, except in the Second Circuit, permits the use of prior inconsistent statements of a witness for impeachment only. Rule 801(d)(1) as proposed by the Court would have permitted all such statements to be admissible as substantive evidence, an approach followed by a small but growing number of State jurisdictions and recently held constitutional in California v. Green, 399 U.S. 149 (1970). Although there was some support expressed for the Court Rule, based largely on the need to counteract the effect of witness intimidation in criminal cases, the Committee decided to adopt a compromise version of the Rule similar to the position of the Second Circuit. The Rule as amended draws a distinction between types of prior inconsistent statements (other than statements of identification of a person made after perceiving him which are currently admissible, see United States v. Anderson, 406 F.2d 719, 720 (4th Cir.), cert. denied, 395 U.S. 967 (1969)) and allows only those made while the declarant was subject to cross-examination at a trial or hearing or in a deposition, to be admissible for their truth. Compare United States v. DeSisto, 329 F.2d 929 (2nd Cir.), cert. denied, 377 U.S. 979 (1964); United States v. Cunningham, 446 F.2d 194 (2nd Cir.1971) (restricting the admissibility of prior inconsistent statements as substantive evidence to those made under oath in a formal proceeding, but not requiring that there have been an opportunity for cross-examination). The rationale for the Committee's decision is that (1) unlike in most other situations involving unsworn or oral statements, there can be no dispute as to whether the prior statement was made; and (2) the context of a formal proceeding, an oath, and the opportunity for cross-examination provide firm additional assurances of the reliability of the prior statement. House Report No. 93–650.

Note to Subdivision (d)(1)(A). Rule 801 defines what is and what is not hearsay for the purpose of admitting a prior statement as substantive evidence. A prior statement of a witness at a trial or hearing which is inconsistent with his testimony is, of course, always admissible for the purpose of impeaching the witness' credibility.

As submitted by the Supreme Court, subdivision (d)(1)(A) made admissible as substantive evidence the prior statement of a witness inconsistent with his present testimony.

The House severely limited the admissibility of prior inconsistent statements by adding a requirement that the prior statement must have been subject to cross-examination, thus precluding even the use of grand jury statements. The requirement that the prior statement must have been subject to cross-examination appears unnecessary since this rule comes into play only when the witness testifies in the present trial. At that time, he is on the stand and can explain an earlier position and be cross-examined as to both.

The requirement that the statement be under oath also appears unnecessary. Notwithstanding the absence of an oath contemporaneous with the statement, the witness, when on the stand, qualifying or denying the prior statement, is under oath. In any event, of all the many recognized exceptions to the hearsay rule, only one (former testimony) requires that the out-of-court statement have been made under oath. With respect to the lack of evidence of the demeanor of the witness at the time of the prior statement, it would be difficult to improve upon Judge Learned Hand's observation that when the jury decides that the truth is not what the witness says now but what he said before, they are still deciding from what they see and hear in court. [*Di Carlo v. U.S.*, 6 F.2d 364 (2d Cir.1925)].

The rule as submitted by the Court has positive advantages. The prior statement was made nearer in time to the events, when memory was fresher and intervening influences had not been brought into play. A realistic method is provided for dealing with the turncoat witness who changes his story on the stand [see Comment, California Evidence Code § 1235; McCormick, Evidence, § 38 (2nd ed. 1972)].

New Jersey, California, and Utah have adopted a rule similar to this one; and Nevada, New Mexico, and Wisconsin have adopted the identical Federal rule.

For all of these reasons, we think the House amendment should be rejected and the rule as submitted by the Supreme Court reinstated. [It would appear that some of the opposition to this Rule is based on a concern that a person could be convicted solely upon evidence admissible under this Rule. The Rule, however, is not addressed to the question of the sufficiency of evidence to send a case to the jury, but merely as to its admissibility. Factual circumstances could well arise where, if this were the sole evidence, dismissal would be appropriate.]

Note to Subdivision (d)(1)(C). As submitted by the Supreme Court and as passed by the House, subdivision (d)(1)(C) of rule 801 made admissible the prior statement identifying a person made after perceiving him. The committee decided to delete this provision because of the concern that a person could be convicted solely upon evidence admissible under this subdivision.

Note to Subdivision 801(d)(2)(E). The House approved the long-accepted rule that "a statement by a coconspirator of a party during the course and in furtherance of the conspiracy" is not hearsay as it was submitted by the Supreme Court. While the rule refers to a coconspirator, it is this committee's understanding that the rule is meant to carry forward the universally accepted doctrine that a joint venturer is considered as a coconspirator for the purposes of this rule even though no conspiracy has been charged. *United States v. Rinaldi*, 393 F.2d 97, 99 (2d Cir.), cert. denied 393 U.S. 913 (1968); *United States v. Spencer*, 415 F.2d 1301, 1304 (7th Cir., 1969). Senate Report No. 93–1277.

Rule 801 supplies some basic definitions for the rules of evidence that deal with hearsay. Rule 801(d)(1) defines certain statements as not hearsay. The Senate amendments make two changes in it.

Note to Subdivision (d)(1)(A). The House bill provides that a statement is not hearsay if the declarant testifies and is subject to cross-examination concerning the statement and if the statement is inconsistent with his testimony and was given under oath subject to cross-examination and subject to the penalty of perjury at a trial or hearing or in a deposition. The Senate amendment drops the requirement that the prior statement be given under oath subject to cross-examination and subject to the penalty of perjury at a trial or hearing or in a deposition.

The Conference adopts the Senate amendment with an amendment, so that the rule now requires that the prior inconsistent statement be given under oath subject to the penalty of perjury at a trial, hearing, or other proceeding, or in a deposition. The rule as adopted covers statements before a grand jury. Prior inconsistent statements may, of course, be used for impeaching the credibility of a witness. When the prior inconsistent statement is one made by a defendant in a criminal case, it is covered by Rule 801(d)(2).

Note to Subdivision (d)(1)(C). The House bill provides that a statement is not hearsay if the declarant testifies and is subject to cross-examination concerning the statement and the statement is one of identification of a person made after perceiving him. The Senate amendment eliminated this provision.

The Conference adopts the Senate amendment. House Report No. 93–1597.

1987 Amendment

The amendments are technical. No substantive change is intended.

1997 Amendment

Rule 801(d)(2) has been amended in order to respond to three issues raised by *Bourjaily v. United States*, 483 U.S. 171 (1987). First, the amendment codifies the holding in *Bourjaily* by stating expressly that a court shall consider the contents of a coconspirator's statement in determining "the existence of the conspiracy and the participation therein of the declarant and the party against whom the statement is offered." According to *Bourjaily*, Rule 104(a) requires these preliminary questions to be established by a preponderance of the evidence.

Second, the amendment resolves an issue on which the Court had reserved decision. It provides that the contents of the declarant's statement do not alone suffice to establish a conspiracy in which the declarant and the defendant participated. The court must consider in addition the circumstances surrounding the statement, such as the identity of the speaker, the context in which the statement was made, or evidence corroborating the contents of the statement in making its determination as to each preliminary question. This amendment is in accordance with existing practice. Every court of appeals that has resolved this issue requires some evidence in addition to the contents of the statement. *See, e.g., United States v. Beckham*, 968 F.2d 47, 51 (D.C.Cir.1992); *United States v. Sepulveda*, 15 F.3d 1161, 1181–82 (1st Cir.1993), *cert. denied*, 114 S.Ct. 2714 (1994); *United States v. Daly*, 842 F.2d 1380, 1386 (2d Cir.), *cert. denied*, 488 U.S. 821 (1988); *United States v. Clark*, 18 F.3d 1337, 1341–42 (6th Cir.), *cert. denied*, 115 S.Ct. 152 (1994); *United States v. Zambrana*, 841 F.2d 1320, 1344–45 (7th Cir.1988); *United States v. Silverman*, 861 F.2d 571, 577 (9th Cir.1988); *United States v. Gordon*, 844 F.2d 1397, 1402 (9th Cir.1988); *United States v. Hernandez*, 829 F.2d 988, 993 (10th Cir.1987), *cert. denied*, 485 U.S. 1013 (1988); *United States v. Byrom*, 910 F.2d 725, 736 (11th Cir.1990).

Third, the amendment extends the reasoning of Bourjaily to statements offered under subdivisions (C) and (D) of Rule 801(d)(2). In Bourjaily, the Court rejected treating foundational facts pursuant to the law of agency in favor of an evidentiary approach governed by Rule 104(a). The Advisory

Committee believes it appropriate to treat analogously prelim-inary questions relating to the declarant's authority under subdivision (C), and the agency or employment relationship and scope thereof under subdivision (D).

GAP Report on Rule 801. The word "shall" was substitut-ed for the word "may" in line 19. The second sentence of the committee note was changed accordingly.

2011 Amendments

The language of Rule 801 has been amended as part of the general restyling of the Evidence Rules to make them more easily understood and to make style and terminology consis-tent throughout the rules. These changes are intended to be stylistic only. There is no intent to change any result in any ruling on evidence admissibility.

Statements falling under the hearsay exclusion provided by Rule 801(d)(2) are no longer referred to as "admissions" in the title to the subdivision. The term "admissions" is confusing because not all statements covered by the exclusion are admissions in the colloquial sense—a statement can be within the exclusion even if it "admitted" nothing and was not against the party's interest when made. The term "admis-sions" also raises confusion in comparison with the Rule 804(b)(3) exception for declarations against interest. No change in application of the exclusion is intended.

2014 Amendments

Rule 801(d)(1)(B), as originally adopted, provided for sub-stantive use of certain prior consistent statements of a witness subject to cross-examination. As the Advisory Committee noted, "[t]he prior statement is consistent with the testimony given on the stand, and, if the opposite party wishes to open the door for its admission in evidence, no sound reason is apparent why it should not be received generally."

Though the original Rule 801(d)(1)(B) provided for substan-tive use of certain prior consistent statements, the scope of that Rule was limited. The Rule covered only those consis-tent statements that were offered to rebut charges of recent fabrication or improper motive or influence. The Rule did not, for example, provide for substantive admissibility of consistent statements that are probative to explain what otherwise appears to be an inconsistency in the witness's testimony. Nor did it cover consistent statements that would be probative to rebut a charge of faulty memory. Thus, the Rule left many prior consistent statements potentially admis-sible only for the limited purpose of rehabilitating a witness's credibility. The original Rule also led to some conflict in the cases; some courts distinguished between substantive and rehabilitative use for prior consistent statements, while others appeared to hold that prior consistent statements must be admissible under Rule 801(d)(1)(B) or not at all.

The amendment retains the requirement set forth in *Tome v. United States*, 513 U.S. 150 (1995): that under Rule 801(d)(1)(B), a consistent statement offered to rebut a charge of recent fabrication or improper influence or motive must have been made before the alleged fabrication or improper influence or motive arose. The intent of the amendment is to extend substantive effect to consistent statements that rebut other attacks on a witness — such as the charges of inconsis-tency or faulty memory.

The amendment does not change the traditional and well-accepted limits on bringing prior consistent statements before the factfinder for credibility purposes. It does not allow impermissible bolstering of a witness. As before, prior con-sistent statements under the amendment may be brought before the factfinder only if they properly rehabilitate a witness whose credibility has been attacked. As before, to be admissible for rehabilitation, a prior consistent statement must satisfy the strictures of Rule 403. As before, the trial court has ample discretion to exclude prior consistent state-ments that are cumulative accounts of an event. The amend-ment does not make any consistent statement admissible that was not admissible previously — the only difference is that prior consistent statements otherwise admissible for rehabili-tation are now admissible substantively as well.

Changes Made After Publication and Comment

The text of the proposed amendment was changed to clarify that the traditional limits on using prior consistent statements to rebut a charge of recent fabrication or improper influence or motive are retained. The Committee Note was modified to accord with the change in text.

HISTORICAL NOTES

For legislative history and purpose of Pub.L. 94–113, see 1975 U.S.Code Cong. and Adm.News, p. 1092.

Effective and Applicability Provisions

1975 Acts. Section 2 of Pub.L. 94–113 provided that: "This Act [enacting cl. (c) of subd. (d)] shall become effective on the fifteenth day after the date of the enactment of this Act [Oct. 16, 1975]."

CROSS REFERENCES

Attacking and supporting credibility of party-opponent, see Fed.Rules Evid. Rule 806, 28 USCA.

Confrontation with, and cross-examination of, witnesses, see USCA Const. Amend. VI.

Oral testimony in open court, see Fed.Rules Cr.Proc. Rule 26, 18 USCA and Fed.Rules Civ.Proc. Rule 43, 28 USCA.

Prior statements of witnesses, see Fed.Rules Evid. Rule 613, 28 USCA.

Statements, admission of remainder of, see Fed.Rules Evid. Rule 106, 28 USCA.

Rule 802. The Rule Against Hearsay

Hearsay is not admissible unless any of the following provides otherwise:

- a federal statute;

- these rules; or

- other rules prescribed by the Supreme Court.

(Pub.L. 93–595, § 1, Jan. 2, 1975, 88 Stat. 1939; Apr. 26, 2011, eff. Dec. 1, 2011.)

ADVISORY COMMITTEE NOTES

1972 Proposed Rules

The provision excepting from the operation of the rule hearsay which is made admissible by other rules adopted by the Supreme Court or by Act of Congress continues the admissibility thereunder of hearsay which would not qualify under these Evidence Rules. The following examples illus-trate the working of the exception:

Federal Rules of Civil Procedure

Rule 4(g): proof of service by affidavit.

Rule 32: admissibility of depositions.

Rule 43(e): affidavits when motion based on facts not appearing of record.

Rule 56: affidavits in summary judgment proceedings.

Rule 65(b): showing by affidavit for temporary restraining order.

Federal Rules of Criminal Procedure

Rule 4(a): affidavits to show grounds for issuing warrants.

Rule 12(b)(4): affidavits to determine issues of fact in connection with motions.

Acts of Congress

10 U.S.C. § 7730: affidavits of unavailable witnesses in actions for damages caused by vessel in naval service, or towage or salvage of same, when taking of testimony or bringing of action delayed or stayed on security grounds.

29 U.S.C. § 161(4): affidavit as proof of service in NLRB proceedings.

38 U.S.C. § 5206: affidavit as proof of posting notice of sale of unclaimed property by Veterans Administration.

2011 Amendments

The language of Rule 802 has been amended as part of the restyling of the Evidence Rules to make them more easily understood and to make style and terminology consistent throughout the rules. These changes are intended to be stylistic only. There is no intent to change any result in any ruling on evidence admissibility.

CROSS REFERENCES

Affidavits,

Motion on facts not appearing of record, see Fed.Rules Civ.Proc. Rule 43, 28 USCA.

Motions, determination of issues of fact on, see Fed.Rules Cr.Proc. Rule 12, 18 USCA.

Process, proof of service, see Fed.Rules Civ.proc. Rule 4, 28 USCA.

Proof of posting notice of sale of unclaimed property by Veterans' Administration, see 38 USCA § 8506.

Proof of service in National Labor Relations Board proceedings, see 29 USCA § 161.

Summary judgment proceedings, see Fed.Rules Civ.Proc. Rule 56, 28 USCA.

Temporary restraining order, see Fed.Rules Civ.Proc. Rule 65, 28 USCA.

Unavailable witnesses in actions for damages caused by vessel in naval service, or towage or salvage of same, when taking of testimony or bringing of action delayed or stayed on security grounds, see 10 USCA § 7730.

Warrants, issuance upon showing grounds, see Fed.Rules Cr.Proc. Rule 4, 18 USCA.

Depositions, admissibility of in court proceedings, see Fed. Rules Civ.Proc. Rule 32, 28 USCA.

Rule 803. Exceptions to the Rule Against Hearsay—Regardless of Whether the Declarant Is Available as a Witness

The following are not excluded by the rule against hearsay, regardless of whether the declarant is available as a witness:

(1) Present Sense Impression. A statement describing or explaining an event or condition, made while or immediately after the declarant perceived it.

(2) Excited Utterance. A statement relating to a startling event or condition, made while the declarant was under the stress of excitement that it caused.

(3) Then–Existing Mental, Emotional, or Physical Condition. A statement of the declarant's then-existing state of mind (such as motive, intent, or plan) or emotional, sensory, or physical condition (such as mental feeling, pain, or bodily health), but not including a statement of memory or belief to prove the fact remembered or believed unless it relates to the validity or terms of the declarant's will.

(4) Statement Made for Medical Diagnosis or Treatment. A statement that:

(A) is made for—and is reasonably pertinent to—medical diagnosis or treatment; and

(B) describes medical history; past or present symptoms or sensations; their inception; or their general cause.

(5) Recorded Recollection. A record that:

(A) is on a matter the witness once knew about but now cannot recall well enough to testify fully and accurately;

(B) was made or adopted by the witness when the matter was fresh in the witness's memory; and

(C) accurately reflects the witness's knowledge.

If admitted, the record may be read into evidence but may be received as an exhibit only if offered by an adverse party.

(6) Records of a Regularly Conducted Activity. A record of an act, event, condition, opinion, or diagnosis if:

(A) the record was made at or near the time by—or from information transmitted by—someone with knowledge;

(B) the record was kept in the course of a regularly conducted activity of a business, organization, occupation, or calling, whether or not for profit;

(C) making the record was a regular practice of that activity;

(D) all these conditions are shown by the testimony of the custodian or another qualified witness, or by a certification that complies with Rule 902(11) or (12) or with a statute permitting certification; and

(E) the opponent does not show that the source of information or the method or circumstances of preparation indicate a lack of trustworthiness.

(7) Absence of a Record of a Regularly Conducted Activity. Evidence that a matter is not included in a record described in paragraph (6) if:

(A) the evidence is admitted to prove that the matter did not occur or exist;

(B) a record was regularly kept for a matter of that kind; and

(C) the opponent does not show that the possible source of the information or other circumstances indicate a lack of trustworthiness.

(8) Public Records. A record or statement of a public office if:

(A) it sets out:

(i) the office's activities;

(ii) a matter observed while under a legal duty to report, but not including, in a criminal case, a matter observed by law-enforcement personnel; or

(iii) in a civil case or against the government in a criminal case, factual findings from a legally authorized investigation; and

(B) the opponent does not show that the source of information or other circumstances indicate a lack of trustworthiness.

(9) Public Records of Vital Statistics. A record of a birth, death, or marriage, if reported to a public office in accordance with a legal duty.

(10) Absence of a Public Record. Testimony— or a certification under Rule 902—that a diligent search failed to disclose a public record or statement if:

(A) the testimony or certification is admitted to prove that

(i) the record or statement does not exist; or

(ii) a matter did not occur or exist, if a public office regularly kept a record or statement for a matter of that kind; and

(B) in a criminal case, a prosecutor who intends to offer a certification provides written notice of that intent at least 14 days before trial, and the defendant does not object in writing within 7 days of receiving the notice—unless the court sets a different time for the notice or the objection.

(11) Records of Religious Organizations Concerning Personal or Family History. A statement of birth, legitimacy, ancestry, marriage, divorce, death, relationship by blood or marriage, or similar facts of personal or family history, contained in a regularly kept record of a religious organization.

(12) Certificates of Marriage, Baptism, and Similar Ceremonies. A statement of fact contained in a certificate:

(A) made by a person who is authorized by a religious organization or by law to perform the act certified;

(B) attesting that the person performed a marriage or similar ceremony or administered a sacrament; and

(C) purporting to have been issued at the time of the act or within a reasonable time after it.

(13) Family Records. A statement of fact about personal or family history contained in a family record, such as a Bible, genealogy, chart, engraving on a ring, inscription on a portrait, or engraving on an urn or burial marker.

(14) Records of Documents That Affect an Interest in Property. The record of a document that purports to establish or affect an interest in property if:

(A) the record is admitted to prove the content of the original recorded document, along with its signing and its delivery by each person who purports to have signed it;

(B) the record is kept in a public office; and

(C) a statute authorizes recording documents of that kind in that office.

(15) Statements in Documents That Affect an Interest in Property. A statement contained in a document that purports to establish or affect an interest in property if the matter stated was relevant to the document's purpose—unless later dealings with the property are inconsistent with the truth of the statement or the purport of the document.

(16) Statements in Ancient Documents. A statement in a document that was prepared before January 1, 1998, and whose authenticity is established.

(17) Market Reports and Similar Commercial Publications. Market quotations, lists, directories, or other compilations that are generally relied on by the public or by persons in particular occupations.

(18) Statements in Learned Treatises, Periodicals, or Pamphlets. A statement contained in a treatise, periodical, or pamphlet if:

(A) the statement is called to the attention of an expert witness on cross-examination or relied on by the expert on direct examination; and

(B) the publication is established as a reliable authority by the expert's admission or testimony, by another expert's testimony, or by judicial notice.

If admitted, the statement may be read into evidence but not received as an exhibit.

(19) Reputation Concerning Personal or Family History. A reputation among a person's family by blood, adoption, or marriage—or among a person's associates or in the community—concerning the person's birth, adoption, legitimacy, ancestry, marriage, divorce, death, relationship by blood, adoption, or marriage, or similar facts of personal or family history.

(20) Reputation Concerning Boundaries or General History. A reputation in a community—arising before the controversy—concerning boundaries of land in the community or customs that affect the land, or concerning general historical events important to that community, state, or nation.

(21) Reputation Concerning Character. A reputation among a person's associates or in the community concerning the person's character.

(22) Judgment of a Previous Conviction. Evidence of a final judgment of conviction if:

    (A) the judgment was entered after a trial or guilty plea, but not a nolo contendere plea;

    (B) the conviction was for a crime punishable by death or by imprisonment for more than a year;

    (C) the evidence is admitted to prove any fact essential to the judgment; and

    (D) when offered by the prosecutor in a criminal case for a purpose other than impeachment, the judgment was against the defendant.

The pendency of an appeal may be shown but does not affect admissibility.

(23) Judgments Involving Personal, Family, or General History, or a Boundary. A judgment that is admitted to prove a matter of personal, family, or general history, or boundaries, if the matter:

    (A) was essential to the judgment; and

    (B) could be proved by evidence of reputation.

(24) [Other Exceptions.] [Transferred to Rule 807.]

(Pub.L. 93–595, § 1, Jan. 2, 1975, 88 Stat. 1939; Pub.L. 94–149, § 1(11), Dec. 12, 1975, 89 Stat. 805; Mar. 2, 1987, eff. Oct. 1, 1987; Apr. 11, 1997, eff. Dec. 1, 1997; Apr. 17, 2000, eff. Dec. 1, 2000; Apr. 26, 2011, eff. Dec. 1, 2011; Apr. 13, 2013, eff. Dec. 1, 2013; Apr. 25, 2014, eff. Dec. 1, 2014; Apr. 27, 2017, eff. Dec. 1, 2017.)

ADVISORY COMMITTEE NOTES

1972 Proposed Rules

The exceptions are phrased in terms of nonapplication of the hearsay rule, rather than in positive terms of admissibility, in order to repel any implication that other possible grounds for exclusion are eliminated from consideration.

The present rule proceeds upon the theory that under appropriate circumstances a hearsay statement may possess circumstantial guarantees of trustworthiness sufficient to justify nonproduction of the declarant in person at the trial even though he may be available. The theory finds vast support in the many exceptions to the hearsay rule developed by the common law in which unavailability of the declarant is not a relevant factor. The present rule is a synthesis of them, with revision where modern developments and conditions are believed to make that course appropriate.

In a hearsay situation, the declarant is, of course, a witness, and neither this rule nor Rule 804 dispenses with the requirement of firsthand knowledge. It may appear from his statement or be inferable from circumstances. See Rule 602.

Note to Paragraphs (1) and (2). In considerable measure these two examples overlap, though based on somewhat different theories. The most significant practical difference will lie in the time lapse allowable between event and statement.

The underlying theory of Exception [paragraph] (1) is that substantial contemporaneity of event and statement negate the likelihood of deliberate or conscious misrepresentation. Moreover, if the witness is the declarant, he may be examined on the statement. If the witness is not the declarant, he may be examined as to the circumstances as an aid in evaluating the statement. Morgan, Basic Problems of Evidence 340–341 (1962).

The theory of Exception [paragraph] (2) is simply that circumstances may produce a condition of excitement which temporarily stills the capacity of reflection and produces utterances free of conscious fabrication. 6 Wigmore § 1747, p. 135. Spontaneity is the key factor in each instance, though arrived at by somewhat different routes. Both are needed in order to avoid needless niggling.

While the theory of Exception [paragraph] (2) has been criticized on the ground that excitement impairs accuracy of observation as well as eliminating conscious fabrication, Hutchins and Slesinger, Some Observations on the Law of Evidence: Spontaneous Exclamations, 28 Colum.L.Rev. 432 (1928), it finds support in cases without number. See cases in 6 Wigmore § 1750; Annot. 53 A.L.R.2d 1245 (statements as to cause of or responsibility for motor vehicle accident); Annot., 4 A.L.R.3d 149 (accusatory statements by homicide victims). Since unexciting events are less likely to evoke comment, decisions involving Exception [paragraph] (1) are far less numerous. Illustrative are *Tampa Elec. Co. v. Getrost*, 151 Fla. 558, 10 So.2d 83 (1942); *Houston Oxygen Co. v. Davis*, 139 Tex. 1, 161 S.W.2d 474 (1942); and cases cited in McCormick § 273, p. 585, n. 4.

With respect to the *time element*, Exception [paragraph] (1) recognizes that in many, if not most, instances precise contemporaneity is not possible and hence a slight lapse is allowable. Under Exception [paragraph] (2) the standard of measurement is the duration of the state of excitement. "How long can excitement prevail? Obviously there are no pat answers and the character of the transaction or event will largely determine the significance of the time factor." Slough, Spontaneous Statements and State of Mind, 46 Iowa L.Rev. 224, 243 (1961); McCormick § 272, p. 580.

Participation by the declarant is not required: a non-participant may be moved to describe what he perceives, and one may be startled by an event in which he is not an actor. Slough, *supra;* McCormick, *supra;* 6 Wigmore § 1755; Annot. 78 A.L.R.2d 300.

Whether *proof of the startling event* may be made by the statement itself is largely an academic question, since in most cases there is present at least circumstantial evidence that something of a startling nature must have occurred. For cases in which the evidence consists of the condition of the declarant (injuries, state of shock), see *Insurance Co. v. Mosely*, 75 U.S. (8 Wall.) 397, 19 L.Ed. 437 (1869); *Wheeler v. United States*, 93 U.S. App.D.C. 159, 211 F.2d 19 (1953), cert. denied 347 U.S. 1019, 74 S.Ct. 876, 98 L.Ed. 1140; *Wetherbee v. Safety Casualty Co.*, 219 F.2d 274 (5th Cir.1955); *Lampe v. United States*, 97 U.S.App.D.C. 160, 229 F.2d 43 (1956). Nevertheless, on occasion the only evidence may be the content of the statement itself, and rulings that it may be sufficient are described as "increasing," Slough, *supra* at 246, and as the "prevailing practice," McCormick § 272, p. 579. Illustrative are *Armour & Co. v. Industrial Commission*, 78 Colo. 569, 243 P. 546 (1926); *Young v. Stewart*, 191 N.C. 297, 131 S.E. 735 (1926). Moreover, under Rule 104(a) the judge is not limited by the hearsay rule in passing upon preliminary questions of fact.

Proof of declarant's perception by his statement presents similar considerations when declarant is identified. *People v. Poland*, 22 Ill.2d 175, 174 N.E.2d 804 (1961). However, when declarant is an unidentified bystander, the cases indicate hesitancy in upholding the statement alone as sufficient, *Garrett v. Howden*, 73 N.M. 307, 387 P.2d 874 (1963); *Beck v. Dye*, 200 Wash. 1, 92 P.2d 1113 (1939), a result which would under appropriate circumstances be consistent with the rule.

Permissible *subject matter* of the statement is limited under Exception [paragraph] (1) to description or explanation of the event or condition, the assumption being that spontaneity, in the absence of a startling event, may extend no farther. In Exception [paragraph] (2), however, the statement need only "relate" to the startling event or condition, thus affording a broader scope of subject matter coverage. 6 Wigmore §§ 1750, 1754. See *Sanitary Grocery Co. v. Snead*, 67 App. D.C. 129, 90 F.2d 374 (1937), slip-and-fall case sustaining admissibility of clerk's statement. "That has been on the floor for a couple of hours," and *Murphy Auto Parts Co., Inc. v. Ball*, 101 U.S.App.D.C. 416, 249 F.2d 508 (1957), upholding admission, on issue of driver's agency, of his statement that he had to call on a customer and was in a hurry to get home. Quick, Hearsay, Excitement, Necessity and the Uniform Rules: A Reappraisal of Rule 63(4), 6 Wayne L.Rev. 204, 206–209 (1960).

Similar provisions are found in Uniform Rule 63(4)(a) and (b); California Evidence Code § 1240 (as to Exception (2) only); Kansas Code of Civil Procedure § 60–460(d)(1) and (2); New Jersey Evidence Rule 63(4).

Note to Paragraph (3). Exception [paragraph] (3) is essentially a specialized application of Exception [paragraph] (1), presented separately to enhance its usefulness and accessibility. See McCormick §§ 265, 268.

The exclusion of "statements of memory or belief to prove the fact remembered or believed" is necessary to avoid the virtual destruction of the hearsay rule which would otherwise result from allowing state of mind, provable by a hearsay statement, to serve as the basis for an inference of the happening of the event which produced the state of mind. *Shepard v. United States*, 290 U.S. 96, 54 S.Ct. 22, 78 L.Ed. 196 (1933); Maguire, The Hillmon Case—Thirty-three Years After, 38 Harv.L.Rev. 709, 719–731 (1925); Hinton, States of Mind and the Hearsay Rule, 1 U.Chi.L.Rev. 394, 421–423 (1934). The rule of *Mutual Life Ins. Co. v. Hillmon*, 145 U.S. 285, 12 S.Ct. 909, 36 L.Ed. 706 (1892), allowing evidence of intention as tending to prove the doing of the act intended, is, of course, left undisturbed.

The carving out, from the exclusion mentioned in the preceding paragraph, of declarations relating to the execution, revocation, identification, or terms of declarant's will represents and *ad hoc* judgment which finds ample reinforcement in the decisions, resting on practical grounds of necessity and expediency rather than logic. McCormick § 271, pp. 577–578; Annot. 34 A.L.R.2d 588, 62 A.L.R.2d 855. A similar recognition of the need for and practical value of this kind of evidence is found in California Evidence Code § 1260.

Note to Paragraph (4). Even those few jurisdictions which have shied away from generally admitting statements of present condition have allowed them if made to a physician for purposes of diagnosis and treatment in view of the patient's strong motivation to be truthful. McCormick § 266, p. 563. The same guarantee of trustworthiness extends to statements of past conditions and medical history, made for purposes of diagnosis or treatment. It also extends to statements as to causation, reasonably pertinent to the same purposes, in accord with the current trend. *Shell Oil Co. v. Industrial Commission*, 2 Ill.2d 590, 119 N.E.2d 224 (1954); McCormick § 266, p. 564; New Jersey Evidence Rule 63(12)(c). Statements as to fault would not ordinarily qualify under this latter language. Thus a patient's statement that he was struck by an automobile would qualify but not his statement that the car was driven through a red light. Under the exception the statement need not have been made to a physician. Statements to hospital attendants, ambulance drivers, or even members of the family might be included.

Conventional doctrine has excluded from the hearsay exception, as not within its guarantee of truthfulness, statements to a physician consulted only for the purpose of enabling him to testify. While these statements were not admissible as substantive evidence, the expert was allowed to state the basis of his opinion, including statements of this kind. The distinction thus called for was one most unlikely to be made by juries. The rule accordingly rejects the limitation. This position is consistent with the provision of Rule 703 that the facts on which expert testimony is based need not be admissible in evidence if of a kind ordinarily relied upon by experts in the field.

Note to Paragraph (5). A hearsay exception for recorded recollection is generally recognized and has been described as having "long been favored by the federal and practically all the state courts that have had occasion to decide the question." *United States v. Kelly*, 349 F.2d 720, 770 (2d Cir.1965), citing numerous cases and sustaining the exception against a claimed denial of the right of confrontation. Many additional cases are cited in Annot., 82 A.L.R.2d 473, 520. The guarantee of trustworthiness is found in the reliability inherent in a record made while events were still fresh in mind and accurately reflecting them. *Owens v. State*, 67 Md. 307, 316, 10 A. 210, 212 (1887).

The principal controversy attending the exception has centered, not upon the propriety of the exception itself, but upon the question whether a preliminary requirement of impaired memory on the part of the witness should be imposed. The authorities are divided. If regard be had only to the accuracy of the evidence, admittedly impairment of the memory of the witness adds nothing to it and should not be required. McCormick § 277, p. 593; 3 Wigmore § 738, p. 76; *Jordan v. People*, 151 Colo. 133, 376 P.2d 699 (1962), cert. denied 373 U.S. 944, 83 S.Ct. 1553, 10 L.Ed.2d 699; *Hall v. State*, 223 Md. 158, 162 A.2d 751 (1960); *State v. Bindhammer*, 44 N.J. 372, 209 A.2d 124 (1965). Nevertheless, the absence of the requirement, it is believed, would encourage the use of statements carefully prepared for purposes of litigation under the supervision of attorneys, investigators, or claim adjusters. Hence the example includes a requirement that the witness not have "sufficient recollection to enable him to testify fully and accurately." To the same effect are California Evidence Code § 1237 and New Jersey Rule 63(1)(b), and this has been the position of the federal courts. *Vicksburg & Meridian R.R. v. O'Brien*, 119 U.S. 99, 7 S.Ct. 118, 30 L.Ed. 299 (1886); *Ahern v. Webb*, 268 F.2d 45 (10th Cir.1959); and see *N.L.R.B.*

v. Hudson Pulp and Paper Corp., 273 F.2d 660, 665 (5th Cir.1960); *N.L.R.B. v. Federal Dairy Co.*, 297 F.2d 487 (1st Cir.1962). But *cf. United States v. Adams*, 385 F.2d 548 (2d Cir.1967).

No attempt is made in the exception to spell out the method of establishing the initial knowledge or the contemporaneity and accuracy of the record, leaving them to be dealt with as the circumstances of the particular case might indicate. Multiple person involvement in the process of observing and recording, as in *Rathbun v. Brancatella*, 93 N.J.L. 222, 107 A. 279 (1919), is entirely consistent with the exception.

Locating the exception at this place in the scheme of the rules is a matter of choice. There were two other possibilities. The first was to regard the statement as one of the group of prior statements of a testifying witness which are excluded entirely from the category of hearsay by Rule 801(d)(1). That category, however, requires that declarant be "subject to cross-examination," as to which the impaired memory aspect of the exception raises doubts. The other possibility was to include the exception among those covered by Rule 804. Since unavailability is required by that rule and lack of memory is listed as a species of unavailability by the definition of the term in Rule 804(a)(3), that treatment at first impression would seem appropriate. The fact is, however, that the unavailability requirement of the exception is of a limited and peculiar nature. Accordingly, the exception is located at this point rather than in the context of a rule where unavailability is conceived of more broadly.

Note to Paragraph (6). Exception [paragraph] (6) represents an area which has received much attention from those seeking to improve the law of evidence. The Commonwealth Fund Act was the result of a study completed in 1927 by a distinguished committee under the chairmanship of Professor Morgan. Morgan et al., The Law of Evidence: Some Proposals for its Reform 63 (1927). With changes too minor to mention, it was adopted by Congress in 1936 as the rule for federal courts. 28 U.S.C. § 1732. A number of states took similar action. The Commissioners on Uniform State Laws in 1936 promulgated the Uniform Business Records as Evidence Act, 9A U.L.A. 506, which has acquired a substantial following in the states. Model Code Rule 514 and Uniform Rule 63(13) also deal with the subject. Difference of varying degrees of importance exist among these various treatments.

These reform efforts were largely within the context of business and commercial records, as the kind usually encountered, and concentrated considerable attention upon relaxing the requirement of producing as witnesses, or accounting for the nonproduction of, all participants in the process of gathering, transmitting, and recording information which the common law had evolved as a burdensome and crippling aspect of using records of this type. In their areas of primary emphasis on witnesses to be called and the general admissibility of ordinary business and commercial records, the Commonwealth Fund Act and the Uniform Act appear to have worked well. The exception seeks to preserve their advantages.

On the subject of what witnesses must be called, the Commonwealth Fund Act eliminated the common law requirement of calling or accounting for all participants by failing to mention it. *United States v. Mortimer*, 118 F.2d 266 (2d Cir.1941); *La Porte v. United States*, 300 F.2d 878 (9th Cir.1962); McCormick § 290, p. 608. Model Code Rule 514 and Uniform Rule 63(13) did likewise. The Uniform Act, however, abolished the common law requirement in express terms, providing that the requisite foundation testimony might be furnished by "the custodian or other qualified witness." Uniform Business Records as Evidence Act, § 2; 9A U.L.A. 506. The exception follows the Uniform Act in this respect.

The element of unusual reliability of business records is said variously to be supplied by systematic checking, by regularity and continuity which produce habits of precision, by actual experience of business in relying upon them, or by a duty to make an accurate record as part of a continuing job or occupation. McCormick §§ 281, 286, 287; Laughlin, Business Entries and the Like, 46 Iowa L.Rev. 276 (1961). The model statutes and rules have sought to capture these factors and to extend their impact by employing the phrase "regular course of business," in conjunction with a definition of "business" far broader than its ordinarily accepted meaning. The result is a tendency unduly to emphasize a requirement of routineness and repetitiveness and an insistence that other types of records be squeezed into the fact patterns which give rise to traditional business records. The rule therefore adopts the phrase "the course of a regularly conducted activity" as capturing the essential basis of the hearsay exception as it has evolved and the essential element which can be abstracted from the various specifications of what is a "business."

Amplification of the kinds of activities producing admissible records has given rise to problems which conventional business records by their nature avoid. They are problems of the source of the recorded information, of entries in opinion form, of motivation, and of involvement as participant in the matters recorded.

Sources of information presented no substantial problem with ordinary business records. All participants, including the observer or participant furnishing the information to be recorded, were acting routinely, under a duty of accuracy, with employer reliance on the result, or in short "in the regular course of business." If, however, the supplier of the information does not act in the regular course, an essential link is broken; the assurance of accuracy does not extend to the information itself, and the fact that it may be recorded with scrupulous accuracy is of no avail. An illustration is the police report incorporating information obtained from a bystander: the officer qualifies as acting in the regular course but the informant does not. The leading case, *Johnson v. Lutz*, 253 N.Y. 124, 170 N.E. 517 (1930), held that a report thus prepared was inadmissible. Most of the authorities have agreed with the decision. *Gencarella v. Fyfe*, 171 F.2d 419 (1st Cir.1948); *Gordon v. Robinson*, 210 F.2d 192 (3d Cir. 1954); *Standard Oil Co. of California v. Moore*, 251 F.2d 188, 214 (9th Cir.1957), cert. denied 356 U.S. 975, 78 S.Ct. 1139, 2 L.Ed.2d 1148; *Yates v. Bair Transport*, Inc., 249 F.Supp. 681 (S.D.N.Y.1965); Annot., 69 A.L.R.2d 1148. Cf. *Hawkins v. Gorea Motor Express, Inc.*, 360 F.2d 933 (2d Cir.1966); *Contra*, 5 Wigmore § 1530a, n. 1, pp. 391–392. The point is not dealt with specifically in the Commonwealth Fund Act, the Uniform Act, or Uniform Rule 63(13). However, Model Code Rule 514 contains the requirement "that it was the regular course of that business for one with personal knowledge * * * to make such a memorandum or record or to transmit information thereof to be included in such a memorandum or record * * *." The rule follows this lead in requiring an informant with knowledge acting in the course of the regularly conducted activity.

Entries in the form of opinions were not encountered in traditional business records in view of the purely factual nature of the items recorded, but they are now commonly encountered with respect to medical diagnoses, prognoses, and test results, as well as occasionally in other areas. The Commonwealth Fund Act provided only for records of an "act, transaction, occurrence, or event," while the Uniform Act, Model Code Rule 514, and Uniform Rule 63(13) merely added the ambiguous term "condition." The limited phrasing of the Commonwealth Fund Act, 28 U.S.C. § 1732, may account for the reluctance of some federal decisions to admit diagnostic entries. *New York Life Ins. Co. v. Taylor,* 79 U.S.App.D.C. 66, 147 F.2d 297 (1945); *Lyles v. United States,* 103 U.S.App. D.C. 22, 254 F.2d 725 (1957), cert. denied 356 U.S. 961, 78 S.Ct. 997, 2 L.Ed.2d 1067; *England v. United States,* 174 F.2d 466 (5th Cir.1949); *Skogen v. Dow Chemical Co.,* 375 F.2d 692 (8th Cir.1967). Other federal decisions, however, experienced no difficulty in freely admitting diagnostic entries. *Reed v. Order of United Commercial Travelers,* 123 F.2d 252 (2d Cir.1941); *Buckminster's Estate v. Commissioner of Internal Revenue,* 147 F.2d 331 (2d Cir.1944); *Medina v. Erickson,* 226 F.2d 475 (9th Cir.1955); *Thomas v. Hogan,* 308 F.2d 355 (4th Cir.1962); *Glawe v. Rulon,* 284 F.2d 495 (8th Cir.1960). In the state courts, the trend favors admissibility. Borucki v. MacKenzie Bros. Co., 125 Conn. 92, 3 A.2d 224 (1938); *Allen v. St. Louis Public Service Co.,* 365 Mo. 677, 285 S.W.2d 663, 55 A.L.R.2d 1022 (1956); *People v. Kohlmeyer,* 284 N.Y. 366, 31 N.E.2d 490 (1940); *Weis v. Weis,* 147 Ohio St. 416, 72 N.E.2d 245 (1947). In order to make clear its adherence to the latter position, the rule specifically includes both diagnoses and opinions, in addition to acts, events, and conditions, as proper subjects of admissible entries.

Problems of the motivation of the informant have been a source of difficulty and disagreement. In *Palmer v. Hoffman,* 318 U.S. 109, 63 S.Ct. 477, 87 L.Ed. 645 (1943), exclusion of an accident report made by the since deceased engineer, offered by defendant railroad trustees in a grade crossing collision case, was upheld. The report was not "in the regular course of business," not a record of the systematic conduct of the business as a business, said the Court. The report was prepared for use in litigating, not railroading. While the opinion mentions the motivation of the engineer only obliquely, the emphasis on records of routine operations is significant only by virtue of impact on motivation to be accurate. Absence of routineness raises lack of motivation to be accurate. The opinion of the Court of Appeals had gone beyond mere lack of motive to be accurate: the engineer's statement was "dripping with motivations to misrepresent." *Hoffman v. Palmer,* 129 F.2d 976, 991 (2d Cir.1942). The direct introduction of motivation is a disturbing factor, since absence of motive to misrepresent has not traditionally been a requirement of the rule; that records might be self-serving has not been a ground for exclusion. Laughlin, Business Records and the Like, 46 Iowa L.Rev. 276, 285 (1961). As Judge Clark said in his dissent, "I submit that there is hardly a grocer's account book which could not be excluded on that basis." 129 F.2d at 1002. A physician's evaluation report of a personal injury litigant would appear to be in the routine of his business. If the report is offered by the party at whose instance it was made, however, it has been held inadmissible, *Yates v. Bair Transport, Inc.,* 249 F.Supp. 681 (S.D.N.Y.1965), otherwise if offered by the opposite party, *Korte v. New York, N.H. & H.R. Co.,* 191 F.2d 86 (2d Cir.1951), cert. denied 342 U.S. 868, 72 S.Ct. 108, 96 L.Ed. 652.

The decisions hinge on motivation and which party is entitled to be concerned about it. Professor McCormick believed that the doctor's report or the accident report were sufficiently routine to justify admissibility. McCormick

§ 287, p. 604. Yet hesitation must be experienced in admitting everything which is observed and recorded in the course of a regularly conducted activity. Efforts to set a limit are illustrated by *Hartzog v. United States,* 217 F.2d 706 (4th Cir.1954), error to admit worksheets made by since deceased deputy collector in preparation for the instant income tax evasion prosecution, and *United States v. Ware,* 247 F.2d 698 (7th Cir.1957), error to admit narcotics agents' records of purchases. See also Exception [paragraph] (8), *infra,* as to the public record aspects of records of this nature. Some decisions have been satisfied as to motivation of an accident report if made pursuant to statutory duty, United States v. New York Foreign Trade Zone Operators, 304 F.2d 792 (2d Cir.1962); Taylor v. Baltimore & O.R. Co., 344 F.2d 281 (2d Cir.1965), since the report was oriented in a direction other than the litigation which ensued. Cf. Matthews v. United States, 217 F.2d 409 (5th Cir.1954). The formulation of specific terms which would assure satisfactory results in all cases is not possible. Consequently the rule proceeds from the base that records made in the course of a regularly conducted activity will be taken as admissible but subject to authority to exclude if "the sources of information or other circumstances indicate lack of trustworthiness."

Occasional decisions have reached for enhanced accuracy by requiring involvement as a participant in matters reported. *Clainos v. United States,* 82 U.S.App.D.C. 278, 163 F.2d 593 (1947), error to admit police records of convictions; *Standard Oil Co. of California v. Moore,* 251 F.2d 188 (9th Cir.1957), cert. denied 356 U.S. 975, 78 S.Ct. 1139, 2 L.Ed.2d 1148, error to admit employees' records of observed business practices of others. The rule includes no requirement of this nature. Wholly acceptable records may involve matters merely observed, e.g. the weather.

The form which the "record" may assume under the rule is described broadly as a "memorandum, report, record, or data compilation, in any form." The expression "data compilation" is used as broadly descriptive of any means of storing information other than the conventional words and figures in written or documentary form. It includes, but is by no means limited to, electronic computer storage. The term is borrowed from revised Rule 34(a) of the Rules of Civil Procedure.

Note to Paragraph (7). Failure of a record to mention a matter which would ordinarily be mentioned is satisfactory evidence of its nonexistence. Uniform Rule 63(14), Comment. While probably not hearsay as defined in Rule 801, *supra,* decisions may be found which class the evidence not only as hearsay but also as not within any exception. In order to set the question at rest in favor of admissibility, it is specifically treated here. McCormick § 289, p. 609; Morgan, Basic Problems of Evidence 314 (1962); 5 Wigmore § 1531; Uniform Rule 63(14); California Evidence Code § 1272; Kansas Code of Civil Procedure § 60–460(n); New Jersey Evidence Rule 63(14).

Note to Paragraph (8). Public records are a recognized hearsay exception at common law and have been the subject of statutes without number. McCormick § 291. See, for example, 28 U.S.C. § 1733, the relative narrowness of which is illustrated by its nonapplicability to nonfederal public agencies, thus necessitating resort to the less appropriate business record exception to the hearsay rule. *Kay v. United States,* 255 F.2d 476 (4th Cir.1958). The rule makes no distinction between federal and nonfederal offices and agencies.

Justification for the exception is the assumption that a public official will perform his duty properly and the unlikelihood that he will remember details independently of the record. *Wong Wing Foo v. McGrath,* 196 F.2d 120 (9th Cir.1952), and see *Chesapeake & Delaware Canal Co. v. United States,* 250 U.S. 123, 39 S.Ct. 407, 63 L.Ed. 889 (1919). As to items (a) and (b), further support is found in the reliability factors underlying records of regularly conducted activities generally. See Exception [paragraph] (6), supra.

(a) Cases illustrating the admissibility of records of the office's or agency's own activities are numerous. *Chesapeake & Delaware Canal Co. v. United States,* 250 U.S. 123, 39 S.Ct. 407, 63 L.Ed. 889 (1919), Treasury records of miscellaneous receipts and disbursements; *Howard v. Perrin,* 200 U.S. 71, 26 S.Ct. 195, 50 L.Ed. 374 (1906), General Land Office records; *Ballew v. United States,* 160 U.S. 187, 16 S.Ct. 263, 40 L.Ed. 388 (1895). Pension Office records.

(b) Cases sustaining admissibility of records of matters observed are also numerous. *United States v. Van Hook,* 284 F.2d 489 (7th Cir.1960), remanded for resentencing 365 U.S. 609, 81 S.Ct. 823, 5 L.Ed.2d 821, letter from induction officer to District Attorney, pursuant to army regulations, stating fact and circumstances of refusal to be inducted; *T'Kach v. United States,* 242 F.2d 937 (5th Cir.1957), affidavit of White House personnel officer that search of records showed no employment of accused, charged with fraudulently representing himself as an envoy of the President; *Minnehaha County v. Kelley,* 150 F.2d 356 (8th Cir.1945); Weather Bureau records of rainfall; *United States v. Meyer,* 113 F.2d 387 (7th Cir.1940), cert. denied 311 U.S. 706, 61 S.Ct. 174, 85 L.Ed. 459, map prepared by government engineer from information furnished by men working under his supervision.

(c) The more controversial area of public records is that of the so-called "evaluative" report. The disagreement among the decisions has been due in part, no doubt, to the variety of situations encountered, as well as to differences in principle. Sustaining admissibility are such cases as *United States v. Dumas,* 149 U.S. 278, 13 S.Ct. 872, 37 L.Ed. 734 (1893), statement of account certified by Postmaster General in action against postmaster; *McCarty v. United States,* 185 F.2d 520 (5th Cir.1950), reh. denied 187 F.2d 234, Certificate of Settlement of General Accounting Office showing indebtedness and letter from Army official stating Government had performed, in action on contract to purchase and remove waste food from Army camp; *Moran v. Pittsburgh–Des Moines Steel Co.,* 183 F.2d 467 (3d Cir.1950), report of Bureau of Mines as to cause of gas tank explosion; Petition of W——, 164 F.Supp. 659 (E.D.Pa.1958), report by Immigration and Naturalization Service investigator that petitioner was known in community as wife of man to whom she was not married. To the opposite effect and denying admissibility are *Franklin v. Skelly Oil Co.,* 141 F.2d 568 (10th Cir.1944), State Fire Marshal's report of cause of gas explosion; *Lomax Transp. Co. v. United States,* 183 F.2d 331 (9th Cir.1950), Certificate of Settlement from General Accounting Office in action for naval supplies lost in warehouse fire; *Yung Jin Teung v. Dulles,* 229 F.2d 244 (2d Cir.1956), "Status Reports" offered to justify delay in processing passport applications. Police reports have generally been excluded except to the extent to which they incorporate firsthand observations of the officer. Annot., 69 A.L.R.2d 1148. Various kinds of evaluative reports are admissible under federal statutes: 7 U.S.C. § 78, findings of Secretary of Agriculture prima facie evidence of true grade of grain; 7 U.S.C. § 210(f), findings of Secretary of Agriculture prima facie evidence in action for damages against stockyard owner; 7 U.S.C. § 292, order by Secretary of Agriculture prima facie evidence in judicial enforcement proceedings against producers association monopoly; 7 U.S.C. § 1622(h), Department of Agriculture inspection certificates of products shipped in interstate commerce prima facie evidence; 8 U.S.C. § 1440(c), separation of alien from military service on conditions other than honorable provable by certificate from department in proceedings to revoke citizenship; 18 U.S.C. § 4245, certificate of Director of Prisons that convicted person has been examined and found probably incompetent at time of trial prima facie evidence in court hearing on competency; 42 U.S.C. § 269(b), bill of health by appropriate official prima facie evidence of vessel's sanitary history and condition and compliance with regulations; 46 U.S.C. § 679, certificate of consul presumptive evidence of refusal of master to transport destitute seamen to United States. While these statutory exceptions to the hearsay rule are left undisturbed, Rule 802, the willingness of Congress to recognize a substantial measure of admissibility for evaluative reports is a helpful guide.

Factors which may be of assistance in passing upon the admissibility of evaluative reports include: (1) the timeliness of the investigation, McCormick, Can the Courts Make Wider Use of Reports of Official Investigations? 42 Iowa L.Rev. 363 (1957); (2) the special skill or experience of the official, *id.,* (3) whether a hearing was held and the level at which conducted, *Franklin v. Skelly Oil Co.,* 141 F.2d 568 (10th Cir.1944); (4) possible motivation problems suggested by *Palmer v. Hoffman,* 318 U.S. 109, 63 S.Ct. 477, 87 L.Ed. 645 (1943). Others no doubt could be added.

The formulation of an approach which would give appropriate weight to all possible factors in every situation is an obvious impossibility. Hence the rule, as in Exception [paragraph] (6), assumes admissibility in the first instance but with ample provision for escape if sufficient negative factors are present. In one respect, however, the rule with respect to evaluative reports under item (c) is very specific: they are admissible only in civil cases and against the government in criminal cases in view of the almost certain collision with confrontation rights which would result from their use against the accused in a criminal case.

Note to Paragraph (9). Records of vital statistics are commonly the subject of particular statutes making them admissible in evidence, Uniform Vital Statistics Act, 9C U.L.A. 350 (1957). The rule is in principle narrower than Uniform Rule 63(16) which includes reports required of persons performing functions authorized by statute, yet in practical effect the two are substantially the same. Comment Uniform Rule 63(16). The exception as drafted is in the pattern of California Evidence Code § 1281.

Note to Paragraph (10). The principle of proving nonoccurrence of an event by evidence of the absence of a record which would regularly be made of its occurrence, developed in Exception [paragraph] (7) with respect to regularly conducted activities, is here extended to public records of the kind mentioned in Exceptions [paragraphs] (8) and (9). 5 Wigmore § 1633(6), p. 519. Some harmless duplication no doubt exists with Exception [paragraph] (7). For instances of federal statutes recognizing this method of proof, see 8 U.S.C. § 1284(b), proof of absence of alien crewman's name from outgoing manifest prima facie evidence of failure to detain or deport, and 42 U.S.C. § 405(c)(3), (4)(B), (4)(C), absence of HEW [Department of Health, Education, and Welfare] record prima facie evidence of no wages or self-employment income.

The rule includes situations in which absence of a record may itself be the ultimate focal point of inquiry, e.g. People v. Love, 310 Ill. 558, 142 N.E. 204 (1923), certificate of Secretary of State admitted to show failure to file documents required by Securities Law, as well as cases where the absence of a record is offered as proof of the nonoccurrence of an event ordinarily recorded.

The refusal of the common law to allow proof by certificate of the lack of a record or entry has no apparent justification, 5 Wigmore § 1678(7), p. 752. The rule takes the opposite position, as to Uniform Rule 63(17); California Evidence Code § 1284; Kansas Code of Civil Procedure § 60–460(c); New Jersey Evidence Rule 63(17). Congress has recognized certification as evidence of the lack of a record. 8 U.S.C. § 1360(d), certificate of Attorney General or other designated officer that no record of Immigration and Naturalization Service of specified nature or entry therein is found, admissible in alien cases.

Note to Paragraph (11). Records of activities of religious organizations are currently recognized as admissible at least to the extent of the business records exception to the hearsay rule, 5 Wigmore § 1523, p. 371, and Exception [paragraph] (6) would be applicable. However, both the business record doctrine and Exception [paragraph] (6) require that the person furnishing the information be one in the business or activity. The result is such decisions as Daily v. Grand Lodge, 311 Ill. 184, 142 N.E. 478 (1924), holding a church record admissible to prove fact, date, and place of baptism, but not age of child except that he had at least been born at the time. In view of the unlikelihood that false information would be furnished on occasions of this kind, the rule contains no requirement that the informant be in the course of the activity. See California Evidence Code § 1315 and Comment.

Note to Paragraph (12). The principle of proof by certification is recognized as to public officials in Exceptions [paragraphs] (8) and (10), and with respect to authentication in Rule 902. The present exception is a duplication to the extent that it deals with a certificate by a public official, as in the case of a judge who performs a marriage ceremony. The area covered by the rule is, however, substantially larger and extends the certification procedure to clergymen and the like who perform marriages and other ceremonies or administer sacraments. Thus certificates of such matters as baptism or confirmation, as well as marriage, are included. In principle they are as acceptable evidence as certificates of public officers. See 5 Wigmore § 1645, as to marriage certificates. When the person executing the certificate is not a public official, the self-authenticating character of documents purporting to emanate from public officials, see Rule 902, is lacking and proof is required that the person was authorized and did make the certificate. The time element, however, may safely be taken as supplied by the certificate, once authority and authenticity are established, particularly in view of the presumption that a document was executed on the date it bears.

For similar rules, some limited to certificates of marriage, with variations in foundation requirements, see Uniform Rule 63(18); California Evidence Code § 1316; Kansas Code of Civil Procedure § 60–460(p); New Jersey Evidence Rule 63(18).

Note to Paragraph (13). Records of family history kept in family Bibles have by long tradition been received in evidence. 5 Wigmore §§ 1495, 1496, citing numerous statutes and decisions. See also Regulations, Social Security Administration, 20 C.F.R. § 404.703(c), recognizing family Bible entries as proof of age in the absence of public or church records. Opinions in the area also include inscriptions on tombstones, publicly displayed pedigrees, and engravings on rings. Wigmore, *supra.* The rule is substantially identical in coverage with California Evidence Code § 1312.

Note to Paragraph (14). The recording of title documents is a purely statutory development. Under any theory of the admissibility of public records, the records would be receivable as evidence of the contents of the recorded document, else the recording process would be reduced to a nullity. When, however, the record is offered for the further purpose of proving execution and delivery, a problem of lack of firsthand knowledge by the recorder, not present as to contents, is presented. This problem is solved, seemingly in all jurisdictions, by qualifying for recording only those documents shown by a specified procedure, either acknowledgement or a form of probate, to have been executed and delivered. 5 Wigmore §§ 1647–1651. Thus what may appear in the rule, at first glance, as endowing the record with an effect independently of local law and inviting difficulties of an *Erie* nature under *Cities Service Oil Co. v. Dunlap,* 308 U.S. 208, 60 S.Ct. 201, 84 L.Ed. 196 (1939), is not present, since the local law in fact governs under the example.

Note to Paragraph (15). Dispositive documents often contain recitals of fact. Thus a deed purporting to have been executed by an attorney in fact may recite the existence of the power of attorney, or a deed may recite that the grantors are all the heirs of the last record owner. Under the rule, these recitals are exempted from the hearsay rule. The circumstances under which dispositive documents are executed and the requirement that the recital be germane to the purpose of the document are believed to be adequate guarantees of trustworthiness, particularly in view of the nonapplicability of the rule if dealings with the property have been inconsistent with the document. The age of the document is of no significance, though in practical application the document will most often be an ancient one. See Uniform Rule 63(29), Comment.

Similar provisions are contained in Uniform Rule 63(29); California Evidence Code § 1330; Kansas Code of Civil Procedure § 60–460(aa); New Jersey Evidence Rule 63(29).

Note to Paragraph (16). Authenticating a document as ancient, essentially in the pattern of the common law, as provided in Rule 901(b)(8), leaves open as a separate question the admissibility of assertive statements contained therein as against a hearsay objection. 7 Wigmore § 2145a. Wigmore further states that the ancient document technique of authentication is universally conceded to apply to all sorts of documents, including letters, records, contracts, maps, and certificates, in addition to title documents, citing numerous decisions. *Id.* § 2145. Since most of these items are significant evidentially only insofar as they are assertive, their admission in evidence must be as a hearsay exception. But see 5 *id.* § 1573, p. 429, referring to recitals in ancient deeds as a "limited" hearsay exception. The former position is believed to be the correct one in reason and authority. As pointed out in McCormick § 298, danger of mistake is minimized by authentication requirements, and age affords assurance that the writing antedates the present controversy. See *Dallas County v. Commercial Union Assurance Co.,* 286 F.2d 388 (5th Cir.1961), upholding admissibility of 58–year-old newspaper story. Cf. Morgan, Basic Problems of Evidence 364 (1962), but see *id.* 254.

For a similar provision, but with the added requirement that "the statement has since generally been acted upon as true by persons having an interest in the matter," see California Evidence Code § 1331.

Note to Paragraph (17). Ample authority at common law supported the admission in evidence of items falling in this category. While Wigmore's text is narrowly oriented to lists, etc., prepared for the use of a trade or profession, 6 Wigmore § 1702, authorities are cited which include other kinds of publications, for example, newspaper market reports, telephone directories, and city directories. *Id.* §§ 1702–1706. The basis of trustworthiness is general reliance by the public or by a particular segment of it, and the motivation of the compiler to foster reliance by being accurate.

For similar provisions, see Uniform Rule 63(30); California Evidence Code § 1340; Kansas Code of Civil Procedure § 60–460(bb); New Jersey Evidence Rule 63(30). Uniform Commercial Code § 2–724 provides for admissibility in evidence of "reports in official publications or trade journals or in newspapers or periodicals of general circulation published as the reports of such [established commodity] market."

Note to Paragraph (18). The writers have generally favored the admissibility of learned treatises, McCormick § 296, p. 621; Morgan, Basic Problems of Evidence 366 (1962); 6 Wigmore § 1692, with the support of occasional decisions and rules, *City of Dothan v. Hardy,* 237 Ala. 603, 188 So. 264 (1939); *Lewandowski v. Preferred Risk Mut. Ins. Co.,* 33 Wis.2d 69, 146 N.W.2d 505 (1966), 66 Mich.L.Rev. 183 (1967); Uniform Rule 63(31); Kansas Code of Civil Procedure § 60–460(cc), but the great weight of authority has been that learned treatises are not admissible as substantive evidence though usable in the cross-examination of experts. The foundation of the minority view is that the hearsay objection must be regarded as unimpressive when directed against treatises since a high standard of accuracy is engendered by various factors: the treatise is written primarily and impartially for professionals, subject to scrutiny and exposure for inaccuracy, with the reputation of the writer at stake. 6 Wigmore § 1692. Sound as this position may be with respect to trustworthiness, there is, nevertheless, an additional difficulty in the likelihood that the treatise will be misunderstood and misapplied without expert assistance and supervision. This difficulty is recognized in the cases demonstrating unwillingness to sustain findings relative to disability on the basis of judicially noticed medical texts. *Ross v. Gardner,* 365 F.2d 554 (6th Cir.1966); *Sayers v. Gardner,* 380 F.2d 940 (6th Cir.1967); *Colwell v. Gardner,* 386 F.2d 56 (6th Cir.1967); *Glendenning v. Ribicoff,* 213 F.Supp. 301 (W.D.Mo.1962); *Cook v. Celebrezze,* 217 F.Supp. 366 (W.D.Mo.1963); *Sosna v. Celebrezze,* 234 F.Supp. 289 (E.D.Pa.1964); and see *McDaniel v. Celebrezze,* 331 F.2d 426 (4th Cir.1964). The rule avoids the danger of misunderstanding and misapplication by limiting the use of treatises as substantive evidence to situations in which an expert is on the stand and available to explain and assist in the application of the treatise if desired. The limitation upon receiving the publication itself physically in evidence, contained in the last sentence, is designed, to further this policy.

The relevance of the use of treatises on cross-examination is evident. This use of treatises has been the subject of varied views. The most restrictive position is that the witness must have stated expressly on direct his reliance upon the treatise. A slightly more liberal approach still insists upon reliance but allows it to be developed on cross-examination. Further relaxation dispenses with reliance but requires recog-

nition as an authority by the witness, developable on cross-examination. The greatest liberality is found in decisions allowing use of the treatise on cross-examination when its status as an authority is established by any means. Annot., 60 A.L.R.2d 77. The exception is hinged upon this last position, which is that of the Supreme Court, *Reilly v. Pinkus,* 338 U.S. 269, 70 S.Ct. 110, 94 L.Ed. 63 (1949), and of recent well considered state court decisions, *City of St. Petersburg v. Ferguson,* 193 So.2d 648 (Fla.App.1967), cert. denied Fla., 201 So.2d 556; *Darling v. Charleston Memorial Community Hospital,* 33 Ill.2d 326, 211 N.E.2d 253 (1965); *Dabroe v. Rhodes Co.,* 64 Wash.2d 431, 392 P.2d 317 (1964).

In Reilly v. Pinkus, *supra,* the Court pointed out that testing of professional knowledge was incomplete without exploration of the witness' knowledge of and attitude toward established treatises in the field. The process works equally well in reverse and furnishes the basis of the rule.

The rule does not require that the witness rely upon or recognize the treatise as authoritative, thus avoiding the possibility that the expert may at the outset block cross-examination by refusing to concede reliance or authoritativeness. Dabroe v. Rhodes Co., *supra.* Moreover, the rule avoids the unreality of admitting evidence for the purpose of impeachment only, with an instruction to the jury not to consider it otherwise. The parallel to the treatment of prior inconsistent statements will be apparent. See Rules 613(b) and 801(d)(1).

Note to Paragraphs (19), (20) and (21). Trustworthiness in reputation evidence is found "when the topic is such that the facts are likely to have been inquired about and that persons having personal knowledge have disclosed facts which have thus been discussed in the community; and thus the community's conclusion, if any has been formed, is likely to be a trustworthy one." 5 Wigmore § 1580, p. 444, and see also § 1583. On this common foundation, reputation as to land boundaries, customs, general history, character, and marriage have come to be regarded as admissible. The breadth of the underlying principle suggests the formulation of an equally broad exception, but tradition has in fact been much narrower and more particularized, and this is the pattern of these exceptions in the rule.

Exception [paragraph] (19) is concerned with matters of personal and family history. Marriage is universally conceded to be a proper subject of proof by evidence of reputation in the community. 5 Wigmore § 1602. As to such items as legitimacy, relationship, adoption, birth, and death, the decisions are divided. *Id.* § 1605. All seem to be susceptible to being the subject of well founded repute. The "world" in which the reputation may exist may be family, associates, or community. This world has proved capable of expanding with changing times from the single uncomplicated neighborhood, in which all activities take place, to the multiple and unrelated worlds of work, religious affiliation, and social activity, in each of which a reputation may be generated. *People v. Reeves,* 360 Ill. 55, 195 N.E. 443 (1935); *State v. Axilrod,* 248 Minn. 204, 79 N.W.2d 677 (1956); Mass.Stat.1947, c. 410, M.G.L.A. c. 233 § 21A; 5 Wigmore § 1616. The family has often served as the point of beginning for allowing community reputation. 5 Wigmore § 1488. For comparable provisions see Uniform Rule 63(26), (27)(c); California Evidence Code §§ 1313, 1314; Kansas Code of Civil Procedure § 60–460(x), (y)(3); New Jersey Evidence Rule 63(26), (27)(c).

The first portion of Exception [paragraph] (20) is based upon the general admissibility of evidence of reputation as to land boundaries and land customs, expanded in this country to include private as well as public boundaries. McCormick § 299, p. 625. The reputation is required to antedate the controversy, though not to be ancient. The second portion is likewise supported by authority, *id.*, and is designed to facilitate proof of events when judicial notice is not available. The historical character of the subject matter dispenses with any need that the reputation antedate the controversy with respect to which it is offered. For similar provisions see Uniform Rule 63(27)(a), (b); California Evidence Code §§ 1320–1322; Kansas Code of Civil Procedure § 60–460(y), (1), (2); New Jersey Evidence Rule 63(27)(a), (b).

Exception [paragraph] (21) recognizes the traditional acceptance of reputation evidence as a means of proving human character. McCormick §§ 44, 158. The exception deals only with the hearsay aspect of this kind of evidence. Limitations upon admissibility based on other grounds will be found in Rules 404, relevancy of character evidence generally, and 608, character of witness. The exception is in effect a reiteration, in the context of hearsay, of Rule 405(a). Similar provisions are contained in Uniform Rule 63(28); California Evidence Code § 1324; Kansas Code of Civil Procedure § 60–460(z); New Jersey Evidence Rule 63(28).

Note to Paragraph (22). When the status of a former judgment is under consideration in subsequent litigation, three possibilities must be noted: (1) the former judgment is conclusive under the doctrine of res judicata, either as a bar or a collateral estoppel; or (2) it is admissible in evidence for what it is worth; or (3) it may be of no effect at all. The first situation does not involve any problem of evidence except in the way that principles of substantive law generally bear upon the relevancy and materiality of evidence. The rule does not deal with the substantive effect of the judgment as a bar or collateral estoppel. When, however, the doctrine of res judicata does not apply to make the judgment either a bar or a collateral estoppel, a choice is presented between the second and third alternatives. The rule adopts the second for judgments of criminal conviction of felony grade. This is the direction of the decisions, Annot., 18 A.L.R.2d 1287, 1299, which manifest an increasing reluctance to reject *in toto* the validity of the law's factfinding processes outside the confines of res judicata and collateral estoppel. While this may leave a jury with the evidence of conviction but without means to evaluate it, as suggested by Judge Hinton, Note 27 Ill.L.Rev. 195 (1932), it seems safe to assume that the jury will give it substantial effect unless defendant offers a satisfactory explanation, a possibility not foreclosed by the provision. But see *North River Ins. Co. v. Militello,* 104 Colo. 28, 88 P.2d 567 (1939), in which the jury found for plaintiff on a fire policy despite the introduction of his conviction for arson. For supporting federal decisions see Clark, J., in *New York & Cuba Mail S.S. Co. v. Continental Cas. Co.,* 117 F.2d 404, 411 (2d Cir.1941); *Connecticut Fire Ins. Co. v. Farrara,* 277 F.2d 388 (8th Cir.1960).

Practical considerations require exclusion of convictions of minor offenses, not because the administration of justice in its lower echelons must be inferior, but because motivation to defend at this level is often minimal or nonexistent. *Cope v. Goble,* 39 Cal.App.2d 448, 103 P.2d 598 (1940); *Jones v. Talbot,* 87 Idaho 498, 394 P.2d 316 (1964); *Warren v. Marsh,* 215 Minn. 615, 11 N.W.2d 528 (1943); Annot., 18 A.L.R.2d 1287, 1295–1297; 16 Brooklyn L.Rev. 286 (1950); 50 Colum.L.Rev. 529 (1950); 35 Cornell L.Q. 872 (1950). Hence the rule includes only convictions of felony grade, measured by federal standards.

Judgments of conviction based upon pleas of *nolo contendere* are not included. This position is consistent with the treatment of *nolo* pleas in Rule 410 and the authorities cited in the Advisory Committee's Note in support thereof.

While these rules do not in general purport to resolve constitutional issues, they have in general been drafted with a view to avoiding collision with constitutional principles. Consequently the exception does not include evidence of the conviction of a third person, offered against the accused in a criminal prosecution to prove any fact essential to sustain the judgment of conviction. A contrary position would seem clearly to violate the right of confrontation. *Kirby v. United States,* 174 U.S. 47, 19 S.Ct. 574, 43 L.Ed. 890 (1899), error to convict of possessing stolen postage stamps with the only evidence of theft being the record of conviction of the thieves. The situation is to be distinguished from cases in which conviction of another person is an element of the crime, e.g. 15 U.S.C. § 902(d), interstate shipment of firearms to a known convicted felon, and, as specifically provided, from impeachment.

For comparable provisions see Uniform Rule 63(20); California Evidence Code § 1300; Kansas Code of Civil Procedure § 60–460(r); New Jersey Evidence Rule 63(20).

Note to Paragraph (23). A hearsay exception in this area was originally justified on the ground that verdicts were evidence of reputation. As trial by jury graduated from the category of neighborhood inquests, this theory lost its validity. It was never valid as to chancery decrees. Nevertheless the rule persisted, though the judges and writers shifted ground and began saying that the judgment or decree was as good evidence as reputation. See *City of London v. Clerke,* Carth. 181, 90 Eng.Rep. 710 (K.B. 1691); *Neill v. Duke of Devonshire,* 8 App.Cas. 135 (1882). The shift appears to be correct, since the process of inquiry, sifting, and scrutiny which is relied upon to render reputation reliable is present in perhaps greater measure in the process of litigation. While this might suggest a broader area of application, the affinity to reputation is strong, and paragraph [paragraph] (23) goes no further, not even including character.

The leading case in the United States, *Patterson v. Gaines,* 47 U.S. (6 How.) 550, 599, 12 L.Ed. 553 (1847), follows in the pattern of the English decisions, mentioning as illustrative matters thus provable: manorial rights, public rights of way, immemorial custom, disputed boundary, and pedigree. More recent recognition of the principle is found in *Grant Bros. Construction Co. v. United States,* 232 U.S. 647, 34 S.Ct. 452, 58 L.Ed. 776 (1914), in action for penalties under Alien Contract Labor Law, decision of board of inquiry of Immigration Service admissible to prove alienage of laborers, as a matter of pedigree; *United States v. Mid–Continent Petroleum Corp.,* 67 F.2d 37 (10th Cir.1933), records of commission enrolling Indians admissible on pedigree; *Jung Yen Loy v. Cahill,* 81 F.2d 809 (9th Cir.1936), board decisions as to citizenship of plaintiff's father admissible in proceeding for declaration of citizenship. *Contra,* In re Estate of Cunha, 49 Haw. 273, 414 P.2d 925 (1966).

1974 Enactment

Note to Paragraph (3). Rule 803(3) was approved in the form submitted by the Court to Congress. However, the Committee intends that the Rule be construed to limit the doctrine of *Mutual Life Insurance Co. v. Hillmon,* 145 U.S. 285, 295–300 (1892), so as to render statements of intent by a declarant admissible only to prove his future conduct, not the future conduct of another person.

Note to Paragraph (4). After giving particular attention to the question of physical examination made solely to enable a physician to testify, the Committee approved Rule 803(4) as submitted to Congress, with the understanding that it is not intended in any way to adversely affect present privilege rules or those subsequently adopted.

Note to Paragraph (5). Rule 803(5) as submitted by the Court permitted the reading into evidence of a memorandum or record concerning a matter about which a witness once had knowledge but now has insufficient recollection to enable him to testify accurately and fully, "shown to have been made when the matter was fresh in his memory and to reflect that knowledge correctly." The Committee amended this Rule to add the words "or adopted by the witness" after the phrase "shown to have been made", a treatment consistent with the definition of "statement" in the Jencks Act, 18 U.S.C. 3500. Moreover, it is the Committee's understanding that a memorandum or report, although barred under this Rule, would nonetheless be admissible if it came within another hearsay exception. This last stated principle is deemed applicable to all the hearsay rules.

Note to Paragraph (6). Rule 803(6) as submitted by the Court permitted a record made "in the course of a regularly conducted activity" to be admissible in certain circumstances. The Committee believed there were insufficient guarantees of reliability in records made in the course of activities falling outside the scope of "business" activities as that term is broadly defined in 28 U.S.C. 1732. Moreover, the Committee concluded that the additional requirement of Section 1732 that it must have been the regular practice of a business to make the record is a necessary further assurance of its trustworthiness. The Committee accordingly amended the Rule to incorporate these limitations.

Note to Paragraph (7). Rule 803(7) as submitted by the Court concerned the *absence* of entry in the records of a "regularly conducted activity." The Committee amended this Rule to conform with its action with respect to Rule 803(6).

Note to Paragraph (8). The Committee approved Rule 803(8) without substantive change from the form in which it was submitted by the Court. The Committee intends that the phrase "factual findings" be strictly construed and that evaluations or opinions contained in public reports shall not be admissible under this Rule.

Note to Paragraph (13). The Committee approved this Rule in the form submitted by the Court, intending that the phrase "Statements of fact concerning personal or family history" be read to include the specific types of such statements enumerated in Rule 803(11). House Report No. 93–650.

Note to Paragraph (4). The House approved this rule as it was submitted by the Supreme Court "with the understanding that it is not intended in any way to adversely affect present privilege rules." We also approve this rule, and we would point out with respect to the question of its relation to privileges, it must be read in conjunction with rule 35 of the Federal Rules of Civil Procedure which provides that whenever the physical or mental condition of a party (plaintiff or defendant) is in controversy, the court may require him to submit to an examination by a physician. It is these examinations which will normally be admitted under this exception.

Note to Paragraph (5). Rule 803(5) as submitted by the Court permitted the reading into evidence of a memorandum or record concerning a matter about which a witness once had knowledge but now has insufficient recollection to enable him to testify accurately and fully, "shown to have been made when the matter was fresh in his memory and to reflect that knowledge correctly." The House amended the rule to add the words "or adopted by the witness" after the phrase "shown to have been made," language parallel to the Jencks Act [18 U.S.C. § 3500].

The committee accepts the House amendment with the understanding and belief that it was not intended to narrow the scope of applicability of the rule. In fact, we understand it to clarify the rule's applicability to a memorandum adopted by the witness as well as one made by him. While the rule as submitted by the Court was silent on the question of who made the memorandum, we view the House amendment as a helpful clarification, noting, however, that the Advisory Committee's note to this rule suggests that the important thing is the accuracy of the memorandum rather than who made it.

The committee does not view the House amendment as precluding admissibility in situations in which multiple participants were involved.

When the verifying witness has not prepared the report, but merely examined it and found it accurate, he has adopted the report, and it is therefore admissible. The rule should also be interpreted to cover other situations involving multiple participants, e.g., employer dictating to secretary, secretary making memorandum at direction of employer, or information being passed along a chain of persons, as in *Curtis v. Bradley* [65 Conn. 99, 31 Atl. 591 (1894); see, also, *Rathbun v. Brancatella*, 93 N.J.L. 222, 107 Atl. 279 (1919); see, also, McCormick on Evidence, § 303 (2d ed. 1972)].

The committee also accepts the understanding of the House that a memorandum or report, although barred under this rule, would nonetheless be admissible if it came within another hearsay exception. We consider this principle to be applicable to all the hearsay rules.

Note to Paragraph (6). Rule 803(6) as submitted by the Supreme Court permitted a record made in the course of a regularly conducted activity to be admissible in certain circumstances. This rule constituted a broadening of the traditional business records hearsay exception which has been long advocated by scholars and judges active in the law of evidence.

The House felt there were insufficient guarantees of reliability of records not within a broadly defined business records exception. We disagree. Even under the House definition of "business" including profession, occupation, and "calling of every kind," the records of many regularly conducted activities will, or may be, excluded from evidence. Under the principle of ejusdem generis, the intent of "calling of every kind" would seem to be related to work-related endeavors— e.g., butcher, baker, artist, etc.

Thus, it appears that the records of many institutions or groups might not be admissible under the House amendments. For example, schools, churches, and hospitals will not normally be considered businesses within the definition. Yet, these are groups which keep financial and other records on a regular basis in a manner similar to business enterprises. We believe these records are of equivalent trustworthiness and should be admitted into evidence.

Three states, which have recently codified their evidence rules, have adopted the Supreme Court version of rule 803(6), providing for admission of memoranda of a "regularly conducted activity." None adopted the words "business activity" used in the House amendment. [See Nev.Rev.Stats. § 15.135; N.Mex.Stats. (1973 Supp.) § 20–4–803(6); West's Wis.Stats. Anno. (1973 Supp.) § 908.03(6).]

Therefore, the committee deleted the word "business" as it appears before the word "activity". The last sentence then is unnecessary and was also deleted.

It is the understanding of the committee that the use of the phrase "person with knowledge" is not intended to imply that the party seeking to introduce the memorandum, report, record, or data compilation must be able to produce, or even identify, the specific individual upon whose first-hand knowledge the memorandum, report, record or data compilation was based. A sufficient foundation for the introduction of such evidence will be laid if the party seeking to introduce the evidence is able to show that it was the regular practice of the activity to base such memorandums, reports, records, or data compilations upon a transmission from a person with knowledge, e.g., in the case of the content of a shipment of goods, upon a report from the company's receiving agent or in the case of a computer printout, upon a report from the company's computer programmer or one who has knowledge of the particular record system. In short, the scope of the phrase "person with knowledge" is meant to be coterminous with the custodian of the evidence or other qualified witness. The committee believes this represents the desired rule in light of the complex nature of modern business organizations.

Note to Paragraph (8). The House approved rule 803(8), as submitted by the Supreme Court, with one substantive change. It excluded from the hearsay exception reports containing matters observed by police officers and other law enforcement personnel in criminal cases. Ostensibly, the reason for this exclusion is that observations by police officers at the scene of the crime or the apprehension of the defendant are not as reliable as observations by public officials in other cases because of the adversarial nature of the confrontation between the police and the defendant in criminal cases.

The committee accepts the House's decision to exclude such recorded observations where the police officer is available to testify in court about his observation. However, where he is unavailable as unavailability is defined in rule 804(a)(4) and (a)(5), the report should be admitted as the best available evidence. Accordingly, the committee has amended rule 803(8) to refer to the provision of [proposed] rule 804(b)(5) [deleted], which allows the admission of such reports, records or other statements where the police officer or other law enforcement officer is unavailable because of death, then existing physical or mental illness or infirmity, or not being successfully subject to legal process.

The House Judiciary Committee report contained a statement of intent that "the phrase 'factual findings' in subdivision (c) be strictly construed and that evaluations or opinions contained in public reports shall not be admissible under this rule." The committee takes strong exception to this limiting understanding of the application of the rule. We do not think it reflects an understanding of the intended operation of the rule as explained in the Advisory Committee notes to this subsection. The Advisory Committee notes on subsection (c) of this subdivision point out that various kinds of evaluative reports are now admissible under Federal statutes. 7 U.S.C. § 78, findings of Secretary of Agriculture prima facie evidence of true grade of grain; 42 U.S.C. § 269(b), bill of health by appropriate official prima facie evidence of vessel's sanitary history and condition and compliance with regulations.

These statutory exceptions to the hearsay rule are preserved. Rule 802. The willingness of Congress to recognize these and other such evaluative reports provides a helpful guide in determining the kind of reports which are intended to be admissible under this rule. We think the restrictive interpretation of the House overlooks the fact that while the Advisory Committee assumes admissibility in the first instance of evaluative reports, they are not admissible if, as the rule states, "the sources of information or other circumstances indicate lack of trustworthiness."

The Advisory Committee explains the factors to be considered:

*   *   *   *

Factors which may be assistance in passing upon the admissibility of evaluative reports include: (1) the timeliness of the investigation, McCormick, Can the Courts Make Wider Use of Reports of Official Investigations? 42 Iowa L.Rev. 363 (1957); (2) the special skill or experience of the official, id.; (3) whether a hearing was held and the level at which conducted, *Franklin v. Skelly Oil Co.,* 141 F.2d 568 (19th Cir.1944); (4) possible motivation problems suggested by *Palmer v. Hoffman,* 318 U.S. 109, 63 S.Ct. 477, 87 L.Ed. 645 (1943). Others no doubt could be added.

*   *   *   *

The committee concludes that the language of the rule together with the explanation provided by the Advisory Committee furnish sufficient guidance on the admissibility of evaluative reports.

Note to Paragraph (24). The proposed Rules of Evidence submitted to Congress contained identical provisions in rules 803 and 804 (which set forth the various hearsay exceptions), admitting any hearsay statement not specifically covered by any of the stated exceptions, if the hearsay statement was found to have "comparable circumstantial guarantees of trustworthiness." The House deleted these provisions (proposed rules 803(24) and 804(b)(6)[(5)]) as injecting "too much uncertainty" into the law of evidence and impairing the ability of practitioners to prepare for trial. The House felt that rule 102, which directs the courts to construe the Rules of Evidence so as to promote growth and development, would permit sufficient flexibility to admit hearsay evidence in appropriate cases under various factual situations that might arise.

We disagree with the total rejection of a residual hearsay exception. While we view rule 102 as being intended to provide for a broader construction and interpretation of these rules, we feel that, without a separate residual provision, the specifically enumerated exceptions could become tortured beyond any reasonable circumstances which they were intended to include (even if broadly construed). Moreover, these exceptions, while they reflect the most typical and well recognized exceptions to the hearsay rule, may not encompass every situation in which the reliability and appropriateness of a particular piece of hearsay evidence make clear that it should be heard and considered by the trier of fact.

The committee believes that there are certain exceptional circumstances where evidence which is found by a court to have guarantees of trustworthiness equivalent to or exceeding the guarantees reflected by the presently listed exceptions, and to have a high degree of prolativeness [sic] and necessity could properly be admissible.

The case of *Dallas County v. Commercial Union Assoc. Co., Ltd.,* 286 F.2d 388 (5th Cir.1961) illustrates the point.

The issue in that case was whether the tower of the county courthouse collapsed because it was struck by lightning (covered by insurance) or because of structural weakness and deterioration of the structure (not covered). Investigation of the structure revealed the presence of charcoal and charred timbers. In order to show that lightning may not have been the cause of the charring, the insurer offered a copy of a local newspaper published over 50 years earlier containing an unsigned article describing a fire in the courthouse while it was under construction. The court found that the newspaper did not qualify for admission as a business record or an ancient document and did not fit within any other recognized hearsay exception. The court concluded, however, that the article was trustworthy because it was inconceivable that a newspaper reporter in a small town would report a fire in the courthouse if none had occurred. See also *United States v. Barbati*, 284 F.Supp. 409 (E.D.N.Y.1968).

Because exceptional cases like the *Dallas County* case may arise in the future, the committee has decided to reinstate a residual exception for rules 803 and 804(b).

The committee, however, also agrees with those supporters of the House version who felt that an overly broad residual hearsay exception could emasculate the hearsay rule and the recognized exceptions or vitiate the rationale behind codification of the rules.

Therefore, the committee has adopted a residual exception for rules 803 and 804(b) of much narrower scope and applicability than the Supreme Court version. In order to qualify for admission, a hearsay statement not falling within one of the recognized exceptions would have to satisfy at least four conditions. First, it must have "equivalent circumstantial guarantees of trustworthiness." Second, it must be offered as evidence of a material fact. Third, the court must determine that the statement "is more probative on the point for which it is offered than any other evidence which the proponent can procure through reasonable efforts." This requirement is intended to insure that only statements which have high probative value and necessity may qualify for admission under the residual exceptions. Fourth, the court must determine that "the general purposes of these rules and the interests of justice will best be served by admission of the statement into evidence."

It is intended that the residual hearsay exceptions will be used very rarely, and only in exceptional circumstances. The committee does not intend to establish a broad license for trial judges to admit hearsay statements that do not fall within one of the other exceptions contained in rules 803 and 804(b). The residual exceptions are not meant to authorize major judicial revisions of the hearsay rule, including its present exceptions. Such major revisions are best accomplished by legislative action. It is intended that in any case in which evidence is sought to be admitted under these subsections, the trial judge will exercise no less care, reflection and caution than the courts did under the common law in establishing the now-recognized exceptions to the hearsay rule.

In order to establish a well-defined jurisprudence, the special facts and circumstances which, in the court's judgment, indicates that the statement has a sufficiently high degree of trustworthiness and necessity to justify its admission should be stated on the record. It is expected that the court will give the opposing party a full and adequate opportunity to contest the admission of any statement sought to be introduced under these subsections. Senate Report No. 93–1277.

Rule 803 defines when hearsay statements are admissible in evidence even though the declarant is available as a witness. The Senate amendments make three changes in this rule.

Note to Paragraph (6). The House bill provides in subsection (6) that records of a regularly conducted "business" activity qualify for admission into evidence as an exception to the hearsay rule. "Business" is defined as including "business, profession, occupation and calling of every kind." The Senate amendment drops the requirement that the records be those of a "business" activity and eliminates the definition of "business." The Senate amendment provides that records are admissible if they are records of a regularly conducted "activity."

The Conference adopts the House provision that the records must be those of a regularly conducted "business" activity. The Conferees changed the definition of "business" contained in the House provision in order to make it clear that the records of institutions and associations like schools, churches and hospitals are admissible under this provision. The records of public schools and hospitals are also covered by Rule 803(8), which deals with public records and reports.

Note to Paragraph (8). The Senate amendment adds language, not contained in the House bill, that refers to another rule that was added by the Senate in another amendment ([proposed] Rule 804(b)(5)—Criminal law enforcement records and reports [deleted]).

In view of its action on [proposed] Rule 804(b)(5) (Criminal law enforcement records and reports) [deleted], the Conference does not adopt the Senate amendment and restores the bill to the House version.

Note to Paragraph (24). The Senate amendment adds a new subsection, (24), which makes admissible a hearsay statement not specifically covered by any of the previous twenty-three subsections, if the statement has equivalent circumstantial guarantees of trustworthiness and if the court determines that (A) the statement is offered as evidence of a material fact; (B) the statement is more probative on the point for which it is offered than any other evidence the proponent can procure through reasonable efforts; and (C) the general purposes of these rules and the interests of justice will best be served by admission of the statement into evidence.

The House bill eliminated a similar, but broader, provision because of the conviction that such a provision injected too much uncertainty into the law of evidence regarding hearsay and impaired the ability of a litigant to prepare adequately for trial.

The Conference adopts the Senate amendment with an amendment that provides that a party intending to request the court to use a statement under this provision must notify any adverse party of this intention as well as of the particulars of the statement, including the name and address of the declarant. This notice must be given sufficiently in advance of the trial or hearing to provide any adverse party with a fair opportunity to prepare to contest the use of the statement. House Report No. 93–1597.

1987 Amendment

The amendments are technical. No substantive change is intended.

1997 Amendment

The contents of Rule 803(24) and Rule 804(b)(5) have been combined and transferred to a new Rule 807. This was done to facilitate additions to Rules 803 and 804. No change in meaning is intended.

GAP Report on Rule 803. The words "Transferred to Rule 807" were substituted for "Abrogated."

2000 Amendment

The amendment provides that the foundation requirements of Rule 803(6) can be satisfied under certain circumstances without the expense and inconvenience of producing time-consuming foundation witnesses. Under current law, courts have generally required foundation witnesses to testify. *See, e.g., Tongil Co., Ltd. v. Hyundai Merchant Marine Corp.*, 968 F.2d 999 (9th Cir. 1992) (reversing a judgment based on business records where a qualified person filed an affidavit but did not testify). Protections are provided by the authentication requirements of Rule 902(11) for domestic records, Rule 902(12) for foreign records in civil cases, and 18 U.S.C. § 3505 for foreign records in criminal cases.

GAP Report—Proposed Amendment to Rule 803(6)

The Committee made no changes to the published draft of the proposed amendment to Evidence Rule 803(6).

2011 Amendments

The language of Rule 803 has been amended as part of the restyling of the Evidence Rules to make them more easily understood and to make style and terminology consistent throughout the rules. These changes are intended to be stylistic only. There is no intent to change any result in any ruling on evidence admissibility.

2013 Amendments

Rule 803(10) has been amended in response to *Melendez–Diaz v. Massachusetts*, 557 U.S. 305 (2009). The *Melendez–Diaz* Court declared that a testimonial certificate could be admitted if the accused is given advance notice and does not timely demand the presence of the official who prepared the certificate. The amendment incorporates, with minor variations, a "notice-and-demand" procedure that was approved by the *Melendez–Diaz* Court. See Tex. Code Crim. P. Ann., art. 38.41.

Changes Made After Publication and Comment

No changes were made to the proposed amendment or Committee Note as they were issued for public comment.

2014 Amendments

[Subdivision (6)] The Rule has been amended to clarify that if the proponent has established the stated requirements of the exception—regular business with regularly kept record, source with personal knowledge, record made timely, and foundation testimony or certification—then the burden is on the opponent to show that the source of information or the method or circumstances of preparation indicate a lack of trustworthiness. While most courts have imposed that burden on the opponent, some have not. It is appropriate to impose this burden on the opponent, as the basic admissibility requirements are sufficient to establish a presumption that the record is reliable.

The opponent, in meeting its burden, is not necessarily required to introduce affirmative evidence of untrustworthi-ness. For example, the opponent might argue that a record was prepared in anticipation of litigation and is favorable to the preparing party without needing to introduce evidence on the point. A determination of untrustworthiness necessarily depends on the circumstances.

Changes Made After Publication and Comment

In accordance with a public comment, a slight change was made to the Committee Note to better track the language of the rule.

[Subdivision (7)] The Rule has been amended to clarify that if the proponent has established the stated requirements of the exception—set forth in Rule 803(6)—then the burden is on the opponent to show that the possible source of the information or other circumstances indicate a lack of trustworthiness. The amendment maintains consistency with the proposed amendment to the trustworthiness clause of Rule 803(6).

Changes Made After Publication and Comment

In accordance with a public comment, a slight change was made to the Committee Note to better track the language of the rule.

[Subdivision (8)] The Rule has been amended to clarify that if the proponent has established that the record meets the stated requirements of the exception—prepared by a public office and setting out information as specified in the Rule—then the burden is on the opponent to show that the source of information or other circumstances indicate a lack of trustworthiness. While most courts have imposed that burden on the opponent, some have not. Public records have justifiably carried a presumption of reliability, and it should be up to the opponent to "demonstrate why a time-tested and carefully considered presumption is not appropriate." *Ellis v. International Playtex, Inc.*, 745 F.2d 292, 301 (4th Cir. 1984). The amendment maintains consistency with the proposed amendment to the trustworthiness clause of Rule 803(6).

The opponent, in meeting its burden, is not necessarily required to introduce affirmative evidence of untrustworthiness. For example, the opponent might argue that a record was prepared in anticipation of litigation and is favorable to the preparing party without needing to introduce evidence on the point. A determination of untrustworthiness necessarily depends on the circumstances.

Changes Made After Publication and Comment

In accordance with a public comment, a slight change was made to the Committee Note to better track the language of the rule.

2017 Amendments

The ancient documents exception to the rule against hearsay has been limited to statements in documents prepared before January 1, 1998. The Committee has determined that the ancient documents exception should be limited due to the risk that it will be used as a vehicle to admit vast amounts of unreliable electronically stored information (ESI). Given the exponential development and growth of electronic information since 1998, the hearsay exception for ancient documents has now become a possible open door for large amounts of unreliable ESI, as no showing of reliability needs to be made to qualify under the exception.

The Committee is aware that in certain cases—such as cases involving latent diseases and environmental damage—parties must rely on hardcopy documents from the past. The ancient documents exception remains available for such cases for documents prepared before 1998. Going forward, it is anticipated that any need to admit old hardcopy documents produced after January 1, 1998 will decrease, because reliable ESI is likely to be available and can be offered under a reliability-based hearsay exception. Rule 803(6) may be used for many of these ESI documents, especially given its flexible standards on which witnesses might be qualified to provide an adequate foundation. And Rule 807 can be used to admit old documents upon a showing of reliability—which will often (though not always) be found by circumstances such as that the document was prepared with no litigation motive in mind, close in time to the relevant events. The limitation of the ancient documents exception is not intended to raise an inference that 20–year–old documents are, as a class, unreliable, or that they should somehow not qualify for admissibility under Rule 807. Finally, many old documents can be admitted for the non-hearsay purpose of proving notice, or as party-opponent statements.

The limitation of the ancient documents hearsay exception is not intended to have any effect on authentication of ancient documents. The possibility of authenticating an old document under Rule 901(b)(8)—or under any ground available for any other document—remains unchanged.

The Committee carefully considered, but ultimately rejected, an amendment that would preserve the ancient documents exception for hardcopy evidence only. A party will often offer hardcopy that is derived from ESI. Moreover, a good deal of old information in hardcopy has been digitized or will be so in the future. Thus, the line between ESI and hardcopy was determined to be one that could not be drawn usefully.

The Committee understands that the choice of a cut-off date has a degree of arbitrariness. But January 1, 1998 is a rational date for treating concerns about old and unreliable ESI. And the date is no more arbitrary than the 20–year cutoff date in the original rule. *See* Committee Note to Rule 901(b)(8) ("Any time period selected is bound to be arbitrary.").

Under the amendment, a document is "prepared" when the statement proffered was recorded in that document. For example, if a hardcopy document is prepared in 1995, and a party seeks to admit a scanned copy of that document, the date of preparation is 1995 even though the scan was made long after that—the subsequent scan does not alter the document. The relevant point is the date on which the information is recorded, not when the information is prepared for trial. However, if the content of the document is *itself* altered after the cut-off date, then the hearsay exception will not apply to statements that were added in the alteration.

HISTORICAL NOTES
Revision Notes and Legislative Reports
1975 Acts. House Report No. 94–599, see 1975 U.S. Code Cong. and Adm. News, p. 1585.

CROSS REFERENCES
Alien crewman, prima facie evidence of failure to deport, see 8 USCA § 1284.

Certification written by Attorney General of no record entries as admissible evidence, see 8 USCA § 1360.

Character evidence,

Methods of proving character, see Fed.Rules Evid. Rule 405, 28 USCA.

Opinion and reputation evidence and specific conduct, see Fed.Rules Evid. Rule 608, 28 USCA.

Proof of character, see Fed.Rules Evid. Rule 404, 28 USCA.

Confrontation with, and cross-examination of, witnesses, see USCA Const. Amend. VI.

Construction of these rules to secure fairness and development of law of evidence, see Fed.Rules Evid. Rule 102, 28 USCA.

Distribution and marketing of agricultural products, certificates of inspection of products as prima facie evidence, see 7 USCA § 1622.

Findings and orders of Secretary of Agriculture as prima facie evidence,

Associations of agricultural products producers, see 7 USCA § 292.

Official grade designation of grain, see 7 USCA § 78.

Packers and stockyards, see 7 USCA § 210.

Government records and papers, admissibility of, see 28 USCA § 1733.

Naturalization of aliens through active-duty service in Armed Forces, revocation, see 8 USCA § 1440.

Personal knowledge of witness, necessity of, see Fed.Rules Evid. Rule 602, 28 USCA.

Plea of guilty or nolo contendere, admissibility of pleas, discussions, and related statements, see Fed.Rules Evid. Rule 410, 28 USCA.

Preliminary questions as to admissibility, privileges, etc., see Fed.Rules Evid. Rule 104, 28 USCA.

Prior statements of witnesses, extrinsic evidence, see Fed. Rules Evid. Rule 613, 28 USCA.

Production of documents and things and entry upon land for inspection, see Fed.Rules Civ.Proc. Rule 34, 28 USCA.

Quarantine and inspection of ports of entry, bills of health as evidence of statements therein, see 42 USCA § 269.

Records in regular course of business, see 28 USCA § 1732.

Report of examining physician on person's physical or mental condition, discovery of, see Fed.Rules Civ.Proc. Rule 35, 28 USCA.

Self-authentication of public records, documents, etc., see Fed.Rules Evid. Rule 902, 28 USCA.

Social Security, etc., benefits, records of Commissioner of Social Security as evidence, see 42 USCA § 405.

Rule 804. Exceptions to the Rule Against Hearsay—When the Declarant Is Unavailable as a Witness

(a) Criteria for Being Unavailable. A declarant is considered to be unavailable as a witness if the declarant:

(1) is exempted from testifying about the subject matter of the declarant's statement because the court rules that a privilege applies;

(2) refuses to testify about the subject matter despite a court order to do so;

(3) testifies to not remembering the subject matter;

(4) cannot be present or testify at the trial or hearing because of death or a then-existing infirmity, physical illness, or mental illness; or

(5) is absent from the trial or hearing and the statement's proponent has not been able, by process or other reasonable means, to procure:

(A) the declarant's attendance, in the case of a hearsay exception under Rule 804(b)(1) or (6); or

(B) the declarant's attendance or testimony, in the case of a hearsay exception under Rule 804(b)(2), (3), or (4).

But this subdivision (a) does not apply if the statement's proponent procured or wrongfully caused the declarant's unavailability as a witness in order to prevent the declarant from attending or testifying.

(b) The Exceptions. The following are not excluded by the rule against hearsay if the declarant is unavailable as a witness:

(1) Former Testimony. Testimony that:

(A) was given as a witness at a trial, hearing, or lawful deposition, whether given during the current proceeding or a different one; and

(B) is now offered against a party who had—or, in a civil case, whose predecessor in interest had—an opportunity and similar motive to develop it by direct, cross-, or redirect examination.

(2) Statement Under the Belief of Imminent Death. In a prosecution for homicide or in a civil case, a statement that the declarant, while believing the declarant's death to be imminent, made about its cause or circumstances.

(3) Statement Against Interest. A statement that:

(A) a reasonable person in the declarant's position would have made only if the person believed it to be true because, when made, it was so contrary to the declarant's proprietary or pecuniary interest or had so great a tendency to invalidate the declarant's claim against someone else or to expose the declarant to civil or criminal liability; and

(B) is supported by corroborating circumstances that clearly indicate its trustworthiness, if it is offered in a criminal case as one that tends to expose the declarant to criminal liability.

(4) Statement of Personal or Family History. A statement about:

(A) the declarant's own birth, adoption, legitimacy, ancestry, marriage, divorce, relationship by blood, adoption, or marriage, or similar facts of personal or family history, even though the declarant had no way of acquiring personal knowledge about that fact; or

(B) another person concerning any of these facts, as well as death, if the declarant was related to the person by blood, adoption, or marriage or was so intimately associated with the person's

family that the declarant's information is likely to be accurate.

(5) [Other Exceptions.] [Transferred to Rule 807.]

(6) Statement Offered Against a Party That Wrongfully Caused the Declarant's Unavailability. A statement offered against a party that wrongfully caused—or acquiesced in wrongfully causing—the declarant's unavailability as a witness, and did so intending that result.

(Pub.L. 93–595, § 1, Jan. 2, 1975, 88 Stat. 1942; Pub.L. 94–149, § 1(12), (13), Dec. 12, 1975, 89 Stat. 806; Mar. 2, 1987, eff. Oct. 1, 1987; Pub.L. 100–690, Title VII, § 7075(b), Nov. 18, 1988, 102 Stat. 4405; Apr. 11, 1997, eff. Dec. 1, 1997; Apr. 28, 2010, eff. Dec. 1, 2010; Apr. 26, 2011, eff. Dec. 1, 2011.)

ADVISORY COMMITTEE NOTES
1972 Proposed Rules

As to firsthand knowledge on the part of hearsay declarants, see the introductory portion of the Advisory Committee's Note to Rule 803.

Note to Subdivision (a). The definition of unavailability implements the division of hearsay exceptions into two categories by Rules 803 and 804(b).

At common law the unavailability requirement was evolved in connection with particular hearsay exceptions rather than along general lines. For example, see the separate explications of unavailability in relation to former testimony, declarations against interest, and statements of pedigree, separately developed in McCormick §§ 234, 257, and 297. However, no reason is apparent for making distinctions as to what satisfies unavailability for the different exceptions. The treatment in the rule is therefore uniform although differences in the range of process for witnesses between civil and criminal cases will lead to a less exacting requirement under item (5). See Rule 45(e) of the Federal Rules of Civil Procedure and Rule 17(e) of the Federal Rules of Criminal Procedure.

Five instances of unavailability are specified:

(1) Substantial authority supports the position that exercise of a claim of privilege by the declarant satisfies the requirement of unavailability (usually in connection with former testimony). *Wyatt v. State,* 35 Ala.App. 147, 46 So.2d 837 (1950); *State v. Stewart,* 85 Kan. 404, 116 P. 489 (1911); Annot., 45 A.L.R.2d 1354; Uniform Rule 62(7)(a); California Evidence Code § 240(a)(1); Kansas Code of Civil Procedure § 60–459(g)(1). A ruling by the judge is required, which clearly implies that an actual claim of privilege must be made.

(2) A witness is rendered unavailable if he simply refuses to testify concerning the subject matter of his statement despite judicial pressures to do so, a position supported by similar considerations of practicality. *Johnson v. People,* 152 Colo. 586, 384 P.2d 454 (1963); *People v. Pickett,* 339 Mich. 294, 63 N.W.2d 681, 45 A.L.R.2d 1341 (1954). *Contra, Pleau v. State,* 255 Wis. 362, 38 N.W.2d 496 (1949).

(3) The position that a claimed lack of memory by the witness of the subject matter of his statement constitutes unavailability likewise finds support in the cases, though not without dissent. McCormick § 234, p. 494. If the claim is successful, the practical effect is to put the testimony beyond reach, as in the other instances. In this instance, however, it will be noted that the lack of memory must be established by

the testimony of the witness himself, which clearly contemplates his production and subjection to cross-examination.

(4) Death and infirmity find general recognition as grounds. McCormick §§ 234, 257, 297; Uniform Rule 62(7)(c); California Evidence Code § 240(a)(3); Kansas Code of Civil Procedure § 60–459(g)(3); New Jersey Evidence Rule 62(6)(c). See also the provisions on use of depositions in Rule 32(a)(3) of the Federal Rules of Civil Procedure and Rule 15(e) of the Federal Rules of Criminal Procedure.

(5) Absence from the hearing coupled with inability to compel attendance by process or other reasonable means also satisfies the requirement. McCormick § 234; Uniform Rule 62(7)(d) and (e); California Evidence Code § 240(a)(4) and (5); Kansas Code of Civil Procedure § 60–459(g)(4) and (5); New Jersey Rule 62(6)(b) and (d). See the discussion of procuring attendance of witnesses who are nonresidents or in custody in *Barber v. Page*, 390 U.S. 719, 88 S.Ct. 1318, 20 L.Ed.2d 255 (1968).

If the conditions otherwise constituting unavailability result from the procurement or wrongdoing of the proponent of the statement, the requirement is not satisfied. The rule contains no requirement that an attempt be made to take the deposition of a declarant.

Note to Subdivision (b). Rule 803, *supra*, is based upon the assumption that a hearsay statement falling within one of its exceptions possesses qualities which justify the conclusion that whether the declarant is available or unavailable is not a relevant factor in determining admissibility. The instant rule proceeds upon a different theory: hearsay which admittedly is not equal in quality to testimony of the declarant on the stand may nevertheless be admitted if the declarant is unavailable and if his statement meets a specified standard. The rule expresses preferences: testimony given on the stand in person is preferred over hearsay, and hearsay, if of the specified quality, is preferred over complete loss of the evidence of the declarant. The exceptions evolved at common law with respect to declarations of unavailable declarants furnish the basis for the exceptions enumerated in the proposal. The term "unavailable" is defined in subdivision (a).

Exception (1). Former testimony does not rely upon some set of circumstances to substitute for oath and cross-examination, since both oath and opportunity to cross-examine were present in fact. The only missing one of the ideal conditions for the giving of testimony is the presence of trier and opponent ("demeanor evidence"). This is lacking with all hearsay exceptions. Hence it may be argued that former testimony is the strongest hearsay and should be included under Rule 803, supra. However, opportunity to observe demeanor is what in a large measure confers depth and meaning upon oath and cross-examination. Thus in cases under Rule 803 demeanor lacks the significance which it possesses with respect to testimony. In any event, the tradition, founded in experience, uniformly favors production of the witness if he is available. The exception indicates continuation of the policy. This preference for the presence of the witness is apparent also in rules and statutes on the use of depositions, which deal with substantially the same problem.

Under the exception, the testimony may be offered (1) against the party *against* whom it was previously offered or (2) against the party *by* whom it was previously offered. In each instance the question resolves itself into whether fairness allows imposing, upon the party against whom now offered, the handling of the witness of the earlier occasion. (1) If the party against whom now offered is the one against

whom the testimony was offered previously, no unfairness is apparent in requiring him to accept his own prior conduct of cross-examination or decision not to cross-examine. Only demeanor has been lost, and that is inherent in the situation. (2) If the party against whom now offered is the one *by* whom the testimony was offered previously, a satisfactory answer becomes somewhat more difficult. One possibility is to proceed somewhat along the line of an adoptive admission, i.e. by offering the testimony proponent in effect adopts it. However, this theory savors of discarded concepts of witnesses' belonging to a party, of litigants' ability to pick and choose witnesses, and of vouching for one's own witnesses. Cf. McCormick § 246, pp. 526–527; 4 Wigmore § 1075. A more direct and acceptable approach is simply to recognize direct and redirect examination of one's own witness as the equivalent of cross-examining an opponent's witness. Falknor, Former Testimony and the Uniform Rules: A Comment, 38 N.Y.U.L.Rev. 651, n. 1 (1963); McCormick § 231, p. 483. See also 5 Wigmore § 1389. Allowable techniques for dealing with hostile, double-crossing, forgetful, and mentally deficient witnesses leave no substance to a claim that one could not adequately develop his own witness at the former hearing. An even less appealing argument is presented when failure to develop fully was the result of a deliberate choice.

The common law did not limit the admissibility of former testimony to that given in an earlier trial of the same case, although it did require identity of issues as a means of insuring that the former handling of the witness was the equivalent of what would now be done if the opportunity were presented. Modern decisions reduce the requirement to "substantial" identity. McCormick § 233. Since identity of issues is significant only in that it bears on motive and interest in developing fully the testimony of the witness, expressing the matter in the latter terms is preferable. *Id.* Testimony given at a preliminary hearing was held in *California v. Green*, 399 U.S. 149, 90 S.Ct. 1930, 26 L.Ed.2d 489 (1970), to satisfy confrontation requirements in this respect.

As a further assurance of fairness in thrusting upon a party the prior handling of the witness, the common law also insisted upon identity of parties, deviating only to the extent of allowing substitution of successors in a narrowly construed privity. Mutuality as an aspect of identity is now generally discredited, and the requirement of identity of the offering party disappears except as it might affect motive to develop the testimony. Falknor, *supra*, at 652; McCormick § 232, pp. 487–488. The question remains whether strict identity, or privity, should continue as a requirement with respect to the party against whom offered. The rule departs to the extent of allowing substitution of one with the right and opportunity to develop the testimony with similar motive and interest. This position is supported by modern decisions. McCormick § 232, pp. 489–490; 5 Wigmore § 1388.

Provisions of the same tenor will be found in Uniform Rule 63(3)(b); California Evidence Code §§ 1290–1292; Kansas Code of Civil Procedure § 60–460(c)(2); New Jersey Evidence Rule 63(3). Unlike the rule, the latter three provide either that former testimony is not admissible if the right of confrontation is denied or that it is not admissible if the accused was not a party to the prior hearing. The genesis of these limitations is a caveat in Uniform Rule 63(3) Comment that use of former testimony against an accused may violate his right of confrontation. *Mattox v. United States*, 156 U.S. 237, 15 S.Ct. 337, 39 L.Ed. 409 (1895), held that the right was not violated by the Government's use, on a retrial of the same case, of testimony given at the first trial by two witnesses since deceased. The decision leaves open the questions (1) whether direct and redirect are equivalent to cross-examination for purposes of confrontation, (2) whether testimony given in a different proceeding is acceptable, and (3) whether the accused must himself have been a party to the earlier proceeding or whether a similarly situated person will serve the purpose. Professor Falknor concluded that, if a dying declaration untested by cross-examination is constitutionally admissible, former testimony tested by the cross-examination of one similarly situated does not offend against confrontation. Falknor, *supra*, at 659–660. The constitutional acceptability of dying declarations has often been conceded. *Mattox v. United States*, 156 U.S. 237, 243, 15 S.Ct. 337, 39 L.Ed. 409 (1895); *Kirby v. United States*, 174 U.S. 47, 61, 19 S.Ct. 574, 43 L.Ed. 890 (1899); *Pointer v. Texas*, 380 U.S. 400, 407, 85 S.Ct. 1065, 13 L.Ed.2d 923 (1965).

Exception (2). The exception is the familiar dying declaration of the common law, expanded somewhat beyond its traditionally narrow limits. While the original religious justification for the exception may have lost its conviction for some persons over the years, it can scarcely be doubted that powerful psychological pressures are present. See 5 Wigmore § 1443 and the classic statement of Chief Baron Eyre in Rex v. Woodcock, 1 Leach 500, 502, 168 Eng.Rep. 352, 353 (K.B.1789).

The common law required that the statement be that of the victim, offered in a prosecution for criminal homicide. Thus declarations by victims in prosecutions for other crimes, e.g. a declaration by a rape victim who dies in childbirth, and all declarations in civil cases were outside the scope of the exception. An occasional statute has removed these restrictions, as in Colo.R.S. § 52–1–20, or has expanded the area of offenses to include abortions, 5 Wigmore § 1432, p. 224, n. 4. Kansas by decision extended the exception to civil cases. *Thurston v. Fritz*, 91 Kan. 468, 138 P. 625 (1914). While the common law exception no doubt originated as a result of the exceptional need for the evidence in homicide cases, the theory of admissibility applies equally in civil cases and in prosecutions for crimes other than homicide. The same considerations suggest abandonment of the limitation to circumstances attending the event in question, yet when the statement deals with matters other than the supposed death, its influence is believed to be sufficiently attenuated to justify the limitation. Unavailability is not limited to death. See subdivision (a) of this rule. Any problem as to declarations phrased in terms of opinion is laid at rest by Rule 701, and continuation of a requirement of firsthand knowledge is assured by Rule 602.

Comparable provisions are found in Uniform Rule 63(5); California Evidence Code § 1242; Kansas Code of Civil Procedure § 60–460(e); New Jersey Evidence Rule 63(5).

Exception (3). The circumstantial guaranty of reliability for declarations against interest is the assumption that persons do not make statements which are damaging to themselves unless satisfied for good reason that they are true. *Hileman v. Northwest Engineering Co.*, 346 F.2d 668 (6th Cir.1965). If the statement is that of a party, offered by his opponent, it comes in as an admission, Rule 803(d)(2) [sic; probably should be "Rule 801(d)(2)"], and there is no occasion to inquire whether it is against interest, this not being a condition precedent to admissibility of admissions by opponents.

The common law required that the interest declared against be pecuniary or proprietary but within this limitation demonstrated striking ingenuity in discovering an against-interest aspect. Higham v. Ridgway, 10 East 109, 103 Eng.Rep. 717 (K.B.1808); Reg. v. Overseers of Birmingham, 1 B. & S. 763, 121 Eng.Rep. 897 (Q.B.1861); McCormick, § 256, p. 551, nn. 2 and 3.

The exception discards the common law limitation and expands to the full logical limit. One result is to remove doubt as to the admissibility of declarations tending to establish a tort liability against the declarant or to extinguish one which might be asserted by him, in accordance with the trend of the decisions in this country. McCormick § 254, pp. 548–549. Another is to allow statements tending to expose declarant to hatred, ridicule, or disgrace, the motivation here being considered to be as strong as when financial interests are at stake. McCormick § 255, p. 551. And finally, exposure to criminal liability satisfies the against-interest requirement. The refusal of the common law to concede the adequacy of a penal interest was no doubt indefensible in logic, see the dissent of Mr. Justice Holmes in *Donnelly v. United States*, 228 U.S. 243, 33 S.Ct. 449, 57 L.Ed. 820 (1913), but one senses in the decisions a distrust of evidence of confessions by third persons offered to exculpate the accused arising from suspicions of fabrication either of the fact of the making of the confession or in its contents, enhanced in either instance by the required unavailability of the declarant. Nevertheless, an increasing amount of decisional law recognizes exposure to punishment for crime as a sufficient stake. *People v. Spriggs*, 60 Cal.2d 868, 36 Cal.Rptr. 841, 389 P.2d 377 (1964); *Sutter v. Easterly*, 354 Mo. 282, 189 S.W.2d 284 (1945); Band's Refuse Removal, Inc. v. Fairlawn Borough, 62 N.J.Super. 522, 163 A.2d 465 (1960); *Newberry v. Commonwealth*, 191 Va. 445, 61 S.E.2d 318 (1950); Annot., 162 A.L.R. 446. The requirement of corroboration is included in the rule in order to effect an accommodation between these competing considerations. When the statement is offered by the accused by way of exculpation, the resulting situation is not adapted to control by rulings as to the weight of the evidence, and hence the provision is cast in terms of a requirement preliminary to admissibility. Cf. Rule 406(a). The requirement of corroboration should be construed in such a manner as to effectuate its purpose of circumventing fabrication.

Ordinarily the third-party confession is thought of in terms of exculpating the accused, but this is by no means always or necessarily the case: it may include statements implicating him, and under the general theory of declarations against interest they would be admissible as related statements. *Douglas v. Alabama*, 380 U.S. 415, 85 S.Ct. 1074, 13 L.Ed.2d 934 (1965), and *Bruton v. United States*, 389 U.S. 818, 88 S.Ct. 126, 19 L.Ed.2d 70 (1968), both involved confessions by codefendants which implicated the accused. While the confession was not actually offered in evidence in *Douglas*, the procedure followed effectively put it before the jury, which the Court ruled to be error. Whether the confession might have been admissible as a declaration against penal interest was not considered or discussed. *Bruton* assumed the inadmissibility, as against the accused, of the implicating confession of his codefendant, and centered upon the question of the effectiveness of a limiting instruction. These decisions, however, by no means require that all statements implicating another person be excluded from the category of declarations against interest. Whether a statement is in fact against interest must be determined from the circumstances of each case. Thus a statement admitting guilt and implicating another person, made while in custody, may well be motivated by a desire to curry favor with the authorities and hence fail to qualify as against interest. See the dissenting opinion of Mr. Justice White in *Bruton*. On the other hand, the same words spoken under different circumstances, e.g., to an acquaintance, would have no difficulty in qualifying. The rule does not purport to deal with questions of the right of confrontation.

The balancing of self-serving against dissenting aspects of a declaration is discussed in McCormick § 256.

For comparable provisions, see Uniform Rule 63(10); California Evidence Code § 1230; Kansas Code of Civil Procedure § 60–460(j); New Jersey Evidence Rule 63(10).

Exception (4). The general common law requirement that a declaration in this area must have been made *ante litem motam* has been dropped, as bearing more appropriately on weight than admissibility. See 5 Wigmore § 1483. Item (i)[(A)] specifically disclaims any need of firsthand knowledge respecting declarant's own personal history. In some instances it is self-evident (marriage) and in others impossible and traditionally not required (date of birth). Item (ii)[(B)] deals with declarations concerning the history of another person. As at common law, declarant is qualified if related by blood or marriage. 5 Wigmore § 1489. In addition, and contrary to the common law, declarant qualifies by virtue of intimate association with the family. *Id.,* § 1487. The requirement sometimes encountered that when the subject of the statement is the relationship between two other persons the declarant must qualify as to both is omitted. Relationship is reciprocal. *Id.,* § 1491.

For comparable provisions, see Uniform Rule 63(23), (24), (25); California Evidence Code §§ 1310, 1311; Kansas Code of Civil Procedure § 60–460(u), (v), (w); New Jersey Evidence Rules 63–23), 63(24), 63(25).

1974 Enactment

Note to Subdivision (a)(3). Rule 804(a)(3) was approved in the form submitted by the Court. However, the Committee intends no change in existing federal law under which the court may choose to disbelieve the declarant's testimony as to his lack of memory. See *United States v. Insana*, 423 F.2d 1165, 1169–1170 (2nd Cir.), cert. denied, 400 U.S. 841 (1970).

Note to Subdivision (a)(5). Rule 804(a)(5) as submitted to the Congress provided, as one type of situation in which a declarant would be deemed "unavailable", that he be "absent from the hearing and the proponent of his statement has been unable to procure his attendance by process or other reasonable means." The Committee amended the Rule to insert after the word "attendance" the parenthetical expression "(or, in the case of a hearsay exception under subdivision (b)(2), (3), or (4), his attendance or testimony)". The amendment is designed primarily to require that an attempt be made to depose a witness (as well as to seek his attendance) as a precondition to the witness being deemed unavailable. The Committee, however, recognized the propriety of an exception to this additional requirement when it is the declarant's former testimony that is sought to be admitted under subdivision (b)(1).

Note to Subdivision (b)(1). Rule 804(b)(1) as submitted by the Court allowed prior testimony of an unavailable witness to be admissible if the party against whom it is offered or a person "with motive and interest similar" to his had an opportunity to examine the witness. The Committee considered that it is generally unfair to impose upon the party

against whom the hearsay evidence is being offered responsibility for the manner in which the witness was previously handled by another party. The sole exception to this, in the Committee's view, is when a party's predecessor in interest in a civil action or proceeding had an opportunity and similar motive to examine the witness. The Committee amended the Rule to reflect these policy determinations.

Note to Subdivision (b)(2). Rule 804(b)(3) as submitted by the Court (now Rule 804(b)(2) in the bill) proposed to expand the traditional scope of the dying declaration exception (i.e. a statement of the victim in a homicide case as to the cause or circumstances of his believed imminent death) to allow such statements in all criminal and civil cases. The Committee did not consider dying declarations as among the most reliable forms of hearsay. Consequently, it amended the provision to limit their admissibility in criminal cases to homicide prosecutions, where exceptional need for the evidence is present. This is existing law. At the same time, the Committee approved the expansion to civil actions and proceedings where the stakes do not involve possible imprisonment, although noting that this could lead to forum shopping in some instances.

Note to Subdivision (b)(3). Rule 804(b)(4) as submitted by the Court (now Rule 804(b)(3) in the bill) provided as follows:

Statement against interest.—A statement which was at the time of its making so far contrary to the declarant's pecuniary or proprietary interest or so far tended to subject him to civil or criminal liability or to render invalid a claim by him against another or to make him an object of hatred, ridicule, or disgrace, that a reasonable man in his position would not have made the statement unless he believed it to be true. A statement tending to exculpate the accused is not admissible unless corroborated.

The Committee determined to retain the traditional hearsay exception for statements against pecuniary or proprietary interest. However, it deemed the Court's additional references to statements tending to subject a declarant to civil liability or to render invalid a claim by him against another to be redundant as included within the scope of the reference to statements against pecuniary or proprietary interest. See *Gichner v. Antonio Triano Tile and Marble Co.*, 410 F.2d 238 (D.C.Cir.1968). Those additional references were accordingly deleted.

The Court's Rule also proposed to expand the hearsay limitation from its present federal limitation to include statements subjecting the declarant to criminal liability and statements tending to make him an object of hatred, ridicule, or disgrace. The Committee eliminated the latter category from the subdivision as lacking sufficient guarantees of reliability. See *United States v. Dovico*, 380 F.2d 325, 327 nn. 2, 4 (2nd Cir.), cert. denied, 389 U.S. 944 (1967). As for statements against penal interest, the Committee shared the view of the Court that some such statements do possess adequate assurances of reliability and should be admissible. It believed, however, as did the Court, that statements of this type tending to exculpate the accused are more suspect and so should have their admissibility conditioned upon some further provision insuring trustworthiness. The proposal in the Court Rule to add a requirement of simple corroboration was, however, deemed ineffective to accomplish this purpose since the accused's own testimony might suffice while not necessarily increasing the reliability of the hearsay statement. The Committee settled upon the language "unless corroborating circumstances clearly indicate the trustworthiness of the statement" as affording a proper standard and degree of discretion. It was contemplated that the result in such cases as *Donnelly v. United States*, 228 U.S. 243 (1912), where the circumstances plainly indicated reliability, would be changed. The Committee also added to the Rule the final sentence from the 1971 Advisory Committee draft, designed to codify the doctrine of *Bruton v. United States*, 391 U.S. 123 (1968). The Committee does not intend to affect the existing exception to the *Bruton* principle where the codefendant takes the stand and is subject to cross-examination, but believed there was no need to make specific provision for this situation in the Rule, since in that event the declarant would not be "unavailable". House Report No. 93–650.

Note to Subdivision (a)(5). Subdivision (a) of rule 804 as submitted by the Supreme Court defined the conditions under which a witness was considered to be unavailable. It was amended in the House.

The purpose of the amendment, according to the report of the House Committee on the Judiciary, is "primarily to require that an attempt be made to depose a witness (as well as to seek his attendance) as a precondition to the witness being unavailable."

Under the House amendment, before a witness is declared unavailable, a party must try to depose a witness (declarant) with respect to dying declarations, declarations against interest, and declarations of pedigree. None of these situations would seem to warrant this needless, impractical and highly restrictive complication. A good case can be made for eliminating the unavailability requirement entirely for declarations against interest cases. [Uniform rule 63(10); Kan.Stat.Anno. 60–460(j); 2A N.J.Stats.Anno. 84–63(10).]

In dying declaration cases, the declarant will usually, though not necessarily, be deceased at the time of trial. Pedigree statements which are admittedly and necessarily based largely on word of mouth are not greatly fortified by a deposition requirement.

Depositions are expensive and time-consuming. In any event, deposition procedures are available to those who wish to resort to them. Moreover, the deposition procedures of the Civil Rules and Criminal Rules are only imperfectly adapted to implementing the amendment. No purpose is served unless the deposition, if taken, may be used in evidence. Under Civil Rule (a)(3) the Criminal Rule 15(e), a deposition, though taken, may not be admissible, and under Criminal Rule 15(a) substantial obstacles exist in the way of even taking a deposition.

For these reasons, the committee deleted the House amendment.

The committee understands that the rule as to unavailability, as explained by the Advisory Committee "contains no requirement that an attempt be made to take the deposition of a declarant." In reflecting the committee's judgment, the statement is accurate insofar as it goes. Where, however, the proponent of the statement, with knowledge of the existence of the statement, fails to confront the declarant with the statement at the taking of the deposition, then the proponent should not, in fairness, be permitted to treat the declarant as "unavailable" simply because the declarant was not amenable to process compelling his attendance at trial. The committee does not consider it necessary to amend the rule to this effect because such a situation abuses, not conforms to, the rule. Fairness would preclude a person from introducing a hearsay statement on a particular issue if the person taking the

deposition was aware of the issue at the time of the deposition but failed to depose the unavailable witness on that issue.

Note to Subdivision (b)(1). Former testimony.—Rule 804(b)(1) as submitted by the Court allowed prior testimony of an unavailable witness to be admissible if the party against whom it is offered or a person "with motive and interest similar" to his had an opportunity to examine the witness.

The House amended the rule to apply only to a party's predecessor in interest. Although the committee recognizes considerable merit to the rule submitted by the Supreme Court, a position which has been advocated by many scholars and judges, we have concluded that the difference between the two versions is not great and we accept the House amendment.

Note to Subdivision (b)(3). The rule defines those statements which are considered to be against interest and thus of sufficient trustworthiness to be admissible even though hearsay. With regard to the type of interest declared against, the version submitted by the Supreme Court included inter alia, statements tending to subject a declarant to civil liability or to invalidate a claim by him against another. The House struck these provisions as redundant. In view of the conflicting case law construing pecuniary or proprietary interests narrowly so as to exclude, e.g., tort cases, this deletion could be misconstrued.

Three States which have recently codified their rules of evidence have followed the Supreme Court's version of this rule, i.e., that a statement is against interest if it tends to subject a declarant to civil liability. [Nev.Rev.Stats. § 51.345; N.Mex.Stats. (1973 Supp.) § 20–4–804(4); West's Wis.Stats. Anno. (1973 Supp.) § 908.045(4).]

The committee believes that the reference to statements tending to subject a person to civil liability constitutes a desirable clarification of the scope of the rule. Therefore, we have reinstated the Supreme Court language on this matter.

The Court rule also proposed to expand the hearsay limitation from its present federal limitation to include statements subjecting the declarant to statements tending to make him an object of hatred, ridicule, or disgrace. The House eliminated the latter category from the subdivision as lacking sufficient guarantees of reliability. Although there is considerable support for the admissibility of such statements (all three of the State rules referred to supra, would admit such statements), we accept the deletion by the House.

The House amended this exception to add a sentence making inadmissible a statement or confession offered against the accused in a criminal case, made by a codefendant or other person implicating both himself and the accused. The sentence was added to codify the constitutional principle announced in *Bruton v. United States*, 391 U.S. 123 (1968). Bruton held that the admission of the extrajudicial hearsay statement of one codefendant inculpating a second codefendant violated the confrontation clause of the sixth amendment.

The committee decided to delete this provision because the basic approach of the rules is to avoid codifying, or attempting to codify, constitutional evidentiary principles, such as the fifth amendment's right against self-incrimination and, here, the sixth amendment's right of confrontation. Codification of a constitutional principle is unnecessary and, where the principle is under development, often unwise. Furthermore, the House provision does not appear to recognize the exceptions to the *Bruton* rule, e.g. where the codefendant takes the stand and is subject to cross examination; where the accused confessed, see *United States v. Mancusi*, 404 F.2d 296 (2d

Cir.1968), cert. denied 397 U.S. 942 (1907); where the accused was placed at the scene of the crime, see *United States v. Zelker,* 452 F.2d 1009 (2d Cir.1971). For these reasons, the committee decided to delete this provision.

Note to Subdivision (b)(5). See Note to Paragraph (24), Notes of Committee on the Judiciary, Senate Report No. 93–1277, set out as a note under rule 803 of these rules. Senate Report No. 93–1277.

Rule 804 defines what hearsay statements are admissible in evidence if the declarant is unavailable as a witness. The Senate amendments make four changes in the rule.

Note to Subdivision (a)(5). Subsection (a) defines the term "unavailability as a witness". The House bill provides in subsection (a)(5) that the party who desires to use the statement must be unable to procure the declarant's attendance by process or other reasonable means. In the case of dying declarations, statements against interest and statements of personal or family history, the House bill requires that the proponent must also be unable to procure the declarant's *testimony* (such as by deposition or interrogatories) by process or other reasonable means. The Senate amendment eliminates this latter provision.

The Conference adopts the provision contained in the House bill.

Note to Subdivision (b)(3). The Senate amendment to subsection (b)(3) provides that a statement is against interest and not excluded by the hearsay rule when the declarant is unavailable as a witness, if the statement tends to subject a person to civil or criminal liability or renders invalid a claim by him against another. The House bill did not refer specifically to civil liability and to rendering invalid a claim against another. The Senate amendment also deletes from the House bill the provision that subsection (b)(3) does not apply to a statement or confession, made by a codefendant or another, which implicates the accused and the person who made the statement, when that statement or confession is offered against the accused in a criminal case.

The Conference adopts the Senate amendment. The Conferees intend to include within the purview of this rule, statements subjecting a person to civil liability and statements rendering claims invalid. The Conferees agree to delete the provision regarding statements by a codefendant, thereby reflecting the general approach in the Rules of Evidence to avoid attempting to codify constitutional evidentiary principles.

Note to Subdivision (b)(5). The Senate amendment adds a new subsection, (b)(6) [now (b)(5)], which makes admissible a hearsay statement not specifically covered by any of the five previous subsections, if the statement has equivalent circumstantial guarantees of trustworthiness and if the court determines that (A) the statement is offered as evidence of a material fact; (B) the statement is more probative on the point for which it is offered than any other evidence the proponent can procure through reasonable efforts; and (C) the general purposes of these rules and the interests of justice will best be served by admission of the statement into evidence.

The House bill eliminated a similar, but broader, provision because of the conviction that such a provision injected too much uncertainty into the law of evidence regarding hearsay and impaired the ability of a litigant to prepare adequately for trial.

The Conference adopts the Senate amendment with an amendment that renumbers this subsection and provides that a party intending to request the court to use a statement under this provision must notify any adverse party of this intention as well as of the particulars of the statement, including the name and address of the declarant. This notice must be given sufficiently in advance of the trial or hearing to provide any adverse party with a fair opportunity to prepare to contest the use of the statement. House Report No. 93–1597.

1987 Amendments

The amendments are technical. No substantive change is intended.

1997 Amendments

Subdivision (b)(5). The contents of Rule 803(24) and Rule 804(b)(5) have been combined and transferred to a new Rule 807. This was done to facilitate additions to Rules 803 and 804. No change in meaning is intended.

Subdivision (b)(6). Rule 804(b)(6) has been added to provide that a party forfeits the right to object on hearsay grounds to the admission of a declarant's prior statement when the party's deliberate wrongdoing or acquiescence therein procured the unavailability of the declarant as a witness. This recognizes the need for a prophylactic rule to deal with abhorrent behavior "which strikes at the heart of the system of justice itself." *United States v. Mastrangelo,* 693 F.2d 269, 273 (2d Cir.1982), *cert. denied,* 467 U.S. 1204 (1984). The wrongdoing need not consist of a criminal act. The rule applies to all parties, including the government.

Every circuit that has resolved the question has recognized the principle of forfeiture by misconduct, although the tests for determining whether there is a forfeiture have varied. *See, e.g., United States v. Aguiar,* 975 F.2d 45, 47 (2d Cir. 1992); *United States v. Potamitis,* 739 F.2d 784, 789 (2d Cir.), *cert. denied,* 469 U.S. 918 (1984); *Steele v. Taylor,* 684 F.2d 1193, 1199 (6th Cir.1982), *cert. denied,* 460 U.S. 1053 (1983); United States v. Balano, 618 F.2d 624, 629 (10th Cir.1979), *cert. denied,* 449 U.S. 840 (1980); *United States v. Carlson,* 547 F.2d 1346, 1358–59 (8th Cir.), *cert. denied,* 431 U.S. 914 (1977). The foregoing cases apply a preponderance of the evidence standard. *Contra United States v. Thevis,* 665 F.2d 616, 631 (5th Cir.) (clear and convincing standard), *cert. denied,* 459 U.S. 825 (1982). The usual Rule 104(a) preponderance of the evidence standard has been adopted in light of the behavior the new Rule 804(b)(6) seeks to discourage.

GAP Report on Rule 804(b)(5). The words "Transferred to Rule 807" were substituted for "Abrogated."

GAP Report on Rule 804(b)(6). The title of the rule was changed to "Forfeiture by wrongdoing." The word "who" in line 24 was changed to "that" to indicate that the rule is potentially applicable against the government. Two sentences were added to the first paragraph of the committee note to clarify that the wrongdoing need not be criminal in nature, and to indicate the rule's potential applicability to the government. The word "forfeiture" was substituted for "waiver" in the note.

2010 Amendments

Subdivision (b)(3). Rule 804(b)(3) has been amended to provide that the corroborating circumstances requirement applies to all declarations against penal interest offered in criminal cases. A number of courts have applied the corroborating circumstances requirement to declarations against penal interest offered by the prosecution, even though the text of the Rule did not so provide. *See, e.g., United States v. Alvarez,* 584 F.2d 694, 701 (5th Cir. 1978) ("by transplanting the language governing exculpatory statements onto the analysis for admitting inculpatory hearsay, a unitary standard is derived which offers the most workable basis for applying Rule 804(b)(3)"); *United States v. Shukri,* 207 F.3d 412 (7th Cir. 2000) (requiring corroborating circumstances for against-penal-interest statements offered by the government). A unitary approach to declarations against penal interest assures both the prosecution and the accused that the Rule will not be abused and that only reliable hearsay statements will be admitted under the exception.

All other changes to the structure and wording of the Rule are intended to be stylistic only. There is no intent to change any other result in any ruling on evidence admissibility.

The amendment does not address the use of the corroborating circumstances for declarations against penal interest offered in civil cases.

In assessing whether corroborating circumstances exist, some courts have focused on the credibility of the witness who relates the hearsay statement in court. But the credibility of the witness who relates the statement is not a proper factor for the court to consider in assessing corroborating circumstances. To base admission or exclusion of a hearsay statement on the witness's credibility would usurp the jury's role of determining the credibility of testifying witnesses.

2011 Amendments

The language of Rule 804 has been amended as part of the general restyling of the Evidence Rules to make them more easily understood and to make style and terminology consistent throughout the rules. These changes are intended to be stylistic only. There is no intent to change any result in any ruling on evidence admissibility.

No style changes were made to Rule 804(b)(3), because it was already restyled in conjunction with a substantive amendment, effective December 1, 2010.

HISTORICAL NOTES

Revision Notes and Legislative Reports

1975 Acts. House Report No. 94–599, see 1975 U.S. Code Cong. and Adm. News, p. 1585.

CROSS REFERENCES

Confrontation with, and cross-examination of, witnesses, see USCA Const. Amend. VI.

Depositions, use of at trials, see Fed.Rules Civ.Proc. Rule 32, 28 USCA and Fed.Rules Cr.Proc. Rule 15, 18 USCA.

Subpoena of witnesses for a hearing or trial, see Fed.Rules Civ.Proc. Rule 45, 28 USCA.

Rule 805.   Hearsay Within Hearsay

Hearsay within hearsay is not excluded by the rule against hearsay if each part of the combined statements conforms with an exception to the rule.

(Pub.L. 93–595, § 1, Jan. 2, 1975, 88 Stat. 1943; Apr. 26, 2011, eff. Dec. 1, 2011.)

ADVISORY COMMITTEE NOTES

1972 Proposed Rules

On principle it scarcely seems open to doubt that the hearsay rule should not call for exclusion of a hearsay statement which includes a further hearsay statement when both conform to the requirements of a hearsay exception. Thus a hospital record might contain an entry of the patient's age based on information furnished by his wife. The hospital record would qualify as a regular entry except that the person who furnished the information was not acting in the routine of the business. However, her statement independently qualifies as a statement of pedigree (if she is unavailable) or as a statement made for purposes of diagnosis or treatment, and hence each link in the chain falls under sufficient assurances. Or, further to illustrate, a dying declaration may incorporate a declaration against interest by another declarant. See McCormick § 290, p. 611.

2011 Amendments

The language of Rule 805 has been amended as part of the restyling of the Evidence Rules to make them more easily understood and to make style and terminology consistent throughout the rules. These changes are intended to be stylistic only. There is no intent to change any result in any ruling on evidence admissibility.

CROSS REFERENCES

Character and conduct of witness, opinion and reputation evidence, see Fed.Rules Evid. Rule 608, 28 USCA.

Extrinsic evidence of prior statements of witnesses, see Fed.Rules Evid. Rule 613, 28 USCA.

Impeachment by evidence of conviction and crime, see Fed.Rules Evid. Rule 609, 28 USCA.

Rule 806.   Attacking and Supporting the Declarant's Credibility

When a hearsay statement—or a statement described in Rule 801(d)(2)(C), (D), or (E)—has been admitted in evidence, the declarant's credibility may be attacked, and then supported, by any evidence that would be admissible for those purposes if the declarant had testified as a witness. The court may admit evidence of the declarant's inconsistent statement or conduct, regardless of when it occurred or whether the declarant had an opportunity to explain or deny it. If the party against whom the statement was admitted calls the declarant as a witness, the party may examine the declarant on the statement as if on cross-examination.

(Pub.L. 93–595, § 1, Jan. 2, 1975, 88 Stat. 1943; Mar. 2, 1987, eff. Oct. 1, 1987; Apr. 11, 1997, eff. Dec. 1, 1997; Apr. 26, 2011, eff. Dec. 1, 2011.)

ADVISORY COMMITTEE NOTES

1972 Proposed Rules

The declarant of a hearsay statement which is admitted in evidence is in effect a witness. His credibility should in fairness be subject to impeachment and support as though he had in fact testified. See Rules 608 and 609. There are however, some special aspects of the impeaching of a hearsay declarant which require consideration. These special aspects center upon impeachment by inconsistent statement, arise from factual differences which exist between the use of hearsay and an actual witness and also between various kinds of hearsay, and involve the question of applying to declarants the general rule disallowing evidence of an inconsistent statement to impeach a witness unless he is afforded an opportunity to deny or explain. See Rule 613(b).

The principal difference between using hearsay and an actual witness is that the inconsistent statement will in the case of the witness almost inevitably in the nature of things be a *prior* statement, which it is entirely possible and feasible to call to his attention, while in the case of hearsay the inconsistent statement may well be a *subsequent* one, which practically precludes calling it to the attention of the declarant. The result of insisting upon observation of this impossible requirement in the hearsay situation is to deny the opponent, already barred from cross-examination, any benefit of this important technique of impeachment. The writers favor allowing the subsequent statement. McCormick § 37, p. 69; 3 Wigmore § 1033. The cases, however, are divided. Cases allowing the impeachment include *People v. Collup*, 27 Cal.2d 829, 167 P.2d 714 (1946); *People v. Rosoto*, 58 Cal.2d 304, 23 Cal.Rptr. 779, 373 P.2d 867 (1962); *Carver v. United States*, 164 U.S. 694, 17 S.Ct. 228, 41 L.Ed. 602 (1897). *Contra, Mattox v. United States*, 156 U.S. 237, 15 S.Ct. 337, 39 L.Ed. 409 (1895); *People v. Hines*, 284 N.Y. 93, 29 N.E.2d 483 (1940). The force of *Mattox*, where the hearsay was the former testimony of a deceased witness and the denial of use of a subsequent inconsistent statement was upheld, is much diminished by *Carver*, where the hearsay was a dying declaration and denial of use of a subsequent inconsistent statement resulted in reversal. The difference in the particular brand of hearsay seems unimportant when the inconsistent statement is a *subsequent* one. True, the opponent is not totally deprived of cross-examination when the hearsay is former testimony or a deposition but he is deprived of cross-examining on the statement or along lines suggested by it. Mr. Justice Shiras, with two justices joining him, dissented vigorously in *Mattox*.

When the impeaching statement was made prior to the hearsay statement, differences in the kinds of hearsay appear which arguably may justify differences in treatment. If the hearsay consisted of a simple statement by the witness, e.g. a dying declaration or a declaration against interest, the feasibility of affording him an opportunity to deny or explain encounters the same practical impossibility as where the statement is a subsequent one, just discussed, although here the impossibility arises from the total absence of anything resembling a hearing at which the matter could be put to him. The courts by a large majority have ruled in favor of allowing the statement to be used under these circumstances. McCormick § 37, p. 69; 3 Wigmore § 1033. If, however, the hearsay consists of former testimony or a deposition, the possibility of calling the prior statement to the attention of the witness or deponent is not ruled out, since the opportunity to cross-examine was available. It might thus be concluded that with former testimony or depositions the conventional foundation should be insisted upon. Most of the cases involve depositions, and Wigmore describes them as divided. 3 Wigmore § 1031. Deposition procedures at best are cumbersome and expensive, and to require the laying of the foundation may impose an undue burden. Under the federal practice, there is no way of knowing with certainty at the time of taking a deposition whether it is merely for discovery or will ultimately end up in evidence. With respect to both former testimony and depositions the possibility exists that knowledge of the statement might not be acquired until after the time of the cross-examination. Moreover, the expanded admissibility of former testimony and depositions under Rule 804(b)(1) calls for a correspondingly expanded approach to impeachment. The rule dispenses with the requirement in all hearsay situations, which is readily administered and best calculated to lead to fair results.

Notice should be taken that Rule 26(f) of the Federal Rules of Civil Procedure, as originally submitted by the Advisory Committee, ended with the following:

" * * * and, without having first called them to the deponent's attention, may show statements contradictory thereto made at any time by the deponent."

This language did not appear in the rule as promulgated in December, 1937. See 4 Moore's Federal Practice ¶¶ 26.01[9], 26.35 (2d ed.1967). In 1951, Nebraska adopted a provision strongly resembling the one stricken from the federal rule:

"Any party may impeach any adverse deponent by self-contradiction without having laid foundation for such impeachment at the time such deposition was taken." R.S.Neb. § 25–1267.07.

For similar provisions, see Uniform Rule 65; California Evidence Code § 1202; Kansas Code of Civil Procedure § 60–462; New Jersey Evidence Rule 65.

The provision for cross-examination of a declarant upon his hearsay statement is a corollary of general principles of cross-examination. A similar provision is found in California Evidence Code § 1203.

1974 Enactment

Rule 906, as passed by the House and as proposed by the Supreme Court provides that whenever a hearsay statement is admitted, the credibility of the declarant of the statement may be attacked, and if attacked may be supported, by any evidence which would be admissible for those purposes if the declarant had testified as a witness. Rule 801 defines what is a hearsay statement. While statements by a person authorized by a party-opponent to make a statement concerning the subject, by the party-opponent's agent or by a coconspirator of a party—see rule 801(d)(2)(c), (d) and (e)—are traditionally defined as exceptions to the hearsay rule, rule 801 defines such admission by a party-opponent as statements which are not hearsay. Consequently, rule 806 by referring exclusively to the admission of hearsay statements, does not appear to allow the credibility of the declarant to be attacked when the declarant is a coconspirator, agent or authorized spokesman. The committee is of the view that such statements should open the declarant to attacks on his credibility. Indeed, the reason such statements are excluded from the operation of rule 806 is likely attributable to the drafting technique used to codify the hearsay rule, viz. some statements, instead of being referred to as exceptions to the hearsay rule, are defined as statements which are not hearsay. The phrase "or a statement defined in rule 801(d)(2)(c), (d) and (e)" is added to the rule in order to subject the declarant of such statements, like the declarant of hearsay statements, to attacks on his credibility. [The committee considered it unnecessary to include statements contained in rule 801(d)(2)(A) and (B)—the statement by the party-opponent himself or the statement of which he has manifested his adoption—because the credibility of the party-opponent is always subject to an attack on his credibility]. Senate Report No. 93–1277.

The Senate amendment permits an attack upon the credibility of the declarant of a statement if the statement is one by a person authorized by a party-opponent to make a statement concerning the subject, one by an agent of a party-opponent, or one by a coconspirator of the party-opponent, as these statements are defined in Rules 801(d)(2)(C), (D) and (E). The House bill has no such provision.

The Conference adopts the Senate amendment. The Senate amendment conforms the rule to present practice. House Report No. 93–1597.

1987 Amendments

The amendments are technical. No substantive change is intended.

1997 Amendments

The amendment is technical. No substantive change is intended.

GAP Report. Restylization changes in the rule were eliminated.

2011 Amendments

The language of Rule 806 has been amended as part of the restyling of the Evidence Rules to make them more easily understood and to make style and terminology consistent throughout the rules. These changes are intended to be stylistic only. There is no intent to change any result in any ruling on evidence admissibility.

Rule 807. Residual Exception

(a) **In General.** Under the following circumstances, a hearsay statement is not excluded by the rule against hearsay even if the statement is not specifically covered by a hearsay exception in Rule 803 or 804:

(1) the statement has equivalent circumstantial guarantees of trustworthiness;

(2) it is offered as evidence of a material fact;

(3) it is more probative on the point for which it is offered than any other evidence that the proponent can obtain through reasonable efforts; and

(4) admitting it will best serve the purposes of these rules and the interests of justice.

(b) **Notice.** The statement is admissible only if, before the trial or hearing, the proponent gives an adverse party reasonable notice of the intent to offer the statement and its particulars, including the declarant's name and address, so that the party has a fair opportunity to meet it.

(Added Apr. 11, 1997, eff. Dec. 1, 1997; Apr. 26, 2011, eff. Dec. 1, 2011.)

ADVISORY COMMITTEE NOTES

1997 Amendments

The contents of Rule 803(24) and Rule 804(b)(5) have been combined and transferred to a new Rule 807. This was done to facilitate additions to Rules 803 and 804. No change in meaning is intended.

GAP Report on Rule 807. Restylization changes in the rule were eliminated.

2011 Amendments

The language of Rule 807 has been amended as part of the restyling of the Evidence Rules to make them more easily understood and to make style and terminology consistent throughout the rules. These changes are intended to be stylistic only. There is no intent to change any result in any ruling on evidence admissibility.

ARTICLE IX. AUTHENTICATION AND IDENTIFICATION

Rule
901. Authenticating or Identifying Evidence.
902. Evidence That Is Self–Authenticating.
903. Subscribing Witness's Testimony.

Rule 901. Authenticating or Identifying Evidence

(a) **In General.** To satisfy the requirement of authenticating or identifying an item of evidence, the proponent must produce evidence sufficient to support a finding that the item is what the proponent claims it is.

(b) **Examples.** The following are examples only—not a complete list—of evidence that satisfies the requirement:

(1) **Testimony of a Witness with Knowledge.** Testimony that an item is what it is claimed to be.

(2) **Nonexpert Opinion About Handwriting.** A nonexpert's opinion that handwriting is genuine,

based on a familiarity with it that was not acquired for the current litigation.

(3) **Comparison by an Expert Witness or the Trier of Fact.** A comparison with an authenticated specimen by an expert witness or the trier of fact.

(4) **Distinctive Characteristics and the Like.** The appearance, contents, substance, internal patterns, or other distinctive characteristics of the item, taken together with all the circumstances.

(5) **Opinion About a Voice.** An opinion identifying a person's voice—whether heard firsthand or through mechanical or electronic transmission or recording—based on hearing the voice at any time under circumstances that connect it with the alleged speaker.

(6) **Evidence About a Telephone Conversation.** For a telephone conversation, evidence that a call was made to the number assigned at the time to:

(A) a particular person, if circumstances, including self-identification, show that the person answering was the one called; or

(B) a particular business, if the call was made to a business and the call related to business reasonably transacted over the telephone.

(7) Evidence About Public Records. Evidence that:

(A) a document was recorded or filed in a public office as authorized by law; or

(B) a purported public record or statement is from the office where items of this kind are kept.

(8) Evidence About Ancient Documents or Data Compilations. For a document or data compilation, evidence that it:

(A) is in a condition that creates no suspicion about its authenticity;

(B) was in a place where, if authentic, it would likely be; and

(C) is at least 20 years old when offered.

(9) Evidence About a Process or System. Evidence describing a process or system and showing that it produces an accurate result.

(10) Methods Provided by a Statute or Rule. Any method of authentication or identification allowed by a federal statute or a rule prescribed by the Supreme Court.

(Pub.L. 93–595, § 1, Jan. 2, 1975, 88 Stat.1943; Apr. 26, 2011, eff. Dec. 1, 2011.)

ADVISORY COMMITTEE NOTES

1972 Proposed Rules

Note to Subdivision (a). Authentication and identification represent a special aspect of relevancy. Michael and Adler, Real Proof, 5 Vand.L.Rev. 344, 362 (1952); McCormick §§ 179, 185; Morgan, Basic Problems of Evidence 378 (1962). Thus a telephone conversation may be irrelevant because on an unrelated topic or because the speaker is not identified. The latter aspect is the one here involved. Wigmore describes the need for authentication as "an inherent logical necessity." 7 Wigmore § 2129, p. 564.

This requirement of showing authenticity or identity falls in the category of relevancy dependent upon fulfillment of a condition of fact and is governed by the procedure set forth in Rule 104(b).

The common law approach to authentication of documents has been criticized as an "attitude of agnosticism," McCormick, Cases on Evidence 388, n. 4 (3rd ed. 1956), as one which "departs sharply from men's customs in ordinary affairs," and as presenting only a slight obstacle to the introduction of forgeries in comparison to the time and expense devoted to proving genuine writings which correctly show their origin on their face, McCormick § 185, pp. 395, 396. Today, such available procedures as requests to admit and pretrial conference afford the means of eliminating much of the need for authentication or identification. Also, significant inroads upon the traditional insistence on authentication and identification have been made by accepting as at least prima facie genuine items of the kind treated in Rule 902, *infra.* However, the need for suitable methods of proof still remains, since criminal cases pose their own obstacles to the use of preliminary procedures, unforeseen contingencies may arise, and cases of genuine controversy will still occur.

Note to Subdivision (b). The treatment of authentication and identification draws largely upon the experience embodied in the common law and in statutes to furnish illustrative applications of the general principle set forth in subdivision (a). The examples are not intended as an exclusive enumeration of allowable methods but are meant to guide and suggest, leaving room for growth and development in this area of the law.

The examples relate for the most part to documents, with some attention given to voice communications and computer printouts. As Wigmore noted, no special rules have been developed for authenticating chattels. Wigmore, Code of Evidence § 2086 (3rd ed. 1942).

It should be observed that compliance with requirements of authentication or identification by no means assures admission of an item into evidence, as other bars, hearsay for example, may remain.

Example (1). Example (1) contemplates a broad spectrum ranging from testimony of a witness who was present at the signing of a document to testimony establishing narcotics as taken from an accused and accounting for custody through the period until trial, including laboratory analysis. See California Evidence Code § 1413, eyewitness to signing.

Example (2). Example (2) states conventional doctrine as to lay identification of handwriting, which recognizes that a sufficient familiarity with the handwriting of another person may be acquired by seeing him write, by exchanging correspondence, or by other means, to afford a basis for identifying it on subsequent occasions. McCormick § 189. See also California Evidence Code § 1416. Testimony based upon familiarity acquired for purposes of the litigation is reserved to the expert under the example which follows.

Example (3). The history of common law restrictions upon the technique of proving or disproving the genuineness of a disputed specimen of handwriting through comparison with a genuine specimen, by either the testimony of expert witnesses or direct viewing by the triers themselves, is detailed in 7 Wigmore §§ 1991–1994. In breaking away, the English Common Law Procedure Act of 1854, 17 and 18 Vict., c. 125, § 27, cautiously allowed expert or trier to use exemplars "proved to the satisfaction of the judge to be genuine" for purposes of comparison. The language found its way into numerous statutes in this country, e.g., California Evidence Code §§ 1417, 1418. While explainable as a measure of prudence in the process of breaking with precedent in the handwriting situation, the reservation to the judge of the question of the genuineness of exemplars and the imposition of an unusually high standard of persuasion are at variance with the general treatment of relevancy which depends upon fulfillment of a condition of fact. Rule 104(b). No similar attitude is found in other comparison situations, e.g., ballistics comparison by jury, as in *Evans v. Commonwealth,* 230 Ky. 411, 19 S.W.2d 1091 (1929), or by experts, Annot., 26 A.L.R.2d 892, and no reason appears for its continued existence in handwriting cases. Consequently Example (3) sets no higher standard for handwriting specimens and treats all comparison situations alike, to be governed by Rule 104(b). This approach is consistent with 28 U.S.C. § 1731: "The admitted or proved handwriting of any person shall be admissible, for purposes of comparison, to determine genuineness of other handwriting attributed to such person."

For Complete Annotation Materials, see United States Code Annotated

Precedent supports the acceptance of visual comparison as sufficiently satisfying preliminary authentication requirements for admission in evidence. *Brandon v. Collins*, 267 F.2d 731 (2d Cir.1959); *Wausau Sulphate Fibre Co. v. Commissioner of Internal Revenue*, 61 F.2d 879 (7th Cir.1932); *Desimone v. United States*, 227 F.2d 864 (9th Cir.1955).

Example (4). The characteristics of the offered item itself, considered in the light of circumstances, afford authentication techniques in great variety. Thus a document or telephone conversation may be shown to have emanated from a particular person by virtue of its disclosing knowledge of facts known peculiarly to him; *Globe Automatic Sprinkler Co. v. Braniff*, 89 Okl. 105, 214 P. 127 (1923); California Evidence Code § 1421; similarly, a letter may be authenticated by content and circumstances indicating it was in reply to a duly authenticated one. McCormick § 192; California Evidence Code § 1420. Language patterns may indicate authenticity or its opposite. *Magnuson v. State*, 187 Wis. 122, 203 N.W. 749 (1925); Arens and Meadow, Psycholinguistics and the Confession Dilemma, 56 Colum.L.Rev. 19 (1956).

Example (5). Since aural voice identification is not a subject of expert testimony, the requisite familiarity may be acquired either before or after the particular speaking which is the subject of the identification, in this respect resembling visual identification of a person rather than identification of handwriting. Cf. Example (2), *supra*, *People v. Nichols*, 378 Ill. 487, 38 N.E.2d 766 (1942); *McGuire v. State*, 200 Md. 601, 92 A.2d 582 (1952); *State v. McGee*, 336 Mo. 1082, 83 S.W.2d 98 (1935).

Example (6). The cases are in agreement that a mere assertion of his identity by a person talking on the telephone is not sufficient evidence of the authenticity of the conversation and that additional evidence of his identity is required. The additional evidence need not fall in any set pattern. Thus the content of his statements or the reply technique, under Example (4), *supra*, or voice identification under Example (5), may furnish the necessary foundation. Outgoing calls made by the witness involve additional factors bearing upon authenticity. The calling of a number assigned by the telephone company reasonably supports the assumption that the listing is correct and that the number is the one reached. If the number is that of a place of business, the mass of authority allows an ensuing conversation if it relates to business reasonably transacted over the telephone, on the theory that the maintenance of the telephone connection is an invitation to do business without further identification. *Matton v. Hoover Co.*, 350 Mo. 506, 166 S.W.2d 557 (1942); *City of Pawhuska v. Crutchfield*, 147 Okl. 4, 293 P. 1095 (1930); *Zurich General Acc. & Liability Ins. Co. v. Baum*, 159 Va. 404, 165 S.E. 518 (1932). Otherwise, some additional circumstance of identification of the speaker is required. The authorities divide on the question whether the self-identifying statement of the person answering suffices. Example (6) answers in the affirmative on the assumption that usual conduct respecting telephone calls furnish adequate assurances of regularity, bearing in mind that the entire matter is open to exploration before the trier of fact. In general, see McCormick § 193; 7 Wigmore § 2155; Annot., 71 A.L.R. 5, 105 id. 326.

Example (7). Public records are regularly authenticated by proof of custody, without more. McCormick § 191; 7 Wigmore §§ 2158, 2159. The example extends the principle to include data stored in computers and similar methods, of which increasing use in the public records area may be expected. See California Evidence Code §§ 1532, 1600.

Example (8). The familiar ancient document rule of the common law is extended to include data stored electronically or by other similar means. Since the importance of appearance diminishes in this situation, the importance of custody or place where found increases correspondingly. This expansion is necessary in view of the widespread use of methods of storing data in forms other than conventional written records.

Any time period selected is bound to be arbitrary. The common law period of 30 years is here reduced to 20 years, with some shift of emphasis from the probable unavailability of witnesses to the unlikeliness of a still viable fraud after the lapse of time. The shorter period is specified in the English Evidence Act of 1938, 1 & 2 Geo. 6, c. 28, and in Oregon R.S.1963, § 41.360(34). See also the numerous statutes prescribing periods of less than 30 years in the case of recorded documents. 7 Wigmore § 2143.

The application of Example (8) is not subject to any limitation to title documents or to any requirement that possession, in the case of a title document, has been consistent with the document. See McCormick § 190.

Example (9). Example (9) is designed for situations in which the accuracy of a result is dependent upon a process or system which produces it. X rays afford a familiar instance. Among more recent developments is the computer, as to which see *Transport Indemnity Co. v. Seib*, 178 Neb. 253, 132 N.W.2d 871 (1965); *State v. Veres*, 7 Ariz.App. 117, 436 P.2d 629 (1968); *Merrick v. United States Rubber Co.*, 7 Ariz.App. 433, 440 P.2d 314 (1968); Freed, Computer Print–Outs as Evidence, 16 Am.Jur.Proof of Facts 273; Symposium, Law and Computers in the Mid–Sixties, ALI–ABA (1966); 37 Albany L.Rev. 61 (1967). Example (9) does not, of course, foreclose taking judicial notice of the accuracy of the process or system.

Example (10). The example makes clear that methods of authentication provided by Act of Congress and by the Rules of Civil and Criminal Procedure or by Bankruptcy Rules are not intended to be superseded. Illustrative are the provisions for authentication of official records in Civil Procedure Rule 44 and Criminal Procedure Rule 27, for authentication of records of proceedings by court reporters in 28 U.S.C. § 753(b) and Civil Procedure Rule 80(c), and for authentication of depositions in Civil Procedure Rule 30(f).

2011 Amendments

The language of Rule 901 has been amended as part of the restyling of the Evidence Rules to make them more easily understood and to make style and terminology consistent throughout the rules. These changes are intended to be stylistic only. There is no intent to change any result in any ruling on evidence admissibility.

CROSS REFERENCES

Authentication,

　Acts of legislature of State, Territory, or possession for evidence, see 28 USCA § 1738.

　Consul, documents and papers in office for evidence, see 28 USCA § 1740.

　Extradition proceedings, evidence, see 18 USCA § 3190.

　Foreign documents, commission to consular officers to authenticate, see 18 USCA §§ 3492 to 3496.

Foreign documents, evidence, see 18 USCA §§ 3491 and 3492.

Foreign patent documents, etc., copies, evidence, see 28 USCA § 1745.

Foreign records, etc., copies, etc., as evidence, see 28 USCA § 1741.

Patent Office documents, evidence, see 28 USCA § 1744.

Plant Variety Protection Office, documents and certificates evidencing protection authenticated with seal of, see 7 USCA § 2322.

Postal Service, records of, seal used for, see 39 USCA § 207.

Records or books of State, Territory, or possession for use as evidence, see 28 USCA § 1739.

Vice consul, documents and papers in office for evidence, see 28 USCA § 1740.

Court reporters, shorthand or mechanical recording, see 28 USCA § 753.

Depositions, certification and filing by officer, see Fed. Rules Civ.Proc. Rule 30, 28 USCA.

Handwriting, admitted or proved, see 28 USCA § 1731.

Official record, proof of, see Fed.Rules Cr.Proc. Rule 27, 18 USCA.

Proof of official record, authentication, see Fed.Rules Civ. Proc. Rule 44, 28 USCA.

Relevancy conditional on fact, see Fed.Rules Evid. Rule 104, 28 USCA.

Stenographic report or transcript as evidence, see Fed. Rules Civ.Proc. Rule 80, 28 USCA.

Rule 902. Evidence That Is Self–Authenticating

The following items of evidence are self-authenticating; they require no extrinsic evidence of authenticity in order to be admitted:

(1) Domestic Public Documents That Are Sealed and Signed. A document that bears:

(A) a seal purporting to be that of the United States; any state, district, commonwealth, territory, or insular possession of the United States; the former Panama Canal Zone; the Trust Territory of the Pacific Islands; a political subdivision of any of these entities; or a department, agency, or officer of any entity named above; and

(B) a signature purporting to be an execution or attestation.

(2) Domestic Public Documents That Are Not Sealed but Are Signed and Certified. A document that bears no seal if:

(A) it bears the signature of an officer or employee of an entity named in Rule 902(1)(A); and

(B) another public officer who has a seal and official duties within that same entity certifies under seal—or its equivalent—that the signer has the official capacity and that the signature is genuine.

(3) Foreign Public Documents. A document that purports to be signed or attested by a person who is authorized by a foreign country's law to do so. The document must be accompanied by a final certification that certifies the genuineness of the signature and official position of the signer or attester—or of any foreign official whose certificate of genuineness relates to the signature or attestation or is in a chain of certificates of genuineness relating to the signature or attestation. The certification may be made by a secretary of a United States embassy or legation; by a consul general, vice consul, or consular agent of the United States; or by a diplomatic or consular official of the foreign country assigned or accredited to the United States. If all parties have been given a reasonable opportunity to investigate the document's authenticity and accuracy, the court may, for good cause, either:

(A) order that it be treated as presumptively authentic without final certification; or

(B) allow it to be evidenced by an attested summary with or without final certification.

(4) Certified Copies of Public Records. A copy of an official record—or a copy of a document that was recorded or filed in a public office as authorized by law—if the copy is certified as correct by:

(A) the custodian or another person authorized to make the certification; or

(B) a certificate that complies with Rule 902(1), (2), or (3), a federal statute, or a rule prescribed by the Supreme Court.

(5) Official Publications. A book, pamphlet, or other publication purporting to be issued by a public authority.

(6) Newspapers and Periodicals. Printed material purporting to be a newspaper or periodical.

(7) Trade Inscriptions and the Like. An inscription, sign, tag, or label purporting to have been affixed in the course of business and indicating origin, ownership, or control.

(8) Acknowledged Documents. A document accompanied by a certificate of acknowledgment that is lawfully executed by a notary public or another officer who is authorized to take acknowledgments.

(9) Commercial Paper and Related Documents. Commercial paper, a signature on it, and related documents, to the extent allowed by general commercial law.

(10) Presumptions Under a Federal Statute. A signature, document, or anything else that a federal statute declares to be presumptively or prima facie genuine or authentic.

(11) Certified Domestic Records of a Regularly Conducted Activity. The original or a copy of a domestic record that meets the requirements of Rule 803(6)(A)–(C), as shown by a certification of the custodian or another qualified person that complies with a federal statute or a rule prescribed by the

Supreme Court. Before the trial or hearing, the proponent must give an adverse party reasonable written notice of the intent to offer the record—and must make the record and certification available for inspection—so that the party has a fair opportunity to challenge them.

(12) Certified Foreign Records of a Regularly Conducted Activity. In a civil case, the original or a copy of a foreign record that meets the requirements of Rule 902(11), modified as follows: the certification, rather than complying with a federal statute or Supreme Court rule, must be signed in a manner that, if falsely made, would subject the maker to a criminal penalty in the country where the certification is signed. The proponent must also meet the notice requirements of Rule 902(11).

(13) Certified Records Generated by an Electronic Process or System. A record generated by an electronic process or system that produces an accurate result, as shown by a certification of a qualified person that complies with the certification requirements of Rule 902(11) or (12). The proponent must also meet the notice requirements of Rule 902(11).

(14) Certified Data Copied from an Electronic Device, Storage Medium, or File. Data copied from an electronic device, storage medium, or file, if authenticated by a process of digital identification, as shown by a certification of a qualified person that complies with the certification requirements of Rule 902(11) or (12). The proponent also must meet the notice requirements of Rule 902(11).

(Pub.L. 93–595, § 1, Jan. 2, 1975, 88 Stat. 1944; Mar. 2, 1987, eff. Oct. 1, 1987; Apr. 25, 1988, eff. Nov. 1, 1988; Apr. 17, 2000, eff. Dec. 1, 2000; Apr. 26, 2011, eff. Dec. 1, 2011; Apr. 27, 2017, eff. Dec. 1, 2017.)

ADVISORY COMMITTEE NOTES

1972 Proposed Rules

Case law and statutes have, over the years, developed a substantial body of instances in which authenticity is taken as sufficiently established for purposes of admissibility without extrinsic evidence to that effect, sometimes for reasons of policy but perhaps more often because practical considerations reduce the possibility of unauthenticity to a very small dimension. The present rule collects and incorporates these situations, in some instances expanding them to occupy a larger area which their underlying considerations justify. In no instance is the opposite party foreclosed from disputing authenticity.

Note to Paragraph (1). The acceptance of documents bearing a public seal and signature, most often encountered in practice in the form of acknowledgments or certificates authenticating copies of public records, is actually of broad application. Whether theoretically based in whole or in part upon judicial notice, the practical underlying considerations are that forgery is a crime and detection is fairly easy and certain. 7 Wigmore § 2161, p. 638; California Evidence Code § 1452. More than 50 provisions for judicial notice of official seals are contained in the United States Code.

Note to Paragraph (2). While statutes are found which raise a presumption of genuineness of purported official signatures in the absence of an official seal, 7 Wigmore § 2167; California Evidence Code § 1453, the greater ease of effecting a forgery under these circumstances is apparent. Hence this paragraph of the rule calls for authentication by an officer who has a seal. Notarial acts by members of the armed forces and other special situations are covered in paragraph (10).

Note to Paragraph (3). Paragraph (3) provides a method for extending the presumption of authenticity to foreign official documents by a procedure of certification. It is derived from Rule 44(a)(2) of the Rules of Civil Procedure but is broader in applying to public documents rather than being limited to public records.

Note to Paragraph (4). The common law and innumerable statutes have recognized the procedure of authenticating copies of public records by certificate. The certificate qualifies as a public document, receivable as authentic when in conformity with paragraph (1), (2), or (3). Rule 44(a) of the Rules of Civil Procedure and Rule 27 of the Rules of Criminal Procedure have provided authentication procedures of this nature for both domestic and foreign public records. It will be observed that the certification procedure here provided extends only to public records, reports, and recorded documents, all including data compilations, and does not apply to public documents generally. Hence documents provable when presented in original form under paragraphs (1), (2), or (3) may not be provable by certified copy under paragraph (4).

Note to Paragraph (5). Dispensing with preliminary proof of the genuineness of purportedly official publications, most commonly encountered in connection with statutes, court reports, rules, and regulations, has been greatly enlarged by statutes and decisions. 5 Wigmore § 1684. Paragraph (5), it will be noted, does not confer admissibility upon all official publications; it merely provides a means whereby their authenticity may be taken as established for purposes of admissibility. Rule 44(a) of the Rules of Civil Procedure has been to the same effect.

Note to Paragraph (6). The likelihood of forgery of newspapers or periodicals is slight indeed. Hence no danger is apparent in receiving them. Establishing the authenticity of the publication may, of course, leave still open questions of authority and responsibility for items therein contained. See 7 Wigmore § 2150. Cf. 39 U.S.C. § 4005(b), public advertisement prima facie evidence of agency of person named, in postal fraud order proceeding; Canadian Uniform Evidence Act, Draft of 1936, printed copy of newspaper prima facie evidence that notices or advertisements were authorized.

Note to Paragraph (7). Several factors justify dispensing with preliminary proof of genuineness of commercial and mercantile labels and the like. The risk of forgery is minimal. Trademark infringement involves serious penalties. Great efforts are devoted to inducing the public to buy in reliance on brand names, and substantial protection is given them. Hence the fairness of this treatment finds recognition in the cases. *Curtiss Candy Co. v. Johnson,* 163 Miss. 426, 141 So. 762 (1932), Baby Ruth candy bar; *Doyle v. Continental Baking Co.,* 262 Mass. 516, 160 N.E. 325 (1928), loaf of bread; *Weiner v. Mager & Throne, Inc.,* 167 Misc. 338, 3 N.Y.S.2d 918 (1938), same. And see W.Va.Code 1966, § 47–3–5, trademark on bottle prima facie evidence of ownership. *Contra, Keegan v. Green Giant Co.,* 150 Me. 283, 110 A.2d 599 (1954);

Murphy v. Campbell Soup Co., 62 F.2d 564 (1st Cir.1933). Cattle brands have received similar acceptance in the western states. Rev.Code Mont.1947, § 46–606, *State v. Wolfley*, 75 Kan. 406, 89 P. 1046 (1907); Annot., 11 L.R.A.(N.S.) 87. Inscriptions on trains and vehicles are held to be prima facie evidence of ownership or control. *Pittsburgh, Ft. W. & C. Ry. v. Callaghan*, 157 Ill. 406, 41 N.E. 909 (1895); 9 Wigmore § 2510a. See also the provision of 19 U.S.C. § 1615(2) that marks, labels, brands, or stamps indicating foreign origin are prima facie evidence of foreign origin of merchandise.

Note to Paragraph (8). In virtually every state, acknowledged title documents are receivable in evidence without further proof. Statutes are collected in 5 Wigmore § 1676. If this authentication suffices for documents of the importance of those affecting titles, logic scarcely permits denying this method when other kinds of documents are involved. Instances of broadly inclusive statutes are California Evidence Code § 1451 and N.Y.CPLR 4538, McKinney's Consol.Laws 1963.

Note to Paragraph (9). Issues of the authenticity of commercial paper in federal courts will usually arise in diversity cases, will involve an element of a cause of action or defense, and with respect to presumptions and burden of proof will be controlled by *Erie Railroad Co. v. Tompkins*, 304 U.S. 64, 58 S.Ct. 817, 82 L.Ed. 1188 (1938). Rule 302, *supra.* There may, however, be questions of authenticity involving lesser segments of a case or the case may be one governed by federal common law. *Clearfield Trust Co. v. United States*, 318 U.S. 363, 63 S.Ct. 573, 87 L.Ed. 838 (1943). Cf. *United States v. Yazell*, 382 U.S. 341, 86 S.Ct. 500, 15 L.Ed.2d 404 (1966). In these situations, resort to the useful authentication provisions of the Uniform Commercial Code is provided for. While the phrasing is in terms of "general commercial law," in order to avoid the potential complications inherent in borrowing local statutes, today one would have difficulty in determining the general commercial law without referring to the Code. See *Williams v. Walker–Thomas Furniture Co.*, 121 U.S.App.D.C. 315, 350 F.2d 445 (1965). Pertinent Code provisions are sections 1–202, 3–307, and 3–510, dealing with third-party documents, signatures on negotiable instruments, protests, and statements of dishonor.

Note to Paragraph (10). The paragraph continues in effect dispensations with preliminary proof of genuineness provided in various Acts of Congress. See, for example, 10 U.S.C. § 936, signature, without seal, together with title, prima facie evidence of authenticity of acts of certain military personnel who are given notarial powers; 15 U.S.C. § 77f(a), signature on SEC registration presumed genuine; 26 U.S.C. § 6064, signature to tax return prima facie genuine.

1974 Enactment

Note to Paragraph (8). Rule 902(8) as submitted by the Court referred to certificates of acknowledgment "under the hand and seal of" a notary public or other officer authorized by law to take acknowledgments. The Committee amended the Rule to eliminate the requirement, believed to be inconsistent with the law in some States, that a notary public must affix a seal to a document acknowledged before him. As amended the Rule merely requires that the document be executed in the manner prescribed by State law.

Note to Paragraph (9). The Committee approved Rule 902(9) as submitted by the Court. With respect to the meaning of the phrase "general commercial law", the Committee intends that the Uniform Commercial Code, which has

been adopted in virtually every State, will be followed generally, but that federal commercial law will apply where federal commercial paper is involved. See *Clearfield Trust Co. v. United States*, 318 U.S. 363 (1943). Further, in those instances in which the issues are governed by *Erie R. Co. v. Tompkins*, 304 U.S. 64 (1938), State law will apply irrespective of whether it is the Uniform Commercial Code. House Report No. 93–650.

1987 Amendments

The amendments are technical. No substantive change is intended.

1988 Amendments

These two sentences were inadvertently eliminated from the 1987 amendments. The amendment is technical. No substantive change is intended.

2000 Amendments

The amendment adds two new paragraphs to the rule on self-authentication. It sets forth a procedure by which parties can authenticate certain records of regularly conducted activity, other than through the testimony of a foundation witness. See the amendment to Rule 803(6). 18 U.S.C. § 3505 currently provides a means for certifying foreign records of regularly conducted activity in criminal cases, and this amendment is intended to establish a similar procedure for domestic records, and for foreign records offered in civil cases.

A declaration that satisfies 28 U.S.C. § 1746 would satisfy the declaration requirement of Rule 902(11), as would any comparable certification under oath.

The notice requirement in Rules 902(11) and (12) is intended to give the opponent of the evidence a full opportunity to test the adequacy of the foundation set forth in the declaration.

GAP Report—Proposed Amendment to Rule 902

The Committee made the following changes to the published draft of the proposed amendment to Evidence Rule 902:

1. Minor stylistic changes were made in the text, in accordance with suggestions of the Style Subcommittee of the Standing Committee on Rules of Practice and Procedure.

2. The phrase "in a manner complying with any Act of Congress or rule prescribed by the Supreme Court pursuant to statutory authority" was added to proposed Rule 902(11), to provide consistency with Evidence Rule 902(4). The Committee Note was amended to accord with this textual change.

3. Minor stylistic changes were made in the text to provide a uniform construction of the terms "declaration" and "certifying."

4. The notice provisions in the text were revised to clarify that the proponent must make both the declaration and the underlying record available for inspection.

2011 Amendments

The language of Rule 902 has been amended as part of the restyling of the Evidence Rules to make them more easily understood and to make style and terminology consistent throughout the rules. These changes are intended to be stylistic only. There is no intent to change any result in any ruling on evidence admissibility.

2017 Amendments

[Paragraph (13)] The amendment sets forth a procedure by which parties can authenticate certain electronic evidence other than through the testimony of a foundation witness. As with the provisions on business records in Rules 902(11) and (12), the Committee has found that the expense and inconvenience of producing a witness to authenticate an item of electronic evidence is often unnecessary. It is often the case that a party goes to the expense of producing an authentication witness, and then the adversary either stipulates authenticity before the witness is called or fails to challenge the authentication testimony once it is presented. The amendment provides a procedure under which the parties can determine in advance of trial whether a real challenge to authenticity will be made, and can then plan accordingly.

Nothing in the amendment is intended to limit a party from establishing authenticity of electronic evidence on any ground provided in these Rules, including through judicial notice where appropriate.

A proponent establishing authenticity under this Rule must present a certification containing information that would be sufficient to establish authenticity were that information provided by a witness at trial. If the certification provides information that would be insufficient to authenticate the record if the certifying person testified, then authenticity is not established under this Rule. The Rule specifically allows the authenticity foundation that satisfies Rule 901(b)(9) to be established by a certification rather than the testimony of a live witness.

The reference to the "certification requirements of Rule 902(11) or (12)" is only to the procedural requirements for a valid certification. There is no intent to require, or permit, a certification under this Rule to prove the requirements of Rule 803(6). Rule 902(13) is solely limited to authentication, and any attempt to satisfy a hearsay exception must be made independently.

A certification under this Rule can establish only that the proffered item has satisfied the admissibility requirements for authenticity. The opponent remains free to object to admissibility of the proffered item on other grounds—including hearsay, relevance, or in criminal cases the right to confrontation. For example, assume that a plaintiff in a defamation case offers what purports to be a printout of a webpage on which a defamatory statement was made. Plaintiff offers a certification under this Rule in which a qualified person describes the process by which the webpage was retrieved. Even if that certification sufficiently establishes that the webpage is authentic, defendant remains free to object that the statement on the webpage was not placed there by defendant. Similarly, a certification authenticating a computer output, such as a spreadsheet, does not preclude an objection that the information produced is unreliable—the authentication establishes only that the output came from the computer.

A challenge to the authenticity of electronic evidence may require technical information about the system or process at issue, including possibly retaining a forensic technical expert; such factors will affect whether the opponent has a fair opportunity to challenge the evidence given the notice provided.

The reference to Rule 902(12) is intended to cover certifications that are made in a foreign country.

[Paragraph (14)] The amendment sets forth a procedure by which parties can authenticate data copied from an electronic device, storage medium, or an electronic file, other than through the testimony of a foundation witness. As with the provisions on business records in Rules 902(11) and (12), the Committee has found that the expense and inconvenience of producing an authenticating witness for this evidence is often unnecessary. It is often the case that a party goes to the expense of producing an authentication witness, and then the adversary either stipulates authenticity before the witness is called or fails to challenge the authentication testimony once it is presented. The amendment provides a procedure in which the parties can determine in advance of trial whether a real challenge to authenticity will be made, and can then plan accordingly.

Today, data copied from electronic devices, storage media, and electronic files are ordinarily authenticated by "hash value." A hash value is a number that is often represented as a sequence of characters and is produced by an algorithm based upon the digital contents of a drive, medium, or file. If the hash values for the original and copy are different, then the copy is not identical to the original. If the hash values for the original and copy are the same, it is highly improbable that the original and copy are not identical. Thus, identical hash values for the original and copy reliably attest to the fact that they are exact duplicates. This amendment allows self-authentication by a certification of a qualified person that she checked the hash value of the proffered item and that it was identical to the original. The rule is flexible enough to allow certifications through processes other than comparison of hash value, including by other reliable means of identification provided by future technology.

Nothing in the amendment is intended to limit a party from establishing authenticity of electronic evidence on any ground provided in these Rules, including through judicial notice where appropriate.

A proponent establishing authenticity under this Rule must present a certification containing information that would be sufficient to establish authenticity were that information provided by a witness at trial. If the certification provides information that would be insufficient to authenticate the record if the certifying person testified, then authenticity is not established under this Rule.

The reference to the "certification requirements of Rule 902(11) or (12)" is only to the procedural requirements for a valid certification. There is no intent to require, or permit, a certification under this Rule to prove the requirements of Rule 803(6). Rule 902(14) is solely limited to authentication, and any attempt to satisfy a hearsay exception must be made independently.

A certification under this Rule can only establish that the proffered item is authentic. The opponent remains free to object to admissibility of the proffered item on other grounds—including hearsay, relevance, or in criminal cases the right to confrontation. For example, in a criminal case in which data copied from a hard drive is proffered, the defendant can still challenge hearsay found in the hard drive, and can still challenge whether the information on the hard drive was placed there by the defendant.

A challenge to the authenticity of electronic evidence may require technical information about the system or process at issue, including possibly retaining a forensic technical expert;

---

such factors will affect whether the opponent has a fair opportunity to challenge the evidence given the notice provided.

The reference to Rule 902(12) is intended to cover certifications that are made in a foreign country.

HISTORICAL NOTES

Termination of Trust Territory of the Pacific Islands

For termination of Trust Territory of the Pacific Islands, see note set out preceding 48 U.S.C.A. § 1681.

CROSS REFERENCES

Acts of legislature of State, Territory, or possession, see 28 USCA § 1738.

Armed forces, authority to administer oaths and to act as notary, see 10 USCA § 936.

Documents of Patent and Trademark Office, copies of, see 28 USCA §§ 1744 and 1745.

Forfeiture proceedings in custom actions, marks, labels, brands, stamps, as evidence, see 19 USCA § 1615.

Fraudulent and lottery matter, public advertisement that remittances may be made by mail as prima facie evidence, see 39 USCA § 3005.

Government records and papers, see 28 USCA § 1733.

Proof of official foreign record, see Fed.Rules Civ.Proc. Rule 44, 28 USCA.

Proof of official record, see Fed.Rules Cr.Proc. Rule 27, 18 USCA.

Public records, proof of, see Fed.Rules Evid. Rule 1005, 28 USCA.

Securities, signing of registration statements, see 15 USCA § 77f.

State law, applicability of in civil actions and proceedings, see Fed.Rules Evid. Rule 302, 28 USCA.

Tax returns, signature presumed authentic, see 26 USCA § 6064.

Rule 903.   Subscribing Witness's Testimony

A subscribing witness's testimony is necessary to authenticate a writing only if required by the law of the jurisdiction that governs its validity.

(Pub.L. 93–595, § 1, Jan. 2, 1975, 88 Stat.1945; Apr. 26, 2011, eff. Dec. 1, 2011.)

ADVISORY COMMITTEE NOTES

1972 Proposed Rules

The common law required that attesting witnesses be produced or accounted for. Today the requirement has generally been abolished except with respect to documents which must be attested to be valid, e.g. wills in some states. McCormick § 188. Uniform Rule 71; California Evidence Code § 1411; Kansas Code of Civil Procedure § 60–468; New Jersey Evidence Rule 71; New York CPLR Rule 4537.

2011 Amendments

The language of Rule 903 has been amended as part of the restyling of the Evidence Rules to make them more easily understood and to make style and terminology consistent throughout the rules. These changes are intended to be stylistic only. There is no intent to change any result in any ruling on evidence admissibility.

ARTICLE X.   CONTENTS OF WRITINGS, RECORDINGS, AND PHOTOGRAPHS

Rule

Rule 1001.   Definitions That Apply to This Article

In this article:

(a) A "writing" consists of letters, words, numbers, or their equivalent set down in any form.

(b) A "recording" consists of letters, words, numbers, or their equivalent recorded in any manner.

(c) A "photograph" means a photographic image or its equivalent stored in any form.

(d) An "original" of a writing or recording means the writing or recording itself or any counterpart intended to have the same effect by the person who executed or issued it. For electronically stored information, "original" means any printout—or other output

readable by sight—if it accurately reflects the information. An "original" of a photograph includes the negative or a print from it.

(e) A "duplicate" means a counterpart produced by a mechanical, photographic, chemical, electronic, or other equivalent process or technique that accurately reproduces the original.

(Pub.L. 93–595, § 1, Jan. 2, 1975, 88 Stat. 1945; Apr. 26, 2011, eff. Dec. 1, 2011.)

ADVISORY COMMITTEE NOTES

1972 Proposed Rules

In an earlier day, when discovery and other related procedures were strictly limited, the misleading named "best evidence rule" afforded substantial guarantees against inaccuracies and fraud by its insistence upon production or original documents. The great enlargement of the scope of discovery and related procedures in recent times has measurably reduced the need for the rule. Nevertheless important areas of usefulness persist: discovery of documents outside the jurisdiction may require substantial outlay of time and money; the unanticipated document may not practically be discoverable; criminal cases have built-in limitations on discovery. Cleary and Strong, The Best Evidence Rule: An Evaluation in Context, 51 Iowa L.Rev. 825 (1966).

Note to Paragraph (1). Traditionally the rule requiring the original centered upon accumulations of data and expressions affecting legal relations set forth in words and figures. this meant that the rule was one essentially related to writings. Present day techniques have expanded methods of storing data, yet the essential form which the information ultimately assumes for usable purposes is words and figures. Hence the considerations underlying the rule dictate its expansion to include computers, photographic systems, and other modern developments.

Note to Paragraph (3). In most instances, what is an original will be self-evident and further refinement will be unnecessary. However, in some instances particularized definition is required. A carbon copy of a contract executed in duplicate becomes an original, as does a sales ticket carbon copy given to a customer. While strictly speaking the original of a photograph might be thought to be only the negative, practicality and common usage require that any print from the negative be regarded as an original. Similarly, practicality and usage confer the status of original upon any computer printout. *Transport Indemnity Co. v. Seib,* 178 Neb. 253, 132 N.W.2d 871 (1965).

Note to Paragraph (4). The definition describes "copies" produced by methods possessing an accuracy which virtually eliminates the possibility of error. Copies thus produced are given the status of originals in large measure by Rule 1003, *infra.* Copies subsequently produced manually, whether handwritten or typed, are not within the definition. It should be noted that what is an original for some purposes may be a duplicate for others. Thus a bank's microfilm record of checks cleared is the original as a record. However, a print offered as a copy of a check whose contents are in controversy is a duplicate. This result is substantially consistent with 28 U.S.C. § 1732(b). Compare 26 U.S.C. § 7513(c), giving full status as originals to photographic reproductions of tax returns and other documents, made by authority of the Secretary of the Treasury, and 44 U.S.C. § 399(a), giving original status to photographic copies in the National Archives.

1974 Enactment

Note to Paragraph (2). The Committee amended this Rule expressly to include "video tapes" in the definition of "photographs." House Report No. 93–650.

2011 Amendments

The language of Rule 1001 has been amended as part of the restyling of the Evidence Rules to make them more easily understood and to make style and terminology consistent throughout the rules. These changes are intended to be stylistic only. There is no intent to change any result in any ruling on evidence admissibility.

CROSS REFERENCES

Copies of government records and papers, admissibility, see 28 USCA § 1733.

National archives, legal status of photographic copies as originals, see 44 USCA § 2116.

Records made in regular course of business, admissibility, see 28 USCA § 1732.

Rule 1002. Requirement of the Original

An original writing, recording, or photograph is required in order to prove its content unless these rules or a federal statute provides otherwise.

(Pub.L. 93–595, § 1, Jan. 2, 1975, 88 Stat. 1946; Apr. 26, 2011, eff. Dec. 1, 2011.)

ADVISORY COMMITTEE NOTES
1972 Proposed Rules

The rule is the familiar one requiring production of the original of a document to prove its contents, expanded to include writings, recordings, and photographs, as defined in Rule 1001(1) and (2), *supra.*

Application of the rule requires a resolution of the question whether contents are sought to be proved. Thus an event may be proved by nondocumentary evidence, even though a written record of it was made. If, however, the event is sought to be proved by the written record, the rule applies. For example, payment may be proved without producing the written receipt which was given. Earnings may be proved without producing books of account in which they are entered. McCormick § 198; 4 Wigmore § 1245. Nor does the rule apply to testimony that books or records have been examined and found not to contain any reference to a designated matter.

The assumption should not be made that the rule will come into operation on every occasion when use is made of a photograph in evidence. On the contrary, the rule will seldom apply to ordinary photographs. In most instances a party *wishes* to introduce the item and the question raised is the propriety of receiving it in evidence. Cases in which an offer is made of the testimony of a witness as to what he saw in a photograph or motion picture, without producing the same, are most unusual. The usual course is for a witness on the stand to identify the photograph or motion picture as a correct representation of events which he saw or of a scene with which he is familiar. In fact he adopts the picture as his testimony, or, in common parlance, uses the picture to illustrate his testimony. Under these circumstances, no effort is made to prove the contents of the picture, and the rule is inapplicable. Paradis, The Celluloid Witness, 37 U.Colo. L.Rev. 235, 249–251 (1965).

On occasion, however, situations arise in which contents are sought to be proved. Copyright, defamation, and invasion of privacy by photograph or motion picture falls in this category. Similarly as to situations in which the picture is offered as having independent probative value, e.g. automatic photograph of bank robber. See *People v. Doggett,* 83 Cal.App.2d 405, 188 P.2d 792 (1948), photograph of defendants engaged in indecent act; Mouser and Philbin, Photographic Evidence—Is There a Recognized Basis for Admissibility? 8 Hastings L.J. 310 (1957). the most commonly encountered of this latter group is of course, the X ray, with substantial authority calling for production of the original. *Daniels v. Iowa City,* 191 Iowa 811, 183 N.W. 415 (1921); *Cellamare v. Third Acc. Transit Corp.,* 273 App.Div. 260, 77 N.Y.S.2d 91 (1948); *Patrick & Tilman v. Matkin,* 154 Okl. 232, 7 P.2d 414 (1932); *Mendoza v. Rivera,* 78 P.R.R. 569 (1955).

It should be noted, however, that Rule 703, *supra,* allows an expert to give an opinion based on matters not in evidence, and the present rule must be read as being limited accordingly in its application. Hospital records which may be admitted as business records under Rule 803(6) commonly contain reports interpreting X-rays by the staff radiologist, who qualifies as an expert, and these reports need not be excluded from the records by the instant rule.

The reference to Acts of Congress is made in view of such statutory provisions as 26 U.S.C. § 7513, photographic reproductions of tax returns and documents, made by authority of the Secretary of the Treasury, treated as originals, and 44 U.S.C. § 399(a), photographic copies in National Archives treated as originals.

2011 Amendments

The language of Rule 1002 has been amended as part of the restyling of the Evidence Rules to make them more easily understood and to make style and terminology consistent throughout the rules. These changes are intended to be stylistic only. There is no intent to change any result in any ruling on evidence admissibility.

CROSS REFERENCES

National archives, legal status of photographic copies as originals, see 44 USCA § 2116.

Rule 1003. Admissibility of Duplicates

A duplicate is admissible to the same extent as the original unless a genuine question is raised about the original's authenticity or the circumstances make it unfair to admit the duplicate.

(Pub.L. 93–595, § 1, Jan. 2, 1975, 88 Stat. 1946; Apr. 26, 2011, eff. Dec. 1, 2011.)

ADVISORY COMMITTEE NOTES

1972 Proposed Rules

When the only concern is with getting the words or other contents before the court with accuracy and precision, then a counterpart serves equally as well as the original, if the counterpart is the product of a method which insures accuracy and genuineness. By definition in Rule 1001(4), *supra*, a "duplicate" possesses this character.

Therefore, if no genuine issue exists as to authenticity and no other reason exists for requiring the original, a duplicate is admissible under the rule. This position finds support in the decisions, *Myrick v. United States*, 332 F.2d 279 (5th Cir. 1964), no error in admitting photostatic copies of checks instead of original microfilm in absence of suggestion to trial judge that photostats were incorrect; *Johns v. United States*, 323 F.2d 421 (5th Cir.1963), not error to admit concededly accurate tape recording made from original wire recording; *Sauget v. Johnston*, 315 F.2d 816 (9th Cir.1963), not error to admit copy of agreement when opponent had original and did not on appeal claim any discrepancy. Other reasons for acquiring the original may be present when only a part of the original is reproduced and the remainder is needed for cross-examination or may disclose matters qualifying the part offered or otherwise useful to the opposing party. *United States v. Alexander*, 326 F.2d 736 (4th Cir.1964). And see *Toho Bussan Kaisha, Ltd. v. American President Lines, Ltd.*, 265 F.2d 418, 76 A.L.R.2d 1344 (2d Cir.1959).

1974 Enactment

The Committee approved this Rule in the form submitted by the Court, with the expectation that the courts would be liberal in deciding that a "genuine question is raised as to the authenticity of the original." House Report No. 93–650.

2011 Amendments

The language of Rule 1003 has been amended as part of the restyling of the Evidence Rules to make them more easily understood and to make style and terminology consistent throughout the rules. These changes are intended to be stylistic only. There is no intent to change any result in any ruling on evidence admissibility.

Rule 1004. Admissibility of Other Evidence of Content

An original is not required and other evidence of the content of a writing, recording, or photograph is admissible if:

(a) all the originals are lost or destroyed, and not by the proponent acting in bad faith;

(b) an original cannot be obtained by any available judicial process;

(c) the party against whom the original would be offered had control of the original; was at that time put on notice, by pleadings or otherwise, that the original would be a subject of proof at the trial or hearing; and fails to produce it at the trial or hearing; or

(d) the writing, recording, or photograph is not closely related to a controlling issue.

(Pub.L. 93–595, § 1, Jan. 2, 1975, 88 Stat. 1946; Mar. 2, 1987, eff. Oct. 1, 1987; Apr. 26, 2011, eff. Dec. 1, 2011.)

ADVISORY COMMITTEE NOTES

1972 Proposed Rules

Basically the rule requiring the production of the original as proof of contents has developed as a rule of preference: if failure to produce the original is satisfactorily explained, secondary evidence is admissible. The instant rule specifies the circumstances under which production of the original is excused.

The rule recognizes no "degrees" of secondary evidence. While strict logic might call for extending the principle of preference beyond simply preferring the original, the formulation of a hierarchy of preferences and a procedure for making it effective is believed to involve unwarranted complexities. Most, if not all, that would be accomplished by an extended scheme of preferences will, in any event, be achieved through the normal motivation of a party to present the most convincing evidence possible and the arguments and procedures available to his opponent if he does not. Compare McCormick § 207.

Note to Paragraph (1). Loss or destruction of the original, unless due to bad faith of the proponent, is a satisfactory explanation of nonproduction. McCormick § 201.

Note to Paragraph (2). When the original is in the possession of a third person, inability to procure it from him by resort to process or other judicial procedure is a sufficient explanation of nonproduction. Judicial procedure includes subpoena duces tecum as an incident to the taking of a deposition in another jurisdiction. No further showing is required. See McCormick § 202.

Note to Paragraph (3). A party who has an original in his control has no need for the protection of the rule if put on notice that proof of contents will be made. He can ward off secondary evidence by offering the original. The notice procedure here provided is not to be confused with orders to produce or other discovery procedures, as the purpose of the procedure under this rule is to afford the opposite party an opportunity to produce the original, not to compel him to do so. McCormick § 203.

Note to Paragraph (4). While difficult to define with precision, situations arise in which no good purpose is served by production of the original. Examples are the newspaper in an action for the price of publishing defendant's advertisement, *Foster–Holcomb Investment Co. v. Little Rock Publishing Co.*, 151 Ark. 449, 236 S.W. 597 (1922), and the streetcar transfer of plaintiff claiming status as a passenger, *Chicago City Ry. Co. v. Carroll*, 206 Ill. 318, 68 N.E. 1087 (1903). Numerous cases are collected in McCormick § 200, p. 412, n. 1.

1974 Enactment

Note to Paragraph (1). The Committee approved Rule 1004(1) in the form submitted to Congress. However, the Committee intends that loss or destruction of an original by another person at the instigation of the proponent should be considered as tantamount to loss or destruction in bad faith by the proponent himself. House Report No. 93–650.

1987 Amendments

The amendments are technical. No substantive change is intended.

2011 Amendments

The language of Rule 1004 has been amended as part of the restyling of the Evidence Rules to make them more easily understood and to make style and terminology consistent throughout the rules. These changes are intended to be stylistic only. There is no intent to change any result in any ruling on evidence admissibility.

Rule 1005. Copies of Public Records to Prove Content

The proponent may use a copy to prove the content of an official record—or of a document that was recorded or filed in a public office as authorized by law— if these conditions are met: the record or document is otherwise admissible; and the copy is certified as correct in accordance with Rule 902(4) or is testified to be correct by a witness who has compared it with the original. If no such copy can be obtained by reasonable diligence, then the proponent may use other evidence to prove the content.

(Pub.L. 93–595, § 1, Jan. 2, 1975, 88 Stat. 1946; Apr. 26, 2011, eff. Dec. 1, 2011.)

ADVISORY COMMITTEE NOTES

1972 Proposed Rules

Public records call for somewhat different treatment. Removing them from their usual place of keeping would be attended by serious inconvenience to the public and to the custodian. As a consequence judicial decisions and statutes commonly hold that no explanation need be given for failure to produce the original of a public record. McCormick § 204; 4 Wigmore §§ 1215–1228. This blanket dispensation from producing or accounting for the original would open the door to the introduction of every kind of secondary evidence of contents of public records were it not for the preference given certified or compared copies. Recognition of degrees of secondary evidence in this situation is an appropriate *quid pro quo* for not applying the requirement of producing the original.

The provisions of 28 U.S.C. § 1733(b) apply only to departments or agencies of the United States. The rule, however, applies to public records generally and is comparable in scope in this respect to Rule 44(a) of the Rules of Civil Procedure.

2011 Amendments

The language of Rule 1005 has been amended as part of the restyling of the Evidence Rules to make them more easily understood and to make style and terminology consistent throughout the rules. These changes are intended to be stylistic only. There is no intent to change any result in any ruling on evidence admissibility.

CROSS REFERENCES

Code and supplements to Code of Laws of United States, and District of Columbia, prima facie evidence of original, see 1 USCA § 204.

Government records and papers, admissibility of authenticated copies or transcripts, see 28 USCA § 1733.

Proof of official domestic records, see Fed.Rules Civ.Proc. Rule 44, 28 USCA.

Statutes at Large, admissibility in evidence, see 1 USCA § 112.

Treaties, public acts, etc., admissibility in evidence, see 1 USCA § 113.

Rule 1006. Summaries to Prove Content

The proponent may use a summary, chart, or calculation to prove the content of voluminous writings, recordings, or photographs that cannot be conveniently examined in court. The proponent must make the originals or duplicates available for examination or copying, or both, by other parties at a reasonable time and place. And the court may order the proponent to produce them in court.

(Pub.L. 93–595, § 1, Jan. 2, 1975, 88 Stat. 1946; Apr. 26, 2011, eff. Dec. 1, 2011.)

ADVISORY COMMITTEE NOTES

1972 Proposed Rules

The admission of summaries of voluminous books, records, or documents offers the only practicable means of making their contents available to judge and jury. The rule recognizes this practice, with appropriate safeguards. 4 Wigmore § 1230.

2011 Amendments

The language of Rule 1006 has been amended as part of the restyling of the Evidence Rules to make them more easily understood and to make style and terminology consistent throughout the rules. These changes are intended to be stylistic only. There is no intent to change any result in any ruling on evidence admissibility.

Rule 1007. Testimony or Statement of a Party to Prove Content

The proponent may prove the content of a writing, recording, or photograph by the testimony, deposition, or written statement of the party against whom the evidence is offered. The proponent need not account for the original.

(Pub.L. 93–595, § 1, Jan. 2, 1975, 88 Stat. 1947; Mar. 2, 1987, eff. Oct. 1, 1987; Apr. 26, 2011, eff. Dec. 1, 2011.)

ADVISORY COMMITTEE NOTES

1972 Proposed Rules

While the parent case, *Slatterie v. Pooley*, 6 M. & W. 664, 151 Eng.Rep. 579 (Exch.1840), allows proof of contents by evidence of an oral admission by the party against whom offered, without accounting for nonproduction of the original, the risk of inaccuracy is substantial and the decision is at odds with the purpose of the rule giving preference to the original. See 4 Wigmore § 1255. The instant rule follows Professor McCormick's suggestion of limiting this use of admissions to those made in the course of giving testimony or in writing. McCormick § 208, p. 424. The limitation, of course, does not call for excluding evidence of an oral admission when nonproduction of the original has been accounted for and secondary evidence generally has become admissible. Rule 1004, supra.

A similar provision is contained in New Jersey Evidence Rule 70(1)(h).

1987 Amendments

The amendment is technical. No substantive change is intended.

2011 Amendments

The language of Rule 1007 has been amended as part of the restyling of the Evidence Rules to make them more easily understood and to make style and terminology consistent throughout the rules. These changes are intended to be stylistic only. There is no intent to change any result in any ruling on evidence admissibility.

CROSS REFERENCES

Depositions, see Fed.Rules Cr.Proc. Rule 15, 18 USCA.

Depositions and discovery, see Fed.Rules Civ.Proc. Rule 26 et seq., 28 USCA.

Rule 1008. Functions of the Court and Jury

Ordinarily, the court determines whether the proponent has fulfilled the factual conditions for admitting other evidence of the content of a writing, recording, or photograph under Rule 1004 or 1005. But in a jury trial, the jury determines—in accordance with Rule 104(b)—any issue about whether:

(a) an asserted writing, recording, or photograph ever existed;

(b) another one produced at the trial or hearing is the original; or

(c) other evidence of content accurately reflects the content.

(Pub.L. 93–595, § 1, Jan. 2, 1975, 88 Stat. 1947; Apr. 26, 2011, eff. Dec. 1, 2011.)

ADVISORY COMMITTEE NOTES

1972 Proposed Rules

Most preliminary questions of fact in connection with applying the rule preferring the original as evidence of contents are for the judge, under the general principles announced in Rule 104, *supra*. Thus, the question whether the loss of the originals has been established, or of the fulfillment of other conditions specified in Rule 1004, supra, is for the judge. However, questions may arise which go beyond the mere administration of the rule preferring the original and into the merits of the controversy. For example, plaintiff offers secondary evidence of the contents of an alleged contract, after first introducing evidence of loss of the original, and defendant counters with evidence that no such contract was ever executed. If the judge decides that the contract was never executed and excludes the secondary evidence, the case is at an end without ever going to the jury on a central issue. Levin, Authentication and Content of Writings, 10 Rutgers L.Rev. 632, 644 (1956). The latter portion of the instant rule is designed to insure treatment of these situations as raising jury questions. The decision is not one for uncontrolled discretion of the jury but is subject to the control exercised generally by the judge over jury determinations. See Rule 104(b), *supra*.

For similar provisions, see Uniform Rule 70(2); Kansas Code of Civil Procedure § 60–467(b); New Jersey Evidence Rule 70(2), (3).

2011 Amendments

The language of Rule 1008 has been amended as part of the restyling of the Evidence Rules to make them more easily understood and to make style and terminology consistent throughout the rules. These changes are intended to be stylistic only. There is no intent to change any result in any ruling on evidence admissibility.

ARTICLE XI. MISCELLANEOUS RULES

Rule 1101. Applicability of the Rules

(a) To Courts and Judges. These rules apply to proceedings before:

- United States district courts;
- United States bankruptcy and magistrate judges;
- United States courts of appeals;
- the United States Court of Federal Claims; and
- the district courts of Guam, the Virgin Islands, and the Northern Mariana Islands.

(b) To Cases and Proceedings. These rules apply in:

- civil cases and proceedings, including bankruptcy, admiralty, and maritime cases;
- criminal cases and proceedings; and
- contempt proceedings, except those in which the court may act summarily.

(c) Rules on Privilege. The rules on privilege apply to all stages of a case or proceeding.

(d) Exceptions. These rules—except for those on privilege—do not apply to the following:

(1) the court's determination, under Rule 104(a), on a preliminary question of fact governing admissibility;

(2) grand-jury proceedings; and

(3) miscellaneous proceedings such as:

- extradition or rendition;
- issuing an arrest warrant, criminal summons, or search warrant;
- a preliminary examination in a criminal case;
- sentencing;
- granting or revoking probation or supervised release; and
- considering whether to release on bail or otherwise.

(e) Other Statutes and Rules. A federal statute or a rule prescribed by the Supreme Court may provide for admitting or excluding evidence independently from these rules.

(Pub.L. 93–595, § 1, Jan. 2, 1975, 88 Stat. 1947; Pub.L. 94–149, § 1(14), Dec. 12, 1975, 89 Stat. 806; Pub.L. 95–598, Title II, §§ 251, 252, Nov. 6, 1978, 92 Stat. 2673; Pub.L. 97–164, Title I, § 142, Apr. 2, 1982, 96 Stat. 45; Mar. 2, 1987, eff. Oct. 1, 1987; Apr. 25, 1988, eff. Nov. 1, 1988; Pub.L. 100–690, Title VII, § 7075(c), Nov. 18, 1988, 102 Stat. 4405; Apr. 22, 1993, eff. Dec. 1, 1993; Apr. 26, 2011, eff. Dec. 1, 2011.)

ADVISORY COMMITTEE NOTES

1972 Proposed Rules

Note to Subdivision (a). The various enabling acts contain differences in phraseology in their descriptions of the courts over which the Supreme Court's power to make rules of practice and procedure extends. The act concerning civil actions, as amended in 1966, refers to "the district courts * * * of the United States in civil actions, including admiralty and maritime cases. * * *" 28 U.S.C. § 2072, Pub.L. 89–773, § 1, 80 Stat. 1323. The bankruptcy authorization is for rules of practice and procedure "under the Bankruptcy Act." 28

U.S.C. § 2075, Pub.L. 88–623, § 1, 78 Stat. 1001. The Bankruptcy Act in turn creates bankruptcy courts of "the United States district courts and the district courts of the Territories and possessions to which this title is or may hereafter be applicable." 11 U.S.C. §§ 1(10), 11(a). The provision as to criminal rules up to and including verdicts applies to "criminal cases and proceedings to punish for criminal contempt of court in the United States district courts, in the district courts for the districts of the Canal Zone and Virgin Islands, in the Supreme Court of Puerto Rico, and in proceedings before United States magistrates." 18 U.S.C. § 3771.

These various provisions do not in terms describe the same courts. In congressional usage the phrase "district courts of the United States," without further qualification, traditionally has included the district courts established by Congress in the states under Article III of the Constitution, which are "constitutional" courts, and has not included the territorial courts created under Article IV, Section 3, clause 2, which are "legislative" courts. *Hornbuckle v. Toombs*, 85 U.S. 648, 21 L.Ed. 966 (1873). However, any doubt as to the inclusion of the District Court for the District of Columbia in the phrase is laid at rest by the provisions of the Judicial Code constituting the judicial districts, 28 U.S.C. § 81 et seq., creating district courts therein, id. § 132, and specifically providing that the term "district court of the United States" means the court so constituted. *Id.* § 451. The District of Columbia is included. *Id.* § 88. Moreover, when these provisions were enacted, reference to the District of Columbia was deleted from the original civil rules enabling act. 28 U.S.C. § 2072. Likewise Puerto Rico is made a district, with a district court, and included in the term. *Id.* § 119. The question is simply one of the extent of the authority conferred by Congress. With respect to civil rules it seems clearly to include the district courts in the states, the District Court for the District of Columbia, and the District Court for the District of Puerto Rico.

The bankruptcy coverage is broader. The bankruptcy courts include "the United States district courts," which includes those enumerated above. Bankruptcy courts also include "the district courts of the Territories and possessions to which this title is or may hereafter be applicable." 11 U.S.C. §§ 1(10), 11(a). These courts include the district courts of Guam and the Virgin Islands. 48 U.S.C. §§ 1424(b), 1615. Professor Moore points out that whether the District Court for the District of the Canal Zone is a court of bankruptcy "is not free from doubt in view of the fact that no other statute expressly or inferentially provides for the applicability of the Bankruptcy Act in the Zone." He further observes that while there seems to be little doubt that the Zone is a territory or possession within the meaning of the Bankruptcy Act, 11 U.S.C. § 1(10), it must be noted that the appendix to the Canal Zone Code of 1934 did not list the Act among the laws of the United States applicable to the Zone. 1 Moore's Collier on Bankruptcy ¶ 1.10, pp. 67, 72, n. 25 (14th ed. 1967). The Code of 1962 confers on the district court jurisdiction of:

"(4) actions and proceedings involving laws of the United States applicable to the Canal Zone; and

"(5) other matters and proceedings wherein jurisdiction is conferred by this Code or any other law." Canal Zone Code, 1962, Title 3, § 141.

Admiralty jurisdiction is expressly conferred. *Id.* § 142. General powers are conferred on the district court, "if the course of proceeding is not specifically prescribed by this

Code, by the statute, or by applicable rule of the Supreme Court of the United States * * *" *Id.* § 279. Neither these provisions nor § 1(10) of the Bankruptcy Act ("district courts of the Territories and possessions to which this title is or may hereafter be applicable") furnishes a satisfactory answer as to the status of the District Court for the District of the Canal Zone as a court of bankruptcy. However, the fact is that this court exercises no bankruptcy jurisdiction in practice.

The criminal rules enabling act specified United States district courts, district courts for the districts of the Canal Zone and the Virgin Islands, the Supreme Court of the Commonwealth of Puerto Rico, and proceedings before United States commissioners. Aside from the addition of commissioners, now magistrates, this scheme differs from the bankruptcy pattern in that it makes no mention of the District Court of Guam but by specific mention removes the Canal Zone from the doubtful list.

The further difference in including the Supreme Court of the Commonwealth of Puerto Rico seems not to be significant for present purposes, since the Supreme Court of the Commonwealth of Puerto Rico is an appellate court. The Rules of Criminal Procedure have not been made applicable to it, as being unneeded and inappropriate, Rule 54(a) of the Federal Rules of Criminal Procedure, and the same approach is indicated with respect to rules of evidence.

If one were to stop at this point and frame a rule governing the applicability of the proposed rules of evidence in terms of the authority conferred by the three enabling acts, an irregular pattern would emerge as follows:

Civil actions, including admiralty and maritime cases— district courts in the states, District of Columbia, and Puerto Rico.

Bankruptcy—same as civil actions, plus Guam and Virgin Islands.

Criminal cases—same as civil actions, plus Canal Zone and Virgin Islands (but not Guam).

This irregular pattern need not, however, be accepted. Originally the Advisory Committee on the Rules of Civil Procedure took the position that, although the phrase "district courts of the United States" did not include territorial courts, provisions in the organic laws of Puerto Rico and Hawaii would make the rules applicable to the district courts thereof, though this would not be so as to Alaska, the Virgin Islands, or the Canal Zone, whose organic acts contained no corresponding provisions. At the suggestion of the Court, however, the Advisory Committee struck from its notes a statement to the above effect. 2 Moore's Federal Practice ¶ 1.07 (2nd ed. 1967); 1 Barron and Holtzoff, Federal Practice and Procedure § 121 (Wright ed. 1960). Congress thereafter by various enactments provided that the rules and future amendments thereto should apply to the district courts of Hawaii, 53 Stat. 841 (1939), Puerto Rico, 54 Stat. 22 (1940), Alaska, 63 Stat. 445 (1949), Guam, 64 Stat. 384–390 (1950), and the Virgin Islands, 68 Stat. 497, 507 (1954). The original enabling act for rules of criminal procedure specifically mentioned the district courts of the Canal Zone and the Virgin Islands. The Commonwealth of Puerto Rico was blanketed in by creating its court a "district court of the United States" as previously described. Although Guam is not mentioned in either the enabling act or in the expanded definition of "district court of the United States," the Supreme Court in 1956 amended Rule 54(a) to state that the Rules of Criminal Procedure are applicable in Guam. The Court took this step following the enactment of legislation by Congress in 1950 that rules there-

tofore or thereafter promulgated by the Court in civil cases, admiralty, criminal cases and bankruptcy should apply to the District Court of Guam, 48 U.S.C. § 1424(b), and two Ninth Circuit decisions upholding the applicability of the Rules of Criminal Procedure to Guam. *Pugh v. United States,* 212 F.2d 761 (9th Cir.1954); *Hatchett v. Guam,* 212 F.2d 767 (9th Cir.1954); Orfield, The Scope of the Federal Rules of Criminal Procedure, 38 U. of Det.L.J. 173, 187 (1960).

From this history, the reasonable conclusion is that Congressional enactment of a provision that rules and future amendments shall apply in the courts of a territory or possession is the equivalent of mention in an enabling act and that a rule on scope and applicability may properly be drafted accordingly. Therefore the pattern set by Rule 54 of the Federal Rules of Criminal Procedure is here followed.

The substitution of magistrates in lieu of commissioners is made in pursuance of the Federal Magistrates Act, P.L. 90–578, approved October 17, 1968, 82 Stat. 1107.

Note to Subdivision (b). Subdivision (b) is a combination of the language of the enabling acts, supra, with respect to the kinds of proceedings in which the making of rules is authorized. It is subject to the qualifications expressed in the subdivisions which follow.

Note to Subdivision (c). Subdivision (c) singling out the rules of privilege for special treatment, is made necessary by the limited applicability of the remaining rules.

Note to Subdivision (d). The rule is not intended as an expression as to when due process or other constitutional provisions may require an evidentiary hearing. Paragraph (1) restates, for convenience, the provisions of the second sentence of Rule 104(a), *supra.* See Advisory Committee's Note to that rule.

(2) While some states have statutory requirements that indictments be based on "legal evidence," and there is some case law to the effect that the rules of evidence apply to grand jury proceedings, 1 Wigmore § 4(5), the Supreme Court has not accepted this view. In *Costello v. United States,* 350 U.S. 359, 76 S.Ct. 406, 100 L.Ed. 397 (1965), the Court refused to allow an indictment to be attacked, for either constitutional or policy reasons, on the ground that only hearsay evidence was presented.

"It would run counter to the whole history of the grand jury institution, in which laymen conduct their inquiries unfettered by technical rules. Neither justice nor the concept of a fair trial requires such a change." *Id.* at 364. The rule as drafted does not deal with the evidence required to support an indictment.

(3) The rule exempts preliminary examinations in criminal cases. Authority as to the applicability of the rules of evidence to preliminary examinations has been meagre and conflicting. Goldstein, The State and the Accused: Balance of Advantage in Criminal Procedure, 69 Yale L.J. 1149, 1168, n. 53 (1960); Comment, Preliminary Hearings on Indictable Offenses in Philadelphia, 106 U. of Pa.L.Rev. 589, 592–593 (1958). Hearsay testimony is, however, customarily received in such examinations. Thus in a Dyer Act case, for example, an affidavit may properly be used in a preliminary examination to prove ownership of the stolen vehicle, thus saving the victim of the crime the hardship of having to travel twice to a distant district for the sole purpose of testifying as to ownership. It is believed that the extent of the applicability of the Rules of Evidence to preliminary examinations should be

appropriately dealt with by the Federal Rules of Criminal Procedure which regulate those proceedings.

Extradition and rendition proceedings are governed in detail by statute. 18 U.S.C. §§ 3181–3195. They are essentially administrative in character. Traditionally the rules of evidence have not applied. 1 Wigmore § 4(6). Extradition proceedings are accepted from the operation of the Rules of Criminal Procedure. Rule 54(b)(5) of Federal Rules of Criminal Procedure.

The rules of evidence have not been regarded as applicable to sentencing or probation proceedings, where great reliance is placed upon the presentence investigation and report. Rule 32(c) of the Federal Rules of Criminal Procedure requires a presentence investigation and report in every case unless the court otherwise directs. In *Williams v. New York*, 337 U.S. 241, 69 S.Ct. 1079, 93 L.Ed. 1337 (1949), in which the judge overruled a jury recommendation of life imprisonment and imposed a death sentence, the Court said that due process does not require confrontation or cross-examination in sentencing or passing on probation, and that the judge has broad discretion as to the sources and types of information relied upon. Compare the recommendation that the substance of all derogatory information be disclosed to the defendant, in A.B.A. Project on Minimum Standards for Criminal Justice, Sentencing Alternatives and Procedures § 4.4, Tentative Draft (1967, Sobeloff, Chm.). Williams was adhered to in *Specht v. Patterson*, 386 U.S. 605, 87 S.Ct. 1209, 18 L.Ed.2d 326 (1967), but not extended to a proceeding under the Colorado Sex Offenders Act, which was said to be a new charge leading in effect to punishment, more like the recidivist statutes where opportunity must be given to be heard on the habitual criminal issue.

Warrants for arrest, criminal summonses, and search warrants are issued upon complaint or affidavit showing probable cause. Rules 4(a) and 41(c) of the Federal Rules of Criminal Procedure. The nature of the proceedings makes application of the formal rules of evidence inappropriate and impracticable.

Criminal contempts are punishable summarily if the judge certifies that he saw or heard the contempt and that it was committed in the presence of the court. Rule 42(a) of the Federal Rules of Criminal Procedure. The circumstances which preclude application of the rules of evidence in this situation are not present, however, in other cases of criminal contempt.

Proceedings with respect to release on bail or otherwise do not call for application of the rules of evidence. The governing statute specifically provides:

"Information stated in, or offered in connection with, any order entered pursuant to this section need not conform to the rules pertaining to the admissibility of evidence in a court of law." 18 U.S.C.A. § 3146(f). This provision is consistent with the type of inquiry contemplated in A.B.A. Project on Minimum Standards for Criminal Justice, Standards Relating to Pretrial Release, § 4.5(b), (c), p. 16 (1968). The references to the weight of the evidence against the accused, in Rule 46(a)(1), (c) of the Federal Rules of Criminal Procedure and in 18 U.S.C.A. § 3146(b), as a factor to be considered, clearly do not have in view evidence introduced at a hearing under the rules of evidence.

The rule does not exempt habeas corpus proceedings. The Supreme Court held in *Walker v. Johnston*, 312 U.S. 275, 61 S.Ct. 574, 85 L.Ed. 830 (1941), that the practice of disposing of matters of fact on affidavit, which prevailed in some circuits, did not "satisfy the command of the statute that the judge shall proceed 'to determine the facts of the case, by hearing the testimony and arguments.'" This view accords with the emphasis in *Townsend v. Sain*, 372 U.S. 293, 83 S.Ct. 745, 9 L.Ed.2d 770 (1963), upon trial-type proceedings, *id.* 311, 83 S.Ct. 745, with demeanor evidence as a significant factor, *id.* 322, 83 S.Ct. 745, in applications by state prisoners aggrieved by unconstitutional detentions. Hence subdivision (3) applies the rules to habeas corpus proceedings to the extent not inconsistent with the statute.

Note to Subdivision (e). In a substantial number of special proceedings, *ad hoc* evaluation has resulted in the promulgation of particularized evidentiary provisions, by Act of Congress or by rule adopted by the Supreme Court. Well adapted to the particular proceedings, though not apt candidates for inclusion in a set of general rules, they are left undisturbed. Otherwise, however, the rules of evidence are applicable to the proceedings enumerated in the subdivision.

1974 Enactment

Note to Subdivision (a). Subdivision (a) as submitted to the Congress, in stating the courts and judges to which the Rules of Evidence apply, omitted the Court of Claims and commissioners of that Court. At the request of the Court of Claims, the Committee amended the Rule to include the Court and its commissioners within the purview of the Rules.

Note to Subdivision (b). Subdivision (b) was amended merely to substitute positive law citations for those which were not. House Report No. 93–650.

1987 Amendments

Subdivision (a) is amended to delete the reference to the District Court for the District of the Canal Zone, which no longer exists, and to add the District Court for the Northern Mariana Islands. The United States bankruptcy judges are added to conform the subdivision with Rule 1101(b) and Bankruptcy Rule 9017.

1988 Amendments

The amendments are technical. No substantive change is intended.

1993 Amendments

This revision is made to conform the rule to changes in terminology made by Rule 58 of the Federal Rules of Criminal Procedure and to the changes in the title of United States magistrates made by the Judicial Improvements Act of 1990.

2011 Amendments

The language of Rule 1101 has been amended as part of the restyling of the Evidence Rules to make them more easily understood and to make style and terminology consistent throughout the rules. These changes are intended to be stylistic only. There is no intent to change any result in any ruling on evidence admissibility.

HISTORICAL NOTES

Revision Notes and Legislative Reports

1975 Acts. House Report No. 94–599, see 1975 U.S. Code Cong. and Adm. News, p. 1585.

1982 Acts. Senate Report No. 97–275, see 1982 U.S. Code Cong. and Adm. News, p. 11.

Effective and Applicability Provisions

1982 Acts. Amendment by Pub.L. 97–164 effective Oct. 1, 1982, see section 402 of Pub.L. 97–164, set out as a note under section 171 of this title.

1978 Acts. Amendment of subds. (a) and (b) of this rule by section 251 of Pub.L. 95–598 effective Oct. 1, 1979, see section 402(c) of Pub.L. 95–598, set out as a note preceding section 101 of Title 11, Bankruptcy.

Change of Name

United States magistrate appointed under section 631 of Title 28, Judiciary and Judicial Procedure, to be known as United States magistrate judge after Dec. 1, 1990, with any reference to United States magistrate or magistrate in Title 28, in any other Federal statute, etc., deemed a reference to United States magistrate judge appointed under section 631 of Title 28, see section 321 of Pub.L. 101–650, set out as a note under section 631 of Title 28.

Pending Actions

Amendments of Supreme Court to the Federal Rules of Evidence effective December 1, 1993, applicable, insofar as just and practicable, in all proceedings then pending, pursuant to the Order of April 22, 1993.

CROSS REFERENCES

Applicability of rules to all criminal proceedings in United States district courts, see Fed.Rules Cr.Proc. Rule 1, 18 USCA.

Bankruptcy Rules, power of Supreme Court to prescribe, see 28 USCA § 2075.

District courts,

Creation and composition of, see 28 USCA § 132.

Guam, applicability of rules to, see 48 USCA § 1424.

Northern Mariana Islands, applicability of rules to, see 48 USCA § 1821.

Supreme court, power to prescribe rules of procedure, see 28 USCA § 2072.

Territorial composition, see 28 USCA § 81 et seq.

Virgin Islands, applicability of rules to, see 48 USCA § 1614.

Extradition, see 18 USCA § 3181 et seq.

General provisions applicable to courts and judges, see 28 USCA § 451 et seq.

Judicial power, tenure, and compensation, generally, see USCA Const. Art. III, § 1.

Scope of rules, see Fed.Rules Evid. Rule 101, 28 USCA.

Rule 1102. Amendments

These rules may be amended as provided in 28 U.S.C. § 2072.

(Pub.L. 93–595, § 1, Jan. 2, 1975, 88 Stat.1948; Apr. 30, 1991, eff. Dec. 1, 1991; Apr. 26, 2011, eff. Dec. 1, 2011.)

ADVISORY COMMITTEE NOTES

1991 Amendments

The amendment is technical. No substantive change is intended.

2011 Amendments

The language of Rule 1102 has been amended as part of the restyling of the Evidence Rules to make them more easily understood and to make style and terminology consistent throughout the rules. These changes are intended to be stylistic only. There is no intent to change any result in any ruling on evidence admissibility.

Rule 1103. Title

These rules may be cited as the Federal Rules of Evidence.

(Pub.L. 93–595, § 1, Jan. 2, 1975, 88 Stat.1948; Apr. 26, 2011, eff. Dec. 1, 2011.)

ADVISORY COMMITTEE NOTES

2011 Amendments

The language of Rule 1103 has been amended as part of the restyling of the Evidence Rules to make them more easily understood and to make style and terminology consistent throughout the rules. These changes are intended to be stylistic only. There is no intent to change any result in any ruling on evidence admissibility.

HISTORICAL NOTES

Short Title

1978 Amendments. Pub.L. 95–540, § 1, Oct. 28, 1978, 92 Stat. 2046, provided: "That this Act [enacting rule 412 of these rules and a provision set out as a note under rule 412 of these rules] may be cited as the 'Privacy Protection for Rape Victims Act of 1978'."

FEDERAL RULES OF APPELLATE PROCEDURE

SELECTED FEDERAL RULES OF APPELLATE PROCEDURE

Amendments received to December 1, 2018

Rule

Rule 1. Scope of Rules; Definition; Title

(a) Scope of Rules.

(1) These rules govern procedure in the United States courts of appeals.

(2) When these rules provide for filing a motion or other document in the district court, the procedure must comply with the practice of the district court.

(b) Definition. In these rules, "state" includes the District of Columbia and any United States commonwealth or territory.

(c) Title. These rules are to be known as the Federal Rules of Appellate Procedure.

(As amended Apr. 30, 1979, eff. Aug. 1, 1979; Apr. 25, 1989, eff. Dec. 1, 1989; Apr. 29, 1994, eff. Dec. 1, 1994; Apr. 24, 1998, eff. Dec. 1, 1998; Apr. 29, 2002, eff. Dec. 1, 2002; Apr. 28, 2010, eff. Dec. 1, 2010.)

ADVISORY COMMITTEE NOTES

1967 Adoption

These rules are drawn under the authority of 28 U.S.C. § 2072 as amended by the Act of November 6, 1966, 80 Stat. 1323 (1 U.S.Code Cong. & Ad.News, p. 1546 (1966)) (Rules of Civil Procedure); 28 U.S.C. § 2075 (Bankruptcy Rules); and 18 U.S.C. §§ 3771 [§ 3771 of Title 18, Crimes and Criminal Procedure] (Procedure to and including verdict) and 3772 [§ 3772 of Title 18] (Procedure after verdict). Those statutes combine to give to the Supreme Court power to make rules of practice and procedure for all cases within the jurisdiction of the courts of appeals. By the terms of the statutes, after the rules have taken effect all laws in conflict with them are of no further force or effect. Practice and procedure in the eleven courts of appeals are now regulated by rules promulgated by each court under the authority of 28 U.S.C. § 2071. Rule 47 expressly authorizes the courts of appeals to make rules of practice not inconsistent with these rules.

As indicated by the titles under which they are found, the following rules are of special application: Rules 3 through 12 apply to appeals from judgments and orders of the district courts; Rules 13 and 14 apply to appeals from decisions of the Tax Court (Rule 13 establishes an appeal as the mode of review of decisions of the Tax Court in place of the present petition for review); Rules 15 through 20 apply to proceedings for review or enforcement of orders of administrative agencies, boards, commissions and officers. Rules 22 through 24 regulate habeas corpus proceedings and appeals in forma pauperis. All other rules apply to all proceedings in the courts of appeals.

1979 Amendment

The Federal Rules of Appellate Procedure were designed as an integrated set of rules to be followed in appeals to the courts of appeals, covering all steps in the appellate process, whether they take place in the district court or in the court of appeals, and with their adoption Rules 72 to 76 of the F.R.C.P. [rules 72 to 76, Federal Rules of Civil Procedure] were abrogated. In some instances, however, the F.R.A.P. provide that a motion or application for relief may, or must, be made in the district court. See Rules 4(a), 10(b) and 24. The proposed amendment would make it clear that when this is so the motion or application is to be made in the form and manner prescribed by the F.R.C.P. or F.R.Cr.P. [Federal Rules Criminal Procedure] and local rules relating to the form and presentation of motions and is not governed by Rule 27 of the F.R.A.P. See Rule 7(b) of the F.R.C.P. [rule 7(b), Federal Rules of Civil Procedure] and Rule 47 of the F.R.Cr.P. [rule 47, Federal Rules of Criminal Procedure].

1989 Amendment

The amendment is technical. No substantive change is intended.

1994 Amendment

Subdivision (c). A new subdivision is added to the rule. The text of new subdivision (c) has been moved from Rule 48 to Rule 1 to allow the addition of new rules at the end of the existing set of appellate rules without burying the title provision among other rules. In a similar fashion the Bankruptcy Rules combine the provisions governing the scope of the rules and the title in the first rule.

1998 Amendments

The language and organization of the rule are amended to make the rule more easily understood. In addition to changes made to improve the understanding, the Advisory Committee has changed language to make style and terminology consistent throughout the appellate rules. These changes are intended to be stylistic only. The Advisory Committee recommends deleting the language in subdivision (a) that describes the different types of proceedings that may be brought in a court of appeals. The Advisory Committee believes that the language is unnecessary and that it s omission does not work any substantive change.

2002 Amendments

Subdivision (b). Two recent enactments make it likely that, in the future, one or more of the Federal Rules of Appellate Procedure ("FRAP") will extend or limit the jurisdiction of the courts of appeals. In 1990, Congress amended the Rules Enabling Act to give the Supreme Court authority to use the federal rules of practice and procedure to define when a ruling of a district court is final for purposes of 28 U.S.C. § 1291. *See* 28 U.S.C. § 2072(c). In 1992, Congress amended 28 U.S.C. § 1292 to give the Supreme Court authority to use the federal rules of practice and procedure to provide for appeals of interlocutory decisions that are not already authorized by 28 U.S.C. § 1292. *See* 28 U.S.C. § 1292(e). Both § 1291 and § 1292 are unquestionably jurisdictional statutes, and thus, as soon as FRAP is amended to define finality for purposes of the former or to authorize interlocutory appeals not provided for by the latter, FRAP will "extend or limit the jurisdiction of the courts of appeals," and subdivision (b) will become obsolete. For that reason, subdivision (b) has been abrogated.

Changes Made After Publication and Comments No changes were made to the text of the proposed amendment or to the Committee Note.

2010 Amendments

Subdivision (b). New subdivision (b) defines the term "state" to include the District of Columbia and any commonwealth or territory of the United States. Thus, as used in these Rules, "state" includes the District of Columbia, Guam, American Samoa, the U.S. Virgin Islands, the Commonwealth of Puerto Rico, and the Commonwealth of the Northern Mariana Islands.

HISTORICAL NOTES

Pending Actions

Amendments of Supreme Court to Federal Rules of Appellate Procedure effective December 1, 1993, applicable, insofar as just and practicable, in all proceedings then pending, pursuant to the Order of April 22, 1993.

CROSS REFERENCES

Authority to create courts inferior to Supreme Court, see USCA Const. Art. III § 1.

"Court of the United States" as including courts of appeals, see 28 USCA § 451.

Creation and composition of courts, see 28 USCA § 43.

Forging or counterfeiting seals of courts, penalties, see 18 USCA § 505.

Number and composition of circuits, see 28 USCA § 41.

Writs and process issued by court to be under seal, see 28 USCA § 1691.

Rule 6.   Appeal in a Bankruptcy Case

(a) Appeal From a Judgment, Order, or Decree of a District Court Exercising Original Jurisdiction in a Bankruptcy Case. An appeal to a court of appeals from a final judgment, order, or decree of a district court exercising jurisdiction under 28 U.S.C. § 1334 is taken as any other civil appeal under these rules.

(b) Appeal From a Judgment, Order, or Decree of a District Court or Bankruptcy Appellate Panel

Exercising Appellate Jurisdiction in a Bankruptcy Case.

(1) Applicability of Other Rules. These rules apply to an appeal to a court of appeals under 28 U.S.C. § 158(d)(1) from a final judgment, order, or decree of a district court or bankruptcy appellate panel exercising appellate jurisdiction under 28 U.S.C. § 158(a) or (b), but with these qualifications:

(A) Rules 4(a)(4), 4(b), 9, 10, 11, 12(c), 13–20, 22–23, and 24(b) do not apply;

(B) the reference in Rule 3(c) to "Form 1 in the Appendix of Forms" must be read as a reference to Form 5;

(C) when the appeal is from a bankruptcy appellate panel, "district court," as used in any applicable rule, means "appellate panel"; and

(D) in Rule 12.1, "district court" includes a bankruptcy court or bankruptcy appellate panel.

(2) Additional Rules. In addition to the rules made applicable by Rule 6(b)(1), the following rules apply:

(A) Motion for Rehearing.

(i) If a timely motion for rehearing under Bankruptcy Rule 8022 is filed, the time to appeal for all parties runs from the entry of the order disposing of the motion. A notice of appeal filed after the district court or bankruptcy appellate panel announces or enters a judgment, order, or decree—but before disposition of the motion for rehearing—becomes effective when the order disposing of the motion for rehearing is entered.

(ii) If a party intends to challenge the order disposing of the motion—or the alteration or amendment of a judgment, order, or decree upon the motion—then the party, in compliance with Rules 3(c) and 6(b)(1)(B), must file a notice of appeal or amended notice of appeal. The notice or amended notice must be filed within the time prescribed by Rule 4—excluding Rules 4(a)(4) and 4(b)—measured from the entry of the order disposing of the motion.

(iii) No additional fee is required to file an amended notice.

(B) The Record on Appeal.

(i) Within 14 days after filing the notice of appeal, the appellant must file with the clerk possessing the record assembled in accordance with Bankruptcy Rule 8009—and serve on the appellee—a statement of the issues to be presented on appeal and a designation of the record to be certified and made available to the circuit clerk.

(ii) An appellee who believes that other parts of the record are necessary must, within 14 days after being served with the appellant's designation, file with the clerk and serve on the appellant a designation of additional parts to be included.

(iii) The record on appeal consists of:
- the redesignated record as provided above;
- the proceedings in the district court or bankruptcy appellate panel; and
- a certified copy of the docket entries prepared by the clerk under Rule 3(d).

(C) Making the Record Available.

(i) When the record is complete, the district clerk or bankruptcy-appellate-panel clerk must number the documents constituting the record and promptly make it available to the circuit clerk. If the clerk makes the record available in paper form, the clerk will not send documents of unusual bulk or weight, physical exhibits other than documents, or other parts of the record designated for omission by local rule of the court of appeals, unless directed to do so by a party or the circuit clerk. If unusually bulky or heavy exhibits are to be made available in paper form, a party must arrange with the clerks in advance for their transportation and receipt.

(ii) All parties must do whatever else is necessary to enable the clerk to assemble the record and make it available. When the record is made available in paper form, the court of appeals may provide by rule or order that a certified copy of the docket entries be made available in place of the redesignated record. But any party may request at any time during the pendency of the appeal that the redesignated record be made available.

(D) Filing the Record. When the district clerk or bankruptcy-appellate-panel clerk has made the record available, the circuit clerk must note that fact on the docket. The date noted on the docket serves as the filing date of the record. The circuit clerk must immediately notify all parties of the filing date.

(c) Direct Review by Permission Under 28 U.S.C. § 158(d)(2).

(1) Applicability of Other Rules. These rules apply to a direct appeal by permission under 28 U.S.C. § 158(d)(2), but with these qualifications:

(A) Rules 3–4, 5(a)(3), 6(a), 6(b), 8(a), 8(c), 9–12, 13–20, 22–23, and 24(b) do not apply;

(B) as used in any applicable rule, "district court" or "district clerk" includes—to the extent appropriate—a bankruptcy court or bankruptcy appellate panel or its clerk; and

(C) the reference to "Rules 11 and 12(c)" in Rule 5(d)(3) must be read as a reference to Rules 6(c)(2)(B) and (C).

(2) Additional Rules. In addition, the following rules apply:

(A) The Record on Appeal. Bankruptcy Rule 8009 governs the record on appeal.

(B) Making the Record Available. Bankruptcy Rule 8010 governs completing the record and making it available.

(C) Stays Pending Appeal. Bankruptcy Rule 8007 applies to stays pending appeal.

(D) Duties of the Circuit Clerk. When the bankruptcy clerk has made the record available, the circuit clerk must note that fact on the docket. The date noted on the docket serves as the filing date of the record. The circuit clerk must immediately notify all parties of the filing date.

(E) Filing a Representation Statement. Unless the court of appeals designates another time, within 14 days after entry of the order granting permission to appeal, the attorney who sought permission must file a statement with the circuit clerk naming the parties that the attorney represents on appeal.

(Added Apr. 25, 1989, eff. Dec. 1, 1989; amended Apr. 30, 1991, eff. Dec. 1, 1991; Apr. 22, 1993, eff. Dec. 1, 1993; Apr. 24, 1998, eff. Dec. 1, 1998; Mar. 26, 2009, eff. Dec. 1, 2009; Apr. 25, 2014, eff. Dec. 1, 2014.)

ADVISORY COMMITTEE NOTES

1989 Addition

A new Rule 6 is proposed. The Bankruptcy Reform Act of 1978, Pub.L. No. 95–598, 92 Stat. 2549, the Supreme Court decision in *Northern Pipeline Construction Co. v. Marathon Pipe Line Co.*, 458 U.S. 50 (1982), and the Bankruptcy Amendments and Federal Judgeship Act of 1984, Pub.L. No. 98–353, 98 Stat. 333, have made the existing Rule 6 obsolete.

Subdivision (a). Subdivision (a) provides that when a district court exercises original jurisdiction in a bankruptcy matter, rather than referring it to a bankruptcy judge for a final determination, the appeal should be taken in identical fashion as appeals from district court decisions in other civil actions. A district court exercises original jurisdiction and this subdivision applies when the district court enters a final order or judgment upon consideration of a bankruptcy judge's proposed findings of fact and conclusions of law in a non-core proceeding pursuant to 28 U.S.C. § 157(c)(1) or when a district court withdraws a proceeding pursuant to 28 U.S.C. § 157(d). This subdivision is included to avoid uncertainty arising from the question of whether a bankruptcy case is a civil case. The rules refer at various points to the procedure "in a civil case", *see*, e.g. Rule 4(a)(1). Subdivision (a) makes it clear that such rules apply to an appeal from a district court bankruptcy decision.

Subdivision (b). Subdivision (b) governs appeals that follow intermediate review of a bankruptcy judge's decision by a district court or a bankruptcy appellate panel.

Subdivision (b)(1). Subdivision (b)(1) provides for the general applicability of the Federal Rules of Appellate Procedure, with specified exceptions, to appeals covered by subdivision (b) and makes necessary word adjustments.

Subdivision (b)(2). Paragraph (i) provides that the time for filing a notice of appeal shall begin to run anew from the entry of an order denying a rehearing or from the entry of a subsequent judgment. The Committee deliberately omitted from the rule any provision governing the validity of a notice of appeal filed prior to the entry of an order denying a rehearing; the Committee intended to leave undisturbed the current state of the law on that issue. Paragraph (ii) calls for a redesignation of the appellate record assembled in the bankruptcy court pursuant to Rule 8006 of the Rules of Bankruptcy Procedure. After an intermediate appeal, a party may well narrow the focus of its efforts on the second appeal and a redesignation of the record may eliminate unnecessary material. The proceedings during the first appeal are included to cover the possibility that independent error in the intermediate appeal, for example failure to follow appropriate procedures, may be assigned in the court of appeals. Paragraph (iii) provides for the transmission of the record and tracks the appropriate subsections of Rule 11. Paragraph (iv) provides for the filing of the record and notices to the parties. Paragraph (ii) and Paragraph (iv) both refer to "a certified copy of the docket entries". The "docket entries" referred to are the docket entries in the district court or the bankruptcy appellate panel, not the entire docket in the bankruptcy court.

1993 Amendments

Note to Subparagraph (b)(2)(i). The amendment accompanies concurrent changes to Rule 4(a)(4). Although Rule 6 never included language such as that being changed in Rule 4(a)(4), language that made a notice of appeal void if it was filed before, or during the pendency of, certain posttrial motions, courts have found that a notice of appeal is premature if it is filed before the court disposes of a motion for rehearing. See, e.g., *In re X-Cel, Inc.*, 823 F.2d 192 (7th Cir.1987); *In re Shah*, 859 F.2d 1463 (10th Cir.1988). The Committee wants to achieve the same result here as in Rule 4, the elimination of a procedural trap.

1998 Amendments

The language and organization of the rule are amended to make the rule more easily understood. In addition to changes made to improve the understanding, the Advisory Committee has changed language to make style and terminology consistent throughout the appellate rules. These changes are intended to be stylistic only.

Subdivision (b). Language is added to Rule 6(b)(2)(A)(ii) to conform with the corresponding provision in Rule 4(a)(4). The new language is clarifying rather than substantive. The existing rule states that a party intending to challenge an alteration or amendment of a judgment must file an amended notice of appeal. Of course, if a party has not previously filed a notice of appeal, the party would simply file a notice of appeal not an amended one. The new language states that the party must file "a notice of appeal or amended notice of appeal."

2009 Amendments

Subdivision (b)(2)(B). The times set in the former rule at 10 days have been revised to 14 days. See the Note to Rule 26.

2014 Amendments

Subdivision (b)(1). Subdivision (b)(1) is updated to reflect the renumbering of 28 U.S.C. § 158(d) as 28 U.S.C. § 158(d)(1). Subdivision (b)(1)(A) is updated to reflect the renumbering of Rule 12(b) as Rule 12(c). New subdivision (b)(1)(D) provides that references in Rule 12.1 to the "district court" include—as appropriate—a bankruptcy court or bankruptcy appellate panel.

Subdivision (b)(2). Subdivision (b)(2)(A)(i) is amended to refer to Bankruptcy Rule 8022 (in accordance with the renumbering of Part VIII of the Bankruptcy Rules).

Subdivision (b)(2)(A)(ii) is amended to address problems that stemmed from the adoption — during the 1998 restyling project — of language referring to challenges to "an altered or amended judgment, order, or decree." Current Rule 6(b)(2)(A)(ii) states that "[a] party intending to challenge an altered or amended judgment, order, or decree must file a notice of appeal or amended notice of appeal ..." Before the 1998 restyling, the comparable subdivision of Rule 6 instead read "[a] party intending to challenge an alteration or amendment of the judgment, order, or decree shall file an amended notice of appeal ..." The 1998 restyling made a similar change in Rule 4(a)(4). One court has explained that the 1998 amendment introduced ambiguity into that Rule: "The new formulation could be read to expand the obligation to file an amended notice to circumstances where the ruling on the post-trial motion alters the prior judgment in an insignificant manner or in a manner favorable to the appellant, even though the appeal is not directed against the alteration of the judgment." *Sorensen v. City of New York*, 413 F.3d 292, 296 n.2 (2d Cir. 2005). Though the *Sorensen* court was writing of Rule 4(a)(4), a similar concern arises with respect to Rule 6(b)(2)(A)(ii). Rule 4(a)(4) was amended in 2009 to remove the ambiguity identified by the *Sorensen* court. The current amendment follows suit by removing Rule 6(b)(2)(A)(ii)'s reference to challenging "an altered or amended judgment, order, or decree," and referring instead to challenging "the alteration or amendment of a judgment, order, or decree."

Subdivision (b)(2)(B)(i) is amended to refer to Rule 8009 (in accordance with the renumbering of Part VIII of the Bankruptcy Rules).

Due to the shift to electronic filing, in some appeals the record will no longer be transmitted in paper form. Subdivisions (b)(2)(B)(i), (b)(2)(C), and (b)(2)(D) are amended to reflect the fact that the record sometimes will be made available electronically.

Subdivision (b)(2)(D) sets the duties of the circuit clerk when the record has been made available. Because the record may be made available in electronic form, subdivision (b)(2)(D) does not direct the clerk to "file" the record. Rather, it directs the clerk to note on the docket the date when the record was made available and to notify the parties of that date, which shall serve as the date of filing the record for purposes of provisions in these Rules that calculate time from that filing date.

Subdivision (c). New subdivision (c) is added to govern permissive direct appeals from the bankruptcy court to the court of appeals under 28 U.S.C. § 158(d)(2). For further provisions governing such direct appeals, see Bankruptcy Rule 8006.

Subdivision (c)(1). Subdivision (c)(1) provides for the general applicability of the Federal Rules of Appellate Procedure, with specified exceptions, to appeals covered by subdivision (c) and makes necessary word adjustments.

Subdivision (c)(2). Subdivision (c)(2)(A) provides that the record on appeal is governed by Bankruptcy Rule 8009. Subdivision (c)(2)(B) provides that the record shall be made available as stated in Bankruptcy Rule 8010. Subdivision (c)(2)(C) provides that Bankruptcy Rule 8007 applies to stays pending appeal; in addition, Appellate Rule 8(b) applies to sureties on bonds provided in connection with stays pending appeal.

Subdivision (c)(2)(D), like subdivision (b)(2)(D), directs the clerk to note on the docket the date when the record was made available and to notify the parties of that date, which shall serve as the date of filing the record for purposes of provisions in these Rules that calculate time from that filing date.

Subdivision (c)(2)(E) is modeled on Rule 12(b), with appropriate adjustments.

Changes Made After Publication and Comment
No changes were made after publication and comment.

HISTORICAL NOTES

References in Text
The Bankruptcy Rules, referred to in subd. (b)(2)(A)(i), (B)(i), (c)(2)(A)–(C), are set out in the Appendix to Title 11, Bankruptcy.

Form 5. Notice of Appeal to a Court of Appeals from a Judgment or Order of a District Court or a Bankruptcy Appellate Panel

United States District Court for the ....
District of ....

```
In re                             )
                                  )
................................, )
           Debtor                 )
                                  )  File No...........
................................, )
           Plaintiff              )
                                  )
            v.                    )
                                  )
................................, )
           Defendant              )
```

Notice of Appeal to
United States Court of Appeals
for the .... Circuit
......................., the plaintiff [or defendant or other party] appeals to the United States Court of Appeals for the .... Circuit from the final judgment [or order or decree] of the district court for the district of ... [or bankruptcy appellate panel of the .... circuit], entered in this case on ...., 20.... [here describe the judgment, order, or decree] ....
The parties to the judgment [or order or decree] appealed from and the names and addresses of their respective attorneys are as follows:

Dated ....
Signed ....
Attorney for Appellant

Address: ....
....

*[**Note to inmate filers:** If you are an inmate confined in an institution and you seek the timing benefit of Fed. R. App. P. 4(c)(1), complete Form 7 (Declaration of Inmate Filing) and file that declaration along with this Notice of Appeal.]*

(Added Apr. 25, 1989, eff. Dec. 1, 1989; amended Mar. 27, 2003, eff. Dec. 1, 2003; Apr. 28, 2016, eff. Dec. 1, 2016.)

RELATED PROVISIONS
OF THE
CODE OF FEDERAL REGULATIONS

Current through November 2, 2018

TITLE 28—JUDICIAL ADMINISTRATION

CHAPTER I—DEPARTMENT OF JUSTICE

§ 58.1 Authorization to establish panels of private trustees.

(a) Each U.S. Trustee is authorized to establish a panel of private trustees (the "panel") pursuant to 28 U.S.C. 586(a)(1).

(b) Each U.S. Trustee is authorized, with the approval of the Director, Executive Office for United States Trustees (the "Director") to increase or decrease the total membership of the panel. In addition, each U.S. Trustee, with the approval of the Director, is authorized to institute a system of rotation of membership or the like to achieve diversity of experience, geographical distribution or other characteristics among the persons on the panel.

[62 FR 30183, June 2, 1997]

§ 58.2   Authorization to appoint standing trustees.

Each U.S. Trustee is authorized, subject to the approval of the Deputy Attorney General, or his delegate, to appoint and remove one or more standing trustees to serve in cases under chapters 12 and 13 of title 11, U.S. Code.

[Order No. 921–80, 45 FR 82631, Dec. 16, 1980, as amended by Order No. 960–81, 46 FR 52360, Oct. 27, 1981; 51 FR 44288, Dec. 9, 1986]

§ 58.3   Qualification for membership on panels of private trustees.

(a) To be eligible for appointment to the panel and to retain eligibility therefor, an individual must possess the qualifications described in paragraph (b) of this section in addition to any other statutory qualifications. A corporation or partnership may qualify as an entity for appointment to the private panel. However, each person who, in the opinion of the U.S. Trustee or of the Director, performs duties as trustee on behalf of a corporation or partnership must individually meet the standards described in paragraph (b) of this section, except that each U.S. Trustee, with the approval of the Director, shall have the discretion to waive the applicability of paragraph (b)(6) of this section as to any individual in a non-supervisory position. No professional corporation, partnership, or similar entity organized for the practice of law or accounting shall be eligible to serve on the panel.

(b) The qualifications for membership on the panel are as follows:

(1) Possess integrity and good moral character.

(2) Be physically and mentally able to satisfactorily perform a trustee's duties.

(3) Be courteous and accessible to all parties with reasonable inquiries or comments about a case for which such individual is serving as private trustee.

(4) Be free of prejudices against any individual, entity, or group of individuals or entities which would interfere with unbiased performance of a trustee's duties.

(5) Not be related by affinity or consanguinity within the degree of first cousin to any employee of the Executive Office for United States Trustees of the Department of Justice, or to any employee of the office of the U.S. Trustee for the district in which he or she is applying.

(6)(i) Be a member in good standing of the bar of the highest court of a state or of the District of Columbia; or

(ii) Be a certified public accountant; or

(iii) Hold a bachelor's degree from a full four-year course of study (or the equivalent) of an accredited college or university (accredited as described in part II, section III of Handbook X118 promulgated by the U.S. Office of Personnel Management) with a major in a business-related field of study or at least 20 semester-hours of business-related courses; or hold a master's or doctoral degree in a business-related field of study from a college or university of the type described above; or

(iv) Be a senior law student or candidate for a master's degree in business administration recommended by the relevant law school or business school dean and working under the direct supervision of:

(A) A member of a law school faculty; or

(B) A member of the panel of private trustees; or

(C) A member of a program established by the local bar association to provide clinical experience to students; or

(v) Have equivalent experience as deemed acceptable by the U.S. Trustee.

(7) Be willing to provide reports as required by the U.S. Trustee.

(8) Have submitted an application under oath, in the form prescribed by the Director, to the U.S. Trustee for the District in which appointment is sought: *Provided*, That this provision may be waived by the U.S. Trustee on approval of the Director.

§ 58.4   Qualifications for appointment as standing trustee and fiduciary standards.

(a) As used in this section—

(1) The term standing trustee means an individual appointed pursuant to 28 U.S.C. 586(b).

(2) The term relative means an individual who is related to the standing trustee as father, mother, son, daughter, brother, sister, uncle, aunt, first cousin, nephew, niece, husband, wife, father-in-law, mother-in-law, son-in-law, daughter-in-law, brother-in-law, sister-in-law, stepfather, stepmother, stepson, stepdaughter, stepbrother, stepsister, half brother, half sister, or an individual whose close association to the standing trustee is the equivalent of a spousal relationship.

(3) The term financial or ownership interest excludes ownership of stock in a publicly-traded company if the ownership interest in not controlling.

(4) The word region means the geographical area defined in 28 U.S.C. 581.

(b) To be eligible for appointment as a standing trustee, an individual must have the qualifications for membership on a private panel of trustees set forth in §§ 58.3(b)(1)–(4), (6)–(8). An individual need not be an attorney to be eligible for appointment as a standing trustee. A corporation or partnership may be appointed as standing trustee only with the approval of the Director.

(c) The United States Trustee shall not appoint as a standing trustee any individuals who, at the time of appointment, is:

(1) A relative of another standing trustee in the region in which the standing trustee is to be appointed;

(2) A relative of a standing trustee (in the region in which the standing trustee is to be appointed), who, within the preceding one-year period, died, resigned, or was removed as a standing trustee from a case;

(3) A relative of a bankruptcy judge or a clerk of the bankruptcy court in the region in which the standing trustee is to be appointed;

(4) An employee of the Department of Justice within the preceding one-year period; or

(5) A relative of a United States Trustee or an Assistant United States Trustee, a relative of an employee in any of the offices of the United States Trustee in the region in which the standing trustee is to be appointed, or a relative of an employee in the Executive Office for United States Trustees.

(d) A standing trustee must, at a minimum, adhere to the following fiduciary standards:

(1) Employment of relatives.

(i) A standing trustee shall not employ a relative of the standing trustee.

(ii) A standing trustee shall also not employ a relative of the United States Trustee or of an Assistant United States Trustee in the region in which the trustee has been appointed or a relative of a bankruptcy court judge or of the clerk of the bankruptcy court in the judicial district in which the trustee has been appointed.

(iii)(A) Paragraphs (d)(1)(i) and (ii) of this section shall not apply to a spouse of a standing trustee who was employed by the standing trustee as of August 1, 1995.

(B) For all other relatives employed by a standing trustee as of August 1, 1995, paragraphs (d)(1)(i) and (ii) of this section shall be fully implemented by October 1, 1998, unless specifically provided below:

(1) The United States Trustee shall have the discretion to grant a written waiver for a period of time not to exceed 2 years upon a written showing by the standing trustee of compelling circumstances that make the continued employment of a relative necessary for a standing trustee's performance of his or her duties and written evidence that the salary to be paid is at or below market rate.

(2) Additional waivers, not to exceed a period of two years each, may be granted under paragraph (d)(1)(iii)(B)(1) of this section provided the standing trustee makes a similar written showing within 90 days prior to the expiration of a present waiver and the United States Trustee determines that the circumstances for waiver are met.

(3) No waivers will be granted for a relative of the United States Trustee or of an Assistant United States Trustee.

(2) Related Party Transactions.

(i) A standing trustee shall not direct debtors or creditors of a bankruptcy case administered by the standing trustee to an individual or entity that provides products or services, such as insurance or financial counseling, if a standing trustee is a relative of that individual or if the standing trustee or relative has a financial or ownership interest in the entity.

(ii) A standing trustee shall not, on behalf of the trust, contract or allocate expenses with himself or herself, with a relative, or with any entity in which the standing trustee or a relative of the standing trustee has a financial or ownership interest if the costs are to be paid as an expense out of the fiduciary expense fund.

(iii)(A) The United States Trustee may grant a waiver from compliance with paragraph (d)(2)(ii) of this section for up to three years following the appointment of a standing trustee if the newly-appointed standing trustee can demonstrate in writing that a waiver is necessary and the cost is at or below market.

(B) The United States Trustee may grant a provisional waiver from compliance with the allocation prohibition contained in paragraph (d)(2)(ii) of this section if one of the following conditions is present:

(1) A standing trustee has insufficient receipts to earn maximum annual compensation as determined by the Director during any one of the last three fiscal years and provides the United States Trustee with an appraisal or other written evidence that the allocation is necessary and the allocated cost is at or below market rate for that good or service, or

(2) A chapter 13 standing trustee also serves as a trustee in chapter 12 cases and provides the United States Trustee with an appraisal or other written evidence that the allocation is necessary and the allocated cost is at or below market rate for that good or service.

(C) Except as otherwise provided in this paragraph, a standing trustee may seek a reasonable extension of time from the United States Trustee to comply with paragraph (d)(2)(ii) of this section. To obtain an extension, a standing trustee must demonstrate by an appraisal or other written evidence, satisfactory to the United States Trustee, that the expense is necessary and at or below market rate. In no event shall an extension be granted for the use and occupation of real estate beyond October 1, 2005. For personal property and personal service contracts, no extension shall be granted beyond October 1, 1998.

(3) Employment of other standing trustees. A standing trustee shall not employ or contract with

another standing trustee to provide personal services for compensation payable from the fiduciary expense fund. This section does not prohibit the standing trustee from reimbursing the actual, necessary expenses incurred by another standing trustee who provides necessary assistance to the standing trustee provided that the reimbursement has been pre-approved by the United States Trustee.

(e) Paragraph (d) of this section is effective July 2, 1997. As to those standing trustees who are appointed as of July 2, 1997, paragraph (d) will be applicable on the first day of their next fiscal year (i.e., October 1, 1997, for chapter 13 trustees and January 1, 1998, for chapter 12 trustees).

[62 FR 30183, June 2, 1997]

§ 58.5   Non-discrimination in appointment.

The U.S. Trustees shall not discriminate on the basis of race, color, religion, sex, national origin or age in appointments to the private panel of trustees or of standing trustees and in this regard shall assure equal opportunity for all appointees and applicants for appointment to the private panel of trustees or as standing trustee. Each U.S. Trustee shall be guided by the policies and requirements of Executive Order 11478 of August 8, 1969, relating to equal employment opportunity in the Federal Government, section 717 of the Civil Rights Act of 1964, as amended (42 U.S.C. 2000e–16), section 15 of the Age Discrimination in Employment Act of 1967, as amended (29 U.S.C. 633a), and the regulations of the Office of Personnel Management relating to equal employment opportunity (5 CFR part 713).

[Order No. 921–80, 45 FR 82631, Dec. 16, 1980, as amended by Order No. 960–81, 46 FR 52360, Oct. 27, 1981]

§ 58.6   Procedures for suspension and removal of panel trustees and standing trustees.

(a) A United States Trustee shall notify a panel trustee or a standing trustee in writing of any decision to suspend or terminate the assignment of cases to the trustee including, where applicable, any decision not to renew the trustee's term appointment. The notice shall state the reason(s) for the decision and should refer to, or be accompanied by copies of, pertinent materials upon which the United States Trustee has relied and any prior communications in which the United States Trustee has advised the trustee of the potential action. The notice shall be sent to the office of the trustee by overnight courier, for delivery the next business day. The reasons may include, but are in no way limited to:

(1) Failure to safeguard or to account for estate funds and assets;

(2) Failure to perform duties in a timely and consistently satisfactory manner;

(3) Failure to comply with the provisions of the Code, the Bankruptcy Rules, and local rules of court;

(4) Failure to cooperate and to comply with orders, instructions and policies of the court, the bankruptcy clerk or the United States Trustee;

(5) Substandard performance of general duties and case management in comparison to other members of the chapter 7 panel or other standing trustees;

(6) Failure to display proper temperament in dealing with judges, clerks, attorneys, creditors, debtors, the United States Trustee and the general public;

(7) Failure to adequately monitor the work of professionals or others employed by the trustee to assist in the administration of cases;

(8) Failure to file timely, accurate reports, including interim reports, final reports, and final accounts;

(9) Failure to meet the eligibility requirements of 11 U.S.C. 321 or the qualifications set forth in 28 CFR 58.3 and 58.4 and in 11 U.S.C. 322;

(10) Failure to attend in person or appropriately conduct the 11 U.S.C. 341(a) meeting of creditors;

(11) Action by or pending before a court or state licensing agency which calls the trustee's competence, financial responsibility or trustworthiness into question;

(12) Routine inability to accept assigned cases due to conflicts of interest or to the trustee's unwillingness or incapacity to serve;

(13) Change in the composition of the chapter 7 panel pursuant to a system established by the United States Trustee under 28 CFR 58.1;

(14) A determination by the United States Trustee that the interests of efficient case administration or a decline in the number of cases warrant a reduction in the number of panel trustees or standing trustees.

(b) The notice shall advise the trustee that the decision is final and unreviewable unless the trustee requests in writing a review by the Director, Executive Office for United States Trustees, no later than 20 calendar days from the date of issuance of the United States Trustee's notice ("request for review"). In order to be timely, a request for review must be received by the Office of the Director no later than 20 calendar days from the date of the United States Trustee's notice to the trustee.

(c) A decision by a United States Trustee to suspend or terminate the assignment of cases to a trustee shall take effect upon the expiration of a trustee's time to seek review from the Director or, if the trustee timely seeks such review, upon the issuance of a final written decision by the Director.

(d) Notwithstanding paragraph (c) of this section, a United States Trustee's decision to suspend or terminate the assignment of cases to a trustee may include, or may later be supplemented by an interim directive, by which the United States trustee may immediately discontinue assigning cases to a trustee during the review period. A United States Trustee may issue such an interim directive if the United States Trustee specifically finds that:

(1) A continued assignment of cases to the trustee places the safety of estate assets at risk;

(2) The trustee appears to be ineligible to serve under applicable law, rule, or regulation;

(3) The trustee has engaged in conduct that appears to be dishonest, deceitful, fraudulent, or criminal in nature; or

(4) The trustee appears to have engaged in other gross misconduct that is unbefitting his or her position as trustee or violates the trustee's duties.

(e) If the United States Trustee issues an interim directive, the trustee may seek a stay of the interim directive from the Director if the trustee has timely filed a request for review under paragraph (b) of this section.

(f) The trustee's written request for review shall fully describe why the trustee disagrees with the United States Trustee's decision, and shall be accompanied by all documents and materials that the trustee wants the Director to consider in reviewing the decision. The trustee shall send a copy of the request for review, and the accompanying documents and materials, to the United States Trustee by overnight courier, for delivery the next business day. The trustee may request that specific documents in the possession of the United States Trustee be transmitted to the Director for inclusion in the record.

(g) The United States Trustee shall have 15 calendar days from the date of the trustee's request for review to submit to the Director a written response regarding the matters raised in the trustee's request for review. The United States Trustee shall provide a copy of this response to the trustee. Both copies shall be sent by overnight courier, for delivery the next business day.

(h) The Director may seek additional information from any party in the manner and to the extent the Director deems appropriate.

(i) Unless the trustee and the United States Trustee agree to a longer period of time, the Director shall issue a written decision no later than 30 calendar days from the receipt of the United States Trustee's response to the trustee's request for review. That decision shall determine whether the United States Trustee's decision is supported by the record and the action is an appropriate exercise of the United States Trustee's discretion, and shall adopt, modify or reject the United States Trustee's decision to suspend or terminate the assignment of future cases to the trustee. The Director's decision shall constitute final agency action.

(j) In reaching a determination, the Director may specify a person to act as a reviewing official. The reviewing official shall not be a person who was involved in the United States Trustee's decision or a Program employee who is located within the region of the United States Trustee who made the decision. The reviewing official's duties shall be specified by the Director on a case by case basis, and may include reviewing the record, obtaining additional information from the participants, providing the Director with written recommendations, or such other duties as the Director shall prescribe in a particular case.

(k) This rule does not authorize a trustee to seek review of any decision to increase the size of the chapter 7 panel or to appoint additional standing trustees in the district or region.

(*l*) A trustee who files a request for review shall bear his or her own costs and expenses, including counsel fees.

[62 FR 51750, Oct. 2, 1997]

§ 58.7   Procedures for Completing Uniform Forms of Trustee Final Reports in Cases Filed Under Chapters 7, 12, and 13 of the Bankruptcy Code.

(a) UST Form 101–7–TFR, Chapter 7 Trustee's Final Report. A chapter 7 trustee must complete UST Form 101–7–TFR final report (TFR) in preparation for closing an asset case. This report must be submitted to the United States Trustee after liquidating the estate's assets, but before making distribution to creditors, and before filing it with the United States Bankruptcy Court. The TFR must contain the trustee's certification, under penalty of perjury, that all assets have been liquidated or properly accounted for and that funds of the estate are available for distribution. Pursuant to 28 U.S.C. 589b(d), the TFR must also contain the following:

(1) Summary of the trustee's case administration;

(2) Copies of the estate's financial records;

(3) List of allowed claims;

(4) Fees and administrative expenses; and

(5) Proposed dividend distribution to creditors.

(b) UST Form 101–7–NFR Chapter 7 Trustee's Notice of Trustee's Final Report. After the TFR has been reviewed by the United States Trustee and filed with the United States Bankruptcy Court, if the net proceeds realized in an estate exceed the amounts specified in Fed. R. Bankr. P. 2002(f)(8), UST Form 101–7–NFR (NFR) must be sent to all creditors as the notice required under Fed. R. Bankr. P. 2002(f). The NFR must show the receipts, approved disbursements, and any balance identified on the TFR, as well as the information required in the TFR's Exhibit D. In addition, the NFR must identify the procedures for objecting to any fee application or to the TFR.

(c) UST Form 101–7–TDR Chapter 7 Trustee's Final Account, Certification The Estate Has Been Fully Administered and Application of Trustee To Be Discharged. After distributing all estate funds, a trustee must submit to the United States Trustee and file with the United States Bankruptcy Court the trustee's final account, UST Form 101–7–TDR (TDR). The TDR must contain the trustee's certification, under penalty of perjury, that the estate has been fully administered and the trustee's request to be discharged as trustee. Pursuant to 28 U.S.C. 589b(d), the TDR must also include the following:

(1) The length of time the case was pending;

(2) Assets abandoned;

(3) Assets exempted;

(4) Receipts and disbursements of the estate;

(5) Claims asserted;

(6) Claims allowed; and,

(7) Distributions to claimants and claims discharged without payment, in each case by appropriate category.

(d) UST Form 101–7–NDR Chapter 7 Trustee's Report of No Distribution. In cases where there is no distribution of funds the case trustee must submit to the United States Trustee and file with the United States Bankruptcy Court UST Form 101–7–NDR (NDR). The NDR must contain the trustee's certification that the estate has been fully administered, that the trustee has neither received nor disbursed any property or money on account of the estate, and that there is no property available for distribution over and above that exempted by law. In addition, the NDR must set forth the trustee's request to be discharged as trustee. Pursuant to 28 U.S.C. 589b(d), the NDR must also include the following information:

(1) The length of time the case was pending;

(2) Assets abandoned;

(3) Assets exempted;

(4) Claims asserted;

(5) Claims scheduled; and,

(6) claims scheduled to be discharged without payment.

(e) UST Form 101–12–FR–S, Chapter 12 Standing Trustee's Final Report and Account and UST Form 101–13–FR–S, Chapter 13 Standing Trustee's Final Report and Account. After the final distribution to creditors in a chapter 12 or 13 case in which a standing trustee has been appointed, a trustee must submit to the United States Trustee and file with the United States Bankruptcy Court either UST Form 101–12–FR–S for chapter 12 cases or UST Form 101–13–FR–S for chapter 13 cases, which are the trustee's final report and account. In these forms, a trustee must include a certification that the estate has been fully administered if not converted to another

chapter and a request to be discharged as trustee. Pursuant to 28 U.S.C. 589b(d), these forms must also include the following information:

(1) The length of time the case was pending;

(2) Assets abandoned;

(3) Assets exempted;

(4) Receipts and disbursements of the estate;

(5) Expenses of administration, including for use under section 707(b), actual costs of administering cases under chapter 12 or 13 (as applicable) of title 11;

(6) Claims asserted;

(7) Claims allowed;

(8) Distributions to claimants and claims discharged without payment, in each case by appropriate category;

(9) Date of confirmation of the plan;

(10) Date of each modification thereto; and,

(11) Defaults by the debtor in performance under the plan.

(f) UST Form 101–12–FR–C, Chapter 12 Case Trustee's Final Report and Account, and UST Form 101–13–FR–C, Chapter 13 Case Trustee's Final Report and Account. After the final distribution to creditors in a chapter 12 or 13 case in which a case trustee has been appointed, the trustee must submit to the United States Trustee and file with the United States Bankruptcy Court either UST Form 101–12–FR–C for chapter 12 cases, or UST Form 101–13–FR–C for chapter 13 cases, which are the trustee's final report and account. In these forms, a trustee must include a certification, submitted under penalty of perjury, that the estate has been fully administered if not converted to another chapter and the trustee's request to be discharged from further duties as trustee. Pursuant to 28 U.S.C. 589b(d), these forms must also include the following information:

(1) The length of time the case was pending;

(2) Assets abandoned;

(3) Assets exempted;

(4) Receipts and disbursements of the estate;

(5) Expenses of administration, including for use under section 707(b), actual costs of administering cases under chapter 12 or 13 (as applicable) of title 11;

(6) Claims asserted;

(7) Claims allowed;

(8) Distributions to claimants and claims discharged without payment, in each case by appropriate category;

(9) Date of confirmation of the plan;

(10) Date of each modification thereto; and,

(11) defaults by the debtor in performance under the plan.

(g) Mandatory Usage of Uniform Forms. The Uniform Forms associated with this rule must be utilized by trustees when completing their final reports and final accounts. All trustees serving in districts where a United States Trustee is serving must use the Uniform Forms in the administration of their cases, in the same manner, and with the same content, as set forth in this rule:

(1) All Uniform Forms may be electronically or mechanically reproduced so long as all the content and the form remain consistent with the Uniform Forms as they are posted on EOUST's Web site;

(2) The Uniform Forms shall be filed via the United States Bankruptcy Courts Case Management/Electronic Case Filing System (CM/ECF) as a "smart form" meaning the forms are data enabled, unless the court offers an automated process that has been approved by EOUST, such as the virtual NDR event through CM/ECF.

[73 FR 58444, Oct. 7, 2008]

§ 58.11   **Procedures governing administrative review of a United States Trustee's decision to deny a Chapter 12 or Chapter 13 standing Trustee's claim of actual, necessary expenses.**

(a) The following definitions apply to this section. These terms shall have these meanings:

(1) The term claim of actual, necessary expenses means the request by a chapter 12 or chapter 13 standing trustee for the United States Trustee's approval of the trustee's projected expenses for each fiscal year budget, or for an amendment to the current budget when an increase in an individual expense line item is greater than both 10% of the budgeted amount and $5,000.00. Expenses for certain items require prior United States Trustee approval regardless of amount;

(2) The term director means the person designated or acting as the Director of the Executive Office for United States Trustees;

(3) The term final decision means the written determination issued by the Director based upon the review of the United States Trustee's decision to deny all or part of a trustee's claim of actual, necessary expenses;

(4) The term notice means the written communication from the United States Trustee to a trustee that the trustee's claim of actual, necessary expenses has been denied in whole or in part;

(5) The term request for review means the written communication from a trustee to the Director seeking review of the United States Trustee's decision to deny, in whole or in part, the trustee's claim of actual, necessary expenses;

(6) The term trustee means an individual appointed by the United States Trustee under 28 U.S.C. 586(b) to serve as the standing trustee for chapter 12 or chapter 13 cases in a particular region; and

(7) The term United States Trustee means, alternatively:

(i) A United States Trustee appointed under 28 U.S.C. 581; or

(ii) A person acting as a United States Trustee under 28 U.S.C. 585.

(b) The United States Trustee may issue a decision to deny a trustee's claim of actual, necessary expenses. Reasons for denial include, but are not limited to, finding that the trustee failed to do any of the following:

(1) Provide to the United States Trustee sufficient justification for the expense;

(2) Demonstrate to the United States Trustee that the expense is a cost effective use of funds;

(3) Demonstrate to the United States Trustee that the expense is reasonably related to the duties of the trustee;

(4) Obtain authorization from the United States Trustee prior to making an expenditure that was not provided for in the current budget;

(5) Provide the United States Trustee with documents, materials, or other information pertaining to the expense;

(6) Timely submit to the United States Trustee accurate budgets or requests for amendment of budgets to cover the additional expense; or

(7) Demonstrate to the United States Trustee that the expense is directly related to office operations.

(c) Before issuing a notice of denial, the United States Trustee shall communicate in writing with the trustee in an attempt to resolve any dispute over a claim of actual, necessary expenses:

(1) For disputes involving the trustee's projected expenses for the upcoming fiscal year budget, the United States Trustee shall either resolve the dispute or issue a notice of denial no later than July 30 of the current calendar year for a chapter 12 standing trustee or October 31 of the current calendar year for a chapter 13 standing trustee, or if the United States Trustee has requested additional information, 30 calendar days from submission of the additional information if such submission is after July 1 for a chapter 12 standing trustee or October 1 for a chapter 13 standing trustee, unless the trustee and United States Trustee agree to a longer period of time. Any projected expenses not specifically disputed shall be approved in the ordinary course and the trustee's fee shall be set on an interim basis;

(2) For disputes over amendments to the current year budget, the United States Trustee shall either resolve the dispute or issue a notice of denial no later than 30 calendar days after the trustee's amendment request, or if the United States Trustee has requested additional information, 30 calendar days from submis-

sion of the additional information, unless the trustee and the United States Trustee agree to a longer period of time. Any portion of the amendment not specifically disputed shall be approved in the ordinary course;

(3) If the United States Trustee does not resolve the dispute or issue a notice of denial within the time frames identified in (c)(1) or (2) of this section, the trustee's claim of actual, necessary expenses shall be deemed denied on the next business day following expiration of the time frames identified in (c)(1) or (2) of this section.

(d) The United States Trustee shall notify a trustee in writing of any decision denying a trustee's claim of actual, necessary expenses. The notice shall state the reason(s) for the decision and shall reference any documents or communications relied upon in reaching the decision. The United States Trustee shall provide to the trustee copies of any such non-privileged documents that were not supplied to the United States Trustee by the trustee. The notice shall be sent to the trustee by overnight courier, for delivery the next business day.

(e) The notice shall advise the trustee that the decision is final and unreviewable unless the trustee requests in writing a review by the Director no later than 21 calendar days from the date of the notice to the trustee. If the United States Trustee did not issue a notice of denial, and the expenses were deemed denied under (c)(3) of this section, the trustee shall have 21 calendar days from the date on which the expenses were deemed denied to submit a request for review to the Director.

(f) The decision to deny a trustee's claim of actual, necessary expenses shall take effect upon the expiration of a trustee's time to seek review from the Director or, if the trustee timely seeks such review, upon the issuance of a final decision by the Director.

(g) The trustee's request for review shall be in writing and shall fully describe why the trustee disagrees with the United States Trustee's decision, and shall be accompanied by all documents and materials the trustee wants the Director to consider in reviewing the United States Trustee's decision. The trustee shall send the original and one copy of the request for review, including all accompanying documents and materials, to the Office of the Director by overnight courier, for delivery the next business day. In order to be timely, a request for review shall be received at the Office of the Director no later than 21 calendar days from the date of the notice to the trustee or the date the expenses were deemed denied. The trustee shall also send a copy of the request for review to the United States Trustee by overnight courier, for delivery the next business day.

(h) The United States Trustee shall have 21 calendar days from the date of the trustee's request for review to submit to the Director a written response regarding the matters raised in the trustee's request for review. The United States Trustee shall provide a copy of this response to the trustee by overnight courier, for delivery the next business day.

(i) The Director may seek additional non-privileged information from any party, in the manner and to the extent the Director deems appropriate.

(j) In reviewing the decision to deny a trustee's claim of actual, necessary expenses, the Director shall determine:

(1) Whether the decision is supported by the record; and

(2) Whether the decision constitutes an appropriate exercise of discretion.

(k) The Director shall issue a final decision no later than 90 calendar days from the receipt of the trustee's request for review, or, if the Director has requested additional information, 30 calendar days from submission of the additional information, unless the trustee agrees to a longer period of time. The Director's final decision on the trustee's request for review shall constitute final agency action.

(l) In reaching a final decision the Director may specify a person to act as a reviewing official. The reviewing official may not be under the supervision of the United States Trustee who denied the trustee's claim of actual, necessary expenses. The reviewing official's duties shall be specified by the Director on a case-by-case basis, and may include reviewing the record, obtaining additional information from the participants, providing the Director with written recommendations, and such other duties as the Director shall prescribe in a particular case.

(m) This rule does not authorize a trustee to seek review of any decision to change maximum annual compensation, to decrease or increase appointments of trustees in a region or district, to change the trustee's percentage fee, or to suspend, terminate, or remove a trustee.

(n) A trustee must exhaust all administrative remedies before seeking redress in any court of competent jurisdiction.

[76 FR 31228, May 31, 2011]

§ 58.12 Definitions.

(a) The following definitions apply to §§ 58.12 through and including 58.24 of this Part and the applications and other materials agencies submit in an effort to establish they meet the requirements necessary to become an approved nonprofit budget and credit counseling agency.

(b) These terms shall have these meanings:

(1) The term "accreditation" means the recognition or endorsement that an accrediting organization bestows upon an agency because the accrediting organiza-

tion has determined the agency meets or exceeds all the accrediting organization's standards;

(2) The term "accrediting organization" means either an entity that provides accreditation to agencies or provides certification to counselors, provided, however, that an accrediting organization shall:

(i) Not be an agency or affiliate of any agency; and

(ii) Be deemed acceptable by the United States Trustee;

(3) The term "adequate counseling" means the actual receipt by a client from an approved agency of all counseling services, and all other applicable services, rights, and protections specified in:

(i) 11 U.S.C. 109(h);

(ii) 11 U.S.C. 111; and

(iii) This part;

(4) The term "affiliate of an agency" includes:

(i) Every entity that is an affiliate of the agency, as the term "affiliate" is defined in 11 U.S.C. 101(2), except that the word "agency" shall be substituted for the word "debtor" in 11 U.S.C. 101(2);

(ii) Each of an agency's officers and each of an agency's directors; and

(iii) Every relative of an agency's officers and every relative of an agency's directors;

(5) The term "agency" and the term "budget and credit counseling agency" shall each mean a nonprofit organization that is applying under this part for United States Trustee approval to be included on a publicly available list in one or more United States district courts, as authorized by 11 U.S.C. 111(a)(1), and shall also mean, whenever appropriate, an approved agency;

(6) The term "application" means the application and related forms, including appendices, approved by the Office of Management and Budget as form EOUST–CC1, Application for Approval as a Nonprofit Budget and Credit Counseling Agency, as it shall be amended from time to time;

(7) The term "approved agency" means an agency currently approved by a United States Trustee under 11 U.S.C. 111 as an approved nonprofit budget and credit counseling agency eligible to be included on one or more lists maintained under 11 U.S.C. 111(a)(1);

(8) The term "approved list" means the list of agencies currently approved by a United States Trustee under 11 U.S.C. 111, as currently published on the United States Trustee Program's Internet site, which is located on the United States Department of Justice's Internet site;

(9) The term "audited financial statements" means financial reports audited by independent certified public accountants in accordance with generally accepted accounting principles as defined by the American Institute of Certified Public Accountants;

(10) The term "certificate" means the certificate identified in 11 U.S.C. 521(b)(1) that an approved agency shall provide to a client after the client completes counseling services;

(11) The term "client" means an individual who both seeks and receives (or sought and received) counseling services from an approved agency;

(12) The term "counseling services" means all counseling required by 11 U.S.C. 109(h) and 111, and this part including, without limitation, services that are typically of at least 60 minutes in duration and that shall at a minimum include:

(i) Performing on behalf of, and providing to, each client a written analysis of that client's current financial condition, which analysis shall include a budget analysis, consideration of all alternatives to resolve a client's credit problems, discussion of the factors that caused such financial condition, and identification of all methods by which the client can develop a plan to respond to the financial problems without incurring negative amortization of debt; and

(ii) Providing each client the opportunity to have the agency negotiate an alternative payment schedule with regard to each unsecured consumer debt under terms as set forth in 11 U.S.C. 502(k) or, if the client accepts this option and the agency is unable to provide this service, the agency shall refer the client to another approved agency in the appropriate federal judicial district that provides it;

(13) The term "counselor certification" means certification of a counselor by an accrediting organization because the accrediting organization has determined the counselor meets or exceeds all the accrediting organization's standards for counseling services or related areas, such as personal finance, budgeting, or credit or debt management;

(14) The term "criminal background check" means a report generated by a state law enforcement authority disclosing the entire state criminal history record, if any, of the counselor for whom the criminal background check is sought, for every state where the counselor has resided or worked during any part of the immediately preceding five years. If a criminal background check is not available for, or is not authorized by state law in, each of the states where the counselor has resided or worked during any part of the immediately preceding five years, the agency shall instead obtain at least every five years a sworn statement from each counselor attesting to whether the counselor has been convicted of a felony, or a crime involving fraud, dishonesty, or false statements;

(15) The term "debt repayment plan" means any written document suggested, drafted, or reviewed by an approved agency that either proposes or implements any mechanism by which a client would make payments to any creditor or creditors if, during the

time any such payments are being made, that creditor or those creditors would forbear from collecting or otherwise enforcing their claim or claims against the client; provided, however, that any such written document shall not constitute a debt repayment plan if the client would incur a negative amortization of debt under it;

(16) The term "Director" means the person designated or acting as the Director of the Executive Office for United States Trustees;

(17) The term "entity" shall have the meaning given that term in 11 U.S.C. 101(15);

(18) The term "fair share" means payments by a creditor to an approved agency for administering a debt repayment plan;

(19) The terms "fee" and "fee policy" each mean the aggregate of all fees, contributions, and payments an approved agency charges clients for providing counseling services; "fee policy" shall also mean the objective criteria the agency uses in determining whether to waive or reduce any fee, contribution, or payment;

(20) The term "final decision" means the written determination issued by the Director based upon the review of the United States Trustee's decision either to deny an agency's application or to remove an agency from the approved list;

(21) The term "financial benefit" means any interest equated with money or its equivalent, including, but not limited to, stocks, bonds, other investments, income, goods, services, or receivables;

(22) The term "governmental unit" shall have the meaning given that term in 11 U.S.C. 101(27);

(23) The term "independent contractor" means a person or entity who provides any goods or services to an approved agency other than as an employee and as to whom the approved agency does not:

(i) Direct or control the means or methods of delivery of the goods or services being provided;

(ii) Make financial decisions concerning the business aspects of the goods or services being provided; and

(iii) Have any common employees;

(24) The term "languages offered" means every language other than English in which an approved agency provides counseling services;

(25) The term "legal advice" shall have the meaning given that term in 11 U.S.C. 110(e)(2);

(26) The term "limited English proficiency" refers to individuals who:

(i) Do not speak English as their primary language; and

(ii) Have a limited ability to read, write, speak, or understand English;

(27) The term "material change" means, alternatively, any change:

(i) In the name, structure, principal contact, management, counselors, physical location, counseling services, fee policy, language services, or method of delivery of an approved agency; or

(ii) That renders inapplicable, inaccurate, incomplete, or misleading any statement an agency or approved agency previously made:

(A) In its application or related materials; or

(B) To the United States Trustee;

(28) The term "method of delivery" means one or more of the three methods by which an approved agency can provide some component of counseling services to its clients, including:

(i) "In person" delivery, which applies when a client primarily receives counseling services at a physical location with a credit counselor physically present in that location, and with the credit counselor providing oral and/or written communication to the client at the facility;

(ii) "Telephone" delivery, which applies when a client primarily receives counseling services by telephone; and

(iii) "Internet" delivery, which applies when a client primarily receives counseling services through an Internet Web site;

(29) The term "nonprofit" means, alternatively:

(i) An entity validly organized as a not-for-profit entity under applicable state or federal law, if that entity operates as a not-for-profit entity in full compliance with all applicable state and federal laws; or

(ii) A qualifying governmental unit;

(30) The term "notice" in § 58.24 means the written communication from the United States Trustee to an agency that its application to become an approved agency has been denied or to an approved agency that it is being removed from the approved list;

(31) The term "potential client" means an individual who seeks, but does not receive, counseling services from an approved agency.

(32) The term "qualifying government unit" means any governmental unit that, were it not a governmental unit, would qualify for tax-exempt status under 26 U.S.C. 501(c)(3), or would qualify as a nonprofit entity under applicable state law;

(33) The term "referral fees" means money or any other valuable consideration paid or transferred between an approved agency and another entity in return for that entity, directly or indirectly, identifying, referring, securing, or in any other way encouraging any client or potential client to receive counseling services from the approved agency; provided, however, that "referral fees" shall not include fees paid to the agency under a fair share agreement;

(34) The term "relative" shall have the meaning given that term in 11 U.S.C. 101(45);

(35) The term "request for review" means the written communication from an agency to the Director seeking review of the United States Trustee's decision either to deny the agency's application or to remove the agency from the approved list;

(36) The term "state" means state, commonwealth, district, or territory of the United States;

(37) The term "tax waiver" means a document sufficient to permit the Internal Revenue Service to release directly to the United States Trustee information about an agency;

(38) The term "trust account" means an account with a federally insured depository institution that is separated and segregated from operating accounts, which an approved agency shall maintain in its fiduciary capacity for the purpose of receiving and holding client funds entrusted to the approved agency; and

(39) The term "United States Trustee" means, alternatively:

(i) The Executive Office for United States Trustees;

(ii) A United States Trustee appointed under 28 U.S.C. 581;

(iii) A person acting as a United States Trustee;

(iv) An employee of a United States Trustee; or

(v) Any other entity authorized by the Attorney General to act on behalf of the United States under this part.

[78 FR 16150, March 14, 2013]

§ 58.13 Procedures all agencies shall follow when applying to become approved agencies.

(a) An agency applying to become an approved agency shall obtain an application, including appendices, from the United States Trustee.

(b) The agency shall complete the application, including its appendices, and attach the required supporting documents requested in the application.

(c) The agency shall submit the original of the completed application, including completed appendices and the required supporting documents, to the United States Trustee at the address specified on the application form.

(d) The application shall be signed by an agency representative who is authorized under applicable law to sign on behalf of the applying agency.

(e) The signed application, completed appendices, and required supporting documents shall be accompanied by a writing, signed by the signatory of the application and executed on behalf of the signatory and the agency, certifying the application does not:

(1) Falsify, conceal, or cover up by any trick, scheme or device a material fact;

(2) Make any materially false, fictitious, or fraudulent statement or representation; or

(3) Make or use any false writing or document knowing the same to contain any materially false, fictitious, or fraudulent statement or entry.

(f) The United States Trustee shall not consider an application, and it may be returned if:

(1) It is incomplete;

(2) It fails to include the completed appendices or all of the required supporting documents; or

(3) It is not accompanied by the certification identified in paragraph (e) of this section.

(g) The United States Trustee shall not consider an application on behalf of an agency, and it shall be returned if:

(1) It is submitted by any entity other than the agency; or

(2) Either the application or the accompanying certification is executed by any entity other than an agency representative who is authorized under applicable law to sign on behalf of the agency.

(h) By the act of submitting an application, an agency consents to the release and disclosure of its name, contact information, and non-confidential business information relating to the services it provides on the approved list should its application be approved.

[78 FR 16150, 16152, March 14, 2013]

§ 58.14 Automatic expiration of agencies' status as approved agencies.

(a) Except as provided in § 58.15(c), if an approved agency was not an approved agency immediately prior to the date it last obtained approval to be an approved agency, such an approved agency shall cease to be an approved agency six months from the date on which it was approved unless the United States Trustee approves an additional one year period.

(b) Except as provided in § 58.15(c), if an approved agency was an approved agency immediately prior to the date it last obtained approval to be an approved agency, such an agency shall cease to be an approved agency one year from the date on which it was last approved to be an approved agency unless the United States Trustee approves an additional one year period.

[78 FR 16150, 16152, March 14, 2013]

§ 58.15 Procedures all approved agencies shall follow when applying for approval to act as an approved agency for an additional one year period.

(a) To be considered for approval to act as an approved agency for an additional one year term, an approved agency shall reapply by complying with all the requirements specified for agencies under 11 U.S.C. 109(h) and 111, and under this part.

(b) Such an agency shall apply no later than 45 days prior to the expiration of its six month probationary period or annual period to be considered for approval for an additional one year period, unless a written extension is granted by the United States Trustee.

(c) An approved agency that has complied with all prerequisites for applying to act as an approved agency for an additional one year period may continue to operate as an approved agency while its application is under review by the United States Trustee, so long as either the application for an additional one year period is timely submitted, or an agency receives a written extension from the United States Trustee.

[71 FR 38078, July 5, 2006; 78 FR 16152, March 14, 2013]

§ 58.16   Renewal for an additional one year period.

If an approved agency's application for an additional one year period is approved, such renewal period shall begin to run from the later of:

(a) The day after the expiration date of the immediately preceding approval period; or

(b) The actual date of approval of such renewal by the United States Trustee.

[71 FR 38078, 38080, July 5, 2006; 78 FR 16152, March 14, 2013]

§ 58.17   Mandatory duty of approved agencies to notify United States Trustees of material changes.

(a) An approved agency shall immediately notify the United States Trustee in writing of any material change.

(b) An approved agency shall immediately notify the United States Trustee in writing of any failure by the approved agency to comply with any standard or requirement specified in 11 U.S.C. 109(h) or 111, this part, or the terms under which the United States Trustee approved it to act as an approved agency.

(c) An approved agency shall immediately notify the United States Trustee in writing of any of the following events:

(1) Notification by the Internal Revenue Service or by a state or local taxing authority that the approved agency has been selected for audit or examination regarding its tax-exempt status, or any notification of a compliance check by the Internal Revenue Service or by a state or local taxing authority;

(2) Revocation or termination of the approved agency's tax-exempt status by any governmental unit or by any judicial officer;

(3) Cessation of business by the approved agency or by any office of the agency, or withdrawal from any

federal judicial district(s) where the approved agency is approved;

(4) Any investigation of, or any administrative or judicial action brought against, the approved agency by any governmental unit;

(5) Termination or cancellation of any surety bond or fidelity insurance;

(6) Any administrative or judicial action brought by any entity that seeks recovery against a surety bond or fidelity insurance;

(7) Any action by a governmental unit or a court to suspend or revoke the approved agency's articles of incorporation, or any license held by the approved agency, or any authorization necessary to engage in business;

(8) A suspension, or action to suspend, any accreditation held by the approved agency, or any withdrawal by the approved agency of any application for accreditation, or any denial of any application of the approved agency for accreditation;

(9) A change in the approved agency's nonprofit status under any applicable law;

(10) Any change in the banks or financial institutions used by the agency; and

(11) [Reserved]

(d) An agency shall notify the United States Trustee in writing if any of the changes identified in paragraphs (a) through (c) of this section occur while its application to become an approved agency is pending before the United States Trustee.

(e) An approved agency whose name or other information appears incorrectly on the approved list shall immediately submit a written request to the United States Trustee asking that the information be corrected.

[71 FR 38078, 38081, July 5, 2006; 78 FR 16152, March 14, 2013]

§ 58.18   Mandatory duty of approved agencies to obtain prior consent of the United States Trustee before taking certain actions.

(a) By accepting the designation to act as an approved agency, an agency agrees to obtain approval from the United States Trustee, prior to making any of the following changes:

(1) Cancellation or change in the amount of the surety bond or employee fidelity bond or insurance;

(2) The engagement of an independent contractor to provide counseling services or to have access to, possession of, or control over client funds;

(3) Any increase in the fees, contributions, or payments received from clients for counseling services or a change in the agency's fee policy;

(4) Expansion into additional federal judicial districts;

(5) Any changes to the method of delivery the approved agency employs to provide counseling services; or

(6) Any changes in the approved agency's counseling services.

(b) An agency applying to become an approved agency shall also obtain approval from the United States Trustee before taking any action specified in paragraph (a) of this section. It shall do so by submitting an amended application. The agency's amended application shall be accompanied by a contemporaneously executed writing, signed by the signatory of the application, that makes the certifications specified in § 58.13(e).

(c) An approved agency shall not transfer or assign its United States Trustee approval to act as an approved agency.

[78 FR 16153, March 14, 2013]

§ 58.19 Continuing requirements for becoming and remaining approved agencies.

(a) To become an approved agency, an agency must affirmatively establish, to the satisfaction of the United States Trustee, that the agency at the time of approval:

(1) Satisfies every requirement of this part; and

(2) Provides adequate counseling to its clients.

(b) To remain an approved agency, an approved agency shall affirmatively establish, to the satisfaction of the United States Trustee, that the approved agency:

(1) Has satisfied every requirement of this part;

(2) Has provided adequate counseling to its clients; and

(3) Would continue to satisfy both paragraphs (b)(1) and (2) of this section in the future.

[78 FR 16153, March 14, 2013]

§ 58.20 Minimum qualifications agencies shall meet to become and remain approved agencies.

To meet the minimum qualifications set forth in § 58.19, and in addition to the other requirements set forth in this part, agencies and approved agencies shall comply with paragraphs (a) through (p) of this section on a continuing basis:

(a) Compliance with all laws. An agency shall comply with all applicable laws and regulations of the United States and each state in which the agency provides counseling services including, without limitation, all laws governing licensing and registration.

(b) Prohibition on legal advice. An agency shall not provide legal advice.

(c) Structure and organization. An agency shall:

(1) Be lawfully organized and operated as a nonprofit entity; and

(2) Have a board of directors, the majority of which:

(i) Are not relatives;

(ii) Are not employed by such agency; and

(iii) Will not directly or indirectly benefit financially from the outcome of the counseling services provided by such agency.

(d) Ethical standards. An agency shall:

(1) Not engage in any conduct or transaction, other than counseling services, that generates a direct or indirect financial benefit for any member of the board of directors or trustees, officer, supervisor, or any relative thereof;

(2) Ensure no member of the board of directors or trustees, officer, or supervisor receives any commissions, incentives, bonuses, or benefits (monetary or non-monetary) of any kind that are directly or indirectly based on the financial or legal decisions any client makes after requesting counseling services;

(3) Ensure no member of the board of directors or trustees, officer or supervisor is a relative of an employee of the United States Trustee, a trustee appointed under 28 U.S.C. 586(a)(1) or (b) for any federal judicial district where the agency is providing or is applying to provide counseling services, a federal judge in any federal judicial district where the agency is providing or is applying to provide counseling services, a federal court employee in any federal judicial district where the agency is providing or is applying to provide counseling services, or a certified public accountant that audits the agency's trust account;

(4) Not enter into any referral agreement or receive any financial benefit that involves the agency paying to or receiving from any entity or person referral fees for the referral of clients to or by the agency, except payments under a fair share agreement;

(5) Not enter into agreements involving counseling services that create a conflict of interest; and

(6) Not provide counseling services to a client with whom the agency has a lender-borrower relationship.

(e) Use of credit counselors. An agency shall have a credit counselor provide the counseling services to each of the agency's clients. The credit counselor shall interact with the client regarding the accuracy of the information obtained from the client and the alternatives available to the client for dealing with his or her current financial situation, including the plan developed to address such financial situation.

(f) Credit counselor training, certification and experience. An agency shall:

(1) Use only counselors who possess adequate experience providing credit counseling, which shall mean that each counselor either:

(i) Holds a counselor certification and who has complied with all continuing education requirements necessary to maintain his or her counselor certification; or

(ii) Has successfully completed a course of study and worked a minimum of six months in a related area such as personal finance, budgeting, or credit or debt management. A course of study shall include training in counseling skills, personal finance, budgeting, or credit or debt management. A counselor shall also receive annual continuing education in the areas of counseling skills, personal finance, budgeting, or credit or debt management;

(2) Demonstrate adequate experience, background, and quality in providing credit counseling, which shall mean that, at a minimum, the agency shall either:

(i) Have experience in providing credit counseling for the two years immediately preceding the relevant application date; or

(ii) For each office providing counseling services, employ at least one supervisor who has met the qualifications in paragraph (f)(2)(i) of this section for no fewer than two of the five years preceding the relevant application date;

(3) If offering any component of counseling services by a telephone or Internet method of delivery, use only counselors who, in addition to all other requirements, demonstrate sufficient experience and proficiency in providing such counseling services by those methods of delivery, including proficiency in employing verification procedures to ensure the person receiving the counseling services is the client, and to determine whether the client has completely received counseling services.

(g) No variation in services. An agency shall ensure that the type and quality of services do not vary based on a client's decision whether to obtain a certificate in lieu of other options that may or may not be suggested by the agency.

(h) Use of the telephone and the Internet to deliver a component of client services. An agency shall:

(1) Not provide any client diminished counseling services because the client receives any portion of those counseling services by telephone or Internet;

(2) Confirm the identity of the client before receiving counseling services by telephone or Internet by:

(i) Obtaining one or more unique personal identifiers from the client and assigning an individual access code, user ID, or password at the time of enrollment; and

(ii) Requiring the client to provide the appropriate access code, user ID, or password, and also one or more of the unique personal identifiers during the course of delivery of the counseling services.

(i) Services to hearing and hearing-impaired clients and potential clients. An agency shall furnish toll-free telephone numbers for both hearing and hearing-impaired clients and potential clients whenever telephone communication is required. The agency shall provide telephone amplification, sign language services, or other communication methods for hearing-impaired clients or potential clients.

(j) [Reserved]

(k) Services to clients and potential clients with special needs. An agency that provides any portion of its counseling in person shall comply with all federal, state and local laws governing facility accessibility. An agency shall also provide or arrange for communication assistance for clients or potential clients with special needs who have difficulty making their service needs known.

(l) Mandatory disclosures to clients and potential clients. Prior to providing any information to or obtaining any information from a client or potential client, and prior to rendering any counseling service, an agency shall disclose:

(1) The agency's fee policy, including any fees associated with generation of the certificate;

(2) The agency's policies enabling clients to obtain counseling services for free or at reduced rates based upon the client's lack of ability to pay. To the extent an agency publishes information concerning its fees on the Internet, such fee information must include the agency's policies enabling clients to obtain counseling for free or at reduced rates based upon the client's lack of ability to pay;

(3) The agency's policy to provide free bilingual counseling services or professional interpreter assistance to any limited English proficient client;

(4) The agency's funding sources;

(5) The counselors' qualifications;

(6) The potential impacts on credit reports of all alternatives the agency may discuss with the client;

(7) The agency's policy prohibiting it from paying or receiving referral fees for the referral of clients, except under a fair share agreement;

(8) The agency's obligation to provide a certificate to the client promptly upon the completion of counseling services;

(9) A statement that the client has the opportunity to negotiate an alternative payment schedule with regard to each unsecured consumer debt under terms as set forth in 11 U.S.C. 502(k), and a statement whether or not the agency will provide this service. If the agency does not provide this service, it shall disclose that it may refer the client to another approved agency, and shall disclose that clients may incur additional fees in connection with such a referral;

(10) The fact that the agency might disclose client information to the United States Trustee in connection with the United States Trustee's oversight of the agency, or during the investigation of complaints, during on-site visits, or during quality of service reviews;

(11) The fact that the United States Trustee has reviewed only the agency's credit counseling services (and, if applicable, its services as a provider of a personal financial management instructional course pursuant to 11 U.S.C. 111(d)), and the fact that the United States Trustee has neither reviewed nor approved any other services the agency provides to clients; and

(12) The fact that a client will receive a certificate only if the client completes counseling services.

(m) Complaint Procedures. An agency shall employ complaint procedures that adequately respond to clients' concerns.

(n) Background checks. An agency shall:

(1) Conduct a criminal background check at least every five years for each person providing credit counseling, and

(2) Not employ anyone as a counselor who has been convicted of any felony, or any crime involving fraud, dishonesty, or false statements, unless the United States Trustee determines circumstances warrant a waiver of this prohibition against employment.

(o) Agency records. An agency shall prepare and retain records that enable the United States Trustee to evaluate whether the agency is providing adequate counseling and acting in compliance with all applicable laws and this part. All records, including documents bearing original signatures, shall be maintained in either hard copy form or electronically in a format widely available commercially. Records that the agency shall prepare and retain for a minimum of two years, and permit review by the United States Trustee upon request, shall include:

(1) Upon the filing of an application for probationary approval, all information requested by the United States Trustee as an estimate, projected to the end of the probationary period, in the form requested by the United States Trustee;

(2) After probationary or annual approval, and for so long as the agency remains on the approved list, semi-annual reports of historical data (for the periods ending June 30 and December 31 of each year), of the type and in the form requested by the United States Trustee; these reports shall be submitted within 30 days of the end of the applicable periods specified in this paragraph;

(3) Annual audited financial statements, including the audited balance sheet, statement of income and retained earnings, and statement of changes in financial condition;

(4) Books, accounts, and records to provide a clear and readily understandable record of all business conducted by the agency, including, without limitation, copies of all correspondence with or on behalf of the client, including the contract between the agency and the client and any amendments thereto;

(5) Records concerning the delivery of services to clients and potential clients with limited English proficiency and special needs, and to hearing-impaired clients and potential clients, including records:

(i) Of the number of such clients and potential clients, and the methods of delivery used with respect to such clients and potential clients;

(ii) Of which languages are offered or requested and the type of language support used or requested by such clients or potential clients (e.g., bilingual instructor, in-person or telephone interpreter, translated web instruction);

(iii) Detailing the agency's provision of services to such clients and potential clients; and

(iv) Supporting any justification if the agency did not provide services to such potential clients, including the number of potential clients not served, the languages involved, and the number of referrals provided;

(6) Records concerning the delivery of counseling services to clients for free or at reduced rates based upon the client's lack of ability to pay, including records of the number of clients for whom the agency waived all of its fees under § 58.21(b)(1)(i), the number of clients for whom the agency waived all or part of its fees under § 58.21(b)(1)(ii), and the number of clients for whom the agency voluntarily waived all or part of its fees under § 58.21(c);

(7) Records of complaints and the agency's responses thereto;

(8) Records that enable the agency to verify the authenticity of certificates their clients file in bankruptcy cases; and

(9) Records that enable the agency to issue replacement certificates.

(p) Additional minimum requirements. An agency shall:

(1) Provide records to the United States Trustee upon request;

(2) Cooperate with the United States Trustee by allowing scheduled and unscheduled on-site visits, complaint investigations, or other reviews of the agency's qualifications to be an approved agency;

(3) Cooperate with the United States Trustee by promptly responding to questions or inquiries from the United States Trustee;

(4) Assist the United States Trustee in identifying and investigating suspected fraud and abuse by any party participating in the credit counseling or bankruptcy process;

(5) Not exclude any client or creditor from a debt repayment plan because the creditor declines to make a fair share contribution to the agency;

(6) Take no action that would limit, inhibit, or prevent a client from bringing an action or claim for damages against an agency, as provided in 11 U.S.C. 111(g)(2);

(7) Refer clients and prospective clients for counseling services only to agencies that have been approved by a United States Trustee to provide such services;

(8) Comply with the United States Trustee's directions on approved advertising, including without limitation those set forth in Appendix A to the application;

(9) Not disclose or provide to a credit reporting agency any information concerning whether a client has received or sought instruction concerning credit counseling or personal financial management from an agency;

(10) Not expose the client to commercial advertising as part of or during the client's receipt of any counseling services, and never market or sell financial products or services during the counseling session provided, however, this provision does not prohibit an agency from generally discussing all available financial products and services;

(11) Not sell information about any client or potential client to any third party without the client or potential client's prior written permission;

(12) If the agency is tax-exempt, submit a completed and signed tax waiver permitting and directing the Internal Revenue Service to provide the United States Trustee with access to the Internal Revenue Service's files relating to the agency;

(13) Comply with the requirements elsewhere in this part concerning fees for credit counseling services and fee waiver policies; and

(14) Comply with the requirements elsewhere in this part concerning certificates.

[78 FR 16153, March 14, 2013]

§ 58.21　Minimum requirements to become and remain approved agencies relating to fees.

(a) If a fee for, or relating to, credit counseling services is charged by an agency, such fee shall be reasonable:

(1) A fee of $50 or less for credit counseling services is presumed to be reasonable and an agency need not obtain prior approval of the United States Trustee to charge such a fee;

(2) A fee exceeding $50 for credit counseling services is not presumed to be reasonable and an agency must obtain prior approval from the United States Trustee to charge such a fee. The agency bears the burden of establishing that its proposed fee is reasonable. At a minimum, the agency must demonstrate that its cost for delivering such services justify the fee. An agency that previously received permission to charge a higher fee need not reapply for permission to charge that fee during the agency's annual review. Any new requests for permission to charge more than previously approved, however, must be submitted to EOUST for approval; and

(3) The United States Trustee shall review the amount of the fee set forth in paragraphs (a)(1) and (2) of this section one year after the effective date of this part and then periodically, but not less frequently than every four years, to determine the reasonableness of the fee. Fee amounts and any revisions thereto shall be determined by current costs, using a method of analysis consistent with widely accepted accounting principles and practices, and calculated in accordance with the provisions of federal law as applicable. Fee amounts and any revisions thereto shall be published in the Federal Register.

(b)(1) An agency shall waive the fee in whole or in part whenever a client demonstrates a lack of ability to pay the fee.

(i) A client presumptively lacks the ability to pay the fee if the client's household current income is less than 150 percent of the poverty guidelines updated periodically in the Federal Register by the U.S. Department of Health and Human Services under the authority of 42 U.S.C. 9902(2), as adjusted from time to time, for a household or family of the size involved in the fee determination.

(ii) The presumption shall be rebutted, and the agency may charge the client a reduced fee, if the agency determines, based on income information the client submits in connection with counseling services, that the client is able to pay the fee in a reduced amount. Nothing in this section requires an agency to charge a fee to clients whose household income exceeds the amount set forth in paragraph (b)(1)(i) of this section, or who are able to demonstrate ability to pay based on income as described in this section.

(iii) An agency shall disclose its fee policy, including the criteria on which it relies in determining a client's eligibility for reduced fees, and the agency's policy for collecting fees pursuant to paragraph (b)(1)(ii) of this section, in accordance with § 58.20(l)(2).

(2) The United States Trustee shall review the basis for the mandatory fee waiver policy set forth in paragraph (b)(1) of this section one year after the effective date of this part and then periodically, but not less frequently than every four years, to determine the impact of that fee waiver policy on clients and agencies. Any revisions to the mandatory fee waiver policy set forth in paragraph (b)(1) of this section shall be published in the Federal Register.

(c) Notwithstanding the requirements of paragraph (b) of this section, an agency may also waive fees based upon other considerations, including, but not limited to:

(1) The client's net worth;

(2) The percentage of the client's income from government assistance programs;

(3) Whether the client is receiving pro bono legal services in connection with a filed or anticipated bankruptcy case; or

(4) If the combined current monthly income, as defined in 11 U.S.C. 101(10A), of the client and his or her spouse, when multiplied times twelve, is equal to or less than the amounts set forth in 11 U.S.C. 707(b)(7).

(d) An agency shall not require a client to purchase counseling services in connection with the purchase of any other service offered by the agency.

[78 FR 16153, 16156, March 14, 2013]

§ 58.22   Minimum requirements to become and remain approved agencies relating to certificates.

(a) An approved agency shall send a certificate only to the client who took and completed the counseling services, except that an approved agency shall instead send a certificate to the attorney of a client who took and completed counseling services if the client specifically directs the agency to do so. In the case of Internet counseling and automated telephone counseling, counseling is not complete until the client has engaged in interaction with a counselor, whether by electronic mail, live chat, or telephone, following the automated portion of the counseling session.

(b) An approved agency shall attach to the certificate the client's debt repayment plan (if any).

(c) An approved agency shall send a certificate to a client no later than one business day after the client completed counseling services. If a client has completed counseling services, an agency may not withhold certificate issuance for any reason. An agency may not consider counseling services incomplete based solely on the client's failure to pay the fee.

(d) If an approved agency provides other financial counseling in addition to counseling services, and such other financial counseling satisfies the requirements for counseling services specified in 11 U.S.C. 109(h) and 111, and this part, a person completing such other financial counseling is a client and the approved agency shall send a certificate to the client no later than one business day after the client's request. The approved agency shall not charge the client any additional fee except any separate fee charged for the issuance of the certificate, in accordance with § 58.20(l)(1).

(e) An approved agency shall issue certificates only in the form approved by the United States Trustee, and shall generate the form using the Certificate Generating System maintained by the United States Trustee, except under exigent circumstances with notice to the United States Trustee.

(f) An approved agency shall have sufficient computer capabilities to issue certificates from the United States Trustee's Certificate Generating System.

(g) An approved agency shall issue a certificate to each client who completes counseling services. Spouses receiving counseling services jointly shall each receive a certificate.

(h) An approved agency shall issue a replacement certificate to a client who requests one.

(i) An approved agency shall not file certificates with the court.

(j) Only an authorized officer, supervisor or employee of an approved agency shall issue a certificate, and an approved agency shall not transfer or delegate authority to issue certificates to any other entity.

(k) An approved agency shall implement internal controls sufficient to prevent unauthorized issuance of certificates.

(l) An approved agency shall ensure the signature affixed to a certificate is that of an officer, supervisor or employee authorized to issue the certificate, in accordance with paragraph (j) of this section, which signature shall be either:

(1) An original signature; or

(2) In a format approved for electronic filing with the court (most typically in the form/s/name of counselor).

(m) An approved agency shall affix to the certificate the exact name under which the approved agency is incorporated or organized.

(n) An approved agency shall identify on the certificate:

(1) The specific federal judicial district requested by the client;

(2) Whether counseling services were provided in person, by telephone or via the Internet;

(3) The date and time (including the time zone) on which counseling services were completed by the client; and

(4) The name of the counselor that provided the counseling services.

(o) An approved agency shall affix the client's full, accurate name to the certificate. If the counseling services are obtained by a client through a duly authorized representative, the certificate also shall set forth the name of the legal representative and legal capacity of that representative.

(p) If an individual enters into a debt repayment plan after completing credit counseling, upon the client's request after the completion or termination of the debt repayment plan, the approved agency shall:

(1) Provide such additional credit counseling as is necessary at such time to comply with the requirements specified in 11 U.S.C. 109(h) and 111, and this

part, including reviewing the client's current financial condition and counseling the client regarding the alternatives to resolve the client's credit problems;

(2) Send a certificate to the client no later than one business day after the client completed such additional counseling; and

(3) Not charge the client any additional fee except any separate fee charged for the issuance of the certificate, in accordance with § 58.20(*l*)(1).

[78 FR 16153, 16156, March 14, 2013]

§ 58.23   **Minimum financial requirements and bonding and insurance requirements for agencies offering debt repayment plans.**

If an agency offers or has offered debt repayment plans, an agency shall possess adequate financial resources to provide continuing support services for such plans over the life of any debt repayment plan, and provide for the safekeeping of client funds, which shall include:

(a) Depositing all client funds into a deposit account, held in trust, at a federally insured depository institution. Each such trust account shall be established in a fiduciary capacity and shall be in full compliance with federal law such that each client's funds shall be protected by federal deposit insurance up to the maximum amount allowable by federal law.

(b) Keeping and maintaining books, accounts, and records to provide a clear and readily understandable record of all business conducted by the agency, including without limitation, all of the following:

(1) Separate files for each client's account that include copies of all correspondence with or on behalf of the client, including:

(i) All agreements with all entities, including the contract between the agency and the client and any amendments thereto;

(ii) The analysis of the client's budget;

(iii) Correspondence between the agency and the client's creditors;

(iv) The notice given to creditors of any debt repayment plan; and

(v) All written statements of account provided to the client and subsidiary ledgers concerning any debt repayment plan;

(2) A trust account general ledger reflecting all deposits to and disbursements from all trust accounts, which shall be kept current at all times;

(3) A reconciliation of the trust accounts, prepared at least once a month; and

(4) An operating account general ledger reflecting all of the agency's financial transactions involving the agency's operating account, which shall be kept current at least on a monthly basis.

(c) Allowing an independent certified public accounting firm to audit the trust accounts annually in accordance with generally accepted accounting principles as defined by the American Institute of Certified Public Accountants and any Statement of Work prepared by the United States Trustee, which audit shall include:

(1) A report of all trust account activity including:

(i) The balance of each trust account at the beginning and end of the period;

(ii) The total of all receipts from clients and disbursements to creditors during the reporting period;

(iii) The total of all disbursements to the agency; and

(iv) The reconciliation of each trust account;

(2) A report of all exceptions (e.g., discrepancies, irregularities, and errors) found, regardless of materiality; and

(3) An evaluation of the agency's trust account internal controls and its computer operations to determine whether it provides a reasonable assurance that the trust funds are safeguarded against loss from unauthorized use or disposition.

(d) Obtaining a surety bond payable to the United States, as follows:

(1) Subject to the minimum amount of $5,000, the amount of such surety bond shall be the lesser of:

(i) Two percent of the agency's disbursements made during the twelve months immediately prior to submission of the application from all trust accounts attributable to the federal judicial districts (or, if not feasible to determine, the states) in which the agency seeks approval from the United States Trustee; or

(ii) Equal to the average daily balance maintained for the six months immediately prior to submission of the application in all trust accounts attributable to the federal judicial districts (or, if not feasible to determine, the states) in which the agency seeks approval from the United States Trustee;

(2) The agency may receive an offset or credit against the surety bond amount determined under paragraph (d)(1) of this section if:

(i) The agency has previously obtained a surety bond, or similar cash, securities, insurance (other than employee fidelity insurance), or letter of credit in compliance with the licensing requirements of the state in which the agency seeks approval from the United States Trustee;

(ii) Such surety bond, or similar cash, securities, insurance (other than employee fidelity insurance), or letter of credit provides protection for the clients of the agency;

(iii) Such surety bond, or similar cash, securities, insurance (other than employee fidelity insurance), or letter of credit, is written in favor of the state or the appropriate state agency; and

(iv) The amount of the offset or credit shall be the lesser of:

(A) The principal amount of such surety bond, or similar cash, securities, insurance (other than employee fidelity insurance), or letter of credit; or

(B) The surety bond amount determined under paragraph (d)(1) of this section;

(3) If an agency has contracted with an independent contractor to administer any part of its debt repayment plans:

(i) Except as provided in paragraphs (d)(3)(ii) and (d)(3)(iii) of this section, the independent contractor shall:

(A) Be an approved agency; or

(B) If the independent contractor is not an approved agency, then the independent contractor shall:

(1) Be specifically covered under the agency's surety bond required under paragraph (d)(1) of this section; or

(2) Have a surety bond that meets the requirements of paragraph (d)(1) of this section; and

(3) Agree in writing to allow the United States Trustee to audit the independent contractor's trust accounts for the debt repayment plans administered on behalf of the agency and to review the independent contractor's internal controls and administrative procedures;

(ii) If the independent contractor holds funds for transmission for five days or less, then the amount of the required surety bond under paragraph (d)(3)(i)(B) of this section shall be $500,000;

(iii) If the independent contractor performs only electronic fund transfers on the agency's behalf, then the independent contractor need not satisfy the requirements of paragraph (d)(3)(i) of this section during such time as the independent contractor is authorized by the National Automated Clearing House Association to participate in the Automated Clearing House system.

(e) Obtaining either adequate employee bonding or fidelity insurance, as follows:

(1) Subject to the minimum amount set forth below, the amount of such bonding or fidelity insurance shall be 50 percent of the surety bond amount calculated under paragraph (d)(1) of this section, prior to any offset or credit that the agency may receive under paragraph (d)(2) of this section; provided, however, that at a minimum, the employee bond or fidelity insurance must be $5,000;

(2) An agency may receive an offset or credit against the employee bond or fidelity insurance amount determined under paragraph (e)(1) of this section if:

(i) The agency has previously obtained an employee bond or fidelity insurance in compliance with the requirements of a state in which the agency seeks approval from the United States Trustee; and

(ii) The deductible does not exceed a reasonable amount considering the financial resources of the agency; and

(iii) The amount of the offset or credit shall be the lesser of:

(A) The principal amount of such employee bond or fidelity insurance; or

(B) The employee bond or fidelity insurance amount determined under paragraph (e)(1) of this section.

(f) An agency that ceases to offer debt repayment plans to individuals who receive counseling from such agency pursuant to 11 U.S.C. 109(h) shall, concerning any debt repayment plans it services that remain in existence with respect to such individuals as of the date it ceases to offer debt repayment plans to new clients, continue to comply with all of the requirements of this section.

(1) The agency may seek a waiver of the bonding and insurance requirements set forth in paragraphs (d) and (e) of this section if:

(i) The agency has in effect, as of the date it ceases to offer debt repayment plans, a written agreement to transfer all such debt repayment plans to another approved agency for servicing, provided that:

(A) Transfers to another approved agency pursuant to such agreements must be completed within 60 days of the date the agency ceases to offer debt repayment plans to individuals who receive counseling from such agency pursuant to 11 U.S.C. § 109(h); and

(B) The agency provides written notice to clients whose debt repayment plans it intends to transfer within the time described in paragraph (f)(1)(i)(A) of this section, identifying the approved agency to which the clients' plans will be transferred, any fees associated with servicing by the approved agency, and any fees associated with the transfer; or

(ii) In the reasonable determination of the United States Trustee, taking into account the facts and circumstances surrounding the agency's business and the terms of the bond, compliance with the bonding and insurance requirements set forth in paragraphs (d) and (e) of this section would impose an undue hardship on the agency.

[78 FR 16153, 16157, March 14, 2013]

§ 58.24 Procedures for obtaining final agency action on United States Trustees' decisions to deny agencies' applications and to remove approved agencies from the approved list.

(a) The United States Trustee shall remove an approved agency from the approved list whenever an approved agency requests its removal in writing.

(b) The United States Trustee may issue a decision to remove an approved agency from the approved list, and thereby terminate the approved agency's authorization to provide counseling services, at any time.

(c) The United States Trustee may issue a decision to deny an agency's application or to remove an agency from the approved list whenever the United States Trustee determines that the agency has failed to comply with the standards or requirements specified in 11 U.S.C. 109(h) or 111, this part, or the terms under which the United States Trustee designated it to act as an approved agency, including, but not limited to, finding any of the following:

(1) The agency is not employing adequate procedures for safekeeping of client funds or paying client funds, which could result in a loss to a client;

(2) The agency's surety bond has been canceled;

(3) Any entity has revoked the agency's nonprofit status, even if that revocation is subject to further administrative or judicial litigation, review or appeal;

(4) Any entity has suspended or revoked the agency's license to do business in any jurisdiction; or

(5) Any United States district court has removed the agency under 11 U.S.C. § 111(e).

(d) If the Internal Revenue Service revokes an agency's tax exempt status, the United States Trustee shall promptly commence an investigation to determine whether any of the factors set forth in paragraphs (c)(1) through (5) of this section exist.

(e) The United States Trustee shall provide to the agency in writing a notice of any decision either to:

(1) Deny the agency's application; or

(2) Remove the agency from the approved list.

(f) The notice shall state the reason(s) for the decision and shall reference any documents or communications relied upon in reaching the denial or removal decision. To the extent authorized by law, the United States Trustee shall provide to the agency copies of any such documents that were not supplied to the United States Trustee by the agency. The notice shall be sent to the agency by overnight courier, for delivery the next business day.

(g) Except as provided in paragraph (i) of this section, the notice shall advise the agency that the denial or removal decision shall become final agency action, and unreviewable, unless the agency submits in writing a request for review by the Director no later than 21 calendar days from the date of the notice to the agency.

(h) Except as provided in paragraph (i) of this section, the decision to deny an agency's application or remove an agency from the approved list shall take effect upon:

(1) The expiration of the agency's time to seek review from the Director, if the agency fails to timely seek review of a denial or removal decision; or

(2) The issuance by the Director of a final decision, if the agency timely seeks such review.

(i) The United States Trustee may provide that a decision to remove an agency from the approved list is effective immediately and deny the agency the right to provide counseling services whenever the United States Trustee finds any of the factors set forth in paragraphs (c)(1) through (5) of this section.

(j) An agency's request for review shall be in writing and shall fully describe why the agency disagrees with the denial or removal decision, and shall be accompanied by all documents and materials the agency wants the Director to consider in reviewing the denial or removal decision. The agency shall send the original and one copy of the request for review, including all accompanying documents and materials, to the Office of the Director by overnight courier, for delivery the next business day. To be timely, a request for review shall be received at the Office of the Director no later than 21 calendar days from the date of the notice to the agency.

(k) The United States Trustee shall have 21 calendar days from the date of the agency's request for review to submit to the Director a written response regarding the matters raised in the agency's request for review. The United States Trustee shall provide a copy of this response to the agency by overnight courier, for delivery the next business day.

(l) The Director may seek additional information from any party in the manner and to the extent the Director deems appropriate.

(m) In reviewing the decision to deny an agency's application or remove an agency from the approved list, the Director shall determine:

(1) Whether the denial or removal decision is supported by the record; and

(2) Whether the denial or removal decision constitutes an appropriate exercise of discretion.

(n) Except as provided in paragraph (o) of this section, the Director shall issue a final decision no later than 60 calendar days from the receipt of the agency's request for review, unless the agency agrees to a longer period of time or the Director extends the deadline. The Director's final decision on the agency's request for review shall constitute final agency action.

(o) Whenever the United States Trustee provides under paragraph (i) of this section that a decision to remove an agency from the approved list is effective immediately, the Director shall issue a written decision no later than 15 calendar days from the receipt of the agency's request for review, unless the agency agrees to a longer period of time. The decision shall:

(1) Be limited to deciding whether the determination that the removal decision should take effect immediately was supported by the record and an appropriate exercise of discretion;

(2) Constitute final agency action only on the issue of whether the removal decision should take effect immediately; and

(3) Not constitute final agency action on the ultimate issue of whether the agency should be removed from the approved list; after issuing the decision, the Director shall issue a final decision by the deadline set forth in paragraph (n) of this section.

(p) In reaching a decision under paragraphs (n) and (o) of this section, the Director may specify a person to act as a reviewing official. The reviewing official's duties shall be specified by the Director on a case-by-case basis, and may include reviewing the record, obtaining additional information from the participants, providing the Director with written recommendations, and such other duties as the Director shall prescribe in a particular case.

(q) An agency that files a request for review shall bear its own costs and expenses, including counsel fees.

(r) When a decision to remove an agency from the approved list takes effect, the agency shall:

(1) Immediately cease providing counseling services to clients and shall not provide counseling services to potential clients;

(2) No later than three business days after the date of removal, send all certificates to all clients who completed counseling services prior to the agency's removal from the approved list;

(3) No later than three business days after the date of removal, return all fees to clients and potential clients who had paid for counseling services, but had not completely received them; and

(4) Transfer any debt repayment plans that the agency is administering to another approved agency.

(s) An agency must exhaust all administrative remedies before seeking redress in any court of competent jurisdiction.

[78 FR 16153, 16158, March 14, 2013]

§ 58.25   Definitions.

(a) The following definitions apply to §§ 58.25 through and including 58.36 of this part, as well as the applications and other materials providers submit in an effort to establish they meet the requirements necessary to become an approved provider of a personal financial management instructional course.

(b) These terms shall have these meanings:

(1) The term "accreditation" means the recognition or endorsement that an accrediting organization bestows upon a provider because the accrediting organization has determined the provider meets or exceeds all the accrediting organization's standards;

(2) The term "accrediting organization" means either an entity that provides accreditation to providers or provides certification to instructors, provided, however, that an accrediting organization shall:

(i) Not be a provider or affiliate of any provider; and

(ii) Be deemed acceptable by the United States Trustee;

(3) The term "affiliate" means:

(i) Every entity that is an affiliate of the provider, as the term "affiliate" is defined in 11 U.S.C. 101(2), except that the word "provider" shall be substituted for the word "debtor" in 11 U.S.C. 101(2);

(ii) Each of a provider's officers and each of a provider's directors; and

(iii) Every relative of a provider's officers and every relative of a provider's directors;

(4) The term "application" means the application and related forms, including appendices, approved by the Office of Management and Budget as form EOUST–DE1, Application for Approval as a Provider of a Personal Financial Management Instructional Course, as it shall be amended from time to time;

(5) The term "approved list" means the list of providers currently approved by a United States Trustee under 11 U.S.C. 111 as currently published on the United States Trustee Program's Internet site, which is located on the United States Department of Justice's Internet site;

(6) The term "approved provider" means a provider currently approved by a United States Trustee under 11 U.S.C. 111 as an approved provider of a personal financial management instructional course eligible to be included on one or more lists maintained under 11 U.S.C. 111(a)(1);

(7) The term "certificate" means the document an approved provider shall provide to a debtor after the debtor completes an instructional course, if the approved provider does not notify the appropriate bankruptcy court in accordance with the Federal Rules of Bankruptcy Procedure that a debtor has completed the instructional course;

(8) The term "debtor" shall have the meaning given that term in 11 U.S.C. 101(13), to the extent that individual has sought an instructional course from an approved provider;

(9) The term "Director" means the person designated or acting as the Director of the Executive Office for United States Trustees;

(10) The term "effective instruction" means the actual receipt of an instructional course by a debtor from an approved provider, and all other applicable services, rights, and protections specified in:

(i) 11 U.S.C. 111; and

(ii) this part;

(11) The term "entity" shall have the meaning given that term in 11 U.S.C. 101(15);

(12) The terms "fee" and "fee policy" each mean the aggregate of all fees an approved provider charges debtors for providing an instructional course, including the fees for any materials; "fee policy" shall also mean the objective criteria the provider uses in determining whether to waive or reduce any fee, contribution, or payment;

(13) The term "final decision" means the written determination issued by the Director based upon the review of the United States Trustee's decision either to deny a provider's application or to remove an approved provider from the approved list;

(14) The term "financial benefit" means any interest equated with money or its equivalent, including, but not limited to, stocks, bonds, other investments, income, goods, services, or receivables;

(15) The term "governmental unit" shall have the meaning given that term in 11 U.S.C. 101(27);

(16) The term "independent contractor" means a person or entity who provides any goods or services to an approved provider other than as an employee and as to whom the approved provider does not:

(i) Direct or control the means or methods of delivery of the goods or services being provided;

(ii) Make financial decisions concerning the business aspects of the goods or services being provided; and

(iii) Have any common employees;

(17) The term "instructional course" means a course in personal financial management that is approved by the United States Trustee under 11 U.S.C. 111 and this part, including the learning materials and methodologies in § 58.33(f), which is to be taken and completed by the debtor after the filing of a bankruptcy petition and before receiving a discharge under 11 U.S.C. 727(a)(11), 1141(d)(3) or 1328(g)(1);

(18) The term "instructor" means an individual who teaches, presents or explains substantive instructional course materials to debtors, whether provided in person, by telephone, or through the Internet;

(19) The term "languages offered" means every language other than English in which an approved provider offers an instructional course;

(20) The term "legal advice" shall have the meaning given that term in 11 U.S.C. 110(e)(2);

(21) The term "limited English proficiency" refers to individuals who:

(i) Do not speak English as their primary language; and

(ii) Have a limited ability to read, write, speak, or understand English;

(22) The term "material change" means, alternatively, any change:

(i) In the name, structure, principal contact, management, instructors, physical location, instructional course, fee policy, language services, or method of delivery of an approved provider; or

(ii) That renders inapplicable, inaccurate, incomplete, or misleading any statement a provider previously made:

(A) In its application or related materials; or

(B) To the United States Trustee;

(23) The term "method of delivery" means one or more of the three methods by which an approved provider can provide some component of an instructional course to debtors, including:

(i) "In person" delivery, which applies when a debtor primarily receives an instructional course at a physical location with an instructor physically present in that location, and with the instructor providing oral and/or written communication to the debtor at the facility;

(ii) "Telephone" delivery, which applies when a debtor primarily receives an instructional course by telephone; and

(iii) "Internet" delivery, which applies when a debtor primarily receives an instructional course through an Internet Web site;

(24) The term "notice" in § 58.36 means the written communication from the United States Trustee to a provider that its application to become an approved provider has been denied or to an approved provider that it is being removed from the approved list;

(25) The term "provider" shall mean any entity that is applying under this part for United States Trustee approval to be included on a publicly available list in one or more United States district courts, as authorized by 11 U.S.C. 111(a)(1), and shall also mean, whenever appropriate, an approved provider;

(26) The term "referral fees" means money or any other valuable consideration paid or transferred between an approved provider and another entity in return for that entity, directly or indirectly, identifying, referring, securing, or in any other way encouraging any debtor to receive an instructional course from the approved provider;

(27) The term "relative" shall have the meaning given that term in 11 U.S.C. 101(45);

(28) The term "request for review" means the written communication from a provider to the Director seeking review of the United States Trustee's decision either to deny the provider's application or to remove the provider from the approved list;

(29) The term "state" means state, commonwealth, district, or territory of the United States;

(30) The term "United States Trustee" means, alternatively:

(i) The Executive Office for United States Trustees;

(ii) A United States Trustee appointed under 28 U.S.C. 581;

(iii) A person acting as a United States Trustee;

(iv) An employee of a United States Trustee; or

(v) Any other entity authorized by the Attorney General to act on behalf of the United States under this part.

[71 FR 38082, July 5, 2006; 78 FR 16170, March 14, 2013]

§ 58.26   Procedures all providers shall follow when applying to become approved providers.

(a) A provider applying to become an approved provider shall obtain an application, including appendices, from the United States Trustee.

(b) The provider shall complete the application, including its appendices, and attach the required supporting documents requested in the application.

(c) The provider shall submit the original of the completed application, including completed appendices and the required supporting documents, to the United States Trustee at the address specified on the application form.

(d) The application shall be signed by a representative of the provider who is authorized under applicable law to sign on behalf of the applying provider.

(e) The signed application, completed appendices, and required supporting documents shall be accompanied by a writing, signed by the signatory of the application and executed on behalf of the signatory and the provider, certifying the application does not:

(1) Falsify, conceal, or cover up by any trick, scheme or device a material fact;

(2) Make any materially false, fictitious, or fraudulent statement or representation; or

(3) Make or use any false writing or document knowing the same to contain any materially false, fictitious, or fraudulent statement or entry.

(f) The United States Trustee shall not consider an application, and it may be returned if:

(1) It is incomplete;

(2) It fails to include the completed appendices or all of the required supporting documents; or

(3) It is not accompanied by the certification identified in the preceding subsection.

(g) The United States Trustee shall not consider an application on behalf of a provider, and it shall be returned if:

(1) It is submitted by any entity other than the provider; or

(2) Either the application or the accompanying certification is executed by any entity other than a representative of the provider who is authorized under applicable law to sign on behalf of the provider.

(h) By the act of submitting an application, a provider consents to the release and disclosure of its name, contact information, and non-confidential business information relating to the services it provides on the approved list should its application be approved.

[71 FR 38082, 38084, July 5, 2006; 78 FR 16170, 16172, March 14, 2013]

§ 58.27   Automatic expiration of providers' status as approved providers.

(a) Except as provided in § 58.28(c), if an approved provider was not an approved provider immediately prior to the date it last obtained approval to be an approved provider, such an approved provider shall cease to be an approved provider six months from the date on which it was approved unless the United States Trustee approves an additional one year period.

(b) Except as provided in § 58.28(c), if an approved provider was an approved provider immediately prior to the date it last obtained approval to be an approved provider, such a provider shall cease to be an approved provider one year from the date on which it was last approved to be an approved provider unless the United States Trustee approves an additional one year period.

[71 FR 38082, 38084, July 5, 2006; 78 FR 16170, 16172, March 14, 2013]

§ 58.28   Procedures all approved providers shall follow when applying for approval to act as an approved provider for an additional one year period.

(a) To be considered for approval to act as an approved provider for an additional one year term, an approved provider shall reapply by complying with all the requirements specified for providers under 11 U.S.C. 111, and under this part.

(b) Such a provider shall apply no later than 45 days prior to the expiration of its six month probationary period or annual period to be considered for approval for an additional one year period, unless a written extension is granted by the United States Trustee.

(c) An approved provider that has complied with all prerequisites for applying to act as an approved provider for an additional one year period may continue to operate as an approved provider while its application is under review by the United States Trustee, so long as either the application for an additional one year period is timely submitted, or a provider receives a written extension from the United States Trustee.

[78 FR 16172, March 14, 2013]

§ 58.29   Renewal for an additional one year period.

If an approved provider's application for an additional one year period is approved, such renewal period shall begin to run from the later of:

(a) The day after the expiration date of the immediately preceding approval period; or

(b) The actual date of approval of such renewal by the United States Trustee.

[78 FR 16172, March 14, 2013]

§ 58.30   Mandatory duty of approved providers to notify United States Trustees of material changes.

(a) An approved provider shall immediately notify the United States Trustee in writing of any material change.

(b) An approved provider shall immediately notify the United States Trustee in writing of any failure by the approved provider to comply with any standard or requirement specified in 11 U.S.C. 111, this part, or the terms under which the United States Trustee approved it to act as an approved provider.

(c) An approved provider shall immediately notify the United States Trustee in writing of any of the following events:

(1) Cessation of business by the approved provider or by any office of the provider, or withdrawal from any federal judicial district(s) where the approved provider is approved;

(2) Any investigation of, or any administrative or judicial action brought against, the approved provider by any governmental unit;

(3) Any action by a governmental unit or a court to suspend or revoke the approved provider's articles of incorporation, or any license held by the approved provider, or any authorization necessary to engage in business; or

(4) A suspension, or action to suspend, any accreditation held by the approved provider, or any withdrawal by the approved provider of any application for accreditation, or any denial of any application of the approved provider for accreditation; or

(5) [Reserved]

(d) A provider shall notify the United States Trustee in writing if any of the changes identified in paragraphs (a) through (c) of this section occur while its application to become an approved provider is pending before the United States Trustee.

(e) An approved provider whose name or other information appears incorrectly on the approved list shall immediately submit a written request to the United States Trustee asking that the information be corrected.

[78 FR 16172, March 14, 2013]

§ 58.31   Mandatory duty of approved providers to obtain prior consent of the United States Trustee before taking certain actions.

(a) By accepting the designation to act as an approved provider, a provider agrees to obtain approval from the United States Trustee, prior to making any of the following changes:

(1) The engagement of an independent contractor to provide an instructional course;

(2) Any increase in the fees received from debtors for an instructional course or a change in the provider's fee policy;

(3) Expansion into additional federal judicial districts;

(4) Any changes to the method of delivery the approved provider employs to provide an instructional course; or

(5) Any changes in the approved provider's instructional course.

(b) A provider applying to become an approved provider shall also obtain approval from the United States Trustee before taking any action specified in paragraph (a) of this section. It shall do so by submitting an amended application. The provider's amended application shall be accompanied by a contemporaneously executed writing, signed by the signatory of the application, that makes the certifications specified in § 58.26(e).

(c) An approved provider shall not transfer or assign its United States Trustee approval to act as an approved provider.

[78 FR 16172, March 14, 2013]

§ 58.32   Continuing requirements for becoming and remaining approved providers.

(a) To become an approved provider, a provider must affirmatively establish, to the satisfaction of the United States Trustee, that the provider at the time of approval:

(1) Satisfies every requirement of this part; and

(2) Provides effective instruction to its debtors.

(b) To remain an approved provider, an approved provider shall affirmatively establish, to the satisfaction of the United States Trustee, that the approved provider:

(1) Has satisfied every requirement of this part;

(2) Has provided effective instruction to its debtors; and

(3) Will continue to satisfy both paragraphs (b)(1) and (2) of this section in the future.

[78 FR 16172, March 14, 2013]

§ 58.33   Minimum qualifications providers shall meet to become and remain approved providers.

To meet the minimum qualifications set forth in § 58.32, and in addition to the other requirements set forth in this part, providers and approved providers shall comply with paragraphs (a) through (n) of this section on a continuing basis:

(a) *Compliance with all laws.* A provider shall comply with all applicable laws and regulations of the United States and each state in which the provider provides an instructional course including, without limitation, all laws governing licensing and registration.

(b) *Prohibition on legal advice.* A provider shall not provide legal advice.

(c) *Ethical standards.* A provider shall:

(1) Ensure no member of the board of directors or trustees, officer or supervisor is a relative of an employee of the United States Trustee, a trustee appointed under 28 U.S.C. 586(a)(1) for any federal judicial district where the provider is providing or is applying to provide an instructional course, a federal judge in any federal judicial district where the provider is providing or is applying to provide an instructional course, or a federal court employee in any federal judicial district where the provider is providing or is applying to provide an instructional course;

(2) Not enter into any referral agreement or receive any financial benefit that involves the provider paying to or receiving from any entity or person referral fees for the referral of debtors to or by the provider; and

(3) Not enter into agreements involving an instructional course that create a conflict of interest; and

(4) Not contact any debtor utilizing the United States Postal Service, or other mail carrier, or electronic mail for the purpose of soliciting debtors to utilize the provider's instructional course, unless:

(i) Any such solicitations include the phrase "This is an advertisement for services" or "This is a solicitation;"

(ii) Prominently displayed at the beginning of each page of the solicitation;

(iii) In a font size larger than or equal to the largest font size otherwise used in the solicitation;

(iv) Any such solicitations include only logos, seals, or similar marks that are substantially dissimilar to the logo, seal, or similar mark of any agency or court of the United States government, including but not limited to the United States Trustee Program.

(d) *Instructor training, certification and experience.* A provider shall:

(1) Use only instructors who possess adequate experience providing an instructional course, which shall mean that each instructor either:

(i) Holds one of the certifications listed below and who has complied with all continuing education requirements necessary to maintain that certification:

(A) Certified as a Certified Financial Planner;

(B) Certified as a credit counselor by an accrediting organization;

(C) Registered as a Registered Financial Consultant; or

(D) Certified as a Certified Public Accountant; or

(ii) Has successfully completed a course of study or worked a minimum of six months in a related area such as personal finance, budgeting, or credit or debt management. A course of study must include training in personal finance, budgeting, or credit or debt management. An instructor shall also receive annual continuing education in the areas of personal finance, budgeting, or credit or debt management;

(2) Demonstrate adequate experience, background, and quality in providing an instructional course, which shall mean that, at a minimum, the provider shall either:

(i) Have experience in providing an instructional course for the two years immediately preceding the relevant application date; or

(ii) For each office providing an instructional course, employ at least one supervisor who has met the qualifications in paragraph (d)(2)(i) of this section for no fewer than two of the five years preceding the relevant application date; and

(iii) If offering any component of an instructional course by a telephone or Internet method of delivery, use only instructors who, in addition to all other requirements, demonstrate sufficient experience and proficiency in providing such an instructional course by those methods of delivery, including proficiency in employing verification procedures to ensure the person receiving the instructional course is the debtor, and to determine whether the debtor has completely received an instructional course.

(e) *Use of the telephone and the Internet to deliver a component of an instructional course.* A provider shall:

(1) Not provide any debtor a diminished instructional course because the debtor receives any portion of the instructional course by telephone or Internet;

(2) Confirm the identity of the debtor before commencing an instructional course by telephone or Internet by:

(i) Obtaining one or more unique personal identifiers from the debtor and assigning an individual access code, user ID, or password at the time of enrollment;

(ii) Requiring the debtor to provide the appropriate access code, user ID, or password, and also one or more of the unique personal identifiers during the course of delivery of the instructional course; and

(iii) Employing adequate means to measure the time spent by the debtor to complete the instructional course.

(f) *Learning materials and methodologies.* A provider shall provide learning materials to assist debtors in understanding personal financial management and that are consistent with 11 U.S.C. 111, and this part, which include written information and instruction on all of the following topics:

(1) Budget development, which consists of the following:

(i) Setting short-term and long-term financial goals, as well as developing skills to assist in achieving these goals;

(ii) Calculating gross monthly income and net monthly income; and

(iii) Identifying and classifying monthly expenses as fixed, variable, or periodic;

(2) Money management, which consists of the following:

(i) Keeping adequate financial records;

(ii) Developing decision-making skills required to distinguish between wants and needs, and to comparison shop for goods and services;

(iii) Maintaining appropriate levels of insurance coverage, taking into account the types and costs of insurance; and

(iv) Saving for emergencies, for periodic payments, and for financial goals;

(3) Wise use of credit, which consists of the following:

(i) Identifying the types, sources, and costs of credit and loans;

(ii) Identifying debt warning signs;

(iii) Discussing appropriate use of credit and alternatives to credit use; and

(iv) Checking a credit rating;

(4) Consumer information, which consists of the following:

(i) Identifying public and nonprofit resources for consumer assistance; and

(ii) Identifying applicable consumer protection laws and regulations, such as those governing correction of a credit record and protection against consumer fraud; and

(5) Coping with unexpected financial crisis, which consists of the following:

(i) Identifying alternatives to additional borrowing in times of unanticipated events; and

(ii) Seeking advice from public and private service agencies for assistance.

(g) *Course procedures.*

(1) Generally, a provider shall:

(i) Ensure the instructional course contains sufficient learning materials and teaching methodologies so that the debtor receives a minimum of two hours of instruction, regardless of the method of delivery of the course;

(ii) Use its best efforts to collect from each debtor a completed course evaluation at the end of the instructional course. At a minimum, the course evaluation shall include the information contained in Appendix E of the application to evaluate the effectiveness of the instructional course;

(2) For an instructional course delivered in person, the provider shall:

(i) Ensure that an instructor is present to instruct and interact with debtors; and

(ii) Limit class size to ensure an effective presentation of the instructional course materials;

(3) For instructional courses delivered by the telephone, the provider shall:

(i) Ensure an instructor is telephonically present to instruct and interact with debtors;

(ii) Provide learning materials to debtors before the telephone instructional course session;

(iii) Incorporate tests into the curriculum that support the learning materials, ensure completion of the course, and measure comprehension;

(iv) Ensure review of tests prior to the completion of the instructional course; and

(v) Ensure direct oral communication from an instructor by telephone or in person with all debtors who fail to complete the test in a satisfactory manner or who receive less than a 70 percent score;

(4) For instructional courses delivered through the Internet, the provider shall:

(i) Comply with § 58.33(g)(3)(iii), (iv), and (v); provided, however, that to the extent instruction takes place by Internet, the provider may comply with § 58.33(g)(3)(v) by ensuring direct communication from an instructor by electronic mail, live chat, or telephone; and

(ii) Respond to a debtor's questions or comments within one business day.

(h) *Services to hearing and hearing-impaired debtors.* A provider shall furnish toll-free telephone numbers for both hearing and hearing-impaired debtors whenever telephone communication is required. The provider shall provide telephone amplification, sign language services, or other communication methods for hearing-impaired debtors.

(i) [Reserved]

(j) *Services to debtors with special needs.* A provider that provides any portion of its instructional course in person shall comply with all federal, state and local laws governing facility accessibility. A provider shall also provide or arrange for communication assistance for debtors with special needs who have difficulty making their service needs known.

(k) Mandatory disclosures to debtors. Prior to providing any information to or obtaining any information from a debtor, and prior to delivering an instructional course, a provider shall disclose:

(1) The provider's fee policy, including any fees associated with generation of the certificate;

(2) The provider's policies enabling debtors to obtain an instructional course for free or at reduced rates based upon the debtor's lack of ability to pay. To the extent an approved provider publishes information concerning its fees on the Internet, such fee information must include the provider's policies enabling debtors to obtain an instructional course for free or at reduced rates based upon the debtor's lack of ability to pay;

(3) The provider's policy to provide free bilingual instruction or professional interpreter assistance to any limited English proficient debtor;

(4) The instructors' qualifications;

(5) The provider's policy prohibiting it from paying or receiving referral fees for the referral of debtors;

(6) The provider's obligation to provide a certificate to the debtor promptly upon the completion of an instructional course;

(7) The fact that the provider might disclose debtor information to the United States Trustee in connection with the United States Trustee's oversight of the provider, or during the investigation of complaints, during on-site visits, or during quality of service reviews;

(8) The fact that the United States Trustee has reviewed only the provider's instructional course (and, if applicable, its services as a credit counseling agency pursuant to 11 U.S.C. 111(c)), and the fact that the United States Trustee has neither reviewed nor approved any other services the provider provides to debtors; and

(9) The fact that a debtor will only receive a certificate if the debtor completes an instructional course.

(l) Complaint Procedures. A provider shall employ complaint procedures that adequately respond to debtors' concerns.

(m) Provider records. A provider shall prepare and retain records that enable the United States Trustee to evaluate whether the provider is providing effective instruction and acting in compliance with all applicable laws and this part. All records, including documents bearing original signatures, shall be maintained in either hard copy form or electronically in a format widely available commercially. Records that the provider shall prepare and retain for a minimum of two

years, and permit review of by the United States Trustee upon request, shall include:

(1) Upon the filing of an application for probationary approval, all information requested by the United States Trustee as an estimate, projected to the end of the probationary period, in the form requested by the United States Trustee;

(2) After probationary or annual approval, and for so long as the provider remains on the approved list, semi-annual reports of historical data (for the periods ending June 30 and December 31 of each year), of the type and in the form requested by the United States Trustee; these reports shall be submitted within 30 days of the end of the applicable periods specified in this paragraph;

(3) Records concerning the delivery of services to debtors with limited English proficiency and special needs, and to hearing-impaired debtors, including records:

(i) Of the number of such debtors, and the methods of delivery used with respect to such debtors;

(ii) Of which languages are offered or requested, and the type of language support used or requested by such debtors (e.g., bilingual instructor, in-person or telephone interpreter, translated Web instruction);

(iii) Detailing the provider's provision of services to such debtors; and

(iv) Supporting any justification if the provider did not provide services to such debtors, including the number of debtors not served, the languages involved, and the number of referrals provided;

(4) Records concerning the delivery of an instructional course to debtors for free or at reduced rates based upon the debtor's lack of ability to pay, including records of the number of debtors for whom the provider waived all of its fees under § 58.34(b)(1)(i), the number of debtors for whom the provider waived all or part of its fees under § 58.34(b)(1)(ii), and the number of debtors for whom the provider voluntarily waived all or part of its fees under § 58.34(c);

(5) Records of complaints and the provider's responses thereto;

(6) Records that enable the provider to verify the authenticity of certificates their debtors file in bankruptcy cases; and

(7) Records that enable the provider to issue replacement certificates.

(n) Additional minimum requirements. A provider shall:

(1) Provide records to the United States Trustee upon request;

(2) Cooperate with the United States Trustee by allowing scheduled and unscheduled on-site visits, complaint investigations, or other reviews of the provider's qualifications to be an approved provider;

(3) Cooperate with the United States Trustee by promptly responding to questions or inquiries from the United States Trustee;

(4) Assist the United States Trustee in identifying and investigating suspected fraud and abuse by any party participating in the instructional course or bankruptcy process;

(5) Take no action that would limit, inhibit, or prevent a debtor from bringing an action or claim for damages against a provider, as provided in 11 U.S.C. 111(g)(2);

(6) Refer debtors seeking an instructional course only to providers that have been approved by a United States Trustee to provide such services;

(7) Comply with the United States Trustee's directions on approved advertising, including without limitation those set forth in Appendix A to the application;

(8) Not disclose or provide to a credit reporting agency any information concerning whether a debtor has received or sought instruction concerning personal financial management from a provider;

(9) Not expose the debtor to commercial advertising as part of or during the debtor's receipt of an instructional course, and never market or sell financial products or services during the instructional course provided, however, this provision does not prohibit a provider from generally discussing all available financial products and services;

(10) Not sell information about any debtor to any third party without the debtor's prior written permission;

(11) Comply with the requirements elsewhere in this part concerning fees for the instructional course and fee waiver policies; and

(12) Comply with the requirements elsewhere in this part concerning certificates.

[78 FR 16172, March 14, 2013]

§ 58.34   Minimum requirements to become and remain approved providers relating to fees.

(a) If a fee for, or relating to, an instructional course is charged by a provider, such fee shall be reasonable:

(1) A fee of $50 or less for an instructional course is presumed to be reasonable and a provider need not obtain prior approval of the United States Trustee to charge such a fee;

(2) A fee exceeding $50 for an instructional course is not presumed to be reasonable and a provider must obtain prior approval from the United States Trustee to charge such a fee. The provider bears the burden of establishing that its proposed fee is reasonable. At a minimum, the provider must demonstrate that its cost for delivering the instructional course justifies the fee. A provider that previously received permission to

charge a higher fee need not reapply for permission to charge that fee during the provider's annual review. Any new requests for permission to charge more than previously approved, however, must be submitted to EOUST for approval; and

(3) The United States Trustee shall review the amount of the fee set forth in paragraphs (a)(1) and (2) of this section one year after the effective date of this part and then periodically, but not less frequently than every four years, to determine the reasonableness of the fee. Fee amounts and any revisions thereto shall be determined by current costs, using a method of analysis consistent with widely accepted accounting principles and practices, and calculated in accordance with the provisions of federal law as applicable. Fee amounts and any revisions thereto shall be published in the Federal Register.

(b)(1) A provider shall waive the fee in whole or in part whenever a debtor demonstrates a lack of ability to pay the fee.

(i) A debtor presumptively lacks the ability to pay the fee if the debtor's household current income is less than 150 percent of the poverty guidelines updated periodically in the Federal Register by the U.S. Department of Health and Human Services under the authority of 42 U.S.C. 9902(2), as adjusted from time to time, for a household or family of the size involved in the fee determination.

(ii) The presumption shall be rebutted, and the provider may charge the debtor a reduced fee, if the provider determines, based on income information the debtor submits to the provider, that the debtor is able to pay the fee in a reduced amount. Nothing in this subsection requires an provider to charge a fee to debtors whose household income exceeds the amount set forth in paragraph (b)(1)(i) of this section, or who are able to demonstrate ability to pay based on income as described in this subsection.

(iii) A provider shall disclose its fee policy, including the criteria on which it relies in determining a debtor's eligibility for reduced fees, and the provider's policy for collecting fees pursuant to paragraph (b)(1)(ii) of this section, in accordance with § 58.33(k)(2).

(2) The United States Trustee shall review the basis for the mandatory fee waiver policy set forth in paragraph (b)(1) of this section one year after the effective date of this part and then periodically, but not less frequently than every four years, to determine the impact of that fee waiver policy on debtors and providers. Any revisions to the mandatory fee waiver policy set forth in paragraph (b)(1) of this section shall be published in the Federal Register.

(c) Notwithstanding the requirements of paragraph (b) of this section, a provider also may waive fees based upon other considerations, including, but not limited to:

(1) The debtor's net worth;

(2) The percentage of the debtor's income from government assistance programs;

(3) Whether the debtor is receiving pro bono legal services in connection with a bankruptcy case; or

(4) If the combined current monthly income, as defined in 11 U.S.C. 101(10A), of the debtor and his or her spouse, when multiplied times twelve, is equal to or less than the amounts set forth in 11 U.S.C. 707(b)(7).

(d) A provider shall not require a debtor to purchase an instructional course in connection with the purchase of any other service offered by the provider.

(e) A provider who is also a chapter 13 standing trustee may only provide the instructional course to debtors in cases in which the trustee is appointed to serve and may not charge any fee to those debtors for the instructional course. A standing chapter 13 trustee may not require debtors in cases administered by the trustee to obtain the instructional course from the trustee. Employees and affiliates of the standing trustee are also bound by the restrictions in this section.
[78 FR 16172, 16175, March 14, 2013]

§ 58.35   Minimum requirements to become and remain approved providers relating to certificates.

(a) An approved provider shall send a certificate only to the debtor who took and completed the instructional course, except that an approved provider shall instead send a certificate to the attorney of a debtor who took and completed an instructional course if the debtor specifically directs the provider to do so. In lieu of sending a certificate to the debtor or the debtor's attorney, an approved provider may notify the appropriate bankruptcy court in accordance with the Federal Rules of Bankruptcy Procedure that a debtor has completed the instructional course.

(b) An approved provider shall send a certificate to a debtor, or notify the appropriate bankruptcy court in accordance with the Federal Rules of Bankruptcy Procedure, that a debtor has completed the instructional course no later than three business days after the debtor completed an instructional course and after completion of a debtor course evaluation form that evaluates the effectiveness of the instructional course. The approved provider shall not withhold the issuance of a certificate or notice of course completion to the appropriate bankruptcy court because of a debtor's failure to submit an evaluation form, though the provider should make reasonable effort to ensure that debtors complete and submit course evaluation forms.

(c) If a debtor has completed instruction, a provider may not withhold certificate issuance or notice of course completion to the appropriate bankruptcy court for any reason, including, without limitation, a debtor's failure to obtain a passing grade on a quiz, examination, or test. A provider may not consider instruction-

al services incomplete based solely on the debtor's failure to pay the fee. Although a test may be incorporated into the curriculum to evaluate the effectiveness of the course and to ensure that the course has been completed, the approved provider cannot deny a certificate to a debtor or notice of course completion to the appropriate bankruptcy court if the debtor has completed the course as designed.

(d) An approved provider shall issue certificates only in the form approved by the United States Trustee, and shall generate the form using the Certificate Generating System maintained by the United States Trustee, except under exigent circumstances with notice to the United States Trustee.

(e) An approved provider shall have sufficient computer capabilities to issue certificates from the United States Trustee's Certificate Generating System.

(f) An approved provider shall issue a certificate, or provide notice of course completion to the appropriate bankruptcy court in accordance with the Federal Rules of Bankruptcy Procedure, with respect to each debtor who completes an instructional course. Spouses receiving an instructional course jointly shall each receive a certificate or notice of course completion to the appropriate bankruptcy court shall be made for both individuals.

(g) An approved provider shall issue a replacement certificate to a debtor who requests one.

(h) Only an authorized officer, supervisor or employee of an approved provider shall issue a certificate, or provide notice of course completion to the appropriate bankruptcy court, and an approved provider shall not transfer or delegate authority to issue a certificate or provide notice of course completion to any other entity.

(i) An approved provider shall implement internal controls sufficient to prevent unauthorized issuance of certificates.

(j) An approved provider shall ensure the signature affixed to a certificate is that of an officer, supervisor or employee authorized to issue the certificate, in accordance with paragraph (h) of this section, which signature shall be either:

(1) An original signature; or

(2) In a format approved for electronic filing with the court (most typically in the form /s/ name of instructor).

(k) An approved provider shall affix to the certificate the exact name under which the approved provider is incorporated or organized.

(*l*) An approved provider shall identify on the certificate:

(1) The specific federal judicial district requested by the debtor;

(2) Whether an instructional course was provided in person, by telephone or via the Internet;

(3) The date and time (including the time zone) when instructional services were completed by the debtor; and

(4) The name of the instructor that provided the instructional course.

(m) An approved provider shall affix the debtor's full, accurate name to the certificate. If the instructional course is obtained by a debtor through a duly authorized representative, the certificate shall also set forth the name of the legal representative and legal capacity of that representative.

[78 FR 16172, 16176, March 14, 2013]

§ 58.36   **Procedures for obtaining final provider action on United States Trustees' decisions to deny providers' applications and to remove approved providers from the approved list.**

(a) The United States Trustee shall remove an approved provider from the approved list whenever an approved provider requests its removal in writing.

(b) The United States Trustee may issue a decision to remove an approved provider from the approved list, and thereby terminate the approved provider's authorization to provide an instructional course, at any time.

(c) The United States Trustee may issue a decision to deny a provider's application or to remove a provider from the approved list whenever the United States Trustee determines that the provider has failed to comply with the standards or requirements specified in 11 U.S.C. 111, this part, or the terms under which the United States Trustee designated it to act as an approved provider, including, but not limited to, finding any of the following:

(1) If any entity has suspended or revoked the provider's license to do business in any jurisdiction; or

(2) Any United States district court has removed the provider under 11 U.S.C. 111(e).

(d) The United States Trustee shall provide to the provider in writing a notice of any decision either to:

(1) Deny the provider's application; or

(2) Remove the provider from the approved list.

(e) The notice shall state the reason(s) for the decision and shall reference any documents or communications relied upon in reaching the denial or removal decision. To the extent authorized by law, the United States Trustee shall provide to the provider copies of any such documents that were not supplied to the United States Trustee by the provider. The notice shall be sent to the provider by overnight courier, for delivery the next business day.

(f) Except as provided in paragraph (h) of this section, the notice shall advise the provider that the denial or removal decision shall become final agency action, and unreviewable, unless the provider submits in writing a request for review by the Director no later than 21 calendar days from the date of the notice to the provider.

(g) Except as provided in paragraph (h) of this section, the decision to deny a provider's application or to remove a provider from the approved list shall take effect upon:

(1) The expiration of the provider's time to seek review from the Director, if the provider fails to timely seek review of a denial or removal decision; or

(2) The issuance by the Director of a final decision, if the provider timely seeks such review.

(h) The United States Trustee may provide that a decision to remove a provider from the approved list is effective immediately and deny the provider the right to provide an instructional course whenever the United States Trustee finds any of the factors set forth in paragraphs (c)(1) or (2) of this section.

(i) A provider's request for review shall be in writing and shall fully describe why the provider disagrees with the denial or removal decision, and shall be accompanied by all documents and materials the provider wants the Director to consider in reviewing the denial or removal decision. The provider shall send the original and one copy of the request for review, including all accompanying documents and materials, to the Office of the Director by overnight courier, for delivery the next business day. To be timely, a request for review shall be received at the Office of the Director no later than 21 calendar days from the date of the notice to the provider.

(j) The United States Trustee shall have 21 calendar days from the date of the provider's request for review to submit to the Director a written response regarding the matters raised in the provider's request for review. The United States Trustee shall provide a copy of this response to the provider by overnight courier, for delivery the next business day.

(k) The Director may seek additional information from any party in the manner and to the extent the Director deems appropriate.

(l) In reviewing the decision to deny a provider's application or to remove a provider from the approved list, the Director shall determine:

(1) Whether the denial or removal decision is supported by the record; and

(2) Whether the denial or removal decision constitutes an appropriate exercise of discretion.

(m) Except as provided in paragraph (n) of this section, the Director shall issue a final decision no later than 60 calendar days from the receipt of the provider's request for review, unless the provider agrees to a longer period of time or the Director extends the deadline. The Director's final decision on the provider's request for review shall constitute final agency action.

(n) Whenever the United States Trustee provides under paragraph (h) of this section that a decision to remove a provider from the approved list is effective immediately, the Director shall issue a written decision no later than 15 calendar days from the receipt of the provider's request for review, unless the provider agrees to a longer period of time. The decision shall:

(1) Be limited to deciding whether the determination that the removal decision should take effect immediately was supported by the record and an appropriate exercise of discretion;

(2) Constitute final agency action only on the issue of whether the removal decision should take effect immediately; and

(3) Not constitute final agency action on the ultimate issue of whether the provider should be removed from the approved list; after issuing the decision, the Director shall issue a final decision by the deadline set forth in paragraph (m) of this section.

(*o*) In reaching a decision under paragraphs (m) or (n) of this section, the Director may specify a person to act as a reviewing official. The reviewing official's duties shall be specified by the Director on a case-by-case basis, and may include reviewing the record, obtaining additional information from the participants, providing the Director with written recommendations, and such other duties as the Director shall prescribe in a particular case.

(p) A provider that files a request for review shall bear its own costs and expenses, including counsel fees.

(q) When a decision to remove a provider from the approved list takes effect, the provider shall:

(1) Immediately cease providing an instructional course to debtors;

(2) No later than three business days after the date of removal, send all certificates to all debtors who completed an instructional course prior to the provider's removal from the approved list; and

(3) No later than three business days after the date of removal, return all fees to debtors who had paid for an instructional course, but had not completely received the instructional course.

(r) A provider must exhaust all administrative remedies before seeking redress in any court of competent jurisdiction.

[78 FR 16172, 16176, March 14, 2013]

Appendix A to Part 58—Guidelines for Reviewing Applications for Compensation and Reimbursement of Expenses Filed Under 11 U.S.C. 330

(a) General Information. (1) The Bankruptcy Reform Act of 1994 amended the responsibilities of the United States Trustees under 28 U.S.C. 586(a)(3)(A) to provide that, whenever they deem appropriate, United States Trustees will review applications for compensation and reimbursement of expenses under section 330 of the Bankruptcy Code, 11 U.S.C. 101, et seq. ("Code"), in accordance with procedural guidelines ("Guidelines") adopted by the Executive Office for United States Trustees ("Executive Office"). The following Guidelines have been adopted by the Executive Office and are to be uniformly applied by the United States Trustees except when circumstances warrant different treatment.

(2) The United States Trustees shall use these Guidelines in all cases commenced on or after October 22, 1994.

(3) The Guidelines are not intended to supersede local rules of court, but should be read as complementing the procedures set forth in local rules.

(4) Nothing in the Guidelines should be construed:

(i) To limit the United States Trustee's discretion to request additional information necessary for the review of a particular application or type of application or to refer any information provided to the United States Trustee to any investigatory or prosecutorial authority of the United States or a state;

(ii) To limit the United States Trustee's discretion to determine whether to file comments or objections to applications; or

(iii) To create any private right of action on the part of any person enforceable in litigation with the United States Trustee or the United States.

(5) Recognizing that the final authority to award compensation and reimbursement under section 330 of the Code is vested in the Court, the Guidelines focus on the disclosure of information relevant to a proper award under the law. In evaluating fees for professional services, it is relevant to consider various factors including the following: the time spent; the rates charged; whether the services were necessary to the administration of, or beneficial towards the completion of, the case at the time they were rendered; whether services were performed within a reasonable time commensurate with the complexity, importance, and nature of the problem, issue, or task addressed; and whether compensation is reasonable based on the customary compensation charged by comparably skilled practitioners in non-bankruptcy cases. The Guidelines thus reflect standards and procedures articulated in section 330 of the Code and Rule 2016 of the Federal Rules of Bankruptcy Procedure for awarding compensation to trustees and to professionals employed under section 327 or 1103. Applications that contain the information requested in these Guidelines will facilitate review by the Court, the parties, and the United States Trustee.

(6) Fee applications submitted by trustees are subject to the same standard of review as are applications of other professionals and will be evaluated according to the principles articulated in these Guidelines. Each United States Trustee should establish whether and to what extent trustees can deviate from the format specified in these Guidelines without substantially affecting the ability of the United States Trustee to review and comment on their fee applications in a manner consistent with the requirements of the law.

(b) Contents of Applications for Compensation and Reimbursement of Expenses. All applications should include sufficient detail to demonstrate compliance with the standards set forth in 11 U.S.C. § 330. The fee application should also contain sufficient information about the case and the applicant so that the Court, the creditors, and the United States Trustee can review it without searching for relevant information in other documents. The following will facilitate review of the application.

(1) Information about the Applicant and the Application. The following information should be provided in every fee application:

(i) Date the bankruptcy petition was filed, date of the order approving employment, identity of the party represented, date services commenced, and whether the applicant is seeking compensation under a provision of the Bankruptcy Code other than section 330.

(ii) Terms and conditions of employment and compensation, source of compensation, existence and terms controlling use of a retainer, and any budgetary or other limitations on fees.

(iii) Names and hourly rates of all applicant's professionals and paraprofessionals who billed time, explanation of any changes in hourly rates from those previously charged, and statement of whether the compensation is based on the customary compensation charged by comparably skilled practitioners in cases other than cases under title 11.

(iv) Whether the application is interim or final, and the dates of previous orders on interim compensation or reimbursement of expenses along with the amounts requested and the amounts allowed or disallowed, amounts of all previous payments, and amount of any allowed fees and expenses remaining unpaid.

(v) Whether the person on whose behalf the applicant is employed has been given the opportunity to review the application and whether that person has approved the requested amount.

(vi) When an application is filed less than 120 days after the order for relief or after a prior application to the Court, the date and terms of the order allowing leave to file at shortened intervals.

(vii) Time period of the services or expenses covered by the application.

(2) Case Status. The following information should be provided to the extent that it is known to or can be reasonably ascertained by the applicant:

(i) In a chapter 7 case, a summary of the administration of the case including all moneys received and disbursed in the case, when the case is expected to close, and, if applicant is seeking an interim award, whether it is feasible to make an interim distribution to creditors without prejudicing the rights of any creditor holding a claim of equal or higher priority.

(ii) In a chapter 11 case, whether a plan and disclosure statement have been filed and, if not yet filed, when the plan and disclosure statement are expected to be filed; whether all quarterly fees have been paid to the United States Trustee; and whether all monthly operating reports have been filed.

(iii) In every case, the amount of cash on hand or on deposit, the amount and nature of accrued unpaid administrative expenses, and the amount of unencumbered funds in the estate.

(iv) Any material changes in the status of the case that occur after the filing of the fee application should be raised, orally or in writing, at the hearing on the application or, if a hearing is not required, prior to the expiration of the time period for objection.

(3) Summary Sheet. All applications should contain a summary or cover sheet that provides a synopsis of the following information:

(i) Total compensation and expenses requested and any amount(s) previously requested;

(ii) Total compensation and expenses previously awarded by the court;

(iii) Name and applicable billing rate for each person who billed time during the period, and date of bar admission for each attorney;

(iv) Total hours billed and total amount of billing for each person who billed time during billing period; and

(v) Computation of blended hourly rate for persons who billed time during period, excluding paralegal or other paraprofessional time.

(4) Project Billing Format. (i) To facilitate effective review of the application, all time and service entries should be arranged by project categories. The project categories set forth in exhibit A should be used to the extent applicable. A separate project category should be used for administrative matters and, if payment is requested, for fee application preparation.

(ii) The United States Trustee has discretion to determine that the project billing format is not necessary in a particular case or in a particular class of cases. Applicants should be encouraged to consult with the United States Trustee if there is a question as to the need for project billing in any particular case.

(iii) Each project category should contain a narrative summary of the following information:

(A) a description of the project, its necessity and benefit to the estate, and the status of the project including all pending litigation for which compensation and reimbursement are requested;

(B) identification of each person providing services on the project; and

(C) a statement of the number of hours spent and the amount of compensation requested for each professional and paraprofessional on the project.

(iv) Time and service entries are to be reported in chronological order under the appropriate project category.

(v) Time entries should be kept contemporaneously with the services rendered in time periods of tenths of an hour. Services should be noted in detail and not combined or "lumped" together, with each service showing a separate time entry; however, tasks performed in a project which total a de minimis amount of time can be combined or lumped together if they do not exceed .5 hours on a daily aggregate. Time entries for telephone calls, letters, and other communications should give sufficient detail to identify the parties to and the nature of the communication. Time entries for court hearings and conferences should identify the subject of the hearing or conference. If more than one professional from the applicant firm attends a hearing or conference, the applicant should explain the need for multiple attendees.

(5) Reimbursement for Actual, Necessary Expenses. Any expense for which reimbursement is sought must be actual and necessary and supported by documentation as appropriate. Factors relevant to a determination that the expense is proper include the following:

(i) Whether the expense is reasonable and economical. For example, first class and other luxurious travel mode or accommodations will normally be objectionable.

(ii) Whether the requested expenses are customarily charged to non-bankruptcy clients of the applicant.

(iii) Whether applicant has provided a detailed itemization of all expenses including the date incurred, description of expense (e.g., type of travel, type of fare, rate, destination), method of computation, and, where relevant, name of the person incurring the expense and purpose of the expense. Itemized expenses should be identified by their nature (e.g., long distance telephone, copy costs, messengers, computer research, airline travel, etc.) and by the month incurred. Unusual items require more detailed explanations and should be allocated, where practicable, to specific projects.

(iv) Whether applicant has prorated expenses where appropriate between the estate and other cases (e.g., travel expenses applicable to more than one case) and has adequately explained the basis for any such proration.

(v) Whether expenses incurred by the applicant to third parties are limited to the actual amounts billed to, or paid by, the applicant on behalf of the estate.

(vi) Whether applicant can demonstrate that the amount requested for expenses incurred in-house reflect the actual cost of such expenses to the applicant. The United States Trustee may establish an objection ceiling for any in-house expenses that are routinely incurred and for which the actual cost cannot easily be determined by most professionals (e.g., photocopies, facsimile charges, and mileage).

(vii) Whether the expenses appear to be in the nature nonreimbursable overhead. Overhead consists of all continuous administrative or general costs incident to the operation of the applicant's office and not particularly attributable to an individual client or case. Overhead includes, but is not limited to, word processing, proofreading, secretarial and other clerical services, rent, utilities, office equipment and furnishings, insurance, taxes, local telephones and monthly car phone charges, lighting, heating and cooling, and library and publication charges.

(viii) Whether applicant has adhered to allowable rates for expenses as fixed by local rule or order of the Court.

Exhibit A—Project Categories

Here is a list of suggested project categories for use in most bankruptcy cases. Only one category should be used for a given activity. Professionals should make their best effort to be consistent in their use of categories, whether within a particular firm or by different firms working on the same case. It would be appropriate for all professionals to discuss the categories in advance and agree generally on how activities will be categorized. This list is not exclusive. The application may contain additional categories as the case requires. They are generally more applicable to attorneys in chapter 7 and chapter 11, but may be used by all professionals as appropriate.

Asset Analysis and Recovery: Identification and review of potential assets including causes of action and non-litigation recoveries.

Asset Disposition: Sales, leases (§ 365 matters), abandonment and related transaction work.

Business Operations: Issues related to debtor-in-possession operating in chapter 11 such as employee, vendor, tenant issues and other similar problems.

Case Administration: Coordination and compliance activities, including preparation of statement of financial affairs; schedules; list of contracts; United States Trustee interim statements and operating reports; contacts with the United States Trustee; general creditor inquiries.

Claims Administration and Objections: Specific claim inquiries; bar date motions; analyses, objections and allowances of claims.

Employee Benefits/Pensions: Review issues such as severance, retention, 401K coverage and continuance of pension plan.

Fee/Employment Applicants: Preparation of employment and fee applications for self or others; motions to establish interim procedures.

Fee/Employment Objections: Review of and objections to the employment and fee applications of others.

Financing: Matters under §§ 361, 363 and 364 including cash collateral and secured claims; loan document analysis.

Litigation: There should be a separate category established for each matter (e.g., XYZ Litigation).

Meetings of Creditors: Preparing for and attending the conference of creditors, the § 341(a) meeting and other creditors' committee meetings.

Plan and Disclosure Statement: Formulation, presentation and confirmation; compliance with the plan confirmation order, related orders and rules; disbursement and case closing activities, except those related to the allowance and objections to allowance of claims.

Relief From Stay Proceedings: Matters relating to termination or continuation of automatic stay under § 362.

The following categories are generally more applicable to accountants and financial advisors, but may be used by all professionals as appropriate.

Accounting/Auditing: Activities related to maintaining and auditing books of account, preparation of financial statements and account analysis.

Business Analysis: Preparation and review of company business plan; development and review of strategies; preparation and review of cash flow forecasts and feasibility studies.

Corporate Finance: Review financial aspects of potential mergers, acquisitions and disposition of company or subsidiaries.

Data Analysis: Management information systems review, installation and analysis, construction, maintenance and reporting of significant case financial data, lease rejection, claims, etc.

Litigation Consulting: Providing consulting and expert witness services relating to various bankruptcy matters such as insolvency, feasibility, avoiding actions, forensic accounting, etc.

Reconstruction Accounting: Reconstructing books and records from past transactions and bringing accounting current.

Tax Issues: Analysis of tax issues and preparation of state and federal tax returns.

Valuation: Appraise or review appraisals of assets.

[61 FR 24890, May 17, 1996]

INDEX TO
BANKRUPTCY CODE, RULES AND FORMS

References are to U.S. Code sections unless otherwise indicated.
CFR Title 28 Bankruptcy Reform Regulations foll. FRAP.

CITATIONS

BKR	.Bankruptcy Rule
BKR Form	.Bankruptcy Form
FRAP	.Federal Rules of Appellate Procedure
FRCVP	.Federal Rules of Civil Procedure
FRE	.Federal Rules of Evidence

ALPHAMEPRODINE

Controlled Substances, generally, this index

ALPHAMETHADOL

Controlled Substances, generally, this index

ALPHAPRODINE

Controlled Substances, generally, this index

ALTERATION OF INSTRUMENTS

Crimes and offenses, 18 § 1519

Fines and penalties, 18 § 1519

ALTERNATIVE DISPUTE RESOLUTION

Generally, 28 § 651 et seq.

Administration, 28 § 651

Confidential or privileged information, 28 § 652

Consent, arbitration referrals, 28 § 654

Damages, arbitration referrals, 28 § 654

Definitions, 28 § 651

Exemptions, 28 § 652

Jurisdiction, 28 § 652

Neutrals, 28 § 653

Referrals, arbitration referrals, 28 § 654

AMPHETAMINES

Controlled Substances, generally, this index

ANALOGUES

Controlled Substances, generally, this index

Drugs and Medicine, generally, this index

ANILERIDINE

Controlled Substances, generally, this index

ANIMALS

Bankruptcy, this index

ANNUITIES

Administrative Office of United States Courts, 28 § 604

Bankruptcy, exemptions, 11 § 522

Exemptions, bankruptcy, 11 § 522

ANTHRANILIC ACID

Controlled Substances, generally, this index

ANTICRAMDOWN LAW

Bankruptcy, chapter 13 proceedings, 11 § 1325

APPEAL AND REVIEW

Bankruptcy, this index

Courts of Appeals, generally, this index

Rules of Appellate Procedure, generally, this index

Rules of Civil Procedure, this index

APPELLATE PROCEDURE RULES

Rules of Appellate Procedure, generally, this index

APPRAISAL AND APPRAISERS

Bankruptcy, this index

ARBITRATION

Arbitrators,

Certificates and certification, 28 § 655

Compensation and salaries, 28 § 658

Disqualification, 28 § 655

ARBITRATION—Cont'd

Arbitrators—Cont'd

Privileges and immunities, 28 § 655

Referrals, 28 § 655

Awards,

Referrals, 28 §§ 655, 657

Sealing, 28 § 657

Certificates and certification, arbitrators, 28 § 655

Compensation and salaries, 28 § 658

Disqualification, arbitrators, 28 § 655

Dockets and docketing, new trial, 28 § 657

Hearings, referrals, 28 § 655

Judgments and decrees, 28 § 657

Neutrals, compensation and salaries, 28 § 658

New trial, 28 § 657

Oaths and affirmations, 28 § 655

Powers and duties, arbitrators, 28 § 655

Privileges and immunities, arbitrators, 28 § 655

Process, awards, 28 § 657

Production of books and papers, 28 § 656

Referrals, 28 §§ 654, 655

Sealing, awards, 28 § 657

Subpoenas, 28 § 656

Time, new trial, 28 § 657

Traveling expenses, 28 § 658

Trial de novo, 28 § 657

ARBITRATORS

Arbitration, this index

ARIZONA

Bankruptcy, judges or justices, appointments, 28 § 152

Judicial districts, bankruptcy, 28 § 581 nt

United States trustees, appointments, 28 § 581

ARKANSAS

Bankruptcy, judges or justices, appointments, 28 § 152

Judicial districts, bankruptcy, 28 § 581 nt

United States trustees, judicial districts, appointments, 28 § 581

ARMED FORCES

Application of law, bankruptcy, reserves, chapter 7 proceedings, 11 § 707 nt

Bankruptcy,

Chapter 7 proceedings, abuse, 11 § 707

Counseling services, exemptions, 11 § 109

Reserves, chapter 7 proceedings, 11 § 707

Counseling services, bankruptcy, exemptions, 11 § 109

Reserves, bankruptcy, chapter 7 proceedings, 11 § 707

ARMED SERVICES

Armed Forces, generally, this index

ASSASSINATION

Interception of wire, oral, or electronic communications, 18 § 2516

Justices of Supreme Court, 18 § 2516

ASSAULT AND BATTERY

Cabinet departments, interception of wire, oral, or electronic communications, 18 § 2516

BANKRUPTCY CODE, RULES AND FORMS

INDEX

BANKRUPTCY CODE, RULES AND FORMS

INDEX

BANKRUPTCY CODE, RULES AND FORMS

INDEX

INDEX

I-31

INDEX

BANKRUPTCY CODE, RULES AND FORMS

INDEX

BANKRUPTCY CODE, RULES AND FORMS

INDEX

INDEX

INDEX

INDEX

DIVORCE
Bankruptcy, this index

DOCKETS AND DOCKETING
Administrative Office of U.S. Courts, information, **28 § 604**
Bankruptcy, this index
Examinations and examiners, **28 § 604**
Information, Administrative Office of U.S. Courts, **28 § 604**
Rules of Civil Procedure, this index

DOCUMENTARY EVIDENCE
Racketeer influenced and corrupt organizations, **18 § 1961**

DOMESTIC VIOLENCE
Bankruptcy, automatic stay, **11 § 362**

DOMICILE AND RESIDENCE
Bankruptcy, this index

DOMICILIARY CARE
Nursing Homes, generally, this index

DOWER AND CURTESY
Bankruptcy, sales, **11 § 363**
Sales, bankruptcy, **11 § 363**

DRUGS AND MEDICINE
Bankruptcy, trafficking, chapter 7 proceedings, dismissal and nonsuit, **11 § 707**
Controlled Substances, generally, this index
Interception of wire, oral, or electronic communications, **18 § 2516**
Racketeering, generally, this index
Trafficking, bankruptcy, chapter 7 proceedings, dismissal and nonsuit, **11 § 707**

EAVESDROPPING
Interception of Wire, Oral, or Electronic Communications, generally, this index

EDUCATION
Bankruptcy, this index
Colleges and Universities, generally, this index
Coverdell education savings accounts, bankruptcy, **11 §§ 521, 541**
Income Tax, this index
Postsecondary education. Colleges and Universities, generally, this index
Scholarships, generally, this index
Secretary of Education, generally, this index

EDUCATION DEPARTMENT
Secretary of Education, generally, this index

EDUCATION INDIVIDUAL RETIREMENT ACCOUNTS
Bankruptcy, **11 §§ 521, 541**

EDUCATION SECRETARY
Secretary of Education, generally, this index

ELECTIONS
Bankruptcy, this index

ELECTRONIC SURVEILLANCE
Interception of Wire, Oral, or Electronic Communications, generally, this index

EMBEZZLEMENT
Bankruptcy, **11 § 523; 18 § 153**
Interception of wire, oral, or electronic communications, Pension and Welfare Fund, **18 § 2516**

EMIGRATION
Immigration, generally, this index

EMINENT DOMAIN
Rules of Civil Procedure, this index

EMPLOYEE RETIREMENT INCOME SECURITY PROGRAM
Bankruptcy, this index
Theft, **18 § 2516**

ENERGY
Interception, wire and oral communications, **18 § 2516**
Secretary of Energy, generally, this index

ENERGY DEPARTMENT
Head of Department. Secretary of Energy, generally, this index
Secretary of Energy, generally, this index

ENERGY SECRETARY
Secretary of Energy, generally, this index

ENGINE HOUSES
Railroads, generally, this index

ENTIRETIES, ESTATES BY
Bankruptcy, sales, **11 § 363**

ENTRY UPON LAND
Rules of Civil Procedure, this index

EQUITY
Receivers and receivership, **28 § 959**
Rules of Civil Procedure, this index
Trusts and trustees, **28 § 959**

EQUITY SECURITY HOLDERS
Bankruptcy, this index

ERGONOVINE
Controlled Substances, generally, this index

ERGOTAMINE
Controlled Substances, generally, this index

ESCAPE
Interception of wire, oral, or electronic communications, **18 § 2516**

ESPIONAGE
Interception of wire, oral, or electronic communications, **18 § 2516**

ESTATE TAX
United States Tax Court, generally, this index

ETHCHLORVYNOL
Controlled Substances, generally, this index

ETHINAMATE
Controlled Substances, generally, this index

ETHYL ETHER
Controlled Substances, generally, this index

ETHYLMETHYLTHIAMBUTENE
Controlled Substances, generally, this index

ETHYLMORPHINE
Controlled Substances, generally, this index

ETONITAZENE
Controlled Substances, generally, this index

ETORPHINE
Controlled Substances, generally, this index

ETOXERIDINE
Controlled Substances, generally, this index

EVICTIONS
Bankruptcy, this index

EVIDENCE
Bankruptcy, this index
Federal Rules of Evidence. Rules of Evidence, generally, this index
Rules of Civil Procedure, this index
Rules of Evidence, generally, this index
Witnesses, generally, this index

EXAMINATIONS AND EXAMINERS
Bankruptcy, this index
Rules of Civil Procedure, this index

EXECUTION
Bankruptcy, this index
Rules of Civil Procedure, this index

EXECUTIVE DEPARTMENTS
Justice Department, generally, this index
President of the United States, generally, this index
Secretary of Agriculture, generally, this index
Secretary of Commerce, generally, this index
Secretary of Energy, generally, this index
Secretary of Housing and Urban Development, generally, this index
Secretary of Labor, generally, this index
Secretary of State, generally, this index
Secretary of the Interior, generally, this index
Secretary of the Treasury, generally, this index

EXECUTIVE MANSION
White House, generally, this index

EXECUTORS AND ADMINISTRATORS
Disqualification, judges or justices, 28 § 455
Judges or justices, disqualification, 28 § 455

EXEMPTIONS
Bankruptcy, this index
New markets venture capital companies, bankruptcy, 11 § 109

EXHIBITS
Rules of Civil Procedure, this index

EXPENSES AND EXPENDITURES
Administrative Office of U.S. Courts, **28 § 604**
Bankruptcy, this index
Court officers and employees, payment, Administrative Office of U.S. Courts, **28 § 604**
Rules of Civil Procedure, this index
Subsistence, generally, this index
Traveling Expenses, generally, this index

EXPERTS
Rules of Civil Procedure, this index

EXPLOSIVES
Crimes and offenses, communications, interceptions, **18 § 2516**
Interception of wire, oral, or electronic communications, **18 § 2516**

EXPORTS AND IMPORTS
Courts. International Trade Court, generally, this index
International Trade Court, generally, this index

EXTENDED CARE SERVICES
Nursing Homes, generally, this index

EXTORTION
Credit (payment of indebtedness), **18 § 2516**
Interception of wire, oral, or electronic communications, credit (payment of indebtedness), **18 § 2516**

FAMILY FARMERS PROTECTION ACT OF 2002
Generally, **11 §§ 101 nt, 1201 et seq.**

FATHERS
Children and Minors, generally, this index

FEDERAL AGENCIES
Arbitration, generally, this index
Interception of wire, oral, or electronic communications, **18 § 2516**
Notice, bankruptcy, debtors and creditors, **28 § 1930 nt**
Officers and employees. Federal Officers and Employees, generally, this index
Rules of Civil Procedure, this index

FEDERAL BUREAU OF INVESTIGATION
Bankruptcy, powers and duties, **18 § 158**
Interception of wire, oral, or electronic communications, **18 § 2516**

FEDERAL CLAIMS COURT
Court of Federal Claims, generally, this index

FEDERAL JUDICIAL CENTER
Judicial Center, generally, this index

FEDERAL OFFICERS AND EMPLOYEES
Bribery and corruption, interception of wire, oral, or electronic communications, **18 § 2516**
Disqualification, judges or justices, **28 § 455**
Influence, injuries, interception of wire, electronic or oral communications, **18 § 2516**
Interception of wire, oral, or electronic communications, **18 § 2516**
Judges or justices, disqualification, **28 § 455**

INDEX

INDEX

LYSERGIC ACID
Controlled Substances, generally, this index

LYSERGIC ACID AMIDE
Controlled Substances, generally, this index

MAGISTRATES
United States Magistrate Judges, generally, this index

MAIL AND MAILING
Bankruptcy, this index
Counterfeiting, interception of wire, oral, or electronic
    communications, **18 § 2516**
Rules of Civil Procedure, this index

MAINE
United States trustees, judicial districts, appointments,
    28 § 581

MALICIOUS MISCHIEF
Energy facilities, destruction, **18 § 2516**
Interception of wire, oral, or electronic communications,
    18 § 2516

MARGINS
Bankruptcy, this index

MARIANA ISLANDS
Northern Mariana Islands, generally, this index

MARSHALS
United States Marshals Service, generally, this index

MARYLAND
Bankruptcy, judges or justices, appointments, **28 § 152**
Judicial districts, bankruptcy, **28 § 581 nt**
United States trustees, judicial districts, **28 § 581**

MASSACHUSETTS
Bankruptcy, judges or justices, appointments, **28 § 152**
United States trustees of judicial districts, appointment,
    28 § 581

MASTER AGREEMENTS
Bankruptcy, this index

MASTERS
Rules of Civil Procedure, this index

MEDIATION AND MEDIATORS
Alternative Dispute Resolution, generally, this index

MEDICAL CARE AND TREATMENT
Drugs and Medicine, generally, this index
Hospitals, generally, this index
Long term care. Nursing Homes, generally, this index
Nursing Homes, generally, this index

MEDICAL DEVICES
Bankruptcy, exemptions, **11 § 522**

MEDICAL FACILITIES
Hospitals, generally, this index

MEDICARE
Bankruptcy, automatic stay, **11 § 362**

MEDICINE
Drugs and Medicine, generally, this index

MENTAL HEALTH
Bankruptcy, this index
Rules of Civil Procedure, this index

MEPROBAMATE
Controlled Substances, generally, this index

MESCALINE
Controlled Substances, generally, this index

MESSENGERS
Courts, compensation and salaries, **28 § 604**

METAZOCINE
Controlled Substances, generally, this index

METHADONE
Controlled Substances, generally, this index

METHOHEXITAL
Controlled Substances, generally, this index

METHYLDESORPHINE
Controlled Substances, generally, this index

METHYLHYDROMORPHINE
Controlled Substances, generally, this index

METHYLPHENIDATE
Controlled Substances, generally, this index

METHYLPHENOBARBITAL
Controlled Substances, generally, this index

METHYPRYLON
Controlled Substances, generally, this index

MEXICO
Boundaries,
    Interception of wire, oral, or electronic communications,
        tunnels, **18 § 2516**
    Tunnels, interception of wire, oral, or electronic
        communications, **18 § 2516**
Interception of wire, oral, or electronic communications,
    border tunnels, **18 § 2516**

MICHIGAN
Bankruptcy, judges or justices, appointments, **28 § 152**
Judicial districts, bankruptcy, **28 § 581 nt**
United States trustees, judicial districts, appointments,
    28 § 581

MILEAGE
Traveling Expenses, generally, this index

MILITARY FORCES
Armed Forces, generally, this index

MINITRIALS
Alternative Dispute Resolution, generally, this index

MINNESOTA
Bankruptcy, judges or justices, appointments, **28 § 152**
United States trustees, judicial districts, appointments,
    28 § 581

MINORS
Children and Minors, generally, this index

INDEX

INDEX

INDEX

RULES OF CIVIL PROCEDURE—Cont'd

Examinations and examiners—Cont'd
  Depositions, generally, ante
  Jury, **FRCVP 47**
  Masters, **FRCVP 53**
  Mental health, **FRCVP 35, 37**
  Physical examinations, **FRCVP 35, 37**
  Sanctions, **FRCVP 37**
Excusable neglect, **FRCVP 6, 60**
Execution,
  Admiralty, **FRCVP E**
  Discovery, **FRCVP 69**
  Dockets and docketing, **FRCVP 79**
  Masters, **FRCVP 53**
  Possession, **FRCVP 70**
  Stay of proceedings, **FRCVP 62**
  Time, **FRCVP 62**
Executors and administrators, **FRCVP 17**
Exemptions,
  Depositions, **FRCVP 32**
  U.S. vessels, arrest, supplemental rules, **FRCVP C**
Exhibits,
  Depositions, **FRCVP 30**
  Discovery, **FRCVP 26**
  Masters, **FRCVP 53**
  Written instruments, **FRCVP 10**
Exoneration, admiralty, **FRCVP A, F**
Expenses and expenditures,
  Admiralty, **FRCVP E**
  Admissions, requests, **FRCVP 36**
  Depositions, **FRCVP 37**
  Discovery, **FRCVP 37**
  Documents, genuineness, **FRCVP 37**
  Entry upon land, **FRCVP 37**
  Interrogatories, **FRCVP 37**
  Production of documents or things, **FRCVP 37**
Experts, **FRCVP 43**
  Depositions, **FRCVP 26**
  Discovery, **FRCVP 26**
  Pretrial conferences, **FRCVP 16**
Facsimile transmissions, **FRCVP 5**
Fair conduct, class actions, **FRCVP 23**
Federal agencies,
  Answers, **FRCVP 12**
  Appeal and review, **FRCVP 62**
  Depositions, **FRCVP 32, 37**
  Injunctions, **FRCVP 65**
  Interrogatories, **FRCVP 33**
  Process, **FRCVP 15**
  Subpoenas, **FRCVP 45, 81**
  Temporary restraining orders, **FRCVP 65**
Federal officers and employees,
  Answer, **FRCVP 12**
  Appeal and review, **FRCVP 62**
  Compelling testimony, **FRCVP 81**
  Definitions, **FRCVP 81**
  Injunctions, **FRCVP 65**
  Process, **FRCVP 15**
  Subpoenas, **FRCVP 45**

RULES OF CIVIL PROCEDURE—Cont'd

Federal officers and employees—Cont'd
  Temporary restraining orders, **FRCVP 65**
Fellow servant, pleading, affirmative defenses, **FRCVP 8**
Filing, **FRCVP 5**
  Complaints, **FRCVP 3**
  Definitions, **FRCVP 5**
  Electronic filing, **FRCVP 5**
  Eminent domain, **FRCVP 71.1**
  Facsimile transmissions, **FRCVP 5**
  Masters, **FRCVP 53**
  Numbers and numbering, dockets and docketing, **FRCVP 79**
  Pleading, **FRCVP 3 et seq.**
  Privacy protection, **FRCVP 5.2**
Findings, **FRCVP 52, 53**
  Admiralty, **FRCVP F**
  Amendments,
    Extension of time, **FRCVP 6**
    New trial, motions, **FRCVP 59**
    Stay of proceedings, **FRCVP 62**
  Class actions, **FRCVP 23**
  Jury, unanimity, **FRCVP 48**
  New trial, **FRCVP 59**
  Special verdict, **FRCVP 49**
  Stay of proceedings, **FRCVP 62**
Fines and penalties,
  Admiralty, **FRCVP A, C, G**
  Conferences, **FRCVP 16**
  Depositions, **FRCVP 30**
  Disclosure, parties, **FRCVP 37**
  Discovery, **FRCVP 37**
  Motions, **FRCVP 11**
  Pleading, **FRCVP 11**
  Pretrial conferences, **FRCVP 16**
  Pretrial orders, **FRCVP 16**
  Subpoenas, **FRCVP 45**
  Witnesses, **FRCVP 53**
Foreign countries,
  Depositions, **FRCVP 28**
  Discovery, **FRCVP 37**
  Judgments and decrees, **FRCVP 9**
  Laws, **FRCVP 44.1**
  Official records, authentication, **FRCVP 44**
  Records and recordation, official records, authentication, **FRCVP 44**
  Subpoenas, **FRCVP 45**
  Summons, **FRCVP 4**
Foreign diplomatic and consular officers,
  Authentication, **FRCVP 44**
  Depositions, **FRCVP 28**
Forms,
  Depositions, **FRCVP 32**
  Evidence, **FRCVP 43**
  Masters, **FRCVP 53**
  Pleading, **FRCVP 10**
  Sanctions, nonuse, **FRCVP 83**
  Subpoenas, **FRCVP 45**
  Summons, **FRCVP 4**

INDEX

INDEX

INDEX

INDEX

BANKRUPTCY CODE, RULES AND FORMS

TAXATION—Cont'd

Income Tax, generally, this index

United States Tax Court, generally, this index

TELECOMMUNICATIONS

Interception of Wire, Oral, or Electronic Communications, generally, this index

Wiretapping. Interception of Wire, Oral, or Electronic Communications, generally, this index

TENANTS

Landlord and Tenant, generally, this index

TENANTS IN COMMON

Bankruptcy, sales, 11 § 363

TENEMENTS

Landlord and Tenant, generally, this index

TENNESSEE

Bankruptcy, judges or justices, appointments, 28 § 152

Judicial districts, bankruptcy, 28 § 581 nt

United States trustees, judicial districts, appointment, 28 § 581

TERMINALLY ILL

Hospices, generally, this index

TERRITORIES

Guam, generally, this index

Northern Mariana Islands, generally, this index

Virgin Islands, generally, this index

TERRORISTS AND TERRORISM

Interception of wire, oral, or electronic communications, 18 § 2516

Racketeering, 18 § 1961

TETRAHYDROCANNABINOLS

Controlled Substances, generally, this index

TEXAS

Bankruptcy, judges or justices, appointments, 28 § 152

Judicial districts, bankruptcy, 28 § 581 nt

United States trustees, judicial districts, appointments, 28 § 581

THEBACON

Controlled Substances, generally, this index

THIRD PARTIES

Bankruptcy, this index

Rules of Civil Procedure, this index

TIMESHARES

Bankruptcy, this index

TITLE TO PROPERTY

Bankruptcy, this index

TOLUENE

Controlled Substances, generally, this index

TOYS

Bankruptcy, exemptions, 11 § 522

TRADEMARKS AND TRADE NAMES

Trafficking, interception of wire, oral, or electronic communications, 18 § 2516

TRAFFICKING

Human trafficking, racketeering, 18 § 1961

Racketeering, traffickers in persons, 18 § 1961

TRAINS

Railroads, generally, this index

TRANSCRIPTS

Bankruptcy, this index

TRANSPORTATION

Aircraft, generally, this index

Expenses and expenditures. Traveling Expenses, generally, this index

Mass transportation. Railroads, generally, this index

Planes. Aircraft, generally, this index

Railroads, generally, this index

Secretary of Commerce, generally, this index

Secretary of Transportation, generally, this index

TRANSPORTATION DEPARTMENT

Bankruptcy, railroads, appearances, 11 § 1164

Secretary of Transportation, generally, this index

TRANSPORTATION SECRETARY

Secretary of Transportation, generally, this index

TRAVELING EXPENSES

See, also, Subsistence, generally, this index

Arbitration, 28 § 658

Bankruptcy, this index

Court officers and employees, 28 § 604

National Bankruptcy Review Commission, 11 nt prec § 101

TREASON

Interception of wire, oral, or electronic communications, 18 § 2516

TREASURY DEPARTMENT

Secretary of the Treasury, generally, this index

TREASURY OF UNITED STATES

Bankruptcy, this index

TREASURY SECRETARY

Secretary of the Treasury, generally, this index

TREATIES

Bankruptcy, 11 § 1503

TRIAL

Bankruptcy, this index

Disqualification, judges or justices, 28 § 455

Judges or justices, disqualification, 28 § 455

Jury, generally, this index

Rules of Civil Procedure, this index

Speedy trial, 28 § 604

TRIBUNALS

Courts, generally, this index

TRIMEPERIDINE

Controlled Substances, generally, this index

TRUST TERRITORY OF PACIFIC ISLANDS

Northern Mariana Islands, generally, this index

BANKRUPTCY CODE, RULES AND FORMS

INDEX